Chambers Dictionary of Etymology

Chambers Dictionary of Etymology

EDITOR
Robert K. Barnhart

MANAGING EDITOR
Sol Steinmetz

Chambers

CHAMBERS
An imprint of Chambers Harrap Publishers Ltd
338 Euston Road, London, NW1 3 BH

Chambers Harrap Publishers Ltd is an Hachette UK Company

Reprinted 2000, 2001, 2002, 2003, 2004, 2005, 2008, 2010, 2011

This edition published by arrangement with The H. W. Wilson Company

Previously published as the *Barnhart Dictionary of Etymology*

A CIP catalogue record for this book is available from the British Library.

ISBN 978 0550 14230 6

www.chambers.co.uk

Designed by Chambers Harrap Publishers Ltd
Printed and bound by CPI Group (UK) Ltd, Croydon CR0 4YY

Table of Contents

Preface to the Chambers edition

This *Dictionary of Etymology* was first published to critical acclaim as the *Barnhart Dictionary of Etymology,* and we are pleased to include it now as part of the authoritative range of Chambers dictionary and reference titles.

This dictionary was compiled over several years by a team of eminent scholars led by Robert K Barnhart. Their intentions were two-fold: to explain where English words come from and how they have changed over time, and to do so in such a way that the subject may be understood by those with no specialized knowledge of linguistics or language study. Thus this *Dictionary of Etymology* is for everyone interested in the history of the English language; it is an essential work of reference for scholars and students, and a fascinating work of reference for the general reader.

The Editor
Chambers Dictionaries

Preface

The *Barnhart Dictionary of Etymology* records the roots of our language and shows its many points of contact with the other cultures from which it has absorbed new words and new ideas. It is truly an American reference work not only because it pays particular attention to the American aspect of semantic development of English words but also because it bases much of its material on points of view developed by American scholars. This is the first dictionary of etymology to be produced by an editorial staff in collaboration with American scholars from various fields of language study.

Explanations about the development of particular words in a language are probably as ancient as language itself. In western Europe such explanations occur in the writings of Aristotle, Plato, Cicero, and Varro. Though the ancients apparently held many misconceptions about language development, among them that Latin was derived as a form of Greek, their fundamental interest in the workings of language is evidenced by the commentaries and grammars they produced. Even in Anglo-Saxon Britain, we find Ælfric's *Grammar* and *Colloquy*, which to this day remain clear statements of the study and acquisition of language.

In Middle English times men began to travel farther, to make new contacts with other cultures, and to write practical grammars that facilitated commercial contacts. Early glossaries found in Old and Middle English were succeeded by attempts to show the origins of many new words that were introduced into English in the 1400's to 1600's. The subject of etymology was considered on a consistent basis in Blount's *Glossographia* (1656), preceded by earlier works devoted to the subject, such as Minsheu's *Guide into Tongues* (1617), and by a sense of borrowing evident in Cawdrey's *A Table Alphabeticall* (1604) and the Latin-English dictionaries from *Promptorium Parvulorum* (1440) on. Linguistic awareness was so developed by the early 1600's that the languages of Europe had already been classified, although more by accident than systematic study. In the early 1700's the great philosopher Leibniz attempted an intuitive analysis that built a system of "linguistic genealogy," which in part paved the way for a more rational system of explaining relationships among languages.

Other scholars of the 1700's were comparing the structure of languages. Hiob Ludolf's work in Semitic is of particular interest, as is the later work of Samuel Gyármathi, who proved the relationship of Finnish and Hungarian. By 1786, when the English jurist and Oriental scholar Sir William Jones stated that Sanskrit "bears a stronger affinity [to Latin and Greek] both in roots of verbs and in forms of grammar, than could possibly have been produced by accident," ideas about language development and the relationships among various languages were already in the air.

Jones' remarks, based on his comparison of Sanskrit with Latin and Greek, and the work of Friedrich and August von Schlegel in the early nineteenth century, led to the further comparative studies among nineteenth-century philologists. Much of their work is concerned with the study of language development from a stock of reconstructed Indo-European ancestral word elements or roots.

This work and the early work of Rasmus Rask, Franz Bopp, and Jacob Grimm made it possible to systematize these explanations, which later reached their most comprehensive form in the etymology dictionary. Such books in English contain accumulated findings about language interpreted by various English-language scholars including Walter Skeat and James Murray in England and William Dwight Whitney in the United States. These men worked from the research of the comparative philologists and much of that research has further benefited from the findings and interpretations of linguistic scientists in the tradition of Edward Sapir, Edgar Sturtevant, Roland G. Kent, and Kemp Malone, and later specialists such as Zelig Harris, Yakov Malkiel, and Joseph Greenberg.

This dictionary is an interpretation of current scholarship, much of it based indirectly on their work. In specific instances not all of our conclusions represent agreed-upon knowledge, but the etymologies are formulated upon the standards and practices used in the working methods of most linguistic scholars today.

In our etymologies we have tried to forge a closer association between the elements of dating the first recorded appearance of a word and its semantic development and its development of form. We have also reexamined the function of affixation and of compounding. In both of these undertakings Professor Sherman Kuhn and his assistants on the *Middle English Dictionary* staff have provided generously of their time and help. In numberless instances the chronological record has been revised from that of the *Oxford English Dictionary,* drawing the year of first recorded appearance back sometimes as much as two to three hundred years. The existence and the sources of early compounds and the tracing of forms to Old English have also been improved by Professor Kuhn's work. As dictionary makers, we examined not only the extensions of semantic development and borrowing, but also the shift in function from noun to verb, adjective to noun, and so forth, and again the *Middle English Dictionary* provided a broad base of evidence that permitted a systematic study of this process.

So much of English, particularly from the 1500's and 1600's, is composed of many borrowings from Latin and French that one might be tempted to describe our language in very broad terms as having a largely Romance vocabulary built upon a Germanic structure. While such a statement does not take into account the Scandinavian element in English nor the elements from the Low Countries close to England, it is in large measure true of our vocabulary. And in studying the borrowing process of the Romance words in English we have been fortunate to have the guidance of Professor Ralph de Gorog.

In addition to Professor de Gorog's contribution, we have had the guidance of Professor Ralph L. Ward, who has worked out many of the problems in etymology for the Thorndike-Barnhart dictionary series. His study of Latin and of the borrowing processes from Latin into the Romance languages has made it possible to supply forms (especially in Gallo-Romance and Vulgar Latin) that have provided logical steps in tracing many derivations.

Beyond the Romance and Latin borrowings into English, Professor Ward has also reconstructed the Proto-Germanic forms for native words and supplied Indo-European roots. For native English words, reconstruction of the Proto-Germanic forms makes it possible to show the underlying relationships among the Germanic cognates. The inclusion of cognates in Germanic languages, especially those cognates obviously related in form and meaning, demonstrates that English is a Germanic language. Cognates outside Germanic reinforce the Indo-European character of English. Precisely because English has borrowed so extensively from Indo-European languages outside Germanic, it is useful to show the relationship of English vocabulary development to the non-Germanic languages.

Cognates may also show that many developments of meaning are not inventions of English alone and that meanings in English may even derive from senses in other languages long after the word itself was originally borrowed into English. If, for instance, certain of the Germanic cognates are old enough, some words in Old English may actually have derived from them, originally brought to England by the "Continentals" (Angles, Saxons, or Jutes). The processes of borrowing and the relationships to the cognates emphasize the fact that communication as a human enterprise is based upon previous linguistic experience.

In this dictionary, two articles about language development discuss these processes. Professor Ward explains the application of the cognates, the Proto-Germanic forms, and the

Indo-European roots to the study of the development of English. In a history of English, Professor Einar Haugen explains the various events and influences that have affected the language. His remarks relate language processes to the cultural background against which change in the English language has occurred. Though Professor Haugen's work on the Scandinavian element in English is markedly evident throughout this book, it is perhaps from his carefully constructed historical statement that most students will immediately benefit.

Many people contribute to the compiling of a reference book. Without the help of any single one, this book in particular could not have been completed. Probably no one has contributed more to the early drafts of the manuscript than Sol Steinmetz, who worked closely with Professor Ward and the late Dr. Reason A. Goodwin to carry out concepts that were gradually formulated into editorial policy.

The original conception of this dictionary was shared by two language scholars: my father, Clarence Barnhart, who is chiefly responsible for the application of principles of linguistic science to dictionary making; and Professor Kemp Malone, who wrote the first modern etymologies to appear in a general-purpose English-language dictionary.

For many years their ideas were developed by criticism and advice from a group of scholars that included Elliott V. K. Dobbie, Ralph L. Ward, Henry and Renée Kahane, Yakov Malkiel, A. E. Alexander, Harry Hoijer and many others. Now, with the efforts of The H. W. Wilson Company and particularly Bruce R. Carrick, the Editor of General Publications, who encouraged and nurtured this project, we have been able to draw this work into a finished form. Our aim throughout has been to make examples of the development of English an understandable subject for those with no specialized knowledge of language study. We also hope this work will serve as a ready reference for language scholars, and that it will contribute to greater interest in serious study of language, but our chief purpose remains to explain to students of English how our present-day language has evolved.

Robert K. Barnhart

Bronxville, New York

Editorial Committee of Contributing Scholars

RALPH PAUL de GOROG

Professor Emeritus of Romance Philology, University of Georgia; author of *The Scandinavian Element in French and Norman, La Sinonimia en La Celestina, Lexique français moderne-ancien français, Concordancias del Arcipreste del Talavera, Dictionnaire inverse de l' ancien français;* Member of the Editorial Board, *The Georgia Review*, and University of Georgia Press

EINAR HAUGEN

Victor S. Thomas Professor of Scandinavian and Linguistics, Emeritus, Harvard University; author of *Beginning Norwegian, Spoken Norwegian, Norwegian-English Dictionary, Life of Ibsen, The Norwegian Language in America: A Study in Bilingual Behavior, Bilingualism in America, The Ecology of Language*, and *The Scandinavian Languages: An Introduction to Their History;* past president of the American Dialect Society and the Linguistic Society of America, and member of the American Academy of Arts and Sciences

GARY B. HOLLAND

Assistant Professor, Department of Linguistics, University of California, at Berkeley; author of *Word Order Change in Indo-European* (forthcoming 1987–88); also contributor of numerous articles on topics in Indo-European linguistics, among them: "Word Order Change: Typology vs. Reconstruction" (1984), "Nominal Sentences and the Origin of Absolute Constructions in Indo-European" (1984), "Transitivity, Causativity, and Surface Case in Old Norse" (1987), and "The Relative Chronology of the Indo-European Relative Stems **kwi*- and **yo*-" (1987).

SHERMAN M. KUHN

Professor Emeritus of English, University of Michigan; Editor Emeritus of the *Middle English Dictionary* and former Editor-in-Chief. Editor, *The Vespasian Psalter*, 1965; author of *Studies in the Language and Poetics of Anglo-Saxon England;* member of the Advisory Board, *Michigan Germanic Studies;* Fellow of the Medieval Academy of America and Dictionary Society of North America.

—assisted by

DAVID RUDDY, Department of English Language and Literature (Medieval Studies), University of Michigan

MICHAEL DELAHOYDE, Department of English Language and Literature (Middle English Literature), University of Michigan

RICHARD SMITH, formerly of the Department of English Language and Literature, University of Michigan

RALPH LAWRENCE WARD

Professor Emeritus of Classics, Hunter College, City University of New York; formerly Director, Master-of-Arts Program in Linguistics. Co-author, with Henry and Renée Kahane, of *Spoken Greek;* consultant in etymology to the Thorndike-Barnhart dictionary series

Original Committee of Contributing Scholars

ELLIOTT V. K. DOBBIE
Formerly Professor of English, Columbia University

C. WILLIAM DUNMORE
Formerly Associate Professor in Classics, University College, New York University

F. F. FALES
Formerly Associate Professor of Romance Languages, Queens College, New York

JOSEPH H. GREENBERG
Professor of Anthropology, Stanford University

HARRY J. HOIJER
Formerly Professor of Anthropology and Sociology, University of California, at Los Angeles

ROMAN JAKOBSON
Formerly Professor of Slavic Languages, Literature, and General Linguistics, Harvard University, and Institute Professor, Massachusetts Institute of Technology

GEORGE A. KENNEDY
Formerly Director, Institute of Far Eastern Languages

ALO RAUN
Professor of Uralic and Altaic Languages, Indiana University

BENJAMIN SCHWARTZ
Formerly Chairman, Classics Department, Lincoln University

Editorial Staff

Managing Editor:
Sol Steinmetz
General Editors:
Cynthia A. Barnhart
Benjamin B. Normark
Senior Associate Editor:
Anne L. Bartling
Associate Editors:
Carol Braham
Gerald Dalgish
George S. Waldo

Assistant Editors:
Shirley Abramson
Maria Bastone
Rowena Summers Fenstermacher
Editorial Assistants:
Maria Aiello
Katherine E. Barnhart
Rebecca L. Barnhart
Julie Van Brocklin
Office Assistant:
Albert S. Crocco

Explanatory Notes

This dictionary traces the origins of the basic vocabulary of modern English. It contains over 30,000 entries, more than twice the reported vocabulary of Shakespeare, who was writing in the first period of modern English. The dictionary examines not only the antecedents of modern English, but emphasizes its development, especially from the point of view of American English.

Articles and Glossaries

Two scholars have contributed special articles to this book. Einar Haugen has written a "Short History of the English Language," that will serve as background against which specific cultural influences in an entry can be compared. Ralph L. Ward has provided a "General Statement of Proto-Germanic Forms and Indo-European Roots," which will aid the student in assessing the relationship of reconstructed forms with known historical materials.

Two glossaries are included. One lists language names and terms used in the etymologies. The second glossary consists of a list of titles of early literary sources cited in the dictionary to give the reader some idea of the context of a word's first recorded appearance in English. Sometimes only the author is cited, especially where a word is confined to the minor works of an author, or conversely is found throughout an author's writings.

Dates of Words and Meanings

Every word and meaning entered in this dictionary is given the year of its earliest recorded appearance or use as far as the editors and critics can ascertain. We consulted not only historical dictionaries (and general-purpose dictionaries of the 17th, 18th, and 19th centuries) but the Barnhart files of citations as well and the *Middle English Dictionary* (*MED*) made accessible by its editors.

In using the carefully framed system of dating in the *MED* we have substituted the word *probably* for their question mark, and cited the presumed date of composition whereas the *MED* gives both the date of composition and the date of the manuscript used by the *MED* editors.

The dates in most cases probably show no more than relative occurrence in English, and in other cases may be no more than an accident of the record. In many sources where citations from early writings were found by reading only odd or even pages or half pages, we have a very imperfect record of English; despite such practice, English remains the best recorded language.

Development, Borrowing, and Word Formation

An important feature of this dictionary is the distinction drawn between development within English and borrowing from other languages. Sometimes native words have been influenced in their development by the existence of words in neighboring languages (e.g., *bush* and *she*), and sometimes they have even been reinforced or revived by the existence of foreign terms (*atone* and *capon*). In either case, for the most part the distinction between foreign and native elements is maintained in this work. The editors have also taken into consideration the fact that many English words have been absorbed from more than one language, particularly when Medieval Latin flourished as the international language of Europe alongside the various national languages.

In addition to borrowing, many internal processes were at work in English that expanded its vocabulary. Among them, back formation played at least as prominent a part in forming new words earlier as it does today (as in *gyrate* from *gyration*). One of the contributions of this dictionary is to show the significant productive role played by back formation in creating new forms (*admire, assert, liberate,* etc.). Also carefully noted are the shifts in function from noun to verb, noun to adjective, verb to noun, etc., functional shift always having been an active process in English (even today we find this process in such a usage as "the book is a good *read*").

Diacritic Marks

Among the practices followed in this dictionary to account for the development of form and meaning is the use of diacritic marks, especially in Greek and Latin, where vowel quantity is phonemic. However, absence of such marking in Medieval Latin words is the result of its widespread use, as Medieval Latin became the common scholarly language of Europe and was known in the Near East, and was probably known even in parts of Asia and India. Consequently any marking of vowel quantities in Medieval Latin is only parochial.

Scandinavian Forms

Where borrowing into English comes from a probable Scandinavian source, relevant forms from Scandinavian languages (Swedish, Danish, Norwegian, Icelandic) are given. These words show several possible forms from which the English word may have been borrowed. In other instances words borrowed from Scandinavian and attributable to ancient formation are given in Old Icelandic, the classic literary language of the North, which is the language of record for the sagas and poetry.

Influence of Dutch and the Low Countries

Closely involved with Scandinavian loans is the borrowing from other Germanic languages, particularly of the coastal areas of the Continent near England. In the languages of Friesland and the Frisian Islands, the Netherlands, and the Low German areas, words are often similar to the Scandinavian forms, and it is sometimes difficult to determine whether an early borrowing is from Scandinavian or from one of the coastal languages. We have been mindful of the possibility of a greater influence of this cultural contact than others have in the past, especially by listing possible sources of borrowing among Frisian, Middle Dutch, and Low German cognates.

Development from Anglo-French

During the early years of the Middle English period, a dialect of Old French developed as the language of government, the law courts, and the social life of the new aristocracy. This became the dialect of the French residents in England and of their descendants and is designated *Anglo-French* (the French of England). Originally it was probably a dialect known as Old Norman French, spoken in Normandy by the gallicized Viking settlers who had not entirely given up their native Scandinavian dialects. It was also in part a mixture of other closely related dialects of the north French coastal region. We have, in so far as evidence shows, differentiated the antecedents of Anglo-French from Old French by using the term "Old North French" to indicate a basis for the French dialect brought to England.

French and Latin Borrowings

Both French and English have borrowed directly from Latin, and in this dictionary we have made a particular effort to show where the borrowing from Old and Middle French was probably augmented by direct borrowing from Latin, and similarly in French where learned borrowing took place directly from Latin.

French words in which regular phonetic development did not take place, and which are truly Latinisms, constitute a cultural group by themselves. These learned borrowings are important for the understanding of English vocabulary as they are the heritage of the age of the humanists.

The emphasis on Latin was evident in French and English before the 1300's but gained an increasing momentum in both languages after that time, gradually dying out in France towards 1550 but remaining as an active process in English throughout the 1600's. In French the trend was partly a result of the influence of literary Italian, and coincided with the spread of the Renaissance movement and its attendant admiration for the classical languages.

Where French did not adopt a form directly from Latin and the Old French word developed more or less regularly from a locally differentiated form of the Vulgar Latin of the late Roman Empire, we have tried to reconstruct the necessary hypothetical Gallo-Romance form. These phonetic and morphological conceptions explain the normal process of development of Latin into French and represent unattested Late Latin words which were probably limited to the territory of Gaul.

Replacement in English

In English much of the later borrowing from Latin, especially in the late 1400's through the 1600's, is often characterized as an attempt to "purify" the language by replacing what were considered corrupting influences, principally derived from adoption of French forms and the normalizing processes of Anglicization. In fact it was also perhaps originally as much the reflection of a desire to introduce familiar spellings (even to standardize spelling) by individuals who were more familiar with Latin than with English.

Whenever writers in English reached back into Latin for a new formation, a replacement occurred (e.g., *advance, advise, advocate*). The concept of replacement in the development of English often explains spelling changes that at first seem inconsistent by giving immediate evidence of the source of new spelling patterns. A replacement may also indicate continued or revived use of a word or even of an intellectual concept (e.g., *appreciation, fault, scent,* and *victuals*).

Doublets

In the process of borrowing, the factors of time and replacement of forms often resulted in a further association of terms known as doublets, which involve two or more related words in English. These are words of different form in English (such as *frail* and *fragile, forge* and *fabric*) that were derived from the same original source but came into English by different routes. Many doublets are marked in this dictionary and cross-referred to each other. While some reinforce the evidence of a learned borrowing, others illustrate the rules of phonetic change in borrowing through specific languages.

American English

Special emphasis in this work is placed on American English. Words or meanings that, as far as it is known, originated in the United States or are now commonly current only in the United States, are identified as American English. See, for example, such Americanisms as *amigo, ante-bellum, bobolink, boob, caballero, copacetic, dope, gobbledygook, icky, jambalaya, kibitz, lollygag, Mace, narc, O.K., shyster, smart aleck.*

Affixes and Combining Forms

Particular attention is given to word elements. We have separated and analyzed all living prefixes and suffixes in English and indicated combining forms where they appear. Sometimes this dictionary also includes word elements that are no longer active in word formation but are of particular interest. To the native speaker, many will seem obvious, but their systematic treatment reinforces the formative processes in English and explains their proper semantic function.

Where such derivatives are especially numerous, they are listed alphabetically, as under *out-*, *over-*, *psycho-*, *un-*[1], *un-*[2] and *under-*.

Cross References

This dictionary has a system of cross references that extends the association of cognates within a group of words and suggests some of the more remote connections of Proto-Germanic and Indo-European. Cross references are given in SMALL CAPITAL LETTERS. They deserve attention if the user is studying ultimate source as well as more immediate information.

Abbreviations and Symbols

As a rule, this dictionary does not use abbreviations beyond those for the parts of speech (*n.*, *v.*, *adj.*). The exceptions are references to a few scholarly books that were continuously consulted throughout the editing of this dictionary. While they are standard abbreviations for these works, a list appears below to avoid confusion.

DA	Dictionary of Americanisms (Mathews)
DAE	Dictionary of American English (Craigie and Hulbert)
FEW	Französisches Etymologisches Wörterbuch (von Wartburg)
MED	Middle English Dictionary (Kurath, Kuhn, Lewis)
OED	Oxford English Dictionary (Murray, et al.)
OEDS	Supplement to the Oxford English Dictionary (Burchfield)
Pok.	Indogermanisches Etymologisches Wörterbuch (Pokorny)

We have also eschewed the use of symbols except for the traditional asterisk (*) to indicate hypothetical forms. The chief function of hypothetical forms is to serve as a bridge in tracing an etymology. To be sure, a hypothetical form must be reconstructed by rules of sound change on the basis of parallel formations and other comparative evidence. It must also be of appropriate construction to fit logically as a missing link. The same is true of Proto-Germanic forms and Indo-European roots, whose reconstruction is discussed in Professor Ward's article.

Language Periods

The dates given to various periods in the history of a language are broad periods generally agreed upon by most scholars. By and large they indicate the end of one stage and the beginning of another in the development of a given language. Following are the dates of language periods frequently cited in this book (all the dates are A.D., except where noted; those in parentheses refer to dates preferred by some scholars):

Modern refers to the period in any language after the *Middle* period, except for Latin (called *New Latin*, see below) and Greek, where the accepted term before modern Greek is *Medieval Greek*.

Late refers to the language period following the Classical period of Greek and Latin and to the end of a language period such as Old English:

Late Greek 300–700
Late Latin 300–700

Middle refers to an intermediate language period before *Modern:*

Middle Dutch	1100–1500
Middle English	1100–1500 (1475)
Middle French	1400–1600 (1350–1600)
Middle High German	1100–1500 (1450)
Middle Low German	1100–1500 (1450)

Old refers to the earliest known or recorded period of a language:

Old English	before 1100
Old French	before 1400 (before 1350)
Old Frisian	before 1500
Old High German	before 1100 (before 1450)
Old Icelandic	before 1500 (from the Viking period to about 1300)
Old Provençal	before 1500 (before 1350)
Old Saxon	before 1100
Old Slavic	before 800
Anglo-French	1066–1400, but especially to about 1164
Greek	from Homer to A.D. 300
Latin, Classical Latin	200 B.C.–A.D. 300
Medieval Greek	700–1500
Medieval Latin	700–1500
New Latin	after 1500

Pronunciation

Since this dictionary will be used by students of language who have a certain familiarity with English, phonetic respellings are given (in parenthesis) only for hard or unusual words, occasionally for words with several pronunciations, and for pairs or a series of homographs with different pronunciations. The pronunciation system used in this dictionary was developed, under the guidance of Miles Hanley and a group of linguistic scholars, from the International Phonetic Alphabet for the Thorndike-Barnhart school dictionaries and is, in one form or another, found in most American, and some British, dictionaries today. The full key with traditional representation of the consonants and foreign sounds is given below.

COMPLETE PRONUNCIATION KEY

a	cap	h	he	ou	out	yu̇	uric
ā	face						
ã	air	i	pin	p	paper	v	very
ä	father	ī	five	r	run	w	will
		j	jam	s	say	y	yet
b	bad	k	kin	sh	she	z	zero
ch	child	l	land			zh	measure
d	did	m	me	t	tell		
		n	no	th	thin	ə	represents:
e	best	ng	long	ŦH	then	a	in about
ē	be			u	cup	e	in taken
ėr	term	′ o	rock	u̇	put	i	in pencil
		ō	go	ü	rule	o	in lemon
f	fat	ô	order, all	yü	use	u	in circus
g	go	oi	oil				

Foreign Sounds

Y as in French *lune*, German *süss*. Pronounce ē as in *equal* with the lips rounded as for ü, as in *rule*.

N as in French *bon*. The N is not pronounced, but shows that the vowel before it is nasal.

œ as in French *peu*, German *König*. Pronounce ā as in *age* with the lips rounded for ō as in *open*.

H as in German *ach*, Scottish *loch*. Pronounce *k* without closing the breath passage.

(The mark ′ is placed after a syllable with a primary or strong accent; the mark ′ after a syllable indicates a secondary or lighter accent in a multisyllable word).

Short History of the English Language

The etymology of a word is essentially an account of its history. The present book recounts what is known today about the history of the basic vocabulary of English. This history opens vast perspectives on the past, not only of the English-speaking peoples but also of the many others who have interacted with them. There are words that can be traced back thousands of years and others that sprang into being just yesterday. Everyday words are used quite unconsciously which, if their full stories were known, would reveal the panorama of the glory and the shame of the past, its fears and hopes, its prejudices and its faith.

The framework of our knowledge of language we owe to the diligent and sometimes inspired labors of *historical linguists,* or *philologists,* over the past two centuries. Through the pioneering work of such men as the Dane Rasmus Rask (1787–1832), and the Germans Jakob Grimm (1785–1863), and Franz Bopp (1791–1867), a discipline known as comparative philology (or linguistics) was born. Since their time the growing insights gained from the studies of hundreds of linguists have made it possible to place English in its proper relationship to the other languages of the world. One aspect of their work has been to compile etymological dictionaries, not only of English, but also of other languages. This dictionary is a continuation of that tradition, a distillation of many older scholars' detailed studies, and an explanation of how English has developed from Proto-Germanic and Indo-European to its present (and still changing) form.

The Tradition of Writing

English has been written only since about 700 A.D., when Roman missionaries introduced the Latin alphabet into Great Britain. The language of these early texts was formerly often described as *Anglo-Saxon*—since it was largely Angles and Saxons who became the English people—but is now more properly referred to as *Old English.* This language soon became quite distinct from the other Germanic dialects that followed divergent development on the Continent. In the eighth century the Anglo-Saxons suffered an invasion by their old northerly neighbors, the Vikings, Scandinavian marauders who overran the northern and eastern sections of England. Ultimately halted by an army of men from Wessex under King Alfred the Great, the invading Scandinavians in the course of time settled down with the natives in what became the Danelaw. Though the English language survived, its vocabulary absorbed numerous words from the invaders' Scandinavian dialects (*awkward, birth, egg, sky, thrive, window*). Not until the Norman Conquest, some 250 years later, in 1066, was the survival of English threatened. The use of the new invaders' native Old French dialect in government and literature brought the Old English period to a close.

Old English

Old English was a language of many dialects by the time of the Norman Conquest, but much of the surviving literature is found only in the West Saxon tongue. This includes such classics as the *Anglo-Saxon Chronicle,* the epic poem *Beowulf,* the shorter poems of the Battle of Maldon and of Brunanburh, as well as a host of Christian writings. Nevertheless, outside West Saxon, some of the finest writing is to be found in works of Caedmon and Cynewulf, in the Northumbrian dialect.

To modern users of English, the language of all of these texts seems strange and remote because of its older Germanic structure. In spite of obvious word elements that are a part of Modern English and loans that are recognizably Latin and Scandinavian forms, Old English has an outward appearance that resembles German or Icelandic. Nouns are inflected for four cases (nominative, accusative, genitive, dative) in the singular and plural in a variety of declensions. Every noun is also marked for gender (masculine, feminine, and neuter), which determines the form of accompanying articles and adjectives. Verbs are inflected for each person (first, second, third) of their subject in the singular and to some extent in the plural. Both nouns and verbs have *strong* and *weak* forms of their inflections.

However, there is abundant evidence that the inflectional system of Old English was beginning to break down some time before William of Normandy ever set foot on English soil. A certain simplification in verbal inflection had already occurred by then, and the complicated system of inflections of nouns and adjectives was beginning to break down. What the Norman Conquest did do was to eliminate the influence of the Anglo-Saxon upper classes, and in so doing, destroy many of the forces of language conservatism which tend to slow down linguistic change. In other words, the Norman Conquest accelerated the process of linguistic change that presumably would have occurred in any case.

Transition to Middle English

The end of the Old English period marked a great sea-change in English. The conquest by the Norman French imposed a new political and cultural life on the insular land of the Anglo-Saxons and dramatically altered the development of their language. After 1066, the Germanic language that was Old English was relegated to an inferior position. For three centuries it remained only the spoken tongue of the common people. Norman French was the language of supremacy: the power of the Court and its administration was expressed in a tongue foreign to the subject Anglo-Saxon citizenry. Likewise the Church, which continued to conduct all its affairs in Latin, was another "foreign" presence. Nevertheless, this grotesque situation greatly benefited the English language which, in a mostly unwritten form as the language of the common people, was gradually adapted to necessity and circumstance. Vocabulary swelled with borrowing that resulted from wider and closer contact with Old French and its Anglo-French dialect, and the structure changed with the gradual substitution of word order for inflectional endings. The language of Robert Mannyng, Geoffrey Chaucer, and John Gower reveal this process taking place in a language too deeply rooted to be replaced by French. These two languages operated in parallel for a long time, as French was the language of the law courts until 1362 and was still used widely for writing documents well past the 1450's.

The Middle English that emerged had lost most of the inflections of noun and verb, becoming much more like Modern English. Nouns had only the suffix *-s*, functioning both as a possessive and a plural (*boy's*, *boys*); verbs had only *-s* to mark the third person singular in the present (competing with *-th*) and an *-ed* or *-t* for the past tense (*wanted*, *swept*). There were still anomalies in both classes: such plurals as *men*, *mice*, or past tense verb forms like *thought*, *sang*, both reminders that English was still a Germanic language in structure. But the vocabulary was transformed as borrowing added a huge number of French and Latin loanwords to the old Germanic word stock. This process continued at an ever-quickening pace into early Modern English. There was no inner, linguistic necessity for this; Anglo-Saxon literature was at a high point prior to the Norman Conquest, and manuscript illumination and metalwork had achieved such a state of perfection that England became the training ground for many European apprentices.

The flowering of English through the borrowing process occurred as a consequence of two languages of different cultures in intimate day-to-day contact. In contrast, languages, such as German and especially Icelandic, have managed with much less outside influence to coin words from their native linguistic stock to satisfy their modern needs. For English the most marked result has been that, while retaining its Germanic structure, it acquired a large Romance element in its vocabulary and thereby assimilated a great deal from the Classical world, to become a more sophisticated and cosmopolitan language than it was before the Norman Conquest. Another and less favorable result has been a loss of predictability in its spelling, which now reflects numerous and conflicting spelling patterns. These developed from the often imperfect interpretations of English writers transcribing words from the various languages of borrowing. Thus many Old and Middle English spellings have been retained in the vocabulary (as in the *gh* of *dough*, *bough*, and *rough*) against all phonetic reason. In addition, the influence of French has left many ways to write the same sound, such as the sound traditionally represented by *sh—conscience*, *sure*, *ocean*, *machine*, *nation*, *tissue*, and *fuchsia*.

The Middle English of the 1300's and 1400's was still split into dialects of Northern or Northumbrian, Midland, Southern, and Kentish. But in the fifteenth century the center of English cultural and political life began to shift to London and its environs. This meant that the East Midlands exerted a new dominance in the history of English. London was the seat of the Court and the center of an expanding government; as the center of English commercial life, it attracted people from all parts of the country. Courtiers and civil servants became the élite whose fashion of speaking and writing was normative. Accents leveled out into a more or less standard form used by the gentry, but the cement that held English together was primarily its written form, which was more conservative than the spoken form.

Modern English

In the 1500's and 1600's, the introduction of printing democratized literacy within all language groups, and literary enterprise was no longer largely restricted to the scribes of the Church and Courts. Coupled with the intellectual enthusiasms of the Renaissance, printing forced attention to the written form of language and encouraged standardization. In English especially, the rediscovery of Classical literature and widespread familiarity with it among the intellectuals of the day led to the introduction of innumerable terms from Latin (and Greek) into the English of learned men. Although some contemporary critics regarded the plethora of Classical borrowings with much disfavor, calling the Latinisms "inkhorn terms" in reference to their somewhat self-conscious introduction into English, many of the terms were nonetheless accepted, adding richness and variety to the English vocabulary.

If Chaucer was the quintessential Middle English writer, then Shakespeare, by virtue of his creative use of the English vocabulary, must occupy a similar position during the Elizabethan period. He and other great stylists—Donne, Bacon, Sidney, Spenser, Raleigh, among others—produced a flowering of literature such as English had never before experienced. They made full use of the syntactical and grammatical resources that the language provided, often using forms that later ages have branded as "ungrammatical," such as the double negative. It was left to the 1700's, the "Age of Reason," to create an atmosphere where grammarians and lexicographers could achieve success in a campaign to standardize the language. The Italians and French had set up academies to regulate development of their languages, and under that influence many English writers (Dryden, Defoe, Swift, etc.) called for similar measures in England. As it turned out, the English "Academy" took the form of a dictionary, compiled by an individual, not by a government-sponsored committee. Samuel Johnson's great Dictionary of 1755, originally conceived as a prescriptive work, was adopted as a standard of acceptable English well into the nineteenth century.

One aspect of the language that resisted all standardizing and that no dictionary, in spite of the several attempts by Walker and Sheridan, could regulate, was pronunciation. From the Middle English period to the Modern, changes continued to occur which altered the relation of sound to symbol. In Old and Middle English the letters represented much the same sounds as in other European languages. But toward the end of the Middle English and well into the Modern period the long vowels changed drastically. This *Great Vowel Shift* was marked by a systematic series of changes in which the pronunciation of vowels resulted in the vowel system of Modern English. Old ī became *ai* as in *mine*, ū became *aw* as in *house* (from *hūs*), ē became the *i* of *machine* (as in *beet*) and ō became the *u* of *sue* (as in *boot*), while ā turned into *ey* (as in *mate*). The short vowels were more consistent with the past, but *a* shifted to *æ* (as in *can, chance*), with some examples restored to *ah* in London English (*chance, path*). Unstressed final *-e* (representing the sound of *a* in *sofa*) was lost in words such as *name, rate*, with the result that thousands of words which once had two syllables became monosyllabic in Modern English. Interestingly, the pronunciation of Latin by Englishmen followed the same path, so that in legal English we still have idiosyncratic pronunciations of *sine die, habeas corpus*, instead of the assumed classical sounds.

Though Modern English can be dated from 1500, the real expansion and extension of the language commenced in the 1700's. Even though English was largely standardized, its vocabulary did not remain static. Within England the language responded to the rapid proliferation of scientific and technological developments that led to the Industrial Revolution. One need only mention Sir Isaac Newton as a key to the spirit that resulted eventually in the thousands of words required to describe the new knowledge of the times. Physics and astronomy led the way in giving humanity an entirely novel view of the universe. Technological advances brought railroads and led to factories and machines and products that required naming. Outside the British Isles English spread with the voyages of discovery and the colonization of North America, Australia, South Africa, and dominion in India.

American English

The United States secured its political freedom from England in 1783, but in spite of independence and an open reception of immigrants from many other lands, America's language remained English. Though not precisely the English of England, American English did not depart in structure from its English model. The new nation's need to establish a separate identity did not go unnoticed, however. By 1813 Thomas Jefferson was admonishing his fellow citizens to create a "new language" fit for the new nation; he referred specifically to the need for a vocabulary that would describe the innumerable different aspects of the American landscape and social order. Old words were extended in meaning: the name *robin* was used for a bird that was not the same as the English robin. American Indian names were adopted for plants and animals, and words from the languages of other immigrants were borrowed. In addition, there were borrowings from the established vocabulary of the French explorers and traders who had preceded even the early colonists in their push West, as well as from the American Spanish of the southwest. The new *American English* was first recorded in 1828 by Noah Webster, who compiled a prescriptive American counterpart to Johnson's Dictionary, and the name Webster signified a standard of its own as the first fruits of American lexicography.

Webster's dictionary and spellers were significant in the standardization of American English through the schools. Printing had made the written form of English readily available. The common citizen learned to read and sent his children to school to follow suit. Both in England and America (and in western Europe generally) the nineteenth century was a time when reading and writing became a widely acquired accomplishment important to the dissemination of information and ideas. Development of a popular press and an increasingly rapid pace of scientific, social, and cultural advancement have accelerated the growth of English in the twentieth century. Modern inventions of travel and communication (the telephone and telegraph, automobile and airplane, radio, television, and satellite) have brought almost instantaneous contact and interchange of information. In this context, modern technology, because it is largely couched in American English, has assured American English of a major role throughout the world as a language of international communication, supplanting French which, in a much earlier era, replaced Latin.

The Roots of English

The English language is of course much more than its written tradition; it is first and foremost spoken, although the present-day emphasis on writing has caused many to forget the significance of speech. Every child learns to speak before he or she can read and write; most people spend a great deal more time talking than either reading or writing. A distinguishable form of English was spoken in Great Britain long before it was ever written, and we are fortunate in being able to trace the origins of English back far beyond the dawn of its writing. While all users of English read and write in much the same way, their speech may vary widely, and certainly deviates a great deal from what they read and write. Modern English speech obviously varies regionally by local dialects; but it also varies more subtly by social status: the "Cockney" London speech and the distinctive "Brooklynese" and "New Yorkese" of New York City are but a few examples. Similarly there are marked differences between British and American English, and within American English one distinguishes the New England dialect from Midwestern or Western and both from the Midland speech of Pennsylvania and western settlement areas, and all from Southern.

In spite of the variation in English, it is possible to trace much of the language back to its earliest known roots through the discipline of comparative linguistics. Built upon a study of the relationships between languages, comparative linguistics was in large measure founded by Sir William Jones. A distinguished English orientalist, Jones called attention to the kinship of Sanskrit and Old Persian to Greek and Latin and thence to English and other European languages. His observation, made in 1786, was of overwhelming importance to language studies by stimulating inquiry into the relationships between languages.

Once this astonishing relationship was recognized, it led scholars to the realization that most of the languages of Europe, and several in Asia, are apparently descended from a common ancestor, the Indo-European. It is not known exactly when or where this mother tongue was spoken, but it has to be older than the oldest known texts, which date as far back as 1700 B.C. (Hittite). The earliest writings are so distributed that they suggest an area in the Caucasus, straddling the Eurasian border.

The details that establish Indo-European as a family, and distinguish it from other families such as Semitic, Finno-Ugric, Sino-Tibetan, and Niger-Congo, are mainly the work of a great many nineteenth-century linguists, some mentioned earlier. These scholars determined that the relationships between the European languages could be stated in precise formulas reflecting their divergent development from common, primitive roots. Lacking a written record from so far back, the roots are hypothetical (and are generally so indicated by asterisks). Thus the originals of *father* and *mother* are **pəter* and **māter*. These original forms reflect Grimm's rule, based on the work of Rask, by which Grimm described the regular correspondence of consonants in the older Germanic languages and in Greek and Latin. He also postulated predictable changes in sounds from one Germanic language to another. Thus, we can derive English *father* from Old English *fæder* and English *mother* from Old English *mōdor* and relate these two to the corresponding Latin *pater* and *māter*. Beginning with the modern vocabulary, it is possible to thread through the series of variant forms and cognates to the original form and to account for most of the forms still retained by the languages of the Indo-European family. The line of descent goes from the (Proto-) Indo-European language to (Proto-) Germanic to West Germanic to Old English and on to Modern English, constituting an unbroken spoken tradition from the dim past of at least four thousand years ago to the English of today. There is no certainty about such roots, but they represent the best of our present-day knowledge in the judgment of the contemporary scholars who have contributed to this book.

It is important to understand that linguistic descent does not imply biological descent: only a tiny proportion of the present-day millions who speak English are descended from the original Indo-Europeans. As we have seen, English has also been enormously affected in its development by many languages with which it has been in contact. Language contact (either face-to-face contact or indirect contact through the written word) has made English a singularly heterogeneous language, in which the majority of its words have been borrowed and are not lineally descended from earlier native forms. The most important sources of borrowing have been Old and Middle French, Latin, and Greek, as well as the early infusion from the Scandinavian languages. Almost by historical accident, the Indo-European element has been strengthened in English, because many such words that are lost in Germanic have been restored in English by borrowing from other members of the Indo-European family.

Borrowing is a more haphazard process of vocabulary development than lineal descent within a family, but insofar as external factors induce borrowing, the resulting forms are relatively predictable.

Those branches of Indo-European that are still represented in one or more languages are Indo-Iranian (Sanskrit, Hindi-Urdu, Iranian), Greek, Armenian, Balto-Slavic (Lithuanian-Latvian, Polish, Ukrainian, Russian, Czech), Albanian, Celtic (Irish, Welsh, Gaelic, Breton), Italic (Latin and its Romance descendants, Italian, Spanish, Portuguese, French, Romanian), and Germanic (English, German, Dutch-Flemish, Icelandic, Norwegian, Swedish, Danish). In recent times two extinct Asian languages also have been recognized as members of the Indo-European family: Hittite and Tocharian. Whenever any of these have influenced English or show a direct or parallel relationship to the development of a word in English, their forms are included in the etymologies given in this book, so that the evidence of their ultimate contribution to the English of our times is available for comparative study.

Any dictionary of etymology is to a great extent the by-product of language studies, a compilation of the research of many linguistics scholars. The work in Indo-European etymology is particularly widespread, and the scholarship over the years has been an international enterprise. Among the scholars who have contributed most extensively to that knowledge are Karl Brugmann (1849–1919) of Germany, Antoine Meillet (1866–1936) of France, Julius Pokorny (1887–1970) of Germany, and Jerzy Kurylowicz (1895–1978) of Poland. An account of this and other work in Comparative Linguistics is to be found in Holger Pedersen's *Linguistic Science in the Nineteenth Century* (1924; reissued as *The Discovery of Language* 1962).

A discussion of Indo-European roots and Proto-Germanic forms in the context of this etymological dictionary is found in Professor Ward's statement.

Einar Haugen

Harvard University

Proto-Germanic and Indo-European

Scholars in Romance linguistics have long traced back related cognates (such as Italian *figlio* "son," Spanish *hijo*, Portuguese *filho*, Old French *filz*) to an attested Latin original (in this case *filius*); where no (satisfactory) Latin original was to be found, they have quite legitimately resorted to reconstructing a Vulgar Latin source, such as **pariculus* for Italian *parecchio* (usually plural *parecchi* "some"; in Old Italian "similar"), Spanish *parejo* "similar," Provençal *parelh*, French *pareil* (historically a diminutive of Latin *pār*, genitive *paris* "equal").

Reconstructing Proto-Germanic

Students of the Germanic languages, wishing similarly to get back to an original for a set of cognates (say, Old High German *lōh* "a clearing," Middle Low German *lōch* "a stretch of low-bush country," Old English *lēah* "open land, meadow"—all these being masculine) can provisionally arrive at the Proto-Germanic stem **lauH-*, but not feel fully confident of the

TABLE 1: THE SOUNDS OF PROTO-GERMANIC

Vowels:

	short			long		
	i		u	ī		ū
		e			ǣ	ō
		a				

(Note: Proto-Germanic had also a long, close ē of very rare occurrence, as in Old English *hēr* "here.")

Diphthongs:	ai	au
		eu

Consonants:	*labial*	*dental*	*velar*	*labiovelar*
stops	p	t	k	kw
	b	d		
spirants	f	th	H	Hw
	ƀ	đ	ʒ	ʒ^{w}
		s		
		z		
nasals	m	n	ŋ	
liquids				l, r
semivowels	w		j	

Note the absence of *g* (i.e. a hard velar stop) from the repertory of Proto-Germanic stops. Though the former ʒ may have hardened into a *g* earlier in some positions (e.g. initially, or after ŋ) than in others, such hardening probably took place only later in the history of the individual languages. In Dutch the *g* is still a voiced (or half-voiced) velar spirant; while in English such words as *yellow* have a *y* from an earlier palatal spirant.

whole Proto-Germanic word without adducing cognates from other Indo-European languages, namely Latin *lūcus* (Old Latin accusative *loucom*) "grove," and Lithuanian *laũkas* "field": hence Proto-Germanic **lauHaz*, from Indo-European **loúkos*; Sanskrit *loká-s* "space, world" would demand a variant **loukós*. Note, in this reconstruction (See Table 1), that, of the three *u*-diphthongs of Indo-European (*eu*, *au*, and *ou*), only the *ou* (i.e: **loukos*) is available here, since the Germanic cognates cannot call for *eu* (which would have yielded Old High German *io* and Old English *ēo*), and Latin *lūcus* cannot call for *au* (which would have remained Latin *au*). Note also how Indo-European short *o*, whether as a separate vowel or as part of a diphthong, became Proto-Germanic short *a*; how, as part of Grimm's Law (See Table 4), the Indo-European velar *k* became the Proto-Germanic spirant *H* (as in Scottish *loch* or German *ach*); and how, as affected by Verner's Law (See Table 5)—i.e. when the original accent did not fall on the next-preceding vowel—the earlier Proto-Germanic voiceless spirant *s* became the later Proto-Germanic voiced spirant *z*.

The fact that *sound correspondences are regular* makes all work in historical and comparative linguistics possible; stated in another way, when a given phonetic change occurs in a certain language or dialect it affects all words of identical structure. Until this principle was grasped and applied, few persuasive or convincing etymologies were attainable; of course, to be satisfactory, etymologies must also meet the criterion of being plausible as regards meaning and changes of meaning.

As to the approximate date of Proto-Germanic we may refer to Eduard Prokosch's *Comparative Germanic Grammar* (Philadelphia, 1939, p. 26) for the statement, "Shortly before the beginning of our era, the Germanic group appears to have been a fairly homogeneous linguistic and cultural unit. This is the period that is termed *Urgermanisch*, Primitive [we should say Proto-] Germanic."

Reconstructing Indo-European

The relative abundance of documents and recorded forms of ancient and medieval languages stretching all the way from Ireland to India (and indeed to Chinese Turkestan for Tocharian) and the inspired and patient work of a multitude of scholars have made possible the substantially accurate reconstruction, over the course of the last two hundred years, of an astonishing number of words of the ancient parent language, Indo-European, the date of whose unity can hardly be later than 3000 or 4000 B.C. in view of the fact that some documents of the Hittites in Asia Minor go back to the 1700's B.C.

TABLE 2: THE SOUNDS OF INDO-EUROPEAN

Vowels:

	short	long
	i e ə, e a o u	ī ē ā ō ū

Vocalic liquids and nasals:

	short	long
	l̥, r̥ m̥, n̥	l̥̄, r̥̄ m̥̄, n̥̄

Consonants:	*labial*	*dental*	*palatal*	*velar*	*labiovelar*	
stops	p, ph	t, th	k̂, k̂h	k, kh	kw, kwh	
	b, bh	d, dh	ĝ, ĝh	g, gh	gw, gwh	
spirants		s				
		z				
nasals	m	n		ŋ		
liquids						l, r
semivowels	w		y			

A couple of examples, one simpler, one more complex, illustrate the method of reconstruction pursued. (1) Greek *agrós* "field, country" (in contrast to city), Latin *ager* (genitive *agrī*), Sanskrit *ájra-s* "open country," Gothic *akrs*, Old English *æcer* (Modern English *acre*), from Indo-European **aĝros*. Here the first consonant must have been a palatal *ĝ*, for a velar *g* would have yielded Sanskrit *g*; either guttural, by Grimm's Law, would have yielded the *k* of the Germanic (Gothic and Old English) words. Greek faithfully keeps the *o*-vowel, while Sanskrit changes it to *a*. Final syllables are subject to considerable loss or change: Latin *ager* has grown from earlier **agerr*, from still earlier **agr̥s*, like Gothic *akrs* from earlier **akraz* (whose final *s* had changed to *z* by Verner's Law, after an unaccented vowel); Old English *æcer* has undergone a similar development, after losing the Proto-Germanic final syllable *az*. Note that since Sanskrit *ájra-s* has accent on one syllable and Greek *agrós* on the other, we have no way to determine where the Indo-European accent originally fell.

(2) Sanskrit *śatá-m* "hundred" (in form, a neuter singular), Avestan *satəm*, Greek *hekatón*, Latin *centum*, Old Irish *cēt*, Welsh *cant*, Gothic *hund*, Lithuanian *šim̃tas*. Here (putting aside for the moment the curious *he-* of the Greek word), the first consonant must have been a palatal *k̂*, to have given Sanskrit *ś*, Avestan *s*, and Lithuanian *š*, while by Grimm's Law the *k̂* would have yielded Gothic *h*. The great Karl Brugmann was the one who established that the correspondence of preconsonantal Sanskrit *a*, Greek *a*, Latin *en*, Old Irish *ē*, Welsh *an*, Gothic *un*, and Lithuanian *in* (as in *mintìs* "thought") represented Indo-European vocalic *n̥*, but that where the Lithuanian shows *im*, as in *šim̃tas*, Indo-European had vocalic *m̥*. With the exception of Gothic *hund*, all the cognates point immediately to Indo-European *t* as the consonant following the vocalic *m̥*. By Grimm's Law every *t* of Indo-European first developed into voiceless *th* (as in Gothic *threis* "three" beside Sanskrit *tráyas*, from Indo-European **tréyes*). But now, as proved by the accents of Sanskrit *śatá-m* and Greek *hekatón*, Verner's Law came into play, by which, if the Indo-European accent did not come on the next-preceding vowel (or vocalic element), a voiceless spirant of Proto-Germanic turned into the corresponding voiced spirant—hence the changes from Indo-European **k̂m̥tóm* to early Proto-Germanic **Humthám* to later **Hunđán*, whence Gothic *hund*. As for Greek *he-katón*, its *he-* is a prefixal form of *hén* (neuter) "one"—thus one hundred, with the vowel color of the prefix altered (by influence of *hén*) from earlier **ha-*, from Indo-European **sm̥-* (zero grade of the neuter **sem* "one"); compare Sanskrit *sa-hásra-m* "one thousand."

As users of this dictionary will observe, a great many of the English words etymologized here are traced back to one or more of the Indo-European forms or roots systematically listed in Julius Pokorny's standard work, *Indogermanisches Etymologisches Wörterbuch* (abbreviated Pok., followed by the page number under which the indicated form or root is found).

In this work of Pokorny's, designed primarily for scholars but not beyond the capacity of anyone interested in languages, all the comparative vocabulary of the Indo-European languages is listed under an alphabetical series of reconstructed roots. For example, the first of the two items discussed above is found in Pokorny on page 6 under the heading *aĝ-ro-s*, glossed as "field, meadow" and parenthetically linked to the root **aĝ-* "to drive" (page 4), with the original sense of "place where cattle are driven; pasture, meadow." (For the semantics here, compare German *Trift* "pasture, cattle run" with the related verb *treiben* "to drive".) This general statement is followed by a full list of the forms in the cognate languages from which the Indo-European **aĝ-ro-s* was reconstructed.

Similarly, the second example listed above is found in Pokorny under the form **k̂m̥tóm* (on page 192), glossed as "hundred" and derived from earlier **dk̂m̥tóm*, a derivative of **dék̂m̥* "ten" (page 191).

Derivatives of roots are also listed in Pokorny, using a systematic terminology for the various forms, especially those involving ablaut or vowel gradation. Ablaut is usually divided into *Abstufung* or quantitative gradation of vowels (on the one hand, lengthened as opposed to normal; on the other hand, reduced or even lost), and *Abtönung* or their qualitative gradation (in Indo-European, typically *o*-color as opposed to *e*-color). Over the long history of Indo-European as an evolving language there was ample time for varying conditions of accent. Many believe that both *Abstufung* and *Abtönung* could have arisen under an original system of stress accent. Be that as it may, at the end of the Indo-European period the accent of the language had surely become one of pitch, to judge from the striking absence of syncope from any inherited syllables of Sanskrit or Greek words. It will now be useful to illustrate the Indo-European ablaut system with derivatives of the root **bher-* bear, carry (See Table 3).

TABLE 3: INDO-EUROPEAN ABLAUT GRADES

Lengthened:	*bhēr-*	*Lengthened ō:*	bhōr-
Gothic	*bērusjōs* parents	Greek	*phṓr* thief
		Latin	*fūr* thief
Normal:	*bher-*	*Short o*:	*bhor-*
Greek	*phérein* carry	Greek	*phóros* tribute
Latin	*ferre* carry	Sanskrit	*bhára-s* booty
Sanskrit	*bhárati* carries		
Gothic	*baírith* carries		
Reduced:	*bh*$_e$*r-*		
Greek	*pharétrā* a quiver		
Zero:	*bhr̥-*		
Sanskrit	*bhr̥tí-s* a carrying, support		
Latin	*fors* (ablative *forte*) chance, accident		
Gothic	*ga-baúrths* birth		
	bhr-		
Greek	*dí-phr-o-s* chariot (a "two-carrier" for a combatant and his driver)		

The outline formulations given below are included for purposes of reference, because one can understand the peculiar consonantism of Proto-Germanic (and therefore of English) only by constantly bearing in mind the details of Grimm's and Verner's Laws.

TABLE 4: GRIMM'S LAW

Indo-European stops	became	Proto-Germanic spirants
p		f
t		th
k̂, k		H
kw		Hw
voiced stops	became	voiceless stops
b		p
d		t
ĝ, g		k
gw		kw
stops	became	spirants
bh		ƀ
dh		đ
ĝh, gh		ʒ
gwh		ʒ^w

TABLE 5: VERNER'S LAW

When the (Indo-European) accent did not fall on the next-preceding vowel, Proto-Germanic

voiceless spirants	became	voiced spirants
f		ƀ
th		đ
s		z
H		ʒ
Hw		ʒ^w

Shelter Island, New York

Ralph L. Ward

A

a, a form of the indefinite article before words beginning with consonant sounds, including sounded *h* (as in *a hotel*). *A* is a reduced form of *an* (from Old English *ān* one); the process of losing the nasal sound began before 1160, perhaps as early as 1130. The *n* was frequently lost before sounded *h* in the 1300's and 1400's.

The development of the forms *a/an* has occurred in south German dialects and also in Yiddish, quite independently of any contact with English. The distribution is the same as in English, *a* before a word beginning with a consonant sound, *an* before a word beginning with a vowel sound. And *an* is in these other dialects a development of the numeral *one* as well.

a-[1] a prefix forming adjectives and adverbs from nouns, as in *abed, afire,* especially verbal nouns, as in *a-hunting.*

The prefix is a survival of a low-stressed variant *a* of the Old English preposition *on* (or *an*) meaning on, in. Occasionally in late Old English and commonly in Middle English this *a* occurred in prepositional phrases such as those which developed into the compounds (in modern form) *alive, afloat, afield, asleep,* and the like. As *a* dropped out of use as a preposition (separate word), it survived in special uses, one of which is the prefix in these compounds.

a-[2] a prefix in a few words of Latin origin as a variant of *ab-*[1] from, away from. Latin *ā-* replaced *ab-* before *m-, p-,* and *v-,* and in English this *a-* is seen in *avert* and related words.

a-[3] a prefix taking the place of *ad-* to, toward, in words of Latin origin, especially before *sc-, sp-,* and *st-,* as in *ascribe, aspire, astringent.*

a-[4] a prefix having the general meaning of not, without, lacking, as in *apolitical* (= not political), *atonal* (= without tone). It has the form *an-* before vowels.

The prefix *a-* came into English from Greek *a-, an-,* meaning not, without, and is found in words taken directly, or through Latin, from Greek, as in *amorphous* (Greek *ámorphos* without form), *anonymous* (Greek *anṓnymos* nameless), and *apathy* (Greek *apátheia* lack of feeling). As a naturalized English prefix, *a-* is also found in new formations, such as *amoral, asocial,* and *areligious.*

The Greek prefix is called "alpha privative" from *alpha,* the name of the Greek letter corresponding to our letter *a,* and *privative,* meaning "taking away, depriving." It is cognate with Sanskrit *a-, an-,* Latin *in-,* and English *un-,* from Indo-European **n̥-* (Pok.756).

In English the form *a-* occurs before *h-* in a new coinage, as in *ahistorical;* in Greek an initial *h-* (the "rough breathing") was dropped and the prefix was *an-,* as in *anaimíā* bloodlessness (from *haîma* blood) which came into English as *anemia;* but the *h-* is sometimes restored by analogy with English words with *h-* of Greek origin, as in *anhydrous* (from Greek *ánydros* waterless, from *hýdōr* water), patterned after *hydrous.*

a-[5] a prefix marking an act as momentary, as a single event, added to verbs, and found in such words as *alight*[1], *abide, arise, amaze, ashamed,* and *ago.* Old English *ā-* (originally *or-*), cognate with Old Saxon *ur-, ar-,* Old High German *ar-, ir-, ur-* (modern German *er-*), Gothic *us-, ur-,* meaning away, out, also usable as an intensive prefix. Old English *ā-* is an unaccented variant of accented *or-;* see ORDEAL. These prefixes are from Proto-Germanic **uz-,* Indo-European **us-* from still earlier **ud-s,* an extension of **ud* OUT (Pok. 1103).

A 1 or **A-1** *adj.* first-class, excellent. 1837, in Dickens' *Pickwick Papers;* originally a symbol used by Lloyd's of London, a marine insurance corporation, to denote ships in first-class condition, *A* denoting the hull and *1* the stores of the ship. Popular at first among merchants, meaning of the highest commercial credit, *A 1* was further extended to signify excellence in general.

aardvark (ärd′värk) *n.* a burrowing South African mammal. 1833, borrowed from earlier Afrikaans *aardvark,* meaning literally "earth pig," a compound of *aard* earth + *vark* pig. In modern Afrikaans the word is spelled *erdvark.* See EARTH and FARROW.

ab-[1] a prefix that entered English as a component of many words taken from Latin or French, and used also to some extent in forming words in English.

Latin *ab-* is a special use of the preposition *ab* (with variants *ā, abs*), meaning from, away from, an ancient Indo-European word cognate with English *of* and *off,* Old English *æf,* Greek *apó* from, Sanskrit *ápa* away, from Indo-European **ápo* (Pok. 53). Combined with a verbal stem Latin *ab-* adds meanings of separation, removal, motion away from, and the like. In these formations, the prefix has the form *ab-* before a vowel or *h,* as in *abhor* shrink from; *a-* before *m, p,* or *v,* as in *avert* turn away; and *abs-* before *c* or *t,* as in *abstract* draw out.

In a rarer instance, the prefix converted from a Latin phrase that keeps the underlying function of the preposition, along with its object. This is seen in the case of *aborigines,* which is possibly formed on the Latin phrase *ab orīgine* from the beginning.

In a few adjectives formed in English, *ab-* recalls its prepositional function of "away from" with an object. An example is *aboral* away from the mouth (antonym of *adoral* toward the mouth). Similar in force is *abnormal* (refashioned in English) deviating from the normal.

ab-[2] a form of the prefix *ad-,* meaning to, toward, before *b* in words of Latin or French origin, as in *abbreviate.* In words from Latin the form is due to the assimilation of the *d* to the following consonant (*b*).

aback *adv.* Probably before 1200 *abac,* in Layamon's *Chronicle of Britain* (later *abak*), developed from Old English (11th century) *on bæc* at or toward the back.

The idiom **taken aback** was originally a nautical term meaning (of a ship) caught by a head wind that presses the sails back against the mast. The figurative sense "caught suddenly by surprise" appeared in 1840 in Hood's *Up the Rhine.*

abacus (ab'əkəs) *n.* frame with beads for counting. Before 1387, in Trevisa's translation of Higden's *Polychronicon,* borrowed from Latin *abacus,* from Greek *ábax* (stem *ábak-* as in the genitive form *ábakos*) counting table; board sprinkled with fine sand for marking on. Possibly Greek *ábax* was borrowed from Hebrew *'ābhāq* dust.

abaft *prep., adv.* behind, aft. 1594, developed from Middle English *baft* behind, and the prefix *a-* on, on the model of adverbs like *about, around, aside. Baft* developed from Old English (before 800) *bæftan,* formed of *bi-* BY, + *æftan* AFT.

There is also before 1325 a Middle English word *obaft* from the phrase *on baft* or *of baft,* but there is a gap of almost three centuries between the examples of *obaft* and the earliest recorded example of *abaft,* which makes it doubtful that they are the same word.

abalone (ab'əlō'nē) *n.* shellfish of the Pacific coast. 1888, American English *abalone,* alteration of earlier (1850) *avalone,* borrowed from Mexican Spanish *aulone,* from Costanoan (an American Indian language of the California coast) *aūlun* red abalone.

abandon *v.* 1390 *abandonen,* in Chaucer's *Canterbury Tales;* borrowed from Old French *abandoner* leave to one's mercy or discretion, from *abandon* surrender, from the phrase *a bandon* at the power of (*a* at, from Latin *ad*) + (*bandon* power, jurisdiction, of Frankish origin and related to the source of BAN² edict). **—abandon** *n.* freedom from restraint. 1850, borrowed from modern French, from Old French *abandon.* The noun was a reborrowing of a word that existed in Middle English (probably before 1400) as *abandoun,* borrowed from Old French *abandon.* **—abandoned** *adj.* immoral. 1692, formed from English *abandon,* v. in imitation of modern French *abandonné* immoral, past participle of *abandonner.*

abase *v.* Alteration in 1539 (influenced by *base* ² low) of Middle English *abaishen, abassen* (before 1338, in Manning's *Chronicle of England*); borrowed from Old French *abaissier* bring low (*à* to, from Latin *ad-*) + (*baissier* make lower, from Vulgar Latin **bassiāre,* seen in Medieval Latin *bassus* low, humble; see BASE² low). **—abasement** *n.* 1561, formed from English *abase* + *-ment.*

abash *v.* About 1303 *abaishen, abassen* to lose one's composure, be upset, borrowed through Anglo-French *abaiss-,* from Old French *esbaiss-,* stem of *esbaïr,* also *esbaer* be astonished (*es-* out, from Latin *ex-*) + (*baïr, baër* to be open, gape; see BAY³ space, division). Related to ABEYANCE.

abate *v.* About 1300 *abaten,* borrowed from Old French *abatre, abattre* beat down, from Vulgar Latin **abbattere* (Latin *ab-* to, toward, variant of *ad-* before *b*) + (**battere,* from Latin *battuere* to beat). Related to BAT³ wink and BAT¹ stick.

The sense "to become less, diminish" appeared probably before 1325.

—abatement *n.* Before 1340, borrowed from Middle French *abatement,* from Old French *abatre;* for suffix see -MENT.

abbess *n.* About 1300 *abbesse,* borrowed through Old French *abbeësse,* from Late Latin *abbātissa,* feminine of *abbās* (stem *abbāt-* as in the genitive form *abbātis*). *Abbess* alternated with and finally replaced the earlier forms *abbatess* and *abbotess.* See ABBOT.

abbey *n.* About 1300 *abbeye,* borrowed through Old French *abaïe,* from Late Latin *abbātía,* from *abbās* (genitive *abbātis*). See ABBOT.

abbot *n.* About 1123, in the *Anglo-Saxon Chronicle,* Middle English *abbot,* also *abbat,* alteration of Old English (about 880, in Alfred's translation of Bede's *Ecclesiastical History*) *abbod,* also *abbad,* borrowed from Late Latin *abbās* (genitive *abbātis*), from Late Greek *abbâs,* from Aramaic *'abbā* father.

abbreviation *n.* Probably before 1425 *abbreviacioun* a shortening, borrowed through Middle French *abréviation* from Late Latin *abbreviātiōnem* (nominative *abbreviātiō*), from *abbreviāre* make brief (Latin *ab-* to, variant of *ad-* before *b* + *breviāre* shorten, from *brevis* short; see BRIEF); for suffix see -TION. **—abbreviate** *v.* Before 1425, possibly a back formation of *abbreviation,* or borrowed from Late Latin *abbreviātus,* past participle of *abbreviāre;* for suffix see -ATE ¹. Doublet of ABRIDGE.

abdicate *v.* 1541, borrowed from Latin *abdicātus,* past participle of *abdicāre* renounce, reject (*ab-* away + *dicāre* proclaim; see DICTION); for suffix see -ATE¹. **—abdication** *n.* 1552, borrowed from Latin *abdicātiōnem* (nominative *abdicātiō*) renunciation, from *abdicāre;* for suffix see -TION.

abdomen *n.* 1601, borrowed from Latin *abdōmen;* also known in 1541 from a translation by Robert Copland from the French. Perhaps the original meaning is concealment (of viscera); if so, the word is very likely derived from Latin *abdere* conceal (*ab-* away + *-dere* combining form meaning to put, place; see DO¹ perform). **—abdominal** *adj.* 1746, borrowed from New Latin *abdominalis,* from Latin *abdōminis* (genitive of *abdōmen*); for suffix see -AL¹.

abduction *n.* 1626, borrowed from Latin *abductiōnem* (nominative *abductiō*), from *abdūcere* lead away (*ab-* away + *dūcere* to lead; see TOW¹ pull); for suffix see -TION. **—abduct** *v.* 1834, probably borrowed from Latin *abductus.* Alternatively *abduct* may be a back formation in English from *abduction.*

aberration *n.* departure from an expected course. 1594, borrowed from Latin *aberrātiōnem* (nominative *aberrātiō*), from *aberrāre* wander away, go astray (*ab-* away + *errāre* wander; see ERR); for suffix see -TION.

abet *v.* About 1380 *abetten,* borrowed from Old French *abeter* (*à* to + *beter* hound on, from a Germanic source: 1) either Middle or Low Franconian *bētan* incite; compare Old English *bǣtan* to hunt, bait, or 2) Scandinavian, compare Old Icelandic *beita* cause to bite, from *bīta* to BITE).

Use in the sense of to instigate or encourage in a crime appeared in 1590, in Shakespeare's *Comedy of Errors.*

abeyance *n.* suspension. 1528, borrowed from Anglo-French *abeiance* (legal) expectation, from Old French *abeër* covet (*à* at, after + *beër, baër* to be open, gape expectantly; see ABASH).

abhor *v.* feel disgust for. Probably before 1425 *abhorren,* borrowed from Latin *abhorrēre* shrink away from in horror (*ab-* from + *horrēre* bristle with fear; see HORROR).

abide *v.* remain, endure. Probably before 1200 *abiden,* developed by fusion (about 1000) of Old English *ābīdan* remain, (*ā-* a-[5] + *bīdan*) and *abīdan* (earlier *onbīdan*) stay on, both compounds with *bīdan* stay, wait; see BIDE. —**abidance** *n.* 1647, formed from English *abide* + *-ance.*

ability *n.* Before 1398, in Trevisa's translation of Bartholomew's *De Proprietatibus Rerum,* Middle English *ablete,* borrowed from Old French *ableté.* The spelling *ablete* was replaced in Middle English in the 1400's by *abilite,* from Old French *habilité,* a learned borrowing from Latin *habilitātem* (nominative *habilitās*) aptitude, from *habilis* easy to manage, handy, see ABLE.; for suffix see-ITY.

The *h* in the Old French and Latin forms was never established in English, and though scholars, such as Bacon, More, and Hooker, tried to impose the Latin form, the case for initial *h* was dropped by the end of the 1600's.

abject *adj.* miserable. Before 1415, in Wycliffe's *The Lantern of Light,* Middle English *abiect, abject* outcast, wretched, borrowed from Latin *abjectus,* past participle of *abicere* throw away, cast off (*ab-* away, off + *-icere,* combining form of *jacere* to throw, cast; see JET[1] stream).

abjure *v.* reject solemnly. 1430, borrowed through Middle French *abjurer,* or directly from Latin *abjūrāre* deny on oath (*ab-* away + *jūrāre* swear; see JURY). —**abjuration** *n.* Before 1439, borrowed from Latin *abjūrātiōnem* (nominative *abjūrātiō*), from *abjūrāre;* for suffix see -TION.

ablation *n.* removal or wearing away. Probably before 1425, borrowed from Latin *ablātiōnem* (nominative *ablātiō*) a taking away, see ABLATIVE (def. 1); for suffix see -TION. —**ablate** *v.* 1902, back formation from *ablation.* This is a new formation of a word that was originally borrowed in the 1500's from Latin *ablātus* but became obsolete by the early 1600's.

ablative *n.* **1** (ab'lətiv) case in grammar, originally denoting the case of taking away. About 1434, in the Wycliffe Bible, borrowed from Middle French *ablatif* (feminine *ablative*), from Latin *cāsus ablātīvus* case of removal, once thought to be coined by Julius Caesar. The grammatical case that expresses direction from a place and derives its application from Latin *ablātus* removed, a form serving as past participle of *auferre* carry away (*au-* away, cognate with Sanskrit *ava-* away from, down; see AB-[1]) + (*ferre* carry; see BEAR[2] carry); for suffix see -IVE. The Latin past participle *lātus* (related to the perfect *tulī* I have borne) is from Indo-European **tl̥tós,* cognate with Greek *tlân* to bear, from Indo-European **telə-* (Pok.1060). **2** (ablā'tiv) a substance that ablates. 1959, formed from English *ablate* + *-ive.*

able *adj.* Probably about 1375, borrowed from Old French *hable, able,* from Latin *habilis* easily managed, held, or handled, from *habēre* to have, hold; see HABIT. The *h* of the Old French and Latin forms was never established in English, though Classical scholars tried to restore it in the 1500's and 1600's. In the 1400's *habile* was refashioned from Latin and is current today as a different form: *able* in modern use meaning capable, *habile* meaning skillful. Derivative forms, such as *habilitate* retain the *h; ability* has lost it.

-able a suffix freely forming adjectives from verbs, with a generally passive meaning "able, liable, fit, etc., to be ____ed" (as in *enjoyable* = able to be enjoyed, *breakable* = liable to be broken); in some older words it has an active meaning "able to ____" (as in *suitable* = able to suit); it is also used to form nouns meaning "giving or inclined to ____" (as in *pleasurable* = giving pleasure, *peaceable* = inclined to peace).

The suffix has only a superficial resemblance and no historical connection with the adjective *able,* although the latter undoubtedly has affected productivity of the suffix in English in such modern coinages as *jumpable, actable, actionable,* and even verbal phrases, such as *get-at-able.*

As a suffix *-able* came into the language in words from Old French, or directly from Latin *-ābilis.* In Latin the suffix is actually *-bilis,* which shows up in *-ābilis* in adjectives derived from verbs with infinitives in *-āre* (first conjugation) such as *amāre* to love: *amābilis* lovable. In other conjugations the form was *-ibilis,* English *-ible.* On that account, there has been uncertainty and competition between spellings in *-able* and *-ible;* the uncertainty was probably compounded by the extension of *-able* to verbs of all conjugations in French.

In English *-able* is the spelling when added to native English words. The general practice is to spell with *-ible* when the underlying verb is clearly derived from a Latin verb in *-ēre, -ere, -ire* (such as *terrible* (Latin infinitive *terrēre*) or from the past participle of such a verb *(permissible:* Latin *permissus,* past participle of *permittere).*

ablution *n.* a washing. About 1395 *ablucioun,* in Chaucer's *Canterbury Tales,* meaning cleansing of impurities, borrowed through Old French *ablution,* or directly from Latin *ablūtiōnem* (nominative *ablūtiō*) a washing away, from *abluere* wash away (*ab-* away + *-luere,* combining form of *lavere, lavāre* to wash; see LAVE); for suffix see -TION.

abnegation *n.* denial, renunciation. Before 1398 *abnegacioun,* borrowed from Late Latin *abnegātiōnem* (nominative *abnegātiō*), from Latin *abnegāre* refuse (*ab-* off, from + *negāre* deny; see NEGATE); for suffix see -TION. —**abnegate** *v.* 1657, possibly a back formation from *abnegation,* or borrowed from Latin *abnegātus,* past participle of *abnegāre;* for suffix see -ATE[1].

abnormal *adj.* Formed about 1835 from English *ab-* off + *normal.* Under the influence of Latin *abnormis* deviating from a rule (*ab-* off, away from + *norma* rule), *abnormal* outlived the now obsolete *anormal,* which came through French from Medieval Latin *anormalis* (Latin *ā-* away from + *normālis* NORMAL); for suffix see -AL[1]. —**abnormality** *n.* 1854, formed from English *abnormal* + *-ity.*

abode *n.* Probably about 1200 *abad;* later *abod* (probably about 1300) a stay, delay, continuance (verbal noun with the same vowel alternation as the past tense of *abiden* to abide, developed from Old English *ābīdan* ABIDE).

The extended meaning "habitual residence, dwelling" appeared in 1576.

abolish *v.* 1459 *abolisshen,* borrowed from Middle French *aboliss-,* stem of *abolir* to abolish, learned borrowing from Latin *abolēre* destroy, cause to die out, related to *abolēscere* die out (*ab-* off + *-olēscere,* as in *adolēscere* grow up; see ADOLESCENT); for suffix see -ISH[2].

abolition *n.* 1529, in Sir Thomas More's *Supplycacyon of Soulys,* borrowed through Middle French *abolition,* or directly from Latin *abolitiōnem* (nominative *abolitiō*), from *abolēre* destroy, ABOLISH; for suffix see -TION. —**abolitionist** *n.* 1788, in Thomas Clarkson's *Impolicy of the African Slave Trade,* formed from English *abolition* + *-ist.*

abominable *adj.* arousing disgust, abhorrent. 1340, in *Ayenbite of Inwyt,* borrowed from Old French *abominable,* and from Late Latin *abōminābilis* (from the stem of Latin *abōminārī* deplore as an evil omen; see ABOMINATION); for suffix see -ABLE.

An alternative spelling *abhominable* came into use in the 1300's because the word was thought to be derived from Latin *ab homine* inhuman, beastly; this spelling was gradually abandoned during the 1600's.

abomination *n.* object of intense aversion, feeling of disgust, vile action. About 1350, in *Midland Prose Psalter,* borrowed from Old French *abomination,* from Latin *abōminātiōnem* (nominative *abōminātiō*), from *abōminārī* deplore as an evil omen (*ab-* off, away from + *ōminārī* prophesy, foreboding, from *ōmin-,* stem of *ōmen;* see OMEN); for suffix see -TION. —**abominate** *v.* 1644, possibly a back formation from *abomination,* or borrowed from Latin *abōminātus,* past participle of *abōminarī;* for suffix see -ATE[1].

aborigines *n.pl.* the earliest inhabitants of a country. 1547, borrowed from Latin *Aborīginēs* the first inhabitants, especially of Latium, possibly formed from the phrase *ab orīgine* from the beginning. The tendency to regard this word as a normal English plural produced the singular **aborigine** (1858) by back formation. This form replaced the singular use of *aboriginal,* which appeared in the late 1700's and was used by Darwin and others as the singular for *aborigines. Aborīginēs* is a proper noun in early Latin histories. Perhaps it is an ancient tribal name altered by popular etymology. See ORIGIN.

abortive *adj.* Before 1382, in Wycliffe's translation of the Bible, borrowed from Latin *abortīvus* causing abortion, from *abortus,* past participle of *aborīrī* disappear, miscarry (*ab-* amiss + *orīrī* appear, be born, arise; see RISE); for suffix see -IVE. —**abort** *v.* 1580, borrowed from Latin *abortāre,* from *abortus,* past participle of *aborīrī.* —**abortion** *n.* 1547, borrowed from Latin *abortiōnem* (nominative *abortiō*), from *abortus,* past participle of *aborīrī;* for suffix see -TION. —**abortionist** *n.* 1872, formed from English *abortion* + *-ist.*

abound *v.* About 1325, borrowed from Old French *abunder,* learned borrowing from Latin *abundāre* to overflow (*ab-* off + *undāre* rise in waves, from *unda* a wave; see UNDULATE).

about *adv., prep.* Old English *abūtan* about 1000, in Ælfric's *Manual of Astronomy*). The form *abūtan* developed from earlier (about 880) *onbūtan* (*on* on + *būtan* outside of, a compound of *bī, be* by + *ūtan* outside, from *ūt* out. See BUT). In Old English *ymbe* and the compound *ymbūtan* served the function of about, around. *Onbūtan* meant on the outside of, but it changed in meaning as the original Old English words disappeared by the 1200's.

above *adv., prep.* Old English (about 896) *abufan,* reduction of earlier *onbufan* (*on* on + *bufan* over, a compound of *bī, be* by + *ufan* over, related to Old English *upp* UP). Old English *ufan* is cognate with Old Saxon *oƀan(a),* Old High German *oban(a)* (modern German *oben*), and Old Icelandic *ofan,* from Proto-Germanic **ufan-,* **uƀan-,* formed on the basic adverb represented by Old English *ufe-* and Gothic *uf* under, cognate with Greek *hypó* under and Sanskrit *úpa* towards, from Indo-European **úpo* (Pok.1106).

abrade *v.* 1677, borrowed from Latin *abrādere* (*ab-* off + *rādere* to scrape; see RAZE).

abrasion *n.* 1656, borrowed through French, or directly from Medieval Latin *abrasionem* (nominative *abrasio*) a scraping, from Latin *abrāsus,* past participle of *abrādere* scrape off; see ABRADE; for suffix see -SION.

abridge *v.* About 1303 *abregen* curtail, lessen, borrowed from Old French *abregier* or *abreger,* from Late Latin *abbreviāre* make brief. For an explanation of *-g-* in French *abréger* see ASSUAGE. Doublet of ABBREVIATE.

The sense "to make shorter, condense" appeared about 1384 in the Wycliffe Bible. —**abridgment** *n.* 1494, borrowed from Old French *abregement,* from *abreger;* for suffix see -MENT.

abrogate *v.* annul, repeal. 1526, in Tyndale's translation of the New Testament, verb use of earlier *abrogate* archaic adjective and participle borrowed before 1464 in Middle English as *abrogat* abolished, from Latin *abrogātus,* past participle of *abrogāre* (*ab-* away + *rogāre* propose a law, request; see RIGHT); for suffix see -ATE[1]. Middle English had a verb *abrogen* by 1427 borrowed from Old French *abroger,* but it seems to have died out quickly in favor of the form *abrogate.*—**abrogation** *n.* 1535, borrowed from Latin *abrogātiōnem* (nominative *abrogātiō*), from *abrogāre;* for suffix see -TION.

abrupt *adj.* 1583, broken away, borrowed from Latin *abruptus,* past participle of *abrumpere* break off (*ab-* off + *rumpere* to break; see RUPTURE).

The meaning sudden, hasty appeared in 1591, in Shakespeare's *1 Henry VI.*

abs- a prefix appearing instead of *ab-*[1] from, away from, before *c* or *t* in words of Latin or Latin and French origin, as in *abscond, abstract, abstain.*

abscess *n.* 1615, borrowed from Latin *abscessus* a going away; in medicine, a congestion, an abscess, from *abscessus;* (genitive *abscessūs*), from *abscess-,* stem of *abscēdere* withdraw (*abs-* away, variant of *ab-* before *c* + *cēdere* go; see CEDE).

abscond *v.* 1565, borrowed through Middle French *abscondre,* or directly from Latin *abscondere* hide, conceal (*abs-* away, variant of *ab-* before *c* + *condere* put together, store, from *con-* together + *-dere* put).

absence *n.* About 1380, in Chaucer's translation of Boethius' *De Consolatione Philosophiae,* borrowed from Old French *absence, ausence,* learned borrowing from Latin *absentia,* from *absentem* (nominative *absēns*), present participle of *abesse* be away; see ABSENT[1].

absent[1] (ab′sənt) *adj.* being away, not present. About 1382, in the Wycliffe Bible, borrowed from Old French, learned borrowing from Latin *absentem* (nominative *absēns*), present participle of *abesse* be away (*ab-* away + *esse* be, the source of English ESSENCE).

absent[2] (absent′) *v.* take or keep (oneself) away. Probably before 1400, in Chaucer's probable translation of *Roman de la Rose,* borrowed from Middle French *absenter,* learned borrowing from Late Latin *absentāre* cause to be away, from Latin *absentem* (nominative *absēns*), present participle of *abesse* be away; see ABSENT[1]. —**absentee** *n.* 1537, formed from English *absent*

+ *-ee.* —**absenteeism** *n.* 1829, formed from English *absentee* + *-ism.*

absinthe *n.* a liqueur flavored with wormwood. 1842, borrowed from French *absinthe,* learned borrowing from Latin *absinthium* the plant wormwood, from Greek *apsínthion,* of non-Indo-European origin.

In the sense of the plant, *absinthe* came into English from French before 1500.

absolute *adj.* free from defect; complete, perfect. About 1380, in Chaucer's translation of Boethius' *De Consolatione Philosophiae,* borrowed from Latin *absolūtus,* past participle of *absolvere* to set free, make separate or complete; see ABSOLVE.

absolution *n.* About 1200, *absolucion,* borrowed from Old French *absolution,* from Latin *absolūtiōnem* (nominative *absolūtiō*) completion, acquittal, from *absolū-*, stem of *absolvere,* see ABSOLVE; for suffix see -TION.

The Middle English spelling was replaced by a reborrowing from Latin *absolūtiōnem* sometime in the 1300's or, more likely, in the 1400's.

absolve *v.* Probably before 1425, borrowed from Latin *absolvere* to set free, acquit (*ab-* from + *solvere* loosen; see SOLVE).

absorb *v.* Probably about 1425, borrowed from Middle French *absorber,* refashioned from Old French *assorbir,* after Latin *absorbēre* swallow up (*ab-* from + *sorbēre* suck in, cognate with Greek *rhopheîn* sip up, from Indo-European **srebh-/srobh-/sr̥bh-;* Pok.1001). —**absorbent** *adj.* 1718, borrowed from Latin *absorbentem* (nominative *absorbēns*), present participle of *absorbēre;* for suffix see -ENT.

absorption *n.* 1597, borrowed from Latin *absorptiōnem* (nominative *absorptiō*) a sucking in, from *absorbēre;* see ABSORB; for suffix see -TION.

abstain *v.* About 1380, Middle English *abstenen, absteynen,* borrowed from Old French *abstenir,* learned borrowing from Latin *abstinēre* withhold (*abs-* away, variant of *ab-* before *t* + *tenēre* to hold; see TENANT).

abstemious *adj.* 1610, in Shakespeare's *The Tempest,* borrowed from Latin *abstēmius* (*abs-* off + **tēmus,* base of *tēmētum* intoxicating drink); for suffix see -OUS.

abstention *n.* 1521, act of withholding, borrowed from Middle French *abstention,* from Late Latin *abstentiōnem* (nominative *abstentiō*), from Latin *absten-*, stem of *abstinēre* withhold; see ABSTAIN; for suffix see -TION.

The meaning act of abstaining or refraining appeared between 1624 and 1647, in Bishop Hall's *Works.*

abstinence *n.* 1340, in *Ayenbite of Inwyt,* borrowed from Old French *abstinence, astinence,* from Latin *abstinentia,* from *abstinentem* (nominative *abstinēns*), present participle of *abstinēre* withhold; see ABSTAIN; for suffix see -ENCE.

abstract *adj.* Before 1398, in Trevisa's translation of Bartholomew's *De Proprietatibus Rerum,* borrowed from Latin *abstractus,* past participle of *abstrahere* draw away (*abs-* away, variant of *ab-* before *t* + *trahere* to draw; see TRACT).

The noun *abstract* appeared before 1456, the verb in 1542, both from the adjective.

—**abstraction** *n.* Before 1400, borrowed from Old French *abstraction,* from Latin *abstractiōnem* (nominative *abstractiō*), from *abstrac-*, stem of *abstrahere;* for suffix see -TION.

The sense of an abstract idea appeared in 1644, in Milton's *Of Education.* The modern sense of a work of abstract (nonrepresentational) art came into use about 1915.

abstruse *adj.* hard to understand. 1599, borrowed through Middle French *abstrus,* or directly from Latin *abstrūsus,* past participle of *abstrūdere* conceal (*abs-* away, variant of *ab-* before *t* + *trūdere* to thrust, push; see THREAT).

absurd *adj.* 1557, borrowed from Middle French *absurde,* from Latin *absurdus* out of tune, senseless (*ab-* off, amiss + *surdus* deaf, dull, mute). —**n. the absurd** 1954, translation of French *l'absurde* (in the existential philosophy of Albert Camus). —**absurdity** *n.* Probably in 1472, borrowed from Middle French *absurdité,* from Late Latin *absurditātem* (nominative *absurditās*), from Latin *absurdus;* see SURD; for suffix see -ITY.

abundance *n.* 1340, in *Ayenbite of Inwyt,* Middle English *aboundance, aboundaunce,* borrowed from Old French *abundance,* learned borrowing from Latin *abundantia* fullness, plenty, from *abundantem* overflowing; see ABUNDANT; for suffix see -ANCE.

There is also evidence that some writers in the 1300's and 1400's borrowed directly from the Latin form *abundantia.*

The form *habundance* was often used in Middle English in the 1300's because the word was thought to have been derived from Latin *habēre* to have. (The ancient Roman writers occasionally made that connection too and wrote *habundantia,* etc.)

Later in the 1400's and 1500's a form *boundance* appeared probably from the mistaken notion that *a* in *aboundance* was an indefinite article.

abundant *adj.* About 1380, in Chaucer's translation of Boethius' *De Consolatione Philosophiae,* Middle English *aboundaunt,* borrowed from Old French *abundant,* learned borrowing from Latin *abundantem* (nominative *abundāns*), present participle of *abundāre* to overflow, see ABOUND; for suffix see -ANT.

Some writers in the 1300's and 1400's probably borrowed directly from the Latin form *abundantem.*

For an explanation of the form *habundant* see usage note under ABUNDANCE.

abuse *v.* Probably before 1425 *abusen,* borrowed from Middle French *abuser,* from Vulgar Latin **abūsāre,* from Latin *abūsus,* past participle of *abūtī* use up, misuse (*ab-* away + *ūtī* to use; see USE). —**n.** 1439, in the *Rolls of Parliament,* Middle English *abus,* borrowed from Middle French *abus,* from Latin *abūsus* (genitive *abūsūs*) a using up, from past participle of *abūtī;* see ABUSE. —**abusive** *adj.* 1583, formed from English *abuse* + *-ive.*

abut *v.* Before 1250 *abutten* to end at, border on; a fusion of Old French *abouter* join end to end (*à* to + *bout* end) with Old French *abuter* touch with an end (*à* to + *but* end); see BUTT[2] target. —**abutment** *n.* 1644, in John Evelyn's *Memoirs,* formed from English *abut* + *-ment.*

abysmal *adj.* 1656, in Blount's *Glossographia,* formed from English *abysm* + *-al*[1]. The now obsolete word *abysm,* meaning an abyss, is first recorded in English as *abime* before 1325 in *Cursor Mundi* and as *abysm* in 1483 in Caxton. The earlier form was borrowed from Old French *abisme,* from Vulgar Latin **abismus,* an alteration of Late Latin *abyssus* ABYSS. The *m* in *abis-*

mus was introduced by the influence of nouns ending in Latin *-ismus* -ism.

abyss *n.* 1534, borrowed from Late Latin *abyssus* as a "more correct" or learned substitute for *abysm* (see *abysmal*). Late Latin *abyssus* is from Greek *ábyssos* (*a-* without + *byssós* bottom, possibly related to Greek *báthos* depth; see BATHOS).

In Middle English, the word appeared as *abyssus* (before 1398, in Trevisa's translation of Bartholomew's *De Proprietatibus Rerum*); the Anglicized form *abisse* appeared in 1534.

ac- a form of the prefix *ad-*, meaning to, toward, before *c* and *q* in words of Latin or French origin, as in *accept, account, acquaint.* In words from Latin the form is due to the assimilation of the *d* to the "k" sound of a following *c* (which in Latin represented a "k" sound even when followed by *e* or *i*) or *q*. In Old French this prefix was reduced to *a-*, which is the form in the early (Middle) English borrowings; but in or around the 1500's the spelling *ac-* was restored in the drive for words to resemble more closely the Latin original.

acacia *n.* a tree or shrub of the pea family. Before 1398, in Trevisa's translation of Bartholomew's *De Proprietatibus Rerum,* Middle English *acacia* a medicinal gum, borrowed from Latin *acacia,* from Greek *akakíā* a thorny Egyptian tree, probably related to Greek *akḗ* point; see EDGE.

Alternatively the Greek word *akakíā* may have been borrowed from an Egyptian word and modified on the model of Greek words with *ak-*, such as *akmḗ, ákros,* etc.

academy *n.* 1474, in Caxton's *Game and Play of Chess,* borrowed from Latin *acadēmīa,* name of a park near Athens and of a school held in a grove of the park where Plato taught, from Greek *Akadḗmeia,* the grove belonging to *Akádēmos,* a Greek hero of the Trojan War.

In the sense of any school or place for training, *academy* came into English in the 1500's probably through Middle French *académie,* from Italian *accademia;* or from New Latin *academia,* both ultimately from Latin *acadēmīa.* However, it is not absolutely certain by which path this latter meaning entered English, as the term was introduced into several countries at the same time during the period of Humanism in Europe. **—academic** *adj.* 1588, borrowed from Medieval Latin *academicus;* or from Middle French *académique;* for suffix see -IC.

acanthus *n.* a prickly plant. 1667, in Milton's *Paradise Lost,* borrowed from Latin *acanthus,* from Greek *ákanthos* (compound of *akḗ* point, spine, thorn + *ánthos* blossom, flower; see EDGE and ANTHER).

accede *v.* agree (to). Probably before 1425, in a translation of Higden's *Polychronicon,* Middle English *acceden* become adapted, come near to, borrowed from Latin *accēdere* approach, enter upon (*ac-* to, variant of *ad-* before *c* + *cēdere* move, go; see CEDE).

accelerate *v.* 1525-30, in Sir Thomas More's *Treatise Upon These Words of Holy Scripture,* perhaps modeled on Latin from Middle French *accélérer,* but more likely borrowed directly from Latin *accelerātus,* past participle of *accelerāre* quicken (*ac-* to, variant of *ad-* before *c* + *celerāre* quicken, from *celer* swift; see CELERITY); for suffix see -ATE[1]. It is also possible that *accelerate* is a back formation from *acceleration.* **—acceleration** *n.* 1531, perhaps borrowed from Middle French *accélération,* but more likely from Latin *accelerātiōnem* (nominative *accelerātiō*), from *accelerāre;* for suffix see -TION. **—accelerator** *n.* 1611, formed from English *accelerate* + *-or*[2].

accent *n.* Before 1398, in Trevisa's translation of Bartholomew's *De Proprietatibus Rerum,* borrowed from Middle French *accent,* from Old French *acent,* from Latin *accentus* song added to speech (*ac-* to, variant of *ad-* before *c* + *cantus* (genitive *cantūs*) a singing, from *canere* sing; see CHANT).

Latin *accentus* was a loan translation of Greek *prosōidíā* PROSODY.

—*v.* 1530, in Palsgrave's *Lesclarcissement,* borrowed from Middle French *accenter,* from *accent* ACCENT *n.*

accentuate *v.* 1731, borrowed from Medieval Latin *accentuatus,* past participle of *accentuare* to accent, from Latin *accentus* ACCENT; for suffix see -ATE[1].

accept *v.* About 1380, in Chaucer's *Canterbury Tales,* borrowed from Latin *acceptāre* take or receive willingly (a Latin form indicating repeated action) derived from *acceptus,* past participle of *accipere* receive (*ac-* to, variant of *ad-* before *c* + *-cipere,* combining form of *capere* to take; see CAPTIVE). Some scholars derive *accept* from Old French *accepter,* which may be a parallel borrowing with the Latin. **—acceptable** *adj.* About 1384, in Wycliffe's translation of the Bible, borrowed from Old French *acceptable,* learned borrowing from Latin *acceptābilis* worthy of acceptance, from *acceptāre;* for suffix see -ABLE. **—acceptance** *n.* 1574, borrowed from Middle French *acceptance,* from *accepter;* for suffix see -ANCE.

access *n.* About 1300 *acces* an attack of fever, borrowed from Old French *acces* onslaught, attack, learned borrowing from Latin *accessus* (genitive *accessūs*) a coming to, an approach, from past participle of *accēdere* to approach; see ACCEDE.

The revival of the original meaning in Latin, approach, entrance, appeared in Middle English about 1384, in the Wycliffe Bible.

—*v.* obtain access to. 1970, from the noun.

—accessible *adj.* Before 1400, borrowed from Old French *accessible,* learned borrowing from Late Latin *accessibilem,* from Latin *accessum,* past participle of *accēdere;* for suffix see -IBLE. **—accession** *n.* 1646, borrowed from French *accession,* learned borrowing from Latin *accessiōnem* (nominative *accessiō*) a going to, joining, from *accēdere;* for suffix see -SION. **—accessorize** *v.* 1939, formed from English *accessory* + *-ize.* **—accessory** *n.* something added. 1414, in *Rolls of Parliament,* Middle English *accessorie* an accessory to a crime, borrowed from Middle French *accessoire* accomplice, learned borrowing from Medieval Latin *accessorius* additional, from Latin *accessus* a coming to; for suffix see -ORY.

accident *n.* About 1380, in Chaucer's *House of Fame,* borrowed from Old French *accident,* from Latin *accidentem* (nominative *accidēns*), present participle of *accidere* happen, fall out (*ac-* to, variant of *ad-* before *c* + *-cidere,* combining form of *cadere* to fall; see CADENCE); for suffix see -ENT. **—accidental** *adj.* 1386, in the *Rolls of Parliament,* borrowed from Middle French *accidental,* or directly from Medieval Latin *accidentalis,* from Latin *accidentem* (nominative *accidēns*); for suffix see -AL[1].

acclaim *v.* 1633, perhaps borrowed from Middle French *acclamer,* but more likely from Latin *ac-*

clāmāre shout approval or disapproval of (*ac-* toward, variant of *ad-* before *c* + *clāmāre* cry out; see LOW², v.). The spelling was initially influenced by *claim.*

acclamation *n.* 1541, perhaps borrowed from Middle French *acclamation,* but more likely from Latin *acclāmātiōnem* (nominative *acclāmātiō*) shout of approval, from *acclāmāre* ACCLAIM; for suffix see -TION.

acclimate *v.* accustom to a new climate. 1792, in Arthur Young's *Travels in France,* borrowed from French *acclimater (à* to, from Latin *ad-)* + (*climat* CLIMATE).

acclivity *n.* an upward slope. 1614, borrowed from Latin *acclīvitātem* (nominative *acclīvitās*), from *acclīvis* (or *acclīvus*) ascending, steep (*ac-* toward, variant of *ad-* before *c* + *clīvus* rising ground, related to *clīnāre* to bend; see LEAN¹ slant); for suffix see -ITY.

accolade *n.* praise or award. 1623, a ceremony bestowing knighthood with a kiss, embrace, or tap on the shoulder with the blade of a sword, borrowed from French *accolade* an embracing about the neck. The modern French and English spellings are an alteration (after nouns in *-ade*) of Old French *acolée,* from *acoler* to embrace, from Vulgar Latin **accollāre* (Latin *ac-* to, variant of *ad-* before *c* + *collum* neck; see COLLAR).

The current meaning of praise or award appeared in the late 1800's from the idea of a public recognition of merit, such as that of bestowing knighthood upon a deserving person.

accommodate *v.* 1525, as a participial adjective, Wolsey quoted in Strype's *Ecclesiastical Memorials;* 1531, in Sir Thomas Elyot's *The Boke Named the Governour,* as a verb; both forms probably borrowed from Latin *accommodātus,* past participle of *accommodāre* fit one thing to another (*ac-* to, variant of *ad-* before *c* + *commodāre* make fit, from *commodus* fit; see COMMODE); for suffix see -ATE¹. **—accommodation** *n.* 1611, borrowed from French *accommodation,* from Latin *accommodātiōnem* (nominative *accommodātiō*), from *accommodāre;* for suffix see -TION.

accompany *v.* 1426 *accompanien,* borrowed from Middle French *accompagner,* from Old French *acompaignier* take as a companion (*à* to, from Latin *ad-*) + (*compaignier* from *compain* companion, from Late Latin *compāniō* COMPANION).

accomplice *n.* 1589, perhaps arising from the phrase *a complice* in which the indefinite article was absorbed into the noun *complice* by assimilation as *accomplice* on analogy with *accomplish, accompany,* etc. *Complice* a confederate, 1485, in Caxton's *Charles the Great,* is the earlier word, from Middle French *complice,* learned borrowing from Late Latin *complicem,* accusative of *complex* partner, confederate, from Latin *complicāre* fold together; see COMPLICATE.

accomplish *v.* About 1380, in Chaucer's translation of Boethius' *De Consolatione Philosophiae,* Middle English *accomplisshen,* borrowed from Old French *acompliss-,* stem of *acomplir* to fulfill, from Vulgar Latin **accomplēre* (Latin *ac-* to, variant of *ad-* before *c* + *complēre* fill up; see COMPLETE); for suffix see -ISH². **—accomplishment** *n.* About 1425, in *Proceedings of the Privy Council,* Middle English *accomplisshement,* borrowed from Old French *acomplissement;* for suffix see -MENT.

accord *v.* Before 1121 *acorden,* borrowed from Old French *acorder,* from Vulgar Latin **accordāre* make agree, be of one heart (Latin *ac-* to, variant of *ad-* before *c* + *cor, cordis* heart; see HEART). The Vulgar Latin form **accordāre* was patterned on Latin *discordāre* to disagree and *concordāre* to agree.

Though the Middle English form *acorden* appeared sporadically with *-cc-* before 1400, the spelling *accorden* became fixed in the 1400's when the word was refashioned after the Latin spelling.

The noun *accord* came into English about 1300 as *acord,* borrowed from Old French *acord,* from *acorder* to accord.

—accordance *n.* About 1303, borrowed from Old French *acordance,* from *acorder;* for suffix see -ANCE.

accordion *n.* 1831, borrowed from earlier German *Akkordion,* from *Akkord* concord of sounds, from French *accord,* from Old French *acord* accord; see ACCORD. The instrument was invented in 1829 in Vienna. The *-ion* ending was apparently patterned on German *Orchestrion* an instrument resembling a barrel organ.

The word is now spelled *Akkordeon* in German though often still pronounced as if spelled *-ion.*

accost *v.* to approach and speak to first. 1578, borrowed from Middle French *accoster* move up to, from Late Latin *accostāre* come up to the side (Latin *ac-* to, variant of *ad-* before *c* + *costa* side, rib; see COAST).

account *n.* About 1300 *acount, acunt,* borrowed from Old French *acont, acunt,* and later (in imitation of Latin) *acompt* account (*à* to + *cont* count, from Late Latin *computus* a calculation, from Latin *computāre* calculate, COMPUTE). Old French also had the forms *aconte, acunte,* from *acounter, acunter* to count, which were a parallel source of borrowing into English. **—v.** About 1300, Middle English *acounten, acunten,* borrowed from Old French *aconter, acunter* to count (*à* to + *conter, cunter,* from Latin *computāre* COMPUTE.). **—accountable** *adj.* Probably before 1387, formed in Anglo-French from *acounte* (Old French *aconte*); for suffix see -ABLE. **—accountant** *n.* 1453, borrowed from Old French *acontant, acuntant,* present participle of *aconter, acunter* to count; for suffix see -ANT. In the 1400's the then prevailing English spelling *acount* was frequently replaced by *accompt,* from Old French *acompt,* from *compter* to count, an artificial form after Latin *computāre.* The spelling *accompt* then prevailed in English for several centuries until, through the influence of *count,* it was finally displaced by *account* in the 1800's.

accouter or **accoutre** (əkü′tər) *v.* equip. 1596, in Shakespeare's *Merchant of Venice,* borrowed from Middle French *accoustrer, accoutrer,* from Old French *acostrer* arrange, (originally meaning sew up), from Vulgar Latin **accōstūrāre* to arrange, sew, from **cōstūra, *cōnsūtūra* a sewing; see COUTURIER. **—accouterment** or **accoutrement** *n.* 1549, borrowed from Middle French *accoustrement,* from *accoustrer;* for suffix see -MENT.

accredit *v.* 1620, in Shelton's first English translation of *Don Quixote,* borrowed from French *accréditer* (*à* to + *crédit* credit, from Middle French; see CREDIT). **—accreditation** *n.* 1806, formed possibly from obsolete English (1654) *accreditate* + *-ion.*

accretion *n.* growth by gradual addition. 1615, borrowed from Latin *accrētiōnem* (nominative *accrētiō*) a growing larger, from *accrē-,* stem of *accrēscere* grow larger, see ACCRUE; for suffix see -TION.

accrue *v.* grow or increase by gradual addition. 1440 *acreuen,* borrowed from Old French *acreüe* growth, increase, from *acreü*, past participle of *acreistre* to increase, from Latin *accrēscere* (*ac-* to, variant of *ad-* before *c* + *crēscere* grow; see CRESCENT). *Accrue* was originally said to be from the obsolete noun *accrue*, but no evidence is available to support this contention, as the first citations of noun use appear more than 135 years later in 1577. —**accrual** *n.* 1880, formed from English *accrue* + *-al*[2].

accumulate *v.* 1529, borrowed from Latin *accumulātus*, past participle of *accumulāre* heap up in a mass (*ac-* in addition, variant of *ad-* before *c* + *cumulāre* heap up, from *cumulus* a heap; see CUMULATE); for suffix see -ATE[1]. —**accumulation** *n.* 1490, in Caxton's translation of *The Book of Eneydos*, perhaps borrowed from Middle French *accumulation*, or more likely from Latin *accumulātiōnem* (nominative *accumulātiō*), from *accumulāre*; for suffix see -TION.

accurate *adj.* 1612, borrowed from Latin *accūrātus* prepared with care, exact, past participle of *accūrāre* take care of (*ac-* to, variant of *ad-* before *c* + *cūrāre* take care; see CURE); for suffix see -ATE[1]. —**accuracy** *n.* 1662, formed from English *accurate* + *-acy.*

accusative *adj.* case in grammar indicating goal of action. About 1434, borrowed through Anglo-French *accusatif* (feminine *accusative*), corresponding to Old French *acusatif*, or borrowed directly from Latin *cāsus accūsātīvus* case of accusing, from *accūsātus*, past participle of *accūsāre* ACCUSE; for suffix see -IVE.

The Latin *cāsus accūsātīvus* arose out of a mistranslation of Greek *ptôsis aitiātikḗ* case of that which is caused or effected, because of the coexistence of Greek *aitiâsthai* accuse.

accuse *v.* About 1300 *acusen*, borrowed through Old French *acuser*, or directly from Latin *accūsāre* (*ac-* against, variant of *ad-* before *c* + *causārī* give as a cause or motive, plead a case, from *causa* motive, reason, CAUSE). In the late 1300's the original English and French forms with the prefix *a-* were refashioned to *ac-* after the Latin. —**accusation** *n.* Before 1387, borrowed through Old French *accusation*, or directly from Latin *accūsātiōnem* (nominative *accūsātiō*), from *accūsāre* ACCUSE; for suffix see -TION.

accustom *v.* 1422, in *Proceedings of the Privy Council*, Middle English *acustumen*, borrowed from Middle French *acostumer* (*à* to + *costume* CUSTOM). In the 1400's the original English and French forms with the prefix *a-* were refashioned to *ac-* in conformity with Latin spelling.

ace *n.* a side of dice, playing cards, etc., having one spot. Before 1250 *as* (later, about 1450, *ace*), borrowed from Old French *as*, from Latin *as* (genitive *assis*) a unit, especially the smallest unit of coinage, measure, etc., a word possibly borrowed from Etruscan. The *as* (plural *assēs*) was the ancient Roman pound, originally equal to twelve ounces, but by subsequent devaluation equal to ½ ounce.

The meaning "best or highest" developed in English in the 1700's from the fact that in some card games the ace is the most valuable. *Ace* in the sense of a crack combat pilot appeared in World War I. *Ace* in sports, in the meaning "to score a point, etc." against an opponent, appeared in the 1920's.

Ace as a verb, in the phrase "ace out" appeared about 1970.

-aceous an adjective suffix, borrowed from Latin *-āceus*, and meaning of or like, having the appearance of, containing, as in *arenaceous* looking like or composed of sand (Latin *arēna* sand), *cretaceous* like chalk (Latin *crēta* chalk), and *tuffaceous* like tuff.

-Aceous is used in botany in adjectives relating to families of plants named in *-aceae* (in New Latin, the feminine plural of *-aceus*, from Latin *-āceus*), as in *liliaceous* relating to New Latin *Liliaceae*, the lily family, and *rosaceous* relating to New Latin *Rosaceae*, the rose family. In zoology *-aceous* is used in adjectives relating to classes or orders of animals named in *-acea* (in New Latin, the neuter plural of *-aceus*, from Latin *-āceus*), as in *cetaceous* relating to the order *Cetacea*, including the whales and related animals.

acerbity *n.* sourness, severity. 1572, borrowed from Middle French *acerbité*, from Latin *acerbitātem* (nominative *acerbitās*) bitterness, from *acerbus* sharp or harsh to the taste, bitter, related to *ācer* sharp; see ACRID; for suffix see -ITY. —**acerbic** *adj.* 1865, formed in English from Latin *acerbus* + the English suffix *-ic.*

acetic *adj.* of vinegar or the acid responsible for the taste of vinegar. 1808, borrowed from French *acétique*, or formed in English from Latin *acētum* vinegar (originally past participle of *acēre* be sour; related to *ācer* sharp; see ACRID) + the English suffix *-ic.*

ache *v., n.* The Old English verb (about 1000, in Ælfric's *Grammar*) was *acan*, spelled in Middle English *ake* or *aken* and pronounced with *k*, as in *make;* cognate with Low German *äken* to hurt, from Proto-Germanic **akanan.*

The Old English noun (before 899) was *æce*, spelled in Middle English *ache, eche* and pronounced with *ch*, as in *match.* Old English *ǣce*, from Proto-Germanic **akiz*, is probably cognate with Greek *ágos* guilt, from Indo-European **ag-/ōg-* (Pok.8).

The present identical spelling and pronunciation of verb and noun became widespread in the 1700's, when the noun was confused in pronunciation with the verb and was pronounced with a *k*-sound, while the verb, influenced by the spelling of the noun, was changed in form from *ake* to *ache.* The fixing of this change in spelling is usually attributed to Samuel Johnson, who mistakenly derived the older forms from the Greek word *áchos* pain. However, later evidence has shown that in the 1400's the noun was already frequently spelled *ake.*

achieve *v.* About 1300 *acheven*, borrowed from Old French *achever* finish, from the phrase *à chef* at an end, or perhaps from Vulgar Latin **accapāre* bring to a head, either form from Latin *ad* to + Vulgar Latin **capum*, from Latin *caput* HEAD.

The spelling *achieve* was influenced by the Old French variant spelling *achiever* as well as by *chief*, the older form of *chef.*

—**achievement** *n.* 1475, in Caxton's translation of *History of Jason*, borrowed from Middle French *achèvement*, from Old French *achever;* for suffix see -MENT.

acid *adj.* 1626, in Francis Bacon's *Sylva Sylvarum*, probably borrowed through French *acide*, a learned borrowing from Latin; or borrowed directly from Latin *acidus* sour, from *acēre* be sour, related to *ācer* sharp; see ACRID. —**n.** 1696, noun use of *acid*, adj. —**acidity** *n.* 1620, probably borrowed through French *acidité*, a learned borrowing from Latin; or borrowed directly from Late Latin *aciditātem* (nominative *aciditās*), from Latin *acidus;* for suffix see -ITY.

acknowledge *v.* 1481, in Caxton's *Mirror of the World*,

Middle English *acknowlechen,* formed from a blend of *acknow* admit + *knowlechen* admit, from *knowleche,* n., KNOWLEDGE. *Acknow* developed from Old English *oncnāwan,* a compound of *on* and *cnāwan* recognize, see KNOW. —**acknowledgment** *n.* 1594, in Richard Hooker's *Of the Laws of Ecclesiastical Polity,* formed from English *acknowledge* + *-ment.*

acme *n.* highest point, peak. 1620, borrowed from Greek *akmḗ* (highest) point, related to *akḗ* point; see EDGE.

Though *acme* first appears in 1570 in an English text, it is written with Greek letters and appears in the same form as late as the mid-1700's. Few words borrowed into English have retained a spelling in the letters of a foreign alphabet from which they were borrowed for almost 200 years.

acne *n.* 1835, New Latin (medical term), borrowed from Late Greek *aknḗ,* misspelling (in the 6th century author Aëtius) of Greek *akmḗ* (highest) point; see ACME.

acolyte *n.* altar boy, assistant. About 1300, borrowed through Old French *acolite,* or directly from Medieval Latin *acolytus,* alteration of Late Latin *acolūthos,* from Medieval Greek *akólouthos* following, attendant, from Greek *akólouthos* following, attending on, earlier **hakólouthos,* from *ha-* (cognate with Sanskrit *sa-,* from Indo-European **sm̥-*) SAME + Greek **-kolouthos,* variant of *kéleuthos* road, path, journey, of uncertain origin.

aconite *n.* monkshood or wolfsbane (plants of the crowfoot family). 1578, borrowed from Middle French *aconit,* Old French *aconita, aconite,* from Latin *aconītum,* from Greek *akóníton,* of uncertain origin.

acorn *n.* The Old English form (about 1000, in Ælfric's *Genesis*) was *æcern,* from which Middle English *akern, akkorn, accorn, acorn* developed. The word's original meaning in Old English was fruit of the field, mast of the oak, beech, etc., with cognates in Old High German *ackeran,* pl., Old Icelandic *akarn,* and Gothic *akran* fruit, Old Slavic *agoda, jagoda* fruit, and Lithuanian *úoga* berry, from Indo-European **ōg-/əg-* grow (Pok.773). However, in the 1400's and 1500's, the Middle English forms *akorn, akkorn,* etc., were popularly taken to be a compound of *ake* oak (Old English *āc*) and *corn* kernel; hence the modern spelling *acorn.*

acoustic *adj.* 1605, in Francis Bacon's *Of the Advancement of Learning,* borrowed from French *acoustique,* from Greek *akoustikós,* from *akoustós* heard, audible, from *akoúein* hear, see HEAR; for suffix see -IC. —**acoustics** *n.* 1683, formed from English *acoustic* + *-s* on analogy with *mathematics,* etc.

acquaint *v.* Probably before 1200, in *Ancrene Riwle,* Middle English *aqueynten, acointen,* borrowed from Old French *acointer, acointier,* from Vulgar Latin **accognitāre* make known, from Latin *accognitus,* past participle of *accognōscere* know well (*ac-* to, variant of *ad-* before *c* + *cognōscere* come to know; see COGNIZANCE). Related to QUAINT. —**acquaintance** *n.* Probably before 1200, in *Ancrene Riwle,* Middle English *aqueyntance, acointance,* borrowed from Old French *acointance,* from *acointer;* for suffix see -ANCE.

acquiesce *v.* agree to passively. 1620, borrowed from French *acquiescer,* from Latin *acquiēscere* remain at rest, be satisfied with (*ac-* to, variant of *ad-* before *q* + *quiēscere* become quiet, rest; see QUIESCENT). —**acquiescence** *n.* About 1631, in Donne's *Selections,* borrowed from French *acquiescence,* from *acquiescer;* for suffix see -ENCE. —**acquiescent** *adj.* 1697, borrowed from Latin *acquiēscentem* (nominative *acquiēscēns*), present participle of *acquiēscere;* for suffix see -ENT.

acquire *v.* 1601, in Shakespeare's *All's Well That Ends Well,* borrowed from Latin *acquīrere* get in addition (*ac-* to, variant of *ad-* before *q* + *quærere* seek; related to QUERY). Latin *acquīrere* shows the regular result of the "weakening" of *quærere* to *-quīrere* in derivatives, in very early Latin. The connection with the simple verb *quærere* was restored by "recomposition" in Vulgar Latin **acquærere,* which yielded Old French *acquerre,* borrowed in Middle English *acqueren* in 1450. However, this Middle English form was ultimately replaced by *acquire* in an effort to restore the connection with the literary Latin form.

acquisition *n.* Before 1400, borrowed perhaps through Old French *acquisition,* or more likely directly from Latin *acquīsītiōnem* (nominative *acquīsītiō*), from *acquīsī-,* stem of *acquīrere* get in addition, see ACQUIRE; for suffix see -TION. —**acquisitive** *adj.* 1637, formed in English from Latin *acquīsītus,* past participle of *acquīrere* + the English suffix *-ive.*

acquit *v.* Probably before 1200, in *Ancrene Riwle,* Middle English *acwiten, aquiten* settle a claim or discharge a debt, borrowed from Old French *acquitter* settle a claim (*à* to + *quite* free, clear; see QUIT).

The Middle English form *aquiten* began to be replaced in the 1400's by *acquit* (with a *c*) in imitation of Latin forms with the prefix *ac-* when followed by a *q.*

The meaning clear of a charge, declare not guilty appeared about 1390, in Chaucer's *Canterbury Tales.* —**acquittal** *n.* 1430, in *Proceedings of the Privy Council,* probably formed from English *acquit* + *-al*[2]. The word also appears in Anglo-French.

acre *n.* Old English (about 975) *æcer* tilled field, a measure of land, from which *acer, aker* developed in Middle English before 1124. Under the influence of Old French *acre* and Medieval Latin *acra* (both from Old English *æcer*), the spellings *acer, aker* were changed to *acre.*

Old English *æcer* is cognate with Old High German *achar,* Old Icelandic *akr,* Gothic *akrs,* from Proto-Germanic **akraz,* and with Latin *ager,* Greek *agrós*—all in the sense of "field" or earlier a pasture and originally a hunting ground or wild area, untenanted and open, from Indo-European **agros* (Pok.6).

Greek *agrós* is from the root *aĝ-,* as in *ágein* to lead (as cattle were driven to the field), hence the meaning "drive" underlies all of the cognates. For instance, Latin *ager* is akin to *agere* to drive and to Sanskrit *ájra-s* field, and *ájati* drives, leads, which attests to the antiquity of the connection.

—**acreage** *n.* 1859, formed from English *acre* + *-age.*

acrid *adj.* bitterly harsh or sharp. 1712, borrowed from Latin *ācer,* (feminine *ācris*) sharp, related to Greek *akḗ* point; see EDGE.

The suffixal ending *-id* was probably added by influence of earlier *acid.*

acrimony *n.* bitterness of manner or temper. 1542, pungency of taste, borrowed through Middle French *acrimonie,* or directly from Latin *ācrimōnia,* from *ācer, ācris* sharp + *-monia* suffix signifying action, state, condition; see ACRID.

The current English meaning appeared in 1618.

acrobat *n.* 1825, borrowed from French *acrobate,* from

Greek *akrobátēs,* related to *akróbatos* going on tiptoe, climbing up high (*ákros* tip, high point + *-batós,* from *baínein* go; see EDGE and COME).

acronym *n.* word made up of the first letters or syllables of other words, as *NATO* or *radar.* 1943, coined from *acro-* combining form from Greek *ákros* tip, end + English *-onym* name, as in SYNONYM. —**v.** make an acronym of. 1967, from the noun.

acropolis *n.* citadel of a Greek city, especially the one in Athens. 1662, in Henry A. More's *Antidote Against Atheism,* borrowed from Greek *akrópolis* (*ákros* highest, upper + *pólis* city).

acrostic *n.* arrangement of words whose first letters spell a word. 1587, perhaps borrowed through Middle French *acrostiche,* or directly from Medieval Latin *acrostichis,* from Greek *akrostichís* (*ákros* highest, upper + *stichos* row, line of verse ; see STAIR). The spelling might logically have developed as *acrostich,* as in *distich, hemistich,* etc., but development of the present spelling was probably influenced by other nouns in *-ic,* such as *mastic, rustic,* etc.

across *adv.* About 1325 *acros* from one side to another; earlier *a-croiz* in a crossed position (about 1300), and *o cros* in the shape of a cross (probably before 1200); all alterations of Anglo-French phrase *an cros* (*an* in, from Latin *in* + *cros* CROSS). —**prep.** from side to side of, over. 1591, in Shakespeare's *Henry VI;* from the adverb.

acrylic (əkril′ik) *adj.* relating to synthetic substances used in fibers, plastics, etc. 1855, formed from English *acryl* + *-ic* a suffix meaning "containing". *Acryl,* denoting a unit of atoms in the allyl group derived especially from garlic and onion, was abstracted from *acrolein* (Latin *ācer, ācris* sharp + *olēre* to smell + English *-yl;* see ACRID). —**n.** acrylic material. 1960, from the adjective.

act *n.* About 1380, in Chaucer's *House of Fame,* borrowed, perhaps especially in a legal sense, from Old French *acte,* from Latin *āctus* a doing, and *āctum* a thing done, both from *agere* do, set in motion, drive. Latin *agere* is cognate with Greek *ágein* lead, draw; Old Icelandic *aka* drive; Sanskrit *ájati* drives, and *ajirá-s* active; related to ACRE. —**v.** About 1460, probably in part influenced by the noun already used in English and Latin *āctus,* past participle of *agere* to do.

ACTH hormone that stimulates the adrenal cortex. 1944, formed in English from *a*(dreno)*c*(ortico)*t*(ropic) *h*(ormone).

actinic *adj.* producing chemical changes by radiation. 1844, Sir John Herschel in *British Association Report,* formed from Greek *aktís* (genitive *aktînos*) ray (of light) + the English suffix *-ic.* Greek *aktís* is cognate with Gothic *ūhtwō* early morning (from Proto-Germanic **unHtwōn-*) and with Sanskrit *aktú-s* ray, twilight, from Indo-European **n̥kwt-* (root **nokwt-* night) (Pok. 762).

actinium *n.* chemical element found in pitchblende. 1881, New Latin, formed from Greek *aktís* (genitive *aktînos*) ray + New Latin *-ium* (suffix of chemical elements). The element was originally thought to occur in zinc, and because of a peculiar action of light upon its salts the Greek word for ray of light was used to form the new name.

action *n.* Before 1338, borrowed from Old French *action,* learned borrowing from Latin *āctiōnem* (nominative *āctiō*), from stem of *agere* ACT; for suffix see -TION. —**actionable** *adj.* 1591, formed from English *action* + *-able.*

active *adj.* 1340, in *Ayenbite of Inwyt,* borrowed through Old French *actif* (feminine *active*), or borrowed directly from Latin *āctīvus,* from *āctus* ACT; for suffix see -IVE. —**activate** *v.* 1626, in Francis Bacon's *Sylva Sylvarum,* probably formed from English *active* + *-ate*[1]. —**activity** *n.* Probably before 1400, probably borrowed from Old French *activité,* from Medieval Latin *activitatem* (nominative *activitas*), from Latin *āctīvus* active; for suffix see -ITY.

actor *n.* About 1384 *actour,* in the Wycliffe Bible, borrowed from Latin *āctor* an agent or doer, from stem of *agere* ACT; for suffix see -OR[2].

In the sense of one who acts in plays *actor* was first used in 1581, in Sidney's *Defence of Poesie,* and was applied to both men and women.

—**actress** *n.* 1589, a female doer, probably formed from English *actor* + *-ess* female agent suffix; not used of a female stage actor until 1666, in Pepys' *Diary.*

actual *adj.* Before 1333 *actual, actuel,* borrowed from Old French *actuel* and (before 1398) from Late Latin *āctuālis* active, practical, from Latin *āctus* (genitive *āctūs*) a doing, see ACT; for suffix see -AL[1]. —**actuality** *n.* Before 1398 *actualite,* in Trevisa's translation of Bartholomew's *De Proprietatibus Rerum,* perhaps borrowed from an Old French form, but traditionally recorded as a borrowing from Medieval Latin *actualitatem* (nominative *actualitas*), from Late Latin *āctuālis;* for suffix see -ITY. —**actually** *adv.* Probably before 1425, Middle English *actualli,* formed from English *actual* + *-ly*[1].

actuary *n.* statistician for an insurance company. 1553, a registrar or clerk, borrowed from Latin *āctuārius* copyist, account keeper, from *āctus* public business, see ACT; for suffix see -ARY.

In the current sense of one who figures rates, etc., for insurance companies, the word was first used in 1849 in Macaulay's *History of England.*

—**actuarial** *adj.* 1869, formed from English *actuary* + *-al*[1].

actuate *v.* activate, impel. 1596, borrowed from Medieval Latin *actuatus,* past participle of *actuare,* from Latin *āctus* a doing, see ACT; for suffix see -ATE[1].

acuity *n.* Probably before 1425 *acuite,* borrowed through Middle French *acuité,* or directly from Medieval Latin *acuitatem* (nominative *acuitas*) sharpness, from Old French *agüeté,* from *agu* sharp, from Latin *acūtus* ACUTE; for suffix see -ITY.

acumen *n.* keenness of mind. 1531, in Sir Thomas Elyot's *The Boke Named the Governour,* borrowed from Latin *acūmen* sharp point, sharpness, shrewdness, from *acuere* sharpen; see ACUTE.

acupuncture *n.* insertion of fine needles in the body to anesthetize or treat illness. 1684, formed from Latin *acus* needle + English *puncture;* see ACUTE. —**v.** 1972, verb use of *acupuncture,* n. —**acupuncturist** *n.* 1952, formed from English *acupuncture* + *-ist.*

acute *adj.* Before 1398, in Trevisa's translation of Bartholomew's *De Proprietatibus Rerum,* in Middle English used in medicine to describe a brief and severe disease, fever, etc., as opposed to a chronic condition, from Latin *acūtus* sharp-pointed, past participle of *acuere* sharpen to a point, related to *acus* needle; see EDGE.

After the Middle English period, *acute* began to develop figurative and other extended meanings: sharp, pointed (by 1570); penetrating, sharp-witted (by 1588, in Shakespeare's *Love's Labour's Lost*); intense, sharply felt (by 1727, in Swift's *Poisoning of Curll*).

-acy a suffix forming abstract nouns with a general meaning of quality, state, or condition (such as *accuracy, intricacy, lunacy*) or of activity or function (such as *advocacy, candidacy*). It often takes the place of *-ate* or other suffix in the noun or adjective from which it is formed (*accuracy* from *accurate, lunacy* from *lunatic*); occasionally it is simply added to the other word (as in *supremacy*, from *supreme*).

The suffix *-acy* is one of the special forms of the suffix *-cy*. The form in Middle English was *-cie;* it entered English in words borrowed from Old or Middle French words in *-acie* or *-atie*, or directly from Latin words in *-ācia* or *-ātia*. Especially frequent among the Latin sources are words in which *-āt-* is the participial stem which supplies many English adjectives and nouns in *-ate*, and *-ia* is the suffix equivalent to *-y*[3]. Occasional sources are Greek words in *-kia, -keia, -tia* or *-teia* (such as *pharmacy*, Greek *pharmakeíā*).

A.D. in the year of our Lord. 1538, abbreviation of Medieval Latin *Anno Domini*.

ad *n. Informal.* advertisement. 1841, in Thackeray's *Britannia*, shortening of *advertisement*. **—adman** *n.* 1909, formed from English *ad* + *man*.

ad- a prefix that entered English as a component of many words taken from Latin (directly or through French); it has had some use, furthermore, in forming words in English.

Latin *ad-* is a special use of the preposition *ad* to, toward, cognate with English *at*, Old English *æt*, Gothic *at*, Proto-Germanic **at*, Indo-European **ad* (Pok. 3). As a prefix to verbs it adds a meaning of direction toward, addition, or the like. When it was prefixed to words beginning with certain consonants, it changed form by assimilation of the *d* to the following consonant. This was followed in spelling in later texts, and in the form in which such words appear in English: *ad-* becomes *ab-* before *b: abbreviate; ac-* before *c, q: accede, acquaint; af-* before *f: affix; ag-* before *g: agglutinate; al-* before *l: ally; an-* before *n: annul; ap-* before *p: apprehend; ar-* before *r: arrogant; as-* before *s: assist; a-* before *sc, sp, st: ascribe, aspire, astringent; at-* before *t: attract*.

Words formed with *ad-* found in modern English do not always reflect a direct passage from Latin into English. The prefix *ad-* was transformed to *a-* in Old French, and so appeared in words that entered Middle English through Old French. In the 15th century many of these words were respelled with the *ad-* to restore the connection with Latin. (See REPLACEMENT in the Glossary Section) When the process went too far, as in *advance*, English acquired a *d* that had no historical justification.

In English, *ad-* is sometimes employed in adjective formations in its ancient prepositional sense, as in *adoral* at or near the mouth, and *adrenal* at (above) the kidneys.

adage *n.* saying or proverb. 1548, borrowed from Middle French *adage*, learned borrowing from Latin *adagium* (*ad-* to, and root *ag-*, related to *aiō* I say and, in turn, to Greek *ê* said (he), and to Armenian *asem* I say, from Indo-European **ēĝ-/ōĝ-/əg-* (Pok. 290).

adagio *adv. Music.* slowly. About 1746, in Garrick's *Musical Lady*, borrowed from Italian *adagio*, from the phrase *ad agio* at ease (*ad*, from Latin *ad* at) + (*agio* ease, from Provençal *aize* comfort, Old French *aise;* see EASE).

adamant *adj.* firm, unyielding. 1677, extended from the earlier meaning "extremely hard; unbreakable," recorded before 1387 in Trevisa's translation of Higden's *Polychronicon*.

The adjective derived from *adamant*, n., 1345, meaning "a hard rock or mineral," which came from a confusion of meaning: either very hard (diamond) or magnetic (loadstone), recorded as early as 885 in Alfred's translation of St. Gregory's *Pastoral Care*.

The word in Alfred's translation was borrowed from Old French *adamant* the hardest stone, from Latin *adamantem*, accusative of *adamās*, from Greek *adámās* (genitive *adámantos*) the hardest metal, (later) diamond (perhaps from *a-* not + *damnánai* conquer; see TAME; but very possibly of foreign origin). Doublet of DIAMOND.

adapt *v.* Probably before 1425 (as past participle *adapted* meaning "fitted"), borrowed from Middle French *adapter*, from Latin *adaptāre* adjust (*ad-* to + *aptāre* join, from *aptus* fitted, joined, APT).

The evidence of the use of *adapt* in Middle English is weak. Apparently the word did not become current in English until the 1600's, with the first reliable attestation occurring before 1616, in Ben Jonson's *Discoveries*.

—adaptable *adj.* 1800, formed from English *adapt* + *-able*. **—adaptation** *n.* 1610, borrowed from Medieval Latin *adaptationem* (nominative *adaptatio*), from Latin *adaptāre;* for suffix see -ATION.

add *v.* About 1380 *adden*, in Chaucer's translation of Boethius' *De Consolatione Philosophiae*, borrowed from Latin *addere* add to, join (*ad-* to + *-dere*, combining form meaning to put, place; see DO[1] perform).

addendum *n.* 1878, in Oliver Wendell Holmes' memoir of John Motley, borrowed from Latin *addendum* something to be added, gerund of *addere* ADD. **—addenda** *pl.* 1684, in Boyle's *History of Blood*, borrowed from Latin *addenda*, plural of *addendum*.

Note that the plural *addenda* was recorded almost two hundred years before the first recorded use of the singular *addendum*.

adder *n.* a snake. The Old English form (about 950) was *nædre*, with cognates in Old Saxon *nādara*, Old High German *nātra, nātara* (modern German *Natter*), from Proto-West-Germanic **næđrṓ*, Indo-European **nētrā́;* Old Icelandic *nadhr*, Gothic *nadrs*, from Proto-North-Germanic **nađrás;* cognate with Old Irish *nathir*, Welsh *neidr*, Old Cornish *nader*, and Latin *natrīx*, all in the sense of "a snake," from Indo-European **nətr-* (Pok. 767).

During the period about 1300-1400 in Middle English, the initial *n* was lost by mistaken division of *a nadder* as *an adder*. Compare APRON for a similar instance of misdivision.

The form is ultimately traceable to the Indo-European base **(s)nē*, reduced grade **(s)nə-*, to wind, thread, weave.

addict (ədikt′) *v.* 1534, in Sir Thomas More's *On the Passion*, borrowed from Latin *addictus*, past participle of *addīcere* deliver, yield, devote (*ad-* to + *dīcere* say, declare; see DICTION). —**n.** (ad′ikt). About 1909, noun use of *addict,* v. —**addiction** *n.* 1641, borrowed from Latin *addictiōnem* (nominative *addictiō*), from *addic-,* stem of *addīcere;* for suffix see -ION.

addition *n.* Before 1388, borrowed from Old French, learned borrowing from Latin *additiōnem* (nominative *additiō*), from *addi-,* stem of *addere* ADD; for suffix see -TION. —**additive** *adj.* 1699, borrowed from Latin *additīvus,* from *addi-,* stem of *addere;* for suffix see -IVE. —*n.* 1945, noun use of *additive,* adj.

addle *adj.* **1** muddled. **2** rotten. About 1250, rotten (in reference to eggs), an attributive use of Old English *adela* mud, mire, liquid filth, (about 1000, in Ælfric's *Homilies*), cognate with Middle Dutch *adel* liquid manure and Old Swedish *-adel* urine, of unknown origin.

The phrase *adel eye* rotten egg, in *The Owl and the Nightingale,* is a translation of Medieval Latin *ovum urinae* egg of urine or putrid liquid, an erroneous rendering of Latin *ōvum ūrinum,* Greek *oúrinon ōión* wind egg (an addle egg, formerly supposed to be caused by impregnation by the wind).

By the end of the 1500's the usage had been extended to mean confused, muddled, on analogy with the decomposed condition of an addle egg, and at the same time the adjective use in *addle brain, addle pate* was evinced.

—**v.** (at first used chiefly in the past participle, as *addled*), 1646, from the adjective.

address *v.* Before 1325 *adressen* to guide, direct, borrowed from Old French *adresser* (earlier *adrecier*), from Vulgar Latin **addīrēctiāre* make straight (Latin *ad-* to) + (**dīrēctiāre* straighten, from Latin *dīrēctus* straight, DIRECT).

The present spelling with *-dd-* is a refashioning of the prefix *a-* into *ad-* in English, after the Latin form, and occasionally occurs in Middle French.

—**n.** 1539, act of addressing or directing; noun use of *address,* v. The sense "direction written on a letter" appeared in 1712.

adduce *v.* bring forward (reasons or arguments). Probably before 1425, borrowed from Latin *addūcere* lead to, bring to (*ad-* to + *dūcere* to lead; see TOW[1] pull).

-ade suffix meaning an act or process (as in *blockade*), a product or result (as in *lemonade*), or a person or thing acting (as in *cavalcade*). Borrowed from French *-ade,* related to Provençal, Spanish, and Portuguese *-ada* or Italian *-ata,* all from Latin *-āta,* originally the feminine of the past participle *-ātus.*

adenine (ad′ənīn) *n.* substance in nucleic acid of cells. 1885, borrowed from German *Adenin,* from Greek *adḗn* (genitive *adénos*) gland, because it was first isolated from the pancreatic gland of an ox.

adenoid *adj.* glandular. 1839, borrowed from Greek *adenoeidḗs* (*adḗn,* genitive *adénos,* gland + *eîdos* form). Greek *adḗn,* cognate with Latin *inguen* (genitive *inguinis*) groin, is from Indo-European *n̥gwḗn* (Pok.319). —**adenoids** *n.pl.* glandlike tissues in the upper part of the throat. 1891, from the adjective.

While borrowed from Greek as a medical term, the word has existed in French since 1541.

adenosine (əden′əsēn) *n.* substance in muscle tissue important in muscle contraction. 1909, borrowed from German *Adenosin* (blend of *Aden(in)* adenine + *(Rib)-ose* ribose, a kind of sugar in nucleic acid).

adept *adj.* expert, skillful. Before 1691, borrowed from Latin *adeptus,* past participle of *adipīscī* to attain to, acquire (*ad-* to + *apīscī* grasp, obtain, related to *aptus* fitted, APT). —**n.** an expert. 1663, in Samuel Butler's *Hudibras,* borrowed from New Latin *adeptus* alchemist claiming attainment of the philosopher's stone, from *adeptus,* adj., skilled in one's art, from Latin *adeptus,* past participle.

adequate *adj.* Before 1617, borrowed from Latin *adaequātus,* past participle of *adaequāre* equalize (*ad-* to + *aequāre* make level, from *aequus* EQUAL); for suffix see -ATE[1].

adherent *n.* 1425, in the *Rolls of Parliament,* borrowed from Middle French *adhérent,* or directly from Latin *adhaerentem* (nominative *adhaerēns*), present participle of *adhaerēre* stick to (*ad-* to + *haerēre* stick, cling; see HESITATE); for suffix see -ENT. —**adhere** *v.* 1597, in Francis Bacon's *Essays,* borrowed from Middle French *adhérer,* or directly from Latin *adhaerēre.*

adhesion *n.*1624, borrowed from French *adhésion,* or directly from Latin *adhaesiōnem* (nominative *adhaesiō*) an adhering, from *adhaes-,* stem of *adhaerēre* ADHERE; for suffix see -ION.

ad hoc for a particular purpose; special. 1659, as an adverbial phrase, New Latin *ad hoc* (literally) for this. Since the late 1800's *ad hoc* has been commonly used as an adjective meaning assigned or devoted to a particular purpose (as in *ad hoc committee*).

adidas (ədē′dəz) *n.* trademark for athletic equipment. 1975, from the name of *Adi Dassler,* a German manufacturer who in 1948 founded the company that produces the athletic equipment, especially footwear and garments.

The trademark is spelled in lower-case to distinguish it from other nouns in German, but in common English usage it is spelled with an initial capital.

adieu *interj., n.* good-by, farewell. About 1385, in Chaucer's *Troilus and Criseyde,* Middle English *adew,* borrowed from Old French *adieu,* earlier *a dieu (vous) commant* I commend (you) to God (*a* to, from Latin *ad* + *dieu* God, from Latin *deum,* accusative of *deus;* see DEITY). Compare ADIOS.

The original English spelling *adew* (with variants *adewe, adeu, adue*) was gradually replaced with the French form, beginning in the late 1300's.

adios (ä′dēōs′) *interj.* good-by. 1837, American English, borrowed from Spanish *adiós,* earlier *a dios,* in *a dios vos acomiendo* I commend you to God (*a* to, from Latin *ad* + *dios* God, from Latin *deus* ; see DEITY).

adipose (ad′əpōs) *adj.* fatty. 1743, borrowed from New Latin *adiposus,* perhaps also influenced by a parallel form in French *adipeux* (feminine *adipeuse*), both New Latin and French from Latin *adeps* (genitive *adipis*) fat of animals, parallel to Umbrian *ařepes, ařipes, ařpes.* Both the Latin and the Umbrian were borrowed from Greek *áleipha* unguent, fat (construed as an accusative **alipa,* to which a nominative **alips* was formed and altered to *adeps*). Greek *áleipha,* related to *lípos* grease, cognate with Sanskrit *lipyate* is smeared and Latin *lippus* blear-eyed, is from Indo-European **leip-*/*lip-* (Pok. 670).

adjacent *adj.* Before 1420, in Lydgate's *Troy Book,* borrowed from Latin *adjacentem* (nominative *adjacēns*), present participle of *adjacēre* lie near (*ad-* near + *ja-*

cēre lie, rest, related to *jacere* to throw; see JET[1] stream).

adjective *n.* Probably before 1387, in a version of *Piers Plowman,* borrowed through Old French *adjectif* (feminine *adjective*), from Latin *adjectīvum;* see *adj.* below. **—adj.** Before 1398, in Trevisa's translation of Bartholomew's *De Proprietatibus Rerum,* in the phrase *noun adjective,* borrowed as a translation of Late Latin *nōmen adjectīvum,* from Latin *adjectīvum,* neuter of *adjectīvus* added, from *adjectus,* past participle of *adicere* add to (*ad-* + *-icere,* combining form of *jacere* to throw; see JET[1] stream); for suffix see -IVE.

The Late Latin phrase was a translation of Greek *ónoma epítheton* adjectival noun. This was the term used by Dionysius Thrax. It was not until the Middle Ages that the categories of noun and adjective were clearly separated into two.

adjoin *v.* About 1303, in Mannyng's *Handlyng Synne,* Middle English *ajoinen,* borrowed from Old French *ajoin-,* stem of *ajoindre,* from Latin *adjungere* join to (*ad-* to + *jungere* join; see YOKE).

The Middle English spelling was refashioned in the 1400's to *adjoinen* in imitation of the Latin form.

adjourn *v.* Before 1338 *ajornen* assign a day, especially a day to appear in court, borrowed from Old French *ajorner,* from the phrase *a jorn* to a stated day, (*a-* to, from Latin *ad-*) + (*jorn* day, from Latin *diurnum,* neuter of *diurnus* daily; see DIURNAL).

The present English spelling with *ad-* was influenced by the occasional Middle French form *adjorner,* which did not survive in modern French but has been retained in English since the 1500's.

The sense "to put off until a later time (originally, to another day)" appeared in 1427, in *Proceedings of the Privy Council of England.*

—adjournment *n.* 1444, borrowed from Middle French *adjournement,* from Old French *ajornement* from *ajorner;* for suffix see -MENT.

adjudge *v.* About 1380, in Chaucer's translation of Boethius' *De Consolatione Philosophiae,* Middle English *ajuggen, adjuggen,* borrowed from Old French *ajugier,* from Latin *adjūdicāre;* see the doublet ADJUDICATE.

adjudicate *v.* 1700, borrowed from Latin *adjūdicātus,* past participle of *adjūdicāre* grant or award as a judge (*ad-* to + *jūdicāre* to judge; see JUDGE); for suffix see -ATE[1]. Doublet of ADJUDGE.

—adjudication *n.* 1691, borrowed from French *adjudication,* or directly from Late Latin *adjūdicātiōnem* (nominative *adjūdicātiō*), from Latin *adjūdicāre;* for suffix see -TION.

adjunct *n.* 1588, in Shakespeare's *Love's Labour's Lost,* borrowed from Latin *adjūnctus,* past participle of *adjungere* join to; see ADJOIN. **—adj.** 1595, in Shakespeare's *King John,* joined to another, subordinate; adjective use of *adjunct,* n.

The title *adjunct professor* appeared in 1826 in American English (Catalogue of Harvard University).

adjure *v.* request earnestly. 1382, in the Wycliffe Bible, Middle English *adjuren* put to an oath, borrowed from Latin *adjūrāre* confirm by oath, (later) put to an oath (*ad-* to + *jūrāre* swear; see JURY). **—adjuration** *n.* About 1390, in Chaucer's *Canterbury Tales,* borrowed from Late Latin *adjūrātiōnem* (nominative *adjūrātiō*), from Latin *adjūrāre;* for suffix see -TION.

adjust *v.* About 1380, in Chaucer's translation of Boethius' *De Consolatione Philosophiae,* Middle English *ajusten,* borrowed from Old French *ajoster, ajuster,* from Vulgar Latin **adjuxtāre* to set beside, add (Latin *ad-* to + *juxtā* next, related to *jungere* join; see YOKE).

Later, probably before 1611, *adjust* was reborrowed from Middle French *adjuster* (modern *ajuster*), where it had already been refashioned as if from Latin *jūstus* right, JUST (the connection with Latin *juxtā* was obscured when Old French *ajoster, ajuster* became Middle French *adjouter,* modern *ajouter* to add).

—adjustment *n.* 1644, in Milton's *Works,* formed from English *adjust* + *-ment.*

adjutant *n.* 1600, in Philemon Holland's translation of Livy's *Roman History,* army officer assisting a superior officer, borrowed from Latin *adjūtantem* (nominative *adjūtāns*), present participle of *adjūtāre* to help; see AID; for suffix see -ANT.

adlib (ad lib′) *v. Informal.* to improvise. 1919, formed from (1811), abbreviation of AD LIBITUM. **—n.** something improvised. 1925, noun use of *adlib,* v.

ad libitum *Music.* free to change a passage at one's pleasure. 1610, as an adverbial phrase, New Latin *ad libitum* at one's pleasure, from Latin *ad* at, and New Latin *libitum* pleasure, from Latin *libēre* to please. In Latin the singular *libitum* does not exist. It was formed in New Latin when needed on the basis of the already existing plural *libita,* not altogether unlike the coining of *pea* from the long-established form *peas.*

admass (ad′mas′) *n., adj. British.* (of or relating to) high-pressure advertising and publicity in the mass media. 1955, from *ad* (vertisement) and *mass.* The word was coined by the English writer J.B. Priestley.

administer *v.* to serve, manage. About 1380, *amynistren, administren,* both spellings appearing in Chaucer's translation of Boethius' *De Consolatione Philosophiae,* borrowed from Old French *aministrer, administrer,* from Latin *administrāre* serve, manage (*ad-* to + *ministrāre* serve, MINISTER).

The spelling *administren* was thought to have replaced *amynistren* by imitation of the Latin form, but that is not strictly the case, for both spellings appeared in the Chaucer text.

—administrate *v.* 1651, possibly a back formation of *administration* or borrowed from Latin *administrātus,* past participle of *administrāre;* for suffix see -ATE[1]. Modern use of *administrate* seems to be confined chiefly to the U.S. and Canada and is almost certainly a back formation from *administration.* **—administration** *n.* About 1333, borrowed from Latin *administrātiōnem* (nominative *administrātiō*), from *administrāre;* for suffix see -TION. **—administrator** *n.* 1434, borrowed through Middle French *administrateur,* or directly from Latin *administrātor* manager, servant, from *administrāre;* for suffix see -OR[2].

admirable *adj.* About 1450, borrowed from Latin *admīrābilis,* from *admīrārī* ADMIRE; for suffix see -ABLE.

admiral *n.* commander of a fleet of ships. 1297 *amiral,* borrowed from Old French, traditionally said to come from Arabic *ămīr-al-* chief of the ____ (appearing in such titles as *ămīr-al-bahr* chief of the sea) and misinterpreted by Christian writers to be a word with the ending *-al*[2]. However, later scholars have suggested that the source in Arabic is more likely through cultural contact to be *ămīr-ar-raḥl* chief of the transport, referring to the fleet plying between North Africa and Andalusia.

The spelling *admiral* with *d,* in the sense of a Moslem

emir or prince, came into Middle English before 1200 borrowed from Medieval Latin *admiralis.* The Medieval Latin, which was influenced by earlier Latin *admīrābilis* ADMIRABLE, is an alteration of *amiralis,* borrowed through Old French *amiral,* or borrowed directly from Arabic.

The spelling *admiral* alternated with *amiral* until the 1500's, when *admiral* became the usual literary form. See AMIR, EMIR.

—**admiralty** *n.* 1419 *Admiralte, Amiralte* a department of State, borrowed from Middle French *amiralté,* from Old French *amiral* admiral; for suffix see -TY². The meaning of an office or command was not recorded until 1436.

admiration *n.* About 1425 *admiraciou*n, borrowed through Middle French *admiration* and Old French, or directly from Latin *admīrātiōnem* (nominative *admīrātiō*), from *admīrārī* ADMIRE; for suffix see -TION. —**admire** *v.* About 1590, borrowed through Middle French *admirer* and Old French *amirer,* or perhaps directly from Latin *admīrārī* wonder at (*ad-* at + *mīrārī* wonder, from *mīrus* wonderful, remarkable; see MIRACLE).

admissible *adj.* allowable. 1611, borrowed from Middle French *admissible,* from Latin *admissus* (past participle of *admittere* ADMIT); for suffix see -IBLE.

admission *n.* About 1430, borrowed from Latin *admissiōnem* (nominative *admissiō),* from *admiss-,* stem of *admittere* ADMIT; for suffix see -ION.

admit *v.* Before 1387 *admitten,* borrowed from Latin *admittere* (*ad-* to + *mittere* let go, send; see MISSION).

Contrary to some sources, from a phonetic standpoint transmission from French does not seem likely, because Old French forms have *e (ametre, amettre, admettre)* rather than *i.*

admixture *n.* 1605, borrowed from Latin *admixtus,* past participle of *admiscēre* (*ad-* in addition + *miscēre* MIX); for suffix see -URE.

admonish *v.* warn or reprove. 1340, in *Ayenbite of Inwyt,* Middle English *amonesten,* from Old French *amonester,* from Vulgar Latin **admonestāre,* alteration of Latin *admonēre* advise, remind (*ad-* to + *monēre* advise, warn; see MONITOR).

The ending *-ish* developed because the *-t* in Middle English *amonest-* from *amonesten* was thought to be the past participial ending that would produce the stem *amoness-,* from the pattern of English verbs like *abolish* (from Middle French *aboliss-*); the form *amonesh,* later *admonish,* was constructed by imitation.

Sometime later the prefix *a-* was replaced by *ad-* after the Latin form.

The alteration in Latin from *admonēre* to *admonestāre* was perhaps influenced by a form like *obtestārī* implore, in a phrase such as *Tē obtestor atque admonestō, nē. . .* I implore you and warn you not to. . .

admonition *n.* About 1380, in Chaucer's translation of Boethius' *De Consolatione Philosophiae,* Middle English *amonicioun,* borrowed from Old French *amonicion,* from Latin *admonitiōnem* (nominative *admonitiō)* from *admonēre* advise, see ADMONISH; for suffix see -TION.

The original Middle English form was fully replaced in the 1600's by *admonition* after the Latin, but the earliest spelling with *ad-* appeared probably before 1425.

ado *n.* doings, bustle, fuss. About 1380, contraction of *at do,* recorded about 1280 as a Northern dialectal form of *to do.* Northern English dialectal use of *at do* (as in *We have other things at do*) may have been influenced by Old Icelandic, in which the preposition *at* was used with the infinitive form of the verb, the way *to* is used in modern English.

adobe (ədō'bē) *n.* brick made of sun-dried clay. 1739, American English, borrowed from Spanish *adobe,* from Arabic (oral form) *aṭ-ṭōb,* (written form) *aṭ-ṭūb* the brick (*al-* the + *ṭūb* brick, probably from Coptic *tōb* brick).

adolescence *n.* Probably before 1425, borrowed from Middle French *adolescence,* from Latin *adolēscentia,* from *adolēscentem* (nominative *adolēscēns*), present participle of *adolēscere* grow up (*ad-* to + *-olēscere* grow up, derived from *-olēre,* related to *alere* nourish; see OLD); for suffix see -ENCE. —**adolescent** *n.* 1459, borrowed through Middle French *adolescent,* or directly from Latin *adolēscentem.*

adoption *n.* 1340, in *Ayenbite of Inwyt,* Middle English *adopciou*n, borrowed through Old French *adoption,* or directly from Latin *adoptiōnem* (nominative *adoptiō*), from *adopt-,* the stem of *adoptāre* choose for oneself, especially a child (*ad-* to + *optāre* choose, wish; see OPTION); for suffix see -TION. —**adopt** *v.* Before 1500, perhaps as a back formation of English *adoption,* traditionally considered as a borrowing through Middle French *adopter,* or directly from Latin *adoptāre.*

adore *v.* About 1375, in Chaucer's *Canterbury Tales,* Middle English *adouren, aouren,* borrowed from Old French *adourer, adorer,* from Latin *adōrāre* speak to formally, beseech, and in Late Latin, to worship (*ad-* to + *ōrāre* speak formally, pray; see ORATION).

Middle English *adouren* gradually replaced *aouren,* in use before 1300 and borrowed from Old French *aörer,* from Latin *adōrāre.*

In both Middle English and Old and Middle French two forms competed with each other through the 15th century. In French it was *adorer, adourer* and *aörer,* the forms in *d* finally being preferred probably partly because of the learned influence of the Latin *adoremus* let us pray. How much of this influenced English is debatable.

—**adoration** *n.* 1543, borrowed from Middle French, learned borrowing from Latin *adōrātiōnem* (nominative *adōrātiō*), from *adōrāre;* for suffix see -TION.

adorn *v.* About 1385, in Chaucer's *Troilus and Criseyde,* Middle English *adournen,* borrowed from Old French *adourner, adorner,* from Latin *adōrnāre* equip, embellish (*ad-* to + *ōrnāre* prepare, furnish; see ORNATE).

Middle English *adournen* gradually replaced *aournen,* in use before 1325 and borrowed from Old French *aourner, aorner,* from Latin *adōrnāre.*

—**adornment,** *n.* About 1385, borrowed from Old French *adournement, aournement,* from *adourner* to adorn, from Latin *adōrnāre;* for suffix see -MENT.

adrenal *adj.* on or near the kidneys. 1875, formed in English from Latin *ad-* at, by + Late Latin *rēnālis* of or pertaining to the kidneys, from Latin *rēnēs* kidneys; for suffix see -AL¹.

adrenalin *n.* hormone of the adrenal glands. 1901, formed in English from *adrenal* + *-in* (chemical suffix).

The term was coined by Jokichi Takamine, 1853-1922, Japanese chemist, who discovered the hormone.

adroit *adj.* 1652, borrowed from French, from Old

French *adroit, adreit,* from *a-* to (from Latin *ad-*) + (*droit, dreit* right, from Late Latin *dīrēctum* right, justice, from Latin, accusative of *dīrēctus* straight, DIRECT).

adsorb *v.* (distinguished from *absorb*). 1882, formed in English from *ad-* + *-sorb,* abstracted from earlier *absorb,* from Latin *sorbēre* suck in; *or* possibly a back formation from *adsorption.* **—adsorbent** *n.* 1928, formed in English from the verb + -ENT. **—adsorption** *n.* 1882, formed in English from *ad-* + *-sorption,* abstracted from earlier *absorption.*

adulate *v.* 1777 back formation from ADULATION; perhaps influenced by French and Middle French *aduler* to flatter, used by Diderot in the *Encyclopédie* (published 1751-1771).

adulation *n.* Before 1400, borrowed from Old French *adulacion,* from Latin *adūlātiōnem* (nominative *adūlātiō*), from *adūlārī* to flatter, fawn upon (like a dog), a word of uncertain origin); for suffix see -TION.

adult *adj.* 1531, borrowed from Latin *adultus,* past participle of *adolēscere* grow up, mature; see ADOLESCENCE. **—n.** 1658, noun use of *adult,* adj.

adulterate *v.* 1531, possibly a back formation from *adulteration,* or borrowed from Latin *adulterātus,* past participle of *adulterāre* to corrupt, give an altered form to (*ad-* to + Late Latin *alterāre* to alter; see ALTER); for suffix see -ATE[1]. **—adulterant** *n.* 1755, in Johnson's *Dictionary,* borrowed from Latin *adulterantem* (nominative *adulterāns*), present participle of *adulterāre;* for suffix see -ANT. **—adulteration** *n.* 1505, borrowed from Latin *adulterātiōnem* (nominative *adulterātiō*), from *adulterāre;* for suffix see -TION.

adultery *n.* About 1415, in Chaucer's *Canterbury Tales,* Middle English *adultrie, adulterie,* borrowed through Middle French and Old French *adulterie,* or directly as a learned borrowing from Latin *adulterium,* from *adulterāre* to corrupt, ADULTERATE; for suffix see -Y[3].

Middle English *adultrie, adulterie* was a replacement of *advoutrie* and earlier (about 1303) *avoutrie,* borrowed from Old French *avoutrie,* which coexisted with *adulterie* into the 16th century in French, from *avoutre* adulterer, from Latin *adulterum,* accusative of *adulter,* from *adulterāre* to corrupt, ADULTERATE. **—adulterous** *adj.* replaced (before 1400) Middle English *avoutrious,* from *avouter,* borrowed from Old French *avoutre;* for suffix see -OUS.

adumbrate *v.* to foreshadow. 1581, borrowed from Latin *adumbrātus,* past participle of *adumbrāre* to cast a shadow over, shade in sketching (*ad-* to + *umbra* shade); for suffix see -ATE[1]. The formation of *adumbrate* in English was probably influenced by a tendency to back formation from *adumbration,* which appeared fifty years earlier but in a different sense. **—adumbration** *n.* 1531, shading in printing, borrowed from Latin *adumbrātiōnem* (nominative *adumbrātiō*), from *adumbrāre;* for suffix see -TION. The meaning "a foreshadowing" is recorded in English in 1552.

ad valorem (ad vəlôr′əm), (of duty or tax on goods) according to the value (of the goods). 1698, New Latin, from Latin *ad* to + Medieval Latin *valorem* worth; see VALOR.

advance *v.* Before 1200, in *Ancrene Riwle,* Middle English *avauncen* move forward, borrowed from Old French *avancer, avancier,* from Vulgar Latin **abanteāre,* from Latin *abante* from before (*ab* from + *ante* before; see ANTE-).

The form *advance* resulted during the 1500's and 1600's because the initial *a* was thought to represent Latin *ad* and was therefore refashioned after Latin words in *ad-*. This occurred in the French word occasionally, but in English it became a permanent adoption. The same error led to the spelling *advantage* in place of *avantage.*

—advancement *n.* About 1300 *avauncement,* borrowed from Old French *avancement,* from *avancer;* for suffix see -MENT.

advantage *n.* About 1300 *avantage, avauntage* a being ahead, superiority, borrowed from Old French *avantage,* from *avant* before, from Latin *abante,* see ADVANCE; for suffix see -AGE.

The occasional Middle French spelling *advantage,* as if from Latin *ad-,* became permanently adopted in English in the late 1500's. **—advantageous** *adj.* 1598, formed in English from *advantage* + -OUS.

advent *n.* Old English *Advent* the season of devotion before Christmas (963, in *The Anglo-Saxon Chronicle*), borrowed from Latin *adventus* (genitive *adventūs*) arrival, from *adven-,* stem of *advenīre* arrive, come to (*ad-* to + *venīre* come; see COME).

In the middle of the 1400's *Advent* was extended to the Second Coming, and in the 1700's extended to any important or epoch-making arrival, as the *advent* of the Normans or of spring, a sense influenced in part by the primary sense of "arrival" in Latin.

adventitious (ad′vəntish′əs) *adj.* coming from outside; additional; accidental. 1603, borrowed from Medieval Latin *adventitius,* alteration of Latin *adventīcius,* from *adventum,* past participle of *advenīre* arrive, see ADVENT; for suffix see -ITIOUS.

The meaning in biology, "appearing outside the normal place," is recorded in English in 1676.

adventure *n.* Before 1200, in *Ancrene Riwle,* Middle English *aventure* that which comes by chance, borrowed from Old French *aventure,* from Vulgar Latin **adventūra* a happening, from the Latin future participle of *advenīre* to come about, see ADVENT; for suffix see -URE.

In the 1400's and 1500's the French form was often respelled *adventure* in imitation of Latin, and though the fashion soon died out in France, the respelled form passed permanently into English. **—adventurous** *adj.* About 1380, in Chaucer's translation of Boethius' *De Consolatione Philosophiae,* Middle English *aventurous,* borrowed from Old French *aventuros,* from *aventure;* for suffix see -OUS.

An older spelling (about 1330) exists *(aunterous)* but in the available citations is confined to describing the knight errant in the phrase *aunterous knigt* or *knyght auntrous.*

adverb *n.* About 1425, borrowed perhaps through Old French *averbe,* or more likely directly from Latin *adverbium* (*ad-* to + *verbum* word, verb; translation of Greek *epírrhēma,* from *epi-* on, to + *rhêma* verb). Greek *rhêma* (originally) word, cognate with Latin *verbum* and Old English *weord* WORD, is from Indo-European **were-/wrē-* (Pok. 1162).

adversary *n.* 1340, in *Ayenbite of Inwyt,* borrowed through Old French *adversaire,* or directly from Latin *adversārius,* from *adversus* turned against, ADVERSE; for suffix see -ARY.

adverse *adj.* About 1385, in Chaucer's *Troilus and Criseyde,* borrowed from Old French *avers, advers,* from Latin *adversus* turned against, past participle of *advertere;* see ADVERT. **—adversity** *n.* Before 1200, in *Ancrene Riwle,* Middle English *adversite,* borrowed from Old French *adversité,* from Latin *adversitātem* (nominative *adversitās*) opposition, from *adversus* turned against; for suffix see -ITY.

advert (advėrt′) *v.* to refer to. Before 1420, in Lydgate's *Troy Book,* Middle English *averten* turn toward, notice; borrowed from Old French *avertir,* from Latin *advertere* (*ad-* to + *vertere* to turn; see VERTEX). Compare AVERT.

The spelling *advert* replaced the Middle English form in the 1500's, partly in imitation of the Latin form, partly by influence of Middle French *advertir* warn (see ADVERTISE).

advertise *v.* Probably before 1425, in a translation of Higden's *Polychronicon,* Middle English *advertisen* take notice (of), borrowed from Middle French *advertiss-,* stem of *advertir,* variant of Old French *avertir* warn, from Vulgar Latin **advertīre,* corresponding to Latin *advertere* turn toward (*ad-* toward + *vertere* to turn; see VERTEX). **—advertisement** *n.* 1426, in *Proceedings of the Privy Council,* borrowed from Middle French *advertissement,* from *advertiss-,* stem of *advertir;* for suffix see -MENT.

advice (advīs′) *n.* About 1300 *avis* opinion, borrowed from Old French *avis,* from the phrase *a vis,* as in *ce m'est a vis* my view is, an alteration of *(ce) m'est vis* it seems to me, from Vulgar Latin **mī est vīsum,* corresponding to Latin *mihī vidētur* seems (best) to me.

While the phrases explain the development, the source of the borrowing is Latin *ad* to + *vīsum,* neuter past participle of *vidēre* to see; see WIT[2] know.

The spelling *advis* was popularized in English by Caxton in the late 1400's, from the occasional French spelling *advis,* in imitation of the Latin. In the 1500's final *-e* was added to show vowel quantity of *i;* and in the 1700's the *s* was changed to *c* apparently to distinguish the word from the verb *advise.*

advise (advīz′) *v.* give advice. About 1300 *avisen* examine, find out, consider, decide, devise, borrowed from Old French *aviser,* from *avis* opinion; see ADVICE.

The spelling *advise* replaced *avisen* in the late 1400's by influence of the occasional Middle French spelling *adviser,* in imitation of the Latin.

The later form *advisor* is a back formation from *advisory,* or a direct borrowing of the Late Latin *advīsor.* **—adviser** *n.* 1611, formed from English *advise* + *-er,* perhaps after Late Latin *advīsor.***—advisory** *adj.* 1778, formed from English *advise* + *-ory,* as if an adaptation of Late Latin **advīsōrius,* from Late Latin *advīsor.*

advocacy *n.* About 1385, in Chaucer's *Troilus and Criseyde,* Middle English *advocacie,* borrowed from Old French *advocacie,* learned borrowing from Medieval Latin *advocatia,* from Latin *advocātus* ADVOCATE; for suffix see -ACY.

advocate *n.* 1340, in *Ayenbite of Inwyt,* Middle English *avocat,* borrowed from Old French, learned borrowing from Latin *advocātus,* originally past participle of *advocāre* call to, as a witness or advisor (*ad-* to + *vocāre* to call, related to *vōcem* voice; see VOICE); for suffix see -ATE[1]. The original Middle English spelling was largely replaced after 1380 by *advocat* after the Latin form. **—v.** 1641, from the noun.

adz or **adze** *n.* cutting tool similar to an ax. Old English (before 830, in the *Vespasian Psalter*) *adesa, eadesa,* whose origin is unknown.

In Middle English the term was spelled *adese, adse;* the current forms with *z* appeared in the 1700's.

aegis (ē′jis) *n.* protection, auspices. 1793, figurative sense of earlier (1611, in Coryat's *Crudities*) *aegis* shield, especially the shield of Jupiter or Minerva, borrowed from Latin *aegis,* from Greek *aigís* the shield of Zeus (said to be made of goatskin, and therefore popularly derived from *aig-,* the stem of *aíx* goat).

aeolian (ēō′lēən) *adj.* carried by the wind. 1605, formed in English from Latin *Aeolius* (from *Aeolus* the god of the winds, from Greek *Aíolos,* from *aiólos* quickly moving) + English *-an.*

aeon or **eon** (ē′on) *n.* very long period of time; age. 1647, borrowed from Latin *aeōn,* from Greek *aiṓn* age, lifetime; see AGE.

Since the early 1970's *aeon* has been used in geology and astronomy to mean a period of one billion years.

aer- a combining form meaning air, in a few derivatives and compounds, used before a vowel, as in *aerate, aerify.* Borrowed from Latin *āēr* (from Greek *āḗr*), *āer-* (as in *āerius* aerial). Much more productive in derivatives is *aero-,* ultimately borrowed from Greek *āero-.*

aerate (ār′āt) *v.* 1794, formed in English after Latin *āēr* air (from Greek *āḗr*) + English suffix *-ate*[1].

The formation of *aerate* was perhaps influenced indirectly by Old French *aérer.*

aerial (ār′ēəl) *adj.* of or like the air. 1604, in Shakespeare's *Othello,* formed in English after Latin *āerius* airy (from Greek *āérios,* from *āḗr* air) + English suffix *-al*[1]; see AIR. **—n.** radio or television antenna. 1902, noun use of *aerial,* adj.

aerie or **aery** (ãr′ē *or* ir′ē) *n.* nest of a bird of prey. Before 1475 *eyre,* later *airie* (1581); borrowed from Medieval Latin *aeria,* from Old French *aire,* from Latin *ārea* level ground, garden bed, AREA. The common variant spelling *eyrie* (used by Milton, Joyce, Tolkien, etc.) was introduced in the 1600's in the belief that the word was derived from Middle English *ey(e),* meaning egg, and its literal meaning was "a repository for eggs."

aero- a combining form meaning: **1** air: *Aerometer = air meter.* **2** atmosphere: *Aerology = science of the atmosphere.* **3** gas: *Aerodynamics = dynamics of gases.* **4** aircraft: *Aerodrome = landing field for aircraft.* Before 1393, in Gower's *Confessio Amantis,* abstracted in Middle English from *aeromance* divination by studying the air, borrowed from Old French *aeromancié,* or from Medieval Latin *aeromantia.* The combining form is ultimately from Greek *āero-,* from *āḗr, āéros* air. Most of the *aero-* compounds are relatively late coinages. Some that date from the late 1700's were coined in France, reflecting concern with flight, especially in lighter-than-air craft; the earliest balloon ascent was in France in 1783. Some examples, in form adapted into English, are *aerology* 1736, *aeronaut* 1784, *aerostatics* 1784, and *aerostat* (the original term for a balloon) 1784.

aerobic *adj.* living on atmospheric oxygen. 1884, formed in English after French *aérobic* (coined in 1863 by Louis Pasteur, 1822-1895, from Greek *āḗr, āéros* air + *bíos* life) + English suffix *-ic.* **—aerobics** *n.* system of exercises designed for maximum use of oxygen. 1968 (coined by Kenneth H. Cooper, American physician), formed in English from *aerobic* + *-s*, on analogy with *gymnastics, calisthenics,* etc.

aeronautics *n.* 1824, formed in English from *aeronautic* + *-s* on analogy with *aerostatics,* etc.; or from New Latin *aeronautica* (1753 in *Chambers Cyclopaedia*) + English suffix *-ics.* **—aeronautic** *adj.* 1784, borrowed from French *aéronautique,* from *aéro-* (from Greek *āero-*, from *āḗr, āéros* air) + *nautique* of ships, nautical (from Latin *nautica,* feminine singular and neuter plural of *nauticus,* from Greek *nautikós*); for suffix see -IC.

aeroplane *n.* Originally the accepted spelling in American and British English, now considered British and replaced in American English, especially after World War II, by *airplane.* 1873, borrowed from French *aéroplane,* from *aéro-* of air (from Greek *āero-*) + *plane,* stem of *planer* to soar; see PLANE[1], v.

aerosol (ãr′əsol) *n.* fine particles of a solid or liquid substance suspended in air or a gas. 1923, formed in English from *aero-* of air + *sol* (1899) colloidal solution, shortened from *solution.*

aerospace *n.* 1958, formed in American English from *aero-* atmosphere + (outer) *space.*

aesthetic *adj.* 1798, of or having to do with sensuous perception (after Immanuel Kant), borrowed from French *esthétique* and German *ästhetisch,* from Greek *aisthētikós* perceptible to the senses, from *aisthánesthai* perceive, see AUDIBLE; for suffix see -IC.

The broad sense pertaining to an appreciation of beauty (after Alexander Baumgarten) was already established in German (1750-58) by the time Kant (1781) used the word, but the meaning did not develop in English until sometime between 1803 and 1825. It is first recorded in the OED as used by Coleridge in 1821. **—aesthetics** *n.* 1803, possibly formed in English from *aesthetic* + *-s,* on analogy with *athletic* + *-s;* or borrowed from German *Ästhetik,* from Greek *aisthētikós;* or from New Latin *aesthetica;* see AESTHETIC; for suffix see -ICS. **—aesthete** *n.* person with appreciation of beauty. 1881, borrowed from Greek *aisthētḗs* person who perceives; cited in most sources as a formation on analogy with *athlete, athletic.*

af- a form of the prefix *ad-*, meaning to, toward, before *f,* as in *affect, affirm.* In words from Latin the form is due to the assimilation of the *d* to the following consonant *(f).*

affable *adj.* Probably about 1475, borrowed from Middle French *affable,* learned borrowing from Latin *affābilis* easy to speak to, from *affārī* speak to (*af-* to, variant of *ad-* before *f* + *fārī* speak; related to FABLE); for suffix see -ABLE.

affair *n.* Probably before 1300 *afer,* in the plural use *aferes* things to do, activities, borrowed from Anglo-French *afere,* from Old French *afaire* (*à faire* to do, from Latin *ad* to + *facere* DO[1] perform).

The Old French spelling with one *f* was refashioned in Middle French as *affaire* after Latin words with *aff-*, and this spelling was popularized in England by Caxton.

The development of the French word parallels that of English *ado.*

affect[1] *v.* have an effect on. 1410 *affecten,* borrowed from Latin *affectus,* past participle of *afficere* act on, exert influence on (*af-* to, variant of *ad-* before *f* + *facere* DO[1] perform).

affect[2] *v.* make a pretense or show of. Probably before 1425 *affecten* to desire, aim at, aspire to, borrowed from Middle French *affecter,* learned borrowing from Latin *affectāre* strive for, frequentative verb form of *afficere* act on; see AFFECT[1]). **—affectation** *n.* 1548, borrowed through Middle French *affectation,* or directly from Latin *affectātiōnem* (nominative *affectātiō*), from *affectāre;* for suffix see -TION.

affection *n.* Probably before 1200, in *Ancrene Riwle,* emotion or feeling, borrowed from Old French *affection,* learned borrowing from Latin *affectiōnem* (nominative *affectiō*) inclination, influence, from *affec-*, stem of *afficere* act on, AFFECT[1]; for suffix see -TION.

afferent (af′ərənt) *adj. Physiology.* conducting inward. 1839-47, borrowed from Latin *afferentem* (nominative *afferēns*), present participle of *afferre* bring to (*af-* to, variant of *ad-* before *f* + *ferre* bring; see BEAR[2] carry); for suffix see -ENT.

affiance (əfī′əns) *n.* betrothal. Before 1338, borrowed from Old French *afiance,* from *afi-* stem of *afier, affier* to trust, from Medieval Latin *affidare* (Latin *af-* to, variant of *ad-* before *f* + Vulgar Latin **fidāre* to trust, from Latin *fīdus* faithful; see FAITH); for suffix see -ANCE. **—v.** betroth. 1555, borrowed from Middle French *afiancer,* from Old French *afiance,* n. betrothal.

affidavit *n.* 1598, in Ben Jonson's *Every Man in His Humor,* borrowed from Medieval Latin *affidavit* he has stated on oath, third person singular perfect of *affidare* to trust; see AFFIANCE.

affiliation *n.* 1751, adoption; (later) joining in association, borrowed from French *affiliation,* from Medieval Latin *affiliationem* (nominative *affiliatio*), from *affiliare* adopt as a son (Latin *af-* to, variant of *ad-* before *f* + *filius* son; see FILIAL); for suffix see -ATION. **—affiliate** *v.* join in association. 1761, in Smollett's *Gil Blas,* borrowed after French *affilier,* from Medieval Latin *affiliatus,* past participle of *affiliare;* for suffix see -ATE[1]. Alternatively *affiliate* may be a back formation in English from earlier *affiliation.* **—n.** 1879, from the verb.

affinity *n.* About 1303, in Mannyng's *Handlyng Synne,* relationship by marriage, borrowed from Old French *afinité, affinité,* learned borrowing from Latin *affīnitātem* (nominative *affīnitās*), from *affīnis* kin by marriage (*af-* to, variant of *ad-* before *f* + *fīnis* border, end; see FINE); for suffix see -ITY.

affirm *v.* Probably before 1300 *affermen* make firm, borrowed from Old French *afermer,* from Latin *affirmāre* (*af-* to, variant of *ad-* before *f* + *firmāre* strengthen, affirm, from *firmus* strong, FIRM). In the 1500's the original spellings were refashioned after the Latin as French *affirmer* and English *affirm.* **—affirmation** *n.* About 1410, borrowed through Middle French, or directly from Latin *affirmātiōnem* (nominative *affirmātiō*), from *affirmāre;* for suffix see -TION. **—affirmative** *adj., n.* About 1400, through Middle French, or directly from Late Latin *affirmātīvus,* from Latin *affirmātus* past participle of *affirmāre* affirm; for suffix see -ATIVE.

affix *v.* 1533, borrowed from Medieval Latin *affixare,* frequentative verb form of Latin *affigere* fasten to (*af-* to, variant of *ad-* before *f* + *figere* fasten; see FIX). **—n.** 1612, borrowed from French *affixe,* from Latin *affixum,* past participle of *affigere* fasten to.

affliction *n.* About 1303, in Mannyng's *Handlyng Synne,* Middle English *affliccioun,* borrowed from Old French *afflicion,* from Latin *afflīctiōnem* (nominative *afflīctiō*), from *afflīgere;* for suffix see -TION. —**afflict** *v.* Before 1393, in Gower's *Confessio Amantis,* to cast down or deject, borrowed from Old French *afflicter,* from Latin *afflīctus,* past participle of *afflīgere* to dash down, distress (*af-* to, variant of *ad-* before *f* + *flīgere* to dash, strike; see CONFLICT). The meaning of trouble, distress is first recorded in Sir Thomas More's *Works* (1535). In this meaning *afflict* takes the place of *aflight,* recorded before 1393 and borrowed from Old French *aflit* distressed, from Latin *afflīctus,* past participle of *afflīgere.*

affluent *adj.* 1413, flowing in abundance, copious; borrowed through Middle French, or directly from Latin *affluentem* (nominative *affluēns*), present participle of *affluere* flow towards (*af-* to, variant of *ad-* before *f* + *fluere* to flow; see FLUENT); for suffix see -ENT. The currently commonest meaning of abounding in riches, wealthy, appeared in the 1700's. —**affluence** *n.* About 1350, borrowed from Middle French, from Latin *affluentia,* from *affluentem* (nominative *affluēns*), present participle of *affluere;* for suffix see -ENCE.

afford *v.* 1588, in Shakespeare's *Love's Labour's Lost,* (spelled with two *f's* after words in Latin beginning with *af-*) an alteration of Middle English *aforthen* (probably before 1387, in a version of *Piers Plowman*) and earlier *ivorthen* (probably before 1200, in Layamon's *Chronicle of Britain*). These forms were reduced from Old English *geforthian* to further, accomplish (*ge-,* prefix implying completeness + *forthian* to further, from *forth* forward, onward, FORTH).

The change from *th* to *d,* which occurred in the 1500's, was similar to the earlier change of such forms as *burthen* to *burden* and *murther* to *murder.*

affray *n.* noisy quarrel, brawl. About 1303, in Mannyng's *Handlyng Synne,* disturbance, alarm, fright, borrowed from Old French *effrei* disturbance, fright, from *effreer, esfreer* disturb, frighten, from Vulgar Latin **exfridāre* (literally) to take out of peace. The Vulgar Latin is formed of Latin *ex-* out of + Frankish **frithu* peace, represented in Old High German *fridu,* Old Saxon *frithu,* and Old English *frithu* peace, from Proto-Germanic **fríthuz* consideration, forbearance, cognate with Sanskrit *príti-s* joy, pleasure, *priyá-s* dear, from Indo-European **prī-/pri-* (root **prāi-*) love (Pok.844).

affront (əfrunt′) *v.* insult to one's face. About 1330, borrowed from Old French *afronter,* from Vulgar Latin **affrontāre* to face, confront (literally) strike on the forehead, from Latin *ad frontem* to the face. —**n.** an insult. 1598, noun use of *affront,* v. See FRONT.

aficionado (əfis′yənä′dō), *n.* devotee of some sport, hobby, etc. 1845, borrowed from Spanish *aficionado* amateur, (literally) fond of, from *afición* affection, from Latin *affectiōnem;* see AFFECTION. Most sources derive this word from the Spanish verb *aficionar;* however, according to Corominas, the verb does not appear in Spanish before 1555, and the word *aficionado* is recorded in the 1400's.

aflatoxin (af′lətok′sən) *n.* poisonous substance produced by a common mold. 1962, formed in English from New Latin *A(spergillus) fla(vus),* the species of mold (Latin *aspergere* to sprinkle, and *flāvus* yellow) + English *toxin.*

afraid *adj.* Probably about 1300, in *The Romance of Guy of Warwick,* originally the past participle of the archaic verb *afray* frighten, borrowed through Anglo-French *afrayer, effrayer* disturb, frighten, from Old French *effreer, esfreer;* see AFFRAY.

The form *afraid* as a past participle is similar in construction to *laid,* past participle of *lay, said,* past participle of *say,* etc.

Afrikaans *n.* language of South Africa developed from Dutch. 1908, borrowed from obsolete Dutch *Afrikaansch,* from *Afrikaan* African, from Latin *Āfricānus,* from *Āfrī,* plural of *Āfer,* the name of an ancient people of North Africa, the ancestors of the modern Berbers.

Afro- a combining form for *African,* from the stem *Āfr-* of Latin *Āfer, Āfrī* African. The form *Afr-* sometimes occurs before a vowel, as in *Aframerican.*

aft *adv. Nautical.* at or toward the stern; abaft. Before 1325, Middle English *afte* back, developed from Old English (937) *æftan* from behind; cognate with Old High German *aftan* from behind, Old Icelandic *aptan* (*pt* represents sounds *ft*), and Gothic *aftana.* Related to AFTER.

after *adv., prep.* Old English *æfter* next or following in time (before 735, in *Bede's Death Song*).

Originally *æfter* was a comparative form meaning "farther back, more away." Compare AFT.

Old English *æfter* is cognate with Old High German *aftar* back, behind, Old Icelandic *aptr* back, aft, *eptir* after (*pt* represents sounds *ft*), and Gothic *aftra* back, *aftarō* from behind, from Proto-Germanic **afteraz,* from the Indo-European **opiteros,* formed from **opi* back (found in Greek *ópithen* from behind) (Pok. 323).

aftermath *n.* 1523, a second or later mowing of grass; formed from English *after* + dialectal *math* a mowing, Old English *mǣth,* cognate with Old High German *mād* (modern German *Mahd* mowing, hay crop), from Proto-Germanic **mǣthan;* also cognate with Greek *ámētos* harvest, from Indo-European **mē-/mə-* (Pok. 703). From Old English *mǣth* the expected modern resultant would be **meath,* but lack of accent led to shortening and modification of the vowel of the second member of the compound in *aftermath.*

The current meaning is a figurative sense occurring before 1658.

afterward *adv.* Old English (about 1000) *æfterweard* (*æfter* after + *-weard* -ward, suffix indicating direction).

The form **afterwards** appeared about 1300 in Middle English as a derivative of *afterward* with the adverbial genitive ending *-s* and *-es.*

ag- a form of the prefix *ad-,* meaning to, towards, before *g,* as in *aggress, aggrieve.* In words from Latin the form is due to the assimilation of the *d* to the following consonant *(g).*

again *adv.* Late Old English (1031) *agan,* (1052) *agean* back (to a starting point), reduced before 830 from Old English *ongegn, ongēan* toward, opposite, against, back, again (*on* on + *gegn* against, toward).

The Old English *ongegn, ongēan* are cognate with Old High German *ingegin, ingagan* against, in opposition to (modern German *entgegen*).

The Old English forms *-gegn, -gēan* are found only in compounds and are cognate with Old High German *gegin, gagan* against, toward (modern German *gegen*), and with Old Icelandic *gegn* toward, again. The Proto-

Germanic root *$\mathfrak{z}$a$\mathfrak{z}$- of these adverbs (often altered later to *$\mathfrak{z}$e$\mathfrak{z}$-) is of unknown origin.

against *prep.* Probably before 1160 *agenes* in opposition to, against, from *agen* again (Old English *ongegn* opposite, AGAIN) + the ending *-s, -es* adverbial genitive suffix. The ending *-st* was added in the late 1300's to this word and to others, such as *among (amongst)* and *amid (amidst),* probably by confusion with superlatives ending in *-st.* Traditionally the ending *-s* in *against* is said to come from a change in pronunciation that developed in southern English dialect, influenced by a confusion with superlatives ending in *-st* (an example of the added *-st* often given is *amid, amidst,* an example of the *-t* is *betwyx, betwixt*). Forms in *-st* began to appear about 1300, according to the *Middle English Dictionary,* and "are abstracted from the sequence *agen(e)s the.*"

agape (ag′əpē) *n.* brotherly love. 1690, love feast held by early Christians, perhaps influenced by early French *agape,* but borrowed from Greek *agápē* love, from *agapân* to love.

agar (ä′gər) *n.* gelatinlike extract made from seaweeds. 1889, short for earlier (1813) *agar-agar* an East Indian seaweed, borrowed from Malay *agar-agar.*

agaric (ag′ərik) *n.* a kind of fungus. 1422, perhaps through French *agaric,* or borrowed directly from Latin *agaricum,* from Greek *agarikón,* from *Agariā* a place in Sarmatia, ancient region in Europe comprising much of Poland and Russia; for suffix see -IC.

agate *n.* 1570, borrowed from Middle French *agate,* alteration of Old French *acate,* learned borrowing from Latin *achātes,* from Greek *achā́tēs,* named after Achates, a river in Sicily where Pliny reports the mineral was first found. But the Hellenist Hjalmar Frisk thinks that *achā́tēs* was a non-Greek word of unknown origin, and that the river got its name from the stone.

agave (əgä′vē) *n.* any of various American desert plants. 1797, New Latin *agave,* from Greek *Agaúē,* a proper name in mythology, from *agaué* feminine of *agaués* noble, perhaps from *ágasthai* wonder at.

age *n.* About 1275, borrowed from Old French *aage,* earlier *eage,* from Vulgar Latin **aetāticum,* from Latin *aetātem* (nominative *aetās*) period of life. The Latin word is a contraction of *aevitās,* from *aevum* lifetime, eternity, age.

The Latin *aevum* is cognate with Greek *aión* age, Sanskrit *ā́yus* life, and in the Germanic languages is cognate with Old English *ā, ō* always, ever, Old High German *eo, io* (modern German *je* ever), and Gothic *aiws* time, eternity. The word is traceable to the Indo-European base **aiw-, *ayu-,* meaning vitality, life (Pok. 17).

—v. make old. Before 1420, in Lydgate's *Troy Book;* from the noun.

-age a suffix acquired in many words borrowed from French, especially Old French, such as *message, tonnage, umbrage, voyage,* and extensively used in English to form nouns from other nouns, expressing various relations (as in *baggage, parsonage, peerage, postage, poundage*), and from verbs, expressing action or the result of action (as in *breakage, cleavage, wreckage*). Old French *-age* is from Latin *-āticum,* neuter of the adjective suffix *-āticus,* that originated as the form with *-ā* stem nouns of *-ticus,* from Greek *-tikós.*

ageism *n.* discrimination against old people. 1970, coined by R.N. Butler, American gerontologist, from (old) *age* + *-ism,* on the pattern of such words as *sexism* and *racism,* in which particular cases *-ism* implies discriminatory practice or behavior.

agency *n.* 1658, borrowed from Medieval Latin *agentia,* from Latin *agentem* (nominative *agēns*), present participle of *agere,* to do, see AGENT; for suffix see -ENCY. French *agence,* recorded in 1653, though probably not the source of the English borrowing, shows that this word, like so many others, was "in the air" in cultivated circles in mid-17th century Europe, and that exact histories of borrowing are not possible to trace, but only patterns of cultural contact can be described.

agenda *n.* 1657, borrowed from Latin *agenda,* plural of *agendum,* neuter gerundive of *agere* to drive, lead, do; see AGENT.

agent *n.* 1471, in Ripley's *The Compend of Alchemy,* perhaps influenced by Old French *agent,* but probably borrowed from Latin *agentem* (nominative *agēns*), present participle of *agere* to do, act, lead, drive; for suffix see -ENT.

The Latin *agere* is cognate with Greek *ágein* to lead, Sanskrit *ájati* (he) drives, Tocharian *āk-* to travel, lead, and Old Icelandic *aka* to travel —all traceable to the Indo-European base *aĝ-,* with the meaning "drive."(Pok. 4).

aggiornamento (əjôr′nəmen′tō) *n.* modernization of practices and institutions of the Roman Catholic Church. 1963, borrowed from Italian *aggiornamento,* from *aggiornare* bring up to date (*a-* to + *giorno* day, from Latin *diurnum,* neuter of *diurnus* daily; see DIURNAL).

agglomerate *v.* gather together in a mass. 1684, borrowed from Latin *agglomerātus,* past participle of *agglomerāre* to wind or add onto a ball (*ag-* on, variant of *ad-* before *g* + *glomerāre* wind up into a ball, from *glomus,* genitive *glomeris,* ball; see CLAM; for suffix see -ATE[1]. —**agglomeration** *n.* 1774, formed in English from *agglomerate* + *-ion;* or borrowed from French *agglomération,* from Latin *agglomerātus,* past participle of *agglomerāre;* for suffix see -ATION.

agglutinate *v.* fasten as with glue. 1586, in Bright's *Treatise on Melancholie,* verb use of earlier *agglutinate,* adj., glued, (1541, in Copland's translation of Galen's *Terapeutyke*), borrowed from Latin *agglūtinātus,* past participle of *agglūtināre* fasten with glue (*ag-* to, variant of *ad-* before *g* + *glūtināre* to glue, from *glūten,* genitive *glutinis,* glue, related to Late Latin *glūs* glue; see CLAY); for suffix see -ATE[1].

It is possible that *agglutinate* is a back formation from *agglutination,* and also that formation of *agglutinate* was influenced by earlier Middle French *s'aglutiner* join morally or mentally, used in the 1300's, and *aglutiner* bring together (two people), used in the 1400's. —**agglutination** *n.* 1541, in Copland's translation of Galen's *Terapeutyke,* probably formed in English from Latin *agglūtināre* + English *-ation.*

aggrandize *v.* make greater. 1634, borrowed from French *agrandiss-,* extended stem of *agrandir* (Old French *a-* to + *grandir* to increase, from Latin *grandīre* make great, from *grandis* great, GRAND). The doubling of the *g* was influenced by Middle French *aggrandir* and Italian *aggrandire* and the attempt to correct what may have been considered a corrupted Latin prefix by supplying *ag-* in place of *a-* before *grandiss-.*

The suffix *-ize* was used with the original French

verb stem *-is, -iss,* in imitation of Greek verbs or verbs thought to derive from Greek.

aggravate *v.* 1530, in Palsgrave's *Lesclarcissement,* the meaning is "make heavy, burden down," verb use of Middle English *aggravate,* adj., meaning weighed down, burdened, attested in 1471 in Ripley's *The Compend of Alchemy.* The Middle English word was borrowed possibly through influence of Old French *aggraver,* from Latin *aggravātus,* past participle of *aggravāre* make heavier (*ag-* to, variant of *ad-* before *g* + *gravāre* weigh down, from *gravis* heavy; see GRAVE[2] weighty); for suffix see -ATE[1]. Doublet of AGGRIEVE.

The sense of "exasperate, annoy" was first recorded in 1611, in Cotgrave's *Dictionary.*

—aggravation *n.* 1481, in Caxton's *Mirror of the World,* borrowed from Old French *aggravation,* from Late Latin *aggravātiōnem* (nominative *aggravātiō*), from Latin *aggravāre* make heavy; for suffix see -TION.

aggregate *adj.* About 1400 *aggregat* collected into a mass, borrowed from Latin *aggregātus,* past participle of *aggregāre* add to (*ag-* to, variant of *ad-* before *g* + *grex,* genitive *gregis* flock, herd, see GREGARIOUS); for suffix see -ATE[1]. **—v.** Probably before 1400, in Wycliffe's writings, borrowed from Latin *aggregātus.* **—n.** Before 1425, in Wycliffe's sermons, borrowed from Latin *aggregātum,* neuter past participle of *aggregāre.* **—aggregation** *n.* Probably before 1425, borrowed through Middle French *agrégation,* or directly from Medieval Latin *aggregationem* (nominative *aggregatio*), from Latin *aggregāre;* for suffix see -TION.

aggress *v.* About 1575, approach or march forward, borrowed through French *aggresser,* or directly from Latin *aggressus,* past participle of *aggredī* to approach, attack (*ag-* to, variant of *ad-* before *g* + *gradī* to step, walk, see GRADE). The meaning to attack or commit aggression is recorded before 1714, in Prior's *Ode to Queen Anne.* **—aggressive** *adj.* 1824, formed in English from *aggress* + *-ive.*

aggression *n.* 1611, borrowed through French *agression,* or directly from Latin *aggressiōnem* (nominative *aggressiō*), from *gress-,* stem of *aggredī* to attack; see AGGRESS; for suffix see -ION.

aggrieve *v.* Now rare in English except in the passive use. Probably before 1300, Middle English *agreven,* borrowed from Old French *agrever* bear heavily on, make heavier or more severe, from Latin *aggravāre* make heavier. Doublet of AGGRAVATE. In the 1300's the French form, and in the 1400's the English form, began to be written *agg-,* after the Latin.

aghast *adj.* Probably before 1325 *agast* terrified, from the past participle of earlier *agasten* terrify, probably before 1200, in Layamon's *Chronicle of Britain.* Middle English *agasten* was formed from *a-,* intensive prefix + *gasten* frighten, Old English *gǣstan,* from *gǣst, gāst* spirit, ghost; see GHOST.

The spelling *aghast* became widespread in the 1700's, probably by influence of *ghastly* and *ghost.*

agile *adj.* 1581, borrowed from Middle French *agile,* from Latin *agilis,* from *agere* to move; see AGENT. **—agility** *n.* 1413, borrowed from Middle French *agilité,* from Latin *agilitātem* (nominative *agilitās*), from *agilis;* for suffix see -ITY.

agitate *v.* 1586, verb use of Middle English *agitat,* adj. 1449, borrowed from Latin *agitātus,* past participle of *agitāre* move to and fro, frequentative form of *agere* to drive, lead, do; see AGENT; for suffix see -ATE[1]. **—agitation** *n.* 1596, in Shakespeare's *Merchant of Venice,* borrowed from Latin *agitātiōnem* (nominative *agitātiō*), from *agitāre;* for suffix see -TION.

agnostic (agnos′tik) *n.* person who believes that nothing can be known outside human experience. 1870, coined by Thomas Huxley in 1869 from Greek *ágnōstos* unknown, unknowable (*a-* not + *gnōstós* (to be) known; see GNOSTIC) + English suffix *-ic.* **—agnosticism** *n.* 1870, formed in English from *agnostic* + *-ism.*

ago *adj.* Probably about 1300, originally Middle English past participle of *agon* go away, go forth, developed from Old English *āgān,* about 897, in *Anglo-Saxon Chronicle* (from *ā-* a-[5], prefix meaning away, forth, out + *gān* GO).

agog *adv., adj.* excited. Before 1405, borrowed from the Middle French phrase *en gogues* in good humor, of uncertain origin.

agonize *v.* 1583, to subject to agony, borrowed from Middle French *agoniser* torment, from Late Latin *agōnizāre,* from Greek *agōnízesthai* to contend, struggle, from *agṓn* (genitive *agônos*) a contest, see AGONY; for suffix see -IZE.

agony *n.* About 1384, in the Wycliffe Bible, perhaps borrowed from Old French *agonie,* or directly from Late Latin *agōnia,* from Greek *agōníā* a struggle, from *agṓn* a contest, assembly, from *ágein* to conduct, celebrate; originally "to lead"; see AGENT; for suffix see -Y[3].

agora (ag′ərə) *n.* marketplace of an ancient Greek city. 1598, in Hakluyt's *Voyages,* borrowed from Greek *agorā́* marketplace, place of assembly, from *ageírein* to gather together, related to Latin *grex* (genitive *gregis*) flock. Greek *ageírein* is built on a stem *ager-,* a compound of *a-* (from Indo-European *n̥-,* weak form of *en* in) + *ger-* (Indo-European *ger-* gather, Pok. 382).

agoraphobia (ag′ərəfō′ bēə) *n.* fear of public places and unfamiliar situations. 1873, coined by German psychiatrist Carl Westphal in 1871 as German *Agoraphobie,* formed from Greek *agorā́* marketplace + *-phobíā* fear.

agouti (əgü′tē) *n.* tropical American rodent. 1625, borrowed from French *agouti,* from Spanish *agutí,* from a Tupi name.

agrarian *adj.* 1618, borrowed through Middle French in the phrase *loy agrarienne* agrarian law, from Latin *agrārius* of the land, from *ager* (genitive *agrī*) field, see ACRE; for suffix see -IAN.

agree *v.* About 1385, in Chaucer's *Troilus and Criseyde,* to please, borrowed from Old French *agréer* to please, from *a gré* to (one's) liking, from Latin *ad* to, and *grātum* pleasing, neuter of *grātus;* see GRACE. **—agreeable** *adj.* About 1380, in Chaucer's translation of Boethius' *De Consolatione Philosophiae,* borrowed from Old French *agréable,* from *agréer* to please; for suffix see -ABLE. **—agreement** *n.* 1425, in *Proceedings of the Privy Council,* borrowed from Old French *agrément,* from *agréer* to please; for suffix see -MENT.

agriculture *n.* Probably 1440, in Middle English translation of Palladius' *De re rustica,* probably influenced by Old French *agriculture,* but borrowed from Late Latin *agricultūra* (compound formed with short *i* by analogy with Latin *agricola* farmer), from Latin *agrī cultūra* cultivation of land (*agrī,* genitive of *ager* land, field; see ACRE, CULTURE).

agro- a combining form meaning field, land, soil, as in *agrology,* or agriculture, as in *agrochemical.* Borrowed from Greek *agro-*, combining form of *agrós* field, land; see ACRE.

agronomy (əgron′əmē) *n.* science of managing farmland. 1814, borrowed from French *agronomie,* from Greek *agronómos* overseer of land (*agrós* land + *-nómos* dispensing or administering, related to *némein* manage; see NIMBLE).

ague (ā′gyü) *n.* malarial fever or an attack of fever. About 1300, borrowed from Old French *aguë,* from Latin *acūta* severe (in the phrase *febris acūta* severe fever), feminine of *acūtus* sharp; see ACUTE.

-aholic a combining form meaning a person with an addiction such as that of a *workaholic,* a person with a compulsive desire to work. Abstracted in 1972 from *workaholic,* coined in 1971 by Wayne Oates, an American pastoral counselor. The new form *-aholic* took the place of *-oholic,* abstracted from *alcoholic.* From *workaholic,* the new combining form freely extended to numerous ad hoc compounds, such as *bookaholic, sweetaholic,* and *wheataholic.* It is also found in the form *-holic,* as in *colaholic* and *chocoholic.*

aid *v.* Probably before 1400, borrowed from Old French *aidier,* from Latin *adjūtāre,* frequentative form of *adjuvāre* give help to (*ad-* to + *juvāre* to help, of uncertain origin). —**n.** Probably 1419, a wartime tax to the Crown; 1430, help or support; borrowed from Old French *aide* (earlier *aiude*), from Late Latin *adjūta,* from the stem of the past participle of *adjuvāre* give help to.

aide (ād) *n.* assistant. 1777, short for AIDE-DE-CAMP. In the 1950's *aide* began to be frequently applied to any assistant or helper (a *Red Cross aide,* a *White House aide*).

aide-de-camp (ād′ dəkamp′) *n.* military officer who assists a superior officer. 1670, borrowed from French *aide-de-camp,* literally, camp assistant.

aikido (īkē′ dō) *n.* Japanese art of self-defense derived from judo. 1968, borrowed from Japanese *aikidō* (*ai-* with each other, together + *ki* spirit + *dō* mastery, art).

ail *v.* Before 1300 *ailen, eilen,* developed from Old English (about 940) *eglan, eglian,* related to *egle* troublesome, oppressive, from Proto-Germanic **azljaz.* It is cognate with Gothic *(us-)agljan* harass, Middle Low German *egelen* cause trouble, and perhaps also with Old High German *egi* fear, punishment, Old Icelandic *agi* fear, and Greek *áchos* pain. The form is traceable to the Indo-European base **agh-* to be oppressed, be afraid (Pok. 7). —**ailment** *n.* 1706, formed from English *ail* + *-ment.*

ailanthus (ālan′thəs) *n.* Asian shade tree. 1845, alteration (influenced by Greek *ánthos* flower) of New Latin *ailantus,* borrowed from Amboinese *ai lanto,* from *ai lanit* tree of heaven.

aileron *n.* movable flap on an airplane wing. 1909, borrowed from French *aileron,* alteration (influenced by *aile* wing) of Old French *aleron,* diminutive of *ele* wing, from Latin *āla;* see AISLE.

aim *v.* About 1303, in Mannyng's *Handlyng Synne,* estimate, calculate, reckon; borrowed from Old French *esmer,* from Latin *aestimāre* appraise, and also from Old French *aesmer,* from Vulgar Latin **adaestimāre* (Latin *ad-* to + *aestimāre* appraise). Doublet of ESTEEM. The current meaning developed in the 1400's from the sense of calculating or estimating the direction of something, such as an object or a blow, about to be delivered. —**n.** Probably about 1380, from the noun, influenced by Old French *esme* and *aesme* aim.

air *n.* A combination of three senses from different origins: **1** mixture of gases; atmosphere. Probably before 1200, in *Ancrene Riwle,* borrowed from Old French *air,* from Latin *āerem,* accusative of *āēr,* from Greek *āḗr* (earlier **āwḗr*), genitive *āéros,* earliest meaning: mist, clouds; of unknown origin.
2 appearance; manner; bearing. 1596, in Shakespeare's *1 Henry IV,* borrowed from Middle French *air,* perhaps influenced by Old French *aire* quality, disposition, place, from Vulgar Latin **arja,* from Latin *āera,* from Greek *āéra,* accusative of *āḗr.*
3 melody; tune. 1590, in Shakespeare's *Midsummer Night's Dream,* borrowed from or influenced by Italian *aria* melody, ARIA. The Italian word, meaning air (mixture of gases) and coming from Vulgar Latin **arja,* developed the sense of "melody, aria" from the earlier meaning "manner, appearance," taken from Middle French *air* (cited in def. 2).

airplane *n.* 1907, alteration of AEROPLANE. The spelling *airplane* soon replaced *aeroplane* in official American publications and in some official British publications (OED Supplement cites *King's Regulations R.A.F.* 1918, and curiously, the BBC committee on pronunciation advised use of "airplane" as early as 1928). Dr. Woodford Heflin, in *The U.S. Air Force Dictionary,* refers to Professor Skeat's recommendation "in 1911 that the British adopt 'airplane' in preference to 'aeroplane'."

aisle *n.* About 1370 *ele, eill* wing of a church, borrowed from Old French *ele,* from Latin *āla* wing, earlier **aeslā,* related to Latin *axilla* armpit.

Latin *axilla* is cognate with Old High German *ahsala* shoulder (modern German *Achsel*), Old Icelandic *ǫxl,* Old English *eaxl,* and Latin *axis* AXIS. Compare AXLE.

In the 1700's the original spelling was confused with and replaced by *isle.* In the 1800's, through the influence of French *aile* wing, it was respelled *aisle,* and this became the standard form.

ajar *adj., adv.* 1718, alteration of Scottish dialect *a char,* contracted from earlier (about 1500-1512) *on char* slightly open, ajar; Middle English *on char* ajar (literally) on the turn; see CHAR² turn, chore.

akimbo *adj., adv.* with hand on hip and elbow bent outward. About 1400 *in kenebowe,* later (1611) *a kenbow,* of uncertain origin. There has been much speculation about where this term comes from: one traditional explanation is from the Middle English phrase *in keen bow* at a sharp angle; another possible source is a Scandinavian word related to Icelandic *kengboginn* crooked, (literally) bent hookwise.

al- a form of the prefix *ad-,* meaning to, toward, before *l,* as in *alloy, allude.* In words from Latin the form is due to the assimilation of the *d* to the following consonant *(l).*

-al¹ a suffix forming adjectives from nouns or other adjectives and meaning of, like, related to, as in *natural, ornamental, historical.*

Middle English had the forms *-al* and *-el,* borrowed in part from Old French *-al, -el,* and in part directly from Latin *-ālis* (adjective suffix meaning of the kind of, pertaining to). Later the form *-el* was refashioned after the Latin as *-al,* and since then Latin adjectives in *-ālis* and French in *-el* have been regularly Anglicized to *-al.*

The form *-al* is freely applied to words with different endings from Latin *(funereal, terrestrial),* Greek *(musical, rhomboidal),* and other languages, including English itself *(operational, genocidal,* etc.*).*

-al[2] a suffix forming nouns of action from verbs, chiefly from Latin or French, and meaning act of ______ing, as in *revival, survival, removal, approval.*

Middle English had the forms *-aille,* later *-aile, -al,* borrowed from Old French feminine singular *-aille* (see ESPOUSAL), from Latin *-ālia* (neuter plural of *-ālis,* adjective suffix also used as noun suffix; see -AL[1]).

In modern English *-al*[2] also forms nouns from verbs of Germanic origin, as in *bestowal, betrothal.* (See *bridal* and *burial* for words that simulate this ending but actually have a different origin.)

à la, in the manner or style of. 1589, borrowed from French *à la,* as in *à la mode, Française,* etc. (*à* to, in, from Latin *ad* + French *la* the, ultimately from Latin *illa,* feminine of *ille* that one).

alabaster *n.* 1375, in John Barbour's *The Bruce,* borrowed from Old French *alabastre,* from Latin *alabaster,* from Greek *alábastros,* alteration of *alábastos* vase (of alabaster) with round or pointed bottom. A possible source of the Greek word may be from Egyptian **a-labaste* vessel of the goddess Bast in the city of Bubastis in northern Egypt.

alacrity *n.* liveliness. Before 1460, borrowed from Latin *alacritātem* (nominative *alacritās*), from *alacer* (genitive *alacris*) brisk, lively, eager. Perhaps cognate with Old English and Old High German *ellen* zeal, Old Icelandic *eljan* courage, power, and Gothic *aljan* zeal, as burning, from Indo-European **al-* burn (Pok. 28); for suffix see -ITY.

alarm *n.* Probably about 1380, a call to arms, borrowed from Old French *alarme,* from Italian *allarme,* from *all'arme!* to (the) arms! —**v.** About 1590, in Marlowe's *Tamburlane,* verb use of *alarm,* n.

alas *interj.* Probably before 1200, in *Ancrene Riwle,* borrowed from Old French phrase *a las* ah, miserable (*las,* from Latin *lassus* weary); see LET[1] allow.

alb *n.* white linen robe. Old English (before 1100) *albe,* borrowed from Medieval Latin *alba,* from Latin *vestis alba* white vestment, feminine of *albus* white (surviving in Romanian *alb* white). Cognate with Greek *alphós* a white leprosy, Old High German *albiz, elbiz* swan, Russian *lebed'* swan, and Armenian *ałauni* dove, from Indo-European **albh-* (Pok. 30). The French *aube* was the usual spelling in English in the 14th and early 15th centuries, according to OED and citations in the *Middle English Dictionary.*

albacore *n.* large fish related to the tuna. 1579, borrowed from Portuguese *albacor, albacora,* from Arabic *al-bakūra* the young camel.

albatross *n.* 1672, probably an alteration of earlier *alcatras* a large sea bird related to the petrels. The name, first recorded in 1681, had various spellings: *albitross, algatross, albetross, alb-* perhaps influenced by Latin *albus* white. *Alcatras* is an obsolete name, recorded from the Portuguese in 1564 by Sir John Hawkins and borrowed from Portuguese *alcatraz* pelican, in 1593, which came from Arabic *al-ghaṭṭās* a sea eagle.

The figurative meaning of a burden, such as one of guilt, is an allusion to the albatross shot by the ancient mariner and hung about his neck by his shipmates as a sign of his guilt in Coleridge's *The Rime of the Ancient Mariner* (1798).

albedo (albē'dō) *n. Astronomy.* the ratio of light reflected to light received. 1859, borrowed from Late Latin *albēdō* whiteness, from *albus* white; see ALB.

albeit (ôlbē'it) *conj.* although. Before 1325, in *Cursor Mundi,* from the phrase in Middle English *al be it* although it be.

albino *n.* person or animal lacking coloring pigment. 1777, borrowed from Portuguese *albino,* or from Spanish *albino,* from *albo* white, from Latin *albus;* see ALB.

Traditionally said to be borrowed from Portuguese, as the Portuguese were thought to have applied the term albino to white Negroes they encountered on the western coast of Africa. However, later research by Corominas has shown that the term appears earlier in Spanish than in Portuguese, but because the Portuguese and the Spanish word appeared earlier than the English word *albino,* it is not possible to determine which language was the source of borrowing for the English word.

album *n.* 1651, through German use as applied to a book of friends' or colleagues' signatures, verses, drawings, etc., borrowed from Latin *album* white tablet on which things were inscribed (neuter of *albus* white; see ALB).

albumen *n.* white of an egg. 1599, borrowed from Latin *albūmen* (genitive *albūminis*) white of an egg, (literally) whiteness, from *albus* white; see ALB.

albumin *n.* protein found in milk, egg white, etc. 1869, borrowed from French *albumine* white of an egg, from Latin *albūmin-,* stem of *albūmen* ALBUMEN; for suffix see -IN[2].

alchemy *n.* Medieval chemistry combining the study of chemistry, philosophy, and magic. Probably before 1387 *alconomye, alkenamye,* in a version of *Piers Plowman;* about 1378 *alkemonye, alkamye,* in Wycliffe; borrowed from Old French *alkemie,* learned borrowing from Medieval Latin *alkimia.* Some spellings of the word were also influenced by association with other sciences, in particular astronomy, which produced endings in *-onomie, -onye,* etc.

Medieval Latin *alkimia* was borrowed from Arabic *al-kīmiyā'* (*al* the + Late Greek *chymeíā* art of alloying metals, from Greek *chýma,* genitive *chýmatos* that which is poured out, ingot, from *cheîn* pour; see FOUND[2] cast metal).

Traditionally there has been speculation that Arabic *kīmiyā'* and Greek *chymeíā* were associated with *Chymeía* the ancient name of Egypt, meaning "the land of black earth." This was later set aside in favor of a probable closer relationship with Greek *chymeíā* pouring, as it applied to the mixing of juices from various plants among the Alexandrian alchemists, perhaps then picked up by the Arabs and introduced by them into European culture through Spain. —**alchemist** *n.* Probably about 1425, *alkemyst,* borrowed from Medieval Latin *alkimista* (from *alkimia*) and Middle French *alkemiste,* from Old French *alkemie;* for suffix see -IST.

alcohol *n.* 1543, fine powder, borrowed from Medieval Latin *alcohol* powdered ore of antimony, from Arabic *al-koḥ'l* the powdered metal, kohl (metallic powder used in the Orient to stain the eyelids).

The original sense of a powder refined by heating to a vapor and condensing to a solid was extended in 1672 to fluids: distillate of a liquid, essence; and finally, in 1753, to spirit of wine and by extension to the spirit of any fermented liquor.

—**alcoholic** *adj.* 1790, formed from English *alcohol* + *-ic.* —**alcoholism** *n.* 1852, formed from English *alcohol* + *-ism.*

alcove *n.* 1676, borrowed from French *alcôve,* from Spanish *alcoba,* from Arabic *al-qubba* the vaulted chamber, from *qubba* to vault. There is no connection in the historical development of *alcove* and *cove,* which is a native English word from Old English *cofa* chamber.

alderman *n.* Old English Mercian dialect (before 810) *aldormonn* a nobleman or leader of high rank; before 891, in Old English, West Saxon *ealdormann;* formed from *aldor, ealdor* patriarch, chief (from *ald* old + *-or* as in *baldor* prince, from *bald* bold) + *mann* man; see OLD, MAN.

ale *n.* a strong beer. Old English (about 940) *ealu, alu;* cognate with Old Saxon *alo,* Old Icelandic *ǫl* ale, from Proto-Germanic **aluth-,* from Indo-European **alu-* bitter; beer (Pok. 33). Until the growing of hops was introduced to England in the first half of the 1400's, ale and beer were synonymous terms in Middle English according to MED.

aleatory (ā′ lēətôr′ ē) *adj.* dependent on uncertain or random elements. 1693, borrowed through French *aléatoire* relating to the game of dice, (later) dependent on an uncertain event, or directly from Latin *āleātōrius* having to do with the throwing of dice, from *aleātor* dice player, from *ālea* a die, chance; for suffix see -ORY. —**aleatoric** *adj.* 1961, formed in English from Latin *āleātōrius* + English suffix *-ic.*

alee (əlē′) *adv., adj.* on or toward the lee side of a ship. About 1399, from Scandinavian; compare Old Icelandic *ā hlē* (*ā* on + *hlē* shelter, LEE).

alert *adj.* 1618, borrowed from French *alerte* vigilant, alert, from *à l'herte, à l'erte* on one's guard, from the Italian military phrase *all'erta* on the watch (*erta* lookout, high tower, steep slope, originally feminine of *erto,* past participle of *ergere* raise up, from Latin *ērigere* raise; see ERECT). —**v.** 1868, in Whitman's *Poems,* verb use of *alert,* adj.

alewife *n.* fish of the herring family. 1633, formed in American English, of uncertain origin. Perhaps *alewife* is an altered form of an American Indian name, or an alteration (influenced by *alewife* meaning a woman who keeps an alehouse, about 1400) of English dialect *allowes* the allice-shad (a herring), borrowed from French *alose* shad, from Late Latin *alausa,* from a Gaulish word adopted by the Gallo-Roman author Ausonius in his *Mosella,* a travel narrative.

alfalfa *n.* 1845, in Darwin's *The Voyage of the Beagle,* borrowed from Spanish *alfalfa,* from Arabic *al-'faṣfaṣa, al-fiṣfiṣa* the best kind of fodder.

alfresco *adv., adj.* in the open; outdoors. 1753, borrowed from Italian *al fresco* (literally) in the fresh, in the cool air; see FRESH.

algae *n.pl.* of **alga.** 1551 *alga,* borrowed from Latin *alga* seaweed, of uncertain origin.

The plural form *algae* appeared in English in 1794.

algebra *n.* branch of mathematics that uses symbols and letters. 1551, in Recorde's *The Pathway to Knowledge,* borrowed from Medieval Latin *algebra,* from Arabic *al-jabr, al-jebr,* "the bone setting," reintegration, as of broken parts, i.e. restoration or reduction of parts to make a whole, as in computation (*al* the + *jabara* reunite, consolidate, restore).

The earliest sense in English was of the surgical treatment of fractures, bone setting, used before 1400 in Lanfranc's *Science of Surgery.*

The use of the Arabic *al-jabr* in a famous work on algebra (*Kitāb al-Jabr wal-Muqābala* Rules of Reintegration and Reduction) popularized the word in its mathematical sense. See ALGORISM.

ALGOL or **Algol** (al′gol) *n.* algebraic computer language. 1959, acronym formed in English from *Algo*(rithmic) *L*(anguage).

algorism (al′gərizəm) *n.* the Arabic or decimal system of numerals. Probably before 1200, *augrim,* in *Ancrene Riwle;* 1340, *algorisme,* in *Ayenbite of Inwyt;* borrowed from Old French *augorisme, algorisme,* learned borrowing from Medieval Latin *algorismus,* from Arabic *al-Khuwārizmī,* literally, the native of *Khuwārizm* (Khiva).

Khuwārizm was the surname of Abū 'Abdullāh Muḥammad ibn Mūsā, a 9th-century mathematician and author of a famous work on algebra, *Kitāb al-Jabr wal-Muqābala* (Rules of Reintegration and Reduction), which popularized the use of Arabic numerals in Europe. See ALGEBRA; for suffix see -ISM.

algorithm (al′gəriᴛʜəm) *n.* formal procedure in mathematics. 1699, either influenced by or borrowed from French *algorithme* and perhaps separately formed in English as an alteration of *algorism,* influenced by Greek *arithmós* number; see ARITHMETIC.

alias (ā′ lēəs) *adv.* otherwise called or named. About 1432, borrowed from Latin *aliās* at another time, from *alius* (an)other; see ELSE. —**n.** an assumed name. 1605, from the adverb.

alibi *n.* 1743, developed from an adverb meaning "elsewhere," 1727, perhaps influenced by French *alibi* subterfuge, poor excuse, having been elsewhere during a crime, borrowed from Latin *alibī* elsewhere, locative adverb of *alius* (an)other. —**v.** *Informal.* make an excuse (for). 1909, American English, from the noun.

alien *n., adj.* Before 1338, in Mannyng's *Chronicle of England,* stranger, foreigner; *adj.* probably before 1300, in *Kyng Alisaunder* strange, foreign. *Alien* was borrowed through Old French *alien,* or directly from Latin *aliēnus* of or belonging to another person or place, from *alius* (an)other; see ELSE.

alienate *v.* **1** transfer property to another, 1573, possibly a back formation from *alienation,* or borrowed by influence of Middle French *aliéner* transfer property to another, from Latin *aliēnātus* (see def. 2).

2 turn away in feeling or affection, estrange, 1548; verb use of the earlier adjective form *alienate* estranged, before 1420 in Lydgate's *Troy Book;* borrowed from Latin *aliēnātus,* past participle of *aliēnāre* to make another's, estrange, from *aliēnus* of or belonging to another person or place, from *alius* (an)other; see ELSE; for suffix see -ATE[1]. —**alienation** *n.* About 1395, in the Wycliffe Bible, borrowed through Old French *aliénacion,* or directly from Latin *aliēnātiōnem* (nominative *aliēnātiō*), from *aliēnāre;* for suffix see -TION. —**alienist** *n.* psychiatrist. 1864, from French *aliéniste,* from Latin *aliēnus* insane, an earlier meaning of strange; for suffix see -IST.

alight[1] *v.* jump down, dismount. Old English (about 1000 in Ælfric's *Grammar*) *ālihtan,* formed from *ā-* a-[5]

+ *līhtan* get off, make light, from *līht* light in weight; originally said of taking one's weight off a horse or vehicle; see LIGHT[2], adj. and LIGHT[3], v.

alight[2] *adj.* lighted up. About 1300, adjective use of early Middle English *alight,* probably before 1200, past participle of *alighten* light up, developed from Old English *onlīhtan,* formed from *on-* up + *līhtan* to light; see LIGHT[1], v.

align *v.* bring into line. About 1410 *alinen* of wolves, bitches, etc., to copulate; borrowed from Middle French *aligner,* from Old French *alignier* (*a-* to, from Latin *ad-* + *lignier* to line, from Latin *līneāre,* from *līnea* LINE).

The spelling *align* became widespread in the 1800's in imitation of the French, making a variant spelling out of the original English form *aline.* **—alignment** *n.* 1790, borrowed from French or formed in English from French *aligner* to align + English suffix *-ment.*

alike *adv., adj.* About 1175 *iliche,* probably about 1300 *aliche,* Middle English forms developed from Old English *gelīce* and *onlīce,* from *gelīc* and *onlīc,* adjectives meaning similar, like; see LIKE[1].

Old English *gelīc, gelīce* are cognate with Old Saxon *gilīk, gilīkō,* Old Frisian *gelīk, līk,* Gothic *galeiks* Middle Dutch *ghelijc* (modern Dutch *gelijk*), Old High German *galīh, gilīh, gelīh,* (modern German *gleich*), Old Icelandic *glīkr* (modern Icelandic *līkur*), and Gothic *galeiks,* from Proto-Germanic **ʒaltkaz* (*ʒa-* together + *līkan* body), from Indo-European **līg-* shape (Pok.667).

Alike is not a compound of *a-*[1] and Old English **līc* as is often supposed. On the contrary, *like*[1] is an abbreviated form of *alike,* for Old English did not have the adjective form **līc.*

alimentary *adj.* 1615, borrowed from Latin *alimentārius* (*alimentum* nourishment + *-ārius* -ary); or formed in English from *aliment* nourishment, food (1477, borrowed through Middle French *aliment* food, from Latin *alimentum,* from *alere* nourish) + English suffix *-ary.* Latin *alere* is cognate with Gothic *alan* to grow, Old Irish *alim* I nourish, and Greek *althainein* heal, from Indo-European **al-* grow; nourish (Pok. 26).

alimony (al'əmō'nē) *n.* money paid for support of a spouse. 1655, borrowed from Latin *alimōnia* nourishment, sustenance, support, from *alere* nourish + *-monia* suffix signifying action, state, condition.

alive *adj.* Probably about 1175, reduced form of the Old English phrase *on līfe* in life, living, from *on* in, and *līfe,* dative of *līf* LIFE.

alkaline *adj.* About 1330, perhaps borrowed independently of *alkali,* in the phrase *sal alkalin* (retaining the foreign word order), from Medieval Latin. Later it became *sal alkali* and was finally reduced to *alkali.* **—alkali** *n.* any substance with the properties of soda, such as lye and potash. About 1395, in Chaucer's *Canterbury Tales,* borrowed from Medieval Latin *alkali,* from Arabic *al-qalī* the ashes of saltwort (plant growing on alkaline soil).

Many sources derive *alkali* through French, but it is not recorded in French until almost 115 years after *alkali* appeared in English.

all *adj.* Old English *eall, al* (about 725, in *Beowulf*). *All* is common to Germanic languages such as Old Saxon *all, al,* Old Frisian *al, ol,* Old High German *al,* Old Icelandic *allr,* and Gothic *alls,* from Proto-Germanic **alnaz,* from Indo-European **alnos/olnos* (Pok. 24).

Allah (äl'ə) *n.* name of God among Moslems and Christian Arabs. 1584, borrowed from Arabic*Allāh,* contraction of *al-ilāh* the (true) god, corresponding to Hebrew *'elōah* God.

allay *v.* put to rest; quiet. About 1150 *aleyen* to put down; developed from Old English *ālecgan* (about 725, in *Beowulf*) (*ā-* a-[5] + *lecgan* to LAY[1] put down); cognate with modern German *erlegen* lay low, and Gothic *uslagjan* lay out, from Proto-Germanic **uz-laʒjanan.*

The spelling with two l's was introduced in the 1600's by mistakenly identifying the Old English prefix *ā-* with *al-,* which is the assimilated form of *ad-* in words adopted or formed from Latin. This came about quite naturally as *allay* was early confused in spelling and sense with several other words of Latin origin, among them *allege.*

allege (əlej') *v.* assert, declare. About 1300, to plead before a court, borrowed through Anglo-French *aleger,* an alteration, partially influenced in meaning and in form by Latin *allēgāre* to charge, of Old French *esligier* to clear at law, from Latin *ex-* out + *litigāre* bring suit; see LITIGATE. **—allegation** *n.* Probably before 1425, borrowed through Middle French *allégation,* from Latin *allēgātiōnem* (nominative *allēgātiō*), from *allēgāre* to charge, send a message (*al-,* form of *ad-* before *l,* to + *lēgāre* to commission, see LEGATE); for suffix see -ATION.

allegiance (əlē' jəns) *n.* About 1399, in Langland's *Richard the Redeles,* Middle English *alegeaunce* loyalty of a liegeman to his lord, borrowed through Anglo-French *alegaunce,* alteration of Old French *lijançe, liejance, legeance,* from *liege* LIEGE; for suffix see -ANCE.

The Old French forms were also confused in England with another word *allégeance* alleviation, relief to contribute to the development of the English spelling *allegiance.*

allegory (al'əgôr'ē) *n.* story with an underlying meaning. About 1384, in the Wycliffe Bible, probably borrowed from Latin *allēgoria,* from Greek *allēgoríā,* from *allēgoreîn* speak otherwise than one seems to speak, (*állos* another, different + *agoreúein* speak openly, from *agorā́* public place, AGORA); for suffix see -Y[3].

The word appears in Old French about 250 years before the Wycliffe translation and may have been used by English writers before his time. **—allegorical** *adj.* 1528, in Tyndale's *Obedience of a Christian Man,* from earlier *allegoric* (about 1395, in a later version of Wycliffe's translation of the Bible), borrowed from Latin *allēgoricus,* from Greek *allēgorikós,* from *allēgoríā;* for suffix see -ICAL.

allegro (əleg'rō) *adj., adv. Music.* quick, lively. 1683, in Purcell's *Sonnata's Three Parts,* borrowed from Italian *allegro,* probably from Vulgar Latin **alicrum,* from early Latin **alicer* (genitive **alecris*), corresponding to Latin *alacer* (genitive *alacris*) brisk, glad; see ALACRITY.

allele (əlēl') *n.* one of a pair of alternative genetic characters. 1931, possibly borrowed from German *Allel,* or developed independently in English, both the German and the English forms then being a shortened form of **allelomorph,** 1902 borrowed from the stem of Greek *allḗlōn* of one another (from *állos* other, ELSE) + *morphḗ* form.

alleluia (al'əlü'yə) *n.* variant of HALLELUJAH. Probably before 1200, borrowed from Latin *allēlūja,* from Greek *allēloúia,* from Hebrew *halləlū-yāh* praise Jehovah, HALLELUJAH.

allergy *n.* 1911, borrowed from German *Allergie* (coined in 1906 by Clemens von Pirquet, 1874-1929, Austrian pediatrician), from Greek *állos* different, strange + *érgon* action; for suffix see -Y[3]. **—allergic** *adj.* 1911, though formed in English from *allergy* + *-ic,* the word is attested earlier (1906) in French *allergique.* **—allergen** *n.* substance causing allergy. 1912, formed in English from *aller(gy)* + *-gen.*

alleviate (əlē′vēāt) *v.* lessen, lighten. Probably before 1425, in a translation of Higden's *Polychronicon;* possibly a back formation from *alleviation,* or borrowed perhaps through influence of Middle French *allevier,* from Late Latin *alleviātus,* past participle of *alleviāre* to lighten (Latin *al-,* form of *ad-* before *l,* to + *levis* light in weight; see LIGHT[2] not heavy); for suffix see -ATE[1]. **—alleviation** *n.* Probably before 1425, borrowed possibly through Middle French *alleviation,* from Late Latin *alleviātiōnem* (nominative *alleviātiō*), from *alleviāre;* for suffix see -TION.

alley *n.* 1360-61 *aley, aleye* open passage between buildings, alley; borrowed from Old French *allée* a path, passage (also meaning "a going") from *alé,* past participle of *aler* to go, probably from Gallo-Romance *allārī,* back formation from Latin *allātus* having been brought to (*al-,* form of *ad-* before *l,* to + *lātus,* serving as past participle to *ferre* bring; see BEAR[2] carry).

A contrary point of view is expressed by Bloch-Wartburg, who maintain that Old French *aler* developed from Latin *ambulāre* to walk, since *aler* is found in the Latinized form *alare* in a glossary of the 700's titled the *Reichenau Glosses. Alare* is cited as a possible development from the hypothetical form **amlare* that could have developed from **amblāre,* from Latin *ambulāre.* The two forms *ambler* and *aler* are considered as doublets: *ambler* remaining for some time fixed in meaning "walk as a horse does," while *aler* developed from *ambulāre* in the common meaning "to go."

alliance *n.* About 1300, borrowed from Old French *aliance,* from *alier* ally with, see ALLY; for suffix see -ANCE.

alligator *n.* reptile of the crocodile family. 1623 *allegater,* in Shakespeare's *Romeo and Juliet* (First Folio), alteration of earlier *aligarto,* borrowed from Spanish *el lagarto (de Indias)* the lizard (of the Indies), from *el* the + *lagarto,* from Latin *lacertus* LIZARD.

An earlier form, *lagarto,* appeared in English in 1568 and 1577; it was borrowed from Spanish without the article *el* or *al* and was replaced in 1591 by *aligarto.*

alliteration (əlit′ərā′shən) *n.* repetition of the same first sound. 1656, probably borrowed from New Latin *alliterationem* (nominative *alliteratio*), from Latin *al-* (form of *ad-* before *l*) to, + *lītera* LETTER, on the pattern of Latin *oblīterātiōnem* obliteration. **—alliterate** *v.* 1816, in Southey's *Letters,* back formation from *alliteration,* on the pattern of *obliteration, obliterate.*

allo- a combining form meaning "other," as in *allocentric,* or "different, varying," as in *allochromatic,* and otherwise involving variance, in generally technical compounds. Borrowed from Greek *allo-* combining form of *állos* (see ELSE). Before a vowel the form is *all-,* as in *allergy.*

allocate *v.* set aside for a special purpose. 1640-41, verb use of earlier *allocate,* adj.; 1438, in *Proceedings of the Privy Council;* borrowed from Medieval Latin *allocate* (the word with which writs authorizing payment often began). It is the imperative plural of *allocare* allocate (Latin *al-,* form of *ad-* before *l* + *locāre* to place, see LOCATE); for suffix see -ATE[1]. **—allocation** *n.* 1447-48, borrowed possibly through Middle French *allocation,* from Medieval Latin *allocationem* (nominative *allocatio*), from *allocare;* for suffix see -TION.

It is also possible that *allocation* was formed in English from earlier *allocate,* adj. + *-ion.*

allot *v.* 1474, in *Rolls of Parliament,* Middle English *alotten,* borrowed from Old French *aloter* (*a-* to + *lot* LOT from a Germanic word). **—allotment** *n.* 1574, possibly borrowed from Middle French *allotement,* but more likely formed in English from *allot* + *-ment.*

allow *v.* Before 1325, in *Cursor Mundi,* Middle English *allouen,* borrowed through Anglo-French *allouer, alouer,* from Old French *alouer* approve, from Latin *allaudāre* (*al-,* form of *ad-* before *l,* + *laudāre* praise, LAUD).

In Old French *alouer,* meaning approve, was confused with *alouer* meaning assign, from Medieval Latin *allocare* allocate, and both were considered different senses of the same word by the time *alouer* was adopted in English.

—allowance *n.* Probably before 1387, in a version of *Piers Plowman,* borrowed from Old French *alouance,* from *alouer* approve; for suffix see -ANCE.

alloy *n.* Before 1325 *alai, allai,* borrowed through Anglo-French *alei,* from Old French *alei,* from *aleier* mix with a baser metal; literally, to combine, unite, from Latin *alligāre* bind to (*al-,* form of *ad-* before *l* + *ligāre* bind; see LIGAMENT). Doublet of ALLY.

Middle English *alai* was later replaced (1604) by *alloy,* from French *aloi.*

—*v.* About 1378 *alaien, allaien,* borrowed through Anglo-French *allaier,* from Old French *aloiier, aliier,* from older *aleier,* from Latin *alligāre.* Middle English *alaien, allaien* was later replaced (1691) by *alloy,* from French *aloyer,* now *allier.*

allude *v.* refer indirectly. 1533, Henry VIII quoted in Strype's *Ecclesiastical Memorials,* mock, (later) refer fancifully to, possibly borrowed through Middle French *alluder,* from Latin *allūdere* make a mocking allusion to; play with (*al-,* form of *ad-* before *l,* to, + *lūdere* play; see LUDICROUS).

allure *v.* 1402, borrowed from Anglo-French *alurer,* corresponding to Old French *aleurer* (*a-* to + *loirre* falconer's LURE, from a Frankish word).

allusion *n.* 1548, in Udall's translation of Erasmus' *Upon the New Testament,* borrowed from Latin *allūsiōnem* (nominative *allūsiō*), from *allūs-,* stem of *allūdere* ALLUDE; for suffix see -SION.

alluvium *n.* deposit of sand, etc., left by flowing water. 1665-66, borrowed from Medieval Latin *alluvium,* neuter of *alluvius* washed against, from Latin *alluere* wash against, (*al-,* form of *ad-* before *l,* to, against, + *-luere,* combining form of *lavere* to wash, LAVE). **—alluvial** *adj.* 1802, borrowed from French *alluvial,* or formed in English from *alluvium* + -AL[1].

ally (əlī′) *v.* About 1300 *allien* combine, unite, borrowed from Old French *alier, allier,* from a different stem of *aleier,* from Latin *alligāre* bind to; see the doublet ALLOY.

—*n.* (al′ī). Probably about 1375, in Chaucer's *Canterbury Tales,* Middle English *allie,* noun use of *allien,* v., to ally.

alma mater, school where one was a student. 1710,

Latin *alma māter* bountiful or nourishing mother (*alma,* feminine of *almus* nourishing, from *alere* nourish, related to ALUMNUS and OLD, and *māter* MOTHER).

Alma māter was a title given by the ancient Romans to various goddesses, especially Ceres and Cybele, and was used in this sense in English in 1398. In the 1700's the title was first used in reference to British universities such as Oxford, which were regarded as nourishing or fostering their alumni.

The term is also used in other countries, notably Germany and Holland, and probably dates from the time when the language of instruction was Latin in European universities.

almanac *n.* Before 1388, borrowed from Medieval Latin *almanach,* from Spanish *almanaque,* earlier Catalan *almanac,* from Spanish-Arabic *al-manākh* calendar, almanac, apparently from Late Greek *almenichiakón,* probably of Coptic origin.

Some sources dispute the existence of *al-manākh* but Corominas cites two Spanish-Arabic sources for the word.

almighty *adj.* Old English (about 725, in *Beowulf*) *ælmihtig (æl-* ALL + *mihtig* MIGHTY). Cognate with Old Saxon *alomahtig,* Old High German *alamahtīc* (modern German *allmächtig*) and Old Icelandic *almāttigr,* all of which are evidently loan translations based on Latin *omnipotēns,* accusative *omnipotentem* OMNIPOTENT.

almond *n.* Probably about 1300, borrowed from Old French *almande, alemande, amande,* from Medieval Latin *amandola,* alteration (influenced by Latin *amandus* lovable) of Latin *amygdala,* from Greek *amygdálē,* a foreign word of unknown origin.

The initial *al-* may have developed through influence of Spanish *almendra* almond, a form which probably arose from the influence of the Arabic article *al* appearing in many Spanish words.

almoner (al'mənər) *n.* distributor of alms. 1264 as a surname; about 1303 *aumener,* in Mannyng's *Handlyng Synne,* borrowed from Old French *aumosnier, almosnier,* from Vulgar Latin **almosinārius,* variant of Late Latin *eleēmosi-, elēmosinārius,* from *eleēmosyna* ALMS.

During the 1400's spellings with *l* occurred sporadically, but in the 1500's the spelling with *l* became the accepted spelling by analogy with *alms* (Middle English *almes*) or Latin *elēmosinārius.*

almost *adv.* Old English (before 1000) *ealmǣst* nearly (a compound of *eal, al* ALL + *mǣst* MOST).

Over a period of about 130 years, from 1123 to 1250, Middle English *almest, ealmest* developed into modern *almost,* but it was not until the 1400's that the spelling *almost* predominated.

alms *n.* Old English (before 810) *ælmesse,* corresponding to Old Saxon *alamosna* alms, Old High German *alamuosan,* and Old Icelandic *ölmusa, almusa,* all from a Germanic word going back to Vulgar Latin **alemosyna,* an alteration of Late Latin *eleēmosyna,* from Greek *eleēmosýnē* alms, pity, ultimately from *éleos* pity, of unknown origin.

aloe (al'ō) *n.* plant of the lily family. Old English (about 950) *alwe,* borrowed from Latin *aloē,* from Greek *alóē,* of uncertain (perhaps Semitic) origin.

aloft *adv.* Probably about 1200, in *The Ormulum, o loft,* borrowed from Scandinavian; compare Old Icelandic *ā lopti* up above (*ā* in, on + *lopt* sky, LOFT).

alone *adj., adv.* Probably about 1200, in *The Ormulum,* literally, all by oneself (*al* ALL + *on, one,* Old English *āna* adv., by oneself). Compare German *allein* and Dutch *alleen,* both meaning alone; also late Old Icelandic *all-einna.*

along *prep.* Old English (887) *andlang,* alongside of (*and-* opposite, against + *lang* long; see ANTI-, LONG).

aloof *adv.* 1532, in Sir Thomas More's works, away to the windward (*a-* on + *loof* windward, probably from Old French *lof,* from Germanic; see LUFF).

alpaca (alpak'ə) *n.* 1792, borrowed from Spanish, probably from Aymara *allpaca, aḷpáka,* possibly related to Quechua *p'áko* alpaca.

The form *pacos* appears in *Chambers Cyclopaedia* supplement, 1753.

alpha *n.* first letter of the Greek alphabet. Probably about 1200, in *The Ormulum,* borrowed from Latin *alpha,* from Greek *álpha,* from Semitic; compare Hebrew *'aleph* the first letter of the Hebrew alphabet, literally meaning an ox, originally formed from the hieroglyph of an ox's head.

alphabet *n.* Probably before 1425, in a translation of Higden's *Polychronicon;* borrowed from Late Latin *alphabētum,* from Greek *alphábētos,* from *álpha* the letter A (see ALPHA) and *bêta* the letter B (see BETA), the first two letters of the Greek alphabet.

alphanumeric (al'fənümer'ik) *adj.* using both letters and numerals. 1955, formed in English from *alpha(bet)* + *numeric(al).*

Alpine *adj.* Probably before 1425, in a translation of Higden's *Polychronicon,* borrowed perhaps through Middle French *alpin,* from Latin *Alpīnus,* from *Alpēs* the Alps, ultimately a name of non-Indo-European origin.

The sports meaning, "of or having to do with skiing events" appeared in 1973, and was so called because such events were popularized in the Alps.

—**Alpinist** *n.* 1881, borrowed from French *alpiniste.*

already *adv.* About 1300, from the adjective phrase *all ready* fully ready. Compare Norwegian and Danish *allerede* already.

All ready as an adjective phrase in "The men were all ready to work." has been used as two words in English since before the 1200's, and has existed sporadically as one word at least since the 1450's. The parallel form *all right,* used either as an adjective or an adverb, has never fully established itself as one word, though the now obsolete adverbial meaning "just exactly" existed as one word in early Middle English and perhaps in Old English.

also *adv.* Before 1131 *alswa* likewise, similarly, Middle English form of Old English, in Ælfric's *Grammar, ealswā* (and, occasionally, *alswā*) entirely so, quite so (a compound of *eall, all* ALL + *swā* SO). Doublet of AS.

altar *n.* Old English (about 1000), borrowed from Latin *altāre,* earlier *altāria,* plural, perhaps related to Latin *adolēre* burn up, consume, cognate with Sanskrit *alāta-m* firebrand, a coal, from Indo-European **al-/ol-* burn (Pok. 28).

From about 1200 to 1500 the Old English form was generally replaced by *auter,* borrowed from Old French *auter,* from Latin *altāre.* During the 1500's *altar,* reintroduced from Latin, quickly replaced *auter.*

alter *v.* change. About 1385, in Chaucer's *Troilus and*

Criseyde, borrowed from Old French *altérer,* learned borrowing from Late Latin *alterāre,* from Latin *alter* the other.

The *al-* of Latin *alter* is also found in such words as Latin *alius* other (English *alias*); see ELSE. The *-ter* is from an Indo-European contrastive suffix found in words such as *after* and in the form *-ther* in words such as *whether* and *other.*

—alteration *n.* Before 1398, in Trevisa's translation of Bartholomew's *De Proprietatibus Rerum,* borrowed from Old French *alteracion* and Medieval Latin *alterationem* (nominative *alteratio*), from Late Latin *alterāre* alter; for suffix see -TION.

altercation *n.* quarrel. About 1390, in Chaucer's *Canterbury Tales,* borrowed through Old French *altercacion,* or directly from Latin *altercātiōnem* (nominative *altercātiō*), from *altercārī* altercate; for suffix see -TION. **—altercate** *v.* 1530, created in English from a back formation of *altercation,* or borrowed directly from Latin *altercātus,* past participle of *altercārī* from **altercus* in turn, from *alter* the other, see ALTER; for suffix see -ATE[1].

alter ego (ôl'tər ē'gō), aspect of one's nature; intimate friend. 1537, borrowed from Latin *alter ego* the other I, translation of Greek *héteros egṓ.*

alternate *adj.* 1513, in Sir Thomas More's *History of King Richard III,* borrowed from Latin *alternātus,* past participle of *alternāre,* from *alternus* every other, from *alter* the other, see ALTER; for suffix see -ATE[1]. **—n.** 1718, in Pope's translation of the *Iliad,* noun use of *alternate,* adj. **—v.** 1599, from the adjective.

By a curious fact of happenstance or incomplete records the derivative form *alternately* appears in English in 1432, about 80 years before *alternate,* and *alternation* appears in 1443, which gives rise to speculation that *alternate* may have been derived by back formation from *alternation* or that *alternate* may have existed earlier than the formal records indicate, perhaps even as a verb replacing earlier Middle English *alternen* (1447), especially since underlying forms appear in Old French as early as 1380.

although *conj.* About 1325 *althagh,* Middle English compound of Old English *al, eall* ALL, and *thāh,* variant of *thēah* THOUGH.

The original two-word phrase in Old English was equivalent to "all though" and more emphatic than *though,* but the stress on the first syllable was lost in the 1300's and the word became a mere variant of *though.*

altitude *n.* About 1386, borrowed from Latin *altitūdō* (genitive *altitūdinis*), from *altus* high; see OLD.

alto (al'tō) *n.* highest male singing voice. 1784, man with alto voice, borrowed from Italian, from Latin *altus* high.

Though originally applied to a man's voice, and therefore explaining the connection with "high," *alto* is now usually applied to a woman's voice and is thought of as "low" because the word is generally considered to be a clipped form of *contralto.*

altogether *adv.* Before 1200 *altogeder* completely, developed from Middle English phrase (about 1150) *al togedere* all together (Old English *eall, al* ALL + *tōgædere* TOGETHER).

altruism (al' trüizəm) *n.* unselfishness. 1853, in George H. Lewes' *Comte's Philosophy of the Sciences,* borrowed from French *altruisme,* possibly from French *autrui* for another or others, (Old French *altrui,* from Vulgar Latin **alterui,* altered under the influence of *cui* for whom, from Latin *alterī,* dative of *alter* the other; see ALTER) + French *-isme* -ism. **—altruistic** *adj.* 1853, formed in English from French *altruiste* altruistic + English -IC.

French sources dispute traditional attribution of the coinage in 1830 to the French philosopher Auguste Comte but do not agree on whom to credit. Several works cite Italian *altrui* as the source of French *altruisme.*

alum (al'əm) *n.* white mineral salt. 1373, borrowed from Old French *alum,* from Latin *alūmen* an astringent substance, probably a sulfate, related to *alūta* dressed leather, and Old English *ealu* ale, from Indo-European **alu-* bitter (Pok.33).

aluminum *n.* Coined in 1812 by its discoverer, the British chemist Sir Humphry Davy, as alteration (influenced by Latin *alūmen, alūminis* alum) of earlier (1808) New Latin *alumium* (also coined by Davy from *alumina* a mineral occurring in nature as corundum + *-ium* a suffix meaning "metal").

The variant form *aluminium,* preferred in British usage, also appeared in 1812 as a deliberate alteration of *aluminum* on the analogy of other names of elements, such as *sodium, potassium, magnesium,* all coined earlier by Davy.

alumna (əlum'nə) *n., pl.* **alumnae** (-nē). woman graduate of a school. 1882, American English, borrowed from Latin *alumna,* feminine of ALUMNUS.

alumnus (əlum'nəs), *n., pl.* **alumni** (-nī). graduate of a school. 1645, in John Evelyn's *Diary,* borrowed from Latin *alumnus,* literally, foster child, vestigial present passive participle of *alere* nourish; see ALMA MATER and OLD.

alveolus (alvē'ələs) *n.* small cavity, sac, or socket. 1706, borrowed from Latin *alveolus,* diminutive of *alveus* cavity, related to *alvus* belly (metathesized form by shift of *l,* of earlier **aulos*) and cognate with Greek *aulós* hollow tube, from Indo-European **aulos* (Pok. 88).

always *adv.* Probably about 1350, a compound of *all* and *way* (the *s* comes from Middle English *wayes,* the adverbial genitive form of *way*).

Beginning as separate phrases with different meanings and different grammatical application, Old English *ealne weg,* originally meaning "all the way, the whole way," was an adverbial accusative phrase; *alles weis* originally meaning "at every time" was an adverbial genitive phrase. However, *ealne weg* adopted the additional meaning of "at every time, continually" in Old English before 899 and survived in Middle English as *alne way,* along with the later phrase *alles weis,* until about 1350. The later phrase *alles weis* with the same meaning (i.e. continually) was used probably before 1200 but quickly disappeared.

Dropping its inflection, the phrase *alne way* became a compound before 1375, *alway* always, and survived until well into the 1800's, although its uses after the 1600's seem to be conscious archaisms. With the addition of the adverbial suffix *-s, -es alway* became *always* probably about 1350, and gradually gained ground on *alway* from the 1400's onward.

am *v.* form of the verb *be.* Developed from Old English (about 725, in *Beowulf*) *eom,* altered from earlier **em* (compare Old Icelandic *em*), probably on the model of *bēom, bēon* BE, Mercian (before 830) *eam,* Northumbrian (about 950) *am.*

In Old English the verb *am* had only a present tense; all other forms were part of a separate verb with the stem *wes-* meaning "to remain." The two verbs supplemented each other in Old English and constituted the verb *am-was* showing "existence" as the substantive verb. However, by the 1200's parts of *am-was* became obsolete (the infinitive, participle, imperative, etc.) and corresponding parts of *be* took their place, thus making up a verb *am-was-be.* Since *be* supplied the infinitive form, the name was applied to the whole verb, though *be* was separate from the original verb, *am-was.* See BE for further explanation and ARE[1], IS, and WAS for particular details.

English *am* is cognate with Gothic *im,* Old Icelandic *em,* Old Irish *am,* Latin *sum* (irregular), Attic and Homeric Greek *eimí,* Aeolic *émmi* from Proto-Greek **esmi,* Old Lithuanian *esmi,* Latvian *esmu,* Armenian *em,* Old Persian *amiy,* Sanskrit *ásmi,* Hittite *esmi* (*e-eš-mi* in the cuneiform writing).

am- a prefix taking the place of *ambi-* in a few borrowings from Latin, especially *amputate.*

amalgam *n.* mixture, blend. Before 1400, an alloy of mercury, borrowed perhaps through Old French *amalgame,* or directly from Medieval Latin *amalgama,* perhaps alteration of Latin *malagma* poultice or plaster, from Greek *málagma* softening substance, from *malássein* to soften, from *malakós* soft, from Indo-European **meləkós* (Pok. 719). **—amalgamate** *v.* 1660, in Boyle's *New Experiments,* verb use of earlier (1642-47) participle *amalgamate,* probably borrowed from Medieval Latin **amalgamatus,* past participle of *amalgamare,* from *amalgama;* for suffix see -ATE[1].

It is also possible that *amalgamate* is a back formation from earlier *amalgamation.* **—amalgamation** *n.* 1612, probably formed from English *amalgam* (archaic *v.* to alloy with mercury, in Boyle's *Works*) + *-ation.*

Alternatives present themselves: French *amalgamation* was earlier (1578), and may have been the source of borrowing, or the record of English may be incomplete and not include a possibly earlier use of *amalgamate,* to which *-ation* could easily have been applied.

Whatever the facts of the matter, it was during these early developmental years of chemistry, when Boyle and others were active in both England and Europe, that a new vocabulary was developing to meet the needs of describing what these men did.

amanuensis (əman′ yüen′sis) *n.* person who writes what another says or has written. 1619, borrowed from Latin *āmanuēnsis,* a shortened form of *servus ā manū* secretary (originally "servant from the hand," from *ā* from, *manū,* ablative of *manus* hand).

amaranth (am′əranth) *n.* 1616, borrowed perhaps through French *amarante,* from Latin *amarantus,* from Greek *amárantos,* literally, everlasting (*a-* not + *maraínesthai* wither, decay, die out; related to *márnasthai* fight; cognate with Sanskrit *mṛṇāti* seizes, steals, from Indo-European **merə-,* Pok.735).

The form with *-th* probably developed from the influence of Greek *ánthos* flower, as now evident in such later words as *polyanthus.*

amaryllis (am′əril′is) *n.* lilylike plant. 1794, borrowed from Latin, from Greek *Amaryllís,* typical name of a country girl (in Theocritus, Ovid, Vergil, etc).

amass *v.* 1481, in Caxton's translation of *Mirror of the World,* borrowed from Old French *amasser* (*à-* to + *masser,* from *masse* MASS[1] lump).

amateur *n.* 1784, lover of (some activity or thing), borrowed from French and Old French *amateur,* learned borrowing from Latin *amātōrem* (nominative *amātor*) lover, from *amāre* to love, of uncertain origin.

amatory (am′ətôr′ē) *adj.* 1599, borrowed from Latin *amātōrius,* from *amātōrem* lover; see AMATEUR.

amaze *v.* Probably before 1200, in *Ancrene Riwle, amasen,* Middle English form of Old English (about 1000) *āmasian* (*ā-* a-[5] + **masian* to confuse; related to MAZE).

amb- a form of the prefix *ambi-* before a vowel, in borrowings from Latin or French, as in *ambient* and *ambiguous.*

ambassador *n.* About 1385, in Chaucer's *Troilus and Criseyde,* borrowed from Middle French *ambassadeur,* Old French *embassator,* from Italian *ambasciatore,* from Old Provençal *ambaisador,* from *ambaisa(da)* office of an ambassador, EMBASSY; for suffix see -OR[2].

The variant spellings *embassador, ambassador* fluctuated in use throughout the 1600's and 1700's in English and once fixed with the spelling *a* would seem to the casual observer to conflict with *e* in the spelling of *embassy.*

amber *n.* yellowish translucent fossil resin. 1365, earlier meaning (probably about 1350) ambergris, borrowed from Old French *ambre,* learned borrowing from Medieval Latin *ambar, ambara,* from Arabic *ʿanbar* ambergris.

The original meaning of *amber,* "*ambergris*" (the product of whales) was extended to the fossil resin "amber," by influence of the distinction in French between *ambre jaune* the resin and *ambre gris* the whale sperm oil. English retained the differentiation omitting the French identifying color name *jaune* yellow.

ambergris (am′bərgrēs) *n.* grayish waxlike substance used in perfumes. Probably before 1425, borrowed from Middle French *ambre gris,* literally, gray AMBER.

ambi- a prefix borrowed from Latin *ambi-* around, both, in two ways; cognate with Greek *amphi-* around, about, on both sides, Old English *ymb-* around, and Old High German *umbi* (modern German *um* around), and related to Latin *ambō,* Greek *ámphō* both, from Indo-European **ambhi/m̥bhi* (Pok.34). The meaning "around" is preserved in borrowings with the shorter forms *am-* and (before vowels) *amb-,* but as a living word-forming element in English *ambi-* has a general meaning of both, double, as in *ambilateral, ambisexual, ambivalence.*

ambiance (am′bēans) *n.* surroundings. 1923, borrowed from French *ambiance,* but influenced by earlier (1889) English *ambience;* English spelling now follows the French form *-ance.* French *ambiance,* from *ambiant* surrounding, from Latin *ambientem;* see AMBIENT. English *ambience* was formed from *ambient* + *-ence.*

ambidextrous (am′bədek′strəs) *adj.* 1646, borrowed through French *ambidextre,* or directly from Late Latin *ambidexter* (Latin *ambi-* both + *dexter* right-handed, see DEXTERITY); for suffix see -OUS.

ambient (am′bēənt) *adj.* surrounding. 1596, borrowed through Middle French *ambiant, ambient,* or directly from Latin *ambientem* (nominative *ambiēns*), present participle of *ambīre* go about (*amb-* around, form of *ambi-* before a vowel + *īre* go; see EXIT); for suffix see -ENT. —**ambience** *n.* See AMBIANCE.

ambiguity *n.* Probably about 1400, borrowed from Old French *ambigüité,* from Medieval Latin *ambiguitatem* (nominative *ambiguitas),* from Latin *ambiguus* ambiguous; see AMBIGUOUS. —**ambiguous** *adj.* 1528, in Sir Thomas More's *A Dialogue Concerning Heresyes,* borrowed perhaps through French *ambigu,* but more likely directly from Latin *ambiguus,* from *ambigere* dispute about (*amb-,* form of *ambi-* before a vowel, in two ways + *agere* to drive, lead, act; see AGENT); for suffix see -OUS.

ambition *n.* 1340, in *Ayenbite of Inwyt,* borrowed through Middle French *ambition,* or directly from Latin *ambitiōnem* (nominative *ambitiō*) a going about, from *ambīre* go about; see AMBIENT; for suffix see -TION.

The meaning "eager desire for honor, power, etc." developed already in Latin from the literal meaning "a going about," from the going about of candidates for office in ancient Rome soliciting the votes of individual citizens, which led to the meaning "a striving for favor or good will," and finally to "a desire for popularity, fame, etc."

—**ambitious** *adj.* 1382, in the Wycliffe Bible, borrowed through Old French *ambitieux,* or directly from Latin *ambitiōsus,* from *ambitiō* (accusative *ambitiōnem*) a going about; for suffix see -OUS.

ambivalence *n.* 1924, formed in English from earlier (1912) *ambivalency,* or borrowed directly from German *Ambivalenz* (coined about 1910 by the German psychiatrist Eugen Bleuler), from Latin *ambi-* in two ways + *valentia* strength, vigor, from present participle of *valēre* be worth, be strong; see VALUE, —**ambivalent** *adj.* 1916, formed in English from *ambivalency,* on the analogy of *equivalent, equivalency.*

amble *v.* Probably about 1300, in *The Romance of Guy of Warwick,* borrowed through Anglo-French *aumbler,* from Old French *ambler,* from Latin *ambulāre* to walk, from *amb-,* form of *ambi-* before a vowel, around, in two ways + *-ulāre,* cognate with Greek *álē* wandering, roaming, *alâsthai* wander about, Latvian *aluôt* go around or astray, and Tocharian *āl-* remove, detach, from Indo-European **al-* wander aimlessly (Pok. 27).

ambrosia *n.* 1555, borrowed perhaps through Middle French *ambroysie,* or directly from Latin *ambrosia,* from Greek *ambrosíā,* a feminine of *ambrósios* of the immortals (i.e. gods), from *ámbrotos* immortal (*a-* not + *brotós,* from earlier **mrotós* mortal; see MORTAL).

ambulance *n.* 1809, in the *Annual Register 1807,* borrowed from French *ambulance,* from *hôpital ambulant* mobile hospital, literally, walking hospital, from Latin *ambulantem* (nominative *ambulāns),* present participle of *ambulāre* to walk; see AMBLE.

The meaning of a vehicle, such as a wagon or cart to carry the injured, did not develop until the Crimean War (1853-56) when ambulances came into general use, as cited in 1854 in the *Manchester Guardian.*

ambuscade (am′bəskād′) *n.* ambush. 1582-88, borrowed from Middle French *embuscade,* alteration (influenced by Old French *embuscher* to ambush) of Italian *imboscata,* from *imboscare* to ambush, lie in wait in the woods (*im-* in + *bosco* woods, from Provençal *bosc,* from Frankish **busk;* see AMBUSH).

ambush *v.* About 1300 *ambushen, embushen,* borrowed from Old French *embuscher* (*en-* in + *busche* wood, bush, apparently from Frankish **busk;* compare Old High German *busc* BUSH[1]. —**n.** 1489, in Caxton's *Faytes of Armes,* Middle English *embushe,* from the verb, or borrowed from Middle French *embusche,* from Old French *embusche,* from *embuscher;* see AMBUSH, *v.*

ameba *n.* See AMOEBA.

ameliorate (əmēl′yərāt) *v.* 1767, formed from English *a-*[3] to + *meliorate.* The word is patterned on French *améliorer,* from Old French *ameillorer* (from *a-* to + *meillorer* to better, from Late Latin *meliōrāre* improve; see MELIORATE).

amen *interj.* Frequent in Old English (before 1000) as a closing word of vernacular texts, as in Cynewulf and Ælfric, borrowed from Late Latin *āmēn,* from Greek *āmḗn,* from Hebrew *āmēn* truly, verily, surely.

The word is used as an expression of affirmation or agreement in the Bible (Deuteronomy 27:15-26) and adopted in Greek in the Septuagint, from which it passed into early Christian use in Greek and Latin.

amenable (əmē′nəbəl) *adj.* 1596, in Spenser's *A View of the Present State of Ireland,* answerable (to the law), borrowed through Anglo-French *amenable,* from Middle French *amener* (*à* to + *mener* to lead, from Latin *mināre* to drive with shouts, variant of *minārī* threaten; see MENACE; for suffix see -ABLE.

amend *v.* Probably before 1200 *amenden,* in *Ancrene Riwle,* borrowed from Old French *amender,* alteration (influenced by Vulgar Latin **am-,* for Latin *ad-* to) of Latin *ēmendāre* to free from fault (*ē-,* variant of *ex-* out + *menda* fault, blemish). Latin *menda* is cognate with Sanskrit *mindā́* (altered from earlier **mandā́*), from Indo-European **mendā́* (compare also Old Irish *mind* mark, from Indo-European **mndu*) and Welsh *man geni* birthmark (Pok.729). Doublet of EMEND.

—**amendment** *n.* Probably before 1200, in *Ancrene Riwle,* borrowed from Old French *amendement,* from *amender* amend; for suffix see -MENT. —**amends** *n.* compensation. Probably before 1300, borrowed from Old French *amendes* penalties, plural of *amende* reparation, from *amender* to AMEND.

amenity *n.* pleasantry. Before 1398, in Trevisa's translation of Bartholomew's *De Proprietatibus Rerum,* borrowed from Old French *amenité,* or directly from Latin *amoenitātem* (nominative *amoenitās),* from *amoenus* pleasant, of uncertain origin, but according to traditional etymology, perhaps related to *amāre* to love.

American *adj.* 1598, borrowed from New Latin *Americanus,* from *America,* the continent, named after *Americus Vespucius,* in Italian *Amerigo Vespucci,* 1454-1512, Italian navigator who made three voyages to America between 1499 and 1504 and claimed to have discovered it. In 1507 a German geographer and humanist, Martin Waldseemüller, named the land *America* after him in a Latin treatise entitled *Cosmographiae Introductio.*

americium (am′ərish′ēəm) *n.* chemical element discovered in 1945. 1946, New Latin, formed from *Americ(a)* + *-ium.*

Ameslan (am′əslan) *n.* American Sign Language. 1974, formed in English as an acronym for *Ame(rican) S(ign) Lan(guage).*

amethyst *n.* Before 1300 *amatiste,* borrowed from Old French *ametiste* and Medieval Latin *amatistus,* from

Latin *amethystus,* from Greek *améthystos* the amethyst, thought to be a preventive of intoxication (*a-* not + *methýskein* make drunk, from *méthy* wine; see MEAD[2] drink).

amiable *adj.* good-natured and friendly. Before 1375, borrowed from Old French *amiable,* from Late Latin *amīcābilis,* from Latin *amīcus,* n. friend; see the doublet AMICABLE.

A later sense of the word meaning "lovely, lovable" which is now archaic, developed from a confusion of earlier *amiable* "friendly" with Old French *amable* lovable, from Latin *amābilis,* from *amāre* to love.

amicable *adj.* showing a friendly attitude; peaceable. Probably before 1425, borrowed from Late Latin *amīcābilis,* from Latin *amīcus,* n. friend, related to *amāre* to love. Doublet of AMIABLE.

amicus curiae (əmē′kəs kyu̇r′ēē), *Law.* person invited to give information in court. 1612, in Bacon's *Essays,* as *amici curiae,* plural of New Latin *amicus curiae,* literally, friend of the court.

amid *prep.* Probably before 1200, in Layamon's *Chronicle of Britain,* Middle English *amidde, amid,* developed from the Old English phrase (about 725, in *Beowulf*) *on middan* in the middle, possibly on analogy with Latin *in mediō;* see MID.

amidst *prep.* amid. 1391 *amyddes,* formed from *amidde* AMID + adverbial genitive *-s* or *-es.*

The ending was changed in the 1500's to *-st,* probably by association with superlatives in *-st* and *-est* (compare *amongst* and *against*); alternatively, the final *-t* may have been added to the ending *-s* or *-es* for phonetic or articulatory reasons (compare *betwixt*).

amigo (əmē′gō) *n.* friend. 1837, American English, borrowed from Spanish *amigo,* from Latin *amīcum,* accusative of *amīcus* friend; see AMICABLE.

amino (əmē′nō) *adj.* 1887, formed in English as a word and a combining form from earlier (1863) *amine* chemical compound formed from ammonia (*am(monia)* + *-ine* [2] chemical suffix denoting basic substances).

amir (əmir′) *n.* 1614, borrowed from Arabic *amīr* commander, EMIR. Related to ADMIRAL.

Amish *adj.* 1844, American English, apparently borrowed from German *amisch,* derived from the name of Jacob *Amman,* a Swiss Mennonite preacher of the 1600's who founded the sect, + *-isch* -ish[1]. **—n.** 1884, noun use of *Amish,* adj.

amiss *adv.* About 1250, in *The Owl and the Nightingale,* Middle English *amis, amisse* in a wrong or mistaken manner, in fault (*a-*[1] in + *missen* fail to hit, MISS[1]).

amity *n.* friendliness. 1450, in *Rolls of Parliament,* Middle English *amyte,* borrowed from Middle French *amitié,* from Old French *amistié,* from Vulgar Latin **amīcitātem* (nominative **amīcitās*), from Latin *amīcus,* adj. friendly, related to *amāre* to love, of uncertain origin; for suffix see -TY[2].

ammeter *n.* instrument for measuring the strength of electric current. 1882, formed from English *am(pere)* + *-meter.*

ammonia *n.* 1799, New Latin. Ammonia was so named because it was obtained from *sal ammoniac* ammonium chloride, in Middle English (about 1330) *armoniac;* borrowed through Old French *armoniac,* or directly from Medieval Latin *armoniacum,* alteration of Latin *ammōniacum,* from Greek *ammōniakós,* literally salt of *Ammon.*

The connection with Ammon, an Egyptian god identified by the Romans with Jupiter, developed because sal ammoniac was brought from the region of Libya near the shrine of Ammon.

ammunition *n.* Before 1626, in writings of Francis Bacon, borrowed from obsolete French *amunition, ammunition,* and an altered form *amonition,* all from Middle French *munition.*

It has been proposed that French *amunition, amonition* developed from a misdivision of *la munition* into *l'ammunition* and that *amonition* was a further alteration of *munition* by confusion with *admonition.*

amnesia (amnē′zhə) *n.* 1786, Benjamin Rush in *Medical Inquiries and Observations,* New Latin, from Greek *amnēsíā* forgetfulness, from *amnḗmōn* forgetful (*a-* not + *mimnḗskesthai* to recall; see MIND).

amnesty *n.* general pardon of past offenses against a government. 1605, in Francis Bacon's *Of the Advancement of Learning,* forgetfulness, intentional overlooking, borrowed from French *amnestie,* from Latin *amnēstia,* from Greek *amnēstíā* oblivion (*a-* not + *mimnḗskesthai* to recall; see MIND).

The current meaning of pardon for a past offense appeared in 1693.

amniocentesis (am′nēōsentē′sis) *n.* withdrawal of amniotic fluid from the sac enclosing an embryo. 1970, New Latin, formed from *amnion* + *centesis* surgical puncture, borrowed from Greek *kéntēsis* a pricking, from *kenteîn* to prick, related to *kontós* pole, and cognate with Lettish *sīts* hunting spear (corresponding to Lithuanian **šiñtas*), and Old High German *hantag* pointed, from Indo-European **k̑ent-/k̑ont-/k̑n̥t* (Pok.567).

amnion (am′nēən) *n.* sac enclosing an embryo. 1667, New Latin, from Greek *amníon* membrane around a fetus; originally, bowl in which the blood of victims was caught; of unknown origin. **—amniotic** *adj.* 1822, formed from English *amnion* + *-otic,* as in *sclerotic* and *narcotic.*

amoeba or **ameba** *n.* 1855, borrowed from New Latin *Amoeba* (1841) the genus name, from Greek *amoibḗ* change, in reference to its continually changing shape, from *ameíbein* to change; see MIGRATE.

amok *adv., adj.* See AMUCK.

among *prep.* Before 1121, reduced from Old English (before 899, in Alfred's translation of St. Gregory's *Pastoral Care*) *onmang, ongemang,* originally a phrase *on gemang, gemong* in a crowd, from *on* in + *gemang, gemong* mingling, crowd, from the same root as *gemengan* mix or mingle (*ge-* together, collective prefix + *mengan* to mix, MINGLE). Compare Old Saxon *angimang* among, amid; Old Frisian *mong* among.

amongst *prep.* Before 1250, formed from *among* + adverbial genitive *-s* or *-es.*

The ending was changed in the 1500's to *-st,* probably by association with superlatives in *-st* and *-est* (compare *amidst* and *against*); alternatively, the final *-t* may have been added to the ending *-s* or *-es* for phonetic or articulatory reasons (compare *betwixt*).

amontillado (əmon′təlä′dō) *n.* pale dry sherry. 1825, borrowed from Spanish *amontillado* (*a-* to, from Latin *ad-* + *Montilla* town in Spain where the sherry was produced + *-ado* noun suffix, originally past participle, from Latin *-ātus* -ATE[1]).

amorous *adj.* About 1303, in Mannyng's *Handlyng Synne,* borrowed from Old French *amorous, amoureus,* from *amour* love, see AMOUR; for suffix see -OUS.

amorphous (əmôr′fəs) *adj.* formless. 1731, in Bailey's *Dictionary,* borrowed from Greek *ámorphos* (*a-* without + *morphḗ* form).

amortize *v.* Probably before 1387, in a version of *Piers Plowman,* Middle English *amortisen* hold property in mortmain, that is without right of disposal; borrowed from Old French *amortiss-,* stem of *amortir* deaden, from Vulgar Latin **admortīre* (Latin *ad-* to + *mortem,* nominative *mors,* death; related to MORTAL and MORTGAGE); for suffix see -IZE. —**amortization** *n.* 1672, formed in English from *amortize* + *-ation,* or borrowed through Medieval Latin *amortizationem* (nominative *amortizatio*), from *amortizare;* for suffix see -TION.

amount *v.* About 1275, go up, rise, mount, borrowed from Old French *amonter,* from *a mont* upward (literally, to the mountain), from Latin *ad montem* (*ad-* to + *montem,* nominative *mōns* MOUNT[2] mountain). The meaning "be equal (to), reach (to)" appeared in Middle English about 1350. —**n.** 1710, noun use of *amount,* v.

amour *n.* love affair. Probably before 1300, in *Kyng Alisaunder,* borrowed from Old French *amour,* from Latin *amōrem* (nominative *amor)* love, from *amāre* to love.

ampere *n.* 1881, unit of electric current adopted by Paris Electric Conference in 1881, borrowed from French *ampère,* named after André M. *Ampère,* 1775-1836, a French physicist. —**amperage** *n.* 1894, formed in English from *ampere* + *-age,* after *voltage.*

ampersand *n.* the sign &, meaning "and." 1835, formed in English by alteration of *and per se (=) and,* a phrase formerly found in glossaries, meaning *"&" by itself = "and."*

The phrase developed from the use of Latin *per se,* meaning "by itself", which was formerly used in naming a letter that stood by itself to form a word, such as *A per se A* (*a* by itself equals or makes the word *A*), *I per se I* means *I is I* the personal pronoun. The formula is also used for symbols which by themselves stand for a word.

The sign *&* is almost certainly a stylized blend of the letters *E* and *t,* representing Latin *et* and.

amphetamine (amfet′əmēn) *n.* drug used as a stimulant. 1938, acronym formed in English from *a(lpha)-m(ethyl-beta)-ph(enyl)-et(hyl)-amine* the chemical constituents.

amphibian *adj.* 1637, having two modes of existence, or of doubtful nature; (later, probably after 1847) of or having to do with the *Amphibia* (class of animals that live both on land and in water). Both senses derive from New Latin *Amphibia* (1607), from Greek *amphíbia,* neuter plural of *amphíbios* AMPHIBIOUS; for suffix see -AN. —**n.** 1835, noun use of *amphibian,* adj.

amphibious *adj.* 1643, in Sir Thomas Browne's writings; borrowed from Greek *amphíbios* living a double life, amphibious (*amphi-* both + *bíos* life); see AMBI- and BIO-

amphitheater *n.* 1546, borrowed through Middle French *amphithéâtre,* or directly from Latin *amphitheātrum,* from Greek *amphithéātron,* neuter of *amphithéātros* with seats for spectators all round (*amphi-* around, on both sides + *théātron* THEATER).

amphora (am′fərə) *n.* two-handled jar. 1323, borrowed from Latin *amphora,* from Greek *amphoreús,* earlier *amphiphoreús* (*amphi-* on both sides + *phoreús* bearer, ultimately from *phérein* to bear; see BEAR[2] support).

ample *adj.* 1437, in *Proceedings of the Privy Council,* borrowed from Middle French *ample,* from Latin *amplus* large, wide, spacious; possibly related to *ampla* handle, grip, which is cognate with Armenian *aman* vessel, and with Sanskrit *ámatra-m* vessel, pitcher, from Indo-European **am-* grasp, hold (Pok. 35).

amplify *v.* Probably before 1425, in a translation of Higden's *Polychronicon,* borrowed from Middle French *amplifier,* learned borrowing from Latin *amplificāre,* from *amplificus* splendid, from *amplus* ample + the root of *facere* make, DO[1]; for suffix see -FY.

amplitude *n.* 1549, borrowed perhaps through Middle French *amplitude,* or directly from Latin *amplitūdō* (genitive *amplitūdinis),* from *amplus* ample; for suffix see -TUDE.

ampoule (am′pül) *n.* small sealed glass container. 1907, borrowed from French, from Latin *ampulla,* diminutive of *amphora* AMPHORA.

amputate *v.* 1638, possibly a back formation from *amputation,* or borrowed from Latin *amputātus,* past participle of *amputāre* (*am-* variant of *ambi-* about + *putāre* to prune, trim, see PUTATIVE); for suffix see -ATE[1]. —**amputation** *n.* 1611, in Cotgrave's *Dictionary,* borrowed through Middle French *amputation,* or directly from Latin *amputātiōnem* (nominative *amputātiō),* from *amputāre;* for suffix see -TION. —**amputee** *n.* 1910, formed from English *amput(ate)* + *-ee.*

amuck or **amok** *adv., adj.* 1672 *amuck,* 1772 *amock,* borrowed from Malay *amok* in a murderous frenzy, mad with a desire to attack.

amulet (am′yəlit) *n.* charm. 1584, borrowed perhaps through Middle French *amulette,* but more likely from Latin *amulētum,* of unknown origin.

amuse *v.* 1480, in Caxton's translation of Ovid's *Metamorphoses,* borrowed from Middle French *amuser* divert, cause to muse, from Old French *amuser* (*a-* to + *muser* ponder, MUSE). —**amusement** *n.* 1603, in Holland's translation of Plutarch's *Moralia,* borrowed from French, from *amuser;* for suffix see -MENT.

an a form of the indefinite article before words beginning with vowel sounds. *An* is the older and fuller form of *a.* It originated in Old English as an unstressed form of the numeral *ān* one; see ONE. By 1150 it was reduced in the midland dialect of England to *a* before a consonant; but in the southern dialect *an* before a consonant was found as late as 1340. Before *w* and *y* it was used until the 1400's *(an woman),* and before *h* in a stressed syllable *(an hundred)* down to the 1600's and is still affected occasionally before *h* today.

an-[1] a prefix meaning not, as in *analphabetic, anastigmatic,* or without, as in *anhydrous;* the form before vowels and sometimes *h-,* corresponding to *a-* [4] before consonants.

an-[2] a form of the prefix *ad-,* meaning to, toward, before *n,* as in *annex.* Formed in Latin by assimilation of the *d* to the following consonant *(n).*

an-[3] a form of the prefix *ana-* before a vowel, as in *anode.*

-an a suffix of adjectives and nouns meaning: "(person or thing) being of or belonging to," as in *American, European, crustacean;* "person expert or skilled in," as in *historian, magician.* Derived either from Latin *-ānus,* adjective suffix, or by alteration of Middle English *-ain, -en,* borrowed from Old French, from Latin *-ānus.*

From the same sources (Latin *-ānus,* Old French *-ain*) English in a few cases acquired a variant in *-ane,* sometimes in a word distinguished in meaning from the form in *-an (humane: human, urbane: urban),* sometimes without any such contrast *(arcane, mundane).*

ana- a prefix meaning up, again, back, backward, in words borrowed directly or indirectly from Greek *ana-,* as in *anachronism, analysis, anathema,* and much used in technical coinages of various kinds, as in *anabolism, anagram, anaplastic.*

-ana, with a common variant **-iana,** a suffix added to a proper noun, meaning lore (anecdotes, sayings, publications) or a collection of objects, documents, etc.) concerning a person or place, as in *Americana, Lincolniana.* Borrowed from Latin *-āna, -iāna,* neuter plural of the adjective suffixes *-ānus, -iānus,* through such a phrase as *Dicta Vergiliana* Sayings of Vergil, and thence (in France and England in the 1600's and early 1700's) the use of *Vergiliana* alone as a noun and the extension of the suffix *-ana* or *-iana* to other names.

anabolism (ənab′əliz′əm) *n.* process by which food is changed into tissue. 1886, coined from *metabolism* by substitution of Greek *ana-* up, back, on, from *aná,* prep.; see ON.

anachronism *n.* Before 1646, borrowed through French *anachronisme* and Latin *anachronismus,* from Greek *anachronismós,* from *anachronízesthai,* literally, be "timed back", from *anachronízein* refer to a wrong time (*ana-* back + *chronízein* spend time, from *chrónos* time; see CHRONIC); for suffix see -ISM.

anaconda *n.* 1768, a large snake of Ceylon, modification of New Latin (1693) *Anacandaia,* probably from Singhalese *henakandayā* a kind of whip snake, (literally) lightning stem.

The name was mistakenly applied as *Boa anacondo* in 1802 by the French naturalist F.M. Daudin to the South American boa now classified as *Eunectes murinus.*

anaerobic *adj.* 1884, formed in English by adding the common English adjective suffix *-ic* to noun and adjective use of French *anaérobie* (coined in 1863 by Louis Pasteur from Greek *an-* without + *ā̃ḗr, āéros* air + *bíos* life).

anagram *n.* word or phrase formed from another by rearranging the letters. 1589, borrowed probably through French *anagramme,* or adapted directly from New Latin *anagramma,* from Greek *anagrammatízein* transpose letters (*ana-* up or back + *grámma* letter; see GRAMMAR).

analgesic *adj.* causing deadening of pain. *n.* drug that deadens pain. 1875, formed in English from *analgesia* + *-ic.* New Latin *analgesia* was adopted in English (1706) and is derived from Greek *analgēsiā* (*an-* without + *álgēsis* sense of pain, from *algeîn* feel pain, from *álgos* pain, related to *alégein* to care about, originally to feel pain, from Indo-European ***aleg-/alg-,*** Hjalmar Frisk, *Griechisches etymologisches Wörterbuch,* I.67).

analogous *adj.* 1646, borrowed perhaps through French *analogue* adj., or directly from Latin *analogus,* from Greek *análogos* proportionate (*anà lógon* according to due ratio, *aná* up, upon + *lógon,* accusative of *lógos* ratio, reason; see LOGIC); for suffix see -OUS.

analogue *n.* 1826, borrowed from French *analogue,* from Greek *análogon,* neuter singular of *análogos;* see ANALOGOUS.

analogy *n.* Probably before 1425, borrowed through Old French *analogie,* or directly from Latin *analogia,* from Greek *analogíā* proportion, relation, from *análogos* proportionate; see ANALOGOUS; for suffix see -LOGY.

analysis *n.* 1581, Kirke in preface to Spenser's *The Shepheardes Calender,* borrowed from Medieval Latin *analysis,* from Greek *análysis* a breaking up, from *analýein* unloose (*ana-* up + *lýein* loosen, untie; see LOOSE). **—analyst** *n.* 1656, in Hobbes' *Elements of Philosophy,* borrowed from French *analyste,* from *analyse* analysis, from Greek *análysis.* **—analytic** *adj.* 1601, in Ben Jonson's *The Poetaster,* from earlier (about 1590) noun use in Marlowe's *Doctor Faustus,* borrowed through French *analytique,* or directly from Late Latin *analyticus,* from Greek *analytikós,* from *análysis.* **—analyze** *v.* 1601, in Ben Jonson's *The Phoenix Analysde,* early spelling *analyse,* formed in English probably by back formation from *analysis,* influenced by verb suffix *-ize.*

anarchy *n.* 1539, borrowed through French *anarchie* and Medieval Latin *anarchia,* from Greek *anarchíā,* from *ánarchos* rulerless (*an-* without + *archós* ruler, related to *arche-, archi-* chief, first, ARCH-). **—anarchic** *adj.* 1790, in Burke's *Reflections on the Revolution in France,* probably borrowed through French *anarchique,* from Greek *ánarchos;* or formed in English from earlier *anarch* (1667) leader of revolt, borrowed from Greek *ánarchos* + *-ic.* **—anarchist** *n.* 1678, probably formed in English from earlier *anarch* (1667) leader of revolt + *-ist.*

anathema (ənath′əmə) *n.* accursed person or thing. 1526, in Tyndale's translation of the Bible; borrowed from Latin, from Greek *anáthema* thing dedicated or devoted, especially to evil, related to *anatithénai* to set up (*ana-* up + *tithénai* to set, put, place); see DO[1] perform.

Though the word is recorded in French before 1200, it is unlikely that it entered English through French in view of the fact that Tyndale was translating a Latin Bible. However, Tyndale probably knew of the word in French.

anatomy *n.* Before 1398, in Trevisa's translation of Bartholomew's *De Proprietatibus Rerum,* borrowed through Old French *anatomie* and Late Latin *anatomia,* from Greek *anatomḗ* dissection, related to *anatémnein* to cut up, dissect (*ana- up* + *témnein* to cut); for suffix see -TOMY. **—anatomist** *n.* 1543, borrowed from Middle French *anatomiste,* from Old French *anatomie* anatomy; for suffix see -IST.

-ance a suffix forming nouns (chiefly from verbs) and meaning action, process, state, or quality, as in *allowance = action of allowing, annoyance = state or quality of being annoyed. -Ance* is borrowed through Old French or directly from Latin *-antia* (*-ant-* participial stem, as in *cōnstantem* steady, firm + *-ia* suffix corresponding to English *-y*[3]). Compare -ENCE.

ancestor *n.* About 1300 *auncestre, ancestre,* borrowed from Old French *ancestre,* from Late Latin *antecessor* predecessor, from Latin *antecess-,* stem of *antecēdere* precede, go before, (*ante-* before + *cēdere* go; see CEDE). The original ending *-re* would be expected to change to *-er,* but it was Latinized to *-or* in the1500's; for suffix see -OR[2]. **—ancestry** *n.* Before 1338, in Mannyng's *Chronicle of England,* borrowed with alteration (influenced by Middle English *ancestre* ancestor) from Old French *ancesserie, from ancessour,* from Late Latin *antecessōrem* (nominative *antecessor*), from Latin *antecess-*, stem of *antecēdere.*

anchor *n.* Middle English *ancre, anker,* developed from Old English (before 899, in Alfred's translation of Boethius' *De Consolatione Philosophiae*) *ancor,* borrowed from Latin *ancora,* from Greek *ánkȳra,* related to Greek *ankýlos* crooked, curved; see ANGLE[2]. —**v.** Probably before 1200 Middle English *ancren,* verb use of *ancre,* n., anchor.

Anchor was rarely spelled with *-ch-* before the end of the 1500's. It is an example of an attempt to impose Latinate forms in place of natural linguistic development. The adoption of *-ch-* was an imitation of Latin *anchora,* which was itself a corrupt variant of *ancora.*

anchorite (ang'kərīt) *n.* recluse; hermit. About 1433, borrowed from Medieval Latin *anachorita,* alteration of Late Latin *anachōrēta,* from Late Greek *anachōrētḗs,* from Greek *anachōreîn* to retire, retreat (*ana-* back + *chōreîn* withdraw, give place, from *chôros* place, space); for suffix see -ITE[1].

In the 1500's *anchorite* completely replaced the older *ancre* (in use before 1121), which developed from Old English *ancra* (before 900), a shortening of Late Latin *anchōrēta.*

anchovy *n.* 1596, in Shakespeare's *1 Henry IV,* borrowed from Spanish *anchova,* (earlier) *anchoa,* from Italian dialect of Genoa *anciua* and dialect of Corsica *anchiua,* apparently from Vulgar Latin **apiuva,* corresponding to Latin *apua* a small fish, possibly the anchovy, from Greek *aphýē* small fish of various kinds.

ancient *adj.* Middle English *auncien* (probably about 1390, in *Sir Gawain and the Green Knight*), borrowed from Old French *ancien, auncien,* from Vulgar Latin **anteānus* meaning "from before" (Latin *ante* before + *-ānus* -an).

The addition of final *-t* to English *auncien* occurred in the 1400's by mistaken association of the word with adjectives in *-ant* and *-ent* that had dropped the final *-t.*

ancillary *adj.* subordinate, dependent, auxiliary. 1667, borrowed from Latin *ancillāris* of a handmaid, from *ancilla* handmaid, diminutive of *ancula,* feminine of *anculus* manservant (*an-*, variant of *ambi-* around + *-culus,* from *colere* attend to, cultivate); for suffix see -ARY.

-ancy a suffix forming nouns (chiefly corresponding to adjectives in *-ant,* such as *buoyant, constant*) and meaning state or quality, as in *buoyancy = state or quality of being buoyant, constancy = state or quality of being constant; vacancy = state or quality of being vacant.*

-Ancy is a variant form of *-ance* and is borrowed from Latin *-antia.* It became differentiated from *-ance* probably to emphasize the sense of state or quality. Compare the older form -ANCE, which forms nouns meaning state or quality and also nouns meaning action and process.

and *conj.* Old English (about 700, in Caedmon's *Hymn*) *and, end, ond.*

The word is cognate with Old Frisian *anda, enda* and, Old Saxon *ande, endi,* Old High German *endi, anti, enti, unti* (modern German *und*), Middle Dutch *ende, end, enn* (modern Dutch *en*), and Old Icelandic *enn* and, but, from Proto-Germanic **unđá.* Cognates also occur in Avestan *atha* likewise, and in Sanskrit *átha* then, from Indo-European **n̥tha* (Pok.50). It is presumably the unaccented character of the word that has led to most of the variations in the vowels.

andante (ändän'tā) *adv., adj.* 1724, borrowed from Italian *andante* going, verbal adjective of *andare* go, perhaps from Vulgar Latin **ambitāre* (Latin *amb-*, variant of *ambi-* around + *itāre,* frequentative of *īre* go).

andiron *n.* 1309 *aundiren, aundirne,* borrowed from Old French *andier, aundier.*

The ending *-iron* developed after *andier* was borrowed from Old French and was influenced by Middle English *iren* iron.

It has been proposed, in order to take account of certain shapes or decorations of medieval andirons, that Old French *andier* may have developed from Gaulish **andero-* bullock, represented by Basque loan words from Celtic *andre, andere, anre* young woman; also compare Welsh *anner* heifer, and Middle Irish *ainner* young woman.

androgynous (androj'ənəs) *adj.* being both male and female. 1651, borrowed from Latin *androgynus,* from Greek *andrógynos* male and female in one, hermaphrodite (*anḗr,* genitive *andrós* man, male + *gynḗ* woman, female); for suffix see -OUS. Greek *anḗr* is cognate with Sanskrit *nā́* (accusative *náram*), Armenian *air* (genitive *aṙn*), Oscan *nerum* of men, and Sabine *Nerō* "the manly," all from Indo-European **ner-/aner-* (Pok. 765); see QUEEN.

-ane a suffix designating a saturated hydrocarbon of the methane series (as in *butane, propane*), one of the coinages in the systematic nomenclature of organic chemistry, contrasting with *-ene, -ine, -one.*

-Ane also occurs as an occasional variant of the suffix *-an,* as in *humane, germane, urbane,* adding force or emphasis to a quality described by an adjective, as in *human, german, urban.*

anecdote *n.* 1686, private or unpublished historical fact; borrowed through French *anecdote,* or directly from Medieval Latin *anecdota,* from Late Greek *anékdota* things unpublished (in reference to the title of memoirs by the Greek historian Procopius, which consisted chiefly of gossip about the court of Justinian). Late Greek *anékdota,* neuter plural of Greek *anékdotos* unpublished, is from *an-* not + *ékdotos* published, from *ekdidónai* give out, publish, (*ex-* out + *didónai* give; see DATE[1] time).

anemia *n.* 1876 *anemia;* before 1824 *anaemia,* influenced by earlier French *anémie* (1722), but adopted from New Latin, from Greek *anaimíā* lack of blood, from *ánaimos* bloodless (*an-* without + *haîma* blood). The spelling *anemia* appeared in English by 1876. —**anemic** *adj. anemic* after 1839; *anaemic* sometime before 1847, perhaps influenced by earlier French *anémique* (1833), but formed from English *anaemia* + *-ic.*

anemometer (an'əmom'ətər) *n.* instrument for measuring wind velocity. 1727, in *Chambers Cyclopaedia,* borrowed from French *anémomètre,* a compound formed from Greek *ánemos* wind + *métron* a measure. Cognate with Sanskrit *ániti* breathes; Greek *ánemos* wind is also cognate with Latin *animus* spirit and *anima* breath and with Gothic *uz-anan* breathe out, from Indo-European **anə-* (Pok. 38).

anemone (ənem'ənē) *n.* windflower. 1548, borrowed through Middle French *anemone,* Old French *anem-*

oine, or directly from Latin *anemōnē,* from Greek *anemṓnē,* (*ánemos* wind + *-ōnē* daughter of, a feminine patronymic suffix).

The name was applied to the flowerlike sea polyp in 1773.

anent (ənent′) *prep.* concerning. The term is literary, if not archaic, in modern English. Old English (about 725, in *Beowulf*) *on efn,* (before 899, in Alfred's translation of Orosius) *on emn* alongside, on a level with (*on* on + *efn* EVEN).

The final *-t* was added, probably before 1200, perhaps by association of some other word or as a result of the reduction of a following article, as *oneman (anemn) the,* to *anen-te,* to *anent.*

Anent is cognate with Old Saxon *on eban* alongside, and Middle High German *eneben, neben* alongside.

aneroid *adj.* using no liquid, as in *aneroid barometer* that works by air pressure. 1848, borrowed from French *anéroïde* (Greek *a-* without + Late Greek *nērón* water + French *-oïde* -oid). The word *nērón* derived from the Late Greek phrase *nēròn hýdōr* fresh water, from Greek *nearón,* neuter of *nearós* fresh, from *néos* new; see NEW.

anesthesia *n.* 1721 *anaesthesia,* New Latin, from Greek *anaisthēsíā* insensibility (*an-* without + *aísthēsis* sensation, from *aisthánesthai* to feel, perceive; see AUDIBLE). **—anesthetic** *adj.* 1846 *anaesthetic* (proposed by Oliver Wendell Holmes, 1809-94, American physician and author), borrowed from Greek *anaísthētos* insensible (*an-* without + *aisthētós* sensible, from *aisthánesthai* to feel) + English *-ic.*

Noun use of *anesthetic* with the spelling *anaesthetic,* a substance that causes anesthesia, appeared by 1848.

aneurysm or **aneurism** (an′yəriz′əm) *n.* permanent swelling of an artery or vein. Probably before 1425 *aneurisma,* borrowed from Medieval Latin *aneurisma,* from Greek *aneúrysma,* from *aneurýnein* dilate (*ana-* up + *eurýnein* widen, from *eurýs* wide, from earlier **werýs,* cognate with Sanskrit *urú-s* wide, fro· . Indo-European **wer-,* (Pok.1165).

The spelling with *y* is a later etymological reversion.

angel *n.* About 1300 *angel, aungel,* replacing earlier Middle English *angel, angles,* a fusion of Old English *engel* and Latin *angelus.* The later Middle English *angel, aungel* are a fusion of Old English *engel* and Old French *angele, angel, aungel,* from Latin *angelus,* from Greek *ángelos,* originally meaning "messenger."

The Greek word was a loan translation in the Septuagint of Hebrew *mal'akh* messenger, angel; and *ángelos* may have been suggested by the related Greek *ángaros* royal mounted courier (which is another loan word, but from Old Persian, probably from Akkadian *agāru* to hire, *agru* hireling).

The Old English *engel* was a borrowing of Latin *angelus.* Other Germanic languages made a similar borrowing of the Latin: Old Frisian *angel, engel,* Old High German *angil, engil,* Old Icelandic *engill.* **—angelic** *adj.* About 1385, in Chaucer's *Troilus and Criseyde,* borrowed from Old French *angélique,* from Latin *angelicus,* from Greek *angelikós,* from *ángelos* angel; for suffix see -IC.

Angelus *n.* 1658, in *Chambers Cyclopaedia,* borrowed from Medieval Latin, from Latin *angelus* angel; so called from the opening word of the service, *Angelus domini nuntiavit Mariae* An angel of the Lord announced to Mary.

The meaning of the bell that sounds the call to the service was used in 1847 by Longfellow in *Evangeline.*

anger *n.* Probably about 1250 *anger, angre* distress, affliction, grief, pain, sorrow, borrowed from a Scandinavian source represented in Old Icelandic *angr* grief.

The word is cognate in Germanic with Old English *enge* narrow, Old High German *engi* (modern German *eng*), Old Icelandic *ǫngr,* Gothic *angwus,* from Proto-Germanic **anȝús.* It is cognate outside Germanic with Latin *angere* to press, choke, distress, and its development may have been influenced further by Latin *angor* anxiety, anguish. It is also cognate with Greek *ánchein* to squeeze, strangle, and Sanskrit *áṅhas* distress, anxiety, *aṅhós,* ablative of **aṅhú-s* narrow, from Indo-European **anĝh-* (Pok. 42). Related to ANGUISH, ANXIETY. **—v.** Probably about 1200, in *The Ormulum,* Middle English *angren* to distress, irritate, annoy, provoke; borrowed from Scandinavian represented in Old Icelandic *angra* to grieve, from *angr* grief.

angina *n.* **1** inflammation of the throat. **2** = angina pectoris. 1578, influenced by French *angine,* but borrowed from Latin *angīna* infection of the throat accompanied by choking, from *angere* to choke; see ANGER.

angina pectoris heart condition marked by sharp chest pains. 1744, New Latin *angina pectoris* sudden constriction of the chest (Latin *pectoris,* genitive of *pectus* chest).

angio- before vowels **angi-,** a combining form adopted from Greek *angeîon* receptacle (formed from *ángos* vessel, of unknown origin). New Latin *angio-, angi-* is used in scientific coinage referring to a covering or enclosure, as in *angiocarpous* (having a fruit enclosed in a covering), and especially to blood and lymph vessels, as in *angiogram* (X-ray of blood-vessels).

angiosperm (an′jēəspėrm′) *n.* flowering plant. 1828, borrowed from New Latin *angiospermus,* from Greek *angeîon* vessel + *spérma* seed.

angle[1] *n.* space between two lines that meet. About 1380, in Chaucer's *The House of Fame,* corner, borrowed through Old French *angle,* or directly from Latin *angulus* corner, angle.

Latin *angulus* is cognate with Greek *ánkos* bend, valley, Armenian *ankiun, angiun* corner, Sanskrit *áṅga-m* limb, and *aṅká-s* a bend, hook, from Indo-European **ang-/ank-* (Pok. 45); and *angle*[1] is related to ANGLE[2] and ANKLE.

angle[2] *v.* fish with hook and line. About 1450, verb use of *angle,* n., fishhook, developed from Old English *angel* (before 899, in Alfred's translation of Boethius' *De Consolatione Philosophiae*); related to *anga* hook.

Old English *angel* is cognate with Old High German *angul* fishhook, *ango* hook, Old Icelandic *ǫngull* fishhook, Latin *ancus* crooked, Greek *ánkos* a bend, hollow, *ankýlos* crooked, curved, and Sanskrit *aṅká-s* a bend, hook.

Ultimately *angle*[1], *angle*[2], and *ankle* are traced to the Indo-European base **ank-/ ang-* (Pok.45).

Anglican *adj.* of the Church of England. 1635, borrowed from Medieval Latin *Anglicanus,* from *Anglicus* of the English people, of England, from Latin *Anglī* the Angles; see ANGLO-.

The word was used in its Latin form *Anglicana* in the Magna Charta 1215. The noun use did not appear in English until sometime before 1797 in a collection of Burke's letters.

Anglicize *v.* 1710, in a collection of Samuel Sewall's letters; formed in English from Medieval Latin *Anglicus* of the English people + English suffix *-ize.* —**Anglicism** *n.* Anglicized idiom or language. 1642, in James Howell's *Instructions for Foreign Travel;* formed in English from Medieval Latin *Anglicus* + English *-ism.*

Anglo (ang′glō) *n. Informal.* **1** *U.S. (Southwest)* an American white who speaks English. 1941, abstracted from *Anglo-American* (1787). **2** *Canadian.* a Canadian of English descent. 1959, abstracted from *Anglo-Canadian* (1832). **3** *British.* a British citizen of English descent. 1964, abstracted from *Anglo-Saxon* (1610). *Anglo* is sometimes used as a term of contempt by French Canadians in Canada and by Hispanic people in the U.S. and Latin America.

Anglo- a combining form meaning English, as in *Anglo-Catholic, Anglo-American.* Borrowed from Medieval Latin *Anglo-*, combining form of *Angli* the English, from Latin *Anglī* the Angles (a Germanic tribe that, accompanied by Saxons, Jutes, and Frisians, crossed over into Britain in the 400's and 500's A.D. and colonized the greater part of it). The name of the tribe is also of Germanic origin (compare Old English *Engle* the Angles).

Angles referred originally to the people of *Angul,* now called *Angeln,* a region of northern Schleswig-Holstein in Germany (Old Icelandic *Ǫngull*), which was so called because of its hooklike shape.

Anglo-Saxon *adj., n.* Old English *Angul-Saxon* (about 885) with the meaning "English Saxons" to distinguish them from the Saxons of the Continent, sometimes now referred to as Old Saxons.

The development of the term *Anglo-Saxon* parallels the historical comings of various groups to Britain. At first there was no record of a collective name for the colonizers who came to Britain from the Continent in the 400's and 500's A.D, but later the term *Englisc* (English) appeared from the dialect of the Angles. Subsequently *Englisc* applied to all dialects of the Angles and the Saxons, probably sometime before 700 A.D. Then in the struggle with the Danes *English* was used probably by 800 A.D. to describe all speakers of any dialect of the Angles and the Saxons.

After the Norman Conquest (1066) the invaders were referred to as French and the natives as English, but in a few generations *English* no longer served as a term of distinction, and *Saxon* was used to distinguish the natives from before the Norman Conquest.

This distinction was diluted, however, by the chroniclers of the 1100's and later, who were often of Franco-Latin background, and to whom a historical distinction between the Angles and the Saxons was not very clear so that the meaning *Anglo-Saxon* was easily extended to all English. However, this use of *Anglo-Saxon* was not adopted in English until about 1610 when scholars needed a term to distinguish between the Saxons of England and the Saxons of the Continent, or Germany.

The modern use of *Anglo-Saxon* has evolved another meaning *"Anglo* and *Saxon",* that is "a union of Angle and Saxon". This in turn has given rise to the popular use of *Anglo-* as meaning "English and ______" so that numerous combinations have developed; see ANGLO-.

Angostura (ang′gəstůr′ə) *n.* Trademark for a kind of aromatic bitters. 1879, named after *Angostura,* now the port city of Ciudad Bolívar in eastern Venezuela, where the substance was originally made.

There is a tree of South America, whose bitter bark is *angostura* (1791 *angustura,* borrowed from Spanish). However, this bark is not the source of *Angostura* bitters and so the two words are not in that way related.

angry *adj.* 1375, in John Barbour's *The Bruce,* vexing, fierce, severe, inflamed (referring to things and events); about 1385, in Chaucer's *Troilus and Criseyde,* incensed, resentful, angered (referring to people), formed from Middle English *anger* + *-y*[1].

angst (ängst) *n.* dread, panic, anxiety. 1956, in C.P. Snow's *Homecomings,* borrowed from German *Angst,* from Old High German *angust.* The word is cognate with Latin *angere* to choke, distress, *angustus* narrow; see ANGER, ANGUISH.

Angst was first recorded in a collection of George Eliot's letters, in a letter written in 1849. For the next 100 years the word slowly made its way into English and was given special prominence after translations of Freud's work in psychology were circulated in the U.S. during the 1920's and 1930's. But it was not until after World War II that writers, such as C.P. Snow, felt the word was widely enough known among their readership to use *angst* without any special identification (such as italics or quotation marks). Much of the later familiarity with *angst* comes from books, such as that of Cyril Connolly in *The Unquiet Grave* (1944), in which the word was still capitalized, as in German, and from discussions in the popular press, such as the *Sunday Times* of London, Jan. 1, 1959.

angstrom (ang′strəm) *n.* unit of measurement of the wavelength of light. 1951, altered from earlier *Ångström* (1906), shortened from (1897) *Ångström unit,* named after A.J. *Ångström,* 1814-1874, Swedish physicist.

anguish *n.* Probably before 1200, in *Ancrene Riwle,* borrowed through Old French *anguisse, angoisse,* from Latin *angustia* tightness, from *angustus* narrow. The word is related to *anger* through Latin *angere* to choke, see ANGER; for suffix see -ISH[2].

angular *adj.* having angles. Before 1398, in Trevisa's translation of Bartholomew's *De Proprietatibus Rerum,* borrowed, perhaps through influence of earlier Old French *angulaire,* from Latin *angulāris,* from *angulus* ANGLE[1] (space); for suffix see -AR.

aniline (an′əlin) *n.* liquid obtained from coal tar and nitrobenzene to make dyes, plastics, etc. 1850, borrowed from French *aniline,* also perhaps reinforced by German *Anilin.* Both forms are from French *anil,* from Portuguese *anil,* from Arabic *an-nīl* (*al-* the + *nīl* indigo, from Sanskrit *nīlī,* originally the feminine of *nīla-s* dark blue, of unknown origin); for suffix see -INE[2].

It is also possible that *aniline* is a formation in English of *anil* indigo dye, the word known in English from 1581, + *-ine*[2], because the name *aniline* was applied to the dyes when a process for making it was invented in 1826.

animadversion *n.* unfavorable comment, criticism. 1599, borrowed through Middle French *animadversion,* from Latin *animadversiōnem* (nominative *animadversiō*), from *animadvers-*, stem of *animadvertere* (*animum,* accusative of *animus* mind + *advertere* turn to; see ADVERT refer to); for suffix see -SION.

animal *n.* About 1330, in *Sir Orfeo,* borrowed perhaps through Old French, or more likely directly from Latin *animal.* The Latin word was originally the neuter form of *animālis* having the breath of life, animate, from *anima* life, breath, which is related to *animus* mind, spirit. Latin *animus* is cognate with Greek *ánemos* wind, breath, and with Sanskrit *ániti* he breathes, from Indo-European *ənə- (Pok.38).

animate (an'əmit) *adj.* Before 1398, in Trevisa's translation of Bartholomew's *De Proprietatibus Rerum,* borrowed from Latin *animātus,* past participle of *animāre,* from *anima* life, breath, see ANIMAL; for suffix see -ATE[1]. —**v.** (an'əmāt) 1538, in writings of Miles Coverdale, verb use of the adjective.

Both adjective and verb are recorded in French prior to their use in English, and the verb may have come into use in English by influence of French, because Coverdale spent time in Paris in 1538-39 supervising a translation of the Bible into English.

animism *n.* belief that natural objects have souls. 1866, formed from Latin *anima* life, breath, soul + English *-ism.*

The development of the term in English was probably influenced by an earlier sense of a doctrine that animal life is produced by an immaterial soul (1832), borrowed from German *Animismus* (coined by the German physicist G.E. Stahl, 1660-1734).

animosity *n.* violent hatred, enmity. Probably before 1425, in a translation of Higden's *Polychronicon,* meaning vigor; borrowed through Middle French *animosité,* or directly from Latin *animōsitātem* (nominative *animōsitās*), from *animōsus* spirited, from *animus* spirit, see ANIMAL; for suffix see -ITY.

The current meaning of *animosity* appeared in 1605, in Francis Bacon's *Of the Advancement of Learning.*

animus *n.* = animosity. 1816, borrowed from Latin *animus* spirit, feeling; see ANIMAL.

anion (an'ī'ən) *n.* negatively charged ion. 1834 (a term applied by the English physicist and chemist Michael Faraday, 1791-1867), borrowed from Greek *anión* (thing) going up, neuter present participle of *aniénai* go up (*aná* up + *iénai* go; see EXIT). The term is related to CATION and ION.

anise (an'is) *n.* Probably about 1300, in *The Romance of Guy of Warwick,* borrowed from Old French *anis,* learned borrowing from Latin *anīsum, anēsum,* from Greek *ánnēson,* of unknown origin.

ankle *n.* About 1350 *ancle;* probably before 1300 *anclowe,* in *Arthour and Merlin;* before 1150 *ancleowe;* developed from Old English *onclēow* (before 800, in *Corpus Glossary*).

The word is cognate with Old High German *anchal, enchil* ankle (in modern German *Enkel*), Middle Dutch *ankel* (modern Dutch *enkel*), Old Icelandic *ǫkkla* (from **ankulan*), and Latin *angulus* corner, angle, from Indo-European **ang-* (Pok. 45); see ANGLE[1] space.

Old English had another form *anclēow* (cognate with Old High German *anchlāo,* and apparently due to influence of Proto-Germanic **klāwa-* claw), but eventually this was supplanted by the simpler *ancle.*

A later form in Middle English *ankel* was borrowed ultimately from Old Icelandic *ǫkkla.*

annals *n.pl.* 1563, borrowed perhaps through Middle French *annales,* but more likely directly from Latin *annālēs librī,* literally, annual books or records, plural form of *annālis* annual, from *annus* year; see ANNUAL.

anneal (ənēl') *v.* Before 1382 *anelen,* developed from Old English (before 725) *onǣlan* to set on fire, kindle (*on-, an-* on + *ǣlan* to burn, bake, Proto-Germanic **ailjanan* from *āl* fire, a burning, Proto-Germanic **ailan*). The Old English term *-āl* was a rare word and is related to the more common Old English *ǣld, ǣled* fire, which is cognate with Old Saxon *ēld,* Old Icelandic *eldr* fire, Swedish *eld,* and Danish *ild* fire, Proto-Germanic **ailiđaz,* from Indo-European **ai-l-* (root **ai-* burn) (Pok. 11,12).

The spelling with the double *n* is an imitation of Latin and was introduced in the early 1600's, becoming generally fixed by the next century.

The meaning "to temper by heating and then cooling" appeared before 1382 in Wycliffes' translation of the Bible.

annelid (an'əlid) *n.* 1834, borrowed from French *annélide.* The term in French developed from New Latin *Annelida,* the scientific name for the phylum of worms in a system of classifying animals developed by the French naturalist Lamarck in 1801 and in which he proposed the French word *annelés* ringed ones, from which the New Latin term came. Ultimately *annelés* developed from Old French *annel* ring, from Latin *ānellus,* a diminutive form of *ānulus* small ring, itself a diminutive form of *ānus* ring, ANUS.

annex *v.* About 1370, in Chaucer's *Pity,* borrowed through Old French *annexer,* from Medieval Latin *annexare,* frequentative form of Latin *annectere* to bind to (*an-* to, variant of *ad-* before *n* + *nectere* to bind; related to CONNECT). —**n.** 1540, probably borrowed from Middle French *annexe,* from Latin *annexus,* past participle of *annectere.*

There is a possibility that in the 170 years between the first record of the verb and that of the noun, the noun use developed in English from the verb, perhaps influenced by the existence of the previous French noun, and was not a borrowing. However, the meaning "an addition to an existing building" apparently is an adoption in 1861 from French *annexe.* —**annexation** *n.* 1611, in Cotgrave's *Dictionary,* probably formed from English *annex,* v. + *-ation.*

Annie Oakley *Slang.* free ticket. 1922 in American English, named after *Annie Oakley,* 1860-1926, a noted American sharpshooter and showman. The ticket is supposed to have gotten its name from the resemblance between punched tickets and her small perforated targets.

annihilate *v.* 1525, verb use of Middle English past participle *annihilate,* in Wycliffe (*adnichilat*); borrowed perhaps through influence of Middle French *annihiler* from *anichiler,* or directly from Late Latin *annihilātus,* past participle of *annihilāre* to cause to be nothing (from Latin *an-* to, variant of *ad-* before *n* + *nihil* nothing; see NIL); for suffix see -ATE[1]. —**annihilation** *n.* Before 1638, formed from English *annihilate* + *-ation,* or alternatively either borrowed from Middle French *annihilation,* or directly from Late Latin *annihilātiōnem* (nominative *annihilātiō*), from *annihilāre;* for suffix see -TION.

anniversary *n.* Probably before 1200, in *Ancrene Riwle,* borrowed through Anglo-French *anniversarie* and Medieval Latin *anniversarium,* from Latin *anniversārius* returning annually (*annus* year + *versus,* past participle of *vertere* to turn; see ANNUAL and VERSION); for suffix see -ARY.

announce *v.* 1483, in Caxton, borrowed from Old

French *annoncier,* from Latin *annūntiāre* (*an-* to, variant of *ad-* before *n* + *nūntiāre* announce, relate, from *nūntius* messenger, of unknown origin). Doublet of ANNUNCIATE. —**announcement** *n.* 1798, either borrowed from French *annoncement,* or formed in English from *announce* + *-ment.*

annoy *v.* About 1275, Middle English *anoien,* borrowed through Anglo-French *anuier, anoier,* from Old French *anoier, enoier, enuier* to weary, vex, from Late Latin *inodiāre* make loathsome, from Latin *esse in odiō* be hateful or in hatred (*odiō,* ablative of *odium* hatred; see ODIUM). —**annoyance** *n.* About 1390, in Chaucer's *Canterbury Tales,* borrowed from Old French *anoiance,* from *anoier* to weary, vex; for suffix see -ANCE.

annual *adj.* Before 1382, in Wycliffe's translation of the Bible, borrowed perhaps through Old French *annuel,* or more likely as a learned borrowing from Late Latin *annuālis.* The Late Latin form is an alteration of Latin *annālis* annual, and was influenced by Latin *annuus* yearly, both forms from *annus* year; for suffix see -AL.

annuity *n.* About 1412, in Hoccleve's *Regement of Princes* (a version in English of a treatise in Latin); borrowed through Anglo-French *annuité,* or directly from Medieval Latin *annuitatem* (accusative of *annuitas*), from Latin *annuus* yearly, see ANNUAL; for suffix see -ITY.

annul *v.* 1395, in writings of Wycliffe, borrowed through Old French *annuler,* or directly from Late Latin *annūllāre* (Latin *an-* to, variant of *ad-* before *n* + *nūllus* of no value, NULL).

annular *adj.* ring-shaped. 1571, borrowed from Latin *anularis* of or having to do with a ring, from *ānulus,* diminutive of *ānus* ring, ANUS.

annunciate *v.* Before 1536, in writings of Tyndale, verb use of Middle English past participle *annunciat* (about 1375, in Chaucer's *Canterbury Tales*) or borrowed directly from Latin *annūntiātus,* past participle of *annūntiāre* make known, proclaim, announce. See the doublet ANNOUNCE; for suffix see -ATE[1].

There is also a possibility *annunciate* may be a back formation in English from earlier *annunciation.*—**annunciation** *n.* Before 1325, in *Cursor Mundi,* referring to Lady Day, which is the festival of the Annunciation. The word was borrowed through Anglo-French *annunciacioun,* from Late Latin *annūntiātiōnem* (nominative *annūntiātiō*), from Latin *annūntiāre* announce; for suffix see -TION.

Annunciation in the primary sense of an announcement appeared in 1563.

anode *n.* positive electrode. 1834, borrowed from Greek *ánodos* way up (*aná* up + *hodós* way); so called from the path that the electric current was thought to take from the positive pole.

Anode and *cathode* were introduced, though apparently not coined, by the English chemist and physicist Michael Faraday, 1791-1867. Compare ELECTRODE.

anodyne (an'ədin) *adj., n.* (thing) that soothes. 1543, borrowed from Medieval Latin *anodynus* pain-removing, from Latin *anōdynus, anōdynos* painless, from Greek *anṓdynos* (*an-* without + *odýnē* pain). Greek *odýnē,* earlier *odýnā,* altered by a kind of assimilation from *edúnā* (found in Aeolic), related to *édesthai* to be going to eat (compare Horace's *cūrae edācēs* gnawing cares), cognate with Latin *edere* EAT, from Indo-European **ed-* (Pok.287).

The word was known in Middle French *anodin* as early as 1503 but was probably not the immediate source of English borrowing, rather it was a parallel development in French from Latin, because the first recorded appearance of the word in English is from a book on surgery translated from Latin.

anoint *v.* About 1303, in Mannyng's *Handlyng Synne,* Middle English *anointen, enointen;* borrowed from Old French *enoint* smeared on, past participle of *enoindre* smear on, from Latin *inunguere* (*in-* on + *unguere* to smear; see UNGUENT).

anomaly *n.* something irregular or abnormal. 1571, borrowed from Latin *anōmalia,* from Greek *anōmalíā,* from *anṓmalos* anomalous (*an-* not + *homalós* even, probably from *homós* SAME); for suffix see -Y[3]. —**anomalous** *adj.* 1646, borrowed from Late Latin *anōmalus,* from Greek *anṓmalos* anomalous; for suffix see -OUS.

anon *adv.* Middle English *anan, anon, onan.* **1** shortly, soon (probably before 1200, in *Ancrene Riwle,* etc.). **2** onward, all the way (before 1121, in *Peterborough Chronicle*). Both senses developed from Old English *on ān* in or into one (probably about 800, meaning "at once"); see ON and ONE.

anonymous *adj.* 1601, in Holland's translation of Pliny's *Natural History,* borrowed from Late Latin *anōnymus,* from Greek *anṓnymos* (*an-* without + *ónyma,* dialectal form of *ónoma* name; see NAME); for suffix see -OUS.

anorak (ä'nəräk) *n.* arctic jacket. 1924, borrowed from Eskimo (Greenlandic) *ánorâq* clothing, dress.

anorexia *n.* lack of appetite for food. 1626, perhaps influenced by earlier French *anorexie;* New Latin, from Greek *anorexíā* (*an-* without + *órexis* appetite, desire, from *orégein* to desire, reach after, stretch out; see RIGHT). —**anorexic** *adj., n.* 1974, formed in English from *anorexia* + suffix *-ic.*

answer *n.* Middle English *andswere,* developed from Old English (about 725, in *Beowulf*) *ondswere, andswaru* (*and-* against + *-swaru* affirmation, swearing, from *swerian* swear). Old English *andswaru* is cognate with Old Frisian *ondser,* Old Saxon *antswōr,* and Old Icelandic *andsvar,* all with the original sense of rebutting a charge or accusation; see ANTI and SWEAR. —**v.** Middle English *answeren,* developed from Old English (about 725, in *Beowulf*) *andswarian,* from *andswaru* answer.

ant *n.* Before 1500 *ant,* developed from earlier *ampte, empte* (1382, in the Wycliffe Bible), and still earlier *amete, emete* (about 1300), developed from Old English *ǣmette* (before 899, as in the form *ǣmethyl* ant hill, in Alfred's translation of St. Gregory's *Pastoral Care*).

The Old English *ǣmette,* literally, one that cuts off (leaves), is cognate with Old High German *āmeiʒa* ant, in modern German *Ameise.* The Old English prefix *ǣ-* off, and Old High German *ā-* are from Proto-Germanic **ai-,* which has no known cognates. Both Old English *ǣmette* (*ǣ-* off, away + *-mette* one that cuts) and Old High German *āmeiʒa* (*ā-* off + *-meiʒa* a cutter) have elements of their compound forms (*-mette* and *-meiʒa*) that are cognate with Old Icelandic *meita* and Gothic *maitan* to cut, from Proto-Germanic **maitanan,* Indo-European **mai-d-* (Pok.697).

-ant a suffix forming adjectives and nouns from verbs, as in *compliant* (from *comply*), *assistant* (from *assist*).

Borrowed through Old French *-ant,* or directly from Latin *-antem,* present participle suffix. Compare -ENT.

antagonize *v.* 1634, borrowed from Greek *antagōnízesthai* to struggle against (*anti-* against + *agōnízesthai* to struggle, contend, from *agṓn* contest; see AGONY). —**antagonism** *n.* 1838, borrowed from French *antagonisme,* from Late Greek *antagṓnisma,* from Greek *antagōnízesthai* to contend. —**antagonist** *n.* 1599, in Ben Jonson's *Cynthia's Revels,* borrowed perhaps through French *antagoniste,* or directly from Late Latin *antagōnista,* from Greek *antagōnistḗs* opponent, rival, from *antagōnízesthai* to contend.

antarctic (antärk'tik *or* antär'tik) *adj.* 1601 *antarcticke,* in Holland's translation of Pliny's *Natural History,* alteration (influenced by Latin *antarcticus*) gradually replacing earlier Middle English *antartik,* about 1400, in Chaucer's *Astrolabe.* The word was borrowed through Old French *antartique,* from Medieval Latin *antarticus.* The Medieval Latin word followed the same process of sound change by dissimilation as the parallel term *arctic* and dropped the *c* in *-arc-* which was in the original Latin *antarcticus,* from Greek *antarktikós* opposite the north (*anti-* opposite + *arktikós* of the north; see ARCTIC.

The variant pronunciation (antär'tik) is reminiscent of the original spelling *antartik.*

ante *n.* stake in poker put up before the deal. 1838, American English, apparently from *ante-* before. —**v.** put up an ante. 1846, from the noun.

ante- a prefix meaning before, as in *antedate,* or in front of, as in *anteroom.* Borrowed from Latin prefix *ante-,* from *ante* before, in front of. The prefix is cognate with Greek *antí* against, instead of; see ANTI-.

ante-bellum *adj.* 1862, American English (referring to the Civil War, 1861-65), borrowed from Latin *ante bellum* before the war.

antecedent *n.* Probably before 1387, in a version of *Piers Plowman,* borrowed perhaps through Old French *antécédent,* or directly from Latin *antecēdentem* (nominative *antecēdēns*), present participle of *antecēdere* go before (*ante-* before + *cēdere* go; see CEDE); for suffix see -ENT. —**adj.** 1543, adjective use of *antecedent,* n. (influenced by French *antécédent*); or borrowed directly from French *antécédent,* from Latin *antecēdentem.*

antediluvian (an'tidəlü'vēən) *adj.* 1646, in Sir Thomas Browne's *Pseudodoxia Epidemica,* existing before the Deluge, formed in English from *ante-* before + Latin *dīluvium* DELUGE; for suffix see -IAN and -AN.

The extended meaning "very old or old-fashioned" appeared before 1726.

antelope *n.* About 1417, referring to a picture of a beast on a coat of arms, borrowed from Old French *antelop* mythical savage beast with long, sawlike horns living on the banks of the Euphrates, from Medieval Latin *antalopus,* from Late Greek *anthólops* (genitive *anthólopos*), of unknown origin.

The modern meaning of a deerlike animal appeared in English in 1607, and is probably the source of the term in modern French according to scholars such as Kluge, Bloch, and von Wartburg.

antenna *n.* 1646, in Sir Thomas Browne's *Pseudodoxia Epidemica,* meaning "sensory organ"; borrowed from Medieval Latin in the plural form *antennae,* used in a translation of Aristotle as an equivalent to Greek *keraîai* (meaning "horns" of an insect). The earlier Latin *antenna, antemna* sail yard, probably in reference to the long yard that sticks up on the lateen sail, is of uncertain origin.

The modern meaning of a radio, and later television, aerial appeared in 1902.

anterior *adj.* 1611, in Cotgrave's *Dictionary,* toward the front, fore, borrowed perhaps through French *antérieur,* or more likely directly from Latin *anterior,* used as a contrastive adjective as if from *anterus, from *ante* before.

The word was formed in Latin as an opposite to *posterior* after; see ANTE-.

anthem *n.* Old English (before 899, in Alfred's translation of Bede's *Ecclesiastical History*) *ontemn, antefn* antiphon (verses of a hymn, church service, etc. sung or chanted in alternate parts).

The word was borrowed from Late Latin *antefana,* an alteration of *antiphōna* antiphon. The change in spelling from *anti* to *ante* was influenced by Late Latin *ante* before, which was probably considered to fit the meaning better than *anti* against. See the doublet ANTIPHON.

The Middle English spellings *antefne, antimne, antempne, antimpne, antim, antem* shifted in the late 1500's to *anthem.* The change from *t* to *th* was probably introduced in an attempt to restore what was thought to be a more accurate reflection of the Greek ancestry of the word. Such attempts came about because of a Renaissance fondness for spellings that "looked Greek," as in *author, theater,* and *sympathy.* The spelling change gave rise to the modern pronunciation (an'thəm).

anther *n.* part of the stamen bearing the pollen. Indeterminately applied between 1706 and 1759, but generally fixed in meaning and form by 1791, in Erasmus Darwin's *Botanic Garden;* borrowed from French *anthère* and from New Latin *anthera,* from Latin *anthēra* medicine extracted from flowers. The Latin word was borrowed from Greek *anthērá,* feminine of *anthērós* flowery, from *ánthē* full bloom, from *ánthos* flower.

The Greek word is cognate with Sanskrit *ándhas* herb, Armenian *and* field, and Albanian *ënde* bloom, from Indo-European *ándhos (Pok.40).

anthology*n.* collection of writings. 1640, collection of the "flowers" of verse (i.e. small, choice poems) by various authors, borrowed, perhaps by influence of French *anthologie,* from Greek *anthologiā́* flower-gathering (*ánthos* flower + *légein* gather; see ANTHER and LEGEND); for suffix see -LOGY. —**anthologize** *v.* 1892, formed from English *anthology* + *-ize.*

anthracite *n.* 1601, in Holland's translation of Pliny's *Natural History,* meaning "a mineral resembling coals of fire"; 1812, in writings of Sir Humphry Davy, meaning "hard coal"; borrowed from Latin *anthracītēs* a kind of semiprecious gem known as bloodstone, from Greek *anthrakítēs,* from *ánthrax* (genitive *ánthrakos*) live coal, charcoal, ANTHRAX; for suffix see -ITE[1].

anthrax *n.* Before 1398, in Trevisa's translation of Bartholomew's *De Proprietatibus Rerum, antrax* carbuncle, malignant boil, developed through Medieval Latin and Anglo-French *antrax,* from Greek *ánthrax* carbuncle, live coal, charcoal; of unknown origin.

The modern spelling with *th* is a replacement in

English from the 1500's, made in an effort to restore a classical spelling.

As the name of the disease, the word first appeared in 1876, the year Robert Koch established its cause.

anthropo-, anthrop- a combining form meaning man, human being, as in *anthropology, anthropomorphic;* borrowed from Greek *anthrōpo-*, combining form of *ánthrōpos* man, human being.

Anthrop- is used before vowels, as in *anthropoid.*

anthropoid *adj.* manlike. Before 1837, probably from adjective use of the noun (1832); borrowed from Greek *anthrōpoeidés* (*ánthrōpos* man + *eîdos* shape); for suffix see -OID. The origin of Greek *ánthrōpos* is uncertain.

anthropology *n.* 1593, probably borrowed from New Latin *anthropologia,* or formed directly in English from Greek *anthrōpo-*, combining form of *ánthrōpos* man, human being + *-logy.*

anthropomorphic *adj.* attributing human qualities or form to gods, animals, and things. 1827, formed in English from earlier *anthropomorphism, anthropomorphous* (both 1753, in *Chambers Cyclopaedia*) + suffix *-ic. Anthropomorphous* is an Anglicization of Late Latin *anthrōpomorphus* having human form, or of Greek *anthrōpómorphos* (*ánthrōpos* human being + *morphḗ* form).

anti- a prefix meaning against, opposed to, or opposite of, as in *antiaircraft, antifreeze, antisocial.* Borrowed through Old French, or directly from Latin *anti-*, representing Greek *anti-*, from *antí* against, instead.

Anti- is cognate with Latin *ante,* in front of, Sanskrit *ánti* opposite, Gothic *and, anda-* against, along, Old High German *ant-* against, and Old English *and-* against, related to Old English *ende* END.

Related in function to Old English *and-*, first recorded in Middle English before 1150, the prefix was generally confined to words such as *anticrist (Antecrist), antipope (Antepope), antidot, antidotum.* The formation does not appear to have become popularized until well into the period of modern English. The OED reports, "Shakespeare has no *anti-* combinations," and it may not have been until after its use in English political sloganeering about 1650, and especially at the time of the Anti-corn-law in the 1830's, that *anti-* became a popular form in coinages.

antibiotic *adj.* 1894, borrowed from French *antibiotique* (*anti-* against + *biotique* of microbial life, from Late Latin *biōticus* of life; see BIOTIC); for suffix see -IC. **—n.** 1944, noun use of *antibiotic,* adj.

antibody *n.* substance in the body that weakens or destroys bacteria and neutralizes the toxins they produce. 1901, translation of German *Antikörper* (*anti-* opposing + *Körper* body, substance).

antic *n.* Often **antics,** *pl.* 1529, originally *antike, anticke,* and only later *antique,* borrowed from Italian *antico* antique, from Latin *antīquus* ANTIQUE.

Antic was originally used as an equivalent to Italian *grottesco* grotesque, from *grotta* grotto, in reference to fantastic representations of human, animal, and plant forms running into each other in murals unearthed in the ancient Baths of Titus in Rome. The term was later extended to anything similarly bizarre.

anticipation *n.* Before 1397, in a prologue to the Wycliffe Bible, borrowed from Latin *anticipātiōnem* (nominative *anticipātiō*), from *anticipāre* take care of ahead of time (*anti-*, variant of *ante-* before + *-cipāre,* form of *capere* to take); for suffix see -TION. **—anticipate** *v.* 1532, in writings of Sir Thomas More; possibly a back formation from *anticipation,* or borrowed from Latin *anticipātus,* past participle of *anticipāre* take care of ahead of time; for suffix see -ATE[1]. Alternatively *anticipate* may be a back formation in English from earlier *anticipation.*

antidote *n.* Probably before 1425, in a translation of Chauliac's *Grande Chirurgie;* borrowed through Old French *antidote,* from Latin *antidotum,* from Greek *antídoton* given as a remedy, verbal adjective of *antididónai* give in return (*anti-* against + *didónai* to give); see DOSE.

antigen (an'təjən) *n.* substance that stimulates production of antibodies. 1908, borrowed from German *Antigen,* formed from *Anti(körper)* antibody + *-gen* thing that produces.

antimony *n.* metallic chemical element. Probably about 1425, borrowed apparently through Old French *antimoine,* or directly perhaps from Medieval Latin *antimonium.*

Several explanations have been offered for the derivation of the Medieval Latin *antimonium,* but none is altogether satisfactory because there are missing links in the chain of forms and requisite meanings. The most widely offered explanation is that *antimonium* developed through a process of Latinization from some Arabic word such as *'othmud* (originally *'ithmid*). Perhaps the Arabic was borrowed from, or at least influenced by, Greek *stímmis* (variant of *stímmi* powdered antimony used to paint the eyelids), which can be traced back to Egyptian *stm.*

antipasto *n.* Italian hors d'oeuvre. 1625, borrowed from Italian *antipasto,* literally, before food (*anti-* before + *pasto* food, from Latin *ante* + *pāstus,* genitive *pāstūs,* from *pāscere* to feed; see FOOD).

Earlier English *antepast* (1590), meaning "an appetizer," was formed from the prefix *ante-* before + Latin *pāstus* food, but *antepast* and *antipasto* are doublets of Latin *pāstus* and developed independently of each other.

antipathy *n.* 1601 *antipathie* contrary feeling, in Holland's translation of Pliny's *Natural History;* borrowed (perhaps by influence of French *antipathie,* 1542), from Latin *antipathīa,* from Greek *antipátheia,* from *antipathḗs* opposed in feeling (*anti-* against + *páthos* feeling).

antiphon (an'təfon) *n.* verses of a hymn, church service, etc. sung or chanted in alternate parts. About 1500, borrowed perhaps from Middle French *antiphone, antifone* hymn, or, more likely, directly from Late Latin *antiphōna,* from Greek *antíphōna* musical accords, neuter plural of *antíphōnos* sounding in response (*anti-* in response to, opposed to + *phōnḗ* sound, song). Doublet of ANTHEM.

antipodes (antip'ədēz) *n.pl.* places on opposite sides of the earth. Before 1398, in Trevisa's translation of Bartholomew's *De Proprietatibus Rerum,* those who dwell on opposite sides of the earth; borrowed from Latin *antipodes,* from Greek *antípodes,* plural of *antípous* with feet opposite ours (*anti-* opposite + *poús,* genitive *podós,* foot; see FOOT).

The meaning "things that are opposite or contrary" did not begin to appear before the middle of the 1600's (1641), though it appeared in the obsolete form *antipos* in 1631.

antique *adj.* 1536, aged, venerable (but recorded in 1530 in Palsgrave's *Lesclarcissement* as a noun meaning "a relic of ancient art"); borrowed probably through Middle French *antique,* from Latin *antīquus* former, ancient, an earlier form of *antīcus,* from *ante* before; see ANTE-. Latin *antīquus,* with its variant *antīcus* lying in front, is a resultant of Indo-European **antīkwos* "looking forward" or "looking toward", compounded of *anti* + **ekw-*, the reduced grade of **okw-* see (the root of Latin *oculus* eye). It is paralleled by such Sanskrit compounds as *prátika-m* face, from *práti* toward. (Walde-Hofmann, *Lateinisches etymologisches Wörterbuch* I, 55, Pok.776). —**antiquarian** *n.* 1610; *adj.* 1771, either (1) formed in English from Latin *antīquārius* of antiquity + *-an;* or (2) developed in English from earlier *antiquary* (1563) + *-an.* If *antiquarian* developed from *antiquary,* then the root form *antiquary* was borrowed (perhaps through Middle French *antiquaire*) from Latin *antīquārius* of antiquity, from *antīquus,* the Latin being the common source of both *antiquary* and *antiquarian;* for suffix see -ARY. —**antiquity** *n.* Probably about 1280, borrowed through Anglo-French and Old French *antiquité,* from Latin *antīquitātem* (nominative *antīquitās*), from *antīquus;* for suffix see -ITY.

antithesis *n.* direct opposite, contrast of ideas. 1529, borrowed from Late Latin *antithesis,* from Greek *antíthesis,* from *antitithénai* to set against, oppose (*anti-* against + *tithénai* to set, place); see DO[1] perform.

antler *n.* Before 1398 *aunteler,* in Trevisa's translation of Bartholomew's *De Proprietatibus Rerum;* borrowed through Anglo-French *auntiler,* variant of Old French *auntoillier,* from Northern Gallo-Romance *cornū *antoculāre* horn in front of the eyes, neuter of **antoculāris* before the eyes (Latin *ante* before + Late Latin *oculāris* of the eyes, OCULAR).

A similar pattern of senses is found in German *Augensprosse* meaning "antler" with the literal sense of "eye sprout."

antonym *n.* 1870, perhaps borrowed from French *antonyme* (1866), or formed in English from *anti-* (variant of *anti-* opposite of) + *-onym,* as in *synonym.* If the term was formed independently in English, it was coined, as in French, as an opposite of *synonym, French synonyme,* probably suggested at least in part by Greek *antōnymíā* pronoun, in Late Greek meaning interchange of names.

anus *n.* Probably before 1425, in a translation of Chauliac's *Grande Chirurgie;* borrowed through Old French *anus,* from Latin *ānus* ring, circular form, anus.

The word is possibly cognate with Old Irish *ānne, āinne* ring or rump, and with Armenian *anur* necklace, ring, from Indo-European **āno-* (Pok.47).

anvil *n.* Middle English *anvelt, anfelt, anvild,* developed from Old English *anfilte* (about 1000, in Ælfric's *Grammar*) and earlier *onfilti,* before 800 (*an, on* on + *-filte* or *-filti* something beaten, related to Old English *felt* FELT).

The *f* and *t* in the Old English and early Middle English forms changed mostly to *v* and *d* by the late 1400's; the final *d* was dropped in the 1600's.

The word is cognate with Old High German *anafalz,* dialectal Middle Dutch *anevilt,* and with modern Low German: *afilts* (Aachen district), *amfilt* (Solingen district), and *anefilt,* all meaning "anvil." Compare also German *falzen* to groove, fold, welt, *Falzamboss* coppersmith's anvil, and *Filz* felt, from Proto-Germanic **(ana-)felt-, (ana)falt-,* from Indo-European **peld-/pold-* (Pok.801).

Contrary to some opinion, the Germanic scholar Kluge pointed out that there is no need to regard the parallel term German *Amboss* (Old High German *anabōz*) meaning literally "beaten on," as patterned on Latin *incūs* (genitive *incūdis*), also meaning literally "beaten on," since the activity of the smith is of ancient origin in the North, as evidenced by the number of cognates, and quite independent of Latin influence.

anxiety *n.* About 1525, in Sir Thomas More's works, probably borrowed from Latin *ānxietātem* (nominative *ānxietās*), from *ānxius* ANXIOUS; for suffix see -TY[2].

The word was known in French *(anxiété)* as a medical term from the 1100's, but it is unknown whether it was familiar to More or other English authors, who would have been familiar with the Latin.

anxious *adj.* 1623, probably borrowed from Latin *ānxius,* from *angere* choke, cause distress, see ANGER; for suffix see -OUS.

The French *anxieux* was known from 1375; whether it was known to writers in English in the early 1600's has not been determined. Therefore, Latin is a more probable source of the English term than French.

any *adj., pron.* Middle English *ani* or *eni,* developed from Old English (about 725, in *Beowulf*) *ǣnig* any, anyone, (*ān* one + *-ig* -y[1]; see ONE and for suffix see -Y[1]).

The word is cognate with Old Saxon *ēnig* any, Old Frisian *ēnig,* Old High German *einag* some, any (modern German *einige,* Dutch *enig*), Old Icelandic *einigr* no one, anyone, Latin *ūnicus* only, sole and Old Slavic *inokŭ* monk, from Proto-Germanic **ainazás, ainizás,* Indo-European **oinokós, oinikós* (Pok.286).

Any is an adjective derivative of *an, a,* the so-called weakened forms of *one.*

Combinations of *any* appeared early and frequently in English writing. In Old English *anything* appears by 1000 as *ǣnig thing* and is well established as one word by the Middle English period. Others include: *anybody,* as a compound about 1300; *anyone,* but only as a phrase, by 1380; *anyway* or *anyways,* for "anyhow" or "in any way," probably about 1200; *anywhere,* as one word before 1400. However, the common term *anyhow* is not recorded before 1740.

aorta *n.* 1578, perhaps borrowed by influence of earlier French *aorte* (1546), or more likely taken as New Latin *aorta,* from Greek *aortḗ* the aorta (the term applied by Aristotle to the great artery of the heart); earlier, the bronchial tubes (the term applied by Hippocrates).

According to the Classics scholars Frisk, Boisacq, and others, the original meaning of *aortḗ* was "that which is hung onto or attached," and the word was derived from a Greek verb *-aeírein* tie or couple (found only in the compound *syn-aeírein* tie or harness together), earlier **awerye-,* cognate with Lettish *veŕu* I rank, I embroider, and Albanian *vjer* hang up, from Indo-European **wer-* attach (Pok.1150).

ap-[1] a form of the prefix *ad-,* meaning to, toward, before *p,* as in *apportion.* Formed in Latin by assimilation of *d* to the following consonant *(p).*

ap-[2] a form of the prefix *apo-* before a vowel, as in the astronomical term *apastron* (*ap-* away + Greek *ástron* star), also before (and merged in pronunciation with) *h,* as in *aphelion, aphorism.*

apace *adv.* About 1385 *a paas* step by step, at a walking pace, in Chaucer's *Canterbury Tales;* borrowed from

Old French phrase *à pas,* literally, on step; see PACE. The current sense of rapidly, fast, promptly, appeared in Middle English before 1400.

apache (əpäsh′ *or* əpash′) *n.* rowdy or gangster, especially of Paris or Brussels. 1902, borrowed from French in which, according to the French scholar Quemada, it appeared, also in 1902, as a term created by journalists of *Le Matin* and *Le Journal* to refer to the criminal element of the outer boulevards of Paris. The French term was originally borrowed from English *Apache* (pronounced ə pach′ē), member of a North American Indian tribe. This meaning was used in American English by 1745 as a borrowing through American Spanish of Zuñi *ápachu* enemy (the Zuñi name for the Navajo Indians).

apart *adv.* Before 1325, in *Cursor Mundi,* borrowed from Old French *à part* to the side, from Latin *ad partem* to one side or part (*ad* to + *partem,* accusative of *pars* PART).

apartheid (äpär′tīd) *n.* racial segregation, especially in South Africa. 1947, borrowed from Afrikaans *apartheid* (literally) separateness, apartness (used in Afrikaans in the sense of "racial segregation" since about 1929), from Dutch *apart* separate, apart + *-heid* -hood.

apartment *n.* 1641, in John Evelyn's *Memoirs,* borrowed from French *appartement,* from Italian *appartamento,* literally, separate part, from *appartare* to separate (*a parte* to the side, from Latin *ad partem;* see APART); for suffix see -MENT.

apathy *n.* 1603, in Holland's translation of Plutarch's *Moralia,* borrowed from French *apathie* and Latin *apathīa,* from Greek *apátheia,* from *apathḗs* without feeling (*a-* without + *páthos* feeling; for suffix see -Y[3]). **—apathetic** *adj.* 1744, formed in English from *apathy* + *-ic,* on analogy with the already existing word *pathetic.*

ape *n.* Old English *apa* (about 700, in various Old English glossaries). Related to and probably cognate with Old Saxon *apo* ape, Frisian *apa,* Middle Dutch *āpe, aep* (modern Dutch *aap*), Old High German *affo* (modern German *Affe*), Old Icelandic *api,* Swedish *apa,* Danish *abe;* of uncertain origin.

It has been proposed that the word is a borrowed form, perhaps through contact in trading, and is in that way related to Irish *ap, apa;* Welsh *ab, epa;* Old Russian *opica;* all borrowed in very early times apparently with loss of an original *k* found in Sanskrit *kapí-s* ape.

—v. to imitate; mimic. 1632, in Massinger's *The City Madam,* verb use of the noun sense, "an imitator or mimic" (probably developed before 1200).

apéritif (əper′ətēf′) *n.* alcoholic drink to stimulate appetite (presumably by getting the digestive juices flowing). 1894, reborrowed from French but not Anglicized in spelling, from Medieval Latin *aperitivus,* from Latin *aperīre* to open; see APERTURE.

An earlier borrowing of *apéritif,* meaning "opening the intestines" (1582) and "a medicine that opens the bowels" (1671) was fully Anglicized as *aperitive,* but apparently remained a technical term so that the modern use is a separate borrowing of the same word about 300 years later. Latin, as early as the 200's A.D. had a form *apertīvus,* meaning "purgative".

aperture *n.* 1649, borrowed perhaps through Middle French *aperture,* or directly from Latin *apertūra,* from *apertus,* past participle of *aperīre* to open, uncover, earlier **ap-verīre,* cognate with Sanskrit *ápa-vṛṇoti* (he) opens, from Indo-European **apo* off, away (Pok.53); **wer-/wṛ-* to close, cover (Pok.1160); for suffix see -URE. Doublet of OVERTURE.

apex *n.* 1601, borrowed from Latin *apex* (genitive *apicis*) peak, tip, in reference to the small rod at the top of a Roman priest's cap, possibly from *apere* connect; see APT.

aphasia (əfā′zhə) *n.* total or partial loss of ability to use or understand words. 1867, New Latin, from Greek *aphasíā* (*a-* without + *phásis* utterance, from *phánai* to speak; see BAN[1] forbid).

The word *aphasie* was known in French by 1826, but the form of the word introduced into English was Latinate.

aphelion (əfē′lēən) *n.* point of an orbit farthest from the sun. 1676, borrowed as a form of *aphelium* patterned on Greek with the Greek ending *-on* from New Latin *aphelium.* The earlier New Latin *aphelium* (1656, from a translation of Hobbes' *Elements of Philosophy*) was coined by the German astronomer Johann Kepler writing in Latin about the findings of Ptolemaic astronomy, which were written in Greek, and therefore show the connection for the Greek origin of many terms in astronomy. Kepler coined his term on the basis of Greek *apò hēlíou* away from the sun (*apó* away from, off + *hēlíou,* genitive of *hḗlios* sun) and was prompted by the pattern of Greek *apógeion* APOGEE.

aphid *n.* plant louse. 1884, in Robert Browning's *Ferishtah's Fancies,* an alteration of New Latin *aphides,* plural of *aphis* (a term of uncertain origin coined or, at least first applied, by Linnaeus and attested in English since 1771).

aphorism *n.* 1528, borrowed from Middle French *aphorisme,* from Late Latin *aphorismus,* from Greek *aphorismós* definition, pithy sentence (*ap-* off, form of *apo-* before *h* + *hóros* boundary of uncertain origin); for suffix see -ISM.

aphrodisiac *n.* 1719, borrowed from Greek *aphrodisiakós* inducing sexual desire, sexual, from *aphrodísios* pertaining to *Aphrodítē* Aphrodite, the Greek goddess of love, a name of non-Indo-European origin. Compare VENEREAL.

apiary *n.* place where bees are kept. 1654, in John Evelyn's *Memoirs,* borrowed from Latin *apiārium,* neuter of *apiārius* of bees, from *apis* bee, of unknown origin; for suffix see -ARY.

apical *adj.* of, at, or forming the apex of something. 1828, formed in English from Latin *apic-* (stem of *apex*) + English *-al*[1].

apiculture *n.* beekeeping. 1864, formed in English from Latin *apis* bee + English *culture.*

An identical form *apiculture* was known in French as early as 1845, but the English *apiculture* was probably formed independently.

aplomb *n.* 1828, borrowed from French *aplomb,* from earlier *à plomb* according to the plummet (i.e., poised upright); see PLUMB.

apo- a prefix meaning: **1** from, off, away, as in *apogeotropic* = *turning away from the earth.* **2** free from, without, as in *apochromatic* = *free from chromatic aberration.* **3** formed from or related to, as in *apoenzyme* = *protein portion of an enzyme* or *enzyme system.* **4** apart, separate, detached, as in *aposepalous* = *having separate sepals.*

Apo- was borrowed from Greek *apo-,* from *apó* away, from, off; cognate with Latin *ab,* Sanskrit *ápa,* Gothic *af,* and English *of,* from Indo-European *ápo* (Pok.53). It was acquired in English through French or directly from Latin in borrowings, such as *apocalypse, apologia, apology, apoplexy, apostasy, apostle, apostrophe,* and *apotheosis.*

Its later use in English is particularly productive as an element in word formation of technical vocabulary, as evidenced above in the definitions.

apocalypse (əpok′əlips) *n.* revelation of future upheaval, etc. Middle English *apocalips* a vision or hallucination, about 1384, in the Wycliffe Bible, developed in English from earlier *Apokalypsis* (name of the last book of the New Testament, usually called *Revelation*), probably about 1200, in *The Ormulum.* The name of the biblical text in Middle English was borrowed through Anglo-French *apocalipse,* from Old French *apocalypse,* and from Late Latin *apocalypsis* revelation, from Greek *apokálypsis,* literally meaning "uncovering," from *apokalýptein* uncover (*apo-* off, un- + *kalýptein* to cover, veil; see CONCEAL and CELL). **—apocalyptic** *adj.* 1663, borrowed through French *apocalyptique,* from Greek *apokalyptikós,* from *apokalýptein* uncover; for suffix see -IC.

apocope (əpok′əpē) *n.* dropping of the end of a word, usually a final vowel. 1591, borrowed possibly through Middle French *apocope,* or directly from Late Latin *apocopē,* from Greek *apokopḗ,* from *apokóptein* to cut off (*apo-* off + *kóptein* to cut; see CAPON).

apocrypha *n.pl.* writings of doubtful authorship. Before 1387, in Trevisa's translation of Higden's *Polychronicon,* and by 1539 *Apocrypha,* books excluded from the Bible because they were not considered genuine in the Old Testament. Borrowed from Medieval Latin, from Late Latin *apocrypha,* neuter plural of *apocryphus* secret, not approved for public reading in the church, from Greek *apókryphos* hidden, as of hidden or unknown authorship (*apo-* away + *krýptein* to hide; see CRYPT).

Apocrypha replaced the earlier form *apocrif* about 1445, which had been borrowed from Old French *apocrife.* **—apocryphal** *adj.* of doubtful authenticity. 1590, formed in English from *apocrypha* + *-al*[1].

apogee *n.* 1594, point in the orbit of a planet, comet, etc., at its greatest distance from the earth or from any other heavenly body about which it orbits, in John Davy's *The Seamens Secrets,* later meaning figuratively "furthermost point; highest point" (1600, in a translation from Italian). Probably borrowed from French *apogée,* from Greek *apógeion sēmeîon* point far from the earth, neuter of *apógeios* far from the earth, from *apò gês* (*apó* off, away + *gês,* genitive of *gê* earth, of unknown origin).

Until the Space Age this term was usually applied to the orbit of the moon about the earth. Now it is also applied to space flight and rocket trajectories.

apologia (ap′əlō′jēə) *n.* defense, justification. 1784, borrowed from Late Latin *apologia* APOLOGY.

The currency of the term is attributed to onetime general familiarity with the title of Cardinal Newman's *Apologia pro Vita Sua* (1864, in which he recounts his spiritual development). The book was prominent because its author wrote it, first in serial form, as an answer to a personal attack on him in the 19th century religious controversy involved in the Oxford Movement. Later the book gained recognition as a literary masterpiece.

apology *n.* words of regret. 1533, defense, justification, in the title of Sir Thomas More's *Apologie of Syr Thomas More, Knyght;* borrowed from Late Latin *apologia,* from Greek *apologíā* a speech in defense, from *apologeîsthai* defend oneself, give an account of oneself, from *apólogos* an account, story, from *apolégein* to tell fully (*apo-* away, from, off + *légein* to tell, speak; see LEGEND).

Whether the term came into English by way of French or was modeled after the French is questionable, but *apologie* has been recorded in French since 1488. **—apologetic** *adj.* 1649, defensive; borrowed through French *apologétique,* from Late Latin *apologēticus,* from Greek *apologētikós,* from *apologeîsthai* defend oneself. **—apologize** *v.* 1597, formed from English *apology* + *-ize.*

apoplexy (ap′əplek′sē) *n.* stroke. About 1390, in Chaucer's *Canterbury Tales,* borrowed through Old French *apoplexie,* or directly from Late Latin *apoplēxia,* from Greek *apoplēxíā,* from *apoplḗssein* disable by a stroke (*apo-* off, from + *plḗssein* to strike, earlier **plākye-,* cognate with Lithuanian *plõkis* a blow, a stroke, from Indo-European **plāk-* (Pok.832).

apostasy *n.* forsaking of one's religion, etc. Perhaps about 1348, in Richard Rolle's *Form of Living,* borrowed from Late Latin *apostasia,* from Greek *apostasíā* defection, desertion of one's faith, from *apostênai* to defect, stand off (*apo-* away from + *stênai* STAND); for suffix see -Y[3].

The word may have been borrowed also from French *apostasie,* which is recorded from about 1250 and which also existed in Anglo-French *apostasye.* **—apostate** *n.* 1340, in *Ayenbite of Inwyt,* borrowed through Old French *apostate,* or directly from Late Latin *apostata,* from Greek *apostátēs* defector, deserter, rebel, from *apostênai* to defect.

apostle *n.* The term as we know it today comes from two sources in Middle English. *Apostle* is a fusion of: 1) Old English *apostol* one of the disciples of Christ (before 899, in Alfred's translation of Bede's *Ecclesiastical History,* etc.); borrowed from Late Latin *apostolus;* and 2) Middle English *apostle* disciple of Christ (probably before 1200, in *Ancrene Riwle*); borrowed through Anglo-French *apostle,* from Old French *apostle,* learned borrowing from Late Latin *apostolus,* from Greek *apóstolos* messenger, from *apostéllein* send away (*apo-* away + *stéllein* to send; see STALL[1] place).

apostrophe[1] *n.* the sign ('), indicating omission of a letter or a sound in a word, or showing possessive forms (as *lion's den, John's book*), or forming certain plurals (as in *2 o's*). 1530, in Palsgrave's *Lesclarcissement,* borrowed from Middle French *apostrophe,* learned borrowing from Late Latin *apostrophus,* from Greek *apóstrophos prosōidíā* omission mark, related to *apostréphein* avert, turn away (*apo-* away + *stréphein* to turn; see STROPHE).

In the case of possessives, the apostrophe was originally used to show dropping of the *-e* in *-es,* which was the possessive ending in English.

apostrophe[2] *n.* rhetorical address to one not present or to an idea or thing as if it could hear or reply. 1533, in Sir Thomas More's *Apologie of Syr Thomas More, Knyght;* borrowed from Late Latin *apostrophē,* from Greek *apostrophḗ,* literally, a turning away, related to *apostréphein* turn away; see APOSTROPHE[1]. **—apostrophize** *v.* 1725, in Pope's translation of Homer's *Odyssey,* formed from English *apostrophe* + *-ize.*

apothecary *n.* druggist, pharmacist. About 1387-95, in the general prologue to Chaucer's *Canterbury Tales;* borrowed probably through Old French *apothicaire, apotecaire,* or directly from Late Latin *apothēcārius* shopkeeper, from Latin *apothēca* storehouse, from Greek *apothḗkē,* related to *apotithénai* put away (*apo-* away + *tithénai* to put; see DO[1] act); for suffix see -ARY.

apothegm (ap′əthem) *n.* short saying, maxim. 1542 *apophthegm,* in Nicholas Udall's translation of Erasmus' *Apothegms;* borrowed perhaps from Medieval Latin **apothegma,* from Greek *apóphthegma* (*apo-* from + *phthéngesthai* to utter, related to *phthóngos* sound, voice, of unknown origin; compare DIPHTHONG).

apotheosis (əpoth′ēō′sis) *n.* a glorified ideal. 1573-80, a raising to the status of a god, in Gabriel Harvey's *Letter Book,* borrowed from Late Latin *apotheōsis,* from Greek *apothéōsis,* from *apotheoûn* deify (*apo-* special use of prefix indicating change + *theós* god); see THEOLOGY.

appall *v.* Before 1333 *appallen, apallen* to fade, become feeble, borrowed from Old French *apallir* become or make pale (*a-* to, from Latin *ad-* + *pale,* from Latin *pallidus* PALE[1] wan).

The meaning "to dismay, shock, discomfit" appeared in 1532, in writings of Sir Thomas More.

appanage (ap′ənij) *n.* accompaniment, adjunct. 1602, provision made for the support of the younger children of royalty; borrowed from French and Old French *apanage,* from *apaner* provide for a younger child, literally, provide with bread, (*a-* to + *pain* bread, from Latin *pānis* bread; see FOOD); for suffix see -AGE.

apparat (äpärät′) *n.* political party machine, especially Communist. 1950, in Arthur Koestler's *The God that Failed,* borrowed from Russian *apparat,* from German *Apparat* apparatus, from Latin *apparātus* APPARATUS. **—apparatchik** (äpärät′chik) *n.* 1941, in Koestler's *Scum of the Earth,* borrowed from Russian *apparatchik* (*apparat* + *-chik* agent suffix).

apparatus *n.* Before 1628, in Fulke Greville's *Life of Sidney,* borrowed from Latin *apparātus* (genitive *apparātūs*) equipment, preparation, from *apparāre* prepare (*ap-* to, variant of *ad-* before *p* + *parāre* make ready); see PARE.

apparel *n.* Probably before 1300 *appareil, apareil,* borrowed through Anglo-French *apareil, apparraille,* from Old French *apareil,* from *apareiller* to clothe, prepare, fit out.

Beyond this point two possible courses have been suggested: 1) That Old French *apareiller* is derived from a supposed Vulgar Latin form **appariculāre,* built on a noun **appariculum* preparation, formed from Latin *apparāre* prepare, make ready; 2) That Old French *apareiller* is derived from an earlier hypothetical Vulgar Latin form **adpariculāre* make equal, fit (*ad-* to + **pariculus,* a diminutive of Latin *pār* equal).

apparent *adj.* Before 1393, in Gower's *Confessio Amantis,* borrowed from Old French *aparant,* also later *apparent,* learned borrowing from Latin *appārentem* (nominative *appārēns),* present participle of *appārēre* APPEAR; for suffix see -ENT.

apparition *n.* Probably before 1425, Middle English *aparicion* appearance, especially of something strange, in a translation of Higden's *Polychronicon;* borrowed through Anglo-French *aparicion,* perhaps from Old French *apparition* (though this does not fit the chain of meaning, because the word in Old French referred to Epiphany and the act of making oneself visible).

The word in Old French comes from Late Latin *appāritiōnem* (nominative *appāritiō*), meaning "an appearance," and "attendants." In Classical Latin the meaning was restricted to "service, servants, attendants," from *appāri-,* stem of Latin *appārēre* APPEAR, serve; for suffix see -TION.

In English, according to the OED, the sense of a specter, phantom, or ghost first appears in 1601, in Shakespeare's *Julius Caesar,* but earlier (about 1525) Sir Thomas More used the word in "The aparicion of a very ghost."

appeal *v.* Before 1338 *apelen, appelen* to call to a higher court, in Mannyng's *Chronicle of England;* borrowed through Anglo-French and Old French *apeler* to call upon, accuse, from Latin *appellāre* accost, address, call upon, appeal to (originally, to drive to court for payment of debt). The Latin is related to another form *appellere* drive to, direct toward (*ap-* up to, variant of *ad-* before *p* + *pellere* to drive; see PULSE[1] beat). **—n.** About 1300, Middle English *apel, appel* an appealing to a higher court; borrowed from Old French *apel,* from *apeler,* v.

The change of spelling from *-el* to *-eal* was a product of spelling reform that took place in the 1500's.

appear *v.* About 1275, Middle English *aperen, apperen,* borrowed from Old French *aper-,* a stem of *apareir, aparoir,* from Latin *appārēre* (*ap-* to, variant form of *ad-* before *p* + *pārēre* come in sight, come forth). **—appearance** *n.* About 1380, Middle English *apparence,* in Chaucer's *House of Fame;* borrowed through Anglo-French *apparaunce* and Old French *aparence,* from Late Latin *appārentia,* from Latin *appārentem* (nominative *appārēns*), present participle of *appārēre* APPEAR; for suffix see -ANCE.

The change in spelling from *-er* to *-ear* was a product of spelling reform in the 1500's. In the case of *appearance* the change in spelling was further influenced by the verb.

appease *v.* About 1300 *apesen, appesen,* borrowed through Anglo-French *apeser, apeiser,* from Old French *apeiser, apaisier* bring to peace, pacify (*a-* to, from Latin *ad-*) + (*pais* peace; see PEACE). **—appeasement** *n.* 1439, in *Proceedings of the Privy Council,* borrowed from Middle French *apeisement, apaisement,* from Old French *apaisement,* from *apeiser, apaisier* pacify; for suffix see -MENT.

Like other words from Middle English spelled with *e* in the stem, *apesen* became *appease* in the process of spelling reform during the 1500's.

appellate (əpel′it) *adj.* of or for appeals. 1726, appealed against, borrowed from Latin *appellātus,* past participle of *appellāre* APPEAL; for suffix see -ATE[1].

append *v.* 1646, borrowed from Latin *appendere* (*ap-* on, variant of *ad-* before *p* + *pendere* to cause to hang, weigh; see PENDANT). **—appendage** *n.* 1649, formed from English *append* + *-age.*

appendix *n.* subsidiary addition. 1542 *appendex,* meaning "something added of an immaterial nature, such as a consequence"; borrowed from Latin *appendix* (genitive *appendicis*) something attached, from *appendere* attach; see APPEND.

The meaning "section added to a book" appeared in 1549. The meaning "organ, especially the intestinal appendix," appeared in 1615 and was perhaps borrowed from, or at least influenced by the French, in which the term was known by 1541.

—appendectomy *n.* surgical removal of the intestinal appendix. 1894-95, formed in American English from *appendix* + *-ectomy.* **—appendicitis** *n.* inflammation of the intestinal appendix. 1886, formed in American English from New Latin *appendic-*, stem of *appendix* + *-itis.*

apperception (ap′ərsep′shən) *n.* clear perception. 1753, in *Chambers Cyclopaedia, adperception,* later *apperception;* borrowed as a learned reconstruction of French *aperception,* applied as a term for New Latin *apperceptionem* (nominative *apperceptio*), a term used by Leibnitz to describe a phenomenon of his philosophy, in which the mind is supposed to be conscious of its own perception.

The French *aperception* is from *apercevoir* perceive clearly (*a-* to, from Latin *ad-*) + (*percevoir* perceive, from Latin *percipere* PERCEIVE); for suffix see -TION.

The double *p,* and the curious *adperception* from Chambers, reflect the influence of the spelling change introduced in the 1400's to imitate Latin *ap-, ad-* as a replacement for the French *a-,* because of a mistaken notion of refining or purifying English.

appertain *v.* pertain. About 1380, in Chaucer's translation of Boethius' *De Consolatione Philosophiae;* borrowed through Anglo-French *apartenir, appurtenir,* from Old French *apertenir, apartenir.* The Old French came through Vulgar Latin **appartenēre* which is an alteration (influenced by Latin *pars,* genitive *partis* part) of Late Latin *appertinēre* belong to, pertain to (Latin *ap-* to, variant of *ad-* before *p* + *pertinēre* belong to, PERTAIN). Related to APPURTENANCE.

The doubling of *p* came about in the spelling changes of the 1400's; see note at *apperception.*

appetite *n.* About 1303, in Mannyng's *Handlyng Synne,* borrowed through Anglo-French *apetit, appetit,* from Old French *apetit,* learned borrowing from Latin *appetītus* desire, appetite, from *appetere* to long for (*ap-* to, variant of *ad-* before *p* + *petere* seek, ask, go toward).

For the doubling of *p* see note at *apperception.*

applaud *v.* About 1475, borrowed from Latin *applaudere* approve by clapping hands (*ap-* upon, variant of *ad-* before *p* + *plaudere* clap, applaud, approve). **—applause** *n.* About 1425, borrowed from Latin *applausus* (genitive *applausūs*), from *applaudere* applaud.

apple *n.* Old English *æppel* (before 899, in Alfred's translation of St. Gregory's *Pastoral Care*). The word is cognate with many older words for *apple* in other northern European languages: Old Frisian *appel,* Old High German *apful* (modern German *Apfel*), Old Icelandic *epli,* Old Swedish *æpl,* Crimean Gothic *apel,* from Proto-Germanic **aplu-*.

It is also represented in other languages, though sometimes considered a foreign or borrowed term, such as in Celtic: Old Irish *ubull,* Old Welsh *abel,* Cornish and Breton *aval;* in Slavic: Old Slavic *ablŭko,* Polish *jabłko,* Russian *yabloko;* and in Baltic: Old Prussian *woble,* and Lithuanian *óbuolas,* Latvian *ābols;* all from Indo-European **abel-/ābōl-/ābol-* (Pok.1).

A connection with Latin has been offered through a place name found in Vergil's *Aeneid* (VII, 740): *māliferae . . . moenia Abellae* the walls of apple-bearing Abella (a town in Campania, which is a fertile agricultural region of Italy at times occupied by Goths, Byzantines, and Normans). The Latin and Greek words for apple were, respectively, *mālum* and *mêlon,* related words of unknown origin.

Culturally there is a mythology involving apples and dragons that is recorded from Central Asia to Celtic lands and invites some comparison between the Latin *mālum* and *Alma Ata* (Father of Apples), capital of Kazakhstan, and also Turkish *elma* apple. It is, therefore, too narrow to confine the apple to Germanic culture as has been done occasionally.

appliance *n.* 1561, formed in English from *apply* + *-ance.*

In 1561 the meaning was confined to "application"; by 1597 the meaning was extended to an apparatus or device.

applicant *n.* About 1485, borrowed from Latin *applicantem* (nominative *applicāns*), present participle of *applicāre* APPLY; for suffix see -ANT.

application *n.* Before 1398, in Trevisa's translation of Bartholomew's *De Proprietatibus Rerum,* borrowed from Old French *application,* from Latin *applicātiōnem* (nominative *applicātiō*) a joining to, from *applicāre* APPLY; for suffix see -TION.

appliqué (ap′ləkā′) *n.* ornament made of one material sewed or otherwise fastened on another. 1801, borrowing of French *appliqué* (not Anglicized even though the term is inflected in English as *appliquéd, appliquéing*), from past participle of *appliquer* apply, from Old French *apliquier,* learned borrowing from Latin *applicāre* APPLY.

apply *v.* About 1380 *aplien, applien* join to (in Chaucer's translation of Boethius' *De Consolatione Philosophiae*); borrowed from Old French *aplier,* from Latin *applicāre* (*ap-* on, variant of *ad-* before *p* + *plicāre* to fold, lay; see PLY[2] fold).

For the doubling of *p* see the note under *apperception.*

appoint *v.* About 1385 *apointen, appointen* come to a point about a matter, agree (in Chaucer's *Troilus and Criseyde*); borrowed through Anglo-French *appointer,* from Old French *apointer* (*a-* to, from Latin *ad-*) + (*point,* from Latin *pūnctum* POINT). **—appointment** *n.* 1417 *apointment,* in *Proceeding of the Privy Council,* borrowed from Middle and Old French *apointment,* from Old French *apointer* appoint; for suffix see -MENT.

For the doubling of *p* see the note under *apperception.*

apportion *v.* 1574, borrowed through Middle French, from Old French *apportionner* (*a-* to, from Latin *ad-*) + (*portionner* to portion, from *portion* PORTION). **—apportionment** *n.* 1628, in Sir Edward Coke's *Institutes: a commentarie upon Littleton,* probably formed in English from *apportion* + *-ment;* but influenced by French *apportionnement.*

appose *v.* place side by side. 1593, to put or apply one thing to another; borrowed from Middle French *apposer* (*a-* to, from Latin *ad-*) + (*poser* to put; see POSE[1] position).

apposite *adj.* appropriate. 1621, in Burton's *Anatomy of*

Melancholy, borrowed from Latin *appositus,* past participle of *appōnere* apply to, put near (*ap-* near, variant of *ad-* before *p* + *pōnere* to place; see POSITION). —**apposition** *n.* 1440, referring to "grammatical parallelism," in *Gesta Romanorum;* borrowed from Latin *appositiōnem* (nominative *appositiō*), from *appōnere;* for suffix see -TION.

appraise *v.* to estimate the value of, set a price on. Before 1420 *apreisen, apraisen,* in Lydgate's *Troy Book;* probably borrowed from Middle French **apreis-*, stem of *apriser, aprisier,* from Late Latin *appretiāre* value, estimate, appraise (Latin *ap-* to, variant of *ad-* before *p* + *pretium* price).

It has been offered that there was influence of *praise* v. to praise, value, prize, in English formation of *appraise;* the extent of this is unknown. English *apprize,* also meaning "appraise," did not serve as a pattern, because *apprize* (Middle English *apprisen* appraise) and *appraise* are simultaneous borrowings. —**appraisal** *n.* 1817, in Coleridge's *Biographia Literaria,* formed from English *appraise* + *-al*[2].

appreciate *v.* to value, enjoy. 1655, borrowed from Late Latin *appretiāre* value, estimate, appraise (Latin *ap-* to, variant of *ad-* before *p* + *pretium* price); for suffix see -ATE[1]. —**appreciation** *n.* Probably about 1400, in Wycliffe's works, borrowed through Anglo-French *appréciation,* or directly from Late Latin *appretiātiōnem* (nominative *appretiātiō*), from *appretiāre* appraise; for suffix see -TION.

apprehend *v.* Before 1398, grasp mentally, comprehend, in Trevisa's translation of Bartholomew's *De Proprietatibus Rerum;* borrowed perhaps through Old French *appréhender,* or directly from Latin *apprehendere* take hold of, grasp (*ap-* upon, variant of *ad-* before *p* + *prehendere* seize; see PREHENSILE). —**apprehension** *n.* Before 1398, in Trevisa's translation of Bartholomew's *De Proprietatibus Rerum;* borrowed perhaps through Old French *appréhension,* or directly from Latin *apprehēnsiōnem* (nominative *apprehēnsiō*), from *apprehendere;* for suffix see -SION.

The meaning "fear of what may happen, dread" appeared in 1648.

apprentice *n.* 1307, borrowed through Anglo-French *aprentiz,* from Old French *aprentiz, aprentis,* from Gallo-Romance **apprēnditīcius* learner of a trade, from Latin *apprēndere* grasp mentally, learn, a contraction of *apprehendere* APPREHEND.

For the doubling of the *p,* see note under *apperception.*

—**v.** 1631, from the noun.

apprise *v.* inform. 1694, borrowed from French *appris,* past participle of *apprendre* learn, inform, from Latin *apprēndere,* contraction of *apprehendere* APPREHEND.

approach *v.* About 1300, borrowed through Anglo-French *approcher* from Old French *aprochier,* from Late Latin *appropiāre* come near to (Latin *ap-* to, variant of *ad-* before *p*) + (Late Latin *propiāre* come nearer, from Latin *propius* nearer, comparative of *prope* near; see APPROXIMATE). —**n.** Before 1460, noun use of *approach,* v.

approbation *n.* Before 1393, in Gower's *Confessio Amantis,* borrowed through Old French *aprobacion,* or directly from Latin *approbātiōnem* (nominative *approbātiō*) from *approbāre* APPROVE; for suffix see -TION.

For the doubling of *p,* see note under *apperception.*

appropriate *adj.* suitable. Probably before 1425, belonging to as an attribute, quality, etc., borrowed from Late Latin *appropriātus,* past participle of *appropriāre* (Latin *ap-* to, variant of *ad-* before *p* + *propriāre* take as one's own, from *proprius* one's own; see PROPER.); for suffix see -ATE[1]. —**v.** set apart (as one's own). Probably before 1425, to attribute as belonging to, (in a translation of Higden's *Polychronicon*), borrowed from Late Latin *appropriātus,* past participle of *appropriāre;* for suffix see -ATE[1].

By the 1600's a Latinate form *appropriate,* v. had established itself in English and superseded the older *appropre* from Old French *aproprier,* both the new and the older term in English being derived from Latin *appropriāre.*

approve *v.* About 1380, to confirm, commend (in Chaucer's translation of Boethius' *De Consolatione Philosophiae*); earlier, about 1300, to show to be true, prove; borrowed from Old French *aprover,* from Latin *approbāre* (*ap-* to, variant of *ad-* before *p* + *probāre* PROVE).

In Middle English the spelling *apreven* was common. It developed from a stem form of the Old French verb, but later died out.

For the doubling of *p,* see note under *apperception.* —**approval** *n.* 1690, formed from English *approve* + *-al*[2].

The OED indicates that this term was rare before 1800, but that it generally replaced the older term *approvance.*

approximate *adj.* Probably before 1425, borrowed from Latin *approximātus,* past participle of *approximāre* (*ap-* to, variant of *ad-* before *p* + *proximāre* come near, from *proximus* nearest, superlative of *prope* near, probably assimilated from **pro-que,* although the sense-development from *-que* and, and *pro-* forward is not at all clear); for suffix see -ATE[1]. —**v.** Before 1425, borrowed from Latin *approximātus,*past *approximāre;* for suffix see -ATE[1]. —**approximation** *n.* Probably before 1425, borrowed from Middle French *approximation,* from Latin *approximātiōnem* (nominative *approximātiō*), from *approximāre;* for suffix see -TION.

appurtenance *n.* added thing, accessory. Probably before 1300, a minor right or privilege that is part of a more important one, such as a lordship or manor (in *Kyng Alisaunder*); borrowed through Anglo-French *apurtenance,* variant of Old French *apartenance,* from *apertenir* APPERTAIN; for suffix see -ANCE.

For the doubling of *p,* see note under *apperception.*

apricot *n.* 1551 *abrecock,* borrowed probably from Catalan *abercoc* (related to Spanish *albaricoque* and Portuguese *albricoque*), from Arabic *al-barqūq* (*al-* the + *barqūq* apricot).

The Arabic *barqūq* is believed to have come ultimately from Latin through Greek. But instead of coming into English from Latin by way of the traditional borrowings through the Romance languages in Europe, the word traveled across the Mediterranean from Latin *praecoquis,* variant of *praecox* early-ripe, through the variant *praecoquum* to its Greek form *praikókion.* The Greek had a variant plural *berikókkia,* and either by trade or by Ptolemaic influence in Arabic culture, it came into Arabic as *barqūq.* Subsequently the Arabic word was carried into southwestern Europe in the time of the Moslem domination of Spain.

The Latin *praecoquis* early-ripe, can probably be attributed to the fact that the fruit was considered a variety of peach that ripened sooner than other peaches; the Latin word was formed from *prae* before, pre- + *coquere* to ripen, COOK.

The change in spelling from *abrecock* to *apricot* (1580 and through the 1600's) was probably influenced by French *abricot* apricot, itself from Catalan *abercoc,* and there is further influence traditionally offered from Latin *aprīcus* sunny, though the connection is not established.

April *n.* About 1375, Middle English *April, Aperill,* etc., in Chaucer's *Anelida and Arcite;* reborrowed, possibly through Anglo-French *Aprille,* from Latin *Aprīlis* the second month in the ancient Roman calendar, dedicated to the goddess Venus (Aphrodite). Connections beyond this point are conjectural.

The various forms cited above in the works of Chaucer and others, borrowed again from Latin, replaced an earlier form in English, *Averil* (probably before 1200), borrowed from Old French *avrill,* from Gallo-Romance **Aprīlius,* an alteration of Latin *Aprīlis.*

a priori (ā prīôr′ī) from a general rule to particular cases. 1618, borrowed from Medieval Latin *a priori* from (something) previous (Latin *ā* from + *priōrī,* ablative of *prior;* see PRIOR).

apron *n.* Middle English *napron,* originally spelled *naperon* (1307), borrowed from Old French *naperon,* diminutive of *nape, nappe* cloth, tablecloth, from Latin *mappa* napkin, MAP. Later in Middle English, between about 1450 and 1485, the initial *n* was lost, through the mistaken division of *a napron* as *an apron.* Compare ADDER, NICKNAME, and UMPIRE for similar misdivisions.

The shift from *m* in Latin *mappa* to *n* in French *nappe* and then *naperon* is seen in several Old French words and is a matter of continuous change in Medieval Latin.

apropos (ap′rəpō′) *adv.* 1668, in Dryden's *Essay on Dramatic Poesy,* borrowed from French *à propos* to the purpose (Old French *a* to + *propos* purpose, plan, the verbal noun of *proposer* offer, set before, PROPOSE).

apse *n.* arched recess in a church. 1846, borrowed from Medieval Latin *apsis,* from Latin *apsis* arch, vault, from Greek *apsís,* dialectal variation of *hapsís* loop, arch, from *háptein* fasten, of uncertain origin.

apt *adj.* Probably about 1350, borrowed perhaps through Old French *apte,* or directly from Latin *aptus* joined, fitted, originally past participle of *apere* connect, and later used as the past participle of *apīscor, apiscī* to reach, attain, a form that is probably cognate with Sanskrit *āptá-s* skilled, fit, and Hittite *ēpmi* I take, from Indo-European **ēp-/əp-* (Pok.50).

apteryx (ap′təriks) *n.* New Zealand bird; kiwi. 1813, New Latin *apteryx* (Greek *a-* without + *ptéryx* wing; related to *pterón* wing, FEATHER).

aptitude *n.* Probably before 1425, in a translation of Chauliac's *Grande Chirurgie,* borrowed through Middle French *aptitude,* or directly from Late Latin *aptitūdō* (genitive *aptitūdinis*) fitness, from Latin *aptus* joined, fitted, see APT; for suffix see -TUDE. Doublet of ATTITUDE.

aquacade *n.* 1937, American English, used as a generic term after *Aquacade,* a water spectacle presented by the American showman Billy Rose in 1937 in Cleveland, Ohio. The term was coined from Latin *aqua* water + English *-cade,* a form abstracted from words such as *cavalcade,* and apparently first used as a combining form in *motorcade.*

aqua fortis (ak′wə fôr′tis) nitric acid. Before 1500, New Latin *aqua fortis* (literally) strong water.

aqualung *n.* 1950, formed in English from Latin *aqua* water + English *lung.* The original device was developed by Jacques Cousteau and Emile Gagnan in 1943, but the elements of this term were long in the air. As early as 1881 W.D. Hay's *300 Years Hence* was writing about 'the aquanaut's lungs'.

aquamarine *n.* bluish-green semiprecious stone. 1727, in *Chambers Cyclopaedia,* perhaps influenced by earlier French *aigue-marine,* borrowed through Provençal from Latin *aqua marīna* sea water (for its color).

aquanaut (ak′wənôt) *n.* underwater explorer. 1960, formed in English from Latin *aqua* water + English *-naut,* a form abstracted from earlier *aeronaut, Argonaut.*

An early, futuristic use of this word, in W.D. Hay's *300 Years Hence* (1881), is recorded in the OED.

aquaplane (ak′wəplān) *n.* board on which a rider is towed by a speedboat. 1914, formed in American English, from Latin *aqua* water + English *plane*[1] level surface. —*v.* ride on such a board. 1941, verb use of *aquaplane,* n. A new sense of the verb, meaning "to skid out of control in an automobile on a wet road," appeared in 1961. Compare HYDROPLANE, v.

aquarium *n.* 1854, borrowed from Latin *aquārium* watering place for cattle, neuter of *aquārius* of water, from *aqua* water; see AQUATIC.

The term may have been stimulated by earlier attempts to combine *vivarium* with Latin words suggesting "water," such as *aquatic vivarium* and *marine vivarium.*

aquatic *adj.* 1490, in Caxton's translation of *The Book of Eneydos;* borrowed from Middle French and Old French *aquatique,* learned borrowing from Latin *aquāticus* watery, inhabiting water, from *aqua* water.

Latin *aqua* is cognate within a wide range of ancient Germanic languages: Gothic *ahwa* river, Old High German *aha,* Old Icelandic *ā,* Old Frisian *ā,* and Old English *ēa* river, flowing water, from Proto-Germanic **áʜwō,* Indo-European **əkwā́,* root *ēkw-* (found in Hittite *e-ku-uz-zi* drinks) (Pok.23).

aqua vitae (ak′wə vī′tē) alcoholic liquor. Probably before 1425, in a translation of Chauliac's *Grande Chirurgie,* borrowed from Medieval Latin *aqua vitae* (literally) water of life. Compare the etymology of WHISKEY.

aqueduct *n.* 1538, in Leland's *The Itinerary,* borrowed from Latin *aquaeductus* (*aquae,* genitive of *aqua* water + *ductus,* genitive *ductūs,* from stem *duc-* of *dūcere* to lead, convey).

aqueous *adj.* watery. 1643, in reference to the aqueous humor inside the eye; borrowed from Medieval Latin *aqueus,* from Latin *aqua* water; for suffix see -OUS. The Medieval Latin term *aqueus* was probably formed by analogy of Latin *terreus* earthy, from *terra* earth.

aquiline *adj.* curved, hooked. 1646, curved like an eagle's beak; borrowed from Latin *aquilīnus* of or like an eagle, from *aquila* EAGLE; for suffix see -INE[1].

ar- a form of the prefix *ad-,* meaning to, toward, before *r* in words of Latin or French origin, as in *arrogant.* Formed in Latin by assimilation of *d* to the following consonant *(r)*. In words formed in Old French with the prefix *a-* (from Latin *ad-*) and borrowed in that form, the spelling before *r* was changed to *ar-* (as in *arrange, array, arrive*) in or about the 1600's on the model of the Latin.

-ar a suffix forming adjectives from nouns and meaning: **1** of or having to do with, as in *molecular = having to do with molecules*. **2** like, as in *oracular = like an oracle*. **3** of the nature of, as in *spectacular = of the nature of a spectacle*.

The suffix was borrowed from Latin *-āris,* altered by dissimilation from original *-ālis* -AL[1] in words that contain an *l,* as seen from the Latin originals of words such as *angular, familiar, jocular, peculiar, popular, stellar,* and *polar*. The adjectives formed in English, especially from Latin nouns, follow the same pattern, such as *curricular, granular*.

Arab *n.* Before 1398, a native of Arabia (in Trevisa's translation of Bartholomew's *De Proprietatibus Rerum*); borrowed from Old French *Arabe,* a learned borrowing from Latin *Arabs,* from Greek *Áraps* (genitive *Árabos*), from Arabic *ʿarab,* the indigenous name of the people. **—Arabian** *n., adj.* Probably before 1300, in *Kyng Alisaunder,* borrowed from Old French *Arabien* and Latin *Arabius;* for suffix see -IAN. **—Arabic** *n.* About 1325, in the phrase "gum arabic"; borrowed from Old French *Arabic,* from Latin *Arabicus,* adj., from *Arabs* (genitive *Arabis*) Arab; for suffix see -IC. In the sense of "language of the Arabs" *Arabic* appeared in Middle English about 1400.

arabesque *n.* 1611, Arabian ornamental design, borrowed from French *arabesque,* from Italian *arabesco* (known in the Renaissance to such as Raphael), from *Arabo* Arab, ultimately borrowed from Latin *Arabus* Arabian, from *Arabs* Arab; for suffix see -ESQUE.

arable *adj.* fit for plowing. About 1410, borrowed through Anglo-French *arrable,* variant of Old French *arable,* from Latin *arābilis,* from *arāre* to plow; for suffix see -ABLE.

Latin *arāre* is cognate with Old English *erian* to plow, Old High German *erran,* Old Icelandic *erja,* Gothic *arjan* (Proto-Germanic **arjanan*), Greek *aroûn,* and Lithuanian *árti,* from Indo-European **ar(ə)-* (Pok.62).

The current term *arable* may have been introduced in an effort to "correct" the equivalent, earlier native English term *erable, earable* (derived from Old English *erian* to plow) by replacing it with a Latinate spelling. By the 1700's *erable* and its variants dropped out of use.

arachnid *n.* 1869, in Thomas Huxley's *An Introduction to the Classification of Animals,* borrowed (perhaps through influence of earlier French *arachnide,* 1806) from New Latin *Arachnida* the class of arachnids (a name introduced by Lamarck). The New Latin term came from Greek *aráchnē* spider, web, (earlier **arák-snā*), which is cognate with Latin *arānea* spider, cobweb, (earlier **araksneyā*).

arbiter *n.* Probably before 1387, in a version of *Piers Plowman,* Middle English *arbitour,* borrowed perhaps through Old French *arbitre,* or directly from Latin *arbiter,* originally, one who approaches (two disputants), from *ar-,* dialectal variant of *ad-* to + *baetere* to go, from a root **bait-/bit-,* of uncertain origin.

arbitrary *adj.* Before 1400 *arbitrarie,* borrowed perhaps through Old French *arbitraire,* or directly from Latin *arbitrārius* of arbitration, from *arbiter;* for suffix see -ARY.

arbitrate *v.* 1590, replacing earlier *arbitren* (1425, in *Rolls of Parliament*); borrowed perhaps through influence of Old French *arbitrer,* (from Latin *arbitrārī*), from Latin *arbitrātus,* past participle of *arbitrārī* to act as arbiter, examine, give judgment, from *arbiter* ARBITER; for suffix see -ATE; or possibly a back formation in English from earlier *arbitration*. **—arbitration** *n.* About 1390, in Chaucer's *Canterbury Tales,* borrowed from Old French *arbitracion,* from Latin *arbitrātiōnem* (nominative *arbitrātiō*), from *arbitrārī;* for suffix see -TION.

arbitrator *n.* About 1426 *arbitratour,* in *The Paston Letters;* borrowed from Old French *arbitrateur, arbitratour,* from Latin *arbitrātōrem,* accusative of *arbitrātor* from *arbitrārī* to act as arbiter; for suffix see -OR[2].

arbor[1] *n.* shady place formed by trees or shrubs. Probably before 1300, in the *Thrush and the Nightingale,* Middle English *erber, herber* a garden area of grass and flowers, garden of herbs; borrowed through Anglo-French *erber, herber* from Old French *erbier, herbier,* from Late Latin *herbārium,* from Latin *herba* herb, grass. Doublet of HERBARIUM.

According to OED the sense development began to separate "the garden of herbs" from "the shady place formed by trees" about the middle of the 1500's. This was furthered by a tendency to connect the word with Latin *arbor* "tree".

The change of initial *er-,* as in *erber, herber,* to *ar-* before consonants took place in many Middle English words, affecting the pronunciation, as well as the spelling. For example, *carve* was earlier *kerven, farm* earlier *ferme*. However, sometimes there was a shift in pronunciation, as in *sergeant,* pronounced with the sound of *-ar-* while the older *-er-* spelling was retained, as is also seen in *clerk* and *Derby* in Britain.

The shift of *-er, -or* in the final syllable follows a common practice of interchanging spellings of *-er, -or,* and *-our* in the 1500's.

arbor[2] *n.* main axle of a machine. 1659, borrowed from French *arbre* (originally) tree, axis, from Latin *arbor* tree, of unknown origin.

arbor[3] *n.* tree (especially in *Arbor Day* for planting trees, or *arbor vitae,* now Anglicized from the Latin meaning literally "tree of life," but in English referring specifically to various evergreen trees, especially a white cedar). 1646, borrowed from Latin *arbor* tree, beam, of unknown origin. **—arboreal** *adj.* Before 1667, formed in English from Latin *arboreus,* from *arbor* tree; for suffix see -AL[1].

arboretum *n.* place where trees and shrubs are cultivated for exhibition and scientific study. 1838, borrowed from Latin *arborētum* place grown with trees, from *arbor* tree.

arbovirus *n.* virus causing such diseases as yellow fever and a form of encephalitis, transmitted by mosquitoes, ticks, and other arthropods. 1963, alteration of earlier *arborvirus* (1959), *arbor virus* (1957), from *ar(thropod)-bor(ne) virus*.

arc *n.* any part of a circle or other curved line. About 1390, in Chaucer's *Canterbury Tales,* Middle English *ark, arc* part of a circle which the sun appears to pass through from the eastern to western horizons, especially in the phrase *days arc;* borrowed through Anglo-

French *arc, ark, arche* from Old French *arc,* from Latin *arcus* arch, bow; see ARROW. Doublet of ARCH[1].

The general application to any segment of a circle appears in 1570.

arcade *n.* 1731, in Pope's *Moral Essays,* borrowed from French *arcade* an arch, half circle, from Italian *arcata* arch of a bridge, from Medieval Latin *arcata* an arch, from Latin *arcus* arch, bow; for suffix see -ADE.

arcane *adj.* understood only by a few; secret; mysterious. 1547, borrowed from Latin *arcānus* closed, hidden, from *arca* chest; see ARK.

arch[1] *n.* curved structure. About 1300, borrowed from Old French *arche* arch of a bridge, from Northern Gallo-Romance **arca* arch, feminine (earlier neuter plural) form corresponding to Latin *arcus* arch, bow; see ARROW.Doublet of ARC.—**v.** About 1400, *archen* provide with an arch; from the noun.

arch[2] *adj.* **1** chief, leading, as in *arch rebel.* 1547, formed in English by abstraction from the prefix *arch-*. **2** mischievous in a playful way, saucy, waggish, as in *an arch look.* 1662, developed in English from def. 1, and in such use as *arch knave* the term has acquired some negative connotations.

arch- a prefix meaning: **1** chief, principal, as in *archenemy = chief enemy, archbishop = chief or highest ranking bishop.* **2** extreme, ultra-, especially in a derogatory sense, as in *archconservative = extreme conservative, archfool = extreme fool.* **3** early, primal, primitive, as in *archencephalon = primitive encephalon* (primitive part of the brain).

The prefix developed from Middle English *arche-, erche-* (influenced in form by Old French *arche-* and earlier *arce-*), forms of Old English *arce-, erce-, ærce-.* Both Old English and Old French forms were borrowed from Latin *archi-,* from Greek *arche-, archi-,* related to *archós* ruler, *arché* a beginning, and *árchein* to begin, take the lead, rule, of unknown origin. See also ARCHI-.

archaebacteria (är′kēbaktir′ēə) *n.pl.* group of microorganisms thought to have evolved before bacteria. 1977, coined by Carl R. Woese, American biophysicist, from English *archae-* ancient, borrowed from Greek *archaîos,* from *arché* a beginning + English *bacteria.*

archaeology *n.* 1607, ancient history, study of antiquities; borrowed, perhaps by influence of French *archéologie* (1599), from Greek *archaiologíā,* from *archaîos* ancient, from *arché* a beginning, see ARCH-; for suffix see -LOGY.

The meaning of "the scientific study of ancient people, customs, and life, especially by unearthing and examining artifacts where written records do not exist" appeared in English in 1837.

archaic *adj.* no longer in general use, old-fashioned, out-of-date. 1832, perhaps developed in English from earlier *archaical* (before 1804), or possibly by influence of French *archaïque* (1776), ultimately borrowed from Greek *archāïkós* old-fashioned, from *archaîos* ancient, from *arché* a beginning, see ARCH-; for suffix see -IC. —**archaism** *n.* word no longer in general use. 1643, borrowed from New Latin *archaismus,* from Greek *archāïsmós,* from *archāïzein* to give an archaic flavor to, from *archaîos* ancient; for suffix see -ISM.

Archaic must have been somehow influenced by the existence of *archaism,* which appeared in the language about 200 years before *archaic,* but our records are wanting in this instance.

archangel *n.* Probably before 1200, gradually replacing Old English *hēah-engel* high angel. Middle English *archangel* was borrowed through Old French *archangel* (1155), or directly from Latin *archangelus,* from Greek *archángelos* (*arch-* chief + *ángelos* ANGEL).

archbishop *n.* Before 1121, *archebishop, erchebishop,* and earlier *arce biscop, erce biscop,* developed from Old English *ærce biscop, erce biscop* (about 850, written as either one word or two). The later forms in Middle English *archebishop,* etc., were influenced by Old French *archevesque* and Late Latin *archiepiscopus,* according to MED (Middle English Dictionary). The Old English *ærce biscop, erce biscop* (or *bisceop*) are borrowed from Late Latin *archiepiscopus,* from Late Greek *archiepískopos* (from Greek *archi-* chief + *epískopos* overseer).

The Old English *ærce biscop* was probably a replacement for earlier Old English *hēah biscop* (or *bisceop*) high bishop; see ARCHI- and BISHOP.

archer *n.* About 1300, borrowed through Anglo-French *archer,* from Old French *archier,* from Late Latin *arcārius* archer, alteration of *arcuārius* maker of bows, from Latin *arcus* bow, see ARROW; for suffix see -ER[2]. —**archery** *n.* Probably before 1400 in writings of Wycliffe, borrowed through Anglo-French *archerye,* from Old French *archerie,* from *archier* archer; for suffix see -Y[3].

archetype (är′kətīp) *n.* original model or pattern from which copies are made. 1605, in Francis Bacon's *Of the Advancement of Learning,* borrowed possibly from French *archétype* (Old French *architipe*), or directly from Latin *archetypum,* from Greek *archétypon* pattern, model, the neuter form of adjective *archétypos* original (*arch-* first + *týpos* stamp, mold, TYPE).

archi- a form of the prefix *arch-* borrowed from Greek *archi-,* and occurring in words borrowed from Greek (sometimes through Latin), such as *architect* = Greek *archi-* chief + *téktōn* builder, as well as in modern scientific coinages patterned on Greek, such as *archibenthos* = Greek *archi-* primal + *bénthos* depth (of the sea).

Archi- also occurs in a few adjectives based on nouns that occur in Greek. These Greek nouns, through development in Latin and sometimes French, became different forms in English from what they are in Greek; thereby earlier English *archbishop* (about 850) acquired the adjective form *archiepiscopal* (about 1600), a borrowing from the Greek original through Latin. Therefore, both *archbishop* (ultimately from Greek *archi-* chief + *epískopos* overseer) and *archiepiscopal* have a commonly discernible root in Greek.

In Greek a variant form of the prefix *archi-* was *arche-,* which in English survives in *archetype* = *arche-* first, primal + *týpos* stamp.

archipelago *n.* group of many islands. 1502 *archpelago* the Aegean sea, borrowed from Italian *arcipelago* (*arci-* chief, from Greek *archi-* + Italian *pelago* sea, from Latin, from Greek *pélagos;* see PELAGIC). The present meaning developed in the 1600's from the generalized meaning, any sea with many islands (such as the Aegean sea).

The Italian word *Arcipelago* first occurs in the 1200's as the name of the Aegean sea, yet the word does not appear before that in Greek or Latin. It has been suggested that the word was altered in Italian (by influence of the prefix *arci-*) from the Medieval Latin name for the Aegean, *Egiopelagus,* representing Greek *Ai-*

gaîon pélagos Aegean Sea, and further that the spelling with *-ch-* is a learned restoration of the Greek after *archi-*.

architect *n.* 1563, borrowed from Middle French *architecte,* possibly influenced by Italian *architetto,* from Latin *architectus,* from Greek *architéktōn* chief builder (*archi-* chief + *téktōn* builder); see TECTONIC.
—**architecture** *n.* 1555, borrowed from Middle French *architecture,* possibly influenced by Italian *architettura,* from Latin *architectūra,* from *architectus* architect; for suffix see -URE. See *architrave* for note.

architrave *n.* the main beam resting on the top of a column. 1563, borrowed from Italian *architrave* (*archi-* chief, learned borrowing from Greek *archi-* principal + Italian *trave* beam, from Latin *trabs, trabis,* related to *taberna* hut, shed; see TAVERN).

All of these terms: *architect, architecture, architrave* in the field of architecture were first recorded in English from John Shute's *The First and Chief Grounds of Architecture.*

archives *n.pl.* 1603 *archive,* 1638 *archives,* borrowed from French *archives,* a learned borrowing from Latin singular *archīvum,* variant of *archīum,* from Greek *archeîon* governmental building, public office, from *arché* government.

The singular form *archive* is now generally archaic except in names, such as *Bettman Archive,* and in reference to a particular source, as in *Some rotten archive, rummaged out of some seldom explored press* (Charles Lamb).

arcology (ärkol′əjē) *n.* planned city or environment housed within a single structure. 1969, coined by Paolo Soleri, an American architect; blend of *ar(chitectural)* and *(e)cology.*

arctic (ärk′tik *or* är′tik) *adj.* 1556 *arctike,* in Robert Recorde's *The Castle of Knowledge,* alteration (influenced by Latin *arcticus*) gradually replacing earlier Middle English *artic,* about 1400, in Chaucer's *Treatise on the Astrolabe.* Middle English *artic* was borrowed through Old French *artique,* from Medieval Latin *articus.* The Medieval Latin word followed the same process of sound change by dissimilation as the parallel term *antarticus* (antarctic) and dropped the *c* in *arc-* which was in the original Latin *arcticus,* from Greek *arktikós* of the north, of the Bear (the northern constellation Ursa Major), from *árktos* bear. Greek *árktos* is related to Latin *ursus,* Sanskrit *ṛ́kṣa-s,* Avestan *arša-,* Armenian *arǰ* and Irish *art,* all meaning bear, from Indo-European **ṛ́k̑pos,* and Hittite *ḫartagga-* beast of prey (Pok.875). See BEAR[1] animal.

The spelling *arc-* and its pronunciation (ark′-) reflect the ultimate Latin origin, but the now variant pronunciation (är′tik) is not recent, having occurred in Chaucer's time and even in later stages of Latin itself.

-ard a suffix forming nouns and meaning one who does (something) excessively or conspicuously, as in *drunkard, laggard, stinkard.* Borrowed from Old French *-ard, -art,* of Germanic origin, as in Old High German *-hart, -hard* hardy, found in personal names such as *Reginhart* Reynard, and cognate with Old English *heard* HARD.

The suffix appeared originally in Middle English in words from Old French, such as *bastard, coward, mallard,* and *placard,* where it functioned as an intensive, augmentative, and often pejorative form. It later became a living suffix in English, forming such words as *dastard, sluggard,* and *wizard.*

ardent *adj.* impassioned, very enthusiastic, fiery, glowing. Probably before 1425, fiery, glowing, in a translation of Chauliac's *Grande Chirurgie.* The spelling with *e, ardent,* is an alteration of earlier *ardaunt, ardant* (before 1333). The later form *ardent* was influenced by Latin *ārdentem* (nominative *ārdēns*), present participle of *ārdēre* to burn, and gradually replaced the earlier *ardaunt, ardant,* borrowed through Anglo-French *ardante,* from Old French *ardant,* present participle of *ardoir* to burn, from Latin *ārdēre* to burn, related to *āridus* ARID.

ardor *n.* warmth of emotion. About 1390, in Chaucer's *Canterbury Tales,* Middle English *ardour, ardure,* borrowed through Anglo-French *ardour, ardure* from Old French *ardour,* from Latin *ārdōrem* (nominative *ārdor*), from *ārdēre* to burn, related to *āridus* ARID. The later spelling *ardor* was influenced by the Latin and gradually replaced the earlier *ardour, ardure* in the 1500's.

arduous *adj.* hard to do. 1538, borrowed from Latin *arduus* steep, difficult; for suffix see -OUS. Latin *arduus* is cognate with Old Irish *ard* high, Welsh *hardd* handsome, and Avestan *ərədva-* high, from Indo-European **er(ə)d-/erəd/r̥̄d-* (Pok.339). English *arduous* may have been influenced in its borrowing from Latin by the Old French *ardu* steep, difficult (1365).

are[1] *v.* form of the verb *be.* Old English (before 950), in the Mercian dialect (before 830) *earun,* in Northumbrian *aron* (about 1100), together with (*thū*) *eart* (thou) art. These are ancient perfect active (preterite present) forms from Proto-Germanic **ar-,* cognate with Latin *orīrī* to arise, come to be, come into existence, and Greek *órnysthai* to arise, from Indo-European **or-/r̥-* (Pok.326).

In Old English *am* had two forms in the plural: *sind, sindon* and *earon, aron.* Of these *sind, sindon* gradually fell out of use in the first half of the 1200's, and were replaced by forms of *be (beth, ben, be)* which remained through Middle English and are still found in dialect and some literary expressions today. At the same time *aron* and its forms *(aren, arn, are)* continued in use and spread until early in the 1500's, *are* became a part of standard English, replacing forms of *be* partly through influence of Tyndale's use, though *be,* which was first used as a substitute form in the 1200's, is still found in expressions such as "the powers that be." See AM for further explanation and BE for a differentiation of all parts of the verb *am-was-be.*

are[2] *n.* metric measure equal to 100 square meters. 1819, borrowed from French *are,* coined in 1795 from Latin *ārea* open space, piece of level ground, AREA.

area *n.* 1538, borrowed from Latin *ārea* open space, piece of level ground, vacant space; ultimate origin uncertain.

There has been an attempt to derive Latin *ārea* from *ārēre* meaning "be dry" but this is not generally accepted.

arena *n.* 1600, a variant of Latin *harēna* sand, sandy place (generally considered to be in reference to the floor of Roman arenas that were strewn with sand); cognate with Sabine *fasēna.*

argent *n. Archaic or Poetic.* silver. Probably before 1425, quicksilver or mercury, in a translation of Chauliac's *Grande Chirurgie;* borrowed through Middle French *argent,* from Old French, from Latin *argen-*

tum. The Latin word is cognate with Old Irish *argat* silver, Welsh *arian,* Greek *árgyros* silver, *argós* (earlier **argrós*) white, Sanskrit *árjuna-s* white, *rajatá-s* silvery, and Tocharian A *ārkyant,* from Indo-European **areĝ-/ arĝ-/reĝ-/r̥ĝ-* shining, whitish (Pok.64).

argon *n.* 1894, New Latin *argon,* borrowed from Greek *ārgón,* neuter of *ārgós* idle (*a-* without + *érgon* WORK).

The chemical element was so called by its discoverers, Baron Rayleigh and Sir William Ramsay, from its inert qualities.

argosy *n.* large merchant ship. 1587, alteration of earlier *ragusye* (1577), borrowed from Italian *Ragusea* ship of *Ragusa* (now Dubrovnik, but formerly an Italian port which traded extensively with England in the 1500's). No connection can be established with the *Argo,* the boat that Jason used in his search for the Golden Fleece.

As early as 1517, or seventy years before the spelling *argosy* is recorded in place of *ragusye,* an English writer was referring to the town as *Aragouse* which strongly implies that the word for the ship came into English influenced by the name of the town.

argot (är′gō) *n.* jargon. 1860, borrowed from French, from Middle French *argot* a group of beggars, of unknown origin. Originally the term applied to the slang or jargon of thieves.

argue *v.* About 1303, in Mannyng's *Handlyng Synne,* borrowed through Anglo-French *arguer,* from Old French, from Latin *argūtāre* chatter shrilly, prattle, frequentative of *arguere* accuse, assert, make clear. **—argument** *n.* About 1330, reasoning, disputation, borrowed from Old French *argument* proof, from Latin *argūmentum,* from *arguere* assert, make clear; for suffix see -MENT.

aria (ä′rēə) *n.* 1724, borrowed from Italian *aria* melody, song, air, musical mode; possibly an extension of the meaning "manner, appearance, mode," that meaning being itself an extension of *aire, aere, aria* the atmosphere. However, this development of meaning is disputed and not fully understood (some sources referring to Middle French *air* as the influence for the meaning "manner, appearance" in Italian), though the Italian is generally agreed to have come through Vulgar Latin **arja,* from Latin *āera* (accusative of *āēr,* from Greek *āéra* accusative of *āḗr* AIR).

arid *adj.* 1652, borrowed probably through French *aride,* or directly from Latin *āridus,* from *ārēre* be dry; related to *ārdēre* to burn, *āra* altar, earlier *āsa.* Cognate with Sanskrit *ā́sa-s* ashes, dust. Related to ASH[1]. **—aridity** *n.* 1599, borrowed probably through Middle French *aridité,* from Latin *āriditātem* (nominative *āriditās*), from *āridus;* for suffix see -ITY.

It is interesting to note that the form *aridité* was recorded in Anglo-French as early as 1120, yet was not recorded in English for almost 480 years, and that it was over 500 years before the "root" form *arid* was first recorded in Blount's *Glossographia* (1656).

aristocracy *n.* 1561, borrowed from Middle French *aristocratie,* or directly from Late Latin *aristocratia,* from Greek *aristokratíā* rule of the best-born (*áristos* best + *krátos* rule, power, strength; see HARD). **—aristocrat** *n.* 1789, borrowed from French *aristocrate,* from Greek *aristokrátēs* aristocrat.

The word *aristocrate* came into French in the mid-1500's, apparently then dropped out of use, and was reintroduced in French in 1778, becoming popularized during the French Revolution. Its introduction to English in 1789 shows how closely events in France at that time were discussed in England.

arise *v.* Probably before 1200 *arisen* stand up, rise; developed from Old English *ārīsan* (before 830, in the *Vespasian Psalter*); cognate with Old Saxon *ārīsan,* Old High German *ur-, ar-, irrīsan,* Gothic *urreisan,* from Proto-Germanic **uz-rīsanan;* see A-[5], RISE.

arithmetic *n.* About 1250 *arsmetike,* borrowed from Old French *arsmetique, arismetique,* a learned borrowing from Latin *arithmētica,* from Greek *arithmētikḕ téchnē* art of reckoning, from *arithmeîn* to count, from *arithmós* number, cognate with Latin *ars* (genitive *artis*) ART.

About 1300 the form *arsmetrike* appeared from Medieval Latin *arsmetrica* art of measure, arithmetic, which resembles in form and meaning the earlier, but independently formed, *arsmetike.* Other sources contributed spellings, such as Anglo-French *arismatike, aritmetike* and in 1270 Old French *aritmétique* in *Roman de la Rose,* a work translated by Chaucer about 1370. These and other intermediate variants *arismetrik, arithmetik* (before 1410), and *arithmetricke* were generally standardized to *arithmetyke,* (1543), probably in an attempt to return to the etymological source, Greek *arithmētikḕ.*

ark *n.* boat (as in Noah's *ark*); chest or cabinet (as in *ark* of the Covenant). Old English *erc* before 830, in the *Vespasian Psalter;* elsewhere in Old English *ærca, earc, arc;* an early borrowing (like Old High German *arahha* ark, Old Icelandic *ǫrk* (genitive *arkar*), and Gothic *arka*), from Latin *arca* chest, box, coffer, which is related to *arcēre* hold in, restrain, enclose.

arm[1] *n.* limb of the body from the shoulder to the hand. Old English *earm,* about 725, in *Beowulf,* cognate with Old Frisian *arm, erm* arm, Old High German *arm, aram,* Old Icelandic *armr,* Gothic *arms,* from Proto-Germanic **armaz,* and with Latin *armus* shoulder (of an animal), Greek *harmós* joint, and Sanskrit *īrmá-s* arm, Avestan *arəma* arm, Old Prussian *irmo* arm, Armenian *armukn* elbow, all of which show a derivative with *m-* suffix of the Indo-European **ar-* to join, fit (Pok.58).

arm[2] *n.* weapon, now generally confined in the singular to the terms *side arm* referring to a pistol, bayonet, or other weapon carried on a belt around the waist, or *short arm* a handgun, and *firearm* a rifle, pistol, or other gun.

The term is more usual as **arms,** *n.pl.* weapons. Before 1250, in *The Proverbs of Alfred, armes,* borrowed through Anglo-French and Old French *armes,* from Latin *arma* tools, weapons; related to *ars* (accusative *artem*) skill; see ART[1] skills.

Latin had no singular form, but Vulgar Latin **arma* became a feminine singular form in Old French, showing the same need for a singular form as was felt in English, which then produced *arm* by the mid-1800's. —v. Probably before 1200, in *Ancrene Riwle,* borrowed perhaps through Anglo-French and Old French *armer,* from Latin *armāre,* from *arma* weapons. **—armament** *n.* 1699, borrowed from French *armement,* from Late Latin *armāmentum* arms, from Latin *arma* tools, weapons; for suffix see -MENT.

armada *n.* 1533 *armado,* a misspelling, used among others by Shakespeare in *Comedy of Errors* (1590), but gradually corrected in the 1600's to *armada* (first appearing in 1599 in Hakluyt's *Principal Navigations, Voyages and Discoveries of the English Nations*); borrowed from Spanish *armada,* from Medieval Latin *armata* armed force; see the doublet ARMY.

The word acquired much currency in reference to the "Invincible Armada" sent by Philip II of Spain against England in 1588.

armadillo *n.* 1577, borrowed from Spanish *armadillo,* diminutive of *armado* armed (with reference to its bony armorlike shell), from Latin *armātus,* past participle of *armāre* to arm; see ARM², v.

Armageddon (är′məged′ən) *n.* a great and final conflict. 1811, in a letter of Shelley's, figurative use of the name from the Bible (Revelation 16:16) meaning the place of the great and final conflict of good and evil at the end of the world (1611, in King James Bible); borrowed from Late Latin *Armageddōn,* from Greek *Armageddṓn* (translated by Luther as *Harmagedon,* also in the Revised Version), probably from Hebrew *Har Megiddōn* Mount of Megiddo, a city in central Palestine which was the site of important battles in the history of the Israelites.

armature *n.* **1a** a coil of wire that rotates in a magnetic field causing an electric motor to move (1835), a meaning developed from **b** the iron bar placed between poles of a horseshoe magnet to protect or contain its magnetic field (1752) which is an extension of **2** a protective covering of a plant or animal (1662), an extension of **3** protection provided by God (1542). Before 1450, an armed force, borrowed from Middle French *armature,* learned borrowing from Latin *armātūra* armor, from *armāre* to arm; for suffix see -URE. Doublet of ARMOR.

armistice *n.* 1707, borrowed after the pattern of French *armistice* (1688), from New Latin *armistitium* (recorded in English as early as 1664), from Latin *arma* arms + *-stitium,* from *sistere* to stop, stand.

Solstice is another word that follows this pattern of borrowing through French.

armor *n.* Probably before 1300, in *The Romance of Guy of Warwick,* Middle English *armure, armour, armeur;* borrowed from Old French *armeüre,* from Latin *armātūra,* from *armāre* to arm, from *arma* arms, gear. Doublet of ARMATURE.

arms *n.pl.* See ARM².

army *n.* About 1387-95 *armee,* in Chaucer's *Prologue* to *The Canterbury Tales,* borrowed through Anglo-French *armee* from Old French *armée,* from Medieval Latin *armata* armed force. The Medieval Latin developed from Latin *armāta,* feminine of *armātus,* past participle of *armāre* to arm, from *arma* weapons; for suffix see -Y⁴. Doublet of ARMADA.

aroma *n.* fragrance (1814), influenced by or reborrowed directly from Latin *arōma* sweet odor. The new meaning in English extended the older meaning of, or replaced earlier *aroma (aromat, aromaz)* fragrant substance (recorded probably before 1200 in *Ancrene Riwle*). These earlier Middle English forms were borrowed through Anglo-French and Old French *aromat,* a learned borrowing from Medieval Latin *aromatum,* alteration of Latin *arōma* sweet odor, spice, from Greek *árōma* (genitive *arṓmatos*) spice, of unknown origin. —**aromatic** *adj.* About 1400, in *The Voiage of Sir John Maundeville,* probably borrowed through Old French *aromatique,* from Late Latin *arōmaticus,* from Greek *arōmatikós,* from *árōma* spice; for suffix see -IC.

The adjective *aromatic* referred to the scent some 400 years before the noun *aroma.*

around *prep., adv.* Probably before 1300, in *Kyng Alisaunder,* developed from the phrase *on round.*

arpeggio (ärpej′ēō) *n.* the sounding of the notes of a chord in rapid succession instead of together. 1724, borrowed from Italian *arpeggio,* from *arpeggiare* play the harp, from *arpa* harp, from an indeterminate word of Germanic origin (compare Old High German *harpha* harp; see HARP).

arraign *v.* Probably about 1380 *araynen, areinen, arreinen,* borrowed through Anglo-French *arainer, areiner* from Old French *araisnier* (*a-* to, from Latin *ad-*) + (*raisnier* speak, reason, from Vulgar Latin **ratiōnāre* reason, from Latin *ratiōnem,* accusative of *ratiō,* argumentation, REASON).

The *g* in *arraign* came about in the late 1400's and early 1500's probably from an effort to restore what was thought to be a correct spelling of Latin origin, such as in *reign* or in the replacement of earlier *fain, fein* by *feign.* That was a mistake or overcorrection, because though *reign* derived from Old French *reigne* and Latin *rēgnum* and *fein, feign* from Old French *feign-* and Latin *fingere,* the English *arraign* was already correct in its Middle English form *araynen, arreinen,* since the source was Old French *araisnier* (Latin *ad-* + *ratiōnem*) with no *g.*

The introduction of the second *r* in English was likewise a mistaken attempt to restore what was thought to be a Latin form by adding the prefix *ar-,* variant of *ad-* before *r.*

arrange *v.* 1375, in John Barbour's *The Bruce,* Middle English *araingen* draw up in ranks, borrowed from Old French *arangier* (*a-* to, from Latin *ad-*) + (*rangier, ranger* place in ranks, assemble, from *rang* rank¹, earlier *renc,* from Frankish **hring,* cognate with RING; see RANGE). —**arrangement** *n.* 1727-51, in *Chambers Cyclopaedia,* borrowed from French *arrangement,* from *arranger* arrange, from Old French *arangier;* for suffix see -MENT.

The introduction of the second *r* in English was an effort to restore what was thought to be a Latin form.

arrant *adj.* thoroughgoing, downright. 1550, at first a variant of *erraunt* roving, vagabond, as a special use of *errant,* as in *knight-errant.*

For 150 years from about 1390 (in Chaucer's *Canterbury Tales,* in phrases such as *thief erraunt* and *arrant thief,* meaning "a roving robber, one that is outlawed") the term was used in a derogatory sense, until about 1570 when it began to take on a generalized meaning of "thoroughgoing, downright, unmitigated."

array *v.* Probably before 1325, *araien, arraien* arrange in order, borrowed through Anglo-French *arraier, arayer,* from Old French *arëer,* from Vulgar Latin **arrēdāre* (from Latin *ad-* to + Frankish **rǣđ-,* the source of Old English *(ge)rǣde* ready, and Old High German *reiti;* see READY).

—**n.** Before 1338, in Mannyng's *Chronicle of England,* Middle English *arai, arrai* order, arrangement, borrowed through Anglo-French *arraie, arai,* from Old French *arei,* from *arëer* to array.

arrears *n.* money due but not paid. About 1300, *arere* behind; 1340, in *Ayenbite of Inwyt* in the phrase *in arriers,* meaning "in time past;" borrowed through Anglo-French *arere,* from Old French *ariere* behind, backward, from Vulgar Latin **ad retrō* backward (Latin *ad* to + *retrō* back, behind). The meaning of "balance due" appeared in 1432; the phrase *in arrears,* meaning "behind in payments, in debt," appeared in 1620.

The introduction of the second *r* in English was an effort to restore what was thought to have been the original Latin form.

arrest *v.* Before 1375, stay, stop; 1375, in John Barbour's *The Bruce,* Middle English *aresten* seize, restrain legally, borrowed through Anglo-French *arester,* from Old French *arester* to stay, stop, from Vulgar Latin **arrestāre* (Latin *ad-* to + *restāre* stay back, remain, from *re-* back + *stāre* to stand; see STAND). **—n.** 1375, in John Barbour's *The Bruce,* a staying, stopping, borrowed through Anglo-French *arest, areste,* from Old French *areste,* from *arester* to stay, stop.

The introduction of the second *r* in English was an effort to restore what was thought to have been the original Latin form.

arrive *v.* Probably before 1200, in Layamon's *Chronicle of Britain,* Middle English *ariven* come to land on the shore, borrowed through Anglo-French *ariver,* from Old French *ariver, arriver* to come to land, from Vulgar Latin **arripāre,* from Latin *ad rīpam* to the shore (*ad* to + *rīpam,* accusative of *rīpa* shore; see RIVER). **—arrival** *n.* About 1380, in Chaucer's *House of Fame,* Middle English *arivaile* landing, disembarkation, borrowed through Anglo-French *arivail, aryvaille,* from Old French *arivaille, arrivaille,* from *ariver, arriver* to come to land.

The introduction of the second *r* in English was an effort to restore what was thought to have been the original Latin form.

arrogance *n.* haughtiness. 1340, in *Ayenbite of Inwyt,* borrowed through Old French *arrogance,* from Latin *arrogantia* arrogance, overbearing quality, from *arrogantem* (nominative *arrogāns*) assuming, overbearing, insolent, present participle of *arrogāre* claim for oneself, assume (*ar-,* variant of *ad-* before *r,* to + *rogāre* ask, propose; see RIGHT); for suffix see -ANCE. **—arrogant** *adj.* haughty. About 1390, in Chaucer's *Canterbury Tales,* borrowed from Latin *arrogantem* assuming, overbearing, insolent; for suffix see -ANT. **—arrogate** *v.* claim or take without right. Probably about 1530, borrowed from Latin *arrogātus,* past participle of *arrogāre* claim for oneself; for suffix see -ATE.

While *arrogance* came into English through Old French *arrogance* (recorded since 1160 in French), *arrogant* is found in English (1390) before it is recorded in French (1398) and *arrogate* is recorded in English (1530) before its French equivalent *arroger* (1538). Therefore, one may assume that *arrogant* and *arrogate* were borrowings modeled on Latin, probably suggested by the already available English *arrogance.*

arrow *n.* Old English, before 800 in writings of Cynewulf *earh,* especially in *earh-faru* flight of arrows, and before 835 *arwan,* singular and plural; these forms developed into Middle English *aro* and *arow* before 1325, in *Cursor Mundi.*

The word is cognate with Old Icelandic *ǫr* arrow (genitive *ǫrvar*), from Proto-Germanic **arHwō;* Gothic **arhwazna* dart (attested only in accusative plural *arhwaznōs*), and Latin *arcus* bow (the source of English ARC, ARCH[1] curved structure, and the derivative word ARCHER), from Indo-European **arku-* (Pok.67).

arroyo (əroi′ō) *n.* dry bed of a stream; gully. 1807 (in a place name), American English, borrowed from Spanish *arroyo* small stream, perhaps from Medieval Latin *arrogium* (compare Medieval Latin *rogium, rogia* a stream for irrigation); or perhaps Spanish *arroyo* came ultimately from Latin *arrugia* a kind of galleried mine.

arsenal *n.* place for building or storing weapons. 1506, a dock with naval stores, borrowed from Italian *arsenale,* earlier *arsena,* Medieval Latin *arsana,* from Arabic *dār aṣ-ṣinā'a* house of manufacturing (*ṣinā'a* art, craft, skill, from *ṣana'a* make, fabricate).

French also had the form *arsenal* (recorded in 1250); Spanish is later (1610), but the original English borrowing was almost certainly from Italian, because the earliest sources were descriptions of Italy, especially in reference to the Arsenal at Venice, and the earliest forms of the word in English were Italianate *arsenale, arzenale.*

arsenic *n.* Before 1393, in Gower's *Confessio Amantis,* borrowed from Latin *arsenicon,* from Greek *arsenikón* yellow arsenic (orpiment) literally meaning "masculine," neuter form of *arsenikós, arrhenikós* masculine, from *ársēn, árrhēn* (genitive *ársenos, árrhenos*) male, strong (the word supposedly referring to the powerful qualities of arsenic). But the Greek *arsenikón* is actually merely a folk-etymological adoption of a Middle Persian word **zarnīk* golden, gold-colored, probably by Semitic transmission (Syriac *zarnīqā* arsenic).

Traditionally regarded as being borrowed from French and Latin, evidence now suggests little French influence initially, for *arsenic* is not recorded in French before 1398.

arson *n.* Before 1680, borrowed through Anglo-French *arsoun, arson,* from Old French *arson, arsion,* from Late Latin *ārsiōnem* a burning, from Latin *ārsum,* past participle of *ārdēre* to burn. **—arsonist** *n.* 1864, formed from English *arson* + *-ist.*

art *n.* About 1250, in *King Horn,* meaning "cunning, trickery"; borrowed through Anglo-French *art,* from Old French *art,* from Latin *artem,* accusative of *ars* skill. The Latin *ars* is related to *artus* joint, *arma* tools, weapons, and is cognate with Greek *ararískein* to fit, *artýein* arrange, prepare, and Sanskrit *ṛtá-s* fit, from Indo-European **ar-/ṛ-* (Pok.56).

The early use of the word in English centered upon the meaning of skill, scholarship, and learning. The application of "skill" to the arts, such as music, dancing, drama, and literary composition does not appear before 1600. The specific meaning of painting, sculpture, etc., does not appear before the latter 1600's or early 1700's.

—artful *adj.* 1613, formed from English *art* + *-ful.*

art deco ornate style of decoration originating in France in the early 1920's. 1967, borrowed from French *Art Déco,* shortened from *Arts Décoratifs* decorative arts, part of the name of an exposition of decorative and industrial arts held in Paris in 1925.

artery *n.* Before 1398, in Trevisa's translation of Bartholomew's *De Proprietatibus Rerum,* borrowed perhaps through Anglo-French *arterie,* from Old French *artaire* (1213), or more likely directly from Latin *artēria* windpipe, artery, from Greek *ārtēríā* (earlier **aertēríā*) an artery, as distinct from a vein; originally windpipe (arteries were regarded by some of the ancients as air ducts branching from the trachea, since the arteries do not contain blood after death); perhaps related to *aortḗ* AORTA. **—arterial** *adj.* Probably before 1425, in a translation of Chauliac's *Grande Chirurgie,* formed in English from Latin *artēria* + English suffix *-al*[1].

The word does not derive from French, because the corresponding French *artériel* was not recorded before 1503.

artesian well 1830 *artesian,* adj., borrowed from French *artésien* of Artois (in Old French *Arteis*), region in northern France where such wells were first drilled in the 1700's, though the descriptive term *artésien* is not recorded as being applied in French to such wells before 1803.

arthritis *n.* 1544, borrowed from Latin *arthrītis,* abstracted from Greek *nósos arthrîtis* disease of the joints, from *árthron* joint, from *araráskein* to fit, see ART; for suffix see -ITIS, though *arthritis* is one of the original borrowings into English (along with *nephritis* and a few others) from which the suffix *-itis* was abstracted in the 1800's to mean "inflammation."—**arthritic** *adj.* Before 1398, as a noun *arthetica* in Trevisa's translation of Bartholomew's *De Proprietatibus Rerum;* by 1400 as an adjective *artetik, artetica;* borrowed through Old French *goute artetique* arthritic gout and Medieval Latin *gutta artetica,* from Latin *arthrīticus,* from Greek *arthrītikós* of the joints, gouty, from *arthrîtis.*

For almost 150 years some form of the adjective (*artetik, arthretik,* etc.) was also used as a noun so that the need for a noun form, such as the later *arthritis* (1544), was not felt (nor had the suffix *-itis* assumed importance in medical terminology). This accounts for the adjective form of today *(arthritic)* seeming to come into English before the modern noun *arthritis.*

arthropod *n.* 1877, earlier (1870) *Arthropoda* the name given in biological classification to the invertebrate animals with jointed bodies and legs which constitute a phylum. *Arthropoda* is New Latin, formed from Greek *árthron* joint + *poús* (genitive *podós*) foot.

artichoke *n.* 1530 *archicokk,* borrowed from northern dialect forms of Italian such as *articiocco, arciocco, arcicioffo,* etc., from Old Provençal *arquichaut,* from older Spanish *alcarchofa,* from Spanish-Arabic *al-ḥarshōfa,* variant of Arabic *al-ḥarshūf* the artichoke.

The word was introduced into Europe during the 1500's, but the plant was known in Italy by the 1450's.

The variant names abound, from *hortichock* and *horty-chock* to *archychok* and *artychough,* and the explanations for them are as numerous, from choking the garden to choking the heart. The unfamiliar foreign origin of the term seems to have stimulated associations with some familiar element in the native tongue to produce any of a number of alterations in spelling.

article *n.* Probably before 1200, in *Ancrene Riwle,* referring to a clause or section, as in a set of rules or a creed, borrowed through Anglo-French from Old French *article,* a learned borrowing from Latin *articulus* small section or joint, diminutive of *artus* (genitive *artūs*) joint; see ART.

articulation *n.* Probably before 1425 meaning (1) a joint (2) setting of bones, both in a translation of Chauliac's *Grande Chirurgie;* borrowed through Old French *articulation* (1363), from Medieval Latin *articulationem* (nominative *articulatio*), from Latin *articulāre* to divide (meat, etc.) into single joints; for suffix see -TION. —**articulate** *v.* 1563-83, in one of various versions of John Foxe's *Book of Martyrs* meaning "to draw up articles of charges," and serving as an alternate form for earlier *articlen* (1448) *articulen* 1454) meaning "to draw up articles of a claim," later (1616) developing the meaning "to connect by joints" and 1691 "to speak distinctly". Earlier *articlen, articulen* was borrowed perhaps through Old French *articuler* (1265) and Italian *articolare* (before 1321) to move parts of the body, from Latin *articulāre;* modern English *articulate* replaced earlier *articulen* and may have been borrowed directly from Latin *articulātus,* past participle of *articulare* to divide (meat, etc.) into joints, from *articulus,* diminutive of *artus* joint, see ART; for suffix see -ATE[1].

It is also possible that *articulate,* developing almost 140 years after *articulation,* is a back formation in English. —*adj.* 1586, uttered in distinct syllables; borrowed from Latin *articulātus* jointed, past participle of *articulāre* to divide into joints; for suffix see -ATE[1]. The sense of speaking clearly or intelligibly appeared in 1829.

artifact *n.* 1821 *artefact,* in writings of Coleridge, formed probably by influence of Italian *artefatto,* from Latin *arte,* ablative of *ars* art + *factus* made, past participle of *facere* to make, DO[1]. The form *artifact* appeared in English in 1884, probably an alteration of *artefact* influenced by Latin *arti-,* stem of *ars* art.

artifice *n.* clever device, trickery, craft. 1534, the making of anything by craft or skill, earlier (probably before 1425) *artificie* technical skill, art; borrowed through Anglo-French *artefice, artifice,* from Middle French *artifice* meaning "skill, cunning," learned borrowing from Latin *artificium* meaning "craft, employment, art, cunning," from *artifex* (genitive *artificis*) craftsman (*arti-,* stem of *ars* art + *facere* to make, DO[1] act).

The sense "clever stratagem, trick" first appeared in 1656.

artificial *adj.* About 1390, in Chaucer's *Canterbury Tales,* in the phrase *artificial day* meaning "the part of the day from sunrise to sunset," later (probably about 1425) meaning "made by man, not natural"; borrowed through Old French *artificial, artificiel,* from Latin *artificiālis* of or belong to art, from *artificium* art, skill, craft; for suffix see -AL[1].

artillery *n.* About 1390, in Chaucer's *Canterbury Tales,* Middle English *artelrie, artyllerye,* borrowed through Anglo-French *artillerie* and Medieval Latin *artillaria,* both forms from Old French *artillerie* implements of war, specifically ballistic machines to throw arrows or other missiles, from *artillier* equip (with implements of war); for suffix see -ERY.

Old French *artillier,* a spelling influenced by *art* skill, may derive from *atilier,* an alteration of *atirier* arrange (*a-* to, from Latin *ad-* + Old French *tire* order, rank); alternatively some sources refer the word to Medieval Latin *articula, articulum* art, skill, a diminutive form of Latin *ars* (genitive *artis*) art. This connection is not accepted by all authorities, however,

artisan *n.* craftsman. 1538, borrowed probably from Italian *artesano* (*arte* art, from Latin *artem* (nominative *ars*) + suffix *-esano,* from Latin *-ēnsiānus*); also compare Spanish *artesano* (about 1440); for suffix see -AN. Compare COURTESAN, PARTISAN.

Though Middle French *artisan* is often cited as the source for English, the word is not recorded in French before 1546 and was probably itself borrowed from Italian.

artist *n.* 1581, in Sidney's *Defence of Poesie,* borrowed from Middle French *artiste,* from Italian *artista,* from Medieval Latin *artista,* from Latin *ars* (genitive *artis*)

ART skill; for suffix see -IST. **—artistic** *adj.* 1753, in *Chambers Cyclopaedia,* formed from English *artist* + *-ic.*

The French source *artistique* traditionally cited is not recorded before 1808. **—artistry** *n.* 1868, in Robert Browning's *Ring and the Book,* formed from English *artist* + *-ry.*

-ary 1 a suffix forming nouns meaning: **a** a place for, as in *infirmary = a place for the infirm.* **b** a collection of, as in *statuary = a collection of statues.* **c** a person or thing that, as in *boundary = a thing that bounds or limits.*
2 suffix forming adjectives meaning: **a** of or having to do with, as in *legendary = of legend.* **b** being, having the nature of, as in *secondary = being second.* **c** characterized by, as in *customary = characterized by custom.*

Borrowed from Latin *-ārius* (feminine *-āria,* neuter *-ārium*), and in part influenced by Old French *-arie, -aire,* from Latin *-ārius.* The suffix *-ary* was also reinforced in English by many words that were direct borrowings from Latin, such as *infirmary* (from Medieval Latin *infirmaria*) and *statuary* (from Latin *statuāria*). On the other hand, words such as *cautionary* and *inflationary* are purely English formations.

Some loan words from French retain the French *-aire,* such as *concessionaire* from French *concessionnaire, solitaire* from French *solitaire, legionnaire* from French *légionnaire,* and *millionaire* from French *millionnaire.*

Aryan *adj.* 1847, earlier *Arian* (1839): referring to a national name 'comprising the worshippers of the gods of the Brahmans' (1861, by Max Müller), and also applied (1858, by Whitney; 1847, by Pritchard) to the Indo-European languages as a group, including Sanskrit which was associated with the Brahmans and Hindu literature. The word was borrowed through Latin *Ariānus* belonging to *Ariāna* or *Aria* and Greek *Areíā, Aríā* the eastern part of ancient Persia, from Sanskrit *Ārya-* (earlier *Āria-*) noble, the name the Sanskrit-speaking immigrants into India called themselves. The ancient Persians gave themselves the same title, Old Persian *Ariya-,* and it appears in Pahlevi and modern Persian *Iran.* Sanskrit *ā̀rya-s* honorable, respectable, meant originally "belonging to the hospitable," a derivative of *aryà-s* lord, hospitable lord, originally "protecting the stranger," from *arí-s* stranger, earlier **alí-s,* cognate with Latin *ali-quis* someone, *aliēnus* strange, foreign (Pok.24,25).

The spelling *Aryan,* argued by some to be *Arian* as more closely representing the earlier Sanskrit form *āria-,* was used by the scholars William Dwight Whitney and A.H. Sayce and by Friedrich Max Müller in the 1850's and following, but was gradually replaced by what is now the standard term *Indo-European* (first attested for this group of languages in 1814).
—n. 1601 *Arian,* in Holland's translation of Pliny's *Natural History.*

The term was later popularized by Max Müller (1861) and used from then until the 1940's, when it began to die out because of the repugnance of its use associated with Hitler's racism of the 1930's and 1940's.

as, *adv., prep., conj., pron.* Probably before 1200 *ase* and earlier *als, alse,* developed as weakened phonetic forms of Old English *ealswā, allswā* (before 950) meaning "all so, wholly so, quite so," in which *swā* meaning "so" was a demonstrative adverb qualified by the intensive adverb *all.* Through weakening of force and accent *allswā* gradually became *alsa, alse, als, ase,* finally being reduced to *as.* Historically *as* is equivalent to *so* and has all the relational uses of *so,* the differences being largely idiomatic. With many common adjectives and adverbs, *as* was formerly written in combination (*asmuch, aswell, assoon*) and survives in *forasmuch, inasmuch, whereas.* Doublet of ALSO.

as- a form of the prefix *ad-,* meaning to, toward, before *s,* as in *assign.* Formed in Latin by assimilation of *d* to the following consonant *(s).*

asbestos *n.* 1607 *asbest,* 1658 *asbestos* mineral that does not burn, borrowed from Latin *asbestos,* and replacing earlier *albeston* applied to quicklime (before 1387, in Trevisa's translation of Higden's *Polychronicon*), still earlier *abestus* (before 1100). These Middle English forms were borrowed from Old French *abeste, abeston, albeston* and Medieval Latin *albeston,* from Latin *asbestos,* from Greek *ásbestos* unquenchable (*a-* not + *sbestós,* verbal adjective of *sbennýnai* to quench), cognate with Sanskrit *jásate* is exhausted, Lithuanian *gèsti* be extinguished, and Old High German *quist* ruin, from Indo-European **gwes-/sgwes-* (Pok.479).

The Latin word was mistakenly applied by Pliny to a noncombustible mineral capable of being woven into a fabric and originally thought to be a vegetable. In English the word originally referred to the phenomena observed when pouring cold water on quick lime (the "unquenchable" stone).

ascend *n.* Before 1382, in the Wycliffe Bible, borrowed from Anglo-French *ascendre* and from Latin *ascendere* (*a-* to, up, variant of *ad-* before *sc* + *scandere* to climb). Latin *scandere* is cognate with Middle Irish *sescaind* he sprang, Sanskrit *skāndati* leaps, Greek *skándalon* trap, *skandálēthron* the bait-stick in a trap, which when touched by an animal springs up and shuts the trap, from Indo-European **skand-* (Walde-Hofmann, *Lateinisches etymologisches Wörterbuch* II, 488). **—ascendant** *n., adj.* About 1380 *ascendent,* in Chaucer's *House of Fame;* 1548 *ascendant* borrowed from Middle French *ascendant* and from Latin *ascendentem* (nominative *ascendēns*), present participle of *ascendere;* for suffix see -ANT. **—ascension** *n.* Before 1333, borrowed from Anglo-French *ascensium* and from Latin *ascēnsiōnem* (nominative *ascēnsiō*), from *ascēnsus,* past participle of *ascendere;* for suffix see -SION. **—ascent** *n.* 1600, In Philemon Holland's translation of Livy's *Roman History,* formed in English from *ascend,* on the analogy of earlier *descend, descent.*

ascertain *v.* find out with certainty. 1417 *assertenyng* a giving assurance, later *ascertenen* to inform, give assurance (1425, in *Proceedings of the Privy Council*); borrowed through Anglo-French *acerteiner* from Old French *acertener* (*a-* to, from Latin *ad-*) + *(certener,* from *certain* CERTAIN*).* The modern meaning of *ascertain* is not attested until the 1700's.

The introduction of the *s* in the 1400's and 1500's is a mistaken attempt to Latinize the word as though formed from Latin *as-,* variant of *ad-* before *s* or *c* + *certus* certain.

ascetic *adj.* practicing self-denial; austere. 1646, borrowed from Greek *askētikós* laborious, from *askētḗs* hermit, monk; an earlier meaning in Greek was "one who practices a spiritual exercise to attain perfection and virtue," which developed from a still earlier meaning "one who practices any art or trade," from *askeîn* to exercise (of uncertain origin); for suffix see -IC. **—n.**

1660, noun use of *ascetic,* adj. —**asceticism** *n.* 1646, formed from English *ascetic* + *-ism.*

ascorbic acid vitamin C. 1933, formed from English *a-*[4] not + *scorbutic* (1655) having to do with scurvy, affected with scurvy, borrowed from New Latin *scorbuticus,* from *scorbutus* scurvy, from French *scorbut,* from Russian *skrobota,* through some Germanic language.

ascot *n.* 1908 *ascot tie,* developed in English from *Ascot,* an English village and racetrack, scene of an annual horse race attended by royalty, at which guests in the royal enclosure are fashionably dressed, some of the men wearing cutaways and a type of neckwear somewhat like a short silk scarf. Later a colorful type of this tie was worn with any dress shirt open at the collar. Before 1957 *ascot* replaced *ascot tie,* especially in the United States.

ascribe *v.* Probably before 1425 *ascriben,* in a translation of Higden's *Polychronicon,* developed by influence of Latin *ascrībere* as a replacement of earlier *ascriven,* first recorded about 1340 in Rolle's translation of the *Book of Psalms.* Middle English *ascriven* was borrowed from Old French *ascrivre* to attribute, inscribe, from Latin *ascrībere, adscrībere,* originally meaning "to write in, inscribe," later "to attribute" (*ad-* to + *scrībere* write; see SCRIBE).

The form *ascriven* continued to be used in English as an occasional form or in a derivative word, such as *ascrivable,* into the 1600's.

—**ascription** *n.* 1597, borrowed from Latin *ascriptiōnem* (nominative *ascrīptiō*), from *ascrībere* ascribe; for suffix see -TION.

-ase a suffix used in organic chemistry to name enzymes, such as *maltase = an enzyme that decomposes malt. -Ase* is a form abstracted from *diastase,* adopted in French from Greek *diástasis* separation.

ash[1] *n.* remains after burning. Middle English *asshe, esse,* usually in the plural *asshen, esken,* developed from Old English (before 800) *æsce, asce, esce.* The Old English is cognate with Old High German *asca* ash (modern German *Asche*), Old Icelandic *aska,* earlier Dutch *asch* (now *as*), Danish *aske,* Swedish *aska,* from Proto-Germanic **askōn,* Indo-European **asgōn-;* Gothic *azgō,* is from Proto-Germanic **azgōn,* Indo-European **asghōn-* (Pok.69); these are cognate with Latin *ārēre* be dry; see ARID.

ash[2] *n.* a tree of Europe, western Asia, and North Africa well-known for the tough, springy qualities of its wood used in various implements, and mentioned widely in older literature, especially as a shaft for a spear. Middle English *asshe, assh, ash,* developed from Old English *æsc* spear made of ash wood (about 725, in *Beowulf*). The word is cognate with Old High German *ask* ash tree (modern German *Esche,* earlier *Asche*), Old Icelandic *askr* ash, spear, boat, Swedish, Danish, Norwegian *ask* ash, box or container, Middle Dutch *essce* (modern Dutch *es,* earlier *esch*), all of these forms implying Proto-Germanic **askaz* or **askiz,* from Indo-European **os-k-.* Outside the Germanic languages it is cognate with Greek *oxýē, oxýā* beech (altered from earlier **oskíā* by influence of *oxýs* pungent, acid), Armenian *haçi* ash tree, Albanian *ah* beech; Old Irish *(h)uinnius,* Welsh *onn* ash trees, Latin *ornus* (earlier **osenos*) mountain ash; Lithuanian *úosis* ash tree, Latvian *uôsis,* Old Prussian *woasis,* Russian *yasen',* from Indo-European **ōs, ōs-i-s,ōsen-, os(e)n-, osk-* (Pok.782).

ashamed *adj.* Old English (before 1000) *āsceamod,* past participle of *āsceamian* feel shame (*a-* a-[5] + *sceamu* SHAME).

asinine *adj.* stupid, silly. About 1610, borrowed from Latin *asinīnus* of or like an ass, from *asinus* ASS, also dolt, blockhead; for suffix see -INE[1].

The meaning "of or having to do with an ass or asses" is recorded in English later than the meaning "characteristic of an ass or asses, stupid, silly," but note that the meaning "stupid" is also in Latin. In Old French and Middle French *asinin* adj. meant "pertaining to asses" and French *asinine* appeared in the 1500's, but it does not seem to be connected to the English borrowing.

ask *v.* Old English *āhsian* (before 725), *ācsian* (before 800), *āscian* (about 885). In Old English the word is cognate with Old Frisian *āskia* to request, demand, ask, Old Saxon *ēscōn,* Old High German *eiscōn, heiscōn,* from Proto-Germanic **aiskōjanan,* and with Latin *aeruscāre* beg, request, Old Slavic *iskati* to seek, and Sanskrit *iccháti* he seeks, desires, from Indo-European **ais-/is-* (Pok.16).

The Old English variant, *ācsian* (formed by interchanging the consonants) or *axian,* became *axen* in Middle English and later *ax,* which was an accepted literary form of the verb until about 1600, and survives to this day in dialectal speech. Forms of *asken* are frequent in literary Middle English beside *axen,* and *ask* occurs in the late 1500's, especially in Shakespeare.

askance *adv.* 1530, sideways, obliquely, askew, developed from earlier *ascaunce,* conjunction, meaning "as if, pretending that," about 1395 in Chaucer's *Canterbury Tales;* Middle English *ascaunce* appears to be an alteration of earlier *ase quances* meaning "in such a way that, even as" (before 1333), formed from *ase* as, and a borrowing from Old French *quanses* as though, from Latin *quamsī,* variant of *quasi* as if, as it were; see QUASI.

Though contrary to most sources, this etymology through the earliest forms cited in English follows the semantic and structural evidence of the Middle English Dictionary.

asp[1] *n.* poisonous snake. 1526, in Tyndale's translation of the Bible, borrowed perhaps through Middle and Old French *aspe, aspis,* or more likely directly from Latin *aspis,* from Greek *aspís,* of uncertain origin. The Latin and Old French form *aspis* was used in English from the 1300's until the early 1500's.

asp[2] *n. Poetic.* aspen, poplar tree. Old English (about 700) *æspe, æpse,* a word cognate with Old High German *aspa* aspen (modern German *Espe*), Old Icelandic *ǫsp,* Swedish, Danish, Norwegian *asp,* Dutch *esp,* from Proto-Germanic **aspō,* Latvian *apse,* Old Prussian *abse,* Lithuanian *apušē;* all from an Indo-European base **apsā,* (Pok.55), though the Germanic words have undergone a metathesis: *-sp-* for the original *-ps-.*

asparagus *n.* Before 1398, Middle English *asperages, aspergy,* in Trevisa's translation of Bartholomew's *De Proprietatibus Rerum;* borrowed from Old French *asperge, asparge* and Medieval Latin **asperagi,* from Latin *asparagus,* from Greek *aspáragos, aspháragos,* probably borrowed from some foreign source.

The current form is a reborrowing about 1597 of Latin *asparagus* and replaced the earlier *sparage, sperge* (existing probably before 1300), borrowed through Anglo-Latin *spargus* (before 1250), from Medieval Latin *sparagus, sparagi* (alterations of Latin *asparagus*).

In the mid 1500's when the asparagus plant became familiar, a shortened form *'sparagus* displaced *sperage, sparage.* This short form was then itself altered by folk etymology (before 1650) to *sparagrass, sparrow-grass.* During the early 1800's the spelling *asparagus* gained ground so that by the late 1800's it was the popular form.

aspect *n.* About 1385, meaning "relative position in planets as they appear," in Chaucer's *Canterbury Tales;* borrowed from Latin *aspectus* (genitive *aspectūs*) seeing, look, appearance, from *aspec-,* stem of *aspicere, adspicere* look at (*ad-* at + *specere* to look; see SPY).

aspen *n.* the poplar tree, but originally confined to the European aspens. Used as an adjective about 1385, in Chaucer's *Canterbury Tales,* especially in *aspen leaf,* the *-en* being an old adjective ending found in German *espen* and Old Frisian *ęspen;* or perhaps a survival of the old English genitive *æspan* of the ASP[2] (from about 1000).

Used as a noun in 1596 as *aspine,* in Spenser's *Faerie Queene,* and in 1703 as *aspen,* probably from the adjective misconstrued as a noun used attributively.

asperity *n.* harshness of manner; severity. Before 1535, in the works of Sir Thomas More; *asperity* is an alteration (influenced by Latin *asperitās*) of earlier *asperete,* in use probably before 1200, in *Ancrene Riwle;* borrowed from Old French *asperеté,* learned borrowing from Latin *asperitātem* (nominative *asperitās*), from *asper* rough, of uncertain origin; for suffix see -ITY.

aspersion *n.* 1448, meaning "shedding (of Christ's blood)"; borrowed from Latin *aspersiōnem* (nominative *aspersiō*), from *aspers-,* stem of *aspergere, adspergere* to sprinkle (*ad-* on + *spargere* to scatter; see SPARSE); for suffix see -SION.

A later meaning "the act of sprinkling with water, dust, etc." was extended by 1596, in Spenser's *A View of the Present State of Ireland* to mean "a damaging or false statement" and by 1633 "the action of casting such statements."

—asperse *v.* slander. 1490, in Caxton's *The Book of Eneydos,* meaning "to sprinkle (a person or thing) with dust, water, etc.," developing probably before 1611 to mean "spatter (a person or his character) with damaging reports," borrowed from Latin *aspersus,* past participle of *aspergere,* or perhaps a back formation in English from *aspersion.*

asphalt *n.* Before 1398, in Trevisa's translation of Bartholomew's *De Proprietatibus Rerum,* borrowed from Late Latin *asphaltum,* from Greek *ásphalton,* variant of *ásphaltos* (*a-* not + **sphaltós* able to be thrown down, so called from its use as a binding material assuring the solidity of walls; **sphaltós* is taken to be a verbal adjective of *sphállein* to throw down.

There was also *asphaltoun* (probably about 1380, in *Cleanness*), from the Greek *ásphalton.* Latinate *asphaltus, asphaltum,* and pseudo-Greek *asphaltos* were popular in the 1600's.

asphyxia *n.* suffocation. 1706, meaning "stoppage of the pulse," New Latin *asphyxia,* borrowed from Greek *asphyxíā* a stopping of the pulse (*a-* without + *sphýxis* pulse, from *sphýzein* to throb, of uncertain origin). The current sense appeared in 1778 and was regarded as a misnomer, because the original sense referred to the pulse, which in victims of suffocation continues long after the outward signs of respiratory action have ceased. **—asphyxiate** *v.* 1836, formed from English *asphyxia* + *-ate*[1]. **—asphyxiation** *n.* 1866, formed from English *asphyxia* + -TION.

aspic *n.* a gelatin made from meat or fish stock with tomato juice, etc., usually molded. 1789, borrowed from French *aspic* jelly, literally meaning "asp." The word *aspic* is an expansion of Old French *aspe,* influenced by *basilic* basilisk. The meaning in French may come from the phrase *froid comme un aspic,* meaning "cold, like an asp (serpent)," or from the various colors in the gelatin resembling those of the asp, or from the shape of the mold, usually curled like a serpent. See ASP[1].

aspirate (as′pərāt) *v.* pronounce with a breathing or *h*-sound prefixed, added, or blended. Before 1700, in writings of Dryden, borrowed probably through influence of earlier French *aspirer* (1529) to aspirate in pronunciation, from Latin *aspīrātus,* past participle of *aspīrāre, adspīrāre* breathe upon, see ASPIRE; for suffix see -ATE[1].

Note however that *aspiration,* Middle English *aspiracioun,* referring to pronunciation, existed probably before 1398, as recorded in Trevisa's translation of Bartholomew's *De Proprietatibus Rerum;* see ASPIRATION at ASPIRE. This points to an incomplete record of English or *aspirate* as a back formation of *aspiration.* It is also possible that Dryden or some author of his time is responsible for borrowing directly from the Latin verb form *aspīrāre.*

aspire *v.* desire earnestly. Before 1400, borrowed from Old French *aspirer* aspire to, inspire, from Latin *aspīrāre, adspīrāre* breathe upon, seek to reach (*ad-* to, upon + *spīrāre* breathe; see SPIRIT). **—aspiration** *n.* Probably before 1398, meaning "act of aspirating;" probably about 1425, meaning "inspiration;" borrowed from Old French *aspiration* divine inspiration, from Latin *aspīrātiōnem* (nominative *aspīrātiō*), from *aspīrāre* aspire; for suffix see -TION. The meaning "earnest desire" appeared in 1606, in Shakespeare's *Troylus and Cressida.*

See note at *aspirate.*

aspirin *n.* Probably before 1922, borrowed (1899) as a trademark in German *Aspirin,* from *A(cetylirte) (säure)* acetylated spiraeic acid + *-in*[2] (chemical suffix). Spiraeic acid is an old name of salicylic acid, originally obtained from the leaves of *Spiraea ulmaria.*

ass *n.* Old English *assa,* masculine (before 830, in the *Vespasian Psalter*); *assen,* feminine (about 1000); *assan,* plural; perhaps developed from either (1) the source of Middle Welsh *asen,* or (2) from Middle Irish *assan.* Old English *assa,* whether it came through these Celtic forms or not, is ultimately borrowed from Latin *asinus* (masculine), *asina* (feminine), from a language of Asia Minor (compare Greek *ónos,* Armenian *ēš,* Sumerian *anšu* ass). If, as is likely from Latin *asinus,* the original form of the Greek word was **osonos,* that would have yielded first **ohonos,* then **hoonos,* at which point it was evidently construed as *ho ōnos* the ass.

The masculine and feminine forms in Old English were superseded in Middle English (before 1382, in Wycliffe's translation of the Bible) by *he-ass* and *she-ass.* The usual equivalents now are jackass and jenny ass.

assail *v.* Probably before 1200, in *Ancrene Riwle,* borrowed from Old French *assaillier, asaillir,* from Vulgar Latin **assalīre,* alteration of Latin *assilīre* to leap at (*as-*

at, variant of *ad-* before *s* + *salīre* to leap; see SALLY). **—assailant** *n.* About 1532, borrowed from Middle French *assaillant,* present participle of *assaillir,* from Old French *assaillier.* English *assailant* gradually replaced earlier *assailer, assailour* (recorded before 1400); borrowed from Old French *assailleur,* from *assaillier* ASSAIL.

assassin *n.* 1531, meaning "murderer," borrowed through Middle French *assassin* (Old French *assassis* hashish eaters who committed murder) and through Italian *assassino* murderer (earlier meaning "hashish eater"), from Arabic *hashshāshīn,* literally, hasish eaters, in reference to a religious and military order located chiefly in the mountains of Lebanon, who were remarkable for their secret murders in blind obedience to their leader, a condition brought on because the members selected to commit a murder, especially of a king or public figure, were first intoxicated with hashish. The term in current use still refers chiefly to a murderer of a public figure.

The singular form was established before the word was borrowed into English but in all cases is based on the Arabic plural form, as are the words (Arabic) *Bedouin,* (Hebrew) *cherubim* and *seraphim.*

—assassinate *v.* 1618, perhaps borrowed by influence of French *assassiner* to murder, from Medieval Latin *assassinatus,* past participle of *assassinare* to assassinate.

Assassinate could also be a back formation of earlier *assassination.* **—assassination** *n.* 1605, in Shakespeare's *Macbeth,* formed in English, probably from French *assassinat* assassination + English *-ion.*

assault *n.* 1375, in John Barbour's *The Bruce,* alteration of earlier *asaut* (probably before 1200, in *Ancrene Riwle*); borrowed from Old French *asaut, assaut,* from Vulgar Latin **assaltus* assault, attack, alteration of Latin *assultus* (genitive *assultūs*), from stem *assul-* of *assilīre, adsilīre* leap at, assail (*as-* at, variant of *ad-* before *s* + *salīre* to leap); see SALLY.

The original English form *asaut* was altered to *saulte* (1530, in Palsgrave's *Lesclarcissement*) after the Latin form, as in *fault, vault.* However, Palsgrave reads: *make a saulte.* The *a* could be the article *a* but could just as well be part of *assaulte,* incorrectly divided by the printer.

—v. About 1410, *asauten* to attack, assault, borrowed from Middle French *asauter, assauter,* from Vulgar Latin **assaltāre* (Latin *as-* at, variant of *ad-* before *s* + *saltāre* to leap).

assay *n.* analysis to determine the quantity of metal in an ore. Before 1338, in Mannyng's *Chronicle of England,* a trying, trial, ordeal; borrowed through Anglo-French *assai,* alteration (influenced by the prefix *a-* to, from Latin *ad-*) of Old French *essai* trial; see the doublet ESSAY. The current sense appeared about 1386 (in Chaucer's *Canterbury Tales*).

—v. Probably before 1300, *assaien* to try, borrowed from Anglo-French *assaer, assaier,* from *assai, n.*

assemble *v.* Before 1325 (but used as a gerund *assemblinge* meaning "a coming together, gathering or meeting" about 1300); borrowed through Anglo-French from Old French *assembler,* from Vulgar Latin **assimulāre* bring together (Latin *as-* to, variant of *ad-* before *s* + *simul* together, at the same time; see SAME). **—assembly** *n.* Probably before 1300, in *Kyng Alisaunder,* borrowed through Anglo-French *assemblé,* from Old French *assemblée,* feminine past participle of *assembler* assemble; for suffix see -Y[3]. **—assembly line** (1914, American English).

assent *v.* give consent. About 1300, borrowed through Anglo-French *assentir,* from Old French *assentir, assenter,* from Latin *assentārī,* serving as a frequentative form to *assentīre* (*as-* to, along with, variant of *ad-* before *s* + *sentīre* feel, think; see SENSE). **—n.** Probably before 1300, in *Kyng Alisaunder,* borrowed from Old French *assent,* from *assentir,* v.

assert *v.* state positively, declare. Before 1604, formed in English either as (1) a word modeled on Latin, as if borrowed from Latin *assertus,* past participle of *asserere* claim (rights over something), state, but originally meaning "attach to oneself" (*as-* to, variant of *ad-* before *s* + *serere* join, put; see SERIES). The meaning in Latin "to lay claim," is said to have arisen from the practice among the Romans of laying one's hand on a slave and declaring the slave free (*asserere in libertatem*), or in servitude (*asserere in servitutem*); or (2) a word created by back formation from earlier *assertion.* **—assertion** *n.* 1424, borrowed through Middle French *assertion,* or directly from Late Latin *assertiōnem* (nominative *assertiō*), from Latin *asserere* claim (rights over something); for suffix see -TION. **—assertive** *adj.* 1562, formed in English as if from Medieval Latin **assertivus,* from Latin past participle *assertus;* for suffix see -IVE.

assess *v.* 1423, in *Rolls of Parliament,* borrowed through Anglo-French *assesser,* from Medieval Latin *assessare* fix a tax upon, originally a frequentative form of Latin *assidēre* sit, especially as assistant judge or assessor, literally meaning "to sit beside another" (*as-* to, by, variant of *ad-* before *s* + *sedēre* sit; see SIT and compare ASSIZE). **—assessment** *n.* 1548, formed from English *assess* + *-ment.* **—assessor** *n.* 1427, in *Rolls of Parliament,* borrowed through Anglo-French from Old French *assessour,* or directly from Latin *assessōrem* (nominative *assessor*) a tax assessor, earlier meaning "an assistant judge," from *assess-,* stem of *assidēre* sit, especially as assessor.

assets *n.pl.* things of value; property. 1531, sufficient estate to pay off debts and legacies, borrowed through Anglo-French *assez, assetz,* from Old French *assez, asez* enough, from Vulgar Latin phrase **ad satis* to sufficiency (Latin *ad* to + *satis* enough; see SAD).

The English use originated in the Anglo-French legal phrase *aver assetz* to have enough (to meet a claim), from which *assets* as a technical term later passed into general use. It was originally singular but because of the final *-s* in imitation of the pronunciation (asets) in French and its collective sense, *assets* came to be treated as a plural, with the singular *asset* appearing in the 1800's.

assiduity *n.* careful and steady attention, diligence. Probably before 1425, persistence, continual recurrence, in: (1) translation of Chauliac's *Grande Chirurgie,* borrowed through Old French *assiduité,* from Latin *assiduitātem* (nominative *assiduitās*); and (2) a translation of Higden's *Polychronicon,* borrowed from Latin *assiduitās,* from *assiduus* sitting down to, constantly occupied, unremitting, from *assidēre* sit at or near (*ad-* at + *sedēre* SIT); for suffix see -ITY. **—assiduous** *adj.* careful and attentive, diligent. 1538, in Leland's *The Itinerary,* borrowed from Latin *assiduus,* from *assidēre* sit at; for suffix see -OUS.

The word *assidu* meaning "careful, diligent," appears in Old French in the 1200's but does not seem to have found a need in English.

assign *v.* About 1300, borrowed through Anglo-French from Old French *assigner,* a learned borrowing from Latin *assignāre* mark out (*as-* to, for, variant of *ad-* before *s* + *signāre* make a sign, mark, from *signum* mark; see SIGN. —**assignment** *n.* 1389, borrowed through Anglo-French from Old French *assignement,* from *assigner* assign; for suffix see -MENT); *or* formed in Middle English from earlier *assign* + *-ment.*

assimilate *v.* Probably before 1425, borrowed through influence of Old French *assimiler,* from Latin *assimilātus,* past participle of *assimilāre,* variant of *assimulāre* compare, liken (*as-* to, variant of *ad-* before *s* + *simulāre* make similar, imitate, from *similis* like); see SIMILAR; for suffix see -ATE[1]. —**assimilation** *n.* Probably before 1425, borrowed through Old French *assimilation,* from Latin *assimilātiōnem* (nominative *assimilātiō*), variant of *assimulātiōnem,* from *assimulāre* compare; for suffix see -TION.

assist *v.* 1426, in *Proceedings of the Privy Council,* borrowed through Middle French *assister,* a learned borrowing from Latin *assistere* to assist (*as-* to, by, variant of *ad-* before *s* + *sistere* take a stand, from *stāre* to stand; see STAND). —**n.** 1597, from the verb. —**assistance** *n.* 1424, in *Proceedings of the Privy Council,* borrowed from Middle French *assistance,* from *assister* to assist, and from Medieval Latin *assistentia* assistance, from Latin *assistere* to assist; for suffix see -ANCE. —**assistant** *n., adj.* 1433, in *Rolls of Parliament,* borrowed from Middle French *assistent,* present participle of *assister* to assist, and from Latin *assistentem* (nominative *assistēns*) assisting, present participle of *assistere* to assist; for suffix see -ANT.

assize (əsīz′) *n.* session of a law court. About 1300 *assise* session of a law court, a legal suit, a legal regulation, standard of quality or measure, custom or practice, in several sources including *Kyng Alisaunder,* various early chronicles, *Rolls of Parliament* etc.; borrowed through Anglo-French from Old French *assise* court session; also, a setting (of taxes, etc.), from the feminine past participle of Anglo-French *aseeir,* later Old French *asseoir* to sit at, settle, assess, from Medieval Latin *assedere* sit at, alteration of Latin *assidēre;* see ASSESS.

associate (əsō′shēit) *adj.* Probably before 1425, developed from past participle *associat* associated; the past participial form in English was borrowed from Latin *associātus,* past participle of *associāre* join with (*as-* to, variant of *ad-* before *s* + *sociāre* keep company or join with, from *socius* companion; see SOCIAL); for suffix see -ATE[1]. —**v.** (əsō′shēāt) About 1450, gradually replacing earlier *associen* (in existence about 1383 in writings of Wycliffe). The form *associate* is a verb use of the Middle English past participle *associat,* later an adjective, that was borrowed from Latin *associātus,* past participle of *associāre* join with. The earlier Middle English *associen* was borrowed through Old French *associer, associier,* from Latin *associāre.* —**n.** (əsō′shēit) 1533, in Sir Thomas More's *The Apology Made by Him,* developed from *associate,* adj. used absolutely. —**association** *n.* 1535, borrowed perhaps through Middle French *association,* or directly from Medieval Latin *associationem* (nominative *associatio*), from Latin *associāre* join with; for suffix see -TION. —**associative** *adj.* 1812, in writings of Coleridge, formed from English *associate* + *-ive.*

assonance *n.* resemblance in sound. 1727, in *Chambers Cyclopaedia,* borrowed from French *assonance,* from Latin *assonāre* respond to, sound in answer (*as-* to, variant of *ad-* before *s* + *sonāre* to sound); for suffix see -ANCE.

assort *v.* sort out; classify (now used chiefly in the form *assorted* as an adjective, first found before 1797 in writings of Burke). 1490, in Caxton's *The Book of Eneydos,* borrowed from Middle French *assortir,* from Old French *assorter* (*a-* to, from Latin *ad-*) + (*sorte* kind, SORT). —**assortment** *n.* 1611, formed from English *assort* + *-ment,* probably influenced in its formation by earlier French *assortiment* (1532).

assuage (əswāj′) *v.* make easier or milder. About 1300 *aswagen, asswagen;* borrowed through Anglo-French *asuager, assuager, asswager,* from Old French *assouagier,* from Northern Gallo-Romance **assuāviāre* (from Latin *as-* to, variant of *ad-* before *s* + *suāvis* sweet, agreeable; see SWEET).

The development of the sound represented by *vi* in *assuāviāre* to /dʒ/ represented by *g* in Old French *cage* is parallel to the development in Old French of *déluge* from Latin *dīluvium* and *abregier* to abridge, from *abbreviāre.*

assume *v.* Before 1420, in Lydgate's *Troy Book,* borrowed from Latin *assūmere* take up, receive, assume (*as-* to, up, variant of *ad-* before *s* + *sūmere* to take, formed from **sus-* (from earlier **subs-,* variant of *sub-* up) + *emere* to take; see REDEEM). —**assumption** *n.* About 1300, *Assumpcion* the taking up of the Virgin Mary to heaven, borrowed perhaps through Anglo-French *asompcyon,* or directly from Old French *assumpcion, assomption* and from Latin *assūmptiōnem* (nominative *assūmptiō*) a taking up, adoption, from *assūmere* take up; for suffix see -TION. See also CONSUMPTION.

assure *v.* About 1375, in Chaucer's *Anelida and Arcite;* borrowed from Old French *aseürer,* from Vulgar Latin **assēcūrāre* (from Latin *as-* to, variant of *ad-* before *s* + *sēcūrus* safe, SECURE). —**assurance** *n.* About 1385, in Chaucer's *Canterbury Tales,* borrowed from Old French *aseürance,* from *aseürer* assure; for suffix see -ANCE.

aster *n.* plant having daisylike flowers. 1706, New Latin *aster,* from Latin *astēr* star, aster, starflower, from Greek *astḗr* star; see STAR.

The original meaning in English was "star," borrowed from Latin (1603), but now obsolete.

asterisk *n.* the star-shaped mark (*). Before 1382 *asterich,* in Prologue to the Wycliffe Bible; before 1387 *asterisc,* in Trevisa's translation of Higden's *Polychronicon;* borrowed from Late Latin *asteriscus,* from Greek *asterískos,* literally, little star, diminutive of *astḗr* (genitive *astéros*) star; see STAR.

asteroid *n.* any of the thousands of very small objects that orbit the sun. 1802, borrowed from Greek *asteroeidḗs* starlike (*astḗr,* genitive *astéros,* star + *eîdos* form).

asthma *n.* Before 1398, *asma,* in Trevisa's translation of Bartholomew's *De Proprietatibus Rerum;* borrowed, perhaps by influence of Old French *asmat,* from Latin *asthma* (genitive *asthmatis*), from Greek *ásthma* panting, probably related to Greek *áēmi* I breathe hard, blow, and *ánemos* wind; see ANIMAL.

The introduction of *th* to the spelling in English oc-

curred in the 1500's in an effort to restore Latinate forms to English.
—asthmatic *adj.* 1542, borrowed from Latin *asthmaticus,* from Greek *asthmatikós,* from *ásthma* (genitive *ásthmatos*); for suffix see -IC.

astigmatism (əstig'mətizəm) *n.* eye defect that prevents focusing. 1849, formed from English *a-* without + Greek *stígmat-* (stem of *stígma* mark, spot) + English suffix *-ism;* see STIGMA. The word was coined by the English scientist and philosopher William Whewell, 1794-1866, while he was Master of Trinity College. **—astigmatic** (as'tigmat'ik) *adj.* 1849, formed at the same time as *astigmatism* from English *a-* without + Greek *stígmat-* + English suffix *-ic.*

astonish *v.* 1530, in Palsgrave's *Lesclarcissement,* alteration of Middle English *astonen, astonien, astounen, astunen* (in existence probably before 1300); borrowed from Old French *estoner, estuner* to stun, astonish, from Vulgar Latin **extonāre* (Latin *ex-* out + *tonāre* to thunder). The Vulgar Latin **extonāre* corresponds to Latin *attonāre* to strike with a thunderbolt, stun, stupefy (*at-* to, variant of *ad-* before *t* + *tonāre* to thunder); see THUNDER.

The alteration of Middle English *astonen* to *astonish* may have been influenced by a pattern of verbs already existing in *-ish,* e.g. *admonish, distinguish, famish;* no form now is known to have existed in Old French *estoner* to supply the *-iss-* that traditionally evolved into the English verb suffix *-ish.* **—astonishment** *n.* 1576, formed from English *astonish* + *-ment.*

astound *v.* 1600, developed from Middle English *astouned, astoned,* (in existence probably before 1300), past participle of *astounen, astonen* to stun, astonish; see ASTONISH.

Astonish is taken from the verb *astonen, astounen,* while *astound* developed from the past participle *astouned, astoned* of the same verb *astounen, astonen.*

astrakhan (as'trəkən) *n.* fine fur and skin of young lambs. 1766, adopted in English from *Astrakhan,* a city and region in southern Russia, on the Volga, where this lambskin is produced from the very young or still-born lambs of that region.

astral *adj.* of the stars. 1605, borrowed from Late Latin *astrālis,* from Latin *astrum* star, from Greek *ástron,* see STAR; for suffix see -AL[1].

astray *adv., adj.* Middle English *astrai, o stray* (before 1325, in *Cursor Mundi*); earlier *astraied,* past participle (about 1300); borrowed from Old French *estraié* strayed, past participle of *estraier, estrayer;* see STRAY.

The loss of the initial *e* in borrowing from Old French *estraié* gave rise to a belief that the word was formed in English from *a-*[1] + *stray,* n., but no earlier English noun form *stray* has been found. Originally Middle English *astrai* was a past participle *astraied* and developed into a prepositional phrase and later an adverb, being confused with forms like *afloat, asleep, aloft.*

astringent (əstrin'jənt) *adj.* shrinking or contracting. 1541, in Copland's translation of Galen's *Terapeutyke,* borrowed from Latin *astringentem* (nominative *astringēns*), present participle of *astringere* bind fast (*a-* to, from *ad-* + *stringere* to tie, bind; see STRAIN[1] stretch).

astro-, a combining form meaning: **1** star or other heavenly body or bodies, as in *astrophysics = the study of the physics* (temperature, size, density) *of heavenly bodies.* **2** outer space, space travel, as in *astronautics = science of space travel.* Appearing by 1740 as a combining form in English abstracted from a host of earlier words, such as *astronomy* (before 1200), *astrology* (1375), and ultimately borrowed from Greek *astro-,* from *ástron* star; see STAR.

astrobleme (as'trəblēm) *n.* scar on the earth's surface from a meteorite. 1961, formed in English from *astro-* heavenly body + Greek *blêma* throw of a missile, or the resulting wound, from *bállein* to throw, hit; see BALL[2] dance.

astrolabe (as'trəlāb) *n.* astronomical instrument for measuring altitude of the sun or stars, precursor of the sextant. About 1390 *astrelabie,* in Chaucer's *Canterbury Tales;* borrowed through Anglo-French from Old French *astrelabe,* a learned borrowing of Medieval Latin *astrolabium,* from Greek *astrolábos* celestial sphere, originally meaning "taking (position of) stars" (*astro-* star + *lambánein* to take). The form *astrolabe* is a remodeling after the Latin.

astrology *n.* 1375 *astrologie,* in John Barbour's *The Bruce,* the medieval study of heavenly bodies, practical astronomy; borrowed from Old French *astrologie,* and from Latin *astrologia* astronomy, from Greek *astrologíā,* from *astrológos* astronomer (*astro-* star + *-lógos* treating of, from *légein* speak of; see LEGEND); for fuller explanation of suffix see -LOGY. See note at ASTRONOMY. **—astrologer** *n.* About 1385, in Chaucer's *Canterbury Tales,* used in the phrase *comune astrologer* in reference to the cock as announcer of sunrise; formed in English after Latin *astrologus* astrologer + English suffix *-er.* Another form *astrologien* (about 1400, in Chaucer's *Treatise on the Astrolabe*) was for a time contemporaneous with *astrologer.*

astronaut *n.* 1929, but widely popularized in 1961, traveler in outer space, formed in English from *astro-* the heavens, outer space + *-naut,* from Greek *naútēs* sailor; see NAUTICAL. An earlier use, *Astronaut* (1880) was the name of a fictional spaceship, and therefore the ending *-naut* was patterned on earlier formations, others of which include *aeronaut* (1784) and *aquanaut* (1881). **—astronautics** *n.* art or science of space vehicles or space flight. 1929, borrowed from French *astronautique,* coined by J.H. Rosny aîné, French writer, in 1927, on the pattern of *aéronautique* aeronautics.

astronomy *n.* Probably before 1200 *astronomie,* borrowed from Old French *astronomie,* from Latin *astronomia,* from Greek *astronomíā,* from *astronómos* one who arranges or classifies the stars (*astro-* star + *-nómos* arranging, regulating, from *némein* administer, dictate the laws of, manage; see NIMBLE).

Originally *astronomy* included the observation of the stars and planets and their influence upon the tides, climate, and other natural phenomena, together with the supposed influence of the stars and planets on human affairs. In Medieval Latin, Old French, and for the most part in Middle English of the 1300's and 1400's the terms *astronomy* and *astrology* were interchangeable, but as the study of the stars and planets in relation to human destiny came into increasing dispute during the late 1400's, a distinction developed between scientific study of astronomy (called *natural astronomy*) and the philosophical study of human destiny (called *judicial astronomy* or *astrology*). The distinction became generally established in the 1600's. **—astronomer** *n.* Before 1398, in Trevisa's translation of

Bartholomew's *De Proprietatibus Rerum,* gradually replacing earlier *astronomien,* probably existing before 1300, *astromyen* in *Kyng Alisaunder;* formed in Middle English after Medieval Latin *astronomus* astronomer (from Greek *astronómos*) + English suffix *-er.*[1] The earlier *astronomien* was borrowed from Old French *astronomien.*

astrophysics *n.* Before 1890, perhaps as early as 1869, formed from English *astro-* + *physics.*

astute *adj.* 1611, borrowed perhaps through influence of Middle French *astu, astut,* from Latin *astūtus* crafty, cunning, from *astus* (genitive *astūs*) craft, guile, of uncertain origin.

asylum *n.* Probably before 1439, *asilum,* in Lydgate's *Falls of Princes,* place of refuge, sanctuary; borrowed from Latin *asȳlum* sanctuary, from Greek *ásylon* refuge, from the neuter of *ásȳlos* inviolable, safe from violence (*a-* without + *sȳlē* right of seizure, a word of uncertain origin). Middle English *asilum* was a Latinate replacement of earlier *asile* (about 1384), a borrowing from Old French.

The meaning of an institute for special care, as of the insane or orphans, appeared in 1776.

at *prep.* Old English (before 725) *æt,* from which Middle English *at* developed by about 1200. Old English *æt* is cognate with Old Saxon *at, æt,* Old High German *az,* Old Icelandic and Gothic *at,* Old Frisian *et,* and Latin *ad* to, from Indo-European **ad-* (Pok.3).

In Middle English *at* combined with the definite article to produce *atte, atten, attere* meaning "at the" and *attam* meaning "at them." *At* also formed a part of many verbs which are now obsolete, but is found in the Welsh prefix *add-* and was also found in Old Irish *ad-* and Gaulish *ad-.*

In modern German, *zu* (to) has replaced Old High German *az* (at); in Scandinavian, on the other hand, the word corresponding to English *to* has been lost, and its place largely taken by forms of Old Icelandic *at,* such as Swedish *åt.*

at- a form of the prefix *ad-,* meaning to, toward, before *t,* as in *attend, attest, attribute.* Formed in Latin by assimilation of *d* to the following consonant *(t).*

atavism (at'əvizəm) *n.* resemblance to a remote ancestor. 1833, borrowed from Latin *atavus* ancestor, great-grandfather's grandfather (*at-* an element of undetermined origin + *avus* grandfather; see UNCLE and AVUNCULAR); for suffix see -ISM.

Said to have been a borrowing of French *atavisme;* but the word is not recorded in French before 1838.

ataxia (ətak'sēə) *n.* inability to coordinate voluntary movements. 1878, borrowed possibly through French *ataxie,* or adopted directly as New Latin *ataxia,* especially in the phrase *locomotor ataxia,* from Greek *ataxíā* (*a-* without + *táxis* order, from a stem of *tássein* arrange, see TACTICS.

-ate[1] suffix forming: **1** adjectives meaning: **a** of or having to do with, as in *collegiate = having to do with college.* **b** having, containing, as in *compassionate = having compassion.* **c** having the form of, like, as in *stellate = having the form of a star.* **2** verbs meaning: **a** become, as in *maturate = become mature.* **b** cause to be, as in *alienate = cause to be alien.* **c** produce, as in *ulcerate = produce ulcers.* **d** supply or treat with, as in *aerate = treat with air.* **e** combine with, as in *oxygenate = combine with oxygen.* **3** nouns derived from adjectives or participial forms often already found in English with *-ate,* as in *delegate, mandate, prelate, advocate.*

The suffix *-ate* was borrowed into Middle English largely in words that are part of verb phrases (and only later as adjectives) by translation of Latin texts containing first-conjugation verbs with the past passive participial ending *-ātus* and infinitives ending in *-āre.*

Another path of borrowing was ultimately from Latin, but immediately by way of Old French forms ending in *-é,* as in *sené* senate, refashioned in Old French to *-at* as in *senat* in the 1200's and 1300's. In Middle English these words were originally adopted in their French form, as *senat,* but after 1400 an *-e* was added to show a long vowel sound in the suffix *-at,* and it appears that all forms borrowed from Old and Middle French took *-ate* thereafter.

The same process is evident in later forms taken from modern French where the infinitive ends in *-er* and the past participle in *-é.* Here English substitutes the suffix *-ate* as in French *aérer,* English *aerate,* and French *affectionné,* English *affectionate.*

Adjectives, such as *desolate,* came into English as participial adjectives (that is, where English would now say, "the land was desolated by war," the early usage would have been "the land was desolate by war"). This prompted the formation of many English verbs, such as *desolate* that had an equivalent Latin infinitive *dēsōlāre,* and the convention of making English verbs in *-ate* after Latin verbs in *-āre* became a common practice among writers so familiar with Latin as the medieval scribes and scholars.

Other adjectives are sometimes formed in English with *-ate* from Latin participial adjectives ending in *-ātus,* such as English *foliate* from Latin *foliātus.*

Some nouns are furnished in English from the participial forms in *-ate.* For instance, *associate,* the noun, meaning "a person associated with another," developed from the Middle English participial form *associat,* which was borrowed from Latin *associātus.* Other words were originally adjectives; while many more were borrowed from nouns that already existed in Latin or were created after the pattern of fourth-declension nouns in Latin.

-ate[2] a suffix in chemical terms, denoting a salt formed by reaction of an acid with a base, such as *nitrate* from nitric acid. A specialized use of *-ate*[1], in that it is a particular application of the adjective form that takes the place of older chemical terminology, as in the forms *acetatum,* now *acetate.*

-ate[3] a suffix forming nouns naming an occupation, position, condition or the like, or the persons serving or being in it, such as *consulate = office of a consul, professorate = position of a professor.*

Borrowed from Latin *-ātus,* ending of fourth-declension nouns that have genitive ending *-ātūs.* This is not a part of the noun formations under *-ate*[1].

atheism *n.* 1587, borrowed from Middle French *athéisme,* from Greek *átheos* denying the gods (*a-* without + *theós* a god + Middle French *-isme* -ism). —**atheist** *n.* 1571, borrowed from Middle French *athéiste,* from Greek *átheos* + Middle French *-iste* -ist. —**atheistic** *adj.* 1634, formed from English *atheist* + suffix *-ic.*

athlete *n.* Probably before 1425 *athletez,* borrowed probably from Greek *āthlētḗs.* 1528 *athelete,* borrowed from Latin *āthlēta,* from Greek *āthlētḗs* contestant, combatant, from *āthleîn* contend, compete for a prize, from *âthlos* (earlier *áethlos*) contest, and *âthlon* (earlier *áethlon*) prize, contest; of uncertain origin. —**athletic** *adj.* 1636, borrowed probably from Latin *āthlēticus,* from Greek *āthlētikós,* from *āthlētḗs* athlete; for suffix see -IC.

The borrowing from Latin may have been influenced by earlier French *athlétique* (1534). —**athletics** *n.* 1727-51, in *Chambers Cyclopaedia,* formed from English *athletic* + *-s* on analogy with *gymnastics* (1652); for suffix see -ICS.

-athon or **-thon** a combining form abstracted from *marathon* meaning "any prolonged or extended activity, event, etc., of a specified kind, usually involving endurance," as in *walkathon* (1932), *talkathon* (1948), and *telethon* (1952); very productive in the United States since about 1972 in forming nonce words such as *bikeathon, singathon, workathon,* etc. The form *-athon* is used after a consonant, while *-thon* follows a vowel, as in *discothon.*

-ation a suffix forming nouns, and meaning act or state of ____ing, as in *admiration;* condition or state of being ____ed, as in *agitation;* result of ____ing, as in *civilization.* English *-ation* was borrowed from Latin *-ātiōnem* (nominative *-ātiō*) which is formed of *-ā-* (stem of verbs ending in *-āre,* such as Latin *ōrāre,* English *orate*) + *-tiōnem* (accusative of noun suffix *-tiō* -TION).

Often *-ation* is a spelling replacement of Middle English *-acion, -acioun,* borrowed from Old French *-aciun,* from Latin *-ātiōnem,* and forms nouns from a wide variety of words modeled on derivatives from Latin and French (*create, creation* and *moderate, moderation*), but for some there is no underlying verb form (*constellation*).

Another source of borrowings is from Greek verbs ending in *-ize* (*civilize, civilization* and *organize, organization).*

There is also a large group of words that are derived through French (*modify, modification; apply, application; form, formation*). The latter are usually considered to be formed in English, though in fact they are borrowings, but by their existence the general speaker has come to consider *-ation* as an active suffix and so to produce words in English such as *flirtation, starvation,* and *botheration.*

Thus formations in English generally take on the meaning of verbs in *-ing,* as evidenced by the definitions above, and in turn lend force to creating back formations of new verbs, a process that occurs with some regularity in English from words ending in *-ation* where no underlying verb form has been previously attested, specifically *administrate* (1651) from *administration* (1333), *evaluate* (1842) from *evaluation* (1755), *hibernate* (before 1802) probably from *hibernation* (1664), *legislate* (1719) probably from *legislation* (before 1655), *medicate* (1623) probably from *medication* (before 1425), *narrate* (1656) probably from *narration* (before 1425), and *syllabicate* (1775) from *syllabication* (1631). Of course, a Latin past participial stem exists for a few of these verbs, but the evidence seems to point to the noun in *-ation* as the source in English for these verbs ending in *-ate*[1].

-ative a suffix forming adjectives, and meaning: **1** tending to, as in *talkative = tending to talk.* **2** having to do with, as in *qualitative = having to do with quality.* English *-ative* was borrowed directly from Latin *-ātīvus* (*-āt-,* past participial stem in *-ātus, -ātum* of verbs ending in *-āre,* such as *dēmōnstrāre,* English *demonstrate*) + *-īvus* (the adjective suffix, see -IVE). Many English words were also borrowed through French and Old French *-atif* (masculine), *-ative* (feminine) from Latin *-ātīvus,* such examples include *affirmative* and *representative.* Still others are formed in English directly from nouns in *-ty* but based on the Latin noun stem, such as *authoritative* from Latin stem *auctōritāt-,* and *qualitative* from *quālitāt-.*

Atlantic *adj.* Probably before 1425 *Atlantik,* in a translation of Higden's *Polychronicon,* from earlier noun use *Atlant* 1387, in Trevisa's translation of Higden's *Polychronicon,* both uses referring to the sea on the west coast of Africa, named after Mount *Atlas* in Mauretania, which, according to Classical mythology, supported the heavens (an extension of the Classical idea of the heavens resting on the shoulder of the Titan *Atlas*); later extended to the entire ocean between Europe and Africa on the east and America on the west.

English *Atlantic* was borrowed from Latin *Atlanticus,* from Greek *Atlantikós* having to do with Atlas (*Átlant-,* stem of *Átlās* ATLAS + *-ikós* English suffix -IC). —**Atlanticism** *n.* a policy of cooperation among western European and North American nations. 1964, formed in English by influence of the *Atlantic* Charter (1941) and later the *Atlantic* Pact (1949), which was the basis of the North *Atlantic* Treaty Organization (1950) + English suffix -ISM. —**Atlanticist** *n.* (1963)

Atlas or **atlas** *n.* **1** chief supporter; mainstay. 1589, in Nashe's preface to *Menaphon,* adopted in English from the name *Atlas,* a Titan in Greek mythology who bore the heavens or world on his shoulders, from Latin *Atlās,* from Greek *Átlās.*

2 Usually **atlas,** book of maps. 1636, title of Mercator's and Hondt's *Atlas; or a Geographical Description of the World;* adopted in English from New Latin *Atlas,* said to have been used originally in the sense "book of maps" by Gerhardus Mercator, the Flemish mapmaker of the 1500's, from the practice of placing a picture of Atlas supporting the heavens on the front page of collections of maps. However, this application of *atlas* may have been borrowed from the earlier French use, recorded in 1595.

atmosphere *n.* 1677, perhaps influenced by French *atmosphère* (1665), but probably suggested by Bishop John Wilkins' use of New Latin *atmosphaera* in *Discovery of a World in the Moone* (1638), a compound formed from Greek *ātmós* vapor + *sphaîra* sphere; see WIND[1] air. According to the OED, the word originally applied to a ring of vapor supposedly exhaled from the body of a planet, was later extended to the air very near the planet, and eventually included all the surrounding air.

The figurative sense of "surrounding influence" appeared sometime between 1797 and 1803.
—**atmospheric** *adj.* 1783, formed from English *atmosphere* + suffix *-ic.*

atoll *n.* ring-shaped coral island. 1625 *atollon,* in *Purchas his Pilgrimes,* borrowed from *aṭolu,* a word of the Maldive Islands in the Indian Ocean (apparently applied in the Maldives to the islands themselves), perhaps from Malayalam *aḍal* uniting, closing.

French had an earlier form *attollon* (1611), borrowed from Portuguese *attollon,* and Singhalese *ätull* meaning "interior" has been cited as a possible source, but no relationship to English *atoll* has been formally established, especially with the modern French word, which was apparently reborrowed from English as *atoll* in 1848.

atom *n.* About 1477 *attome,* the smallest part of a substance, in Thomas Norton's *Ordinal of Alchemy,* borrowed from Middle French *atome,* learned borrowing from Latin *atomus* (a word used, especially by Lucretius, about 96-55 B.C., in describing an atomic theory of materialism), from Greek *átomos* (used especially in reference to the founding of an atomic philosophy of material constituents of all matter by Leucippus, about 500 B.C., later enhanced by Democritus, about 460-357 B.C.), noun use of *átomos* indivisible (*a-* without + *tómos* a cutting, from *témnein* to cut; see TOME).

The use of *atom* in the scientific sense of the smallest particle of an element in a chemical reaction was published in a paper by the British chemist John Dalton in 1805, and *atomic* in this sense may have appeared at the same time, though the form was known in English as early at 1678. The term *atomic energy* appeared in 1906, *atomic bomb* in H.G. Wells' *The World Set Free* (1914), and *atomic number* in 1821, *atomic weight* in 1820.

Atomic in some compounds is perhaps being replaced slowly in popular use by *nuclear,* as in *nuclear energy* and *nuclear power.*

atonal *adj.* 1922, formed from English *a-*[4] + *tonal.*

atone *v.* make amends (*for*). Probably about 1300 *atonen* to reconcile; developed in English from the adverbial phrase *at on* in agreement (probably about 1225). The verb *atone* may have been influenced by a translation of the Latin phrase *ad unum,* underlying Medieval Latin *adunare* to unite. **—atonement** *n.* 1513, in writings of Sir Thomas More, reconciliation, possibly developed in English from the phrase *at onement* a being at one, i.e., in accord; but more likely formed in English from earlier *atone* + *-ment.*

atrium (ā'trēəm) *n.* **1** hall or court. 1577, borrowed from Latin *ātrium,* of uncertain origin. **2** either of the two upper cavities of the heart, sometimes called *auricles.* 1870, an extension of the meaning of definition 1.

atrocity *n.* great wickedness or cruelty. 1534, in writings of Sir Thomas More, borrowed, perhaps through influence of Middle French *atrocité,* from Latin *atrōcitās,* from *atrōx* gloomy, cruel, fierce, originally meaning "having a gloomy face," (stem *atr-,* related to *āter,* black, dark + a lost noun *ōqws* eye, face); for suffix see -ITY. **—atrocious** *adj.* 1669, formed in English from Latin *atrōci-* (stem of *atrōx* gloomy, cruel) + English suffix *-ous.*

atrophy (at'rəfē) *n.* wasting away of the body. 1620, borrowed probably through French *atrophie,* from Late Latin *atrophia,* from Greek *atrophíā* (*a-* without + *trophḗ* nourishment, from *tréphein,* curdle, fatten, nourish); for suffix see -Y[3]. Greek *tréphein* is cognate with Russian *drobá* brewer's yeast, German *Treber* brewer's grains, from Indo-European **dherebh-/dhrebh-/dhrobh-* curdle (Pok.257) **—v.** to waste away. 1865, from the noun.

attach *v.* Before 1338, in Mannyng's *Chronicle of England,* take or seize by law, borrowed perhaps through an Anglo-Latinized form *attachiare* (1258) of Old French *atachier* (1080) hold fast, fasten, earlier *estachier* fasten, from *estache* post, door jamb; ultimately from a Germanic source (compare Old English *staca* STAKE[1] post). The general sense of "to fasten" came into English in the 1400's. **—attachment** *n.* (1) the act of attaching or seizing by law. Before 1400, borrowed through an Anglo-Latinized form *attachimentis* (1258), from Old French *atachier;* for suffix see -MENT. (2) something that is attached. Before 1797, in writings of Walpole.

attaché (at'əshā') *n.* person on the official staff of a diplomat. 1829, borrowed from French, originally past participle of *attacher,* in Old French *atachier* ATTACH.

The term *attaché case,* a small case (originally used by attachés to carry documents), appeared in English in 1904, though it was not adopted in French until 1960.

Though *attaché* is a borrowing from French and is used in a compound with English *case,* the spelling remains unanglicized.

attack *v.* 1600, in Philemon Holland's translation of Livy's *Roman History,* borrowed from French *attaquer,* from Italian *attaccare* (from the same source as Old French *atachier;* see ATTACH, which was used occasionally from the 1400's to the 1600's to mean "to attack"). **—n.** 1667, in Milton's *Paradise Lost,* from the verb (perhaps influenced by French *attaque*). *Attack* is a re-formation in English taking the place of *attach,* n., a seizure or attack of fever, a use lost sometime in the 1400's.

attain *v.* reach. Probably before 1300, in *Kyng Alisaunder,* borrowed from Old French *ataign-,* stem of *ataindre* to touch upon, seize, affect, from Vulgar Latin **attangere,* alteration of Latin *attingere* (*at-* to, variant of *ad-* before *t* + *tangere* to touch; see TANGENT). **—attainment** *n.* 1384, formed from English *attain* + *-ment,* probably by influence of Old French *ataignement.* **—attainable** *adj.* 1647, formed from English *attain* + *-able.*

attainder *n.* loss of property and civil rights as the result of being sentenced to death or being outlawed. 1444, in *Rolls of Parliament,* borrowed through noun use of Anglo-French *ateindre,* Old French *ataindre* to touch upon, seize; see ATTAIN. English *attainder* is related to earlier *attaint,* v. condemn to loss of property and civil rights (about 1390) and still earlier *ateynt* (probably before 1300); borrowed from Old French *ataint,* past participle of *ataindre.*

Originally, *attainder* referred to the detection of a crime, and in later usage to the legal consequences of a crime, such as loss of property and rights. The underlying meaning was "the stain on a criminal," which was influenced by mistaken association with Old French *taindre* to stain, TAINT.

attempt *v.* Before 1393, in Gower's *Confessio Amantis,* borrowed from Old French *attempter, attenter,* or directly from Latin *attemptāre* (*at-* to, upon, variant of *ad-* before *t* + *temptāre* to try; see TEMPT). **—n.** About 1534, noun use of *attempt* v.

attend *v.* Before 1325, in *Cursor Mundi,* Middle English *attenden, atenden* observe, consider, pay attention; borrowed through Old French *atendre* pay attention, and directly from Latin *attendere* pay attention to, listen to; literally, stretch to, especially in the phrase *attendere animum* stretch or apply the mind to (*at-* toward, variant of *ad-* before *t* + *tendere* to stretch; see TEND[1] incline). **—attendance** *n.* About 1380, *attendaunce* duty, service, in Chaucer's translation of Boethius' *De Consolatione Philosophiae;* borrowed from Old French *atendance,* from *atendre* pay attention, and Anglo-Latin *attendentia,* from Latin *attendentem* (nominative *attendēns*), present participle of *attendere;* for suffix see -ANCE. —**attendant** *n.* Before 1422, from earlier adjective use, borrowed from Middle French *attendant,* present participle of *attendre* attend (Old French *atendre*); for suffix see -ANT.

attention *n.* About 1380, in Chaucer's translation of Boethius' *De Consolatione Philosophiae;* borrowed from Latin *attentiōnem* (nominative *attentiō*), from *attendere* ATTEND; for suffix see -ION. The word was used by Chaucer in translation from Latin, and in one other translation from Latin of the late 1400's, but it is not found thereafter in English until 1593 and in French until 1535, so that subsequent use in English, in Shakespeare's *Richard II* (1593), was probably a reborrowing. —**attentive** *adj.* About 1449, borrowed from Middle French *attentif* (feminine *attentive*), probably from Latin *attentus,* past participle; for suffix see -IVE. *Attentive* may have existed in English sometime before 1449 and not been recorded because of a defect in our records; certainly its derivative forms *attentively* (before 1382) and *attentiveness* (probably before 1400) point to such a conclusion.

attenuate (əten′yüāt) *v.* weaken, dilute. 1530, in Palsgrave's *Lesclarcissement,* replacing Middle English *attenuen* (probably existing before 1425). *Attenuate* is a verb use of Middle English *attenuate,* adj., emaciated, thin (probably existing before 1425); borrowed from Latin *attenuātus,* past participle of *attenuāre* (*at-* to, variant of *ad-* before *t* + *tenuāre* make thin, from *tenuis* thin; see THIN).

The earlier Old French *atténue* (1130) may have influenced the introduction of this word into English. —**attenuation** *n.* Probably before 1425, borrowed from Latin *attenuātiōnem* (nominative *attenuātiō*), from *attenuāre* attenuate; for suffix see -TION.

attest *v.* give proof of; testify to. 1596, in Spenser's *Faerie Queene,* borrowed through Middle French *attester,* Old French *atester,* from Latin *attestārī* confirm, bear witness (*at-* to, in addition, variant of *ad-* before *t* + *testārī* bear witness, from *testis* witness; see TESTAMENT). —**attestation** *n.* 1451, borrowed, perhaps through Middle French *attestation,* or directly from Latin *attestātiōnem* (nominative *attestātiō*), from *attestārī* bear witness; for suffix see -TION.

attic *n.* space just below the roof in a house and above the other rooms. 1696, a low decorative story above the main facade of a building, later referred to as the *attic storey* (1724, in writings of Defoe), which was shortened to *attic* by 1855 in Macaulay's *History of England* (vol. 3); borrowed from French *attique,* learned borrowing from Latin *Atticus,* from Greek *Attikós* of Attica, a region in ancient Greece whose style of architecture was represented by this structure.

attire *v.* to dress, array. Probably before 1300, in *Sir Tristrem,* Middle English *atiren* to dress (meat), also to dress, adorn, or equip for war; borrowed from Old French *atirer, atirier* arrange, equip, dress (*a-* to, from Latin *ad-*) + (*tire* order, rank; see TIER). —**n.** Probably before 1300, in *Arthour and Merlin,* dress, fine apparel, equipment for war; apparently noun use of *attire,* v.

attitude *n.* manner of feeling, thinking, etc. 1695, in Dryden's translation of DuFresnoy's *Art of Painting,* posture of a figure in a statue or painting; borrowed from French *attitude,* from Italian *attitudine* fitness, disposition, from Late Latin *aptitūdinem,* accusative of *aptitūdō* fitness, from Latin *aptus* joined, fitted; see APT; for suffix see -TUDE. Doublet of APTITUDE.

Originally a technical term in the fine arts, according to OED, the term was written *aptitude* and so introduced from the French *attitude* by the English writer John Evelyn in 1668. Curiously, though *attitude* was establishing itself in the early 1700's, the modern meaning developing around it was that of the earlier word *aptitude.* Therefore, Defoe's extension of *attitude* (1725) to mean "posture of the body implying a mental state," and Carlyle's further extension (1837) to mean "manner of acting representative of a mental state," and Herbert Spencer's use (1862) introducing the phrase "attitude of mind," were all encompassed in the earlier use of *aptitude* (before 1425) to mean "disposition, likelihood."

atto- a combining form meaning "one quintillionth (10^{-18})," as in *attosecond.* 1962, borrowed from Danish *atten* eighteen (related to Old Icelandic *ātjān;* cognate with Old English *eahtatēne* eighteen) + the connective form *-o-,* as in *quadro-, sexto-.*

attorney *n.* About 1303 *aturne,* in Mannyng's *Handlyng Synne,* later *atournei* (about 1440); borrowed through Anglo-French *aturné, atturné,* from Old French *aturné, atorné,* past participle of *aturner, atorner* to decree, assign, appoint, prepare (*a-* to, from Latin *ad-*) + (*torner, turner* to turn; see TURN).

The doubling of the *t,* about 1440, was an attempt to correct the spelling by Latinizing the form to what was thought to be its original Latin elements (*at-,* variant of *ad-* before *t* + *tornāre* turn). —**attorney general,** 1533, legal officer of the State, from earlier meaning of a legal representative acting under power of attorney (1292, in translation from French).

attract *v.* Probably before 1425, in a translation of Chauliac's *Grande Chirurgie,* to draw out (diseased matter) as a means of treatment, perhaps developed in Middle English by back formation from earlier *attraction,* or borrowed directly from Latin *attractus,* past participle of *attrahere* draw to (*at-* to, variant of *ad-* before *t* + *trahere* to draw; see TRACT). —**attraction** *n.* Before 1400, the action of drawing out diseased matter, extraction; borrowed probably through Anglo-French *attraction,* Old French *attraction,* from Latin *attractiōnem* (nominative *attractiō*), from *attractus,* past participle of *attrahere;* for suffix see -TION. —**attractive** *adj.* Before 1398, in Trevisa's translation of Bartholomew's *De Proprietatibus Rerum,* having the ability to draw off and ingest nutriment, borrowed perhaps through Middle French *attractif* (feminine *attractive*), from Medieval Latin *attractivus,* from Latin *attractus;* for suffix see -IVE. —**attractant** *n.* 1926, formed from English *attract* + *-ant.*

attribute (at′rəbyüt) *n.* quality considered as belonging to a person or thing. 1373, borrowed from Latin *attribūtus,* past participle of *attribuere* assign to (*at-* to, variant of *ad-* before *t* + *tribuere* assign, give, bestow; see TRIBUTE). —**v.** (ətrib′yüt) consider (something) as belonging or appropriate to. 1523, developed in English from earlier participial adjective *attribut* (probably before 1425, in a translation of Higden's *Polychronicon*); borrowed from Latin *attribūtus,* past participle of *attribuere.* The verb was usually pronounced like the noun until the 1600's. —**attribution** *n.* 1467, borrowed from Middle French *attribution,* from Latin *attribūtiōnem* (nominative *attribūtiō*), from *attribuere;* for suffix see -TION. —**attributive** *adj.* 1606, in

Shakespeare's *Troylus and Cressida,* that attributes, later, that expresses an attribute (about 1840); borrowed from French *attributif* (feminine *attributive*), from Latin *attribūtus,* past participle of *attribuere;* for suffix see -IVE. —*n.* 1750, noun use of *attributive,* adj.

attrition *n.* a wearing away or wearing down. Probably before 1425, a rubbing away by friction; earlier, meaning "regret," a form of contrition; borrowed from Latin *attrītiōnem* (nominative *attrītiō*), from *attritus,* past participle of *atterere* rub against (*at-* to, against, variant of *ad-* before *t* + *terere* to rub; see THROW); for suffix see -TION.

The military sense of wearing down the enemy's strength, especially in the phrase *war of attrition,* appeared in 1914.

auburn *adj.* reddish brown. Before 1420, in Lydgate's *Troy Book,* yellowish or whitish, blond; borrowed through Anglo-French *auburn,* Old French *auborne,* from Medieval Latin *alburnus* whitish, from Latin *albus* white; see ALB. In the 1400's to the 1600's the word was often spelled *abron, abrune, abroun,* which probably gave rise to the idea that *auburn* was a kind of brown, especially if influenced by the Old French *aubornaz* dark blond; this use contributed to modifying the meaning of the word.

auction *n.* public sale. 1595, borrowed from Latin *auctiōnem* (nominative *auctiō*) sale by increase of bids, literally meaning "an increase," from *aug-,* stem of *augēre* to increase; see EKE; for suffix see -ION. —**v.** sell at an auction. 1807, from the noun. —**auctioneer** *n.* 1708, developed from English *auction* n. + *-eer.*

Note that the usual formation of *auctioneer* would develop from the verb use + the suffix *-eer* (one who auctions), but the verb is not recorded in English until 100 years after *auctioneer* is recorded.

audacity *n.* Probably before 1425, in a translation of Higden's *Polychronicon;* borrowed from Medieval Latin *audacitas* boldness, from Latin *audāx* (genitive *audācis*) bold, from *audēre* be bold, dare; for suffix see -ITY. —**audacious** *adj.* 1550, probably borrowed from Middle French *audacieux,* from *audace* boldness, learned borrowing from Latin *audācia;* for suffix see -OUS.

audible *adj.* capable of being heard. 1529, in writings of Sir Thomas More, borrowed perhaps through Middle French *audible* (1488), or more likely directly from Late Latin *audībilis,* from Latin *audīre* to hear; cognate with Greek *aíein* hear, *aisthánesthai* feel, perceive, Old Church Slavic *aviti* reveal, and Sanskrit *āvís* openly, from Indo-European **awis-/āwis-* perceive (Pok.78); for suffix see -IBLE.

audience *n.* Probably before 1387, in a version of *Piers Plowman,* an opportunity to be heard, later a group of listeners; borrowed through Anglo-French *audience,* from Old French, learned borrowing from Latin *audientia* a hearing, from *audientem* (nominative *audiēns*), present participle of *audīre* hear; see AUDIBLE; for suffix see -ENCE.

audio (ô'dēō) *n.* sound signals or reproduction. 1940, abstracted from English AUDIO-.

The form was influenced by earlier *video* (1935).

audio- a combining form meaning sound or hearing, as in *audiology* (1947, the science of hearing), *audiophile* (1951, a devotee of high-fidelity sound reproduction), *audiovisual* (1937). Modern coinage (1913) from the stem of Latin *audīre* hear + the connective form *-o-.*

audit *n.* official examination of accounts. 1431, probably formed in English by influence of earlier *auditor* (before 1333), on the basis of a borrowing from Latin *audītus* (genitive *audītūs*) a hearing, from *audīre* to hear; see AUDIBLE. —**v.** examine accounts. 1457, verb use of Middle English *audit,* n. —**auditor** *n.* person who audits accounts. Before 1333, an official who examines accounts, and before 1382, in the Wycliffe Bible, a hearer or listener; borrowed through Anglo-French *auditour,* from Old French *auditeur,* or directly from Latin *audītor* a hearer, listener, from *audīre* to hear; for suffix see -OR[2].

audition *n.* 1599, power or faculty of hearing, borrowed through Middle French *audicion,* from Latin *audītiōnem* (nominative *audītiō*), from *audīre* hear, see AUDIBLE; for suffix see -TION. The sense of a trial hearing of a performer appeared in 1881. —**v.** give a trial hearing to (a performer). 1935, from the noun.

auditorium *n.* 1727-51, in *Chambers Cyclopaedia,* gradually replacing earlier *auditory,* developed from Middle English *auditorie* (about 1384, in the Wycliffe Bible); borrowed from Latin *audītōrium* lecture room, audience, neuter of the adjective *audītōrius* of or for hearing, from *audītor* a hearer, listener, from *audīre* to hear. —**auditory** *adj.* of the sense of hearing. 1578, borrowed from Latin *audītōrius* of or for hearing; for suffix see -ORY.

auger *n.* tool for boring holes. Old English (about 700) *nafogār, nabogār,* in Middle English (down to 1500) spelled *nauger, nawger, navger.* Old English *nafogār, nabogār,* developed from a Germanic compound made from the words for nave, hub (Old English *nafu*) and spear, borer (Old English *gār*), with cognate descendants in Old Icelandic *nafarr,* Old High German *nabugēr, nabagēr,* Old Saxon *naƀugēr,* and early Middle Dutch *navegheer,* from Proto-Germanic **naƀōʒaizaz.*

In Middle English, as in late Middle Dutch also, the initial *n* was dropped through analysis of *a nauger* as *an auger;* compare Modern Dutch *avegaar.* ADDER and APRON show similar loss of *n.* Related to NAVE[2], NAVEL, CORE[3].

aught *n.* anything whatever. Before 1300 *ought, aught, awiht,* Middle English forms of Old English (before 1000) *āht,* contraction of *āwiht* (*ā* ever + *wiht* anything; literally, anything whatever); see AY and WIGHT.

augment *v.* increase, enlarge. Before 1400, borrowed through Anglo-French, from Old French *augmenter,* learned borrowing from Late Latin *augmentāre,* from Latin *augmentum* an increase, from *augēre* to increase.

augur *n.* prophet, fortuneteller. Before 1393, in Gower's *Confessio Amantis,* borrowed from Latin *augur,* a religious official in ancient Rome who foretold events by omens to advise other government officials, probably originally meaning an increase in growth (as of crops) enacted in ritual, from *augēre* to increase; see EKE. The general sense of one who predicts the future appeared in 1593, probably as a natural extension of the original meaning in English, even though the general meaning was recorded in French as early as 1213. —**v.** predict; be a sign or promise of. 1601, in Ben Jonson's *The Poetaster,* from the noun, or borrowed from Latin *augurārī* to predict from signs or omens, from *augur,* n. —**augury** *n.* prediction; omen. About 1385, in Chaucer's *Troilus and Criseyde,* borrowed from Old French *auguré, augurie,* or directly from Latin *augurium* divination, omen, from *augur,* n.

august (ôgust′) *adj.* majestic, venerable. 1664, borrowed from Latin *augustus* venerable, worthy of honor (assumed as a title by the Roman emperors after Julius Caesar) and probably originally meaning "consecrated by the augurs" or "consecrated with favorable auguries." The Latin *augustus* developed from **augus* (genitive **augoris*) increase, power (a Latin form which later produced *augur*), from *augēre* to magnify, increase; see EKE.

August *n.* eighth month. Old English (1097 in *Old English Chronicle*), borrowed from Latin *Augustus* the sixth month in the ancient Roman calendar, named after *Augustus* Caesar, the first Roman emperor, from *augustus* majestic, AUGUST.

The earlier Old English name was *Wēodmōnath* the Month of Weeds.

auk *n.* northern sea bird. 1674, borrowed from a Scandinavian source (compare Norwegian *akle,* modern Icelandic *alka,* Old Icelandic *álka*); cognate with Latin *olor* (earlier **elōr*), Middle Irish *ela,* and Welsh *alarch* (plural *elyrch*), all meaning swan, from Indo-European **el-/ol-/olg-* (Pok. 304).

aunt *n.* About 1300, borrowed through Anglo-French *aunte,* from Old French *ante,* from Latin *amita* father's sister; probably cognate with Greek *ammá* mother, nurse, Old Icelandic *amma* grandmother, and Old High German *amma* mother, nurse, all apparently from a root imitating the babbling of infants as in *mamma* MAMMA[1] mother.

au pair (ō pãr′) *Chiefly British.* (an arrangement) providing room and board, originally in exchange for tutoring in language, later in exchange for domestic work, child care, etc. 1897, borrowed from French, literally, on equality, on equal terms; *noun use* 1960, person who tutors or works under such an arrangement; *verb use* 1963, to be or serve as an au pair.

aura *n.* 1859, subtle emanation or atmosphere, in a figurative sense. 1732 (in writings of Bishop Berkeley) meaning "subtle emanation from any substance," earlier (before 1398, in Trevisa's translation of Bartholomew's *De Proprietatibus Rerum*) meaning a gentle breeze; borrowed from Latin *aura* breeze, a breath of air, from Greek *aúrā* breeze, breath, from Indo-European **aurā* (Pok.82). Greek *aúrá* is apparently related to *āḗr* mist, air.

aural *adj.* of the ear or hearing. 1847, formed in English from Latin *auris* ear + English suffix *-al*[1]; see EAR.

aureole (ô′rēōl) *n.* halo. Before 1396, borrowed through Old French *auréole,* from Late Latin phrase *aureola corōna* golden crown; *aureola* is feminine of Latin *aureolus,* diminutive of *aureus* golden, from *aurum* gold, cognate with Sabine *ausom* and Old Lithuanian *ausas,* from Indo-European **auso-* gold (Pok.86).

aureomycin (ôr′ēōmī′sin) *n.* antibiotic substance used to treat lung and rickettsial diseases. 1948, formed in English from Latin *aureus* golden (abstracted from *Streptomyces aureofaciens* name of the fungus from which the drug is produced) + English *-mycin* (from Greek *mýkēs* fungus + English *-in*[2]).

auricle *n.* **1** chamber of the heart, probably before 1425, in a translation of Chauliac's *Grande Chirurgie,* the meaning borrowed through Old French *auricule,* from Latin *auricula* ear, traditionally attributed to the shape of the auricles of the heart, which it was said are supposed to resemble the ear of a dog, bear, or some other quadruped.
2 outer part of the ear, 1653; apparently borrowed separately from Latin *auricula* ear, diminutive of *auris* ear; see EAR.

aurochs (ôr′oks) *n.* European bison. 1835, by misinterpretation of earlier use (1766) referring to an extinct species of wild ox living in and near the forests of Europe as described by Caesar and Aristotle. This distinction between the European bison and the extinct wild ox was later (1869) more carefully drawn and is now generally reestablished. The term was borrowed from German *Aurochs,* obsolete form of *Auerochs,* from Old High German *ūrohso* (*ūro* aurochs + *ohso* OX). Old High German *ūro* is cognate with Old English *ūr* and Old Icelandic *ūrr,* both meaning aurochs.

The French word *aurox* appears in Cotgrave (1611) but seems to be an independent borrowing with no influence on the English *aurochs.*

aurora *n.* dawn. About 1386, in Chaucer's *Legend of Good Women,* borrowed perhaps through Old French *aurore,* or directly from Latin *aurora* dawn, *Aurora* the goddess of dawn; see EAST. **—aurora borealis** 1621, as originally described by the French physicist and astronomer Pierre Gassendi in *Physics,* to mean "northern dawn," later (1727-51, in *Chambers Cyclopaedia*) "northern light."

auspices *n.* helpful influence, approval, support, favor; especially in the phrase *under the auspices of.* 1533, in Bellenden's translation of Livy's *Roman History,* sign or omen given by birds; later (before 1637, in writings of Ben Jonson) favor, influence; borrowed from Middle and Old French *auspice, auspices,* a learned borrowing from Latin *auspicium* divination by observing the flight of birds, from *auspex* (genitive *auspicis*) one who takes signs from the flight of birds (*avi-,* stem of *avis* bird + *-spex* observer, from *specere* look, observe; see AVIARY and SPY).

The plural *auspices* became the primary usage in the 1800's. **—auspicious** *adj.* showing favor; propitious. 1601, in Shakespeare's *All's Well That Ends Well,* formed from Latin *auspicium* + English suffix *-ous.*

austere *adj.* stern, strict. Before 1338, in Mannyng's *Chronicle of England,* borrowed through Old French *austere,* or directly from Latin *austērus,* from Greek *austērós* making the tongue dry; hence, harsh, severe, related to *haûos* dry; see SERE. **—austerity** *n.* About 1380, in writings of Wycliffe, borrowed through Old French *austerité,* or directly from Latin *austēritātem* (nominative *austēritās*), from *austērus* austere; for suffix see -ITY.

austral *adj.* southern. 1541, borrowed from Latin *austrālis,* from *auster* the south wind; see EAST.

Austral was known in Old French (1372) but the English word appears to be a separate borrowing from Latin.

The name *Australia* was derived by mapmakers of the 1600's from the New Latin phrase *Terra Australis* Southern Land.

authentic *adj.* 1369 *autentyk* authoritative, in Chaucer's *Book of the Duchesse,* borrowed through Anglo-French *autentic,* from Old French *autentique* and from Medieval Latin and Late Latin *authenticus,* from Greek *authentikós,* from *authéntēs* one acting on one's own authority, master, perpetrator (*aut-* stem of *autós* self + *-héntēs* doer, related to *hanýein* accomplish, and cognate with Sanskrit *sanóti* he gains); for suffix see -IC.

The Greek and Latin *-th-* was restored in the 1600's. **—authenticity** *n.* 1657, formed from English *authentic* + *-ity,* perhaps by influence of Middle French *autentiquité* (1557). **—authenticate** *v.* 1653, borrowed, perhaps by influence of Old French *authentiquer* (1265), from Medieval Latin *authenticatus,* past participle of *authenticare,* from *authenticus* authentic; for suffix see -ATE[1]. **—authentication** *n.* 1788, in writings of Thomas Jefferson, formed from English *authenticate* + *-ion.*

author *n.* 1529, in writings of Sir Thomas More, alteration by influence of Middle French variant *author* of earlier *autour, auctour* (probably about 1350); borrowed through Anglo-French *auctour, autour, autor,* from Old French *auctor, autor,* learned borrowings from Latin *auctōrem* (nominative *auctor*), literally one who causes to grow; hence, founder, author, backer, from *augēre* to increase, see EKE; for suffix see -OR[2].

The spelling *author* was a scribal variant of *autor* in Middle French, and came about during the Renaissance partly by analogy with words in *th* thought to come ultimately from Greek. The spelling *author* appeared in English in the early 1500's, and ultimately resulted in effecting a change to our present pronunciation. **—v.** write, compose. 1596, to originate, verb use of *author,* n. The verb disappeared after the 1630's but was revived, at first chiefly in the United States, in the 1940's. **—authorship** *n.* 1710, formed from English *author* + *-ship.*

authority *n.* Before 1535, in writings of Sir Thomas More, alteration by influence of Middle French *authorité* of Middle English *autorite, auctorite* book or quotation that settles a question (probably before 1200 in *Ancrene Riwle*); borrowed through Anglo-French *auctorité, autorité,* from Old French *auctorité, autorité,* learned borrowings from Latin *auctōritātem* (nominative *auctōritās*), from *auctor* AUTHOR; for suffix see -ITY. See *author* for note on *-th-* spelling.

—authoritative *adj.* 1605, formed from English *authority* + *-ative.* **—authorize** *v.* set up as authoritative. 1579, alteration of Middle English *autorisen, auctorisen)* (about 1383, in writings of Wycliffe); borrowed from Old French *autoriser, auctorisier,* from Medieval Latin *auctorizare,* from Latin *auctor* AUTHOR; for suffix see -IZE. **—authorization** *n.* 1610, re-formed in English from *authorize* + *-ation;* the earlier *auctorisation* (1472-73), probably adapted from an Anglo-Latin formation, appears to have dropped out of English shortly after use in *Rolls of Parliament.*

autism (ô'tizəm) *n. Psychology.* condition of total self-absorption. 1912, borrowed from German *Autismus* (coined by Paul Eugen Bleuler, 1857-1939, Swiss psychiatrist), from New Latin *autismus* (*aut-,* from Greek *autós* self + *-ismus* -ism). **—autistic** adj. 1912, formed from English *aut-* (from *autism* + *-istic,* as in *characteristic,* the ending *-istic* being imitative of Greek *-istikós.* **—n.** 1968, noun use of *autistic,* adj.

auto *n.* 1899, American English, shortened from AUTOMOBILE.

auto-[1] a combining form meaning self, one's own, by oneself, as in *autobiography, autograph, autointoxication.* Sometimes spelled *aut-* before vowels and *h,* as in *autopsy, authentic.* Borrowed from Greek *auto-, aut-,* combining form of *autós* self, of uncertain origin.

auto-[2] a combining form meaning automobile or vehicle, as in *autodrome, automaker;* a clipped form of English *automobile.*

autobiography *n.* 1809, in writings of Southey, formed from English *auto-*[1] + *biography.*

autocrat *n.* ruler with absolute power. 1803, in writings of Southey, borrowed from French *autocrate,* from Greek *autokratḗs* ruling by oneself, absolute (*autós* self + *krátos* strength, power). **—autocratic** *adj.* 1823, in Byron's *Don Juan,* borrowed from French *autocratique;* for suffix see -IC.

auto-da-fé (ô'tōdəfā') *n.* burning a person condemned as a heretic. 1723, borrowed from Portuguese, literally, act of (the) faith; also found in French 1714. The term was first used to refer to the public ceremony accompanying a sentence passed by the Spanish Inquisition.

autograph *n.* a person's signature. 1791-1817, in writings of Isaac Disraeli, earlier (1640-44) an author's own manuscript; borrowed by influence of earlier French *autographe* (1580), from Latin *autographum, autographus,* from Greek *autógraphos* written with one's own hand (*autós* self + *gráphein* write). **—v.** 1837, to write one's autograph on or in (a book, etc.), verb use of *autograph,* n.

automat *n.* self-service cafeteria with coin-operated food compartments. 1903 *Automat,* American English, a trademark for such a service; borrowed from German *Automat* automatic machine, automaton, from French *automate,* from Latin *automaton* AUTOMATON.

automatic *adj.* self-acting. 1748, like an automaton, mechanical; formed in English from Greek *autómatos* self-acting, spontaneous + English suffix *-ic;* see AUTOMATON. **—n.** automatic pistol. 1902, noun use of *automatic,* adj., having a mechanism for continuous loading and firing (1877).

automation *n.* the use of automatic machines and controls in place of human labor. 1948, American English, from *autom(atic oper)ation,* coined by Delmar S. Harder, a manufacturing executive of the Ford Motor Company who organized in 1947 a group of specialists he named "automation engineers."**—automate** *v.* convert to automation. 1954, American English, back formation from *automation.*

automaton (ôtom'əton) *n.* person or thing having mechanical actions. Before 1625, in John Fletcher's *The Bloody Brother,* borrowed from Latin *automaton,* from Greek *autómaton,* neuter of *autómatos* self-acting, spontaneous (*autós* self + *-matos* thinking, animated, cognate with Sanskrit *matá-s* (having been) thought, Latin *com-mentus* having thought up, and Lithuanian *miñtas,* from Indo-European **mn̥tós,* Pok.727; see MIND).

automobile *n.* 1895, motor vehicle, probably developed from the adjective use (1883), as in *auto-mobile car;* borrowed from French *automobile,* adj. (1861), and at least influenced by French *automobile,* n. (1890). The word is a compound of French *auto-* self (from Greek *auto-,* from *autós* self) + *mobile* moving (learned borrowing from Latin *mōbilis,* from *movēre* to move). **—automotive** *adj.* 1898, formed from English *auto-*[1] + *motive.* As a noun *automotive* appeared in 1865, referring to a kind of flying machine.

autonomy *n.* independence, self-government. 1623, borrowed, perhaps by influence of earlier French *autonomie* (1596), from Greek *autonomiā,* from *autónomos* living under one's own laws, independent (*auto-* self + *nómos* custom, law, related to *némein* manage); for suffix see -Y[3]. **—autonomic** *adj.* 1832, but especially in *autonomic nervous system* (1896), formed from English *autonomy* + *-ic*. **—autonomous** *adj.* 1800; borrowed, perhaps by influence of earlier French *autonome* (1751), from Greek *autónomos* independent; for suffix see -OUS.

autopsy (ô′topsē) *n.* examination of a body to determine cause of death. 1651, eyewitnessed observation, borrowed from New Latin *autopsia*, from Greek *autopsíā* a seeing with one's own eyes, from *autóptēs* an eyewitness (*autós* + *op-* root meaning "to see"; see OPTIC). The meaning "dissection of a body" appeared in 1678, probably by influence of earlier Middle French *autopsie* (1573).

autumn *n.* the fall season. 1596 *autumne*, in Shakespeare's *Taming of the Shrew*, and 1526, mistakenly as *authum* in writings of Tyndale, both forms alterations of earlier Middle English *autumpne* (about 1380, in Chaucer's translation of Boethius' *De Consolatione Philosophiae*); borrowed from Old French *autompne*, learned borrowing from Latin *autumnus*, of uncertain origin.

The uses in Shakespeare, Tyndale, and others of the 1500's may also be direct borrowings through Old French, which had the forms *autonne* and *auton;* however, Tyndale's use, in particular, seems to be a conscious attempt to return to the Latin. **—autumnal** *adj.* 1574, maturing or blooming in autumn; borrowed from Latin *autumnālis*, from *autumnus*.

auxiliary *adj.* helping, assistant. 1603, in Holland's translation of Plutarch's *Moralia*, borrowed from Latin *auxiliārius, auxiliāris*, from *auxilium* help, probably from a lost adjective **auxilis* serving to strengthen, from *augēre* to increase; see EKE; for suffix see -ARY.

The earlier Middle French *auxiliaire* (1512) may also have been borrowed by English or influenced the English formation.

avail *v.* be of value; benefit. About 1300 *availen*, apparently formed from *a-* to (from Latin *ad-*) + *vailen* to avail (borrowed from Old French *vaill-*, stem of *valoir* be worth, from Latin *valēre;* see VALUE). **—n.** help; benefit. About 1400, either (1) noun use of *avail*, v. or (2) a possible mistaking Old French *de vaille* of value, as *d'availle* (an explanation offered in the Middle English Dictionary). **—available** *adj.* 1417, in *Proceedings of the Privy Council*, valid, effective; 1444, in *Rolls of Parliament*, beneficial, serviceable; hence, 1827, in writings of Faraday, capable of being made use of, at one's disposal; formed from English *avail* + *-able*.

avalanche (av′əlanch) *n.* 1771, borrowed from French *avalanche*, from Swiss French *avalantse* descent, possibly an alteration by transposition of *l* resulting from *lavanche*, from a pre-Latin Alpine language.

The formation of this word was further influenced by Old French *avaler* go down, from *à val* down, from Latin *ad vallem* to the valley; and is felt by some to be ultimately from Vulgar Latin **lābīna*, from Latin *lābī* to slide; see LAPSE.

Earlier forms appear in English as *valancas* (1765), borrowed from Italian *valanca;* or *valanche* (1766), borrowed from dialectal French *valanche* or by misanalysis of standard French *l'avalanche*.

avant-garde (ä′väNgärd′, əvänt′gärd′) *n.* pioneers or innovators in the arts. 1910, borrowed from French, literally, advance guard. Doublet of VANGUARD. In the literal sense of the foremost part of an army, vanguard, *avant-garde* was used in English between the 1400's and 1700's. **—adj.** 1925, attributive use of *avant-garde*, n.

avarice *n.* greedy desire for money. Probably about 1300, borrowed from Old French *avarice*, learned borrowing from Latin *avāritia*, from *avārus* greedy, related to *avēre* crave, long for; see AVID. **—avaricious** *adj.* About 1390, in Chaucer's *Canterbury Tales*, borrowed from Old French *avaricieux* (masculine), *avaricieuse* (feminine), from *avarice*.

avenge *v.* get revenge for; take vengeance on. Probably before 1387, in a version of *Piers Plowman*, borrowed through Anglo-French *avenger*, from Old French *avengier* (*a-* to, from Latin *ad-*) + (*vengier* take revenge; see VENGEANCE).

avenue *n.* 1600, an approach, passage, pass, in Holland's translation of Livy's *Roman History;* borrowed from Middle French *avenue* a way of access or approach. In Old French *avenue* meant, "act of approaching, arrival," from feminine of *avenu*, past participle of *avenir* arrive, from Latin *advenīre;* see ADVENT. The extended meaning "broad, tree-lined roadway" appeared in 1654, in John Evelyn's *Diary*, leading to the current sense of a wide main street, which probably appeared before 1858.

aver (əvėr′) *v.* state to be true. Before 1400, Middle English *averren, oueren*, in writings of Wycliffe, borrowed through Anglo-French *averer*, from Old French *averer* verify, from Vulgar Latin **advērāre* make true, prove to be true (from Latin *ad-* to + *vērus* true; see VERY).

average *n.* arithmetic mean; hence, any mean. Originally (1540), *average* meant an extra charge or expense of shipment, and was an alteration (influenced by the ending *-age* in words like *damage, cartage*, etc.) of the earlier form (1491) *averag*, meaning a duty or tax on goods, and specifically, an expense or loss arising from damage at sea to goods; the English word developed sometime between 1250 and 1490 and was borrowed from Old French *avarie*, from Italian *avaria*, and ultimately from Arabic *ʿarwārīya* damaged goods, from *ʿawār* damage, defect, from *ʿāra* to spoil.

The current sense of the word developed from the special sense of "an equal distribution of expense or loss among all the interested parties in proportion to their interests" (1598); any similar distribution based on a median estimate (1735); the arithmetic mean so obtained; "a medium, a mean proportion" (1755, Johnson's *Dictionary*), and so extended to "any mean." **—adj.** 1770, adjective use of *average*, n. **—v.** 1769, in George Washington's *Diaries*, verb use of *average*, n.

averse *adj.* opposed; unwilling. Before 1450, borrowed through Old French *avers*, or directly from Latin *āversus*, past participle of *āvertere* AVERT. **—aversion** *n.* 1596, borrowed from Middle and Old French *aversion*, from Latin *āversiōnem* (nominative *āversiō*), from *āversus*, past participle; for suffix see -ION.

avert *v.* turn away, prevent. Probably before 1439, in Lydgate's *Falls of Princes*, borrowed from Old French *avertir*, from Latin *āvertere* turn aside (*ā-* from, variant of *ab-*[1] + *vertere* to turn).

aviary (ā′vēer′ē) *n.* birdhouse. 1577, borrowed from Latin *aviārium*, neuter of *aviārius* of birds, from *avis* bird; for suffix see -ARY. Latin *avis* is cognate with Sanskrit *ví-s* bird and Greek *aietós* eagle (earlier **awye-tós*), from Indo-European **awei-/awi-/wi-* (Pok.86).

aviation *n.* flying by airplane. 1866, borrowed from French *aviation* (1863), from Latin *avis* bird + French *-ation.* **—aviator** *n.* 1887, in a translation of Jules Verne's *Clipper of the Clouds,* borrowed from French *aviateur,* from *aviation.*

avid *adj.* eager, greedy. 1769; borrowed, perhaps through influence of earlier French and Middle French *avide* (1470), from Latin *avidus,* from *avēre* desire eagerly; or, more likely, as a back formation in English from *avidity,* or perhaps from the now obsolete *avidous* (formed in English about 1542 from Latin *avid(us)* + English suffix *-ous).* Latin *avēre* desire eagerly, crave, is related to *avārus* greedy; cognate with Sanskrit *ávati* desires, Armenian *aviun* libido, and Welsh *ewyllys* will, from Indo-European **aw-/awē-/awēi-* (Pok.77). **—avidity** *n.* 1449, borrowed from Middle French *avidité,* from Latin *aviditātem* (nominative *aviditās*), from *avidus* greedy, eager; for suffix see -ITY.

avocado *n.* pear-shaped tropical fruit. 1763, *avocato, avocado,* in a list of terms that by the 1860's had not replaced earlier variants, such as *avogato* (1697). The name is borrowed from Spanish *avocado,* alteration of an earlier form similar to the preferred form *aguacate,* from Nahuatl *ahuacatl* testicle.

The name *alligator pear* (also 1763), a synonym of *avocado,* was apparently an English formation by folk etymology.

avocation *n.* minor occupation, hobby. Before 1617, a calling away from one's occupation, diversion; borrowed from Latin *āvocātiōnem* (nominative *āvocātiō*), from *āvocāre* (*ā-* away, variant of *ab-* + *vocāre* to call, related to *vōcem* voice).; for suffix see -TION

avoid *v.* Before 1325, in *Cursor Mundi,* clear out, withdraw (oneself); borrowed probably from Anglo-French *avoider,* variant of Old French *esvuidier* to empty, quit (*es-* out, from Latin *ex-*) + (*vuidier* to empty, void, from Vulgar Latin **vocitāre,* from **vocitus* void; see VOID). **—avoidance** *n.* Before 1398, in Trevisa's translation of Bartholomew's *De Proprietatibus Rerum,* formed from English *avoid* + suffix *-ance.*

avoirdupois (av′ərdəpoiz′) *n.* system of weight. 1656, alteration of earlier *avoir-de-peise* (probably before 1325), borrowed from Old French *avoir de pois, aveir de peis* goods of weight (*aveir* property, goods, a noun use of *aveir* have, from Latin *habēre* have) + (*de* of, from Latin *dē* of) + (*peis* weight, from Latin *pēnsum,* from *pendere* weigh).

avouch *v.* declare to be true. 1494, borrowed from Middle French *avochier* call upon as an authority, from Old French, from Latin *advocāre* call to (as a witness); see ADVOCATE.

avow *v.* admit, acknowledge. Probably before 1300, in *Arthour and Merlin,* borrowed through Anglo-French *avoer, avouer,* from Old French *avöer, avouer* acknowledge, accept, especially as a protector (*a-* to, from Latin *ad-*) + (*vouer* to affirm, vow, from *vou* VOW. **—avowal** *n.* 1727-31, in Bailey's *Dictionary,* formed from English *avow,* v. + suffix *-al*[2].

avuncular *adj.* of or resembling an uncle. 1831; formed in English, perhaps through influence of earlier French *avunculaire* (1801), from Latin *avunculus* mother's brother (diminutive of *avus* grandfather) + English suffix *-ar;* see UNCLE.

awake (əwāk′) *v.* Probably before 1200 *awaken* wake up; developed from Old English *āwacan* (*ā-* a-[5] + *-wacan,* cognate with Gothic *wakan* stay awake, watch), from Proto-Germanic **wak-;* see WAKE[1]. **—adj.** Before 1300, short for *awaken,* original past participle of *awaken* wake up.

award *v.* grant (a prize, honor, etc.). About 1390, in Chaucer's *Canterbury Tales,* decide after careful consideration; borrowed from Anglo-French *awarder,* variant of Old French *esguarder* decide, examine, watch out (*es-* out, from Latin *ex-*) + (*guarder* to watch; see GUARD). The sense "to confer, grant" appeared (in judicial use) in 1523. **—n.** About 1390, in Chaucer's *Canterbury Tales,* decision after careful consideration; borrowed from Anglo-French *award,* variant of Old French *esguard,* from *esguarder* decide, examine. The sense "something awarded" appeared in 1596, in Spenser's *Faerie Queene.*

aware *adj.* Probably before 1325 *a ware* watchful, conscious; developed from earlier *iwar* (about 1175, in Layamon's *Chronicle of Britain*), found in Old English (about 950, in *Lindisfarne Gospels*) *gewær* (*ge-* an intensive prefix + *wær* wary; see WARY).

The Old English *gewær* is of West Germanic origin as shown by the cognates in Old Saxon *giwar,* Middle Dutch *gheware,* Old High German *giwar* (modern German *gewahr*), all meaning "aware," from Proto-Germanic **ʒa-waraz;* see WARY.

away *adv.* Probably before 1300 *awey, away;* developed from earlier *awei, a-wei* (about 1150), found in Old English *aweg* and (about 725, in *Beowulf*) *on weg* (*on* on + *weg* way). The sense of the original compound was "on one's way," that is, to another place, and can be compared with Old High German *in wëg* on the way, Middle High German *enwëc* away (modern German *weg* away).

awe *n.* Probably before 1300, in *Arthour and Merlin;* developed from earlier *age* (about 1250, in *The Story of Genesis and Exodus*) and *aghe* (probably about 1200, in *The Ormulum*), borrowed from a Scandinavian source (compare Old Icelandic *agi* fear; cognate with Gothic *agis* fright (Proto-Germanic **aʒ-*) and Greek *áchos* pain, distress, from Indo-European **agh-* (Pok.7).

Old Icelandic *agi* is also cognate with Old English *ege* fear, awe; and it was this Old English *ege* which yielded *eie* and *aye* meaning "fear, terror" in early Middle English, before being replaced finally in the 1400's by the form *awe,* borrowed from Scandinavian. Related to AIL.

—awful *adj.* Before 1425, developed from *agheful* (probably about 1200, in *The Ormulum*) (*aghe* awe + *-ful*). In the 1400's Middle English *awful, agheful* replaced Old English *egefull* (recorded before 899, in works of King Alfred). **—awesome** *adj.* 1598, formed from English *awe,* n. + *-some*[1].

awkward *adj.* Before 1400, in the wrong direction; formed from *awk* untoward, backhanded + *-ward.* The old word *awk,* which appeared in Middle English before 1400 and became obsolete in the 1600's, was borrowed from a Scandinavian source (compare Old Icelandic *ǫfugr* turned the wrong way, back foremost, and Swedish and Norwegian *avig*).

The sense of "clumsy" appeared in 1530, in Palsgrave's *Lesclarcissement.*

awl *n.* tool for making small holes. Old English *awel* (about 700), *æl* (about 885, in *Laws of Alfred*), *awul* (about 1000, in Ælfric's *Glossary*).

Though the Old English forms *awel* and *awul* have not been explained, the inherited Old English form appears to be *ǣl,* and it is cognate with Old High German *āla* awl (modern German *Ahle*), Middle Dutch *āl,* from Proto-Germanic **ǣlō,* and Sanskrit *ā́rā.* Possibly Old English *awel, awul* represent a borrowing from a Scandinavian word, as might be evidenced by the Old Icelandic *alr* and modern Icelandic *alur,* from Proto-Germanic **alás.*

awning *n.* 1624, cover above ship's deck, in Captain John Smith's *The Generall Historie of Virginia;* of unknown origin.

The extended meaning of a canvas cover in front of a tent first appeared in American English in 1806, in the *Journals* of Lewis and Clark, and that of a cover over a window or porch, in 1852, in *Harper's Magazine.*

ax or **axe** *n.* Old English *æces* (before 830, in the *Vespasian Psalter*); *æcs, æx* (before 899, in Alfred's works); *acas* (about 950, in Northumbrian dialect).

The word is cognate with Old Frisian *axa* ax, Old Saxon *akus,* Old High German *acchus* (modern German *Axt*), Old Icelandic *øx,* Gothic *aqizi,* from Proto-Germanic forms **akwiz-* and **akus-,* reflecting Indo-European **ag-wes-ī/ag-us-yā-.* But Latin *ascia* ax (earlier **acsiā*) and Greek *axínē* are from Indo-European **aksī* (Pok.9). **—v.** 1677, from the noun.

axil *n.* upper angle between a leaf or stem and the supporting stem or branch. 1794, borrowed from New Latin *axilla,* from Latin *axilla* armpit, related to *axis* axle, AXIS.

axiom *n.* self-evident truth. 1485, in Caxton's translation of *Paris and Vienne,* borrowed from Middle French *axiome,* from Latin *axiōma,* from Greek *axíōma* something thought worthy or fit, from *axioûn* think worthy or fit, from *áxios* worthy, built on a lost noun **ak-tis* weight, from *ágein* weigh, pull, from Indo-European **aĝ-* (Pok.4). **—axiomatic** *adj.* 1797, borrowed from French *axiomatique,* from Greek *axiōmatikós,* from *axiṓmatos* (genitive of *axíōma* axiom); for suffix see -IC.

axis *n.* straight line. Before 1398, in Trevisa's translation of Bartholomew's *De Proprietatibus Rerum;* borrowed from Latin *axis:* (1) axle (of a wheel), (2) axis (of the earth, heavens, etc.).

The cognates include Old English *eax, æx* axle, axis, Old High German *ahsa,* from Proto-Germanic **aHsō,* Indo-European **aḱsā,* with Greek *áxōn* axis, axle, and Sanskrit *ákṣa-s* axis, axle, formed from Indo-European **aḱs-* by other suffixes (Pok.6).

Axis and its cognates derive ultimately from the Indo-European base **aĝ-* "to drive" (Pok.4).

axle *n.* bar on which a wheel turns. 1367-68, earlier in the compound *axeltre* axletree (1290). The form *eaxl* is found in Old English, but *axle* and *axel* are thought to come by way of the earlier compound *axeltrē,* borrowed from Old Icelandic *ǫxultrē* (*ǫxull* axis, axle + *trē* tree). Old Icelandic *oxull* is from Proto-Germanic **aHsulaz* (Pok.6), root **aHsō;* see AXIS.

axon *n.* elongated part of nerve cell. 1899, New Latin *axon,* from Greek *áxōn* AXIS.

ay[1] or **aye**[1] (ā) *adv.* always, ever. Probably about 1200, in *The Ormulum, ai,* borrowed from a Scandinavian source (compare Old Icelandic *ei*). The word is cognate with Old English *ā, ō* always, ever; see AGE.

ayatollah (ä'yətō'lə) *n.* religious leader of the highest rank in the Shiite sect of Islam. 1963 *ayatullah,* borrowed from Persian, from Arabic *āyātollāh, āyātullāh* (*āyāt,* plural of *āya* sign, model, paragon + *allāh* God).

The term became widely known outside of Iran in 1979 in the title Ayatollah Khomeini, after the deposition of the Shah.

aye[2] or **ay**[2] (ī) *adv., interj.* yes. 1576, spelled *I,* 1714 *ay;* developed perhaps by alteration of Middle English *yai* (existing before 1225), variant of *ye, ya* yea, yes; see YEA. **—n.** affirmative answer or vote. 1589, spelled *I,* 1669 *aye;* from the adverb.

azalea (əzāl'yə) *n.* shrub with showy flowers. 1753, in *Chambers Cyclopaedia,* New Latin *azalea,* borrowed from Greek *azaléā,* feminine of *azaléos* dry, from *ázein* parch, cognate with Czech *ozd* malt-kiln, from Indo-European **as-d-* to dry (Pok.69). The plant was so named from the dry soil in which it grows, or, possibly, from its dry, brittle wood.

azimuth (az'əməth) *n.* arc of the horizon measured to obtain the angular distance between an object and a reference point. Before 1388 *azimut* arc of the heavens from the zenith to the horizon which it cuts at right angles; borrowed from Arabic *as-sumūt* the ways, plural of *as-samt* the way, direction (*as-,* variant of *al-* the + *samt* way). Compare ZENITH.

The *-th-* spelling arose in the 1500's.

azure (azh'ər) *n., adj.* sky blue. Probably before 1300, in *Arthour and Merlin;* borrowed from Old French *azur,* from Arabic *lāzuward,* from Persian *lā́zward* lapis lazuli (or its blue color).

The word passed from Arabic into the Romance languages (Spanish and Portuguese *azul,* French and Romanian *azur,* etc.) without the initial *l-,* apparently because it was mistakenly thought to be the definite article *l'* or *la* or some variant of it.

B

Babbitt *n.* a complacent middle-class businessman. 1923, allusion to George F. *Babbitt,* the central character in the novel *Babbitt* (1922) by the American writer Sinclair Lewis, 1885-1951. —**Babbittry** *n.* adherence to narrow middle-class ideals of respectability and success. 1928, formed from English *Babbitt* + *-ry.*

babble *v.* prattle. Before 1250, *babelen, bablen,* in *Ancrene Riwle;* probably of imitative origin. Similar forms are found in many languages: compare Middle Low German *babbelen* to babble, Icelandic *babbla,* Latin *babulus* babbler, *balbus* stammering, and Sanskrit *balbalā-kr-* to stammer; all probably formed on the repeated syllables *ba, ba,* or *bar, bar,* sounds typically made by infants and used to express childish prattle; though the *l* is not accounted for.

The sounds may also be used typically to imitate inarticulate speech or to represent unintelligible foreign speech sounds. Folk etymology has connected this word with the Tower of *Babel,* and this association may have influenced its sense of meaningless or confusing chatter.

babe *n.* baby. Before 1393, in Gower's *Confessio Amantis,* apparently from *baban* (probably before 1200, in *Ancrene Riwle*); of uncertain origin, perhaps ultimately from a child's word.

baboon *n.* large ape. About 1400 *babewyn,* in Sir John Maundeville's *Travels;* earlier *babeweis* grotesque figures (probably about 1320); borrowed from Old French *babouin* baboon, fool; perhaps related to Old French *babine* lip, and *babiller* to babble, probably ultimately imitative of the looks and the chatter of these apes; for ending see -OON.

babushka (bəbüsh′kə) *n.* kerchief. 1934; borrowed from Russian *bábushka* grandmother, diminutive of *baba* old woman (a common word in Slavic languages).

The meaning of kerchief arose in English from association with the typical head covering of Russian women.

baby *n.* About 1378, *baby, babi, babee,* in a version of *Piers Plowman,* a diminutive form of BABE.

baccalaureate (bak′əlôr′ēit) *n.* bachelor's degree. 1625-49, borrowed from Medieval Latin *baccalaureatus,* from *baccalaureus* student with the first or bachelor's degree; for suffix see -ATE³.

The form *baccalaureus* was altered by a pun or play on words from *baccalarius* (see BACHELOR) as if connected with *bacca lauri* laurel berry.

bacchanal (bak′ənəl) *n.* drunken revelry; orgy. 1536, in a sermon of Bishop Latimer's; borrowed from Latin *bacchānālis* having to do with *Bacchus* (Dionysus), the god of wine, from Greek *Bákchos,* a name of unknown origin.

bachelor *n.* Probably before 1300 *bacheler:* (1) a young man, (2) a young aspirant knight, squire, both meanings in *Arthour and Merlin;* about 1300: (3) a young unmarried man, (4) a young knight, especially one in the service of another; before 1376, in a version of *Piers Plowman,* a university graduate with the lowest degree; 1418, a junior member of a guild. The word is borrowed from Old French *bacheler, bachelier,* from Medieval Latin **baccalaris,* probably a variant of *baccalarius* helper or tenant on a *baccalaria,* section of land; later in Medieval Latin *baccalarius* also had the meaning "junior member of a guild, university student," the latter meaning seen in the pun on *baccalaureus* under BACCALAUREATE. The ultimate origin of *bachelor* is uncertain.

bacillus *n.* rod-shaped bacterium. 1883, New Latin *bacillus,* prompted by French *bacille* (1842), from Late Latin *bacillus* little rod, variant of Latin *bacillum,* diminutive form of *baculum* rod, staff. Latin *baculum* is cognate with Greek *baktḗrion* small staff; see BACTERIA, from Indo-European **bak-* (Pok.93).

back *n.* Old English (about 885) *bæc.* The word is cognate with Old Frisian *bek,* Old Saxon and Middle Dutch and Old Icelandic *bak,* Old High German *bah* back, from Proto-Germanic **bakan,* with no connections outside Germanic; probably related to Old High German *bahho* side of bacon; see BACON. —**adj.** Probably before 1200, in *Ancrene Riwle.* —**adv.** Before 1390. Both the adverb and the adjective developed from *abak,* Old English *on bæc.* —**v.** Before 1376, in a version of *Piers Plowman.*

Various compounds include: **backache,** *n.* 1601; **backbiting,** *n.* probably before 1200, in *Ancrene Riwle;* **backbone,** *n.* before 1325; **background,** *n.* 1672; **backlash,** *n.* adverse reaction, 1921; **backlog,** *n.* 1684, American English, in writings of Increase Mather (figurative sense 1883); **backpack,** American English, *n.* 1914, *v.* 1916; **backwater,** *n.* a backward place, 1820; **backwoods,** *n.* American English, remote place, 1709; **backyard,** *n.* 1659, American English.

backgammon *n.* 1645, probably developed from *back,* adj. + Middle English *gamen* to GAME, GAMBLE. Originally called *tables* (1297, but known before 700) because the pieces, when taken up, had to go back and reenter at the table (i.e. the board).

backward or **backwards** *adj., adv.* Before 1325 *bakward,* in *Cursor Mundi,* developed from *abakward,* modeled on *hindeward, foreward,* using Old English adjective and adverbial suffix *-weard* expressing direction toward. The word is cognate with Old Frisian *bekward, bekwardich* backward.

bacon *n.* About 1330 *bacoun,* borrowed from Old French *bacon, bacun* (perhaps through Medieval Latin *baconem*), from a word of a Germanic source; compare Old High German *bahho* side of bacon, Middle High German *bache* ham, bacon (modern German *-backe,* as in *Hinterbacke* buttock), and Middle Dutch *baken* side of bacon, from Proto-Germanic **bakōn-.* Compare BACK.

bacteria *n.,* plural of **bacterium,** single-celled organisms. 1847-49, New Latin *bacteria,* plural of *bacterium,* prompted by French *bactérie* (1842), from Greek *baktḗrion* small staff, diminutive of *báktron* stick, rod. Compare BACILLUS.

bacteriology *n.* 1884, formed probably through influence of earlier German *Bakteriologie,* from English *bacteri(um)* + connective form *-o-* + *-logy.*

bad *adj.* 1203 *badde,* in the surname *Baddecheese;* origin uncertain.

Middle English *badde* is more probably an adjective developed from a shortened form of Old English *bǣdling* an effeminate man, pederast, from Proto-Germanic **baiđlingaz;* cognate with Latin *foedāre* to defile, pollute (compare Latin *foedus* foul, filthy), from Indo-European **bhoidh-* (Pok.161).

The meaning "pederast" in Old English may account for the small number of written examples up to the early 1400's, the word *evil* being more popular in use until the 1700's. The forms *badder, baddest* occurred from the 1300's to the 1700's, though Shakespeare used *worse, worsest.*

badge *n.* Probably before 1400 *bage, bagge* in *Morte Arthur;* borrowed perhaps from Anglo-French *bage* (1334), or Anglo-Latin *bagis,* plural of *bagia* (about 1370), both meaning emblem; of unknown origin.

badger *n.* burrowing animal. 1523. Traditionally it is offered that *badger* is perhaps related to *badge* (because of the white blaze on its forehead), but it is *blaze* rather than *badge* that exists in this meaning; so the origin of *badger* is unknown. The Middle English *brok* and Old English *broc* were the terms for this animal, as in Tommy Brock, in Beatrix Potter's *The Tale of Mr. Tod.*—v. 1794, to bait like a badger, pester, tease; from the noun.

badminton *n.* 1874, after *Badminton,* an estate in Gloucestershire, the country seat of the Duke of Beaufort, where the game may have been first played, after British officials stationed in India introduced the game, which in India is often called *poona.*

baffle *v.* confound. 1548, originally Scottish, meaning to disgrace publicly. In the later sense of confound, bewilder (about 1590), probably related to French *bafouer* to abuse, hoodwink, baffle. **—n.** a device for changing the flow of air, water, etc. 1913, developed from earlier meaning of *baffle,* v. (1885) to control by changing the flow of air, water, etc.

bag *n.* Probably before 1200 *bagge,* in *Ancrene Riwle;* borrowed from an indeterminate word of Scandinavian source (compare Old Icelandic *baggi* pack, bundle). Medieval Latin *baga* and Old French *bague* sack, chest, are probably from a word of Germanic source. **—v.** About 1412 *baggen* to put into a bag, developed from Middle English *bagge,* n. **—bagman** *n.* This word, known today primarily as a slang term for "a person who collects graft or protection money," was also known in Middle English, one of its senses being "tax collector (1377)." It has long been a part of English vocabulary with various meanings; especially one who makes bags (1329), one who carries a bag (1531), a peddler and a traveling salesman (1765).

bagatelle *n.* trifle. 1637, borrowed from French *bagatelle,* from Italian *bagatella,* probably a diminutive of *bagata* a trifle, Italian dialect *baga* berry, from Latin *bāca* berry, pearl, probably from a non-Indo-European language, and very likely related to the name of the Thracian wine god *Bacchos.*

bagel (bā′gəl) *n.* ring-shaped roll of bread. 1919 *beigel,* 1932 *bagel,* borrowed from Yiddish *beygl,* from Middle High German *boug-* ring, bracelet, from Old High German *boug,* related to *biogan* to bend, from Proto-Germanic **biuȝanan,* Indo-European **bheugh-* (Pok.153).

baggage *n.* Probably about 1440, in writings of Lydgate; borrowed from Old French *bagage,* from *bague* pack, bundle, from Medieval Latin *baga,* perhaps from a word of Germanic source (compare Old Icelandic *baggi* pack, bundle, BAG); for suffix see -AGE.

bail[1] *n.* bond money. 1485, developed from an earlier meaning "temporary release from jail or custody" (1423, in *Rolls of Parliament*), a sense that developed from a still earlier meaning "captivity, custody, stewardship" (before 1338, in Mannyng's *Chronicle of England*); borrowed through Anglo-French *bail,* from Old French *baillier* hand over, control, guard, from Latin *bajulāre* bear (a burden for pay), from *bajulus* porter, of unknown origin.

bail[2] *n.* curved handle of a pail or kettle. 1447 *beyl,* borrowed probably from an indeterminate Scandinavian source (compare Old Icelandic *beygla* bending, hoop, ring, and *beyla* hump, swelling, and *beyglast* to bend; Danish *bøjle* bar, strap, Swedish *bögel* hoop, ring). The Old Icelandic *beyglast* is probably cognate with Old English *būgan* to BOW[1] bend.

bail[3] *v.* throw out (water). 1613, verb use developed from *baille* (1353), *balie* 1336 bucket, borrowed from Old French *baille* bucket, from Vulgar Latin **bajula,* from Latin *bajulus* porter, of unknown origin.

bailiff *n.* About 1242, as a surname, later an administrator of a district (about 1300); borrowed from Old French *baillif,* accusative of *baillis* administrative official, deputy, from Vulgar Latin **bajulīvus,* from Latin *bajulus* porter. Compare BAIL[1].

bailiwick (bā′ləwik) *n.* district of a bailiff. 1444 *Baillywyke,* in *Rolls of Parliament,* apparently by alteration of earlier *baillifwyke* (1431), formed from *bailiff* + *wick* village. *Wick* is found in Old English *wīc,* a word surviving mainly in place names, as in *Hardwick* and *Wickham,* ultimately a borrowing of Latin *vicus* village.

The extended sense "one's field of knowledge, authority, etc.," first appears in American English (1843).

bairn (bārn) *n. Chiefly Scottish.* child. Middle English *barn* (probably about 1150), developed from Old English *bearn* (about 725, in *Beowulf*), probably related to *beran* BEAR[2] (carry, give birth).

The Middle and Old English forms have cognates in a wide variety of ancient and modern Germanic languages, including Gothic, Old and modern Icelandic, Swedish, Danish, Norwegian, Old and Middle High German, Old Saxon *barn,* all meaning "child," from Proto-Germanic **barnan,* and with similar formations in Baltic, including Latvian *bērns* child and Lithuanian *berniùkas* boy (diminutive of *bérnas* lad, fellow), from Indo-European **bher-/bhor-* to bear (Pok.131). Thus, though the word resides now chiefly in Scottish, it was once a word of widespread use in older forms of English.

bait *n.* About 1300, food used to entice prey; borrowed from an indeterminate Scandinavian source (compare Old Icelandic *beita* food, especially to entice prey, *beit* pasture, related to *bīta* to bite). **—v.** About 1300, in *Havelok the Dane,* to attack or torment with a dog; borrowed from a Scandinavian source (compare Old

Icelandic *beita* to cause to bite, hunt, a causative of *bīta* to bite, cognate with Old English *bǣtan* to cause to bite, a form of *bītan* to bite, and with Old and Middle High German *beizen* and Gothic **baitjan* to bait, from Proto-Germanic **baitjanan*; see BITE).

bake *v.* Old English *bacan, bōc, bacen* (before 893, in a translation of St. Gregory's *Dialogues*).

The Old English *bacan* is cognate with Old High German *bahhan* to bake, Middle High German *bachen,* Old Icelandic *baka,* Norwegian *bake,* Danish *bage,* Swedish *baka,* from Proto-Germanic **bakanan,* and with Old High German *backan* (modern German *backen*) and Middle Dutch *backen* (modern Dutch *bakken*), from Proto-Germanic **bakkanan* and with Greek *phṓgein* to roast; from the Indo-European base **bhōg-/bhəg-* (Pok.113). Compare BATCH. **—baker** *n.* 1177 *bakere* in a surname; developed from Old English *bæcere, bæcestre;* cognates in Germanic are shaped with appropriate derivatives of the languages listed under BAKE. **—bakery** *n.* 1545, work of a baker, formed from English *baker* + *-y* [3], and 1826, shop where baked goods are sold, formed from English *bake* + *-ery,* formed independently of earlier Middle English *bakern* (before 1000, in Ælfric's *Glossary*), from Old English *bæcern.*

balance *n.* Probably about 1200 *balaunce* instrument for weighing, scale; borrowed through Anglo-French *balaunce,* variant of Old French *balance,* from Medieval Latin *bilancia,* from Late Latin *bilānx* (accusative *bilancem*) referring to a scale having two plates (possibly Latin *bi-* two + *lānx,* accusative *lancem,* shallow pan; or perhaps a borrowing in Latin from some unknown foreign source). **—v.** 1583, in writings of Bishop Stubbs, either: (1) borrowed from Old French *balancer* (1100's), or (2) from English *balance,* n.

balcony *n.* 1618, borrowed from Italian *balcone,* derived from *balco* scaffold + *-one,* the Italian augmentative suffix indicating something large and often grossly unattractive or awkward. Italian *balco* was probably a loan word from a Germanic source (compare Old High German *balcho, balko* beam, scaffold; related to Old English *balca* beam, ridge); see BALK.

bald *adj.* **1** wholly or partly without hair on the head. Before 1292 *bal-* in a surname; about 1300 *balled.* **2** having a white spot or blaze on the head, as some animals are marked. Before 1325, especially in combination as *balled coot* a water bird with a noticeable white mark on the forehead.

It is unclear just how one sense developed from the other; Middle English *balled* probably developed from Celtic *bal* a white mark + *-ed* adjectival suffix (compare Middle Irish, modern Irish, and Gaelic *ball* a spot, mark; Middle Irish *ballach* spotted; Breton *bal* a white mark on an animal's face; Welsh *bal* having a white spot on the forehead, used of horses. The word is also possibly related to Danish *bældet* bald). As a reborrowing in the 1600's in the now obsolete *ball,* meaning "white spot or streak," the word occurs twice in English: 1523, meaning "a white streak or spot"; 1573, meaning "a white-faced horse."

There is also speculation that *bald* may be related to English *ball* a round protuberance, but examples for this course of development are wanting, and the relation to cognates in other languages through the sense of "white, shining, having a white spot on the forehead," is questionable. However, the latter path leads to Gothic *bala-* pale (horse), Greek *phalós* white, *phálāros* having a white patch, Latin *fulica* coot (from the white mark on its head), Old High German *belihha* coot, Old Icelandic *bāl* fire, flame, Old English *bǣl* fire, flame, Old Slavic *bělŭ* white, and Sanskrit *bhāla-m* luster, forehead, from Indo-European **bhel-* white, shining (Pok.118).

bale *n.* large bundle. About 1380, in *Patience* and *Sir Ferumbras,* borrowed from Old French *bale* and Medieval Latin *bala* ball, round package, from a Germanic source (compare Old High German *balla* ball); see BALL[1].

baleen *n.* whalebone. About 1312 *balayn* whalebone (about 1300 *bleine,* 1333 *balayn* whale); borrowed from Old French *baleine, balaine* whale, whalebone, from Latin *balēna,* dialectal variant of *balaena* whale, borrowed from the same source as Greek *phálaina, phállaina* whale, from Indo-European **bhel-* blow up, swell up (Pok.120).

baleful *adj.* Old English (before 1000) *bealuful, bealoful* (*bealu, bealo* evil + *ful* full). The now archaic *bale* evil, is found in Old English (about 725, in *Beowulf*) *bealu, bealo, balu* evil, misfortune, and is cognate with Old High German *balo* destruction, Old Icelandic *bǫl* misfortune, damage, and Gothic *balwa-wēsei* wickedness, *balwjan* to torment, Old Slavic *bolěti* ail, be sick, Old Cornish *bal* pestilence, from Indo-European **bheleu-* strike, hurt, weak, sick (Pok.125).

balk *n.* Old English *balca* ridge (before 900, in Alfred's translation of Boethius' *De Consolatione Philosophiae*). Cognates, all meaning "beam" are abundant in the Germanic languages, including Old Frisian *balka,* Old Saxon *balko,* Old High German *balco, balko* (modern German *Balken*), Middle Dutch *balc* (modern Dutch *balk*), and Old Icelandic *bjalki* (compare also Old Icelandic *bālkr* partition), from Proto-Germanic **balkan-, *belkan-.* Cognates also appear in Latin *fulcīre* to support, and Greek *phálanx* trunk, log; line of battle, from Indo-European **bheləĝ-/bhelĝ-/bholĝ* (Pok.122).

The meaning "hindrance" is first recorded about 1405, in *Mum Sothseger,* and developed as a figurative sense from "ridge, mound," that existed probably about 1380, first recorded in *Pearl.* The earliest recorded meaning for *balk* in Middle English is "strip of unplowed land," 1202, perhaps as a place name or location, and later "strip of land left unplowed by accident," which took on the figurative meaning "an oversight," probably before 1430, in *Pilgrimage of Man.* It is curious that the meaning "beam," found in so many cognates, was not recorded in Middle English until sometime before 1325, in *Cursor Mundi.*

—v. Before 1393, in Gower's *Confessio Amantis,* Middle English *balken* make ridges in plowing; from verb use of Middle English *balke,* n., developed from Old English *balca* ridge.

ball[1] *n.* round object, ball. Probably before 1200 *bal,* in Layamon's *Chronicle of Britain;* perhaps developed from Old English **beal, *beall,* borrowed from a Scandinavian source (compare Old Icelandic *bǫllr* ball), from Proto-Germanic **balluz* (earlier **ƀalnus*), and related to Old High German *ballo, balla* ball, from Proto-Germanic **ballōn* (earlier **ƀalnōn*), Old English *beallucc* testicle, and more remotely to *bulluc* little bull; see BULL[1].

ball[2] *n.* dancing party. 1632, borrowed from French *bal* a dance, from *baller* to dance, Old French *baler* to dance, from Late Latin *ballāre* to dance, which derives from Greek *ballízein* to jump, throw the legs about, dance, ultimately from *bállein* to throw, Arcadian Greek **dellen,* cognate with Old High German *quellan* spurt up, from Indo-European **gwel-* (Pok.471).

ballad *n.* a poem that tells a story, simple song, sentimental popular song, music for a ballad or folk song. Before 1393 *balade* a poem or song in a form of strict or varied stanzas, in Gower's *Confessio Amantis;* borrowed from Old French *ballade,* from Old Provençal *balada* song for dancing, dance, from *balar* to dance, from Late Latin *ballāre* to dance. In the 1500's and 1600's the termination *-ad* was commonly changed to *-et, -at,* as is seen in *salad,* formerly *sallet* and *ballet.* OED says the form *ballet* has probably tended to reinforce restoration of the spelling *ballad.* —**ballade** *n.* a musical composition without strict form especially for piano; a poem, usually of strict form, with three stanzas. About 1386, in Chaucer's *Legend of Good Women,* Middle English *ballade* a poem of three or more stanzas in rhyme royal, perhaps a separate borrowing from Old French *ballade,* or a specialized meaning that retained the Old French spelling. The modern meaning of an instrumental musical composition was first used by Frédéric Chopin (d. 1849).

ballast *n.* 1530, in Palsgrave's *Lesclarcissement;* borrowed from Low German *ballast,* probably from a Scandinavian source (compare Old Danish and Old Swedish and Norwegian *barlast,* before 1400, possibly a compound of *bar* bare + *last* load; that is, lading which is a bare or mere load, for the sake of weight only).

ballerina *n.* 1792, but first recorded as an English form by Byron (1815); borrowed from Italian *ballerina,* feminine of *ballerino* a dancer, from *ballare* to dance, from Late Latin *ballāre* to dance.

ballet *n.* 1667, borrowed from French *ballet,* from Italian *balletto,* diminutive of *ballo* ball (dance), from *ballare* to dance, from Late Latin *ballāre* to dance.

ballistics *n.* science of projectiles in motion. 1753, in *Chambers Cyclopaedia;* probably formed in English from Latin *ballista* machine for hurling stones or other missiles (from Greek *ballistḗs,* from *ballízein,* in the sense of *bállein* to throw) + English suffix *-ics,* as in *physics, athletics,* etc.; see BALL[2] dance. —**ballistic** *adj.* having to do with the motion or, originally, the hurling of projectiles. 1775, adjective use of *ballistics,* n. with loss of *s;* or perhaps borrowed from earlier French *balistique* (1647), from Latin *ballista* + French adjective suffix *-ique.* Alternatively, formed in English from Latin *ballista* + English suffix *-ic.*

There is also the possibility that *ballistics* developed from *ballistic,* adj., which may have existed earlier but was not recorded by some defect in the record of English.

—**ballistic missile,**1954, earlier *ballistic rocket* (1949).

balloon *n.* 1579, *ballone* game played with a large leather ball, in a version of Plutarch's *Lives;* borrowed perhaps partly from earlier French *ballon* (1549), and from northern Italian dialect *ballone* (derived from *balla* ball, from a Germanic source; compare Old High German *balla* ball + Italian *-one* augmentative suffix indicating something large); for ending see -OON. The sense of a large gas-filled bag for carrying a basket with a passenger first appeared in 1783 after the flights of the Montgolfier brothers, especially the one before the French court at Versailles in September, 1783.

ballot *n.* 1549, small ball used for secret voting, in William Thomas' *The Historie of Italie;* borrowed from Venetian Italian dialect *ballotta,* diminutive form of *balla* ball; see BALLOON. *Ballotta* is now the standard term in Italian. —**ballot box** (before 1680)

balm *n.* aromatic resin, healing ointment. 1373 *balme;* before 1300 *baum;* probably before 1200 *basme,* in *Ancrene Riwle;* borrowed from Old French *basme* or *baume,* from Latin *balsamum,* from Greek *bálsamon.* The Greek word is probably of Semitic origin (compare Hebrew *bāśām* spice, balsam, Syriac *besmā,* Aramaic *bsem* be sweet, pleasant).

The English spelling with *l* was influenced by the Latin *balsamum* in an attempt to correct the spelling.

baloney *n., interj. Slang.* nonsense. 1928 *boloney,* American English, probably related in meaning to earlier use as a term of contempt for an inferior prizefighter (1920), alteration of *bologna* (1850) type of sausage traditionally stuffed with odds and ends from slaughter and, in some quarters, reputed to be stuffed with asses' meat, from *Bologna,* city in Italy where these sausages were made.

Baloney and *bologna* are pronounced bəlō′nē, and the spelling *baloney* is used both for the sausage and to mean nonsense. Why "nonsense" is a matter of conjecture, but it follows a long history of applying names of food to human attributes and conditions: ham, chicken, goose, puddinghead, molasses, vinegar, hot dog.

balsa *n.* 1593, a raft of the South American Indians; 1917, in *Scientific American,* a very light wood; both terms apparently borrowed from Spanish *balsa.*

balsam *n.* fragrant, sticky resin, balm. The form *balsam* is found in Old English (about 1000, in Ælfric's *Glossary*), but was superseded by *basme* BALM, until late in the 1300's (before 1398, in Trevisa's translation of Bartholomew's *De Proprietatibus Rerum* by the Latin form *balsamum*). The modern form *balsam* was reintroduced in 1579; see BALM.

baluster *n.* supporting post of a railing on a balcony, staircase, etc. 1602 (also *ballister*), borrowed from Italian *balaustro,* from *balaustra* wild pomegranate flower, from Latin *balaustium,* from Greek *balaústion;* so called from the resemblance of a baluster to the double-curving calyx tube of the wild flower.

Apparently the word did not come into English through French, because French *balustre* is not recorded as an architectural term before 1633, though the flower was known in French by 1529.

balustrade *n.* banister. 1644, in John Evelyn's *Diary,* borrowed from French *balustrade,* from Italian *balaustrata* balustrade, from *balaustro* BALUSTER.

bamboo *n.* woody grass. 1598, borrowed from Dutch *bamboe, bamboes,* from Portuguese *bambu,* from Malay *bambu,* perhaps introduced from Kanarese, a Dravidian language of southern India.

bamboozle *v.* cheat, deceive. 1703, in writings of Colley Cibber; origin uncertain (but compare Scottish *bumbaze, bombaze* to confuse, probably from *bombase* stuff with cotton, pad, borrowed from Old French *bombace,* n.; see BOMBAST).

ban[1] *v.* forbid, prohibit. Formed in Middle English about 1378, in a version of *Piers Plowman,* perhaps from fusion of a word of Scandinavian origin (compare

Old Icelandic *banna* curse, prohibit) + Old English *bannan* summon, proclaim (before 800, in poetry of Cynewulf). Old English *bannan* is cognate with Old Frisian *banna, bonna* command, proclaim; Old Dutch *bannen* prohibit (modern Dutch, banish, exile); Old High German *bannan,* Middle High German (modern German) *bannen* banish, expel; Gothic **bannan* proclaim, command, forbid; and is probably related to Latin *fāri* speak and Greek *phánai* speak on the basis of an Indo-European **bhā-/bhə-*(Pok.106).

There is also evidence that the meaning "forbid, prohibit" could have developed from a fusion of meanings already recorded in Middle English: (1) curse, condemn (probably about 1150), and (2) summon (probably before 1200, in Layamon's *Chronicle of Britain*).

ban² *n.* edict, proclamation. About 1300; earlier meaning "a troop of warriors summoned by proclamation" (about 1250, in *The Owl and the Nightingale*); and still earlier in the phrase *bane cruces* crosses marking a boundary (1228). Formed in Middle English by fusion of Old English (1051-52) *ban,* earlier *geban, gebann* a summons, proclamation (before 800, in poetry of Cynewulf) + Old North French *ban* a summoning of the king's vassals for military service, proclamation, from Frankish **ban* (compare Old High German *ban* proclamation commanding or forbidding, from *bannan* proclaim, command); see BAN¹ in which the cognates listed for the verb occur in the same languages for the noun, except possibly for the hypothetical Gothic form. Related to ABANDON.

banal (bā'nəl) *adj.* commonplace, trite. 1840, borrowed from French *banal* common, ordinary, without originality, developed from an earlier sense "open to the use of the whole community, owned in common," from Middle French *banal* of or belonging to compulsory feudal service, from Old French *ban* a summoning of the king's vassals for military service, see BAN²; for suffix see -AL. —**banality** *n.* 1861, borrowed from French *banalité,* from *banal;* for suffix see -ITY.

banana *n.* 1597, borrowed through Portuguese or Spanish *banana,* from a word of West African origin (compare Mandingo and Wolof *banäna, barända* plantain).

band¹ *n.* group acting together. 1490, in Caxton's translation of *The Book of Eneydos,* borrowed from Middle French *bande,* from Old French *bande,* from a Germanic source (compare Gothic *bandwa* sign, signal). The meaning probably derived from the use of a band of cloth as a mark of identification by members of a group of soldiers (before 1470, *band²,* variant of *bond*), or from a banner as a sign of the group as a whole (*banere,* probably before 1200, in *Ancrene Riwle*); see BANNER. The meaning "a group of musicians" first appeared about 1660. —**v.** to unite, join together in a group. 1530, in Palsgrave's *Lesclarcissement,* borrowed from Middle French *bander* to join, from *bande* a group. The senses of *band¹* and *band²* run together in the verb.

band² *n.* strip of material. 1552 *band* a strip, developed from Middle English *band* (1126), dialect variant of *bond;* fusion of a borrowing from a Scandinavian word (compare Old Icelandic *band,* from Proto-Germanic **bandan,* Indo-European **bhondhom*), and from Old French *bande* strip, Old North French *bende* flat strip, from a Germanic source (compare Old High German *binta* band, Old English *bindan* to bind); see BIND. —**v.** to bind or fasten with a band or bands. 1530, in Palsgrave's *Lesclarcissement,* borrowed from Middle French *bander* to band, from Old French *bande,* n.

bandage *n.* 1599, borrowed from Middle French *bandage,* from Old French *bander* to bind, from *bande* a strip, see BAND²; for suffix see -AGE. —**v.** 1774, in Goldsmith's *A History of the Earth and Animated Nature;* from the noun.

bandana *n.* gaily colored kerchief. 1752, borrowed from Hindi *bāndhnū* way of tying cloth to produce designs when dyed, tie-dyeing, from *bādhnā* to tie, bind, from Sanskrit *badhnā̆ti* binds; see BIND.

bandit *n.* 1591 *bandito;* 1593 *bandetto,* in Shakespeare's *2 Henry VI,* borrowed from Italian *bandito* outlaw; literally, proscribed, from the past participle of *bandire* proscribe, banish, from Medieval Latin *bannire* proclaim; see BANISH. —**banditry** *n.* 1922, formed from English *bandit* + *-ry.*

bandy *v.* toss, exchange. 1577, in Holinshed's *Chronicle,* figurative meaning of to throw or hit (a ball) back and forth; borrowed perhaps from Middle French *bandé,* past participle of *bander* return a ball from one's side, to side with, from Old French *bander,* from *bande* side, group; see BAND¹ a group. The meanings "to talk about from one to another," as in *bandy gossip about,* and "to toss about," as in *fortune bandied him about,* were first recorded in the very late 1500's and the 1600's. —**bandy-legged** *adj.* 1687 *bandy-leg* with the legs curved outward; formed perhaps from English *bandy,* n. (1629), in reference to the curved lower end of a stick *(bandy)* used for striking the ball in the game *bandy,* which was much like field hockey.

bane (bān) *n.* cause of death, ruin, or harm, curse. Old English *bana* slayer, cause of death, (less often) murderer (about 725, in *Beowulf*). Old English *bana* is cognate with Old Saxon *bano,* Old Frisian *bana, bona,* Old High German *bano,* Middle High German *bane, ban,* Old Icelandic *bani,* all meaning "death, murder," from Proto-Germanic **banōn,* and related to Gothic *banja* blow, wound, sore, and Old English *benn* wound, from Proto-Germanic **banjō,* Indo-European **bhen-/bhon-* (Pok.126).

The current common meaning "cause of ruin or harm" is first recorded in 1577.

bang¹ *v.* to make a loud noise. Probably about 1550, to strike violently often with a resounding blow; perhaps borrowed from a word of Scandinavian origin (compare Old Icelandic *banga* to strike, hammer, Old Swedish *banga* to strike, cognate with Low German *bangen, bangeln* to strike, beat). —**n.** Probably about 1550, a heavy resounding blow; probably borrowed from a noun of the same Scandinavian source as English *bang¹*, v.

Most of the uses cited in the OED that refer to loud noise occur from the late 1700's onward, indicating that this sense is a relatively recent development in English. Only the meaning "beat or hit violently" occurs earlier.

bang² *n.* Usually, **bangs,** *pl.* fringe of hair cut squarely across the forehead. 1878, American English, perhaps influenced by adverb use of *bang¹* (1828), in the meaning of abruptly, as in *hair cut bang off;* some sources offer a relation to earlier *bangtailed* (1861) of a horse's tail that has been cut horizontally across.

bangle *n.* 1787, borrowed from Hindi *bangrī* wrist- or ankle-ring (originally made of colored glass).

banish *v.* About 1385 *banysen, banysshen* to condemn, exile, in Chaucer's *Canterbury Tales*; earlier, *forbanishen* (about 1300); borrowed from Old French *baniss-*, stem of *banir* proclaim, from Medieval Latin *bannire* proclaim, from *bannum* proclamation, from a Germanic source (compare Old High German *ban* proclamation commanding or forbidding, see BAN[2] edict); for ending see -ISH[2]. The extended meaning "to drive away, as of kindness, or to force out" developed almost simultaneously with "condemn, exile" and is found in *Piers Plowman* (before 1376). —**banishment** *n.* 1507, formed from English *banish* + *-ment.*

banister *n.* 1851, the handrail and its balusters on a staircase; earlier *bannister* (1667), an unexplained alteration of BALUSTER.

The word was possibly influenced in its formation by the earlier form *barrister* (1662) of the same meaning, but through just what connection is unknown.

banjo *n.* 1774, earlier *banshaw* (1764), American English, perhaps of African origin, from a Bantu language of West Africa (compare Kimbundu *mbanza* and Tshiluba *mbanzi* stringed musical instruments). The earliest citations for this word, from 1764 through 1845, associate it with the music of American Black slaves. Whether the word developed from a mispronunciation of *bandore* (an old lutelike instrument) is difficult to establish, but certainly many observers, such as Jefferson, probably equated the *bandore,* which he wrote *bajor,* with the *banjo.*

bank[1] *n.* pile, heap, ridge. Probably about 1200, in *The Ormulum.* The development of this word is uncertain. It does not appear in Old English. A compound Old English *hō-banca,* literally, heel-bench, couch, or footstool, is often cited for its similarity of form but has no real semantic relationship, except that if **banca, banc* existed as a variant of *benc* bench, its connection would be through the sense "shelf," as in the turf-covered mounds used for seats in a garden (about 1385, in Chaucer's *Troilus and Criseyde*).

The word is probably of Scandinavian origin (compare Danish *banke,* Swedish *bank* sandbank), but it has other Germanic cognates, from Germanic **banki-*; see BENCH. The meanings of Middle English *bank, banke* (ridge, cliff or coast by water, embankment), as well as its early appearance in northern English dialect, suggest the possibility of a Scandinavian source.
—**v.** 1590, earlier *banked* provided with an embankment (before 1400); from the noun.

bank[2] *n.* place for keeping money. 1474, in Caxton's *Game and Play of Chess,* borrowed through Middle French *banque,* from Italian *banca;* and 1475, in a *Treaty of Edward IV* (in a phrase *the banke de Medicys*), borrowed directly from Italian *banca,* perhaps by influence of Middle French *banque.* Whether by way of Middle French or directly from Italian *banca,* originally a counter on which money-changers transacted their business, bench, Middle English also had *bench* (about 1390, in Chaucer's *Canterbury Tales*) as a counting table, which is derived from a Germanic source (compare Old High German *bank* bench); see BENCH. —**v.** 1727-51, in *Chambers Cyclopaedia,* from the noun. —**banking** *n.* 1735, from earlier *banking,* participial adjective (1641, in Milton's *Church Discipline*).

bank[3] *n.* row of things. Probably before 1200, in Layamon's *Chronicle of Britain,* meaning "bench"; borrowed from Old French *banc,* from a Germanic source (compare Old High German *bank* bench); see BENCH. The current meaning seems to have been first applied to a row or a group of rows of keys on an organ (1884) and to have developed from the sense of a row or tier of oars in a galley (1614), and earlier, the *bench* occupied by the rowers of each oar (1599).

bankrupt *n.* insolvent person. 1533 *bank roupte,* in Sir Thomas More's *Apologie of Syr Thomas More, Knyght,* later *bankrupt* (1543); borrowed through Middle French *banqueroute,* and directly from Italian *banca rotta* bankruptcy, (literally, bank broken; *rotta,* feminine past participle of *rompere* to break, from Latin *rumpere* break; the modern form *-rupt* is an alteration of Medieval Latin *ruptus* broken, also as a noun "a bankrupt").

The original meaning in Italian was the ruin or breaking up of a trader's business because of failure to pay creditors, or the abandonment of business to avoid paying debts. (Transfer of this sense to mean "an insolvent person" is peculiar to English.)
—**adj.** 1566, from the noun. —**v.** 1552, from the noun. —**bankruptcy** *n.* 1700, formed from English *bankrupt* + suffix *-cy,* as in *insolvency* (with the *-t* curiously retained in the spelling instead of being absorbed into the suffix *-cy*).

banner *n.* flag, standard. Probably before 1200 *banere,* in *Ancrene Riwle* (also, probably before 1300 *baner* troops under a particular banner); borrowed from Old French *banere, baniere,* alteration of a Germanic word corresponding to Gothic *bandwa, bandwō* sign, signal. The formation of the Old French from the Germanic was influenced by another Old French word *ban* a proclamation summoning vassals for military service. See BAN[2] edict, and BAND[1] group.

banns *n.pl.* notice of marriage. 1549 *bannes,* in *Book of Common Prayer,* plural of *banne,* alteration (influenced by Medieval Latin *bannum* ban) of earlier *bane* (about 1440), variant of *ban* proclamation; see BAN[2] edict.

A proclamation of intent to marry was known in the councils of Canterbury before 1328 and reference to such a proclamation appears in English literature before 1333. Banns were made a part of ecclesiastical legislation in 1215.

banquet *n.* feast. Probably before 1475 *banket,* borrowed from Middle French *banquet,* from Italian *banchetto,* diminutive of *banco* bench, (in reference to benches placed at a table around which people are eating), variant of *banca;* see BANK[2].

bantam *n.* small domestic fowl. 1749, named after *Bantam,* a town in Java, from which these small fowl were supposed to have first been imported.

The sense of a small, cocky person first appeared in Dickens' *Pickwick Papers* (1837) in reference to the bantam cocks' spirited fighting qualities.

banter *v.* tease, joke. 1676, origin unknown. —**n.** playful teasing or joking. 1690, possibly from the verb.

baptize *v.* immerse in water; christen. About 1280 *baptyzen,* later *baptisen* (about 1300); borrowed from Old French *baptizier, baptisier, batizier, baptizer,* learned borrowings from Latin *baptizāre,* from Greek *baptízein* to dip, bathe, from *báptein* to dip; for suffix see -IZE. Greek *báptein* (earlier **baphye-*), related to *baphḗ* a dipping, cognate with Old Icelandic *kvefja* to press under, drown, is from Indo-European **gwēbh-/gwəbh-* (Pok.465). —**baptism** *n.* About 1303 *bapteme,* in Mannyng's *Handlyng Synne,* later *baptisme* (1357);

borrowed from Old French *baptisme, baptesme, batesme, bapteme,* learned borrowings from Late Latin *baptisma,* from Greek *báptisma,* from *baptízein* to dip; for suffix see -ISM. —**baptist** *n.* Probably before 1200, in *Ancrene Riwle,* borrowed from Old French *baptiste,* learned borrowing from Latin *baptista,* from Greek *baptistḗs,* from *baptízein* to dip; for suffix see -IST.

Until the 1600's *baptist* was used only in reference to St. John the Baptist. The name of the sect *Baptist* is first recorded in 1654, the name perhaps originating in the form Baptized Church, Baptized Believers, etc.

bar *n.* straight piece of wood, iron, etc. Probably before 1200 *barre* barrier, later a bolt for a door or gate (probably before 1300), still later a metal bar, a pole or shaft (1364, 1380 in *Sir Ferumbras*); borrowed from Old French *barre,* from Vulgar Latin **barra,* of uncertain origin. —**v.** fasten with a bar. About 1280 *barren,* borrowed from Old French *barrer,* from *barre* bar.

barb *n.* point on fishhook or arrowhead. About 1390 *barbe,* in *Sir Gawain and the Green Knight;* earlier, piece of pleated cloth forming part of a headdress of widows and nuns (1305); borrowed from Old French *barbe* beard, beardlike appendage, from Latin *barba* BEARD. The figurative sense of something that wounds or stings is first recorded in Sheridan's *School for Scandal* (1777). —**v.** 1483, from the noun, perhaps influenced by Middle French *barber* shave. —**barbed** *adj.* 1611, formed from verbal adjective use of *barb,* v.

barbarian *n.* uncivilized person. Before 1338 *barbaryn* an infidel, especially a Moslem, in Mannyng's *Chronicle of England;* later, a foreigner (1384, in the Wycliffe Bible); borrowed through Old French *barbarin,* or directly from Medieval Latin *barbarinus,* probably from Latin *barbaria* foreign country. English *barbarian* also existed as an adjective probably before 1400.

A related form existed about the same time in Middle English *barbariene,* both as an adjective meaning "foreign, heathen" (probably before 1350) and later, as a noun meaning "a foreigner" (1422). It was borrowed through Anglo-French *barbarie* Barbary Coast or directly from Latin *barbaria* foreign country.

Latin *barbaria* derives from *barbarus* foreign, from Greek *bárbaros* foreign, rude; originally, stammering. Ultimately the Greek may be of imitative origin like Sanskrit *barbara-s* stammering (applied to non-Aryans) and *balbalā-kr-* to stammer, see BABBLE; for suffix see -IAN.

—**barbaric** *adj.* About 1395 *barbarik,* in the Wycliffe Bible; borrowed through Old French *barbarique* like a foreigner, or directly from Latin *barbaricus,* from Greek *barbarikós,* from *bárbaros* foreign, rude; for suffix see -IC. —**barbarism** *n.* Before 1447, borrowed through Old French *barbarisme,* or directly from Latin *barbarismus,* from Greek *barbarismós* foreign mode of speech. —**barbarity** *n.* 1570, formed from English *barbarous* + *-ity.* The older meaning "barbarism" became obsolete in English in the early 1800's; the current meaning "savage cruelty, inhumanity" is first recorded in 1685. —**barbarous** *adj.* 1405 *barbarus* uncultured, ignorant, gradually replacing *barbar* heathen, non-Christian (about 1390, in Chaucer's *Canterbury Tales;* a form that was used into the early 1500's, but was first used in Middle English as a noun meaning "one who speaks a foreign tongue or is a foreigner, especially not a Greek, Roman, or Christian," recorded in 1384, in the Wycliffe Bible). The form became *barbarouse* (1526, in Wynkyn de Worde's printing of *Pilgrimage of Perfection*), either developed from earlier English *barbar* + *-ous,* by influence of Latin *barbarus,* or perhaps reborrowed directly from Latin *barbarus,* with Anglicization of the Latin suffix *-us* to English *-ous.*

The earlier *barbar* was a borrowing from Old French *barbare,* from Latin *barbarus* barbarous (meaning not Latin or Greek, pertaining to those outside the Roman Empire; therefore, uncivilized; later, non-Christian, especially in reference to the Saracen; and by extension, savage, inhuman). The source of the Latin was Greek *bárbaros* also with the same type of sense development (foreign, non-Hellenic in speech; later, outlandish, rude, brutal).

barbecue *n.* 1697, borrowed from Spanish *barbacoa* framework for roasting meat or fish, from Arawak (Haiti) *barbakoa* tree-house, perhaps in relation to the framework of poles or sticks supporting such a structure. The current sense of an outdoor meal of roasted meat or fish appeared in 1733. —**v.** 1661, to dry or cure on a barbecue; later, to roast or broil meat or fish over an open fire (1690). Though the verb in both senses is recorded earlier than the noun, the OED states that the verb developed from the noun.

barber *n.* Probably before 1300 *barbour,* in *Sir Tristrem,* borrowed through Anglo-French *barbour,* from Old French *barbeor* and *barbier,* from *barbe* beard, from Latin *barba* BEARD; so called from the barber's business of shaving. The modern spelling in *-er* is a further Anglicization of the older *barbour,* influenced by *barberie* occupation of a barber (about 1400 in Lydgate's *Troy Book*) and also perhaps influenced by *barbier,* common in French to the late 1700's; for further discussion of suffix see -ER[1].

barberry *n.* type of thorny shrub used in hedges. Before 1400 *barbaryn, barbare, berber* common barberry, borrowed through Middle French *berbere, berberis;* also before 1400 *berberie* fruit of the common barberry; influenced by Middle English *berie* berry; both forms borrowed from Medieval Latin *barbaris* and *berberis,* probably from Arabic *barbāris.*

The OED and the Century Dictionary dispute the Arabic origin, but the Spanish scholar Corominas confirms an ultimate Arabic source.

barbiturate (bärbich′ərāt) *n.* sedative drug made from barbituric acid. 1928, formed from *barbitur(ic acid)* + suffix *-ate* [2] forming nouns and meaning "salt made from a specific acid." *Barbituric acid* (1866) is a loan translation *(barbit-* + *uric* and *acid)* of French *barbiturique acide,* from German *Barbitursäure* barbitur(ic) acid, coined in 1863 by the German chemist Adolf von Baeyer.

bard *n.* minstrel, poet. 1449, Scottish *baird,* probably developed from Gaelic *bàrd,* from an earlier Celtic form (compare Irish *bárd,* Cornish *bardh,* Welsh *bardd,* Breton *barz,* Middle Irish *bard,* Gaulish *bardos*); cognate with Sanskrit *gṛṇā́ti* sings, from Indo-European **gwer(ə)-* (Pok.478). Latin *bardus* and Greek *bárdos,* both meaning bard, are borrowings from Gaulish, but as imports from a respected Classical source the Latin and Greek words influenced the use of the word in English literature as a poetic term among such authors as Shakespeare 1606, Milton 1667, Pope 1704, and Byron 1809, where once *bard* had fallen into a term of contempt chiefly by way of the Scots, who considered *bards* itinerant troublemakers for the most part. Among the Welsh, on the other hand, *bardd* was an exalted title, awarded in recognition of outstanding achievement.

bare *adj.* uncovered, naked. Old English (probably about 725) *bær.* The word has cognates within a variety of Germanic languages, including Old and Middle High German *bar* bare (modern German *bar,* as in *barfuss* barefoot), Old Saxon *bar,* Old Frisian *ber,* Middle Dutch *baer,* Old Icelandic *berr,* from Proto-Germanic **bazás,* and is possibly cognate with Old Slavic *bosŭ,* Lithuanian *bãsas* barefoot, and Armenian *bok* naked (from **bhos-ko-*), from Indo-European **bhosó-s* (Pok.163). —**v.** Old English **barian,* found in the compound *ābarian* (about 725, in *Beowulf*), possibly verb use of Old English *bær,* adj. The word is cognate with Old High German *barōn,* Old Icelandic *bera.* —**barely** *adv.* About 950, in *Lindisfarne Gospels.*

bargain *n.* Before 1338 *bergayn, bargayne,* in Mannyng's *Chronicle of England;* borrowed through Anglo-French *bargayne, bergain,* from Old French *bargaine, bargaigne,* from *bargainier, bargaignier* to bargain. —**v.** About 1380 *bargeyne, bargayne,* in writings of Wycliffe; borrowed from Old French *bargainier, bargaignier,* to haggle, bargain; perhaps from Frankish **borganjan* borrow and lend (compare Old High German *borgēn* to take care, modern German *borgen* to borrow, lend, from Proto-Germanic **burʒ-,* Indo-European **bherĝh-/bhr̥ĝh-* keep safe, secure, Pok.145), or perhaps from Medieval Latin *barcaniare* to trade, probably from Germanic.

barge *n.* large flat boat. Probably before 1300, in *Kyng Alisaunder,* borrowed from Old French *barge,* from Vulgar Latin **bārica,* from Greek *bâris;* see BARK[3].

The early meaning in Middle English was "a boat or small ship with sail." After the introduction of *bark* the use of *barge* in English became specialized to "a boat with a flat bottom for carrying freight."

bargello (bärjel′ō) *n.* any one of a variety of zigzag stitches in needlework. 1972, named after *Bargello,* a museum in Florence, Italy, containing work of Andrea della Robbia, noted for its highly decorative borders that inspired the design of various stitches used in this needlework. The museum's name comes from Italian *bargello* chief constable, temporary prison in a police station (originally the museum was the residence of a bargello, then a prison).

baritone *n.* male voice. 1609, borrowed from Italian *baritono,* learned borrowing from Greek *barýtonos* deep-sounding (*barýs* heavy, deep + *tónos* pitch, sound); see BAROMETER, TONE.

In the 1800's the prevalent spelling in English was *barytone,* influenced by French *baryton.*

barium (bãr′ēəm) *n.* metallic chemical element. 1808, New Latin, formed from *bar(ytes)* sulfate of barium + suffix *-ium,* as in *sodium.* Sulfate of barium was named *barytes* in 1791, from Greek *barýtēs* weight, from *barýs* heavy.

Barium was coined by its discoverer, the English chemist Sir Humphry Davy, 1778-1829, on a pattern he established in naming *aluminum,* (at first *alumium*).

bark[1] *n.* outer covering of trees. Before 1325, in *Cursor Mundi,* borrowed from a Scandinavian source (compare Old Icelandic *bǫrkr,* genitive *barkar* bark, and Swedish, Danish, Norwegian *bark*). The word is cognate with Middle High German and Low German *borke* and Middle Dutch *barc,* all meaning bark of a tree, from Indo-European **bhorĝus* (Pok.166).

bark[2] *v.* make the short, sharp sound of a dog. Middle English *berken* (probably before 1200, in *Ancrene Riwle*), and earlier *borcen* (about 1150), developed from Old English *beorcan* (before 899, in Alfred's translation of St. Gregory's *Pastoral Care*), from Proto-Germanic **berkanan.* The Old English word is cognate with Old Icelandic *berkja* to boast, Lithuanian dialect *burgĕti* to growl, quarrel, from Indo-European **bhereg-* (Pok.138). —**n.** About 1250 *berk,* developed from Old English *beorc,* noun use of Old English *beorcan,* v.

bark[3] *n.* three-masted ship. About 1420 *barke* a boat, an early synonym for *barge;* borrowed perhaps from Old French *barque,* from Old Provençal *barca,* from Latin *barca* small boat, developed through Vulgar Latin **bārica* from Latin *bāris* flat-bottomed Egyptian boat, from Greek *bâris,* from Egyptian (compare Coptic *barī* small pleasure boat), although the OED and the Century Dictionary dismiss this, both favoring a possible Celtic origin, the OED citing Old Irish *barc* representing a possible original **barga.*

barley *n.* 1184-85 *barli* (in compound *barli-bred* bread made of barley flour), Middle English form of Old English *bærlīc* (966). The Old English *bærlīc* was originally an adjective meaning "of barley" (*bar-* root form of *bere* barley + *līc* -ly, adjective suffix) but was later used as a noun in Middle English, appearing as late as 1250 in the form *barlic,* 1425 as *barlich,* and 1459 as *barleche.* Old English *bere* (from Proto-Germanic **bariz*) has cognates in Old Icelandic *barr* barley (from Proto-Germanic **baraz*), Gothic *barizeins* of barley; Latin *far* grain, *farīna* ground meal, flour, from Indo-European **bhares-/bhars-* (Pok.111).

bar mitzvah (bar mits′və) celebration of a Jewish boy's reaching the age of religious responsibility. 1861, borrowed from Medieval Hebrew *bar miṣwah* son of the commandment (Aramaic *bar* son, and Hebrew *miṣwah* commandment). The verb form, usually in the passive "to be *bar mitzvahed,*" appeared in the 1940's and was derived from the noun in English.

barn *n.* Middle English *bern* (probably about 1200, in *The Ormulum*), developed from Old English (about 950) *berern,* literally, barley house (*bere* barley + *ærn* house, building, storeroom). It is possible that *ærn,* in its older form *ræn,* is cognate with Old English *ræsn* plank, rafter, ceiling, Old Icelandic *rann,* and Gothic *razn,* both meaning house, from Proto-Germanic **rasnan,* Indo-European **rosnom* (Pok.339).

barnacle *n.* a kind of shellfish seen especially on rocks and wharves exposed at low tide and on ship bottoms. Before 1581, developed from earlier *bernacle* (about 1353) and *barnakylle* (1440) referring to a wild goose, now called barnacle goose, because it was believed to be produced by the shellfish whose feathery stalks suggested the plumage of the geese.

The earliest forms included *bernek, bernake,* which existed before 1217 to the late 1400's and referred to a kind of wild goose, probably the barnacle goose. These older forms, especially *bernake,* were borrowed through Anglo-Latin *bernaca, berneca* and probably Old French *bernaque,* ultimately perhaps from a Gallo-Romance source, but this is by no means certain, because the origin of the word may be Celtic (perhaps in Gaulish **bernos*). However, Scottish *bàirneach* and Irish *báirneac* limpet, Welsh *brennig* limpets, and even Breton *bernic, bernique, brenique* barnacle, are apparently late borrowings from English.

barometer *n.* instrument for measuring pressure of the atmosphere. 1665, formed in English from Greek *báros* weight (see GRAVE² weighty) + *métron* MEASURE.

The term *barometer* was probably coined by the great English scientist Robert Boyle (1627-1691); it was certainly popularized by him. The figurative meaning is first attributed to the philosopher David Hume (1752, in *Political Discourses*). **—barometric** *adj.* 1802, formed in English, perhaps through influence of earlier French *barométrique* (1752), by clipping of earlier *barometrical* (1665, in writings of Robert Boyle).

baron *n.* nobleman. Probably before 1200 *baron, baroun, barun,* in Layamon's *Chronicle of Britain,* a tenant of the king or other nobleman holding title by virtue of military or other service; borrowed probably through Anglo-French, from Old French *baron;* also probably overlapping with Middle English *bern* nobleman, lord (1190), found in Old English *beorn.*

The Old French *baron* is a noun in the accusative case of *ber* military leader, borrowed from Medieval Latin *baro* man, or directly from Frankish **baro* king's man (compare Old High German *baro* man, freeborn warrior; cognate with English BAIRN).

A connection with earlier Latin *bārō* fool, is not supportable as the underlying meanings clustered around *baron* are that of a warrior.

—baronet *n.* Probably before 1400, formed in English from *baron* + *-et* (diminutive suffix), perhaps by influence of Medieval Latin *baronettus.* **—baronial** *adj.* 1767, formed from English *baron* + *-ial.*

baroque (bərōk′) *adj.* having to do with a style of lavish ornamentation in art, music, architecture, etc. 1765, borrowing of French *baroque,* a term used in the 1600's to describe a style of architecture, and by 1700 to refer to something irregular and grotesque, from Middle French *baroque* irregular, in reference to the surface of a pearl, from Portuguese *barroco* pearl of irregular shape, of unknown origin.

There is no historical basis for the word being derived from Federigo *Barocci* (or *Baroccio*), 1528-1612, an Italian painter, as Barocci's paintings were not in the baroque style.

barracks *n.pl. or sing.* 1686, originally a temporary hut, as for soldiers during a siege; later, buildings to lodge soldiers (1697); borrowed from French *baraque,* originally, wooden hut or a shed, from Italian *baracca* hut, or Spanish *barraca* a tent or hut for soldiers, of unknown origin.

barracuda (bar′əkü′də) *n.* large, tropical fish. 1678, borrowed from American Spanish *barracuda,* perhaps from a Carib word.

barrage *n.* barrier of artillery fire. 1916, borrowed from French *tir de barrage,* literally, barrier fire; earlier, 1859, the action of barring, as by putting artificial barriers in a watercourse to raise its level; borrowed from French *barrage* act of barring, barrier, from *barrer* to bar, block, from *barre* bar, from Old French *barre* BAR, n.

barrel *n.* Probably before 1300, in *Kyng Alisaunder,* borrowed from Old French *baril,* of uncertain origin.

barren *adj.* unproductive. Before 1200, sterile, said especially of women; borrowed through Anglo-French *barain, baraine,* Old French *baraigne, brahaine,* feminine forms of *baraign, brahain* not fertile (applied especially to barren land), of uncertain origin (perhaps derived from a Germanic source).

The figurative sense "bare, meager" is first recorded about 1385.

barrette (bəret′) *n.* clasped pin to hold the hair. 1901, borrowed from French *barrette,* diminutive of *barre* bar.

The earlier English *barret* a little bar (1577 in Holinshed's *Chronicle*) is now obsolete, but demonstrates the easy practice in English of borrowing to suit the needs of the moment.

barricade *n.* 1642, noun use of earlier English *barricade,* v. (1592); or borrowed from Middle French *barricade* (1570), possibly with influence of earlier English *barricado,* n. (1590), probably borrowed from Spanish *barricada.* Both French *barricade* and Spanish *barricada* derive either from French *barrique* or Spanish *barrica* cask (from the root of Old French *baril* barrel), in reference to the first barricades put up in the streets of Paris and composed chiefly of casks filled with earth, cobblestones, and other debris. **—v.** 1592, borrowed from Middle French *barricader* (1558), possibly with influence of verb use of earlier English *barricado,* n. (1590). The use of *barricado,* v. does not appear before 1598; so, unless there is a defect in the record of English, *barricado,* v. could not be a possible source for the verb use of *barricade* in English.

No matter which form appeared first the prevailing usage in the 1600's seems to have been *barricado,* giving the impression that it is the older form.

barrier *n.* About 1380 *barer,* in *Sir Ferumbras,* later *barrer* (before 1420, in Lydgate's *Troy Book*); borrowed through Anglo-French *barrer,* Old French *barriere,* from *barre* obstacle, BAR. The influence of the French spelling with *i* was introduced gradually during the late 1400's and through the 1500's.

barrio (bär′ēō) *n.* a section of a city in which the population is predominantly Spanish speaking. Before 1909, American English, borrowed from Spanish *barrio,* from Arabic *barrī* exterior (feminine *barrīya* open country), from *barr* outside (of a city).

barrow¹ *n.* handcart, wheelbarrow. About 1300 *barewe* handbarrow, litter; later *barowe* wheelbarrow (1335); but note earlier *barwer, barewer* one who makes barrows (1264); developed from Old English *bearwe* basket; compare *meoxbearwe* basket for carrying dung (before 1100), *bærwan* baskets (before 1000, perhaps an altered spelling). The Old English is cognate with East Frisian *barwe* barrow (from Proto-Germanic **barwōn*), Old Icelandic *barar* handcart, bier, and Old High German *beran* to bear; see BEAR² carry.

barrow² *n.* mound of earth. Before 1425 *berwe* hill, mound; earlier *bergh* (probably before 1387, in a version of *Piers Plowman*); in place names, *Berweham* (1313) and *Bergham* enclosure on a hill (1277); developed from Old English (about 725 in *Beowulf*) *beorg, beork* (West Saxon) and *berg* (Anglian) hill, mound. The Old English is cognate with Old Saxon and Old High German *berg* mountain (modern German *Berg*), Middle Dutch *berch* (modern Dutch *berg*), Old Icelandic *bjarg, berg* mountain, rock (from Proto-Germanic **berʒaz*), Gothic *baírgahei* mountain region, Armenian *berj* height, Old and Middle Irish *bri* (accusative *brig*) mountain, Welsh *bera* stack, heap, *bryn, bre* hill, and Sanskrit *bṛhánt-* high, lofty; from Indo-European **bherĝh-* (Pok.140).

Except for its popularization by archaeologists, the

word has been rarely used in literary English since the mid-1400's.

barter *v.* About 1440 *bartren,* borrowed from Middle French *barater, bareter* cheat, exchange, barter, do business; of uncertain origin. **—n.** 1465, from the verb.

baryon (bar'ēon) *n.* heavy elementary particle. 1953, formed in English from Greek *barýs* heavy (see GRAVE[2] weighty) + *-on* (suffix for elementary particle, as in *electron*).

basal *adj.* 1610, in the phrase *basal area,* formed from English *base* [1] + *-al* [1]. The word was probably reformed in 1828, the next date of its appearance in print.

basalt *n.* 1601 *basaltes,* in Holland's translation of Pliny's *Natural History,* borrowed from Late Latin *basaltēs,* a manuscript alteration of Latin *basanītēs* a very hard stone, touchstone, from Greek *basanítēs,* from *básanos* touchstone, test. Pliny, who used the form *basanītēs,* claimed the word is of African origin. The word is from Egyptian *baḫan* slate. The form *basalt* appeared in English in 1769.

bascule *n.* 1678, device that operates on the principle of a seesaw, by levering heavy moving parts with weights, later applied specifically to lift-bridges or drawbridges called *bascule bridge* (1884). Borrowed from French *bascule* seesaw, from *bas* low (see BASE[2]) + *cul* the buttocks (from Latin *cūlus*).

base[1] *n.* part on which something rests, foundation. Before 1300 *bas,* borrowed (perhaps through some confusion with Old French adjective *bas, basse* low), from Old French *bas, basse* pedestal, foundation, learned borrowing from Latin *basis* foundation. The English borrowing was also influenced directly by Latin *basis,* from Greek *básis* thing to step or stand on, step, foundation, from *baínein* to go, step. See the doublet BASIS. **—adj.** 1605, from the noun.**—v.** 1587, from the noun.

base[2] *adj.* low, inferior. About 1390 *bace* in imitation of Old French; later, as a separate formation, before 1393 *bass,* in Gower's *Confessio Amantis;* borrowed from Old French *bas, basse,* from Medieval Latin *bassus* low, Late Latin *bassus* thick, fat, stumpy. Compare BASS[1] low.

baseball *n.* 1850, American English, formed from *base*[1], n. + *ball*[1]. According to Mathews' *A Dictionary of Americanisms,* "the first mention so far found of 'baseball' is in *A Little Pretty Book* brought out in London in 1744." But this word, like that cited in the OED from Jane Austen's *Northanger Abbey* (1803-1815), refers to a game known more generally as *rounders,* which is roughly similar in concept to baseball and was played by New England colonists in the 1700's. The theory that baseball was originated by Abner Doubleday at Cooperstown, N.Y., in 1839 is now generally held to be part of American folk legend.

basement *n.* 1730, probably formed from English *base* [1], n. + *-ment,* and perhaps influenced by French *soubassement* subfoundation (1362). A parallel form also exists in Middle Low German *basement* base, pedestal, and probably Italian *bassamento* abasement.

bash *v.* smash. 1641, of uncertain origin. Speculation on the source of this word ranges from an origin in some Scandinavian source (compare Swedish *basa* whip, beat, Danish *baske* beat, strike) to an imitative origin, with the *b* of *beat, bang,* etc. + the ending of *lash, smash,* etc. The other words in this group, including *dash, flash, lash,* and *smash* are all compared with words in the Scandinavian languages, but are also ultimately of uncertain origin. **—n.** 1805, first recorded in Scottish as noun use of *bash,* v.

bashful *adj.* 1548, developed from earlier *baishen* to abash (before 1338, in Mannyng's *Chronicle of England;* borrowed from Old French *baissier* to bring down, lower, humiliate) + English suffix *-ful;* see ABASE.

basic *adj.* 1842, formed from English *base* [1], n. + *-ic.* **—n.** About 1927, American English, from the adjective.

BASIC (bā'sik) *n.* computer programming language. 1965, formed as an acronym in English for *B(eginners) A(ll-purpose) S(ymbolic) I(nstruction) C(ode).*

basil (baz'əl) *n.* sweet-smelling plant. About 1450, borrowed from Middle French *basile,* learned borrowing from Medieval Latin *basilicum;* also influenced by Middle English *basilicon* (1373), borrowed through Anglo-French *basilicon,* from Medieval Latin *basilicum, basilicon,* from Greek *basilikòn phytón* royal plant, neuter of *basilikós* royal, from *basileús* king, of uncertain origin.

basilica (bəsil'əkə) *n.* oblong hall, church. 1541, borrowed from Latin *basilica* building housing a court of justice, from Greek *stoà basilikḗ* stoa or roofed portico of the archon basileus (the official who dispensed justice in Athens), feminine of *basilikós* royal, from *basileús* king, of uncertain origin.

basin *n.* Probably about 1200 *bacin,* borrowed from Old French *bacin,* from Late Latin *bachīnus, bacchīnus,* apparently also spelled *bacchinon* wooden vessel used by the Gauls according to Gregory of Tours, writing in the 500's. Some sources have traced the word further to a supposed Latin **baccinus, *baccīnum,* thought to be derived from *bacca* vessel, probably originally used for wine (compare Late Latin *baccārium* wine vessel; perhaps of Gaulish origin).

basis *n.* 1571, borrowed from Latin *basis* foundation, from Greek *básis* thing to step or stand on, from *baínein* go, step, from earlier **gwamye-,* cognate with Latin *venīre* come, Sanskrit *gam-,* and Old English *cuman* COME. Doublet of BASE[1].

bask *v.* warm pleasantly. Before 1393 *basken* to wallow in blood or warm water, in Gower's *Confessio Amantis;* perhaps borrowed from a Scandinavian source (compare Old Icelandic *badhask* bathe oneself, reflexive form of *badha* BATHE). The figurative meaning "to revel or take great delight in" is first recorded in 1647.

basket *n.* 1229, in the compound *basketwricte* basket maker, borrowed from Anglo-French *bascat,* of uncertain origin; compare Old French *baschoe, baschoue* wooden or wicker container, and dialectal French (Gascon) *bascojo,* (Béarnais) *bascoyes* kind of basket, all possibly from Latin *bascauda* a kind of basin. The Latin word is generally thought to be of British, maybe Celtic, origin; the Roman writer Martial refers to Britain as the source of the *bascauda.*

basketball *n.* 1892, American English, coined after the invention of the game (1891) by James A. Naismith, a physical education instructor in Springfield, Massachusetts.

bas-relief (bä'rilēf' *or* bä'rilēf') *n.* carving in which figures stand out slightly from the background. 1667 *basse relieve,* borrowed first perhaps through influence of French *basse,* from Italian *basso-rilievo* low relief or raised work, and later modified to *bas-relief* (1762) by influence of French *bas-relief* or by being borrowed from the French as a second source of the word.

bass[1] (bās) *adj.* low in sound. About 1390 *bace* low (see BASE[2]); applied to music before 1450, and later altered in spelling to *bass* (1596, in Shakespeare's *1 Henry IV*) by influence of Italian *basso* bass, from Medieval Latin *bassus* low, short, Latin (name) *Bassus* fat.—**n.** lowest musical voice. Before 1500, noun use of *base*[2], adj., later altered in spelling (1674) after the Italian influence of *basso* on the spelling of the adjective in English. The spelling was not fixed until the 1800's.

bass[2] (bas) *n.* any of various fishes, especially of the perch family. 1602 *basse,* earlier *bace* (about 1410), a variant form of dialectal *barse* perch, found in Old English (about 700) *bærs, bears,* cognate with Middle High German *bars,* probably related to Old English *byrst* BRISTLE. The modern form *bass* was not fully established until the mid-1800's.

basset *n.* short-legged dog; now commonly *basset hound* (since 1883). 1616, borrowed from French *basset* a dog developed from crossing the French bloodhound and short-legged white hounds; originally, in Old French, a diminutive adjective formed from *bas* low and the diminutive suffix *-et.*

bassinet *n.* hooded cradle. 1854, in Thackeray's *The Newcomes,* borrowed from French *bassinet,* a diminutive of *bassin* basin, from Old French *bacin;* see BASIN.

bassoon *n.* deep-toned wind instrument. 1727 *basson, bassoon,* in *Chambers Cyclopaedia;* borrowed from French *basson,* from Italian *bassone,* augmentative form of *basso* BASS[1]; for ending see -OON.

bastard *n.* illegitimate child. About 1300, earlier as an epithet in names Peter *Bastard* (1250); borrowed through Anglo-French, as in William le *Bastard* (1223), from Old French *bastard* child of a nobleman and a woman other than his wife, synonym of *fils de bast* child born in a barn, or more usually child of the packsaddle. Old French *bastard* was probably derived from *bast* usually glossed as "packsaddle" (often used as a bed while traveling) and perhaps also meaning "barn" + *-ard* hard, bold, hardy (having the disparaging sense "one who does what is discreditable"). Old French *bast* may ultimately be derived from Proto-Germanic **banstiz,* source of Gothic *bansts* barn (from Indo-European **bhondh-sti-s;* see BIND), and would emphasize that the child was born in a barn or of low origin on the mother's side.

The figurative senses are now largely confined to adjective use with the meanings: not genuine, inferior (1530, in Palsgrave's *Lesclarcissement*); irregular, unusual (1418); resembling but not identical (1558, in writings of Knox).

—bastardize *v.* 1587, formed from English *bastard* + *-ize,* or perhaps from obsolete *abastardize* (1580), borrowed from Middle French *abastardir* to bastardize; for suffix see -IZE. *Abastardize* and *bastardize* coexisted in English through the 1600's, after which *abastardize* became obsolete.

baste[1] *v.* drip melted fat on (meat). Probably before 1475, of uncertain origin (compare Old French *basser* to soak).

baste[2] *v.* sew with loose stitches. Probably before 1400, Middle English *basten,* in Chaucer's translation of *Roman de la Rose;* borrowed from Old French *bastir* to baste (sew), from Frankish (compare Old High German *bestan* patch, Middle High German *besten* to lace, tie, sew with bast, from *bast* tough fiber of the inner bark of certain trees), from Proto-Germanic **basta-.*

baste[3] *v.* beat soundly. 1533, of uncertain origin; occurring first as *basit, baist,* apparently a past tense or past participle, perhaps of a form such as *bas* or *base,* possibly borrowed from a Scandinavian source (compare Swedish *basa* beat, strike; or if *baste* was the original form, compare Icelandic *beysta,* Swedish *bösta,* Danish *bøste* beat, drub).

The other possibility may be that *baste*[3] is a figurative extension of *baste*[1], v., perhaps even by distant influence of some Scandinavian word, such as those cited above.

bastion (bas′chən) *n.* part of a fortification, stronghold. 1562, borrowed from Middle French *bastion* (perhaps influenced by Italian *bastione*), variant of *bastillon,* a diminutive form developed from *bastille* fortress, from Old French *bastille* fortress, tower. The Old French is an alteration of Old Provençal *bastida* (which as *Bastide* was often used in the 1400's in France to refer to the famous Bastille) from *bastir* to build; Old French *bastir* to baste (sew) and Old Provençal *bastir* to build, are probably derived from the same Germanic source; see BASTE[2].

bat[1] *n.* stick, club. Probably before 1200 *batte* mace, cudgel, in Layamon's *Chronicle of Britain,* found in Old English *batt* (date not recorded), probably borrowed from Late Latin *battere,* Latin *battuere* to beat, possibly from a Gaulish word (compare Gaulish *anda-bata* blind fighter, gladiator), cognate with Latin *fatuus* silly, from Indo-European **bhāt-/bhət-* (Pok.111).

Bat is sometimes attributed to Celtic origin; however, Irish *bata* is a borrowing from Old French, first occurring in a Middle Irish translation of the French romance *Fierabras (Ferumbras),* and reinforced by borrowing Middle English *batte, bat* bat. Welsh *bat* is also from English.

—**v.** strike, as with a bat. About 1200, from the noun *bat*[1], and also as a borrowing from Old French *battre* to beat, from Late Latin *battere,* Latin *battuere.*

bat[2] *n.* flying mammal. About 1575 *bat,* replacing the earlier Middle English *bakke* (before 1325), both apparently from a Scandinavian source (compare Old Swedish *-backa* in *natt-backa* night bat, Old Danish *-bakkæ* in *nath-bakkæ* night bat).

It is suggested that the change from *k* to *t* may have been influenced by confusion with another meaning of *bakke* a kind of nocturnal insect, that derives from Latin *blatta* moth.

bat[3] wink. 1838, developed from earlier meaning "to flutter" (1615), variant of Middle English *baten* to flutter, beat the wings, before 1333; borrowed from Old French *batre, battre* to beat, strike, from Late Latin *battere,* Latin *battuere;* see BAT[1] stick.

batch *n.* quantity, lot. Probably before 1475 *bach* process of baking, quantity of bread produced in one baking, developed through Old English *gebæc* baking, from *bacan* to bake; see BAKE. The probable form in Old English **bæcce* gave rise to Middle English *bach* and *bache* with the spelling *batch* finally developing in the 1500's as a reflection of the pronunciation.

bate *v.* hold back, lessen (in phrases *bate one's breath* or *with bated breath*). Probably before 1300 *baten,* in *Kyng Alisaunder,* apparently shortened form of *abaten* ABATE.

bateau (batō′) *n.* light flat-bottomed riverboat. 1711, American English *batteau,* borrowed through Canadian French *bateau,* from French *bateau* boat, from Old French *batel,* generally considered to be derived from Old English *bāt* BOAT.

bath *n.* Old English (about 725) *bæth.* Some form of the word is found in all Germanic languages except Gothic; cognates include Old High German *bad* bath (modern German *Bad*), Old Icelandic *badh,* and Dutch, Swedish and Danish *bad,* from Proto-Germanic **bathan;* see BATHE. These forms are associated with the verb represented by Old High German *bājan, bāen* to warm, toast, and *bahhan* BAKE. —**bathhouse** *n.* (1363) —**bathrobe** *n.* (1902) —**bathroom** *n.* (1780) —**bathtub** *n.* 1870, earlier *bathing tub* (1594). —**bathwater** *n.* (about 1300).

bathe *v.* Old English *bathian* (before 899, in Alfred's translation of *Orosius*). This word is also widespread in the Germanic language with cognates in Old High German *badōn* bathe (modern German *baden*), Old Icelandic *badha,* and modern Dutch *baden,* Swedish *bada,* Danish *bade;* all ultimately from the same root as Old English *bæth* BATH, from Proto-Germanic **bathōn,* from Indo-European **bhē-/bhə-* (Pok.113). The difference in pronunciation of *bath* (bath) and *bathe* (bāᴛʜ) has developed since the Old English period by adding the verbal ending with its additional syllable. —**bathing suit** (1873).

bathos (bā′thos) *n.* comic or ridiculous descent of elevated speech or writing to the commonplace or trivial. 1727, in Pope's *Peri Bathous* (a parody on *Perì Hýphous* "On the Sublime," treatise on literary criticism); borrowed, with satirical awareness of the parallel to English *pathos,* from Greek *báthos* depth, of unknown origin. —**bathetic** *adj.* Before 1834, in writings of Coleridge, formed in English on analogy of the pattern *pathos, pathetic* (though *pathetic* is not derived from *pathos*).

batik (bətēk′) *n.* the art of dyeing cloth only part at a time while protecting the rest with a wax coating; also, cloth dyed in this manner. 1880, borrowed probably through Dutch *batik* (because of the Dutch colonial control of Indonesia), from Javanese *mbatik* writing, drawing. The art of *batik* was introduced to Europe by way of the Dutch, who lectured widely about the art in the mid-1800's, but whether it came into English solely from Dutch, or also by way of the French *batik* (1845) because of their influence in fashion on design of material, is not known.

batiste (bətēst′) *n.* fine, thin linen or cotton cloth. 1697, borrowed from French *batiste,* from Middle French *baptiste,* reputedly from the name of *Baptiste* of Cambrai (in French Flanders), a textile maker of the 1200's who is said to have made this cloth. Compare CAMBRIC.

baton (bəton′) *n.* staff, stick. 1548, gradually through the 1600's replacing earlier *baston* (recorded before 1325, in *Cursor Mundi*), and *batoon* through the 1700's. The word in all its forms was borrowed ultimately from Old French *baston,* a form cognate with Spanish *bastón,* Portuguese *bastão,* Italian *bastone,* the sum of which suggests a Vulgar Latin **bastōnem* a stick, though others cite Late Latin *bastum* stout staff, from **bastāre* beat or drive with a stick.

The musical sense of a conductor's stick to indicate time was first recorded in 1785.

battalion *n.* military unit. 1589 (perhaps influenced by, and replacing, earlier *bataille* a company of troops; recorded probably about 1225); borrowed from Middle French *bataillon, battaillon* a company of troops, from Italian *battaglione* battle squadron, an augmentative form of *battaglia* troop; originally, battle array, from Late Latin *battālia* BATTLE.

batten *n.* strip of wood nailed across adjoining boards to form a door, wall, ship's hatch cover, etc. 1658, an Anglicized variant of *baton.* —*v.* 1775, furnish with battens; 1823 *batten down* fasten with battens; from the noun.

batter[1] *v.* strike with repeated blows. About 1330 *bateren* beat repeatedly, in *Sir Degare;* borrowed from Old French *batre, battre* to beat, strike, from Late Latin *battere,* Latin *battuere* strike; see BAT[1] stick.

In Middle English the *r* in the infinitive of verbs borrowed from French is not normally retained, but in this case the *-re* or *-er* may have been equated with the English suffix *-er*[4] (showing repeated action), that suffix appearing in many Middle English verbs. Compare RENDER, TENDER, v. —**battered child** (1962) —**battering ram** (1611)

batter[2] *n.* flour and milk mixture. 1381 *batour, bater, bature,* either borrowed from Old French *batëure,* n. a beating, from *batre* to beat, strike; or developed from English *batter*[1], v. to strike; for suffix see -ER[4].

batter[3] *n.* player who bats in baseball, cricket, etc. 1773, formed from English *bat*[1], n. + *-er*[1].

battery *n.* 1531 *batrye, batery, batterie* act of beating or battering; borrowed from Middle French *batterie* a beating, battering, group of cannon, from Old French *baterie* a beating, from *batre* to beat, Late Latin *battere,* Latin *battuere* beat, strike; see BAT[1]; for suffix see -ERY.

The meaning "set of mounted guns" is recorded in 1555, developed from the sense "bombardment" (1548). The meaning "set of electrical cells" appeared in 1748, in letters of Benjamin Franklin, and the modern sense "container holding one or more cells that produce electricity" in 1801, in writings of Sir Humphry Davy. The meaning "percussion section of an orchestra" is recorded in 1926.

batting *n.* cotton fiber in sheets to stuff quilts, furniture, etc. 1875 *batting,* specific use of gerund (1611), or formed from earlier *batt* (1830), obsolete variant of *bat*[1], n. felted mass of fur, wool, etc. + *-ing,* from *bat*[1], v., describing the action of batting or beating the fibers to make such material.

battle *n.* Before 1250 *bataille, bataile* single combat, especially for settling an issue, in *The Owl and the Nightingale;* borrowed from Old French *bataille* battle, arrayed troops, from Late Latin *battālia* battle, variant of *battuālia,* neuter plural, fencing exercises, from Latin *battuere* to strike, beat; see BAT[1] stick. —**v.** Probably before 1300 *bataillen* to fight, in *Kyng Alisaunder* and *Arthour and Merlin;* borrowed from Old French *bataillier* to fight, from *bataille* battle. —**battle cry** (1814) —**battlefield** *n.* (1812) —**battleground** *n.* (1815) —**battleship** *n.* (1705)

battlement *n.* low wall with openings, used for defense at the top of a tower or wall of a castle, fort, etc. Probably about 1380 *batilment, batelment;* borrowed from Old French *batillement,* earlier *bastillement* fortification, derived from *bataille* battlement, from *bateiller,* earlier *bastillier* fortify, from *bastille* fortress, tower, see BASTION; for suffix see -MENT.

bauble (bô′bəl) *n.* trifle. About 1330 *babel,* borrowed from Old French *babel, baubel* child's toy, trinket, of uncertain origin.

baud (bôd) *n.* unit of speed in telegraphy and data processing. 1932, borrowed from French *baud* (1929), from the name of J.M.E. *Baudot* (1845-1903), a French engineer who invented the Baudot code, a telegraph transmission code.

bauxite *n.* claylike mineral from which aluminum is extracted. 1868, borrowed from French *bauxite* (1847), from Les *Baux,* town near Arles in southern France; the mineral is so called from its being found there in 1821; for suffix see -ITE[1].

bawdy *adj.* lewd, obscene. 1513, formed from English *bawd* procurer, pander + adjective suffix *-y*[1], but probably influenced by an earlier and separate form *bawdy,* Middle English *baudy* dirty, filthy (1378, in a version of *Piers Plowman*).

Modern English *bawd,* developed from Middle English *baude* a procurer or prostitute, also in another version of *Piers Plowman* (before 1376), perhaps by shortening of earlier *baude-strote* procurer (about 1300); borrowed from Old French *baudetrot, baudrestote* (probably *baud,* merry, licentious, bold, a meaning confirmed in *fille de joie* prostitute + *-trot* one who runs errands, from Old French *troter* to TROT, as in *Trotaconventos* name of a go-between in Juan Ruiz's *Libro de Buen Amor*).

Some sources suggest Middle English *baude* may have been borrowed directly from Old French *baud* merry, licentious, dissolute, thence from earlier *bald* bold, from a Frankish word, (compare Old High German *bald*). This is difficult to sustain, because there is no semantic relationship in the borrowing to be found in Middle English or in French, and the Old French *baud* functioned as an adjective rather than a noun.

bawl *v.* cry, wail. About 1440 *bawlynge* barking (of dogs), a bark, in *Promptorium Parvulorum;* later *baull* cry out, yell (1570); borrowed perhaps from a Scandinavian source (compare Icelandic *baula,* Swedish *böla* to low like a cow, Old Icelandic *baula* cow); all forms apparently of imitative origin.

The form *bawlynge* could also be from Medieval Latin *baulare* to bark, and *baulatus* a bark; but these forms are very rare and may, themselves, be derived from a Scandinavian source.
—n. 1792, from the verb.

bay[1] *n.* inlet of a sea. Probably before 1400 *bay, baye,* in Trevisa's translation of Higden's *Polychronicon;* borrowed from Old French *baie,* of uncertain origin.

Whether the Old French is derived from a Late Latin form *baia* or from a Frisian form **baga* is a matter of controversy among scholars. It seems likely that Old French *baie* developed from *baër, baïr* to open, from Medieval Latin *batare* as Corominas suggests, and that Late Latin *baia,* which appears only in the work of Isidor of Seville, developed because he misunderstood the name of the port of *Baiae,* in Campania, to be a common noun *baia,* according to Ernout and Meillet. The Frisian origin has the problem of cultural contact which remains unexplained.

bay[2] *n.* long, deep bark. Before 1400 *bay* barking of dogs, in *Ipomedon,* earlier *bay* cornering of a hunted animal (before 1375, in *William of Palerne*), still earlier *abay, abai* at bay with barking dogs (probably about 1300, in *The Romance of Guy of Warwick*); borrowed from Old French *abai* barking, from *abaier, baier* to bark, probably imitative of the sound, but perhaps remotely influenced by Medieval Latin *batare* to open the mouth, and therefore to be open-mouthed or agape. —v. Probably about 1390 *bayen, baien* to bark, in *Sir Gawain and the Green Knight,* earlier *abayen, abaien* bark at someone, speak rudely (probably before 1300, in *Kyng Alisaunder*), borrowed from Old French *abaier* to bark.

bay[3] *n.* space in a wall between columns, or furnished with windows; space in a barn, warehouse, etc.; compartment. Probably about 1380, borrowed from Old French *baëe, beëe* opening, cave, from *baée,* past participle of *baër, beër, baïr* stand open, gape, yawn, from Medieval Latin *batare* gape. **—bay window** (1405)

bay[4] *adj.* reddish-brown. 1341, borrowed through Anglo-Latin and Anglo-French *bai,* from Old French *bai,* from Latin *badius* reddish-brown (probably as a technical term confined to horses).

bay[5] *n.* shrub with leaves used for flavoring. 1373, the fruit of various plants; later, bayberry (before 1400) and bay leaf (about 1450); the shrub itself (probably about 1425); borrowed from Old French *baie* berry, seed, from Latin *băca* berry, probably from a non-Indo-European language, and very likely related to the name of the Thracian wine god *Bacchos.*

bayonet *n.* blade attached to a rifle. 1672, earlier *bayonnette* a short dagger (1611, in Cotgrave's *Dictionary*); borrowed from French *baïonnette,* probably derived from *Bayonne,* city in southern France where the weapon was first made; for suffix see -ETTE.

bayou (bī′yü) *n.* inlet or outlet of a lake, etc. 1766, American English *Bayoue,* later *bayou* (1803), borrowed through American French *Bayoue,* from Choctaw *bayuk* small stream.

bazaar *n.* marketplace. 1588 *bazar,* in Thomas Hickock's translation of *The Voyage of M.C. Frederick into the East India,* perhaps influenced by earlier French *Bathzar* (1432), but borrowed through obsolete Italian *bazarra,* from Persian *bāzār* market. **—bazaari** *n.* bazaar merchant. 1978, borrowed, by influence of earlier English *bazaar,* from Persian *bāzārī* merchant.

bazooka (bəzü′kə) *n.* tubular gun for firing small rockets. 1942, American English, special use of earlier *bazooka* a trombone-like instrument popularized (about 1935) by the American comedian Bob Burns (1896-1956), and invented and named possibly in the early 1900's; probably formed by alteration of older *bazoo* a voice or mouth trumpet (1877), from Dutch *bazuin* trumpet, trombone.

The formation of *bazoo* is said to be influenced by *kazoo,* but the first recorded use of *kazoo* is 1884. Whether *palooka* an inferior boxer (1925), popularized in the comic strip *Joe Palooka* of the 1930's and 1940's and earlier meaning "an inferior race horse," reinforced the formation of *bazooka* is not possible to determine.

BB *n.* a shot or size of shot used in a BB gun or as part of a larger charge to shoot birds, etc. 1874, American English, designation of a size of shot. **—BB gun** air rifle that shoots BB shot. 1932, American English, in oral use since about 1928.

be *v.* irregular verb (serving as a linking verb and the chief auxiliary verb of English). One of three distinct verbs of Germanic origin (*be, am, was*) gradually combined under *be,* because *be* later supplied the infinitive form. Middle English *been* (about 1200), developed from Old English *bēon, bēom, bīon* be, exist, come to be, become (before 830, in the *Vespasian Psalter*).

In Old English *bēon, bēom* was a distinct verb, but with no past tense, though through its meaning "come to be," it often served as the future tense of the separate verb *am-was.* Later, in the 1200's, Middle English *be, been* gradually took the place of the infinitive, participial, and imperative forms of *am-was;* see AM and WAS.

Later, the plural forms of *be,* that is, we *beth,* ye *ben,* they *be* (after 1250), became standard forms in Middle English, and also for a time made inroads on the singular, that is, I *be,* thou or you *beest,* he, she, it *beth.* However, forms of *are (aron, aren, arn, are)* spread in use, until in the 1500's they began to take over in standard English, and finally replaced *be* in the plural (we, you, they *are*); see ARE[1].

In Old English the substantive verb, showing existence (I *am* before 950, he *is* about 885), was derived from a Germanic stem **es-,* whose form existed only in the present tense in Old English; all other parts of that verb were supplied by the form **wes-* meaning "to remain." (The form **wes-* was still a complete verb only in Gothic.) The two verbs, already coalesced in Old English, supplemented each other and constituted the verb **es-wes- (am-was),* showing existence. The form *art* (thou or you *art*) was the singular, second-person present tense for this verb until it became an archaic form in the 1800's. For other parts of this verb see IS and WAS.

English *be* (Old English *bēon, bēom*) is cognate with Old Saxon *bium,* Old High German *bim,* Middle High German and modern German *bin* I am, all derived from a Germanic form **beu-* and cognate in other Indo-European languages with Lithuanian *búti,* Old Slavic *byti,* Russian *byt',* Old Irish *buith,* Welsh *bod,* all meaning "to be."

Other farther ranging cognates include some forms in Latin (*fuī* I have been, *futūrus* about to be), Greek *phýein* bring forth, produce, and Sanskrit *bhávati* exists, happens, is. The widespread existence of these cognates attests to the ancientness of this form, from Indo-European **bhew(ə)-* grow, come to be (Pok.146).

be- prefix meaning: **1** thoroughly, completely, all around or all over, as in *bespatter* = to spatter all over; *becalmed* = thoroughly or completely calmed. **2** to make, cause to seem, as in *belittle* = cause to seem little or unimportant. **3** to provide with, adorn, as in *bejewel* = to adorn with jewels. **4** at, on, to, for, about, against, as in *bewail* = to wail about. **5** (in words from Middle and Old English) *because* Middle English *bi cause* = by cause; *beneath* Old English *beneothan* = *be-* be, in the sense by, about + *neothan* below; *beside* Old English *bi sīdan* = *bi* by and *sīdan* side; *between* Old English *betwēonum, betwēon* = *be-* by + *twā* two. Other forms, such as *before* and *behind,* which appear to be formations in English are perhaps actually borrowings in Old English from some indeterminate source beyond English, as they appear in Old Saxon, Old High German, and other languages contemporary with or antedating Old English.

The prefix *be-* developed from the Old English prefix *bi-, be-* an unstressed form of the preposition and adverb *bī* by, and is represented in other Germanic languages (compare Old High German *bi-,* Middle High German and modern German *be-,* Gothic *bi-*), from Indo-European **bhi* (Pok.34).

beach *n.* About 1535, the loose, water-worn pebbles of the sea shore; 1596, in Shakespeare's *Merchant of Venice,* the sea shore; possibly a transferred sense of Middle English *bech, beche* stream, brook, developed from Old English *bece* brook, stream, cognate with Old Saxon *beki,* from Proto-Germanic **bakiz;* related to Middle English *bek, bec* brook, stream, borrowed from a Scandinavian source (compare Old Icelandic *bekkr*); it is also related to Middle English *bach, bache,* developed from Old English *bæc* brook, cognate with Old High German *bah* brook, and Middle Irish *būal* flowing water, from Indo-European **bhog-* (Pok.161).

beacon *n.* 1338, *beken* signal fire, developed from Old English *bēacen* sign, signal (about 725, in *Beowulf*). The Old English is cognate with Old Frisian *bāken* sign, Old Saxon *bōcan,* and Old High German *bouhhan,* from Proto-Germanic **bauknan,* of unknown origin. Compare BECKON.

bead *n.* small ball or bit of glass. About 1175 *bede* prayer, developed from Old English *bed* prayer, (before 900, from Proto-Germanic **beđan,* Indo-European **bhedh-* to bend, Pok.114); and earlier *gebed* (about 725, in the book of *Daniel*), and cognate with Old Saxon *gibed* prayer, Old High German *gibet* (modern German *Gebet*), Gothic *bida* prayer, *bidjan* to ask; see BID.

The current meaning of "glass ball" for a bead used in a necklace, bracelet, etc., appeared in the 1300's, when a series of small perforated balls, threaded on a string, formed the *rosary* or *paternoster,* used for keeping count of the number of prayers said.

beadle *n.* minor parish officer. About 1300 *bedel* minor official of a lord, manor, town, or court of law, constable, borrowed from Old French *bedel,* from Frankish (compare Old High German *butil* bailiff, beadle, Middle High German *bütel;* modern German *Büttel*).

The Middle English form *bedel,* borrowed from Old French, replaced earlier Middle English *bidel* herald, messenger (about 1200, in *The Ormulum*) and dialect variants, such as *budel,* which had developed from Old English *bydel* (about 1000, in works of Ælfric), related to *bēodan* to announce, offer, BID.

beagle *n.* small hunting dog. Probably about 1475 *begle,* of uncertain origin; possibly borrowed from Old French *beegueulle* noisy shouting person (*beër* gape, open wide + *gueulle, goule* throat; see GULLET) in allusion to the noise made by a person shouting.

beak *n.* bill of a bird. Before 1250 *bec,* later *bek* (about 1380); borrowed from Old French *bec,* from Gaulish *beccus* (possibly related to the Celtic stem *bacc-,* meaning hook).

beaker *n.* large cup, goblet. Probably about 1380 *bekyr,* borrowed perhaps from Middle Dutch *bēker* goblet, corresponding to Old High German *behhāri* (modern German *Becher*); replacing earlier *biker* (1348), borrowed from Medieval Latin *bicarium,* probably from Greek *bîkos* earthen vessel, of Egyptian origin. Compare PITCHER.

beam *n.* Old English *bēam* tree, piece of timber, ray (about 725, in a version of *Genesis*); cognate with Old Frisian *bām,* Old High German *boum* (modern German *Baum*), Middle Dutch *boom,* and perhaps Old Icelandic *badhmr,* and Gothic *bagms,* all meaning "tree"; of uncertain origin.

The sense "ray of light" apparently developed as a literal translation of Latin *columna lucis* column or pillar of light, found in Bede's writing in Old English. —v. Before 1425, from the noun.

bean *n.* Old English (about 1000) *bēan;* cognate with Old High German *bōna* bean (modern German *Bohne),* and Old Icelandic *baun* that point to Proto-Germanic **baunō,* with no further cognates.

The slang meaning "head" is first recorded in American English in 1905, perhaps from the phrase *bean ball,* used in baseball, and the verb meaning "to hit someone on the head" is first recorded in American English in 1910.

bear[1] *n.* large, heavy mammal. About 1150 *bere* (genitive *beran*), developed from Old English *bera* (before 893, in a translation of St. Gregory's *Dialogues*). Cognates appear in Old High German *bero* (modern German *Bär*), Middle Dutch *bere* (modern Dutch *beer*), from Proto-Germanic **beron-,* Old Icelandic *bjǫrn,* all meaning "bear," literally, "brown (animal)" (a designation shared with *beaver*) going back to the Indo-European base **bher-* light brown (Pok.136), which is related to the source of Old English *brūn* BROWN.

The actual name of the European brown bear considered "the brown animal" by the Germanic, Baltic, and Slavic peoples goes back to the Indo-European base that was the source of Latin *ursus* (see URSINE), Greek *árktos* (see ARCTIC), and Old Irish *art.* Compare the related words BRUIN and BEAVER[1] rodent.

Bear in the sense of a speculator who sells short, hoping for a fall in stocks (from which we derived *bearish,* 1881), was first recorded in 1709, in an article in the *Tatler* by Steele, as a shortening of *bearskin jobber,* supposed to be from the phrase "to sell the bearskin," in allusion to the proverb "sell the bear's skin before one has caught the bear" (recorded since the 1500's); see also BULL[1].

bear[2] *v.* carry, bring forth. Before 1123 *beren,* developed from Old English *beran* (about 725, in *Beowulf*). The word is cognate with Old Saxon *beran,* Old Frisian *bera,* Old High German *beran* to carry, (from Proto-Germanic **beranan*), *giberan* bring forth, give birth to (modern German *gebären*), Old Icelandic *bera* to carry, and Gothic *baíran,* all from the same Indo-European base (**bher-,* Pok.128) that is common to Latin *ferre* to carry, bring, Greek *phérein,* Armenian *berem* I carry, Old Irish *berid, beirid,* and Sanskrit *bhárati* (he) carries. —**bearable** *adj.* About 1454, formed from English *bear* + *-able*[2]. —**bearer** *n.* 1255, developed from Old English, in phrases such as *wæter-berere.* —**bearing** *n.* About 1250 *bering* behavior, conduct, formed from Middle English *beren,* v. + *-ing.*[1] —**bearings** *n.pl.* 1711, formed from English *bearing* + *-s*[1].

beard *n.* Old English *beard* (before 830, in the *Vespasian Psalter*). The correspondence in spelling between Old English and modern English is accidental, as the modern form developed from Middle English, first recorded as the surname *Berd* (1165). The word is cognate with Old Frisian *berd,* Old High German *bart* (modern German *Bart*), Middle Dutch *baert* (modern Dutch *baard*), late Old Icelandic *bardh,* from Proto-Germanic **barđaz,* and with Latin *barba* beard, Old Slavic *brada,* and Lithuanian *barzdà,* from Indo-European **bhardhā* (Pok.110).
—**v.** About 1303, *berden* to grow or have a beard, reach the age of puberty, in Mannyng's *Handlyng Synne;* later, to face boldly, defy (1525), a meaning already known in the Middle English phrase *rennen in berd* oppose openly, and *in the berd* to one's face, directly.

beast *n.* Probably before 1200 *beste,* in *Ancrene Riwle* (compare English *bestial,* which retained the Middle English spelling), borrowed from Old French *beste,* from Vulgar Latin **besta,* from Latin *bēstia* wild animal, of uncertain origin. Middle English *beste* a living being, an animal as distinct from "man," was used to translate the Latin word *animal* and took the place of Old English *dēor* deer (which became specialized), just as in this sense *beast* was replaced in the 1500's by *animal.* —**beastly** *adj.* Probably about 1200. Compare BESTIAL.

beat *v.* strike repeatedly. Probably before 1200 *beten,* in *Ancrene Riwle,* developed from Old English *bēatan* (about 725, in *Beowulf*). Though the word is not found in Gothic it is cognate with other Germanic forms, such as Old High German *bōzan* to beat, kick, and Old Icelandic *bauta,* from Proto-Germanic **bautanan,* from Indo-European **bhau-/bhu-* (Pok.112). The past tense *beat* developed in the 1500's as a shortened form from Middle English *beted.* The old past participle *beat* is still found in *dead-beat* all tired out. —**n.** About 1300, from the verb. —**beater** *n.* (1200) —**beating** *n.* (probably about 1200).

beatific (bē'ətif'ik) *adj.* blissful, making blessed. 1639, borrowed from French *béatifique,* or perhaps directly from Late Latin *beātificus,* derived from Latin *beātus* happy, blessed; see BEATITUDE; for suffix see -FIC. —**beatification** *n.* 1502, borrowed from Middle French *béatification,* from Late Latin *beātificāre;* for suffix see -ATION. —**beatify** *v.* make blessed. 1535, in a version of Trevisa's translation of *De Proprietatibus Rerum,* borrowed from Middle French *béatifier,* learned borrowing from Late Latin *beātificāre,* from *beātificus* beatific; for suffix see -FY.

The appearance of *beatification* about 130 years before *beatific* suggests that *beatific* is possibly a back formation of *beatification.*

beatitude (bēat'ətüd) *n.* bliss, blessing. Probably before 1425, borrowed through Middle French *béatitude,* and directly from Latin *beātitūdō* state of blessedness, from *beātus* happy, blessed, past participle of *beāre* make happy; whether related to Latin *bene* well, and to *bonus* good, is a matter of doubt; for suffix see -TUDE.

The reference to *the Beatitudes* in the New Testament books of Matthew and Luke is first recorded in 1526.

beatnik *n.* Bohemian, especially of the 1950's. 1958, formed in English from *beat generation* (name coined by American novelist Jack Kerouac, 1922-1969, for the post-World War II group of young artists and writers) + Yiddish suffix *-nik,* as in *nudnik,* from Russian *-nik* agent suffix, as in *sputnik* (1957); for suffix see -NIK.

beau (bō) *n.* suitor, dandy. 1684, borrowed from French *beau,* noun use of earlier adjective meaning "fine, handsome," from Old French *bel,* from Latin *bellus* handsome, fine, originally a diminutive form of *bonus* good; see BONUS. The meaning "lover, sweetheart" is not recorded in English before 1720. The original Middle English *beau* became obsolete in the early 1500's, so that the current use is a reborrowing of modern French. —**beau geste,** 1920, borrowed from French.

beautility *n.* the qualities of fine design, combining usefulness and beauty or elegance. 1973, formed in

English as a blend of *beauty* and *utility* (coined by Ada Louise Huxtable, American architectural critic).

beauty *n.* Before 1325 *bealte, beute,* in *Cursor Mundi,* borrowed from Old French *biauté, beauté, belté* (earlier *beltet*), from Vulgar Latin **bellitātem* state of being handsome, from Latin *bellus* fine, handsome, see BEAU; for suffix see -TY. —**beautiful** *adj.* About 1443, formed from English *beauty* + *-ful.* —**beautify** *v.* 1526, formed from English *beauty* + *-fy.* —**beautician** *n.* 1924, formed from English *beauty* + *-ician* (as in *physician, optician*). —**beauteous** *adj.* About 1400, formed from Middle English *beaute* (about 1330) + *-ous.*

beaver *n.* amphibious mammal. Old English *beofor* (about 1000, in Ælfric's *Glossary*), earlier *bebr* (about 720). The word has cognates in Old High German *bibar* beaver (modern German *Biber*), Old Saxon *bibar,* Middle Dutch and modern Dutch *bever,* Old Icelandic *björr;* from Proto-Germanic **beƀrús;* and outside Germanic with Latin *fiber,* Old Slavic *bebrŭ,* Lithuanian *bebrùs,* and Sanskrit *babhrú-s* large mongoose, all meaning literally "brown (animal)," from Indo-European **bhe-bhrú-s* (Pok.136), and ultimately derived from the same root as Old English *brun* BROWN.

bebop *n.* style of jazz. 1944 (but said to go back to the 1920's), originally imitative of the continually shifting accents in the music of a group of jazz players.

because *conj.* About 1375, in Chaucer's *Canterbury Tales,* Middle English *by cause* for the reason (that); later *bycause* (1380), *because* (1425). —**adv.** Probably about 1380, *bi cause* on account (of), for the sake (of); later *because* (about 1385); see BY and CAUSE.

beck *n.* calling gesture, as in *at one's beck and call.* Before 1382 *bek,* in the Wycliffe Bible, noun use of Middle English *bekken,* v., beckon to; see BECKON.

While the Middle English Dictionary derives *beck* (Middle English *bek*) from *bekken,* which is not recorded in English before 1385, in Chaucer's *Troilus and Criseyde,* it is possible that formation of *beck* (Middle English *bek*) was influenced by Middle English *bekenen* beckon, recorded in *The Ormulum* (probably about 1200), which would account for the appearance of *beck,* n. before *bekken,* v. However, a lapse of three years in a record of such antiquity may be simply a defect in the availability of source material.

beckon *v.* signal by a gesture. Old English *bēcnian* (before 830, in the *Vespasian Psalter*), West Saxon *bēacnian,* developed from *bēacen, bēcen* a sign, BEACON.

As alluded to at *beck,* n. Middle English had two forms that meant "beckon": 1) *bekken* (about 1385) derived from 2) *bekenen* (before 1200), developed from Old English; both related to *beken* a signal fire, beacon.

become *v.* Old English *becuman* happen, come about (about 725, in *Beowulf*), formed from *be-, bi-* + *cuman* come. This is a common Germanic compound cognate with Old Frisian *bikuma* come about, Old High German *biqueman* obtain, Gothic *biqiman* come upon suddenly. —**becoming** *adj.* About 1475, developed from English *become,* v.

bed *n.* Old English (about 700) *bed.* The Germanic cognates include Old Frisian and Old Saxon *bed,* Old High German *betti* bed, Middle High German *bette, bet* (modern German *Bett*), Old Icelandic *bedhr,* and Gothic *badi* bed, from Proto-Germanic **bađja-.* As the Germanic cognates derive from the same source as Latin *fodere* to dig, *fossa* ditch, Greek *bóthros* pit, Welsh *bedd* grave, and Lithuanian *bedù* dig, from Indo-European **bhedh-/bhodh-* to dig (Pok.113), the semantic connection with "dig" is supposed to be either a hole or ditch to lie in or soft ground to lie on; however, that idea disappeared in Germanic, which had only two senses: a sleeping place for man, and a garden bed for plants.

bedlam *n.* scene of noisy confusion. 1667, figurative use of an earlier sense of a lunatic asylum, madhouse (1663), in allusion to *Bedlam,* the popular name of St. Mary of *Bethlehem,* insane asylum in London, England (founded 1247). *Bethlehem* appeared as *Betleem* (town of Bethlehem in Judea) before 971, and, in reference to the hospital, as *Bedlem,* in 1418.

Bedouin (bed′üin) *n.* a wandering desert Arab. About 1400, *Bedoyn,* in Sir John Maundeville's *Travels;* borrowed from Old French *bedüin,* from colloquial Arabic *badāwīn,* plural of *badāwīy* desert dweller. Later apparently reborrowed (1603) from French *bedouin,* a spelling which was fully established only in the late 1800's. The transferred sense "a wanderer" is recorded in 1863.

bee *n.* insect. Old English *bēo* (before 900, in Alfred's translation of Boethius' *De Consolatione Philosophiae*), earlier *bīo-wyrt* bee wort, a plant (about 700) and *Bēo-wulf* Bee-wolf, a personal name (about 725, in *Beowulf*).

The word is cognate with Old High German *bīa, bini* bee (modern German *Biene*), Old Icelandic *bӯ* (usually in compounds), Middle Dutch *bie* (modern Dutch *bij*), and is found in many other of the older European languages, such as Old Slavic *bĭčela,* Old Prussian *bitte,* and Welsh *bydaf* nest of wild bees, from Indo-European **bhei-/bhi-* (Pok.116).

beech *n.* tree. 1296 *beche,* developed from Old English (about 700) *bœce,* later *bēce* (from Proto-Germanic **bōkjōn*), a derivative form of older *bōc* beech (from Proto-Germanic **bōkō).*

The fruit of the tree is an ancient food source for agricultural animals so that the tree was widely known in ancient Europe, and the word is therefore cognate with many of the older Germanic languages, including Old Icelandic *bōk* beech, Old High German *buohha,* Middle High German *buoche* (modern German *Buche*), Middle Dutch *boeke.* The Germanic forms are cognate with Latin *fāgus* and Greek *phēgós* oak, from Indo-European **bhāgó-s* beech (Pok.107); see also BOOK.

beef *n.* Probably before 1300 *bef,* in *Kyng Alisaunder,* borrowed from Old French *buef, boef* beef, ox, from Latin *bovem,* accusative of *bōs* ox. The Latin *bōs* (actually an Umbrian dialect form) is cognate with Greek *boûs* ox, Old Irish *bō* cow, Middle Welsh *buw,* and Sanskrit *gāú-s (go-)* cow, which in turn is cognate with Old English *cū* cow; thus *cow* is ultimately related to *beef.* From Indo-European **gwōu-s* (Pok.482).

beep *n.* 1929, formed in English in imitation of the sound of a horn, especially of an automobile; later extended to the sound emitted in radar tracking and other signals. —**v.** 1936, from the noun. —**beeper** *n.* 1946, formed from English *beep,* n. + *-er* [1].

beer *n.* Probably about 1225 *ber,* in *King Horn,* developed from Old English *bēor* (about 725, in *Beowulf*). Cognates include Old Frisian *biar, bier* beer, Old High German *bior,* Middle High German *bier* and modern

German *Bier,* Middle Dutch and modern Dutch *bier,* and Old Icelandic *bjǭrr* (from West Germanic). The native Scandinavian word, as seen in Old Icelandic *ǫl,* is cognate with English *ale.*

Whether English *beer* and its West Germanic cognates are connected with Latin *bibere* to drink, is a matter of conjecture, but the phonology is difficult.

beet *n.* plant with edible root. Old English (about 1000) *bēte,* borrowed from Latin *bēta,* a name adopted into other Germanic languages such as Old Frisian *bete,* Old High German *bieza,* Low German *bete* (modern German *Beete*) and Middle Dutch *bēte.*

The possibility of Celtic origin of Latin *bēta* is remote, because the Irish is borrowed from Latin and the Welsh from Middle English, and there is no Gaulish or other word that is unquestionably the source of the Latin.

beetle[1] *n.* insect. About 1440 *bytylle,* later *betylle* (before 1500), developed from Old English (about 700) *bitula,* later *bitela,* from *bītan* to bite, and *bita* a bite, morsel; see BITE.

beetle[2] *v.* project, overhang. 1602, in Shakespeare's *Hamlet,* apparently a back formation by Shakespeare from earlier *beetyl-browde* beetle-browed, having prominent, overhanging brows (1562), from *bitelbrouwed, betilbrowed* (before 1376), (Middle English *bitel* sharp-edged, sharp, probably Old English **bitol* sharp, biting + *browed*).

befall *v.* About 1225 *bifallen* to fall out in the course of events, to happen, developed from Old English *befeallan* to fall (probably about 875, in a version of *Genesis*), formed from *be-* by, about + *feallan* to FALL. The word is cognate with Old Saxon and Old High German *bifallan* (modern German *befallen*), and Old Frisian *bifalla.*

before *prep., adv., conj.* About 1175 *beforen,* developed from Old English *beforan* (about 725, in *Beowulf*) and *biforan* (about 750, in poetry of Cynewulf), both Old English forms meaning "in front, ahead" (*be-, bi-* by, about + *foran* before, from *fora* FORE).

This is a Common Germanic compound cognate with Old Frisian *bifara,* Old Saxon *biforan,* Old High German *bifora,* Middle High German *bevor* (modern German *bevor,* conj.).

beg *v.* Probably before 1200 *beggen* ask as charity, in *Ancrene Riwle;* probably related to or formed from BEGGAR.

The Anglo-French *begger* to beg, is first recorded somewhat later than the Middle English verb. It may be a borrowing from Middle English, but we cannot exclude the possibility that Middle English *beggen* was from Anglo-French.

beget *v.* bring forth, produce. About 1250 *begeten,* alteration of earlier *biyeten* (before 1121) through influence of *geten* to GET. Middle English *biyeten* developed from Old English *begietan, bigeotan* to get (by effort), acquire. A similar form is found in Gothic *bigitan.*

beggar *n.* Probably before 1200, in *Ancrene Riwle,* person who lives by begging; borrowed perhaps from Old French *begart, begard,* originally, a member of the *Beghards,* lay brotherhoods of mendicants that arose in the Low Countries in the early 1200's, from Middle Dutch *beggaert* mendicant; for the suffix *-aert* see -ARD. It is a matter of conjecture whether the Middle Dutch stem *beg-* was derived from *begīne* a member of the *Beguines* lay sisterhoods devoted to religious life.

begin *v.* Old English (about 1000, in Ælfric's version of *Genesis*) *beginnan* (*be-* by, about + *-ginnan* to begin, recorded only in compounds, such as Old English *onginnan* and *āginnan* to begin.).

The Old English is cognate with Old Frisian *biginna* to begin, Old Saxon and Old High German *biginnan* (modern German *beginnen*), and Gothic *duginnan;* further connections are uncertain.

begonia (bigōn′yə) *n.* tropical plant. 1751, probably borrowed through French (1706), from New Latin, formed on the name of Michel *Bégon,* 1638-1710, French governor of Haiti and patron of botany + *-ia,* New Latin suffix used in taxonomy.

behalf *n.* **on** (or **in**) **behalf of,** in the interest of. About 1303 *behalve,* in Mannyng's *Handlyng Synne;* later, *behalf,* literally meaning "beside" (about 1386, in Chaucer's *Legend of Good Women*); fusion of Old English *(him) be healfe* by (his) side, and *on (his) healfe* on (his) side, from *healfe* side, HALF. From the latter part of the 1400's onward, the form *behalve* gave way to *behalf,* paralleling the displacement of the singular *halve* by *half.*

Comparable development appears in German *meinethalben* on my behalf, developed from Middle High German *von mīnen halben* on my half or side, where *halbe* means "side" as in Middle English.

behave *v.* About 1410, formed from *be-* thoroughly + *have* to have or bear oneself (in a specified way).

Old English *behabban* to encompass, contain (*be-* + *habban* have, hold) is only coincidentally similar in form and no direct connection exists between Old English *behabban* and the form *behave* of the 1400's. **—behavior** *n.* Probably before 1425 *behaver,* in a translation of Higden's *Polychronicon,* later *behavour* (probably before 1475), influenced by the synonymous *haver, havour* (about 1450); developed from *behave* + *-our* -or[1]. The spelling *behavior* with *i* appeared in 1538, influenced by the synonymous *havior* (1478), earlier *havour, haver* (about 1450), an alteration (by association with Middle English *haven* to have) of Middle French and Old French *avoir, aveir,* noun use of verb meaning to have, from Latin *habēre* (see HABIT).

—behaviorism *n.* 1913, coined by John B. Watson, 1878-1958, American psychologist, founder of this school of psychology.

behemoth (bihē′məth) *n.* large, powerful animal or thing. Before 1382 *bemoth* an animal mentioned in Job, in the Wycliffe Bible, later *behemot* (1388, in a second version of the Wycliffe Bible); borrowed from Latin *behēmōth,* from Hebrew *bəhēmōth* beasts or beast.

behest (bihest′) *n.* command, bidding. Probably before 1200 *biheste* promise, command, request, in Layamon's *Chronicle of Britain,* alteration of Old English *behǣs* promise, from *behātan* to promise (*be-* by, about + *hātan* to call, command). Old English *behǣs* represents Proto-Germanic *bi-Haissiz,* and the Old English *hātan* is cognate with Old High German *heizan* and Gothic *haitan* to order, command, from Proto-Germanic **Haitanan,* Indo-European **kəi-,* root *kēi-* (Pok.538).

The addition in Middle English of *-t* to Old English *behǣs* was influenced by the *-t* of the synonymous word *behight,* on a pattern also seen in such words as *amongst.*

behind *prep., adv., adj.* Old English (about 725, in a version of *Exodus*) *behindan* (*be-, bi-* by + *hindan* in back, behind; see HIND[1] back). The word is identical with Old Saxon *bihindan,* and cognate with Old High German *hintana* (modern German *hinten*), and Gothic *hindana* back of, behind of, from the root *hind-* in *hinder* and *hindmost.*

behold *v.* Before 1200 *biholden,* in *Ancrene Riwle,* developed from Old English *bihaldan* (before 830, in the *Vespasian Psalter*), corresponding to West Saxon *behealdan* give regard to, hold in view, watch (*be-, bi-* by + *haldan, healdan* HOLD). The word is identical with Old Saxon *bihaldan* hold, keep, Old Frisian *bihalda,* Old High German *bihaltan* (modern German *behalten*).

The meaning "indebted" as in *beholden to* is first recorded in Middle English probably about 1390, in *Sir Gawain and the Green Knight.*

behoove (bihüv′) *v.* be necessary (or proper) for. Probably before 1200 *bihoven,* in Layamon's *Chronicle of Britain* and *Ancrene Riwle;* developed from Old English *behōfian* have use for (about 725, in *Beowulf*), from **behōf* advantage, use, (only recorded in derivatives such as *behōflic* useful). The Old English is cognate with Old Frisian *behōf* advantage, and Middle High German *behuof* useful thing, *beheben* take, hold (related to Old English *hebban* raise, as seen in its past tense *hōf;* see HEAVE).

beige (bāzh) *adj., n.* pale-brown. 1858, borrowed from French *beige,* earlier *baige,* from Old French *bege* of the natural color (of cotton and wool), of uncertain origin. Several dictionaries suggest a borrowing of Old French from Italian *bambagia* cotton, from Medieval Latin *bambax* (genitive *bambacis*), but this raises the problem of the disappearance of the first syllable *bam-.* Another suggestion is that the first syllable, *bam-, bom-,* in Old French *bambais,* and particularly *bombace* cotton, was taken to be *bon* good, and that the syllable was easily eliminated because of its weak meaning (compare, for instance, *bonhomme —homme* fellow, *boneurté — eureté* happiness, *bonaventure — aventure* lucky).

being *n.* person, thing that exists. 1380, in Chaucer's *Canterbury Tales,* from earlier use meaning "existence" (1340, in *Ayenbite of Inwyt*), developed from verbal noun of *be,* v.

belay (bilā′) *v.* fasten (a rope) by winding. 1549, developed from Middle English *beleggen* encircle, surround (before 1250, in *The Owl and the Nightingale*); developed from Old English *belecgan* to lay over (about 725, in a version of *Genesis*), from *be-, bi-* by, over, against + *lecgan* to LAY[1] put down.

belch *v.* An altered form *belchen* (1483) of earlier *belken* (about 1350), both variants of Middle English *bolken* to belch, vomit, overflow; developed from Old English *bilkettan* (about 950), later *bealcan, balcettan, bylcettan* to belch, vomit, utter (words) vehemently (about 1025).

The word is cognate with Middle Dutch *belken* bellow, roar, cry out, and possibly related to Old English *bellan* to roar (see BELLOW), but is almost certainly imitative in origin.

The phonetic alteration of *belken* to modern English *belch* came about by palatalization.
—n. 1513, from the verb.

beleaguer (bilē′gər) *v.* surround, besiege. 1589, probably from Low German *belegeren* (*be-* around + *leger* camp). The word is cognate with Swedish *belägra* to besiege, German *Belagerung* siege, and *belagern* beleaguer, and Dutch *belegeren* besiege, of which the Dutch *leger* encamping army, lair, bed, is related to English LAIR.

belfry *n.* bell tower. 1272 *belfrey* bell tower; probably before 1300, *berefrei* movable tower for besieging fortifications, in *Kyng Alisaunder;* borrowed through Anglo-French *berefrei, berfrei,* Old North French *berfroi, belfroy, belefroy,* probably from Middle High German *bercfrit* portable shelter, originally used to protect a besieging force, from Proto-Germanic **berʒan* protect, and **frithuz* peace, shelter, meaning a protective shelter.

According to Bloch and Wartburg, "The loan cannot go back to the period of the Frankish invasion [of France] because at that time siege warfare was hardly practiced." Therefore, the often cited hypothetical Frankish source is probably not relevant.

belief *n.* Before 1400 *belyefe,* earlier *bileve* (before 1225) and *bileave* (probably before 1200, in *Ancrene Riwle*); all forms replacing Old English *gelēafa* by influence of later Old English *belȳfan* (about 1000, in works of Ælfric), *belēfan* believe. The Old English *gelēafa* is cognate with Old Saxon *gilōbo* belief, Old High German *giloubo* (modern German *Glaube*), and Gothic *galaubeins* belief, *galaubjan* to believe; see BELIEVE. Old High German *giloubo* is from Proto-Germanic **ʒalauƀen.*

By the 1400's the distinction in the final consonant was developing to differentiate *belief* and *believe,* as seen in the pattern *proof — prove* and *grief — grieve.*

believe *v.* Before 1393 *believen,* in Gower's *Confessio Amantis,* earlier *beleven* (about 1386, in Chaucer's *Legend of Good Women*) and *bileven* (1225, in *King Horn*). The Middle English forms developed from Old English *belȳfan* (about 1000, in works of Ælfric) and *belēfan* believe, which replaced a variety of Old English dialectal forms including Mercian *gelēfan,* Northumbrian *gelēfa,* and West Saxon *gelȳfan* believe. These Old English words are cognate with Old Saxon *gilōbian* believe, Old High German *gilouben* (modern German *glauben*), and Gothic *galaubjan* to believe, literally, to make palatable to oneself, accept, approve, from Proto-Germanic **ʒa-lauƀjanan,* from Indo-European **leubh-/loubh-* (Pok.683).

belittle *v.* 1781, American English, in writings of Thomas Jefferson, formed from *be-* + *little.*

bell *n.* Old English *belle* (before 900, in works of Alfred); cognate with Middle Low German and Middle Dutch *belle* bell; perhaps related to Old English *bellan* to roar, BELLOW.

belladonna (bel′ədon′ə) *n.* poisonous plant or the drug made from it. 1597, as an Italian term introduced into an English work on plants, literally, fair lady. According to one source (1757), the plant got its name because women made a cosmetic from its juice.

belle (bel) *n.* beautiful girl or woman. 1622, in Fletcher's *The Beggars Bush,* borrowed from French *belle,* as a noun use of *belle,* adj., beautiful, from Old French *belle* (feminine of *bel* fine, handsome); see BEAU.

belles-lettres (bellet′rə) *n.pl.* finer forms of literature. 1665, borrowed from French *belles lettres* literary studies, literally, fine letters, being parallel to *beaux arts* fine arts.

bellicose *adj.* warlike, belligerent. Probably before

1425, in a translation of Higden's *Polychronicon,* borrowed perhaps through influence of Italian *bellicoso* (1363), from Latin *bellicōsus,* from *bellicus* of war, from *bellum* war; see DUEL; for suffix see -OSE.[1]

belligerent *adj.* fond of fighting, warlike. 1577 *belligerant,* borrowed perhaps through influence of Italian *belligerante* (1480) from Latin *belligerantem* (nominative *belligerāns),* from *belligerāre* wage war, from *belliger* waging war (*bellum* war + *gerere* to conduct). **—n.** 1811, from the adjective. **—belligerence** *n.* 1814, formed from English *belliger(ent)* + *-ence.*

bellow *v.* roar. About 1300 *belewen* be enraged, roar, developed from Old English (about 750) *belgan* become angry; cognate with Old Icelandic *belgja* to swell up, Old High German *belgan* swell up, be angry, Old Saxon *belgan* become angry; related to Anglian *bælg* (compare *blǣstbælg* a bellows, *bēanbælg* bean pod) and West Saxon *bylg* bag; see BELLOWS, BELLY. **—n.** 1779, from the verb.

bellows *n. sing. or pl.* instrument for producing air current. 1372-74 *belowes,* earlier *beliges* (about 1125), plural of *beli* (about 1200) and *bali* (about 1250), both meaning "stomach, abdomen, BELLY." The Old English word for bellows was *blǣstbælg,* literally, blowing bag.

belly *n.* About 1200 *beli* abdomen, bowels, developed from Old English (about 700) *bælg* (with dialect variants *belg, bylg*) bag; cognate with Old High German *balg* bag, skin, Old Icelandic *belgr,* Gothic *balgs* wineskin, (from Proto-Germanic **balʒiz*), Old Irish *bolg* bag, and Welsh *bola, boly* belly, bag, from Indo-European **bhelĝh-/bholĝh-* to swell (Pok.125). Related to BILLOW, BELLOW. **—v.** 1606, in Shakespeare's *Troylus and Cressida,* from the noun.

belong *v.* 1340 *belongen,* in *Ayenbite of Inwit,* formed from *bi-* thoroughly + *longen* go along with, be appropriate to, from *long,* adj., dependent (on), belonging (to); formed after Old English *gelang, gelong* (about 725, in *Beowulf*), from *ge-* (prefix expressing completion of action) + **lang* of uncertain meaning. Old English *gelang* is cognate with Old High German and Old Saxon *gilang* nearby, at hand, but no trace can be found in Old English of a form corresponding to Old High German *bilangen,* Middle Dutch *belanghen* (modern German and Dutch *belangen*), all meaning "to concern, interest, belong to." **—belongings,** *n.pl.* 1603, in Shakespeare's *Measure for Measure,* formed from English *belonging,* verbal noun, + plural suffix *-s*[1].

below *adv.* About 1325, Middle English *biloughe* (*bi-,* variant of *be-* by, about + *looghe,* variant of *lou, lowe* LOW[1], adj.). *Below* was very rare in Middle English and only appeared as an adverb; it began apparently as a variant of the earlier *a-lowe,* the parallel form to *an-high* (now *on high*); the synonymous forms *a-low, below* were analogous to *a-fore, be-fore. Below* gained currency in the 1500's, and is frequent in Shakespeare. **—prep.** 1575, from the adverb.

belt *n.* Old English (about 1000) *belt,* found also in Old High German *balz* and Old Icelandic *belti,* all borrowed ultimately from Latin *balteus* girdle, belt, perhaps of Etruscan origin.

bench *n.* Before 1200, developed from Old English *benc* (about 725, in *Beowulf*), and cognate with Old Frisian *bank, benk* bench, Old High German *bank,* and Old Icelandic *bekkr,* in which *-kk-* is the North Germanic correspondence of *-nk-.*

bend *v.* Probably before 1300, in *Arthour and Merlin,* developed from Old English (probably about 1000) *bendan* tighten (a bow); originally, constrain; causative of Old English *bindan* to BIND. Old English *bendan* developed from Proto-Germanic **bandjanan.* **—n.** About 1434, from the verb.

beneath *adv., prep.* 1125 *benethan,* developed from Old English (854) *beneothan* (*be-, bi-* by, about + *neothan* below; cognate with Old Saxon *nithana* below, Old High German *nidana,* and Old Icelandic *nethan;* related to Old English *nithera, niothera* lower, NETHER).

benediction *n.* blessing. Probably before 1400 *benediccioun,* in *Sir Ferumbras;* borrowed, perhaps by influence of rare Old French *benedicion,* from Latin *benedictiōnem* (nominative *benedictiō*), from *benedīcere* to bless; literally, speak well of (*bene* well + *dīcere* to say); for suffix see -TION. Doublet of BENISON.

benefactor *n.* one who gives help or money. 1451, in *The Paston Letters,* borrowed, probably by influence of Middle French *bienfacteur,* from Late Latin *benefactor,* from the Latin phrase *bene facere* do well + *-tor* the agent suffix. **—benefaction** *n.* Before 1662, from Late Latin *benefactiōnem* (nominative *benefactiō*), from *benefacere,* in Classical Latin always written as two words; for suffix see -TION.

benefice *n.* office or position in the church, fief. About 1300, borrowed through Old French *benefice,* and directly as a learned borrowing from Latin *beneficium* kindness, promotion, from *beneficus* obliging, kind, from *bene* well + the root of *facere* do. **—beneficence** *n.* kindness, gift. About 1454, from Latin *beneficentia,* from a variant stem of *beneficus* kind; for suffix see -ENCE. **—beneficent** *adj.* 1616, probably formed in English from *beneficence,* on the pattern of earlier English *benevolent, magnificent;* for suffix see -ENT.

benefit *n.* advantage. Before 1376 *benfet* good deed, in *Piers Plowman,* borrowed through Anglo-French *benfet, benfait,* from Old French *bienfait,* and directly from Latin *benefactum* good deed (*bene* well + *factum,* neuter past participle of *facere* to do). **—v.** 1472, from the noun. **—beneficial** *adj.* 1464, borrowed through Middle French *bénéficial* and directly from Latin *beneficiālis,* from *beneficium* a benefit, kindness; for suffix see -AL[1]. **—beneficiary** *n.* 1611, borrowed probably from French *bénéficiaire,* from Latin *beneficiārius,* from *beneficium;* for suffix see -ARY.

benevolent *adj.* kindly, charitable. About 1443, borrowed from Middle French *benivolent,* and directly from Latin *benevolentem* (*bene* well + *volentem* (nominative *volēns*), present participle of *velle* to wish); for suffix see -ENT. **—benevolence** *n.* Probably about 1400, borrowed from Old French *benivolence,* and directly from Latin *benevolentia* well-wishing, from *benevolentem.*

benign *adj.* kindly. Probably before 1325, borrowed from Old French *benigne,* a learned borrowing from Latin *benignus* good-natured (*bene* good, well + *-gnus,* from *gignere* to bear, beget; see KIN). **—benignant** *adj.* Before 1782, formed in English from Latin *benignus,* on the pattern of earlier *malignant.* **—benignity** *n.* About 1380 *benignite,* in Chaucer's *Canterbury Tales,* borrowed from Old French *benignité,* learned borrowing from Latin *benignitātem* (nominative *benignitās*), from *benignus;* for suffix see -ITY.

benison (ben′əzən) *n.* blessing. Probably before 1300 *benisoun,* borrowed from Old French *beneiçon, beneison,* a learned borrowing from Latin *benedictiōnem;* see the doublet BENEDICTION.

bent[1] *adj.* not straight, crooked. Probably before 1300 *ibent,* in *Arthour and Merlin;* later *bent* (about 1370, in Chaucer's *An A.B.C.*), developed from *bent,* past participle of BEND. **—n.** inclination, tendency. 1586, developed from earlier *bent,* adj., being turned or inclined in some direction (1534, in writings of Sir Thomas More), probably as a translation of Latin *inclīnātiō* inclination.

bent[2] *n.* stiff grass. 1364; an earlier meaning, "grassy place," is attested in 1327; an earlier form *Benet-* (1136 and after, in place names), developed from Old English *Beonet-* (851), as in *Beonet-lēah* Bentley, and is cognate with Old Saxon *binet* and Old High German *binuz* (early modern German *Bintze,* German *Binse*) meaning "rush, marshy grass," from Proto-Germanic **binut-,* of unknown origin.

benzene or **benzine** *n.* volatile chemical compounds obtained from hydrocarbons. 1835 *benzine,* borrowed from German *Benzin* (coined in 1833 by E. Mitscherlich, German chemist), from *Benz(oesäure)* benzoic acid (1791, in English) the acid obtained from benzoin (from *Benzoe* benzoin + *Säure* acid), + *-in* -ine[2], chemical suffix. The form *benzene* is attested since 1872.

benzoin (ben′zōin) *n.* resin used in cosmetics, incense, etc. 1562 *benzoin,* earlier (1558) *bengewine,* which probably gave rise to the alteration *benjamin* (a variant name current from the late 1500's to the 1800's); also English *benjoin* (1601), borrowed from Middle French *benjoin* and Italian *benzoi,* from which English assimilated the *z.* The source of the word in European languages is Arabic *lubān jāwī* incense of Jāwā (Java); *lu* of the first element in Arabic, being mistaken as the definite article in Arabic, was omitted in the borrowing process.

bequeath *v.* leave or give in a will. Probably before 1200 *biquethen,* in Layamon's *Chronicle of Britain,* developed from Old English *becwethan* give by will (800-885, in Alfred's Will); earlier, to say, speak (probably about 750, in *Andreas*), a compound of *be-, bi-* by, about + *cwethan* say, from Proto-Germanic **kwethanan.*

bequest *n.* legacy, bequeathing. Before 1338 *biqueste,* in Mannyng's *Chronicle of England;* later occasionally *biquyst,* as in the 1378 version of *Piers Plowman* (*be-, bi-* be- + *quiste,* about 1300; later *quest,* between 1330 and 1350, with the *-e-* spelling by analogy with Middle English *biquethen;* Middle English *quiste, quest* developed from Old English **cwis, *cwiss* something said, utterance —compare Old English *andcwis* an answer, *uncwisse* speechless, forms cognate with Gothic *anaquiss* slander, *missaquiss* dispute —all from the Indo-European base **gwet-* (Pok. 480) of Old English *cwide* saying, speech + a suffix beginning with *t-;* the *tt* becoming *ss* (from Proto-Germanic **kwessís,* Indo-European *gwet-tís*). The new *t* in Middle English is probably due to analogy between *biquethen—biquiste, quiste* and pairs such as *give—gift, freeze—frost,* etc.).

berate (birāt′) *v.* scold sharply. 1548, formed from English prefix *be-* thoroughly + *rate* to scold (about 1390, in Chaucer's *Canterbury Tales*), perhaps borrowed from a Scandinavian source (compare Norwegian dialect and Swedish *rata* reject, find fault).

bereave (birēv′) *v.* leave desolate and alone, rob. About 1175 *bireaven,* developed from Old English *berēafian,* about 725, in a version of *Genesis* (*be-, bi-* thoroughly + *rēafian* rob, about 725, in *Beowulf*); cognate with Old Frisian *birāva* despoil, Old Saxon *biroban,* Old High German *biroubōn* (modern German *berauben*), and Gothic *biraubōn,* from Proto-Germanic **rauƀojanan,* cognate with Sanskrit *ropayati* breaks off from Indo-European **reup-/roup-* (Pok.870). **—bereavement** *n.* 1731, in Bailey's *Dictionary,* formed from English *bereave* + *-ment.* **—bereft** *adj.* About 1375, in Chaucer's *Canterbury Tales,* developed from *bereaved, bireved,* later *bereft,* past participle of Middle English *bireaven.*

The two forms *bereaved* and *bereft* have existed side by side since the latter 1300's, *bereaved* being the earlier form; however, the usage is not now interchangeable: *bereaved* is applied to loss of a beloved one, *bereft* is applied to circumstances, especially in such phrases as *bereft of hope.*

beret (bərā′) *n.* cap with no visor. 1827, borrowed from French *béret,* earlier *berret,* Old Gascon *berret,* from Medieval Latin *birretum,* from Vulgar Latin **birrittum* (diminutive form of Late Latin *birrus* cape with a hood), perhaps of Gaulish origin.

beriberi (ber′ēber′ē) *n.* disease affecting nerves. 1703, borrowed from Singhalese *beriberi* (reduplication of *beri* weakness).

berkelium (bėrkē′lēəm) *n.* radioactive metallic chemical element. 1950, New Latin *berkelium,* formed from *Berkeley,* California, site of University of California, where it was first produced + New Latin *-ium* (suffix of chemical elements).

berm *n.* bank of a canal; side of a road; later, terrace along a river bank or beach (1891). 1729, borrowed from French *berme,* from Dutch *berm* and German *Berme;* see BRIM.

berry *n.* Old English *berie* (about 1000, in Ælfric's translation of *Deuteronomy*). Though the early history of this word is uncertain, it is found in various forms in all Germanic languages, and is cognate with Old Saxon *-beri* in *wīnberi* grape, and Old High German *beri* berry (modern German *Beere*), Middle High German and Middle Dutch *bere,* Old Icelandic *ber,* Danish *bær,* Swedish *bär,* and Gothic *-basi* in *weinabasi* grape.

The form with *s,* seen in Gothic, is preserved in modern Dutch *bes,* and through the Proto-Germanic **basja-, *bazja-* may possibly be connected with a root form represented by Sanskrit *bhas-* to eat, in *bábhasti* chews thoroughly, from Indo-European **bhes-/bhos-* (Pok.145). **—v. berrying** *vbl.n.* the producing or gathering of berries. 1845, American English, in writings of James Fenimore Cooper.

berserk (bėrsėrk′) *adj.* violently angry, mad. 1851, developed in English either as a shortening of earlier *berserker* (1822, in Scott's *The Pirate*) or more probably a back formation of *berserker,* from a misunderstanding of the function of the final *-r* in the Scandinavian *berserkr* where the *-r* is a case ending of the masculine singular, rather than an agent noun suffix for one who goes *berserk.*

The word is of uncertain etymology, though its reference to the Norse warriors who fought with ferocious and frenzied fury is undisputed. *Berserker* is borrowed from a Scandinavian source (compare Old Icelandic *berserkr,* probably, bear shirt).

berth *n.* 1622, safe room or space necessary to keep ships from running afoul of each other, of uncertain origin; perhaps related to BEAR[2] in the sense "bearing-off room," that is "room or way made by keeping a safe distance from the shore." The extended sense of "a sleeping place" is first recorded for a ship's passenger (1796) and a railroad passenger (1806). —**v.** 1667, in Pepys' *Diary,* from the noun.

beryl (berʹəl) *n.* hard blue-green mineral used as a gem. Before 1300, borrowed from Old French *beril,* and from Latin *bēryllus,* from Greek *bḗryllos.*

According to the Greek scholar Frisk, *bḗrýllos* is a back formation from *bērýllion,* from Prakrit *veruliya,* variant of Pali *veluriya* (formed in Sanskrit as *váiḍūrya-m* lapis lazuli), from Dravidian, and probably formed on *Vēḷūr* (now Bēlūr) the name of a town in southern India.

beryllium (bərilʹēəm) *n.* metallic chemical element. 1863, New Latin *beryllium,* formed from Latin *bēryllus* BERYL + New Latin *-ium* (suffix of chemical elements).

beseech *v.* beg. Probably before 1200 *bisechen,* in *Ancrene Riwle* and Layamon's *Chronicle of Britain;* formed from Middle English *be-, bi-* about, or perhaps meaning "thoroughly" + *sechen* seek, developed from Old English *sēcan* (about 725, in *Beowulf*); earlier *sōhte* (about 700, in early glossaries, past tense only). The word is cognate with Old Frisian *bisēka* and modern German *besuchen* to seek out, visit; see SEEK.

beset *v.* set upon, attack. Old English *besettan* surround, about 725, in *Beowulf* (*be-, bi-* about + *settan* SET); cognate with Old Frisian *bisetta* surround, Old Saxon *bisettjan,* Old High German *bisezzan,* Middle High German *besetzen* (modern German *besetzen* occupy, settle), and Gothic *bisatjan,* from Proto-Germanic *bi-satjanan. The meaning "to assail, attack" appeared in Middle English before 1200.

beside *prep., adv.* Probably before 1200 *bisiden, biside,* in Layamon's *Chronicle of Britain,* formed from Old English *bī sīdan* by the side; earlier, *besīdan,* probably about 725 (*be, bi* by + *sīdan,* dative case of *sīde* SIDE).

The adverbial use is now generally replaced by *besides.*

besides *adv., prep.* Probably before 1200 *bisides,* in Layamon's *Chronicle of Britain,* but generally of later use about 1390 and after, formed of Middle English *bisiden* beside + *-s,* variant form of the adverbial genitive ending *-es.*

besom (bēʹzəm) *n.* broom of twigs. Old English (about 800) *besma,* later *besema* bundle of twigs (used as a broom or as a flail); cognate with Old Frisian *besma,* Old Saxon *besmo,* Middle Dutch *besem, bessem* (modern Dutch *bezem*) and Old High German *besmo, besamo* (modern German *Besen*), from Proto-Germanic **besmōn.*

best *adj., adv.* superlative of *good* and *well.* Probably before 1200 *beste* or *best,* in *Ancrene Riwle,* earlier *betste* (before 1121); found in Old English *betst, betsta* (about 725, in *Beowulf*). Forms of *best* are common in Germanic as seen in the variety of cognates, such as Old Frisian, Old Saxon, and Middle Dutch *best,* Old High German *bezzist* best (modern German *best*), Old Icelandic *beztr,* and Gothic *batists*—all ultimately from the Germanic base **bat-* (see also BETTER) + the superlative suffix represented by Old English *-st* -est.

Old English *betst* was reduced to *best* by assimilation of the *t* to the following *s* (and similarly in German and other modern Germanic languages).

The relationship of *best* and *better* with *good* and *well* developed outside of Old English.
—**n.** Probably before 1200 *best,* in Layamon's *Chronicle of Britain,* earlier *beste, betste* (probably before 1175); from the adjective. —**v.** 1863, verb use of *best,* n.

bestial (besʹchəl) *adj.* Before 1393, in Gower's *Confessio Amantis;* borrowed from Old French *bestial* and from Latin *bēstiālis* like a beast, from *bēstia* BEAST; for suffix see -AL[1].

bestow *v.* Before 1375 *bestowen, bistowen* give (alms, etc.), mete out, from *be-, bi-* be- + *stowen* to place, spend, STOW. —**bestowal** *n.* 1773, act of bestowing, formed from English *bestow* + *-al*[2].

bet *v.* to wager. The origin of this word is uncertain. The verb is first recorded in 1597, in Shakespeare's *2 Henry IV,* and it is suggested that it derived from *beet,* v., to make good, developed from Middle English *beten* to mend, remedy; improve, make better; kindle or replenish (a fire); arouse (emotion), stimulate (action), Old English *bǣtan,* cognate with Old Saxon *bōtian,* Old High German *beizen* and Old Icelandic *beita,* from Proto-Germanic **baitjanan.*

The shortened *e* of *bet* is due to the presence of short *-e* forms in Middle English *beten,* as signaled by rimes and by *tt-* spellings. *Betting* (1599, in Shakespeare's *Henry V*) was very likely thought of as "improving a game or contest, stimulating action, etc." The means or material with which to *beet* is frequently indicated in a phrase with *mid* or *with,* but Shakespeare's turning the means (*i.e.* money) into the direct object of the verb seems to be without precedent.
—**n.** 1592, probably from the verb. The later date for the verb (1597) may be a defect in the record of English.

With similarity of form, it is tempting to draw a connection between modern English *bet* and Middle English *bet* advantage (noun use of *bet,* adv., the earlier form of BETTER). However, no accepted connection has been established.

beta (bāʹtə) *n.* second letter of the Greek alphabet. Before 1325, in *Cursor Mundi,* borrowed from Latin *bēta,* from Greek *bêta,* from Semitic; compare Hebrew *bēth* the second letter of the Hebrew alphabet, literally meaning a house, originally formed from the hieroglyph of a house.

betel (bēʹtəl) *n.* East Indian pepper plant whose leaves are wrapped around a nut *(betel nut)* and chewed as a stimulant. 1553, borrowed from Portuguese *betele, vitele,* from Malayalam *veṭṭila,* or Tamil *veṭṭilei.*

bête noire (bātʹ nwärʹ) thing dreaded or detested, bugbear. 1844, as a French phrase introduced in Thackeray's *Barry Lyndon;* French *bête noire,* literally, black beast.

betray *v.* be disloyal to. About 1280 *bitrayen* mislead, deceive, betray, formed from Middle English *bi-* be-, thoroughly + *trayen* betray, borrowed from Old French *traïr,* from Latin *trādere* hand over (*trāns-* across + *dare* give; see DATE[1] period). —**betrayal** *n.*

1816, in Southey's *Essays,* formed from English *betray* + *-al* ².

betroth *v.* promise in marriage. About 1303 *betrouthen,* variant of *bitreuthen,* in Mannyng's *Handlyng Synne* (*be-, bi-* by + *treuth* a pledge, TROTH). —**betrothal** *n.* 1844, formed from English *betroth* + *-al* ².

better *adj., adv.* comparative of *good* and *well.* Probably before 1300 *better,* earlier *bettre* (about 1250) and *betre* (1131); developed from Old English *bettra* (before 900, in writings of Alfred), earlier *betra* (about 750, in Cynewulf's *Elene*) and *betera* (about 725, in *Beowulf*). The word was used as the comparative of *good* in older Germanic languages and is cognate with Old Frisian *betera,* Old Saxon *betiro,* Old High German *bezziro* better (modern German *besser*), Old Icelandic *betri,* and Gothic *batiza* —all from Proto-Germanic **batizōn,* containing the comparative suffix represented by Old English *-ra* -er.

The Proto-Germanic base **bat-* is represented by the Old and Middle English adverb *bet* better, which is cognate with Old Frisian *bet,* Old High German *baz,* Old Icelandic *betr,* from Proto-Germanic *batiz,* and is possibly related to Old English *bōt* remedy, compensation; modern English BOOT² (now used only in *to boot*). —**n.** About 1175, but developed in Old English from the adjective in such phrases as *the better and the worse.* —**v.** Before 1400, from the adjective, and analogous to Old English *beterian, gebeterian* be or make better; cognate with Old Frisian *beteria,* Old High German *bezzirōn,* Middle High German *bezzern,* and modern German *bessern.*

between *prep., adv.* 1225 *bitwene,* earlier *bitwenen* (probably before 1200, in Layamon's *Chronicle of Britain*) and *betwenen* (about 1200); developed from Old English *betwēonum* (about 750, in Cynewulf's *Elene*); formed from *bi-, be-* by + *twēonum* two each (about 725, in *Beowulf*).

Between combines two earlier forms in Old English: *betwēonum* (Mercian *betwīnum*) and *betwēon, betwīn.* The elements *twēonum* and *twēon* partially correspond through **tweohnum* and **tweohn* (Proto-Germanic **twiHn*) to Gothic *tweihnáim* and *tweihna,* grammatical cases of *tweihnái* two each, a derivative of *twā* TWO, cognate with Sanskrit *dviká-s* double, from Indo-European **dwei-k-/dwi-k-* (Pok.231).

betwixt (bitwikst′) *prep., adv.* between. Before 1333 *bytwixte,* earlier *betwix* (1127); developed from Old English *betweox* (before 899, in writings of Alfred), formed from *bi-, be-* by + *tweox* for two. Old English *betweox* is probably a shortened form of **betweoxum* twofold, the element **-tweoxum* from **twiscum,* dative plural of **twisc,* cognate with Old Frisian *twiska,* Old Saxon *twisc,* and Old High German *zwiski* two each, from Proto-Germanic **twiska-,* formed from the adverb **twis* twice (compare Old High German *zwis,* Sanskrit *dvís,* Greek *dís* and Latin *bis,* from Indo-European **dwis*); see TWO.

The final *t* in *betwixt* developed in Old English but was infrequently used until after 1500 when it gradually became the regular spelling.

bevel *n.* edge, angle. 1677 *bevil,* earlier *bevile,* adj. (1562), possibly borrowed from Old French **bevel,* a form implied by French *biveau, béveau* (in which Middle and modern French *-eau* come from Old French *-el*). The supposed Old French **bevel* may have developed from *baïf* gaping (*beër, baër* to open, gape, from Medieval Latin *batare* + *-if* -ive; see BAY³ space).

The problem here lies in the dates of borrowing. Since the word is first recorded in English (1562), there appears to be a gap of about 150 years between the assumed borrowing from Old French (a period ending in 1400) and the appearance of *bevile* in English. —**v.** 1677, probably from the noun.

beverage *n.* liquid for drinking. About 1300, earlier as a surname (1237); borrowed from Old French *bevrage,* from *bevre* to drink, variant of *boivre,* from Latin *bibere,* see IMBIBE; for suffix see -AGE.

bevy (bev′ē) *n.* group, flock. About 1425, applied to quails; before 1450, applied to a group of ladies; borrowed from Anglo-French *bevée,* of unknown origin. It has been conjectured that the word corresponds to Old French *bevee, buvee* drink, drinking, and thence to Italian *bevuta* drinking bout or party, "but of this there is no known evidence"—OED.

beware *v.* Developed from the imperative phrase *be ware* (probably about 1200, in the plural *beth warre*), from *be,* v., and *ware,* adj., careful; see AWARE.

Old English had the compound *bewarian* to defend, not found in Middle English, and the verb *warian* to guard, keep clear of, which survived only in certain specialized phrases in modern English, such as "ware holes," in the sense of "keep clear of the holes," and a use commonly mistaken as a contraction of *beware.* Old English also had *wær* on one's guard, from Proto-Germanic **warás,* Indo-European **worós* (Pok.1164), and Middle English *war, ware* appeared regularly in the phrase *to be ware* to be on one's guard. From such constructions *be ware* soon began to be treated as a single word.

bewilder *v.* perplex, confuse. 1684, first occurring in the past participial form *bewildered* (*be-* thoroughly + now archaic *wilder* lead astray or into the wilds, probably back formation from *wilderness,* on the analogy of *wander*).

beyond *prep., adv.* Before 1325 *biyond,* in *Cursor Mundi,* earlier *beionde* (1154), developed from Old English *begeondan* (probably about 885, in the *Anglo-Saxon Chronicle*), from *bi-, be-* by + *geond* yonder, prep. + *-an* from or at (a place, position, direction), compare Old Icelandic *-an,* Old High German and Gothic *-ana;* see YONDER.

bi-, prefix meaning: **1a** twice, as in *bimonthly* = twice each month. **b** once every two, as in *bimonthly* = once every two months. **2** having two, or doubly, as in *bipolar* = having two poles, *biconvex* = doubly convex. **3** two, as in *bisect* = section or divide in two. About 1250, borrowed through Old French *bi-,* or directly from Latin *bi-,* from Old Latin *dvi- (dui-*); cognate with Greek *di-* twice, two; see DI-. *Bi-,* though once confined largely to adjective and verb stems of Latin origin, is today a free-forming prefix added to nouns, adjectives, verbs, and adverbs as the situation suits.

bias *n.* slant, prejudice. 1530, in Palsgrave's *Lesclarcissement,* borrowed from Middle French *biais* slant, from Old Provençal *biais,* of uncertain origin.

According to Bloch and Wartburg, the Old Provençal form is possibly from Greek *epikársios* oblique, which may have come into Provençal through the Greek colonies on the coast of France through a form **bigassius, *ebigassius* (compare *Marseilles* and *Nice,* names of Greek origin).

—**v.** 1622, from the noun. —**biased** *adj.* 1649, prejudiced, earlier (1611) as a participial of *bias,* v. Note the participial adjective is recorded before the verb, suggesting that the earlier use of *biased* was influenced by the French verb *biaiser* (1402).

bib *n.* cloth worn under the chin to protect clothing. 1580, developed from earlier verb *bibben* to drink (probably about 1380), perhaps borrowed from Latin *bibere;* see IMBIBE.

Bible *n.* Before 1325, in *Cursor Mundi,* borrowed in part through Anglo-Latin *biblia* (replacing Old English *bibliothece* the Scriptures, after use in Jerome) from Medieval Latin *Biblia,* and in part from Old French *bible,* a learned borrowing from Medieval Latin *Biblia,* neuter plural, though interpreted as feminine singular of Late Latin *biblia* (usually *biblia sacra* holy books), probably from the habit of considering the Scriptures as one work. *Biblia* was the popular name as evidenced by the wide variety of its use in European languages: Provençal *bibla,* Spanish and Portuguese *biblia,* Italian *bibbia;* Middle High German *bibel* (modern German *Bibel*), Dutch *bijbel,* and Old Icelandic *bibla* (later, *biblia*).

Late Latin *biblia* was borrowed from Greek *biblía,* plural of *biblíon* (often *byblíon*) originally, little book, but later the ordinary word for "book," and so diminutive of *býblos* book, writing, scroll (literally meaning "paper" and the same as *býblos* Egyptian papyrus, the inner bark of which paper was made; compare similar processes of formation in Latin *liber* book, also derived from *liber* the inner bark of a tree, and English *book,* from Old English *bōc,* related to *bōc* beech tree).

The general meaning "book or treatise, especially a lengthy one" is recorded 1387, in a version of *Piers Plowman.*

—biblical *adj.* 1790, replacing earlier *Biblic* (1684), from which it was formed + *-al*[1].

biblio- combining form meaning: **1** book or books, as in *bibliophile* = lover of books. **2** the Bible, as in *bibliolatry* = excessive reverence for the Bible.

Biblio- has been an element of a few English words since about 1000 in the Old English period. As a naturalized combining form in English it began to appear with some frequency in the 1800's, in imitation of the Greek element *biblio-* from *biblíon* book; see BIBLE and BIBLIOGRAPHY for further explanation.

bibliography *n.* list of books. 1678, borrowed perhaps through influence of French *bibliographie* (1633), from Greek *bibliographíā* the writing of books (*biblíon* book + *-graphíā* record, account, from *gráphein* write). **—bibliographer** *n.* 1656, formed in English from Greek *bibliographíā* + English suffix *-er*[1]. **—bibliographical** *adj.* 1679, formed possibly from English *bibliography* + *-ical.*

The form *biblio-* was already known in English through earlier *bibliotheke* library (1549), and *bibliotheca* the Scriptures (about 1000, in writings of Ælfric) and other forms so that it is quite possible *biblio-* was a natural formation from established Greek elements in the great literary flowering of England during the period after the mid-1500's, and became a naturalized combining form in English by the early 1800's when most words in *biblio-* are first recorded in English. It is also possible that the utility of *bibliography* and *bibliographer* were largely responsible for promoting *biblio-* as a combining form in modern English.

bicameral (bīkam′ərəl) *adj.* having two legislative chambers. Before 1832, in writings of Jeremy Bentham, formed in English from *bi-* two + Late Latin *camera* chamber + English suffix *-al*[1]; see CAMERA.

biceps (bī′seps) *n.* muscle having two heads or origins, especially the large muscle in the upper part of the arm. 1634, borrowed probably from French *biceps* (1562), and from Latin *biceps* (genitive *bicipitis*) two-headed (*bi-* two + *-ceps, -cipit-, caput* HEAD).

bicker *v.* to quarrel. Probably before 1300 *bikeren* (*bikering,* in *Arthour and Merlin*) to attack; formed in English perhaps from Middle Dutch *bicken* to slash, stab, attack + English suffix *-er*[4] frequently, again and again. The suggested Middle Dutch *bicken* is supported by Middle English *biker,* n.; see noun below. Middle Dutch *bicken* to slash, attack has cognates in Old High German *bicchan* to thrust, attack, Middle Low German *bicken,* Old English *becca* pickax, Gaulish *beccus* beak; see BEAK). **—n.** Probably before 1300 *biker* battle, attack, in *Arthour and Merlin;* later, quarrel (1350), probably developed from *bikeren,* v.

bicycle *n.* 1868 (perhaps 1866, in U.S. Patents), probably formed in English from *bi-* two + *-cycle* wheel, on the pattern of earlier *tricycle,* applied to carriages (1828).

According to most sources *bicycle* is borrowed from French; however, it is not recorded in French until 1869 and is held by French scholars to be a borrowing from English (see *Petit Robert,* 1978). The confusion apparently comes from the fact that it was a workman, Lallement, in a French carriage works who, in 1865, made the improvements in Macmillan's version (1839) of the pedal velocipede and went to America with his invention.

—v. 1869, from the noun.

bid *v.* command, offer, proclaim. Before 1121 *bidden* beg, request, influenced by and often confused in meaning with *beden* offer, announce, command, but developed from Old English *biddan* ask for, demand (about 725, in *Beowulf*). Of the two forms, Middle English *bidden* (Old English *biddan*) is cognate with Old Frisian *bidda,* Old High German *bitten* ask for, beseech (modern German *bitten*), Old Icelandic *bidhja,* and Old Saxon and Gothic *bidjan,* from Proto-Germanic **biđjanan,* cognate with Sanskrit *jñu-bā́dh-* bending the knees, from Indo-European **bhedh-* bend (Pok.114); and *beden* (Old English *bēodan*) is cognate with Old Frisian *biada,* Old High German *biotan* to offer (modern German *bieten*), Old Icelandic *bjōdha,* Old Saxon *biodan,* and Gothic *anabiudan* to command, from Proto-Germanic **biuđanan,* cognate with Greek *peúthesthai* inquire, from Indo-European **bheudh-* be awake, be aware (Pok.150). **—n.** offer. 1788, in correspondence of Thomas Jefferson, from the verb.

bide *v.* wait, abide. Old English *bīdan* stay, wait (about 725, in a version of *Genesis*). Old English *bīdan* is cognate with Old Saxon *bīdan,* Middle Dutch *bīden,* Old High German *bītan* to wait, Old Frisian *bīda,* Old Icelandic *bīdha,* and Gothic *beidan* to wait. Except in such use as *bide one's time,* the word has been largely displaced by *abide.* The Germanic meaning "to wait" has grown from an earlier one "to trust." Compare the cognate Greek *peíthesthai* obey and Latin *fīdere* trust, from Indo-European **bheidh-* convince (Pok.117).

biennial (bīen′ēəl) *adj.* requiring or occurring (every) two years. 1621, borrowed perhaps from French *biennal* (1550), or formed in English from Latin *biennium* two-year period (*bi-* two + *annus* year) + English suffix *-al* [1].

bier (bir) *n.* stand for a coffin or corpse. Probably before 1200 *bere,* in Layamon's *Chronicle of Britain,* developed from Old English (before 900) West Saxon *bǣr* litter or stretcher; earlier, Anglian *bēr,* formed from the stem of *beran* to bear; see BEAR² carry.

Since about 1600 the modern spelling *bier* has developed, apparently influenced by French **bière* coffin, from Old French *biere* litter, bier, ultimately from Frankish **bēra* (compare Old High German *bāra* bier, a cognate of Old English *bǣr, bēr*), from Proto-Germanic **bǣrō,* Indo-European **bhērā* (Pok.131).

bifocal *adj.* 1888, formed from English *bi-* + *focal.* **—bifocals** *n. pl.* 1888 or 1889, formed from noun use of *bifocal,* adj. + *-s* in such phrases as *perfection bifocals.* Though bifocals were conceived by Benjamin Franklin who used the term *double spectacles* (1784), the name *bifocals* did not appear until over 100 years later.

big *adj.* About 1300, strong or sturdy (in reference to persons and animals); of obscure origin, perhaps borrowed from a Scandinavian source (compare Norwegian dialect *bugge* strong man).

Its use much before 1400 is rare, the general sense "of great size, large" appearing earlier (about 1380) in *Patience,* and *Pearl,* slightly later in Chaucer's *Troilus and Criseyde* (about 1385).

—adv. 1563, from the adjective.

bigamy (big′əmē) *n.* practice of having two spouses at the same time. About 1250, borrowed from Old French *bigamie* and from Medieval Latin *bigamia,* from Late Latin *bigamus* twice married (forming a hybrid of Latin *bi-* two, twice + Greek *gámos* marriage, a form equivalent to Greek *dígamos* twice-married person). The Greek *gámos* is related to *gameîn* to marry, and to *gambrós* relative by marriage, in-law; cognate with such forms as Latin *gener* son in law, and Sanskrit *jāmí-s* blood-brother (or -sister), and thus to the Indo-European base **ĝem(ə)-* marry (Pok.369). **—bigamous** *adj.* 1864, formed from English *bigamy* + *-ous,* after Medieval Latin *bigamus.*

bight *n.* curve or bend in coastline. 1278, in a place name (*Syde biht* in Lancashire), developed from Old English (825) *byht* a bend, related to *būgan* to bend, bow; see BOW¹ bend. Old English *byht* (from Proto-Germanic **buHtís,* Indo-European **bhugh-tís,* (Pok. 153) is cognate with Middle Low German *bucht* (modern German *Bucht*), Middle Dutch and modern Dutch *bocht* bend, bight.

bigot (big′ət) *n.* prejudiced person. 1598, hypocrite, especially a hypocritical professor of religion; borrowed from Middle French *bigot* hypocrite, of uncertain origin. Possibly a term of Germanic origin (compare Old High German *bī got* by God), and originally in Old French (1155) a proper name among the Normans and also a term of disparagement for Normans and some others. According to the French scholar Gamillscheg, and others, the name may have been inspired by an excessive use of profanity adopted by the Norman soldiers from the English oath, and it is suggested that a comparison exists with Middle French *godon* an Englishman, again probably inspired by the English fondness for *God damn.*

The sense of a prejudiced person first appeared in 1661, but the development of this sense and the earlier meaning "hypocrite," in French or in English, have never been successfully accounted for.

—bigoted *adj.* 1645, formed from English *bigot* + *-ed* ². **—bigotry** *n.* Before 1674, borrowed from French *bigoterie,* from *bigot;* for suffix see -RY.

bijou (bē′zhü) *n.* jewel, trinket. 1668, borrowed from French *bijou,* from Breton *bizou,* earlier *besou* finger ring, from *biz* finger (like other native Breton words, it is common in Celtic; compare Cornish *bis, bes,* and Welsh *bys* finger), cognate with Old Icelandic *kvistr* twig, from Indo-European **gwistis* finger (Pok.481).

bike *n.* 1882, American English, shortened and altered form of *bicycle.*

bikini (bikē′nē) *n.* women's very brief two-piece bathing suit. 1948, borrowed from French *bikini,* named after *Bikini* atoll in the Marshall Islands of the Pacific, where several atomic bomb tests were carried out after 1946.

The name of the bathing suit, once a registered trade name of Louis Reard, has been attributed to an analogy with the shape of the mushroom cloud of an atomic explosion and to the "explosive" effect of the skimpy suit on men, but no concrete evidence is available.

bile *n.* bitter secretion, gall. 1665, borrowed from French *bile,* a learned borrowing from Latin *bīlis* bile, anger; cognate with Welsh *bustl,* Old Cornish *bistel,* and Breton *bestl,* all meaning bile, from Indo-European **bistli-s* (Pok.102). **—bilious** *adj.* 1541, of or having to do with bile, in a translation of Galen's *Terapeutyke;* later, ill-tempered (1561); borrowed from Middle French *bilieux,* a learned borrowing of Latin *bīliōsus* full of bile, from *bīlis* bile; for suffix see -OUS. Note that in the record of English the adjective preceded the noun by some 120 years.

bilge *n.* bottom of a ship's hull. 1513, probably variant of earlier *bulge* a ship's hull, a leather bag (about 1200); borrowed from Old North French *boulge,* originally meaning "leather sack," from Late Latin *bulga* leather sack, apparently from Gaulish *bulga,* from Indo-European **bholĝhā,* root **bhelĝh-* to swell (Pok.125).

bilk *v.* defraud, cheat. 1672, in Andrew Marvell's *The Rehearsal Transposed,* developed as an extended sense of the earlier meaning "to balk or spoil one's score in the game of cribbage" (1651, in a collection of Cleveland's poetry), perhaps as a verb use of *bilk,* n. (1633, in Ben Jonson's *A Tale of a Tub*), either the verb or the noun possibly being an alteration in the pronunciation of the verb BALK.

bill¹ *n.* written statement. About 1370 *bille,* in Chaucer's *An A.B.C.,* a formal plea or charge in law, and about 1378, in a version of *Piers Plowman,* a petition or legislative measure; borrowed from Anglo-French *bille* list, schedule, account (blend of Old French *bille* stick of wood, with *bulle* a decree) and Anglo-Latin *billa* (similar blend of Medieval Latin *billia* tree trunk, with *bulla* seal, document with a seal attached); both *bille* and *billa* ultimately derive from Gaulish (compare Old Irish *bile* tree, tree trunk); see BILLET¹,² and BULL² decree. It has been suggested that the English may originally have applied *bille* and *billa* to a wooden tally.

The meaning "account or invoice" is first recorded in 1404, the meaning "paper money, note" from *paper bill* (1670), curiously before *dollar bill* (1774), is first recorded in American English in 1682. The meaning "broadside," as in the phrase *post no bills,* is first recorded about 1426, in *The Paston Letters.*

bill[2] *n.* beak. Probably before 1200, in *Ancrene Riwle,* developed from Old English (about 1000) *bile* beak; possibly related to another form, *bill* spear with a hooked blade, developed from Old English *bil* a kind of sword (about 725, in *Beowulf*) and earlier in the compound *wudu-bil* pruning hook (about 700).

billet[1] (bil′it) *n.* written order for soldier's food and lodging. 1644; earlier meaning "an official record or register" (probably before 1425, in a translation of Higden's *Polychronicon*); borrowed from Anglo-French *billette* list, schedule (a diminutive form of *bille;* see BILL[1]), perhaps influenced by Middle French *billette,* variant of Old French *bullette* certificate (a diminutive form of *bulle* document, learned borrowing from Medieval Latin *bulla* document, seal; see BULL[2] decree).

billet[2] (bil′it) *n.* thick stick of wood. 1437, in *Proceedings of the Privy Council,* borrowed from Middle French *billette,* a diminutive form of *bille* stick of wood, from Medieval Latin *billia* tree trunk, possibly of Gaulish origin (compare Old Irish *bile* sacred tree, trunk of a tree, from Indo-European **bhelyom,* root **bhel-* swell, Pok.122); see BLADE.

billiards *n.* 1591, earlier used as an adjective in *billiard stick* (1588); borrowed from Middle French *billard* cue stick (a diminutive form of *bille* stick of wood; see BILLET[2]). The *-s* added to the English word parallels use in the names of other games, such as *checkers, skittles,* and *bowls.*

billion *n.* 1690, (in Great Britain) second power of a million, in Locke's *Essay Concerning Human Understanding,* borrowed from French *billion,* formed from *bi-* two + *(m)illion,* from Old French *millon* MILLION.

The difference between British and German use (one million millions) and American, Canadian and modern French use (one thousand millions) comes from British and German use of the original meaning in French, while the later meaning, that resulted from change by French mathematicians to dividing the numerals of long numbers in groups of threes rather than groups of sixes, was adopted elsewhere.

—billionaire *n.* 1860, American English, in Oliver Wendell Holmes' *Elsie Venner,* patterned on *millionaire.*

billow *n.* great wave, surge of the sea. 1552, probably borrowed from a Scandinavian source (compare Old Icelandic *bylgja* billow, Danish *bølge,* and Swedish *bölja*). The Scandinavian words are cognate with Old Dutch *bolghe, bulghe,* Middle Dutch *bulge* bubble, blister, Middle High German *bulge* billow, probably related to Old High German *bulgā* (modern German *Bulge* leather bag), from Proto-Germanic **bulʒ-,* Indo-European **bhl̥ĝh-,* root **bhelĝh-* to swell (Pok.125).

The connections with *bellow* (except as a roaring of the sea) and *belly* are not substantiated by semantic links in Middle English.

—v. surge, swell. 1597, from the noun. **—billowy** *adj.* About 1615, formed from English *billow* + *-y*[1].

billy *n.* club or stick. 1848, American English (burglar's slang), a crowbar; 1856, a policeman's club; probably from *Billy* nickname of William. Like the names *Jack* and *Jenny, Billy* was used to name various implements and machines as early as 1795, and is recorded as a common appellation about 1500.

billy goat *Informal.* male goat. 1861; earlier *Billy* (1849), an application of the male name *Billy* (nickname of William), after the earlier *nanny goat* (1788).

bin *n.* box. Old English *binne* manger (about 750, in poetry of Cynewulf), probably of Celtic origin (compare Medieval Latin *benna* basket and Late Latin *benna* cart with a basket top, the latter form said to be a Gaulish word for a kind of vehicle, perhaps a wicker or basket cart, and Welsh *ben* wagon, cart), from Indo-European **bhendh-nā,* root **bhendh-* BIND (Pok.127).

binary *adj.* consisting of two parts, dual. Before 1464, borrowed through Anglo-Latin *binarius,* from Late Latin *bīnārius* (from Latin *bīnī* two at a time; related to *bis* twice, from Old Latin *dvis* and thence to Latin *duo* TWO); for suffix see -ARY. **—binary digit** (1946) **—binary number** (before 1796) **—binary system** (1835, of biological classification; 1802, of a binary star).

bind *v.* Old English *bindan* (about 725, in a translation of *Exodus*). The word was pronounced with a short vowel in Old and Middle English, as it is in its cognates: Old Saxon *bindan* to bind, Old Frisian and Old Icelandic *binda,* Old High German *bintan* (modern German *binden*), and Gothic *bindan.* The Sanskrit cognate *badhnā́ti* (he) binds, is of the same Indo-European base **bhendh-* to bind (Pok.127), which probably appears in *-fend-* of Latin *offendīx* knot, band, and Greek *peîsma* cable, rope. *Bind* is thereby ultimately related to BAND[2] fasten. **—n.** 1295, developed from Old English *binde* band (about 1000), probably from the verb. The two modern English forms *band* and *bind* were probably confused at first; until Middle English *band* (1126) supplanted *bind* except in specialized usages and in the curious modern popular usage *to be in a bind* (1950's and later), both forms may have had some interchangeable usage or been differentiated by dialect use rather than semantic applications. **—binder** *n.* 1218, in surnames, earlier *bindere* (before 1000), formed from Old English *bindan,* v. + *-ere* -er[1]. **—bindery** *n.* 1810, American English, formed from *bind* + *-ery.*

binge *n.* spree (of drinking, eating, etc.). 1854, English dialect, apparently a special use of dialectal *binge* to soak (a wooden vessel); and so by extension "to drink heavily" in allusion to soaking up alcohol, perhaps reminiscent of a popular and long-established connection between alcoholic drink and *soak* with reference to drink in such phrases as *an old soak* for a drunk.

bingo *n.* 1929, game developed from lotto, probably from earlier use as an exclamation indicating the suddenness with which something happens (1927). Before that, it is possible only to guess at various connections, such as *bingo* a slang term for brandy, in Hughes' *Tom Brown* (1861).

binnacle (bin′əkəl) *n.* box or stand for ship's compass. 1762, alteration of earlier *bittacle* (1622), borrowed from French *bitacle* binnacle, from Old French *habitacle* dwelling, later, *binnacle,* from Latin *habitāculum* dwelling place, from *habitāre* dwell. Contrary to traditional sources, the Spanish scholar Corominas finds that the Spanish term *bitácula* (now *bitácora*) is derived from French.

binocular (bənok′yələr) *adj.* of, for, or using both eyes. 1738, perhaps developed from the earlier meaning having two eyes (1713); borrowed from French *binoculaire,* ultimately from Latin *bīnī* two at a time + *oculī* eyes; for suffix see -AR. **—binoculars** *n. pl.* 1877, from earlier singular *binocular* (1871), noun use of *binocular,* adj.

binomial (bīnō′mēəl) *n.* expression consisting of two terms or names. 1557, borrowed from New Latin *binomialis,* from Medieval Latin *binomius* having two names, alteration of Latin *binōminis* (*bi-* two + *nōmen,* genitive *nōminis* NAME); for suffix see -AL[1]. **—adj.** consisting of two terms or names. 1570, from the noun.

bio- a combining form meaning: **1** life, living things, as in *biology* = science of life or living things. **2** biological, as in *biochemistry* = biological chemistry. The combining form probably entered English through New Latin *bio-* as a borrowing of Greek *bio-,* combining form of *bíos* life, way of living, which is cognate with Latin *vīvus* living, and with Old English *cwic, cwicu* quick, in the archaic sense "living," and Gothic *qius.* The Indo-European root has the various stems **gwiy(ə)-, gwi-wo-, gwī-wo-, gwi-gwo-* (Pok.467).

biography *n.* account of a person's life. 1683, in Dryden's translation of Plutarch's *Lives,* borrowed perhaps through New Latin *biographia,* from Late Greek *biographíā* (from Greek *bio-* life + *-graphíā* record, account, from *gráphein* write). **—biographer** *n.* 1715, in writings of Addison, probably formed from English *biography* + *-er*[1], perhaps by influence of Medieval Greek *biográphos* writer of lives.**—biographical** *adj.* 1738, formed from English *biography* + *-ical.*

biology *n.* study of living things. 1819; borrowed from German *Biologie,* also used by Lamarck, 1802, from *bio-* (from Greek *bíos* life, way of living) + *-logie* study of, from Greek *-logíā,* from *-lógos* one who treats of). The word appears earlier in English with the meaning "study of human life and character" (1813, and now obsolete), perhaps as an independent borrowing of Greek elements cited above. **—biological** *adj.* 1859, formed from English *biology* + *-ical.* **—biologist** *n.* 1874, formed from English *biology* + *-ist,* perhaps by influence of earlier French *biologiste* (1836), and earlier English *biologist* (1813) but in reference to the study of human life and character.

bionics (bīon′iks) *n.* the making of electronic devices modeled on biological systems. 1959, formed from English *bio-* living, life, biological + *-onics,* as in *electronics.* **—bionic** *adj.* (1970)

biopsy (bī′opsē) *n.* medical examination of living tissue. 1895, borrowed from French *biopsie* (*bio-* living, life + Greek *ópsis* a viewing). —**v.** perform a biopsy on. 1964, from the noun.

biotic *adj.* 1600, borrowed from Late Latin *biōticus,* from Greek *biōtikós* related to life, lively, from *biônai,* a form of *bioûn* to live, from *bíos* life; for suffix see -IC.

biped (bī′ped) *n.* animal having two feet. 1646, borrowed, perhaps through French *bipède,* or directly from Latin *bipedem* two-footed (*bi-* two + *pedem,* nominative *pēs* FOOT).

birch *n.* About 1385, in Chaucer's *Canterbury Tales,* developed from Old English (about 700) *birce;* cognate with Old Saxon *birka, berka,* Middle Low German and Middle Dutch *berke* (modern Dutch *berk*), Old High German *biricha, birca* (modern German *Birke*), from Proto-Germanic **berkjōn,* Old Icelandic *bjǫrk,* from Proto-Germanic **berkō,* all meaning "birch"; also cognate with Old Prussian *berse,* Lithuanian *béržas,* Latvian *bęr̃zs, Russian berëza,* Serbian *breza,* Old Slavic *brěza* birch, and Sanskrit *bhūrjá-s* a species of birch, from Indo-European **bherəĝ-/bhr̥̄ĝ-* (Pok.139).

Latin *farnus, fraxinus,* meaning ash tree, have been associated by some with the word for *birch,* although the phonology is not clear.
—birchbark *n.* (1643, American English).

bird *n.* 1353 *bird,* variant of *brid* (before 1200, in *Ancrene Riwle,* the form predominating until the later 1400's); found in Old English *brid* young fowl (probably about 750, in *Phoenix*); of uncertain origin, with no corresponding form in any other Germanic language.

birth *n.* About 1250 *birthe,* in a translation of *The Story of Genesis and Exodus;* earlier *burthe, burde* (probably before 1200, in *Ancrene Riwle*) and *birde* (probably about 1200, in *The Ormulum*). The Middle English forms were influenced by, and perhaps borrowed from, a Scandinavian source (compare Old Icelandic *burthr,* Old Swedish *byrth* birth), that affected the previously Old English *gebyrd* birth (cognate with Old High German *giburt,* modern German *Geburt,* and Gothic *gabaúrths*), from Proto-Germanic **(ʒa)ƀurđís,* cognate with Sanskrit *bhr̥tís,* from Indo-European **bhr̥-tís* (Pok.131).

The early spellings with *d,* found up to the mid-1200's, show how the Old English *-byrd* was displaced by the Scandinavian forms with *th.*
—v. About 1250, from the noun. **—birthday** *n.* About 1384, in the Wycliffe Bible; earlier Old English *byrddæg.*

biscuit *n.* hard cookie or cracker (now only in British use). A spelling reborrowed from French in the 1800's to replace English *bisket,* developed in the 1500's from *besquite* (before 1338, in Mannyng's *Chronicle of England*). Middle English *besquite* was borrowed from Old French *bescuit,* literally meaning "twice-cooked" in reference to how it was prepared (*bes-* twice, from Latin *bis* + Old French *cuit,* past participle of *cuire* to cook, from Vulgar Latin **cocere,* from Latin *coquere;* see COOK). The American use applied to "a soft bun raised by baking powder" is first recorded in 1818.

bisect *v.* divide in two. 1646, in writings of Sir Thomas Browne; formed in English from *bi-* two + Latin *sectus,* past participle of *secāre* to cut; see SECTION.

bishop *n.* clergyman in charge of a diocese. Old English *biscop* (before 830, in the *Vespasian Psalter*) and *bisceop* (before 900); cognate with Old Saxon *biscop* and Old High German *biscof;* all borrowed from Late Latin *espiscopus* bishop, overseer, from Greek *epískopos* overseer (*epi-* over + *skopós* watcher, related to *sképtesthai* look at; see SCOPE[1]). **—bishopric** *n.* diocese. Old English (about 890) *bisceoprīce,* a compound of *bisceop* bishop + *rīce* realm, province, dominion, power (cognate with Gothic *reiki* realm, rule; see RICH).

bismuth (biz′məth) *n.* reddish-white metallic chemical element. 1668, borrowed from earlier German *Bismuth,* from *Wismuth, Wismut* (the forms to which the modern German has reverted).

Though the origin is unknown it is possible the German is a compound of *Wiesen,* Saxony, where the element was first found + *muten* claim, sue for.

bison *n.* wild ox. 1611, in King James Bible, (although the Latinized plural form *bysontes* appeared before 1398, in Trevisa's translation of Bartholomew's *De Proprietatibus Rerum*), borrowed through French *bison,* or more likely directly from Latin *bisōn* (accusative *bisontem*), from a Germanic source (compare Old High German *wisunt* aurochs, a species of wild ox, modern German *Wisent,* Old English *wesend,* and Old Icelandic *visundr*).

bisque[1] (bisk) *n.* thick, rich soup. 1647 *bisk,* later *bisque* (1731, in Bailey's *Dictionary*), borrowed from French *bisque* a soup; said to be an altered form of *Biscaye* Biscay.

bisque² (bisk) *n.* kind of pottery. 1664, alteration of English *biscuit.*

bissextile (bisek'stəl) *adj., n.* (containing or designating) the extra day of leap year. 1581 n., 1594 adj.; borrowed from Late Latin *bissextīlis, bisextīlis,* adj., from Latin *bisextus diēs* intercalary day (*bi-* two + *sextus* sixth).

The Julian calendar added an extra day after the *sixth* day (thereby doubling it) before the calends of March, or the 24th of February.

bistro (bēstrō') *n.* wineshop and restaurant; bar or nightclub. 1922 *bistrot,* 1924 *bistro,* borrowed from French *bistrot, bistro* (1884), originally Parisian slang for "little wineshop or restaurant"; origin uncertain, for the French sources cannot satisfactorily account for the ending *-ot* or *-o,* nor can they show a root word that conforms sufficiently with the stem *bistr-,* except in *bistringue* cabaret (1909) which is too late, and *bistraud* little shepherd which is not semantically related.

bit¹ *n.* small piece; fragment; morsel. Probably about 1200 *bite,* in *The Ormulum,* developed from Old English *bita* piece bitten off, morsel, mouthful (before 1050, in *West Saxon Gospels*), from *bītan* to bite; see BITE. Old English *bita* is cognate with Old Frisian *bita,* Old Icelandic *biti* bit, and Old High German *bizzo* biting (modern German *Bissen* a bite), from Proto-Germanic **bitōn.*

bit² *n.* tool for drilling; part of a bridle in the horse's mouth. About 1150, a bite, biting, found in Old English *bite* a bite (about 725, in *Beowulf*), (compare modern German *Gebiss* horse's bit, from *beissen* to BITE).

Old English *bite* is cognate with Old Frisian *bit, bite, biti,* Old Saxon *biti,* Old High German *biz* piece bitten off (modern German *Biss* a bite), Old Icelandic *bit* bite, biting, from Proto-Germanic **bitiz.* As can be seen from comparing the cognates for *bit¹* and *bit²*, the senses "act of biting" and "piece bitten off" were not uniformly distinguished in different languages. And even in English, the Old English *bite* and *bita* were finally merged in Middle English, to be distinguished only by tracing the history of their senses.

By about 1386 *bit²* was applied to the part of a horse's bridle in the mouth, and about 1594 to the tool for drilling (from the meaning "cutting edge," used probably before 1300, in *Arthour and Merlin*).

bit³ *n.* binary digit (unit of information in computers). 1948 (a word coined by J.W. Tukey), short for *bi(nary) (digi)t.* Compare BYTE.

bitch *n.* female dog. Probably about 1150 *bicche,* developed from Old English (about 1000) *bicce,* cognate with and, perhaps originally borrowed from, a Scandinavian word such as Old Icelandic *bikkja* female dog or Old Danish *bikke.*

The oath *bikkju-sonr* in Old Icelandic and *biche sone* in Middle English (probably before 1300, in *Arthour and Merlin*) further establish a close connection between the English word and a possible borrowing from Scandinavian.

—**v.** to grumble, complain. Before 1930, probably by extension from an earlier verb meaning, such as to bungle, spoil (1823).

bite *v.* Probably about 1150 *biten,* developed from Old English *bītan* (about 725, in *Beowulf*). Old English *bītan* is cognate with Old Saxon *bītan* to bite, Old Frisian *bīta,* Middle Dutch *bīten* (modern Dutch *bijten*), Old High German *bīzan* (modern German *beissen*), Old Icelandic *bīta,* (Swedish *bita,* Danish *bide*), and Gothic *beitan,* from Proto-Germanic **bītanan.* Cognates outside Germanic include Latin *findere* to cleave, split, and Sanskrit *bhinádmi* I split, from Indo-European **bheid-* (Pok.116). —**n.** Probably before 1200, in *The Ormulum;* see BIT¹.

bitter *adj.* About 1175, developed from Old English *biter* (about 725, in *Beowulf*) and *bitre, bittreste* (before 830, in the *Vespasian Psalter*). The Old English forms are cognate with Old Saxon and Old High German *bittar* bitter (modern German, Dutch, Swedish, and Danish *bitter*), Old Icelandic *bitr* (from Proto-Germanic **bitrás,* Indo-European **bhid-rás*), and Gothic *baitrs* bitter (with a different vowel); all derived from the Proto-Germanic root that was the source of Old English *bītan* to BITE. —**bittersweet** *adj.* 1611, in Cotgrave's *Dictionary,* adjective use of *bittersweet,* n. a kind of tree, its fruit, or a drink made from it (before 1393, in Gower's *Confessio Amantis*).

bittern (bit'ərn) *n.* small heron with a booming cry. 1515, alteration of *bitore* (about 1395, in Chaucer's *Canterbury Tales);* earlier *butur* (about 1353) and *botor* (probably before 1300, in *Arthour and Merlin*); borrowed probably from Anglo-Latin *butorius, bitorius,* and Old French *butor,* both apparently from Gallo-Romance **būtitaurus,* from Latin *būtiō* bittern + *taurus* bull, so called from its booming voice (compare use of *bull* in the popular English name for this bird, *bull of the bog,* which appeared in 1815; also Pliny's use of *taurus* to designate the bittern of southern France).

bitumen (bətü'mən) *n.* mineral that burns. Before 1464 *bitumen* mineral pitch used as mortar, borrowed from Latin *bitūmen* asphalt, probably from a Celtic source (compare Gaulish *betulla* birch, a name used by Pliny for the tree that was supposedly the source of bitumen; from the Gaulish base *betu-;* cognate with Sanskrit *játu* lac, gum and Old English *cwidu* resin, from Indo-European **gwētu, gwēt-,* Pok.480). —**bituminous** *adj.* 1620, borrowed through French *bitumineux,* or directly from Latin *bitūminōsus,* from *bitūmen;* for suffix see -OUS.

bivalent (bivā'lənt) *adj.* having a valence of two. 1869, formed from English *bi-* two + *-valent,* from Latin *valentem* (nominative *valēns*), present participle of *valēre* be worth; for suffix see -ENT.

bivouac (biv'wak) *n.* outdoor camp. 1702, a night watch by an army, borrowed from French *bivouac,* probably from Low German *bīwake* (*bi-* by + *wake* watch; related to English WAKE). Alternatively, as the French scholar Dauzat suggests, the French word might have come from Swiss German *Biwacht* extra night patrol. The current sense is first recorded in English in 1853, in writings of De Quincey. —**v.** camp outdoors. 1809, to post troops or remain in the open during the night; verb use of *bivouac,* n. The meaning "camp outdoors" first appeared in 1814, in writings of Sir Walter Scott.

bizarre (bizär') *adj.* fantastic, grotesque. Before 1648, borrowed from French *bizarre* odd, fantastic; formerly, brave, from Spanish *bizarro* brave (perhaps influenced by Basque *bizar* beard, taken as a symbol of energy and individuality as in Spanish *hombre de bigote* moustached man, implying "man of spirit"), but ultimately from Italian *bizzarro* angry, wrathful.

The Spanish scholar Corominas emphasizes early Italian use of the word (in the 1200's) and the late first example in Spanish, implying a possible borrowing of the French from Italian rather than from Spanish and further concludes that it was the prestige of the scholar Diez that caused the Basque etymology to gain acceptance.

black *adj.* About 1150 *blac* and (in place name) *Blakeberge,* developed from Old English (about 700) *blæc, blec.* The Old English is cognate with Old High German *blah, blach,* Old Icelandic *blakkr* black, dun-colored, and is sometimes confused with Old English *blāc* shining, white and thence Old Icelandic *bleikr* pale, whitish. Old Icelandic *blakkr* is from Proto-Germanic **blak-*, cognate with Greek *phlóx,* genitive *phlogós* flame, from Indo-European **bhlog-*, root **bhleg-* burn (Pok.124). **—n.** Probably before 1200, in *Ancrene Riwle;* Old English *blæc,* n. The meaning "a black person," in reference to race, is perhaps a translation of Spanish *Negro* (1625). **—v.** Also, *blacken.* Probably about 1200; from the adjective; for suffix of *blacken* see -EN[1]. **—blackberry** *n.* Probably about 1125. **—blackbird** *n.* 1279 (in a surname). **—blackboard** *n.* (1823) **—black eye** 1327 (in a surname). **—blackguard** *n.* (1535, kitchen help; 1736, scoundrel) **—blacklisted** *adj.* 1457 (edged with black), ostracized (1884). **—blackmail** *n.* 1552, money paid outlaws for protection (*black,* adj. + *mail* tax, tribute, Old English *māl*); payment extorted by threats (before 1826). **—black market** (1931) **— blacksmith** *n.* 1248 (in a surname).

bladder *n.* soft bag in the body that receives urine. About 1200 *bladdre,* earlier *bladre* (about 1150), developed from Old English *blǣdre* (West Saxon) and *blēdre* (Anglian, about 700). The Old English words are cognate with Old Saxon *blādara,* Old High German *blātara* bladder, and Old Icelandic *blādhra* bladder, blister, from the same base as Old English *blāwan* to blow; see BLOW[2] puff.

blade *n.* broad, flattened part of anything (as of a sword or oar or a stalk of grass). About 1380 *blad,* in *Sir Ferumbras,* earlier in compound *shuldre blade* shoulder blade (about 1300), found in Old English *blæd* leaf, (but usually) any leaflike part (about 725, in a version of *Genesis*).

The Old English is cognate with Old Frisian *bled,* Old Saxon *blad,* Old and Middle High German *blat* leaf (modern German *Blatt*), Old Icelandic *bladh,* from Proto-Germanic **bladán,* Indo-European **bhlətóm,* and through the Indo-European base **bhlō-* (Pok.122), is cognate with Latin *folium* leaf, *flōs* flower, *flōrēre* to bloom, and Greek *phýllon* leaf; related to English BLOOM.

blame *v.* find fault with; accuse. Probably before 1200, borrowed from Old French *blamer,* earlier *blasmer,* from Vulgar Latin **blastēmāre,* alteration of Late Latin *blasphēmāre* revile, reproach. According to the OED the word was introduced into Latin in language of the New Testament which used Greek *blasphēmeîn.* See the doublet BLASPHEME.

—n. Probably about 1200, borrowed from Old French *blame,* earlier *blasme,* from *blamer,* v.

blanch *v.* whiten. Before 1398 *blaunchen* to remove the hull of (almonds, etc.) after soaking, in Trevisa's translation of Bartholomew's *De Proprietatibus Rerum;* borrowed from Old French *blanchir,* from *blanche,* feminine of *blanc* white; see BLANK.

The Anglo-French *blaunche,* feminine of *blaunk,* and the earlier Middle English *blauncher* cosmetic powder for whitening (about 1303, in Mannyng's *Handlyng Synne*), suggest the possibility of earlier use of the verb *blaunchen.*

bland *adj.* 1667, soft, mild, gentle, in Milton's *Paradise Lost;* perhaps borrowed from Italian *blando* delicate (before 1321, in Dante, an author read by Milton who traveled in Italy long before writing *Paradise Lost*); earlier 1661, smooth in manner, suave, in Pepys' *Diary,* also in Milton's *Paradise Lost.* Either Milton borrowed Italian *blando,* or used the earlier meaning of Pepys that was an extension of earlier English "flattering," now seen in *blandish,* also in French as far back as Old French *bland* flattering. All forms are ultimately borrowings from Latin *blandus* smooth-tongued, flattering, soothing, pleasant; of uncertain origin.

blandish *v.* persuade gently, coax, flatter. About 1340, earlier *blaundishing,* verbal noun (about 1300); borrowed from Old French *blandiss-*, stem of *blandir,* from Latin *blandīrī* flatter, from *blandus* smooth-tongued, flattering, BLAND; for suffixal ending see -ISH[2]. **—blandishment** *n.* 1591, in poetry of Edmund Spenser; probably formed from English *blandish* + *-ment,* or, less likely, borrowed from Middle French *blandissement.*

blank *adj.* 1230 *Blanc-heved* (a surname), white, pale, colorless; borrowed from Old French *blanc* white, shining, of West Germanic origin (compare Old High German *blanch* bright, shining, Old English *blanca* white horse), from Proto-Germanic **blank-* shining, pale, from a nasalized form of Indo-European **bhlog-* burning (Pok.125). The meaning "having empty spaces to be filled in" is first recorded in 1399. **—n.** Before 1392, in the obsolete sense referring to a small French coin; later, a blank space (about 1570).

blanket *n.* About 1300 *blaunket* white woolen stuff used for clothing, borrowed from Old French *blanchet, blanquet,* from *blanc* white, see BLANK; for suffix see -ET. The sense of a bed covering appeared in 1303.

blare *v.* make a loud, harsh sound. About 1400 *blaren* to cry, bellow, wail; earlier *bleren* (1390). Though probably developed from Old English **blæren,* it is also possible that *bleren* was borrowed from Middle Dutch *blēren* to bleat, cry, bawl, shout, roar; or from Middle Low German *blarren* (Low German *blarren*) and is cognate with Middle High German *blēren* to shout, yell, scream (modern German *plärren* cry, whine, bellow). Whatever the immediate source, the word is probably of imitative origin. **—n.** 1809, from the verb.

blarney *n.* flattering, coaxing talk. 1766, Lady *Blarny* (for *Blarney*), a smooth-talking flatterer in Goldsmith's the *Vicar of Wakefield,* her name being a literary contrivance in allusion to *Blarney Stone,* a stone in a castle near Cork, Ireland. Anyone kissing the stone is supposed to become skillful in flattering and coaxing. The word is used in its general sense in a letter of Sir Walter Scott (1796).

blasé (bläzā′) *adj.* bored, tired of pleasures. 1819, in Byron's *Don Juan,* borrowed from French *blasé,* past participle of *blaser* exhaust with pleasure, satiate; said to be of unknown origin, but probably from Dutch *blasen* to blow, cognate with Old High German *blāsan* to blow; see BLAST.

blaspheme (blasfēm′) *v.* speak about God or sacred things with contempt. 1340 *blasfemen,* in *Ayenbite of Inwyt,* borrowed from Old French *blasfemer,* learned borrowing from Late Latin *blasphēmāre,* from Greek *blasphēmeîn* to speak profanely (*blas-* probably with the meaning "false" + *phḗmē* speech, related to *phánai* speak. Doublet of BLAME.

—blasphemy *n.* Probably before 1200, in *Ancrene Riwle,* borrowed from Old French *blasfemie, blasphemie,* learned borrowing from Late Latin *blasphēmia,* from Greek *blasphēmíā* profane speech, slander, formed beside the verb *phēmeîn;* for suffix see -Y[3]. It may be noted that though *blasphemy* appears in recorded English 140 years before *blaspheme,* yet the spelling *-ph-* had greater currency in this word than did the form with the spelling *-f-,* which was more popular in the verb *blaspheme (blasfemen).* **—blasphemous** *adj.* Before 1415 *blasfemouse,* in Wycliffe's *The Lantern of Light,* borrowed from Medieval Latin *blasphemus,* from Late Latin *blasphēmus,* or perhaps immediately through Middle French *blasphemeus* from Medieval Latin; for suffix see -OUS.

blast *n.* Probably before 1200, the call of a trumpet, in Layamon's *Chronicle of Britain;* developed from Old English *blǣst* strong gust of wind (about 725, in a version of *Exodus*); cognate with Old High German *blāst* blast, gust of wind, *blāsan* to blow (modern German *blasen*), Old Icelandic *blāstr* blast, *blāsa* to blow, and Gothic *-blēsan* blow (in compounds); from Indo-European **bhlē-s-* (Pok.121), the same Indo-European root as that of Old English *blāwan* to blow. **—v.** to blow. Probably before 1300, in *Kyng Alisaunder,* developed from Old English *blǣstan,* perhaps from the noun. **—blastoff** *n.,* **blast off** *v.* (1951)

blatant (blā′tənt) *adj.* offensively loud or noisy. 1596 *blatant, blattant,* used in the phrase "blatant beast" or "blattant beast" in Spenser's *Faerie Queene.* The word was apparently an invention of Spenser's to describe a monster representing slander with a thousand tongues.

The OED questions the suggestion that the word is an archaic form of *bleating.* Others suggest a connection with Latin *blatīre* to babble, or compare English *blatter* to chatter, babble (recorded before 1555), borrowed from Latin *blaterāre* to babble.

blather *v.* talk nonsense. 1524 *blether* (in Scottish use), borrowed from a Scandinavian source (compare Old Icelandic *bladhra* to chatter, babble). **—n.** foolish talk. 1787, in poetry of Burns, *blether,* noun use of *blether,* v.

blaze[1] *n.* bright flame or fire. Probably before 1200 *blase,* in Layamon's *Chronicle of Britain,* developed from Old English *blæse* torch, firebrand (before 893, in Werfrith's translation of St. Gregory's *Dialogues*), from Proto-Germanic **blasōn.* The word is cognate with Middle High German *blas* torch, candle, fire, from Indo-European **bhles-/bhlos-* shine (Pok.158). **—v.** Probably before 1200 *blasen,* in *Ancrene Riwle,* from the noun.

blaze[2] *n.* white mark on face of an animal. 1639; later, mark made on a tree by cutting off a piece of bark (1662, American English); of uncertain origin. The word may have been borrowed in a north English dialect at some early date from Old Icelandic *blesi* white mark on the forehead of an animal, and later came into general use. Another possibility is that *blaze* [2] was borrowed from Middle High German *blasse* white spot on the forehead of an animal, bald forehead, related to Middle Low German *blesse, bles* (modern German *Blässe, Blesse*) and cognate with Old Icelandic *blesi,* Gothic *bala-* pale (horse), and Middle High German *blas* bald; see BALD. **—v.** 1750, American English, to mark a tree or trail; from the noun.

blaze[3] *v.* proclaim. About 1380, in Chaucer's *House of Fame,* to blow (as a musical instrument); borrowed probably from Middle Dutch *blāsen* to blow; cognate with Old Icelandic *blāsa* to blow, Old High German *blāsan* (modern German *blasen*), related to Old English *blāwan* to BLOW [2], puff, and *blǣst* BLAST.

The current sense "proclaim" is probably also associated with *blaze* [1], v. as if "to expose to the blaze of publicity," according to the OED.

blazer *n.* a sports jacket (in the U.S. it is usually of blue flannel, sometimes with a school seal on the breast pocket, in Great Britain it is often brightly colored as with stripes). 1880, formed from English *blaze* [1], v. (from the red color of the original jackets worn by a boating club of Cambridge University) + *-er* [1].

blazon (blā′zən) *n.* shield in heraldry. 1278 *blazoun;* borrowed from Old French *blason* shield, of uncertain origin.

bleach *v.* whiten. Probably before 1200 *blechen,* developed from Old English *blǣcan* to bleach (before 899, in Alfred's translation of Bede's *Ecclesiastical History*), from *blāc* pale, shining. Old English *blāc* is cognate with Old High German *bleih* pale, shining (modern German *bleich* pale), and Old Icelandic *bleikr* pale; in turn *blǣcan* is cognate with Old High German *blīhhan* (modern German *bleichen*) and Old Icelandic *bleikja* to bleach, from Indo-European **bhleiĝ-/bhloiĝ-* (Pok.156). For an explanation of the spelling see CH. **—n.** Before 1425, probably as a noun use of earlier and now obsolete adjective. **—bleachers** *n.pl.* (originally uncovered) seats at sports events or the occupants of such seats. 1889, American English; so called from the bleaching of the benches (called *bleaching boards,* 1888) by the sun.

bleak *adj.* bare, cold, dreary. About 1300 *bleike* pale, in *Havelok the Dane,* borrowed from a Scandinavian source (compare Old Icelandic *bleikr* pale); see BLEACH.

The extended sense "bare, windswept" appeared in 1538, and the figurative sense "cheerless, dreary" appeared in writings of Addison before 1719.

blear *v.* make dim or blurred. Probably before 1325 *bleren* have watery eyes, of uncertain origin (but compare Middle High German *blerre* having blurred vision). The Middle English compound *blereighed* blear-eyed (about 1378, in a version of *Piers Plowman*) corresponds in form and meaning to Low German *bleer-oged.* The adjective *blear* arose probably before 1387, in a later version of *Piers Plowman,* and *bleary* in 1495, in Wynkyn de Worde's edition of Trevisa's translation of Bartholomew's *De Proprietatibus Rerum.* The word *blear* is perhaps related to BLUR.

bleat *v.* cry of sheep, goat, or calf. Before 1300 *bleten,* in *Sumer is icumen in,* developed from Old English (before 800) *blǣtan;* cognate with Old High German *blāzan* to bleat, modern Dutch *blaten,* and Greek **phlēdônta* babbling, from Indo-European **bhléd-* (Pok.155). **—n.** 1590, in Shakespeare's *Much Ado About Nothing,* from the verb. The earlier noun use *blet* (1382) refers to a ewe.

bleed *v.* lose blood. Old English (about 900) *blēdan;* cognate with Old Frisian *blēda,* Old High German *bluotēn* (modern German *bluten*), and Old Icelandic *blœdha,* from Proto-Germanic **blōđjanan;* related to Old English *blōd* BLOOD.

The figurative sense "to feel pity or sympathy for" is

first recorded about the time of Chaucer's *Troilus and Criseyde* (before 1385, actually in minor poems of 1377).

blemish *v.* stain, spot, scar. About 1380 *blemishen,* in Chaucer's translation of Boethius' *De Consolatione Philosophiae;* earlier *blemis* (probably before 1350); borrowed from Old French *blemiss-,* stem of *blemir,* from earlier *blesmir* make pale, harm, probably from Frankish; for suffixal see -ISH². **—n.** 1526, from the verb.

blench *v.* draw back, shrink away. Probably before 1200 *blenchen* move suddenly, wince, dodge, in Layamon's *Chronicle of Britain,* developed from Old English (before 1000) *blencan* deceive; cognate with Old Icelandic *blekkja* to cheat, from Proto-Germanic **blankjanan,* of uncertain origin.

The form and meaning of this word were confused in its development with *blanch.* For an explanation of the spelling see CH.

blend *v.* mix. Before 1325 *blenden,* in *Cursor Mundi,* developed from Old English *blondan* to mix (a form in Mercian corresponding to West Saxon **blandan*) and a Scandinavian form (compare Old Icelandic *blanda* to mix). The words are cognate with Old High German *blantan* to mix, Gothic *blandan,* Lithuanian *blandùs* thick, dark, and Sanskrit *bradhná-s* reddish, pale yellowish-brown. In Middle English, the form was usually *blenden,* probably because of confusion with another form *blenden* to deprive of sight, from Old English *blendan* to BLIND. **—n.** 1883, from the verb.

bless *v.* Probably about 1225 *blessen,* in *King Horn,* developed from Old English *blœdsian* (an early form, although preserved only in Northumbrian about 950), and also found in various other forms, such as *blēdsian* (before 830, in the *Vespasian Psalter;* from Proto-Germanic **blōđisōjanan*), *blētsian* (about 725, but preserved in "modernized" copy about 1000), *blesian* (about 1000); all meaning "to make holy or sacred by some sacrificial rite" (originally, "to mark with blood" and hence related to *blōd* BLOOD).

The sense development was probably influenced by the use of this verb in versions of the English language Bible to translate Latin *benedīcere* to bless (literally, speak well of), resulting in such meanings as "to praise or extol, as in *bless God"* and "to speak well of or wish well to, as in *bless them for their kindness."*

—blessed *adj.* Probably before 1200, adjective use of *blessed,* past tense of *bless,* v. **—blessing** *n.* 1123, developed from Old English *blēdsung* (before 830, in the *Vespasian Psalter*), later *blētsunge* (in a version of the *Anglo-Saxon Chronicle*) and *bletsunga* (1070).

blight *n.* 1611, in Cotgrave's *Dictionary,* plant disease such as mildew, rust, or smut; a word of uncertain origin, apparently first used by farmers and gardeners; perhaps ultimately related to Old English *blāc* pale, shining (from the appearance of blighted plants). The common figurative sense, "anything that withers, destroys, or mars," is first recorded before 1661. **—v.** affect with blight. 1695, from the noun. The figurative sense of the verb first appeared in 1712, in Addison's writings in *The Spectator.*

blimp *n.* dirigible airship. 1916, of uncertain origin; the most convincing explanation is that the word derives from (British) Type *B-limp,* a designation for "limp dirigible," without a rigid internal structure, in early experiments, as opposed to the Type *A-rigid* lighter-than-air craft with a rigid framework; by some sources said to have been coined by the British aviator Horace Shortt.

blind *adj.* Old English *blind* (about 725, in an early version of *Genesis*). The word had both literal and figurative meanings even in Old English. Its cognates include Old Frisian and Old Saxon *blind,* Old High German and Middle Dutch *blint* blind (modern German and Dutch *blind*), Old Icelandic *blindr* (modern Swedish, Danish, and Norwegian *blind*), Gothic *blinds* blind, from Proto-Germanic **blindaz,* from Indo-European **bhlendh-o-s* (Pok.157). By some sources also related to Old English and Gothic *blandan* to mix; see BLEND. **—n.** About 1200, in *The Ormulum,* from the adjective. The meaning "covering for a window" is first recorded in 1730. **—v.** Middle English *blinden* (about 1225, in *Ancrene Riwle*); gradually, probably by influence of *blind,* adj., replacing earlier *blenden* (before 1200, in Layamon's *Chronicle of Britain*), developed from Old English *blendan.* Middle English *blinden* is cognate with Old Frisian *blindia,* modern Dutch *verblinden,* Danish *forblinde,* Gothic *gablindjan;* also cognate outside Germanic with Lettish *blendu* I see dimly, and Old Slavic *blędǫ* go blindly. **—blinder** *n.* 1809, American English, formed from *blind,* v. + *-er* ¹, replacing earlier *blind halter* (1711).

blindfold *v.* 1526, in Tyndale's translation of the Bible, alteration (influenced by *fold* ¹ wrap) of earlier *blindfeld, blindfelled* (1483), past participle of *blindfellen* to strike blind, to blindfold (probably before 1200, in *Ancrene Riwle*), developed from Old English (about 1000) *geblindfellian* (*blind* + *gefeollan* to strike down, FELL¹; an Anglian form corresponding to West Saxon *gefyllan*). **—n.** 1880, in Wallace's *Ben Hur,* from the verb.

blink *v.* move the eyelids; twinkle. 1590, in Shakespeare's *Midsummer Night's Dream;* borrowed from Middle Dutch *blinken* to glitter, of uncertain origin. The word has been sometimes confused with Middle English *blenchen,* v. meaning "to avert the eyes"; see BLENCH. **—n.** 1594, from the verb. **—blinker** *n.* 1923, something that blinks a light; earliest use 1636, one who blinks.

blip *n.* a small dot on a radar screen. 1945, perhaps from earlier meaning "a quick popping sound, sudden blow" (1894, in writings of Mark Twain). **—v.** to rap or tap briskly. 1924, in A.A. Milne's *When We Were Very Young.* Both the noun and verb are of uncertain origin, perhaps imitative of the sound.

bliss *n.* happiness. Old English *blis* (about 725, in an early version of *Genesis*), alteration of *blīths* (a form not recorded earlier but associated with *blithe;* compare archaisms *bliths,* in a translation of Psalm 50 (900's), and *blithsian,* v. in Alfred's translation of St. Gregory's *Pastoral Care* (before 899). The Old English is cognate with Old Saxon *blīdsea, blīzza* bliss; derived from the root of BLITHE.

blister *n.* swelling under the skin. Before 1325 *blester, blister,* in *Cursor Mundi,* borrowed from Old French *blestre* a boil, lump, from a Scandinavian source (compare Old Icelandic *blāstr* a blowing, dative *blǣstri* swelling, from *blāsa* to blow); or possibly the Old French is derived from a West Germanic source (compare Old High German *blāst* breathing, blowing, from *blāsan* to blow); see BLAST. **—v.** Probably before 1425, in an anonymous translation of Chauliac's *Grande Chi-*

rurgie; from the noun, influenced by Middle French verb.

blithe *adj.* happy. About 1175, joyful, gentle, and by 1200, bright, beautiful, found in Old English *blīthe* joyous, kind (about 725, in *Beowulf*). The word is cognate with Old High German *blīdi* joyous, bright, Old Saxon *blīdhi,* Middle Dutch *blīde* (modern Dutch *blijde*), Old Icelandic *blīdhr* cheerful, bright, and Gothic *bleiths* kind, merciful, from Proto-Germanic **blīthiz,* and is perhaps related to Old English *blēoh* color, itself cognate with Old High German *blīo,* Old Icelandic *blȳ* lead, and Lithuanian *blývas* lilac, from Indo-European **bhlī-ti-s, bhlī-wo-s* (Pok.155).

blitz *n., v.* attack. Probably before 1940 (noun), 1939 (verb); borrowed from German *Blitz* lightning, and originally short for German *Blitzkrieg* (before 1939) rapid warfare or offensive (*Blitz* lightning + *Krieg* war).

blizzard *n.* snowstorm with high wind. 1859, American English. There is some question as to whether the word is derived from earlier dialectal *blizz* violent rainstorm (1770) + the intensive suffix *-ard* one that does to excess, as in *drunkard.* The origin of *blizz* is uncertain.

In the sense of "a violent blow" *blizzard* is recorded in American English in 1829. For further discussion of this word see Allen Walker Read's articles in *American Speech,* vol. III, pp. 191-217 and vol. V, pp. 232-35.

bloat *v.* swell up. Probably a fusion of two words: 1) *bloat* (1611, in Cotgrave's *Dictionary*) to half-cure herring (by a process that leaves them soft and less shriveled than fully cured herring), from earlier *blote,* adj. (as in *blote herring,* before 1586, in poetry of Sidney), developed from Middle English *blot, blout* soft, pliable (about 1300, in *Havelok The Dane*); borrowed from a Scandinavian source (compare Old Icelandic *blautr* soft, Old Swedish *blöter*); and 2) *bloat* (1677, in Dryden's Prologue to *Circe*) to inflate, from earlier *blowt,* adj. puffed up (1603), also developed from Middle English *blot, blout* in form, but with meaning developed from Middle English *blouen* to blow (probably about 1175, in *Poema Morale*) and later "to inflate" (about 1380, in Chaucer's *Canterbury Tales*), developed from Old English *blāwan;* see BLOW[2] puff.

blob *n.* 1725, a drop or globule; earlier, pimple or spot (1597), and bubble (1536); from the verb. **—v.** 1429, make or mark with blobs. According to the OED and others, some relation may exist between *blob* and *bubble* in the meaning "blister," through such forms as Middle English *blober* a bubble (about 1438), bubbling (1296).

bloc *n.* group combined, often for a political purpose. 1903, borrowed from French *bloc* group, block, from Old French *bloc* piece of wood; see BLOCK.

block *n.* **1** solid piece. 1390; earlier, in the compound *blockbord* (1323) and in the derivative form *Blocker* as an Anglo-French surname (1212); borrowed from Old French *bloc* piece of wood, from Middle Dutch *blok.* Alternatively, it has been suggested that Old French *bloc* is borrowed from Old High German *bloh* block, which is also cognate with Middle Dutch *blok,* and both it and the Old High German are cognate with Middle Low German *block* (sometimes cited as the source of English *block*), Swedish *block,* Danish *blok,* and Gothic *bliggwan* to strike; see BLOW[1] stroke. A further relationship with Old Irish *blog* fragment, Welsh *bloc* block, and Gaelic *ploc* round mass, block, is uncertain. The meaning of a section of land, or group of buildings, as in a city block, is first recorded in 1796. **2** an obstruction. 1649, earlier in the literal sense of a lump of wood, stone, etc. that obstructs the way (before 1500); developed from noun use of English *block,* v. **—v. 1** form into blocks, strengthen, support. 1585, developed from verb use of *block,* n. (def. 1). **2** to obstruct. 1580, borrowed from French *bloquer* block, stop up, from Old French *bloc* block, barrier. **—blockade** *n.* blocking of a harbor, etc. 1693 (but probably used before 1680, when the verb appeared), from *block,* v. + *-ade;* perhaps formed by influence of French *blocus* blockade (1547; earlier, 1507, fort used in a siege, from Middle Dutch *blochuus* blockhouse).

blond or **blonde** *adj.* light in color. 1481, in Caxton's translation of *The Mirror of the World,* borrowed from Old French *blonde, blont,* adj., from Medieval Latin *blundus,* probably from Frankish (compare Middle High German *blunde, blunt*). **—n.** 1822, noun use of *blonde,* adj.; earlier, *blond,* referring to a type of silk lace (about 1755).

blood *n.* About 1150 *blod,* developed from Old English *blōd* (about 725, in *Beowulf*); cognate with Old Frisian and Old Saxon *blōd,* Dutch *bloed,* Old High German *bluot* blood (modern German *Blut*), Old Icelandic *blōdh,* and Gothic *blōth,* from Proto-Germanic **blōđan,* from a base not found outside Germanic but perhaps related to the root of Old English *blōwan* to flower; see BLOOM.

Old English *blōd* would normally have been expected to change in Middle English to a pronunciation that rhymes with *food,* but in the early 1500's the vowel was shortened to rhyme with *good* and later with *flood.* **—bloody** *adj.* Probably before 1200 *blodi,* developed from Old English *blōdig* (about 725, in a translation of *Exodus*), from *blōd* blood; for suffix see -Y[1].

bloom *n.* blossom. Probably about 1200 *blom, blome,* in *The Ormulum;* borrowed from a Scandinavian source (compare Old Icelandic *blōm* blossom, *blōmi* prosperity).

The word does not appear in Old English, which had *blōstma, blōstm* flower, blossom, but has cognates in a variety of other Germanic languages including late Old Frisian *blœm, blam,* Middle Dutch *bloeme* (modern Dutch *bloem*), Old Saxon *blōmo,* Old High German *bluomo, bluoma* flower, blossom (modern German *Blume*), and Gothic *blōma,* from Proto-Germanic **blōmōn.*

The word is further related to the now archaic and technical sense *blow* to blossom or flower, found in Old English *blōwan* to flower, from which we retain such common collocations as *full blown* meaning "fully developed." Old English *blōwan* is cognate with Old Saxon *blōjan,* Old High German *bluoen* (modern German *blühen*), and with Latin *flōs* (accusative *flōrem*), flower, *flōrēre* to bloom, from Indo-European **bhlō-* (Pok.122).
—v. Probably about 1200 *blomen* to flower, blossom, in *The Ormulum,* from *blome,* n., influenced by and perhaps in part borrowed from a Scandinavian source (compare Old Icelandic *blōmandi* blooming).

bloomers *n.pl.* women's loose underpants. 1895, earlier *bloomer* (1889), American English, from *Bloomer* (1851, in a women's magazine *Lily*) a woman's garment of loose trousers gathered at the ankles and worn under a short skirt (after Amelia J. *Bloomer,* 1818-1894, who promoted this garment as an equivalent to male attire; but introduced earlier by E.S. Miller).

blooper *n.* 1937, in *New York Times,* American English, a looping fly ball that is not caught by a fielder and is considered an error in fielding; 1926, an early radio receiver that emits a signal interfering with nearby sets by causing a howling sound. Either use providing a meaning for the extended sense of "a blunder or howler" (1940's).

blossom *n.* flower. Probably before 1200 *blosme, blostme,* developed from Old English (probably about 725) *blōstm, blōstma.* The Old English is cognate with Middle Dutch and modern Dutch *bloesem* blossom, Middle Low German *blōsem, blossem,* and Old High German *bluomo, bluoma* blossom, *bluoen* to bloom; the Old Icelandic *blōmstr* a flower, suggests some possibility of metathesis in Old English; all apparently derived from the same base as English BLOOM. Yet Latin *flōrēre* to bloom, earlier **flōsēre,* would point to an extended stem **bhlō-s-* in Indo-European. **—v.** About 1378 *blosmen,* in a later version of *Piers Plowman,* developed from Old English (about 900) *blōstmian,* from *blōstm, blōstma,* n., blossom.

blot *n.* spot, stain. 1373 *blot* spot; 1375, disgrace, blemish, of uncertain origin (compare Old Icelandic *blettr* blot, stain, spot of ground, and Danish *plet* speck, spot; however, the OED points out that phonetic relationship is wanting; also compare Old French *blotre, blostre* a boil, lump, variant of *blestre* a boil; see BLISTER). **—v.** Before 1420 *blotten,* in Lydgate's *Troy Book,* from the noun. **—blotter** *n.* 1591. The meaning in American English of an arrest record in a police *blotter* (1887) is derived from the earlier meaning of a day book or journal (1678).

blotch spot, stain. **—v.** 1604 *blotched* marked with spots, of uncertain origin, perhaps a blend of *blot* and *botch* (1530, to spoil by unskilled work). **—n.** 1669, probably from the verb. **—blotchy** *adj.* 1824, formed from English *blotch* + *-y*[1].

blouse *n.* 1828, a workman's short tunic or smock; borrowed from French *blouse* (1788), of uncertain origin; compare Provençal *(lano) blouso* short (wool). In 1870 the word was applied to a woman's loose shirtwaist, a meaning also found in French at the end of the 1800's, which is the most common meaning today.

The English word has a spelling pronunciation (blous) quite different from its French origin (blüz).

blow[1] *n.* hard hit, stroke. Before 1500: 1) *blow* a blow with the fist, in East Midland dialect, and 2) *blaw* a blast of wind, in Northern dialect (before 1460). The word is in part developed from Middle English *blouen* to blow a current of air (compare *thay blowe a boffet* they struck a blow, probably about 1380), and in part borrowed from Middle Dutch *blouwen, blauwen* to beat; cognate with Old High German *bliuwan* (modern German *bleuen*) beat, and with Gothic *bliggwan* to beat (with *-ggw-* from *-ww-*).

blow[2] *v.* send a current of air; puff. Before 1250 *blowen,* in a version of *Ancrene Riwle,* earlier *blawen* (1127); developed from Old English (probably about 725) *blāwan* to produce a current of air, sound a wind instrument (all other meanings developed after the Old English period). The word is cognate with Old High German *blāen* to blow, (from Proto-Germanic **blǣ-anan*), Middle High German *blœwen* (modern German *blähen*) to blow, puff up, swell, and Latin *flāre* to blow, perhaps related to *follis* bellows. This word and its cognates are traced back to the Indo-European base **bhlē-, *bhelē-,* from **bhel-,* meaning "to swell, blow up" (Pok. 120).

—n. 1660, from the verb. **—blower** *n.* Before 1131, a horn blower; later, a blowing device (before 1398, in Trevisa's translation of Bartholomew's *De Proprietatibus Rerum*).

blubber *n.* Probably about 1380 *bluber* bubble, foam, and perhaps earlier in *Blobermere,* a surname (1296), apparently with some reference to bubbling water or foaming waves, from which a derivation of imitative origin is perhaps justified. The sense of whale fat or fish oil is first recorded in 1467. **—v.** Probably about 1380 *blubren* to bubble, probably from the noun. The figurative meaning "to weep copiously" is first recorded about 1400.

bludgeon (bluj′ən) *n.* short club. 1730, in Bailey's *Dictionarium Britannicum;* of unknown origin. **—v.** 1868, verb use of *bludgeon,* n. The figurative sense "to bully or threaten" is first recorded in 1888.

blue *adj., n.* Probably before 1300 *bleu,* in *Sir Tristrem;* taking the place of the corresponding Old English *blāw.* Middle English *bleu* was borrowed from Old French *blo, bleu,* from Frankish (compare Old High Germanic *blāo* blue (modern German *blau*); cognate with Old Frisian *blaw* blue, Middle Dutch *blaeuw,* and Old Icelandic *blā* livid (where the meaning survives in English *black and blue*) and *blār* blue; all developing from Proto-Germanic **blǣwaz,* probably cognate with Latin *flāvus* yellow, from Indo-European **bhlē-wo-s* (Pok.160), and distantly related to Greek *phalós* white, and Sanskrit *bhāla-m* luster; see BALD.

The name of one color often shifted to another color in the various Indo-European languages so that different colors (here yellow, white, pale or livid) have related forms from the same base.

The modern spelling *blue* developed largely by influence of French in the 1700's, though it is occasionally seen as early as 1220 in the form *blu* and 1366 in the form *blue.*

—blues *n.* slow, melancholy jazz song or style. 1905 (but known in jazz circles about 1895, perhaps by influence of earlier *blue-devil* to make despondent, 1817), from earlier *blues* low spirits, despondency (1741, in a letter of David Garrick), from the adjective *blue* low-spirited, depressed, dejected (about 1385, in Chaucer's *The Complaint of Mars*), as in the phrase *to look blue,* originally, to look livid or leaden-colored from anxiety, depression, etc. (about 1600). **—blue chip** (1929, American English) **—blue-collar** *adj.* of industrial or manual workers (about 1950). **—blue law** (1781, American English) **—blueprint** *n.* (1886)

bluegrass *n.* traditional country music. 1958, in allusion to the *Bluegrass* Boys, a country-music band of 1940's and 1950's, after the *Bluegrass* State (Kentucky, where *bluegrass,* a kind of grass with a bluish-green stem, is widely grown, though it did not originate there).

blue jeans or **bluejeans** *n.pl.* 1901, American English; from earlier use meaning a twilled cotton cloth dyed blue (1843).

bluff[1] *n.* high, steep bank or cliff. 1687, American English, from the adjective. **—adj.** rising with a straight, broad front. 1627, in writings of Captain John Smith; origin uncertain (but compare obsolete Dutch *blaf* broad, flat, a connection with English favored by the nautical use in Smith's *Seaman's Glossary*).

The figurative meaning "good-naturedly blunt" is first recorded in 1808, in Scott's *Marmion.*

bluff[2] *v.* deceive by a show of confidence. 1839, American English, perhaps developed from earlier English *bluff* to blindfold (1674), probably borrowed from Dutch *bluffen* to make a trick at cards; but possibly borrowed from Low German *bluffen, blüffen* to frighten by menacing conduct, or borrowed from Dutch *bluffen* to boast, (formerly) to make a trick at cards, from Middle Dutch *bluffen* to strike. **—n.** 1873, from earlier phrase *the game of bluff* (1859) in figurative reference to *bluff* meaning "the game of poker" (1845).

blunder *v.* Before 1378 *blondren* act blindly or irrationally, in Trevisa's translation of Higden's *Polychronicon;* borrowed from a Scandinavian source (compare Old Icelandic *blunda* to shut the eyes, Norwegian and Swedish *blundra* act blindly; from Indo-European **bhlndh-* zero grade of **bhlendh-* blind (Pok. 157); related to Old English *blind* BLIND); for suffix see -ER[4]. The common meaning "to make a stupid mistake" is first found in 1711, in letters of Swift. **—n.** Probably about 1390, confusion, bewilderment, trouble, in *Sir Gawain and the Green Knight;* from the verb. The meaning "stupid mistake" is first recorded in Phillips' *Dictionary* (1706).

blunt *adj.* Probably about 1200, dull, obtuse, in *The Ormulum,* later meaning "dull-edged, not sharp," in the surname *Blundspure* Bluntspur (about 1285); probably borrowed from a Scandinavian source (compare Old Icelandic *blunda* to shut the eyes, to doze, *blundr* dozing, related to *blindr* blind; see BLIND).

With the original meaning of dull, referring to the mind, some sources have suggested a connection with *blunder* in relation to the use of *blunt* which is found in *Promptorium Parvulorum;* however, the late date of this use (1440) seems to belie this connection.

—v. make dull. Before 1398, in Trevisa's translation of Bartholomew's *De Proprietatibus Rerum;* from the adjective.

blur *n.* dimness. 1548, a smear, stain; origin uncertain; commonly considered to be a possible variant of BLEAR. **—v.** make dim or indistinct. 1581, in the phrase *blur out* erase or darken by a smear, from the noun. The meaning "to make dim or indistinct" appeared in 1611, in Shakespeare's *Cymbeline.*

blurb *n.* brief advertisement or description of something, especially an advertisement full of praise. 1914, American English, supposed to have been coined in 1907 by Gelett Burgess, 1866-1951, an American humorist and illustrator, to satirize the excessive praise found on book jackets.

blurt *v.* say suddenly. 1573, apparently imitative of a discharge of breath after an effort to retain it, with the *bl-* element of *blow* or *blast* combined with another element of *spurt, squirt,* and the like.

blush *v.* become red in the face. Probably about 1350 *blissen, blishen* to glance, look, stare; later, *blussen,* (about 1405 in *Mum and the Sothsegger),* and *blisshen* (before 1450). These Middle English forms apparently developed from: 1) Old English **blysian* (found in compound *āblysian* blush); cognate with Middle Dutch *blōzen* (modern Dutch *blozen*) blush, and Middle Low German *blosen, bloschen;* and from: 2) Old English *blyscan* (earlier **bluskjan*) become red, glow, also cognate with Middle Low German *blōsen* blush. Both words in Old English are connected with Old English *blysa* torch, flame; distantly related to Old Icelandic *blys* torch, light. Many related forms are found, as in Middle Low German *blūs* flame, torch, Swedish *bloss* and Danish *blus* torch, and Low German *blüsen* set on fire, from Indo-European **bhleu-s-/bhlu-s-* burn (Pok.159). **—n.** 1593, a reddening of the face, in Shakespeare's *3 Henry VI;* earlier, a rosy color or glow (1590); and a glance, glimpse (probably about 1350, now obsolete except in the phrase *at first blush*); from the verb. **—blusher** *n.* 1665, one who blushes, in writings of Robert Boyle; later, a cosmetic to give the cheeks a rosy color (1965).

bluster *v.* 1463, to blow violently; earlier, to speak or shout noisily or threateningly (about 1400, in Lydgate's *Troy Book*), and to stray blindly, wander blunderingly (before 1376, in *Piers Plowman*); borrowed probably from Middle Low German *blüstern* blow violently; related to Old Icelandic *blāsa* to blow; see BLAST. **—n.** 1583, noisy blowing, from the verb. **—blusterer** *n.* 1597, formed from English *bluster* + *-er* [1], in Shakespeare's *A Lovers Complaint.* **—blustery** *adj.* 1739, formed from English *bluster* + *-y* [1].

boa *n.* large snake. Before 1398, in Trevisa's translation of Bartholomew's *De Proprietatibus Rerum,* borrowed from Latin *boa* type of serpent (mentioned in Pliny's *Natural History*); of unknown origin.

boar *n.* male hog. About 1209 *Bor* as a surname, and before 1250 *bor;* earlier *bar* (1150), developed from Old English (about 700) *bār.* The Old English word is cognate with Old Saxon and Old High German *bēr* boar (modern dialectal German *Bär*), Middle Dutch and Dutch *beer* male pig, and Langobardic (the West Germanic language of the Lombards) *-pair* boar, from Proto-Germanic **bairaz,* of unknown origin.

board *n.* 1228 *bord* board, plank; earlier, table, shield, side of a ship (probably before 1200, in Layamon's *Chronicle of Britain*); found in Old English *bord* board, plank (about 1000, in Ælfric's version of *Genesis*); earlier *bord* table, shield, side of a ship (about 725). The word is cognate with Old Saxon *bord* table, shield, Old High German *bort* side of a ship, rim, border, Middle High German *bort* board, plank, table, Old Icelandic *bordh* board, plank, table, side of a ship, rim, and Gothic *baúrd* (in compound *fōtubaúrd* footstool), from Proto-Germanic **burđan,* Indo-European **bhrdhom,* root **bheredh-* to cut (Pok.138). The development of *bord* was reinforced in Middle English by the presence of Anglo-French *bord;* Old French *bort* border, side of a ship, table, from Germanic.

Some evidence suggests that the Germanic word was a fusion of two different but related words: one that had senses related to "plank, table, shield"; the other with senses related to "border, rim, side of a ship."

The shift in spelling to modern *board* came about in the 1500's.

—v. Before 1475 *borden* to come up alongside a ship, and *borden* board up (probably 1440); verb use of *bord,* n.; also evidenced by the past participle *borded* in *bordidbed* a bedstead (1387).

—boarder *n.* 1201, in a surname *Border* signifying a feudal tenant, earlier *bordario* (1130, in *Pipe Rolls* of Henry I); borrowed from Old French *bordier.*

boast *n.* 1265 *bost* arrogance, bragging, ostentation; possibly borrowed through Anglo-French *bost* boasting, ostentation, from a Scandinavian source (compare Norwegian *baus* proud; cognate with Old High German *bōsi* wicked, bad, modern German *böse*). —**v.** About 1350 *bosten* to show off, brag, probably from the noun. —**boaster** *n.* About 1280, probably formed from Middle English *bost,* v. (though as of 1280 unrecorded) + *-er*[1].

boat *n.* About 1200 *bote;* earlier *bat* (probably before 1200, in Layamon's *Chronicle of Britain*); developed from Old English *bāt* (about 725, in *Beowulf*). The West Germanic languages have no corresponding form, but it is supposed that a Proto-Germanic form **baita-* is probably preserved in Old Icelandic *beit* and Old English *bāt* and was adopted in Middle Low German *bōt* (modern German *Boot*) and Middle Dutch and modern Dutch *boot,* from Indo-European **bhoido-* dug-out canoe, root **bheid-* split (Pok.117).

Some form of *bot, bote* must have existed well before the first recorded date, because the word is seen in the surname *Botere* (boater, boatman) by 1168.
—**v.** 1613, developed from the noun. —**boat people** (1977) —**boatyard** *n.* (1805, American English).

boatswain *n.* ship's deck officer in charge of ropes, anchor, etc. 1304 *botswayn,* found in late Old English *bātswegen* (*bāt* boat + **swegen,* probably borrowed from Old Icelandic *sveinn* boy; see SWAIN).

bob[1] *v.* move quickly up and down. About 1390 *bobben,* in Chaucer's *Canterbury Tales;* perhaps the same word as earlier Middle English *bobben* to strike or beat (probably before 1325), in expressing short jerking or rebounding motion of striking. —**n.** About 1550, from the verb.

bob[2] *n.* short haircut or horse's docked tail. 1688, a knot or bunch of hair; earlier *bobbe* bunch or cluster, as of leaves or flowers (probably about 1390, in *Sir Gawain and the Green Knight*); of uncertain origin; perhaps from Celtic (compare Irish *baban* bobbin, Gaelic *bab* tassel, cluster). The meaning "a woman's short haircut" is first recorded in 1926, in Galsworthy's *Silver Spoon,* but probably existed earlier (compare the date of the verb meaning). —**v.** cut short. 1822, American English, verb use of *bob*[2], n. The meaning "to cut a woman's hair short all around" is first recorded in 1918. —**bobby pin** 1936, perhaps connected with *bob*[2] the cut of a woman's hair. —**bobcat** *n.* 1888, American English, in writings of Theodore Roosevelt, in allusion to the short tail of the lynx. —**bobsled** *n.* 1839, American English, in allusion to the sled's short runners; *v.* 1883, from the noun.

bobbin *n.* reel or spool. 1530, in Palsgrave's *Lesclarcissement,* borrowed from Middle French *bobine, babine* small instrument used in sewing or tapestry making, from Old French *balbiner* (recorded once in 1396), probably an alteration of *baubier, balbeier, baboier* to stutter, stammer (the name of the instrument being due, perhaps, to the rattling noise it made), from *baube,* adj. stuttering, stammering, from Latin *balbus;* see BABBLE.

bobby *n. British Slang.* policeman. 1844, as a nickname *Bobby* in allusion to Sir *Robert* Peel, who as Home Secretary in 1829 organized the Metropolitan Police Force of London (originally called *peelers,* after *Peel,* replacing the earlier *Charlies* or watchmen).

bobolink (bob′əlingk) *n.* kind of American songbird. Before 1801, American English, alteration of earlier *bob-o-Lincoln* (1774), probably a fanciful rendering of the call of the bird.

bode *v.* be a sign of. Before 1200 *boden* to be an omen, developed from Old English *bodian* announce, foretell (about 725, in a translation of *Exodus*), from *boda* messenger, which is cognate with Old Frisian *boda,* Old Saxon *bodo,* Old High German *boto* (modern German *Bote*), and Old Icelandic *bodhi,* all meaning "a messenger", from Proto-Germanic **buđōn,* from Indo-European **bhudh-,* related to **bheudh-* the source of Old English *bēodan* to offer, proclaim, command; see BID.

bodice (bod′is) *n.* close-fitting waist of a dress. 1566 *bodies* (bod′ēz), considered as the plural of *body* tight-fitting part of a garment covering the trunk of the body (originally in *a pair of bodies* analogous to *a pair of stays*). The spelling changed to *bodice* in the late 1600's, though the word was treated as a plural (like *pence* and *dice*) until the late 1800's; meanwhile the spelling pronunciation (bod′is) became established.

body *n.* Before 1200 *bodi,* in *Ancrene Riwle* and Layamon's *Chronicle of Britain;* developed from Old English *bodıg,* with substitution of the suffix *-ig* for *-ag, -æg* in earlier *bodæi, bodeg* (about 700). The Old English word is cognate with Old High German *botah, potach, botch* body, Middle High German *botech, botich,* though it appears to have no relatives outside West Germanic. The High German word disappeared in standard German, its place being taken by *Leib* (originally meaning life, and cognate with English *life*) and *Körper,* from Latin *corpor-,* stem of *corpus* body.

Some sources observe an apparent discrepancy between the final consonants of Old English *bodig* and Old High German *botah,* but for the High German development of the final consonant, compare Old High German *balg, palc, balch* bag, cognate with Old English *belg, bylg* bag (modern English BELLY), and Old High German *honag, honak,* Middle High German *honec, honick* honey, cognate with Old English *hunig.* —**bodily** *adj., adv.* About 1300, in Mannyng's *Handlyng Synne,* formed from Middle English *bodi* + *-ly*[1,2].

Boer (bôr *or* bůr) *n.* 1824 *Boor,* 1834 *Boer* South African of Dutch descent; earlier, *Boor* Dutch or German peasant (1581) and countryman, peasant (1551). Both forms are related to Middle Dutch *boer* farmer, but the South African use is derived from modern Dutch *boer* farmer, from Middle Dutch, while the earlier uses in the 1500's may possibly have been a development in English from Middle English *boveer,* but influenced by Dutch *boer.*

The Middle Dutch *boer,* earlier *geboer,* is cognate with Old English *gebūr* dweller, farmer, peasant, and *būr* dwelling; see BOWER.

bog *n.* soft, spongy ground. Before 1450 *bog,* earlier *Bogge* (1327, as a surname); borrowed from Irish and Gaelic *bog-* (in *bogach* marsh), from *bog* soft, from Old Irish *bog, boc;* cognate with Old Breton *buc* rotten, crumbling, and related to Old English *būgan* to BOW[1], bend, Old High German *biogan,* and Gothic *biugan.* —**v.** 1603, especially in the passive *to be bogged* to be mired, in Ben Jonson's *Sejanus;* from the noun. —**boggy** *adj.* 1586, formed from English *bog,* n. + *-y*[1].

bogey *n.* **1** goblin. 1836 *Bogey* the Devil, as in *old Bogey* the Devil; see BOGY goblin. **2a** a system of scoring in golf equal to par. About 1892, said to be a description of the system, thought of as an imaginary adversary, that is as a "real *bogey* man," from a popular song of the day entitled "The Bogey Man." **b** in American golf (after 1918), *bogie* one stroke over par, probably from the idea of losing holes to Bogey (par) in playing.

boggle *v.* blunder, hesitate, overwhelm. 1598, to startle, scare, alarm, in Chapman's translation of the *Iliad,* probably related to BOGY as a variant of Scottish *bogill* goblin, bugbear; or, according to the OED, a variant of *bogle* a ghost, specter (at which horses were reputed to shy). The OED goes further to say, "In later times there has been a tendency to associate the word with *bungle* (1536 *buggle*) to fumble, make a clumsy attempt."

The meaning "to blunder, hesitate" appeared before 1638; the current sense "overwhelm" (as in *boggle the mind*) is an extended use of the original sense "to startle or be startled."

bogus *adj.* counterfeit, fraudulent. 1838, American English, adjective use of earlier *Bogus* a machine for making counterfeit money (1827), and probably of *bogus* counterfeit money made on a Bogus (first recorded 1839, but probably used earlier). The origin of *bogus* as a noun has been traced to *tantrabobus* and *tantarabobus* a name for the devil or bogie, as recorded in Wright's *English Dialect Dictionary,* and to a variant *trantrabogus,* cited in correspondence of a Dr. Samuel Willard of Chicago with Sir James Murray, first editor of the OED. Whether this is related to *bogus* a liquor made of rum and molasses (1848, in reference to sugar cane refuse) is a matter of conjecture.

bogy *n.* 1857, goblin, bugbear; earlier, 1836, *Bogey,* as in *old Bogey* the Devil. The word is of uncertain origin, though connections have been proposed with *bogle* a phantom, goblin common in Scottish (first recorded about 1505) as *bogill,* perhaps ultimately from *bogge,* variant of *bugge* terror, BUGBEAR; and possibly related to Welsh *bwg* (obsolete) ghost, goblin, *bwgwl* fear.

bohemian *n.* carefree, unconventional artist, writer, etc. 1848 *Bohemian,* in Thackeray's *Vanity Fair;* possibly influenced by or even a borrowing of the same meaning that existed in French *bohémien* as early as 1559 and was popularized in France by its appearance in Henri Murger's *Scènes de la vie de Bohème* (1848, the same year as Thackeray's use). However, development of the sense in English may have been a coincidental extension of an earlier sense, "gypsy," which appeared in English in 1696 and was perhaps a development of the meaning "a native of Bohemia" (1603, in Shakespeare's *Measure for Measure*).

The meaning "gypsy" appeared in French in the 1300's. apparently because gypsies were thought, in France, to have come from Bohemia or, according to the OED, to have perhaps entered Europe through Bohemia.

The name of the country (Middle English *Beeme, Boeme*) was known in English about 1449, and is a borrowing from Middle French *Boheme;* the sense "a native of Bohemia" was recorded in English before 1398, in Trevisa's translation of Bartholomew's *De Proprietatibus Rerum* as a gloss of Latin *Boiohaemum,* from *Boii* a people of ancient Gaul who settled in Bohemia (former country in Europe, now part of Czechoslovakia) + *-haemum,* cognate with HOME; for suffix see -AN.

boil[1] *v.* bubble up and steam. About 1300 *boillen,* borrowed from Old French *boillir, bolir, boulir, buillir,* from Latin *bullīre* to bubble, seethe, from *bulla* a bubble; see BULL[2] decree. —**n.** Probably about 1425, from the verb. —**boiler** *n.* 1305 *Boyllur* surname of a cook; borrowed from Old French *boillir.* The meaning of a container in which to boil is recorded in 1725, in writings of Defoe. —**boiler plate** formulaic writing or filler material. 1893, American English.

boil[2] *n.* painful swelling. 1529, in writings of Sir Thomas More, alteration (perhaps influenced by *boil*[1] in the sense "inflammation" found in Middle English *boillinge*) of earlier *bile* a festering sore (about 1300, in Mannyng's *Handlyng Synne*), developed from Old English *bȳl, bȳle* (about 1000), from Proto-Germanic **būlja-*; cognate with Old High German *būlla* lump, swelling (modern German *Beule*), Middle Low German and Middle Dutch *būle* (modern Dutch *buil*), Icelandic *beyla* hump, Swedish *bula,* Danish *bule, bugle* swelling, and Gothic *ufbauljan* swell up, from Indo-European **bheu-l-/bhou-l-/bhū-l-* (Pok. 99).

boisterous *adj.* rough, violent, noisy. About 1400 *boistreous* rough, coarse, especially in manner, variant of earlier *boistous* crude, awkward, rough, roughly vigorous; also, brutal, violent (probably before 1300, in *Kyng Alisaunder*); of uncertain origin. It has been suggested that Middle English *boistous* is borrowed from Old French *boistos, boisteus* limping, rough, clumsy, perhaps from *boiste* box, from Medieval Latin *buxis, buxida,* from Latin *buxus* something made of box tree wood.

Alternatively, French scholars propose that Middle English *boistous* is borrowed from Anglo-French *boistous* rough, having a rough surface, *boistousement* roughly, (also glossed as "noisily"), either related to Old French *boitous* noisy, or (according to the Französisches Etymologisches Wörterbuch) related to Old French *boiteaux* curved, Middle French *boiteux* imperfect, ultimately from Latin *pyxis,* the source of French *boîte* BOX[1].

Connections with *boast* are generally rejected by modern sources.

bola (bō′lə) *n.* or **bolas** *n.pl.* weapon of stone or metal balls tied at the ends of a long cord. 1826 *bolas,* American English, from Spanish and Portuguese *bolas,* plural of *bola* ball, from Latin *bulla* bubble; see BULL[2] decree.

bold *adj.* fearless, daring. About 1250, developed from Old English *bald* (about 725, an Anglian form in a translation of *Exodus*), and *beald* (before 893, a West Saxon form in Werfrith's translation of St. Gregory's *Dialogues*). The Old English word is cognate with Old Saxon and Old High German *bald* bold, swift (modern German *bald* quickly, soon), Old Dutch *baldo* confidently, Old Icelandic *ballr* terrible, dangerous, and Gothic *balthaba* boldly, from Proto-Germanic **balthaz,* from Indo-European **bhol-to-s,* from **bhel-* to swell (Pok.121).

bole *n.* trunk of a tree. Probably about 1300, in *The Romance of Guy of Warwick,* borrowed from a Scandinavian source (compare Old Icelandic *bolr* bole); cognate with Middle Dutch *bolle* bole, Middle Low German *bolle* plank, from Proto-Germanic **bulás,* Indo-European **bhelós,* root **bhel-* to swell (Pok.121).

bolero (bəlãr′ō) *n.* lively Spanish dance. 1787, in Joseph Townsend's *A Journey Through Spain,* borrowed from Spanish *bolero,* possibly from *bola* ball, in reference to the dance's whirling motion, see BOLA; or, according to the Spanish scholar Corominas, Spanish *bolero* is possibly derived from *vuelo* flight, referring to the gracefulness of the dance, from *volar* to fly (note that *b* and *v* are initially pronounced alike in Spain).

The meaning of a short jacket coming to the waist appeared about 1892.

boll *n.* rounded seed pod. Probably before 1450, earlier meaning a round vessel, such as a bowl or cup (probably before 1200, in Layamon's *Chronicle of Britain*); developed from Old English *bolla* bowl (about 700); cognate with Old Saxon *bollo,* Old Icelandic *bolli,* and probably influenced in meaning by Latin *bulla* bubble, ball; see BOWL[1] dish. **—boll weevil** 1895, American English; the extended political sense of a renegade Democrat is first recorded in 1906.

bologna *n.* = baloney. 1850, variant of *Bologna sausage* (1750, in Fielding's *Tom Jones*); from earlier *Bolognian sausage* (1596, in works of Thomas Nashe).

Bolshevik or **bolshevik** (bōl′shəvik) *n.* member of the wing of the Russian Social Democratic Party that seized power in 1917. 1917, borrowed from Russian *bol'shevik* (*ból'she* more, greater, a comparative form of *bol'shói* large, great, as in *Bolshoi Ballet* + *-evik* suffix meaning "one that is"); cognate with Sanskrit *bála-m* strength and Greek *beltīōn* better, from Indo-European **bol* strong (Pok.96). The name is in allusion to the radical group within the Russian Socialist Democratic Party which held a temporary majority in 1903, in contrast to the *Mensheviks,* the members of the more moderate wing.

The meaning "Communist" developed in 1918 when the Bolsheviks became the Communist Party and the extended meaning "extreme radical" appears in the works of William Inge in 1926.

bolster *n.* long pillow. Old English *bolster* (about 725, in *Beowulf*); cognate with Old High German *bolstar, polstar* bolster (modern German *Polster*), Middle Dutch *bolster, bulster,* Old Icelandic *bolstr* (Swedish *bolster* bed, Danish *bolster* bed ticking), from Proto-Germanic **bulHstran,* cognate with Old Prussian *balsinis* pillow, from Indo-European **bhl̥k-/bholĝ-,* root **bheleĝ-* (Pok.122). **—v.** prop up, as with a bolster. 1508, from the noun, but implied in earlier verbal use in *bolstering* (1451) and *bolstered* (about 1460).

bolt[1] *n.* rod for fastening. 1425; earlier, part of a door lock (1396); a length of cloth (1310); a bundle (1266), and the blunt-headed arrow for a crossbow, found in Old English *bolt,* about 950; cognate with Old High German *bolz* (modern German *Bolzen*) short arrow, bolt, Dutch *bout,* Danish *bolt,* Swedish *bult,* from Proto-Germanic **bultás,* Indo-European **bhl̥dós,* and Lithuanian *beldù* I knock, from Indo-European **bheld-, bhl̥d-* (Pok.124).

The idiom *shoot one's bolt* echoes the saying *A fool's bolt is soon shot,* referring to the arrow of a crossbow (probably about 1150, in an early edition of *The Proverbs of Alfred*).

—v. move suddenly. About 1425, in Scottish use; later, "to fasten with a bolt" (1580); the Americanism "to break away from a political party," appears in 1833. The earliest meaning "to restrain, fetter" (1378, in a version of *Piers Plowman*) is from the noun.

bolt[2] *v.* sift. Probably about 1200 *bulten,* in *The Ormulum,* borrowed from Old French *bulter,* earlier *buleter,* probably from a Germanic source (compare Middle High German *biuteln* to sift, from Old High German *būtil* sack, modern German *Beutel*).

bomb *n.* 1684, explosive projectile filled with gunpowder (earlier *bome,* 1588, as a translation of Spanish *bomba* in a history of China); the current use, however, is borrowed from French *bombe,* from Italian *bomba,* from Latin *bombus* a booming sound, from Greek *bómbos* a deep hollow sound, probably of imitative origin. Compare BOOM[1]. The meaning "atomic bomb" in *the bomb* is first recorded in 1945. **—v.** to attack with bombs. 1688, from the noun. **—bomber** *n.* 1915, formed from English *bomb,* v. + *-er*[1]. **—bombshell** *n.* (1708)

bombard *v.* 1598, to fire a cannon; probably verb use of earlier *bombard, bumbard,* n. 1436, a catapult; borrowed from Old French *bombarde* (1363) a siege weapon, catapult, probably from Latin *bombus* booming sound; see BOMB. A parallel French verb *bombarder* to attack with a cannon or catapult, is recorded from 1515. The transferred sense, to batter with shot and shell, appeared in English in 1686; the figurative sense, to attack vigorously, appeared in 1765. **—bombardment** *n.* 1702, formed from English *bombard,* v. + *-ment.*

bombast *n.* 1589, inflated language, either noun use of earlier archaic *bombast,* v. to inflate with grandiose language (1573); or figurative use of earlier obsolete noun meaning "cotton wadding" (1547), a variant of *bombace* (1553), borrowed from Middle and Old French *bombace* cotton, cotton wadding, from Medieval Latin *bambacem,* accusative of *bambax* cotton, from Late Greek *bámbax* (genitive *bámbakos*) or *pámbax,* from Pahlavi *pambak* cotton. The first syllable of French *bombace* was influenced by Latin *bombȳx* silk, from Greek *bómbȳx* silk, silkworm.

The *t* may have been supplied to earlier *bombace,* n. by influence of a past participial *bombast* of obsolete *bombase,* v., to stuff with cotton (1558).

—bombastic *adj.* 1704, earlier *bombastical* (1649), formed from English *bombast,* n. + *-ic, -ical.*

bona fide (bō′nə fīd) in good faith; genuine. 1542-43, in *Acts of Henry VIII,* and later in adjective use (1788, in *bona fide purchaser or driver*); borrowed from Latin *bonā fidē,* the ablative form of the noun phrase *bona fidēs* good faith. This Latin noun phrase later came into English as *bona fides* in the original Latin sense of "good faith" (1845), but nearly a century later, this singular noun phrase was mistakenly analyzed as a plural, because of the *s* in *fides,* and came to mean "guarantees of good faith."

bonanza *n.* rich source of profit. 1844, American English, borrowed from American Spanish *bonanza* a rich lode, from Spanish *bonanza* fair weather at sea, prosperity (compare Italian *bonaccia* a calm at sea), from Vulgar Latin **bonacia,* from the word elements of Latin *bon-* in *bonus* good + *-acia* in *malacia* calm at sea, in the mistaken belief that *malacia* derived from *malus* bad, whereas it actually was a borrowing of Greek *malakíā* calm at sea, (literally) softness, from *malakós* soft; see BONUS.

bonbon *n.* piece of candy. 1796, in Fanny Burney's *Camilla,* borrowed from French *bonbon* a small candy or confection, reduplication of *bon* good, from Latin *bonus;* see BONUS.

bond *n.* thing that binds; tie, fetter. Probably about 1200; earlier variant of *band* (1126), presumably also influenced by Middle English *bond,* n. serf, tenant farmer holding land under a lord, developed from Old English *bōnda* householder, farmer; see BONDAGE. The meaning "a binding agreement or commitment" appeared in the 1300's (as early as 1303, in Mannyng's *Handlyng Synne* referring to a marriage contract). **—v.** Before 1460; from the noun. **—bonded** *adj.* 1597, in

Shakespeare's *A Lovers Complaint.* —**bondsman** *n.* 1713, one who gives a bond for another.

bondage *n.* servitude, slavery. 1303, in Mannyng's *Handlyng Synne,* borrowed from Anglo-French *bondage* and from Anglo-Latin *bondagium.* The Anglo-Latin word appeared before 1221, possibly a Latinized form of Old French **bondage* (as Medieval Latin *-agium* is a Latinized form of Old French *-age*), or based on Middle English *bond* a serf, tenant farmer as distinct from a freeholder + Medieval Latin *-agium* -age.

The now largely archaic *bond* meaning "serf" from Middle English *bond* a serf, tenant farmer (1180, as a surname) developed from Old English *bōnda* householder, farmer (about 1025, in Laws of King Canute, Danish ruler of England); borrowed from a Scandinavian source (compare Old Icelandic **bōnda, bōndi* free-born farmer, householder, landowner; earlier *būandi,* noun use of present participle of *būa* dwell, live); see BOWER.

bone *n.* Probably before 1200 *bone,* in Layamon's *Chronicle of Britain,* and *bon* (also before 1200) from earlier *ban* (about 1150), developed from Old English (about 700) *bān.* The word is cognate with Old Frisian and Old Saxon *bēn* bone, Old High German *bein* (modern German *Bein* leg; but "bone" in compounds using *-bein*), Old Icelandic *bein* bone, from Proto-Germanic **bainan*; but no cognate appears in Gothic and, unlike other names of parts of the body, it is not related to any word for "bone" outside Germanic. —**v.** 1494, from the noun (compare *boned,* adj. 1297). —**boner** *n.* 1912, American English, a blunder, formed from *bone,* n. + *-er* [1]. —**boneless** *adj.* Probably about 1200.

bonfire *n.* 1556, open-air fire; earlier, a fire to burn corpses (1552), and *banefire* a fire to burn bones (before 1415), a compound of *bone* (or its northern dialectal form *bane*) + *fire.* The spelling *bonfire* became more common as the etymological sense was forgotten, as evidenced by Johnson's derivation from French *bon* good + English *fire.*

bongo *n.* small drum. 1920, in Hergesheimer's *San Cristóbal de la Habana,* borrowed from American Spanish of the West Indies *bongó,* a word of West African (Bantu) origin (compare Lokele, a Bantu language in Zaire, *boungu, bongungu*).

bonnet *n.* 1375 (Scottish) *bonat* brimless hat for men, in John Barbour's *The Bruce;* later, *bonet* brimless hat for men and women (before 1425); borrowed from Old French *bonet* hat, fabric for hats, in the phrase *chapel de bonet* hat or cap of "bonet," from Medieval Latin *boneta, bonetus* material for hats, perhaps from Germanic (compare Middle High German *bonit* bonnet).

bonus *n.* extra gift. 1773, borrowed from Latin *bonus,* adj., good, from Old Latin *dvonos,* earlier *dvenos* and related to Latin *bene* well, *bellus* fine.

The use of Latin *bonus,* adj. in place of *bonum,* n., a good thing (intending to refer to a *boon* or extra gift or gratuity) was perhaps originally an ignorant or humorous application coined in traders' parlance of the London Exchange.

boob *n.* stupid person. 1909, American English, probably a shortening of *booby,* n. —**booby** *n.* stupid person; fool. 1599-1603, possibly borrowed from Spanish *bobo* fool, seabird; cognate with Portuguese *bobo* buffoon, Old French *baube* a stammerer; all from Latin *balbus* stammering, inarticulate; see BABBLE.

However, the word is of uncertain origin, and the phonetic connection between the English and Spanish is distant enough to have prompted some etymologists to speculate on a borrowing of German *Bube* worthless wretch, found in the writings of Luther. But whether Luther's works were read sufficiently in English to adopt *booby* from *Bube* is questionable, though Shakespeare did pun on the Diet of Worms of 1521 and made references to Wittenberg in *Hamlet,* so that some acquaintance with Luther and his part in the Reformation must have been common knowledge to Shakespeare's audiences.

boogie-woogie *n.* style of playing the blues. 1928 (as a song title), but current among black jazzmen since about 1920; of uncertain origin, perhaps a reduplication of a word from a West African language (compare Hausa *buga,* as an attributive, *bugi* and Mandingo *bugc,* both meaning to beat drums). —**boogie** *n.* 1941, short for *boogie-woogie;* 1972, applied to disco music and dancing. —**v.** 1955, enjoy oneself thoroughly; 1974, dance uninhibitedly, as to disco music.

book *n.* Before 1121 *boke, bok,* developed from Old English *bōc* writing tablet, written document; collectively, writings, a written work (about 725, in a translation of the book of *Daniel*). The word is cognate with Old Frisian and Old Saxon *bōk,* Old High German *buoh,* Middle High German *buoch* written work, book (modern German *Buch*), Old Icelandic *bōk* (Swedish *bok*), and Gothic *bōka* letter of the alphabet, *bōkōs* (plural) books; Proto-Germanic **bōks;* related to Old English *bōc, bēce* beech, on the supposition that early inscriptions may have been made on tablets of beech wood; see BEECH. The modern spelling *book* appeared as early as 1375 for the noun in Chaucer's *Canterbury Tales* and about 1390 for the verb. —**v.** Probably before 1200 *boken, bocken* to record, in *Ancrene Riwle,* developed from Old English (966) *bōcian* assign land, etc. by charter, from Old English *bōc,* n.

boom[1] *v.* make a loud, deep sound. About 1430, in Chaucer's *Canterbury Tales;* earlier *bommen* drink with a gurgling sound (before 1376, in *Piers Plowman*), of imitative origin (compare German *bummen,* Dutch *bommen,* etc.); compare BOMB. —**n.** Before 1500, from the verb.

boom[2] *n.* long pole or beam. 1543 (Scottish) *boun,* borrowed from Dutch *boom* tree, pole, beam, from Middle Dutch; cognate with Old High German *boum* tree (modern German *Baum*). The analogous form in Old English was *bēam* and in modern English is also *beam,* the sense of *boom* in English being borrowed from Dutch to supply meanings in which English *beam* was not used; see BEAM.

boom[3] *n.* a sudden increase in value, activity, price, etc. 1879, American English; noun use of earlier *boom* [3], v. 1873, to increase suddenly in value, activity, price, etc.

Though dictionaries traditionally connect these meanings of *boom* with *boom*[1] to make a loud, deep noise, the meanings seem more closely connected semantically to a meaning of *boom*[2], v. to go under full sail, usually at full speed (probably 1617), in the OED defined as to rush with violence, as a ship is said "to come booming, when she makes all the sail she can."

boomerang *n.* curved throwing club. 1827, an adoption or modification of a name for this weapon in the language of the aborigines of New South Wales, Australia. The form *wo-mur-rang* was recorded in a glossary of aboriginal words (1798) by an official of the Port Jackson colony.

boon[1] *n.* Probably about 1350 *bone* benefit (in *Ywain and Gawain*); earlier, prayer, request, grant, (probably before 1200, in *Ancrene Riwle*); borrowed from a Scandinavian source (compare Old Icelandic *bōn* petition; cognate with Old English *bēn* prayer), from Proto-Germanic **bōniz,* and probably cognate with Latin *fārī* to speak, from Indo-European **bhā-* (Pok.105).

boon[2] *adj.* jolly, as in *boon companion.* Probably about 1380 *bone, boon* good, in Chaucer's *House of Fame;* borrowed from Old French *bon* (feminine *bone*) good, from Latin *bonus;* see BONUS.

boondocks *n.pl. Slang.* backwoods. 1944, American English, borrowed (through American soldiers' contact in the Philippines during World War II) from Tagalog *bundók* mountain. Since 1965 often altered to **boonies.**

boondoggle *n. Informal.* useless or wasteful work. 1935, American English, origin uncertain; said to have been coined about 1925, as a name for the braided lanyard made and worn by boy scouts; however, the occupation of braiding leather scraps for saddle trappings is also said to have been known among cowboys.

boor *n.* rude person. Probably before 1410, in poetry of Lydgate, *boveer* peasant, countryman; earlier, as a surname in *Buver* (1236) and *Bover* (1268); borrowed from Old French *bovier* herdsman (compare Old French *buef* ox; see BEEF), from Latin *bovis,* genitive of *bōs* cow, ox.

The later forms *bour* (1551) and *boor* (1581) were probably borrowed from Dutch *boer* farmer, peasant; see BOER. The current sense of a rude, ill-bred person appeared in 1598.

—boorish *adj.* 1562, formed from English *boor,* n. + *-ish.* The meaning pertaining to a rude, ill-bred person appeared in 1660, in Pepys' *Diary.*

boost *n., v.* lift or push up. 1815 verb, 1825 noun, American English, of unknown origin. First appearance of the form was in a book published in 1815 by David Humphreys, entitled *The Yankey in England,* where it is defined as a glossary word: *"Boost,* raise up, lift up, exalt."

Any connection with earlier (1593) *bouse,* v. to haul (rigging of a ship) seems strained, because the sense of *boost* when first defined was connected with raising a person or some thing in rank, honor, character, or quality, as evidenced by the word "exalt" in the early definition cited above.

—booster *n.* 1890, formed from English *boost,* v. + *-er*[1].

boot[1] *n.* large shoe. About 1300 *bote,* in *King Horn,* borrowed from Old French *bote* (modern French *botte*), corresponding to Provençal, Spanish, and Portuguese *bota;* of uncertain origin. —**v.** 1468, to put boots on; later, in American English, to kick or remove as if by kicking (1877) and to kick out, eject (1880).

boot[2] *n.* profit; use (an archaism that survives in the phrase *to boot* meaning "in addition, besides," which appeared in Old English before 1000).

The old use of *boot,* Middle English *bōte* relief, remedy (1131, in the *Peterborough Chronicle*), developed from Old English *bōt* expiation for a crime or sin, compensation, remedy; literally, making better (about 725, in *Beowulf*). The Old English is cognate with Old Frisian *bōte* compensation, atonement, Old High German *buoz, buoza* improvement, remedy, Old Icelandic *bōt* remedy, compensation, and Gothic *bōta* advantage, benefit, good, from Proto-Germanic **bōtō,* Indo-European **bhādā,* root **bhad-/bhād-* (Pok.106); related to the Proto-Germanic root of Old English *bet* and *betera* BETTER.

booth *n.* About 1145 in a proper name *Bouthum;* later *Buthum* (about 1150) and *Bothon* (about 1449). The word as a common noun is first recorded about 1200, in *The Ormulum,* with the spelling *bothe;* later *bouthe* (before 1400) and *buth* (probably about 1475); gradually *booth* appears about 1450 and is established in the 1500's. The word is probably borrowed from a Scandinavian source (compare Old Icelandic *būdh* dwelling, Old Swedish and Old Danish *bōth* booth, stall). Cognates exist in Middle High German *buode* hut, tent (modern German *Bude* booth, hut), Middle Dutch *boede* booth, from Proto-Germanic **bōthō,* Indo-European **bhōtā,* root **bheu-/bhō(u)-* (Pok.149). The word is ultimately related to Old English *būr* dwelling; see BOWER.

bootleg *n.* illegal liquor or other goods. Before 1889, American English, coined in reference to the practice of smuggling liquor as if in the tall legs of boots. —**v.** sell or make illegally. 1903, from the noun. —**bootlegger** *n.* (1889)

booty *n.* plunder. 1474 *botye,* in Caxton's *Game and Play of Chess;* later *buty* (1491 in Caxton's translation of *Four Sons of Aymon*), perhaps from earlier *boti,* adj. profiting (by plunder), probably about 1439, or *bottyne* booty (about 1450); borrowed in part from Old French *butin* booty, from Middle Low German *būte, buite* exchange, barter, booty (modern German *Beute*), of uncertain origin; and perhaps borrowed also in part directly from Middle Low German *būte, buite* or earlier Dutch *buyt, buet* booty (modern Dutch *buit*).

booze *v.* drink heavily. 1768, in letters of Walpole, probably a variant of earlier *bouse* (pronounced büz), with the same meaning (probably before 1325); borrowed from Middle Dutch *būsen* drink heavily, which is related to Middle Low German *būsen* to revel, carouse, drink heavily, both of uncertain origin. —**n.** drink, especially intoxicating drink. 1732, from the verb.

borax *n.* a white crystalline powder. 1543 *borax,* an alteration (influenced by Anglo-Latin *borax*) of earlier Middle English *boras* (about 1387, in *Prologue* to Chaucer's *Canterbury Tales*); Middle English *boras* was borrowed from Anglo-French *boras,* which itself is a learned borrowing from Anglo-Latin *borax,* Medieval Latin *baurach, borac, borax,* from Arabic *būraq,* from Persian *būrah.*

border *n.* side, edge, boundary. Probably about 1400, variant spelling (by weakening of *-ure* to *-er*) of earlier *bordure* (about 1350); borrowed from Old French *bordëur* seam, edge, border, from *bord, bort* side, boundary, from Frankish (compare Old High German *bort;* cognate with Old English *bord* border, side; see BOARD). The earlier spelling *bordure* is now confined to use in heraldry. —**v.** About 1400, put a border on, in Sir John Maundeville's *Travels;* from the noun.

bore[1] *v.* pierce, drill. Before 1200 *boren,* developed from Old English *borian* (about 1000). The Old English is cognate with Old High German *borōn* to bore (modern German *bohren*), Old Icelandic *bora,* from Proto-Germanic **burōn,* and through the Indo-European base **bher-/bhor-* to cut (Pok.133), cognate with Latin *forāre* to bore, *ferīre* to knock, strike, and Greek *pháros* a plow. —**n.** a hole, especially one made by drilling. Probably before 1300, in *Sir Tristrem,* partly developed from Old English *bor* (before 800); cognate with Old High German *bora* auger, gimlet (modern German *Bohr*), Old Icelandic *borr* (Swedish *borr,* Danish *bor*); probably in part derived from *boren* to bore, and partly a borrowing from a Scandinavian source (compare Old Icelandic *bora* a hole). —**borer** *n.* 1318, as a surname *Boriere;* later, a tool for making holes; formed from English *bore* [1], v. + *-er* [1].

bore[2] *v.* make weary by being dull or tiresome. 1768, of unknown origin. —**n.** 1766, a fit of boredom or ennui (suggested as a specifically French malady); later, a tiresome person or thing (1778). Suggestions that the word is a figurative use of BORE[1], in allusion to persistent drilling and, therefore, annoyance, or "being in a deep hole" (as in the original phrase *in a long bore*) cannot be established in fact. —**boredom** *n.* 1852, in Dickens' *Bleak House,* formed from English *bore* [2], n. + *-dom.*

boreal (bō′rēəl) *adj.* northern. 1450; borrowed perhaps through Italian *boreale* from Latin *boreālis,* from *boreās* the north wind, *Boreās* god of the north wind, from Greek *Boréās* north wind; for suffix see -AL[1].

boric *adj.* of or from boron. 1869, perhaps borrowed from French *borique* (1818), or influenced by French in the formation of the term, from *bor(on),* n. + *-ic,* as in *boric acid,* replacing earlier *boracic acid* (1801), formed from English *borax* + *-ic* (the *-x-* being replaced by *-c-).*

born *adj.* Old English *boren* (and *geboren*) brought forth (about 725, in a version of *Genesis*), past participle of *geberan, beran* to carry, bring forth; see BEAR[2] carry.

boron *n.* nonmetallic chemical element. Probably before 1812, formed from English *bor(ax)* + *(carb)on.* The element was first isolated from *boracic acid* by Sir Humphry Davy, in 1807, and the next year by Gay-Lussac and Thénard in France.

borough *n.* incorporated or chartered town. 1100 *burg;* later *burgh,* in proper name *Goldesburgh,* and probably before 1350 *borough* town, city. In Middle English the word also meant "dwelling, refuge, and stronghold," as well as "a castle or fortified dwelling," and was used in the legal term *burgbriche* the crime of burglary or of disturbing the peace, recorded in 1235. The Old English *burh,* which carried over into Middle English for about 200 years, and *burg,* both meaning "city, fortress" (recorded about 725, in a version of *Genesis* and in *Beowulf*) are cognate with Old High German *burg* fortress, citadel (modern German *Burg* castle), Old Saxon *burg, burug,* Old Frisian *burch, burich,* Old Icelandic *borg* wall, fortress, Gothic *baúrgs* city, from Proto-Germanic **burȝs;* and are related to Old English *beorg* hill, mound, from Indo-European **bherĝh-/ bhr̥ĝh-* (Pok.140); see BARROW[2] mound.

Of the early spellings, Old English *burg* is still evident, as in *Gettysburg,* while *burgh* is established in Scotland (accounting for the American and English pronunciation of *Edinburgh* as if it were "*Edinborough,*" though natives say ed′ən brə), and the dative case of Old English *burg (byrig)* resulted in *-buri, -bury,* as in *Canterbury.*

borrow *v.* Probably before 1300 *borowen,* in *Kyng Alisaunder,* and *borwen,* in *The Romance of Guy of Warwick;* earlier *boruwen* (before 1250); developed from Old English *borgian* (about 950, in a version of *The Psalter*), from *borg* pledge, surety. Old English *borgian* is cognate with Old High German *borgēn* take heed, give surety (German *borgen* borrow, lend), Old Frisian *borga* borrow, Old Icelandic *borga* become surety for, guarantee, from Proto-Germanic **burȝ-;* and is related to Old English *beorgan* to save, preserve; see BURY. —**borrower** *n.* Before 1415, formed from English *borrow,* v. + *-er* [1].

bosh *n.* nonsense. 1834, as the Turkish word *bosh* (now written *bos*) empty, worthless, introduced into English in the novel *Ayesha* by J.J. Morier (1780-1849), British novelist and diplomat who traveled in Asia Minor and wrote popular romances with settings there. The word was popularized after the novel was reissued and widely circulated in a later edition (1846). —**interj.** 1852, in Dickens' *Bleak House,* from *bosh,* n., used as an interjection.

bosom *n.* breast. Probably before 1200 *bosum,* in *Ancrene Riwle,* developed from Old English *bōsm* (about 725, in a version of *Genesis*); cognate with Old Frisian *bōsm,* Old Saxon *bōsom,* Old High German *buosam* breast (modern German *Busen*), from West Germanic **bōsm-,* of unknown origin. —**adj.** 1590, from the noun.

boss[1] *n.* employer, chief, master. Before 1649 *base,* in John Winthrop's *The History of New England,* 1653 *basse,* American English, borrowed from Dutch *baas* master; further connections are doubtful (German *Baas,* Swedish, Danish, and Norwegian *bas* are all borrowed from Dutch). The modern spelling was thoroughly established in English by the beginning of the 1800's. —**v.** 1856, from the noun. —**bossy** *adj.* 1882, formed from English *boss* [1], n. + *-y* [1].

boss[2] *n.* raised ornament of a flat surface; knoblike mass. Before 1325 *boce* swelling, in *Cursor Mundi;* later, a raised ornament, architectural ornament (1382, in the Wycliffe Bible); borrowed through Anglo-Latin *boci* and Anglo-French *bose, busse,* from Old French *boce, boche* hump, perhaps from Frankish **botja* blow, swelling caused by a blow, from **botan* to strike, the source of Old French *boter* to thrust, push; see BUTT[3] strike. Alternatively, Old French *boce, boche* may have developed from Vulgar Latin **bottia,* represented also by Old Provençal *bossa* swelling, ball, Italian *bozza, boccia,* and Romanian *bot* ball, but of uncertain origin. —**v.** Probably before 1400 *bocen, bosen* to project, stand out, borrowed from Old French *bocier,* from *bocė* hump.

botanical *adj.* of plants. 1658, variant of earlier *botanic* (1656), borrowed from French *botanique,* from Greek *botanikós* of herbs, from *botánē* plant, related to *bóskein* to pasture, and cognate with Lithuanian *gúotas* herd, from Indo-European **gwō(u)-/gwə-* (Pok.483); for suffix see -ICAL. —**botanist** *n.* Before 1682, borrowed from French *botaniste;* for suffix see -IST. Both *botanical* and *botanist* were introduced into English in the writings of Sir Thomas Browne. —**botany** *n.* study of plants. 1696, formed from *botanic, botanical,* on the analogy of *history, historic, historical,* etc.

botch *v.* spoil, bungle. Before 1382, to mend or patch, in the Wycliffe Bible; later, to spoil by unskillful work (1530, in Palsgrave's *Lesclarcissement*); of uncertain origin.

A proposed ultimate relationship with *patch* is doubtful.

—**n.** 1605, a botched part, in Shakespeare's *Macbeth;* from the verb.

both *adj., adv.* two together. 1124 *bathe;* later, about 1225 *bothe,* in *King Horn;* probably developed from Old English **bā thā* both those (compare Old English *bā the,* in late manuscripts of the *West Saxon Gospels,* replacing *bū tū* (neuter) or *bā twā* (masculine or feminine) both two, in earlier manuscripts).

The word is cognate with Old Saxon *bēthie, bēthe* both, Old High German *beide, bēde* (modern German *beide*), Old Icelandic *bādhir,* and Gothic *bai thai* both those. All these forms apparently derive from an alteration of an Indo-European dual form **bhōu-,* meaning both (Pok.35), found perhaps in the second element of Latin *ambō* both, Greek *ámphō,* and Sanskrit *ubhāú,* and represented by Old English *bā, bū* both, Gothic *bai, ba,* plus the addition of a demonstrative form from Indo-European **to-* that, the, the source of Old English *thā* and modern English THE.

There are difficulties in reconciling the *-ōu-* of Indo-European **bhōu-* with the vowels of the Germanic words, but perhaps the alteration results from the replacement of a dual form by the plural form in Germanic.

The influence of the Scandinavian word represented by Old Icelandic *bādhir* during late Old English and early Middle English times undoubtedly affected the native expression and helped to fix its form. It would not be inaccurate to describe Middle English *bathe, bothe* as a blend of the Old English and the Scandinavian forms.

bother *v.* pester, annoy. 1718, bewilder with noise, confuse, in writings of Sheridan; of uncertain origin. Earliest use is by Irish writers: Sheridan, Swift, Sterne, suggesting Irish origin (compare Irish *bodar* deaf, confused, annoyed, with *d* pronounced as *th* in *wither,* Gaelic *bodhar* deaf, *bodhair* to deafen, with *dh* pronounced like the Irish *d,* and Old Irish *bodar* deaf, cognate with Cornish *bodhar,* Welsh *byddar,* and Breton *bouzar,* from Indo-European **bhud-* strike, hit (Pok.112). The current meaning appeared before 1745 (in Swift's works). —**n.** petty trouble; annoyance. 1834; from the verb, earlier, possibly meaning "nonsense, meaningless chatter" (1803); from the verb. —**bothersome** *adj.* (1834)

bottle *n.* About 1380 *botel,* in *Sir Ferumbras;* earlier in compound *botelmaker* (1346), also certainly related to *boteler,* occurring as early as 1171 in the form *butiller* (according to MED an occupational term and personal name, as in *Alexander le butiller,* some examples of which may mean bottlemaker) and further related to *boteler* chief servant in charge of drink and food, or one who serves wine (probably before 1300, in *Kyng Alisaunder*), a term that became modern English *butler.*

Middle English *botel* was borrowed from Old French *boteille, bouteille* wine vessel, from Medieval Latin *butticula,* diminutive of Late Latin *buttis* cask, BUTT[4] barrel.

—**v.** 1622, to store up as if in a bottle; later, to put in bottles (1641). With the figurative meaning recorded some 20 years before the literal meaning and the verb recorded some 250 years after the noun, a defect in the record of English is suggested.

The spelling with two *t's* begins to appear in the late 1400's, earlier though in proper names.

bottom *n.* 1294-95 *butme;* earlier, in place names referring to a valley floor or land along a stream *bothem,* in *Keldebothem* (1153) and *botme,* in *Botmeshil* (1190); developed from Old English *botm* lowest part, bottom (about 725, in *Beowulf*). Old English *botm* is cognate with Old Frisian *bodem* bottom, Old Saxon *bodam,* Old High German *bodam* (modern German *Boden*), Old Icelandic *botn,* from Proto-Germanic **buthm-, buthn-,* and through the common Indo-European base **bhudh-* (Pok.174), is cognate with Latin *fundus* (and therefore English *foundation*), Greek *pythmḗn* bottom, and Sanskrit *budhná-s* depth, ground.

The spelling with *-tt-* gradually replaced the older spelling after 1400 (*bottum* appearing as early as 1399). —**adj.** 1561, developed from attributive use of noun as early as 1175. —**v.** 1544, from the noun (implied in the verbal noun *bottoming* as early as 1526).

botulism (boch′əlizəm) *n.* bacterial food poisoning. 1887, Anglicizing of earlier *botulismus* (1878), borrowed from German *Botulismus,* from Latin *botulus* sausage (because the disease was associated with eating tainted sausages) see BOWEL; for suffix see -ISM.

The root form of *botulism* was already familiar in English language scientific circles in *botuliform* (1861).

boudoir (bü′dwär) *n.* woman's sitting or dressing room. 1777, as a French term introduced into English; the French, literally meaning a place to sulk in, derives from *bouder* to sulk, pout, of imitative origin.

bouffant (büf änt′) *adj.* puffed out, as a skirt (1880) or hairdo (1955). 1880, a French term introduced into writing about fashion, from the present participle of *bouffer* to puff or swell out, from Old French *bouffer,* of imitative origin.

bough *n.* branch of a tree. About 1385 *hough,* in Chaucer's *Canterbury Tales;* earlier *bogh* (1305) and *bowe* (before 1250, in *The Owl and the Nightingale*); developed from Old English *bōg* bough, shoulder (probably about 875, in a version of *Genesis*) and *boog* (about 700, earliest glossaries). The Old English is cognate with Old High German *buog* shoulder (modern German *Bug* shoulder joint of an animal, bow of a ship), Old Icelandic *bōgr* shoulder, ship's bow, from Proto-Germanic **bōʒaz.* Outside Germanic cognates are found in Greek *pêchys* forearm, and Sanskrit *bāhú-* forearm, from Indo-European **bhāĝhú-s* (Pok.108). The sense "branch of a tree" is, according to the OED "of exclusively English development, [though] *bow* of a ship is ultimately the same word, but of recent adoption"; compare BOW[3].

bouillabaisse (bül′yəbās′) *n.* fish chowder. 1855, in Thackeray's *Ballad of Bouillabaisse,* borrowed from French *bouillabaisse;* earlier variant *Bouille-à-baisse,* from Provençal *bouiabaisso* (*boui* boil + *abaisso* (go) down, bring quickly to a boil and let simmer down, with stem *baiss-* from Vulgar Latin **bassiāre* to lower; see ABASE.).

bouillon (bül′yon) *n.* clear, thin soup. 1725, earlier in Blount's *Glossographia* listed as a French word (1656), from *bouillir* to boil, from Old French *boillir;* see BOIL[1] bubble.

boulder *n.* large rock. 1421 *bulder,* shortened from earlier *bulderston* (about 1300, in *Havelok the Dane*); borrowed from a Scandinavian source (compare Swedish *bullersten* large stone in a stream causing the water to make noise, a compound of *bullra* roar, rumble + *sten* stone).

boulevard *n.* broad street. 1769, a French term introduced into English in correspondence of Walpole; originally the French meant "the passageway along a rampart," from Middle Low German *bolwerk* or Middle Dutch *bolwerc* BULWARK.

bounce *v.* Probably before 1225 *buncin* to beat, thump, in a version of *Ancrene Riwle*); later, *bonchen* (before 1376, in *Piers Plowman*); extended to various actions producing a noise, especially to the action of moving with a sudden bound (1519, in which sense the use was probably influenced by *bound*[2] leap); perhaps ultimately of imitative origin, like Dutch *bonzen* to thump, *bons* a thump. **—n.** 1523, a leap, from the verb.

bound[1] *adj.* fastened, confined, compelled. Before 1449 *bound,* earlier *bounde* (probably before 1300), shortened from *bounden,* past participle of BIND.

bound[2] *v.* leap, spring. 1586, borrowed from Middle French *bondir* to rebound, spring, from Old French *bondir* make a resounding noise, from Vulgar Latin **bombitīre,* from Late Latin *bombitāre,* a frequentative form of Latin *bombīre* to buzz, from *bombus* a buzzing or booming sound; see BOMB. **—n.** Before 1553, in Udall's *Ralph Roister Doister,* borrowed from Middle French *bond* leap, from *bondir* to leap.

Note the noun is recorded almost 35 years before the verb.

bound[3] *n.* Usually, **bounds.** boundary, limit. About 1380, in Chaucer's translation of Boethius' *De Consolatione Philosophiae;* earlier *bounde* boundary marker (probably before 1300, in *Kyng Alisaunder*); borrowed through Anglo-Latin *bunda,* probably from Old French (compare *bonde, bodne,* variant forms of Old French *borne, bone*), perhaps from Gaulish. The word is also related to Middle English *boune* a boundary stone (probably before 1200, in Layamon's *Chronicle of Britain*), also borrowed from Old French (compare Old French *bodne, boune* boundary stone). **—v.** to set boundaries, limit, enclose. 1391, in Chaucer's *Treatise on the Astrolabe;* from the noun, or perhaps borrowed from Old French (compare *bodner* to bound). **—boundary** *n.* 1626, in Francis Bacon's *Sylva Sylvarum,* formed from English *bound*[3], n. + *-ary.* **—boundless** *adj.* 1592, in Shakespeare's *Romeo and Juliet,* formed from English *bound*[3], n. + *-less.*

bound[4] *adj.* ready or intending to go. Before 1400 *bownde;* earlier *bun* (probably about 1200, in *The Ormulum*); borrowed from a Scandinavian source (compare Old Icelandic *būinn,* past participle of *būa* dwell, live, get ready, and Old Danish *bōen,* Old Swedish *boin*); see BOWER. The final *-d* that appears largely after the mid-1500's may have been added on the analogy of English past participles and by some confusion with *bound*[1] made fast.

bounden *adj.* required, obliged. Before 1325 *bunden,* in *Cursor Mundi,* past participle of *bind;* see BOUND[1].

bounteous *adj.* generous, abundant. 1542, in writings of Udall, alteration, on analogy of *bounty,* of earlier *bountevous* (about 1385, in Chaucer's *Troilus and Criseyde*); borrowed from Middle French *bontif, bontive,* from *bonté* goodness, gift; see BOUNTY; for suffix see -OUS.

bounty *n.* generous gift, reward, generosity in bestowing gifts. Before 1325 *bounte,* in *Cursor Mundi;* earlier *bunte* (about 1275), also meaning "goodness"; borrowed through Anglo-French *bunté,* Old French *bonté* goodness, bounty, gift, from Latin *bonitātem* (nominative *bonitās*), from *bonus* good; see BONUS; for suffix see -TY[2]. **—bountiful** *adj.* 1508, formed from English *bounty* + *-ful.*

bouquet *n.* bunch of flowers. 1716-18, as a French word introduced in correspondence of Lady Mary Montagu, from Middle French *bouquet* thicket, from Old French *boschet, boscet, bosket,* originally diminutive of Old French *bois* forest or Medieval Latin *boscus,* from Frankish (compare Old High German *bosc, busc* bush; see BUSH[1] shrub).

bourgeois (bůrzhwä′) *adj.* 1564-65, of or belonging to the French middle class, borrowed from Middle French *bourgeois,* from Old French *borjois, burgeis* citizen of a town or village, from *borc* town, village, from Latin *burgus* fortress, castle, borrowed earlier from Greek *pýrgos,* of Germanic origin, then later influenced by Germanic (compare Old High German *burg* fortress); see BOROUGH. **—n.** Before 1562, member of the French middle class; later, any member of the middle class (1704), from the adjective. See the doublet BURGESS. **—bourgeoisie** *n.* middle class. 1707, borrowed from French *bourgeoisie* the French middle class, from *bourgeois.*

bourn[1] or **bourne**[1] *n.* brook (now, British Southern dialect variant of *burn*). Before 1376 *bourne,* in *Piers Plowman;* earlier *borne* (before 1338, in Mannyng's *Chronicle of England*) and *burne* (probably about 1175); developed from Old English *burna, burne* spring, stream, brook (about 725, in *Beowulf*). The word is cognate with Old Frisian *burna* spring, well, and (by metathesis or a shift in position of the *r*) with Old High German *brunno* spring, well (modern German *-born* in place names, poetic German *Born* spring, well), Old Icelandic *brunnr,* Gothic *brunna,* Greek *phréār,* all representatives of an Indo-European *r/n* stem **bhrēw-r̥/bhrēw-n̥-/bhru-n-* (Pok.144).

bourn[2] or **bourne**[2] *n. Archaic.* boundary, limit. 1523, borrowed from Middle French *bourne,* from Old French *bourne,* earlier *bodne;* see BOUND[3] boundary.

The introduction of the *r* in Old French has not been fully explained, but the use of the term in English is largely because of its appearance in passages of Shakespeare, particularly in *Hamlet* (Act III, scene 1) "...The undiscovered country, from whose *bourne* no traveler returns."

bout *n.* trial of strength, contest. 1591, in Shakespeare's *1 Henry VI;* earlier, a spell of any kind of work or other activity (1575), and a circuit, orbit (before 1541, in poetry of Wyatt); probably a variant of obsolete *bowt* a bend or curve, loop (1468), *bought* (probably before 1400), developed perhaps from Old English **buht,* (from Proto-Germanic **buHta-*)variant of *byht* a bend; see BIGHT.

boutique (bütēk′) *n.* small shop. 1767, borrowed from French *boutique,* earlier *bouticle* workshop, from Old Provençal *botica,* an adaptation of Latin *apothēca,* from Greek *apothḗkē* storehouse; see APOTHECARY.

boutonniere or **boutonnière** (bü′tənyãr′) *n.* flower worn in a buttonhole. 1877, a French word introduced in a short story of Bret Harte's, borrowed from French *boutonnière* buttonhole, from *bouton;* see BUTTON.

bovine (bō′vin) *adj.* of an ox or cow. 1817, borrowed from, or at least in part suggested by French *bovin, bovine* (1352), learned borrowing from Late Latin *bovīnus,* from Latin *bōs* (genitive *bovis*) ox, COW[1].

bow[1] (bou) *v.* bend the head or body. Before 1325 *bow-*

en, earlier *bouwen* (1300), *buwen, buhen* (1250), developed from Old English *būgan* to bend (about 725, in *Beowulf*). The Old English *būgan* is cognate with Old High German *biogan* to bend (modern German *biegen*), Old Icelandic *boginn* bent, *bjúgr* bent, bowed, Gothic *biugan* to bend, and Sanskrit *bhujáti* bends, from Indo-European **bheugh-/bhugh-* (Pok.152).

In the 1200's the now obsolete verb *bey* (Middle English *beighen*) to bend, cause to bow or bow out, was confused with *bughen, buhen* to bend the head or body, so that by the end of the 1300's the latter took the place of both verbs.

—n. Before 1656, from the verb.

bow² (bō) *n.* weapon for shooting arrows. Probably before 1200 *bowe,* in Layamon's *Chronicle of Britain;* developed from Old English *boga* bend (only in compounds, such as *elnboga* elbow, and *rēnboga* rainbow); also a weapon, bow (about 725, in *flanboga* arrow bow), and something curved, arch, vault (about 700). Old English *boga* is cognate with Old High German *bogo* and Old Icelandic *bogi,* both meaning a bow, from Proto-Germanic **buʒōn,* and related to Old English *būgan* to bend; see BOW¹.

The sense of "a looped knot" is not found in English before 1671.

bow³ (bou) *n.* forward part of a ship, prow. 1342, in the name of a ship *Swetebowe,* later 1409-11 *bowe;* perhaps borrowed from a Low German or Scandinavian source (compare Middle Dutch *boech,* modern Dutch *boeg,* Low German *būg,* and Old Icelandic *bógr,* all meaning "shoulder of an animal" and "bow of a ship"; cognate with Old English *bōg* shoulder; see BOUGH).

bowdlerize (boud'ləriz) *v.* expurgate. 1836, formed from *Bowdler* (English editor, 1754-1825, of an expurgated edition of Shakespeare designed for "family" reading, published in 1818) + *-ize.*

bowel *n.* **bowels,** intestines. Probably before 1300, in *Kyng Alisaunder,* borrowed from Old French *böel, bouele,* from Medieval Latin *botellus* intestine, from Latin *botellus,* diminutive form of *botulus* sausage (borrowed from Oscan-Umbrian), which is cognate with Old English *cwith, cwitha* belly, womb, from the Indo-European root **gwet-* (Pok.481).

bower *n.* shelter of leafy branches. Probably before 1400; earlier *boure* small room (before 1325, in *Cursor Mundi*), *bure* dwelling, bedroom (probably before 1200, in Layamon's *Chronicle of Britain*), and *bur-* (1121, in compounds: *burthenas* chamberlain); all developed from Old English *būr* dwelling (about 725, in *Beowulf*) thereby related to *neighbor, boor,* and indirectly to *boer;* also related to Old English *būan* dwell. Old English *būr* is cognate with Old High German *būr* dwelling (modern German *Bauer* cage, also *-beuren* in place names: *Benediktbeuren* dwellings of the Benedictines), Old Icelandic *būr* chamber, storeroom, (from Proto-Germanic **būra-*), Old High German *būan* dwell, Old Icelandic *būa* dwell, get ready, Gothic *bauan* dwell, inhabit, live, from Indo-European **bheu-/bhōu-/bhū-* (Pok.146).

The spelling *bower* began to appear gradually after 1350, developing from a tendency to pronounce a second syllable after "long" *u, i,* or diphthong before *-r,* as in *flower/flour* and even in the spelling *hower* for *hour,* that existed for a time in the 1500's and 1600's.

bowie knife (bō'ē *or* bü'ē) hunting knife. 1836, American English, in allusion to Jim *Bowie,* American pioneer and supposed inventor of this heavy sheath knife.

bowl¹ *n.* hollow, rounded dish. 1471 *bowle;* earlier, about 1150 *bolle,* developed from Old English (about 700) *bolla;* cognate with Old Frisian *bolla* (in compounds), Old Icelandic *bolli* bowl (Danish *bolle* bowl), Old High German *bolla* blister, bowl, bud (modern German *Bolle* bulb, onion), from Proto-Germanic **bullōn,* Indo-European **bhl̥-nōn-,* root **bhel-* swell, round out, (Pok.121).

The Middle English *bolle* is still evident in modern English *boll* a round seed pod, but the shift in spelling of *-owl* for *-oll,* that reflects the temporary early modern English change in pronunciation and the confusion with *bowl²* from French *boule,* has remained in modern spelling.

bowl² *n.* wooden ball used in games. Probably before 1400 *bowle,* borrowed from Middle French *boule,* from Gallo-Romance *bulla* ball, from Latin *bulla* bubble; see BULL² decree. The name of the game is *bowls* (1495). **—v.** play at bowls; roll a bowl in cricket, etc. 1440, either verb use of *bowl²,* n., or borrowed from Middle French *bouler* to bowl, from *boule* bowl. **—bowling** *n.* About 1500, from gerund of *bowl²,* v. **—bowling alley** (1555)

bowlegged *adj.* 1552, formed from English *bow¹,* v. + *legged* (1470).

bowsprit *n.* pole projecting from the bow of a ship. 1296 *bousprete,* probably borrowed from Middle Low German *bōchsprēt* (*bōch* bow + *sprēt* pole).

Since the word appears in English as early as 1296 and *bow³* was not in regular use in English before 1400, it is not possible to regard *bowsprit* as a compound of *bow³* and *sprit.*

box¹ *n.* container. About 1150, a jar; found in Old English *box* (before 1000, in works of Ælfric), probably borrowed from Late Latin *buxis* box, corresponding to Latin *pyxis,* from Greek *pyxís* box, as if originally made of the wood of the box tree, from *pýxos* BOX³ tree. **—v.** About 1450, from the noun.

box² *n.* blow, stroke. Probably about 1300, in *Sir Bevis of Hamtoun;* of unknown origin (often compared with Middle Dutch *bōke,* Middle High German *buc,* and Danish *bask* all meaning "blow," though without evidence of intermediate links or explanation of the formation in English; another supposition is based on possible figurative use of *box¹,* n.). **—v.** 1390 *boxen* to beat an animal; later, meaning to strike with the fist, beat, thrash (1519); from the noun. The sense "to fight with the fists" appeared in 1567. **—boxer** *n.* 1472, a person who engages in the sport of boxing, formed from English *box²,* v. + *-er¹.* **—boxing** *n.* 1711, the sport of fighting with the fists. The late date is accounted for by the fact that boxing died out as a sport in ancient Rome and was not reintroduced until the late 1600's, and not popularized until the early 1700's by the English athlete James Figg.

box³ *n.* small, bushy evergreen tree. Old English *box* (before 800, in an early glossary), borrowed from Latin *buxus,* from Greek *pýxos* box tree, of unknown origin.

boy *n.* Probably before 1300 *boye* male child, in *Kyng Alisaunder;* earlier, servant (about 1225, in *King Horn*) and *boi, boie* (1154); of uncertain origin: 1) compare Frisian *boi* boy, young man, though not easily connected with Middle Low German *bove* boy, knave; cognate with Middle Dutch *boef* boy (modern Dutch "knave"),

Middle High German *buobe* boy (modern dialectal German *Bube*). The relation of Old English *Bōia, Bōfa, Bōba* a masculine personal name, to any of these forms or to the Middle English is obscure. 2) the wide variety of vowels appearing in the Middle English forms (*boi, bey, beye, bay, bye*) suggests by form and by meaning (servant) that the word is possibly a borrowing of Old French *buié* (*embuié*), *boié* (*emboié*) meaning "fettered, shackled," past participial forms of *embuiier,* from *buie* shackle, from Latin *boia* leg iron, yoke; of uncertain origin. **—boyhood** *n.* Before 1745, in writings of Swift, formed from English *boy,* n. + *-hood.* **—boyish** *adj.* 1548, formed from English *boy,* n. + *-ish*[1].

boycott *v.* 1880, in allusion to Captain Charles *Boycott,* 1832-1897, an English land agent over Irish tenant farmers, who refused to lower rents in hard times and was subjected to an organized campaign by local people who refused to have any dealings with him; *boycotting* (1883). The practice was widely instituted towards others and the term was quickly adopted by newspapers in almost all European and many non-European languages: French *boycott, boycotter,* German *Boykott, boykottieren,* Russian *boikót, boikotirovat′* (probably through German), Spanish *boicoteo, boicotear,* Polish *bojkot, bojkotować,* Croatian *bojkotirati,* Japanese *boikotto.* **—n.** 1880, from the verb.

boysenberry *n.* hybrid of blackberry and other berries. 1935, American English, in allusion to Rudolph *Boysen* (American horticulturist who developed it in California) + *berry.*

brace *n.* 1313-14, a fastening; later, armor covering the arms (1333); borrowed from Old French *brace* the two arms, from Latin *brachia, bracchia,* plural forms of *bracchium* arm, from Greek *brachíōn* upper arm, from *brachýs* short (as being shorter than the forearm), cognate with Latin *brevis,* from Indo-European **mrĝhú-s* (Pok.750). The meaning "a support" is first recorded in 1348. **—v.** Probably about 1350, borrowed from Old French *bracier* embrace, gird tightly, from *brace* the two arms. **—bracing** *n.* (1461); *adj.* (1750)

bracelet *n.* 1437, borrowed from Middle French diminutive form of Old French *bracel* bracelet, from Latin *bracchiāle,* from *bracchium* arm, see BRACE, n.; for suffix see -LET.

bracken *n.* large type of fern. Probably before 1300 *brakan,* apparently borrowed from a Scandinavian source (compare Swedish *bräken* kind of fern, Danish *bregne* and, by alteration, Icelandic *burkni* common fern; also English BRAKE[3] bracken).

bracket *n.* support projecting from a wall. 1627, in writings of Captain John Smith, alteration of earlier *bragget* (1580); borrowed probably from Middle French *braguette* codpiece (because of the resemblance of the codpiece of breeches to the architectural bracket), diminutive form of *brague* breeches, from Provençal *braga,* from Latin *brāca,* from Gaulish, which had borrowed it from Germanic (compare Old English *brōc* garment for the legs and trunk); see BREECHES. It is also possible that the word was influenced by Spanish *bragueta* meaning both "codpiece" and "bracket," from Spanish *bragas* breeches.

The meaning of squarish or rounded punctuation marks to set off written matter appeared in 1750.
—v. 1823, implied in *bracketing,* later 1861, from verb use of *bracket,* n.

brackish *adj.* somewhat salty. 1538, formed from earlier English *brack* (1513, probably borrowed from Dutch *brak* brackish, possibly the same as Middle Dutch *brak* worthless) + *-ish*[1].

bract *n.* small leaf at the base of a flower or stalk. 1770, borrowed from New Latin *bractea,* variant spelling of Latin *brattea* thin plate or leaf of metal, gold leaf; of uncertain origin.

brad *n.* small thin nail. 1455 (in *bradsmyth* maker of nails or goads), variant of *brod* (1295); earlier, a sprout or shoot (probably about 1200, in *The Ormulum*); borrowed from a Scandinavian source (compare Old Icelandic *broddr* spike, shaft; cognate with Old English *brord* spike, point, spire, Old High German *brort* edge, margin, apparently from Proto-Germanic **brozda-,* and thereby related to Old Irish *brot* sting, prick, Middle Irish *brostaim* I goad, spur, Old High German *burst* bristle; see BRISTLE), from Indo-European **bḥrosdh-/ bhṛsdh-* (Pok.110).

brag *n., v.* boast. 1387 (noun), in Trevisa's translation of Higden's *Polychronicon;* 1378 (verb), in a version of *Piers Plowman;* both perhaps developed from *brag,* adj., adv., boastful, boastfully (about 1325), of uncertain origin; possible sources include Gaulish or Celtic *brāca* kind of trousers, and thence Provençal *braga* to wear rich clothes, and French (Swiss dialect) *braguâ* to boast or strut, but the French forms appear much later than the English by some 300 years; alternatively a Scandinavian source has been proposed (compare Old Icelandic *bragga sig* recover heart, *bragr* the best, the boast or toast of anything and Old Icelandic *brak* creaking noise; however, the Scandinavian is weak in semantic association).
—bragger *n.* Before 1376, in *Piers Plowman,* probably formed from *braggen,* v. (even though the verb is not recorded before 1378, which is not a significant gap in such an ancient record) + *-er*[1].

braggadocio (brag′ədō′shēō) *n.* boasting, boaster. 1590 *Braggadocchio,* a name coined by Spenser for a character personifying boastfulness in *The Faerie Queene* (from *brag* + *-occio* the Italian suffix showing increased importance or size, probably reformed by Spenser as *-occhio* with the intent of insuring the pronunciation -dō′chē ō).

braggart *n.* boastful person. Before 1577, borrowed from Middle French *bragard,* from *braguer* to brag; properly, show off one's fine clothes, especially one's new breeches, from *brague* breeches, see BRACKET; for suffix see -ARD of which *-art* is an occasional variant.

Though related to *brag* in meaning, *braggart* and its immediate French sources *bragard* and *braguer* are not related as underlying forms of English *brag* because *braguer* does not appear in French until almost 300 years after *brag* is recorded in English.

Brahmin (brä′mən) *n.* intellectual of the upper class, especially from New England. 1859 (in Oliver Wendell Holmes' *The Brahmin Caste of New England*), in allusion to *Brahman* (1481, in Caxton's translation of *The Mirror of the World*) the name for a member of the highest of priestly Hindu caste; borrowed from Sanskrit *bráhmaṇa-s,* from *brahmán-* sacrifice-priest; of unknown origin.

braid *v.* intertwine, plait. Probably before 1200 *breiden* move quickly; later, to plait, braid (about 1200), the forms *breide,* present tense, and *braide,* past tense, being merged about 1300; both developed from a form *breyden* of Old English *bregdan* move quickly, draw (a sword, etc.), twist in and out, intertwine (about 725, in *Beowulf*). The Old English is cognate with Old Saxon *bregdan,* Old High German *brettan* draw (a sword etc.), Old Icelandic *bregdha* move quickly, draw (a weapon), braid, from Proto-Germanic **brezđanan* and possibly Greek *phorkón* something white, gray, or shriveled, from Indo-European **bherək̑-/bhrēk̑-* shine (Pok.141). (Sanskrit *bhrā́śate* it blazes, glows, is also occasionally cited as a cognate, but it is unattested and perhaps a contrivance among lexicographers.) **—n.** Probably before 1200 *brede* a deceptive act, in Layamon's *Chronicle of Britain;* later, *breide* (before 1250) and, a quick movement (about 1300). Some meanings developed from *breiden,* v.; others developed from Old English *brægd* craft, fraud, which is cognate with Old Icelandic *bragd* deed, trick.

Braille or **braille** *n.* 1853, from the name of Louis *Braille,* 1809-1852, a blind French musician and teacher of the blind who developed this system of writing and printing for the blind and published it in 1829.

brain *n.* Probably before 1200, in Layamon's *Chronicle of Britain,* developed from Old English (about 1000) *brægen;* cognate with Old Frisian *brein* brain, Middle Low German *bregen* brain (dialectal German *Brägen*), from Proto-Germanic **braznan,* and probably with Greek *bréchma, brechmós* front part of the head, and Avestan *mərəzu-* crown of the neck and back, from Indo-European **mregh-/mrogh-* skull, brain (Pok.750). The word is not found in Scandinavian or Gothic. —**v.** dash one's brains out. Before 1382, in the Wycliffe Bible, from the noun. **—brainless** *adj.* 1434, formed from English *brain,* n. + *-less.* **—brainwashing** *n.* 1950, American English, possibly a loan translation of Chinese *xǐ* wash + *nao* brain. **—brainy** *adj.* clever. 1845; earlier meaning, cerebral (probably before 1425, in a translation of Chauliac's *Grande Chirurgie*), formed from English *brain,* n. + *-y*[1].

braise *v.* cook slowly in a covered pan. 1797, borrowed from French *braiser,* from *braise* hot charcoal, from Old French *brese* embers (the source of Middle English *brase* embers, especially as used to roast meat, found in the phrase *in brase,* before 1399, in an early cookbook); of uncertain origin (but compare Swedish *brasa* stake, fire; ultimately perhaps from West Germanic **brasa,* according to the French scholar von Wartburg). Compare BRAZE[2] solder.

brake[1] *n.* device that slows or stops motion (of a wheel, etc.). 1772-82, possibly an extended sense of earlier, and now obsolete, *brake* a bridle or curb (1552), borrowed probably from Middle Low German or Middle Dutch *brake* nose ring to control draft animals, a toothed machine for breaking up flax into fibers (a meaning also known in Middle English about 1450); related to Middle Dutch *breken* to break, which is cognate with Old English *brecan* to BREAK. Alternatively, *brake* may be an application of earlier *brake* a lever or handle for working a device, such as a crossbow (about 1380), or a pump (1626); borrowed from Old French *brac,* a form of *bras* arm from Latin *bracchium;* see BRACE. The OED also suggests a connection by popular etymology with BREAK. —**v.** apply a brake to. 1868, from the noun.

brake[2] *n.* thicket, clump of bushes. About 1440 (in compound *ferne-brake* a fern thicket, in *Promptorium Parvulorum*); later, a clump or thicket of ferns (probably about 1450); borrowed from Middle Low German *brake,* related to *breken* to break (which is cognate with Old English *brecan* to BREAK) and originally meaning tree stumps or broken branches.

brake[3] *n.* bracken. Before 1325, probably a variant of *bracken,* which may have been taken (dialectally) as a plural (as *chick* singular, from *chicken* plural) and thus shortened to *brake.*

bramble *n.* prickly shrub. About 1390 *brambel,* in Chaucer's *Canterbury Tales;* earlier *brembel* (before 1325, in *Cursor Mundi*), and in place names *Brambeley* (about 1128), developed from Old English (about 1000) *brǣmbel,* variant of *brēmel,* from *brōm* BROOM; for suffix see -LE[1].

The *b,* between *m* and *l,* and consequent shortening of the *e,* follows the pattern in English of the development of *thimble, mumble* and even the dialectal *chimbly* for *chimney.*

bran *n.* broken husks of grains. Before 1325, in *Cursor Mundi;* borrowed from Old French *bran, bren,* from a Gaulish word (probably surviving in Vulgar Latin **brennus;* also compare Breton *brenn,* but not recorded in other Celtic languages).

branch *n.* About 1300 *braunche,* borrowed from Old French *braunche, branche,* from Late Latin *branca* paw of an animal, from a Gaulish word of unknown origin. —**v.** Before 1375, in *The Romance of William of Palerne,* from the noun.

brand *n.* Before 1325, northern Middle English *brand,* in *Cursor Mundi;* earlier, *brond* (probably before 1200, in *Ancrene Riwle,* but not fully replaced by *brand* until the 1500's); found in Old English *brond, brand* piece of burning wood, firebrand, blade of a sword, in allusion to its glint (about 725, in *Beowulf*). The Old English is cognate with Old Frisian *brand,* Old High German *brant* brand, sword (modern German *Brand*), and Old Icelandic *brandr* (Swedish, Danish *brand*), from Proto-Germanic **brandaz,* earlier **brandás,* Gothic *brinnan* burn (*bran* in past tense), and thereby related through Proto-Germanic **brenwanan* to Old English *beornan, byrnan* be on fire; see BURN.

The meaning "a sign or mark, as of ownership, made by burning with a hot iron" appeared in 1552; this meaning evolved into "a trademark" applied to goods (1827), and in turn to a particular sort or class of goods, as indicated by the trademark on them (1854).

—**v.** 1422, to set on fire; later, to burn with a hot iron (1440, in *Promptorium Parvulorum*); from the noun.

brandish *v.* wave or shake threateningly. About 1340 *braundishen,* borrowed from Old French *brandiss-,* stem of *brandir,* from *brand, brant* sword, from Frankish (compare Old High German *brant* sword); see BRAND; for suffix see -ISH[2].

brand-new *adj.* About 1570, formed from English *brand* + *new,* apparently as if fresh from the fire (Shakespeare's comparable use was *fire-new,* 1594, in *Richard III,* and *brand-fire-new* is found in American English of the 1800's).

brandy *n.* strong alcoholic liquor. 1657, shortened from earlier *brand-wine, brandy-wine* (1622, in John Fletcher's *The Beggar's Bush*); borrowed from Dutch *brandewijn* burnt (i.e., distilled) wine; cognate with Middle High German *brantwein* (modern German *Branntwein*) and Middle Low German *brannewin.*

brash *adj.* hasty, rash, impetuous. 1824, perhaps connected with the older *brash* fragile, brittle (used to describe timber as early as 1566), possibly in association with *break* and *rash* or *crash;* alternatively, the association may be with earlier *brash* an attack or assault (1573), a Scottish use (compare Gaelic *bras* hasty, impetuous).

brass *n.* yellow metal, an alloy of copper and zinc. Probably about 1200 *brass,* in *The Ormulum,* developed from Old English *bræs,* originally meaning an alloy of copper and tin, now called "bronze" (about 1000, in Ælfric's *Grammar*); of uncertain origin (probably cognate with Old Frisian *bras,* in compound *bras-penning* copper penny, and Middle Low German *bras* metal). **—brassy** *adj.* forward in manner. 1576; later, strident (1865, in writings of Matthew Arnold); formed from English *brass,* n. + *-y*[1].

brat *n.* unpleasant child. About 1505, also in dialects of northern, midlands, and western England meaning "an apron, woman's or child's pinafore, a rag," perhaps a special use of Middle English *brat* coarse garment (about 1395, in Chaucer's *Canterbury Tales*), developed from Old English *bratt* cloak, covering (about 950, in *Lindisfarne Gospels*); probably borrowed from a Celtic source (compare Old Irish *bratt* cloak, cloth, Welsh *brethyn* cloth, Breton *broz* petticoat).

bravado (brəvä′dō) *n.* a great show of boldness. 1583, in writings of Bishop Stubbes wherein is also found the earlier *bravade* (1579), borrowed from French *bravade* bragging, boasting, though *bravado* is assumed to be borrowed from Spanish *bravada, bravata;* both the French and the Spanish were borrowed from Italian *bravata* bragging, boasting, from *bravare* brag, boast, be defiant, from *bravo* BRAVE.

brave *adj.* 1485, in a translation of Caxton's from Middle French, borrowed from Middle French *brave* splendid, valiant, from Italian *bravo* fine, splendid, bold, and from Spanish *bravo* wild, savage, possibly from Latin *barbarus* foreign; see **BARBARIAN**; or possibly through Medieval Latin *bravus* cutthroat, daring villain, from Latin *prāvus* crooked, depraved (since the derivation from Latin *barbarus* is phonetically highly dubious). —v. 1546, borrowed from Middle French *braver* to brave, affront, defy, from *brave.* **—bravery** *n.* 1548, borrowed probably from Middle French *braverie* action of braving, from *braver* to brave.

bravo *interj.* well done! 1761, borrowed from Italian *bravo* fine, splendid; see **BRAVE**. The term may have also been influenced by existence of the earlier English *bravo,* n. 1597, a daring villain.

brawl *v.* quarrel noisily. 1375 (Scottish) *brallen,* in John Barbour's *The Bruce;* later, 1450, in *York Plays;* of uncertain origin (compare Dutch *brallen* to brag, boast, German dialect *brallen* to shout, roar, perhaps from the same ultimate source). **—n.** noisy quarrel. Probably 1445 *braule;* later, before 1460 *brall,* from the verb.

brawn *n.* strong muscles. Before 1325; earlier, carcass of a hog, side of pork (1290); borrowed from Old French *brāon, brāoun* fleshy part suitable for roasting, Old Provençal *brazon* fat on the arm, from Frankish **brādo* ham (compare Old High German *brātan* to roast, modern German *braten,* and *brāt, brāto* meat without bones or fat, Old English *brǣdan* to roast, and Old Icelandic *brǣdha* to melt), from Proto-Germanic **brǣđ-,* from Indo-European **bhrē-* (Pok.133). **—brawny** *adj.* Before 1400, formed from Middle English *brawn* + *-y*[1].

bray *v.* make a loud, harsh sound. About 1303, in Mannyng's *Handlyng Synne,* borrowed from Old French *braire* cry out, from Gallo-Romance **bragere* cry, squall, perhaps from a Celtic source cognate with Latin *frangere* to break (compare Middle Irish *braigid* he breaks wind, Gaelic *bragh* an explosion), from Indo-European **bhreĝ-/bhreg-* (Pok.165). **—n.** Probably before 1300, in *Kyng Alisaunder,* borrowed from Old French *brait,* from *braire* cry out.

braze[1] (brāz) *v.* harden like brass. 1602, in Shakespeare's *Hamlet;* earlier, *brasen* to cover with brass or bronze (before 1400), developed from Old English *brasian* (about 1000, in Ælfric's *Grammar*), probably from *bræs* BRASS, on the analogy of *glass* and *glaze, grass* and *graze.*

braze[2] *v.* solder with brass. 1581, probably borrowed from Middle French *braser* to solder, from Old French *braser* to burn, possibly from, or at least related to, *brese* embers; see **BRAISE**.

It has also been conjectured that *braze*[2] was taken from or influenced by *braze*[1], because it is difficult to establish a semantic link between Old French *braser* to burn and thence to Middle French *braser* and English *braze* to solder.

brazen *adj.* shameless, bold. Probably before 1200 *brasen* made of brass, in *The Ormulum,* developed from Old English (about 1000) *bræsen* made of brass (*bræs* BRASS + *-en*[2]). The current meaning is a figurative extension that arose about 1573 from the idea of having a countenance that is unabashed or hardened like brass. **—v. brazen (out** or **through)** act as if unashamed. Before 1555, in sermons of Bishop Latimer, from the adjective.

brazier[1] (brā′zhər) *n.* metal container to hold burning coals. 1690, borrowed from French *brasier* a pan of hot coals, from Old French *brasier,* from *brese* embers, hot charcoal; see **BRAISE**.

brazier[2] (brā′zhər) *n.* person who works with brass. 1307 *brasier,* formed from *bras,* Middle English form of *brass* + *-ier* (as in *glazier, clothier*).

breach *n.* a breaking, break, gap. 1237-38 *breche,* earlier (1208, in proper name), formed from a fusion of: 1) Old English *brǣc* a breaking, breach (about 750, in compound *unbrǣc* unbroken, unblemished; cognate with Old High German *brācha,* Middle Low German *brāke,* from Proto-Germanic **brǣkō;* related to Old English *bryce* breaking and *brecan* BREAK); and 2) Old French *breche* breach, fracture, from Frankish (compare Old High German *brecha, brehha,* related to *brehhan* BREAK). **—v.** make a breach. 1547, from the noun.

bread *n.* Old English *brēad* bit, piece, morsel (about 950, in *Lindisfarne Gospels*); cognate with Old Frisian *brād,* Old Saxon *brōd,* Old High German *brōt* (modern German *Brot*), Middle Dutch *broot* (modern Dutch *brood*), and Old Icelandic *braudh,* all meaning bread, from Proto-Germanic **brauđan;* related to Old English *brēowan* to BREW, apparently by virtue of the fermenting action of yeast in leavening. In Old English this word was rare (though it is found to refer to food in the compound *bēobrēad,* modern *beebread*); the common word was *hlāf,* which survives in modern LOAF. But by about 1200 *bread* had displaced *loaf* as the name for a piece of the substance. According to the OED, sense development of the word was from "bit, piece," to "piece of bread," to "bread."

The pronunciation of Middle English *bread* (brēd) gradually began to shift in Shakespeare's time until it

was fully established in its modern form (bred) in the middle of the 1700's. Exceptions to this change include *break, great,* and *steak.*
—v. 1629, to cover with bread crumbs; from the noun.

breadth *n.* width. Probably before 1425 *breadeth,* alteration of earlier *brede* breadth (probably before 1300, in *Sir Tristrem*), developed from Old English *brǣd, brǣdu,* from *brād* BROAD. Old English *brǣd, brǣdu* derive from Proto-Germanic **braiđjōn.* The final *-th* was probably added on the analogy of earlier *length.*

break *v.* Early Middle English *breken* (before 1121, in *Peterborough Chronicle*), developed from Old English *brecan* (about 725, in *Beowulf*). The Old English is cognate with Old Frisian *breka,* Old Saxon *brekan,* Old High German *brehhan* to break (modern German *brechen*), Gothic *brikan,* which correspond to Latin *frangere* (perfect tense *frēgī),* and Sanskrit *-bhraj-* breaking out, through the Indo-European base **bhreĝ-* (Pok.165). The relationship to BRAKE[1] device, comes probably by way of popular etymology with *break* in a variety of meanings, such as "to tame an animal" and "to apply force suddenly," through the old past tense *brak* and the late Middle English singular and plural form *brake.* The form *broke* began to appear in the 1500's as a replacement for the Middle English past tense *brak* by influence of the past participle *broken,* which is retained in modern English.

The original short vowel of the present tense and past participle was gradually lengthened in Middle English.
—n. act of breaking, breach. 1296-97 *breck,* from Middle English *breken* to break.

breakfast *n.* 1472 *brekefaste;* earlier variant *breffast* (1463), from the earlier verb phrase *breken faste* (before 1393, in Gower's *Confessio Amantis*), in reference to *break* and *fast*[2], in the sense of ending one's fast of the night before. **—v.** 1679, from the noun, and probably influenced by the earlier verb phrase.

A specific name for the first meal of the day does not appear in Old English glossaries, and some sources refer to French *déjeuner* morning meal (1100's), and to have the morning meal (also 1100's) as a possible source of influence or even loan translation, especially for the verb. This does not seem likely, since, as a noun, English *breakfast* is recognized as a formation from the earlier verb phrase, and, as a verb phrase, of course, already existed on its own.

breast *n.* 1380 *breest,* in sermons of Wycliffe; earlier *brest* (probably about 1200, in *The Ormulum*), developed from Old English *brēost* (about 725, in a version of *Genesis*). The Old English is cognate with Old Frisian *briast* breast, Old Saxon *breost, briost,* Old Icelandic *brjōst* (from Proto-Germanic **breustan*), and Old High German *brust* (modern German *Brust*), Gothic *brusts* breasts (no singular, the form probably representing a dual ending that was later lost). Outside Germanic cognates are found in Old Irish *brū* bosom, Welsh *broa* breast, Russian *brjukho* belly, from Indo-European **bhreus-/bhrus-* (Pok.170).

Old English *ēo* became normally *ee* in Middle English (with the sound of *ee* in *feet*); but in this word Old English *ēo* was shortened in later Middle English to *e* (brest) before the two consonants, so that a spelling showing a "long" vowel remained (*ea* as in *feast, least*) fixed in modern English but reflected the earlier pronunciation, though a variant spelling *brest* was current into the 1700's.

—v. to press on confidently, struggle with. 1599, in Shakespeare's *Henry V,* an extension (possibly by confusion of meaning and closeness of form) of Middle English *bresten* to overcome, conquer (probably before 1200, in Layamon's *Chronicle of Britain*); developed from Old English *berstan* burst and Old Icelandic *bresta.*

breath *n.* Early Middle English *breth* (pronounced *brēth,* and first recorded as *breath,* probably before 1200, in *Ancrene Riwle*), developed from Old English *brǣth* odor, exhalation as of something cooking or burning (before 900, in Alfred's translation of Orosius' *Historia adversus Paganos*). Old English *brǣth* (from Proto-Germanic **brǣthaz)* is cognate with Old High German *brādam* breath, steam (modern German *Brodem* steam); related, through the Indo-European base **bhrē-* to burn, heat (Pok. 133), to Old English *brǣdan* to roast, Old High German *brātan,* Old Icelandic *brædha, brādhna* to melt. **—v. breathe** About 1300 *brethen;* earlier, *breathen* (probably before 1200, in Layamon's *Chronicle of Britain*), from *breth* breath. The verb retains the original Old English "long" vowel (ē); the "long" vowel of the noun was shortened to (e) probably as late as the 1600's (compare the pairs *sheath/sheathe, teeth/teethe*).

breeches (brich′iz) *n.pl.* short trousers. Probably before 1200, in Layamon's *Chronicle of Britain, breches,* a later plural formed from *brech, breche* breeches, developed from Old English (before 1000) *brēc,* plural of *brōc* garment for the legs and trunk (before 900); from Proto-Germanic *brōkiz,* plural of **brōks,* from Indo-European **bhrōĝ-* (Pok.165). Old English *brōc* is cognate with Old High German *bruoh* and Old Icelandic *brōk,* both meaning breeches, originally crotch, from the root of BREAK.

breed *v.* produce (young). Old English *brēdan* bring young to birth, carry (a child), hatch (before 1000, in Ælfric's *Homilies*), from earlier *brœ̄dan* (before 850, in an Old English glossary), from Proto-Germanic **brōđjanan;* related to *brōđ* BROOD. *Breed* and *brood* are related in the same way as *feed, food,* and *bleed, blood.* **—n.** race, stock. 1465 (in compound *breedgoose* goose for breeding), from the verb. **—breeder** *n.* 1531, in Sir Thomas Elyot's *The Boke Named the Governour,* formed from English *breed* + *-er*[1]. **—breeder reactor** (1948) **—breeding** *n.* Before 1325, in *Cursor Mundi,* from *breed,* v. + *-ing*[1]

breeze *n.* 1565 *brise* a northeast wind; later, such a wind applied to the trade winds of the American tropics (1595, in writings of Sir Walter Raleigh), and a gentle wind (1626, in writings of Captain John Smith), apparently borrowed from Old Spanish and Portuguese *briza* (now *brisa*) northeast wind; but compare Italian *brezza* cold wind, French *brize* (now *brise*) a breeze, German *Brise;* of uncertain origin. The slang "something easy to do," appeared in American English about 1928. **—v.** 1907, to move quickly and casually; earlier, to blow gently (1682, implied in participial adjective *breezing*), from *breeze,* n. **—breezy** *adj.* 1718, exposed to breezes, in Pope's translation of the *Iliad;* later, having a carefree manner (1873, in writings of Mark Twain); formed from English *breeze,* n. + *-y*[1].

brevet (brəvet′) *n.* commission promoting an army officer without increase in pay. Before 1376, official message in writing, in *Piers Plowman,* borrowed from Anglo-French *brevet,* Old French *brievet,* diminutive form of *bref, brief* letter; see BRIEF; for suffix see -ET.

breviary (brē′vēer′ē) *n.* book of prescribed prayers. 1547, a summary, borrowed through Old French *breviaire,* or directly from Latin *breviārium,* from neuter of *breviārius* abridged, from *brevis* short, see BRIEF; for suffix see -ARY.

brevity *n.* briefness. 1509 *brevitie,* in Barclay's *The Ship of Fools,* borrowed from Middle French *briéveté* (earlier, *briété*), or directly from Latin *brevitātem,* (nominative *brevitās*), from *brevis* short, see BRIEF; for suffix see -ITY.

brew *v.* make beer, ale, and the like by boiling, fermentation, etc. About 1250 *brewen* (in *The Story of Genesis and Exodus*), developed from Old English *brēowan* (before 900, in Alfred's translation of Orosius' *Historia adversus Paganos*). The Old English is cognate with Old Frisian *briūwa,* Old Saxon *breuwan,* Middle Low German *brūwen,* Old High German *briuwan* to brew, modern German *brauen,* and Old Icelandic *brugga* to brew. Through the Germanic base **breu-* (Indo-European **bhreu-*) the word is also possibly related to Latin *dēfrutum* must (new wine) boiled down, *fermentum* leaven, yeast, *fervēre* to boil, Middle Irish *bruith* to boil, Welsh *berwi* to boil, seethe, and Greek *phréār* a spring, well. The full Indo-European root **bhereu-* (Pok.143) has variants **bheru-, bhreu-, bhrēu-, bhru-,* and *bhruw-.* See also BREAD, BROTH. **—n.** About 1510, from the verb. **—brewer** *n.* 1203-04, formed from Middle English *brewen* + *-er*[1]. **—brewery** *n.* 1166, formed from Middle English *brewen* + *-ery,* later replaced by *breuern,* developed from Old English *brēawern* (*brēaw-,* stem of *brēowan* to brew + *-ern* place). This latter term gradually fell out of use by the 1500's.

bribe *n.* About 1425, in a late version of Chaucer's *Canterbury Tales,* something given to a beggar; later, a gift given to influence corruptly (probably before 1439, in Lydgate's *Falls of Princes*); borrowed from Old French *bribe* morsel of bread given to a beggar, of uncertain origin. A meaning "something extorted or stolen" appeared about 1450. **—v.** About 1390, in Chaucer's *Canterbury Tales,* to extort, steal, borrowed from Old French *briber* to go begging, from Old French *bribe,* n. The meaning "to influence corruptly by giving a gift," is not recorded in English before 1528. **—bribery** *n.* Before 1387, in Trevisa's translation of Higden's *Polychronicon,* borrowed from Old French *briberie* mendicancy, or perhaps formed from Middle English *briber* a vagabond, strolling vagrant (earlier *bribour,* also in Trevisa's translation cited above) + *-y*[3].

The origin of Old French *bribe, briber* is in dispute. Bloch and Wartburg state it is of onomatopoeic origin. Corominas thinks the word spread from Spain with pilgrims and beggars who went to France (though French *bribe* is attested earlier than the Spanish form).

bric-a-brac or **bric-à-brac** *n.* knickknacks, trinkets. 1840, in Thackeray's *Paris Sketch Book,* borrowed from French *bric-à-brac,* perhaps related to the phrase *à bric et à brac* any old way.

brick *n.* block used in building. 1416 *bryke,* borrowed from Middle Dutch *bricke* a tile, brick; cognate with Middle Low German *bricke* disk, plate, Old Danish *bricke* wooden plate.

The Middle French *brique* a form of loaf, from Old French *brique, briche* is probably derived from Middle Low German *bricke* or a Frankish word.

The English *brickel* brittle, brittle candy, is not related but is instead derived through Middle English *brekil* from *brekken* to break, developed from Old English *brecan* to break.
—v. 1648, from the noun. **—bricklayer** *n.* (1443) **— brickwork** *n.* (1580)

bridal *n.* wedding celebration. About 1200 *bridale,* in *The Ormulum,* developed from late Old English *brȳdealo* wedding feast (about 1075, in *Anglo-Saxon Chronicle,* a compound of *brȳd* bride + *ealo* ale, because ale was drunk at such feasts).

In the 1500's the spelling adopted final *-al* or *-all,* reflecting the loss of the "long" a (ā) sound, and with it a loss of the sense of "ale." The word then became thought of as *bride* + *-al*[2] (noun suffix), as in *espousal,* and later as if from *bride* + *-al*[1] (adjective suffix), as in *nuptial,* which gradually led to the use of *bridal* as an adjective. **—adj.** nuptial. 1748, from the noun, but earlier as an attributive of *bridale* in the form *bridall* (1596, in Spenser's *Faerie Queene*).

bride *n.* Probably before 1200 *brid, brude,* in *Ancrene Riwle* and Layamon's *Chronicle of Britain,* developed from Old English *brȳd* (about 725, in *Beowulf*). The Old English is cognate with Old Frisian *breid,* Old Saxon *brūd,* Old High German *brūt* bride (modern German *Braut),* Old Icelandic *brūdhr* bride, young woman, and Gothic *brūths* daughter-in-law (*brūth-* bride, in *brūth-faths* bridegroom), from Proto-Germanic **brūđiz.* The word is unknown outside Germanic. **—bridegroom** *n.* 1526 *bridegrome,* in Tyndale's translation of the Bible; an alteration (influenced by *grome* groom, boy, lad) of earlier *bridegome* (before 1300), and *bridgume* (probably about 1200); developed from Old English *brȳdguma* (about 750, in Cynewulf's *Juliana,* a compound of *brȳd* bride + *guma* man); see BRIDE, GROOM. The Old English compound is cognate with Old Saxon *brūdigumo* bridegroom, Old Frisian *breidgoma,* Old High German *brūtigomo* (modern German *Bräutigam*), and Old Icelandic *brūdhgumi,* from Proto-Germanic **brūđizumōn.*

bridge[1] *n.* structure built over a river, road, etc. Before 1114 *brigge,* in *Peterborough Chronicle,* developed from Old English *brycg* (about 1000, in Ælfric's *Grammar*); cognate with Old Frisian *bregge, brigge,* Old High German *brucca* bridge (modern German *Brücke*), Old Icelandic *bryggja* gangway (from Proto-Germanic **bruȝjō*), also *brū* bridge, and probably with Old Slavic *brŭvŭno* beam, Gaulish *brīva* bridge, from Indo-European **bhrēu-/bhrū-*(Pok.173). **—v.** 1375 (Scottish) *briggen,* developed from Old English *brycgian* (probably about 750, in *Andreas*), from *brycg,* n., bridge.

bridge[2] *n.* card game similar to whist. Possibly 1843 (though the citation is of undetermined application), probably alteration (influenced by *bridge*[1]) of *biritch,* a word of unknown origin. The word *biritch* appeared in a pamphlet "Biritch, or Russian whist" (London, 1886), in which *biritch* was a call of "no trumps." The game, played in the Near East in 1870's, does not appear at that time in any other language except possibly in Turkish **bir-üc* one, three (advanced as a theoretical explanation that describes the play: one player showing his hand, the other three making tricks with it).

bridle *n.* head part of a harness. About 1175, found in Old English *brīdel* (before 900, in Alfred's translations), earlier *brīdels* (about 750, in Cynewulf's *Elene*), and *brigdels,* (probably about 700); related to *bregdan* move quickly, see BRAID; for suffix see -LE[1].

The word is found in other West Germanic lan-

guages; compare Old Frisian *bridel,* Middle Low German and Middle Dutch *breidel,* Old High German and Middle High German *brittel,* from Proto-Germanic **breʒđilaz.*
—**v.** curb or restrain. Probably before 1200, in *Ancrene Riwle,* developed from Old English *(ge)brīdlian* (before 900, in Alfred's translations); probably from Old English *brīdel* bridle, n.

brief *adj.* short. Probably before 1300 *bref,* in *Arthour and Merlin,* borrowed through Old French *bref, brief,* and directly from Latin *brevis* short; cognate with Greek *brachýs* short, Avestan *mǝrǝzu-* short, and Gothic *gamaúrgjan* cut short, from Indo-European **mreĝhu-/mr̥ĝhu-* (Pok.750). —**n.** short statement; summary. Before 1338 *bref* a letter, in Mannyng's *Chronicle of England,* borrowed through Old French *bref, brief,* and directly from Late Latin *breve* (genitive *brevis*) letter, summary, originally in *breve scriptum* short written note, from Latin *breve* (neuter of *brevis* short). This word passed from the official Latin used in European countries into all the Germanic languages, except perhaps Old English, where it is not recorded, and where it entered only later into Middle English. Germanic cognates include Old Frisian and Old Saxon *bref,* Old High German *briaf* (modern German *Brief*), and Old Icelandic *brēf,* all meaning letter. —**v.** 1837, put (information) in the form of a lawyer's brief; later, to give information (1866); from the noun.

brier[1] or **briar**[1] *n.* thorny bush. Probably before 1200 *brer,* in *Ancrene Riwle,* developed from Old English (about 1000) *brǣr* (West Saxon), *brēr* (Anglian), of unknown origin.

The OED says it is hard to account for the modern spelling *brier,* but that it is parallel to *friar, frier* which developed from Middle English *frere* about the same time. *Briar* is a later variant.

brier[2] or **briar**[2] *n.* heath whose root is used in making pipes. 1868, borrowed from French *bruyère* (dialectal *brière*) heath, heath plant, from Old French *bruyere,* from Gallo-Romance **brūcāria,* from **brūcus* heather, from Gaulish (compare Breton *brug* heath, and Welsh *brwg* a thicket). The sense of a pipe made from this root appeared in English in 1882.

brig *n.* 1720, short for *brigantine;* later, a square-rigged ship with two masts. The sense of a place of detention (1852) is of obscure origin, possibly because such ships were originally used as prison ships.

brigade *n.* part of an army. 1637, borrowed from French *brigade* (since 1300's), from Italian *brigata* company, crew, from *brigare* to brawl, fight, from *briga* strife; possibly of Germanic origin (compare Gothic *brikan* to BREAK). —**brigadier** *n.* military officer. 1678, probably borrowed from French *brigadier* formerly meaning "a military officer," from *brigade,* though possibly also formed in English from *brigade* + *-ier.*

brigand (brig'ǝnd) *n.* robber, bandit. Probably before 1400 *bregaund, in Morte Arthur;* earlier, *brigant* (probably before 1387, in Trevisa's translation of Higden's *Polychronicon*); borrowed from Old French *brigand* (originally) foot-soldier, from Italian *brigante* trooper, skirmisher, from *brigare;* see BRIGADE.

brigantine (brig'ǝntēn) *n.* a ship with two masts. 1553 (probably influenced by later French spelling *brigantin*), but earlier *brigandyn* (1525), borrowed from Middle French *brigandin,* from Italian *brigantino* perhaps meaning "skirmishing vessel, a pirate ship," from *brigante* skirmisher, pirate, brigand, from *brigare* fight; see BRIGAND and BRIGADE; for suffix see -INE[1].

bright *adj.* Before 1325 *bright,* in *Cursor Mundi;* earlier *briht* (probably before 1200, in Layamon's *Chronicle of Britain*), developed from Old English *bryht* (about 1000), by metathesis of an altered form *beorht* (before 900, in writings of Alfred) and *berht* (before 830, in the *Vespasian Psalter*); earlier in names *Erconbercht* (before 800) and *Erconberct* (about 737). The Old English is cognate with Old Saxon *berht, beraht,* Old High German *beraht* bright, Middle High German *berht* (surviving in the altered form of modern German proper names *Albrecht,* etc.), Old Icelandic *bjartr* Gothic *baírhts* (from Proto-Germanic **berHtaz*), and the root of Sanskrit *bhrā́jate* it shines, from Indo-European **bherǝg-/bhrēĝh-* shine (Pok.139). —**adv.** Before 1385 bright, in Chaucer's *Canterbury Tales;* earlier *brighte,* developed from Old English *beorhte* (about 725, in *Beowulf*). —**brighten** *v.* Before 1450 *bryghten;* earlier *brihten* (probably before 1200, in *Ancrene Riwle*), possibly developed from Old English *gebrehtnian* to shine (about 950, in *Lindisfarne Gospels*), and Anglian *gebrihtan* to make bright; or the word may be, according to the OED, a new formation of modern English from *bright* + *-en*[1] (1583), though *brihtin* appears in Middle English (probably before 1200, in *Ancrene Riwle*).

brilliant *adj.* 1681, borrowed from French *brillant* shining, present participle of *briller* to shine, from Italian *brillare* to glitter, probably from obsolete *brillo* brilliant, imitation diamond, from *berillo* beryl, from Latin *bēryllus* BERYL.

The English spelling *-lli-* represents the former sound of French *-ll-.*

—**brilliance** *n.* 1755, formed from English *brilliant* + *-ance.*

brim *n.* Probably before 1200 *brimme* edge of the sea, coast, in Layamon's *Chronicle of Britain;* of uncertain origin, but related to Middle High German *brem* and Old Icelandic *barmr,* both meaning edge (and the Old Icelandic being itself cognate with German *Berme,* Dutch *berm,* and English *berm*), from Indo-European **bhrem-, *bhrom-, bhorm-* (Pok.142).

The form was perhaps influenced by Old English *brim* sea, surf (about 725, in *Beowulf*); cognate with Old Icelandic *brim* sea, surf.

brimstone *n.* sulfur. About 1250 *brimeston;* earlier, *brynstan* (1125), literally, burn-stone (*brin-,* stem of *brinnen* to BURN + *stan, ston* STONE); compare Old Icelandic *brennusteinn, brennisteinn,* Dutch *barnsteen,* German *Bernstein,* of similar formation, all meaning "amber."

brindled *adj.* gray or tawny with dark streaks or spots. 1678, alteration of earlier *brinded* (1589), probably by influence of such words as *kindled, mingled,* etc.; *brinded* was an alteration of earlier *brended,* found in Middle English *brend* brown color, horse of this color (about 1426, and in surname *Brendeskyn,* 1262) noun use of past participle of *brennen* to BURN. —**brindle** *adj.* 1676; *n.* 1696, apparently shortening of *brindled,* adj. though the record is wanting in listing the dates.

brine *n.* salty water. Before 1325, in *Cursor Mundi,* found in Old English *brȳne* (before 1000, in Ælfric's *Glossary*); of unknown origin, but cognate with Middle Dutch *brīne* brine. —**briny** *adj.* 1608, formed from English *brine* + *-y*[1].

bring *v.* Old English *bringan* (about 725, in *Beowulf*); cognate with Old Frisian *bringa, brenga* to bring, Old Saxon *brengian,* Old High German *bringan* (modern German *bringen*), Gothic *bringan,* from Proto-Germanic **brenganan,* and with Welsh *he-brwng* to conduct, from Indo-European **bhrenk-/bhronk-* (Pok. 168).

Old English had an infrequent past participle *brungen* (found in modern dialectal *brung*) to which has been added *brang* (found in dialect and children's speech), on analogy of so-called strong verbs, such as *ring: ring, rang, rung.*

brink *n.* edge or border. Probably about 1225, in *King Horn,* Middle English *brinke* seashore, bank of a stream, borrowed probably from a Scandinavian source (compare Danish *brink* edge, and Old Icelandic *brekka* steep hill, with *-kk-* from *-nk,* from Proto-Germanic **brenkōn*); cognate with Middle Low German *brink* edge, and Middle Dutch *brinc* (modern Dutch *brink*), from Indo-European **bhreng-* (Pok.167). The word does not appear in Old English, but in sense is parallel to *brim.*

briquette *n.* block of coal or charcoal dust. 1883, borrowed as French *briquette,* diminutive form of French *brique* BRICK; for suffix see -ETTE.

brisk *adj.* quick and active. 1560; of uncertain origin (perhaps a variant of BRUSQUE, as a gloss given by Cotgrave in his *Dictionary of the French and English Tongues,* the two words, according to the OED, appearing to have influenced each other in early use). The word in several senses was used by Shakespeare.

brisket *n.* breast of an animal. 1338 *brusket;* cognate with Middle High German *brūsche* lump, swelling, and Old Icelandic *brjōsk* gristle, related to *brjōst* BREAST; for suffix see -ET.

The Old French *bruschet, brichet* is widely attested (Normandy, Anjou, Poitou, Maine, and Vendôme) as early as 1385, and may have been borrowed from English, but is more likely a borrowing from Scandinavian.

bristle *n.* stiff hair. Probably before 1300, in *Kyng Alisaunder,* Middle English *brustel, bristel,* developed, with diminutive form *-el,* from Old English (about 700) *byrst* bristle, by transposition of *r* (metathesis), and possibly even found in Old English **brystl,* which would have been a direct source of the Middle English form. Old English *byrst* is cognate with Old High German *burst* bristle (modern German *Borste*), Old Icelandic *burst* bristle, and Sanskrit *bhṛṣṭí-s* point, peak, border, edge, from Indo-European **bhṛstí-s;* also cognate with Latin *fastīgium* top, peak, and Old Irish *barr* point, peak, from the Indo-European base **bhars-* (Pok.109); for suffix see -LE[1]. —*v.* stand stiff or up straight. 1480 *brustelen,* in Caxton's translation of Ovid's *Metamorphoses;* from the noun.

britches *n.pl.* 1905, in writings of H.G. Wells, modern English *britches,* originally an old variant of *breeches,* also spelled *briches* (1727) and found in *britch* (1630).

British *adj.* of Great Britain or its people. Old English *Brittisc, Brettisc, Bryttisc* of or relating to the ancient Britons (before 855, in *Anglo-Saxon Chronicle*), developed from *Brittas, Brettas, Bryttas* natives of ancient Britain, the Britons; see BRITON. The word acquired its current sense shortly before 1387.

Briton *n.* native of Great Britain. Before 1387, in Trevisa's translation of Higden's *Polychronicon,* Middle English *Briton;* earlier *Bretoun* (probably before 1300) and *Brutun* (probably before 1200, in Layamon's *Chronicle of Britain*) one of the Celtic people who occupied Britain to the southern part of Scotland before the Anglo-Saxons; borrowed through Anglo-French *Bretun, britun, bruton,* and Anglo-Latin (plural) *Brittonēs,* from Latin *Brittō* (from the Celtic name of the people).

The forms in Middle English, Anglo-French, and Anglo-Latin were generally reshaped through the influence of Old English *Brittas* and its variants; see BRITISH. The word acquired its current sense after the union of England and Scotland in 1707.

brittle *adj.* easily broken. Before 1382 *britil* easily broken, feeble, in the Wycliffe Bible; earlier, *brotil* (probably before 1325), developed through Old English *bryttian* tear to pieces, shatter, from Proto-Germanic **brutilo-,* also the source of Old English *brēotan* to break; cognate with Old High German *brōdi* fragile, and Old Icelandic *brjōta* to break from Proto-Germanic **breutanan,* from Indo-European **bhreu-d-/bhrou-d-/bhru-d-* (Pok.169); for suffix see -LE[2]. The vowel in Middle English *brotil,* however, suggests development from Old English *brēotan* + suffix *-le*[2], and two words fused in later Middle English *britil* may actually be the case here.

broach *n.* pointed tool. About 1310 *broche* skewer, spit; earlier, an ornament, clasp (probably before 1200, in *Ancrene Riwle,* as an older variant of Middle English *brooch*); borrowed from Old French *broche* a spit, awl, pointed tool, from Vulgar Latin **brocca* pointed tool, originally feminine of Latin *broccus* projecting, having projecting teeth, perhaps of Gaulish origin (compare Gaelic *brog* awl and Welsh *broch* badger). —*v.* begin to talk about. 1579, figurative use of the earlier verb *brochen* to pierce (about 1380), as in broaching a new cask in order to insert a bung, and to spur or to charge into action (before 1338); probably from the noun, but influenced by Old French *brochier* to spur.

broad *adj.* wide across. Probably before 1200, in Layamon's *Chronicle of Britain,* Middle English *brod,* developed from Old English *brād* (about 725, in *Beowulf*); earlier, in compound *brādlāstæcus* a broadax (about 700). The Old English is cognate with Old Frisian and Old Saxon *brēd* broad, Middle Dutch *breet, breed* (modern Dutch *breed*), Old High German and modern German *breit,* Old Icelandic *breidhr,* and Gothic *braiths,* from Proto-Germanic **braiđaz;* no related words are known outside Germanic.

The vowel sound in words such as *boat* and *road* represents a pronunciation today associated with "long" *o,* which developed in the 1500's and 1600's from a Middle English pronunciation approximating the sound associated with the *a* of present-day *call.* However, *broad* retained the Middle English pronunciation "possibly. . .on account of [the influence] of a shortened [variant] form, now extinct; the shortening would naturally occur before consonant groups, as in *broadly, broadcloth. . .*but would by no means be unparalleled before *d* (compare *dead*)"—*Jesperson.*

—**broaden** *v.* 1726, implied in past participle *broadened,* formed from English *broad,* adj. + *-en*[1]. —**broadcloth** *n.* (about 1412) —**broadcast** *v.* 1813, formed from English *broad* wide across + *cast,* v., on the basis of earlier *broadcast,* adj. (of seeds) scattered (1767), itself formed from *broad,* adj. + *cast,* past participle. —*n.* 1796, developed from *broadcast,* adj. The meaning (noun and verb) relating to transmission of radio waves is first recorded in 1921.

brocade *n.* cloth with raised designs. 1563-99, in Hakluyt's *Voyages,* borrowed from Spanish *brocado,* from Catalan *brocat,* corresponding to Italian *broccato* embossed cloth, originally past participle of *broccare* to stud, set with nails, from *brocco* small nail, protruding tooth, sprout, from Latin *broccus* having projecting teeth, see BROACH; for suffix see -ADE. However, the Spanish scholar Corominas maintains that Catalan *brocat,* probably of Celtic origin, is the source of Italian *broccato.* Bloch and Wartburg cite Middle French *brocat* (1549), earlier *brocart* (1519), from Italian *broccato* with a change in suffix.

broccoli *n.* green vegetable. 1699, borrowed from Italian *broccoli,* plural of *broccolo* cabbage, sprout, diminutive form of *brocco* sprout, shoot, protruding tooth, from Latin *broccus* having projecting teeth; see BROACH. Earlier French *brocoli* (1560), also borrowed from the Italian, was apparently not influential in introducing *broccoli* into English, as corroborated by the identity of the English and Italian spellings.

brochure *n.* pamphlet. 1748, borrowed from French *brochure* a stitched work (because originally these were pages stitched together), from *brocher* to stitch, from Old French *brocher* to prick, from *broche* pointed tool, awl, see BROACH; for suffix see -URE.

brogue[1] *n.* a strongly marked pronunciation or accent, especially one peculiar to Irish. 1705, of uncertain origin. Most sources conjecture that it is a special use of *brogue*[2] stout shoe worn by Irish or Scottish highlanders, and therefore originally in the sense of "speech characteristic of those who call their shoes brogues." This may be pure fancy.

brogue[2] *n.* stout shoe made with perforated decorations. 1586, rough, stout shoe worn by the rural Irish and by Scottish highlanders, borrowed from Irish *bróg* or Gaelic *bròg* shoe, from Old Irish *brōce* shoe. In a later, but now obsolete sense of hose, trouser (1615, in plural), this word was probably confused with Old English *brōc* and Old Icelandic *brōk* garment for the legs and trunk; see BREECHES.

broil[1] *v.* cook on fire, grill. About 1387-95, in Chaucer's *Canterbury Tales,* Middle English *broillen;* earlier *brulen* (about 1350); borrowed from Old French *bruller,* earlier *brusler* to burn, alteration (by influence of Germanic *br-,* as in Old High German *brant* BRAND and *brinnan* to BURN), of Latin *ustulāre* to scorch, from *ustus,* past participle of *ūrere* to burn, cognate with Sanskrit *óṣati* (it) burns, and Greek *heúein* to singe, from Indo-European **eus-* (Pok.347).

The vowel shift in Middle English from *brulen* to *broillen* is paralleled by Middle English *fullen, foilen* to foil, borrowed from Old French *fouler* to trample, and by English *reculen, recoilen* to recoil, borrowed from Old French *reculer.*

broil[2] *v.* engage in a quarrel, fight. 1402, mix up, present in disorder, borrowed through Anglo-French *broiller* mix up, confuse, Old French *bröoillier,* from *breu, bro* broth, brew, from Frankish (compare Old High German *brod* broth); see BROTH. **—n.** quarrel, fight. 1525, from the verb.

broker *n.* person who buys and sells stock. About 1378 *brokour* commercial agent, middleman; earlier *Brokur* (1260 as surname), borrowed through Anglo-French *abrokur, brocour* retailer of wine, tapster; also, a broker, from Old North French *brokeor,* variant of Old French *brocheor,* from *brochier* to tap, pierce (a keg), from *broche* pointed tool; see BROACH.

bromide *n.* drug used to calm. 1836, formed from English *brom(ine)* + *-ide.* The pair *bromine/bromide* is parallel in construction to Sir Humphry Davy's *chlorine/chloride* (about 1816). The figurative sense of "a dull, conventional person or a trite saying" was popularized by the American humorist Gelett Burgess (1866-1951) in his book *Are You A Bromide?* (1906). **—bromidic** *adj.* trite. American English, 1906 (in work cited above), formed from *bromide* + *-ic.*

bromine *n.* chemical element that gives off an irritating vapor. 1827, formed in English from French *brome* (from Greek *brômos* bad smell, stench) + English *-ine*[2].

bronchi (brong′kī) *n.pl.* of **bronchus.** the branching tubes of the windpipe. 1782, New Latin plural of *bronchus,* from Late Latin *bronchus* windpipe, from Greek *brónchos* windpipe, throat. *Bronchi* is parallel with older *bronchia* (1674), borrowed from Late Latin *bronchia* the bronchial tubes, from Greek *brónchia,* perhaps related to *bróxai* to gulp down, cognate with English *craw,* from Indo-European **gwrogh-* (Pok.475). **—bronchial** *adj.* Before 1735, probably formed from English or New Latin *bronchia* + *-al*[1], also found in New Latin *bronchialis,* from Late Latin *bronchium* branch of the bronchi in the lungs. It is also possible the word was borrowed immediately from earlier French *bronchial* (1666). **—bronchitis** *n.* inflammation of bronchial tubes. Before 1814, New Latin (introduced in 1808 by Charles Badham), formed from *bronchi, bronchia* + *-itis* inflammation.

bronco (brong′kō) *n.* wild or half tamed horse. Probably 1850, American English, borrowed from American Spanish *bronco,* from Spanish *bronco* rough (applied to wood), rude, and, as a noun meaning "a knot in wood."

According to the Spanish scholar Corominas, the Spanish was derived from Vulgar Latin **bruncus* knot, projection, apparently a blend of Latin *broccus* projecting, and *truncus* trunk of a tree.

bronze *n.* brown alloy of copper and tin. Before 1721, in Prior's *Alma,* work of art done in bronze, borrowed from French *bronze* from Italian *bronzo* bell metal, brass, of uncertain origin (possibly from Latin *aes Brundisium* copper of Brundisium, ancient seaport in southeastern Italy).

The concept of *bronze* as an alloy of copper and tin was not differentiated in Middle English vocabulary from *brass* an alloy of copper and zinc, for both alloys were described by Middle English *bras,* a word that is recorded as early as 1200, in *The Ormulum.* This is not surprising, as the ancient alloying was often achieved by mixing in tin, lead, zinc, etc., with copper without distinction. Though bronze is the oldest alloy known to man, the noun *bronze* was not introduced into English before the 1700's, when it was used in reference to the material of ancient works of art.

—v. make or become like bronze. 1645, in John Evelyn's *Memoirs,* borrowed from French *bronzer,* from French *bronze,* n.

Since Middle English also had a verb use *brasen* to make (something) out of, or cover with plates of copper alloy (before 1400), it is not surprising that the new word *bronze* is recorded in English as a verb 75 years before it is recorded as a noun.

brooch (brōch) *n.* ornamental pin. Before 1382, in the

Wycliffe Bible, Middle English *brooch;* earlier *brouche* (before 1333) and *broche* (probably before 1200, in *Ancrene Riwle*); see BROACH. This is the same word as *broach* (with specialized meaning), which accounts for the first pronunciation (brōch); but the spelling pronunciation (brüch) has also gained currency, perhaps aided by the Scottish and Northern English dialectal pronunciation (compare Yorkshire and Scottish *bruche* of the 1400's).

brood *n.* the young of birds, etc. Before 1387, in Trevisa's translation of Higden's *Polychronicon,* Middle English *brood;* earlier *brod* (before 1250, in *The Owl and The Nightingale*), developed from Old English *brōd* (about 1000, in works of Ælfric), from Proto-Germanic *brōđ-; cognate with Middle Dutch *broet* (modern Dutch *broed*), Old High German *bruot* heat, warmth, brood (modern German *Brut* brood), appearing in English with formative *-d* from the Proto-Germanic base **brō-* to warm, heat, from Indo-European *bhrō- (Pok. 133).—**v.** sit on to hatch. 1440, in *Promptorium Parvulorum,* Middle English *brodyn,* from the noun. The figurative meaning "to meditate moodily or closely" from the idea of nursing (anger or some other emotion) appears in 1571.

brook[1] *n.* small stream. Probably before 1200, in Layamon's *Chronicle of Britain,* Middle English *brok,* developed from Old English (about 847) *brōc,* originally, a strong, flowing stream. The Old English is cognate with Middle Dutch and modern Dutch *broek,* Middle Low German *brōk* and Low German *brook* marsh, pool, Old High German *bruoh* marshy ground, morass (modern German *Bruch* marsh, bog, fen), from Proto-Germanic **brōka-,* cognate with Old Irish *meirc* rust, and Welsh *merydd* damp, from Indo-European **merəĝ-/mrōĝ-* (Pok.740).

brook[2] *v.* tolerate. 1530, in Palsgrave's *Lesclarcissement;* earlier in Middle English *bruken, broken* to use, enjoy (probably before 1200, in Layamon's *Chronicle of Britain*); developed from Old English (about 950) *bruccan;* earlier *brūcan* (about 725, in *Beowulf*). The word is cognate with Old Saxon *brūkan* to use, Old Frisian *brūka,* Old Icelandic *brūka* (Swedish *bruka* use, be accustomed to), Middle Dutch *brūken* to use, Old High German *brūhhan* (modern German *brauchen),* Gothic *brūkjan* to use, enjoy, from Proto-Germanic **brūk-* to make use of, enjoy, corresponding to Indo-European **bhrūg-* (Pok.173), represented in Latin *fruī* to use, enjoy, ultimately the source of English *fruit.*

The meaning "tolerate" is thought of as a figurative extension of the earlier meaning "to stomach, digest," as in "So fat that men can hardly brook them (1598)."

broom *n.* 1346, *brome* implement for sweeping, originally made of twigs of a shrub abundant in Britain and also called *broom,* Middle English *brom* (probably about 1125); developed from Old English *brōm* the shrub (about 700, in Old English glossaries). The word is cognate with Old High German *brāmo, brāma* bramble (modern German *Brom-,* in the compound *Brombeere* blackberry), Middle Dutch *brāme* bramble (modern Dutch *braam* bramble), and Old Saxon *brāmal-* bramble, in the compound *brāmalbusk* blackberry bush, from Proto-Germanic **brǣma-z,* from Indo-European **bhrēmo-s* (Pok.142). Related to BRAMBLE. —**v.** sweep with a broom. 1838, from the noun. —**broomstick** *n.* 1683, concurrent with, but eventually replacing, earlier *broomstaff* (1613, in Shakespeare's *Henry VIII*).

broth *n.* thin soup. Old English (before 1000); cognate with Old High German *brod* broth, Old Icelandic *brodh,* from Proto-Germanic **bruthan,* related to Old English *brēowan* to BREW. The Medieval Latin *brodum, brodium* was a borrowing of the Old High German *brod* and is the origin of this term in Old French (*breu*), Italian (*brodo*), and other Romance languages.

brothel *n.* Before 1593, house of prostitution; by confusion of Middle English *bordel* (also *bordel house*), house of prostitution (about 1300), and *brothel's house* wherein *brothel* had the meaning prostitute (1493); earlier, a worthless, abandoned person (1376, in *Piers Plowman*), from *brothen* ruined, degenerate (probably before 1325), developed from Old English *brothen,* past participle of *brēothan* go to ruin, from Proto-Germanic **breuthanan,* variant of **breutanan* to break; see BRITTLE.

brother *n.* Before 1121, in *Peterborough Chronicle,* developed from Old English *brōthor* (about 725, in *Beowulf*). One of the classic words of Indo-European etymology whose cognates have been traced in a wide variety of languages, including the Germanic group of Old Frisian *brōther* brother, Middle Dutch and modern Dutch *broer,* Old Saxon *brōthar,* Old High German *bruoder* and modern German *Bruder,* Old Icelandic *brōdhir,* and Gothic *brōthar,* from Proto-Germanic **brōthar.* Outside Germanic cognates appear in the Celtic languages, including Old Irish *brāthair* and Welsh *brawd* with the plural *brodyr;* the Italic languages, including Latin *frāter,* Oscan *fratrúm* (genitive plural), and Umbrian *frater* brothers; the Hellenic languages, of which the principal form is found in Greek *phrā́tēr* clansman, member of a brotherhood; the Baltic languages, including Old Prussian *brāti* and Lithuanian *broterẽlis;* the Slavic languages, including Old Slavic *bratrŭ, bratŭ* and Russian *brat';* the Indo-Iranian languages, including Old Persian *brātā* (accusative *brātaram*) and Sanskrit *bhrā́tā* (accusative *bhrā́taram*); and Tocharian A *pracar* and Tocharian B *procer,* from Indo-European **bhrā́ter-* (Pok.163).

The special plural *brethren* appeared in early Middle English, before 1200, and became standard until *brothers* replaced it in the 1600's. *Brethren* then acquired the specialized meaning of fellow members of a church, sect, etc.

—**brotherhood** *n.* (probably about 1300) —**brother-in-law** *n.* (probably before 1300) —**brotherly** *adj.* (about 1325)

brouhaha (brü'hähä) *n.* confused uproar. 1890, in Oliver Wendell Holmes' *Over the Tea-cups,* borrowed from French *brouhaha* (1552), of uncertain origin. Bloch and Wartburg suggest as a possible source the Hebrew phrase *bārūkh habbā'* blessed be the one who comes, used in Synagogue prayers and as a greeting at Jewish weddings and other public occasions; parallel instances occur in Italian dialect of Arezzo *barruccaba* confusion, disorder, derived from the Hebrew phrase, and Italian *badani* noise of people chattering, derived from Hebrew *ānnā 'adōnāi* Oh Lord, found in prayers.

brow *n.* forehead. Middle English (usually in the plural) before 1325 *browes, brues* brow, forehead; also eyebrows; earlier *brouwes* (about 1300) and *bruwen* (probably before 1200, in Layamon's *Chronicle of Britain*), developed from Old English *brū,* probably originally "eyebrow," but extended at an early date to "eyelash" and then to "eyelid," by association of the hair of the eyebrow with the hair of the eyelid, the eyebrow then becoming Old English *ofer-brūa* "over-brows" along with the unrelated form *brǣw* (West Saxon).

The earliest recorded meanings in Middle English (probably before 1200) refer to the eyelid and to movement of the eyebrows or forehead that shows emotion or attitude. The general word for "eyebrow" in Middle English was *brew, breowen* (probably before 1200, in Layamon's *Chronicle of Britain*), developed from West Saxon *brǣw;* cognate with Old Frisian *brē* in *āg-brē* eyebrow, Old Saxon *brāwa, brāha,* Middle Dutch *brauwe, brouwe* eyelid, Old High German *brāwa* eyebrow, and Old Icelandic *brā* eyebrow.

Old English *brū,* from the Proto-Germanic base **brū-* that was lost in some Germanic languages but retained in others, is cognate with Old Icelandic *brūn,* and through **bhrū-s* (Pok.172) with Greek *ophrȳ́s,* Old Slavic *brŭvĭ,* Lithuanian *bruvis,* and Sanskrit *bhrū́-s,* all meaning eyebrow. Middle English *browe* also meaning "brow of a hill" is closely related to Middle English *brō* bank of a stream, and thence to Old Icelandic *brā* eyelash.

—browbeat *v.* to bully. 1581, formed from English *brow + beat.*

brown *adj.* Probably before 1300, in *Kyng Alisaunder,* Middle English *broun;* earlier *Brunloc* brown-haired (before 1130, in surname), developed from Old English *brūn* (about 700, in glossaries). The Old English is cognate with Old Frisian *brūn* brown, Middle Dutch *bruun* (modern Dutch *bruin*), Old High German *brūn* (modern German *braun*), Old Icelandic *brūnn* (Swedish *brun,* Danish *brun*), all from Proto-Germanic **brūnəz-;* and through the Indo-European base **bhrū-* (Pok. 136) cognate with Greek *phrȳ́nē* toad (originally descriptive of its brown color) and Sanskrit *babhrú-s* reddish-brown (also, as a noun meaning beaver or large mongoose); compare BEAR[1] animal, and BEAVER. **—n.** About 1300, in *Havelok the Dane,* Middle English *browne,* from the adjective. **—v.** Probably before 1300, in *Kyng Alisaunder,* Middle English *brounen,* from the adjective.

The Germanic word was adopted in Medieval Latin as *brunus,* by Italian, Spanish, and Portuguese as *bruno,* and by Provençal and French as *brun.* **—brownstone** *n.* (1836, American English)**—brown sugar** (1704)

brownie *n.* a friendly goblin. 1513, formed as a diminutive (Scottish) of English *brown;* for suffix see -IE.

browse *v.* feed on grass, graze. 1523, probably borrowed from Middle French *brouster* (modern French *brouter*), from Old French *broster* to sprout, bud, from *brost* sprout, shoot, probably from a Germanic source (compare Middle High German *broz* a bud, Old Saxon *brustian* to sprout, from Indo-European **bhreus-/ bhrus-,* Pok.171).

In English the loss of the final *-t* in the Middle French word is difficult to explain, unless *broust* appeared in English and was perhaps considered the past participle, so that *brouse* (which is recorded) was the infinitive, etc.

The figurative meaning "to look through a book casually" first appeared in American English in Lowell's *Among My Books* (1870).

bruin *n.* bear. 1481, in Caxton's translation of *Reynard the Fox,* borrowed from Middle Dutch *Bruin, Bruun,* the name of the bear in the Dutch version of the fable *Reynard the Fox,* literally meaning "Brown," from *bruun* brown; cognate with Old English *brūn* BROWN.

A parallel instance occurs in French, in which *reynard,* from this Medieval epic, has become the word for *fox.*

bruise *v.* injure. Probably before 1200 *brisen* (also, in surname *Brusebarre,* 1203), and gradually after about 1300 *bruse,* and later *brus* in the 1400's and *bruise* from the mid-1500's; borrowed through Anglo-French *bruser, bruiser, briser* to break, smash, from Old French *bruisier, brisier,* replacing and fusing with earlier Middle English *brisen* and early modern English *brise,* developed from Old English *brȳsan* to crush (appearing before 900), from Proto-Germanic **brūsjanan,-* Indo-European **bhreus-/bhrus-/bhrūs-* (Pok.171). The two forms (*brise* from English, and *bruse* from French) existed side by side, at least from 1200 onward, till the form *bruise,* derived from French, was generally established by the mid-1600's.

Old French *bruisier, brisier* is perhaps of Gaulish origin (compare Old Irish *bruid* he smashes, and Welsh *brau* brittle, fragile).

—n. injury. 1541, in Copland's translation of Galen's *Terapeutyke;* earlier, a breaking, breach (1441); from the verb.

brunch *n.* combined breakfast and lunch. 1896, formed from English *br(eakfast) + (l)unch.* The word is quoted in *Punch* (the British humor magazine) as coined in 1895 by Guy Beringer, a British author.

brunette or **brunet** *n.* brown-haired person. 1669, borrowed from French *brunette, brunet,* from Old French *brunet,* feminine diminutive of *brun* brown, from Germanic (compare Old High German *brūn* BROWN); for suffix see -ET. **—adj.** 1712, probably developed from English *brunette, brunet,* n.

brunt *n.* Probably about 1380, in *Pearl,* Middle English *brunt* a sharp blow; later, a sudden attack, a rush (probably about 1400), a violent attack (about 1410), and main force or violence (probably about 1420, in Lydgate's *Troy Book*); of uncertain origin, but perhaps borrowed from a Scandinavian source (compare Old Icelandic *bruna* to advance in battle with the speed of fire), and modeled on *dont, dunt,* variants of Middle English *dint* an assault, blow.

brush[1] *n.* implement for sweeping or scrubbing. About 1378, in a version of *Piers Plowman,* borrowed from Old French *broisse, brouesse* a brush, usually regarded as derived from Vulgar Latin **bruscia* bunch of new shoots, used to sweep away dust, from Latin *bruscum* excrescence on a maple, of unknown origin. **—v.** use a brush (on). Before 1475, from the noun.

brush[2] *n.* shrubs, bushes, etc. Before 1338, in Mannyng's *Chronicle of England,* borrowed through Anglo-French *bruce* brushwood, bushes, Old North French *broche,* and Old French *brosse,* earlier *broce,* from Gallo-Romance **brocia,* perhaps from **brūcus* heather; see BRIER[2] heath.

The presence of many forms in English and French and the concurrent Anglo-French *bruce* and Anglo-Latin *brusca, bruscia* suggests a confusion of meaning among the various forms and perhaps points to an artificial separation of the words *brush*[1] and *brush*[2] in modern English, so that these two words may actually be one word after all.

brusque *adj.* abrupt. 1651, borrowed from French *brusque* and earlier meaning "tart," in Holland's translation of Pliny's *Natural History* (1601); the French was borrowed from Italian *brusco* coarse, rough, of uncertain origin, but also found in Spanish and Portuguese *brusco* rude, peevish. In English the word is sometimes regarded as the source of BRISK.

brute *adj.* senseless, stupid, cruel. Probably before 1425, in a translation of Higden's *Polychronicon*, borrowed from Middle French *brute, brut* coarse, brutal, from Latin *brūtus* heavy, dull, stupid, from an Oscan word probably cognate with Latin *gravis* heavy; see GRAVE[2] weighty. —**n.** 1611, lower animal, borrowed from Medieval Latin *brutus*, from Latin *brūtus* dull, stupid. —**brutal** *adj.* About 1450 (Scottish), borrowed from Middle French *brutal*, from Medieval Latin *brutalis*, from *brutus* brute; for suffix see -AL[1]. —**brutality** *n.* 1549, in sermons of Bishop Latimer, formed from English *brutal* + *-ity*. —**brutalize** *v.* Before 1704, formed from English *brutal* + *-ize*.

bubble *n., v.* About 1325 *bobel*, n., borrowed from Middle Dutch *bobbel;* about 1440 *bobelen*, v., from the noun or borrowed from Middle Low German *bubbeln* to bubble.

bubonic (byübon′ik) *adj.* having swelling of the lymph glands. 1871, formed in English from Latin *būbō* swelling of the lymph glands in the groin, genitive *būbōnis*, (from Greek *boubṓn* groin, swelling in the groin, of unknown origin) + English *-ic*.

The term *bubo*, meaning a swelling of the lymph glands, was borrowed in Middle English as early as 1398 from Latin *būbō*, but the adjective *bubonic* did not appear until almost 500 years later.

buccal *adj.* of the cheek or mouth. 1831, borrowed probably from French *buccal*, from Latin *bucca* cheek, mouth; for suffix see -AL[1]. A noun use meaning "mouthpiece" is recorded in English in 1605, but probably did not influence the adjective.

buccaneer *n.* 1661, a French settler employed as a hunter of wild oxen on the Spanish coasts of America, borrowed from French *boucanier* one who dries and smokes meat on a *boucan*, a barbecue, after the manner of the Indians, from an Indian word of the Caribbean area (perhaps Tupi *mocaém*, transcribed as *mukem* in a Portuguese travel account, 1587); for suffix see -EER. By 1690 the word was applied to French and then to British piratical rovers who were driven from their business of hunting wild oxen by the Spanish authorities and turned to plundering goods. In the 1800's it was extended to any pirate or sea rover.

buck[1] *n.* male deer, goat, etc. Before 1375 *bucke* male deer, earlier *bocke* (about 1300), new application of meaning derived from *bucke* male goat (probably before 1200, in *Ancrene Riwle*), also found in surname *Buckeshorn* (1184-85), developed from Old English *bucca* male goat (before 830, in the *Vespasian Psalter*). The often-cited Old English *buc* is a ghost word, or scribal error, and so it is Old English *bucca* (from Proto-Germanic **bukkōn*) that is cognate with Old Saxon *buck* male goat, Middle Dutch *boc, buc* (modern Dutch *bok*), Old High German *boc* (modern German *Bock*), Old Icelandic *bukkr*, and with Iranian *buz* goat, and Armenian *buz* lamb, from Indo-European **bhuĝ-* (Pok.174). —**buckskin** *n.* 1306, also found in the surname *Bucskin* (1274-75), formed from Middle English *bucke* + *skin*. —**buckshot** *n.* shot used to shoot large animals. 1775, American English, formed from *buck*[1] + *shot*.

buck[2] *v.* (of horses and mules) jump with arched back and land with stiff legs. 1848, in Haygarth's *Bush Life in Australia*, verb use of BUCK[1], originally apparently in the sense "to jump like a buck." In 1857 the sense of "fight against, resist stubbornly" arose as a figurative use, possibly influenced by the earlier meaning of "to butt, push or hit with the head" (1750). The idiom **buck up** is probably also related; in 1844 it meant to cheer up, encourage.

buck[3] *n. Slang.* dollar. 1856, American English, probably a development of the earlier sense of a deerskin used as a unit of exchange, especially among Indians and frontiersmen (1748); hence a special use of BUCK[1] male deer.

buck[4] *n.* **pass the buck** shift responsibility. 1912, American English, from an earlier meaning in the game of poker, *buck* article put in the jackpot and taken by the winner to remind him that when he gets the deal he must order another jackpot, perhaps shortened from *buckhorn* handles of knives, used as counters.

buck[5] *n.* sawhorse. 1817, American English, apparently borrowed from Dutch *bok* trestle, vaulting frame; see SAWBUCK; the spelling was influenced by *buck*[1].

buckaroo (buk′ərü′) *n.* cowboy. 1889, American English, alteration of earlier *bakhara* (1827), borrowed from Spanish *vaquero* cowboy, from *vaca* cow, from Latin *vacca;* see VACCINE.

The alteration of the original spelling *bakhara* was influenced by *buck*[1]. (See "Another Look at *Buckaroo*" F.G. Cassidy, *American Speech*, Spring 1978.) The end of the word *(-aroo)* is a modification of the Spanish *-ero*.

buckboard *n.* 1839, American English, formed from dialectal English *buck* body of a cart (1691) + *board*.

bucket *n.* 1248 *buket*, borrowed from Anglo-French *buket* bucket, pail, from Middle English *buc, buk* belly, trunk, body (probably before 1200, in *Ancrene Riwle*), developed from Old English *būc* vessel, pitcher, belly (about 700); cognate with Old High German *būh* belly (modern German *Bauch*), Old Icelandic *būkr* belly, body, from Proto-Germanic **būkaz*, and perhaps Greek *phōídes* blisters, from Indo-European **bheu-/bhōu-/bhū-g-* to swell up (Pok.100). —**bucketful** *n.* (before 1563) —**bucket seat** (1908)

buckle *n.* clasp for fastening a belt or strap. 1300 *bukel*, also later Middle English *bokel;* borrowed from Old French *bucle, bocle*, from Latin *buccula* cheek strap on helmet, diminutive form of *bucca* cheek. —**v.** fasten with a buckle. About 1386 *bokelen*, in Chaucer's *Canterbury Tales*, from the noun. The sense "to bend out of shape or warp under pressure" appeared about 1525, and may be a separate borrowing from Middle French *boucler* to bulge.

buckler *n.* small round shield. Probably before 1300, in *Kyng Alisaunder*, Middle English *bokler, bokeler*, borrowed from Old French *bocler, bucler*, from *bocle, bucle* boss of a shield, BUCKLE.

buckram *n.* coarse, stiff cloth. 1222 *bukeram* a fine cloth of linen or cotton, borrowed from Old French *bouquerant*, and Italian *bucherame*, probably from *Bukhara* (city in central Asia) from where it was imported.

bucksaw *n.* 1856, American English, formed from *buck*[5] a sawhorse + *saw*[1].

bucolic (byükol′ik) *adj.* of shepherds, pastoral. 1613, variant of earlier *bucolical* (1523), borrowed, perhaps by influence of earlier French *bucolique* (1265), from Latin *būcolicus*, from Greek *boukolikós* rustic, from *boukólos* herdsman, from *boûs* COW + *-kólos* from

Indo-European **-kwoló-s* tending, from the base **kwel-* (Pok.639); for suffix see -IC.

bud *n.* swelling on a plant that develops to a flower, leaf, etc. Before 1398 *budde,* in Trevisa's translation of Bartholomew's *De Proprietatibus Rerum,* and *bodde* (about 1450). The origin of English *bud* is uncertain, but possible cognates exist in Middle Low German *buddech* thick, swollen, Old Saxon *būdil,* Old High German *pūtil,* Middle High German *biutel* bag, sack (modern German *Beutel*), probably related to Middle Low German *būle* and Middle Dutch *buil* lump, swelling; see BOIL² swelling. **—v.** Probably about 1408 *budden,* in writings of Lydgate; verb use developed from *budde,* n.

buddy *n. Informal.* close friend. 1850, American English, apparently an alteration of BROTHER, possibly influenced by or a variant of earlier *butty* companion (1802), itself a possible alteration of *booty* in *booty fellow* a confederate who shares plunder (1530, in Palsgrave's *Lesclarcissement*). The short form *bud* appeared in 1851 in American English. **—v.** *Informal.* be or become close friends. 1931, American English, from the noun.

budge *v.* move, stir. 1590, borrowed from Middle French *bouger, bougier* to stir, from Vulgar Latin **bullicāre* to bubble, boil, from Latin *bullīre* to bubble, seethe; see BOIL¹ bubble up.

budget *n.* estimate of money to be spent. Probably before 1425 *bowgette* small bag, wallet, in a version of Higden's *Polychronicon;* borrowed from Middle French *bougette,* diminutive form of Old French *bouge* leather bag, from Latin *bulga,* probably from Gaulish (compare Old Irish *bolc, bolg* bag), related to BULGE and BELLY.

The modern sense appeared in 1733, in *open the budget,* said of the British Chancellor of the Exchequer in presenting his annual statement.

—v. 1618, to store up; from the noun. The modern sense appeared about 1884.

buff¹ *n.* dull-yellow leather. 1580 *buffe leather,* earlier, *buffalo* (1552), apparently borrowed from Middle French *buffle,* from Italian *bufalo,* probably because this leather was originally obtained from buffaloes; see BUFFALO. The transferred sense "bare skin, naked" appeared in such phrases as *in* or *to the buff,* about 1602. **—adj.** of the color of buff leather, dull yellow. 1599, in a version of Hakluyt's *Diverse Voyages,* from the noun. **—v.** polish with a buff. 1885, from the noun.

buff² *n. Informal.* enthusiast, devotee, fan. 1903, American English, an enthusiast about fighting fires, said to be so called because the uniforms of the volunteer firemen (in New York City at the time) were buff-colored; see BUFF¹. By 1931 the meaning was extended to any enthusiast or devotee.

buffalo *n.* wild ox, bison. 1588, borrowed from Italian *bufalo* or possibly from Spanish *búfalo,* from Late Latin *būfalus,* variant of Latin *būbalus* wild ox, (earlier) African gazelle, from Greek *boúbalos* African gazelle, wild ox, of uncertain origin. The spelling *buffalo* gradually replaced the earlier *buffel, buffle* (about 1511-1808) and *buffe* (1552-1706); both forms borrowed from Middle French *buffle;* cognate with Dutch *buffel,* Middle High German *buffel* (modern German *Büffel*). **—v.** *Slang.* intimidate or overawe. 1903, American English, from the noun, perhaps originally transferred from the verb *cow* to frighten.

buffer¹ *n.* anything that softens a blow or shock. 1835, apparently formed from obsolete or dialectal English verb *buff* (before 1550) make a dull sound when struck + *-er*¹. The verb *buff* developed in Middle English from *buff* a blow (about 1420), borrowed perhaps from Middle French *buffe* a blow, from Old French; see BUFFET¹.

The figurative sense of a person or country acting as a *buffer* between opponents appeared in 1858; hence, *buffer state* (1876).

buffer² *n.* a person or device that polishes. 1854, formed from English *buff*¹, v. + *-er*¹. The noun *buffer* precedes *buff*¹, v. by about 30 years in the record of English; *buffing,* n. appears in 1856, about the same time as *buffer.* This suggests that use of *buff*¹, v. was unrecorded and its record is incomplete.

buffet¹ (buf′it) *n.* blow, stroke. Probably before 1200, in *Ancrene Riwle,* borrowed from Old French *buffet,* diminutive of *buffe* a blow, of uncertain origin. According to Bloch and Wartburg, the meaning "blow, slap" may be of onomatopoeic development. **—v.** hit, strike. Probably before 1200, in *Ancrene Riwle,* borrowed from Old French *buffeter,* from *buffet*¹, n.

buffet² (bu̇fā′) *n.* piece of furniture for holding dishes, silver, and table linen. 1718, borrowed from French *buffet,* possibly from Italian *buffeto,* of uncertain origin. It has been suggested that French *buffet* is a special use of Old French *buffet* a blow, in some dialects meaning "bellows" but the semantic connection is not apparent.

The sense of refreshments or a meal set out on tables or buffets from which guests serve themselves appeared (usually attributively as in *a buffet dinner* or *luncheon*) in the late 1800's.

buffoon (bəfün′) *n.* 1585, clown; earlier, 1549, a pantomime dance; borrowed from Middle French *bouffon,* from Italian *buffone* jester, from *buffa* a jest, from *buffare* blow out the cheeks (as a comic gesture), of imitative origin; for suffixal ending see -OON. Compare BOUFFANT. **—buffoonery** *n.* 1621, formed from English *buffoon* + *-ery.*

bug *n.* crawling insect. 1622, in reference to the bedbug, though of uncertain origin, but probably influenced by Middle English *bugge* bugbear, hobgoblin (1395, in the Wycliffe Bible); see BUGBEAR. It has been suggested that *bug* a crawling insect is a dialectal alteration of earlier *budde* beetle (1440, in *Promptorium Parvulorum*), developed from Old English *budda* (in a version of Ælfric's *Glossary*). The Old English is cognate with Low German dialect *budde* louse, grub, and Middle Low German *buddech* thick, swollen; see BUD.

The slang sense of a defect or flaw in a machine, plan, etc., was originally American English and appeared in 1889, probably from the idea of a small insect getting inside machinery and interfering with its action.

—v. *Slang.* **1** put a concealed microphone in. 1919, American English, verb use of *bug,* n. (from the resemblance of the microphone to a small insect). **2** annoy, irritate. 1949, American English, probably originally in allusion to insect pests.

bugaboo *n.* bugbear. 1843, in Poe's *Premature Burial,* alteration of earlier *buggybow* (1740), probably related to BUGBEAR.

bugbear *n.* imaginary thing feared, goblin, ghost. 1580, in Sidney's *The Arcadia,* a compound formed from obsolete English *bug* goblin, scarecrow (earlier *bugge,* about 1395) + *bear* BEAR[1]. Middle English *bugge* is of uncertain origin, though Celtic origin has been suggested (compare Middle Irish *bocanách* supernatural being associated with battlefields, perhaps a goatlike creature, apparently from *bocán* he-goat, Irish and Gaelic *bocan* hobgoblin; the often-cited Welsh *bwg* goblin, ghost, cannot be traced further than the 1500's and is now generally assumed to be a borrowing from Middle English *bugge.*)

buggy[1] *n.* light carriage. 1773 *Buggies* light one-horse vehicles; of unknown origin.

buggy[2] *adj.* infested with bugs. 1714, formed from English *bug,* n. + *-y*[1].

bugle *n.* trumpetlike musical instrument. Probably about 1350, shortened from earlier *bugle horn* (probably before 1300, in *Kyng Alisaunder*), from *bugle* wild ox, borrowed from Old French *bugle* wild ox, instrument made from the horn of the ox, learned borrowing from Latin *būculus,* diminutive form of *bōs* ox; see COW[1] female of cattle. —**v.** play a bugle. 1862, in writings of Thackeray; earlier *bugling,* verbal noun (1847), from the noun. —**bugler** *n.* 1840, formed from English *bugle,* n. + *-er*[1], in the sense of a person who works (blows) a bugle.

build *v.* About 1330, in *Sir Orfeo,* Middle English *bilden;* earlier *bulden* (probably before 1200, in Layamon's *Chronicle of Britain*); developed from late Old English *byldan* (1016), from *bold* dwelling, from Proto-Germanic **buthlan,* from Indo-European **bhu-tlo-m,* from the base **bheu-* be, live (Pok.149). The Old English is cognate with Old Frisian *bōdel* dwelling, Old Saxon *bodl,* Old Icelandic *bōl,* and related to Old English *būan* to dwell; see BOWER. The modern spelling *build* did not appear before 1550, and then only rarely; an earlier spelling *buylden* appears in Chaucer's *Canterbury Tales* (1395), but it was not until the late 1500's that our spelling begins to appear with frequency. Even so, the spelling is not accounted for, unless it is simply a composite of the two earlier spellings *bilden* and *bulden.* —**n.** form in which something is put together, shape or lines of construction. 1667, from the verb, replacing the now obsolete noun *built* (about 1615), also from the verb in the sense of something *built* (past participle). —**builder** *n.* (about 1280) —**building** *n.* (about 1300)

bulb *n.* 1568, onion, borrowed perhaps through Middle French *bulbe,* from Latin *bulbus* bulb, bulbous root, onion, from Greek *bolbós* tassel-hyacinth, or one of certain other bulbous plants, possibly cognate with Latin *bulla* bubble; see BULL[2] decree. The sense of an object with a rounded, swollen end appeared about 1800, and *electric bulb* appeared in 1856. —**bulbous** *adj.* 1578, borrowed from Latin *bulbōsus,* from *bulbus* bulb; for suffix see -OUS.

bulge *n.* Probably about 1200, leather bag or pouch, borrowed from Old French *bouge, boulge,* from Latin *bulga,* probably from Gaulish (compare Old Irish *bolc, bolg* bag, Breton *bolc'h*); related to BUDGET. —**v.** swell out. 1677, from the noun.

bulk *n.* largest part, main mass. About 1454 *bulk;* earlier *bolke* a heap (1440, in *Promptorium Parvulorum*) and the cargo of a ship (before 1350), probably borrowed from a Scandinavian source (compare Old Icelandic *bulki* cargo or hold of a ship). —**v.** 1540, swell out (in the phrase *bulk out*); probably a confusion of *bolken* spill over (before 1352, in the Wycliffe Bible) and *bulken* of undetermined meaning (before 1325, in *Cursor Mundi*), but reinforced by *bulked* having bulk, big (probably 1440). —**bulky** *adj.* About 1450, plump, stout, formed from English *bulk,* n. + *-y*[1].

bull[1] *n.* male of cattle, etc. Probably before 1200, in Layamon's *Chronicle of Britain,* Middle English *bule* (about 1280 *bole*), and earlier *Bule-* and *Bulla* (1130, 1166, in surnames); developed from Old English (972) *bula* (from Proto-Germanic **bulōn*), related to *bulluc* young bull. The Old English *bula* is cognate with Middle Low German *bulle* bull, Middle Dutch *bul, bulle* (modern Dutch *bul*), and Old Icelandic *boli* bull, from Indo-European **bhel-/bhḷ-* swell (Pok.120). The sense of a speculator who anticipates a rise in prices on the stock exchange appeared in 1714, probably in contrast to *bear;* see BEAR[1] animal. —**v.** to get by force, push. 1884, American English, in Mark Twain's *Huckleberry Finn,* from the noun. —**bullish** *adj.* anticipating a rise in prices. 1882, formed from English *bull*[1] + *-ish*[1].

bull[2] *n.* papal decree or edict. About 1300, borrowed from Old French *bulle* and Medieval Latin *bulla* papal decree, document, seal, from Latin *bulla* amulet, bubble (in reference to the amulet used to impress the seal on the paper); of uncertain origin.

bulldoze *v.* 1876, American English, to intimidate by violence; of uncertain origin. The word *bulldozer,* meaning one who intimidates by violence, appeared also in 1876 (the current sense of a machine for clearing or leveling came much later, in 1930). The etymology usually suggested is that the word is a compound of *bull* (the animal) and an altered form of *dose,* i.e. that a whipping given to coerce voters was a dose suitable for a bull. The reference was to a supposed practice carried out during the Tilden campaign, especially among Blacks in the South.

bullet *n.* 1557, borrowed from Middle French *boullette* small ball, diminutive form of *boule* ball; see BOWL[2] ball. The idiom **bite the bullet** act with courage, submit without protest, is first recorded in 1923 (earlier, 1891 *bite on the bullet),* perhaps in reference to the practice of giving a wounded person something to bite down on while undergoing a painful operation without anesthesia.

bulletin *n.* 1651, official certificate, borrowed from French *bulletin,* from Old French *bullette* certificate, from *bulle* document, BULL[2]. French *bulletin* was probably modeled after Italian *bollettino, bullettino,* diminutive form of *bulletta* small ball, itself a diminutive form of *bulla* papal decree, from Medieval Latin; see BULL[2] decree. The earliest uses of *bulletin* are apparently borrowed directly from Italian and use the Italian spelling, but modern senses are an adoption of the French.

The meaning "a short account of news" appeared in English in 1791, in writings of Edmund Burke.

bullion (bu̇l′yən) *n.* bar of gold or silver. 1429 *billon* a bar of precious metal, in *Rolls of Parliament;* also, *bullion* a mint (1433, in *Proceedings of the Privy Council*), borrowed through Anglo-French *bullion, billon* a bar of precious metal, or a mint, and *buillir* to melt down, from Old French *boillir* to boil, in reference to the practice of melting down gold or silver and casting it into bars; see BOIL[1] to heat.

In pronunciation of modern English *bullion* and *boullion* are often confused, a situation which reflects the close historical connection, both words coming into

English ultimately from Old French *boillir* to boil (in essence, *boullion* is boiled soup, *bullion* is "boiled" metal).

bullock *n.* ox, steer, young bull. Old English *bulloc* (901), *bulluc* (about 1000) young bull, from Proto-Germanic **bull-*, earlier **buln-;* see BULL[1] male of cattle.

bully[1] *n.* person who teases or hurts the weak. 1688, probably extracted from such earlier terms as *bully-huff* a boaster who bullies (1680), *bully roister* a swaggering reveler (1687), and *bully-ruffian* (1653), on the pattern of *bully boy* (1609), in which *bully* means "good friend, fine fellow". Earlier (1538), *bully* was applied to both men and women as a term of endearment equivalent to "sweetheart, darling" (often found in Shakespeare). By popular etymology the word is now associated with *bull*[1], but originally it was probably a borrowing from Dutch *boel* lover, brother, from Middle High German *buole,* of uncertain origin. **—v.** intimidate. 1710, from the noun, also influenced by BULL[1]. **—adj.** very good, excellent. 1681, worthy, admirable, developed from the noun sense "good fellow," which was often used attributively, again in Shakespeare ("bully Bottom" and "bully Doctor"), and so abstracted from such phrases to mean worthy or admirable; popularized in part by Theodore Roosevelt's phrase describing the presidency as a *bully pulpit* because of its prestige and power.

bully[2] *n.,* or **bully beef** canned or pickled beef. 1753, in Smollett's *Count Fathom,* perhaps borrowed from French *boeuf bouilli* boiled beef; *bouilli,* past participle of *bouillir* to boil, from Old French *boillir;* see BOIL[1] bubble up.

bulwark *n.* defense, protection. Probably about 1416 *bulwerke* rampart, fortification; borrowed from Middle Dutch *bolwerc* or Middle Low German *bolwerk* (*bolle* plank, tree trunk + *werc, werk* work). The figurative sense appeared in English in 1577, in Holinshed's *Chronicle.*

bum *n.* vagrant, loafer. 1864, in American English, of disputed origin: 1) possibly identical with earlier Scottish *bum* (1540) lazy, dirty person, a special use of *bum* rump (before 1387), perhaps borrowed from Middle Dutch *bonne* (modern Dutch *bom*) bung; 2) perhaps reinforced by and fusing with a shortened form of earlier English *bummer* loafer, idle person (1855), apparently alteration of German *Bummler,* from *bummeln* to loaf.

The origin from earlier Scottish *bum* makes it easier to account for the verb and adjective uses, which otherwise unaccountably precede the noun use (even *bumming* is recorded before the noun in American English). However, appearance of the noun, adjective, and verb in such close proximity (within seven years), points to the German borrowing in American English, perhaps by influence of German immigrants at the time.

—v. beg, obtain by begging. 1863, American English, perhaps back formation from *bummer* loafer, or from the noun (reinforced by *bumming,* n., 1857). **—adj.** of poor condition or quality. 1859, American English, apparently from the noun. The slang expression *bum steer* bad advice, appeared in the 1920's.

bumble *v.* bungle, botch. 1532 *bumble, bomble* to blunder about, flounder, referring to the noise of booming or buzzing about, both forms appearing in the writings of Sir Thomas More, the words being used in a disparaging way to describe theological points made by Tyndale. The Middle English *bumblen, bomblen* to boom, as a bittern does, and to buzz, are first recorded about 1395 in Chaucer's *Canterbury Tales.* For suffix see -LE[3]. **—n.** awkward mistake. 1648, confusion, jumble; probably from the noun.

bumblebee *n.* 1530, in Palsgrave's *Lesclarcissement,* formed from Middle English *bumblen, bomblen* to buzz, boom (about 1395, in Chaucer's *Canterbury Tales*) + *bee. Bumblebee* is a partial replacement of the earlier term *humbulbe* HUMBLEBEE (before 1475).

bump *v., n.* push, throw, or strike. 1611 *bumpe* blow, strike or knock, both verb and noun, in Cotgrave's *Dictionary,* of imitative origin, and possibly related to obsolete *bum* to make a booming noise; to strike. **—bumper** *n.* 1676, a cup or glass of wine filled to the brim, formed from English *bump* (in the sense of a "bumping" or "thumping" large glass) + *-er*[1]. By 1759 this meaning was extended to anything unusually large or abundant, sometimes used attributively as in *bumper crop.* The sense of a bar of metal to protect an automobile appeared in 1926, from the earlier sense of a device on railroad cars (1839). **—bumpy** *adj.* 1865, formed from English *bump,* n. + *-y*[1].

bumpkin *n.* awkward person from the country. 1570 *bunkin,* of uncertain origin, possibly borrowed from Middle Dutch *bommekijn* little barrel, used in a humorous sense in referring to a man with a short stumpy figure.

bumptious *adj.* unpleasantly assertive. 1803, probably derived from *bump* + suffixal ending *-tious* from *-ous,* on the pattern of such words as *captious, facetious, fractious, scrumptious,* etc., some of these being humorous formations in English and others borrowings into English.

bun *n.* sweet roll. 1371 *bunne,* of uncertain origin; perhaps an altered borrowing from Old French *buignet* a fritter, originally a diminutive form of *buigne* swelling from a blow, bump on the head, probably of pre-Roman origin; also, compare Spanish *buñelo* a fritter, apparently of the same ultimate origin as the French.

bunch *n.* About 1350 *bunche* a little bundle; later, protuberance, hump on the back (about 1390), borrowed from Old French (Walloon) *bonge* bundle, from Flemish *bondje* little bundle. **—v.** Before 1398 *bunchen* form a bunch, in Trevisa's translation of Bartholomew's *De Proprietatibus Rerum,* developed from *bunche,* n.

bunco *Slang.* **—n.** a swindle. 1872, American English, dice and card game, apparently borrowed from American Spanish *banca, banco* card game, bank in gambling game, from Italian *banca* BANK[2]. **—v.** 1875, from the noun.

bundle *n.* About 1331 *bondell* collection of things bound, probably borrowed from Middle Dutch *bondel,* or perhaps alteration (influenced by Middle Dutch) of Old English *byndele* a binding, (from Proto-Germanic **bundilīn*); related to *bindan* BIND. **—v.** Before 1628, from the noun. The word in many cases is now superseded by *bunch* (Caxton refers to "a bondel of keyes"), which is currently undergoing even wider application, as in "a bunch of people."

bung *n.* About 1440, in *Promptorium Parvulorum,* borrowed (probably because of the wine trade) from Middle Dutch *bonge;* cognate with Middle High German *bunge* stopper, and probably with Middle Low German *bunken* to strike, beat, hammer, Old Swedish *bunka* (Norwegian and Swedish *banka* to knock, strike), Old Icelandic *bang* hammering (Icelandic and Swedish *banga* make a loud noise); see BANG[1] make noise. —**v.** 1589, to stop or stop up, later (by 1829) said of the eyes after a boxing match, and in modern times extended to a dilapidated or injured condition.

bungalow (bung′gəlō) *n.* one-story house. 1676 *bungales,* as a native word introduced into English from Hindi *bangla* one-story thatched cottage, literally, of Bengal, from Bengali *banglā,* from *Banga* Bengal.

bungle *v.* do or make clumsily. 1530, probably borrowed from a Scandinavian source (compare Swedish dialect *bangla* work ineffectually, related to Old Swedish *banga* to strike; see BANG[1] make noise). —**n.** 1656, from the verb. —**bungler** *n.* 1533, in writings of Sir Thomas More, formed from English *bungle,* v. + *-er*[1].

bunion *n.* swelling on the foot. Before 1718 *bunnian,* apparently alteration of earlier *bunnye* lump, hump, swelling (1552), and possibly related to Middle English *bony, boni* a swelling, bump (1440, in *Promptorium Parvulorum*), both words probably borrowed from Middle French *buigne* swelling from a blow, from Old French *buigne;* see BUN.

bunk[1] *n.* narrow bed. 1758, probably shortened from BUNKER seat or bench. —**v.** occupy or sleep in a bunk. 1840, in Dana's *Two Years Before the Mast,* from the noun. —**bunkhouse** *n.* (1876, American English)

bunk[2] *n.* nonsense, humbug. 1900, American English, in writings of George Ade, shortened from BUNKUM, or remotely BUNCO.

bunker *n.* Before 1758, Scottish, seat or bench, of uncertain origin; possibly a variant of *banker* bench (1677). The meaning of a sandy hollow or bank of earth forming an obstacle on a golf course appeared in 1824, and by 1939 (but probably as early as 1915-1918) this sense was extended to a dug-out fortification or obstacle used in battle.

bunkum or **buncombe** (bung′kəm) *n.* humbug, nonsense. 1847, American English, originally (1828, 1841) in the phrase *talk to* or *for Bunkum* (or *Buncombe*) talk long-windedly about nothing, said to be in allusion to *Buncombe* County, North Carolina. The phrase is supposed to have originated in a speech given in Congress by Felix Walker, congressman (1817-23) from a district that included Buncombe County. Once during the 16th Congress (1819-21), over the protests of his colleagues, he made a long and pointless speech and excused himself by explaining that the people of his district expected him to make a speech, and so he had to make it "for Buncombe."

bunny *n.* rabbit. 1690, earlier a term of endearment for a woman or child (1606), perhaps formed from Scottish *bun* tail of a hare (about 1538) + *-y*[2]. The Scottish word has been compared with Gaelic *bun* stump, root, and Middle English *bone, boni* swelling, bump, which is reminiscent of earlier *bunny* swelling, lump (1440, in *Promptorium Parvulorum*).

bunt *v.* hit (a baseball) lightly so that it rolls a short distance. 1889, American English, probably from earlier *bunt* (1825) strike, push; also, to strike with the head as a goat does, alteration of BUTT[3] hit. —**n.** action of bunting. 1889, possibly from the verb, though the noun meaning "a push, butt" is recorded in American English in 1767, some 60 years before the verb use of the same meaning.

bunting[1] *n.* thin cloth. 1742, perhaps derived from an earlier verb *bonten* (1340, in *Ayenbite of Inwyt*) to sift meal, because the cloth was used for sifting; of uncertain origin; for suffix see -ING[1]. Compare BOLT[2], n.

bunting[2] *n.* bird. Probably before 1300, of uncertain origin; perhaps a name derived from *buntin* plump, as possibly seen in the phrase *baby bunting,* or from an unrecorded word referring to speckled plumage, cognate with Middle High, Middle Low German, and modern German *bunt* spotted, speckled, Middle Dutch and modern Dutch *bont.*

buoy (boi *or* bü′ē) *n.* floating object anchored to warn or guide ships. 1296 *boye,* borrowed either from Old French **boie, buie* (compare later Old French *boue,* Middle French *bouée* buoy, dialectal *bouie*), or from Middle Dutch *boye, boeye,* both the French and Dutch forms probably derived from West Germanic **baukn* (compare Dutch *baken* beacon, buoy, Old High German *bouhhan* signal, BEACON). The modern English spelling reflects the Dutch pronunciation (bü′ē), though the pronunciation among sailors generally has been, and remains (boi). —**v.** 1596, mark with a buoy, in writings of Sir Walter Raleigh, from the noun. The senses "to rise up, uplift, sustain" appear in the 1600's, perhaps influenced by Spanish *boyar* to float, from *boya* buoy, n., from Dutch *boei,* from Middle French *bouée.* —**buoyant** *adj.* floating, light, cheerful. 1578, floating, perhaps borrowed from Spanish *boyante,* from the present participle of *boyar* to float. The figurative sense is not recorded until about 1748. —**buoyancy** *n.* 1713, formed from English *buoyant* + *-cy.*

bur *n.* prickly seed case or flower. Probably before 1300, in *Arthour and Merlin,* borrowed from a Scandinavian source (compare Old Icelandic *burst* bristle, related to Dutch *burre* bur, and Old English *byrst* BRISTLE).

burden[1] *n.* load (of things, care, etc.). Probably before 1200 *burthen, birden,* in Layamon's *Chronicle of Britain;* later *burden* (about 1250) and *birthen* (about 1300); developed from Old English *byrthen* (before 830, in the *Vespasian Psalter*). The Old English is derived from the root of *beran* to carry, BEAR[2], and is cognate with Old Saxon *burthinnia* burden (from Proto-Germanic **burthinjō-*), Old High German *burdī,* Old Icelandic *byrdhr,* and Gothic *baúrthei.* —**v.** put a burden on, load. 1541, from the noun. —**burdensome** *adj.* 1578, formed from English *burden,* n. + *-some* [1], and replacing earlier *burdenous* (1529).

burden[2] *n.* main idea or message. 1591, fusion of *burden*[1] and earlier *burdoun* (probably about 1300, in *Caiphas*) low undersong or accompaniment, borrowed from Old French *bourdon* bumblebee, bagpipe, drone, of imitative origin.

The figurative sense of chief theme, main idea, appeared in 1649, in the phrase *the burden of my song;* an earlier, literal sense (1598, in Francis Bacon's *Sacred Meditations*) was "the refrain or chorus of a song."

bureau (byůr′ō) *n.* 1699, desk with drawers, borrowed from French *bureau* office, desk, originally, covering cloth for a desk, from Old French *burel* woolen cloth (used as a table or desk covering), diminutive form of *bure* coarse woolen cloth, of uncertain origin; possibly from Vulgar Latin **būra,* variant of Late Latin *burra* coarse wool; alternatively, Old French *bure* may be related to *buire* dark brown, from Vulgar Latin **burreus, *burrius,* from Latin *burrus* red, probably from Greek *pyrrhós* red. The sense of an office or division of a government department appeared in 1720, in the *London Gazette.* —**bureaucracy** (byùrok′rəsē) *n.* government by bureaus. 1818 *Bureaucratie,* used as a French term in Lady Morgan's autobiography; 1834 *bureaucracy* (thereafter popularized by John Stuart Mill); borrowed from French *bureaucratie* (coined by the French economist Vincent de Gournay, from *bureau* + *-cratie* -cracy). —**bureaucrat** *n.* 1842, in John L. Motley's correspondence, borrowed from French *bureaucrate* (1792). —**bureaucratic** *adj.* 1836, borrowed from French *bureaucratique* (1798).

burg *n. Informal.* town or city. 1843, American English, ultimately a spelling alteration of Middle English *burgh* BOROUGH, but in common usage probably abstracted from the names of numerous American towns and cities ending in *-burg,* such as *Blackburg, Plattsburg, Hartsburg.*

burgeon (bėr′jən) *v.* bud, sprout. About 1350 *burjunen,* either borrowed from Anglo-French *burjuner,* Old French *borjoner* to bud, sprout; or developed in Middle English from the earlier noun *burjoin* a bud, sprout (probably before 1300), borrowed from Anglo-French *burjun,* Old French *borjon,* of uncertain origin (perhaps from Vulgar Latin **burriōnem,* accusative of **burriō* bud, sprout, from Late Latin *burra* coarse wool; so called from the downy look of some buds).

burger *n.* 1939, American English, by shortening of *hamburger.* The element *-burger* was quickly abstracted from HAMBURGER (even though a hamburger is not a "burger" of *ham*) and appeared in words like *beefburger* (1940) and *cheeseburger* (1938); by 1941 *burger* was recognized as a distinct word element or combining form.

burgess (bėr′jis) *n.* magistrate or head of a borough. Probably before 1200, in *Ancrene Riwle,* Middle English *burgeis* inhabitant of a borough, borrowed from Old French *borgeis, borjois* citizen of a town or village, from *borc* town, village; see BOURGEOIS. The sense of a member of a legislature appeared in English in 1472, in *The Paston Letters,* and the *House of Burgesses,* the first representative legislative body in America, initially met in 1619 in Jamestown, Virginia. Doublet of BOURGEOIS.

burgh (bėr′ō *or* bėrg) *n.* chartered town in Scotland. 1375, Scottish and obsolete English variant of BOROUGH.

In Scotland the original pronunciation corresponding to *borough* (bėr′ō) is retained from *burgh,* accounting for the unexpected pronunciation of *Edinburgh* (city of Scotland) with final -bėr′ə or -brə, not -bėrg. —**burgher** (bėr′gər) *n.* citizen. 1590, in Marlowe's *Tamburlane the Great,* inhabitant of a borough or town, borrowed from Middle Dutch *burgher,* from Middle High German *burger, burgære* (modern German *Bürger*), from Old High German *burgāri* inhabitant of a fortress, from *burg* fortress, citadel; see BOROUGH.

burglar *n.* 1541, one who breaks into a house to commit a crime, borrowed as Anglo-French *burgler* (1516), alteration of earlier Anglo-French *burgesour, burgeysour* burglar, by influence of Anglo-Latin *burglator* (before 1260), itself a contributing source of English *burglar* and an altered form of Medieval Latin *burgator* burglar. The intrusive *l* is not satisfactorily accounted for by available evidence, though the notion has grown up that the ending *-lar* represents Anglo-French *-ler* from Latin *latrō,* nominative of *latrōnem* a robber.

The Medieval Latin *burgator* is from *burgare* to break open, commit burglary in, from Latin *burgus* fortress, castle; the Anglo-French *burgesour* is of obscure origin, but *burg-* is probably ultimately from Old French *borg* borough. Both the Latin and Old French forms are probably related through a Germanic source (compare Old High German *burg* fortress); see BOROUGH.

A Middle English form *burgur* is found in *Ancrene Riwle* (probably about 1200) but is unrecorded thereafter.

—**burglarize** *v.* 1871, American English, formed from *burglar* + *-ize.* —**burglary** *n.* 1532-33, borrowed as a legal term from Anglo-French *burglarie,* alteration of Anglo-Latin *burgaria, burgeria,* found in the early 1200's; for suffix see -Y[1]. —**burgle** *v.* 1872, back formation from *burglar,* though as a legal term Anglo-Latin *burgulare* was recorded in 1354.

burial *n.* act of burying. Probably before 1400, in Mannyng's *Chronicle of England,* Middle English *beryell, biriel* burial place, tomb, formed as a singular from earlier *buriles* (about 1200, in a version of Ælfric's *Glossary*), *berieles* (before 1225), *birigeles* (about 1250, in *The Story of Genesis and Exodus*), all of these forms being taken as plurals, though developed from Old English (725) *byrgels* burial place (from Proto-Germanic **burʒisli-*), from *byrgan* to bury + the suffix *-els* (as in *hydels* hiding place, *fætels* bag, etc.); see BURY. The sense of act of burying, interment, funeral, is not recorded before 1250.

The spelling with *-al* was due to the influence of the noun suffix *-al*[2] in words like *espousal.*

burl *n.* knot in wool, etc. 1440, in *Promptorium Parvulorum,* borrowed from Anglo-French *burle,* perhaps from Vulgar Latin **burrula,* diminutive of Late Latin *burra* coarse wool.

burlap *n.* 1695-96 *borelapp,* of uncertain origin; possibly borrowed from Dutch **boerenlap* (*boeren* coarse + *lap* piece of cloth).

burlesque (bėrlesk′) *n.* literary or dramatic parody. 1667, from earlier adjective, (1656) meaning droll, jocular; borrowed from French *burlesque,* from Italian *burlesco,* from *burla* a jest, joke, ridicule, from Spanish *burla,* of uncertain origin (possibly an alteration of Late Latin *burrae* trifles, nonsense); for suffix see -ESQUE.

The modern sense of a variety show, frequently with striptease acts, appeared in 1870 in American English. —**v.** to parody or caricature. 1676, from the noun or adjective.

burly *adj.* strong, sturdy, big. Probably before 1400, Northern dialectal *burli* noble, stately, variant of earlier *borlich* (before 1250), developed from an unattested Old English adjective with corresponding adverb *borlīce* excellently, verily, apparently related to Old English *beran* to BEAR[2] carry.

burn *v.* Probably before 1200 *burnen,* in Layamon's *Chronicle of Britain,* but not the prevailing form before the 1550's, representing two forms originally distinct: a strong intransitive verb and a weak transitive verb, each of which underwent a transposition of sounds. The strong intransitive verb, appearing in Middle English as *bernen* (probably about 1175) and *brinnen* (before 1325) is found in Old English as *beornan, bior-*

nan, byrnan to be on fire; the weak transitive verb, appearing in Middle English as *brennen* (probably before 1160), is found in Old English as *bernan, bærnan* to set on fire, consume with fire. The distinction between the two verbs began to break down in late Old English, but note that metathesis (reversal of the *r*) is frequent and fluctuating in the variety of both Middle and Old English forms.

Both verb forms had cognates respectively in Old Saxon, Old High German, and Gothic *brinnan* to be on fire, from Proto-Germanic **brenwanan,* and Old Saxon and Old High German *brennian,* Old Icelandic *brenna,* and Gothic *-brannjan* to set on fire. The word is related through an Indo-European present stem **bhre-n-u-* to the root **bhreu-* (Pok.144) of Old English *brēowan* to BREW. Compare RUN for a similar development.
—n. 1523 *brenne* mark made by burning, noun use developed from Middle English *brennen* to set on fire, replacing the original noun *bryne, brene* a burn (probably before 1200, in *Ancrene Riwle*), developed from Old English *bryne,* from the root of Old English *byrnan* to burn. **—burner** *n.* 1280, as a surname *Brenner* person who makes bricks, formed from Middle English *brennen* burn + *-er*[1].

burnish *v.* polish, shine. About 1330, in *Sir Orfeo,* Middle English *burnishen,* borrowed from Old French *burniss-,* stem of *brunir, burnir* make bright, polish, from *brun* brown, polished, from a Germanic source (compare Old High German *brūn* and Old Icelandic *brúnn,* both meaning either bright, polished or brown; see BROWN); for suffixal ending see -ISH[2].

burnoose or **burnous** (bėrnüs′) *n.* hooded cloak worn by Arabs. 1695, borrowed from French *burnous,* earlier *barnusse,* from Arabic *burnus,* from Greek *bírros* hooded cloak, from Latin **birrus* (found in Late Latin *birrus*); see BERET.

burp *n., v. Informal.* belch. 1932, American English, apparently imitative of the sound of belching.

burr[1] *n.* rough ridge or edge made by a tool. 1611, in Florio's *A World of Words,* variant of BUR. The sense of "a tool shaped like a bur" appeared in 1794.

burr[2] *n.* rough (uvular) pronunciation or *r.* 1760, in Samuel Foote's *The Minor,* probably imitative, but perhaps associated with *bur* prickly seed case, in allusion to its roughness. **—v.** 1798, in Wordsworth's *Idiot Boy,* from the noun.

burro *n.* donkey. 1800, in Southey's correspondence, borrowed from Spanish *burro,* back formation from *borrico* donkey, from Late Latin *burrīcus* little horse, of uncertain origin (possibly from Germanic).

burrow *n.* About 1300 *borewe,* earlier *borwgh* (probably before 1200, in Layamon's *Chronicle of Britain*), developed from Old English *burg* stronghold, fortress, town (about 725, in *Beowulf*), possibly related to Old English *beorg* hill, mound; see BARROW[2] mound, and BOROUGH. **—v.** 1614, from the noun.

bursar *n.* treasurer, especially of a college. 1857, earlier, in Scottish schools, a student with a scholarship (1567), perhaps a reborrowing of Middle English *bouser* treasurer (1450), earlier in Anglo-Latin *burser* treasurer (1234) and *burser* purse maker (in the surname *Rob le Burser,* 1208), borrowed from Medieval Latin *bursarius,* and Old French *borsier, boursier,* from *bourse* purse; both the Medieval Latin and the Old French forms ultimately derived from Medieval Latin *bursa* PURSE; see also BURSITIS. Doublet of PURSER.

bursitis *n.* 1857, formed from English *bursa* + *-itis,* also found in New Latin *bursitis.* The English *bursa* (1803) was apparently abstracted from the New Latin phrase *bursa mucosa* mucous pouch, from Medieval Latin *bursa* bag, purse, from Late Latin *bursa,* a variant of *byrsa* hide, from Greek *býrsa,* of unknown origin.

burst *v.* About 1300 *bursten,* in a version of Layamon's *Chronicle of Britain;* earlier *bersten* (about 1150), developed from Old English *berstan* (about 725, in *Beowulf*); cognate with Old Frisian and Old Saxon *bersta* to burst, Old High German *brestan* (modern German *bersten*), and Old Icelandic *bresta,* from Proto-Germanic **brestanan,* from Indo-European **bhres-* (Pok.169). **—n.** 1611, in Shakespeare's *Cymbeline,* an act of bursting; earlier *berst* (probably about 1300, in *Sir Bevis of Hamtoun*); from the verb.

bury *v.* Probably before 1200 *burien,* in Layamon's *Chronicle of Britain;* earlier, probably before 1160 *birien,* in *Peterborough Chronicle;* developed from Old English (before 1000) *byrgan,* from Proto-Germanic **burȝjanan,* related to *beorgan* save, preserve. The Old English is cognate with Old High German *bergan* protect, shelter, conceal (modern German *bergen*), Old Icelandic *bjarga,* Gothic *baírgan* protect, save; also cognate with Old Slavic *brěšti* to care for, and eastern Lithuanian *bir̃ginti* save, spare, from Indo-European **bherĝh-/bhr̥ĝh-* (Pok.145).

bus *n.* 1832, short for OMNIBUS. **—v.** travel or transport by bus. 1838, from the noun. **—busing** *n.* 1888, transportation by bus, verbal noun from *bus,* v. The specific use in American English of transporting students by bus to schools outside their neighborhoods (as a means of integrating the schools), is first recorded in 1964, though the verbal form *bussed* appeared in 1961.

bush *n.* shrub. Before 1375 *bussh,* in Chaucer's *Canterbury Tales,* earlier *busk* (about 1250, in *The Story of Genesis and Exodus*), in part developed from Old English *busc* (recorded only in *Withibuscemære,* before 1022, in a charter of Peterborough Abbey); and, in part a borrowing from a Scandinavian source (compare Norwegian, Danish *busk,* Swedish *buske* bush), and probably from Old French *busche* firewood, apparently from Frankish (compare Old High German and Old Saxon *busc* bush, modern German *Busch,* and Middle Dutch *busch, bosch,* bush). However, the MED says that Middle English *busk* reflects Anglo-Latin *bosca, busca* firewood, from Medieval Latin *busca,* rather than Scandinavian influence.

The sense of woodland or open forest appeared in 1657 in American English.
—v. exhaust utterly. 1870, American English *bushed,* past participial form, perhaps figurative use of earlier (1856) *bushed* lost in the bush.
—bushy *adj.* Before 1382, in the Wycliffe Bible, formed from English *bush,* n. + *-y*[1].

bushel *n.* About 1330 *busshel* a dry measure, borrowed from Old French *boissel,* probably a derivative of *boisse* a measure of grain (attested only in Middle French), from Gallo-Romance **bostia* handful, from Gaulish (compare Middle Irish *bas, boss* palm of the hand, handful, and Breton *boz*).

bushing *n.* 1839, metal lining for a hole; earlier, the fitting of a metal lining in a hole (1794), gerund of *bush,* v.; and 1566 *busch* provide with a bushing, apparently from *busch,* n., borrowed from Middle Dutch *busse* box (modern Dutch *bus*), from Late Latin *buxis;* see BOX[1] container.

bushwack *v.* 1866, to ambush; earlier, 1836, speak with gesticulation, in Davy Crockett's *Exploits,* and 1834, to pull a boat against the current by grasping undergrowth along the side of a stream. However, the concept of ambush or marauding is recorded earlier in the verbal noun *bushwacking* (1841), and of grasping shoreline undergrowth to move a boat (1826); formed from *bushwacker.* —**bushwacker** *n.* 1809, in Irving's *Knickerbocker's History of New York.* The word was formed in American English from *bush* + *whacker,* possibly after the Dutch *bosch-wachter* forest keeper.

business *n.* Before 1325, in *Cursor Mundi,* Middle English *bisines* state of being busy, eager, or anxious, developed from Old English (about 950) *bisignisse* care, anxiety, from *bisig* careful, anxious, busy, occupied (see BUSY); for suffix see -NESS.

The sense of work, occupation, profession appeared before 1387, in Trevisa's translation of Higden's *Polychronicon,* but was still closely related to *busy* and pronounced with three syllables as (bu.si.ness); the present pronunciation in two syllables developed in the 1600's.

buskin *n.* high thick-soled shoe. 1503, perhaps an alteration (influenced by *buckskin,* 1433) of Middle English *brussekyn* (1349), borrowed from Old French *brosequin* small leather boot, of uncertain origin.

Because buskins were worn by actors in ancient Greek tragedy, the word assumed the figurative sense "tragic drama, tragedy" by 1579 in Spenser's *The Shepheardes Calender.*

bust[1] *n.* sculpture of a head, shoulders, and chest. 1691, borrowed from French *buste,* from Italian *busto,* from Latin *bustum* funeral monument, tomb; originally, funeral pyre, crematory, probably shortened from *ambustum,* neuter of *ambustus* burned around, past participle of *ambūrere* burn around, scorch (*amb-* around + *ūrere* to burn; see COMBUSTION).

The sense development from "funeral pyre" and "tomb" in Latin to "sculpture of a person's head, shoulders, and chest" in Italian *busto* resulted from the custom among the ancient Etruscans of keeping the ashes of the dead in an urn shaped like the person when alive. The Romans partly copied the Etruscans, and later Italian *busto* was applied to the bust of the deceased placed on a grave, long after cremation ceased to be an approved practice.

The transferred sense "upper front part of the body, the bosom (applied to a woman)" appeared in English in 1727-51, in *Chambers Cyclopaedia.*

bust[2] *v., n. Slang.* burst, break. 1764 noun, 1806 verb, American English, alteration of BURST. The sense of "an arrest or raid" appeared about 1938, and the verb sense "to arrest" about 1953, (especially in the past participle *busted*), both perhaps influenced by an earlier (1918) sense "to demote or dismiss."

bustle[1] *v.* be noisily busy, be excessively active. About 1350 *bustelen* to act or move vigorously but blunderingly, thrash about, from earlier *bisten* to thrash, beat; developed, in part, from Middle English *bresten* to rush, gush forth, break, from Old English *bersten* (see BURST), and, in part, as a borrowing from a Scandinavian source (compare Old Icelandic *beysta* to beat; see BASTE[3]); for suffix see -LE[3]. —**n.** stir, fuss. 1634, in Milton's *Comus;* from the verb.

bustle[2] *n.* pad to puff out the back of a skirt. 1788, perhaps a special use of *bustle*[1], n. as something that makes a stir or fuss.

busy *adj.* Before 1375 *busy* (and variants *besy, bisy,* 1387), earlier *bisi* (probably before 1200, in *Ancrene Riwle* and Layamon's *Chronicle of Britain*); developed from Old English (before 1000) *bisig* careful, anxious, busy, occupied. The Old English is cognate with Middle Low German *besich* occupied, busy, and Middle Dutch *bezich* (modern Dutch *bezig*) busy, but no other related words are known.

The spelling with *u, busy,* in contrast with the pronunciation, is very rare in Middle English. It became common in the 1500's for no apparent reason, but perhaps was popularized by some printer.

—**v.** Probably about 1380 *busy,* in *Sir Gawain and the Green Knight* (and variants *besien* before 1393, and *bisien* about 1390); developed from Old English (before 725) *bisgian,* derived from *bisig,* n., busy.

but *conj., prep., adv.* unless, except. Old English *būtan* on the outside, without, unless, used as an adverb and preposition, about 725, in *Beowulf* (*bī, be* by + *ūtan* outside, from *ūt* out; see BY and OUT). —**n.** an objection. About 1390, in Chaucer's *Canterbury Tales,* from the conjunction.

butane *n.* 1875, formed from English *but(yl)* + *ane; butyl,* a hydrocarbon acting as a group of atoms in fractioning butane, from *butyric* (acid) a product of fermentation found in rancid butter, borrowed from Latin *būtȳrum* BUTTER; for suffix see -ANE.

butch *n. Slang.* tough boy or man. 1930, American English, in Damon Runyon's *Guys and Dolls,* nickname of a tough character, originally popularized by the nickname of George "Butch" Cassidy, American outlaw of the early 1900's, probably from dialectal *butch* vendor (as in "news butch"), short for *butcher* (1882); see BUTCHER.

butcher *n.* Probably before 1300, in *Kyng Alisaunder,* Middle English *bocher* slaughterer of animals, borrowed from Old French *bochier, bouchier* one who slaughters and sells he-goats, from *bouc* he-goat, buck, apparently from a fusion of two Celtic and Frankish words (compare Old Irish *boc, bocc* male goat, deer, etc., and Old High German *boc* male goat; see BUCK[1] male deer). The modern spelling begins to appear gradually after the 1550's.

The figurative sense of a brutal murderer appeared in English about 1350. A specifically American usage, *butcher* or *butcher boy,* meaning a vendor of candy, fruit, newspapers, etc. appeared in 1882; its connection with the primary meaning of *butcher* is obscure.

—v. to slaughter. 1562, from the noun.

—**butchery** *n.* About 1450, slaughter, execution, borrowed from Old French *bochierie, bouchierie,* from *bochier, bouchier.*

butler *n.* manservant. About 1250, in *The Story of Genesis and Exodus,* Middle English *butuler* chief servant in charge of the wine; earlier, *butiller* (1171, as an occupation listed in an ancient charter); borrowed through Anglo-French *butiller* cupbearer, variant of Old French *bouteillier,* from *bouteille* wine vessel; see BOTTLE.

butt[1] *n.* thicker end of anything. About 1400 *botte* thicker end of a spear opposite the head, in Lydgate's *Troy Book,* 1422 *butte,* related to Old English *buttuc* end, small piece of land, which may be cognate with Old Icelandic *būttr* short, and possibly *būtr* log of wood, stump, block, Middle Low German *but* and Middle Dutch *bot* blunt, short, stumpy, and Old High German *bōzan* to beat, kick; see BEAT.)

butt² *n.* target of ridicule or scorn. 1345-46 *but* mark for target practice; a fusion in Middle English of Old French *bout, bot* end (from Frankish; compare Old High German *bōzan* and Old Icelandic *bauta* to beat), and of Old French *but* aim, goal, end, also from Frankish (compare Old Icelandic *būtr* log of wood, stump, block); see BEAT and BUTT¹.

butt³ *v.* strike or thrust with the head. Probably about 1200 *butten,* in *The Ormulum,* borrowed from Old French *bouter,* earlier *boter* to thrust, from Frankish (compare Old High German *bōzan* and Old Icelandic *bauta* to strike, beat; see BEAT). **—butt in** *Slang.* meddle, interfere. 1900, American English, in George Ade's *Fables in Slang.*

—n. 1647, from the verb, possibly by influence of French *botte* a thrust in fencing.

butt⁴ *n.* barrel for wine or beer. 1393 *butt,* earlier *bote* (1385), borrowed from Old French *bot, bout,* from Late Latin *buttis* cask, probably of Greek origin (compare Greek dialect *býtinē,* used in Greek colonial city of Tarentum in ancient Italy, from Greek *pýtínē* decorated flask).

butte *n.* a steep, flat-topped hill standing alone. 1805 *butte,* as a French word introduced into Clark's *Journals of the Lewis Expedition.*

butter *n.* Old English (about 1000) *butere,* borrowed from Latin *būtȳrum,* from Greek *boútȳron,* apparently meaning originally cow's milk curds, formed from *boûs* ox, COW¹ + *tȳrós* cheese, cognate with Avestan *tūiri* curdled milk, whey, Middle Indic *tūra-* cheese, and Old English *ge-thweor* curds, related to *thweran* to churn, from Indo-European **twer-/tūr-* twirl (Pok.1100).

Some, following the ancients, claim Scythian origin for Greek *boútȳron.* It is true that both the Hellenic and Italic civilizations were oil-cultures, and butter was not a native product. But the elements of the Greek word look as if they had Greek meanings, unless they were remodeled; or, conceivably, the Greek word is a loan translation of a word in another language such as Scythian.

—v. put butter on. Before 1475, from the noun. **—buttercup** *n.* (1777), earlier **butterflower** (1578). **—buttermilk** *n.* (before 1500) **—butterscotch** *n.* 1855 *butterscot,* later *butterscotch* (1865).

butterfly *n.* Before 1325 *buterfleie,* earlier *buterflige* (about 1250), developed from Old English *buturfliogæ, buturfliogo, buterflege* (about 700, in early glossaries), all forms ultimately being a compound of *butere* BUTTER + *flēoge* FLY; the origin of this name for the insect is obscure.

buttocks *n.pl.* rump. About 1300 *buttok, buttokes,* earlier (in surname *Briddebuttok,* 1268), probably related to Old English *buttuc* end, small piece of land; see BUTT¹ thick end.

button *n.* Before 1325 *botoun* a button; earlier, something insignificant or small (probably before 1300, in *Sir Tristrem*); borrowed from Old French *bouton, boton* bud, knob, from *bouter, boter* to thrust; see BUTT³ strike. Note that *botouner* a maker or seller of buttons, is recorded as early as 1265, suggesting that the usual sense of button existed at least 50 years before it was recorded and that the meaning "something small or insignificant" may be a later figurative extension, not an earlier use. **—v.** furnish or fasten with buttons. About 1380, in *Sir Ferumbras,* either borrowed from Old French *boutonner* to button, earlier meaning "to bud," from *bouton* bud; or developed from Middle English *botoun,* n. The figurative sense "close tightly, fasten" (*button up*) appeared in 1590, in Shakespeare's *Comedy of Errors,* followed by the sense "to silence (a person)," about 1647. **—buttonhole** *n.* 1561, *v.* to corner in conversation (1862), earlier *buttonhold* (1834) and *buttonholder* (1806).

buttress *n.* About 1330 *butras,* in *Sir Orfeo,* 1344-45 *boterace,* borrowed from Old French *bouterez,* from *bouter* to thrust against; see BUTT³ strike. **—v.** strengthen with or as if with a buttress. About 1378, in a version of *Piers Plowman,* from the noun.

buxom (buk′səm) *adj.* plump and comely. About 1250 *buxum,* in the poems *Genesis* and *Exodus;* earlier *buhsum* (probably before 1200) pliant, compliant, obedient, found in Proto-Germanic **būHsamaz,* but refashioned in English from the native elements *buh-,* stem of Old English *būgan* to bend + *-sum* -some¹; see BOW¹ bend.

The present meaning, which appeared in 1589, evolved from the obsolete sense (before 1375) "indulgent, obliging, gracious," later "jolly, lively, wholesome."

buy *v.* About 1300 *beyen,* in *Havelok the Dane;* earlier *biggen* get or redeem for a price, purchase (probably about 1200, past tense *boghte*); developed from Old English *bycgan* (past tense *bohte*); cognate with Old Saxon *buggian* buy, Old Icelandic *byggja* lend, buy, and Gothic *bugjan* buy, from Proto-Germanic **buȝjanan,* but with no cognates outside Germanic.

The present spelling *buy* did not become standard until near the end of the 1500's. It originated in a dialectal variant from southwestern England *buggen* (probably about 1175, in *Poema Morale*) and *buyen* (about 1300). Middle English *-gg-* and Old English *-cg-* in this word were pronounced *-dg-* (j) as in *bridge.*

—n. 1879, American English, from the verb.

—buyer *n.* 1303 *byer,* in Mannyng's *Handlyng Synne;* earlier *biggere* (probably before 1200), from the Middle English *biggen,* v.

buzz *v.* 1530 *buss,* in Palsgrave's *Lesclarcissement,* imitative of the sound made by bees and other insects. The verbal noun *bussing* is attested earlier (1495, in Wynkyn de Worde's version of Trevisa's translation of Bartholomew's *De Proprietatibus Rerum*). The modern sense "fly low and close (in an aircraft)" appeared in 1941.

—n. 1605, in Shakespeare's *King Lear,* a groundless fancy, whim; later, busy talk, hum (1627), and a humming sound (1645, in writings of Milton); all from the verb.

buzzard *n.* bird of prey. Probably before 1300 *bosard, busard,* borrowed from Old French *buisart, busart,* from *buson, buison,* from Latin *būteōnem,* accusative form of *būteō* a kind of hawk.

by *prep., adv.* near, beside. Old English *bī,* unstressed *be* (about 725, in *Beowulf*); cognate with Old Saxon and Old Frisian *bī, be* by, near, Old High German *bī, bi* (modern German *bei*), Gothic *bi* about, by, from Proto-Germanic **bi,* Indo-European **bhi* (Pok.34); also cognate with the second element in Latin *ambi-* about, around, Greek *amphí* around, and Sanskrit *ábhi* toward, to. **—bygone** *adj.* (1442) **—bypath** *n.* (probably before 1325) —**byway** *n.* (before 1338) —**byword** *n.* (before 1131)

bylaw *n.* 1370 *bilawe,* earlier *bilage* local ordinance (1280), alteration of still earlier *birelage* body of local ordinances (1257), probably influenced by *bī* dwelling, village, town, and *lawe, lage* law (late Old English *bӯ,* in the *Lindisfarne Gospels,* and Old English *lagu,* in writings of Ælfric), both forms borrowed from a Scandinavian source (compare Old Icelandic *bӯr,* genitive *bӯar,* dwelling, town, related to *būa* dwell, see BOWER, and Old Icelandic *lǫg* laws, see LAW).

The current meaning of a secondary or subordinate law appeared in 1541, in writings of Coverdale, through confusion of the element *by-* with English *by,* adv., aside, near.

byte (bīt) *n.* unit of eight bits in a computer memory. 1964, American English, irregular blend of *bit* binary digit (see BIT³), and *bite* morsel. On the pattern of *bit* and *byte,* recent coinages have been *nibble* unit of four bits (i.e. a half byte) and *gulp* group of bytes (i.e., large byte). The suggested etymology of *byte* as an acronym formed from *b* (inar)*y* (digi)*t e*(ight) is an ingenious but unproven conjecture.

C

cab *n.* carriage, taxicab. 1826, in Disraeli's *Vivien Grey,* horse-drawn carriage, shortened from *cabriolet* (1763, in works of Smollett), borrowed as French *cabriolet,* from *cabrioler* to caper, leap; so called for its bouncing motion. French *cabrioler* was an alteration (influenced by *cabri* kid, from Provençal *cabrit*) of obsolete French *caprioler* to caper, leap, from Italian *capriolare,* from *capriolo* roebuck, from Latin *capreolus* wild goat, roebuck, diminutive of *caprea* wild she-goat, from *caper* (genitive *caprī*) he-goat. Latin *caper* is cognate with Old English *hæfer* and Greek *kápros* boar, from Indo-European **kápro-s* (Pok.529).

The word was first applied to motor-driven vehicles in 1899 and to the part of a locomotive where the engineer sits in 1859.

—**cabby** *n. Informal.* cab driver. 1859, formed from English *cab* + *-y*².

cabal (kəbal′) *n.* small group working or plotting in secret. 1660; earlier, an intrigue (1646-47), a secret tradition or private interpretation (1637), Jewish tradition or interpretation of the Old Testament (1616); borrowed from French *cabale* secret group, intrigue, or tradition, cabala, from Medieval Latin *cabala, cabbala,* from post-Biblical Hebrew *qabbālāh* received teachings, tradition, from Hebrew *qibbēl* he received.

The word *cabala, cabbala* is also recorded in English as early as 1521 meaning "mystical interpretation of the Old Testament," with the extended sense "mystery, secret or esoteric doctrine or art" appearing in 1665.

caballero (kab′əlyär′ō) *n.* gentleman, gallant. 1835, American English, borrowed from Spanish *caballero* knight, gentleman, from Late Latin *caballārius* horseman, from Latin *caballus* horse. Doublet of CAVALIER and CHEVALIER.

cabana (kəban′ə *or* kəbän′yə) *n.* cabin. 1898, American English, borrowed from Spanish *cabaña,* from Late Latin *capanna* hut (in Medieval Latin, often "tent"). Doublet of CABIN.

cabaret *n.* restaurant with entertainment. 1655, tavern, borrowing of French *cabaret,* probably from Middle Dutch *cabret, cambret, cameret,* from Old Picard (dialect of Picardy) *camberete,* diminutive of *cambre* room, from Late Latin *camera;* see CAMERA and CHAMBER.

The meaning was extended to the entertainment itself (floor show) in the 1920's.

cabbage *n.* Before 1475 *cabage,* earlier *caboge* (before 1450), *caboche* head of cabbage (1391), borrowed from Middle French *caboche,* variant of Old French *caboce,* from Medieval Latin *caputium* head-cabbage, from Latin *caput* HEAD.

Originally the plant may have been *cabbage cole* (compare Dutch *kabuis-kool*); the word *cole* was a general term for a variety of leafy vegetable greens including kale and mustard and is found in Old English *cāl* (modern English *cole*). The distinction, if it existed, between head of cabbage and the plant was apparently lost before the end of the 1300's.

cabin *n.* 1346 *caban,* borrowed from Old French *cabane, cabine* hut, cabin, from Old Provençal *cabana,* from Late Latin *capanna* hut, of uncertain origin. The spelling *cabin* appeared about 1598 and was established in the 1600's. Doublet of CABANA.

cabinet *n.* 1549, secret receptacle, case used especially for safekeeping; private chamber (1565); borrowed in all of these senses from Middle French *cabinet,* diminutive of Old Picard (dialect of Picardy) *cabine* a house or room for gambling, variant of Old French *cabane* (see CABIN); but perhaps influenced by earlier Italian *gabinetto* closet, chest of drawers, suggesting the Middle French form *cabinet;* for suffix see -ET. An early diminutive formed from English *cabin* seems to be confined to the meaning "a little hut, cottage, etc." (1572, 1579) while the modern senses are borrowed from French.

The sense of a group of persons meeting in a private chamber (originally in the phrase *cabinet council*) appeared in 1607-12, in writings of Francis Bacon.

cable *n.* Probably before 1200, in Layamon's *Chronicle of Britain,* borrowed through Anglo-French and Old North French *cable,* from Medieval Latin *capulum* rope, line, bridle, from Latin *capere* to seize, take; see CAPTIVE.

A *cable* for conducting electricity is recorded in 1854; *cable* meaning a message sent by underwater cable (1883), was shortened from *cablegram* (1868), which was formed in American English on the analogy of *telegram.* In the sense of the transmission of television programs by coaxial cable, *cable* was a shortening (1972) of *cable television* or *cable TV* (1963).

—**v.** About 1500, tie up; from the noun. The sense "transmit (a message) by cable" appeared as an Americanism in 1871.

caboodle *n.* group of persons or things. Before 1848, American English, of unknown origin. English *boodle* was probably borrowed as *boedel* (1699) from Dutch *boedel* goods, property. Phrases such as *kit and boodle* (before 1861) and *the whole kit and caboodle* (1888) are the only examples of use.

caboose *n.* 1747, American English, ship's cookhouse, probably borrowed from Early Modern Dutch *kabuyse,* from or related to Middle Low German *kabūse* wooden cabin on ship's deck (modern German *Kabuse, Kombüse* ship's mess), conjectured to be formed from *kab-* (related to Old French *cabane* hut, CABIN) + Middle High German *hūs* house.

The sense "rear car on a freight train, used by the crew" appeared in English in 1861.

cacao (kəkā′ō) *n.* seed from which cocoa and chocolate are made. 1555, borrowed from Spanish *cacao,* from Nahuatl *cacáua,* root form of *cacáuatl* cacao seed.

cache *n.* hiding place. 1797, American English, borrowed from French *cache* hiding place, from Old

French *cacher* to hide; see CACHET. The meaning "anything stored in a hiding place", is first recorded in the 1830's or perhaps earlier as a borrowing from French Canadian *cache* (about 1669). —**v.** put in a cache. 1805, in Lewis and Clark's *Journals,* American English, borrowed from French *cacher* to hide, from Old French.

cachet (kashā') *n.* private seal or stamp. Before 1639, borrowed from French *cachet* seal, stamp (as in *lettre de cachet* letter under seal of the French king), from Old French *cacher* press on or crowd together (later, to hide), from Northern Gallo-Romance **coācticāre,* a frequentative form of Latin *coāctāre* constrain, showing continued action, from *coāctus,* past participle of *cōgere* bring or drive together, collect, press; see COGENT.

cachinnation *n.* 1623, borrowed from Latin *cachinnātiōnem* (nominative *cachinnātiō*), from *cachinnāre* laugh loudly; for suffix see -TION. Latin *cachinnāre* has comparable forms in Greek *kacházein* laugh loudly, Old High German *kachazzen,* Old English *ceahhetan,* and Old Slavic *chochotati,* all possibly derived ultimately from an interjection representing the sound of laughter.

cackle *v.* Probably before 1200, in *Ancrene Riwle,* Middle English *cakelin* to cackle like a hen, probably imitative (of the sounds made by fowls), but compare possible earlier Middle Dutch *cakelen.* Swedish *kakla,* Norwegian *kakle,* and Danish *kagle* seem to be late borrowings from Dutch or English. —**n.** 1676, probably developed from the verb. Earlier use of *cakele* (probably before 1200) is adjectival, meaning cackling, talkative.

cacophony (kəkof'ənē) *n.* harsh, clashing sound. 1656, borrowed from Greek *kakophōníā,* from *kakóphōnos* ill-sounding (*kakós* bad + *phōnḗ* sound).

English borrowing may have been influenced by earlier French *cacophonie* (1587), attested also in Italian (1585).

—**cacophonous** *adj.* 1797, borrowed from Greek *kakóphōnos* ill-sounding; for suffix see -OUS.

cactus *n.* Originally (1607) used of the Spanish artichoke or cardoon, borrowed from Latin *cactus* cardoon. Later (1767) the current sense of a kind of succulent plant, often with sharp spines, appeared (as the genus name given by Linnaeus in his system of plant classification, using New Latin *Cactus*), from Latin *cactus* cardoon, from Greek *káktos* a prickly plant, of non-Indo-European origin.

cad *n.* ill-mannered person. 1790, passenger on a coach who pays the driver privately, without a ticket; shortened from Scottish *caddie* errand boy, porter, an earlier variant (1730) of CADET. The modern meaning (1838) may have originated at Oxford University (1831) in referring to one of the townspeople, especially those who assisted at sports.

cadaver *n.* About 1500, borrowed from Latin *cadāver,* from *cadere* to fall, fall dead, die; see CADENCE. Earlier occurrence of *cadaver* (before 1398, in Trevisa's translation of Bartholomew's *De Proprietatibus Rerum*) is probably Latin. —**cadaverous** *adj.* Probably before 1425, in a translation of Guy de Chauliac's *Grande Chirurgie,* from Latin *cadāverōsus,* from *cadāver;* for suffix see -OUS.

caddie or **caddy**[1] *n.* person who carries a golfer's clubs. 1634-46, Scottish use of *cadet* a young gentleman who entered the military without a commission, borrowed from French *cadet* younger brother; see CADET. The current meaning appeared in 1857, from the earlier Scottish sense of "messenger, errand boy" (1730). The English pronunciation (kad'ē) reflects the French pronunciation of *cadet.* —**v.** to serve as a caddie. 1908, from the noun.

caddy[2] *n.* small box, can, or chest, especially for holding tea. 1792, apparently the meaning derived from a transfer of the name for the weight or measure of tea to the chest it was carried in, and is an alteration of earlier English *catty* (1598) the measure of weight set by the East India Company (1770) for tea and other commodities in China and Malaysia to standardize the Asian unit of weight, about 1-1/3 lbs., from Malay-Indonesian *kati.*

cadence *n.* About 1380, rhythm of prose or poetry, a rhetorical passage, in Chaucer's *House of Fame,* borrowed from Old French *cadence* rhythm, from Italian *cadenza* conclusion of a movement in music; literally, a falling, from Vulgar Latin **cadentia* a falling, from Latin *cadere* to fall. Latin *cadore* is perhaps cognate with Sanskrit *śad-* to fall, and Armenian *çacnum* to fall, from Indo-European **kad-* (Pok.516). Doublet of CHANCE.

cadenza *n.* a flourish or elaborate passage usually near the end of a piece or movement of music. 1836, borrowed from Italian; see CADENCE.

cadet *n.* trainee in a military academy. 1610, younger son or brother, borrowed from French *cadet,* from Gascon (a Gallo-Romance dialect) *capdet* chief, from Latin *capitellum* small head, diminutive form of *caput* (genitive *capitis*) HEAD.

The original meaning "younger son or brother" arose because Gascon officers in the French army were usually younger sons or lesser heads of noble families; the meaning "young career officer in the army" came into English in 1651 (and by way of *caddie* from Scottish use in 1634-46) and led to the current sense of a student in a military academy (1775).

cadge *v. Informal.* beg. 1812, in Vaux's *Flash Dictionary,* a slang verb of uncertain origin; perhaps related to earlier *cadge* (originally in Scottish and North English dialect) to carry, as a peddler does (1607), apparently a back formation from *cadger* (about 1450) originally in Scottish itinerant peddler; perhaps also related to Middle English *caggen* to fasten, tie (probably about 1325, in *The Pearl*), also of uncertain origin.

cadmium *n.* metallic chemical element. 1822, New Latin, from Latin *cadmīa,* earlier *cadmēa* zinc ore, from Greek *Kadmeíā gê,* literally, Cadmean or Theban earth, from *Kádmos* Cadmus, the legendary founder of Thebes.

Cadmium was coined in 1817 by Friedrich Stromeyer, 1786-1835, a German chemist who discovered this element.

cadre (kad'rā) *n.* group of people around which an organization is formed in military, political, or general use; framework or core of an organization. 1830, in Scott's Introduction to *The Lay of the Last Minstrel,* framework, borrowed from French *cadre* frame (as of a picture), officers' group, from Italian *quadro* framework, from Latin *quadrum* a square, related to *quattuor* FOUR.

caduceus (kədü'sēəs) *n.* staff of Mercury or Hermes; emblem of the medical profession. 1591, in writings of

Spenser, borrowed from Latin *cādūceus,* variant of *cādūceum,* alteration of Doric Greek *kā́rȳkeion* herald's staff, from *kā́rȳx* (genitive *kā́rȳkos*) a herald; cognate with Sanskrit *carkṛtí-s* glory, praise, *kārú-s* one who praises, poet, from Indo-European **kar-* and **kāru-s* (Pok.530).

caecum *n.* See CECUM.

Caesar *n.* absolute ruler, emperor, dictator. Probably before 1200 *kaisere, cæiser,* in Layamon's *Chronicle of Britain,* corresponding to Old English *Cāsere,* but probably reborrowed from Medieval Latin *Caesar* and Old French *Cesar,* the surname of the Roman general and statesman Caius Julius *Caesar,* 102?-44 B.C. Caesar's name was transferred as a title to the emperors from Augustus to Hadrian (30 B.C. to A.D. 138) and later often applied to all the emperors until the fall of Constantinople in 1453. Doublet of CZAR and KAISER. —**Caesarean** or **Caesarian** *adj.* 1615 *Caesarian section,* surgical delivery of young through the abdominal wall; so called from the belief (often disputed) that Julius Caesar was born by means of this operation.

caesura (sizhůr′ə) *n.* pause in poetry. 1556 (Anglicized *ceasure*), borrowed from Latin *caesūra* a cutting, from *caesus,* past participle of *caedere* to cut; see EXCISE[2] cut.

cafe or **café** *n.* restaurant. 1802, borrowed as French *café* coffee house, coffee, from Italian *caffè* COFFEE. The modern British slang term is now *caf,* a shortening of *café.*

cafeteria *n.* 1839, American English, coffee house; borrowed from Mexican Spanish *cafetería* coffee shop (*café* coffee, from Italian *caffè* COFFEE + Spanish *-tería* place where something is done usually as a business).

caffeine or **caffein** *n.* stimulating drug in coffee and tea. 1830, borrowed from French *caféine,* from *café* COFFEE; for suffix see -INE[2] (chemical suffix).

cage *n.* Probably before 1200, in *Ancrene Riwle,* borrowed from Old French *cage,* from Latin *cavea* coop, cage, from *cavus* hollow, CAVE. Related to JAIL. —**v.** to put or keep in a cage. 1577, from the noun.

cagey *adj. Informal.* shrewd; wary; devious. 1893, American English, of uncertain origin.

cahoots *n. Slang.* Usually, **in cahoots.** partnership. 1829 *cohoot,* American English, of uncertain origin; occasionally thought to be borrowed from French *cahute* cabin.

cairn (kãrn) *n.* pile of stones heaped up as a memorial, tomb, or landmark. 1535, Scottish *carne,* developed from Gaelic *carn* heap of stones, rocky hill, from Old Irish *carn.* Also found in Welsh *carn* 1) heap 2) hoof and handle of a knife, the latter possibly pointing to an earlier sense "horn" and therefore to Gaulish *karnon* horn, and top or horn of a mountain, according to the OED.

caisson (kā′son) *n.* box or wagon for ammunition. 1704, borrowed from French *caisson,* from Middle French *caisson* large box, alteration of *casson* box, from Italian *cassone* large box, augmentative form of *cassa,* from Latin *capsa* box, CASE[2]. The change from Middle French *casson* to *caisson* was influenced by Middle French *caisse* chest, from Provençal *caissa,* from Vulgar Latin **capsea,* from Latin *capsa* box, CASE[2].

The meaning of a watertight chamber used for underwater construction was first recorded in 1753.

cajole *v.* 1645, borrowed from French *cajoler* persuade by flattery, possibly a blend of Middle French *cageoler* chatter like a jay, from *geai* JAY, and Old French *gaioler* to cage, entice into a cage, from *gaiole* cage. The French word, if a blend, was probably influenced in spelling by *enjôler* coax, imprison, from Old French *enjaoler,* from *jaole, jaiole* JAIL. —**cajoler** *n.* 1677, in Hobb's translation of the works of Homer, formed from English *cajole* + *-er*[1]. —**cajolery** *n.* 1649, in a translation by Evelyn, borrowed from French *cajolerie* persuasion by flattery, from *cajoler.*

cake *n.* Probably about 1200 *kake* kind of flat cake or loaf, probably borrowed from a Scandinavian source (compare Old Icelandic *kaka* cake). The word is cognate with Old English *cēcel* small cake, Old High German *kuocho* cake (modern German *Kuchen*), and Middle Dutch *kōke,* from Indo-European **gag-/gōg-* something round and lumpy (Pok.349). —**v.** form into a flat, compact mass. 1607, in Shakespeare's *Timon of Athens,* from the noun.

cakewalk *n.* 1863, American English, probably originally so named in allusion to a cake given as a prize at a social gathering for the fanciest steps in a dancelike procession. Curiously, the figurative meaning of something easy appears about 15 years before the literal meaning (1879). —**v.** Before 1909, in O. Henry's *Roads of Destiny,* from the noun.

calabash (kal′əbash) *n.* gourd. 1596, either the gourd or the tree it grows on, in writings of Raleigh, borrowed from French *calebasse,* from Middle French *calabasse,* from Spanish *calabaza,* and possibly from **calapaccia,* of pre-Roman (Iberian) origin, as suggested by the Spanish scholar Corominas. Also, compare Persian *kharbuz* melon.

calaboose (kal′əbüs) *n.* jail. 1792, American English, borrowed from Louisiana French *calabouse,* from Spanish *calabozo* dungeon, probably from Vulgar Latin **calafodium,* (pre-Roman **cala* protected place, den + Latin *fodere* to dig, see BED).

calamine (kal′əmin) *n.* ore of zinc. 1601, in Holland's translation of Pliny's *Natural History,* borrowed probably from French *calamine,* in Old French *calemine,* learned borrowing from Medieval Latin *calamina,* alteration of Latin *cadmīa* zinc ore, from Greek *kadmeíā;* see CADMIUM.

calamity *n.* About 1425 *calamyte,* borrowed from Middle French *calamité,* from Latin *calamitātem* (nominative *calamitās*) damage, disaster, adversity, which is perhaps related to Latin *incolumis* undamaged, unharmed, from Indo-European **kelə-* hit, cut (Pok.545); for suffix see -ITY. — **calamitous** *adj.* 1545, borrowed from Middle French *calamiteus,* from Latin *calamitōsus,* contraction of **calamitātōsus,* adjective form of *calamitātem.*

calcareous (kalkãr′ēəs) *adj.* containing lime or limestone. 1677 *calcarious,* borrowed from Latin *calcārius,* from *calx* (genitive *calcis*) lime, see CHALK; for suffixes see -ARY and -OUS. The spelling with *-eous* (1792) appeared by influences of other substances spelled with *-eous.*

calci-, or (before vowels) **calc-,** a combining form meaning lime, limestone, calcium, or calcium salts, as in *calcic, calcify.* Borrowed from Latin *calx* (genitive *calcis*) lime; see CHALK.

calcify *v.* to change into bone by deposits of calcium

salts. 1836, to change into lime, formed in English from Latin *calx* (genitive *calcis*) lime + English *-fy*. **—calcification** *n.* 1849-52, formed from English *calcify*, on the analogy of earlier *petrify, petrification*, etc.; for suffix see -ATION.

calcium *n.* metallic chemical element. 1808, New Latin *calcium*, from Latin *calx* (genitive *calcis*) lime, limestone, see CHALK + New Latin *-ium* (chemical suffix); so called because calcium is found in limestone. It was first separated from it and named by Sir Humphry Davy, though the ancients knew of its qualities of strength in mortar.

calculate *v.* compute, reckon, figure. 1570, borrowed from Late Latin *calculātus*, past participle of *calculāre*, from Latin *calculus* reckoning or account, originally, small stone used in counting, diminutive of *calx* (genitive *calcis*) small stone, limestone, see CHALK; for suffix see -ATE[1]. In the late 1500's and 1600's *calculate* replaced earlier Middle English *calculen* (before 1378, in a version of *Piers Plowman*), borrowed from Old French *calculer* and Late Latin *calculāre*. Another form of this verb, *calk*, Middle English *calken* (probably before 1400) existed, originally, as a shortened form of *calculen*, and was in use at least into the 1650's. **—calculation** *n.* Before 1393, in Gower's *Confessio Amantis*, borrowed from Anglo-French *calculation*, from Late Latin *calculātiōnem* (nominative *calculātiō*), from *calculāre* calculate; for suffix see -TION. **—calculator** *n.* Before 1425 *calkelatour* mathematician, in writings of Wycliffe, borrowed from Latin *calculātor* person versed in arithmetic; for suffix see -OR[2]. The meaning "calculating device, such as a set of numerical tables" appeared in English in 1784; the term *calculating machine* (about 1832) was gradually replaced by *calculator* with the advent of the small electronic devices for figuring.

calculus *n.* system of calculation in higher mathematics. 1666, borrowed from Latin *calculus* pebble, small stone used in counting, calculation, counting; see CALCULATE.

caldron or **cauldron** *n.* Before 1393, in Gower's *Confessio Amantis*, alteration (influenced by Latin *caldus* hot) of earlier *caudroun* (about 1300), borrowed from Anglo-French *caudrun* or Old North French *caudron, cauderon*, diminutive form of *caudiere* cooking pot. Old North French *caudiere* came from Late Latin *caldāria* cooking pot, (originally) *calidāria*, feminine of Latin *calidārius* for heating, from *caldus, calidus* hot, from *calēre* be warm or hot, cognate with Lithuanian *šilti* become warm, and Sanskrit *śarád-* autumn, from Indo-European **k̂el-* warm (Pok.551).

calendar *n.* Probably before 1200 *kalender* system of divisions of the year, in Layamon's *Chronicle of Britain;* about 1350, table showing the divisions; borrowed from Anglo-French *calender*, corresponding to Old French *kalendier* list, register, learned borrowing from Latin *calendārium* account book, from *calendae* calends.

Calends, kalends, meaning the first day of the month, gradually disappeared from use in English after the 1500's and has been retained only in reference to Latin use where its meaning "first day of the month" signified the day Romans proclaimed the order of the days that were to follow, derived from **calēre*, variant of *calāre* call out, proclaim, cognate with Greek *kaleîn* to call; see LOW[2], v. make the sound of a cow.

calender *n.* machine in which cloth, paper, etc., is pressed under rollers. 1513, person who presses cloth, paper, etc., borrowed probably through Anglo-French *kalender* (1278), from Old French *calandre, calendre,* from Vulgar Latin **colondra*, alteration (influenced by Latin *columna* column) of Latin *cylindrus* roller, CYLINDER. The sense of a machine for pressing cloth, etc., is first recorded in 1688. —v. 1513, borrowed from Middle French *calandrer*, from Old French *calandre*.

calf[1] *n.* young cow, bull, etc. Old English *cælf* (before 800), *cealf* (before 830), plural *calfur*, all Anglian forms corresponding to West Saxon *cealf* (about 1000), plural *cealfru*. The Old English is cognate with Old Saxon and Middle Dutch *calf* (modern Dutch *kalf*), Old High German *kalb* calf (modern German *Kalb*), from Proto-Germanic **kalƀan*, related to Old Icelandic *kālfr* (masculine) male calf, Danish and Swedish *kalv*, and Gothic *kalbō* female calf, from Indo-European **golbh-*, from root **gelebh-* (Pok.359).

calf[2] *n.* hind part of the leg below the knee. Before 1325, borrowed from Old Icelandic *kālfi*, related to *kālfr* CALF[1].

caliber or **calibre** *n.* inside diameter of a gun barrel. 1588, borrowed from Middle French *calibre*.

Italian and Spanish words are proposed to continue the derivation from Middle French *calibre* to Arabic *qālib* mold for casting metal, model, shoemaker's last. However, the possible existence of intermediate forms to connect the French and the Arabic is not documented by Italian *calibro* (1606) or by Spanish *calibre* (1594) which are recorded later than the English (1588).

The earliest attested meaning in English was the figurative sense "degree of merit or importance" (1567).

—calibrate *v.* determine the caliber of, test or adjust a measuring device. 1864, formed from English *caliber* + *-ate*[1]. **—calibration** *n.* (1871)

calico *n.* 1540 *kalyko*, 1541 *Callicutt*, from *Calicut*, a city and port on the Malabar coast in southwestern India, from which various cotton cloths were imported by European merchants.

californium *n.* radioactive chemical element. 1950, New Latin, formed from *California* (in reference to the University of California, where it was discovered) + *-ium* (chemical suffix).

calipers or **callipers** *n.pl.* instrument to measure diameter or thickness. 1627, in a glossary of Captain John Smith, from earlier *calliper compasses* device used to measure caliber (1588); variant of CALIBER. The OED remarks "that from the beginning the words were spelt differently."

caliph (kā'lif) *n.* former title of a Moslem ruler, as successor of Mohammed. Before 1393, in Gower's *Confessio Amantis*, borrowed from Old French *calife* and Medieval Latin *califa*, from Arabic *khalīfa* successor, vicar, from *khalafa* he succeeded, was behind. **—caliphate** *n.* 1614, formed from English *caliph* + *-ate*[1], perhaps by influence of French *caliphat*.

calisthenics or **callisthenics** *n.pl.* 1847, formed in English from Greek *kalli-* (combining form of *kállos* beauty) + *sthénos* strength, of unknown origin + English *-ics*. The Greek *kállos* is cognate with Sanskrit *kalyāṇa-s* beautiful, from Indo-European **kal-, *kali-* (Pok.524). The earliest attested use in English was in the singular *calisthenic* (1839) and the derivative *callisthenical* (1837). **—calisthenic** *adj.* 1847, from *calisthen-*

ic, n., or possibly from *calisthenics,* on the analogy of *gymnastics, gymnastic.*

calk[1] or **caulk** *v.* make watertight. About 1378 *cauken* to tread, in a version of *Piers Plowman;* perhaps before 1500 *caulke* to calk; borrowed from Old North French *cauquer* to tread, press in, from Latin *calcāre* to tread, stamp, press in, from *calx* (genitive *calcis*) heel; possibly cognate with Lithuanian *kulnìs* heel, and Greek *kôlon* limb, member, COLON[1] punctuation mark.

The spelling has varied between *caulk* and *calk* since the 1400's, possibly because of confusion with the word *calk*[2] in the meaning "a sharp iron spike" and the use of the word in blacksmithing. The spelling *calk* has been established as the preferred form in American English since the late 1800's, though British *caulk* still appears occasionally.

calk[2] (kôk) *n.* projecting piece on a horseshoe to prevent slipping. 1587, apparently back formation from earlier (1447) *kakun,* borrowed from Old North French *calkain* heel, from Late Latin *calcāneum,* from Latin *calx* (genitive *calcis*) heel; see CALK[1]. **—v.** put calks on. 1624, from the noun.

call *v.* Old English (about 725) **callian* (implied in *hilde-calla* war herald), variant of Old English (before 1000) *ceallian.* The Old English **callian* is cognate with Old Icelandic *kalla* to call, Old High German *kallōn* talk much, chatter (Proto-Germanic **kallōjanan*), Welsh *galw* call, and Old Slavic *glasŭ* voice, from Indo-European **galso-,* extended from the root **gal-* call, cry (Pok. 350). Middle English *callen, kallen* (probably about 1200) is thought to be a fresh borrowing from Scandinavian (compare Old Icelandic *kalla* to call). **—n.** Before 1325, in *Cursor Mundi,* developed from *callen,* v., to call. **—caller** *n.* 1435, from Middle English *callen* to call + *-er*[1]. **—calling** *n.* occupation (1551) from earlier meaning "summons to a way of life" (probably before 1250), from Middle English *callen* to call + *-ing.*

calligraphy *n.* handwriting, especially as an art or a study. 1613, in Cawdrey's *Table Alphabeticall,* borrowed ultimately from Greek *kalligraphíā,* from *kalligráphos* good penman (*kalli-,* combining form of *kállos* beauty + *gráphein* write; see CARVE), but perhaps coming into English through French *calligraphie* or directly from New Latin *calligraphia.*

calliope (kəlī′əpē) *n.* musical instrument made of a series of steam whistles pitched to various tones. 1858, in allusion to *Calliope* the ninth and chief Muse of eloquence and epic poetry, borrowed from Latin *Calliopē,* from Greek *Kalliópē* (*kalli-,* a combining form of *kállos* beauty + **óps,* genitive *opós* VOICE).

callous *adj.* Before 1400, borrowed through Middle French *calleux,* or directly from Latin *callōsus,* from *callus, callum* hardened skin; cognate with Old Irish *calath, calad* hard, Old Slavic *kaliti* to cool, harden, Albanian *akul* ice, and Sanskrit *kiṇa-s* callus. from Indo-European **kal-, *kalno-, *kḷno-* (Pok.523); for suffix see -OUS.

The figurative sense "unfeeling, not sensitive" appeared in English in 1679.

callow *adj.* Before 1230 *calewe* bald, developed from Old English (before 1000) *calu* bald; cognate with Old High German *kalo, kalwer, kalawe* bald, bare (modern German *kahl*), Middle Dutch *calu* bald, bare (modern Dutch *kaal*), and outside Germanic with Old Slavic *golŭ* bare, from Indo-European **galwo-s* (Pok.349).

The sense "young and inexperienced" appeared in English in 1580 as a synonym of "unfledged (being bare or bald, without feathers, like a young bird, hence young and inexperienced)."

In spite of the coincidence in form and meaning, the Germanic words are apparently not borrowed from Latin *calvus* bald.

callus *n.* hard, thickened place on the skin. 1563, borrowed as Latin *callus;* see CALLOUS.

calm *adj.* 1380, in Chaucer's translation of Boethius' *De Consolatione Philosophiae.* **—v.** Probably before 1400, in *The Destruction of Troy.* **—n.** Probably before 1400, in Chaucer's translation of *Roman de la Rose.* Traditionally said to be borrowed through Old French *calme,* from Italian *calma,* or directly from Medieval Latin *cauma* (with substitution of *al* for *au* by possible influence of Latin *calēre* be warm or hot), from Greek *kaûma* heat of the day; hence, time for rest, stillness, from *kaíein* to burn, from Indo-European **kēu-/ kəu-* (Pok.595).

However, available evidence does not altogether support borrowing from the French. While Old French *calme,* n. is recorded in 1418, Middle English *calme* is at least 20 years earlier, the Middle English adjective is recorded 20-40 years earlier, and the verb probably developed from *calme,* n.

Chaucer's translation of *Roman de la Rose* suggests a French source for the noun, but his earlier translation of Boethius also suggests his familiarity with *calm* from Latin and points to an original borrowing from Medieval and Late Latin *cauma,* which may have developed into Vulgar Latin **calma* (and thence into Italian *calma*).

calorie *n.* unit of heat. 1866, borrowing of French *calorie,* learned borrowing from Latin *calor* (genitive *calōris*) heat, from *calēre* be warm or hot, see CALDRON; for suffix see -Y[3]. **—caloric** *adj.* 1853, in *caloric-engine* heat or hot-air engine, borrowed from French *calorique,* n. (1791), from Latin *calor* (genitive *calōris*) heat + *-ique* -ic.

calque (kalk) *n.* loan translation of a foreign word or phrase. 1937, borrowed from French *calque,* literally, a copy, from *calquer* to trace (a design, etc.) by rubbing a pencil on paper placed over an object (a meaning also found in English *calk* 1662), from Italian *calcare* to press under, from Latin *calcāre* to tread; see CALK[1].

calumet (kal′yəmet) *n.* long pipe smoked by the North American Indians as a symbol of peace or friendship. 1665, Canadian English, borrowed from Canadian French *calumet,* special use of Norman French *calumet* pipe, related to *calumo* (corresponding to French *chalumeau,* Old French *chalemel*), from Late Latin *calamellus,* diminutive of Latin *calamus* reed, from Greek *kálamos:* (by assimilation from **kolamos*), cognate with Latin *culmus* stalk, stem, and Old High German *hal(a)m,* from Indo-European **k̑oləmo-s* (Pok. 612).

calumny *n.* false statement, slander. 1447 *calumnye,* borrowed from Middle French *calomnie* and from Latin *calumnia* trickery, artifice, false accusation, ultimately from *calvī* to trick, deceive; possibly cognate with Greek *kēleîn* to bewitch, beguile, Gothic *hōlōn* to slander, deceive, Old High German *huolen* to deceive, and Old English *hōl* slander, from Indo-European **kēl-/kōl-/kəl-* (Pok.551). Doublet of CHALLENGE. **—calumniate** *v.* 1554, borrowed from Latin *calumniātus,* past participle of *calumniārī* to slander, from *calumnia* calumny; for suffix see -ATE[1]. —**calumnious** *adj.* 1490, borrowed from Latin *calumniōsus,* from *calumnia;* for suffix see -OUS.

calve *v.* give birth to a calf. About 1395 *calven,* in the Wycliffe Bible, developed from Old English *cealfian* (about 1000, in Ælfric's writings), from *cealf* CALF[1]. Possible cognates of Old English *cealfian* (from Proto-Germanic **kalbōjanan*) include Middle High German *kalben,* Old Icelandic *kelfa,* Swedish *kalva,* Norwegian *kalve,* Danish *kælve, kalve,* and Dutch *kalven,* all meaning to calve.

calypso *n.* West Indian improvised song with an African rhythm. 1934, in Aldous Huxley's *Beyond Mexique Bay,* of uncertain origin. No connection has been found with the name *Calypso,* a nymph *(Kalypsṓ)* in Greek mythology who detained Odysseus on her island for seven years.

calyx (kā'liks) *n.* part of a flower that holds the petals. 1693, borrowed from Latin *calyx,* from Greek *kályx* seed pod, husk; possibly cognate with Sanskrit *kalikā* bud, from Indo-European **kel-* cup (Pok.550).

cam *n.* projection on a shaft that changes regular circular motion of a separate part it rubs against into an irregular circular motion or into a back-and-forth motion. 1777, borrowed from: 1) Dutch *kam* cog, comb, from Middle Dutch *cam* comb, toothed wheel, cog (see COMB); or perhaps from 2) French *came* cam or cog (itself from German *Kamm*); or possibly 3) reminiscent of, or even a shortened form of, English *camber* (1618) in the sense of having a slight arch, from the eccentric form of a *cam* that has an arch, as its outside surface projects from the circular form of a wheel.

camaraderie *n.* comradeship. 1840, in writings of Thackeray, borrowed from French *camaraderie,* from *camarade,* from Middle French, from Spanish *camarada* COMRADE; for suffix see -ERY.

camass or **camas** (kam'əs) *n.* plant of the lily family. 1805, American English, borrowed from Chinook jargon *kamass,* from Nootka *chamass* sweet.

camber *n.* slight arch. Before 1618, in writings of Raleigh, *camber-keeled* in reference to ship construction, borrowed from Middle French (North) *cambre* bent, from Latin *camurum,* accusative of *camur* crooked, related to *camera* vault; see CAMERA. —**v.** arch slightly. 1627, in writings of Captain John Smith, borrowed from French *cambrer* arch slightly, from Middle French *cambre.*

cambium (kam'bēəm) *n. Botany.* layer of tissue between the bark and wood. 1671, developed from an earlier sense of *cambium* (1643), in reference to sap that becomes or exchanges form with vegetative cambium, New Latin *cambium* exchange, special use of Medieval Latin *cambium* exchange, from Latin *cambīre* to exchange; see CHANGE.

cambric *n.* fine linen or cotton cloth. 1385, borrowed from Flemish *Kameryk, Kamerijk* (French *Cambrai*), city in Flanders (now in northern France) where the cloth was originally made. Compare CHAMBRAY.

camel *n.* Old English *camel, camella* (about 950, in *Lindisfarne Gospels*), borrowed from Latin *camēlus,* from Greek *kámēlos,* of Semitic origin; compare Hebrew *gāmāl* camel, Assyrian *gammalu,* Arabic *jamal.*

camellia (kəmēl'yə) *n.* flowering shrub or tree. 1753, borrowed from New Latin *Camellia* the genus name given by Linnaeus and Latinized as *Camellus* after G.J. *Kamel,* 1661-1706, a Moravian Jesuit missionary who described the flora on the island of Luzon.

cameo *n.* semiprecious stone with a figure carved on it in relief. 1670, borrowing of Italian *cameo, cammeo;* of uncertain origin. The word was borrowed into English earlier from different sources, such as *camfeo* (1554, from Spanish *camafeo*) and as *camew* (1437, from Middle French *camahieu,* Old French *cameu*). The Italian, Spanish, and French words were all ultimately borrowed from the unidentified source.

The sense of "a short literary or dramatic sketch" appeared in English in 1851.

camera *n.* 1708, an arched roof or vaulted room, as in the Camera, a building at Oxford; later, a legislative or council chamber (1712) borrowed from Italian and Spanish; later still, in the Latin phrase *camera obscura* dark chamber (1727), applied to the Daguerreotype photographic process (1840); all forms borrowed from Late Latin *camera* chamber, room, from Latin *camera* vault, arch, from Greek *kamárā* anything with an arched cover, cognate with Latin *camur(us)* curved or arched inward, and Avestan *kamarā* girdle, from Indo-European **kam-er-* to arch, bend (Pok.524). Doublet of CHAMBER. Apparently, the word was used chiefly as a conscious Latinism until it was popularized by its use in photography.

camisole *n.* woman's undergarment. 1816, sleeved jacket, borrowed from French *camisole,* from Provençal *camisola,* diminutive of *camisa* shirt, from Late Latin *camisia* shirt, nightgown; see the doublet CHEMISE.

camomile (kam'əmīl) *n.* plant whose dried leaves are used in medicine and tea. Before 1398 *camomil,* in Trevisa's translation of Bartholomew's *De Proprietatibus Rerum,* borrowed through Anglo-French *camemille,* or directly from Late Latin *camomilla,* alteration of Latin *chamaemēlon.* Also found in Old English *camemalon,* borrowed from Latin *chamaemēlon,* from Greek *chamaímēlon,* literally, earth apple (*chamaí* on the ground + *mêlon* apple; named from the apple-like scent of the blossoms; see HUMUS and MELON).

camouflage (kam'əfläzh) *n.* disguise, concealment. 1917, borrowed from French *camouflage,* from *camoufler* to disguise, from Italian *camuffare* (with influence of French *camouflet* snub; earlier, smoke blown in someone's face), probably from Medieval Latin *muffula* manipulation; for suffix see -AGE. —**v.** 1917, from the noun.

camp[1] *n.* group of tents, huts, or shelters. 1528, borrowed from Middle French *camp,* from Italian *campo,* from Latin *campus* plain, field of battle or other contest, from which probably came an earlier Old English word *camp* contest (about 725, in *Beowulf*) that existed in Middle English until about 1440, also found in Old Frisian *camp,* Middle Dutch *camp* (modern Dutch *kamp*), Middle Low German *kamp,* Old High German *champf* (modern German *Kampf*) combat, Old Icelandic *kapp (pp* from *mp)* contest, and West Germanic **kampaz.* Latin *campus* is cognate with Greek *kampḗ* a bend, turn, Lithuanian *kam̃pas* corner, angle, *kum̃pti* become twisted, from Indo-European **kam-p-* to bend, **kampo-s* a bend (Pok.525). Doublet of CAMPUS. —**v.** 1543, borrowed from Middle French *camper* to encamp, from *camp,* n. —**camper** *n.* (1856, earlier in reference to soldiers or others belonging to a military camp, 1631). **—campfire** *n.* (1675) **—campground** *n.* (1805)

camp² *adj. Slang.* amusing or clever for its exaggerated, banal, mediocre, or outmoded quality that is artistically unsophisticated. 1909, actions or gestures of exaggerated emphasis (applied to homosexuals); of unknown origin. The word was popularized in 1964 by the American writer Susan Sontag in the essay "Notes on 'Camp'," published in *Partisan Review.* **—n.** 1931, a homosexual; 1964, something amusingly or cleverly artificial, exaggerated, or outmoded. **—v.** especially in the phrase *camp it up* 1931. **—campy** *adj.* 1959, formed from English *camp²* + *-y¹*.

campaign *n.* 1647, the operations of an army in the field or open country for a season (originally the summer, since during winter it remained in quarters in towns, garrisons, camps, etc.), borrowed from French *campagne* open country, from Italian *campagna,* from Late Latin *campānea, campānia* level country, from Latin *campus* plain, field; see CAMP¹. Earliest use in English (1591, 1598) is *campania* from the Latin in reference to open country. Doublet of CHAMPAIGN.

By 1770 *campaign* was applied to any series of actions to obtain an end, and in 1809, in American English, to the political activities designed to get someone elected.

—v. 1701, participate in a military campaign, from the noun.

campanile (kam′pənē′lē) *n.* bell tower. 1640, borrowed through French *campanile,* and directly from Italian *campanile,* from *campana* bell, from Late Latin *campāna* bell, originally bronze ware of *Campania* (ancient territory around Naples).

camphor *n.* white crystalline substance used in medicine, and to protect clothes from moths. Probably about 1425 *camphor,* in a translation of Guy de Chauliac's *Grande Chirurgie,* alteration of earlier spelling *caumfre* (1313), borrowed from Anglo-French *camphor,* learned borrowing from Medieval Latin *camphora,* from Arabic *kāfūr,* from Malay *kāpūr,* probably ultimately from Persian. **—camphorated** *adj.* 1641, formed in English as if from New Latin *camphoratus,* from Medieval Latin *camphora* camphor; for suffix see -ATE¹ and -ED².

campus *n.* grounds of a college, university, or school. 1774, American English, borrowed from Latin *campus* plain, field. The word was first used at Princeton University in New Jersey. Doublet of CAMP¹.

can¹ *v.* be able to. Old English (about 725, in *Beowulf*) *can, con* know, know how, can (infinitive *cunnan*).

Can is an irregular verb that belongs to a group of Germanic verbs (chiefly auxiliary verbs, such as *may* and *shall*) which now have a present tense that was originally a form of the past tense. This shift in use was accompanied by development of a new form for the past tense: for *can (cunnan)* the new form became in Old English *cūthe,* which developed into Middle English *coud, coude* (before 1325, in *Cursor Mundi*) and later *could* (about 1500), the *l* inserted on analogy of the earlier spellings *should, would.*

The original past participle *cūth* known remains today as *couth,* principally found in *uncouth* unmannerly, strange in the sense of "unusual or unknown." Its form in Old English *cūth* developed from **cunth* and parallels the loss of *n* in *mūth* mouth, *tōth* tooth. Old English *cūth* developed from Proto-Germanic **kúnthəz* from Indo-European **ĝn̄tó-s* (Pok.377).

The present participle and the gerund *cunning* (about 1300) survive in modern English with the meanings "clever or cleverness in deceiving" and in the literary senses "skillful" and "expertness," the latter of which was one of the senses in Middle English. The form is not recorded in Old English, its equivalent there being *cunnand.*

The meaning "know," from Old English, was current in Middle English and remained so into the 1600's; the meaning "be able to" which is evident throughout Middle English from at least 1123, in the *Peterborough Chronicle,* is found to be rare in Old English, the use being supplied by *mæg* may.

The Old English *can* (infinitive *cunnan*) know, is cognate with Old Saxon *can (cunnan)* and Old Frisian *kan (kunna),* Old High German *kan (kunnan)* and modern German *kann (können),* Old Icelandic *kan (kunna),* Gothic *kann (kunnan).* Old English *cunnan* is also related to Old English *cnāwan* KNOW, perceive, get knowledge of. In the formation of its present tense, it is striking that Old English *cun-no-n* we know (Gothic *kun-nu-m*) exactly parallels Sanskrit *jā-nī-más* we know (from earlier **jā-ni-más*), from Indo-European **ĝn̥-nə-més,* root **ĝenə-/ĝnē-/ĝn̥ō-* (Pok.376).

can² *n.* metal container. Old English (before 1000, in Ælfric's writings) *canne* container, vessel; cognate with Old Saxon *kanna* container, vessel, Old High German *channa* (modern German *Kanne*), Middle Dutch *kanne,* and Old Icelandic *kanna,* all probably early borrowings from Late Latin *canna* container, vessel, from Latin *canna* reed, tube, CANE. **—v.** put or preserve in a can. 1861, American English developed from the noun.

canal *n.* Probably before 1425, in a translation of Guy de Chauliac's *Grande Chirurgie,* pipe for liquid, borrowed from Middle French *canal,* learned borrowing from Latin *canālis* trench, pipe, from *canna* CANE. Doublet of CHANNEL. The modern sense of a waterway is first recorded in English in 1673.

canapé (kan′əpā) *n.* cracker or bread spread with fish paste, cheese, etc. 1890, in *Mrs. Beeton's Cookery Book,* borrowed from French *canapé,* originally, a sofa or couch (with mosquito netting), from Old French *conopé;* see CANOPY. The connection between the French and English meanings supposedly arises because the bread or cracker is taken as a "seat" for the delicacy spread on it.

canard (kənärd′) *n.* false rumor. Before 1850, borrowed from French *canard,* literally, duck, from Old French *quanart,* from *caner* to cackle, quack, of imitative origin. The sense of a false or exaggerated story comes from a French expression of the late 1500's, *vendre un canard à moitié* to half-sell a duck (i.e., not to sell it at all), hence to take in, deceive, make a fool of. The sense of "false news spread to deceive the public" appeared in French in 1750.

canary *n.* 1584, light wine of the *Canary* Islands; 1655, a songbird of the *Canary* Islands, earlier *canary bird* (1576), borrowed from French *Canarie* (the chief island of the group), from Spanish *Canaria,* from Latin *Canāria Īnsula* Isle of Dogs, because of the large dogs found there, from *canis* dog; see HOUND.

cancan *n.* 1848, borrowed from French *cancan* dance of extravagant motion often suggestive in nature (about

1836); of uncertain origin, possibly from the meaning "gossip, scandal" or a childish pronunciation of *canard* duck, the dance imitating a duck's waddle.

cancel *v.* 1399, cross out or strike with lines, in *Rolls of Parliament;* borrowed through Anglo-French *canceler,* Old French *canceller* cross out, or directly from Latin *cancellāre* to strike out writing with crossed lines, from *cancellī* crossbars, grating, diminutive form of *cancrī* lattices, barriers, plural of *cancer* lattice or barrier, an alteration of *carcer* barrier, prison, (originally) network, grating, of uncertain origin. Compare CHANCEL. The figurative meaning "nullify an obligation" appeared shortly before 1443. —**cancellation** *n.* Probably before 1425, borrowed from Old French *cancellation,* from Medieval Latin *cancellationem* (nominative *cancellatio*), from Latin *cancellāre* cancel; for suffix see -TION.

cancer *n.* **1** malignant tumor, carcinoma. 1601, in Holland's translation of Pliny's *Natural History,* found in Old English (about 1000, in writings of Ælfric) in the sense of "spreading sore, either malignant or benign," and reinforced by Anglo-French *cancre* after 1100. **2** sign of the Zodiac representing the constellation of the Crab. About 1380, in Chaucer's translation of Boethius' *De Consolatione Philosophiae.* In both senses *cancer* was borrowed from Latin *cancer* crab, tumor, constellation Cancer, a form patterned after and cognate with Greek *karkínos* crab, tumor, constellation Cancer, also cognate with Sanskrit *karkaṭa-s* crab (from a Middle Indic source) and *karkara-s* HARD, from Indo-European **kar-*, reduplicated **karkar-* (Pok.531). Doublet of CANKER.

The sense of a spreading sore developed, according to the Greek physician Galen, from the resemblance of the swollen veins surrounding the sore to the legs of a crab, CHANCRE.

—**cancerous** *adj.* 1563, borrowed from Middle French *cancereux,* and directly from Medieval Latin *cancerosus,* from Latin *cancer;* for suffix see -OUS. The word is also found in Middle English as *cancrose* (probably before 1425, in a translation of Chauliac's *Grande Chirurgie*); borrowed from Medieval Latin *cancrosus,* variant of *cancerosus* cancerous.

candelabrum *n.* ornamental candlestick. 1811, reborrowed from Latin *candēlābrum* candlestick; originally meaning candlestick (before 1400) with the spelling *chaundelabre,* borrowed from Old French *chaundelabre* from Latin *candēlābrum,* from *candēla* CANDLE.

candescent (kandes′ənt) *adj.* glowing with heat. 1824, borrowed from Latin *candēscentem* (nominative *candēscēns*), present participle of *candēscere* begin to glow (especially white hot), from *candēre* to shine; glow; see CANDLE.

candid *adj.* 1630, white, borrowed from Latin *candidus* white, clear; hence, pure, sincere, from *candēre* to shine, glow; see CANDLE. The meaning "frank, sincere" is first recorded in English in 1675.

candidate *n.* person seeking some office or honor. 1600, in Holland's translation of Livy's *Roman History,* borrowed from Latin *candidātus,* (originally) clothed in white (so called because in ancient Rome candidates for political office wore white togas), from *candidus* white, see CANDID; for suffix see -ATE[1].

In Middle English (before 1460, in a translation of Vegetius' *De Re Militari*), *candidate* was used in the special sense of a class of soldiers in the Roman army. —**candidacy** *n.* 1864, formed from English *candidate* + *-acy.*

candle *n.* Probably before 1160, in *Peterborough Chronicle,* developed from Old English *candel* (about 725, in *Beowulf*); earlier, in compound the *candeltwist* an instrument for snuffing candles (about 700); borrowed from Latin *candēla,* from *candēre* to shine, glow. The Latin is cognate with Greek *kándaros* charcoal, Albanian (Tosk dialect) *hënë* moon, and Welsh *can, cannaid* white, bright, shining, from Indo-European **kand-* (Pok.526).

According to the OED, *candle* came into English with the adoption of Christianity.

—**candlelight** *n.* (before 1000) —**candlestick** *n.* (about 970)

candor *n.* frankness. 1610, in Ben Jonson's *The Alchemist,* purity, integrity; earlier *candoure* extreme whiteness (before 1500); borrowed, perhaps before 1398, in Trevisa's translation of Bartholomew's *De Proprietatibus Rerum* from Latin *candor* sincerity, purity; originally, whiteness, from *candēre* to shine; see CANDLE and also the parallel formation CANDID; for suffix see -OR[1]. Middle French *candeur* (1488) may have influenced the use in English.

candy *n.* 1274 *candy,* borrowed from Anglo-Latin and Old French *candi,* from Arabic *qandī* crystallized into sugar, from *qand* cane sugar, apparently of Proto-Munda (pre-Aryan) origin (like Sanskrit *khaṇḍa-s* sugar lump). —**v.** 1533, from the noun, by influence of French *candir* to candy, possibly because earlier French *candi* was considered a past participle in the phrase *sucre candi* sugar candy. —**candied** *adj.* 1600, formed from English *candy* + -ED[2].

cane *n.* jointed stem of various large reeds, such as bamboo and sugar cane. Before 1398 *canne,* in Trevisa's translation of Bartholomew's *De Proprietatibus Rerum* (but with many examples in other translations of Medieval Latin texts); borrowed through Anglo-French *cane,* Old French *canne, cane,* from Old Provençal *cana,* from Latin *canna* reed, cane, from Greek *kánna* reed, from Babylonian-Assyrian *qanū* reed, from Sumerian *gin* (compare Hebrew *qāneh* and Arabic *qanāh* reed).

The meaning "stick for walking or beating" appeared in English in 1590.

—**v.** beat with a cane. Before 1667, from the noun.

canine *adj.* of or like a dog. 1607, borrowed from Latin *canīnus,* from *canis* dog, HOUND; for suffix see -INE[1]. —**n.** a pointed tooth like that of a dog. Before 1425, in a translation of Guy de Chauliac's *Grande Chirurgie,* possibly by influence of earlier use of Latin *canīnus* (before 1398, in Trevisa's translation of Bartholomew's *De Proprietatibus Rerum*). The informal sense "a dog" appeared in 1869.

canister *n.* Probably 1474, basket, borrowed from Latin *canistrum* basket for bread, flowers, or fruit, from Greek *kánastron* wicker basket, from *káneon* basket made of reed, from *kánna* reed, CANE.

canker *n.* spreading sore, especially of the mouth. About 1150 *cancor,* later *cankre* (before 1400); developed from Old English *cancer* CANCER (about 1000, in Ælfric). Doublet of CANCER, CHANCRE. —**cankerous** *adj.* 1541, formed from English *canker* + *-ous.*

cannabis (kan′əbis) *n.* hemp plant. 1798, borrowing of

earlier New Latin *Cannabis* the genus name given by Linnaeus, 1728, in *Chambers Cyclopaedia,* from Latin *cannabis* hemp, from Greek *kánnabis,* perhaps of Scythian or Thracian origin and related to the source of English HEMP. Doublet of CANVAS.

The sense "a preparation from the hemp plant smoked or chewed for its hallucinatory or intoxicating effects" appeared in 1848.

cannibal *n.* 1553, borrowed from Spanish *caníbal, caríbal,* from *Caniba, Carib,* names cited by Columbus as belonging to the Indians of Cuba and Haiti, who were thought to eat human flesh. The names were apparently local variant forms of Carib *Galibi* the Caribs, literally, brave men. **—cannibalism** *n.* 1796, in writings of Burke, probably borrowed from French *cannibalisme* (1796), from *cannibale* cannibal (1515), from Spanish *caníbal* + French *-isme* -ism.

cannon *n.* big mounted gun. 1400, borrowed through Anglo-French *canon* tube for projectiles, Old French *canon,* from Italian *cannone* barrel, great tube, an augmentative form of *canna* tube, from Latin *canna* reed, tube, CANE.

The differentiation in spelling *cannon* and *canon* began to appear by 1650 but was not firmly fixed before 1800.

canny *adj.* shrewd, knowing. 1637, Scottish and Northern English, apparently formed as a variant from English CAN[1] in the older sense "to know, know how" + *-y*[1].

canoe *n.* 1590 *canow,* earlier *canoa* (1555), borrowed from Spanish, from Arawakan (Haiti) *canoa* (the form cited by Columbus), from Carib *canoua, canaoua.* In the 1600's various forms appeared in English from modern European languages (*cano, cannoe, canoe,* etc.) of which English adopted *canoe,* first occurring in a translation from French in 1600. **—v.** 1842, from the noun. **—canoeist** *n.* 1865, formed from English *canoe* + *-ist.*

canon[1] *n.* law of a church. Old English *canon* (before 900, in writings of Alfred); borrowed from Late Latin *canon,* from Latin *canon* rule, model; and in part borrowed from Old French *canon,* learned borrowing of Latin *canōn,* from Greek *kanṓn* rule, (straight) rod, probably from *kánna* reed, CANE.

The sense of "a criterion, standard of judging" appeared in English in 1601.

—canonical *adj.* Probably before 1425, in a translation of Higden's *Polychronicon,* borrowed from Medieval Latin *canonicalis,* from Latin *canonicus* according to rule, (in Late Latin, according to church law), from Greek *kanonikós,* from *kanṓn* (genitive *kanónos*) rule; for suffix see -AL[1] and -ICAL. **—canonize** *v.* About 1384, in Wycliffe's Bible, borrowed from Old French *canonisier* and directly from Medieval Latin *canonizare,* from Late Latin *canōn* church law; for suffix see -IZE.

canon[2] *n.* clergyman belonging to a cathedral or collegiate church. Probably before 1200, in Layamon's *Chronical of Britain,* borrowed probably through Anglo-French *canun,* from Old North French *canonie,* from Late Latin *canonicus* clergyman living under a rule, from Latin *canonicus,* adj., according to rule, canonical, from Greek *kanonikós,* from *kanṓn,* (genitive *kanónos*) rule, CANON[1]; for suffix see -IC. According to the OED, Middle English *canon* (represented in Old English in *canonic*) was temporarily replaced in the 1300's and 1400's by *chanun, chanoun,* borrowed from the Old French *chanoine,* which disappeared in the 1500's when *canon* reappeared and has since often been confused with *canon*[1] meaning "church law."

canopy *n.* Before 1382, in the Wycliffe Bible, borrowed from Old French *canapé, conopé,* learned borrowing from Medieval Latin *canapeum, canopeum,* and directly from Latin *cōnōpēum, cōnōpium* couch with curtains of mosquito netting. The Latin forms are from Greek *kōnṓpion, kōnōpeṓn,* an alteration of **kanōpion,* influenced by *kṓnōps* mosquito, gnat, of uncertain origin. Ultimately Greek **kanōpion* is from the name of the Egyptian town *Canopus.* **—v.** About 1600, in Shakespeare's *Sonnets,* from the noun.

cant[1] *n.* insincere talk. 1709; earlier, "a whining manner of speaking, especially of beggars" (1640), developed from *cant,* v. (1567) to speak in a whining or singsong tone used by beggars; borrowed from Old North French *canter* to sing, chant, from Latin *cantāre,* a frequentative form of *canere* sing; see the doublet CHANT. The Latin *cantāre* was used at least by 1180 as a contemptuous reference to church services.

The disparaging meaning "special language of a group, jargon" is recorded in English in 1681, in works of Dryden.

cant[2] *n.* slant, slope, bevel. About 1375 (Scottish), in Barbour's *The Bruce,* edge, brink, borrowed probably from Middle Dutch or Middle Low German *cant* border, edge, side, or directly from Old North French *cant,* from Vulgar Latin **cantus,* **canthus* corner, edge, possibly from Latin *cantus, canthus* rim of a wheel, tire; see DECANT. **—v.** to slant, slope. 1542-43, from the noun.

cantaloupe or **cantaloup** *n.* 1739, borrowed from French *cantaloup,* apparently from Italian *Cantalupo* or *Cantaluppi,* former papal estate near Rome, where it was cultivated.

cantankerous *adj.* 1772, in Goldsmith's *She Stoops to Conquer,* probably dialectal alteration (influenced by *rancorous*) of Middle English *conteckour* troublemaker, quarrelsome person (about 1300); borrowed through Anglo-French *contecker,* perhaps from Old North French *contekier* to touch, feel (with the hands), Old French *contechier* (*con-* with + *teche,* related to *atachier* hold fast, ATTACH); for suffix see -OUS.

cantata *n.* story or play set to music to be sung by a chorus. 1724, borrowed from Italian *cantata,* from past participle of *cantare* sing, from Latin *cantāre*; see CANT[1].

canteen *n.* small container for carrying water, commissary. Before 1744 (probably 1710-11), borrowed from French *canteen* sutler's shop; also (1737) small case for carrying bottles, from Italian *cantina* cellar, perhaps from *canto* corner (for storage), from Vulgar Latin **cantus;* see CANT[2] slant.

canter *v.* gallop gently. 1706, shortened from earlier *Canterbury,* v., to gallop gently (1673, in Marvell's *The Rehearsal Transposed*), from the noun phrase *Canterbury gallop* or *pace,* an allusion to the easy pace of pilgrims riding to *Canterbury* (1631). **—n.** 1755, from the verb.

canticle (kan′təkəl) *n.* short song or hymn. Before 1225, borrowed from Latin *canticulum,* diminutive of *canticum* song, from *cantus* song; see CANTO.

cantilever *n.* 1667, a support that projects from a wall to hold up a beam, balcony, etc. Probably formed from English *cant*² slope, slant + connecting *-i-* + *lever.* The meaning applied to bridge building appears in 1850 and echoes an earlier formation *flying lever bridge* to describe a cantilever bridge that appeared in a book on bridges published in 1811.

cantle *n.* part of the saddle that sticks up at the back. 1592, earlier meaning "support, brace" (1426-27), and "part, piece set off, rim" (about 1300); borrowed from Old French *cantel,* from Medieval Latin *cantellus,* diminutive form of Vulgar Latin **cantus* corner; see CANT² slant.

canto *n.* main division of a long poem. 1590, in writings of Spenser, borrowed from Italian *canto* song, singing, from Latin *cantus* (genitive *cantūs*) song, from *canere* sing, CHANT.

canton *n.* political division or part of a country. 1522, probably borrowed from Middle French *canton* piece, portion of a country, from dialectal Italian (Lombard) *cantone* region, especially in the mountains, an augmentative form of *canto* corner, from Vulgar Latin **cantus;* see CANT².

cantonment (kanton′mənt) *n.* soldiers' quarters. 1756, borrowed from French *cantonnement,* from Middle French *cantonner* to apportion, from *canton* piece; see CANTON.

cantor *n.* 1538, borrowed from Latin *cantor* singer, from *canere* sing, see CHANT; for suffix see -OR².

canvas *n.* strong cloth used in tents, sails, etc. 1354 *canevace,* borrowed from Anglo-French *canevaz,* Old French *canevas* (fusion of Old North French *canevach* and Old French *chenevas*), and from Medieval Latin *canavasium, canebacium,* both the Old French and the Medieval Latin forms from Vulgar Latin **cannapāceus* made of hemp, from *cannapus,* variant of Latin *cannabis* hemp, from Greek *kánnabis;* see the doublet CANNABIS.

A spelling with two *s*'s developed in the 1500's and lasted into the 1800's, and from that now obsolete spelling for the cloth came the verb *canvass* to toss in a canvas sheet, which now has the seemingly unrelated meaning "to solicit votes" and "to examine, inspect," both new meanings producing their own noun uses spelled with two *s*'s.

canvass *v.* ask for votes or support. 1508 *canvas* or *canvass* toss someone in a canvas sheet as a sport or punishment, from CANVAS, n. The sense development seems to have been from "toss in a sheet" to "shake out, discuss, examine carefully" (1530, in Palsgrave's *Lesclarcissement*) to "solicit votes" (before 1555, in sermons of Bishop Latimer), but the last connection is unclear. **—n.** 1608-11, from the verb.

canyon or **cañon** *n.* 1834 *cañon,* American English, borrowed from Mexican Spanish *cañón,* an extended sense of Spanish *cañón* tube, pipe, of uncertain origin. Since the Spanish word was attested in 1560-75 as *callón,* it is possible that it comes from *calle* street (from Latin *callis* a rough track, path), in the sense "narrow way."

cap *n.* Probably before 1200 *cappe,* in *Ancrene Riwle,* developed from Old English *cæppe* (about 1000, in Ælfric's *Glossary*), a borrowing from Late Latin *cappa* cap, hood, mantle, of uncertain origin (perhaps related to Latin *caput* HEAD). Doublet of CAPE¹ garment. **—v.** Probably about 1400 *cappen* put a cap on, (though the verbal noun appears in a surname as early as 1270), developed from *cappe,* n. The meaning "cover, as with a cap" appeared in 1602 (though, again, the verbal noun appears with this meaning in 1368). The meaning "to excel, outdo, surpass" is first recorded (in Northern dialectal use) in 1821.

capable *adj.* able. 1561, able to take in, perceive, borrowed through Middle French *capable* capable, able, sufficient, or directly from Late Latin *capābilis* capacious, capable of, fit, from Latin *capere* to take, contain, hold; see CAPTIVE. **—capability** *n.* 1587, formed in English from Late Latin *capābilis* + English *-ity.*

capacious *adj.* able to hold much. 1614, in writings of Sir Walter Raleigh, borrowed from Latin *capāx* (genitive *capācis*) able to take in, from *capere* to take, hold, contain, see CAPTIVE; for suffix see -OUS.

capacity *n.* Probably before 1425, in translations of Guy de Chauliac's *Grande Chirurgie* and Higden's *Polychronicon,* borrowed from Middle French *capacité,* from Latin *capācitātem* (nominative *capācitās*), from *capāx* (genitive *capācis*) able to take in; for suffix see -ITY.

caparison *n.* ornamental covering for a horse. 1579, borrowed from Middle French *caparasson, caparaçon,* from Spanish *caparazón,* perhaps from Old Provençal *caparasso* cape with hood, from *capa* CAPE¹ garment. **—v.** put trappings on; deck. 1594, in Shakespeare's *Richard III,* probably borrowed from Middle French *caparaçonner,* from *caparaçon* caparison.

cape¹ *n.* outer garment without sleeves. Probably before 1200, in Layamon's *Chronicle of Britain,* not distinguished from *cope* the ecclesiastical garment, but in a thesaurus (1565-78) and later Cotgrave's *Dictionary* (1611) set apart as a sleeveless garment. The early use was borrowed from Medieval Latin *cappa* cloak, but the later use and the current sense of sleeveless garment are borrowed from, or at least influenced by, Middle French *cape,* partly from Old Provençal *capa* hooded mantle, partly from Spanish *capa, cape* cloak, both from Late Latin *cappa;* see CAP.

cape² *n.* point of land extending into the water. About 1387-95, in the *Prologue* to Chaucer's *Canterbury Tales,* borrowed from Middle French *cap* cape, head, from Old Provençal *cap,* literally, head, from Latin *caput* HEAD.

Several languages use a word for "head" to mean "headland, cape": for example, Arabic *rā's,* Danish *hoved,* Welsh and Cornish *pen.*

caper¹ *v.* dance or leap playfully; prance; frolic. 1588, in Shakespeare's *Love's Labour's Lost,* apparently short for earlier English *capriole* to leap, skip, caper (1580), borrowed from Italian *capriolare,* from *capriolo* roebuck; see CAB. **—n.** 1592, playful leap or jump, probably from the verb.

The current usual sense of "a prank, trick, or scheme" appeared in 1840.

caper² *n.* prickly shrub. Before 1398 *capar,* in Trevisa's translation of Bartholomew's *De Proprietatibus Rerum,* back formation from earlier *caperis,* taken as plural (before 1382, in the Wycliffe Bible), borrowed from Latin *capparis,* from Greek *kápparis,* of uncertain origin.

Possibly *caper* came into English twice: 1) borrowed from Latin *capparis,* and 2) later (about 1551), borrowed from Middle French *câpre,* from Italian *cappero,* from Latin *capparis.*

capillary *n.* blood vessel with tiny, hairlike opening. 1667, noun use of *capillary,* adj. **—adj.** 1664, hairlike, very slender; earlier, of or having to do with hair (1656, in Blount's *Glossographia*) borrowed from French *capillaire,* and replacing earlier *capillar* (before 1400, in works of Lanfranc), both borrowed from Latin *capillāris* of hair, from *capillus* hair (of the head), of uncertain origin; for suffix see -ARY. A connection with Latin *caput,* meaning "head," is not supported by the form of Latin *capillus.* **—capillary attraction** (1813)

capital[1] *adj.* Probably before 1200, in *Ancrene Riwle,* of or relating to the head, borrowed from Old French *capital,* from Latin *capitālis* relating to the head, chief, from *caput* (genitive *capitis*) HEAD; for suffix see -AL[1]. Various other senses soon began to develop: 1) chief, principal, head (as in *capital city*) appeared probably before 1425, in a translation of Guy de Chauliac's *Grande Chirurgie.* 2) involving loss of the head or life, deadly, mortal (as in *capital punishment*) appeared in 1395, in writings of Wycliffe. 3) upper-case or *capital* letters, so called because they appear at the head or beginning of a sentence, appeared before 1387, in Trevisa's translation of Higden's *Polychronicon.* **—n.** Probably before 1430, in Lydgate's *The Pilgrimage of Man,* a capital letter, from the adjective; later, fund of money (1611, in Cotgrave's *Dictionary*), in this latter sense borrowed from Medieval Latin *capitale* assets, from Latin *caput,* another meaning of which was "principal, money laid out, capital." The sense "chief city or town" appeared in 1667, in Milton's *Paradise Lost.* Doublet of CATTLE and CHATTEL. **—capitalism** *n.* 1854, in Thackeray's *The Newcomes,* formed from English *capital*[1] + *-ism.* **—capitalist** *n.* 1791, in writings of Washington, formed from English *capital*[1] + *-ist.*

capital[2] *n.* top part of a column. Before 1300, borrowed through Anglo-French *capitel,* Old French *chapitel,* or directly from Latin *capitellum* small head, diminutive of *caput* (genitive *capitis*) HEAD. Doublet of CADET.

Capitol *n.* Congressional building in Washington, D.C. 1793, in writings of Jefferson, referring to the Congressional building then under construction; earlier, colonial Statehouse of Virginia (1699), from earlier *capitol* (about 1450), and *capitolie* (about 1375) both referring to the Temple of Jupiter in Rome; borrowed from Old North French *capitolie,* Old French *capitoile,* both learned borrowings from Latin *Capitōlium* temple of Jupiter on the Capitoline Hill in Rome, possibly related to *caput* (genitive *capitis*) head (because the temple was built on the top or head of the hill).

capitulate *v.* 1580, make conditions, stipulate, agree, either developed in English from earlier *capitulate,* adj. stipulated, borrowed from Medieval Latin *capitulatus,* past participle of *capitulare* draw up under separate heads, arrange in chapters; or borrowed directly from the Medieval Latin past participle of *capitulare,* from Latin *capitulum* chapter, section, diminutive of *caput* (genitive *capitis*) HEAD; for suffix see -ATE[1]. It is also possible that *capitulate* may have been in part a back formation of earlier *capitulation.*

The current sense "surrender under stipulated terms" appeared in English in 1689; the sense may have been influenced by earlier French *capituler* agree on terms, from Medieval Latin *capitulare.*

—capitulation *n.* 1535, agreement on specified terms, borrowed from Middle French *capitulation,* from *capituler* agree on specified terms, from Medieval Latin *capitulare* arrange in chapters; for suffix see -TION.

capon *n.* castrated rooster. Before 1250 *capun,* developed from Old English *capūn* (about 1000, in Ælfric's *Glossary*), probably reinforced by Old North French *capon,* from Latin *cāpōnem* (nominative *cāpō*), perhaps better **cappōnem*; cognate with Greek *kóptein* to strike, cut off, *skáptein* dig out, Old Slavic *kopati* to dig, *skopiti* castrate, and Lithuanian *kapóti* to cut small, *skōpti* dig out, from Indo-European **kap-/kop-* (Pok.930).

capriccio (kəprē′chēō) *n.* lively piece of music. 1696; earlier meaning "caprice," in Shakespeare's *All's Well that Ends Well* (1601); borrowed from Italian *capriccio* CAPRICE.

caprice *n.* 1667, borrowed from French *caprice* whim, from Italian *capriccio* whim, sudden start, (earlier) shiver, horror, raising of hackles, possibly a blend of *capo* head (from Latin *caput* HEAD) and *riccio* frizzled (hair), hedgehog, from Latin *ēricius* hedgehog; see URCHIN. **—capricious** *adj.* 1594, borrowed from French *capricieux* whimsical, from Italian *capriccioso,* from *capriccio* caprice; for suffix see -OUS.

Capricorn *n.* 10th sign of the Zodiac; southern constellation represented in ancient times in the form of a goat. Before 1387 *Capricorne,* in Trevisa's translation of Higden's *Polychronicon,* borrowed through Old French *capricorne,* or directly from Latin *Capricornus,* literally, having horns like a goat (*caper,* genitive *caprī,* goat + *cornū* horn). The Latin *Capricornus* is a translation of Greek *Aigó-kerōs.*

capsize *v.* 1788, of uncertain origin. The OED says that apparently the word was originally sailor's cant, and cites Skeat's proposal that *capsize* is a possible borrowing of Spanish *cabezar* pitch, as a ship does, and *capuzar* sink a ship by the head.

capstan *n.* winch for lifting or pulling, especially on a boat. Probably about 1380, borrowed from Old French *cabestant,* from Old Provençal *cabestan,* from *cabestran,* present participle of **cabestrar* roll up cables, from *capestre* pulley cord. The Old Provençal derives from Latin *capistrum* halter, from *capere* to hold, take; see CAPTIVE.

Although Old French *cabestant* is not attested until 1382, it is a possible source of English *capstan,* because nautical terms are known to have existed even though they are often missing from French literature.

capsule *n.* 1652, borrowed from French *capsule* a membranous sac, from Latin *capsula* little box, diminutive of *capsa* box, CASE[2]. The sense of a gelatin case enclosing a dose of medicine appeared in 1875. The aerospace use (space *capsule*) was first recorded in 1958. **—adj.** compact. 1938, American English, from the noun.

captain *n.* leader, chief. About 1375 *capitayn,* in Chaucer's *Canterbury Tales,* borrowed from Old French *capitain, capitaine,* learned borrowing from Late Latin *capitāneus* commander, noun use of *capitāneus,* adj., prominent, chief, from Latin *caput* (genitive *capitis*) HEAD. The sense of a naval officer (*captain* of the fleet) appeared in 1554; that of master of any vessel, before 1649; and that of an army officer, in 1567. The meaning applied to a pilot of an aircraft is first recorded in 1929. The meaning of head of a sports team appeared in 1857. Doublet of CHIEFTAIN. **—v.** 1598, from the noun.

caption *n.* 1789, in writings of James Madison, American English, borrowed from Latin *captiōnem* (nominative *captiō*) a taking, from *capere* to take, see CAPTIVE;

for suffix see -TION. The meaning was strongly influenced by Latin *caput* HEAD, as well as by the earlier (1670) legal use of *caption,* in the phrase "certificate of caption" (referring to a part of a document stating where it was *taken* to be executed), which was sometimes interpreted as "the beginning or heading of a warrant, indictment, etc." The word originally appeared in Middle English (about 1384) as *capcioun,* borrowed from Anglo-French and Old French *capcion* in the now obsolete sense of seizure or capture.

captious *adj.* hard to please, finding fault. Probably about 1408 *capcyus,* in Lydgate's *Reson and Sensuallyte,* borrowed from Middle French *captieux,* from Latin *captiōsus,* from *captiō* a deceiving, fallacious argument; literally, a taking (in), from *capere* to catch, take, see CAPTIVE; for suffix see -OUS.

The meaning "designed to entrap, fallacious, sophistical" appeared in 1447, in Bokenham's *Legends of Holy Women.*

captive *adj.* Probably about 1425 *captif,* in a translation of Higden's *Polychronicon,* borrowed from Latin *captīvus,* from *captus,* past participle of *capere* to take, hold, seize; cognate with Greek *káptein* gulp down, Albanian *kap* I grasp, seize, Low German *happen* swallow, Gothic *hafjan* to raise, lift, and Old English *hebban* HEAVE; for suffix see -IVE. —**n.** Probably before 1400 *captif,* in *Morte Arthur,* from the adjective. —**captivate** *v.* About 1526, hold captive, borrowed from Late Latin *captīvātus,* past participle of *captīvāre,* from Latin *captīvus* captive; for suffix see -ATE[1]. —**captivity** *n.* About 1380, in Chaucer's translation of Boethius' *De Consolatione Philosophiae,* borrowed from Old French *captivité,* from Latin *captīvitātem* (nominative *captīvitās,* from *captīvus* captive; for suffix see -ITY.

capture *n.* 1541-42, in a record of criminal trials, borrowed from Middle French *capture* a taking, catching, learned borrowing from Latin *captūra* a taking, from *captus,* past participle of *capere* to take, capture, see CAPTIVE; for suffix see -URE. —**v.** 1795, in Southey's *Joan of Arc,* from the noun. —**captor** *n.* 1688; earlier meaning "censor" (1646), borrowed from Latin *captor,* from *capere* to take, capture; for suffix see -OR[2].

car *n.* 1301 (in surname) *Careman;* later, *carre* any wheeled vehicle (about 1350, in a psalter); borrowed through Anglo-French *carre,* Old North French *carre,* and directly from Latin *carra,* plural of *carrus, carrum* two-wheeled vehicle for carrying loads, wagon, of Gaulish origin (compare Old Irish *carr* wagon, chariot); cognate with Latin *currere* to run; see CURRENT.

The word was first applied to the automobile in 1896.

carafe *n.* glass bottle for water, etc. 1786, borrowed from French *carafe,* either from Italian *caraffa,* or possibly from Spanish *garrafa,* perhaps from Arabic *gharrāf,* from *gharafa* draw water.

caramel *n.* 1725, borrowed from French *caramel* burnt sugar, from archaic Spanish *caramel* sugar candy, alteration of Provençal *canamel* sugar cane, from Medieval Latin *cannamellis* (apparently by folk etymology from Latin *canna* CANE + *mel,* genitive *mellis* honey). The Spanish *caramel* was influenced in its formation by *caramillo* reed, from Late Latin *calamellus,* a diminutive form of Latin *calamus* reed, cane.

The meaning "a small piece of chewy candy flavored with browned or burnt sugar" first appears in English in 1884.

carapace *n.* shell of a turtle, lobster, etc. 1836, borrowed from French *carapace,* from Portuguese *carapaça,* of uncertain origin.

carat or **karat** *n.* 1469 *carat* a measure of the fineness of gold; borrowed from Middle French *carat,* from Italian *carato,* from Arabic *qīrāṭ,* from Greek *kerátion* carat, the small carob seed used as a weight, originally, the horn-shaped pod of the carob tree; a diminutive form of *kéras* (genitive *kérātos*) HORN. The meaning "unit of weight for precious stones" is first recorded in English in 1555.

caravan *n.* 1588, borrowed from Middle French *caravane* or from Medieval Latin *caravana,* both from Persian *kārwān.*

The meaning of a covered carriage or wagon is first recorded in English in 1674; from this developed the British sense of a house trailer (1872).

caravansary *n.* inn or hotel where caravans rest. 1712, in writings of Addison in *The Spectator;* earlier *cavarzara, carvanzara* (1599, in Hakluyt's *Discoveries of the English Nation*); borrowed from Middle French *caravansera,* from Persian *kārwānsarāī* (from *kārwān* caravan + *sarāī* inn).

caravel (kar′əvel) *n.* small, fast ship. 1527, borrowed from Middle French *caravelle,* from Portuguese *caravela* a kind of small vessel, and a diminutive form of *cáravo* kind of ship, from Late Latin *cārabus,* from Late Greek *kárabos* kind of light ship, Greek *kárabos* horned beetle, spiny lobster, probably used in allusion to the outline of the ship.

While *caravel* is a borrowing from Middle French *caravelle,* it also replaces the earlier *carvel* (about 1425) meaning a fast, light ship, a term which disappeared after the 1650's, except in historical context and in the compound *carvel-built* that still exists, referring to a type of ship construction in which the edges of the planks of the hull are flush rather than overlapping each other as in the clinker-built construction.

caraway *n.* 1281-82, spicy seed of a plant; later, the plant itself (1373), through Anglo-Latin *carvi, carwi* or Old French *carvi, caroi,* both probably borrowed from Old Spanish *alcarahueya,* variant of *alcaravea,* from Spanish-Arabic *karawía,* Arabic *karawiyā,* perhaps from Greek *karṓ,* variant of *káron* caraway, of uncertain origin.

carbide *n.* About 1865, formed from English *carb-* (combining form of *carbon*) + *-ide.*

carbine *n.* short rifle. 1605 and eventually replacing earlier *carabin* (1590); *carbine* was borrowed through French *carabine* a small harquebus; *carabin* was borrowed directly from Middle French *carabin* cavalryman armed with this weapon; origin uncertain (perhaps from Middle French, southern dialect, *escarrabin* gravedigger during the plague, possibly referring to black uniforms of the gravediggers, or from Old French *calabrin* one who operated an ancient engine of war, and according to the OED perhaps the name was transferred to those who carried these firearms).

carbo-, or (before vowels) **carb-**, a combining form meaning carbon, as in *carbide = an oxide of carbon, carbohydrate = a hydrate of carbon.* 1810, coined from CARBON.

carbohydrate *n.* 1869, formed from English *carbo-* carbon + *hydrate* a compound produced when certain substances combine with water, borrowed from Greek *hýdōr* water + English *-ate*[2].

carbon *n.* nonmetallic chemical element. 1789 *carbone,* borrowed from French *carbone,* coined by Lavoisier from Latin *carbō* (genitive *carbōnis*) charcoal; see HEARTH.

The spelling *carbon* (without the final e) appeared in English in 1808. In Middle English (1415) *carbon* was borrowed in the sense of charcoal from Anglo-French, but this usage did not survive into the modern period.

carbonate *n.* 1794, borrowed from French *carbonate* salt or ester of carbonic acid, from New Latin *carbonatum* a carbonated substance (Latin *carbō,* genitive *carbōnis* + *-ātum* -ate[2]). **—v.** 1805, from the noun, probably by influence of French *carbonater* transform into a carbonate. **—carbonation** *n.* 1881, formed in English from *carbonate* + *-ion.*

carboniferous *adj.* 1799, formed in English from Latin *carbō* (genitive *carbōnis*) coal + *-iferous* combining form of English suffix *-ferous* producing, containing. **—n. Carboniferous** After the 1940's the noun use, shortened from the phrase *Carboniferous period.*

carbonize *n.* 1806, formed perhaps as a back formation of earlier English *carbonization* (1804), or from English *carbon* + *-ize.*

carborundum *n.* hard compound of carbon and silicon. 1892, American English, *Carborundum,* a trademark formed from *carbo(n)* + *(co)rundum.*

carbuncle *n.* inflamed swelling under the skin. Before 1300, a red or fiery colored jewel; also *charbugle* (about 1250) and *charbucle* (about 1200); borrowed from Old French *charboucle, carbuncle,* from Latin *carbunculus* a gem, of which Pliny describes several types, and a red tumor or boil; also, literally, a little coal, diminutive of *carbō* (genitive *carbōnis*) charcoal; see HEARTH.

The meaning "inflamed tumor," that is, in allusion to the fiery red color of the jewel, appeared probably before 1425, in a translation of Chauliac's *Grande Chirurgie.*

carburetor *n.* 1866, originally a device to enhance a gas flame; formed from English *carburet* to combine with carbon (*carb-* + *-uret,* an archaic suffix used in chemistry, from New Latin *-uretum,* after French words in *-ure*) + English suffix *-or*[2].

carcass *n.* dead body of a man or animal. Probably before 1400 *carcas,* earlier, *carkas* (before 1330); borrowed from Anglo-French *carkeis, carcois,* Old French *charcois,* and Anglo-Latin *carcasium, carcosium,* of uncertain origin.

carcinoma *n.* 1721, in Bailey's *Dictionary,* borrowed from Latin *carcinōma,* from Greek *karkínōma* a cancer, from *karkínos* crab; see CANCER. **— carcinogen** (kärsin′əjən) *n.* cancer-producing substance. 1936, probably back formation from *carcinogenic,* adj. (1926, formed from English *carcino(ma)* + *-genic*).

card[1] *n.* piece of stiff paper or pasteboard. Probably before 1425 *cardes* playing cards, borrowed from Middle French *carte,* from Latin *charta, carta* leaf of paper or papyrus, see CHART. It is not known how the original English form came to be *carde* instead of *carte,* which was established in Scottish; possibly the form was influenced by the earlier *kard* CARD[2]. The sense of a piece of paper to write on, etc., is first recorded in 1596. **—v.** 1548, from the noun. **—cardboard** *n.* (1848; earlier, *card paper,* 1777). **—card catalogue** (1854; earlier, *card index,* 1849). **—cardsharp** *n.* (1884; earlier, *card sharper,* 1859, and *sharper,* 1797). **—card table** (1713)

card[2] *n.* toothed tool or wire brush. 1375 *kard* (in legal document), earlier, 1351 (in surname) *Cardmaker;* borrowed from Anglo-Latin *cardo,* from Medieval Latin *cardo* a teasel, from Latin *carduus* thistle, related to *carrere* to clean or comb with a card. The Latin *carduus* is cognate with Middle Low German *harst* a rake, Lithuanian *karšti* to comb, curry, and Sanskrit *kaṣati* (he) scrapes, scratches, from Indo-European **kars-* (Pok.532). **—v.** About 1378 *karden* to comb (wool, etc.) from spinning, from *kard,* n. card[2].

cardiac *adj.* of or having to do with the heart. 1601, in Holland's translation of Pliny's *Natural History,* borrowed, perhaps by influence of French *cardiaque,* from Latin *cardiacus,* from Greek *kardiakós,* from *kardíā* HEART. The form was known in Middle English times: *cardiac* about 1440, noun meaning "a vein associated with the heart," but that sense dropped out of use apparently by the 1500's, and the meaning of a medicine for the heart disappeared in the 1800's.

cardigan *n.* 1868, named after Brudenell, Earl of *Cardigan* (1797-1868), who wore such a jacket during the charge of the Light Brigade.

cardinal *n.* high official of the Roman Catholic Church. Before 1126, in a chronicle, borrowed from Medieval Latin *cardinalis* a cardinal, from *episcopus cardinalis* chief bishop, from Late Latin *cardinālis,* adj., chief, pivotal. **—adj.** main, chief. Probably before 1325, in *Cursor Mundi,* borrowed from Old French *cardinal,* from Late Latin *cardinālis* chief, or pivotal in the sense of having to do with something a thing turns or hinges on, in Latin *cardinālis* having to do with a door hinge, from *cardō* (genitive *cardinis*) pivot, turning point; for suffix see -AL[1].

Latin *cardō* is considered to be cognate with Greek *kradân* to swing, wave, brandish, and Welsh *cerdded* to walk, from Indo-European **kerd-/kr̥d-* (Pok.934).

cardio- a combining form meaning heart, as in *cardiogram* (1876), *cardiology* (1847). Borrowed from Greek *kardio-,* combining form of *kardíā* heart, cognate with Latin *cor* (genitive *cordis*) and English HEART.

care *n.* trouble, worry, concern. Old English *caru, cearu* sorrow, anxiety, grief (about 725, in *Beowulf*). The word is cognate, in the primary sense of inward grief, with Old Saxon *kara* care, Old High German *chara* wail, lamentation, Middle High German *kartac* day of mourning (modern German *Karfreitag* Good Friday), and Gothic *kara* sorrow, trouble, care, from Proto-Germanic **karó.* Though not connected with Latin *cūra* care, in the sense of pains or troubles bestowed on others, the word is cognate outside Germanic with Latin *garrīre* to chatter, Greek *gêrys* (Doric *gârys*) voice, Old Irish *gāir* call, outcry, and *do-gar* sad, from Indo-European **ĝar-/ĝār-* cry (Pok.352). **—v.** Old English *carian, cearian* to be anxious (about 725, in *Beowulf*), from *caru, cearu,* n. The Old English verb corresponds to Old Saxon *karōn* to care, Old High German *karōn, karēn* to lament, and Gothic *karōn* to care, *ga-karōn* be concerned about, from Proto-Germanic **karōjanan.* **—careful** *adj.* Old English *carful* (about 1000, in homilies of Ælfric); earlier, *cearful* (before 750, in Cynewulf), formed from *caru, cearu* care + *-ful* full. **—carefree** *adj.* (1795) **—careless** *adj.* Old English *carlēas* (before 1000, in writings of Caedmon), formed from *caru, cearu* care + *-lēas* -less. **—caretaker** *n.* (1858) **—careworn** *adj.* (1828, in writings of Carlyle).

careen *v.* heel over, sway, lurch. 1600, in Hakluyt's *Discoveries of the English Nations,* lean (a ship) on its side, from earlier *careen,* n. (1591), position of a ship when laid on one side; borrowed from Middle French *carène* keel, from Italian (Genoese) *carena,* from Latin *carīna* keel; originally, nutshell. The Latin word is cognate with Greek *káryon* nut, Sanskrit *karaka-s* coconut, *karkara-s* hard, and probably Old English *heard* HARD.

career *n.* occupation, profession. About 1534, a run, usually at full speed, a course or course of action, borrowed from Middle French *carrière* race course, stretch, from Old Provençal *carriera* road for vehicles, from Medieval Latin *via carraria* carriageway, from Latin *carrum* cart, CAR. The sense "occupation or profession through the course of one's life" appeared in 1803, in writings of the Duke of Wellington. **—v.** 1594, to charge at a tournament; from the noun. In 1647 the sense "run at full speed" is first recorded.

caress *n.* affectionate touch or stroke. 1651; earlier, a show of regard (1647); borrowed from French *caresse* a caress, from Italian *carezza* endearment, fondness, from *caro* dear, from Latin *cārus* dear. See CHARITY. **—v.** 1658, in writings of Milton, borrowed from French *caresser* to caress, from Italian *carezzare,* from *carezza* caress, endearment, fondness.

caret *n.* mark (ʌ) to show where something should be put in. 1681, borrowed from Latin *caret* there is lacking, 3rd person singular present indicative of *carēre* to be without, lack; related to *castrāre* CASTRATE.

cargo *n.* 1657, borrowed from Spanish *cargo* a loading, burden, or perhaps from *carga* load, cargo, from *cargar* to load, from Late Latin *carricāre* to load on a cart, from Latin *carrum* cart, CAR. The older term for a load or burden of a ship, wagon, etc., in Middle English was *charge* (about 1300, in an old chronicle); the general meaning of *charge* a burden and, therefore, of something produced (cited in OED) is first recorded probably before 1200, in *Ancrene Riwle.*

caribou *n.* About 1665, American English, borrowed through Canadian French *caribou,* from Algonquian *xalibû,* literally, pawer, scratcher, in reference to the animal's habit of pawing snow to find grass.

caricature (kar′əkəchůr) *n.* cartoon that ridiculously exaggerates a person or thing. 1748, in letters of Horace Walpole, borrowed from French *caricature,* from Italian *caricatura,* from *caricare* overload, exaggerate, from Late Latin *carricāre* to load. The Italian spelling *caricatura* appeared frequently in English before 1682 and into the 1800's. —v. 1749, in writings of Walpole, from the noun, probably by influence of French *caricaturer* to represent in caricature. **—caricaturist** *n.* 1798, formed from English *caricature,* n. + *-ist.*

caries (kãr′ēz) *n.* decay of teeth, bones, or tissues. 1634, borrowed, perhaps by influence of French *carie* (1537), from Latin *cariēs* decay; cognate with Greek *kḗr* death, *akḗratos* inviolate, intact, Old Irish *crīn* withered, decayed, Tocharian A *kāryap* damage, Avestan *asarəta-* intact, and Sanskrit *śṛṇā́ti* (he) breaks, crushes, from Indo-European **k̑er-/k̑erə-/k̑rē-* (Pok.578).

carillon *n.* set of bells arranged for playing melodies. 1775, borrowed from French *carillon,* from Old French *quarellon* a chime of bells, alteration of *quarregnon, carignon* set of four bells, from Northern Gallo-Romance *quadriniōnem,* and corresponding to Latin *quaterniōnem* a set of four, from *quaternī* four each, *quater* four times, *quattuor* four. **—carillonneur** *n.* 1772, as a French term introduced into an English work on music.

carmine *n.* deep red with a tinge of purple. 1712, borrowed from French *carmin,* from Medieval Latin *carminium,* from a fusion of Arabic *qirmiz* the kermes insect, and Latin *minium* red lead; see CRIMSON. **—adj.** 1737-59, from the noun.

carnage *n.* slaughter, massacre. 1600, in Holland's translation of Livy's *Roman History,* borrowed from Middle French *carnage,* from Italian *carnaggio* slaughter, murder, from Medieval Latin *carnaticum* flesh, often as meat in tribute to a feudal lord, from Latin *carō* (accusative *carnem*) flesh; see CARNAL; for suffix see -AGE.

carnal *adj.* bodily, sensual. Probably about 1400, borrowed through Old French *carnal,* and directly from Medieval Latin *carnalis* natural, of the same blood or descent, Latin *carnālis* of the flesh, from *carō* (genitive *carnis*) flesh, related to Latin *corium* skin, hide, and *cortex* bark, rind, CORTEX; for suffix see -AL[1].

carnation *n.* red, white, or pink flower. 1538, borrowed from Middle French *carnation* person's color or complexion, probably adapted from Italian (originally Northern dialect) *carnagione* flesh color, from Late Latin *carnātiōnem* (nominative *carnātiō*) fleshiness, from Latin *carō* (genitive *carnis*) flesh; for suffix see -TION.

carnival *n.* 1549, time of feasting and merrymaking before Lent, borrowed from Italian *carnevale* the last three days before Lent, alteration of dialectal (Milanese) **carnelevale* and (Old Pisan) *carnelevare* a leaving off of eating meat (*carne* flesh, meat, from Latin *carnem* + Italian *levare* to remove, from Latin *levāre* lift up). The Italian dialect forms were influenced by Medieval Latin *carnelevamen, carnilevamen* a form equivalent in use to English Shrovetide.

The sense "any celebration, festival" is first recorded in 1916, in Joyce's *Portrait of an Artist;* the sense "place of amusement, circus" appeared in American English in 1931.

carnivorous *adj.* flesh-eating. 1646, in writings of Sir Thomas Browne, borrowing of Latin *carnivorus* flesh-eating (*carō,* genitive *carnis* flesh + *vorāre* devour; see VORACIOUS). English use was patterned after earlier *carnivora* a name applied to a large order of flesh-eating mammals (1627, in Francis Bacon's *Natural History*), Latin *carnivorus* was possibly a loan translation of Greek *sarkobóros* flesh-eating.

carol *n.* Probably before 1300, in *Arthour and Merlin,* borrowed from Old French *carole,* probably alteration of Latin *choraula* one that accompanies a choral dance on a flute, from Greek *choraúlēs* (*chorós* dance + *aulós* hollow tube, flute). See CHORUS, HYDRAULIC.

The meaning "hymn of joy, especially one sung at Christmas" appeared in 1502.

—v. sing joyously. About 1303, in Mannyng's *Handlyng Synne,* borrowed from Old French *caroler,* from *carole,* n.

carom *n.* billiard shot in which the ball strikes two balls. 1779, in an edition of *Hoyle's Games,* shortened from earlier *carambole* (1775), apparently borrowed from French *carambole,* from Spanish *carambola* a red ball in billiards, originally meaning a snare, trap, or trick, of uncertain origin; perhaps from earlier Spanish *carambola* name of an orange fruit from tropical Asia, borrowed through Portuguese from Mahratti (a language of India) *karambal,* from Sanskrit *karmarañga-s.* —**v.** glance off, rebound. 1860, in Oliver Wendell Holmes' *Professor at the Breakfast-Table,* from the noun.

carotid *adj.* having to do with a large neck artery. 1667, borrowed, perhaps by influence of earlier French *carotide,* n. (1541), from Greek *karōtídes* carotid arteries, from *karoûn* stupefy, whence *káros* stupor, a state thought to be produced by compression of carotid arteries. —**n.** 1741, probably developed in English from the adjective.

carouse *v.* revel. 1567, drink freely, drain; probably borrowed from Middle French *carrousser* drink, quaff, swill, from *carous* a bout of drinking. It is also possible that the verb was abstracted from the phrase *drink carouse* (also *quaff* or *pledge carouse*), in which *carouse* appears as an adverb meaning "to the bottom, all out, or all up." The words (both English and French) are said to derive from German *garaus,* adv. all out, from a German phrase *(trink) gar aus!* (drink) all up! —**n.** revelry. 1559, probably borrowed from French *carous* a bout of drinking. The word in English has been largely superseded by *carousal.* —**carousal** *n.* 1765, in Sterne's *Tristram Shandy,* formed from English *carouse,* v. + *-al*[2].

carp[1] *v.* find fault with, complain. About 1225 *carpen* to talk, discourse, borrowed from a Scandinavian source (compare Old Icelandic *karpa* to boast; possibly earlier, to speak, talk, and *karp* boasting).

The sense "find fault with" developed in Middle English and is first recorded in about 1378, apparently influenced by Latin *carpere* to pluck, tear to pieces, (figurative) to slander, revile; see HARVEST.
—**carper** *n.* 1440, talker, in *Promptorium Parvulorum,* from earlier *carp,* n. (probably about 1350).

carp[2] *n.* freshwater fish. 1393, borrowed through Old French *carpe,* from Old Provençal *carpa,* and directly from Medieval and Late Latin *carpa,* probably from a Germanic source; compare Old High German *karpfo* carp (modern German *Karpfen*), Middle Dutch *carpe* carp (modern Dutch *karper*), probably from a pre-Germanic (Alpine) word.

carpel *n. Botany.* modified leaf from which a pistil is formed. 1835, borrowed from New Latin *carpellum* (1817), diminutive from Greek *karpós* fruit; see HARVEST.

carpenter *n.* About 1300; earlier, as a surname (1175); borrowed from Anglo-French *carpenter,* Old French *charpentier,* from Late Latin *artifex carpentārius* carriage maker, from Latin *carpentum* two-wheeled carriage, from Gaulish.

Latin borrowed several names for carriage, chariot from Gaulish: *carrum* (see CAR), *cisium* (a kind of light, two-wheeled chariot), and *carpentum.*
—**carpentry** *n.* About 1378, in a version of *Piers Plowman,* borrowed from Anglo-French *carpenterie,* from *carpenter* carpenter.

carpet *n.* 1345 *karpete* cloth to cover floors, tables, beds, etc., borrowed from Old French *carpite* and from Medieval Latin *carpita;* both from Old Italian *carpita* (thick cloth, often used for a cover, originally made of shreds, derived from past participle of Vulgar Latin **carpīre* to pick, pluck, card (wool), for Latin *carpere* to pluck; see HARVEST. —**v.** Before 1626, in Francis Bacon's *New Atlantis,* from the noun. —**carpetbagger** *n.* 1868, American English, formed from *carpetbag,* n. (1830), originally, a traveling bag made out of carpet + *-er*[1]. —**carpet sweeper** (1858)

carriage *n.* Before 1387, in Trevisa's translation of Higden's *Polychronicon,* Middle English *cariage* wheeled vehicles collectively; earlier in the compound *carriageman* carter (1374); borrowed through Anglo-French *cariage,* Old North French *cariage,* from *carier* CARRY; for suffix see -AGE. The word was used in Middle English about 1398 to refer to an individual wheeled vehicle; in 1596 the sense "a way of carrying one's body, bearing" appeared, paralleling an earlier meaning referring to the act or condition of carrying, and specifically to a feudal service or duty to provide transportation, first recorded in 1253 (Anglo-Latin).

Gradually during the late 1500's and into the 1600's the spelling became fixed with two *r*'s.

carrion *n.* dead and decaying flesh. Before 1325 *carion,* in *Cursor Mundi,* alteration of earlier *caroine, charoine* (probably before 1200, in *Ancrene Riwle*), borrowed through Anglo-French *careine, caroine,* Old French *charoigne, caroigne,* from Vulgar Latin **carōnia,* from Latin *carō* (genitive *carnis*) flesh; see CARNAL. —**carrion crow** (1528, in writings of Sir Thomas More).

The spelling with two *r*'s was established after the 1550's.

carrot *n.* 1533, borrowed from Middle French *carotte,* learned borrowing from Latin *carōta,* from Greek *karōtón* a carrot, possibly from *kárā* head, top. The earlier forms included *carot, carette, caret,* which were superseded by *carrot* about 1680.

carrousel or **carousel** (kar′əsel′) *n.* merry-go-round. 1673, developed from the earlier meaning "tournament in which companies of knights engaged in exercises, including chariot races" (1650, in writings of Marvell), borrowed from French *carrousel* a tilting match, from Italian *carosello* a kind of joust or feat on horseback, of uncertain (perhaps dialectal) origin.

carry *v.* Before 1338 *carien,* in Mannyng's *Chronicle of England,* borrowed from Anglo-French or Old North French *carier* to transport in a vehicle, Old French *charier,* from Gallo-Romance **carrizāre* (=**carridiāre*), from Latin *carrum* cart, CAR. See the doublet CHARGE.

The spelling *carry* (with two *r*'s) was established by the early 1600's.
—**n.** 1605, from the verb.
—**carrier** *n.* Before 1398 *cariere,* in Trevisa's translation of Bartholomew's *De Proprietatibus Rerum,* formed from Middle English *carien,* v. to carry and, in part, borrowed from or at least influenced in formation by Anglo-French *cariour* one who carries, from Old North French *carier* to carry. —**carrier pigeon** (1647; earlier *carrier,* 1641).

cart *n.* About 1200 *carte,* in *The Ormulum,* borrowed probably from a Scandinavian source (compare Old Icelandic *kartr* cart) and replacing Old English (before 800) *cræt* cart. Both Middle English *carte* and Old English *cræt* are cognate with Middle Dutch *cratte* woven mat, wagon basket, and Old High German *kratto* basket, from Indo-European **gord-,* **grod-* (Pok. 386); further, Old English *cræt* is related to Old English *cradol* CRADLE. —**v.** Probably about 1387 *carten,* in a version of *Piers Plowman,* from the Middle English noun. —**cartage** *n.* (1305) —**carter** *n.* (1193, in part borrowed from Anglo-French *careter,* and in part formed from English *cart* + *-er*[1]). —**cartwheel** *n.* (about 1395)

cartel *n.* 1560, written challenge, borrowed from Middle French *cartel,* from Italian *cartello* little card, diminutive of *carta* paper, letter, bill, from Latin *charta* CHART. In 1889, the word was extended to mean "written agreement between challengers or belligerents, coalition," and in 1902 to mean "agreement between rival businesses to fix prices, restrict production, etc.," under the influence of German *Kartell,* from French *cartel,* from Middle French.

cartilage *n.* substance forming parts of a skeleton. Probably before 1425, in a translation of Chauliac's *Grande Chirurgie,* borrowed through Middle French *cartilage,* or directly as a learned borrowing from Latin *cartilāgō* (genitive *cartilāginis*) cartilage, gristle, possibly related to Latin *crātis* wickerwork, CRATE. **—cartilaginous** *adj.* 1541, borrowed from French *cartilagineux,* or directly from Latin *cartilāginōsus,* from *cartilāgō;* for suffix see -OUS.

cartography *n.* the making of maps or charts. Before 1843, borrowed from French *cartographie* (from Medieval Latin *carta* CHART, map + French *-graphie* -graphy). **—cartographer** *n.* (before 1843)

carton *n.* pasteboard box. 1816, borrowed from French *carton* pasteboard, papier-mâché, from Italian *cartone* pasteboard, an augmentative form of *carta* paper, from Latin *charta* paper, CHART. —**v.** 1921, implied in the past tense *cartoned* used as an adjective.

cartoon *n.* sketch or drawing. 1671, in John Evelyn's *Diary,* drawing or painting used as model for another work, borrowed from French *carton* pasteboard (because it was originally drawn on paper), from Italian *cartone* pasteboard; see CARTON; for suffix see -OON. The meaning "amusing sketch," is first recorded in 1843 from *Punch.* —**v.** 1884, from the noun. **—cartoonist** *n.* (1880)

cartridge *n.* 1626, in writings of Captain John Smith, alteration of earlier (1579) *cartage,* borrowed from French *cartouche* a full charge for a pistol, held in paper, from Italian *cartuccia* a cartridge, cylinder or cone of paper, from *carta* paper, from Latin *charta* paper, CHART.

carve *v.* cut into slices. Probably before 1200 *kerven,* in Layamon's *Chronicle of Britain,* partly developed from Old English (about 725 *ceorfan* and *beceorfan,* and partly borrowed from or influenced by a Scandinavian word (compare Old Icelandic *kurfla* cut to pieces, Norwegian *karve* to carve). The word is cognate with Old Frisian *kerva* to notch, carve, Middle Low German and Middle Dutch *kerven* to cut, carve, and Middle High German *kerben* to notch, carve, from Proto-Germanic **kerƀanan;* also probably cognate with Greek *gráphein* to write, scratch, engrave, Old Slavic *žrěbĭjĭ* lot (probably originally in the sense of a small notched stick), and Old Prussian *gīrbin* number, from Indo-European **gerbh-/gṛbh-* (Pok. 392). **—carver** *n.* (about 1275, in a surname). **—carving** *n.* (probably before 1200, in *Ancrene Riwle*) **—carving knife** (about 1415)

caryatid (kar′ēat′id) *n. Architecture.* female figure used in a column. 1563, *cariatide,* borrowed from Middle French *cariatide,* from Latin *caryātides,* from Greek *Karyátides* priestesses of Artemis (Diana) at Caryae (Greek *Karýai*), a town in Laconia where dance festivals were held in the temple of Artemis.

casaba (kəsä′bə) *n.* kind of muskmelon. 1889, American English, from *Kasaba,* the place from which the fruit was first imported (a city, now called Turgutlu, near Izmir, Turkey).

Casanova *n.* lady's man, lover. 1888, in allusion to *Casanova,* 1725-1798, Italian adventurer famous for his escapades and love affairs, described in his memoirs, written in French and published 1826-38.

cascade *n.* small waterfall. 1641, in John Evelyn's *Diary,* borrowed from French *cascade,* from Italian *cascata* waterfall, from *cascare* to fall, from Vulgar Latin **cāsicāre,* from Latin *cāsum,* past participle of *cadere* to fall; see CADENCE; for suffix see -ADE. —**v.** 1702, from the noun.

cascara (kaskär′ə) *n.* kind of dried bark used as a laxative. 1903, American English, short for *cascara sagrada,* from Spanish *cáscara sagrada* sacred bark (*cáscara* bark, from *cascar* to crack, break + *sagrada* sacred, feminine of *sagrado,* from Latin *sacrātus* consecrated); see CASK.

case[1] *n.* instance, example. Before 1250, in *Ancrene Riwle,* state of affairs, situation, borrowed from Old French *cas* circumstance, event, chance, learned borrowing from Latin *cāsus* (genitive *cāsūs*) a falling, event, chance, from *cās-,* past participle stem of *cadere* to fall; see CADENCE. The meaning "instance or example" is first recorded in Middle English about 1300.

case[2] *n.* box, container, receptacle. Before 1325, in *Cursor Mundi,* borrowed from Anglo-French *casse,* Old French *chasse,* from Latin *capsa* box, container, from *capere* to take, hold; see CAPTIVE. —**v.** to put in a case or box. 1575, from the noun. The meaning "to examine, inspect" is first recorded in 1915. **—casing** *n.* covering (1839).

casein (kā′sēn) *n.* protein present in milk. 1841 *caseine,* borrowed from French *caséine,* formed from Latin *cāseus* cheese + French *-ine* -ine[2].

casement *n.* Before 1420, in Lydgate's *Troy Book,* hollow molding; borrowed from Anglo-Latin *cassementum,* from *casse* frame, CASE[2] box, or frame; for suffix see -MENT.

The sense "a frame or sash that forms a window" is first recorded in 1556.

cash *n.* 1593, borrowed from Middle French *caisse* money box, coffer, from Provençal *caissa,* from Vulgar Latin **capsea* box, from Latin *capsa* box; see CASE[2] box. —**v.** convert into cash. 1811, from the noun. **—cash book** (1622) **—cashbox** *n.* (1855) **—cash register** (1879, American English).

cashew (kash′ü) *n.* 1703; earlier *caju,* borrowed from French *cajou, acajou,* from Brazilian Portuguese *cajú, acajú,* from Tupi-Guarani *acajú* the tree producing this nut.

cashier[1] *n.* person in charge of money in a bank or business. 1596, in writings of Thomas Nashe, borrowed from Middle French *caissier* treasurer, from *caisse* money box; see CASH; for suffix see -IER.

cashier[2] *v.* dismiss from service, especially in disgrace. 1592, *casseere,* in Robert Greene's *Groatsworth of Wit,* borrowed from Middle Dutch *casseren,* to cast off, discharge, from French *casser* to discharge, annul, from Late Latin *cassāre* annul, from Latin *cassus* void, empty; see QUASH[2] annul. The OED suggests that *cashier* came into English from Dutch because of the contact of British soldiers with the Dutch during the campaign in the Netherlands in 1585.

cashmere *n.* fine soft wool. 1684, originally in the sense of a shawl made of cashmere, from *Cashmere,* variant of *Kashmir,* region in the Himalayas north of India; so called because the wool was obtained from a breed of long-haired goats of Kashmir.

casino *n.* 1744, in letters of Walpole, building or room for dancing, etc.; borrowed from Italian *casino,* diminutive of *casa* house, from Latin *casa* hut, cabin, of uncertain origin.

The sense "building used for gambling" is first recorded in English in 1851.

cask *n.* barrel. 1458, borrowed from Middle French *casque* a cask, helmet, from Spanish *casco* skull, helmet, cask; originally, potsherd, fragment, or broken piece, from *cascar* to crack, break, shatter, from Vulgar Latin **quassicāre,* a frequentative form showing repeated action of *quassāre* to break, shatter, shake; see QUASH[1] crush.

casket *n.* 1461, small box for valuables, perhaps formed from English *cask* + *-et* or, possibly, an alteration of Middle French *casset* small box or chest; see CASSETTE. The meaning "coffin" appeared in 1849 in American English, as a figurative sense of a small box containing something valuable, in the specific case cited, a dear friend.

cassava *n.* tropical plant with starchy roots. 1565 *casava,* borrowed from Middle French *cassave,* from Spanish *casabe,* and earlier *cazabbi* (1555), borrowed directly from Spanish, from Taino (Haiti) *caçábi.*

casserole *n.* covered baking dish. 1706, borrowed from French *casserole* stew pan or saucepan, a diminutive form of Middle French *casse* pan, from Provençal *cassa,* from Medieval Latin *cattia* pan, vessel, possibly from Greek *kyáthion,* diminutive of *kýathos* cup, formed from *kýar* hole; see CAVE.

cassette *n.* 1793, in writings of Southey, small box, casket, borrowed from French *cassette* little box, from Middle French *casset,* diminutive of Old North French *casse* box, from Latin *capsa;* see CASE[2] box.

The meaning "cartridge of photographic film" appeared in 1875. The sense of a container of magnetic tape to be used in a tape recorder or the like, appeared in 1960.

cassock *n.* long garment worn by clergymen. About 1550, long coat or gown worn by men and women, borrowed from Middle French *casaque* long coat, perhaps from Arabic *kazāgand,* from Persian *kazhāgand* padded coat (*kazh, kaj* raw silk + *āgand* stuffed).

cassowary (kas′əwer′ē) *n.* large bird like an ostrich. 1611, borrowed from Malay *burong kĕsuari* cassowary bird.

cast (kast) *v.* throw. Probably before 1200 *casten,* in *Ancrene Riwle,* borrowed from a Scandinavian source (compare Old Icelandic *kasta* to throw, related to *kǫs* heap thrown up, pile). **—n.** About 1250, partly developed from *casten,* v., and, in part, borrowed from Scandinavian (compare Old Icelandic *kast,* n.). The earliest recorded sense of the Middle English noun was "a throw," with the idea of the form into which a thing is thrown, which was applied in such varied senses as arrangement, plan, design, conformation, bearing, appearance, and the like. **—castaway** *n.* (probably before 1475). **—casting** *n.* (before 1300; later, with the meaning of a metal casting, before 1398).

castanet (kas′tənet′) *n.* small wood or ivory cymbal. 1647, borrowed from Spanish *castañeta* a castanet, diminutive of *castaña* chestnut, from Latin *castanea* CHESTNUT.

caste (kast) *n.* hereditary social class, as among the Hindus. 1555, race, breed, lineage, borrowed from Spanish and Portuguese *casta* (earlier *casta raça* unmixed race) originally feminine of *casto* chaste, from Latin *castus* pure, related to *castrāre* to cut off, CASTRATE. See the doublet CHASTE.

In 1613 Purchas, in his *Pilgrimage,* introduced the word in the sense of one of the hereditary classes in India.

castellated *adj.* 1679, formed in English after Medieval Latin *castellatus,* past participle of *castellare* to fortify as a castle with turrets and battlements (from Latin *castellum* CASTLE) + English past participial suffix *-ed*[2].

caster *n.* formed from English *cast,* v. + *er*[1]. **1** a small wheel on a piece of furniture or machinery to make it move easier (1748). **2** bottle containing seasoning, etc., for table use (1676). **3** a person or thing that casts (before 1382, in the Wycliffe Bible). The variant spelling *castor* probably arose from confusion with Latin *castor* beaver, or in an effort to Latinize the earlier *-er* form. In the U.S. usage favors the spelling *-or* for the shaker used at the table.

castigate *v.* criticize severely, punish. 1607, in Shakespeare's *Timon of Athens,* probably borrowed from Latin *castīgātus,* past participle of *castīgāre* to correct, chastise, formed (perhaps by influence from *fatigāre* to weary), from *castus* pure, CHASTE, for suffix see -ATE[1]. Doublet of CHASTEN. It is also possible that *castigate* is a back formation from earlier English **castigation** *n.* punishment. About 1390 *castigacioun,* in Chaucer's writings, borrowed from Latin *castīgātiōnem* (nominative *castīgātiō*), from *castīgāre* to chastise; for suffix see -TION.

castle *n.* Old English *castel* (about 1000) in early Gospels, first borrowed from Latin *castellum* fortified village, and later, as a reborrowing from Old North French *castel* fortress, castle, from Latin *castellum,* diminutive of *castrum* fort (plural *castra* camp, encampment), related to Latin *castrāre* cut off, CASTRATE. See the doublet CHATEAU.

castor *n.* beaver, oily substance secreted by glands in the groin of the beaver and known as castoreum. Both senses appeared in Middle English before 1398, in Trevisa's translation of Bartholomew's *De Proprietatibus Rerum,* borrowed through Old French *castor,* or directly from Latin *castor* beaver from Greek *kástōr,* from *Kástōr* Castor (originally, he who excels), one of the Twins of Greek mythology (the other being Pollux).

Castor was worshipped by women of Ancient Greece as their healer and preserver (*sōtḗr*) from disease. Later Castor was involved by Roman women in an oath (using *ēcastor* or *mēcastor* as the first word). It was because of the healing effect of the beaver's secretion (known as *castoreum*) in the treatment of women's diseases that the name of Castor was carried over to the beaver, completely displacing the native Greek word and almost entirely eliminating the native Latin one *(fiber).*

The name of another substance, *castor oil* (the extract of a plant), appeared in 1746, and though never obtained from a beaver, was associated with the "oil of a castor," i.e., castoreum, perhaps because both have similar medicinal properties and were noted for their bitter or acrid taste.

castrate *v.* remove the male glands from. 1633, probably developed from earlier English *castrate,* n. a castrated man (1639), from *castrated,* participial adj., gelded, diminished (1613, in a later edition of Robert Cawdrey's A *Table Alphabeticall*); borrowed from Latin *castrātus,* past participle of *castrāre* cut off, curtail, castrate (formed from **castrum* knife, cognate with Sanskrit *śastrá-m* knife); for suffix see -ATE. The Latin *castrāre* is cognate with Greek *keázein* to split, Middle Irish *cess* spear, Old Slavic *kosa* sickle, scythe, and Sanskrit *śásti, śásati* (he) cuts, chops up, from Indo-European **k̂es-* (Pok.586). It is also possible that *castrate* is a back formation of earlier *castration.* —**castration** *n.* Probably before 1425 *castracioun,* borrowed from Latin *castrātiōnem* (nominative *castrātiō*), from *castrāre* castrate; for suffix see -TION.

casual *adj.* not planned or expected. About 1384 *casuel* accidental, fortuitous, borrowed from Old French *casuel,* learned borrowing from Latin *cāsuālis,* from *cāsus* (genitive *cāsūs*) chance; see CASE[1] instance; for suffix see -AL[1]. —**casualty** *n.* 1422 *casueltee* a casual or incidental charge or payment; later, chance, accident, misfortune (1442), formed from Middle English *casuel* + -*tee* -ty[2], by influence of earlier Old French *casualité,* and Medieval Latin *casualitas,* from Latin *cāsuālis* depending on chance. In the 1600's the word was applied to losses resulting from accidents; the sense "one who has been killed or wounded" appeared in 1844.

casuist (kazh'üist) *n.* one who reasons cleverly but falsely, quibbler, sophist. In 1609, in Ben Jonson's writings, a person who studies and resolves questions of right and wrong; borrowed from French *casuiste* or directly from Spanish *casuista,* from Latin *cāsus* (genitive *cāsūs*) a falling, chance, CASE[1] instance; for suffix see -IST.

The pejorative meaning of this word developed in the mid-1600's, and probably led to the formation of **casuistry** *n.* quibbling, sophistry. 1725, in Pope's *Rape of the Lock,* formed from English *casuist* + *-ry.* From its first use, the word was contemptuous, implying by its suffix "the casuist's trade".

cat *n.* Old English (before 800, in an early glossary) *cat, catte,* corresponding to Old Frisian *katte* cat, Old High German *kazza* (modern German *Katze*), and Old Icelandic *köttr* (Danish *kat,* Norwegian and Swedish *katt*) all of which probably came from the same source as Late Latin *catus, cattus, catta* cat, Old Irish *cat,* Old Slavic *kotŭka,* Lithuanian *katė̃,* perhaps ultimately from an Afro-Asiatic source (compare Nubian *kadis* and Berber *kaddiska* cat).

The related words in the Romance languages, such as Spanish and Portuguese *gato, gata* and (Italian *gatto, gatta*), came from Medieval Latin *gattus, gatta,* variants of Late Latin *cattus, catta.* French *chat, chatte* came directly from Late Latin *cattus, catta.*

cata- or (before vowels) **cat-** a prefix meaning: **1** down, downward, as in *cataract* = violent rush, downpour (Greek *kata-* down + *rhā́ttein* to dash). **2** against, as in *catapult* = a weapon for hurling darts or missiles (Greek *kata-* against + *pállein* hurl). **3** wrongly, amiss, as in *catachresis* = misuse of words (Greek *kata-* amiss + *chrêsthai* to use). **4** completely, as in *catalogue* = complete list of (things) counted or said (Greek *kata-* completely + *légein* to count or speak).

Most English words with *cata-* were borrowed, often through Latin, after the 1500's as part of Greek words. Other words in English that have *cata-* as a prefix are made on analogy with Greek words or follow similar forms of compounding as derivatives. Though *cata-* was known in Latin (as in *catacomb*), it is a borrowing from Greek *kata-,* from *katá* down, against, over, and is cognate with Old Welsh *cant* with, Old Irish *cēt,* Hittite *katta* down, under, with, and possibly with Latin *com-* with, COM-.

catabolism *n.* process of breaking down living tissues. 1889; earlier, *katabolism* (1876), probably formed in English after METABOLISM, with the substitution of *cata-* down, for *meta-* (*bolism* thereby being taken as a derivative combining form in English, formed of Greek *bolḗ* a throw + English *-ism*).

cataclysm *n.* upheaval. 1633, borrowed from French *cataclysme,* from Latin *cataclysmos,* from Greek *kataklysmós* flood, ultimately from *kata-* down + *klýzein* to wash, related to *klýdōn* billow, cognate with Old Latin *cluere* clean out, Gothic *hlūtrs* clear, pure, and Lithuanian *šlúoti* sweep, from Indo-European **k̂leu-/k̂lō(u)-/k̂lū-* (Pok.607).

catacomb *n.* Usually, **catacombs.** underground burying place. Old English (before 900) *catacumbas,* borrowed from Late Latin *catacumbae,* plural, possibly alteration (influenced by Latin *-cumbere* to lie) of the phrase *cata tumbās* among the tombs (*cata* among, from Greek *katá* down, over) + (*tumbās,* plural accusative of *tumba* TOMB).

In the four occurrences in Old English and one in Middle English, the word is treated as a foreign word and the inflections are not clearly English. The first instance in which it is treated as an English word is in Caxton's *Golden Legend,* 1483.

catafalque (kat'əfalk) *n.* stand or frame for a coffin. 1641, borrowed from French *catafalque,* from Italian *catafalco* scaffold, from Vulgar Latin **catafalicum* (Latin *cata-* down + *fala* scaffolding, possibly of Etruscan origin). Compare SCAFFOLD.

catalepsy (kat'əlep'sē) *n.* trancelike paralytic seizure. Before 1398 *catalempcia,* in Trevisa's translation of Bartholomew's *De Proprietatibus Rerum,* borrowed from Medieval Latin *catalepsia,* alteration of Late Latin *catalēpsis,* from Greek *katálēpsis* seizure, ultimately from *kata-* down + *lambánein* to take, seize; see DILEMMA.

catalogue or **catalog** *n.* list of items in a collection. Probably before 1425 *cathologe,* borrowed in a translation of Chauliac's *Grande Chirurgie,* from Old French *catalogue,* and directly as a learned borrowing from Late Latin *catalogus,* from Greek *katálogos* list, ultimately from *kata-* completely + *légein* to count, speak; see LEGEND. —*v.* 1598, in a translation of the *Iliad,* from the noun.

catalysis *n.* regulation of a chemical reaction by the presence of a catalyst. 1655, dissolution, in John Evelyn's *Memoirs,* borrowed from Greek *katálysis,* ultimately from *kata-* completely, down + *lýein* loosen; see LOSE. Use of the term in chemistry was introduced in 1836 by the Swedish chemist Jöns Jakob Berzelius.

catalyst *n.* 1902, formed from English *catalysis,* on the pattern of *analysis, analyst.* —**catalytic** *adj.* 1836 (introduced by Jöns Jakob Berzelius), borrowed from Greek *katalytikós,* from *katálysis* catalysis; for suffix see -IC. —**catalyze** *v.* 1890, formed from English *catalysis,* on the pattern of *analysis, analyze;* probably influenced in its formation by French *catalyser* (1842).

catamaran (kat′əmәran′) *n.* boat or raft with two hulls side by side. 1673, borrowed from Tamil *kaṭṭu-maram,* literally, tie-wood (*kaṭṭu* to tie + *maram* tree, wood).

catamount (kat′əmount) *n.* wildcat, panther. 1664, short for *cat-o'-mountain* (1616), in John Fletcher's *Custom of the Country* and for *cat of the mountain* leopard (probably before 1425, in a translation of Higden's *Polychronicon*).

catapult *n.* ancient weapon for shooting stones, arrows, etc. 1577, borrowed from Middle French *catapulte,* or directly from Latin *catapulta* war machine for throwing darts, from Greek *katapéltēs,* alteration of earlier *katapáltēs,* ultimately from *kata-* against + *pállein* to hurl; see POLEMIC. —**v.** 1848, to hurl or shoot; as if from a catapult; from the noun.

cataract *n.* large, steep waterfall, violent downpour or rush of water. Before 1420, in Lydgate's *Troy Book,* floodgate, portcullis, waterfall; borrowed from Latin *cataracta* and *catarrhācta* waterfall; Latin *cataracta* derives from Greek *kataráktēs* (ultimately from *kat-* cat-, down + *aráttein* to strike hard, break into pieces), and Latin *catarrhācta* derives from Greek *katarrắktēs* (ultimately from *kata-* down + *rhắttein* to dash, break). The Greek roots *arach-* (of *aráttein*) and *rhāch-* (of *rhắttein*) probably both go back to one Indo-European root **wrāĝh/werəĝh* (Pok.1181).

The sense "an eye disease" appeared probably before 1425 in a translation of Chauliac's *Grande Chirurgie,* and was borrowed from Middle French *cataracte* or Medieval Latin *cataracta* (both from Latin *cataracta*), supposedly from the sense "portcullis," as of an obstruction to one's eyesight.

catarrh *n.* discharge of mucus from the nose or throat. Probably before 1425 *catarre,* in a translation of Chauliac's *Grande Chirurgie;* borrowed from Medieval Latin *catarrus,* from Late Latin *catarrhus,* from Greek *katárrhous* a catarrh; literally, a flowing down, earlier *katárrhoos,* ultimately from *kata-* down + *rheîn* to flow; see STREAM.

catastrophe *n.* sudden disaster. 1540, concluding action of a drama, often a reversal of what is expected, in Palsgrave's translation of Fullonius' *Comedy of Acolastus;* borrowed from Greek *katastrophḗ* an overturning, ultimately from *kata-* down + *stréphein* to turn; see STROPHE.

The current sense appeared in 1748, from the earlier meaning (1601, in Shakespeare's *All's Well That Ends Well*) "conclusion which is generally unhappy." —**catastrophic** *adj.* 1837, formed from English *catastrophe* + *-ic.*

catatonic *adj.* of or characterized by muscular rigidity associated with schizophrenia. 1908, formed in English from New Latin *catatonia* (earlier in English *katatonia,* 1880's, from Greek *kata-* down + *tónos* tone) + English *-ic.*

catch *v.* Probably before 1200 *cacchen, cahten* capture, ensnare, receive, chase, in Layamon's *Chronicle of Britain* and *Ancrene Riwle,* borrowed from Anglo-French or Old North French *cacher, cachier* catch or capture (animals), chase, hunt, from Vulgar Latin **captiāre,* (attested only in the form of Medieval Latin *caciare*), from Latin *captāre*), try to catch, seek, chase, frequentative form conveying repeated or continued action of *capere* to take; see CAPTIVE. Doublet of CHASE[1] hunt. —**n.** 1399, earlier, a trap in the compound *mouscacche* (before 1382 in the Wycliffe Bible); from the verb.

The past tense of the verb, *caught,* is a rare instance of a strong verb in a root of French origin. Its development probably stems from the influence of the native verb *latch* (Middle English *lacchen, lachen,* Old English *læccan, læcan*) which also had the meaning "to catch, ensnare, lie in wait for" and very early was treated as a synonym of *catch,* gradually replacing the Old and Middle English forms of the verb after 1300. Hence the Middle English past tense *cahte, cauhte, caughte, caught* was apparently patterned on *lahte, lauhte, laughte, laught,* the past tense of *lacchen.* But while in modern English *latch* became a weak verb (*latched, latching*), the regular past tense form of *catch* (*cacched, catchte, catched*) was superseded in the 1800's by *caught* in literary use, though *catched* is still heard in dialectal or untutored speech. In the noun it will be noted that *catch* and *latch* are still synonymous in the meaning "a thing that catches as in The catch on the gate is not fastened."
—**catcher** *n.* 1200 (in a surname); borrowed from Anglo-French *cachëour,* from *cacher.*

Catch-22 *n.* a hidden difficulty involving a paradox. 1961, *Catch-22,* title of a novel by the American writer Joseph Heller. The allusion to the story involves a rule that a pilot is judged insane if he flies combat missions without asking to be relieved; if he does make such a request, he is considered sane and may not be relieved.

catchup *n.* sauce made from tomatoes, etc. 1690, borrowed from Malay *kĕchap,* with the spelling influenced by English *catch* and *up,* later, *cat* and *sup.* Compare the variant KETCHUP.

The spelling *catsup* appeared in 1730, in Swift's writings.

catechism (kat′əkiz′əm) *n.* book of questions and answers about religion. 1509; earlier, instruction in the elementary principles of Christianity (1502); borrowed, perhaps by influence of Middle French *catéchisme,* from Late Latin *catēchismus* book of instruction, from *catēchizāre* CATECHIZE; for suffix see -ISM. —**catechize** (kat′əkīz) *v.* teach by questions and answers. Probably about 1425, borrowed, perhaps by influence of Old French *catéchiser,* from Latin *catēchizāre,* from Greek *katēchízein* teach orally, variant of *katēcheîn* (*kata-* toward, against + *ēcheîn* to sound, related to *ēchṓ* ECHO); for suffix see -IZE. —**catechist** *n.* Before 1563, borrowed from Late Latin *catēchista,* from Late Greek *katēchistēs* one who teaches orally; for suffix see -IST.

category (kat′əgôr′ē) *n.* 1588, borrowed from Middle French *catégorie,* learned borrowing from Late Latin *catēgoria,* from Greek *katēgoríā* assertion, ultimately from *kata-* down to + the root of *agoreúein* to assert, speak (in the assembly), from *agorā́* place of assembly, AGORA. Originally in English the term was used in reference to Aristotle's *Categories* (a term applied to ten classes of terms, things, or nations) and is found in the form *Categories* as early as 1450. —**categorical** *adj.* 1598, borrowed from Late Latin *catēgoricus,* from Greek *katēgorikós,* from *katēgoríā* category; for suffix see -ICAL. —**categorization** *n.* 1886, probably formed from English *categorize* + -ATION, perhaps by influence of earlier French *catégorisation* (1845). —**categorize** *v.* 1705, formed from English *category* + *-ize.*

cater *v.* 1600, in Shakespeare's *As You Like It,* developed from Middle English *catour,* n., buyer of provisions borrowed from Anglo-French *catur,* short for *acatur,* from *acater* to buy, Old French *acheter, aceter,* from Vulgar Latin **accaptāre* (from Latin *ac -,* variant of *ad -* to before *c*) + Latin *captāre,* frequentative form showing continued action of *capere* to take; see CAPTIVE). **—caterer** *n.* 1281, *Katerer* (as a surname), formed from English *cater* + *-er*[1]. The later forms *catourer* (1469) and *catour* (about 1350, earlier, *Katur* 1270 as a surname) were borrowings of Anglo-French.

cater-cornered or **catty-cornered** *adj., adv.* diagonal, diagonally. 1838, formed from earlier English *cater* to set or move diagonally (1577), developed from English *cater* four (probably before 1400); borrowed from Middle French *catre, quatre* four, from Latin *quattuor* FOUR + *cornered.*

caterpillar *n.* About 1440 *catyrpel,* in *Promptorium Parvulorum,* alteration of Old North French **catepelose,* literally, hairy cat, Old French *chatepelose* and modern Norman *catepelouse* (*cate* cat, from Late Latin *catta* + *pelose* hairy, from Latin *pilōsus,* from *pilus* hair; related to PILE). The alteration of the original English form *catyrpel* was probably influenced by obsolete *piller* plunderer (related to *pillage*).

caterwaul *v.* yowl like a cat. 1610 *catterwall,* 1630 *catterwaule,* formed from English *cater-* (from Middle Dutch *cater* tomcat) + *waul,* v. to yowl (1557), from Middle English *wrawlen, wrawen* be angry, from *wrah, wrau* angry, apparently from Old English **wrāg, *wrāh,* of uncertain origin, perhaps related to *wrecan* punish.

Chaucer used *a-caterwawed (a-caterwrawed* in two manuscripts) as an adverbial phrase in *gon a-caterwawed* go caterwauling. This usage points to a Middle English verb **caterwawen, *caterwrawen* in Chaucer's vocabulary, the second element from *wrawlen* or *wrawen* or a combination of both.

catharsis *n.* a purging. 1803, New Latin *catharsis,* from Greek *kátharsis* purging, cleansing, from *kathaírein* to purge, cleanse, from *katharós* clean, pure, of uncertain origin. The sense "a purging of emotions through drama" appeared in 1872. **—cathartic** *adj.* 1612, borrowed from Latin *catharticus,* from Greek *kathartikós* purgative, from *kathairein* to purge; for suffix see -IC.

cathedral *n.* church of a bishop. 1587; earlier in the phrase *cathedral church,* translation of Medieval Latin *ecclesia cathedralis* (before 1387, in Trevisa's translation of Higden's *Polychronicon*). **—adj.** of a bishop's throne or church. About 1300, borrowed from Old French *cathedral* and from Medieval Latin *cathedralis* of or belonging to the (bishop's) chair, from Latin *cathedra* chair, from Greek *kathédrā* chair, see CHAIR; for suffix see -AL[1].

catheter *n.* slender tube. 1601, borrowed from French *cathéter,* and perhaps replacing earlier *cathirum* (probably before 1425), a borrowing of Medieval Latin *cathirum;* both French and Medieval Latin derived from Late Latin *cathetēr* a catheter, from Greek *kathetḗr* a catheter, plug (*kata-* down + *he-,* stem of *hiénai* to send + agent suffix *-tēr;* see JET[1] stream).

cathode *n.* negative electrode. 1834, borrowed from Greek *káthodos* a way down (*kata-* down + *hodós* way); so called from the path that the electric current was thought to take from the negative pole. The term was introduced by the English chemist and physicist Michael Faraday. Compare ANODE, ELECTRODE. **—cathode ray** (1880, but first known in 1859) **—cathode-ray tube** (1905)

catholic *adj.* About 1350, in a Medieval Psalter, of or pertaining to the doctrines of the ancient (undivided) Christian Church; universally accepted; borrowed from Medieval Latin *catholicus,* from Late Latin *catholicus* relating to all, universal, from Greek *katholikós* universal, general, from *kathólou* in general, from the phrase *kath' hólou (katá* down, about + the genitive of *hólos* whole*);* for suffix see -IC.

The specific sense, since the Reformation, "of or pertaining to the Church of Rome, Roman Catholic," appeared about 1554-55 in capitalized form. The general sense "of interest or use to all people, universal, common" appeared in 1551.

—n. 1594, in Hooker's *Ecclesiastical Polity,* an orthodox member of the ancient (undivided) Christian Church, or one faithful to the beliefs of that Church. Specific reference to a member of the Roman Church appeared by 1570. **—catholicism** *n.* (1609)

cation (kat'ī'ən) *n.* positively charged ion. 1834, borrowed from Greek *katión* (thing) going down, neuter present participle of *katiénai* go down (*kata-* down + *iénai* go; see EXIT).

The term is related to ANION and ION and was introduced by the English chemist and physicist Michael Faraday. For semantic connection with "going down" see *cathode.*

catkin *n.* downy spike of flowers. 1578, borrowed from Dutch *kàtteken,* literally, little cat; apparently so called from the soft downy appearance suggesting a kitten's fur.

catnip *n.* 1712, American English, a compound of *cat* + *nip,* English dialect variant of *nep* a name for catmint and a variant of Old English *nepte,* borrowed from Latin *nepeta* calamint (an aromatic herb). The older name is Middle English *catmint* (before 1300).

cattle *n.* About 1250, property; later, livestock (before 1325, in *Cursor Mundi*); borrowed through Anglo-French, Old North French *catel* property, from Medieval Latin *captale, capitale* property; also cattle; originally neuter of Latin *capitālis* of the head, principal; see the doublets CAPITAL[1] city, and CHATTEL. The current meaning "cows, bulls, and steers" appeared in 1555, and since that time the English words *cattle* and *chattel,* represented by Norman French *catel* and its central French variant *chatel,* have developed into two distinctly different words in English. **—cattleman** *n.* (1864)

Caucasian *n.* 1807, after New Latin *Caucasianus,* from *Caucasus* name of mountains between the Caspian and Black seas. The connection with "white race" came from the first anthropological division of mankind by physical features and the belief that these people came originally from this region.

caucus *n.* meeting of members of a political party. 1763, in John Adams' *Diary;* earlier *Corcus* (1745); American English, possibly borrowed from an Algonquian source (compare Algonquian *caucauasu* elder, adviser, a dialect term of Virginia). **—v.** to hold a caucus. 1850, in Carlyle's writing's, from the noun.

caudal *adj. Zoology.* of, at, or near the tail. 1661, borrowed from New Latin *caudalis,* from Latin *cauda* tail, of uncertain origin; for suffix see -AL[1].

cauliflower *n.* 1597 *cole florie,* perhaps a fusion of New

Latin *cauliflora* with elements of Middle English *cole, coul, caul* cabbage, and other leafy vegetables. New Latin *cauliflora* was formed from Latin *caulis* cabbage, COLE, (originally) stalk + *flōs* (genitive *flōris*) FLOWER.

caulk *v.* = calk[1].

cause *n.* Probably before 1200, in *Ancrene Riwle,* borrowed from Old French *cause* matter, thing, and directly as a learned borrowing from Latin *causa* reason, purpose, cause, of uncertain origin. Compare BECAUSE.

The popular form developed in Old French from Latin *causa* is *chose* thing, corresponding to Old North French *cose.* Old French *cause* was a learned form borrowed from the Latin.

—v. About 1385 *causen,* in Chaucer's *Canterbury Tales,* from *cause,* n., or possibly borrowed from Old French *causer,* from *cause,* n. **—causative** *adj.* (about 1412)

causeway *n.* 1571, variant of Middle English *cauceweye* (about 1440, in *Promptorium Parvulorum*), a compound of *cauce, cauci* causeway (probably before 1330, in *Arthour and Merlin*) + *weye* way. The older Middle English *cauce, cauci* was borrowed through Anglo-French *calcee, cauce,* perhaps from Old North French, from Vulgar Latin **calciāta via* paved way, ultimately from Latin *calcis,* genitive of *calx* limestone, CHALK.

caustic *adj.* burning, corrosive. Before 1400, borrowed, perhaps through Old French *caustique,* from Latin *causticus,* from Greek *kaustikós* capable of burning, from *kaustós* combustible, from *kaíein* to burn, future *kaúsō;* from Indo-European **kéu-kəu-*(Pok.595); for suffix see -IC.

The figurative sense "biting, sarcastic" appeared in writings of Smollett (1771).

—n. Before 1425, probably from the adjective.

cauterize *v.* Before 1400 *cauterizen,* borrowed perhaps through Old French *cauteriser* or directly from Late Latin *cautērizāre,* from Latin *cautērium* branding iron, from Greek *kautḗrion,* diminutive of *kautḗr* burner, from *kaíein* to burn, see CAUSTIC; for suffix see -IZE. **—cauterization** *n.* Before 1400, borrowed perhaps from Old French *cauterisation* (1314), or directly from Late Latin *cautērizātiōnem* (nominative *cautērizātiō*), from *cautērizāre;* for suffix see -TION.

caution *n.* About 1300 *caucioun* precaution, guarantee or pledge; borrowed through Old French *caution,* and directly as a learned borrowing of Latin *cautiō* (accusative *cautiōnem*), from *cautus,* past participle of *cavēre* to beware; for suffix see -ION. See CAVEAT. The present-day common meaning "taking care to be safe," is first recorded in Shakespeare's *Macbeth* (1605). **—v.** 1641, to give warning, from the noun, perhaps by influence of earlier French *cautionner* (1360). **—cautionary** *adj.* 1597, formed from English *caution* + *-ary.* **—cautious** *adj.* Before 1640, formed from English *caution* + *-ous.*

cavalcade *n.* 1591, a ride, march, raid on horseback, borrowed from Middle French *cavalcade,* from Italian *cavalcata,* from *cavalcare* to ride on horseback, from Late Latin *caballicāre,* from Latin *caballus* horse, nag, see CAVALRY; for suffix see -ADE. The current meaning "a procession on horseback" is first recorded in English in 1644, in John Evelyn's *Memoirs.*

cavalier *n.* 1589, a courteous gentleman, usually one trained to arms, borrowed originally in the form *cavaliero, cavallero,* from Spanish and Italian; later adopting the French spelling in the 1640's, from Middle French *cavalier* horseman, from Italian *cavalliere* knight, horseman, from Late Latin *caballārius* horseman; see CAVALRY. Doublet of CABALLERO and CHEVALIER. **—adj.** haughty, arrogant. Before 1641, gallant, from the noun. The meaning "disdainful, haughty, and offhand" appeared in 1657.

cavalry *n.* 1546 *cavallery,* borrowed from Middle French *cavalerie,* from Italian *cavalleria* mounted militia, horsemanship, knighthood, from *cavalliere* knight, horseman. The Italian word developed from Late Latin *caballārius* horseman, from Latin *caballus* horse, nag; compare Greek *kabállēs* nag, and Old Slavic *kobyla* female horse, of Asiatic origin. For suffix see -RY, -ERY.

cave *n.* Before 1250, borrowed from Old French *cave* a cave, learned borrowing of Latin *cava* hollow (places), neuter plural of *cavus* hollow, adj. The Latin is cognate with Greek *koîlos* hollow, Middle Irish *cūa* hollow, *cūass* cave, Avestan *sūra-* hole, gap, and Greek *kýar* hole, from Indo-European **k̑eu-/k̑ou-, k̑ewə-/k̑ū-* (Pok.592).**—v. 1** usually **cave in,** to collapse, especially leaving a hollow. 1707, American English, probably from the noun, though the verb has been associated with earlier verbs *cave* to fall in a heap (1513), and to hollow out (1541) and *calve* to fall (1755). The figurative sense "yield to pressure" is first recorded in 1837. **2** usually **caving,** gerund, the action exploring caves as a sport (1932). **—cave man** (1865)

caveat (ka'vēät) *n.* a warning. 1549, earlier, in the phrase *caveat emptor* (1523), borrowed from Latin *caveat* let him beware, 3rd person singular present subjunctive of *cavēre* to beware; cognate with Greek *koeîn* notice, and Sanskrit *kaví-s* wise, seer, from Indo-European **keu/kou* (Pok.587).

cavern *n.* About 1380, in Chaucer's translation of Boethius' *De Consolatione Philosophiae,* borrowed from Old French *cavern* cave, learned borrowing from Latin *caverna* cave, cavity, from *cavus* hollow, adj.; see CAVE. **—cavernous** *adj.* Before 1400, borrowed from Latin *cavernōsus* full of hollows or cavities, perhaps by influence of Old French *caverneux;* for suffix see -OUS.

caviar or **caviare** (kav'ēär) *n.* About 1560, borrowed from French *caviar,* from Turkish *ḥavyār,* from Iranian, bearer of eggs.

cavil *v.* find fault unnecessarily. 1548, borrowed from Middle French *caviller* to mock, jest, learned borrowing from Latin *cavillārī* to jeer, from *cavilla* a jeering, scoffing, alteration of **calvilla,* related to *calumnia* CALUMNY. Earlier use of the now rare or literary *cavillation* is attested probably in 1388. **—n.** 1570, a finding fault, from the verb.

cavity *n.* 1541, in Copland's translation of Galen's *Terapeutyke,* borrowed from Middle French *cavité,* learned borrowing from Late Latin *cavitās* hollowness, cavity, from Latin *cavus* hollow, adj., see CAVE; for suffix see -ITY.

cavort *v.* prance about. 1829, earlier *cauvaut* (1793), American English, perhaps alteration of still earlier CURVET leap about, frisk (1600, in Shakespeare's *As You Like It*).

caw *v.* 1590, in Shakespeare's *Midsummer Night's Dream,* imitative of the cry. **—n.** 1666, in Dryden's writings, from the verb.

cayenne (kāen') *n.* red pepper. 1756 *cayan* associated with *Cayenne,* city in French Guiana, but apparently borrowed from Tupi (Brazil) *quiýnha* or *kyýnha.*

cayman or **caiman** *n.* 1577, borrowed probably through Spanish *caimán* and French *caïman,* from a native Guianan or Carib name meaning "crocodile."

cayuse (kīyüs′) *n.* any horse, especially an Indian pony. 1841, American English, originally a kind of pony bred by the *Cayuse* Indians (1825) of Washington and Oregon.

cease *v.* Probably about 1300 *cesen,* borrowed from Old French *cesser,* from Latin *cessāre* to cease, go slowly, loiter, frequentative form of *cēdere* go away, withdraw, CEDE. **—cease-fire** *n.* (1918) **—ceaseless** *adj.* (1586, in Marlowe's *Tamburlane the Great*)

cecum or **caecum** (sē′kəm) *n.* first part of the large intestine. 1721, in Bailey's *Dictionary,* New Latin *intestinum caecum* blind intestine (because it is closed at one end), from Latin *caecum* neuter of *caecus* blind. The Latin is cognate with Gothic *haihs* one-eyed, Old Irish *caech* squinting, one-eyed, blind, and Sanskrit *kekara-s* squinting, from Indo-European **kaiko-s* (Pok.519).

cedar *n.* 1325 *cedre,* in *Cursor Mundi,* blending with and partially replacing Old English *ceder* (about 1000), but found earlier in *ceder-bēam* cedar tree (before 830, in the *Vespasian Psalter*). The Middle English was borrowed from Old French *cedre,* learned borrowing from Latin *cedrus,* from Greek *kédros* cedar, juniper, probably of Semitic origin (compare Hebrew *qāṭar* it smoked, *qəṭōret* smoke, incense) and originally meaning "wood used for incense."

The spelling *cedar* began to appear in the mid-1500's, in imitation of what was mistakenly thought to be the Latin form.

cede *v.* 1633, borrowed from Latin *cēdere* to go, proceed, yield, withdraw. Latin *cēdō* I go, proceed, etc., derives from earlier **ke-sd-ō* I move in this direction (*ke* here, compare Latin *ce-do* give [it] here! + *sd-* of the root *sed-, sod-* "sit," which, with directional adverb *ke,* could convey motion, as in Sanskrit *ā-sad-* go to, and modern English *set out*). Latin *cēdō,* then, could be cognate with Greek *hodós* way, journey (compare compounds such as *éx-hodos* a going out and *án-hodos* a going up).

cedilla (sədil′ə) *n.* mark under the letter *c* (ç) to show sound of *s* in *sit.* 1599, borrowed from Spanish *cedilla, zedilla* little *z,* diminutive of *ceda, zeda* the letter *z,* from Latin *zēta,* from Greek *zêta.* The association with *z* comes from a mark derived from *z* and formerly written after *c* to indicate the sound of *s* (in French) and, originally *ts* (in Spanish). The cedilla is no longer used in Spanish.

ceiling *n.* About 1380 *celynge* paneling, from earlier *celyng* act of lining or paneling (1347-48), gerund of *celyn* to cover with paneling and *selen over* to put a cover on (probably before 1400); borrowed from Middle French *celer, cieler,* from *ciel* canopy, sky, from Latin *caelum* sky; see CELESTIAL.

The common meaning of the word (the ceiling of a room) is first recorded in 1535, in Coverdale's *Song of Solomon.*

celebrate *v.* 1465, borrowed from Latin *celebrātus,* past participle of *celebrāre,* originally, attend in great numbers, from *celeber, celebris, celebre* thronged, frequented, well-known, perhaps related to Latin *celer* swift; see CELERITY. **—celebrant** *n.* 1839, borrowed through French *célébrant,* or directly from Latin *celebrantem* (nominative *celebrāns*), present participle of *celebrāre.* **—celebrated** *adj.* 1586, in Marlowe's *The Great Tamburlane,* formed from English *celebrate* + *-ed.* **—celebration** *n.* 1529, in Sir Thomas More's writings, probably borrowed from Latin *celebrātiōnem* (nominative *celebrātiō*), from *celebrāre* celebrate; or formed from English *celebrate* + *-tion.* **—celebrity** *n.* About 1380 *celebrete* fame, notoriety, in Chaucer's translation of Boethius' *De Consolatione Philosophiae,* borrowed from Old French *celebrité,* from Latin *celebritātem* (nominative *celebritās*) a multitude, fame, renown, from *celeber, celebris, celebre* well-known; for suffix see -ITY.

celerity *n.* swiftness, speed. 1483, borrowed from Middle French *célérité,* from Latin *celeritātem* (nominative *celeritās*), from *celer, celeris, celere* swift; probably cognate with Greek *kéllein* drive on, *kélēs* race horse, racing boat, and Sanskrit *kaláyati* (he) drives, carries, holds, from Indo-European **kel-* (Pok.548); for suffix see -ITY.

celery *n.* 1664, borrowed from French *céleri,* from Italian (Lombard dialect) *seleri* (plural), from Late Latin *selīnon* parsley, from Greek *sélīnon.*

celesta *n.* a musical instrument resembling a small upright piano, having the sound of bells. 1899, as a French word introduced into an English work on orchestration, adapted from Latin *cælestis* of heaven, from *cælum* heaven. By the 1930's a variant form *celeste,* also borrowed from the French, began to appear.

celestial *adj.* About 1380, in Chaucer's translation of Boethius' *De Consolatione Philosophiae,* borrowed from Old French *celestial,* from Latin *caelestis* heavenly, from *caelum* sky, heaven, of uncertain origin; for suffix see -AL[1].

celibate *adj.* 1829, in letters of Southey, formed in English from Latin *caelebs, caelibis* unmarried + English *-ate.* **—n.** person taking a vow not to marry. 1869, from the adjective, but perhaps influenced by another use of *celibate* state of celibacy, order of celibates, that developed quite apart from the later adjective use cited above. The earlier form *celibate* is first recorded in English in 1614, borrowed from Latin *caelibātus,* from *caelebs* (genitive *caelibis*) unmarried, from **kaiwilibs,* earlier **kaiwilo-libs* living alone (cognate with Sanskrit *kévala-s* alone) from Indo-European **kaiwelo-s* + **leibh-/libh-* LIVE (Pok.519, 670). **—celibacy** *n.* 1663, formed in English from Latin *caelibātus* state of being unmarried + English *-acy.*

cell *n.* Before 1131, small monastery, in the *Peterborough Chronicle;* later, probably before 1300, small room, in *Arthour and Merlin,* found in Old English *cell,* borrowed from Latin *cella* small room, and later reinforced as a borrowing from Old French *celle,* from Latin *cella* small room (in Late Latin, monk's cell). Latin *cella* (probably earlier **cēlā-,* compare Sanskrit *śā́lā* hut, hall) especially in the sense of a cloistered cell, is related to Latin *cēlāre* to hide, conceal, which is cognate with Welsh *celu* to conceal, Old High German *helan* (modern German *hehlen*), Greek *kalýptein* to cover, conceal from Indo-European **k̂el-/k̂al-/k̂ēl-* hide, enclose (Pok.553); see HALL.

The sense in biology "a unit of protoplasm in an organism" appeared in 1672-73 as one of a number of cavities, but was not recorded in its scientific applica-

tion to living organisms as the basic structure before 1845. Curiously, the figurative sense of brain cells in relation to reason was used as early as 1393 in Gower's *Confessio Amantis,* as a reference to the compartments into which the brain was believed to be separated.
—**cell membrane** 1870, replacing earlier *cellular membrane* (1773). —**cellular** *adj.* 1753, borrowed probably from New Latin *cellularis* of little cells, from *cellula* little cell, diminutive of Latin *cella,* perhaps by influence of earlier French *cellulaire* (1740, though not recorded in use in biology before 1860). —**cell wall** (1847-49)

cellar *n.* Probably before 1200 *celer,* in *Ancrene Riwle,* borrowed through Anglo-French *celer,* Old French *celier,* from Latin *cellārium* storeroom, from *cella* small room, CELL.

The spelling with two *l's* was always a variant spelling in Middle English, but did not become the preferred spelling until the 1550's. The spelling *-ar,* also in imitation of the Latin, became fixed in the 1600's.

cello or **'cello** *n.* 1876, shortened from VIOLONCELLO. —**cellist** *n.* 1888, formed from English *cello* + *-ist.*

cellophane *n.* 1912 *Cellophane,* a trademark, probably formed in French from *cell(ulose)* + connecting *-o-* + *-phane,* suffix meaning "substance having a (specified) appearance," from Greek *-phanēs* appearing, shining, from *phaínein* to show; see FANTASY.

celluloid (sel'yəloid) *n.* 1871, American English, formed from English *cellul(ose)* + *-oid.*

The transferred sense "motion pictures, films" appeared in 1934, from the fact that photographic film was then made on a celluloid base.

cellulose *n.* 1835, noun use of earlier *cellulose,* adj., consisting of cells (1753), borrowed from New Latin *cellulosus,* from Latin *cellula* cell, diminutive of *cella* small room, CELL; for suffix see -OSE[2].

Celsius *adj.* of or on the centigrade scale. 1850, earlier *Celsius's thermometer* (1797), in allusion to Anders *Celsius* (1701-1744), Swedish astronomer, who invented the centigrade temperature scale.

cement *n.* Probably before 1300 *cyment,* in *Kyng Alisaunder,* later *siment* (about 1330), borrowed from Old French *ciment,* from Latin *caementum* rough stone, rubble, earlier **caidmentom,* from *caedere* to cut; see EXCISE[2] cut. The spelling *cement* appeared before 1398, influenced by French *cément,* itself a learned borrowing from Latin *caementum.* The noun *cement* was accented on the first syllable until modern times; now it is usually accented as the verb is on the second syllable.

The meaning in English was always a pasty mixture that hardens into rocklike substance, but originally the word referred to rubble mixed with lime and water to form mortar, and later to the mortar itself.
—v. Before 1400 *cymenten,* from the noun, in Sir John Maundeville's *Travels.*

cemetery *n.* About 1425 *cymytory;* earlier (in compound) *simeterigarth* cemetery yard or plot (1377), borrowed from Old French *cimetiere, cimitere* graveyard, from Late Latin *coemētērium,* (also *cīmitērium*), from Greek *koimētḗrion* sleeping room, (but used among early Christian ecclesiastical writers to mean "burial ground"), from *koimân* put to sleep, related to *keîsthai* to lie down. The Greek is cognate with Latin *cūnae* cradle, Sanskrit *śéte* he lies, rests, and Hittite *kitta* (he) lies, from Indo-European **ḱei-/ḱoi-* (Pok.539).

cenacle (sen'əkəl) *n.* artistic or literary clique; coterie. 1889, reborrowed from French *cénacle,* from Latin *cēnāculum* dining room, garret, attic, from *cēna* dinner, supper, cognate with Oscan *kersnu* (from **kert-snā* a portion), and Sanskrit *kṛntáti* he cuts, from Indo-European **kert-/kṛt-* (Pok.941).

Cenacle appeared earlier in Middle English (about 1386) meaning "dining room," specifically where the Apostles gathered but it disappeared after 1500.

cenotaph *n.* monument of a person buried elsewhere. 1603, borrowed from French *cénotaphe,* learned borrowing from Latin *cenotaphium,* from Greek *kenotáphion* an empty tomb (*kenós* empty + *táphos* tomb. Greek *kenós,* earlier **kenwós,* is cognate with Armenian *sin,* from Indo-European **ḱen-* (Pok.564); and *táphos* tomb (root **thaph-*), is cognate with Armenian *damban* tomb, from Indo-European **dhembh-/dhm̥bh-* (Pok.248).

censer *n.* container to burn incense. About 1250, borrowed from Old French *censier, encensier,* from *encens* incense, a learned borrowing from Late Latin *incēnsum* INCENSE[1].

censor *n.* official who removes objectionable parts in books, before publishing or broadcasting. 1531, in Sir Thomas Elyot's *The Boke Named the Governour,* Roman magistrate who took the census and supervised public morals; borrowed through Middle French *censor,* or directly from Latin *cēnsor,* from *cēnsēre* appraise, estimate, assess. The Latin is cognate with Albanian *thom* I say, and Old Slavic *sętŭ* he says, from Indo-European **ḱens-* (Pok.566). —v. act as a censor. 1882, from the noun. —**censorious** *adj.* 1536, formed from English *censor* + *ous,* after the Latin pattern of *censōrius* of a censor. —**censorship** *n.* 1591, formed from English *censor* + *ship.*

censure *n.* adverse judgment, criticism. Probably about 1378, in Wycliffe's writings, borrowed from Latin *cēnsūra* judgment, censorship, from *cēnsēre* appraise, estimate, assess. —v. 1589, from the noun, or borrowed from Middle French *censurer,* from *censure* criticism, learned borrowing from Latin *cēnsūra.*

census *n.* 1613, poll-tax; later, registration of citizens and their property in ancient Rome (1634); borrowed from Latin *cēnsus* (genitive *cēnsūs*), from *cēnsēre* appraise; see CENSOR. The meaning "official count of citizens or population" is first recorded in 1769, in writings of Goldsmith.

cent *n.* penny; 1/100 of a dollar. Before 1375, a hundred; later, in the phrase *per cent* (1568), and a hundredth part of (1685). This latter meaning was carried over by Robert Morris, American financier (1734-1806), in a suggestion on the proposed units of American currency before the Congress in 1782. The term is not recorded before 1786 in American English, and was borrowed in the 1300's from Old French *cent* hundred, from Latin *centum* HUNDRED.

In 1786 the Continental Congress designated the *cent* to be 1/100 of a dollar, with Morris' idea in mind and probably influenced by French *centime,* a coin equal to 1/100 of a franc.

centaur *n.* mythical monster that is half man and half horse. About 1375, in Chaucer's *Canterbury Tales,* borrowed through Old French *centaure,* and directly from Latin *centaurus,* from Greek *kéntauros,* of uncertain origin. In early Greek literature the name occurs as that of a savage people of Thessaly, who were supposed to have been expert horsemen.

centenary *n.* period of 100 years. 1607, borrowed from Latin *centēnārius* consisting of or containing a hundred, from *centēnī* a hundred each, from *centum* HUNDRED; for suffix see -ARY. This word is a reborrowing of Latin *centēnārius,* which is found in Middle English *centener, centenarie* Roman centurion, officer in command, leader (before 1325, in *Cursor Mundi*). **—centenarian** *n.* person 100 years old. 1846, formed in English from Latin *centēnārius* of a hundred + English *-an.*

centennial *adj.* of a hundred years, especially a hundredth anniversary. Before 1797, formed in English from Latin *cent(um)* HUNDRED + English *(bi)ennial.* **—n.** hundredth anniversary. 1876, Howells writing in *Atlantic Monthly,* from the adjective.

center *n.* About 1380 *centre* middle point of a circle, in Chaucer's translation of Boethius' *De Consolatione Philosophiae;* borrowed from Old French *centre,* learned borrowing from Latin *centrum,* from Greek *kéntron* sharp point, goad, stationary point of a compass, middle point of a circle. Greek *kéntron* is formed from the stem of *kenteîn* to prick, goad, stab, which is probably cognate with Old High German *hantag* sharp, pointed, and Gothic *handugs* wise (from Proto-Germanic **Handaʒás*), and with Old Icelandic *hannarr* skillful, smart (from Proto-Germanic **Hántheraz*), from Indo-European **k̂ent-/k̂ont-* prick (Pok.567).

The meaning "player in a game who is in the center of a line, such as in football, basketball, or hockey" is first recorded in 1866; the meaning "a main point, especially where people go or come from, as in a "cultural center, shopping center" is first recorded in 1685 (perhaps even 1626); the group of a lawmaking body having moderate views is first recorded in 1837, from use in the French National Assembly in 1789.

—v. Probably before 1590, but first recorded in writings of Spenser, from the noun. **—centerboard** *n.* (1867) **—centerpiece** *n.* (1803, American English)

From the 1500's to the 1700's the prevalent spelling was *center,* used by Shakespeare, Milton, Pope, Addison, Hobbes, and others. But the technical volume (1727) of Bailey's *Dictionary* had the spelling *centre* and Johnson followed it in his dictionary, so that *centre* was generally adopted in Great Britain while *center* remained the spelling in the United States.

centi- a combining form meaning a hundred or a hundredth part of, as in *centimeter, centillion.* Borrowed from French *centi-* hundredth and from Latin *centum* HUNDRED. Many metric units of measure derive from this combining form. **—centigrade** *adj.* (1812; curiously is not found in French before 1820) **—centigram, centiliter, centimeter,** *n.* (1801, borrowed from French)

centipede *n.* 1646; earlier, in Holland's translation of Pliny's *Natural History,* as the Latin *centipeda* (*centum* HUNDRED + *pēs,* genitive *pedis,* FOOT).

central *adj.* at or near the center. 1647, popularized and reintroduced to English by influence of French *central,* Latin *centrālis,* from *centrum* CENTER; for suffix see -AL[1]. An adverb, *centraly,* recorded apparently before 1425 possibly implies the use of *central* in Middle English and if so, shows a defect in the record of English. **—n.** *Archaic.* telephone operator or exchange. American English, 1889, in Mark Twain's *Connecticut Yankee,* from the adjective. **—centralize** *v.* 1800, formed from English *central* + *-ize,* probably by influence of earlier French *centraliser* (1790). **—centralization** *n.* 1801, formed from English *centralize* + *-ation,* probably by influence of earlier French *centralisation* (1798).

centrifugal (sentrif′əgəl) *adj.* moving away from a center. Before 1721, in the phrase *centrifugal force,* formed in English from New Latin *centrifugus* (coined in 1687 by Sir Isaac Newton) + English *-al*[1]. New Latin *centrifugus* was formed from Latin *centrum* CENTER + *fugere* to flee; see FUGITIVE. **—centrifuge** *n.* machine using centrifugal force to separate substances. 1887, originally an adjective meaning centrifugal (1801), borrowed from French *centrifuge,* from New Latin *centrifugus.*

centripetal (sentrip′ətəl) *adj.* moving towards a center. 1709, in the phrase *centripetal force,* in Steele's writings in *The Tatler,* formed in English from New Latin *centripetus* (coined in 1687 by Sir Isaac Newton) + English *-al*[1]. New Latin *centripetus* was formed from Latin *centrum* CENTER + *petere* go toward, seek; see FEATHER.

centurion *n.* commander of 100 soldiers in the ancient Roman army. About 1384, in the Wycliffe Bible, earlier as a proper name (before 1300); borrowed through Old French *centurion,* or directly from Latin *centuriō* (accusative *centuriōnem*), from *centuria* CENTURY; for suffix see -ION.

century *n.* Before 1398, a measure of land, in Trevisa's translation of Bartholomew's *De Proprietatibus Rerum;* later a division of the Roman army of about a hundred men (about 1450), borrowed from Latin *centuria* division of 100 units, company of 100 men, from *centum* HUNDRED. In the late 1500's the word developed a meaning "any group of a hundred things" as in *a century of prayers* (1611, Shakespeare's *Cymbeline*). By 1626 the application is extended to *a century of years,* and before 1638 *century* has adopted the specific sense of a period of one hundred years.

cephalic (səfal′ik) *adj.* near, on, or in the head. Probably before 1425, earlier Anglo-Latin *cephalca* the cephalic vein (before 1398); borrowed from Latin *cephalicus,* from Greek *kephalikós* belonging to the head, from *kephalḗ* head; for suffix see -IC.

Greek *kephalḗ* is cognate with Old High German *gebal* skull, *gibil* gable, pole of the earth, Gothic *gibla* gable, pinnacle, Old Icelandic *gafl* gable, and Tocharian A *śpāl-* head, from Indo-European **ghebh(e)l-/ghobh(e)l-* (Pok.423).

ceramic *adj.* 1850 *keramic,* borrowed from Greek *keramikós,* from *kéramos* potter's clay, earthen vessel (a pre-Greek word possibly borrowed from a language of Asia Minor); for suffix see -IC.

The spelling *ceramic* appeared in 1859 in *ceramics* (a plural noun meaning ceramic art) and was probably influenced by earlier French *céramique* (1806).

cereal *n.* 1832, grass yielding edible corn or grain, from earlier adjective meaning "having to do with corn or edible grain" (1818); borrowed from French *céréale,* from Latin *Cereālis* of or having to do with the cultivation of land or the growing of grain; originally, of or having to do with *Cerēs,* the goddess of agriculture and growth, for suffix see -AL[1].

The meaning of a breakfast food made from cereal grain appeared in 1899, in American English.

cerebellum (ser′əbel′əm) *n.* hind part of the brain. 1565, borrowed from Medieval Latin and Latin *cerebellum* small brain, diminutive of *cerebrum* brain; see CEREBRUM.

The earlier existence of *cerebellar,* adj. (probably before 1425) suggests that *cerebellum* was in use some time before its recorded date.

cerebrum (sərē′brəm) *n.* main part of the brain. 1615, borrowed from Latin *cerebrum* brain, (from earlier **keras-rom*); cognate with Greek *kárā* head and *kéras* HORN, Sanskrit *śíras* head, Old High German *hirni* brain (modern German *Hirn*), Old Icelandic *hjarni* brain, and modern Dutch *hersen* brain, from Indo-European **k̂er-/k̂erə-* (Pok.574). —**cerebral** *adj.* 1816, borrowed from French *cérébral,* from Latin *cerebrum* brain + French *-al* -al[1].

cerement (sir′mənt) *n.* cloth used to wrap the dead, originally of wax. 1602, in Shakespeare's *Hamlet,* from earlier *cere,* v. (about 1425) to wrap in a cloth covered with wax + *-ment.*

The earlier *cere* developed from Middle English *ciren* to wax (about 1395), which was borrowed from Middle French *cirer* to wax, from Latin *cērāre,* from *cēra* wax, from Greek *kērós,* probably from an oriental source.

ceremony *n.* rite, ritual. Before 1382 *ceremoyn,* later *cerymonye* (1384), both forms in the Wycliffe Bible; borrowed from Old French *ceremonie,* and Medieval Latin *ceremonia,* from Latin *caerimōnia* sanctity, reverence, show of reverence, religious rite, ritual, of uncertain origin. Ancient scholars derived the Latin word from the Etruscan name *Caere,* a city (now Cerveteri) that was once the capital of Etruria. —**ceremonial** *adj.* 1402, from earlier noun meaning "a ceremonial practice or usage" (before 1397, in the Wycliffe Bible); borrowed from Medieval Latin **ceremonialis,* from Late Latin *caerimōniālis* pertaining to ceremony, from Latin *caerimōnia* ceremony. —**ceremonious** *adj.* 1553, borrowed from Late Latin *caerimōniōsus* celebrated by rites, from Latin *caerimōnia* ceremony, possibly by influence of Middle French *cérémonieux.*

cerise (sərēs′) *adj., n.* bright, pinkish red. 1858, borrowed from French *cerise,* literally, cherry, from Old French *cerise,* from Vulgar Latin **ceresia;* see CHERRY.

cerium (sir′ēəm) *n.* grayish metallic element. 1804, New Latin, formed from *Ceres* an asteroid discovered in 1801 and named after *Cerēs,* the Roman goddess of agriculture + *-ium* (suffix of chemical elements). The word was coined in 1803 by its Swedish discoverers Jöns Berzelius, a chemist, and Wilhelm Hisinger, a geologist.

certain *adj.* sure, settled, fixed. Probably before 1300 *certein,* in *Arthour and Merlin,* borrowed from Old French *certain,* from Vulgar Latin **certānus,* from Latin *certus* sure, determined, resolved, certain. Originally *certus* was a variant past participle (the other being *crētus*) of *cernere* to separate, sift, distinguish, discern, decide, which is related to Latin *crībrum* sieve, and cognate with Greek *krī́nein* to separate, distinguish, decide, and Gothic *hrains* clean, pure, from Indo-European **krei-/kroi-/kri-* (Pok.946). —**certainly** *adv.* About 1300, with the emphatic meaning "yes, assuredly" formed from English *certain* + *-ly*[1]. —**certainty** *n.* About 1300 *certeynte,* in Mannyng's *Handlyng Synne,* borrowed from Anglo-French *certainté,* Old French *certaineté,* from Old French *certain* + *-té* -ty[2].

certify *v.* Before 1338, in Mannyng's *The Story of England;* borrowed from Old French *certifier* make certain, learned borrowing from Late Latin *certificāre,* from a lost adjective **certi-ficus,* from Latin *certus* sure (see CERTAIN) + the root of *facere* to make, DO[1] perform; for suffix see -FY. —**certificate** *n.* 1439, document that certifies; earlier, act of certifying (about 1419, in *Proceedings of the Privy Council*); borrowed from Middle French *certificat,* learned borrowing from Medieval Latin *certificatum,* from neuter of Late Latin *certificātus,* past participle of *certificāre* certify. —**certification** *n.* Probably 1424, borrowed from Middle French *certification,* learned borrowing from Medieval Latin *certificatio* (accusative *certificationem*), from Late Latin *certificāre;* for suffix see -TION. —**certified** *adj.* 1611, as a loan translation of French *certifié* assured, ascertained.

certitude *n.* certainty. Probably before 1425, in a version of Higden's *Polychronicon,* borrowed from Middle French *certitude* certainty, learned borrowing from Late Latin *certitūdō* (accusative *certitūdinem*) that which is certain, from Latin *certus* CERTAIN; for suffix see -TUDE.

cerulean (sərü′lēən) *adj.* sky-blue. 1667, formed in English from Latin *caeruleus* dark blue (from *caelum* sky, heaven) + English *-an.* —**n.** 1756, from the adjective.

cervix (sėr′viks) *n.* necklike part, especially of the womb. Probably before 1425, in a translation of Chauliac's *Grande Chirurgie,* borrowed from Latin *cervīx* (genitive *cervīcis*) neck; of uncertain origin, possibly originally a compound meaning "that which binds the head," whose components are akin to Latin *cerebrum* brain (see CEREBRUM), and *vincīre* to bind, from Indo-European **weik-/wik-* bend (Pok.1130). —**cervical** *adj.* of the neck or cervix. 1681, borrowed from French *cervical,* from Latin *cervīx* (genitive *cervīcis* neck) + French *-al* -al[1].

cesium (sē′sēəm) *n.* silvery metallic element. 1861, New Latin; earlier *caesium* (1860), from neuter of Latin *caesius* bluish gray; so called by its discoverers, the German chemists Bunsen and Kirchhoff, in reference to the two blue lines visible in its spectrum.

cessation *n.* 1447 *cessacyoun, cessacion,* borrowed from Old French *cessation,* learned borrowing from Latin *cessātiōnem* (nominative *cessātiō*) a delaying, idling, ceasing, from *cessāre* to delay, CEASE; for suffix see -TION.

cession *n.* a ceding. 1399, in *Rolls of Parliament,* borrowed from Old French *cession,* learned borrowing from Latin *cessiōnem* (nominative *cessiō*), from *cess-,* stem of *cēdere* to yield, CEDE; for suffix see -ION.

cesspool *n.* pool or pit for drains to empty into. 1671 *cestpool,* possibly alteration (with *pool*[1]) of earlier *cesperalle* (1583), variant of *suspiral* cesspool (about 1512), breathing hole, vent, conduit (about 1400); borrowed from Old French *souspirail* air hole, vent, from *souspirer* breathe, sigh, from Latin *suspīrāre* breathe deep. An alternative derivation suggests that *sesspool* is the original spelling from dialectal *suspool* (*suss, soss* puddle, anything foul or muddy + *pool*). It is also possible there is some connection with *cess* a bog on the banks of a tidal river where pools of water form.

cetacean (sətā′shən) *n.* 1836, formed in English from New Latin *Cetacea* the order of mammals including whales, dolphins, and porpoises (from Latin *cētus* large sea animal such as whale or dolphin, from Greek *kêtos* sea monster, whale, of unknown origin) + English *-an.*

ch as the spelling used to represent the last consonant of *bleach, blench,* and similar native English words, was introduced into English from France after the Norman Conquest (1066). In Old English the digraph *ch* was not used, although the sound of *ch* in words like *bleach* was already developed in English before the 900's. But after many new French words with *ch,* such as *charity* and *riches,* were introduced into English, the digraph began to be widely applied also to native English words, as in *chin, chink,* etc., which in Old English had been spelled with *c* and pronounced with the sound of *k.* See also, SH, TH, WH.

The spelling is also found in: 1) *chasm, chimera,* and *chyle,* taken from Greek directly or through Latin, Italian, or French and representing the sound of *k* in *kind.* 2) *chivalry, champaign,* borrowed from French, and representing the sound of *sh* in *shin.* 3) Scottish *loch,* Yiddish *chutzpah,* German *ach,* and other words in which the guttural sound pronounced *k* without closing the breath passage, is imitative of a foreign sound.

chafe *v.* Probably before 1300 *chaufen* to inflame, warm, heat, in *Arthour and Merlin;* borrowed from Old French *chaufer,* from Vulgar Latin **calefāre,* alteration of Latin *calefacere* to make hot, make warm, from *calēre* be warm (see CALDRON) + *facere* make, DO[1] perform.

Two common senses evolved separately: 1) to make sore by rubbing, developed by 1526 from the sense "to rub so as to make warm" (about 1410); 2) to anger, vex, or irritate, developed probably before 1387 from the earliest sense "to inflame, excite, make hot in temper" (probably before 1300).

chaff[1] *n.* husks of grain. Probably before 1200 *chaf, chef,* in *Ancrene Riwle* and Layamon's *Chronicle of Britain;* developed from Old English *ceaf* (in Ælfric's *Glossary*); cognate with Middle Dutch *caf* chaff, and Old High German *cheva* pod, husk, from Proto-Germanic **kaf-/kef-,* of unknown origin.

chaff[2] *n.* good-natured joking. Probably 1648, of uncertain origin, possibly from *chaff*[1], n. something trivial or worthless (about 1390, in Chaucer's *Canterbury Tales*), from earlier meaning "something evil" (probably before 1200, in *Ancrene Riwle*).

chaffer (chaf′ər) *n.* bargaining. Probably before 1200 *chaffere,* (1440) *cheapfare,* in *Ancrene Riwle* (*cheap* bargain, see CHEAP + *fare* journey, FARE).

chaffinch *n.* European songbird. About 1440 *caffynche,* in *Promptorium Parvulorum,* developed from Old English *ceaffinc* (*ceaf* CHAFF, because it feeds on chaff or grain + *finc* FINCH).

chagrin *n.* 1716-18, feeling of irritation from disappointment, in Pope's writings; earlier, melancholy, worry (1656, in Blount's *Glossographia*); borrowed from French *chagrin* melancholy, anxiety, vexation, from Old French *chagrin* grief, vexation (1389), of uncertain origin; perhaps related to Old North French *chagreiner* become gloomy, in terms of weather (*cha-,* a pejorative prefix + *grain* sorrow, from Germanic; compare Old High German *gram* angry, hostile, related to *grimm* savage, GRIM).

The traditional reference (to English *shagreen*) to French *chagrin* grained leather, as a metaphorical term for abrasive feelings in English and in French does not pertain to the etymology of this word and accordingly is treated as a separate entry in French dictionaries.

—**v.** 1727, in Fielding's writings, possibly borrowed from French *chagriner* to be vexed, grieve, but more likely a back formation from earlier *chagrined* (1665, in Pepys' *Diary*) or from the noun.

chain *n.* Probably before 1300 *chaene, cheine,* in *Kyng Alisaunder;* borrowed from Old French *chäeine, chaine,* from Latin *catēna* (originally **cates-nā*) chain, fetter; related to *cassis* (originally **kat-s-is*) hunting net, snare. Latin *cassis* is cognate with Old English *heathor* a locking in, imprisonment, and Old Slavic *kotici* a cell, from Indo-European **kat-* twist together by plaiting (Pok.534).

The meaning of a group of related stores is first recorded in 1846, in American English.

—**v.** Before 1376 *cheynen,* in *Piers Plowman,* from the noun. —**chain gang** (1834) —**chain reaction** (*nuclear physics* 1938; the concept was applied by Max Bodenstein, in 1916, to explain high quantum yields in gas reactions, but the word was known earlier in chemistry). —**chain stitch** (1598)

chair *n.* Probably about 1225 *chaere, chayere,* in *King Horn,* borrowed from Old French *chaiere, chaëre,* from Latin *cathedra,* from Greek *kathédrā* seat (*katá* down + *hédrā* seat, base; see SIT).

Old French *chaiere* represents regular phonetic development in borrowing from Latin *cathedra* with the loss of *th* between two vowels and the suppression of *d* before *r.*

—**v.** put in a chair, install in authority. Probably about 1450, implied in the form *chairing,* from the noun. The sense "be chairman of, preside over (a meeting)" is first recorded in 1921. —**chairman** *n.* (1654) —**chairwoman** *n.* (1681) —**chairperson** *n.* (1971, American English)

chaise (shāz) *n.* lightweight carriage. 1701, borrowed from French *chaise,* (earlier) sedan chair, chair; originally a Parisian dialectal variant of *chaire,* from Old French *chaiere* CHAIR.

chaise longue (shāz′ lông′) chair with a long seat and a back. 1800, borrowed from French *chaise longue* long chair. The English spelling **chaise lounge** also occurs, along with its spelling pronunciation (shāz′ lounj′). The alteration by confusion of form and meaning of English *lounge* for French *longue* is first recorded in the late 1800's.

chalet (shalā′) *n.* house or villa in the style of a Swiss cottage. 1782, borrowed from Swiss French, apparently a diminutive related to Old Provençal *cala* small shelter for ships, ultimately from a pre-Latin word, perhaps of the Mediterranean region, meaning "sheltered place."

The word is attested in French as early as 1723 but was popularized by Rousseau in the novel *La Nouvelle Héloïse,* 1761.

chalice *n.* cup. Before 1325, in *Cursor Mundi,* borrowed through Anglo-French *chalice,* as a learned borrowing from Latin *calix* (accusative *calicem*) cup. *Chalice* replaced earlier Middle English *calice* (1102), and *caliz* (about 1300), borrowed from Old North French, and also a learned borrowing from Latin *calix* (accusative *calicem*). The Latin is cognate with Greek *kýlix* cup, and Sanskrit *kalásá-s* pot, cup, from Indo-European **kel-/kol-* (Pok.550).

The word is also found in Old English as *celic* and *calic, cælc,* etc. Both borrowings are from Latin *calix, calicem* (see above), but the latter forms came apparently at the time of early Christian use. The earliest dates of recorded use appear before 830, in the *Vespasian Psalter*.

chalk *n.* About 1325 *chalk;* earlier in compound *chalcston* chalkstone (before 1200), developed from Old English *calc* (about 700), later *cealc* (before 900, in a different dialect); borrowed from Latin *calx* (genitive *calcis*) small stone, limestone, chalk, from Greek *chálix* small stone, pebble, of unknown origin, **—v.** write or draw with chalk. 1571, from the noun.

challenge *v.* **1** to call in question, dispute (about 1395, in Chaucer's *Canterbury Tales*); earlier, to challenge to combat (about 1380, in *Sir Ferumbras*), and to rebuke (probably before 1200, in *Ancrene Riwle*). **2** to lay claim to. Middle English *chalengen, calengen,* borrowed from Old French *chalengier, chalongier* (rarely *calengier*), from Latin *calumniārī* accuse falsely, from Latin *calumnia* trickery, false accusation, CALUMNY. **—n.** Probably before 1325 *chalange* accusation, charge, objection; later, but rarely, *calenge* (before 1333); borrowed from Old French *chalenge,* from Latin *calumnia* trickery, false accusation, calumny. **—challenger** *n.* About 1350, in part borrowed through Anglo-French *chalengeour,* from Old French *chalenger,* and in part developed from Middle English *chalengen* + *-er*[1].

chamber *n.* room. Probably before 1200 *chaumbre,* in *Ancrene Riwle,* borrowed from Old French *chambre,* from Latin *camera* vault, arch, from Greek *kamárā* vaulted chamber, vault, anything with an arched cover; see the doublet CAMERA. **—v.** Before 1402, from the noun. **—chambered** *adj.* (before 1387) **—chamber music** (before 1789)

chamberlain *n.* high official of a royal court. Probably before 1200 *chamberleng,* in *Ancrene Riwle;* later *chaumberlein* (about 1250); borrowed from Old French *chamberlenc,* from a Germanic source; compare Old High German *chamarling* (*chamara* chamber, from Latin *camera* vault, in Medieval Latin, room, chamber + *-ling* -ling[1]).

chambray (sham′brā) *n.* kind of fine gingham. 1814, American English, alteration (perhaps by influence of *champagne, champaign,* etc.) of French *cambrai,* or Spanish *cambray,* named after *Cambrai,* a city in northern France where the cloth was originally made. Compare CAMBRIC.

chameleon (kəmē′lēən) *n.* Before 1387 *camelion,* in Trevisa's translation of Higden's *Polychronicon,* borrowed from Old French *caméléon,* from Latin *chamaeleōn,* from Greek *chamailéōn,* literally, ground lion (*chamaí* on the ground, see HUMBLE + *léōn* LION).

The spelling with *ch* in imitation of the Greek begins to appear in the early 1800's. The figurative sense of a changeable or fickle person is first recorded in 1586.

chamois (sham′ē) *n.* small goatlike antelope. 1560, borrowed from Middle French *chamois,* from Late Latin *camōx* (genitive *camōcis*), probably from a pre-Romance Alpine word, represented also by Old High German *gamiza* (modern German *Gemse*).

champ[1] *v.* bite or chew noisily. 1530, in Palsgrave's *Lesclarcissement,* probably of imitative origin. **—n.** 1604, from the verb.

champ[2] *n.* champion. 1868, American English, shortened from CHAMPION.

champagne (shampān′) *n.* bubbly wine. 1664, borrowing of French *champagne,* from the name of the former province *Champagne,* in northwestern France, where it was originally made, from Late Latin *campānia* level country; see CHAMPAIGN.

champaign (shampān′) *n.* wide plain, level country. Probably before 1400 *champayne,* in *Morte Arthur,* borrowed from Old French *champaigne* open country, from Late Latin *campānia* level country, from Latin *campus* plain, field; see CAMP[1]; see the doublet CAMPAIGN.

champion *n.* Probably before 1200 *champiun* fighting man, combatant, in *Ancrene Riwle,* borrowed from Old French *champiun, champion* a champion, combatant in a duel, from Late Latin *campiō* (accusative *campiōnem*) combatant in the athletic field or arena, from Latin *campus* field, CAMP[1]. The meaning "one who holds first place in a sport" appeared in 1730. **—v.** 1605, in Shakespeare's *Macbeth,* to challenge to a contest; from the noun. The meaning "defend, support," in a general sense, is first recorded in 1844 from the earlier meaning "to defend or protect as a champion" (1820). **—championship** *n.* 1825, formed from English *champion,* n. + *-ship.*

chance *n.* Probably before 1300, in *Arthour and Merlin,* Middle English *chaunce, cheance* something that takes place, especially unexpectedly, fortune, luck; borrowed from Old French *cheance* accident, the falling of dice, dice game, from Vulgar Latin **cadentia* a falling, from Latin *cadentem* (nominative *cadēns*), from *cadere* to fall; see the doublet CADENCE. **—v.** happen. Before 1393, in Gower's *Confessio Amantis,* Middle English, *chauncen,* from the noun.

chancel (chan′səl) *n.* space around the altar of a church. About 1303 *chaunsel,* in Mannyng's *Handlyng Synne;* later *chauncel* (about 1390, in Chaucer's *Canterbury Tales*); borrowed from Old French *chancel,* from Late Latin *cancellus,* originally, lattice, from Latin *cancellī* (plural) grating, bars see CANCEL. The extension in meaning from the latticework that set off the altar space to the altar itself, took place in Latin.

chancellor *n.* title of various high officials. 1123 *canceler,* in *Peterborough Chronicle;* earlier found in Late Old English, in the *Anglo-Saxon Chronicle* (1093) and in documents of the reign of Edward the Confessor (before 1066); borrowed from Old Norman French *cancheler* and later Anglo-French *canceler.* Another form *chaunceler* appears in Middle English (probably before 1300, in *Arthour and Merlin*) and is a borrowing of the Anglo-French variant *chanceler,* Old French *chancelier.* Both forms in Old French are derived from Latin *cancellārius* court secretary, but originally meaning officer stationed at the bar or latticework separating the judges from the public in a basilica or other court of law, from *cancellī* a grating, bars (enclosing the area); see CHANCEL. The meaning applied to the head of a university is first recorded about 1300. **—chancellery** *n.* office of a chancellor. About 1300 *chauncelerie,* borrowed from Old French *chauncelerie* from *chancelier* chancellor.

chancery *n.* court of equity, court of the Lord Chancellor of England. About 1378, in a version of *Piers Plowman,* contraction of CHANCELLERY.

chancre (shang′kər) *n.* ulcer. Before 1605, borrowed

from French *chancre* cancer, from Latin *cancer* (genitive *cancrī*) cancer, originally, crab; see CANCER. See the doublet CANKER.

chandelier *n.* Probably before 1382 *chaundeler* candlestick or chandelier, in the Wycliffe Bible; earlier, one who makes or sells candles (1332); borrowed from Old French *chandelier* candlestick; see CHANDLER. The word was respelled in the 1600's after the French fashion.

chandler (chan′dlər) *n.* maker or seller of candles. 1389, earlier *Shaundeler,* (1332, as a surname); borrowed from Anglo-French *chandeler,* variant of Old French *chandelier* candlemaker, candlestick, from Vulgar Latin **candēlārius* candlemaker, *candēlāria* candlestick, from Latin *candēla* CANDLE; for suffix see -ER[1].

change *v.* Probably before 1200 *changen* make different, alter, in *Ancrene Riwle,* borrowed from Old French *changier,* from Latin *cambiāre* to barter, exchange, from a Gaulish source (compare Old Irish *camm* crooked, bent, cognate with Greek *skambós* crooked, bent, from Indo-European **(s)kamb-* (Pok.918).). **—n.** Probably before 1200, in *Ancrene Riwle,* borrowed from Old French *change,* from *changier,* v. **—changeable** *adj.* About 1250 *chaungable,* borrowed from Old French *chaungable,* from *changier,* v.; for suffix see -ABLE. **—changer** *n.* 1325, in part borrowed from Old French *changeour,* and in part formed from Middle English *changen* to change + *-er*[1].

channel *n.* Before 1325 *chanel,* in *Cursor Mundi,* borrowed from Old French *chanel,* from Latin *canālis* waterpipe, canal, channel. See the doublet CANAL. The figurative sense "medium of transmission or communication, means, agency" appeared in 1537, in sermons of Bishop Latimer. **—v.** 1596, in Shakespeare's *1 Henry IV,* from the noun.

chant *v.* About 1390 *chaunten,* in Chaucer's *Canterbury Tales,* borrowed from Old French *chanter* to sing, from Latin *cantāre,* frequentative form of *canere* to sing. The Latin *canere* is cognate with Greek *kanássein* to flow with a gurgling sound, *kanachḗ* sharp sound, ring, clang, *ēï-kanós* rooster; (originally), early singer, Old Irish *canim* I sing; and is also cognate with Gothic *hana,* Old Saxon and Old High German *hano,* and Old Icelandic *hani,* all meaning rooster, and Tocharian A *kan* melody, rhythm, from Indo-European **kan-* sing, sound (Pok.525). See the doublet CANT[1]. **—n.** 1671, in Milton's *Paradise Lost,* borrowed from French *chant* song, from Old French *chant,* from Latin *cantus* a singing, song, from *canere* to sing.

chantey or **chanty** (shan′tē) *n.* song sung by sailors. 1856, borrowed probably by alteration of French *chanter* to sing, or of *chantez,* imperative plural of *chanter,* from Old French; see CHANT. Also variant of *shanty*[2].

chanticleer (chan′təklir) *n.* rooster. Probably before 1300 *chauntecler,* borrowed from Old French *chantecler,* name of the rooster in the medieval epic *Reynard the Fox* (*chanter* to sing, crow, see CHANT + *cler* CLEAR). Compare BRUIN.

chaos (kā′os) *n.* great confusion. Before 1396 *cahos,* later *chaos* (1494), borrowed through Old French *chaos,* (1377) or directly from Latin *chaos,* from Greek *cháos* gulf, chasm, abyss, empty space (earlier **cháwos*), related to *chaûnos,* spongy, loose, empty, and cognate with Old High German *goumo* (modern German *Gaumen* gums), originally space (for teeth), from Indo-European **ĝhō(u)-/ĝhəu-* gape (Pok.449). **—chaotic** *adj.* 1713, irregularly formed from English *chaos* + ending *-otic,* found in other words derived from Greek, such as *erotic* (compare *eros*), *hypnotic.*

chap[1] *v.* crack open, become rough. Probably 1440 *chappen* to burst open, split, possibly a variant form of *choppen* to strike, cut off, chop, break (before 1376); of uncertain origin. Perhaps related to Middle Dutch *cappen* to chop, cut, Danish *kappe* and Swedish *kappa* to cut, cut off, and German dialect (northern Alsace) *kchapfe* chop into small pieces. **—n.** place where the skin is rough. Before 1398, in Trevisa's translation of Bartholomew's *De Proprietatibus Rerum;* from the verb.

chap[2] *n. Informal.* fellow, man, boy. 1577, buyer, purchaser, short for *chapman* purchaser, trader, developed from Old English *cēapman* tradesman (*cēap* trade, see CHEAP + *man* MAN). In the 1700's the sense shifted to person, lad, fellow, similar to extended meaning of the word *customer* a purchaser, which developed colloquially to mean "a character," as in "tough customer."

chaparral (chap′əral′) *n.* thicket of low shrubs. 1845, American English, borrowed from Spanish *chaparral* grove of evergreen oaks, thicket, from *chaparro* evergreen oak, probably of pre-Roman origin and related to Basque dialect *txaparra,* variant of Basque *txapar,* diminutive of *saphar* thicket, hedge.

chapel *n.* building for worship. Probably about 1200 *chapele, chapelle,* borrowed from Old French *chapele,* from Medieval Latin *cappella* chapel, sanctuary for relics, canopy, literally, little cape, diminutive of Late Latin *cappa* CAPE[1] garment. The Medieval Latin *cappella* is said to have been an extended use of the sense "canopy" referring to the altar cover, but *chapel* was a meaning of *cappella* from at least 796. A traditional explanation of the relation to "cape" is that it refers to the shrine in which the Frankish kings preserved the *cappella* or cloak of St. Martin of Tours (patron saint of France), using it as a sacred relic carried before them in battle. The name was then generally applied to a sanctuary containing holy relics.

chaperon or **chaperone** (shap′ərōn) *n.* 1720, older woman accompanying a young or unmarried woman; earlier meaning hooded cloak (about 1400, and 1130 in a surname); borrowed from French *chaperon* female companion to a young woman, literally, a hood, from Old French *chaperon* diminutive form of *chape* cape, from Late Latin *cappa* CAPE[1] garment. **—v.** act as a chaperone to. 1796, in Jane Austen's *Sense and Sensibility,* probably borrowed from French *chaperonner,* from French *chaperon,* n.

chaplain *n.* Before 1376 *chapeleyn,* in a version of *Piers Plowman,* borrowed from Old French *chapelain* clergyman, from Medieval Latin *cappellanus* clergyman, originally a keeper of the cloak or *cappella* of St. Martin; see CHAPEL.

Middle English *chapeleyn* replaced the earlier *capelein* (1114), which had developed from Old English *capellane,* a form borrowed from Medieval Latin *cappellanus.*

chaplet *n.* wreath worn on the head. 1375, Scottish, in John Barbour's *The Bruce,* borrowed from Old French *chapelet* little headdress, rosary, diminutive of *chapel* headdress, hat, from Medieval Latin *cappellus* hood, from Late Latin *cappa* CAPE[1] garment.

chaps *n.pl.* strong leather leggings without a back, fitted to a belt and worn over trousers. 1844, American English, borrowed and shortened from Mexican Spanish *chaparreras* leather leggings to protect trousers from *chaparro* evergreen oak, a kind of scrubby vegetation; see CHAPARRAL.

chapter *n.* Probably before 1200 *chapitre,* in *Ancrene Riwle,* borrowed from Old French *chapitre, chapitle,* learned borrowing from Late Latin *capitulum,* section of a book, from Latin, little head, diminutive of *caput* (genitive *capitis*) head. The sense of a local division or branch developed from the Middle English (about 1300) meaning convocation of the canons of a cathedral church or the members of a religious order (also attested with this sense in Old French and Medieval German). At such a meeting it was the practice to read a *capitulum* or chapter of the Scriptures or rules of the order, so that the assembled canons or monks themselves came to be called in a body the *capitulum* or chapter, and their meeting place the chapter house.

char[1] *v.* burn to charcoal, scorch, 1679, probably back formation from CHARCOAL.

char[2] or **chare** *n.* odd job, chore. Before 1250 *char* occasional turn of work, odd job; earlier *cherre* (probably before 1200, in Layamon's *Chronicle of Britain*) and in a surname *Chareman* (1183), developed from Old English (before 900) *cerr, cierr, cyrr* turn, occasion, related to *cerran, cierran* to turn. The Old English is cognate with Middle High German *kerren* turn (earlier **karzjan*), and Greek *gérron* wicker shield, from Indo-European **ĝers-/ĝors-* turn, bend (Pok.392). Compare CHORE. **—charwoman** *n.* woman doing odd jobs of household work. 1379 (in surname) *Alicia Charwoman,* formed from Middle English *char* + *woman.*

character *n.* Before 1333 *caracter* a symbol marked on the body or an imprint on the soul, borrowed from Old French *caractere,* from Latin *charactēr,* from Greek *charaktḗr* instrument for marking, distinctive mark, or distinctive nature, personal feature, from *charássein* engrave, cut furrows in, scratch. The spelling with *ch-* appeared in English in the 1500's, in imitation of the Latin and Greek forms. The meaning "person in a play or book" is first recorded in works of Dryden (1664). **—characteristic** *n.* 1664; *adj.*1665, surviving and ultimately replacing earlier *characteristical* (1621, in Burton's *Anatomy of Melancholy*). *Characteristic* may be a clipped form of *characteristical* or may have been an independent formation. It has a parallel form in French *caractéristique* (1550) and an ultimate source in Greek *charaktēristikós,* from *charaktḗr* character; for suffix see -IST and -IC. **—characterize** *v.* 1591, perhaps formed in English: 1) from *character* + *-ize,* or 2) as a back formation of earlier *characterization* (1570); or possibly borrowed: 1) by influence of French *caractériser* (1512) from Medieval Latin *characterizare* 2) or directly from Medieval Latin *characterizare,* from Greek *charaktērízein,* from *charaktḗr* character; for suffix see -IZE.

charade *n.* guessing game. 1776, borrowed from French *charade,* from Provençal *charrado* a chat, chatter, from *charra* to chatter, of imitative origin.

charcoal *n.* 1371 *charcole,* from *char-,* of uncertain origin, + *cole* COAL. It is suggested that *char-* comes from *char* to turn (in reference to wood being "turned" or "converted" into coal); another possible source of *char-* is by shortening of Middle French *charbon* charcoal, from Latin *carbōnem,* accusative of *carbō* charcoal, CARBON.

charge *v.* Before 1250 *chargen* load, fill, in a version of *Ancrene Riwle;* borrowed from Old French *chargier, charger* to load, charge, from Late Latin *carricāre* to load, carry, from Latin *carrum* wagon, CAR. Doublet of CARRY.

The meanings "to burden, entrust, command, accuse" appeared in Middle English. The extended sense "to attack impetuously" appeared in 1583, perhaps from an earlier sense "to load or ready a weapon (1541). A later meaning, "to subject to a monetary obligation," is found before 1626, in writings of Francis Bacon. **—n.** Probably before 1200, load, weight, in an earlier version of *Ancrene Riwle;* borrowed from Old French *charge* a load, from *chargier,* v., to load, charge. The meaning "burden of expense" appeared about 1460, developing into "liability to pay money" by about 1570.

chariot *n.* 1358, any vehicle, borrowed from Old French *chariot* wagon, augmentative of *char* chariot, from Latin *carrum* chariot, wagon, CAR. The sense of a two-wheeled cart pulled by horses applies chiefly to vehicles of the Greeks, Romans, and others that were used in ancient warfare. It is first recorded in 1581. **—charioteer** *n.* Before 1382 *charieter* in the Wycliffe Bible, a fusion of Old French *charioteur* and *charetier,* both meaning drivers of vehicles; for suffix see -EER.

charisma *n.* 1875, grace, talent bestowed by God, gift, replacing the earlier spelling *charism* (first recorded *before* 1641), borrowed from Greek *chárisma,* from *charízesthai* show favor, from *cháris* favor, grace, related to *chaírein* rejoice. Later a specific sense developed, "gift of leadership or power of authority" (1947) and was extended to "strong personal appeal or magnetism," especially in reference to political figures (in the early 1960's). **—charismatic** *adj.* 1882-83, formed in English from Greek *charísmata* favors given (plural of *chárisma* charisma)+English *-ic.* **—n.** Christian who believes in divine gifts, such as the power to heal by the laying on of hands. 1970, from the adjective.

charity *n.* 1137 *carited,* in *Peterborough Chronicle,* (pronounced *kariteth,* rhyming with *faith*), gradually replaced by later Middle English *chearite, cherite* (before 1200, in *Ancrene Riwle*) and *charite* (about 1200). Earlier Middle English *carited* loving-kindness, hospitality, almsgiving, was borrowed from Old North French *carité, caritét,* Old French *charité;* later Middle English *chearite, cherite,* and *charite* love of God and fellow men, kindness, especially to the poor, were borrowed from Old French *cherité, charité,* learned borrowing from Latin *cāritās* (accusative *cāritātem*) dearness (in price), costliness, affection, fondness, from *cārus* dear, costly, valued, loved; for suffix see -ITY.

Latin *cārus* is cognate with Old Irish *caraim* I love, *carae* friend, Latvian *kārs* desirous, Sanskrit *kāma-s* love, Gothic *hōrs* adulterer, and Old English *hōre* whore, from Indo-European **kā-ro-s, *kə-r-, *kā-mo-s* (Pok. 515).

—charitable *adj.* Probably before 1200, in *Ancrene Riwle,* borrowed from Old French *charitable,* from *charité;* for suffix see -ABLE.

charlatan (shär′lətən) *n.* pretender, quack. 1618, borrowed from French *charlatan* mountebank, tattler, babbler, from Italian *ciarlatano* mountebank, babbler, alteration (influenced by *ciarlare* to babble) of earlier *cerretano* charlatan, literally, inhabitant of *Cerreto,* Italy; for suffix see -AN.

charlotte (shär′lət) *n.* dessert of cake or bread filled with fruit or custard. 1796, probably in allusion to *Charlotte,* a woman's name. In French, *charlotte* in the sense of this dessert has been attested only since 1804. **—charlotte russe** (rüs), dessert of sponge cake filled with whipped cream. Before 1845, borrowed as a French term, literally, Russian charlotte.

charm *n.* Probably before 1300 *charm, charme* incantation, magic spell, in *Kyng Alisaunder;* borrowed from Old French *charme* a charm, enchantment, from Latin *carmen* song, enchantment, incantation. Latin *carmen* was formed by dissimilation of *n* to *r* before *m* in **canmen,* from *canere* to sing, CHANT. The sense "a pleasing quality" probably first appears in 1598, in Shakespeare's *Merry Wives of Windsor.* The meaning of a trinket worn on a chain or bracelet is first recorded in 1865 as an extension of the older meaning "anything worn to avert evil" (1596, in Spenser's *Fairie Queene*). **—v.** please greatly. Probably before 1300 *charmen* to recite or cast a magic spell, in *Kyng Alisaunder;* borrowed from Old French *charmer* to charm, enchant, from Late Latin *carmināre* enchant, sing, from Latin *carmen* song.

chart *n.* 1571, borrowed from Middle French *charte* card, map, from Latin *charta, carta* paper, card, map, from Greek *chártēs* leaf of paper, roll of papyrus, a borrowed word, perhaps from Egyptian. Doublet of CARD[1]. The meaning "a diagram of information" is first recorded in 1840. **—v.** 1842, in Tennyson's works, from the noun.

charter *n.* written grant of certain rights or privileges. Probably before 1200 *chartre,* in *Ancrene Riwle,* borrowed from Old French *chartre* charter, from Latin *chartula, cartula* a little paper or writing, diminutive of *charta, carta* paper, document, CHART. **—v.** grant a charter to. About 1425 (Scottish) *chartren,* from the noun. The sense "to hire some conveyance for transportation" appeared in 1806.

chartreuse (shärtrüz′) *n.* 1806, an ornamental meat or vegetable dish prepared in a mold; earlier, liqueur first made by Carthusian monks (1866); borrowed from French *chartreuse* (masculine *chartreux,* earlier *charteus*), associated by popular etymology with *La Grande Chartreuse* chief monastery of the Carthusian monks, at Chartreuse, France. The sense of a pale, green color appeared in 1884.

The word is related to *Charterhouse* (Middle English *Charterhous, Chartirhous,* probably before 1425, in writings of Wycliffe), an alteration of Anglo-French *chartrouse* Carthusian house, Old French *chartreus* (feminine *chartreuse*), both forms being earlier alterations of *charteus* (feminine *charteuse*), from Medieval Latin *cartusius, carthusius,* ultimately from *Catorissium, Chatrousse* the village of *Chartreuse,* France; but according to the OED *La Grande Chartreuse* comes from the name of the Carthusian order.

chary *adj.* careful. Probably about 1200 *charig,* in *The Ormulum,* developed from Old English (probably about 750) *cearig* sorrowful, in the sense of "with care or trouble," from *cearu, caru* CARE. This meaning shifted to "careful" (with the idea of caring about one's work) in the 1500's. The Old English *cearig* is cognate with Old Saxon *carag* (found in *mōdcarag*) and Old High German *charag* sorrow, trouble, care.

chase[1] *v.* run after, hunt. Before 1338 *chasen* to hunt, in Mannyng's *Chronicle of England;* earlier *chacen* (probably before 1300, in *Sir Tristrem*), borrowed from Old French *chacier* to catch, seize, from Vulgar Latin **captiāre* to take, seize, catch, Latin *captāre* to try to catch. Doublet of CATCH. The meaning "to run after" developed in Middle English probably about 1350. **—n.** About 1300 *chas* a hunt; earlier *chace* (probably about 1250), borrowed from Old French *chace, chas,* from *chacier,* v. The meaning "pursuit, as of an enemy" developed in Middle English about 1330. **—chaser** *n.* 1204, in surname *Chacur,* later *chacer* (1275), in part borrowed from Old French *chaceor,* and in later spellings developed from Middle English *chacen* + *-er*[1]. The meaning "water or other mild drink taken after strong alcoholic drink", is first recorded in American English, in 1897.

chase[2] *v.* engrave, emboss. 1414, variant form developed by shortening of *enchase* borrowed from Middle French *enchasser* to set (gems), enclose, encase (Old French *en-* in, into + *chasse* casket, case, setting, from Latin *capsa* CASE[2] box).

chasm (kaz′əm) *n.* abyss, gulf. 1596, borrowed from Latin *chasma,* from Greek *chásma* yawning hollow, gulf, any wide space or expanse, related to *cháskein, chainein* to gape, YAWN. The spelling *chasma* after the Latin and Greek appears in English until the late 1600's.

chassis (chas′ē) *n.* frame, wheels, and machinery of a motor vehicle. 1903, in American English, earlier, window frame, sash (1664, in works of John Evelyn, borrowed from French *châssis* frame (*châsse* frame, from Latin *capsa* box, CASE[2]) + suffix *-is,* used in a collective sense of a number of parts taken together).

chaste *adj.* pure, virtuous. Probably before 1200, in *Ancrene Riwle,* borrowed from Old French *chaste* morally pure, from Latin *castus* pure, chaste, holy, related to *castrāre* to cut off, CASTRATE. Doublet of CASTE. **—chastity** *n.* purity, virtue. Probably before 1200 *chastete,* borrowed from Old French *chasteté,* from Latin *castitātem* (nominative *castitās*) purity, from *castus* pure; for suffix see -ITY.

chasten *v.* punish to improve. 1526, in Tyndale's translation of the Bible; developed by extension with *-en*[1] from an obsolete English verb *chaste* to correct (a person's) behavior, from earlier *chastien* chastise (probably before 1200); borrowed from Old French *chastier,* from Latin *castigāre* chastise, correct, punish; literally, make pure, formed (perhaps by influence of *fatigāre* to weary) from *castus* pure, CHASTE. Doublet of CASTIGATE.

chastise *v.* to inflict punishment on; punish (an offense). About 1303 *chastysen,* in Mannyng's *Handlyng Synne,* probably alteration of *chastien* CHASTEN. Middle English probably developed by influence of *-isen,* as in *baptyzen, baptisen* to baptize; a parallel word formation occurs in French: Old French *favorer* to favor, modern French *favoriser.*

chasuble (chaz′yəbəl) n. sleeveless outer vestment worn by the priest at mass. 1611, in Cotgrave's *Dictionary,* borrowed from Old French *chasuble,* from Late Latin *casubla,* an unaccounted alteration of Latin *casula,* literally, little house, diminutive of *casa* cottage, hut, of uncertain origin.

The form *chasuble* replaced the earlier *chesible,* (about 1300), borrowed through Anglo-French, Old French *chesible,* from Medieval Latin *cassibula.*

chat *v.* Before 1450, shortened from CHATTER. **—n.**

1530, in works of Sir Thomas More, from the verb. **—chatty** *adj.* Before 1762, formed from English *chat,* v. + *-y*[1].

château (shatō′) *n.* large home, especially country residence. About 1739, borrowing of French *château* country mansion, large country house, from Old French *chastel,* from Latin *castellum* CASTLE. Doublet of CASTLE.

chattel *n.* property that is not real estate; movable possession. About 1225 *chatel,* also *chetel* (before 1250) property, goods, borrowed from Old French *chatel,* from Medieval Latin *capitale* property, originally neuter of Latin *capitālis;* see CAPITAL[1] city. Doublet of CAPITAL, CATTLE.

According to the OED the word adopted in general use in English was *catel* (*cattell, cattle*) from Norman French, but in the 1500's *catel* was gradually restricted to farm animals and *chattel* to other articles of property.

chatter *v.* talk constantly. Before 1250 *cheateren,* in a version of *Ancrene Riwle,* and *chiteren;* later *chateren* (about 1250) to twitter, jabber, gossip, mumble, of imitative origin, as in English *chitter, twitter, jabber* (compare Dutch *koeteren* to jabber, *kwetteren* to chatter, and Danish *kvidre* to twitter, chirp). **—n.** About 1250, in *The Owl and the Nightingale,* probably from the verb.

chauffeur (shō′fər) *n.* person whose work is driving a car. 1899, a motorist, borrowed from French *chauffeur* stoker (originally, one who fuels the fire of a steam engine), from *chauffer* to heat, from Old French *chaufer;* see CHAFE. **—v.** to drive as a chauffeur. 1917, from the noun.

chauvinism (shō′vənizəm) *n.* 1870, boastful, warlike patriotism, borrowed from French *chauvinisme* (1843), from the surname of Nicolas *Chauvin;* for suffix see -ISM. Chauvin, in spite of being severely wounded in the Napoleonic wars, expressed devotion to the Emperor and the Empire that was at first celebrated but, after the fall of Napoleon, was ridiculed and considered the attitude of old soldiers who had blindly idolized the Emperor. Chauvin's name was popularized as that of an excessively nationalistic character in the French vaudeville *La Cocarde Tricolore* (1831), and until the 1970's *chauvinism* was used in English to denote exaggerated loyalty to one's country; about 1970 the term was extended in English, but not in French, to sexism, chiefly in the phrase *male chauvinism.* **—chauvinist** *n.* 1877, borrowed from French *chauviniste,* from *Chauvin;* for suffix see -IST. **—chauvinistic** *adj.* (1870)

cheap *adj.* 1509 *chepe* low-priced, inexpensive, a shortened form of earlier *good chep, goode chepe* good bargain, good price (about 1280); earlier, as a surname *Godchep* (1166), formed after the noun *chep, chepe* bargain, barter, price, developed from Old English *cēap* trade, barter, purchase, sale (about 725, in *Beowulf*).

Old English *cēap* is cognate with Old Frisian *kāp* trade, purchase, Old Saxon *kōp,* Old High German *kouf, koufo* trader (modern German *Kauf*), and Old Icelandic *kaup* bargain, pay, with derivatives in Old English *cēapian* to buy, Old Saxon *kōpian,* Old High German *koufōn* (modern German *kaufen*), Old Icelandic *kaupa,* and Gothic *kaupōn.* The noun forms probably represent an early Germanic borrowing from Latin *caupō* (genitive *caupōnis*) petty tradesman, huckster, innkeeper, which is perhaps from the same foreign source as Greek *kápēlos* retail dealer, huckster, innkeeper.

The Middle English and early modern English noun use survives in some place names, such as *East Cheap* and *Cheapside.* The idiom *to live on the cheap* is a later development (1888) of a noun construction of the adverb use meaning "cheaply". The sense "of little value or esteem, contemptible", is first recorded in 1596, in Shakespeare's *1 Henry IV.*

cheat *v.* 1440 *cheten* confiscate, seize, in *Promptorium Parvulorum,* shortened form of *acheten,* a variant of *escheten* ESCHEAT. The current sense "deceive or trick" is first recorded in 1590, in Shakespeare's *Comedy of Errors* with reference to unscrupulous actions, especially of those who confiscated lands *(escheats)* for the state, and this became generalized to any deceptive act. **—n.** About 1378 *chet* forfeited property, in a version of *Piers Plowman,* shortened of *achet,* a variant of *eschet* ESCHEAT (property that goes to a lord by forfeit). The sense of a deceptive act appeared about 1641, in writings of Milton; the sense of a fraud or trick, in 1648, and that of a swindler, one who cheats, about 1664, all probably from the verb. **—cheater** *n.* (1607; earlier as a shortened form of *escheater* an officer in charge of escheats, 1327).

check *n.* sudden stop. Probably about 1300 *chek* a call in the game of chess giving notice that one's move has exposed the opponent's king; borrowed from Old French *eschec, eschac,* from Arabic *shāh* (especially in the phrase *shāh māt* CHECKMATE), from Persian *shāh* king, from Old Persian *xšāyathiya-;* cognate with Avestan *xšayati* (he) has power, he rules, Sanskrit *kṣáya ti* (he) possesses, rules, *kṣatrá-m* rule, dominion, and Greek *kéktēmai* I possess, from Indo-European **kþē(i)-/kþə(i)-* (Pok.626).

Out of usage in chess came the sense of attack (probably about 1380), the sense of an adverse event, repulse, rebuff (before 1303, in Mannyng's *Chronicle of England*), the sense of a sudden stoppage (1526, seen earlier perhaps in the figurative sense of *check* used in chess 1338). The use of a bank *check* appeared in 1798, in correspondence of John Jay, from the earlier sense of a receipt stub or counterfoil used to *check* forgery or alteration (1706, spelled *cheque,* probably from *exchequer*). The meaning "a pattern of squares" is first recorded about 1400, as a shortening of CHECKER. The check mark to show something has been examined or compared is from earlier verb use of *check* (1885). **—v.** stop the motion of. Probably before 1387 *cheken,* in a version of *Piers Plowman;* borrowed from Old French *eschequier* play chess, put a check to, from *eschec,* n., check.

checker *n.* pattern of squares. 1389 *cheker;* earlier, a chessboard or checkerboard (probably before 1300), and a game of chess or checkers (about 1250); borrowed from Old French *eschekier, eschequier* chessboard, from *eschec* CHECK; for suffix see -ER[1]. The meaning is also found in "a table covered with a checked cloth for counting" (1179, in Anglo-Latin). **—v.** Probably before 1400 *chekeren* (implied in *checkered,* in *Morte Arthur*) to vary with a different color, from *cheker* chessboard. **—checkers** *n.* game played with round pieces on a checkered board. 1712, American English, plural of *checker.*

checkmate *n.* move in chess that ends the game. Before 1346 *chekmat,* borrowed from Old French *eschecmat,* from Arabic *shāh māt* the king died (a misinterpretation of Persian *māta* to die, for *mat* be astonished), from Persian *shāh mat* the king is astonished or stumped (*shāh* king + *mat* astonished). —**v.** to put (an opponent's king) in check to end the game. Before 1375 *chekmaten,* developed from *chekmat* checkmate.

cheek *n.* Probably before 1200 *cheke* jaw, jawbone, cheek, in *Ancrene Riwle,* developed from Old English *cēace* (before 899, in Alfred), *cēce* (before 830, in the *Vespasian Psalter*); cognate with Middle Low German *kāke, kēke* jaw, jawbone, and Middle Dutch *kāke* jaw (modern Dutch *kaak*), from Proto-Germanic **kaukōn,* from Indo-European **geu-g-ōn* (Pok.400). Related to CHEW.

The informal sense "impudence, insolence" is first recorded in 1852, in Dickens's *Bleak House,* from the earlier phrase *give cheek* speak impudently (1840). —**cheeky** *adj.* (1859)

cheep *v.* make short, sharp sounds. 1513, a Scottish use of imitative origin. —**n.** Before 1774, from the verb.

cheer *n.* Probably before 1200 *chere* the face, expression or mood shown by the face, in *Ancrene Riwle;* later, gladness (before 1393, in Gower's *Confessio Amantis*); borrowed from Old French *chere* face, from Late Latin *cara* face, countenance, from Greek *kárā* head (from earlier **kárasa*); see CEREBRUM. The present-day phrase *be of good cheer* seems to be tautological, for *cheer* now means "gladness" but the meaning of *cheer* in this phrase is reminiscent of the original meaning "expression or mood shown on the face," in Middle English *maken god chere* be of good cheer. —**v.** About 1390 *cheren* comfort oneself, cheer up, developed from *chere,* n., cheer. —**cheers** *n.pl.* salutation before drinking. 1919, from earlier meaning "a shout of support or encouragement" (1720, in writings of Defoe). —**cheerful** *adj.* (probably before 1400, in *Destruction of Troy*). —**cheerily** *adv.* (1616) —**cheery** *adj.* (1448)

cheese *n.* food made from curds of milk. 1186 *chese* (in surname *Chesemangere*); earlier *ceose* (1131, in *Peterborough Chronicle*), developed from Old English *cēse* (800, in an early glossary) and *cȳse* (before 1000, in Ælfric's *Colloquy*), an early borrowing from Latin *cāseus* cheese, of uncertain origin. Other languages that derive a term borrowed from Latin *cāseus* include Old Saxon *kāsi,* Old High German *chāsi, kāsi* (modern German *Käse*), and Middle Dutch *cāse, kāse* (modern Dutch *kaas*).

cheesy *adj. Slang.* cheap, inferior. 1896, student slang, possibly from earlier slang meaning "showy" (1858), formed from English *cheese* (1818, probably in an Anglo-Indian phrase *the real chīz,* borrowed from Urdu *čīz* thing, from Persian) + *-y*[1].

cheetah *n.* 1781, borrowed from Hindustani *chītā* a hunting leopard, from Sanskrit *citraka-s* tiger or hunting leopard; literally, spotted, from *citrá-s* distinctive, marked, bright, clear. The Sanskrit *citrá-s* is cognate with Old High German *heitar* bright, shining, from Indo-European **kāi-/kəi-/ki-* (Pok.916).

chef *n.* head cook. 1826, in Disraeli's *Vivian Grey,* borrowed from French *chef,* from Old French *chief* head, CHIEF.

chela (kē′lə) *n. Zoology.* claw. 1646, New Latin *chela* claw, from Greek *chēlḗ* claw, hoof, Doric *chālā́,* of unknown origin.

chemical *adj.* 1576 *chimical,* formed in English probably from New Latin *chimicus* (short for Medieval Latin *alchimicus* of alchemy, from *alchimia* ALCHEMY) + English *-al*[1]; possibly influenced by earlier French *chimique* (1558). The spelling with *e* became established in the 1800's.

chemise (shəmēz′) *n.* women's shirtlike undergarment. Probably before 1200, borrowed from Old French *chemise,* a half-learned development from Late Latin *camisia* shirt. Late Latin *camisia* was taken from Gaulish, which in turn had borrowed it from Proto-Germanic **Hamíthjan* (compare Old English *hemethe,* Old Saxon *hemiđi,* Old High German *hemidi,* modern German *Hemd*); cognate with Sanskrit *śāmulyà-m* woolen shirt, from Indo-European **k̑em-/k̑om-/k̑ēm-* to cover (Pok.556). Doublet of CAMISOLE.

chemist *n.* 1562 *chymist, chimist* alchemist, alteration of *alkemyst* ALCHEMIST. The word was influenced in its formation by Middle French *chimiste* alchemist, and Late Greek *chymeíā* ALCHEMY. The modern sense of one who makes chemical investigations was introduced by Francis Bacon in 1626. —**chemistry** *n.* 1605 *chymistrie* alchemy, formed from English *chymist* chemist + *-rie* -ry. The modern sense was introduced in 1646 by Sir Thomas Browne, and reinforced in use by Joseph Priestley (1788). The spelling with *e* became established in the 1800's.

chemo- or (before vowels) **chem-** a combining form meaning chemistry or chemical, as in *chemosynthesis, chemotherapy.* Formed by clipping *chem(ical)* + connecting vowel *-o-,* on the pattern of *bio-, chromo-,* etc.

chemotherapy (kē′mōther′əpē) *n.* treatment of disease, especially cancer, by means of chemicals. 1907, borrowed from German *Chemotherapie* (*chemo-* chemical + *Therapie,* from Greek *therapeíā* THERAPY). The word was coined by the German biochemist Paul Ehrlich.

chenille (shənēl′) *n.* velvety cord used in embroidery. 1738, borrowed from French *chenille,* from Old French *chenille,* literally, hairy caterpillar, from Latin *canīcula* little dog, from *canis* dog, HOUND, so called from the cord's furry look.

cherish *v.* Probably before 1325 *chersen,* later *cherisen, cherischen;* borrowed from Old French *chériss-,* stem of *chérir* to hold dear, from *cher, chier* dear, from Latin *cārus;* see CHARITY; for suffixal ending see -ISH[2].

cheroot (shərüt′) *n.* cigar cut off square at both ends. 1759, probably borrowed from Portuguese *charuto* cigar, from Tamil *curuṭṭu* roll (of tobacco), from *curuḷ* to roll, curl.

cherry *n.* Probably before 1300, in compound *chirston* cherry stone or pit; earlier, in surname *Chyrimuth* (1266). These forms and the later spelling *cherie* (before 1393, in Gower's *Confessio Amantis*) are replacements of Old English *ciris, cirse* found only in compounds, as *cirisbēam* cherry tree. The early Middle English forms were pronounced with the vowel of the Old English forms, but like the later Middle English *cherie,* were borrowings of Anglo-French and Old North French *cherise* (by influence of Old French *cerise*) though mistaken as a plural (thought to be *cheri* + *-se*) as *pea* is a back formation of *peas.* The Old North French *cherise* was derived from Vulgar Latin **ceresia, *cerasia,* from Late Greek *kerasíā* cherry tree, from Greek *kerasós* cherry tree. Possibly Greek *kerasós* was borrowed from a language of Asia Minor. Doublet of CERISE.

The OED points out that lack of a native name for *cherry* in Celtic and Germanic languages "confirms the opinion of botanists that the tree is not indigenous to Britain and Western Europe."

The spelling with two *r*'s was not established in England until the late 1500's.

cherub *n.* one of an order of angels. About 1384, in the Wycliffe Bible, borrowed from Late Latin *cherub* (plural *cherūbim*), from Greek *cheroúb,* from Hebrew *kərūbh,* probably related to Akkadian *karābu* be gracious.

Modern English *cherub* (a new singular form) replaced the earlier *cherubin* (also a singular form, recorded probably before 1200, in *Ancrene Riwle*) that developed from Old English *cerubin* (recorded before 830, in the *Vespasian Psalter*). The Old English form was borrowed from Greek *cheroubín, cheroubím,* plural forms of *cheroúb.* For some time the forms *cherubin, cherubim,* and *cherub* competed because of confusion of the Latin plural *cherūbim* and the Middle English *cherubin,* but the plural *cherubs* began to appear about 1526, and gradually *cherubims* became the literary plural and *cherubim* the collective form (about the 1600's, in writings of Bacon and Milton).

chess *n.* Probably before 1300, in *Sir Tristrem,* shortened borrowing from Anglo-French and Old French *esches,* (earlier) *eschecs,* plurals of *eschec* check; see CHECK.

chest *n.* box, thorax. Before 1200 *cheste* box, developed from Old English (about 700) *cest, cist* box, coffer, casket, an early borrowing from Latin *cista* box, basket, from Greek *kístē* basket. The Greek is cognate with Old Irish *cess* basket, from Indo-European **kistā* woven container (Pok. 599). Other languages and their forms that borrowed from Latin *cista* include Old Frisian and Middle Dutch *kiste* box, chest, Old High German and Old Icelandic *kista.*

The sense "part of the body enclosed by ribs, thorax" is recorded in 1530, in Palsgrave's *Lesclarcissement,* but stems from figurative, and probably some concrete use of *chest* in Middle English in reference to the body is recorded as early as 1385 by Chaucer, and before 1405 by Lydgate.

chesterfield *n.* kind of overcoat. 1852, probably named after the fourth Earl of *Chesterfield,* 1694-1773, an Englishman noted for the *Letters to His Son* (1774) and for his supposedly unintentional neglect of Johnson in support of his *Dictionary.* The word *chesterfield,* in British and Canadian usage, also refers to a large overstuffed sofa (1900).

chestnut *n.* 1519 *chesten nut* nut of the chestnut tree; *chesten* developed from obsolete *chestein* (about 1390) and *chesteine* (probably about 1300); *chastein* (about 1330), borrowed from Old French *chastaigne,* from Latin *castanea,* from Greek *kastanéā,* chestnut tree from *kástanon* chestnut, probably borrowed from a language of Asia Minor.

chevalier (shev′əlir′) *n.* knight. About 1399 *chevaler,* also *chivaler* (about 1378, in a version of *Piers Plowman*), borrowed through Anglo-French *chevaler,* Old French *chevalier* knight, horseman, from Late Latin *caballārius,* horseman. Doublet of CAVALIER.

The modern spelling *chevalier* after the French, does not appear in English until the 1500's.

chevron (shev′rən) *n.* 1395, heraldic device of a bar bent like two meeting rafters, borrowed from Old French *chevron* rafter, from Vulgar Latin **capriōnem,* from Latin *caper* (genitive *caprī*) goat; perhaps so called from the angular shape of a goat's hind legs. However, similar semantic developments are often found in French; for example, *chevalet* easel (from *cheval* horse), *poutre* beam (from a word for mare), *bélier* battering ram (from the word for ram).

chew *v.* Probably before 1200 *chewen,* in *The Ormulum,* developed from Old English *cēowan* (before 1000, in Ælfric's writings); cognate with Middle Low German *keuwen* to chew, modern Dutch *kauwen,* Old High German *kiuwan* (modern German *kauen*), and Old Icelandic *tyggva,* from Proto-Germanic **keuwjanan.* Cognates outside Germanic include Old Slavic *žĭvati* to chew, Russian *ževát',* Persian *jāvīdan* to chew, Pashto *žoval* to bite, gnaw, and Tocharian A and B *śwātsi* to eat, from Indo-European **ĝeu-* chew (Pok.400).

chez (shā) *prep.* at the house (or home) of. 1740, as a French word introduced into English correspondence. The French *chez* developed from Old French, unstressed form of *chies,* from Latin *casa* cottage, hut, probably dialectal, from earlier **katjā* wickerwork, from Indo-European **kat-* twist together by plaiting (Pok.534).

chic (shēk) *n.* 1856, as a French word in an English novel. French *chic* is perhaps borrowed from German *Schick* fitness, skill, from Middle High German *schicken* arrange, put in order, send (modern German *schicken* to send), of uncertain origin. **—adj.** stylish. 1865, from the noun.

chicanery (shikā′nərē) *n.* trickery, deception. Before 1613, borrowed from French *chicanerie* trickery, from Middle French *chicanerie,* from *chicaner* to quibble, quarrel, to confuse with crafty argument; of uncertain origin; for suffix see -ERY.

Chicano (chēkä′nō) *n.* Mexican American. 1969 (about 1954, American English); earlier in Chicano English, borrowed from a Mexican Spanish dialectal pronunciation of *Mexicano* Mexican, with the loss of the initial unaccented syllable *me* in *mechēkä′nō* (wherein the original Nahuatl *sh-* sound is replaced by Spanish *ch-*).

chichi (shē′shē′) *n.* affected or pretentious chic, artiness. 1908, borrowed from French *chichi,* of unknown origin. **—adj.** elaborately chic; arty. 1932, from the noun.

chick *n.* 1342 *cheke* young bird; earlier *chike* child (about 1330), and as surname (1214); shortened form of *chiken* CHICKEN. The slang sense of a girl or young woman appeared in 1927 in American English. **—chickweed** *n.* 1373 *chekwede;* later *chekyn-wede* chicken weed (about 1450); all replacing earlier *chikenmete, chicnemete* (before 1300), developed from Old English *cīcene mete, cīcena mete* chicken food.

chickadee *n.* small American bird. 1838, in Thoreau's *Journal,* American English; imitative of its call.

chicken *n.* Before 1200 *chikene* young chicken, and probably also with the meaning of any chicken (possibly an Old English form); later *cheken* (probably before 1325) and *chyken* (before 1382, in the Wycliffe Bible); developed from Old English *cīcen* (about 950, in *Lindisfarne Gospels*). Old English *cīcen* (earlier **cīecen*) is cognate with Middle Dutch *kieken, kiekijen, kūken* young fowl, chicken (modern Dutch *kuiken*), Middle Low German *kuken* (modern German *Küken*), from Proto-Germanic **kiukīnan,* imitative, like Old English *cocc* of the sound of the bird; see COCK[1].

The word was applied in a disparaging sense in Middle English as early as 1330 and had the meaning of cowardly person in the phrase *cherles chekyn* probably before 1400, in *Morte Arthur.*

—**v.** *Slang.* Also, **chicken out,** act as a coward. 1943, American English, from the noun. —**chicken pox** 1727-38, in *Chambers Cyclopaedia,* possibly in allusion to the mild form of the disease when compared with *small pox.*

chicle (chik'əl) *n.* substance used in making chewing gum. 1889, American English (in the compound *chicle-gum*), borrowed from Mexican Spanish *chicle,* from Nahuatl *tzictli.*

chicory *n.* plant used to flavor coffee or ground as a substitute for coffee. 1605 *chicory,* as a replacement (influenced by French *chicorée*) of earlier *cicoree* (before 1450); borrowed from Middle French *cichorée,* from Latin *cichorēum,* from Greek *kichórion, kichóreia* (plural) endive, of uncertain origin.

chide *v.* Probably 1150 *chiden* scold, nag, rail; developed from Old English (about 1000) *cīdan* to quarrel, wrangle; not known in other Germanic languages.

chief *n.* About 1300 *chef, chief,* borrowed from Old French *chef, chief* leader, ruler, head (of something), along with other forms such as Spanish and Portuguese *cabo,* Italian *capo* that suggest a Late Latin **capum,* from Latin *caput* (genitive *capitis*) HEAD. Doublet of CHEF. —**adj.** About 1300 *chef, chief* highest in rank, from the noun. Both spellings are found in an early chronicle. —**chief justice** (about 1395)

chieftain (chēf'tən) *n.* chief of a tribe or clan. Before 1338 *cheftayne* ruler, chief, head (of something), in Mannyng's *Chronicle of England,* also *chieftayn* (about 1385, in Chaucer's *Canterbury Tales*) and *chevetaine* (about 1300); borrowed through Anglo-French *chiefteyn, cheftain,* and directly from Old French *chevetain, chevetaine,* from Late Latin *capitāneus* commander, from Latin *caput* (genitive *capitis*) HEAD. Doublet of CAPTAIN.

chiffon (shifon') *n.* very thin silk, or now rayon, cloth. 1756, any bit of feminine finery, as ribbon or lace, borrowed from French *chiffon,* from *chiffe* a rag, flimsy stuff, of uncertain origin.

The meaning in pastry cooking referring to being whipped to a lighter consistency, as in lemon chiffon pie or chiffon cake, is first recorded in 1929.

chiffonier (shif'ənir') *n.* high bureau. 1765, borrowed from French *chiffonnier* chest of drawers for needlework, cloth (but originally meaning rag collector), from *chiffon* CHIFFON.

chigger *n.* mite whose larva sticks to the skin. 1756, American English, variant form of earlier *chigoe,* especially in West Indies (1668); *chigoe* is borrowed from the Indian name in the West Indies possibly of Carib origin, or from a West African language; the variant *chigger* is almost surely influenced by, if not borrowed from a West African language (compare Yoruba *jígà* chigger, Wolof *jiga* insect, and Tshiluba *njiga* sand flea).

chignon (shēn'yon) *n.* coil or lump of hair worn on the back of the head. 1783, borrowed from French *chignon* bun or coil of hair, nape of the neck, an alteration of Old French *chaignon* collar, chain, nape, which is a variant of *chaînon* ring or link of a chain, from *chaine, chäeine* CHAIN.

chilblain (chil'blān') *n.* Usually, **chilblains.** itching sore or redness on the hands or feet caused by cold. 1547, formed from English CHILL + *blain* an inflamed swelling or sore on the skin; Old English *blegen* (about 1000), from Proto-Germanic **blajinōn,* from Indo-European **bhlei-/bhloi-* swell up (Pok.156).

child *n.* About 1175 *child,* developed from Old English *cild* (about 750, in Cynewulf's *Elene*). Old English *cild* is cognate with Old Swedish *kulder, kolder* litter (modern Swedish and Norwegian *kull*), Danish *kuld* offspring, brood, Gothic *kilthei* womb, *inkilthō* pregnant, and Sanskrit *jaṭhára-m* belly, (from Indo-European **gel-t-/gl̥-t-,* Pok.358), but Old Frisian, Old Saxon and Old High German *kind* child, offspring, is a form not satisfactorily related to Old English *cild.*

The original Old English nominative plural was the same as the singular *cild,* but about 975 the plural *cildru* (genitive *cildra*) developed, which became *children,* about 1175, through influence of the plural ending *-en,* as in *brethren.*

—**childbed** *n.* (probably before 1200) —**childbirth** *n.* (probably before 1450) —**childhood** *n.* (probably before 1200) —**childish** *adj.* Old English *cildisc* (before 1000). —**child's play** (about 1350)

chile con carne or **chili con carne** (chil'ē kon kär'nē) meat cooked with red peppers and usually beans. 1857, American English (earlier *chili, chilli,* 1846); borrowed from American Spanish *chile con carne* CHILI with meat.

chili or **chilli** (chil'ē) *n.* hot-tasting red pepper used for seasoning. 1662 *chille,* borrowed from Mexican Spanish *chile, chilli,* from Nahuatl *chilli,* native name for these peppers. The word was also applied to *chile con carne,* or a dish like it, as early as 1846.

chill *v.* About 1378 *chillyng* gerund of *chillen* become cold, in a version of *Piers Plowman;* formed on the basis of earlier *chele, chile,* n., coldness of weather, frost (about 1175), developed from Old English *cele, ciele* (before 830, in the *Vespasian Psalter*), from Proto-Germanic **kaliz,* related to *ceald, cald* COLD. —**n.** 1601, from the verb. —**chilly** *adj.* 1570, formed from English *chill* + *-y*[1].

chime *n.* Probably before 1300 *chymbe* cymbal, in *Kyng Alisaunder;* later, set of bells (1453), this latter meaning probably a back formation from earlier *chymbe bellen* chime bells (probably before 1300); borrowed from Old French *chimbe,* a back formation of *chimble,* learned borrowing from Latin *cymbalum* CYMBAL. —**v.** About 1340, from the noun.

chimera or **chimaera** (kəmir'ə) *n.* mythical monster with a serpent's tail, goat's body, and a lion's head. Before 1387 *chimera,* in Trevisa's translation of Higden's *Polychronicon;* borrowed from Medieval Latin *chimera* and from Old French *chimère,* both forms from Latin *Chimaera,* from Greek *chímaira* monster, supposed to have been a personification of the snow or winter; originally, she-goat, feminine form of *chímaros* he-goat (that is one winter old), related to *cheîma, cheimṓn* winter season. The Greek is cognate with Sanskrit *hímā* winter, *himá-s* snow, from Indo-European **ĝhei-m-/ĝhi-m* (Pok.425). The meaning "wild fantasy" is first recorded in 1587. —**chimeric** *adj.* (1653) —**chimerical** *adj.* (1638)

chimney *n.* About 1280 *chymenay,* in figurative uses meaning "the furnace of hell, the mouth of a volcano"; later, a chimney (about 1330), and a fireplace (about 1380); borrowed from Old French *cheminee* fireplace, chimney, from Late Latin *camīnāta* fireplace, room with a fireplace, from Latin *camīnus* hearth, oven, furnace, flue, from Greek *kámīnos* oven, furnace, of uncertain origin. —**chimney pot** (1830, in poetry of Tennyson). —**chimney sweep** (1611; earlier, *chimney sweeper,* about 1500).

chimpanzee *n.* 1738, borrowed from a West African Bantu language of Angola, perhaps from Tshiluba *kivili-chimpenze* ape.

chin *n.* Probably before 1200, in Layamon's *Chronicle of Britain,* developed from Old English *cin* (probably before 832) and earlier in the compound *cinberg* (about 725). The word is cognate with a variety of forms in the Germanic languages often with wider meaning than in later English: Old Frisian *zin, kin* (in compounds) chin, Old Saxon *kinni* chin, jaw, Old High German *kinni* (modern German *Kinn*), Old Icelandic *kinn* cheek, and Gothic *kinnus* cheek; also cognate with Old Irish *gin* mouth, Welsh *gen* jaw, chin, Latin *gena* cheek, (usually plural *genae*), Greek *génys* and *gnáthos* jaw, Lithuanian *žándas* jawbone, Sanskrit *hánu-s* chin, and Tocharian A *śanwem* (dual) jaws, from Indo-European **ĝénu-* and **ĝonədh-/ĝnədh-* (Pok.381).—**v.** 1599, from the noun. The meaning of to talk, gossip first appears in American English (1883) and the meaning of a gymnastic exercise of drawing the body up to an overhead bar (1903).

china *n.* earthenware. 1579, as an early reference to Drake's voyages, in Hakluyt's *Voyages,* used in compound *China-dishes;* later, *China* (1653); borrowed from Persian *chīnī* China porcelain. The earthenware was originally manufactured in China and brought to Europe in the 1500's by the Portuguese.

chinch *n.* small bug. 1616, bedbug; borrowed from Spanish *chinche,* and from Portuguese *chinche* bug, from Latin *cīmex* (accusative *cimicem*) bedbug, cognate with Sanskrit *śyāmá-s* dark-colored, from Indo-European **k̂yē-m-/k̂ī-m-* dark-gray (Pok.541).

chinchilla *n.* a South American rodent with valuable fur. 1593, borrowed from Spanish *chinchilla,* literally, little bug, probably alteration influenced by *chinche* bug, of a word from Aymara or Quechua (compare Quechua *č'ičiļa* fringe, flounce, *čiphciļa* shining, lustrous).

Chinese *adj.* 1577, from the name of the country *China* (1555, of uncertain origin, but found in Sanskrit *Cīnā-s* the Chinese, probably from the name of the emperor *Chin* Shihnangdi, who ruled from 246 to 207 B.C.) + -ESE. The word was probably formed in English by influence of French *chinois* Chinese.

chink[1] *n.* narrow opening, split, crack. 1535, apparently an altered form of Middle English (before 1382, in the Wycliffe Bible); developed from *chin, chine* cleft, split, crack, Old English (about 888) *cinu,* related to *cīnan* to crack, split, gape. Cognate with Old Saxon and Old High German *kīnan* to burst open, sprout, Gothic *uskeinan* to sprout out, and Old High German *kīmo* sprout (modern German *Keim* germ, bud, sprout), from Indo-European **ĝēi-/ĝī/ĝi-* (Pok.355). —**v.** 1552, to crack, later, in American English, to fill in cracks (1748).

chink[2] *n.* 1573, pieces of money, cash in coins; later, short, sharp sound (1581); probably imitative of the sound. —**v.** 1589, probably from the noun.

chinook *n.* warm wind that blows from the Rocky Mountains across the Plains. 1860, American English, said to be from the jargon of Hudson Bay Company traders in reference to the wind that blew from an encampment of Chinook Indians. The tribe's name is from Salishan *Tsinúk.*

chinos (chē'nōs) *n.pl.* khaki trousers made of cotton twill fabric. 1943, borrowed from American Spanish *chino* toasted; earlier male Indian of white parent, in reference to light-brown skin color (feminine *china*), from Quechua *čina* female animal, servant.

chintz *n.* cotton cloth of various colors and often glazed. 1719; originally a plural form of *chint* a printed calico from India (1614), borrowed from Hindi *chīnt,* from Sanskrit *citrá-s* distinctive, marked, bright, clear; see CHEETAH. —**chintzy** *adj.* unfashionable, cheap, petty (because the fabric was inexpensive). 1851, in George Eliot's letters formed from English *chintz* + *-y*[1].

chip *n.* small piece of wood, stone, etc. Before 1338, in Mannyng's *Chronicle of England,* probably developed from Old English *cipp, cyp* small piece of wood, beam, log, apparently an early borrowing (like Old Saxon *kipp* stick, staff, Old High German *kipfa* wagon pole, and Old Icelandic *keppr* stick, staff) from Latin *cippus* stake, post, pillar. —**v.** break off in small pieces. 1425 *chippen,* in *The Paston Letters,* probably developed from Old English *forcippian* to cut off, which corresponds to East Frisian *kippen* to cut, Middle Low German *kippen* to hatch (modern German *kippen* cut the edges off, clip); probably ultimately related to Old English *cipp* small piece of wood, chip. Alternatively, it has been suggested that all of these verbs may have been borrowed from a Latin verb **cippāre* (formed on *cippus*) seen in French *recéper* to cut down close to the ground, and in some other forms, including the verbs listed above.

chipmunk *n.* small, striped American squirrel. 1841, in J. Fenimore Cooper's *Deerslayer,* American English; earlier, *chitmunk* (1832); borrowed from Algonquian (probably Ojibwa) *atchitamon* squirrel, literally, one who descends trees headlong.

chipper *adj.* lively, cheerful. 1837, perhaps a form of English dialect *kipper* nimble, frisky; but now thought to be associated with *chipper,* v. to twitter, possibly an imitative origin of the sound of birds, and also thought to be formed from *chirrup,* by metathesis of *r* and *p.*

chiropodist (kərop'ədist) *n.* person who treats the feet, especially painful growths on them. 1785, one who treats diseases of the hands and feet, formed in English from Greek *cheír* (genitive *cheirós*) hand + *poús* (genitive *podós*) FOOT + English *-ist.*

chiropractic (kī'rəprak'tik) *adj.* 1898, American English, of or having to do with treatment by spinal manipulation. According to the Dictionary of Americanisms, the word was coined by an early patient of Daniel Palmer, founder of the Chiropractic School & Cure, from Greek *cheír* (genitive *cheirós*) hand + *prāktikós* concerned with practice, practical, and freely translated as "done by hand". —**n.** 1903, from the adjective. —**chiropractor** *n.* 1904, formed from English *chiropract(ic)* + *-or*[2].

chirp *v.* make a short, sharp sound like a bird. 1566; earlier *cyrpinge, chyrpyinge,* gerund (1440, in *Promp-*

torium Parvulorum), perhaps variant of Middle English *chirk, chirken* to creak, crackle, chirp (1380, in works of Chaucer); developed from Old English *cearcian* to creak (about 1000, in Ælfric's *Grammar*), related to *cracian* to CRACK. **—n.** 1802, in Southey's *Thalaba,* from the verb.

chirrup (chir'əp) *v.* to chirp. 1579, implied in *chirruping* gerund, in Spenser's *Shepheardes Calender;* probably alteration of *chirp.* **—n.** a chirp. 1788, in poetry of Cowper, from the verb.

chisel *n.* cutting tool. 1323, borrowed from Old French *chisel, cisel* a chisel, from Vulgar Latin **cīsellum,* a variant form of *caesellum* (compare Italian *cesello*) a cutting tool, diminutive from Latin *caesus* (genitive *caesūs*) a cutting, from *caes-,* stem of *caedere* to cut; see EXCISE² cut. —**v.** cut or shape with a chisel. 1509, from the noun. The slang sense "to cheat" is first recorded in Jamieson's Scottish dictionary (1808) and spelled *chizzel;* perhaps it is not the same word as *chisel.* **—chiseler** *n.* (1918)

chit *n.* voucher of a debt, as for food. 1776, shortened form of earlier Anglo-Indian *chitty* letter, note, certificate (1673), borrowed from Hindi *chiṭṭhī,* from Sanskrit *citrá-s* distinctive, marked; see CHEETAH.

chit-chat *n.* 1710, reduplication of *chat;* influenced by *chit* twitter (before 1639), *chit-chit-chat* a squeaking (before 1618). **—v.** 1821, from the noun.

chitin (kī'tin) *n.* horny outer covering of beetles, lobsters, crabs, etc. 1836, borrowed from French *chitine,* from Greek *chitṓn* coat of mail, tunic, from Phoenician *k-t-n* linen garment (compare Hebrew *kuttōneth* coat, Assyrian *kitinnu* linen).

chitter *v.* twitter, chatter. Probably before 1200 *chiteren,* in *Ancrene Riwle,* imitative of the call of birds. **—chitter-chatter** *n.* 1712, reduplication of *chatter* influenced by *chitter; v.* 1928, from the noun.

chitterlings (chit'ərlingz) *n.pl.* intestines of pigs, cooked as food. About 1280 *cheterlingis;* earlier, in a surname *Chiterling;* probably cognate with Sanskrit *gudá-s* intestines; or perhaps from Old English **cīeterlingas;* for suffix see -LING.

The variants *chitlins* (1845) and *chitlings,* (1880, in Mark Twain's writings) are also recorded with a figurative sense "shreds, tatters".

chivalry *n.* About 1385 *chivalrye,* in Chaucer's *Canterbury Tales;* earlier *chevalrie* body of warriors, knighthood (probably before 1300, in *Kyng Alisaunder*), borrowed from Old French *chevalerie* horsemanship, from *chevalier* knight, CHEVALIER; for suffix *-ry* see -ERY. **—chivalrous** *adj.* Probably about 1350 *chevalrous,* in *Ywain and Gawain;* borrowed from Old French *chevalerous,* from *chevalier;* for suffix see -OUS.

chive *n.* plant related to the onion. About 1390 *chyve,* (also *cyve, cive,* probably a transferred sense from earlier word *civey, cive* meaning "sauce containing chives or onions" (apparently before 1300); and in part a borrowing of Anglo-French *chive;* both the earlier Middle English *civey* and Anglo-French *chive* from Old French *cive* any of several small species of onion, from Latin *cēpa* onion, of unknown origin.

chlor- a combining form, the form of *chloro-* before vowels, as in *chloride* (1812, on analogy of *oxide*).

chloral *n.* 1838, borrowed as French *chloral,* formed from *chlor(ine)+ al(cohol).* The word was coined by the German chemist Justus Liebig, 1803-1873, after the earlier *ethal* and is now found chiefly in the commercial preparation *chloral hydrate* (1874).

chlorine (klôr'ēn) *n.* poisonous gaseous element. 1810, formed in English from Greek *chlōrós* pale green, greenish yellow + English *-ine²* (chemical suffix). *Chlorine* was discovered by the Swedish chemist Carl Scheele in 1774 and called oxymuriatic acid gas, but the name *chlorine* was coined by the English chemist Sir Humphry Davy, 1778-1829, who first identified it as an element and named *chlorine* after the color of the gas. **—chlorinate** *v.* combine or treat with chlorine. 1856, formed from English *chlorine* + *-ate².*

chloro- a combining form meaning: 1) green, as in *chlorophyll.* 2) chlorine, as in *chloroform.* Borrowed from Greek *chlōro-,* combining form of *chlōrós* pale green, greenish yellow, related to *chlóē* young grass; cognate with Latin *helvus* dull yellow, and Old English *geolu* YELLOW, from Indo-European **ĝhel-wo-s, *ĝhlou-/ĝhlō(u)-* (Pok.429).

chloroform (klôr'əfôrm) *n.* colorless liquid used as an anesthetic, solvent, refrigerant, etc. 1838, borrowed from French *chloroforme* (*chloro-* chlorine + *-forme,* from *formique* formic (acid). The substance was discovered in 1831 and 1832 by three chemists working independently, but the source of the English word was not coined in French until 1834 by the French chemist Jean Baptiste Dumas. **—v.** administer chloroform to. 1848, in an article by Sir James Simpson, from the noun.

chlorophyll or **chlorophyl** (klôr'əfil) *n.* green coloring matter of plants. 1819, borrowed from French *chlorophyle,* from Greek *chlōrós* pale green, CHLORO- + *phýllon* leaf; altered (probably by influence of *phýein* to grow) from earlier **phóllon,* cognate with Latin *folium* leaf, from Indo-European **bhol-* bloom (Pok.122). The name was coined by the French chemists J. B. Caventou and P. J. Pelletier. **—chloroplast** *n.* plant cell containing chlorophyll. 1887, in a translation of a German textbook by Strasburger, who in 1884 shortened the original German *chloroplastid* (1883) formed from *chloro-* + *plastid.* (OEDS)

chock *n.* block, wedge. 1674 *chuck* lumpy piece of wood, found in a glossary of ruralisms, apparently borrowed from Old North French *choque* log (Picard dialect *choke*), Old French *çoche* log, block of wood, related to Old French *souche* stump, from Gaulish **tsukka.* The latter corresponds to Old High German *stoc* stump (ancient *st-* changing to *ts-* in Celtic); see STOCK. **—chock-full** *adj.* Probably before 1400 *chokkefull* crammed full, in *Morte Arthur,* formed from *chokken,* in the phrase *chokken togeder* crammed together + *full.* Middle English *chokken* was borrowed from Old French *choquier* collide, thrust, according to the MED. A variant *chuck-full* appeared by 1770.

This compound and the spellings in Middle English suggest that *chock* has been influenced in its development by *choke* with which it is confused.

chocolate *n.* 1604, in a translation of a Dutch history of the West Indies, drink made from the seeds of the cacao tree; later, paste or cake made by roasting and grinding the seeds (1640); borrowed from Mexican Spanish *chocolate,* from Nahuatl *chocolatl,* now written *xocoatl,* literally, bitter water. Though *chocolate* is not connected by derivation with the Mexican word *cacáuatl* cacao, the latter was probably often confused with *chocolatl.*

choice *n.* selection, alternative. About 1300 *chois,* borrowed from Old French *chois,* from *choisir* to choose, from a Germanic source (compare Gothic *kausjan* examine, test, prove, taste, derivative of *kiusan* CHOOSE). The later borrowed form *chois* replaced the early Middle English *cure, kire* choice, developed from Old English *cyre* (from Proto-Germanic **kuzis*) because the new form sounded closer to Middle English *chosen* choose than the noun forms *kire, cure* then in use. **—adj.** About 1350, from the noun, in the sense "distinguished, excellent."

choir (kwīr) *n.* 1643, in correspondence of Cromwell; spelling alteration (influenced by Latin *chorus* and by French *choeur*) of Middle English *quyre* (about 1405), or earlier *quer, queor* the part of a church where the choir sings (about 1300); borrowed from Old French *cuer* choir of a church, from Medieval Latin *chorus* part of a church, especially the chancel, and body of church singers; in Latin *chorus* band of dancers; see CHORUS. The spelling *choir* was not fully established until after the 1850's, though the pronunciation is still as if spelled *quire.*

choke *v.* Before 1387 *choken,*in Trevisa's translation of Higden's *Polychronicon,* variant of earlier *cheken,* (about 1303, in Mannyng's *Handlyng Synne*), a shortened form of *acheken* (probably before 1200). Middle English *acheken* developed from Old English *ācēocian* (from Proto-Germanic **us-keukōjanan*) to suffocate, strangle, choke (about 1000, in Ælfric's *Homilies*) and is probably related in Old English to *cēoce* CHEEK. Middle English *choken,* variant of *cheken,* developed by shift of stress in the diphthong *éo/eó* of the Old English *ācēocian.* **—n.** 1562, that which chokes, from the verb. **—choker** *n.* 1928 a necklace or ribbon worn close about the throat, developed from earlier meaning of a neckerchief or high collar (1848, in writings of Thackeray).

choler (kol′ər) *n.* irritable disposition. About 1390 *colre, colere,* in Chaucer's *Canterbury Tales,* one of the humors, bile (supposed to cause irascibility or temper), also a digestive disorder (before 1382, in the Wycliffe Bible); borrowed from Old French *colre* bile, anger, learned borrowing of Late Latin *cholera* bile; see CHOLERA. Middle English *coler* was respelled *choler* in the 1500's and 1600's in imitation of the Latin spelling. **—choleric** *adj.* 1340 *colrik* irascible, temperamental, in *Ayenbite of Inwyt,* borrowed from Old French *colerique, colorik,* learned borrowing of Late Latin *cholericus* bilious, from Greek *cholerikós* bilious.

cholera (kol′ərə) *n.* acute disease of the stomach and intestines. 1565-78; earlier probably not differentiated from, and perhaps, often the same as Middle English *choler* (before 1382, in the Wycliffe Bible); borrowed from Middle French *choléra,* or directly from Latin *cholera,* from Greek *cholérā* a digestive disorder, especially biliousness, jaundice, from *cholḗ* bile; see GALL[1] bile.

cholesterol (kəles′tərōl) *n.* fatty substance found in the blood and tissues. 1894, formed from English *cholester(in)* from French *cholestrine* (from Greek *cholḗ* bile + *stereós* solid, stiff) + English *-ol* (chemical suffix).

choose (chüz) *v.* make a choice. 1545, respelling of Middle English *chosen* (probably about 1390), variant form of earlier *cheosen* (probably before 1200, in Layamon's *Chronicle of Britain*) and *chesen* (probably about 1150) and *cesen* (1123); developed from Old English *cēosan* (about 725, in *Beowulf*). Middle English *chosen,* variant of *chesen, cheosen,* developed by shift of stress in the diphthong *éo/eó* of Old English *cēosan.* The Old English is cognate with Old Frisian *ziāsa, kiāsa* choose, Old Saxon *kiosan,* Old High German *kiosan* (modern German *kiesen*), Old Icelandic *kjōsa,* and Gothic *kiusan* choose, from Proto-Germanic **keusanan,* which is cognate with Sanskrit *jóṣati* (he) tastes, Greek *geúesthai* to taste, Latin *gustus* taste, from Indo-European **ĝeus-/ĝus-* (Pok.399). **—choosy** or **choosey** *adj.* fastidious. 1862, American English, formed from *choose* + *-y*[1].

Choose is only indirectly related to *choice,* since the latter came into Middle English from Old French, and is unknown in Old English, though both are ultimately Germanic.

chop[1] *v.* cut into pieces. Before 1376, in *Piers Plowman,* Middle English *choppen* cut with a quick and heavy blow, probably early variant of *chappen* CHAP[1] crack open; not found in Old English. **—n.** cutting blow. Before 1376, in *Piers Plowman,* probably developed from *chappen,* v. The change in vowel has been explained as analogous to the shift in *strap/strop.* **—chopper** *n.* 1552, formed from English *chop*[1] + *-er*[1]. The meaning of a helicopter is first recorded in 1951. **—choppy** *adj.* jerky. 1867; earlier full of chops or clefts (1605, in Shakespeare's *Macbeth*), formed from English *chop*[1] + *-y*[1].

chop[2] *n.* Usually, **chops,** *pl.* the jaws. About 1400 *choppe* jaw, earlier variant *cheppe* (1373), perhaps related to *choppen* CHOP[1].

chop[3] *v.* change suddenly; shift or veer quickly. Before 1438, implied in the gerund *chopping* bargaining, apparently a variant spelling of obsolete *chap* to bargain, barter, buy and sell; developed from earlier *chapen,* (probably before 1200), variant of *chepen,* developed from Old English *cēapian* to buy; see CHEAP. In the 1500's the phrase *chop and change* to barter and exchange, was generalized to mean "change about, change often," which developed into the nautical usage referring to the wind, "to change, veer, or shift in direction suddenly" in the 1600's. The figurative expression *chop logic* to exchange logical arguments, bandy logic, argue (1577) survives from the early sense of *chop* to exchange, barter. **—choppy** *adj.* veering; shifting; unstable. 1865, formed from English *chop*[3] + *-y*[1].

chopsticks *n.pl.* **1** pair of sticks used to raise food to the mouth. 1699, formed from Chinese Pidgin English *chop* quick (related to Cantonese *kap*) + English *sticks,* plural of STICK[1] piece of wood. The word is a free translation of Chinese *k′wai tse* quick ones, nimble ones. **2** simple, fast-paced piece played on the piano, the treble part played with the forefingers. 1893, probably from the resemblance of the quick-moving fingers to the sticks.

chop suey (chop′ sü′ē) Chinese dish of meat and vegetables. 1888, American English, borrowed from Chinese (Cantonese dialect) *tsap sui* odds and ends, mixed bits.

choral (kôr′əl) *adj.* of a choir or chorus. 1587, borrowed from Middle French *choral* or Medieval Latin *choralis* belonging to a chorus or choir, from Latin *chorus* CHORUS; for suffix see -AL[1].

chorale (kəral′) *n.* choral hymn or song. 1841, borrowed from German *Choral* metrical hymn that developed in the reformed church of Germany, and shortened form of *Choralgesang,* originally, plain song, choral song, favored by Luther; translation of Medieval Latin *cantus choralis* (Latin *cantus* song, CHANT + Medieval Latin *choralis* CHORAL).

chord[1] *n.* two or more musical notes sounded together. 1608, alteration (influenced by *chord*[2]) of Middle English *cord* (before 1398), shortened form of ACCORD, n.

English *chord*[2] and Latin *chorda,* both meaning a string of a musical instrument have influenced this word by association of form and meaning.

chord[2] *n.* a structure of the body, emotions figuratively considered as a string on a musical instrument, straight line connecting two points on a circumference. 1543, structure in an animal resembling a string, alteration (influenced by Greek *chordḗ* gut, string) of CORD. **—chordate** *n., adj.* 1889, from earlier *Chordata* phylum of animals having a spinal cord (1880), from Latin *chorda* chord + *-ate*[1].

chore *n.* odd job, small task. 1751 (recorded earlier as verb, 1746), variant of *chare* CHAR[2] odd job.

chorea (kôrē′ə) *n.* nervous disease characterized by involuntary twitching of muscles. 1806, shortened from New Latin *chorea* (sic *chorus*) *Sancti Viti* St. Vitus dance (1621), from Latin *chorēa,* from Greek *choreíā* dance, from *chorós;* see CHORUS. The name *St. Vitus's dance* or *St. Vitus dance* was originally a form of mass hysterical behavior in Medieval Europe, and was characterized by tortuous, convulsive dancing. In the 1600's the name was extended to the nervous disease.

choreography (kôr′ēog′rəfē) *n.* art of creating or composing dances. Before 1789 *choregraphy,* borrowed from French *chorégraphie* from Greek *choreiā* dance, from *chorós* CHORUS; for combining form see -GRAPHY. **—choreograph** *v.* arrange or create dancing (for). 1943, American English, probably borrowed from French *chorégraphier* (since 1827), with the spelling influenced by English *choreography,* or perhaps a back formation of *choreograph.* **—choreographer** *n.* 1886; earlier *choreograph* (1876) and *choreographist* (1923); formed from *choreograph(y)* + *-er,* by influence of French *chorégraphier.*

chorister *n.* 1595, in Spenser's writings; earlier *coruster* (1563), alteration (influenced by Middle French *choristre*) of Middle English *queristre* (before 1400), borrowed from Anglo-French *cueristre, cueriste,* learned borrowing from Medieval Latin *chorista* chorister, from Latin *chorus* CHORUS; for suffixes see -IST and -ER[1]. Though the current spelling appeared early in modern English (1614), it was not fully established until after the 1850's.

chortle *v.* chuckle or snort with glee. 1872, coined by Lewis Carroll in *Through the Looking Glass,* a blend of *chuckle* and *snort.* **—n.** 1903, from the verb.

chorus *n.* choir, group of singers. 1561, person who speaks the prologue and comments upon events in a drama, borrowed from Late Latin *chorus* choir, from Latin *chorus* dance, band of dancers and singers, from Greek *chorós,* from Indo-European **ĝhoró-s* enclosed place, from root **ĝher-* take in (Pok.442). Related to CHOIR. The senses in music appear later: 1) choir in 1656, in Blount's *Glossographia;* 2) a vocal composition, in 1744; 3) a refrain, in 1599, in Ben Jonson's *Cynthia's Revels.*

Apparently there is no connection between this borrowing from Latin and the earlier borrowing in Old and Middle English *chor* a group or company, choir; a troupe of dancers (in a late edition of Ælfric's *Glossary,* 1200, and the Wycliffe Bible, 1382). **—v.** 1703, in Defoe's writings, from the noun.

chow *n.* **1** *Slang.* food. 1856, American English, shortened from earlier Chinese Pidgin English *chow-chow* food (1795), perhaps reduplication of Chinese *cha* or *tsa* mixed, as evidenced in the English use Pidgin *chow-chow* mixture of any kind. **2** breed of dog, originally from China. 1889, earlier *chow-chow* (1886), of uncertain origin.

chowder *n.* soup or stew of sea food. 1751, American English, apparently borrowed from French *chaudière* pot, from Late Latin *caldāria, calidāria* CALDRON. According to the OED the practice of making chowder spread from the fishermen of Brittany to Newfoundland and thence to Nova Scotia and New England.

chow mein (chou′ mān′) Chinese dish of fried noodles. 1903, American English, borrowed from Chinese *ch'ao mien* fried flour.

chrism (kriz′əm) *n.* consecrated oil used in church rites. About 1250 *crisme,* developed from Old English (before 1000) *crisma,* borrowed from Late Latin *chrīsma,* from Greek *chrîsma* an anointing, unction, from *chríein* anoint, smear; cognate with English *grime,* from Indo-European **ghri-* (Pok.457).

The spelling with *ch* was introduced in the 1500's after the Latin and Greek forms.

Christ *n.* Middle English and Old English *Crist* the anointed one, the Lord's Anointed, Jesus Christ, (about 830, in *Vespasian Psalter;* 675, according to the *Peterborough Chronicle*); borrowed from Latin *Chrīstus,* from Greek *Chrīstós,* noun use of *chrīstós* anointed, from *chríein* anoint (see CHRISM). The Greek is a translation of Hebrew *māshīah* anointed (of the Lord), MESSIAH. This word and its derivatives and related forms, such as *chrism,* were rarely spelled with *ch* in Middle English even after the 1400's. The spelling *Christ* did not become standard until after 1500. The more frequent name in Old English is *Hǣlend* healer, Savior; the pronunciation of Old and Middle English *Crist* with a "long" *i* is a result of Irish missionary work in England during the 600's and 700's. Sometime in the late 1300's it became common to write the name Christ and words associated with it, such as *Christian,* with a capital letter, but the practice did not become fixed until the 1600's.

christen *v.* Probably about 1200 *cristnen* to baptize, in *The Ormulum,* developed from Old English (before 900) *cristnian* make Christian, from *cristen* Christian; borrowed from Latin *chrīstiānus* CHRISTIAN. **—Christendom** *n.* Old English (before 900) *cristendōm* condition of being Christian, Christianity, formed from *cristen* Christian (from Latin *chrīstiānus*) + *-dōm* -dom. The sense "Christian domain or realm" is recorded before 900, in Alfred's translation of Orosius. The sense "that part of the world ruled by Christians" is first recorded in Middle English about 1300.

Christian *n., adj.* Middle English and Old English *cristen* (about 750, in Cynewulf's *Elene*), borrowed from Latin *chrīstiānus,* from Greek *chrīstiānós,* from *Chrīstós* Christ. In the 1500's the entire word was respelled after the Latin and Greek forms. **—Christianity** *n.* Probably before 1300 *cristiante,* borrowed from Old French *crestienté,* from Late Latin *chrīstiānitātem* (nominative *chrīstiānitās*), from Latin *chrīstiānus*

Christian; for suffix see -ITY. —**Christianize** *v.* 1593, formed from English *Christian* + *ize,* perhaps influenced by Medieval Latin *christianizare.* —**Christian name** (about 1330)

Christmas *n.* 1100 *Cristesmessa,* literally, Christ's festival, Christmas Day, found in Old English *Cristes mæsse* (*Cristes,* genitive of *Crist* Christ and *mæsse* festival, feast day, MASS[2]. Unlike other words associated with Christ, *Christmas* in its various spellings seems to have been spelled with a capital *C* from its first recorded use. —**Christmastide,** *n.* (1626) —**Christmas tree** (1835, earlier reference to an illuminated tree as a Christmas decoration, 1789). —**Christmas Eve** (probably before 1300 *Cristenmesse even*).

chrom- a combining form, the form of *chromo-* before vowels, as in *chrominance* (the difference between colors of equal luminance or brightness).

chromatic (krōmat′ik) *adj.* of a musical scale, of color or colors. 1603, of or relating to a kind of four-tone chord in Greek music, borrowed (possibly by influence of earlier Middle and Old French *chromatique*) from Greek *chrōmatikós,* from *chrôma* (genitive *chrṓmatos*) color of the skin, complexion, character, style or form of music; for suffix see -IC. Greek *chrôma* is related to *chrṓs* skin, color of the skin, *chroïzein* touch a surface or the skin, from Indo-European **ghrō(u)-/ghrəu-* rub hard against (Pok.460). The adjective sense "of or relating to color or colors" is first recorded in English in 1831, from the noun meaning "science of color" (about 1790), probably from the obsolete sense "art of coloring" (1695, in works of Dryden), but recorded in Middle English *cromatik* in a figurative sense relating to color, 1464, from Medieval Latin *chromaticus*). —**chromatic scale** (before 1789, but the concept is alluded to in *chromatic tones,* 1680). —**chromatin** *n.* 1882, formed in English from Greek *chrôma* color + English suffix *-in*[2].

chrome *n.* chromium, especially as the source of pigments or as component of steel. 1800, borrowed from French *chrome,* from Greek *chrôma* color; see CHROMATIC. The term was coined in 1797 by the French chemist Louis Vauquelin and so called from the brilliant colors of its compounds. —**v.** 1876, from the noun.

chromium (krō′mēəm) *n.* hard metallic element. 1807, New Latin, formed from French *chrome* + New Latin *-ium* (suffix of chemical elements). The term was coined by Vauquelin after he established that *chrome* was a chemical element; see CHROME.

chromo- a combining form meaning color, as in *chromophotography, chromodynamics, chromosphere.* Adapted from Greek *chrôma* color; see CHROMATIC. The combining form of Greek *chrôma* was *chrōmato-,* based on the stem as seen in the genitive *chrṓmatos;* this appears in some borrowings, such as *chromatic,* and coinages such as *chromatography.*

chromosome (krō′məsōm) *n.* threadlike structure in a cell's nucleus that carries genes. 1889, borrowed from German *Chromosom,* from Greek *chrôma* color + *sôma* body, -SOME[3]. The borrowed term *Chromosom* was coined in 1888 by the German anatomist Wilhelm von Waldeyer, because the threadlike structures contain a substance that stains readily with basic dyes.

chron- a combining form, the form of *chrono-* before vowels, as in *chronic.*

chronic (kron′ik) *adj.* continuing a long time. Probably before 1425 *cronic,* in a translation of Chauliac's *Grande Chirurgie,* borrowed from Old French *cronique,* learned borrowing from Latin *chronicus,* from Greek *chronikós* pertaining to time, from *chrónos* time, of uncertain origin; for suffix see -IC. The spelling *chronic* is first found in 1655, after the Latin.

chronicle *n.* 1303 *kronikel,* (about 1330) *cronikle, cronicle, kronikel,* in Mannyng's *Handlyng Synne,* borrowed from Anglo-French *cronicle,* alteration of Old French *cronique,* learned borrowing from Latin *chronica.* The Latin form is abstracted from the Greek phrase *chronikà biblía* books of annals, in which *chronikà* is neuter plural of *chronikós* pertaining to time, CHRONIC. The ending *-icle* may have been introduced in the Anglo-French *cronicle* on the analogy of words like *article.* Middle English did have *cronyke,* which is etymologically a more regular formation, but it was in active use for only about 100 years, though it existed sporadically until the 1670's. —**v.** Probably about 1400 *croniclen,* from the noun. —**chronicler** *n.* Before 1420 *cronicler,* in Lydgate's *Troy Book,* formed from Middle English *cronicle* + *-er*[1].

chrono- a combining form meaning time, as in *chronology, chronometer* (before 1735). Borrowed from Greek *chrono-,* combining form of *chrónos* time.

chronology *n.* 1593 (but implied before 1572 in *chronologer* and perhaps influenced by Middle French *chronologie,* 1579), borrowed from New Latin *chronologia,* from Greek *chrónos* time; for suffix see -LOGY. —**chronological** *adj.* 1614, in Sir Walter Raleigh's *History of the World,* formed from English *chronology* + *-ic* and *-al*[1], perhaps by influence of Middle French *chronologique,* 1584.

chrysalis (kris′əlis) *n.* form of an insect when it is in a case. 1601, in Holland's translation of Pliny's *Natural History,* borrowed from Latin *chrȳsallis,* from Greek *chrȳsallís* golden pupa of a butterfly, from *chrȳsós* gold, from Phoenician; compare Hebrew *ḥārus,* Assyrian *ḫurāšu,* both meaning gold. The variant *chrysalid* appears in 1621, in Burton's *Anatomy of Melancholy,* perhaps borrowed from Middle French *chrysalide,* 1593.

chrysanthemum *n.* 1551, borrowed, perhaps by influence of Middle French *chrysanthemon,* from Latin *chrȳsanthemum,* from Greek *chrȳsánthemon,* literally, gold flower (*chrȳsós* gold, see CHRYSALIS + *ánthemon* flower, for *ánthos* flower; see ANTHER).

chrysolite (kris′əlīt) *n.* green or yellow gem. Before 1300 *crisolite,* in *Kyng Alisaunder,* borrowed from Old French *crisolite,* or directly from Medieval Latin *crisolitus,* from Latin *chrȳsolithus,* from Greek *chrȳsólithos* a yellow stone, probably topaz (*chrȳsós* gold, see CHRYSALIS + *líthos* stone, of unknown origin).

The Middle English spelling was refashioned with *ch* in the 1600's, after the Latin and Greek forms.

chub *n.* thick freshwater fish. About 1450 *chobe,* of unknown origin.

chubby *adj.* 1611, in Cotgrave's *Dictionary,* short and thick like a chub; later, round-faced, plump (1722), formed from English *chub* + *-y*[1]. —**chubbiness** *n.* 1850, in Stowe's *Uncle Tom's Cabin,* formed from English *chubby* + *-ness.*

chuck[1] *v.* toss, throw. 1593, variant form of earlier *chock* give a blow under the chin (1583), perhaps borrowed from Middle French *choquer* to jolt, SHOCK[1]. —**n.** 1611, perhaps borrowed from Middle French *choc* a knock or blow.

chuck² *n.* 1674, chunk of wood or meat, variant of CHOCK, and perhaps CHUNK; the meaning "a cut of shoulder meat" is first recorded in 1723; the meaning "device for holding a piece of work in a machine" is first recorded as *chock* (1703), later *chuck* (1807). **—chuck wagon** (1890, American English)

chuckle *v.* laugh to oneself. 1598, probably frequentative form of earlier Middle English *chukken* make a clucking noise (1390, in Chaucer's *Canterbury Tales*); for suffix see -LE³. Middle English *chukken* is also the source of *chuck,* v. (1598) laugh to oneself, which may even be the immediate source of *chuckle,* since both *chuck* and *chuckle* are first recorded in use by the same author (Florio). *Chuckle* is also reminiscent of Middle English *chokelen* make a clucking or warbling sound, and is related to it in meaning, if not in form. The Middle English forms are probably of imitative origin. **—n.** Before 1754, in Fielding's writings; from the verb.

chug *n.* loud burst of sound. 1866, imitative of a sound such as a thump or that from a steam engine. **—v.** make this sound. 1896, from the noun.

chum *n. Informal.* very close friend. 1684, roommate, in early British students' slang, sometimes suggested as a shortened form of *chamber-fellow* (1580) roommate. **—chummy** *adj.* 1884, formed from English *chum* + *-y*¹.

chunk *n.* lump. 1691, possibly nasalized variant of CHUCK² cut of meat. **—chunky** *adj.* stocky. 1751, American English, formed from English *chunk* + *-y*¹.

church *n.* Probably before 1200 *chirche,* in Layamon's *Chronicle of Britain,* developed from Old English *cirice* public place of worship, Christians collectively (about 750, in Cynewulf), an early borrowing (like Old Frisian *zerke, ziurke* church, Old Saxon *kirika,* and Old High German *kirihha,* whence modern German *Kirche*) from Greek *kȳriakòn dôma* the Lord's house, from *kȳ́rios* master, from *kȳ́ros* power; cognate with Sanskrit *śū́ra-s* hero, from Indo-European **k̑ewə-/k̑ū-* to swell, become strong (Pok.592). The phonetic spelling *church* for Middle English *chirche* begins to appear at the end of the 1200's but is only rarely seen; it began to appear with greater frequency after 1450 and became the established spelling in the 1500's.

The Slavic forms of this word, such as Old Slavic *crŭky,* Russian *tserkov',* and Bulgarian *cherkva,* were probably borrowed from Germanic.
—churchgoer *n.* (1687, implied in earlier *churchgoing,* probably before 1200). **—churchman** *n.* (1259) **—churchwarden** *n.* (1443, earlier *churchward* sacristan, before 1121) **—churchyard** *n.* (1137)

churl (chėrl) *n.* rude, surly person. Probably about 1200 *cherl,* in Layamon's *Chronicle of Britain,* developed from Old English *ceorl* man, husband (before 800); later, freeman of the lowest rank (before 1000). Old English *ceorl* is cognate with Old Frisian *zerl* man, fellow, Middle Low German *kerle* (modern German *Kerl*), Old High German *karal* man, husband, lover, (modern German *Karl,* proper name), and Old Icelandic *karl* man, old man, from Proto-Germanic **kerlaz/karlaz.* Outside Germanic the word is cognate with Sanskrit *járant-* old, and Greek *gérōn* old man, from Indo-European **ĝer-, ĝor-/ĝerə-* grow up, ripen, age (Pok.390).

The current disparaging sense appeared in Middle English about 1250. The predominant spelling in Middle English was *cherl,* and while *churl* appeared before 1400, it did not become the established form before the 1500's.
—churlish *adj.* Before 1382, in the Wycliffe Bible, of or pertaining to a churl or freeman of the lowest rank, developed from Old English *cierlisc, ceorlisc* (before 1000 *ceorl* churl + *-isc* -ish¹).

churn *n.* About 1350 *chirne;* earlier, *kirne* (1339), developed from Old English *cyrin* (about 1000); cognate with Middle Low German *kerne, kirne* churn, Middle Dutch *kerne* (modern Dutch *karnen*), and Old Icelandic *kirna, kjarni,* from Proto-Germanic **kernjōn,* of unknown origin. The spelling *churn* developed in Middle English but did not become the established form until the 1500's. **—v.** About 1440 *chyrnen,* in *Promptorium Parvulorum,* from the noun.

chute¹ *n.* inclined trough, tube, etc., for dropping things down. 1804, American English, rapid fall or descent of water, borrowing of French *chute, cheüte* fall, and replacing earlier *shoot* (before 1613); also the source of variant *shute* (1790). The French form came into American English through contact with early French-speaking explorers and settlers in North America, as evidenced in the early diary entry (1793) with the spelling "*chute* a Blondeau." French *chute, cheüte* are alterations of Old French *cheoite* fall, influenced in form by *chu* (from Vulgar Latin **cadūtum),* past participle of *cheoir* to fall, from Vulgar Latin **cadēre.* Old French *cheoite* derives from Gallo-Romance **cadēcta,* feminine past participle of **cadēre* to fall, from Latin *cadere;* see CADENCE.

chute² *n.* parachute. 1920, shortened from PARACHUTE.

chutney *n.* spicy sauce or relish. 1813, borrowed from Hindi *chaṭnī.*

chutzpah (hůts′pə) *n. Slang.* brazen audacity, nerve. 1892 *chutzbah,* in Israel Zangwill's *Children of the Ghetto,* borrowed from Yiddish *khutspe* impudence, gall, from Hebrew *ḥutspāh.*

chyle (kīl) *n.* milky liquid of digested fat and lymph. 1541, borrowed from Middle French *chyle,* from Late Latin *chȳlus,* from Greek *chȳlós* (earlier **chyslós*) juice, chyle, from the stem of *cheîn* to pour, from Indo-European **ĝheu-/ĝhu-* (Pok.447). Compare CHYME.

chyme (kīm) *n.* Probably before 1425, any of various bodily fluids, in a translation of Chauliac's *Grande Chirurgie;* later, semi-liquid mass of food in the stomach (1681, earlier *chymus,* 1607, borrowed directly from Latin). The form and meaning of *chyme,* as we know it today, were borrowed from Middle French *chyme,* from Latin *chȳmus,* from Greek *chȳmós* (earlier **chysmós*) juice, from the stem of *cheîn* to pour; differentiated by the Greek physician Galen (130-200 A.D.) from CHYLE as being natural (i.e., semi-digested) juice.

ciao (chou) *interj.* greetings, good-by. 1957, borrowing of Italian *ciao,* from Northern Italian dialect *ciau, ciaou.* The dialectal form is an alteration of Italian *schiavo* slave (originally in the salutation *sono vostro schiavo* I am your slave), from Medieval Latin *Sclavus Slav, sclavus* SLAVE. Compare the German greeting *Servus,* literally, servant, slave, from Latin *servus.*

ciborium (səbôr′ēəm) *n.* vessel holding the consecrated Eucharist. 1651, in John Evelyn's *Diary,* borrowed from the special use in Medieval Latin of earlier Latin *cibōrium* cup, from Greek *kibṓrion* cup, originally, cup-shaped seed vessel of the Egyptian water lily; probably of Egyptian origin.

cicada (səkā′də) *n.* large insect with transparent wings. Before 1387, in Trevisa's translation of Higden's *Polychronicon,* borrowed from Latin *cicāda* tree cricket, probably derived from a word in a Mediterranean language.

-cide[1] a combining form meaning killer, and **-cide**[2] a combining form meaning (the act of) killing; often the same words can be cited for the two derivations and the two meanings (*homicide, fratricide,* and so on), but occasional examples such as *insecticide* illustrate only the meaning of killer. The forms were the same in Old French and Middle French *(-cide)* when words containing them were borrowed into Middle English. French *-cide* meaning "killer" is a borrowing of Latin *-cīda* and French *-cide* meaning "the killing" from Latin *-cīdium,* in each word with adjustments to French form. Each of the Latin forms is derived from *-cīdere,* the usual form in compounds of *caedere* to cut, kill; see EXCISE[2] to cut.

cider *n.* fermented apple juice. Probably about 1280 *sider,* before 1325 *cidar,* before 1400 *cidre* strong drink, borrowed from Old French *sidre* pear or apple cider (earlier *cisdre*), from Late Latin *sīcera,* from Greek *síkera,* from Semitic; compare Hebrew *shēkhār* intoxicating drink, from *shākhar* he got drunk. The Late Latin and Greek words were used in the Vulgate and the Septuagint to translate the Hebrew word.

The Old Spanish *sizra* (modern Spanish *sidra*) is probably representative of a general shift in the spelling, originally borrowed from Latin *sīcera,* that took place in other Romance languages. If the intermediate link is represented by *sizra (sitsra, sidzra),* then the change parallels French *ladre* leprous, from *Lazarus.*

cigar *n.* 1730, borrowed from Spanish *cigarro,* of uncertain origin; perhaps derived from Spanish *cigarra* grasshopper (by comparison with the dark cylindrical shape of this insect), ultimately from Latin *cicāda* CICADA; or possibly from Mayan *sī'c* tobacco, (and by extension) cigar, or its derivative *sicar* to perfume, smoke.

cigarette *n.* 1835, American English, borrowed from French *cigarette,* diminutive form of *cigare,* from Spanish *cigarro* CIGAR.

cilia (sil′ēə) *n.pl.* hairlike projections. 1794, New Latin *cilia,* plural of earlier *cilium* eyelid (1715), from Latin *cilium* eyelid, cover, probably a back formation from *supercilium* eyebrow, ridge; see SUPERCILIOUS.

cinch *n.* saddle girth. 1859 *sinche,* American English, replacing earlier English *surcingle, cingle,* borrowed from Spanish *cincha* girth, from Latin *cīnctus* (genitive *cīnctūs*) and *cingula* saddle-girth, girdle, from *cingere* to bind, gird; see CINCTURE. The sense "a sure or easy thing; dead certainty" is first recorded in 1898, as a further extension of the figurative use "a strong or sure hold" (1888). **—v.** 1866, in a speech by Mark Twain, American English, fix securely with a cinch, from the noun. The figurative sense "to make sure of (something)" was first recorded as college slang in 1900.

cinchona (sinkō′nə) *n.* South American tree whose bark yields quinine and other alkaloids. 1800, earlier *cinquona* (1742), New Latin *Cinchona* genus name of the tree (coined in 1742 by Linnaeus after the Countess of *Chinchón,* wife of the Spanish viceroy of Peru, who was cured of a fever by powdered cinchona bark, and was instrumental in introducing the drug in Europe).

cincture (singk′chər) *n.* belt, girdle. 1587, process of girding, specifically in a ceremony in which a sword and belt is put on; borrowed from Latin *cīnctūra* girdle, from *cīnctus,* past participle of *cingere* to bind, gird; cognate with Greek *kinklís* lattice, Lithuanian *kinkýti* to harness (horses), and Sanskrit *káñcate* (he) binds, from Indo-European **kenk-* (Pok.565).

cinder *n.* 1530, small bits of coal or wood left from burning, in Palsgrave's *Lesclarcissement;* earlier, *cyndre* ashes (about 1400, in Sir John Maundeville's *Travels*), slag of metal, dross, variant of *synder* (before 1398, in Trevisa's translation of Bartholomew's *De Proprietatibus Rerum*), and *Synderhelle* a place name (1239); developed from Old English *sinder* (before 800). Old English *sinder* is cognate with Old Saxon *sinder* slag, dross, Old High German *sintar* (modern German *Sinter*), Old Icelandic *sindr,* from Proto-Germanic **sindran,* and Old Slavic *sędra* hardened fluid, stalactite, from Indo-European *sendhro-m, *sendhrā* (Pok.906). The original Middle English spelling *synder* was altered to *cyndre* by influence of Old French *cendre* ashes, from Latin *cinerem,* accusative of *cinis;* see INCINERATE.

cinema *n.* motion picture, motion-picture theater. 1899 *cinéma* a motion-picture projector, a borrowing of French *cinéma,* shortened form of *cinématographe* motion-picture projector and camera; see CINEMATOGRAPHY. The Anglicized form *cinema* is first recorded in 1909, and the senses of motion-picture theater (1913), and a motion picture (1922). **—cinematic** *adj.* 1927, an Anglicized form of French *cinématique* (1917, though used earlier by Ampère, in studies of motion, 1834); see CINEMATOGRAPHY.

cinematography *n.* 1897, apparently derived from *cinematograph* + *-y*[3] (on analogy of *photograph, photography*). French *cinématographie* is first recorded in 1898. The now archaic English *cinematograph* motion-picture projector, is first recorded in 1896, as a borrowing of French *cinématographe* (coined by its French inventors, A. and L. Lumière), from Greek *kínēma* (genitive *kīnḗmatos*) motion + French *-graphe* -graph. Greek *kínēma* derives from *kīneîn* to move, which is related to earlier *kíō* I move, go, cognate with Latin *ciēre* to stir up, rouse, from Indo-European **kī-/kiy-* (Pok.538).

cinerary *adj.* of or for ashes (of a cremated body). 1750, borrowed from Latin *cinerārius,* from *cineris,* genitive of *cinis* ashes, see INCINERATE; for suffix see -ARY.

cinnabar (sin′əbär) *n.* reddish mineral; mercuric sulfide. Probably 1440 *cynabare,* in a translation of Palladius' *De Re Rustica;* borrowed from Latin *cinnabaris,* from Greek *kinnábari,* of uncertain origin (compare Persian *šängärf* cinnabar, Arabic *zinjafr, zunjufr,* and Turkish *zinjifre*). An earlier form *cynoper* (1382, in the Wycliffe Bible) and *sinopre* are apparently not the same word as *cinnabar.*

cinnamon *n.* About 1390 *cynamome,* in Chaucer's *Canterbury Tales,* borrowed from Old French *cinnamome,* from Latin *cinnamōmum, cinnamon,* from Greek *kinnámōmon, kínnamon,* from Phoenician (compare Hebrew *qinnāmōn* cinnamon).

cinquefoil (singk′foil′) *n.* plant with leaves divided into five parts. Probably before 1300 *cynkfoil,* borrowed from Old French *cincfoille,* from Latin *quīnquefolium* (formed from *quīnque* FIVE + *folium* leaf, BLADE). The

Latin word was a loan translation of Greek *pentáphyllon* (*pénte* FIVE + *phýllon* leaf, BLADE).

cipher *n.* 1399 *siphre* zero, borrowed from Middle French *cifre,* from Medieval Latin *cifra, ciphra,* from Arabic *ṣifr* empty, null, zero, a loan translation of Sanskrit *śūnyá-s* empty. Doublet of ZERO. The sense "secret writing, cryptographic code" is first recorded in English in 1528, about the time when *cipher* was extended to mean any of the numerals, not just zero, since early cryptography made much use of numerals ("ciphers") as substitutes for letters. **—v.** 1530, in Palsgrave's *Lesclarcissement,* from the noun.

circa *adv., prep.* about, approximately. 1861, borrowed from Latin *circā,* adv., around, from *circum* round about; see CIRCUM-. Latin *circā* was patterned on *suprā* above, *extrā* outside, *intrā* within, and similar adverbs.

circadian *adj.* functioning or recurring in 24-hour cycles. 1959, formed in English from Latin *circā* around + *diēs* day + English *-an.*

circle *n.* About 1300 *cercle* figure of a circle drawn on a surface, borrowed from Old French *cercle,* from Latin *circulus,* diminutive form of *circus* circle, ring, probably from Greek *kírkos,* an altered form of earlier *kríkos* ring, perhaps changed from **kikro-s,* reduplicated form of the Indo-European root **ker-* turn, bend (Pok.935). Old English (about 1000) *circul* astronomical sphere or orbit, also borrowed from Latin *circulus,* was a separate borrowing and, while recorded in the *Anglo-Saxon Chronicle* as late as 1104, did not influence the formation or later borrowing from Old French. The modern spelling *circle* was gradually established in the 1500's, though the adjective *circuler* is recorded about 1370 and appears in that spelling thereafter. **—v.** About 1385 *cerclen,* in Chaucer's *Troilus and Criseyde,* to surround, encircle, from the noun. **—circlet** *n.* About 1400, borrowed from Middle French *cerclet;* for suffix see -ET.

circuit *n.* Before 1382 *circuyt,* in the Wycliffe Bible, borrowed from Old French *circuit,* from Latin *circuitus* (genitive *circuitūs*) a going around, from stem of *circuīre, circumīre* go around (*circum* around + *īre* to go; see EXIT). The sense "path of an electric current" is first recorded in 1746. **—v.** About 1410, from the noun. **—circuit breaker** (1872) **—circuitous** *adj.* 1664, borrowed from Medieval Latin *circuitōsus,* from Latin *circuitus* (genitive *circuitūs*) a going around; for suffix see -OUS. **—circuit rider** 1837, a formation based on *to ride the circuit* (1718). **—circuitry** *n.* 1946, formed from English *circuit* + *-ry.*

circular *adj.* 1370 *circuler,* in Chaucer's translation of Boethius' *De Consolatione Philosophiae;* borrowed from Anglo-French *circuler,* Old French *circulier,* learned borrowing from Latin *circulāris,* from *circulus* CIRCLE; for suffix see -AR. The spelling *circular* is first recorded in the late 1500's in imitation of Latin *circulāris,* probably influenced by new English formations, such as *circularity* that were formed directly as if Latin derivatives. **—n.** 1560 *circuler* a circular figure, from the adjective. The sense of notice circulated or distributed is first recorded in 1818. **—circularity** *n.* 1582, formed from English *circular* + *-ity.* **—circularize** *v.* 1799, in correspondence of Southey, formed from English *circular* + *-ize.*

circulate *v.* 1545, from earlier *circulate,* past participle (1471); borrowed from Latin *circulātus,* past participle of *circulāre* make circular, encircle, from *circulus* CIRCLE. **—circulation** *n.* 1440 *circulacion,* borrowed from Middle French *circulation,* or directly from Latin *circulātiōnem* (nominative *circulātiō*), from *circulāre* circulate; for suffix see -TION. **—circulatory** *adj.* 1605 (perhaps 1597), borrowed perhaps from French *circulatoire,* or directly from Latin *circulātōrius* having to do something that circulates, from *circulātor* one who or that which circulates, from *circulāre.*

circum- a prefix meaning around, on all sides, as in *circumpolar* = *around the pole.* Many words came into English with the Latin prefix, such as *circumnavigate,* which was later abstracted as if an English formation. Borrowed from Latin *circum* around, about, originally accusative of *circus* circle.

circumcise *v.* About 1250, in *The Story of Genesis and Exodus,* borrowed from Latin *circumcīsus,* past participle of *circumcīdere,* literally, cut around (*circum-* around + *caedere* cut; see EXCISE[2]). **—circumcision** *n.* Probably before 1200, borrowed from Latin *circumcīsiōnem* (nominative *circumcīsiō*), from *circumcīs-,* stem of *circumcīdere;* for suffix see -ION.

circumference *n.* Before 1393, in Gower's *Confessio Amantis,* borrowed (possibly by influence of Old French *circonference*), from Latin *circumferentia,* from *circumferēns* (genitive *circumferentis*), present participle of *circumferre* to carry around (*circum-* around + *ferre* to carry, BEAR[2]).

circumflex *n.* **circumflex accent**. accent mark placed over a vowel, as in â, î, ê. Before 1577 as an adjective, borrowed from Latin *circumflexus* bent around, past participle of *circumflectere* (*circum-* around + *flectere* to bend, FLEX). In reference to the accent mark, the word is a loan translation from Greek *perispṓmenos* drawn around (in allusion to its shape); a term used by the grammarian Dionysius of Halicarnassus to designate the rising and falling tone on certain Greek vowels (*perí* around + *spân* to draw, pull).

circumlocution *n.* Before 1401, borrowed from Latin *circumlocūtiōnem* (*circum-* around + *locūtiōnem,* nominative *locūtiō* a speaking, from stem of *loquī* speak, of uncertain origin); for suffix see -TION. Latin *circumlocūtiō* was a loan translation of Greek *periphrasis* PERIPHRASIS. The adoption of the term in English may have been influenced by Old French *circonlocution.*

circumnavigate *v.* 1634, borrowed from Latin *circumnāvigāre* to sail around; for suffix see -ATE[1]. **—circumnavigator** *n.* 1770, formed from English *circumnavigate* + *-or*[2].

circumscribe *v.* About 1385, in Chaucer's *Troilus and Criseyde,* borrowed from Latin *circumscrībere* to draw a line around, limit, confine (*circum-* around + *scrībere* write; see SCRIBE). **—circumscribed** *adj.* 1571, from the verb.

circumspect *adj.* Before 1420, in Lydgate's *Troy Book,* borrowed from Latin *circumspectus,* past participle of *circumspicere* look around, take heed (*circum-* around + *specere* to look; see SPY). **—circumspection** *n.* Before 1387, in Trevisa's translation of Higden's *Polychronicon,* borrowed from Latin *circumspectiōnem* (nominative *circumspectiō*), from *circumspicere* look around; for suffix see -TION. The adoption of these words in English may have been influenced by Old French *circonspect* and *circonspection.*

circumstance *n.* Probably before 1200, in *Ancrene*

Riwle, borrowed from Latin *circumstantia* surrounding condition, from *circumstāns* (genitive *circumstantis*), present participle of *circumstāre* stand around (*circum-* around + *stāre* to stand). **—circumstantial** *adj.* 1600, in Shakespeare's *As You Like It,* formed in English from Latin *circumstantia* + English *-al*[1]. **—circumstantial evidence** (1736)

circumvent *v.* About 1450, borrowed from Latin *circumventus,* past participle of *circumvenīre* surround, get around, deceive (*circum-* around + *venīre* come). The sense "get the better of" is first recorded before 1564. **—circumvention** *n.* 1424, borrowed from Latin *circumventiōnem* (nominative *circumventiō*), from *circumvent-,* stem of *circumvenīre* circumvent; for suffix see -TION.

circus *n.* About 1380, in Chaucer's translation of Boethius' *De Consolatione Philosophiae,* probably in reference to the Circus Maximus in ancient Rome; a borrowing of Latin *circus,* literally, ring; see CIRCLE. The meaning of a traveling show is first attested in 1791.

cirrhosis (sərō′sis) *n.* diseased condition of the liver. 1839-47, in an edition of an anatomy text, New Latin *cirrhosis* from Greek *kirrhós* orange-yellow (of uncertain origin); for suffix see -OSIS. The name was coined by the French physician Laënnec, because of the yellowish appearances of the diseased liver.

cirrus (sir′əs) *n. Meteorology.* thin, fleecy cloud. 1803; earlier tendril of a plant, New Latin *cirrus,* Latin *cirrus* curl, fringe, of uncertain origin. The spelling *cirrus* gradually replaced the earlier *cirrous* (1681).

cis- a prefix meaning on the near side of, on this side of, as in *cislunar, cisalpine,* used chiefly to form scientific terms. Borrowed from Latin *cis-,* from the preposition *cis* on this side of, related to *citrā,* adv., on this side, cognate with Old English *hider* hither and *him* him, from Indo-European **k̂i-* (Pok.609).

cislunar (sislü′nər) *adj.* of the space between earth and moon. 1867, formed from English *cis-* on this side + *lunar* of the moon.

cistern *n.* tank for storing water. About 1250, borrowed from Old French *cisterne,* from Latin *cisterna* underground reservoir, from *cista* box, CHEST.

citadel *n.* fortress. Before 1586, borrowed from Middle French *citadelle,* from Italian *cittadella* (diminutive form of *cittade* city, later *città*) from Latin *cīvitātem;* see CITY.

cite *v.* quote, refer to. 1438 *citen* to summon, in *Proceedings of the Privy Council,* borrowed from Old French *citer,* learned borrowing from Latin *citāre* move, excite, summon, a frequentative form of *ciēre* set in motion, call. The Latin *ciēre* is cognate with Greek *kíō* I go, move, travel, *kīneîn* set in motion, move, *seúein* set in violent motion, and Sanskrit *cyávate* he moves, goes forth, from Indo-European **kī-/kiy-/ky-eu-* (Pok.538).

The Middle English sense "summon, call" was extended by 1535 to "quote or refer to as an authority." **—citation** *n.* About 1300, a summons, written notice to appear; borrowed through Old French *citation* or, as a learned borrowing, directly from Latin *citātiōnem* (nominative *citātiō*), from *citāre* to summon; for suffix see -TION. The sense "quotation" appeared in English in 1548.

cithara (sith′ərə) *n.* ancient musical instrument somewhat like a lyre. Before 1789, borrowed from Latin *cithara,* from Greek *kithárā* lyrelike instrument with triangular box and 7 to 11 strings. Doublet of GUITAR and ZITHER.

An earlier form *cither* (1606) is an Anglicized form of Latin *cithara,* and is also applied to the *cithern,* variant of *cittern,* and to *zither* and *guitar.*

cithern or **cittern** *n.* musical instrument similar to the guitar. 1566 *cithren,* 1575 *cittern,* alteration (possibly influenced by *gittern,* about 1350) of Latin *cithara* CITHARA.

citizen *n.* Probably before 1300 *citisein* inhabitant of a city, in *Arthour and Merlin;* borrowed from Anglo-French *citesein, citezein,* alteration of Old French *citeain, citeien* (*cite* CITY + *-ien* -ian). The spelling with *z,* probably not influenced by later *denizen* (1419), was more likely due to Anglo-French *citezein,* a spelling influenced by words such as Old French *denzein* interior, *sozain* superior, whose suffix may have been misunderstood as *-zain* rather than *-ain,* though actually these forms derive from *denz* (*dans* within) and *soz* (from Latin *sūrsum* upwards) respectively.

The extended sense "inhabitant of a country" appeared in Middle English about 1380, in Chaucer's translation of Boethius' *De Consolatione Philosophiae.* **—citizenry** *n.* 1819, formed from English *citizen* + *-ry.* **—citizenship** *n.* 1611, in Cotgrave's *Dictionary,* formed from English *citizen* + *-ship.*

citron *n.* lemonlike fruit. 1391, implied in *citronade* candied citron, also later *citrine* (probably about 1425), and *citron* (1526); borrowed from Old French *citron,* possibly from Old Provençal *citron,* alteration (influenced by *limon* LEMON) of Latin *citrus* CITRUS. Middle English *citrine* may have been a separate borrowing from Middle French *citrin,* probably from Medieval Latin **citrina,* from Latin *citrus,* but the citations in the Middle English Dictionary refer to the citron. **—citric** *adj.* 1800, formed in English from Latin *citr(us)* + English suffix -IC.

citronella (sitrənel′ə) *n.* fragrant Asian grass, oil from this grass. 1858, New Latin *citronella,* and French *citronnelle* citronella, lemon liquor, from *citron;* so called from its citronlike smell.

citrus *n.* tree bearing lemons, limes, oranges, or similar fruit. 1882, borrowed from New Latin *Citrus* the genus name, from Latin *citrus* a lemon or citron, citron tree; of uncertain origin (compare Greek *kítron* citron and *kédros* CEDAR).

cittern *n.* See CITHERN.

city *n.* Probably before 1200 *cite* town, borough, especially a walled town or city and its government; also a cathedral town with its bishopric, in *Ancrene Riwle;* borrowed from Old French *cité,* earlier *citet,* from Latin *cīvitātem* (nominative *cīvitās*) condition of a citizen, citizenship, citizenry, the state, city, from *cīvis* citizen; for suffix see -TY[2]. Latin *cīvis* is cognate with Sanskrit *śivá-s* trusty, worthy, and Old English *hīwen* household, family, from Indo-European *k̂ei-uo-,* root **k̂ei-* lie down (Pok. 539); related to HOME.**—citified** *adj.* 1828, American English, formed from English *city* + *-fied,* past participial form of *-fy,* as if from the later formation *citify* (1865). **—cityward** *adv., adj.* Probably about 1375, formed from Middle English *cite* + *-ward.*

civet (siv′it) *n.* cat producing a secretion used in making perfume; the secretion. 1532, borrowed from French *civette,* from Italian *zibetto,* from Medieval Latin *zibe-*

thum, Medieval Greek *zapétion,* from Arabic *zabād* musk. **—civet cat** (1607)

civic *adj.* 1542, borrowed from Latin *cīvicus* of or for a citizen (chiefly in the phrase *corōna cīvica* civic crown or garland, awarded to one who saved the life of a fellow citizen in war), from *cīvis* citizen, see CITY; for suffix see -IC.

It is unlikely that Middle French *civique* (1504) was a part of the borrowing process, as the first recorded use in English is in Udall's translation of Erasmus' *Apothegms* written in Latin. The earliest use in English referred to the civic crown or garland. The meaning "of or having to do with a citizen or citizens" is first recorded in 1790, in Burke's works on the French Revolution.

—civics *n.pl.* 1886, American English, formed from English *civic* + *s,* on analogy with *politics.*

civil *adj.* Before 1387, in Trevisa's translation of Higden's *Polychronicon;* borrowed through Old French *civil,* and directly as a learned borrowing from Latin *cīvīlis* of or proper to a citizen, relating to private rights, state law, and public life, urbane in manner, from *cīvis* citizen; see CITY. Though distinctions of meaning were already known in Latin, the meaning "polite" is not recorded in English before 1606, "not barbarous, civilized" before 1553, and the distinction between military and ecclesiastical function and that of the ordinary citizen was not recorded as drawn before 1592. **—civil defense** (1939) **—civil law** (about 1380) **—civil liberty** (1788) **—civil rights** (1721) **—civil servant** (1800) **—civil service** (about 1785) **—civil war** (probably before 1439) **—civilian** *n.* Before 1397, judge or authority on civil law, in *Prologue* to the Wycliffe Bible; borrowed from Old French *civilien* of the civil law, from *civil* civil; for suffix see -IAN. The meaning "nonmilitary person" is first recorded in 1829, formed from English *civil* + *-ian.* —*adj.* 1645, in Milton's writings, from the noun. **—civility** *n.* About 1384, in the Wycliffe Bible, borrowed from Old French *civilité,* from Latin *cīvīlitātem* (nominative *cīvīlitās*) courteousness, politeness, from *cīvīlis;* for suffix see -ITY.

civilize *v.* make civil, refine, polish. 1601, apparently borrowed from French *civiliser, civilizer,* from Old French *civil* civil; for suffix see -IZE. It is possible that the Old French word was based upon Medieval Latin **civilizare* to consider a criminal action as a civil matter. **—civilization** *n.* 1704, law which makes a criminal process civil, formed from English *civilize* + *-ation.* The sense "civilized condition or state" is first recorded in 1772, in Boswell's *The Life of Samuel Johnson,* in a conversation about entering the meaning in Johnson's fourth edition of the *Dictionary.* The meaning was probably known to Johnson in this sense from the French *civilisation* used by Mirabeau in 1756.

clabber *n.* thick, sour milk. 1634, borrowed from Gaelic *clabar* mud; sometimes short for *bainne clabair,* from *bainne* milk, and *clabair,* genitive of *clabar* mud.

clack *v.* make a short, sharp sound. Before 1250 *clacken,* in *The Owl and the Nightingale,* probably of imitative origin like Dutch *klakken* to clack, crack, Old High German *kleken* to crack, and Old Icelandic *klaka* to twitter, chatter (compare CLUCK). **—n.** Before 1450, from the verb.

clad *adj.* clothed. About 1250, in *The Story of Genesis and Exodus,* developed from Old English *geclǣthd* (about 950, in *Lindisfarne Gospels*), past participle of *clǣthan* to clothe, from *clāth* CLOTH.

claim *n.* assertion to a right. Before 1325, in *Cursor Mundi,* borrowed from Old French *claime,* from *clamer* to call, appeal, claim, from Latin *clāmāre* cry out, call, proclaim; see LOW², v. **—v.** Probably about 1300 *cleimen* lay claim to; later *claymen* (before 1338); borrowed from Old French *claim-,* accented stem of *clamer,* from Latin *clāmāre* proclaim. **—claimant** *n.* 1747, formed from English *claim* + *-ant.*

clairvoyant (klãrvoi'ənt) *adj.* able to see things that are out of sight. 1850; earlier, having insight (1671); borrowing of French *clairvoyant,* clear-sighted, literally, clear-seeing (*clair* clear, from Latin *clārus* CLEAR + *voyant,* present participle of *voir* to see, from Latin *vidēre;* see WIT² know). **—n.** clairvoyant person. 1851; earlier, a clear-sighted person (1794); borrowing of French *clairvoyant,* n., from French *clairvoyant,* adj. **—clairvoyance** *n.* 1847, borrowing of French *clairvoyance,* from *clairvoyant,* adj.

clam *n.* 1500, in the compound *clam-shell,* apparently special use of earlier *clam* pincers, vise, clamp (1399), developed from Old English (971) *clamm* fetter, bond, chain. The Old English is cognate with Old High German *klamma* cramp, fetter, constriction (modern German *Klamm*), Lithuanian *glomóti* to embrace, Old Irish *glomar* fence, Latin *glomus* (genitive *glomeris*), originally **glemos,* ball of yarn; from Indo-European **glem-,* also **glembh-/glombh-* (Pok.360), possibly suggesting a Proto-Germanic form **klam-, *klamm-,* or **klamb-* to press or squeeze together (Pok.360). **—v.** dig for clams. 1636, American English, from the noun. The meaning "be silent" in the idiom *clam up* is American English (1916), from the idea of closing the mouth like a clamshell, but a similar use is found in Middle English *clam!* be silent (probably about 1350). **—clambake** *n.* (1835) **—clam chowder** (1836)

clamber *v.* climb, scramble. About 1375 *clambren,* possibly a frequentative form of *climben* to CLIMB, by way of its Middle English preterit *clamb.*

clammy *adj.* moist and sticky, damp. Before 1398, in Trevisa's translation of Bartholomew's *De Proprietatibus Rerum,* from earlier *clam* viscous, sticky, muddy (about 1340); developed from Old English *clām* mud, sticky clay, from Indo-European **gloi-mo-s* (Pok. 364); (compare Flemish *klammig,* Low German *klamig* sticky, damp; for suffix see -Y¹. Compare also Old English *clǣg* CLAY.

clamor *n.* uproar. About 1385 *clamour,* in Chaucer's *Canterbury Tales,* borrowed from Old French *clamour,* from Latin *clāmor* a shout, from *clāmāre* cry out; see LOW² (of cattle); for suffix see -OR¹. **—v.** About 1385, from the noun. **—clamorous** *adj.* 1402, borrowed, probably by influence of Middle French *clamoreux,* from Medieval Latin *clamorosus,* from Latin *clāmor;* for suffix see -OUS.

clamp *n.* brace, band, or clasp. 1402, earlier in compound *clampchute* (1304), probably borrowed from Middle Dutch *clampe* (modern Dutch *klamp*); cognate with Middle Low German *klampe* clasp, hook, Old High German *klampfer* clip, clamp (from Indo-European **glemb-/glomb-* Pok. 360), and Old English *clamm* fetter; see CLAM. —v. 1677, from the noun.

clan *n.* tribe. About 1425 (Scottish), from Gaelic *clann* family, stock, offspring, a borrowing (like Old Irish *cland, clann* stock, offspring, and Welsh *plant* children) from Latin *planta* sprout, root, scion, see PLANT. The Gaelic branch (Goidelic) of the Celtic languages having no initial *p* regularly substituted *k* or *c* for Latin *p*. **—clannish** *adj.* 1776, formed from English *clan* + *-ish.* **—clansman** *n.* 1810, in Scott's *The Lady of the Lake,* formed from English *clan's,* genitive of *clan* + *man.*

clandestine (klandes'tən) *adj.* secret, concealed. 1566, borrowed, perhaps by influence of earlier French *clandestin* (about 1355), from Latin *clandestīnus* secret, hidden, from *clam* secretly, related to *cēlāre* to hide; see CELL.

Latin *clandestīnus* was apparently formed from **clam-de* (compare *unde* from where), on the model of *intestīnus* internal; see INTESTINE.

clang *v.* make a loud ringing sound. 1576, apparently borrowed from Latin *clangere* resound, ring, clang; cognate with Greek *klangḗ* sharp sound, din, *klázein* make a sharp sound, scream, bark, Old Icelandic *hlakka* to shout, scream, and Lithuanian *klagė́ti* to cackle, from Indo-European **klang-*, **klag-* (Pok.599). It is also possible that *clang* is an independent imitative formation related to *clank* (compare modern German *Klang*). **—n.** loud ringing sound. 1596, in Shakespeare's *Taming of the Shrew,* probably from the verb. **—clangor** *n.* continuous clanging. 1593, in Shakespeare's *3 Henry VI,* borrowed from Latin *clangor* sound, clang, noise, from *clangere* to clang; for suffix see -OR¹. **—clangorous** *adj.* 1712, formed from English *clangor* + *-ous,* possibly on the model of Medieval Latin *clangorosus.*

clank *n.* sharp, harsh sound. 1656, possibly borrowed from Dutch *klank* sound, ring, from Middle Dutch *clank;* cognate with Middle Low German *klank,* Old High German *klanc* (modern German *Klang*), and perhaps Latin *clangor.* **—v.** make a sharp, harsh sound. 1656, apparently from the noun. But *clank,* v., in the sense of "put down resoundingly" is found once before 1614, suggesting an imitative origin such as that of *clink*¹, v. and possibly *clang,* v.

clap *v.* About 1300 *clappen,* in *Havelok the Dane,* perhaps earlier, about 1150, developed from Old English *clæppan, clappian* to beat, throb, probably of imitative origin like Old Frisian *klapa* to beat, Middle Low German *klappen* to chatter, Old High German *klaphōn* to beat, and Old Saxon *klapunga* clatter. Middle English *clappen* may also be borrowed from Old Icelandic *klappa* to beat, at least in some meanings which are common to the modern Scandinavian sense (Danish and Norwegian *klappe,* Swedish *klappa*). **—n.** Probably before 1200 *cleappe, claippe* thing that makes a clapping noise, stroke or blow, loud talking, in *Ancrene Riwle,* from the verb; the form is not found in Old English. **—clapboard** *n.* About 1520, partial loan translation replacing earlier *clapholt* (1378) with English *board* for Low German *holt* wood. **—clapper** *n.* About 1280, developed from Old English *clipur,* by influence of Middle English *clappen,* v. **—claptrap** *n.* 1727-31, in an edition of Bailey's *Dictionary,* formed from English *clap* + *trap,* in its earliest sense of an actor's stage device to get applause.

claret (klar'ət) *n.* red wine of Bordeaux. About 1440, in *Promptorium Parvulorum,* light-colored yellow or reddish wine (as opposed to red or white wine); earlier, wine sweetened and spiced (before 1398), borrowed from Middle French *claret* in the phrase *vin claret* light-colored wine (*vin* wine, and *claret* light-colored, in Old French also a noun meaning "wine mixed with honey and spices," diminutive of Old French *cler* CLEAR). About 1600, the word was used in English for any of the red wines and only later (gradually after 1700) for red wine of Bordeaux.

clarify *v.* make clear. Before 1325 *clarifien* make illustrious, make known, borrowed from Old French *clarifier,* learned borrowing from Late Latin *clārificāre* make clear, from *clārificus* brilliant (Latin *clārus* CLEAR + the root of *facere* make, DO¹ perform); for suffix see -FY. **—clarification** *n.* 1612, borrowed from French *clarification,* from Late Latin *clārificātiōnem* (nominative *clārificātiō*) from *clārificāre* to clarify; for suffix see -TION.

clarinet *n.* 1796, borrowed from French *clarinette,* diminutive of *clarine* bell; earlier, clarion, from Old French noun *clarine,* from the feminine of the adjective *clarin,* from *clair, cler,* CLEAR; for suffix see -ET. **—clarinetist, clarinettist** *n.* 1864, borrowed from French *clarinettiste.*

clarion *n.* kind of trumpet with clear tones. Before 1338 *clarioun,* in Mannyng's *Chronicle of England,* borrowed through Old French *clarion,* or directly from Medieval Latin *clarionem* (nominative *clario*) trumpet, from Latin *clārus* CLEAR, for suffix see -ET. **—clarion call** (1838)

clarity *n.* clearness. About 1425 *clarite* brightness, splendor, glory; earlier *clerte, clarte* (probably about 1300); borrowed from Old French *clarté,* from Latin *clāritātem* (nominative *clāritās*) clearness, brightness, splendor, from *clārus* CLEAR; for suffix see -ITY. The later Middle English form *clarite* was influenced by or a reborrowing from Latin *clāritās.*

clash *v.* About 1500, probably of imitative origin. The figurative meaning "come into conflict with" is first recorded in 1622, in Bacon's writings. **—n.** 1513, probably imitative like the verb. The figurative meaning "hostile encounter, conflict" is first recorded in 1646, and "conflict of opinions" in 1781, in Cowper's writings. An echoic element, as in *bash* and *smash,* is present in several English words ending in *-ash.*

clasp *n.* 1307 *claspe,* probably an alteration (by metathesis of *p* and *s*) of *clapse,* which may have been the older form even though it is not recorded until 1388; probably related to Old English *clyppan* encircle, embrace, CLIP². **—v.** About 1387-95 *claspen, clapsen,* in the *Prologue* to Chaucer's *Canterbury Tales,* from the noun.

class *n.* 1602 *classe* group of students, borrowed from French *classe,* learned borrowing from Latin *classis* class, division, army, fleet. The ancient Romans related this word to *calāre* call out, proclaim, from Indo-European **kel-/kal-* to call, shout; see LOW² (of cattle). Within the forms of this root, Latin *classis* goes even more closely with Greek *kélados* noise, clamor, as being from Indo-European **kləd-tí-s* (Pok.549).

The spelling *class* appeared in English by 1664, but it and *classe* were preceded by an earlier form *classis* (1593) meaning "a division according to rank" a borrowing of Latin *classis,* as seen above.

—v. 1705, divide into classes; 1776, in Adam Smith's *Wealth of Nations,* to place in a class; from the noun. **—classmate** *n.* (1713) **—classroom** *n.* (1870) **—classy** *adj.* 1891, formed from English *class* high quality, 1847 + *-y*¹.

classic *adj.* 1613, in Cawdrey's *A Table Alphabeticall,* borrowed from French *classique,* from Latin *classicus* pertaining to the highest class (of Romans), from *classis* CLASS. The sense "of or relating to the ancient Greek or Roman writers or arts," appeared in English in 1628. —**n.** 1711, in **classics** *pl.* ancient Greek or Latin writings, from the adjective, a formation probably influenced by earlier French *classiques.* —**classical** *adj.* 1599, of the highest rank, formed in English from Latin *classicus* + English *-al*[1]. —**classicism** *n.* 1837, formed from English *classic* + *-ism.*

classify *v.* 1799, borrowed from French *classifier,* from *classe* class; for suffix see -FY. —**classification** *n.* 1790, borrowed from French *classification,* from *classifier* + *-fication,* a formation similar to that in English from pairs, such as *falsify/falsification, purify/purification, beautify/beautification.* —**classifiable** *adj.* 1846, formed from *classify* + *-able.* —**classified** *adj.* (1889)

clatter *v.* Probably about 1200 *clateren,* found in Old English (about 1050) *clatrung* a clattering, of imitative origin and corresponding to Middle Dutch *klāteren* to clatter, chatter, East Frisian *klatern,* and Low German *klāteren.* —**n.** Probably about 1350, from the verb.

clause *n.* Probably before 1200, in *Ancrene Riwle,* borrowed from Old French *clause,* learned borrowing from Medieval Latin *clausa* close of a rhetorical period, conclusion, from Latin *clausa,* feminine past participle of *claudere* to CLOSE[1]. The meaning "an article or section of a text" is first recorded about 1300.

claustrophobia (klôs'trəfō'bēə) *n.* abnormal fear of enclosed spaces. 1879, New Latin *claustrophobia,* formed from Latin *claustrum* closed place (see CLOISTER) + New Latin *phobia* fear, PHOBIA. —**claustrophobic** *adj.* 1889, formed in English from New Latin *claustrophobia* + English *-ic; n.* person who has claustrophobia. 1953, from the adjective.

clavichord (klav'əkôrd) *n.* a stringed musical instrument with a keyboard. 1457-58 *clavecord,* borrowed from Medieval Latin *clavichordium* (Latin *clāvis* key, see CLAVICLE + *chorda* string, CORD).

clavicle (klav'əkəl) *n.* collarbone. 1615, borrowed from Middle French *clavicule* small key, tendril, collarbone, learned borrowing from Latin *clāvīcula* small key, bolt, diminutive form of *clāvis* key (supposedly because of the shape of the bone), related to *claudere* to fasten, CLOSE[1], v.

clavier *n.* musical instrument with keyboard and strings. 1845; earlier, the keyboard of a musical instrument (1708); borrowed from German *Klavier,* from French *clavier* keyboard, from Old French *clavier* key bearer, from Latin *clāvis* key, see CLAVICLE; for suffix see -ER[1].

claw *n.* About 1250 *clawe,* in *The Owl and the Nightingale,* developed from Old English (about 700) *clawu,* alteration of *clēa* claw, talon (influenced by *clawe* the oblique form). Old English *clawu, clēa* is cognate with Old Frisian *klāwe, klē* claw, hoe, Middle Dutch *klouwe* (modern Dutch *klauw*), Old High German *klāwa* claw (modern German *Klaue*), from Proto-Germanic **klawō* related to Old Icelandic *klō* claw. Cognates outside Germanic are also found in Greek *gínglymos* hinge, joint, possibly Old Irish *glūn* knee, and Sanskrit *glāú-s* bundle, round mass, from Indo-European **gleu-/glēu-/glou-/glōu-/glu-*(Pok.361). Sanskrit *glāú-s* is further related to *gula-s* ball, sphere; see GALL[3] gallnut. —**v.** tear with the claws. About 1250 *clawen,* in *The Owl and the Nightingale,* developed from Old English (about 1000, in Ælfric's *Grammar*) *clawen, clawian,* derived from the Germanic root of *claw,* n.

clay *n.* Before 1325 *clai,* in *Cursor Mundi,* also *cley* (about 1325); earlier in compound *cleyputh* clay pit (about 1241); developed from Old English *clǣg* stiff, sticky earth, clay (about 1000, in Ælfric's *Glossary*). Old English *clǣg* is related to *clām* mud, clay (see CLAMMY) and is cognate with Old Frisian *klai* clay, Old Saxon *klei,* Middle Dutch *clei* clay, from Proto-Germanic **klaijaz* related to Old High German *klīwa* bran (modern German *Kleie*). Cognates outside Germanic are found in Greek *gliā* glue, *gloiós* sticky matter, Latin *glūten* glue, Old Irish *glenim* I stick, adhere, and Lithuanian *gliēti* to smear, *glitùs* smooth, slippery, from Indo-European **glei-/gloi-/gli-* (Pok.363). —**clay pigeon** (1888)

claymore *n.* heavy, two-edged sword, formerly used by Scottish Highlanders. 1722, Gaelic *claidheamh mor* great sword (from Old Irish *claidheb* sword + *mōr* great). The military term **claymore mine,** or **claymore,** a mine that sprays small metal pellets, is first recorded in 1962.

-cle a suffix in various words of French and Latin origin, as in *clavicle, obstacle, spectacle, vehicle,* sometimes with diminutive force, as in *cubicle, particle.* Borrowed from Old French *-cle,* from Latin *-culus, -cula, -culum.*

clean *adj.* 1110 *clene* clear, pure, in *Peterborough Chronicle,* developed from Old English *clǣne* (about 750, in a reference to Cynewulf); cognate with Old Saxon *klēni* dainty, delicate, Old Frisian *klēne* small, and Old High German *kleini* delicate, fine, small (modern German *klein* small), from Proto-Germanic **klainiz;* also cognate with Greek *gelân* to laugh, *galēnós* calm, and Armenian *calr* laughter, *calic* flower, from Indo-European **ĝel-, ĝelə-, ĝləi-,* bright (Pok.366). —**adv.** completely, entirely. Old English *clǣne* (before 900, in Alfred), from the adjective. —**v.** About 1450, from the adjective, in part taking the place of *cleanse* in the more literal senses of modern English. —**clean-cut** *adj.* (1843) —**cleaner** *n.* 1466, formed from Middle English *clene* + *-er*[1]. —**cleanup** *n.* (1866)

cleanly[1] (klen'lē) *adj.* clean, habitually clean. About 1340, in *Ayenbite of Inwyt,* developed from Old English *clǣnlīc* (*clǣne* clean + *līc* body, having a clean body); for suffix see -LY[2].

cleanly[2] (klēn'lē) *adv.* in a clean manner. Probably before 1200, in *Ancrene Riwle,* developed from Old English *clǣnlīce* (*clǣne* clean + *līce, -līc* -ly[2]); for suffix see -LY[1].

cleanse (klenz) *v.* make clean, purify. Probably about 1200 *cleansen,* in *Ancrene Riwle,* also *clennsen,* in *The Ormulum,* developed from Old English *clǣnsian* (about 750, in Cynewulf's *Elene*), from *clǣne* CLEAN. The modern spelling *cleanse* appeared in the 1500's, but the word retained the pronunciation represented in the Middle English spelling. —**cleanser** *n.* (1373)

clear *adj.* About 1280 *cler* bright, borrowed from Old French *cler,* from Latin *clārus* clear, bright, distinct, illustrious, related to *clāmāre* cry out, call, proclaim; see LOW[2], v. —**adv.** About 1303, in Mannyng's *Handlyng Synne,* from the adjective. —**v.** About 1380 *cleren* to enlighten, in Chaucer's translation of Boethius' *De Consolatione Philosophiae,* from the adjective. —**n.** 1237, the phrase *in the clear* is first recorded in 1715, as a figurative sense (1928). —**clearance** *n.* Before 1563, formed from English *clear,* v. + *-ance.* —**clear-cut** *adj.*

(1885) **—clear-eyed** *adj.* (1530) **—clear-headed** *adj.* (1709) **—clearing** *n.* a piece of open land (1678, American English).

cleat *n.* strip of wood or metal. 1302 *clete* wedge, wedge-shaped piece (from Old English **clēat*), probably related to Old English *clott* and *clūt* CLOT. The sense of a fixture to stop a rope from slipping is first recorded in 1377, but such a fixture to wrap a rope around is not recorded until 1768. **—v.** 1794, from the noun.

cleave[1] *v.* split, divide. Probably before 1200 *cleven,* developed from Old English (about 1000) *clēofan* (910 and 937, in forms of the past tense and past participle). Old English *clēofan* is cognate with Old Saxon *kliohan* to split, Old High German *klioban, chliuban* (modern German *klieben*), and Old Icelandic *kljūfa* to split, from Proto-Germanic **kleuhanan.* Cognates outside Germanic include Latin *glūbere* to peel, Greek *glýphein* to hollow out, carve, engrave, and Old Prussian *gleuptene* moldboard of a plow, from Indo-European **gleubh-/glubh-*(Pok.401). The early Middle English and Old English past tense plural form *cloven* (*clufon,* etc.) is now seen mostly in the form *cloven-footed* (1415) and as a separate past participle in *cloven foot* or *hoof* (about 1200). The modern past tense form *cleft* is first recorded probably before 1500. **—cleavage** *n.* 1816, action of cleaving, formed from English *cleave* + *-age.* **—cleaver** *n.* About 1360, formed from English *cleave* + *-er*[1].

cleave[2] *v.* stick, cling. Probably about 1200 *cleovien,* in Layamon's *Chronicle of Britain,* developed from Old English *cleofian, clifian* (before 899 in Alfred's translation of Boethius' *De Consolatione Philosophiae*). The Old English forms are cognate with Old Saxon *klibhōn* to stick, cling, from West-Germanic **klihōjanan,* related to Old High German *klebēn* to stick (modern German *kleben*), Old Icelandic *klīfa* to climb, clamber, and Old Irish *glenim* I stick, adhere, from Indo-European **glei-bh-/gli-bh-* (Pok.363); see CLAY. The Middle English variants *cleve, cleeve* developed as the predominate forms shifting in spelling to *cleave* (1530) and thus producing the form *cleaved.*

clef *n.* symbol indicating the pitch of the musical notes on a staff. Before 1577, borrowed from Middle French *clef* key, from Latin *clāvis* key; see CLAVICLE.

cleft *n.* space or opening made by splitting. 1576, replacement of earlier *clift* (recorded before 1325, in *Cursor Mundi*), developed from Old English *geclyft,* adj. split, cleft. The spelling *cleft* was influenced by *cleft,* a form of the past participle of CLEAVE[1] split. Old English **clyft (geclyft)* is cognate with Old High German *kluft* (modern German *Kluft*) cleft, Norwegian *kluft, klöft,* Danish *kløft* cleft, from Proto-Germanic **kluftis.*

clematis (klem′ətis) *n.* vine with clusters of fragrant flowers. 1597, earlier a name for periwinkle (1551); borrowed from Latin *clēmatis,* from Greek *klēmatís* a climbing vine, from *klêma* (genitive *klḗmatos*) vine, branch, related to *klṓn* twig, earlier probably **klaṓn,* from Indo-European **kel-* and **klā-/klə-* split (Pok.545).

clement (klem′ənt) *adj.* merciful, mild. 1459, earlier (1230 as surname) *Clement,* borrowed from Old French *clement,* learned borrowing from Latin *clēmentem* (nominative *clēmēns*) calm, mild, of uncertain origin. Roman writers connected *clēmēns* with *clīnāre* to bend, and also thought that *clēmēns* contained *mēns* (genitive *mentis*) mind; both contentions are unsupportable. **—clemency** *n.* 1553, in a proclamation of Queen Mary's, borrowed from Latin *clēmentia* calmness, gentleness, from *clēmentem* calm; for suffix see -CY.

clench *v.* About 1250 *clenchen,* in *The Owl and the Nightingale,* developed from Old English *beclencan* hold fast, from Proto-Germanic **klankjanan;* cognate with Old High German *chlankhan, klenkan,* and Middle High German *klenken* to fasten closely together, tie, knot, entwine, from Indo-European **glenĝ-/glonĝ-* (Pok.358). Related to CLINCH. **—n.** a grasp, grip. 1779; earlier perhaps meaning "a swaddling band" (about 1250), from the verb.

clerestory (klir′stôr′ē) *n.* upper part of the wall of a church, with windows that admit light to the center of the building. 1412, possibly formed from Middle English *clere* CLEAR + STORY[2] floor.

clergy *n.* Before 1300 *clergie* a group of persons ordained for religious work; earlier, learning, branch of learning (probably about 1200); borrowed from two words in Old French: 1) *clergié, clergé* clerics, learned men, from Medieval Latin *clericatus,* from Latin *clēricus* CLERIC, and 2) *clergie* also meaning "clerics" and "learning" (literally) clerkship, from *clerc* cleric, CLERK + *-ie* -Y[3]. Confusion of *clergié* and later *clergie* so that both finally came to mean "cleric" in Old French was prompted by substitution of *g* for *c* in **clercie* on the pattern of earlier *clergié.* The earlier meaning of learning in Middle English seems to point to a separate borrowing from Old French *clergie* and the later meaning "group of clerics" to a borrowing from Old French *clergié,* but this cannot be substantiated, as both words meant "clerics" in Old French, though *clergie* was used in reference to "the condition of a cleric." **—clergyman** *n.* (1577) **—clergywoman** *n.* (1673)

cleric *n.* clergyman. 1621, borrowed from Latin *clēricus* clergyman, priest; (literally as an adjective) priestly, from Greek *klērikós* of the clergy, from *klêros* the clergy; (originally, inheritance, lot, allotment), related to *klêma* branch; for suffix see -IC. Greek *klêros* was originally applied (in the Septuagint) to the Levites, the service of God being the priest's lot, and was a loan translation of Hebrew *naḥalāh* inheritance, lot. Compare CLERK.

According to the available record Old English *clēric* member of a holy order merged with Old French *clerc* to become Middle English *clerc,* modern English CLERK, and was reborrowed into English in the 1600's with the specific meaning "clergyman."

—clerical *adj.* 1592; earlier (about 1475), learned borrowing of Old French *clerical* and from Latin *clēricālis,* from *clēricus* clergyman, priest; for suffix see -AL[1].

clerk *n.* Probably before 1200 *clerc* member of the clergy, clergyman, in Layamon's *Chronicle of Britain* and *Ancrene Riwle;* in part developed from Old English (about 975) *clēric* clergyman, (later) secretary, scribe; and in part borrowed from Old French *clerc* clergyman, both Old English and Old French borrowed from Latin *clēricus* CLERIC. Since scholarship in the Middle Ages was often limited to clergymen, who performed writing and secretarial work, the word *clerk* and its Old English equivalent *cleric* came to mean "scribe," and later in Middle English, "scholar" and was applied to a notary, secretary, recorder, accountant, or writer. The specific sense of shop, office, or warehouse assistant who keeps written accounts, is first recorded in 1512. —v. 1551, from the noun.

clever *adj.* 1580-95, in correspondence of Southwell, handy, dexterous, found earlier in Middle English (before 1250) *cliver* nimble-handed, possibly related to Middle English *clivre* claw, talon (earlier, *cleavre*) and to Old English *clifian* CLEAVE[2] to stick.

cliché (klēshā′) *n.* 1832 as a French word introduced into an English work on manufacturing. French *cliché* stereotype (printing plate cast from a mold), from past participle of *clicher* to click, strike melted lead to obtain a cast or mold, perhaps variant of Old French *cliquer* to click, probably of imitative origin. The figurative meaning "worn out expression, trite idea" appeared in 1888, parallel to the figurative extension of earlier *stereotype* (1850), meaning "a fixed, conventional, unoriginal expression."

click *v.* 1581, of imitative origin, and perhaps related to Dutch *klik* click, German *klicken* to click, Old French *clique* tick of a clock, and *cliquer* to click. The figurative sense "to fit together, agree, harmonize" is first recorded in 1915. —**n.** light, sharp sound. 1611, in Cotgrave's *Dictionary,* perhaps from the verb, or formed independently of imitative origin like the verb.

client *n.* Probably before 1387, in a version of *Piers Plowman,* one who engages the services of a lawyer, borrowed through Anglo-French *clyent* (1306), learned borrowing from Latin *cliēns* (accusative *clientem*) retainer, follower, dependent, perhaps literally one who bends before or leans on another, and so possibly related to *clīnāre* to bend; see LEAN[1] slant.

The original meaning in Middle English was extended to "one who obtains any professional or business service, a customer" (1608, in Shakespeare's *Pericles*). —**clientele** *n.* 1563-68, in an edition of John Foxe's *Book of Martyrs,* group of dependents, borrowed from Latin *clientēla* relationship between dependent and patron, body of dependents, from *cliēns* CLIENT.

The word was reborrowed into English in 1854, in Thackeray's *The Newcomes,* this time from French *clientèle* clients of a professional person, customers in general, also from Latin *clientēla,* and retains the meaning from French.

cliff *n.* Old English *clif* (about 725, in *Beowulf*); cognate with Old Saxon *clif* cliff, Middle Dutch *klippe* (modern Dutch *klip*), Old High German *klep* promontory, and Old Icelandic *klif* cliff, *klīfa* to climb, clamber; see CLEAVE[2] stick, though by some scholars related to *cleave*[1] to split, because in several Indo-European languages a number of words for rock, cliff, etc., are from forms meaning split, cut, break. —**cliff dweller** (1881, American English).

climacteric *adj.* crucial, critical. 1601, in Holland's translation of Pliny's *Natural History,* borrowed from Latin *clīmactēricus,* from Greek *klīmaktērikós* of a critical period, from *klīmaktḗr* rung of a ladder, from *klîmax* ladder; see CLIMAX. —**n.** 1630, critical stage in life, borrowed from French *climatérique,* but with a spelling change to *climacteric,* influenced by the adjective. In the 1800's the term became identified with menopause.

climactic *adj.* 1872, from *climax,* apparently derived on the analogy of *syntax, syntactic* rather than from a Greek form (the genitive of Greek *klîmax* is *klī́makos*); see CLIMAX.

climate *n.* 1375 (Scottish) *climat* zone of the earth lying between two parallels of latitude, in John Barbour's *The Bruce;* borrowed through Old French *climat,* learned borrowing from Latin *clima* (genitive *climatis* region, slope of the earth, from Greek *klíma* (genitive *klímatos*) inclination, slope of the earth, from *klī́nein* to incline, LEAN[1] slant.

The meaning "a region of the earth" was often used in reference to the region's atmospheric conditions. It later evolved into the current sense "weather conditions of a region" (1611, in Shakespeare's *A Winter's Tale*).

—**climatic** *adj.* Before 1828, formed from English *climate* + *-ic.*

climax *n.* highest point. 1589, in Puttenham's *The Arte of English Poesie,* rhetorical series of expressions in ascending order of effectiveness; borrowed from Late Latin *clīmax* (genitive *clīmacis*), from Greek *klîmax* (genitive *klī́makos*) rhetorical climax, literally, ladder, something that slopes or inclines, from *klī́nein* to incline, LEAN[1] slant. Greek *klîmax, klī́nein* and Old English *hlǣder* are related through Indo-European **k̂lei-/k̂loi-/k̂lī-* (Pok.600). The term is first recorded as meaning "highest point, as reached by gradual ascent" by 1789, but the editors of the OED writing in the 1800's, label that meaning a misuse of the learned word due to "popular ignorance." —**v.** 1835, bring to a climax or culmination; from the noun.

climb *v.* Probably before 1200 *climben,* in Layamon's *Chronicle of Britain,* developed from Old English (before 1000) *climban;* cognate with Middle and modern Dutch *klimmen* to climb, Old High German *klimban* (modern German *klimmen*), from West Germanic **klimbanan* from Indo-European **glembh-* (Pok. 360). —**n.** 1577-87, in Raphael Holinshed's *Chronicles,* from the verb.

The *b* present in the older forms is generally silent and has been dropped from the form of the word in most languages where it did occur (compare Old High German and modern German above). The *i* is long only in standard English, and is analogous to the *i* in *find, mind,* etc.

clime *n.* region. 1542, borrowed from Latin *clima;* see CLIMATE.

clinch *v.* fasten firmly. 1570, variant of CLENCH. The figurative sense "settle decisively" is recorded before 1716. —**n.** 1627, from the verb. The sense "a struggle or scuffle at close quarters" appeared first in the phrase *clinch fight* (1849, American English); and later developed into a meaning "a tight grasp in fighting" first recorded in 1875. —**clincher** *n.* 1330, a workman who puts in clinching nails, a variant of *clencher,* in a surname; formed from English *clinch* + *-er*[1]. The meaning "a conclusive argument or statement" is first recorded in 1737.

cling *v.* stick, hold fast. Before 1280; earlier, shrivel, shrink (about 1150); developed from Old English *clingan* hold fast, contract, shrivel (about 1000, in Ælfric's *Grammar*). The word is cognate with Middle Dutch *klingen* to stick, adhere, Old High German *klinga* narrow gorge, Middle High German *klingen* to climb, Old Icelandic *klengjask* press onward, push upward, *klungr* thornbush (Norwegian *klenge* cling, Swedish *klänga* climb).

Another form appears in Middle English *clengen* to cling, adhere, and in *clengen doun* to shrink, disappear, developed from Old English *clengan,* from Indo-European **glenk-/glonk-/gln̥k-* (Pok.357).

clinic *n.* Before 1626, a bedridden person, borrowed from Latin *clīnicus* physician (also as an adjective, meaning "of or having to do with bed"), from Greek *klīnikós* physician who visits bed patients (and, as in Latin, with adjective meaning "of bed"), from *klī́nē* bed, from *klī́nein* to incline, LEAN[1] slant.

The modern meaning "place for medical treatment" is first recorded in 1884, a meaning that developed in English probably by influence of German *Klinik,* from earlier French *clinique.* English had already adopted the meaning "medical instruction at the bedside of hospital patients," by 1843 from French *clinique,* itself a borrowing from Greek *klīnikḗ (téchnē)* art or method of treating the bedridden, from *klīnikós (iātrós)* physician who visits bedridden patients.

The old adjective use of *clinic,* first recorded in 1626, in a sermon of Donne's, has generally given way to **clinical** *adj.* 1780, of or pertaining to a sickbed, formed in English from Latin *clīnicus* (from Greek *klīnikós* of a bed) + English *-al*[1].

clink[1] *v.* make a light, ringing sound. Before 1325 *clinken,* probably of imitative origin, similar to Middle and modern Dutch *klinken,* and Old High German *klingan* (modern German *klingen*) to sound, ring, clink, and to Old High German *klinken* to clink glasses. **—n.** Probably before 1400, from the verb.

clink[2] *n. Informal.* jail. 1515, from *the Clink,* a noted prison in the south of London. The name might have come from *clink*[1], in some lost allusion to sound, or perhaps from *clink* to fasten securely, Middle English *clinken,* Northern British English form of *clenchen* to CLENCH.

clinker *n.* large, rough cinder. 1769, alteration of earlier *klincard* kind of paving brick made in Holland (1641), borrowed from earlier Dutch *klinkaerd* (modern Dutch *klinker*), from *klinken* to ring (as it does when struck), from Middle Dutch; see CLINK.

The sense "bad or stupid mistake" is first recorded in 1950 in American English.

clip[1] *v.* trim, cut. Probably about 1200 *clippen,* in *The Ormulum,* apparently borrowed from a Scandinavian source (compare Old Icelandic *klippa* to clip, pinch, modern Icelandic and Swedish *klippa* to cut, shear, clip, Danish and Norwegian *klippe;* probably imitative). **—n.** Possibly 1465, shears, from the verb. **—clippers** *n.pl.* 1876, formed from English *clip*[1], v. + *-er(s),* replacing earlier *clipping shears* (1435). **—clipping** *n.* something cut off or out. 1324-25, formed from Middle English *clippen* + *-ing*[1].

clip[2] *v.* hold tight, fasten. Probably before 1200 *clippen,* in Layamon's *Chronicle of Britain* and *Ancrene Riwle,* developed from Old English (about 725) *clyppan* encircle, embrace, grasp; cognate with Old Frisian *kleppa* to embrace, and Latin *globus* compact mass, throng, from Indo-European **glob-/gleb-* (Pok. 359). **—n.** device that clips objects. 1354, hook for holding pots, developed from *clippen* to hold tight. **—clipboard** *n.* (1907)

clique (klēk) *n.* small, exclusive set of people. 1711, borrowed from French *clique,* from Old French *cliquer* to click (of indeterminate sense); at one time the French word apparently equivalent to *claque* group hired to applaud in a theater.

clitoris (klit′əris) *n.* organ of the genitals of female mammals. 1615, New Latin *clitoris,* from Greek *kleitorís,* diminutive of **kleítōr* hill, related to *kleitýs* hill, and *klī́nein* to LEAN[1] slant. **—clitoral** *adj.* 1946, formed from English *clitoris* + *-al*[1].

cloaca (klōā′kə) *n. Zoology.* excretory cavity or canal. 1834, New Latin *cloaca,* from Latin *cloāca* sewer, drain, cognate with Greek *klýzein* to clean, wash; see CATACLYSM. The word is first recorded in English in Blount's *Glossographia* (1656), in the sense of sewer, borrowed directly from Latin; the usage is now rare. **—cloacal** *adj.* 1656, in Blount's *Glossographia,* borrowed from Latin *cloācālis* of a cloaca, from *cloāca;* for suffix see -AL[1].

cloak *n.* loose outer garment. 1293 *cloke,* borrowed from Old North French *cloque,* from Medieval Latin *clocca* cape worn by horsemen and travelers, literally meaning bell and so called from its shape; see CLOCK. **—v.** to cover with a cloak; conceal. 1509, from the noun. **—cloakroom** *n.* (before 1852)

clobber *v. Slang.* hit, beat, defeat. 1941 (first recorded as British Air Force slang) *clobbering* a bombing, possibly imitative.

cloche (klōsh) *n.* 1882, bell-shaped glass to cover a plant; also later, woman's bell-shaped hat (1907); borrowed from French *cloche* bell, bell glass, from Old French *cloche* bell, from Medieval Latin *clocca* bell; see CLOCK.

clock *n.* About 1370 *clocke* timepiece in which the hours are sounded by a bell, borrowed either from Middle Dutch *clocke* clock, bell, or from Old North French *cloque,* both forms from Medieval Latin *clocca* bell. The Medieval Latin word probably came from a Celtic source (compare Middle Irish *clocc* bell, Breton *kloc'h,* Welsh *cloch*), though it is also possible that the Celtic words were borrowed from Medieval Latin; ultimately the word is apparently of imitative origin and cognate with Greek *klṓssein* to cluck, Old Slavic *klokotati* to cluck, cackle, and Old English *hliehhan* to LAUGH. The Middle Dutch form is also cognate with Old Frisian *klocka, klocke,* Old High German *klocka, glocka, glogga* (modern German *Glocke* bell), Old Icelandic *klocka* bell (Swedish *klocka,* Norwegian and Danish *klokke* bell, clock). **—v.** 1872, to sound a bell; later, to time by the clock (1883); from the noun. **—clockwise** *adj., adv.* (1888) **—clockwork** *n.* (1662)

clod *n.* Before 1398 *cludde* clot (of blood), in Trevisa's translation of Bartholomew's *De Proprietatibus Rerum;* developed from Old English *clodd-, clod-* (as in *clod-hamer* field goer), from Proto-Germanic **kludda-,* from Indo-European **glut-* (Pok. 362). The meaning became differentiated to "lump of earth" and the spelling shifted to *clodde* (1440, in *Promptorium Parvulorum*). Later a figurative sense of the human body or a person, as being a mere lump of earth is recorded (1595, in Spenser's *Epithalamion*), and the sense "blockhead, clumsy person" (1605, in Ben Jonson's *Volpone*).

clog *n.* Before 1325 *clogge* block, lump, of uncertain origin. The sense "shoe with a thick wooden sole" is first recorded in the compound surname *Clogmaker* (1367). **—v.** obstruct, hinder. Before 1398 *cloggen* fasten a clog or block of wood to something (as a hindrance), in Trevisa's translation of Bartholomew's *De Proprietatibus Rerum,* from the noun.

cloister *n.* Before 1225 *cloistre* place of religious seclusion, monastery or convent, borrowed from Old French *cloistre.* The spelling of Old French *cloistre* was an alteration of earlier *clostre* by influence of *cloison* partition, probably from Vulgar Latin **clausiōnem* (nominative **clausiō*), from Latin *clausus* closed. The early Old French *clostre* was derived from Latin *claustrum* closed place, lock (in Medieval Latin, monastery, room in a monastery), from *claus-,* past participial stem of *claudere* to CLOSE[1].

The sense of a covered walk or arcade is first recorded in Middle English before 1300, and that of any enclosed place or space, probably about 1380.
—**v.** shut up, enclose, or seclude (as in a cloister). Probably about 1408, implied in *cloistered,* past participle, from the noun.

clone *n.* group of individuals produced asexually from a single ancestor. 1903, pertaining to plants, borrowed from Greek *klṓn* twig (earlier probably **klaṓn*), related to *klêma* vine, branch, *kládos* sprout, and *klân* to break, from Indo-European **kel-/kl-, klā-/klə-* (Pok. 545).

The application of the term to bacterial cells is first recorded in 1929, and the figurative extension "exact duplicate, carbon copy, replica" is first recorded about 1978. —**v.** to reproduce or propagate asexually. 1959, from the noun.

close[1] (klōz) *v.* to shut. About 1280 *closen,* gradually replacing earlier *clusen* (recorded probably before 1200 in Layamon's *Chronicle of Britain*) developed from Old English *beclȳsan* close, enclose. The new Middle English *closen* was borrowed from Old French *close, clos-,* stem of *clore* to shut, from Latin *claudere* stop up an opening, fasten, shut, related to *clāvis* bar, key. The Latin forms are cognate with Greek *kleíein* to close, bar, shut (from *kleís,* earlier *klēís* bar, bolt, key), Old Irish *clō* nail, Old Slavic *ključĭ* key, *ključiti* to close, from Indo-European **klāu-, *klēu-,* hook, little peg (Pok.604).—**n.** About 1399 *clos* a closing, conclusion, end, from the verb.

close[2] (klōs) *adj.* with little space between, confined, near. Probably about 1380 *clos* (past participle) closed, shut, borrowed from Old French *clos,* from Latin *clausus,* past participle of *claudere* to CLOSE[1]. —**n.** an enclosed space, especially the grounds around an abbey. About 1250, a dwelling or apartment; perhaps later, an enclosed space (about 1280), borrowed from Old French *clos* enclosure; see CLOSET. —**close call** (1881, also earlier **close shave,** 1834, American English). —**close-fisted** *adj.* (1608) —**close-mouthed** *adj.* (1881) —**close quarters** (1753) —**close-up** *adj.* (1913)

closet *n.* About 1385, private room for study or prayer, in Chaucer's *Troilus and Criseyde,* borrowed from Old French *closet,* diminutive form of *clos* enclosure, from Latin *clausum* closed space, from neuter past participle of *claudere* to CLOSE[1]; for suffix see -ET.

The meaning "case or cabinet for valuables" (as in *china closet*) is first recorded in 1601, in Shakespeare's *Julius Caesar,* and "small room, cupboard," in 1616.
—**adj.** 1685, private, secluded; later hidden, covert, secret (1968); from the noun. —**v.** 1595, to shut up in (or as though in) a closet, from the noun.

closure (klō′zhər) *n.* a closing. About 1390, an encircling barrier or fence, enclosure, in Chaucer's *Canterbury Tales;* borrowed from Old French *closure* that which encloses, from Late Latin *clausūra* lock, fortress, from *claus-,* stem of Latin *claudere* to CLOSE[1]; for suffix see -URE.

The meaning "act of closing or shutting (an establishment, a debate, etc.)" appeared in Middle English in 1423 (closure of a gate) and about 1450 (closure of life).

clot *n.* lump, mass. Probably before 1200, in *Ancrene Riwle,* developed from Old English (about 1000) *clott;* cognate with Middle High German *kloz, klotzes* lump, ball (modern German *Klotz*), from Proto-Germanic **kluttə-,* related to Middle Low German *klōt,* and Middle Dutch *klotte, klūte* lump, clod; from Indo-European **gloud-/glūd-/glud-* (Pok.362). —**v.** to form into clots, coagulate. About 1440 *cloted* coagulated, as a variant form in Chaucer's *Canterbury Tales;* earlier *cloten* to break up clods (before 1425); from the noun.

cloth *n.* Before 1200 *cloth,* in Layamon's *Chronicle of Britain,* developed from Old English (before 800) *clāth* woven or felted material, article of clothing, garment. The Old English is cognate with Old Frisian *klāth* cloth, Middle Dutch *cleet* (modern Dutch *kleed* garment, dress), Middle High German *kleit* (modern German *Kleid* garment, dress), Old Icelandic *klædhi* cloth, clothing (Danish *klæde,* Norwegian *klede,* Swedish *kläde*), from Proto-Germanic **klaithaz;* probably related to Old English *ǣt-clīthan* to adhere, from Indo-European **glei-t-/gloi-t-* (Pok.364).

Originally the plural of *cloth* was *clothes;* but after *cloth* meaning "article of clothing" became obsolete, the plural *cloths* (*cloth* + *-s*) was formed in the 1800's to distinguish *cloths* materials of wool, felt, etc., from *clothes* garments.
—**clothes** (klōz) *n.pl.* Old English (before 800) *clāthes,* plural of *clāth* cloth, garment.

clothe (klōᴛʜ) *v.* Old English (about 950) *clāthian,* from *clāth* cloth, garment. —**clothesline** *n.* (1830) —**clothespin** *n.* (1846, American English) —**clothier** *n.* (about 1470), earlier *Clother* (1286, as a surname) —**clothing** *n.* (probably about 1200).

cloture (klō′chər) *n.* closure of debate in a legislature. 1871, borrowed from French *clôture* (used in the French Assembly), from Middle French *clôture.* It is posited that the Middle French developed from Old French *closure* closure as an alteration, influenced by nouns ending in *-ture,* such as *ligature, investiture;* or that the Middle French developed from Old French *closture* either through Vulgar Latin **clausitūra,* or directly from Late Latin *claustūra,* a variant form of *clausūra* lock, fortress, from *claus-,* stem of Latin *claudere* to close.

cloud *n.* Probably before 1200 *clude* mass of rock, hill, cloud, in Layamon's *Chronicle of Britain;* later *cloude* (about 1280); developed from Old English *clūd* rock, hill (about 893 , in Alfred's translation of Orosius), from Proto-Germanic **klūđás.* The Old English is cognate with Greek *gloutós* buttock, Slovenian *glûta, glúta* lump, swelling, from Indo-European **glout-/glūt-/glut-* (Pok.362). —**v.** Before 1420 *clouden* to dim, darken, in Lydgate's *Troy Book;* from the noun.

Cloud replaced Old English *wolcen* cloud and differentiated in meaning from Middle English *skie* which originally also meant cloud: see SKY.
—**cloudburst** *n.* 1872 (earlier reference "bursting of a cloud", before 1817). —**cloudy** *adj.* Probably about 1200 *cludig,* in *The Ormulum,* later *cloudi* (about

1300), developed in part from Old English *clūdig* and in part from Middle English *clude, cloude;* for suffix see -Y[1].

clout *n.* Probably before 1325 *cloute* a stroke, blow, a special sense of earlier *clout* piece of cloth, rag (probably before 1300) and *clut* (probably before 1200, in *Ancrene Riwle*); found in Old English (about 700) *clūt* small piece (of cloth, metal, etc.). Old English *clūt* (from Proto-Germanic **klūtaz*) is cognate with Middle Low German *klōt, klūte* and Middle Dutch *klūt, klūte* lump, clod (modern Dutch *kluit*), Old and Middle High German *klōz* lump, clod (modern German *Kloss*), and late Old Icelandic *klūtr* kerchief (if not borrowed from some other Germanic language); from Indo-European **gloud-/glūd-* (Pok.362).

The sense "a blow, as with a sword or the fist" developed from, or was influenced by, the earlier verb sense "to beat or strike" (probably about 1300). The figurative sense "political power or influence," appeared in 1963 in American English.

—**v.** strike heavily. Probably about 1300, to beat or strike, in *The Romance of Guy of Warwick,* apparently an extension of the earlier meaning to add patches (of cloth, metal, etc.), add (something untrue) by means of a change (probably before 1200, in *Ancrene Riwle*) from the noun and formed partly by influence of Old English, implied in the past participle *geclūtod* patched.

clove[1] *n.* fragrant spice. Probably before 1200 in the Anglo-French phrase *clowes de gilofre,* in *Ancrene Riwle;* later *clowes of gylofre* (about 1400); borrowed from Old French *clo de girofle* spike of the gillyflower, or with the variant *gilofre,* a form with the common change of *r* to *l;* a compound phrase of *clo,* from Latin *clāvus* nail, spike, and *girofle,* ultimately from Greek *karyóphyllon* nut leaf; see GILLYFLOWER. In the 1300's the forms *clowes, clawes, clowys* began to appear by themselves, finally yielding *cloves,* probably before 1475, but the two words *clove*[1] and *clove*[2] were frequently confused in Middle English.

clove[2] *n.* section of a bulb of garlic, etc. Probably about 1300 *clof,* in *The Romance of Guy of Warwick,* developed from Old English (about 1000) *clufu* clove, from Proto-Germanic **kluƀō,* Indo-European **glubhā;* cognate with Old Saxon *kluflōk* garlic, Old High German *klobilouh* (modern German *Knoblauch,* by dissimilation of the two l's of *klobilouh*), Middle Low German *klōf, klōve* a cleft, Old Icelandic *klofi* cleft, cloven thing, related to *kljūfa* to split; see CLEAVE[1] split.

clover *n.* plant with leaves in three small parts. Before 1300 *clovere,* developed from Old English (about 1000) *clāfre;* cognate with Middle Low German *klēver,* Middle Dutch *clāver* (modern Dutch *klaver*), from Proto-Germanic **klaiƀrōn,* from Indo-European **gloi-bhrōn,* while Old High German *klēo* (modern German *Klee*), and Old Saxon *klē* clover, developed from a simpler derivative (**gloi-wó-s*) of the root **glei-* (Pok.363). The spelling *clover,* representing the Old English *clāfre,* became the established form about 1700, according to the OED, finally replacing the more common Middle English *claver.* —**cloverleaf** *n.* (1882, first recorded to describe a highway intersection, 1933).

clown *n.* 1600 *clowne* a fool or jester, apparently the same word as earlier *clowne* a rustic, boor, peasant (1567), also spelled *cloyne* (1563, 1565). The origin of the word is uncertain; but possibly it was borrowed from a Scandinavian source (compare Icelandic *klunni* clumsy, boorish fellow, Swedish dialect *kluns* hard knob, clumsy fellow, Danish *klunt* a log, block, related to Danish and Swedish *klump* lump, and to Old Icelandic *klumba* CLUB).

The notion that *clown* is derived from Latin *colōnus* husbandman, farmer, colonist, suggested by Ben Jonson in 1633, is not likely phonetically and without any evidence to support it.

—**v.** 1599, in Ben Jonson's *Every Man Out of His Humour,* from the noun.

cloy *n.* weary by too much, too sweet, or too rich food. 1530, in Palsgrave's *Lesclarcissement,* an extended sense of Middle English *cloyen* to stop or hinder movement, obstruct; also to encumber (probably before 1387, in a version of *Piers Plowman*); shortened from earlier *acloyen,* (about 1330) and *encloyen* to lame a horse, cripple by driving a nail into the hoof; borrowed from Old French *encloer, enclouer,* from Vulgar Latin **inclāvāre,* from Latin *clāvus* nail, related to *clāvis* key; see CLAVICLE. Middle English *cloyen* was also influenced in its development by Anglo-French *cloyé* hurt by a nail and, thereby, Old French *clöer* fasten with a nail.

club *n.* Probably before 1200 *clubbe* thick stick used as a weapon, in Layamon's *Chronicle of Britain,* probably borrowed from a Scandinavian source (compare Old Icelandic *klubba, klumba* heavy stick, Norwegian *klubbe* club, Swedish *klubba* gavel), from Proto-Germanic **klumbōn,* from Indo-European **glm̥bh-,* root **glembh-* (Pok.360).

The general outline of the development of senses in the OED is to trace the meaning "a social club" (1670) back to an "association or combination of people," (1648) which developed from the verb senses "gather into a clublike mass," and "collect, combine" (1625). The suit of cards (clubs) is a translation of Spanish *basto* or Italian *bastone* from the picture on Spanish cards, though the picture has been replaced by the trefoil of French cards.

—**v.** 1593, beat with a club, from the noun.

cluck *v.* 1481, in Caxton's translation of *The History of Reynard the Fox,* an alteration of earlier *clokken* to cluck (about 1350), developed from Old English *cloccian.* The Old English verb is apparently cognate with Middle Dutch *klokken* to cluck, Middle High German *klucken, glucken* to cluck (modern German *glucken*), Old Icelandic *klaka* to cackle (Danish and Norwegian *klukke,* Swedish *klucka*), Latin *glōcire* to cluck, and Greek *klṓzein* make the sound of a jackdaw, *klṓssein* to cluck; see CLOCK. —**n.** 1703, from the verb.

clue *n.* guide to solving a mystery or problem. 1596, ball of thread, variant of *clew* (about 1250, in *The Owl and the Nightingale,* developed from Old English, about 750 *clīewen* ball, skein; cognate with Old Saxon *kleuwin* ball of thread, skein, from West Germanic **kleuwīn,* related to Old High German *kliuwa* ball, skein, and Sanskrit *glāús* ball, round lump, from Indo-European **gleu-/glōu-/glu-* (Pok.361).

In Greek legend Theseus was guided by a ball or clew of thread through the Cretan Labyrinth, thus the sense of "guide to solving a mystery or problem" is in allusion to the Greek myth, and is first recorded in 1628 with the spelling *clue,* but appears much earlier (about 1386, in Chaucer's *Legend of Good Women*) with the spelling *clew.* The spelling was changed probably by influence of change in other words, such as *hue, rue, true.* —v. 1934, from the noun.

clump *n.* Before 1586, recorded in the sense "cluster of trees," but also surely meaning "lump"; developed from Middle English *clompe* a lump (about 1300) in turn probably developed with influence of Middle Low German *klumpe* and Middle Dutch *klompe* (modern Dutch *klomp*) lump, mass, from Old English *clympre* lump, mass of metal, from Indo-European **glemb-/glm̥b-* (Pok.360). —v. form a clump; earlier, to walk with heavy tread (1665), from the noun.

clumsy *adj.* 1597, acting as if numb, moving awkwardly, probably derived from the Middle English verb *clomsen* 1) become numb with cold (about 1378, in a version of *Piers Plowman*) and 2) as a past participle, stupefied, overcome, dazed (before 1325, in *Cursor Mundi*). This verb may have been borrowed from a Scandinavian source (compare Icelandic *klumsa* lock-jawed, Swedish dialect *klumsen* benumbed with cold, Norwegian *klumsen* speechless); for suffix see -Y[1].

cluster *n.* Before 1382 *clustre,* in the Wycliffe Bible, developed from Old English (before 800) *clyster, cluster,* probably from the same root as CLOT. —v. Probably about 1380 *clustren,* from the noun.

clutch[1] *v.* grasp tightly. Probably before 1325 *cluchen* to bend or crook, clench, a dialectal variant of *clicchen* (probably before 1200); developed from late Old English (about 1025) *clyccan* bring together. The Old English is cognate with Swedish *klyka* clamp, fork, from Proto-Germanic **klukja-,* from Indo-European **gleĝ-* (Pok.358). —n. About 1300 *cloche* claw, alteration of earlier *cloke* (probably before 1200, in *Ancrene Riwle*) and Scottish and Northern English *cluke;* both words related to *clicchen,* v. clutch. The sense of this word has developed in English from that of claw to the meaning of grasping hand (1525), and thence to "tight grasp" (1784, in Cowper's *The Task*). The mechanical sense of a coupling device to engage and disengage gears of machinery appeared in 1814, and was applied to such a device on a motor vehicle in 1899.

clutch[2] *n.* nest of eggs, brood of chickens. 1721, variant of earlier *cletch* (1691), from the Middle English verb (1402) *clekken* to hatch (parallel to the relation *bake—batch*). The verb was borrowed from a Scandinavian source (compare Old Icelandic *klekja* to hatch, perhaps related to *klaka* to cackle, Danish *klække,* Norwegian *klekke,* Swedish *kläcka;* see CLUCK).

clutter *v.* 1556, to collect in heaps, apparently developed from Middle English *clutteren* (about 1425), variant of *cloteren* to form clots, to heap on (about 1400), derived from CLOT. The sense "to litter with things" appeared in 1674. —n. 1580, from the verb. The sense "a crowded and confused collection, a litter" appeared in 1666.

co- a prefix, originally the form of *com-* before vowels and *h* (as in *coalesce, cohere*) and meaning: 1) with, together, as in *cooperate, coproduce;* 2) joint, fellow, as in *coauthor, copilot;* 3) equally, same, as in *coexisting, coextensive;* 4) in mathematics, complement, as in *cosine, cosecant.* The prefix was borrowed from Latin *co-,* variant of *com-,* and is related to *cum* with, together with; it is cognate with Greek *koinós* (from earlier **komyós*) common, general, Old Irish *com-, con-* with, together, and Albanian *kë-* with, together. Indo-European had only the form **kom* (Pok.612) for this ancient adverb (or prefix). The variant *co-* developed under particular conditions in Italic and Celtic.

Though *co-* has been a productive prefix in English since the 1600's, and can be used to create new forms, such as *copilot, coordinate,* it has been a part of many borrowed words and cannot strictly be analyzed as an English prefix in *cooperate, coadjutor,* etc.

coach *n.* 1556, borrowed from Middle French *coche,* from earlier German *Kotsche* (now *Kutsche*), from Hungarian *kocsi,* short for *kocsi szekér* Kocs cart, meaning "a cart made in (of or from) *Kocs,*" a town in northern Hungary where such carriages were made. The vehicle has been known since the reign of King Matthias Corvinus (1458-90) and its name was introduced into European culture in connection with the marriage of his son to a duchess of Milan. Since the 1500's the word has been adopted in nearly all the European languages: Spanish and Portuguese *coche,* Italian *cocchio,* Dutch *koets,* Polish *kocz,* etc. The sense of a private tutor is first recorded in 1848 in informal British university usage and that of an athletic trainer in 1861. —v. 1849, in Thackeray's *Pendennis,* to tutor, train; earlier, to convey in a coach (1612); from the noun. —**coachman** *n.* (1579)

coagulate (kōag′yəlāt) *v.* to change into a thickened mass, curdle, clot. Probably before 1425 *coagulen, coagulaten,* both forms appear in the translation of Chauliac's *Grande Chirurgie.* The Middle English *coagulaten* is a verb use of earlier *coagulat,* adj. clotted (1395, in Chaucer's *Canterbury Tales*), borrowed from Latin *coāgulātus,* past participle of *coāgulāre.* The Middle English *coagulen* was formed as a borrowing from Middle French *coaguler,* from Latin *coāgulāre.* Latin *coāgulāre* to coagulate, curdle, is from *coāgulum* rennet, means of curdling, literally, thing that presses or drives together (*co-* together + *agere* to drive; see AGENT); for suffix see -ATE[1]. —**coagulation** *n.* Before 1400 *coagulasion,* borrowed from Latin *coāgulātiōnem* (nominative *coāgulātiō*), from *coāgulāre* coagulate; for suffix see -TION.

coal *n.* Probably before 1200 *col, cole* charcoal, in Layamon's *Chronicle of Britain,* developed from Old English *col* (before 830, in the *Vespasian Psalter*); earlier in compound *colthred* blackened thread, plumb line (about 700). The Old English is cognate with Old Frisian *kole* charcoal, coal, Middle Dutch *cole* (modern Dutch *kool*), Old High German *kolo, kol* (modern German *Kohle*), Old Icelandic *kol* (Swedish and Norwegian *kol,* Danish *kul*), from Proto-Germanic **kula(n)-,* Irish *gúal,* and Welsh *glo* coal, from Indo-European **geu-lo-/gu-lo-* glowing coal (Pok.399). —v. 1602, from the noun. —**coal bin** (1423) —**coal-black** *adj.* (about 1250) —**coal cellar** (1281) —**coal mine** (1475) —**coal oil** (1858, American English) —**coal tar** (1785)

coalesce (kō′əles′) *v.* grow together. 1541, in Copland's translation of Galen's *Terapeutyke,* borrowed from Latin *coalēscere* (*co-* together + *alēscere* grow up, from *alere* nourish; see OLD). —**coalescence** *n.* 1541, borrowed possibly from Middle French *coalescence* (1537), from Latin *coalēscentem* (nominative *coalēscēns*), present participle of *coalēscere* coalesce; for suffix see -ENCE. —**coalescent** *adj.* 1655, borrowed from French *coalescent* (1539), from Latin *coalēscentem* (nominative *coalēscēns*), present participle of *coalēscere* coalesce; for suffix see -ENT.

coalition *n.* 1612, the growing together of parts, coalescence, borrowed from French *coalition* (1544), formed to the participle *coalitus* of Latin *coalēscere* COALESCE; for suffix see -TION.

The sense of a political coalition (as of parties or states) is first recorded in English in 1715.

coarse *adj.* not fine, rough, crude. 1582, spelling alteration of Middle English *cors* ordinary, coarse, inferior (1424, referring to cloth), variant of earlier *cours* (1398, probably an adjectival use of the noun *cours* COURSE ordinary or habitual way, in the sense of the ordinary run or sort, probably before 1300). Both the OED and the MED concur that *coarse* was probably used to describe the type of rough cloth used for ordinary wear; the OED going on to say that the sense "not fine, heavy or rough" became closely associated with the word. The MED suggests connection with *of course* meaning "of the ordinary sort" but also mentions Medieval Latin *cursorius* ordinary, current. The sense of unrefined, uncivil, rude, developed about 1510, and that of vulgar, gross, obscene, in 1711, Addison in *The Spectator.* **—coarsen** *v.* 1805, formed from English *coarse* + *-en*[1].

coast *n.* Before 1338 *coste* seashore, in Mannyng's *Chronicle of England;* earlier, a rib as part of the side of the body (probably about 1125); borrowed from Old French *coste* (modern French *côte*) coast, hill, from Latin *costa* side, rib (and in Medieval Latin, coast), cognate with Old Slavic *kostĭ* bone, from Indo-European **kost-* (Pok.616). **—v.** Probably about 1390 *costen* go by the side of, skirt the border of, in *Sir Gawain and the Green Knight;* developed from the noun. The sense of slide down the side of a slope or hill (1836, but implied in *coasting* 1775) and the figurative extension of do or achieve effortlessly (1934), both came from American English. **—coastal** *adj.* (1883) **—coaster** *n.* (1574) **—Coast Guard** (1833) **—coastline** *n.* (1860) **—coastwise** *adv., adj.* (1691)

coat *n.* About 1330 *cote* tuniclike garment, borrowed from Old French *cote,* from Frankish (compare Old High German *chozza* cloak of coarse wool, German dialect *Kotze,* and Old Saxon *kot* woolen coat).

Probably about 1390, as in *Sir Gawain and the Green Knight,* the original Middle English sense was transferred to an animal's natural covering, and later to a layer of paint, tar, or other substance (1663).

—v. Before 1376 *coten* provide with a coat, in *Piers Plowman,* from the noun. The sense "cover with a layer or coating" is first recorded in Benjamin Franklin's letters (1753). **—coating** *n.* (1768) **—coat of arms** (before 1338) **—coatroom** *n.* (1870)

coati (kōä'tē) *n.* small raccoonlike animal. 1676, as a word of Brazilian Portuguese introduced into an article in an English journal; borrowed from Tupi *coati, cuati, cuatim* (apparently from *cua* belt + *tim* nose).

coax *v.* 1586 *cokes* to blandish, coddle; from earlier noun, meaning "silly fellow, simpleton" (1567), of uncertain origin.

The sense "persuade by soft words" appeared in 1663; the spelling *coax* is first found in 1706 (in Farquhar's *The Recruiting Officer*).

coaxial (kōak'sēəl) *adj.* having a common axis. 1881 formed from English *co-* + *axis* + *-al*[1]. **—coaxial cable** (1936; earlier *coaxial line,* 1934).

cob[1] *n.* center of an ear of corn, corncob. 1684, in writings of Increase Mather; earlier, head of a herring (1594), thick nut of a hazel (1589), headman, chief (about 1412); possibly borrowed from a Scandinavian source (compare Icelandic *kubbi* block, lump, in Old Icelandic, *-kubbi,* related to Old Icelandic *kūfr* round point, heap; see COVE). According to the MED the word is recorded as a surname from about 1200.

cob[2] *n.* male swan. 1406 *cobbe;* probably cognate with Old Icelandic *kobbi* seal, and Icelandic *kubbi* block, lump; see COB[1].

cobalt *n.* silvery metallic element. 1683, borrowed from German *Kobalt,* dialectal variant of *Kobold* goblin (so called by miners from their belief that it was a worthless substance put in silver ore by goblins after stealing the silver and because of the ill effects the arsenic and sulphur that the rock contained had on the health of the miners). The various forms *Kobalt, Kobald, Kobold* derived in German from Middle High German *kobolt* household goblin, probably formed from *kobe* hut, shed (see COVE) + **holt* goblin, in Old High German *holdo* ghost, from *hold* gracious, friendly (from the superstitious practice of referring to evil beings by complimentary names to avoid their wrath), related to *halda* inclined; see HEEL[2] tilt. Compare the etymology of NICKEL.

Though known as a substance since perhaps the 1400's, cobalt was not identified chemically before 1735.

cobble[1] *n.* rounded stone used in paving. 1600, shortened from earlier *cobelstone* (about 1440, from *cobel-,* possibly diminutive of *cob*[1], in the sense of block, lump + *stone*). A Northern English dialectal variant *kobilstane* is found about 1375. **—v.** pave with cobbles. 1691, from the noun.

cobble[2] *v.* mend (shoes, etc.). 1496 *coblen,* apparently back formation from earlier *cobelere* one who mends shoes, cobbler (1287), of uncertain origin.

cobbler[1] *n.* one who mends shoes. 1287, see COBBLE[2].

cobbler[2] *n.* a kind of pie baked in a deep dish. 1859, American English, but perhaps ultimately related to, or even developed from unrecorded use of *cobeler,* n. 1385, a kind of wooden bowl or dish.

COBOL or **Cobol** (kō'bôl) *n.* computer programming language. 1960, formed as an acronym in English for *Co(mmon) B(usiness) O(riented) L(anguage).*

cobra *n.* snake. 1802, shortened form of *cobra capello* (1671), borrowed from Portuguese *cobra de capello* snake with a hood (*cobra,* from Latin *colubra* snake, of uncertain origin, and *capello,* from Vulgar Latin **cappellus* little cape, from Late Latin *cappa* CAPE[1] garment).

cobweb *n.* 1323, *coppewebbe,* a compound of Middle English *coppe* spider and WEB. Middle English *coppe* developed from Old English *-coppe* (as in *āttorcoppe* poison spider, from *āttor* poison + *-coppe*), possibly from *copp* top, head, of uncertain origin.

Old English *-coppe* is cognate with Middle Dutch and modern Flemish *coppe, cobbe,* modern Dutch *spinnecop,* and Danish *(edder)kop,* all meaning spider. Old English *āt(t)or* is cognate with Old High German *eit(t)ar* (modern German *Eiter* pus), from Proto-Germanic **aitra-* poisonous ulcer; cognate also with Greek *oîdos* a swelling, and Old Slavic *jadro* a swelling and *jadŭ* poison, from Indo-European **oid-* (Pok.774).

coca (kō'kə) *n.* tropical shrub whose dried leaves are used to make cocaine and other alkaloids. 1577, borrowed from Spanish *coca,* from Quechua *cúca,* perhaps from Aymara (language of a group of South American Indians of Bolivia and Peru).

cocaine *n.* drug used to deaden pain and as a stimulant. 1874, probably borrowed from French *cocaïne* (1856), from *coca,* from Spanish *coca;* for suffix see -INE².

coccus *n.* spherical bacterium. 1883, from New Latin *Coccobacteria* (1874), ultimately from Greek *kókkos* seed, berry, a loanword of unknown origin. Its earlier application (1753) is to a type of insect.

coccyx (kok′siks) *n.* bone at the lower end of the spine. 1615, borrowed, possibly through French *coccyx,* or directly from Latin *coccyx,* from Greek *kókkȳx,* originally, cuckoo; so called because of its supposed resemblance to the beak of a cuckoo.

cochlea (kok′lēə) *n.* a spiral-shaped cavity of the inner ear. 1688; earlier, in reference to Archimedes' screw (1641), borrowed from New Latin and Latin *cochlea* snail, snail shell, from Greek *kochlíās,* from *kóchlos* shellfish with a spiral shell; related to *kónchē* mussel, cockle; see CONCH.

cock¹ *n.* male chicken, rooster. Before 1250 *coc,* in *The Owl and the Nightingale;* earlier in surname *Bulecoc* (1221); developed from Old English *cocc* (recorded before 900, in Alfred's translation of St. Gregory's *Pastoral Care*) ; of imitative origin, like Old Icelandic *kokr* cock, borrowed from Old French *coc* (modern French *coq*), Old Slavic *kokotŭ,* and Sanskrit *kukkuṭá-s* cock.

The origin of the use of *cock* in such technical senses as a tap or faucet (about 1425) and the hammer or firing pin of a gun (1566), is unclear. In German, *Hahn* (cock) has been used in the sense of a spout or tap for an equally long period.

—v. to draw back the hammer or cock of (a gun). 1649, in Milton's *Ikonoklastes;* earlier, to fire the cock of a matchlock gun (1598); from the noun.

—cock-a-doodle-doo *n.* 1573, formed in English in imitation of the crowing sound of a cock. **—cockscomb** *n.* About 1400, in Maundeville's *Travels.* **—cocky** *adj.* vain. 1768; earlier, lecherous (1549); formed from English *cock¹* + *-y¹*.

cock² *v.* to set or turn up, especially in an alert manner or in a jaunty way. About 1600, from earlier to swagger (1575), and *cocken* to wrangle, fight (probably about 1150), apparently all from COCK¹, especially referring to fighting cocks. **—n.** 1711, an upward turn of the brim of a hat, in Sir Richard Steele's writings in *The Spectator;* later, a turn of the eye, ear, nose, hat, etc. (1824, in Scott's writings), this later meaning is from the verb sense "to cock the ears, nose, eye" (about 1600, apparently in reference to the stiff and assertive posture of a cock's neck when crowing). **—cocked hat,** 1673, especially in the phrase *knocked into a cocked hat* (1833). The original meaning was of a hat with an upward turn of the brim; the phrase is of unknown origin. **—cockeyed** *adj.* 1821, squint-eyed, in Byron's *The Vision of Judgment,* apparently from *cock²,* v. to set or turn the head or eye in such a direction as to see; later *cockeyed* was applied to things tilted to one side and extended to anything askew or foolish and silly (1896).

cock³ *n.* cone-shaped pile of hay in a field. Before 1398, in Trevisa's translation of Bartholomew's *De Proprietatibus Rerum,* of uncertain origin, but probably cognate with dialectal German *Kocke* heap (of hay or dung), Norwegian *kok* heap, pile, cognate with Lithuanian *gugà* hump, hill, from Indo-European **gugā* ball (Pok.394). **—v.** Probably before 1387, in a version of *Piers Plowman,* probably from the noun, despite the earlier date.

cockade *n.* 1709, in Sir Richard Steele's writings in *The Tatler,* alteration (influenced by *-ade*) of earlier *cockard* (1660), borrowed from French *cocarde (earlier coquarde),* feminine of *cocard* foolishly proud, cocky, from *coq* COCK¹. According to Cotgrave *coquarde* in *bonnet à la coquarde* was a Spanish cap, especially one worn proudly, and cocked at an angle.

cockamamie or **cockamamy** (kok′əmā′mē) *adj. Slang.* foolish, absurd, or nonsensical. 1960, from earlier *cockamamie* decal (probably before 1926), apparently an alteration of DECALCOMANIA though the phonetic process is not certain.

cock-and-bull *adj.* especially *cock-and-bull story.* 1621, in Burton's *Anatomy of Melancholy,* in the phrase "to talk of Cock and Bull", either in allusion to the strain on credulity produced by the fables of Aesop and his imitators, in which cocks moralize and bulls debate; or perhaps derived from the idea in the parallel French expression *coq-à-l'âne* a cock-and-bull story, earlier *du coq à l'asne* a libel, satire (a tale of the cock to the ass).

cockatoo *n.* brightly colored parrot. 1634 *cacatoe,* (but known earlier, evidenced by a facetious reference in a play of Beaumont and Fletcher, 1616); borrowed from Dutch *kaketoe,* from Malay *kakatùa* a cockatoo, perhaps in imitation of its call. The later spelling *cockatoo* (before 1732) was apparently influenced by COCK¹.

cocker *n.* (especially *cocker spaniel*). Before 1811, a breed of bird dog; earlier, Middle English *cocker* a fighter or quarrelsome man (probably about 1150); formed from English *cock, cok* + *-er¹*.

cockhorse *n.* 1540, as a term for anything a child rides in the manner of a horse. The origin and reference is uncertain; perhaps it resides in the phrase *on a cockhorse* in which the reference may be to the bent knee or may simply be to "astride".

cockle¹ *n.* saltwater mollusk with two ridged shells. 1311-12 *cokel,* borrowed from Old French *coquille,* alteration (influenced by *coque* shell) of Vulgar Latin **conchīlia,* neuter plural taken to be feminine singular of Latin *conchȳlium* shellfish, from Greek *konchȳ́lion,* diminutive of *konchýlē,* from *kónchē* mussel, CONCH. See COCOON. **—cockleshell** *n.* (about 1420) a weed that grows in grain fields.

cockle² *n.* a weed that grows in grain fields. Probably before 1300 *cockel,* found in Old English *coccel,* perhaps from Medieval Latin **cocculus* little berry, diminutive form of *coccus,* from Greek *kókkos* grain, seed. **—cocklebur** *n.* (1804, American English)

cockney *n.* inhabitant of a section of London; dialect of such a person. 1600; earlier, a city dweller generally (perhaps as early as 1521, in a reference to the pampered city child), from *cokeney* pampered child, literally, cock's egg (about 1390, in Chaucer's *Canterbury Tales*); formed, possibly by derisive use of *cokenei* on the model of *chiken ei, ey* chicken egg), (*cok, coc* COCK¹ + *ei, ey* egg, from Old English *ǣg*). It is also possible that some popular association existed with *Cockaigne* name of an imaginary country of luxury and idleness (from Old French *Cocagne*), and that this word was humorously applied to the *Cockney* area of London. **—adj.** characteristic of a London cockney. 1632; earlier, effeminate (1573), from the noun.

cockpit *n.* place where the pilot sits in an airplane. 1914; earlier, the part of a warship where junior officers were quartered (1706); the buildings housing the

Treasury and Privy Council, built on the site of a former London theater known as *The Cockpit* (before 1635) where a *cockpit* (1587) once stood, a pit for cockfighting.

cockroach *n.* 1624, in writings of Captain John Smith, alteration (by influence of a *cock*[1] and *roach*) of Spanish *cucaracha,* from *cuca* kind of caterpillar, of imitative origin and originally in children's language.

cocktail *n.* 1806, American English, apparently formed from *cock*[1] + *tail,* but the allusion is uncertain (origins of *cocktail* are discussed in Mencken's *The American Language,* Supplement I).

In American English the word is applied to non-alcoholic appetizers, such as *fruit cocktail* (1928), *oyster cocktail* (about 1938), and, by extension, to any concoction, such as *Molotov cocktail* (1940).

coco (kō′kō) *n.* palm tree on which coconuts grow. 1582; borrowed from Spanish *coco,* from Portuguese *côco* grinning face, bugbear, coco; so called from the coconut shell's base, with its hollows resembling a grimacing face. An earlier Latinized form *cocus* a name for the coconut (1555) was Anglicized to *cocos* gradually from 1579. Both the later *coco* and *cocoa* were confused in Johnson's *Dictionary* and to some extent the confusion still exists. **—coconut** *n.* (1613)

cocoa (kō′kō) *n.* powder made from cacao seeds; drink made of this powder. 1707, variant of earlier CACAO (1555), by confusion with COCO.

cocoon *n.* 1699, borrowed from French *cocon, coucon,* from *coque* shell of a clam, mussel, etc., or of an egg, husk, nut, from Old French *coque* shell, from Latin *coccum* oak gall, berry, from Greek *kókkos* seed, berry; a loan word of unknown origin. Some sources have related the word to Latin *concha* shell, shellfish, but the relationship is closer semantically than phonetically.

cod *n.* food fish. 1357, earlier, *cotfish* (1273), origin uncertain, perhaps related to *cod,* n. a capsule or seed pod, bag or wallet (1131), through *codnet* probably meaning "bag-shaped fishing net" (1299).

coddle *v.* 1598, boil gently, stew, in Ben Jonsons' *Every Man in His Humour,* perhaps alteration of Middle English *caudle* a hot, thin gruel mixed with wine or ale (about 1300); borrowed through Anglo-French *caudel,* Old French *chaudel,* from Late Latin *calidellum* measure for hot drink, from Latin *calidum* hot drink, neuter of *calidus* hot, from *calēre* be warm; see CALDRON.

The transferred sense "treat tenderly" appeared in 1815, in Jane Austen's *Emma.*

code *n.* About 1303, system of laws, in Mannyng's *Handlyng Synne,* borrowed from Old French *code,* learned borrowing from Latin *cōdex,* dialect variant of *caudex* tree trunk, block of wood split into flat tablets for writing, book, code of laws, related to Latin *cūdere* to beat; see HEW.

The sense "system of secret writing" appeared in English in 1808, in a dispatch of Wellington's.

—v. 1815, enter in a legal code; later, to encode (1885); from the noun.

codeine (kō′dēn) *n.* drug, obtained from opium. 1881, borrowed from French *codéine,* from Greek *kṓdeia* poppy head (probably related to *kṓdōn* bell, for the bell-shaped flower of the poppy) + French *-ine* -ine[2]. The word was coined in French, in 1832, by its discoverer, the French chemist Robiquet.

codex *n.* volume of manuscript, especially of the Scriptures. 1581, collection of statutes, borrowed from Latin *cōdex* ledger; see CODE.

codicil (kod′əsəl) *n.* something added to a will to change it. About 1419, borrowed from Middle French *codicille,* from Latin *cōdicillus* a short writing, especially in a will, diminutive form of *cōdex* (genitive *cōdicis*) ledger; see CODE.

codon (kō′don) *n. Biology.* group of three chemical substances forming the genetic code for a particular amino acid. 1962, formed from English *code* + *-on* unit of genetic material (as in *operon*).

coed or **co-ed** (kō′ed′) *n. Informal.* female student at a college or school. 1893, American English, from earlier sense, coeducational institution (1886, in Alcott's *Jo's Boys*), shortened from *coeducation* (1852) *coeducational* (1881). **—adj.** *Informal.* coeducational. 1889, American English, shortened from *coeducational.*

coefficient *n.* 1708-15, in an edition of Kersey's *Dictionary,* earlier as an adjective (1665-66), formed from English *co-* + *efficient,* perhaps by influence of French *coefficient,* n. or by New Latin *coefficiens,* which was used as a term in mathematics apparently before 1600.

coelenterate (silen′tərāt) *adj.* belonging to a group of saltwater animals with saclike bodies. 1872, in Herbert Spencer's *Principles of Psychology,* borrowed from New Latin *Coelenterata* the phylum name, from Greek *koîlos* hollow (see CAVE) + *énteron* intestine (see INTER-). **—n.** coelenterate animal. 1888, borrowed from New Latin *Coelenterata.*

coerce *v.* Probably about 1451 *cohercen,* borrowed from Middle French *cohercer,* from Latin *coercēre* confine, control (*co-* together + *arcēre* shut in, keep off). Latin *arcēre* is cognate with Greek *arkeîn* ward off, defend, assist, Old High German *rigil* bar, and Lithuanian *rãktas* key, from Indo-European *arek-/ark-/rek-/rok- (Pok.65).

There is no record of the use of this verb in English between the late 1400's and mid-1600's. In its new spelling *coerce* (1659, implied in *coercing*) it was probably a back formation from *coercion.*

—coercion *n.* 1414 *cohercion,* in *Rolls of Parliament;* borrowed from Middle French *cohercion,* from Latin *coerctiōnem,* variant of *coercitiōnem* (nominative *coercitiō*), from *coercēre;* for suffix see -TION. The spelling *coercion* (without the *h*) appeared in 1467. The ending *-cion* was retained when other words with this medieval spelling were changed to the Latin type *-tion,* because it was mistakenly assumed that *coercion* was formed from the verb *coerce.* **—coercive** *adj.* Before 1600, in Richard Hooker's *Ecclesiastical Polity,* formed from English *coerce* + *-ive.*

coeval (kōē′vəl) *adj.* of the same age, date, or duration. 1622-62, in one of the editions of a geography by Peter Heylyn, formed in English from Late Latin *coaevus* (from Latin *co-* equal + *aevum* AGE) + English *-al*[1]. **—n.** person of the same period as another; a contemporary. 1605, in Francis Bacon's *Of the Advancement of Learning,* apparently noun use of *coeval,* adj., though recorded earlier than the adjective.

coexistence *n.* 1459, formed from English *co-* together + *existence.*

coffee *n.* 1598 *chaoua,* 1601 *coffe,* 1603-30 *coffa,* borrowed from Turkish *kahveh,* or directly from Arabic *qahwah* coffee, originally, wine. Two forms of this word (with *a* and with *o*) came into most modern languages about 1600: the first is represented by French, Spanish, and Portuguese *café,* Italian *caffè,* German *Kaffee,* Danish, Norwegian, and Swedish *kaffe.* The second form is represented by English *coffee,* Dutch *koffie,* Russian *kofe.* The forms with *o* may have had earlier *au* (see the earliest English form *chaoua*), from Turkish *-ahv-* or Arabic *-ahw-.* **—coffee house** (1615) **—coffeepot** *n.* (1705)

coffer *n.* box, chest, or trunk. About 1250 *cofre,* borrowed from Old French *cofre,* from Latin *cophinus* basket; see COFFIN.

coffin *n.* Before 1338, chest, case, in Mannyng's *Chronicle of England;* borrowed from Old French *cofin* sarcophagus; earlier, basket, from Latin *cophinus,* from Greek *kóphinos* basket, of uncertain origin. The ordinary current sense of a burial casket appeared in English in 1525.

cog *n.* Before 1300, in a version of *The Owl and the Nightingale,* probably borrowed from a Scandinavian source (compare Swedish and Norwegian *kugg* cog); cognate with Middle High German *kugel* ball; see CUDGEL. **—cogwheel** *n.* (1354)

cogent *adj.* forcible, convincing. 1659, borrowed from French *cogent* necessary, urgent, from Latin *cōgentem* (nominative *cōgēns*), present participle of *cōgere* compel, constrain (*co-* together + *agere* to drive, lead, act; see AGENT). **—cogency** *n.* 1690, in Locke's *Essay Concerning Human Understanding,* formed from English *cogent* + *-cy.*

cogitate *v.* think over, consider with care. 1563-83, in an edition of John Foxe's *Book of Martyrs,* borrowed, perhaps by influence of Middle French *cogiter* to meditate, from Latin *cōgitātus,* past participle of *cōgitāre* to think (*co-* intensive or reinforcing prefix + *agitāre* consider, set in motion, frequentative form showing renewed action of *agere* to drive, lead; see AGENT). **—cogitation** *n.* Probably before 1200, in *Ancrene Riwle,* borrowed from Old French *cogitation,* from Latin *cōgitātiōnem* (nominative *cōgitātiō*) from *cōgitāre;* for suffix see -TION.

cognac (kōn′yak) *n.* 1594 *Coniackc* wine produced in Cognac, borrowed from French *Cognac,* in allusion to the town and region in the department of Charente, western France, where it is made. The sense of a brandy distilled from Cognac wine appeared in 1755 and earlier as *cognac brandy* (1687). The French spelling and its pronunciation appear to be adoptions of mid-1800's.

cognate *adj.* About 1645, related by family or origin; borrowed, perhaps by influence of French *cognat,* from Latin *cognātus* of common descent (*co-* together + *gnātus,* past participle of *gnāscī,* later *nāscī* be born; see NATIVE.

The sense "descended from the same original language, or the same word or root" appeared in English in 1827.
—n. 1754, from the adjective.

cognition *n.* awareness, sensation. 1447, probably before 1425, in a translation of Higden's *Polychronicon,* borrowed from Latin *cognitiōnem* (nominative *cognitiō*) a getting to know, acquaintance, from *cogni-,* stem of *cognōscere* to come to know, see COGNIZANCE; for suffix see -TION. **—cognitive** *adj.* involving cognition. 1586, formed from English *cognition* + *-ive.*

cognizance *n.* About 1350 *conissaunce* recognition; later, knowledge, understanding (probably before 1400), borrowed from Anglo-French *conysance, conusance,* from Old French *connissance, connussance,* from *conoissance,* from past participle *conoistre* to know, from Latin *cognōscere* to come to know (*co-* intensive + *gnōscere* KNOW).

From the 1300's to the 1500's, the spelling in French was often partially Latinized as *cognoissance,* but the *g* was never pronounced, and after 1600 was entirely dropped. In English the *g* appeared in the late 1400's and has gradually affected the pronunciation, which today is (kog′nəzəns) though in law the older (kon′əzəns) was used into this century.
—cognizant *adj.* 1820, in Southey's poems, from the noun, on analogy of *assistance, assistant, distance, distant,* etc.

cohabitation *n.* About 1454, borrowed perhaps from Middle French *cohabitation,* from Late Latin *cohabitātiōnem* (nominative *cohabitātiō*), from *cohabitāre* to dwell together. **—cohabit** *v.* About 1530, probably a back formation from *cohabitation,* but possibly borrowed directly from Late Latin *cohabitāre.*

cohere *v.* stick together. 1598, borrowed from Latin *cohaerēre* (*co-* together + *haerēre* cling, cleave to; see HESITATE). **—coherence** *n.* About 1580, borrowed from Middle French *cohérence,* from Latin *cohaerentia,* from *cohaerentem* (nominative *cohaerēns*), present participle of *cohaerēre* cohere; for suffix see -ENCE.
—coherent *adj.* About 1555, borrowed from Middle French *cohérent,* from Latin *cohaerentem* (nominative *cohaerēns*), present participle of *cohaerēre* cohere; for suffix see -ENT.

Note that the first word to appear in the record of English is the derivative from *coherent,* which in fact may have prompted the use of *coherence* and the relatively rare *cohere.* If that is the case, then *cohere* may be technically a back formation of *coherent* or *coherence* though the writer was surely aware of the Latin *cohaerēre* when he used *cohere.*
—cohesion *n.* 1678, formed as if borrowed from Latin **cohaesiōnem* (nominative **cohaesiō*), formed to *cohaesus,* past participle of *cohaerēre* to stick together.
—cohesive *adj.* 1727-31, in an edition of Bailey's *Dictionary,* implied in the derivative *cohesiveness.* Formed in English from *cohes-* as if it were a stem of *cohesion* + *-ive.*

cohort (kō′hôrt) *n.* group or company. 1422, in Lydgate's writings, borrowed from Middle French *cohorte,* from Latin *cohortem,* accusative of *cohors* a tenth part of a Roman legion; any group of persons enclosed together; an enclosure; see COURT.

The modern informal sense "colleague, accomplice" appeared in 1952 in American English, from the earlier sense of a group united in a common cause (1719, in correspondence of Swift).

coif *n.* close-fitting cap. About 1330 *koife,* borrowed from Old French *coife, coiffe,* from Late Latin *cofia,* of West Germanic origin (compare Middle High German *kupfe, kuffe* cap). **—v.** About 1450 *coifen* cover with a cap, borrowed from Middle French *coiffer,* from *coiffe* coif, from Old French. The sense "arrange the hair" is first recorded in English in 1835. **—coiffeur** (kwäfėr′) *n.* hairdresser. 1850 in writings of Thackeray, borrowed from French, from *coiffer* + *-eur* -er[1]. **—coiffure** (kwäfyůr′) *n.* hair style. Before 1631, in writings of Donne, borrowed from French *coiffure,* from *coiffer* to arrange the hair; for suffix see -URE.

coil *v.* 1611, in Cotgrave's *Dictionary,* borrowed from Middle French *coillir* to gather, collect, cull, from Latin *colligere* gather together, COLLECT. **—n.** 1627, from the verb.

coin *n.* 1304, a wedge; borrowed from Old French *coin* wedge, corner, stamp, piece of money, from Latin *cuneus* wedge; see CUNEIFORM.

The meaning "piece of money" is first recorded about 1380, in Chaucer's *The Former Age;* this sense developed first in Old French from the wedge-shaped die used for stamping coin and from the die, also called a coin.

—v. About 1338 *coinen* to mint (money), in Mannyng's *Chronicle of England,* borrowed from Old French *coignier,* from *coin,* n. The figurative sense "invent a new word or phrase" is first recorded in English in 1589. **—coinage** *n.* About 1380, in *Sir Ferumbras,* borrowed from Old French *coigniage,* from *coignier* to coin + *-age* -age; for suffix see -AGE. The sense "something devised or invented (such as a new word)" is first recorded in 1602, in Shakespeare's *Hamlet.*

coincide *v.* correspond exactly. 1715, borrowed from French *coïncider,* from Medieval Latin *coincidere* (Latin *co-* together + *incidere* fall upon, itself a compound of *in* upon, and *cadere* to fall; see CADENCE). **—coincidence** *n.* 1605, in Francis Bacon's *Sylva Sylvarum,* exact agreement or correspondence; borrowed from French *coïncidence,* from Middle French *coincidance,* from *coincider* coincide, from Medieval Latin *coincidere;* for suffix see -ENCE. **—coincident** *adj.* 1563-83, in an edition of John Foxe's *Book of Martyrs,* borrowed from French *coïncident,* from *coïncider;* for suffix see -ENT. *—n.* 1626, from the adjective, probably by confusion of *coincidence* with *coincidents,* as attested in available citations. **—coincidental** *adj.* 1800, formed from English *coincident* + *-al*[1].

coitus (kō′ətəs) *n.* sexual intercourse. 1855, borrowed from Latin *coitus,* from the stem of *coīre* come together (*co-* together + *īre* come, go; see EXIT).

The word also appeared in Middle English as *coite* (probably before 1425, in a translation of Chauliac's *Grande Chirurgie*).

—coition (kōish′ən) *n.* coitus. 1615; earlier, coming together (1541, in Copland's translation of Galen's *Terapeutyke*); borrowed from Late Latin *coitiōnem* (nominative *coitiō*), from *coīre* come together; for suffix see -TION.

coke[1] *n.* residue from coal used as fuel. 1669, perhaps variant of *colk* core, in Middle English *colke* (before 1400) and specifically in reference to charcoal (1430). If the sense development has been from "pit" to "what is in the pit," the source may be Old English *-colc* a hole, cognate with Old Frisian *kolk* pit, hole, Middle Low German *kolk, kulk* water hole, gulf, Danish *kulk* throat (from Proto-Germanic **kulkaz*), and Old English *ceole* throat, which is cognate with Old High German *kela* (modern German *Kehle*) throat, from Indo-European **gel-/gḷ-/gḷ-g-* to swallow (Pok.365).

—v. convert into coke. 1804 (earlier, implied in gerund *coking,* 1791), from the noun.

coke[2] *n. Slang.* cocaine. 1908, American English, shortening and alteration of COCAINE.

col- a prefix meaning with, together, the form of *com-* before *l,* as in *collinear* = *together on the same line.* The Latin form *col-* resulted from sound change by assimilation of *con-, com-* to *l* before word elements beginning with *l,* though the spelling *conl-* persisted in Latin. The spellings in Middle English that were reduced to one *l* were later changed to include two *l's* during the revival of learning and its emphasis on Classical Latin forms, and it is these latter forms that largely survive today.

cola *n.* See KOLA.

colander (kul′əndər *or* kol′əndər) *n.* dish full of holes to draw off liquids from solid matter. 1368 *coloundour,* alteration of Medieval Latin *colatorium* strainer, from Latin *cōlātus,* past participle of *cōlāre* to strain, from *cōlum* strainer, filter, sieve, of uncertain origin.

cold *adj.* Before 1200 *cold, colde,* in Layamon's *Chronicle of Britain,* developed from Old English, probably about 725 (Anglian) *cald,* (West Saxon) *ceald;* cognate with Old Frisian and Old Saxon *kald* cold, Old High German (and modern German) *kalt,* Old Icelandic *kaldr,* Gothic *kalds,* from Proto-Germanic **kaldás.* Outside Germanic the word is cognate with Latin *gelū* frost, *gelāre* to freeze, *gelidus* cold, and more distantly *glaciēs* ice, from Indo-European **gel-/gol-,* and **glə-g-* (Pok.365), and perhaps Old Slavic *chladŭ* cool, cold. See COOL, CHILL.

Cold and its Germanic cognates may have been originally past participial formations, hence the endings *d* and *t.*

—n. Before 1300, coldness, in *Havelok the Dane;* from the adjective. The sense of the common cold (respiratory infection) appeared in 1537, from the earlier senses of a physical indisposition caused by exposure to cold (before 1338) and the discomfort or pain caused by cold (about 1300). **—cold-blooded** *adj.* (1595, in Shakespeare's *King John*). **—cold cream** (1709) **—cold cuts** (1945, from earlier *cold cut,* 1770, American English). **—cold feet** (1893, American English, in writings of Stephen Crane). **—cold front** (1921) **—cold-hearted** *adj.* (1606, in Shakespeare's *Antony and Cleopatra*). **—cold war** (1945, in writings of Orwell).

cole *n.* kind of cabbage. Before 1325 *col,* in *Cursor Mundi,* developed from Old English (about 1000) *cāl,* variant of *cāwel,* from Latin *caulis,* dialectal variant *cōlis* cabbage, stalk of a plant; see HOLE and COLESLAW.

coleopterous (kō′lēop′tərəs) *adj.* of a group of insects including beetles and weevils. 1791, borrowed from Greek *koleópteros* sheath-winged (*koleós* sheath + *pterón* wing; see FEATHER); for suffix see -OUS.

coleslaw *n.* salad of shredded cabbage. 1794 *cold slaw,* American English, borrowed from Dutch *kool sla,* literally, cabbage salad, from *kool* cabbage (from Latin *caulis* cabbage, stalk) and *sla,* variant of *salade* salad, from French. Related to COLE and SALAD.

The common spelling of this word was *cold slaw* up to the 1860's when the spelling with *cole* appeared, probably through association with the word *cole.*

colic *n.* abdominal pains. Probably about 1421, borrowed through Middle French *colique,* or directly from Late Latin *cōlicus,* from Greek *kōlikós* colicky, literally, of the colon, from *kólon* COLON; so called because the pain was associated with the lower part of the intestine.

Greek *kōlikós* is the sole surviving example in Greek of a system of forming secondary derivatives in Indo-European in which the root vowel of the basic noun undergoes lengthening while the accent shifts to the

opposite end of the word. The system is strong in Sanskrit and there are examples of it in Germanic. An example in Sanskrit is *śváśura-s* father-in-law: *śvāśurá-s* belonging to the father-in-law.
—**colicky** *adj.* 1742, formed from English *colic* + *-y*[1]. The spelling with *k* was due to the convention of changing the derivatives of a word with final *c* (as *traffic, picnic, mimic*) to *ck* whenever the *c* was followed by *e* or *i*, as in *trafficker, trafficking, picnicker, mimicking,* etc. An exception is *arced, arcing,* the past tense and present participle of *arc;* however, this verb also has the variant forms *arcked, arcking.*

coliseum (kol′əsē′əm) *n.* stadium, arena. 1708-15, in an edition of Kersey's *Dictionary,* borrowed from Medieval Latin, variant of *colosseum* COLOSSEUM.

collaborate *v.* work together. 1871, borrowed from Latin *collabōrātum,* past participle of *collabōrāre* work with (*col-,* form of *com-* before *l* + *labōrāre* to work, from *labor,* genitive *labōris,* work, LABOR); for suffix see -ATE[1]. During World War II the word was associated with those who cooperated with the Nazis or Fascists, especially in France (1941, probably translation of French *collaborer,* 1940). —**collaboration** *n.* 1860, in writings of Charles Reade, borrowed from French *collaboration,* from *collaborer* collaborate, from Latin *collabōrāre;* for suffix see -ATION. —**collaborator** *n.* 1802, in writings of Bentham, borrowed from French *collaborateur,* from *collaboration;* for suffix see -OR[2].

collage (kəläzh′) *n.* form of art consisting of odd parts and pieces glued to a canvas, etc. 1919, in writings of Wyndham Lewis, borrowed from French *collage,* literally, a pasting, gluing, from Old French *coller* to glue, *colle* glue, from Vulgar Latin **colla,* from Greek *kólla* glue, cognate with Old Slavic *klějĭ* glue, from Indo-European **koly-/kolei-* (Pok.612); for suffix see -AGE. —**v.** form or compose as a collage. 1964, from the noun.

collagen (kol′əjən) *n.* protein fiber that is a main constituent of connective tissues. About 1865, borrowed from French *collagène,* from Greek *kólla* glue; for suffix see -GEN.

collapse *v.* fall in. 1732, borrowed from Latin *collāpsus,* past participle of *collābī* fall together (*col-,* form of *com-* before *l,* + *lābī* to fall, slip, slide); related to LAPSE. —**n.** 1801, from the verb. —**collapsible** *adj.* 1843, formed from English *collapse* + *-ible.*

collar *n.* About 1300 *coler* neck piece in armor, borrowed from Old French *coler,* from Latin *collāre* band for the neck, collar, from *collum* neck. The Latin word is cognate with Old English *heals neck,* Old Saxon, Old Frisian, Old High German, Old Icelandic, and Gothic *hals,* from Indo-European **kwolsom,* Lithuanian *kāklas* neck (as "that which turns"), Greek *kýklos* cycle, wheel; see WHEEL.

By gradual approximation to the Latin form *collāre,* Middle English *coler* changed to modern English *collar.*
—**v.** Before 1555, seize a person's collar or neck; from the noun. The generalized sense "to take hold of, seize" is first recorded about 1700. —**collar bone** (perhaps 1500)

collate *v.* compare carefully. 1612, in Francis Bacon's *Essays,* borrowed from Latin *collātus,* a form serving as past participle of *cōnferre* bring together (*con-,* variant of *com-* together + *ferre* bring, carry, BEAR[2]); for suffix see -ATE[1].

collateral *adj.* secondary. About 1378, in a version of *Piers Plowman,* borrowed from Old French *collateral,* learned borrowing from Medieval Latin *collateralis* accompanying, concomitant; literally, side by side (Latin *col-,* form of *com-* before *l,* + *laterālis* pertaining to the side, LATERAL). —**n.** 1513-75, in an early Scottish almanac, colleague, associate; from the adjective. The current sense "anything given as collateral security" appeared in 1832 in American English, from the phrase *collateral security* (1720).

collation[1] *n.* act of collating. About 1380, act of bringing together for comparison, in Chaucer's translation of Boethius' *De Consolatione Philosophiae;* borrowed from Old French *collation,* learned borrowing from Latin *collātiōnem* (nominative *collātiō*), from the verbal stem of *collātus,* a form serving as past participle of *cōnferre* bring together; for suffix see -TION.

collation[2] *n.* light meal. Before 1300, borrowed from Medieval Latin *collationem* light meal or refreshments taken by members of a monastery after reading of the *Collationes* Conferences of the Church Fathers (a work by John Cassian, A.D. 410-420), from Late Latin *collātiōnem* conference, from Latin *collātiōnem* (nominative *collātiō*) act of bringing together, from the verbal stem of *collātus* (see COLLATE); for suffix see -TION.

colleague *n.* Before 1533, borrowed from Middle French *collègue,* learned borrowing from Latin *collēga* associate, colleague; literally, one chosen together with another (*col-* together, form of *com-* before *l,* + *lēgāre* send or choose as deputy; see LEGATE).

collect *v.* Probably before 1425, in a version of Higden's *Polychronicon, collecten* to accumulate, gather; borrowed from Old French *collecter* and Latin *collēctus,* past participle of *colligere* gather together (*col-* together, form of *com-* before *l,* + *legere* gather; see LEGEND). —**n.** a prayer said for a specific purpose. Probably before 1200, in *Ancrene Riwle,* borrowed from Old French *collecte* and directly from Latin *collēcta* a gathering, from *collēctus;* see the verb. —**collectible** *adj.* 1662 (1660 *-able*), formed from English *collect* + *-ible.* —**collectibles** *n.pl.* item(s) suitable for collecting. 1952, from *collectible,* adj. —**collection** *n.* 1387, in Trevisa's translation of Higden's *Polychronicon,* borrowed from Old French *collection,* learned borrowing from Latin *collēctiōnem* (nominative *collēctiō*), from the stem of *colligere* gather together; for suffix see -TION. —**collective** *adj.* Probably before 1425, borrowed from Middle French *collectif, collective,* learned borrowing from Latin *collēctīvus,* from *collēctus,* see *collect,* v.; for suffix see -IVE. —*n.* collective farm, etc. 1925, from the adjective. —**collector** *n.* About 1405, borrowed through Anglo-French *collectour,* Old French *collecteur* and Medieval Latin *collector,* from Latin *collēctus,* see *collect,* v.; for suffix see -OR[2].

colleen *n.* 1828, borrowed from Irish *cailīn* girl, diminutive of *caile* girl, woman.

college *n.* Probably about 1378, a body of scholars and students within a university (as at Oxford or Cambridge), in writings of Wycliffe; borrowed from Old French *college,* learned borrowing from Latin *collēgium* a fellowship, company, from *collēga* COLLEAGUE.

The meaning "educational institution beyond secondary school or high school" appeared in 1563.
—**collegiate** *adj.* 1514, borrowed from Medieval Latin *collegiatus* of or having to do with a college, from Latin *collēgium;* for suffix see -ATE[1].

collide *v.* 1621, in Burton's *Anatomy of Melancholy,* borrowed from Latin *collīdere* strike together (*col-* together, form of *com-* before *l,* + *laedere* to strike, of uncertain origin).

collie *n.* Before 1651, possibly *Colle,* about 1386, in Chaucer's *Canterbury Tales* as a proper name, origin uncertain; the conjecture is that Middle English *Colle* may have had a diminutive form *collie* and that the form is equivalent to "coaly" meaning black in color, the original color of the breed.

collier (kol′yər) *n.* coal miner; ship for carrying coal. 1276 *collere* charcoal maker and seller; later *colier* (1408-09), formed from Middle English *col* coal + *-ere, -ier* -er[1]. **—colliery** *n.* 1635, formed from English *collier* + *-y*[3], as in -ERY.

collision *n.* clash. Probably before 1425, in a translation of Higden's *Polychronicon,* borrowed from Middle French *collision,* learned borrowing from Latin *collīsiōnem* (nominative *collīsiō*), from *collīdere* COLLIDE; for suffix see -SION.

collocation *n.* 1605, in Francis Bacon's *Of the Advancement of Learning,* probably borrowed from French *collocation,* learned borrowing from Latin *collocātiōnem* (nominative *collocātiō*), from *collocāre* place together; for suffix see -TION. The reference to a particular combination of words established by usage is first recorded in Southey's *The Doctor* (1834-47), though as a technical term it does not appear before 1940; but general references to arrangement of words or sounds in language appear as early as 1750. It is also possible that *collocation* is a back formation from earlier *collocate,* v., to place. 1513, in Sir Thomas More's *History of King Richard III,* borrowed from Latin *collocātus,* past participle of *collocāre* (*col-* together, form of *com-* before *l,* + *locāre* to place, put, LOCATE); for suffix see -ATE[1]. Doublet of COUCH.

colloid (kol′oid) *n.* substance composed of particles larger than molecules, that remain in a suspension of gas, liquid, or solid. 1849-52, jelly-like substance, in an edition of an anatomy text; earlier, as an adjective (1847-49); borrowed from French *colloïde* (1845), from Greek *kólla* glue (see COLLAGE); for suffix see -OID. **—colloidal** *adj.* 1861, probably borrowed from French *colloïdal* (1855), from *colloïde;* for suffix see -AL[1]; or perhaps formed from English *colloid* + *-al*[1].

colloquy (kol′əkwē) *n.* a talking together. 1459, a discourse; later, a conversation (1581); borrowed from Latin *colloquium* conference, conversation, from *colloquī* speak together (*col-* together, form of *com-* before *l,* + *loquī* speak, of uncertain origin). **—colloquial** *adj.* 1751-52, Samuel Johnson in an issue of *The Rambler,* conversational, belonging to common speech, formed from English *colloquy* + *-al*[1]. **—colloquialism** *n.* 1810, formed from English *colloquial* + *-ism.*

collusion *n.* 1389, borrowed from Old French *collusion,* learned borrowing from Latin *collūsiōnem* (nominative *collūsiō*) a playing together, act of colluding, from *collūdere* collude; for suffix see -SION. **—collude** *v.* 1525, borrowed from Latin *collūdere* play together, collude (*col-* together, form of *com-* before *l,* + *lūdere* to play, from *lūdus* game; see LUDICROUS).

cologne *n.* 1814 *cologne water,* American English, loan translation of French *eau de Cologne,* literally, water of Cologne, from *Cologne,* Germany, where it is made. The word has been used to describe articles made in Cologne (before 1399).

colon[1] *n.* punctuation mark. 1589, in George Puttenham's *The Arte of English Poesie,* borrowed from Latin *cōlon* part of a poem, member of a verse, from Greek *kôlon* limb, member of the body or of a sentence, clause, related to *skélos* leg, from Indo-European **(s)kel-/kōl-* (Pok.928).

The punctuation mark (:) was so called because it was originally used to separate independent clauses (Greek *kôlon* clause). See COMMA.

colon[2] *n.* lower part of the large intestine. Before 1398, in Trevisa's translation of Bartholomew's *De Proprietatibus Rerum,* borrowed from Latin *colon,* from Greek *kólon* part of the large intestine; apparently cognate with Armenian *k'ałird* intestines, and Lithuanian *skìlvis* belly.

colonel (kėr′nəl) *n.* Originally (1548) spelled *coronel,* borrowed from Middle French *coronel, coronnel,* which with Spanish *coronel* came from Italian *colonnello* the commander of a column of soldiers at the head of a regiment, from *colonna* column, from Latin *columna* pillar, post, COLUMN.

The change of the first *l* in Italian *colonnello* to *r* in French *coronnel, coronel* is due to dissimilation of two identical neighboring sounds.

Later (1583) the form *colonel* came into English from Middle French *colonel,* a variant spelling of the commoner *coronel.* This variant spelling became established primarily through familiar literary use and in translations of Italian military treatises in the late 16th century.

Two pronunciations (koləneľ, korəneľ) existed until the early years of the 19th century when the popular pronunciation (kėr′ənəl) gave way to kėr′nəl and began to gain prominence at all levels, though the familiar literary form *colonel* remained firmly established in printing.

colonnade *n.* series of columns, usually supporting a roof, etc. 1718, borrowed from French *colonnade,* alteration of earlier *colonnate* (1675), from Italian *colonnato,* from *colonna* column, from Latin *columna* pillar, COLUMN; for suffix see -ADE.

colony *n.* About 1384, in the Wycliffe Bible, *colonie* a Roman settlement; borrowed through Old French *colonie,* or directly from Latin *colōnia,* from *colōnus* cultivator, settler, from *colere* cultivate, till, inhabit; cognate with Sanskrit *karṣū́-s* furrow, *cárati* he moves, Greek *télos* end, (originally a turning), *pólos* axis, from Indo-European **kwel-/kwol-* turn (Pok.639).
—colonial *adj.* 1776, formed in American English from Latin *colōnia* colony + English *-al*[1]; or perhaps from English *colony* + *-ial,* on the pattern of *barony, baronial.* **—colonialism** *n.* 1853, formed from English *colonial* + *-ism.* **—colonist** *n.* 1701, formed from English *colony* + *-ist.* **—colonization** *n.* 1770, in Burke's writings, formed from English *colonize* + *-ation.* **—colonize** *v.* 1622, in Francis Bacon's writings, formed from English *colony* + *-ize.* **—colonizer** *n.* 1781, formed in American English from *colonize* + *-er.*[1]

colophon (kol′əfon) *n.* 1774, publisher's inscription at the end of a book (corresponding to the modern title page); borrowed from Latin *colophōn,* from Greek *kolophṓn* summit, final touch. Since the first use of this word was as the name of a town in Lydia it is probably best to consider it as non-Indo-European. The sense of a publisher's imprint on a book is attested in English since 1930.

color *n.* About 1225 *colur* skin color, complexion, in *King Horn;* visible color, color of an object (probably before 1300, in *Kyng Alisaunder* and *Sir Tristrem*); probably borrowed through Old French *colour,* from Latin *color* (accusative *colōrem*) color, hue, related to *cēlāre* to hide, conceal; see CELL. **—v.** Probably about 1375-90 *colouren* give color to, in a version of one of Chaucer's *Canterbury Tales,* probably borrowed through Old French *colorer,* from Latin *colōrāre* to give color to, color, from *color* color. **—coloration** *n.* 1626, in Francis Bacon's *Sylva Sylvarum,* possibly borrowed from French *coloration,* but more likely from Late Latin *colōrātiōnem* (nominative *colōrātiō*) act or fact of coloring, from Latin *colōrāre* to color. **—color-blind** *adj.* 1854, but implied in earlier *color-blindness* (1844). **—colored** *adj.* (probably about 1375-90, see *color,* v.). **—colorful** *adj.* 1889, formed from English *color* + *-ful.* **—coloring** *n.* (probably before 1425) **—colorless** *adj.* About 1380, in *Sir Ferumbras,* formed from English *color* + *-less.*

coloratura *n.* ornamental vocal passages in music. 1740, an Italian word used in a translation of a book on music, from Late Latin *colōrātūra* coloring, from Latin *colōrāt-* (past participial stem of *colōrāre* to COLOR); for suffix see -URE. The meaning of soprano who sings such passages is first recorded in English in 1944.

Colosseum (kol′əsē′əm) *n.* large amphitheater in Rome, completed in A.D. 80; compare COLISEUM. 1563, borrowed in reference to the *Colosseum* in Rome from Latin *colossēum,* neuter of *colossēus* gigantic, from *colossus* COLOSSUS.

colossus *n.* huge statue. Before 1398, a Latin word used in Trevisa's translation of Bartholomew's *De Proprietatibus Rerum,* in reference to the *Colossus of Rhodes;* from Greek *kolossós* gigantic statue (in reference to Egyptian statues referred to by Herodotus), later specifically that of Apollo at Rhodes. The word was apparently borrowed from an Aegean language. The transferred sense of anything vast or gigantic is first recorded in English in 1794. **—colossal** *adj.* like a colossus; huge. 1712, borrowed from French *colossal,* from *colosse* colossus, from Latin *colossus;* for suffix see -AL[1].

colostomy (kəlos′təmē) *n.* surgical opening into the colon through the abdominal wall. 1888, formed in English from *colon*[2] + Greek *stóma* opening + *-y*[3].

colt *n.* young horse. Developed in Middle English, probably before 1382, from Old English *colt* young donkey or camel (about 1000, in Ælfric's paraphrase of *Genesis*); probably cognate with dialectal Swedish *kult* young boar, piglet, boy, Norwegian *kult* stout person, block, stump, and Danish *kuld* offspring, brood, from Proto-Germanic **kultaz,* from Indo-European **gl̥-d-os* fetus (root **gel-/gl̥-* to swell, Pok.358); see CHILD.

columbine (kol′əmbin) *n.* plant whose flowers have petals shaped like hollow spurs. Before 1310, borrowed perhaps through Old French *columbin,* from Medieval Latin *columbina,* apparently transferred sense from Late Latin *columbīna* vervain, feminine of Latin *columbīnus* dovelike, from *columba* dove (because the inverted flower supposedly resembles a cluster of five doves). The Latin word is possibly cognate with Greek *kólymbos* a diver (kind of bird), from Indo-European **kel-/kal-* (Pok. 547).

column *n.* About 1440, in *Promptorium Parvulorum,* a vertical division of a page; also, a pillar, post (before 1449); borrowed from Old French *colombe, colompne,* and Latin *columna* column, pillar, post, related to *columen, culmen* top, summit, *celsus* high, *collis* hill, Greek *kolōnós* hill, and Old English *hyll* HILL, from Indo-European **kel-/kol-/kl̥-* (Pok.544).

The specific sense of matter written for a newspaper or magazine column, is recorded since 1785. **—columnar** *adj.* 1728, probably formed from English *column* + *-ar,* on the pattern of *curricular;* but possibly a borrowing from Late Latin *columnāris,* from Latin *columna* column. **—columnist** *n.* 1920, American English, formed from (newspaper) *column* + *-ist.*

com- a prefix added primarily to verbs, meaning with, together, as in *combine, compress,* or serving as an intensive to strengthen the force of the verb, as in *comminute, complete. Com-* is also added to nouns and adjectives, meaning joint, fellow, as in *compatriot.* English *com-* was borrowed from Latin *com-,* from the preposition *com,* early form of *cum* with, which is cognate with Greek *koinós* common, general (from earlier **komyós*), Old Irish *com-, con-* with, together, and Albanian *kë-* with, together, from Indo-European **kom* along, with (Pok.612).

In Latin, the form *com-* survived when followed by *b, m, p,* as illustrated by examples of English borrowings *(combine, commute, compete);* before other consonants *com-* became *con-* or was assimilated (as *con-* would be) to *col-* and *cor-.* Before a vowel or *h* the *m* (apparently weakly sounded as final *m* generally was) dropped out, and *co-* became the form before vowels or *h* as in *coagulate, coerce, cohere;* this form has had a vigorous life in English as a prefix added especially to nouns and verbs, and before consonants as well as before vowels *(copilot, coworker, coauthor, coedit).* See also CO-, COL-, CON-, COR-.

coma[1] (kō′mə) *n.* unconsciousness. 1646, borrowed from New Latin, from Greek *kôma* (genitive *kṓmatos*) deep sleep, perhaps related to *kámnein* to toil, be sick or worn out, suffer. The Greek word is cognate with Middle Irish *cuma* trouble, sorrow, and Sanskrit *śámati, śamyati* he exerts himself, works, from Indo-European **k̂em-/k̂om-/k̂ōm-* (Pok.557). **—comatose** *adj.* 1755, either formed in English from Greek *kôma* (genitive *kṓmatos*) coma + English adjective suffix *-ose*[1]; or borrowed from earlier French *comateux,* feminine *comateuse* (1616).

coma[2] (kō′mə) *n.* head of a comet. 1669, tuft of hairs on foliage, borrowed from Latin *coma* hair of the head, mane, from Greek *kómē,* of uncertain origin. The sense in astronomy is first recorded in 1765.

comb *n.* Old English (about 700) *camb,* later (chiefly Anglian) *comb;* cognate with Old Saxon and Old High German *camb* comb (modern German *Kamm*), Middle Dutch *cam* (modern Dutch *kam*), Old Icelandic *kambr* comb (Swedish *kamm,* Norwegian and Danish *kam*), from Proto-Germanic **kambaz.* Outside Germanic the word is cognate with, and semantically related as a toothed implement, to Greek *gómphos* bolt, *gomphíos* molar tooth, Albanian *dhëmb* tooth, Old Slavic *zǫbŭ,* Lithuanian *žam̃bas* sharp edge, Sanskrit *jámbha-s,* and Tocharian A *kam,* Tocharian B *keme* tooth, from Indo-European **ĝombho-s* (Pok.369) **—v.** 1495, from the noun; earlier *kombid,* past participle, before 1398, in Trevisa's translation of Bartholomew's *De Proprietatibus Rerum.* **—comber** *n.* About 1200, one who cards wool, formed from Middle English *comben* to card wool + *-er*[1].

combat *v.* do battle, fight. 1564, in Hakluyt's *Voyages,* borrowed from Middle French *combattre,* learned borrowing from Late Latin *combattere* (Latin *com-* with each other + Late Latin *battere* to beat, strike; see BAT[1] stick). **—n.** 1567, borrowed from Middle French *combat,* from *combattre* to combat. **—combatant** *n.* 1489, in a translation by Caxton, from Middle French *combattant,* from present participle of *combattre* to combat; probably influenced by Middle English *combattant,* adj. (about 1460); borrowed from Middle French, present participle. **—combative** *adj.* Before 1834, in correspondence of Lamb, formed from English *combat* + *-ive.*

combine (kəmbīn′) *v.* Before 1420, in Lydgate's *Troy Book,* borrowed probably through Middle French *combiner,* from Late Latin *combīnāre* join two by two, yoke together, combine (Latin *com-* together + *bīnī* two each, two by two; see BINARY). **—n.** (kom′bīn) 1887, American English, a combination or alliance of persons, especially for fraudulent purposes; from the verb. The sense "machine for harvesting" appeared in 1910, though the use of a mower and a thresher as a combined harvesting operation is recorded as early as 1857. **—combination** *n.* Before 1398 *combinacyoun,* in Trevisa's translation of Bartholomew's *De Proprietatibus Rerum,* borrowed from Late Latin *combīnātiōnem,* (nominative *combīnātiō*), from *combīnāre* combine; for suffix see -TION.

combustion *n.* act or process of burning. Probably before 1425, in a translation of Chauliac's *Grande Chirurgie;* borrowed from Old French *combustion,* learned borrowing from Latin *combustiōnem* (nominative *combustiō*), from *combūrere* burn up; for suffix see -TION. Latin *combūrere* was formed from *com-* completely + *-būrere,* an alteration (influenced by *ambūrere* burn around, scorch) of *ūrere* to burn, which is cognate with Greek *heúein* to singe, Old Icelandic *ysja* fire, Old English *ysel, ysle* spark, cinder, ember, and Sanskrit *óṣati* (he) burns, *uṣṇá-s* hot, from Indo-European **eus-/us-* burn (Pok.347). Related to BROIL[1] (cook), BUST[1] (sculpture), and EMBER.

An earlier use of this word in Middle English (before 1398, in Trevisa's translation of Bartholomew's *De Proprietatibus Rerum*) referred to an obscuring by the sun.

—combustible *adj.* 1529, in Sir Thomas More's works, but implied earlier in *combustibility* (1471), borrowed probably from Middle French *combustible* and Late Latin *combustibilis,* from Latin *combustum,* past participle of *combūrere* burn up.

come *v.* About 1175 *comen;* earlier *cumen* (before 1121), developed from Old English *cuman* (before 830, in the *Vespasian Psalter*) and having the forms in the past tense *cuōm, cōm,* past participle *cumen.* The Old English *cuman* is cognate with Old Saxon *cuman* to come, Old Frisian *kuma,* Middle Dutch *comen* (modern Dutch *komen,* past tense *kwam*), Old High German *queman, coman,* past tense *quam* (modern German *kommen,* past tense *kam*), Old Icelandic *koma* (Swedish *komma,* Danish and Norwegian *komme*), and Gothic *qiman,* all from a Germanic base **kwem-,* from Proto-Germanic **kwemanan,* corresponding to Indo-European **gwem-.* The latter, whose initial consonant cluster became in Latin *v,* in Greek *b,* and in Sanskrit *g,* is represented by Latin *venīre* to come, Greek *baínein* to go (from an earlier stem *bamy-*), Sanskrit *gámati* (he) goes, *gáti-s* a going, course, and Tocharian A, Tocharian B *käm-* to come, from Indo-European **gwem-/gwom-/gwm̥-* (Pok.464).

The Old English past tense *cuōm,* later *cōm,* became *com, come* in Middle English, but was soon replaced, perhaps through the influence of Scandinavian (compare Old Icelandic past tense form *kvam*) by *cam, came* (modern English *came*). The Old English past participle *cuman* was used occasionally down to the 1600's as *comen,* but the loss of the final *-n* (which began in the 1200's) finally caused this form to be leveled with the infinitive form as *come.*

—comer *n.* Before 1376, in *Piers Plowman,* formed from Middle English *comen* + *-er*[1]. **—coming** *n.* (1280); *adj.* (about 1460). **—comeuppance** *n.* 1859, American English, from special use of the verb phrase *come up* get the better of (1856) + *-ance.*

comedy *n.* About 1385, a narrative, especially a poem, with a happy ending, a humorous work, in Chaucer's *Troilus and Criseyde;* borrowed from Old French *comedie,* from Latin *cōmoedia,* from Greek *kōmōidíā* a comedy, amusing spectacle, from *kōmōidós* actor or singer in a comic chorus (*kômos* merrymaking, festive procession + *aoidós* singer, from *aeidein* to sing, member of the compound related to Greek *ōidḗ* ODE). The modern sense of an amusing play or theatrical performance is the same as that used by the ancient Greek and Roman writers, but in the Middle Ages the application was chiefly to poems and stories, though a "happy ending" continued to be an essential part of the meaning. The ancient sense of an amusing performance reappeared in English in the 1500's. **—comedian** *n.* 1581, writer of comedies, in Sidney's *Apology for Poetry;* borrowed from Middle French *comédien,* from Old French *comedie;* for suffix see -IAN. The sense "comic actor" is first recorded in 1601, in Shakespeare's *Twelfth Night.*

comely *adj.* Before 1400 *comly* beautiful, handsome; earlier, noble (probably before 1300, in a version of *The Romance of Guy of Warwick*), and *kumelich* becoming, appropriate (probably about 1200); possibly shortened from *bicumelic* (probably before 1200), from BECOME fitting, seemly, attractive; for suffix see -LY. Compare Middle High German *komlich* suitable (beside *bekōme* suitably) and German dialect *kommlich, kömmlich.*

The traditional point of view is that Middle English *kumelich* developed from Old English *cȳmlīc* finely made, handsome (about 1000, but recorded earlier as an adverb, about 725, in *Beowulf*), from Old English *cȳme* fine, exquisite. The phonological connection is explained by a shortening of *cȳmlīc* to *cymlīc* by influence of *ml;* this form with short *y* was then associated by similarity of *cym-* forms of *cuman* to come, and thus with "becoming."

The development of the form in Middle and modern English *comely* is associated with Middle English *cumen, comen* to come; the sense development parallels *become becoming,* but in Middle English, *become,* v. be attractive, suitable, etc. is not recorded earlier than *bicumlic,* adj. becoming (probably before 1200); so it is still not definite that *bicumlic* is the source of Middle English *kumelich* comely.

comestible *n.* thing to eat. 1837, in Theodore Hook's *Jack Brag,* noun use of earlier adjective meaning fit to eat, edible (1483, in Caxton's translation of *Golden Legend*); borrowed from Middle French *comestible,* a learned borrowing from Late Latin *comēstibilis,* from

Latin *comēstus,* an alteration (under the influence of *pōtus* drunk) of earlier *comēsus,* past participle of *comedere* eat up, consume (*com-* thoroughly + *edere* EAT; for suffix see -IBLE.

comet *n.* Probably before 1200 *comete,* in Layamon's *Chronicle of Britain,* borrowed from Old French *comete,* learned borrowing from Latin *comēta,* from Greek *komḗtēs* comet, (originally) wearing long hair (because a comet's tail resembles long hair), from *komân* let the hair grow long, from *kómē* hair; see COMA[2]. Earlier citation in *The Anglo-Saxon Chronicle* is Latin.

comfit (kum′fit) *n.* confection. Before 1399 *confyt,* borrowed from Old French *confit, confite,* from Latin *cōnfectum, cōnfecta,* neuter and feminine of *cōnfectus,* past participle of *cōnficere* put together, prepare (*com-* together + *facere* make, DO[1]). The spelling *comfyte* (with *m*) appeared before 1450.

comfort *v.* About 1280 *conforten* cheer up, console, borrowed from Old French *conforter* to help, strengthen, from Late Latin *cōnfortāre* strengthen (Latin *con-*, variant of *com-* altogether + *fortis* strong; see FORT). **—n.** Probably before 1200 *cunfort* a feeling of consolation, in *Ancrene Riwle;* later *confort* (about 1200 and about 1280); borrowed probably through Anglo-French from Old French *cunfort, confort,* from earlier noun use derived from the stem of Latin *cōnfortāre* strengthen. Apparently the noun and verb were borrowed separately in English, though the noun replaced earlier Old English *frōfor;* however, it is possible that the later verb is from the noun. The phonetic change of *con-* to *com-* before *f* took place in English. **—comfortable** *adj.* About 1340 *comfortabil* pleasant, enjoyable, borrowed from Anglo-French *confortable* from *conforter* to help, strengthen + *-able.* **—comforter** *n.* Before 1382, in the Wycliffe Bible; earlier, one who gives solace such as the Holy Ghost or Jesus (about 1350); borrowed through Anglo-French *confortour* from Old French *comforteor,* from Late Latin **cōnfortātōrem,* from *cōnfortāre;* for suffix see -ER[1]. **—comfortless** *adj.* Before 1387, in Trevisa's translation of Higden's *Polychronicon;* formed from English *comfort* + *-less.*

comic *adj.* Before 1387 *comice* of or belonging to comedy, in Trevisa's translation of Higden's *Polychronicon;* borrowed from Latin *cōmicus,* from Greek *kōmikós* of or pertaining to comedy, from *kômos* merrymaking, see COMEDY; for suffix see -IC. The modern sense of humorous, laughable, is first recorded in 1751 in Samuel Johnson's *The Rambler,* though *comical* had been used in this sense since the late 1600's. **—n.** 1581, writer of comedies; 1619, actor in comedies, comic actor; from the adjective. The sense of "comic strip" (usually *comics*) is first recorded in 1910, in H.G. Wells' *Mr. Polly.* **—comical** *adj.* Probably before 1425, formed in English from Latin *cōmicus* + English *-al*[1]. An earlier meaning "epileptic" (before 1398) was borrowed from Latin *morbus comitiālis* epilepsy. **—comic strip** 1920, American English, in Carl Sandburg's *Smoke and Steel.*

comity (kom′ətē) *n.* courtesy, civility. 1543, borrowed from Latin *cōmitās* friendliness, from *cōmis* friendly, courteous, probably from Old Latin *cosmis,* of uncertain origin; for suffix see -ITY. Old Latin *cosmis* is believed by some to derive possibly from *co-* with, together + *-smi-s* smile, cognate with Sanskrit *smita-s* smiling; see SMILE.

An early use of this word is found in a translation of Chauliac's *Grande Chirurgie* (probably before 1425) in Middle English *comite* association, borrowed from Medieval Latin *comitas,* from Latin *cōmitās* friendliness.

comma *n.* 1586, short part of a sentence, division of a period or full sentence, in Angel Day's *The English Secretary;* borrowed probably through Middle French *comma,* from Latin *comma,* from Greek *kómma* stamp, short clause; literally, piece cut off, related to *kóptein* to cut off, strike; see CAPON. The sense of the punctuation mark is first recorded in English in 1599.

The words *colon, comma,* and *period* originally denoted divisions in Greek rhetoric and prosody. The period meant a complete or rounded sentence, the colon a member or clause of a sentence, and the comma a short segment of a sentence. The comparative length of the parts of the sentence evolved into terms of punctuation indicating shorter or longer parts, just as the period, or full stop, marks the end of the "period" or sentence itself.

command *v.* Probably before 1300 *comanden,* in *Arthour and Merlin,* borrowed from Old French *comander* to order, enjoin, entrust, from Vulgar Latin **commandāre,* alteration (influenced by Latin *mandāre* command, entrust) of Latin *commendāre* to recommend, COMMEND. **—n.** Before 1400, in a version of *Cursor Mundi;* borrowed from Old French *comande,* from *comander* to command. **—commandant** *n.* 1687, borrowed from French *commandant,* originally in the sense of commanding, present participle of *commander* to command, from Old French *comander* to command; for suffix see -ANT. **—commander** *n.* Before 1325 *comandur,* in *Cursor Mundi;* borrowed from Old French *comandeor,* from *comander* to command; for suffix see -ER[1]. **—commandment** *n.* About 1275, borrowed from Old French *comandement,* from Vulgar Latin **commandāmentum,* from **commandāre;* for suffix see -MENT. Originally, Middle English *commandement,* and later into the 1600's by some users, the word was pronounced with four syllables, though the OED says "the trisyllabic form appeared already in the 13th c. and became prevalent in the literary language in 17-18th c."

commandeer (kom′əndir′) *v.* 1881, in the London *Times,* borrowed from Afrikaans *kommandeer,* from French *commander* to command, from Old French *comander;* see COMMAND.

commando *n.* 1791, a military expedition or raid, borrowed from Afrikaans *kommando,* from Dutch *commando* a troop under a commander, from Portuguese *commando* a command, from *commandar* to command, from Vulgar Latin **commandāre;* see COMMAND.

The meaning of a soldier who makes daring raids appeared in World War II and is first attested in 1940, in Winston Churchill's *Second World War,* in reference to a body of British troops specially trained to repel a German invasion of Britain, and later for carrying out raids in other theaters of war.

commemorate *v.* 1599, to recall, possibly borrowed through Old French *commemorer,* or directly from Latin *commemorātus,* past participle of *commemorāre* bring to remembrance, mention (*com-* together + *memorāre* bring to mind, from *memor* mindful of, remembering; see MEMORY); for suffix see -ATE[1]. Alternatively, the verb may have been a back formation of earlier *commemoration.* The sense "to honor or preserve the memory of" appeared before 1638. **—com-**

memoration *n.* About 1384, a calling to remembrance, in the Wycliffe Bible; borrowed through Old French *commemoration,* or directly from Latin *commemorātiōnem* (nominative *commemorātiō*), from *commemorāre* commemorate; for suffix see -TION. —**commemorative** *adj.* 1612-19, formed from English *commemorate* + *-ive.*

commence *v.* begin. Probably about 1300, in *The Romance of Guy of Warwick,* borrowed from Old French *comencier,* from Vulgar Latin **cominitiāre* (Latin *com-* together + Late Latin *initiāre* begin, from Latin *initiāre* INITIATE). The doubling of the *m* started in Old French, and was fully established in English by 1500. —**commencement** *n.* About 1275, borrowed from Old French *comencement,* from *comencier* commence; for suffix see -MENT. The sense of ceremony at which academic degrees are conferred appeared before 1387, in Trevisa's translation of Higden's *Polychronicon,* and is derived from the verb sense of be admitted to the title of an academic degree, which was a translation of Medieval Latin *incipere,* from Latin, to begin; see INCIPIENT.

commend *v.* Probably about 1350 *comenden,* borrowed from Latin *commendāre* recommend, praise (*com-* with, intensive form + *mandāre* commit, entrust, MANDATE). —**commendable** *adj.* Probably about 1350, borrowed from Middle French *commendable,* from Latin *commendābilis* praiseworthy, from *commendāre;* for suffix see -ABLE. —**commendation** *n.* About 1390, expression of approval, in Chaucer's *Canterbury Tales;* earlier, eulogy (probably before 1200, in *Ancrene Riwle*); borrowed from Old French *commendation,* learned borrowing from Latin *commendātiōnem* (nominative *commendātiō*), from *commendāre* commend; for suffix see -TION.

commensurate *adj.* 1641, borrowed from Late Latin *commēnsūrātus* (Latin *com-* together + Late Latin *mēnsūrātus,* past participle of *mēnsūrāre* to measure, from Latin *mēnsūra* MEASURE); for suffix see -ATE[1]. —**commensurable** *adj.* 1557, borrowed through Middle French or directly from Late Latin *commēnsūrābilis* having a common measure (Latin *com-* together + Late Latin *mēnsūrābilis* that can be measured, from *mēnsūrāre* to measure); for suffix see -ABLE.

comment *n.* Before 1387, in Trevisa's translation of Higden's *Polychronicon,* borrowed possibly through Old French *comment,* or directly from Late Latin *commentum* comment, interpretation, from Latin *commentum* invention, contrivance, originally neuter past participle of *comminīscī* think up, invent (*com-* thoroughly + *-minīscī* to think, related to *mēns,* genitive *mentis* MIND). —**v.** 1591, in Shakespeare's *The Two Gentlemen of Verona,* from the noun; earlier *commenten* explain (probably before 1425); borrowed from Latin *commentārī* think about, discuss, frequentative form of *comminīscī* think up, invent. —**commentary** *n.* Probably before 1425, in a version of Higden's *Polychronicon,* borrowed possibly through Old French *commentaire,* or directly from Latin *commentārius,* originally as adjective with the meaning of relating to comment, from *commentum* comment; for suffix see -ARY. —**commentator** *n.* Before 1398, in Trevisa's translation of Bartholomew's *De Proprietatibus Rerum,* borrowed, possibly by influence of Old French *commentateur,* from Late Latin and Latin *commentātor* inventor, author, from Latin *commentārī* think about, discuss, frequentative form of *comminīscī* think up, invent. —**commentate** *v.* 1794, back formation from *commentator* + *-ate*[1].

commerce *n.* 1537, borrowed from Middle French *commerce,* learned borrowing from Latin *commercium* trade, trafficking (*com-* together, with + *merx,* genitive *mercis* wares, merchandise; see MARKET). —**commercial** *adj.* Before 1687, formed in English from Latin *commercium* trade + English *-al*[1]. —**commercialize** *v.* 1830, formed from English *commercial* + *-ize.*

commingle *v.* Before 1616, in writings of Francis Bacon; formed from English *com-* with, together + *mingle,* replacing earlier *comingle.*

commiserate *v.* 1606, to pity, borrowed from Latin *commiserātus,* past participle of *commiserārī* to pity (*com-* with, together + *miserārī* bewail, lament, from *miser* wretched, MISERABLE); for suffix see -ATE[1]. —**commiseration** *n.* 1585, borrowed from Middle French *commisération* and directly from Latin *commiserātiōnem* (nominative *commiserātiō*) act or fact of pitying, from *commiserārī* to pity.

commissar *n.* 1918, head of a government department in the Soviet Union, borrowed from Russian *komissar,* from German *Kommissar* commissioner, from Old French *commissaire,* from Medieval Latin *commissarius;* see COMMISSARY. The word appeared in Middle English with the meaning of delegate or commissioner of a ruler (before 1376, in *Piers Plowman*), but is not recorded after 1709, until its present use.

commissariat (kom′əsãr′ēat) *n.* department of an army that supplies food, etc. 1779, in correspondence of Thomas Jefferson; earlier use in Scottish law, a court, the office, or the jurisdiction of a commissioner (1609); borrowed from French *commissariat,* from Medieval Latin *commissarius* COMMISSARY + French *-at* -ate[1].

commissary *n.* Before 1376 *comissarie* one entrusted with certain duties, representative or delegate, in *Piers Plowman;* borrowed from Medieval Latin *commissarius,* from Latin *commissus* entrusted, past participle of *committere* entrust, COMMIT; for suffix see -ARY. In 1489 (in writings of Caxton) the word appears in the sense of a military officer in charge of food and supplies. The sense of store for provisions, is first recorded in 1882 in American English, and that of a dining room in a film studio or business establishment in 1929.

commission *n.* 1344, authority committed or entrusted to anyone, borrowed from Old French or directly from Latin *commissiōnem,* accusative of *commissiō,* from *commiss-,* past participle stem of *committere* COMMIT; for suffix see -ION. The sense of a document conferring authority is first recorded in 1418, and that of a body of persons charged with a trust, an investigation, etc., is first recorded in 1494. —**v.** Before 1661, from the noun. —**commissioner** *n.* 1427, in *Rolls of Parliament,* formed from English *commission* + *-er*[1], possibly by influence of Middle French *commissioner.*

commit *v.* About 1390 *committen* give in charge, entrust, in Chaucer's *Canterbury Tales,* borrowed from Latin *committere* put together, join (*com-* with + *mittere* send, put; see MISSION). The meaning "perpetrate" appeared in 1449. —**commitment** *n.* 1611, commission of sin or crime, formed from English *commit* + *-ment.* The sense of a pledge, promise, appeared in 1793, in Thomas Jefferson's writings.

committee *n.* 1621, body of persons charged or entrusted in Parliament with a special assignment, formed from English COMMIT to entrust + *-ee.* A now obsolete use of this word was recorded earlier in 1495, and applied to an individual charged with a special duty. It was an Anglo-French form replacing Old French *commis,* from Latin *commissus,* past participle of *committere* COMMIT.

commode *n.* chest of drawers. 1786; earlier, a fashionable ladies' headdress (before 1688); borrowed from French noun use of adjective *commode* suitable, convenient, learned borrowing from Latin *commodus* convenient, appropriate, fit (*com-* with + *modus* measure, MODE[1]).

commodious (kəmō'dēəs) *adj.* conveniently roomy, spacious. 1423, beneficial, advantageous, borrowed from Medieval Latin *commodiosus,* from Latin *commodus* convenient (see COMMODE); for suffix see -OUS. The current sense appeared in 1553.

commodity *n.* 1410 *commoditee* benefit, profit, welfare; later, a convenient or useful product (before 1420); borrowed from Middle French *commodité,* learned borrowing from Latin *commoditātem* (nominative *commoditās*) due measure, fitness, convenience, from *commodus* suitable, convenient, see COMMODE; for suffix see -ITY. The specific sense in commerce "article produced for use or sale" is first found in 1436.

commodore *n.* 1694 *commandore,* probably borrowed from Dutch *kommandeur* commander, from French *commandeur,* from Old French *comandeor* commander, from *comander* to COMMAND.

common *adj.* Before 1300 *commune* belonging to all, general, borrowed from Old French *comun,* from Latin *commūnis* common, public; originally, sharing burdens (*com-* together + *mūnia* duties, related to *mūnus* office, duty; see MEAN[2] low). **—n.** About 1300, a fellowship or brotherhood; later, free citizens of a town or country (before 1325, in *Cursor Mundi*), see COMMUNE[2]; 1347-48, the right to use land held in common, in *Rolls of Parliament;* later, land held in common (before 1475); borrowed from Old French *comun, commun* common, and from Medieval Latin *communia* common, public; and in some senses developed from English *common,* adj. The Old French and Medieval Latin forms are from Latin *commūnis* common, public. **—common cold** (1786) **—common denominator** (1594) **—commoner** *n.* (1357 one who has a share; later, citizen, about 1378). **—common law** (about 1378) **—commonplace** *adj.* (1609) **—commons** *n.pl.* (land, 1600; Parliament, 1415) **—common sense** (1535) **—commonweal** *n.* (before 1338) **—commonwealth** *n.* (1549; earlier as a noun phrase about 1425).

commotion *n.* About 1390, borrowed from Middle French *commocion* learned borrowing from Latin *commōtiōnem* (nominative *commōtiō*) violent motion, agitation, from *commovēre* move violently, agitate (*com-* thoroughly + *movēre* MOVE); for suffix see -TION.

commune[1] (kəmyün') *v.* talk intimately. About 1303 *comonen* have dealings with, in Manning's *Handlyng Synne;* later *comounen* talk together (before 1387, in Trevisa's translation of Higden's *Polychronicon*); borrowed from Old French *communer* make common, share, from *comun* COMMON.

commune[2] (kom'yün) *n.* division of local government. 1792, borrowed from French, from Middle French *commune* free city, group of citizens, from Medieval Latin *communia,* originally neuter plural of Latin *commūnis* COMMON. The sense "communal division or settlement in a Communist country" appeared in English in 1919. In 1967, the term came to be widely used in the sense "a group or community of hippies." **—communal** *adj.* 1811, borrowed from French, from Late Latin *commūnālis,* from Latin *commūnis* common; for suffix see -AL[1].

communication *n.* About 1384 *communicacioun* an imparting or transmitting of something, in the Wycliffe Bible; borrowed from Old French *communicacion,* learned borrowing from Latin *commūnicātiōnem* (nominative *commūnicātiō*) from *commūnicāre* make common to many, share, impart (*com-* together + a lost adjective ***moinicos** carrying an obligation, from *mūnia,* Old Latin *moenia* duties; see COMMON); for suffix see -ATION. The specific sense of the imparting or transmitting of ideas, knowledge, information, etc., is first found in English in Locke's *Essay Concerning Human Understanding* (1690). **—communicate** *v.* 1526, partake in common, share; either 1) a back formation from English *communication,* or 2) borrowed from Latin *commūnicātus,* past participle of *communicare* make common, share, impart; for suffix see -ATE[1]. **—communicable** *adj.* Before 1398, borrowed probably through Old French *communicable* or directly as if from Latin ***commūnicābilis,** from Latin *commūnicāre;* for suffix see -ABLE. **—communicant** *n.* 1552, in *Book of Common Prayer,* borrowed from stem of Latin *commūnicantem* (nominative *commūnicāns*) communicating, from *commūnicāre;* for suffix see -ANT. **—communicative** *adj.* Before 1398, borrowed probably through Old French *communicatif* (feminine *communicative*) or directly from stem of Late Latin *commūnicātivus,* from *commūnicātus,* past participle of *commūnicāre;* for suffix see -IVE.

communion *n.* Before 1382, in the Wycliffe Bible, borrowed from Old French *communion,* learned borrowing from Latin *commūniōnem* (nominative *commūniō*) mutual participation, from *commūnis* COMMON; for suffix see -ION. The sense of the Lord's Supper or Eucharist is first recorded in English in 1440, in *Promptorium Parvulorum,* and was borrowed through Old French from Late Latin *commūniōnem* Christian communion, the Eucharist, from Latin *commūniōnem* mutual participation.

communiqué (kəmyü'nəkā') *n.* official communication. 1852, a French word introduced into a news story about the French government, originally past participle of *communiquer* communicate, from Latin *commūnicāre* COMMUNICATE.

communism *n.* theory advocating elimination of private ownership. 1843, borrowed from French *communisme* (1840), from *commun* common, communal (from Old French *comun* COMMON); for suffix see -ISM. As the name of the political system or movement (usually capitalized), it was translated in 1850 from German *Kommunismus* in Marx and Engels' *Manifesto of the German Communist Party* (1848); the German word came from French *communisme.* **—communist** *n.* 1841-42, borrowed from French *communiste* (1840), from *commun* COMMON; for suffix see -IST. In the sense of "co-owner" *communiste* is attested in French from 1769.

community *n.* 1375 (Scottish) *comminite,* in John Barbour's *The Bruce;* borrowed from Old French *communité,* learned borrowing from Latin *commūnitātem* (nominative *commūnitās*) fellowship, community, from *commūnis* COMMON; for suffix see -ITY.

commute (kəmyüt′) change, exchange. About 1450 *commuten,* borrowed from Latin *commūtāre* change altogether, exchange, interchange (*com-* altogether + *mūtāre* to change, MUTATE). The sense "make less severe," is first recorded in 1633, and "travel regularly to or from work" in 1889 (in the *Century Dictionary*). —**commutation** *n.* 1435 *commutacion* exchange, borrowed from Middle French, learned borrowing from Latin *commūtātiōnem* (nominative *commūtātiō*), from *commūtāre* commute; for suffix see -TION. —**commutative** *adj.* 1531, borrowed from Medieval Latin *commutativus,* from stem of Latin *commūtātus,* past participle of *commūtāre* commute; for suffix see -IVE. —**commuter** *n.* person who commutes. 1865, formed from English *commute,* v. + *-er*[1].

compact[1] *adj.* closely packed together. Before 1398, in Trevisa's translation of Bartholomew's *De Proprietatibus Rerum,* borrowed through Old French *compact,* or directly from Latin *compāctus,* past participle of *compingere* to confine (*com-* together + *pangere* fasten; see PACT). —**v.** Probably before 1425 *compacten* consolidate, pack together, in a translation of Higden's *Polychronicon;* from the adjective. —**n.** 1921, small case for face powder; later, small, compact car (1960); both from the adjective.

compact[2] *n.* agreement. 1591, in Shakespeare's *1 Henry VI,* borrowed from Latin *compactum* a compact, agreement; originally neuter past participle of *compacīscī* to contract together (*com-* together + *pacīscī* make an agreement, contract; see PACT).

companion *n.* Probably before 1300 *companioun,* in *Arthour and Merlin,* borrowed from Old French *compaignon* fellow, mate, from Late Latin *compāniōnem* (nominative *compāniō*) literally, one who takes bread with someone (Latin *com-* together + *pānis* bread; see FOOD). The Late Latin word, found only in the Lex Salica, a Frankish document of the 500's, is probably a translation of a Germanic word related to Gothic *gahlaiba* and Old High German *galeipo,* both meaning mess mate (*ga-* with, together + Gothic *hlaifs,* Old High German *hleib* LOAF). —**companionable** *adj.* 1627, formed from English *companion* + *-able.* —**companionship** *n.* 1548, formed from English *companion* + *-ship.*

company *n.* 1275 *compainie* companionship, fellowship, society; earlier *companie* a (large) group of people (probably about 1150); borrowed through Anglo-French *compaynie,* Old French *compagnie* body of soldiers, companion, from *compain* companion, from Late Latin *compāniō* COMPANION; for suffix see -Y[3]. *Company* in the military sense was first used probably before 1300, in *Kyng Alisaunder,* as a synonym of "army" or "host"; in 1590 it was used to refer to a subdivision of an infantry regiment. The modern sense of an association for business or commerce appeared in 1553, but was preceded by a more general sense that included the trade guilds, recorded as early as 1303 in Mannyng's *Handlyng Synne.*

compare *v.* 1375 *comparen,* in John Barbour's *The Bruce,* borrowed from Old French *comparer,* learned borrowing from Latin *comparāre* make equal with, liken, compare, from *compār* like, equal with (*com-* with + *pār* equal; see PAIR). Doublet of COMPEER. —**comparable** *adj.* 1410, borrowed from Middle French *comparable,* from Latin *comparābilis,* from *comparāre;* for suffix see -ABLE. —**comparative** *adj.* About 1434 *comparatif,* (in grammar) expressing a higher degree of the quality described, borrowed from Middle French *comparatif* (feminine *comparative*), from Latin *comparātīvus,* from *comparātus,* past participle of *comparāre* compare; for suffix see -IVE. —**comparison** *n.* 1340, in *Ayenbite of Inwyt,* borrowed from Old French *comparaison,* from Latin *comparātiōnem* (nominative *comparātiō*) act of comparing, from *comparāt-,* past participle stem of *comparāre* compare.

compartment *n.* 1564, borrowed from Middle French *compartiment* part partitioned off, from Italian *compartimento,* from *compartire* divide, from Late Latin *compartīrī* (Latin *com-* with + *partīrī* to share, from *pars* PART); for suffix see -MENT.

compass *n.* Before 1325 *compas* circumference, in *Cursor Mundi,* borrowed from Old French *compas,* from *compasser* to measure, divide equally, from Vulgar Latin **compassāre* measure off, from **compassus* equal step (Latin *com-* with + *passus,* genitive *passūs* a step, PACE[1]). The sense of an instrument for drawing circles appeared in 1349, and that of an instrument for showing directions perhaps before 1422. —**v.** About 1380 *compasen* encircle, encompass, in Chaucer's translation of Boethius' *De Consolatione Philosophiae;* borrowed from Old French *compasser* to measure, divide equally.

compassion *n.* 1340 *compassioun,* in *Ayenbite of Inwyt,* borrowed through Old French *compassion* sympathy, pity, or directly from Late Latin *compassiōnem* (nominative *compassiō,* loan translation of Greek *sympátheia*), and formed from *compass-,* stem of *compatī* suffer together with, feel pity (*com-* with + *patī* suffer, see PATIENT); for suffix see -SION. —**compassionate** *adj.* 1587, formed from English *compassion* + *-ate*[1].

compatible *adj.* 1459, sympathetic, borrowed from Middle French *compatible,* from Medieval Latin *compatibilis,* from Latin *compatī* suffer, see COMPASSION; for suffix see -IBLE. The meaning of able to exist together, is first recorded in 1532, in Sir Thomas More's writings. —**compatibility** *n.* 1611, in Cotgrave's *Dictionary,* borrowed from French *compatibilité;* for suffix see -ITY.

compatriot *n.* 1611, borrowed from French *compatriote,* from Latin *compatriōta* fellow countryman, partial translation of Greek *sympatriṓtēs;* see PATRIOT.

compeer (kəmpir′) *n.* equal, companion. Before 1375 *comper,* borrowed from Old French *comper* an equal, from Latin *compār* equal with; see the doublet COMPARE.

compel *v.* Probably about 1350 *compellen* oblige, force, borrowed from Old French *compeller, compellir* to compel, learned borrowing from Latin *compellere* to force; literally, drive together, collect (*com-* together + *pellere* to drive; see PULSE[1] beat).

compendium (kəmpen′dēəm) *n.* abridgment, condensation, abstract. 1589, in Thomas Nashe's writings; a separate reborrowing from Latin *compendium* a shortening, saving; literally, thing weighed or kept together (*com-* together + *pendere* weigh; see PENDANT). Middle English had a form *compendi* (about 1441), the original borrowing from Latin *compendium,* but the word apparently did not survive. —**compendious** *adj.* concise, succinct. About 1395, in the Wycliffe Bible, borrowed from Latin *compendiōsus* abridged, brief, from *compendium;* for suffix see -OUS.

compensate *v.* make up for. 1646, in Sir Thomas Browne's writings, borrowed, perhaps through influence of French *compenser,* from Latin *compēnsātus,* past participle of *compēnsāre* weigh one thing against another, balance out (*com-* with + *pēnsāre* weigh out, frequentative form of *pendere* weigh; see PENDANT); for suffix see -ATE[1]. The development of *compensate* is probably a back formation from the earlier *compensation* in some of its uses. **—compensation** *n.* Before 1387 *compensacioun,* in Trevisa's translation of Higden's *Polychronicon;* borrowed from Old French *compensation* or directly from Latin *compēnsātiōnem* (nominative *compēnsātiō*), from *compēnsāre* compensate; for suffix see -TION.

compete *v.* 1620, borrowed from French *compéter,* probably in the sense of be in rivalry with, strive against others, or directly from Late Latin *competere* strive in common; in Latin, coincide, agree, be fit for (*com-* together + *petere* seek, aim at, go toward; see FEATHER). The commercial usage "to strive for command of a market" appeared in the 1840's, perhaps as a back formation from earlier *competition* (1793 in this sense). The use in athletics appeared late in the 1800's, also perhaps back-formed from *competition* (in the sense of contest, 1618). **—competition** *n.* 1605, in Francis Bacon's *Of the Advancement of Learning,* borrowed from Late Latin *competītiōnem* (nominative *competītiō*) rivalry, from *competere* strive in common; for suffix see -TION. **—competitive** *adj.* 1829, in Southey's letters, formed (as if from Latin **competītīvus*) from English *compete* + *-ive.* **—competitor** *n.* 1534, borrowed, probably by influence of Middle French *compétiteur,* from Latin *competītor* rival, from *competī-,* a stem of *competere* strive in common + Latin suffix *-tor.*

competent *adj.* Before 1398, suitable, sufficient, in Trevisa's translation of Bartholomew's *De Proprietatibus Rerum;* borrowed through Old French *competent* from Latin *competentem* (nominative *competēns*), present participle of *competere* coincide, agree, be fit for; see COMPETE; for suffix see -ENT. The sense of being legally qualified appeared in 1483 (in Caxton's writings), and the general sense of able, fit for, in 1647. **—competence** *n.* 1594, rivalry; later, adequate supply (1597, in Shakespeare's *2 Henry IV*), and legal power, admissibility (1708-15, in a printing of Kersey's *Dictionary*); borrowed from French *competence* aptness, fitness, learned borrowing from Latin *competentia* agreement, meeting, from *competēns,* present participle of *competere* coincide, agree; for suffix see -ENCE. The sense of ability, capacity to deal with a subject, appeared in 1790. **—competency** *n.* 1594, rivalry, form as a variant of COMPETENCE; for suffix see -ENCY.

compile *v.* collect in one list or book. Probably before 1325 *compilen,* borrowed from Old French *compiler,* learned borrowing from Latin *compīlāre* steal, pillage, plagiarize, snatch together; originally, pile up (*com-* together + *pīlāre* to press, from *pīla* PILE[1] heap). **—compilation** *n.* 1426 *compilacioun,* in Lydgate's *Falls of Princes,* borrowed from Middle French *compilation,* learned borrowing from Latin *compīlātiōnem* (nominative *compīlātiō*) a compilation; literally a pillaging, from *compīlāre;* for suffix see -TION. **—compiler** *n.* Before 1338, in Mannyng's *Chronicle of England,* borrowed through Anglo-French *compilour,* Old French *compileor* author or chronicler, from Latin *compīlātōrem,* from *compīlāre;* for suffix see -ER[1]. English *compilator* (about 1400) is also borrowed through Anglo-French *compilatour,* from Latin *compīlātōrem.*

complacent *adj.* 1660, pleasing, borrowed from Latin *complacentem* (nominative *complacēns*), present participle of *complacēre* be very pleasing (*com-* completely + *placēre* PLEASE); for suffix see -ENT. The sense of pleased with oneself, is first recorded in 1767. See the note at *complaisant, complaisance.* **—complacence** *n.* 1436, pleasure; later, self-satisfaction (before 1500); borrowed from Medieval Latin *complacentia* satisfaction, pleasure, from Latin *complacentem* (nominative *complacēns*), present participle of *complacēre;* for suffix see -ENCE. **—complacency** *n.* 1643, in Milton's writings, borrowed from Medieval Latin *complacentia* satisfaction, pleasure; see COMPLACENCE; for suffix see -ENCY.

complain *v.* About 1370 *compleinen* find fault, accuse, in Chaucer's writings, later in the record of English but probably of simultaneous development, to lament, bewail (about 1375, in Chaucer's *Canterbury Tales*); borrowed from Old French *complaign-,* stem of *complaindre,* from Vulgar Latin **complangere* (Latin *com-* thoroughly + *plangere* to lament; see PLAINT). **—complaint** *n.* About 1380, lamentation, grief, in Chaucer's translation of Boethius' *De Consolatione Philosophiae;* borrowed from Old French *complainte,* from feminine past participle of *complaindre* complain. **—complainer** *n.* 1473, formed from Middle English *compleinen* + *-er*[1].

complaisant (kəmplā'zənt) *adj.* obliging, gracious. 1647, borrowed from French *complaisant,* from Middle French *complaisant* pleasing, present participle of *complaire* acquiesce in order to please, learned borrowing from Latin *complacēre* be very pleasing (with influence of Old French *plaire* gratify); see COMPLACENT. **—complaisance** *n.* obligingness, courtesy. 1651, in Hobbes' *Leviathan,* borrowed from French *complaisance,* from Middle French *complaisance* care or desire to please, learned borrowing from Medieval Latin *complacentia* COMPLACENCE.

In English of the 1600's to at least the 1850's, *complaisance, complaisant* and *complacent, complacence* overlapped in the sense of obliging, graciousness.

compleat or **compleet** *adj.* perfect, accomplished, consummate. 1384, see COMPLETE; later, revived as an archaic spelling of *complete* for humorous effect, to refer to a person engaged in a particular hobby or pursuit (1954 and earlier, as in *the compleat handyman* or in titles, as *The Compleat Bachelor,* 1900); all of these later uses are ultimately in allusion to *The Compleat Angler* (1653, by Izaak Walton).

complement *n.* Before 1398, in Trevisa's translation of Bartholomew's *De Proprietatibus Rerum,* borrowed from Old French *complement,* from Latin *complēmentum* that which fills up or completes, from *complēre* fill up, COMPLETE; for suffix see -MENT. Doublet of COMPLIMENT (an approving remark). **—v.** 1612, exchange courtesies; later, make complete (1641); from the noun. **—complementary** *adj.* 1628, ceremonious; later, forming a complement, as of colors (1829), formed from English *complement* + *-ary.* The word was used as a noun in English as early as 1599 by Ben Jonson.

complete *adj.* About 1384, in Wycliffe's writings, borrowed from Old French *complet* (feminine *complete*) full, complete, learned borrowing from Latin *complētus,* past participle of *complēre* fill up, finish, fulfill (*com-* completely + *plēre* to fill; see FULL). —**v.** About 1390 *completen,* in Chaucer's *Canterbury Tales,* from the adjective. —**completion** *n.* Before 1398 *compleci-oun,* in Trevisa's translation of Bartholomew's *De Proprietatibus Rerum,* borrowed from Latin *complētiōnem* (nominative *complētiō*), from *complēre* to complete; for suffix see -TION.

complex *adj.* Before 1652, combining various parts; borrowed from French *complexe,* from Latin *complexus,* past participle of *complectī* encompass, embrace, comprise (*com-* together + *plectere* to braid, twine; see PLY² fold). The sense "complicated, involved, intricate," is first recorded in 1715. —**n.** Before 1652, a whole comprising various parts; borrowed from Latin *complexus* (genitive *complexūs* a surrounding, compass, embrace, from *complex-,* stem of *complectī* encompass. —**complexity** *n.* Before 1721, composite structure; formed from English *complex,* adj. + *-ity.*

complexion *n.* 1340, in *Ayenbite of Inwyt;* bodily constitution, individual balance of the humors, borrowed from Old French *complexion,* learned borrowing from Late Latin *complexiōnem* (nominative *complexiō*) physical constitution, from classical Latin also with the meaning of combination, connection, from *complex-,* stem of *complectī* to embrace, encompass, related to *complexus* COMPLEX; for suffix see -XION. The sense of general appearance of the skin, especially the face is first recorded before 1450, originally implying that the complexion indicated a person's temperament or health.

complicate *v.* 1621, in Burton's *Anatomy of Melancholy,* unite, combine, possibly verb use of earlier *complicate,* participial adjective meaning involved, complicated (probably before 1425, in a translation of Chauliac's *Grande Chirurgie*); borrowed from Latin *complicātus,* past participle of *complicāre* fold together (*com-* together + *plicāre* to fold; see PLY² fold); for suffix see -ATE¹. The sense "to entangle, combine in a complex way" is first recorded in 1673 (possibly before 1631, in Donne's writings), and from it "to make complex or intricate" (1832). —**complication** *n.* Probably before 1425 *complicacioun* a complication in the medical sense, in a translation of Chauliac's *Grande Chirurgie;* later, in a general sense of a complicated state, matter, or structure (1647); borrowed from Middle French *complication,* from Latin *complicātiōnem* (nominative *complicātiō*), from *complicāre* fold together, an obsolete meaning also found in English, first recorded in 1611; for suffix see -TION.

complicity *n.* 1656, in Blount's *Glossographia,* borrowed from French *complicité,* from Middle French *complicité,* from Old French *complice* ACCOMPLICE, learned borrowing from Late Latin *complicem,* accusative of *complex* partner, confederate, from Latin *complicāre* fold together (*com-* together + *plicāre* to fold, see PLY² fold); for suffix see -ITY.

compliment *n.* 1578 *complement* courtesy paid to another; restyled as *compliment* gradually after about 1650, in imitation of French *compliment* expression of respect, from Italian *complimento,* from Spanish *cumplimiento,* from *cumplir* fulfill, accomplish (from Latin *complēre* fill up) + *-miento* -ment; for suffix see -MENT. Doublet of COMPLEMENT (something that completes). Development of the sense of something good said about another, gentle praise, is difficult to distinguish from the original sense of courtesy and respect paid to another, but the modern sense of praise alone seems to have developed in the early 1700's. —**v.** 1612 *complement,* in Beaumont and Fletcher's *Coxcomb,* restyled as *compliment,* see the noun (1668, in Pepys' *Diary*), borrowed from French *complimenter,* from *compliment,* n. The verb sense of to praise, is recorded perhaps earlier than the noun, in the 1640's. The evidence demonstrates that the distinction in spelling between *complement* and *compliment* was not fully established for about 100 years, as both words contained the idea of fulfilling or completing the requirements and forms of courtesy. —**complimentary** *adj.* 1628 *complementary* ceremonious, restyled as *complimentary* by 1716; formed originally from English *complement* + *-ary,* but by perhaps the early 1700's, considered to be formed from English *compliment* + *-ary.*

comply *v.* Before 1333 *complien* to fulfill, carry out, accomplish, in poems of William of Shoreham; borrowed from Old French *complir,* past participle *compli* (a form occurring in Middle English rhymes), from Latin *complēre* fill up, COMPLETE. The meaning "consent, accede, yield" is first recorded in 1650, but may also have been implied as early as 1631, in Donne's letters. —**compliance** *n.* 1641, act of courtesy; formed from English *comply* + *-ance.* The sense of consent, submission, is first recorded in 1647.

component *n.* 1645, constituent element or part; earlier, with the possible meaning of one who is involved in making up a group of persons (1563); borrowed from Latin *compōnentem* (nominative *compōnēns*), present participle of *compōnere* put together, compose (*com-* together + *pōnere* put, place; see POSITION); for suffix see -ENT. —**adj.** composing; constituting. 1664, borrowed from Latin *compōnentem,* present participle of *compōnere* compose; for suffix see -ENT.

comport (kəmpôrt′) *v.* About 1385 *comporten* tolerate, endure, in Chaucer's *Troilus and Criseyde,* borrowed from Middle French *comporter* endure, bear, behave (oneself), learned borrowing from Latin *comportāre* carry together (*com-* together + *portāre* carry; see PORT⁴ bearing). The sense of behave is first recorded in 1616, though see *comportment* behavior, for earlier date. —**comportment** *n.* 1599, borrowed from Middle French *comportement,* from *comporter;* for suffix see -MENT.

compose *v.* Probably before 1402 *compousen,* borrowed from Old French *composer* put together, arrange, compose (*com-* together + *poser* to put, place, see POSE; influenced by the perfect stem, *compos-* of Latin *compōnere* put together, arrange; see COMPONENT). —**composer** *n.* 1597 formed from English *compose* + *-er*¹. —**composition** *n.* Before 1382 *composicioun,* in the Wycliffe Bible, borrowed from Old French *composition,* learned borrowing from Latin *compositiōnem* (nominative *compositiō*) act of putting together, connection, from *compōnere* put together; for suffix see -TION.

composite *adj.* Probably before 1400, borrowed from Old French *composite,* from Latin *compositus,* past participle of *compōnere* put together, arrange (*com-* together + *pōnere* to put, place; see POSITION). Doublet of COMPOST and COMPOTE. —**n.** Probably before 1400, a compound number; from the adjective.

compost *n.* Before 1399, compote; later, prepared mixture of manure, leaves, etc. to fertilize land (1587); borrowed from Middle French *compost* mixture of leaves, etc. for fertilizing land, from Latin *compositus,* past participle of *compōnere* put together; see the doublets COMPOSITE and COMPOTE. —**v.** treat with compost. 1499, in a version of *Promptorium Parvulorum,* borrowed from Middle French *composter,* from the noun.

composure *n.* composed condition; calmness. 1667, in Milton's *Paradise Lost,* formed from English *compose* + *-ure.* This word was coined earlier (along with *exposure,* 1605) on the analogy of *enclosure* and similar words. Earlier meanings of *composure* included that of composition (1599, in Ben Jonson's *Cynthia's Revels*), constitution, temperament (1606, in Shakespeare's *Antony and Cleopatra*), and of form, style (1659, in Evelyn's *Diary*).

compote *n.* 1693, in John Evelyn's writings, borrowed from French *compote* stewed fruit, from Old French *composte* mixture, compost, from Latin *composita* mixture, feminine of *compositus,* past participle of *compōnere* put together; see the doublets COMPOSITE and COMPOST. The sense of a dish with a supporting stem for fruit or candy is first recorded before 1904, but appears earlier in the misspelled form *comport* (1881).

compound[1] *v.* About 1380 *compounen* mix, combine, compose, in Chaucer's *House of Fame* and in his translation of Boethius' *De Consolatione Philosophiae;* borrowed from Old French *componre, compondre* arrange, direct, from Latin *compōnere* put, place, or bring together (*com-* together + *pōnere* to put, place; see POSITION).

The *-d* in *compound* began to appear gradually during the 1500's partly on analogy of the earlier *expound,* and also through the influence of the past participle *compouned,* which lost the vowel of its third syllable before 1400 and became the adjective *compound,* see next. —**adj.** Before 1387, in Trevisa's translation of Higden's *Polychronicon,* originally *compouned,* past participle of *compounen,* v. —**n.** About 1434, a compound word; from the adjective.

compound[2] *n.* fenced-in area, enclosure. 1679, borrowed from Malay *kampong, kampung* enclosure, village, quarter of a town occupied by a particular nationality. The word, according to Yule and Burnell in the *Anglo-Indian Glossary,* as stated in the OED, was first used by Englishmen in the early factories of the Malay Archipelago and from there spread to India and other parts of the former British Empire. The English spelling of the word was apparently largely due to the influence of *compound*[1].

comprehend *v.* About 1340 *comprehenden* understand, in an early Psalter; borrowed from Latin *comprehendere* to grasp, seize, comprise (*com-* completely + *prehendere* seize; see PREHENSILE). —**comprehensible** *adj.* 1529, in writings of Sir Thomas More, borrowed from Latin *comprehēnsibilis,* from *comprehēnsus,* past participle of *comprehendere.* —**comprehension** *n.* About 1445, borrowed from Middle French *compréhension,* learned borrowing from Latin *comprehēnsiōnem* (nominative *comprehēnsiō*) a seizing, from *comprehendere* comprehend; for suffix see -SION. —**comprehensive** *adj.* 1614, comprising much, of great scope; perhaps earlier implied in Middle English *comprehensively* comprehendingly, thoroughly (about 1454); borrowed from French *compréhensif* (feminine *compréhensive*), and from Late Latin *comprēhēnsīvus,* from Latin *comprehēnsus,* past participle of *comprehendere;* for suffix see -IVE.

compress (kəmpres′) *v.* About 1380 *compressen* press together, in Chaucer's translation of Boethius' *De Consolatione Philosophiae;* borrowed from Old French *compresser,* from Latin *compressāre* to press together, oppress, frequentative form of *comprimere* press together, restrain (*com-* together + *premere* to PRESS[1] push). —**n.** (kom′pres) 1599, pad applied to stop bleeding; borrowed from Middle French *compresse,* from Latin *compressa,* from *compressus,* past participle of *comprimere* compress. —**compressible** *adj.* Before 1691, in Boyle's works, formed from English *compress* + *-ible,* as if from Latin **compressibilis,* from *compressus,* past participle of *comprimere.* —**compression** *n.* Before 1400, borrowed from Middle French *compression,* learned borrowing from Latin *compressiōnem* (nominative *compressiō*), from *comprimere* press together; for suffix see -SION.

comprise *v.* About 1425, to be included, developed from *comprised* included, borrowed from Old French *compris,* past participle of *comprendre* to contain, comprise, comprehend, from Latin *comprehēnsus,* past participle of *comprehendere* grasp, seize, COMPREHEND. The word may have been formed in analogy of *apprise, surprise,* older verbs with the ending *-prise* formed from other compounds of French *prendre.*

compromise *n.* a coming to terms, settlement, adjustment. 1426, in *Rolls of Parliament;* joint promise or agreement, borrowed from Middle French *compromis,* learned borrowing from Latin *comprōmissum,* originally neuter past participle of *comprōmittere* promise together, as to abide by an arbiter's decision (*com-* together + *prōmittere* PROMISE). The sense of a coming to terms, settlement, adjustment, is first recorded probably about 1435. —**v.** Probably before 1450; earlier be agreed (1437); from the noun.

comptroller (kəntrōl′ər) *n.* a variant spelling of CONTROLLER, introduced probably before 1400, because of the mistaken analogy with earlier *compter* (now *counter*), and *accompt* (now *account*), artificial respellings after Latin *computāre* COMPUTE and its related forms; see ACCOUNT.

compulsion *n.* Probably before 1425, use of force, coercion, in a translation of Higden's *Polychronicon,* borrowed from Middle French *compulsion,* learned borrowing from Latin *compulsiōnem* (nominative *compulsiō*), from *compellere* COMPEL; for suffix see -SION. The psychological sense of an uncontrollable impulse to behave a certain way is first recorded in 1909 as part of the compound *compulsion neurosis,* a loan translation of *Zwangsneurose,* in Brill's translation of Freud's *Interpretation of Dreams.* —**compulsive** *adj.* 1602, in Shakespeare's *Hamlet,* probably borrowed from French *compulsif,* from Latin *compulsus* (past participle of *compellere* compel); for suffix see -IVE. The psychological sense of acting from, or related to a compulsion is first recorded in 1902, in a text on clinical psychiatry. —**compulsory** *adj.* involving compulsion; obligatory; enforced. 1581, borrowed from Medieval Latin *compulsorius,* from Latin *compulsus,* past participle of *compellere* compel; for suffix see -ORY. —*n.* 1968, required demonstration of skill in gymnastics, etc., earlier, a compulsory means, constraining authority (1516); from the adjective.

compunction *n.* regret, remorse. About 1340, in an early psalter; borrowed from Old French *compūnction,* learned borrowing from Late Latin *compūnctiōnem* (nominative *compūnctiō*) a pricking, remorse, from Latin *compūnct-,* past participle stem of *compungere* to prick severely, sting (*com-* thoroughly + *pungere* prick, see PUNGENT); for suffix see -ION.

compute *v.* 1631, borrowed from French *computer,* learned borrowing from Latin *computāre* to count, sum up (*com-* together + *putāre* count, reckon, consider; see PUTATIVE). Doublet of COUNT[1] add. **—computation** *n.* Probably about 1408 *computacion,* borrowed from Old French *computation,* learned borrowing from Latin *computātiōnem* (nominative *computātiō*), from *computāre* compute; for suffix see -TION. **—computer** *n.* 1646, person who computes; later, mechanical calculating machine (1897); and electronic machine (1946, perhaps 1941); formed from English *compute* + *-er*[1]. **—computerize** *v.* 1960, formed from English *computer* + *-ize.*

comrade *n.* 1591 *camerade* one who shares the same room, also with the sense of close companion (1593); borrowed from Middle French *camarade* partner, comrade, from Spanish *camarada* roommate; originally, roomful, from *cámara* room, from Latin *camera* vault; see CAMERA. The term, used before surnames in a conscious effort to avoid such conventional titles as "Mr." is first recorded in English in 1884.

comsat *n.* communication satellite. 1962, American English, formed from *com(munication)* and *sat(ellite),* originally as an acronym for Communications Satellite Corporation, a commercial system for satellite communication, authorized by the U.S. Congress.

con[1] *adv.* against (a proposition, opinion, etc.). 1572, shortened from Latin *contrā* against; originally, in the phrase *pro and con.* **—n.** reason or argument against. 1589, from the adverb.

con[2] *v.* pore over, study, memorize. About 1425, in Andrew of Wyntoun's *Chronicle of Scotland,* variant of Middle English *cunnen* to know, developed from Old English *cunnan* know, know how, the infinitive form of *cann* know; see CAN[1]; also related to CUNNING.

The earliest unambiguous example of the meaning "to know," in the sense of study, memorize seems to be about 1425, and in the phrase *to cun thanks* to acknowledge or express thanks, a past tense *cunde, conned* is found by 1325, in *Cursor Mundi* so that by a differentiation of forms the weak verb *con* with accompanying past tense *conned* is fully formed in the 1400's.

con[3] *adj.* duping, swindling, as in *con game, con man.* 1889, American English, shortened from *confidence game, man,* etc. (1849), in which the victim is induced to hand over money or other valuables as a token of "confidence" in the swindler. **—v.** dupe, swindle. 1896, American English, from the adjective.

con[4] *n. Slang.* convict. 1893, shortened form of *convict.*

con- a prefix meaning with, together, as in *concentrate, congeneric,* or used as an intensive, as in *concave, conceal.* Borrowed from Latin *con-,* the form of COM- before most consonants except *h* and the labials *b, m, p; con-* in Latin was also the form which by assimilation yielded *col-* and *cor-.*

This prefix appears in Middle English words taken from Latin and Old French, or from both sources, such as *conceive, conception, confirm, confess, conquer, conquest.* Since the prefix had little meaning of its own in Middle English, it was not productive; words formed in English rather used the form *co-,* as in *copilot.* So also in Old French *con-* was often reduced to *co-,* especially before *v,* for example in such words as in *covenant;* on the other hand some words were later respelled with *con-,* such as *convent.*

concave *adj.* Probably before 1425, in a translation of Chauliac's *Grande Chirurgie,* borrowed probably through Old French *concave,* or directly from Latin *concavus* (*con-* intensive + *cavus* hollow; see CAVE). **—n.** a hollow, cavity. Before 1398, in Trevisa's translation of Bartholomew's *De Proprietatibus Rerum,* borrowed from Old French *concave,* n., from Old French *concave,* adj. **—concavity** *n.* Before 1400, concave surface or side, borrowed from Old French *concavité,* or directly from Late Latin *concavitātem* (nominative *concavitās*), from Latin *concavus* concave; for suffix see -ITY.

conceal *v.* Before 1325 *concelen* to keep secret, in *Cursor Mundi;* later, to hide (probably before 1420); borrowed from Old French *conceler* to hide, from Latin *concēlāre* conceal completely (*con-* intensive + *cēlāre* to hide; see CELL). **—concealment** *n.* Before 1325, borrowed from Old French *concelement,* from *conceler* conceal; for suffix see -MENT.

concede *v.* admit, grant. 1632, borrowed through French *concéder* or directly from Latin *concēdere* give way, yield, grant (*con-* intensive + *cēdere* to yield, CEDE).

conceit *n.* About 1380, something conceived in the mind, thought, notion, conception, in Chaucer's translation of Boethius' *De Consolatione Philosophiae;* apparently formed from earlier *conceiven* CONCEIVE on the analogy of *deceive, deceit,* and *receive, receipt.* The sense of fanciful action, ingenious, or witty notion is first recorded about 1513 and was much used in literature until this century. Now the word is used with the primary meaning of vanity, in the sense of a high opinion of oneself, pride (1605), which developed from the sense of a favorable opinion of oneself (1581), especially in *self-conceit* (1588); earlier with the meaning of a favorable opinion (1462), and a personal opinion or judgment (about 1395). **—conceited** *adj.* 1542, having intelligence; later, vain (1608-11), shortened form of *self-conceited* (1595), from *self-conceit* favorable opinion of oneself + the suffix *-ed.*

conceive *v.* Probably about 1280 *conceiven* receive (seed) in the womb, become pregnant; later, take into or form in the mind (1340, in *Ayenbite of Inwyt*); borrowed from Old French *conceiv-,* stem of *conceveir,* from Latin *concipere* take in, receive, conceive, perceive (*con-* intensive + *-cipere,* combining form of *capere* to take; see CAPTIVE). **—conceivable** *adj.* About 1454 (but implied earlier in *conceivabliness,* about 1443), formed from English *conceive* + *-able.*

concentrate *v.* 1640, come to a common center or focus, developed as a variant of *concenter, concentre* meet in a common center (before 1591) + suffix *-ate*[1]. The earlier *concenter, concentre,* was probably borrowed from Italian *concentrare* (*con-* together + *centro,* from Latin *centrum* CENTER). In English the original meaning evolved into the sense of condense to, increase intensity or power (1689), and later of focus the attention or mind on (about 1860). **—n.** something concentrated. 1883, from the verb. **—concentration** *n.* 1634, the act or state of bringing to a common center or focus; probably formed from English *concentrate* (or less likely, *concenter, concentre*) + *-ation.* Even though *concentration* appears six years before *concentrate,* the defect is probably in the record of English. The term *concentration camp* appeared in the Second Anglo-Boer War (1899-1902) referring to an internment camp for South African civilians. In the 1930's the term referred to a prison camp for political opponents in Germany, Russia, etc., and during World War II to forced-labor and extermination camps of the Nazis in Europe.

concentric *adj.* About 1400, in Chaucer's *Treatise on the Astrolabe,* borrowed from Old French *concentrique* and Medieval Latin *concentricus* (from *con-* together + *centrum* circle, center).

concept (kon′sept) *n.* idea, thought. 1556, borrowed from Middle French *concept,* or directly from Late Latin *conceptus* (genitive *conceptūs*) draft or abstract, from classical Latin with the meaning of a taking in, a conceiving, fetus, from *concep-,* stem of *concipere* take in, CONCEIVE. **—conception** *n.* Before 1333 *concepcioun* act of conceiving, in poetry of William of Shoreham; borrowed from Old French *conception,* learned borrowing from Latin *conceptiōnem* (nominative *conceptiō*), from *concipere* CONCEIVE; for suffix see -TION. The sense of the mental processes forming concepts, is first recorded about 1380, in Chaucer's translation of Boethius' *De Consolatione Philosophiae.* The specific sense of an idea or notion is first recorded in 1603, but is earlier found in allusion to that which is conceived, specifically a child (1526). **—conceptive** *adj.* 1640, conceiving (in the mind), in Hobbes' writings; borrowed from Latin *conceptīvus,* from *conceptus,* past participle of *concipere* conceive; for suffix see -IVE. **—conceptual** *adj.* 1662, borrowed from Medieval Latin *conceptualis,* from Late Latin *conceptus* (genitive *conceptūs*) concept; for suffix see -AL[1].

concern *v.* Before 1420 *concernen* perceive, distinguish; later, refer to, relate (1420); borrowed through Middle French *concerner* concern, touch, belong to, or directly from Medieval Latin *concernere* relate to, belong to, regard, in Late Latin with the meaning of mingle with, mix, as for sifting (Latin *con-* together + *cernere* separate, distinguish, sift; see CERTAIN). The sense of cause to worry, trouble, appeared probably about 1408, in Lydgate's works. **—n.** 1589, regard, reference, relation; from the verb. The meaning of a business organization, is first recorded in 1681, and developed from the meanings of affairs or matters of interest (1675), and of that which relates to or is of interest to someone (1655). **—concerned** *adj.* 1656, from *concern,* v. **—concerning** *prep.* Before 1425, developed from English *concerning,* present participle of *concern.*

concert[1] (kon′sərt) *n.* 1665, agreement, accord, harmony, in John Evelyn's *Memoirs,* borrowed from French *concert,* from Italian *concerto* concert, harmony, from *concertare* to accord together; see CONCERT[2] and the doublet CONCERTO. The sense of a public musical performance or entertainment appeared in English in 1689; in French it is attested since 1608, and in Italian since 1623. The word *concert* was regularly confused with *consort,* according to the OED, "down to the Restoration, and often later: *e.g.* 1611 [in Cotgrave's *Dictionary*] *Concert de Musique,* a consort of Musicke."

concert[2] (kənsėrt′) *v.* 1598, to unite; later to arrange by agreement (1694), borrowed from French *concerter* contrive, adjust, from Italian *concertare* accord together, settle, adjust, possibly from Latin *concertāre* contend zealously or warmly, discuss, debate (*con-* together + *certāre* strive for primacy, contend, frequentative form from *certus,* variant past participle of *cernere* distinguish, separate, decide; see CERTAIN).

concertina *n.* instrument similar to a small accordion. 1837, formed from English *concert* + *-ina,* borrowed from Italian diminutive suffix *-ina;* for suffix see -INE[1]. The instrument was invented (and apparently named) by Sir Thomas Wheatstone in 1829. The word's coinage may have been influenced by Italian *concertino* a short concerto (diminutive of *concerto*). The Italian word for a concertina or accordion is *fisarmonica.*

concerto (kəncher′tō) *n.* musical composition. 1730, an Italian word introduced in an English work on music, from Italian *concertare* accord together; see the doublet CONCERT[2], v.

concession *n.* 1464, borrowed through Middle French *concession* or directly from Latin *concessiōnem* (nominative *concessiō*), from *concēdere* CONCEDE; for suffix see -SION. The meaning of a right or privilege granted to an individual or company is first recorded in 1856, by extension of the earlier meaning of a grant of land (1656). **—concessionaire** *n.* 1862, borrowed from French *concessionnaire,* from *concession* + *-aire,* from Latin *-ārius;* see English suffix -ARY.

conch *n.* 1391, shallow bowl; later shell (1410), and shellfish (about 1520); borrowed from Latin *concha* shellfish, mollusk, from Greek *kónchē* mussel, cockle, which is perhaps cognate with Sanskrit *śaṅkhá-s* conch shell, mussel, from Indo-European **k̂onkho-s* (Pok. 614).

The earlier English forms were *conke, congh* which accord with the English pronunciation of Latin *concha* (kongk). The more common pronunciation with *ch* was probably influenced by French *conche.*

concierge (kon′sēėrzh′) *n.* custodian or janitor. 1646, custodian of a palace, prison, etc.; a French word used in a work referring to an individual in France, from Old French *cumcerges* guard, warden, from Vulgar Latin **cōnservius* keeper, guardian, alteration of Latin *cōnservus* fellow servant, slave (*con-* with + *servus* slave; see SERVE). The general sense of a custodian or janitor is recorded in English before 1697.

conciliate *v.* win over, soothe. 1545, from Latin *conciliātus,* past participle of *conciliāre* unite in feeling, make friendly, from *concilium* convocation, COUNCIL; for suffix see -ATE[1]. **—conciliation** *n.* 1543, borrowed from Old French *conciliation,* learned borrowing from Latin *conciliātiōnem* (nominative *conciliātiō*), from *conciliāre;* for suffix see -TION. **—conciliatory** *adj.* 1576, formed from English *conciliate* + *-ory.*

concise *adj.* About 1590, in Marlowe's *The Tragical History of Dr. Faustus,* borrowed, perhaps through Middle French *concis* (feminine *concise*), or directly as a learned borrowing from Latin *concīsus* cut off, brief, past participle of *concīdere* cut up, cut short (*con-* completely + *-cīdere,* combining form of *caedere* to cut; see EXCISE[2] cut). **—concision** *n.* About 1384, the act of cutting to pieces, mutilation, in the Wycliffe Bible; later, conciseness (1774); borrowed from Late Latin *concīsiōnem* (nominative *concīsiō*) a cutting to pieces, from Latin *concīdere* cut up, cut short.

conclave *n.* Before 1393, meeting of cardinals to elect a pope, in Gower's *Confessio Amantis;* borrowed through Old French, or perhaps Italian *conclave,* learned borrowing from Latin *conclāve* room that can be locked up (*con-* with + *clāvis* key, bar; see CLAVICLE). The generalized meaning of a private meeting or assembly is first recorded in English in 1568, probably developed from the sense of a private meeting room (about 1450).

conclude *v.* Before 1325, in *Cursor Mundi,* to shut off an argument, borrowed from Latin *conclūdere* shut up closely, close up, end (*con-* completely + *-clūdere,* combining form of *claudere* shut, CLOSE[1]). The meaning of finish, end, is recorded in English before 1420 and that of reach a conclusion, infer, deduce, about 1380, in Chaucer's translation of Boethius' *De Consolatione Philosophiae.* **—conclusion** *n.* Probably about 1370, destiny, fate, in Chaucer's works; later, outcome, result (about 1380, in Chaucer's *Canterbury Tales*), borrowed from Old French *conclusion,* from Latin *conclūsiōnem* (nominative *conclūsiō*), from *conclūdere* conclude; for suffix see -SION. **—conclusive** *adj.* 1590, summary; later, concluding, closing (1612), and decisive, convincing (1649); borrowed from French *conclusif* (feminine *conclusive*), learned borrowing from Late Latin *conclūsīvus,* from Latin *conclūs-,* past participle stem of *conclūdere* close up; for suffix see -IVE.

concoct *v.* 1533, digest (food), borrowed from Latin *concoctus,* past participle of *concoquere* boil together, digest, ripen (*con-* together + *coquere* to COOK). It is not convincing that *concoct,* v. was derived from the obsolete English past participle *concoct,* because both forms are first recorded in use by Elyot in writings only a year apart. And for the same reasons *concoct* is probably not a back formation of *concoction.* The sense of make up or prepare a soup, drink, etc., is first recorded in English in 1675, in John Evelyn's *Terra*), and that of make up or devise a story, scheme, etc., in 1792, in Mary Wollstonecraft's *Vindication of the Rights of Woman.* **—concoction** *n.* 1531, digestion, borrowed possibly from Middle French *concoction,* but more likely directly from Latin *concoctiōnem* (nominative *concoctiō*), from *concoquere* digest; for suffix see -TION. The sense of something concocted or made up, is first recorded in English in 1823, in Isaac Disraeli's *Curiosities of Literature.*

concomitant *adj.* accompanying, attendant. 1607, borrowed from French *concomitant,* learned borrowing from Latin *concomitantem* (nominative *concomitāns*), present participle of *concomitārī* accompany, attend (*con-* with, together + *comitārī* join as a companion, from *comes,* genitive *comitis* companion; see COUNT[2] nobleman). **—n.** accompaniment. 1621, in Burton's *Anatomy of Melancholy,* from the adjective, though in Francis Bacon's Of the *Advancement of Learning* the Latin *concomitantia* appears, suggesting a direct connection between the English noun and Latin. **—concomitance** *n.* Before 1530, in writings of Sir Thomas More, borrowed from Middle French *concomitance,* from Medieval Latin *concomitantia,* from Latin *concomitantem* (nominative *concomitāns*), present participle of *concomitārī* accompany; for suffix see -ANCE.

concord *n.* agreement, harmony. Before 1325, in *Cursor Mundi,* borrowed from Old French *concorde,* learned borrowing from Latin *concordia* agreement, union, harmony, from *concors* (genitive *concordis*) of one mind, agreeing (*con-* together + *cor,* genitive *cordis* HEART). **—concordance** *n.* Before 1387, alphabetical list of principal words in a book, in Trevisa's translation of Higden's *Polychronicon;* borrowed from Old French *concordance,* from Medieval Latin *concordantia,* from Latin *concordantem* (nominative *concordāns*), present participle of *concordāre* be of one mind, agree, from *concors* (genitive *concordis*) of one mind; for suffix see -ANCE. The meaning "agreement, concord" is recorded probably before 1439.

concordat (konkôr′dat) *n.* agreement, pact. 1616, borrowed from French *concordat,* from Middle French *concordat,* learned borrowing from Medieval Latin *concordatum,* noun use of Latin *concordātum,* neuter past participle of *concordāre* be of one mind, agree, from *concors* (genitive *concordis*) of one mind; see CONCORD.

concourse *n.* 1384, confluence of people, crowd, in the Wycliffe Bible; borrowed from Old French *concours,* learned borrowing from Latin *concursus* (genitive *concursūs*) a running together, crowd, from past participle of *concurrere* run together; see CONCUR. The sense of an open space through which many people pass, as in a park, boulevard, or railroad station, is first recorded in 1862 in American English.

concrete *adj.* Before 1398, denoting an actual or solid substance rather than a quality, in Trevisa's translation of Bartholomew's *De Proprietatibus Rerum,* borrowed from Latin *concrētus,* past participle of *concrēscere* grow together (into a mass), harden, solidify (*con-* together + *crēscere* grow; see CRESCENT). The word was chiefly a term of logicians and grammarians to contrast with *abstract,* but from the 1600's it gradually spread in the sense of not abstract or general; particular; real, as used by Milton, Hobbes, Burke, Carlyle, Lowell, and others. **—n.** 1834, mixture of sand, gravel, etc., formed into a mass with cement; earlier, solid mass (1656), from the adjective. **—concretion** *n.* solidification, solid mass. 1603, the process of growing together into a mass, coalescence; borrowed perhaps from French *concrétion,* or directly as a learned borrowing from Latin *concrētiōnem* (nominative *concrētiō*), from *concrēscere* grow together; for suffix see -TION.

concubine (kong′kyəbīn) *n.* About 1300, borrowed from Old French *concubine,* or directly from Latin *concubīna* a concubine (*con-* with + *cubāre* to lie; see CUBICLE).

Originally the term was used in reference to polygamous societies, but the generalized meaning of a kept mistress was used as early as Chaucer.

concupiscent (konkyü′pəsənt) *adj.* lustful. Before 1500 (implied in *concupiscently*), probably borrowed from Latin *concupīscentem* (nominative *concupīscēns*), present participle of *concupīscere* be very desirous of, long for, covet (*con-* intensive + *cupīscere* to wish, a form of *cupere* to desire, COVET); for suffix see -ENT. Related to CUPIDITY. It is also possible that *concupiscent* is back-formed from earlier *concupiscence.* The word is not recorded in French before 1588. **—concupiscence** *n.* lust. Probably about 1350, eager desire; later, sexual appetite, lust (about 1390, in Chaucer's *Canterbury Tales*); borrowed probably through Old French *concupiscence* (1265), from Late Latin *concupīscentia,* from Latin *concupīscentem* (nominative *concupīscēns*), present participle of *concupīscere* be very desirous of; for suffix see -ENCE.

concur *v.* agree, coincide. 1410 *concurren,* borrowed from Latin *concurrere* run or come together, meet coincide (*con-* together + *currere* to run; see CUR

RENT). **—concurrence** *n.* Probably before 1425, in a translation of Higden's *Polychronicon,* borrowed through Old French *concurrence,* or directly from Medieval Latin *concurrentia,* from Latin *concurrentem,* (nominative *concurrēns*), present participle of *concurrere* concur; for suffix see -ENCE. **—concurrent** *adj.* Before 1398, in Trevisa's translation of Bartholomew's *De Proprietatibus Rerum,* borrowed through Old French *concurrent,* or directly from Latin *concurrentem* (nominative *concurrēns*), present participle of *concurrere* concur; for suffix see -ENT.

concussion *n.* Before 1400, in a translation of Lanfranc's *Science of Surgery;* borrowed from Latin *concussiōnem* (nominative *concussiō*), from *concutere* shake violently; for suffix see -SION. The medical sense of injury to the brain by a blow, is first recorded in 1541. **—concuss** *v.* shake or shock, as by a blow. 1597, either: 1) borrowed from Latin *concuss-,* past participle stem of *concutere* shake violently (*con-* intensive + *-cutere,* combining form of *quatere* to shake; see QUASH[1] crush), or 2) a back formation from earlier Middle English *concussion.*

condemn *v.* Probably before 1325 *condempnen,* in *Cursor Mundi;* later, *condemnen* to blame, censure (1340, in *Ayenbite of Inwyt*); borrowed from Old French *condemner, condempner,* learned borrowing from Latin *condemnāre* to sentence, convict, accuse, blame (*con-* intensive + *damnāre* cause loss to, condemn, from *damnum* loss, injury; see DAMN). **—condemnation** *n.* About 1384, in the Wycliffe Bible, borrowed from Latin *condemnātiōnem* (nominative *condemnātiō*), from *condemnāre* condemn; for suffix see -TION.

condense *v.* Probably before 1425, borrowed through Middle French *condenser,* or directly as a learned borrowing from Latin *condēnsāre* make dense, compress, thicken (*con-* together + *dēnsāre* make thick, from *dēnsus* thick, DENSE). **—condensation** *n.* 1603, a making dense, borrowed through French *condensation,* or directly from Late Latin *condēnsātiōnem* (nominative *condēnsātiō*), from *condēnsāre* make thick; for suffix see -TION.

condescend *v.* 1340, to comply, acquiesce, in *Ayenbite of Inwyt,* borrowed from Old French *condescendre,* learned borrowing from Late Latin *condēscendere* to stoop, let oneself down, condescend (Latin *con-* together + *dēscendere* DESCEND). The meaning of stoop to the level of inferiors, deign, patronize, is first recorded probably about 1435. **—condescension** *n.* 1642, borrowed possibly from Middle French *condescension,* or formed in English after Late Latin *condēscensiōnem* (nominative *condēscensiō*), from *condēscendere* condescend; for suffix see -SION.

condigne (kəndīn′) *adj.* deserved, fitting. 1410, borrowed from Middle French *condign,* learned borrowing from Latin *condignus* very worthy (*con-* completely + *dignus* worthy; see DIGNITY).

condiment *n.* seasoning. Before 1500; earlier, a pickling fluid (probably 1440); borrowed from Middle French *condiment,* from Latin *condīmentum* spice, from *condīre* to preserve, pickle, season, spice, a variant (perhaps influenced by *sallīre* to salt in the sense of preserve) of *condere* to make, build, lay up, store, preserve (*con-* together + *-dere* to put, place; see DO[1] perform); for suffix see -MENT.

condition *n.* Before 1333 *condicioun* provision, stipulation, in William of Shoreham's poetry; borrowed from Old French *condition, condicion,* learned borrowing from Latin *condiciōnem* (in Late Latin sometimes spelled *conditiōnem*) (nominative *condiciō, conditiō*) stipulation, compact, agreement, apparently from *condīcere* talk over together, agree upon (*con-* together + *dīcere* to say; see DICTION). A common meaning of this word, "mode of being, state, position," appeared about the same time (1340, in *Ayenbite of Inwyt*) as the earliest recorded meaning. **—v.** 1494, make conditions, stipulate, borrowed from Middle French *conditionner,* from Old French, from *condition,* n. The sense of make fit, bring to a desired condition, is first recorded in 1849. **—conditional** *adj.* About 1380 *condicional, condicionel,* in Chaucer's translation of Boethius' *De Consolatione Philosophiae,* borrowed probably from Old French *condicionel,* and directly from Latin *condiciōnālis,* from *condiciōnem;* for suffix see -AL[1]. **—conditioner** *n.* 1598, formed from English *condition* + *-er*[1].

condole *v.* express sympathy (with). 1588, to grieve, lament, borrowed from Late Latin *condolēre* suffer greatly, suffer with (Latin *con-* with + *dolēre* grieve, suffer pain; see DOLOR). The sense of to express sympathy (with) is recorded before 1603, in correspondence of Queen Elizabeth I. Formation of a verb in English may have been influenced by earlier Middle English *condolent* sympathizing, contrite (before 1500), and perhaps remotely by Old French *condouloir.* **—condolence** *n.* 1603, sympathetic grief, in Holland's translation of Plutarch's *Moralia;* probably formed in English from Late Latin *condolēre* + English *-ence.* For a time, roughly 1600 to 1800, the spelling *condoleance* was used for the meaning of an expression of sympathy, borrowed from French *condoléance,* from Old French *condouloir* condole, from Late Latin *condolēre* + *-ance* -ance, but by 1800 *condoleance* had been leveled to *condolence.* The plural *condolences* an expression of sympathy, is recorded before 1674.

condom *n.* contraceptive. 1706, of unknown origin. The popular belief that it was named for an 18th-century physician who invented the device has no basis in fact. The word's history is traced in detail in William E. Kruck's *Looking for Dr. Condom* (1981, Publication of the American Dialect Society No. 66).

condominium (kon′dəmin′ēəm) *n.* Before 1714, joint rule or sovereignty, New Latin *condominium* (from Latin *con-* together + *dominium* property, ownership; see DOMAIN). Until 1962 this was chiefly a term of politics and international law (and among stamp collectors for the Anglo-French condominium in New Hebrides); but in American English (1962) a new sense appeared of individual ownership of an apartment unit with common ownership of the grounds and the building. By 1963 the term also meant an apartment house with this type of ownership and an apartment in such a building. *Condo,* a popular shortened form of this word, is first recorded in 1964.

condone *v.* forgive or overlook. 1857, borrowed as a legal term from Latin *condōnāre* to grant, permit, forgive (*con-* intensive + *dōnāre* give, present, pardon, from *dōnum* gift; see DONATION).

Apparently the word is not a back formation of the earlier legal and philosophical term *condonation* (1623), which probably produced the obsolete *condonate* (1656-81, in editions of Blount's *Glossographia*). *Condone* appeared in early English dictionaries, such as that of Blount (1656) and Bailey (1731), but until the

1850's it remained an Anglicized form for a term in law, and was omitted in later dictionaries, such as that of Johnson (1755), Webster (1828), and Craig (1847). The use of *condone* in common vocabulary may have been popularized by De Quincey, who first used it in 1859.

condor *n.* large vulture. 1604, borrowed from Spanish *cóndor,* from Quechua *cúntur,* the native name.

conduce *v.* lead, contribute. About 1400, borrowed from Latin *condūcere* to lead or bring together, collect, contribute, serve (*con-* together + *dūcere* to lead; related to TOW[1] pull). **—conducive** *adj.* favorable. 1646, formed from English *conduce* + *-ive,* on analogy with *conduct, conductive* and *abuse, abusive.*

conduct (kəndukt′) *v.* Before 1422 *conducted* guided or directed, borrowed from Latin *conductus,* past participle of *condūcere* lead or bring together, conduce; see CONDUCE. The sense of to behave in a certain way, is first recorded in 1706-10 and was an extension of the earlier sense of to direct, manage a transaction, business, etc. (1632). The sense of convey, especially in science, is first recorded in 1740.

Middle English *conducten* replaced *conduiten* to guide, escort, control oneself; earlier *condyten, conduyten* (about 1400), from *conduit,* n.

—n. (kon′dukt) About 1441, escort, guide, in the phrase *sauf conducte* safe conduct; borrowed from Latin *conductus* (genitive *conductūs*), from the stem *conduc-* of *condūcere* conduce. The sense of behavior is first recorded in 1673.

Middle English *conduct,* n. replaced earlier *conduit,* n., a guide, escort; earlier *conduyt* a channel or pipe to convey water, etc. (about 1300); see CONDUIT.

—conduction *n.* 1538, hiring; later, conveying (1541), borrowed from Middle French *conduction,* from Latin *conductiōnem* (nominative *conductiō*), from *condūcere.* **—conductivity** *n.* 1837, formed from English *conductive* (possibly from Middle French *conductif,* or English *conduct* + *-ive*) + *-ity.* **—conductor** *n.* 1526 *conductour* leader, borrowed from Middle French *conducteur,* and directly from Medieval Latin *conductor,* both from Latin *conductor* one who hires, from *conduct-,* past participle stem of *condūcere* bring together, hire, conduce; for suffix see -OR[2]. *Conductor* replaced earlier *conduitor* a guide or leader (about 1410); borrowed from Old French *conduitor,* from Latin *conductor.*

The sense of an orchestra director is first recorded in English in 1784-85; that of a person in charge of a railroad train, etc., in American English in 1832; and that of a wire or other device for conducting electricity, in 1737.

conduit *n.* channel. About 1300 *conduyt* (differentiated in meaning from *conduct* in the 1400's); borrowed from Old French *conduit,* from Medieval Latin *conductus* a leading, a pipe, from Latin *conduc-,* stem of *condūcere* lead or bring together, CONDUCE.

cone *n.* 1562, cone-shaped fruit, in a book on horticulture; borrowed from Middle French *cone, cône,* or directly from Latin *cōnus* cone, from Greek *kônos* cone, peak, pine cone; see HONE. The meaning of the geometrical shape is first recorded in 1570, but implication of this meaning is found in Middle English *cone* angle or corner of a quadrant (probably before 1400, in *Treatise of Geometry*). **—conic** *adj.* 1570, formed in English after Greek *kōnikós,* from *kônos* cone; for suffix see -IC. **—conical** *adj.* 1570, formed in English after Greek *kōnikós* conic + English *-al*[1]. If the words (*conic, conical*) were first used in English in 1570, they were formed independently by different authors.

confab *Informal.* **—n.** 1701, shortened form of *confabulation* (before 1500, borrowed, possibly by influence of earlier Middle French *confabulation,* from Late Latin *cōnfābulātiōnem,* nominative *cōnfābulātiō,* from *cōnfābulārī;* for suffix see -TION. **—v.** 1741, in Richardson's *Pamela,* shortened form of *confabulate* (1613, in Cawdrey's *A Table Alphabeticall,* borrowed, possibly by influence of earlier Middle French *confabuler,* from Latin *cōnfābulātus,* past participle of *cōnfābulārī* converse, chat, *con-* together + *fābulārī* speak, see FABLE; for suffix see -ATE[1]).

confection *n.* piece of candy. Before 1387 *confeccioun* anything prepared by mixing ingredients, in Trevisa's translation of Higden's *Polychronicon;* earlier *confescioun* (1345-46); borrowed from Old French *confeccion* a confection, learned borrowing from Late Latin *cōnfectiōnem* (nominative *cōnfectiō*), from Latin *cōnfectiōnem* a making, preparing, from *cōnficere* put together, prepare; see COMFIT; for suffix see -TION. **—confectioner** *n.* 1591, formed from English *confection* + *-er*[1]. **—confectionery** *n.* 1769, confused with earlier *confectionary* (1599), both words formed in English: *confectionery,* from *confectioner* + *-y*[1] and *confectionary,* from *confection* + *-ary.*

confederate *v.* unite, join together. About 1370 *confederen,* in Chaucer's poetry, borrowed through Old French *confédérer,* from Late Latin *cōnfoederātus,* past participle of *cōnfoederāre* unite in a league (*con-* together + Latin *foederāre* establish by treaty or league, from *foedus,* genitive *foederis,* league, compact, see FEDERAL); for suffix see -ATE[1]. **—adj.** joined together. Before 1387 *confederat,* in Trevisa's translation of Higden's *Polychronicon;* borrowed from Late Latin *cōnfoederātus,* past participle of *cōnfoederāre;* for suffix see -ATE[1]. **—n.** ally, accomplice. 1495, from the adjective. **—confederacy** *n.* About 1380, league, alliance, in Chaucer's translation of Boethius' *De Consolatione Philosophiae,* borrowed from Anglo-French *confederacie,* as if a from Late Latin **cōnfoederātia,* from *cōnfoederāre* unite in a league; for suffix see -ACY. **—confederation** *n.* About 1422 *confederacion* league, alliance, borrowed through Middle French *confédération,* or directly from Late Latin *cōnfoederātiōnem* (nominative *cōnfoederātiō*), from *cōnfoederāre;* for suffix see -TION.

confer *v.* give, grant. 1570; earlier, contribute (1528); borrowed perhaps through Middle French *conférer* to give, converse, compare, from Latin *cōnferre* bring together, gather, contribute, consult together, compare (*con-* together + *ferre* bring, carry; see BEAR[2] carry). Although the meaning of to compare is now obsolete, the abbreviation *cf.* (for Latin *cōnfer* compare) is widely used. **—conference** *n.* 1555, act of conferring, conversation; earlier, comparison (1538); borrowed from Middle French *conférence,* or directly from Medieval Latin *conferentia,* from Latin *cōnferentem* (nominative *cōnferēns*), present participle of *cōnferre* confer; for suffix see -ENCE.

confess *v.* admit. About 1378 *confessen,* in a version of *Piers Plowman,* borrowed from Old French *confesser,* from Latin *cōnfessus,* past participle of *cōnfitērī* acknowledge, avow, confess (*con-* intensive + *fatērī* to utter, declare, disclose, related to *fātus,* past participle of *fārī* to speak; see BAN[1] forbid). **—confession** *n.* About 1378, in a version of *Piers Plowman,* borrowed from Old French *confession,* from Latin *cōnfessiōnem* (nominative *cōnfessiō*), from *cōnfitērī* confess; for suffix see -ION. **—confessional** *n.* 1727, small booth where a priest hears confession; earlier, a fee for confession (1596); the sense of the booth is borrowed from French *confessional,* from Medieval Latin *confessionale* a confessional, from *confessionalis,* from Latin *cōnfessiōnem.* **—confessor** *n.* priest who hears confession. Before 1376, in a version of *Piers Plowman;* earlier, person who avows Christianity (about 1200); borrowed through Anglo-French *confessour,* Old French *confessor,* or directly from Late Latin *cōnfessor* a confessor (of Christianity), a martyr, from Latin *cōnfessus,* past participle of *cōnfitērī;* for suffix see -OR[2].

confetti (kənfet′ē) *n.pl.* bits of colored paper thrown by celebrators on festive occasions. 1895; earlier, candy, or paper, or plaster imitations of candy, thrown during carnivals in Italy, borrowed from Italian *confetti,* plural of *confetto* sweetmeat, candy, adapted from Old French *confit* confection; see COMFIT.

confide *v.* Before 1455 (Scottish), to trust, borrowed from Latin *cōnfīdere* have full trust, rely completely (*con-* completely + *fīdere* to trust; see FAITH). The sense of to entrust secrets to is first recorded in 1735. **—confidant** (kon′fədant′) *n.* close friend, intimate. 1714; earlier, also *confident* (1619 to about 1870); borrowed from French *confident* close friend, from Italian *confidente,* from Latin *cōnfīdentem* (nominative *cōnfīdēns*), present participle of *cōnfīdere* have full trust, rely completely; for suffix see -ANT and -ENT.

The spelling with *-ant* may have been an erroneous effort to correct the earlier spelling in *-ent* to what was thought to be French *-ant,* or *-ant* may have replaced *-ent* in an attempt to emphasize the French pronunciation, with stress on the final syllable.

—confidence *n.* Before 1400, borrowed from Old French *confidence* and directly from Latin *cōnfīdentia,* from *cōnfīdentem* (nominative *cōnfīdēns*), present participle of *cōnfīdere* have full trust; for suffix see -ENCE. **—confidence man** (1849, American English) **—confident** *adj.* 1576, borrowed from Middle French *confident,* learned borrowing from Latin *cōnfīdentem* (nominative *cōnfīdēns*) firmly trusting, bold, present participle of *cōnfīdere* have full trust; for suffix see -ENT. **—confidential** *adj.* 1759, perhaps borrowed from French *confidentiel,* as if from Latin **cōnfīdentiālis,* from *cōnfīdentia;* see CONFIDENCE.

configuration *n.* 1559, perhaps borrowed from Latin *cōnfigūrātiōnem* (nominative *cōnfigūrātiō*), from *cōnfigūrāre* (*con-* together + *figūrāre* to shape), see FIGURE; for suffix see -TION. A representative of the family of words to which *configuration* belongs existed in earlier *configured* (about 1384, in the Wycliffe Bible).

confine (kon′fīn) *n.* Usually, **confines.** boundary, limit. About 1400, region, territory, borrowed from Old French *confins,* pl., boundaries, learned borrowing from Medieval Latin *confines,* from Latin *cōnfīnia,* plural of *cōnfīnium* boundary, from *cōnfīne,* neuter of *cōnfīnis* having the same boundary (*con-* together + *fīnis* boundary, limit; see FINAL). —*v.* (kənfīn′) 1523, border on, borrowed from Middle French *confiner,* from Old French *confiner,* from *confins,* pl., bounds, confines. The sense of to keep within limits, restrain, is first recorded in 1595 in Shakespeare's *King John.* **—confinement** *n.* 1646, borrowed from French *confinement,* from *confiner* confine + *-ment* -ment.

confirm *v.* Probably before 1250 *confirmyen* to ratify; later *confermen* (about 1300); borrowed from Latin *cōnfirmāre,* and from Old French *confermer,* learned borrowing from Latin *cōnfirmāre* make firm, strengthen, establish (*con-* intensive + *firmāre* strengthen, from *firmus* FIRM). **—confirmation** *n.* About 1303, ceremony admitting person to church membership, in Mannyng's *Handlyng Synne;* borrowed from Old French *confirmacion,* from Latin *cōnfirmātiōnem* (nominative *cōnfirmātiō*), from *cōnfirmāre* confirm; for suffix see -TION. The sense of verification, proof, is first recorded about 1382, in the Wycliffe Bible. **—confirmed** *adj.* (about 1350)

confiscate *v.* seize, appropriate. 1552, verb use of earlier past participle or adjective (1553); perhaps influenced by Middle French *confisquer,* but borrowed from Latin *cōnfiscātus,* past participle of *cōnfiscāre* seize for the public treasury, originally, lay away in a chest (*con-* together + *fiscus* public treasury, chest; see FISCAL); for suffix see -ATE[1]. **—confiscation** *n.* 1543, borrowed from Middle French *confiscation,* learned borrowing from Latin *cōnfiscātiōnem* (nominative *cōnfiscātiō*), from *cōnfiscāre* confiscate; for suffix see -TION.

conflagration *n.* 1555, consumption by fire, borrowed from Middle French *conflagration,* learned borrowing from Latin *cōnflagrātiōnem* (nominative *cōnflagrātiō*), from *cōnflagrāre* burn up (*con-* intensive + *flagrāre* to burn; see FLAGRANT); for suffix see -TION.

conflict (kon′flikt) *n.* Probably before 1425, in a translation of Higden's *Polychronicon;* borrowed from Latin *cōnflīctus* (genitive *cōnflīctūs*), from *cōnflīc-,* stem of *cōnflīgere* strike together, clash, fight (*con-* together + *flīgere* to strike, dash, cognate with Aeolic or Ionic Greek *phlíbein* to press, squeeze, and Middle Welsh *blif* catapult, from Indo-European **bhlīgw-* smite, Pok.160). —*v.* (kənflikt′) Probably before 1425, in a translation of Higden's *Polychronicon,* borrowed from Latin *cōnflīctus,* past participle of *cōnflīgere* to conflict, fight.

confluence *n.* Probably before 1425, in a translation of Higden's *Polychronicon;* borrowed from Late Latin *cōnfluentia,* from Latin *cōnfluentem* (nominative *cōnfluēns*), present participle of *cōnfluere* flow together (*con-* together + *fluere* to flow; see FLUENT); for suffix see -ENCE. **—confluent** *adj.* Probably 1473, borrowed from Middle French *confluent,* learned borrowing from Latin *cōnfluentem* (nominative *cōnfluēns*), present participle of *cōnfluere;* for suffix see -ENT.

conform *v.* About 1340 *confourmen,* borrowed from Old French *conformer* make or be similar, learned borrowing from Latin *cōnfōrmāre* to form or shape symmetrically, make of the same form (*con-* with + *fōrmāre* to shape, from *fōrma* a shape, FORM). **—conformation** *n.* 1511, borrowed from Latin *cōnfōrmātiōnem* (nominative *cōnfōrmātiō*), from *cōnfōrmāre.* **—conformist** *n.* 1634, formed from English *conform* + *-ist.* **—conformity** *n.* Probably before 1425 *conformite* correspondence in form or manner, likeness, resemblance, in a translation of Higden's *Polychronicon;* borrowed from Middle French *conformité,* from Late Latin *cōnfōrmitātem* (nominative *cōnfōrmitās*), from *cōnfōrmis* similar in shape (Latin *con-* with + *fōrma* form); for suffix see -ITY. The sense of behavior according to some standard, compliance, acquiescence, is first recorded in 1494.

confound *v.* confuse, perplex. About 1300 *confounden* make uneasy and ashamed, borrowed through Anglo-French *confoundre,* Old French *confondre,* from Latin *cōnfundere* pour or mingle together, mix up, confuse (*con-* together + *fundere* pour; see FOUND[2] cast). The sense of to confuse, perplex is first recorded before 1376, in a version of *Piers Plowman.*

confrere (kon′frār) *n.* fellow member, colleague. About 1425 (Scottish), borrowed from Middle French and Old French *confrere,* from Medieval Latin *confrater* (Latin *con-* together + *frāter* BROTHER).

As a naturalized English word *confrere* apparently became obsolete in the 1600's, but has been revived as a reborrowing of modern French *confrère.*

confront *v.* About 1568, stand in front of, face, borrowed from Middle French *confronter,* learned borrowing from Medieval Latin *confrontare* assign limits, adjoin (Latin *con-* together + *frontem,* nominative *frōns,* forehead; see FRONT). The sense of to face in defiance or hostility, is first recorded in 1580. **—confrontation** *n.* 1632, action of bringing persons face to face, borrowed from French *confrontation,* from *confronter* confront + *-ation* -ation. The sense of an encounter between hostile persons or groups is first recorded in English about 1955, in a context of international relations.

confuse *v.* About 1330, to defeat, frustrate; later implied in *confused* bewildered (1378, in *Piers Plowman*); borrowed from Old French *confus* confused, from Latin *cōnfūsus,* past participle of *cōnfundere* pour together, mix up, confuse; see CONFOUND. **—confusion** *n.* About 1300, discomfiture, overthrow; borrowed from Old French *confusion,* learned borrowing from Latin *cōnfūsiōnem* (nominative *cōnfūsiō*), from *cōnfundere* confuse; for suffix see -SION. The sense of a confounding, confusing, or throwing into disorder is first recorded about 1380, in Chaucer's translation of Boethius' *De Consolatione Philosophiae.*

confute *v.* prove (something) false. 1529, in writings of Sir Thomas More, borrowed from Latin *cōnfūtāre* disprove, restrain, silence (*con-* intensive + *-fūtāre* to beat, earlier **-fautāre,* cognate with Gothic *bauths* deaf, dumb, from Indo-European **bhau-t-* strike, Pok.112); or possibly a back formation from earlier English *confutation.* **—confutation** *n.* 1459 *confutacioun,* borrowed from Latin *cōnfūtātiōnem* (nominative *cōnfūtātiō*), from *cōnfūtāre* confute; for suffix see -TION.

conga (kong′gə) *n.* Cuban dance of African origin. 1935, borrowed from American Spanish, from Spanish *conga,* feminine of *congo* of or pertaining to the *Congo,* region and river in central Africa, from *Kongo* a Bantu people.

congeal (kənjēl′) *v.* About 1380 *congelen,* in Chaucer's *House of Fame,* borrowed from Old French *congeler* freeze; thicken, learned borrowing from Latin *congelāre* (*con-* together + *gelāre* freeze, from *gelū* frost, ice; see COLD).

congenial *adj.* kindred, sympathetic. About 1625, probably formed in English from *con-* together + Latin *geniālis* of birth or generation; see GENIAL. Alternatively *congenial* may have been borrowed from New Latin **congenialis* (*con-* together + *genialis* of birth, from *genius*); or formed from English *con-* together + *genius* + *-al*[1]. The sense "agreeable, suited to" is first recorded in 1711.

congenital *adj.* present at birth. 1796, borrowed from Latin *congenitus* born with (*con-* with + *genitus* born, past participle of *gignere* beget, bear; see GENUS, GENITAL; for suffix see -AL[1].

conger (kong′gər) *n.* large ocean eel. 1310 *cunger,* later *kongyr* (1324); borrowed from Old French *congre,* from Late Latin *congrus,* from Latin *conger,* from Greek *góngros* conger, eel, tubercular growth on a tree, probably of Mediterranean origin.

congest *v.* Probably before 1425, borrowed from Latin *congestus,* past participle of *congerere* bring together, collect, heap up (*con-* together + *gerere* to carry, wage; see GESTURE). **—congestion** *n.* Probably before 1425, borrowed from Middle French *congestion* accumulation, learned borrowing from Latin *congestiōnem* (nominative *congestiō*), from *congerere* bring together; for suffix see -TION.

conglomerate (kənglom′ərit) *adj.* gathered into a mass. 1572, borrowed from Latin *conglomerātus,* past participle of Latin *conglomerāre* heap together (*con-* together + *glomerāre* form into a ball, from *glomus,* genitive *glomeris* ball, as of yarn; see CLAM); for suffix see -ATE[1]. **—n.** large business corporation. 1961, from the adjective. **—v.** (kənglom′ərāt) gather into a mass. 1596, borrowed from Latin *conglomerātus,* past participle of *conglomerāre* heap together; for suffix see -ATE[1]. **—conglomeration** *n.* 1626, in Francis Bacon's *Sylva Sylvarum,* borrowed from Late Latin *conglomerātiōnem* (nominative *conglomerātiō*), from Latin *conglomerāre;* for suffix see -TION.

congratulate *v.* 1548, borrowed, perhaps through Middle French *congratuler,* from Latin *congrātulātus,* past participle of *congrātulārī* congratulate, wish joy (*con-* together + *grātulārī* give thanks, show or express joy, from earlier **grātitulāri,* from a lost adjective **grātitulos* thanks-bringing, from *grātēs* thanks, related to *grātus* pleasing + *-tulos,* related to *tulī* I have brought); see GRACE; for suffix see -ATE[1]. Alternatively *congratulate* may be a back formation in English from the earlier *congratulation.* **—congratulation** *n.* 1438 *congratulacion,* in *Proceedings of the Privy Council;* borrowed from Middle French *congratulation,* or directly from Latin *congrātulātiōnem* (nominative *congrātulātiō*), from *congrātulārī;* for suffix see -TION. The plural noun *congratulations* is first recorded in 1632, and the informal clipped form *congrats* in 1884.

congregate *v.* Probably before 1450, verb use of earlier *congregat,* past participle or adjective (probably before 1425, in a translation of Higden's *Polychronicon*); borrowed from Latin *congregātus,* past participle of *congregāre* collect, assemble (*con-* together + *grex,* genitive *gregis* flock, herd, crowd; see GREGARIOUS); for suffix see -ATE[1]. It is also possible that in some early instances *congregate* may have been a back formation of earlier *congregation.* **—congregation** *n.* About 1380 *congregacioun* a gathering, assemblage, in Chaucer's *House of Fame;* borrowed from Old French *congregation,* from Latin *congregātiōnem* (nominative *congregātiō*), from *congregāre;* for suffix see -TION. The sense of a group of persons assembled for religious worship, a church, appeared before 1415 (in writings of Wycliffe).

The words referring to *Congregationalism* as a sect of Christian worship are first recorded for *Congrega-*

tional (1639), *Congregationalist* (1692, in writings of Cotton Mather), *Congregationalism* (1716, in writings of Increase Mather).

congress *n.* lawmaking body. Before 1400 *congrece* body of attendants; later *congresse* meeting of armed forces (before 1460), and *congress* a coming together of people, a meeting (1528); borrowed from Latin *congressus* (genitive *congressūs*) a coming together, assembly, encounter, from past participle of *congredī* meet with, fight with (*con-* together + *gradī* to step, walk; see GRADE). The sense of a meeting of delegates for discussion or settlement of some question is first recorded in English in 1678; the meaning of a lawmaking body of a country, in 1765, and with specific reference to the *Congress* of the United States, in correspondence of Samuel Adams, in 1775. **—congressional** *adj.* Before 1691, formed in English from Latin *congressiōnem* (nominative *congressiō*) a meeting, encounter (from the stem of *congredī* meet with) + English *-al*[1]. Application to the United States Congress is first recorded in 1775. **—Congressman** *n.* (1780) **Congresswoman** *n.* (1918)

congruent (kong′grüənt) *adj.* Probably before 1425, suitable, proper; borrowed from Latin *congruentem* (nominative *congruēns*), present participle of *congruere* agree, correspond with, fit (*con-* together + *-gruere,* as in *ingruere* rush into, fall upon, attack, combining form of a lost verb **gravere,* compare *ab-luere* wash off, with *lavere* wash, cognate with Greek *échrae* it fell upon, attacked, with corresponding **chra(w)eîn* to fall upon, from Indo-European **ghrəu-,* root **ghrēu-,* Pok.460); for suffix see -ENT. The sense in geometry of exactly coinciding, is first recorded in 1706. **—congruence** *n.* About 1443, borrowed from Latin *congruentia,* from *congruentem* (nominative *congruēns*), present participle of *congruere* agree, correspond with; for suffix see -ENCE. The application in geometry is first recorded in 1879. **—congruity** *n.* Before 1393, in Gower's *Confessio Amantis,* borrowed from Latin *congruitātem* (nominative *congruitās*) agreement, coincidence, from *congruus* agreeing, coinciding; for suffix see -ITY. **—congruous** *adj.* 1599, formed (on the model of Latin *congruus*) from Latin stem *congru-* + English *-ous.*

conic, conical. See CONE.

conifer *n.* cone-bearing tree or shrub. 1851, borrowed probably by influence of French *conifère,* from Latin *cōnifer* cone-bearing (*cōnus* CONE + *ferre* to carry, BEAR[2]). **—coniferous** *adj.* 1664, in John Evelyn's *Sylva,* formed in English from Latin *cōnifer* cone-bearing + English *-ous.*

conjecture (kənjek′chər) *n.* About 1384, interpretation of signs, forecast, in the Wycliffe Bible; borrowed through Old French *conjecture,* or directly from Latin *conjectūra* a casting together of facts and indications, conjecture, from the stem of *conicere* discuss, throw together (*con-* together + *-icere,* combining form of *jacere* to throw; see JET[1] stream); for suffix see -URE. The current generalized sense of guess, surmise, is first recorded in Middle English about 1395, in Chaucer's *Canterbury Tales.* **—v.** Probably before 1425 *coniecturen* to infer from signs and omens, forecast, in a translation of Higden's *Polychronicon;* borrowed from Old French *conjecturer,* from *conjecture,* n. **—conjectural** *adj.* 1553, implied in earlier *conjecturally* (1447), formed (on the model of Latin *conjectūrālis,* from *conjectūra*), from English *conjecture* + *-al*[1].

Originally *conjecture* existed alongside *conjecten,* v. (and *conjecte,* n.) in Middle English, both words meaning "to suppose, assume, surmise," but *conjecten* also meant "to plot, contrive, scheme." The noun *conjecte* disappeared in the 1500's and gradually during the 1600's *conjecture* took the place of *conjecten.*

conjoin *v.* About 1380, in Chaucer's translation of Boethius' *De Consolatione Philosophiae,* borrowed from Old French *conjoign-,* stem of *conjoindre,* from Latin *conjungere* to join together (*con-* together + *jungere* to join). **—conjoint** *adj.* Before 1393, in Gower's *Confessio Amantis,* implied in earlier *conjointly* (before 1325), borrowed from Old French *conjoint,* past participle of *conjoindre.*

conjugal (kon′jəgəl), *adj.* of marriage, matrimonial. 1545, borrowed from Middle French *conjugal,* or directly from Latin *conjugālis,* from *conjūnx* (genitive *conjugis*) wife or husband, consort, spouse, from *conjungere* join together, see CONJUNCTION; for suffix see -AL[1].

conjugate *v.* inflect (a verb). 1530, in Palsgrave's *Lesclarcissement,* verb use of earlier *conjugate,* adj., combined, united (1471); borrowed from Latin *conjugātus,* past participle of *conjugāre* to yoke together (*con-* together + *jugāre* to yoke, from *jugum* YOKE); for suffix see -ATE[1]. **—conjugation** *n.* About 1450 *conjugacion,* borrowed perhaps through influence of Old French *conjugaison,* from Latin *conjugātiōnem* (nominative *conjugātiō*), from *conjugāre* conjugate; for suffix see -TION.

conjunction *n.* 1375, an apparent proximity of two planets, in John Barbour's *The Bruce;* later, act of joining together, union (about 1380, in Chaucer's translation of Boethius' *De Consolatione Philosophiae*), and a word that connects words, phrases, and sentences in grammar (before 1397, in the Wycliffe Bible); borrowed from Old French *conjunction, conjonction,* from Latin *conjūnctiōnem* (nominative *conjūnctiō*), from *conjungere* join together (*con-* together + *jungere* JOIN); for suffix see -TION. The meaning in grammar was probably a direct borrowing from Latin, where the meaning existed as a loan translation borrowed from Greek *sýndesmos.* **—conjunctive** *adj.* About 1475 *conjunctyf* connective; earlier (before 1450) in the grammatical sense "subjunctive," from Latin *conjūnctīvus,* from *conjūnct-,* past participle stem of *conjungere* join together; for suffix see -IVE. **—conjunctivitis** *n.* 1835, New Latin, formed from *conjunctiva* connecting (as of the membrane over the eye) + *-itis* inflammation.

conjure *v.* About 1280 *conjuren* command or charge on oath, adjure; borrowed from Old French *conjurer,* learned borrowing from Latin *conjūrāre* swear together, make a compact, also in Late Latin with the meaning of adjure, entreat, exorcise (Latin *con-* together + *jūrāre* swear; see JURY). The sense of compel to appear or disappear by magic is first recorded in about 1300. The phrase *conjure up* cause to appear (in the mind) by magic, appeared in 1590, in Shakespeare's *Midsummer Night's Dream.* **—conjuration** *n.* About 1380 conspiracy, in the Wycliffe Bible; later, magic spell (1390, in Chaucer's *Canterbury Tales*); borrowed from Old French *conjuration,* from Latin *conjūrātiōnem* (nominative *conjūrātiō*), from *conjūrāre.* By 1500 the older *conjurisoun* (about 1250), borrowed from Old French *conjurison* was replaced by *conjuration.* **—conjurer, conjuror** *n.* Probably about 1350, from Middle English *conjuren* + *-er*[1], *-or*[2].

connect *v.* Probably 1440 *connecten;* borrowed from Latin *cōnectere* join together (*cō-* together, perhaps by analogy with *cō-nīvēre* close tightly, + *nectere* to tie, bind, probably altered, on the analogy of *plectere* to braid, twine, from earlier **nedere* and related to *nōdus* knot, NODE).

Alternatively the early form *connect* may be a back formation in English from the earlier *connection.* The spelling *connex* replaced *connect* in the 1500's and 1600's, modeled on the Latin **connexāre* a supposed frequentative form of *connectere,* possibly influenced by Middle French *connexer;* but this Latinate form was gradually itself replaced by *connect* in the late 1600's and 1700's.
—connection *n.* About 1385 *conneccion;* later *connexioun* (before 1447); borrowed from Old French *connexion,* learned borrowing from Latin *cōnexiōnem* (nominative *cōnexiō*), from *cōnectere* connect; for suffix see -TION. The spelling with *-tion* became prevalent in the 1700's, especially in American English, influenced by words such as *affection, collection, direction,* which were formed etymologically with final *-tion.* **—connective** *adj.* 1655-60; earlier *connexive,* borrowed from Latin *cōnexīvus* serving to connect, from *cōnex-* past participle stem of *cōnectere* + *-ive.* The spelling with *-tive* was influenced perhaps by French *connectif* (feminine *connective*) and by words such as *effective,* after the spelling *connect* began to replace *connex.*

conniption *n. Informal.* (fit of) rage or hysteria. 1833 *conniption-fit,* American English, perhaps a euphemism for *corruption* in the sense of anger, temper (1799).

connive *v.* cooperate in wrongdoing, especially by taking no notice of something, and thus to wink at. 1602, borrowed from French *conniver,* or directly from Latin *connīvēre,* spelling variant of the Classical *cōnīvēre* wink at, shut the eyes, overlook, connive (*con-* together + earlier **cnīvēre,* with its frequentative form *nictāre* to blink, wink constantly, cognate through Indo-European **kneigwh-* (Pok.608) with Old English, Old Saxon, and Old High German *hnīgan* to bend, bow, modern German *neigen,* Old Icelandic *hnīga,* and Gothic *hneiwan* to bow, from Proto-Germanic **Hnīȝanan*). **—connivance** *n.* 1596 *connivence,* borrowed from Middle French, from Latin *cōnīventia,* from *cōnīventem* (nominative *cōnīvēns*), present participle of *cōnīvēre* connive; for suffix see -ANCE, -ENCE. The modern English spelling *connivance* appeared in the 1700's. **—conniver** *n.* 1639, formed from English *connive* + *-er*[1].

connoisseur *n.* 1714, borrowed from French, from Old French *connoisseur* (since the early 1800's spelled *connaisseur*), from *connoistre* know, from Latin *cognōscere* become well acquainted with (*con-* with + *gnōscere* recognize, KNOW).

connote *v.* suggest in addition to the literal meaning. Before 1665, imply; borrowed from French *connoter,* from Medieval Latin *connotare* signify in addition to the main meaning (Latin *con-* with + *notāre* to note, from *nota* a mark, sign, NOTE). Alternatively, *connote* may have been a back formation in English from the earlier *connotation.* **—connotation** *n.* 1532, in Sir Thomas More's writings, borrowed from Medieval Latin *connotationem* (nominative *connotatio*), from *connotare* connote; for suffix see -TION.

connubial (kənü′bēəl) *adj.* of marriage; conjugal. 1656, in Blount's *Glossographia,* borrowed from Latin *connūbiālis,* a spelling variant of the Classical *cōnūbiālis,* from *cōnūbium* marriage (*con-* together + *nūbere,* earlier **sneubere* marry, see NUPTIAL); for suffix see -AL[1].

conquer *v.* Probably about 1200 *cunquearen,* borrowed through Old French *conquerre,* from Vulgar Latin **conquaerere,* re-formed from Latin *conquīrere* seek for, procure by effort, win (*con-* completely + *quaerere* seek, procure, gain; related to QUERY). **—conqueror** *n.* Probably before 1300 *conquerur,* borrowed through Anglo-French *cunquerrur,* Old French *conquereor,* from *conquerre* conquer; for suffix see -OR[2]. **—conquest** *n.* Before 1325, in *Cursor Mundi,* borrowed from Old French *conqueste* (from Vulgar Latin **conquaesita,* re-formed from Latin *conquīsīta),* feminine past participle of *conquerre* conquer.

conquistador (konkēs′tədôr) *n.* Spanish plunderer in North or South America during the 1500's. 1830, as a Spanish word introduced into Scott's writing; borrowed from Spanish *conquistar* conquer, from *conquista* conquest, originally feminine past participle (altered by influence of *visto* seen) of archaic Spanish *conquerir* conquer, from Vulgar Latin **conquaerere* seek, gain; see CONQUER.

consanguineous (kon′sanggwin′ēəs) *adj.* descended from the same ancestor. 1601, in Shakespeare's *Twelfth Night,* borrowed from Latin *cōnsanguineus* of the same blood (*con-* together + *sanguineus* of blood; see SANGUINE); for suffix see -OUS. **—consanguinity** *n.* About 1400 *consanguinyte,* in writings of Wycliffe, borrowed from Old French *consanguinité,* or directly from Latin *cōnsanguinitātem* (nominative *cōnsanguinitās*), from *cōnsanguineus* consanguineous; for suffix see -ITY.

conscience *n.* Probably before 1200, in *Ancrene Riwle,* borrowed from Old French *conscience,* learned borrowing from Latin *cōnscientia* knowledge, consciousness, conscience, from *cōnscientem* (nominative *cōnsciēns*), present participle of *cōnscīre* know, be conscious (*con-* intensive + *scīre* to know, see SCIENCE); for suffix see -ENCE.

Latin *cōnscientia* is probably a loan translation of Greek *syneídēsis* (literally) with knowledge. The Latin (and Greek) word was translated into German as *Gewissen,* which provided the model for Scandinavian words like Swedish *samvete* (with + know) and Icelandic *samvizka.* Similar loan translations are seen in Middle English *inwyt* (especially in the Middle English work *Ayenbite of Inwyt* Remorse of Conscience), in Dutch *geweten* (probably imitating German), and in Welsh *cydwybod* (with + knowing). Russian *sóvest'* is probably a direct loan translation from Greek.
—conscientious *adj.* 1611, borrowed from earlier French *conscientieux* (now spelled *consciencieux*), learned borrowing from Medieval Latin *conscientiosus,* from Latin *cōnscientia* conscience; for suffix see -OUS.

conscious *adj.* 1601, knowing, privy to (some knowledge), in Ben Jonson's *The Poetaster;* borrowed from Latin *cōnscius* knowing (something) with another (*con-* intensive + *scīre* know; see SCIENCE). The sense of having perception, being aware is first recorded in English in 1632.

Latin *cōnscius* was probably a loan translation of Greek *syneidṓs.* The sense resulting from "with" + "know" developed from "knowing (along with others)"

and then to "privy to a crime, accomplice, guilty," and also "inwardly aware."
—**consciousness** *n.* 1632, formed from English *conscious* + *-ness.*

conscript *n.* drafted soldier or sailor. 1800, back formation from CONSCRIPTION; influenced by French *conscrit,* noun use of Old French *conscrit,* adj., drafted, from Latin *cōnscrīptus,* past participle of *cōnscrībere* enter in a list, enroll, draw up (*con-* together + *scrībere* write; see SCRIBE). —**v.** to draft into the armed forces. 1813, American English, from the noun. —**conscription** *n.* 1382 *conscripcioun* written agreement or record; later, enrollment or enlistment of soldiers (1529); borrowed from Middle French *conscription,* learned borrowing from Latin *cōnscrīptiōnem* (nominative *cōnscrīptiō*) a drawing up of a list, enrollment, a levying of soldiers, from *cōnscrībere* enter in a list, enroll; for suffix see -TION.

consecrate *v.* set apart as sacred, dedicate. Before 1387, in Trevisa's translation of Higden's *Polychronicon;* borrowed, possibly by influence of Old French *consacrer,* from Latin *cōnsecrātus,* past participle of *cōnsecrāre* devote, dedicate (something) as sacred to a deity, deify (*con-* intensive + *sacrāre* make sacred, consecrate, from *sacr-,* stem of *sacer* SACRED); for suffix see -ATE[1]. —**consecration** *n.* Before 1382, in the Wycliffe Bible, borrowed from Old French *consécration,* learned borrowing from Latin *cōnsecrātiōnem* (nominative *cōnsecrātiō*) from *cōnsecrāre* consecrate; for suffix see -TION.

consecutive *adj.* successive. 1611, in Cotgrave's *Dictionary,* borrowed from French *consécutif* (feminine *consécutive*), from Middle French, learned borrowing from Medieval Latin *consecutivus,* from Latin *cōnsecūtus* following closely, past participle of *cōnsequī* follow closely (*con-* intensive + *sequī* follow; see SEQUEL); for suffix see -IVE.

consensus *n.* general agreement. 1633, as a nonce coinage; later, as a Latin borrowing (1843, in John Stuart Mill's *System of Logic*); Latin *cōnsēnsus* (genitive *cōnsēnsūs*) agreement, accord, common feeling, from *cōnsens-,* stem of *cōnsentīre* feel together, agree; see CONSENT. —**consensual** *adj.* 1754, of or having to do with consent; later, by consent (1800); formed from English *consensus* + *-al*[1]; the formation influenced by *sensual.*

consent *v.* Probably before 1200, in *Ancrene Riwle,* borrowed from Old French *consentir* agree, comply, learned borrowing from Latin *cōnsentīre* feel together, agree, accord (*con-* together + *sentīre* feel, think; see SENSE). —**n.** About 1300, borrowed from Old French *consente* agreement, compliance, from *consentir,* v.

consequent *adj.* 1410, borrowed from Middle French *conséquent* following, resulting, learned borrowing from Latin *cōnsequentem* (nominative *cōnsequēns*), present participle of *cōnsequī* to follow closely; see CONSECUTIVE; for suffix see -ENT. —**consequence** *n.* About 1380, an inference or conclusion, in Chaucer's translation of Boethius' *De Consolatione Philosophiae,* borrowed from Old French *consequence* result, learned borrowing from Latin *cōnsequentia,* from *cōnsequentem* (nominative *cōnsequēns*), present participle of *cōnsequī;* for suffix see -ENCE. —**consequential** *adj.* 1626, implied in earlier *consequentially* (1607), formed in English from Latin *cōnsequentia* thing resulting, from *cōnsequentem* (nominative *cōnsequēns*), present participle of *cōnsequī* + *-al*[1].

conserve *v.* About 1380 *conserven,* in Chaucer's *Canterbury Tales,* borrowed from Old French *conserver* protect, preserve, learned borrowing from Latin *cōnservāre* preserve (*con-* intensive + *servāre* keep, watch, maintain; cognate with Avestan *haurvaiti* he keeps watch, guards, from Indo-European **ser-w-* (Pok.910). —**n.** Often, **conserves.** Before 1393, a preservative, in Gower's *Confessio Amantis;* borrowed from Old French *conserve,* from *conserver* conserve. The sense of a medicinal preparation of fruit preserved in sugar as a confection or as jam, appeared probably about 1425, and as the plural noun *conserves* confections (before 1425), influenced in meaning by Medieval Latin or Italian *conserva.*
—**conservation** *n.* About 1380 *conservacioun* preservation, in Chaucer's translation of Boethius' *De Consolatione Philosophiae;* borrowed from Old French *conservacion,* and directly from Latin *cōnservātiōnem* (nominative *cōnservātiō*), from *cōnservāre* preserve; for suffix see -TION. —**conservationist** *n.* 1870, in letters of John Stuart Mill, formed from English *conservation* + *-ist.* —**conservative** *adj.* tending to preserve; opposed to change. About 1380 *conservatyf,* in Chaucer's *House of Fame,* borrowed from Middle French *conservatif* (feminine *conservative*), learned borrowing from Late Latin *cōnservātīvus,* from Latin *cōnservātus,* past participle of *cōnservāre* conserve; for suffix see -IVE. J. W. Croker, British writer and politician, used this word in the *Quarterly Review* (1830); Peel used the word in reference to the British party (1831) and general application to a political point of view is first recorded in American English (1832, in *Congressional Debates*). —*n.* 1831, Sir Robert Peel in *Croker Papers,* member of the Conservative party; from the adjective. The term was extended to general attitudes in politics, religion, etc., in 1843, in Carlyle's *Past and Present.*
—**conservatism** *n.* (1835, in reference to the British party; 1850, in general application). —**conservatory** *n.* 1563, a preservative, borrowed from New Latin *conservatorium,* from Medieval Latin, from the past participle stem of Latin *cōnservāre* conserve; for suffix see -ORY. The sense of a greenhouse is first recorded in 1664, in John Evelyn's *Sylva.* The sense of a school for music, drama, etc., is first recorded in 1842.

consider *v.* think about. 1375, in John Barbour's *The Bruce,* borrowed from Old French *considerer,* learned borrowing from Latin *cōnsīderāre* look at closely, examine, contemplate, consider; probably originally meaning "examine the stars," in reference to augury or navigation (*con-* with + *sīdus,* genitive *sīderis* constellation; see SIDEREAL). —**considered** *adj.* (probably before 1400) —**considering** *prep.* (about 1390, in Chaucer's *Canterbury Tales*). —**considerable** *adj.* About 1449, that can be considered, borrowed from Medieval Latin *considerabilis,* from Latin *cōnsīderāre* consider; for suffix see -ABLE. The meaning "worthy of consideration, significant" is first recorded before 1619, in Donne's writings, and then extended to "somewhat large" in 1651, in Hobbes' *Leviathan.* —**considerate** *adj.* 1572, well-considered, deliberate; earlier in Middle English *considerat* observed, noted (probably before 1425); borrowed from Latin *cōnsīderātus,* past participle of *cōnsīderāre* consider; for suffix see -ATE[1]. —**consideration** *n.* Probably about 1350, a beholding, contemplation, borrowed from Old French *considération,* learned borrowing from Latin *cōnsīderātiōnem* (nominative *cōnsīderātiō*), from *cōnsīderāre* consider; for suffix see -TION.

consign *v.* Before 1449, ratify or attest (as with a sign or seal), borrowed from Middle French *consigner,* learned borrowing from Latin *cōnsignāre* furnish or mark with a seal (*con-* with + *signum* seal, SIGN). The sense "hand over, deliver, commit" is first recorded in 1528. **—consignment** *n.* 1563, a sealing with a sign, formed from English *consign* + *-ment.* The general sense of a handing over or delivery, is first recorded before 1668.

consist *v.* 1526, exist, consist, borrowed through Middle French *consister,* or directly from Latin *cōnsistere* take a standing position, remain firm, exist (*con-* intensive + *sistere* cause to stand, place, related to *stāre* be standing, STAND). **—consistence** *n.* 1598 *consistence* a standing fast, firmness; borrowed from Middle French *consistence* (modern French *consistance*), from Medieval Latin *consistentia,* from Latin *cōnsistentem* (nominative *cōnsistēns*), present participle of *cōnsistere,* see CONSIST; for suffix see -ENCE. **—consistency** *n.* 1594, borrowed from Medieval Latin *consistentia* or from Latin *cōnsistentem,* see CONSISTENCE; for suffix see -ENCY. **—consistent** *adj.* 1574, standing still, borrowed from Latin *cōnsistentem* (nominative *cōnsistēns*), present participle of *cōnsistere;* see CONSIST. The sense of agreeing, compatible, congruous, is first recorded in 1646.

consistory *n.* Probably before 1300, a secular tribunal, in *Sir Tristrem;* borrowed from Old French *consistorie, consistoire,* and directly from Late Latin *cōnsistōrium* waiting room, meeting place of the emperor's council, the emperor's cabinet, from Latin *cōnsistere,* see CONSIST; for suffix see -ORY. The meaning of a church council is first recorded before 1325.

console[1] (kənsōl′) *v.* comfort. 1693, in Dryden's *Juvenal,* borrowed from French *consoler,* learned borrowing from Latin *cōnsōlārī* offer solace, console (*con-* intensive + *sōlārī* soothe; see SOLACE). Alternatively the word might possibly be a back formation in English from the earlier *consolation,* influenced in its formation by French *consoler.* **—consolation** *n.* About 1385, in Chaucer's *Troilus and Criseyde,* borrowed through Old French, or directly from Latin *cōnsōlātiōnem* (nominative *cōnsōlātiō*), from *cōnsōlārī* console; for suffix see -TION.

console[2] (kon′sōl) *n.* case, cabinet, or panel. 1706, ornamental bracket serving as a structural support, borrowed from French *console* a bracket, from Middle French, of uncertain origin.

According to Bloch-Wartburg the word was probably shortened from *consolateur* a sculptured figure of a man bearing a cornice, literally, meaning a consoler, from Latin *cōnsōlātor* (from *cōnsōlārī* CONSOLE[1]), so called because such figures were originally used as supports in church architecture; (compare Medieval Latin *misericordia* the name of such a carved figure in a church; literally, mercy, compassion). Dauzat and others refer the word to Old French *sole* beam, formed by folk etymology on *consoler* to console, with influence of *consolider* consolidate.

English *console* is first recorded in 1881 with the meaning of a case enclosing the keyboard, knobs, etc., of an organ. This sense was extended to the cabinet enclosing a radio, phonograph (1925), later, to that of a television, tape recorder, or computer set, and to a control panel or switchboard (1944).

consolidate *v.* 1511-12, borrowed from Latin *cōnsolidātus,* past participle of *cōnsolidāre* make solid (*con-* intensive + *solidus* SOLID); for suffix see -ATE[1]. Alternatively, *consolidate* may be a back formation of earlier *consolidation. Consolidate* replaced the Middle English verb *consouden, consolden* (recorded before 1400); borrowed from Old French *consolider,* learned borrowing from Latin *cōnsolidāre.* **—consolidation** *n.* Before 1400, uniting of a broken bone, healing of a wound, borrowed from Old French *consolidation* and from Latin *cōnsolidātiōnem* (nominative *cōnsolidātiō*), from *cōnsolidāre* make firm, consolidate; for suffix see -TION. The general sense of the action of consolidating, is first recorded in 1603, in Holland's translation of Plutarch's *Moralia.*

consommé (kon′səmā′) *n.* clear soup. 1815, as a French word introduced by a French author into a travel book; noun use of past participle of *consommer* finish, complete (as noun, in the sense of "extracted completely"), from Latin *cōnsummāre* to complete, CONSUMMATE.

consonant *n.* Probably before 1325, a sound other than a vowel, borrowed through Old French, from Latin *cōnsonantem* (nominative *cōnsonāns*), present participle of *cōnsonāre* sound together, i.e. with the vowels (*con-* together + *sonāre* to sound, from *sonus* a SOUND[1]); for suffix see -ANT. Latin *cōnsonāns* (*littera*) was a loan translation of Greek *sýmphōnon* sounding or voicing together. **—adj.** 1410, agreeing, consistent, borrowed from Middle French *consonant,* from Latin *cōnsonantem* (nominative *cōnsonāns*), present participle of *cōnsonāre* sound together. **—consonance** *n.* Before 1420, in Lydgate's *Troy Book,* borrowed through Old French *consonance,* from Latin *cōnsonantia* harmony, agreement, from *cōnsonantem,* see CONSONANT; for suffix see -ANCE.

consort *n.* husband or wife. 1419, colleague, partner, borrowed from Middle French *consort* mate, fellow, partner, wife, learned borrowing from Latin *cōnsortem,* accusative of *cōnsors* sharer, partner, comrade (*con-* with + *sortem,* accusative of *sors* lot; see SORT). The sense of husband or wife is first recorded in 1634. **—v.** 1588, in Shakespeare's *Love's Labour's Lost,* to escort, attend; from the noun. The meaning "to associate (with)" also appeared in Shakespeare, in *A Midsummer Night's Dream* (1590) and *Macbeth* (1605). **—consortium** (kənsôr′shəm) *n.* association, partnership. 1829, borrowed from Latin *cōnsortium* partnership, from *cōnsors* (genitive *cōnsortis*) partner; see CONSORT.

conspicuous *adj.* 1545, borrowed from Latin *cōnspicuus* visible, striking, from *cōnspicere* catch sight of, see, notice (*con-* thoroughly + *specere* look at; see SPY); for suffix see -OUS.

conspire *v.* plot, plan. Before 1376 *conspiren,* in *Piers Plowman;* borrowed from Old French *conspirer,* learned borrowing from Latin *cōnspīrāre* accord, agree, combine for a purpose, plot together, literally, breathe together (*con-* together + *spīrāre* breathe; see SPIRIT). **—conspiracy** *n.* 1357, borrowed from Anglo-French *conspiracie,* Old French *conspiratie,* replacing earlier *conspiration* (before 1325), borrowed from Old French *conspiration,* from Latin *cōnspīrātiōnem* (nominative *cōnspīrātiō*) act of plotting, conspiracy, from *cōnspīrāre* conspire; for suffix see -TION. **—conspirator** *n.* 1403, borrowed through Anglo-French *conspiratour,* Old French *conspirateur,* from Latin *cōnspīrātōrem,* from *cōnspīrāre;* for suffix see -OR[2].

constable *n.* Probably about 1200, chief household officer; also later, high military officer, governor of a royal domain or castle, justice of the peace (all about 1300), borrowed from Old French *conestable,* from Late Latin *comes stabulī* count or officer of the stable, marshal (*comes* COUNT[2] nobleman + Latin *stabulī,* genitive of *stabulum;* see STABLE[1] stall). The sense of a police officer is first recorded before 1836, preceded by various senses referring to different types of peace officers: king's peace officer, as of a county or town (about 1300), parish constable (1472), high constable (1543), officer of the peace (1597). **—constabulary** *n.* Before 1461, an adaptation of Medieval Latin *constabularia,* replacing earlier *constablerie* (1333); borrowed from Old French *conestablerie,* from *conestable,* see CONSTABLE; for suffix see -ARY.

constant *adj.* About 1390 *constaunt* steadfast, in Chaucer's *Canterbury Tales;* borrowed from Old French *constant* and directly from Latin *cōnstantem* (nominative *cōnstāns*) standing firm, immovable, stable, present participle of *cōnstāre* stand together, stand firm (*con-* intensive + *stāre* to STAND); for suffix see -ANT. **—n.** unvarying quantity (in mathematics or physics). 1832, from the adjective (1753). **—constancy** *n.* 1526, probably developed from earlier *constance, constaunce* + *-y* (as if *constaunce/constauncy*), after the pattern *-ance/-ancy* as in *fragrance/fragrancy,* but ultimately influenced by Latin *cōnstantia,* from *cōnstantem* (nominative *cōnstāns*), present participle, see CONSTANT; for suffix see -ANCY. *Constancy* replaced Middle English *constaunce* (1340, in *Ayenbite of Inwyt);* borrowed from Old French *constaunce,* from Latin *cōnstantia,* from *cōnstantem,* see CONSTANT. **—constantly** *adv.* (probably about 1425)

constellation *n.* About 1330, configuration of stars supposedly influencing a person; borrowed from Old French *constellation,* from Late Latin *cōnstēllātiōnem* (nominative *cōnstēllātiō*), from *cōnstēllātus* starred, studded with stars (Latin *con-* with + *stēllātus* covered with stars, from *stēlla* STAR); for suffix see -TION. The sense of a group of stars is first recorded before 1398, in Trevisa's translation of Bartholomew's *De Proprietatibus Rerum,* and the figurative extension of noteworthy persons or things appeared before 1631, in Donne's *Epithalamium.*

consternation *n.* 1611, in Cotgrave's *Dictionary,* borrowed from French *consternation* dismay, confusion, learned borrowing from Latin *cōnsternātiōnem* (nominative *cōnsternātiō*), from *cōnsternāre* overcome, alarm, confuse, dismay (*con-* with + *-sternāre,* probably related to *sternāx,* genitive *sternācis,* liable to throw a rider of a horse, cognate with Greek *stereós* solid, see STARE); for suffix see -TION.

constipate *v.* 1533, implied in earlier *constipat,* adj., constipated (probably before 1425, in a translation of Chauliac's *Grande Chirurgie*); borrowed from Latin *cōnstīpātus,* past participle of *cōnstīpāre* press closely together (*con-* together + *stīpāre* press, cram full; see STIFF); for suffix see -ATE[1]. Doublet of COSTIVE. *Constipate,* v. replaced earlier *constipen* (before 1398, in Trevisa's translation of Bartholomew's *De Proprietatibus Rerum*); borrowed from Old French *constiper,* from Latin *cōnstīpāre.* Modern English *constipate* is probably, in part, a back formation from the earlier *constipation.* **—constipation** *n.* Before 1400 *constipacioun* constriction of tissues; borrowed through Old French, or directly from Late Latin *cōnstīpātiōnem* (nominative *cōnstīpātiō*), from Latin *cōnstīpāre* press closely together; for suffix see -TION.

constitute *v.* make up, form. 1442, verb use of earlier adjective *constitute* made up, formed (before 1398, in Trevisa's translation of Bartholomew's *De Proprietatibus Rerum*); borrowed from Latin *cōnstitūtus,* past participle of *cōnstituere* set up, establish, appoint, ordain (*con-* intensive + *-stituere,* combining form of *statuere* set up; see STATUTE). **—constituency** *n.* 1831, in letters of Macaulay, formed from English *constituent* + *-cy* of *-ency.* **—constituent** *n.* 1622 *constituent, constituant* one who constitutes another as an agent (in 1714, one who elects another to public office); borrowed from, or by influence of French *constituant,* from Latin *cōnstituentem* (nominative *cōnstituēns*), present participle of *cōnstituere* set up, establish. **—*adj.*** 1660, probably from the noun, or perhaps influenced by French *constituant,* also used as a noun. **—constitution** *n.* Probably about 1350 *constitucion* law, regulation, edict; borrowed from Old French *constitution, constitucion,* learned borrowing from Latin *cōnstitūtiōnem* (nominative *cōnstitūtiō*) disposition, nature, constitution, order, arrangement, from *cōnstituere* set up; for suffix see -TION. **—constitutional** *adj.* 1682, formed from English *constitution* + *-al*[1]. **—constitutionality** *n.* 1787, in Alexander Hamilton's works, formed from English *constitutional* + *-ity.* **—constitutionally** *adv.* 1742, formed from English *constitutional* + *-ly*[1] or *constitution* + *-ally.*

constrain *v.* force, compel. Probably before 1325 *constreynen,* borrowed from Old French *constreign-, constraign-,* stem of *constreindre, constraindre,* from Latin *cōnstringere* tie tightly together, compress (*con-* together + *stringere* pull tightly; see STRAIN[1] stretch). **—constraint** *n.* restraint, restriction. About 1385 *constreinte,* in Chaucer's *Troilus and Criseyde,* borrowed from Old French *constreinte, constrainte,* originally feminine past participle of *constreindre, constraindre* CONSTRAIN.

constrict *v.* draw together. 1732 (though implied earlier in *constrict,* past participle and adjective, probably before 1425); borrowed from Latin *cōnstrictus,* past participle of *cōnstringere* compress, CONSTRAIN. Alternatively *constrict* may be a back formation in English from the earlier *constriction.* **—constriction** *n.* Before 1400 *constriccion,* borrowed through Middle French or directly from Latin *cōnstrictiōnem* (nominative *cōnstrictiō*), from *cōnstrict-,* past participle stem of *cōnstringere* constrain; for suffix see -ION. **—constrictive** *adj.* Before 1400, borrowed from Latin *cōnstrictīvus,* from *cōnstrictus,* see CONSTRICT; for suffix see -IVE. **—constrictor** *n.* Before 1735, formed in English from *constrict* + *-or*[2] on the pattern of Latin *conductor* from *condūcere.*

construct (kənstrukt′) *v.* 1663 (though implied earlier in *construct,* past participle, probably before 1425); borrowed from Latin *cōnstrūctus,* past participle of *cōnstruere* pile together, build up (*con-* together + *struere* pile, build; see STRUCTURE). Alternatively *construct* may be a back formation in English from the earlier *construction.* **—n.** (kon′strukt′) 1871, group of words forming a phrase; from the verb. **—construction** *n.* Before 1387 *construccioun* act of construing or translating, in Trevisa's translation of Higden's *Polychronicon;* borrowed through Old French *construction* or directly from Latin *cōnstrūctiōnem* (nominative *cōnstrūctiō*), from *cōnstrūct-,* past participle stem of *cōnstruere* build up; for suffix see -ION. The sense of building, putting together appeared probably before 1425. **—constructive** *adj.* Before 1425; borrowed through Old French *constructif* or directly from Latin *cōnstrūctīvus,* from *cōnstrūctus,* from *cōnstruere;* for suffix see -IVE.

construe *v.* show the meaning of, explain. Before 1376 *construen* analyze parts of a sentence, translate, in a version of *Piers Plowman;* borrowed from Late Latin *cōnstruere* relate grammatically, in Classical Latin meaning build up; see CONSTRUCT.

consul *n.* About 1384, a magistrate in ancient Rome, in the Wycliffe Bible; borrowed through Old French *consul* or directly from Latin *cōnsul,* probably originally meaning one who consults the senate, from *cōnsulere* CONSULT. *Consul* was used in the Middle Ages and after as the title of magistrates and other officials in Italy, France, England, and elsewhere, and by 1599 was used in reference to a representative of a government in a foreign country. **—consular** *adj.* Probably before 1425, in a version of Higden's *Polychronicon;* borrowed perhaps by influence of Old French *consulaire,* from Latin *cōnsulāris,* from *cōnsul;* for suffix see -AR. **—consulate** *n.* Before 1387, government by consuls, in Trevisa's translation of Higden's *Polychronicon;* borrowed from Latin *cōnsulātus* (genitive *cōnsulātūs*), from *cōnsul;* for suffix see -ATE[1]. The modern sense of a consul's office or residence is first recorded in 1702.

consult *v.* 1527, borrowed through Middle French *consulter* or directly from Latin *cōnsultāre* consult, frequentative form of *cōnsulere* take counsel, consult, probably meaning originally to gather (the senate) together (*con-* together + **selere* take, gather; see SELL). Alternatively *consult* may be a back formation in English from the earlier *consultation.* **—consultation** *n.* About 1425 (Scottish); borrowed from Middle French *consultation,* from Latin *cōnsultātiōnem* (nominative *cōnsultātiō*), from *cōnsultāre* consult; for suffix see -TION. **—consultant** *n.* 1697, probably formed from English *consult* + *-ant,* perhaps by influence of Latin *cōnsultantem* (nominative *consultāns*), present participle of *cōnsultāre* or, more likely, French *consultant.*

consume *v.* use up, devour. About 1380, in Chaucer's translation of Boethius' *De Consolatione Philosophiae;* borrowed through Old French *consumer,* and directly from Latin *cōnsūmere* take up completely, do away with, use up, consume (*con-* intensive + *sūmere* take up, formed from **sus-,* from earlier **subs-,* variant of *sub-* up, + *emere* to take; see REDEEM). **—consumer** *n.* About 1425, one who consumes or destroys, formed from English *consume* + *-er*[1]. The sense of one who makes use of goods (opposite of *producer*) is first recorded in 1745. **—consumerism** *n.* 1944, American English, emphasis on economic consumption, formed from English *consumer* + *-ism.* The sense of a movement advocating safer and better manufactured products, is first recorded about 1970.

consummate (kənsum′it *or* kon′səmət) *adj.* complete, perfect. 1447 *consummat,* adjective or participle, borrowed from Latin *cōnsummātus,* past participle of *cōnsummāre* sum up, make up, complete (*con-* intensive + *summa* highest degree, total; see SUM). **—v.** (kon′səmāt) 1530, fulfill, complete, in Palsgrave's *Lesclarcissement;* from the adjective. **—consummation** *n.* Before 1398 *consummacioun* completion, borrowed through Old French *consommation,* and directly from Latin *cōnsummātiōnem* (nominative *cōnsummātiō*), from *cōnsummāre* make up, complete; for suffix see -TION.

consumption *n.* Before 1398, a wasting of the body by disease, specifically after the 1650's, pulmonary consumption or tuberculosis, borrowed probably through Old French *consomption, consumption,* from Latin *cōnsūmptiōnem* (nominative *cōnsūmptiō*) a using up, wasting, from the stem of *cōnsūmere* use up, CONSUME; for suffix see -TION. The literal sense of the use of material appeared before 1535, in writings of Sir Thomas More, and the sense in economics (opposite of *production*), in 1662.

The *p* in Latin *cōnsūmptus, cōnsūmptiōnem,* etc., was inserted in those forms of *cōnsūmere* where an *m* was assimilated to a following stop (t).

—consumptive *adj.* Probably before 1425, in a translation of Chauliac's *Grande Chirurgie; n.* Before 1398, in Trevisa's translation of Bartholomew's *De Proprietatibus Rerum;* both functions of the word ultimately probably formed in English as if from Latin *cōnsūmpt-,* participial stem of *cōnsūmere* + English *-ive.* It is difficult to determine which derived from a functional shift of the other.

contact *n.* 1626, in Francis Bacon's *Sylva Sylvarum,* action of touching, borrowed perhaps through French *contact,* or directly from Latin *contāctus* (genitive *contāctūs*) a touching, from past participle of *contingere* touch closely (*con-* intensive + *tangere* to touch; see TANGENT). The figurative sense of connection, communication (as in *come in contact with*), appeared in 1818, in Byron's *Childe Harold's Pilgrimage.* **—v.** 1834, put in contact. The sense of get in touch with (someone) is first recorded in 1927 in American English.

contagion *n.* About 1380, corrupting influence, contamination, in Chaucer's *Canterbury Tales;* later, a communicable disease (before 1398); borrowed from Old French *contagion,* from Latin *contāgiōnem* (nominative *contāgiō*) a touching, contact, contagion, related to *contingere* touch closely (see CONTACT); for suffix see -ION. **—contagious** *adj.* About 1380, in Chaucer's translation of Boethius' *De Consolatione Philosophiae;* borrowed from Old French *contagieus,* from Late Latin *contāgiōsus,* from *contāgiō* a touching; for suffix see -OUS.

contain *v.* Probably before 1300 *conteinen* behave in a certain way, restrain (oneself), in *Arthour and Merlin;* borrowed from Old French *contenir,* from Latin *continēre* hold together, restrain, contain (*con-* together + *tenēre* to hold; see TENANT). **—container** *n.* About 1443 *conteiner,* formed from Middle English *conteinen* contain + *-er*[1]. **—containment** *n.* 1655, formed from English *contain* + *-ment.*

contaminate *v.* make impure. Probably before 1425, in a translation of Chauliac's *Grande Chirurgie;* borrowed by influence of Old French *contaminer,* from Latin *contāminātus,* past participle of *contāmināre* bring into contact, contaminate, from a lost noun **con-tāmen,* from earlier **com-tag-smen,* related to *tangere* touch; see TANGENT; for suffix see -ATE[1]. **—contaminant** *n.* 1934, formed from English *contaminate* + *-ant.* **—contamination** *n.* Probably before 1425, borrowed possibly through Middle French *contamination,* or directly from Latin *contāminātiōnem* (nominative *contāminātiō*), from *contāmināre* contaminate; for suffix see -TION.

contemn (kəntem′) *v.* treat with contempt, despise

About 1425 *contempnen;* borrowed from Middle French *contempner, contemner,* from Latin *contemnere* (*con-* intensive + pre-Latin **temnere* to slight, scorn, of uncertain origin; the later Classical Latin *temnere* is an artificial form abstracted from *contemnere* by Roman poets.

contemplate *v.* meditate. 1592, probably in part a back formation in English from the earlier *contemplation,* and a borrowing from Latin *contemplātus,* past participle of *contemplārī* survey, observe (originally, an augury), consider, contemplate (*con-* intensive + *templum* restricted area marked off for the taking of auguries, consecrated place, sanctuary, TEMPLE); for suffix see -ATE[1]. —**contemplation** *n.* Probably before 1200 *contemplaciun* devout meditation, in *Ancrene Riwle,* borrowed through Old French *contemplacion, contemplation,* or directly from Latin *contemplātiōnem* (nominative *contemplātiō*) the act or fact of looking at or considering, from *contemplari* contemplate; for suffix see -TION. —**contemplative** *adj.* 1340, in *Ayenbite of Inwyt,* borrowed from Old French *contemplatif* (feminine *contemplative*), from Latin *contemplātivus,* from *contemplātus;* see CONTEMPLATE.

contemporaneous *adj.* contemporary. 1656, in Blount's *Glossographia;* borrowed from Late Latin *contemporāneus* (from Latin *con-* together + *tempor-,* stem of *tempus* time + *-āneus,* from *-ānus* -an; see TEMPORAL); for suffix see -OUS.

contemporary *adj.* belonging to the same period. 1631, originally borrowed on the model of Medieval Latin *contemporarius,* from Latin *con-* together + *temporārius* pertaining to time (*tempor-,* stem of *tempus* time + *-ārius* -ary; compare TEMPORARY). From about the mid-1600's to sometime after the 1750's the form *cotemporary* largely replaced *contemporary,* according to the OED, but gradually during the latter half of the 1700's *contemporary* again became the common form. —**n.** Before 1635, *cotemporary;* later *contemporary* (1646, though not fully established until the 1800's); from the adjective.

contempt *n.* scorn. Before 1393, in Gower's *Confessio Amantis,* borrowed from Latin *contemptus* (genitive *contemptūs),* from past participle of *contemnere* to scorn, despise, CONTEMN. —**contemptible** *adj.* About 1384, worthy of contempt, despicable, in the Wycliffe Bible; borrowed from Latin *contemptibilis,* from *contemptus* (genitive *contemptūs*) contempt; for suffix see -IBLE. —**contemptibly** *adv.* About 1575, formed from English *contemptible* + *-ly*[1]. —**contemptuous** *adj.* 1595, showing contempt, disdainful, in Shakespeare's *King John;* formed in English from Latin *contemptus* (genitive *contemptūs*) contempt + English *-ous.*

contend *v.* struggle, fight. Probably 1440 *contenden,* borrowed through Middle French *contendre,* or directly from Latin *contendere* exert oneself, strain, strive (*con-* intensive + *tendere* to stretch; see TEND). —**contender** *n.* 1547, formed from English *contend,* v. + *-er*[1].

content[1] (kon′tent) *n.* what is contained. Probably before 1425 *contents,* in a translation of Higden's *Polychronicon,* and of Chauliac's *Grande Chirurgie* (about 1425); borrowed through Middle French, and directly from Latin *contentum,* neuter past participle of *continēre* CONTAIN. The singular *content* is recorded earlier (before 1420, in Lydgate's *Troy Book*).

content[2] (kəntent′) *v.* satisfy, please. 1418 *contenten,* in *Proceedings of the Privy Council;* borrowed from Middle French *contenter,* from *content,* adj., satisfied, from Latin *contentus* contained, self-contained, satisfied, from past participle of *continēre* CONTAIN. —**adj.** Probably before 1400 (adjective or past participle), borrowed from Old French *content,* from Latin *contentus* contained, satisfied, past participle of *continēre.* —**contented** *adj.* About 1445, from *content*[2], v. —**contentment** *n.* 1437, satisfaction of a claim or payment of a debt; borrowed from Old French *contentement,* from *contenter,* see CONTENT[2], v.; for suffix see -MENT.

contention *n.* act of contending, strife, dispute. About 1384 *contencioun,* in the Wycliffe Bible, borrowed from Old French *contention,* learned borrowing from Latin *contentiōnem* (nominative *contentiō*), from the stem of *contendere* CONTEND; for suffix see -TION. —**contentious** *adj.* Before 1500, borrowed through Middle French *contentieux,* and directly from Latin *contentiōsus,* from *contentiōnem* contention, see CONTENTION; for suffix see -OUS.

contest (kəntest′) *v.* 1603, borrowed from French *contester* dispute; oppose, also Middle French, from Latin *contestārī (lītem)* introduce (a lawsuit) by calling witnesses, bring an action (*con-* intensive + *testārī* be a witness, bear witness, testify, from *testis* witness; see TESTAMENT). A past participial form occurs only in the phrase *the strif lawfully contestat* having brought suit (before 1475), according to the *Middle English Dictionary,* which may be the source of *contest,* v. in English. —**n.** (kon′test) 1643, from the verb, but perhaps influenced by French *conteste,* from *contester* to contest, if the noun use in French is earlier than 1643. —**contestant** *n.* 1665, borrowed from French *contestant,* present participle of *contester* to contest.

context *n.* Probably before 1425, literary composition put together in a translation of Higden's *Polychronicon;* borrowed from Latin *contextus* (genitive *contextūs*), from past participle of *contexere* weave together, join, connect (*con-* together + *texere* to weave; see TEXT). The sense of surrounding parts of a text, is first recorded about 1568.

contiguous *adj.* touching each other, adjoining. 1611, borrowed, perhaps by influence of French *contigu,* from Latin *contiguus* adjacent, near, touching from *contingere* to touch (*con-* together + *tig-* in compounds the form of *tag-,* root of *tangere* to touch; see TANGENT); for suffix see -OUS; related to CONTINGENT and CONTAGION. —**contiguity,** *n.* 1641, borrowed, probably through French *contiguité,* from Latin *contiguitās,* from *contiguus;* see CONTIGUOUS.

continent[1] *n.* continuous land mass. Probably about 1425, that which is contained, content; borrowed from Latin *continentem* component part, noun use of *continentem* (nominative *continēns*) holding together, continuous, the present participle of *continēre* hold together, CONTAIN; for suffix see -ENT. The sense of a continuous tract of land, is first recorded in English in 1559, extended by the sense "mainland", a meaning borrowed from Latin and first recorded in English in 1576; followed by "one of the main continuous land masses of the earth", first recorded in English in 1614. —**continental** *adj.* 1760, formed from English *continent* + *al*[1]. The form *Continental* of or having to do with the American Colonies at the time of the American Revolution, is first recorded in 1774, in John Adams' works. —**Continental Divide** (1868)

continent[2] *adj.* showing restraint. Before 1382, in the

Wycliffe Bible, borrowed from Old French *continent* and from Latin *continentem* (nominative *continēns*), present participle of *continēre* hold together, restrain, CONTAIN; for suffix see -ENT. —**continence** *n.* self-restraint. Before 1387, in Trevisa's translation of Higden's *Polychronicon;* borrowed through Old French *continence* and directly from Latin *continentia,* from *continentem,* present participle of *continēre* contain; for suffix see -ENCE. Doublet of COUNTENANCE.

contingent *adj.* conditional, depending on something not certain. About 1385, borrowed through Old French *contingent* or directly from Latin *contingentem* (nominative *contingēns*) befalling, happening, touching, coming into contact, present participle of *contingere* befall, happen, touch; see CONTACT; for suffix see -ENT. Related to CONTIGUOUS and CONTAGION. —**n.** 1548, thing happening by chance; from the adjective. The sense of an additional part, group, etc., sent out to augment another part or group, is first recorded in English in 1727. The meaning of an unexpected event is first recorded in 1623. —**contingency** *n.* 1561, formed from English *contingent* + *-cy* in *-ency,* or possibly on a model of Late Latin *contingentia,* from Latin *contingentem* befalling, happening, touching; see CONTINGENT, adj.; for suffix see -ENCY.

continue *v.* About 1340 *contynuen,* borrowed from Old French *continuer,* learned borrowing from Latin *continuāre* join together, connect, continue, from *continuus* joining, connecting, uninterrupted, continuous, from *continēre* hold together, see CONTAIN. —**continual** *adj.* Before 1325 *continuel,* borrowed from Old French *continuel,* from Latin *continuus;* for suffix see -AL[1]. —**continuance** *n.* Before 1349, a keeping up, a going on; borrowed from Old French *continuance,* from *continuant* continuing, from Latin *continuantem* (nominative *continuāns*), present participle of *continuāre* continue. —**continuation** *n.* About 1380, in Chaucer's translation of Boethius' *De Consolatione Philosophiae;* borrowed through Old French *continuation, continuacion,* or directly from Latin *continuātiōnem* (nominative *continuātiō*), from *continuāre* continue; for suffix see -TION. —**continuity** *n.* Probably before 1425 *continuite,* borrowed from Middle French *continuité,* from Latin *continuitātem* (nominative *continuitās*), from *continuus* continuous; for suffix see -ITY. —**continuous** *adj.* 1642, borrowed, possibly through French *continueus,* or directly from Latin *continuus* hanging together, uninterrupted from *continēre* hang together, contain; for suffix see -OUS. —**continuum** (kəntin′yüəm) *n.* continuous quantity, series, etc. 1650, a borrowing of Latin *continuum* a continuous thing, neuter of *continuus* continuous.

contort *v.* Probably before 1425, borrowed from Latin *contortus,* past participle of *contorquēre* to twist, twirl, whirl (*con-* intensive + *torquēre* to twist; see TORTURE). —**contortion** *n.* Probably before 1425 *contorsioun,* borrowed from Middle French *contorsion,* from Latin *contortiōnem* (nominative *contortiō*), from the stem of *contorquēre* contort; for suffix see -TION. The spelling *contortion* is first recorded in English in 1615. —**contortionist** *n.* 1859, formed from English *contortion* + *-ist.*

contour *n.* 1662, borrowed from French *contour* circuit, circumference, outline, from *contourner* go around, perhaps through Italian *contorno,* from Italian and Medieval Latin *contornare* encircle go round, turn around (Latin *con-* with + *tornāre* to turn, round off, turn on a lathe, from *tornus* lathe; see TURN). The word was probably known earlier with the meaning of bedspread or quilt, in reference to its falling over the sides of the mattress (1423).

contra- a prefix meaning in opposition, counter, against, as in *contradistinction, contraindication.* Borrowed from Latin *contrā-,* from *contrā,* preposition and adverb, originally meaning "in comparison with," from an old ablative singular feminine form of a pre-Latin contrastive adjective **com-teros* (**com-terā, *com-terom*); it was a contrastive form of *com-* with, together; see COM-. As a prefix *contra-* existed in Middle English alongside the earlier *countre-* (about 1303).

contraband *n.* Before 1529 *counterbande* smuggling, borrowed from Middle French *contrebande,* from early Italian *contrabando* (now *contrabbando*) unlawful dealing against law or proclamation (*contra-* against, from Latin *contrā* + *bando* proclamation, of Germanic origin and related to the source of English BAN[2] edict); compare ABANDON. The meaning "smuggled goods" appeared in English in 1599.

contrabass *n.* the lowest voice or musical instrument, especially the largest instrument of the violin class. 1598-1611 *counterbase,* in an edition of Florio's *A World of Words,* originally a loan translation of Italian *contrabasso* (*contra-* opposite, from Latin *contrā-,* + *basso* bass).

contraception *n.* 1886, formed from English *contra-* against + *(con)ception.* —**contraceptive** *n.* device or drug preventing conception. 1891, formed from English *contra-* against + *(con)ceptive.* —*adj.* 1918, from the noun.

contract (kəntrakt′) *v.* Probably before 1425 *contracten* make an agreement or contract; occurring in English in part as: 1) a development from verb use of earlier participle and adjective *contract* incurred, contracted (1390, in Chaucer's *Canterbury Tales*), borrowed from Latin *contractus;* and 2) a borrowing from Middle French *contracter,* from Latin *contractus,* past participle of *contrahere* draw together, collect, combine, make an agreement or contract (*con-* together + *trahere* to pull; see TRACT). The sense of make narrow, draw together, is first recorded before 1398, usually with reference to the drawn-up or shrunken appearance of paralyzed limbs. —**n.** (kon′trakt) Before 1333, borrowed from Old French *contract* (modern French *contrat*), learned borrowing from Latin *contractus* (genitive *contractūs*) agreement, from past participle of *contrahere* to contract. —**contraction** *n.* Before 1398 *contraccioun* a coming or drawing together; later contraction, compression (probably before 1425); borrowed through Old French *contraction,* or directly from Latin *contractiōnem* (nominative *contractiō*), from the past participle stem of *contrahere* to contract; for suffix see -TION. —**contractor** *n.* 1548, borrowed from Late Latin *contractor* one who makes a contract, from Latin *contrahere;* for suffix see -OR[2].

contradict *v.* 1570-76, speak against, oppose in speech; borrowed from Latin *contrādictus,* past participle of *contrādīcere* speak against, from *contrā dīcere* say in opposition (*contrā* against, CONTRA- + *dīcere* say; see DICTION). The sense of assert the contrary, deny, is first recorded in 1582. Alternatively *contradict* may be a back formation in English from earlier *contradiction.* —**contradiction** *n.* Before 1382, in the Wycliffe Bible, borrowed through Old French *contradiction,* or directly from Latin *contrādictiōnem* (nominative *contrādictiō*), from *contrādīcere* speak against; for suffix see -TION. —**contradictory** *adj.* 1534, from earlier noun use (about 1385); borrowed from Late Latin *contrādictōrius,* from *contrādictor* one who opposes, from *contrādīcere;* for suffix see -ORY.

contrail (kon′trāl′) *n.* vapor trail left by an airplane. 1945, formed from English *con(densation)* + *trail.*

contralto (kəntral′tō) *n.* the lowest female voice. 1730 *contrealt,* later *contralto* (1740); borrowed from Italian *contralto* (*contra-* counter to, from Latin *contrā* + *alto* high, from Latin *altus;* see OLD).

contraption *n. Informal.* contrivance, gadget. 1825, dialect use (western England), a formation of unknown origin, possibly suggested by *contrivance,* in unexplained combination with *trap,* and the ending *-tion.* Perhaps the use of *trap* has some association with the small, lightly sprung, horse-drawn carriage (also found in *rattletrap*).

contrapuntal (kon′trəpun′təl) *adj.* of or having to do with musical counterpoint. 1845, formed in English probably from early Italian *contrapunto* counterpoint (although recorded by 1724, in English) + English *-al*[1]. The Italian word is derived from the Medieval Latin phrase *punctum contra punctum* point, or musical note against note. Though known in Middle English *countrepoint* (before 1450), which was borrowed through Anglo-French, the word remains unrecorded for almost 400 years, which suggests a reborrowing in the 1800's.

contrary *adj.* 1340, *contrarie,* in *Ayenbite of Inwyt;* borrowed through Anglo-French *contrarie,* also in early Old French, from Latin *contrārius* opposite, hostile, from *contrā* against (see CONTRA-); for suffix see -ARY. Another spelling, *contraire,* from Old French, is found after 1370 and into the late 1400's, but except for dialectal use in English the spelling disappeared by 1500. —**n.** About 1275 *contrarie,* borrowed through Anglo-French *contrarie,* also in early Old French, from absolute use of the adjective in Old French.

contrast (kəntrast′) *v.* 1695, in Dryden's translation of Dufresnoy's *The Art of Painting;* borrowed from French *contraster,* from Italian *contrastare* strive, contend, stand out against, from Vulgar Latin **contrāstāre* (Latin *contrā-* against + *stāre* to STAND). —**n.** (kon′trast) 1711, borrowed from French *contraste,* from Italian *contrasto,* from *contrastare* to contrast. —**contrastive** *adj.* 1816, formed from English *contrast,* v. + *-ive.*

The verb *contrast* was reintroduced in English as a term of art after having become obsolete. Earlier the term spelled *contrest,* used in a translation of Caxton's from Middle French *contrester* (from Vulgar Latin **contrāstāre*), was recorded in the verb sense of withstand, strive, fight against, by the late 1400's, and as a noun in the late 1500's.

contravene (kon′trəvēn′) *v.* go counter to, conflict with. 1567, borrowed from Middle French *contravenir* to transgress, decline, depart, learned borrowing from Late Latin *contrāvenīre* oppose, also in Medieval Latin, transgress (Latin *contrā-* against + *venīre* to COME). —**contravention** *n.* 1579, borrowed from Middle French *contravention,* from Late Latin **contrāventiōnem* (nominative **contrāventiō*), from *contrāvenīre* contravene); for suffix see -TION.

contretemps (kôNtrətäN′) *n.* 1684, pass or thrust in fencing made at a wrong moment; borrowed from French *contretemps,* literally, bad or false time, inopportuneness, unexpected accident (*contre* against, from Latin *contrā,* + *temps* time, from Latin *tempus;* see TEMPORAL). The sense of an untoward incident, mishap, was first recorded in 1802.

contribute *v.* 1530, give jointly with others, in Palsgrave's *Lesclarcissement;* probably a back formation in English from the earlier *contribution,* and in part a borrowing from Latin *contribūtus,* past participle of *contribuere* bring together, add, collect (*con-* together + *tribuere* bestow, assign, allot; see TRIBUTE). —**contribution** *n.* Before 1387, tax, in Trevisa's translation of Higden's *Polychronicon;* borrowed through Old French *contribution,* or directly from Latin *contribūtiōnem* (nominative *contribūtiō*), from *contribuere* collect; for suffix see -TION. —**contributor** *n.* 1433, in *Rolls of Parliament,* borrowed through Anglo-French *contributour,* formed as if from Latin **contribūtor,* from *contribuere* + *-tor;* for suffix see -OR[2]. —**contributory** *adj.* 1410, in a version of Chaucer's *Canterbury Tales,* formed as if from Latin **contribūtōrius,* from *contribūtus,* past participle of *contribuere;* for suffix see -ORY.

contrite *adj.* penitent. Probably before 1300 *contrit,* borrowed through Old French *contrit,* or directly from Latin *contrītus* (thoroughly) crushed, past participle of *conterere* to wear down, crush (*con-* thoroughly + *terere* rub, grind, wear; see THROW). —**contrition** *n.* penitence. About 1303 *contrycyun,* in Mannyng's *Handlyng Synne;* borrowed through Old French *contricion,* or directly from Latin *contrītiōnem* (nominative *contrītiō*), from the stem *contrī-* of *conterere* to crush; for suffix see -TION.

contrive *v.* invent, design, scheme. Before 1338 *contreven, controven,* in Mannyng's *Chronicle of England;* borrowed from Old French *contreuver, controver,* from Late Latin *contropāre* compare, search out (Latin *con-* together, with + Vulgar Latin **tropāre* to compose, from Latin *tropus* song, musical mode, from Greek *trópos* mode, style, TROPE).

In the 1400's the prevailing form *contreve* gradually changed to *contrive,* representing a phonetic change that is unexplained; compare *brier*[1], *friar* and *choir* for a similar change.

—**contrivance** *n.* 1627-28, artifice, trick, formed from English *contrive* + *-ance.* The sense of a mechanical device or arrangement appeared in 1667.

control *v.* direct, have power over. 1422 *countrollen* check or verify (payments or accounts), in *Rolls of Parliament;* borrowed from Anglo-French and Old French *contreroller,* from *contrerolle* copy of a register, for checking, verification (*contre* against + *rolle* ROLL). The sense of to direct, dominate, is first recorded in 1451. —**n.** 1590, restraint, check, in Shakespeare's *Comedy of Errors,* probably in part developed from the verb, and in part borrowed from Middle French *contrôle,* from Old French *contrerolle.* —**controller** *n.* person who supervises expenditures and accounts. Probably before 1387 *contreroller,* in a version of *Piers Plowman;* borrowed from Anglo-French *countrerollour,* Old French *contrerolleur,* from *contrerolle.* See COMPTROLLER.

controversy *n.* dispute. About 1384, in the Wycliffe Bible, borrowed through Old French *controversie,* or directly from Latin *contrōversia,* from *contrōversus* turned against, disputed (*contrō-* against, from a lost adverb **contrō*, from an old ablative singular masculine form of a pre-Latin contrastive adjective **comteros* + Latin *versus,* past participle of *vertere* to turn; see CONTRA- and VERTEX). —**controversial** *adj.* 1583, borrowed from Latin *contrōversiālis,* from *contrōversia;* see CONTROVERSY. —**controvert** *v.* dispute, deny. 1609, derived from English *controversy,* on the assumed analogy of Latin *contrōversus* with such words as *conversus,* past participle of *convertere* to convert, *perversus,* past participle of *pervertere* to pervert, etc.

contumacy (kon′tủməsē) *n.* stubborn resistance. About 1390, in Chaucer's *Canterbury Tales,* borrowed from Latin *contumācia* arrogance, from *contumāx* (genitive *contumācis*) insolent (*con-* intensive + *tumēre* to swell, see THUMB); for suffix see -ACY. The form *contumacy* replaced the earlier *contumace* (recorded probably before 1200, in *Ancrene Riwle*); borrowed from Old French, from Latin *contumācia.* —**contumacious** (kon′tủmā′shəs) *adj.* 1603, formed from English *contumacy* + *-ous.*

contumely (kon′tủməlē) *n.* insulting words or actions. About 1390, in Chaucer's *Canterbury Tales;* borrowed from Old French *contumelie,* from Latin *contumēlia* abuse, originally, insolent action, built on a lost adjective **contumēlis* (probably influenced in its ending by *crūdēlis* cruel), related to *contumāx* (genitive *contumācis*) insolent; see CONTUMACY. —**contumelious** *adj.* Probably about 1425 *contumilious* full of contumely, borrowed from Middle French *contumelius,* from Latin *contumēliōsus,* from *contumēlia* contumely; for suffix see -OUS.

contusion (kəntü′zhən) *n.* a bruise. Before 1400, borrowed from Middle French *contusion,* learned borrowing from Latin *contūsiōnem* (nominative *contūsiō*) crushing, bruising, from the participle stem *contūs-* of *contundere* to crush, bruise (*con-* intensive + *tundere* to beat; see STUDY).

conundrum (kənun′drəm) *n.* riddle. 1605, a whim, in Ben Jonson's *Volpone;* earlier *Cunundrum,* a name for a pedant (1596); of unknown origin. In 1645, in the sense of a pun or word play, it was referred to as an Oxford term, hence possibly it originated as a parody of some Latin term. The current meaning of a riddle involving a pun appeared in 1790.

convalesce (kon′vəles′) *v.* make progress toward health. 1483, in Caxton's version of the *Golden Legend;* borrowed from Latin *convalēscere* thrive, convalesce (*con-* intensive + *valēscere* grow strong, from *valēre* be strong, be well, be worth; see VALUE). —**convalescence** *n.* About 1489, in Caxton's translation of *Blanchardyn and Eglantine,* borrowed from Middle French, from Late Latin *convalēscentia* regaining of health, from Latin *convalēscentem* (nominative *convalēscēns*), present participle of *convalēscere* convalesce; for suffix see -ENCE. —**convalescent** *adj.* 1656, in Blount's *Glossographia,* borrowed from French *convalescent,* from Latin *convalēscentem* (nominative *convalēscēns*), present participle of *convalēscere;* for suffix see -ENT. —*n.* 1758, in Lord Chesterfield's letters, from the adjective.

convection *n.* act of conveying. 1623, borrowed from Latin *convectiōnem* (nominative *convectiō*), from *convect-,* past participle stem of *convehere* to carry together (*con-* together + *vehere* to carry; see WEIGH); for suffix see -ION.

Despite the relationship of meaning, *convection* and *convey* are not related in formation, as *convey* is ultimately from Latin *con-* and *via* road.

convene *v.* come or bring together. About 1425 (Scottish), borrowed from Middle French *convenir,* from Latin *convenīre* come together, unite, agree, suit (*con-* together + *venīre* COME).

convenient *adj.* About 1380, in Chaucer's translation of Boethius' *De Consolatione Philosophiae;* borrowed from Latin *convenientem* (nominative *conveniēns*), present participle of *convenīre* come together, agree, suit, see CONVENE; for suffix see -ENT.

Convenient is not recorded in Middle French before 1450; this may be only a defect in the record so that French may be the immediate source of this borrowing, especially since Chaucer is the first author of record and his translation may have been influential in establishing the word.

—**convenience** *n.* Before 1398, conformity, suitability, borrowed through Old French *convenience,* and directly from Latin *convenientia* agreement, meeting together, from *convenientem* (nominative *conveniēns*), present participle; for suffix see -ENCE.

convent *n.* Probably before 1425, assemblage, alteration (influenced by Latin *conventus*) of earlier *cuvent* (probably before 1200); borrowed through Anglo-French *covent,* from Old French *convent,* from Latin *conventus* (genitive *conventūs*) assembly, from past participle of *convenīre* come together, CONVENE. The sense of a group of nuns living together, is first recorded before 1450, but an earlier sense of a group of men *or* women living as a religious order, is first recorded about 1230 as *cuvent,* which became obsolete by the late 1600's.

convention *n.* Before 1420 *convencioun* agreement, in Lydgate's *Troy Book;* borrowed through Middle French *convention,* or directly from Latin *conventiōnem* (nominative *conventiō*) meeting, assembly, covenant, from *convenīre* CONVENE; for suffix see -TION. Latin *conventiō* is a new formation taking the place of the old *cōntiō,* from earlier **co-ventiō,* from pre-Latin **com-ventiō.* —**conventional** *adj.* Before 1475, borrowed from Late Latin *conventiōnālis,* from Latin *conventiōnem* convention; for suffix see -AL[1]. —**conventionality** *n.* Before 1834, in Lamb's letters, formed from English *conventional* + *-ity.*

converge *v.* 1691, borrowed from Late Latin *convergere* to incline together (Latin *con-* together + *vergere* to incline; see WRENCH). —**convergence** *n.* 1713, formed from English *converge* + *-ence.* —**convergent** *adj.* 1727-51, in *Chambers Cyclopaedia,* borrowed from Medieval Latin *convergentem* (nominative *convergens*), present participle of *convergere* converge.

conversant *adj.* familiar by use or study. About 1390 *conversaunt,* borrowed from Old French *conversant,* from Latin *conversantem* (nominative *conversāns*), present participle of *conversārī* associate with; see CONVERSE[1].

converse[1] (kənvėrs′) *v.* talk informally. About 1380 *conversen* live, dwell, in Chaucer's translation of Boethius' *De Consolatione Philosophiae;* borrowed from Old French *converser* to live with, learned borrowing from Latin *conversārī* associate with, keep company with, the frequentative form of *convertere* to turn about, change, CONVERT. The current sense is first recorded in English in 1615; in French it is found in 1537 and in Italian, before 1306. —**conversation** *n.* 1340, a living together, manner of behaving, in *Ayenbite of Inwyt;* borrowed from Old French *conversation,* from Latin *conversātiōnem* (nominative *conversātiō*) act of living with, from *conversārī* associate with; for suffix see -TION. The sense of familiar or informal talk, is first recorded in 1580, in Sidney's *The Arcadia.* **—conversational** *adj.* 1779, formed from English *conversation* + *-al*[1]. **—conversationalist** *n.* 1836, formed from English *conversational* + *-ist.*

converse[2] (kon′vėrs) *adj.* opposite, reversed. 1570, in mathematics; borrowed from Latin *conversus* turned around, past participle of *convertere* CONVERT. **—n.** something reversed. 1570, in mathematics, borrowed from Latin *conversus* turned around; earlier *convers* someone who has converted to a religious faith, a convert (before 1325).

conversion *n.* act of converting. About 1340, turning of a sinner to righteousness, in a Middle English Psalter; later, transformation (probably before 1425); borrowed from Old French *conversion,* from Latin *conversiōnem* (nominative *conversiō*), from past participle stem *convers-* of *convertere* CONVERT; for suffix see -ION.

convert (kənvėrt′) *v.* About 1300 *converten,* borrowed from Old French *convertir,* learned borrowing from Latin *convertere* turn about, transform, translate (*con-* intensive + *vertere* to turn; see VERTEX). **—n.** (kon′-vėrt) person who has been converted. 1561, from the verb; replacing earlier *convers* a convert (before 1325, in *Cursor Mundi*); borrowed through Old French *convers,* from Latin *conversus,* past participle of *convertere* convert. **—convertible** *adj.* About 1385, borrowed from Old French *convertible,* from Late Latin *convertibilis,* from Latin *convertere;* for suffix see -IBLE. — *n.* automobile with a folding top. 1916, American English, from the adjective.

convex *adj.* 1571, borrowed from Middle French *convexe,* from Latin *convexus* vaulted, arched (probably from *con-* intensive + *-vexus,* found also in *subvexus* sloping upwards from below; cognate with Sanskrit *váñcati* moves crookedly, from Indo-European **wek-* to bend, Pok.1135).**—convexity** *n.* 1600, probably formed in English from *convex* + *-ity,* but perhaps also influenced by French *convexité,* from Latin *convexitās,* from *convexus;* for suffix see -ITY.

convey *v.* Before 1393 *conveien* carry, transport, in Gower's *Confessio Amantis;* earlier, go along with, accompany (before 1325, in *Cursor Mundi*); borrowed through Anglo-French *conveier,* Old French *convoier,* from Vulgar Latin **conviāre,* literally, go together on the road (Latin *con-* with + *via* road; see VIA). Doublet of CONVOY, verb. **—conveyance** *n.* About 1437, formed from English *convey* + *-ance.* **—conveyer** *n.* 1513-14, **conveyor** *n.* 1647, formed from English *convey* + *-er*[1], *-or*[2].

convict (kənvikt′) *v.* About 1340 *convicten,* borrowed from Latin *convictus,* past participle of *convincere* overcome (in argument), convict, CONVINCE. **—n.** (kon′ vikt) About 1475, from the verb. **—conviction** *n.* 1437, borrowed from Late Latin *convictiōnem* (nominative *convictiō*) proof, refutation, from *convict-,* participle stem of Latin *convincere* convince; for suffix see -ION. The sense of a firm belief, is first recorded in 1699, in Pepys' *Diary.*

convince *v.* 1530, overcome in argument, in Palsgrave's *Lesclarcissement;* borrowed from Latin *convincere* overcome, convict, convince (*con-* intensive + *vincere* conquer; see VICTOR). The sense of persuade is first recorded in 1606, in Shakespeare's *Troylus and Cressida*). **—convincing** *adj.* 1624, formed from the verb *convince* + *-ing*[1].

convivial *adj.* Before 1668, belonging to a feast, festive, borrowed through French *convivial,* or directly from Late Latin *convīviālis,* from Latin *convīvium* social feast, entertainment (*con-* with + *vīvere* to live, see VIVID); for suffix see -AL[1]. The sense of being fond of eating and drinking with friends, jovial, sociable, is first recorded in the 1700's.

convoke *v.* call together. 1598, in Florio's Italian-English dictionary; borrowed from Middle French *convoquer,* learned borrowing from Latin *convocāre* call together (*con-* together + *vocāre* to call, related to *vōx,* genitive *vōcis* VOICE). **—convocation** *n.* Before 1387, assembly of persons, in Trevisa's translation of Higden's *Polychronicon;* borrowed from Old French *convocation* and from Latin *convocātiōnem* (nominative *convocātiō*), from *convocāre* call together; for suffix see -TION.

convolute *v.* to coil, twist. 1698, probably a back formation from English *convolution,* and possibly also formed in English as if borrowed from Latin *convolūtus,* past participle of *convolvere* roll together (*con-* together + *volvere* to roll; see VOLUME). **—adj.** 1794, possibly from the verb, especially in botany; otherwise, more likely formed in English as if from Latin *convolūtus,* past participle of *convolvere.* **—convolution** *n.* 1545, a fold, twist, coiled form, formed in English, as if from Latin *convolūt-,* past participle stem of *convolvere* to roll up, roll together + *-ion.*

convoy *v.* 1375 *convoyen* accompany, escort, in John Barbour's *The Bruce;* borrowed from Old French *convoier,* from Vulgar Latin **conviāre,* literally, go together on the road; see the doublet CONVEY. **—n.** 1500-20, conduct, in an edition of William Dunbar's *Poems;* borrowed from Middle French *convoi,* from *convoier* to convoy, from Old French.

convulse *v.* shake violently. 1643, borrowed, perhaps by influence of Middle French *convulsé,* past participle of *convulser* (not recorded before 1829), from Latin *convulsus,* past participle of *convellere* tear violently (*con-* intensive + *vellere* tear away, pull, pluck; see VULTURE). Alternatively *convulse* may also have been a back formation in English from *convulsion.* **—convulsion** *n.* 1585, cramp; borrowed from Middle French *convulsion,* or directly from Latin *convulsiōnem* (nominative *convulsiō*), from *convuls-,* past participle stem of *convellere* tear violently; for suffix see -ION. The sense of a violent, involuntary contracting and relaxing of the muscles, is first recorded in English in 1650, but was known in Latin in Pliny's writings. **—convulsive** *adj.* 1615, formed from English *convulse* + *-ive,* modeled on New Latin **convulsivus,* from Latin *convulsus;* see CONVULSE.

cony or **coney** (kō′nē *or* kun′ē) *n.* rabbit, rabbit fur. Probably about 1175 *koning, cunig,* borrowed from Anglo-French *conyng,* Old French *conin,* variant of *conil,* from Latin *cunīculus* rabbit, possibly of Iberian origin (compare Basque *untxi* rabbit, Basque dialect *untxarta* ferret). The spelling *cony* is first recorded before 1338, in Mannyng's *Chronicle of England.*

coo *v.* to make the murmuring sound of doves and pigeons. 1670, in Dryden's *Conquest of Granada,* coined in imitation of the sound. The sense of to murmur softly, is first recorded in English in 1736. **—n.** 1729, from the verb.

cook *n.* Probably before 1200 *coke* man charged with the preparation of food, in Layamon's *Chronicle of Britain;* developed from Old English (about 700) *cōc,* borrowing from Latin *cocus* a cook. The Latin form *cocus* is a variant of *coquus,* related to *coquere* to cook, from pre-Latin **quequ-,* formed by assimilation producing an initial *qu-* from the original **pequ-.* Though Latin *cocus* shows the expected change of forms in *-quo-* to *-co-* and the declension should have stayed *cocus, coquī,* etc., the form *coquus* was restored by analogy to genitive *coquī* and the verb *coquere.*

For English, cognates exist in Old Saxon *kok* cook, Middle Dutch *coc* (plural *cōke*) and modern Dutch *kok,* Old High German *choh, koch* (modern German *Koch*), Swedish *kock.*

Cognates of Latin *coquere* (pre-Latin **quequ-, *pequ-*) are found in Greek *péttein* (Ionic *péssein*) to cook, Sanskrit *pácati* he cooks, Old Bulgarian *pekǫ* I cook, Albanian *pjek* I bake, Tocharian A and Tocharian B *päk-* to ripen, cook, and Welsh *pobi* to bake, from Indo-European **pekw-, pokwo-s* (Pok.798).

—v. Before 1387 *coken* act as a cook, in a version of *Piers Plowman,* from the noun. **—cookbook** *n.* 1809, probably American English, but earlier *cookery book* (1639). **—cooker** *n.* 1884, formed from English *cook,* v. + *-er*[1]. **—cookery** *n.* Before 1393, in Gower's *Confessio Amantis,* formed from English *cook,* v. *or* n. + *-ery.* **—cookhouse** *n.* 1296, in surname *Cokehuse,* Middle English *coken* + *huse.* **—cookout** *n.* 1947, American English, formed from *cook,* v. + *out,* developed from the sense of to cook outside.

cookie or **cooky** *n.* 1703, American English, probably borrowed from Dutch *koekje* little cake, diminutive of *koek* cake, from Middle Dutch *kōke;* see CAKE. In Scotland, where the word means "a bun" (1701), the history of the word is uncertain and the *Scottish National Dictionary* refers to a comparison with Dutch *koekje* but gives the source as probably English *cook* + *-ie.*

cool *adj.* About 1150 *cole,* developed from Old English *cōl* (about 725, in *Beowulf*); cognate with Middle Dutch *coel* (modern Dutch *koel*), from Proto-Germanic **kōluz,* related to Old High German *kuoli* cool (modern German *kühl*), and Old Icelandic *kala* be cold. The Old English *calan* be cold, and *cald, ceald* are related to Old Icelandic *kalr* through *ceald,* an old past participial adjective of *kala,* cognate with Latin *gelū* cold, from Indo-European **gel-/gol-/gōl-* (Pok.365). **—v.** Probably about 1200 *colen,* developed from Old English *cōlian* become cool (about 750), from Old English adjective *cōl* cool, replacing earlier *kele* to make cool. **—n.** Probably before 1400, from the adjective. **—coolant** *n.* 1930, formed from English *cool,* v. + *-ant,* after such formation as *lubricant.* **—cooler** *n.* 1575, formed from English *cool,* v. + *-er*[1]. **—coolheaded** *adj.* 1575, a parasynthetic derivative formed by adding *-ed* to earlier *coolhead,* developed from *coolhede* coolness (before 1400).

coolie *n.* laborer in India or China. 1598, borrowed from *qūlī* a day laborer, probably from Dravidian (compare Tamil *kūli* daily hire, payment for menial labor). The Middle French *culi* is recorded as early as 1575, suggesting by its form influenced by the Portuguese contact with Western India and the Gujarat peoples (known as *Kuli, Kolis, Kolas*), who served as laborers. The OED says that "these (Gujarati) carried the name both to Southern India and to China . . . It is probable that the similarity between *Kuli* (of Gujarat) and the Tamil word *kūli* 'hire' may have led to the use of *coolie* in Southern India."

coon *n.* 1742, American English, shortened form of RACCOON.

coop *n.* 1342 *cowpe* coop for chickens; earlier, *cupe* a wicker basket (about 1250); developed apparently through Old English **cūpe,* a dialectal variant of Old English *cȳpe, cȳpa* basket, cask, probably ultimately a borrowing (like Middle Low German *kupe* large pot, Middle Dutch *cupe* cask, and Norwegian *kupe,* Swedish *kupa,* Icelandic *kúpa* bowl, hive, vessel) from Latin *cūpa* tub, cask; see CUP. **—v.** 1563-87, in an edition of John Foxe's *Book of Martyrs,* from the noun.

cooper *n.* maker of barrels, casks, etc. 1176 *Cupere,* as surname; later *coupere* (before 1376, in a version of *Piers Plowman*), and *cooper* (1589); an early borrowing (like Middle Dutch *cuper* and Middle Low German *kuper*) from Latin *cūpārius,* from *cūpa* cask; see CUP.

cooperate *v.* 1604, possibly implied in earlier *cooperante,* present participle (apparently before 1425, in a translation of Higden's *Polychronicon*), borrowed from Latin *cooperantem,* present participle of *cooperārī;* but probably borrowed through influence of French *coopérer* from Late Latin *cooperātus,* past participle of *cooperārī* to work together (Latin *co-* together, variant of *com-* + *operārī* to work, OPERATE); for suffix see -ATE[1]. Alternatively *cooperate* may be a back formation in English from earlier *cooperation.* **—cooperation** *n.* 1495, in a version of Trevisa's translation of Bartholomew's *De Proprietatibus Rerum;* borrowed possibly through Middle French *coopération,* or directly from Late Latin *cooperātiōnem* (nominative *cooperātiō*) a working together (Latin *co-* together, variant of *com-* + *operātiōnem* OPERATION); for suffix see -TION. **—cooperative** *adj.* 1603, in Holland's translation of Plutarch's *Moralia;* borrowed possibly through French *coopératif* (feminine *coopérative*), or directly from Late Latin *cooperātīvus* collaborating, from *cooperātus,* past participle of *cooperārī* cooperate; for suffix see -IVE. **—n.** 1829, member of a cooperative society, in Southey's letters; from the adjective. **—co-op** *n.* 1872, clipped form of *cooperative (store);* earlier, a clipped form of *cooperator* (1861).

co-opt *v.* elect into a body as a member. 1651, borrowed as a shortened form of Latin *cooptāre* (*co-* together + *optāre* choose; see OPTION). The usually expected English form borrowed from a Latin verb ending in *-āre* would be *cooptate,* but this form that appeared in English in 1623 is archaic or obsolete today.

The extended sense of take over, adopt, commandeer, is first recorded about 1953.

coordinate (kōôr′dənit) *adj.* equal in importance, 1641, formed from English *co-* together, equal + *-ordinate,* as a parallel to *subordinate,* adj. **—n.** 1823, from the adjective. —v. (kōôr′dənāt) 1665, either from the adjective, or formed from English *co-* together, equal + *-ordinate,* as a parallel to *subordinate,* v. It is also possible that *coordinate* is a back formation in English from earlier *coordination.* **—coordination** *n.* 1605, orderly combination, in Francis Bacon's *Of the Advancement of Learning;* borrowed probably through French *coordination,* and directly from Late Latin *coōrdinātiōnem* (nominative *coōrdinātiō*), from Latin *co-* together +

ōrdinātiōnem (nominative *ōrdinātiō*) arrangement, ORDINATION; for suffix see -ATION. The sense of act of coordinating is first recorded in English about 1643. **—coordinator** *n.* 1864, formed from English *coordinate,* v. + *-or*².

coot *n.* wading and swimming bird. About 1300 *cote,* corresponding to Dutch *koet,* also earlier Dutch *meercoet* lake coot; of unknown origin.

cop *v. Slang.* capture, catch, nab, steal. 1704, perhaps a variant of obsolete *cap* to arrest (1589); borrowed from Middle French *caper* seize, perhaps from Sicilian *capere,* from Latin *capere;* see CAPTIVE. The informal phrase *cop out* to escape, withdraw, drop out, appeared in American English (about 1967), probably from the earlier slang meaning of plead guilty, especially to a lesser charge in order to avoid a trial, chiefly in the phrase *cop a plea* (about 1925). The compound noun *cop-out* has been recorded since 1942. **—n.** *Informal.* policeman. 1859, probably a shortening of earlier *copper* policeman (1846), from *cop,* v. to capture + *-er*¹.

copacetic (kō'pəset'ik) *adj. Slang.* very good, all right. 1919 *copasetic,* in I.A. Bacheller's *A Man for the Ages,* American English, said to have originated among southern blacks in the 1800's, of uncertain origin.

The suggestion that *copacetic* came from a Hebrew phrase such as *(hā)kōl b'sēder* all in order, or (unrecorded) *kōl b'ṣedek* all with justice, is not accepted among scholars in American English, such as Frederic G. Cassidy.

cope¹ *v.* contend or deal with, face. Before 1400 (earlier as a verbal noun *coupyng,* before 1375), *coupen* come to blows, strike; borrowed from Old French *couper, coper* (earlier *colper*) to strike, cut, from *coup, colp* a blow; see COUP. The modern figurative sense of contend or deal with successfully, is first recorded in 1641, in Milton's *Church Discipline,* an essay on church government. In Shakespeare's *Merchant of Venice, Venus and Adonis,* etc., the word is used in the now obsolete sense of come into contact, meet, match.

cope² *n.* long cape worn by priests. Probably before 1200 *cope,* in *Ancrene Riwle,* developed from earlier *cāpe* as in compound *cantelcāpe* (before 1121); borrowed from Medieval Latin *capa* cloak, from Late Latin *cappa* hood, mantle; see CAP. —**v.** cover with or as with a cape. Before 1376, in a version of *Piers Plowman,* from the noun.

copilot *n.* 1927, formed from *co-* + *pilot.*

coping *n.* top arching or sloping layer of a masonry wall. 1601, formed from *cope,* v. to provide with a cope + *-ing.* **—coping saw** 1931, from *coping* arching, of an arched or vaulted form.

copious *adj.* plentiful. Probably about 1350, in the Wycliffe Bible, borrowed from Latin *cōpiōsus* plentiful, from *cōpia* plenty, from *cōpis* well supplied (*co-* with + *ops,* genitive *opis* power, wealth, resources; see OPULENT); for suffix see -OUS. It is possible that *copious* was reinforced in English by Old French *copieux* or that it was borrowed into English through Old French.

copper¹ *n.* reddish-brown metallic element. Probably about 1225, developed from Old English (about 1000) *coper,* an early borrowing (like Middle Dutch *koper* copper, Old Icelandic *koparr,* and Old High German *kupfar,* modern German *Kupfer*) from Late Latin *cuprum* copper, for Latin *cyprum* from *aes Cyprium* metal of Cyprus, from *Cyprium,* neuter of *Cyprius* of Cyprus, from Greek *Kýprios,* from *Kýpros* Cyprus, island in the eastern Mediterranean where copper was found in ancient times. **—copperhead** *n.* (1775, American English) **—copperplate** *n.* (1663) **—coppery** *adj.* 1791, formed from English *copper*¹ + *-y*¹.

copper² *n. Slang.* policeman. 1846, formed from English *cop,* v., to capture, nab + *-er*¹.

copra (kop'rə) *n.* dried meat of coconuts. 1584, borrowed from Portuguese *copra,* from Malayalam *koppara,* probably from Hindi *khoprā* coconut.

copse *n.* 1578, contraction of earlier *koppis* (before 1398), borrowed from Old French *coupeïz, copeïz* a cut-over forest, from Gallo-Romance **colpāticium,* from Vulgar Latin **colpāre* to cut, strike, from Late Latin *colpus* a blow; see COUP. The original forms *koppis, copies,* etc., developed into modern *coppice,* which is the variant form used especially in British English.

copula (kop'yələ) *n. Grammar.* linking verb, such as *is.* 1619, borrowed from Latin *cōpula* bond; see the doublet COUPLE.

copulate *v.* 1425, to join; later, join sexually (1632); borrowed, possibly by influence of Middle French *copuler,* from Latin *cōpulātus,* past participle of *cōpulāre* join together, link, couple, from *cōpula* bond; for suffix see -ATE¹. **—copulation** *n.* About 1385, act of coupling; later, coupling sexually (1483); borrowed from Old French *copulation,* and directly as a learned borrowing from Latin *cōpulātiōnem* (nominative *cōpulātiō*), from *cōpulāre* join together; for suffix see -TION. **—copulative** *adj.* 1397, in the Wycliffe Bible, *copulatif;* borrowed from Old French *copulatif* (feminine *copulative*), and directly from Late Latin *cōpulātīvus,* from Latin *cōpulātus,* past participle of *cōpulāre* join together; for suffix see -IVE. Latin *cōpulātīvus* as a grammatical term is evidently a translation of Greek *symplektikós,* literally, twined together.

English use of Latin *cōpula* a band, bond, link, as a grammatical term for "linking verb" is first recorded in 1619; see the doublet COUPLE.

copy *n.* Before 1338 *copie* a written account or record, in Mannyng's *Chronicle of England;* later *kopy* a transcript, about 1385 in Chaucer's *Troilus and Criseyde;* borrowed from Old French *copie,* from Medieval Latin *copia* reproduction, transcript, from Latin *cōpia* plenty, abundance, opportunity, means; see COPIOUS. According to the OED, origins of the sense of transcript, copy, are found in such Medieval Latin phrases as *dare vel habere copium legendi* to give or have the power of reading, and *facere copiam description* to allow a transcription to be made.

In English, the sense of a written transcript was extended by the 1500's to any written or printed specimen of writing ("clean copy") and, figuratively, to any reproduction, imitation, or duplicate.

—**v.** Before 1376 *copien* make a copy of, transcribe, in a version of *Piers Plowman;* borrowed from Old French *copier,* from Medieval Latin *copiare* transcribe, from *copia* transcript.

—copier *n.* (1597) **—copybook** *n.* (1557) **—copyright** *n.* (1735); *v.* (1806, implied in *copyrighted*)

coquette *n.* woman who flirts. 1669, as a French term used in Dryden's *An Evening's Love,* from feminine of French *coquet* male flirt, from Old French *coq* COCK¹ + *-et* -et; so called from the male flirt's supposed similarity to the cock's strutting gait and interest in the opposite sex. **—coquetry** *n.* 1656 *coquetterie* pertness;

coqueterie, later, behavior intended to attract a man's attentions (1673); borrowed from French *coquetterie,* from *coquette;* for suffix see -ERY. —**coquettish** *adj.* 1702, formed from English *coquette* + *-ish.*

cor- a prefix, meaning with, together, altogether. It is the form of *com-* before *r,* as in *correlation.* In words from Latin the form *cor-* resulted from assimilation of *com-, con-* to the following consonant (*r*).

coracle (kôr′əkəl) *n.* small boat made of wicker and leather. 1547, borrowed from Welsh *corwgl, cwrwgl,* alteration of *corwg, cwrwg* coracle, skiff, cognate with Middle Irish *curach* coracle, which was the source of earlier Middle English *currok* coracle (probably about 1450), possibly cognate with Greek *kṓrykos* leather bag, and Latin *corium* leather, from Indo-European **ker-/kor-/kōr-* cut (Pok.939).

coral (kôr′əl) *n.* Before 1300, borrowed from Old French *coral,* from Latin *corallium,* from Greek *korállion;* of uncertain origin, perhaps Semitic (compare Hebrew *gōrāl* lot, originally, pebble or small stone used for casting lots, Arabic *jaral* pebble).

corbel (kôr′bəl) *n.* bracket on a wall to support a beam, ledge, etc. 1428; earlier, in the compound *corbeiltable* stone used as a corbel (1360); borrowed from Old French *corbel,* diminutive of *corp* raven, from Latin *corvus* RAVEN; probably so called because originally the corbel was cut at a slant, so that its profile resembled a raven's beak. Compare CORNICE.

cord *n.* Probably before 1300, in *Arthour and Merlin;* earlier, in the compound surname *Cordemaker* (1199); borrowed from Old French *corde,* from Latin *chorda* string, gut, from Greek *chordḗ,* altered (perhaps by influence of *kardíā* heart) from **chornḗ*; cognate with Sanskrit *hira-s* band, Old Icelandic *gǫrn* gut, Latin *haru-spex* one who divines from inspection of entrails, Lithuanian *žarnà,* from Indo-European **ĝhor-/ĝher-* (Pok.443). Doublet of CHORD[2] straight line. —**v.** tie with a cord. 1610; earlier, to string, as a bow (about 1450); from the noun. —**cordage** *n.* 1490, borrowed from Middle French *cordage,* from *corde* cord; for suffix see -AGE.

cordate *adj.* heart-shaped. 1769, borrowed from New Latin *cordātus,* from Latin *cor* (genitive *cordis*) HEART; for suffix see -ATE[1]. Earlier use of *cordate* with the meaning of wise, prudent, is first recorded in English in 1651 as a borrowing of Latin *cordātus* wise, prudent, from *cor, cord-* judgment.

cordial *adj.* Before 1400, of the heart; later, hearty (1458); borrowed from Middle French *cordial,* learned borrowing from Medieval Latin *cordialis* of or for the heart, from Latin *cor* (genitive *cordis*) HEART; for suffix see -AL[1]. —**n.** liqueur. About 1386, medicine, food, or drink that stimulates the heart, in Chaucer's *Prologue* to *The Canterbury Tales;* borrowed from Medieval Latin *cordialis* of or for the heart. —**cordiality** *n.* 1611, borrowed from French *cordialité,* from *cordial* hearty; for suffix see -ITY.

cordillera (kôrdil′ərə) *n.* 1704, American English, borrowed from Spanish *cordillera,* from *cordilla,* diminutive of *cuerda* string, rope, from Latin *chorda* string, CORD. The plural, *cordilleras,* was applied originally by the Spaniards to the parallel chains of the Andes in South America (*Cordilleras de los Andes*), later extended to the continuation of the same system through Central America and Mexico.

cordon (kôr′dən) *n.* 1440, in *Promptorium Parvulorum,* cord or ribbon worn as an ornament or badge, borrowed from Middle French *cordon* ribbon, diminutive of Old French *corde* CORD. The sense of a line or circle of people or things enclosing or guarding a place, appeared in 1758 in military usage. —**v.** 1561, to ornament with a cord or ribbon, borrowed from French *cordonner* decorate with a cord or ribbon, from French *cordon,* n. The later sense of to enclose or guard with a cordon, is first recorded in 1891 and is from English *cordon,* n.

cordovan *adj.* 1591, of or having to do with Cordova, Spain, or a kind of leather originally manufactured there; borrowed from Spanish *cordován, cordobán,* from *Córdoba,* Spain, from Latin *Corduba.*

The earlier form *cordewan* is recorded as early as 1303, from Old French *cordewan, cordöan,* but the spelling developed into English *cordwain* in the 1400's. —**n.** 1599, from the adjective.

corduroy *n.* 1780, American English, in compound *corduroy road;* later, *corduroys* corduroy trousers (1787-91); perhaps formed from English CORD (mentioned in an English patent, 1776) + *duroy* obsolete name for a kind of coarse woolen cloth, of uncertain origin. The word *corduroy* and the supposed connection with **corde du roi* do not appear in French, early reference being confined to *kings-cordes* (1807), probably from English. —**adj.** 1789, from the noun.

core (kôr) *n.* the central part. Probably before 1400; earlier *kore* central part of an apple, pear, etc. (probably before 1325); borrowed probably from Old French *cuer, coeur* core of fruit, heart of lettuce or other vegetable, but literally, heart, from Latin *cor* HEART. The form *core* is traditionally thought to have replaced *colk* heart of an apple, onion, etc., but *colk* is not recorded in Middle English until about 1400. The form *cork* also meaning core of an apple is recorded in Middle English probably about 1300.

The sense "the part of a nuclear reactor containing fissionable material" is first recorded in 1949.
—**v.** Before 1450, take out the core of fruit; from the noun.

corgi (kôr′gē) *n.* short-legged dog of Welsh origin. 1926, borrowed from Welsh *corgi,* a compound of *cor* dwarf + *ci* dog; see HOUND. Welsh *cor* is from Indo-European **kor-so-s* shrunken, root **ker-* cut (Pok.945).

coriander (kôr′ēan′dər), *n.* plant with aromatic seedlike fruits used as a spice. 1373, borrowed from Old French *coriandre,* learned borrowing from Latin *coriandrum,* from Greek *koríandron,* variant of *koríannon,* of unknown (perhaps Mediterranean) origin.

cork *n.* outer bark of a kind of oak tree. 1303, borrowed probably in North Africa and Spain from Arabic *qurq,* from Latin *cortex* (genitive *corticis*) bark, CORTEX. The early sense of cork sandal or slipper (1391) may have been influenced by Spanish *alcorque,* of the same meaning, which derived from Arabic *qurq.* —**v.** 1580, furnish (a shoe) with a cork sole or heel; from the noun. —**corkscrew** *n.* (1720)

corm *n.* bulblike underground stem. 1838, borrowed from New Latin *cormus* (about 1800), from Greek *kormós* stripped tree trunk, from *keírein* to cut; see SHEAR.

cormorant *n.* large, voracious sea bird. About 1330 *cormeraunt,* borrowed as an alteration of Old French *cor-*

maran, cormoran, (earlier) *cormareng,* literally, raven of the sea, from *corb, corp* raven (see CORBEL) + **ma-renc* of the sea (attested in dialectal French *pie marenge* sea magpie), from Latin *mare* sea + a suffix *-enc, -enge* from Germanic *-ing;* compare Late Latin *corvus marīnus* sea raven.

corn[1] *n.* Old English (probably about 750) *corn* seed, grain; earlier in compound *berecorn* barleycorn, grain of barley (about 700); cognate with Old Frisian and Old Saxon *korn* grain, Middle Dutch *coren* (modern Dutch *koren* corn, grain), Middle High German *korn* (modern German *Korn*), Old Icelandic, Swedish, Norwegian, and Danish *korn,* Gothic *kaúrn,* Crimean Gothic *korn.* Cognates of this word outside Germanic include Latin *grānum* grain, Old Irish *grān,* Welsh *grawn,* Old Slavic *zrŭno,* Serbian *zŕno* grain, seed, and with restricted meaning Lithuanian *žìrnis* and Latvian *zir̃nis* pea, from Indo-European **ĝr̥̄-nó-m,* root **ĝerə-* (Pok.390). It is noteworthy that this word for "grain" is lacking in the eastern Indo-European languages, including Indic, Iranian, Armenian, and Greek.

In the United States the word became restricted to Indian corn or maize (corn growing in large ears), a sense first attested in 1608. The restriction to a single type of grain also occurs in other countries: *corn* usually means wheat in England and oats in Scotland and Ireland, and in parts of Germany *Korn* refers to rye.

—v. 1456, to provision with corn; later, to granulate (1560) and to salt (1565-73); from the noun.

—corned *adj.* (1577) **—corn bread** (1750) **—corncob** *n.* (1787) **—cornfield** *n.* (1297, as a surname) **—cornflower** *n.* (1578) **—cornhusk** *n.* (1712) **—corn meal** (1749) **—corn popper** (1874) **—cornstalk** *n.* (1645) **—corn syrup** (1903) **—corny** *adj.* About 1390, tasting strongly of malt, in Chaucer's *Canterbury Tales;* later, of or producing corn (1580); formed from English *corn*[1] + *-y*[1]. The informal sense "old-fashioned, trite, or sentimental" appeared in the 1930's in American English, originally (about 1932) with the meaning "of a kind that appeals to country people; provincial, rustic, unsophisticated," perhaps with allusion to earlier *corn-fed,* of the same meaning (1929).

corn[2] *n.* horny hardening of the skin, usually on a toe. Probably before 1425 *corne,* in a translation of Chauliac's *Grande Chirurgie;* borrowed from Old French *corn* horn, (later) corn on the foot, from Latin *cornū* (genitive *cornūs*) HORN.

cornea *n.* transparent part of the coat of the eyeball. Before 1398, in Trevisa's translation of Bartholomew's *De Proprietatibus Rerum;* borrowed as a shortening of Medieval Latin *cornea tela* or *tunica* horny web or sheath, from Latin *cornū* (genitive *cornūs*) HORN. The shortening of the Medieval Latin form was probably influenced by the earlier Old French *cornee* (1314). **—corneal** *adj.* 1808, formed from English *cornea* + *-al*[1].

corner *n.* About 1280, borrowed through Anglo-French *corner,* variant of Old French *cornere, corniere,* from *corne* horn, corner, from Vulgar Latin **corna,* from Latin *cornua,* plural of *cornū* (genitive *cornūs*) point, end, HORN. The sense of a difficult position is first recorded in 1548. **—adj.** 1535, from the noun. **—v.** Before 1387, furnish with corners, in Trevisa's translation of Higden's *Polychronicon;* from the noun. The sense of going around a corner, as in a race, is first recorded in 1864. The figurative sense of force into a difficult position, is first recorded in 1824 in American English. **—cornerstone** *n.* About 1280; the figurative sense of a foundation or basis, is first recorded before 1325, in *Cursor Mundi.*

cornet *n.* wind instrument. Probably before 1400 *cornette,* in *Morte Arthur;* borrowed from Middle French *cornet,* diminutive of *corn* horn, from Latin *cornū* HORN. In ancient times the cornet was either made of, or similar to, the horn of an animal.

cornice *n.* 1563 *cornishe,* borrowed from Middle French *corniche* ornamental molding along a wall, etc., from Italian *cornice,* originally a crow, then (from the bird's curved beak or feet) an ornamental molding, cornice, from Latin *cornīcem,* accusative of *cornīx* crow; see RAVEN. For the sense development, compare CORBEL.

cornucopia (kôr′nəkō′pēə) *n.* horn-shaped container. 1508, borrowed from Late Latin *cornūcōpia,* from Latin *cornū cōpiae* horn of plenty (*cornū* HORN + *cōpiae,* genitive of *cōpia* plenty; see COPIOUS). The original cornucopia was fabled to be the horn of the goat Amalthea, who suckled the infant Zeus; it became later a symbol of fruitfulness and plenty.

corolla (kərol′ə) *n.* the petals of a flower. 1671, crown, cornet, borrowed from Latin *corōlla* small garland, diminutive of *corōna* garland, wreath, CROWN. The botanical sense appeared in 1753.

corollary (kôr′əler′ē) *n.* About 1380, in Chaucer's translation of Boethius' *De Consolatione Philosophiae;* borrowed through Old French *corollaire,* and directly from Late Latin *corōllārium* corollary, consequence, in Latin *corōllārium* money paid for a *corōlla* or small garland, gratuity, gift, from *corōlla* small garland, see COROLLA; for suffix see -ARY.

corona (kərō′nə) *n.* ring of light or halo. 1658, borrowed from Latin *corōna* garland, wreath, CROWN. The form and the meaning in Latin also developed into Middle English *coroune* (1340) with the meaning "halo," but this word became *crown* in modern English.

coronary *adj.* 1610, of or suitable for garlands, borrowed possibly from Middle French *coronaire,* and directly from Latin *corōnārius* of a crown, from *corōna* garland, wreath, CROWN; for suffix see -ARY. By 1679 the word was applied to blood vessels which encircle a part of the body, such as the heart, like a crown (*e.g.* the *coronary arteries*). The noun *coronary* was originally a shortening of *coronary artery* (1893), and *coronary thrombosis* (1955).

coronation *n.* About 1400 *coronacioun,* borrowed from Late Latin *corōnātiōnem* (nominative *corōnātiō*) a wreathing, from Latin *corōnāre* to wreathe, crown, from *corōna* CROWN; for suffix see -TION.

coroner *n.* Probably about 1350 *corowner* officer of the crown (originally charged with protecting property of the royal family); borrowed from Anglo-French *curuner,* from *coroune* CROWN + *-er*[1] (corresponding to Old French *-ier,* from Latin *-ārius* -ary). Gradually the coroner's original duties were narrowed, until by the 1600's his chief function was to hold inquests as to the cause of death.

coronet *n.* small crown. Probably before 1400 *crownet,* in Chaucer's translation of *Roman de la Rose,* later, *coronette;* borrowed from Old French *coronete, couronnette,* diminutive of *corone, couronne* crown, from Latin *corōna* CROWN; for suffix see -ET.

corporal[1] *adj.* of the body, bodily. About 1390 *corporel* secular, temporal, in Chaucer's *Canterbury Tales;* perhaps later, of the body, physical, in Chaucer's translation of *Roman de la Rose* (probably before 1400); borrowed from Old French *corporal,* learned borrowing from Latin *corporālis* of the body, corporeal, from *corpus* (genitive *corporis*) body, see CORPSE; for suffix see -AL[1].

corporal[2] *n.* lowest ranking noncommissioned army officer, usually in charge of a squad. 1579, borrowed from Middle French *corporal,* variant (perhaps influenced by *corps* body) of *caporal* a corporal, from Italian *caporale* a corporal, from *capo* head, from Latin *caput* HEAD; for suffix see -AL[1].

corporate *adj.* forming a corporation. 1425 *corporat,* in *Rolls of Parliament;* borrowed from Latin *corporātus,* past participle of *corporāre* form into a body, from *corpus* (genitive *corporis*) body, see CORPSE; for suffix see -ATE[1]. **—corporation** *n.* 1439, a legal corporate body, the governing body of an incorporated town, in *Rolls of Parliament;* borrowed from Late Latin *corporātiōnem* (nominative *corporātiō*), in Classical Latin, an embodying, physical makeup, from *corporāre* form into a body; for suffix see -TION. The sense, act of incorporating, is first recorded in 1447-48.

corporeal (kôrpôr′ēəl) *adj.* of the body, physical, material. Probably before 1425, in a translation of Higden's *Polychronicon;* formed in English from Latin *corporeus* belonging to the body (from *corpus,* genitive *corporis* body) + English *-al*[1]; see CORPSE.

corps *n.* 1a) About 1275 *cors* dead body; later, *corps* (before 1333); and b) probably before 1300 *cors* a live body; later, *corps* (about 1378). 2) 1429 *corps* a body of citizens; later, a band of knights (1464). Borrowed from Old French *corps, cors* body, and directly from Latin *corpus;* doublet of CORPSE.

The meaning "a military unit" is first recorded in the writings of Addison in *The Spectator,* in 1711. The phrase *diplomatic corps* is a translation of French *corps diplomatique.* A number of French phrases formed on *corps* came into English in the 1700's and early 1800's: *corps de ballet* (1829), *corps diplomatique* (1764), *esprit de corps* (1780), etc.

corpse *n.* 1542, variant spelling of earlier Middle English *corps* (before 1333); borrowed from Old French *corps, cors,* from Latin *corpus* body, cognate with Sanskrit *kr̥pā́* (instrumental case) form, beauty, from Indo-European *kr̥p-* (Pok.620); doublet of CORPS and CORPUS.

The *p* was not pronounced in Middle English *corps* until the late 1400's.

corpulent *adj.* Before 1398, in Trevisa's translation of Bartholomew's *De Proprietatibus Rerum;* borrowed from Old French *corpulent* stout, fat, from Latin *corpulentus* fleshy, fat, large, from *corpus* body + *-ulentus,* suffix meaning abounding in, full of. **—corpulence** *n.* Before 1500 *corpolence* carnal nature; later *corpulence* stoutness; obesity (1581); borrowed from Middle French *corpulence,* from Latin *corpulentia,* from *corpulentus* stout, fat; for suffix see -ENCE. It is possible *corpolentes* (1398) is the earliest recorded use, but the spelling is suspicious.

corpus *n.* About 1390, in oaths such as *goddes corpus* and *by corpus bones* with reference to the body of Christ, in Chaucer's *Canterbury Tales;* later, body of a person or animal (about 1450); borrowed from Latin *corpus* body; see the doublet CORPSE. The sense of a body of writings and literature appeared in *Chambers Cyclopaedia,* in 1727. **—Corpus Christi** About 1378, in a version of *Piers Plowman,* Latin phrase for Christ's Body. **—corpus delicti** evidence of a crime, especially the body of a person. 1832, New Latin *corpus delicti,* literally, body of the crime, from Latin *corpus* body (see CORPSE) + *dēlictī,* genitive of *dēlictum* offense, fault, crime, from past participle of *dēlinquere* fail, commit a fault; see DELINQUENT.

corpuscle *n.* 1660, small particle or body of matter, in writings of Boyle; borrowed from French *corpuscle,* and from Latin *corpusculum,* diminutive of *corpus* body; see CORPSE. The word was not recorded in English with reference to blood cells until 1845-46. **—corpuscular** *adj.* 1667, formed in English, as if from Latin **corpuscularis,* from *corpusculum* + English *-ar.*

corral *n.* 1582, as a Spanish term for an enclosed yard or pen, used in an English translation, perhaps from Vulgar Latin **currāle,* from Latin *currus* (genitive *currūs*) chariot, cart, from *currere* to run; see CURRENT. —**v.** 1847, from the noun. The meaning "capture, secure" appeared in 1860 in American English.

correct *v.* 1345-46, borrowed from Latin *corrēctus,* past participle of *corrigere* make straight (*cor-* intensive, variant of *com-* before *r* + *-rigere* combining form of *regere* to direct, lead straight; see RIGHT). **—adj.** 1676, in writings of Dryden, borrowed from French *correct* right, proper, from Latin *corrēctus,* past participle of *corrigere.* **—correctable** *adj.* 1450, formed from English *correct,* v. + *-able.* **—correction** *n.* 1340, borrowed through Anglo-French *correccioun,* Old French *correction,* from Latin *corrēctiōnem,* from *corrigere* make straight; for suffix see -TION. **—corrective** *adj.* 1531, borrowed from French *correctif* (feminine *corrective*), from Latin *corrēct-,* stem of past participle of *corrigere;* for suffix see -IVE.

correlate *v.* put in relation, show the relation between. Before 1742, back formation from *correlation,* or verb use of the earlier noun. **—n.** either of two related things. 1643, back formation from *correlation,* or possibly borrowed from or suggested by New Latin **correlatum,* according to OED. **—correlation** *n.* mutual relation of two or more things. 1561, borrowed from Middle French *corrélation,* formed from *cor-* together, variant of *com-* before *r* + *relation* relation. **—correlative** *adj.* having a mutual relation. 1530, borrowed from Middle French *correlatif* (feminine *correlative*), formed from *cor-,* variant of *com-* before *r* + *relatif* relative; perhaps suggested by New Latin **correlativus* according to OED. *—n.* either of two things having a mutual relation. 1545, from the adjective.

correspond *v.* 1529, borrowed through Middle French *correspondre* be in harmony, agree, or directly from Medieval Latin *correspondere* (Latin *cor-* together, with + *respondēre* RESPOND). The sense "communicate by exchanging letters" is first recorded in 1645. **—correspondence** *n.* 1413, harmony, agreement; borrowed through Middle French *correspondance,* or directly from Medieval Latin *correspondentia,* from *correspondentem* (nominative *correspondens*), present participle of *correspondere* correspond; for suffix see -ENCE. The sense of communication by letters is first recorded in 1644, in Milton's writings. **—correspondent** *adj.* Probably before 1425, analogous; borrowed from Medieval Latin *correspondentem,* present participle of *correspondere* correspond; for suffix see

-ENT. —*n.* 1630, one who communicates by letters; from the adjective, but probably influenced by French *correspondant,* of the same meaning. The extended sense of one who contributes news (originally through letters) and other material to a newspaper, is first recorded in 1711, in Steele's writings in *The Spectator.* —**corresponding** *adj.* (1579)

corridor *n.* 1591, a covered way of a fortification; later, passage (1620), and a long hallway (1814, in Byron's *The Corsair*); borrowed from French *corridor,* from Italian *corridore,* alteration (by influence of *corridore* runner) of *corridoio,* from Vulgar Latin **curritōrium* running place (Latin *currere* to run + *-tōrium* -ory; see CURRENT).

corrigible *adj.* that can be corrected. 1451, in *The Paston Letters;* borrowed from Middle French *corrigible* correctable, learned borrowing from Medieval Latin *corrigibilis,* from Latin *corrigere* make straight, CORRECT; for suffix see -IBLE.

corroboration *n.* 1459 *corroboracion* strengthening or support; borrowed through Middle French *corroboration* or directly from Late Latin *corrōborātiōnem* (nominative *corrōborātiō*), from Latin *corrōborāre* strengthen (*cor-* intensive, variant of *com-* before *r* + *rōborāre* make strong, from *rōbur,* genitive *rōboris* oak tree, strength; see ROBUST); for suffix see -TION. The sense "confirmation" is first recorded in 1768, in critical writings of Samuel Johnson. —**corroborate** *v.* 1530, probably back formation of English *corroboration,* possibly influenced by Middle French *corroborer* confirm, from Latin *corrōborātus,* past participle of *corrōborāre;* for suffix see -ATE[1]. —**corroborative** *adj.* 1583, probably borrowed from Middle French *corroboratif* (feminine *corroborative*), formed as if from Latin **corrōborātīvus,* from *corrōborāt-,* past participle stem of *corrōborāre;* for suffix see -IVE.

corrode *v.* Before 1400, borrowed through Old French *corroder,* or directly from Latin *corrōdere* gnaw away (*cor-* intensive, variant of *com-* before *r* + *rōdere* gnaw; see RODENT). —**corrosion** *n.* Before 1400, borrowed through Middle French *corrosion,* or directly from Late Latin *corrōsiōnem* (nominative *corrōsiō*), from the stem of Latin *corrōdere;* for suffix see -SION. —**corrosive** *adj.* About 1395, in Chaucer's *Canterbury Tales,* borrowed from Old French *corosif* (feminine *corosive*), or directly as if from Medieval Latin **corrosivus,* from Latin *corrōsus,* past participle of *corrōdere.*

corrugate *v.* 1620; earlier, *corrugate* as a past participle or adjective (probably about 1425); borrowed from Latin *corrūgātus,* past participle of *corrūgāre* (*cor-* intensive, variant of *com-* before *r* + *rūgāre* to wrinkle, from *rūga* wrinkle, of unknown origin); for suffix see -ATE[1]. —**corrugated** *adj.* 1623, from *corrugate,* v. —**corrugated paper** (1897) —**corrugation** *n.* 1528, formed from English *corrugate,* v. + *-ion.*

corrupt *adj.* 1340 *corupt,* in *Ayenbite of Inwyt;* borrowed from Old French *corrupt,* and directly from Latin *corruptus,* past participle of *corrumpere* break into pieces, destroy, spoil, falsify, corrupt (*cor-* intensive, variant of *com-* before *r* + *rumpere* break, RUPTURE). —v. About 1385, pervert, debase, in Chaucer's *Canterbury Tales;* possibly from English *corrupt,* adj. and later considered as a borrowing from Latin *corruptus,* past participle of *corrumpere.* —**corruption** *n.* Before 1340, destruction, decomposition, in *Ayenbite of Inwyt;* borrowed from Old French *corruption,* or directly from Latin *corruptiōnem* (nominative *corruptiō*), from *corrumpere* corrupt; for suffix see -TION. —**corruptible** *adj.* Before 1382, in the Wycliffe Bible; borrowed from Old French *corruptible,* and directly from Late Latin *corruptibilis* from Latin *corrupt-,* past participle stem of *corrumpere;* for suffix see -IBLE. —**corruptibility** *n.* Before 1475, borrowed from Middle French *corruptibilité,* from Late Latin *corruptibilitās,* from *corruptibilis;* for suffix see -ITY.

corsage *n.* 1843, body of a woman's dress, bodice; earlier, trunk of the body (1510-20), and size of the body (1481); borrowed from Old French *corsage* upper part of the body, bust (*cors* body + *-age* -age). The sense of a bouquet worn on the bodice appeared in 1911 in American English, apparently from the French phrase *bouquet de corsage* bouquet of the bodice or blouse.

corsair *n.* 1549, borrowed from Middle French *corsaire* pirate, from Italian *corsaro,* from Medieval Latin *cursarius* runner, from *cursus* hostile excursion, booty, from Latin *cursus* (genitive *cursūs*) a race, journey, from past participle of *currere* to run; see CURRENT. Doublet of HUSSAR.

corselet (kôrs′lit) *n.* About 1500, tight garment covering the trunk; borrowed from Middle French *corselet,* diminutive of Old French *corsel,* itself a diminutive of *cors* body, see CORPSE; for suffix see -ET. The sense of an armor for the body is first recorded in 1563, replacing earlier *corset* (1306-1489); the sense of a woman's foundation garment (originally spelled *corselette*) is first recorded in 1926.

corset (kôr′sit), *n.* woman's undergarment. 1299, tight body garment worn in the Middle Ages, a kind of laced bodice, borrowed from Old French *corset,* diminutive of *cors* body; see CORPSE. The ordinary sense of a stiff supporting undergarment is first recorded in 1795.

cortege or **cortège** (kôrtezh′) *n.* procession. 1648, in letters of John Evelyn; borrowed from French *cortège* retinue, procession, from Italian *corteggio* a train of followers, from *corteggiare* make up the court, from *corte* court, from Latin *cohortem* enclosure, crowd in an enclosure, retinue, accusative of *cohors* enclosure, COURT.

cortex *n.* bark, outer layer (of a plant, animal body, or organ). 1653, outer shell, husk; borrowed from Latin *cortex* (genitive *corticis*) bark, related to *corium* skin, hide, from Indo-European **ker-/kor-* (Pok.938). The form *cortex* replaced earlier *cortice,* n. first recorded probably before 1425 in a translation of Chauliac's *Grande Chirurgie.* —**cortical** *adj.* 1671, borrowed from Latin *corticālis* of the bark, skin, or hide, from *cortex;* for suffix see -AL[1].

cortisone (kôr′təzōn) *n.* hormone obtained from the cortex of the adrenal glands. 1949, coined as an abbreviation of its chemical name, *17-hydroxy-11 dehydro-cortico-sterone,* ultimately from Latin *corticis* (genitive of *cortex* CORTEX) + English *sterol* + *-one.* When it was discovered in 1936, it was named Compound E, but was renamed by its discoverer, the American biochemist Edward Calvin Kendall, 1886-1972.

corundum *n.* Before 1728, borrowed through Anglo-Indian, from Tamil *kurundam,* also found in Telugu *kuruvindam* and Hindi *kuruṇḍ* referring to various kinds of sapphire found in India and China; and earlier in Sanskrit *kuruvinda-s* ruby.

corvette or **corvet** *n.* small warship. 1636, borrowed from French *corvette* warship smaller than a frigate, from Middle French *corvette, corvot,* probably from Middle Dutch *corver* a fishing boat, also a privateer, of uncertain origin, though the form *corver* was known in Middle English by 1420. The form *corbe* was used in French in 1520 to designate Dutch and Flemish boats. The modern meaning of a light, fast warship of the destroyer class is first recorded in 1940.

cosine *n.* ratio in mathematics of sides of a right triangle. 1635, but coined in 1620 by the English mathematician Edmund Gunter, from *co-* + Medieval Latin *sinus* sine.

cosmetic *n.* 1605, art of beautifying, in Francis Bacon's *Of the Advancement of Learning;* borrowed from Greek *kosmētikē téchnē,* from feminine of *kosmētikós* skilled in ordering or adorning, from *kosmētós* well-ordered, from *kosmeîn* to order, arrange, adorn, from *kósmos* order, universe, cosmos; for suffix see -IC. The sense "preparation for beautifying" is first recorded in 1650, probably from the adjective. **—adj.** of or for beautifying. 1650, borrowed from French *cosmétique,* from Greek *kosmētikós* skilled in ordering or adorning.

cosmic *adj.* universal. 1649, borrowed from Greek *kosmikós* of the world or universe; later, as a parallel form of *cosmical* (1583). Modern use of *cosmic* is first recorded in 1846, in George Grote's *History of Greece,* borrowed from French *cosmique,* from Greek *kosmikós,* from *kósmos* cosmos; see COSMOS; for suffix see -IC. **—cosmic rays** (1925)

cosmo- a combining form meaning: **1** world, universe, as in *cosmology = science or study of the universe, cosmopolis = city of the world.* **2** cosmic rays, as in *cosmogenic = originating from cosmic rays.* **3** Since 1957 it has had the further meaning of outer space, especially the Russian activities in it, and is sometimes equivalent to English *astro-,* as in *cosmonaut,* an adaptation of Russian *kosmonavt* astronaut, and *cosmonautics,* Russian *kosmonavtika* astronautics. Borrowed from Greek *kosmo-,* combining form of *kósmos* world, universe.

cosmography *n.* description of the universe. About 1433 *cosmagraffie* (perhaps earlier, before 1387, in Trevisa's translation of Higden's *Polychronicon*); borrowed from Late Latin *cosmographia,* from Greek *kosmographíā* (title of a work by Democritus), from *kósmos* universe + *-graphíā* drawing, delineation, from *gráphein* write, mark; see CARVE.

cosmology *n.* science or theory of the universe. 1656, in Blount's *Glossographia,* borrowed from French *cosmologie,* from New Latin *cosmologia,* from Greek *kósmos* universe + *-logíā* treatment of, -logy.

cosmonaut *n.* astronaut, especially of the Soviet Union. 1959, borrowed from Russian *kosmonavt,* from *kosmos* universe, outer space (from Greek *kósmos* cosmos) + *-navt,* from Greek *naútēs* sailor; see NAUTICAL. The word appears once in French (1934), but is not recorded again before 1961.

cosmopolitan *adj.* 1844, in Emerson's *Essays,* formed from English *cosmopolite* + *-an,* on the pattern of *metropolitan.* **—n.** cosmopolitan person. 1868, from the adjective. (A single earlier use is recorded about 1645, apparently a variant of *cosmopolite.*) **—cosmopolite** *n.* About 1618, citizen of the world; earlier, a man of this world (1614); borrowed from Greek *kosmopolítēs* (*kósmos* world, COSMOS + *polítēs* citizen, from *pólis;* see POLICE). The word apparently dropped out of use in English during the 1700's (though in French it appears in Voltaire's letters, 1742) and was revived in English in the 1800's (1809, in Washington Irving's *Knickerbocker's History of New York*).

cosmos (koz′məs) *n.* universe. Probably about 1200, in *The Ormulum,* borrowed from Greek *kósmos* order, ornament; world, universe (so called by Pythagoras or his disciples, who regarded the physical world as a perfectly ordered and harmonious system), of uncertain origin. Except for the use in 1200, the word disappears from the record until 1848, in a translation of Humboldt's *Kosmos.*

Cossack (kos′ak) *n.* one of a former group of warlike frontiersmen of southwestern Russia, noted as horsemen. 1598 *Cassacke,* borrowed through Middle French *cosaque* or Italian *cosacco,* from Russian *kazák, kozák,* from Turkic *kazak* free man, free lance.

cosset (kos′it) *n.* pet lamb, pet. 1579 *Cosset* a pet lamb, in Spenser's *The Shepheardes Calender,* of uncertain origin, perhaps in Middle English *cotsete* dweller in a cottage (1125), used figuratively of a lamb (probably an orphan) kept in the cottage and brought up by the cotter's family, found in Old English *cot-sǣta.* See COT²; the element *-sǣta* is cognate with Latin *sēdāre* to quiet, from Indo-European **sed-/sēd-* sit (Pok.884).

cost *n.* Probably about 1200, borrowed from Old French *cost,* from *coster* to cost, from Latin *cōnstāre* stand together, stand firm, be settled or fixed, stand at a price, cost (*con-* together + *stāre* to STAND). **—v.** About 1378 *costen* to involve great expenditure, in a version of *Piers Plowman;* earlier, to buy, in *Cursor Mundi;* borrowed from Old French *coster* to cost. The verb is widely represented in the Romance languages: Provençal and Spanish *costar,* Portuguese *custar,* Italian *costare,* etc. Both the verb and noun (Spanish *costo, coste,* Italian *costo,* Portuguese *custa,* etc.) were widely adopted in Germanic, Slavic, and Celtic: German *kosten,* v., *Kosten,* n.pl., Polish *koszt,* Irish *cost,* etc. **—costly** *adj.* Probably about 1384, in writings of Wycliffe, formed from *cost,* n. + *-ly*¹.

costive *adj.* constipated. Before 1400 *costif,* probably borrowed through Anglo-French **costif* (with loss of final *-é*), from Old French *costivé* (past participle of *costiver* to constipate, from Latin *cōnstīpāre*), from Latin *cōnstīpātus,* past participle of *cōnstīpāre;* see the doublet CONSTIPATE.

costume *n.* style of dress, etc. 1715, borrowed from French *costume,* from Italian *costume* fashion, habit, custom, from Vulgar Latin **cōnsuētūmen,* corresponding to Latin *cōnsuētūdinem,* accusative of *cōnsuētūdō* habit, custom, usage; see the doublet CUSTOM. **—v.** 1823, from the noun. **—costume jewelry** (American English, 1933)

cot¹ *n.* portable bed. 1634, borrowed through Anglo-Indian *cot* light bedstead, from Hindi *khaṭ* bedstead, couch, hammock, bier, from Sanskrit or Prakrit *kháṭvā,* probably from Dravidian (compare Tamil *kaṭṭil* bedstead).

cot² *n.* cottage. Old English (about 893) *cot* small house, cottage, lair of wild animal; cognate with Old Icelandic *kot* hut, Middle Dutch *cot* cottage, and Middle Low German *kot* cottage, all evidently from a word for the earliest, lowliest shelter, a lair, a hollow in the ground covered over with branches, a recess (Proto-Germanic **kutan,* Indo-European **gudom,* Pok.393); for another use with the meaning of something bent or crooked, we find Middle Low German *kūt* and ancient Macedonian *góda,* both meaning intestines, and Sanskrit *gudá-m* bowel.

cote *n.* shelter for doves, small animals, etc. Old English (before 1034) *cote* cottage for poor people, variant of *cot* COT².

coterie (kō′tərē) *n.* circle of acquaintances. 1738, borrowed from French *coterie,* in Middle French meaning an association of tenant-farmers holding land in common from the same owner, from Old French *cotier* cottager, cotter, from *cote* hut, COTTAGE.

cotillion (kōtil′yən) *n.* 1766 *cotillon* a dance with complicated steps and much changing of partners; borrowed from French *cotillon* a kind of country dance, from Middle French *cotillon* petticoat, peasant girl's frock, from diminutive of Old French *cotte, cote* COAT. The sense of a formal dance or ball derives from a shortening of *cotillion ball* (1811), *cotillion party* (1827).

cottage *n.* About 1390 *cotage* small house, in Chaucer's *Canterbury Tales,* borrowed through Anglo-French **cotage* and directly from Old French *cotage* (*cote* hut, cottage + *-age*). Anglo-French and Old French *cote* is probably of Scandinavian origin (compare Old Icelandic *kot* hut, COT²). The term originally meant a dwelling occupied by a peasant or farm laborer under the feudal system. **—cottager** *n.* person living in a cottage, especially a peasant or farm laborer. 1555, formed from English *cottage* + *-er*¹. **—cottage cheese** (1848)

cotter¹ or **cottar** *n.* tenant farmer or laborer, feudal peasant. 1199 *Coterfaude,* a place name; later *cotyer* (before 1387, in a version of *Piers Plowman*). The word in English is attributable to a borrowing from Old French *cotier* cottager, see COTERIE; and from Medieval Latin *cotarius* cottager; and is perhaps also in part a formation of English *cot*² + *-ar,* variant of *-er*¹, as in *scholar, vicar.*

cotter² *n.* a pin, wedge, bolt, inserted through a rod, etc. that is sticking through a hole. Before 1338 *coter,* in Mannyng's *Chronicle of England,* perhaps a shortened form of *cotterel* cotter pin or bolt, bracket to hang a pot over the fire; both of uncertain origin, perhaps a borrowing of Old French *coterele* piece of armor, possibly attached to a helmet. **—cotter pin** 1881, but implied much earlier by *cotter hole* (1649).

cotton *n.* 1286 *coton,* borrowed from Old French *coton,* from Arabic *quṭun,* variant of *quṭn.* The Arabic is the source of Dutch *katoen,* German *Kattun,* Provençal *coton,* Italian *cotone,* and with the prefixed article *al-* the, Spanish *algodón* and Portuguese *algodão.* **—v.** 1488 (Scottish) form down or a nap on; from the noun. The informal sense "get on together, agree," is first recorded in 1567; the sense "to take a liking to" is first recorded in 1805. **—cotton candy** (1926) **—cotton gin** (1796) **—cottonmouth** *n.* (American English, 1832) **—cottontail** *n.* (1869; earlier *Molly Cottontail* 1835).

cotyledon (kot′əlē′dən) *n. Botany.* embryo leaf in the seed of a plant. 1776, New Latin (named by Linnaeus in 1751), from Latin *cotylēdōn* navelwort (a plant) from Greek *kotylēdṓn* cup-shaped hollow, from *kotýlē* small vessel, cup, hollow; probably borrowed from some Mediterranean source, perhaps cognate with Latin *catīnus* bowl, dish, pot; see KETTLE.

couch *n.* 1340, in *Ayenbite of Inwyt,* borrowed from Old French *couche,* earlier *culche,* from *coucher* lay in place, from Latin *collocāre* put in place, put together (*col-* together, variant of *com-* before *l* + *locāre* to place, put, LOCATE). Doublet of COLLOCATE. **—v.** Probably before 1300, to overlay as with gold; inlay, in *Arthour and Merlin;* borrowed from Old French *coucher* lay in place. The sense "to frame or express in words" appeared in 1529 (in writings of Sir Thomas More), and that of "express in a veiled or obscure way" in 1563.

cougar *n.* wildcat, puma, mountain lion. 1774, borrowed from French *couguar* (coined in 1761 by the French naturalist Buffon probably on the model of earlier *jaguar*), by contraction of New Latin *cuguacuara,* apparently a misreading of Brazilian Portuguese *çuçuarana,* from Tupi *suasuarana* (*suasu* deer + *rana* false; apparently so called from its tawny color).

cough *v.* Before 1325 *kouwen,* later *coughen* (about 1378, in a version of *Piers Plowman*); related to Old English *cohhettan* to bluster, probably of imitative origin, as in Middle Dutch *kochen* to cough, Middle High German *kūchen* breathe on, exhale, and Old English *ceahhettan* laugh loudly. The phrase *cough up,* meaning hand over (money), is first recorded in 1894 in American English.

The original sound represented by *gh,* in *cough, laugh, rough,* etc., was a guttural *ch,* as in Scottish *loch* or German *ach.* As the pronunciation shifted to the sound of *f* in *off* the spelling of many words also changed to reflect this process in *dwarf* and *draft* for *draught,* etc.; but a group of spellings remained fixed. For spelling see ROUGH.

—n. About 1300, from the verb. Though the verb is recorded after the noun, scholars show the noun as coming from the verb, the dating being a defect of the record.

could *v.* past tense of CAN¹. Old English *cūthe,* past tense of *cunnan* (about 725, in *Beowulf*). In Middle English the form was *coude, cowde* (about 1350), but in the early 1400's the *l* was inserted on analogy with *should* and *would,* where it is etymologically justified. The earliest recorded instance spelled with *l* is probably *colde,* about 1400, in *Destruction of Troy.*

coulee (kü′lē), *n.* deep ravine or gulch. 1804, Canadian English, borrowed through Canadian French *coulée* a small stream or bed of such a stream when dry, from French *coulée* flow, flow of lava, from feminine past participle of *couler* to flow, glide, from Old French *couler,* from Latin *cōlāre* to filter, strain, from *cōlum* strainer, COLANDER.

coulomb (külom′) *n.* unit of electrical quantity. 1881, from the name of Charles Augustin de *Coulomb* (1736-1806), a French physicist who devised a method of measuring the quantity of electricity.

council *n.* meeting, assembly. 1125 *concilie* assembly of churchmen; later *counseil* (about 1300) and *councel* (probably before 1400); borrowed from Old North French *concilie,* Old French *concile, cuncile,* learned borrowing from Latin *concilium* gathering, assembly (*con-* together, variant of *com-* before *c* + *-cilium,* related to *calāre* call out; see LOW², v. sound of cattle).

In early English *council* and *counsel* were frequently confused. In the 1500's *council* became established as a deliberative body, and *counsel* was restricted to the giving of advice and related senses. **—council chamber** (1407) **—council house** (before 1393) **—councilman** *n.* (before 1637, in writings of Ben Jonson). **—councilor** *n.* (before 1325 *counsalour priue,* in *Cursor Mundi;* later *councillor,* 1586).

counsel *n.* consultation, advice. Probably before 1200 *cunsail* advice, direction, in *Ancrene Riwle;* borrowed probably through Anglo-French **cunseil,* and directly from Old French *cunseil, conseil,* from Latin *cōnsilium* counsel, deliberation, from *cōnsulere* to CONSULT. The sense of a body of advisers is first recorded probably before 1300, in *Arthour and Merlin;* the sense of a single adviser, probably about 1250, and of a legal adviser, advocate, lawyer, before 1393, in Gower's *Confessio Amantis.* —**v.** About 1280 *counsaylen* take counsel with oneself, consider; later, to give or seek advice (probably before 1300, in *Kyng Alisaunder* and *Arthour and Merlin*); borrowed probably through Anglo-French *cunseiler,* and directly from Old French *conseiller,* from Latin *cōnsiliārī,* from *cōnsilium* counsel. —**counselor** *n.* Probably before 1200, in *Ancrene Riwle,* borrowed probably through Anglo-French *cunseiler,* and directly from Old French *conseillëor.*

count[1] *v.* name numbers, reckon. Probably about 1380; earlier, to value (1369, in Chaucer's *Book of the Duchesse*) and implied in *counting* reckoning, accounting (1341-42); borrowed from Old French *cunter, conter,* from Latin *computāre* calculate, compute (*com-* together + *putāre* to count, think, consider; see PUTATIVE). Doublet of COMPUTE. —**n.** Before 1325, a reckoning, an accounting; borrowed from Old French *conte, cunte,* from Late Latin *computum* calculation, reckoning, from Latin *computāre.* —**countless** *adj.* 1588, in Shakespeare's *Titus Andronicus,* formed from English *count,* n. + *-less.* —**countinghouse** *n.* (before 1443)

count[2] *n.* nobleman. Probably about 1425 *counete,* but implied in earlier *counte* a shire (about 1303) and a territory ruled by a count (about 1378); borrowed through Anglo-French *counte* (about 1290), Old French *conte, cunte,* from Latin *comitem,* accusative of *comes* member of the imperial court, attendant, associate, companion (*com-* with, together + *it-,* from the root of *īre* to go; see EXIT).

countenance *n.* look, expression, appearance. About 1250 *cuntenaunce* demeanor, borrowed from Old French *cuntenaunce, contenance* bearing, behavior, countenance, learned borrowing from Medieval Latin *continentia,* from Latin *continentia* self-control, from *continentem* (nominative *continēns*), present participle of *continēre* CONTAIN; for suffix see -ANCE. Doublet of CONTINENCE. —**v.** 1486, to behave or act (as if one were doing something), look upon with favor, approve; borrowed from Middle French *contenancer,* from *contenance* countenance, from Old French.

counter[1] *n.* table, case, or shelf. 1345 *countour* table used for counting money or making accounts, counting table; borrowed through Anglo-French *counteour,* Old French *conteoir,* from Medieval Latin *computatorium* place for counting or making accounts (Latin *computātus,* past participle of *computāre* compute, COUNT[1] + *-ōrium* -ory). The sense of a disk of metal, etc., used in counting is first recorded about 1390.

counter[2] *n.* person or machine that counts. About 1300 *countour* accountant, tax collector; earlier *Cunter* (as a proper name); borrowed from Anglo-French *countour,* Old French *conteor* one who counts, from Latin *computātōrem* (nominative *computātor*) computer, reckoner, from *computāre* compute, COUNT[1]; for suffix see -ER[1].

counter[3] *adv.* in the opposite direction, opposed. About 1450, borrowed from Middle French *countre* facing, opposite (to), from Latin *contrā* against; see CONTRA-. —**v.** go counter to, oppose. Before 1397 *countren,* in the Wycliffe Bible; borrowed from Old French *countre* opposite (to). —**adj.** opposed, opposite. 1596, in Spenser's *Faerie Queene,* from English *counter-,* prefix.

counter- a prefix meaning: **1** against, in opposition to, as in *counteract = act against.* **2** in return, as in *counterattack = attack in return.* **3** corresponding, as in *counterpart = corresponding part.* Middle English and Anglo-French *countre-,* borrowed from Old French *contre, countre* facing, opposite (to), from Latin *contrā* against; see CONTRA-. —**counteract** *v.* (1678) —**counterattack** *n.* (1893, perhaps suggested by earlier French *contre-attaque*); *v.* (1916). —**counterclaim** *n.* (1784); *v.* (1881). —**counterclockwise** *adv., adj.* (1888) —**counterintelligence** *n.* (1940) —**counterrevolution** *n.* (1793, perhaps suggested by earlier French *contre-révolution*). —**countersink** *v., n.* (1816) —**counterspy** *n.* (1939)

counterbalance *v.* 1580, borrowed from Middle French *contre-balancer* (*contre-* against, counter-, from *contre, countre* facing, opposite (to) + *balancer* BALANCE). —**n.** 1603, either noun use of English verb, or borrowed from French *contre-balance,* n., from the French verb.

counterespionage *n.* 1899, borrowed from French *contre-espionnage* (*contre-* against, counter- + *espionnage* ESPIONAGE), and later (1919) also formed from English *counter-* + *espionage* possibly after French *contre-espionnage.*

counterfeit *adj.* deceptive, sham, false. Before 1393, *contrefet,* in Gower's *Confessio Amantis;* borrowed from Old French *contrefait* imitated, past participle of *contrefaire* imitate (*contre-* against, counter- + *faire* make, from Latin *facere* to DO[1] act); perhaps also formed from English *countrefet, counterfet,* a past participial form of earlier English *countrefeten,* v. —**v.** imitate, deceive. About 1300 *countrefeten,* borrowed from Old French *contrefait,* past participle of *contrefaire* imitate. —**n.** counterfeit copy. 1397, from the adjective.

countermand *v.* cancel or change an order. Before 1420, in Lydgate's *Troy Book;* borrowed from Middle French *contremander* reverse an order or command (*contre-* against, counter- + *mander,* from Latin *mandāre* to order, MANDATE). —**n.** 1548, borrowed from Middle French *contremand,* from *contremander* countermand, and possibly from English *countermand,* v.

countermarch *n.* 1598, borrowed from Middle French *contre-marche* (*contre-* against, counter-, from *contre, countre* facing, opposite (to) + *marche* MARCH[1]). —**v.** 1625, either verb use of English noun, or borrowed from French *contre-marcher,* v., from the French noun.

counterpane *n.* quilt, coverlet. 1603, alteration of earlier *counterpoynte* quilt (1467); borrowed from Old French *cuilte contrepointe* quilt stitched through and through. Old French *contrepointe* itself was an alteration of *coute pointe,* representing Medieval Latin *culcita puncta* quilted mattress (Latin *culcita* cushion, mattress, see QUILT + *pūncta,* feminine past participle of *pungere* to prick, stab; see PUNGENT). The substitution of *pane* coverlet, for *pointe* was a semantic development, English *pane* being a borrowing from Old French *pan* cloth, from Latin *pannus* PANE.

counterpart *n.* 1451 *countre part* duplicate of a legal document, borrowed from Old French *contrepartie* (*contre, countre* facing, opposite (to), from Latin *contrā* against, + *partie* duplicate or exact copy of a person or thing, originally, feminine past participle of *partir* to divide; see PARTY).

counterpoint *n.* melody added to another as an accompaniment. Before 1450, art of singing an accompaniment; borrowed probably through Anglo-French and Old French *contrepoint,* from Medieval Latin **contrapunctum* (in music, *cantus contrapunctus* song or melody pointed against, explained as the accompaniment or second melody indicated by notes jotted down over or under the primary melody), from Latin *contrā* against + *pūnctus* dotted, *pūnctum* dot, POINT.

counterpoise *v.* counterbalance, compensate. 1586, alteration of earlier *countrepesen* (1385, in Chaucer's *Troilus and Criseyde*); borrowed from Old French *contrepeser* (*contre-* against, counter- + *peser* to weigh; see POISE). **—n.** weight balancing another weight. 1598, alteration of earlier *countrepeis* (about 1400); borrowed from Old French *contrepeis* (*contre-* against, counter- + *peis* weight, from Latin *pēnsum,* neuter past participle of *pendere* weigh, cause to hang; see PENDANT; compare AVOIRDUPOIS). The English spelling with *-poise* was probably influenced by Middle French *contrepois,* but this does not account for the earlier English verb spelling with *-poise.*

countersign *n.* a special mark to identify something, secret signal. 1591, borrowed from Middle French *contresigne,* from Italian *contrasegno,* from Latin *contrā* against + *signum* mark, token. **—v.** 1662; earlier probably French *contresigner,* in Cotgrave's *Dictionary of the French and English Tongues* (1611), from French *contresigner,* possibly from Italian *contrasegnare* to countermark, from Latin *contrā* against + *signāre* to mark, from *signum* mark, token.

counterweight *n.* 1693, formed from English *counter-* + *weight,* possibly influenced in its formation by earlier *counterweigh,* v. (probably before 1439, *countirweien*).

country *n.* Probably before 1250 *contre* one's native land; borrowed from Old French *contree, cuntree,* from Vulgar Latin **contrāta regiō* region lying opposite, i.e., spread out before one (Latin *contrā* opposite, against, see CONTRA- + *regiō* REGION).

German *Gegend* region, from *gegen* against, was formed as a loan translation of Old French *contree* or the corresponding Italian *contrada* country region (also from Vulgar Latin **contrāta*). The sense of a tract of land is recorded probably before 1300, and that of a national territory, about 1300.

—adj. Before 1387, from the noun.

—countrify *v.* (usually in the past participle form *countrified*) 1653, formed from English *country* + *-fy.* **—country club** (1894, American English) **—countryfolk** *n.* (about 1300) **—countryman** *n.* (1279, as a surname *Contreman*). **—country music** (1968) **—countryside** *n.* (about 1450) **—countrywoman** *n.* (1440)

county *n.* district of a state or country. About 1378 *counte* domain of a count, in a version of *Piers Plowman;* earlier, a shire (before 1338, in Mannyng's *Chronicle of England*), and a shire court (about 1303, in Mannyng's *Handlyng Synne*); borrowed through Anglo-French *counté,* Old French *conté, cunté* territory or domain of a lord, from Late Latin *comitātus* court or palace, from Latin *comitātus* train, retinue, from *comes* (accusative *comitem*) a state officer; earlier, attendant of the emperor, associate, companion; see COUNT[2] nobleman. **—countyseat** *n.* (1803, American English)

coup (kü) *n.* unexpected, clever move. Probably before 1400, borrowed from Old French *coup, colp* a blow, from Late Latin *colpus,* from Latin *colaphus* a blow with the fist, from Greek *kólaphos* a blow, slap. The meaning of *coup* in the sense of coup d'état, is first recorded in 1852, by shortening from *coup d'état.* **—coup de grâce** (kü′ də gräs′) action that quickly kills a suffering person or animal; finishing stroke. 1699, borrowing of French *coup de grâce,* literally, stroke of grace. **—coup d'état** (kü′ dā tä′) sudden and decisive act in politics, especially the overthrow of a government. 1646, borrowing of French *coup d'état,* literally, stroke of state.

coupe or **coupé** (küp *or* küpā′) *n.* closed two-door automobile. 1834, four-wheeled closed carriage, borrowed from French *coupé,* originally past participle of *couper* to cut, from Old French, from *coup* a blow; see COUP; so called from its being a *carrosse coupé* a cut or shortened carriage. 1908 is the first recorded application of the word to an automobile.

couple *n.* About 1280, a married couple or pair of lovers; later, a pair of things (1338, in Mannyng's *Chronicle of England*); borrowed from Old French *cople* couple, from Latin *cōpula* bond; later, pair, from **coapla* connected together (*co-* together **apla,* noun showing means by which something is fastened or connected, derived from *apere* fasten, connect; see APT. Doublet of COPULA. **—v.** Probably before 1200 *cuplen,* in *Ancrene Riwle;* borrowed from Old French *copler,* from *cople,* n., couple. **—coupler** *n.* 1552, formed from English *couple* + *-er*[1]. **—couplet** *n.* 1580, pair of successive lines of verse, borrowed from Middle French *couplet,* diminutive of *couple,* from Old French *cople* couple, couplet.

coupon *n.* 1822, certificate of interest due on an investment bond which can be cut from the bond and presented for interest; borrowed from French *coupon,* from Old French *coupon* piece cut off, from *couper* to cut, from *coup* a blow; see COUP. The sense of a certificate or one of a series of tickets that gives the holder certain rights, such as to a ride, a discount in price, etc., was introduced by the travel agent Thomas Cook in 1864.

courage *n.* Probably before 1300 *corage* spirit, disposition, nature, in *Kyng Alisaunder;* borrowed from Old French *corage, curage* (corresponding to Provençal and Catalan *coratge,* Spanish *coraje,* Portuguese *coragem,* and Italian *coraggio*), from Vulgar Latin **corāticum,* from Latin *cor* HEART; for suffix see -AGE. The ordinary sense of bravery, fearlessness is first recorded in English before 1338, in Mannyng's *Chronicle of England.* All senses of the word stem from the notion that the heart is the center of feeling, thought, and character. **—courageous** *adj.* Probably before 1300 *corageus* brave, fearless, in *Kyng Alisaunder;* borrowed from Old French *corageus,* from *corage* courage; for suffix see -OUS.

courier (kėr′ēər) *n.* special messenger, usually sent in haste. Probably before 1350 *currur,* borrowed through Anglo-French *courrier,* Old French *coreor, corier,* from Italian *corriere,* from *correre* to run, from Latin *currere;* see CURRENT.

The spelling *courier* is first recorded in English in

1770, altered from earlier *courrier* (1718), which was borrowed from or influenced by modern French *courrier,* from Old French *corier.*

course *n.* Probably before 1300 *cours* onward movement, in *Kyng Alisaunder,* borrowed from Old French *cours, curs,* from Latin *cursus* (genitive *cursūs*), a running race or course, from past participle stem *curs-* of *currere* to run; see CURRENT. The sense of a planned or prescribed series of classes, lectures, etc., is first recorded in English in 1605; the sense existed in French in the 1300's and earlier. The earliest instances of the adjectival and adverbial phrase *of course* (literally, of or in the ordinary or due course) are dated 1541 and 1542 respectively, replacing earlier *bi cours* with the same meaning (probably before 1300). —**v.** 1466, to pursue; from the noun.

courser *n.* a swift horse. Probably about 1300, in *The Romance of Guy of Warwick,* borrowed from Old French *coursier, cursier, corsier,* from Medieval Latin *cursarius,* from Latin *cursus,* see COURSE; for suffix see -ER[1].

court *n.* Probably before 1200 *curt* princely residence or household; borrowed from Old French *cort, curt,* from Latin *cōrtem,* accusative of *cōrs* (earlier *cohortem,* accusative of *cohors*) enclosure, courtyard, company, cohort or retinue, a compound of *co-* together, and a stem *hort-* (Indo-European **ĝhr̥-tis*); related to *hortus* garden, plot of ground; see YARD[1]. Doublet of COHORT. The sense of homage such as offered at court, attention or courtship (especially in the phrase *pay court to*), is first recorded in 1589, in Spenser's *Faerie Queene.* —**v.** 1515 (implied in *courting*); later play or act the courtier (1553); seek to win or attract (1571), pay amorous attention to, woo (1580), and pay court to, pay courteous attention to (1590); from the noun. —**courthouse** *n.* (probably about 1475) —**courtly** *adj.* (before 1475) —**court-martial** (probably 1435); *v.* (1859). —**court order** (1650, American English) —**courtroom** *n.* (1677, American English) —**courtship** *n.* (1588)

courteous *adj.* polite. Probably about 1350 but rare before 1500, alteration of earlier *curteis* (before 1300) with substitution of *-ous, -eous* for *-is, -eis.* Early Middle English *curteis* was borrowed from Old French *curteis, corteis* having such manners as befit a princely court, having courtly bearing or manners (*cort, curt* COURT + *-eis* adjective suffix, from Latin *-ēnsis*). —**courtesy** *n.* Probably before 1200 *curteisie,* in *Ancrene Riwle;* borrowed from Old French *curtesie, cortesie,* from *curteis, corteis;* for suffix see -Y[3].

courtesan (kôr′təzən), *n.* woman of loose morals among the nobility or the wealthy. 1549; earlier *courtezane* (1426); borrowed from Middle French *courtisane, courtisan,* from Italian *cortigiana* prostitute; originally, woman of the court, feminine of *cortigiano, cortegiano* one attached to a court, from *corte* court, from Latin *cōrtem* COURT. Compare ARTISAN, PARTISAN.

courtier *n.* 1228-29, as a surname *Curtier;* later *courteoures* (about 1300); borrowed through Anglo-French *courteour, curteour* courtier, Old French *courtier, cortier* judge, from *cort, curt* COURT; for suffix see -IER.

cousin *n.* 1160 *Cusin,* as a surname; later, *cosin* a relative, by blood or marriage (probably about 1225, in *King Horn*) and, a cousin (about 1300); borrowed from Old French *cosin, cusin,* from Latin *cōnsobrīnus* mother's sister's child, cousin (*con-* together + *sobrīnus,* from earlier **sosrīnos* cousin on mother's side, from *soror,* genitive *sorōris* SISTER).

couth (küth) *adj.* cultured, well-mannered. 1896, reintroduced as a back formation from *uncouth,* adj. Earlier, in Middle English *couth* courteous, polite (before 1325, in *Cursor Mundi* and surviving to the 1500's); in Old English (before 1000) *cūth* known, well-known, renowned, was a past participle of *cunnan* to know (see CAN[1]), corresponding to Old Frisian *kūth* known, Old Saxon *cūth,* Old High German *kund, chund* (modern German *kund*), and Gothic *kunths* known. Old English *cūth* developed from Proto-Germanic **kúnthaz* from Indo-European **ĝn̥tó-s* (Pok.377). The form *couth* survived in English only in *uncouth,* and in Scottish use in the sense of kind, pleasant, into the 1700's; its reemergence in standard English is an independent formation from *uncouth,* with its meaning also taken from the word.

couturier (kütůr′ēər) *n.* dressmaker or fashion designer. 1899, as a modern French term used in writings of Max Beerbohm; earlier *couturière* (1818), from Old French *cousturier, costurier* dressmaker, from *costure* a sewing, seam, from Vulgar Latin **cōnsūtūra,* from past participle of Latin *cōnsuere* sew (*con-* together + *suere* SEW). Related to ACCOUTER and SUTURE.

cove *n.* small, sheltered bay. Before 1325, a den or cave, in *Cursor Mundi;* later, a narrow valley (probably before 1400), developed from Old English (before 800) *cofa* small chamber, cell. The Old English word is cognate with Middle Low German *kove* hut, Old High German *kubisi, chubisi* tent, hut, Middle High German *kobe* pen, stall (modern German *Koben*), and Old Icelandic *kofi* hut, shed, cell (Norwegian *kove* small room); and is probably also cognate with Greek *gýpē* cave, from Indo-European **gupā* cave (Pok.395). The sense of a small bay is first recorded in English in 1590.

coven (kuv′ən) *n.* gathering of witches. 1500-20, meeting, variant of earlier *covent, cuvent* (probably before 1200, in *Ancrene Riwle*), earlier form of CONVENT, as found in *Covent Garden* (London). The sense of a gathering of witches appeared in 1662.

covenant *n.* solemn agreement, compact. Probably before 1300 *covenaunt,* in *Kyng Alisaunder;* borrowed from Old French *covenant* agreement, (originally) present participle of *covenir* agree or meet, from Latin *convenīre* come together, CONVENE. —**v.** agree formally. Probably before 1300, from the noun.

cover *v.* Probably about 1150 *coveren* protect or shelter, from Old French *covrir,* from Late Latin *cōperīre,* from Latin *cooperīre* to cover over (*co-* intensive + *operīre* to close, cover, from earlier **op-werī-;* see WEIR). —**n.** 1223, in compound *kovrechief* kerchief, a woman's covering for the head or veil; later, *koverchef* a wrapping, protective covering (1245), and in *bancover, bankcover* protective covering (1346-47); in compounds borrowed from Old French *cuevre-chief* head covering, and *covert* table furnishings and utensils for a meal, but also, especially as a single word, influenced by Middle English *coveren,* v. —**coverage** *n.* 1462, a charge for a booth at a fair, borrowed possibly from Middle French *couvrage* a cover; later, reintroduced in American English in the sense of risk covered by insurance (1912), formed from English *cover* + *-age.* —**coverall** *n.* (1830) —**covered wagon** (1745) —**covering** *n.* (1303) —**coverlet** *n.* (1303)

covert (kōvėrt′) *adj.* covered, concealed, secret. About

1303, in Mannyng's *Handlyng Synne,* borrowed from Old French *covert* (past participle of *covrir* to cover), from Latin *coopertus,* past participle of *cooperīre* to COVER. **—n.** Probably before 1300, a covering; later, a shelter (1338), and an animal's shelter, den or nest (before 1398), borrowed from Old French *covert, coverte* cover or shelter, from Medieval Latin *coopertum* a cover, from Latin *coopertus,* past participle; see *covert,* adj.

covet *v.* desire eagerly. Before 1250 *cuveiten,* in a version of *Ancrene Riwle;* later *coveiten* (about 1300); borrowed from Old French *coveitier.* The Old French form is probably derived from Gallo-Romance **cupidietāre,* from **cupidietās,* alteration (influenced by Latin *pietās, ānxietās, medietās*) of Latin *cupiditās* passionate desire, from *cupidus* very desirous, from *cupere* long for, desire; see CUPID. **—covetous** *adj.* About 1250 *covetus;* borrowed from Old French *coveitous* (compare Old Provençal *cobeitos*), probably from Gallo-Romance **cupidietōsus,* from **cupidietās,* alteration of Latin *cupiditās* passionate desire, CUPIDITY; for suffix see -OUS.

covey *n.* brood of partridges, quail, etc. About 1350, borrowed from Middle French *covée,* from feminine past participle of *cover* incubate, brood, from Latin *cubāre* be in a lying position; see CUBICLE.

cow[1] *n.* female of cattle. Middle English *ku* (before 1200); later, in a place name *Cowmede* (1227); developed from Old English (before 800) *cū.* The Old English *cū* is cognate with Old Frisian *kū* cow, Old Saxon *kō,* Middle Dutch *coe* (modern Dutch *koe*), Old High German *kuo* (modern German *Kuh*), Old Icelandic *kýr* (Norwegian *ku,* Danish and Swedish *ko*), from Proto-Germanic **kwōn,* earlier **kwōm.* Cognates outside Germanic are found in Old Irish *bō* cow (*b-* from *gw-*), Middle Welsh *buw,* Latin *bōs* ox, bull, cow. The Latin shows *b-* for expected *v-,* suggesting a borrowing from some other Italic language. Other cognates include Greek *boûs,* Latvian *gùovs* cow, Armenian *kov,* Sanskrit *gāú-s* ox, bull, cow, Avestan *gāuš,* and Tocharian A *ko* cow (plural *kowi*), Tocharian B *kau,* from Indo-European **gwōu-s* with accusative **gwōm* (Pok.482).

The Old English plural *cȳ, cȳe* became *ky, kye* in Middle English, with an extended form *kyn,* later *kyne, kine* (the latter still found as an archaic or dialectal variant of *cows*); this extended form probably developed on analogy with *oxen,* though the Old English genitive plural *cūna, cȳna* (later *cuna, kyne*) possibly contributed to use of *kine, kyne.*

—cowbell *n.* (1652, American English) **—cowbird** *n.* (1810, American English) **—cowboy** *n.* (1725) **—cowhand** *n.* (1886, American English) **—cowherd** *n.* 1222, developed from Old English *cū-hyrde, -hierde,* etc. **—cowhide** (before 1399) **—cowlick** *n.* (1598) **—cowpox** *n.* (1798) **—cowpuncher** *n.* (1878, American English) **—cowslip** *n.* Before 1325, developed from English (about 1000) *cūslyppe,* literally, cow slime.

cow[2] *v.* intimidate, frighten. 1605, in Shakespeare's *Macbeth,* probably borrowed from a Scandinavian source (compare Danish and Norwegian *kue* to cow, subdue, Old Icelandic *kūga* to force, oppress); of unknown origin.

coward *n.* Before 1250 *couard,* borrowed from Old French *coart,* from *coe* tail, from Latin *cōda,* dialectal variant of *cauda* tail, of uncertain origin; for suffix see -ARD. According to the OED, perhaps reference to the tail is in allusion to an animal "turning tail" in fright or to the habit of a frightened animal of drawing the tail between the hind legs. In the Old French version of *Reynard the Fox,* the name of the hare is *Coart,* possibly in reference to its timidity. **—cowardice** *n.* Probably before 1300, in *Kyng Alisaunder;* borrowed from Old French *couardise* (*couard, coart* coward + *-ise* noun suffix, from Latin *-itia*). **—cowardly** *adv.* (before 1375)

cower *v.* crouch in fear or shame. Before 1300 *couren* to skulk, apparently borrowed from a Scandinavian source (compare Old Icelandic *kūra* doze, lie quiet, Danish and Norwegian *kure* and Swedish *kura* to squat); cognate with Middle Low German *kūren* lie in wait (modern German *kauern* to crouch, squat); and probably also cognate with Greek *gȳrós* rounded, curved, crooked, and Armenian *kor* crooked, bent, from Indo-European **gūró-s, *gowero-* (Pok.397).

cowl *n.* monk's cloak with a hood. Probably before 1200 *cule,* in Layamon's *Chronicle of Britain;* later, *couel;* developed from Old English *cūle,* earlier *cugele* (about 961), borrowed from Late Latin *cuculla* monk's cowl, variant of Latin *cucullus* hood, of uncertain origin. **—v.** cover with or as with a cowl. 1536, from the noun. **—cowling** *n.* covering of an aircraft engine (1917).

cowrie or **cowry** *n.* shell used as money in parts of Africa and Asia. 1698, borrowed from Hindi and Urdu *kaurī, kauṛī,* from Sanskrit *kaparda-s,* from Dravidian; compare Tamil *kōṭu* mussel shell, (originally) curved, bent, crooked.

coxcomb *n.* vain, empty-headed man. 1573, also with the meaning "cap worn by clowns," variant of *cock's comb* (1562), since the cap resembled the comb of a cock; earlier *cokkes comb* crest of a cock (about 1400), in Sir John Maundeville's *Travels.*

coxswain (kok'sən) *n.* 1327, officer in charge of a ship's boat and its crew (*cock* ship's boat + *swain* boy, young man, as in *boatswain*).

coy *adj.* Before 1338, quiet, still, in Mannyng's *Chronicle of England;* earlier, in surname *Coyman* (1230); borrowed from Old French *coi,* earlier *quei,* from Vulgar Latin **quētus,* from Latin *quiētus* resting, at rest; see the doublets QUIET and QUIT, *adj.* The sense shy or modest, is first recorded about 1386, in Chaucer's *Canterbury Tales.*

coyote (kī'ōt) *n.* 1759, American English, borrowed from Mexican Spanish *coyote,* from Nahuatl *coyotl.*

coypu (koi'pü) *n.* water rodent of South America. 1793, borrowed from American Spanish *coipú,* from Araucanian (Chile) *koypu.*

cozen (kuz'ən) *v.* cheat. 1573; earlier, *cozener* a cheater (1561); perhaps 1) borrowed from French *cousiner* claim to be a cousin for some advantage, cheat on the pretext of being a cousin, from *cousin,* n.; or 2) developed from Middle English *cosyn* fraud, trickery (1453), of uncertain origin (compare Old French *coçon* dealer, from Latin *cōciōnem* horse dealer. **—cozenage** *n.* fraud. 1583, formed from English *cozen* + *-age.*

cozy or **cosy** *adj.* comfortable, snug. 1728; earlier, *colsie* (1709), originally Scottish; possibly borrowed from a Scandinavian source (compare Norwegian *kose* (*seg*) enjoy (oneself), be cozy, *koselig* cozy). **—n.** covering to keep a teapot, etc., warm. 1863 *cosy,* probably from the adjective. **—v.** *Informal.* snuggle. 1937, American English, from the adjective.

crab[1] *n.* shellfish. Probably before 1200 *crabbe;* earlier as a surname (1188); developed from Old English (about 1000) *crabba;* cognate with Middle Low German *krabbe* crab, Old High German *krebiz* (modern German *Krabbe*), Old Saxon *krebit,* Old Icelandic *krabbi* (Danish and Norwegian *krabbe,* Swedish *krabba*) crab, from Indo-European **grobh-* scratch (Pok.392). —**v.** Probably before 1400 *crabben* to vex, irritate, anger, either from earlier *crabbed,* adj., or from *crabbe* crab[1] or crab[2] used figuratively. The sense of complain irritably, find fault appeared before 1500. —**crab grass** 1743; earlier, possibly a marine grass of salt marshes (1597).

crab[2] *n.* small, sour wild apple; (crab apple, 1712). Probably before 1300 *crabbe,* of uncertain origin (perhaps a transferred use of CRAB[1] the animal, its disposition compared with the sour taste of the fruit). The sense of a sour person is first recorded in 1580, in part a figurative use of *crab* the apple, and later, according to the OED, in reference to an ill-tempered person, as a back formation from *crabbed* and also directly from *crab* the animal. —**crabby** *adj.* 1550, crooked, gnarled, cross-grained; formed from English *crab[2]* sour apple + *-y[1]*. The sense of peevish, is first recorded in 1776, in American English, in Paine's *Common Sense.*

crabbed *adj.* peevish, ill-natured. Before 1376, in a version of *Piers Plowman,* formed from Middle English *crabbe* crab[1] (shellfish) + *-ed,* with reference to the crab's crooked motion, and the perverse disposition expressed by it; later, the sense of harsh, unpleasant, and bitter to the taste, is recorded (probably about 1390), evolving into the figurative use of sour-tempered, peevish (about 1565), most likely under influence of *crab[2]* wild apple.

crack *v.* Probably before 1200 *craken* make a bursting or splitting sound, in Layamon's *Chronicle of Britain;* developed from Old English (about 1000) *cracian* make a sharp noise, crack. Old English *cracian* is related to *cearcian* to creak, and cognate with Middle Dutch *craken* to crack, creak (modern Dutch *kraken*), Old High German *krahhōn* (modern German *krachen*), *krach* loud noise (modern German *Krach*), and with Sanskrit *gárjati* roars, from Indo-European **gorg-* (Pok.384). The sense of break something hard with a sharp noise, is first recorded probably before 1300. —**n.** Probably before 1300 *crak* sharp noise, in *Kyng Alisaunder;* related to Old English *cracian* make a sharp noise. The meaning "split, opening" is first recorded about 1450. —**adj.** first-class. 1793, from the noun sense of that which is superior (1637). —**cracked** *adj.* About 1440; later, specifically of the mind (1611). —**cracker** *n.* 1440; specifically a thin crisp biscuit (1739). —**cracker barrel** (1877) —**cracker box** (1857); *adj.* (1911) —**crackerjack** *n.* (1895) —**crackpot** *n.* 1883, from *crack* (1614) to collapse, be of unsound mind; and earlier, *cracked* + *pot* skull. —**crack-up** *n.* (1926) from *crack,* v., collapse (1658).

crackle *v.* Before 1450 *crackelen,* frequentative form of *cracken* to crack; for suffix see -LE[3].

-cracy a combining form meaning rule or ruling body or class, as in *aristocracy, bureaucracy, theocracy.* Borrowed from Greek *-kratíā* (in words such as *aristokratíā* rule of the best-born, aristocracy, and *dēmokratíā* rule of the people, democracy) from *krátos* power, rule, through Latin *-cratia* and Middle French *-cratie.*

Since the 1800's *-cracy* has become productive in English, especially in the form *-ocracy,* possibly by influence of *bureaucracy* (borrowed in 1818 from French) and the earlier *mobocracy* rule of the mob, coined in 1754. Often *-cracy* is used to form nonce words, such as *snobocracy* and *rabbleocracy,* but some coinages with *-cracy* have become established, for example *technocracy* rule of technical experts (1932) and *meritocracy* class of people ruling by merit (1958).

cradle *n.* Probably before 1200 *cradel,* in *Ancrene Riwle,* developed from Old English *cradol* little bed or cot (about 1000, in Ælfric's *Glossary*) from Proto-Germanic **kradulás* ; cognate with Old High German *kratto, krezzo* basket, and Sanskrit *grathnā́mi* I wind, and *grantha-s* knot, from Indo-European *greth-* to weave, plait; **groth-uló-s* (Pok.386).—**v.** put in a cradle. Before 1500 *credelen,* from the noun. —**cradlesong** *n.* (before 1398) —**cat's cradle** (1768)

craft *n.* Old English *cræft* skill or art (before 899, in Alfred's translation of Boethius' *De Consolatione Philosophiae*), but originally with the meaning of power, strength, might (also in Alfred's works). The word is cognate with Old Frisian *kreft* strength, skill, Old Saxon *kraft,* Old High German *chraft* (modern German *Kraft*), and Old Icelandic *kraptr* strength, virtue (Danish, Norwegian, and Swedish *kraft* strength), with no cognates outside Germanic but related to CRAVE. The sense *craft* for boat, as in *small craft* is first recorded in 1671-72. —**v.** 1436, make skillfully; earlier, to attain; from the noun. The verb, even in its later principal meaning of act craftily, became obsolete after the 1500's, but was revived in the late 1950's, especially by American manufacturers who advertised products "crafted or carefully put together" by craftsmen. —**craftsman** *n.* Probably before 1200, in Layamon's *Chronicle of Britain.* —**craftsmanship** *n.* Before 1652, variant **craftmanship** (1839). —**crafty** *adj.* Probably before 1200 *crafti* skillful, developed from Old English *cræftig* strong, powerful (about 893, in a translation of Alfred's); formed from *cræft* craft + *-ig* -y[1]. The sense "skillful" appeared in 971, and that of "cunning, wily," probably about 1200.

crag *n.* Before 1325, in *Cursor Mundi;* earlier, in place name *Cragdal* (1218); borrowed from a Celtic source (compare Old Irish *crec, carrac* rock, cliff, Irish *carraig,* and Welsh *craig* rock, stone). —**craggy** *adj.* Probably about 1400, formed from English *crag* + *-y[1]*.

cram *v.* Before 1325 *crommen* fill, stuff, dialectal variant of *crammen* (about 1353); developed from Old English *crammian* (about 1000, in Ælfric's *Grammar*), derivative of *crimman* to insert. Old English *crimman* is cognate with Old High German *krimman* to press or pinch, Middle High German *krammen* to claw, Old Icelandic *kremja* to squeeze or pinch (Danish, Norwegian *kramme,* Swedish *krama*), and outside Germanic with Old Slavic *gromada* heap, and Sanskrit *grā́ma-s* heap, crowd, village, from Indo-European **grem-/grom-/grōm-* (Pok.383).

cramp[1] *n.* metal bar bent at both ends. 1423, borrowed from Middle Dutch *crampe* or Middle Low German *krampe* hook. The Middle Dutch and Low German are cognate with Old Saxon *kramp* cramp or clamp, Old High German *kramph, krampho* bent or crooked (modern German *Krampe*), Old Icelandic *krappr* (with *-pp-* from *-mp-*) narrow, from Indo-European **gremb-/gromb-* (Pok.387).

The figurative sense of something that confines or hinders, constraint, is first recorded in 1719.

—**v.** Probably about 1408 *crawmpen* to bend or twist; later *crampe* compress forcibly (before 1555); in part from *cramp*[1], n., and in part from *cramp*[2], n. The figurative sense of restrict, limit or confine, is first recorded in 1625, in Francis Bacon's *Essays.*

cramp[2] *n.* painful contraction of muscles. About 1378 *crampes,* in a version of *Piers Plowman;* borrowed from Old French *crampe,* from a Frankish word (compare Old High German *kramph, kramphe* cramp, spasm, related to *kramph* bent, crooked, Old Icelandic *krappa* to clench; see CRAMP[1]). **—v.** Probably about 1425 *crampen,* in a translation of Chauliac's *Grande Chirurgie;* from the noun. **—writer's cramp** (1853)

cranberry *n.* 1647 *cranberry;* 1648 *craneberry;* both forms are American English, apparently borrowed from Low German *Kraanbere* (*Kraan* crane, from Middle Low German *krān* + *bere* berry; of unknown origin). **—cranberry bog** (1807) **—cranberry sauce** (1767, in John Adams' *Diary*)

crane *n.* large wading bird. 1177, as surname *Crane,* developed from Old English *cran* (about 1000, in Ælfric's *Glossary*); cognate with Old Saxon *krano* crane, Old High German *krano* and *chranuh* (modern German *Kranich*), Old Icelandic *trani,* Danish, Norwegian, and Swedish *trane* (with unexplained change of *k-* to *t-*). Outside Germanic the word is cognate with Latin *grūs* crane, battering ram, Greek *géranos* crane, device imitating the movements of a crane, Welsh, Breton and Cornish *garan* crane, Gaulish *tri-garanos* having three cranes, Lithuanian *garnỹs* stork, Old Prussian *gerwe* crane, and Armenian *kṙunk* crane; all from an Indo-European base of imitative origin (**gerō-/gerə-; grənon-, grə-nu-g-, gerəno-s, grū-s,* Pok.383), represented also by Old English *ceorran* to creak, Old High German *carron* to screech, scream, and possibly Sanskrit *járate* (he) cries, sounds, calls. Related to CROW[1] and CROW[2].

The use of *crane* for a machine with a long arm for moving heavy weights, is first recorded as early as 1349 (earlier, in compound *creneman,* 1299); a similar meaning existed in the Latin, Greek, and Old High German cognates.

—v. 1570, hoist or lower with a crane; from the noun.

cranium *n.* Probably before 1425 *craneum,* in a translation of Chauliac's *Grande Chirurgie;* borrowed from Medieval Latin *cranium,* from Greek *krāníon,* related to *kárā* head; see CEREBRUM. **—cranial** *adj.* 1800, formed from English *cranium* + *-al*[1].

crank *n.* About 1440 *cranke,* in *Promptorium Parvulorum;* earlier *cronk* (1295); developed from Old English (about 1000) *cranc-,* in compound *crancstæf* weaver's instrument, related to *crincan* to bend, yield; see CRINKLE. The sense of a person with a mental twist, an eccentric, is first recorded in 1833, probably as a back formation of *cranky.* **—v.** 1592, to zigzag, in Shakespeare's *Venus and Adonis;* from the noun. The sense of turn a crank, is first recorded in 1908. **—crankshaft** *n.* (1854) **—cranky** *adj.* 1821, capricious, cross-tempered; later, queer, eccentric (1850); formed from English *crank,* n. + *-y*[1].

cranny *n.* small, narrow opening. About 1440 *crayne,* scribal error for *cranye,* in *Promptorium Parvulorum;* possibly borrowed as an alteration of Middle French *cran, cren* notch, fissure, from *crener* to notch, split, from Medieval Latin *crenare,* from Vulgar Latin **crināre* to split, probably related to Latin *cernere* to separate, sift; see CERTAIN.

crap *n.* rubbish. 1898; earlier, chaff (before 1425); borrowed from Middle French *crape* siftings, Old French *crappe,* from Medieval Latin *crappa, crapinium* chaff, perhaps from Old Dutch *krappen* cut off, pluck. **—v.** 1930, talk nonsense; spoil; earlier, defecate (1846). **—crappy** *adj.* 1846, formed from English *crap,* n. + *-y*[1].

crape *n.* piece of crepe used in mourning. 1446, variant of *crepe,* possibly borrowed from Middle French *crespe;* see CREPE.

crappie *n.* kind of fish. 1856, American English; apparently borrowed from dialectal Canadian French *crappé.*

craps *n.* gambling game played with dice. 1843, American English, borrowing of Louisiana French *craps* the game of hazard (the ancestor of *craps*), from English *crabs* the lowest throw in hazard, being two aces (1768), from CRAB[1] shellfish.

crash *v.* Probably before 1400 *crasschen, craschen* break in pieces, in *Morte Arthur;* earlier, make a crashing sound (about 1390); probably ultimately of imitative origin, like *clash, dash, smash,* etc.; but compare Middle English *crāsen* to shatter, borrowed from Old French *crasir,* and Middle English *cruschen* to crush, borrowed from Old French *croissir.*

The sense of wreck a vehicle (or originally an airplane), have a collision, is first recorded in 1910.

—n. 1580, sudden loud noise; from the verb.

The sense of a sudden business failure or financial ruin, is first recorded in 1817.

—crash landing (1928)

crass *adj.* 1545, thick, fat, gross, borrowed from Middle French *crasse,* from Latin *crassus* solid, thick, dense, related to *crātis* wickerwork, hurdle; see CRATE.

The extended sense of grossly dull or stupid, is first recorded in English in 1660, though it was used earlier in French (as in *ignorance crasse*).

crate *n.* 1397-98, hurdle, grillwork, borrowed from Latin *crātis* wickerwork, lattice, HURDLE, from Indo-European **kṛtis* (Pok.584). Doublet of GRATE[1] framework. The sense of large box is first recorded in 1688 with the spelling *creat.* **—v.** 1871, from the noun.

crater *n.* 1613, mouth of a volcano, borrowed from Latin *crātēr,* from Greek *krātḗr* bowl for mixing wine with water, from *kerannýnai* to mix, cognate with Sankskrit *śrā́yati* boils, from Indo-European **kerə-/ krā-/kṝ-* (Pok.582).—**v.** to form a crater. 1884, from the noun.

cravat (krəvat′) *n.* necktie. 1656 *crabbat,* in Blount's *Glossographia;* borrowed from French *cravate,* from special use of *Cravate* Croat (in Régiment de *Royal-Cravate*), from German dialect *Krabate,* from Serbo-Croatian *Hrvat* a Croat. The cravat came into fashion in France in the 1600's in imitation of the linen scarf worn by Croatian mercenaries in the French military service.

crave *v.* Probably before 1200 *craven,* in *Ancrene Riwle;* developed from Old English (about 1000) *crafian* demand with authority or by right; cognate with Old Icelandic *krefja* to demand, require, (Danish *kræve,* Norwegian *kreve,* and Swedish *kräva*). The sense of long for is first recorded before 1375.

craven *adj.* Probably before 1200 *cravant* vanquished, defeated, in *Ancrene Riwle;* perhaps borrowed from Old French *crevanté* (with loss of final *-é*), past participle; or even *crevant,* present participle of *crever* burst, rattle, from Latin *crepāre* to crack, creak; possibly cognate with Sanskrit *kr̥pate* (he) wails, from Indo-European **krep-/krop-/kr̥p-* (Pok.569). The sense of cowardly, is first recorded probably before 1400, in *Morte Arthur.*

craw *n.* pouchlike enlargement of a bird's gullet. About 1395 *crawe,* in the Wycliffe Bible; earlier *crei* neck or throat (about 1250, in *The Owl and the Nightingale*); developed from Old English **cræg, *craga.* The Old English is cognate with Middle Dutch *crāghe* neck, throat (modern Dutch *kraag* collar), Middle High German *krage* neck, throat (modern German *Kragen* collar, neck). Outside Germanic cognates are found in Old Irish *brāgae* neck, Middle Welsh *breuant* windpipe (from **gwrogh-*), Greek *brónchos* windpipe, from Indo-European **gwrogh-, *gwr̥g-n̥t-* (Pok.475).

crawfish *n.* 1624, in Captain John Smith's *The Generall Historie of Virginia;* American English, variant of CRAYFISH. **—v.** *Informal.* retreat, back out. 1842, American English, from the noun (in allusion to the animal's manner of moving backward).

crawl *v.* Before 1400 *crawlen;* earlier *crewlen* (about 1200), borrowed from a Scandinavian source (Old Icelandic *krafla,* Danish, Norwegian *kravle,* Swedish *kravla* to crawl); see CRAB[1] shellfish. **—n.** slow movement. 1818, in Shelley's *Revolt of Islam,* from the verb.

crayfish *n.* 1555 *crefisshe,* alteration (influenced by *fish* in some confusion with *-vis, *-vish*) of earlier *crevis* (1311-12); borrowed from Middle French *crevice,* from a Frankish word (compare Old High German *krebiz* CRAB[1] shellfish).

crayon *n.* 1644, in John Evelyn's *Diary*; borrowed from French *crayon* pencil, (originally) chalk pencil, from *craie* chalk, from Latin *crēta,* of uncertain origin. **—v.** draw with crayon. 1662, also in Evelyn's *Diary,* from French *crayonner,* from French *crayon,* n.

craze *n.* About 1369 *crasen* perforate, in Chaucer's *Book of the Duchesse;* later, break in pieces, shatter (about 1399); borrowed from a Scandinavian source (compare Swedish *krasa* to crack, crunch, Norwegian *krase* to crush), apparently of imitative origin.

A figurative sense of break down in health, is first recorded in Middle English before 1450, and from it followed the sense of break down mentally, drive mad, make insane (1496-97). The early literal meanings developed into the sense of become minutely cracked (1832), said of the glaze on the surface of pottery.

—n. 1534, a flaw or defect; from the verb, but earlier with the meaning of a shattering attack (1410). The sense of a mania, is first recorded in 1813 and that of a fad in 1877.

—crazy *adj.* 1576, broken down, sickly; later, insane, mad (1617); formed from English *craze,* n. + *-y*[1]. **—crazy bone** (1876, American English) **—crazy quilt** (1886, American English)

creak *v.* Before 1325 *creken* utter a harsh cry, croak, apparently of imitative origin. The sense of squeak loudly, is first recorded in 1583. **—n.** creaking noise. 1605, from the verb. **—creaky** *adj.* 1834, formed from English *creak* + *-y*[1].

cream *n.* 1378 *creem,* in a version of *Piers Plowman;* earlier *creyme* (1332); borrowed from Old French *cresme, craime, creme,* a blending of Late Latin *chrisma* ointment, from Greek *chrîsma* an anointing, unguent (see CHRISM) + Late Latin *crāmum* cream, of uncertain origin, perhaps from Gaulish (compare Welsh *cramen* scab, Breton *crammen, cremmen,* Middle Irish *screm* surface, skin), from Indo-European **krəm-, *skrəm-* (Pok. 945). The Middle English word replaced Old English *rēam* cream. **—v.** 1440, to foam, froth, in *Promptorium Parvulorum;* later, to separate as cream (1615), to add cream to (1834), and to apply cream to (1921); from the noun. **—cream cheese** (1583) **—creamer** *n.* 1858, a dish for skimming cream; later, in American English, a pitcher for cream (1877); formed from English *cream* + *-er*[1]. **—creamery** *n.* 1858, in American English; formed from English *cream* + *-ery.* **—cream pitcher** 1860, in American English; earlier implied in *devil's cream pitcher* a plant (1838). **—creamy** *adj.* About 1450; formed from English *cream* + *-y*[1]. **—cold cream** (1381, as a custard; later, a preparation for the skin, 1709).

crease *n.* 1665, alteration of earlier *creaste* furrow, wrinkle, fold, or ridge, perhaps a variant of *crest* CREST; found in Middle English *creste* fold in a length of cloth (1433); earlier, bony ridge (before 1398). **—v.** 1588 *cressed,* past participle, perhaps alteration of *crested,* past participle of *crest,* v.

create *v.* About 1380, in Chaucer's translation of Boethius' *De Consolatione Philosophiae,* borrowed from Latin *creātus,* past participle of *creāre* to make, produce, from a lost noun *krē-yā* growth, related to *crēscere* arise, grow; see CRESCENT; for suffix see -ATE[1]. **—creation** *n.* About 1390 *creacion* a created thing, borrowed through Old French *création,* or directly from Latin *creātiōnem* (nominative *creātiō*), from *creāre* create; for suffix see -TION. **—creationism** *n.* 1880, in reference to, and contrasted with, *Darwinism;* earlier, the theory that God immediately creates a soul for every human born (1847). **—creative** *adj.* 1678, probably borrowed from French *créatif* (feminine *créative*), from Latin *creātus,* past participle of *creāre* create; for suffix see -IVE. **—creator** *n.* About 1300 *creatour, creatur* God, borrowed through Anglo-French *creatour,* Old French *creator, creatur, creatour,* and directly as a learned borrowing from Latin *creātōrem* (nominative *creātor*), from past participle stem of *creāre* create; for suffix see -OR[2]. The word was not generally capitalized *Creator* until the appearance of the King James Bible (1611).

creature *n.* About 1280, human being, borrowed from Old French *creature,* and probably directly as a learned borrowing from Latin *creātūra,* from past participle stem of *creāre* create; for suffix see -URE. **—creature comforts** (1659)

crèche (kresh) *n.* representation of the infant Jesus in the manger. 1792, borrowed from French *crèche,* from Old French *creche* manger, from Frankish **kripja* (compare Old High German *krippa* manger, CRIB).

credence (krē′dəns), *n.* belief, testimonial. About 1338, in Mannyng's *Chronicle of England,* borrowed from Medieval Latin *credentia,* from Latin *crēdentem* (nominative *crēdēns*), present participle of *crēdere* believe, trust, see CREDIT; for suffix see -ENCE. **—credential** *adj.* 1470, recommending for credit, accrediting; borrowed from Medieval Latin *credentialis,* from *credentia* credence; for suffix see -AL[1]. **—credentials** *n.pl.* Before 1674, letters of recommendation or introduction; earlier, testimonial (1660, in singular); from *credential,* adj.

credible *adj.* believable. About 1380, in Chaucer's translation of Boethius' *De Consolatione Philosophiae;*

borrowed from Latin *crēdibilis,* from *crēdere* believe, trust, see CREDIT; for suffix see -IBLE. —**credibility** *n.* 1594, borrowed from Medieval Latin *credibilitas,* from Latin *crēdibilis* credible; for suffix see -ITY.

credit *n.* 1542, borrowed from Middle French *crédit* belief, trust, from Italian *credito,* learned borrowing from Latin *crēditum* a loan, thing entrusted to another, from past participle of *crēdere* to trust, entrust, believe. The Latin is cognate with Old Irish *cretim* I believe, Sanskrit *śraddhā́* confidence, belief, Avestan *zrazdā-* belief, and Sanskrit *śrád-dadhāti* he trusts, believes, all going back to Indo-European base **k̑red-dhē-* to put power in, place belief or trust in (Pok.580). —**v.** 1541, trust (a person) with goods or money; formed in some senses from the noun and in others borrowed directly from Latin *crēditus,* past participle of *crēdere* believe, trust. —**creditable** *adj.* 1526 *cridible;* later, bringing credit or honor (1659); formed from English *credit,* v., n. + *-able.* —**creditor** *n.* Probably 1435 *creditour,* borrowed through Anglo-French *creditour,* Old French *crediteur,* learned borrowing from Latin *crēditōrem* (nominative *crēditor*), from *crēdere* to trust; for suffix see -OR².

credo (krē′dō) *n.* creed. Probably before 1200, the Apostles' Creed or the Nicene Creed, in *Ancrene Riwle;* borrowed from Latin *crēdō* I believe, 1st person singular present indicative of *crēdere* to believe, trust; see CREDIT. Doublet of CREED.

Credo is the first word of the Apostles' and Nicene Creeds in Latin; hence it became the name for either of these Creeds. The general sense "formula or statement of belief" is first recorded in 1587.

credulous *adj.* too ready to believe, easily deceived. 1576, borrowed from Latin *crēdulus* from *crēdere* to believe, see CREDIT; for suffix see -OUS. —**credulity** *n.* Probably before 1425 *credulite* readiness to believe; borrowed through Middle French *credulité* or directly from Latin *crēdulitātem* (nominative *crēdulitās*), from *crēdulus* credulous; for suffix see -ITY.

creed *n.* Before 1225 *crede,* developed from Old English (before 1000) *crēda* Christian article or statement of belief, such as the Apostles' Creed or Nicene Creed, from Latin *crēdō* I believe; see the doublet CREDO. The sense of any statement of belief or cherished opinion is first recorded in 1613, in Shakespeare's *Henry VIII.*

creek *n.* 1449 *creke* inlet; earlier in *Krekeset* (place name, 1198). Middle English *creke* is an alteration (by influence of Middle Dutch *kreke* creek) of the earlier *kryk* (1220-30), also found in place name *Sayercrik* (1160-80). The term was probably borrowed from a Scandinavian source (compare dialectal Swedish *krik* corner, bend, creek, cove, Old Icelandic *kriki* corner, nook, related to *krikr* bend, creek, and *krōkr* hook; see CROOK). The word in its form *crike,* in Middle English, may have been reinforced by Anglo-French *crique* (1386), from the Normans, who were of Scandinavian origin. The sense of small stream or brook, is first recorded in 1622, in American English, probably as an extension of the earlier meaning of a short arm or inlet of a river (1557), which is in itself an extension of the original meaning of inlet of a sea, estuary of a river, etc.

creel *n.* wicker basket. 1323-24 *crele,* borrowed perhaps from Old French **creïlle* (compare Middle French *crille* latticework, lattice), from Latin *crāticula,* diminutive of *crātis* wickerwork, lattice, HURDLE.

creep *v.* Probably before 1200 *crepen,* in Layamon's *Chronicle of Britain;* developed from Old English *crēopan* (about 899, in Alfred's translation of Boethius' *De Consolatione Philosophiae*). The Old English is cognate with Old Frisian *kriāpa* to creep, Middle Low German *krūpen,* Middle Dutch *crūpen,* Old Icelandic *krjūpa* (Danish *krybe,* Norwegian *krype,* and Swedish *krypa* to creep, from Proto-Germanic **kreupanan,* from Indo-European **greub-* (Pok.389). —**n.** 1818, a creeping motion, in Keats' *Endymion;* from the verb. The slang sense of a despicable person is first recorded in 1935, in American English, perhaps an extension of the earlier slang meaning of a robber or sneak thief (1914). —**creeper** *n.* 1440 *crepere,* in *Promptorium Parvulorum;* developed from Old English (before 1000) *crēopere* (*crēopan* to creep + *-ere* -er¹). The meaning of a plant that creeps along the ground or up a wall, is first recorded in 1626, in Francis Bacon's *Sylva Sylvarum.* —**creepy** *adj.* 1831, having a feeling of horror; earlier, having a creeping motion (1794), formed from English *creep* + *-y*¹.

cremate *v.* burn (a body) to ashes. 1874, probably a back formation in English of the earlier *cremation;* occasionally, perhaps also an artificial borrowing from Latin *cremātus,* past participle of *cremāre* to cremate, burn, and then possibly from Indo-European **k(e)r-em-* burn, extended from the root **ker-* as found in Old High German *herd,* Old English *heorth* hearth (Pok.572). —**cremation** *n.* 1623, borrowed from Latin *cremātiōnem* (nominative *cremātiō*), from *cremāre* to burn, cremate; for suffix see -TION. —**crematory** *n.* 1876, **crematorium** *n.* 1880, from New Latin *crematorium,* from Latin *cremātus* (past participle of *cremāre* cremate) + *-ōrium* -ory.

crenelated (kren′əlā′tid) *adj.* furnished with battlements. 1823, formed from English *crenel* one of the open spaces of a battlement (1481, from Middle French *crenel* notch, a diminutive form of Old French *cren* notch, fissure; see CRANNY) + *-ate*¹ + *d* in *-ed*². —**crenelation** *n.* 1849, formed from English *crenelate* + *-ation.*

Creole or **creole** (krē′ōl) *n.* 1697 *Cirole* a native of the West Indies, etc., of European or African descent; later *Creole* (1737); borrowed from French *créole,* from Spanish *criollo* person native to a locality, from Portuguese *crioulo,* diminutive of *cria* person (especially a servant) raised in one's house, from *criar* to raise or bring up, from Latin *creāre* to produce, CREATE.

In 1792 the word is recorded in American English as applied to a descendant of early French or Spanish settlers in Louisiana. The sense of a creolized language is first recorded in 1879.

—**adj.** 1748, from the noun.

—**creolize** *v.* 1818, to lounge or pass time quietly; later, to naturalize in the West Indies, etc. (1834); formed from English *creole* + *-ize.* A *creolized language* (1932) is a language developed from a mixture of two or more languages.

creosote (krē′əsōt) *n.* oily liquid used to preserve wood. 1835, borrowing of German *Kreosot,* from Greek *kreo-,* combining form of *kréas* flesh (see RAW) + *sōtḗr* savior, preserver, from *sṓizein* save, preserve, from *sôs* safe, earlier *sáwos,* from Indo-European **twə-wo-s* (Pok. 1080). According to the OED, the formation was supposed to mean "flesh saving" and was used in surgery and medicine as a powerful antiseptic, but was later replaced by the more cheaply-produced carbolic acid, its chief use now being as a wood preservative. —**v.** 1846, from the noun.

crepe (krāp) *n.* material with a crinkled surface. 1797, borrowed from French *crêpe,* from Old French *crespe,* from Latin *crispa,* feminine of *crispus* curled, CRISP.

The sense of a thin pancake, usually curled or rolled up before serving, is first recorded in 1877, and later in reference to *Suzette* (1907), as in the term *crêpe Suzette* (about 1922); now used chiefly in the plural *crepes* since about 1951.

—**crepe paper,** (1897; earlier *crepe tissue paper* 1895).

crescendo *n.* 1776, borrowed from Italian *crescendo* increasing, from Latin *crēscendō,* ablative case of the gerund of *crēscere* arise, grow; see CRESCENT. The figurative sense of an increase in force or effect, is first recorded in 1785. —**adj.** 1859, from the noun. —**v.** 1900, from the noun.

crescent *n.* 1399 *cressaunt* crescent-shaped ornament; later, crescent of the moon (before 1460); borrowed through Anglo-French *cressaunt,* from Middle French *creissant* growing (*creistre* to grow), from Latin *crēscentem* (nominative *crēscēns*), present participle of *crēscere* arise, grow, and related to *creāre* produce, make; cognate with Lithuanian *šérti* feed, and Greek *korésai* satiate, from Indo-European **k̑erə-/k̑orə-/k̑rē-* grow, nourish (Pok.577); for suffix see -ENT. The sense of referring to the shape of a waxing moon, apparently developed in medieval French, according to the OED.

cress *n.* any of various plants of the mustard family. Old English (before 700) *cresse, cressa, cærse;* cognate with Middle Low German *kerse, karse* cress, Middle Dutch *kersse* (modern Dutch *kers*), Old High German *kresso, kressa* (modern German *Kresse*). The shift of *r* (by metathesis) in Old English *cræse* and Middle Low German *karse,* is similar to that in GRASS.

Old English *cresse, cressa* is also cognate with Greek *grástis* green fodder, grass, *grân* to gnaw, (of animals) to eat, Sanskrit *grásati* (he) eats, devours, *grāsa-s* mouthful, fodder, and Old Icelandic *krās* dainty morsel, from Indo-European **gres-/gros-/gr̥s-/grēs-* (Pok.404).

cresset *n.* metal container to give light by burning oil or wood. 1370, borrowed from Old French *cresset, craisset,* alteration (influenced by *-et,* diminutive suffix) of *croisuel,* probably from northern Gallo-Romance *croceolus* kind of small lamp, from a Frankish word (compare Old Icelandic *krōkr* hook); see CROOK.

crest *n.* About 1312, replacing Old English *hrīs;* borrowed from Old French *creste* tuft, comb, summit, from Latin *crista* tuft or plume, related to *crīnis* hair, from pre-Latin **crisnis;* cognate with Old Frisian, Old Saxon, Old High German, and Old Icelandic *hrīs* twig, brush (wood), Old Prussian *craysi* stalk, *crays* hay, from Indo-European **kreis-/kris-* shake, swing (Pok.937). —**v.** About 1380, put a crest on, in *Sir Ferumbras;* from the noun. —**crestfallen** *adj.* (1589)

cretaceous (kritā′shəs) *adj.* chalky. About 1675, borrowed from Latin *crētāceus* chalky, from *crēta* chalk, see CRAYON; for suffix see -OUS. —**Cretaceous** *adj.* of or having to do with the geological period when flowering plants began to appear (1832). —*n.* 1851, from the adjective.

cretin *n.* person who is deformed and mentally deficient. 1779, borrowed from French *crétin,* from French Alpine dialect (probably of Savoy or Valais) *crétin* a kind of dwarfed and deformed idiot, from Vulgar Latin **christiānus,* from Latin *chrīstiānus* CHRISTIAN. In many Romance languages the equivalents of *Christian* have the general meaning of human being, but as a euphemism carry the sense of poor fellow. A parallel sense development is found in French *benêt* simpleton, from Old French *benoit* blessed, traced to the Gospel according to St. Matthew: "Blessed are the poor in spirit." —**cretinism** *n.* 1801, probably formed from English *cretin* + *-ism,* but reinforced by French *crétinisme.*

crevasse (krəvas′) *n.* deep crack or crevice in a glacier, the ground, etc. 1823, borrowed from French *crevasse,* from Old French *crevace* a burst or split; see the doublet CREVICE.

crevice *n.* narrow split or crack. About 1380 *crevace;* earlier *crevice* (probably about 1350) and *crevesse* (probably before 1350); borrowed from Old French *crevace,* from Vulgar Latin ***crepācea,* from Latin *crepāre* to crack, creak. According to the OED, the accent shifted to the first syllable during the 1300's, which allowed for the later adoption of the doublet CREVASSE.

crew *n.* About 1437 *crewe* group of soldiers, increase or reinforcement of a military force; borrowed from Middle French *crue,* from Old French *creüe* an increase, recruit, from feminine past participle of *creistre* grow, from Latin *crēscere;* see CRESCENT.

The sense of any group of people working or acting together, is first recorded in English in 1570.

—**v.** 1935, from the noun.

crewel *n.* embroidery done originally with worsted yarn. 1598; earlier, a thin worsted yarn (1494). The embroidery was repopularized in the 1860's, but the word is of unknown origin.

crib *n.* Old English (before 1000) *cribbe, crib* manger; cognate with Old Saxon *kribbia* manger, Old High German *krippa* (modern German *Krippe*), perhaps Old Icelandic *kjarf* bundle, and Sanskrit *grapsa-s* bundle, from Indo-European **grebh-* (Pok.386).

The sense of a child's bed, is first recorded in English in 1649.

—**v.** Before 1460, to eat from a manger; later to confine as in a crib (1605, in Shakespeare's *Macbeth*); from the noun. The sense of to steal, is first recorded in 1748, perhaps originating in thieves' slang, and of plagiarizing in 1778.

cribbage *n.* card game in which players keep score on a board fitted with movable pegs. 1630, probably formed from English *crib,* n. + *-age.* English *crib,* n. cards discarded by players into a dealer's pot, is not recorded before 1680, but this may be a simple defect in the record of English, as the meaning is probably a simple extension of *crib,* n.

crick *n.* painful muscular cramp. About 1424 *crikke,* of uncertain origin (perhaps imitative of the sudden check or spasm in a muscle).

cricket[1] *n.* insect of the grasshopper family. Before 1325 *criket;* earlier as a surname (1198); borrowed from Old French *criquet* a cricket, from *criquer* to creak rattle, crackle, of imitative origin; found also in Middle Dutch *crekel* (modern Dutch *krekel*) and Low German *Krekel* cricket.

cricket[2] *n.* a popular ball game of England, played with bats and wickets. 1598, apparently borrowed from Old French *criquet* goal post in game of bowls, stick, perhaps from Middle Dutch *cricke* stick, staff; cognate with, but not derived from, Old English *crycc* CRUTCH. The sense of fair play, good sportsmanship, is first recorded in English in 1851, apparently from the idea of how cricket should be properly played. —**v.** play cricket. About 1809, in Byron's *Letters and Journals;* from the noun.

crime *n.* About 1250 *cryme* sinfulness; later, offense punishable by law (1384, in the Wycliffe Bible); borrowed from Old French *crime, crimne,* from Latin *crīmen* (genitive *crīminis*) charge, indictment, offense, related to *cernere* to distinguish, decide, decree; see CERTAIN. —**criminal** *adj.* About 1400; borrowed through Middle French *criminel,* or directly from Latin *crīminālis* of or pertaining to crime, from *crīmen* (genitive *crīminis*) crime; for suffix see -AL[1]. —*n.* Before 1626, in Francis Bacon's writings; from the adjective.

crimp *v.* wrinkle or crumple minutely. 1698, to compress, curl, shrink; earlier, in a single use *crympen* be drawn together (before 1398, in Trevisa's translation of Bartholomew's *De Proprietatibus Rerum*); possibly originally developed from Old English *gecrympan* to crimp, curl, but generally agreed to have been reintroduced from Dutch or Low German *krimpen* to shrink, crimp, from Middle Dutch *crimpen* or Middle Low German *krimpen* to shrink, shrivel, crimp; cognate with Old Icelandic *kropna* draw together, from Indo-European **gremb-/grm̥b-* (Pok.387); see CRUMPLE. The word *crimplen* to wrinkle, shrivel up (about 1378, in a version of *Piers Plowman*) is associated with *crumple,* but may also have some connection with *crimp.* —**n.** 1863, American English, natural curl in wool fiber; from the verb.

crimson *n., adj.* deep red. 1416 *crymesyn, cremesin;* borrowed from early Spanish *cremesín,* early Italian *cremesino,* or directly from Medieval Latin *cremesinus,* all from Arabic *qirmazī* of or belonging to the kermes (insect from which a deep red dye was obtained). The adjective form in Arabic is from *qirmiz* kermes, which came probably through Persian from Sanskrit *kṛ́mi-s* worm. Related to CARMINE and parallel semantically with VERMILION. —**v.** make crimson. 1601, in Shakespeare's *Julius Caesar;* from the adjective.

cringe *v.* shrink or crouch in fear. Probably about 1200 *crengen* twist or bend, often haughtily; possibly in Old English **crengan,* a causative form derived from Old English *cringan* give way, fall (in battle), shrink into a bent position, draw oneself together. Old English *cringan* is the source of *crinkle* and possibly of *crank* and is cognate with Middle High German *krinc* ring, circle, *kranc* weak, frail (modern German *krank* sick), and Old Icelandic *kringr, kringla* ring, circle, *krangr* weak, frail, from Indo-European **grenk-/gronk-* (Pok.385). —**n.** 1597, from the verb.

crinkle *v.* wrinkle. About 1386 *krynkelen* turn or wind repeatedly, in Chaucer's *Legend of Good Women;* developed from the stem of Old English *crincan* to bend, yield; for suffix see -LE[3]. Old English *crincan* is cognate with Lithuanian *grįžti* go back, from Indo-European **grenĝ-* (Pok.386). —**n.** wrinkle. 1596, probably from the verb. An apparent noun form is found in Middle English place names, such as *Krinkelker* (1212).

crinoline (krin′əlin) *n.* stiff cloth used as a lining, etc. 1830, borrowed from French *crinoline* hair cloth, from Italian *crinolino* (*crino* horsehair, from Latin *crīnis* hair + *lino* flax, thread, from *līnum,* see LINEN; so called from the original mixture of these fibers).

cripple *n.* Probably about 1200 *crupel;* later *cripel* (about 1330), developed from Old English *crypel* (about 950), related to *cryppan* to crook, bend. The Old English *crypel* is cognate with Old Frisian *kreppel* cripple, Middle Dutch *cropel, crepel* (modern Dutch *kreupele*), Middle Low German *kroppel, kreppel,* Middle High German *krüppel* (modern German *Krüppel*), and Old Icelandic *kryppill* cripple from Proto-Germanic **krupilaz.* —**v.** Before 1250 *criplen* move or walk lamely, from Middle English *cripel,* n., cripple. The sense "make a cripple of, lame," is first recorded before 1325, and the figurative extension "to disable or impair," in 1694.

crisis *n.* Probably about 1425, turning point in a disease, in a translation of Chauliac's *Grande Chirurgie;* borrowed from Latin *crisis,* from Greek *krísis* a separating, discrimination, decision, from *krínein* to separate, decide, judge; see CERTAIN. The word appears in the first translation of Chauliac's as Old French *crise,* and in the second version as Latin *crisis,* which is the form that became established in English.

The sense of decisive moment, is first recorded in English in 1627 as a figurative extension of the original medical meaning.

crisp *adj.* **1** curly. Before 1325 *crisp* having a curled or fretted surface; earlier, *crips* (about 1300) and as a surname *Crips* (about 1200), *Crispe* (1279); developed from Old English (about 900) *crisp* curly; borrowed from Latin *crispus* curled, and cognate with Gaulish *Crixos* and Welsh *crych* curly, Middle High German *rispen* to curl, Old High German *hrispahi* bush (modern German *Rispe* panicle), from Indo-European **krisp-,* root **krei-s-* (Pok.937). **2** brittle. Before 1530, in Palsgrave's *Lesclarcissement,* origin uncertain; perhaps imitative of the sound made by things described as "crisp," such as the burning of dry sticks on a fire, or brittle food breaking between the teeth. The noun use in Middle English, as early as 1381, for a kind of crisp pastry is suggestive of a possible source for the adjective meaning of brittle. The sense of short or brisk in manner, is recorded in English in 1814. —**v. 1** to curl. Probably about 1390, from the adjective, though possibly influenced by Old French *crespir* and Latin *crispāre* to curl. **2** to make or become brittle. 1805, from the adjective. —**crispy** *adj.* **1** curly (before 1398). **2** brittle (1611). Both senses from English *crisp* + *-y*[1].

crisscross *v.* 1818, in Keats' *Life and Letters,* alteration of Middle English *Crist-crosse* (about 1475) and earlier *Cros-Kryst* (probably about 1390) referring to the mark of a cross formerly written before the alphabet in hornbooks. The mark itself stood for the phrase *Crist-cross me speed* ("May Christ's cross give me success"), a formula said before reciting the alphabet. Now that the earlier associations are lost, the word is often thought to be a mere reduplication of *cross* similar to *mishmash.* —**adj.** 1846, in Hawthorne's *Mosses from an Old Manse,* from the verb. —**n.** 1848, American English, the game of tick-tack-toe, from the verb. The sense of a transverse crossing, is first recorded in 1876, and of a network of intersecting lines, in 1881.

criterion (krītir′ēən) *n.* yardstick, standard. 1661, borrowed from Greek *kritḗrion* means for judging, standard, from *kritḗs* judge; see CRITIC. Earlier, the word is recorded in English spelled with the Greek letters (1613, 1622, etc.). The Latinized form *criterium* is recorded before 1631, in Donne's writings, and was used occasionally until the late 1800's.

critic *n.* 1588, one who passes judgment, in Shakespeare's *Love's Labour's Lost;* later, one who judges the merits of books, plays, etc. (1605, in Francis Bacon's *Of the Advancement of Learning*); borrowed from Middle French *critique,* learned borrowing from Latin *criticus* literary critic, from Greek *kritikós* one who is able to judge, noun use of adjective, from *krités* judge, from *krínein* to separate, decide, judge, see CERTAIN; for suffix see -IC. —**adj.** 1544, relating to the crisis of a disease, etc.; later, skillful in judging literary or artistic work; borrowed from Latin *criticus* literary critic, from Greek *kritikós* critical. —**critical** *adj.* 1590, given to passing judgment, in Shakespeare's *Midsummer Night's Dream,* formed in English from Latin *criticus,* from Greek *kritikós* able to judge + English *-al*[1]. The sense "of the nature of a crisis, decisive, crucial," is first recorded in English in 1649, influenced by now obsolete English *critic,* adj. and Late Latin *criticus* (in medical use) decisive, critical, from Greek *kritikós* suitable for deciding, able to judge. —**criticism** *n.* 1607, in Thomas Dekker's *A Knights Conjuring,* formed from English *critic* + *-ism.* —**criticize** *v.* 1649, in Milton's *Eiconoclastes,* formed from English *critic* + *-ize.*

critique (kritēk′) *n.* critical essay or review. 1702, in Addison's *Dialogue upon the Usefulness of Ancient Medals,* alteration of earlier *critick* art of criticism (1656) and essay in criticism (1709); borrowed from French *critique,* from Greek *kritikḕ technḗ* the critical art, feminine of *kritikós* critical, able to judge; see CRITIC. After Addison introduced *critique,* Pope altered *critick* to *critique* in *The Dunciad* (1729). Thereafter Cowper, Byron, and others popularized *critique,* though dictionaries to the end of the 1700's kept *critick* until Todd's 1818 edition of Johnson's *Dictionary* introduced *critique.* The pronunciation in the French manner appeared in 1815, replacing (krit′ik) associated with the old spelling. —**v.** write a critique upon, review, criticize. 1751, from the noun.

croak *v.* 1547, from Middle English *crok* (before 1460), *crouken* (before 1325), perhaps imitative, but possibly developed from Old English *crāc(ettan)* to croak; cognate with early modern German *krachitzen* to cry hoarsely (modern German *krächzen)* and related to Old English *cracian* make a sharp noise, CRACK. —**n.** 1561, deep hoarse cry; from the verb.

crochet (krōshā′) *n.* knitting done with a hooked needle. 1846, borrowed from French *crochet,* from Old French *crochet,* diminutive of *croche, croc* hook, from a Germanic source (compare Old Icelandic *krōkr* hook; see CROOK). Doublet of CROQUET and CROTCHET. —**v.** knit with a hooked needle. 1858, from the noun.

crock *n.* Old English (about 1000) *crocc, crocca;* related to *crūce* pitcher, and cognate with Old Frisian *krocha* pot, Old Saxon *krūka,* Middle Dutch *crūke* (modern Dutch *kruik*), Middle High German *krūche* pot, Old High German *kruog* pitcher (modern German *Krug*), and Old Icelandic *krukka* (Danish, Norwegian *krukke,* and Swedish *kruka)* pot, from Proto-Germanic **krōgu-,* ultimately from Indo-European **greu-g-* (Pok.389). —**crockery** *n.* 1719, formed from English *crock* + *-ery.*

crocodile *n.* 1563, alteration (influenced by Latin *crocodilus*) of Middle English *cokedrille* (probably before 1300, in *Kyng Alisaunder*); borrowed from Old French *cocodrille,* from Medieval Latin *cocodrillus,* itself an alteration of Latin *crocodīlus,* from Greek *krokódīlos* crocodile, lizard, probably a non-Greek word of unknown origin, but by folk etymology, meaning literally pebbleworm (*krókē* pebble, cognate with Sanskrit *śárkarā* gravel + *drîlos* earthworm).

crocus *n.* Before 1398, in Trevisa's translation of Bartholomew's *De Proprietatibus Rerum;* borrowed through Old French *crocus,* or directly from Latin *crocus,* from Greek *krókos* saffron, crocus, from a Semitic source (compare Hebrew *karkōm* crocus, saffron, Aramaic *kurkĕmā* saffron, and Arabic *kurkum* saffron).

croissant (krwäsäɴ′) *n.* 1899, borrowed as French *croissant* crescent-shaped roll, crescent, from *croissant* growing (as of a waxing moon), present participle of *croître* grow, from Old French *creistre,* from Latin *crēscere;* see CRESCENT.

Cro-Magnon (krōmag′non) *adj.* designating a pre-historic people of western Europe. 1869, borrowing of the name of a cave in the Dordogne department of France, where the first remains were found in 1868.

crone *n.* shrunken old woman. About 1390, in Chaucer's *Canterbury Tales;* earlier, as a surname *Hopcrone* (1323-24); borrowed through Anglo-French *carogne,* as a term of abuse, from Old North French *carogne, caroigne* cantankerous woman, literally, CARRION. According to the OED, the term was rare in English until it was revived by Southey, Scott, and their contemporaries. Both MED and OED refer to a meaning "old ewe," but question it as a transferred sense.

crony *n.* very close friend, chum. 1665 *chrony,* in Pepys' *Diary,* said to be originally a term of college or university slang, perhaps as a borrowing from Greek *chrónios* lasting, from *chrónos* time.

crook *n.* hook, bend, or curve. Probably before 1200 *crok,* borrowed from a Scandinavian source (compare Old Icelandic *krōkr* hook, Danish *krog,* Norwegian, Swedish *krok*); cognate with Old High German *krācho* hooked tool, from Indo-European* *grēg-/grōg-* (Pok. 385).

The figurative sense of a person who is crooked, a swindler or criminal, is first recorded in 1879 in American English.

—**v.** Probably before 1200 *croken* to bend, curve; apparently from *crok,* n.

—**crooked** *adj.* Probably before 1200 *croked* bent, curved, in *Ancrene Riwle;* formed in part from the past participle of *croken* to crook, and in part from *crok* crook + *-ed,* as in *hunched,* etc. The figurative sense of dishonest, not straightforward, is first recorded in 1708, in American English.

croon *v.* hum, sing, or murmur in a low tone. Probably about 1400 *crownen;* later, *croynen* (about 1460), borrowed from Middle Dutch *krōnen* to lament, mourn, groan; cognate with Old High German *krōnan* to chatter, prattle, of imitative origin.

crop *n.* Old English (about 700) *cropp* rounded head or top of an herb, sprout; later, craw of a bird (about 1000); cognate with Old High German *kropf* swelling on a bird's throat, craw of a bird (modern German *Kropf*), Old Icelandic *kroppr* (Danish *krop,* Norwegian, Swedish *kropp)* body, from Indo-European **grub-* (Pok.389).

The sense of the produce of a field, harvest, is first recorded about 1300.

—**v.**Probably before 1200 *croppen* remove the top of a plant, in *Ancrene Riwle;* from the noun. The general meaning of cut off is first recorded probably before 1440.

croquet (krōkā′) *n.* game played with wooden balls and mallets. 1858, borrowed from Northern French dialect *croquet* hockey stick, from Old North French *croquet* shepherd's crook, originally variant of Old French *crochet;* see the doublet CROCHET.

croquette (krōket′) *n.* small mass of chopped meat, fish, etc., coated with crumbs and fried. 1706 *croquet,* borrowed from French *croquette* (*croquer* to crunch, of imitative origin + *-ette* -ette).

Curiously, the earliest recorded form of *croquette* in French is in 1740, more than three decades after its appearance in English.

crosier (krō′zhər) *n.* ornamental staff carried by a bishop. 1203 *crozer;* later *crosier* (1483) having several meanings: one who carries a cross before a prelate, one who carries the pastoral staff or crook of a bishop or other prelate, and (about 1400, in writings of Wycliffe) *crocer* the pastoral staff itself; borrowed through Anglo-French *crosser,* from Old French *crosier, crocier* crook bearer, from *crosse, croce* hook, pastoral staff, from a Frankish word (compare Old High German *krucka* CRUTCH); for suffix see -IER. The meaning of one who carries a cross before a prelate, is borrowed from Old French *croisier,* from *crois* CROSS.

cross *n.* Old English (963-84) *cros,* replacing earlier Old English *rōd,* and borrowed from Old Irish *cros* (probably through Scandinavian; compare Old Icelandic *kross*), from Latin *crux* (genitive *crucis*) stake, cross; originally, a tall, round pole; cognate with Sanskrit *krúñcati* (it) curves, Welsh *crug* knoll, Old Icelandic *hryggr* backbone, Old English *hrycg* spine, top, from Indo-European *krouk-/kruk-* (Pok.938). Doublet of CRUX.

Other forms of the word are also recorded in English: Old English *crūc,* borrowed from Latin *crucem,* and Middle English *croiz, crois,* borrowed through Anglo-French *cros,* and from Old French *croiz, crois,* but these Middle English forms became obsolete after 1450. —**v.** Probably before 1200 *crossen* make the sign of the cross over, in *Ancrene Riwle;* from the noun. The sense of to cancel by drawing lines across, strike out, is first recorded in 1443, in *Proceedings of the Privy Council,* and that of go across, probably before 1400. —**adj.** 1523, from the noun and elliptical use of the earlier adverb (probably before 1400). The sense of ill-tempered, peevish, is first recorded in 1639, from the earlier sense of contrary, opposed to (1565).
—**crossbar** *n.* (1466) —**crossbow** *n.* (1415) —**cross-examination** *n.* (1827) —**cross-examine** *v.* (1664) —**cross-eyed** *adj.* (1791) —**crossing** *n.* (probably before 1425) —**cross-purposes** *n.pl.* (1666, in Pepys' *Diary*). —**cross-question** *v.* (1769); *n.* (before 1694). —**crossroad** *n.* (1719) —**cross street** (1661, American English) —**crossways** *adj., adv.* (1300) —**crosswise** *adv.* (about 1410) —**crossword puzzle** (1914)

crotch *n.* forked piece or part. 1539, fork, probably in part a variant of CRUTCH, and in part a variant of *croche* crook, crosier, borrowed from Old North French *croche* shepherd's crook, variant of *croc* hook; see CROCHET.

The word is recorded in English before 1592 for the part of the body where the legs meet.

crotchet (kroch′it) *n.* odd notion or whim. Probably about 1395, architectural ornament usually in the form of curled leaves; borrowed from Old French *crochet,* diminutive of *croche, croc* hook; see the doublet CROCHET.

The sense "whim or fancy" appeared in 1573, perhaps influenced by the idea of a mental twist or crook, although Cotgrave (1611) connects it with the musical quarter note (1440), citing the saying "his head is full of crotchets."
—**crotchety** *adj.* 1825, formed from English *crotchet* + *-y*[1].

crouch *v.* stoop low. Probably about 1395; probably borrowed from Old French *crochir* become bent, crooked, from *croche* hook; see CROCHET, but it is suggested that *crouch* may be a blend of *couchen* lie down and *croken* bend, bow. —**n.** 1597, from the verb.

croup[1] (krüp) *n.* disease of the throat and windpipe. 1765, noun use of obsolete verb *croup* to cry hoarsely, croak (1513); probably of imitative origin. —**croupy** *adj.* 1834, formed from English *croup* + *-y*[1].

croup[2] (krüp) *n.* rump of a horse, etc. Probably before 1300 *croupe,* in *Arthour and Merlin,* borrowed from Old French *croupe, crope,* from a Frankish word (compare Old High German *kropf* swelling on a bird's throat; see CROP).

croupier (krü′pēər) *n.* 1707, person who stands behind and assists a game player; borrowed from French, from *croupe,* originally, one who rides behind on the CROUP[2] (of a horse, etc.). The meaning of attendant at a gambling table, is first recorded in 1731.

crouton (krü′ton) *n.* small piece of toast used as a garnish in soups, salads, etc. 1806, borrowed from French *croûton* small piece of toasted or fried bread, from *croûte* crust, from Old French *crouste;* see CRUST.

crow[1] *v.* make a cry of a rooster. About 1250 *crowen,* developed from Old English (about 1000) *crāwan;* cognate with Old High German *krāen* to crow (modern German *krähen*), and Old Slavic *grajati* to crow, all ultimately from the Indo-European base ***grā-**, ***grāg-** (Pok.384); of imitative origin; see CRANE.

The figurative sense to show one's happiness and pride, is first recorded in English in 1522.
—**n.** cry of a rooster. Probably before 1200 *crau;* later *crowe,* from *crowen* to crow.

crow[2] *n.* large glossy black bird. About 1250 *crowe,* in *The Owl and the Nightingale;* earlier, as a surname (1188); developed from Old English (before 700) *crāwe;* cognate with Old High German *krāwa* crow (modern German *Krähe*), Old Saxon *krāia,* and Old Icelandic *krāka* crow, *krākr* raven (Danish *krage,* Norwegian *kråke,* and Swedish *kråka* crow); derived from the Proto-Germanic root of Old English *crāwan* CROW[1].
—**crowbar** *n.* 1748, in American English; formed from English *crow* bar of iron used as a lever (before 1400) + *bar.* —**crow's-feet** *n.* About 1385, in Chaucer's *Troilus and Criseyde.* —**crow's-nest** *n.* 1818, a small lookout near the top of a ship's mast; earlier, the nest of a crow (probably before 1300).

crowd *v.* About 1380 *crouden* to push, jostle, crowd, in Chaucer's *House of Fame;* earlier, to press on, hurry (probably about 1225); developed from Old English *crūdan* to press, drive, hasten (937, in the *Anglo-Saxon Chronicle*). The Old English is cognate with Middle Dutch *crūden* to press, push, Middle High German *kroten* to press, oppress, Norwegian *kryda* to crowd, and Old Irish *gruth* curds, from Indo-European *greut-/grūt-/grut- (Pok.406). —**n.** 1567, large number of people pressing against each other, throng; from the verb, and replacing earlier *press.*

crown *n.* 1111 *coronan* royal crown; later *crune* wreath placed on the head of a victor, diadem, royal crown (probably before 1200, in *Ancrene Riwle*), and *croune* (1300); borrowed through Anglo-French *coroune,* from Old North French *curune* (Old French *corone*), from Latin *corōna* wreath, garland, crown, from Greek *korṓnē* anything curved, kind of crown; cognate with Latin *curvus* curved; see CURVE. Doublet of CORONA. The two forms *crune, coroune* existed together in Middle English but only the shortened or syncopated *crune, crown* survived after the 1500's. —**v.** Probably before 1200 *crunen* place a crown on the head of (a person), in *Ancrene Riwle;* borrowed through Anglo-French *corouner,* from Old French *coroner,* from Latin *corōnāre,* from *corōna* crown. —**crowning** *adj.* 1611, that crowns or bestows a crown, in the King James Bible; later, that makes perfect or complete (1651, in correspondence of Oliver Cromwell).

crucial *adj.* 1706, cross-shaped, as of an incision in the body; borrowing of French *crucial* (used as a medical term), from Latin *crux* (genitive *crucis*) CROSS; for suffix see -AL[1]. The sense of decisive, critical, is first recorded in 1830 and was a translation of Francis Bacon's phrase *instantia crucis* crucial instance (1620, in Bacon's *Novum Organum*), the Latin word *crucis* referring to the cross-signpost at a fork in a road at which point one must make a decision.

crucible *n.* container in which metals, ores, etc. can be melted; melting pot. Probably before 1425 *crusible;* borrowed from Medieval Latin *crucibulum* melting pot for metals, originally a night lamp, possibly Latinization of a Romance word like Old French *croisuel;* see CRESSET.

The figurative sense of a severe test or trial, is first recorded about 1645, in allusion to the melting pot, which must endure great heat in order to fuse metals.

crucify *v.* Before 1325 *crucifien* put to death by nailing or tying to a cross, in *Cursor Mundi;* borrowed from Old French *crucifier,* from Vulgar Latin **crucificāre* replacing Late Latin *crucifigere,* literally, fasten to a cross (*crucī,* dative of Latin *crux* CROSS + *figere* fasten; see DIKE); for suffix see -FY.

The figurative sense of to torment is first recorded in English in 1621.

—**crucifix** *n.* cross with the figure of Christ crucified. Probably before 1200, in *Ancrene Riwle;* borrowed through Old French *crucifix,* or directly from Late Latin *crucifixus,* from past participle of *crucifigere* crucify. —**crucifixion** *n.* act of crucifying. Before 1410, borrowed from Late Latin *crucifixiōnem* (nominative *crucifixiō*), from *crucifigere* crucify; for suffix see -ION.

crude *adj.* About 1395, in a raw state, unrefined, in Chaucer's *Canterbury Tales;* borrowed from Latin *crūdus* rough, RAW.

The extended sense of rude, lacking grace or refinement, is first recorded in English in 1650.

—**crudity** *n.* Probably before 1325 *crudite,* borrowed through Middle French *crudité* or directly from Latin *crūditātem* (nominative *crūditās*), from *crūdus* crude; for suffix see -ITY.

cruel *adj.* Probably before 1200, severe, strict, in *Ancrene Riwle;* later pitiless, heartless (about 1300); borrowed from Old French *cruel,* from Latin *crūdēlem* morally rough, unfeeling, cruel, related to *crūdus* rough, RAW. —**cruelty** *n.* Probably before 1200 *cruelte,* in *Ancrene Riwle;* borrowed from Old French *cruelté,* from Latin *crūdēlitātem* (nominative *crūdēlitās*), from *crūdēlem* cruel; for suffix see -TY[2].

cruet (krü'it) *n.* glass bottle to hold vinegar, oil, etc. About 1300, a church vessel to hold wine or water; borrowed possibly through Anglo-French *cruet,* or directly from Old French *cruet,* diminutive of *cruie* pot, from a Frankish word (compare Middle High German *krūche* pot; see CROCK).

cruise *v.* sail about. 1651, borrowed from Dutch *kruisen* to cross, sail crossing to and fro, from *kruis* cross, from Latin *crux* CROSS. —**n.** 1706, act of cruising; from the verb. —**cruiser** *n.* 1695, ship that cruises, privateer; borrowed from Dutch *kruiser,* from *kruisen* to cruise; for suffix see -ER[1]. An earlier use *crosier, croiser* (1679) refers to pirates, perhaps from French *croiseur* ship and captain, which may have influenced the noun use in English.

cruller (krul'ər) *n.* twisted doughnut. 1805, American English; borrowed apparently from Dutch *kruller,* from *krullen* to curl, from Middle Dutch *crullen;* see CURL.

crumb *n.* About 1150 *crume* a small bit of bread, developed from Old English *cruma* (about 975); cognate with Middle Dutch *crūme* crumb (modern Dutch *kruim*), Middle Low German *krōme,* Middle High German *krume* (modern German *Krume*); also Albanian *grimɛ* crumb, Greek *grȳ́mēā, grȳmeíā* rubbish, trash, riffraff, and Latin *grūmus* little heap, mound, from Indo-European **grum-/grūm-* what is scratched together (Pok.388)

The final *b* began to be added to Middle English *crume* about 1450, by analogy with Old English words such as *dumb.*

—**crumby** or **crummy** *adj.* 1767 *crumby* like crumbs; 1579 *crummy* like crumbs, earlier, easily crumbled (1567); formed from English *crum(b)* + *-y*[1]. The slang sense of inferior, disagreeable, is first recorded in 1859.

crumble *v.* break into crumbs. 1577, variant (probably influenced by the new spelling *crumb*) of earlier *kremelen* (about 1475); developed from Old English **crymelan,* a frequentative form of *gecrymman* to break into crumbs, from *cruma* crumb; for suffix see -LE[3]. An analogous form is also found in Dutch *kruimelen,* German *krümeln,* and Low German *krömeln* to crumble.

crumpet *n.* small cake baked on a griddle and toasted. 1769; earlier, a thin griddlecake (1694); perhaps developed from *crompid cake* wafer, literally, curled-up cake (1382, in the Wycliffe Bible, and a variant of *cramcake*), from *crompid,* past participle of *crumpen* curl up; see CRUMPLE.

crumple *v.* crush together, wrinkle. Before 1325 *crumplen,* in *Cursor Mundi,* apparently a frequentative form of *crumpen* to curl up; developed from Old English (before 800) *crump* bent, crooked; cognate with Old Icelandic *kropna* draw together, *krappr* narrow (*-pp-* from *-mp-*), see CRAMP[1] bent bar; for suffix see -LE[3].

The cognates cited are from the Indo-European root **gremb-/gromb-/gr̥mb-;* others traditionally cited with Old English *crumb* crooked, include Old Saxon *crumb* crooked, Old High German *krump* (modern German *krumm*) and Latvian *grumbt* become wrinkled, from the Indo-European root **grup-* or **gru(m)b-*.

crunch *v.* 1814, alteration of earlier *craunch* (1631), probably of imitative origin, but perhaps influenced by *crush, munch.* **—n.** 1836, in Marryat's *Mr. Midshipman Easy;* from the verb. The sense of a critical point or crisis was popularized by Winston Churchill, whose use of it was first recorded in 1939. **—crunchy** *adj.* 1892, formed from English *crunch,* v. + *-y*[1].

crupper *n.* strap attached to the back of a harness and passing under a horse's tail. About 1330 *cropper;* borrowed perhaps through Anglo-French *cropere* from Old French *cropiere,* from *crope* CROUP[2] rump; for suffix see -ER[1].

crusade *n.* 1706, historical military expedition of Christians to recover the Holy Land, alteration of earlier *croisade* (1577), influenced by the stem *cruz-* of Spanish *cruzada.* In the 1500's early modern English *croisade* was borrowed from Middle French *croisade,* alteration of Old French *croisee* crusade, also influenced by Spanish *cruzada* in adapting the suffix *-ada* to Middle French *-ade.* Old French *croisee* from *crois* cross, derived from Latin *crux;* Spanish *cruzada,* literally, a marking with the cross, derived from the feminine past participle of *cruzar,* from Medieval Latin *cruciare,* from Latin *crux* (genitive *crucis*) CROSS.

The Middle English forms *croiserie, creiserie* (about 1300) were borrowed from Old French *croiserie* and were replaced by *croisade* in the 1500's.

The figurative sense of an aggressive movement or campaign against some public evil, is first recorded in 1786, in Jefferson's writings.

—v. 1732, engage in a crusade; from the noun.

—crusader *n.* 1743, formed from English *crusade* + *-er*[1], and replacing earlier *croisader,* borrowed from, or imitative of, French *croisadeur.*

crush *v.* Before 1349 *crowsen;* later, *cruschen* (probably before 1400); borrowed from Old French *croissir, cruissir* to crash, smash, from a Frankish word (compare Gothic *kriustan,* Old Swedish *krȳsta,* both meaning to gnash), from Indo-European **greus-* (Pok.405). **—n.** 1599, act of crushing; earlier, *crusche* a crash (before 1338, in Mannyng's *Chronicle of England*); from the verb.

crust *n.* Probably before 1325, hard outer part of bread; borrowed through Old French *crouste,* or directly from Latin *crusta* rind, crust, shell. Latin *crusta* is cognate with Greek *krýstallos* ice, Old Icelandic *hriōsa* to shudder, and Old High German *hroso* ice, from Indo-European **kreus-/krus-* (Pok.621).

The geological sense of the outer portion of the earth, is first recorded in English in 1555.

—v. cover with crust. Before 1382, in the Wycliffe Bible; borrowed from Old French *crouster,* from *crouste* crust.**—crusty** *adj.* Before 1400, formed from English *crust,* n. + *-y*[1].

crustacean (krustā'shən) *n.* any of a class of water animals with hard shells, jointed bodies and appendages. 1835, formed in English from New Latin *Crustacea* the name of this class of animals (introduced in 1801 by Lamarck), from neuter plural of *crustaceus* having a hard shell (from Latin *crusta* shell, CRUST) + English *-an.* **—adj.** 1858, from the noun. The use of the word was preceded in English by *crustaceous* (1646).

crutch *n.* staff to support a lame or disabled person. Probably before 1200 *crucche,* in Layamon's *Chronicle of Britain;* developed from Old English (about 900) *cryc;* cognate with Old Saxon *krukka* crutch, Middle Dutch *crucke,* Old High German *krucka* (modern German *Krücke*), from Proto-Germanic **krukjō,* from Indo-European **gru-g-,* root **greu-g* (Pok.389).

The figurative sense of a prop or support is first recorded in English in 1602.

—v. 1642, from the noun.

crux *n.* essential part, main point. 1718, used by Sheridan and Swift in the sense of a difficulty, riddle, puzzling question, probably shortened from the Medieval Latin phrase *crux interpretum* interpreters' cross, torment of interpreters, from Latin *crux* (genitive *crucis*) cross; see the doublet CROSS. The extended sense of the critical or central point is first recorded in 1888.

cry *v.* Probably before 1200 *crien* beg, implore, in *Ancrene Riwle;* borrowed from Old French *crier,* from Vulgar Latin **crītāre,* from Latin *quirītāre* cry out, wail, of uncertain origin (folk etymology refers to a meaning of to implore the aid of the *Quirītēs* or Roman citizens, plural of *Quirīs* Roman citizen, originally with the meaning of citizen of the Sabine town of *Curēs*).

The meaning of make a noise of grief or pain is first recorded about 1280. In this sense *cry* has replaced *weep* in everyday speech.

—n. About 1280, borrowed from Old French *cri,* from Vulgar Latin **crītum,* from **crītāre* to cry.**—crier** *n.* 1221, as a surname *Criur;* later *crior, criour* an officer who makes public announcements, town crier (probably about 1350); and *crier* (before 1387); borrowed from Old French *criere,* from *crier,* v. **—crybaby** *n.* (1851, American English) **—crying** *n.* (probably before 1300); *adj.* Before 1398, shouting or roaring; later, demanding attention, very bad (1607).

cryo- a combining form meaning very cold, freezing, very low temperature, as in *cryobiology* (study of the effects of freezing on living things), *cryogenic, cryonics.* Borrowed from Greek *kryo-,* combining form of *krýos* icy cold, related to *kryerós* chilling, cognate with Sanskrit *krūrá-s* raw, cruel, and Lettish *kruvesis* frozen mud, from Indo-European **kruw-es-* (Pok.622). *Cryo-* has become very productive in science and technology since the 1960's.

cryogenic (krī'əjen'ik) *adj.* having to do with the production of very low temperatures. 1902, formed from English *cryo-* freezing + *-genic* having to do with production.

crypt *n.* 1667, in John Evelyn's *Diary;* borrowed through French *crypte,* or directly from Latin *crypta* vault, cavern, from Greek *kryptḗ,* feminine of *kryptós* hidden, from *krýptein* to hide, cognate with Old Slavic *kryti* to hide, from Indo-European **kru-bh-,* **krū-* (Pok.616). Doublet of GROTTO. An earlier isolated instance of this word is recorded as *cripte* a grotto or cavern (probably before 1425, in a translation of Higden's *Polychronicon*), borrowed from Latin *crypta.* **—cryptic** *adj.* having a hidden meaning. Before 1638, borrowed from Late Latin *crypticus,* from Greek *kryptikós,* from *kryptós* hidden; for suffix see -IC.

crypto- or **crypt-** (before vowels) a combining form meaning: **1** hidden, secret, as in *cryptogram = secret writing,* or *cryptology = the study of secret writing.* **2** secretly, disguised, not open or acknowledged, as in *crypto-fascist = secretly fascist.* Borrowed from Greek *kryptós* secret, hidden; see CRYPT.

cryptography *n.* writing in secret codes or ciphers. 1658, borrowed from French *cryptographie* (from Greek *kryptós* hidden + *-graphiā* writing, -graphy). **—cryptogram** *n.* something written in a secret code or cipher. 1880, probably formed from English *crypto* + *-gram.*

crystal *n.* Old English *cristal* clear ice, transparent mineral (about 1000, in Ælfric's writings); borrowed from Old French *cristal,* learned borrowing from Latin *crystallum* ice, crystal, from Greek *krýstallos* ice, rock crystal (so called from its resemblance to ice, of which it is supposed to be a modified and permanent form); see CRUST. Between the 1400's and 1600's the English spelling gradually adopted the Latin form *crystal.* **—adj.** Probably about 1380, composed of crystal; from the noun. **—crystalline** *adj.* Before 1398 *cristalline,* in Trevisa's translation of Bartholomew's *De Proprietatibus Rerum;* borrowed from Old French *cristalin* like crystal, and directly as a learned borrowing from Latin *crystallinus,* from Greek *krystállinos* of crystal, from *krýstallos;* see CRYSTAL. **—crystallization** *n.* 1665, formed from English *crystallize* + *-ation.* **—crystallize** *v.* 1598, formed from English *crystal* + *-ize.*

cub *n.* young fox, bear, lion, etc. 1530 *cubbe* young fox, in Palsgrave's *Lesclarcissement;* of unknown origin, but perhaps cognate with Old Icelandic *kobbi* seal, *-kubbi* block, lump; see COB[1] corncob, and possibly related to Old Irish *cuib* cub, whelp, *cū* dog; see HOUND. The native English word for *cub* is *whelp.*

cubbyhole *n.* 1825, of uncertain origin; possibly formed from English *cub* pen, coop, hutch (1546) + *-y*[2] + *hole,* and perhaps related to, or influenced by, *cuddy* small room, closet, cupboard (1793; earlier, small cabin on a boat, 1660).

cube *n.* solid with six equal, square sides. 1551, borrowed through Middle French *cube,* or directly from Latin *cubus,* from Greek *kýbos* cube, a hollow above the hips of cattle; see HIP[1] haunch. The mathematical sense of the third power of a quantity, is first recorded in 1557. **—v.** 1588, raise to the third power, find the cube of; borrowed from Middle French *cuber,* from *cube,* n., and replacing earlier *cubicen* (before 1500), from earlier *cubik,* adj. (before 1500). The sense of cut into cubes, is first recorded in 1947. **—cubic** *adj.* Before 1500, borrowed from Middle French *cubique,* from Latin *cubicus,* from Greek *kybikós,* from *kýbos* cube; for suffix see -IC. **—cubical** *adj.* Before 1500, probably formed from English *cubic* + *-al*[1]. **—cubism** *n.* art characterized by the use of cubes and other geometric shapes. 1911, borrowed from French *cubisme* (coined in 1908, reportedly by a member of the Hanging Committee of the Salon des Indépendants in Paris), from French *cube* cube + *-isme* -ism. **—cubist** *n.* 1911, borrowed from French *cubiste,* from *cube* + *-iste* -ist.

cubicle *n.* very small room or compartment. About 1450, bedroom, borrowed from Latin *cubiculum,* from *cubāre* to lie down, (originally) bend oneself; see HIP[1] haunch. The word in its original sense of "bedroom" became obsolete in the 1500's, but it was reintroduced in the 1800's, especially in English public schools, for a small sleeping compartment in a dormitory; from this evolved the current sense (attested since 1926) of any small compartment or partitioned space.

cubit *n.* ancient measure of length. Before 1338, in Mannyng's *Chronicle of England;* borrowed from Latin *cubitum* elbow, cubit, distance from the elbow to the end of the middle finger, related to *cubāre* to lie down, be lying; see HIP[1] haunch. For the sense development, compare ELL[1] measure of length.

cuckold (kuk′əld) *n.* husband of an unfaithful wife. About 1250 *kukeweld,* in *The Owl and the Nightingale;* apparently borrowed from Old French *cucuault* cuckold, from *cucu* CUCKOO + pejorative suffix *-ault;* supposedly so called either because the female cuckoo changes mates frequently or because she lays her eggs in the nests of other birds. **—v.** make a cuckold of. 1589, from the noun.

cuckoo *n.* Before 1300 *cuccu* cry of the cuckoo bird, the bird itself; earlier, as a surname *Kuku* (1191); borrowed from or influenced by Old French *cucu,* which is of imitative origin, like Middle Dutch *cucūc* (modern Dutch *koekoek*), Middle Low German *kukuk* (modern German *Kuckuck*), Latin *cucūlus,* Greek *kókkȳx* (genitive *kókkȳgos*), and Sanskrit *kokilá-s* **—adj.** 1627, from the noun. The slang sense of crazy, silly, is first recorded in 1918 in American English, from the earlier noun meaning of a foolish or stupid person (1581), probably so called in reference to the bird's monotonous call, and its habit of laying eggs in the nests of other birds.

cucumber *n.* About 1384 *cucumer,* in the Wycliffe Bible; later *cucumber* (probably 1440); borrowed from Old French *cocombre, coucombre,* from Latin *cucumerem,* accusative of *cucumis* cucumber or a sea plant of similar color and odor, perhaps of Mediterranean origin. Compare GOURD.

cud *n.* Probably about 1200 *cude* food that cattle and similar animals return to the mouth to rechew, in *The Ormulum;* earlier, gum or resin; developed from Old English (about 1000) *cudu,* earlier *cwidu, cwudu* cud or tree resin. The Old English is cognate with Old High German *quiti, kuti* glue, Middle High German *küte, küt* cement (modern German *Kitt* cement, putty), Old Icelandic *kvātha* (Norwegian *kvae,* Swedish *kåda*) resin, Old Danish *kvade* birch sap, Middle Irish *beithe, bethe* box tree, Welsh *bedw* birch, Latin *bitūmen* asphalt, and Sanskrit *játu* lac, gum, from Indo-European **gwētu, *gwēt-* (Pok.480).

cuddle *v.* About 1520 *cudle,* implied in *cudlyng* in a song but not found again until 1719; apparently a dialectal word of nursery or baby-talk origin. **—cuddlesome** *adj.* 1876, formed from English *cuddle* + *-some*[1]. **—cuddly** *adj.* 1863, in Charles Kingsley's *The Water-Babies,* formed from English *cuddle* + *-y*[1].

cudgel *n.* short thick stick used as a weapon; club. Probably before 1200 *cuggel,* in *Ancrene Riwle;* earlier as a surname (1187); developed from Old English *cycgel* (about 897, in Alfred's writings). The Old English bears a certain resemblance to Middle Dutch *koghele* stick with a round end (modern Dutch *kogel* bullet, ball) and Middle High German *kugele, kugel* ball, sphere (modern German *Kugel*), but this group of words cannot be traced to an Indo-European source. **—v.** 1596, beat with a cudgel, in Shakespeare's *1 Henry IV;* used figuratively in *Hamlet* (1602).

cue[1] *n.* hint or signal for an actor. 1553 *q,* letter said to have been used to mark the point at which an actor was to enter or begin a speech, and explained as an abbreviation of Latin *quandō* when, related to *quantum* how much; see QUANTUM. In 1565 it was spelled out *quew;* in the context of speeches in Shakespeare's works it is found both as *Q* in *Richard III* and as *cue* in *Hamlet* and *Midsummer Night's Dream,* but no use of *q* or *Q* has been found as a stage direction. —**v.** 1928, from the noun.

cue[2] *n.* long stick used in billiards, pool, etc. 1731, pigtail, in writings of Colley Cibber, variant of *queue* (1592); borrowed from French *queue,* literally, tail, from Old French; see QUEUE. The sense of a billiard cue is first recorded in 1749.

cuff[1] *n.* band or fold of the sleeve around the wrist. Before 1376 *coffe* mitten, glove; later, *cuffe* (1410); of uncertain origin, but similar in form to Medieval Latin *cuphia, cuffia* head covering, and Old English *cuffie* cap, head covering, and French *coiffe* close-fitting cap; all, however, lacking a semantic connection. The sense of a band around the sleeve, is first recorded in 1522, and that of turned-up hems on the legs of trousers, about 1911, chiefly in American English. —**cuff links** (1897)

cuff[2] *v.* hit with the hand, buffet. 1530 *cuffe,* in Palsgrave's *Lesclarcissement,* of uncertain origin; perhaps borrowed from Swedish *kuffa* to thrust, push, or, less likely, verb use of *cuffe* mitten, glove; see CUFF[1]. —**n.** 1570 *cuffe* a blow with the hand, buffet, apparently from the verb.

cuirass (kwiras′) *n.* armor for the chest and the back. 1464, borrowed from Middle French *cuirasse,* from Late Latin *coriācea vestis* garment of leather, from Latin *corium* leather, hide, related to *carō* (genitive *carnis*) meat (originally, a cut); cognate with Greek *keírein* cut off, from Indo-European **ker-/kor-* cut (Pok.938).

The word is traditionally thought to have been borrowed into Middle French from Italian *corazza,* but that is impossible because of the age of the French word; see FEW II, part 2 p. 1187, note 4.

cuisine (kwizēn′) *n.* style of cooking or preparing food. 1786, borrowed from French *cuisine,* literally, kitchen, from Vulgar Latin **cocīna,* variant of Latin *coquīna* cookery, kitchen, from *coquere* to COOK.

cul-de-sac (kul′dəsak′) *n.* blind alley. 1738, vessel closed at one end, borrowed from French *cul-de-sac,* literally, bottom of the sack (*cul* bottom, from Latin *cūlus* bottom, backside; *de* of, from Latin *dē from;* and *sac* sack, bag, from Latin *saccus* SACK[1] bag). Latin *cūlus* is cognate with Old Irish *cūl* hiding place, and Welsh *cil* back, corner, from Indo-European *kū-lo-s,* root *keu-/*kewə-* cover up (Pok.951.) The meaning of a blind alley, especially in its figurative sense, is first recorded in 1800.

culinary (kul′əner′ē) *adj.* having to do with cooking or the kitchen. 1638, borrowed perhaps through French *culinaire* (1546, in Rabelais), from Latin *culīnārius,* from *culīna* kitchen, of uncertain origin; for suffix see -ARY.

cull *v.* pick out, select. About 1225 *culen* choose, select; earlier *cullen* put through a strainer (probably before 1200, in *Ancrene Riwle*); borrowed from Old French *cueill-,* stem of *cuillir, coillir* collect, gather, select, from Latin *colligere* COLLECT. The sense of to gather, pluck (flowers, fruits, etc.), is first recorded in 1634, in Milton's *Comus;* this sense has been known in French since about 1080. —**n.** Before 1618; from the verb.

culminate *v.* reach the highest point, climax. 1647, borrowed from Late Latin *culminātus,* past participle of *culmināre* to crown, from Latin *culmen* (genitive *culminis*) top, related to *celsus* high, see HILL; for suffix see -ATE[1]. It is also possible that *culminate* is a back formation of earlier English *culmination.* —**culmination** *n.* 1633, probably borrowed from French *culmination,* from Late Latin *culmināre* culminate; for suffix see -ATION.

culottes (kü′lots) *n.pl.* woman's skirt divided like trousers. 1911, American English, borrowed from French *culottes* knee breeches, from *cul* bottom, backside; see CUL-DE-SAC. Compare SANS-CULOTTE.

culpable *adj.* deserving blame. Before 1338, in Mannyng's *Handlyng Synne;* earlier *coupable* (about 1280); borrowed from Old French *coupable, coulpable,* from Latin *culpābilis,* from *culpāre* to blame, from *culpa* fault, crime, blame, of uncertain origin; for suffix see -ABLE. The spelling *culpable* developed in imitation of the Latin form.

culprit *n.* one guilty of a fault or crime, offender. 1678 (at the trial of the Earl of Pembroke for murder), used in the formula *"Culprit,* how will you be tried?" Apparently this word was formed by the accidental running together of two words (a fusion facilitated by the use of abbreviations in legal writing): Anglo-French *culpable* guilty, abbreviated *cul.,* and *prit* or *prist,* variant of Old French *prest* ready, from Latin *praestō* see PRESTO. The original unabbreviated phrase had been *Culpable: prest d'averrer* (*nostre bille*) Guilty: ready to aver (our indictment). The abbreviated form, *Cul. prit,* was later mistaken for an appellation addressed to the accused, so that by 1700 Dryden used it in the sense of "the accused" and by 1769 it was used (partly by influence of Latin *culpa* fault, offense) to mean "an offender."

cult *n.* 1617, worship or homage; later, system of religious worship (1679, in writings of William Penn); borrowed through French *culte,* learned borrowing from Latin, and directly from Latin *cultus* (genitive *cultūs*) cultivation, care, attention, worship, from *cult-,* stem of *colere* to till, cultivate, attend to; see COLONY.

cultivate *v.* 1620-55, in an edition of Inigo Jones' writings; formed (probably through influence of French *cultiver* and Spanish *cultivar*) from Medieval Latin *cultivat-,* past participle stem of *cultivare,* from *cultivus* under tillage, from Latin *cultus,* past participle of *colere* to till; see COLONY; for suffix see -ATE[1]. The figurative sense of train, refine, is first recorded in English in 1681-86. —**cultivation** *n.* Before 1700, in writings of Dryden, formed from English *cultivate* + *-ion.* Though cited as a borrowing from French, no record of *cultivation* appears in French before 1700.

culturati (kul′chərä′tē) *n.pl.* cultured people, often considered as a group. 1971, formed in English from *culture,* on the analogy of LITERATI.

culture *n.* Probably 1440, tillage; borrowed from Middle French *culture,* learned borrowing from Latin, and directly from Latin *cultūra* a tending, care, cultivation, from *cult-,* the past participle stem of *colere* to till, see COLONY; for suffix see -URE.

The figurative sense of cultivation of the mind or body through education or training, is first recorded about 1510, in works of Sir Thomas More; the sense of intellectual or artistic side of civilization in 1805, in Wordsworth's *The Prelude.* —**cultural** *adj.* 1868, relating to the cultivation of plants, etc.; probably formed from English *culture* + *-al*[1], possibly by influence of earlier French *cultural* (1863). The sense relating to culture of the mind, manners, etc., is first recorded in English in 1875, in William D. Whitney's *The Life and Growth of Language.*

culvert *n.* conduit. 1773 (used in connection with canal construction), of uncertain origin.

The word is possibly of English dialectal origin. A connection with French *couloir* passage, corridor, track, from *couler* to flow, has not been established.

cum *prep.* with (often used in hyphenated phrases, as in *a country-cum-sea vacation*). 1871, abstracted from Latin phrases such as *cum privilegio* with privilege (1589 in English use), from Latin *cum* with; related to the prefix COM-.

cumber *v.* burden, trouble. About 1300 *cumberen,* also *comberen* (1348); borrowed probably from Old French *combrer* prevent, impede, from *combre* barrier, especially of a river, from Gallo-Latin **comboros* that which is carried together (*com-* together + *-boros,* related to the source of Latin *ferre* to carry), and Old English *beran* BEAR² carry. Related to ENCUMBER. —**cumbersome, cumbrous** *adj.* Both forms: 1375, in John Barbour's *The Bruce,* formed from English *cumber* + *-some*¹, and + *-ous.*

cum laude (kům lou′dē), with distinction (added to the diploma of a superior student). 1893 (but used at Harvard University as early as 1872), American English, borrowed from New Latin or Medieval Latin *cum laude,* literally with praise (Latin *cum* with + *laude,* ablative of *laus,* genitive *laudis* praise; see LAUD). The phrase probably came into American usage from the academic Latin of Germany (as at the University of Heidelberg) and ultimately from the terminology of the medieval universities of Europe.

cummerbund (kum′ərbund) *n.* wide sash around the waist. 1616, borrowed from Hindi *kamarband,* from Persian (*kamar* waist, loins + *band, bandh* band, tie, cognate with Sanskrit *bandhá-s* BAND², tie).

cumulate *v.* accumulate. 1534, borrowed perhaps through Middle French *cumuler,* or directly from Latin *cumulātus,* past participle of *cumulāre* heap up, from *cumulus* heap, of uncertain origin; for suffix see -ATE¹. —**cumulative** *adj.* 1605, in Francis Bacon's *Of the Advancement of Learning,* formed in English from Latin *cumulātus* (past participle of *cumulāre* to heap) + English *-ive.*

cumulus (kyü′myələs) *n.* cloud formation of rounded heaps with a flat bottom. 1659, heap or pile; borrowed from Latin *cumulus* heap. The meteorological use is first recorded in 1803.

cuneiform (kyünē′əfôrm) *adj.* wedge-shaped. 1677 (used in anatomy); borrowed from French *cunéiforme* (from Latin *cuneus* wedge, of unknown source, + French *-forme* -form). In 1818 the word is first recorded in English as applied to the wedge-shaped characters of the ancient inscriptions of Persia, Assyria, etc., perhaps influenced by the same meaning found in French *cunéiforme* (1813). —**n.** 1862, cuneiform character or writing; from the adjective.

cunning *adj.* Before 1338 *konnyng, konnynge* skillful, clever, in Mannyng's *Chronicle of England,* present participle of *connen* to know, developed from Old English *cunnan* to know (how), see CAN¹ be able; for suffix see -ING². The southern Middle English form *konnyng* replaced the earlier northern present participle form *konnand, connand* (about 1300), found in Old English *cunnand,* borrowed from a Scandinavian source (compare Old Icelandic *kunnandi,* from *kunna* know; see CAN¹).

The pejorative sense of sly, sharp, crafty, developed probably before 1402. The informal sense of attractive, cute, is first recorded in 1844 in American English, perhaps modeled after earlier *cute* (1834).

—**n.** Probably about 1300 *kunning* knowledge; later *konnyng* cleverness, shrewdness (before 1375); from gerund of *connen* to know.

cup *n.* Old English *cuppe* drinking vessel (about 1000, in Ælfric's *Glossary*); borrowed from Late Latin *cuppa* cup, a variant of Latin *cūpa* tub, cask; see HIVE. The Late Latin word is also the source of Old Frisian *kopp* cup, head, Middle Low German *kopp* cup, Middle Dutch *coppe* (modern Dutch *kopje* cup, head), Old High German *kopf, chuph* cup (modern German *Kopf* head). In the Romance languages, Late Latin *cuppa* was the source of Italian *coppa,* Provençal, Spanish, and Portuguese *copa,* and Old French *coupe,* all meaning cup.

—**v.** Before 1398, in Trevisa's translation of Bartholomew's *De Proprietatibus Rerum,* to draw blood by applying a glass cup ("cupping glass") to the skin; from the noun. The sense of form a cup, become cup-shaped, is first recorded in 1830. —**cupbearer** *n.* (before 1425) —**cupboard** *n.* (1375) —**cupcake** *n.* (1828, American English) —**cupful** *n.* (about 1150)

cupid or **Cupid** *n.* 1380 *Cupid,* the Roman god of love, often represented as a winged child with a bow and arrow, in Chaucer's *Parlement of Foules;* borrowed, perhaps by influence of Old French *Cupidon,* from Latin *Cupīdō,* personification of *cupīdō* desire or love, from *cupere* to desire or long for, COVET. Latin *cupere* is cognate with Sanskrit *kúpyati* gets excited, is angry, and Old Slavic *kypěti* boil, from Indo-European **kup-/ kūp-* (Pok.596).

The sense of a sculptured figure or representation of Cupid is first recorded in 1611, in Shakespeare's *Cymbeline.*

—**cupidity** *n.* eager desire, greed. 1436 *cupidite,* borrowed from Middle French *cupidité,* learned borrowing from Latin *cupiditātem* (nominative *cupiditās*) passionate desire, from *cupidus* desirous, from *cupere* to desire; for suffix see -ITY.

cupola (kyü′pələ) *n.* rounded roof, dome. 1549, borrowed from Italian *cupola,* from Late Latin *cūpula* little cask, small vault, diminutive of Latin *cūpa* cask, barrel.

cupreous (kyü′prēəs) *adj.* of or having to do with copper. 1666, in writings of Robert Boyle; borrowed from Late Latin *cupreus,* from *cuprum,* alteration of Latin *cyprum* COPPER; for suffix see -OUS. —**cupric** *adj.* containing copper. 1799, in writings of Sir Humphry Davy, formed from English *cupr(eous)* + *-ic,* or from Late Latin *cuprum* copper + English *-ic.*

cur *n.* Probably before 1200, in *Ancrene Riwle,* both *curre* vicious dog, cowardly dog, and *cur-dogge* the Devil (in later Middle English use, both terms could mean either a bad dog or a good dog); perhaps borrowed from a Scandinavian source (compare dialectal Swedish *kurre* house dog, related to Old Icelandic *kurra* to grumble); cognate with Middle Dutch *corre* house dog, literally, grumbling animal, and Middle High German *kurren* to growl, grunt, probably ultimately of imitative origin.

The figurative sense of contemptible person, is first recorded in 1590, in Shakespeare's *Midsummer Night's Dream.*

curare (kyůrä′rē) *n.* poisonous substance obtained from a tropical vine, used in medicine. 1777, this substance used by South American Indians to poison their arrows; borrowed from Spanish or Portuguese *curare,* from the Carib, Arawakan, or Tupi name.

curate (kyůr′it) *n.* Probably 1382, spiritual guide, one who cures, in writings of Wycliffe; borrowed from Medieval Latin *curatus* person having the cure of souls, from *cura* cure (of souls), from Latin *cūra* care; see CURE. Doublet of CURÉ.

The meaning of a clergyman who assists a pastor, rector, or vicar was first recorded in 1557, and originated in the Church of England.

curator (kyůrā′tər) *n.* Probably about 1375 *curature* person having the care of souls, borrowed from Anglo-French *curatour,* Old French *curateur,* learned borrowing from Latin *cūrātōrem* (nominative *cūrātor*) overseer, guardian, from *cūrāre* care for, from *cūra* care, see CURE; for suffix see -OR².

The general meaning of a manager or overseer (borrowed directly from Latin *cūrātor*) is first recorded in English in 1632, later, the specialized sense of a person in charge of a museum, library, etc., is found in John Evelyn's *Diary* (1661).

curb *n.* A fusion of two related words: 1) 1477 *corbe* strap used to restrain a horse, from earlier verb *courben* to bow down, make stop (about 1378, in a version of *Piers Plowman*); borrowed from Old French *corber, courber,* from Latin *curvāre,* from *curvus* curved; see CURVE. The figurative sense of a check or restraint is first recorded in 1613. 2) 1511 *corbe* curved border, as of a well; earlier *curb* a curved piece of timber (1324); borrowed from Old French *corbe, courbe* curved object, curve, from *corp, corbe,* adj., curved, from Latin *curvus* curved.

The extended sense of a border of a sidewalk, is first recorded in 1836.
—**v.** 1530, put a curb on a horse, in Palsgrave's *Lesclarcissement;* from the noun (1). The figurative sense of to check, restrain, is first recorded in 1588. —**curbing** *n.* (1838) —**curbstone** *n.* (1791)

curd *n.* Often **curds.** thick part of milk separated when milk sours. Before 1500 *curd,* alteration (by metathesis of *u* and *r*) of earlier *crud* (before 1376, in *Piers Plowman*); probably related to Old English *crūdan* to press, drive; see CROWD. —**v.** 1471 *curden* make into curd, curdle, alteration of earlier *crudden* (before 1382, in the Wycliffe Bible); from *crud,* n., curd. —**curdle** *v.* 1627-47, alteration of earlier *crudle* (1590, in Spenser's *Faerie Queene*); frequentative form of *crud* curd; for suffix see -LE³.

cure *n.* Probably before 1300 *coure,* in *Arthour and Merlin,* and *cure,* in *Kyng Alisaunder,* care, heed, charge; borrowed through Old French *cure,* or directly from Latin *cūra* care, concern, attention, management, from Old Latin *coirā-.* The Old Latin form is cognate with Paelignian (early Italic dialect) *coisā-* care, and perhaps even with Gothic *ushaista* needy, if originally meaning neglected, from Indo-European **kois-* care for (Pok.611).

The sense of medical care or treatment, healing, restoration to health, is first recorded in English about 1380.
—**v.** About 1378 *curen* take care of, in a version of *Piers Plowman;* later, to restore to health, heal (about 1384, in the Wycliffe Bible); borrowed from Old French *curer,* from Latin *cūrāre* take care, care for, attend, manage, from *cūra* care.
—**curable** *adj.* Before 1398, in Trevisa's translation of Bartholomew's *De Proprietatibus Rerum;* borrowed through Old French *curable,* or directly from Latin *cūrābilis,* from *cūrāre* take care; for suffix see -ABLE. —**cure-all** *n.* (1821, in American English) —**curative** *adj.* Probably before 1425, borrowed from Old French *curatif* (feminine *curative*), from Latin *cūrāt-,* past participle stem of *cūrāre* take care.

curé (kyůrā′) *n.* 1655, borrowing of French *curé,* found in Old French since the 1200's, from Medieval Latin *curatus;* see the doublet CURATE.

curette or **curet** (kyůret′) *n.* small surgical instrument in the shape of a scoop. 1753, borrowing of French *curette* (*curer* to cleanse, heal, CURE + *-ette* -ette). —**curettage** (kyůret′ij *or* kyůr′ətäzh′) *n.* scraping or cleaning by means of a curette. 1897, borrowing of French *curettage* (*curette* curette + *-age* -age). The earlier word was *curetting* (1888).

curfew *n.* About 1330 *corfu* the ringing of a bell at a fixed hour in the evening (originally, as a signal to cover or put out fires); borrowed through Anglo-French *coeverfu,* Old French *covrefeu,* literally, cover fire (*covrir* to COVER + *feu* fire, from Latin *focus* hearth; see FOCUS).

The custom or practice of ringing a bell at a fixed hour in the evening continued long after the original purpose of putting out fires and lights became obsolete. It was often used as a signal to observe various municipal or communal regulations. In time the signal was used in various communities to regulate the movements of inhabitants after dark, especially in periods of political disorder and war. By the 1800's the word *curfew* meant chiefly an official order or regulation to keep off the streets at fixed hours.

curia (kyůr′ēə) *n.* 1600, the Roman senate, (originally) one of the ten divisions of each of the three ancient Roman tribes; the Latin word *cūria,* used in Holland's translation of Livy's *Roman History,* came probably from Old Latin **co-viria* coalition of men (*co-* together + *vir* man), but considered by some as possibly a borrowing from Etruscan.

Before the 1600's the word is recorded in Middle English *curie* one of the divisions of the city of Rome in ancient times (before 1425).

In Medieval Latin *curia* was used to render French *cour* court, and English historians have used it thus since 1706 in referring to the court of the Norman kings of England. Now English *Curia* commonly refers to the Papal court (1840).

curie (kyůr′ē) *n.* unit for measuring the intensity of radioactivity. 1910, in an article in *Nature* by Lord Rutherford; named for Pierre *Curie* who, with his wife Marie, discovered the element radium.

curio (kyůr′ēō) *n.* 1851, American English, in Melville's *Moby Dick;* informally shortened form of *curiosity.*

curious *adj.* About 1340 *curiouse* eager to know, inquisitive, borrowed from Old French *curios,* learned borrowing from Latin, and directly from Latin *cūriōsus* full of care, taking pains, curious, from *cūra* care, see CURE; for suffix see -OUS. The sense of exciting curiosity, singular, odd, queer, is first recorded in 1715, probably a development from the Middle English sense of subtle, abstruse, occult (1350), though a similar sense is found in French *curieux* in the 1600's and in Italian *curioso,* about 1535. **—curiosity** *n.* Probably about 1378 *curiousite* inquisitiveness, in writings of Wycliffe; borrowed from Old French *curiosité,* learned borrowing from Latin *cūriōsitātem* (nominative *cūriōsitās*), from *cūriōsus* curious; for suffix see -ITY. The meaning of an object of interest, something valued as curious, rare, or strange, is first recorded in English about 1645.

curium (kyůr′ēəm) *n.* artificial radioactive chemical element. 1946, New Latin, formed in allusion to Pierre *Curie* and his wife Marie, discoverers of radium, + *-ium* (suffix of chemical elements). The word was coined by American physicist Glenn T. Seaborg, who discovered curium (element 96) in 1945.

curl *v.* 1440 *curlen,* in *Promptorium Parvulorum,* alteration (by metathesis of *u* or *o* and *r*) of earlier *crollen* (about 1380), from *crolle, crul,* adj., curly (probably before 1300), and earlier *Crul* (1191, as surname). The Middle English word probably developed from an unrecorded Old English word. The early Middle English forms are cognate with Frisian *krull, krulle* lock of hair, curl, Middle Dutch *crulle* curl, *crullen* to curl, Middle High German *krol, krolle,* Norwegian *krull,* and Danish *krølle,* all meaning curl, and with Middle High German *krūs* (modern German *kraus* curly-haired), from Indo-European **grus-lo-, grūs-* (Pok.390). **—n.** 1602, in Shakespeare's *Hamlet;* from the verb. **—curler** *n.* 1748, one who or that which curls hair; earlier, player at the game of curling (1638). **—curling** *n.* 1440, action of curling the hair; later, a game of sliding special stones over ice (1620). **—curly** *adj.* 1772-84, in writings of Captain James Cook; formed from English *curl,* n. + *-y*[1].

curlew *n.* wading bird. About 1340 *curlu* a quail; later, *corlue* a wading bird (about 1378); borrowed from Old French *corlieu, corlue,* probably imitative of the bird's cry. According to Bloch-Wartburg, the form *corlieu* was perhaps modeled on the Old French *corlieu* runner, messenger (from *corre* to run; see CURRENT), since this bird is a good runner.

curlicue *n.* 1843 *curlycue,* formed in American English from *curly* + *cue*[2], as corresponding to French *queue* tail; possibly also influenced by the name and form of the letter Q.

curmudgeon (kərmuj′ən) *n.* churlish and miserly person. 1577 *curmudgen,* of unknown origin. It has been suggested that the first syllable is the word *cur* dog; the ending is similar to those of *bludgeon* and *dudgeon,* also of unknown origin. Another suggestion is that the word meant "one who withholds corn," considered as a type of churlish avarice. But the use of *cornmudgin,* in Holland's translation of Livy, is considered a play on words by the OED, which notes that *curmudgeon* was cited "a quarter of a century before Holland's date." It is also tempting to associate *-mudgeon* with Middle English *margon* (later *mudgeon*) dirt, refuse, dregs, but there is no known evidence for this connection. Johnson's *coeur méchant* (French *méchant coeur* evil or malicious heart) is now considered an equally unfounded source.

currant (kėr′ənt) *n.* small seedless raisin. 1540 *currante,* shortened from earlier *Raysyn of Curans* raisin of Corinth (1391), *raysyn of coraunce* (probably about 1425), and *Reyssin of Corent* (1432-33), the *-s* and *-ce* endings probably mistaken for the plural inflection. The Middle English was borrowed through Anglo-French *reisin de Corauntz* raisin of Corinth, from *Corauntz* Corinth, city in Greece, from Old French *Corinthe,* from Latin *Corinthus,* from Greek *Kórinthos;* so called because currants were produced chiefly in Greece and probably exported from Corinth.

currency *n.* 1657, a flow or course; probably developed from: 1) obsolete *currence,* modeled on Medieval Latin **currentia* a current of a stream, from Latin *currentem,* present participle of *currere* to run; for suffix see -ENCY; or 2) from *current,* on the pattern of *decent, decency, potent, potency,* etc. The sense of circulation of money is first recorded in 1699, in Locke's writings (suggested by earlier use of *current* with the meaning of in circulation as a medium of exchange (1481), and followed by that of money in circulation in 1729, in Benjamin Franklin's *Essays.*

current *adj.* Probably before 1300 *curraunt* running, flowing, in *Kyng Alisaunder,* borrowed from Old French *corant, curant* running, present participle of *corre, curre* to run, from Latin *currere* to run; for suffix see -ENT. Latin *currere* is cognate with *carrus* wagon (Gaulish **carros),* and Greek *epí-kouros* running to (help), from Indo-European **k̑ers-/k̑ors-/k̑r̥s-* (Pok. 583).

The sense of in general circulation, prevalent, is first recorded in 1563, and that of occurring in the present, in 1608. Both of these meanings may have developed from the Middle English legal sense of presently in effect (1438, in *Proceedings of the Privy Council*).

The spelling *current* appeared in 1555, replacing the earlier spelling by influence of Latin *currentem* (nominative *currēns*), present participle of *currere* to run.

—n. stream. Before 1425, in Wycliffe's writings; borrowed from Middle French *corant, curant,* from Old French *corant, curant,* present participle of *corre, curre* to run.

curriculum *n.* 1824, borrowing of New Latin (1633, at the University of Glasgow), from Latin *curriculum* a running, course, career, from *currere* to run; see CURRENT. **—curricular** *adj.* 1798, having to do with the driving of carriages; formed in English from Latin *curriculum* (race) course + English *-ar.* The transferred sense of having to do with a school's curriculum, is first recorded before 1913 (about 1909 in Webster).

curry[1] *v.* rub or dress (a horse, leather, etc.). About 1300 *coureyen,* borrowed probably through Anglo-French *curreier, cunreier,* from Old French *correier,* originally *conreier* put in order, prepare, curry a horse (*con-* intensive + *reier* arrange, make ready, from *rei* order, preparation, from Germanic; compare Old English *rǣde* READY). **—curry favor** About 1510, alteration by folk etymology of earlier *curry favel* (probably about 1400), a phrase apparently borrowed from Old French *correier fauvel* to be false, be hypocritical (about 1310); literally, to curry the fallow-colored horse. The *favel* or fallow horse was used in medieval allegories as a symbol of fraud, cunning, or deceit, perhaps because of its indefinite color; Middle English *favel, fauvel* (before 1338, in Mannyng's *Chronicle of England*) was borrowed from Old French *fauvel,* which was of Germanic origin and ultimately from the same source as English *fallow.*

Middle English *favel, fauvel* was also confused with *favel* flattery or guile; borrowed from Old French *favele* lying, deception, from Latin *fābella* story, fable, diminutive of *fābula* FABLE.

—currycomb *n.* (1678, in American English)

curry[2] *n.* kind of sauce made from a mixture of spices, seeds, etc. 1681, borrowed from Tamil *kari* sauce, relish for rice. An earlier form *carriel* (1598) came through Portuguese *caril* from Kannada (a Dravidian language of India) *karil.* —**v.** prepare or flavor with curry. 1839, from the noun. —**curry powder** (1810)

curse *n.* Late Old English (before 1050) *curs* a prayer or wish that evil or harm befall one (contrasted with *blessing*), of uncertain origin.

Various connections to other words have been proposed, for example to the word *cross,* to Old French *coroz* anger, or to Old Irish *cūrsaigim* I scold, but none seems to bridge satisfactorily the great gap in meaning between any of them and the Old English word *curs,* which, in addition to the basic meaning of malediction, also meant a formal sentence of excommunication (before 1121) and a profane oath or imprecation (probably before 1200). However, the *Middle English Dictionary* suggests a possible borrowing of the Old English noun from Latin *cursus* COURSE in the medieval church sense of the set of daily liturgical prayers, applied to "the set of imprecations," especially in *the grete curse,* a formula read in churches four times a year setting forth the offenses which entailed excommunication.

—**v.** Probably before 1160 *cursen;* developed from late Old English (about 1050) *cursian* to utter a curse or curses, blaspheme; apparently from the noun.

—**cursed** *adj.* Probably before 1200, condemned; later, "damned" as an expression (about 1386) or deserving a curse (before 1300).

cursive *adj.* written with the letters joined together. 1784, borrowed from French *cursif* (feminine *cursive*), from Medieval Latin *cursivus,* from Latin *cursus* (genitive *cursūs*) a running, from past participle of *currere* to run, see CURRENT; for suffix see -IVE. —**n.** cursive character or type. 1861, probably borrowed from French *cursive,* feminine noun, from the adjective in French.

cursor *n.* movable square of light serving as an indicator on the display screen of an electronic computer, typesetter, etc. 1972, extended sense of the earlier term (1594) for a sliding part of any instrument (such as a slide rule or, later, a filter placed on a radar screen) that facilitates computing or sighting, a use probably influenced by Middle French *curseur* (1562); in Middle English (1305) used in the sense of a runner or messenger; borrowed from Latin *cursor* runner, see CURSORY; for suffix see -OR[2].

cursory *adj.* 1601, probably borrowed from Middle French *cursoire* rapid (used of boats, winds, rumors), from Late Latin *cursōrius* of a race or running, from Latin *cursor* runner, from *cursum,* past participle of *currere* to run, see CURRENT; for suffix see -ORY.

curt *adj.* 1425, in writings of Chaucer; earlier, *Courtehose* (1366, in a surname); borrowed through Old French *court, cort,* or directly from Latin *curtus* (cut) short, shortened, from Indo-European *kr̥-tó-s* (Pok.939); cognate with Old English *sc(e)ort* SHORT, from Proto-Germanic **skurtás,* and *scieran* to cut, SHEAR, from Indo-European **skr̥-dó-s,* root **sker-* (Pok.941).

The meaning of concise, brief, condensed, terse, is first recorded in Ben Jonson's *New Inn* (1630), and the extended sense of so brief as to be impolite or rude, in Benjamin Disraeli's *The Young Duke* (1831).

curtail *v.* Probably about 1471 *curtaylen* to restrict, limit, apparently an alteration (influenced by *taylen* to cut, from Old French *tailler;* see TAILOR) of Middle French *courtault* made short, docked (*court* short, from Latin *curtus* CURT + *-ault,* pejorative suffix of Germanic origin). The meaning of shorten by cutting off a part is first recorded in English in 1553, followed by the sense of diminish, lessen, in 1589.—**curtailment** *n.* 1794, formed from English *curtail* + *-ment.*

curtain *n.* About 1303 *curteyn* piece of hanging cloth (enclosing a bed); borrowed from Old French *curtine, cortine,* from Late Latin *cōrtīna* a curtain, from Latin *cōrtem,* earlier *cohortem* enclosure, courtyard, COURT. Late Latin *cōrtīna* was a loan translation in the Vulgate, perhaps misapplied to render Greek *aulaíā* curtain (from *aulḗ* court, courtyard), used in the Septuagint (Exodus 26:1, etc.) to render Hebrew *yerī'āh.* —**v.** Probably before 1300 *curtynen* surround or cover with a curtain, in *Kyng Alisaunder,* from the noun.

curtsy *n.* 1546, expression of respect by action or gesture, variant of COURTESY. The specific reference to a bow made by bending the knees is first recorded in 1575. —**v.** Before 1553, make a curtsy, show courtesy to; from the noun.

curve *v.* Probably before 1425 *curved,* past participle form of unrecorded verb, from *curve,* adj., bent (also probably before 1425); borrowed from Latin *curvus* curved, crooked, bent. The Latin is cognate with Greek *kyrtós* bent, *korṓnē* anything bent, crown, Middle Irish *cor* circle, Russian *kórtochki* a crouching, cowering, and Avestan *skarəna-* round, from Indo-European **kor-/kr̥-/(s)kor-* turn, bend (Pok.935).

The unrecorded Middle English verb was probably also borrowed from Latin *curvāre* to bend, from *curvus* curved.

—**n.** 1696, probably from the earlier adjective *curve* bent, curved.

—**curvaceous** (kėrvā'shəs) *adj.* full of curves, well-rounded. 1936, American English, formed from *curve,* n. + *-aceous* (adjective suffix chiefly used in botany, from Latin *-āceus,* but here used facetiously). —**curvature** *n.* Probably before 1425, perhaps later reinforced by Middle French *curvature,* both the Middle English and Middle French from Latin *curvātūra* bending, from *curvātus,* past participle of *curvāre* to curve; for suffix see -URE.

cushion *n.* 1302-03 *quissin;* later, *qwyschen* (before 1350) and *cussheon* (1397); borrowed from Old French *coissin, coussin* seat cushion, probably variants from Vulgar Latin **coxīnum,* from Latin *coxa* hip, thigh, cognate with Sanskrit *kákṣā* armpit, Avestan *kaša-* shoulder, from Indo-European **koksā, koksos* (Pok.611). —**v.** 1735-38, from the noun.

cushy *adj. Informal.* easy, comfortable. 1915, Anglo-Indian, formed from Hindi *khūsh* pleasant, healthy, happy (from Persian *khūsh*) + English *-y*[1].

cusp *n.* pointed end, point. 1585, entrance to an astrological house or division of the heavens; later, peak, apex or pointed ornament; borrowed from Latin *cuspis* a point, spear, pointed end of anything, of uncertain origin.

cuspid *n.* 1743, geometrical point, borrowed from Latin *cuspidem* (nominative *cuspis*) point. The sense of a tooth with a point, canine tooth, is first recorded in English in 1878; earlier, referred to in the Latin plural *cuspidati* (1771).

cuspidor *n.* spittoon. 1871 *cuspador,* American English, borrowed from Portuguese *cuspidor* spittoon, from *cuspir* to spit, from Latin *cōnspuere* spit on (*con-* intensive, variant of *com-* before *s,* + *spuere* to spit; see SPEW).

cuss *n. Informal.* troublesome person or animal. 1775, American English, an alteration of *curse,* but often used without consciousness of the origin; in some dialects the alteration may represent a regular phonetic development, as *ass* from *arse, sasparilla* from *sarsaparilla,* etc. In the literal sense of curse, the word has been recorded since 1843. **—v.** to curse. 1815, American English, alteration of *curse.* **—cussed** *adj.* 1840, American English, alteration of *cursed.*

custard *n.* About 1353 *custadis,* pl.; later *crustarde* meat or fruit pie (1399), borrowed probably from Old Provençal *croustado,* from *crosta* crust, from Latin *crusta* CRUST.

The spelling *custard* is first recorded about 1450, and the sense of a baked or boiled pudding about 1600.

custody *n.* Before 1449 *custodye,* borrowed from Latin *custōdia* guarding or keeping, from *custōs* (genitive *custōdis*) guardian, keeper, of uncertain origin; for suffix see -Y³. **—custodial** *adj.* 1772, formed in English from Latin *custōdia* + English *-al*¹. **—custodian** *n.* 1781, formed from English *custody* + *-an,* replacing Middle English *custode* custodian of a friary (about 1400); borrowed through Old French *custode* from Latin *custōdem,* accusative of *custōs.*

custom *n.* Probably before 1200 *custume,* borrowed from Old French *costume, custume,* from Vulgar Latin *cōnsuētūmen, corresponding to Latin *cōnsuētūdinem,* accusative of *cōnsuētūdō* habit or usage, from *cōnsuētus,* past participle of *cōnsuēscere* accustom (*con-* intensive, variant of *com-* before *s,* + *suēscere* become used to, accustom oneself, related to *suī* of oneself). Latin *suī* is cognate with Sanskrit *svadhā́* inclination, custom, Greek *éthos* custom, *ēthos* character, *heós* his own, Latin *suus* his own, from Indo-European *sewó-s, swe-dh-, swē- (Pok.882). Doublet of COSTUME. The word *customs* meaning taxes on imports, was originally applied (about 1390) to a tax levied by a lord or local authority on goods on their way to the market. Earlier (about 1330) the singular, *costome* had the general sense of an exaction of a tax or tribute and gradually replaced the Old English term *toll.*

—customary *adj.* 1523, held by custom rather than law; borrowed through Anglo-Latin *custumarius* subject to tax, from *custuma,* from Anglo-French *custume* CUSTOM; for suffix see -ARY. The general sense of usual or habitual, is first recorded in 1607, in Shakespeare's *Coriolanus.* **—customer** *n.* 1409, formed from Middle English *custom* + *-er*¹. An earlier sense, "customs official" appeared before 1399. The extended informal sense of a fellow or chap (usually with some pejorative qualifier, such as tough, ugly, strange) appeared in 1589. **—custom house** (before 1490) **—custom-made** *adj.* (1855, in American English)

cut *v.* Probably before 1300 either as: *cutten,* in *Kyng Alisaunder,* or *kitten* in *Arthour and Merlin;* of uncertain origin (possibly borrowed from a Scandinavian source; compare Swedish dialect *kuta, kata* to cut, *kuta* knife, and Icelandic *kuti* knife. **—n.** 1530, gash, wound, in Palsgrave's *Lesclarcissement;* from the verb. The sense of a stroke or blow with a knife, sword, etc., is first recorded in 1601, in Shakespeare's *Julius Caesar.* **—cutaway** *n.* a coat (1894); *adj.* showing something cut away, as a cutaway coat (1841). **—cutback** *n.* (1897) **—cutoff** *n.* (1647) **—cutout** *n.* (1851) **—cutter** *n.* (1177) **—cutthroat** *n.* (1535); *adj.* (1567) **—cutting** *n.* (about 1350); *adj.* (about 1400) **—cutup** *n.* (1782)

cutaneous (kyütā'nēəs) *adj.* having to do with the skin. 1578, borrowed from New Latin *cutaneus,* from Latin *cutis* skin, HIDE²; for suffix see -OUS.

cute *adj.* 1731, in Bailey's *Dictionary,* acute, clever, shortened from ACUTE. The informal sense of attractive, pleasing, is first recorded in 1834, in American English students' slang, and was perhaps the model for the same sense attached to *cunning* (1844).

cuticle (kyü'təkəl) *n.* outer skin. 1615, borrowed from Latin *cutīcula,* diminutive of *cutis* skin; see HIDE² animal skin. The specific sense of skin at the base of a nail, is first recorded in 1907. Earlier Middle French *cuticule* was borrowed in Robert Boyle's writings, but does not appear elsewhere. Middle English *cuticles* (before 1475) probably refers to membranes of the intestines.

cutlass or **cutlas** *n.* 1594 *coutelace,* borrowed from Middle French *coutelas,* probably from Italian *coltellaccio* large knife, from *coltello* knife, from Latin *cultellus* small knife, diminutive of *culter* knife, plowshare, cognate with Armenian *čelk'em* I split, Gothic *skilja* butcher, from Indo-European* *kel-tro-s,* root *(s)kel-* cut (Pok.923).

cutler *n.* person who makes, sells, or repairs knives, scissors, etc. Before 1400 *coteler,* in Lanfranc's *Science of Surgery;* perhaps earlier, in an Anglo-French surname *Cuteler* (1207); borrowed from Old French *coutelier,* from *coutel* knife, from Latin *cultellus,* see CUTLASS; for suffix see -ER¹. **—cutlery** *n.* 1340 *cotellerie,* borrowed from Old French *coutelerie* cutting utensils, from *coutel* knife; for suffix see -ERY.

cutlet *n.* 1706, borrowed from French *côtelette,* from Old French *costelette* cutlet, little rib; diminutive with *-ette* of original diminutive *costele* with *-el,* diminutive of *coste* rib, side, from Latin *costa;* see COAST. The English spelling has been influenced by *cut* and the diminutive form *-let,* as if *cutlet* = a small cut (of meat).

cuttlefish or **cuttle** *n.* saltwater mollusk. Probably before 1425 *cutyl,* variant of *codel* (before 1425), developed from Old English (about 1000) *cudele* the cuttlefish. In form the Old English is sometimes associated with Middle Low German *küdel* container, pocket, Middle High German *kiutel* dewlap, jowl, Old High German *kiot* bag, pocket, Old Icelandic *koddi* cushion, testicle, and with Old English *codd,* from Indo-European *geu-t-/gu-t- (Pok.394).

The compound *cuttlefish* is first recorded in 1591 and its first component was either drawn from English *cuttle* or borrowed from German *Kutteln* entrails.

-cy a suffix forming abstract nouns and meaning: **1** office, position, or rank, as in *captaincy* = *rank of a captain,* and *chaplaincy* = *office or position of a chaplain,* **2** quality, condition, or fact of being, as in *delicacy* = *quality of being delicate, bankruptcy* = *condition of being bankrupt.* Borrowed from Latin *-cia, -tia* (often through French *-cie, -tie*), from the stem endings *-c-* or *-t-* and the suffix *-ia,* equivalent to English *-y*³; or from Greek *-kíā, -keia, -tíā, -teia,* from the stem endings *-k-* or *-t-* and the suffix *-íā, -eia,* equivalent to English *-y*³. The suffix occurs in English chiefly in the forms *-acy, -ancy,* and *-ency.*

cyanide (sī'ənīd) *n.* 1826, formed from English *cyan-, cyano-* combining forms for carbon and nitrogen compounds (from Greek *kýanos* dark-blue enamel, lapis lazuli, of uncertain origin) + *-ide* (chemical suffix); so called because the compound radical (*cyanogen*) enters into the composition of Prussian blue, a common dark-blue pigment.

cybernetics (sī'bərnet'iks) *n.* study of the automatic controls governing the operation of complex electronic machines and animal nervous systems. 1948, American English, formed from Greek *kybernḗtēs* steersman, pilot (from *kybernân* to steer) + English *-ics;* see GOVERN. The word was coined by Norbert Wiener, 1894-1964, American mathematician. **—cybernetic** *adj.* 1951, back formation from *cybernetics.* **—cybernate** *v.* 1962, back formation from *cybernation.* **—cybernation** *n.* automation through the use of computers. 1962, formed as a blend of English *cybern(etics)* + *(autom)ation.*

cyborg (sī'bôrg) *n.* human body or other organism whose functions are taken over in part by electromechanical devices. 1962, formed from English *cyb(ernetic) org(anism).*

cyclamen (sik'ləmen) *n.* plant of the primrose family. About 1550, borrowed possibly through Middle French *cyclamen,* and directly from New Latin *cyclamen* (remodeled by analogy with other botanical words in *-men,* such as *legumen*), from Latin *cyclamīnos,* from Greek *kykláminos* species of cyclamen, probably from *kýklos* circle, WHEEL; so called, it is supposed, from the plant's rounded or swollen roots.

cycle *n.* Before 1387 *cicle* recurrent period of time, in Trevisa's translation of Higden's *Polychronicon,* borrowed through Old French *cycle,* or directly from Late Latin *cyclus,* from Greek *kýklos* circle, ring, WHEEL. —*v.* 1842, revolve in cycles, in Tennyson's *Two Voices;* from the noun. The meaning of to ride a bicycle is first recorded in 1883. **—cyclic** *adj.* 1794, borrowed through French *cyclique,* or directly from Latin *cyclicus,* from Greek *kyklikós,* from *kýklos* circle; for suffix see -IC. **—cyclist** *n.* 1882, one who rides a bicycle; formed from English *cycle,* v. + *-ist.*

cyclo-, before vowels **cycl-,** a combining form meaning: **1** circle, ring, used especially with reference to rotation, as in *cyclometer = instrument that measures arc of a circle or rotation of a wheel.* **2** cycle, alternation, as in *cyclothymia = alternation of liveliness and depression.* **3** in chemistry, arrangement of atoms in a ring, cyclic, as in *cyclohexane = form of hexane considered as a ring of six bivalent radicals.* Borrowed from Greek *kyklo-,* combining form of *kýklos* ring, circle, WHEEL.

cyclone *n.* 1848, borrowed from Greek *kyklôn* moving in a circle, whirling around, present participle of *kykloûn* move in a circle, whirl, from *kýklos* circle, WHEEL; so called because the cyclone's winds move in a circular course. The word was coined by Henry Piddington, 1797-1858, English meteorologist. **—cyclonic** *adj.* 1860, formed from English *cyclone* + *-ic.*

cyclopedia *n.* book giving information on all branches of one subject; encyclopedia. 1636 *cyclopaedia,* shortened form of *encyclopaedia* ENCYCLOPEDIA; later, book on all branches of one subject (1728). The Anglicized spelling *cyclopedia* is first recorded in 1676, in Hobbes' preface to his translation of the *Iliad.* **—cyclopedic** *adj.* Before 1843, in writings of Southey, formed from English *cyclopedia* + *-ic.*

cyclorama (sī'klərä'mə) *n.* large picture of a landscape, battle, etc., on the wall of a circular room. 1840, formed from English *cyclo-* circle, ring + *(pan)orama;* probably influenced by the earlier *diorama.* The theatrical sense of a large curved backdrop on a stage to give the illusion of distance, is first recorded in 1915.

cyclotron (sī'klətron) *n.* particle accelerator, atom smasher. Before 1935, American English, formed from *cyclo-* + *-tron,* as if from Greek **kýklōtron,* from *kykloûn* to whirl; so called from the circular path of the accelerated particles. The name was coined by American physicist E.O. Lawrence, 1901-1958, and his associates, who developed the cyclotron in 1930.

cygnet (sig'nit) *n.* young swan. 1400 *cignet,* borrowed from Anglo-French diminutive of Old French *cisne, cigne* swan, from Latin *cygnus,* variant of *cycnus,* from Greek *kýknos;* for suffix see -ET. Greek *kýknos* is cognate with Sanskrit *śukrá-s* shining, white, from Indo-European **k̂uk-,* root **k̂euk-* (Pok.597). Old French *cigne* was an alteration, influenced by Latin *cygnus,* of earlier *cisne,* which, like Old Italian *cecino,* came from Late Latin *cicinus,* from Latin *cycnus.*

The spelling *signet* prevailed in English until the 1600's (Shakespeare used it in *1 Henry VI*), when it was gradually replaced by *cygnet,* after the French and Latin forms.

cylinder *n.* 1570, in Sir Henry Billingsley's translation of Euclid's *Elements;* borrowed probably through Middle French *cylindre,* from Latin *cylindrus* roller, cylinder, from Greek *kýlindros* a cylinder, roller, roll, from *kylíndein* to roll, of uncertain origin. **—cylindrical** *adj.* 1646, formed in English from French *cylindrique* (from Greek *kylindrikós,* from *kýlindros* cylinder) + English *-al*[1]; for suffix see also -ICAL.

cymbal *n.* About 1340, in an early psalter, partly developed from Old English *cimbal* (about 825, in the *Vespasian Psalter*); and partly borrowed from Old French *cymbale.* Both the Old English and Old French derived from Latin *cymbalum,* from Greek *kýmbalon* a cymbal, from *kýmbē* hollow of a vessel, bowl, drinking cup; cognate with Welsh *cwm* valley, from Indo-European **kumb-* (Pok.592).

cyme (sīm) *n.* flower cluster. 1725 *cime* sprout of a plant, such as cabbage; borrowed from French *cime* shoot or sprout of cabbage, and directly from Latin *cȳma* a sprout, from Greek *kŷma* young sprout, anything swollen, from *kyeîn* become pregnant. Greek *kyeîn* is cognate with Sanskrit *śváyati* swells up, Latin *cavus* hollow, from Indo-European **k̂ou-/k̂ū-* (Pok.592).

The word appeared in 1794 with the spelling *cyme* and the meaning of flower cluster, by influence of the original Latin *cȳma.*

cynic *n.* 1547-64, in an edition of William Baldwin's *A Treatise of Moral Philosophy,* one of a group of ancient Greek philosophers who sneered at wealth and personal comfort; borrowed through Middle French *cynique,* or directly from Latin *Cynicus,* from Greek *Kynikós,* literally, doglike, from *kýōn* (genitive *kynós*) dog, HOUND.

The sense of a sneering, sarcastic person is first recorded in English in 1596, but was already implicit in the name of the philosophical sect associated with its principles of asceticism. Probable association of *kynós*

dog's and *kynikós* doglike with *Kynósarges,* the school of this group, led to the Greek word for dog becoming the nickname for a member of the sect.
—**cynical** *adj.* 1588, formed from English *cynic* + *-al*[1].
—**cynicism** *n.* 1672, formed from English *cynic* + *-ism.*

cynosure (sī′nəshůr) *n.* 1601, center of attraction or attention; earlier, guiding star (1596); borrowed from Middle French *cynosure,* from Latin *Cynosūra* Ursa Minor, a constellation containing the North Star, formerly used as a guide by sailors, from Greek *kynósoura,* literally, dog's tail (*kýōn,* genitive *kynós* dog, HOUND; *ourá* tail; see SQUIRREL).

cypress *n.* evergreen tree. About 1175, borrowed from Old French *cipres,* learned borrowing from Latin *cyparissus, from Greek kypárissos,* which was apparently a borrowing, like Latin *cupressus* cypress, from a language of the Mediterranean region (compare Hebrew *gōfer* a kind of tree mentioned in the Bible, Genesis 6:14).

cyst *n.* 1713, saclike growth, shortened form of New Latin *cystis* (the form cited in English from 1543 to 1758), from Greek *kýstis* bladder, pouch (what is or can be blown up); cognate with Sanskrit *śvásiti* blows, snorts, Latin *querī* complain, and Old Icelandic *hvæsa* wheeze, from Indo-European **kwes-/kus-/k̑wēs-* (Pok.631). — **cystic** *adj.* 1634, borrowed from French *cystique,* from New Latin *cysticus,* from *cystis* cyst; for suffix see -IC.

cyt- the form of *cyto-* before vowels, as in *cytaster* (star-shaped structure of a cell).

-cyte a combining form meaning cell of an organism, as in *leucocyte* (white blood cell). Borrowed from Greek *kýtos* hollow container; see HIDE[2] skin.

cyto- a combining form meaning cell or cells of organisms, as in *cytology = study of cells* and *cytoplasm = protoplasm of a cell.* Borrowed from Greek *kyto-*, combining form of *kýtos* a hollow, a hollow space or container.

cytology (sītol′əjē) *n.* study of the cells of organisms. 1889, possibly borrowed from French *cytologie* (*cyto-* cell + *-logie* -logy). —**cytologist** *n.* (1895)

cytosine (sī′təsin) *n.* substance in nucleic acids of cells. 1894, formed in English from *cyto-* cell + *(rib)ose* ribose (a sugar), + *-ine*[2] (chemical suffix).

czar (zär) *n.* former emperor of Russia. 1555, in Richard Eden's translation of Peter Martyr's *De Orbe Novo;* borrowed through earlier Polish *czar,* from Russian *tsar',* from Old Slavic *tsēsarĭ,* from Gothic *kaisar* (*-ai-* denoting an open e sound), from Greek *Kaîsar,* from Latin *Caesar;* see the doublets CAESAR and KAISER.

The transferred sense of a person with dictatorial power, such as a baseball czar, is first recorded in 1866 in American English, when the word was applied to President Andrew Johnson; but it was popularized in the 1890's as the nickname of Speaker Thomas B. Reed of the House of Representatives, who gained notoriety for his dictatorial use of parliamentary rules.
—**czarina** *n.* 1717, borrowed from Italian *czarina,* from German *Zarin* (earlier *Czarin*), feminine of *Zar,* from Russian *tsar'.* The feminine form in Russian is *tsaritsa.*
—**czarist** *adj.* (1954)

D

dab *n.* Probably before 1300, heavy blow with a weapon, in *Kyng Alisaunder.* —v. Before 1307, deliver a heavy blow with a weapon. Both noun and verb are of uncertain origin; perhaps Middle English *dabben* is related to *tappen* which is conjectured to be of imitative origin.

The verb meaning of strike lightly, peck, is first recorded in 1532, in Sir Thomas More's writings, followed by the sense of pat with something soft or moist, recorded in 1562. The noun meaning of a light blow or tap is first recorded in 1658.

dabble *v.* 1557, wet by splashing, probably a frequentative form of DAB. Middle English *dable* in the surname *Dablewife* (1336) is of uncertain meaning, perhaps meddler, dabbler. The modern sense of do superficially is first recorded in 1625, in Ben Jonson's *The Staple of News.* —**dabbler** *n.* 1611, formed from English *dabble,* v. + *-er*[1].

dachshund (däks'hůnt') *n.* German dog with a long body and very short legs. About 1881, borrowed from German *Dachshund* (*Dachs* badger + *Hund* hound); perhaps so called for its use in hunting badgers. German *Dachs* badger is cognate with Dutch *das* and Norwegian svin-*toks* (Proto-Germanic **thaHsuz,* which seems to have meant originally "the builder", and to have been cognate also with Sanskrit *tákṣati* he builds, Greek *téktōn* carpenter, and Latin *texere* weave; see TEXT).

dactyl (dak'təl) *n. Poetry.* metrical foot of three syllables. Before 1382, in the Wycliffe Bible, borrowed from Latin *dactylus,* from Greek *dáktylos* finger, dactyl, of unknown origin; so called from its three parts, suggesting the three joints of the finger. Doublet of DATE[2] fruit.

dad or **daddy** *n.* Before 1529 *dadye* and 1553 *dad,* of uncertain origin, but probably from children's speech. Similar forms occur independently in many languages, as in Welsh *tad* father, Latin *tata,* Greek *tétta, tatâ,* and Sanskrit *tata-s.* —**daddy-longlegs** *n.* (before 1814).

Dada (dä'də) *n.* radical anti-traditional movement in modern art and literature. 1920, in Aldous Huxley's correspondence; borrowed from French *dada* hobbyhorse (a child's word), from the title of a literary periodical, *être sur son dada* to be on (that is, ride) one's hobbyhorse, founded in Zürich in 1916 by Tristan Tzara, a Rumanian poet, and Jean Arp, a French artist and poet; the name was chosen for its nonsensical sound and meaning. —**Dadaism** *n.* (1920) —**Dadaist** *n., adj.* (1920).

dado (dā'dō) *n.* cube forming body of a pedestal. 1664, borrowing of Italian *dado* cube or pedestal, DIE[2]. The meaning of a wood rail or paneling around the lower part of the walls of a room, is first recorded in 1787.

daffodil *n.* 1548, variant of (obsolete) *affodill* (before 1400); borrowing of Medieval Latin *affodillus,* from Latin *asphodelus,* from Greek *asphódelos,* of unknown origin. The initial *d* has not been satisfactorily accounted for, but may be a union with a clipped form (*th'*) of English *the* or of the French preposition *de.*

daffy *adj.* 1884, perhaps formed from DAFT, or from *daff, daffe* a halfwit, simpleton (about 1330, earlier as a surname *Daf,* 1253; of unknown origin) + *-y*[1].

daft *adj.* Probably about 1200 *daffte* mild, gentle, meek, in *The Ormulum;* developed from Old English (about 1000) *gedæfte* gentle, becoming, from Proto-Germanic **ʒadaftjaz.* Old English *gedæfte* is related to *gedafen* fit or suitable, past participle of a lost verb **dafan* be fit, and Gothic *gadaban* be fit; cognate with Latin *faber* craftsman, Old Slavic *dobrŭ* fine, good, Lithuanian *dabinti* to adorn, from Indo-European **dhabh-* to fit suitably (Pok. 233). See the doublet DEFT.

About 1300 the meaning of dull appeared, perhaps because a person who is mild or gentle might be taken as dull or stupid, a development that parallels SILLY. The later sense of foolish, silly (1440), probably developed from analogy with *daffe,* n. a halfwit and *daffish,* adj. dull-witted.

dagger *n.* Before 1375 *dagare* (in an Anglo-Latin text), apparently altered form of Old French *dague* dagger, from Old Provençal *dague* or Italian *daga,* of uncertain origin. Both Kluge and Corominas trace the word to a possible Celtic origin in the British Isles.

daguerreotype (dəger'ətīp) *n.* early method of photography. 1839, borrowing of French *daguerréotype,* from the name of Louis *Daguerre,* 1789-1851, its inventor + French *type* type.

dahlia (dal'yə) *n.* tall flowering plant of the aster family. 1804, New Latin, named (in 1791) after Anders *Dahl,* a Swedish botanist of the 1700's, a pupil of Linnaeus, who found the plant in Mexico in 1788.

daily *adj.* 1421 *daly,* also *dayly* (1423), and *daily* (1447), found in Old English *dæglīc* (in compounds, such as *twādæglīc* once in two days); cognate with Old High German *tagalīh* (modern German *täglich*) and Old Icelandic *dagligr;* for suffix see -LY[2]. The equivalent Old English word for "daily" was *dæghwāmlic,* which survived as *daiwamliche* in Middle English into the 1200's.

dainty *adj.* delicate, delicious. About 1300 *deinte* delightful, pleasing, in *Arthour and Merlin;* developed from a noun meaning esteem, affection (before 1250, in *Ancrene Riwle*), and found as a surname *Deintie* (1199); borrowed from Old French *daintee, daintié* price, value, delicacy, good dish, pleasure, joy, from Latin *dignitātem* (nominative *dignitās*) worthiness, worth, beauty, from *dignus* worthy; see the doublet DIGNITY.

The noun sense of a choice bit of food, a delicacy, is first recorded about 1300.

dairy *n.* place where milk and cream are kept. About 1300 *deierie,* formed with Anglo-French *-erie* -ery from *deie, daie* maid, dairymaid, corresponding to Old English *dǣge* kneader of bread, which is cognate with Old Icelandic *deigja* housekeeper, female servant (from Proto-Germanic **daizjōn*), and Gothic *deigan* knead, and Old English *dāg* DOUGH. —**dairymaid** *n.* 1599; earlier, in Middle English *daie* (probably before 1200). —**dairyman** *n.* 1784; earlier, in Middle English *daieman,* recorded as a surname *Deyman* (1428), and *Dai* (1196).

dais (dā′is) *n.* raised platform. Probably before 1300 *deys,* in *Kyng Alisaunder,* and *deis* (about 1300), borrowed from Anglo-French *deis,* in Old French *dais* table, platform, canopy, from Latin *discus* disk-shaped object, discus, from Greek *dískos* quoit, dish, disk. Doublet of DESK, DISCUS, DISH, and DISK. The modern spelling *dais* is from modern French *dais,* the two-syllable pronunciation in English being influenced by the spelling. According to the OED the word died out in English about 1600, but was revived after 1800.

daisy *n.* Before 1300 *daiseie;* earlier, as surname *Dayeseye* (1281); developed from Old English *dægesege* (about 1000, in Ælfric's *Glossary*), and *dæges ēage* day's eye, in allusion to closing of the petals in the evening, and their opening again in the morning; see DAY and EYE.

dale *n.* Probably before 1200 *dale,* in Layamon's *Chronicle of Britain,* developed from Old English *dæl* (before 899, in Alfred's translation of Orosius' *Historiarum Adversus Paganos*). Old English *dæl* (from Proto-Germanic **dalan*) is cognate with Old Saxon, Middle Dutch, and modern Dutch *dal* valley, Old High German *tal* (modern German *Tal*), Old Icelandic *dalr,* Gothic *dal* valley. The word is also cognate with Greek *thólos* round building, Welsh *dol* dale, Old Slavic *dolŭ* pit, valley, and Russian *dol, dolina* valley, from Indo-European **dhol-* (Pok. 245). The basic meaning is "something curved." It is used in geographical names, such as *Annandale* and in German *Joachimstal* (see DOLLAR), and has a poetical use in literary English.

dally *v.* act in a playful manner. Probably before 1300 *daylen* to talk, converse; later, to chat, converse idly (probably about 1390); possibly borrowed from Anglo-French *dalier* to amuse oneself, of uncertain origin. According to FEW, however, the Anglo-French word could be a loan from an unattested Old English word related to Middle English *daylen.* The meaning of act in a frivolous manner, is first recorded about 1440. —**dalliance** *n.* Before 1349, formed from English *dally* + *-ance.*

dam[1] *n.* wall built to hold back water. Probably before 1400; earlier, body of water (about 1340, and as a surname *Dam,* 1230). The Middle English *dam* is cognate with Old Frisian *damm* dam, Middle High German *tam, tamm* (modern German *Damm*), Old Icelandic *damm,* from Proto-Germanic **dammaz* (perhaps from Indo-European **dhob-mó-s,* Pok. 239), from which have been formed the verbs represented in Old English *fordemman* to dam up, Old High German *temmen,* Old Frisian and Old Icelandic *demma,* Gothic *faúrdammjan* to stop up. —**v.** provide with a dam. Probably before 1475 *dammen* to stop up or block, from the noun.

dam[2] *n.* female parent of four-footed hoofed animals. Before 1325 *dame;* earlier *dam* mother, mother superior (probably before 1200, in *Ancrene Riwle*); see DAME. Originally *dam* was used in all the senses of *dame* (i.e. lady, female ruler, housewife, schoolmistress, mother), but in the 1500's the sense of mother was differentiated to *dam.*

damage *n.* Probably before 1300, in *Arthour and Merlin,* borrowed from Old French *damage* loss caused by injury (*dam* damage, from Latin *damnum* loss, hurt, damage + *-age* -age); see DAMN. —**v.** About 1330, borrowed from Old French *damagier,* from Old French *damage,* n.

damascene (dam′əsēn) *n.* 1481-90, ornament made with inlaid gold or silver or with a wavy design (in an early collection of books); earlier, inhabitant of Damascus (1375, in Chaucer's *Canterbury Tales*); borrowed from Latin *Damascēnus* of Damascus, Syria, from Greek *Damaskēnós,* from *Damaskós* Damascus; see the doublet DAMSON. The wavy pattern of the design was characteristic of the steel of swords made in Damascus, and of damask cloth. —**v.** to ornament with a wavy pattern, as by inlaying. Perhaps, 1585; from the noun.

damask (dam′əsk) *n.* silk woven with an elaborate pattern. 1378; earlier, name for Damascus (about 1250); borrowed from Medieval Latin *damascus,* from Latin *Damascus* the ancient city and capital of Syria, famous for its steel and silk fabrics, from Greek *Damaskós* Damascus.

dame *n.* lady, madam, (as slang) woman. Probably before 1200, mother superior, in *Ancrene Riwle;* about 1200, lady or female ruler; later, housewife (before 1338, in Mannyngs *Chronicle of England*); borrowed from Old French *dame,* from Late Latin *domna,* Latin *domina* lady, mistress of the house, from *domus* house; see DOME. Compare MADAM for a related etymology. In Old French *dame* the *a* developed from *o* in Latin *domina* when the word was unaccented before the next word. The slang sense of woman is attested in American English since 1902, but has also been recorded in English dialect.

damn *v.* About 1280 *dampen* to condemn, borrowed from Old French *damner,* from Latin *damnāre,* from *damnum* damage, loss, hurt. Latin *damnum* is related to *daps* sacrificial meal, which is cognate with Greek *dapánē* cost, expenditure, Old Icelandic *tafn* sacrifice, booty, nourishment, Armenian *tawn* festival, feast, from Indo-European **dāp-/dəp-* (Pok. 176); possibly from an ancient religious term. —**n.** 1619, in John Fletcher's *Monsieur Thomas;* from the verb. —**adj.** 1775, shortened from *damned* (probably before 1405); earlier, *dampned* (about 1378, in a version of *Piers Plowman*), from the past participle of *damn,* v. —**damnable** *adj.* Before 1333 *dampnable* deserving punishment; borrowed from Old French *damnable,* from Latin *damnābilis,* from *damnāre,* see DAMN; for suffix see -ABLE. —**damnation** *n.* Before 1300 *dampnacioun* consignment to hell; borrowed from Old French *dampnation,* from Latin *damnātiōnem* (nominative *damnātiō*), from *damnāre;* for suffix see -TION.

damp *n.* 1316, noxious vapor; possibly found in Old English **damp;* cognate with Middle Dutch or Middle Low German *damp* vapor and with Old High German *damph* vapor, steam (modern German *Dampf*), Middle High German *dimpfen* to steam, smoke, and Old Icelandic *dumba* dust, *dimma* darkness, *dimmr* dark; see DIM. Old High German *damph* derives from Proto-Germanic **dampaz,* Indo-European **dhombos,* root **dhem-b-* (Pok. 248). The meaning of dampness, humidity, moisture, is not recorded in English until 1706, with a single possible, but ambiguous use, in 1586. —**v.** 1380, to suffocate; from the noun. The meaning of moisten is first recorded in English in 1671, though a sense of deaden, depress, "wet down" spirits or zeal is recorded in 1548, in writings of Udall. **—adj.** 1590, dazed or stupefied; from the noun. The meaning of moist or slightly wet is first recorded in 1706. **—dampen** *v.* (1380) surviving Middle English form of *damp,* v. **—dampener** *n.* 1887, formed from English *dampen* + *-er*[1].

damsel *n.* Probably about 1225, in *King Horn;* borrowed from Old French *dameisele,* from Gallo-Romance **domnicella,* diminutive of Latin *domina* lady, mistress of the house; see DAME.

damson *n.* small plum. Before 1475 *damson,* developed from earlier *damesene* plum tree (about 1390); borrowed from Latin *prūnum damascēnum* plum of Damascus, from Greek *Damaskēnón,* neuter of *Damaskēnós* of Damascus, from *Damaskós* Damascus; see DAMASK. Doublet of DAMASCENE.

dance *v.* Probably before 1300 *dauncer,* in *Kyng Alisaunder;* borrowed from Old French *dancier,* of uncertain origin; perhaps: 1) from Frankish **dintjan* (compare Middle Dutch *deinsen, densen* to shrink back), based on the conjecture that the Latin word for dance was lost in France because of the religious ban on dancing in the Middle Ages; *or* 2) from Vulgar Latin **deanteāre,* from Late Latin *deante* in front of, from Latin *dē* from, and *ante* before. **—n.** Probably before 1300 *daunce,* in *Kyng Alisaunder;* borrowed from Old French *daunce,* from *dancier* to dance. **—dancer** *n.* 1440 *dauncere;* earlier as a surname *Dancere* (1130); borrowed from Old French **dauncier,* or formed from Middle English *dauncen* + *-er*[1].

dandelion *n.* Probably about 1425 *dandelyon;* developed from earlier *dent-de-lyon* (1373) and *Daundelyon* (1363, as a surname); borrowed from Middle French *dent de lion,* literally, lion's tooth (from its toothed leaves), a translation of Medieval Latin *dens leonis* (Latin *dēns* tooth + *leōnis,* genitive of *leō* lion); see TOOTH and LION.

dander *n.* angry temper. 1832, possibly a figurative use of *dander* dandruff, alteration of DANDRUFF; or a figurative use of *dander* ferment.

dandle *v.* move up and down playfully. 1530 *dandyll,* in Palsgrave's *Lesclarcissement,* of uncertain origin; compare Italian *dandolare,* variant of *dondolare* to rock, swing, dangle.

dandruff *n.* scurf. 1545; the origin of the first element, *dand-,* is unknown; the second element probably came from Northumbrian or East Anglian dialect *huff, hurf* scab, from a Scandinavian source (compare Old Icelandic *hrūfa* scab, *hrjūfr* scabby, leprous). The word is cognate with Old English *hrēof* rough, scabby, leprous, Old High German *hruf* scab, *riob* leprous (from Proto-Germanic **Hreufaz/Hrufaz*), Latvian *kraũpa* scab, and Lithuanian *kraupùs* rough, from Indo-European **kreup-/kroup-/krup-* (Pok. 623).

dandy *n.* fop, fashionable person. About 1780, of uncertain origin; possibly shortened from earlier *Jack-a-dandy,* with the same meaning (1659). The earliest form of the latter is *Jack O'Dandy* (1632). These usages originated in Scotland, where *Dandy* is a variant or diminutive of the name *Andrew.* According to the OED *dandy* came into vogue in London around 1813-19. **—adj.** 1792, fine, superior, in American English; probably from the noun.

danger *n.* Before 1250 *daunger* arrogance, insolence, in a version of *Ancrene Riwle;* later *dangere* (before 1338 in Mannyng's *Chronicle of England;* borrowed through Anglo-French *daunger,* from Old French *dangier* power to harm, mastery, alteration (influenced by *dam* damage; see DAMAGE) of *dongier,* from Vulgar Latin **domniārium* or **dominiārium* power, from Latin *dominium* sovereignty; see DOMINION. The meaning of something that causes harm, a risk or peril, is first recorded in English in about 1378, in a version of *Piers Plowman.* **—dangerous** *adj.* Before 1200 *dangerus* difficult to deal with, haughty or aloof, in *Ancrene Riwle;* borrowed through Anglo-French *dangerous,* from Old French *dangeros, dangereus,* from *dangier;* for suffix see -OUS.

dangle *v.* hang loosely. About 1590, probably borrowed from a Scandinavian source (compare Norwegian and Danish *dingle,* Swedish and Icelandic *dingla,* both meaning to dangle), from Indo-European **dhen-gh-/dhon-gh-* (Pok. 250).

Danish *adj.* Before 1387 *Danysche,* formed from *Danes,* pl., people of Denmark (before 1338) + *-ische* -ish[1]. Middle English *Danes* was borrowed from Old Icelandic *Danir,* found also in Late Latin *Danī.* Middle English also had earlier *Densce* (probably before 1200) and *Denescæ* (1070), found in Old English *Denisc.* The phrase *Danish pastry* is first recorded in Webster (1934) and its clipped form *Danish* in 1963.

dank *adj.* moist, wet. Probably before 1400, in *Morte Arthur;* borrowed probably from a Scandinavian source (compare Swedish *dank* marshy spot, related to Old Icelandic *dǫkk* pool), cognate with Lettish *danga* muddy slough, from Indo-European **dhongwā,* root *dhem-* (Pok. 248).

dapper *adj.* neat, trim. About 1440 *dapyr* elegant, in *Promptorium Parvulorum;* borrowed from Middle Dutch *dapper* agile, strong, sturdy, which is cognate with Middle Low German *dapper* heavy, stout, Old High German *tapfar* heavy, Middle High German *tapfer, dapfer* firm, full, weighty, bold (modern German *tapfer* brave), Old Icelandic *dapr* sad, dreary (from Proto-Germanic **dapraz*). Outside Germanic cognates are found in Old Slavic *debelŭ* thick, and Tocharian A *tsopats* big, *täppo* courage, from Indo-European **dheb-/dhob-* thick, stout (Pok. 239).

dapple *adj.* 1551, marked with round spots. **—n.** 1580, in Sidney's *The Arcadia.* **—v.** 1599, in Shakespeare's *Much Ado About Nothing.* Both noun and verb apparently from the participial adjective *dappled* (about 1400) and *dapple,* adj. (1551); of uncertain origin.

dare *v.* Old English (about 950) *darr, dear,* originally the 1st and 3rd person singular present indicative of *durran* to dare; the form *dearst* 2nd person singular is recorded earlier in *Beowulf,* about 725. The Old English verb *durran* is cognate with Old High German *giturran* to dare, Gothic *gadars* I dare (from Proto-Germanic **ders-/dars-/durs-*). Outside Germanic cognates are found in Ionic Greek *tharseîn* be bold, and Sanskrit *dhárṣati* (he) is bold, dares, from Indo-European **dhers-/dhors-/dhr̥s-* (Pok. 259). **—n.** 1594, from the verb. **—daredevil** *n.* (1794); *adj.* (1832). **—daring** *n.* About 1385, in Chaucer's *Troilus and Criseyde,* from *dare,* verb, in Middle English *durren.*

dark *adj.* Probably about 1200 *dork;* later *derk* (about 1280); developed from Old English *deorc* (about 725, in *Beowulf*), from Proto-Germanic **derkaz;* cognate with Old High German *tarchannen* to hide something (in a dark place), Middle Irish *derg* red, from Indo-European *dherg-/dhorg- (Pok. 251). —**n.** About 1225 in *King Horn,* from the Middle English verb. —**Dark Ages** (1876; earlier **dark ages,** 1748). —**darken** *v.* About 1300, found in Old English *deorcian.* —**dark horse** (1831) —**darkly** *adv.* 1380, in Chaucer's *House of Fame,* found in Old English *deorclīce.* —**darkness** *n.* Before 1325 *derkenes,* found in Old English *deorcnes.*

darling *n.* Probably about 1150 *derling;* later *darlyng* (before 1450); developed from Old English *dēorling* (before 899, in Alfred's translation of Boethius' *De Consolatione Philosophiae*); formed from *dēor, dēore* DEAR + *-ling,* noun suffix. —**adj.** 1509, from the noun.

darn[1] *v.* mend. About 1600, borrowed from Middle French dialect *darner* mend, from *darne* piece, from Breton *darn,* related to Welsh *darn* piece, fragment, part; cognate with Greek *dérein* to skin, flay, and Old English *teran* to tear; see TEAR[2] pull apart. It is possible that some connection exists between *darn* and *dern* to conceal, hide, but it has not been established. —**n.** 1720, from the verb.

darn[2] *v.* curse. 1781, American English, euphemism for *damn;* probably influenced by *tarnal* (shortened variant of *eternal*). —**darned** *adj.* 1815, confounded (used as an expletive, 1808); *adv.* 1806, extremely.

dart *n.* Probably before 1300, in *Sir Tristrem;* borrowed from Old French *dart,* from a Germanic source (compare Old English *daroth* dart, from Proto-Germanic **darōthuz,* Old High German *tart* dart or javelin, and Old Icelandic *darradhr* dart, javelin, or peg); cognate with Sanskrit *dhā́rā* edge, blade, from Indo-European **dhō-/dhə-* sharp (Pok. 272). —**v.** About 1385, pierce with a dart, in Chaucer's *Troilus and Criseyde;* from the noun.

dash *v.* Probably before 1300, in *Arthour and Merlin,* of uncertain origin, but probably formed like other verbs, such as *clash, bash, smash,* etc., from some imitative notion of sound of striking or motion (compare Swedish *daska* to slap, strike, Danish *daske* to drub, Dutch *daske* to beat, strike). —**n.** About 1390, from the verb. —**dashboard** *n.* (1846) —**dasher** *n.* (1790, a person who dashes; earlier, a brush for sprinkling holy water, probably before 1325). —**dashing** *n.* (about 1450, splashing).

dashiki (dəshē'kē) *n.* loose, shirtlike pullover garment, originally worn in Africa. 1968, borrowed from a West African language (compare Yoruba *danshiki,* Akan (Ghana) *dánta* underclothing).

dastard *n.* About 1440, coward, dullard (stupid person), in *Promptorium Parvulorum;* apparently formed from **dast* dazed, past participle of *dasen* to daze + *-ard;* see DAZE. —**dastardly** *adj.* (1567).

data *n.pl.* of **datum,** which see.

date[1] *n.* time or period when something happens. About 1330, borrowed from Old French *date,* probably a learned borrowing from Medieval Latin *data,* noun use of the feminine singular form of Latin *datus* given, past participle of *dare* give. In Latin *data,* agreeing with the unexpressed or omitted *epistula* letter, was abstracted from such a phrase as the following, found in Cicero: *d. pr. K. Iūn. Athēnīs,* abbreviated form of *data prīdiē Kalendās Iūniās Athēnīs,* with the meaning (letter) given (to a messenger) the day before the calends of June at (or from) Athens. Since such a formula was employed so often, usually at the close of a letter, the first word of the formula, *data,* became the term for the time stated. Latin *dare* is related to *dōnum* gift (the source of English DONATION) and cognate with Greek *didónai* to give, and Sanskrit *dádāti* (he) gives, from Indo-European **dō-/də-* (Pok. 223).

The meaning of an appointment or engagement, especially with a person of the opposite sex, is first recorded in 1885 in American English. The related informal sense of a person of the opposite sex with whom one has made a date, is first recorded in 1925, also in American English.

—**v.** Apparently before 1400 *daten* to mark (a letter, etc.) with a date, fix the date or time of (an event, etc.); from *date,* n. The meaning of mark as old-fashioned or outdated, is first recorded in 1895. The informal sense of make or have a date (social engagement) with, especially regularly, is first recorded in 1902 in American English.

date[2] *n.* fruit of a palm tree. About 1300, borrowed from Old French *date,* from Old Provençal *datil,* from Latin *dactylus,* from Greek *dáktylos* date; originally, finger. The leaves and fruit of the date palm are shaped somewhat like fingers. Doublet of DACTYL. —**date palm** (1837; earlier *date tree,* probably before 1400).

dative *n.* case in grammar denoting an indirect object. About 1434 *datif,* borrowed from Latin *datīvus cāsus* case of giving, from *datus,* past participle of *dare* to give (translation of Greek *dotikḗ ptôsis,* from *dotikós* related to giving, from *dotós* given); see DATE[1] time; for suffix see -IVE.

datum *n., pl.* **data.** thing given or assumed; information or fact. 1646, in plural *data,* borrowing of Latin *datum* (thing) given, past participle (neuter) of *dare* give; see DATE[1] time.

daub (dôb) *v.* cover with plaster or soft material. Probably about 1380, borrowed from Old French *dauber,* originally, to whitewash, plaster, probably from Latin *dealbāre* (*dē-* thoroughly + *albāre* whiten, from *albus* white; see ALB). —**n.** material for daubing. 1446, from the verb. —**dauber** *n.* Before 1382 *daubere,* in the Wycliffe Bible; earlier, as a surname *Daubour* (1263).

daughter *n.* About 1385 *doughter,* in Chaucer's *Troilus and Criseyde;* earlier *dohter* (1110); developed from Old English *dohtor* (about 725, in *Beowulf*); cognate with Old Saxon *dohtar* daughter, Old Frisian *dochter,* Old and Middle High German *tohter* (modern German *Tochter*), Old Icelandic *dōttir* (with *-tt-* for *-ht-*), and Gothic *daúhtar* (from Proto-Germanic **doHtḗr,* earlier **dhuktḗr*). Cognates outside Germanic include Greek *thygátēr* (accusative *thygatéra*) daughter, Sanskrit *duhitā́* (accusative *duhitáram*), Persian *duxtar,* Lithuanian *duktė̃,* Old Slavic *dŭšti,* Tocharian A *ckācar,* Tocharian B *tkācer,* from Indo-European **dhug(h)ətér-* (Pok. 277). —**daughter-in-law** *n.* (before 1382, in the Wycliffe Bible).

daunt *v.* Before 1325 *danten* frighten or discourage, in *Cursor Mundi;* earlier, overcome, vanquish (before 1300, in *Kyng Alisaunder*); borrowed from Old French *danter,* variant of *donter,* from Latin *domitāre,* frequentative form of *domāre* to tame; see TAME. —**dauntless** *adj.* (1593, in Shakespeare's *3 Henry VI*).

dauphin (dô'fēn) *n.* title of the oldest son of the king of France. 1418, in *Proceedings of the Privy Council;* borrowed from Middle French *dauphin,* from Old French *daufin,* originally, a family name, from Medieval Latin *Dalphinus,* for Latin *delphīnus,* literally, DOLPHIN (because their banners bore a dolphin as their symbol).

The last lord of *Dauphiné* (a province ruled by the family *Delphinus*) wished the title to be perpetuated, and upon ceding the province to Philip of Valois in 1349, made it a condition that the title be borne by the oldest son of the French king.

davenport *n.* long couch. 1902 *Davenport Bed Couch,* in *Sears Catalogue;* earlier, a small ornamental writing table (1853); apparently from the name of its manufacturer.

davit *n.* one of a pair of curved arms at side of a ship for holding a small boat. 1373 *daviot,* borrowed from Anglo-French *daviot,* in Old French *daviet,* originally, a diminutive of the name *Davi* David. In English this device was also called a *david* in the 1600's.

Davy Jones 1751, the spirit of the sea; also **Davy Jones's locker** bottom of the sea (1803); nautical slang of unknown origin.

daw *n.* small bird (commonly called jackdaw). Probably before 1425 *dawe,* (from Proto-Germanic **dazwṓ*); cognate with Old High German *taha.* Old High German *taha* derives from Proto-Germanic **dáHwō,* Indo-European **dhakw-* (Friedrich Kluge, *Etymologisches Wörterbuch der deutschen Sprache,* p.136), and Middle High German *tahe* jackdaw.

dawdle (dô′dəl) *v.* loiter. Before 1656, origin uncertain; perhaps dialectal variant of *daddle* walk unsteadily, be slow in motion. **—dawdler** *n.* (1818)

dawn *v.* 1499, a back formation from *dawninge* (about 1250), probably from a Scandinavian source (compare Danish *dagning,* from *daga* to dawn). Middle English *dawninge* was a replacement of Old English *dagung* (also found in Middle English as *dawoing* dawn), from *dagian* to become day, derived from the root of *dæg* DAY, and cognate with Old High German *tagēn* and Old Icelandic *daga,* both meaning to dawn. **—n.** 1599, in Shakespeare's *Henry V,* from the verb *dawn.* Although Old Icelandic had similar forms *dœgun, dagan* dawn (from *daga* to dawn), the noun apparently developed within English.

day *n.* Probably before 1200 *dai,* in Layamon's *Chronicle of Britain;* developed from Old English *dæg* (about 725, in *Beowulf*). Old English *dæg* is cognate with Old Saxon, Middle Dutch and modern Dutch *dag* day, Old Frisian *dei, dī* (plural *degar*), Old High German *tag* (modern German *Tag*), and Gothic *dags,* (all from Proto-Germanic **dazaz,*), and also cognate with Gothic *fidur-dōgs* of four days, Old Icelandic *døgr* day (*-r-* stem) and *døgn* day, half-day (12 hours), (*-n-* stem). All of these forms owe their initial consonant to the influence of a Germanic representative of an Indo-European base **dhegwh-* (Pok. 240) meaning heat, burning, found in Sanskrit *dáhati* burns, *dāha-s* heat, *nidāghá-s* heat, summer, Greek *téphrā* ashes, Latin *fovēre* to warm, heat, *favilla* ashes, *febris* fever, Lithuanian *dègti* to burn, *dāgas* summer heat. But from the nature of the final consonant of the Germanic words and especially from the striking three-fold stem (*-r-, -n-, -es-*) displayed, scholars are convinced that the cognates of English *day* are Sanskrit *áhar* day (*-r-* stem nominative), *áhāni* (*-n-* stem nominative plural), *áhobhis* (*-es-* stem instrumental plural), and Avestan *azan-* (*-n-* stem), with Indo-European base **ăĝh-* or **ŏĝh-* (Pok. 7).

English *day* is not related to Latin *diēs* day. **—daybreak** *n.* (1530, in Palsgrave's *Lesclarcissement*). **—daydream** *n.* (1685, in a translation of Dryden's); *v.* (1820, in Washington Irving's *Sketch Book*). **—daylight** *n.* Probably about 1150 *daies liht;* later, *dæi-liht* (probably before 1200) and *dailigt* (about 1300). **—daytime** *n.* (1533)

daze *v.* stun. Probably about 1380 *dasen;* borrowed probably from a Scandinavian source (compare Old Icelandic **dasa, dasask* become exhausted, related to *dāsi* blunderer); cognate with Middle Dutch *dasen* act silly and perhaps with Latin *famēs* hunger, and *fatīgāre* to tire; see FATIGUE. **—n.** dazed condition. 1825, from the verb; earlier, an old name for mica, from its glitter (1671).

dazzle *v.* 1481 *dasel,* in Caxton's translation of *The History of Reynard the Fox, dasle,* frequentative form of Middle English *dasen* DAZE. **—n.** 1627, from the verb. **—dazzler** *n.* (before 1800) **—dazzling** *adj.* (1571)

D-day *n.* 1918, the date set for the beginning of a military operation, *D* being an abbreviation for *day,* probably on the pattern of (1918) *H-hour.*

de- a prefix derived mainly from Latin *dē-* (from preposition *dē* down, down from, away from) or the French equivalent *de-, dé-,* in words borrowed from Latin or French, and meaning: **1** down, lower, as in *depress = press down.* **2** off, away, as in *derail = off the rails.* **3** thoroughly, completely, as in *despoil = spoil completely,* or some other extended meaning, as in *deceive, delay, deride,* and so on.

In a few words English *de-* and French *dé-* are from Old French *des-* representing Latin *dis-* (also meaning away), as in *debauch* (Old French *desbaucher*), or apart, as in *deploy* (French *déployer,* Old French *desploier,* Latin *displicāre*).

In English, *de-* is productive especially in the meaning of undoing or doing the opposite of an underlying verb, as in *depopulate, decentralize,* and forming verbs from nouns to mean get rid of, as in *debug, defog,* or to move from, as in *deplane, detrain.*

deacon *n.* Old English *dēacon, dīacon* (before 899, in Alfred's translation of Bede's *Ecclesiastical History*); learned borrowing from Latin *diāconus,* from Greek *diā́konos* servant of the church, religious official; originally, servant, related to *enkoneîn* be quick and active, especially in service, from *koneîn* hurry, which is cognate with Latin *cōnārī* to try, endeavor, from Indo-European **kon-/kōn-* (Pok. 564).

dead *adj.* Old English *dēad* (about 725, in *Beowulf*); cognate with Old Frisian *dād* dead, Old Saxon *dōd,* Middle Dutch *doot, dood* (modern Dutch *dood*), Old High German *tōt* (modern German *tot*), Old Icelandic *daudhr,* and Gothic *dauths,* from Proto-Germanic **dauđás,* from Indo-European **dhou-tó-s* (Pok. 260); related to DIE[1] become dead. **—adv.** completely, absolutely. Before 1393, in Gower's *Confessio Amantis,* a figurative extension of the primary adverbial meaning of in the manner characteristic of death. **—n.** Old English (about 950), from the adjective by absolute use. **—deaden** *v.* 1723; earlier, inferred from *deadened* (1720); formed from English *dead,* adj. + *-en*[1].

deaf *adj.* Old English *dēaf* (about 750, in Cynewulf's *Juliana*); cognate with Old Frisian *dāf* deaf, Middle Dutch and modern Dutch *doof,* Middle Low German *dōf,* Old High German *toup, toub* deaf (modern German *taub*), Old Icelandic *daufr,* Gothic *daufs* unperceptive, (from Proto-Germanic **dauƀaz*). Outside Germanic cognates are found in Old Irish *dub* black, Welsh *du* black, and ultimately Greek *typhlós* blind, from Indo-European **dhoubh-/dhubh-* dark (Pok. 264). **—deafen** *v.* (1597, in Shakespeare's *2 Henry IV).*

deal *n.* part, portion. Old English (before 700) *dǣl;* cognate with Old Frisian and Old Saxon *dēl* part, Middle Dutch and modern Dutch *deel,* Old High German *teil* (modern German *Teil*), Old Icelandic *deild,* and Gothic *dails.* Outside Germanic only Slavic has comparable words: Old Slavic *dělŭ* part, *děliti* to divide (but it is uncertain whether these are cognates or loans). The Proto-Germanic word (**dailiz*) was perhaps an early borrowing from Venetic-Illyrian (compare Greek *daíesthai* to divide, apportion), from Indo-European **dāi-/dəi-* (Pok. 175). Related to DOLE.

The meaning of an act of dealing in business, a transaction, bargain (as in *a fair deal, make a deal*), derived from the verb and is first found in 1837.
—**v.** divide, distribute. Old English (about 725) *dǣlan;* cognate with Old High German *teilan* distribute (modern German *teilen*), Old Icelandic *deila,* and Gothic *dailjan.* The sense of have to do with, ("deal with") is first recorded about 1200, in *The Ormulum.* **—dealer** *n.* About 1000, in Ælfric's *Glossary.* **—dealing** *n.* (1378)

dean *n.* About 1330 *den* head of a chapter of canons; earlier, in a surname *Denesclerk* (1285); borrowed from Old French *deien,* from Late Latin *decānus* master, commander of ten soldiers, monks, etc., from Latin *decem* TEN. Doublet of DOYEN.

The meaning of head of a college division is first recorded in English in 1524, although its usage is found in the Medieval Latin of England and Scotland from the 1200's. The meaning of doyen is first recorded in English in 1687.

dear *adj.* About 1250 *dere,* later *deere* (about 1380, in Chaucer's *Canterbury Tales*); developed from Old English (about 725) *dēore* precious, valuable, costly; cognate with Old High German *tiuri* and Old Icelandic *dȳrr,* both meaning costly (Proto-Germanic **deurijaz*); of unknown origin. In polite forms of address, *dear* (as in "Dear Sir") is first recorded about 1450. The modern spelling *dear* appeared in the 1500's.—**adv.** Old English (about 1000) *dēore;* cognate with Old High German *tiuro;* see the adjective. —**n.** Before 1375, probably shortened from *dear one, my dear,* originally as a term of address, and then a noun; possibly by influence of similar use of Old French *chier* and Latin *carus.* The interjection *O dear* is first found in 1694 (in Congreve's *The Double-Dealer)* and *Dear me!* is first attested in 1773, in Goldsmith's *She Stoops to Conquer.* But according to Olivia Vlahos, *The Battle-Ax People,* p. 201, the English exclamation "Dear me!" was taken from Italian *dio mio* my God, during the Renaissance. **—dearly** *adv.* Probably about 1300 *dere,* later *deere* (about 1385, in Chaucer's *Canterbury Tales*); developed from Old English *dēorlīce* (about 750, in Cynewulf's *Elene*).

dearth (dėrth) *n.* scarcity. Probably about 1300 *derthe,* with the likely original meaning of costliness; formed from the root of Old English *dēore* DEAR. Middle English *derthe* is cognate with Old Saxon *diuritha* splendor, glory, love, Middle Dutch *dierte* (modern Dutch *duurte*), Old High German *tiurida, diurida* glory, Middle High German *tiurde* great value, costliness, and Old Icelandic *dȳrdh* glory, from Proto-Germanic **deuríthō.*

The original sense of the Middle English word referred to a famine, when food is scarce and costly, but the word was extended to the meaning of scarcity of anything, about 1330.

death *n.* Old English *dēath* (about 725, in *Beowulf*); cognate with Old Frisian *dāth* death, Old Saxon *dōth,* Middle Dutch *doot, dood* (modern Dutch *dood*), Old High German *tōd* death (modern German *Tod*), Old Icelandic *daudhi,* and Gothic *dauthus,* from Proto-Germanic **dauthuz,* from Indo-European **dhoú-tu-s* (Pok. 260); related to DIE[1] become dead. **—deathbed** *n.* (about 725, in *Beowulf,* meaning the grave; later, the bed on which one dies, about 1300). **—deathblow** *n.* (1795; replacing *deth* or *dethes dint,* recorded probably before 1300). **—deathless** *adj.* (1598)

debacle (dābä′kəl) *n.* disaster. 1848, in Thackeray's *Vanity Fair;* originally, breaking up of ice in a river (1802); borrowed from French *débâcle* breaking up of ice, disaster, from *débâcler* to free, from Middle French *desbacler* to unbar (*dé-* off, un-, from Latin *dis-* + *bâcler* to bar, from Old Provençal *baclar* from Vulgar Latin **bacculāre,* from **bacculum* bar, staff, variant of Latin *baculum* stick; see BACILLUS).

debar *v.* shut out, prevent. Probably before 1405, borrowed through Anglo-French *debarrer,* from Old French *desbarer* to unbar (*des-* de- + *barer, barrer* to BAR).

debark *v.* disembark. 1654, borrowed from French *débarquer* (*dé-* off from Latin *dis-* + *barque* BARK[3] ship).

debase *v.* 1568, formed in English from *de-* down + BASE[2] low, on the analogy of *abase.* **—debasement** *n.* (1593)

debate *n.* Before 1325 *debat* quarrel, dispute, in *Cursor Mundi;* borrowed from Old French *debat,* from *débatre* to fight, contend (*de-* down, completely + *batre* to beat; see BATTER[1] strike). —**v.** About 1380 *debaten* to fight, oppose, in writings of Chaucer; borrowed from Old French *débatre* to fight. **—debatable** *adj.* (1536) **—debater** *n.* (about 1395)

debauch (dibôch′) *v.* Before 1595, borrowed from Middle French *débaucher* entice from work or duty, but earlier, to split or separate, and, originally, to trim (wood) to make a beam out of it; from Old French *desbaucher* (*des-* de- + *bauch* beam, earlier *balc,* from Frankish **balk;* compare Old High German *balko* beam; see BALK). —**n.** 1603, borrowed from French *débauche,* from *débaucher* to debauch. **—debauchee** *n.* Before 1661, borrowed from French *débauché* debauched person, noun use of the past participle of *débaucher* to debauch. **—debauchery** *n.* 1642, in Milton's writings, formed from English *debauch,* v. + *-ery.*

debenture *n.* written acknowledgment of a debt. 1437 *debentur,* in *Proceedings of the Privy Council;* borrowed from Latin *dēbentur* they are owing (occurring at the head of a list of sums owed), 3rd person plural present passive of *dēbēre* to owe; see DEBT. The spelling with *-ure* appeared in 1469, probably by influence of the suffix *-ure,* as in *nature* and *picture.*

debility *n.* Probably before 1425 *debilite,* in an anonymous translation of Chauliac's *Grande Chirurgie;* borrowed from Middle French *débilité,* from Latin *dēbilitātem* (nominative *dēbilitās*), from *dēbilis* weak (*dē-* from, away + *-bilis* strength; cognate with Sanskrit *bála-m* strength and Greek *beltíōn* better, from Indo-European **bel-/bol-,* Pok. 96); for suffix see -ITY. **—debilitate** *v.* 1533, borrowed from Latin *dēbilitātus,* past participle of *dēbilitāre* weaken, from *dēbilis* weak; for suffix see -ATE[1].

debit *n.* Before 1455 *dubete* debt, in *The Paston Letters;* later *debyte* (before 1475); borrowed through Middle French *débet,* or directly from Latin *dēbitum* thing owed, neuter past participle of *dēbēre* to owe; see DEBT. As a bookkeeping term, it is first found in 1776, in the records of the trial (for forgery) of the Maharaja of Nuncomar. —**v.** 1682, from the noun.

debonair or **debonaire** (debənãr′) *adj.* cheerful, pleasant, courteous. Probably before 1200 *debonere,* in *Ancrene Riwle;* borrowed from Old French *debonaire,* from the phrase *de bon aire* of good origin or character (*aire* area, site, situation; origin, race; character; see AERIE), contrasted with *de put aire* of bad origin or character, in the *Song of Roland.*

debouch (dibüsh′) *v.* come out into the open. 1745, borrowed from French *déboucher* emerge from, issue, open, from Old French *desbouchier* open out (*dé-* away, off + *bouche* opening, mouth, from Latin *bucca* mouth, originally, puffed out cheek or mouth), perhaps borrowed from Celtic (compare the Gaulish names *Buccus, Buccō, Bucciō*); cognate with Old English *pohha* bag, from Indo European **bu-k-* (Pok.100).

debris or **débris** (dəbrē′) *n.* 1708, borrowing of French *débris,* from obsolete French *débriser* break down, crush, from Old French *debrisier* (*de-* away, down + *brisier* to break, from Vulgar Latin **brisiāre,* from Late Latin *brisāre,* possibly of Gaulish origin; compare Old Irish *brissim* I break (*-ss-* for *-st-*), and Latin *friāre* to crumble, from Indo-European **bhrēi-/bhrī-/bhri-* (Pok.166); see FRIABLE and BURST).

debt *n.* About 1280 *dette;* earlier, *deatte* (probably before 1200, in a different dialect); borrowed from Old French *dete,* from Latin *dēbitum* thing owed, neuter past participle of *dēbēre* to owe, originally, keep something from someone (*dē-* away + *habēre* to have; see HABIT). About 1405 the spelling *debtes,* pl., is first recorded in English in imitation of the Latin form *dēbitum.* —**debtor** *n.* Probably before 1200 *dettour;* borrowed possibly through Anglo-French *detour,* in Old French *detor, dettor, detour,* etc., from Latin *dēbitor* a debtor, from *dēbitus,* past participle of *dēbēre* to owe.

debut or **début** (dā′byü) *n.* first public appearance. 1751, in correspondence of Chesterfield; borrowing of French *début,* from *débuter* make the first appearance, play first as in billiards, fire as in artillery (*dé-* from + *but* starting point, goal, from Old French; see BUTT[2] target). —**v.** 1830, from the noun, or from French *débuter* to debut. —**debutante** or **débutante** (deb′yətänt) *n.* 1801, borrowing of French *débutante,* present participle of *débuter.*

deca- or (before a vowel) **dec-** a combining form meaning ten, as in *decasyllable, decathlon;* and in the terminology of the metric system, ten times a basic unit, as in *decaliter, decameter.* Borrowed from Greek *déka* TEN.

decade *n.* Probably about 1451, a group of ten things; borrowed from Middle French *décade,* learned borrowing from Late Latin *decas* (accusative *decadem*), from Greek *dekás* (accusative *dekáda*) group of ten, from *déka* TEN. The meaning of a period of ten years is first recorded in English in 1605.

decadence (dek′ədəns) *n.* 1549, borrowed from Middle French *décadence,* learned borrowing from Medieval Latin *decadentia* decay, from *decadentem* (nominative *decadens*) decaying, present participle of *decadere* to decay (Latin *dē-* apart, down + *cadere* to fall; see CADENCE); for suffix see -ENCE. Doublet of DECAY. —**decadent** *adj.* 1837, in Carlyle's *The French Revolution,* borrowed from French *décadent,* back formation from *décadence;* for suffix see -ENT.

decagon *n.* plane figure having ten angles and ten sides. 1613-39, borrowed from New Latin *decagonum,* from Greek *dekágōnon* (*déka* TEN + *gōníā* angle). —**decagonal** *adj.* 1571 *decagonall,* formed in English from New Latin *decagonum* + English *-al*[1].

decalcomania (dikal′kəmā′nēə) *n.* art of transferring pictures from treated paper to glass, etc. 1864, borrowed from French *décalcomanie,* from *décalquer* transfer a tracing (*dé-* off, un- + *calquer* to press, from Italian *calcare,* from Latin *calcāre* tread on, press + *-manie* mania, craze; see CAULK and MANIA). It was so called because the practice was much in vogue in France during the 1840's, and in England some twenty years later. —**decal** *n.* design or picture treated with glue to stick on something. 1937, in Webster's; a shortening formed from *decalcomania.*

decamp *v.* leave suddenly, abscond. 1676, break camp, borrowed from French *décamper* (*dē-* away, off + *camp* CAMP). The meaning of abscond is first recorded in English in 1792.

decant (dikant′) *v.* pour off (liquid) gently. 1633, perhaps borrowed from Medieval Latin *decanthare* (*de-* down + Latin *canthus, cantus* ring or tire of a wheel, in transferred sense of "lip of a jug," from Gaulish **kantos* rim, tire, cognate with Greek *kanthós* corner of the eye, ring or tire of a wheel, from Indo-European **kamtho-s,* Pok. 526). —**decanter** *n.* a container for wine, etc. 1712, formed from English *decant*[1] + *-er*[1]. —**v.** to pour wine in a decanter. 1825, from the noun.

decapitate *v.* behead. 1611, in Cotgrave's *Dictionary;* borrowed probably through French *décapiter,* from Late Latin *dēcapitātus,* past participle of *dēcapitāre* (Latin *dē-* off + *caput,* genitive *capitis* HEAD); for suffix see -ATE. —**decapitation** *n.* 1650, borrowed from French *décapitation,* from Medieval Latin *decapitationem* (nominative *decapitatio*) a beheading, from Late Latin *dēcapitāre* decapitate; for suffix see -ION.

decathlon (dikath′lon) *n.* Olympic contest of ten events. 1912, from *deca-* ten, from Greek *déka,* + *âthlon* (earlier *áethlon*) contest, prize; patterned on PENTATHLON. —**decathlete** *n.* competitor in a decathlon. 1968, blend of *decathlon* and *athlete.*

decay *v.* rot, decline. 1475 *decayen* to decrease, in *Rolls of Parliament;* borrowed from Middle French *decäir,* from Old French *decäir* fall away or decline, apparently from Old Provençal or Norman dialect (*de-* off, away + *cäir* fall, from Vulgar Latin **cadēre,* from Latin *cadere* to fall; see CADENCE). Doublet of DECADENCE. The meaning of decline or deteriorate, is first recorded before 1500, followed by decompose or rot, in 1580. —**n.** 1442, deterioration or decline; probably from the verb (though the noun is attested somewhat earlier).

decease *n.* death. Before 1338 *desces,* in Mannyng's *Chronicle of England;* later, *deces* (before 1393); borrowed from Old French *decès,* from Latin *dēcessus* (genitive *dēcessūs*) death, departure, from the past participle stem of *dēcēdere* (*dē-* away + *cēdere* go; see

CEDE). —**v.** die. 1433, in *Rolls of Parliament;* from the noun. —**deceased** *adj.* 1489, in a translation of Caxton's, from *decesed,* past participle (1458); *n.,* **the deceased** (1625). —**decedent** *n.* 1599, borrowed from Latin *dēcēdentem* (nominative *dēcēdēns*), present participle of *dēcēdere* to die.

deceit *n.* Probably before 1300 *disceyte;* later *deceyte* (about 1325, in *Kyng Alisaunder*); borrowed from Old French *deceite,* feminine past participle of *deceveir* DECEIVE. —**deceitful** *adj.* (about 1450 *disseytful*)

deceive *v.* About 1300 *deceiven,* borrowed from Old French *deceiv-,* stem of *deceveir,* from Vulgar Latin **dēcipēre,* corresponding to Latin *dēcipere* ensnare, catch in a trap (*dē-* away + *capere* to take; see CAPTIVE). —**deceiver** *n.* About 1384, borrowed from Old French *deceveur* (with influence of stem *deceiv-* in earlier Middle English verb *deceiven*) which, in part, makes *deceiver* a Middle English derivative of *deceive,* v. + *-er*[1].

deceleration *n.* 1897, formed from English *de-* do the opposite of + *acceleration* a speeding up. —**decelerate** *v.* 1899, either a back formation of *deceleration,* or formed from English *de-* do the opposite of + *accelerate* speed up.

December *n.* twelfth month. 1122, in *Peterborough Chronicle;* borrowed from Old French *decembre,* from Latin *December,* from *decem* TEN, this being originally the tenth month of the early Roman calendar (which began with March). Most scholars derive the ending *-ber* from an earlier ending *-bris* in a form such as **decemembris,* from earlier **decem-mēns-ris,* an adjective based on the root of Latin *mēnsis* month.

decent *adj.* 1539, borrowed through Middle French *décent,* or directly from Latin *decentem* (nominative *decēns*) becoming, fitting, present participle of *decēre* be fitting, proper, or suitable. Latin *decēre* is cognate with Greek *dokeîn* seem good, think, suppose, and Sanskrit *dákṣate* (he) is able, strong, from Indo-European **dek̂-/dok̂-* receive, be acceptable (Pok. 189). Related to DECORATE, DEXTER, DIGNITY, and DOCILE. —**decency** *n.* 1567; borrowed, perhaps by influence of earlier French *décence,* from Latin *decentia,* from *decentem,* present participle of *decēre* be fitting; for suffix see -CY.

decentralize *v.* 1851, formed from English *de-* + *centralize,* or perhaps a back formation of *decentralization.* —**decentralization** *n.* (1846)

deception *n.* About 1412 *decepcioun;* borrowed through Middle French *déception* and directly from Late Latin *dēceptiōnem* (nominative *dēceptiō*), from Latin *dēceptus,* past participle of *dēcipere* DECEIVE; for suffix see -TION. —**deceptive** *adj.* 1611, borrowed from obsolete French *déceptif* (feminine *déceptive*), from Late Latin *dēceptīvus,* from Latin *dēcept-,* past participle stem of *dēcipere* deceive; for suffix see -IVE.

deci- a combining form meaning tenth, especially in the terminology of the metric system a tenth part of a basic unit, as in *decigram, decimeter.* Coined by abbreviation of Latin *decimus* tenth, from *decem* TEN.

decibel *n.* unit of sound or loudness. 1928, formed from English *deci-* tenth, from Latin *decimus* + *bel* unit of sound equal to 10 decibels, from the name of Alexander Graham *Bell,* Scottish-American scientist who invented the telephone. See DECIMAL.

decide *v.* Before 1393 *deciden,* in Gower's *Confessio Amantis;* borrowed perhaps through Old French *decider,* and directly from Latin *dēcīdere* to decide; literally, cut off, terminate (*dē-* off + *caedere* to cut; see EXCISE[2] cut). Another form of the verb existed in Middle English, *decisen* (recorded probably before 1425), borrowed from Latin *dēcīsus,* past participle of *dēcīdere* to decide, but it was displaced by *deciden.* —**decided** *adj.* (1790) —**decidedly** *adv.* (1790)

deciduous (disij'ůəs) *adj.* (of leaves) falling off at a particular season. 1688; earlier, falling off or down (1757); borrowed from Latin *dēciduus* that falls off or down, from *dēcidere* fall off (*dē-* away, off + *cadere* to fall, see CADENCE); for suffix see -OUS.

decimal *adj.* based on ten. 1608, borrowed from Medieval Latin *decimalis* of tithes or tenths, from Latin *decima pars* tenth part; Latin *decima,* feminine of *decimus* tenth, from *decem* TEN; for suffix see -AL[1]. Latin *decima* tenth, tithe, was also borrowed into Middle English as *desime* (before 1475) through Old French *disime, diseme.* —**n.** 1641, tenth part, from the adjective. —**decimal point** (1873, but cited in use as early as 1704). —**decimal system** (1842)

decimation *n.* Before 1449, the demanding and paying of tithes; later, the killing of every tenth man as punishment of mutiny or other military offence (1580), and destruction on a large scale (1682); borrowed probably through Middle French *décimation,* from Late Latin *decimātiōnem* (nominative *decimātiō*) the taking of a tenth or tithing, from Latin *decimāre* to take the tenth, from *decimus* tenth, from *decem* TEN; for suffix see -TION. —**decimate** *v.* destroy. 1600, probably a back formation of *decimation,* and in some sources a borrowing, perhaps through influence of French *décimer,* from Latin *decimātus,* past participle of *decimāre;* for suffix see -ATE[1]. Curiously, *decimate,* v. is not recorded in the general sense of destroy a large proportion of, until 1848, in correspondence of Charlotte Brontë, perhaps influenced by the use of French *décimer* in this sense in 1820 by the poet Lamartine.

decipher *v.* 1528 *discipher* to discover, 1529 *decypher* to reveal; later *decipher* to decode (1545); formed from English *dis-, de-* + *cipher,* probably as a loan translation of Middle French *déchiffrer, deschiffrer* to decode or reveal (*de-, des-* de- + *chiffre* CIPHER). —**decipherable** *adj.* (1607)

decision *n.* About 1454 *decisioun,* borrowed from Middle French *décision,* from Latin *dēcīsiōnem* (nominative *dēcīsiō*), from *dēcīdere* DECIDE; for suffix see -SION. —**decisive** *adj.* 1611, in Cotgrave's *Dictionary;* borrowed from French *décisif* (feminine *décisive*), from Medieval Latin *decisivus,* from Latin *dēcīs-,* past participle stem of *dēcīdere* DECIDE; for suffix see -IVE.

deck *n.* 1466 *dekke* a covering over part of a boat; the meaning may have developed in English from the general sense of a covering, borrowed probably from Middle Dutch *dec* roof, covering, cloak, from *decken* to cover. The sense of a deck on a boat, is not recorded in Dutch until 160 years after its appearance in English. By 1513 the sense was extended in English to the platform of a ship, and later to a pack of cards (about 1593, in Shakespeare's *3 Henry VI*). —**v.** 1513, to cover, 1514 to clothe, adorn; borrowed from Dutch *dekken,* from Middle Dutch *decken* to cover. *Deck* replaced and is cognate with Old English *theccan* to cover; see THATCH. The slang sense of to knock down, floor, is first recorded about 1953. —**deckhand** *n.* (1844, in American English)

declaim *v.* recite. About 1385 *declamen,* in Chaucer's *Troilus and Criseyde;* borrowed through Middle French *déclamer,* or directly from Latin *dēclāmāre* (*dē-* away, out +*clāmāre* to cry, call, shout; see LOW², v.) The current spelling *declaim* replaced the earlier spelling in the 1600's by influence of *claim.* —**declamation** *n.* Before 1387 *declamacioun,* borrowed perhaps through Middle French *déclamation,* or directly from Latin *dēclāmātiōnem* (nominative *dēclāmātiō*), from *dēclāmāre* declaim; for suffix see -TION.

declare *v.* Before 1338 *declaren* decide a legal question, in Mannyng's *Chronicle of England;* borrowed perhaps through Old French *declarer,* or directly from Latin *dēclārāre* make evident or clear (*dē-* off, away + *clārāre* make clear, from *clārus* CLEAR). The meaning of proclaim or state, is first recorded in English in 1399. —**declaration** *n.* About 1380, in Chaucer's translation of Boethius' *De Consolatione Philosophiae;* borrowed probably through Old French *declaration,* from Latin *dēclārātiōnem* (nominative *dēclārātiō*), from *dēclārāre* declare; for suffix see -ATION. —**declarative** *adj.* About 1445, borrowed perhaps through Middle French *déclaratif* (feminine *déclarative*), or directly from Late Latin *dēclārātīvus,* from Latin *dēclārāt-,* past participle stem of *dēclārāre* DECLARE; for suffix see -IVE. —**declaratory** *adj.* 1440, borrowed from Medieval Latin *declaratorius,* from Latin *dēclārator* a declarer, from *dēclārāre* DECLARE; for suffix see -ORY.

declension *n. Grammar*. the system or the act of giving various forms or endings of such a system of nouns, pronouns, and adjectives according to their case, gender, number. About 1434 *declenson,* an irregular formation borrowed (through Old French *declinaison,* learned borrowing from Latin), from Latin *dēclīnātiōnem* (nominative *dēclīnātiō*) grammatical variation, inflection, a turning away, from *dēclīnāre* DECLINE; for suffix see -SION.

Etymologically, the word *declension* reflects the ancient notion that the nominative was the "upright case" (*cāsus rēctus* = Greek *ptôsis orthíā*) while the other cases, vocative, genitive, etc., leaned or fell away from it, so that they were *cāsūs oblīquī* (= Greek *ptṓseis plágiai*) "oblique cases."

decline *v.* Before 1376 *declinen,* in *Piers Plowman,* borrowed from Old French *decliner* turn aside, from Latin *dēclīnāre* to bend, turn aside, inflect, decline (*dē-* from + *clīnāre* to bend; see LEAN¹ slant; see DECLENSION for source of grammatical sense. The sense of turn or bend downward is first recorded in English before 1420; and that of refuse politely or turn down, about 1631. —**n.** Before 1325, borrowed from Old French *declin,* from *decliner* decline, from Latin *dēclīnāre.* —**declination** *n.* 1395, in Chaucer's *Canterbury Tales;* borrowed from Old French *declination,* from Latin *dēclīnātiōnem* (nominative *dēclīnātiō*), from *dēclīnāre* decline; for suffix see -ATION.

declivity *n.* downward slope. 1612, borrowed probably through influence of French *déclivité,* from Latin *dēclīvitātem* (nominative *dēclīvitās*), from *dēclīvis* sloping downward (*dē-* down + *clīvus* slope, related to *clīnāre* to bend; see LEAN¹ slant; for suffix see -ITY.

decode *v.* 1896, formed from English *de-* + *code,* n. or v.

décolleté(dā'koltā') *adj.* (of a dress) low-necked. 1831, from French *décolleté,* past participle of *décolleter* bare the neck (*dé-* from + *collet,* diminutive of *col* neck, from Latin *collum;* see COLLAR). Reference to this style of dress appeared earlier in Middle English *decoloured* cut low at the neck to expose the neck and breast (about 1450). —**décolletage** (dā'koltäzh') *n.* 1894, borrowed from French *décolletage,* from *décolleté;* for suffix see -AGE.

decompose *v.* Before 1751, formed from English *de-* + *compose,* v., possibly by influence of earlier French *décomposer,* from parallel constituents in French. —**decomposition** *n.* 1762, as if formed from English *decompose* + *-tion* after the earlier use of *decomposition* (1659) a further compounding of already composite things, from *decomposite* (1622, borrowed from Late Latin *dēcompositus,* loan translation of Greek *parasýnthetos* with the meaning of formed or derived from a compound word) (*de-* in the Latin use acquiring the meaning of formed or derived from).

decompression *n.* 1905, formed from English *de-* + *compression.*

décor (dākôr') *n.* decoration. 1897, scenery or furnishing of a theater stage, surroundings, in writings of George Saintsbury; borrowing of French *décor,* from *décorer* to ornament, from Latin *decorāre;* see DECORATE. The sense of decoration, furnishings, etc. of a room, is first recorded in 1926, probably influenced by *decorate,* v.

decorate *v.* 1530, in Palsgrave's *Lesclarcissement;* originally, a past participle and adjective (probably before 1425, in a translation of Chauliac's *Grande Chirurgie*); borrowed from Latin *decorātus,* past participle of *decorāre* to ornament, from *decus* (genitive *decoris*) adornment, related to *decēre* be fitting or suitable, see DECENT; for suffix see -ATE¹. Existence of the word in English was also influenced by earlier Middle French *décorer* to ornament. —**decoration** *n.* Probably before 1425 *decoracioun,* borrowed through Middle French and directly from Late Latin *decorātiōnem* (nominative *decorātiō*), from Latin *decorāre* to ornament; for suffix see -ATION. —**decorative** *adj.* Probably before 1425, borrowed from Middle French *décoratif* (feminine *décorative*) and directly from Latin *decorātivus,* from *decorāt-,* past participle stem of *decorāre;* for suffix see -IVE. —**decorator** *n.* 1755, borrowed from Latin *decorāre;* for suffix see -OR².

decorum (dikôr'əm) *n.* appropriate behavior. Before 1568, borrowing of Latin *decōrum* that which is proper or seemly, noun use of the neuter singular of the adjective *decōrus* seemly, from *decor* (genitive *decōris*) grace, related to *decēre* be proper; see DECENT. —**decorous** *adj.* well-behaved. 1664, proper or seemly, from Latin *decōrus* proper or seemly; see DECORUM.

decoy *n.* lure. 1625, place for luring wild ducks, but recorded earlier in prison slang with the meaning of swindler (1618), though the OED says it is very doubtful that there is any connection with *decoy duck.* It is possible that *decoy* was formed from earlier *coy* (1621) place for luring ducks, (appearing first in the combination *coy-duck*), from Dutch *kooi* cage, from Latin *cavea* enclosure, cavity; see CAGE. The origin of *de-* is uncertain; it may be the Dutch definite article *de.* —**v.** 1660 *duckoy,* from the noun.

decrepit *adj.* Before 1439, borrowed from Middle French *décrépit,* from Latin *dēcrepitus* (*dē-* down + **crepitus,* past participle of *crepāre* crack, break; see CREPITATE). —**decrepitude** *n.* 1603, borrowed from French *décrépitude,* ultimately from Latin *dēcrepitus* decrepit; for suffix see -TUDE. Modern English *decrepitude* replaced earlier *decrepitus* (about 1433), borrowed directly from the Latin.

decry *v.* denounce. 1617, borrowed from French *décrier,* from Old French *descrier* cry out, proclaim, announce (*des-* down, out, from Latin *dis-* + *crier* to CRY). Related to DESCRY.

dedicate *v.* Probably before 1425 *dedicaten,* in a translation of Higden's *Polychronicon;* developed from earlier *dedicat* adjective and past participle meaning of consecrated or hallowed (about 1390, in Chaucer's *Canterbury Tales*); borrowed from Latin *dēdicātus,* past participle of *dēdicāre* consecrate, proclaim, affirm (*dē-* away + *dicāre* proclaim, related to *dīcere* speak, say; see DICTION); for suffix see -ATE. **—dedication** *n.* Before 1382 *dedicacioun,* in the Wycliffe Bible; borrowed through Old French *dedicacion,* or directly from Latin *dēdicātiōnem* (nominative *dēdicātiō*), from *dēdicāre* consecrate, proclaim; for suffix see -TION. **—dedicatory** *adj.* 1565, formed in English as if from Late Latin **dēdicātōrius,* from Latin *dēdicātor* dedicator + English *-y*[1].

deduce *v.* 1410 *deducen* demonstrate, argue or infer from a text; borrowed from Latin *dēdūcere* lead down, derive; later, in Medieval Latin with the meaning of infer logically (*dē-* down + *dūcere* to lead).

deduct *v.* take away, subtract. 1419, in *Proceedings of the Privy Council;* borrowed from Latin *dēductus,* past participle of *dēdūcere* lead down, derive; see DEDUCE. From the 1500's *deduct* and *deduce* had nearly all senses in common, but gradually during the 1600's *deduct* became restricted to the sense of subtract, which is now obsolete for *deduce.* **—deduction** *n.* Probably before 1425 *deduccioun,* borrowed through Middle French *déduction,* or directly from Latin *dēductiōnem* (nominative *dēductiō*), from *dēdūcere* lead down; for suffix see -TION. *Deduction* serves as the agent noun for both *deduce* and *deduct* in all their senses. **—deductive** *adj.* 1646, possibly formed from English *deduct* + *-ive;* or borrowed through French *déductif* (feminine *déductive*), or directly from Late Latin *dēductivus,* from *dēduct-,* past participle stem of *dēdūcere.* **—deductible** *adj.* 1856, formed from English *deduct* + *-ible.*

deed *n.* Before 1200 *dede,* developed from Old English *dǣd* a doing, act (about 725, in *Beowulf*); cognate with Old Frisian *dēd, dēde* deed, Old Saxon *dād,* Middle Dutch *daet* (modern Dutch *daad*), Old High German *tāt* (modern German *Tat*), Old Icelandic *dādh,* Gothic *ga-dēths,* from Proto-Germanic **dǣđis,* from Indo-European **dhē-tí-s* (Pok. 237); related to DO[1] act. The meaning of a written document containing a contract is first recorded before 1338. **—v.** 1806, in American English, from the noun.

deep *adj.* Before 1150 *dep;* earlier, in place name *Depehill* (1119), developed from Old English *dēop* (about 725, in a version of the poem *Genesis*); cognate with Old Frisian *diap* deep, Old Saxon *diop, diap,* Middle Dutch and modern Dutch *diep,* Old High German *tiuf, tiof* (modern German *tief*), Old Icelandic *djūpr,* and Gothic *diups,* from Proto-Germanic **deupaz;* also represented in the Baltic languages by Lithuanian *dubùs* deep, hollow, and Latvian *duõbs* deep, from Indo-European **dheub-/dhub-/dhōub-* (Pok. 267), related to Old English *dyppan* to DIP. **—adv.** Probably about 1200 *depe,* developed from Old English (before 1000) *dēope* deeply. **—n.** About 1250 *depe,* developed from Old English (before 1000) *dēop* deep water, especially of the sea, a meaning now known in the phrase *the deep* (before 1333, in Shoreham's poetry). **—deepen** *v.* Before 1605, formed from English *deep,* adj. + *-en*[1]. **—deep-rooted** *adj.* (about 1412) **—deep-sea** *adj.* (1626) **—deep-seated** *adj.* (1741) **—deep-set** *adj.* (before 1393)

deer *n.* Probably about 1200 *der* animal, beast, in *The Ormulum;* developed from Old English *dēor* (before 899, in Alfred's translation of Orosius' *Historiarum Adversus Paganos;* cognate with Old Frisian *diar, dier* animal, beast, Old Saxon, Middle Dutch and modern Dutch *dier,* Old High German *tior* (modern German *Tier*), Old Icelandic *dýr,* and Gothic **dius* (dative plural *diuzam*), from Proto-Germanic **deuzán,* from Indo-European **dheus-ó-m,* root **dheus-* (Pok. 270).

During the Middle English period, when the stag or hind was considered the most desirable animal to hunt, specific application of the word to the antlered, hoofed mammals of the deer family became distinct (before 1200, in *Bestiary*), and by the 1400's it became the usual sense of the word in English.

Though the word *deer* is not connected with Greek *thḗr* wild beast, it is traceable to the Indo-European base **dheus-/dhous-/dhus-* (Pok. 270) whirl, storm, blow, breathe, the source of Old Slavic *dukhŭ* breath, spirit, *duša* breath, soul (compare the similar sense development of *animal,* from Latin *anima* life, breath). **—deerskin** *n.* (1396)

deface *v.* disfigure. 1340 *defacen* to blot out, obliterate; later, to mar or make ugly (about 1385, in Chaucer's *Troilus and Criseyde*); borrowed from Old French *defacier, desfacier* (*de-, des-* away from + *face* FACE). **—defacement** *n.* 1561, formed from English *deface,* v. + *-ment.*

de facto 1602, used as an adverbial phrase; 1696, used as an adjective. The phrase is a borrowing of Latin *de facto* from the fact, and generally used in English with the meaning of in fact, in reality, or actually existing whether or not lawfully.

defame *v.* About 1303 *defamen,* in Mannyng s *Handlyng Synne;* borrowed from Old French *defamer, difamer,* from Latin and probably from Medieval Latin *defamare,* from Latin *diffāmāre* to spread abroad by ill report (*dif-,* variant of *dis-* before *f* + *fāma* a report, rumor). **—defamation** *n.* 1303 *dyffamacyun;* borrowed from Old French *difamacion,* from Medieval Latin *defamation,* from Latin *diffāmātiōnem* (nominative *diffāmātiō*), from *diffāmāre;* for suffix see -ATION. **—defamatory** *adj.* 1592, borrowed probably from Middle French *diffamatoire,* from Medieval Latin *diffamatorius,* from Latin *diffāmāre;* for suffix see -ORY. **—defamer** *n.* About 1340, formed from English *defame,* v. + *-er*[1], perhaps by influence of Old French *difameur* and Medieval Latin *diffamator, defamator.*

default *n.* 1250 *defaute* an offense, crime or sin, in *Ancrene Riwle;* later, failure (about 1280); borrowed from Old French *defaute,* from *defaillir* (by influence of *faute* and *faillir*), and from Medieval Latin *defalta* a deficiency or failure, possibly a form of **defallere, *defallire* fail (Latin *dé-, dis-* away + *fallere* to be wanting). **—v.** Before 1382 *defauten* to be lacking, in the Wycliffe Bible; from the noun, possibly by influence of Old French *defaut, defalt,* 3rd person singular present tense of Old French *defaillir.* Though spellings *default* and *defalt* are recorded as early as 1393, the *l* was not generally pronounced until at least 200 years later, according to the OED.

defeat *v.* About 1380 *deffeten* overcome, in Chaucer's translation of Boethius' *De Consolatione Philosophiae;* borrowed from Old French *defait, desfait,* past participle of *defaire, desfaire,* from Vulgar Latin **diffacere* undo, destroy (from Latin *dis-* un-, not + *facere* to DO[1] perform). **—n.** 1599, in Shakespeare's *Much Ado About Nothing* and *Henry V;* from the verb. **—defeatism,** *n.* acceptance of defeat. 1918, borrowed from French *défaitisme,* from *défaite* defeat; for suffix see -ISM. **—defeatist** *n.* 1918, borrowed from French *défaitiste* (applied to the Russians), from *défaite* a defeat; for suffix see -IST.

defecate (def′əkāt) *v.* excrete. 1575, to clear of impurities; earlier *defecate* purified (1533), past participle; borrowed from Latin *dēfaecātus,* past participle of *dēfaecāre* (re-formed from *dēficāre*) cleanse from dregs, purify, from the prepositional phrase *dē faece* from dregs (*dē* from and *faex,* genitive *faecis* dregs, plural *faecēs,* the Latin original of FECES); for suffix see -ATE. It is possible that English verb use of the earlier past participle was influenced by Middle French *deféquer* to defecate. The sense of excrete, was first recorded in the 1860's in the United States. **—defecation** *n.* 1656, a clearing of impurities, borrowed from Late Latin *dēfaecātiōnem* (nominative *dēfaecātiō*), from Latin *dēfaecāre* cleanse from dregs; for suffix see -TION. The sense of discharge of feces appeared in 1830, in a textbook of anatomy translated from French *défécation* (1754, from Late Latin *dēfaecātiōnem*).

defect (dē′fekt) *n.* flaw. Probably before 1425, a lack; later, a flaw or fault (about 1450), borrowed from Middle French *defect,* and directly from Latin *dēfectus* (genitive *dēfectūs*) failure, revolt, from past participle of *dēficere* to fail, desert, be DEFICIENT. —v. (difekt′) to desert. 1579, to damage; later to rebel or desert; borrowed from Latin *dēfectus,* past participle of *dēficere* fail, desert. **—defection** *n.* 1544, borrowed from Latin *dēfectiōnem* (nominative *dēfectiō*), from *dēficere* fail, desert; for suffix see -TION. **—defective** *adj.* 1345-46, borrowed from Middle French *défectif* (feminine *défective*), and directly from Late Latin *dēfectīvus,* from *dēfec-,* stem of Latin *dēficere* fail, desert; for suffix see -IVE. **—defector** *n.* 1662, perhaps borrowed from Latin *dēfector* revolter, from *dēficere, or* more likely, formed from English *defect,* v. + *-or*[2].

defend *v.* About 1250 *defenden,* from Old French *defendre,* and directly from Latin *dēfendere* ward off, protect (*dē-* from, away + *-fendere* to strike, push). Latin *-fendere* is from the Indo-European base **gwhen-/gwhn̥-* (Pok. 491) which is also the source of Old English *gūth* combat (from Proto-Germanic **ʒwúnthijō*), Old Saxon *gūthea,* Old High German *gund-* (as in *gundfano* war banner, GONFALON), Old Icelandic *gunnr* battle, Old Irish *gonim* I injure, kill, Greek *theínein* to strike, kill, Armenian *ganem* I strike, Sanskrit *hánti* he strikes, kills and Hittite *kuenzi* strikes. Related to FEND and OFFEND. **—defendant** *n.* Before 1400, person defending himself in a lawsuit; earlier, *defense* (about 1390, in Chaucer's *Canterbury Tales*), and as an adjective (probably about 1300); borrowed from Old French *defendant,* present participle of *defendre* defend; for suffix see -ANT. **—defender** *n.* About 1300 *defendour;* earlier in a surname *Defendur* (1222); borrowed through Anglo-French, from Old French *defendeor,* from *defendre;* for suffix see -ER[1].

defense *n.* Probably before 1300, in *Kyng Alisaunder,* fusion of 1) *defens, defence* a fortified place; borrowed from Old French *defens,* from Latin *dēfēnsum* thing protected or forbidden, from neuter past participle of *dēfendere* ward off, protect, and 2) *defense* act of defending oneself; borrowed from Old French *defense* defense, prohibition, from Latin *dēfēnsa* defense, vengeance, from feminine past participle of *dēfendere* ward off, DEFEND. **—defenseless** *adj.* (about 1530) **—defensible** *adj.* About 1300 *defensable* ready to fight; borrowed from Old French *defensable,* from Late Latin *dēfensābilem,* from Latin *dēfensāre* to ward off, frequentative form of *dēfendere* to defend. Later *defensable* was gradually replaced after the 1450's by *defensible,* borrowed directly from Late Latin *dēfensibilem,* from *dēfens-,* past participle stem of Latin *dēfendere,* so that by the 1700's the current spelling was fully established; for suffix see -ABLE and -IBLE. **—defensive** *adj., n.* Before 1400, borrowed from Old French *defensif* (feminine *defensive*), and directly from Medieval Latin *defensivus,* from *defens-,* past participle stem of Latin *dēfendere;* for suffix see -IVE.

defer[1] *v.* delay. About 1375 *differren;* later *deferren* (about 1382); borrowed from Old French *differer,* learned borrowing from Latin *differre* set apart, put off, delay; (also) be different, differ (*dif-* apart, variant of *dis-* before *f* + *ferre* carry; see BEAR[2] carry). Originally *defer* was the same word as DIFFER but the two words separated in meaning, and the spelling with *def-* developed as the stress shifted to the second syllable, and as confusion arose by association with *defer*[2] and the form of the prefix.

defer[2] *v.* yield. Before 1447 *differren* to refer; borrowed from Middle French *déférer,* learned borrowing from Latin *dēferre* carry away, refer (matter) to anyone, transfer, grant (*dē-* down, away + *ferre* carry; see BEAR[2] carry). **—deference** *n.* Before 1660, a respectful or courteous yielding; borrowed from French *déférence,* from *déférer* defer. **—deferential** *adj.* 1880, formed from English *deference,* as if from Medieval Latin *deferentia* + *-ial; or* possibly from English *deferent,* adj. + *-ial.*

defiance *n.* Probably before 1300, in *Kyng Alisaunder,* borrowed from Old French *defiance, desfiance* challenge, from *defiant, desfiant,* present participle of *defier, desfier* DEFY. **—defiant** *adj.* Before 1837, borrowed from French *défiant,* present participle of *défier* defy, from Old French *defier, desfier.*

deficient *adj.* 1581, borrowed from Latin *dēficientem* (nominative *dēficiēns*), present participle of *dēficere* to desert, fail (*dē-* down, away + *facere* to DO[1] perform); for suffix see -ENT. **—deficiency** *n.* 1634, either formed from English *deficience* + *-cy,* or formed as if borrowed from Late Latin *dēficientia,* from Latin *dēficientem,* present participle; for suffix see -ENCY.

deficit *n.* 1782, borrowing of French *déficit,* from Latin *dēficit* it is wanting, 3rd person singular present indicative of *dēficere* to be DEFICIENT.

defile[1] *v.* make filthy. Before 1400 *defilen,* alteration of earlier *defoulen* (about 1280); borrowed from Old French *défouler* trample down, violate (*dé-* down + *fouler* to tread, thicken cloth, from Vulgar Latin **fullāre,* from Latin *fullō* FULLER). Generally it is held that the earlier English *defoulen* was probably re-formed as *defile* by analogy with the synonymous pairs *filen* (Old English *fȳlan,* from *fūl* foul) and *foulen* to FOUL, for which a parallel synonymous pair is found in *befilen, befoulen* to pollute. The association of *defoulen* with *foul* contributed to the sense of pollute materially or morally, a meaning not inherent in the Old French word. **—defilement** *n.* 1571, formed from English *defile* + *-ment.*

defile[2] *n.* narrow passage. 1685, borrowed from French *défilé,* noun use of past participle of *défiler* march by files (*dé-* off + *file* FILE[2] row). **—v.** march in a line or by files. 1705, borrowed from French *défiler.*

define *v.* about 1380 *diffynen* to specify, in Chaucer's translation of Boethius' *De Consolatione Philosophiae* and in *House of Fame,* to end, behave at the end; borrowed through Anglo-French, from Old French *definir,* (earlier) *diffinir* to end, terminate, determine, and directly from Latin *dēfīnīre* to limit, determine, explain (*dē-* completely + *fīnīre* to bound, limit, from *fīnis* boundary; see FINAL). **—definite** *adj.* Before 1500 *diffinyte* defined; borrowed from Latin *dēfīnītus,* past participle of *dēfīnīre* to limit. **—definition** *n.* About 1384 *diffinicioun* decision, in the Wycliffe Bible; borrowed from Old French *deffinition,* and directly from Latin *dēfīnītiōnem* (nominative *dēfīnītiō*), from *dēfīnīre* to limit; for suffix see -TION. **—definitive** *adj.* About 1390 *diffynytif* decisive, conclusive, in Chaucer's *Canterbury Tales;* borrowed from Old French *definitif* (feminine *definitive*), from Latin *dēfīnītīvus,* from *dēfīnī-,* past participle stem of *dēfīnīre* to limit; for suffix see -IVE.

deflate *v.* 1891, release air from something inflated (*de* do the reverse of + *(in)flate*). **—deflation** *n.* (1891)

deflect *v.* About 1555, borrowed from Latin *dēflectere* to bend aside or downward (*dē-* away, aside + *flectere* to bend; see FLEX). **—deflection** *n.* 1603 *deflexion* modification of the meaning or form of a word, in Philemon Holland's translation of Plutarch's *Moralia;* later, a twin or deviation from a usual course or expected result (1605, in Francis Bacon's *Of the Advancement of Learning*), originally formed in British English as *deflexion,* rendered after Latin as *deflex-* + *-ion;* or borrowed from Late Latin *dēflexiōnem* (nominative *dēflexiō*) from *dēflectere* deflect; for suffix see -TION.

defoliate *v.* strip a tree or plant of leaves. 1793, formed in English as a back formation of *defoliation, or* possibly borrowed from Late Latin *dēfoliātus,* past participle of *dēfoliāre* shed leaves (Latin *dē-* from, away + *folium* leaf; see BLADE). **—defoliant** *n.* chemical used to defoliate. 1943, formed from English *defoliate* + *-ant.* **—defoliation** *n.* 1659, formed in English from Late Latin *dēfoliāre* defoliate + English *-tion.*

deforest *v.* 1538, to designate as ordinary land by removing the legal protection of forested land; later, as a term reintroduced into English, to clear or strip of trees (1880); formed from English *de-* remove or take away + *forest.* **—deforestation** *n.* 1884, formed from English *deforest* + *-ation.*

deform *v.* About 1400 *difform* mar or disfigure; borrowed from Old French *deformer, desformer,* a blend of Latin *dēfōrmāre* put out of shape, disfigure, and the variant **disfōrmāre,* and Medieval Latin *difformare.* **—deformation** *n.* Before 1449, transformation, borrowed from Old French *deformation,* and directly from Latin *dēfōrmātiōnem* (nominative *dēfōrmātiō*), from *dēfōrmāre* deform; for suffix see -ATION. **—deformity** *n.* 1413, borrowed from Old French *deformité,* from Latin *dēfōrmitās* deformity, from *dēfōrmis* deformed, from *dēfōrmāre* disfigure.

defraud *v.* Before 1376, in a version of *Piers Plowman;* borrowed from Old French *defrauder,* and from Latin *dēfraudāre* to cheat (*dē-* completely + *fraudāre* to cheat, from *fraus,* accusative *fraudem* deceit, FRAUD).

defray *v.* pay, settle. 1543, borrowed from Middle French *defraier, desfraier* (*de-, des-* out + *fraier* spend, from Old French *frais,* plural, costs; probably damages caused by breakage, from Latin *frāctum,* neuter of past participle of *frangere* to BREAK).

defrost *v.* 1895, formed from English *de-* to remove, take away + *frost.*

deft *adj.* skillful. Before 1450 *defte* adept, apt; earlier, mild or gentle (before 1250), from *daffte* (probably before 1200, in *The Ormulum*); see the doublet DAFT. Both *deft* and *daft* developed from Old English *gedæfte* mild, gentle, becoming, but differentiated in later development; *daft* used in the sense of meek and gentle with later semantic development of dull, foolish, and *deft* used in the sense of apt, adept, skillful.

defunct *adj.* 1599, in Shakespeare's *Henry V;* earlier *the defunct,* as a noun (1548); borrowed possibly through Old French *defunct,* or directly from Latin *dēfūnctus* dead, deceased, discharged, from past participle of *dēfungī* to discharge, finish (*dē-* off, completely + *fungī* perform or discharge a duty); see FUNCTION.

defy *v.* Probably before 1300 *defyen* renounce faithfulness to, reject, in *Kyng Alisaunder;* borrowed from Old French *defier, desfier,* from Vulgar Latin **disfīdāre* (Latin *dis-* away + *fīdus* faithful, related to *fidēs* FAITH). The meaning withstand or challenge is first recorded before 1338, in Mannyng's *Chronicle of England.*

degenerate (dijen′ərit) *adj.* degraded, debased. 1494, borrowed (perhaps through influence of Middle French *dégénérer*), from Latin *dēgenerātus,* past participle of *dēgenerāre* depart from one's race or kind, fall from ancestral quality, from the prepositional phrase *dē genere* down from one's noble descent (*dē* down from and *genus,* genitive *generis* birth or descent; see GENUS and KIN); for suffix see -ATE[1]. **—n.** 1555, from the adjective. **—v.** 1545, from the adjective, probably by influence of Latin *dēgenerāre,* and also probably borrowed in some instances directly from Latin *dēgenerāt-,* past participle stem of *dēgenerāre* + English *-ate*[1]. **—degeneracy** *n.* 1664, formed from English *degenerate,* adj. + *-acy.* **—degeneration** *n.* 1607, borrowed through French *dégénération,* or directly from Late Latin *dēgenerātiōnem* (nominative *dēgenerātiō*), from Latin *dēgenerāre;* for suffix see -ATION.

degrade *v.* Before 1387, in Trevisa's translation of Higden's *Polychronicon;* borrowed from Old French *degrader,* learned borrowing from Late Latin *dēgradāre* reduce the rank of (Latin *dē-* down + *gradus,* genitive *gradūs,* step, GRADE). **—degradation** *n.* Before 1535, borrowed through Middle French *dégradation,* or directly from Late Latin *dēgradātiōnem* (nominative *dēgradātiō*), from *dēgradāre* degrade; for suffix see -ATION.

degree *n.* Probably about 1200, borrowed from Old French *degre* a degree, step, rank, earlier *degret,* from Vulgar Latin **dēgradus* a step, from Late Latin *dēgradāre* used in the unrecorded meaning of step down (Latin *dē-* down + *gradus,* genitive *gradūs* step, GRADE).

dehydrate *v.* take water from. 1876, borrowed from French *déshydrater* (*dé-* un- + Greek *hýdōr, hydr-* water; for suffix see -ATE[1]). Alternatively, the verb may be a back formation from earlier English *dehydration.* **—dehydration** *n.* 1854, formed from English *de-* + *hydration* (1854) a combining with water, from *hydrate,* v., combine with water (1850).

deify *v.* About 1340, make godlike, in an early psalter; borrowed from Old French *deifier,* from Late Latin *deificāre,* from *deificus* making godlike, divine, holy, from Latin *deus* god, DEITY; for suffix see -FY. **—deification** *n.* Before 1393 *deificacion,* in Gower's *Confessio Amantis;* borrowed from Late Latin *deificātiōnem* (nominative *deificātiō*), from *deificāre* deify; for suffix see -ATION.

deign (dān) *v.* condescend. About 1300 *deignen, deinen* consider something fit or worthy, borrowed from Old French *deignier,* from Latin *dignārī* to deem worthy or fit, from *dignus;* see DIGNITY. The meaning of condescend (to reply, answer, etc.), is first recorded in 1589, developing from a related meaning of take or accept graciously (1576).

deism *n.* belief in God without accepting any particular religion. 1682, in Dryden's *A Layman's Faith;* formed from English *de(ist)* + *-ism,* by influence of French *déisme* (coined by Pascal before 1660), from Latin *deus* god, DEITY; for suffix see -ISM. **—deist** *n.* 1621, in Burton's *Anatomy of Melancholy;* borrowed from French *déiste* (1564), from Latin *deus* god; for suffix see -IST. The word was originally synonymous with *theist,* both *deist* and *theist* being antonyms of *atheist,* but in the late 1700's *deist,* with its rejection of the supernatural doctrines of Christianity, acquired a negative connotation.

deity *n.* About 1385 *deite,* in Chaucer's *Troilus and Criseyde;* earlier, divine nature or divinity (probably about 1300); borrowed from Old French *deité,* learned borrowing from Late Latin *deitātem* (nominative *deitās*) divine nature, a term coined by St. Augustine, from Latin *deus* god; for suffix see -ITY.

Latin *deus* and its cognates Sanskrit *devá-s* god, and the Germanic resultants (Old English *Tīw, Tīg,* Old High German *Zīo,* and Old Icelandic *Týr*) of Proto-Germanic **Tīwaz* god of the sky, are from Indo-European **deiwos* (Pok. 185), from the Indo-European base **deyeu-* (Pok. 184) bright sky, day, an extension of **dei-, deyə-, dī-* (Pok. 183) to shine, glitter.

A different derivative of the same base **deyeu-* was Indo-European **dyēu-s* (with vocative **dyeu* and accusative **dyēm*) sky, day, god of the sky, whence Sanskrit *dyāú-s,* Greek *Zeús,* and Latin *Jūpiter, Juppiter* (originally the vocative **pater* father).

déjà vu (dā'zhä vü') a feeling of having already experienced something occurring at the present. 1903, borrowing of French *déjà vu* already seen (*déjà* already, from Old French *des ja* from the present (Latin *dē* + *ex* from, *jam* now, already, from Indo-European *yām,* Pok. 285), and *vu* seen, past participle of *voir* to see, from Latin *vidēre;* see WIT). A generalized sense of tiresome familiarity, is first recorded in English in 1953.

deject *v.* Before 1420 *deiecten* throw or cast down, in Lydgate's *Troy Book;* borrowed, probably by influence of Old French *degeter, dejeter, dejecter,* from Latin *dējectus,* past participle of *dēicere* to cast down (*dē-* down + *-icere,* combining form of *jacere* to throw; see JET[1] stream). The sense of depress or dispirit is first recorded before 1500. **—dejection** *n.* About 1420 *deieccion* unhappiness or humiliation, in Lydgate's *Troy Book;* borrowed from Old French *dejection,* and directly from Latin *dējectiōnem* (nominative *dējectiō*), from *dējec-,* stem of *dēicere* to cast down; for suffix see -TION. The sense of depression of spirits is first recorded before 1500.

delay *v.* put off. Probably before 1300 *deleien,* in *Arthour and Merlin;* from Old French *delaier* (*de-* from, away + *laier* leave, let, of unknown origin. **—n.** Before 1250, borrowed from Old French *delai,* from *delaier,* v.

delectable *adj.* Before 1396, borrowed from Old French *delectable,* learned borrowing from Latin *dēlectābilis,* from *dēlectāre* to DELIGHT.

delegate (del'əgit) *n.* representative. Before 1475, borrowed through Old French *delegat,* or directly from Latin *dēlēgātus,* past participle of *dēlēgāre* to send or assign as a representative (*dē-* from, away + *lēgāre* send with a commission; see LEGATE); for suffix see -ATE[3]. **—v.** (del'əgāt) 1530, in Palsgrave's *Lesclarcissement,* possibly developed in English from *delegate,* n. (or, *obsolete,* adj.); *or* borrowed, by influence of Middle French *deléguer,* from Latin *dēlēgātus,* past participle of *dēlēgāre;* for suffix see -ATE[1]. **—delegation** *n.* 1611, charge given to a delegate; possibly formed from English *delegate,* v. + *-ion,* replacing earlier *delegacie* (recorded about 1460); *or* borrowed through French *délégation,* or directly from Latin *dēlēgātiōnem* (nominative *dēlēgātiō*), from *dēlēgāre* to delegate; for suffix see -TION. The meaning of a group or body of delegates appeared in 1818.

delete *v.* cross out. 1534 (possibly 1495) destroy, eradicate; later, erase, as printed matter (about 1605); borrowed from Latin *dēlētus,* past participle of *dēlēre* destroy, blot out, efface, back formation from *dēlēvī,* originally perfect tense of *dēlinere* to daub, erase by smudging (*dē-* from, away + *linere* to smear; wipe; see LINIMENT). **—deletion** *n.* 1590, from Latin *dēlētiōnem* (nominative *dēlētiō*), from *dēlēre* destroy; for suffix see -TION.

deleterious (del'ətir'ēəs) *adj.* harmful, noxious. 1643, borrowed from New Latin *deleterius,* from Greek *dēlētḗrios,* from *dēlētḗr* destroyer, from *dēleîsthai* to hurt, injure; cognate with Sanskrit *dálati* bursts, *dālayati* splits, Latin *dolāre* hew, Old Irish *delb* form, Welsh *delw* image, from Indo-European **del-/dol-/dēl-/dōl-* split, cut (Pok. 194); for suffix see -OUS.

deliberate (dəlib'ərit) *adj.* Probably before 1425; borrowed from Latin *dēlīberātus,* past participle of *dēlīberāre* weigh, consider well (*dē-* entirely + *-līberāre,* apparently an alteration, perhaps influenced by *līberāre* liberate, of *lībrāre* to balance, weigh, from *lībra* scale, of uncertain origin). **—v.** (dəlib'ərāt) 1550, borrowed from Latin *dēlīberātus,* past participle of *dēlīberāre;* replacing earlier *deliberen,* borrowed through Old French *deliberer,* or directly from Latin *dēlīberāre;* for suffix see -ATE[1]. **—deliberation** *n.* About 1385 *deliberacioun,* in Chaucer's *Troilus and Criseyde;* borrowed through Old French *deliberation,* or directly from Latin *dēlīberātiōnem* (nominative *dēlīberātiō*), from *dēlīberāre;* for suffix see -TION. **—deliberative** *adj.* 1553, borrowed through Middle French *délibératif* (feminine *délibérative*), or directly from Latin *dēlīberātīvus,* from *dēlīberāt-,* past participle stem of *dēlīberāre;* for suffix see -IVE.

delicate *adj.* About 1375, in Chaucer's *Canterbury Tales,* self-indulgent, loving ease; borrowed through Old French *delicat,* or directly from Latin *dēlicātus* alluring, delightful, luxurious, dainty, probably related (at least by folk etymology) to *dēliciae* a pet, and *dēlicere* to allure, entice, DELIGHT.

The meaning of fine, soft (applied to cloth) is recorded in Middle English probably before 1425, and that of sensitive, feeble, is recorded about 1390, in Chaucer's *Canterbury Tales.*

—delicacy *n.* About 1375, pleasure, gratification, in Chaucer's *Canterbury Tales,* formed from English *delicate* + *-cy.* The meaning of something that pleases the palate, a fine food, appeared in Middle English before 1450. The meaning of exquisite fineness of texture, substance, etc., occurs before 1586, and the transferred sense of exquisite fineness of expression, touch, etc., in 1675.

delicatessen *n.* 1889, American English, borrowing of German *Delikatessen,* plural of *Delikatesse* a delicacy, fine type of food, from French *délicatesse,* from *délicat* delicate, fine, from Latin *dēlicātus* DELICATE.

delicious *adj.* Probably before 1300 *delicious,* in *Kyng Alisaunder;* borrowed from Old French *delicieus,* from Late Latin *dēliciōsus* delicious, delicate, from Latin *dēliciae, pl.,* a delight, from *dēlicere* to allure, entice, DELIGHT.

delight *n.* Probably before 1200 *delit,* in *Ancrene Riwle;* borrowed from Old French *delit,* from *delitier* please greatly, charm, from Latin *dēlectāre* to allure, delight, charm, frequentative form of *dēlicere* entice (*dē-* away + *lacere* entice; see LACE). **—v.** Probably before 1200 *deliten,* in *Ancrene Riwle,* from Old French *delitier* please greatly, from Latin *dēlectāre* to allure. **—delightful** *adj.* Before 1400, formed from Middle English *delite* + *-ful.*

According to the OED the spelling *delight* came into use in the late 1500's under the influence of such words as *light, flight,* etc.

delineate *v.* outline, draw, sketch. 1559, borrowed from Latin *dēlīneātus,* past participle of *dēlīneāre* (*dē-* completely + *līneāre* draw lines, from *līnea* LINE); for suffix see -ATE[1]. **—delineation** *n.* 1570, either formed from English *delineate* + *-ion,* or borrowed from Latin *dēlīneātiōnem* (nominative *dēlīneātiō*) sketch, description, from *dēlīneāre* to outline, sketch; for suffix see -ATION.

delinquent *n.* 1484 *delinquaunt,* in Caxton's *Chivalry,* borrowed from Middle French *délinquant,* from present participle of *délinquer* be at fault, fail, offend, and directly from Latin *dēlinquentem* (nominative *dēlinquēns*), present participle of *dēlinquere* (*dē-* off + *linquere* to leave; see LOAN); for suffix see -ENT. **—adj.** 1603, in Philemon Holland's translation of Plutarch's *Moralia;* borrowed from Latin *dēlinquentem* (nominative *dēlinquēns*), present participle of *dēlinquere* be at fault, fail, offend. **—delinquency** *n.* 1636, probably borrowed from Latin *dēlinquentia,* from *dēlinquentem,* present participle of *dēlinquere;* for suffix see -ENCY.

delirum *n.* 1599, borrowing of Latin *dēlīrium* madness, from *dēlīrāre* be crazy, rave, literally, go off the furrow, from the prepositional phrase *dē līrā* (*dē* off, away and *līra* furrow, Latin *līra* being cognate with Old High German *leisa* track, modern German *Gleis, Geleise,* and Old English *lāst* footprint, track, *læste* LAST[3] block). **—delirious** *adj.* 1703, formed from English *deliri(um)* + *-ous.* **—delirium tremens** (trē′mənz) alcoholic delirium. 1813, New Latin, literally, trembling delirium.

deliver *v.* Probably before 1200 *delivren* set free, liberate, in *Ancrene Riwle;* borrowed from Old French *delivrer,* from Late Latin *dēlīberāre* (Latin *dē-* away + *līberāre* to free, LIBERATE). The sense of hand over, transfer, convey, is first recorded about 1280; the sense of bring (a woman) to childbirth (that is, unburdened or set free), about 1300; and to give forth, project, throw, is found in 1597. **—deliverance** *n.* About 1300, borrowed from Old French *deliverance* (*delivrer* set free + *-ance*). **—delivery** *n.* 1425 *delevery,* and *delyvere* (1442); noun use in Middle English of Middle French *delivrée,* feminine past participle of *delivrer* deliver, from Old French *delivrer.*

dell *n.* small valley. Before 1250 *dele;* earlier, in place name *Brixisdelle* (1225); developed from Old English *dell;* cognate with Middle Dutch *delle* dell, Middle High German *telle* (modern German *Delle* dent, depression), and Gothic *ib-dalja* slope of mountain, from Proto-Germanic **daljō,* from Indo-European **dhol-yā,* root **dhel-* (Pok. 245). Related to DALE. See also DELVE.

delta *n.* Probably about 1200, the fourth letter of the Greek alphabet, shaped like a triangle (Δ), in *The Ormulum;* later as a place name *Delta,* alluvial land shaped like a triangle at the mouth of the Nile river (1555, a sense introduced into Greek in the 400's B.C. by Herodotus); both senses borrowed from Greek *délta,* from Semitic (compare Hebrew *dāleth* fourth letter of the Hebrew alphabet, from *deleth* door, originally formed from the hieroglyph of a door, as of a tent). It is just possible that the sense of a geographic *delta* was introduced into English partly through the earlier Old French *delta.*

delude *v.* Probably about 1408 *delluden,* in writings of Lydgate; borrowed from Latin *dēlūdere* (*dē-* down, to one's detriment + *lūdere* to play; see LUDICROUS). **—delusion** *n.* Probably about 1421 *dilusioun,* in writings of Lydgate; borrowed from Latin *dēlūsiōnem* (nominative *dēlūsiō), from dēlūs-,* past participle stem of *dēlūdere* delude; for suffix see -SION. **—delusive** *adj.* 1605, formed from English *delus(ion)* + *-ive;* or from Latin *dēlūs-,* past participle stem of *dēlūdere* + English suffix *-ive.*

deluge (del′yüj) *n.* flood. About 1380, in Chaucer's translation of Boethius' *De Consolatione Philosophiae;* later *Deluge* the great Biblical flood (probably before 1430, in Lydgate's translation of De Guileville's *Pilgrimage of the Life of Man*); borrowed from Old French *deluge* (earlier *deluve*), and from Latin *dīluvium,* from *dīluere* wash away (*dis-* away + *-luere,* combining form of *lavere* to wash, LAVE). Doublet of DILUVIAL. **—v.** flood. 1649, from the noun.

de luxe or **deluxe** *adj.* 1819, borrowing of French *de luxe,* literally, of luxury (*de* of and *luxe* luxury, from Latin *luxus,* genitive *luxūs* excess, abundance, LUXURY).

delve *v.* search deeply. Probably before 1200 *delven,* in Layamon's *Chronicle of Britain;* developed from Old English (before 830) *delfan* to dig; cognate with Old Saxon *bi-deltban* bury, Middle Low German, Middle Dutch, and modern Dutch *delven* to dig, Flemish *delv* ditch, ravine, and Old High German *bi-telban* to dig; also cognate with Lithuanian *délba, dálba* crowbar, and Russian *dolbit'* to chisel, make hollow, from Indo-European *dhelbh-/dholbh-* (Pok. 246).

demagogue (dem'əgôg) *n.* unprincipled political leader who stirs up the masses. 1648, borrowed from Greek *dēmagōgós* leader of the people, popular leader, (also) demagogue (*dêmos* people, see DEMOCRACY + *agōgós* leader, leading, from *ágein* to lead, see AGENT). The earliest English sense was pejorative. The spelling *-agogue* developed from the influence of French words with this ending (seen in French *démagogue,* 1361) borrowed from Latin words in *-agōgus* (from Greek words in *-agōgós*). There is also the possibility that this word was borrowed into English by influence of Old French *demagogue.* **—demagogic** (dem'əgoj'ik) *adj.* 1831, borrowed from Greek *dēmagōgikós,* from *dēmagōgós* demagogue; for suffix see -IC. **—demagoguery** *n.* 1855, American English, formed from *demagogue* + *-ery.*

demand *v.* Before 1382 *demaunden* ask, make an inquiry, in the Wycliffe Bible; borrowed from Old French *demander* to request, from Latin *dēmandāre* entrust, charge, with a commission (*de-* completely + *mandāre* to order, MANDATE). The English sense of ask for as a right (1434) arose from an Anglo-French legal sense (about 1292), and may have been influenced by the Medieval Latin sense of *demandare* to demand, request, from Latin. **—n.** About 1280 *demaunde,* borrowed from Old French *demande,* from *demander.*

demarcation *n.* 1727-52, borrowed (perhaps through French *démarcation*) from Spanish *demarcación,* from *demarcar* to delimit, mark out the bounds of (*de-* off + *marcar* to mark, from Germanic; compare Old High German *marca, marcha* MARK); for suffix see -TION. The Spanish *demarcación* was first used in 1493 in the phrase *línea de demarcación,* a boundary laid down by Pope Alexander VI to divide the New World between the Spanish and Portuguese. Even in English, the word is often used in the phrase "line of demarcation". **—demarcate** *v.* 1816, back formation from *demarcation.*

demean[1] *v.* lower in dignity. 1601, formed from *de-* down + MEAN[2] low in quality or social position; probably patterned on DEBASE, and perhaps developing also out of occasional confusion with *demean*[2].

demean[2] *v.* behave in a certain way. Probably before 1300 *demaynen* to handle, manage, conduct, in *Kyng Alisaunder;* borrowed from Old French *demener* (*de-* completely + *mener* to lead, direct, from Late Latin *mināre* to drive (animals, from Latin *minārī* threaten, drive with shouts, MENACE). The current sense of behave in a certain way evolved (before 1420) from the now obsolete meanings of conduct (a business), manage (a person or thing), and treat someone (in a specified way). **—demeanor** *n.* behavior. Probably before 1472 *demenure,* formed from Middle English *demenen, demaynen* behave + *-or*[1].

demented *adj* 1644, from now archaic *dement* drive mad + *-ed*[2] (1545). The verb *dement* was borrowed probably through Middle French *démenter,* from Late Latin *dēmentāre,* from Latin *dēmentem* out of one's mind, from the prepositional phrase *dē mente* (*dē* out of and *mēns,* ablative *mente* MIND). **—dementia** (dəmen'shə) *n. Psychiatry.* mental deterioration. 1806, borrowing of Latin *dēmentia* (*dēmentem* out of one's mind + *-ia* abstract noun suffix).

demerit *n.* fault, defect, black mark on one's record. 1421, blameworthy act, offense; earlier, worthiness of reward or punishment (1399); borrowed from Old French *desmerite* (Old French *des-* not, opposite of + *merite* MERIT), and from Latin *dēmeritum,* from past participle stem of *dēmerērī* to merit, deserve (*dē-* thoroughly + *merērī* to merit, deserve). According to the OED, the Latin prefix *dē-* was mistaken for meaning not, opposite, and so in Old French *desmerite* has both the sense of merit, desert and of demerit, fault, and Medieval Latin *demeritum* has the meaning of a fault.

demesne (dimān') *n.* possession of land, domain. 1491, respelling of earlier *demeyne* (probably before 1300, in *Arthour and Merlin*); borrowed from Old French *demeine, demaine,* noun use of an adjective with the meaning of belonging to a lord, from Latin *dominicus,* from *dominus* lord; see the doublet DOMAIN. The respelling is a borrowing from Anglo-French legal scribes to show that the vowel preceding a "silent *s*" was long, perhaps influenced also by *mesne* as a legal term familiar to them in such a phrase as "mesne lord".

demi- a prefix meaning: **1** half, half-sized, or partial, as in *demigod = half god.* **2** smaller than usual, as in *demitasse = smaller than the usual cupful.* Borrowed from Middle French, from Old French *demi* half, from Late Latin *dīmedius,* re-formed for Latin *dīmidius* (*dis-* apart + *medius* MIDDLE).

demigod *n.* 1530, loan translation of Latin *sēmideus.*

demijohn (dem'ējon) *n.* bottle enclosed in wicker; now often, a pitcher with a thermos lining. 1769, a partial loan translation, a play on words of French *damejeanne* Lady Jane, its popular fanciful name.

demilitarize *v.* 1883, formed from English *de-* the opposite of + *militarize.* **—demilitarization** *n.* 1883, formed from English *de-* the opposite of + *militarization.*

demimonde (dem'ēmond) *n.* class of women of doubtful reputation. 1855, borrowing of French *demi-monde* (*demi-* half, DEMI- + *monde,* learned borrowing from Latin *mundus* world; see MUNDANE). The term was popularized in the title of a successful play by Alexandre Dumas fils.

demise (dimīz') *n.* death. 1442 *dimisse* transfer of an estate by will, in *Proceedings of the Privy Council;* borrowed from Middle French *demise,* feminine past participle of *demettre* dismiss, put away (*des-* away, from Latin *dis-* + Middle French *mettre* put, from Latin *mittere* let go, send; see MISSION). Compare DISMISS. The meaning of death is first recorded about 1754 because a person's estate is transferred upon his death. **—v.** 1447 *dimisen* to transfer an estate by will, in *Rolls of Parliament;* borrowed from Middle French *demise,* past participle of *demettre.* The meaning of die is first recorded in 1727.

demitasse (dem'ētas') *n.* small coffee cup. 1842, borrowing of obsolescent French *demi-tasse* half-cup (*demi-* half + *tasse* cup, from Old French *tasse,* from Arabic *ṭāsah,* from Persian *tāsht*). In French it is now called *tasse à moka.*

demobilization *n.* 1866, formed from English *de-* the opposite of + *mobilization* (1866). **—demobilize** *v.* 1882, back formation from *demobilization.*

democracy *n.* government by the people who live

under its rule. 1574, borrowed through Middle French *démocratie,* learned borrowing from Medieval Latin *democratia,* from Greek *dēmokratíā,* from *dêmos* common people, district + *krátos* rule, strength; for suffix see -CRACY. Greek *dêmos* was originally *dâmos,* cognate with Old Irish *dām* a following, crowd, Welsh *daw* son-in-law, from Indo-European **dāmos* division of the people, root **dā-/də-* divide (Pok. 175).

The early spelling in English *democratie* was gradually replaced by *democracy* in the 1600's and early 1700's. **—democrat** *n.* 1790, a republican of the French Revolution, as opposed to an *aristocrat,* borrowed from French *démocrate,* from *démocratie* democracy. The use of *Democrat* for the name of a member of one of the current principal U.S. political parties is first recorded in 1839. **—democratic** *adj.* 1602, borrowed from French *démocratique,* from Medieval Latin *democraticus,* from Greek *dēmokratikós,* from *dēmokratíā* democracy; for suffix see -IC. The use of *Democratic* to designate one of the current U.S. political parties is first recorded in 1829.

democratize *v.* 1790, probably borrowed from French *démocratiser,* from *démocrate* + *-iser* -ize; or formed from English *democrat,* n. + *-ize.*

demolish *v.* 1570-76, borrowed from Middle French *démoliss-,* stem of *démolir* to destroy, tear down, learned borrowing from Latin *dēmōlīrī* tear down (*dē-* down + *mōlīrī* build, construct, from *mōlēs,* genitive *mōlis* massive structure, MOLE[3] breakwater); for suffix see -ISH[2]. **—demolition** *n.* 1549, borrowed from Middle French *démolition* destruction, from Latin *dēmōlītiōnem* (nominative *dēmōlītiō), from dēmōlīrī* to demolish; for suffix see -TION.

demon *n.* Probably before 1200, in Layamon's *Chronicle of Britain;* borrowed from Late Latin *daemōn, dēmōn* evil spirit, from Latin *daemōn* spirit, from Greek *daímōn* (genitive *daímonos*) lesser god, good or bad spirit, probably originally with the meaning of one that distributes destinies, related to *daíesthai* divide, allot; see DEAL.**—demoniac** *adj.* About 1405 *demonyak;* earlier, as a noun (about 1395), both uses in Chaucer's *Canterbury Tales;* borrowed from Late Latin *daemoniacus,* as if from Greek **daimoniakós,* for which only *daimonikós* exists; see DEMONIC. **—demonic** *adj.* 1662, borrowed from Late Latin *daemonicus,* from Greek *daimonikós,* from *daímōn* god, spirit; for suffix see -IC.

demonstrate *v.* 1552, borrowed, possibly by influence of Middle French *demonstrer,* from Latin *dēmōnstrātus,* past participle of *dēmōnstrāre* (*dē-* entirely + *mōnstrāre* to point out, show, from *mōnstrum* divine omen; wonder; see MONSTER); for suffix see -ATE[1]. Alternatively, *demonstrate* may be a back formation of *demonstration.* **—demonstration** *n.* About 1380, in Chaucer's translation of Boethius' *De Consolatione Philosophiae;* borrowed from Old French *demonstration,* or directly from Latin *dēmōnstrātiōnem* (nominative *dēmōnstrātiō*), from *dēmōnstrāre;* for suffix see -TION. **—demonstrable** *adj.* Probably before 1400, in Chaucer's translation of *Roman de la Rose;* borrowed from Old French *demonstrable,* from Late Latin *dēmōnstrābilis,* from Latin *dēmōnstrāre;* for suffix see -ABLE. **—demonstrative** *adj., n.* About 1395, in Chaucer's *Canterbury Tales;* borrowed from Old French *demonstratif* (feminine *demonstrative*), from Latin *dēmōnstrātivus,* from past participle stem of *dēmōnstrāre;* for suffix see -IVE. **—demonstrator** *n.* 1611, probably formed from English *demonstrate,* v. + *-or[2];* but usually said to be borrowed through French *démonstrateur,* from Latin *dēmōnstrātor,* from *dēmōnstrāre;* for suffix see -OR[2].

demoralize *v.* About 1793, to corrupt the morals of; Anglicized by Noah Webster as a borrowing of French *démoraliser,* a word, according to the OED, born of the French Revolution, from *de-* remove, take + *moral,* adj. + *-iser* -ize. The sense of lower the morale of, is first recorded in 1848.

demote *v.* reduce to a lower rank. About 1891, American English, from *de-* down + *(pro)mote.* **—demotion** *n.* 1901, American English, from *de-* down + *(pro)motion.*

demotic (dimot′ik) *adj.* of the common people. 1822, of or relating to the simplified, popular form of ancient Egyptian writing; borrowed from Greek *dēmotikós* of or for the common people, from *dêmos* common people; see DEMOCRACY; for suffix see -IC. The sense of relating to the popular written or spoken form of Modern Greek, is first recorded in English in 1927.

demur (dimėr′) *v.* to object. Probably before 1200 *demeorien* linger or wait, in *Ancrene Riwle;* borrowed from Old French *demorer, demourer* delay or retard, from Latin *dēmorārī* (*dē-* + *morārī* to delay, from *mora* a pause, delay, cognate with Sanskrit *smárati* remembers, thinks of, Latin *memor* mindful, from Indo-European **(s)mer-/(s)mor-,* Pok.969). The legal sense of put in a demurrer, is first recorded in 1620, the meaning object, about 1639. **—n.** About 1250 *demure* a delay, objection; borrowed from Old French *demor, demore, demoure,* from *demorer, demourer.* **—demurrer** *n.* plea to dismiss a lawsuit. 1533, pause; borrowed through Anglo-French, as a noun use of the Old French infinitive *demorer, demourer* to linger.

demure (dimyůr′) *adj.* reserved, coy. 1377 *dimuir;* later *demure* calm, still (before 1420, in Lydgate's *Troy Book*); probably formed in English from *di-, de-* (origin and meaning uncertain) + Old French *meür* discreet, from Latin *mātūrus* MATURE.

An alternative etymology derives English *demure* perhaps from Anglo-French *demuré* (Old French *demoré*), past participle of *demorer* stay (compare English *staid,* from *stay*), influenced by Old French *meür.* See DEMUR.

den *n.* Old English *denn* (about 725, in *Beowulf*), from Proto-Germanic **danjan;* related to *denu* valley; cognate with a variety of words, some with a semantic connection which include Middle Low German *denne* lair, depression, valley, Old Dutch *denne* cave, den, and Sanskrit *dhánu-s* sandbank, shore, from Indo-European **dhen-/dhon-* flat surface (Pok. 249). The sense of a small, cozy room for work is first recorded in 1771, in Smollett's *The Expedition of Humphry Clinker,* developed from *denne* a private chamber (about 1340). **—v.** Before 1250, to seek shelter; from the noun.

denarius *n.* ancient Roman silver coin. Before 1398, the weight of a denarius, in Trevisa's translation of Bartholomew's *De Proprietatibus Rerum;* borrowing of Latin *dēnārius* containing ten, from *dēnī* ten at a time, (earlier **dex-noi,* formed by analogy with **sex-noi,* whence *sēnī* six at a time), related to Latin *decem* TEN. The letter *d* was used in Britain as a symbol of *denarius* for penny and for pence (Latin *dēnāriī, pl.*) from 1387 until 1970.

denature *v.* 1685, to make unnatural; later, to make

unfit for eating or drinking (1878); borrowed from French *dénaturer,* from Old French *desnaturer* (*des-, dé-* do the opposite of + *nature*). **—denatured** *adj.* 1878, from past participle of English *denature,* v.

dendrite *n.* 1727-51, treelike marking on stones, borrowed from Greek *dendrítēs* of a tree, from *déndron* tree, related to *drŷs* TREE. The anatomical sense of a branching part of a nerve cell, is first recorded in 1893.

dengue (den′gā) *n.* a type of infectious fever. 1828, American English, borrowed from West Indian Spanish *dengue* (1827), from an African source; compare Swahili *kidingapopo* dengue; and possibly Giryama (an East African language) *kidhinghidyo* fever. It was identified with the Spanish word *dengue* fastidiousness, prudery, and an altered form, *dandy,* appeared in 1828 in the British West Indies, both words probably from a folk etymology suggested by the stiffness in the joints that causes the victims to walk carefully or daintily like a dandy.

denial *n.* See under DENY.

denigrate (den′əgrāt) *v.* blacken or stain the reputation of; defame. 1526, probably from earlier past participle *denigrate* blackened, discolored (before 1425); borrowed possibly by influence of Old French *denigrer,* from Latin *dēnigrātus,* past participle of *dēnigrāre* to blacken (*dē-* completely + *nigr-,* stem of *niger* (glossy) black; see NEGRO); for suffix see -ATE[1]. **—denigration** *n.* Probably before 1425 *denigracioun,* borrowed from Late Latin *dēnigrātiōnem* (nominative *dēnigrātiō*) a blackening, from Latin *dēnigrāre* to blacken; for suffix see -ATION.

denim *n.* coarse cotton cloth. 1695, a type of serge, a borrowing shortened from French *serge de Nîmes,* serge from Nîmes, town in southern France where it was primarily manufactured. The meaning of a coarse cotton cloth with a diagonal weave, is probably first recorded in an adjective use in 1850 in American English, and the plural *denims,* meaning overalls or trousers made of denim, is first recorded in 1868. Compare JEANS and BLUE JEANS.

denizen (den′əzən) *n.* inhabitant, resident. 1419 *densyn;* later *denizeine* (1433); borrowed from Anglo-French *deinzein* (*deinz* within or inside, from Late Latin *deintus,* from Latin *dē* from, and *intus* within + *-ein,* from Latin *-ānus* -an). The three-syllable form arose probably by influence of *citizen.*

denomination *n.* name, designation, or title. Before 1398 *denominacioun* a mentioning by name, in Trevisa's translation of Bartholomew's *De Proprietatibus Rerum;* borrowed from Old French *denomination,* or directly from Latin *dēnōminātiōnem* (nominative *dēnōminātiō*) a calling by other than the proper name, metonymy, from *dēnōmināre* to name (*dē-* completely + *nōmināre* to name, NOMINATE); for suffix see -TION. The sense of a value or kind of money, is first recorded in 1660; that of a religious sect or group, before 1716. **—denominational** *adj.* 1838, formed from English *denomination* + *-al*[1]. **—denominator** *n.* number below the line in a fraction. 1542, borrowed, possibly by influence of Middle French *dénominateur,* from Medieval Latin *denominator,* from Latin *dēnōmināre* to name; for suffix see -OR[2].

denote *v.* 1592, in Shakespeare's *Romeo and Juliet;* borrowed from Middle French *dénoter,* learned borrowing from Latin *dēnotāre* denote, mark out (*dē-* completely + *notāre* to mark, from *nota* a mark, NOTE). **—denotation** *n.* About 1532, indication, borrowed perhaps through Middle French *dénotation,* or directly from Latin *dēnotātiōnem* (nominative *dēnotātiō*), from *dēnotāre* denote; for suffix see -ATION. In 1843 the sense of exact, literal meaning (contrasted with *connotation*) appeared in John Stuart Mill's *Logic.*

denouement or **dénouement** (dā′nümäN′) *n.* outcome or unraveling of a plot, etc. 1752, in Lord Chesterfield's letters; borrowing of French *dénouement* an untying, from *dénouer* untie, from Old French *desnouer* (*des-* un-, out, from Latin *dis-* + *nouer* to tie, knot, from Latin *nōdāre,* from *nōdus* a knot, NODE).

denounce *v.* Before 1325 *denuncen* proclaim someone to be something bad, in *Cursor Mundi;* later *denounce* (probably about 1380) to inform; borrowed through Old French *denoncier, denuntier,* from Latin *dēnūntiāre* (*dē-* down + *nūntiāre* proclaim, announce, from *nūntius* messenger, of uncertain origin). Two forms exist in English *denounce* and *denunciate,* both borrowed ultimately from Latin *dēnūntiāre,* but *denunciate* is not widely used and only its noun form *denunciation* is generally found to complement the verb *denounce.* **—denunciation** *n.* Probably before 1425, public proclamation, borrowed, perhaps by influence of Old French *denonciation,* from Latin *dēnūntiātiōnem* (nominative *dēnūntiātiō*), from *dēnūntiāre* denounce; for suffix see -TION.

dense *adj.* Probably before 1425, borrowed from Middle French *dense,* and directly from Latin *dēnsus* thick, crowded; possibly cognate with Greek *dasýs* hairy, shaggy, bushy, from Indo-European **dens-/dṇs-* (Pok. 202). The sense of stupid, thick-headed, is first recorded in English in 1822. **—density** *n.* 1603, in Philemon Holland's translation of Plutarch's *Moralia;* borrowed from French *densité,* from Latin *dēnsitātem* (nominative *dēnsitās*) thickness, from *dēnsus* thick; for suffix see -ITY.

dent *n.* hollow made by a blow. Probably about 1225, stroke or blow, in *King Horn,* dialectal variant of DINT, n.; later, wound made by a blow (1373). The meaning of an indentation, hollow impression made on a surface, is first recorded in 1565, apparently influenced by INDENT, v., make a dent in. **—v.** make a dent in. 1440 *denten,* dialectal variant of *dinten* to beat with blows (about 1225), from *dint,* n. The verb *dent* probably existed earlier, as can be inferred from the gerund *dentyng* an indentation (about 1395, in the Wycliffe Bible).

dental *adj.* 1594, borrowed through Middle French *dental* of or for teeth, from Late Latin *dentālis,* from Latin *dēns* (genitive *dentis*) TOOTH; for suffix see -AL[1]. **—dentifrice** (den′təfris) *n.* toothpaste or toothpowder. Probably before 1425 *dentifricie,* borrowed from Latin *dentifricium* (*dēns,* genitive *dentis* tooth + *fricāre* to rub; see FRICTION). **—dentist** *n.* 1759, borrowed from French *dentiste,* from *dent* tooth, from Latin *dentem* (nominative *dēns*) tooth; for suffix see -IST. **—dentistry** *n.* 1838, formed from English *dentist* + *-ry.*

denture *n.* a set of artificial teeth. 1874, borrowed from French *denture* a set of teeth, from Middle French *denteüre* (*dent* tooth + *-ure*).

denude *v.* uncover, make bare. Probably before 1425 *denuden,* borrowed through Middle French *dénuder,* from Latin *dēnūdāre* (*dē-* away + *nūdāre* to strip, from *nūdus* bare, NUDE).

denunciate *v.* 1593, to make a denunciation against. For *denunciation* see DENOUNCE.

deny *v.* Before 1325 *denyen,* borrowed from Old French *denier, denoier,* from Latin *dēnegāre* (*dē-* away + *negāre* refuse, say no, NEGATE). **—denial** *n.* 1528, formed from English *deny* + *-al*[2]; replacing earlier *denyance* (1468), a blend of *deny* and Old French *denoiance,* from *denoier,* variant of *denier;* for suffix of this older form see -ANCE.

deodorant *n.* 1869, formed in English, as if from Latin **deodōrantem,* present participle of **deodōrāre* to remove the smell, from *odōrem* smell or odor, the OED suggests on analogy of *dēcolōrāre.* **—deodorize** *v.* 1858, formed in English from *de-* take away + Latin *odōrem* smell + *-ize.* Of course it is also possible that both *deodorant* and *deodorize* are purely English formations.

deoxyribonucleic acid (dēok′sərī′bōnüklē′ik) acid found in the nuclei of all living cells; DNA. 1931, formed from English *deoxyribo(se)* sugar component of this acid (from *deoxy-* having fewer atoms in the molecule than the specified compound + RIBOSE a sugar), and *nucleic acid.*

depart *v.* About 1250 *departen* part from each other; borrowed from Old French *departir,* from Late Latin *departīre* divide (Latin *dē-* from + *partīre, partīrī* to part, divide, from *pars,* genitive *partis,* PART). **—departure** *n.* 1441, borrowed from Middle French *departeüre, desparteüre,* from Old French *departeüre,* formed (as if from Late Latin **dispartītūra*) from Old French *departir* + *-ure* -ure.

department *n.* 1450 *departement* departure; borrowed from Middle French *département, despartement,* from *departir;* for suffix see -MENT. The Middle and Old French words also had the meaning of a group of people, from which English later borrowed the senses of a separate division or part (before 1735). **—departmental** *adj.* 1791, borrowed from French *départemental,* from *departement* + *-al*[1]. **—department store** (1887, from an earlier concept of specialized departments in a large store, 1847).

depend *v.* 1410 *dependen* be conditioned on, be because of; later, to be uncertain or in suspense (before 1420), and to hang down, grow down (about 1450); borrowed from Middle French *dependre* to hang from, hang down, from Vulgar Latin **dēpendere,* from Latin *dēpendēre* (*dē-* from, down + *pendēre* to hang, be suspended; see PENDANT). **—dependable** *adj.* 1735, in Pope's correspondence; formed from English *depend* + *-able.* **—dependence** *n.* 1414 *dependance,* borrowed from Middle French *dépendance,* from *dépendre* depend; for suffix see -ANCE. Respelling of the ending *-ence,* which was established by the early 1800's, was influenced by the Latin and, to a limited extent, by *dependent.* **—dependency** *n.* 1594, formed from English *dependence, dependance* + *-cy.* **—dependent** *adj.* Before 1398 *dependaunt,* borrowed from Old French *dependant,* present participle of *dependre* depend. From the 1400's on, the spelling *dependent* gradually became dominant, after Latin *dēpendentem* (nominative *dēpendēns*), present participle of *dēpendēre* depend, and was fully established by 1700. *—n.* 1425, from the adjective, generally spelled *-ent,* especially in American English.

depict *v.* show, portray. Before 1420 *depicten* to disguise, in Lydgate's *Troy Book;* later, to portray, paint, draw (probably about 1430); borrowed from Latin *dēpictus,* past participle of *dēpingere* (*dē-* down + *pingere* to PAINT). **—depiction** *n.* 1688, borrowed from French *depiction,* from Latin *dēpictiōnem* (nominative *dēpictiō*), from *dēpic-,* stem of *dēpingere;* for suffix see -TION.

depilatory (dəpil′ətôr′ē) *adj.* that removes hair. 1601 *depilatorie,* borrowed from French *dépilatoire,* adj., from Latin *dēpilātus* having one's hair plucked (*dē-* completely + *pilātus,* past participle of *pilāre* deprive of hair, from *pilus* hair; see PILE[3] nap); for suffix see -ORY. English *depilatory* replaced earlier *depilative,* adj. (1562, formed in English from Latin *dēpilāt-,* past participle stem of *dēpilāre* + English suffix *-ive*). **—n.** preparation for removing hair. 1606 *depilatorie,* borrowed from French *dépilatoire,* n.

deplete *v.* empty out. 1807, empty the blood vessels; borrowed from Latin *dēplētus,* past participle of *dēplēre* to empty (*dē-* off, away + *plēre* to fill; see FULL). **—depletion** *n.* 1656, from Late Latin *dēplētiōnem* (nominative *dēplētiō*) bloodletting, from Latin *dēplēre* to empty; for suffix see -TION.

deplore *v.* regret deeply. 1559, to give up as hopeless; later, to regret deeply (1567); borrowed from Middle French *deplorer,* or directly from Latin *dēplorāre* deplore, bewail (*dē-* entirely + *plōrāre* weep, cry out, perhaps imitative of the sound, Pok. 831). **—deplorable** *adj.* 1612, borrowed through French *déplorable,* or directly from Late Latin *dēplōrābilis* mournful, lamentable, from *dēplōrāre* deplore; for suffix see -ABLE.

deploy *v.* spread out (troops, etc.) in a line. 1786, borrowed from French *déployer* unroll, unfold, from Old French *desployer* unfold (earlier *despleier*) from Latin *displicāre* unfold, scatter; see the doublet DISPLAY. The form *deploy* appears earlier in Caxton's works with the meaning of unfold, display; borrowed, according to the OED, from Parisian French, but this use was not apparently established at the time in English. **—deployment** *n.* 1796, borrowed from French *déploiement,* from *déployer* deploy; for suffix see -MENT.

deponent (dipō′nənt) *adj.* (of verbs) passive in form but active in meaning, or middle in form (intermediate between active and passive, as a voice of Greek verbs which represents the subject as acting on or for itself, as reflexive verbs do). About 1450, borrowed from Latin *dēpōnentem,* present participle of *dēpōnere* put off or aside (*dē-* off, aside + *pōnere* to put, place; see POSITION). The term was used by Latin grammarians for verbs which, though passive in their forms, had "put aside" their passive meanings. The term is a translation of Greek *apothetikós,* literally, laying aside, from *apotithénai* to lay or put aside. **—n.** 1548, one who gives a sworn testimony or deposition; earlier, a deponent verb (1530); borrowed from Medieval Latin *deponentem* (nominative *deponens*), present participle of *deponere* to testify, (also) to lay aside, from Latin *dēpōnere* to put down, deposit.

deport *v.* 1474, behave or conduct oneself in a certain way, in Caxton's *Game and Play of Chess;* borrowed from Middle French *deporter* (*de-* thoroughly, formally, from Latin *dē-* away + *porter* to carry, bear oneself from Latin *portāre* carry; see PORT[4] bearing). The sense of banish, expel from a country, is first recorded before 1641; borrowed from French *déporter,* from Latin *dēportāre* carry off, transport, banish (*dē-* off away + *portāre* carry). **—deportation** *n.* banishment 1595, borrowed from Middle French *déportation,* from Latin *dēportātiōnem* (nominative *dēportātiō*), from *dēportāre* transport, banish; for suffix see -TION. **—deportment** *n.* behavior. 1601, borrowed from French *déportement,* from *déporter* behave, from Middle French *deporter;* for suffix see -MENT.

depose *v.* remove from authority. Probably before 1300 *deposen,* in *Kyng Alisaunder;* borrowed from Old French *deposer* (*de-* down + *poser* put, place, see POSE). **—deposition** *n.* removal from authority. 1399, in *Rolls of Parliament;* borrowed from Latin and Late Latin *dēpositiōnem* (nominative *dēpositiō*) a putting down, removal, testimony, from *dēposi-,* past participle stem of *dēpōnere* put down, deposit; for suffix see -TION. The sense of sworn testimony in writing, is first recorded in 1425; see DEPONENT, n.

deposit v. 1624, borrowed from Latin *dēpositus,* past participle of *dēpōnere* lay aside, put down, deposit (*dē-* away + *pōnere* to put; see POSITION). **—n.** 1624, in writings of Francis Bacon, borrowed from Latin *dēpositum,* neuter past participle of *dēpōnere.* Doublet of DEPOT. **—depositor** *n.* 1565, borrowed from Latin *dēpositor* one who deposes. 1624, borrowed from French *dépositeur* one who deposits. **—depository** *n.* 1656, borrowed from or patterned on Medieval Latin *depositorium,* from Latin *déposi-,* past participle stem of *dēpōnere;* for suffix see - ORY.

depot (dē′pō) *n.* warehouse, railroad station (in U.S.). 1794, a depositing; 1795, warehouse; borrowing of French *dépôt* a deposit or place of deposit, from Middle French, from Old French *depost* a deposit or pledge, learned borrowing from Latin *dēpositum* a deposit, neuter past participle of *dēpōnere* lay aside, deposit; see the doublet DEPOSIT, n.

deprave *v.* corrupt, pervert. Before 1376 *depraven* vilify, in a version of *Piers Plowman;* later, corrupt (before 1382, in the Wycliffe Bible); borrowed through Old French *depraver,* or directly from Latin *dēprāvāre* corrupt (*dē-* completely + *prāvus* crooked; possibly related to Latin *prātum* meadow, perhaps originally a hollow, and hence to English *prairie,* cognate with Old Irish *rāth* earth wall, from Indo-European **prā-* to bend, Pok. 843). **—depravity** *n.* 1641, in Milton's *Of Reformation,* formed from English *deprave* + *-ity,* on the model of earlier *pravity* corruption (1550), from Latin *prāvitās* (accusative *prāvitātem*), from *prāvus* crooked.

deprecate (dep′rəkāt) *v.* protest against, disapprove of. 1624, supplicate, pray, back formation from earlier *deprecation* (1566), or borrowed from Latin *dēprecātus,* past participle of *dēprecārī* plead in excuse, avert by prayer (*dē-* away + *precārī* PRAY); for suffix see -ATE[1]. The sense of protest against, show disapproval of, is first recorded in 1641. **—deprecation** *n.* 1566, prayer, borrowed from Middle French *déprécation,* from Latin *dēprecātiōnem* (nominative *dēprecātiō*), from *dēprecārī* avert by prayer; for suffix see -TION. The sense of a strong expression of disapproval, is first recorded in 1612-15.

depreciate (dəprē′shēāt) *v.* to lower in value or estimation. 1564 *depreciaten,* borrowed from Latin *dēpretiātus,* past participle of *dēpretiāre* (*dē-* down + *pretium* PRICE); for suffix see -ATE[1]. Latin *dēpretiāre* developed in Medieval Latin the spelling *depreciare.* **—depreciation** *n.* 1767, in Benjamin Franklin's writings; formed from English *depreciate* + *-ion.*

depredation (dep′rədā′shən) *n.* act of plundering. 1483, in Caxton's *Golden Legend;* borrowed through Middle French *déprédation,* or directly from Late Latin *dēpraedātiōnem* (nominative *dēpraedātiō),* from Latin *dēpraedārī* to pillage, plunder thoroughly; for suffix see -TION. **—depredate** *v.* 1626, in Francis Bacon's *Sylva Sylvarum,* either a back formation from earlier *depredation* (1483), or borrowed from Latin *dēpraedātus,* past participle of *dēpraedārī* to pillage (*dē-* thoroughly + *praedārī* to plunder, from *praeda* booty, PREY); for suffix see -ATE[1].

depress *v.* Probably about 1380, *depressen* put down by force, overcome; borrowed from Old French *depresser,* learned borrowing from Late Latin *dēpressāre,* frequentative form of Latin *dēprimere* press down (*dē-* down + *premere* to PRESS[1] push). The literal sense of push down, press down, is first recorded probably about 1425; that of deject, make gloomy, in 1621, in Burton's *Anatomy of Melancholy,* and the economic sense of to lower in value, about 1878. **—depressant** *n.* sedative drug. 1876 formed from English *depress* + *-ant.* **—depression** *n.* About 1391, angular distance of a heavenly body below the horizon, in Chaucer's *Treatise on the Astrolabe;* borrowed through Old French *depression,* or directly from Medieval Latin *depressionem,* from Latin *dēpressiōnem* (nominative *dēpressiō*) a pressing down, from *dēpress-,* past participle stem of *dēprimere* press down; for suffix see -ION. The sense of a state of dejection is first recorded probably about 1425, but the formal sense of psychology did not appear until 1905. The sense of a downturn in business, is first recorded in 1793, with the formal sense in economics (originally with reference to the Great Depression) appearing after 1929.

deprive *v.* Before 1338 *depriven* force to give up, rob, divest, exclude, dismiss; borrowed from Medieval Latin *deprivare* (Latin *dē-* entirely + *prīvāre* release from, deprive; see PRIVATE). **—deprivation** *n.* 1445 *deprivacion,* borrowed from Medieval Latin *deprivationem* (nominative *deprivatio*), from *deprivare* deprive; for suffix see -TION.

depth *n.* Before 1382 *depthe,* in the Wycliffe Bible; cognate with Old Saxon *diupitha* depth, Middle Dutch *diepde* (modern Dutch *diepte*), Middle Low German *dēpede,* Middle High German *tiufede,* Old Icelandic *dýpt,* and Gothic *diupitha,* from Proto-Germanic **deupíthō;* derived from the root of Old English *dēop* DEEP.

depute *v.* Probably about 1350 *deputen* to appoint, assign, select (for a certain purpose); borrowed from Middle French *deputer,* learned borrowing from Late Latin *dēputāre* to destine, allot, from Latin *dēputāre* consider as (*dē-* away + *putāre* to think, count, consider, prune, trim; see PUTATIVE). **—deputation** *n.* Before 1393, delegation of responsibilities to deputies, in Gower's *Confessio Amantis;* borrowed from Medieval Latin *deputationem* (nominative *deputatio*), from Latin *dēputāre* to allot; for suffix see -ATION. **—deputize** *v.* 1730-36, formed from English *deputy* + *-ize.* **—deputy** *n.* 1406 *depute,* in the *Rolls of Parliament,* borrowed through Anglo-French *deputé,* noun use of the past participle of Middle French *deputer* appoint, assign; for suffix see -Y[4].

derange *v.* 1776, to disturb the order of arrangment of, throw into confusion, in Adam Smith's *Wealth of Nations;* borrowed, possibly by influence of earlier English *derangement,* from French *déranger,* from Old French *desrengier* disarrange (*des-* do the opposite of, from Latin *dis-* + *reng, renc* line, row, RANK). The sense of disorder the mind, make insane, is first recorded in 1825, in Southey's *Tale of Paraguay.* **—derangement** *n.* 1737, borrowed from French *dérangement,* from *déranger;* for suffix see -MENT.

derby (dėr′bē) *n.* stiff hat first manufactured in the U.S. in 1850, but not recorded in American English until 1870. The hat derives its name from the *Derby* a horse race run annually in England, at which this type of hat was worn, apparently after the fashion of the Earl of Derby (see WELLINGTON for a similar style and fashion set by a leading social figure). The general sense of any important race, is first recorded in 1875, in American English, for the *Kentucky Derby.* The original Derby horse race was founded by the twelfth earl of *Derby* in 1780, whose title is from the name of a county in central England, called in Old English (959) *Dēorbȳ* deer village or homestead (*dēor* DEER + *bȳ* habitation, homestead, from a Scandinavian source; compare Old Icelandic *bȳr* court, town, Norwegian, Swedish, Danish *by,* related to *būa* to dwell, and hence to English BOWER; the ending *-by* is found in Old English names of places where Scandinavians settled; see also BYLAW).

derelict *adj.* abandoned, delinquent. 1649, borrowed perhaps through obsolete French *derelict,* or directly from Latin *dērelictus,* past participle of *dērelinquere* abandon (*dē-* entirely + *relinquere* leave behind, RELINQUISH). **—n.** person or thing that is abandoned, especially a ship abandoned at sea. 1670, from Latin *dērelictus.* The sense of a derelict person, is first recorded in 1728, in Savage's *The Bastard.* **—dereliction** *n.* 1597, borrowed perhaps through obsolete French *dereliction,* or directly from Latin *dērelictiōnem* (nominative *dērelictiō*), from *dērelic-,* past participle stem of *dērelinquere* abandon; for suffix see -TION.

deride *n.* ridicule. 1530, in Palsgrave's *Lesclarcissement,* borrowed from Middle French *derider,* learned borrowing from Latin *dērīdēre* (*dē-* down + *rīdēre* to laugh; see RIDICULOUS). **—derision** *n.* Probably about 1408, in writings of Lydgate; borrowed from Old French *derision,* learned borrowing from Latin *dērīsiōnem* (nominative *dērīsiō*) from *dērīdēre* deride; for suffix see -SION. **—derisive** *adj.* Before 1662, formed in English, probably by influence of French *dérisif* (feminine *dérisive*), from *deris(ion)* or Latin *dērīs-,* past participle stem of *dērīdēre* + English suffix *-ive.*

derive *v.* About 1385, in Chaucer's *Canterbury Tales;* borrowed from Old French *deriver,* learned borrowing from Latin *dērīvāre* lead or draw off (a stream of water), from the prepositional phrase *dē rīvō* (*dē* from and *rīvus* the stream; see RIVULET and RIVAL). The sense of trace the origin of (a word) is first recorded in 1559. **—derivation** *n.* Probably before 1425, a draining off; in an anonymous translation of Chauliac's *Grande Chirurgie;* later, the tracing of the origin of a word (1447); borrowed from Middle French *dérivation,* from Latin *dērīvātiōnem* (nominative *dērīvātiō*), from *dērīvāre* derive; for suffix see -TION. **—derivative** *adj.* Probably before 1425 *derivatif* drawing off (blood), in an anonymous translation of Chauliac's *Grande Chirurgie.* —*n.* About 1450 *derivative* a derived word or form. Both noun and adjective borrowed from Middle French *dérivatif* (feminine *dérivative*), from Late Latin *dērīvātīvus,* from Latin *dērīvāre* derive; for suffix see -IVE.

derma *n.* layer of skin beneath the epidermis. 1706, borrowed, possibly by influence of French *derme,* from Greek *dérma* (genitive *dérmatos*) skin, from *dérein* to flay; see TEAR pull.**—dermatologist** *n.* (1861) **—dermatology** *n.* 1819, formed from English *dermat-, dermato-,* combining form, borrowed from Greek *dérma* (genitive *dérmatos*) skin + *-ology.*

dermis *n.* derma. 1830, New Latin *dermis,* back formation from Greek *epidermís* EPIDERMIS.

derogatory *adj.* detracting. 1502-03 *derogatorie;* perhaps borrowed through Middle French *dérogatoire,* or directly from Latin *dērogātōrius,* from *dērogāre* detract from; for suffix see -ORY. Alternatively, *derogatory* may have been formed from English *derogate* + *-ory,* possibly by influence of Middle French *dérogatoire.* **—derogate** (der′əgāt) *v.* detract. Before 1420 *derogaten,* in Lydgate's *Troy Book;* borrowed from Latin *dērogātus,* past participle of *dērogāre* repeal in part, detract from (*dē-* away from + *rogāre* ask, question, propose a law; see RIGHT); for suffix see -ATE[1].

derrick *n.* 1727, stationary machine for hoisting heavy weights, in *Chambers Cyclopaedia;* originally, a gallows, a hanging, or a hangman (early 1600's); formed from *Derick* surname of a hangman at the Tyburn gallows, London, during the reign of Elizabeth I (often referred to in contemporary theatrical productions).

derrière or **derriere** (de′rēār′) *n.* the rump, backside. 1774, French word introduced as a euphemism, from Old French *deriere* back, behind, from Late Latin *dēretrō* behind, in the rear (Latin *dē-* from + *retrō* backwards).

derring-do *n.* daring feats. The phrase appeared originally about 1385 in Chaucer's *Troilus and Criseyde* as *dorrying don,* literally, daring to do, from *durriing* daring, present participle of *durren* to DARE, and *don* (infinitive) to do. In the 1500's, by misspelling it became *derring do* and developed as a compound noun with the meaning of daring deeds, desperate courage. Scott and others borrowed the phrase from Spenser's *The Shepheardes Calender* (1579), and printing it *derring-do* popularized its use as a noun.

derringer *n.* short-barreled pistol. 1853, American English, in allusion to the name of Henry *Deringer,* 1786-1868, an American gunsmith who invented and manufactured this pistol in the 1840's. Its popularity spawned many imitations that often bore the misspelled name "Derringer" on their locks.

dervish *n.* Moslem religious mendicant. 1585 *dervis,* borrowed from Turkish *derviş,* from Persian *darvēš, darvīš* beggar, poor. The native Arabic equivalent is *faqīr* poor (man), FAKIR.

The spelling *dervish* appeared in 1847, in Emerson's poetry.

descant *n.* music for two or more parts, counterpoint. About 1400 *dyscant, deschaunt,* in Wycliffe's writings; borrowed from Anglo-French *deschaunt;* later *descant* (before 1450), borrowed from Old North French *descant.* Both forms in French, and some uses of *descant* in English, were borrowed from Medieval Latin *discantus* (Latin *dis-* asunder, apart + *cantus* song; see CHANT). **—v.** Before 1450 *discanten* to sing in counterpoint; probably borrowed from Medieval Latin *descantare, discantare* to play or sing a descant, from *discantus,* n. The meaning of talk or discuss at length is first recorded in English before 1661.

descend *v.* Probably before 1300 *decenden,* in *Arthour and Merlin;* later *descenden* about 1375, in Chaucer's *Canterbury Tales*); borrowed from Old French *descendre,* learned borrowing from Latin *dēscendere* (*dē-* down + *scandere* to climb; see SCAN). The sense of spring from, originate, is first recorded about 1375, in Chaucer's *Canterbury Tales.* **—descendant** *n.* 1600, borrowed from French *descendant,* from Old French, present participle of *descendre* descend. *—adj.* About 1460, borrowed from Middle French *descendant* (see noun), though when spelled *-ent* was at one time regarded as a form borrowed from Latin. **—descent** *n.* Probably before 1300 *decente,* in *Arthour and Merlin;* borrowed from Old French *descente,* from *descendre* descend.

describe *v.* Probably before 1425 *describen,* in a translation of Higden's *Polychronicon;* borrowed from Latin *dēscrībere* write down, transcribe, copy, sketch. The later Middle English *describen* replaced earlier *descriven* (before 1250, in *Ancrene Riwle*); borrowed from Old French *descrivre,* from Latin *dēscrībere* (*dē-* down, out + *scrībere* write; see SCRIBE). Later use of *describen* in place of *descriven* came from the effort to Latinize the English spelling. **—description** *n.* About 1380, in Chaucer's *House of Fame;* borrowed from Old French *descripcion,* and directly from Latin *dēscriptiōnem,* from *dēscrīpt-,* stem of *dēscrībere* describe; for suffix see -TION. **—descriptive** *adj.* 1751, Samuel Johnson in *The Rambler,* borrowed from Late Latin *dēscrīptīvus* containing a description, from Latin *dēscrīpt-,* stem of *dēscrībere* describe; for suffix see -IVE.

descry[1] (diskrī′) *v.* catch sight of, make out; discern. Probably about 1300 *discrien* see, catch sight of, discover; later *descrien* (1375); borrowed from Old French *descrire, descrivre* describe, explain (rarely), make visible, from Latin *dēscrībere* DESCRIBE. The meaning of catch sight of, probably developed from the Old French sense of make visible.

descry[2] *v.* to cry out, proclaim, announce. About 1350 *discrien* announce, declare; earlier *descrien* to taunt or challenge (before 1338); borrowed from Old French *decrier, descrier* call out, proclaim; see DECRY.

desecrate *v.* destroy the sacredness of. Before 1677; earlier, to dismiss from holy orders, degrade (1674); formed from English *de-* do the opposite of + *-secrate,* in *consecrate,* perhaps influenced by Old French *dessacrer* to profane, violate (*des-,* from Latin *dis-* + *sacrer* consecrate, from *sacrāre,* from *sacer* SACRED). **—desecration** *n.* Before 1717, formed from English *desecrate* + *-ion.*

desegregate *v.* 1953, in American English, formed from English *de-* do the opposite of + *segregate;* or possibly a back formation from *desegregation.* **—desegregation** *n.* 1952, in American English, formed from English *de-* do the opposite of + *segregation* separation of Negroes from white society or institutions (1903, American English, in Booker T. Washington's writings).

desert[1] (dez′ərt) *n.* barren region. Probably before 1200, in *Ancrene Riwle;* borrowed from Old French *desert,* from Late Latin *dēsertum,* literally, thing abandoned, noun use of neuter past participle of Latin *dēserere* forsake, DESERT[2]. **—desertification** (dez′ərtəfəkā′shən) *n.* changing of land into desert. 1973, formed from English *desert* + *-ification* causing to become (as in *calcification* and *stratification*).

desert[2] (dizėrt′) *v.* leave, forsake. About 1380, in Chaucer's translation of Boethius' *De Consolatione Philosophiae,* borrowed from Old French *deserter* to abandon, from Late Latin *dēsertāre,* frequentative form of *dēserere* leave, literally, undo or sever connection (*dē-* undo + *serere* join; see SERIES). **—deserter** *n.* 1635, formed from English *desert*[2], v. + *-er*[1]. **—desertion** *n.* 1591, borrowed from Middle French *désertion,* from Late Latin *dēsertiōnem* (nominative *dēsertiō*), from Latin *dēserere* leave; for suffix see -TION.

desert[3] (dizėrt′) *n.* suitable reward or punishment. About 1300, borrowed from Old French *deserte,* past participle of *deservir* be worthy to have, from Latin *dēservīre* to serve well, devote oneself to; see DESERVE. The plural *deserts,* as found in the phrase *one's just deserts,* is first recorded about 1380, in Chaucer's translation of Boethius' *De Consolatione Philosophiae.*

deserve *v.* be worthy of, merit. About 1225 *deserven,* in *Ancrene Riwle;* borrowed from Old French *deservir,* from Latin *dēservīre* serve well (*dē-* completely + *servīre* to SERVE). **—deserving** *n.* Probably about 1300, from *deserve,* v. *—adj.* 1576, from the noun.

desiccate (des′əkāt) *v.* dry thoroughly. 1575, from earlier *desicatt* dried up (1425, past participle and adjective); borrowed from Latin *dēsiccātus,* past participle of *dēsiccāre* (*dē-* thoroughly + *siccāre* to dry, from *siccus* dry; see SACK[3] sherry); for suffix see -ATE[1]. **—desiccation** *n.* Probably before 1425 *desiccacioun* a drying up, borrowed through Middle French *dessication,* or directly from Late Latin *dēsiccātiōnem* (nominative *dēsiccātiō*), from Latin *dēsiccāre;* for suffix see -TION.

design *v.* Before 1398 *designen* design or shape (something), in Trevisa's translation of Bartholomew's *De Proprietatibus Rerum;* borrowed from Latin *dēsignāre* mark out, trace out, denote, devise (*dē-* out + *signāre* to mark, from *signum* a mark, SIGN). **—n.** 1588, in Shakespeare's *Love's Labour's Lost;* borrowed from Middle French *desseign* purpose, project, design, from Italian *disegno,* from *disegnare* to mark out, from Latin *dēsignāre* mark out, trace out, denote, devise. **—designer** *n.* 1649, a plotter or schemer; later, one who makes artistic designs (1662); formed from English *design,* v. + *-er*[1].

designation *n.* 1398, act of marking or pointing out, in Trevisa's translation of Bartholomew's *De Proprietatibus Rerum;* borrowed through Old French *designation,* and directly from Latin *dēsignātiōnem* (nominative *dēsignātiō*), from *dēsignāre* mark out, denote, devise, appoint; for suffix see -TION. See DESIGN for specific meanings of Latin *dēsignāre* that have been differentiated in English between *designate* and *design.* Some senses of Latin *dēsignāre* have come into English through French and Italian, according to the OED. The sense of appointing or nominating for office or duty, is first recorded in English in 1605, in Francis Bacon's *Of the Advancement of Learning.*
—designate (dez′ignit) *adj.* 1646, appointed, selected; earlier, indicated, manifested (probably borrowed from Latin *dēsignātus,* past participle of *dēsignāre* appoint for office. *—v.* (dez′ignāt) 1791, appoint for duty or office, either from the adjective in English, or a back formation from *designation.*

desire *v.* Probably about 1200, borrowed from Old French *desirer,* from Latin *dēsīderāre* long for, wish for, (originally) await what the stars will bring, from the prepositional phrase *dē sīdere* from the stars or constellation (*dē-* from + *sīdus,* genitive *sīderis* heavenly body, star, constellation; see SIDEREAL). **—n.** Probably before 1300, in *Arthour and Merlin;* borrowed from Old French *desir,* from *desirer* to desire. **—desirable** *adj.* Before 1382, in the Wycliffe Bible; borrowed from Old French, from *desirer* to desire; for suffix see -ABLE. **—desirous** *adj.* Before 1300, in *Kyng Alisaunder;* borrowed through Anglo-French *desirous,* from Old French *desireus, desidros,* from Vulgar Latin **dēsīderōsus,* from the stem of Latin *dēsīderāre;* for suffix see -OUS.

desist (dizist′) *v.* stop, cease. 1459 *desisten,* borrowed from Middle French *désister,* learned borrowing from Latin *dēsistere* (*dē-* off + *sistere* to stop, come to a stand, from *stāre* to STAND).

desk *n.* 1363-64 *deske* a reading desk, lectern, or study desk; borrowed from Medieval Latin *desca* table, from Italian *desco* table, desk, from Latin *discus* quoit, platter, dish, from Greek *dískos.* Doublet of DAIS, DISCUS, DISH, and DISK.

desolate (des′əlit) *adj.* Probably about 1350 *desolat,* borrowed from Latin *dēsōlātus,* past participle of *dēsōlāre* leave alone, desert, (*dē-* completely + *sōlāre* make lonely, from *sōlus* lonely, lone, SOLE[1]); for suffix see -ATE[1]. **—v.** (des′əlāt) make barren. 1384 *desolaten,* in the Wycliffe Bible, borrowed, perhaps by influence of Old French *desoler,* from Latin *dēsōlātus,* past participle of *dēsōlāre* leave alone; for suffix see -ATE[1]; and also perhaps a back formation from *desolation.* **—desolation** *n.* Before 1382, in the Wycliffe Bible, borrowed from Old French *desolation,* from Late Latin *dēsōlātiōnem* (nominative *dēsōlātiō*), from Latin *dēsōlāre* leave alone; for suffix see -TION.

despair *n.* About 1300 *dyspayr;* borrowed probably from Old French **despeir,* earlier form of *despoir* (perhaps on the pattern of Old French *espeir* hope, earlier form of *espoir*), from *desperer* lose hope, despair, from Latin *dēspērāre* (*dē-* without, out of + *spērāre* to hope, from *spēs* hope; see SPEED). **—v.** lose hope. About 1340, borrowed from Old French *despeir-,* accented stem of *desperer,* from Latin *dēspērāre.*

desperado (des′pərä′dō) *n.* 1647, reckless criminal; a person in despair or in a desperate condition (1610); apparently a refashioning of earlier, and now obsolete *desperate* a desperate person (1563), or a reckless criminal (1611, in Chapman's translation of the *Iliad*), from DESPERATE, adj. The ending *-ado* is no doubt purposefully suggestive of Spanish, and the form is found in Old Spanish *desperado,* but what prompted its use in English is unknown.

desperate *adj.* Probably about 1400 *desperat* filled with despair, hopeless; borrowed from Latin *dēspērātus,* past participle of *dēspērāre* lose hope, DESPAIR; for suffix see -ATE[1]. **—desperation** *n.* About 1370, in Chaucer's *An A.B.C.,* borrowed through Middle French *desperacion,* or directly from Latin *dēspērātiōnem* (nominative *dēspērātiō*), from *dēspērāre* lose hope; for suffix see -TION.

despicable *adj.* contemptible. 1553, borrowed from Late Latin *dēspicābilis,* from Latin *dēspicārī* look down on (related to *dēspicere* DESPISE); for suffix see -ABLE.

despise *v.* scorn. Probably before 1300 *despisen,* in *Kyng Alisaunder;* from Old French *despis-,* stem of *despire,* from Latin *dēspicere* look down on, scorn (*dē-* down + *specere* look at; see SPY).

despite *n.* malice, spite. Probably before 1300 *despit,* *despite,* in *Arthour and Merlin* and *Kyng Alisaunder;* borrowed from Old French *despit,* from Latin *dēspectus* (genitive *dēspectūs*) a looking down on, from *dēspicere* DESPISE. **—prep.** in spite of. Before 1420, in Lydgate's *Troy Book,* a shortening of *in despite of* (about 1300), loan translation of Old French *en despit de.*

despoil *v.* rob, plunder. About 1300 *despoilen,* borrowed from Old French *despoillier,* from Latin *dēspoliāre* (*dē-* entirely + *spoliāre* to strip of clothing, rob, from *spolium* armor, booty, SPOIL).

despond *v.* lose heart, become depressed. 1655, Cromwell in a speech to Parliament; borrowed from Latin *dēspondēre* to give up, lose, lose heart (sometimes rendered *dēspondēre animum*), resign, from the sense of promise (a woman) in marriage (*dē-* away + *spondēre* to promise; see SPOUSE). **—despondence** *n.* (1676) **—despondency** *n.* (1653) If the haphazardness of the dating of the derived words is at all accurate it appears likely that *despond* and its accompanying forms were vogue words of the 1600's, and that each was probably formed from *despond* and one of the usual suffixes in English to suit the need of the user. **—despondent** *adj.* (1699) **—despondently** *adv.* (before 1677)

despot *n.* tyrant. 1585, title of a Christian ruler of a province in the Turkish Empire (as the Despot of Morea or Servia), from Middle French *despot, despote,* and Italian *dispoto* a lord or lordlike governor; borrowings from modern Greek, from Greek *despótēs* master of a household, lord, absolute ruler. The Greek word was originally a compound, Indo-European **dems-potās,* meaning lord of the house (cognate with Sanskrit *dámpati-s,* Avestan *dəng patoiš* lord of the house), its two elements corresponding to Greek *dómos* house (see DOME) and *pósis* husband, spouse (see POTENT). The pejorative or hostile sense of the word already existed to some extent in Greek, especially in reference to the Roman emperors, but it became established during the French Revolution, when it was applied by the revolutionaries to Louis XVI. **—despotic** *adj.* 1650, in Hobbes' *De Corpore Politico,* borrowed from French *despotique,* from Greek *despotikós,* from *despótēs* master; for suffix see -IC. **—despotism** *n.* 1727, in *Chambers Cyclopaedia,* borrowed from French *despotisme* (1678, in Fénelon), from *despote* despot; for suffix see -ISM.

dessert (dizėrt′) *n.* course served at end of the meal. 1600 *desert;* later *dessert* (1666, in Pepys' *Diary*); borrowing of Middle French *dessert* last course, literally, removal of what has been served, from *desservir* to remove what has been served (*des-* remove, undo, from Latin *dis-* + Old French *servir* to SERVE).

destine *v.* ordain by fate, intend. About 1340 *destaynen;* earlier, inferred from *destininge,* gerund (before 1300, in *Kyng Alisaunder*); borrowed from Old French *destiner,* from Latin *dēstināre* determine, appoint, choose, make firm or fast (*dē-* completely, formally + *-stināre,* earlier **-stanāre,* related to *stāre* to STAND). **—destination** *n.* Before 1400 *destynacyone* destroy; later intention (before 1656), and place where a person or thing is destined (1787); borrowed from Old French *destinacion,* and directly from Latin *dēstinātiōnem* (nominative *dēstinātiō*), from *dēstināre* determine; for suffix see -TION. **—destiny** *n.* About 1350 *destene,* borrowed from Old French *destinée* (feminine past participle of *destiner*), from Latin *dēstinātus,* past participle of *dēstināre.*

destitute *adj.* About 1384, abandoned, forsaken, in the Wycliffe Bible, borrowed from Latin *dēstitūtus,* past participle of *dēstituere* forsake (*dē-* away + *statuere* put, place, causative of *stāre* to STAND). The sense of lacking necessities, needy, is first recorded in 1539. **—destitution** *n.* About 1425, deprivation or loss; borrowed from Old French *destitution,* and directly from Latin *dēstitūtiōnem* (nominative *dēstitūtiō*) forsaking, abandoning, from *dēstituere.*

destroy *v.* Probably before 1200 *destruen,* in *Ancrene Riwle;* later *destroien* (before 1300, in *Arthour and Merlin*); borrowed from Old French *destruire* (1080, in the *Song of Roland*), from Vulgar Latin **dēstrūgere,* a refashioning (influenced by the Latin past participle *dēstrūctus*) of Latin *dēstruere* tear down, demolish (*dē-* un-, down + *struere* to pile, build; see STRUCTURE). **—destroyer** *n.* Before 1382 *destruyer,* in the Wycliffe Bible, formed from Middle English *destroien* + *-er,* and also borrowed from Old French *destruiere, destruieour;* see DESTROY.

destruction *n.* Probably about 1300 *destruccioun,* borrowed from Old French *destruction* or directly from Latin *dēstrūctiōnem* (nominative *dēstrūctiō*), from *dēstrūc-,* stem of *dēstruere* tear down; see DESTROY; for suffix see -TION. **—destruct** *v.* destroy. 1957, back formation from *destruction.* This verb was first used primarily in military and intelligence jargon (*self-destruct* in reference to the automatic destruction of a rocket or missile that malfunctions), but is now used in the science community. **—destructible** *adj.* 1755, in Johnson's *Dictionary;* probably formed in English from *destruct(ion)* + *-ible* on the model of Late Latin *indēstrūctibilis, dēstrūct-,* past participle stem of Latin *dēstruere* to destroy; for suffix see -IBLE. **—destructive** *adj.* 1490, in Caxton's works, borrowed from Old French *destructif* (feminine *destructive*), from Late Latin *dēstrūctīvus,* from *dēstrūct-,* past participle stem of Latin *dēstruere* to destroy; for suffix see -IVE.

desuetude (des′wətüd) *n.* disuse. Before 1460 *dissuetude,* borrowed from Middle French *désuétude,* learned borrowing from Latin *dēsuētūdō* (genitive *dēsuētūdinis*), from earlier **dēsuētitūdō,* from *dēsuētus,* past participle of *dēsuēscere* become unaccustomed to (*dē-* away, from + *suēscere* become used to; see CUSTOM); for suffix see -TUDE.

desultory *adj.* jumping from one thing to another. 1581, borrowed from Latin *dēsultōrius* pertaining to a *dēsultor* (a rider in a circus who jumped from one horse to another), hasty or casual, superficial, from *dēsul-,* stem of *dēsilīre* jump down (*dē-* down + *salīre* to jump, leap; see SALLY); for suffix see -ORY. The extended sense of without aim or method is first recorded in 1740, but the sense of unconnected is recorded even earlier, before 1704.

detach *v.* separate, send off. 1684, borrowed from French *détacher,* from Old French *destachier* (*des-* apart, from Latin *dis-* + *attachier* ATTACH). From the later date of *detach* it is possible to conclude that *detach* is a back formation from *detachment,* especially since first recorded use of *detach* is in the military use of send off a separate body of troops. **—detachable** *adj.* 1818, formed from English *detach,* v. + *-able.* **—detachment** *n.* 1669, borrowed from French *détachement,* from *détacher* detach; for suffix see -MENT.

detail (ditāl′) *n.* 1603, borrowed from French *détail,* from Old French *detail* small piece or quantity, from *detaillier* cut in pieces (*de-* entirely, from Latin *dē-* + *taillier* to cut in pieces; see TAILOR). The word was first used in the phrase "in detail," from French *en détail* retail. From the sense of a retail, item by item sale, the meaning developed into the dealing with matters item by item. The military meaning of a small group of soldiers sent on specific duty is first recorded in 1780 and can be traced to an earlier sense of a list of particular or general duties for a military force (1703-08). **—v.** (dē′tāl) 1637-50, borrowed from French *détailler* cut up in pieces, retail, narrate in particular, from Old French *detaillier.* **—detailed** *adj.* (1740)

detain *v.* About 1425 *deteynen* hold back; borrowed from Middle French *detenir,* from Old French *detenir* to hold off, keep back, from Gallo-Romance **dētenīre,* replacing Latin *dētinēre* hold off, keep back, detain (*dē-* from, away + *tenēre* to hold; see TENANT). The spelling *detain* was gradually established in the 1600's, in association with words such as *contain, maintain, retain.*

detect *v.* Probably before 1425 *detecten* expose, uncover, in a translation of Higden's *Polychronicon;* borrowed from Latin *dētēctus,* past participle of *dētegere* uncover, disclose (*dē-* un, off + *tegere* to cover; see THATCH). **—detection** *n.* 1427, exposure, accusation, in *Rolls of Parliament;* probably borrowed from Latin *dētēctiōnem,* from *dētegere* uncover; for suffix see -TION. Alternatively, the word may also have been formed from English *detect* + *-ion.* **—detective** *n.* 1856, probably shortened form of earlier *detective police* (1843); formed from English *detect* + *-ive.*

détente (dātänt′) *n.* easing of strained relations. 1908, borrowing of French *détente,* literally, a loosening, slackening, from Old French, from Latin *dētendita,* feminine of the past participle of *dētendere* loosen (*dē-* from, away + *tendere* stretch; see TEND[1] incline). Doublet of DISTEND. An earlier Anglicized use *detent,* borrowed from French *détente,* had the meaning of the catch which regulates the strike in a clock (1688), developed from a misconception of the use of French *détente* as the catch for the string in a crossbow, which in fact meant in French the piece which released or slackened the string of a crossbow.

detention *n.* a holding back, detaining. 1443 *detencion,* borrowed from Middle French *détention,* from Late Latin *dētentiōnem* (nominative *dētentiō*), from Latin *dētinēre* DETAIN; for suffix see -TION. The sense of confinement or arrest appeared about 1570, in a reference to Queen Mary of Scotland's confinement.

deter *v.* restrain by fear. 1579, borrowed from Latin *dēterrēre* (*dē-* away + *terrēre* frighten; see TERROR). **—deterrence** *n.* 1861, formed from English *deterr(ent)* + *-ence.* **—deterrent** *adj., n.* 1829, borrowed from Latin *dēterrentem* (nominative *dēterrēns*), present participle of *dēterrēre;* for suffix see -ENT.

detergent *adj.* cleansing. 1616, borrowed, perhaps through French *détergent,* from Latin *dētergentem,* present participle of *dētergēre* wipe away (*dē-* off, away + *tergēre* to rub, polish, wipe, cognate with Greek *trṓgein* gnaw (with single-act *trageîn*), from Indo-European **ter-g-, trō-g-/trəg-,* extensions of root **ter-* rub, as in Latin *terere,* Pok. 1073). **—n.** cleansing agent. 1676, from the adjective.

deteriorate *v.* depreciate, impair. 1644, borrowed (probably through influence of French *détériorer,* learned borrowing from Latin *dēteriōrāre*), and directly from Late Latin *dēteriōrātus,* past participle of *dēteriōrāre,* from Latin *dēterior* worse, a contrastive form of an earlier adjective **dēter* lower, from *dē* down; for suffix see -ATE[1]. **—deterioration** *n.* 1658, borrowed from French *détérioration,* from Late Latin *dēteriōrātiōnem* (nominative *dēteriōrātiō*), from *dēteriōrāre* deteriorate; for suffix see -TION. It is also possible that *deterioration* was formed from English *deteriorate* + *-ion.*

determinate (ditėr′mənit) *adj.* fixed, with exact limits. 1391, in Chaucer's *Treatise on the Astrolabe;* borrowed from Latin *dēterminātus,* past participle of *dētermināre* DETERMINE; for suffix see -ATE[1].

determine *v.* 1350-54 *determinen* to decide a case, render a verdict; later, to ascertain or interpret; to end or terminate (about 1380, in Chaucer's translation of Boethius' *De Consolatione Philosophiae;* borrowed from Old French *determiner,* learned borrowing from Latin *dētermināre* set limits to (*dē-* off + *termināre* to mark the end or boundary, from *terminus* end, limit; see TERM). **—determination** *n.* 1350-54 *determinacion,* borrowed through Old French *determination,* or directly from Latin *dēterminātiōnem* (nominative *dēterminātiō*), from *dētermināre* determine; for suffix see -ATION.

detest *v.* Before 1535, in writings of Sir Thomas More, borrowed from Middle French *détester,* learned borrowing from Latin *dētestārī* to call down a solemn curse on, express abhorrence for, literally, denounce with one's testimony (*dē-* from, down + *testārī* be a witness, from *testis* witness; see TESTAMENT). **—detestable** *adj.* 1415, borrowed from Middle French *détestable,* and directly from Latin *dētestābilis,* from *dētestārī;* for suffix see -ABLE.

dethrone *v.* 1609, formed from English *de-* remove, take away + *throne,* possibly influenced by Middle French *detroner.*

detonate *v.* 1729, a back formation from English *detonation,* or possibly borrowed (through influence of French *détoner,* learned borrowing from Latin *dētonāre*), from Latin *dētonātus,* past participle of *dētonāre* to release one's thunder, roar out (*dé-* down + *tonāre* to THUNDER); for suffix see -ATE[1]. **—detonation** *n.* 1677-86, borrowed from French *détonation,* probably from Medieval Latin *detonationem* (nominative *detonatio*), from Latin *dētonāre;* for suffix see -ATION. **—detonator** *n.* 1822, formed from English *detonate* + *-or*[2].

detour *n.* roundabout route. 1738, borrowed from French *détour,* from Old French *destour,* from *destourner* turn aside (*des-* aside, from Latin *dis-* + *tourner* to TURN). —*v.* 1836, from the noun.

detract *v.* Probably before 1425, disparage, in a translation of Higden's *Polychronicon,* borrowed through Middle French *détracter,* or directly from Latin *dētractus,* past participle of *dētrahere* take down, pull down, disparage (*dē-* down + *trahere* to pull; see TRACT). In some cases English *detract* was probably a back formation of *detraction.* **—detraction** *n.* 1340, in *Ayenbite of Inwyt,* borrowed from Old French *detractiun,* from Latin *dētractiōnem* (nominative *dētractiō*), from *dētrahere.* **—detractor** *n.* About 1384, in the Wycliffe Bible, borrowed through Anglo-French *detractour,* from Old French *detracteur,* and directly from Latin *dētractor,* from *dētrahere;* for suffix see -OR[2].

detriment *n.* loss or damage. About 1425, borrowed through Middle French *détriment,* or directly from Latin *dētrīmentum,* from stem *dētrī-* of *dēterere* impair, wear away (*dē-* away + *terere* to rub, wear; see THROW). **—detrimental** *adj.* 1656, in Blount's *Glossographia,* formed from English *detriment* + *-al*[1].

detritus (ditrī′təs) *n.* 1795, a wearing away, decomposition; borrowed from Latin *dētrītus* (genitive *dētrītūs*) a wearing away, from stem *dētrī-* of *dēterere* wear away; see DETRIMENT. The sense of matter produced by wearing away, is first recorded in English in 1802, probably borrowed from French *détritus,* from Latin *dētrītus.*

deuce[1] (düs) *n.* two (in dice and card games). About 1475 *deus* two-spot in a game of dice; later, a throw in dice which turns up as two, the lowest and unluckiest throw (1519); borrowed from Middle French *deus,* from Latin *duōs* (nominative *duo*) TWO. The meaning in tennis that both sides need two consecutive points to win a game, is first recorded in English in 1598, influenced by French *à deux de jeu* at two from the game.

deuce[2] (düs) *interj.* exclamation of annoyance. 1651, a plague (on him), probably developed from DEUCE[1] (in the sense of "bad luck" at a throw of dice), with possible influence of Low German *duus* the devil!, (also) unlucky throw at dice, probably from French *deux* DEUCE[1].

deus ex machina (dē′əs eks mak′ənə) person or thing that comes just in time to solve a difficulty. 1697, New Latin, a translation from Greek *theòs apò mēchanês,* literally, god from the *machina* (in reference to a device in Greek theater that lowered an actor playing a god to the stage so that the god might unravel a dilemma in the plot), from *mēchanḗ* device, contrivance, MACHINE.

deuterium (dütir′ēəm) *n.* heavy hydrogen. 1933, borrowed from Greek *deutérion* (neuter of *deutérios*) having second place, from *deúteros* second, see DEUTERONOMY + *-ium* (chemical suffix). The word was coined by Harold C. Urey, an American chemist, because the isotope (H^2) was second with twice the mass of H^1 or protium, the ordinary isotope of hydrogen.

Deuteronomy (dü′təron′əmē) *n.* fifth book of the Old Testament. About 1395 *Deuteronomye,* in the Wycliffe Bible, borrowed from Late Latin *Deuteronomium,* from Greek *Deuteronómion,* literally, second law (*deúteros* second + *nómos* law; see NIMBLE). The book was so called because it contains a repetition of the Decalogue and parts of Exodus, but the name is actually based on a mistranslation into Greek (*tò deuteronómion toûto* this second law) of the Hebrew phrase in the Septuagint *mishnēh hattōrāh hazzōth* a copy of this law. Greek *deúteros* is a contrastive formed early to the root (*deu-*) of *deîn* to lack, fall short (of being first), cognate with Sanskrit *doṣa-s* a lack, fault, from Indo-European **deu-s-* to stop, root *deu-* move far off (Pok. 219).

devalue *v.* 1918, either a shortened form of earlier *devaluate* (1898), or a formation from English *de-* reduce, take away + *value.* Also *devalue* may be a back formation from *devaluation* (1914, *de-* reduce, take away + *valuation*).

devastate (dev′əstāt) *v.* 1634, possibly a reformation of earlier *devast* (1537); borrowed from Middle French *dévaster,* from Latin *dēvāstāre;* also, by traditional pattern, borrowed from Latin *dēvāstātus,* past participle of *dēvāstāre* lay waste completely (*dē-* completely +

vāstāre lay waste, from *vāstus* empty, desolate, WASTE). Alternatively, in some uses, *devastate* may be a back formation from earlier *devastation.* **—devastation** *n.* 1461, borrowed probably through Middle French *dévastation,* from Late Latin *dēvāstātiōnem* (nominative *dēvāstātiō*), from Latin *dēvāstāre* lay waste; for suffix see -TION.

develop *v.* 1656, unfold, unwrap, borrowed from French *développer,* and replacing earlier English *disvelop* (1592, borrowed from Middle French *desveloper*). Both French and Middle French forms derive from Old French *desveloper, desvoloper* (*des-* undo, from Latin *dis-* + *veloper, voloper* wrap up, ENVELOP). **—developer** *n.* 1833, formed from English *develop* + *-er*[1]. **—development** *n.* 1756, formed from English *develop* + *-ment,* on the pattern of French *développement.*

deviate *v.* Before 1633, from Late Latin *dēviātum,* past participle of *dēviāre* turn or go aside, from Latin *dēvius* out of the way, remote; see DEVIOUS. **—n.** person or thing that deviates. 1912, from the verb. **—deviant** *adj.* that deviates. Probably before 1400 *deviaunt,* in Chaucer's translation of *Roman de la Rose;* borrowed from Late Latin *dēviantem* (nominative *dēviāns*), present participle of *dēviāre* deviate; for suffix see -ANT. *—n.* one that deviates. 1471, from the adjective. **—deviation** *n.* About 1385 *deviacion,* borrowed from Medieval Latin *deviationem* (nominative *deviatio*), from Late Latin *dēviāre* deviate; for suffix see -TION. **—devious** *adj.* 1599, out of the way, borrowed from Latin *dēvius,* from the prepositional phrase *dē viā* (*dē* off + *via* way); for suffix see -OUS. The meaning of *diverging* from a course, straying, is first recorded in 1628; and the figurative sense of deviating from the straight way, erring, deceitful, in 1633.

device *n.* Probably before 1300 *devise* intent, desire, in *Arthour and Merlin;* earlier something devised, arrangement or contrivance (about 1300); borrowed from Old French *devis* division, separation, disposition, wish, desire, and *devise* division, separation, plan, design, will, wish, desire, from Latin *dīvīsus* (feminine *dīvīsa*), past participle of *dīvidere* to DIVIDE; see DEVISE.

devil *n.* **1** Satan. Before 1295 *devel* Satan; earlier, *deovel* (probably before 1200). **2** any evil spirit or devil. Probably before 1200 *devel* (often plural *devels*). The Middle English forms developed from Old English *dēoful* (before 1000) and (about 725, in *Beowulf*) *dēofla* evil spirits; earlier, *dīobul* (before 800), *diābul, diavol;* borrowed from Late Latin *diabolus,* from Greek (New Testament) *diábolos* (in Jewish and Christian use, Devil, Satan; in broad use, accuser, slanderer), from *diabállein* to slander, attack, literally, throw across, (*dia-* across, through + *bállein* to throw; see BALL[2] dance). Greek *diábolos* is a loan translation of Hebrew *sātān* in the Old Testament. The English spelling with *dev-, div-* is a shortening of Old English *dēofol, dīobul,* etc., and in some dialects where the *v* was lost, produced shortened forms such as Scottish *deil.* **—v.** 1593, to play the devil; from the noun. The meaning of prepare food with hot condiments, especially in the form *deviled,* is first recorded in 1800, and the meaning of tease or annoy, in 1823, in American English. **—devilish** *adj.* Probably before 1439 *develish* fiendish, wicked, formed from Middle English *devel* devil + *-ish* [1]. **—deviltry** *n.* Before 1825, alteration (probably modeled on *gallantry,* etc.) of earlier *devilry* (probably before 1400), formed from Middle English *devel* + *-ry,* perhaps on the model of Old French *diablerie.*

devious *adj.* See under DEVIATE.

devise *v.* Probably about 1225 *devisen* to form, fashion, in *King Horn;* later, to plan; contrive (about 1300); borrowed from Old French *deviser* dispose in portions, arrange, (also) plan, contrive, from Vulgar Latin **dīvīsāre,* frequentative form of Latin *dīvidere* to DIVIDE.

devoid *adj.* lacking, wanting. Probably before 1400, in Chaucer's translation of *Roman de la Rose,* a shortening or variant of *devoided,* past participle of earlier *devoiden* remove, void, vacate (probably before 1300, in *Arthour and Merlin*); borrowed from Old French *devoidier, desvoidier* (*des-* out, away, from Latin *dis-* + *voidier* to empty, from *voide* empty, VOID).

devolve *v.* pass down or transfer (duty, etc.). Probably 1440 *devolven* roll down, unroll, borrowed from Latin *dēvolvere* (*dē-* down + *volvere* to roll; see VOLUME). **—devolution** *n.* 1545, borrowed probably through Middle French *dévolution,* from Late Latin *dēvolūtiōnem* (nominative *dēvolūtio*), from Latin *dēvolū-,* stem of *dēvolvere* roll down; for suffix see -TION.

devote *v.* 1586, associated in meaning and form with *devout* and possibly developed from earlier *devote, devot,* adj. devoted, dedicated, faithful (about 1449), the forms being early variants of *devout;* borrowed from Latin *dēvōtus,* past participle of *dēvovēre* dedicate by a vow (*dē-* down, away + *vovēre* to vow; see VOTE). Doublet of DEVOUT. **—devotee** *n.* 1645, reformed from English *devote* + *-ee,* replacing an earlier *devote* one devoted (1630), from the verb. **—devotion** *n.* Probably before 1200 *devociun,* in *Ancrene Riwle;* borrowed from Old French *devotion,* from Latin *dēvōtiōnem* (nominative *devotio*), from *dēvō-,* stem of *dēvovēre* devote; for suffix see -TION.

devour *v.* Before 1333 *devouren,* borrowed from Old French *devorer,* learned borrowing from Latin *dēvorāre* swallow down (*dē-* down + *vorāre* swallow; see VORACIOUS).

devout *adj.* Probably before 1200 *devot* pious, in *Ancrene Riwle;* later *devout* (about 1300); borrowed from Old French *devot, devout* devoted, learned borrowing from Latin *dēvōtus* given up by vow, devoted, past participle of *dēvovēre* dedicate by vow; see the doublet DEVOTE.

dew *n.* Probably before 1200 *deu,* developed from Old English *dēaw* (about 725, in the book of *Daniel*); cognate with Old Frisian *dāw* dew, Old Saxon *dou,* Middle Dutch *dau* (modern Dutch *dauw*), Old High German *tou, touwes* (modern German *Tau*), from Proto-Germanic **dawwaz,* from Indo-European **dhówo-s* (Pok. 260), and related to Old Icelandic *dǫgg* (genitive *dǫggvar*). Old English *dēaw* is possibly also cognate with Greek *theîn* to run, flow (future *theúsesthai*), and Sanskrit *dhávate* it runs, flows, from Indo-European **dheu-/dhou-* run (Pok. 259); however, the Greek and Sanskrit are semantically remote. **—dewclaw** *n.* (1576) **—dewdrop** *n.* Probably before 1200, in *Ancrene Riwle.* **—dewy** *adj.* Before 1387 *dewy,* developed from Old English *dēawig* (before 1000, in *Exodus* and *Genesis*).

dewlap. *n.* fold of skin under the throat of some animals. About 1350 *dewe lappe* (*dewe,* origin and meaning uncertain + *lappe* LAP[1] loose piece). A traditional explanation in popular etymology, suggested by the equivalent Danish *doglæp,* Norwegian *dogglapp,* is that the first element may be the word for "dew," the compound being derived from *lap* "hanging piece" which brushes against the *dew* on the grass.

dexterity (dekster'ətē) *n.* skill. 1527 *dexterite,* borrowed from Middle French *dexterité,* from Latin *dexteritātem* (nominative *dexteritās*), from *dexter* skillful, dexter; for suffix see -ITY. English *dexter,* adj., of or on the right-handed side (1562) is a borrowing of Latin *dexter* right, on the right, favorable, skillful; and its appearance in English was probably influenced by earlier use of *dexterity* and possibly by Middle French *destre.* It is also found as a noun in Middle English *dester* the right hand, borrowed from Old French *destre.*

Latin *dexter* is cognate with Greek *dexiterós* right-hand, and *dexiós* on the right side, fortunate, skillful, Gothic *taíhswa* on the right side, Old High German *zeso,* and Sanskrit *dáksina-s* of or on the right side, *dákṣate* he is able, strong, from Indo-European **deḱs-* (Pok. 190); see DECENT. **—dexterous** *adj.* 1622, skillful, clever; earlier convenient, suitable (1605, in Francis Bacon's *Of the Advancement of Learning*); formed in English, either from earlier English *dexter* skillful (1597) or directly from Latin *dexter* skillful + English suffix *-ous.*

dextrose *n.* grape sugar, a form of glucose. 1869, formed from English *dextr-* to the right, from Latin *dexter* right + *-ose,* chemical suffix denoting a sugar. The substance was so called from its turning the plane of polarization of light to the right of spectroscopy.

di-[1] a prefix meaning: **1** twice, double, twofold, as in *dicotyledon;* or two, having two, as in *digraph.* **2** having two radicals, atoms, etc., as in *dioxide.* Borrowed from Latin *di-,* from Greek *di-* (earlier **dwi-*), related to *dýo* TWO.

di-[2] a form of the prefix *dis-* before certain letters (b, d, l, m, n, r, v, *sometimes* g *and* j) in words borrowed from Latin (often through Old French), such as *digest, dilute, direct;* formed as Latin *dī-* before most voiced consonants.

di-[3] a form of the prefix *dia-* before vowels, as in *dielectric, diorama.*

dia- a prefix, mainly in words borrowed from Greek (directly or through Latin or Old French), meaning through, across, apart, by, thoroughly, as in *diagonal, diagnosis, diaphanous, diaphragm.* Borrowed from Greek *dia-,* from the preposition *diá* through, across, by, related to Latin *dis-* apart, DIS-.

diabetes *n.* disease in which proper amounts of sugar and starch are not absorbed, and which is characterized by excessive discharge of urine containing glucose. Probably before 1425 *diabete,* in a translation of Chauliac's *Grande Chirurgie;* borrowed from Middle French *diabète,* from Latin *diabētēs,* from Greek *diabḗtēs* excessive discharge of urine, literally, a passer-through, siphon, from *diabaínein* go through or over (*dia-* through + *baínein* to go; see COME). The spelling *diabetes* (with *s*) is first recorded in English in 1562. **—diabetic** *adj.* 1799, replacing earlier *diabetical* (1603), possibly by shortening, *or* a new formation of *diabetes* + *-ic; or* from French *diabétique,* from *diabète* diabetes; for suffix see -IC.

diabolic *adj.* About 1399 *deabolik,* borrowed from Old French *diabolique,* from Late Latin *diabolicus,* from Greek *diabolikós* devilish, from *diábolos* DEVIL; for suffix see -IC. **—diabolical** *adj.* 1503, formed from English *diabolic* + *-al*[1].

diachronic *adj.* 1857, through the course of time, historical; formed in English from Greek *diá-* through + *chrónos* time + English *-ic,* on the model of earlier *synchronic.* The sense of dealing with the historical development of a language, as opposed to descriptive or synchronic, is first recorded in English in 1922, in the writings of Leonard Bloomfield, and was a reborrowing into English from French *diachronique* (used by Ferdinand de Saussure before 1913).

diacritic *adj.* serving to distinguish (different sounds represented by the same letter). 1699; earlier, critical (1677); borrowed from Greek *diakritikós* that separates or distinguishes, from *diakrínein* to separate, distinguish (*dia-* apart + *krínein* distinguish, separate; see CERTAIN). **—n.** diacritic mark. 1866, from the adjective.

diadem *n.* crown. About 1300 *diademe,* borrowed from Old French *diademe;* and directly from Latin *diadēma* cloth band worn around the head as a sign of royalty, from Greek *diádēma,* from *diadeîn* to bind across (*dia-* across + *deîn* to bind, related to *desmós* band, cognate with Sanskrit *dyáti* binds, and *dāman-* band, from Indo-European **dē-/də-* and **dēi-/dī-/di-,* Pok. 183).

diagnosis *n.* 1681, New Latin, from Greek *diágnōsis* a discerning, distinguishing, from *diagignṓskein* discern, distinguish (*dia-* apart + *gignṓskein* learn to KNOW. **—diagnostic** *adj.* 1625 *diagnosticke,* borrowed from French *diagnostique,* from Greek *diagnōstikós* able to distinguish, from *diagnōstós* to be distinguished, from *diagignṓskein* distinguish; for suffix see -IC. **—diagnose** *v.* 1861, back formation from *diagnosis.*

diagonal *adj.* 1563 *diagonall;* earlier implied in *diagonally,* adv. (1541), and also in Middle English *diagonally,* adv. (probably before 1425, in an anonymous translation of Chauliac's *Grande Chirurgie*); borrowed from Middle French *diagonal,* from Latin *diagōnālis,* from *diagōnus* a slanting line or direction, from Greek *diagṓnios* from angle to angle (*diá* across + *gōníā* angle, related to *góny* KNEE); for suffix see -AL[1].

diagram *n.* 1619, borrowed from French *diagramme,* learned borrowing from Latin *diagramma,* from Greek *diágramma* (genitive *diagrámmatos*) that which is marked out by lines, from *diagráphein* mark out by lines, delineate (*dia-* across, out + *gráphein* write, mark, draw; see CARVE). **—v.** 1840, in writings of Carlyle; from the noun. **—diagrammatic** *adj.* 1853, formed from English *diagram* + *-ic.*

dial *n.* Before 1420, sundial; earlier, the dial of a compass (1338); apparently borrowed from Medieval Latin *dialis* daily, from Latin *diēs* day; see DEITY. Medieval Latin *dialis* was probably abstracted from a phrase such as *rota dialis* daily wheel. A single use is cited in Old French *dyal* time piece, clockwork, and could be the source in Middle English, as acknowledged by the MED, in which the spelling is *dyal,* in Lydgate's *Troy Book* and an early document of the Royal Navy. **—v.** 1653, to survey with the aid of a dial; from the noun. The common use of call by a telephone dial, which will become obscure when buttons have replaced the dial in a sufficient number of years, was first recorded in English in 1921, though the dial was invented in 1879.

dialect *n.* 1577, form of speech peculiar to a region or group; earlier, critical examination (1551); borrowed from Middle French *dialecte,* from Latin *dialectus* local language, way of speaking, conversation, from

Greek *diálektos,* from *dialégesthai* speak alternately, converse with each other (*dia-* across, between + *légein* speak; see LEGEND). **—dialectal** *adj.* 1831, formed from English *dialect + -al*[1].

dialectic (dī′əlek′tik) *n.* logical analysis or discussion. 1586, borrowed from Latin *dialectica;* replacing earlier *dialatik* logic, metaphysics (before 1382, in a preface to the Wycliffe Bible); borrowed from Old French *dialetique, dialectique,* from Latin *dialectica,* from Greek *dialektikḕ téchnē* art of discussion or discourse, from feminine of *dialektikós* skilled in discourse, from *diálektos* discourse, conversation, see DIALECT; for suffix see -IC. **—adj.** 1650, possibly from the noun, or borrowed from Latin *dialecticus,* from Greek *dialektikós,* see noun. **—dialectical** *adj.* **1** argumentative, logical (1548). **2** of or belonging to a speech dialect (1750). Both uses formed from English *dialectic + -al*[1].

dialogue *n.* conversation. Probably before 1200 *dyaloge,* in *Ancrene Riwle;* borrowed from Old French *dialoge,* from Latin *dialogus,* from Greek *diálogos,* related to *dialégesthai* speak alternately, converse with each other (*dia-* across, between + *légein* speak; see LEGEND).

dialysis (dīal′əsis) *n.* the chemical separation of crystalloids from colloids in solution. 1861, borrowed from Greek *diálysis* dissolution, separation, from *dialýein* dissolve, separate (*dia-* apart + *lýein* loosen; see LOSE).

The term was introduced by Thomas Graham, 1805-69, Scottish chemist who discovered the process. The medical sense of separation of waste matter from the blood by a machine that temporarily replaces the kidney, is first recorded in 1914.

diameter *n.* Before 1387, in Trevisa's translation of Higden's *Polychronicon;* borrowed from Old French *diametre,* learned borrowing from Latin *diametrus,* from Greek *diámetros* diagonal of a circle or parallelogram (*dia-* across, through + *métron* a MEASURE). **—diametric** *adj.* 1802, shortening of *diametrical* (1553), formed on English *diameter + -ic.* English *diametrical* was formed from English *diameter + -ical* on the pattern of Greek *diametrikós,* from *diámetros;* see DIAMETER.

diamond *n.* About 1325 *diamaund;* borrowed from Old French *diamant,* learned borrowing from Medieval Latin *diamantem* (nominative *diamas*), alteration (influenced by Greek words in *dia-*) of Vulgar Latin **adimantem,* from Latin *adamantem* (nominative *adamās*) the hardest metal, (later) diamond; see the doublet ADAMANT. The sense of a baseball infield area appeared in American English in 1875.

diapason (dī′əpā′zən) *n.* Before 1387 *dyapasoun* interval of an octave in music; borrowed through Old French *diapason,* and directly from Latin *diapāsōn* octave, from Greek *diapāsôn,* from *dià pāsôn chordôn* across all the notes of the scale. The extended sense of a swelling musical sound, is first recorded in 1599, and of the whole range of a voice or instrument, in 1687, in Dryden's poetry.

diaper *n.* About 1330 *diapre* a fabric with a repeated pattern of figures; borrowed from Old French *diapre,* earlier *diaspre* ornamental cloth, from Medieval Latin *diasprum,* from Medieval Greek *díaspros* (*dia-* entirely, very + *áspros* white; earlier, rough, from Latin *asper* rough, earlier **apsparos* repellent, pushing away, cognate with Sanskrit *apa-sphúra-s* bursting forth, from Indo-European **apo-sphero-s;* compare Sanskrit *sphuráti* spurns, and Latin *spernere,* from Indo-European *spher-* kick away, Pok. 992).

The shift in meaning of Greek *áspros* from rough to white occurred during the time of the Byzantine empire in referring to newly minted pieces of silver, with figures in relief. The Old French word was originally applied to a costly fabric, possibly made of silk. In Middle English after the 1400's, the word referred to a linen or cotton patterned cloth. Shakespeare used the word in 1596 with the meaning of towel, napkin, cloth. The meaning of a folded cloth used as underpants for a baby to absorb waste matter, is first recorded in 1837.

diaphanous (dīaf′ənəs) *adj.* transparent. 1614, borrowed from Medieval Latin *diaphanus,* from Greek *diaphanḗs* (*dia-* through + *phaínesthai,* middle voice, representing the subject as acting upon itself, to *phaínein* to show, see FANTASY); for suffix see -OUS.

An earlier form, *diaphane,* adj. (1561, perhaps suggested by *diaphanite* transparency, about 1477), was borrowed from Middle French *diaphane,* from Greek *diaphanḗs.*

diaphragm (dī′əfram) *n.* partition, as that dividing the chest from the abdominal cavity. 1398 *difragma,* in Trevisa's translation of Bartholomew's *De Proprietatibus Rerum;* borrowed, perhaps by influence of Old French *diaphragme,* from Late Latin *diaphragma,* from Greek *diáphragma* (genitive *diaphrágmatos*) partition, barrier, from *diaphrássein* to barricade (*dia-* across + *phrássein* to fence or hedge in, of unknown origin).

diarrhea *n.* Before 1398 *diarria,* in Trevisa's translation of Bartholomew's *De Proprietatibus Rerum;* borrowed, probably through Old French *diarrie,* from Latin *diarrhoea,* from Greek *diárrhoia* diarrhea, literally, a flowing through, from *diarrheîn* to flow through (*dia-* through + *rheîn* to flow; see STREAM). The word was respelled on the Latin model in the 1500's.

diary *n.* 1581, a daily record of events, a journal; borrowed from Latin *diārium,* from *diēs* day, formed in Latin as a nominative to *diem,* from Indo-European **diyḗm,* variant of **dyḗm,* the ancient accusative of **dyēú-s* sky, day, god of the sky, whence Sanskrit *dyāú-s,* Greek *Zeús,* Latin *Jū-piter* (Pok. 184); for suffix see -ARY.

The sense of a book specially designed for keeping a daily record is first recorded in Ben Jonson's *Volpone* (1605).

diaspora (dīas′pərə) *n.* dispersion, especially of a people, in allusion to the scattering of the Jews after the Babylonian captivity. 1876, borrowing of Greek *diasporá,* from *diaspeírein* to scatter about, disperse (*dia-* about, across + *speírein* to scatter; see SPORE). An earlier form *diaspore* (1805, in the writings of Sir Humphry Davy) is used as a term for aluminum hydrate, in reference to its instantaneous dispersion when heated.

diastase (dī′əstās) *n.* enzyme that changes starch into sugar. 1838, borrowing of French *diastase,* from Greek *diástasis* separation (*dia-* apart + *stásis* a standing, from *sta-,* stem of *histánai* cause to STAND).

The word was coined (1833) by the French chemists A. Payen and J.F. Persoz. Use of the chemical suffix -ASE in English was abstracted from this word.

diastole (dīas′təlē) *n.* normal rhythmical dilation of the heart. 1578, borrowed probably through Middle French *diastole,* from Late Latin *diastolē,* from Greek *diastolḗ* dilation, from *diastéllein* expand, dilate (*dia-* apart + *stéllein* to send; see STALL[1] place).

diatonic *adj.* 1603 *diatonique* of the ancient Greek musical scale; later, of a standard major or minor musical scale (1694); borrowed from French *diatonique,* and, probably also influenced by Italian *diatonico,* from Latin *diatonicus,* from Greek *diatonikós* (*dia-* through + *tónos* tone, from *teínein* to stretch; see TEND).

diatribe *n.* 1643 *diatribe* discourse, critical dissertation; earlier *diatriba* (1581); borrowed from French *diatribe* (from Latin) and directly from Latin *diatriba* learned discussion, from Greek *diatribḗ* discourse, study, pastime, literally, a wearing away of time (*dia-* away + *tríbein* to wear, rub; see TRIBULATION and THROW).

The meaning of a discourse against someone, bitter and violent criticism, invective, is found in the writings of Scott (1804); apparently borrowed from this use in French since Voltaire in 1734.

dibble *n.* pointed tool for making holes to plant seeds, etc. 1352, possibly from *dibben* to dip (about 1300), a variant of *dippen* (about 1150), found in Old English *dyppan* to DIP.

dice *n.pl.* Probably before 1300 *dys,* in *Kyng Alisaunder,* plural of *dy* DIE[2] cube. The form *dys* was altered before 1399 to *dyse, dyce* and by 1479 to *dice. Dice* was sometimes used as a singular (with plural *dices*) between 1400 and 1700. —**v.** Before 1399 *dycen* to cut into cubes; later (about 1440) to play or gamble with dice (about 1415, in Chaucer's *Canterbury Tales*); from *dyce,* n., dice.

dichotomy (dīkot′əmē) *n.* division into two parts. 1610, borrowed from Greek *dichotomíā* a cutting in half (*dícha* in two + *témnein* to cut; see DI-[1] and TOME).

dickens *interj.* the deuce, the devil. 1598, in Shakespeare's *Merry Wives of Windsor,* probably from the surname *Dickens* used as a substitute for *Devil.*

dicker *v.* barter, bargain, haggle. 1802, American English, of uncertain origin. According to the OED *dicker* in American English is perhaps related to earlier *dicker,* n., a unit or package of ten items, especially hides (1799); developed from Middle English *diker,* with the same meaning (1275); earlier *dyker* (1266), suggesting Old English **dicor* (compare German *Decher* bale of ten hides); ultimately an early borrowing from Latin *decuria* company or parcel of ten, from *decem* TEN.

dickey or **dicky** *n.* detachable shirt front. 1811; earlier, a petticoat (1753); of uncertain origin; perhaps from *Dicky,* diminutive of *Dick.*

dicotyledon *n.* 1727, New Latin *dicotyledones,* formed from Greek *di-* twice + *kotylēdṓn* cup-shaped, hollow, from *kotýlē* cup, hollow, of unknown origin.

dictate *v.* 1592, say aloud for another to write down; borrowed from Latin *dictātus,* past participle of *dictāre* say often, pronounce, prescribe, dictate, frequentative form of *dīcere* tell, say; see DICTION; for suffix see -ATE[1]. The sense of to order, command, is first recorded in 1621, in Burton's *Anatomy of Melancholy.* —**n.** 1594, order that must be obeyed; borrowed from Latin *dictātum,* noun use of *dictātus,* past participle of *dictāre*; see verb.

In Latin the word was used largely in the plural *dictāta* things dictated, lessons, rules, precepts, which is found also in English in such usages as listening to the dictates of one's conscience. —**dictation** *n.* Before 1656, authoritative utterance; borrowed from Late Latin *dictātiōnem* (nominative *dictātiō*), from *dictāre* dictate; for suffix see -TION. —**dictator** *n.* absolute ruler. Before 1387, Roman judge invested with absolute power, in Trevisa's translation of Higden's *Polychronicon;* borrowed, perhaps by influence of Old French *dictateur,* from Latin *dictātor,* from *dictāre* dictate; for suffix see -OR[2]. —**dictatorial** *adj.* 1701, perhaps formed from English *dictatory* (1644) + *-ial; or* borrowed from French *dictatorial* or directly from Latin *dictātōrius* of a dictator; for suffix see -AL[1]. —**dictatorship** *n.* 1586, formed from English *dictator* + *-ship.*

diction (dik′shən) *n.* choice of words, manner of expression. 1700, in Dryden's *Fables;* earlier, a word (1542); borrowed through Middle French *diction,* or directly from Late Latin *dictiōnem* (nominative *dictiō*), from Latin, a saying, expression, word, from *dic-,* stem of *dīcere* speak, tell, say; related to Latin *dicāre* proclaim, dedicate; for suffix see -TION. Latin *dīcere* is cognate with Greek *deiknýnai* to show, Sanskrit *disáti* he shows, and in Germanic with Old English *tēon* and Old High German *zīhan,* both meaning to accuse, Old Icelandic *tjā* to show, make known, and Gothic *gateihan* make known, proclaim, from Indo-European **deik-/dik-* show (Pok.188).

dictionary *n.* 1526, borrowed from Medieval Latin *dictionarium* collection of words and phrases, from Latin *dictiōnem* (nominative *dictiō*) word, see DICTION; for suffix see -ARY.

dictum *n.* 1706, formal statement, saying; earlier, edict (1670, in Blount's *Law Dictionary*); replacing earlier *dicte* (recorded probably before 1400). Both English words were borrowed from Latin *dictum* thing said, saying, from neuter of *dictus,* past participle of *dīcere* say; see DICTION.

didactic (dīdak′tik) *adj.* intended to instruct. 1658, borrowed, probably through French *didactique,* from Greek *didaktikós* apt at teaching, from *didaktós* taught, that can be taught (from *didáskein* teach); for suffix see -IC. Greek *didáskein* (**di-das-skein*) is related to *daênai* to learn, *dédae* he taught, and *dḗnea* plans, cognate with Sanskrit *dánsas* clever deed, and *dasrá-s* accomplishing wonderful deeds, from Indo-European **dens-/dṇs-* keen intellect (Pok.201).

didymium (dīdim′ēəm) *n.* mixture of the elements neodymium and praseodymium, formerly thought to be an element. 1842, New Latin *didymium,* from Greek *dídymos* twin (of uncertain origin) + New Latin *-ium* (suffix of chemical elements); so called because it was found usually in association with lanthanum. The word was coined by Carl G. Mosander, Swedish chemist who discovered it in 1841.

die[1] *v.* stop living. About 1300 *dien,* alteration of earlier *deien* (probably about 1200), corresponding to, and possibly borrowed from Old Icelandic *deyja;* cognate with Old Saxon *dōian* to die, Old High German *touwen* (from Proto-Germanic **dawjanan*), Gothic *diwans* mortal, Old Irish *duine* human being, *dīth* end, death, and Armenian *di* corpse, from Indo-European **dheu-/dhou-/dhu-* and **dhw-ēi-/dhw-ī-* pass away (Pok.260). The word *die* was not recorded in Old English, though the related words DEAD and DEATH were, and some scholars have posited an Old English **dīegan, *dēgan.* In Old English the meaning of die was expressed by *steorfan* (see STARVE), *sweltan* die of heat (see SWEL-

TER), and *wesan dēad* be dead. **—die-hard** *n.* (1844); *adj.* (1871)

die[2] *n.* one of a pair of dice. Probably before 1300 *dy* (plural *dys* dice); later *de* (before 1338); borrowed from Old French *de,* of uncertain origin; but represented widely in Romance languages, as in Spanish, Portuguese, and Italian *dado,* and in Provençal *dat* and Catalan *dau.* Some scholars trace these words to Latin *datum* given (see DATE), in the sense of that which is given or decreed, especially by lot or fortune. Others suggest as possible, but unproved sources Arabic *dad* or Persian *dadā,* both meaning game, pastime. In English, *dice* is by far the more frequent word in referring to the game; *die* usually refers to a stamping block or tool, a sense that is first recorded in 1699.

dieresis (dier′əsis) *n.* the sign (¨) over a vowel marking division of a syllable. 1611 *diæresis,* borrowed from Late Latin *diaeresis,* from Greek *diaíresis* division, separation, from *diaireîn* to divide (*dia-* apart + *haireîn* to take, of unknown origin).

diesel or **Diesel** *n.* internal-combustion engine using oil as fuel. 1894, in allusion to Rudolf *Diesel,* German mechanical engineer, who designed this engine in the 1890's **—v.** continue idling after ignition is shut off. 1971, American English, from the noun, because the heat of the engine continues to fire the gasoline in the cylinders, like the action of a diesel engine.

diet[1] *n.* food or special selection of food. Probably before 1200 *diete,* in *Ancrene Riwle;* borrowed from Old French *diete,* borrowed from Medieval Latin *dieta,* from Latin *diaeta* prescribed way of life, from Greek *díaita,* originally, way of life, regimen, dwelling, from *diaitâsthai* lead one's life, live, and from *diaitân,* originally, separate, select (food and drink), also, decide, arbitrate, frequentative form of **di-aínysthai* take apart (*dia-* apart + *aínysthai* take; compare *éx-aitos* picked out, chosen; from Indo-European **ai-,* in the active voice, give; in the middle voice, have given to one, take; Pok.10). **—v.** Before 1376 *dieten,* in a version of *Piers Plowman;* borrowed from Old French *dieter,* from *diete,* n. **—dietary** *adj.* 1614, adjective use of earlier *dietary,* n. (about 1450); borrowed from Medieval Latin *dietarius,* adj., n., from Latin *diaetārius,* from *diaeta,* see *diet,* n.; for suffix see -ARY. **—dietetic** *adj.* 1579, borrowed through Middle French *diététique,* from Greek *diaitētikós,* from *diaítēsis* way of life, from *diaitâsthai* lead one's life, live; for suffix see -IC. **—dietitian** *n.* 1846, formed from English *diet,* n. + *-itian* (alteration of *-ician,* as in *physician*). The spelling *dietician* appeared in 1905; both forms replaced earlier *dietist* (1607). **—diet drink** (1607, drink prepared for medicinal purposes)

diet[2] *n.* formal assembly. About 1450; later, a national lawmaking body (1565); borrowed from Medieval Latin *dieta,* variant of the commoner *diaeta* the ordinary course of the Church, daily office, daily duty, assembly, meeting of councilors. But this word *dieta,* though from Greek *díaita* course of life (and therefore from the same source as DIET[1]), came to be associated in a peculiar way with Latin *diēs* day; see DIARY.

Medieval Latin *dieta* was originally used to translate German *Tag* in the sense of day of assembly (compare *Reichstag, Landstag*) in reference to political assemblies in Germany.

dif- a form of the prefix *dis-* before *f* in a few words borrowed from Latin, as in *differ, diffract, diffuse;* formed in Latin by assimilation of the *s* to the following consonant (*f*).

differ *v.* About 1380 *differen* be different, in Chaucer's translation of Boethius' *De Consolatione Philosophiae;* earlier *differren* put off, defer (about 1375); borrowed from Old French *diferer,* learned borrowing from Latin and directly from Latin *differre* to set apart, differ (*dif-* variant of *dis-* before *f* + *ferre* carry; see BEAR). Doublet of DEFER[1] delay. The differentiation in form in modern English (*defer, differ*) comes from a difference in stress, the transitive senses becoming *defer* and the intransitive senses, related in meaning to *different, difference,* becoming *differ.*

difference *n.* 1340, in *Ayenbite of Inwyt;* borrowed from Old French *difference,* learned borrowing from Latin *differentia,* from *differentem* (nominative *differēns*), present participle of *differre* to set apart, DIFFER. **—different** *adj.* About 1384, in the Wycliffe Bible; borrowed from Old French *different,* from Latin *differentem* (nominative *differēns*), present participle of *differre* DIFFER. **—differential** *adj.* 1647, borrowed from Medieval Latin *differentialis,* from Latin *differentia,* see DIFFERENCE; for suffix see -IAL. **—differentiate** *v.* 1816, in a translation of Lacroix's *Elementary Treatise on the Differential and Integral Calculus;* formed in English on the model of French *différencier,* from *différent* different, from Old French *different,* from Latin *differentem;* for suffix see -ATE[1]. The general meaning of make different, distinguish, is first recorded in English in 1853, in De Quincey's *Autobiographic Sketches.* **—differentiation** *n.* 1802, formed from English *differentiate* + *-ion.*

difficulty *n.* 1380, in Chaucer's translation of Boethius' *De Consolatione Philosophiae;* borrowed from Old French *difficulté,* from Latin *difficultātem* (nominative *difficultās*), from *difficilis* hard (*dif-* not, away from, variant form of *dis-* before *f* + *facilis* easy, FACILE; for suffix see -TY[2]. **—difficult** *adj.* Before 1400, back formation from Middle English *difficulte* difficulty.

diffident *adj.* lacking self-confidence, timid. Before 1460, borrowed from Latin *diffidentem* (nominative *diffidēns*), present participle of *diffidere* to mistrust, lack confidence (*dis-* away + *fidere* to trust; see BIDE). The sense of not confident in oneself is first recorded in English in 1713, in Addison's *Cato.* **—diffidence** *n.* Before 1400, borrowed from Latin *diffidentia* lack of confidence, distrust, from *diffidentem,* present participle of *diffidere.*

diffract *v.* break up a beam of light, sound wave, etc. 1803, probably a back formation from earlier *diffraction;* but analyzed as borrowed from Latin *diffrāct-,* stem of *diffrāctus,* past participle of *diffringere* break in pieces, shatter (*dis-* apart + *frangere* to BREAK). **—diffraction** *n.* 1671, borrowed from French *diffraction,* from New Latin *diffractionem* (nominative *diffractio*), from Latin *diffrāc-,* stem of *diffringere* break in pieces; for suffix see -TION.

diffuse (difyüs′) *adj.* 1413, confused, obscure; implying the concrete sense of scattered, widespread, unrecorded before 1475; borrowed from Latin *diffūsus,* past participle of *diffundere* scatter, pour out (*dif-* apart, in every direction, variant of *dis-* before *f* + *fundere* pour; see FOUND[3] pour). **—v.** (difyüz′) scatter widely. Before 1400, from the adjective. **—diffusion** *n.* About 1385, in Chaucer's *Troilus and Criseyde,* from Latin *diffūsiō-*

nem (nominative *diffūsiō*), from *diffūd-*, stem of *diffundere* scatter; for suffix see -SION.

dig *v.* Probably before 1200 *diggen,* in *Ancrene Riwle,* of uncertain origin; perhaps ultimately related to DIKE and DITCH. Originally the past participle was *digged;* the use of *dug,* on the analogy of *stuck,* arose in the 1500's. The slang sense of understand, appreciate, is first recorded in American English in 1936. **—n.** 1674-91, tool for digging; from the verb. The sense "a sharp poke" is first recorded in English in 1819, and the figurative extension of a sarcastic remark, in 1840. The meaning of an archaeological excavation is first recorded in 1896. **—digger** *n.* 1440, formed from English *dig,* v. + *-er*[1].

digest (dī'jest) *n.* summary. Before 1387, a collection of laws, in Trevisa's translation of Higden's *Polychronicon;* borrowed from Latin *dīgesta* collection of writings arranged under headings, from neuter plural of *dīgestus,* past participle of *dīgerere* to separate, divide, distribute, arrange (*dis-* apart + *gerere* to carry, of uncertain origin). Earliest use in English refers to the *Digest,* a summary of Roman laws better known as the Justinian Code. The sense of a condensation, abridgment, or abstract appeared before 1626 in a proposal by Francis Bacon to King James to make an abstract of the laws of England **—v.** (dəjest'). Before 1398 *digesten* arrange in the mind or in a treatise; assimilate food in the stomach and intestines, in Trevisa's translation of Bartholomew's *De Proprietatibus Rerum;* borrowed from Latin *dīgestus,* past participle of *dīgerere* to separate, arrange (*dis-* apart + *gerere* to carry). **—digestible** *adj.* About 1387-95, in Chaucer's *Prologue* to *the Canterbury Tales,* borrowed from Old French *digestible,* from Latin *dīgestibilis,* from *dīgest-,* past participle stem of *dīgerere* DIGEST; for suffix see -IBLE. **—digestion** *n.* About 1395, process of changing food in the stomach and intestines, in Chaucer's *Canterbury Tales;* borrowed from Old French *digestion,* from Latin *dīgestiōnem* (nominative *dīgestiō*) a dividing or dissolving of food, digestion, from *dīges-,* stem of *dīgerere* to divide, dissolve; for suffix see -TION. **—digestive** *adj.* 1425, in an anonymous translation of Chauliac's *Grande Chirurgie;* earlier, as a noun (about 1390, in Chaucer's *Canterbury Tales*); borrowed from Old French *digestif* (feminine *digestive*), from Latin *dīgestīvus,* from past participle stem of *dīgerere;* for suffix see -IVE.

digit (dij'it) *n.* any cardinal numeral below ten. Probably before 1400, in Trevisa's translation of Bartholomew's *De Proprietatibus Rerum;* borrowed from Latin *digitus* finger (because the numerals below ten were originally counted on the fingers), from earlier **dicitus,* originally meaning pointer, related to Latin *dīcere* tell, say, *indicāre* point out, and cognate with Greek *deiknýnai* to show; see DICTION.

The sense of a finger or toe is first recorded in English in the 1600's.

—digital *adj.* Probably about 1425, of a number below ten; earlier, of or relating to information displayed in digits or numerals (1938); borrowed from Latin *digitālis,* from *digitus* finger; for suffix see -AL[1].

digitalis (dij'ətal'is) *n.* medicine used for stimulating the heart. 1664, the foxglove plant (from which the medicine is derived), New Latin *digitalis,* possibly adopted by influence of Middle French *digitale,* from Latin *digitālis* pertaining to the finger, from *digitus* finger. The name was coined in 1542 by Leonhard Fuchs, German physician and botanist, in allusion to its German name *Fingerhut* thimble (after Medieval Latin *digitale* thimble), so called from the shape of the plant's corolla. The meaning of medicine from this plant is first recorded in English in 1799.

dignify *v.* About 1449 *dignifien* to honor, exalt; earlier, to judge something worthwhile to do (probably before 1425); borrowed from Middle French *dignifier,* learned borrowing from Late Latin *dignificāre* make worthy, from Latin *dignus* worthy, see DIGNITY; for suffix see -FY. **—dignified** *adj.* (1667)

dignity *n.* Probably before 1200 *dignete,* in *Ancrene Riwle;* borrowed from Old French *digneté,* learned borrowing from Latin *dignitātem* (nominative *dignitās*) worthiness, from *dignus* worthy, proper, fitting, related to Latin *decēre* be proper, be DECENT; for suffix see -ITY. Doublet of DAINTY. **—dignitary** *n.* (1672)

digress (dəgres') *v.* 1529, turn aside; get off the main subject, in writings of Sir Thomas More; earlier, to translate, depart from the language of an original; borrowed from Latin *dīgressus,* past participle of *dīgredī* to deviate (*dī-,* from *dis-* apart, aside + *gradī* to step, go; see GRADE). Alternatively, *digress* may be a back formation from *digression.* **—digression** *n.* About 1385, in Chaucer's *Troilus and Criseyde;* borrowed from Old French *digression,* or directly from Latin *dīgressiōnem* (nominative *dīgressiō*), from *dīgredī* to deviate; for suffix see -SION.

dihedral (dīhē'drəl) *adj.* having two plane surfaces. 1799, formed in English from *di-* two + Greek *hédrā* seat, base (see SIT) + English suffix *-al*[1].

dike *n.* About 1250 *dik* a ditch, wall; developed from Old English (847) *dīc* narrow place dug in the earth, trench, DITCH; cognate with Old Saxon and Old Frisian *dīk* mound, dam, Middle Dutch *dijc* (modern Dutch *dijk*), Middle High German *tīch* pond (modern German *Teich*), Old Icelandic *dīki* marsh, ditch, from Proto-Germanic **dīk-;* and probably cognate with Latin *fīgere* to fix, fasten, and Lithuanian *díegti* to prick, *dáiktas* point, from Indo-European **dhēigw-/dhōigw-/dhīgw-* (Pok.243).

The sense of an embankment or dam to resist flooding appeared in English in the 1500's, probably influenced by Middle Dutch *dijc.*

—v. About 1300 *diken* to make a ditch or a dike, developed from Old English *dīcian,* from the noun.

dilapidate *v.* 1570, probably a back formation of *dilapidation,* but usually analyzed as a borrowing, perhaps influenced by Middle French *dilapider,* from Latin *dīlapidātus,* past participle of *dīlapidāre;* see DILAPIDATION. **—dilapidation** *n.* About 1425 (Scottish); borrowed from Late Latin *dīlapidātiōnem* (nominative *dīlapidātiō*), from Latin *dīlapidāre* pelt with stones, ruin, destroy (*dī-, dis-* asunder + *lapidāre* throw stones at, from *lapis,* genitive *lapidis* stone; see LAPIDARY); for suffix see -TION.

dilate *v.* Before 1393, describe at length, in Gower's *Confessio Amantis;* borrowed from Old French *dilater,* learned borrowing from Latin *dīlātāre* make wider, enlarge (*dī-,* from *dis-* apart + *lātus* wide, see LATITUDE). The sense of make wider or larger, is first recorded in English probably before 1400. **—dilation** *n.* a making or becoming wider. 1598, formed from English *dilate* (on the erroneous assumption that the ending is the suffix *-ate*[1]) + *-ion.* This form has largely replaced earlier *dilatation,* n. (about 1390, in Chaucer's

Canterbury Tales; borrowed from Middle French *dilatation*).

dilatory (dil′ətôr′ē) *adj.* tending to delay. Probably before 1450 *delatarye;* later *dilatory* (before 1475); borrowed through Middle French *dilatoire* and directly from Latin *dīlātōrius,* from *dīlātor* a procrastinator, from *dīlātus,* a form serving as past participle of *differre* delay, DEFER[1]; for suffix see -ORY.

dilemma *n.* 1523, borrowed from Late Latin *dilemma,* from Greek *dílēmma* (genitive *dilḗmmatos*) double proposition (*di-* two + *lêmma,* genitive *lḗmmatos* premise, anything taken, from a stem *lēph-,* originally *lāph-,* which figures in some of the forms of *lambánein* to take, but was once part of an entirely different verb, cognate with *láphȳra* spoils, booty, Sanskrit *lábhate* he gets, takes, *lalābha* has gotten, and Lithuanian *lõbis* wealth, from Indo-European **labh-/lābh-* seize, Pok.652).

dilettante (dil′ətänt′) *n.* dabbler, amateur. About 1733, one delighted by or fond of the fine arts, Italian *dilettante* a lover of music or painting, from *dilettare* to delight, from Latin *dēlectāre* DELIGHT. The sense passed from lover of the arts to amateur or nonprofessional (1748), to dabbler (1770).

diligence *n.* careful effort or attention. 1340, in *Ayenbite of Inwyt;* borrowed from Old French *diligence* attention, care, learned borrowing from Latin *dīligentia* attentiveness, carefulness, from *dīligentem* (nominative *dīligēns*) attentive, assiduous, careful, originally the present participle of *dīligere* value highly, love, choose (*dis-* apart + *legere* choose, gather, see LEGEND); for suffix see -ENCE. **—diligent** *adj.* hardworking. 1340, in *Ayenbite of Inwyt;* borrowed from Old French *diligent,* learned borrowing from Latin *dīligentem* (nominative *dīligēns*), present participle of *dīligere* value highly; for suffix see -ENT.

dill *n.* herb with spicy seeds. 1373 *dill;* earlier *dile* (about 1150), found in Old English (before 700) *dile;* cognate with Old Saxon *dilli* dill, Middle Dutch and modern Dutch *dille,* Old High German *tilli* (modern German *Dill* with *D-* from Low German), Danish *dild,* and Swedish *dill,* of uncertain source. **—dill pickle** 1906, American English, in writings of O. Henry.

dilly *n. Slang.* delightful or remarkable person or thing. 1935, in *American Mercury,* American English, from earlier English *dilly* (1909), adj., delightful, delicious, of unknown origin, but reminiscent of *dilly* and *daffy* in *daffydowndilly* and *dilly* (before 1610) in *dilly-dally,* etc.

dilute *v.* About 1555, borrowed from Latin *dīlūtus,* past participle of *dīluere* dissolve, wash away, dilute (*dis-* apart + *-luere,* combining form of *lavere* to wash, LAVE); see DELUGE. **—adj.** 1605, in Francis Bacon's *Of the Advancement of Learning;* borrowed from Latin *dīlūtus,* past participle of *dīluere;* see verb. **—dilution** *n.* 1646, formed from English *dilute* + *-ion.* Late Latin *dīlūtiōnem* (in St. Jerome) had a special sense of refutation, and was probably not the source of the English word, which had the literal sense of act of making thinner or watering down when it appeared.

diluvial (dəlü′vēəl) *adj.* of or having to do with a flood. 1646, borrowed from Late Latin *dīluviālis,* from Latin *dīluvium* flood, DELUGE; for suffix see -AL[1].

dim *adj.* Old English *dimm* dark, gloomy (before 1000, attributed to Caedmon's poetry); cognate with Old Frisian *dimm* dark, dusky, dim, Old Icelandic *dimmr,* from Proto-Germanic **dimbaz,* and, Old High German *timber;* probably also cognate with Greek *themerós* grave, earnest, and Sanskrit *dhámati* he blows, from Indo-European **dhem-, *dhem-bh-* smoky, dark (Pok.247). Related to DAMP and DANK. **—v.** Before 1200, from the adjective. **—dimmer** *n.* 1892, in Kipling's poetry, formed from English *dim* + *-er[1].*

dime *n.* 1786, American English, silver coin worth ten cents; found in Middle English *dime* a tenth, tithe (about 1378, in a version of *Piers Plowman*); borrowed from Old French *dime,* earlier *disme,* from Latin *decima* (*pars*) tenth (part), from *decem* TEN.

dimension *n.* Before 1398 *dimencioun* measurement, size, in Trevisa's translation of Bartholomew's *De Proprietatibus Rerum;* borrowed from Latin *dīmēnsiōnem* (nominative *dīmēnsiō*), from stem of *dīmētīrī* to measure out (*dī-, dis-* + *mētīrī* to MEASURE); for suffix see -SION.

diminish *v.* 1417 *deminishen,* a blend of two verbs of similar meaning: 1) About 1384 *diminuen* detract, disparage; later, reduce, lessen (1410); borrowed from Old French *diminuer* make small, learned borrowing from Latin *dīminuere* break into small pieces, variant of *dēminuere* lessen, diminish (*dē-* completely + *minuere* make small); and 2) Before 1382 *mynushen* make small, diminish; earlier, *menusen* (probably before 1350); borrowed from Old French *menuisier,* from Vulgar Latin **minūtiāre,* altered (by influence of Late Latin *minūtiae* small pieces) from Late Latin *minūtāre,* frequentative form of Latin *minuere* make small, from *minus* smaller, (originally) small. Related to MINCE, MINOR, and MINUTE[2] small; for suffix see -ISH[2].

diminuendo (dəmin′yůen′dō) *n.* gradual lessening of loudness. 1775, borrowing of Italian *diminuendo* lessening, diminishing, present participle of *diminuire* diminish, from the ablative of the gerund of Latin *dīminuere* DIMINISH.

diminution (dim′ənü′shən) *n.* About 1303 *dymynucyun* a lessening or decrease, in Mannyng's *Handlyng Synne;* borrowed from Old French *diminution,* learned borrowing from Latin *dīminūtiōnem,* variant of *dēminūtiōnem* (nominative *dēminūtiō*), from *dēminuere* DIMINISH; for suffix see -TION.

diminutive (dəmin′yətiv) *n.* Before 1398 *dymynutyf,* in Trevisa's translation of Bartholomew's *De Proprietatibus Rerum;* borrowed from Old French *diminutif* (feminine *diminutive*), from Latin *dīminūtīvum,* variant of **dēminūtīvum,* from **dēminūtīvus* small, from *dēminuere* DIMINISH; for suffix see -IVE. **—adj.** Before 1398, borrowed from Old French *diminutif* (feminine *diminutive*), from Latin **dīminūtīvus,* variant of *dēminūtīvus* small.

dimity *n.* thin cotton cloth. 1440 *demyt;* later *dimite;* borrowed probably directly from Late Greek *dímitos* of double thread (Greek *di-* double + *mítos* warp thread, of uncertain origin). It is possible that *dimity* was reinforced in English by later Italian *dimiti* plural of *dimito* (1454).

dimple *n.* small hollow or dent, especially in the cheek. Probably before 1400 *dympull;* earlier in a place name *Kerlingdimpil* (1200-10); of uncertain origin, but perhaps cognate with Old High German *tumphilo* whirlpool (modern German *Tümpel* pool), from Proto-Germanic **dumpilaz* and *tupfen* to wash, see DIP; for suffix see -LE[1]. **—v.** 1602, from the noun.

din *n.* loud noise. Probably before 1200 *dine,* developed from Old English (before 1000) *dyne;* cognate with Old High German *tuni* din, Old Icelandic *dynr,* from Proto-Germanic **dluniz,* and Sanskrit *dhúni-s* roaring, *dhvánati* it roars, resounds, from Indo-European **dhwen-/dhun-* (Pok.277). —**v.** Probably before 1200, dialectal *dunien,* in Layamon's *Chronicle of Britain;* later *dinen* (about 1250, in *The Story of Genesis and Exodus*); developed from Old English *dynnan* to resound (about 725, in *Beowulf*); cognate with Old Saxon *dunnian* sound forth, Middle High German *tünen* to roar, and Old Icelandic *dynja* to rumble; related to the noun. The sense of assail with din, is first recorded in English in 1674 as a new formation from the noun.

dinar (dinär′) *n.* 1634, coin of the Middle East, borrowed from Arabic *dīnār,* from Late Greek *dēnárion,* from Latin *dēnārius;* see the doublet DENARIUS.

dine *v.* About 1300 *dinen,* borrowed from Old French *disner, dîner,* originally, take the first meal of the day, from unaccented stem of Gallo-Romance **disjūnāre,* from **disjejūnāre* to break one's fast (Latin *dis-* undo + Late Latin *jejūnāre* to fast, from Latin *jejūnus* fasting, hungry, of uncertain origin). See BREAKFAST for similar sense development. —**diner** *n.* 1815; earlier, in *diner out* (1807-08); formed from English *dine,* v. + *-er*[1]. —**dinette** *n.* small dining room. 1930, American English, formed from English *dine,* v. + *-ette,* probably on the pattern of *kitchenette* (1910). —**dining room** (1601)

ding *v.* 1819, in Washington Irving's *Sketch Book,* possibly abstracted from earlier *ding-dong,* n. (1659), of imitative origin. —**n.** 1749; possibly earlier in Shakespeare's *As You Like It* (though it is adverbial in use); also possibly abstracted from *ding-dong,* v. (about 1560).

dinghy or **dingey** (ding′ē) *n.* small rowboat. 1810, borrowed from Hindi *ḍiṅgī,* variant of *ḍeṅgī, ḍoṅgī* small boat, perhaps from Sanskrit *dróṇa-m* wooden trough, related to *drú-s* wood, TREE.

dingus *n. Slang.* something whose name is unknown or forgotten. 1876, in American English, borrowed from Dutch *dinges* (usually *Dinges*) so-and-so, from German *Dings,* from *Ding* THING. The South African use cited in the OED is a separate borrowing.

dingy (din′jē) *adj.* 1736, (Kentish dialect), dirty; of uncertain origin; for suffix see -Y[1]. The sense of a dull, drab color or look appeared in 1751. A figurative sense, shabby or squalid, is found in Thackeray's *The Newcomes* (1854) and used in 1881 by Henry James in *Portrait of a Lady.* According to the OED the word may be derived from *dung,* supported by the early sense of "dirty," but the pronunciation ding′gē would be expected, instead of din′jē, and early appearance of the meaning "drab color" is difficult to account for.

dinky (ding′kē) *adj.* small. 1858, earlier, neat or trim (1788), from Scottish dialect *dink* finely dressed, trim (1508); of unknown origin; for suffix see -Y[1].

dinner *n.* About 1300 *diner* midday meal; borrowed from Old French *disner, dîner,* noun use of the infinitive *disner, dîner,* to DINE; for suffix see -ER[3]. —**dinner party** (1815, in Jane Austen's *Emma*). —**dinner table** (1813) —**dinner time** (1370)

dinosaur *n.* 1841, borrowed from New Latin *dinosaurus,* from Greek *deinós* terrible + *saûros* lizard, of unknown origin. Greek *deinós* is related to *deîsai* to fear, *déos* fear, cognate with Sanskrit *dvéṣṭi* he hates. Both concepts, of fear and hate, have grown from "a split," from Indo-European **dwei-/dwi-* (Pok.228), variants of **dwō(u)* TWO.

dint *n.* force. Probably about 1200 *dint,* in *The Ormulum;* earlier dialectal *dunt* (probably before 1200, in Layamon's *Chronicle of Britain*); developed from Old English *dynt,* blow dealt in fighting (before 900, in *Solomon and Saturn*); cognate with Old Icelandic *dyntr* blow, kick (modern Icelandic *dintur* dint), *dyttr* (as in *hnakka-dyttr* shot at the nape of the neck), from Proto-Germanic **duntiz,* from Indo-European **dhen-d-/dhon-d-/dhṇ-d-* (Pok.249). The phrase *by dint of* by force of or by means of, is first recorded probably before 1400, in *Morte Arthur.*

diocese (dī′əsis) *n.* district of a bishop. Before 1338 *dyocise,* in Mannyng's *Chronicle of England;* borrowed from Old French *diocese,* learned borrowing from Late Latin *diocēsis,* variant of *dioecēsis,* from Greek *dioíkēsis* diocese, province; originally, economy, housekeeping, from *dioikeîn* manage a house, administer (*dia-* thoroughly + *oikeîn* live in, manage, from *oîkos* house, dialectal *woîkos,* cognate with Sanskrit *véśa-s* house, Gothic *weihs* village, and Latin *vīcus* village, quarter, from Indo-European **weik-/woik-* dwelling, Pok.1131). —**diocesan** *n.* Before 1443; *adj.* About 1460; both forms were borrowed from Middle French *diocesain,* from Old French *diocise;* for suffix see -AN.

diorama (dī′əram′ə) *n.* exhibit of lifelike figures or objects against a painted or modeled background. 1823, borrowed from French *diorama* (*dia-* through, from Greek + *(pan)orama,* from English). The word was coined in French by Louis Daguerre, inventor of the DAGUERREOTYPE. The diorama was invented about 1788 by a Scotsman, Robert Barker (1739-1806), but it was perfected by Daguerre, who in July, 1822 presented it in Paris in an exhibition he called the Diorama; in September, 1823 the Diorama was exhibited in London. See PANORAMA.

dip *v.* About 1150 *dipen* to immerse in liquid; later *dippen* to baptize (probably about 1200, in *The Ormulum*); developed from Old English (about 975) *dyppan* baptize by immersion (from Proto-Germanic **dupjanan*), related to *dīepan* immerse, dip, from Proto-Germanic **daupijanan.* The Old English forms are cognate with Old High German *tupfen* to wash, *toufen* immerse, dip (modern German *taufen* baptize), Old Icelandic *deypa,* and Gothic *daupjan* immerse, baptize, from Indo-European **dhoub-/dhub-* (Pok. 267); see DEEP. —**n.** 1599, immersion; from the verb. —**dipper** *n.* About 1395 *dippere* a kind of diving waterfowl; earlier, in a surname *Dypere* (1310, and *dypere,* 1296-97); formed from Middle English *dipere,* v. + *-er*[1]. The meaning of a utensil for dipping up water, etc., is not recorded in English before 1783, in American English.

diphtheria *n.* contagious disease of the throat. 1857, New Latin *diphtheria,* from French *diphthérie,* from Greek *diphthérā* hide, leather; from the tough membrane developed in the throat. The French word was coined in 1855 by the French physician P. Bretonneau, replacing earlier *diphthérite* diphtheritis, diphtheria (1821).

diphthong *n.* vowel sound consisting of two sounds pronounced in one syllable. Probably about 1475 *dypon;* later *diptonge* (1483); borrowed from Middle French *diptongue,* from Late Latin *dipthongus,* variant of Latin *diphthongus,* from Greek *díphthongos* (*di-* double + *phthóngos* sound, voice; related to *phthéngesthai* utter, speak loudly, of unknown origin).

diploma *n.* About 1645, official state document, charter; borrowed from Latin *diplōma,* from Greek *díplōma* (genitive *diplṓmatos*) letter of recommendation or license, chart, paper folded double, from *diploûn* to double, fold over, from *diplós* double (cognate with Latin *duplus* double, and Gothic *tweifl* doubt), from *di-* two (Indo-European *dwi-*) + *-plo-s,* cognate with Gothic *falthan* to fold, from Indo-European **pel-/pol-/pl-* (Pok.802).

The meaning "an academic diploma," is first recorded in English in 1682; earlier, in a figurative sense (before 1658).

diplomacy *n.* 1796, in writings of Burke; borrowed from French *diplomatie,* from *diplomate* diplomat, on the pattern of *aristocratie* aristocracy, *aristocrate* aristocrat; for suffix see -CY. **—diplomat** *n.* 1813, either a back formation from English *diplomatic,* or borrowed from French *diplomate,* back formation from *diplomatique* diplomatic, on the pattern of *aristocrate* aristocrat, *aristocratique* aristocratic. **—diplomatic** *adj.* 1711, pertaining to official documents, textual; borrowed from New Latin *diplomaticus* (1695), from Latin *diplōma* (genitive *diplōmatis*) official document conferring a privilege, see DIPLOMA; for suffix see -IC. In the 1780's *diplomatic* referred to official documents exchanged between countries; this meaning came into English from French *diplomatique.* An extended sense tactful, is first recorded in English in 1826, in Benjamin Disraeli's *Vivian Grey.*

dipterous *adj. Biology.* having two wings or winglike parts. 1773, borrowed from New Latin *dipterus* two-winged, after French *diptère,* from Greek *dípteros* (*di-* two + *pterón* wing, see FEATHER); for suffix see -OUS.

dire (dīr) *adj.* 1567, borrowed from Latin *dīrus* fearful, awful, boding ill, from Oscan and Umbrian, from Indo-European **dweiros;* cognate with Greek *deinós* fearful, terrible, *déos* fear, Avestan *dvaēthā* threat, and Sanskrit *dvéṣṭi* he hates; see DINOSAUR. **—direful** *adj.* 1583, formed from English *dire* + *-ful.*

direct *v.* guide, regulate. About 1385 *directen* to address or direct (a letter, document, spoken words) straight to someone, in Chaucer's *Troilus and Criseyde;* borrowed from Latin *dīrēctus* straight, past participle of *dīrigere* set straight (*dī-,* from *dis-* apart + *regere* to guide; see RIGHT). Doublet of DRESS. **—adj.** straight. 1391, in Chaucer's *Treatise on the Astrolabe;* borrowed, possibly through Old French *direct,* and from Latin *dīrēctus,* past participle of *dīrigere* set straight. **—adv.** exactly, directly. About 1392, from the adjective. **—direction** *n.* About 1385, guidance, regulation; borrowed through Old French *direction* and directly from Latin *dīrēctiōnem* (nominative *dīrēctiō*), from *dīrēg-,* stem of *dīrigere* set straight; for suffix see -TION. **—directive** *adj.* About 1454, borrowed through Middle French *directif* (feminine *directive*) and from Medieval Latin *directivus,* from *direct-,* past participle stem of Latin *dīrigere.* **—n.** 1642, from the adjective. For suffix see -IVE. **—director** *n.* About 1454, a guide; formed from Middle English *directen* + *-or²,* and probably borrowed from Anglo-French *directour,* from Late Latin *dīrēctor,* from *dīrigere;* for suffix see -OR². **—directory** *n.* Before 1449, a guide, in Lydgate's writings; borrowed from Late Latin *dīrēctōrium,* from Latin *dīrēctōrius* that directs, from *direct-,* past participle stem of Latin *dīrigere;* for suffix see -ORY.

dirge (dėrj) *n.* funeral song. Probably before 1200 *dirige* memorial service, in *Ancrene Riwle;* borrowed from Latin *dīrige* direct! (imperative of *dīrigere* to DIRECT); generally considered to come from its use as the first word in the Latin antiphon *Dirige, Domine, Deus Meus, in conspectu tuo viam meam* "Direct, O Lord, my God, my way in thy sight," taken from Psalm 5:9 in the Vulgate to open the Matins service in the Office of the Dead. The contracted form *dirge* is first recorded in Middle English in 1430, though an earlier form *derge* exists (1389).

dirigible (dir′əjəbəl) *n.* dirigible balloon, airship. 1885, probably by influence of French *dirigeable,* from the adjective, meaning "capable of being directed or guided" (1581, formed in English from Latin *dīrigere* DIRECT + English *-ible,* as if from a Latin word **dīrigibilis*).

dirk *n.* dagger. 1602, apparently alteration of earlier Scottish *durk* (about 1574), of uncertain origin.

dirndl (dėrn′dəl) *n.* a full, usually brightly colored skirt with tight bodice, originally imitating that of an Alpine peasant girl's costume. 1937, borrowed from German *Dirndlkleid* dirndl dress, from South German dialect *Dirndl* girl, diminutive of *Dirne* maid, wench, from Old High German *thiorna;* cognate with Old Saxon *thiorna* maid, Middle Dutch *dierne* maidservant (modern Dutch *deerne* girl, lass), Old Icelandic *therna* maidservant (from Proto-Germanic **thewernō*), cognate with Gothic *thius* servant; originally, runner, and Sanskrit *tákti* he hurries, *takvá-s* hastening, from Indo-European **tekw-* run (Pok.1059).

dirt *n.* 1434 *dyrt* something worthless or degrading; probably before 1425 *dird, dert,* alteration by transposition of *r* and *i,* of earlier *drit, drytt* mud, dirt, dung (before 1300); borrowed from a Scandinavian source (compare Old Icelandic *drit* excrement, related to *drīta* defecate; cognate with Old English *drītan,* Middle Dutch *drīten,* modern Dutch *drijten,* and Old High German *trīzan,* all meaning to defecate, from Proto-Germanic **drītanan,* from Indo-European **dhr-ei-d-/dhr-i-d-,* root **dher-,* Pok.256, and with Russian dialect *dristat'* have diarrhea, and Lithuanian *der̃kti* make filthy). **—dirty** *adj.* Probably before 1425 *dyrty,* alteration of earlier *dritty* (before 1398), formed from Middle English *drit* dirt + *-y¹.* **—v.** make dirty. 1591, from the adjective.

dis- a prefix meaning: **1** opposite of, lack of, not, as in *dishonest = not honest.* **2** do the opposite of, as in *disallow = do the opposite of allow.* **3** apart, away, as in *discard.* Middle English *dis-* (earlier *des-*), borrowed from Old French *des-,* from Latin *dis-* apart, or directly from Latin *dis-.* Latin *dis-* is cognate with Old English, Old Frisian, and Old Saxon *te-* apart, Old High German *zi-, ze-,* Greek *diá* through, and Albanian *tsh-* apart, all from an Indo-European base **dis-,* a variant form of **dwis* apart, twice, formed from **dwō(u)* TWO (Pok. 232).

In Latin *dis-* became *dif-* before *f* and *dī-* before most of the voiced consonants (*b, d, l, m, n, r, v* and sometimes *g* and *j*); these changes are reflected in words taken from Latin and preserving the Latin form, such as *differ, digest, dilute, divert.*

disabled *adj.* 1444, formed from Middle English *dis-* + *abled,* past participle of *ablen,* v. make able or fit.

disadvantage *n.* Probably 1384, borrowed from Old French *desavantage* (*des-* dis- + *avantage* ADVANTAGE). —**disadvantageous** *adj.* 1603, formed from English *dis-* + *advantageous,* perhaps on the model of French *désavantageux.*

disaffected *adj.* 1632, formed from English *disaffect* to estrange or alienate + *-ed.* —**disaffection** *n.* (1605, formed in English)

disagree *v.* 1473-74, borrowed from Middle French *désagréer* (*dés-* dis- + *agréer* to AGREE). —**disagreeable** *adj.* Probably before 1400, in Chaucer's translation of *Roman de la Rose;* borrowed from Old French *desagreable* (*des-* dis- + *agreable,* see AGREEABLE).

disallow *v.* About 1378, in a version of *Piers Plowman;* borrowed from Anglo-French *desalouer,* Old French *desaloer, desalouer* to blame (*des-* dis- + *aloer, alouer* ALLOW).

disappear *v.* Before 1420, in Lydgate's *Troy Book,* formed from English *dis-* + *appear.*

disappoint *v.* 1494 *disapointen* frustrate the expectation of; earlier, dispossess of appointed office (1434); borrowed from Middle French *desappointer* undo the appointment of (*des-* dis- + *appointer* APPOINT). —**disappointment** *n.* 1614, formed from English *disappoint* + *-ment;* possibly by influence of French *désappointement.*

disapprove *v.* 1481, in Caxton's translations; probably borrowed from Middle French **desaprover* (*des-* dis- + *aprover* APPROVE). —**disapproval** *n.* 1662, formed from English *disapprove* + *-al²* or from English *dis-* + *approval.*

disarm *v.* About 1380, in Chaucer's translation of Boethius' *De Consolatione Philosophiae;* borrowed from Old French *desarmer* (*des-* dis- + *armer* to ARM²). —**disarmament** *n.* 1795, in letters of Burke, formed from English *dis-* + *armament,* possibly influenced by French *désarmement.*

disarray *v.* Before 1387, in Trevisa's translation of Higden's *Polychronicon;* formed from English *dis-* + *array,* v.; probably modeled on Old French *desareer* to put in disorder. —**n.** About 1415, in Chaucer's *Canterbury Tales,* from the verb, perhaps by influence of Old French **desarei.*

disaster *n.* 1591, borrowed from Middle French *désastre,* from Italian *disastro* (*dis-* away, without, from Latin *dis-* + *astro* star, from *astrum,* from Greek *ástron* STAR (because an unfavorable position of a star or planet was thought to cause such mishaps or calamities). —**disastrous** *adj.* 1586 *desastrous* ill-starred; later, calamitous (1603, in Philemon Holland's translation of Plutarch's *Moralia*); borrowed from Middle French *désastreux,* from earlier Italian *disastroso,* from *disastro* disaster; for suffix see -OUS.

disavow *v.* Probably before 1387, in a version of *Piers Plowman;* borrowed from Old French *desavöer* (*des-* + *avöer* AVOW). —**disavowal** *n.* 1748, in Richardson's *Clarissa;* formed from English *disavow* + *-al²,* modeled on English *avowal.*

disbar *v.* Probably before 1430 *dysbarryd* prevented, denied, excluded, in writings of Lydgate, variant form of *debar.*

disburse *v.* pay out, expend. 1530 *disbourse,* in Palsgrave's *Lesclarcissement;* borrowed from Middle French *desbourser* (*des-,* from Latin *dis-* + *bourse;* see BURSAR). —**disbursement** *n.* 1596, in writings of Spenser, formed from English *disburse* + *-ment,* after Middle French *déboursement,* earlier *desboursement,* from *desbourser* disburse; for suffix see -MENT.

disc *n.* variant of DISK, modeled on Latin *discus.*

discard *v.* Before 1586, discharge, dismiss; later, reject a playing card from the hand (1591), and cast aside (1598); formed from English *dis-* away + *card¹,* n. —**n.** 1742, in an edition of Hoyle's *A Short Treatise on the Game of Whist,* from the verb.

discern *v.* About 1380 *discernen* perceive, distinguish, in Chaucer's translation of Boethius' *De Consolatione Philosophiae;* borrowed from Old French *discerner* distinguish, separate, from Latin; and directly as a learned borrowing in English from Latin *discernere* (*dis-* off, away + *cernere* distinguish, separate; see CERTAIN). —**discernible** *adj.* 1586 *discernable,* borrowed from Middle French *discernable,* from Old French *discerner;* for suffix see -IBLE. The early spelling in English with *-able* gradually changed to *-ible* in imitation of Latin (found in Late Latin *discernibilis*) after 1650. —**discernment** *n.* 1586, formed from English *discern* + *-ment,* and probably also borrowed from Middle French *discernement,* from Old French *discerner* discern; for suffix see -MENT.

discharge *v.* Before 1338, in Mannyng's *Chronicle of England;* borrowed from Old French *deschargier* unload, from Late Latin *discarricāre* (*dis-* do the opposite of + *carricāre* load). —**n.** 1390, in Gower's *Confessio Amantis;* borrowed from Old French *descharge* act of unloading, from the Old French verb.

disciple *n.* Probably before 1200 *deciple,* in *Ancrene Riwle;* later *disciple* (before 1225); developed from Old English (about 900, in Alfred's translation of Bede's *Ecclesiastical History*); borrowed from Latin *discipulus* pupil. As *capulus* handle, was formed from *capere* take hold of, so *discipulus* was formed from a lost compound **discipere* to grasp intellectually, analyze thoroughly (*dis-* apart + *capere* take; compare its frequentative form *disceptāre* debate; see CAPTIVE). The Middle English spelling *deciple, disciple* was influenced by Old French *deciple, disciple,* learned borrowing from Latin *discipulus.* —**disciplinarian** *n.* 1593, formed in English from Medieval Latin *disciplinarius* + English -AN. —**disciplinary** *adj.* 1593, borrowed from Medieval Latin *disciplinarius* pertaining to discipline, from Latin *disciplīna* instruction. —**discipline** *n.* Probably before 1200, in *Ancrene Riwle;* borrowed through Old French *descepline,* and directly from Latin *disciplīna* instruction given to a disciple, from *discipulus* DISCIPLE. —**v.** About 1300, probably borrowed through Old French *descepliner* and directly from Medieval Latin *disciplinare* chastise, from Latin *disciplīna* instruction.

disclaim *v.* 1434, in *Proceedings of the Privy Council;* borrowed through Anglo-French *disclaimer,* Old French *desclamer* (*des-* dis- + *clamer* CLAIM); and through Anglo-Latin *disclamare* renounce (Latin *dis-* dis- + *clāmāre* cry out, CLAIM). —**disclaimer** *n.* About 1436, borrowing of Anglo-French *disclaimer,* the infinitive used as a noun.

disclose *v.* Before 1393 *desclosen, disclosen,* in Gower's *Confessio Amantis;* borrowed from Old French *desclos,* past participle of *desclore* (*des-* dis- + *clore* to CLOSE). —**disclosure** *n.* Before 1598, formed from English *disclose* + *-ure,* on the model of *closure.*

disco *n.* 1964, American English, shortened form of

DISCOTHEQUE. In 1975 *disco* was applied to a kind of music played in discotheques.

discolor *v.* About 1380 *discolouren,* in *Sir Ferumbras;* borrowed from Old French *discolourer* (*des-* dis- + *colourer* to color, from Latin *colōrāre* to COLOR). **—discoloration** *n.* 1642, formed from English *discolorate* (probably before 1425, borrowed from Medieval Latin *discolorat-,* past participle stem of *discolorare,* supplanting Latin *dēcolōrāre*) + *-ation.*

discomfit *v.* Probably before 1200 *descumfiten* defeated, overthrown, in *Ancrene Riwle;* borrowed from Old French *desconfit,* past participle of *desconfire* to defeat, destroy (*des-* not, from Latin *dis-* + *confire* make, prepare, accomplish, from Latin *cōnficere* put together, finish up, from *con-,* variant of *com-* before *f* with, together + *facere* make, DO[1] perform). The Old French word *desconfit* was borrowed into English as a participle ("he was *desconfit*") but subsequently (about 1303, in Mannyng's *Handlyng Synne*) was considered as the stem of a verb, *desconfiten,* and a new past participle and past tense, *discomfited,* developed in the 1300's, becoming popular in the 1400's.

The sense of embarrass, disconcert, is first recorded in English in 1530, probably by association with *discomfort,* both words having the same pronunciation in some speech areas.

—discomfiture *n.* Probably before 1350 *discomfitoure* act of being overthrown, defeat, borrowed from Old French *desconfiture,* from *desconfit;* for suffix see -URE.

disconnection *n.* 1735 *disconnexion,* British variant of *disconnection* (1875), in writings of Benjamin Franklin, formed from English *dis-* + *connection,* British *connexion.* **—disconnect** *v.* 1770, in writings of Edmund Burke, possibly a back formation from *disconnection, disconnexion,* but more likely formed from English *dis-* + *connect.*

disconsolate *adj.* About 1385 *disconsolat* cheerless, depressing, in Chaucer's *Troilus and Criseyde;* borrowed, perhaps by influence of Old French *desconseillé* discouraged, from Medieval Latin *disconsolatus* comfortless (Latin *dis-* away + *cōnsōlātus,* past participle of *cōnsōlārī* CONSOLE). The meaning of unhappy, forlorn, is first recorded in English probably before 1400.

discord *n.* About 1230 *descorde,* in *Ancrene Riwle;* later *discord,* in *Cursor Mundi* (1325); borrowed from Old French *discorde* disagreement, learned borrowing from Latin *discordia* discord, from *discors* (genitive *discordis*) disagreeing, discordant; and borrowed from Old French *descord, discord* disagreement, discord, from *descorder, discorder* to disagree, learned borrowing from Latin *discordāre,* from *discors* (genitive *discordis*) disagreeing, discordant (*dis-* apart + *cor,* genitive *cordis* HEART). The musical sense of dissonance is first recorded before 1398, in Trevisa's translation of Bartholomew's *De Proprietatibus Rerum.* **—discordance** *n.* 1340, in *Ayenbite of Inwyt;* borrowed from Old French *descordance, discordance,* from Medieval Latin *discordantia,* from Latin *discordāre.* **—discordant** *adj.* About 1380, in Chaucer's translation of Boethius' *De Consolatione Philosophiae;* borrowed from Old French *descordant, discordant,* present participle of *descorder, discorder.*

discotheque (dis′kətek) *n.* nightclub that provides recorded music for dancing. 1954, borrowing of French *discothèque* nightclub with recorded music for dancing, record library (1932), from Italian *discoteca* (1927) record collection, record library (*disco* phonograph record, disk + *-teca* collection, as in *biblioteca* book collection, library, from Latin *thēca* case, receptacle, from Greek *thḗkē,* from the stem of *tithénai* to put, place; see DO[1] perform). French *discothèque* was applied at first to a café where customers could choose records to be played, and then to a small nightclub for dancing to records.

discount *n.* 1622 *discount* an abatement or deduction, alteration (influenced by English *dis-* + *count*) of French *décompte,* from Old French *descont,* from *desconter* count out (*des-* away, dis- + *conter* to COUNT). The commercial sense of a deduction from the price, is first recorded in English in 1690, borrowed (perhaps through the influence of Italian *disconto*) from French *décompte* (1671). **—v.** deduct. 1629 *discompt,* alteration (influenced by English *dis-*) of French *décompter,* from Old French *desconter* count out. The sense of believe only part of, is first recorded in English in the early 1700's.

discourage *v.* 1437 *discoragen* dishearten; borrowed from Middle French *descourager,* from Old French *descoragier* (*des-* away + *corage* COURAGE). **—discouragement** *n.* 1561, borrowed from Middle French *descouragement,* from Old French *descoragier* discourage; for suffix see -MENT.

discourse *n.* About 1380, process of understanding or reasoning by which one passes from premises to conclusions, in Chaucer's translation of Boethius' *De Consolatione Philosophiae;* alteration (influenced by English *course*) of Latin *discursus* (genitive *discursūs*) a running about, in Late Latin meaning discourse, from the stem of *discurrere* run about (*dis-* apart + *currere* to run; see CURRENT). The sense of a discussion, conversation is first recorded in 1559, and a formal speech or writing, in 1581. **—v.** Before 1547, run or travel over a region (the literal sense of Latin *discurrere*), from *discourse,* n. The sense of hold discourse, converse, is first recorded in 1559, but first recorded use of the verb (before 1547) appears in the Earl of Surrey's translation of two books of the *Aeneid,* in which he introduced blank verse into English.

discourtesy *n.* 1555, formed from English *dis-* + *courtesy,* probably by influence of Middle French *descourtoisie,* and possibly Italian *discortesia.* **—discourteous** *adj.* 1578, perhaps formed from English *discourte(sy)* + *-ous,* or independently from *dis-* + *courteous,* probably by influence of Middle French *descortese,* and possibly Italian *discortese.*

discover *v.* Before 1325, reveal, disclose, uncover, in *Cursor Mundi;* borrowed from Old French *descovrir,* from Late Latin *discooperīre* (Latin *dis-* opposite of + *cooperīre* to cover up; see COVER). **—discoverer** *n.* Before 1325, an informer, in *Cursor Mundi;* borrowed from Old French *descovrëor,* from *descovrir.* **—discovery** *n.* 1553, in Hakluyt's *Voyages;* probably formed in English on analogy with *recover, recovery, deliver, delivery.*

discredit *v.* 1559, formed from English *dis-* + *credit,* probably by influence of Middle French *discréditer,* and possibly Italian *discreditare.*

discreet *adj.* careful, prudent. About 1385 *discret,* in Chaucer's *Troilus and Criseyde;* borrowed from Old French *discret,* learned borrowing from Latin *discrētus* separated, distinct (in Medieval Latin, discerning, careful), from past participle of *discernere* distinguish, DISCERN. Doublet of DISCRETE. During the 1400's *discret, discrete,* and *discreet* were variant spellings for all senses of *discreet* and *discrete,* but gradually into the late 1500's the spelling *discreet* was associated with careful, prudent, possibly patterned on words such as *sweet* (Middle English *swete*). The use of *discrete* remained the spelling of the meanings in music, philosophy, medicine, etc., where knowledge and association of Latin *discrētus* was more widely known.

discrepancy *n.* About 1425, borrowed from Latin *discrepantia* (probably influenced by earlier *discrepant,* adj.; 1450, borrowed from Latin *discrepantem,* and by Old French *discrepance*), from *discrepantem,* present participle of *discrepāre* sound differently, disagree, differ (*dis-* apart, off + *crepāre* to rattle, crack, creak; for suffix see -ANCY.

discrete *adj.* separate, distinct. About 1385, borrowed from Old French *discrete,* learned borrowing from Latin *discrētus* separated, past participle of *discernere* distinguish, DISCERN. Doublet of DISCREET. Although the word is first recorded in English in the sense of separate, distinct, about 1385, in Thomas Usk's *The Testament of Love,* it did not come into general use until the late 1500's.

discretion *n.* quality of being discreet, discernment, prudence. About 1303 *dyscrecyun,* in Mannyng's *Handlyng Synne;* borrowed through Old French *discretion,* or directly from Late Latin *discrētiōnem* (nominative *discrētiō*) discernment, from Latin *discrētiōnem* separation, distinction, from *discrē-,* stem of *discernere* to separate, distinguish, DISCERN; for suffix see -TION. **—discretionary** *adj.* 1698, formed from English *discretion* + *-ary.*

discriminate *v.* distinguish, make or see a difference between. 1628, borrowed from Latin *discrīminātus,* past participle of *discrīmināre* to divide, separate, distinguish, from *discrīmen* (genitive *discrīminis*) separation, formed as the noun to *discernere* distinguish, DISCERN (as *crīmen* was the noun to *cernere*); for suffix see -ATE[1]. The sense of make distinctions prejudicial to people of a different race or color is first recorded in American English in 1866. **—discrimination** *n.* 1646, distinction, 1866, racial distinction; borrowed from Latin *discrīminātiōnem* (nominative *discrīminātiō*), from *discrīmināre* discriminate; for suffix see -TION.

discursive *adj.* rambling. 1599, borrowed through Middle French *discursif* (feminine *discursive*), from Medieval Latin *discursivus,* from Latin *discursus* (genitive *discursūs*), a running about; see DISCOURSE; for suffix see -IVE.

discus *n.* heavy disk thrown in athletic games. 1656, borrowed from Latin *discus* discus, disk of a dial, from Greek *dískos* disk, quoit, platter; see DISH. Doublet of DAIS, DESK, DISH, and DISK.

discuss *v.* About 1380 *discussen* examine, investigate, in Wycliffe's writings; borrowed from Latin *discussus,* past participle of *discutere* strike asunder, break up (*dis-* apart + *quatere* to shake; see QUASH[1] crush). The meaning talk over, debate, is first recorded in 1448, in the gerund *discussyng.* Alternatively, *discuss* may be a back formation from *discussion.* **—discussion** *n.* About 1340, examination, judicial decision; borrowed from Old French *discussion,* from Late Latin *discussiōnem* examination, discussion, from Latin *discussiōnem* a shaking, from *discuss-,* stem of *discutere* strike asunder; for suffix see -SION.

disdain *v.* scorn, despise. About 1380 *disdaignen,* in Chaucer's translation of Boethius' *De Consolatione Philosophiae;* probably borrowed from Old French *desdeignier* (*des-* do the opposite of, from Latin *dis-* + *deignier* treat as worthy, DEIGN). It is also possible that the verb in English is a shift in use from the earlier noun. **—n.** Before 1338 *desdegne,* in Mannyng's *Chronicle of England,* alteration of earlier *dedeyne* (about 1300); borrowed from Old French *desdeign, desdaign,* from *desdeignier* to disdain.

disease *n.* Before 1338 *deses* absence of ease, discomfort, in Mannyng's *Chronicle of England;* borrowed from Old French *desaise* (*des-* without, away, from Latin *dis-* + *aise* EASE).

The sense of sickness (first recorded as *desese* in Gower's *Confessio Amantis,* before 1393) often had to be inferred from the context, with reference to a specific "dis-ease" or discomfort.

—diseased *adj.* Before 1398 *desesed,* in Trevisa's translation of Bartholomew's *De Proprietatibus Rerum,* formed from the past participle of Middle English *disesen,* v., afflict with hardship, vex, injure.

disembody *v.* 1714, in Addison's writing in *The Spectator,* formed from English *dis-* do the opposite of + *embody.*

disenchant *v.* Before 1586, in Sidney's works; borrowed from Middle French *désenchanter* (*dés-* + *enchanter* to enchant).

disfigure *v.* Probably about 1375, disguise; later, deform, in Chaucer's *Canterbury Tales,* borrowed from Old French *desfigurer,* from Medieval Latin *diffigurare,* from Latin *dis-* + *figūra* figure, from *figūrāre* to figure.

disgrace *v.* About 1549, disfigure, from Middle French *disgracier,* from Italian *disgraziare,* from *disgrazia* misfortune, deformity (*dis-* from Latin *dis-,* + *grazia* grace, from Latin *grātia* GRACE). The meaning of bring shame upon is first recorded in 1593, in Shakespeare's *Lucrece.* **—n.** 1581, borrowed from Middle French *disgrace* misfortune, deformity, from Italian *disgrazia.* The meaning of shame or dishonor is first recorded in 1593, in Shakespeare's *Richard II.* **—disgraceful** *adj.* (1591)

disgruntle *v.* 1682, from *dis-* entirely, very + obsolete *gruntle* to grunt, grumble (Middle English *gruntelen,* probably before 1425), frequentative form of GRUNT; for suffix see -LE[3].

disguise *v.* Probably before 1300 *degysen* change appearance to hide identity, in *Kyng Alisaunder;* also *dysgysen* dress up in an elaborate way (about 1303, in Mannyng's *Handlyng Synne*); both forms borrowed from Old French *desguisier* (*des-* away, off, from Latin *dis-* + *guise* style, appearance, GUISE). **—n.** Before 1400, from the verb.

disgust *n.* 1598, borrowed from Middle French *desgoust* strong dislike, repugnance (literally) distaste, from *desgouster-* have a distaste for (*des-* opposite of, from Latin *dis-,* + *gouster* to taste, from Latin *gustāre* to taste); see GUSTO. **—v.** 1601, to dislike; later, offend the taste or smell of (1650); borrowed from Middle French *desgouster* to dislike.

dish *n.* Probably before 1200 *disch,* in *Ancrene Riwle,* developed from Old English (about 700) *disc* plate, bowl, platter, corresponding to, and possibly borrowed through, a West Germanic word, represented by Old Saxon *disk* table, and Old High German *tisc* dish, table (modern German *Tisch* table); all borrowed from Latin *discus* dish, platter, quoit, from Greek *dískos* disk, platter, originally **dik-skos,* from the root of *dikeîn* to throw, cast (infinitive of the aorist, i.e. single-action form, of an ancient verb); related to *deiknýnai* to show, cognate with Sanskrit *diśáti* he points to, Latin *dicāre* proclaim, Gothic *gateihan* proclaim, from Indo-European **deiḱ-/diḱ-* (Pok. 188). Doublet of DAIS, DESK, DISCUS, and DISK.

The meaning of a particular variety of food served, is first recorded about 1450. The sense of an attractive person, especially a woman, is first recorded in 1599, in Shakespeare's *Much Ado About Nothing.*
—v. 1381 *dischen* serve food; from the noun.
—dishcloth *n.* (1828, earlier *dish clout,* before 1529).

dishearten *v.* 1599, in Shakespeare's *Henry V,* formed from English *dis-* + *hearten.*

disheveled *adj.* About 1410 *discheveled,* alteration (with the ending *-ed*[2]) of earlier *dischevele* (about 1380, in Chaucer's *Parlement of Foules*) having disarranged or unkempt hair; borrowed from Old French *deschevelé,* past participle of *descheveler* to disarrange the hair (*des-* apart, from Latin *dis-,* + *chevel* hair, from Latin *capillus,* of uncertain origin). The sense of having untidy dress or appearance is first recorded in English in 1612.

dishonest *adj.* 1390, in Chaucer's *Canterbury Tales,* borrowed from Old French *deshoneste, desoneste,* perhaps from Medieval Latin **dishonestus* (Latin *dis-* not + *honestus* honorable, HONEST). **—dishonesty** *n.* About 1390, in Chaucer's *Canterbury Tales,* borrowed from Old French *deshonesté, desonesté,* from Latin *dis-* not + *honestātem* honorableness. **—dishonor** *v.* About 1250, borrowed from Old French *deshonorer, desonorer,* from Latin *dis-* not + *honōrem* honor. **—dishonorable** *adj.* About 1533, formed from English *dis-* + *honorable,* and from English *dishonor* + *-able,* possibly by influence of Middle French *déshonorable.*

disinherit *v.* About 1450, replacing earlier *disherein* (probably before 1400). *Disinherit* is generally regarded as formed from English *dis-* do the opposite of + *inherit,* while *disherein* was borrowed from Middle French *disheriter, deseriter,* from Latin *dis-* not + *hērēditāre* to inherit.

disinterested *adj.* Before 1612, having no feeling of wanting to know, see, do, etc., unconcerned, in Donne's writings, perhaps replacing his earlier use of *disinteressed* (1610) though Donne may have considered this a different word because he uses *disinteressed* to mean "impartial"; both words formed from English *dis-* not, without + *interested* and *interessed,* the latter alternatively formed possibly from *disinteress* (in spite of its date 1622), borrowed from French *désintéresser* to rid of interest in. First recorded use of the spelling *disinterested* to mean "impartial" is 1659; earlier use meant "unconcerned" (before 1612). First recorded use of *disinteressed* to mean "impartial" is 1610; earlier use meant "unconcerned" (1603).

disjoint *v.* Probably 1440, to disrupt or destroy; from English *disjoint,* n., a dilemma, distress (about 1385, in Chaucer's *Canterbury Tales*), a use of the noun probably influenced by Old French *desjoint,* past participle of *desjoindre* to disjoin.

disk or **disc** *n.* 1664 *disk* a round, flat surface like that which the sun or moon presents; later *disc* a discus or quoit (about 1727); borrowed from Latin *discus* quoit, discus, dish, from Greek *dískos;* see DISH. Doublet of DAIS, DESK, DISCUS, and DISH.

The meaning phonograph record is first recorded in 1888, a year after Emile Berliner patented the Gramophone, which, unlike Edison's phonograph (1877), used a flat disk instead of a cylinder.
—diskette *n.* floppy disk (flexible magnetic disk for storing information electronically). 1975, formed from English *disk* + *-ette* (diminutive suffix).

dislike *v.* About 1555, formed from English *dis-* not + *like.* **—n.** 1577, from the verb.

dislocate *v.* put out of joint. 1605, in Shakespeare's *King Lear,* from earlier adjective or past participle *dislocate* out of joint (before 1408, in a translation of Lanfranc's *Science of Surgery*); borrowed from Medieval Latin *dislocatus,* past participle of *dislocare* put out of place (Latin *dis-* away + *locāre* to place, LOCATE); for suffix see -ATE[1]. **—dislocation** *n.* Before 1400, in a translation of Lanfranc's *Science of Surgery;* borrowed through Old French *dislocation,* and directly from Medieval Latin *dislocationem* (nominative *dislocatio*), from *dislocare* dislocate; for suffix see -TION.

dislodge *v.* Probably about 1408 *disloggen,* in writings of Lydgate; borrowed from Old French *desloger* to leave or cause to leave a lodging place (*des-* do the opposite of + *loger* to LODGE). The English spelling *dislodge* with the combination of letters *dg* (introduced to a wide audience in some of Caxton's printed works) was apparently a spelling device to distinguish the sound represented by the *g* in *page* (especially in words from French, such as *disloggen*) from the *g* in *beg.*

disloyalty *n.* About 1410 *disloyalte* unfaithful or sinful behavior; borrowed from Middle French *desloyaulte,* Old French *desloialteit* (*des-* not + *loial* loyal); for suffix see -TY[2]. **—disloyal** *adj.* 1417 (inferred from *disloyally,* 1417); borrowed from Middle French *desloyal,* Old French *desloial* (*des-* not + *loial* loyal). An obsolete form *disleal* appears in 1590, in Spenser's *Faerie Queene;* borrowed from Italian *disleale,* it apparently did not become a fixed spelling.

dismal *adj.* gloomy, dreary. Probably about 1400, unlucky, unpropitious, in Wycliffe's writings; developed from earlier *dismale,* n., evil days, unlucky days (about 1300, originally in reference to the unpropitious days of the medieval calendar); borrowed from Anglo-French *dismal* (recorded in 1250), corresponding to Old French (*li*) *dis mals* (the) bad days, from Medieval Latin *dies mali* evil or unlucky days (Latin *diēs* days + *malī,* plural of *malus* bad). The native Old French equivalent of *li dis mals* was *li mal jour.*

Calendars of the Middle Ages marked two days of each month as unlucky days; such days were also called in Medieval Latin *dies Aegyptiaci* Egyptian days, perhaps because they originated in the calculations of Egyptian astrologers; or by some writers, such as Chaucer, were associated with the ten plagues of ancient Egypt.

The meaning of gloomy, dreary, is first recorded in English in 1593, relating to a sound that is dreary or woeful, in Shakespeare's *3 Henry VI,* and relating to things in general in 1617.

dismantle *v.* 1579, to tear down fortifications or the like; later, to take apart (1601, in Philemon Holland's translation of Pliny's *Natural History*); borrowed from Middle French *desmanteler* to tear down the walls of a fortress, (literally) divest of a mantle or cloak (*des-* off, away, from Latin *dis-,* + *manteler* to cloak, MANTLE).

dismay *v.* trouble greatly. About 1300 *demayen;* earlier *dismaien* (probably before 1300, in *Kyng Alisaunder*); apparently borrowed from Anglo-French, Old French **demaier,* **desmaier* (from Latin intensive *dē-* + Old French *esmaier* to trouble, disturb, from Vulgar Latin **exmagāre* divest of power or ability, probably from Latin *ex-* from, out of, and the Germanic stem *mag-;* compare Old High German *magan* have strength, be able). **—n.** Probably before 1300 *desmay* consternation, fear, uneasiness, in *Arthour and Merlin;* from the verb.

dismember *v.* About 1300, borrowed from Old French *desmembrer,* from Medieval Latin *dismembrare, demembrare* (Latin *dis-, dē-* take away + *membrum* member). **—dismemberment** *n.* About 1658, a cutting off from membership; later, a cutting into pieces, division, partition (before 1751), formed from English *dismember* + *-ment.*

dismiss *v.* send away or release. About 1432 *dismissen,* apparently borrowed from Latin *dīmissus,* past participle of *dimittere* send away, with the prefix altered in English to *dis-* by analogy with numerous Middle English verbs in *dis-* (*dī-* apart, away, variant of *dis-* + *mittere* send, let go). **—dismissal** *n.* Before 1806, formed from English *dismiss* + *-al*[2], replacing earlier *dismission* (1547).

disobey *v.* About 1390, in Chaucer's *Canterbury Tales;* borrowed from Old French *desobëir,* a re-formation with *dis-* of Late Latin *inoboedīre,* a back formation from *in-oboediēns* not obeying (Latin *in-* not + present participle of *oboedīre* obey). **—disobedience** *n.* Probably before 1400 *dysobediaunce;* later Middle English *disobedience* (probably before 1439); borrowed from Old French *desobedience,* a re-formation with *dis-* of Late Latin *inoboedientia* (Latin *in-* not + *oboedientia* OBEDIENCE); for suffix see -ENCE. **—disobedient** *adj.* About 1412; borrowed from Middle French *desobedient,* a re-formation with *dis-* of Late Latin *inoboedientem* (Latin *in-* not + *oboedientem* OBEDIENT); for suffix see -ENT. The form *disobedient* displaced *disobeissant* (about 1380), *disobeiaunt* (1422), in the 1500's paralleling the spelling of *disobedience.*

disorder *v.* put out of order, throw into confusion. 1503, formed from *dis-* + the verb ORDER, replacing earlier *disordeine* (about 1300); borrowed from Old French *desordainer,* variant of *desordener,* from Medieval Latin *disordinare* throw into disorder, from Latin *dis-* take away + *ōrdināre* to order, regulate. **—n.** 1530, in *Lesclarcissement,* from the verb, patterned on French *désordre.*

disorganize *v.* 1793, in writings of Burke, borrowed from French *désorganiser* (*dés-* not + *organiser* organize). According to the OED *disorganize, disorganization* (also in Burke's writings), etc. entered English at the time of the French Revolution.

disparage *v.* Before 1375 *desparagen* degrade socially, as for marrying below rank, in *The Romance of William of Palerne;* borrowed from Old French *desparagier* (literally) lower in rank, degrade (*des-* away, from Latin *dis-,* + *parage* rank, lineage, from Gallo-Romance **parāticum,* from Latin *pār,* genitive *paris* equal, see PAIR); for suffix see -AGE. The sense of belittle is first recorded in 1536, in writings of Thomas Cranmer, extended from the earlier meaning of dishonor, discredit (about 1390, in Chaucer's *Canterbury Tales*). **—disparagement** *n.* 1486, borrowed from Middle French *desparagement,* from *desparager* disparage, from Old French *desparagier;* for suffix see -MENT.

disparate (dis′pərit) *adj.* unlike, different. 1608, borrowed from Latin *disparātus,* past participle of *disparāre* divide, separate (*dis-* apart + *parāre* get ready, prepare; see PARE). The meaning of unlike, different was apparently influenced by association with Latin *dispār* unequal, unlike, different (*dis-* not + *pār* equal; see PAIR).

disparity *n.* About 1555, borrowed from Middle French *disparité* learned borrowing from Late Latin *disparitātem* (nominative *disparitās*) inequality (Latin *dis-* not + Late Latin *paritās,* genitive *paritātis* PARITY); for suffix see -ITY.

dispatch *v.* 1517, borrowed from Italian *dispacciare* to send off, hasten, or from Spanish *despachar* to send off (Italian *dis-* not + *-pacciare* in *impacciare* impede, trouble; Spanish *des-* not + *-pachar* in *empachar* impede, trouble; both the Italian and Spanish probably from Old Provençal *empachar* impede, from Gallo-Romance **impāctāre,* frequentative form of Latin *impingere* dash against; see IMPINGE). **—n.** 1550, dismissal, borrowed from Italian *dispaccio,* from *dispacciare,* or from Spanish *despacho,* from *despachar;* see verb. **—dispatcher** *n.* About 1547, formed from English *dispatch,* v. + *-er*[1].

dispel *v.* drive away and scatter. Probably before 1400 *dispelen;* borrowed from Latin *dispellere* (*dis-* away + *pellere* to drive, push, from Indo-European **pel-, pelə-,* Pok.801).

dispense *v.* Probably about 1350 *dispencen;* later *dispensen* (1380); borrowed from Old French *dispenser* give out, learned borrowing from Latin *dispēnsāre* disburse, administer, distribute (by weight), frequentative form of *dispendere* pay out (*dis-* out + *pendere* to pay, weigh; see PENDANT). In Medieval Latin *dispensare* had the meaning of deal with the application of church law, in reference to granting a person remission from punishment or exemption from a law (often followed by Latin *cum* with). By 1382 this usage was translated directly into the English phrase *dispense with* having the sense of to exempt, let (someone) off from doing something; *dispense with* eventually evolved into the meaning of do away with (1576), forgo, do without (1607). **—dispensation** *n.* About 1380 *dispensacion* divine ordering of events, Providence, in Chaucer's translation of Boethius' *De Consolatione Philosophiae;* borrowed through Old French *dispensation,* or directly from Latin *dispēnsātiōnem* (nominative *dispēnsātiō*) distribution of money or property, management, regulation (in Medieval Latin, pardon, exemption), from *dispēnsāre* dispense; for suffix see -TION. **—dispensary** *n.* 1699, formed in English, probably by influence of French *dispensaire* book of pharmaceutical composition, from Medieval Latin *dispensarium* (for suffix see -ARY), and eventually replacing earlier *dispensatory* book of pharmaceutical composition (1566), place where medicines are made up (1597).

disperse *v.* Probably before 1425 *dispersen,* in a translation of Higden's *Polychronicon;* borrowed from Middle French *disperser* scatter, learned borrowing from Latin *dispersus.* An earlier *dispers,* adj., in Gower's *Confessio Amantis* (1393) was borrowed directly from

Latin *dispersus,* past participle of *dispergere* to scatter (*dis-* apart, in every direction + *spargere* to scatter; see SPARSE). **—dispersal** *n.* 1821, formed from English *disperse* + *-al*[2]. **—dispersion** *n.* About 1384, dispersion of Jews among the Gentiles, DIASPORA, in the Wycliffe Bible; borrowed through Old French *dispersion* and directly from Latin *dispersiōnem* (nominative *dispersiō*), from the stem of *dispergere* to scatter; for suffix see -SION.

dispirit *v.* 1642, to extract the essence of; later, to lower the spirits of (1647); formed from English *dis-* strip or deprive of + *spirit.* **—dispirited** *adj.* (1647)

displace *v.* 1551, formed from English *dis-* do the opposite of + *place,* by influence of, and possibly in some instances, borrowed from Middle French *displacer* to displace (*dis-* implying removal, negation + *placer* to place). **—displacement** *n.* 1611, removal from office, borrowed from French *déplacement,* Old French *desplacement;* in scientific use, the word is an English formation of *dis-* + *placement.*

display *v.* Probably before 1300 *desplayen* unfurl or display (a banner), in *Arthour and Merlin;* later *displayen* (1338); borrowed from Old French *despleier* unfold, spread out, from Latin *displicāre* to scatter (*dis-* un-, apart + *plicāre* to fold; see PLY[2] fold). Doublet of DEPLOY. The meaning of reveal or exhibit, developed in Middle English, probably about 1380. **—n.** 1583, a description; later, an exhibition or show (1665); from the verb. The meaning of ostentation is first recorded in Byron's *Parisina* (1816).

displease *v.* Probably about 1350, implied in the gerund *displesyng;* later *displesen* (about 1378, in a version of *Piers Plowman*); borrowed from Old French *desplais-,* present tense stem of *desplaisir* to displease, represented in Anglo-French **despleser,* and refashioned in Vulgar Latin **displacēre* for Latin *displicēre* displease (*dis-* not + *placēre* to please). The spelling with *ea* from the late 1400's and the 1500's, first found especially in Caxton's work, was used to represent the Anglo-French and Middle English open *e* (a sound close to that represented by *e* in *met*) from Old French *ai.* **—displeasure** *n.* 1427 *displeser;* borrowed from noun use of Old French *desplaisir* to displease.

Displeasure and *displesaunce* (*displeasaunce*) were competing forms from the late 1300's into the early 1600's; the latter was a borrowing from Old French *displaisance.* But by 1600 *displeasure* was the established form.

disport *v.* play, amuse. About 1380, in Chaucer's *House of Fame;* borrowed through Anglo-French *disporter* divert, amuse, from Old French *desporter,* literally, carry away, as of the attention from serious matters (*des-* away, from Latin *dis-,* + *porter* carry or bear, from Latin *portāre;* see PORT[4] bearing). Compare DEPORT and SPORT.

dispose *v.* arrange. 1373 *disposen* tend or have a natural tendency toward; borrowed from Old French *disposer,* replacement of Old French *despondre,* from Latin *dispōnere* put in order, arrange (*dis-* apart + *pōnere* to put, place; see POSITION). The substitution of *disposer* for *despondre* in Old French was influenced by *poser* to place, lay down, POSE. **—disposable** *adj.* 1643, formed from English *dispose* + *able.* **—disposal** *n.* 1630, formed from English *dispose* + *-al*[2]. **—disposition** *n.* About 1380, in Chaucer's translation of Boethius' *De Consolatione Philosophiae;* borrowed from Old French *disposicion,* and from Latin *dispositiōnem,* from the stem *disposi-* of *dispōnere* arrange; for suffix see -TION.

disproportionate *adj.* 1555, formed from English *dis-* not + *proportionate,* perhaps after Middle French *disproportionné* (1534). **—disproportion,** *n.* 1555, formed from English *dis-* not + *proportion,* perhaps after Middle French *disproportion* (1549).

disprove *v.* Probably about 1380, in Wycliffe's writings; borrowed from Old French *desprover* (*des-* not, from Latin *dis-* + *prover* to prove). **—disproof** *n.* 1531, in Sir Thomas Elyot's *The Boke Named the Governour;* formed from English *dis-* not + *proof.*

dispute *v.* argue, debate. About 1300 *desputen;* later *disputen* (1300); borrowed from Old French *desputer, disputer,* from Latin *disputāre* examine, discuss, argue (*dis-* apart, separately + *putāre* to count, consider). **—n.** 1594, logical argument; later, controversy, debate (1611); borrowed from Middle French *dispute,* from Old French *disputer,* v. An earlier form *disput* action of disputing (before 1325), was perhaps merely the infinitive used as a noun. **—disputation** *n.* Before 1387 *disputacioun,* in Trevisa's translation of Higden's *Polychronicon;* borrowed perhaps through Old French *disputation* and directly from Latin *disputātiōnem* (nominative *disputātiō*) an argument, dispute, from *disputāre; for suffix see* -ATION.

disqualification *n.* 1711-14, Addison and Steele in *The Spectator,* formed from English *dis-* not + *qualification,* possibly on the model of French *déqualification.* **—disqualify** *v.* 1723, either formed from English *dis-* not + *qualify,* or formed as a back formation from *disqualification.*

disquiet *v.* 1530, in Palsgrave's *Lesclarcissement,* formed from English *dis-* not + *quiet.* **—disquietude** *n.* 1709, Addison in *The Tatler,* formed probably from English *dis-* not + *quietude,* influenced in its formation by *disquiet.*

disquisition *n.* 1605, subject for writing; also, examination or investigation (1608-11); borrowed from Latin *disquīsītiōnem* (nominative *disquīsītiō*), from the stem of *disquīrere* inquire (*dis-* apart + *quaerere* seek, ask, QUERY); for suffix see -TION. The meaning of long speech or formal writing about a subject, is first recorded in English in 1647.

disregard *v.* 1641, in Milton's writings, formed from English *dis-* + *regard,* v. **—n.** 1665, from the verb, or formed independently from English *dis-* + *regard,* n.

disrupt *v.* 1657, break up; earlier *disrupt* torn, severed, past participle or adjective (probably before 1425, in an anonymous translation of Chauliac's *Grande Chirurgie*); borrowed from Latin *disruptus,* past participle of *disrumpere* (variant of *dīrumpere*) break apart, split (*dis-* apart + *rumpere* to break; see RUPTURE). The word did not come into common use until the 1800's. **—disruption** *n.* Probably before 1425 *disrupcion* laceration or tearing (of tissue), in an anonymous translation of Chauliac's *Grande Chirurgie;* borrowed from Latin *disruptiōnem* (nominative *disruptiō*), from the stem of *disrumpere;* for suffix see -TION. The meaning of a breaking up, is not recorded in English until 1646. **—disruptive** *adj.* 1842-43, formed from English *disrupt* + *-ive.*

dissatisfy *v.* 1666, in Pepys' *Diary,* formed from English *dis-* do the opposite of + *satisfy,* or as a back formation from *dissatisfaction.* **—dissatisfaction** *n.* 1640, formed from English *dis-* the opposite of + *satisfaction.*

dissect *v.* 1607, to cut in pieces, divide by cutting; later, to cut apart (an animal or plant) to examine or study (1611); borrowed from Latin *dissectus,* past participle of *dissecāre* cut in pieces (*dis-* apart + *secāre* to cut; see SECTION). Alternatively, the verb may be a back formation from *dissection.* The figurative sense of analyze, is first recorded in Donne's writings before 1631. The fairly common American pronunciation (dī sekt′) has probably arisen from the influence of *bisect.* **—dissection** *n.* 1581, that which has been cut to pieces or is in such a condition; later, the act of cutting apart (an animal or plant) for examination or study (1605, in Francis Bacon's *Of the Advancement of Learning*); borrowed through Middle French *dissection,* from Medieval Latin *dissectionem* (nominative *dissectio*), from the stem of Latin *dissecāre* cut in pieces; for suffix see -TION. The figurative sense of examination, is first recorded in Milton's writings in 1642.

dissemble *v.* hide or disguise (feelings or thoughts). Before 1420, in Lydgate's *Troy Book,* alteration of earlier *dissimule* to disguise, make believe (1380, in Chaucer's *Canterbury Tales*); borrowed through Middle French *dissimuler,* and directly from Latin *dissimulāre* to disguise, conceal (*dis-* completely + *simulāre* pretend). The later Middle English *dissemble,* as a replacement of *dissimule,* was apparently influenced in its formation by Middle French *dessembler* to separate, be unlike (*des-* dis- + *-sembler* as in *resembler* resemble), though the semantic connection is somewhat veiled.

disseminate *v.* scatter widely. 1603, in Philemon Holland's translation of Plutarch's *Moralia;* earlier *disseminate,* adj., scattered widely (probably before 1425, in a translation of Higden's *Polychronicon*); borrowed from Latin *dissēminātus,* past participle of *dissēmināre* (*dis-* in every direction + *sēmināre* to plant, propagate, from *sēmen,* genitive *sēminis* seed, SEMEN); for suffix see -ATE[1]. The borrowing of Middle English *disseminate,* adj., was probably influenced by earlier Middle English *dissemen* to scatter (about 1410). **—dissemination** *n.* 1646, either borrowed from Latin *dissēminātiōnem* (nominative *dissēminātiō*), from *dissēmināre* disseminate; for suffix see -ATION; *or* formed from English *disseminate* + *-ion.*

dissension *n.* disagreement, discord. Before 1325, in *Cursor Mundi;* borrowed from Old French *dissension,* and from Latin *dissēnsiōnem* (nominative *dissēnsiō*) disagreement, from *dissēns-,* stem of *dissentīre* disagree, DISSENT; for suffix see -SION.

dissent *v.* disagree, object. About 1425 (Scottish), borrowed possibly through Middle French *dissentir,* from Latin *dissentīre* differ in sentiment (*dis-* apart, differently + *sentīre* think, feel; see SENSE). **—n.** difference of opinion, disagreement. 1585, from the verb.

dissertation *n.* 1611, discussion or debate; borrowed from Latin *dissertātiōnem* (nominative *dissertātiō*) discourse or disquisition, from *dissertāre* debate or argue, frequentative form of *disserere* discuss, examine (*dis-* apart + *serere* to arrange words; see SERIES); for suffix see -ATION. The sense of a formal, written treatise appeared in English in 1651, in Hobbes' *Government and Society.*

dissident *adj.* disagreeing, dissenting. About 1534, borrowed from Latin *dissidentem* (nominative *dissidēns*), present participle of *dissidēre* to sit apart, be remote, disagree (*dis-* apart + *sedēre* to SIT). **—n.** dissenter. 1766, in allusion to the name given in Poland to Protestants and others who did not belong to the established Roman Catholic Church; from the adjective (translation of New Latin *dissidentes,* pl., from Latin *dissidentem,* present participle). **—dissidence** *n.* 1658, in Blount's *Glossographia,* perhaps formed from English *dissident* + *-ence,* after Latin *dissidentia,* from *dissidēns,* see DISSIDENT; for suffix see -ENCE.

dissimilar *adj.* 1621, in Burton's *Anatomy of Melancholy;* formed from English *dis-* not + *similar,* possibly on the model of French *dissimilaire.*

dissimulate *v.* dissemble, disguise. Probably before 1425, in a translation of Higden's *Polychronicon;* probably, in part, borrowed from Latin *dissimulātus,* past participle of *dissimulāre* conceal, disguise (*dis-* completely + *simulāre* pretend, SIMULATE); for suffix see -ATE[1]. The verbs *dissimulate* and *dissemble* gradually replaced earlier Middle English *dissimulen* (1380, in Chaucer's *Canterbury Tales*). By the 1600's use of *dissimulate* became widespread probably, in part, as a back formation of the earlier *dissimulation.* **—dissimulation** *n.* About 1380, in Chaucer's *House of Fame,* borrowed from Old French *dissimulation,* from Latin *dissimulātiōnem* (nominative *dissimulātiō*), from *dissimulāre* dissimulate; for suffix see -ATION.

dissipate *v.* About 1425, probably borrowed from Latin *dissipātus,* past participle of *dissipāre* disperse, squander, disintegrate (*dis-* apart + *supāre* to throw, scatter, cognate with Sanskrit *svapū́-* broom, and Old Slavic *sŭpǫ, suti* shake, from Indo-European **swep-/sup-,* Pok.1049); for suffix see -ATE[1]. It is also possible that *dissipate,* in some instances may have been a back formation from *dissipation.* **—dissipation** *n.* Probably before 1425 *dissipacioun* disintegration, dissolution; borrowed from Latin *dissipātiōnem* (nominative *dissipātiō*), from *dissipāre* dissipate; for suffix see -ATION.

dissociate *v.* 1623, verb use of earlier *dissociate,* adj., separated (1548); borrowed from Latin *dissociātus,* past participle of *dissociāre* to separate from companionship (*dis-* apart + *sociāre* to join, from *socius* companion; see SOCIAL); for suffix see -ATE[1]. **—dissociation** *n.* separation. 1611, in Cotgrave's *Dictionary,* borrowed probably through French *dissociation,* from Latin *dissociātiōnem* (nominative *dissociātiō*), from *dissociāre* dissociate; for suffix see -ATION. It is also possible that *dissociation* was formed from English *dissociate* + *-ion.*

dissolute *adj.* Before 1382 *dissolut* morally loose, lax, negligent, in the Wycliffe Bible; borrowed from Latin *dissolūtus,* past participle of *dissolvere* loosen up, DISSOLVE. The sense of immoral is first recorded in 1433, in the *Rolls of Parliament.* **—dissolution** *n.* 1348 *dissolucioun* laxity, frivolity, in Richard Rolle's writings; later, *dissipation* (1398, in Trevisa's translation of Bartholomew's *De Proprietatibus Rerum*); borrowed from Old French *dissolution* and directly from Latin *dissolūtiōnem* (nominative *dissolūtiō*), from *dissolū-,* stem of *dissolvere* DISSOLVE; for suffix see -TION.

dissolve *v.* About 1380, in Chaucer's translation of Boethius' *De Consolatione Philosophiae;* borrowed from Latin *dissolvere* to loosen up, break apart (*dis-* apart + *solvere* to loose, loosen; see SOLVE).

dissonance *n.* discord, lack of harmony. Probably

before 1425 *dissonaunce,* in a translation of Higden's *Polychronicon;* borrowed through Middle French *dissonance* and directly from Late Latin *dissonantia,* from Latin *dissonantem* (nominative *dissonāns*), present participle of *dissonāre* differ in sound (*dis-* apart + *sonāre* to SOUND); for suffix see -ANCE. —**dissonant** *adj.* Probably before 1425 *dissonaunte,* in a translation of Higden's *Polychronicon;* borrowed through Middle French *dissonant* and directly from Latin *dissonantem* (nominative *dissonāns*), present participle of *dissonāre;* for suffix see -ANT.

dissuade *v.* advise against. 1513 in Sir Thomas More's *History of King Richard III,* borrowed from Middle French *dissuader* and directly from Latin *dissuādēre* (*dis-* off, against + *suādēre* to urge). —**dissuasion** *n.* advice against. Before 1420, in Lydgate's *Troy Book;* borrowed from Middle French *dissuasion* and directly from Latin *dissuāsiōnem* (nominative *dissuāsiō*), from *dissuādēre* dissuade; for suffix see -SION.

distaff *n.* stick that holds flax, etc. for spinning. Before 1325 *distaf,* developed from Old English *distæf,* about 1000, in Ælfric's *Glossary* (*dis-* bunch of flax; see DIZEN + *stæf* stick, STAFF). Probably because spinning was typically done by women in the Middle Ages, *distaff* is recorded in English, by the late 1400's, as a synonym for the female sex, female authority and the female side of a family. In other European languages a similar development occurred.

distant *adj.* About 1391, in Chaucer's *Treatise on the Astrolabe;* borrowed from Old French *distant,* learned borrowing from Latin *distantem* (nominative *distāns*) standing apart, separate, distant, present participle of *distāre* stand apart (*dis-* apart, off + *stāre* to STAND); for suffix see -ANT. —**distance** *n.* About 1300 *destaunce* quarrel, estrangement; earlier, a dispute (probably before 1300); borrowed from Old French *destance, distance,* and directly from Latin *distantia* a standing apart, from *distantem* distant; for suffix see -ANCE. The sense of intervening space, remoteness, is first recorded in 1391, in Chaucer's *Treatise on the Astrolabe.* According to the MED, senses of disagreement or strife were borrowed from Old French, and senses of distance or difference were borrowed chiefly from Latin.

distend *v.* stretch out, swell out. Before 1400, borrowed from Latin *distendere* to swell or stretch out, extend (*dis-* apart + *tendere* to stretch, TEND[1] incline). —**distention** *n.* Probably before 1425 *distension,* in an anonymous translation of Chauliac's *Grande Chirurgie;* borrowed through Middle French *distension* and directly from Latin *distēnsiōnem, distentiōnem* (nominative *distēnsiō, distentiō*), from *distent-,* stem of *distendere;* for suffix see -TION.

distich (dis′tik) *n.* two lines of verse, couplet. 1577-87, in Holinshed's *Chronicles;* earlier *distichon* (1553); borrowed from Latin *distichon,* from Greek *dístichon,* neuter of *dístichos* of two rows, of two verses (*di-* two + *stíchos* row, line of verse, related to *steíchein* stride, Sanskrit *stighnoti* he steps, Lithuanian *steĩgti* to hurry, and Gothic *steigan* to mount, from Indo-European **steigh-/stigh-,* Pok.1017).

distill *v.* Probably about 1378 *distillen* produce (an essence) by condensation given off in drops, in Wycliffe's writings; borrowed from Old French *distiller,* from Latin *distillāre* trickle down in minute drops, as rain or tears (*dis-* apart + *stillāre* to drip, drop, from *stilla,* earlier **stīrelā* drop, diminutive of *stīria* frozen drop, icicle; cognate with Greek *stílē* drop) and Sanskrit *stíyā* standing water, from Indo-European **stāi-/stī-/sti-,* Pok.1010). —**distillation** *n.* Before 1393 *distillacion,* in Gower's *Confessio Amantis;* borrowed perhaps through Old French *distillation* or directly from Latin *distīllātiōnem* (nominative *distīllātiō*), from *distīllāre* trickle down, for suffix see -ATION. Alternatively *distillation* may have been formed from English *distill* + *-ation.* —**distillery** *n.* 1677, the act or art of distilling, in John Evelyn's *Diary;* later, a place for distilling (1759); formed from English *distill* + *-ery* or possibly formed from English *distiller* (1577) + *-y*[3].

distinct *adj.* About 1390, in Chaucer's *Canterbury Tales,* developed from past participle of earlier verb *distincten* to distinguish (about 1303, in Mannyng's *Handlyng Synne*); borrowed from Old French *distincter,* developed from *distinct,* adj., from Latin *distīnctus,* past participle of *distinguere* DISTINGUISH. It is possible that in some instances the adjective *distinct* was also borrowed directly from Old French *distinct,* adj., and, in other instances, directly from Latin *distīnctus.* —**distinction** *n.* Probably before 1200 *distinccioun, destinctiun* division or section, in *Ancrene Riwle;* borrowed through Old French *distinction,* and directly from Latin *distīnctiōnem* (nominative *distīnctiō*), from *distīnct-,* stem of *distinguere* distinguish; for suffix see -TION. —**distinctive** *adj.* Probably before 1425, borrowed through Old French *distinctif* and directly from Medieval Latin *distinctivus,* from Latin *distīnctus,* past participle of *distinguere;* for suffix see -IVE.

distinguish *v.* 1561, borrowed from Middle French *distinguiss-,* stem of *distinguer,* replacing earlier Middle English *distinguen* (about 1340), also borrowed from Old French *distinguer,* learned borrowing from Latin *distinguere* to separate between (*dis-* apart + *-stinguere* to prick); for suffix see -ISH[2]. Latin *-stinguere* is an alteration of **-stingere* on such analogy as *ūnxī: unguere* = *-stīnxī:* **-stingere;* cognate with Greek *stízein* tattoo, mark, Old English *stician* stab, Sanskrit *téjate* is sharp, from Indo-European **(s)teig-/(s)tig-* (Pok.1016). —**distinguishable** *adj.* 1594, in Richard Hooker's *Ecclesiastical Polity,* formed from English *distinguish* + *-able.* —**distinguished** *adj.* 1609, distinct; later, famous or celebrated (1714), developed as a special use of the past participle.

distort *v.* About 1586, borrowed from Latin *distortus,* past participle of *distorquēre* to twist different ways, distort (*dis-* completely + *torquēre* to twist; see TORTURE). —**distortion** *n.* 1581, borrowed, possibly in part by influence of Middle French *distorsion,* from Latin *distortiōnem* (nominative *distortiō*), from *distort-,* stem of *distorquēre;* for suffix see -TION.

distract *v.* About 1340; borrowed from Latin *distractus,* past participle of *distrahere* draw in different directions (*dis-* away + *trahere* to draw; see TRACT). —**distraction** *n.* 1447, borrowed from Old French *distraction,* or directly from Latin *distractiōnem* (nominative *distractiō*), from *distract-,* stem of *distrahere;* for suffix see -TION. It is possible that *distraction* was, in some instances, formed from English *distract* + *-ion.*

distraught *adj.* distracted, bewildered. Before 1393 *distraght,* in Gower's *Confessio Amantis,* alteration in spelling and pronunciation of earlier *distract,* adj., perplexed, confused (about 1340), past participle of *distracten* DISTRACT. According to the OED, the alteration of *distract* to *distraght* and thence to *dis-*

traught may have resulted from an association with other past participial forms with the spelling *-ght* (*caught, bought, taught*), and perhaps immediately influenced by Middle English *straght, straught,* past participial forms of *strecchen* to stretch.

distress *n.* About 1280 *destresse,* borrowed from Old French *destresse, destresce,* from Gallo-Romance **districtia* constraint, restraint, affliction, from Latin *districtus,* past participle of *distringere* draw apart, stretch out, hinder, also, in Medieval Latin, compel, coerce (*dis-* apart + *stringere* draw tight, press together; see STRAIN[1] stretch). **—v.** Probably about 1380, borrowed from Old French *destresser, destrescer* constrain, restrain, afflict, from *destresse, destresce,* n., distress. **—distressful** *adj.* 1591, in Shakespeare's 1 *Henry VI,* formed from English *distress* + *-ful.*

distribute *v.* Probably before 1425, in a translation of Higden's *Polychronicon;* borrowed from Latin *distribūtus,* past participle of *distribuere* deal out in portions or shares (*dis-* apart, individually + *tribuere* assign, allot; see TRIBUTE). **—distribution** *n.* About 1350 *distribucioun,* borrowed through Old French *distribution,* and directly from Latin *distribūtiōnem* (nominative *distribūtiō*), from *distribuere* distribute; for suffix see -TION. **—distributive** *adj.* 1450, borrowed from French *distributif* (feminine *distributive*), from Late Latin *distribūtīvus,* from Latin *distribūtus,* past participle of *distribuere* distribute; for suffix see -IVE. **—distributor** *n.* 1526, formed from English *distribute* + *-er*[1], later, respelled after Late Latin *distribūtor* (1752).

district *n.* 1611, in Cotgrave's *Dictionary;* borrowed from French *district,* also Middle French, from Medieval Latin *districtus* (genitive *districtūs*) restraining of offenders, exercise of justice, jurisdiction, area of jurisdiction, from past participle stem of Latin *distringere* hinder, detain; see DISTRESS. **—district attorney,** American English (1789)

distrust *v.* Before 1420, in Lydgate's *Troy Book;* formed from English *dis-* not + *trust,* v. **—n.** 1513, from the verb. **—distrustful** *adj.* 1591, in Shakespeare's *I Henry VI,* formed from English *distrust* + *-ful.*

disturb *v.* Probably before 1200 *disturben* to prevent, stop, hinder, in *Ancrene Riwle;* later, to stir up, agitate, trouble (about 1300); borrowed from Old North French *distourber,* and directly from Latin *disturbāre* throw into disorder (*dis-* completely + *turbāre* to disorder, disturb, from *turba* turmoil; see TURBID). **—disturbance** *n.* About 1280 *distourbaunce,* borrowed from Old North French *distourbance,* from *distourber* disturb; for suffix see -ANCE.

disuse *n.* Probably before 1408, in Lydgate's writings, from *disuse,* v., 1375, in John Barbour's *The Bruce;* borrowed from Old French *desuser* (*des-* not + *user* use).

ditch *n.* Probably about 1175 *dich,* developed from Old English (847) *dīc* ditch, dike; cognate with Old Frisian and Old Saxon *dīk* ditch, dike, Old Icelandic *dīki;* see DIKE. **—v.** About 1385 *dichen* surround with a ditch, build a ditch, in Chaucer's *Canterbury Tales;* from the noun. The sense of abandon, defeat, discard, jilt, is first recorded in American English in 1899.

According to the OED, Old English *dīc* is probably represented in Middle English by a northern form *dike* and a southern form *dich,* of which the latter developed the spelling with *t* (*ditch*) largely in the 1500's.

dither *v.* waver, hesitate. 1649, tremble, quake, vibrate, apparently a phonetic variation of earlier *didderen* (about 1375), of uncertain origin. The figurative sense of vacillate, waver, is first recorded about 1908. **—n.** 1819, tremulous, confused excitement; figurative extension from the verb.

ditto *n.* 1625, (in) the said (month or year), use of dialectal Italian *ditto,* in Purchas' *Pilgrims.* The word developed from Standard Italian *detto* (literally) said, past participle of *dire* to say; the past participle in Italian parallels Latin *dictus,* past participle of *dīcere* say. The meaning of the same or exactly the same as appeared before, is first recorded in English in 1678; the meaning of a copy or duplicate, is first recorded in 1776. **—v.** produce a copy or duplicate of. 1837-40, from the noun.

ditty *n.* simple poem or song. Probably before 1325 *ditee,* borrowed from Old French *ditié, dité* composition, poem, treatise, from Latin *dictātum* thing dictated, from neuter past participle of *dictāre* DICTATE.

diuretic (dī'yůret'ik) *adj., n.* (of a drug or agent) causing an increased flow of urine. Before 1400 *duretik;* later *diuretic* (probably before 1425), borrowed from Old French *diuretique,* from Late Latin *diūrēticus,* from Greek *diourētikós* prompting urine, from *dioureîn* urinate (*dia-* through + *oureîn* URINATE).

diurnal (dīėr'nəl) *adj.* daily. About 1390, in Chaucer's *Canterbury Tales;* borrowed from Late Latin *diurnālis,* from *diurnum* day, from Latin *diurnus* daily (modeled on *nocturnus* by night), from *diēs* day. Doublet of JOURNAL.

diva (dē'və) *n.* prima donna, principal woman opera singer. 1883, borrowed, possibly by influence of French *diva* or German *Diva,* from Italian *diva* goddess (in Dante), fine lady, from Latin *dīva* goddess, feminine of *dīvus* divine (one); see DIVINE.

divan *n.* 1586, council of state in Turkey or some other Oriental country; borrowed from Turkish *divan,* from Arabic *dīwān,* from Persian *dēvān* council room with a raised cushioned seat; the council; originally an official register of documents. The meaning of a long, low, soft couch or sofa, especially popular in the 1930's and 1940's, developed from the earlier meaning of a long seat or bench set against a wall and furnished with cushions (1702).

dive *v.* About 1250 *diven;* earlier dialectal *duven* (probably before 1200); developed by confusion of synonymous forms in a transitive use of Old English *dūfan* (originally v.i.) to dive, duck, sink, with Old English *dȳfan* (v.t.) to dip, submerge. Vestiges of the Old English strong verb *dūfan* died out in Middle English in the 1200's, so that *diven* carried the meaning to dive. Old English *dȳfan* is cognate with Old Icelandic *dȳfa* to dip, from Proto-Germanic **dūbijanan; dūfan* is cognate with Middle Low German *bedoven* covered over, Old High German *tobal* gorge, and Old Slavic *dupina* cave, from Indo-European **dheup-/dhoup-/dhūp-/dhup-* (Pok.268). It is also possible that Old English *dȳfan,* and *dyppan* to dip, are related. **—n.** 1700, a plunge; from the verb (earlier, implied in the gerundive use *diving;* before 1398, in Trevisa's translation of Bartholomew's *De Proprietatibus Rerum*). The sense of a disreputable tavern or saloon, is first recorded in American English about 1871. **—diver** *n.* 1506, formed from English *dive,* v. + *-er*[1].

diverge *v.* 1665, borrowed from Latin *dīvergere* go in different directions (*dī-,* from *dis-* apart + *vergere* to bend, turn, see WRENCH). **—divergence** *n.* 1656, in

Hobbes' *Elements of Philosophy;* borrowed from Latin *dīvergentem* (nominative *dīvergēns*), present participle of *dīvergere;* for suffix see -ENCE. —**divergent** *adj.* 1696, borrowed through French *divergent,* from Latin *dīvergentem* (nominative *dīvergēns*), present participle of *dīvergere;* for suffix see -ENT. Alternatively *divergent* may be a back formation of earlier *divergence.*

divers *adj.* About 1275, separate, distinct; borrowed from Old French *divers* different or odd, learned borrowing from Latin *dīversus* turned different ways (in Late Latin, various), past participle of *dīvertere* DIVERT. The meaning of various or various kinds, is first recorded probably before 1300, in a version of *Guy of Warwick,* and the meaning of several, numerous, more than one, is recorded before 1400.

diverse *adj.* About 1300 *diverse* separate, distinct; later, various, varied (before 1333, in Shoreham's poetry); a variant of *divers.* The final *-e* may have been added by analogy with converse, traverse, etc. —**diversify** *v.* 1481, in Caxton's translation of *The Mirror of the World;* borrowed from Middle French *diversifier,* from Medieval Latin *diversificare* to render unlike, from *diversus;* for suffix see -FY. —**diversity** *n.* About 1340 *diversite,* borrowed from Old French *diversité,* learned borrowing from Latin *dīversitātem* (nominative *dīversitās*), from *dīversus* diverse; for suffix see -ITY.

diversion *n.* Probably before 1425, act of diverting; borrowed from Middle French *diversion,* from Late Latin *diversiōnem* (nominative *dīversiō*), from Latin *dīvertere* DIVERT; for suffix see -SION.

The meaning of amusement, entertainment, especially in the plural *diversions,* is first recorded in English in 1648, in John Evelyn's *Diary.*

divert *v.* Before 1420 *diverten,* in Lydgate's *Troy Book;* borrowed from Middle French *divertir,* from Old French, learned borrowing from Latin *dīvertere* turn in different directions, and blended with *dēvertere* turn aside (*dī-*, variant of *dis-* aside, apart, and *dē-* from + *vertere* to turn).

The meaning of amuse, entertain, is first recorded in English in 1662 (and in French also in the 1600's), as an extension of the meaning of turning one's mind away from serious or unpleasant thoughts (about 1600, in Shakespeare's *Sonnets*).

divest *v.* 1605, in Shakespeare's *King Lear,* alteration of earlier *devest* to strip (a person or thing) of possessions, rights, etc. (1563); to strip of clothes (1583); borrowed from Middle French *devester, devestir,* from Old French *desvestir (des-,* from Latin *dis-* away, + *vestir* to clothe, from Latin *vestīre;* see VEST). The respelling of English *devest* to *divest* was influenced by Medieval Latin *divestire* undress, remove privileges, from *dis-vestire,* modeled on Latin *dīvellere* to separate, *dīvertere* to divert. English *devest* is an obsolete spelling, except in the field of law in which it means to take away (property), to alienate, convey. —**divestiture** *n.* 1601, formed in English from Medieval Latin *divestit-* (stem of *divestire* remove privileges, from Latin *dī-*, away + *vestīre* to clothe) + English *-ure.*

divide *v.* Probably before 1325, borrowed from Latin *dīvidere* to force apart, cleave, distribute (*dī-* apart, from *dis-* + *-videre* to separate, related to *vidua* WIDOW). —**n.** division, watershed. 1642, from the verb. —**divider** *n.* About 1526, one who distributes, in the Tyndale Bible; later, one who or that which separates (1591); formed from English *divide* + *-er* [1].

dividend *n.* 1557, number divided by another; later, share or portion (1600); borrowed from Middle French *dividende,* from Latin *dīvidendum* thing to be divided, neuter gerundive of *dīvidere* to DIVIDE. The sense of a share of money or profit divided among stockholders, is first recorded in 1623.

By the late 1600's *dividend* had replaced the earlier form *divident* a divider or barrier (first recorded probably before 1425, and borrowed from Latin *dīvidentem,* nominative *dīvidēns,* present participle of *dīvidere* to divide).

divine *adj.* About 1380 *devyne* of God or a god; godlike, in Chaucer's *House of Fame;* borrowed from Old French *devin, divin,* learned borrowing from Latin *dīvīnus* of a god, from *dīvus* a god, related to *deus* god, DEITY; for suffix see -INE[1]. —**n.** Probably before 1300 *devine* soothsayer, in *Arthour and Merlin;* later theologian (about 1387, in Wycliffe's writings); borrowed from Old French *devin,* from Medieval Latin *divinus* theologian, doctor of divinity, from Latin *dīvīnus* soothsayer, from the adjective in Latin. —**v.** About 1378 *devinen* to conjecture, guess, in a version of *Piers Plowman;* earlier *devynen* to foretell, prophesy (before 1376, in an earlier version of *Piers Plowman*); borrowed through Old French *deviner, diviner,* and directly from Latin *dīvīnāre* foretell, predict, from *dīvīnus* soothsayer, from the adjective in Latin. —**divination** *n.* Before 1384 *dyvynacioun* foretelling, in the Wycliffe Bible; borrowed from Old French *divination,* learned borrowing from Latin *dīvīnātiōnem* (nominative *dīvīnātiō*), from *dīvīnāre* foretell, predict; for suffix see -ATION. —**divinity** *n.* About 1300 *divinite* theology; borrowed from Old French *devinité, divinité,* from Latin *dīvīnitātem* (nominative *dīvīnitās*) godhead, divination, from *dīvīnus* of a deity, see DIVINE; for suffix see -ITY.

division *n.* Probably about 1350, borrowed from Old French *division, devisiun,* from Latin *dīvīsiōnem* (nominative *dīvīsiō*), from *dīvīd-*, stem of *dīvidere* DIVIDE); for suffix see -SION. —**divisible** *adj.* Probably before 1425, borrowed from Old French *divisible,* from Late Latin *dīvīsibilis,* from *dīvīs-*, stem of Latin *dīvidere;* for suffix see -IBLE. —**divisor** *n.* Before 1500, borrowed from Middle French *diviseur,* and perhaps directly from Latin *dīvīsōrem,* from *dīvidere;* for suffix see -OR[2].

divorce *n.* About 1378, *devose, devorse,* in a version of *Piers Plowman;* borrowed from Old French *divorce,* from early and legal Latin *dīvortium* (later dīvertium) separation, dissolution of marriage, from *dīvertere* to separate, leave one's husband, turn aside, DIVERT. *Divorce* as spelled in Old French and meaning deprivation, is recorded once in Middle English in 1357 and does not reappear until about 1425. —**v.** Before 1400 *devorsen,* borrowed from Old French *divorcer,* from *divorce,* n. —**divorcé** (dəvôr′sā′) *n.* 1813, a French word used in an English novel to describe a divorced woman, feminine of French *divorcé* divorced man; noun use of the past participle of *divorcer* to divorce, from Old French.

divulge *v.* make publicly known. About 1450, borrowed through Middle French *divulguer* and directly from Latin *dīvulgāre* publish, make common (*dis-* apart + *vulgāre* make common property, from *vulgus* common people; see VULGAR).

Dixie *n.* a name for the Southern States of the U.S.; of uncertain origin, first recorded in American English in 1859 in the folk song *Dixie's Land* by Daniel Decatur Emmett, the title of the song later modified to *Dixie* and *Dixie Land* or *Dixieland.*

According to the DAE and the DA, three sources of the name have been advanced: 1) that *Dixie* is a modification of *Dixon* abstracted from *Mason and Dixon's line* (1779, the boundary between Pennsylvania and Maryland, surveyed 1763-67 by Charles Mason and Jeremiah Dixon; the line was regarded as separating the slave states from the free states). 2) that *Dixie* is an allusion to *Dixies,* pl. (unrecorded), said to be applied to bank notes issued by the Citizens Bank of Louisiana before the Civil War, bearing the French *dix* on the ten-dollar bill. The land of *dixies,* etc., arising as a general term for the area where the bank notes were circulated (disputed by Arthur, 1936). 3) that *Dixie* was formed in allusion to a Mr. *Dixy* or *Dixie,* a slave owner on Manhattan Island in New York City (forced to move South because of the general Northern sentiment against slave holding or because Dixy died and his slaves were moved South) whose slaves were unhappy in the South, and possibly in reference to their remembered contentment, referred to *Dixy's* or *Dixie's* land as a place of contentment (though somewhat fanciful, this is originally the view recorded by Farmer). **—Dixieland** *n.* 1917, abstracted from the *Original Dixieland Jass (Jazz) Band* (the first group to make commercial jazz recordings); perhaps earlier, *Dixieland* a style of jazz developed in New Orleans, according to the *Harvard Dictionary of Music,* beginning about 1910.

dizen *n.* dress with gaudy clothes. 1530, dress a distaff with flax for spinning; borrowed possibly from Middle Dutch *disen;* cognate with Low German *dise, disene* bunch of flax on a distaff. This verb is probably represented by *dis-, dise-* in the compound *distaff,* though no noun or verb form is found in Old or Middle English. The extended sense of to dress in finery, is first recorded in John Fletcher's *Monsieur Thomas* (1619).

dizzy *adj.* Probably about 1150 (dialectal) *dusi;* later *dysy* (before 1400); developed from Old English *dysig* foolish, stupid (before 830). Old English *dysig* is cognate with Old Frisian *dusig* foolish, stupid, from Proto-Germanic **dusīȝaz;* modern Dutch *duizelig* dizzy, giddy; Old High German *tusig* stupid, modern German *Tor* fool, with *r* from *z,* Middle Low German *dūsich* stunned, dizzy, *dwās* foolish, stupid, and Old Icelandic *dūs* calm, lull, *dūsa* to doze; cognate with Latin *furere* be crazy, rave, from Indo-European **dhwēs-/dhūs-/dhus-* (Pok. 268); see DOZE. **—dizziness** *n.* About 1400 *duysenes,* in Lydgate's writings; earlier *desynaiss* (1375, in John Barbour's *The Bruce*); developed from Old English *dysignesse* (about 900, in Alfred's translation of Bede's *Ecclesiastical History*); formed from Old English *dysig* + *nesse.*

do[1] (dü) *v.* Probably before 1200 *do,* in *Ancrene Riwle;* earlier *dou* (before 1121, in *Peterborough Chronicle*); found in Old English *dōn* (about 725, in *Beowulf*). Old English *dōn* is cognate with Old Frisian *duā* to do, Old Saxon *dūan,* Middle Dutch *duon* (modern Dutch *doen*), Old and Middle High German *tuon* to do (modern German *tun*); from the Indo-European base **dhē-/***dhō-/dhə-* (Pok. 235),which is also the source of Latin *facere* (*f* from *dh*) make, do. Outside of Germanic, and except for Latin *facere,* the meaning of cognates from the Indo-European base shifts, as in Latin *-dere* to put, place (as in *abdere* put away, hide), Greek *tithénai* to put, place, or set, Old Slavic *dĕti* to put, Lithuanian *dĕti* put, set, Sanskrit *dádhāti* he puts, places, Hittite *dāi-* puts, places, Armenian *dnem* I place, and Tocharian A *tā-, tas-,* Tocharian B *tes-* to place.

Originally *do* was the first person singular of the indicative mood of Middle Engligh *don*; the form *does* was an adoption of north English *does* (from Old English, about 950) and gradually replaced earlier *doth, doeth* between the 1500's and 1600s.

Past tense *did,* also found in Middle English, developed from Old English *dide, dyde,* cognate with Old Saxon *deda,* Old High German *teta,* Middle High German *tete,* and Gothic only in the suffix *-da.* This past tense form, being a reduplication of the present stem, is the only form in modern Germanic that retains visible traces of that way of indicating past tense. (In earliest Germanic the past tense represented by *did,* was used as a suffix to form the past tense of other verbs and was then reduced in Gothic to *-da,* to *-de* in Old English, and then to *-d* in English, but usually regarded as *-ed*).

The past participle *done,* in Middle English *don, doon* developed from Old English *gedōn.* Middle English retained an altered form of the prefix in *ido, ydo,* but finally dropped the *-n* in the south of England, though a vestige of the prefix is still evident in *ado.* **—doer** *n.* About 1380 *doere,* in Chaucer's translation of Boethius' *De Consolatione Philosophiae;* formed from Middle English *do, don* do + *-er*[1]. **—doings** *n.pl.* About 1378 *doynges,* in a version of *Piers Plowman;* from the gerund *doung* in Middle English (about 1325); for suffix see -ING[2].

do[2] (dō) *n.* the first and last note of the musical scale. 1754, possibly about 1670; borrowing of Italian *do,* used as a substitute for *ut* in the GAMUT. However, about 1450, a treatise on music refers to *Dlasolre, Dsolre.*

dobbin *n.* 1596, a slow, gentle, plodding horse, in Shakespeare's *Merchant of Venice,* familiar use of *Dobbin,* personal name, diminutive of *Dob* (now more frequently in *Dobbins* or *Dobbs*); alteration of *Robin, Rob,* diminutives of *Robert.*

docile *adj.* 1483, easily taught, in Caxton's *Golden Legend,* probably borrowed through Italian *docile,* as a learned borrowing from Latin *docilis* easily taught, from *docēre* teach, related to *doctor* teacher; see DOCTOR. The meaning of obedient, submissive, is first recorded in English in 1774, in Goldsmith's writings.

dock[1] *n.* wharf or pier. 1513, hollow made by a ship run aground, borrowed from Middle Dutch or Middle Low German *docke,* of unknown origin.

The meaning of an artificial basin built for ships is first recorded in English in 1552; the general use as a synonym for pier or wharf is not recorded until 1707, in American English.
—dockyard *n.* (1704) **—dry dock** (1627); **dry-dock** *v.* 1514, from the noun.

dock[2] *n.* fleshy part of an animal's tail. Probably about 1390 *dok,* in *Sir Gawain and the Green Knight;* developed possibly from Old English *-docca,* as in *fingerdocca* finger muscle (before 750), from Proto-Germanic **dokkō,* apparently meaning "something round"; cognate with Frisian *dok* bundle, bunch, Middle Low German *docke* bundle, doll (modern German *Docke*), Old High German *tocka* doll, and Old Icelandic *dokka* doll, of unknown origin. The semantic relationship seems to be built around the concept of something round. **—v.**

Probably about 1378 *dokken* to abridge, reduce, in Wycliffe's writings; later, to cut (hair) short (1387-95, in Chaucer's *Prologue* to the *Canterbury Tales*), and to curtail (probably before 1400); probably from earlier unrecorded use of *dok* dock, n. The meaning of deduct from one's pay is first recorded in 1822.

dock[3] *n.* place where accused person stands in court. 1586, borrowed from Flemish *dok,* earlier *docke* pen or cage for animals, of unknown origin. After 1610, the common term was *bail-dock;* the use of *dock* was revived and popularized in the 1800's largely through the writings of Dickens.

dock[4] *n.* any of various large weeds. Probably before 1300 *docke,* developed from Old English *docce* (about 1000), from Proto-Germanic **dokkōn;* cognate with Middle Dutch and Middle Low German *docke* dock, and Old Danish *dokka.*

docket *n.* Before 1483 *doggette* a summary or abstract; of uncertain origin. A common spelling in the 1500's was *docquet,* perhaps echoing the diminutive ending *-et* or *-ette.* The meaning of a list of lawsuits to be tried, is first recorded in 1709, in American English; the meaning of a list of judgments (1668-69), in Pepys' *Diary*).

doctor *n.* About 1303 *doctour* early teacher or father of the Christian Church, in Mannyng's *Handlyng Synne;* borrowed from Old French *doctour,* learned borrowing from Medieval Latin *doctor* religious teacher, adviser, scholar, from Latin *doctor* (genitive *doctōris*) teacher, from *doct-,* stem of *docēre* to show, teach; originally, make to appear right, causative form of *decēre* be seemly, fitting, DECENT; for suffix see -OR[2]. The meanings of a person having the highest degree from a university and doctor of medicine are first recorded in English probably before 1378, in a version of *Piers Plowman.* —v. 1599, to confer a degree on; later to treat as a doctor (1712, in American English); from the noun. The sense of alter the appearance, disguise, or falsify is first recorded in 1774. —**doctorate** *n.* degree of doctor of philosophy. 1676, borrowed from Medieval Latin *doctoratus,* from *doctorare* take a doctor's degree; from *doctor,* n. Although *doctorat* is recorded in French by 1575, English use of the term is confined to the academic, which supports a direct borrowing from the Latin.

doctrine *n.* About 1380, teaching or offering advice, in Chaucer's translation of Boethius' *De Consolatione Philosophiae;* later, theories, principles, dogma (about 1384, in the Wycliffe Bible); borrowed from Old French *doctrine,* learned borrowing from Latin *doctrīna,* and directly from Latin *doctrīna* teaching, body of teachings, learning, from *doctor* teacher; see DOCTOR. —**doctrinaire** *n.* 1820, a member of a French political party whose doctrines were deemed impractical; borrowing of French *doctrinaire,* from *doctrine* doctrine; for suffix see -ARY. The meaning of an impractical theorist is first recorded in English in 1831. —*adj.* 1834, borrowed from French *doctrinaire* referring to the French political party. The meaning of impractical or stubbornly theoretical, is first recorded in English in 1873. —**doctrinal** *adj.* About 1449, possibly through Middle French *doctrinal,* but more likely borrowed directly from Late Latin *doctrīnālis* theoretical, from Latin *doctrīna;* see DOCTRINE; for suffix see -AL[1].

document *n.* Probably before 1425, teaching or instruction; borrowed from Middle French *document* lesson or written evidence, from Latin *documentum* example, proof, lesson, (in Medieval Latin, official written instrument, from *docēre* to show, teach; see DOCTOR); for suffix see -MENT. The meaning of something written which gives information or evidence of some fact, is first recorded in English in 1727. —**v.** 1648, to teach; from the noun. The meaning to prove by means of documents is first recorded in English in 1711; curiously, before the noun meaning. —**documentary** *adj.* 1802-12, in Jeremy Bentham's writings, formed from *document* + *-ary.* The adjective and noun senses of a motion picture, drama, etc., based on facts or actual events are first recorded in English in 1930-32; probably borrowed from French *film documentaire* (1924) and *documentaire,* n. (1929). —**documentation** *n.* 1754, formed from English *document,* v. + *-ation,* perhaps modeled on Medieval Latin *documentationem* (nominative *documentatio*) a reminding, from *documentum;* see DOCUMENT.

dodder *v.* 1617, shake, totter, a variant of parallel formation of earlier *dadder* (1500's), developed from Middle English *daderen* (about 1353), apparently a frequentative form similar to *patter, totter,* etc. The origin of the Middle English stem *dad-* is obscure.

dodge *v.* 1568, move so as to avoid; of uncertain origin, perhaps related to Scottish dialectal *dodd* to jog; as *sled* is related to *sledge.* —**n.** 1575, from the verb. —**dodger** *n.* 1568, apparently from *dodge,* v. + *-er*[1].

dodo (dō′dō), *n.* large bird, now extinct. 1628, borrowed from Portuguese *doudo,* literally, a fool or simpleton, and as an adjective, foolish or silly, the name being applied to the awkward appearance of the bird. Portuguese *doudo* is said to have been borrowed from Middle English *dold* foolish, stupid, variant of *dolt,* both of them being participles of the verb to DULL.

doe *n.* Before 1200 *do* the fallow deer; later the female of the fallow deer (about 1300), and any deer (probably about 1380); developed from Old English *dā* (about 1000, in Ælfric's *Glossary*); cognate with German dialect (Alemannic) *tē* doe, of unknown origin . The meaning of a female rabbit or other animal is first recorded in English in 1607. —**doeskin** *n.* (1425-26)

doff *v.* Before 1375 *doffen* (imperative *dof*) take off; remove; contraction of *do off.* Compare DON[2] put on.

dog *n.* Probably before 1200 *dogge,* in *Ancrene Riwle;* developed from Old English *docga* (about 1050), specifically the name of a powerful breed of dog. *Docga* was apparently an English word which the Continental languages borrowed (often with the attributive *English*), and is found in French *dogue* mastiff, Spanish *dogo* terrier, Dutch *dog* mastiff, German *Dogge* Great Dane. In Old English, the nonspecific name for this dog was *hund* HOUND. Of Old English *docga* no further connections are known. —v. 1519, to pursue, track, follow like a dog; from the noun. —**dogfight** *n.* Middle English *dogg feghttyng* (probably before 1500). —**dogfish** *n.* About 1450 *dogge fysch.* —**dogged** *adj.* (about 1300) —**doggerel** *n.* (1277); *adj.* About 1390, in Chaucer's *Canterbury Tales.* —**doghouse** *n.* (1611) —**dog sled** (1806-08, American English) —**dog tag** (1918) —**dogtrot** *n.* (before 1450) —**dogwood** *n.* (1617)

doge (dōj) *n.* chief magistrate of the former republics of Genoa or Venice. 1549, an Italian word used in a history of Italy, from dialectal (Venetian) *dose, doxe,* from Latin *ducem* (nominative *dux*) leader; see the doublet DUKE.

dogma *n.* 1638, authoritative opinion, doctrine; used earlier in the plural form *dogmata* (before 1600, in Richard Hooker's *Ecclesiastical Polity*); borrowed, probably by influence of Middle French *dogme,* from Latin *dogma* philosophical tenet, from Greek *dógma* (genitive *dógmatos*) opinion, tenet, from *dokeîn* to seem good, think; see DECENT. **—dogmatic** *adj.* 1678; earlier *dogmatical* (1604); borrowed probably through French *dogmatique,* from Latin *dogmaticus,* from Greek *dogmatikós,* from *dógma* (genitive *dógmatos*) opinion; for suffix see -IC. It is also possible that *dogmatic* was a shortening of earlier English *dogmatical.* **—dogmatism** *n.* 1603, borrowed from French *dogmatisme* teaching of new doctrine, from Medieval Latin *dogmatismus,* modeled after Late Greek *dogmatismós;* from *dógma* (genitive *dógmatos*); for suffix see -ISM.

doily *n.* 1785-95, small ornamental mat, from *doiley-napkin* (1711, in Swift's *Journal to Stella*), from *doily* a thin woolen fabric (1678, in Dryden's *The Kind Keeper*), supposedly from *Doiley* surname of a dry goods dealer in London in the 1600's.

dojo (dō'jō) *n.* place where judo, karate, and other martial arts are practiced. Probably before 1942, borrowed from Japanese *dōjō* (*dō* art + *-jō* ground, ring).

doldrums *n.pl.* dullness, low spirits. 1811, perhaps formed from earlier *dold* dull, foolish, inactive because of age, cold, etc. (before 1460; earlier *dulled,* about 1390, past participle of *dullen, dollen,* v., developed from Old English *dol* foolish, DULL), and the ending *-rum,* perhaps patterned on *tantrum.*

dole[1] *n.* portion of money or food given in charity. About 1200 *dol* part allotted, developed from Old English (before 1000) *dāl,* shortened from *gedāl* (about 725, in *Genesis A*). Old English *dāl* is cognate with Old Frisian and Old Saxon *dēl,* Middle Dutch *deil* (modern Dutch *deel*), Old High German *teil* (modern German *Teil*), Gothic *dails* (Proto-Germanic **dailaz),* modern English DEAL, Old English *dǣl* portion, division, is a parallel umlaut form from **dailiz* in Proto-Germanic. —v. give out alms, charity. 1465, from the noun.

dole[2] *n.* sorrow, grief. About 1225 *dol,* borrowed from Old French *doel, duel,* from Late Latin *dolus* grief, from Latin *dolēre* suffer, grieve; see DOLOR. **—doleful** *adj.* mournful, sorrowful. Probably before 1300 *diolful,* in Layamon's *Chronicle of Britain;* developed from *diol, dol* dole + *-ful* full.

doll *n.* Before 1700, a child's toy baby, a particular application of earlier *doll,* a name of affection for a person, a female pet or a mistress (1560); originally a shortened nickname or endearing form of the name *Dorothy* (as the *l* in *Hal* is a replacement of *r* in Harold, the *l* in *Moll* for the *r* in Mary). **—v.** dress up in a stylish or showy way. 1906 *doll up,* from the noun. **—dollhouse** *n.* 1873, in American English; earlier *doll's house* (1783). **—dolly** *n.* 1790, a name of affection for a child's doll; earlier, a name of affection for *Dorothy* (1610, in Ben Jonson's *The Alchemist*).

dollar *n.* 1553, use in correspondence of Low German *daler,* name for the German *Taler, Joachimstaler,* a coin of the 1500's made of silver from a mine in *Joachimstal* St. Joachim's valley (town in northwestern Bohemia, where this coin was minted beginning in 1519). By 1581 use of *dollar* was recorded in English for the Spanish peso or piece of eight, a coin commonly found in North America at the time of the Revolutionary War. At the suggestion of Jefferson (1782) the Continental Congress established the dollar as the currency of the United States in 1785.

dollop *n.* 1812, dash or splash of something; portion or serving of food; from earlier *dallop* patch, tuft, or clump of grass (1573); of uncertain origin.

dolmen *n.* prehistoric tomb. 1859, borrowed from French *dolmen,* probably a misapplication by Latour d'Auvergne (1790's) and later French archaeologists of Cornish *tolmen* hole of stone (compare Welsh *twll* hole, *maen* stone), from Indo-European **tu-k-slo-* hole (root **(s)teu-*), Pok.1032; **meĝ-* great, Pok. 709.

The initial variation *d-/t-* may be the result of the gradual lessening of the force with which the *t-* was articulated in Celtic leading to the change to *d-.*

dolorous *adj.* Probably before 1400, causing pain, suffering, or hardship, in Chaucer's translation of *Roman de la Rose;* later, sorrowful (about 1450); borrowed from Old French *doloros,* from Late Latin *dolōrōsus,* from Latin *dolor* pain, grief; for suffix see -OUS. **—dolor** *n.* sorrow, grief. Probably before 1300 *dolour,* borrowed from Old French *dolour,* from Latin *dolōrem* (nominative *dolor*) pain, grief, from *dolēre* suffer pain or grief, lament, related to *dolāre* hew, chop; cognate with Sanskrit *dálati* bursts, from Indo-European **del-/dol-* split, cut (Pok. 194).

dolphin *n.* About 1350 *dolfin* sea mammal; borrowed from Old French *daulphin, dalphin, daufin,* through Medieval Latin *dalfinus,* for Latin *delphinus* dolphin, from Greek *delphís* (genitive *delphînos*) dolphin; so called because in the view of the Greeks its body looked like a womb, Greek *delphýs,* cognate with Sanskrit *gárbha-s* womb, fetus, from Indo-European **gwelbh-/gwolbh-* (Pok. 473). Compare DAUPHIN.

dolt *n.* 1551, stupid person (implied in earlier *doltish,* 1543); apparently a variant of *dold* dull, foolish, and perhaps influenced by *dulte, dolte,* past participle forms of *dullen,* v. to dull, make or become dazed or stupid; see DOLDRUMS.

-dom, a suffix forming abstract and collective nouns. **1** added to *adjectives* to show state or condition, as in *freedom = state or condition of being free; wisdom = condition of being wise or smart.* **2** added to *nouns* to show **a** position, rank, or realm of, as in *earldom = rank or realm of an earl; kingdom = realm of a king.* **b** all of those who are, as in *Christendom = all those who are Christian.* In Old English *-dōm* is related to *dōm* judgment, DOOM, and cognate with Old Saxon *-dōm* -dom, Old High German *-tuom* (modern German *-tum*), and Old Icelandic *-dōmr.*

domain *n.* territory, estate, dominion. About 1425 (Scottish), landed property, demesne; borrowed from Middle French *domaine* (a spelling alteration after Medieval Latin *dominium*), from Old French *demaine, demeine,* learned borrowing from Latin *dominium* right of ownership, property, dominion, from *dominus* lord, master, owner, from *domus* house; see DOME. Doublet of DEMESNE and DOMINION.

The spelling *domain* replaced earlier *demeine* (recorded probably before 1300) to restore the Latin form.

dome *n.* 1656, rounded roof, in Blount's *Glossographia,* borrowed from French *dôme,* from Provençal *doma,* from Greek *dôma* house, housetop (a type of roof that came from the East), related to *dómos* house. The various forms of *dome* are cognate with Latin *domus,* Old

Slavic *domŭ,* and Sanskrit *dáma-s,* all meaning house, and with Old English *timber* building, TIMBER.

An earlier and completely distinct English use of *dome* house, home, building, was borrowed directly from Latin *domus* and is first recorded in 1513. A later and equally distinct use meaning a cathedral church (1691) came into English from French *dôme,* which borrowed the word from Italian *duomo,* also from Latin *domus* house.

domestic *adj.* Probably before 1425, made or prepared in the home; borrowed from Middle French *domestique,* learned borrowing from Latin *domesticus* belonging to the household, and directly from Latin *domesticus,* from *domus* house, see DOME; for suffix see -IC. Latin *domesticus* was presumably formed by extension from a lost adjective **domestis,* under the influence of forms such as *rūsticus* rustic; compare *agrestis* rural.

The meaning of or belonging to one's own country, not foreign, is first recorded in 1545, and the meaning of the home or household appears in Shakespeare's *Cymbeline* (1611).
—n. 1539, member of household; later, domestic servant (1613, in Shakespeare's *Henry VIII*), either from the English adjective or borrowed from Middle French *domestique,* adj. and n.
—domesticate *v.* Before 1639, from *domestic,* adj. + *-ate*[1]; possibly influenced by French *domestiquer* live in a family, domesticate, from *domestique,* adj.
—domesticity *n.* 1721, borrowed from French *domesticité,* from *domestique* domestic; for suffix see -ITY.

domicile *n.* 1442 *domicylie* residence, dwelling; borrowed from Middle French *domicile,* learned borrowing from Latin *domicilium,* and directly from Latin *domicilium,* probably from earlier **domo-colyom* house-dwelling (*domus* house + *colere* dwell); see DOME.

domination *n.* About 1375, rule, control, in Chaucer's *Canterbury Tales;* earlier, an angel of the fourth order (probably about 1343); borrowed from Old French *domination,* from Latin *dominātiōnem* (nominative *dominātiō*), from *dominārī* to rule, have dominion over, from *dominus* lord, master, from *domus* home; see DOME; for suffix see -TION. **— dominant** *adj.* Before 1460 *domynaunt,* borrowed from Middle French *dominant,* from Latin *dominantem* (nominative *dominplaces*), present participle of *dominārī*; for suffix see -ANT.
—dominate *v.* 1611, back formation from English *domination;* or borrowed from Latin *dominātus,* past participle of *dominārī* to rule, possibly influenced by Middle French *dominer* dominate.

domineer *v.* 1588, rule or govern arbitrarily, tyrannize, in Shakespeare's *Love's Labour's Lost,* borrowed apparently from Dutch *domineren* to rule, have domination, from Middle French *dominer,* learned borrowing from Latin *dominārī* to rule, DOMINATE. **—domineering** *adj.* (1588)

dominion *n.* Probably before 1425, borrowed from Middle French *dominion,* from Medieval Latin *dominionem* (nominative *dominio*), from Latin *dominium* ownership; for suffix see -ION. Doublet of DOMAIN.

domino[1] *n.* 1694, a hood worn by canons or priests with a cloak, also a mourning veil worn by women; later, cloak with a small mask, worn at masquerades (1730, in Bailey's *Dictionarium Britannicum*), borrowed from French *domino,* apparently from Latin *dominō,* dative form of *dominus* lord, master (see DOMINATE). It is conjectured that the priest's cloak was called, perhaps in jest, a *domino* in French by association with priestly use of such standard phrases as *benedīcāmus Dominō* let us praise the Lord.

domino[2] *n.* Usually **dominoes.** game played with flat, oblong tiles marked with dots. 1801, borrowed from French *domino* (1771), probably an extended sense of *domino*[1] cloak with a small mask (in allusion to the black-colored back of the tiles that resemble the cloak, *or* from resemblance of the white dots on the playing pieces to the masks worn at a masquerade).

A traditional etymology (no longer generally accepted) traces *domino* in French to Latin *dominus* master, in reference to the winner in the game. In Italian, *domino,* as the name of the game, was borrowed from French in 1830.

don[1] *n.* Spanish title of respect for a man. 1523 *Don* (prefixed to a man's Christian name), from Spanish *don,* from Latin *dominus* lord, master; see DOMINATE. The word was later used in the sense of a Spanish gentleman (1610, in Ben Jonson's *The Alchemist*), a meaning extended to any distinguished man (before 1634). From 1660, in English universities, a *don* is the head, fellow, or tutor of a college. The slang sense of a head of an underworld syndicate appears in general use in American English before 1963, as a borrowing of Italian *don,* a title of respect for a man, shortened form of earlier *donno* master, from Late Latin *domnus,* from Latin *dominus* lord, master.

don[2] *v.* put on (clothing, etc.). Probably before 1350, contraction of *do on.* Compare DOFF (from *do off*).

donation *n.* About 1425 (Scottish), borrowed through Middle French *donation* from Latin *dōnātiōnem* (nominative *dōnātio*), from *dōnāre* give as a gift, from *dōnum* gift, related to *dare* to give; see DATE[1] time; for suffix see -TION. **—donate** *v.* 1785, American English, back formation from *donation.*

donjon (dun′jən) *n.* Before 1325 *dunjon* large tower of a castle, in *Cursor Mundi;* an early form of DUNGEON.

Don Juan (don wän′) libertine, rake. 1854, in Thackeray's *The Newcomes,* in allusion to *Don Juan,* name of a legendary Spanish nobleman famous for his many love affairs, popularized by Tirso de Molina, Spanish dramatist (1571-1648), in *El Burlador de Sevilla* The Seville Deceiver, Molière's play *Don Juan ou le Festin de Pierre* (1665), Mozart's opera *Don Giovanni* (1787), and, more immediately perhaps by Lord Byron (1788-1824), in his unfinished epic poem *Don Juan,* though this latter is pronounced don jü′ən.

donkey *n.* 1785, of uncertain slang origin, perhaps from English DUN[2] dull grayish-brown + *-key,* a probable diminutive form, possibly parallel to *monkey;* or perhaps a nickname for *Duncan,* a man's name, from Gaelic, brown head (*cen* head).

Donnybrook or **donnybrook** *n.* 1852, scene of uproar and disorder or great commotion; in allusion to *Donnybrook,* the name of a suburb of Dublin, Ireland, once famous for its annual fair, suppressed in 1855 for its wild brawls.

donor *n.* About 1439 *donour,* borrowed from Anglo-French *donour,* in Old French *doneur,* from Latin *dōnātōrem* (accusative of *dōnātor*), from *dōnāre* give as a gift; see DONATION; for suffix see -OR[2].

don't *contraction.* do not (1670). **—n.** a prohibition (1894).

doodad *n.* 1905, trinket or gadget; American English, originally dialectal use, of uncertain origin.

doodle[1] *n.* 1937, aimless scrawl, apparently from dialectal English *doodle, dudle* fritter away time, trifle, or from association with *dawdle.* **—v.** 1937, from the noun. **—doodler** *n.* (1937)

doodle[2] *n.* a silly or foolish person. 1628, of uncertain origin; compare Low German *Dudeltopf* simpleton.

doom *n.* Before 1325 *dome,* in *Cursor Mundi,* developed from Old English (about 725) *dōm* law, judgment, trial, sentence, condemnation; cognate with Old Frisian and Old Saxon *dōm* statute, law, judgment, Old High German *tuom,* Old Icelandic *dōmr* judgment, decree (Swedish and Danish *dom*), and Gothic *dōms* honor, fame, decree, from Proto-Germanic **dōmaz;* also cognate with Greek *thōmós* heap, and Sanskrit *dhā́man* site, dwelling place, domain, rule. All of the various forms of *doom* are from an Indo-European base **dhē-/*dhō-/dhə-* (Pok. 235) meaning that which is put or set up, statute, ordinance.

The extended meaning of final fate, destruction, ruin, death is first recorded in English about 1600, in Shakespeare's *Sonnets.*

—v. 1382 *domen* pronounce judgment on, from the noun.

—doomsday *n.* Before 1200 *domes dai,* developed from Old English (about 975) *dōmes dæg* judgment day, from *dōmes* (genitive of *dōm* judgment) + *dæg* DAY.

door *n.* Probably before 1200 *dore,* in Layamon's *Chronicle of Britain;* earlier *dure* (about 1150). Middle English *dore* developed from Old English (about 1000) *dor* (pl. *doru*) large door, gate; Middle English *dure* developed from Old English *duru* (feminine) door (first recorded about 725, in *Beowulf*), from Proto-Germanic stem **dur-.* The Old English forms are cognate with Old Saxon *dor* gate, *duri,* pl., door, Old High German *tor* gate (modern German *Tor*), *turi,* pl., door (modern German *Tür*), Old Icelandic *dyrr* (feminine pl.) door, and Gothic *daúr* gate, from Proto-Germanic **duran;* and outside Germanic, cognate with Latin *forēs,* pl., door, Greek *thýrā* door, Old Irish *dorus,* Old Slavic *dvĭrĭ,* Lithuanian *dùrys* (nominative pl.), and Sanskrit *dvā́ras* (nominative pl.), *dúras* (accusative pl.) *dvā́rāu* (dual), from Indo-European **dhwōr-/dhwor-/dhur-* (Pok. 278). The numerous cognates of *door* in the plural suggest that doors consisted of two parts that slid or pivoted together. **—doorbell** *n.* (about 1815, in Jane Austen's *Persuasion*) **—doorknob** *n.* (1846, in American English) **—doorway** *n.* (1799, in Southey's works) **—dooryard** *n.* (about 1764, in American English)

dope *n.* 1807, American English, sauce, gravy, in Washington Irving's *Salmagundi;* borrowed from Dutch *doop* thick dipping sauce, from *dopen* to dip, from Old Saxon *dōpian,* cognate with Gothic *daupjan,* from Indo-European **dhoub-* (Pok. 267). The concept of thick consistency or thickness connects many of the senses of *dope,* as in thick liquid preparation (1800's), thickheaded or stupid person (1851), and preparation of opium, a thick, viscous substance when used for smoking (1889). In the 1890's the latter sense was extended to mean any stupefying narcotic drug, with the derivatives *dope fiend* (1896), *dope addict* (1933), and a preparation of drugs designed to influence a racehorse's performance (1900). Perhaps because the knowledge of which horse had been dosed with dope would be an advantage to a bettor, the sense of inside knowledge, tip, information developed by 1901, with *dope sheet* piece of paper with information about racehorses, first recorded in 1903, in George Ade's writings. **—v.** 1868, smear, lubricate, American English, from the noun. The sense of administer drugs to, is first recorded in 1889; the phrase *dope out* find out (1906, in O. Henry's writings), probably came from *dope,* n., inside information (which is then revealed).

dormant *adj.* About 1387-95 *dormaunt* fixed in place, in Chaucer's *Prologue* to the *Canterbury Tales;* later, inactive, sleeping (1623) and in a resting position (about 1500); borrowed from Old French *dormant,* present participle of *dormir* to sleep, from Latin *dormīre* to sleep. Latin *dormīre* (Indo-European **dr̥m-ī-*) is related most closely to Old Slavic *drěmati* to doze (Indo-European **drēm-*) much less closely to Greek *édrathon, édarthon* I slept, Armenian *tartam* slow, sleepy, and Sanskrit *drā́ti, drāyáte* he sleeps, from Indo-European **der-/dr-* and **drē-/drə-* (Pok. 226).

dormer *n.* 1592, window of a sleeping room; later, the sleeping room itself (1605); borrowed from Middle French *dormeor* sleeping room, formed from *dormir* to sleep, with *-eor* suffix from Latin *-ātōrem;* compare Old French *dresseur* dresser (piece of furniture). The sense of an upright window projecting from a sloping roof or the projecting part of a roof that contains such a window is first recorded, probably, in 1703.

dormitory *n.* 1440 *dormytorye,* borrowed, possibly by influence of Old French *dormitoire,* from Latin *dormitōrium,* from *dormīre* to sleep; see DORMANT; for suffix see -ORY.

dormouse *n.* About 1425 *dormowse,* possibly from Anglo-French **dormouse* tending to be dormant, mistaken as a blend of Middle French *dormir* to sleep (from Latin *dormīre*), and **-mouse* thought to be equivalent to Middle English *mowse* mouse; so called because this small rodent that looks somewhat like a squirrel is inactive through most of winter.

dorsal *adj.* Probably before 1425 *dorsale* back, rear, in an anonymous translation of Chauliac's *Grande Chirurgie;* borrowed through Middle French *dorsal* from Late Latin *dorsālis,* alteration of Latin *dorsuālis* of the back, from Latin *dorsum* back, of uncertain origin. The meaning in anatomy of situated on or towards the back (of an animal) is first recorded in *Chambers Cyclopaedia* (1727).

dory *n.* 1709, small boat, American English; of uncertain origin, compare Miskito (an Indian language of Honduras and Nicaragua) *dóri.*

dose *n.* Probably about 1425, in an anonymous translation of Chauliac's *Grande Chirurgie;* borrowed from Middle French *dose,* learned borrowing from Late Latin *dosis,* from Greek *dósis* a portion prescribed, literally, a giving, from *didónai* to give; see DATE. **—v.** 1654, from the noun, or borrowed from French *doser* (1558), from *dose,* n. **—dosage** *n.* 1867 *doseage, dosage,* formed from English *dose* + *-age,* possibly by influence of French *dosage* (1812), from *dose,* n.; for suffix see -AGE.

dossier (dos'ēā) *n.* 1880, collection of documents or papers about a subject, borrowed from French *dossier* bundle of papers, from *dos* back (said to be so called because the bundle of papers had a label on the back), from Latin *dossum,* a variant of *dorsum* back; see DORSAL.

dot *n.* Old English *dott* speck, head of a boil (about 1000); cognate with Old High German *tutta* nipple, Dutch *dot* knot, tuft, Norwegian *dott* wad, wisp, and Old Icelandic *dytta* to stop up. *Dot* is not found in Middle English documents; after Old English it is not recorded until 1530 with the meaning of a small lump or a clot. *Dot* with the meaning of a minute spot is first recorded in modern English in 1674, and with the sense of a tiny round mark, such as one makes with a pen, in 1748, though reference to this meaning is implied in the earlier usage *to a dot* meaning exactly (1728). **—v.** mark with a dot. 1740, from the noun.

dote *v.* Probably about 1200 *doten* behave foolishly; earlier, be feeble-minded (probably before 1200 *dotien* behave foolishly, in *Ancrene Riwle* and Layamon's *Chronicle of Britain*); borrowed probably from Middle Low German *doten* be foolish, related to Middle Dutch *doten* be childish, of unknown origin. The meaning of be foolishly fond of, as in *dote upon,* is first recorded in 1477. **—dotage** *n.* Probably about 1380, folly, foolish behavior; formed from Middle English *doten* to behave foolishly + *-age.* The sense of senility or a second childhood is first recorded in Chaucer's *Canterbury Tales* (about 1390). **—dotard** *n.* foolish or senile person. About 1390, in Chaucer's *Canterbury Tales;* formed from Middle English *doten* to dote + *-ard.* **—dotty** *adj.* 1402 *doty* (in *dotypolle* fool, simpleton); apparently formed from *dote* + *-y* [1]. The spelling *dotty,* with the meaning of silly, is first recorded in 1870.

double *adj.* Probably before 1200 *duble* twice, twofold, in *Ancrene Riwle;* borrowed from Old French *duble, doble,* from Latin *duplus* twofold (*du-,* from *duo* TWO + *-plus* -FOLD). Doublet of DUPLE. **—v.** Probably before 1300 *dublen* make double, in *Arthour and Merlin;* borrowed from Old French *dobler, doubler,* from Latin *duplāre* to double, fold up, from *duplus* double. **—n.** Before 1325, in *Cursor Mundi,* from the adjective; the noun meaning of a fold or a sharp turn was taken from the verb. **—double bed** (1798, in Jane Austen's letters) **—double cross** act of treachery (1834); **double-cross,** *v.* (1903, in American English) **—double-header** *n.* (1896, in American English) **—double-park** *v.* (1931, in American English) **—double play** (1867, in American English) **—double-take** *n.* (1938, in American English) **—doubletalk** *n.* (1938, in American English); *v.* 1952, in C. Day Lewis' writings.

double-entendre (dübläNtäN′drə) *n.* 1673, word or expression with two meanings, one of which is often indelicate, in Dryden's *Marriage-à-la-Mode;* borrowing of French *double entendre* (obsolete variant of *double entente* double meaning, ambiguity); and *entendre,* noun use of *entendre* to mean, understand, from Latin *intendere* INTEND.

doublet *n.* 1326, close-fitting garment; borrowed from Old French *doublet,* literally, something folded or doubled, from *double, doble* DOUBLE + *-et* (diminutive suffix).

The linguistic sense of two or more different words which ultimately derive from the same language source (as *aptitude* and *attitude, fragile* and *frail*) is first recorded in English in 1869, probably borrowed from the French usage (1864).

doubloon *n.* 1622 *doblon* Spanish gold coin, borrowed from Spanish *doblón;* 1719 *doubloon,* in Defoe's *Robinson Crusoe,* borrowed from French *doublon* (1594), also from Spanish *doblón,* an augmentative form of *doble* double, from Latin *duplus* double; for suffix see -OON.

The *doubloon* was so called because its worth was double the value of a *pistole,* another Spanish gold coin.

doubt *v.* Probably before 1200 *duten,* in *Ancrene Riwle;* later *douten* be afraid of, dread (probably about 1280); borrowed from Old French *douter* doubt, fear, from Latin *dubitāre* hesitate, waver in opinion, related to *dubius* doubtful, DUBIOUS. The *b* was regularly introduced in the spelling *doute* in imitation of the Latin forms as early as 1513 in Sir Thomas More's writings, though it is occasionally recorded earlier, as in Gower's *Confessio Amantis* (1393).

—n. Probably before 1200 *dute,* in *Ancrene Riwle;* later *doute* (about 1300); borrowed from Old French *doute,* from *douter* to doubt. The spelling *doubte* is occasionally recorded, probably before 1425, in imitation of the Latin.

—doubtful *adj.* About 1395 *douteful,* in the Wycliffe Bible, formed from Middle English *doute* doubt + *-ful.*

—doubtless *adj.* About 1380 *douteles,* in Chaucer's translation of Boethius' *De Consolatione Philosophiae,* formed from Middle English *doute* doubt + *-les* -less.

douche (düsh) n. jet of water applied to any part of the body. 1766, borrowed from French *douche,* from Italian *doccia* shower, conduit, from *docciare* to spray, make jet forth, probably from *doccione* conduit, from Latin *ductiōnem* (nominative *ductiō*) a leading, from *duc-,* stem of *dūcere* to lead; see TOW[1] pull. **—v.** administer a douche. 1838, probably borrowed from French *doucher,* from *douche,* n., or from the English noun.

dough *n.* About 1150 *doh* dough for bread or pastry; later *dogh,* 1303, in Mannyng's *Handlyng Synne;* developed from Old English (about 1000) *dāg.* Old English *dāg* is cognate with Middle Low German *dēch* dough, Middle Dutch *deech* (modern Dutch *deeg*), Old High German *teic* (modern German *Teig*), Old Icelandic *deig* (Swedish *deg,* Danish *dej*), and Gothic *daigs* dough, from Proto-Germanic **daiȝaz,* which is cognate with Greek *toîchos, teîchos* wall (originally of mud), Oscan *feíhúss* (accusative plural) walls, Armenian *dēz* heap, and Sanskrit *deha-s* body; all from the Indo-European base **dheiĝh-/dhoiĝh-* (Pok. 244), meaning to knead dough or work clay.

Though the spelling with *g* appeared by the 1300's, *dow* was a common spelling up to the late 1500's when the modern spelling is first recorded in 1596, in Shakespeare's *The Taming of the Shrew.*

The slang meaning of money is first recorded in American English in 1851.

—doughnut *n.* 1809, American English, in Washington Irving's *Knickerbocker's History of New York.*

doughty (dou′tē) *adj.* Probably before 1200 *duhti* brave, strong, in Layamon's *Chronicle of Britain;* later *douhti* (probably before 1300); developed from Old English (1030) *dohtig* and *dyhtig* able, strong, valiant (about 725, in *Beowulf*). The later *dohtig* is probably an alteration (influenced by *dohte,* past tense of *dugan* be worthy) of earlier *dyhtig,* cognate with Middle Low German and Middle Dutch *duchtich* doughty (modern Dutch *duchtig*), Middle High German *tuhtec* able, useful (modern German *tüchtig* capable), from Proto-Germanic **duHtiȝás,* adjective to the noun **duHtiz* (Old High German *tuht* ability, strength). Further cognates are found in Old High German *tugan* be worthy, Old

Icelandic *duga* to avail, help, Gothic *dugan* be worthy, and possibly Greek *teúchein* make, produce, *tynchánein* reach a goal, succeed, from Indo-European **dheugh-/dhugh-* touch, meet with, succeed (Pok. 271).

The spelling with *g* began to appear in the 1300's and was generally established by the 1600's.

dour *adj.* Before 1350 (in northern dialect) severe; later, 1375 (Scottish), in John Barbour's *The Bruce,* stern, fierce; possibly borrowed from Latin *dūrus* hard; related to ENDURE. *Dour* meaning stubborn, gloomy, sullen, is first recorded in English about 1470.

douse *v.* 1600, to plunge in water; 1606, to throw water over; perhaps from an earlier verb *douse* to strike, punch (1559). The word is probably related to Middle Dutch *dossen* or early modern Dutch *doessen* beat with force and noise.

dove *n.* Probably before 1200 *duve* (also in the place name *Duvebrigge,* 1150); probably developed from Old English *dūfe-,* in *dūfe-doppa* dabchick, a water bird; cognate with Old Saxon *dūƀa* dove, Middle Dutch *dūve* (modern Dutch *duif*), Old High German *tūba* (modern German *Taube* dove, pigeon), Old Icelandic *dūfa* (Swedish *duva,* Danish *due*), and Gothic *-dūbō* (in *hraiwa-dūbō* turtledove), from Proto-Germanic **dūƀōn,* from Indo-European **dheubh-/dhūbh-* dark, (Pok. 264). **—dovecote** *n.* (1200) **—dovetail** *n.* 1565-73, a joint in carpentry. —*v.* 1657, to fit together.

dowager *n.* widow who holds title or property from her husband. 1530 *douagier,* in letters of Palsgrave, later *dowager* (1542); borrowed from Middle French *douagere, douagiere,* from *douage* dower, from *douer* endow, from Latin *dōtāre,* from *dōs* (genitive *dōtis*) DOWRY; for suffix see -ER[1]. The meaning of an elderly, dignified lady is first recorded in English in Dickens' *The Mystery of Edwin Drood* (1870).

dowdy *n.* poorly dressed woman. 1581, probably a diminutive form of earlier *doue* poorly dressed woman (about 1338); of uncertain origin. **—adj.** poorly dressed, shabby. 1676, from the noun.

dowel *n.* 1296-97 *dule* rim of a wheel or a section of it, later *doule* (1313-14); of uncertain origin, but perhaps connected with Middle Low German *dovel* plug, tap (of a cask), related to Old High German *tubili* plug (modern German *Döbel, Dübel* peg, plug, dowel), cognate with Greek *týphoi* wedges, from Indo-European **dhubh-* (Pok. 268). The meaning of a headless peg, pin, or bolt of wood is first recorded in English in 1794.

down[1] *adv.* to a lower place. Before 1275 *doun,* developed from an Old English word element *-dūne-* (before 830), as in *ofdūne,* adv., downwards, *ic dūnestīgu* I go down; from *dūne,* dative form of *dūn* hill, DOWN[3]. **—prep.** Before 1382, in the Wycliffe Bible; from the adverb. **—v.** 1562, from the adverb. **—adj.** About 1565, from the adverb. The meaning of depressing is first recorded about 1967. **—n.** 1611, used with an indeterminate meaning as a word to fill out a ballad refrain; later, a descent (1710); from an earlier such use as an adverb (1598, in Shakespeare's *Merry Wives of Windsor*). **—downcast** *adj.* (about 1303, in Mannyng's *Handlyng Synne*) **—downer** *n.* depressant drug. (1968, American English) **—downfall** *n.* (about 1325, in *Cursor Mundi*) **—downhearted** *adj.* (before 1774, in Goldsmith's writings) **—downhill** *adv.* (before 1398); *adj.* (1727, Pope et al. in *The Art of Sinking*) **—downpour** *n.* (1811, earlier *dounshedyng,* probably before 1425) **—downright** *adv.* (probably before 1200); *adj.* (1530) **—downstairs** *adv.* (1597, in Shakespeare's *2 Henry IV*); *adj.* (1819) **—downward** *adv.* (probably before 1200, developed from Old English *adūnweard*); *adj.* (before 1325, in *Cursor Mundi*). **—downwards** *adv.* (probably about 1200)

down[2] *n.* 1345-49 *doune* soft feathers or hair; from a Scandinavian source (compare Old Icelandic *dūnn* down, related to Old Icelandic *dȳja* to shake); cognate with Greek *thȳein* to rage, storm, *thȳnein* to rush, flit, and Sanskrit *dhūnóti* he shakes, moves, from Indo-European **dhewə-dhū-* (Pok. 261).

down[3] *n.* rolling, grassy land. About 1300 *doune* hill, in Layamon's *Chronicle of Britain* (earlier 1254, in surname); developed from Old English *dūn* hill (661, in the *Anglo-Saxon Chronicle*), cognate with Old Irish *dūn* citadel, fortress, Old Welsh *din* fortress, hill fort), from Indo-European **dhūno-* (Pok. 263). English *town* (Old English *tūn* fort, enclosure, town, with *t* for Celtic *d*) and related words are based on very early borrowing from this Celtic group.

In other Germanic languages Old English *dūn* is cognate with a group of words whose meaning is restricted to dune or sandbank, including Old Frisian *dūne,* Old Saxon *dūna,* Middle Dutch *dūnen* (modern Dutch *duin*), Middle Low German *dūne,* and Old Icelandic *dūnn* DOWN[2]. Doublet of DUNE.

dowry *n.* Before 1338 *dowarye* widow's share of her husband's property, in Mannyng's *Chronicle of England;* later, *dowarie* property a bride brings to her marriage (before 1387, in Trevisa's translation of Higden's *Polychronicon*); borrowed from Anglo-French *dowarie,* Old French *douaire,* from Medieval Latin *dotarium,* from Latin *dōs* (genitive *dōtis*) dowry, related to *dōnum* a giving, gift; see DONATION; for suffix see -RY. **—dower** *n.* Before 1387, widow's share of her husband's property, and property a bride brings to her marriage, in Trevisa's translation of Higden's *Polychronicon;* borrowed from Old French *douaire,* see DOWRY. The original distinction in meaning, if there was one intended, was soon lost, and is only recently maintained in English.

dowse *v.* use a divining rod to locate water, etc., underground. 1691 *deusing rod,* in Locke's correspondence; later *dowse* (1838), of uncertain origin; perhaps a dialect term, possibly from south England.

doxology (doksol'əjē) *n.* hymn or statement praising God. 1649, borrowed through French *doxologie,* or directly from Medieval Latin *doxologia,* from Greek *doxologíā,* from *doxológos* praising, glorifying, from *dóxa* glory, praise, from *dokeîn* to seem good, seem, think; see DECENT; for suffix see -LOGY.

doyen (doi'en) *n.* 1422, leader of ten; borrowed from Middle French *doyen,* from Old French *deien;* see the doublet DEAN. The modern meaning of the senior member of a group is first recorded in 1670 and may have been a reborrowing from French. **—doyenne** (doi'en) *n.* 1905, female doyen, borrowed from French *doyenne* (feminine of *doyen*), from Middle French, from Old French *deien.*

doze *v.* sleep lightly. 1693; earlier, make drowsy, stupefy, bewilder (1647); probably borrowed from a Scandinavian source (compare Old Icelandic *dūsa* be quiet doze, also Middle High German *dōsen* be quiet, slumber, *dœsen* to scatter); see DIZZY. **—n.** 1731, from the verb.

dozen *n.* Probably before 1300 *doseyn* group of twelve, in *Kyng Alisaunder;* borrowed from Old French *dozeine, dozaine* a dozen, twelve (*douze, doze* twelve + *-ain,* from Latin *-ānus*). Old French *douze* (pronounced düdzə) is from Latin *duodecim,* altered from earlier *duodicem* by influence of *decem,* (*duo* TWO + *decem* TEN).

drab *adj.* colorless, dull. 1775, dull brown; earlier *drab-colour'd* (1768), and *drapp-colour* (1686), the color of *drap* or *drab* cloth (1541); borrowed from Middle French *drap,* from Old French; see DRAPE. The figurative sense of colorlessness is first recorded in English in 1880.

drachma (drak'mə) *n.* **1** principal silver coin of the ancient Greeks. 1579-80, in Thomas North's translation of Plutarch's *Lives.* **2** a small ancient Greek weight, 1527. Both senses in modern English were borrowed from Latin *drachma,* from Greek *drachmḗ* and both replaced earlier *dragme:* 1) the ancient coin, about 1384, in the Wycliffe Bible; 2) the ancient weight, before 1398, in Trevisa's translation of Bartholomew's *De Proprietatibus Rerum.* Middle English *dragme* was borrowed through Old French *dragme* and Anglo-Latin *dragma, drama,* from Latin *drachma,* from Greek *drachmḗ,* literally, handful (of six obols), from (Ionic) *drássesthai* to grasp, cognate with Armenian *trç-ak* bundle of twigs, from Indo-European **dergh-/dorgh-/dr̥gh-* (Pok. 212). Doublet of DRAM.

draft *n.* 1552, possibly 1543, a privy; later, extract of distillation (1576), and plan, sketch (1579); spelling variant of earlier *draught* from *drahte* (probably before 1200, in Layamon's *Chronicle of Britain*); developed probably from Old English **dreaht, *dræht* (compare Old English *dragan,* v., to DRAW, and the cognates, Old High German *traht* a carrying, Old Icelandic *drāttr* a pulling, a drawing, and Middle Dutch *dracht,* from Proto-Germanic **draHtiz*). The meaning of the action of pulling is first recorded probably before 1200 in reference to drawing in of nets for fishing or catching birds. The sense of the act of drinking in one swallow is also first recorded probably before 1200. Later meanings include a rough copy of a writing (before 1382) and the flow of a current of air (1768-74). —**v.** 1714, select for some special purpose; from the noun. The sense of writing a rough copy of a letter, etc., is first recorded in 1828. —**draftee** *n.* military conscript. 1866, American English, formed from English *draft* + *-ee.*

The form *draft* is a spelling reflecting the shift in pronunciation of *gh* (like the *ch* in Scottish *loch*) to the modern English sound represented by *f* in *fat.* See the note under LAUGH, v.

drag *v.* 1440 *draggen* draw or pull, in *Promptorium Parvulorum;* borrowed from a Scandinavian source (compare Old Icelandic *draga*) or perhaps a dialectal variant of *drawen* (Old English *dragan*) to DRAW. —**n.** 1339-40, heavy harrow; earlier, a dragnet (1300-01); borrowed from a Scandinavian source (compare Swedish *dragg* grapnel, Icelandic *drag-net* dragnet), or perhaps developed from Old English (about 1000) *dræge* dragnet; related to *dragan* DRAW. The slang sense of an annoying, boring person or thing, is first recorded in 1813, probably an extension of the earlier meaning of something heavy or unmoving acting as an impediment (1708). —**dragnet** *n.* Old English *dræg-net,* about 1000 in Ælfric's *Glossary* (*dræge* drag, dragnet, related to *dragan* DRAW + *net*).

draggle *v.* 1513, make or become wet or dirty, as by dragging through mud or water; apparently a frequentative form of DRAG; for suffix see -LE[3]. The meaning of lag behind, straggle, is first recorded in 1577.

dragon *n.* Before 1250 *dragun* huge serpent; later, mythical fire-breathing monster (about 1250), and as a surname *Dragun* (1165-66); borrowed from Old French *dragon,* learned borrowing from Latin *dracōnem* (nominative *dracō*) serpent, dragon, from Greek *drákōn* (genitive *drákontos*) serpent, seafish, literally, the one with the (deadly) glance, from a lost noun **drák* glance (later *-dra*), cognate with Sanskrit *dŕś-* glance, and related to Greek *dérkesthai* to flash or gleam (like the eye), see clearly, look at or on, from Indo-European *derḱ-/dr̥ḱ-* (Pok. 213). —**dragonfly** *n.* (1626, in Francis Bacon's *Sylva Sylvarum*)

dragoon (drəgün') *n.* 1622, mounted soldier armed with a kind of carbine or musket; borrowed from French *dragon* carbine or musket, dragoon, literally, dragon, from Old French; see DRAGON; for suffix see -OON. The soldier was so called because the carbine or musket he carried "breathed fire" like a dragon. —**v.** to force or drive to something or some end. 1689, from the noun.

drain *v.* Before 1398 *dreynen,* strain or filter (a liquid), in Trevisa's translation of *De Proprietatibus Rerum*; later *dreyn* to draw off a liquid (1440); developed from Old English (about 1000) *drēahnian,* from Proto-Germanic **drauȝnōjanan,* apparently from the root **drauȝ-* related to *drȳge* DRY. The word seems to have disappeared from use shortly after the Old English period, reappearing later in the 1500's. The figurative sense of to exhaust is recorded about 1660. —**n.** 1372, from the verb (compare the compound *dreinhole*); earlier as a surname *Drenc* (1327) —**drainage** *n.* 1652, formed from English *drain* + *-age.*

drake *n.* About 1300, male duck, in *Havelok the Dane,* corresponding to Low German *drake* male duck, German dialect *drache,* and the second element in Old High German *anutrehho* (from **anut-trahho*), Middle High German *antrech* (modern German *Enterich*). The first element *anut-, ant-, -ent* derives from Old High German *anut, enit* duck (modern German *Ente*), which is cognate with Middle Dutch *aent* (modern Dutch *eend*), and Old English *ænid, ened* duck, from Proto-Germanic *anidís;* and outside Germanic with Sanskrit *ātí-s* aquatic bird, Greek *nêtta* (earlier **nātya*) duck, Latin *anas,* genitive *anatis,* Lithuanian *ántis,* Old Slavic *ąti,* from Indo-European **anət-/ant-/n̥t-* (Pok. 41). The origin of the element *-trehho* in Old High German *anutrehho* is apparently a West Germanic **drako,* of uncertain meaning. The full forms **endrake, *andrake* expected in Old English are not found there or in Middle English.

dram *n.* About 1373 *dram* and before 1398 *dragme* small weight of apothecary's measure; borrowed through Anglo-Latin *dragma, drama,* and from Middle French *drame, dragme,* both Anglo-Latin and Middle French from Late Latin *dragma,* from Latin *drachma* drachma, from Greek *drachmḗ;* see the doublet DRACHMA.

The figurative sense of a small amount, especially of talent, is first recorded in English about 1425.

drama *n.* 1515 *drame;* later *drama,* in Ben Jonson's *Epigrams* (1616); borrowed from Late Latin *drāma* play, drama, from Greek *drâma* (genitive *drā́matos*) play, action, deed, from *drân* to do, act, perform, cognate with Lithuanian *darýti* to do, from Indo-European *derə-/drā- to work (Pok. 212). —**dramatic** *adj.* 1589 *drammatick,* in Puttenham's *The Arte of English Poesi;* borrowed through Middle French *dramatique,* or directly from Late Latin *drāmaticus,* from Greek *drāmatikós* of or pertaining to plays, from *drâma* (genitive *drā́matos*) drama; for suffix see -IC. —**dramatis personae** (dram′ətis pərsō′nē) 1730, the characters of the drama or play, in Henry Fielding's *The Temple Beau;* borrowed from New Latin *dramatis personae,* literally, persons of the drama. —**dramatist** *n.* 1678, formed in English from Greek *drâma* (genitive *drā́matos*) + English *-ist.* —**dramatize** *v.* 1780-83, formed in English from Greek *drâma* (genitive *drā́matos*) + English *-ize.*

drape *v.* Probably before 1400 *draperen* to decorate with cloth hangings; 1436 *drapen* to weave into cloth; borrowed from Old French *draper,* from *drap* cloth. —**n.** 1665, cloth or hangings, drapery; in some instances borrowed from French *drap* cloth from Old French *drap,* from Late Latin *drappus* cloth, possibly from Gaulish, and in other instances, from the English *drape,* v. The Gaulish word, found in the proper name *Drappus,* is perhaps a variant of **drāpus,* cognate with Sanskrit *drāpí-s* mantle, garment, from Indo-European **drōp-,* root **drep-* (Pok. 211). —**drapery** *n.* Probably before 1325 *draperie* cloth, textile fabric; borrowed from Old French *draperie,* from *drap* cloth; for suffix see -ERY.

drastic *adj.* Before 1691, (of medicines) acting with force, in writings of Robert Boyle; borrowed from Greek *drāstikós* effective, from *drāstéon* (thing) to be done, from *drân* to do, act, see DRAMA; for suffix see -IC. The meaning of extreme, severe, is first recorded in English in 1808, in Jeremy Bentham's writings, possibly suggested by the earlier English noun meaning of a drastic medicine or severe purgative (1783), or borrowed from the French meaning of *drastique* (1741).

draw *v.* pull, tug. Probably before 1200 *drawen,* in Layamon's *Chronicle of Britain,* and *drahen,* in *Ancrene Riwle;* developed from Old English *dragan* (before 900, in Alfred's translation of St. Gregory's *Pastoral Care*). Old English *dragan* is cognate with Old Saxon *dragan,* Old Frisian *draga, drega,* Old High German *tragan* (modern German *tragen*) to carry, bear, with Old Icelandic *draga* to pull, draw, Gothic *gadragan* to pull or carry together, from Proto-Germanic **draʒanan,* and with Russian *doróga* and Polish *droga* road or way, from Indo-European **dhrəgh-* (root **dherāgh-*), Pok. 257. Though there are many constructions and uses that reflect Latin *trahere* to pull or draw, there is no etymological connection in form between the Latin and Old English.

The meaning to trace (a line or figure) by drawing a pencil or pen across a surface, is first recorded in Middle English probably about 1200.

The spelling change in Middle English from *g* to *w* occurred because the sound represented by *a* + *g* of the Old English *dragan* (in the stem *drag-*) developed into the diphthong represented by the spelling *aw* in Middle and modern English.

—**n.** Probably before 1300, in the compound *drawebrigge;* earlier, as a surname *Draespere* (1255); from the verb. The meaning of the action of drawing, as in shooting a bow, is first recorded about 1400-25, and that of a tie in a game or contest, in the phrase *draw game,* in 1825, in American English.

—**drawbridge** *n.* Probably before 1300 *drawebrigge,* in *Kyng Alisaunder;* formed from Middle English *draw, drauht,* etc. + *brigge, brugge,* etc. —**drawer** *n.* About 1385, person who draws (a sword); earlier, as a surname *Drahere* (1327); formed from English *drawen* to draw + *-er*[1]. The sense of a box that can be drawn out of a cabinet, desk, etc., is first recorded in 1580. The plural *drawers* an undergarment, is first recorded in 1567. —**drawing** *n.* Probably before 1300, the pulling of a sword or bowstring, in *Kyng Alisaunder;* the meaning of the act of making pictures, sketches, etc., is first recorded in 1467, and of the picture itself, in 1688-89, in Pepys' *Diary.* —**drawing room** 1642, private room to withdraw to; earlier *drauht chambre* (1435) and probably Anglo-French *drawyng chaumbre* (1410). Traditionally *drawing room* is given as a shortening of *withdrawing room* (1591 *with-drawing roem*); earlier *withdrawyng chambre* (1392-93); however, *withdrawing room* and *drawing room* seem to be parallel terms into the late 1800's when *drawing room* displaced the other term.

drawl *v.* 1597, crawl or draw along; 1598, speak slowly, draw out words, in Shakespeare's *Merry Wives of Windsor;* borrowed probably from Middle Dutch *dralen* to linger, delay (also formed in Low German and East Frisian *dralen,* in the same sense), apparently an intensive form derived from the root of DRAW, v. —**n.** 1760, from the verb.

dray *n.* cart for hauling heavy loads. 1370 *dreye* wheelless sled for logs; later *drey* a little cart (1565-73); a derivative form of Old English *dragan* to DRAW; related to Old English *dræge* dragnet, and cognate with Old Icelandic *draga* (pl. *drǫgur*) timber trailed along the ground. —**drayman** *n.* 1581, formed from English *dray* + *man.*

dread *v.* Probably before 1200 *dreden* fear greatly, in *Ancrene Riwle* and Layamon's *Chronicle of Britain;* shortened form of *adreden;* developed from Old English (about 1000) *adrǣdan,* a contraction of earlier *ondrǣdan* counsel or advise against, fear (900, in a version of *Beowulf*); and cognate with Old Saxon *antdrādan* and Old High German *intrātan* fear, dread. Old English *ondrǣdan* was misconstrued in late Old English as *on* + **drǣdan* (of unknown origin), but is properly analyzed as *ond-, and-,* cognate with Greek *antí* against, ANTI + *rǣdan* advise, cognate with Old High German *rātan* to advise, counsel, Gothic *garēdan* reflect upon.

—**n.** Probably before 1200 *dred,* in Layamon's *Chronicle of Britain,* from *dreden,* v.

dream *n.* About 1250 *drem,* in *The Story of Genesis and Exodus;* probably developed from Old English *drēam* joy, music (influenced in meaning by Old Icelandic *draumr* dream); cognate with Old Saxon *drōm* merriment, noise, Old Frisian *drām* dream, Old High German *troum* (modern German *Traum*), Old Icelandic *draumr* dream, from Proto-Germanic **draumaz,* earlier **đrauȝmas,* and possibly with Old Saxon *bidriogan* deceive, *gidrog* phantom, ghost, Old High German *triogan* deceive (modern German *trügen*), Old High German *gitrog* phantom, ghost, Old Icelandic *draugr,* Middle Irish *aurddrach* phantom, ghost, Avestan *druǰlie,* deception, *družaiti* he lies, deceives, and Sanskrit *drúhyati* he seeks to damage, he hurts, from Indo-European **dhreugh-/dhrough-/dhrugh-* (Pok. 270).

Though *dream* is not recorded in Old English with the meaning of a vision, the number of Germanic cognates of the same meaning strongly suggests that the meaning existed in Old English, but that perhaps the prevailing sense of joy, music, precluded use in literature of the meaning of a vision, especially in sleep, for which *swefn* was substituted.

The two groups of cognates with the meaning of deceive, phantom, ghost, and joy, music, dream, represent a double development of meaning.

—v. Probably before 1200 *dremen,* in *Ancrene Riwle* and Layamon's *Chronicle of Britain;* probably developed from Old English *drēmen, drȳman* rejoice, play music (influenced in meaning by Old Icelandic *dreyma* to dream); cognate with Old High German *troumen* (modern German *träumen*) to dream.

dreary *adj.* Probably about 1150 *dreri* sad, doleful; developed from Old English *drēorig* sorrowful, gory, bloody (about 725, in *Beowulf*), from *drēor* gore, falling blood, from Proto-Germanic **dreuzás;* for suffix see -Y[1]. The Old English is cognate with Middle High German *trūrec* sorrowful, sad (modern German *traurig*), Old High German *trūrēn* be sad (modern German *trauern* mourn), Middle High German *trōr* dripping fluid, Old Icelandic *dreyri* blood, gore. Old English *drēor* is related to Old English *drēosan* to fall, Old Saxon *driosan,* Gothic *driusan* to fall, Welsh *dryll* small piece, fragment, and Greek *thraúein* break in pieces, shatter, *from Indo-European *dhrēus-/dhrəus-/dhrēs-* (Pok. 274).

The sense of dismal, gloomy, is first recorded in 1667, in Milton's *Paradise Lost.*

dredge[1] *n.* machine or net for bringing up objects from a body of water. 1471 (Scottish) *dreg-,* found in the compound *dreg-boat* boat for dredging, apparently a derivative form from the root of DRAG, v. **—v.** to bring up objects with a dredge. 1508 (Scottish) *dreg,* from the noun.

dredge[2] *v.* sprinkle with powdered mixture, especially flour. 1596, apparently from earlier variants *dregge* (1435), *dregy* (1353-54); from *drage, dragge,* n., grain or spice mixture (about 1250); borrowed from Old French *dragie, dragée,* from Latin *tragēmata, pl.,* spices, sweetmeats, from Greek *tragḗmata,* from *trageîn,* (aorist or single-action form) of *trṓgein* to gnaw, nibble, very possibly (in the view of H. Frisk, *Griechisches etymologisches Wörterbuch,* II 939) a verb formed by extension from the root *trō-* of *titrṓskein* to wound, cognate with Middle Welsh *taraw* to strike, from Indo-European **treu-/trou-/trō(u)-* (Pok. 1072).

dregs *n.pl.* sediment, worthless parts. About 1378 *dregges* sediment of liquors, in a version of *Piers Plowman* (earlier in the surname *Dryngedregges,* 1309); borrowed from a Scandinavian source (compare Old Icelandic *dregg* sediment, from Proto-Germanic **draȝ-*). Middle English *dregges* replaced Old English *dræst, dærst* dregs, and is cognate with Old High German *trestir, pl.,* skins, husks, grounds, Old Lithuanian *drãges, pl.,* dregs, and Greek *thrắttein* distrub, trouble, from Indo-European **dhrəgh-/dhr̥gh-* (root **dherāgh-*), Pok. 251; see DROSS.

drench *v.* Probably before 1200 *drenchen* submerge in water, drown, in Layamon's *Chronicle of Britain,* and about 1200, to soak, saturate; earlier, to poison with a drink (probably about 1175); developed from Old English (about 1000) *drencan,* causative form of *drincan* to DRINK. Old English *drencan* is cognate with Old High German *trenken* cause to drink (modern German *tränken*), Old Icelandic *drekkja* drench, drown, and Gothic *drankjan* cause to drink, from Proto-Germanic **drankijanan.*

dress *v.* Probably before 1300 *dressen* to direct, guide, control, in *Arthour and Merlin;* also, to arrange, adjust, and to stand up, sit up, both senses in *Kyng Alisaunder;* borrowed from Old French *dresser,* earlier *drecier* arrange, prepare, from Vulgar Latin **dīrēctiāre,* from Latin *dīrēctus* straight, DIRECT.

The general meaning of decorate, adorn is recorded in Middle English in 1381; the specific sense to put on clothing is first recorded about 1395, in Chaucer's *Canterbury Tales.*

—n. 1606, clothing, especially clothing appropriate to rank or a specific ceremony, in Shakespeare's *Antony and Cleopatra;* from the verb. The meaning of a woman's garment is first recorded in English in 1638.

—dresser[1] *n.* person who prepares or finishes something. 1300, in a surname *Dresceour* (probably Anglo-French); later *dresser* guide, director (about 1445), from *dressen,* v. + *-er*[1]. **—dresser[2]** *n.* table, sideboard. Probably 1393 *dressor,* borrowed from Old French *dresseur, dreceur* a dresser, from *dresser* to prepare, DRESS; for suffix see -ER[1]. The meaning of a kitchen cupboard is first recorded in 1552, and that of a chest, dressing bureau with drawers in 1895, in American English. **—dressing** *n.* About 1350, rule, control, from English *dress,* v. + *-ing*[1]. The meaning of a bandage is first recorded in 1713.

dressage (drəsäzh′) *n.* 1936, guiding of a horse through various maneuvers; borrowed from French, literally, preparation, training, from *dresser* to prepare, train; see DRESS, v.; for suffix see -AGE.

dribble *v.* About 1589, flow in drops, trickle, a frequentative form of obsolete English *drib,* variant of DRIP, perhaps influenced by earlier *dryvelen* to DRIVEL (probably about 1378); for suffix see -LE[3].

The meaning to move (a ball) along with short bounces or kicks, first applied to soccer in 1863, was extended to basketball in the early 1900's, in American English.

—n. About 1680, from the verb.

drift *n.* Probably before 1325, movement as of falling rain or snow, snowdrift; later, movement as of running, beating of wings, etc. (before 1350), and driving cattle to pasture (1426). Though not recorded in Old English, the Middle English *drift* is cognate with Middle Dutch and modern Dutch *drift* passage for cattle, drove, Middle High German *trift* (modern German *Trift*), and Old Icelandic *drift* snowdrift (Norwegian *driv* drift of snow or sand); all from Proto-Germanic **driftiz,* related **drīƀanan* to DRIVE. English *drift* is related to *drive* as *thrift* is to *thrive, shrift* is to *shrive, gift* is to *give,* etc.

—v. 1584, to delay; later, move as driven by a current (probably before 1600); from the noun. **—drifter** *n.* (1864) **—driftwood** *n.* (1633)

drill[1] *n.* instrument for boring holes. 1611, borrowed from Dutch *dril, drille* a hole, instrument for boring holes, from *drillen* to bore (a hole), turn around, whirl, brandish, from Middle Dutch *drillen* to bore, turn in a circle; cognate with Middle High German *drillen* to turn, round off, bore (modern German *drillen*), from Proto-Germanic **threljanan,* an extension of the Indo-European root **ter-,* **terə-,* **trē(i)-* (Pok. 1071) shown in Latin *terere* rub, Greek *tetraínein* bore through, and Old English *thrāwan* THROW.

Before 1637 *drill* also meant a military exercise (probably from the sense turn around as in maneuvers), and by 1815 its meaning was extended to any rigorous

training or strict instruction. These latter senses probably from the verb in English.
—**v.** 1622, train by or as if with military precision, borrowed from Dutch *drillen.* The meaning of bore a hole is first recorded in English in 1649.

drill[2] *n.* twilled cotton or linen cloth. 1743, shortened form of *drilling* (1640), alteration of German *Drillich* a heavy, coarse cotton or linen fabric, from Middle High German *drilich* threefold, in reference to the three-threaded method of weaving this fabric, from Old High German *drilīh.* The Old High German word is itself an alteration (influenced by Old High German *drī* three, and *-līh* -ly[1]) of Latin *trilīx* (genitive *trilīcis*) woven with three sets of threads, triple-twilled (*tri-* three + *līcium* thread, of uncertain origin).

drill[3] *n.* baboon of western Africa. 1644, from the baboon's West African name; see MANDRILL.

drink *v.* Probably about 1150 *drinken,* developed from Old English *drincan* (about 725); cognate with Old Frisian *drinka* to drink, Old Saxon *drinkan,* Middle Dutch and modern Dutch *drinken,* Old High German *trinkan* (modern German *trinken*), Old Icelandic *drekka* (with *kk* from *nk*), Swedish *dricka,* Danish *drikke,* and Gothic *drinkan,* from Proto-Germanic **drinkanan.* The word is not found outside Germanic. —**n.** Probably before 1200 *drinke,* developed from Old English (about 888) *drinc* beverage, from *drincan* to drink. —**drinker** *n.* Probably before 1200, developed from Old English *drincere* (about 950, in *Lindisfarne Gospels*).

drip *v.* fall in drops. Probably about 1300 *drippen* drop down; later, fall in drops (1440, in *Promptorium Parvulorum*), probably borrowed from a Scandinavian source (compare Danish *dryppe* to drip, Old Icelandic *dreypa* let fall in drops); cognate with Middle Low German *druppen* fall in drops, and Old English *dropian* fall in drops; see DROP.

No clear evidence exists for an Old English source for Middle English *drippen.* From an Old English form *drype,* cited in *Leechdoms, Wortcunning, and Starcraft of Early England* (about 1000), an infinitive **dryppan* has been previously inferred, but the form may be taken as a subjunctive. However, Old English had other related verbs: *drypan* to let drop, *dropian* fall in drops, and *drēopan* to drop.
—**n.** 1440 *dryppe,* in *Promptorium Parvulorum,* from the verb.

drive *v.* Probably about 1175 *driven* to chase, drive, developed from Old English (about 725) *drīfan;* cognate with Old Frisian *drīva* to drive, Old Saxon *drīban,* Middle Low German and Middle Dutch *drīven* (modern Dutch *drijven*), Old High German *trīban* (modern German *treiben*), Old Icelandic *drīfa* (Swedish *driva,* Danish *drive*), and Gothic *dreiban* (*ei* = *ī*), from Proto-Germanic **drīƀanan.* The word is not represented outside Germanic. —**n.** 1697, from the verb. The meaning of an excursion in a vehicle is first recorded in 1785, in Boswell's *Tour of the Hebrides.* —**driveway** *n.* (1875, in American English)

drivel *v.* Probably about 1350 *dravelen* dribble (saliva), speak nonsense; 1378 *dryvelen,* in a version of *Piers Plowman;* developed from Old English (about 1000) *dreflian* (earlier **dræflian*) to dribble or run at the nose, from Proto-Germanic **draƀlōjanan.* This Old English word is related to early Middle English *draf* refuse, dregs (probably before 1200, in Layamon's *Chronicle of Britain*), which is cognate with Middle Dutch and Old Icelandic *draf* dregs, and Old High German *trebir* grains, husks (modern German *Treber* husks), from Indo-European **dhrābh-/dhrəbh-* (Pok. 252).—**n.** Probably before 1325 *drivil* spittle, from the verb. The meaning of nonsense, twaddle, is first recorded in English in 1852.

drizzle *v.* 1543 *dryseling* shedding a fine spray of drops; possibly an alteration of earlier *drysning* a falling of dew, etc. (probably before 1400), from *drysnen* to fall; developed from Old English *-drysnian* (about 950), related to *drēosan* to fall; see DREARY; for the possible suffix see -LE[3]. —**n.** 1554, from the verb. The spelling *drizzle* is first recorded in 1590 for the verb and in 1554 for the noun but did not become the established form until the 1800's.

droll *adj.* funny, odd. 1623, borrowed from French *drôle* odd, comical, funny, originally (in Middle French) a noun meaning a merry fellow, possibly from Middle Dutch *drol* fat little fellow, goblin. —**drollery** *n.* 1597, caricature, in Shakespeare's *2 Henry IV;* borrowed from Middle French *drôlerie* grotesque figure, from Middle French *drôle;* for suffix see -ERY. The meaning of something odd or amusing is first recorded in 1610, in Shakespeare's *The Tempest.*

dromedary *n.* one-humped camel. Probably about 1280, a fleet camel bred for riding, usually Arabian or one-humped; borrowed through Old French *dromadaire,* from Late Latin *dromedārius* kind of camel, for Latin *dromas* (genitive *dromados*), from Greek *dromás kámēlos* running camel, from *drómos* a running, course, race course, cognate with Sanskrit *drámati* runs about, from Indo-European **drem-/drom-* (Pok. 204); for suffix see -ARY.

drone *n.* 1127 *drane* male honeybee, developed from Old English *dran* (about 1000 in Ælfric's *Glossary*), *dræn* (about 1050), from Proto-Germanic **dran-;* cognate with (possible Old Saxon *dran, dreno* drone, though perhaps a dictionary word) Middle Low German *drane, drone,* Old High German *treno* drone, Norwegian *drynja* to roar, Gothic *drunjus* sound, Greek *thrênos* dirge, lament, Sanskrit *dhránati* it sounds, and Old Irish *drēcht* song, from Indo-European **dhren-/dhron-/dhrēn-* (Pok. 255).

The form *drone* appeared in 1475 and later in 1508, in Dunbar's poetry (*dron* bee), which is also the first recorded source (between 1500 and 1520) of the sense "a deep continuous humming sound," apparently from the verb.

There is as yet no satisfactory explanation of how *o* replaced *a* in Middle English *drane;* it was pronounced *a,* as in *sat,* later *a,* as in *late,* in all Midland examples of Middle English except one in the MED.

The figurative meaning of a lazy worker (because the male bee is a nonworker) is first recorded in English before 1529 in Skelton's poetry.
—**v.** to hum or buzz. 1500-20, in Dunbar's poetry; probably from the noun, though use of noun and verb, in reference to the bee's hum, are simultaneously used by the same author of record with the spelling *drōn* in the verb and *drāne* in the noun in other poems; this suggests that the *o* spelling might have entered the noun from the verb.

drool *v.* 1802 *drule, dreul;* later *drool* (1867-69); apparently a dialectal variant or contraction of DRIVEL. —**n.** 1867-69, from the verb.

droop *v.* Before 1300 *drupen* to sag or hang down, to be downcast, grieve; later, about 1333-52, *droupen,* borrowed from a Scandinavian source (compare Old Icelandic *drūpa* hang the head; droop); related to Old English *dropian* to DROP. **—n.** 1647, from the verb.

drop *n.* About 1150 *drope* disease characterized by spots; later, smallest quantity of a liquid (before 1200); developed from Old English *dropa* (about 725, in a translation of the book of *Daniel*), from Proto-Germanic **drupōn.* Old English *dropa* is cognate with Old Saxon *dropo* drop, Middle Dutch *droppe* (modern Dutch *drop*), Old High German *tropfo* (modern German *Tropfen*), Old Icelandic *dropi* drop (Swedish *droppe*), *drjūpa* to drop, drip, Old High German *triofan* (modern German *triefen*), from Indo-European **dhreub-/dhrub-* (Pok. 275), and probably Gothic *driusan* to fall; see DREARY. **—v.** About 1300 *droppen,* developed from Old English (about 1000) *dropian* fall in drops, related to *drēopan* to drop, drip, *dropa* a drop. **—droplet** *n.* 1607, in Shakespeare's *Timon of Athens*); formed from English *drop,* n. + *-let.* **—dropper** *n.* 1700, a distiller; later, small glass tube from which liquid may be made to fall in drops (1889, in American English); formed from English *drop,* v. + *-er*[1].

dropsy *n.* About 1250 *dropesie* condition in which watery fluid collects in body tissues, shortened form of *idropesie;* borrowed from Old French *idropisie,* from Latin *hydrōpisis;* also, a shortened from of English *hydropsy,* borrowed from Latin *hydrōpisis,* from Greek *hýdrōps* (genitive *hýdrōpos*) dropsy, from *hýdōr* WATER. The element *ṓps* was originally a noun meaning eye (cognate with Latin *oculus*) or face, but in *hýdr-ōps* "the force of *-ōps* is practically that of a possessive suffix and may be translated as 'having' or 'characterized by'." (Carl D. Buck and Walter Petersen, *A Reverse Index of Greek Nouns and Adjectives,* p. 382)

droshky *n.* four-wheeled open carriage formerly used in Russia. 1808, borrowed from Russian *drózhki,* diminutive of *drógi, pl.,* wagon, related to *doróga* way; see DRAW.

dross *n.* waste, refuse. About 1384 *drosse,* in the Wycliffe Bible; earlier *dros* (probably before 1200, in *Ancrene Riwle*); developed from Old English (about 1050) *drōs* dirt, dregs, which is most closely related to Middle Low German *drōs,* and Middle Dutch *droes;* also to the longer form Old English *drōsna* (genitive plural dregs, which is cognate with Old High German *truosana* lees, dregs (modern German *Drusen, pl.*), Middle Dutch *droesen* lees, dregs. Old English *drōs* and its Middle Low German and Middle Dutch cognates are from Proto-Germanic **drōHs-,* from Indo-European **dhrāk-s-,* root **dherāgh-/ *dhrāgh-* (Pok. 251); see DREGS.

drought *n.* About 1380 *drowghte* dryness, long period of dryness, in Chaucer's translation of Boethius' *De Consolatione Philosophiae;* earlier *drught* (before 1325, Northern dialect); developed from Old English (before 1100) *drūgath, drūgoth,* from Proto-Germanic **drūʒṓthuz,* related to *drūgian* dry up, wither, from *drūg-,* the base of *drȳge* DRY (compare Dutch *droogte* drought, from *droog* dry), from Indo-European **dhreugh-/dhrough-/dhrūgh-* (Pok. 275). The Old English *drūgath, drūgoth* also developed into *drouth, drowth* and the forms with *-th* and *-t* have varied as also found in *highth* and *height.*

drove *n.* animal herd driven along together. About 1250 *drof,* in *The Story of Genesis and Exodus;* earlier, in a place name *Bradedrave* (1220); developed from Old English (971) *drāf* act of driving, from *drīfan* to DRIVE. **—drover** *n.* 1393-94, person who drives livestock, in *Rolls of Parliament;* earlier, as a surname *Drovere* (1287-93).

drown *v.* About 1325 *drounen, drunen* die by submersion in water, in *Cursor Mundi;* perhaps developed from Old English **drūnian* (compare Middle English *druncnen* to drown, probably before 1200; developed from Old English *druncnian,* about 950; cognate with Old Icelandic *drukna* to drown, be drunk or swallowed up by water; from the base of Old English *drincan* to DRINK).

drowsy *adj.* Before 1529 *drowsie,* in Skelton's poetry; probably adapted from Old English *drūsan* (about 725, in *Beowulf*), *drūsian* sink, become low, slow, or inactive, related to *drēosan* to fall (from Indo-European *dhrēus-/dhrūs-,* Pok. 274) + *-y*[1]. **—drowse** *v.* 1596, to be drowsy, in Shakespeare's *1 Henry IV;* earlier, be inactive or sluggish (1573); probably a back formation of *drowsy.* The OED points out that in the record of English there is a gap of almost 600 years between the use of *drowse* in Old English and its appearance in early Modern English.

drub *v.* beat with a stick. 1634, used in an Eastern context to describe a bastinado (a kind of beating with a stick), of uncertain origin; perhaps from Arabic *ḍaraba* he beat up.

drudge *v.* About 1385 *druggen* do menial or monotonous work, in Chaucer's *Canterbury Tales,* earlier (before 1250) *druggunge,* gerund; apparently related to Old English *drēogan* to work, suffer, endure; cognate with Old Icelandic *drȳgja* do, carry out, accomplish, and Gothic *driugan* serve as a soldier, from Indo-European **dhreugh-/dhrūgh-/dhrugh-* endure, serve as a soldier (Pok. 255).

The spelling *drudge,* first recorded as a verb in 1494 and as a noun in 1549 suggests a verb **drycgean* in Old English, or a noun **drycgea,* but no such form is known. The history for such an assertion is based upon the fact that in early Middle English, or perhaps late Old English, the sounds represented by *-cg* in Old English *brycg, ecg, wecg,* and later *-gg* in Middle English *brigge, egge, wegge,* developed into the sound represented by *-dge* or *-ge* in *bridge, edge, wedge.* The spelling change took place for the most part from the 1400's to the 1600's.

—n. one doing menial or monotonous work; hack. 1494, from the verb.

—drudgery *n.* menial or monotonous work. 1550, from English *drudge* + *-ery.*

drug *n.* About 1387-95 *drogge* medicinal substance, in Chaucer's *Prologue* to the *Canterbury Tales;* borrowed from Old French *drogue,* of uncertain origin; perhaps from Middle Dutch *droge,* or Middle Low German *droge-* in *droge-fate* dry-barrels, with *droge-* taken as the name of the barrels' contents; see DRY. In the 1300's and 1400's, there was confusion between *drogge* drug (found in a version of *Piers Plowman*) and *dragge* DREDGE[2] spice mixture (also found in a version of *Piers Plowman*). The specific application to narcotics and opiates is first recorded in the 1880's, although the association of drugs with poisons goes back to the 1500's. **—v.** 1605, mix with a drug, especially a poisonous drug, in Shakespeare's *Macbeth;* from the noun. The meaning of give drugs to a person, especially to stupefy or poison, is first recorded in English in 1730.

—druggist *n.* 1611, formed from English *drug,* n. + *-ist.* **—drugstore** *n.* (1810, in American English)

druid or **Druid** *n.* 1509 *Druydan,* in Barclay's *The Ship of Fools,* translation of Latin *Druidae, pl.;* later *Druid* (1563, in Golding's translation of Caesar's *Gallic Wars*), borrowed from Old French *druide,* learned borrowing of Latin *Druidae, pl.,* from Gaulish *Druides* (compare Old Irish *drūi* wizard). Gaulish *Druides* probably derives from **dru-wid-* very wise, assuredly wise, a compound of *dru-* very assuredly, from Indo-European **dreu-/dru-, *drewə/drū-* firm, true (Pok. 214, 215 + *-wid-* knowing, wise, from Indo-European **weid-/wid-* (Pok. 1126).

drum *n.* 1427-30 *dromme,* probably borrowed from Middle Dutch *tromme* drum; compare Middle High German and Middle Low German *trumme, trummel* drum (modern German *Trommel*), Danish and Norwegian *tromme,* Swedish *trumma,* all probably of imitative origin.

It is not satisfactorily explained how the English word should have *dr-,* while the other Germanic languages have *tr-,* nor is it clear how the meaning of the original sense of Middle High German *trumme* trumpet, is associated with *drum,* unless the OED's explanation of a possible general sense "loud-sounding or booming instrument" is accepted.

—v. 1578, from the noun. To drum up business, to solicit orders, canvass, originated in American English and is first recorded in 1839.

—drummer *n.* 1573-78, formed probably from English *drum,* v. + *-er*[1]. If the record of English is accurate, *drummer* appeared before the verb *drum,* which goes against the usual pattern of such derivative formations in English. **—drumstick** *n.* (1589)

drunkard *n.* 1275, as a surname *Druncard,* formed from Middle English *dronken* participial adjective + *-ard.*

drupe *n.* fruit with seed contained in a hard pit. 1753, borrowed from New Latin *drupa,* from Latin *druppa* very ripe olive, from Greek *drýppā,* shortened from *drypepḗs* tree-ripened (used of black olives), from *dry-* (representing *drŷs* TREE) + *pépōn* ripe; see COOK.

dry *adj.* About 1250 *drie;* earlier in a place name *Driebi* (1130), and dialectal *drue* (before 1200, in *Ancrene Riwle*); developed from Old English *drȳge* (before 900 in Alfred's translation of Boethius' *De Proprietatibus Rerum*). The Old English is cognate with Middle Dutch *druge, drōge* dry (modern Dutch *droog*), Old High German *trucchan* (modern German *trocken*), and probably with Old Icelandic *draugr* dry wood, from Indo-European **dhreugh-/dhrough-/dhrūgh-/dhrugh-* (Pok. 275). Related to DROUGHT and DRUG.

—v. Before 1325 *drien;* earlier dialectal *druyen* (about 1300); developed from Old English *drȳgan* (before 900, in Alfred, see adj.), from *drȳge* dry. **—dry cell** (1893, earlier *dry battery,* 1885) **—dry-clean** *v.* (1817) **—dry cleaner** (1897) **—dry dock** (1627) **—dryer** *n.* a machine for drying (1874), and **drier** *n.* a person or thing that dries (1528); both forms from English *dry,* v. + *-er*[1]. **—dry goods** (1657, in American English) **—dry ice** (1927) **—dry rot** (1855) **—dry wall** (1788)

dryad (drī'ad) *n.* Before 1393 *driad* wood nymph, in Gower's *Confessio Amantis;* later *dryades, pl.* (1555); borrowed from Latin *dryadēs,* plural of *dryas* (genitive *dryadis*), from Greek *Dryás* (genitive *Dryádos*), from *drŷs* (genitive *dryós*) TREE + feminine-noun suffix *-ás* (genitive *-ádos*).

The singular form *dryad* is first recorded in English in Milton's *Paradise Lost* (1667).

dual *adj.* double. 1607, borrowed from Latin *duālis,* from *duo* TWO; for suffix see -AL[1]. Latin *duālis* is supposed to have been a translation by Quintilian of Greek *dyïkós* (in *arithmòs ho dyïkós* the dual number). **—dualism** *n.* 1794, borrowed from French *dualisme,* from Latin *duālis* dual; for suffix see -ISM. **—duality** *n.* About 1385 *dualite,* borrowed from Old French *dualité,* from Late Latin *duālitātem* (nominative *duālitās*), from Latin *duālis* dual; for suffix see -ITY.

dub[1] *v.* give a title to, call, name. Probably before 1200 *dubben* confer knighthood on, in Layamon's *Chronicle of Britain;* developed from Old English *dubbian* (1085, in the *Anglo-Saxon Chronicle*); perhaps borrowed from Old French *aduber, adouber* equip with arms, adorn, a word of uncertain origin but with cognates found in other Romance languages, such as Spanish and Provençal *adobar,* Italian *addobbare,* and Old Portuguese *adubar.* The suggestion that the Romance words are of Germanic origin cannot be supported: no Germanic verb such as **dubban* to strike, exists, and Icelandic and Swedish *dubba* to dub a knight, are late borrowings from English or Romanic. The OED questions even the English borrowing from French on the basis of late dates of the French forms to the 1400's. Before 1338 the sense was extended to that of invest with a new title, and this, in turn, extended by 1599 to that of provide with a name, style, nickname, which is the ordinary current sense, in Shakespeare's *Henry V.*

dub[2] *v.* add or alter sounds on film. 1929, alteration and shortening of DOUBLE, v.; so called because it involves re-recording or doubling of voices on the sound track.

dubious *adj.* 1548, borrowed from Latin *dubiōsus* doubtful, from *dubium* doubt (neuter of *dubius* doubtful from *duo* TWO (i.e. of two minds, undecided between two things). Latin *dubius,* from Indo-European **du-bhw-iyos* of two natures, being double, is a derivative of the ancient root **bheu-/bhu-* to BE (Pok. 146), and is comparable in structure to Latin *pro-b-us* honest, *super-b-us* superior, proud (from **(s)uper-bhw-os*), Greek *hyper-phyḗs* unusually great, and *hyper-phíalos* overweening.

ducal *adj.* of or having to do with a duke or dukedom. 1494, borrowed from Middle French *ducal,* from Late Latin *ducālis,* from Latin *dux* (genitive *ducis*) leader, in Medieval Latin, governor of a province; for suffix see -AL[1].

ducat (duk'ət) *n.* gold or silver coin formerly used in Europe. About 1380, Venetian coin, in Chaucer's *House of Fame;* borrowed from Old French *ducat,* from Italian *ducato,* from Medieval Latin *ducatus* duchy, coin, from *dux* (genitive *ducis*) duke, so called from the title or effigy of the duke who issued it stamped on the coin; see the doublet DUCHY.

Traditionally, it is said that the Byzantine Emperor Constantine Ducas had his name stamped on coins. Later, a silver coin was issued by Roger II of Sicily, as Duke of Apulia, in 1140 with the inscription *R DX AP* (Rogerus Dux Apuliae), followed by a gold ducat struck in Venice.

duchess *n.* Probably before 1300; borrowed from Old French *duchesse,* from Late or Medieval Latin *ducissa,* feminine of *dux;* see DUKE.

duchy *n.* territory of a duke. Before 1338 *duche,* in Mannyng's *Chronicle of England;* borrowed from Old

French *duché,* from Medieval Latin *ducatus,* from *dux* (genitive *ducis*) duke, from Latin *dux* leader; see DUKE. Doublet of DUCAT.

The form *duchy* is first recorded in Middle English probably before 1400.

duck[1] *n.* swimming bird. Probably before 1300 *doke,* in *Arthour and Merlin;* earlier in a surname *Dukeswrd* (1216); developed from Old English (967) *dūce* (found only in the genitive *dūcan*) a duck, literally, a ducker, possibly from **dūcan* to duck, dive; see DUCK[2]. The form *duck* is first recorded in about 1420, but did not become established before the 1500's. **—duckling** *n.* Before 1425, in the erroneous form *dukyng,* formed from Middle English *doke* + *-ling.*

duck[2] *v.* dip, plunge, dive. Before 1325 *duken,* in *Cursor Mundi;* later *douken* (before 1400); developed possibly from Old English **dūcan* to duck, dive (found only in the derivative *dūce* a duck). Middle English *duken* is cognate with Middle Low German and Middle Dutch *dūken* to dip, dive, Old High German *tūhhan* to dip (modern German *tauchen* dive, plunge), but there are no cognates outside Germanic. The sense of bend or stoop quickly, to bob, is first recorded in English in 1530. **—n.** 1554, rapid lowering of head or body; later, quick plunge, dip (1843); from the verb.

duck[3] *n.* cotton cloth. 1640, borrowed from Dutch *doek* linen cloth or light canvas, from Middle Dutch *doec;* cognate with Old Saxon and Old Frisian *dōk,* and Old High German *tuoh* (modern German *Tuch*), all meaning cloth, but of unknown origin.

duct *n.* 1650, course, direction, from Latin *ductus* (genitive *ductūs*) a leading, from the stem *duc-* of *dūcere* to lead; see TOW[1] pull. The meaning of a tube, pipe, or channel conveying fluids, is first recorded in 1667. **—ductless** *adj.* (especially in the term *ductless gland*) 1849-52; formed from English *duct,* n. + *-less.*

ductile (duk′təl) *adj.* pliant, flexible. About 1340 *ductil* hammered or shaped with a hammer; borrowed through Old French *ductile,* or directly from Latin *ductilis* that may be drawn, extended or hammered out thin, from *ductus,* past participle of *dūcere* to lead + *-ilis* an adjective suffix meaning capacity, ability, quality.

dud *n.* 1307 *dudde* cloak or mantle, perhaps made of coarse cloth; later *duds* ragged clothing (1508); of uncertain origin. The meaning was extended in 1825 to a person in ragged clothing, and in 1908 to that of a useless, inefficient person or thing; in World War I it was applied to a shell which failed to explode; hence, failure.

dude *n.* 1883, a man who is very particular or fastidious in dress, speech, and manner, a dandy or fop. The word came into vogue in New York and is of unknown origin. Later it was also applied to a city slicker, especially an Easterner vacationing in the West. The slang sense of any male, is first recorded about 1970. **—dude ranch** (1921)

dudgeon (duj′ən) *n.* anger, resentment (usually in the phrase *in high dudgeon*). 1573 *duggin,* of unknown origin. The spelling *dudgeon* is first recorded in 1599; for the ending compare BLUDGEON, CURMUDGEON.

due *adj.* Probably about 1350 *dewe* customary, regular, suitable, owed as a duty; borrowed from Old French *deü,* past participle of *devoir* to owe, from Latin *dēbēre* to owe, see DEBT. **—adv.** 1597, duly; 1601, directly; both senses first recorded in Shakespeare's writings. **—n.** that which is owed or due. 1423-24, from the adjective.

duel *n.* About 1475 *duelle;* borrowed from Medieval Latin *duellum* combat between two persons (a sense developed from association with Latin *duo* TWO), from Latin *duellum* war (early form of *bellum*), a graphic revival from Old Latin *duellum* (i.e. *dwellum*). **—v.** About 1645, from the noun. **—duelist** *n.* 1592 *dualist,* in Shakespeare's *Romeo and Juliet;* 1616 *duellist,* in Ben Jonson's *Epigrams;* probably formed from English *duel,* n. + *-ist,* on the model of Italian *duellista* and French *duelliste* (from Italian).

duenna (düen′ə) *n.* governess or chaperon in a Spanish or Portuguese family. 1668, borrowed from earlier Spanish *duenna* (now *dueña*) married lady, mistress, from Late Latin *domna,* from Latin *domina.* Doublet of DAME, DOÑA, DONNA.

duet (düet′) *n.* 1740, gradually replacing earlier *duetto* (1724); borrowed from Italian *duetto* short musical composition for two voices, diminutive of *duo* DUO. Both *duet* and *duetto* were preceded in English as well as in Italian by DUO. **—v.** 1822, in Byron's letters; from the noun.

duffel or **duffle** *n.* coarse woolen cloth, camping equipment. 1677, borrowed from Dutch *duffel,* from the name *Duffel,* a town near Antwerp, Belgium, where the cloth was originally sold. The term *duffel bag,* a cylindrical canvas bag, is first recorded in 1917, in American English.

dugout *n.* 1) 1722, American English, boat made by hollowing out a large log. 2) 1855, a rough shelter. Both meanings formed from English *dug,* v. + *out.* The sense of a shelter at the side of a baseball field is first recorded in 1914.

duke *n.* 1129 *duc* sovereign prince, ruler of a duchy, borrowed from Old French *duc,* and from Latin *dux* (genitive *ducis*) leader, commander (in Late Latin, governor of a province), from *dūcere* to lead. Doublet of DOGE. The meaning of a nobleman of high or highest rank, is first recorded in English probably about 1350. **—dukedom** *n.* Probably about 1350, formed from English *duke* + *-dom.*

dulcet (dul′sit) *adj.* About 1450 *dulcet* sweet or pleasant, especially to the ear; earlier *doucet* (probably about 1425), and as a noun (probably about 1408); borrowed from Old French *doucet,* diminutive of *doux* (earlier *dulz*) sweet, from Latin *dulcis,* from Indo-European **dl̥kú-s* (Pok. 222); see GLUCOSE; for suffix see -ET. The form *dulcet* was an alteration of *doucet* influenced by Latin *dulcis* sweet.

dulcimer (dul′səmər) n. musical instrument. Probably 1474 *dowsemer,* borrowed from Middle French *doulce mer,* variant of *doulcemele* and probably *doulz de mer*), said to represent Latin *dulcis* sweet (see DULCET) + *melos* song, from Greek *mélos* MELODY.

In 1864 the form *dulcimer* was borrowed back into French from English.

dull *adj.* not sharp, blunt. Probably about 1200 *dul* not sharp of wit, stupid; later *dulle* blunt, not sharp (about 1230, in *Ancrene Riwle*); apparently related to Old English (about 975) *dol* dull-witted, foolish (from Proto-Germanic **dulaz*) which is cognate with Old Frisian and Old Saxon *dol* foolish, Old High German *tol* (modern German *toll* mad, wild), Gothic *dwals* foolish, Old

Irish *dall* blind, and Greek *tholós* mud, dirt, *tholoûn* make muddy, confound, from Indo-European **dhwol-/dhwḷ-/dhul-* (Pok. 265). The sense of boring is first recorded in 1590, in Shakespeare's *Comedy of Errors.* —**v.** Probably about 1200, to make stupid; from the adjective. —**dullard** *n.* About 1440, in *Promptorium Parvulorum;* earlier as a surname (1225).

duly *adv.* About 1380 *duweliche* rightly, properly, in Chaucer's translation of Boethius' *De Consolatione Philosophiae;* later *duli* (before 1395, in Wycliffe's writings); formed from English *dewe* due + *-liche* -ly[1].

dumb *adj.* unable to speak, mute. Old English *dumb* (about 1000, in Ælfric's writings and an Old English Gospel); cognate with Old Frisian and Old Saxon *dumb* mute, Middle Dutch *dom, domp* (modern Dutch *dom* stupid), Old High German *tumb, tump* mute, stupid, deaf (modern German *dumm* stupid), Old Icelandic *dumbr* mute (Swedish *dum* stupid), and Gothic *dumbs* mute, speechless, from Indo-European **dhumbho-s* dark (Pok. 264). The sense of stupid, foolish, senseless, is first recorded probably before 1200, in Layamon's *Chronicle of Britain.* —**dumbbell** *n.* 1711, exercising device resembling a church bell, in Addison's writings in *The Spectator.* The figurative meaning of a stupid person, blockhead, is first recorded in 1920, in American English. —**dumb show** (1561) —**dumbwaiter** *n.* (1749)

dumfound or **dumbfound** *v.* 1653, formed from English DUMB + (CON)FOUND.

dummy *n.* 1598, mute person, formed from English DUMB + *-y*[3]; by 1796, the meaning was extended to that of blockhead, stupid person, and before 1845 to the sense of a figure representing a person. —**adj.** 1843, from the noun.

dump *v.* About 1333-52 *dompen* to throw down or fall with force; perhaps borrowed from a Scandinavian source (compare Danish *dumpe,* Norwegian *dumpa,* Swedish *dimpa* to fall with a thud), from Indo-European **dhen-,* and **dhem-b-/dhṃ-b-* strike, hit (Pok. 249, 250). The sense of throw down (rubbish, etc.), unload in a mass, is first recorded in 1784, in American English. —**n.** 1784 *dump(s),* American English, place where refuse or other unwanted material is dumped; from the verb. The informal sense of any shabby, dirty, or unpleasant place, is first recorded in 1899, in American English. —**dumps** *n.pl.* low spirits; depression; melancholy. 1529 *dumpes,* in writings of Sir Thomas More, plural of earlier *dumpe* a fit of musing, reverie, abstraction (1523, in writings of Skelton); of uncertain origin. The form corresponds to Dutch *domp* haze, mist, from Middle Dutch *damp* vapor; see DAMP. —**dump truck** (1930, American English, replacing earlier *dump wagon,* 1869). —**dumpy** *adj.* short and fat (1750).

dumpling *n.* About 1600 *dumplin,* of uncertain origin; perhaps formed in English from Low German *dump* damp, moist, heavy + English *-ling,* but since *dump* is not recorded as a noun in English until 1784, it is doubtful that *damp* or *dump* as an adjective was combined with English *-ling.*

dun[1] *v.* persistently demand payment of a debt. Before 1626, in Sir Francis Bacon's works; of uncertain origin, suggested as an allusion to Joe *Dun,* bailiff of Lincoln, England, with the sense of send Dun to catch or arrest a debtor, or perhaps as an extended sense of an earlier verb *dunnen* to sound, resound, make a din (probably before 1200, in Layamon's *Chronicle of Britain*); dialectal variant of DIN. —**n.** 1628, perhaps from the verb, though doubtful according to the OED.

dun[2] *adj.* dull brown. Before 1325 *dune,* in *Cursor Mundi;* developed from Old English (953) *dunn,* perhaps from Celtic (compare Old Irish *donn* dark, Gaulish *Donnos,* a proper name); cognate with Old Saxon *dosan* chestnut brown; see DUSK. —**n.** About 1390, name for a dun horse; earlier as a surname *Dun* (1180); from the adjective.

dunce *n.* 1577 *Duns* stupid person, from earlier *Duns man* a follower or believer in the philosophy of John *Duns* Scotus (1527, in Tyndale's writings). Scotus was a Scottish theologian whose works were textbooks in the Medieval universities, but during the 1500's his teachings were discredited by the humanists, especially the followers of Thomas Aquinas, who ridiculed the Duns men as hairsplitting reasoners and sophists. Later the name meant any student or disciple who showed no capacity to learn, in short, a dull-witted person. The spelling *Dunce* is first recorded in 1530 in Tyndale's writings.

dune *n.* hill or ridges of sand. 1790, borrowed from French *dune,* from Old French *dune,* from Middle Dutch *dūnen* (modern Dutch *duin* or Middle Low German *dūne,* perhaps from Gaulish **dūnom;* cognate with Old Irish *dūn* fort, Welsh *dinas* city, and Old English *tūn* TOWN, from Indo-European **dhūno-m* (Pok. 263); see the doublet DOWN[3] grassy hill.

dung *n.* waste matter, manure. Old English *dung* manure (about 1000 in Ælfric's *Glossary*); cognate with Old Frisian and Old Saxon *dung* manure, Old High German *tunga* manuring, *tung* underground room covered with manure (for protection against cold), modern German *Dung,* and with vowel change Icelandic *dyngja* heap of manure, dung, Swedish *dynga* dung, muck, Danish *dynge* heap, mass, pile, and with Lithuanian *deñgti* to cover, from Indo-European **dhengh-/dhṇgh-* cover, lie upon (Pok. 250). —**dunghill** *n.* About 1330 *donghel,* later *dunghil* (about 1450).

dungaree *n.* coarse cotton cloth. 1696; earlier *dongerijns* (1613); borrowed from Hindi *dungrī.* —**dungarees** *n.pl.* trousers made of dungaree. 1891, in Kipling's *City of the Dreadful Night;* from the singular noun.

dungeon *n.* Before 1325 *dunjon* great tower of a castle, in *Cursor Mundi;* borrowed from Old French *donjon,* from Gallo-Romance **dominiōnem,* from Late Latin *dominium,* from Latin *dominus* master (of the castle); see DOMAIN. The variant DONJON took on the original meaning of this word, the form *dungeon* developed the specialized sense of strong close cell, underground place of confinement, which is first recorded before 1338, in Mannyng's *Chronicle of England.*

dunk *v.* dip into liquid. 1919, American English; borrowed from Pennsylvania German *dunke* to dip, from Middle High German *dunken, tunken,* from Old High German *dunkōn, thunkōn;* see TINGE.

The meaning used in basketball of jump and throw (the ball) down into the basket, is first recorded in 1955.

duo *n.* duet. 1590, song for two voices; borrowed possibly through French *duo,* from Italian *duo* duet, from Latin *duo* TWO. The extended sense of a pair, is first recorded in English in 1802.

duodecimal (dü′ōdes′əməl) *n.* **duodecimals,** a system of numbers based on twelve. 1714; borrowed from Latin *duodecimus* twelfth, from *duodecim* twelve; see DOZEN; for suffix see -AL[1]. **—adj.** 1727, from the noun.

duodenum (dü'ədē'nəm) *n.* first part of the small intestine. Before 1398, in Trevisa's translation of Bartholomew's *De Proprietatibus Rerum;* earlier *duodene* (1379); borrowed from Medieval Latin *duodenum digitorum* space of twelve digits, from Latin *duodēnī* twelve each (from its length, about equal to the breadth of twelve fingers), from *duodecim* twelve; see DOZEN. The Medieval Latin phrase *duodenum digitorum* is a translation of Greek *dōdekadáktylos ékphysis* twelve-finger projection. **—duodenal** *adj.* 1817, composed of twelve members; later, relating to the *duodenum* (1843). The earlier general sense is a formation in English from Latin *duodēnī* twelve each + English *-al*[1]; while the anatomical sense is borrowed perhaps through French *duodénal* from New Latin *duodenalis,* from Medieval Latin *duodenum.*

dupe *n.* person easily deceived. 1681, borrowed from French *dupe* deluded or deceived person, from Middle French *duppe,* probably from the phrase *de huppe* of the hoopoe (a reputedly stupid-looking bird) from *de* of, and *huppe* hoopoe.**—v.** deceive. 1704, in Swift's *A Tale of a Tub;* from the noun in English, or borrowed from French *duper,* from *dupe,* noun in French.

duple (dü'pəl) *adj.* double. 1542-43, borrowed from Latin *duplus* DOUBLE; note that the Medieval Latin feminine *dupla* is used earlier in Middle English as an adjective with the sense of two-fold in a treatise on music (before 1450).

duplex *adj.* double, twofold. 1817, in Peacock's *Melincourt;* borrowed from Latin *duplex* (*du-,* from *duo* TWO + *-plex;* cognate with Greek *díplax* double, twofold, from *di-* two + *pláx,* genitive *plakós* flat surface, from Indo-European **plāk-plək-,* Pok. 831). **—n.** a house accommodating two families; apartment with rooms on two floors. 1922, American English, from the adjective, originally in the phrase *duplex house* and *duplex apartment.*

duplicate (dü'pləkit) *adj.* Probably before 1425, double, consisting of two parts, in a translation of Higden's *Polychronicon;* borrowed from Latin *duplicātus,* past participle of *duplicāre* to double, from *duplex* (genitive *duplicis*) folded double; see DUPLEX; for suffix see -ATE[1]. The meaning of exactly corresponding to something, is first recorded in 1812. **—n.** 1532, from the adjective. **—v.** (dü'pləkāt). 1472 *duplicaten* make a second reply; later, to double (1623); borrowed from Latin *duplicātus,* past participle of *duplicāre* to double; for suffix see -ATE[1]. The meaning of make an exact copy of, is first recorded in 1860, in Emerson's works. **—duplication** *n.* Before 1500 *duplicacioun* the action of doubling; borrowed through Middle French *duplication,* and directly from Latin *duplicātiōnem* (nominative *duplicātiō*), from *duplicāre* to double; for suffix see -TION. The meaning of a counterpart or copy is first recorded in 1872. An earlier form *duplacioun* is found in Middle English (probably about 1425); borrowed directly from Latin *duplātiōnem* (nominative *duplātiō),* from *duplāre.* However, the word had limited use in English.

duplicity *n.* About 1433 *duplycyte* deceitfulness; borrowed from Middle French *duplicité,* from Late Latin *duplicitātem* (nominative *duplicitās*) doubleness (in Medieval Latin, ambiguity), from *duplex* (genitive *duplicis*) twofold, DUPLEX; for suffix see -ITY. **—duplicitous** *adj.* deceitful. 1928, in Webster's *Ninth New Collegiate;* formed from English *duplicity* + *-ous.*

durable *adj.* permanent, lasting. About 1390, in Chaucer's *Canterbury Tales;* borrowed from Old French *durable,* from Latin *dūrābilis* lasting, permanent, from *dūrāre* to last, harden, ENDURE; for suffix see -ABLE. It is also possible that *durable* in English is a back formation from earlier *durability.* **—durability** *n.* About 1380 *durablete,* in Chaucer's translation of Boethius' *De Consolatione Philosophiae;* borrowed from Old French *durabilité,* from Late Latin *dūrābilitātem* (nominative *dūrābilitās*), from Latin *dūrābilis* durable; for suffix see -ITY.

durance *n.* About 1443 *duraunce* duration; later, imprisonment (1513, in Sir Thomas More's writings); borrowed from Old French *durance* duration, from *durer* to last; see ENDURE; for suffix see -ANCE.

duration *n.* About 1380 *duracioun,* in Chaucer's *House of Fame;* borrowed from Old French *duration,* from Medieval Latin *durationem* (nominative *duratio*), from Latin *dūrāre* harden, ENDURE; for suffix see -ATION.

duress *n.* About 1330 *duresse* hardship, cruelty, harm, from Old French *duresse,* from Latin *dūritia* hardness, from *dūrus* hard. See ENDURE. The sense of forcible restraint, confinement, is first recorded in 1414, in *Rolls of Parliament,* and that of coercion, before 1420, in Lydgate's *Troy Book.*

during *prep.* Before 1387, in Trevisa's translation of Higden's *Polychronicon,* developed from the present participle, originally the gerund, of earlier verb *duren* to last, endure (about 1250); borrowed from Old French *durer,* from Latin *dūrāre* ENDURE.

The prepositional use arose in imitation of the Latin ablative absolute construction; for example, Latin *dūrante bellō,* literally, while the war endures, (en)during the war. When the participle *during* started to appear before various nouns, it came to be treated as a preposition of time.

The form *during* gradually replaced the earlier forms: 1) *durand* (recorded probably before 1350), originally the present participle of *duren* to last, endure. 2) *duraunt* (recorded as a surname 1206), an adjective and preposition borrowed from Old French *durant,* participle and preposition, from *durer* to last, endure.

dusk *n.* 1622, noun use of earlier adjective *dosk* dark, dim, dusky (recorded probably before 1200, in *Ancrene Riwle*). In the MED *dosk, dosc* is considered an alteration (by transposition of *k* and *s*) of Old English *dox* dark-colored (before 1000, in Old English glossaries), and cognate with Old Saxon *dosan* chestnut brown, Old High German *tusin* pale yellow. The OED also cites Kluge's reference to Latin *fuscus* dark, dusky, and Sanskrit *dhūsara-s* dust-colored, from Indo-European **dheus-/dhus-, dhus-ko-s* (Pok. 270).

The alteration of spelling may have been in Old English in some literary form, or it may have occurred in earliest Middle English.

Formation of *dusk* is also explained as the adoption of a Northumbrian form of Old English *dox, *dosc.* **—dusky** *adj.* 1588, formed from English *dusk,* adj., dark, dim + *-y*[1]. The OED mentions that the usual source of an adjective in *-y* is a noun. Since the source of *dusky* would be *dusk,* adj. by the dates, the record for *dusk,* n. may be defective.

dust *n.* Old English *dūst* (probably about 725, in *Christ* *and Satan*); cognate with Old High German *tunst, tunist* storm, breath (modern German *Dunst* mist, vapor), from Proto-Germanic **dunstu-z,* cognate with Sanskrit *dhváṅsati* he vanishes, falls to dust, from Indo-European **dhwens-/dhuns-* Pok. 268). **—v.** Probably before 1200 *dusten* rise as dust, in *Ancrene Riwle* ; from the noun. **—dust bowl** (1936, American English) **—duster** *n.* 1576; formed from English *dust,* n. + *-er*[1]. **—dust jacket** (1928, earlier, *jacket,* 1921) **—dustpan** *n.* (1785, American English) **—dust storm** (1879) **—dusty** *adj.* (probably before 1200)

Dutch *adj.* About 1333-52 *Duch* of Germany, German; later *Duch* of Holland and the Netherlands, Dutch (1568); borrowed from Middle Dutch *duutsch, dūtsch* (modern Dutch *Duits* German). The term corresponds to Old English *thēodisc* belonging to the people (in particular reference to the popular or national language), Old Saxon *thiudisc,* Old High German *diutisc* of the German people (modern German *deutsch*), and Gothic *thiudiskō* after the manner of the heathens or gentiles. The Old English *thēodisc* is from *thēod* people, race, nation (from Proto-Germanic **theudṓ*) + the suffix *-isc* -ish, *thēod* being cognate with Gothic *thiuda* people, Gaulish *Teuto-,* Oscan *toutō,* from Indo-European **teutā́* (Pok. 1084). From the Lombard cognate of Old English *thēodisc* has come Italian *tedesco* as the word for German.

The original sense of Middle English *Duch* of Germany, German, survives by coincidence in the name *Pennsylvania Dutch* a people who came to America from Germany, though the name was a misinterpretation of *Deutsch,* meaning German, as *Dutch.* The more accurate term is *Pennsylvania German.*

Various derogatory expressions compounded of *Dutch,* such as *Dutch courage* (1812) and *Dutch treat* (1887), are, according to the OED, largely a legacy of the commercial rivalry between the Dutch and the English in the 1600's and 1700's; however, the later formations are more likely to be simple random ethnic references, as found in any language, or in some cases the result of contact between the Dutch and other settlers in America, such as written about in Washington Irving's works. For instance, *Dutch courage* in the *Annals of the 12th U.S. Congress,* and *Dutch treat* in *Lippincott's Magazine,* are first recorded in American English.

duty *n.* Probably 1383 *dewete* moral or legal obligation, in Wycliffe's writings; borrowed from Anglo-French *dueté,* from *du, due,* variant of Old French *deü* DUE; for suffix see -TY[2]. The sense of a tax, fee, or other charge owed to a government, church, guild, or municipality, is first recorded probably in 1377. **—duteous** *adj.* 1593, in Shakespeare's *Lucrece;* formed from English *duty* + *-ous,* as in *beauteous.* **—dutiable** *adj.* 1774, formed from English *duty* + *-able.* **—dutiful** *adj.* 1552, formed from English *duty* + *-ful.*

dwarf *n.* person much below ordinary size. Probably before 1300 *dwerew,* in *Kyng Alisaunder;* later *dweruf* (before 1325) and *dwergh* (probably before 1350); developed from Old English *dweorh* (Late West Saxon) and from *duerg* (early Mercian, about 700); cognate with Old Frisian *dwerch* dwarf, Old Saxon *dwerg,* Old High German *twerg* (modern German *Zwerg*), Old Icelandic *dvergr* (Swedish *dvärg,* Danish *dverg*), and *dyrgja* female dwarf, from Proto-Germanic **dwerȝaz,* from Indo-European **dhwergh-/dhurgh-* (Pok. 279). The shifts in spelling show the sound development in Old and Middle English represented by final *-g.* **—adj.** 1597, from the noun. **—v.** Before 1626, in Francis Bacon's *The New Atlantis;* from the noun. **—dwarfish** *adj.* 1565-73, formed from English *dwarf,* adj. + *-ish.*

dwell *v.* Probably about 1200 *dwellen* remain, stay, in *The Ormulum;* later, reside or dwell (about 1250, in *The Story of Genesis and Exodus;* developed from Old English (about 725) *dwellan* to hinder, delay, be tardy, linger, tarry; originally, to make a fool of, lead astray. Then Old English *dwellen* is cognate with Old High German *twellen* hinder, delay, Old Icelandic *dvelja* tarry, delay, from Proto-Germanic **dwaljanan,* Middle Low German *dwel, dwal* senseless, foolish, and Gothic *dwals* foolish; see DULL. **—dweller** *n.* Before 1382, in the Wycliffe Bible; formed from English *dwell* + *-er*[1]. **—dwelling** *n.* About 1378, place of residence, in a version of *Piers Plowman;* earlier, the act or fact of staying (in a place), waiting (probably before 1300, in *Sir Tristrem*), and delay, lingering (probably before 1300, in *Kyng Alisaunder*); formed from English *dwell* + *-ing*[1].

dwindle *v.* 1596, in Shakespeare's *1 Henry IV,* apparently a diminutive and frequentative form of Middle English *dwinen* waste away, fade, wither, vanish (about 1150); developed from Old English (about 1000) *dwīnan;* cognate with Middle Dutch *dwīnen* to vanish, disappear, and Old Icelandic *dvīna* grow weaker, faint, from Proto-Germanic **dwīnanan,* from Indo-European **dhw-t-n-* pass away (Pok. 261); see DIE; for suffix see -LE[3].

dye *n.* Before 1300 *dehe;* earlier *deyg* (about 1280); developed from Old English *dēah, dēag* (about 1000, in Ælfric's works), and related to *dēagol, dīegol* secret, hidden, dark, obscure (from Proto-Germanic **dauȝilaz*); cognate with Old Saxon *dōgol* secret, Old High German *tougal* dark, hidden, secret, and probably Latvian *dūkans* dark-colored. **—v.** to color with a dye. About 1325 *deyen;* earlier, implied in the agent noun *deyer* (1260); developed from Old English (about 1000) *dēagian,* from *dēag,* n., dye, from Proto-Germanic **dauȝṓ,* from Indo-European **dhoukā́,* root **dheuk-* color, dark (Pok. 265). The MED shows use of both the noun and verb in the 1400's, so that contrary to earlier known records the word has been in continuous use since Old English.

Chaucer used both *dyen* and *deyen,* but Trevisa is the first writer of record to use *dyen* and *dyed,* the modern form. However, the distinction in spelling between the verbs *die* and *dye* is relatively recent. Johnson in his *Dictionary,* spelled them both *die;* while Addison, his near contemporary, spelled both *dye.* **—dyer** *n.* 1286, in a surname *Dyere;* earlier *Deghar* (1260); from the Middle English *deien,* v. + *-er*[1]. **—dyeing** *n.* 1400, the act or process of dyeing; earlier, a dyed cloth (about 1395, in the Wycliffe Bible).

dynamic *adj.* of energy or force; forceful. 1817, in Coleridge's *Biographia Literaria,* borrowed from French *dynamique,* from New Latin *dynamicus* or German *dynamisch* (introduced by the German philosopher Leibniz in 1691); both from Greek *dynamikós* powerful, from *dýnamis* power, from *dýnasthai* be able, have power; of uncertain origin; for suffix see -IC.

dynamite *n.* 1867, coined as Swedish *dynamit* by the inventor Alfred Nobel (1833-1896), from Greek *dýnamis* power + Swedish *-it* -ite[1]; see DYNAMIC.

dynamo (dī′nəmō) *n.* machine that produces electric current. 1882, short for earlier *dynamo-electric ma-*

chine (1875), invented and named in 1867 as German *Dynamo(elektrische)maschine* by the German engineer Ernst Werner von Siemens (1816-1892), from Greek *dýnamis* power; see DYNAMIC.

dynasty *n.* Before 1464, borrowed from Middle French *dynastie,* and perhaps directly through Late Latin *dynastia,* from Greek *dynasteíā* power, lordship, from *dynástēs* ruler, chief, from *dýnasthai* have power; see DYNAMIC. Late Middle English *dynastie* replaced the earlier *dynastia* (recorded before 1387, in Trevisa's translation of Higden's *Polychronicon*), which was probably borrowed directly from Greek *dynasteíā.* **—dynast** (dī′nast) *n.* hereditary ruler; one in power. 1631, borrowed from Late Latin *dynastēs,* and directly from Greek *dynástēs* ruler. **—dynastic** *adj.* 1828, earlier as a noun (1623); formed from English *dynasty* + *-ic,* on the model of Greek *dynastikós,* from *dynástēs* ruler.

dyne (dīn) *n. Physics.* unit of force. 1873, formed in English from Greek *dýnamis* power; see DYNAMIC.

French *dyne* in this sense was borrowed in 1881 from English. In a related but different sense, however, *dyne* had been proposed in France as the name of a unit as early as 1842, and this proposal may have influenced the English coinage.

dys- a prefix meaning bad, abnormal, difficult, as in *dysfunction, dystopia.* Borrowed from Greek *dys-* bad, difficult, cognate with Sanskrit *dus-,* Gothic *tuz-* (as in *tuz-wērjan* to doubt), and Old English *tor-* (as in *torbegiete* hard to attain); Indo-European **dus-* (Pok. 227).

dysentery *n.* intestinal disease. About 1384 *dissenterie,* in the Wycliffe Bible; borrowed from Old French *dissenterie,* learned borrowing from Latin *dysenteria,* from Greek *dysenteríā* (*dys-* + *éntera* intestines, bowels), cognate with Sanskrit *ántara-s* inner, Latin **interos* (compare *internal*); for suffix see -Y[3].

dyslexia (dislek′sēə) *n.* difficulty in reading caused by neurological impairment. 1886-88, borrowing through German *Dyslexie;* formed from Greek *dys-* bad + *léx(is)* word, from *légein* to speak in reference to reading aloud + *-íā,* denoting condition or quality. **—dyslexic** *adj.* 1961, formed from English *dyslex(ia)* + *-ic.* —*n.* person with dyslexia. 1961, from the adjective.

dyspepsia *n.* indigestion. 1706, possibly a back formation of English *dyspeptic, or* borrowed from Latin *dyspepsia,* from Greek *dyspepsíā* (*dys-* bad + *pépsis* digestion, from *péttein, péssein* to digest, cook + *-íā,* denoting condition or quality. **—dyspeptic** *adj.* 1694, borrowed from Greek *dýspeptos* hard to digest (*dys-* bad + *peptós* digested, from *péttein* to digest; see COOK); for suffix see -IC.

dysprosium (disprō′sēəm) *n.* rare metallic element. 1886, New Latin, from Greek *dysprósiton* (neuter of *dysprósitos* hard to approach, *dys-* bad, difficult + *prósitos* approachable, from *pros* up to + *-itos,* verbal adjective of *iénai* to go) + New Latin *-ium* (suffix for chemical elements); so called from its rarity in nature. *Dysprosium* was named by its discoverer Lecoq de Boisbaudran (1838-1912).

E

e- a form of the prefix *ex-* [1], meaning out of, from, out. *E-* appears in words of Latin origin before consonants other than *c, f, p, q, s,* and *t,* as in *educe, eject, elect, evade.* It also appears without restriction in scientific terms in the meaning of not, without, as in the biological term *ecarinate* without a keel (*e-* without + *carinate,* from Latin *carīna* keel).

each *adj.* Probably before 1200 *elch, æche,* in Layamon's *Chronicle of Britain;* also *euch,* in *Ancrene Riwle,* and *ech;* developed from Old English (before 830) *ǣlc,* originally a compound meaning "ever alike," (*ā* ever + *gelīc* alike); cognate with Old Frisian *ellik, elk* each, and Middle Dutch *ēlic, elc,* modern Dutch *elk;* see AY[1], AGE, and ALIKE. The spelling *each* began to appear gradually in the late 1500's.

eager *adj.* About 1275 *egre* impatient, eager; later, keen, sharp, fierce, impetuous (probably before 1300); borrowed from Old French *aigre,* from Vulgar Latin **ācrus,* corresponding to Latin *ācer* (genitive *ācris*) keen, sharp; see ACRID. The spelling *eager* began to appear gradually at the end of the 1500's, but was not in general use until the later 1600's.

eagle *n.* Before 1338 *egle,* in Mannyng's *Chronicle of England;* borrowed from Old French *egle,* from Old Provençal *aigla,* from Latin *aquila,* originally black eagle, feminine of *aquilus* dark-colored (the color of a storm cloud), probably from *aqua* water; see AQUATIC. The spelling *eagle* was a development of the 1600's.

ear[1] *n.* organ of hearing. Probably before 1200 *ere, eir, eare;* developed from Old English (before 1000) *ēare;* cognate with Old Frisian *āre* ear (modern Frisian *ear*), Old Saxon *ōre, ōra,* Middle Dutch *ōre* (modern Dutch *oor*), Old High German *ōra* (modern German *Ohr*), Old Icelandic *eyra* (Swedish *öra,* Danish and Norwegian *øre*), from Proto-Germanic **auzṓn,* and Gothic *ausō,* from Proto-Germanic **aúsōn.* Outside Germanic the word is also cognate with Old Irish *āu, ō* ear, Latin *auris,* Greek *oûs,* Albanian *veš,* Lithuanian *ausìs,* Old Slavic *ucho,* Russian *úkho,* Armenian *unkn,* Avestan *uši* both ears, and Persian *hoš* ear, from Indo-European **ōus-/əus-/us-* (Pok.785).

It is noteworthy that the word for *ear* in the Romance languages descended from the Latin diminutive *auricula* rather than from *auris:* French *oreille,* Spanish *oreja,* Italian *orecchio,* Portuguese *orelha,* Romanian *ureche,* etc.

—eardrum *n.* (1645) **—earmark** *n.* (before 1460); *v.* (1591, in Spenser's works) **—earring** *n.* Before 1382, developed from Old English *ēarhring* (about 1000). **—earshot** *n.* 1607, in Beaumont and Fletcher's *Woman Hater,* formed from English *ear* + *shot,* modeled on *bowshot,* etc.

ear[2] *n.* part of corn, wheat, etc. containing the grains. Probably before 1200 *ear,* in *Ancrene Riwle,* developed from Old English (before 800) *ēar* (West Saxon), *eher, æher* (Northumbrian); cognate with Old Frisian *ār* ear of grain, Old Saxon *ahar,* Middle Dutch *aer* (modern Dutch *aar*), Old High German *ahir* (modern German *Ähre*), Old Icelandic *ax,* Gothic *ahs, ahana* chaff, from Proto-Germanic **aHaz,* genitive **aHizaz;* also cognate with Latin *acus* (genitive *aceris*) husk of grain, chaff, *agna* ear of grain, Greek *áchnē* chaff, and *akostḗ* barley, from Indo-European **áḱes-/áḱos-/aḱs-* (Pok.21).

earl *n.* About 1300 *erl,* developed from Old English (perhaps before 616) *eorl* man, warrior, nobleman. The Old English *eorl* may be contrasted with a *ceorl* CHURL, or ordinary freeman and is cognate with Old Saxon and Old High German *erl* man, nobleman, Old Icelandic *jarl* chieftain, nobleman, and Runic Norse *erilaR* designation of a magic-religious function. This Germanic word is of unknown origin.

early *adv.* Probably before 1200 *erliche;* later *erli* (before 1382, in the Wycliffe Bible); developed from Old English (about 950) *ǣrlīce* (*ǣr* soon, ERE + *-līce* -ly[1]). Old English *ǣrlīce* may have been formed in imitation of Old Icelandic *ārliga* early. **—adj.** Probably before 1200 *earliche,* in *Ancrene Riwle,* from the adverb.

The spelling *early* of both the adverb and adjective began to appear at the end of the 1500's.

earn *v.* Probably before 1200 *ernen;* developed from Old English *earnian* get as a reward for labor (before 899, in Alfred's translation of Boethius' *De Consolatione Philosophiae*), from Proto-Germanic **aznōjanan;* related to *esne* serf, laborer, man, and cognate with Old Frisian *esna* reward, pay, Old High German *asni* day laborer, *arnōn* to reap, *aren* harvest, crop (modern German *Ernte*), Old Icelandic *ǫnn* harvest, labor, Gothic *asans* harvest, summer, Old Slavic *jeseni̊* autumn, and Greek *opṓrā* early autumn, from a pre-Greek phrase **op(i) ósar* following upon summer, from Indo-European **es-en-/os-en-/os-er-* summer (Pok.343).

The spelling *earn,* found in earlier *earne* (1589), and *yearne* (1591) was gradually adopted in the 1600's.

earnest[1] *n.* seriousness. About 1250 *ernest,* in *The Story of Genesis and Exodus;* developed from Old English (about 1000) *eornost;* cognate with Old Saxon *ernust* seriousness, firmness, struggle, Old High German *ernust* (modern German *Ernst* seriousness), Old Icelandic *ern* able, vigorous, Gothic *arniba* securely, Avestan *arənu-* struggle, and Greek *órnysthai* rise up, from Indo-European **er-/or-/r̥-* rise up (Pok.326). **—adj.** serious. Before 1325 *ernest,* in *Cursor Mundi;* developed from Old English (about 1000) *eornoste,* from *eornost,* n.

earnest[2] *n.* pledge, surety. Probably about 1200 *ernesse,* apparently an alteration (by association with derivatives in *-ness*) of Old French *erres,* plural of *erre* pledge, from Latin *arra, arrha,* short forms of *arrabō, arrhabō,* from Greek *arrhabṓn* earnest money, pledge, surety, from Hebrew *'ērābhōn,* from *'arabh* he gave surety, pledged.

The spelling with *t,* which appeared in Middle English before 1400, was influenced by *earnest*[1], with which this word was confused at an early period in the belief that an *earnest* was so called because a transaction or bargain was supposed to be made "in earnest."

earth *n.* 1137 *erthe,* developed from Old English *eorthe* the ground, soil, earth (about 725, in *Beowulf*); cognate with Old Frisian *erthe* earth, Old Saxon *ertha,* Middle Dutch *aerde* (modern Dutch *aarde*), Old High German *erda* (modern German *Erde*), Old Icelandic *jǫrdh* (Swedish, Danish, and Norwegian *jord*), and Gothic *aírtha,* from Proto-Germanic **erthō,* all containing a dental suffix; compare further without that suffix: Old High German *ero* earth, Welsh *erw* field, Greek *éras* (neuter) earth, *éraze* (adverb) to earth, and perhaps Armenian *erkir* earth (altered from expected *ergin-* on the model of *erkin* heaven, sky), from Indo-European **er-t-,* **er-w-,* root **er-* (Pok.332). **—v.** Probably before 1400, to bury, in *The Wars of Alexander;* from the noun. The spelling *earth* appeared in the last half of the 1500's.

—earthen *adj.* Before 1325 *erthen;* earlier *eorthene* (probably before 1200); formed probably in Middle English from *erthe, eorthe* earth + *-en, -ene* -en[2]. **—earthenware** *n.* (1673) **—earthly** *adj.* Probably before 1200 *erthlike,* formed in Middle English from *erthe* + *-like (-lich)* -ly[1]; and *eorthlic,* developed from Old English *eorthlīc* earthly. **—earthquake** *n.* About 1280 *eorthequakynge;* later *erthe quaque* (about 1325). **—earthward** *adv.* (before 1398) **—earthworm** *n.* (before 1400) **—earthy** *adj.* Before 1398 *earthy,* formed from English *erthe* + *-y*[1].

earwig *n.* beetlelike insect. Probably before 1400 *herewyck;* later *erewygge* (about 1450); developed from Old English (about 1000) *ēarwicga (ēare* ear[1] + *wicga* beetle, worm; probably related to WIGGLE; so called from the former belief that it crawled into people's ears *).* **—v.** whisper insinuations in the ear of. 1837, in Marryat's writings; from the noun.

ease *n.* Probably before 1200 *eise* comfort, opportunity; later *ese* (before 1375); borrowed from Old French *aise* comfort, pleasure, of unknown origin.

Bloch-Wartburg, Meyer-Lübke, etc., derive Old French *aise* from a Vulgar Latin form of Latin *adjacēns* neighboring, adjacent, but the connection is not supported by historical phonetics. Old French *aise* suggests derivation from a word ending in a vowel, but such a form as Vulgar Latin **adjacēs,* **adjacēns* would give Old French **aises* (compare Latin *īnfāns* the source of Old French *enfes*). Moreover, there is a semantic gap between French *aise* comfort, pleasure, and Latin *adjacēns* lying near, neighboring, adjacent, which with the lack of Romance cognates beyond French *aise* and Provençal *aize* (the source of Italian *agio* and Portuguese *azo*) casts further doubt on a Latin derivation.

—v. About 1300 *aisen* to help, assist, borrowed from Old French *aaisier* set at ease (*a-,* from Latin *ad-* at + *aisier* to comfort, ease, from *aise* comfort, opportunity). **—easement** *n.* About 1390 *esement* compensation, redress, in Chaucer's *Canterbury Tales;* borrowed probably through Anglo-Latin *aisiamentum* and Anglo-French *aisement,* from Old French *aaisement* (*aisier* to put at ease + *-ment* -ment). The meaning in law of limited right to use something belonging to another is first recorded in an English document in 1254-67.

easel *n.* 1634, borrowed from Dutch *ezel* easel, ass, from Middle Dutch *esel,* an irregular borrowing (compare Gothic *asilus*) from Latin *asinus* ASS or possibly from its diminutive form *asellus.*

For similar semantic development, compare French *chevalet* easel (1429), from the earlier literal meaning of little horse, diminutive of *cheval* horse, and English *horse (sawhorse)* a frame or structure used as a support.

east *adv.* Probably before 1200 *esten,* in *Ancrene Riwle;* developed from Old English *ēasten,* from the east (about 725), and *ēast* in or toward the east (before 900); cognate with Old Frisian *āst* east, *āster* eastward, from the east, Old Saxon *ōst* east, Middle Dutch and modern Dutch *oost,* Old High German *ōstan* east (modern German *Osten*), *ōstar* eastward, and Old Icelandic *austr* from the east, from Proto-Germanic **austa-, austra-.* Cognates outside Germanic include Latin *aurōra* dawn, *auster* the south wind, Ionic Greek *ēṓs* dawn, Lithuanian *aušrà* dawn, Old Prussian *ausis* gold, and Sanskrit *uṣā́s* dawn, from Indo-European **aus-/us-* shining (Pok.86).

The words for *east* in the Romance languages were borrowed from English: French and Italian *est,* Spanish and Portuguese *este,* and possibly Romanian *est,* unless the latter was borrowed through French.

—adj. Probably before 1200, found in Old English compounds such as *ēast-dǣl* eastern part (the first element regarded as a separate word). **—n.** About 1225 *est,* developed from Old English *ēast* (before 900, in Alfred's works).

—easterly *adj.* 1548, formed from earlier *easter* (before 1387 *ester*) variant of *eastern* + *-ly*[2]. The adverb *easterly,* meaning in an eastern position or direction, appeared in 1635; for suffix see -LY[1]. **—eastern** *adj.* Before 1387 *esterne;* developed from Old English (about 875) *ēasterne (ēast* east + *-erne,* suffix denoting direction); cognate with Old Saxon *ōstroni* eastern, Old High German *ōstrōni,* and Old Icelandic *austrœnn.* **—Easterner** *n.* (1840, person living in the eastern U.S., in Lowell's works). **—eastward** *adv.* Before 1200, developed from Old English (959) *ēastwærde (ēast* + *-weard* -ward).

Easter *n.* 1103 *Eastran* festival commemorating the resurrection of Christ, and corresponding to the Jewish Passover, to which the name *Easter* (Middle English *Esterne, Ester*) was also applied, as recorded before 1387. *Easter* developed from Old English *Ēastre* (before 899, in Alfred's translation of Bede's *Ecclesiastical History*). Originally *Ēastre* was the name of a Germanic goddess whose feast was celebrated at the spring equinox, and is cognate with Old High German *ōstarūn, pl.,* Easter (modern German *Ostern*) and Lithuanian *aušrà* dawn. Old English *Ēastre* ultimately derives from *ēast* east, indicating that it originally referred to the goddess of dawn, corresponding to the Roman goddess *Aurōra* and the Greek goddess *Ēṓs.* **—Easter egg** (1825, replacing earlier *pace egg, paste-egg,* 1611)

easy *adj.* Probably before 1200 *aisie* able, having opportunity; later *esi* (about 1378); borrowed from Old French *aisié* (modern French *aisé*), past participle of *aisier,* to put at ease, from *aise* EASE. The sense of not difficult, is first recorded about 1280, perhaps influenced by *ease,* n. **—adv.** Before 1400, from the adjective. The spelling *easy* began to appear in the first half of the 1400's but was not established until the late 1600's. **—easily** *adv.* About 1290 *aisieliche* with little effort, formed from Middle English *aisie* + *-liche* -ly[1]. **—easiness** *n.* Probably before 1425 *esynez,* formed from Middle English *esy, esi* (later spellings of *aisie*) +

-nez, -nes -ness. **—easy chair** (1707) **—easygoing** *adj.* (1674)

eat *v.* Probably 1140 *eten,* developed from Old English (about 725) *etan,* past tense *ǣt* ate, past participle *eten* eaten; cognate with Old Frisian *īta, eta* to eat (modern Frisian *ite*), Old Saxon *etan,* Middle Dutch *ēten* (modern Dutch *eten*), Old High German *ezzan* (modern German *essen*), Old Icelandic *eta* (Swedish *äta*), and Gothic *itan,* from Proto-Germanic **etanan.* Cognates outside Germanic include Latin *ēsse,* later *edere* to eat, Homeric Greek *édmenai* to eat, Old Irish *esse* eaten, Lithuanian *ė̃sti* to eat, Old Slavic *jastŭ* he eats, Sanskrit *ádmi* I eat, Armenian *utem* I eat, and Hittite *e-it-mi* I eat, from Indo-European **ed-/od-* (Pok.287).

Curiously, Latin *edere* was not transmitted to the Romance languages except in Spanish and Portuguese *comer* from Latin *comedere* eat up (*com-* thoroughly + *edere* eat; see COMESTIBLE); rather *mandūcāre* took its place, yielding French *manger,* Portuguese *manjar,* etc.

—eatable *adj.* About 1384 *etable,* in the Wycliffe Bible, formed from Middle English *eten* + *-able.* **—eatery** *n. Informal.* restaurant; diner. 1901, American English, formed from *eat* + *-ery,* as in *bakery.*

eaves *n.pl.* Probably before 1200 *eovese,* in Southwest Midland dialect; later *evese,* singular (before 1325, in Southeast Midland); developed from Old English *efes* edge of a roof or overhanging thatch on a stack (before 1000); earlier, edge of a woods (894). Old English *efes, yfes* is cognate with Old Frisian *ose* eaves, Old High German *obasa* eaves, porch, Old Icelandic *ups* eaves, and Gothic *ubizwai* (dative singular) porch, from Proto-Germanic **uƀaswa-, uƀiswa-;* probably derived from the same root asOld English *ofer* OVER. In modern English, *eaves* is commonly treated as a plural because of the final *-s,* the form *eave* being occasionally used as the singular. **—eavesdrop** *v.* listen secretly. 1606, probably a back formation from *eavesdropper* one who listens secretly to conversation (probably about 1450), developed from earlier *eavesdrop* space on the ground on which rainwater drops from the eaves (1449). Middle English *evesdrop* is apparently an alteration (influenced by *drop*) of Old English *yfesdrype* the dripping of rainwater from the eaves (*efes, yfes* eaves + *dryppan* to DRIP).

ebb *n.* flowing of the tide away from shore. About 1190 *ebbe,* developed from Old English (before 1000) *ebba;* cognate with Old Frisian *ebba* ebb, Old Saxon *ebbiunga,* Middle Low German and Middle Dutch *ebbe* (modern Dutch *eb*), Old Icelandic *efja* countercurrent in a stream, from Proto-Germanic **aƀjōn;* related to *af* OF and OFF. The figurative sense of a decline, decay, is first recorded before 1398. **—v.** Probably before 1200 *ebben;* developed from Old English *ebbian* (before 1000, in Caedmon's *Genesis and Exodus*), from *ebba* ebb. **—ebb tide** (1837, in Marryat's works).

ebony *n.* 1597, apparently alteration of earlier *hebenyf* (about 1384, in the Wycliffe Bible); borrowed perhaps as *hebenivus* a misreading of Late Latin *hebeninus* of ebony, from Greek *ebéninos,* from *ébenos* ebony, from Egyptian *h-b-ny,* probably also the source of Hebrew *hobhnīm* (in Ezekiel 27:15). **—adj.** 1598, from the noun. The sense of black, dark, is first recorded in 1834.

ebullient (ibul′yənt) *adj.* bubbling over, enthusiastic, exuberant. 1599, boiling, agitated; borrowed from Latin *ēbullientem,* present participle of *ēbullīre* to spout out, burst out (*ē-* out, *e-* + *bullīre* to bubble, BOIL[1]). The figurative sense of enthusiastic, is first recorded in 1664. **—ebullience** *n.* 1749, in Henry Fielding's *Tom Jones,* formed from English *ebullient* + *-ence,* on the analogy of *affluent, affluence,* etc. **—ebullition** *n.* Before 1400 *ebullitiun;* borrowed possibly through Old French *ebullicion,* from Late Latin *ēbullītiōnem* (nominative *ēbullītiō*) a bubbling up or boiling, from Latin *ēbullīre.*

ec- a prefix, form of *ex-*[2], meaning from, out of, appearing in words of Greek origin before consonants, as in *eclectic, eclipse, ecstasy.*

eccentric (eksen′trik) *adj.* 1551, (of a circle) not having the same center, possibly from the earlier noun, but more likely borrowed from Medieval Latin *eccentricus,* from Greek *ékkentros* out of the center (*ek-, ex-* out + *kéntron* CENTER); for suffix see -IC. The figurative sense of deviating from the norm, odd, whimsical, is first recorded about 1630, with particular application to people in 1685. **—n.** Probably before 1430, a circle or orbit not having the earth precisely in its center (a meaning which survived through the 1700's); borrowed from Middle French *excentrique* and Medieval Latin *eccentricus,* both adjectives used as nouns. The meaning of an eccentric person (one who behaves in an unusual manner), is first recorded in 1832, in Sir Walter Scott's *St. Ronan's Well;* also from the adjective, possibly after the French *excentrique* (1611) in the figurative sense. **—eccentricity** *n.* 1551, formed from English *eccentric* + *-ity.* The figurative sense of oddity, is first recorded in 1657.

ecclesiastic (iklē′zēas′tik) *adj* of the church or clergy. 1483, in Caxton's *Cato,* possibly a shortening of earlier *ecclesiastical* (probably before 1425), or borrowed through Middle French *ecclésiastique,* and directly as a learned borrowing from Late Latin *ecclēsiasticus,* from Greek *ekklēsiastikós* of the ancient Athenian assembly, (later) of the church, from *ekklēsiastḗs* speaker in an assembly or church, preacher; for suffix see -IC. Greek *ekklēsiastḗs,* used in the Septuagint to render Hebrew *qōhēleth* (name of the Biblical book of Ecclesiastes), derives from *ekklēsíā* assembly of citizens in ancient Athens, (later) church, from *ekkaleîn* call forth (*ek-* out of, forth, ex-[2] + *kaleîn* to call; see LOW[2], of cattle). **—n.** clergyman. 1651 (in Hobbes' *Leviathan*), from Late Latin *ecclēsiasticus* church officer, noun use of the adjective; replacing earlier *ecclesiast,* n. (1387-95, in Chaucer's *Prologue* to the *Canterbury Tales*).

echelon (esh′əlon) *n.* 1796, steplike arrangement of troops, borrowed from French *échelon* level, echelon, literally, round or rung of a ladder, from Old French *eschelon,* from *eschiele* ladder, from Late Latin *scāla* stair, slope, from Latin *scālae,* pl., ladder, steps; see SCALE[3] steps.

In military usage the generalized sense of a level or subdivision was probably established in English in World War I, and perhaps earlier in French (as in *à l'échelon du régiment* at regimental level). By World War II the usage was extended to administrative levels or grades in the civil service and other professions.

A related form *eschele* a troop of soldiers, appears in Middle English (probably before 1300, in *Arthour and Merlin*), borrowed from Old French *eschiele* ladder, but the meaning is not recorded in English after 1500.

echidna (ikid′nə) *n.* small ant-eating animal. 1847, New Latin, from Latin *echidna* adder, viper, from Greek *échidna,* from *échis* viper, related to *echînos* sea urchin, hedgehog, and cognate with Old English *igil* and *īgil* hedgehog, porcupine, Old Icelandic *igull,* Lithuanian *ežys* hedgehog, and Sanskrit *áhi-s* snake, from Indo-European **eĝhi-* (Pok.292).

echinoderm (ikī'nədėrm) *n.* starfish, sea urchin, or other small sea animal. 1835, borrowed from New Latin *Echinodermata,* the phylum name, from Greek *echînos* sea urchin, originally porcupine, hedgehog (see ECHIDNA) and *dérma* (genitive *dérmatos*) skin; see DERMA. The name refers to the spiny shell of this sea animal.

echo *n.* 1340 *ecko,* in *Ayenbite of Inwit;* later *eccho* (probably before 1430); borrowed from Old French *echo,* and from Latin *ēchō,* from Greek *ēchṓ,* from Indo-European **wāgh-* to cry, shout (Pok. 1110). **—v.** Before 1559, from the noun.

The modern spelling *echo* was introduced in the 1600's in imitation of the Latin.

—echoic *adj.* 1880, formed from English *echo* + *-ic.* The term was proposed by Murray, original editor of the OED, as a substitute for *onomatopoeic* in etymologies.

echovirus *n.* type of virus associated with meningitis, intestinal disturbances, and respiratory illnesses. 1955, acronym formed from *e(nteric) c(ytopathogenic) h(uman) o(rphan) virus;* originally called "orphan virus" because it was not at first known to cause any of the diseases with which it is associated.

éclair (āklãr') *n.* oblong pastry filled with cream or custard. 1861, borrowing of French *éclair,* literally, lightning, from Old French *esclair,* from *esclairer* to light up, make shine, from Gallo-Romance **exclāriāre,* reformed from Latin *exclārāre* light up, illumine (*ex-* out + *clārus* CLEAR).

éclat (āklä') *n.* Before 1674, notoriety in John Evelyn's letters; borrowing of French *éclat* splinter, fragment, (also) flash, brilliance, from *éclater* burst out, splinter, from Old French *esclater;* see SLAT (explained in the OED as adapted from West Germanic or Frankish **slaitan* to tear, slit, causative form of *slītan;* the Germanic *sl-* became *scl-* in Romanic to which *e-* was prefixed before *s* + consonant). The extended meaning of brilliant success, fame, is first recorded in English in 1741.

eclectic *adj.* 1683, in Dryden's translation of *Plutarch's Lives,* designating a group of ancient Greek philosophers who were not attached to a particular school but selected doctrines from every system of thought; borrowed, perhaps through French *éclectique* (1651), from Greek *eklektikós* literally, picking out, selective, from *eklektós* selected, from *eklégein* pick out, select (*ek-, ex-* out + *légein* gather, choose); see LEGEND; for suffix see -IC. The generalized sense of selecting and using what seems best from various sources, consisting of selections from various sources, not narrow, broad in acceptance, is first recorded in 1814. **—n.** 1817, an adherent of the eclectic method of philosophy, in Coleridge's *Biographia Literaria;* probably from the English adjective. **—eclecticism** *n.* formed from English *eclectic,* n. + *ism.*

eclipse *n.* About 1280, darkening of the sun, moon, etc., by another body, borrowed from Old French *eclipse,* learned borrowing from Latin *eclīpsis,* from Greek *ékleipsis* a leaving out, forsaking, an eclipse, from *ekleípein* to forsake its usual place, fail to appear, be eclipsed (*ek-* out of, out, from *ex-* + *leípein* to leave). The figurative sense of loss of brilliance, obscuration, is first recorded about 1385, in Thomas Usk's *The Testament of Love.* **—v.** About 1280 *eclipsen* cause the eclipse of; from the noun. The figurative sense of obscure, overshadow, is first recorded probably before 1387, in Lydgate's writings. **—ecliptic** *n.* great circle which is the apparent path of the sun. 1391, abstracted from *ecliptik lyne,* in Chaucer's *Treatise on the Astrolabe;* borrowed from Latin *līnea ecliptica* ecliptic line, from feminine of *eclīpticus* of an eclipse, from Greek *ekleiptikós,* from *ékleipsis* eclipse; so called because eclipses occur on or near this circle.

eclogue *n.* Probably before 1439, short pastoral poem often written as a dialogue between shepherds, in Lydgate's *Falls of Princes;* borrowed from Latin *ecloga,* from Greek *eklogḗ* selection, from *eklégein* to select; see ECLECTIC.

eco- a combining form, corresponding to Latin *oeco-* and Greek *oiko-,* of Greek *oîkos* house, in words borrowed from Greek, especially *economy* (Greek *oikonomíā* household management); and in *ecology,* a modern coinage, broadened to mean the environment and relation to it; further extended in recent English coinages to mean of the ecology or the environment, as in *ecosystem, ecocide.* Greek *oîkos* is cognate with Latin *vīcus* village, quarter, Sanskrit *víśam,* accusative, house, and Gothic *weihs* village, from Indo-European **weiḱ-/woiḱ-/wiḱ-* (Pok.1131).

ecology *n.* study of the relation of living things to their environment. 1858, in Thoreau's letters, also with the spelling *oecology* (1873); borrowed from German *Ökologie,* and, perhaps by influence of the German word, also formed in English from Greek *oîkos* house, habitation + English *-logy* study of.

economy *n.* Probably 1440 *yconomye* management of a household, possibly influenced in its formation by earlier *iconomique,* n. (before 1393, in Gower's *Confessio Amantis*); but ultimately borrowed through Middle French *économie,* or directly from Latin *oeconomia,* from Greek *oikonomíā,* from *oikonómos* manager, steward (from *oîkos* house + *-nómos* managing, from *némein* manage, see NIMBLE); for suffix see -Y[3]. The extended sense of management of the resources of a country, etc., is first recorded in 1651, in Hobbes' *Leviathan.* **—economic** *adj.* 1592, of household management, possibly a shortening of presumably earlier *economical,* or borrowed through Middle French *économique* or directly from Latin *oeconomicus,* from Greek *oikonomikós,* from *oikonomía* economy; for suffix see -IC. The current sense of having to do with economics is first recorded in English in 1835. As noted under *economy,* the term was used in Middle English as a noun. **—economical** *adj.* 1577, probably formed from English *economy* + *-ical.* The sense of pertaining to the economy of a country, etc., is first recorded in 1781, in Gibbon's *Decline and Fall of the Roman Empire,* preceded by Burke's use (1780), in the sense of thrifty. It is also possible that the date for *economic* is defective and that *economical* was formed from English *economic* + *-al*[1]. **—economics** *n.* 1586, science or art of managing a household, perhaps formed from earlier Middle English *iconomique,* n. + *-s,* as in *physics;* but because there is no record of such use, *economics* is generally considered to be formed in English from Middle French *économique* (from Latin *oeconomica,* from Greek *oikonomiká,* from neuter plural of *oikonomikós* economic) + English *-s.* The sense of the science of managing the resources of a country, etc., is first recorded in 1792. **—economist** *n.* 1586, person who manages a household; later, a student of economics (1804); one of the French Economistes (1776, in Adam Smith's *Wealth of Nations*); probably borrowed from Middle French *économiste,* or formed from English *economy* + *-ist,* by influence of the Middle French. **—economize** *v.* 1648, to manage a household, in Milton's writings; formed from English *economy* + *-ize.* The sense of to spend sparingly, is first recorded in Burke's writings, in 1790.

ecru or **écru** (ek′rü) *adj., n.* pale brown. 1869, borrowed from French *écru* raw, unbleached (variant of *cru* raw), from Old French *escru* (*es-* thoroughly, completely, from Latin *ex-* + *crūdus* raw, CRUDE).

ecstasy *n.* About 1384, thrilling or overwhelming delight, elation, in the Wycliffe Bible; borrowed from Old French *extasie,* from Late Latin *extasis,* from Greek *ékstasis* trance, distraction, from *existánai* put out of place (*ex-* out + *histánai* to place, cause to STAND). **—ecstatic** *adj.* 1630, in Milton's *Passion,* borrowed perhaps through French *extatique* (1546, in Rabelais), and directly from Greek *ekstatikós,* from *ékstasis* trance.

ecto- a combining form meaning outside, outer, in scientific and technical coinages, such as *ectoderm, ectoplasm* (outer portion of the cytoplasm of a cell). Borrowed from Greek *ekto-,* combining form of *ektós* outside, from *ek-, ex-* out, EX-[2].

ectoderm *n.* outer layer of cells formed during development of animal embryos. 1861, formed from English *ecto-* outer + Greek *dérma* skin; see DERMA. The word was coined by the English biologist Thomas H. Huxley, 1825-1895.

-ectomy a combining form designating the surgical removal of a part of the body, as in *appendectomy, tonsillectomy.* Borrowed from Greek *ektomḗ* a cutting out, excision (*ek-, ex-* out, EX-[2] + *-tomíā* a cutting; see TOMY).

ecumenical (ek′yůmen′əkəl) *adj.* general, universal. 1563-87 *œcumenical* representing the entire Christian world, formed in English as if from Latin **oecūmenicālis,* from Latin *oecūmenicus* general, universal, from Greek *oikoumenikós,* from *oikouménē gê* the inhabited world, from *oikoúmenos,* present passive participle of *oikeîn* inhabit, from *oîkos* house, habitation; see VICINITY; for suffix see -AL[1].

eczema (ek′zəmə) *n.* skin inflammation. 1753, New Latin, from Greek *ékzema,* from *ekzeîn* to boil out (*ek-, ex-* out + *zéma* boiling, from *zeîn* to boil; see YEAST). In early use, there was apparently a reference to the boiling over (or out) of the body humors, perhaps because the disease is often characterized by fluid discharges.

-ed[1] an inflectional suffix forming the past tense of many verbs in English, as in *wanted, debated; played, tried; worked, dropped.* The suffix was reduced in Middle English to *-d* from earlier *-ed* and *-ede,* both forms being a development from Old English *-de,* also noted as *-ade, -ede,* and *-ode* for the vowel that occurs between the base and the inflectional ending. The development is evident in such Middle English forms as *herd, hered, herede,* Old English *herede, hierde* (modern English *heard*), and *demed,* earlier *demde,* Old English *dēmde* (modern English *deemed*). Old English *-de* is cognate with Old High German *-ta,* Old Icelandic *-tha,* and Gothic *-da,* from the same Germanic base as -ED[2].

In modern English the suffix appears as *-ed* in spite of the pronunciation: **1** after *t* and *d, -ed* represents the pronunciation /id/, as expected in *wanted, faded,* and also in some words, such as *blessed, beloved, learned* (this latter distinguished in meaning as an adjective from *learned* as a past participle /lėrnd/). **2** after voiceless consonants, except *t, -ed* represents the pronunciation /t/, as in *dressed, washed.* (Many of these forms were often written with *t* from the 1500's to the 1700's, and though this is no longer the general practice, it survives where a long vowel is shortened in the verb stem, as in *crept, slept, swept.*) **3** after vowels and voiced consonants, except *d, -ed* represents the pronunciation /d/, as in *vowed, lagged.*

In other forms the suffix appears without the preceding vowel, where the *-d* is added directly to the base syllable either as *-d* in *sold* (Old English *seald* from *sellan* to sell) or after a voiceless consonant as *-t* in *bought* (Old English *boht* from *bycgan* to buy). This process of contraction that started in Old English was completed in Middle English and Early Modern English where endings in *-ded, -ted* became *d,* as in *bleded, bled* and *t,* as in *seted, set,* and even with *-ded* contracting to *t* in *gilded, gilt.*

-ed[2] a derivational suffix forming the past participle of many verbs in English, as in *(has) rented, (have) echoed,* and used as if from a verb to form adjectives from nouns with various meanings, especially: a) having, provided with, characterized by, as in *renowned, toothed, moneyed, cultured, diseased, long-legged;* b) having the characteristics of, as in *bigoted, crabbed, dogged.*

The suffix appeared in Old English as *-d, -ed, -ad,* or *-od,* with the vowel marking the inflectional class of the verb, so that the actual past participial suffix is *-d,* cognate with Old High German *-t,* Old Icelandic *-th(r),* Gothic *-th(s),* representing the Proto-Germanic base **-đaz.*

The formation of adjectives from nouns by adding *-ed,* as if a verb form existed, when in fact it does not, is an ancient practice of English, and a characteristic of early Germanic (compare Old Icelandic *eyghdhr* eyed, *hyrndr* horned). Nevertheless, words such as *talented* and *cultured* have been the target of objection from Samuel Johnson, Coleridge, and others, even though Old English is noted for such examples as *hringed* (modern English *ringed*), *hōced* (modern English *hooked*), and *ān-ēaged* (modern English *one-eyed*).

The function of the suffix is also identical with that of the Latin past participial suffix *-tus* as used in *caudātus* tailed, and *aurītus* eared; it can also be found in the Greek verbal adjective suffix *-tós,* and Sanskrit past participial suffix *-tá-s* representing Indo-European **-tós.*

eddy *n.* whirlpool or whirlwind. Before 1455 *ydy* Scottish form); later *eddy* (1553); possibly borrowed from a Scandinavian source (compare Old Icelandic *idha* eddy). —v. 1730, from the noun.

edelweiss (ā′dəlvīs) *n.* Alpine plant with white flowers. 1862, in Emerson's *Thoreau;* borrowing of German *Edelweiss* (*edel* noble + *weiss* white). German *edel* is cognate with Old English *æthele* noble (source of the name *Ethel*), from Indo-European **atos,* family word for father (Pok.71).

edema (idē′mə) *n.* watery swelling in body tissues. Probably before 1425 *ydema,* in a translation of Chauliac's *Grande Chirurgie;* borrowed from Greek *oídēma* (genitive *oidḗmatos*) a swelling tumor, from *oideîn* to swell, from *oîdos* tumor, swelling; cognate with Old Icelandic *eitr* purulent matter, pus, Old High German *eiz* pustule, boil, *eitar* poison (modern German *Eiter* pus), Old Slavic *jadŭ* poison, and Sanskrit *índu-s* a drop (of fluid), from Indo-European **oid-/id-* (Pok.774).

edge *n.* Probably before 1200 *egge,* in Layamon's *Chronicle of Britain;* developed from Old English *ecg* corner, edge, sword (about 725, in *Beowulf*); cognate with Old Frisian *egg* edge, Old Saxon *eggia* point, edge, Middle Dutch *egghe* (modern Dutch *eg*), Old High German *ecka* (modern German *Ecke*), Old Icelandic *egg* corner, angle, edge (from Proto-Germanic **azjō*). Outside Germanic cognates are found in Latin *acus* (genitive *acūs*) needle, Greek *akḗ* point, Old Slavic *osla* whetstone, Armenian *aseln* needle, and Sanskrit *áśri-s* edge, corner, from Indo-European *aḱ-* sharp (Pok. 18). **—v.** About 1300, give an edge; implied in the adjective *egged;* from the noun. The sense of advance imperceptibly, is first recorded in 1624, in Captain John Smith's *The Generall Historie of Virginia.*

The spelling *cg* in Old English *ecg* developed into *gg* in Middle English and *dge* in modern English representing a series of sound changes in which the sound represented by *g* developed into that represented by *j,* as in *judge,* because wide-spread use of Old English *brycge, ecge,* etc. (i.e. in genitive, dative, and accusative case of the noun) led to a new nominative form *brigge, egge,* etc. in Middle English, hence *bridge, edge,* etc. in modern English.

—edgeways *adj.* (1566), **edgewise** *adj.* (1715), replacing earlier *eggoling* (probably before 1400); formed from English *edge,* n. + *-ways, -wise.* **—edgy** *adj.* 1775, formed from English *edge,* n. + *-y*[1].

edible *adj.* eatable. 1611, borrowed from Late Latin *edibilis,* from Latin *edere* EAT; for suffix see -IBLE.

edict *n.* 1483, in Caxton's translation of Cato's writings; borrowed from Latin *ēdictum,* originally neuter past participle of *ēdīcere* publish, proclaim (*ē-* out + *dīcere* say; see DICTION). The form *edict* replaced earlier *edit* (recorded about 1300), borrowed from Old French *edit,* from Latin *ēdictum.*

edifice *n.* About 1380, in Chaucer's translation of Boethius' *De Consolatione Philosophiae;* borrowed from Old French *edifice* building, learned borrowing from Latin *aedificium* building, from *aedificāre* to build, from a lost adjective **aedificus* housebuilding (*aedis,* variant of *aedēs* temple, in the plural meaning dwelling or building, originally, hearth + the root of *facere* to make). The earlier meaning of Latin *aedēs* hearth, fireplace, is related to *aestās* summer season, *aestus* fire, heat, and is cognate with Greek *aíthein* to burn, Sanskrit *inddhé* he kindles, *édha-s* kindling wood, Old Irish *aed* fire, and Old English *ād,* Old High German *eit,* both meaning funeral pyre, blaze, from Indo-European **aidh-/idh-* burn (Pok.11).

edify *v.* Before 1338 *edefien* to found or establish; about 1340 *edifien* to build; borrowed from Old French *edifier,* from Latin *aedificāre* to build, construct, and in Late Latin, improve spiritually, instruct; see EDIFICE. The sense of improve (something) or instruct, especially in Christian doctrine, is first recorded in 1340, in the *Ayenbite of Inwyt.* **—edification** *n.* Probably about 1350 *edificacioun;* borrowed perhaps through Old French *edification,* and directly from Latin *aedificātiōnem* (nominative *aedificātiō*) construction, and in Late Latin spiritual improvement, from *aedificāre* to build; for suffix see -ATION.

edit *v.* 1791, to publish; borrowed possibly through French *éditer,* and directly from Latin *ēditus,* past participle of *ēdere* bring forth, produce (*ē-* out, e- + *-dere,* combining form of *dare* to give; see DATE[1] time). In the sense of prepare for publication, *edit* is first recorded in 1793, probably as a back formation from *editor.* **—edition** *n.* Probably before 1425 *edicion* version or translation; borrowed from Latin *ēditiōnem* (nominative *ēditiō*) a bringing forth, producing, from *ēdit-,* stem of *ēdere* put forth, produce; for suffix see -TION. **—editor** *n.* 1649, publisher; borrowed from Latin *ēditor* one who puts forth, from *ēdit-,* stem of *ēdere* put forth, produce; for suffix see -OR[2].

The sense of a person who prepares written matter for publication is first recorded in English in 1712, in Addison in *The Spectator.*

—editorial *adj.* of or having to do with an editor. 1744, formed from English *editor* + *-ial* (variant of *-al*[1]).**—n.** newspaper article by an editor. 1830, in American English; from the adjective.

educate *v.* 1447 *educaten* bring up (children), train; borrowed from Latin *ēducātus,* past participle of *ēducāre* bring up, rear, educate, related to *ēdūcere* bring out, EDUCE; for suffix see -ATE[1]. The specific sense of instruct, provide schooling is first recorded in 1588, in Shakespeare's *Love's Labour's Lost.* **—education** *n.* 1531, child rearing, in Sir Thomas Elyot's *The Boke Named the Governour;* borrowed probably through Middle French *éducation;* learned borrowing from Latin *ēducātiōnem* (nominative *ēducātiō*), from *ēducāre* educate; for suffix see -ATION. The sense of systematic instruction or schooling given to the young, appeared in English in 1616. **—educational** *adj.* 1652, formed from English *education* + *-al*[1]. **—educator** *n.* 1566, borrowed from Latin *ēducātor,* from *ēducāre;* for suffix see -OR[2].

educe (idüs′) *v.* Probably before 1425 *educen* to direct the flow of (a stream), in a translation of Higden's *Polychronicon;* borrowed from Latin *ēdūcere* lead forth, bring out (*ē-* out + *dūcere* to lead; see TOW[1] pull). The sense of bring out, elicit, is first recorded in English in 1603.

-ee a suffix meaning "one who is ______ed," as in *appointee, draftee, trustee,* added to verb stems to form nouns corresponding to agent nouns in *-er* or *-or* (as *payer, trainer, vendor, lessor,* whence *payee, trainee, vendee,* and *lessee*); but also added to intransitive verbs to mean "one who ______s," as in *escapee, standee.* Originally used in technical terms of English law, *-ee* was an adaptation of the *-é* ending of certain Anglo-French past participles used as nouns, from Old French *-é,* masculine past participle ending, from Latin *-ātus* -ATE[1]. In the 1700's *-ee* began to be used as a pseudo-legal and often humorous suffix, chiefly in forming nonce words such as *laughee, educatee, sendee.* Currently it is used in words such as *adaptee, franchisee, mergee.*

eel *n.* Probably about 1200 *ele;* later *eele* (before 1398, in Trevisa's translation of Bartholomew's *De Proprietatibus Rerum*); developed from Old English *ǣl* (about 1000, in Ælfric's works); cognate with Old Frisian *-ēl* eel, Middle Dutch *ael* (modern Dutch *aal*), Old Saxon and Old High German *āl* (modern German *Aal*), and Old Icelandic *āll,* from Proto-Germanic **ǣlaz,* of unknown origin.

-eer a suffix added to nouns to form nouns and verbs meaning: **1** one who directs or operates, as in *auctioneer.* **2** one who produces, as in *pamphleteer.* **3** to be concerned or deal with, as in *mountaineer, electioneer.* This suffix is an Anglicized form of French *-ier,* agent noun suffix showing names of persons or things performing an act or associated with some activity or thing which normally represents Latin *-iārius* but in many words replaces French *-aire* (as in *secrétaire, dictionnaire*), from Latin *-ārius* -ARY. See also -IER.

eerie (ir′ē) *adj.* Before 1325 *eri* fearful, timid, in *Cursor Mundi,* dialectal variant of earlier *ergh* probably about 1175); developed from Old English (about 885) *earg* cowardly, fearful, timid; for suffix see -Y[1]; cognate with Old Frisian *erg* evil, bad, Middle Dutch *arch, erch* bad (modern Dutch *erg*), Old High German *arg* cowardly, worthless (modern German *arg* bad), Old Icelandic *argr* unmanly (from Proto-Germanic **arȝaz*); also cognate with Sanskrit *ṛghāyáti* (he) trembles, rages, and Greek *orcheîsthai* to dance, from Indo-European **ergh-/orgh-/ṛgh-* tremble (Pok.339). The sense of causing fear because of strangeness or weirdness, appeared in Burns' poetry in 1792, and was considered a Scotticism.

ef- a form of the prefix *ex-*[1], meaning out of, from, out, appearing in words of Latin origin before *f,* as in *effect, effluent.*

efface *v.* 1490 *effacen,* in Caxton's works; borrowed from Middle French *effacer,* from Old French *esfacier* (*es-* out, from Latin *ex-* + *face* appearance, FACE). **—effacement** *n.* 1797, formed from English *efface* + *-ment or* possibly borrowed from French *effacement,* from *effacer* efface + *-ment.*

effect *n.* About 1385, in Chaucer's *Treatise on the Astrolabe;* earlier, conclusion or realization (probably about 1350); borrowed from Old French *effect,* from Latin *effectus* (genitive *effectūs*), from *effec-,* stem of *efficere* work out, accomplish (*ef-* out, variant of *ex-* before *f* + *-ficere,* combining form of *facere* to DO[1] perform). **—v.** bring about, accomplish, 1589, from the noun (earlier forms, 1494 and following are a confusion with *affect*). **—effective** *adj.* Before 1398 *effectif* producing results, efficient, in Trevisa's translation of Bartholomew's *De Proprietatibus Rerum;* borrowed from Old French *effectif* (feminine *effective*), from Latin *effectīvus,* from *effec-,* stem of *efficere* to effect; for suffix see -IVE. **—effectual** *adj.* About 1395 *effectuel,* in Chaucer's *Canterbury Tales;* borrowed from Old French *effectuel,* from Late Latin *effectuālis,* from Latin *effectus* effect.

effeminate *adj.* Before 1393 *effeminat,* in Gower's *Confessio Amantis;* borrowed from Latin *effēminātus,* past participle of *effēmināre* make a woman of (*ef-* out, variant form of *ex-* before *f* + *fēmina* woman; see FEMININE); for suffix see -ATE[1]. **—effeminacy** *n.* 1602, formed from English *effeminate* + *-cy.*

efferent (ef′ərənt) *adj. Physiology.* conducting outward. 1856 (but probably earlier, perhaps 1839-47); borrowed from Latin *efferentem* (nominative *efferēns*), present participle of *efferre* bring out (*ef-* out, variant of *ex-* before *f* + *ferre* bring; see BEAR[2] carry; for suffix see -ENT.

effervescence *n.* 1651, a boiling up; borrowed probably through French *effervescence* (1641), from Latin *effervēscere* (*ef-* out, variant of *ex-* before *f* + *fervēscere* begin to boil, from *fervēre* be hot, boil; see BREW); for suffix see -ENCE. The sense of bubbling, is first recorded in 1684-85, and the figurative sense of liveliness, in 1748, in Samuel Johnson's works. **—effervesce** *v.* 1702, to boil up; borrowed from Latin *effervēscere.* The sense of to bubble, is first recorded in 1784, and the figurative sense of be lively, in 1850, in Stowe's *Uncle Tom's Cabin.* **—effervescent** *adj.* 1684, boiling up; borrowed from Latin *effervēscentem* (nominative *effervēscēns*), present participle of *effervēscere;* for suffix see -ENT. The figurative sense of bubbling, exuberant, appeared in 1833, in Macaulay's *Essays.*

effete (ifēt′) *adj.* 1621, unproductive, barren, in Burton's *Anatomy of Melancholy;* borrowed from Latin *effētus* unproductive, worn out (chiefly feminine *effēta*) worn out with bearing offspring, past participle of a lost verb **efferī* become worn out by bearing offspring (*ef-* out, variant of *ex-* before *f* + the root of FEMININE and FETUS).

The general sense of exhausted, depleted, is first recorded in 1662, and figurative sense of intellectually or morally exhausted or depleted, in 1790, in Burke's *Reflections on the Revolution in France.*

efficacy *n.* effectiveness. 1527, borrowed from Latin *efficācia,* from *efficāx* (genitive *efficācis*) effective, from *efficere* work out, accomplish, EFFECT; for suffix see -ACY. *Efficacy* replaced earlier: 1) *efficace* (recorded probably before 1200, in *Ancrene Riwle*); borrowed from Old French *efficace,* from Latin *efficācia,* and 2) *efficacite* recorded probably before 1425, in Higden's *Polychronicon*); borrowed from Old French *efficacité,* from Latin *efficācitātem* (nominative *efficācitās*) effectiveness, from *efficāx* effective. **—efficacious** *adj.* 1528, formed in English from Latin *efficāx* (genitive *efficācis*) effective + English *-ious.*

efficient *adj.* About 1380, producing immediate effect, in Chaucer's translation of Boethius' *De Consolatione Philosophiae;* borrowed through Old French *efficient,* and directly from Latin *efficientem* (nominative *efficiēns*), present participle of *efficere* work out, bring about, accomplish; see EFFECT; for suffix see -ENT. **—efficiency** *n.* 1593, in Richard Hooker's *Ecclesiastical Polity;* borrowed from Latin *efficientia,* from *efficientem* (see EFFICIENT), present participle of *efficere;* for suffix see -ENCY.

effigy *n.* 1539, borrowed from Middle French *effigie* image of a person, learned borrowing from Latin *effigiēs* copy or imitation of an object, likeness; related to *effingere* to mold, fashion (*ef-* out, variant of *ex-* before *f* + *fingere* to form, shape; see DOUGH).

The phrase *in effigy* appeared in 1617, in Donne's *Sermons.* The expression to *burn* (*hang,* etc.) *in effigy,* that is burn, hang, etc. an image of a person to show what he or she deserves, appeared in 1678, in allusion to the former practice of hanging in effigy escaped criminals; now the practice is confined to public figures as an expression of popular hatred or contempt.

effluence *n.* that which flows forth. Before 1398, in Trevisa's translation of Bartholomew's *De Proprietatibus Rerum;* borrowed from Late Latin *effluentia,* from Latin *effluentem* (nominative *effluēns*), present participle of *effluere* flow out (*ef-* out, variant of *ex-* before *f* + *fluere* to flow; see FLUID); for suffix see -ENCE. **—effluent** *adj.* flowing out. Probably 1440, in some instances possibly a back formation of earlier *effluence;* and in others borrowed from Latin *effluentem;* see EFFLUENCE; for suffix see -ENT. **—*n.*** 1859, from the adjective.

effluvium (iflü'vēəm) *n.* 1646, stream of imperceptible particles, in Sir Thomas Browne's *Pseudodoxia Epidemica;* borrowed from Latin *effluvium* a flowing out, from *effluere;* see EFFLUENCE. The sense of a usually noxious odor is first recorded in 1656, in Hobbes' translation of *Elements of Philosophy*.

effort *n.* About 1489, in Caxton's translation of *Fierabras;* borrowed from Middle French *effort,* from Old French *esfort,* from *esforcier* force out, exert, from Vulgar Latin **exfortiāre* (Latin *ex-* out + *fortis* strong; see FORT).

effrontery *n.* shameless boldness. 1715, borrowed from French *effronterie,* from *effronté* shameless, from Old French *esfronté,* possibly from Late Latin *effrontem* (nominative *effrōns*) barefaced (*ef-* out, variant of *ex-* before *f* + Latin *frontem, frōns* brow, FRONT); for suffix see -ERY. Since *effrōns, effrontis* appears only in Late Latin, some scholars compare Italian *sfrontato,* deriving it from a Vulgar Latin **exfrontātus,* formed from the phrase **ex fronte* without a brow (for blushing), from Latin *ex* out of, and *frōns* brow.

Semantic parallels exist in German *Stirn* forehead, brow, (figurative) a bold front, impudence, effrontery, and its Old English cognate *steornede* having a big forehead, (figurative) bold, forward.

effulgence *n.* radiance. 1667, in Milton's *Paradise Lost,* borrowed from Late Latin *effulgentia,* from Latin *effulgentem* (nominative *effulgēns*), present participle of *effulgēre* shine forth (*ef-*, variant of *ex-* before *f* + *fulgēre* to shine; cognate with Latin *flagrāre* to blaze, and Greek *phlégein* to burn, from Indo-European **bhleg-/bhl̥g-* (Pok.124); for suffix see -ENCE. **—effulgent** *adj.* shining brightly, radiant. 1738, possibly a back formation from *effulgence;* or borrowed from Latin *effulgentem* (nominative *effulgēns*), present participle of *effulgēre* shine forth; see EFFULGENCE; for suffix see -ENT.

effusion *n.* 1402, in Hoccleve's writings; borrowed through Middle French *effusion,* and directly from Latin *effūsiōnem* (nominative *effūsiō*), from *effūd-*, stem of *effundere* pour forth (*ef-* out, variant of *ex-* before *f* + *fundere* pour; see FOUND² to cast; for suffix see -SION. **—effuse** *v.* pour out, spill. 1495 *effusen;* in some instances possibly a back formation from *effusion;* in others borrowed from Middle French *effuser,* from Latin *effūsus,* past participle of *effundere;* see EFFUSION.

eft *n.* small newt. Probably about 1175 *evete,* developed from Old English *efete* (about 1000, in Ælfric's *Glossary*); of unknown origin. The unexplained Middle English variant form *ewte,* appearing before 1398, led to the formation of the word NEWT (before 1425).

egalitarian *adj.* believing in equality, democratic. 1885, formed in English from French *égalitaire* (from Old French *egalité,* from Latin *aequālitātem* EQUALITY) + English *-ian.* **—n.** egalitarian person. 1920, from the adjective.

egg¹ *n.* bird's egg, especially that of a hen. About 1340 *eg,* in a Middle English psalter; later *egge* (1366), originally Northern English; borrowed from a Scandinavian source (compare Old Icelandic *egg*). The forms *eg, egge* replaced earlier Middle English *eai* (recorded probably before 1200, in *Ancrene Riwle*), and *aei, ei;* all developed from Old English (805-31) *ǣg,* which is cognate with Old Icelandic *egg,* Old Saxon, Middle Dutch, modern Dutch, and Old High German *ei* (modern German *Ei*) and Crimean Gothic *ada,* from Proto-Germanic **ajjaz.* These Germanic forms are probably cognate with Latin *ōvum* egg, Greek *ōión,* Welsh *wy,* Old Cornish *uy,* Old Slavic *ajĭce,* Armenian *ju,* and Persian *xāya,* all meaning egg, from Indo-European **ō(w)yóm* (Pok.783). Connection of this word with Latin *avis* bird (see AVIARY) is tentative. **—eggbeater** *n.* (1828, in American English) **—eggcup** *n.* (1773) **—eggnog** *n.* drink made of eggs, milk, and sugar, with liquor or wine added. About 1775, American English, formed from *egg¹* + *nog* (1693) strong ale, of unknown origin. **—eggplant** *n.* (1767) **—eggshell** *n.* (1425, *egg-shel*)

egg² *v.* urge, incite. Probably before 1200 *eggen,* in *Ancrene Riwle;* borrowed from a Scandinavian source (compare Old Icelandic *eggja* to goad, from *egg* EDGE).

eglantine (eg'ləntin) *n.* sweetbrier, a wild rose. Probably before 1425 *eglentyn;* earlier, as a personal name *Eglentyne* (about 1387-95, in Chaucer's *Canterbury Tales*); borrowed from Middle French *eglantine,* originally a diminutive adjective of Old French *aiglent,* from Vulgar Latin **aculentus* spiny, from Latin *acus* (genitive *acūs*) needle; see EDGE; for suffix see -INE¹. *Eglantine* replaced earlier *eglentere* (recorded probably about 1300), from Anglo-French.

ego *n.* the self. 1789, in William Cowper's *Letters,* but probably much earlier as suggested by the use of *ego* in formations such as *egotism* (1714); borrowed from Latin *ego* I; see I. The sense of conceit, egotism is first recorded in English in 1891, in Kipling's *The Light that Failed,* but also may have been used much earlier as suggested by *egotism* used in the sense of selfishness, and *egoism* self-interest. The psychoanalytic sense of the conscious part of the mind (contrasted with *id*), appeared in 1910, in a translation from Freud of German *Ich,* literally, I. Compare ID. **—egoism** *n.* 1785, belief that only one's own mind exists, borrowed from French *égoisme* (1755), probably from New Latin *egoismus,* from Latin *ego* I; for suffix see -ISM. The sense of self-interest, is first recorded in English in 1800. **—egoist** *n.* 1785, borrowed from French *égoïste* (1755), probably from New Latin *egoista,* from Latin *ego* I; for suffix see -IST. **—egotism** *n.* 1714, excessive use of *I, me, my,* in writings of Addison in *The Spectator;* formed in English from Latin *ego* I + English *-tism,* a form of *-ism* found in *dogmatism* (1603), *parasitism* (1611), etc. The sense of selfishness is first recorded in English in 1800. The word *egotist* was also introduced by Addison in the same essay in 1714. French *égotisme* was borrowed from English *egotism* in 1726. **—egotist** *n.* 1714, in writings of Addison in *The Spectator;* formed in English from Latin *ego* I + English *-tist,* a form of *-ist* found in *dogmatist* (1541). **—egotistical** *adj.* 1825, in Macaulay's works, formed from English *egotist* + *-ical.* **—egotistic** *adj.* About 1860, probably a back formation from English *egotistical.*

egregious (igrē'jəs) *adj.* very great, remarkable. About 1534, distinguished, eminent; borrowed from Latin *ēgregius,* from the phrase *ē grege* standing out from the flock (*ē* out of, variant of *ex* before *g* + *grege,* ablative of *grex* herd, flock; see GREGARIOUS); for suffix see -OUS. The ironical use of very great (i.e. outrageous, notorious) is first recorded in English in 1573.

egress (ē'gres) *n.* exit, outlet. 1538, a going out; either 1) borrowed from Latin *ēgressus* (genitive *ēgressūs*), from *ēgredī* go out (*ē-* out, variant of *ex-* before *g* + *-gredī,* combining form of *gradī* to step, go, related to *gradus,* genitive *gradūs* step, GRADE); *or* 2) a back formation from earlier *egression* (recorded before 1425, in a translation of Higden's *Polychronicon*); borrowed from Latin *ēgressiōnem* (nominative *ēgressiō*), from *ēgredī* go out; for suffix see -SION. The meaning of exit, outlet, is first recorded in 1677. —v. go forth. 1578, from the noun.

egret (ē'gret) *n.* heron. About 1353, borrowed from Old French *aigrette,* from Old Provençal *aigreta,* from *aigron* heron, corresponding to Old French *hairon* HERON.

eider (ī'dər) *n.* type of duck. 1743, probably borrowed through German *Eider* or Dutch *eider,* from Icelandic *ædhar,* genitive of *ædhr* eider, from Old Icelandic. The compound *eiderdown,* which appeared in 1774, was probably a part translation of German *Eiderdaunen,* Dutch *eiderdons,* or Icelandic *ædhardūn.*

eight *adj.* Probably about 1200 *ehte,* in *The Ormulum;* later *eyhte* (before 1300), and *eighte* (about 1378, in a version of *Piers Plowman*); developed from Old English *eahta* (about 725, in *Beowulf*), *æhta;* cognate with Old Frisian *achta* eight, Old Saxon and Old High German *ahto* (modern German *acht*), Old Icelandic *ātta,* and Gothic *ahtau;* from Proto-Germanic **aHtō(u).* Cognates outside Germanic include Latin *octō* eight, Greek *oktṓ,* Old Irish *ocht,* Old Slavic *asmĭ,* Lithuanian *aštuonì,* Avestan *ašta,* Sanskrit *aṣṭāú,* and Tocharian A *okät,* Tocharian B *okt,* from Indo-European *oḱtṓ(u)* (Pok.775).

The Germanic, Greek, Latin, and Sanskrit forms seem to represent an Indo-European dual form in *-ōu,* possibly = two fours. For the modern spelling with *gh* see FIGHT.

—n. Probably about 1200, in *The Ormulum.*

—eighteen *adj.* Probably before 1200 *ahtene,* in Layamon's *Chronicle of Britain;* later *ehtetene* (about 1300), and *eightene* (before 1398); developed from Old English (about 1000) *eahtatēne* (*eahta* EIGHT + *-tēne* -teen, from *tēn* TEN). **—eighth** *adj.* Before 1250 *eihtuthe,* in a version of *Ancrene Riwle;* later *eighthe* (about 1385, in Chaucer's *Troilus and Criseyde*); developed from Old English *eahtotha;* cognate with Old Frisian *achtund* eighth, Old Saxon and Old High German *ahtodo,* etc. *—n.* Probably before 1200, used as an absolute construction. **—eighty** *adj.* About 1300 *eighteti,* shortened from Old English (before 830) *hundeahtatig* group of eighty (*hund-* ten; see HUNDRED + *eahta* EIGHT + *-tig* group of ten, -TY[1]).

einsteinium *n.* artificial radioactive element. 1955, New Latin; formed from the name of Albert *Einstein,* 1879-1955, German-born physicist, + *-ium,* suffix of chemical elements.

either *pron., adj., adv.* Probably about 1175 *either, aither* both (of two things or persons), every; developed from Old English *ǣgther* (before 900 in Alfred's translation of Orosius), contraction of *ǣghwæther* each of two, both (*ā-* always, see AY and AGE + *ge-* collective prefix + *hwæther* which of two, WHETHER). English *either* is cognate with German *jeder* each (originally of two).

About 1290 *either* assumed the sense of one or the other of two, which has prevailed in modern English. **—conj. either. . .or** About 1250, developed from Old English *ǣgther,* contraction of *ǣghwæther.*

ejaculate *v.* 1578, eject suddenly, borrowed, perhaps by influence of Middle French *éjaculer* ejaculate, from Latin *ējaculātus,* past participle of *ējaculārī* (*ē-* out, variant of *ex-* before *j* + *jaculārī* to throw, dart, from *jaculum* javelin, from *jacere* to throw; see JET[1] stream; for suffix see -ATE[1]. The sense of exclaim is first recorded in 1666, in Pepys' *Diary.* **—ejaculation** *n.* 1603, borrowed from French *éjaculation,* from *éjaculer* ejaculate, from Latin *ējaculārī;* for suffix see -ATION.

eject *v.* Probably before 1425 *ejecten* expel, drive out, in a translation of Higden's *Polychronicon;* borrowed from Latin *ējectus,* past participle of *ēicere* throw out (*ē-* out, variant of *ex-* before *i, j* + *-icere,* combining form of *jacere* to throw; see JET[1] stream). The senses of this word are partly derived from Latin *ējectāre* cast out, throw up, a frequentative form of *ēicere.* **—ejection** *n.* Probably before 1425 *ejeccion,* in a translation of Higden's *Polychronicon;* borrowed probably from Middle French *ejection,* and directly from Latin *ējectiōnem* (nominative *ējectiō*), from *ējec-,* stem of *ēicere* eject; for suffix see -TION. **—ejector** *n.* 1640, formed from English *eject* + *-or*[2].

eke (ēk) *v.* **eke out** supplement, add to, increase. Probably about 1200 *eken* to increase, lengthen, in *The Ormulum;* Northern and East Midland variant of earlier *echen* (probably before 1200); developed from Old English (about 1000) *ēcan, ēacan, ēacian,* probably from *ēaca* an increase (894, in the *Anglo-Saxon Chronicle*). The Old English is cognate with Old Frisian *āka* to increase, Old Saxon *ōkian,* Old High German *ouhhōn,* Old Icelandic *auka,* and Gothic *aukan;* also cognate with Latin *augēre* to increase, augment, Greek *aúxein,* Lithuanian *áugu* I grow, Sanskrit *ójas* strength, and ultimately with WAX[2] increase, from Indo-European **aug-,* root **aweg-* (Pok.84).

elaboration *n.* Probably before 1425, borrowed from Latin *ēlabōrātiōnem* (nominative *ēlabōrātiō*), from *ēlabōrāre* work out, produce by labor (*ē-* out, variant of *ex-* before *l* + *labōrāre* to LABOR); for suffix see -ATION. **—elaborate** (ilab'ərit) *adj.* 1592, accomplished by labor; earlier, as a past participle meaning worked out in detail, firmly crafted (1581); borrowed from Latin *ēlabōrātus,* past participle of *ēlabōrāre* work out, producę by labor; for suffix see -ATE[1]. *—v.* (ilab'ərāt) 1607, to build up (a chemical substance) from simple elements; borrowed from Latin *ēlabōrātus,* past participle of *ēlabōrāre,* probably by influence of French *élaborer* (1534, in Rabelais); for suffix see -ATE[1]. The sense of work out in detail, appeared in English in 1611, in Cotgrave's *Dictionary.* Because of the long preceding use of *elaboration,* it is also possible that the verb, in particular, is a back formation from *elaboration.*

élan (ālän') *n.* enthusiasm, liveliness. 1877, a borrowing of French *élan,* from *élancer* to rush, dart, from Old French *elancer* (*é-* out, variant of Latin *ex-* before *l* + Old French *lancer* to throw a lance, from Late Latin *lanceāre,* from Latin *lancea* LANCE).

The term *élan vital* creative force in life, appears in a letter of William James' (1907) to Henri Bergson, and thence in Bergson's book *L'Évolution créatrice* (Creative Evolution, 1907). The term was later popularized by Shaw, Julian Huxley, etc.

eland (ē'lənd) *n.* large African antelope. 1786; borrowed in a translation from a book on South Africa from Afrikaans use of Dutch *eland* elk, from German *Elen,* (earlier) *Elend,* from a Baltic source (compare Lithuanian *élnis* elk, Old Lithuanian *ellenis*); cognate with Old High German *elaho* ELK.

elapse *v.* slip by. 1644, borrowed from Middle French

elapser, from Latin *ēlāpsus,* past participle of *ēlābī* slip or glide away (*ē-* out, away, variant of *ex-* before *l* + *lābī* to slip; glide; see LAP[1] front part). **—n.** Before 1677, from the verb, possibly influenced by *lapse.*

elastic *adj.* 1653, causing expansion; borrowed from New Latin *elasticus,* from Greek *elastós* ductile, flexible; related to *elaúnein* to strike, beat out; of uncertain origin; for suffix see -IC. The sense of resilient, is first recorded in English in 1674. **—n.** 1847, in American English, elastic cord or string; from the adjective. **—elasticity** *n.* 1664, formed from English *elastic* + *-ity.*

elate *v.* 1578, raise, elevate; developed from earlier *elat,* adj. haughty (about 1375, in Chaucer's *Canterbury Tales*); probably borrowed from Latin *ēlātus* elevated, a form used to make the past participle of *efferre* bring or carry out (*ef-* out, variant of *ex-* before *f* + *ferre* carry; see BEAR[2] carry). Latin *ēlātus* derives from *lātus* (compare *tulī* I have borne) and is cognate with Doric Greek *tlātós* steadfast in suffering and Welsh *tlawd* poor, from Indo-European **tl̥tós,* root **telə-* (Pok.1060). *Elate,* especially in its renewed use in the late 1500's, may have been a back formation from earlier *elation.*

The current sense of raise the spirits of, exalt, stimulate, excite, is first recorded before 1619, in Donne's works.

—elation *n.* Probably about 1350, elevation of mind, pride; borrowed from Old French *elacion,* from Latin *ēlātiōnem* (nominative *ēlātiō*), from *ēlātus* elevated; for suffix see -TION. The sense of elevation of spirits, buoyancy, is first recorded in 1750, in Samuel Johnson in *The Rambler.*

elbow *n.* Before 1200 *elbowe,* developed from Old English (about 1000) *elnboga* (*eln* ELL[1] length of the forearm + *boga* BOW[2] arch); cognate with Middle Dutch *ellenbōghe* elbow (modern Dutch *elleboog*), Old High German *elinbogo* elbow (modern German *Ellenbogen, Ellbogen*), and Old Icelandic *ǫlnbogi.* **—v.** thrust with the elbow; jostle. 1605, in Shakespeare's *King Lear,* from the noun. **—elbow grease** (1672, in Andrew Marvell's writings) **—elbowroom** *n.* (1540)

elder[1] *adj.* older. Probably about 1175, developed from Old English *eldra* (Mercian dialect, about 725, in *Beowulf*), comparative of *eald, ald* OLD; for suffix see -ER[2]. This word was formerly equivalent to the modern form *older,* but is now restricted to special uses, such as *elder statesman.* **—n.** older person. Probably before 1200 *eldre,* in Layamon's *Chronicle of Britain;* developed from Old English (971) *eldra* older person, parent, ancestor; from the adjective. The sense of a member of a ruling body of men, is first recorded before 1382, in the Wycliffe Bible, as a translation of *seniores* (elders, pl.) in the Vulgate, a rendering of the Hebrew *zəqēnīm,* literally, old men. **—elderly** *adv.* 1611, somewhat old; related to *eldernliche* of old time, literally, forefatherly, from the days of our forefathers (*eldern, eldren* forefathers + *-liche* -ly[1]). **—eldest** *adj.* oldest. Old English *eldest* (Mercian dialect, before 900, in Alfred's translation of St. Gregory's *Pastoral Care*), superlative of *eald, ald* OLD; for suffix see -EST. This word is now generally confined to speaking of members of the same family, as in *our eldest daughter.*

elder[2] or **elderberry** *n.* small tree or shrub with white flowers and black or red berries. About 1150 *ellen;* later *ellarn* (before 1300), *ellern* (about 1378), and *eldre* (before 1400); developed from Old English *ellæn, ellærn* elderberry tree (before 800, in an early glossary); of uncertain origin.

elect *adj.* Probably before 1425, voluntary; later, chosen for office (1447), selected or chosen (1477); borrowed from Latin *ēlēctus,* past participle of *ēligere* pick out, select (*ē-* out, variant of *ex-* before *l* + *-ligere,* combining form of *legere* to choose, read; see LEGEND). **—v.** Probably before 1425 *electen* choose, in a translation of Higden's *Polychronicon,* possibly from *elect,* adj., *or* borrowed from Latin *ēlēctus,* past participle of *ēligere.* Alternatively, *elect,* v. may be a back formation from earlier *election.* **—n.** Probably before 1425, from the adjective. **—election** *n.* About 1300 *eleccioun;* later *election* a choosing, election (probably before 1405); borrowed through Anglo-French *eleccioun,* Old French *election,* from Latin *ēlēctiōnem* (nominative *ēlēctiō*), from *ēlēc-,* stem of *ēligere* select; for suffix see -TION. **—election day** (1467) **—electioneer** *v.* 1789, in Jefferson's writings; probably a back formation from earlier *electioneering* (1760, formed from English *election* + *-eer* + *-ing,* on the model of *auctioneering*). **—elective** *adj.* voluntary. Probably before 1425, borrowed from Medieval Latin *electivus* selective, from Latin *ēlēc-,* stem of *ēligere* select; for suffix see -IVE. The meaning pertaining to a course of study taken by choice, is first recorded in 1847 in American English. *—n.* 1701, from the adjective. The meaning of a course of study which may be taken in school, but is not required, is first recorded in 1850 in American English. **—elector** *n.* Before 1464, borrowed from Late Latin *ēlēctor* chooser, selector, from Latin *ēlēc-,* stem of *ēligere* select; for suffix see -OR[2]. **—electoral** *adj.* 1675, formed from English *elector* + *-al*[1]. **—electoral college** (before 1691; specifically referring to U.S. use, 1800) **—electoral vote** (1825) **—electorate** *n.* 1675, in reference to a German Prince Elector, formed from English *elector* + *-ate*[1]. The meaning of the persons having the right to vote is first recorded in 1879.

electr- a combining form, a form of *electro-* before a vowel, as in *electron, electrode.*

electric *adj.* 1646, borrowed from New Latin *electricus* generated from amber, as by friction; from Latin *ēlectrum* amber, from Greek *ḗlektron;* for suffix see -IC. Greek *ḗlektron* is related to *ēléktōr* the beaming sun, and perhaps cognate with Sanskrit *ulkā́* meteor. The New Latin word (in the form *electricam*) was first used in 1600 by William Gilbert, in a treatise on the magnet, but it is quite possible that its popular adoption *electric* was largely a shortening of earlier *electrical.* **—electrical** *adj.* 1635, formed in English from New Latin *electricus* + English *-al*[1]. **—electric blanket** (1930) **—electric chair** (1889, American English) **—electric eye** (1930) **—electrician** *n.* 1751, American English, in Franklin's writings; formed from *electric* + *-ian,* after *physician, magician,* etc. **—electricity** *n.* 1646, in Sir Thomas Browne's writings, formed from English *electric* + *-ity.* In early use, the word referred to the properties of such things as amber and glass, which could attract lightweight objects when excited by friction. **—electrification** *n.* 1748; formed from English *electrify,* on the model of *magnify, magnification.* **—electrify** *v.* 1747, in American English, in Franklin's writings; formed from *electric* + *-fy.*

electro- a combining form corresponding to Greek *ēlektro-,* combining form of *ḗlektron* amber; its use and meaning in English came from the New Latin form *electrum* and the adjective *electricus* in reference to the power of amber to attract lightweight bodies when rubbed. In its compounds *electro-* has meanings that range from electric, electrically, electricity *(electromagnet, electropositive, electromotive)* to electrolysis *(electroplate)*, electronics *(electromusic)*, and the electron *(electrovalence)*. See the entries **electrode, electrolysis, electrolyte.**

electrocute *v.* kill by electricity. 1889, American English, formed from *electro-* + *(exe)cute;* see ELECTRIC. **—electrocution** *n.* 1890, formed from English *electrocute* + *-ion,* on the pattern of *execute, execution.*

electrode *n.* either of the two terminals of a source of electricity. 1834, in Faraday's writings; formed from English *electro-* + *-ode,* as in *cathode. Electrode* was coined by the English chemist and physicist Michael Faraday on the pattern of *anode* and *cathode.*

electrolysis (ilek'trol'əsis) *n.* chemical decomposition by the passage of electric current. 1834, formed from English *electro-* + Greek *lýsis* a loosening, from *lýein* loosen, set free; see LOSE. The word was coined by the English scientist and philosopher William Whewell.

electrolyte *n.* chemical compound whose water solution will conduct an electric current. 1834, in Faraday's writings; formed from *electro-* + *-lyte,* from Greek *lytós* loosened, from *lýein* loosen, set free; see LOSE. The word was coined by Michael Faraday, English physicist and chemist.

electromagnetic *adj.* 1821, in Faraday's writings; formed from English *electro-* + *magnetic.*

electromotive *adj.* 1806, in Sir Humphry Davy's writings; formed from English *electro-* + *motive.*

electron *n.* elementary particle. 1891, formed from English *electric* + *-on* (as in *ion, anion,* etc.), possibly influenced by the earlier English form *electron* amber (1856) and by Greek *élektron* amber (which, when rubbed, produces a negative charge of static electricity); see ELECTRIC. **—electron microscope** (1932) **—electron volt** (1930, in Rutherford's writings) **—electronic** *adj.* 1902, having to do with electrons, formed from English *electron* + *-ic.* The sense of having to do with electronics, is first recorded in 1930. **—electronic music** (1931) **—electronics** *n.* science dealing with the movement of electrons in semiconductors, vacuum tubes, etc. 1910, formed from English *electron* + *-ics,* as in *physics, mechanics,* etc.

eleemosynary (el'əmos'əner'ē) *adj.* of or for charity. Before 1620 borrowed from Medieval Latin *eleemosynarius* pertaining to alms, from Late Latin *eleēmosyna* alms, from Greek *eleēmosýnē* alms, pity; see ALMS; for suffix see -ARY.

elegant *adj.* About 1485, tastefully ornate in dress; borrowed from Middle French *élégant,* learned borrowing from Latin *ēlegantem* (nominative *ēlegāns*) choice, fine, tasteful, usually regarded as the present participle of **ēlegāre,* a parallel form of *ēligere* select with care, choose; see ELECT; for suffix see -ANT. In early Latin *ēlegāns* had an unfavorable sense of choosy, fastidious, foppish, and this was sometimes the early use in English. In Classical Latin the word expressed the notion of refined grace, which is reproduced in modern English usage. **—elegance** *n.* About 1510, borrowed from Middle French *élégance,* from Latin *ēlegantia,* from *ēlegantem* elegant; see ELEGANT; for suffix see -ANCE.

Elegance replaced the earlier form *elegancy* refinement (recorded probably before 1425, in a translation of Higden's *Polychronicon*); borrowed from Latin *ēlegantia* elegance.

elegy *n.* 1514, mournful or melancholy poem; borrowed from Middle French *élégie,* learned borrowing from Latin *elegīa,* from Greek *elegeíā,* ultimately from *élegos* mournful poem, a lament, perhaps of Asiatic (possibly Phrygian) origin, like Armenian *elēgn* flute, reed. **—elegiac** (el'əjī'ak) *adj.* of or for an elegy. 1581, in Sidney's *Defence of Poesie;* borrowed through Middle French *élégiaque,* from Late Latin *elegīacus,* from Greek *elegeiakós,* from *elegeíā* ELEGY.

element *n.* About 1300, one of the four simple substances (earth, water, air, fire); borrowed from Old French *element,* from Latin *elementum* rudiment, first principle; of uncertain origin. The modern chemical sense (in which the simple substances are carbon, oxygen, hydrogen, etc.) is first recorded in 1813, in Sir Humphry Davy's *Elements of Agricultural Chemistry.* The sense of the forces of the atmosphere, is first recorded in the singular form probably about 1300, in the plural, *elements,* probably before 1425, in a translation of Higden's *Polychronicon.* **—elemental** *adj.* About 1477, of the four elements, in Thomas Norton's *Ordinal of Alchemy;* borrowed, possibly through Old French *elementel,* from Medieval Latin *elementalis,* from Latin *elementum;* for suffix see -AL[1].

The sense of as found in physical nature, simple but powerful, is first recorded in English in 1820, in Leigh Hunt's writings and in Shelley's *Prometheus Unbound* (1821).

—elementary *adj.* About 1396 *elementare* material, physical, having the nature of one of the four elements (earth, water, air, fire); borrowed through Middle French *elementaire,* or directly from Latin *elementārius,* from *elementum* element; for suffix see -ARY. The sense of simple, rudimentary, introductory, is first recorded in 1542. **—elementary school** (1841)

elephant *n.* Probably before 1300 *olyfaunt,* in *Kyng Alisaunder;* later *elifans,* in *Ayenbite of Inwyt;* borrowed from Old French *olifant,* and *elefant,* learned borrowing from Latin *elephantus,* from Greek *eléphās* (genitive *eléphantos*) elephant, ivory, a borrowed word of uncertain origin. There is no plausible connection between Greek *eléphās* and Latin *ebur* IVORY, which makes further connection with Egyptian *āb, ābu* elephant, ivory (Coptic *ebou, ebu*), and Hebrew *(shen-)habbīm* (tooth of the) elephant, ivory, and Sanskrit *íbha-s* elephant an unlikely source.

The modern spelling was introduced in imitation of Latin *elephantus* sometime after 1550.

—elephantiasis (el'əfantī'əsis) *n.* disease in which the skin becomes rough, like an elephant's hide. 1581, borrowed through Middle French *éléphantiasis* (1538), and directly from Latin *elephantiāsis,* from Greek *elephantíāsis* (*eléphās,* genitive *eléphantos* ELEPHANT + *-íāsis,* suffix meaning a diseased condition). **—elephantine** *adj.* 1631, perhaps formed from English *elephant* + *-ine*[1]; or borrowed, possibly through French *éléphantin,* or directly from Latin *elephantinus,* from Greek *elephántinos,* from *eléphantos* of an elephant or ivory.

elevate *v.* Before 1410 *elevaten* elate or inflate with pride; later, raise or lift up (probably before 1425); developed from earlier *elevat* high, elevated, past participle and adjective (1391, in Chaucer's *Treatise on the*

Astrolabe); borrowed from Latin *ēlevātus,* past participle of *ēlevāre* lift up, raise (*ē-* out, variant of *ex-* before *l* + *levāre* lighten, raise, from *levis* light; see LIGHT[2] not heavy; for suffix see -ATE[1]. **—elevation** *n.* Before 1398 *elevacioun* a rising, elevating, height, in Trevisa's translation of Bartholomew's *De Proprietatibus Rerum;* borrowed from Old French *elevation,* and directly from Latin *ēlevātiōnem* (nominative *ēlevātiō*) a lifting up, from *ēlevāre* lift up, elevate; for suffix see -ATION. **—elevator** *n.* 1646, a muscle which raises a limb or organ; borrowed from Late Latin *ēlevātor* anything that raises or lifts, from Latin *ēlevāre* elevate; for suffix see -OR[2].

The meaning of a machine that lifts to an upper story, is first recorded in 1787, in American English (as an elevator for lifting grain for storage in a bin, upper story, etc.).

eleven *adj.* Probably before 1200 *elleovene, enleven,* in Layamon's *Chronicle of Britain;* developed from Old English *endleofan,* literally, one left (over ten), before 900 in Alfred's translation of Bede's *Ecclesiastical History.* Old English *endleofan* is cognate with Old Frisian *andlova, elleva* eleven, Old Saxon *ēlleƀan,* Old High German *einlif* (modern German *elf*), Old Icelandic *ellifu,* and Gothic *ainlif;* all developed from a Proto-Germanic compound made up of the root of Old English *ān* ONE + the root *-lif-* of the verb LEAVE[1]; see TWELVE. **—eleventh** *adj., n.* About 1380 *eleventhe,* formed from English *eleven* + *-th*[2]; replacing earlier *ellefte* (about 1300) and *enlefte* (before 1225), developed from Old English *endlyfta, endleofta* (*endleofan* eleven + *-ta* -th[2]). **—eleventh hour** 1829, in Southey's *All For Love,* in allusion to Matthew 20:1-16.

elf *n.* About 1390 *elf,* plural *elves,* in Chaucer's *Canterbury Tales;* earlier *alve* (probably before 1200, in Layamon's *Chronicle of Britain*); developed from Old English *elf* (variant of **ielf*), coexisting with *ælf* (about 725, in *Beowulf*). Middle English *alve* is cognate with Old Saxon and Middle Low German *alf* evil spirit, goblin, Middle High German *alp* (modern German *Alp, Alb*), Old Icelandic *ālfr,* of unknown origin. **—elfin** *adj.* 1596, in Spenser's *Faerie Queene,* probably from *elf.* Spenser may have fashioned the word from the earlier phrase *elvene lond* land of elves (recorded about 1300), or from the name *Elphin,* found in the Arthurian legends, but it is also possible that *elfin* was formed directly from Middle English *elven,* from Old English *-elfen, -ælfen* (as in *wuduelfen* wood nymph and *muntælfen* mountain nymph), from *ælf* elf. **—elfish** *adj.* Probably before 1200 *alvisc,* later *elvyssh* (in Chaucer's *Canterbury Tales*); formed from Middle English *alve* elf + *-isc* -ish.

elicit (ilis′it) *v.* draw forth. 1641, developed from earlier *elicit,* adj. (1624); borrowed from Latin *ēlicitus,* past participle of *ēlicere* draw forth (*ē-* out, variant of *ex-* before *l* + *-licere,* combining form of *lacere* to entice; see LACE). **—elicitation** *n.* 1656, in Hobbes' *Of Liberty and Necessity;* formed in English from Latin *ēlicitus* (past participle of *ēlicere* elicit) + English *-ation;* or formed from English *elicit* + *-ation.*

elide (ilīd′) *v.* omit or slur over. 1593, destroy, in Richard Hooker's *Ecclesiastical Polity;* borrowed, perhaps through Middle French *élider,* from Latin *ēlīdere* strike out (*ē-* out, variant of *ex-* before *l* + *-līdere,* combining form of *laedere* to strike; see COLLIDE). The grammatical sense of omit (a vowel or syllable) in pronunciation is first recorded in English in 1796. Compare ELISION.

eligible *adj.* Probably before 1425, borrowed from Middle French *éligible* fit to be chosen, learned borrowing from Late Latin *ēligibilis* that may be chosen, from Latin *ēligere* choose, ELECT; for suffix see -IBLE. **—eligibility** *n.* 1650, formed from English *eligible* + *-ity.*

eliminate *v.* 1568, cast out, expel, borrowed, perhaps through influence of Middle French *éliminer,* from Latin *ēlīminātus,* past participle of *ēlīmināre* thrust out of doors, expel, from the phrase *ē līmine,* off the threshold (*ē* off, out, variant of *ex* + *līmine,* ablative case of *līmen* threshold, related to *līmes,* genitive *līmitis* LIMIT); for suffix see -ATE[1].

The generalized sense of to exclude, remove, get rid of, is first recorded in 1714.

—elimination *n.* 1601, a casting out, formed from English *eliminate* + *-ion,* after such pairs as *elevate, elevation, attenuate, attenuation,* etc. The sense of expulsion or getting rid of anything, is first recorded in 1627, in Donne's *Sermons.*

elision *n.* suppression of vowel or syllable in pronouncing. 1581, in Sidney's *Apology for Poetry;* borrowed through Middle French *élision* from Latin *ēlīsiōnem* (nominative *ēlīsiō*), from the stem of *ēlīdere* ELIDE; for suffix see -SION.

elite or **élite** (ilēt′ *or* ālēt′) *n.* choice or distinguished part (as of society). 1823, in Byron's *Don Juan,* borrowing of French *élite,* from the Old French feminine past participle of *elire, eslire* pick out, choose, from Vulgar Latin **exlegere,* re-formed (with Latin *ex-* out, + *legere* choose) from Latin *ēligere* choose, ELECT.

Elite, élite is a reborrowing of French in modern English. Middle English *elit, elite* person elected to office, especially a bishop-elect, was borrowed before 1398 from Old French *elit, eslite,* past participle of *elire, eslire* choose, and was still in use in English in 1450, but is unrecorded thereafter.

—elitism *n.* 1951, (coined by David Riesman, born 1909, American social scientist) formed from English *elite* + *-ism.* **—elitist** *n.* 1950, formed from English *elite* + *-ist.*

elixir (ilik′sər) *n.* Before 1393, the philosopher's stone believed by alchemists to change metals into gold, cure diseases, and prolong life, in Gower's *Confessio Amantis;* borrowed through Old French *elixir,* or directly from Medieval Latin *elixir,* from Arabic *al-iksīr* the elixir (*al-* the + *iksīr* elixir, philosopher's stone, probably from Greek *xēríon* powder for drying wounds, from *xērós* dry; see SERENE). The figurative sense of quintessence of a thing, chief principle, is first recorded in English before 1500.

elk *n.* Probably before 1437; earlier, as a surname *Elk* (1297); developed from an alteration probably by sound substitution of *k* in Anglo-French for *h* in Old English *elh, eolh.* The Old English forms are cognate with Old High German *elaho* elk (modern German *Elch*) from Proto-Germanic **elH-,* Old Icelandic *elgr* (from Proto-Germanic **alʒís*), and with Old Irish *elit* deer, roe, Middle Welsh *elain* hind, fawn, Greek *élaphos* deer, Armenian *eɫn* stag, deer, Lithuanian *élnis,* Old Slavic *jelenĭ,* and Sanskrit *ṛ́śya-s* male antelope, from Indo-European **elḱ-/*olḱ-/l̥ḱ-,* root **el-* reddish, brown (Pok.303). Latin *alcēs,* pl., and Greek *álkē* appear only as the name of an animal living in northern

Europe (apparently the elk) and were probably adopted from Germanic or some other northern language, with sound substitution of *c, k,* for the Germanic fricative sound represented by German *Elch.*

ell[1] *n.* old measure of length (about 45 inches in England). About 1250 *elne,* in *The Story of Genesis and Exodus;* later *elle* (about 1330); developed from Old English (about 1000) *eln,* (originally) length of the forearm or of the arm. Old English *eln* is cognate with Old Frisian *elne* ell, Old Saxon and Old High German *elina,* Middle High German *elle* (modern German *Elle),* Old Icelandic *ǫln* (stem *aln-*), and Gothic *aleina.* The old Germanic word (a compound of which is ELBOW) also meant originally arm or forearm, and is cognate with Latin *ulna* elbow, arm, ell, Greek *ōlénē* elbow, Middle Irish *uillind* elbow, Welsh and Old Cornish *elin* elbow, Armenian *oln* spine, shoulder, *aleln* arch, rainbow, and Sanskrit *aratní-s* elbow, from Indo-European **olenā/olīnā,* root **el-* to bend (Pok.307).

The later forms with *-ll-* in Middle English, Middle High and modern German, and in Middle Irish represent assimilation of the older *-ln-.*

ell[2] *n.* extension of a building at right angles to it. 1773, American English; earlier, a shape used to mark a horse's ear (1688); a spelled form of the letter *L;* so called from the resemblance between the shape of the structure and that of the capital letter.

ellipse *n.* a closed plane curve. 1753, in *Chambers Cyclopaedia,* borrowed from French *ellipse,* from Latin *ellīpsis* a falling short, defect, ellipse, from Greek *élleipsis* ELLIPSIS; so called because in the case of a conic section the cutting plane makes a smaller angle with the base than does the side of the cone; thus the idea of falling short of the side of the cone. The earlier term was *ellipsis* (see below).

In some sources it is said that the geometrical meaning of Greek *élleipsis* was brought into Latin *ellīpsis* by the German astronomer Kepler.

ellipsis *n.* omission of a word or words in a sentence. 1570, closed plane curve, ellipse; borrowed from Latin *ellīpsis,* from Greek *élleipsis* a falling short, defect, ellipse, ellipsis, from *elleípein* fall short, leave out (*el-,* assimilated form of *en-* in + *leípein* to leave; see LOAN).

The meaning in grammar is first recorded in English in 1612.

elliptical *adj.* 1656, of an ellipse; 1778 (of a sentence) defective; formed in English from Greek *elleiptikós* (from *élleipsis*) + English *-al*[1].

elm *n.* Old English (about 1000) *elm;* cognate with Old High German *elme, elm* elm, Old Icelandic *almr,* Latin *ulmus,* and Middle Irish *lem.* The modern German *Ulme* and Dutch *olm* were borrowed from or influenced by Latin *ulmus.* The Indo-European source had three variants: **elmos/olmos/ḷmós* (Pok.303).

elocution *n.* Probably before 1439 *ellocucioun* oratorical or literary style, in Lydgate's translation of Bochas' *Falls of Princes;* borrowed from Late Latin *ēlocūtiōnem* (nominative *ēlocūtiō*) voice production, manner of expression, in Classical Latin, oratorical expression, from *ēlocū-,* stem of *ēloquī* speak out; see ELOQUENCE; for suffix see -TION.

The sense of art of reading or speaking clearly in public is first recorded in 1613, in the third edition of Cawdrey's *A Table Alphabeticall,* where it is defined as "good utterance of speech." According to the OED, this is the meaning covered by *pronuntiatio* in Latin.

elongate *v.* About 1540, set at a distance, probably developed from earlier *elongat,* past participle (possibly before 1425); borrowed from Late Latin *ēlongātus,* past participle of *ēlongāre* remove to a distance (Latin *ē-* out, variant of *ex-* before *l* + *longus* LONG[1], adj.); for suffix see -ATE[1].

Alternatively, *elongate,* v. may be a back formation from earlier *elongation.*

In the 1500's *elongate,* v. replaced *elongen* (recorded probably 1440), borrowed from Middle French *élonger* extend, prolong, from Latin *ēlongāre.*

The sense of lengthen, prolong, is first recorded about 1450.

—adj. 1828; re-formed in modern English from the verb, or as a shortened form of *elongated* (recorded 1751).

—elongation *n.* About 1391, angular distance of a heavenly body from a fixed point, in Chaucer's *Treatise on the Astrolabe;* borrowed from Late Latin *ēlongātiōnem* (nominative *ēlongātiō*), from *ēlongāre* elongate; for suffix see -ATION.

elope *v.* 1596, run away, escape, in Spenser's *Faerie Queene,* found in Anglo-French (1338) *aloper* run away from a husband with one's lover, perhaps formed from *a-* away, from Old French *es-,* from Latin *ex-,* + Middle Dutch *(out)lōpen* run away, from *lōpen* to run; see LEAP. The current sense, usually applied to lovers who run away from their homes to marry secretly, is first recorded in the 1800's. **—elopement** *n.* 1641, act of running away from a husband with one's lover, formed from English *elope* + *-ment;* found in Anglo-French *alopement* (1338).

The span of 250 years between Spenser's use and the earlier recorded use in Anglo-French, or the 200 years between the *Nottingham Borough Record* and the Anglo-French, or the even greater spans for derived forms, such as *elopement* and *eloping,* suggests that *elope* is either a direct reborrowing from Dutch or that the term existed in Middle English and remained unrecorded in its development into modern English. This latter seems unlikely, because court and estate records which have been a rich source of such terminology have apparently not yielded such a term.

eloquent *adj.* Before 1393, graceful and forceful in speech, in Gower's *Confessio Amantis,* borrowed from Old French *eloquent,* from Latin *ēloquentem* (nominative *ēloquēns*), present participle of *ēloquī* speak out (*ē-* out, variant of *ex-* before *l* + *loquī* speak, see LOQUACITY); for suffix see -ENT. **—eloquence** *n.* 1369, in Chaucer's *Book of the Duchesse;* borrowed from Old French *eloquence,* from Latin *ēloquentia,* from *ēloquentem,* present participle; for suffix see -ENCE. By the late 1600's *eloquence* replaced the earlier *eloquency* (Middle English *eloquencie,* about 1350).

else *adj., adv.* Before 1175 *elles,* later *ells* (1325); found in Old English (971) *elles* other, otherwise, different; also in the compound *elsewhere* (about 725). Old English *elles* is cognate with Old Frisian *elles* else, besides, Old High German *elles* other, Old Icelandic *elliga, elligar* otherwise, and Gothic *aljis* other; also cognate with Latin *alius* another, other, Greek *állos* other, Old Irish *aile,* Armenian *ail,* and Tocharian A *ālyak,* Tocharian B *alyek* any other, anyone else, from Indo-European **alyos* (Pok.25). **—elsewhere** *adv.* Probably before 1200 *elles hwer,* in *Ancrene Riwle;* later *els-wher* (probably about 1400; found in Old English *elles hwǣr* (about 725, in *Beowulf*). Middle English *elles, ells* developed into *els* during the 1400's and into *else* in the late 1500's and early 1600's.

elucidate *v.* make clear. Before 1568, in Coverdale's letters; borrowed, perhaps through Middle French *élucider,* from Late Latin *ēlūcidātus,* past participle of *ēlūcidāre* make clear (Latin *ē-* out, variant of *ex-* before *l* + *lūcidus* clear, LUCID); for suffix see -ATE[1]. **—elucidation** *n.* 1570, formed from English *elucidate* + *-ion,* possibly by influence of Middle French *élucidation,* from *élucider* make clear; or formed in English from Late Latin *ēlūcidāre* make clear + English *-ation.*

elude *v.* 1538, to fool, delude; borrowed from Latin *ēlūdere* escape from, make a fool of, win from at play (*ē-* out, away, variant of *ex-* before *l* + *lūdere* to play; see LUDICROUS). The sense of slip away from, evade, is first recorded in English in 1612, and later, in a more general sense, in 1667 in Milton's *Paradise Lost.* **—elusive** *adj.* evasive. 1719, formed in English from Latin *ēlūsus* (past participle of *ēlūdere* elude) + English *-ive.*

Elysian *adj.* 1579, in the phrase *Elysian fields,* in Spenser's *The Shepheardes Calender;* formed in English from Latin *Ēlysium* + English *-an.* **—Elysium** *n.* 1590, place or condition of perfect happiness, in Shakespeare's *The Two Gentlemen of Verona* and Marlowe's *Tamburlane the Great;* borrowed through Latin *Ēlysium* from Greek *Ēlýsion pedíon* Elysian field (place where heroes and the virtuous live after death), a name of non-Greek origin.

em-[1] a form of the prefix *en-*[1] before *b, p,* and sometimes *m,* as in *embody, empower,* and *emmesh.*

em-[2] a form of the prefix *en-*[2] before *b, m, p,* and *ph,* as in *emblem, emphasis.*

emaciate *v.* make excessively thin. Before 1626 (implied in *emaciating,* in Francis Bacon's writings); borrowed, probably through influence of French *émacié* emaciated, from Latin *ēmaciātus,* past participle of *ēmaciāre* make lean, waste away (*ē-* out, variant of *ex-* before *m* + *maciēs* leanness, from *macer* lean, MEAGER); for suffix see -ATE[1]. **—emaciation** *n.* 1662, formed in English from Latin *ēmaciāre* emaciate + English *-ation.*

emanate *v.* flow forth, issue. 1756, borrowed, through influence of French *émaner,* from Latin *ēmānātum,* past participle of *ēmānāre* flow out, arise, proceed (*ē-* out, variant of *ex-* before *m* + *mānāre* to flow, of uncertain origin); for suffix see -ATE[1]. It is also possible that in some instances *emanate* was a back formation from *emanation.* **—emanation** *n.* 1570, borrowed from Late Latin *ēmānātiōnem* (nominative *ēmānātiō*), from Latin *ēmānāre* emanate; for suffix see -ATION.

emancipate *v.* set free, release from slavery or restraint. 1625, in Donne's *Sermons,* borrowed, possibly through influence of French *émanciper,* from Latin *ēmancipātus,* past participle of *ēmancipāre* declare free, give up (*ē-* out, away, variant of *ex-* before *m* + *mancipāre* deliver, transfer or sell, from *manceps,* genitive *mancipis,* purchaser or owner, one who takes by hand, from *manus* hand + *-ceps,* genitive *-cipis,* from *capere* to take); see MANUAL and CAPTIVE; for suffix see -ATE[1]. **—emancipation** *n.* Before 1631, in Donne's *Sermons;* either formed from English *emancipate* + *-ion,* or in some instances borrowed from French *émancipation,* from Latin *ēmancipātiōnem* (nominative *ēmancipātiō*), from *ēmancipāre* emancipate; for the suffix of this latter borrowing see -ATION. **—emancipator** *n.* 1782, probably formed from English *emancipate* + *-or*[2], possibly on the model of Late Latin *ēmancipātor,* from Latin *ēmancipāre* emancipate; for suffix see -OR[2].

emasculate *v.* 1607, borrowed, probably through French *émasculer,* from Latin *ēmasculātus,* past participle of *ēmasculāre* remove the male glands of, castrate (*ē-* out, away, variant of *ex-* before *m* + *masculus* MALE, MASCULINE); for suffix see -ATE[1]. The figurative sense of destroy the force of or weaken (something or somebody), has prevailed from the earliest use of this word; the literal sense of castrate (1623, in Cockeram's *Dictionary,* defined as "to geld") is rarely used. **—emasculation** *n.* 1623, in Cockeram's *Dictionary,* formed from English *emasculate* + *-ion,* as if from Latin **ēmasculātiōnem,* from *ēmasculāre* emasculate.

embalm *v.* About 1386 *enbawmen* to treat (a corpse) with spices to prevent decay; probably before 1387 *enbaumen;* later *enbalmen* (1447); borrowed from Old French *embaumer* (*em-,* variant of *en-* + *baume* balm + *-er* verbal suffix). The spelling with *l* became fixed in the 1500's in imitation of Latin *balsamum* balm and parallel to English *balm.* **—embalmer** *n.* 1587, formed from English *embalm* + *-er*[1].

embankment *n.* 1786, in Burke's writings; formed from English *embank* to enclose with a bank (possibly from French *embanquer*) + *-ment.*

embargo *n.* order forbidding ships to enter or leave a port. Possibly about 1593; borrowed from Spanish *embargo,* from *embargar* restrain, embargo, probably from Vulgar Latin **imbarricāre* restrain, impede (*im-,* from Latin *in-* into, upon, + Vulgar Latin **barra* BAR). —*v.* 1650, seize, confiscate, from the noun, though the meaning of suspension is not recorded before 1658. The sense of forbid a ship to enter or leave a port, is first recorded in 1755.

embark *v.* go on board ship. 1550, borrowed from Middle French *embarquer* (*em-,* variant of *en-*[1] before *b* + *barque* BARK[3] ship). **—embarkation** *n.* About 1645, in part probably formed from English *embark* + *-ation,* and in part surely borrowed from earlier French *embarcation* act of embarking, from Spanish *embarcación,* from *embarcar* embark (*em-,* variant of *en-*[1] before *b* + *barca* BARK[3], from Latin).

The spelling with *im-,* widely used in English in the 1600's, may have been influenced by Italian, but the original formation of *embarkation* with *em-* strangely suggests a borrowing from French (with *em-*) because the spelling *im-* would have been the prevailing form as *embarkation* was apparently formed at the time the *im-* spelling was popular.

embarrass *v.* 1672, throw into doubt or unease, shame, perplex; later, to hamper or hinder (1683); borrowed from French *embarrasser,* literally, to block, from *embarras* obstacle, from Italian *imbarrazzo,* from *imbarrare* to bar (*im-,* from Latin *in-* into, upon, + Vulgar Latin **barra* BAR). **—embarrassment** *n.* 1676, hindrance; later, feeling of unease (1774, in Burke's writings); borrowed from obsolete French *embarrassement,* from *embarrasser* embarrass; for suffix see -MENT.

embassy *n.* 1579, the position of ambassador; later, office or residence of an ambassador (1764); borrowed from Middle French *embassée* mission, charge, office of an ambassador, from Italian *ambasciata,* from Old Provençal *ambaisada* office of ambassador, and Medieval Latin *ambactia* service, duty, from Gaulish **ambactos* dependent, servant.

Old English *ambiht* service or office, Old Saxon *ambaht,* Old High German *ampaht* (modern German *Amt* office), Old Icelandic *embætti,* and Gothic *andbahti* service, *andbahts* servant, probably come from an unrecorded Celtic compound which is represented by Latin *ambactus* vassal, retainer, and by Welsh *amaeth* husbandman, farmer (originally perhaps, a tenant, retainer), both literally meaning driven around, and is formed from two words which are cognate with Latin *amb-, ambi-* around, and *agere* to drive; see AGENT.

The form *embassy* replaced earlier *embassade* (1480) and *ambassade* (1417) meaning 1) the position of an ambassador, 2) a diplomatic mission, 3) a deputation, which was borrowed from Old French *ambassade,* from Old Spanish *ambaxada,* from Vulgar Latin **ambactiāta,* a derivation of **ambactiāre* to go on a mission.

embattled *adj.* drawn up ready for battle. 1475, past participle of *embattle,* Middle English *embataillen* (before 1338, in Mannyng's *Chronicle of England*); borrowed from Old French *embataillier* to prepare for battle (*em-,* variant of *en-* before *b* + *bataille* BATTLE).

embed *v.* 1778, imbed; formed from English *em-*[1], *im-*[2] + *bed,* n.

embellish *v.* decorate. About 1380 *embelisen,* in Chaucer's translation of Boethius' *De Consolatione Philosophiae;* borrowed from Old French *embelliss-,* stem of *embelir, embellir* make beautiful, ornament (*em-* en-[1] + *bel* handsome, beautiful; see BEAU); for suffix see -ISH[2]. **—embellishment** *n.* 1623, formed from English *embellish* + *-ment.*

ember *n.* glowing piece of wood or coal. Before 1398 *emer,* in Trevisa's translation of Bartholomew's *De Proprietatibus Rerum;* later *eymbre* (1440, in *Promptorium Parvulorum*); developed from Old English (about 1000) *ǣmerge* and Old Icelandic *eimyrja* ember; cognate with Middle Low German *ēmere* ember and Old High German *eimuria.* The cognates suggest an earlier Germanic compound **aimuzjō* (**aim-* cognate with Old Icelandic *eimr* steam, vapor, of unknown origin + *uzjō,* cognate with Old Icelandic *ysja* fire; see COMBUSTION).

embezzle *v.* steal (money entrusted to one's care). Probably about 1425 *imbesellen,* 1433 *embesilen* carry off secretly; borrowed from Anglo-French *embesiler* to steal, dispose of or destroy fraudulently (apparently *em-,* variant of Old French *en-* + *beseler, besiler,* in Old French *besillier* destroy, gouge, perhaps from *bisel* a gouge, sloping edge, of unknown origin. **—embezzlement** *n.* 1548, probably formed from English *embezzle* + *-ment,* re-formed after Anglo-French *embesilement.* **—embezzler** *n.* 1667, in Pepys' *Diary;* formed from English *embezzle* + *-er*[1].

embitter *v.* Before 1603, formed from English *em-*[1] + *bitter.*

emblazon *v.* 1592, in Thomas Nashe's *Pierce Penilesse,* formed from English *em-*[1] + *blazon.*

emblem *n.* symbol. 1589; borrowed from French *emblème* symbol, representation, learned borrowing from Latin *emblēma* inlaid ornamental work or raised ornaments on a vase, etc., from Greek *émblēma* (genitive *emblḗmatos*) embossed ornament, literally, insertion, from *embállein* throw in, insert (*em-* in + *bállein* to throw; see BALL[2] dancing party). **—emblematic** *adj.* 1645, in John Evelyn's *Memoirs;* borrowed from French *emblématique,* from Greek *emblēmatikós,* from *émblēma* (genitive *emblḗmatos* emblem); for suffix see -IC.

embody *v.* 1548, formed from English *em-*[1] + *body.* **—embodiment** *n.* 1828, in Carlyle's writings; formed from *embody* + *-ment.*

embolden *v.* About 1385, in Thomas Usk's *The Testament of Love;* formed from English *em-*[1] + *bold* + *-en*[1].

embolism (em'bəlizəm) *n. Medicine.* obstruction of a blood vessel by a clot. Before 1387, insertion of days in a calendar to correct errors, in Trevisa's translation of Higden's *Polychronicon;* borrowed through Old French *embolisme* from Late Latin *embolismus* intercalary, altered from Greek *embólimos,* from *embolḗ* insertion, or *émbolos* a plug, wedge, from *embállein* to insert; see EMBLEM; for suffix see -ISM. The medical sense is first recorded in English in 1855.

emboss *v.* decorate with a carved relief. About 1386 *embosen,* in Chaucer's *Legend of Good Women;* borrowed from Old French *embocer* (*em-* en-[1] + *boce* BOSS[2] knoblike mass).

embrace *v.* About 1350 *enbracen* encircle, surround; later *embracen* (about 1380); borrowed from Old French *embracer* clasp in the arms, enclose (*em-* in, en-[1] + *brace* the arms; see BRACE). The sense of fold in the arms, hug, is first recorded in English about 1385, in Chaucer's writings. **—n.** 1592, in Shakespeare's *Romeo and Juliet;* from the verb.

embrasure *n.* opening in a wall for a gun. 1702, borrowed from French *embrasure,* probably from Old French *embraser* to cut at a slant, make a groove or furrow in a door or window (*em-* en-[1] + *braser* to cut at a slant, of unknown origin); for suffix see -URE.

embroider *v.* decorate with needlework. Before 1393 *embroudren,* in Gower's *Confessio Amantis;* developed from earlier *embrouden* (about 1380, in Chaucer's *House of Fame* and in *Sir Ferumbras*) + *-er*[1], and also influenced by Old French *embroder,* from *broder, brosder,* from Frankish **brozđōn,* from Proto-Germanic **bruzđōjanan;* compare Old High German *brort* edge, margin; see BRAD. The earlier Middle English *embrouden* developed, with *em-*[1], and some influence of *brouded* embroidered (1373) from Old English *brogden,* past participle of *bregdan* to weave (from Proto-Germanic **breȝđanan*), and further shows influence of blending with Old French *embrodé* embroidered, from *broder.*

The spelling with *-oi-* became established in the 1600's, after an early appearance in Spenser's *A View of the Present State of Ireland* (1596), and probably developed partly by influence of English *broid* braid, Middle English *broud,* but is found occasionally in *broiderer,* variant of *brouderer* embroiderer, in *broiderie,* variant of *brouderie* embroidery, and *broiden,* variant of *brouden* to pull or twist, attested as early as 1300, in *Body and the Soul,* and 1395, in a version of the Wycliffe Bible. The OED shows spellings with *-oi-* in *broiden* (past participle of *braid*) as early as 1230 and 1250, but these are not cited in the MED.

—embroidery *n.* Before 1393 *embrouderie* art of embroidering, in Gower's *Confessio Amantis,* developed from *embroudren* and *embrouden* embroider (*em-* + *broudren, brouden,* from Old French *broder, brosder*); for suffix see -ERY. The form *brouderie (browdrye)* existed before 1382.

embroil *v.* 1603, throw into disorder, confuse; borrowed from French *embrouiller* (*em-* en-[1] + *brouiller* confuse, from Old French *bröoillier;* see BROIL[2] to fight). The sense of involve in a quarrel, is first recorded in English in 1610.

embryo *n.* undeveloped animal in the womb or plant in the seed. Before 1398 *embrio,* in Trevisa's translation of Bartholomew's *De Proprietatibus Rerum;* borrowed from Medieval Latin *embryo,* from Greek *émbryon* young animal, embryo, fetus (*em-* within, variant of *en-*[2] before *b* + *brýein* to swell, be full). **—embryology** *n.* study of embryos and their development. 1859, in Charles R. Darwin's *Origin of Species;* perhaps borrowed from French *embryologie* (1762); or formed from English *embryo* + *-logy.* **—embryonic** *adj.* 1849, either formed in English from Medieval Latin *embryo* (genitive *embryonis*) + English *-ic; or* formed from English *embryon* (1592, from Greek *émbryon*) + *-ic.*

emcee *n. Informal.* person in charge of ceremony or entertainment. 1933, American English, from the letters *MC* (*Master* of *Ceremonies*). **—v.** *Informal.* serve as an emcee. 1937, American English; from the noun. The transitive use (*to emcee an event*) is first recorded in 1948.

emend *v.* to free from faults or errors. Probably before 1425 *emenden,* in a translation of Higden's *Polychronicon;* borrowed from Latin *ēmendāre* (*ē-* out, ex- + *mendum, menda* fault, blemish, related to *mendāx* lying, deceitful, and *mendīcus* beggar, MENDICANT). Doublet of AMEND. **—emendation** *n.* Before 1460, borrowed from Latin *ēmendātiōnem* (nominative *ēmendātio*), from *ēmendāre* emend; for suffix see -ATION.

emerald *n.* Probably before 1300 *emeraude,* in *Kyng Alisaunder;* later *emeralde* (1413); borrowed from Old French *emeraude, esmeralde,* and directly from Medieval Latin *esmaraldus, esmeraldus, esmeralda,* from Latin *smaragdus,* from Greek *smáragdos,* possibly from Semitic (compare Akkadian *barraqtu,* Hebrew *bāreqet* emerald); but consider also Greek *máragdos* a kind of precious stone, from Sanskrit *marakta-m, marakata-m* emerald.

emerge *v.* 1563–87, in an edition of John Foxe's *Book of Martyrs;* borrowed from Middle French *émerger,* from Latin *ēmergere* rise out or up (*ē-* out, e- + *mergere* to dip, sink, MERGE). **—emergence** *n.* 1649, unforeseen occurrence, emergency; borrowed from French *émergence,* from *émerger;* for suffix see -ENCE. The sense of act of emerging, is first recorded in 1704, in Newton's *Optics.* **—emergency** *n.* unforeseen occurrence; sudden need for action. Before 1631, in Donne's *Selections,* formed from English *emerge* + *-ency.* **—emergent** *adj.* emerging, rising. Before 1460; (earlier, probably before 1425) designating the year of the exodus of the Israelites from Egypt; borrowed from Latin *ēmergentem* (nominative *ēmergēns*), present participle of *ēmergere* emerge; for suffix see -ENT.

emeritus (imer′ətəs) *adj.* honorably retired from service. 1602, borrowing of Latin *ēmeritus,* past participle of *ēmerēre* serve out, complete one's service (*ē-* out + *merēre* to serve, earn; see MERIT). The application of this term to retired professors is first recorded in 1794, in American English.

emery (em′ərē) *n.* hard mineral used for polishing metals and stones. 1481, borrowed from Middle French *émeri,* from Old French *emmery,* (earlier *emeril, esmeril*), from Italian *smeriglio,* from Vulgar Latin **smyrīlium,* from Greek *smýris* abrasive powder, which would appear to be from *smên* to rub, influenced by *mýron* unguent.

emetic (imet′ik) *n.* medicine that causes vomiting. 1657, borrowed from French *émétique,* and as a learned borrowing from Greek *emetikós* causing vomiting, from *émesis* vomiting, from *emeîn* to VOMIT. **—adj.** causing vomiting. 1670, learned borrowing from Greek *emetikós.*

-emia a combining form meaning condition of the blood, as in *toxemia* poisoned condition of the blood, *uremia, leukemia,* etc. New Latin *-emia, -aemia,* as in *anemia, anaemia* ANEMIA, from Greek *anaimíā* lack of blood (*an-* without + *haîma* blood); see HEMO-.

emigration *n.* 1650, migration or departure from a place, borrowed from Late Latin *ēmigrātiōnem* (nominative *ēmigrātiō*) removal from a place, from Latin *ēmigrāre* move away, depart from a place (*ē-* out + *migrāre* to move, MIGRATE); for suffix see -ATION. **—emigrant** *n.* one who emigrates. 1754, borrowed from Latin *ēmigrantem* (nominative *ēmigrāns*), present participle of *ēmigrāre* emigrate. **—emigrate** *v.* move to another country. 1778, in James Boswell's *The Life of Samuel Johnson;* either borrowed from Latin *ēmigrātum,* past participle of *ēmigrāre* move out of a country; *or* a back formation from English *emigration;* for suffix see -ATE[1].

émigré or **emigré** (eməgrā′) *n.* emigrant, refugee. 1792, in Gibbon's writings; borrowing of French *émigré,* from past participle of *émigrer* emigrate, learned borrowing from Latin *ēmigrāre* EMIGRATE. Originally the word was applied to the royalist refugees during the French Revolution. In the 1920's it was particularly applied to refugees of the Russian Revolution and then gradually to any political refugee or exile.

eminent *adj.* prominent; outstanding. About 1425, borrowed through Middle French *éminent,* or directly from Latin *ēminentem* (nominative *ēminēns*), present participle of *ēminēre* stand out, project (*ē-* out + *-minēre,* related to *mōns* MOUNT[2] hill); for suffix see -ENT. **—eminence** *n.* Before 1400, projection or protuberance, in a translation of Lanfranc's *Science of Surgery;* later, a high or exalted position (before 1425, in Higden's *Polychronicon*); borrowed through Old French *eminence,* or directly from Latin *ēminentia,* from *ēminentem* (nominative *ēminēns*), present participle of *ēminēre;* for suffix see -ENCE. **—eminently** *adv.* (about 1425)

emir (əmir′) *n.* Arabian chief, prince, or military leader. 1623; earlier *emeer* (1612); borrowed from French *émir,* from colloquial pronunciation of Arabic *ʾamīr* commander, from *ʾamara* he commanded. See ADMIRAL. The earlier *emeer* may have been a variant spelling of *ameer* AMIR.

emissary *n.* person sent on a mission. 1625, borrowed, probably through French *émissaire,* from Latin *ēmissārius,* literally, that is sent out, from *ēmissus,* past participle of *ēmittere* send forth, EMIT; for suffix see -ARY. This word was used by Ben Jonson in his play *Staple of News* (1625), as the official title of men employed to collect the news.

emission *n.* Probably before 1425, something sent forth, produce or fruit, in a translation of Higden's *Polychronicon;* borrowed from Middle French *émission,* and directly from Latin *ēmissiōnem* (nominative *ēmis-*

-iō) a sending out, from *ēmiss-*, stem of *ēmittere* send out; for suffix see -ION. The sense of a giving off or emitting, is first recorded in English before 1619, in Donne's writings. **—emit** *v.* 1626, in Sir Francis Bacon's *Sylva Sylvarum*, borrowed from Latin *ēmittere* (*ē-* out + *mittere* let go, send; see MISSION). The word was prompted by the need for a verb form of earlier *emission*, possibly by influence of Middle French *émettre*.

Emmy *n.* award given to an outstanding television program or performer. 1949, American English, perhaps an alteration of *immy* (for *image orthicon tube*, used in television cameras until the 1960's), and surely influenced in form by *Emmy*, a diminutive of the name *Emma*, to correspond to the motion picture industry's Oscar award.

emollient (imol′yənt) *adj.* softening; soothing. 1643, borrowed from French *émollient*, from Latin *ēmollientem* (nominative *ēmolliēns*), present participle of *ēmollīre* soften (*ē-* thoroughly + *mollīre* soften, from *mollis* soft; see MOLLIFY); for suffix see -ENT. **—n.** a softening agent. 1656, from the adjective.

emolument (imol′yəmənt) *n.* profit from an office or position. 1435, in *Proceedings of the Privy Council;* borrowed through Middle French *émolument*, and directly from Latin *ēmolumentum* profit, gain, (originally) payment to a miller for grinding corn, from *ēmolere* grind out (*ē-* out + *molere* to grind; see MEAL² grain); for suffix see -MENT.

emotion *n.* 1579, agitation or tumult; borrowed from Middle French *émotion* (perhaps patterned on *motion*, *commotion*), from Old French *emouvoir* stir up, from Latin *ēmovēre*, *exmovēre* move out, remove, agitate (*ē-*, *ex-* out + *movēre* to MOVE); for suffix see -TION. The sense of strong feeling, mental agitation, appeared in English in 1660, when the word began to come into common use. **—emote** *v.* act emotionally. 1917, American English, back formation from *emotion* or *emotive*. **—emotional** *adj.* 1834, in John Stuart Mill's writings, formed from English *emotion* + *-al*¹. **—emotionalism** *n.* 1865, formed from English *emotional* + *-ism*. **—emotive** *adj.* 1735, causing emotion; either formed in English from *emotion* + *-ive;* or formed from Latin *ēmōt-*, participial stem of *ēmovēre* + English *-ive*.

empathy *n.* identification with another's feelings. 1904, borrowed from Greek *empátheia* passion (*em-* in + *páthos* feeling, PATHOS). *Empathy* was a translation of German *Einfühlung* (*ein* in + *Fühlung* feeling), a word introduced in 1903 by the German philosopher and psychologist Theodor Lipps, who originated the theory of aesthetic empathy (that art appreciation depends on the viewer's ability to project his personality into the object). **—empathize** *v.* 1924, in a translation of Kafka's *Growth of the Mind;* formed from English *empathy* + *-ize*, on the analogy of *sympathy*, *sympathize*.

emperor *n.* ruler of an empire. Probably before 1200 *empereur*, in *Ancrene Riwle;* later *emperour* (about 1300); borrowed from Old French (accusative) *empereor*, from Latin *imperātōrem* (nominative *imperātor*) commander, emperor, from the stem of *imperāre* to command; see EMPIRE; for suffix see -OR².

emphasis *n.* special force, stress. 1573, borrowed from Latin *emphasis*, from Greek *émphasis* significance, indirect or implied meaning, from *empha-*, root of *emphaínein* to present, show, indicate (*em-* in + *phaínein* to show; see FANTASY). **—emphasize** *v.* 1828, formed from English *emphasis* + *-ize*. **—emphatic** *adj.* 1708, shortened form of *emphatical*, possibly influenced by earlier *emphatique*. **—emphatically** *adv.* 1584, formed from English *emphatical* (before 1555, from Greek *emphatikós* forcible, vivid + English *-al*¹) + *-ly*.¹

emphysema (em′fəsē′mə) *n.* abnormal enlargement of body tissue, especially the air sacs in the lungs. 1661, New Latin, from Greek *emphýsēma* swelling, from *emphȳsân* blow in, inflate (*em-* in + *phȳsân* to blow, from *phŷsa* breath, blast; see PUSTULE.)

empire *n.* group of states under one ruler. Before 1338 *enpyre;* 1340 *empire*, in *Ayenbite of Inwyt;* borrowed from Old French *empire* imperial rule or dignity, learned borrowing from Latin *imperium* rule, command, from *imperāre* to command, requisition (*im-* in + *-perāre*, combining form of *parāre* to order, prepare; see PARE).

empiric *n.* 1541, member of a school of ancient physicians who based their practice on experience rather than philosophical theory; borrowed from Latin *empīricus*, from Greek *empeirikós* experienced, from *empeiríā* experience, from *émpeiros* skilled (*em-* in + *peîra* trial, experiment; see FEAR). The generalized sense of a person who relies solely on observation and experiment, is first recorded in English in 1578. **—adj.** = empirical. 1605 *emperique*, in Sir Francis Bacon's *Of the Advancement of Learning;* borrowed from French *empirique*, from Latin *empīricus;* and in some instances probably formed by shortening of *empirical*, or adjective use of the noun. **—empirical** *adj.* based on experiment and observation. 1569, formed from English *empiric*, n. + *-al*¹.

emplacement *n.* 1802, borrowed from French *emplacement*, from Old French *emplacier* to place; for suffix see -MENT.

employ *v.* Probably before 1425 *emplien* devote to, apply; 1429 *emploien* make use of; borrowed from Middle French *employer*, *emploier*, from Old French *empleier*, from Latin *implicāre* enfold, involve, be connected with (*in-* in-² + *plicāre* to fold; see PLY² fold). Doublet of IMPLICATE and IMPLY.

The sense of use the services of, hire, engage, is first recorded in English in 1584.

—n. act of employing, employment. 1666, in John Evelyn's *Memoirs;* borrowed from French *emploi*, from Middle French, from *employer* to employ.

—employee *n.* 1850, formed from English *employ* + *-ee*. **—employer** *n.* 1599, in Shakespeare's *Much Ado About Nothing*, formed from English *employ*, v. + *-er*¹. **—employment** *n.* 1437 *employement*, in *Rolls of Parliament;* formed from Middle English *emploien*, v. + *-ment*.

emporium *n.* center of trade, market place. 1586, borrowing of Latin *emporium*, from Greek *empórion*, from *émporos* merchant, traveler (*em-* in + *póros* passage, voyage, ultimately from *peírein* to pass through; see FARE).

empress *n.* 1140 *emperice;* later *emperesse* (about 1300) and *empres* (before 1475); borrowed from Old French *emperesse*, feminine of *empereor* EMPEROR; for suffix see -ESS.

empty *adj.* Probably before 1200 *empti*, in *Ancrene Riwle* (showing the introduction of a euphonic *p* between *m* and *t*); also *emti*, in early homilies; developed from Old English *ǣmettig* at leisure, not occupied (before 899, in Alfred's translation of St. Gregory's *Pastoral Care*), from *ǣmetta* leisure (*ǣ-* not + *-metta*, from *mōtan* have to; see MUST[1], v.); for suffix see -Y[1]. The sense of containing nothing, vacant, is first recorded in Old English in 971. —**v.** 1526, make empty; from the adjective. The verb in modern English took the place left by the obsolete Middle English *empten* (1380), *emten* (1340), *geæmtegian* (probably about 1200) to empty or drain, vacate, exhaust or deprive; developed from Old English (about 1000) *ǣmtian, ǣmetian* be vacant, be at leisure, from *ǣmetta* leisure. The Middle English verb apparently has a dialect remnant *empt* found in a glossary of the Isle of Wight. —**emptiness** *n.* About 1450, formed from English *empty,* adj. + *-ness.*

empyrean (em′pərē′ən) *adj.* of the highest heaven. Probably before 1425 *emperien,* formed from earlier *empire* (about 1350) + *-en,* borrowed from Old French *empirée* and from Medieval Latin *empyreus* of the highest heaven, from Late Latin *empyrius,* from Greek *empýrios,* from *émpyros* burning, fiery (*em-* in + *pŷr,* genitive *pyrós,* FIRE); for suffix see -AN. In ancient times, the heavens were thought to be the sphere of fire. —**n.** 1667, in Milton's *Paradise Lost,* from the adjective. Earlier *empire* (about 1433, in Lydgate's writings); from Old French *empirée,* adj. and n.

emu (ē′myü) *n.* large, flightless Australian bird. 1613 *eme* cassowary (a related bird); borrowed from Portuguese *ema,* probably from *emeu,* a word of the Moluccan language of Indonesia. The current sense is first recorded in 1842.

emulate *v.* try to equal or excel. 1589, either a back formation of earlier *emulation,* or borrowed from Latin *aemulātus,* past participle of *aemulārī* to rival, strive to excel, from *aemulus* striving, rivaling, related to *imitārī* imitate and *imāgō* image (Walde-Hofmann, *Lateinisches etymologisches Wörterbuch,* I, 17); for suffix see -ATE[1]. —**emulation** *n.* 1552, borrowed through Middle French *émulation,* or directly from Latin *aemulātiōnem* (nominative *aemulātiō*), from *aemulārī* emulate; for suffix see -ATION.

emulsion *n.* mixture of liquids that do not dissolve in each other. 1612, borrowed from French *émulsion,* and probably directly from New Latin *emulsionem* (nominative *emulsio*), from Latin *ēmulsus,* past participle of *ēmulgēre* to milk out (*ē-* out + *mulgēre* to milk, see MILK); for suffix see -SION. —**emulsify** *v.* make into an emulsion. 1859, formed from English *emulsion* + *-fy.*

en-[1] a prefix meaning: **1** cause to be, make, as in *enable = cause to be able; enfeeble = make feeble.* **2** put in, put on, as in *encircle = put in a circle; enthrone = put on a throne.* **3** other meanings, as in *enact, encourage.* Borrowed from Old French *en-* (with variants *in-, im-, an-, am-*), from Latin *in-* into, in, prefixal use of the preposition *in* IN. Also spelled *em-* before *b, p, ph,* and sometimes *m.*

In Old French the prevailing use of *en-* was to form verbs from nouns and from adjectives. These verb forms from Old French, and the nouns derived from them, were heavily borrowed in Middle English both in their form in Old French, as for example *enchaunten* enchant, *enchauntement* enchantment, *enchauntour* enchanter, sorcerer, *enchaunteresse* enchantress, *enchaunterie* enchantment, etc., and with the variant *an-,* from Anglo-French, which is evident in words of early borrowing, such as *anointen* anoint.

The prefix also has an intensive force parallel to Latin *in-,* and the spelling *en-* and *in-* are found as variants in numerous terms, such as *encrust, incrust; enclose, inclose; enfold, infold.* Variants in *en-* and *in-* are further complicated by parallel forms in Old French in *as-* and *es-* in which little distinction was made in Middle English, leading to such forms as *assurance, ensurance, insurance,* or *assemble, ensemble,* etc.

en-[2] a prefix meaning in, on, within, chiefly in combinations already formed in Greek, as *endemic, energy, enthusiasm.* Borrowed from Greek *en-,* prefixal use of the preposition *en* IN. Also spelled *em-* before *b, m, p,* and *ph.*

-en[1] a suffix forming verbs from adjectives and nouns, and meaning: **1** to cause to be, make, as in *blacken = to make black.* **2** to cause to have, as in *strengthen = to cause to have strength.* **3** to become, as in *flatten = to become flat; soften = to become soft.* **4** to come to have, gain, as in *lengthen = to gain length.* Chiefly formed in late Middle English or early modern English as *-enen, -nen, -en,* on the analogy of certain old verbs (*fasten, brighten*) which developed from Old English *-nian,* or were borrowed from Old Icelandic *-na.* Both the Old English and Old Icelandic are cognate with Old Frisian *-nia,* Old Saxon and Old High German *-nōn,* and Gothic *-nan,* all suffixes of infinitives of transitive and intransitive verbs.

-en[2] a suffix forming adjectives from nouns, and meaning made of, having the look of, as in *wooden, ashen, flaxen.* Old English *-en* is cognate with Old Saxon *-in* made of, consisting of, Old High German *-īn* (modern German *-en*), Old Icelandic *-inn,* and Gothic *-eins,* corresponding to Latin *-īnus* of, belonging to, like; see -INE[1].

In Old English and Middle English this suffix was extensively used, but modern English tends toward an attributive use of nouns, as in *gold watch, oak tree,* rather than *golden watch, oaken tree,* though in some cases (*earthen, wheaten, wooden,* etc.) these adjectives are still in common use.

-en[3] a suffix forming the past participle of certain strong verbs, as in *broken, fallen, stolen, written.* In some of these verbs the suffix takes the form *-n,* as in *blown, torn.* Found in Middle English and Old English *-en,* the regular ending of most classes of strong verbs.

-en[4] a suffix surviving as the plural ending of a few nouns, as in *brethren, children, oxen.* Middle English *-en,* developed from Old English *-an* (as in *oxan,* plural of *ox; tungan,* plural of *tunge* tongue). In words like *children,* the *-en* was added to a *-re* plural, as in *childre* (Old English *cildru*).

enable *v.* 1415, to make fit or qualified; later, to make able to (1443); formed from Middle English *en-*[1] + *able.*

enact *v.* 1414, to enter in the public records, in the *Rolls of Parliament;* formed from Middle English *en-*[1] + *acte* act, probably after Anglo-Latin *inacticare, inactitare.* —**enactment** *n.* 1817, formed from English *enact* + *-ment.*

enamel *v.* apply a glasslike substance (enamel) to a surface. 1392 *enamelen,* borrowed from Anglo-French *enameler, enamailler* (*en-* in + *amailler* to enamel, variant of Old French *esmaillier,* from *esmail* enamel, from Frankish **smalt;* compare Middle Dutch *smelten* to melt, SMELT[1] melt). —**n.** glasslike substance melted and then cooled to make a smooth hard surface. 1421 *anamell,* literally, a means of enameling, from *enamelen* to enamel.

enamor *v.* captivate, fascinate. Before 1338 *enamouren* fill with love, in Mannyng's *Handlyng Synne;* earlier *anamouren* (probably about 1300, in *The Romance of Guy of Warwick*); borrowed from Old French *enamourer* (*en-* cause to + *amour* love; see AMOUR). **—enamored** *adj.* Before 1631, in Donne's poetry; from the verb.

-ence a suffix forming nouns meaning: **1** action or fact of (when added to verbs), as in *abhorrence = act or fact of abhorring; convergence = act or fact of converging.* **2** state or quality of (when added to adjectives ending in *-ent*), as in *absence = state of being absent; prudence = quality of being prudent. -Ence* was formed in English partially by alteration of Old French *-ance* -ANCE, and partially as a borrowing from Old French *-ence* or directly from Latin *-entia* (*-ent-*, participial stem, as in *ēmergentem* emerging + *-ia,* suffix corresponding to English *-y*[3]). Compare -ANCE.

The varying forms in Latin *-entia* and *-antia* (derived from the participial stems *-ent* and *-ant*) were generally leveled in Old French to *-ance,* especially for nouns showing action or process. Later words were borrowed from Latin usually retaining the vowel found in the Latin word (*absence, diligence; elegance, temperance*), especially for nouns showing state or quality. Both nouns of action or state were borrowed into Middle English, mostly with their French spellings, though some words in *-ance* have later (after 1500) been respelled with *-ence* in imitation of the original Latin spelling. This has produced irregular spelling patterns, such as *assistance, existence; attendance, superintendence; appearance, independence;* and even a divergence between the participial form *apparent, defendant* and the noun *appearance,* (British) *defence.*

encephalon (ensef'əlon) *n.* the brain. 1741, New Latin, from Greek *enképhalos* (*en-* within + *kephalḗ* head; see CEPHALIC). See ENKEPHALIN. **—encephalitis** *n.* 1843; formed, probably by influence of French *encéphalite* (1803), from *encephal(on)* + *-itis.*

enchant *v.* About 1378 *enchaunten* hold spellbound, in a version of *Piers Plowman;* borrowed from Old French *enchanter* put under a magic spell, bewitch, charm, from Latin *incantāre,* literally, chant a magic formula or incantation upon (*in-* upon, into + *cantāre* to sing, CHANT). Alternatively, *enchant* may be a back formation from *enchantment.* **—enchantment** *n.* About 1300 *enchauntment,* borrowed from Old French *enchantement,* from *enchanter* enchant; for suffix see -MENT. **—enchantress** *n.* About 1380 *enchaunteresse,* in Chaucer's translation of Boethius' *De Consolatione Philosophiae;* borrowed from Old French *enchanteresse,* feminine from *enchantour* enchanter, sorcerer; for suffix see -ESS.

enchilada (en'chilä'də) *n.* tortilla with filling and peppery sauce. 1887, American English; borrowed from Mexican Spanish *enchilada,* from feminine past participle of *enchilar* season with chili (*en-* in, from Latin *in-* + *chile* CHILI).

encircle *v.* Probably before 1400, in *Morte Arthur* formed from English *en-* in + *circle.* **—encirclement** *n.* 1919; formed from English *encircle* + *-ment.*

enclave *n.* area surrounded by a foreign territory. 1868, borrowed from French *enclave,* from Middle French, from Old French *enclaver* enclose, from Vulgar Latin **inclāvāre* shut in, lock up (Latin *in-* in + *clāvis* key; see CLAVICLE). Middle English had a related verbal use *enclaved* surrounded, as by land owned by someone else (1435), past participle form apparently developed from a borrowing of Middle French *enclaver* enclose, from Old French.

enclose *v.* Before 1338, in Mannyng's *Chronicle of England;* formed in part from English *en-*[1] + *close,*[1] after *enclos* enclosure (about 1280), borrowed from Old French *enclos,* past participle of *enclore* to surround with a barrier. **—enclosure** *n.* About 1464, the action of fencing in or enclosing land, probably borrowed from Middle French *enclosure,* from Old French *en-* in + *closure* that which encloses, see CLOSURE; it is also possible *enclosure* is a formation in English from *en-*[1] + *closure* (about 1390).

encomium *n.* elaborate expression of praise. 1589, borrowed from Late Latin *encōmium,* from Greek *enkṓmion* laudatory ode, eulogy (*en-* + *kômos* ode, procession, merrymaking; see COMEDY).

encompass *v.* About 1350, formed from Middle English *en-*[1] + *compassen* to surround.

encore (äng'kôr) *interj.* once more, again. 1712, in Steele's writing in *The Spectator;* borrowed from French *encore* still, yet, again, probably from Vulgar Latin **hinc ad hōram* from then to this hour (Latin *hinc* from here, hence + *ad* to + *hōram,* accusative of *hōra* HOUR). **—n.** a call of "encore." 1763, from the interjection. **—v.** call for the repetition of a song, etc. 1748, in Richardson's *Clarissa;* from the interjection.

encounter *v.* meet. About 1300 *encountren* meet as an adversary, confront in battle; borrowed from Old French *encontrer* confront, from *encontre,* prep., adv., against, counter to, from Late Latin *incontrā* in front of (Latin *in-* in + *contrā* against; see CONTRA-). The sense of meet, fall in with (a person or thing) is first recorded in English in 1520. **—n.** About 1300 *encontre* a meeting face to face, confrontation; borrowed from Old French, originally preposition and adverb, against, counter to.

encourage *v.* 1429 *encoragen* inspire with courage, make bold, in *Rolls of Parliament;* borrowed from Middle French *encoragier,* from Old French (*en-* cause to be + *corage* COURAGE). **—encouragement** *n.* 1568, borrowed from Middle French *encoragement,* from *encoragier* encourage; for suffix see -MENT.

encroach *v.* Probably about 1380 *encrochen* acquire, get; later, to seize or acquire illegally; borrowed from Old French *encrochier* seize, fasten on, perch (*en-* cause to be + *croc* hook; see CROCHET). The sense of intrude, trespass, is first recorded about 1534. **—encroachment** *n.* Probably 1469 *encrochments, pl.;* borrowed from Anglo-French *encrochment,* from *encrocher* encroach + *-ment;* also in some instances probably formed from English *encroach* + *-ment.*

encrust *v.* 1641 incrust, probably formed from English *en-, in-* put in or on + *crust,* after French *incruster* or Italian *incrustare* to ornament with a layer of precious material, from Latin *incrustāre* (*in-* upon + *crusta* CRUST).

encumber *v.* Before 1338 *encombren* burden, vex, in Mannyng's *Chronicle of England;* borrowed from Old French *encombrer* obstruct (*en-* put in + *combre* barrier; see CUMBER). The sense of hinder or hamper is first recorded in English about 1386, in Chaucer's *Legend of Good Women.* **—encumbrance** *n.* Probably before 1300 *encombraunce,* borrowed from Old

French *encombrance,* from *encombrer* encumber; for suffix see -ANCE.

-ency a variant form of the suffix *-ence,* meaning: **1** the act or fact of (when added to verbs), as in *dependency = the act or fact of depending.* **2** the quality or condition of (when added to adjectives ending in *-ent*), as in *frequency =condition of being frequent.* **3** other meanings, as in *agency, currency.* Borrowed from Latin *-entia;* see -ENCE.

encyclical (ensik′ləkəl) *adj.* 1647, intended for wide circulation; earlier, general (perhaps 1616); formed in English from Late Latin *encyclicus,* from Greek *enkýklios* circular, general (*en-* in + *kýklos* circle, WHEEL) + English *-al* [1].—**n.** letter from the Pope, stating church opinions. 1837, in Cardinal Newman's writings; from the adjective.

encyclopedia *n.* 1531, general course of instruction, in Sir Thomas Elyot's *The Boke Named the Governour;* borrowed from New Latin *encyclopaedia* (1508), from Greek **enkyklopaideíā,* thought to be a false reading (occurring in manuscripts of certain Roman writers such as Quintilian and Pliny) for the Greek phrase *enkýklios paideíā* general or well-rounded education (*enkýklios* general, see ENCYCLICAL + *paideíā* education, child rearing, from *paîs,* genitive *paidós* child; see FEW).

The modern sense of a work containing information on all branches of knowledge appeared in English in 1632 or 1630.
—encyclopedic *adj.* 1824, either formed from English *encyclopedia* + *-ic,* or borrowed from French *encyclopédique* (1762), from *encyclopédie* (1532) + *-ique* -IC.

end *n.* Old English (about 725) *ende;* cognate with Old Frisian *ende* end, Old Saxon *endi,* Middle Dutch *ende* (modern Dutch *einde*), Old High German *enti* (modern German *Ende*), Old Icelandic *endir, endi* (Danish and Norwegian *ende,* Swedish *ände*), and Gothic *andeis;* also outside Germanic cognate with Greek *antíos* opposite, Sanskrit *antya-s* last, all from Indo-European **antiyó-,* built on **ánto-s,* reflected in Sanskrit *ánta-s* end, boundary, Hittite *hanza* (*-hants*) front, and Tocharian A *antule* outside, beyond, Pok.48.) **—v.** Probably before 1200 *enden,* in Layamon's *Chronicle of Britain;* developed from Old English (about 950) *endian* to finish; complete; cognate with Old Frisian *endia* to end, Old Saxon *endōn,* Old High German *entōn* (modern German *enden*), and Old Icelandic *enda;* derived from the root of Old English *ende* end. **—ending** *n.* Before 1225 *endinge* completion; developed from Old English *endung, ge-endung* (before 1000), formed from Old English *endian, ge-endian,* v. + *-ung* -ing. **—endless** *adj.* Probably before 1200 *endelese,* in *Ancrene Riwle;* developed from Old English *endelēas* (before 900, in Alfred's translation of Boethius' *De Consolatione Philosophiae*), formed from Old English *ende,* n. + *-lēas* -less. **—endways** *adv.* About 1450 *endway;* formed from Middle English *ende* + *-way.*

endanger *v.* 1418, to incur debt, mortgage, in *Proceedings of the Privy Council;* later, to put in peril, cause danger to (1548); formed from Middle English *en-*[1] put in + *daunger* danger.

endear *v.* 1580, to enhance the value of, win the affection of, in Sidney's *The Arcadia;* later, to make dear (1647); formed from English *en-*[1] make + *dear.* **—endearment** *n.* 1612; formed from English *endear* + *-ment.*

endeavor *n.* effort, exertion, attempt. 1417 *endevour,* formed from Middle English *en-*[1] + *dever* duty, from the phrase *put* (oneself) *in dever* make it one's duty (to do something); hence, endeavor (compare the French phrase *mettre en devoir.* **—v.** Before 1450 *endoweren,* before 1500 *indevcren,* from the noun, or directly from the phrase (put) *in dever.*

endemic *adj.* of or belonging to a particular people or locality. 1759, in Oliver Goldsmith's *The Bee;* perhaps from the earlier noun (1662, a disease common to a particular locality). The adjective may also have been a shortened form of earlier *endemical* (1657). Another source of the borrowing from Greek *éndēmos* native (*en-* in + *dêmos* people, district), may have been through French *endémique* (1586); for suffix see -IC.

endive *n.* kind of chicory. 1373 *endyve,* borrowed from Old French *endive,* from Late Latin *endivia,* feminine singular, from Medieval Greek *entýbia* (= *endívia*), plural of *entýbion,* diminutive form of Greek *éntybon,* perhaps from Semitic (compare Arabic *hindab* endive, from Aramaic *hendbā*).

endo- a combining form meaning inside, within, internal, inner, used in scientific and technical coinages, such as *endocrine, endoderm* (inner layer of cells in embryos), *endoskeleton* (internal skeleton). Borrowed from Greek *endo-,* combining form of *éndon* within.

endocrine (en′dōkrin) *adj.* secreting internally (applied to glands which secrete hormones directly into the blood or lymph). 1914, borrowed from French *endocrine* (1912) or Italian *endocrine* (1909), from Greek *endo-* within + *krínein* to separate, distinguish; see CERTAIN.

endogenous (endoj′ənəs) *adj.* originating within. 1830, borrowed from French *endogène,* from Greek *endogenḗs* born in the house (*endo-* within + *génos* birth, from the root of *gígnesthai* to be born; see INK); for suffix see -OUS. Compare EXOGENOUS.

endorphin (endôr′fən) *n.* pain suppressant released by the brain. 1975, formed from English *endo-* internal + *(mo)rphin(e).*

endorse *v.* write one's name, comment, etc. on the back of (a check or other document). 1547 *indorse,* 1581 *endorse,* alteration (influenced by Medieval Latin *indorsare* endorse) of earlier *endossen* (before 1400); borrowed from Old French *endosser* (*en-* put on + *dos* back, from Latin *dossum,* variant of *dorsum,* of uncertain origin). Medieval Latin *indorsare* derived from Latin *in-* in + *dorsum* back. The figurative sense of confirm, approve, is first recorded in English in 1847. **—endorsement** *n.* 1547, formed from English *endorse* + *-ment;* replacing earlier *endosement* (probably 1424); borrowed from Anglo-French, Old French *endossement,* from *endosser;* for suffix see -MENT.

endow *v.* 1375 *indowen,* 1390 *endouwen* provide an income for; borrowed from Anglo-French *endouer,* formed from *en-* + Old French *douer* endow, from Latin *dōtāre* bestow, from *dōs* (genitive *dōtis*) DOWRY. The figurative sense of provide or enrich with a quality, talent, etc., is first recorded in 1402. **—endowment** *n.* 1447 *indowment,* 1450 *endowement;* either borrowed from Anglo-French *endouement,* from *endouer* endow, or formed from English *indowen, endouwen* + *-ment.*

endure *v.* keep on, last. About 1380 *enduren;* borrowed from Old French *endurer,* from Latin *indūrāre* make hard, in Late Latin, harden (the heart) against (*in-* in + *dūrāre* to harden, from *dūrus* hard, probably formed by dissimilation of r. . .r in **drūros,* perhaps cognate with Sanskrit *dāruṇá-s* hard, rough, strong, related to *dáru* wood, Greek *dóry* wood, spear, Welsh *derwen* oak, and Old English *trēow* TREE). **—endurable** *adj.* 1607, formed from English *endure* + *-able.* **—endurance** *n.* 1494, borrowed from Middle French *endurance,* from Old French *endurer* endure; for suffix see -ANCE. **—enduring** *adj.* 1532-33, formed from *endure,* v. + *-ing,* probably by influence of earlier *enduring,* n. duration, continued existence (about 1380, in Chaucer's translation of Boethius' *De Consolatione Philosophiae*).

enema (en'əmə) *n.* injection of liquid to flush the bowels. Probably before 1425, in a translation of Chauliac's *Grande Chirurgie;* borrowed perhaps through Medieval Latin from Greek *énema* (genitive *enématos*) injection, from *eniénai* to send in, inject (*en-* in + *hiénai* send; see JET[1] stream).

enemy *n.* Probably about 1225 *enemi,* in *King Horn;* borrowed from Old French *enemi;* earlier *inimi,* from Latin *inimīcus* (*in-* not + *amīcus* friend; see AMICABLE).

energy *n.* 1599, force of expression; borrowed from Middle French *énergie,* learned borrowing from Late Latin *energīa* and, as found in Sidney's *Defence of Poesie* (1581), borrowed directly from Late Latin *energīa,* from Greek *enérgeia* activity, operation, from *energós* active, working (*en-* in + *érgon* WORK).

The general meaning of power, is first recorded in English in 1665, but the sense of vigor of expression is first recorded in English in 1599, and its general application to action, speech, etc., is first recorded in 1809-10, in Coleridge's writings. In the scientific sense of the power to do work, as in electrical energy or mechanical energy, the word is first recorded in 1807. **—energetic** *adj.* 1651, powerful in activity or effect; probably a shortened form of *energetical* (1603), formed in English from Greek *energētikós* active, energetic (from *energeîn* to operate, effect, from *energós* active) + *-al*[1]*;* for suffix see also -ICAL. The sense pertaining to people as vigorous, is first recorded in 1796, in Burke's works. **—energize** *v.* 1752, in Henry Fielding's *Amelia;* formed from English *energy* + *-ize.*

enervate *v.* weaken. 1610, in Donne's writings; probably developed from earlier *enervate,* adj. lacking strength in character, spiritless (1603); borrowed from Latin *ēnervātus,* past participle of *ēnervāre* weaken, cut the sinews of (*ē-* out + *nervus* sinew, NERVE); for suffix see -ATE[1]. Alternatively, it is possible that in some instances *enervate* was a back formation from earlier *enervation.* **—enervation** *n.* 1429, borrowed, probably through Middle French *énervation,* from Late Latin *ēnervātiōnem* (nominative *ēnervātiō*), from Latin *ēnervāre* weaken; for suffix see -ATION. **—enervator** *n.* 1840, in Thackeray's writings, formed from English *enervate* + *-or*[2].

enfeeble *v.* About 1340 *enfeblen* weaken, be made weaker; borrowed from Old French *enfeblir* (*en-* make + *feble* FEEBLE).

enfilade (en'fəlād') *n.* gunfire directed from the side at a line of troops. 1706, borrowed from French *enfilade,* from Old French *enfiler* to thread on a string, pierce from end to end (*en-* put on + *fil* thread + *-ade;* see FILE[1], v.). **—v.** 1706, from the noun.

enforce *v.* Probably about 1343, to make an effort; 1350, to force or compel; borrowed from Old French *enforcier* to exert force, and *enforcir* to strengthen, from Late Latin *infortiāre, infortīre* (Latin *in-* make + *fortis* strong). **—enforceable** *adj.* 1589; formed from English *enforce* + *-able.* **—enforcement** *n.* 1475, in a translation of Caxton's, borrowed from Middle French *enforcement,* and in some instances formed from English *enforce* + *-ment.*

enfranchise *v.* 1419, borrowed from Middle French *enfranchiss-,* extended stem of *enfranchir* to set or make free (*en-* make + *franchir* set free, from Old French *franche,* feminine of *franc* free; originally, a freeman, from Frankish *Frank* a Frank). **—enfranchisement** *n.* 1595, in Shakespeare's *King John;* formed from English *enfranchise* + *-ment.*

engage *v.* 1430 *engagen* to pledge, in *Proceedings of the Privy Council;* borrowed from Middle French *engagier,* from Old French *en gage* under pledge (*en-* make and *gage* pledge, GAGE[1]). The sense of promise to marry, betroth, is first recorded in 1727, in Henry Fielding's *Love in Several Masques.* The senses of involve (before 1586), attract (the attention (1642), or employ (1648), appear to have developed from the earlier notion of binding or securing as by a pledge. **—engaged** *adj.* (1615, betrothed) **—engagement** *n.* 1624, formed from English *engage* + *-ment.* The sense of a promise or pledge to marry, is first recorded in 1859, in Dickens' letters (but in the plural *engagements,* 1742, in Henry Fielding's writings). **—engaging** *adj.* 1673, but inferred earlier in *engagingly* (1651).

engender *v.* About 1330, beget or procreate; borrowed from Old French *engendrer,* from Latin *ingenerāre* (*in-* in + *generāre* beget, create, GENERATE). The general sense of cause, produce, is first recorded about 1350.

engine *n.* Probably before 1300 *engyne* mechanical device, machine used in warfare, in *Kyng Alisaunder;* also probably about 1300 *engyn, enginne* skill, cleverness, craft, and trickery, snare; borrowed from Old French *engin* skill, cleverness, from Latin *ingenium* inborn qualities, talent (*in-* in + *gen-,* root of *gignere* to beget, produce; see KIN). Related to INGENIOUS.

The broad sense of machine survives in a few compounds, such as *fire engine* and in such literary phrases as *engine of destruction;* the specific application to a machine for converting energy into mechanical power and motion, is first recorded chiefly in compounds, such as *steam engine* (1751) and *internal combustion engine* (1884), but later has had increasing use by itself. **—engineer** *n.* Before 1338 *engynour* builder of military engines, in Mannyngs *Chronicle of England;* borrowed from Old French *engigneor,* from *engignier, enginier* to contrive, build, from *engin* skill, cleverness; for suffix see -EER and -OR[2]. The sense of a designer and builder of bridges, roads, etc. (civil engineer), is first recorded in 1606, but the designer of machines, originally military engines (mechanical engineer), is recorded as early as 1380. The sense of one who operates a locomotive, is first recorded in American English in 1832; a ship's engineer, in 1839. **—v.** 1681, implied in *engineering,* act as an engineer; from the noun.

English *adj.* Probably before 1200 *Englische;* also about 1200 *English,* in *The Ormulum;* developed from Old

English (about 880) *Englisc,* from *Engle, pl.,* the Angles (see ANGLO-); for suffix see -ISH[1]. The Angles were a Germanic people who, with the Saxons and Jutes, crossed over into Britain in the 400's and 500's A.D. When the word first occurred in Old English, it had already lost the etymological sense "of or belonging to the Angles" and the earliest recorded sense had developed the meaning "of or belonging to the group of Germanic peoples comprising the Angles, Saxons, and Jutes." By the time of the Norman Conquest (1066) the name English was applied to the combined West Germanic, Celtic, and Scandinavian population of England as distinguished from the French or Normans. But within a generation or two after the Conquest that distinction, too, had practically disappeared, except in state documents. **—n.** the English language. About 1150 *Englis;* later *English* (probably about 1200); developed from Old English (about 890) *Englisc,* noun use of the adjective. Originally the name was applied to the dialects spoken in Britain by the Angles and Saxons. But early in the Old English period the noun developed the meaning of the aggregate of dialects descended from the language of the Germanic settlers of Britain; now called Anglo-Saxon or Old English. **—v.** Before 1397 *Englishen* to translate into English, in the *Prologue* to the Wycliffe Bible; from *English,* n. **—Englishman** *n.* Probably about 1200, developed from Old English *Engliscman* (about 950). **—Englishwoman** *n.* (about 1400)

engrave *v.* carve artistically. 1509, but earlier implied in *ingraved* (before 1475); formed from English *en-[1]* make + *grave[3]* carve; probably patterned on obsolete French *engraver* (*en-* en-[1] + *graver* engrave, from Frankish; compare Middle Dutch *grāven* to dig; see GRAVE[3] carve).

engross *v.* occupy wholly, take up all the attention of. Before 1400 *engrosen* buy up the whole stock of, borrowed from Old French *en gros* in a large quantity, at wholesale (*en* in and *gros* whole quantity, from *gros* thick; see GROSS). The word was used in a transferred sense by Shakespeare in 1598, *Merry Wives of Windsor,* with the meaning of concentrate in one's possession, monopolize, from which evolved the figurative sense of absorb or engage the whole attention of, 1709 in Steele's writings in *The Tatler.* Other meanings existed in Middle and early modern English, such as to draft a document in law (about 1418), borrowed from Anglo-French *engrosser,* and to increase, thicken (probably before 1425), borrowed from Middle French *engrossier* to enlarge.

enhance *v.* make greater, add to. About 1280 *anhaunsen* to raise, make higher; later *enhauncen* raise in station, wealth, fame (about 1300); borrowed from Anglo-French *enhauncer,* Old French *enhaucier, enhalcier* make greater, from Vulgar Latin **inaltiāre,* alteration of Late Latin *inaltāre* raise, exalt (Latin *in-* on + *altus* high; see OLD). Compare HAWSER.

It has been suggested that the *h* in Old French *enhaucier, enhalcier* (and in the parallel *haucier, halcier* under HAWSER) was possibly the result of the influence of Frankish **hōh* high. The intrusion of *n* in Anglo-French *enhauncer* is parallel to Anglo-Latin *auncerus* as a Latinization of Anglo-French *haucer* hawser, and in 18th-century French *hansière* as a variant of *haussière* hawser (both of the forms with *n* perhaps influenced by such a word as Milanese Italian *antsana* hawser). **—enhancement** *n.* 1577, formed from English *enhance* + *-ment.*

enigma *n.* puzzle, riddle. 1588, in Shakespeare's *Love's Labour's Lost;* earlier, in a partially Latinized plural form *enigmata* (1539), and in an Anglicized form *enigmate* (before 1449); borrowed from Latin *aenigma* riddle, from Greek *aínigma* (genitive *ainígmatos*), from *ainíssesthai* speak allusively or obscurely, speak in riddles, from *aînos* fable, riddle, of uncertain origin. The spelling with initial *e* and even the borrowing of *enigma* may have been influenced by Middle French *énigme,* first attested as *enigmat* (compare Middle English *enigmate*). **—enigmatic** *adj.* 1628-77 *aenigmatic;* in part developed as a shortened form of *enigmaticall* (1576), and in part borrowed from Late Latin *aenigmaticus,* from Latin *aenigma* (genitive *aenigmatis*); for suffix see -IC.

enjoin *v.* order, direct, urge. Probably before 1200 *engoinen* prescribe, impose, in *Ancrene Riwle;* borrowed from Old French *enjoign-,* stem of *enjoindre,* from Latin *injungere* to attach, impose, bestow (*in-* on + *jungere* join; see YOKE).

enjoy *v.* About 1384 *enjoyen* rejoice, be glad, in the Wycliffe Bible; borrowed from Old French *enjoïr* to give joy, enjoy (*en-* make + *joïr* enjoy, from Latin *gaudēre* rejoice; see JOY). The sense of have the use or benefit of, is first recorded about 1430. **—enjoyable** *adj.* 1645, in Milton's *Colasterion;* formed from English *enjoy* + *-able.* **—enjoyment** *n.* 1553, formed from English *enjoy* + *-ment.*

enkephalin (enkef'əlin) *n.* protein substance in the brain that suppresses pain. 1975, formed in English from Greek *enképhalos* brain (see ENCEPHALON) + English *-in,* variant of *-ine[2].* The word was coined by John Hughes and Hans Kosterlitz, of the University of Aberdeen.

enlarge *v.* About 1350 *enlargen* grow fat, increase (pleasure, kindness, etc.); borrowed from Old French *enlargier, enlargir* make large (*en-* make + *large* large). **—enlargement** *n.* 1540, formed from English *enlarge* + *-ment.* The meaning of a photograph increased in size, is first recorded in 1866.

enlighten *v.* About 1384 *inligten* to bring knowledge, stimulate the mind, in the Wycliffe Bible; formed after *inligten* to illuminate, from Old English *inlīhtan* (*in-* make, put in + *līhtan* to shine) and *lighten* to clarify. **—enlightenment** *n.* 1669; formed from English *en-[1]* + *lighten* + *-ment,* except the historical sense referring to the French philosophers of the 1700's where the *Enlightenment* is a loan translation of German *Aufklärung* clarification.

enlist *v.* 1698-99; earlier *inlist* (1665) to enroll on the list or roster of a military unit; formed from *en-[1]* + *list[1],* n. *or* v., possibly suggested by Dutch *inlijsten* to write on a list. **—enlisted man** (1724) **—enlistment** *n.* 1765, formed from English *enlist* + *-ment.*

enmesh *v.* 1604 *enmash,* in Shakespeare's *Othello;* formed from English *en-[1]* + *mesh* (*mash*).

enmity *n.* Before 1382 *enemyte* danger; about 1384 *enmytee* hostility; both forms in different versions of the Wycliffe Bible; borrowed from Old French *enemistie*), from Vulgar Latin **inimīcitātem,* from Latin *inimīcus* ENEMY; for suffix see -ITY.

Loss of *s* in the Middle English forms indicates it was no longer pronounced in French at the time of borrowing. Often *s* continued to be written though no longer pronounced, as is still the case in many proper names: *Du Quesne, Fresnay,* etc.

ennoble *v.* 1502, implied in *ennobled* (about 1475 *ennobeled*); borrowed from Middle French *ennoblir* (*en-* make + *noble* noble).

ennui (än'wē) *n.* boredom. 1667, as a French word used in John Evelyn's *Diary;* developed from Old French *enui* annoyance, from *enuier* ANNOY. The term has resisted adoption into English, still retaining its French vowels and, therefore, appearing in italics through the 1800's, though Gray's is the first recorded use as naturalized term as early as 1742.

enormous *adj.* 1531, borrowed from Latin *ēnormis* irregular, extraordinary, very large (*ē-* out of + *norma* rule, NORM), with substitution of English *-ous* for Latin *-is,* and replacing earlier *enormyous* very great, monstrous; either formed from English *enorme* monstrous act (*adj.* used as a noun before 1464, from Middle French *énorme,* from Latin *ēnormis* irregular, extraordinary + *-ous);* or borrowed from Middle French *énorme* from Latin *ēnormis;* for suffix see -OUS. —**enormity** *n.* 1475, transgression, crime, in a translation of Caxton's; either borrowed from Middle French *énormité,* learned borrowing from Latin *ēnormitātem* (nominative *ēnormitās*) irregularity, vastness, from *ēnormis* irregular; *or* formed from English *enorme* + *-ity.* The sense of extreme wickedness, is first recorded in 1563; that of hugeness, vastness, in 1792.

enough *adj., adv.* Probably before 1200 *inoh,* in Layamon's *Chronicle of Britain;* later *ynough* (about 1303, in Mannyng's *Handlyng Synne*); developed from Old English *genōg* (before 899, in Alfred's translation of Boethius' *De Consolatione Philosophiae*); cognate with Old Frisian *enōch* enough, Old Saxon *ginōg,* Old High German *ginuog,* Old Icelandic *gnōgr,* and Gothic *ganōhs* enough, *ganaúha* sufficiency. All of these Germanic words represent compounds made up of the root of Old English *ge-* with, together (a perfective prefix also found in Old High German *ga-, gi-,* modern German *ge-,* Old Icelandic *g-,* and Gothic *ga-*), and the root *-nah* (as in Old High German *ginah, ganah* suffices), cognate with Sanskrit *náśati* reaches, Greek *podēnekḗs* reaching to the feet, and Latin *nactus* having attained, from Indo-European **(e)neḱ-/noḱ-/neḱ-/nōḱ-* (Pok. 316).

The original sound represented by *gh* in *cough, laugh, rough,* etc., was that of *ch* as in Scottish *loch* or German *ach.* As the pronunciation shifted to the sound of *f* in *off,* the spelling of many words also changed to reflect this process in *dwarf* and *draft* for *draught,* etc.; but a group of spellings remained fixed.

enrage *v.* About 1500, to make violent; but earlier implied in *enraged* (1398, in Trevisa's translation of Bartholomew's *De Proprietatibus Rerum*); borrowed ultimately from Old French *enrager,* but in its earlier use borrowed directly from Old French *enragé* enraged, from *en-* put in + *rage* rage, rabies.

enrapture *v.* 1740, formed from English *en-*[1] put in + *rapture,* probably influenced in its formation by earlier *enrapt* enraptured (1606, in Shakespeare's *Troylus and Cressida*).

enroll *v.* Before 1400 *enrollen* to write in an official list, register; borrowed from Old French *enroller, enrouler,* from Medieval Latin *inrotulare* write in a roll, from Latin *in* in + *rotulus* little wheel; see ROTARY. —**enrollment** *n.* 1440 *enrollement,* borrowed through Anglo-French *enrollement,* from Middle French *enrollement,* from *enroller;* for suffix see -MENT.

ensconce *v.* shelter safely, hide. 1590, to fortify, formed from English *en-*[1] make, put in + *sconce* small fortification, shelter, probably from Dutch *schans* earthwork, brushwood (used as a protective screen), from Middle High German *schanze* bundle of sticks, of uncertain origin.

One explanation offered by Kluge is that Middle High German *schanze* was derived from Italian *scansi,* plural of *scanso* protection, guard, avoidance, from *scansare* avoid, move away, from Vulgar Latin **excampsāre* turn aside (from Latin *ex-* out + Greek *kámpsai,* a form of *kámptein* to bend). The sense of to shelter or conceal safely, is first recorded in 1598, in Shakespeare's *Merry Wives of Windsor,* though the common extended use of settle comfortably is not recorded before 1820, in Washington Irving's *Sketch Book.*

ensemble (änsäm'bəl) *n.* Probably before 1500, a gathering of people; borrowed from Middle French *ensemblée;* later, all the parts of a thing considered together (1703, in the French phrase *tout ensemble*); borrowing of French *ensemble* together, from Late Latin *īnsimul* at the same time (*in-* intensive + *simul* at the same time; see SAME). The sense of a group of musicians playing or singing together, is first recorded in English in 1844, and of a complete, harmonious costume, in 1927.

enshrine *v.* 1395, in Wycliffe's writings; formed from Middle English *en-*[1] make, put in + *shrine, shrinen.*

ensign (en'sən) *n.* banner, naval officer. 1375 (Scottish), a signal, sign, in John Barbour's *The Bruce;* borrowed from Old French *enseigne,* from Latin *īnsignia, pl.;* see the doublet INSIGNIA. The sense of a banner or flag, is first recorded probably before 1400, in Chaucer's translation of *Roman de la Rose.* A soldier who carried the banner was later (1513-75) called an ensign, and from this developed the lowest rank of commissioned officer in the U.S. Navy (1862).

ensnare *v.* 1593, in Shakespeare's *Lucrece;* formed from English *en-*[1] put in + *snare.*

ensue *v.* come after; follow. Before 1400 *insuyen* pursue; later *ensewen* follow, result (1426); borrowed from Old French *ensivre, ensuivre* follow close upon, from Vulgar Latin **insequere,* from Latin *īnsequī* (*in-* upon + *sequī* follow; see SEQUEL).

ensure *v.* Before 1376 *enseuren* to exact a pledge, in a version of *Piers Plowman;* also *ensuren* to give assurance, promise on oath (about 1380, in Chaucer's *House of Fame*); borrowed from Anglo-French *enseurer* (*en-* make + Old French *seür* SURE, probably influenced by Old French *aseürer* ASSURE). The sense of make sure or certain, guarantee, is first recorded in 1440, in *Promptorium Parvulorum.*

-ent a suffix forming adjectives and nouns from verbs, such as *absorbent* (from *absorb*), *correspondent* (from *correspond*). Borrowed through French *-ent,* or directly from Latin *-entem,* present participle ending of verbs in *-ēre, -ere,* and *-īre;* often an alteration of Old French *-ant* -ANT.

Latin present participles *-antem* and *-entem* were leveled in Old French to *-ant,* but later many Latin forms with *-ent* that had assumed an adjective sense were borrowed into French as adjectives with the spelling *-ent*. English kept the French spelling in *-ent* and *-ant* as it borrowed words from French, but after 1500 some English spellings were changed in imitation of what was considered the appropriate Latin ending. This led to a confusion of arbitrary spellings: attendant, superintendent; secant, tangent; convergent, errant.

entablature (entab′ləchůr) *n.* part of a building resting on the top of columns. 1611, in Cotgrave's *Dictionary;* borrowed from obsolete French *entablature* (now *entablement*), from Italian *intavolatura,* from *intavolare* put on a board or tablet (*in-* on, from Latin *in-* in + Italian *tavola* board, tablet, from Latin *tabula* board, plank, TABLE); for suffix see -URE.

entail *v.* involve; require. Probably before 1400 *entaillen* settle (a land estate) on a number of persons in succession, in Wycliffe's writings (*en-* make + *taile* limitation of inheritance to a specified line of heirs; borrowed from Anglo-French *taile,* Old French *taillié,* past participle of *taillier* allot, cut to shape, from Late Latin *tāliāre;* see TAILOR). A transferred and figurative sense of bestow or confer to specified possessors, is first recorded about 1422, and reappeared in 1509, followed by the general sense of attach to someone, from which evolved the sense of bring on as a consequence, involve, necessitate (1829, in Southey's *Sir Thomas More*). **—n.** Probably before 1400, the limitation of inheritance, in Wycliffe's writings; from the verb, probably by influence of Old French *en taille* under a specific condition.

entangle *v.* About 1425 *entanglen* to involve, especially in difficulty, embarrass; formed from Middle English *en-* intensive + *tanglen* to invoke in complex affairs, often ones that embarrass. **—entanglement** *n.* Before 1646; formed from English *entangle* + *-ment.*

entente (äntänt′) *n.* agreement between two or more governments. 1854; earlier in *entente cordiale* (1844); borrowed from French *entente* understanding, from Old French *entente* intent, from feminine past participle of *entendre* INTEND.

enter *v.* About 1275 *entren* go in; borrowed from Old French *entrer,* from Latin *intrāre,* from *intrā* within, related to *inter* between; see INTRA- and INTER-.

entertain *v.* About 1475 *entertienen* maintain, in a translation of Caxton's; borrowed from Middle French *entretenir,* from Old French *entretenir* hold together, support (*entre-* among, from Latin *inter-* INTER- + Old French *tenir* to hold, from Latin *tenēre; see* TENANT*).* The sense of have as a guest, show hospitality to, is first recorded in 1490, in another translation of Caxton's, and that of hold attention of, amuse, in 1626, in Francis Bacon's *Sylva Sylvarum.* **—entertainer** *n.* Before 1535, one who furnishes amusement, in Sir Thomas More's writings; formed from English *entertain,* v. + *-er*[1]. **—entertainment** *n.* 1531, social manners, in Sir Thomas Elyot's *The Boke Named the Governour;* formed from English *entertain* + *-ment;* a re-formation of Middle English *entretenement* maintenance, support (1440); borrowed from Old French *entretenement,* from *entretenir* + *-ment.* The sense of amusement, is first recorded in 1612.

enthusiasm *n.* 1603 *enthusiasme* possession by a god, divine inspiration, prophetic or poetic frenzy, in Holland's translation of Plutarch's *Moralia,* and earlier cited in the Greek (1579); borrowed from Middle French *enthousiasme* (1546), from Greek, also borrowed directly from Late Latin *enthūsiasmus,* and from Greek *enthousiasmós,* from *enthousiázein* be inspired, from *éntheos* inspired, god-possessed (*en-* in + *theós* god; see THEOLOGY). The current sense of fervor, zeal, is first recorded in English in 1716. **—enthusiast** *n.* 1609, one who believes himself divinely inspired; borrowed from French *enthousiaste* (1544), from Greek *enthousiastḗs,* from *enthousiázein* be inspired. The sense of one who is full of enthusiasm for a cause, etc., is first recorded in English in 1764, in Goldsmith's *The History of England.* **—enthusiastic** *adj.* 1603, characterized by divine possession or inspiration, in Holland's translation of Plutarch's *Moralia;* borrowed from Greek *enthousiastikós,* from *enthousiázein* be inspired; for suffix see -IC. The sense of full of enthusiasm, eager, ardent, is first recorded in 1786, in Burke's writings. **—enthuse** *v.* show or fill with enthusiasm. 1827, American English, back formation from *enthusiasm.*

entice *v.* allure, attract, tempt. About 1280 *entycen* incite, stir up; borrowed from Old French *enticier,* perhaps from Vulgar Latin **intītiāre* set on fire, add fuel to a fire (Latin *in-* in + *tītiō,* genitive *tītiōnis,* firebrand, of uncertain origin). The sense of to allure or attract is first recorded about 1300. **—enticement** *n.* Probably before 1300, incitement, in *Arthour and Merlin;* borrowed from Old French, from *enticier;* for suffix see -MENT. The sense of allure or fascination is first recorded in 1549.

entire *adj.* About 1390 *entere* whole or complete, sincere or pure; later *entire* (1449); borrowed from Old French *entier* whole, complete, from Latin *integer* (*in-* not + *tag-,* root of *tangere* to touch; see TANGENT). Doublet of INTEGER. Alternatively it is possible that *entire* is a back formation from *entirety,* particularly as both words have the same spelling in the base form. **—entirety** *n.* completeness. About 1350 *enterete,* borrowed through Anglo-French *entiertie,* Old French *entiereté,* from Latin *integritātem* (nominative *integritās*), from *integer* (genitive *integrī*) whole, complete; for suffix see -TY[2].

entity *n.* something that has a real existence. 1596, being or existence, borrowed through Middle French *entité,* or directly from Medieval Latin *entitatem* (nominative *entitas*), from Latin *ēns* (genitive *entis*), proposed by Caesar as present participle of *esse* be; see IS; for suffix see -TY[2]. The concrete sense now in use is first recorded in English in 1628.

entomology (en′təmol′əjē) *n.* study of insects. 1766, borrowed from French *entomologie,* from New Latin *entomologia,* from Greek *éntomon* insect + *-logíā* study of. Greek *éntomon* derives from the neuter of *éntomos* having a notch or cut at the waist, from *entémnein* to cut into (*en-* in- + *témnein* to cut; see TOME). The meaning of notch in Greek refers to the segmented division of an insect's body.

entourage (än′tůrāzh′) *n.* group of attendants. 1832-34, surroundings, environment, in De Quincey's *The Caesars;* borrowed from French *entourage,* from Middle French, from *entourer* surround, from Old French *entour* that which surrounds (*en* in + *tour* a circuit, TOUR); for suffix see -AGE.

The current sense, which originally conveyed the notion of an assemblage of persons who surround a superior, is first recorded in English in 1860, in Froude's *History of England.*

entr'acte (äntrakt′) *n.* interval between two acts of a play. 1863, borrowing of earlier French *entr'acte* (now written *entracte*), from *entre* between + *acte* performance, action; see INTER- and ACT.

entrails *n.pl.* Probably before 1300 *entraile* inner parts of the body, innards (used as a collective singular form, in *Kyng Alisaunder*); later, *entrailles* (plural, before 1325, in *Cursor Mundi*); borrowed from Old French *entrailles,* from Late Latin *intrālia* inward parts, intestines (alteration of Latin *interānea,* noun use of neuter plural of *interāneus* internal, from *inter* between + *-āneus,* as in *extrāneus* external; see INTER-). The specific sense of intestines, is first recorded in English in 1373.

entrance[1] (en′trəns) *n.* act of entering. 1526, borrowed from Middle French *entrance,* from *entrer* ENTER; for suffix see -ANCE.

The concrete sense of that by which anything is entered, such as a door, gate, or similar passage, is first recorded in English in 1535, in the Coverdale Bible. **—entrant** *n.* 1635, borrowed from French *entrant,* present participle of *entrer* to enter.

entrance[2] (entrans′) *v.* to charm. 1593, to carry away as if in a trance; formed from English *en-*[1] put in + *trance.* The figurative sense of delight, is recorded before 1599, in Spenser's writings.

entrap *v.* 1590-96, in Spenser's *Faerie Queene* (earlier *intrap,* 1534); probably borrowed from Old French *entraper, entrapper* (*en-* make, put in + *trappe* trap).

entreat *v.* About 1400 *entreten* deal with; also, to discuss peace terms; later, to plead with (about 1425); borrowed through Anglo-French *entretier,* Middle French *entraitier,* from Old French *entraiter, entraitier* (*en-* make, cause + *traiter* to TREAT). **—entreaty** *n.* 1448, treatment, negotiation, formed from English *entreat* + *-y*[3]. The current sense of an earnest request, is first recorded in 1573.

entree or **entrée** (än′trā) *n.* 1724, a particular kind of music, especially for a number of short pieces in a ballet; later, a dish served before the main part of a meal (1759), and right to enter, admission (1762); borrowed from French *entrée,* from Old French *entree* ENTRY. This is a reborrowing of the Old French *entree* with somewhat specialized meanings in modern English, including the meaning of the main course of a meal, which developed from the sense of a dish served between the main courses (1759). In Middle English the word was generally spelled *entre* meaning act of entering, admittance, access, entrance to a building, harbor, etc. (about 1300); entrance into office or membership (about 1390); the beginning of an action or period of time, introduction to a book (1300-1400); an item on a list (about 1400). Only the right to entry seems to have been common to the Middle English and modern English terms.

entrench *v.* 1563, earlier *intrench* (1555); formed from English *en-*[1] cause to + *trench,* n., v. **—entrenchment** *n.* 1590, in Spenser's *Faerie Queene;* formed from English *entrench* + *-ment.*

entrepreneur (än′trəprənėr′) *n.* 1828, manager or promoter of a theatrical institution; borrowing of French *entrepreneur,* from Old French, one who undertakes, manager, from *entreprendre* undertake + *-eur* -or[2]; see ENTERPRISE. The modern sense of a business manager or promoter appeared in English in 1852, but the word itself had a much earlier appearance having been borrowed and Anglicized to *entreprennoure* in 1475 and *enterprenour* in 1485, after which it disappeared in recorded English for almost 350 years.

entropy (en′trəpē) *n. Physics.* the part of energy that cannot be converted into work. 1868, borrowed from German *Entropie,* from Greek *entropíā, entropḗ* a turning towards (*en-* in + *tropḗ* a turning; see TROPHY); for suffix see -Y[3]. Between 1868 and 1885 the term was used in English in a sense directly opposite to that of the current meaning; but Maxwell and other physicists later reverted to the original meaning proposed by Clausius. The German word was coined in 1865 by the German physicist Rudolf Julius Emanuel Clausius, on the analogy of German *Energie* energy.

entry *n.* Probably before 1300 *entre* act of entering, in *Arthour and Merlin;* borrowed from Old French *entree,* originally, feminine past participle of *entrer* ENTER. Compare ENTREE.

entwine *v.* 1597, in Richard Hooker's *Ecclesiastical Polity;* formed from English *en-*[1] cause + *twine,* v.

enumeration *n.* 1551, the act of listing or counting; borrowed from Middle French *énumeration,* or directly from Latin *ēnumerātiōnem* (nominative *ēnumerātiō*), from *ēnumerāre* enumerate (*ē-* out + *numerāre* to count, from *numerus* NUMBER); for suffix see -ATION. **—enumerate** *v.* 1647, possibly developed from *enumerate* (1646), past participle and adjective use formed in English on the model of Latin *ēnumerātus,* past participle of *ēnumerāre* to count out; or borrowed (possibly by influence of French *énumérer* to count, number) from Latin *ēnumerātus;* for suffix see -ATE[1]. Alternatively *enumerate* may be a back formation from earlier English *enumeration.*

enunciation *n.* 1551, declaration; borrowed (possibly by influence of Middle French *énonciation*) from Latin *ēnūntiātiōnem* (nominative *ēnūntiātiō*), from *ēnūntiāre* enunciate; for suffix see -ATION. The sense of pronunciation or articulation, is first recorded in English in 1750. **—enunciate** *v.* 1623, declare or express; borrowed from Latin *ēnūntiātus,* past participle of *ēnūntiāre* (*ē-* out + *nūntiāre* ANNOUNCE); for suffix see -ATE[1]. The sense of articulate or pronounce, is first recorded in English in 1759. Alternatively, *enunciate* may be a back formation from earlier *enunciation.*

envelop *v.* wrap, cover on all sides. 1590, in Spenser's *Faerie Queene;* alteration (influenced by Middle French *envelopper*) of earlier *envolupen* be involved in (1390, in Chaucer's *Canterbury Tales*). Middle English *envolupen* was borrowed from Old French *envoluper, envoloper* (*en-* in + *voloper* wrap up; of uncertain origin, but possibly developed from Medieval Latin *faluppa* bundle of straw, ball of grain, with influence of Latin *volvere* to roll; see VOLUME). Related to DEVELOP. **—envelopment** *n.* 1763, formed from English *envelop* + *-ment.*

envelope *n.* cover of a letter. 1705, borrowed from French *enveloppe,* from Middle French, from *envelopper* to ENVELOP. The general sense of a covering or wrapper, is first recorded in English in 1715.

envenom *v.* About 1290 *envenimen* to poison; later *envenomen* to make poisonous (before 1338, in Mannyng's *Chronicle of England*); borrowed from Old French *envenimer* to poison (*en-* cause + *venin* poison from Gallo-Romance **venīmen,* alteration of Latin *venēnum* poison).

environ *v.* surround, enclose. About 1350, surround

beset; borrowed from Old French *environner* surround, from *environ,* adv., around, about (*en-* in + *viron* circle, circuit, from *virer* to turn, VEER). **—n. environs,** *pl.* surrounding area; suburbs. 1665, in John Evelyn's *Memoirs;* borrowed from French *environs,* plural of Old French *environ* compass, circuit, from *environ,* adv., around. **—environment** *n.* 1603, the act or fact of surrounding; later, the surrounding things and conditions affecting an animal or plant (1827, in Carlyle's writings); formed from English *environ,* v. + *-ment.* **—environmental** *adj.* 1887, formed from English *environment* + *-al*[1]. **—environmentalism** *n.* 1923, emphasis on environment in the development of an individual or group; formed from English *environmental* + *-ism.* The ecological sense of concern with the quality of the environment of living things appeared in 1972.

envisage *v.* 1820, look in the face of, in Keats' *Hyperion;* borrowed from French *envisager* (*en-* cause to + *visage* face, VISAGE). The sense of form a mental view of, visualize, is first recorded in English in 1837.

envision *v.* 1921, in Strachey's *Queen Victoria;* formed from English *en-*[1] cause + *vision,* v.

envoy[1] *n.* messenger; diplomat. 1666, in Pepys' *Diary,* alteration of earlier *envoyée* (1660) and *envoyé* (1664); borrowed from French *envoyé* one sent, noun use of past participle of *envoyer* send, from Old French, from Vulgar Latin **inviāre* take the road, send on one's way (Latin *in* on + *via* road; see VIA).

envoy[2] or **envoi** *n.* short concluding passage of a poem, essay, etc.; postscript. About 1380 *envoye* conclusion of a poem, in Chaucer's writings; borrowed from Old French *envoie, envoi* act of sending, message, from *envoyer* send; see ENVOY[1]. The spelling *envoi* appeared in English in the 1800's, adopted from modern French.

envy *n.* About 1280 *envie* feeling of ill will at another's good fortune; borrowed from Old French *envie,* from Latin *invidia,* from *invidus* envious, from *invidēre* look with ill will upon, envy (*in-* upon + *vidēre* to see); for suffix see -Y[3]. **—v.** Before 1382 *envyen* feel envy, in the Wycliffe Bible; borrowed from Old French *envier,* from Latin *invidēre* to envy. **—enviable** *adj.* 1602, possibly borrowed from French *enviable* (*envier* to envy + *-able*); or formed in English from *envy,* v. + *-able.* **—envious** *adj.* About 1303 *envyus,* in Mannyng's *Handlyng Synne;* borrowed through Anglo-French *envious,* Old French *envieus, envius,* from Latin *invidiōsus,* from *invidia* envy; for suffix see -OUS.

enwrap *v.* Before 1382, in the Wycliffe Bible; formed from English *en-*[1] cause + *wrap,* v.

enzyme *n.* protein substance in living cells that can cause changes in other substances without being changed itself. 1881, borrowed from German *Enzym,* from Medieval Greek *énzymos* leavened (Greek *en-* in + *zýmē* leaven; see JUICE). The word was coined in 1877 by the German physiologist Wilhelm Kühne, but appearance of the form in English predates this new and separate borrowing by thirty years, as attested in the OEDS: 1850, the leavened bread of the Greek Orthodox eucharist.

Eocene (ē′əsēn) *adj. Geology.* of the second epoch of the Tertiary period. 1831, formed in English from Greek *ēṓs* dawn (see EAST) + *kainós* new (see RECENT). The word was coined by William Whewell for the use of the geologist Charles Lyell.

eolithic (ē′əlith′ik) *adj.* designating an early or the earliest stage of human culture marked by the use of very primitive stone instruments. 1890, borrowed from French *éolithique* (from Greek *ēṓs* dawn, see EAST + French *-lithique,* as in *néolithique* neolithic, *paléolithique* paleolithic, etc., from Greek *líthos* stone).

eon *n.* See AEON.

ep- a form of the prefix *epi-* before vowels, as in *epaxial* (situated on the axis of the body), *eponym,* and before *h,* as in *ephemeral.*

epaulet or **epaulette** (ep′əlet) *n.* ornament on the shoulder of a uniform. 1783, in a dispatch of Lord Nelson's; borrowed from French *épaulette,* diminutive form of *épaule* shoulder, from Old French *espaule, espale, espalle,* from Latin *spatula, spathula* flat piece of wood, splint, diminutive form of *spatha* two-edged sword, spatula, shoulder blade, from Greek *spáthē* broad blade, shoulder blade; see SPADE[1] tool; for suffix see -ET, -ETTE.

ephemeral (ifem′ərəl) *adj.* very short-lived. 1576, formed in English from Greek *ephḗmeros* subject to what the day may bring + English *-al*[1]. The Greek *ephḗmeros* comes from the phrase *ep' hēmérāi* (*epí* subject to + *hēmérāi,* dative of *hēmérā* day, related to *êmar* day, and cognate with Armenian *aur* day), from Indo-European **āmer-/āmōr/āmr̥* (Pok.35).

The earliest uses of *ephemeral* referred to the course of a disease or the life span of a flower or insect, which encompassed only a few days. Before 1639, *ephemeral* appeared in the extended sense of transitory, short-lived.

An earlier borrowing ultimately of the Greek appeared in Middle English *effimera, effimere* a fever or feverish condition that lasts for a short time (before 1398, in Trevisa's translation of Bartholomew's *De Proprietatibus Rerum*); borrowed from Medieval Latin *ephemera,* feminine of *ephemerus* lasting only a day, from Greek *ephḗmeros* short-lived.

epi- a prefix meaning: **1** on, upon, above, as in *epicenter, epigraph, epiphyte.* **2** in addition, as in *epilogue, episode.* **3** toward, among, as in *epidemic.* Either abstracted from compounds already formed in Greek, or borrowed from Greek *epi-,* related to *epí* on, upon, towards, after, besides, which is further related to *opsé* late in the day, *ópi(s)then* after, behind, and cognate with Latin *ob* before, towards, against, Sanskrit *ápi* also, besides.

epic *adj.* of or denoting a long poem, such as the Iliad or Beowulf, that tells the adventures of great heroes. 1589, in George Puttenham's *The Arte of English Poesie;* borrowed possibly through Middle French *épique,* learned borrowing of Latin or directly from Latin *epicus,* from Greek *epikós,* from *épos* word, story, poem; see VOICE; for suffix see -IC.

The extended sense of grand in style, heroic, is first recorded in English in 1731.

—n. 1706, epic poem; from the adjective. The transferred sense of any composition resembling an epic poem was introduced by Carlyle in 1840, in *On Heroes, Hero Worship, and the Heroic in History.* The figurative sense of any story or account worthy of being the subject of an epic, is first recorded in 1831, in Bulwer-Lytton's *Godolphin.*

epicene (ep′əsēn) *adj.* About 1450 *epycen* denoting either sex (in Latin and Greek grammar), having a common gender; borrowed from Latin *epicoenus* common, from Greek *epíkoinos* (*epi-* on, towards + *koinós* common; see COM-).

The extended sense of having the characteristics of both sexes, is first recorded in English in 1601, and that of adapted to both sexes, in 1624. The figurative sense of effeminate followed in 1633.

epicure *n.* About 1384 *Epicure* disciple of Epicurus, in the Wycliffe Bible; borrowing of the Latin form *Epicūrus,* from Greek *Epíkouros,* Greek philosopher (342?-270 B.C.) who taught that pleasure identified with virtue, is the highest good. In 1565 the word is recorded in English in the pejorative sense of one who gives himself up to sensual pleasure, especially eating as a glutton does (found in *Macbeth*). Soon after the sense of gourmet was recorded (1586), and coexisted with the earlier meaning until the later 1700's when the sense of a glutton gradually receded, existing now chiefly in *epicurean.*

—epicurean *n.* About 1380 *Epicurien* follower of Epicurus, in Chaucer's translation of Boethius' *De Consolatione Philosophiae,* possibly borrowed from Old French *Epicurien,* from *Epicure* Epicure + *-en* -an; or formed in English from *Epicure* + *-an.* The sense of one who gives himself up to sensual pleasure, appeared in English before 1572, in John Knox's writings. *—adj.* 1586, from the noun.

epidemic *adj.* affecting many people at the same time. 1603, borrowed from French *épidémique,* from *épidémie* an epidemic disease, learned borrowing from Medieval Latin *epidemia,* from Greek *epidēmíā* prevalence of an epidemic disease, especially the plague (*epi-* among, upon + *dêmos* people, district; see DEMOCRACY); for suffix see -IC. The concept was known in the English-speaking world 130 years before, as evidenced by the term *epideme* epidemic disease, recorded in *The Paston Letters* in 1472. **—n.** rapid spreading of a disease, idea, or fashion. 1757, anything like an epidemic disease, in Burke's *Abridgement of English History;* from the adjective.

epidermis *n.* outer layer of the skin. 1626, in Francis Bacon's *Sylva Sylvarum;* borrowed from Late Latin *epidermis,* from Greek *epidermís* (*epi-* on + *dérma* skin; see DERMA).

epiglottis *n.* cartilage that covers the entrance to the windpipe during swallowing. 1525, borrowed from Late Latin *epiglōttis,* from Greek *epiglōttís* (*epi-* on + *glōttís,* from *glôtta,* variant of *glôssa* tongue). *Epiglottis* replaced Middle English *epiglote* (recorded before 1400, in a translation of Lanfranc's *Science of Surgery*); borrowed from Old French *epiglotte,* learned borrowing from Late Latin *epiglōttis;* see GLOTTAL.

epigram *n.* short, pointed, or witty saying. Probably before 1439, in Lydgate's translation of Bochas' *Falls of Princes;* borrowed from Middle French *épigramme,* from Latin *epigramma,* from Greek *epígramma* an inscription, epitaph, epigram, from *epigráphein* to write on, inscribe (*epi-* on + *gráphein* write). **—epigrammatic** *adj.* Before 1704, shortened form of earlier *epigrammatical,* adj. (1605, formed in English from Latin *epigrammat-,* stem of *epigrammaticus,* from Late Greek *epigrammatikós,* from *epígramma* + English suffix *-ical*).

—epigraph *n.* 1624, inscription on a building; borrowed from Greek *epigraphḗ* an inscription, from *epigráphein* to write on, inscribe; see EPIGRAM. The meaning of a motto or short pithy sentence of dedication, is first recorded in English in 1844 (in Elizabeth Barrett Browning's *Sonnets from the Portuguese*).

epilepsy *n.* chronic nervous disease causing convulsions and unconsciousness. 1578, borrowed from Middle French *epilepsie,* from Late Latin *epilēpsia,* from Greek *epilēpsíā* seizure (*epi-* upon + *lêpsis* a seizure, from a stem *lēph-* of *lambánein* to take, seize; see DILEMMA); for suffix see -Y[3].

Modern English *epilepsy* replaced Middle English *epilencie,* in use before 1398 and borrowed from Old French *epilencie,* learned borrowing from Medieval Latin *epilempsia* (also found in English, 1540), and *epilentia,* alteration of Late Latin *epilēpsia.*

—epileptic *adj.* affected with epilepsy. 1605, in Shakespeare's *King Lear;* borrowed from French *épileptique,* from Late Latin *epilēpticus,* from Greek *epilēptikós,* from *epilēpsíā* epilepsy; for suffix see -IC. *—n.* epileptic person. 1651, in Hobbes' *Leviathan;* from the adjective.

Modern English *epileptic* gradually replaced *epilentic,* found in modern English in 1542, in use in Middle English before 1398, and borrowed from Old French *epilentique,* from Late Latin *epilenticus,* probably from Greek **epilēmptikós,* variant of *epilēptikós.*

epilogue or **epilog** *n.* concluding part of a literary work. Probably about 1425 *epilog;* borrowed from Middle French *epilogue,* learned borrowing from Latin *epilogus,* from Greek *epílogos* conclusion of a speech (*epi-* upon, in addition + *lógos* a speaking, from *légein* speak; see LEGEND).

epinephrine (ep′ənef′rin) *n.* hormone secreted by the adrenal gland; adrenaline, but the term *epinephrine* appears in the U.S. Pharmacopeia. 1899, formed in English from *epi-* on + Greek *nephrós* kidney (because the adrenal glands are located on the kidneys) + English *-ine*[2] (chemical suffix).

Epiphany (ipif′ənē) *n.* January 6, anniversary of the coming of the Wise Men to honor the infant Jesus at Bethlehem. About 1325 *epyphany* (before 1310, in OED *Epyphany*); borrowed from Old French *epiphanie,* from Late Latin *epiphania,* neuter plural, from Greek *epipháneia* manifestation, striking appearance (in the New Testament, applied to the advent or manifestation of Christ), from *epiphanḗs* manifest, conspicuous, from *epiphainein* to manifest, display (*epi-* on, to + *phainein* to show; see FANTASY).

The general literary sense of any striking manifestation or revelation appeared in English in 1840, in De Quincey's *Works,* but it is rare and a figurative allusion to the appearance of some divine or superhuman being (before 1667), which by itself is a meaning derived from reference to the Epiphany, though in most etymologies this use of the term is derived directly from Greek *epipháneia.*

episcopal *adj.* of or having to do with bishops. About 1460, borrowed from Middle French *épiscopal,* from Late Latin *episcopālis,* from Latin *episcopus* BISHOP; for suffix see -AL[1]. The specific application to a church governed by bishops, such as the Episcopal Church in Scotland or the Protestant Episcopal Church in the United States, appeared in 1752, in David Hume's *Essays and Treatises.* **—Episcopalian** *adj.* belonging to the Episcopal Church. 1768, formed from English *episcopal* + *-ian.* *—n.* member of the Episcopal Church. 1738, formed from English *episcopal* + *-ian.*

episode *n.* 1678 *episod* commentary in a Greek tragedy between two choric songs; 1679 *episode,* in writings of Dryden, an incidental narrative or digression in a story, poem, etc.; borrowed through French *épisode* from Greek *epeisódion* addition, (originally) neuter of *epeisódios* coming in besides (*epi-* in addition + *eísodos* a coming in, entrance, from *eis* into + *hodós* way; see CEDE).

The sense of an incident or experience that stands out from others, is first recorded in English in 1773, in Goldsmith's *She Stoops to Conquer.*
—episodic *adj.* 1711 either a shortened form of earlier *episodical* (1667, from *episode* + *-ical*); or formed from English *episode* + *-ic,* possibly by influence of French *épisodique,* from *épisode;* for suffix see -IC.

epistemology *n.* study or theory of knowledge. 1856, formed in English from Greek *epistḗmē* knowledge (Ionic Greek *epístasthai* understand, know how to do, from *epi-* over, near + *hístasthai* to STAND) + English *-logy.*

epistle *n.* letter. Probably before 1200 *epistel* one of the letters from an apostle forming the apostolic letters of the New Testament, in *Ancrene Riwle;* later, a letter (before 1382, in the Wycliffe Bible); borrowed from Old French *epistle,* learned borrowing from Latin *epistola* letter, from Greek *epistolḗ* message, letter, from *epistéllein* send to (*epi-* to + *stéllein* send; see STALL[1] place). The Old English *pistole, epistol* was borrowed directly from Late Latin *epistola,* and contributed to the formation *epistel* in Middle English. **—epistolary** *adj.* 1656, of letters or letter-writing, borrowed from French *épistolaire,* from Latin *epistolāris,* from *epistola* letter. The earlier Middle English *pistelarie, epistolarie,* n. a book of the epistles read at the Eucharist (1432) was a borrowing from Medieval Latin *epistolarium,* from Latin *epistolāris,* from *epistola.*

epitaph *n.* inscription on a tomb. Before 1338 *epitaf,* in Mannyng's *Chronicle of England;* borrowed from Old French *epitaphe,* learned borrowing from Medieval Latin *epitaphium,* from Latin, funeral oration, eulogy, from Greek *epitáphion,* from neuter of *epitáphios* of a funeral (*epí-* at + *táphos* tomb, funeral rites, related to *tháptein* to bury, and *táphros* ditch), cognate with Armenian *damban* grave, from Indo-European **dhm̥bh-* (Pok.248).

epithelium *n.* layer of cells covering surfaces of the body or the internal cavities of plants. 1748, New Latin, formed from *epi-* on + Greek *thēlḗ* nipple, teat, so called because originally applied to tissue with a nipplelike surface. The term is first recorded in its botanical use in 1870. **—epithelial** *adj.* 1845, formed from English *epithelium* + *-al*[1].

epithet *n.* descriptive word or name. 1579, borrowed through Middle French *épithète,* learned borrowing from Latin, or directly from Latin *epitheton,* from Greek *epítheton,* adjective often used as a noun, from neuter of *epíthetos* attributed, added, from *epitithénai* to add on, put on (*epi-* on, in addition + *tithénai* to put, place; see DO[1]).

epitome (epit′əmē) *n.* 1529, summary or condensation; borrowed through Middle French *épitomé,* learned borrowing from Latin *epitomē,* from Greek *epitomḗ* abridgement, from *epitémnein* cut short, abridge (*epi-* into + *témnein* to cut; see TOME).

The sense of person or thing that is typical or representative of something, is first recorded in 1607, in Shakespeare's *Coriolanus.*
—epitomize *v.* 1599, abridge or condense; formed from English *epitome* + *-ize.* The sense of embody, typify, is first recorded in 1628.

epoch *n.* period of time; era. 1658 *epoch;* earlier *epocha* (1614); borrowed from Medieval Latin *epocha,* from Greek *epochḗ* stoppage, fixed point of time, from *epéchein* to stop, take up a fixed position (*epi-* on + *échein* to hold; see SCHEME). **—epochal** *adj.* 1685, formed from English *epoch* + *-al*[1].

eponymous (epon′əməs) *adj.* giving one's name to a nation, tribe, place, etc. 1846, borrowed from Greek *epṓnymos* given as a name, giving one's name to something or someone (*epi-* upon + *ónyma,* dialectal variant of *ónoma* NAME); for suffix see -OUS. **—eponym** (ep′ənim) *n.* eponymous ancestor, hero, etc. 1846, probably borrowed through French *éponyme* (1755), from Greek *epṓnymos;* but also possibly back formation from English *eponymous.*

equable *adj.* changing little, uniform. 1677, either a back formation from earlier *equability* (1531, borrowed from Latin *aequābilitās,* from *aequābilis* equal, consistent, uniform); *or* borrowed from Latin *aequābilis* equal, consistent, uniform, from *aequāre* make uniform; see EQUATE; for suffix see -ABLE.

equal *adj.* About 1390, in Chaucer's *Canterbury Tales;* borrowed from Latin *aequālis* uniform, identical, equal, from *aequus* level, even, just, of uncertain origin; for suffix see -AL[1].

A parallel form *egal* equal, equivalent (obsolete in English since the 1650's) was widely used in Middle English, first recorded in 1380, in Chaucer's translation of Boethius' *De Consolatione Philosophiae,* and borrowed from Old French *egal, igal,* from Latin *aequālis.* Its derivative in French *égalité* (earlier borrowed into Middle English, 1380, in Chaucer's translation of Boethius' *De Consolatione Philosophiae,* but becoming obsolete by 1650) and thence *égalitare* was used with the suffix *-ian* to form *egalitarian* in English. French *égalité* had also been borrowed into English (Middle English *egalyte,* in Chaucer's Boethius, 1380), but it, too, became obsolete by 1650, until apparently re-formed by Tennyson, in 1864.
—n. 1573, one who is equal to another; from the adjective.
—v. 1586, compare, liken; from the noun. The sense of match, rival, appeared in 1590, in Marlowe's *Tamburlane the Great.*
—equality *n.* 1398 *equalite,* in Trevisa's translation of Bartholomew's *De Proprietatibus Rerum;* borrowed from Old French *equalité* (modern French *égalité*), from Latin *aequālitātem,* from *aequālis* equal; for suffix see -ITY. **—equalize** *v.* 1590 (and perhaps earlier), in Spenser's *Faerie Queene;* formed from English *equal* + *-ize,* perhaps modeled on French *égaliser* (1539), or *equaliser* (1400's), v. **—equalization** *n.* 1793, formed from English *equalize* + *-ation,* perhaps modeled on French *égalisation* (1500's).

equanimity *n.* 1607, fairness, impartiality; borrowed from French *équanimité,* learned borrowing from Latin *aequanimitātem* (nominative *aequanimitās*), from *aequus* even + *animus* mind, spirit; see EQUAL and ANIMAL; for suffix see -ITY.

The sense of evenness of mind or temper, is first recorded in English in Pepys' *Diary* (1663).

equate *v.* Probably before 1425 *equaten* make equal or uniform; earlier, to place a heavenly body in its proper astrological position; borrowed from Latin *aequātus,* past participle of *aequāre* make even or uniform, make equal, from *aequus* level, even, EQUAL; for suffix see -ATE[1]. It may be that *equate,* v. was also formed from earlier *equat, equate* (before 1420), past participle; borrowed from Latin *aequātus.* —**equation** *n.* Probably before 1425 *equacioun* a making even or equal; earlier, dividing the sphere into astrological houses of equal extent; borrowed from Latin *aequātiōnem* (nominative *aequātiō*) an equalizing, equal distribution, from *aequāre* make even or equal; for suffix see -ATION. The mathematical sense of statement of equality of two quantities, appeared in 1570.

equator *n.* 1391, great circle of the celestial sphere, in Chaucer's *Treatise on the Astrolabe;* borrowed from Medieval Latin *aequator diei et noctis* equalizer of day and night (because when the sun is in the celestial equator, day and night are of equal length), from Latin *aequāre* make equal, EQUATE; for suffix see -OR[2]. The geographical sense of great circle of the earth midway between the North and South Poles, is first recorded in English in 1612. —**equatorial** *adj.* 1664; formed from English *equator* + *-ial.*

equerry (ek'wərē) *n.* officer in charge of horses. 1591 *equirrie,* short for *groom of the equirrie* groom of the stables, alteration of earlier *esquirie, esquiry* stables (1552); borrowed from Middle French *escuerie, escuyrie,* cognate with Italian *scuderia* gentleman's stables, reflecting the social change of the *escuier* (E)SQUIRE from shield carrier (from Late Latin *scūtārius* guardsman) through master of horse to stable keeper; for suffix see -Y[3].

The English spelling was influenced by Latin *equus* horse, and so is the meaning horseman, rider of French *écuyer* (Old French *escuier*) as well as of *écurie* stable (for horses).

equestrian *adj.* of horseback riders or horsemanship. 1656-81, in an edition of Blount's *Glossographia,* formed in English from Latin *equester* (genitive *equestris*) of a horseman + English -IAN. Latin *equester* is derived from *eques* horseman, knight, from *equus* horse; see EQUINE.

The sense of mounted on a horse, applied to a statue or portrait, appeared in 1711 (Addison, in *The Spectator*).

—**n.** horseback rider. 1791, from the adjective.

equi- a combining form meaning equal, as in *equidistance,* or equally, as in *equidistant.* Borrowed from Latin *aequi-,* combining form of *aequus* even, EQUAL.

equilateral *adj.* 1570, borrowed from Late Latin *aequilaterālis* (*aequi-,* combining form of *aequus* equal + *latus,* nominative *lateris* side; see LATERAL); for suffix see -AL[1].

equilibrium *n.* balance. 1608, borrowed from Latin *aequilībrium* (*aequus* equal + *lībra* a balance, scale, plummet, of uncertain origin).

equine (ē'kwīn) *adj.* of or like a horse. 1788, borrowed from Latin *equīnus,* from *equus* horse. The Latin *equus* is cognate with Old English *eoh* horse, Old Saxon *ehu-,* Old High German *eha-,* Gothic *aíhwa-,* Old Icelandic *jōr,* Sanskrit *áśva-s,* Greek *híppos,* Old Irish *ech,* and Gaulish *epo-,* from Indo-European **ekwos* (Pok.301); for suffix see -INE[1].

equinox (ē'kwənoks) *n.* either of the two times in the year when the sun crosses the celestial equator and day and night are of equal length. 1391, in Chaucer's *Treatise on the Astrolabe;* borrowed through Old French *equinoxe,* or directly from Medieval Latin *equinoxium* equality between day and night, from Latin *aequinoctium* (*aequus* equal + *nox,* genitive *noctis,* NIGHT). —**equinoctial** *adj.* 1391 *equinoxial,* in Chaucer's *Treatise on the Astrolabe;* borrowed through Old French *equinoxial,* or directly from Medieval Latin *equinoxialis,* from Latin *aequinoctiālis,* from *aequinoctium* equinox; for suffix see -AL[1].

While English, French, Latin, etc. have derived their words for this phenomenon substantially from *nox, noctis* night, in other languages the equivalent of English "day" is part of the formation, as in Russian *ravnod'enstviye,* literally, equidayishness, or both concepts of day and night, as in German *Tagundnachtgleiche,* literally, day and night equality.

equip *v.* 1523, furnish what is needed; borrowed from Middle French *équiper* to fit out, equip, from Old French *esquiper* equip a ship, probably from a Scandinavian source (compare Old Icelandic *skipa* to put in order, arrange, man a ship, from *skip* SHIP). —**equipment** *n.* 1717, possibly formed from English *equip* + *-ment,* but more likely borrowed from French *équipement,* from *équiper* to equip; for suffix see -MENT. *Equipment* has replaced earlier *equipage* (1579), except in the sense of a horse-drawn carriage or such a carriage and all of its appurtenances (probably 1721).

equipoise *n.* 1658, formed from English *equi-* + *poise,* replacing the earlier phrase *equal poise.*

equity *n.* fairness, impartiality, justice. Before 1333, in Shoreham's poetry; borrowed from Old French *equité,* learned borrowing from Latin *aequitātem* (nominative *aequitās*), from *aequus* even, just, EQUAL; for suffix see -ITY. —**equitable** *adj.* fair; impartial; just. 1646, borrowed from French *équitable,* from *équité* equity; for suffix see -ABLE.

equivalent *adj.* equal in value, area, force, effect, meaning, etc. About 1425; borrowed through Middle French *equivalent,* and directly from Late Latin *aequivalentem* (nominative *aequivalēns*) equivalent, present participle of *aequivalēre* have equal power, be equivalent (Latin *aequus* EQUAL + *valēre* be strong, be well, be worth; see VALUE); for suffix see -ENT. —**n.** 1502, from the adjective. —**equivalence** *n.* Before 1541, perhaps back formation from earlier *equivalency* (1535); formed by influence of Middle French *equivalence,* from Medieval Latin *aequivalentia,* from Late Latin *aequivalentem* equivalent; for suffix see -ENCE, -ENCY.

equivocal *adj.* intentionally vague or ambiguous. 1601-02, formed in English from Late Latin *aequivocus* of identical sound + English *-al*[1]. Late Latin *aequivocus* is formed from Latin *aequus* EQUAL + the root *voc-* of *vocāre* to call; see VOICE. —**equivocate** *v.* be equivocal. Probably before 1425 *equivocaten,* in a translation of Higden's *Polychronicon,* either 1) developed from *equivocat,* adj., borrowed from Medieval Latin *equivocatus,* past participle of *equivocare,* from Late Latin *aequivocus* of identical sound; *or* 2) a back formation from *equivocation;* for suffix see -ATE[1]. —**equivocation** *n.* Before 1397 *equivocacoun* ambiguity, in the Wycliffe Bible; borrowed from Old French *equivocation,* from Late Latin *aequivocātiōnem* (nominative *aequivocātiō*), from *aequivocus* of identical sound; for suffix see -TION. The sense of the use of equivocal language to deceive is first recorded in 1605, in Shakespeare's *Macbeth.*

-er[1] a suffix meaning person or thing that does something *(player),* is something *(foreigner),* lives somewhere *(villager),* makes or works with something *(hatter),* has something *(rancher, double-decker),* or is connected with or involved in something *(first-grader); -er* is used to form nouns either from verbs, as *burner, climber, player, thinker,* or from other nouns, as *rancher, cottager, outsider, New Yorker.*

In the sense of a person or thing that is or has something, as in *double-decker* or *double-header* (originally a train with two locomotives or a firework with two explosive heads, and now two baseball games played between the same teams on the same day) the meaning of *-er* perhaps absorbs some of the sense of *-er*[5].

The suffix *-er*[1] is in part a native development, through Middle English *-ere,* from Old English *-ere,* as in *sangere* singer, and *bæcere* baker. It is a common Germanic formative suffixed to verbs to form agent nouns, but was originally probably added mostly to nouns to identify people according to their occupation. The traditional Germanic form given is *-ārijaz* developed as Old High German *-āri* (modern German *-er*), Old Saxon *-eri,* Old Icelandic *-ari,* and Gothic *-areis;* its developmental relationship to Latin *-ārius* is obscure. A vestige of the original Germanic form is evident in *-ar,* as in *beggar, liar,* and its equivalence to Latin *-or* is found in *instructor, advisor,* etc., though this distinction between *-er* and *-or* as an ending of agent nouns is only a matter of convention.

The influence of French is evident in many terms with the formation of Middle English *-ere,* but these terms were often borrowed through Anglo-French *-er* either from Old French *-ier, -iere,* and *-er* after a palatal consonant, from Latin *-ārius, -āria,* or *-ārium* (see -ARY), or from Old French *-eor, -eur* (see -OR[1], also -OUR). Though derivatives of this type already existed in Old English, most such terms are borrowed from Old French and are not usually associated with a verb, terms such as *commissioner, officer, prisoner,* and *carpenter, danger, border.* Later, by analogy, the suffix came to be regarded as a formative of so-called agent nouns. In modern English it may be formed on all verbs, except for those ending in *-or,* and others for which the agent-noun relationship to the verb is fulfilled by *-ent,* as in *correspond/correspondent, -ant,* as in *defend/defendant.*

The English suffix *-er* also has the form *-yer* after nouns ending in *w,* such as *lawyer* and *sawyer,* and appears in English as *-ier* by analogy with English *-yer* and by assimilation of borrowings from French of words ending in *-ier,* such as *clothier, collier,* and *glazier.*

-er[2] a suffix forming the comparative degree of adjectives, as in *softer, smoother,* and of adverbs, as in *slower.* Middle English *-er, -ere* developed from Old English *-ra* (masculine), and *-re* (feminine and neuter for adjectives), and *-or* (for adverbs). Old English *-ra, -re* is cognate with Old Saxon and Old High German *-iro* adjective comparative suffix, German *-er,* Old Icelandic *-ri, -ari,* Gothic *-iza, -ōza,* and also with Latin *-ior,* Greek *-íōn,* and Sanskrit *-īyas.*

In the comparative degree of adjectives few words of Old English retained the vowel changes of the ancient Germanic forms and in modern English they have completely disappeared except for *better* and *elder.* And though the words *worse* and *less* contain ancient comparative forms, they are not now recognized, a fact which has produced the anomaly *worser* and the accepted form *lesser.*

For most comparatives of one or two syllables, dictionaries list and many practiced writers use the *-er* form, but this seems to be a fading usage as the oral element in our society of highly verbal communication tends to rely on *more* before the adjective to express the comparative; thus *prettier* is receding before *more pretty, cooler* before *more cool.*

The Old English comparative suffix for adverbs, *-or,* as in *heardor* more fiercely (English *harder*), comparative of *hearde* (English *hard*), is cognate with Old Saxon and Old High German *-ōr,* Old Icelandic *-r, -ar,* and Gothic *-is, -ōs.* Compare -EST. The *-r-* in most of the Germanic forms is from Indo-European *-s-,* still seen in the superlative *-st.* Gothic *-z-* represents a bridge between the original Indo-European *s* and Germanic *r.* The Greek form has lost the medial *-s-* as a normal development. Latin *-ior* has the same kind of change to *r* as most of the Germanic forms. Sanskrit *-īyas* is exactly the same formation as Latin *-ior.*

In the comparative degree of adverbs the vowel change of Old English in monosyllables died out in Middle English, and was replaced by adjective formations, as *to work harder* (with the exception of *sooner*). Now, as in the case with adjectives, the use of *more* is replacing the adverbial use of *-er* in *friendlier* replaced by *more friendly, oftener* replaced by *more often.*

-er[3] a suffix of nouns that were once French infinitive verb forms (Old French and Anglo-French *-er,* from Latin *-āre*), surviving in certain legal terms from Anglo-French, such as *misnomer* and *waiver,* and in a few nouns of verbal origin in Old French, such as *dinner, supper, surrender, ouster.*

-er[4] a suffix meaning frequently, again and again, in verbs such as *clatter, flutter, jabber, putter.* Middle English *-eren,* developed from Old English *-rian.*

-er[5] a suffix used especially in British slang to form new words by shortening a noun and adding *-er* (sometimes *-ers*) to the stem, as in *Rugger* for *Rugby, rudders* for *rudiments, soccer* for *association* (football). The usage is first recorded in the late 1800's from Rugby School and thence in Oxford University slang, thereafter coming into general currency in words like *bedder* for *bedroom,* especially during the 1920's.

era *n.* age, epoch. 1615 *Æra;* later *era* (1716); borrowed, possibly by influence of French *ère* epoch (1539), from Late Latin *aera, ēra* an era or epoch from which time is reckoned; apparently a special use of the meaning number in Late Latin, referring to a given number upon which a calculation is to be made; probably the same word as Latin *aera* counters used for calculation, plural of *aes* (genitive *aeris*) brass, money; see ORE.

The use of this word in chronology is said to have originated in Spain in the A.D. 400's, where *aera* (more often written *era*) was found in Latin inscriptions prefixed to a specific year reckoned from a base date (usually 38 B.C., suggested by the Spanish Medieval encyclopedist Isidore of Seville, as the year Augustus first ordered the taxation in Spain). This method of reckoning is referred to as *aera Hispanica* Spanish era, a phrase which probably suggested to Renaissance scholars the phrase *aera Christiana* Christian era.

eradicate *v.* Probably before 1425 *eradicaten* pull up by the roots, destroy; borrowed from Latin *ērādīcātus,* past participle of *ērādīcāre* root out (*ē-* out, variant of *ex-* before *r* + *rādīx,* genitive *rādīcis* ROOT[1] plant part); for suffix see -ATE[1]. **—eradication** *n.* Probably before 1425 *eradicacioun;* borrowed from Latin *ērādīcātiōnem* (nominative *ērādīcātiō*), from *ērādīcāre* eradicate; for suffix see -ATION.

erase *v.* 1605, borrowed from Latin *ērāsus,* past participle of *ērādere* scrape out (*ē-* out, variant of *ex-* before *r* + *rādere* to scrape; see RAZE). **—eraser** *n.* 1790, American English; formed from *erase* + *-er*[1]. **—erasure** *n.* 1734, formed from English *erase* + *-ure.*

erbium (ėr′bēəm) *n.* metallic chemical element. 1843, New Latin, formed from *(Ytt)erby,* town in Sweden where the mineral containing erbium (gadolinite) was found + *-ium* (suffix of chemical element). The word was coined by the Swedish chemist C.G. Mosander, who discovered the element.

ere (ãr) *conj., prep.* before. Probably before 1200 *er,* developed from Old English *ǣr,* adv. and conj. (about 725, in *Beowulf*) and Old English *ǣr,* prep. (before 830, in the *Vespasian Psalter*). Old English *ǣr* is cognate with Old Frisian, Old Saxon, and Old High German *ēr* earlier, and Gothic *airis* earlier, from Proto-Germanic **airiz,* comparative of **air,* represented by Old Icelandic *ār* early, Gothic *air* early, and cognate with Greek *êri* in the morning, and Avestan *ayarə* day (from Indo-European **ayer-* day, morning, Pok.12). As an adverb the word is found in modern English *erstwhile,* where the form *erst* developed from the Old English superlative adverb *ǣrest.*

erect *adj.* upright. About 1390, in Chaucer's *Canterbury Tales;* borrowed from Latin *ērēctus,* past participle of *ērigere* raise or set up (*ē-* up, variant of *ex-* before *r* + *regere* to direct, keep straight, guide; see RIGHT). **—v.** Probably about 1408 *erecten* to direct upward; later, to set up, build (1417); formed from the adjective in English, and borrowed from Latin *ērēctus,* past participle of *ērigere* raise or set up. **—erection** *n.* 1450, probably formed in English from *erect* + *-ion* after Late Latin *ērēctiōnem* (nominative *ērēctiō*), from Latin *ērēct-,* participle stem of *ērigere* raise or set up; for suffix see -ION.

erg (ėrg) *n. Physics.* unit for measuring work or energy in the centimeter-gram-second system. 1873, borrowed from Greek *érgon* WORK. This is a made word from formal borrowing first imposed by the British Association (for the Advancement of Science).

ergo *adv., conj.* Before 1376, in a version of *Piers Plowman;* a word in Latin *ergō* therefore, possibly from Latin **ē rogō* or **ē regō* from the direction (*ē* out of, variant of *ex* and the root of *regere* to guide; see RIGHT).

ergot (ėr′gət) *n.* disease of rye and other cereal grains, caused by a fungus. 1683, borrowing of French *ergot,* from Old French *argot* cock's spur, so called from the shape of the diseased grain; of unknown origin.

ermine *n.* weasel of northern climates whose fur in winter is almost wholly white. Probably about 1175, borrowing of Old French *ermine, hermine,* cognate with Old Provençal *ermina, ermeni,* Spanish *armiño,* and Portuguese *arminho.*

The ulterior etymology of *ermine* is in dispute. Scholars such as Dauzat, Bloch-Wartburg, and Corominas believe that the Romance words represent Latin *Armenius* Armenian, the ermine having been abundant in Asia Minor. Other scholars, such as Kluge and Skeat, think that the Romance words are of Germanic origin and compare them to Old High German *harmo* weasel (*harmīn,* adj.), Old Saxon *harmo,* and Old English *hearma* shrew, possibly also meaning weasel. Ultimately it is likely that there was early confusion of the Germanic words and the Romance words because of the similarities in form and meaning.

In Middle English, probably before 1300, *ermine* also referred to the animal's valuable fur.

erode *v.* wear away. 1612, back formation from *erosion,* influenced by French *éroder* but modeled on the Latin pattern *ērōsiōnem, ērōdere* gnaw away (*ē-* away, variant of *ex-* before *r* + *rōdere* gnaw; see RODENT). It is also possible in some instances that *erode* is a direct borrowing from French *éroder.* **—erosion** *n.* 1541, borrowed through Middle French *erosion,* from Latin *ērōsiōnem* (nominative *ērōsiō*) from *ērōdere* gnaw away; for suffix see -SION.

erogenous (iroj′ənəs) *adj.* producing sexual desire. 1889, formed in English from Greek *érōs* love + English *-genous* producing (*-gen* + *-ous*). The variant *erogenic,* borrowed from French *érogénique,* is first recorded in 1887, in a translation of Binet's works, referring to earlier work by Chambard.

erotic *adj.* of sexual desire. 1651, borrowed from French *érotique,* from Greek *erōtikós,* from *érōs* (genitive *érōtos*) love; related to *erâsthai* to love, desire, of uncertain origin; for suffix see -IC. **—erotica** *n.* 1854, borrowed from Greek *erōtiká,* neuter plural of *erōtikós* erotic.

err *v.* go wrong, be in error. Before 1300 *erren;* borrowed from Old French *errer,* learned borrowing from Latin *errāre* wander. The underlying sense is that error and anger are erratic or irregular and a straying from the norm in behavior or practice. Latin *errāre* is cognate with Old English *ierre* angry, straying, Old Frisian *īre* angry, Old Saxon *irri,* Old High German *irri* angry, *irrōn* astray (modern German *irren* err), and Gothic *aírzeis* misled, led astray, from Indo-European **ers-* (Pok. 337).

errand *n.* Probably before 1200 *ernde;* later *erende* (about 1250) and *errand* (before 1325); developed from Old English (about 725) *ǣrende* message, mission, and related to *ār* messenger. Old English *ǣrende* is cognate with Old Frisian *ērende* message or mission, Old Saxon *ārundi,* Old High German *ārunti,* Old Icelandic *erendi, ørendi,* and related to Gothic *airus* messenger of unknown origin. The original sense of an important mission (*an errand of mercy, a secret errand*) still appears occasionally, but the more common sense of a short trip to perform a trivial task, is not recorded in English until 1642.

errant *adj.* wandering, straying from the proper course. About 1369 *erraunt* traveling, roving, in Chaucer's *Canterbury Tales;* earlier in the compound proper name *Bailfesmanerraunt* (1335); borrowed through Anglo-French *erraunt,* Old French *errant,* present participle of *errer* to travel or wander, from Late Latin *iterāre,* from Latin *iter* journey or way, from the root of *īre* to go; see EXIT.

The sense of traveling or wandering, fused in the 1300's with the sense of erring or straying from the right course, from Old French *errant,* present participle of *errer* to ERR. Development of this sense is found in English *arrant* which is recorded in *thief erraunt,* in Chaucer; see ARRANT.

erratic *adj.* About 1385 *erratik* wandering, moving, in

Chaucer's *Troilus and Criseyde;* borrowed through Old French *erratique,* and directly from Latin *errāticus,* from *errātum,* past participle of *errāre* to wander, ERR; for suffix see -IC. The sense of irregular or eccentric in conduct, is first recorded in 1841, in Isaac D'Israeli's *Amenities of Literature,* but the noun sense of an eccentric person, may have appeared as early as 1816.

erratum (erä'təm) *n., pl.* **errata.** error in writing or printing. 1589, borrowing of Latin *errātum,* past participle of *errāre* ERR.

erroneous *adj.* About 1385, in Usk's *Testament of Love;* borrowed through Old French *erroneus,* and directly from Latin *errōneus* vagrant, wandering, from *errōnem* (nominative *errō*) vagabond, from *errāre* to wander, ERR; for suffix see -OUS.

error *n.* Probably before 1300 *errour* condition of erring, in *Arthour and Merlin;* borrowed from Old French *error, errour, errur,* from Latin *errōrem* (nominative *error*) a wandering, straying, uncertainty, mistake, from *errāre* to wander, ERR.

To the end of the 1700's the prevailing spelling, according to the OED, was *errour,* given in Johnson's *Dictionary,* though Bailey's *Dictionary* introduced the spelling *error* in 1753.

The sense of mistake, is first recorded about 1303, in Mannyng's *Handlyng Synne.*

ersatz (erzäts') *adj.* substitute or imitation. 1875, in the *Encyclopaedia Britannica* as an attributive use of a German word describing units of the German army reserve; German *Ersatz* compensation, replacement, substitute, from *ersetzen* to replace. —**n.** a substitute or imitation. 1892, German *Ersatz.*

erstwhile *adv.* formerly, in time past. 1569, in Spenser's *Sonnets,* formed from obsolete English *erst* formerly, before + modern English *while,* adv. Obsolete English *erst,* adj. and adv., developed (probably before 1200) from Middle English *erest* earliest, earlier, former, from Old English *ǣrest* earliest, superlative of *ǣr* ERE (about 725, in *Beowulf*). —**adj.** former, past. 1903, from the adverb.

erudite *adj.* scholarly, learned. Probably before 1425, in a translation of Higden's *Polychronicon;* borrowed from Latin *ērudītus,* past participle of *ērudīre* instruct (*ē-* away or out, variant of *ex-* before *r* + *rudis* unskilled, RUDE).—**erudition** *n.* Probably about 1400 *erudicioun* instruction, education; borrowed from Latin *ērudītiōnem* (nominative *ērudītiō*) an instructing, from *ērudīre* to instruct; for suffix see -TION. The sense of learning, scholarship, is first recorded in English in 1530, in Palsgrave's *Lesclarcissement.*

erupt *v.* 1657, back formation of *eruption,* or in some instances possibly borrowed from Latin *ēruptus,* past participle of *ērumpere* break out, burst forth (*ē-* out, variant of *ex-* before *r* + *rumpere* to break, RUPTURE). —**eruption** *n.* Probably before 1425 *erupcioun* outbreaking (of pustules); borrowed through Middle French *éruption,* and directly from Latin *ēruptiōnem* (nominative *ēruptiō*) a breaking out, from *ērup-,* stem of *ērumpere* break out, burst forth; for suffix see -TION. —**eruptive** *adj.* 1646, formed from English *erupt* + *-ive,* after French *éruptif* (feminine *éruptive*), from Latin *ērupt-,* stem of *ērumpere;* for suffix see -IVE.

-ery a suffix forming nouns meaning: **1** a place for or a place for carrying on the business of: **a** (added to verbs), as in *bakery = a place for baking.* **b** (added to nouns), as in *nunnery = a place for nuns;* or *hennery = a place for hens or chickens.* **2** the art or occupation of, as in *cookery = the art or occupation of a cook.* **3** the condition of, as in *slavery = the condition of a slave.* **4** the qualities or actions of, as in *buffoonery = the qualities or actions of a buffoon.* **5** a group of, as in *machinery = a group of machines.* Though *-ery,* as an independent suffix, is the traditional analysis of many such formations, some are indistinguishable from *-er*[1] + *-y*[3], as in *bakery = a place for or of a baker,* and certainly *tannery = a place of a tanner.* In a formation such as *fishery,* two meanings are immediately evident: a place for carrying on the business of fishing (in this instance, the preparation of what is caught from fishing) and a place for keeping, specifically breeding, fish. Some meanings parallel or are closely associated with *-ary,* as *nunnery* with *infirmary = a place for the infirm,* and *hennery* with *statuary = a collection of statues.* Other meanings are associated with *-ery* but are found under variants, such as *-ry* in *citizenry* and *yeomanry* which developed by omission of *e.*

In Middle English many forms in *-ery* were borrowed from Old and Middle French along with the agent noun ending in *-er,* in such examples as *archer, archier* and *archerie; hosteler* and *hostelerie.* Along with these and other words from Old French, the suffix was borrowed as *-erie,* partly formed from *-ier* (Latin *-ārius,* English *-er*[1]) + *-ie* (Late Latin *-ia,* English *-y*[3]), and more particularly from *-ére, -eor* (Latin *-ātor, ātōrem,* English *-er*[1], *-or*[2]) + *-ie* (Late Latin *-ia,* English *-y*[3]). Other borrowings from Old French include *battery, bravery, cutlery,* and *nursery.*

Other words were formed in Middle English on the model of borrowings from Old French, but in many instances it is uncertain whether such words as *bakery, brewery, fishery* and *pottery* were actually formed from the agent noun *baker, brewer,* etc. + *-y*[3] or from the verb *bake, brew,* etc. + *-ery.* See also -ARY, -RY, and -ER[1].

-es[1] a suffix forming the plural of nouns ending in *s, z, sh, ch* (as in *lasses, whizzes, bushes, witches*), in the plural *-ies* of nouns in *-y* after a consonant (as in *dandies, rubies, duties*), and in most nouns in *-o,* such as *tomatoes, potatoes, mosquitoes;* corresponding to *-s*[1] used in other positions. Middle English *-es,* developed from Old English *-as* (masculine nouns).

-es[2] a suffix forming the third person singular of the present indicative active of verbs in *s, z, sh, ch* (as in *dresses, buzzes, washes, touches*), in *-ies* for the form *-y* (as in *hurries, magnifies*), and in occasional forms such as *does, goes;* corresponding to *-s*[2] used in other verbs. Middle English *-es,* dialectal variant replacing in general use Old English *-eth.*

escalator *n.* a moving stairway. 1900, American English; formed from English *escal-* (from *escalade,* n., 1598, borrowed from Middle French *escalade* an assault with ladders on a fortification, from Spanish *escalada,* Italian *scalata,* from Medieval Latin *scalare* to scale from Latin *scāla* ladder) + *-ator,* in *elevator.* The word was originally a trade name of the Otis Elevator Company. The attributive use of *escalator,* designating a provision that allows an increase or decrease (in wages, etc.), is first recorded in 1930, in American English. —**escalate** *v.* 1922, back formation from *escalator,* and replacing earlier English *escalade,* v. (1801, probably from *escalade,* n., see ESCALATOR). The original sense was that of climb on or by an escalator, but at least by 1959 *escalate* had assumed the figurative sense of *escalation,* that is, to increase or expand by degrees. This has become the primary sense of the verb and may be considered a back formation from *escalation.* **—escalation** *n.* 1938, American English, formed from *escalate* + *-ion.* The earliest and only meaning of *escalation* recorded is a figurative sense of an increase or expansion, climbing by degrees, originally applied to armaments, their costs, etc.

escallop *n.* scalloped edge or decoration. 1472, borrowed from Middle French *escalope* shell; see SCALLOP.

escapade *n.* 1653, an escape, a French word with the meaning of a prank or trick (originally, an escape), found in Sir Thomas Urquhart's translation of works by Rabelais, from either Spanish *escapada* a prank, flight, an escape, from *escapar* to escape; or from Italian *scappata* a prank, an escape, from *scappare* to escape; from Vulgar Latin **excappāre* ESCAPE.

The figurative sense of a breaking loose from restraint or rules, flighty action or conduct, is first recorded in 1814, in Sir Walter Scott's *Waverly,* and became the prevailing meaning.

escape *v.* About 1300 *ascapien,* before 1338 *escapen* get away, get free; borrowed from Old North French *escaper, ascaper,* Old French *eschaper,* from Vulgar Latin **excappāre,* literally, get out of one's cape, leave a pursuer with just one's cape (from Latin *ex-* out of + Late Latin *cappa* mantle, CAP). **—n.** 1402 *escap* act of escaping, probably developed through influence of Anglo-Latin *escapium,* from Middle English *escapen,* v. An earlier form *eschap* (1375, in John Barbour's *The Bruce*) was borrowed from Old French *eschap,* from *eschaper,* v. **—escapee** *n.* 1865, American English, in Walt Whitman's writings; formed from English *escape,* v. + *-ee.* **—escapement** *n.* 1779, earlier *scapement* (1755); formed from English *escape* + *-ment,* modeled after French *échappement.* **—escapism** *n.* 1933, American English; formed from English *escape,* n. + *-ism.*

escarpment *n.* 1802, ground made into a steep slope for fortification; gradually replacing earlier *escarpe* (1688); borrowed from French *escarpement,* from *escarper* make into a steep slope, from *escarpe* slope, from Italian *scarpa* SCARP; for suffix see -MENT.

The meaning in geology of a steep slope or cliff, is first recorded in English in 1813.

-escence a suffix meaning process or state of beginning, becoming, tending to be, as in *adolescence, convalescence, obsolescence;* or act of displaying color or light, as in *phosphorescence, iridescence, fluorescence.* Borrowed from Latin *-ēscentia,* from *-ēscentem* -ESCENT + *-ia* -y[3] (noun suffix).

-escent a suffix meaning beginning, becoming, tending to be, as in *convalescent, effervescent, obsolescent, alkalescent;* or displaying certain qualities or phenomena of color or light, as in *viridescent, phosphorescent, iridescent, opalescent, fluorescent.* Borrowed from Latin *-ēscentem* (nominative *-ēscēns*), the ending of present participles of verbs in *-ēscere.* In older borrowings the underlying verb was commonly borrowed as an English verb in *-esce;* but in the later group *-escent* is added to a noun stem and where a verb in *-esce* exists it is probably a back formation *(fluoresce, phosphoresce).* Abstract nouns in *-escence* exist along with these adjective forms in *-escent.*

escheat (eschēt′) *n.* reversion of property to the state. Before 1338 *eschete,* in Mannyng's *Chronicle of England;* borrowed through Anglo-Latin *escheta, escaeta,* from Vulgar Latin **excadēre,* and from Old French *eschete* inheritance, literally, that which falls to one, from Vulgar Latin **excadecta,* feminine past participle of **excadēre,* re-formed from Latin *excidere* to fall out (Latin *ex-* out + *cadere* to fall; see CADENCE). See CHEAT. **—v.** revert to the state, confiscate. Before 1382 *escheten,* in the Wycliffe Bible; from the noun.

eschew *v.* avoid as bad or harmful. About 1350 *echuen;* later *eschewen* (probably 1375); borrowed from Old French *eschiver, eschever,* from Frankish (compare Old High German *sciuhen* make fearful, Middle High German *schiuhen, schiuwen,* modern German *scheuen* to dread, avoid, shun; see SHY[1] bashful).

An adjective form *eschif* easily frightened, appears in earlier Middle English (probably before 1200, in *Ancrene Riwle*); later, disinclined or averse (about 1390, in Chaucer's *Canterbury Tales*); borrowed from Old French *eschieu* (nominative *eschif*) shy, unwilling, probably from Frankish (compare Old High German **sciuh,* Middle High German *schiech,* modern German *scheu* shy); but it is unclear what influence this earlier word had on the borrowing of the verb *eschew.*

escort *n.* 1579, group of armed men guarding a traveler, baggage, etc.; borrowed from Middle French *escorte,* from Italian *scorta,* literally, a guiding, from *scorgere* to guide, from Vulgar Latin **excorrigere* (*ex-* out + *corrigere* set right, CORRECT).

The wider transferred sense of a person or persons accompanying another for protection, guidance, or courtesy, is first recorded in English in 1745. **—v.** 1708, act as an escort, from the noun; or possibly by influence of French *escorter,* from *escorte,* n. The corresponding transferred sense in the verb is first recorded in 1742, slightly earlier than in the noun.

escrow (es′krō) *n.* written agreement held by a third person until certain conditions are fulfilled. 1598, borrowed through Anglo-French *escrowe,* Old French *escroe, escroue* scrap, roll of parchment, SCROLL, from Germanic (compare Old High German *scrōt* scrap, shred). The phrase *in escrow* (property held) in trust, is first recorded in 1888, in American English; see SHRED.

escutcheon (eskuch′ən) *n.* shield with a coat of arms. 1480, borrowed from Old North French *escuchon,* variant of semi-learned Old French *escusson,* from Gallo-Romance **scūtiōnem* (nominative **scūtiō*), from Latin *scūtum* shield; see SQUIRE; for suffix see -ION, *-eon* being a spelling variant of *-ion* after *ch,* as in *luncheon, puncheon, truncheon.*

-ese a suffix forming adjectives with the meaning "of, belonging to, or originating in (a city or country)," as in *Milanese architect, Vietnamese people,* with corresponding nouns meaning "native or inhabitant of" *(a Viennese, the Japanese),* "language of" *(Chinese, Portuguese),* or, by extension, "typical style or vocabulary of," as in *journalese, bureaucratese, Johnsonese, New Yorkese.*" Borrowed from Old French *-eis* or Italian *-ese,* from Latin *-ēnsis,* of, belonging to, or from (a place).

Eskimo *n.* one of the native people of the arctic regions. 1584 *Esquimawe,* in Hakluyt's *Discourse of Western Planting;* borrowed from Danish *Eskimo* or Middle French *Esquimaux,* pl., probably from an Algonquian source such as the Indians of Labrador who applied this name to the Eskimos of that region (compare Abnaki *esquimantsec,* Ojibwa *ashkimeq,* literally, eaters of raw meat), as opposed to *Innuit,* meaning "men," the Eskimo people's own name for themselves.

esophagus (ēsof′əgəs) *n.* passage for food from the mouth to the stomach. 1392 *ysophagus;* borrowed, perhaps by influence of Old French *ysophague,* from Greek *oisophágos,* a learned formation perhaps with the meaning of what carries and eats (*oiso-,* perhaps from *oísein* used as the future infinitive of *phérein* to carry + *-phágos,* from *phageîn* eat).

esoteric (es′əter′ik) *adj.* understood only by a select few. 1655-60, borrowed from Greek *esōterikós* belonging to an inner circle (originally said to have related to a select few of Pythagoras' disciples), from *esōtérō,* comparative adverb of *ésō* within, from *es* into (from *ens*), related to *en* IN; for suffix see -IC.

espalier (espal′yər) *n.* a trellis or framework of stakes to grow fruit trees or ornamental plants on. 1662, a fruit tree trimmed to grow on a trellis, in a work of John Evelyn's on horticulture; borrowing of French *espalier,* from Italian *spalliera* a support for the shoulders, back of a chair, etc., espalier, from *spalla* shoulder, from Latin *spatula* a broad piece, blade. See SPATULA.

especial *adj.* preeminent, chief. About 1385, in Thomas Usk's *Testament of Love;* borrowed from Old French *especial,* from Latin *speciālis* belonging to a particular kind or species, from *speciēs* kind. See the doublet SPECIAL. It should be noted that Latin words with initial *sp, st, sc* borrowed into French before the 1400's usually add an initial *e-*.

The fine distinction in use between *especial* and *special,* and particularly between *especially* and *specially* has little to do with etymology, *especial* usually being confined to the sense of preeminent, *special* to the sense of particular.
—especially *adv.* Probably before 1400; formed from English *especial* + *-ly*[1].

Esperanto *n.* artificial language for international use. 1892, in allusion to the pen name "Doctor *Esperanto*" (in Esperanto "one who hopes"), used in a book published in 1887 about this language by the Polish physician and language scholar L.L. Zamenhof who invented the language.

espionage *n.* use of spies. 1793, borrowed from French *espionnage,* from Middle French *espionner* to spy, from Old French *espion* spy, probably from Italian *spione,* from a Germanic source (compare Old High German *spehōn* to SPY); for suffix see -AGE.

esplanade *n.* open, level space used for public walks or drives. 1591, borrowed from French *esplanade,* from Middle French, probably from Spanish *esplanada* (influenced by Italian *spianata*), from *esplanar* make level, from Latin *explānāre* to level, EXPLAIN (*ex-* out + *plānus* level, plain); for suffix see -ADE.

espouse *v.* Probably 1435 *espousen* take as spouse, marry; borrowed from Middle French *espouser* marry, betroth, from Latin *spōnsāre* become engaged to marry, from *spōnsa* SPOUSE. The extended sense of adopt, embrace is first recorded in 1622, in Francis Bacon's *Henry VII.* **—espousal** *n.* Before 1393 *esposaile, espousaile,* in Gower's *Confessio Amantis;* borrowed from Old French *espousailles* (plural) act of betrothal, from Latin *spōnsālia,* neuter plural of *spōnsālis* of a betrothal, from *spōnsus* SPOUSE; for suffix see -AL[2].

espresso (espres′ō) *n.* strong coffee brewed under steam pressure. 1945, borrowing of Italian *caffè espresso,* from *espresso* pressed out, from past participle of *esprimere* press out, from Latin *exprimere* press out, EXPRESS.

esprit (esprē′) *n.* lively wit, spirit. 1591; a French word used in a translation of a work on astrology, found in Middle French *esprit* spirit, mind, from Old French *espirit,* learned borrowing from Latin *spīritus* spirit. Doublet of SPIRIT and SPRITE.

-esque a suffix forming adjectives and meaning "resembling or suggesting the style, characteristics, etc., of," as in *arabesque, Romanesque, statuesque, Disneyesque, robotesque.* Borrowed from French *-esque,* from Italian *-esco,* from Vulgar Latin **-iscus,* from Proto-Germanic **-iskaz* (compare Old High German *-isc* -ISH[1]).

esquire *n.* title of courtesy. 1374 *esquier* Englishman ranking next below a knight; borrowed from Middle French *esquier, escuier* squire, literally, shield bearer, from Old French, from Latin *scūtārius* shield bearer, from *scūtum* shield; see SQUIRE. This word was originally applied to a member of the English gentry, but in the 1500's was extended as a general title of courtesy or respect, and in the United States has become especially fashionable among lawyers.

-ess a suffix forming nouns and meaning a female ______, as in *lioness, heiress, hostess, sculptress.* Middle English *-esse,* borrowed from Old French *-esse,* from Late Latin *-issa,* from Greek *-issa,* feminine noun suffix, and replacing Old English *-icge.* Words in Middle English with *-esse,* and particularly with *-isse,* that are found in Old English were direct borrowings from Latin words in *-issa.*

When *-ess* is added to a noun ending in *-tor, -ter,* the vowel before *r* is generally elided, as in *actress* (*actor* + *-ess*), such a derivative with the ending *-tress* (often equivalent to French *-trice*) is usually considered a reduced form of Latin *-trix, -trīcem* and popularly regarded as the equivalent of *-tor* + *-ess.*

In Middle English many words in *-esse* were adopted from French, such as *countess, duchess, mistress, princess,* or formed on nouns in *-er,* such as *enchantress* and *sorceress.* Many have acquired derogatory connotations, such as *Jewess* and *Negress;* others are thought to suggest male condescension, such as *authoress, sculptress,* the terms *author* and *sculptor* associated chiefly with males, but in reality applicable to both male and female. The term *governess* was perhaps substituted for earlier *governoress* on a false analogy with *governor* based upon such formations as *adulterer, adulteress, sorcerer, sorceress,* and, except for *spinster* a rare vestige of Old English feminine agent nouns in *-ster,* and a few others (*goddess, abbess*), the feminine agent nouns are gradually disappearing under social pressure.

essay (es′ā) *n.* literary composition. 1597, as the title of Francis Bacon's *Essays;* borrowed from Middle French *essai* trial, attempt, essay, from Late Latin *exagium* a weighing, weight, from Vulgar Latin **exagere,* a recompounding of Latin *exigere* test (*ex-* out + *agere,* perhaps in a lost meaning of to weigh; compare Latin *exāmen* balance, scale, and *agīna* part of a scales). Doublet and variant of ASSAY.

Though the word as used by Bacon was apparently taken from Montaigne's *Essais* (1580), *essay* was also a variant of earlier *assay* in the meaning of a trial (*essay* about 1600, in Shakespeare; *assay* 1338, in Mannyng) and the meaning of an analysis (*essay* 1614; *assay* 1386, in Chaucer).

—**v.** (esā') try, attempt. 1483 *essayen* to test, assay, in Caxton's translation of *Geoffroi de la Tour l'Andri;* borrowed from Middle French *essaier,* from *essai,* n. The meaning of try, attempt, is first recorded in English with this spelling in 1641; *assay,* v. to try, is first recorded probably before 1300.

—**essayist** *n.* 1609, in Ben Jonson's *The Silent Woman;* formed from English *essay,* n. + *-ist.*

essence *n.* Before 1398 *essencia* substance of the Trinity, in Trevisa's translation of Bartholomew's *De Proprietatibus Rerum;* borrowed from Latin *essentia* being, essence. A later spelling *essence* (1481) is found in Caxton's work, probably the result of his familiarity with French in his many contracted translations, and therefore as a re-spelling in English borrowed from Middle French, from Old French *essence* (1130), from Latin *essentia,* from *esse* to be; see IS. Latin *essentia* was formed in imitation of Greek *ousíā* being or essence, from *ṓn* (genitive *óntos*), present participle of *eînai* to be; see IS. The general sense of the most important or basic element of anything, is first recorded in English in 1656, in Hobbes' translation of *Elements of Philosophy.* The technical sense of extract of a substance in concentrated form, followed in 1660, in Robert Boyle's *New Experiments,* but is common to all Romance languages, possibly from its use by Paracelsus in the 1500's. —**essential** *adj.* Before 1398 *essencyal* of the essence, basic or fundamental, in Trevisa's *Bartholomew;* borrowed, possibly through Old French *essentiel,* or directly from Late Latin *essentiālis,* from Latin *essentia* essence; for suffix see -AL[1]. The sense of absolutely necessary or indispensable, is first recorded in English in 1526. —**essentially** *adv.* 1395; formed from English *essential* + *-ly*[1].

-est a suffix forming the superlative degree of adjectives and adverbs, as in *warmest, slowest.*

Middle English *-est* developed from a blend of: 1) Old English *-ost-, -ust-, -ast-,* found in Old Frisian and Old Icelandic *-ast-,* Old Saxon, Old High German, and Gothic *-ōsts,* from Proto-Germanic **-ōstaz;* and 2) Old English *-est-, -st-,* found in Old Frisian, Old High German, and Gothic *-ists,* from Proto-Germanic **-istaz;* a similar formation is found in Sanskrit *-iṣṭha-s,* considered to be, like the Proto-Germanic suffix **-istaz,* representative of the suffix **-iz-* + Indo-European *-to-,* the Proto-Germanic **-ōstaz* representing **-ōz-* + Indo-European *-to-.*

In Old English the distinction between the two groups of suffixes was already confused, and only two forms with umlaut of the root vowel survive in *eldest* (Old English *eldest, yldest*) and *best,* though *best* is generally analyzed as having the contracted form *-st-,* as in *first, last, worst.*

The Old English ending with the suffix *-m-* resulted in *-mest-,* which was later confused with *most,* adv., producing *foremost* in the pattern *forma, fyrmest* (foremost) and *inmost* in *innema, innemest* (inmost). Compare also -ER[2].

A type *-est,* variant of *-es,* formed adverbs and prepositions as found in *amiddest* and *amongest,* now shortened to *amidst* and *amongst.*

establish *v.* About 1380 *establishen* to fix, settle, set up, in Chaucer's translation of Boethius' *De Consolatione Philosophiae;* borrowed from Old French *establiss-,* stem of *establir,* from Latin *stabilīre* make stable, from *stabilis* STABLE[2] *steady;* for suffix see -ISH[2]. —**establishment** *n.* 1481, a settled arrangement; earlier, property, income or means of support (before 1470); formed from English *establish* + *-ment.* The sense of an institution or a business appeared in 1832. The phrase *the Establishment* meaning the established Church (especially of England and Scotland), is first recorded in English in 1731; it was extended in the 1900's (and became a vogue term, especially in the 1950's and 1960's) to refer to the ruling groups or institutions of a country collectively.

estate *n.* Probably before 1200, special state or condition, status, in *Ancrene Riwle;* borrowed from Anglo-French *astat* and Continental Old French *estat,* learned borrowing from Latin; and directly from Latin *status* (genitive *statūs*) state or condition, from *sta-,* a root form of *stāre* to stand. Doublet of STATE and STATUS.

The sense of property or possessions, fortune, which is first recorded in English about 1385, evolved from an early meaning of STATE "condition with respect to worldly prosperity or fortune" (1325, in *Cursor Mundi*). One of the commonest meanings of *estate,* "landed property," is first recorded in 1623, in American English; with specific reference to the assets of a deceased or bankrupt person, in 1659, also in American English.

esteem *v.* Before 1410 *estymen* estimate the value of; later *estemen* (1449); borrowed from Middle French *estimer,* learned borrowing from Latin *aestimāre* to value, appraise; of unknown origin. Doublet of AIM and ESTIMATE.

The sense of value, respect, is first recorded in 1530, in Palsgrave's *Lesclarcissement.*

—**n.** Before 1338 *steem* account, worth, in Mannyng's *Chronicle of England;* later *extyme* (probably about 1450); borrowed from Old French *estime,* from *estimer,* v. The sense of high regard, is first recorded in 1611, in the Preface to the King James Bible.

ester *n.* compound produced by combination of an acid and an alcohol with elimination of water. 1852, borrowing of German *Ester,* possibly a contraction of *Essigäther* (*Essig* vinegar, from Old High German *ezzīh,* by way of Gothic from **atēcum,* metathesized by shift of *t* and *c* from Latin *acētum;* see ACETIC + German *Äther,* from Latin *aethēr* ETHER). The term was coined in German by the chemist L. Gmelin, to contrast with *ether.*

estimation *n.* 1375 *estimacion* judgment, opinion, in Chaucer's translation of Boethius' *De Consolatione Philosophiae;* borrowed from Old French *estimacion,* from Latin *aestimātiōnem* (nominative *aestimātiō*) a valuation, from *aestimāre* to value; see ESTEEM; for suffix see -ATION. —**estimable** *adj.* Before 1475; borrowed from Old French *estimable,* and directly from Latin *aestimābilis* worthy of estimation, from *aestimāre* to value. —**estimate** (es'timāt) *v.* About 1532, to esteem, consider; earlier *estimat* reputed (before 1500); borrowed from Latin *aestimātus,* past participle of *aestimāre* to value; see ESTEEM; for suffix see -ATE[1]. In some instances *estimate* may be a back formation from earlier *estimation.* The sense of calculate approximately, is first recorded in English in 1669. —*n.* (es'timit) 1563, valuation; earlier *estymate* power of the mind (1464); from the verb in English, or borrowed from Latin *aestimātus,* verbal noun, from *aestimāre* to value. The sense of approximate judgment, is first recorded in

English in 1630, though such a judgment in respect to the character or qualities of a person or thing is first recorded in 1589.

estrange *v.* make unfriendly, alienate. Probably before 1475 *estraungen;* borrowed from Middle French *estrangier* alienate, from Vulgar Latin **extrāneāre* treat as a stranger, from Latin *extrāneus* foreign, STRANGE. Doublet of EXTRANEOUS. **—estrangement** *n.* 1660, formed from English *estrange* + *-ment.*

estrogen (es′trəjən) *n.* female hormone. 1927, formed from English ESTRUS + connective *-o-* + *-gen* producing; so called from the hormone's ability to promote estrus.

estrus (es′trəs) *n.* 1890 *oestrus* rut of animals, heat; earlier, passion or frenzy, as if brought on by a stinging or goading (1850, in FitzGerald's letters), and a gadfly (1697, in Dryden's writings); borrowing of Latin *oestrus* frenzy, gadfly, from Greek *oistros* gadfly, breeze, sting, mad impulse, cognate with Sanskrit *íṣyati* sets in motion; hurries, from Indo-European **eis-/ois-/is-* (Pok.299). **—estrous** *adj.* of the estrus. 1900 *oestrous;* formed from English *oestrus* estrus + *-ous.*

estuary *n.* broad mouth of a river into which the tide flows. 1538, inlet of the sea; borrowed from Latin *aestuārium* a tidal marsh or opening, from *aestus* (genitive *aestūs*) boiling (of the sea), tide, heat; see EDIFICE; for suffix see -ARY.

-et a suffix forming nouns and meaning small, little, as in *islet, owlet.* Borrowed from Old French *-et,* masculine (feminine *-ete*) from Vulgar Latin **-ittum, *-itta,* represented in most Romance languages but of unknown origin. The suffix *-et* occurs chiefly in French words borrowed into Middle English, such as *bullet, pullet, hatchet, sonnet,* and *tablet,* most of which had originally a diminutive sense, of which we are no longer aware. Modern English borrowings from French generally have the form *-ette,* though the related suffix -LET is also active in the formation of diminutives.

et al. and others. 1883, abbreviation of *et alii* (1470, in *The Paston Letters*), Latin *et aliī* and others (*et* and + *aliī* others, plural of *alius* other; see ELSE). Compare ET CETERA.

et cetera About 1150 *& cetera,* borrowed from Latin *et cētera* and the rest (*et* and + *cētera* the rest, neuter plural of *cēterus* remaining over). Latin *cēterus* is probably a result of the fusion of an old phrase *ce *eteros* there, the other (with *ce* as in *illius-ce* of that fellow there, + the pronoun which is found in Old Slavic *eterŭ, jetrŭ* anyone, from Indo-European **eteros,* a contrastive formation from the root *e-* that (Pok.284).

The character &, used in Middle English *&cetera* and in *&c* (written in modern English *etc.*) represents the ligature of *et.* The abbreviation *etc.* appears in Chaucer's *Treatise on the Astrolabe* (1391).

etch *v.* 1634, borrowed from Dutch *etsen,* from German *ätzen* to etch, from Old High German *azzōn, azzen* cause to bite, feed, from Proto-Germanic **atjanan,* causative of **etanan* to EAT (the connection with *eat* evolving from the process of etching which involves treating a metal, etc., with acid or heat which "eats away" the surface). **—etching** *n.* 1762, picture or design printed from an etched plate, in Walpole's writings; earlier, art or process of engraving by means of acid (1634).

eternal *adj.* About 1380, in Chaucer's *Canterbury Tales;* borrowed through Old French *eternal,* or directly from Late Latin *aeternālis,* from Latin *aeternus,* contraction of *aeviternus* of great age, from *aevum* AGE; for suffix see -AL[1]. **—eternally** *adv.* About 1385, in Chaucer's *Canterbury Tales;* formed from English *eternal* + *-ly*[1]. **—eternity** *n.* About 1380 *eternite,* in Chaucer's translation of Boethius' *De Consolatione Philosophiae;* later *eternytie* (probably 1440); borrowed from Old French *eternité,* learned borrowing from Latin *aeternitātem* (nominative *aeternitās*), from *aeternus* eternal; for suffix see -ITY.

-eth[1] a form of the suffix *-th* when the cardinal number to which it is attached ends in *-y,* such as *twentieth* (from *twenty*), *fiftieth* (from *fifty*).

-eth[2] a suffix forming the third person singular, present indicative active, of verbs, now archaic, as in *goeth, sendeth,* but occasionally used as a literary device *(The Iceman Cometh).* The form is sometimes *-th,* as in *doth.* Middle English *-eth,* developed from Old English *-eth, -ath;* cognate with Gothic *-ith, -ōth,* Old High German *-it, -ōt, -ēt,* Latin *-t,* Greek *-ti, -si,* Sanskrit *-ti,* and Old Slavic *-tŭ.*

ether *n.* Before 1398, upper regions of space; constituent substance of stars and planets, in Trevisa's translation of Bartholomew's *De Proprietatibus Rerum;* borrowed from Old French *ether,* learned borrowing from Latin *aethēr,* or borrowed directly from Latin *aethēr* the upper pure, bright air, from Greek *aithḗr* upper air, related to *aíthein* to kindle, burn, glow; see EDIFICE. In 1757 *ether* is first recorded as being applied to a chemical compound, because the chemical's lightness and lack of color suggested a resemblance to air. By 1842 its anesthetic properties were established in use. **—ethereal** *adj.* 1513, of the highest region of the atmosphere, replacing earlier *ethereum, etherum* in the sense of bright, shining (recorded before 1398 in Trevisa's *Bartholomew*); formed in English from Latin *aethereus, aetherius,* from Greek *aithérios,* from *aithḗr* ether) + English *-al*[1]. The sense of light, airy, is first recorded in 1598, and that of spiritlike, immaterial, in 1647. Milton's *Paradise Lost* (1667) contains the first recorded use of the poetic sense "heavenly, celestial."

ethics *n.* morals. 1602, fashioned after Greek *tà ēthiká* the ethics, but formed from plural of earlier Middle English *ethik* study of morals (about 1386, in Chaucer's *Prologue* to *Legend of Good Women*); borrowed from Old French *ethique,* from Late Latin *ēthica,* from Greek *ēthiká;* and directly from Latin *ēthicē,* from Greek *ēthikè philosophíā* moral philosophy, feminine of *ēthikós* (*ēthikē*) ethical; for suffix see -ICS. **—ethical** *adj.* 1607, having to do with morality or ethics; formed in English from Latin *ēthicus* (from Greek *ēthikós,* from *êthos* moral character, related to *éthos* custom) + English *-al*[1].

ethnic *n.* About 1375 (Scottish), a heathen or pagan; probably borrowed directly from a translation of New Testament Greek *tà éthnē* the heathen, from *éthnos* a people, nation, Gentiles, a translation of Hebrew *gōyīm,* plural of *gōy* nation, especially non-Israelites, Gentile nation. The sense of a member of a racial, cultural, or national minority group, is first recorded in 1945 in American English. **—adj.** having to do with different cultural, racial, or national groups. About 1470, heathen or pagan; from the noun, and as a borrowing from Late Latin *ethnicus,* from Greek *ethnikós,* from *éthnos* nation, probably related to *éthos* custom; for suffix see -IC. Greek *éthos* is cognate with Sanskrit *svadhā́* own state, habit, and with Latin *sodālis* companion, from Indo-European **swedh-*, an extension of **swe* self (Pok.883).

The sense of peculiar to a race or nation, is first recorded in 1851, and that of having to do with or belonging to different cultural groups, in 1935.

ethno- a combining form meaning people, race, nation, or culture, as in *ethnology* (the science or study of races or people or their culture), *ethnocentric* (characteristic of those who regard their culture or race as superior to others'). Borrowed from Greek *éthno-*, combining form of *éthnos* people, nation, class; see ETHNIC.

ethnocentric *adj.* of or showing a cultural or racial superiority. 1900, formed from English *ethno-* or Greek *éthno-*, from *éthnos* nation + English *centric.*

ethnography *n.* study of racial and cultural groups. 1834, borrowed possibly through German *Ethnographie* geographical distribution of man, from Greek *éthno-*, from *éthnos* nation + *-graphíā* writing.

ethnology *n.* study of the customs, origins, and distribution of races and cultural groups. 1842, formed from English *ethno-* or Greek *éthno-*, from *éthnos* nation + English *-logy.*

ethos (ē'thos) *n.* characteristic spirit of a people or community. 1851, New Latin, or more likely directly from Greek *êthos* moral character, person's nature or disposition, from Indo-European **swēdhos,* root **swedh-* (Pok.883).

ethyl (eth'əl) *n.* group of atoms forming the radical of ether and other organic compounds. 1850, formed from English *ether* + *-yl,* modeled on German *Äthyl,* from *Äther* ether + *-yl.* The term was coined in 1834 by the German chemist Liebig.

etiology (ē'tēol'əjē) *n.* origin or cause of a disease, etc. Before 1555, science of causes or causation, borrowed from Latin *aetiologia,* from Greek *aitiologíā* statement of the cause, from *aitíā* cause, from **aîtos* one's share, related to *aínysthai* take, from Indo-European **ai-* give (Pok.10); for suffix see -LOGY.

etiquette *n.* conventional rules for conduct or behavior. 1750, used as a French word referring to prescribed behavior, in Lord Chesterfield's *Letters to his Son,* from Old French *estiquette* label, TICKET. The transition from the sense of ticket, label to that of prescribed routine or behavior took place in French, and possibly came from directions for behavior on a soldier's billet for lodgings. Another explanation is that "tickets" given out at court gave directions or information as to prescribed observances to follow on a particular occasion.

-ette a suffix forming nouns and meaning: little, as in *kitchenette, dinette;* female, as in *bachelorette, usherette;* a substitute for, as in *leatherette.* Borrowed from French *-ette,* from Old French *-ete,* feminine of *-et* -ET.

The suffix *-ette* has been preserved in borrowings or added to new formations since the 1600's, but in older words, especially those from Middle English, the form has generally been reduced to *-et,* not much distinction being made between *-et* and *-ette* in earlier times.

étude (ātüd') *n.* piece of music intended to develop technique. Before 1837, borrowing of French *étude,* literally study, from Old French *estudie, estude, estuide,* from Latin *studium.* Doublet of STUDIO and STUDY. The term was popularized in English by the études of Chopin, which were written in recital style.

etymology *n.* derivation of a word or an account of its origin and history. Before 1398 *ethymologye,* in Trevisa's translation of Bartholomew's *De Proprietatibus Rerum;* borrowed from Old French *ethimologie,* learned borrowing from Latin *etymologia,* from Greek *etymologíā,* from *étymon* true sense of a word based on its origin (neuter of *étymos* true, related to *eteós* true; of uncertain origin; for suffix see -LOGY. **—etymologize** *v.* About 1530, borrowed from Middle French *étymologiser,* from Late Latin *etymologizāre,* from Latin *etymologia* etymology; for suffix see -IZE.

eu- a prefix in English words generally borrowed from Greek, and except for modern technical and scientific terms, such as *eucalyptus, eucaryote, eugenic,* not recognized by most users of English as an active suffix in the language. Nonetheless it carries the distinguishable meanings: **1** good or well, as in *eugenic, eulogy, euphoria.* **2** true, as in *eucaryote.* Greek *eu-,* from *eû* well, from neuter of *eys* good, which is cognate with Hittite *aššuš* (= *asus*) good, and probably with Latin *erus* master, from Indo-European **esus* (Pok.342). In Latin the *u* in *eu-* shifted to *v* (then considered the consonantal form of *u*) before vowels, which produced such formations as *evangelium,* for Greek *euangélion* good news (*eu-* good + *angélion,* from *angéllein* to announce). It is, according to the OED, almost the only surviving such formation in English.

eucalyptus (yü'kəlip'təs) *n.* very tall tree that originated in Australia. 1809, New Latin, from Greek *eu-* well + *kalyptós* covered, from *kalýptein* to cover (so called from the covering on the bud), cognate with Latin *cēlāre* to hide, and Old English *helan* to cover, from Indo-European **k̑el-/k̑ēl-* (Pok.553). The term was coined in 1788 by the French botanist Lhéritier.

eucaryote or **eukaryote** (yükar'ēōt) *n.* cell with a visible nucleus. 1963, formed from quasi-English *eu-* true + *caryote* or *karyote* cell nucleus, from Greek *káryon* nut, kernel; see CAREEN.

Eucharist (yü'kərist) *n.* sacrament of the Lord's Supper. Probably about 1350 *Eukaryste;* borrowed from Old French *eucariste,* from Late Latin *eucharistia,* from Greek *eucharistíā* thankfulness, the Lord's Supper, from *euchváristos* grateful (*eu-* well + the stem of *charízesthai* show favor; see CHARISMA); for suffix see -IST.

eugenics *n.* the science of improving the human race. 1883, formed in English on analogy with *economics, physics,* etc., from Greek *eugenḗs* well-born, of good stock (*eu-* good, well + *génos* birth, from the root of *gígnesthai* be born; see KIN) + English *-ics.* The term was coined by the British scientist Francis Galton, in *Inquiries into the Human Faculty and its Development.* **—eugenic** *adj.* having to do with eugenics. 1883, formed in English on the model of *linguistics, linguistic; statistics, statistic;* from *eugenics.*

eulogy (yü'ləjē) *n.* speech or writing in praise of someone, especially a deceased person; high praise. Before 1475 *ewloge;* later *eulogies,* pl. (1591, in Spenser's *Tears of Muses*); borrowed from Latin *eulogium,* adaptation of Greek *eulogíā* praise (*eu-* well + *-logíā* speaking, from *lógos* discourse, word, from *légein* speak, after the phrase *eû légein* speak well of; see LEGEND); for suffix see -Y³. **—eulogistic** *adj.* 1825, formed from English *eulogist,* n. (1808) + *-ic.* **—eulogize** *v.* Before 1810, formed from English *eulogy* + *-ize.*

eunuch (yü'nək) *n.* castrated man. Probably before 1425 *enuch,* in a translation of Chauliac's *Grande Chirurgie;* later *eunuk* (1439); borrowed possibly through Middle French *eunuque,* and directly from Latin *eunūchus,* from Greek *eunoûchos* castrated man (originally, guard of the bedchamber, attendant of a harem), from *euno-,* combining form of *eunḗ* bed + *-óchos,* from the stem of *échein* to have, hold; see SCHEME. In Oriental courts and under the Roman emperors, eunuchs held high offices and were often charged with important affairs of state; hence in Middle English (probably before 1439) the word also meant a chamberlain or other court official.

euphemism (yü'fəmizəm) *n.* use of an indirect expression instead of one that is harsh or direct. 1656-81, in an edition of Blount's *Glossographia;* borrowed from Greek *euphēmismós* euphemism or use of a favorable word in place of an inauspicious one, from *euphēmízein* speak with fair words (*eu-* good + *phḗmē* speaking, from *phánai* speak; see FAME); for suffix see -ISM. **—euphemistic** *adj.* 1856, derived from English *euphemism* + *-ist* + *-ic,* on the analogy of pairs such as *humanism, humanistic* and *egoism, egoistic.*

euphony (yü'fənē) *n.* agreeableness of sound. About 1450 *euphonie;* borrowed from Middle French *euphonie,* from Late Latin *euphōnia,* from Greek *euphōníā,* from *eúphōnos* well-sounding (*eu-* good + *phōnḗ* sound, voice, related to *phánai* speak; see FAME); for suffix see -Y[3]. **—euphonic** *adj.* 1814, in Scott's *Waverley;* formed from English *euphony* + *-ic,* perhaps by influence of earlier French *euphonique* (1756). **—euphonious** *adj.* 1774, formed from English *euphony* + *-ous.*

euphoria (yüfôr'ēə) *n.* extraordinary feeling of well-being and cheerfulness. 1882, in William James' letters; probably by extension of earlier, and now obsolete *euphoria* (1706) or *euphory* (1684) ease or relief coming from the administration of some medical procedure; New Latin, from Greek *euphoríā* power of bearing easily, fertility, from *eúphoros,* literally, bearing well (*eu-* good, well + *phérein* to carry, BEAR[2] carry). **—euphoric** *adj.* 1888, characterized by euphoria, formed from English *euphoria* + *-ic.*

Eur- the form of *Euro-* before vowels, as in *Eurasian.*

eureka (yůrē'kə) *interj., n.* exclamation of triumph at any discovery. 1603, in Holland's translation of Plutarch's *Moralia;* earlier, cited as a Greek form EYPHKA (1570); borrowed from Greek *heúrēka* I have found (it), 1st person singular perfect active indicative form of *heurískein* to find; see HEURISTIC. This exclamation was supposedly uttered by the Greek mathematician, physicist and inventor Archimedes, 287?-212 B.C., when he discovered the means of determining the proportion of base metal in the golden crown of Hiero, the king of Syracuse.

Euro- a combining form created by shortening of *Europe,* meaning Europe or European, with special application to the European money market, as in *Eurodollar, Eurobond, Eurocurrency,* or to the European Community or Common Market, as in *Eurocrat (Euro-* + bureaucrat), *Euromarket;* also (hyphenated) European and, as in *Euro-Asian, Euro-American.* Also spelled *Eur-* before vowels.

europium (yůrō'pēəm) *n.* metallic chemical element. 1901, New Latin, from Latin *Eurōpa* Europe, from Greek *Eurṓpē* + *-ium* (chemical suffix). The word was coined by the French chemist E.A. Demarçay.

Eustachian tube 1755 (earlier as *Eustachian,* adj., in reference to a structure of the kidney, 1741), from *Eustachius,* Latinized form of *Eustachio,* Italian anatomist and physician (died 1574), who first described this structure, in a Latin text published in 1714.

euthanasia (yü'thənā'zhə) *n.* mercy killing. 1606, in Holland's translation of Suetonius' *History of the Caesars;* borrowed from Greek *euthanasíā* an easy or happy death (*eu-* good + *thánatos* death, cognate with Sanskrit *ádhvanīt* (he) vanished, from Indo-European **dhwenə-* (Pok.266)). The sense of act or practice of painlessly putting to death, as the incurably and painfully diseased, is first recorded in 1869; the synonymous *mercy killing* has been used since the 1930's. **—euthanize** *v.* put to death painlessly. 1969, formed from English *euthanasia* + *-ize.*

eutrophic (yütrof'ik) *adj.* (of lakes) rich in nutrients, but lacking sufficient oxygen. 1931, probably suggested by earlier *eutrophic* tending to promote nutrition (probably 1884); formed from earlier English *eutrophy* good nutrition (1721) + *-ic. Eutrophy* was borrowed from Greek *eutrophíā* good nurture, thriving condition, from *eútrophos* thriving, nourishing, well-nourished (*eu-* well, good + *trophḗ* nurture, from *tréphein* to nourish; see ATROPHY). **—eutrophication** *n.* 1947, formed from English *eutrophic* + *-ation.*

evacuate *v.* leave empty, withdraw from. 1542, to empty or deplete (the body), from earlier *evacuate,* adj., depleted or empty of bodily substances (probably before 1425, in a translation of Chauliac's *Grande Chirurgie*); borrowed from Latin *ēvacuātus,* past participle of *ēvacuāre* empty, empty the bowels, also in Late Latin, clear out (*ē-* out, variant of *ex-* + *vacuus* empty; see VACUUM); for suffix see -ATE[1].

Evacuate may have been formed in part also by influence of earlier *evacuation. Evacuate* replaced the Middle English verb *evacuen* (recorded before 1400, in a translation of Lanfranc's *Science of Surgery*); borrowed from Old French *evacuer,* from Latin *ēvacuāre* to empty. The sense of clear out, remove, is first recorded in English before 1639.

—evacuation *n.* Before 1400 *evacuacioun* discharge of humors from the body, in a translation of Lanfranc's *Science of Surgery;* borrowed through Old French *evacuation,* and directly from Late Latin *ēvacuātiōnem* (nominative *ēvacuātiō*), from Latin *ēvacuāre* evacuate; for suffix see -ATION. **—evacuee** *n.* 1934, borrowed from French *évacué,* from *évacuer* cease to occupy, from Latin *ēvacuāre.*

evade *v.* 1513, to escape, borrowed from Middle French *évader,* from Latin *ēvādere* to escape, get away (*ē-* away, variant of *ex-* + *vādere* go, walk; see WADE). The sense of escape by trickery, elude, is first recorded in 1535.

evaluation *n.* 1755, the action of appraising or valuing (goods, etc.); borrowed from French *évaluation,* from *évaluer* to find the value of (*é-* out + *value* VALUE) + *-ation* -ation. **—evaluate** *v.* 1842, back formation from English *evaluation.*

evanescent *adj.* gradually disappearing, soon fading away. 1717, disappearing or vanishing; borrowed from Latin *ēvānēscentem* (nominative *ēvānēscēns*), present participle of *ēvānēscere* disappear or vanish (*ē-* out + *vānēscere* vanish, from *vānus* empty, insubstantial, VAIN); for suffix see -ENT. **—evanesce** *v.* disappear, fade away. 1822, in De Quincey's *Confessions of an English*

Opium-Eater; either a back formation of earlier *evanescence;* or borrowed from Latin *ēvānēscere;* see the doublet VANISH. —**evanescence** *n.* gradual disappearance, fading away. 1751, Samuel Johnson, in *The Rambler,* from *evanescent,* on analogy of *putrescent, putrescence,* etc.; for suffix see -ENCE.

evangelist *n.* Probably about 1200 *ewangeliste* one of the writers of the Four Gospels; borrowed from Old French *evangeliste, evaungeliste,* and directly from Late Latin *evangelista.* The Late Latin form *evangelista,* with the shift from Greek *eu-* to Latin *ev-,* characteristic of many such borrowings from Greek, is derived from Greek *euangelistḗs* bringer of good news, preacher of the gospel, from *euangelízesthai* bring good news, preach the gospel, from *euangélion* good news, from *euángelos* bringing good news (*eu-* good + *angéllein* announce, from *ángelos* messenger, ANGEL). Compare GOSPEL for meaning; see EU- for form. The general sense of one who preaches the gospel, is first recorded in English about 1384, in the Wycliffe Bible. —**evangelic** *adj.* Probably before 1425 *ewangelych,* borrowed from Old French *evangelique,* and directly from Late Latin *evangelicus;* **evangelical** *adj.* 1531, in Tyndale's *Exposition of the Epistles of St. John;* formed in English from Late Latin *evangelicus* (from Late Greek *euangelikós,* from Greek *euangélion* good news) + English *-al*[1]. —**evangelistic** *adj.* 1845, formed from English *evangelist* + *-ic.* —**evangelism** *n.* Before 1626, in Francis Bacon's *The New Atlantis;* borrowed from Medieval Latin *evangelismus* a spreading of the Gospel (found in *Evangelismi festum* (Feast of the Gospels, fifth Sunday after Easter), from Late Latin *evangelium* good news, gospel, from Greek *euangélion* good news; see EVANGELIST. —**evangelize** *v.* Before 1382, in the Wycliffe Bible; borrowed from Old French *evangeliser* to spread or preach the gospel, and directly from Medieval or Late Latin *evangelizāre,* from Greek *euangelízesthai* bring good news, preach the gospel; see EVANGELIST. —**evangelizer** *n.* Before 1382 *euangeliser,* in the Wycliffe Bible; formed in English, by influence of Medieval Latin *evangelizare,* from Greek *euangelíz(esthai)* + English *-er.*

evaporation *n.* Before 1398 *evaporacioun,* in Trevisa's translation of Bartholomew's *De Proprietatibus Rerum;* borrowed from Old French *evaporation,* learned borrowing from Latin, and probably also borrowed into English directly from Latin *ēvapōrātiōnem* (nominative *ēvapōrātiō*), from *ēvapōrāre* disperse in vapor or steam, evaporate (*ē-,* variant of *ex-* + *vapor* steam, VAPOR); for suffix see -ATION. —**evaporate** *v.* turn into vapor. Probably before 1425 *evaporaten,* in a translation of Chauliac's *Grande Chirurgie;* in some instances formed in English as a back formation of earlier *evaporation,* and in others a borrowing from Latin *ēvapōrātum,* past participle of *ēvapōrāre;* for suffix see -ATE[1].

Middle English *evaporen* to draw off (fluids from the body) apparently had more specific application than *evaporaten,* but both terms are found in Chauliac, though *evaporen* was borrowed from Middle French *évaporer,* from Latin *ēvapōrāre.*

evasion *n.* Probably before 1425 *evasioun* means of evading; borrowed through Middle French *évasion,* and directly from Late Latin *ēvāsiōnem* (nominative *ēvāsiō*), from *ēvās-,* stem of Latin *ēvādere* EVADE to escape; for suffix see -SION. —**evasive** *adj.* 1725, in Pope's translation of Homer's *Odyssey;* formed from English *evas(ion)* + *-ive,* perhaps molded on French *évasif* (feminine *évasive*), from *évasion,* from Late Latin *ēvāsiōnem;* or formed in English from Latin past participle stem *ēvās-* + English *-ive.*

eve *n.* evening. Probably before 1200, variant of EVEN[2] (the terminal *n* was apparently regarded as inflectional and not part of the stem; for a similar loss of final *n,* compare *morrow, game,* and *maid*).

The extended sense of the evening, or day, before a festival or holiday (as in *Christmas eve*), appeared about 1300 in the form of *eve,* though the meaning existed earlier in Middle English *even* (1121, in the *Peterborough Chronicle*) and Old English *ǣfen* (about 725, in *Beowulf*).

even[1] *adj.* level, smooth, equal. Probably before 1200 *evene,* developed from Old English *efen, efn* level, even (about 725, in *Beowulf*); cognate with Old Frisian *even, evin* level, plain, smooth, Middle Dutch and modern Dutch *effen,* Old Saxon *eƀan,* Old High German *eban* (modern German *eben*), Old Icelandic *jafn* (Danish *jævn,* Norwegian *jevn,* Swedish *jämn*), and Gothic *ibns,* from Proto-Germanic **eƀnaz,* of unknown origin. —**adv.** indeed, fully; quite. Probably about 1200 *even,* developed from Old English (about 725) *efne,* later *efen,* from Old English *efen, efn,* adj. —**v.** Probably before 1200 *evenen* make level, make equal in rank; developed from Old English (about 975) *efnan* make level with, throw down, from Old English *efen, efn,* adj.

even[2] *n. Archaic.* evening. Probably before 1200, in *Ancrene Riwle;* developed from Old English *ǣfen* (about 725, in *Beowulf*); cognate with Old Frisian *ēvend* evening, Old Saxon *āƀand,* Old High German *āband* (modern German *Abend*), and perhaps Old Icelandic *aptann,* this last altered by influence of *aptan* after, as Old English *ǣfen* has been influenced by its opposite *morgen.* On the basis of Greek *epi* following upon, and *opsé* late (Indo-European **epi/opi,* Pok.323) a quasi-participial **ēp-onto-* has been posited as the source of Old English *ǣfen.* Compare EVE, EVENING. —**evensong** *n.* Probably before 1200, in *Ancrene Riwle;* developed from Old English *ǣfen-sang.* —**eventide** *n.* Probably before 1200, in *Ancrene Riwle;* developed from Old English *ǣfen-tīd.*

evening *n.* Probably before 1200 *evening,* in Layamon's *Chronicle of Britain;* developed from Old English (about 1000) *ǣfnung* (*ǣfnian* become evening, from *ǣfen* evening, EVEN[2]) + *-ung* -ing[1]. —**evening star** 1535, in Coverdale's writings; earlier Middle English *even sterre* (before 1250), developed from Old English *ǣfen-steorra.*

event *n.* 1570-76, outcome or result; borrowed from Middle French *event,* learned borrowing from Latin *ēventus* (genitive *ēventūs*) occurrence, issue, from *ēvenīre* to come out, happen, result (*ē-* out, variant of *ex-* + *venīre* come; see COME).

The sense of a happening, incident, occurrence, is first recorded in 1588, in Shakespeare's *Titus Andronicus.*

—**eventful** *adj.* 1600, in Shakespeare's *As You Like It,* formed from English *event* + *-ful,* but not recorded again until 1755, in Johnson's *Dictionary,* in which appearance of the word may have stimulated its use.

—**eventual** *adj.* 1612-15, borrowed from French *éventuel,* as if formed on the Latin model **ēventuālis,* from *event-,* participle stem of *ēvenīre* to come out, happen.

—**eventuality** *n.* 1828, the power of observing in

phrenology; later, a possible occurrence (1852); formed from English *eventual* + *-ity,* possibly by influence of French *éventualité.*

ever *adv.* About 1250 *euere,* in *The Story of Genesis and Exodus;* developed from Old English *ǣfre* (about 750, in Cynewulf's *Christ*), probably related to Old English *ā* always, ever, see AY[1].

It is a word not found in other Germanic languages, but its form and sense have suggested to some scholars that it is a contraction of the phrase *ā in fēore,* literally, ever in life (*ā* always + *in* in + *feorh* life, in the dative case and cognate with Old High German *ferh, ferah* and Gothic *fairhwus* world, of uncertain origin). Another explanation refers to *ā* always, originally **āw* (with change of *w* to *f*) + *-re* dative feminine adjective suffix, often formative of adverbs. Compare NEVER.

—everglade *n.* (1823, American English) **—evergreen** *n.* (1644); *adj.* (1671, in Milton's *Samson Agonistes*) **—everlasting** *adj.* About 1225, eternal; later, perpetual, about 1303. **—evermore** *adv.* About 1290, developed from Old English *ǣfre mā.*

eversion *n.* Before 1420 *eversioun* an overthrowing, in Lydgate's *Troy Book;* borrowed from Middle French *eversion,* from Latin *ēversiōnem* (nominative *ēversiō*) a turning out, an overthrowing, from *ēvers-,* past participle stem of *ēvertere* to overturn (*ē-* out, variant of *ex-* + *vertere* to turn); for suffix see -SION. The sense of a turning inside out, is first recorded in English in 1751.

every *adj.* Probably about 1200 *eauer-euch,* literally, ever each; later *euerich* (about 1250, in *Ancrene Riwle*) and *euerile* (about 1250, in *The Story of Genesis and Exodus*) and *euery* (about 1303, in Mannyng's *Handlyng Synne*); developed from the Old English phrase *ǣfre ǣlc* ever each (*ǣfre* ever, and *ǣlc* each); see EACH, EVER.

In the OED it is suggested that there was an alternate form in Old English (**ǣfre ylc*), and that *ǣlc* and *ylc* were compounds of Old English *ā* always, which by vowel change and contraction became obscured so that *ǣfre* was added to reinforce the meaning. By the 900's *ǣfre ǣlc* and **ǣfre ylc* were considered compounds in themselves, thus the latter, descending through Middle English was further contracted to *every* by the 1380's.

—everybody *pron.* (about 1390, in Chaucer's *Canterbury Tales*) **—everyday** *adj.* (about 1380, in Chaucer's translation of Boethius' *De Consolatione Philosophiae*) **—everyone** *pron.* (probably about 1200) **—everywhere** *adv.* Probably about 1200, developed from Old English *ǣfre gehwǣr.*

evict *v.* 1447 *evicten* recover (property) by judicial means, in *Rolls of Parliament;* borrowed from Latin *ēvictus,* past participle of *ēvincere* recover property, evict, conquer (*ē-* out, variant of *ex-* + *vincere* conquer; see VICTOR). The sense of to expel by legal process is first recorded in English in 1536. **—eviction** *n.* 1461, in *Rolls of Parliament;* probably borrowed from Middle French *éviction,* from Latin *ēvictiōnem* (nominative *ēvictiō*) recovery of one's property, from *ēvic-,* stem of *ēvincere;* for suffix see -TION. In some early instances *eviction* may have been formed from English *evict* + *-ion.*

evident *adj.* Before 1382, true or faithful, authentic, in the Wycliffe Bible; later, clear, plain, visible, obvious (1393, in Gower's *Confessio Amantis*); borrowed from Old French *evident,* from Latin *ēvidentem* (nominative *ēvidēns*) perceptible, clear, obvious (*ē-* fully, out of, variant of *ex-* + *videntem,* nominative *vidēns,* present participle of *vidēre* to see; see WIT[2] know); for suffix see -ENT. **—evidence** *n.* Probably before 1378, a particular bit of evidence, principles given in support of a belief, in a version of *Piers Plowman;* borrowed from Old French *evidence,* from Late Latin *ēvidentia* proof (also in Latin, clearness or distinctness), from *ēvidentem* perceptible, clear, obvious; for suffix see -ENCE. *–v.* About 1610, show clearly, give evidence of, indicate, manifest; from the noun. **—evidently** *adv.* About 1380, in Chaucer's translation of Boethius' *De Consolatione Philosophiae;* formed from English *evident* + *-ly*[1].

evil *adj.* 1130 *iuele;* later *ufel, euele* (probably before 1200), and *evel* (about 1300), once *evil* (about 1273, in a surname *Evilchild*); developed from Old English *yfel* bad, wicked, vicious (plural *yfla,* about 725 in *Beowulf*); cognate with Old Frisian *evel* evil, Old Saxon *ubil,* Middle Dutch *evel* (modern Dutch *euvel*), Old High German *ubil* (modern German *übel*), Gothic *ubils* evil, from Proto-Germanic **ubilaz,* from Indo-European **upélos,* root **up(o)* under (Pok.1106). **—n.** Probably about 1175 *evel,* developed from Old English *yfel* that which is evil, adjective used absolutely. **—evildoer** *n.* (before 1387) **—evil-minded** *adj.* (1531)

evince *v.* 1608-11, to disprove, confute; borrowed from French *évincer,* from Latin *ēvincere* conquer, elicit by force of argument, prove (*ē-* out, variant of *ex-* + *vincere* conquer, overcome; see VICTOR; EVICT). The sense of make evident, show clearly, reveal, is first recorded in English, in Cook's *Voyages* (1772-84).

eviscerate (ivis′ərāt) *v.* remove the bowels from; disembowel, take out the entrails of. 1621, in Burton's *Anatomy of Melancholy;* borrowed from Latin *ēvīscerātus,* past participle of *ēvīscerāre* (*ē-* out, variant of *ex-* + *vīscera* internal organs, VISCERA); for suffix see -ATE[1]. **—evisceration** *n.* 1628, in Donne's *Sermons;* formed in English from Latin *ēvīscerāre* eviscerate + English *-tion.*

evoke *v.* call forth, bring out. 1623–26, in Cockeram's *Dictionary;* probably borrowed through French *évoquer,* or directly from Latin *ēvocāre* call out, rouse, summon (*ē-* out, variant of *ex-* + *vocāre* to call, related to *vōcem* VOICE); or formed in English as a back formation of *evocation,* on the model of Latin *ēvocāre.* **—evocation** *n.* 1574; earlier, used in a specialized grammatical sense (about 1450, in *Battlefield Grammar*); borrowed, perhaps through Middle French *évocation,* or, more likely, directly from Latin *ēvocātiōnem* (nominative *ēvocātiō*), from *ēvocāre* evoke; for suffix see -ATION. **—evocative** *adj.* 1657, formed in English from Latin *ēvocātus,* past participle of *ēvocāre* evoke + English *-ive.*

evolve *v.* develop gradually. 1664, unfold or set forth in sequence (but implied in earlier *evolved,* before 1641); borrowed from Latin *ēvolvere* unroll (*ē-* out, variant of *ex-* + *volvere* to roll; see VOLUME); or possibly formed in English as a back formation of *evolution,* on the Latin model *ēvolvere* unroll. **—evolution** *n.* 1622, unfolding; borrowed from Latin *ēvolūtiōnem* (nominative *ēvolūtiō*) unrolling of a book, from *ēvolū-,* stem of *ēvolvere* unroll; for suffix see -TION.

This word (as well as *evolve,* v.) was used in 1832 by the British geologist Charles Lyell, 1797-1875, with reference to the theory that animals and plants developed from earlier forms; Darwin adopted the term in *The Origin of Species* (1859).

—evolutionary *adj.* 1846, formed from English *evolution* + *-ary.* **—evolutionist** *n.* 1859, in Darwin's *The*

Origin of Species; formed from English *evolution* + *-ist.*

ewe (yü) *n.* female sheep. About 1300 *ouwe;* earlier, in the compound *ewe-lomb* (probably about 1200); developed from Old English *ēowu* (about 1000, in Ælfric's translation of *Genesis*); cognate with Old Frisian *ei* ewe, Old Saxon *ewi,* Old High German *ouwi, ou,* Old Icelandic *ǣr,* from Proto-Germanic **awī,* genitive **awjōz,* and Gothic *awistr* sheepfold, *awēthi* flock of sheep. Cognates outside Germanic include Old Irish *ōi* sheep, Latin *ovis,* early Greek *óïs,* Lithuanian *āvinas* ram, Old Slavic *ovĭnŭ* ram, *ovĭca* sheep, Sanskrit *ávi-s* sheep, and hieroglyphic Luwian *ḫawis* sheep, from Indo-European **ówis* (Pok.784).

ewer (yü′ər) *n.* water pitcher. Probably about 1380 (but found earlier in the surname *Lewer,* 1219); borrowed from Anglo-French *ewer, ewiere,* Old French *eviere, aiguiere* water pitcher, from Vulgar Latin **aquāria,* as in **aquāria ōlla* water pot, from feminine of Latin *aquārius* of or for water, from *aqua* water; see AQUATIC.

ex[1] *prep.* out of, without, not including (chiefly in commercial use, as in *ex warehouse, ex dividend*). 1845, borrowed from Latin *ex* from, out of; see EX-[1]

ex[2] *n. Informal.* former husband, wife, suitor, officeholder, member of a group, religion, etc. 1827, short for *ex-husband, ex-wife, ex-president,* etc.; see EX-[1].

ex-[1] a prefix meaning: **1** out of, from, out, as in *express* = *press out.* **2** thoroughly, utterly, as in *exterminate* = *terminate utterly.* **3** (usually in words borrowed from Latin) removing, lacking, as in *expatriate.* **4** (free compounding form, usually with a hyphen) former, as in *ex-president, ex-convict, ex-husband.* Borrowed from Latin *ex-,* related to the preposition *ex,* or *ē* out of or from, which is cognate with Greek *ex* out of or from, and with Old Irish *ess-,* Old Prussian *esse, assa,* and Old Slavic *iz, izŭ* out, from Indo-European **eĝhs* (Pok.292).

Latin *ex-* appears before vowels and *h,* and before voiceless consonants such as *c, q, s,* and *t;* before voiced consonants it becomes *ē-;* and before *f* it becomes *ef.*

In Old French and in Middle English, words with the prefix *es-* were sometimes respelled with *ex-,* in imitation of words from Latin; for example, *exchange* for *eschange, exchequer* for *eschequer.*

ex-[2] a prefix meaning out, from, out of, usually in words borrowed from Greek, as in *exodus, exorcise.* Borrowed from Greek *ex-, ex,* cognate with Latin *ex;* see the etymology of EX-[1]. Greek *ex-* appears before vowels; the corresponding form before consonants is *ec-.*

ex-[3] the form of *exo-,* meaning outside, outer, outside of, before vowels, as in *exoccipital.*

exacerbate (egzas′ərbāt) *v.* make worse, embitter, aggravate. 1660, probably formed in English by back formation from earlier *exacerbation,* but also possibly a borrowing, perhaps influenced by French *exacerber,* from Latin *exacerbātus,* past participle of *exacerbāre* exasperate, irritate (*ex-* thoroughly + *acerbus* harsh, bitter; see ACERBITY); for suffix see -ATE[1]. **—exacerbation** *n.* Before 1400 *exacerbacyoun,* in a translation of the Pauline epistles of the New Testament; borrowed from Late Latin *exacerbātiōnem* (nominative *exacerbātiō*), from Latin *exacerbāre* exasperate, irritate; for suffix see -ATION.

exact *v.* to demand; require. 1440 *exacten;* borrowed from Latin *exāctus,* past participle of *exigere,* literally, drive out or force out, also with the extended senses of demand, require, complete, finish, weigh, measure (*ex-* out + *agere* drive, lead, act; see AGENT). **—adj.** precise. 1533, in Sir Thomas More's writings; borrowed from Latin *exāctus* highly perfected or precise, from the past participle of *exigere,* in the senses of weigh accurately, calculate precisely. **—exacting** *adj.* (1583) **—exaction** *n.* About 1380, borrowed from Old French *exaction,* and directly from Latin *exāctiōnem* (nominative *exāctiō*), from *exigere.* **—exactitude** *n.* exactness. 1734, borrowed from French *exactitude,* from *exact,* from Latin *exāctus.* **—exactly** *adv.* Before 1533, though the elliptical use meaning "quite right" is not recorded before 1869.

exacta (egzak′tə) *n.* form of betting in which the bettor must pick the first- and second-place winner of a race. 1964, American English; borrowed from American Spanish *exacta,* shortening of *quiniela exacta,* from Spanish *exacta* exact + American Spanish *quiniela* a game of chance, a bet in horse racing; of unknown origin.

exaggerate *v.* 1533, to pile up, in writings of Sir Thomas More; borrowed from Latin *exaggerātus,* past participle of *exaggerāre* heighten, amplify, magnify (*ex-* out, up + *aggerāre* heap up, from *agger,* genitive *aggeris* heap, from *aggerere* bring together, carry toward; from *ag-* to, toward, variant of *ad-* before *g* + *gerere* carry; see GESTURE); for suffix see -ATE[1].

The sense of magnify or overstate, is first recorded in English in 1564.

—exaggeration *n.* 1565, either: 1) borrowed from Latin *exaggerātiōnem* (nominative *exaggerātiō*), from *exaggerāre* exaggerate; for suffix see -ATION; *or* 2) formed from English *exaggerate* + *-ion.*

exalt *v.* elevate, glorify. Before 1410 *exalten,* borrowed through Middle French *exalter,* and directly from Latin *exaltāre* raise, elevate (*ex-* out, up + *altus* high; see OLD). Alternatively, *exalt* may be a back formation from earlier *exaltation.* **—exaltation** *n.* 1389 *exaltacion,* through Old French *exaltation,* and directly from Late Latin *exaltātiōnem* (nominative *exaltātiō*) elevation, pride, from Latin *exaltāre* raise, exalt; for suffix see -ATION.

examine *v.* About 1303 *examynen* to test or question, in Mannyng's *Handlyng Synne;* borrowed from Old French *examiner* to test or try, learned borrowing from Latin *exāmināre* to test or try, from *exāmen* a means of weighing or testing, tongue of a balance. The probable development in Latin is reconstructed through **exagsmen* a testing, examination, from **exag-,* stem of **exagere,* variant of *exigere* weigh accurately; see EXACT. **—exam** *n.* (1877, shortened form of *examination*) **—examination** *n.* About 1390 *examinacioun,* in Chaucer's *Canterbury Tales;* borrowed from Old French *examination,* learned borrowing from Latin, and borrowed directly from Latin *exāminātiōnem* (nominative *exāminātiō*), from *exāmināre* examine; for suffix see -ATION. **—examiner** *n.* (1530)

example *n.* Before 1382 *exsaumple,* in the Wycliffe Bible; borrowed from Old French *example, essample,* learned borrowing from Latin *exemplum,* originally, that which is taken out, a sample, from *eximere* take out, remove, EXEMPT. An earlier form *asaumple* appeared in Middle English before 1250, in a version of *Ancrene Riwle;* borrowed from Old French *assample,* variant of *essample.*

exasperate *v.* irritate, enrage. 1534, in Sir Thomas More's writings; borrowed, possibly by influence of Middle French *exaspérer,* from Latin *exasperātus,* past participle of *exasperāre* roughen, irritate (*ex-* thoroughly + *asper* rough; related to ASPERITY); for suffix see -ATE[1]. **—exasperation** *n.* 1547, borrowed from Latin *exasperātiōnem* (nominative *exasperātiō*), from *exasperāre* exasperate; for suffix see -ATION.

excavate *v.* 1599, probably developed from earlier *excavate,* adj., hollowed out (1571); borrowed from Latin *excavātus,* past participle of *excavāre* to hollow out (*ex-* out + *cavāre* to hollow, from *cavus* hollow; see CAVE); for suffix see -ATE[1]. **—excavation** *n.* 1611, in Cotgrave's *Dictionary,* either formed from English *excavate,* v. + *-ion;* or borrowed through French *excavation,* or directly from Latin *excavātiōnem* (nominative *excavātiō*), from *excavāre* excavate; for suffix see -ATION. **—excavator** *n.* 1815, formed from English *excavate,* v. + *-or*[2].

exceed *v.* About 1380 *exceden,* in Chaucer's translation of Boethius' *De Consolatione Philosophiae;* borrowed from Old French *exceder,* learned borrowing from Latin *excēdere* depart, go beyond (*ex-* out + *cēdere* go, yield; see CEDE). **—exceeding** *adj.* (1494); *adv.* (1535) **—exceedingly** *adv.* (1535)

excel *v.* do or be better than. Probably about 1408 *excellen,* in Lydgate's *Reson and Sensuallyte;* probably borrowed from Middle French *exceller,* and directly from Latin *excellere* to rise, surpass, be eminent (*ex-* out from + *-cellere* rise high or tower; related to *celsus* high, lofty, great; see HILL). Alternatively, *excel* may have been formed in English as a back formation of *excellence.* **—excellence** *n.* Probably about 1350, borrowed from Old French *excellence,* from Latin *excellentia* superiority, excellence, from *excellentem* (nominative *excellēns*) excellent, present participle of *excellere* excel; for suffix see -ENCE. **—excellency** *n.* Probably about 1200 *excellencie* high rank; borrowed from Latin *excellentia* superiority, excellence. The word is first recorded as a title of honor *(Your excellency)* about 1532, though apparently Latin *Excellentia* was the prior use, as early as 1325. **—excellent** *adj.* Before 1349, surpassing, superior, unexcelled; borrowed from Old French *excellent,* learned borrowing from Latin *excellentem* (nominative *excellēns*), present participle of *excellere* excel; for suffix see -ENT.

excelsior (eksel′sēôr) *adj.* ever upward, higher. 1778, in American English the motto of New York State incorporating the Latin *excelsior* higher, comparative of *excelsus* high, past participle of *excellere* EXCEL. The word was popularized in the United States in the poem *Excelsior* (1841) by Longfellow, in which *excelsior* is a refrain, expressing aspiration toward a higher goal. **—n.** (eksel′sēər) finely curled shavings of soft wood. 1868, American English, originally a trade name; from the adjective.

except *prep.* About 1378 *excepte,* in a version of *Piers Plowman;* borrowed through Old French *excepté,* prep., or directly from Latin *exceptus,* past participle of *excipere* take out (*ex-* out + *capere* take; see CAPTIVE). In Middle English, *except* was used as a participle with the meaning of (being) excepted, and often preceded the noun. In this position it gradually took on the function of a preposition. **—conj.** Before 1387, in a later version of *Piers Plowman;* borrowed directly from Latin *exceptus,* past participle of *excipere.* —**v.** Before 1393 *excepten* take or leave out, exclude, in Gower's *Confessio Amantis;* borrowed from Middle French *excepter,* from Latin *exceptus,* past participle of *excipere.* **—excepting** *prep.* (1549) **—exception** *n.* About 1386 *excepcioun,* in Chaucer's *Legend of Good Women;* borrowed through Anglo-French *excepcioun,* Old French *exception,* or directly from Latin *exceptiōnem* (nominative *exceptiō*), from *excep-,* stem of *excipere* take out; for suffix see -TION. **—exceptionable** *adj.* 1691, implied earlier in *exceptionableness* (1664); formed from English *exception* + *-able.* **—exceptional** *adj.* 1846, forming an exception, unusual, special, formed from English *exception* + *-al*[1], possibly by influence of earlier French *exceptionnel* (1739).

excerpt (eksėrpt′) *v.* About 1536, Cardinal Wolsey, quoted in Ellis' *Original Letters;* borrowed from Latin *excerptus,* past participle of *excerpere* pluck out, excerpt (*ex-* out + *carpere* pluck, gather; see HARVEST). It is possible that *excerpt,* v., was also in part developed from earlier *excerpte* taken or derived (from a book), a past participial use found in a translation of Higden's *Polychronicon* (probably before 1425). **—n.** (ek′sėrpt) Before 1638, borrowed from Latin *excerptum,* neuter past participle of *excerpere* to excerpt; or, in some instances possibly a noun use of the verb.

excess *n.* Before 1382 *exces* extravagant show of emotion, elation or ecstasy, in the Wycliffe Bible; also, more than enough (before 1387, in Trevisa's translation of Higden's *Polychronicon*); borrowed through Old French *excès,* learned borrowing from Latin, or borrowed directly from Latin *excessus* (genitive *excessūs*) departure, going beyond the bounds of reason or beyond the subject, from pre-Latin stem *excesd-* of *excēdere* to depart, go beyond, EXCEED. **—adj.** 1472-75, from the noun. **—excessive** *adj.* Before 1393 *excessif,* in Gower's *Confessio Amantis;* borrowed from Old French *excessif* (feminine *excessive*), from Medieval Latin *excessivus* immoderate, from Latin *excessum,* past participle of *excēdere* exceed; for suffix see -IVE.

exchange *n.* About 1378 *eschaunge,* in a version of *Piers Plowman;* borrowed through Anglo-French *eschaunge,* Old French *eschange,* from *eschangier* to exchange, from Vulgar Latin **excambiāre* (from Latin *ex-* out + *cambiāre* to CHANGE). The original spelling with *es-* was gradually replaced from the 1400's to 1600's with *exchange* after the Latin. **—v.** 1415 *eschaungen,* in Chaucer's *Canterbury Tales;* borrowed through Anglo-French *eschaungier,* Middle French *eschangier* to exchange, from *eschange,* n. The English spelling *exchange* is first recorded in Caxton's *The Curiall* (1484). **—exchangeable** *adj.* 1575, formed from English *exchange* + *-able.*

exchequer (ekschek′ər) *n.* treasury of a city, state, or nation. Before 1338 *escheker* a session of the English king's department of treasury, in Mannyng's *Chronicle of England;* earlier, a chessboard (about 1250); borrowed through Anglo-French *escheker,* from Old French *eschequier* chessboard, from *eschec* a check; see CHECKER. It is disputed whether the term applied to the treasury was first used in Normandy or in England, but the name refers to a cloth divided into squares and covering a table on which so-called accounts of revenue were reckoned with counters.

The spelling *exchequer* developed when *es-* of the original Old French spelling was mistaken as the equivalent of Latin *ex-,* as in *eschaunge,* respelled *exchange.* The shift from *-ker* to *-quer* developed gradually after 1450, modeled on the Anglo-French *-er* for Old French *-ier* in the re-adopted Old French *-quier.*

excise[1] (ek′sīz) *n.* tax on articles made, sold, or used within a country. 1494, borrowed probably from Middle Dutch *excijs,* apparently an altered form of *accijs* tax, by influence of Latin *excīsus* cut out or removed, past participle of *excīdere;* see EXCISE[2]. The Middle Dutch *accijs* is traditionally derived from Old French *acceis* tax or assessment, from Vulgar Latin **accēnsum,* ultimately from Latin *ad-* to + *cēnsus* tax, CENSUS, but further confusion arises in associating Old French *acceis* tax, with Old French *assise* a setting (of taxes), from *asseoir* to assess, ultimately from Latin *assidēre* to sit at, pay attention, especially as a judge or assessor; and the relationship between Medieval Latin *assessare* fix a tax upon, and *assedere* sit at, both derived from Latin *assidēre,* makes the development of *excise* in Middle Dutch and Old French an uncertain matter.

excise[2] (eksīz′) *v.* cut out, remove. 1578, borrowed from Middle French *exciser,* learned borrowing from Latin *excīsus,* past participle of *excīdere* cut out (*ex-* out + *caedere* to cut; cognate with Armenian *xait'* to prick, Sanskrit *khidáti* (he) tears, from Indo-European **khaid-/khid-* to strike, Pok.917). **—excision** *n.* 1490, in Caxton's translation of *The Book of Eneydos,* borrowed through Middle French *excision,* learned borrowing from Latin *excīsiōnem* (nominative *excīsiō*), from *excīs-,* stem of *excīdere* excise; for suffix see -SION.

excite *v.* About 1340 *exciten* urge on; later, to stir up the feelings of (before 1387, in Trevisa's translation of Higden's *Polychronicon*); borrowed through Old French *exciter,* learned borrowing from Latin, or borrowed directly from Latin *excitāre* rouse, excite, frequentative form of *exciēre* call forth, instigate (*ex-* out + *ciēre* set in motion, call; see CITE). **—excitability** *n.* 1788, formed from English *excitable* + *-ity.* **—excitable** *adj.* 1609, formed from English *excite* + *-able.* **—excitation** *n.* 1384, probably borrowed from Old French *excitation,* from Latin *excitātiōnem* (nominative *excitātiō*), from *excitāre* excite; for suffix see -ATION. Alternatively, *excitation* may have been formed from English *excite* + *-ation.* **—excited** *adj.* 1660, magnetically or electrically stimulated, in Robert Boyle's writings; later, disturbed or agitated (1855, in Macaulay's *History of England*); from *excite,* v. **—excitement** *n.* About 1425, encouragement; later, perhaps as a re-formation, in Shakespeare's *Hamlet* (1604); formed from English *excite* + *-ment.* **—exciting** *adj.* 1811, causing disease; later, causing excitement (1826, in Benjamin Disraeli's *Vivian Grey*); from *excite,* v.

exclaim *v.* 1570 *exclame;* probably, at least in part, a back formation from earlier *exclamation;* but traditionally analyzed as a borrowing from Middle French *exclamer,* learned borrowing from Latin, or borrowed directly from Latin *exclāmāre* cry out loud (*ex-* intensive + *clāmāre* cry out, call; see CLAIM). The spelling *exclame* never gained acceptance (even Caxton in an early noun use writes *exclaim,* about 1489) and in spite of the French *exclamer,* the English spelling has been influenced by *claim;* so also *acclaim, acclamation* which follow the same pattern. **—exclamation** *n.* About 1384 *exclamacioun,* in the Wycliffe Bible; borrowed from Old French *exclamation,* learned borrowing from Latin *exclāmātiōnem* (nominative *exclāmātiō*), from *exclāmātus* (past participle of *exclāmāre* exclaim); for suffix see -ATION. **—exclamation mark** or **point** 1824; earlier *note of exclamation* (1657). **—exclamatory** *adj.* 1593, formed from English *exclamat(ion)* + *-ory,* possibly modeled on Latin *exclāmāt-,* participle stem of *exclāmāre* + English suffix *-ory.*

exclude *v.* About 1384 *excluden,* in the Wycliffe Bible; earlier, implied in the gerund *excludyng* (before 1349); borrowed from Latin *exclūdere* keep out, shut out, hinder, from *ex-* out + *claudere* to CLOSE[1] shut. **—exclusion** *n.* Before 1402, borrowed from Middle French *exclusion,* learned borrowing from Latin, or borrowed directly from Latin *exclūsiōnem* (nominative *exclūsiō*), from *exclūdere* exclude; for suffix see -SION. **—exclusive** *adj.* 1515, functioning as an adverb (also recorded in this use about 1450); borrowed, perhaps through Middle French *exclusif,* but more likely from Medieval Latin *exclusivus,* from *exclus-,* participle stem of Latin *exclūdere* exclude; for suffix see -IVE. The noun meaning of news published exclusively by one paper, is first recorded in 1901.

excommunicate *v.* exclude from a religious community or from religious rites. Probably before 1425, in a translation of Higden's *Polychronicon;* borrowed from Late Latin *excommūnicātus,* past participle of *excommūnicāre,* literally, put out of the community (*ex-* out + *commūnis* common; see COMMON, on the analogy of *commūnicāre* communicate; see COMMUNICATE); for suffix see -ATE[1]. **—excommunication** *n.* 1459, in *The Paston Letters;* borrowed possibly through Middle French *excommunication,* earlier *escomination,* or directly from Late Latin *excommūnicātiōnem* (nominative *excommūnicātiō*), from *excommūnicāre* excommunicate; for suffix see -ATION.

excoriate (ekskôr′ēāt) *v.* strip or rub off the skin of; make raw and sore. Probably before 1425 *excoriaten,* in a translation of Chauliac's *Grande Chirurgie;* borrowed from Late Latin *excoriātus,* past participle of *excoriāre* strip off the hide, from Latin *ex-* off + *corium* hide, skin; related to *carō* flesh, meat, cognate with Sanskrit *cárman-* skin, Greek *keírein* to cut, from Indo-European **ker-/kor-* (Pok.938). The figurative sense of denounce or censure violently is first recorded in 1708. **—excoriation** *n.* Probably before 1425 *excoriacioun;* borrowed possibly through Middle French *excoriation,* but more likely directly from Medieval Latin *excoriationem* (nominative *excoriatio*), from Late Latin *excoriāre* strip off the hide; for suffix see -ATION.

excrement (eks′krəmənt) *n.* waste matter discharged from the bowels. 1533, in Sir Thomas Elyot's *The Castel of Helth;* borrowed from Latin *excrēmentum,* from the stem of *excrētus,* past participle of *excernere* to sift out, discharge (*ex-* out + *cernere* sift, separate; see CERTAIN); for suffix see -MENT.

excrescence (ekskres′əns) *n.* abnormal growth of the body. Probably before 1425, in a translation of Chauliac's *Grande Chirurgie;* borrowed through Middle French *excressance,* or directly from Latin *excrēscentia,* pl., abnormal growths, from *excrēscentem* (nominative *excrēscēns*), present participle of *excrēscere* grow out (*ex-* out + *crēscere* grow; see CRESCENT); for suffix see -ENCE. **—excrescent** *adj.* Before 1500 *excressent* resulting from addition; later, growing out of something, especially abnormally (1633); either borrowed from Latin *excrēscentem* (nominative *excrēscēns*), present participle of *excrēscere* grow out; or a back formation in English from *excrescence,* on the model of Latin *excrēscentem;* for suffix see -ENT.

excrete (ekskrēt′) *v.* discharge (waste matter) from the body. 1620, either borrowed from Latin *excrētus,* past participle of *excernere* to discharge; see EXCREMENT; or a back formation in English from *excretion.* **—excretion** *n.* 1603, borrowed probably from French *excrétion,* apparently from Latin *excrē-,* stem of *excernere* to discharge; for suffix see -TION. **—excretory** *adj.* 1681, formed in English from Latin *excrēt-,* past participle stem of *excernere* + English suffix *-ory.*

excruciate (ekskrü′shēāt) *v.* crucify, torture. 1570, borrowed, possibly by influence of Middle French *excrucier,* from Latin *excruciātus,* past participle of *excruciāre* to torture, torment (*ex-* out, thoroughly + *cruciāre* cause pain or anguish to, crucify, from *crux,* genitive *crucis* CROSS); for suffix see -ATE[1]. The participial adjective *excruciating* is first recorded in 1664, and in present-day English is far more common than the verb.

exculpate (eks′kulpāt) *v.* free from blame. 1656-81, in an edition of Blount's *Glossographia;* borrowed from Medieval Latin *exculpatus,* past participle of *exculpare,* from the Latin phrase *ex culpā* (*ex* out of, from + *culpā,* ablative case of *culpa* blame; see CULPABLE); for suffix see -ATE[1]. **—exculpation** *n.* Before 1715, formed from English *exculpate* + *-ion.*

excursion *n.* 1574, digression; borrowed from Middle French *excursion,* learned borrowing from Latin, or borrowed directly from Latin *excursiōnem* (nominative *excursiō*) a running forth, excursion, from *excursum,* past participle of *excurrere* run out (*ex-* out + *currere* to run; see CURRENT); for suffix see -SION. The sense of a trip or journey is first recorded in English in Joseph Glanvill's *Scepsis Scientifica* (1665).

excuse (ekskyüz′) *v.* offer an apology for. About 1225 *escusen,* in *Ancrene Riwle;* later *excusen* (before 1338, in Mannyng's *Chronicle of England*); borrowed from Old French *escuser* (1190), later *excuser,* learned borrowing from Latin *excūsāre* release from a charge, excuse (*ex-* out, away + *causa* accusation, CAUSE). **—n.** (ekskyüs′) About 1375, in Chaucer's *Anelida and Arcite;* borrowed from Old French *excuse,* from *excuser* to excuse. **—excusable** *adj.* About 1385, in Chaucer's *Troilus and Criseyde;* borrowed from Old French *excusable,* from Latin *excūsābilis,* from *excūsāre* to excuse; for suffix see -ABLE.

execrate (ek′səkrāt) *v.* abhor, loathe, detest. 1561, probably borrowed from Latin *execrātus, exsecrātus,* past participles of *execrārī, exsecrārī* to hate, curse (*ex-* out + *sacrāre* to devote to holiness, but also to destruction, consecrate, from *sacer* SACRED); for suffix see -ATE[1]. Alternatively, *execrate* may also be a back formation from the earlier *execration.* **—execrable** (ek′səkrəbəl) *adj.* About 1384, involving a curse, in the Wycliffe Bible; borrowed through Old French *execrable,* and directly from Latin *execrābilis, exsecrābilis,* from *execrārī, exsecrārī* to curse; for suffix see -ABLE. The sense of abominable, detestable, is first recorded in Caxton's translation of *The Book of Eneydos* (1490). **—execrably** *adv.* 1633, formed from English *execrable* + *-ly*[1]. **—execration** (ek′səkrā′shən) *n.* Before 1382 *execracioun* the act of cursing, in the Wycliffe Bible; borrowed through Old French *execration,* and directly from Latin *execrātiōnem* (nominative *execrātiō*), from *execrārī, exsecrārī* to curse; for suffix see -ATION.

execute *v.* About 1385 *executen* carry out, perform, accomplish, in Chaucer's *Canterbury Tales;* borrowed from Old French *executer,* back formation from *executeur* executor, from Latin *execūtor, exsecūtor* doer, performer, agent nouns from *execūt-, exsecūt-,* past participle stems of *exequī, exsequī* follow out (*ex-* out + *sequī* follow; see SEQUEL). The sense of put to death, is first recorded in English in Caxton's translation of Cato's writings (1483); the meaning developed in part from the sense of carry (a law or judgment) into effect (before 1393), and in part from the etymological sense of Latin *exequī, exsequī* follow out, pursue to the end. **—execution** *n.* About 1385 *execucioun* act of carrying out, performance, in Chaucer's *Troilus and Criseyde,* borrowed through Anglo-French *execucioun,* Old French *execution,* from Latin *execūtiōnem, exsecūtiōnem* (nominative *execūtiō, exsecūtiō*), from *execūt-, exsecūt-,* past participle stems of *exequī, exsequī* follow out; for suffix see -TION. The sense of putting to death, is first recorded in 1439, developing from the phrases *do execusion, don execucion of deth* (about 1390), and *puten to execucioun* (before 1393). **—executioner** *n.* 1561, formed from English *execution* + *-er*[1]. **—executive** *adj.* Probably before 1425, intended to be carried out; borrowed from Middle French *exécutif* (feminine *exécutive*), from Old French *executer* execute, as if from a Latin form **execūtīvus;* for suffix see -IVE. The sense pertaining to that branch of a government charged with carrying out the laws, is first recorded in 1649. *—n.* 1776, in American English, person or persons charged with putting laws into effect, in Jefferson's writings; from the adjective. The sense of businessman holding a high administrative position, is first recorded in 1902, also in American English. **—executive committee** (1823) **—Executive Mansion** the White House (1838) **—executive privilege** (1954) **—executive session** (1840) **—executor** *n.* About 1290 *executor* one who executes a will, borrowed through Anglo-French *essecutour,* Old French *executeur,* from Latin *execūtōrem, exsecūtōrem* (nominative *execūtor, exsecūtor*) doer, performer; see EXECUTE.

exegesis (ek′səjē′sis) *n.* scholarly explanation or interpretation, especially of the Bible. 1619, borrowed from Greek *exḗgēsis,* from *exēgeîsthai* explain, interpret (*ex-* out + *hēgeîsthai* to lead, guide; see SEEK).

exemplary *adj.* serving as an example or model. 1589 *exemplarie* of a kind to become an example; probably adjective use of earlier *exemplarie* a model of conduct to be imitated, example (about 1420); the adjective possibly influenced in its development by, and in some instances borrowed from, Middle French *exemplaire,* from Latin *exemplāris* that serves as an example, from *exemplum* example; for suffix see -ARY. **—exemplar** *n.* Before 1398 *exemplar* original model of the universe in the mind of God; later, a model of virtue (1447), and, an original copy of a book (probably before 1425); borrowed from Old French *exemplaire, examplaire,* and directly from Late Latin *exemplārium,* from *exemplum* EXAMPLE.

exemplify *v.* Probably about 1408 *exemplifien* demonstrate by example, in Lydgate's *Reson and Sensuallyte;* borrowed from Middle French *exemplifier,* from Medieval Latin *exemplificare,* from Latin *exemplum* EXAMPLE; for suffix see -FY. **—exemplification** *n.* 1442, attested copy of a document; borrowed through Anglo-French *exemplificacion,* from Medieval Latin, and directly from Medieval Latin *exemplificationem* (nominative *exemplificatio*), from *exemplificare* exemplify; for suffix see -ATION. The sense of act or instance of exemplifying, is first recorded in English before 1461.

exempt *adj.* released, not subject to. About 1380, in Chaucer's translation of Boethius' *De Consolatione Philosophiae;* borrowed from Old French *exempt,* and directly from Latin *exēmptus,* past participle of *eximere* release, remove (*ex-* out + *emere* buy, originally take; see REDEEM). **—v.** About 1443, grant immunity or freedom from (a law or rule); borrowed from Middle French *exempter,* from Old French, from *exempt,* adj. **—exemption** *n.* About 1400, in Wycliffe's writings; borrowed from Old French *exemption,* learned borrowing from Latin; and borrowed directly from Latin *exēmptiōnem* (nominative *exēmptiō*) a taking out, removing, from *exēm-,* stem of *eximere* release, remove; for suffix see -TION.

exercise *n.* About 1340, effort or application, as for virtue, etc.; borrowed from Old French *exercice,* learned borrowing from Latin *exercitium,* from *exercitāre,* frequentative form of *exercēre* keep busy, drive on (*ex-* off + *arcēre* keep away, prevent, enclose; see ARK). The sense of physical exercise, is first recorded in Chaucer's *Canterbury Tales* (about 1390). **—v.** About 1380 *exercisen* put into active use, in Chaucer's translation of Boethius' *De Consolatione Philosophiae;* from the noun. The sense of engage in physical exercise, is first recorded in 1655.

exert *v.* 1660, thrust forth, push out; borrowed from Latin *exertus, exsertus,* past participles of *exerere, exserere* thrust out, put forth (*ex-* out + *serere* attach, join, bind; see SERIES). The sense of put into use, exercise, bring to bear, is first recorded in 1681. **—exertion** *n.* 1668, act of exerting, formed from English *exert* + *-ion.* The meaning of vigorous action, effort, is first recorded in 1777. French *exertion,* attested since 1787, was borrowed from English (FEW III, 293a).

exhale *v.* Before 1400 *exalen* emit vapor, perfume, etc.; borrowed from Middle French *exhaler,* learned borrowing from Latin *exhālāre* breathe out (*ex-* out + *hālāre* breathe, of uncertain origin). **—exhalation** *n.* Before 1393 *exalacion,* in Gower's *Confessio Amantis;* borrowed through Old French, or directly from Latin *exhālātiōnem* (nominative *exhālātiō*), from *exhālāre;* for suffix see -ATION.

In common words beginning with *exh-,* the *h* is generally silent and that therefore probably accounts for its loss in Middle English *exalen* exhale, *exort* exhort, etc. (restored in the 1500's), but in words that were learned borrowings or were borrowed in late Middle English and thereafter (particularly directly from Latin) the *h* is preserved by influence of the Latin spelling which was consciously imitated, especially in the 1500's and 1600's.

exhaust *v.* 1533, use up, consume, in Sir Thomas Elyot's *The Castel of Helth;* probably developed from earlier *exhaust,* past participle; borrowed from Latin *exhaustus,* past participle of *exhaurīre* draw off, take away, use up, from *ex-* out, off + *haurīre* to draw water, etc., probably from earlier **aurīre,* cognate with Greek *exaúein* take out, and Old Icelandic *ausa* dip, from Indo-European **aus-* (Pok.90).

The sense of draw off air is first recorded in 1540, and later that of drain of strength, tire, in 1631.
—n. 1848, escape of steam from an engine; from the verb.
—exhausted *adj.* 1656-81, in an edition of Blount's *Glossographia;* from *exhaust,* v. **—exhaustion** *n.* 1646, fatigue, loss of strength; possibly formed from English *exhaust,* v. + *-ion,* on the model of Late Latin *exhaustiōnem* (nominative *exhaustiō*) a drawing off, emptying, from Latin *exhaurīre* draw off; for suffix see -TION. **—exhaustive** *adj.* 1786-89, in Jeremy Bentham's writings; formed from English *exhaust* + *-ive.* **—exhaust pipe** (1889)

exhibit *v.* 1447, possibly borrowed from Latin *exhibitus,* past participle of *exhibēre* to hold out, show, display (*ex-* out + *habēre* to hold; see HABIT). Alternatively, it is very likely that *exhibit* is a back formation from earlier *exhibition.* **—n.** 1626, legal evidence; borrowed from Latin *exhibitum,* neuter past participle of *exhibēre* to exhibit. The sense of something displayed publicly, is first recorded in 1862. **—exhibitor, exhibiter** *n.* 1599, in Shakespeare's *Henry V;* formed from English *exhibit* + *-or²*, *-er¹*. **—exhibition** *n.* Before 1325 *exhibicion* a display, demonstration; 1442 *exibicioun* maintenance, support; borrowed through Old French *exhibicion,* and directly from Latin *exhibitiōnem* (nominative *exhibitiō*), from *exhibēre* to exhibit; for suffix see -TION. **—exhibitionism** *n.* 1893, indecent exposure, formed from English *exhibition* + *-ism,* on the model of French *exhibitionnisme.* **—exhibitionist** *n.* 1821, a performer, formed from English *exhibition* + *-ist,* on the model of French *exhibitionniste.* The sense of one who indulges in exhibitionism, is first recorded in English in 1813, from the same source as *exhibitionism.*

exhilarate (egzil′ərāt) *v.* make cheerful or lively. 1540, borrowed from Latin *exhilarātus,* past participle of *exhilarāre* gladden, cheer (*ex-* thoroughly + *hilarāre* make cheerful, from *hilarus,* later *hilaris* cheerful, from Greek *hilarós;* see HILARITY); for suffix see -ATE¹. **—exhilarating** *adj.* 1643, in Milton's writings; from *exhilarate,* v. **—exhilaration** *n.* 1623-26, in Cockeram's *Dictionary;* borrowed from Late Latin *exhilarātiōnem* (nominative *exhilarātiō*), from Latin *exhilarāre* exhilarate; for suffix see -ATION.

exhort (egzôrt′) *v.* urge strongly. Probably about 1400 *exorten* encourage or admonish; borrowed through Middle French *exhorter,* and directly from Latin *exhortārī* (*ex-* strongly, thoroughly + *hortārī* encourage, urge; see HORTATORY). **—exhortation** *n.* About 1384, in the Wycliffe Bible; borrowed through Old French *exhortation,* and directly from Latin *exhortātiōnem* (nominative *exhortātiō*), from *exhortārī* exhort; for suffix see -ATION.

The spelling with *h* is first recorded in English about 1425, but did not become established until the 1550's.

exhume (eksyüm′) *v.* dig out of the grave or the ground. 1783, borrowed from French *exhumer,* from Medieval Latin *exhumare* (Latin *ex-* out of + *humāre* bury, from *humus* earth; see HUMBLE). **—exhumation** *n.* 1797, borrowed from French *exhumation,* learned borrowing from Medieval Latin *exhumationem* (nominative *exhumatio*), from *exhumare;* for suffix see -ATION. The words *exhume* and *exhumation* appear earlier once in the record of English, in 1430, in a single source.

exigency (ek′səjənsē) *n.* 1581, that which is urged; replacing Middle English *exigence* (1447); borrowed from Middle French *exigence,* from Late Latin *exigentia,* from Latin *exigentem* (nominative *exigēns*), from *exigere* to demand; for suffix see -ENCY. **—exigencies** *n.pl.* 1659, an urgent need, demand for prompt action; from the noun singular. **—exigent** *adj.* urgent. 1670, possibly a back formation from earlier *exigency,* on the model of Latin *exigentem* (nominative *exigēns*), present participle of *exigere* to demand, EXACT; for suffix see -ENT. Alternatively, *exigent* may be from Middle English *exigent,* n., an emergency (before 1449).

exile *v.* Before 1325, in *Cursor Mundi;* borrowed from Old French *exilier,* learned borrowing from Late Latin *exiliāre,* from Latin *exilium* banishment, from *exul* banished person (*ex-* away + the root *-ul-,* which is possibly related to *ambulāre* to walk; see AMBLE). **—n.** Probably before 1300, in *Arthour and Merlin;* borrowed from Old French *exil,* learned borrowing from Latin *exilium.*

exist *v.* 1602, in Marston's *Antonio's Revenge;* borrowed from French *exister,* from Middle French, learned borrowing from Latin *existere, exsistere* stand forth, appear, exist (*ex-* forth + *sistere* cause to stand, related to *stāre* to STAND), found in English *extant* with the current meaning of in existence, existing). **—existence** *n.* About 1380, reality, in Chaucer's *House of Fame;* borrowed from Old French *existence,* from Late Latin *existentia, exsistentia,* from Latin *existentem, exsistentem* (nominative *existēns, exsistēns*) existent, present participles of *existere, exsistere* exist; for suffix see -ENCE. The sense of fact or state of existing, being, is first recorded about 1430. **—existent** *adj.* 1561, probably a back formation from English *existence,* modeled on Latin *existentem;* see EXISTENCE. **—existential** *adj.* 1693, of or having to do with existence, in a translation of a Latin text; borrowed from Late Latin *existentiālis, exsistentiālis,* from *existentia, exsistentia;* see EXISTENCE; for suffix see -AL[1]. Modern use of the term in philosophy to refer to *existentialism* is first recorded in English before 1937, probably by influence of Kierkegaard's use in German *existential* (1846). **—existentialism** *n.* philosophy that emphasizes the existence of the individual. 1941, borrowed from German *Existentialismus* (1919, replacing earlier *Existentialforhold,* 1849, from Kierkegaard's *Existents-Forhold,* 1846), from Late Latin *existentiālis* existential + German *-ismus* -ism. **—existentialist** *n.* 1945, borrowed from French *existentialiste,* from *existentialisme* (about 1940), from German *Existenzialismus;* for suffix see -IST.

exit *n.* 1538, a direction for leaving the stage, in a play by John Bale; a borrowing of Latin *exit* he or she goes out, 3d person singular present indicative of *exīre* go out (*ex-* out + *īre* to go). The plural form *exeunt* appeared earlier, about 1485, in the Digby Plays.

The original use of *exit* as a stage direction was extended in English with the meaning of departure of a player from the stage, in Shakespeare's *Love's Labour's Lost* (1588) and *As You Like It* (1600), followed by the general sense of a going out, emergence, departure, before 1652. The sense of a way out, passage to the outside, outlet, egress, is first recorded in 1659, apparently borrowed from Latin *exitus* (genitive *exitūs*) a going out, departure, from *exīre* go out.

The base of these forms is Latin *īre* to go, cognate with Greek *iénai* to go, *eîmi* I will go, Lithuanian *eĩti* to go, Old Slavic *iti,* Sanskrit *éti* he goes, Tocharian B *yam* he goes, and Hittite *iya-* go; a Germanic cognate is found in Gothic *iddja* went, from Indo-European **ei-/i-* (Pok.293).

—v. 1607, make one's exit, depart; from the noun.

exo- a combining form meaning outside, outer, outside of, used in new formation of scientific and technical vocabulary, such as *exobiology, exoskeleton, exosphere.* Borrowed from Greek *éxō* outside, related to *ex* out; see EX-[2]. Also EX-[3] before vowels.

exobiology *n.* study of life on other planets. 1960, formed from English *exo-* outer + *biology.*

exodus (ek′sədəs) *n.* departure. Old English (about 1000) *Exodus,* second book of the Old Testament (so named because it contains an account of the departure of the Israelites from Egypt); borrowing of Latin *exodus,* from Greek *éxodos* a going out or departure (*ex-* out + *hodós* way; see CEDE). The general sense of departure, is first recorded in English in Cockeram's *Dictionary* (1623-26); but the application of this meaning to a departure from a place, especially for continuous, or even temporary settlement elsewhere, is not recorded until 1831, in Carlyle's *Sartor Resartus.*

ex officio (eks əfish′ēō). in discharge of one's duty; by virtue of one's office. 1533, in Sir Thomas More's *Apology of Syr Thomas More, Knyght;* borrowing of Latin *ex* out or out of, and *officiō,* ablative case of *officium* OFFICE.

exogenous (eksoj′ənəs) *adj. Botany.* originating from or on the outside. 1830, borrowed probably from French *exogène,* and directly from New Latin *exogenus* (from Greek *éxō* outside, from *ex* out of + *-genḗs* born or produced, from the root of *gígnesthai* be born; see KIN); for suffix see -OUS. Compare ENDOGENOUS.

exonerate (egzon′ərāt) *v.* to free from blame. 1448, borrowed from Latin *exonerātus,* past participle of *exonerāre* remove a burden, discharge (*ex-* off + *onus,* genitive *oneris* burden; see ONUS); for suffix see -ATE[1]. **—exoneration** *n.* 1640-41, perhaps borrowed through French *exonération,* learned borrowing from Latin *exonerātiōnem* (nominative *exonerātiō*) an unloading, lightening, from *exonerāre* remove a burden; for suffix see -ATION; *or* formed from English *exonerate* + *-ion.*

exonumia (ek′sōnü′mēə) *n.pl.* numismatic items other than coins and paper currency, such as medals or coupons. 1966, American English, formed from *exo-* outside of + *-numia,* from *num(ismatics)* + *-ia* plural suffix, as in *paraphernalia.*

exorbitant (egzôr′bətənt) *adj.* 1437, offensive, in *Proceedings of the Privy Council;* borrowed from Latin *exorbitantem* (nominative *exorbitāns*), present participle of *exorbitāre* deviate, go out of the track (*ex-* out of + *orbita* wheel track; see ORBIT); for suffix see -ANT. The sense of excessive or immoderate, is first recorded in 1440. **—exorbitance** *n.* 1449, an offense; formed from *exorbitant* by replacement with *-ance,* possibly after Old French *exorbitance.* The sense of extravagance or excessiveness, is first recorded in English in 1646.

exorcise or **exorcize** (ek′sôrsīz) *v.* drive out (an evil spirit) by prayers, ceremonies, etc. Probably before 1400 *exorcizen* to involve spirits; borrowed from Old French *exorciser,* from Late Latin *exorcizāre,* from Greek *exorkízein* exorcise, bind by oath (*ex-* out of + *horkízein* cause to swear, from *hórkos* oath, also literally, limitation, binding). The sense of driving out evil spirits, is first recorded in English in 1546. **—exorcism** *n.* 1395, a calling up or driving out of spirits; borrowed from Late Latin *exorcismus,* from Greek *exorkismós,* from *exorkízein* exorcise. **—exorcist** *n.* About 1384, in the Wycliffe Bible; borrowed from Late Latin *exorcista,* from Greek *exorkistḗs,* from *exorkízein* exorcise.

exosphere (ek′səsfir) *n.* layer of the atmosphere farthest from the earth. 1951, formed from English *exo-* outer + *sphere.*

exotic *adj.* foreign, alien. 1599, in Ben Jonson's *Every Man Out of His Humor;* borrowed probably from Middle French *exotique* (1548, in Rabelais), and directly from Latin *exōticus,* from Greek *exōtikós,* from *éxō* outside, from *ex* out of; see EX-[1]; for suffix see -IC. The extended general sense of unusual or strange, is first recorded in English in 1629. **—n.** an exotic person or thing. About 1645, an exotic plant; from the adjective. **—exotica** *n.pl.* exotic things. 1876, used in a book title; borrowing of Latin *exōtica,* neuter plural of *exōticus* exotic.

expand *v.* 1422 *expaunden* spread out; borrowed through Anglo-French *espaundre,* Middle French *espandre,* from Latin, and borrowed directly from Latin *expandere* to spread out (*ex-* out + *pandere* to spread, in which the stem *pand-* developed from such a pre-Latin present-tense form as **pa-n-d-més* we spread, from earlier **pa-n-t-més* containing the Latin root *pat-* as in *patēre* lie open, cognate with Greek *petannýnai* to spread, from Indo-European **pet-*, Pok.824; see FATHOM). Doublet of SPAWN. The sense of increase in size, enlarge, swell, is first recorded about 1645. **—expandable** *adj.* 1926, in Fowler's *Modern English Usage;* formed from English *expand* + *-able.* **—expanse** *n.* 1667, that which is spread out, widely extended area, the firmament, in Milton's *Paradise Lost;* borrowed from Latin *expānsum,* from neuter of *expānsus,* past participle of *expandere* spread out. Alternatively, *expanse* may be a back formation from earlier *expansion,* or a noun use of earlier *expanse,* adj. (about 1395, in Chaucer's *Canterbury Tales*). **—expansion** *n.* 1611, anything that is spread out, expanse, firmament, in the King James Bible; borrowed possibly from French *expansion,* learned borrowing from Late Latin, and borrowed directly from Late Latin *expānsiōnem* (nominative *expānsiō*) a spreading out, from Latin *expandere* expand; for suffix see -SION. The sense of the act of expanding, is first recorded in English in 1646. **—expansive** *adj.* 1651, tending to expand; formed in English from Latin *expānsus* (past participle of *expandere* expand) + English *-ive; or* possibly formed from earlier, and then unrecorded, *expanse,* n. + *-ive.*

expatiate (ekspā′shēāt) *v.* write or talk much. 1538, walk about, roam freely; borrowed from Latin *expatiātus, exspatiātus,* past participles of *expatiārī, exspatiārī* wander, digress (*ex-* out + *spatiārī* to walk, spread out, from *spatium* SPACE); for suffix see -ATE[1]. The sense of speak or write at some length, is first recorded in English in 1612.

expatriate (ekspā′trēāt) *v.* banish or withdraw from one's native land. 1768, in Sterne's *Sentimental Journey,* apparently borrowed from French *expatrier* banish (*ex-* out of + *patrie* native land, fatherland); learned borrowing from Latin *patria* one's native country, from *pater* (genitive *patris*) FATHER. **—n.** 1818, expatriated person; from the adjective. The modern sense of a person who takes up residence in a foreign country, is first recorded in 1902, popularized by *The Expatriate,* a novel about wealthy Americans living in Paris, by the American writer Lilian Bell, 1867-1929. **—expatriation** *n.* 1816, borrowed from French *expatriation (expatrier* expatriate + *-ation* -ation*).*

expect *v.* 1560, to wait, defer action; borrowed from Latin *expectāre, exspectāre* await, hope (*ex-* thoroughly + *spectāre* to look, frequentative form of *specere* to look at; see SPY).

The sense of anticipate, is first recorded in English in Shakespeare's *Julius Caesar* (1601). Use as a euphemism for be pregnant, is first recorded in Jane Austen's letters (1817).

—expectancy *n.* 1600, in Holland's translation of Livy's *Roman History;* formed in English from Latin *expectantem* + English suffix *-ancy.* **—expectant** *adj.* Before 1393, in Gower's *Confessio Amantis;* borrowed, perhaps from then unrecorded Old French *expectant,* learned borrowing from Latin, or directly borrowed from Latin *expectantem, exspectantem* (nominative *expectāns, exspectāns*), present participle of *expectāre, exspectāre* expect. **—expectation** *n.* 1538, borrowed from Middle French *expectation,* learned borrowing from Latin *expectātiōnem, exspectātiōnem* (nominative *expectātiō, exspectātiō*) anticipation, from *expectāre, exspectāre* expect; for suffix see -ATION.

Earlier use of *expectation* (1536) was as a variant of *expectative,* shortened form of *expectative grace* an acknowledgment of one's right of succession to a religious position by appointment of a king or pope.

expectorate (ekspek′tərāt) *v.* spit out (phlegm, etc.). 1601, in Holland's translation of Pliny's *Natural History;* borrowed from Latin *expectorātus,* past participle of *expectorāre* expel from the mind (literally, the breast), scorn (*ex-* out of + *pectus,* genitive *pectoris* breast; see PECTORAL); for suffix see -ATE[1].

The Classical Latin verb is attested only in the figurative sense of to banish or expel from the mind. The literal sense came from medical use probably through New Latin. The corresponding French *expectorer* is recorded only since 1701.

—expectoration *n.* 1672, probably borrowed from French *expectoration* (from Latin *expectorāre* + French *-tion* -tion).

expedient *adj.* useful, desirable, advantageous. Before 1400; borrowed through Old French *expedient,* or directly from Latin *expedientem* (nominative *expediēns*) beneficial, present participle of *expedīre* make fit or ready, prepare, bring forward; see EXPEDITE; for suffix see -ENT. **—n.** 1653, contrivance, resource; from the adjective. **—expedience** *n.* Probably 1457, advantage, benefit; borrowed probably through Old French *expedience,* from Late Latin *expedientia,* from *expedientem* (nominative *expediēns*) beneficial, present participle of *expedīre,* see EXPEDIENT. **—expediency** *n.* 1612, formed from English *expedience* + *-y*[3], or from *expedient* + *-cy;* modeled on Late Latin *expedientia;* see EXPEDIENCE.

expedite *v.* speed up. 1602, developed from earlier *expedite,* adj., speedy or prompt (1545), from *expedit,* past participle, accomplished or performed (1471); borrowed from Latin *expedītus,* past participle of *expedīre* make fit or ready, prepare, bring forward, literally, free the feet from fetters, and hence, free from difficulties, be useful (*ex-* out + **pedis* fetter, related to *pēs,* genitive *pedis* FOOT). Compare IMPEDE. **—expedition** *n.* Probably before 1425 *expedicion,* 1430, military journey or campaign, in a translation of Higden's *Polychronicon;* borrowed through Middle French *expédition,* and directly from Latin *expedītiōnem* (nominative *expedītiō*), from *expedīre;* see EXPEDITE; for suffix see -TION. **—expeditionary** *adj.* 1817, formed from English *expedition* + *-ary.* **—expeditious** *adj.* efficient and prompt. About 1475 *expedycius* useful or fitting; later, prompt or speedy (1599); probably formed in English from Latin *expedītus* (past participle of *expedīre;* see EXPEDITE) + English connective *-i-* + *-ous.*

expel *v.* About 1385, in Chaucer's *Canterbury Tales;* borrowed from Latin *expellere* drive out (*ex-* out + *pellere* to drive; see PULSE[1] beat).

expend *v.* About 1413, borrowed from Latin *expendere* pay out (*ex-* out + *pendere* to pay, weigh (out); see PENDANT). Doublet of SPEND. **—expendable** *adj.* 1805, formed from English *expend* + *-able.* **—expenditure** *n.* 1769, in Burke's writings, formed in English from Medieval Latin *expenditus* (irregular past participle of Latin *expendere* expend) + English *-ure.* The irregular Medieval Latin past participle was formed on the analogy of Latin *vēnditus,* past participle of *vēndere* to sell.

expense *n.* Before 1382, money provided for expenses, in the Wycliffe Bible; borrowed through Anglo-French *expense,* Old French *espense,* learned borrowing from Late Latin *expēnsa,* originally, feminine past participle of Latin *expendere* EXPEND. The sense of monetary charge or cost is first recorded in English before 1400. **—v.** 1909, from the noun. **—expense account** (1872) **—expensive** *adj.* 1628, given to profuse expenditure (of anything); formed from English *expense* + *-ive.* The sense of costly is first recorded in 1634.

experience *n.* About 1378, in a version of *Piers Plowman;* borrowed from Old French *experience,* learned borrowing from Latin *experientia* knowledge gained by repeated trials, experience, from *experientem* (nominative *experiēns*), present participle of *experīrī* to try, test (*ex-* out of + a lost verb **perīrī* to go through, with surviving past participle *perītus* experienced, tested, related to *perīculum* risk accompanying an attempt, peril; see FEAR); for suffix see -ENCE. **—v.** 1533, to test, try, in Sir Thomas Elyot's writings; from the noun. The sense of feel, suffer, undergo, is first recorded in 1588. **—experienced** *adj.* 1569, from *experience,* v.

experiment *n.* Probably 1348, a proof or specimen of evidence; also probably before 1350, an investigation, test or trial; borrowed from Old French *experiment,* learned borrowing from Latin *experīmentum* a trial, test, from *experīrī* to try, test; see EXPERIENCE (ultimately from the same Latin verb). **—v.** 1484, ascertain by trial, in Caxton's translation of *Fables of Aesop;* from the noun. The intransitive sense of make an experiment or experiments, is first recorded in English in 1787. **—experimental** *adj.* About 1449, formed from Middle English *experiment* + *-al*[1]. **—experimentation** *n.* 1675, formed from English *experiment* + *-ation.*

expert *adj.* About 1384, very skillful, in the Wycliffe Bible; about 1385, experienced in, having experience of, in Chaucer's *Troilus and Criseyde;* borrowed from Old French *expert,* learned borrowing from Latin, and borrowed directly from Latin *expertus,* past participle of *experīrī* to try, test; see EXPERIENCE. **—n.** Before 1420, person wise through experience, in Lydgate's *Troy Book;* reappears in the record of English in 1825, from the adjective. Noun use possibly from French *expert,* adj., but more likely as a functional shift or conversion of the English adjective. **—expertise** *n.* 1868, expert skill or knowledge, expertness, in Charles Reade's *Foul Play;* borrowed from French *expertise* expert appraisal, expert's report, from French *expert,* adj.

expiate (eks′pēāt) *v.* make amends for (a wrong, sin, etc.). 1600, make atonement, atone, in Holland's translation of Livy's *Roman History;* borrowed, perhaps through influence of Middle French *expier,* from Latin *expiātus,* past participle of *expiāre* make amends (*ex-* completely + *piāre* propitiate, appease, from *pius* faithful, loyal, devout, PIOUS); for suffix see -ATE[1]. Alternatively, *expiate* may be a back formation of earlier *expiation.*

An earlier sense of extinguish (a person's anger), end (one's sorrow) by death (1594, in Marlowe's and Nashe's *The Tragedy of Dido*) became obsolete by the early 1600's. The general sense of make amends or reparation for, appeared in writings of Sir Francis Bacon before 1626.

—expiation *n.* Probably before 1425 *expiacion* act of expiating or making atonement, in a translation of Higden's *Polychronicon;* borrowed, perhaps through Middle French *expiation,* or directly from Latin *expiātiōnem* (nominative *expiātiō*), from *expiāre* expiate; for suffix see -ATION.

expire *v.* 1419 *expiren* terminate, become void, lapse through time, in *Proceedings of the Privy Council;* also before 1420, breathe one's last, die, in Lydgate's *Troy Book;* borrowed from Middle French *expirer, espirer,* from Latin *expīrāre, exspīrāre* breathe out, breathe one's last, die (*ex-* out + *spīrāre* breathe; see SPIRIT). The sense of breathe out (air, etc.), exhale, is first recorded in English in Spenser's *Faerie Queene* (1590). **—expiration** *n.* Probably before 1425, vapor or breath, in a translation of Chauliac's *Grande Chirurgie;* borrowed from Middle French *expiration,* from Latin *expīrātiōnem, exspīrātiōnem* (nominative *expīrātiō, exspīrātiō*), from *expīrāre, exspīrāre* expire; for suffix see -ATION. The sense of termination, end, close, is first recorded in 1562.

explain *v.* About 1425, make clear; borrowed from Latin *explānāre* to make plain or clear, explain, literally, make level, flatten (*ex-* out + *plānus* flat; see PLANE[1] level, and PLAIN). Also, perhaps *explain* is, in some instances, a back formation from earlier *explanation.* **—explainable** *adj.* 1610, formed from English *explain* + *-able.* **—explanation** *n.* Before 1382, in the Wycliffe Bible; borrowed from Latin *explānātiōnem* (nominative *explānātiō*), from *explānāre* explain; for suffix see -ATION. **—explanatory** *adj.* 1618; formed from English *explanat(ion)* + *-ory,* after the model of Late Latin *explānātōrius* having to do with an explanation, from Latin *explānātus,* past participle of *explānāre.*

expletive (eks′plətiv) *n.* obscene or profane exclamation. 1612, word or phrase merely serving to fill out a sentence or metrical line; perhaps developed from an abbreviated or absolute use from earlier *conjunccioun expletif* correlative sentence adverb (1450, in *Battlefield Grammar*); borrowed possibly through Middle French *explétif* (feminine *explétive*), or directly from Late Latin *explētīvus* serving to fill out, from Latin *explēre* fill out (*ex-* out + *plēre* to fill; see FULL); for suffix see -IVE. The sense of meaningless exclamation, often in the form of a profane oath, offensive word, etc., is first recorded in Sir Walter Scott's *Guy Mannering* (1815). **—adj.** 1656-81, serving to fill out, in an edition of Blount's *Glossographia;* perhaps developed from a shortening of *conjunccioun expletif* (1450, in *Battlefield Grammar*); borrowed through Middle French *ex-*

plétif; see the noun above. The sense of serving mainly to fill out a sentence, wordy, is first recorded before 1677.

explicate *v.* clarify, explain. 1531, unfold in words, give a detailed account of, in Elyot's *The Boke Named the Governour;* borrowed from Latin *explicātus,* past participle of *explicāre* unfold, unravel, explain; see EXPLICIT. **—explicable** *adj.* 1556, probably formed from English *explic(ate)* + *-able,* on the model of Latin *explicābilis* capable of being unraveled, from *explicāre* explain; for suffix see -ABLE. **—explication** *n.* 1528, detailed statement or account; borrowed from Middle French *explication,* learned borrowing from Latin *explicātiōnem* (nominative *explicātiō*), from *explicāre* unfold; for suffix see -ATION.

explicit *adj.* clear, definite. 1613 *explicite* made clear, expressed distinctly, in Cawdrey's *A Table Alphabeticall;* borrowed from French *explicite,* from Latin *explicitus,* variant past participle of *explicāre* unfold, unravel, explain (*ex-* out + *plicāre* to fold; see PLY[2] to fold).

explode *v.* 1538, to reject or discard; borrowed from Latin *explōdere* drive out or off by clapping (originally a theatrical word applied to an actor, meaning to drive off the stage by making noise), drive out, reject (*ex-* out + *plaudere* to clap, applaud, of uncertain origin; see APPLAUD and PLAUDIT). The extended sense of drive out with violence and sudden noise, is first recorded in English in Robert Boyle's *New Experiments* (1660), and the sense of go off with a loud noise, as a bomb does, appeared in American English as a quotation of Gouverneur Morris in Jared Spark's *Life of Gouverneur Morris* (1790).

exploit *n.* About 1300 *espleit* outcome of action, literally, something unfolded; borrowed through Anglo-French *espleit,* Old French *esploit* an action, deed, profit, achievement, from Latin *explicitum* a thing settled, ended, displayed, neuter of *explicitus,* past participle of *explicāre* unfold; see EXPLICIT. The spelling *exploit* appeared gradually during the 1400's as an adoption of the French form. The sense of feat or achievement, is first recorded in English about 1400, probably from French. **—v.** Probably before 1400 *espleiten* achieve, fulfill, in Chaucer's translation of *Roman de la Rose;* later *expleiten* accomplish (probably before 1439, in Lydgate's translation of Bochas' *Falls of Princes*); borrowed from Anglo-French *espleiter,* from *espleit,* n., probably formed after Latin *explētum,* past participle of *explēre* fulfill, complete. The form *esploiten* is recorded in 1422 (probably appearing as a parallel to the noun); borrowed from Middle French *esploiter, exploiter,* from Old French *esploit,* n. The sense of make unfair use of, is recorded in 1838, as an adoption from French *exploiter* to make the most of, take advantage of, developed from Old French meaning of facilitate, expedite, a sense also found in Middle English, probably by 1417, in Lydgate's writings. **—exploitation** *n.* 1803, borrowed from French *exploitation* (*exploiter* to exploit + *-ation* -ation).

explore *v.* 1585, in letters of Queen Elizabeth I; possibly a back formation from *exploration* (influenced by Middle French *explorer,* learned borrowing from Latin) and, in some instances, a direct borrowing from Latin *explōrāre* investigate, search out, originally said to be a hunters' term meaning to set up a loud cry (*ex-* out + *plōrāre* to cry) to scare an animal from its hiding place, but later changed to mean beat the bushes. See DEPLORE.

The sense of search or examine a place, a country, etc. for the purpose of discovery, is first recorded in English in poetry of Beaumont (before 1616). **—exploration** *n.* 1543-44, investigation, examination; borrowed from Middle French *exploration,* learned borrowing from Latin *explōrātiōnem* (nominative *explōrātiō*), from *explōrāre* investigate; for suffix see -ATION. **—exploratory** *adj.* Before 1460, borrowed from Latin *explōrātōrius* belonging to scouts, from *explōrātor* scout; from *explōrāre;* for suffix see -ORY. **—explorer** *n.* 1684-85, formed from English *explore* + *-er*[1], and replacing earlier *exploratour* (about 1450), borrowed from Latin *explōrātōrem.*

explosion *n.* 1656-81, rejection, in an edition of Blount's *Glossographia;* borrowed from French *explosion,* learned borrowing from Latin *explōsiōnem* (nominative *explōsiō*), from *explōdere* drive out by clapping; see EXPLODE; for suffix see -SION. The sense of a going off with violence and noise, is first recorded in 1667. The figurative sense of an outburst (of anger, etc.) appears in writings of Coleridge (1817). The modern figurative sense of a rapid increase or development (as in *population explosion*), is first recorded in 1953. **—explosive** *adj.* 1667, tending to explode, probably formed in English from Latin *explōsus* (past participle of *explōdere*) + English *-ive.* **—n.** 1874, an explosive substance; from the adjective.

exponent (ekspō'nənt) *n.* 1706, algebraic symbol or index; borrowed from Latin *expōnentem* (nominative *expōnēns*), present participle of *expōnere* put forth, EXPOUND. The mathematical use may have been influenced by earlier French *exposant* (1680), from *exposer* expose. The sense of one who expounds or sets forth in words is first recorded in English in Southey's *Omniana,* quoting Coleridge (1812). **—exponential** *adj.* 1704 (mathematical sense), in John Harris' *Lexicon Technicum,* probably formed from earlier, and then unrecorded English *exponent* + connective *-i-* + *-al*[1].

export *v.* About 1485 *exsporten* carry out or away, in the Digby Plays; borrowed from Latin *exportāre* (*ex-* away + *portāre* carry; see PORT[4] bearing). The sense of send out (commodities) from one country to another is first recorded in English in 1665. **—n.** 1690, an exported article; from the verb. **—exporter** *n.* 1691, in Locke's writings; formed from English *export,* v. + *-er*[1].

expose *v.* Before 1422 *exposen* lay open, set forth, make known; borrowed from Middle French *exposer,* replacement (by confusion with *poser* to place, lay down, POSE) of Latin *expōnere* set forth, EXPOUND. In some instances, *expose* may be a back formation from earlier *exposition.* **—exposition** *n.* About 1390, act of expounding, explanation; borrowed from Old French *exposition,* learned borrowing from Latin *expositiōnem* (nominative *expositiō*) explanation, narration, from *exposi-,* stem of *expōnere* set forth; for suffix see -TION. The sense of a public exhibition or display, is recorded in 1851, in a letter of George Eliot referring to the Crystal Palace Exposition of London, and in an article in the *Illustrated London News* referring to a showing at the Louvre. **—expositor** *n.* About 1340, a commentator on the Gospel; borrowed through Old French *expositur,* from Latin *expositōrem,* from *expōnere;* for suffix see -OR[2]. **—exposure** *n.* 1605, public exhibition, in Shakespeare's *Macbeth,* formed from

English *expose* + *-ure,* on the analogy of *enclose, enclosure,* etc.

exposé or **expose** (eks′pōzā′) *n.* disclosure of crime, dishonesty, etc. 1803, used as a French word in a diary quoting Pitt, the Younger; past participle of *exposer* lay open, set forth, from Old French; see EXPOSE.

ex post facto (eks′ pōst′ fak′tō) made or done after something but applying to it. 1621, borrowed from the Late Latin legal phrase *ex postfactō* from what is done afterwards, from Latin *ex* out of, from, and *postfactō,* ablative of *postfactum* made or done afterwards (*post* after + *factum* done, neuter past participle of *facere* to do).

expostulate (ekspos′chəlāt) *v.* reason or plead in protest; remonstrate in a friendly manner. About 1534, to demand or claim; borrowed from Latin *expostulātus,* past participle of *expostulāre* to demand urgently, remonstrate (*ex-* from + *postulāre* to demand; see POSTULATE); for suffix see -ATE[1]. The sense of to reason or remonstrate in a friendly manner, is first recorded in English in 1574. **—expostulation** *n.* 1586, action of expostulating, earnest and kindly protest or remonstration; borrowed from Latin *expostulātiōnem* (nominative *expostulātiō*), from *expostulāre* expostulate; for suffix see -ATION.

expound *v.* explain, set forth. About 1340 *expounden,* in Richard Rolle's *The Psalter;* about 1378 *expounen,* in a version of *Piers Plowman;* borrowed from Old French *expondre,* from Latin *expōnere* put forth, explain (*ex-* forth + *pōnere* to put, place; see POSITION). Though Chaucer used both *expounen* and *expounden* in the *Canterbury Tales,* and other authors used a variety of forms (*expownen, exponen,* etc.) the usual form in Middle English was *expounen,* according to the practice of borrowing from the finite part of French verbs rather than the infinitive. In the 1500's *expoune(n)* gradually became obsolete, owing to the phonetic tendency exhibited in *sound* for the earlier *soun,* and the frequent occurrence of *expouned* as past participle. A similar development occurred in such forms as *compoune* and *propone;* both replaced in the 1500's by *compound* and *propound.*

The *d* of the French infinitive *-pondre* developed in the transition of *n* to *r* in *-ponre,* a regular contraction of Latin *pōnere.*

express *v.* About 1384 *expressen* to state, represent, depict, in the Wycliffe Bible; borrowed from Medieval Latin *expressare,* frequentative form of *exprimere* to press out, form by pressure, represent, describe, express (*ex-* out + *premere* to PRESS[1] push). **—adj.** About 1380 *expres* clear, plain, explicit, definite, in Chaucer's *House of Fame;* borrowed through Old French *expres,* or directly from Latin *expressus* clearly presented, from past participle of *exprimere* to express. The sense of direct, distinct, special, is first recorded probably before 1400. The term *express train* (appearing in 1841) originally referred to a special train, and thence to a train running expressly to a place (1845); later, also one stopping at a few stations. **—adv.** Probably about 1380 *expresse* clearly, outright, directly; borrowed from Latin *expressē,* from *expressus* clearly presented. The modern sense of by express messenger, is first recorded in Pepys' *Diary* (1667). **—n.** 1619, special messenger; from the adjective. The sense of a business or system for sending parcels, money, etc., by special messenger, is first recorded in 1794. *Express* as a shortened form of *express train* appeared in Dickens' *Dombey and Son* (1848). **—expression** *n.* Probably before 1425, the action of pressing out; later, a putting into words (1449); borrowed from Middle French *expression,* learned borrowing from Late Latin *expressiōnem* (nominative *expressiō*) expression, vividness, from Latin *expressiōnem* a pressing out, from the stem of *exprimere* to express; for suffix see -SION. **—expressionism** *n.* artistic or literary style in which the artist seeks to express emotional experience. 1908, in *The Edinburgh Review,* formed from English *expression* + *-ism,* perhaps after German *Expressionismus.* **—expressionist** *n.* 1914, in writings of Wyndham Lewis, from *expressionism,* on the analogy of *impressionism, impressionist.* But compare earlier *expressionist* (1850) an artist whose work aims chiefly at expressing character, action, etc., formed from English *expression* + *-ist.* **—expressive** *adj.* Before 1400 *expressif* tending to press out or expel; later *expressyve* serving as evidence (about 1450); possibly borrowed from Middle French *expressif,* from *expres* clear, plain; for suffix see -IVE; or formed from Middle English *expressen* + *-ive.* The sense of expressing feeling, especially in an emphatic manner is first recorded in Shakespeare's *All's Well That Ends Well* (1601). **—expressly** *adv.* Before 1393, directly, outright, in Gower's *Confessio Amantis;* 1395, specifically, in Wycliffe's writings, formed parallel with *expresse,* adv., from the verb *expressen.* **—expressway** *n.* (1945, from earlier *express highway,* in Lewis Mumford's writings, 1938).

expropriate *v.* deprive of property. 1611, in Cotgrave's *Dictionary;* probably a back formation from earlier English *expropriation,* and influenced by Medieval Latin *expropriatus,* past participle of *expropriare* to deprive of property (Latin *ex* away from + *propriāre* to appropriate, from *proprius* one's own); for suffix see -ATE[1]. Alternatively, *expropriate* may have developed in English from earlier *expropriat,* adj. (about 1449); borrowed from Medieval Latin *expropriatus,* past participle. **—expropriation** *n.* About 1443 *expropriacioun* renunciation of worldly goods; borrowed from Medieval Latin *expropriationem* (nominative *expropriatio*), from *expropriare;* for suffix see -ATION. The meaning of action of depriving a person of property, is first recorded in John Stuart Mill's *Principles of Political Economy* (1848), and may have been influenced by French in which this sense is recorded since 1789.

expulsion *n.* act or condition of forcing out or expelling. Before 1400 *expulcioun;* borrowed through Old French *expulsion* from Latin *expulsiōnem* (nominative *expulsiō*), from *expul-,* stem of *expellere* drive out, EXPEL; for suffix see -SION.

expunge (ekspunj′) *v.* remove completely, blot out. 1602, borrowed from Latin *expungere* mark (a name on a list) for deletion by placing dots above or below, mark for deletion by pricking, literally, prick out (*ex-* out + *pungere* to prick, stab; see PUNGENT).

expurgate *v.* 1621, in Burton's *Anatomy of Melancholy,* to purge or clear out; partly a back formation from earlier English *expurgation,* and partly borrowed, probably by influence of earlier English *expurge,* from Latin *expūrgātus,* past participle of *expūrgāre* cleanse out, purify (*ex-* out + *pūrgāre* to PURGE); for suffix see -ATE[1]. The specific sense of remove objectionable passages from a literary work, is first recorded in English in 1678.

Expurgate gradually replaced earlier *expurge* (1483),

borrowed from Middle French *expurger,* learned borrowing from Latin *expūrgāre.*
—expurgation *n.* Probably 1440, a purging or clearing out; borrowed from Latin *expūrgātiōnem* (nominative *expūrgātiō*), from *expūrgāre;* for suffix see -ATION. The sense of removal of objectionable passages from a literary work, is first recorded in 1614.

exquisite (eks'kwizit) *adj.* Probably before 1425, careful, searching; borrowed from Latin *exquīsitus* carefully sought out, choice, from past participle of *exquīrere* search out (*ex-* out + *quaerere* seek, procure, gain, of uncertain origin). The sense of highest degree or excellence, is first recorded in 1530, and that of very lovely, delicate, in 1579.

extant (ekstant') *adj.* 1545, standing out, projecting; borrowed from Latin *extantem, exstantem,* present participles of *extāre, exstāre* stand out, be visible, exist (*ex-* out, forth + *stāre* to STAND; see also EXIST for related forms). The sense of in existence, existing, appeared in English in 1561.

extemporaneous (ekstem'pərā'nēəs) *adj.* spoken or done without preparation. 1656-81, in an edition of Blount's *Glossographia;* borrowed perhaps from French *extemporané* (1535), but more likely borrowed directly from Late Latin *extemporāneus,* from Latin *ex tempore* offhand, in accordance with (the needs of) the moment (*ex* out of, from, and *tempore,* ablative case of *tempus,* genitive *temporis* time; see TEMPORAL[1] of time); for suffix see -OUS. **—extempore** (ekstem'pərē) *adv.* without preparation. Before 1553, in Udall's *Ralph Roister Doister;* borrowed from Latin *ex tempore* in accordance with (the needs of) the moment, offhand. *—adj.* done without preparation. Before 1637, in Ben Jonson's *Leges Convivales,* probably from the adverb in English, by influence of Latin *ex tempore.* **—extemporize** *v.* improvise. 1644 (implied in *extemporizing,* present participle), in Milton's *Areopagitica,* formed from English *extempore,* adv. + *-ize.*

extend *v.* Before 1338 *extenden* to value or assess, calculate the extent of for taxation, in Mannyng's *Chronicle of England;* later, to stretch out, lengthen (1387, in Trevisa's translation of Higden's *Polychronicon*); borrowed, possibly by influence of Old French *estendre* from Latin *extendere* stretch out (*ex-* out + *tendere* to stretch; see TEND). **—extension** *n.* Before 1400 *extencioun* distention, swelling, in Lanfranc's *Science of Surgery;* borrowed through Old French *extension,* or directly from Latin *extēnsiōnem* (nominative *extēnsiō*), from *extendere* extend; for suffix see -SION. **—extensive** *adj.* Probably before 1425, characterized by swelling or distention, in a translation of Chauliac's *Grande Chirurgie;* later, far-reaching, comprehensive (1605, in Francis Bacon's *Of the Advancement of Learning*); both are probably separate borrowings from Late Latin *extēnsīvus,* from Latin *extendere;* for suffix see -IVE. **—extent** *n.* About 1303 *extente* tax on land, in Mannyng's *Handlyng Synne;* later, value assigned to land, assessed value (1338, in Mannyng's *Chronicle of England*); borrowed through Anglo-French *extente, estente* valuation of land, area of land surveyed, stretch of land, in Old French *extente* extension, from feminine past participle of *extendre, estendre* extend, from Latin *extendere* extend. The meaning of amount or degree to which a thing, idea, etc., extends, is first recorded in 1594, and that of extended space, in 1627.

extenuate (eksten'yůāt) *v.* make (guilt, a fault, etc.) seem less. 1529, make light of, lessen, underrate, in Sir Thomas More's writings, developed from earlier past participle and adjective *extenuat* made thin, diminished, lessened (probably before 1425); borrowed from Latin *extenuātus,* past participle of *extenuāre* lessen (*ex-* out + *tenuāre* make thin, from *tenuis* THIN); for suffix see -ATE[1]. The common phrase *extenuating circumstances,* is first recorded in Macaulay's writings (1840). **—extenuation** *n.* Probably about 1425 *extenuacioun* action of making thin or the process of emaciation; later, weakening or mitigation (1542-43); borrowed from Middle French *exténuation,* and directly from Latin *extenuātiōnem* (nominative *extenuātiō*), from *extenuāre* extenuate; for suffix see -ATION.

exterior *adj.* 1528 *exteriour;* borrowed through Middle French *extérieur,* and directly from Latin *exterior,* comparative form of *exter, exterus* outward, outside, from *ex* out of, see EX-; for suffix see -OR[1]. **—n.** 1591, from the adjective.

exterminate *v.* 1541, drive away, in Sir Thomas Elyot's writings; probably borrowed from Latin *exterminātus,* past participle of *extermināre* drive out, expel, also in Late Latin, destroy, from the phrase *ex termine* beyond the boundary (*ex* out of, and *termine,* ablative case of *termen* boundary, end, limit; see TERM); for suffix see -ATE[1]. In some instances *exterminate* may be a back formation from earlier *exterminacioun, extermination.* The form *exterminate* gradually replaced earlier *exterminen* (recorded 1459), borrowed from Middle French *exterminer,* learned borrowing from Latin *extermināre,* and became obsolete in English during the 1600's.

The sense of destroy utterly, is first recorded in English in a translation of the Koran (1649), from the French.

—extermination *n.* 1459 *exterminacioun* expulsion from a country or other place, excommunication; later, utter destruction (1549); borrowed from Middle French *extermination,* learned borrowing from Late Latin, and borrowed directly from Late Latin *exterminātiōnem* (nominative *exterminātiō*), from Latin *extermināre* drive out; for suffix see -ATION. **—exterminator** *n.* Before 1400 *extermynatour,* borrowed through Old French *exterminateur,* learned borrowing from Late Latin, and borrowed directly from Late Latin *exterminātor* destroyer, from Latin *extermināre* drive out; for suffix see -OR[2].

external *adj.* Probably before 1425 *externalle* overt, in a translation of Higden's *Polychronicon;* later *external* outward, outer (1556, in Calvin's *Book of Common Prayer*); formed in English from Middle French *externe,* and from Latin *externus* outside + English *-al*[1]. Latin *externus* is from *exter, exterus* outward; see EXTERIOR. Middle English *externalle* was parallel in meaning with *exterial* (probably before 1425, also found in Higden's *Polychronicon*), which was borrowed from Old French *exterial,* from Latin *exterus,* but *exterial* became obsolete in English after 1550. **—n.pl.** outward appearance. 1635, from the adjective.

extinct *adj.* Probably before 1425 *extincte* extinguished, quenched, in a translation of Higden's *Polychronicon;* borrowed from Latin *extīnctus, exstīnctus,* past participles of *extinguere, exstinguere* EXTINGUISH. The sense of referring to a family line of persons or species of animal, etc., that has died out, is first recorded in English in 1683, though the concept as applied to an institution or title of nobility, is recorded about one hundred years earlier, in 1581, and is probably derived from the same concept as in *extinction* (before 1470). —**extinction** *n.* Probably before 1425 *extinccioun* an extinguishing or quenching; borrowed from Latin *extīnctiōnem, exstīnctiōnem* (nominative *extīnctiō, exstīnctiō*), from *extinguere, exstinguere* extinguish; for suffix see -TION. The sense of the process of coming to an end or fact of dying out, is first recorded before 1470.

extinguish *v.* put out, quench. Probably before 1503, borrowed from Latin *extinguere, exstinguere* quench, wipe out, obliterate (*ex-* out + *stinguere* quench, related to *īnstīgāre* to prick or urge on; see STICK[2] pierce); for suffix see -ISH[2]. *Extinguish* was borrowed directly from Latin and was not formed from the stem of a Middle French verb as did *abolish, banish,* etc., though *extinguish* has the same English suffix.

The new date of borrowing is interpolated from *extinguishable* (1509) and *extinguishment* (1503), both forms which depend on an understanding of *extinguish* for the derivatives to mean anything to the reader, especially since *extinguish* is a formation not found outside of English in the 1500's.

—**extinguisher** *n.* 1560, formed from English *extinguish* + *-er*[1].

extirpate (eks'tərpāt) *v.* root out, eradicate. 1539, perhaps developed from earlier, but then unrecorded *extirpate,* past participle (1541); borrowed from Latin *extirpātus, exstirpātus,* past participles of *extirpāre, exstirpāre* root out (*ex-* out + *stirps,* genitive *stirpis* a root or stock of a tree, perhaps dialectal for **sterps,* cognate with Lithuanian *stir̃pti* to grow up, from Indo-European, **sterp-,* root **ster-* stiff, Pok.1024); for suffix see -ATE[1]. Alternatively, *extirpate* may be a back formation from earlier *extirpation. Extirpate* gradually replaced the earlier form *extirpen* (recorded probably before 1425), which was borrowed, probably through Middle French *extirper,* from Latin *extirpāre, exstirpāre,* and became obsolete in the 1600's. —**extirpation** *n.* Probably before 1425 *extirpacioun* removal; later, a rooting out, eradication (1526); borrowed probably through Middle French *extirpation,* or directly from Latin *extirpātiōnem, exstirpātiōnem* (nominative *extirpātiō, exstirpātiō,*) from *extirpāre, exstirpāre* root out; for suffix see -ATION.

extol or **extoll** (ekstōl') *v.* Before 1400 *extollen* lift up, elevate, exalt; borrowed from Latin *extollere* (*ex-* up + *tollere* to raise; see TOLERATE). The extended sense of praise highly, is first recorded in Middle English probably before 1425, in a translation of Higden's *Polychronicon.*

extort *v.* obtain (money, a promise, etc.) by threats, force, fraud, or wrong use of authority. 1529; developed, in part, from earlier *extort,* adj., acquired wrongfully or by force (before 1420, in Lydgate's *Troy Book*); borrowed from Latin *extortus,* past participle of *extorquēre* wrench out, wrest away, extort (*ex-* out + *torquēre* to twist; see TORTURE). In some instances *extort* is probably also a back formation from earlier *extortion.* —**extortion** *n.* Before 1325 *extorsium* act of extorting, in *Cursor Mundi;* later *extorcion* (about 1390, in Chaucer's *Canterbury Tales*); borrowed from Old French *extorsion,* learned borrowing from Medieval Latin, and borrowed directly from Medieval Latin *extortionem, extorsionem* (nominative *extortio, extorsio*) an extortion, from Late Latin *extortiōnem* torture, from Latin *extorquēre* wrench out; for suffix see -TION. —**extortionate** *adj.* 1789, formed from English *extortion* + *-ate*[1]. —**extortionist** *n.* 1885, formed from English *extortion* + *-ist;* now apparently gradually replacing earlier *extorter* (1591), *extortor* (1579), *extortioner* (about 1375).

extra *adj.* beyond or more than the usual; additional. 1654, outside, without, external; borrowing of Latin *extrā,* adv. and prep., beyond, outside of; later (1776) also developed probably by shortening of EXTRAORDINARY, which in the 1600's was used as an adjective, adverb, and noun in the senses now associated with *extra,* and is felt to have the sense of beyond what was ordinary or normal. —**adv.** 1823, beyond the ordinary degree, unusually; from the adjective. —**n.** 1777-78, person engaged for a minor part in a play, shortening of *extraordinary,* n. (1671), someone outside the regular or ordinary staff, a supernumerary.

extra- a prefix meaning outside, beyond, as in *extraordinary, extraterrestrial.* Borrowed from Latin *extrā,* adv. and prep., beyond, outside of, old feminine ablative case of *exter, exterus* outward, outside, from *ex* out of; see EX-[1].

As a prefix *extra-* is recorded in classical Latin only in the word *extrāordinārius* extraordinary; in Late Latin it is recorded in three or four words; but in Medieval Latin it is more common, though most words that occur in English with this prefix are modern formations.

extract (ekstrakt') *v.* Probably before 1425 *extracten* draw or pull out; borrowed from Latin *extractus,* past participle of *extrahere* draw out (*ex-* out + *trahere* to draw; see TRACT). —**n.** (ek'strakt) About 1443, summary, outline, borrowed from Latin *extractum,* neuter past participle (or from *extracta,* feminine past participle) of *extrahere* to extract. —**extraction** *n.* Probably before 1425 *extraccioun* the action of pulling out or process of withdrawal; later, origin, lineage, descent (about 1477, in Caxton's translation of *History of Jason*); borrowed from Middle French *extraction,* learned borrowing from Late Latin *extractiōnem* (nominative *extractiō*), from the stem of Latin *extrahere* to extract; for suffix see -TION. —**extractor** *n.* 1611, formed from English *extract,* v. + *-or*[2].

extracurricular *adj.* 1925, formed from English *extra-* + *curricular.*

extradition (eks'trədish'ən) *n.* surrender of a fugitive or prisoner by one authority to another. 1839, in writings of De Quincey; borrowed from French *extradition* (1763, in Voltaire), from Latin *ex-* out + *trāditiō* (genitive *trāditiōnis*) a delivering up, handing over, from *trādere* to hand over; see TRADITION. —**extradite** (eks'trədīt) *v.* deliver or surrender by extradition. 1864, back formation from English *extradition,* probably on the analogy of *expedite, expedition.*

extraneous (ekstrā'nēəs) *adj.* of or from outside; not belonging or essential. 1638, of external origin; borrowed from Latin *extrāneus,* from *extrā* outside of, see EXTRA-; for suffix see -OUS. Doublet of STRANGE.

extraordinary *adj.* 1431 *extraordinaire* out of the ordinary, in *Proceedings of the Privy Council;* borrowed from Latin *extrāōrdinārius,* from the phrase *extrā ōrdinem* out of order, especially the usual order (*extrā* out, and *ōrdō, ōrdinem* ORDER); for suffix see -ARY. The sense of outside of or additional to the ordinary or regular staff, is first recorded in 1585 and gave rise to such uses as the formal *ambassador extraordinary* and the informal *musician extraordinary* (the position of the adjective being influenced by that of French *extraordinaire*). *Extraordinary* served also as a noun and as an adverb during the 1600's and 1700's, in such examples as *blank lines left for extraordinaries that occur* (n.), and *extraordinary fine* (adv.), but gradually in the 1800's these functions passed to the shortened form *extra.* —**extraordinarily** *adv.* 1564, formed from English *extraordinary* + *-ly*[1].

extrapolation (ekstrap'əlā'shən) *n.* a calculating and inferring from what is known something that is possible but unknown. 1872, formed from English *extra* + *(inter)polation* insertion of intermediate terms in a mathematical series. In early use, this word applied to a mathematical calculation. —**extrapolate** *v.* 1874, formed from English *extra* + *(inter)polate,* or a back formation from *extrapolation.*

extrasensory *adj.* 1935, in *extrasensory perception;* formed from English *extra-* + *sensory.*

extraterrestrial *adj.* 1868, formed from English *extra-* + *terrestrial.*

extravagant *adj.* Before 1387, with reference to an added part of a papal decree, in Trevisa's translation of Higden's *Polychronicon;* later, extraordinary or unusual (probably before 1425); borrowed through Anglo-French *extravagaunt,* from Middle French *extravagant,* and directly from Medieval Latin *extravagantem,* present participle of *extravagari* wander outside or beyond (Latin *extrā* outside of + *vagārī* wander, roam; see VAGARY); for suffix see -ANT. The extended meaning of flagrantly excessive or extreme, is first recorded in Ben Jonson's *Every Man Out of His Humor* (1599), followed with the sense of spending lavishly or carelessly, wasteful, in Addison's writings in *The Spectator* (1711). —**extravagance** *n.* excess; wastefulness. 1643, a going out of the usual path, digression, in Milton's *Doctrine and Discipline of Divorce;* probably a back formation of earlier *extravagancy* (1601), influenced by French *extravagance,* from *extravagant;* for suffix see -ANCE. The sense of a going beyond the bounds of reason, an absurdity, is first recorded in 1650, and that of excessive wastefulness in spending, etc., in 1727. —**extravaganza** *n.* 1754, extravagance of behavior or language; borrowed from Italian *estravaganza* peculiar behavior (literally, extravagance), from *estravagante* extravagant, from Medieval Latin *extravagantem* EXTRAVAGANT. The English spelling with *x* was influenced by *extravagance.* The sense of a fantastic or extravagant literary, musical, or dramatic work, is first recorded in 1794.

extreme *adj.* Probably before 1425, very severe, utter, farthest, in a translation of Higden's *Polychronicon;* borrowed through Middle French *extreme,* learned borrowing from Latin *extrēmus* outermost, utmost, superlative form of *exter, exterus* outward, outside, from *ex* out of; see EX-[1]. —**n.** 1546, the end, utmost point; from the adjective. —**extremism** *n.* 1865, formed from English *extreme* + *-ism.* —**extremist** *n.* 1846, formed from English *extreme* + *-ist.* —**extremity** *n.* Before 1375 *extremites, pl.,* things as far or as distant as possible from each other, in John Barbour's *The Bruce;* later, extreme or terminal point, end (before 1400); borrowed from Old French *extremité,* learned borrowing from Latin *extrēmitātem* (nominative *extrēmitās*) extremity or end, from *extrēmus* extreme; for suffix see -ITY. The plural form meaning the hands and feet, is first recorded before 1422. The sense of a condition of extreme urgency or need is first recorded about 1425.

extricate *v.* 1614, clear up or unravel; borrowed from Latin *extrīcātus,* past participle of *extrīcāre* disentangle (*ex-* out of + *trīcae,* pl., perplexities, hindrances, of uncertain origin); for suffix see -ATE[1]. The sense of free from difficulties, entanglements, or embarrassment, is first recorded in Donne's *Selections* (1631). —**extrication** *n.* 1650, formed from English *extricate* + *-ion,* modeled on Late Latin *extrīcātiōnem* (nominative *extrīcātiō*) a disentangling, from Latin *extrīcāre* disentangle.

extrinsic (ekstrin'sik) *adj.* 1541, exterior; borrowed from French *extrinsèque,* from Late Latin *extrinsecus,* adj., outer, from Latin *extrīnsecus,* adv., without, on the outside, outwardly, (formed from Old Latin *extrim* from outside, an adverb to Latin *exterus* outside, see EXTERIOR, + Latin *secus* alongside, related to *sequī* to follow; see SEQUEL). The English suffixal ending *-ic* came from confusion between it and the French ending *-que* in *-sèque,* representing Latin *-secus, secus* beside. The sense of coming from the outside, external, is first recorded in 1613, and that of not essential, in 1622.

extrovert (ek'strəvėrt) *n.* person interested mainly in things outside the self; an outgoing, sociable person. 1918, alteration of earlier *extravert* (1916); borrowed from German *Extravert,* coined by the Swiss psychologist Carl Gustav Jung, 1875-1961, from *extra-* outside + Latin *vertere* to turn; see VERTEX. Compare INTROVERT.

The terms *extrovert* and *extravert* have been in the language of English science and technology since the latter part of the 1600's, both as verbs with the sense of turning or thrusting outward. Dr. Jung's coinage in German stimulated or necessitated a noun use in English, eventually based on the old spelling with *extro-* after the contrastive prefix *intro-.* While it is possible that the use of the terms in psychology represents independent coinages, this fitted in neatly with the earlier term *extroversion,* which was already known among doctors in the field of pathology by 1836. *Extravert* and *extraversion,* having been confined to the field of chemistry since their first use, were thus not easily accepted usages and were probably cast aside for the more familiar spelling in medicine.

—**extroversion** *n.* 1920, alteration of *extraversion* (1915); borrowed from German *Extraversion,* coined by Jung from *extra-* outside + *-version* a turning, from Medieval Latin *versionem;* see VERSION. See the note above, referring to earlier use of *extroversion* (1836) in medicine. The term also appeared in an edition of Blount's *Glossographia* (1656-81) with reference to mysticism. —**extroverted** *adj.* 1923, alteration of *extraverted* (1916), formed after the earlier English verb, as a part translation of German *extravertiert,* coined by Jung from *extra-* outside + *-vertiert* turned, from Latin *vertere* to turn.

extrude *v.* thrust or push out, protrude, eject. 1566, borrowed from Latin *extrūdere* (*ex-* out + *trūdere* to thrust, push; see THREAT). —**extrusion** *n.* 1540, expulsion; borrowed from Medieval Latin *extrusionem* (nominative *extrusio*), from Latin *extrūdere* extrude; for suffix see -SION. The sense of the action of pushing out, is first recorded in 1638.

exuberant (egzü'bərənt) *adj.* 1459, luxuriantly fertile, overabundant; later, abounding in health and spirits, overflowing with delight (1503); borrowed, possibly from Middle French *exubérant,* learned borrowing from Latin, and directly from Latin *exūberantem* (nominative *exūberāns*) overabundance, present participle of *exūberāre* be abundant, grow luxuriantly (*ex-* thoroughly + *ūberāre* be fruitful, from *ūber* fertile, from *ūber* UDDER); for suffix see -ANT. **—exuberance** *n.* 1638, overflowing amount; a shortened form of earlier *exuberancy* (1611), perhaps modeled on French *exubérance,* from Latin *exūberantia,* from *exūberantem* (nominative *exūberāns*), present participle of *exūberāre;* for suffix see -ANCE. The sense of quality or condition of being exuberant appeared in 1664.

exude (egzüd′) *v.* ooze. 1574, borrowed from Latin *exūdāre, exsūdāre* ooze out like sweat (*ex-* out + *sūdāre* to sweat, related to *sūdor* SWEAT). **—exudation** *n.* 1612, perhaps formed from English *exude* + *-ation,* modeled on Late Latin *exūdātiōnem, exsūdātiōnem* (nominative *exūdātiō, exsūdātiō*), from Latin *exūdāre, exsūdāre* exude; for suffix see -ATION.

exult (egzult′) *v.* be very glad, rejoice greatly. 1570, leap for joy; borrowed from Middle French *exulter,* from Latin *exultāre, exsultāre,* frequentative forms of *exsilīre* leap out or up (*ex-* forth + *salīre* to leap; see SALLY). The sense of rejoice greatly is first recorded in English in 1594. **—exultant** *adj.* 1653, probably formed from English *exult* + *-ant,* modeled on Latin *exultantem, exsultantem* (nominative *exultāns, exsultāns*), present participle of *exultāre, exsultāre* exult; for suffix see -ANT. **—exultation** *n.* Before 1400, in the phrase *exultacion of the cross;* borrowed, perhaps through Middle French *exultation,* learned borrowing from Latin, and borrowed directly from Latin *exultātiōnem, exsultātiōnem* (nominative *exultātiō, exsultātiō*), from *exultāre, exsultāre* exult; for suffix see -ATION.

exurbanite (eksėr′bənīt) *n.* person who lives between the suburbs and the country. 1955, American English; formed from *ex-* out + *-urbanite,* patterned after *suburbanite.* The word was coined by the American writer A. C. Spectorsky, in *The Exurbanites.* **—exurbia** (eksėr′bēə) *n.pl.* 1955, American English (coined by A. C. Spectorsky); formed from *ex-* out + *-urbia,* patterned after *suburbia.*

-ey a variant form of the suffix *-y*[1], forming adjectives meaning full of, containing, like, as in *clayey, gooey.*

eye *n.* About 1200 *eie;* earlier *ehe* (probably before 1200, in *Ancrene Riwle*); developed from Old English *ēge* (Mercian dialect about 700 in compounds), and from later *ēage* (West Saxon before 800). The forms in Old English are cognate with Old Frisian *āge* eye, Old Saxon *ōga,* Middle Dutch *ōghe* (modern Dutch *oog*), Old High German *ouga* (modern German *Auge*), Old Icelandic *auga,* and Gothic *augō,* from Proto-Germanic **auʒṓn,* earlier **auʒwṓn.*The *au* diphthong is not altogether accounted for but is partly due to influence from Proto-Germanic **auzṓn-* ear (Gothic *ausō*). Outside Germanic there are also cognates in Latin *oculus* eye, Greek *ṓps* (genitive *ōpós*) eye, face, *opḗ* hole, opening, Lithuanian *akis* eye, Old Slavic *oko,* Armenian *akn* eye, opening, Sanskrit *ákṣi* eye, and Tocharian A *ak* eye, from Indo-European *okw-/ōkw-* (Pok. 775). **—v.** Before 1425 *eyen* cause to see, make visible; later, look at or upon, behold, observe (1566); from the noun. **—eyeball** *n.* 1590, in Shakespeare's *Midsummer Night's Dream.* **—eyebrow** *n.* About 1410 (not to be confused with Old English *ēagbrǣw* eyelid). **—eyeglasses** *n.pl.* (1823; earlier *eyeglass,* 1611) **—eyelash** *n.* (1752) **—eyelet** *n.* (1382) **—eyelid** *n.* (before 1325) **—eyesight** *n.* (probably before 1200) **—eyetooth** *n.* (1580)

eyrie *n.* See AERIE.

F

fa (fä) *n.* fourth note of the musical scale. Before 1300; borrowed from Medieval Latin *fa,* from the initial syllable of Latin *famulī* servants, the word sung to this note in the Hymn for St. John the Baptist's day; see GAMUT.

fable *n.* Probably before 1300, a falsehood, lie, pretense, in *Kyng Alisaunder;* later, a fictitious or imaginative story (before 1325, in *Cursor Mundi*); borrowed from Old French *fable,* from Latin *fābula* discourse, story, play, fable, from *fārī* speak, tell; see BAN[1] forbid. **—v.** Before 1400 *fablen* tell fables, in the Wycliffe Bible; borrowed from Old French *fabler,* from Latin *fābulārī* to talk, from *fābula* talk, story. **—fabled** *adj.* 1606, not real, made up; from *fable,* v.

fabric *n.* 1483, something constructed, in Caxton's version of the *Golden Legend;* borrowed from Middle French *fabrique,* learned borrowing from Latin *fabrica* workshop; see the doublet FORGE[1] smithy. The sense of manufactured material, is first recorded in English in 1753, and that of a textile fabric, in 1791. **—fabricate** *v.* About 1450 *fabricaten* to fashion, make, build; borrowed from Latin *fabricātus,* past participle of *fabricāre* to fashion, build, from *fabrica* workshop; for suffix see -ATE[1]. The extended sense of make up (a story), is first recorded in 1779. **—fabrication** *n.* Before 1500, construction; borrowed, perhaps through Middle French *fabrication,* and directly from Latin *fabricātiōnem* (nominative *fabricātiō*), from *fabricāre* to fashion, build; for suffix see -ATION.

fabulous *adj.* Probably before 1425, mythical, legendary, in a translation of Higden's *Polychronicon;* borrowed, probably through Middle French *fabuleux,* learned borrowing from Latin, and in some instances directly from Latin *fābulōsus* celebrated in fable, from *fābula* fable; see FABLE; for suffix see -OUS. The sense of incredible, resembling a fable, is first recorded in English in 1609.

façade or **facade** (fəsäd′) *n.* front part of a building. 1656-81, in an edition of Blount's *Glossographia;* borrowing of French *façade,* from Italian *facciata,* from *faccia* face, from Vulgar Latin **facia;* see FACE. The figurative sense is first recorded in 1875.

face *n.* Probably before 1300 *fas,* in *Arthour and Merlin;* borrowed from Old French *face,* from Vulgar Latin **facia,* corresponding to Latin *faciēs* form, figure, face, and related to *facere* make, DO[1] perform. **—v.** Probably before 1400 *facen* to disfigure; later, show a bold face, boast (1440, in *Promptorium Parvulorum*); from the noun. The sense of confront is first recorded in 1465 in *The Paston Letters.* **—facial** *adj.* 1609, face to face; borrowed from French *facial,* learned borrowing from Medieval Latin *facialis* of the face, from Latin *faciēs* face; for suffix see -AL[1]. The sense "of the face" is first recorded in 1818. **—n.** treatment or massage of the face. 1914, American English; from the adjective. **—facing** *n.* Probably before 1400, disfiguring; later, defiance (1523), and material used in a garment (1566) or as a coating on some structure (1586).

facet *n.* one of the small surfaces of a cut gem. 1625, in Francis Bacon's *Essays;* borrowed from French *facette,* from Old French, a diminutive form of *face* FACE. The figurative sense of any one of several sides or views, is first recorded in 1820.

facetious (fəsē′shəs) *adj.* 1592, polished, urbane; later, given to joking, humorous (1599, in Ben Jonson's *Cynthia's Revels*); borrowed from French *facétieux,* from *facétie* a joke, from Latin *facētia,* from *facētus* witty, elegant; for suffix see -OUS. Latin *facētus,* originally, brilliant, shining, is related to *fax* (genitive *facis*) torch, which is cognate with Greek *phṓps* light, *paiphássein* to wave violently, quiver, and Lithuanian *žvākė* candle, from Indo-European **ĝhwəkw-* twinkle, shine, root **ĝhwōkw-* (Pok.495).

facile *adj.* 1483, in Caxton's translation of *Fables of Aesop;* borrowed from Middle French *facile* easy, learned borrowing from Latin *facilis* easy, easy to do, (of persons) pliant, courteous, from *facere* to DO[1] perform. **—facilitate** *v.* 1611, in Cotgrave's *Dictionary;* borrowed from French *faciliter* make easy, from Italian *facilitare,* from *facilità* facility, from Latin *facilitātem* (nominative *facilitās*); for suffix see -ATE[1]. **—facility** *n.* Probably before 1425 *facilite* gentleness; later, opportunity, favorable condition for doing something (1519) and aptitude, dexterity, ease (1532); borrowed from Middle French *facilité,* from Latin *facilitātem* (nominative *facilitās*), from *facilis* easy; for suffix see -ITY. The sense of a place or means for doing something (as an educational facility) appeared in 1872, in American English.

facsimile (faksim′əlē) *n.* exact copy or likeness. 1662 *fac simile,* borrowing of Latin *fac simile* make similar *(fac,* imperative case of *facere* make, DO[1] perform and *simile,* neuter of *similis* like, SIMILAR).

fact *n.* 1539, action or deed, especially an evil deed or crime; borrowed from Latin *factum* event, occurrence (literally, thing done), from neuter past participle of *facere* to DO[1] perform. Doublet of FEAT. The general sense of thing known to be true or to have really happened, is first recorded in English in 1632. **—factual** *adj.* Before 1834, in Coleridge's *Notes on Southey's Life,* derived from *fact,* on the analogy of *actual.*

faction *n.* 1509, a party or group formed to promote its own interests; borrowed through Middle French *faction,* learned borrowing from Latin, and borrowed directly from Latin *factiōnem* (nominative *factiō*) political party, class of persons (literally, a making or doing), from *facere* to DO[1] perform; for suffix see -TION. Doublet of FASHION. **—factional** *adj.* 1650, formed from English *faction* + *al*[1]. **—factionalism** *n.* 1904, formed in American English from *factional* + *-ism.* **—factious** *adj.* 1532, inclined to form parties, seditious, in Sir Thomas More's *The Confutation of Tyndale's Answer;* borrowed through Middle French *factieux,* and directly from Latin *factiōsus,* from *factiōnem* (nominative *factiō*) faction; for suffix see -OUS.

factitious (faktish′əs) *adj.* artificial. 1646, borrowed from Latin *factīcius* artificial, from *factus,* past participle of *facere* DO[1] perform; for suffix see -OUS. Doublet of FETISH.

factor *n.* 1432 *factour* agent or representative; borrowed through Middle French *facteur,* from Latin *factor* doer or maker, from *facere* to DO[1] perform; for suffix see -OR[2]. The sense of fact or circumstances producing a result, is first recorded in Coleridge's *Lay Sermons* (1816). —**v.** 1611, act as an agent; from the noun. The sense of express a mathematical quantity as a product of two or more numbers, is first recorded in 1848 in American English. —**factotum** *n.* 1618 *factotum* general servant or handyman, developed from earlier phrases (as 1592, *Johannes fac totum* John do everything, and 1566 *Magister fac totum* master factotum); borrowing of Latin *fac,* imperative of *facere* to DO[1] perform + *tōtum* the whole, from neuter of *tōtus* all, entire, TOTAL.

factory *n.* 1560, estate manager's office or position; later, trading post (1582); borrowed through Middle French *factorie,* from Late Latin *factōrium* oil press or mill, from Latin *factor* doer, maker; see FACTOR; for suffix see -Y[3]. The sense of a building for manufactured goods, is first recorded in 1618.

faculty *n.* **1** capability, power to do something. About 1380 *faculte* power, ability, resources, in Chaucer's translation of Boethius' *De Consolatione Philosophiae;* borrowed from Old French *faculté,* and directly from Latin *facultātem* (nominative *facultās*) power, ability, wealth, from earlier **facli-tāt-s,* from *facilis* FACILE; for suffix see -TY[2]. **2** members of a profession; teaching staff. About 1450; earlier, branch of knowledge (about 1380, in Chaucer's *House of Fame*); borrowed from Medieval Latin *facultatem* (nominative *facultas*) branch of learning, from Latin *facultātem* (nominative *facultās*) power, ability; see def. 1.

In the sense of a branch of knowledge, Medieval Latin *facultas* was a translation of Greek *dýnamis* power, a term used by Aristotle to designate an art or branch of learning.

fad *n.* whim, craze. 1834, hobby, pet project; later, fashion, craze (1881). The origin of the word is unknown; it was widely current in British dialects (chiefly Midland) before it was adopted in general use in the 1880's. Some authorities have speculated that *fad* may have been abstracted from *fidfad* (1830), a shortening of *fiddle-faddle.*

fade *v.* Probably before 1325 *faden* to lose brightness, grow pale; borrowed from Old French *fader,* from *fade* pale, weak, insipid, of uncertain origin; probably from Vulgar Latin **fatidus* (a possible blend of Latin *fatuus* silly, tasteless, and *vapidus* flat, flavorless). Both in meaning and in form the term is hard to trace beyond the hypothetical Vulgar Latin.

fag[1] *v.* to tire, flag. 1530, to droop or swerve from, in Palsgrave's *Lesclarcissement;* of uncertain origin. The sense of make fatigued, tire, weary, is first recorded in Sir Walter Scott's *Journal* (1826).

The view that *fag* is an alteration of *flag,* v., would account for the meaning, but *flag* is not recorded in English before 1545, though a defect in the record of English is certainly possible and the gap is only one of 15 years.

fag[2] *n. Slang.* cigarette. 1888, probably a shortening of earlier *fag-end* last part or remnant of anything (1613), either from earlier *fagg* something that hangs loose (1486), or *fagge* a broken thread (1463-64), of uncertain origin.

fagot *n.* bundle of sticks. About 1312, but implied in earlier *fagotter* one who makes fagots of firewood (1279); borrowed from Old French *fagot,* from Old Provençal *fagot,* of uncertain origin; perhaps from Vulgar Latin **facus,* back formation from Greek *phákelos* bundle (of unknown origin), with suffix mistaken for the Latin diminutive *-ellus.*

Fahrenheit *adj.* denoting a temperature scale on which 32 degrees marks the freezing point. 1753, in allusion to the German physicist G.D. *Fahrenheit,* who proposed this scale in 1714. Compare CELSIUS.

fail *v.* Probably before 1200 *failen* cease to exist or function, come to an end, be unsuccessful, in *Ancrene Riwle;* borrowed from Old French *faillir* be lacking, miss, not succeed, from Vulgar Latin **fallire,* corresponding to Latin *fallere* deceive, be lacking or defective; see FALSE. —**n. without fail.** About 1275; borrowed from Old French *faille,* n., from the Old French verb. —**failure** *n.* 1660 *failure,* formed from English *fail* + *-ure,* and gradually replacing earlier *failer* (1643, in Prynne's writings), an Anglicized French word used in a later version (1641) of Rastell's *Exposition of the Terms of the Laws of England* (before 1565), from Old French *faillir* fail. The ending was altered in the 1600's to *failor, failour, faileur,* and did not become fixed until the end of that century.

faille (fil) *n.* ribbed silk or rayon cloth. 1869, borrowing of French *faille,* apparently from Old North French *faille* a kind of cloth head covering worn in Flanders, from Middle Dutch *falie* scarf, of uncertain origin.

fain *adj.* willing, glad. Probably before 1200 *fein,* in Layamon's *Chronicle of Britain;* developed from Old English *fægen, fagen* glad, cheerful, happy (about 725, in *Beowulf*); cognate with Old Saxon *fagin, fagan* glad, Old Icelandic *feginn* glad, Old High German and Gothic *faginōn* rejoice; see FAIR[1]. —**adv.** Probably before 1200 *fein;* from the adjective.

faint *adj.* Probably before 1300 *feinte* cowardly, feigned, spiritless, in *Kyng Alisaunder;* borrowed from Old French *faint* or *feint* cowardly, feigned, sluggish, past participles of *faindre* or *feindre* avoid one's duty by pretending, FEIGN. The extended sense of weak or feeble, is first recorded in *The Romance of Sir Beves of Hamtoun* (probably about 1300). —**v.** Probably before 1300 *feynten* grow weak; from the adjective. The meaning of fall into a swoon, is first recorded in *Siege of Jerusalem* (before 1400). —**faint-hearted** *adj.* 1440, in *Promptorium Parvulorum.*

fair[1] *adj.* Probably before 1200 *feier, fair* pleasing to the eye, beautiful, in *Ancrene Riwle;* developed from Old English *fæger* beautiful, pleasant (before 900, in King Alfred's translation of Boethius' *De Consolatione Philosophiae*). Old English *fæger* is cognate with Old Saxon and Old High German *fagar* beautiful, Old Icelandic *fagr* beautiful, and Gothic *fagrs* fitting, from Proto-Germanic **faʒrás,* and also with Old Icelandic *fāga* to adorn, clean, and Lithuanian *púošti* adorn, from Indo-European **peḱ-/poḱ-/pēḱ-/pōḱ-* (Pok.796). Related to FAIN and FAWN[2] to cringe.

The sense "of a light complexion" is an early development, recorded in Middle English before 1175 and probably used in Old English, the notions of lightness and beauty being closely connected in Germanic. An-

other early meaning was that of free from moral stain, spotless, unblemished (about 1175), from which evolved the now ordinary sense of free from bias, equitable, legitimate (about 1340). The phrase *fair play,* with the meaning of upright conduct, is first recorded in Shakespeare's *King John* (1595).
—adv. Old English (before 1000) *fægre,* from *fæger,* adj.

fair[2] *n.* a gathering of people to buy and sell and to exhibit animals, articles of produce, etc. About 1250 *feire;* borrowed from Old French *feire,* from Vulgar Latin **fēria* holiday, market fair, corresponding to Latin *fēriae* (religious festival, holiday; see FEAST. **—fairground** *n.* (1855, *fairgrounds*)

fairy *n.* Probably before 1300 *fayrye* enchantment, an illusion, in *Kyng Alisaunder;* later, supernatural being (before 1393, in Gower's *Confessio Amantis*); borrowed from Old French *faerie* land of fairies, meeting of fairies, from *fae* FAY. The phrase *fairy tale* (first recorded in Walpole's *Letters,* 1749), is a loan translation of French *Conte de fées* tale of fairies.

faith *n.* About 1250 *feith* loyalty, fealty, allegiance, in *The Story of Genesis and Exodus;* borrowed from Old French *feit, feid* (while still pronounced fāth, fāᴛʜ, from Latin *fidēs* trust, belief; related to *fidere* to trust, and cognate with Greek *peíthesthai* be persuaded, obey, believe, trust, *pístis* trust, faith, Albanian *bē* oath, and Old Slavic *běda* need, *běditi* compel; also cognate with Gothic *baidjan* compel, Old High German *beiten* urge, demand, Old Icelandic *beidha* compel, and Old English *bǣdan* compel, require, solicit, *bīdan* to wait, abide, from Indo-European **bheidh-/ bhoidh-/bhid-* (Pok.117).

The various senses of *faith* came into Middle English from Old French within a relatively short period of time: belief, especially religious belief (before 1325, in *Cursor Mundi*), system of religious belief, especially that of Christianity (probably before 1385), confidence, trust (about 1390, in Chaucer's *Canterbury Tales*). These senses were essentially already present in Latin *fidēs* as well as in its Greek cognate, *pístis,* which was rendered in the Vulgate or New Testament as *fidēs.*
—faithful *adj.* Before 1325, in *Cursor Mundi;* formed from English *faith* + *-ful.* **—faith healer** (1885)

fake *adj.* false, spurious, counterfeit. 1775, in a letter of Sir William Howe; of unknown origin. **—n.** 1851, a dodge, trick, false report, in Henry Mayhew's *London Labour and the London Poor;* possibly from the adjective. The sense of a faker or pretender, is first recorded in 1888. **—v.** 1851, to deceive, falsify; possibly from the adjective. **—faker** *n.* (1885) **—fakery** *n.* (1887)

As a noun and verb *fake* was rare, or at least went unrecorded, until the 1850's, when it was first recorded as a slang term among Londoners, especially those employed in factories and small businesses in trade, though the adjective is recorded 75 years earlier in writing that was certainly of standard English. It is hard to explain how the noun and verb would derive in lower-class speech from upper-class use; the novelty of slang usage usually comes into standard usage in the other direction. The OED connects it with a thieves' slang verb *fake,* meaning to rob, wound, tamper with (recorded in Vaux's *Flash Dictionary* of 1812), but this seems to be a different word judging by its meaning.

fakir (fəkir′) *n.* 1609, Moslem holy man who lives by begging; borrowed from Arabic *faqīr* a poor man, from *fakr, faqr* poverty. In the 1800's *fakir* was applied to Hindu ascetics, notably those who showed their transcendence of physical pain by lying on a bed of nails. Also in the 1800's, in the United States, the word came to be confused with *faker* and took on the latter's meaning of petty swindler, and the pronunciation (fā′kər) in such phrases as *street fakirs, patent-medicine fakirs;* this usage is first recorded in 1882, in Poe's writings, as attested in Mathew's *Dictionary of Americanisms.*

falcon *n.* bird of prey, a kind of hawk. About 1250 *faucun,* in *The Owl and the Nightingale;* borrowed from Old French *faucon, faulcon, falcun,* from Late Latin *falcōnem* (nominative *falcō*), probably from Latin *falx* (genitive *falcis*) sickle; so called from the resemblance of the falcon's hooked claws to a sickle. Latin *falx* is perhaps a loanword from some ancient non-Indo-European language of the Mediterranean area.

The original Middle English spelling *faucun,* (later) *faucon* was refashioned to *falcon* in the 1400's in imitation of the Latin form, but the spelling with *l* is found as early as 1194 in the surname *Falkenar.* The common pronunciations (fal′kən, fôl′kən) developed generally by influence of this spelling change; the older and less common (fô′kən) represents the original spelling; however, the pronunciation with *l* must have existed to some extent in earlier times as evidenced by the surname cited above.

The conjecture that Late Latin *falcōnem* was a borrowing from a Germanic word (represented by Old High German *falco, falcho,* late Old Icelandic *falki,* both meaning falcon, and perhaps found in the Western Gothic masculine proper name *Falco*) is difficult to sustain culturally, especially since falconry, by all historical records, seems to have originated in the East and reached the Germanic tribes through Latin or Romance-speaking peoples.
—falconer *n.* 1194, in the surname *Falkenar,* and in *Johannes le falcuner* (about 1200); later *Faukner* (1252), and *Faconer* (1279); borrowed from Old French *faulconnier* and *fauconnier,* from *faulcon, faucon;* for suffix see -ER[1]. **—falconry** *n.* 1575, alteration (influenced by earlier *falcon,* 1400's) of Middle French *fauconnerie,* from Old French *faucon* falcon; for suffix see -ERY.

falderal or **folderol** *n.* nonsense. About 1820 *falderall,* in James Hogg's *Tales and Sketches;* formed from earlier *fal, al, deral,* a meaningless refrain in songs (1701).

fall *v.* Probably before 1200 *fallen,* in Layamon's *Chronicle of Britain, Ancrene Riwle, The Ormulum,* etc.; developed from Old English *feallan* (before 900, in King Alfred's works); cognate with Old Frisian *falla* to fall, Old Saxon *fallan* (modern Dutch *vallen*), Old High German *fallan* (modern German *fallen*), and Old Icelandic *falla* (from Proto-Germanic **fallanan*); cognates beyond Germanic include Lithuanian *pùlti* to fall, and Armenian *p'ul* downfall, *p'lanim* I fall down, from Indo-European **phol-/phōl-* (Pok.851). See FELL[1]. **—n.** Probably before 1200, a falling, in Layamon's *Chronicle of Britain;* from the verb. The sense of autumn (for which *fall* is the ordinary name in the United States, whereas in Great Britain it is not widely used), is first recorded in 1664, in John Evelyn's *Sylva,* as a shortening of the earlier *fall of the leaf,* in Roger Ascham's *Toxophilus:* "Spring tyme, Somer, faule of the leafe, and winter" (1545). **—fallback** *n.* 1760, a type of carriage; later, something a person may fall back on, reserve (1851). **—fall guy** (1906) **—falling-out** *n.* 1568 disagreement. **—fall line** (1882) **—fall-off** *n.* (1889) **—fallout** *n.* 1950, radioactive particles.

fallacy *n.* false idea, error. 1481, deception, trickery, in Caxton's translation of *The History of Reynard the Fox;* replacement, by influence of Latin *fallācia,* of earlier *fallace* (about 1303, in Mannyng's *Handlyng Synne*); borrowed from Old French *fallace,* learned borrowing from Latin *fallācia* deception, from *fallax* (genitive *fallācis*) deceptive, from *fallere* deceive; see FALSE; for suffix see -ACY. **—fallacious** *adj.* 1509, borrowed by influence of Middle French *fallacieux,* from Latin *fallāciōsus* deceitful, deceptive, fallacious, from *fallācia* deception; for suffix see -OUS. Alternatively *fallacious* may have been formed from English *fallacy* + *-ous,* modeled on Latin *fallāciōsus.*

fallible *adj.* About 1412, unreliable, in Hoccleve's *Regement of Princes;* later, liable to be deceived or mistaken (before 1420, in Lydgate's *Troy Book*); borrowed from Medieval Latin *fallibilis* liable to err, deceitful, that can be deceived, from Latin *fallere* deceive; see FALSE.

Fallopian tubes (fəlō′pēən) pair of tubes through which eggs from the ovaries pass to the uterus. 1706, from *Fallopius,* Latinized name of Gabriello *Fallopio,* 1523-1562, an Italian anatomist who first described them; for suffix see -AN.

fallow[1] *n.* land plowed and left unseeded. Probably before 1300 *falen;* later *falwe* (about 1300), and *falow* (1440, in *Promptorium Parvulorum*); developed from Old English *fealg, fealh* arable land, from Proto-Germanic **falʒṓ.* The Old English forms are cognate with East Frisian *falge* fallow, *falgen* to plow, Middle High German *falgen* plow up (modern German *Felge* plowed-up fallow land), Russian *polosá* tract of land, plot, and probably Gallo-Latin *olca* arable land, from Indo-European **pelḱ-/polḱ-* to turn (Pok.807). **—adj.** uncultivated. 1377 *falwe;* from the noun.

fallow[2] *adj.* pale yellowish-brown, in modern English found in the name *fallow deer* (about 1410). Probably before 1200 *falewe* sallow, faded, yellowish-brown, in Layamon's *Chronicle of Britain;* developed from Old English *fealu* (about 725, in *Beowulf.* Old English *fealu* is cognate with Old Saxon *falu* pale, faded, fallow, Middle Dutch *vale* (modern Dutch *vaal*), Old High German *falo* (modern German *fahl*), and Old Icelandic *fǫlr,* from Proto-Germanic **falwaz.* Cognates outside Germanic include Sanskrit *palitá-s* gray, Greek *poliós* gray, Latin *pallēre* be pale, from Indo-European **pel-/pol-* (Pok.804).

false *adj.* Probably before 1200 *false, fals,* in *Ancrene Riwle;* developed in part from Old English (about 1000) *fals* counterfeit, not genuine, and reinforced by reborrowing in Middle English from Old French *fals, faus,* from Latin *falsus,* past participle of *fallere* deceive, disappoint. Old English *fals* was apparently a rare form also borrowed from Latin *falsus,* from *fallere,* which is probably cognate with Greek *phēlos* deceitful, Lithuanian *žvalùs* clever, Old Slavic *zŭlŭ* bad, wicked, and Sanskrit *hválati* he goes astray, from Indo-European **ĝhwel-* (Pok.489). The continental Germanic languages borrowed the word in an altered form, as found in Middle High German *valsch* (modern German *falsch*), Old Frisian *falsch,* Middle Dutch *valse* (modern Dutch *vals*), Icelandic *falskur,* Danish, Norwegian, and Swedish *falsk.* **—falsehood** *n.* About 1300 *falshede,* formed from Middle English *fals* false + *-hede,* variant of *-hode* -hood. **—falsification** *n.* 1565, borrowed from Middle French *falsification,* or directly from Medieval Latin *falsificationem* (nominative *falsitās*), from Late Latin *falsificāre* falsify; see FALSIFY; for suffix see -ATION. **—falsify** *v.* About 1449 *falsifien;* borrowed from Middle French *falsifier,* learned borrowing from Late Latin *falsificāre* falsify, from Latin *falsificus* making false, from *falsus* false; for suffix see -FY; *falsify* replaced earlier Middle English *falsen,* v., recorded probably before 1200, in *Ancrene Riwle.* **—falsity** *n.* About 1275 *falsete* treachery, fraud; borrowed from Old French *falseté,* learned borrowing from Late Latin *falsitātem* (nominative *falsitās*), from Latin *falsus* false; for suffix see -ITY.

falsetto (fôlset′ō) *n.* unnaturally high-pitched voice. 1774, borrowing of Italian *falsetto,* diminutive of *falso* false, from Latin *falsus* FALSE.

falter *v.* About 1390 *faltren* to stumble, stagger, tremble, in Chaucer's *Canterbury Tales;* borrowed perhaps from a Scandinavian source; compare Old Icelandic *faltrask* be burdened, hesitate, be troubled; for suffix see -ER[4].

Alternatively, *falter* may have originated as a frequentative form of Middle English *falden* (fold up, give way, fail; see FOLD[1]), formed irregularly by influence of verbs like *totter, welter,* etc.

fame *n.* Probably before 1200, character (usually good) attributed to a person or thing, in *Ancrene Riwle;* later, reputation, renown, fame; borrowed from Old French *fame,* from Latin *fāma* talk, rumor, report, reputation; cognate with Greek *phḗmē* voice, report, rumor; see BAN.[1] **—famous** *adj.* About 1380, in Chaucer's *House of Fame;* borrowed from Anglo-French *famous,* Old French *fameus,* learned borrowing from Latin *fāmōsus,* from *fāma* FAME; for suffix see -OUS.

family *n.* Probably before 1425 *familye* household; borrowed from Latin *familia* servants of a household, household (including relatives and servants), from *famulus* servant; cognate with Oscan *famel* servant, Umbrian *fameřiās* families, and Greek *thamées* crowded, thickset, *thōmós* heap, from Indo-European **dhəm-/dhō-m-* (root *dhē-*) (Pok.238); for suffixal form see -Y[3]. **—family planning** (1930) **—family tree** (1807) **—familiar** *adj.* About 1380 *famylier,* in Chaucer's translation of Boethius' *De Consolatione Philosophiae;* borrowed from Old French *familier,* learned borrowing from Latin, and borrowed directly from Latin *familiāris* domestic, from *familia* family; for suffix see -AR. **—familial** *adj.* 1900, borrowed from French *familial,* from Latin *familia;* see FAMILY; for suffix see -AL[1]. **—familiarity** *n.* Probably before 1200 *familiarite,* in *Ancrene Riwle;* borrowed probably from Old French *familiarite,* learned borrowing from Latin, and borrowed directly from Latin *familiāritātem* (nominative *familiāritās*) intimacy, friendship, from *familiāris,* see FAMILIAR; for suffix see -ITY. **—familiarize** *v.* 1608, formed from English *familiar* + *-ize.*

famine *n.* Before 1376 *famyn* extreme and general scarcity of food, in *Piers Plowman;* borrowed from Old French *famine* hunger, from Gallo-Romance **famīna,* from Latin *famēs* hunger, of unknown origin.

famish *v.* Probably before 1400 *famyschen* to starve, in *The Wars of Alexander;* alteration of earlier *famen* to starve (before 1338, in Mannyng's *Chronicle of England*); borrowed as a shortened form of Old French *afamer,* and borrowed directly from Latin *famēs* hunger; for suffix see -ISH². The shift in form of Middle English *famen* to later *famish* was influenced by other verbs ending in *-ish,* such as *ravish, admonish, anguish.*

fan[1] *n.* device to make an air current to cool a room, etc. Before 1325 *fanne* device for winnowing grain; developed from Old English (West Saxon) *fann* a kind of basket or shovel for winnowing grain by throwing it in the air; earlier *fon* (before 800, in Mercian *Corpus Glossary*); borrowed from Latin *vannus,* from pre-Latin **vatnos,* related to Latin *ventus* WIND, from Indo-European **wē-/wə-* blow (Pok.82).

The sense of a device for agitating the air to cool the face, etc., is first recorded in Middle English, in Chaucer's *Canterbury Tales* (about 1390).

—v. Before 1325 *fannen* to winnow (grain), in *Cursor Mundi;* developed from Old English (about 1000) *fannian* to winnow (grain); from the noun. The sense of stir up a current of air to cool something, is first recorded in a version of *Piers Plowman* (before 1425). **—fanlight** *n.* (1819) **—fantail** *n.* (1728) **—fan vaulting** (1835)

fan[2] *n.* enthusiastic devotee. 1889, American English, generally considered to be a revival of obsolete *fan* (1682), itself a shortening of FANATIC. Alternatively, the word may derive from or be influenced by *the fancy* (1735), a collective noun meaning all who "fancy" a certain hobby or pastime, originally applied to pigeon fanciers and later (1807) to boxing fans. *The fancy* was a popular phrase in the 1800's, used by Southey, De Quincey, Thackeray, and Herbert Spencer. **—fan club** (1941) **—fan mail** (1924) **—fan letter** (1932)

fanatic *n.* About 1525, a mad person; borrowed from Latin *fānāticus* mad, frantic, enthusiastic, inspired by divinity (originally pertaining to a temple), from *fānum* temple, related to *fēstus* festive; see FEAST. Alternatively, the noun may have developed from the English adjective (see below), since the latter undoubtedly came from Latin; however, the earliest recorded date of the adjective is 1533.

In current use *fanatic* retains some of its etymological meaning from Latin, often referring to one who is an extremist or zealot in his religious beliefs. This sense is first recorded in Bishop Maxwell's *Sacrosancta Regum* (1644).

—adj. 1533, frantic, furious, mad; borrowed from Latin *fānāticus.* The current sense of extremely zealous, especially in religious matters, is first recorded in 1647. **—fanatical** *adj.* 1550, formed from English *fanatic* + *-al*[1]. **—fanaticism** *n.* 1652, formed from English *fanatic* + *-ism.*

fancy *n.* 1462-65 *fantsy, fansey,* in *The Paston Letters;* formed by contraction of FANTASY.

Fancy and *fantasy* gradually differentiated in form and sense with *fancy* taking on the meaning of inclination, liking, desire, often whimsical, which became obsolete in *fantasy* in the 1600's. Both words, however, retained the sense of imagination, as in *poetic fancy* or *fantasy, a mere fancy* or *fantasy.*

—v. About 1380 *fancyen* take a liking or fancy to; formed by contraction of *fantasien,* v., to fantasy or FANTASIZE. The form was revived by 1545; from the noun.

—adj. Before 1751, fine, ornamental; from the noun. **—fancy dress** (1770) **—fancy-free** *adj.* (1590, in Shakespeare's *Midsummer Night's Dream*) **—fanciful** *adj.* Before 1627, formed from English *fancy,* n. + *-ful.*

fanfare *n.* 1769, military flourish on trumpets, bugles, etc.; borrowed from French *fanfare* (1546, in Rabelais), from *fanfarer* blow a fanfare (also in Rabelais), apparently from the same origin as Spanish *fanfarrón* braggart, Italian *fánfano* babbler, from Arabic *farfār* chatterer, and the parallel term in English *fanfaron* (1622, a braggart), borrowed through French *fanfaron.*

fang *n.* Before 1325 *fang* prey or booty, in *Cursor Mundi,* found in Old English *fang* a seizing or taking; also, probably before 1200 *feng* booty, what is captured or caught, in Layamon's *Chronicle of Britain,* found in Old English *feng* a grasping, prey or booty; both Old English forms derived from *fōn,* v., seize, take, catch (later *fongen, fengen* in Middle English, probably about 1225).

Middle English verb forms *fengen,* and its variants *fongen, fangen,* were formed by analogy with Middle English verbs in *-en,* on the past participle stem *feng-, fong-, fang-* of the earlier *fōn.* Cognates formed by similar development appear in other Germanic languages: Old Frisian *fang, feng* a catch (*fā, fān* to take, catch); Old High German, Middle High German *fang* (modern German *fangen*), Old High German *fāhan,* Middle High German *vāhen, van* (modern German *fahen, fangen*), Dutch *vang,* Icelandic *fang (fā),* Gothic *fāhan;* cognate also with Latin *pacīscī* settle, fix, and Greek *pássalos* peg (earlier **pákyalos*), from Indo-European **pāk-/pak-* (Pok.787).

Fang in the sense of tooth or tusk, is not found so far in Middle English, nor is it in Old English, except in the Old English compound *fæng-tōth* fang-tooth (literally catching or grasping tooth), but this Old English compound probably influenced the semantic development of the sense of *tooth* in modern English though the record is incomplete. Curiously, its application to the venom tooth of a snake is not recorded in English before 1800.

fantasize *v.* 1926, formed from English *fantasy* + *-ize;* see FANTASY.

fantastic *adj.* About 1385 *fantastik* of or pertaining to the faculty of fantasy or imagination, in Chaucer's *Canterbury Tales;* also, before 1387, imaginary or unreal, in Trevisa's translation of Higden's *Polychronicon;* borrowed from Old French *fantastique,* learned borrowing from Late Latin *phantasticus* imaginary, from Greek *phantastikós* able to imagine, from *phantázein* make visible (middle voice *phantázesthai* picture to oneself, in Late Greek, meaning to imagine, have visions), from *phantós* visible, from *phaínesthai* appear; for suffix see -IC.

fantasy *n.* About 1350 *fantasie* use of the imagination; later, apparition or phantom (probably before 1375); borrowed from Old French *fantasie,* learned borrowing from Latin *phantasia,* from Greek *phantasíā* appearance, image, perception, imagination, from *phantázesthai* picture to oneself, from *phantós* visible, from *phaínesthai* appear (middle voice to *phaínein* to show, related to *pháos, phôs* light). The Greek is cognate with Sanskrit *bhā́ma-s* light, Old Irish *bān* white, Albanian (Tosk dialect) *bënj* I make (appear), Armenian *banam* I open, make visible, and Tocharian A *paṃ* clear, from Indo-European **bhā-/bhə-* shine (Pok.104).

The meaning of whimsical or visionary notion, illusion, appeared in Middle English before 1400, followed by the general sense of imagination, especially extravagant or visionary imagination, in early modern English (1539). See also FANCY.

—**v.** About 1430 *fantesien* to fancy, imagine; borrowed from the Old French *fantasier,* from *fantasie* fantasy.

far *adv., adj.* Probably about 1200 *ferr,* in *The Ormulum;* later *farr* (before 1325, in *Cursor Mundi*); developed from Old English (about 725) *feorr* to a great distance. The Old English is cognate with Old Frisian *fēr* far, Old Saxon *ferr,* Old High German *ferro* (modern German *fern*), Middle Dutch *verre* (modern Dutch *ver*), Old Icelandic *fjarri,* and Gothic *faírra* farther (originally a comparative formation, Proto-Germanic **ferrō,* earlier **fer-s-ō*); also cognate with Old Irish *īre* farther, Old Slavic *prĕdŭ* in front, Greek *pérā, pérān* beyond, on the other side of, Armenian *heri* far, Sanskrit *pára-s* beyond, Hittite *parā* out or from within, and Tocharian A *parne* outer, exterior, from Indo-European **per-* (Pok.810).

The comparative form *farther,* whose antecedents in Old English are *fierr, fyrr* replaced in Middle English by *ferrer, ferror,* and later by *ferther* (about 1378), is a variant of *further.* The superlative *farthest* is a modern spelling of Middle English *ferthest,* formed by analogy of *nerer* nearer, *nerest* nearest; see FARTHER, FARTHEST.

—**faraway** *adj.* (before 1250) —**far-fetched** *adj.* Before 1562, replacing earlier *far-fet* forced or strained (about 1400), also with the sense of brought from afar (before 1349). —**far-flung** *adj.* (1895) —**far-reaching** *adj.* (1824) —**far-seeing** *adj.* (1837, in Longfellow's poetry) —**far-sighted** *adj.* (1641, in Milton's works).

farad (far′əd) *n.* unit of electrical capacity. 1881, in Maxwell's *Treatise on Electricity and Magnetism,* formed in English as a shortening in allusion to the English physicist and chemist Michael Faraday. The term was adopted in Faraday's honor at the Electrical Congress in Paris in 1881.

farce *n.* play of ridiculous situations and absurd people meant to be very funny. 1530, in Palsgrave's *Lesclarcissement;* borrowed from Middle French *farce* comic interlude in a mystery play, literally, stuffing, from Old French *farcir* to stuff, interlard (as with humorous skits between acts of a play), from Latin *farcīre* to stuff, related to *frequēns* crowded, and cognate with Greek *phrássein* fence in, hedge round, fill full, from Indo-European **bherekw-* (Pok.110). —**farcical** *adj.* 1716, in John Gay's *What d'ye Call it,* formed from English *farce* + *-ical.*

fare[1] *n.* cost of conveyance; food provided or eaten. 1120 *fare* journey, developed in Middle English from a blend of Old English *fær* journey, road (strong neuter form of *faran*) and *faru* journey, expedition, companions, baggage (strong feminine form of *faran*). Both forms are recorded in Old English about 1000 and are derived from earlier *faran* to journey; see FARE[2]

Old English *fær* and *faru* are cognate with Old Frisian *fere* journey, Middle Low German *vare,* Middle High German *var,* and Old Icelandic *fǫr* journey or travel and *far* trail or passage.

The meaning of food provided or eaten, is first recorded in Middle English probably before 1200, in Layamon's *Chronicle of Britain,* and that of the cost of conveyance, in Scottish about 1425.

fare[2] *v.* to get along, to eat food. 1100 *faren* to depart, journey, travel; developed from Old English (about 725) *faran* to journey, to make one's way; cognate with Old Saxon, Old High German, and Gothic *faran* to journey, Old Frisian and Old Icelandic *fara* (from Proto-Germanic **faranan*), and Latin *portāre* to carry; see PORT[4] bearing.

The meaning of get along, is first recorded in Old English about 1000, and that of be provided with food, in Middle English about 1350.

farewell *v.phr.* Probably before 1200 *faren wel,* in Layamon's *Chronicle of Britain.* —**interj.** About 1378 *farewel,* in a version of *Piers Plowman.* —**n.** About 1425 *farewele;* but in the OED 1393, in Gower's *Confessio Amantis,* though MED analyzes this as an interjection.

farina (fərē′nə) *n.* flour or meal. Before 1398, in Trevisa's translation of Boethius' *De Proprietatibus Rerum;* borrowed from Latin *farīna* ground corn, flour, meal, from *far* (genitive *farris*) grits, a kind of grain; see BARLEY. —**farinaceous** *adj.* 1646, covered with fine dust; later, resembling meal (1664); borrowed from Latin *farīnāceus,* from *farīna* farina; for suffix see -ACEOUS.

farm *n.* About 1300 *ferme* fixed rent or charge; borrowed from Old French *ferme* lease, from Medieval Latin *firma* fixed payment, from Latin *firmāre* to fix, settle, confirm, strengthen, from *firmus* FIRM. The meaning of tract of leased land, is first recorded in *Rolls of Parliament* (1334). —**v.** 1435 *fermen* to rent (land); borrowed through Anglo-French *fermer,* from Old French *ferme* lease. The sense of cultivate, till, practice farming, is first recorded in Defoe's *Robinson Crusoe* (1719). The archaic sense of rent or lease land, is retained in the phrase *farm out* (to lease, subcontract). —**farmer** *n.* About 1384 *fermour* collector of rents or taxes, in the Wycliffe Bible; borrowed through Anglo-French *fermer,* from Old French *fermier,* from Medieval Latin *firmarius* renter of land, tax collector, from *firma;* see FARM, n. According to the OED, the sense of one who works a farm, is now usually considered to be a formation of English *farm* + *-er*[1], and modern uses may be so regarded rather than coming from the older Middle English word, though this sense is recorded in Middle English as early as 1414, in *Rolls of Parliament.* —**farmhand** *n.* (1843) —**farmhouse** *n.* (1598, in Shakespeare's *Merry Wives of Windsor*) —**farmland** *n.* (about 1350) —**farmstead** *n.* (1807) —**farmyard** *n.* (1748)

faro (fãr′ō) *n.* gambling game. Before 1735 in *faro-table,* apparently an alteration of *Pharaoh,* patterned on French *pharaon* faro. Though the allusion is uncertain, it is probable that one of the cards in this game formerly bore a picture of the Pharaoh, a title given to rulers in ancient Egypt.

farrier (far′ēər) *n.* blacksmith who shoes horses. 1562, borrowed from Middle French *ferrier* blacksmith, from Latin *ferrārius* of iron, (also) blacksmith, from *ferrum* iron, of uncertain origin. *Farrier* replaced Middle English *ferrour* (recorded probably before 1400, and as a surname *Ferrour,* 1297); borrowed from Old French *ferreor,* from Medieval Latin *ferrator* blacksmith, from *ferrare* to bind or shoe with iron, from Latin *ferrum* iron.

farrow *n.* litter of pigs. About 1425 *fare* a young pig, in *Kyng Alisaunder,* developed from Old English (about 700) *faerh,* and corresponding to West Saxon *fearh,* from Proto-Germanic **farHaz;* cognate with Old High German *farah, farhilīn* young pig (modern German *Ferkel*), Middle Dutch *verken* (modern Dutch *varken*) pig, and Latin *porcus* tame swine, pig; see PORK.

The sense of a litter of pigs, is first recorded in 1577, but Shakespeare used the word in the older singular sense, in *Macbeth* (1605).

—**v.** produce a litter of pigs. Probably before 1200 *farwen,* in *Ancrene Riwle;* probably developed from Old English **feargian,* from *fearh* young pig.

farther *adv., adj.* Probably before 1300 *ferther,* in *Sir Tristrem;* variant of FURTHER. The variant *ferther* (probably developed by influence of the common vowel sound in Middle English *ferre, ferrer* (comparative of *ferr* FAR) and the confusion with *fertheren, furtheren* to assist, support, promote, advance. The two forms have been used in all senses, but a notion has grown up that *farther* refers to physical distance and *further* to abstractions of degree or quality. It is generally not maintained except in terms such as *farthermost,* adj. (1618).

farthest *adj., adv.* About 1378 *ferthest,* in a version of *Piers Plowman;* formed in English from *ferther* farther + *-est* superlative suffix (on analogy of *nerer* nearer, *nerest* nearest, and other Middle English forms in *-er*[1]); see FARTHER.

farthing *n.* former British coin worth ¼ of a penny. About 1280 *ferthing;* developed from Old English (about 950) *fēorthung,* a derivative form of *fēortha* fourth (from *fēower* FOUR), and corresponding to Old Frisian *fiārdeng* ¼ of a mark, Middle Low German *vērdink* and Middle High German *vierdinc* one fourth, especially ¼ of a mark, and Old Icelandic *fjōrdhungr* one fourth.

farthingale (fär′ᴛʜinggāl) *n.* hooped petticoat. 1552 *verdynggale,* in Bishop Hugh Latimer's *Sermons;* borrowed from Middle French *verdugale,* an alteration of Spanish *verdugado* farthingale, literally, hooped, from *verdugo* hoop, rod, young shoot of a tree, from *verde* green, from Latin *viridis* green; see VERDANT. The petticoat was so called because it was originally held out by cane hoops or rods inserted underneath. The spelling *farthingale* is first recorded in 1607.

fasces (fas′ēz) *n.pl.* bundle of rods containing an ax with the blade projecting. 1598, borrowed from Latin *fascēs,* plural of *fascis* bundle (of wood, etc.); related to *fascia* band, bandage, fillet, and probably cognate with Macedonian *báskioi* bundle of wood, from Indo-European **bhasko-* (Pok.111).

The fasces carried before superior Roman magistrates as a symbol of power over life and limb was a bundle of sticks bound, with an ax blade projecting at the side (the sticks used in punishment by whipping, the axhead for execution). In modern times fasces were a symbol of the Fascist government in Italy (1922-1943), which built much of its propaganda on a return to the "virtues" of Roman times, hoping fasces would evoke some pride in this heritage.

fascicle (fas′əkəl) *n.* bundle, single part of printed work. Before 1500, bunch or bundle; borrowed from Latin *fasciculus,* diminutive of *fascis* bundle; see FASCES. The meaning of part of a work published in installments, is first recorded in 1647.

A variant form *fascicule,* borrowed from French *fascicule,* from Latin *fasciculus,* has produced several derivatives: *fasciculate, fasciculated, fasciculation,* etc., now used chiefly in botany, zoology, and geology.

fascinate *v.* 1598, put under a spell, in Ben Jonson's *Every Man in His Humor;* borrowed, perhaps through influence of Middle French *fasciner,* from Latin *fascinātus,* past participle of *fascināre* bewitch, enchant, from *fascinus* spell, witchcraft, of uncertain origin. Though Latin *fascinus* may have been borrowed from Greek *báskanos* bewitcher or sorcerer, and its form altered by influence of Latin *fārī* to speak, others feel that the resemblance is accidental; Greek *báskanos* may well have been taken from Thracian **bask-* speak, cognate with Greek *pháskein,* frequentative of *phánai* to speak, from Indo-European **bhā-/bhə-* (Pok.104). The sense of delight, attract, is first recorded in Thomas Moore's romance *Lalla Rookh* (1815). —**fascination** *n.* 1605, casting of a spell, in Francis Bacon's *Of the Advancement of Learning;* borrowed from French *fascination,* learned borrowing from Latin *fascinātiōnem* (nominative *fascinātiō*), from *fascināre* bewitch; for suffix see -ATION.

fascist or **Fascist** *n.* 1921 *Fascist* member of a nationalistic Italian party (formed in 1919) which controlled Italy from 1922 to 1943; borrowed from Italian *Fascista,* n. and adj., from *fascista,* adj., of the group, literally, of the bundle, in reference to the party and fasces which were its symbol, from *fascio* grouping or group, literally, bundle, from Latin *fascis* FASCES + Italian *-ista* -ist.

By 1928 the term was used in reference to any person in any country who supported the ideas of the Fascists.

—**fascism** or **Fascism** *n.* 1922 *Fascism* the principles of the Italian Fascists; borrowed from Italian *Fascismo,* formed on the analogy of such terms in Italian as *Comunismo* Communism, *Comunista* Communist, from *Fasc(ista)* + *-ismo* -ism.

fashion *n.* Probably about 1300 *fasoun* form, shape, appearance, in *The Romance of Sir Beves of Hamtoun;* borrowed from Old French *façon,* from Latin *factiōnem* (nominative *factiō*) a making or doing, from *facere* to make; see the doublet FACTION.

The sense of style, fashion, manner (of dress, etc.), is first recorded probably before 1380.

—**v.** 1413 *fascionen* to shape or form, in Lydgate's writings; from *fasoun,* or later *facioun,* n., fashion, possibly by influence of Middle French *façonner,* from Old French *façon,* v. —**fashionable** *adj.* 1606, in Shakespeare's *Troylus and Cressida;* formed from English *fashion,* n. + *-able.*

fast[1] *adj.* quick; held fast. About 1150 *fast* tightly closed; later, secure (probably before 1200), and firmly fixed (about 1290); developed from Old English *fæst* firmly fixed, steadfast (before 900, in Alfred's translation of Boethius' *De Consolatione Philosophiae*); cognate with Old Frisian *fest* firm or firmly fixed, Old Saxon *fast,* Middle Dutch and modern Dutch *vast,* Old High German *festi* (modern German *fest*), and Old Icelandic *fastr;* probably originally from a Proto-Germanic form **fastuz;* also cognate with Armenian *hast* steadfast, and Sanskrit *pastyá-m* dwelling place, from Indo-European **pasto-* (Pok.789). The sense of quick or swift, is first recorded in Chaucer's *Canterbury Tales* (about 1395); from the earlier adjective sense of vigorous (before 1325, in *Cursor Mundi*) and from the adverb. —**adv.** Before 1175 *feste* securely; later *faste* speedily (probably before 1200); developed from Old English *fæste* tightly, securely (before 900, in Alfred's translation of Boethius). The sense of quickly or swiftly, is first recorded about 975, in one of the *Exeter Riddles,* and developed from the sense of firmly, strongly, vigorously (as in *run fast* run with vigor). A similar semantic development occurred in the adjective, based on that in the adverb.

fast[2] *v.* go without food. Before 1175 *festen;* also *fasten* (probably before 1200); developed from Old English (971) *fæstan* (originally) to fast as a religious duty; cognate with Old Frisian *festia,* Middle Dutch and modern Dutch *vasten,* Old High German *fastēn* (modern German *fasten*), Old Icelandic *fasta* (Swedish *fasta,* Danish and Norwegian *faste*), and Gothic *fastan* keep, guard, observe (a fast); all originally meaning "hold firmly"; see FAST[1]. **—n.** About 1200 *fasten,* developed from Old English *fæstan* (about 1000), earlier *festen* (before 830); and before 1175 *feste;* borrowed probably from a Scandinavian source (compare Old Icelandic *fasta* a fasting).

fasten *v.* About 1125 *festnen* attach or tie to; developed from Old English (before 900) *fæstnian* make fast, firm; cognate with Old Frisian *festnia* to make firm, bind fast, Old Saxon *fastnōn,* Old High German *fastinōn,* and Old Icelandic *fastna* to pledge, betroth (all derived from a Proto-Germanic **fastinōjanan,* from **fastu-* the root of Old English *fæst* FAST[1]); for suffix see -EN[1].

fastidious *adj.* Probably before 1425, disdainful or haughty, in a translation of Higden's *Polychronicon;* borrowed from Latin *fastīdiōsus* disdainful, squeamish, exacting, from *fastīdium* loathing, almost certainly formed by contraction from pre-Latin **fastu-taidiom,* a compound of *fastus* contempt or arrogance, and *taedium* aversion or disgust; see TEDIUM. Latin *fastus* appears to be related to *fastīgium* top, peak; see BRISTLE.

Alternatively, the word may have been borrowed into English from Middle French *fastidieux,* learned borrowing from Latin *fastīdiōsus.* The sense of easily disgusted, hard to please, is first recorded in English in 1612-15.

fat *adj.* Probably about 1200 *fatt,* in *The Ormulum;* developed from Old English *fǣtt* (originally) past participle of *fǣtan* to cram, stuff (before 900, in Alfred's translation of Orosius' *Historiarum Adversus Paganos*). The Old English is cognate with Old Frisian *fatt* fat, Old Saxon *feit,* Middle Low German *vet* (modern German *fett*), Old High German *feiz* (modern German *feist*), and Old Icelandic *feitr* (Norwegian *feit,* Swedish *fet,* Danish *fed*). The word is probably also cognate with Latin *opīmus* fat, fertile, Greek *pîar* fat, tallow, *pīdýein* gush forth, *pîdax* fountain, *pīmelḗ* fat, Lithuanian *píenas* milk, and Sanskrit *páyate* it swells, abounds, *pívas* fat, grease, from Indo-European **pei-*/*poi*/*pi-* (Pok.793). **—n.** About 1350; from the adjective. **—fatten** *v.* 1552, formed from English *fat,* adj. + *-en*[1], replacing earlier *fat,* v. (coincidentally in Middle English *fatten*), developed from Old English *fǣttian* (about 1000), from which is retained *fatted calf* in the now largely biblical phrase and literary *kill the fatted calf.*

fatal *adj.* About 1380, destined, fated, in Chaucer's translation of Boethius' *De Consolatione Philosophiae;* borrowed through Old French *fatal,* or directly from Latin *fātālis,* from *fātum* FATE; for suffix see -AL[1]. The sense of causing death, is first recorded in Lydgate's *Troy Book* (before 1420). —**fatalism** *n.* 1678, belief that fate controls everything that happens; formed from English *fatal* + *-ism.* The meaning of acceptance of everything that happens, is first recorded before 1734. **—fatalist** *n.* 1650, formed from English *fatal* + *-ist,* perhaps after Middle French *fataliste.* **—fatalistic** *adj.* 1832, in Coleridge's *Table Talk;* formed from English *fatalist* + *-ic.* **—fatality** *n.* 1490, in Caxton's translation of *How to Die,* borrowed from Middle French *fatalité,* learned borrowing from Late Latin *fātālitātem* (nominative *fātālitās*), from Latin *fātālis* fatal; for suffix see -ITY.

fate *n.* About 1385, lot or destiny of a person, in Chaucer's *Troilus and Criseyde;* borrowed through Old French *fat* fate, destiny, or directly from Latin *fātum* thing spoken (by the gods), one's destiny, from neuter past participle of *fārī* speak; see BAN[1] forbid. The sense of power supposed to control what happens, is first recorded in 1410. **—fateful** *adj.* 1715-20, in Pope's translation of Homer's *Iliad;* formed from English *fate* + *-ful.*

father *n.* Probably about 1175 *fader;* later *father* (before 1464, in the compound *fatherhod*) and *fađer* (before 1250, in *Bestiary,* a spelling reflecting this later pronunciation); developed from Old English (about 825) *fæder.* Another one of the classic words of Indo-European etymology (see *brother, mother,* etc.) whose cognates have been traced in a wide variety of languages, including the Germanic group of Old Frisian *feder* father, Old Saxon *fadar,* Middle Dutch *vader* (modern Dutch *vader*), Old High German *fater* (modern German *Vater*), Old Icelandic *fadhir* (Swedish, Danish, Norwegian *fader, far*), and Gothic *fadar,* from Proto-Germanic **fađḗr.* Outside Germanic cognates appear in Celtic with Old Irish *athir* (genitive *athar*) father; in Italic with Latin *pater,* and Oscan *patir;* in Hellenic with Greek *patḗr;* in Indo-Iranian with Sanskrit *pitár-* and Avestan *pitar-,* Persian *pidhar,* and Tocharian A *pācer,* Tocharian B *pācer,* from Indo-European *pətḗ(r)* (Pok.829). **—v.** Before 1425 *faderen, fadren* be or become the father of, beget; from the noun.

The modern spelling *-ther* (-ᴛʜər) for Middle and Old English *-der* became widespread in the 1500's as a result of a phonetic development common to most English dialects, seen also in such words as *gather, together, weather.* But even while the spelling was still with *d,* the pronunciation with (ᴛʜ) may have been widely current, especially by the 1400's.

—fatherhood *n.* (before 1325 *faderhade;* later *fatherhod,* before 1464). **—fatherland** *n.* (1101 *fæder land*). **—fatherless** *adj.* (1198, in the surname *Faderles,* Old English *fæderlēas*). **—fatherly** *adj.* Before 1420 *faderly,* Old English (before 1000) *fæderlīc; adv.* before 1400.

fathom *n.* unit of measure. Before 1175 *fethme;* later *fathom* (1381-82); developed from Old English (before 800) *fæthm* length of the outstretched arms, grasp, and earlier in a figurative sense of grasp or power (about 725, in *Beowulf*). The Old English term is cognate among the Germanic languages with Old Frisian *fethem* thread, Old Saxon *fathmos* outstretched arms, Middle Dutch *vādem* fathom (modern Dutch *vadem*), Old High German *fadam, fadum* thread (modern German *Faden* thread, fathom), and Old Icelandic *fadhmr* embrace, measure of length, thread (Danish, Norwegian *favn* fathom, embrace, Swedish *famn* fathom, arms), from Proto-Germanic **fathmaz.* In the Celtic languages it is cognate with Scottish-Gaelic *aitheamh* thread, Old Welsh *etem;* in the Italic languages with Latin *patēre* be open, *pandere* spread out; in the Hellenic group with Greek *petannýnai* spread out; in the Baltic group with Lithuanian *petỹs* shoulder, Old Prussian *pettis* shoulder blade; in the Indo-Iranic languages with Avestan *pathana-* wide, broad, and Hittite *pattar* (dative *paddani*) a tray, tablet, etc., from Indo-European **pet-*/*pot-* spread out (Pok.824). **—v.** About 1300 *fadmen;* later *fathmen* to embrace (probably about 1380); developed from Old English *fæthmian* encircle with outstretched arms, embrace (about 725, in *Beowulf*). The term is cognate with Old High German *fademōn* to embrace, and Old Icelandic *fadhma* (Danish *favne,* Swedish *famna*), all derived from the Proto-Germanic **fathmōjanan,* from **fathmaz.*

The figurative sense of get to the bottom of or understand fully, is first recorded in 1625, from the literal sense of to take soundings (1607).

fatigue *n.* 1669, borrowed from French *fatigue* weariness, from *fatiguer* to tire, learned borrowing from Latin *fatīgāre,* (originally) to cause to break down, (later) to tire out, formed from a pre-Latin adjective **fati-agos* driving to the point of breakdown, from Old Latin **fatis* (in Plautus, *ad fatim* to bursting) and the root of *agere* drive; related to *fatīscī* crack, split, of unknown origin.

From the sense of a soldier's nonmilitary duties (1776), the term *fatigues* (clothes for nonmilitary work) appeared in 1836.

—v. 1693, borrowed from French *fatiguer.* **—fatigued** *adj.* 1791, in William Cowper's translation of Homer's *Iliad;* a reappearance formed from English *fatigue,* v., but first recorded as a past participle *fatigate* (probably before 1425, in a translation of Higden's *Polychronicon*); borrowed from Latin *fatīgātus,* past participle of *fatīgāre* to tire out.

fatuous (fach'ùəs) *adj.* stupid, foolish. 1608, tasteless or insipid; later, stupid but self-satisfied, foolish, silly (1633); borrowed, possibly through Italian *fatuo,* and directly from Latin *fatuus* foolish, silly, insipid, of uncertain origin; for suffix see -OUS.

faucet *n.* Probably before 1400, tap or spigot, in *Morte Arthur;* borrowed from Old French *fausset* stopper, plug for a cask, from *fausser* to damage, break into, pierce, earlier *falser* to break or bend, from Late Latin *falsāre* to corrupt, falsify, from Latin *falsus* FALSE.

fault *n.* About 1280 *faute* deficiency, lack, scarcity; borrowed from Old French *faute, faulte,* from Vulgar Latin **fallita* a shortcoming, falling, noun use of feminine past participle, replacing Latin *falsus,* past participle of *fallere* deceive, disappoint; see FALSE. The meaning of a defect or imperfection, is first recorded probably before 1350.

The Middle English spelling *faute* gradually changed to *faulte* in the 1400's, probably by influence of some French writers who inserted the *l* into Old French *faute* in an effort to restore the Latin form. By the 1600's *fault* was the standard spelling though the *l* was not pronounced (in Pope and Swift the word rhymes with *thought*), and according to Johnson in 1755 the sound represented by *l* was not heard in conversation. **—v.** About 1375 (Scottish) *fawt* be deficient; from the noun. The sense of to blame, find fault with, is first recorded about 1450. **—faulty** *adj.* Probably about 1380 *fauty;* formed from Middle English *faute* + *-y*[1].

faun *n.* a minor rustic god in Roman myths. About 1385 *fawn,* in Chaucer's *Canterbury Tales;* borrowed from Latin *Faunus,* name of one of various gods of the countryside, especially some regarded as bogies or goblins.

fauna (fô'nə) *n.* animals of a given region or time. 1771, New Latin *fauna,* from Late Latin *Fauna,* name of a Roman fertility goddess who was the wife, sister, or daughter of *Faunus* FAUN.

The word was popularized in the natural sciences after Linnaeus used it in the title of his work *Fauna Suecica* Swedish Fauna (1746), a companion volume to his *Flora Suecica* (1745).

faux pas (fō' pä') slip in speech, manners, etc. 1674, in Wycherley's *The Plain-Dealer,* borrowing of French *faux pas,* literally, false step. In contemporary French, *gaffe* is used in this sense. See PACE.

favor *n.* Probably before 1300 *favour* attractiveness, charm, in *Kyng Alisaunder;* later, act of kindness (about 1380, in Chaucer's *Parlement of Foules*); borrowed from Old French *favor,* from Latin *favōrem* (nominative *favor*) good will or support, from *favēre* show kindness to. Latin *favēre* (pre-Latin **fovēre*) is cognate with Old Slavic *gověti* to honor, revere, and probably with Gothic *gaumjan* to notice, Old High German *goumen* care for, and Old Icelandic *gā* to heed, from Indo-European **ghou-* notice, pay heed to (Pok.453). **—v.** About 1350 *favuren* approve, support, favor; borrowed from Old French *favorer,* from Old French *favor,* n. **—favorable** *adj.* Before 1376 *faverable,* in *Piers Plowman;* borrowed from Old French *favorable,* from Latin *favōrābilis,* from Latin *favor,* n.; for suffix see -ABLE. **—favorite** *n.* 1583, borrowed from Middle French *favorit* (feminine *favorite*), from Italian *favorito* a favorite, also past participle of *favorire* to favor, support, from *favore* favor, from Latin *favōrem* (nominative *favor*). **—favorite son** 1825, in American English, political candidate supported by his native region, especially a candidate at the party convention. **—favoritism** *n.* 1763, formed from English *favorite* + *-ism.*

fawn[1] *n.* young deer. Before 1338 *fowen,* in Mannyng's *Chronicle of England;* later *fawne* (before 1425); borrowed from Old French *faon* young animal, from Vulgar Latin **fētōnem,* accusative of **fētō,* from Latin *fētus* FETUS.

fawn[2] *v.* cringe and bow, act slavishly. About 1225 *fahenen* to court favor, grovel, in *Ancrene Riwle;* developed from Old English *fagnian* rejoice, from *fagen,* variant of *fægen* glad, FAIN.

The word was widely used in Middle English to refer to expressions of delight, such as a dog's wagging its tail.

fay *n.* fairy. About 1390 *fey* person or place having magical powers; borrowed from Old French *fae, fée,* fairy, from Vulgar Latin *fāta* goddess of fate (recorded in inscriptions), from Latin *fātum* FATE, one of three Roman goddesses who controlled human life.

faze *v.* disturb. 1830, in American English, a dialectal variant of earlier *feeze;* found in Middle English *fesen* frighten, drive away, discomfit (probably before 1325), from Old English (about 890) *fēsian, fȳsian* send forth, drive away, and corresponding to Swedish *fösa* drive away, and Norwegian *föysa,* from Proto-Germanic **fausjanan,* of unknown origin.

fealty *n.* loyalty owed by a vassal to his feudal lord. Probably before 1300 *feute,* in *Kyng Alisaunder;* later *fealtye* (probably before 1425); borrowed from Old French *feaulté, fealté,* from Latin *fidēlitātem* (nominative *fidēlitās*) fidelity, from *fidēlis* loyal, faithful; for suffix see -TY[2]. See the doublet FIDELITY. The general or transferred sense of loyalty, faithfulness, is first recorded about 1530.

fear *n.* Probably about 1280 *fere;* later *feere* (about 1375, in Chaucer's *Canterbury Tales*); developed from late Old English *fǣr* uneasiness caused by possible danger; earlier, danger or peril (about 725, in *Beowulf*). Old English *fǣr* is cognate with Old Saxon *fār* ambush, danger, Middle Dutch *vaer* (modern Dutch *gevaar* danger), Old High German *fāra,* Middle High German *gevǣre* danger (modern German *Gefahr*), Old Icelandic *fār* misfortune, plague, from Proto-Germanic **fǣra-,* and the Gothic derivative form *fērja* one who lies in wait, observer, spy; cognate also with Latin *perītus* experienced, *experīrī* to try, *perīculum* an attempt, danger, Greek *peîra* (pre-Greek **pérya*) trial, proof, from Indo-European **per-/pēr-* try (Pok.818). —**v.** About 1225 *fearen* (occurring once), in *Ancrene Riwle,* but generally found in the spelling *feren*) to frighten or terrify; developed from Old English *fǣran* terrify, frighten (about 1000, in Ælfric's translation of *Deuteronomy*), from *fǣr* danger. The sense of feel fear, is first recorded probably about 1390, in *Sir Gawain and the Green Knight.* The modern spelling was not established before the 1500's. —**fearful** *adj.* About 1350 *ferefull* causing terror, terrible, formed from Middle English *fere* fear + *-full* -ful.

feasible *adj.* 1443 *faisible* capable of being done, in *Proceedings of the Privy Council;* later *feseable* (before 1475); borrowed through Anglo-French *faisible,* Middle French *faisible, faisable,* from *fais-,* stem of *faire* do, make, from Latin *facere* DO[1] perform; for suffix see -IBLE. The modern spelling with *ea* is first recorded in 1614. —**feasibility** *n.* 1624; formed from English *feasible* + *-ity.*

feast *n.* Probably before 1200 *feste, feaste* feast, banquet, rejoicing, in *Ancrene Riwle;* borrowed from Old French *feste* festival, feast, from Vulgar Latin **festa* (feminine singular), from Latin *fēsta* holidays, feasts, from neuter plural of *fēstus* festive, joyous, related to *fēriae* holiday, and *fānum* temple (pre-Latin **fasnem*), from Indo-European **dhēs-/dhəs-* holy (Pok.259). —**v.** Probably before 1300 *festen,* in *Kyng Alisaunder;* borrowed from Old French *fester,* from *feste* feast.

The spelling with *ea* developed among scribes particularly in the late Middle English period as as a device to represent the sound of so-called long *e,* especially before consonants in monosyllables with no terminal vowel, and is found with increasing consistency from then on.

feat *n.* Before 1376 *fet, fait* action or deed; borrowed through Anglo-French *fet,* Old French *fet, fait,* from Latin *factum* thing done; see the doublet FACT. For spelling in *ea* see FEAST. The sense of an exceptional or noble deed, is first recorded probably before 1400, originally often in the phrase *feat of arms,* after Old French *fait d'armes.*

feather *n.* 1280, in compound *fethermongere,* also with old spelling *feđer* (about 1150); found in Old English *fether* wing, feather (about 725, in *Genesis A*). The Old English is cognate with Old Saxon *fethera* feather, Middle Dutch *vēdere* (modern Dutch *veder, veer*), Old High German *fedara* (modern German *Feder*), and Old Icelandic *fjǫdhr* (Swedish *fjäder,* Danish *fjeder*), from Proto-Germanic **fethrō.* Outside Germanic cognates appear in Old Welsh *eterin* bird, Latin *petere* to go to, rush at, seek, *penna* feather, Greek *pterón* feather, wing, *pétesthai* to fly, *píptein* to fall, Armenian *t'ir* flight, Sanskrit *pátra-m* wing, feather, *pátati* he flies, falls, and Hittite *pattar* wing, from Indo-European **pet-/pot-/pt-* (Pok.825). For spelling with *ea* see FEAST. —**v.** Probably before 1300 *fetheren* grow feathers, in *Kyng Alisaunder* (also found with a variant spelling about 1250 in a version of *Ancrene Riwle*); developed from Old English *gefitherian* furnish with feathers (in Alfred's translation of Boethius' *De Consolatione Philosophiae*), from *fether,* n. —**feather bed** 1369 *fether-bed,* in Chaucer's *Book of the Duchesse,* also with old spelling *fether* (about 1300, in Layamon's *Chronicle of Britain*), developed from Old English *fetherbed* (about 1000, in Ælfric's *Glossary*). —**featherless** *adj.* Probably about 1400, formed from Middle English *fether* feather + *-les* -less. —**featherweight** *n.* 1838, in Dicken's *Oliver Twist.* The meaning of a boxer in the lightest weight category, is first recorded in 1889. —**feathery** *adj.* 1580, formed from English *feather* + *-y*[1].

feature *n.* About 1375 *feture* something created in a particular shape or form; also features of the face (1378, in a version of *Piers Plowman*); borrowed through Anglo-French *feture,* Old French *feture, faiture,* from Latin *factūra* a formation, from *facere* make, DO[1] perform; for suffix see -URE. The meaning of characteristic or distinctive part, is first recorded in Dryden's translation of *Saint-Evremond's Miscellaneous Essays* (1692). For spelling in *ea* see FEAST. —**v.** 1755, in Johnson's *Dictionary,* to resemble; from the noun, but implied in earlier *fetured* (before 1420, in the phrase *wel fetured* well built, handsome). The meaning of make a special display or attraction of, is first recorded in American English, in 1888.

febrile (fē'brəl) *adj.* of fever, feverish. 1651; borrowed through French *fébrile,* or directly from Medieval Latin *febrilis,* from Latin *febris* a fever; see FEVER.

February *n.* 1373 *februare* (but originally recorded before 1150, perhaps in Old English *Februarius*); borrowing of Latin *februārius* in *februārius mēnsis* month of purification, in reference to the Roman feast of purification, held in February (the last month of the ancient Roman calendar, and after 450 B.C. becoming the second month, for which the Old English name was *solmōnath,* literally, mud month).

English *February* was a replacement of earlier *feoverel* (about 1225) and *feoverrer* (about 1200); borrowed from Old French *fevriel, fevrier,* from Latin *februārius.* The alternation of *r* and *l* occurred regularly in Old French, an influence probably carried over into Middle English in the forms *laurel* and *laurer,* and reinforced by analogy of *averel* April.

feces *n.pl.* Before 1400 *fecis,* pl., excrement, in a translation of Lanfranc's *Science of Surgery;* later *fecez,* pl. (probably before 1425, in Chauliac's *Grande Chirurgie*); borrowed from Latin *faecēs* sediment or dregs, plural of *faex* (genitive *faecis*), of unknown origin.

feckless *adj.* ineffective, futile. 1599, formed in English from earlier *feck, fek* effect, value, vigor (a meaning occurring about 1500, in the Scottish shortened form of EFFECT) + the suffix *-less.*

fecund (fek'ənd) *adj.* fruitful. About 1425 *fecounde,* 1450 *fecunde;* borrowed from Old French *fecond,* learned borrowing from Latin, and borrowed directly from Latin *fēcundus;* see FEMININE. —**fecundity** *n.* Probably about 1425 *fecundite;* borrowed from Old French *fecondité,* learned borrowing from Latin, and borrowed directly from Latin *fēcunditātem* (nominative *fēcunditās*) fruitfulness, from *fēcundus* fecund.

federal *adj.* 1645 *foederal* pertaining to or based on a treaty, especially a covenant between God and an individual; formed in English from Latin *foedus* covenant, league (genitive *foederis;* related to *fidēs* FAITH) + English *-al*[1]. The Anglicized spelling *federal* is first recorded in 1737 (earlier than French *fédéral,* 1789).

The sense of relating to a government comprising independent states is first recorded in 1707 (in a speech before the Scottish Parliament), and it arose, according to the OED, from the context of phrases such as *federal union,* in which *federal* refers to the earliest sense of a treaty; therefore, a union based on a treaty. **—federalism** *n.* 1789 *Federalism* (in a debate of the U.S. Senate); formed from English *federal* + *-ism.* **—Federalist** *n.* 1787, American English, in Madison's *The Federalist No. 10,* and in George Washington's writings; formed from English *federal* + *-ist.*

federate *v.* 1837, in Carlyle's *The French Revolution,* from English *federate,* adj., allied or united (1710); borrowed from Latin *foederātus* having a treaty, bound by treaty, from *foedus* (genitive *foederis*) covenant; see FEDERAL; for suffix see -ATE[1]. In some instances *federate,* v., may also be a back formation from earlier *federation.* **—federation** *n.* 1721, in Bailey's *Dictionary,* union by agreement, league; borrowed from Late Latin *foederātiōnem* (nominative *foederātiō*), from Latin *foederāre* league together; for suffix see -ATION.

fedora *n.* soft felt hat. 1895, American English, in allusion to *Fédora,* a play that became popular in the United States after 1883. The part of the heroine, a Russian princess named *Fédora* Romanoff, was originally performed by Sarah Bernhardt.

fee *n.* Probably before 1300 *fe* estate held in tenure to a feudal lord, in *Kyng Alisaunder* and *Arthour and Merlin;* borrowed through Anglo-French *fee,* Old French *fié,* both the Anglo-French and Old French forms are variants of Old French *fieu, fief,* from Gallo-Romance *feudum* (also found in Medieval Latin *feudum, feodum*), from Frankish **fehu-ōd* payment-estate. For the first element (**fehu-*) of the compound compare the native, and now obsolete, *fee,* with the meaning of livestock, movable property, money, that is found in Old English *feoh* money, property, cattle, Old Saxon *fehu,* Old Frisian *fiā,* Old High German *fihu* (modern German *Vieh* cattle), Old Icelandic *fē* (Danish *fæ,* Swedish *fä*), and Gothic *faíhu,* from Proto-Germanic **feHu.* These Germanic forms are cognate with a wide variety of forms outside Germanic, but only a few have semantic relationship including Latin *pecus* cattle, *pecūnia* money, property, Old Prussian *pecku* cattle, and Sanskrit *paśú-s* cattle, from Indo-European **peḱu-* (Pok.797). For the second element *(-ōd)* of the compound, compare Old English *ēad* wealth, Old Saxon *ōd,* Old Icelandic *audhr,* and Gothic *auda-,* from Indo-European **audh-* (Pok.76).

The meaning of a payment for professional services, is first recorded in Middle English, in Chaucer's *Prologue* to the *Canterbury Tales* (1387-95).

feeble *adj.* Probably before 1200 *feble* lacking strength, weak, in *Ancrene Riwle;* borrowed from Old French *fieble, foible* weak, *fleible* (with loss of *l* in later forms by dissimilation), from Latin *flēbilis* lamentable, that is to be wept over, from *flēre* weep, cognate with Lettish *blêt* to bleat, Old English *blǣtan,* from Indo-European **bhlē-* (Pok.154). Doublet of FOIBLE. The spelling *feeble* is first recorded probably before 1439, but did not become established until the 1500's. **—feeble-minded** *adj.* 1534, in the Tyndale Bible, replacing earlier *feeble-witted* (about 1385).

feed *v.* About 1125 feden, developed from Old English *fēdan* nourish, feed (about 725, in *Genesis A*); cognate with Old Frisian *fēda* to feed, Old Saxon *fōdian,* Dutch *voeden,* Old High German *fuoten,* Old Icelandic *foedha* (Swedish *föda,* Danish and Norwegian *føde*), and Gothic *fōdjan,* from Proto-Germanic **fōđijanan;* see FOOD. The spelling *feed* is first recorded about 1385, and became established after 1550. **—n.** 1573, right to graze; from the verb. The sense of food for animals is first recorded in Shakespeare's *Titus Andronicus* (1588). **—feed-back** *n.* (1920) **—feeder** *n.* (before 1398)

feel *v.* Probably before 1200 *felen,* developed from Old English *fēlan* to feel (before 900 in Alfred's translation of Orosius' *Historiarum Adversus Paganos*); cognate with Old Frisian *fēla* to feel, Old Saxon *fōlian,* Middle and modern Dutch *voelen,* Old High German *fuolen* (modern German *fühlen*), from Proto-Germanic **fōlijanan.* The term is also cognate with Latin *palpāre* to feel, stroke, *pellere* set in motion with a push, and Greek *pállein* to shake, from Indo-European **pel-/pol-/pōl-* (Pok.801). **—n.** About 1225 *fele* sensation, understanding; from the verb in Middle English. **—feeler** *n.* 1435, formed from Middle English *felen,* v. + *-er*[1]; *n.pl.* 1665, special part of an animal's body for touching. **—feeling** *n.* Probably before 1200 *felunge* act of touching or sense of touch, in *Ancrene Riwle;* formed from *felen* to feel + *-unge* -ing[1]. The meaning of an emotion of joy, sorrow, etc., is first recorded in Chaucer's *Book of the Duchesse* (1369). **—feelings** *n.pl.* 1771, tender or sensitive side of one's nature; from the noun singular.

feign (fān) *v.* pretend. About 1300 *feinen;* borrowed from Old French *feign-,* stem of *feindre,* from Latin *fingere* devise, fabricate, shape, form; see DOUGH. The introduction of *g* into the spelling of Middle English *feinen,* was an imitation of the original French.

feint (fānt) *n.* false appearance. 1679, borrowed from French *feinte* a feint, sham, pretense, from Old French *feint,* (originally) feminine past participle of *feindre* FEIGN. The noun appeared earlier, in the phrase *with feint* falsely, hypocritically (before 1325, in *Cursor Mundi*) as a formation in Middle English from *feint,* adj., in which it was partially confused in spelling with *faint,* adj. The adjective *feint* deceitful, hypocritical (about 1290, borrowed from Old French *feint, faint,* past participle of *feindre*) is now rare or obsolete in English. **—v.** 1833, to make a sham attack, from the noun in English; but the obsolete sense of deceive, is recorded probably about 1300, either from the adjective or borrowed from Old French *feint,* past participle of *feindre.*

feisty *adj.* spirited, excitable, aggressive. 1896, dialectal American English, from *feist* small dog + *-y*[1]. The form *feist* is from earlier dialectal American English *fice, fist* small dog (1805), a shortened form of *fysting curre* stinking cur (1529), from Middle English *fysten, fisten* break wind (1440), and related to Old English *fisting* stink.

feldspar *n.* crystalline mineral. 1785, alteration of earlier *feldspath* (1757); borrowed from German *Feldspath* (now *Feldspat*), a compound of *Feld* field and *Spath* spar. The shift in spelling was influenced by English *spar*[3] mineral.

felicitate *v.* congratulate. 1628, make happy; probably developed from earlier *felicitate* (1605, in Shakespeare's *King Lear*); borrowed from Late Latin *fēlīcitātus,* past participle of *fēlīcitāre* to make happy, from Latin *fēlīx* (genitive *fēlīcis*) happy, fortunate; for suffix see -ATE[1]. The sense of congratulate, is first recorded in English in 1634. It is probable that earlier *felicity* had some effect on the formation of the participial adjective and verb in English. **—felicitation** *n.* 1709, formed from English *felicitate* + *-ion,* probably by influence of French *félicitation.* **—felicitous** *adj.* apt; suited. 1789, formed from English *felicity* + *-ous.*

—**felicity** *n.* happiness. About 1375 *felicitee,* in Chaucer's *Canterbury Tales;* borrowed from Old French *felicité,* learned borrowing from Latin *fēlīcitātem* (nominative *fēlīcitās*) happiness, from *fēlīx* happy, fortunate; for suffix see -ITY.

feline (fē'līn) *adj.* of or like a cat. 1681, borrowed from Late Latin *fēlīnus* of or belonging to a cat, from Latin *fēles* (genitive *fēlis*) cat, wild cat, marten, of uncertain origin; for suffix see -INE[1].

fell[1] *v.* cause to fall, knock down. Probably before 1200 *fellen, feollen, fallen,* in Layamon's *Chronicle of Britain;* developed from Old English *fællan, fellan* make fall, demolish, kill (before 800, in Mercian dialect, corresponding to West Saxon *fyllan*); cognate with Old Frisian *falla, fella* to fell, Old Saxon *fellian,* Old High German *fellen* (modern German *fällen*), and Old Icelandic *fella,* from Proto-Germanic **fallijanan;* see FALL.

fell[2] *adj.* cruel, fierce, terrible. About 1300; borrowed from Old French *fel* cruel, fierce, from Medieval Latin *fello* villain, FELON.

fell[3] *n.* skin or hide of an animal. About 1150 *felle,* developed from Old English *fel, fell* skin, hide (about 725, in *Beowulf*); cognate with Old Frisian *fel* skin, hide, Old Saxon *fel,* Middle and modern Dutch *vel,* Old High German *fell* skin (modern German *Fell*), Old Icelandic *fell,* Gothic *-fill* in *thrūtsfill* leprosy, and Latin *pellis* skin; see FILM.

felloe (fel'ō) or **felly** *n.* outer rim of a wheel. 1411 *felowes,* pl., variant of earlier *felie* (probably about 1200); developed from Old English *felga,* plural of *felg* rim of a wheel (before 899, in Alfred's translation of Boethius' *De Consolatione Philosophiae*); cognate with Old Saxon and Old High German *felga* felloe, harrow (modern German *Felge*), from Proto-Germanic **felʒ-,* from Indo European **pelḱ-/polḱ-* to turn (Pok.807).

fellow *n.* About 1250 *felawe;* earlier *feolahe* companion (probably before 1200, in *Ancrene Riwle*); developed from Old English *fēolaga* partner (1016, in the *Anglo-Saxon Chronicle*); borrowed from a Scandinavian source; compare Old Icelandic *fēlagi* comrade, partner, shareholder, literally, fee layer, one who lays down money in a joint undertaking (*fē* property, money, see FEE + *-lagi,* combining form of *leggja* to LAY[1] set down). —**fellowship** *n.* Probably before 1200 *feolahschipe* companionship, in *Ancrene Riwle;* formed from Middle English *feolah* fellow + *-schipe* -ship.

felon *n.* person who has committed a serious crime. About 1300 *felon, feloun;* from *feloun, felun,* adj., savage, cruel, wicked (now rare or obsolete in English); borrowed from Old French *felon,* n., a wicked person, traitor, rebel, and *felon,* adj., wicked, malignant, from Medieval Latin *fellonem,* from Frankish **fillo, *filljo* person who whips or beats, scourger (compare Old High German *fillen* to flail or scourge, Old Frisian *filla,* Middle and modern Dutch *villen* to flay, fleece, skin, a verb formed from the noun FELL[3] skin). —**felonious** *adj.* 1575, either formed from English *felony* + *-ous,* or a back formation from *feloniously,* adv. (1447-48, probably formed in English from Middle French *felonieus* + *-ly,* not *-liche,* as might be expected). By about 1600 *felonious* had replaced earlier *felonous* (recorded before 1338). —**felony** *n.* About 1290 *felonie* treachery, villainy, crime; borrowed from Old French *felonie,* from *felon,* n., wicked person, traitor; see FELON.

felt *n.* type of cloth made by pressing together wool, etc. Old English *felt* (about 1000, in Ælfric's *Glossary*); cognate with Old Saxon *filt* felt and Old High German *filz* (modern German *Filz*), from Proto-Germanic **peltaz, *peltiz,* Indo-European **peldos, *peldis,* root **pel-* strike (Pok.801).

female *n.* Before 1333 *femele;* borrowed from Old French *femelle,* from Medieval Latin *femella* a female, from Latin *fēmella* young female, girl, a diminutive form of *fēmina* woman; see FEMININE. The spelling *female* is first recorded in 1373, formed by popular etymology on the analogy of *male.* —**adj.** 1382, in the Wycliffe Bible; borrowed from Old French *femelle,* from Medieval Latin *femella* of a female, from *femella,* n.

feminine *adj.* Probably about 1350 *femynyn,* referring to grammatical gender; later, female (in Chaucer's *House of Fame,* about 1380); borrowed from Old French *feminin, feminine,* learned borrowing from Latin *fēminīnus* feminine (in the grammatical sense), from *fēmina* woman, female (Latin base *fē-* to suck, suckle, also found in Latin *fēlāre* to suck, *fīlius* son, *fīlia* daughter, originally suckling, and with *fētus* offspring or fetus; cognate with Sanskrit *dháyati* sucks, Greek *thēsato* he sucked, from Indo-European *dhēi-/dhəi-,* Pok.241). —**femininity** *n.* About 1390 *femynynytee,* in Chaucer's *Canterbury Tales;* formed from Middle English *femynyne* feminine + *-ity.* —**feminism** *n.* 1851, state of being feminine; later, advocacy of women's rights (1895); borrowed from French *féminisme* (1837), formed from Latin *fēmina* woman + French *-isme* -ism. —**feminist** *n.* 1894, borrowed from French *féministe* (1872), from *féminisme* + *-iste* -ist.

femme (fem) *n.* woman. 1814, in Byron's *Journals;* borrowing of French *femme* woman, from Latin *fēmina;* see FEMININE. —**femme fatale** (fàm' fàtàl') dangerously seductive woman. 1912, in letters of George Bernard Shaw; borrowing of French *femme fatale.*

femto- a combining form meaning one quadrillionth (10^{-15}), as in *femtometer* (one quadrillionth of a meter). 1961, borrowed from Danish or Norwegian *femten* fifteen (with connective *-o-*); compare Old Icelandic *fimtān* FIFTEEN.

femur (fē'mər) *n.* 1563, as a term in architecture; later, thighbone (1799); borrowing of Latin *femur* thigh, of uncertain origin. —**femoral** (fem'ərəl) *adj.* 1782, formed in English from Latin *femoris* (genitive of *femur* thigh) + English *-al*[1].

fen *n.* marsh, swamp. Before 1121, developed from Old English *fen, fenn* marsh, dirt, mud (about 725, in *Beowulf*); cognate with Old Frisian *fene, fenne* marsh, swamp, Old Saxon *feni,* Middle Dutch *venne* (modern Dutch *veen*), Old High German *fenna* (modern German *Fenn*), Old Icelandic *fen* quagmire, and Gothic *fani* clay, mud, from Proto-Germanic **fanja-;* cognate outside Germanic with Middle Irish *enach* swamp, Old Prussian *pannean* marsh, and Sanskrit *pánka-s* marsh, mud, from Indo-European **pen-/pon-* (Pok.807).

fence *n.* Before 1338 *fens* action of defending, in Mannyng's *Chronicle of England,* a shortened form of *defens* defense; see DEFENSE. The meaning of enclosure or barrier, is first recorded in *The Paston Letters* (1461). —**v.** 1435, surround with or as with a fence; from the noun. The meaning of use a sword for defense or offense, is first recorded in Shakespeare's *Merry Wives of Windsor* (1598), and developed from the earlier sense of defend oneself or fight with weapons (about 1410, in Lovelich's *History of the Holy Grail*).

—fencer *n.* 1581, formed from English *fence,* v. + *-er*[1]. **—fencing** *n.* 1462, the act of protecting; later, an enclosure (1585) and the materials for an enclosure (1856, in American English). The spelling varied from *c* to *s* in Middle English and became fixed in the later 1500's, though occasionally derivative forms appear with *s* into the mid-1600's.

fend *v.* make an effort. Probably before 1300, in *Arthour and Merlin,* shortened form of DEFEND. The phrase *fend off* ward or keep off, is first recorded about 1380, and the expression *fend for oneself,* in 1629. It is probable that *fend* appeared before 1279, as the derivative *fender* defender, and is recorded at that time.

fender *n.* About 1350 *fendour* defender; earlier as a surname *Fendur* (1279); probably formed from Middle English *fend* + *-er*[1]. The general sense of something that protects by keeping other things off, is first recorded in English in 1615, but the meaning of a boat fender protecting the hull from rubbing a wharf, etc., is first recorded in 1294-95 in a list of Middle English sea terms. Application of the term to automobiles is found first in American English in Sinclair Lewis' *Free Air* (1919).

fennel *n.* plant used in cooking and medicine. Probably before 1300 *fenel,* developed from Old English *fenol* (about 1000, in Ælfric's *Glossary*), a form possibly influenced by Old French *fenoil,* and from Old English *finugl* (about 700); both Old English and Old French were borrowed from Vulgar Latin *fēnuculum,* corresponding to Latin *fēniculum,* from *fēnum* hay (appearing in the overcorrected form *faenum*); apparently so called from its haylike appearance and sweet odor.

feral (fir'əl) *adj.* wild, savage. 1604, probably borrowed from Middle French *feral* wild, from Latin *fera,* in *fera bēstia* wild beast, from *ferus* wild, but traditionally regarded as a formation in English from Latin *fera* + English *-al*[1]*;* see FIERCE.

ferment (fərment') *v.* undergo fermentation, as by the action of leaven or yeast. Before 1398, in Trevisa's translation of Bartholomew's *De Proprietatibus Rerum;* borrowed through Old French *fermenter,* and directly from Latin *fermentāre* to leaven, ferment, from *fermentum* leaven, related to *fervēre* to boil, seethe; see BREW. The sense of agitate, stir up, excite, is first recorded in 1660. **—n.** (fėr'ment) Probably before 1425, leaven or yeast; probably from the verb, and as a borrowing through Middle French *ferment,* from Latin *fermentum* leaven or yeast, drink made of fermented barley; also figuratively, anger or passion. In some instances *ferment* may also be a back formation from *fermentation.* The figurative sense of agitation, excitement, unrest, is first recorded in English in Andrew Marvell's *The Rehearsal Transposed* (1672). **—fermentation** *n.* chemical process of becoming sour or alcoholic and giving off bubbles of gas. About 1395 *fermentacioun,* in Chaucer's *Canterbury Tales;* borrowed from Late Latin *fermentātiōnem* (nominative *fermentātiō*) a leavening, from Latin *fermentāre* to ferment; for suffix see -ATION. The sense of agitation or excitement, is first recorded in English about 1660.

fermion (fėr'mēon) *n.* any of a class of elementary particles, including protons, neutrons, and electrons. 1947, formed in allusion to Enrico *Fermi* + *-on;* see FERMIUM. The term was coined by the English physicist Paul Dirac, and so called because Fermi studied a special type of statistics that govern the behavior of these particles.

fermium (fėr'mēəm) *n.* artificially produced radioactive element. 1955, New Latin, formed in allusion to the Italian atomic physicist Enrico *Fermi* + *-ium.*

fern *n.* Probably before 1300 *ferne,* developed from Old English (about 700) *fearn;* cognate with Old Saxon *farn* fern, Middle Dutch *værn* (modern Dutch *varen*), and Old High German *farn* (modern German *Farn*), from Proto-Germanic **farnan.* Outside the Germanic languages cognates appear in Gaulish *ratis* fern, Middle Irish *raith,* Breton *raden* (collectively) fern, Welsh *rhedyn,* Lithuanian *spar̃nas* wing, *papártis* fern, Russian *páporotnik* fern, Avestan *parəna-* feather, wing, and Sanskrit *parṇá-m* feather, wing, leaf, from Indo-European **por-/prə-* (Pok.850).

ferocious *adj.* 1646, fierce, savage, in Sir Thomas Browne's *Pseudodoxia Epidemica;* formed in English from Latin *ferōcis* (oblique case of *ferōx* fierce, wild-looking) + English *-ious,* variant of *-ous;* perhaps modeled on earlier Middle French *ferocieux,* and prompted in its formation by earlier English *ferocity.* Latin *ferōx* is a derivative of *ferus* wild (see FIERCE) + *-ōx, -ōcem,* a suffix with the meaning of looking, appearing, and possibly related to *oculus* EYE. **—ferocity** *n.* 1606, borrowed through French *férocité,* from Latin *ferōcitātem* (nominative *ferōcitās*) fierceness, from *ferōcis,* oblique case of *ferōx;* for suffix see -ITY.

-ferous suffix added to nouns to form adjectives and meaning producing, containing, conveying, as in *metalliferous, odoriferous.* Formed in English from Latin *-fer* (from *ferre* to BEAR[2]) + English *-ous.*

ferret *n.* weasel. About 1350 *furet;* later *ferrett* (1378); borrowed from Old French *furet, fuiret,* diminutive of *fuiron* weasel, ferret, thief, from Late Latin *fūriōnem* (compare *fūrōnem* cat, thief), probably from Latin *fūr* (genitive *fūris*) thief; see FURTIVE; for suffix see -ET. **—v.** Probably before 1430, to hunt with ferrets, in Lydgate's writings; from the noun, probably modeled on Middle French *fureter* to hunt with ferrets. The sense of search out, discover, in allusion to the use of a ferret to hunt rodents and rabbits, is first recorded in an edition of Holinshed's *Chronicles* (1577-87).

ferric or **ferrous** *adj.* of or containing iron. 1799 *ferric,* in Sir Humphry Davy's writings; about 1865 *ferrous;* both words formed in English from Latin *ferrum* iron + English suffixes *-ic* and *-ous;* see FARRIER.

Ferris wheel large revolving wheel with seats hanging from its rim, used in amusement parks, etc. 1893, American English, in allusion to George W.G. *Ferris,* American engineer who designed it for the World's Columbian Exposition held in Chicago in 1893.

ferro- a combining form meaning iron, especially in the naming of alloys, as in *ferrochrome;* in chemistry it means ferrous (containing iron, especially with a valence of two) as distinguished from ferric (containing iron, especially with a valence of three), as in *ferroconcrete.* Adapted from Latin *ferrum* iron; see FARRIER.

ferrule or **ferule**[1] (fer'əl) *n.* metal cap or band at the end of a stick, etc. 1611 *ferrel,* alteration of earlier *verrel* (1483) and *verol* (1410-11); borrowed from Old French *virelle, virol, virole,* from Latin *viriola* little bracelet, diminutive of *viriae* bracelets, from Gaulish (compare Old Irish *fiar* bent, crooked, and Welsh *gŵyr*), cognate with Sanskrit *váyati* weaves, Latin *viēre* to plait, and

Old English *wīr* wire, from Indo-European **wei-/wi-/wī-* (Pok.1120). The later form *ferrel* developed by influence of Latin *ferrum* iron, in reference to the metal cap.

ferry *v.* 1123 *ferien,* developed from Old English *ferian* to carry, transport (about 725, in *Beowulf*); cognate with Old Frisian *feria* carry, transport, Old Saxon *ferian,* Middle High German *ferien,* Old Icelandic *ferja* to pass over, ferry, and Gothic *farjan* travel by boat, from Proto-Germanic **farjanan*; all from the same Germanic source as Old English *faran* FARE[2] get along. **—n.** 1286 *ferye* place or passage where boats ferry passengers and goods; earlier, in a surname *Blauncheferye* (1279); probably borrowed from a Scandinavian source (compare Old Icelandic *ferja,* n., from *ferja* to ferry).

The meaning of boat for transporting across a ferry, is first recorded in Spenser's *Faerie Queene* (1590), as a shortened form of *ferry boatc* (1580; earlier *feribot,* about 1374-75) ferryboat.

fertile *adj.* 1436 *fertyle,* borrowed through Middle French *fertil* fruitful, from Old French *fertile,* or directly from Latin *fertilis* bearing in abundance, fruitful, productive, from *ferre* to BEAR[2] carry. **—fertility** *n.* Probably before 1425 *fertilite,* in a translation of Higden's *Polychronicon;* borrowed from Middle French *fertilité,* from Latin *fertilitātem* (nominative *fertilitās*) fruitfulness, from *fertilis* fertile; see FERTILE. **—fertilization** *n.* 1857, formed from English *fertilize* + *-ation,* possibly on the model of French *fertilisation.* **—fertilize** *v.* 1648, make fertile; formed from English *fertile* + *-ize,* probably on the model of French *fertiliser.* The biological sense of unite with an egg cell, impregnate, is first recorded in Darwin's *On the Origin of Species* (1859). **—fertilizer** *n.* Before 1661, formed from English *fertilize* + *-er[1].*

ferule[2] (fer′əl) *n.* stick used for punishing children. 1599, earlier in *ferrall rodde* (1528), from *ferula* the fennel plant (before 1398, in Trevisa's translation of Bartholomew's *De Proprietatibus Rerum*); borrowed from Latin *ferula* fennel plant or rod (pre-Latin **fese-lā*), probably related to *festūca* stalk, straw, rod. In ancient Rome, a stalk of this plant was used as an instrument of punishment by schoolmasters. This sense is also attested in Old French *ferule* stick for hitting school children (1385), a use that probably contributed to the appearance of this sense in English.

fervent *adj.* 1340, ardent, earnest, in *Ayenbite of Inwyt;* borrowed from Old French *fervent,* learned borrowing from Latin *ferventem* (nominative *fervēns*), present participle of *fervēre* to boil, glow; see BREW. The etymologically literal sense of boiling or turbulent, is not recorded until shortly before 1398. **—fervency** *n.* 1554, in John Knox's writings; formed from English *fervence* (about 1412, borrowed from Old French *fervence* after Late Latin *ferventia* from Latin *ferventem* boiling, glowing) + -Y[3].

fervid *adj.* 1599, burning, glowing; borrowed from Latin *fervidus* glowing, burning, vehement, from *fervēre* to boil, glow; see BREW. The figurative sense of impassioned, is first recorded in an edition of Blount's *Glossographia* (1656-81).

fervor *n.* intense zeal or passion. About 1384 *fervour,* in the Wycliffe Bible; borrowed from Old French *fervor,* learned borrowing from Latin *fervor* a boiling, violent heat, vehemence, passion, from *fervēre* to boil; see BREW.

fescue *n.* tough grass used for pasture. 1589, piece of straw, twig, in Thomas Nashe's writings; alteration of earlier *festu* (about 1378, in a version of *Piers Plowman*); borrowed from Old French *festue, festu* a kind of straw, from Latin *festūca* straw, stalk, rod, probably related to *ferula;* see FERULE. The meaning of a pasture and lawn grass is first recorded in 1762.

fester *n.* Before 1325, a rankling sore, in *Cursor Mundi;* borrowed from Old French *festre* (with replacement of *r* for *l*), from Latin *fistula* pipe, ulcer; see FISTULA. —v. to form pus; suppurate. Before 1398 *festren,* in Trevisa's translation of Bartholomew's *De Proprietatibus Rerum;* from the noun, or possibly borrowed from Old French *festrir,* from *festre,* n. The figurative sense of cause pain, aggravate, rankle, is first recorded about 1475.

festivity *n.* Before 1387 *festivite,* in Trevisa's translation of Higden's *Polychronicon;* borrowed from Old French *festivité,* learned borrowing from Latin *fēstivitātem* (nominative *fēstīvitās*), from *fēstīvus* festive, from *fēstum* festival or holiday, neuter of *fēstus* of a feast, festal; see FEAST; for suffix see -ITY.

—festival *n.* 1589, a time of festive celebration, holiday, from earlier *festival,* adj., of a feast or holiday (probably before 1380); borrowed from Old French *festival, festivel,* and directly from Medieval Latin *festivalis* of a church holiday, from Latin *fēstīvus* festive; for suffix see -AL. The specialized meaning of a series of concerts, plays, films, etc., held at recurring periods (as a *Mozart Festival* or a *Shakespeare Festival*), is first recorded in 1857, originally in the sense of the celebration of an anniversary, such as a composer's or author's birthday.

—festive *adj.* of or suitable for a feast; in early use (1651), probably borrowed from Latin *fēstīvus* of a feast or holiday, joyous, merry, from *fēstum* festival, neuter of *fēstus;* see FESTIVITY and FEAST; for suffix see -IVE; in later use (1735), possibly re-formed back formation from English *festivity,* perhaps modeled on French *festif* (feminine *festive*). After the single recorded use in 1651, *festive* disappears in the record until 1737.

—festal *adj.* of a feast, festival, or holiday. 1479, borrowed from Middle French *festal, festel,* from Late Latin *fēstālis,* from Latin *fēstum* festival; for suffix see -AL[1]. *Festal* replaced earlier *festial,* adj. (before 1422, and is recorded once later in 1737); formed in English from Latin *fēstum* + English suffix *-ial,* variant of *-al.*

—fest *n. Informal.* festival (usually in compounds, such as *talk fest, songfest, filmfest*). 1889, American English, borrowing of German *Fest* festival, as abstracted from compounds such as *Sängerfest* choral festival, *Volksfest* folk festival, from Middle High German *vëst,* from Latin *fēstum* festival.

festoon *n.* curved hanging ornament. 1630, in Ben Jonson's writings; borrowing of French *feston,* from Italian *festone,* from *festa* celebration, feast, from Vulgar Latin **festa* FEAST; for ending see -OON. **—v.** 1789, to hang with festoons; later decorate with festoons (1800); from the noun.

fetch *v.* Probably before 1200 *fecchen* go and get, in *Ancrene Riwle;* developed from Old English *feccan* (about 1000, in a version of Ælfric's *Genesis*), apparently a variant of *fetian, fatian* to fetch, bring to, marry; cognate with Old Frisian *fatia* to grasp, seize, contain, Middle Low German *vāten,* Middle Dutch *vatten,* Old High German *fazzōn* to climb, mount, take in (modern German *fassen* grasp, contain), from Proto-Germanic **fatōjanan,* from Indo-European **ped-/pod-* grasp, hold (Pok.790). **—fetching** *adj.* 1880, alluring, fascinating; earlier, crafty or scheming (1581); formed in English from *fetch,* v. + *-ing²,* in the modern sense with the idea of taking or catching one's attention.

fête or **fete** (fet) *n.* festival, feast. 1754, in Walpole's *Letters,* borrowing of French *fête* festival, feast, from Old French *feste;* see FEAST. **—v.** 1819, entertain with a fete, feast; borrowed from French *fêter,* v., from *fête* feast.

fetid *adj.* smelling very bad. Probably before 1425, in a translation of Chauliac's *Grande Chirurgie;* borrowed from Latin *foetidus* stinking, from *foetēre* have a bad smell, stink; related to *fimus* manure, and *suf-fire-* fumigate, from Indo-European **dhwoi-/dhwi-* (Pok.263).

fetish *n.* object suppoed to have magic power. 1613 *fatisso, fetisso,* in *Purchas his Pilgrimage;* borrowed from Portuguese *fetiço* charm, sorcery; probably introduced by Portuguese sailors and traders as applied to charms and talismans worshiped by natives on the west coast of Africa; and later *fateish* (1693), *fetiche* (1705); borrowed from French *fétiche,* largely by influence of an early work in anthropology by Charles de Brosses, from Portuguese. The earlier Portuguese term *fetiço* charm, sorcery, was originally *feitiço,* an adjective with the meaning of made artfully, artificial, derived from Latin *facticius* made by art, artificial, from *facere* make.

The figurative sense of something irrationally revered, is first recorded in American English in Emerson's writings (1837). The use in psychology with the meaning of an object that arouses erotic feelings, is first recorded in 1901.

—fetishism *n.* 1801, worship of fetishes; formed from English *fetish* + *-ism;* modeled on French *fétichisme.*

fetlock *n.* tuft of hair above a horse's hoof. About 1330 *fitlok, fetlak,* in *Arthour and Merlin,* corresponding to Dutch *vetlok* fetlock, Middle High German *vizzeloch* (compare modern German *Fessel* fetlock); related to Old High German *fuoz* FOOT. The first element is also compared with Old High German *fizza* (German *Fitze*) a skein of yarn.

The Middle English suffix *-ok* (as in *hillok,* modern English *hillock*) developed from Old English *-oc,* a diminutive suffix, but in the Middle English period *fitlok* was popularly interpreted as a derivative of *feet* and *lock* (of hair).

fetter *n.* Old English (about 700) *feter* chain or shackle for the feet; cognate with Old Saxon *feteros,* pl., fetters, Middle Dutch *veter* fetter (also in modern Dutch, lace or string), Old High German *fezzera,* Old Icelandic *fjǫturr* fetter, from Proto-Germanic **feterō, feteraz,* cognate also with Greek *pédē* fetter, Latin *pedica;* related to Old English *fōt* FOOT.

The transferred sense of anything that confines, shackle, restraint, is first recorded in Old English, about 1000.

—v. About 1300 *feteren* to fasten, chain, or shackle; earlier *fetheren* (probably before 1200, in *Ancrene Riwle*); developed from Old English *gefetrian* to fetter, from *feter,* n.

fettle *n.* condition, trim (especially in the phrase *in fine fettle*). About 1750, dress, case, condition, in English dialect of Lancashire, from earlier Middle English *fettlen, fettelen* to make ready, arrange (probably about 1380); of uncertain origin (compare Old English *fetel* belt, girdle, before 899, in Alfred's translation of Boethius' *De Consolatione Philosophiae*). The OED suggests that the primary meaning derived from Old English *fetel,* would be that of to gird up, and the MED suggests that the suffix would be analogous to *nestlen* from *nesten.* If there is a relation to Old English *fetel,* then the word may ultimately be from the Germanic base **fat-* to hold, and also be cognate with Old High German *fezzil* chain, band, fetter (modern German *Fessel*), Middle Low German *vetel,* and Old Icelandic *fetill;* see FETCH.

fettuccine or fettucine (fet'əchē'nē) *n.* a flat Italian noodle. 1922, an Italian word used in Sinclair Lewis' *Babbitt;* plural of *fettuccina,* diminutive of *fettuccia* ribbon, band, of uncertain origin (possibly derived from Latin *vittae,* plural of *vitta* band, fillet, with influence of Italian *fetta* slice; more plausibly because of the phonology, it has also been suggested in Cortelazzo-Zolli that *fettuccine* ". . . is derived from **offetta,* diminutive of Latin *offa* cake, biscuit, with the passing of **l'offetta* to *la fetta*"). Latin *offa* is of unknown origin.

fetus (fē'təs) *n.* embryo in the later stages of development. Before 1398, in Trevisa's translation of Bartholomew's *De Proprietatibus Rerum;* borrowed from Latin *fētus* (genitive *fētūs*) a bearing, hatching, offspring, young, from the base *fē-* to generate, bear, also to suck, suckle, found in Latin *fēmina* female, woman; see FEMININE, and also found in FECUND. **—fetal** *adj.* 1811, formed from English *fetus* + *-al¹.*

feud *n.* long and deadly quarrel between families, etc. Before 1325 *fede* enmity, hatred, hostility, in *Cursor Mundi,* but considered to be a word generally restricted to northern dialectal use; borrowed from Old French *fede, feide* (as in the phrase *fede mortel* deadly feud), from Old High German *fēhida* (modern German *Fehde* feud); cognate with Old Frisian *feithe* enmity, and related to, though not a derivative of, Old English *fǣhth* enmity (found about 725, in *Beowulf*), (from Proto-Germanic **faiHíthō*) and *fāh* hostile; see FOE.

At first, the word was used largely by Scottish writers with the spelling *fede.* In the 1500's, it was adopted in England as *foode, fewd,* which developed into the current spelling in the 1600's. Several explanations of the modern spelling include an alteration because of a semantic connection with *feud* feudal estate, from Medieval Latin *feudum.* At one time this was rejected because *feud* feudal estate was recorded in English only as early as 1614, but since it is now known to have existed in 1120, the supposition is not as remote as originally thought.

—v. to quarrel. 1673, from the noun.

feudal *adj.* 1614, possibly borrowed through French *féodal,* from Medieval Latin *feudalis, feodalis,* from *feudum, feodum* feudal estate; see FEE; for suffix see -AL¹. **—feudalism** *n.* 1839, in a history text; formed from English *feudal* + *-ism.* **—feudatory** *adj.* 1592, in Francis Bacon's writings; formed in English, as if modeled on Latin **feudātōrius,* or by misspelling of Medieval Latin *feudatarius* the holder of a feudal estate (but earlier an adjective), from *feudat-* (participle stem of *feudare* to give as a fief, from *feudum* feudal estate) + English *-ory.*

fever *n.* Probably before 1200 *feure,* in *Ancrene Riwle;* later *fever* (probably before 1300, in *Arthour and Merlin*); developed from Old English (about 1000) *fēfer, fēfor,* borrowed from Latin *febris* fever, and related to *fovēre* to warm, heat; see DAY. The word also appears in Middle English as *fievre* (1393), borrowed from Old French *fievre,* from Latin *febris.*

The Latin word was adopted in other Germanic languages: Old High German *fiebar* (modern German *Fieber*), Swedish, Norwegian, and Danish *feber,* etc.; and in the Romance languages as the source of French *fièvre,* Portuguese *febre,* Spanish *fiebre,* and Italian *febbre.*

—feverish *adj.* Before 1398 *feverisch* causing fever, in Trevisa's translation of Bartholomew's *De Proprietatibus Rerum;* formed from *fever* + *-isch* -ish. Later the word was re-formed in English with the meaning of excited, restless; first recorded in Milton's works (1634), formed from *fever* + *-ish.*

few *adj.* Probably about 1150 *fewe,* developed from Old English *fēawe,* contracted form *fēa* (about 725, in *Beowulf*); cognate with Old Frisian *fē* little, Old Saxon *fa,* Old High German *fao,* Old Icelandic *fār,* and Gothic *fawai,* pl., few; cognate also with Sanskrit *putrá-s* child, Greek *paîs* child, *paûros* small, Latin *paucī* few, *puer* child, from Indo-European **pōu-/pəu-/pu-* (Pok. 842). **—n.** Probably about 1175 *fewe;* formed from the adjective.

fez *n.* brimless felt cap formerly worn by men in Turkey (now worn in Egypt, in some countries in North Africa, and in Indonesia). 1802, borrowed from French *fez,* from Turkish *fes,* probably in allusion to *Fez,* Morocco (city where this type of cap was principally made).

fiancée or **fiancee** (fē'änsā') *n.* woman engaged to be married. 1853, borrowing of French *fiancée,* feminine form of *fiancé,* past participle of *fiancer* betroth, from Old French *fiancer,* from *fiance* a promise, trust, from *fier* to trust, from Vulgar Latin **fīdāre;* see AFFIANCE. **—fiancé** or **fiance** *n.* man engaged to be married. 1864, borrowing of French *fiancé,* probably by influence of the earlier borrowing *fiancée.* It is no longer sure that the distinction in spelling is always maintained in English.

fiasco (fēas'kō) *n.* 1855, a theatrical or musical failure; later, a dismal failure (1862); borrowed through French, especially in the phrase *faire fiasco* turn out a failure, from Italian *far fiasco,* literally, make a bottle, from *fiasco* bottle, from Late Latin *flascō, flascōnem;* see FLASK.

The sense development is unknown, but one of many explanations refers to the alleged practice of Venetian glassmakers setting aside imperfect glass to make a common bottle or flask.

fiat (fī'ət) *n.* authoritative order, decree. Before 1631, in Donne's *Storm* (in reference to the phrase *Fiat lux* let there be light, in the Book of Genesis); earlier, as a partial Latinism in a document (about 1384); borrowed through Medieval Latin from Latin *fiat* let it be done, 3rd person singular present subjunctive of *fierī,* cognate with Greek *phȳein* cause to grow, and English BE.

fib *n.* 1611, a trivial lie, in Cotgrave's *Dictionary,* of uncertain origin; perhaps from earlier *fibble-fable* nonsense (1581), reduplication of FABLE. **—v.** 1690, in Dryden's *Amphitryon;* from the noun. **—fibber** *n.* 1723, formed from English *fib,* v. + *-er*[1].

fiber *n.* threadlike part. 1540 *fibre,* borrowed from French *fibre,* from Old French *fibre,* learned borrowing from Latin *fibra* a fiber, filament, of uncertain origin (possibly related to Latin *filum* thread, through the Latin base *fi-*). The figurative sense of character or nature, is first recorded in 1855. **—fiberboard** *n.* (1897) **—fiberglass** *n.* (1937) **—fiber optics** (1956) **—fibrous** *adj.* 1626, in Francis Bacon's *Sylva Sylvarum,* probably borrowed by influence of French *fibreux,* as a formation from New Latin *fibrosus,* from Latin *fibra;* for suffix see -OUS.

Fibonacci (fē'bənä'chē) *adj.* of or denoting a series of numbers in which each number is the sum of the preceding two numbers. 1891, in allusion to Leonardo *Fibonacci,* Italian mathematician of the 1200's who first mentioned the series in his book *Liber Abaci* (1202).

fibrin (fī'brin) *n.* 1800, formed from English *fiber, fibre* + *-in*[2].

fibula (fib'yələ) *n.* bone in the lower leg. 1615, New Latin, from Latin *fibula* clasp, brooch, earlier **fīvibula,* from Old Latin fivere, replaced by the analogical Classical form *figere* to fix, fasten; see DIKE. The bone was so called because it resembles a kind of clasp, similar to a modern safety pin, used by the ancient Romans.

In the sense of a clasp or brooch worn in antiquity, *fibula* appeared in English in 1673, borrowed directly from Latin *fibula.*

-fic a suffix forming adjectives and meaning making, doing, causing, as in *pacific* (making peace), *honorific* (doing honor), *terrific* (causing terror). Borrowed (through French *-fique*) from Latin *-ficus,* from the root of *facere* make, DO[1] perform.

-fication a suffix forming nouns and meaning a making, doing, causing, usually corresponding to verbs in *-fy,* as in *pacification, glorification, purification;* sometimes added directly to a noun or adjective, especially in technical and scientific terms, as in *ossification, reification.* Borrowed (through Old French *-fication*) from Latin *-ficātiōnem,* from *-ficātus,* past participle ending of verbs in *-ficāre* -FY.

fiche (fēsh) *n.* 1949, hotel form for registering foreign guests; borrowed from French *fiche* slip of paper or form, from Old French *fiche* point, from *ficher* to fix, fasten, from Vulgar Latin **figicāre,* from Latin *figere;* see DIKE. The meaning of card, strip of film, etc., is first recorded in 1959, as a shortening of *microfiche* (1950).

fickle *adj.* Probably before 1200 *fikel* false, deceitful, treacherous, in *Ancrene Riwle;* developed from Old English (before 1000) *ficol* deceitful, related to *befician* deceive, and *fācen* deceit, treachery; for suffix see -LE[2]. The Old English *fācen* is cognate with Old Saxon *fēkan* deceit, Old High German *feihhan,* Old Icelandic *feikn* deterioration, corruption, and Latin *piget* it irks, from Indo-European **peiḱ-/poiḱ-/piḱ-* hostile (Pok.795). The meaning of changeable, not constant, is first recorded in Mannyng's *Handlyng Synne* (about 1303).

fiction *n.* About 1412 *ficcioun* something made up; invention of the mind; borrowed from Old French *fiction* and from Latin *fictiōnem* (nominative *fictiō*) a fashioning or feigning, from *fingere* to shape, form, devise, feign; see DOUGH. **—fictional** *adj.* 1843, formed from English *fiction* + *-al*[1]. **—fictitious** *adj.* 1615, not real or genuine; formed in English, perhaps on the model of earlier French *ficticieux* hypocritical, from Medieval Latin *fictitius,* a misspelling of Latin *fictīcius* (with substitution of the English spelling *-ous*) artificial, counterfeit, from *fictus,* past participle of *fingere* to devise, fabricate, shape, form.

-fid a combining form meaning split or divided into

parts, as in *bifid.* Borrowed from Latin *-fidus,* related to *findere* to split; see BITE.

fiddle *n.* Probably before 1200 *fithele,* in Layamon's *Chronicle of Britain;* later *fedele* (before 1398, in Trevisa's translation of Bartholomew's *De Proprietatibus Rerum*) and *fydell* (about 1450); developed from Old English *fithele,* corresponding to Old High German *fidula,* Middle Low German *vedel* (modern German *Fiedel*), Middle Dutch *vedel, vedele* (modern Dutch *vedel, veel*), and Old Icelandic *fidhla.*

These words are probably derived from Medieval Latin *vitula, vidula* (for the shift from Latin *v* to *f* compare Old English *fann* from Latin *vannus*) and are supposed by some scholars to have come from Vulgar Latin **vitula,* perhaps related to Latin *vītulārī* be joyful, of uncertain origin. Others suggest that Vulgar Latin **vitula,* represented in Old French *viole,* and Italian and Spanish *viol,* was itself a borrowing from the same Germanic source as Old English *fithele.* A connection has also been suggested with Latin *fidēs* a lyre or lute, but originally a string, the later forms being derived from a diminutive of that word. However, the Latin does not agree with the Germanic forms, nor with those of the Romance languages (Spanish, Portuguese, Italian *viola,* French *viole*).
—v. About 1378 *fithelen* play the fiddle, in a version of *Piers Plowman;* later *fydelen* (1440); from the noun. The meaning of play nervously, fidget, is first recorded in Palsgrave's *Lesclarcissement* (1530). **—fiddler** *n.* Before 1280, in the surname *Fithelare;* developed from Old English *fithelere;* formed from *fithele* + *-ere* -er[1]. **—fiddlestick** *n.* Before 1425; *pl.,* as an interjection (1854).

fidelity *n.* faithfulness. Probably before 1425 *fidelite,* in a translation of Higden's *Polychronicon;* borrowed from Middle French *fidélité,* learned borrowing from Latin *fidēlitātem* (nominative *fidēlitās*) faithfulness, adherence, from *fidēlis* faithful, from *fidēs* FAITH; for suffix see -ITY.

fidget *n.* 1674, *the fidget* uneasiness; later, *the fidgets* (1753); apparently formed from *fidge,* v., move restlessly (1575), perhaps a variant of *fiken* move quickly or restlessly (before 1250); ultimately borrowed from a Scandinavian source (compare Old Swedish *fikja* move briskly). The meaning of a restless person, first recorded in 1837, is from *fidget,* v. **—v.** move restlessly. 1809, American English, in Washington Irving's *Knickerbocker's History of New York;* from the noun. **—fidgety** *adj.* 1730-36, in an edition of Bailey's *Dictionarium Britannicum;* formed from English *fidget,* v. + *-y[1].*

fiduciary (fədü′shēer′ē) *adj.* held in trust. Before 1640, held in trust, borrowed, possibly through French *fiduciaire,* from Latin *fidūciārius* (holding) in trust, from *fidūcia* a trust, from *fidere* to trust; see FAITH; for suffix see -ARY. **—n.** 1631, a trustee; borrowed from Medieval Latin *fiduciarius* trustee, from the adjective use in Latin.

fie *interj.* for shame! About 1300 *fi,* possibly borrowed from Old French *fi, fy,* and perhaps even reinforced by some Scandinavian form (compare Old Icelandic, *fȳ,* Danish *fy*), probably an imitation of the sound of disgust made in response to a disagreeable smell, though *phew* is the commoner English word for this. Latin has the words *fue* and *fi,* which are semantically related; however, these are not necessarily etymologically related, as every language seems to have developed its own terms for such basic expressions, probably independently of others.

fief (fēf) *n.* land held in return for services to a feudal lord. 1611, in Cotgrave's *Dictionary,* borrowed from French *fief,* from Old French, variant of *fieu* fee; see FEE.

field *n.* 1155 *feld;* later *feild* (before 1325, in *Cursor Mundi*), and *field* (before 1393, in Gower's *Confessio Amantis*); developed from Old English (about 725) *feld* field, and probably related to Old English *folde* earth, land, cognate with Old Saxon *folda* earth, and Old Icelandic *fold.* Among the West Germanic languages cognates are found in Old Frisian and Old Saxon *feld* field, Middle Dutch *velt* (modern Dutch *veld*), and Old High German *feld* (modern German *Feld*), from Proto-Germanic **felthuz.* Finnish *pelto* field is considered to be of Germanic origin also. Other cognates occur outside the Germanic languages in Latin *plānus* flat; see PLAIN, and in Old Slavic *polje* field, Russian *pol'e* field, and Polish *pole* field (also found in *Pol-* of Poland), from Indo-European **pelə-/plā-* (Pok.805).

The spelling with *ie* was probably introduced to English from the practice of Anglo-French scribes, who represented the sound of so-called long *e* with the grapheme *ie* in such French words as *brief* and *piece,* from which it spread to native words (*field, fiend,* etc.) from the late 1400's to the 1600's.
—v. 1529, to fight; from the noun (in the sense of battlefield). **—field day** (1747) **—fielder** *n.* 1310, one who works in fields; in baseball, 1868. **—field glasses** (1836, in Wellington's letters)

fiend *n.* evil spirit, devil. Probably about 1200 *fend,* in *The Ormulum;* later *feend* (about 1395, in Chaucer's *Canterbury Tales*); developed from Old English *fēond* enemy, foe (about 725, in *Beowulf*); originally present participle of *fēogan* to hate. The formation of *fiend* is parallel to *friend* and in Old English is cognate with Old Frisian *fiand* enemy, Old Saxon *fiond,* Middle Dutch *vīant* (modern Dutch *vijand*), Old High German *fiant* (modern German *Feind* enemy), *fiēn* to hate, Old Icelandic *fjāndi* enemy, *fjā* to hate, Gothic *fijands* enemy, *fijan* to hate (from Proto-Germanic **fijǣjanan*), *faian* to blame; also cognate with Sanskrit *pīyati* he insults, disdains, from Indo-European **pē(i)-/pī-* do harm, insult (Pok.792). For the spelling with *ie* see FIELD. The sense in American English of a person addicted to some habit, practice, etc., is first recorded in 1886. **—fiendish** *adj.* 1529, in Sir Thomas More's writings; formed from English *fiend* + *-ish[1].*

fierce *adj.* 1240, proud, noble, bold; in the surname *Fiers;* later *fierse* ferocious, wild, savage (about 1378) and *fierce* (before 1393); borrowed from Old French *fers, fiers,* nominative form of *fer, fier* wild, ferocious (modern French *fier* proud), from Latin *ferus* wild, untamed. Latin *ferus* is cognate with Greek *thḗr* (genitive *thērós*) wild animal, Old Slavic *zvěrĭ,* and Lithuanian *žvėris,* from Indo-European **ghwēr-* (Pok. 493).

fiery *adj.* flaming, ardent. About 1300 *fuyri;* later *firy* (about 1385, in Chaucer's *Canterbury Tales*), and *fiery* (about 1443); formed from Middle English *fier* fire (about 1250, in *The Story of Genesis and Exodus;* also *fuyr, fir;* see FIRE) + *-y[1].*

The spelling with *ie* arose by confusion with Old English *fȳr* fire, in which *y,* representing a long *i* sound, was transcribed as *i, y,* and *ie* in Middle English. The *e* was an orthographic indication of the long *i* sound.

Discrepancies with *y* still exist in English: *sirup, syrup; siren, syren.*

fiesta *n.* holiday, festivity. 1844, American English, borrowed from Spanish *fiesta* feast, from Vulgar Latin *festa* FEAST.

fife *n.* small flutelike instrument. 1555, probably borrowed from German *Pfeife* fife or pipe, from Old High German *pfifa,* Middle High German *pfife;* see PIPE. It is also proposed that *fife* may be an alteration of Middle French *fifre* fife, fife player, which was borrowed from Swiss German *pfifer* piper (modern German *Pfeifer*), a derivative of Old High German *pfifa* fife, PIPE. **—v.** 1598; from the noun.

fifteen *adj.* Old English *fiftēne, fiftȳne* (about 725, in *Beowulf*), from *fif* five + *-tēne, -tȳne* -teen, from *tēn* TEN. Old English *fiftēne* is cognate with Old Frisian *fiftine,* Old Saxon *fiftein,* Dutch *vijftien,* Old High German *finfzehan* (modern German *fünfzehn*), Old Icelandic *fimtān,* and Gothic *fimftaíhun.*

fifth *adj.* Before 1325 *fyfthe;* earlier *fifte* (probably about 1200, in *The Ormulum*); developed from Old English *fifta* (827, in the *Anglo-Saxon Chronicle*), from *fif* FIVE + *-ta;* for suffix see -TH². Old English *fifta* is cognate with Old Frisian *fifta,* Old Saxon *fifto,* Dutch *vijfde,* Old High German *fimfto* (modern German *fünfte*), Old Icelandic *fimmti,* and Gothic *fimfta.*

Fifth, with the spelling *-th,* was a re-formation in Middle English of earlier *fifte,* on analogy with *fourth, seventh, ninth,* etc.; the older suffix *-te* (in Old English *-ta*) is from Indo-European *-tos,* attested in Gaulish *pinpetos,* Latin *quīntus,* Greek *pémptos,* Lithuanian *peñktas,* and Sanskrit *pañcatha-s.*

fifth column persons living within a country who secretly aid its enemies. 1936, translation of Spanish *quinta columna.* The phrase developed originally during the Spanish Civil War in allusion to sympathizers with General Franco in Madrid, who were said to constitute a *fifth column* within the city which would join the four columns of troops General Emilio Mola was leading to capture Madrid for the Francoists. The chief propagandist for Franco, General Gonzalo de Llano, is sometimes credited with coining the phrase, but Ernest Hemingway's play *The Fifth Column,* and heavy press coverage and sympathy for the Loyalists in the United States, were the chief instruments that popularized the term.

fifty *adj.* Probably before 1200 *fifti;* developed from Old English *fiftig* (about 725, in *Beowulf*), from *fif* five + *-tig* group of ten, -TY¹. Old English *fiftig* is cognate with Old Frisian and Old Saxon *fiftich,* Dutch *vijftig,* Old Icelandic *fimtigi,* and Old High German *fimfzug* (modern German *fünfzig*). **—fifty-fifty** *adj., adv.* 1913 (in P.G. Wodehouse's writings)

fig *n.* Probably before 1200 *fige,* in *Ancrene Riwle;* borrowed from Old French *fige, figue,* from Old Provençal *figa,* from Vulgar Latin **fica,* from Latin *ficus* fig tree, fig. The Latin *ficus* was probably borrowed from a non-Indo-European language of the Mediterranean region, which is also the source of Greek *sŷkon,* Boeotian *tŷkon,* and Armenian *t'uz,* all with the meaning of fig. In the Middle English period the form *fike* fig, coexisted with *fige* until about 1500. Middle English *fike* (recorded probably about 1300), developed from Old English *fic,* which was borrowed (about 975) from Latin *ficus* fig.

fight *v.* 1122 *fihten,* developed from Old English (about 900) *feohtan* to fight; cognate with Old Frisian *fiuchta* to fight, Middle Dutch and Middle Low German *vechten,* and Old High German *fehtan* to fight (modern German *fechten* to fence, fight), from Proto-Germanic **feuHtanan,* cognate with Greek *eche-peukés* having a sharp point, *pýktēs* boxer, and *pyx* with the fist, from Indo-European **peuk̂-/puk̂-* (Pok.828). **—n.** Probably before 1200 *fihte,* developed from Old English *feoht* a fight (about 725, in *Beowulf*); cognate with Old Frisian *fiucht* a fight, Old Saxon *fehta,* Dutch *gevecht,* and Old High German *gifeht* (modern German *Gefecht*); all derived from the same Germanic source of Old English *feohtan* to fight. **—fighter** *n.* Before 1325 *fighter,* in *Cursor Mundi;* developed from Old English *feohtere.*

The spelling with *gh* developed in Middle English before 1325 after the practice from about 1100 when scribes began to substitute *gh* for *y* and for earlier *ȝ,* especially before *t;* now *gh* stands for *g* (as in *aghast, ghost*), and for an old sound (German *ch*) once found in *night* and *through,* but that is no longer distinguished in English, or that was replaced by the sound associated with *f* in *trough.*

figment *n.* something invented or made up. Probably before 1425, literary myth, in a translation of Higden's *Polychronicon;* borrowed from Latin *figmentum* something formed or fashioned, figure, creation; related through the root **fig-* of *fingere* to shape, form, fashion; for suffix see -MENT.

figure *n.* Probably before 1200, numeral, in *Ancrene Riwle;* borrowed from Old French *figure,* learned borrowing from Latin *figūra* a shape, form, figure; related through the root **fig-* of *fingere* to shape or form; for suffix see -URE. The meanings of a form or shape and of a statue or likeness are first recorded in English in *Kyng Alisaunder* (before 1300); the sense of a literary device appears about 1340. **—v.** 1389 *fyguren* to represent; probably from the noun, by influence of Old French *figurer,* from Latin *figūrāre* to shape or form, from *figūra* figure. **—figurative** *adj.* Before 1397 *figuratif* allegorical, typical, in the Wycliffe Bible; earlier, implied in *figuratively* (probably before 1387, *figuratifliche,* in a version of *Piers Plowman*); borrowed through Old French *figuratif* (feminine *figurative*), or directly from Late Latin *figūrātīvus* figurative (of speech), from Latin *figūrāre* to shape or form; for suffix see -IVE. **—figured** *adj.* Probably before 1400, in *Morte Arthur,* from the past participle of *figure,* v. **—figurehead** *n.* 1765, ornament on the bow of a ship; later, person who is the head of a group, organization, etc., without real authority (1883). **—figurine** *n.* statuette. 1854, borrowed from French *figurine,* from Italian *figurina,* diminutive of *figura* figure, learned borrowing from Latin *figūra* figure.

filament *n.* very fine thread. 1594, borrowed, possibly by influence of Middle French *filament,* from New Latin *filamentum,* from Late Latin *filāre* to spin, draw out in a long line, from Latin *filum* thread; see FILE¹.

filbert *n.* cultivated hazelnut. About 1390, borrowed from Anglo-French *philber,* in allusion to Saint *Philibert,* a Frankish abbot; so called because the nuts ripen near his feast day.

filch *v.* steal, pilfer. About 1300 *filchen* to snatch, take as booty, of unknown origin.

file¹ *v.* to place (papers, etc.) in order. 1473, put (documents) on record; borrowed from Middle French *filer* string documents on a wire for preservation or reference, from *fil* thread or string, from Latin *filum* thread; perhaps *cognate* with Armenian *jil* sinew, string, Lithuanian *gýsla* sinew, Old Slavic *žila* vein, from Indo-European *gwhīslo-* (Pok.489). —**n.** place for keeping papers. 1525, string or wire on which documents are strung for preservation or reference, borrowed from Middle French *fil* string. The extension of meaning to that of a catalog or a collection, as of papers, is first recorded in 1566.

file[2] *n.* line or row. 1598, line of people; borrowed from Middle French *file* row, from *filer* spin (thread), march in file, from Late Latin *filāre* to spin, draw out in a long line, from Latin *filum* thread; see FILE[1]. Although usually associated semantically with *file*[1], n., the word is a separate and later borrowing from French. —**v.** 1598, arrange (people) in a line, from Middle French *filer.*

file[3] *n.* metal instrument for rubbing, smoothing, etc. Probably before 1200 *file, vile,* in *Ancrene Riwle;* developed from Old English *fēol* (before 800 *fil,* in Mercian dialect). The Old English is cognate with Old Saxon *fīla* file, Middle Dutch *vīle* (modern Dutch *vijl*), Old High German *fīhala* (modern German *Feile*), and Old Icelandic *fēl, thēl;* from Proto-Germanic **finHlō,* probably also cognate with Greek *pikrós* sharp, and Sanskrit *piṅśáti* he carves, from Indo-European **peiḱ-/piḱ-* (Pok.794). —**v.** rub, smooth, etc., with a file. Probably before 1200 *filen, vilen,* in *Ancrene Riwle;* developed from Old English *filian;* possibly from the noun in Old English. —**filings** *n.pl.* particles removed by a file. Before 1398, in Trevisa's translation of Bartholomew's *De Proprietatibus Rerum;* from the verb in Middle English.

filet (filā′) *n.* Before 1399, thin slice of meat or bacon; passing into an Anglicized spelling *fillet* after 1475, and appearing as a reborrowing from modern French, in Thackeray's *Miscellaneous Essays* (1841); see FILLET.

filial *adj.* expected from a son or daughter. Before 1425, in a version of *Piers Plowman;* borrowed probably from Middle French *filial,* and directly from Late Latin *filiālis* of a son or daughter, from Latin *filius* son, *filia* daughter; see FEMININE; for suffix see -AL[1].

filibuster *n.* deliberate hindering of legislation by making long speeches, etc. About 1851, in American English *Fillibustier, Flibustier;* later *filibuster* (1855) any American who engaged in uprisings in Latin America, especially in Cuba and later in Mexico and Nicaragua; borrowed from Spanish *filibustero* a freebooter, and from French *flibustier.* The word is recorded earlier in English *flibutor* pirate or adventurer, again in reference to activities of such individuals in the region around the Caribbean (before 1587); borrowed from Dutch *vrijbuiter* freebooter. The relationship of borrowing from Dutch to French and Spanish and English is unclear. Perhaps French *flibustier* came from English *flibutor,* and earlier directly from the Dutch in the form of *fribustier.* The distinction of nomenclature among the adventurers in the Caribbean area during the 1500's and 1600's is confused by the activities they engaged in. The French settlers hired as hunters for the Spanish *(buccaneers),* were driven out and turned to plundering so that *bucaner* took on a new meaning of pirate; this overlapped with the freebooter or *filibuster* (flibustier) or common rover. Doublet of FREE- BOOTER.

Though the meaning of an act or instance of obstructing legislation by prolonging debate, is first recorded in 1890 in the Congressional Record, it is implied earlier in the sense of legislator who prolongs debate, first recorded in 1853. This latter sense has been replaced in the form of *filibusterer* (1855). —**v.** to engage in a legislative filibuster. 1853, in American English; from the noun.

filigree (fil′əgrē) *n.* delicate ornamental work. 1693, in John Evelyn's *Diary,* alteration of *filigreen* (1682) and earlier *filigrane* (1668); borrowed from French *filigrane* filigree, from Italian *filigrana* (from Latin *filum* thread + *grānum* grain). —**v.** to ornament with filigree. 1831; from the noun.

fill *v.* Probably about 1200 *fillen,* in *The Ormulum;* developed from Old English (before 1000) *fyllan;* cognate with Old Frisian *fullia, fella* to fill, Old Saxon *fullian,* Dutch *vullen,* Old High German *fullen* (modern German *füllen*), Old Icelandic *fylla,* and Gothic *fulljan* from Proto-Germanic **fullijanan;* from the same Germanic source of Old English *full* FULL. —**n.** 1250 *fille,* in *Bestiary;* developed from Old English *fylle, fyllu, fyllo* full supply (about 725, in *Beowulf*); cognate with Old High German *fulli* (modern German *Fülle*), Old Icelandic *fyllr,* and Gothic *ufarfullei* great abundance, *fullō* fullness; from the same Germanic source of Old English *full* FULL. —**filler** *n.* 1496, formed from English *fill,* v. + *-er*[1]. —**filling** *n.* 1325-26, from *fill,* v.; *adj.* 1626, in Francis Bacon's *Sylva Sylvarum.*

fillet (fil′it) *n.* narrow band, thin slice. Before 1325 *filet* headband; later, slice of meat or bacon (before 1399); borrowed from Old French *filet,* diminutive of *fil* thread; see FILET; for suffix see -ET. —**v.** 1604, bind with a narrow band; from the noun. The meaning of cut (fish or meat) into fillets, is first recorded in English in 1846.

fillip *v.* About 1450 *philippen* to flip (something) with the fingers or snap the fingers; possibly imitative of the sound. —**n.** 1530, a toss with the fingers or a snap of the fingers, in Palsgrave's *Lesclarcissement;* from the verb. The meaning of thing that rouses or excites, appeared before 1700.

filly *n.* young female horse. 1404 *fyly;* possibly borrowed from a Scandinavian source (compare Old Icelandic *fylja* filly, *fyl* filly or foal; related to *foli* FOAL.

film *n.* Before 1400 *vilm;* later *fylme* (1440); developed from Old English (about 1000) *filmen* membrane, skin; cognate with Old Frisian *filmene* skin (from Proto-Germanic **filminjan*), Greek *pélma* sole of foot, Latin *pellis* skin, Lithuanian *plėnė* skin, and Old Slavic *pelena* covering, from Indo-European **pel-* (Pok.803). The meaning of a thin coat of something is first recorded in English in 1577, and was extended to a coating of chemicals spread on photographic paper, by 1845; then to include the coating and the paper or celluloid, by 1895. The sense of a motion picture was first recorded in 1905. —**v.** 1602, to cover with, or as if with a film, in Shakespeare's *Hamlet;* from the noun. The sense of to photograph is first recorded in 1899. —**filmy** *adj.* 1604, formed from English *film,* n. + *-y*[1].

filter *n.* Probably before 1425 *filtre* felt (used to filter liquids), in a translation of Chauliac's *Grande Chirurgie;* borrowed through Middle French *filtre,* and directly from Medieval Latin *filtrum* felt (used to filter liquids), from a Germanic source (compare Old Saxon *filt* FELT). —**v.** 1576, pass (a liquid) through a filter; borrowed probably from Middle French *filtrer,* from New Latin *filtrare,* from Medieval Latin *filtrum* felt. —**filterable** *adj.* 1908, formed from English *filter,* v. +

-able. **—filtrate** *v.* 1612, probably a back formation from *filtrate;* for suffix see -ATE[1]. **—filtration** *n.* 1605, perhaps borrowed from French *filtration* (1578), from *filtrer* to filter; for suffix see -ATION.

filth *n.* Probably before 1200 *fulthe,* in *Ancrene Riwle;* later *filth* (before 1325, in *Cursor Mundi*); developed from Old English (about 1000) *fȳlth;* cognate with Old Saxon *fūlitha* foulness, filth, Dutch *vuilte,* and Old High German *fūlida* (from Proto-Germanic **fūlithō*); derived from the same Germanic source as Old English *fūl* FOUL. **—filthy** *adj.* Before 1300 *fulthe* corrupt, sinful; later *filthi* unclean (1384, in the Wycliffe Bible); formed from English *filth* + *-y[1]*.

fin *n.* Old English *fin* (about 1000, in Ælfric's works); cognate with Middle Low German *vinne* fin, Middle Dutch *vinne* fin (modern Dutch *vin*), Middle High German *vinne* nail, Swedish *fena* fin, Norwegian *finne* fin, from Proto-Germanic **finnō,* from Indo-European **pi-n-,* root **(s)phēi-/(s)pī-/(s)pi-* (Pok.981). **—finny** *adj.* 1590, in Spenser's *Faerie Queene;* formed from English *fin* + *-y[1]*.

finagle *v. Informal.* use trickery, cheat. 1926, American English, possibly a variant of dialectal *fainaigue* to cheat or renege (at cards), of unknown origin.

final *adj.* Before 1338 *finalle,* in Mannyng's *Chronicle of England;* borrowed through Old French *final,* and directly from Latin *fīnālis* of or pertaining to an end, from *fīnis* end; see FINISH. **—finalist** *n.* 1883, believer in final causes; borrowed from French *finaliste* (Old French *final* + *-iste* -ist). The meaning of competitor in a final contest, is first recorded in 1898. **—finality** *n.* 1541, borrowed through Middle French *finalité,* from Late Latin *fīnālitātem* (nominative *fīnālitās*), from Latin *fīnālis* final; for suffix see -ITY. The word was re-formed in English (1833 or before) from *final* + *-ity.* **—finalize** *v.* 1922, in Australian English, formed from *final* + *-ize.*

finale (fənä′lē) *n.* 1783, borrowed from Italian *finale* final, from Latin *fīnālis* final, from *fīnis* end; see FINISH. The word was first recorded in an English text (1724) as an Italian word in a glossary of terms in music.

finance *n.* Probably about 1400 *fynaunce, fenaunce* settlement, retribution; borrowed from Middle French *finance* ending, settlement of a debt, from Old French *finance* wealth, revenue, extra levy, from Medieval Latin *financia* money, payment, from **finare* pay a fine or tax, from *finis* a payment in settlement, fine or tax (Latin *fīnis* end).

The meaning of management of money, is first recorded in English in 1770, but derived from a similar sense in modern French. **—finances** *pl.* 1730, formed in English on the model of earlier French *finances,* pl., from Old French.

—v. 1827, from *finance,* n. The earlier obsolete meaning of ransom, appeared about 1616. **—financial** *adj.* 1769, in Burke's writings; formed from English *finance,* n. + *-ial,* variant of *-al[1]*. **—financier** *n.* 1618, in Francis Bacon's writings; borrowed from French *financier,* from Middle French *finance* + *-ier* -ER[1].

finch *n.* small songbird. Probably about 1200 *fincq;* later *fynch* (about 1387-95, in Chaucer's *Prologue* to the *Canterbury Tales*); developed from Old English (before 700) *finc;* cognate with Middle Low German and Middle Dutch *vinke* finch (modern Dutch *vink*), Old High German *fincho* (modern German *Fink*), (from Proto-Germanic **finkíz, finkjōn*), Swedish *spink* sparrow, little bird, Greek *spíngos, spíza* chaffinch, and Sanskrit *phiṅgaka-s* kind of hawk, from Indo-European **(s)ping-* (Pok.999).

find *v.* 1013 *finden,* developed from Old English *findan* come upon, alight on (about 725, in *Beowulf*); cognate with Old Frisian *finda* to find, Old Saxon *findan, fithan,* Middle and modern Dutch *vinden,* Old High German *findan* (modern German *finden*), Old Icelandic *finna,* and Gothic *finthan,* from Proto-Germanic **finthanan,* cognate with Sanskrit *pánthā-s* path, Latin *pōns* (genitive *pontis*) bridge, from Indo-European **pent-/pont-* go; arrive at (Pok.808). **—n.** 1825, a discovery, in Southey's *Letters;* from the verb. **—finding** *n.* About 1300, an abandoned child; later, a discovery, that which is found out (often *findings,* 1642; 1644, in Milton's *Areopagitica*).

fine[1] *adj.* of high quality. About 1250 *fin* free from blemish, refined, pure, in *The Story of Genesis and Exodus;* borrowed from Old French *fin* perfected, of highest quality, from Latin *fīnis* end, limit, (hence) acme, peak, height, as in the phrases *fīnis boni* the height of good, the highest good, *fīnis honōrum* the highest of honors; see FINISH.

A number of Romance languages developed this usage from Latin: Provençal *fins,* Spanish and Portuguese *fino,* Italian *fino* (also *fine*), and the Romance word also passed into the Germanic languages, including Old High German *fīn* (modern German *fein*), Middle and modern Dutch *fijn,* Icelandic *fín,* and Swedish *fin.*

Many of the current senses of *fine* in English developed, or were borrowed from Old French; excellent, admirable, pleasing (before 1300); pure, sheer (probably before 1275); delicate, exquisite (probably before 1300); very small or thin (before 1399); subtle, refined (about 1385).

—fine arts (1767) **—finery** *n.* 1680; formed from English *fine[1]*, adj. + *-ery.*

fine[2] *n.* money paid as penalty. About 1250 *fin* ending, conclusion, borrowed from Old French *fin* end, from Latin *fīnis;* see FINISH and FINANCE.

The sense of payment as punishment for an offense, is first recorded about 1399, and developed from a general meaning of payment by way of compensation, especially as a settlement ending a dispute, and so serving as an ending or conclusion. These senses also existed in Medieval Latin and Old French and were probably influential in the development of the English meanings. In English, the original meaning of conclusion, is still used in the phrase *in fine.*

—v. About 1300 *finen* pay as a ransom or penalty; from the noun.

finesse (fənes′) *n.* subtle or tactful strategy. 1528, fineness, delicacy; hence, subtle strategy (1530); borrowed from Middle French *finesse* fineness, subtlety, from Old French *fin* subtle , delicate, FINE[1]. The OED conjectures that many of its early citations may belong to *fineness,* therefore supporting the evidence for an early confusion between *finesse* and *fineness.* **—v.** 1778, to use finesse; from the noun. The earliest (1746) use of the verb was in the game of whist, to denote a special stratagem for taking a trick (1746, in an edition of Hoyle's *A Short Treatise on the Game of Whist*).

finger *n.* Before 1121 *finger;* developed from Old English (about 825) *finger;* cognate with Old Frisian *finger,* Old Saxon *fingar,* Dutch *vinger,* Old High German *fingar* (modern German *Finger*), Old Icelandic *fingr* (Norwegian, Swedish and Danish *finger*), and Gothic *figgrs*, from Proto-Germanic **finȝraz*; perhaps related to Old English *fif* FIVE through the Indo-European form **penkwrós*, from **pénkwe* five (Pok.808). —**v.** Before 1425 *fingren* touch or point at with a finger; from the noun. The meaning of identify a criminal, is first recorded in American English in 1930, and originates from underworld slang. —**fingering** *n.* About 1386 *fyngerynge* the action of using the fingers in playing a musical instrument, in Chaucer's *Legend of Good Women*. —**fingermark** *n.* (1840, in Dickens' *Barnaby Rudge*) —**fingernail** *n.* (about 1225) —**finger paint, finger painting** (1950) —**fingerprint** *n.* (1859); *v.* (1905).

finial (fin′ēəl) *n.* ornament, as on top of a roof, lamp, or post. 1426 *feneal* putting an end to, binding; later *finial*, adj. (1433), variant of FINAL.

finicky *adj.* 1825, dialectal variant, formed either through *finikin, finicking* (1661, dainty, mincing), or directly from *finical* (1592, too dainty or particular) + *-y*[1]; formed from English *fine*[1] delicate + *-ical*, as in *cynical, ironical.*

finis (fin′is) *n.* end. Before 1460, word placed at the end of a book; borrowed from Latin *finis* end; see FINISH. The extended sense of conclusion, end, finish, is first recorded in 1682.

finish *v.* Before 1375 *finischen;* borrowed from Old French *finiss-*, stem of *finir* (alteration of *fenir* to end), from Latin *fīnīre* to limit, set bounds, end, from *fīnis* boundary, limit, border, end; perhaps related to *figere* to fix, fasten; see DIKE; for suffix see -ISH[2]. The alteration of the older French *fenir* to *finir* was influenced by *fin* end, from Latin *fīnis* boundary, limit, end. —**n.** 1779, that which finishes or completes, in a letter of Josiah Wedgwood; from the verb. —**finished** *adj.* (1583; from *finish,* v.)

finite *adj.* 1410, limited in space or time; borrowed from Latin *fīnītus*, past participle of *fīnīre* to limit, set bounds, end; see FINISH.

fink *n. Slang.* unpleasant person, spy or informer; later, strike-breaker. 1903, in George Ade's *People You Know,* American English, of uncertain origin (possibly borrowed from German *Fink* a frivolous or dissolute person, originally a university student who was not a formal member, perhaps abstracted from *Schmierfink* a dirty or low person, or from *Schmierfink* a hack; alternatively, German *Fink* meaning also finch, may have developed the sense of informer, parallel to old slang *sing* to turn informer, and *stool pigeon* an informer, though OED cites a quotation from the *American Mercury* that claims the word appeared earlier during the Homestead Strike in 1892, in reference to the Pinkerton operations called in to break up the strike, *fink* being a term used for *Pinks* or Pinkerton operatives). —**v.** *Slang.* to inform on. 1925, American English, from the noun.

finnan haddie smoked haddock. Before 1861, Scottish, alteration of earlier *Findon haddock* (1707), in allusion to *Findon* (locally *Finnan*), a small fishing village near Aberdeen, noted for its smoked fish.

Finnish *adj.* 1789-96, in an edition of an American geography text; formed from *Finn* + *-ish*[1], and replacing *Finnic* (1668) formed from *Finn* (Old English *Finnas,* pl., corresponding to Old Icelandic *Finnr*) + *-ic.*

fiord or **fjord** (fyôrd) *n.* narrow arm of the sea between high cliffs. 1674, borrowing of Norwegian *fiord, fjord,* from Old Icelandic *fjǫrdhr,* from Indo-European **pertus* (Pok.817); see FORD, and FIRTH.

fir *n.* evergreen tree. Probably about 1300 *fir;* later *firr* (before 1325, in *Cursor Mundi*), *firre,* perhaps developed from Old English *furh-, fyrh-* (found only in *furhwudu* fir-wood), or more likely borrowed from a Scandinavian source (compare Old Icelandic *fȳri* fir forest, *fura* fir, Danish *fyr*); cognate with Old Saxon *furie* pine, Old High German *forha, foraha* pine (modern German *Föhre*), from Proto-Germanic **furHōn, *furHjōn;* also cognate with Latin *quercus* oak, from Indo-European **pérkwus/ pr̥kwus* (Pok.822).

fire *n.* 1122 *fir;* found in Old English (about 725) *fȳr;* cognate with Old Frisian *fiūr, fiōr* fire, Old Saxon *fiur,* Dutch *vuur,* Old High German *fiur, fuir* (modern German *Feuer*), Old Icelandic *fȳri, fūrr* flame, and Gothic *fōn* fire; cognate also with Umbrian *pir* fire, Greek *pŷr,* Old Prussian *panno,* Armenian *hur,* Tocharian A *por,* Tocharian B *puwār,* and Hittite *paḫḫur, paḫḫuwar,* from Indo-European **péwōr/pūr/pur,* genitive *punés* (Pok.828). A Middle English spelling *fier* (about 1250, in *The Story of Genesis and Exodus*) is still found in modern English *fiery,* adj. The spelling *fire* is first recorded in *The Ormulum* (probably about 1200), but did not become fully established until about 1600.
—**v.** Probably about 1200 *furen* arouse, excite, inflame; later *firen* set a fire (before 1393, in Gower's *Confessio Amantis*); from the noun. The Old English verb *fȳrian* to supply with fire (recorded once, about 970) is not recorded in Middle English and apparently was replaced by a new formation from the noun in Middle English. The Old English verb corresponded to Old High German *fiuren* set on fire, whence modern German *feuern.* The informal meaning of dismiss or discharge, is first recorded in 1885 in American English, from the earlier sense of throw (a person) out of a place, recorded in 1871, which is an extension of to discharge a gun, bullet, etc., originally, to apply fire to gunpowder (1530). —**fireboat** *n.* 1826, in correspondence of Mrs. Shelley. —**firebrand** *n.* (probably before 1300) —**fire company** (1777, American English) —**firehouse** *n.* Probably before 1000, house with a fireplace; 1906, American English, building for fire-fighting equipment. —**firelight** *n.* (about 725, in *Beowulf*) —**fireman** *n.* 1377, tender of a fire; 1714, person hired to put out fires. —**firewood** *n.* (1378) —**firing pin** (1874)

firkin *n.* small cask; quarter of a barrel. 1391 *ferdkyn,* apparently borrowed from Middle Dutch **vierdekijn, *veerdelkijn,* diminutives of *vierde, veerdel,* literally, fourth, fourth part; for suffix see -KIN.

firm[1] *adj.* fixed, stable. About 1378 *ferme,* in a version of *Piers Plowman;* borrowed from Old French *ferme,* from Latin *firmus* firm, stable, a dialectal development of pre-Latin **fermos.* In Latin *firmus* is related to *frētus* supported (by), trusting (in); cognate with Greek *thrēsasthai* sit down (originally, prop oneself up), *thrónos* seat, chair, throne, *thrânos* bench, and Sanskrit *dhāráyati* he keeps, holds, *dhárma-s* law, custom, from Indo-European **dher-/dherə-/dhr̥̄-* (Pok.252) —**v.** About 1303 *fermen* make firm, establish, in Mannyng's *Chronicle of England;* borrowed through Old French *fermer,* or directly from Latin *firmāre,* from *firmus,* adj. The spelling with *i* was not established until the late 1500's, modeled on the Latin.

firm[2] *n.* business concern. 1744, name or title of a company; borrowed from German *Firma* a business or name of a business, originally, signature, from Italian *firma* signature, from *firmare* to sign, Latin *firmāre* make firm, affirm, confirm, from *firmus* firm, stable; see FIRM[1].

firmament *n.* arch of the sky. About 1250 *firmament,* in *The Story of Genesis and Exodus;* borrowed from Latin *firmāmentum* firmament, literally, a support or strengthening, from *firmāre* make firm, strengthen, from *firmus* FIRM[1] fixed; for suffix see -MENT.

Latin *firmāmentum* was used in the Vulgate to translate Greek *steréōma* of the Septuagint, with the meaning of firm or solid structure (from *stereoûn* make firm, from *stereós* firm), which was in turn a translation of the Biblical Hebrew *rāqīac'* vault of the sky (literally, expanse, something beaten out which implies coming from something solid).

first *adj.* Probably about 1200 *firste,* in *The Ormulum;* found in Old English *fyrst* earliest, foremost (963, in *Anglo-Saxon Chronicle*); cognate with Old Frisian *ferist, ferost, ferst* first, Old Saxon *furist* first, *furisto* prince, Middle Dutch *vorste* prince (modern Dutch *vorst*), Old High German *furist* first, *furisto* prince (modern German *Fürst*), and Old Icelandic *fyrstr* first. These words are superlatives formed from the same source as Old English *fore* formerly, previously; see FORE and FOREMOST. **—adv.** Before 1121 *first;* found in Old English *fyrst* (963, in *Anglo-Saxon Chronicle*); from the adjective. **—n.** Before 1393 *ferste,* in Gower's *Confessio Amantis,* from the adjective. **—first aid** (1882) **—first base** (1845) **—first-born** *adj., n.* (about 1350) **—first-class** *adj.* (1851) **—first floor** (1663, ground floor) **—first grade** (1818 quality, 1835 grade in school) **—firsthand** *adj., adv.* (1696) **—First Lady** (1861; general meaning 1853) **—first-rate** *adj., adv.* (1666)

firth *n.* narrow arm of the sea. About 1425, Scottish, from a Scandinavian source (compare Old Icelandic *fjǫrdhr,* in the dative case *firdhi;* see FORD; FIORD).

fiscal *adj.* financial. 1563, of or pertaining to a state treasury, in John Foxe's *Book of Martyrs;* borrowed from Middle French *fiscal,* from Late Latin *fiscālis* of or belonging to the state treasury, from Latin *fiscus* treasury, purse, (originally) basket made of twigs; of unknown origin. The general sense of financial, was apparently abstracted in American English from earlier phrases such as *fiscal agent* (1841) and *fiscal year* (1843).

fish *n.* Probably before 1200 *fish;* earlier *fiss* (probably about 1175); developed from Old English (about 750) *fisc.* The Old English is cognate with Old Frisian and Old Saxon *fisc* fish, Middle Dutch *visc* (modern Dutch *vis*), Old High German *fisc* (modern German *Fisch*), Old Icelandic *fiskr* (Norwegian, Swedish and Danish *fisk*), and Gothic *fisks,* from Proto-Germanic **fiskaz;* and outside Germanic with Latin *piscis* fish, and Old Irish *īasc* (with typical Celtic loss of Indo-European *p*), from Indo-European **peisk-/pisk-* (Pok.796). **—v.** Probably about 1225 *fissen, fysshen,* in *King Horn;* developed from Old English (before 899) *fiscian* to catch fish. The Old English verb is cognate with Old Frisian *fiskia* to fish, Old Saxon and Old High German *fiskōn* (modern German *fischen*), Old Icelandic *fiska* (Swedish *fiska,* Norwegian and Danish *fiske*), and Gothic *fiskōn,* from Proto-Germanic **fiskōjanan;* and outside Germanic with Latin *piscārī* to fish; all from the same source as Old English *fisc* fish. **—fishy** *adj.* Probably about 1475, formed from English *fish,* n. + *-y*[1]. The informal sense of doubtful or suspicious, is first recorded in 1840, in American English. **—fisherman** *n.* 1441; formed from English *fisher* (before 1200) + *man.* **—fishhook** *n.* (before 1387) **—fishing** *n.* (probably about 1225) **—fishing line** (1466) **—fishing rod** (1834, in American English) **—fishpond** *n.* (1279) **—fish story** (1819, in American English) **—fishwife** *n.* (1381)

fission *n.* a splitting apart. 1841, division of a cell or organism; borrowed, perhaps by influence of earlier *fissure,* from Latin *fissiōnem* (nominative *fissiō*) a breaking up or cleaving, from *fid-,* root of *findere* to split; for suffix see -SION. The meaning as pertaining to atoms is first recorded in English in 1939. **—v.** to split or divide. 1929; from the noun. **—fissionable** *adj.* 1945, capable of undergoing nuclear fission; formed from English *fission,* v. + *-able.*

fissure *n.* Before 1400, borrowed from Old French *fissure,* or directly from Latin *fissūra,* from *fid-,* root of *findere* to split; for suffix see -URE.

fist *n.* Probably 1200 *fust,* in *Ancrene Riwle* and Layamon's *Chronicle of Britain;* later *fist* (probably before 1300, in *Arthour and Merlin*); found in Old English (before 900) *fȳst.* The Old English is cognate with Old Frisian *fest* fist, Old Saxon and Old High German *fūst* (modern German *Faust*), Middle Dutch *vuust* (modern Dutch *vuist*), from Proto-Germanic **fūHstiz,* earlier **funHstiz,* and Old Slavic *pęstĭ,* from Indo-European **pn̥kstis* (Pok.839). **—fistfight** *n.* (1603) **—fisticuffs** *n.pl.* 1605, fighting with the fists; formed from English *fist* + CUFF(S)[2] hit.

fistula (fis'chùlə) *n.* a passage extending from a deep ulcer. 1373, borrowed from Latin *fistula* pipe, ulcer, of uncertain origin; see FESTER.

fit[1] *n.* the way something fits. Before 1250 *fitte* an adversary of equal power, a match, in *The Owl and the Nightingale;* later, the fitting of one thing to another (1823), and the way something fits (1831).

The early meaning is of obscure origin, possibly derived from Old English **fitta,* from *fitt* a conflict or struggle; the later meanings are from the verb.

—adj. Probably about 1375 *fytt* fitting or suitable; possibly from the noun (though not in the present meaning of the adjective, which may be from **fitte,* past participle of the verb *fitten* to be suitable).

—v. Probably before 1400 *fitten* to marshal troops, in *Morte Arthur;* later, to be suitable (probably before 1420, in Lydgate's *Troy Book*). Early use of the verb may be derived from noun sense of an adversary or match (a meaning which itself may have existed in English longer than the record shows); the later meaning of be suitable, probably came from the adjective sense of fitting or proper, perhaps influenced by or even, in some cases borrowed from, Middle Dutch *vitten* to suit.

If a common Germanic **fitja-* juncture or connection, were present in other languages, a connection could be drawn of cognates among Old Icelandic *fitja* to knit and Old High German *fizzōn* surround, *fizza* yarn, among others, which would point to a source of *fit* in English through the early noun sense of an adversary of equal power, possibly with the still earlier sense of a meeting or coming together.

—fitter *n.* (1660) **—fitting** *adj.* (1535); *n.* (1607; *fittings* fixtures or apparatus, 1864). **—fitness** *n.* (1580)

fit[2] *n.* sudden attack, as of anger. Before 1376 *fitte* an experience of hardship, excitement, pain, etc., in *Piers Plowman,* probably developed from Old English *fitt* conflict, struggle, of uncertain origin, though possibly related to *fit¹*, n. The meaning of a sudden sharp attack, paroxysm, is first recorded in English before 1547. **—fitful** *adj.* characterized by fits, in Shakespeare's *Macbeth;* formed from English *fit²* + *-ful.* The modern sense of shifting, spasmodic, changing, irregular, is first recorded in Scott's *The Lady of the Lake* (1810).

five *adj.* Before 1175 *five,* developed from Old English (about 1000) *fif;* cognate with Old Frisian and Old Saxon *fif* five, Dutch *vijf,* all showing loss of *n,* and with Old High German *finf, fimf, funf* (modern German *fünf*), Old Icelandic *fimm* (Norwegian, Danish, and Swedish *fem*), and Gothic *fimf,* from Proto-Germanic **fimfe.* Outside the Germanic languages cognates exist in Latin *quīnque* five, Gaulish *pempe-* in *pempedoula* cinquefoil, Old Irish *cōic* five, Old Welsh *pimp* (modern Welsh *pump*), Albanian *pesë,* Greek *pénte,* Lithuanian *penkì,* Old Slavic *pętĭ,* Armenian *hing,* Sanskrit *páñca,* and Tocharian A *päñ,* Tocharian B *piś,* from Indo-European **pénkwe* (Pok.808).

fix *v.* About 1370 *fixen* set (one's eyes or mind) on something, in Chaucer's *An A.B.C.;* probably borrowed from Old French *fixer,* from *fixe, fix* fixed, from Latin *fixus,* past participle of *figere* to fix, fasten. Alternatively Middle English *fixen* may have developed from an adjective use in English that was borrowed from Latin *fixus,* past participle of *figere.* This is suggested in several sources, but the later date of the adjective's appearance in English (about 1395, in Chaucer's *Canterbury Tales,* or at least 25 years after the verb) makes this seem untenable, unless the record of English is defective at this point. Another word in Middle English, *fichen* to fix or fasten (about 1350), was borrowed from French *ficher, fichier* (from Vulgar Latin **ficcāre,* earlier **figicāre,* from Latin *figere*), but this was gradually displaced by *fix,* and *fichen* developed into *fitch.*

The meaning of fasten, attach, make firm, is first recorded about 1386, that of establish, settle, assign, is first recorded in the form of *fixed* (before 1500), which evolved into adjust, arrange, put in order (1663, in Pepys' *Diary*), and mend or repair (1737, in American English). The sense of tamper with (a jury, etc.), is also first found in American English, in 1790.

—n. 1809, American English, predicament, condition; from the verb. The meaning of a dose of narcotic drug, is first recorded in American English in 1938. **—fixation** *n.* Before 1393 *fixacion* chemical process, in Gower's *Confessio Amantis;* borrowed from Medieval Latin *fixationem* (nominative *fixatio*), from *fixare* to fix, from Latin *figere;* for suffix see -ATION. The sense of emotional attachment, is first recorded in 1910. **—fixative** *adj.* (1644); *n.* (1870); formed from English *fix,* v. + *-ative.* **—fixings** *n.* trimmings (1820, American English). **—fixity** *n.* 1666, fixed condition; borrowed perhaps from French *fixité,* from Medieval Latin *fixitatem* (nominative *fixitas*) state or condition of being fixed, from Latin *fixus,* past participle; for suffix see -ITY. **—fixture** *n.* 1598, act of fixing, in Shakespeare's *Merry Wives of Windsor;* probably alteration of Late Latin *fixūra* (from Latin *fixus,* past participle), on analogy of *mixture;* for suffix see -URE. The sense of something fixed or securely fastened is first recorded in Southey's *Omniana,* quoting Coleridge (1812).

fizz *v.* 1665, move with a hiss or sputter; imitative of the sound, and perhaps related to *fizzle.* **—n.** 1812, a hissing or sputtering sound; from the verb.

fizzle *v.* About 1532, to break wind without noise, probably an alteration of obsolete *fist* (Middle English *fisten* break wind, 1440) + *-le,* frequentative suffix. The meaning of make a hissing sound or sputtering, is first recorded in 1859, preceded by the figurative use of *fail,* come to a bad conclusion, recorded before 1847, in American English. These extended senses may be derived from earlier noun uses. **—n.** 1598; from the verb, though the senses of the action of hissing or sputtering (1842), and a failure (1846) are recorded before the corresponding senses of the verb and are not considered as derived from the verb.

fjord *n.* See FIORD.

flabbergast *v.* 1772, mentioned in *The Annual Register* as an example of a new fashionable slang word, perhaps an arbitrary formation from *flabby* (or *flapper*) and *aghast.*

It has been suggested that the word is possibly of dialectal origin; but examples of the dialectal forms (such as Scottish *flabrigastit* worn out with exertion) first appeared in the 1800's and are themselves of doubtful or unknown origin.

flabby *adj.* 1697, in Dryden's translation of Vergil's *Georgics,* variant of *flappy* flap + *-y¹.* **—flab** *n.* 1923, back formation from *flabby.*

flaccid (flas′id) *adj.* limp; weak. 1620, borrowed through French *flaccide,* or directly from Latin *flaccidus* flabby, from *flaccus* flabby, of uncertain origin. **—flaccidity** *n.* 1676; formed from English *flaccid* + *-ity,* on the model of French *flaccidité.*

flackery *n. Slang.* publicity, press-agentry. 1967, American English, from *flack* press agent (possible variant of *flak* antiaircraft gunfire, in reference to its similarity to the blusterings of press agents) + *-ery.*

flacon (flak′ən) *n.* small bottle with a stopper. 1824, in Scott's *Redgauntlet;* borrowing of French *flacon,* from Old French *flascon;* see FLAGON.

flag¹ *n.* banner. 1530, in Palsgrave's *Lesclarcissement,* and perhaps as early as 1481; of uncertain origin. This word is found in all modern Germanic languages (for example Danish *flag,* Norwegian *flagg,* Swedish *flagga,* Dutch *vlag,* German *Flagge*), but apparently it was first recorded in English, and that is perhaps the source of the other Germanic words. If the word is English in origin, it might be related to FLAG³ (compare Middle English *flakken* flutter).

—v. 1856, in American English, to stop by waving a flag; from the noun.

flag² *n.* aquatic plant, especially iris. Before 1387 *flagge* reed, rush, in Trevisa's translation of Higden's *Polychronicon;* perhaps borrowed from a Scandinavian source (compare Danish *flæg* yellow iris, and if semantically related to fluttering or waving in the wind, as reeds do, then perhaps related in form to Old Icelandic *flakka* to flicker, flutter, which suggests a possible relationship with English *flag³,* though the date in Middle English is a few years later than *flag²*).

flag³ *v.* get tired, grow weak. 1545, flap about loosely or hang down; perhaps variant of *flakken, flacken* to flap or flutter (1393, in Gower's *Confessio Amantis*), and possibly more remotely *flakeren* to flutter or wave (before 1325); both forms probably borrowed from a Scandinavian source (compare Old Icelandic *flakka* to flicker, flutter), cognate with Latin *plāga* a blow, *plangere* to beat, from Indo-European **plāg-/plag-* (Pok.832). The meaning of become limp or droop is first recorded in Cotgrave's *Dictionary* (1611), followed by that of become feeble or languid, lose strength (1639).

flag[4] *n.* slab of stone, flagstone. 1415-16, probably borrowed from a Scandinavian source (compare Old Icelandic *flaga* slab of stone; see FLAW[1] defect). **—flagstone** *n.* (1730)

flagellate (flaj'əlāt) *v.* to whip, flog. 1623, borrowed from Latin *flagellātus,* past participle of *flagellāre,* from *flagellum* whip, diminutive of *flagrum* whip, scourge, cognate with Old Icelandic *blaka* beat back and forth, from Indo-European **bhlag̑-* (Pok.154); for suffix see -ATE. *Flagellate* replaced the earlier verb *flagellen* (recorded before 1464), which was also borrowed from Latin *flagellāre,* and which became obsolete in the 1500's. **—flagellant** *n.* 1563-87, in an edition of John Foxe's *Book of Martyrs;* borrowed from Latin *flagellantem* (nominative *flagellāns*), present participle of *flagellāre* flagellate; for suffix see -ANT. **—flagellation** *n.* Before 1415 *flagellacyon;* borrowed, perhaps through French *flagellation,* or directly from Latin *flagellātiōnem* (nominative *flagellātiō*), from *flagellāre;* for suffix see -ATION. **—flagellum** *n.* 1807, a whip (later, a long whiplike tail or part, as of certain bacteria, 1852); reborrowed from Latin *flagellum;* see FLAIL. The term is found earlier in Middle English *flagelle* (before 1398, in Trevisa's translation of Bartholomew's *De Proprietatibus Rerum*), but it disappeared from the record of English after 1500.

flageolet (flaj'əlet') *n.* wind instrument somewhat like a flute. 1659, borrowed from French *flageolet,* diminutive of Old French *flageol, flajol* flute, from Vulgar Latin **flābeolum,* from Latin *flāre* to BLOW[2] puff.

flagon *n.* container for liquids. 1459, borrowed from Middle French *flacon,* from Old French *flacon,* (earlier) *flascon,* from Late Latin *flascōnem* bottle; see FLASK.

flagrant (flā'grənt) *adj.* Before 1500 *flagraunt* radiant, glorious; later, flaming, burning (1513); borrowed, probably through French *flagrant,* from Latin *flagrantem* (nominative *flagrāns*) burning, present participle of *flagrāre* to burn, related to *fulgēre* to shine; see EFFULGENT; for suffix see -ANT. The sense of glaringly offensive or scandalous, is first recorded in Defoe's *Jure Divino, A Satyr* (1706).

flail *n.* instrument for threshing grain. Probably about 1200 *flegl,* in *The Ormulum,* suggesting development from Old English **flegel,* of which Late Old English (before 1100) *fligel* seems to be a variant. The Old English form corresponds to Middle Dutch, Dutch, and Middle High German *vlegel* flail, Old High German *flegel,* and modern German *Flegel,* and was probably an early borrowing of Late Latin *flagellum* winnowing tool or flail, from Latin *flagellum* whip, scourge; see FLAGELLATE.

The word is considered rare before the late 1300's, at which time it is recorded in Middle English as *fleil, flail,* influenced in formation by or reborrowed from Old French *flael, flaiel* a scourge, whip, from Late Latin *flagellum.*

—v. to flog or whip. Before 1500 *flaylen;* from the noun.

flair *n.* About 1390 *flayre* fragrance or odor; borrowed from Old French *flair* odor or scent, from *flairer* to smell, from Late Latin *flagrāre,* altered form of Latin *fragrāre* emit (a sweet) odor; see FRAGRANT. The Late Latin spelling with *l* developed from Latin *fragrāre* by dissimilation of *r. . .r* to *l. . .r.*

The meaning of keen perception, literally, power or sense of smell, is first recorded in 1881 as a reborrowing of French *flair,* from Old French, and the extended sense of special ability, natural aptitude or talent, is first recorded in American English, in Sinclair Lewis' novel *Arrowsmith* (1925).

flak *n.* fire from antiaircraft guns. 1938, antiaircraft gun, in Jane's *Fighting Ships;* borrowed from German *Flak,* an acronym formed from the initials of the compound *Fl(ieger)a(bwehr)k(anone),* literally, airplane defense cannon (*Flieger* flier, airplane + *Abwehr* defense + *Kanone* cannon). The meaning of antiaircraft fire, is first recorded in 1940. The informal figurative use of a barrage of criticism, heated argument, etc., is first recorded about 1963, in American English.

flake *n.* Before 1325, a particle; possibly developed from Old English **flacca, *flac-* flakes of snow; probably borrowed ultimately from a Scandinavian source (compare Old Icelandic *flakna* to flake off, peel, *flak* loosened or torn piece, probably related to *flā* to skin, FLAY). The Anglo-German scholar Junius (1589-1667) cites an Old English form **flacca* flakes of snow, in his *Etymologicum Anglicanum,* and the American scholar Kemp Malone cites the apparent derivation as Old English **flac-* which occurs in *flacor* flying (said of arrows); but an Old English form is not found in literature. **—v.** Before 1420 *flaken* fall in flakes, in Lydgate's *Troy Book;* from the noun. **—flaky** *adj.* 1580, formed from English *flake,* n. + *-y*[1].

flambeau (flam'bō) *n.* flaming torch. 1632, borrowing of French *flambeau* torch, flame, from Old French *flambe* FLAME.

flamboyant *adj.* 1832, of an architectural style with flamelike curves; borrowing of French *flamboyant* flaming, wavy, present participle of *flamboyer* to flame, from Old French *flamboier,* from *flambe* FLAME; for suffix see -ANT. The sense of showy or ornate, is first recorded in English in 1879, as an extension of the earlier meaning of brilliantly or flamingly colored, in Longfellow's *The Golden Legend* (1851). **—flamboyance** *n.* 1891, from *flamboyant,* on analogy of such forms as *clairvoyant, clairvoyance;* for suffix see -ANCE.

flame *n.* About 1303 *flamme* blazing fire, in Mannyng's *Handlyng Synne;* later *flawme* (about 1340), and *flambe* (about 1375); borrowed through Anglo-French *flaume, flaumbe,* Old French *flamme, flambe* or *flamble,* from Latin *flammula* small flame, diminutive of *flamma* flame (pre-Latin **flagmā),* and related to *flagrāre* to burn; see FLAGRANT. **—v.** About 1303 *flammen;* later *flaumen* (1350); borrowed through Anglo-French *flaumer, flaumber,* from Old French *flammer, flamer, flamber,* from the noun *flamme, flambe.* **—flammable** *adj.* 1813; formed in English from Latin *flammāre* set on fire (from *flamma* flame) + English *-able.*

flamenco (fləmeng'kō) *n.* a style of music and the traditional dancing that accompanies it, associated with the Gypsies of Spain. 1896, borrowed from Spanish *flamenco,* literally, FLAMINGO. According to Corominas, the term was first applied to the Gypsy singing and dancing of Andalusia, in reference to the "provocative appearance" of the dancers, which was an extension of the "good appearance" of one with a pink complexion, that was associated with the Flemings with their high color and the flamingo with its bright pink coloring.

flamingo (fləming'gō) *n.* bird with bright pink or red feathers. 1565, borrowed from Portuguese *flamengo,* from Spanish *flamengo,* variant of *flamenco* (originally) Fleming, a native of Flanders, from Dutch *Vlaming;* so called from association of the bird's coloring with the pinkish complexion of the Flemish or Dutch in the eyes of Spaniards; Spanish *flamenca* was used by about 1330 as an adjective meaning "of a ruddy complexion, flesh-colored."

flange (flanj) *n.* projecting edge, rim, collar, etc. 1688 *flang* part that widens out, of uncertain origin; perhaps ultimately connected with Old French *flanc;* see FLANK.

flank *n.* side. Probably before 1300 *flaunke,* in *Arthour and Merlin;* developed from Late Old English (before 1100) *flanc* the fleshy part of the side between the ribs and the hip; borrowed from Old French *flanc* (in which there was a replacement of *fl* for *hl*), from Frankish **hlanca* (compare Old High German *hlanca* loin, side; see LANK).

There is some question as to the origin of the Old French form, but the OED states that the shift from Frankish to Old French is probable because a similar change in the spelling of some proper names is believed to have occurred.

The military sense of the extreme left or right side of an army in the field, is first recorded in William Patten's *The Expedition into Scotland of Prince Edward* (1548).

—v. 1548, to shoot on the flank or sideways; from the noun. The sense of guard, protect, or defend on the flank, is first recorded in Spenser's *Faerie Queene* (1596).

flannel *n.* 1300-01 *flaunneol* a kind of woolen cloth or garment, in *Rolls of Parliament;* apparently variant of *flanyn* sackcloth (before 1400); borrowed probably from Old French *flaine* a kind of coarse wool. The alternative and traditional source of *flannel* has been from Welsh *gwlanen* article or piece of woolen material, from *gwlān* wool, but it is difficult to accept English *fl* from the Welsh consonant cluster *gwl,* when compared with the name *Gwladys* which became *Gladys* in English, not **Fladys.*

flap *n.* Probably before 1300 *flappe* a blow, stroke, slap, in *Arthour and Merlin;* probably imitative of the sound of striking. The meaning of anything that hangs down, such as the flap of a coat, is first recorded in 1522, in Skelton's writings; the sense of a flapping motion or noise, such as the flap of a bird's wings, is not recorded before 1774, in Goldsmith's writings, but from this latter meaning evolved the informal sense of excitement, commotion, agitation (1916). **—v.** About 1330 *flappen* dash about, shake; later, beat or strike (about 1350); from *flappe,* n. **—flapjack** *n.* Before 1600; formed from English *flap,* n. + *Jack,* personal name used humorously. **—flapper** *n.* **1** something that flaps. 1570, formed from English *flap,* v. + *-er*[1]. **2** forward and unconventional girl of the 1920's. 1889, in British slang, young immoral girl. The OED considers this meaning to be derived probably from northern English dialect of Northumberland and Durham *flap* woman or girl of loose character (1631), a figurative use of *flap* something that hangs loose; there may also be vestiges of the meaning "youth" in the conventional etymology for this term which cites the sense of a young wild duck or partridge (1773).

flare *v.* About 1550, spread out (hair), of unknown origin; (often compared with Norwegian *flara* to blaze, flaunt in gaudy clothes, but without semantic analogy, because the related sense in English "to blaze, flame up briefly," is not recorded until about 1632, more than 75 years after the word appeared in English). **—n.** bright, unsteady light. 1814, in Scott's *The Lord of the Isles;* from the verb.

flash *v.* Probably before 1200 *flasken* to dash or splash, as water, etc.: later *flaschen* (before 1387, in Trevisa's translation of Higden's *Polychronicon*); probably imitative of the sound. The meaning of give off a sudden short light or flame, is not recorded in English until 1548, but it is found in the earlier phrase *flasshen in a fire* burst into flame (probably before 1400). **—n.** 1566, burst of flame; from the verb. An earlier form, Middle English *flaske* marshy place, pool or puddle (1306, in the place name *Flaiskedaile*), parallels the early verb use of splash (water), but there is no record of its development into the current noun sense of burst of flame; rather it diverged to retain its original association with water in the modern English meaning of a rush of water. **—flashy** *adj.* 1583, splashing; later, sparkling (1609), and showy, cheaply attractive (before 1690).

flask *n.* a glass or metal bottle, especially one with a narrow neck. 1355-56 *flaske* case; later *flask* cask or keg (1393); borrowed from Medieval Latin *flasco, flasca* container, bottle, from Late Latin *flascō, flascōnem* bottle, from a Germanic source (compare Old English *flasce, flaxe* bottle, Middle Dutch *flasce,* modern Dutch *fles,* Old High German *flaska,* modern German *Flasche,* and Old Icelandic *flaska,* (from Indo-European **plok̂-skō,* Pok.834) which in the sense of a plaited or braid-covered bottle are perhaps derived from the same source as Old English *fleohtan* to plait, braid; see PLY[2] fold). The meaning of a glass or metal bottle, especially one with a narrow neck, is first recorded in Southerne's *The Maid's Last Prayer* (1693). The Old English word, *flasce* (more usually *flaxe*) would normally have become *flash* in modern English, but it does not seem to have survived into Middle English.

flat[1] *adj.* level, spread out. Probably about 1300, borrowed from a Scandinavian source (compare Old Icelandic *flatr* flat; cognate with Old Saxon *flat* flat or shallow, Old High German *flaz* even or flat, Latvian *plañdit* make broad, and Greek *platýs* flat, broad; the Germanic adjectives are from Indo-European **plad-os* or **pləd-os,* Pok.833; see PLACE). **—n.** 1167, in the place name *Kirkeflat;* later, level ground (probably about 1390, in *Sir Gawain and the Green Knight*); from the adjective. The musical sense of a half note below natural pitch, is first recorded in Shakespeare's *The Two Gentlemen of Verona* (1594). **—flatboat** *n.* (1660) **—flatfish** *n.* (1710) **—flatfooted** *adj.* (1601) **—flatiron** *n.* (1810, American English, in Franklin's writings) **—flatland** *n.* (1735) **—flatten** *v.* 1375 *flatten* to prostrate oneself; later, to fall flat (before 1400); replaced by the modern English form *flatten* make flat (1630, in Donne's *Progress of the Soul*), re-formed from English *flat,* adj. + *-en*[1].

flat[2] *n. Chiefly British.* 1801, Scottish, floor or story of a house, alteration of Middle English *flet* room or hall (recorded before 1200), found in Old English *flet* a dwelling, floor, ground (about 725, in *Beowulf*); cognate with Old Saxon *flet* (genitive *fletties*) room, house,

Old High German *flezzi* floor in a house, and Old Icelandic *flatr* FLAT[1]. The meaning of a set of rooms or residence on one floor, is first recorded in Scott's *Redgauntlet* (1824).

flatter *v.* Probably before 1200 *flatren* praise insincerely, in *Ancrene Riwle;* later *flatteren* (probably about 1225); borrowed from Old French *flater* to flatter, (originally, stroke with the hand, caress), from Frankish **flat* level, flat (compare Old High German *flaz* FLAT[1]). Middle English *flateren* is an irregular formation, as verbs adapted from Old French in *-er* substituted *-en* for *-er,* and the expected form would be **flaten.* However, there is a class of verbs in Middle English such as *flikeren* to flicker, and *schimeren* to shimmer, which may have influenced the adaptation of Old French *flater* to Middle English *flatren* and later *flatteren.* **—flatterer** *n.* About 1350, formed from Middle English *flatteren* + *-er[1].* An earlier form *flatour* (1340, in *Ayenbite of Inwyt*) was borrowed from Old French *flateor, flatour.* **—flattery** *n.* About 1330 *flaterie,* borrowed from Old French *flaterie,* from *flater* to flatter; for suffix see -ERY.

flatulent (flach′ələnt) *adj.* having gas in the stomach or intestines. 1599, borrowed from Middle French *flatulent,* an irregular formation from Latin *flātus* (genitive *flātūs*) a blowing, a breaking wind, from *flāre* to BLOW[2] puff. The French form was probably patterned on words like *virulent* and *succulent,* which were borrowed from Latin. **—flatulence** *n.* 1711, vanity, pomposity (figurative sense), from *flatulent,* on the analogy of such words as *eminent, eminence;* for suffix see -ENCE.

flaunt *v.* show off. 1566, to display oneself in flashy clothes; of unknown origin. The transitive use of display ostentatiously, show off, is first recorded in 1827. The form of the word points to a French origin, but no likely French source is evident. *Flaunt* has also been compared to Scandinavian dialectal verbs, such as Norwegian *flanta* roam about, Swedish dialect *flanka* flutter or waver, but lack of specific meaning and late appearance of the English word makes such connections doubtful. Another possibility is that *flaunt* may be a coined word, formed from a blending such as *fly[2]* or *flounce[1]* and *vaunt.*

flautist *n.* flutist. 1860, in Hawthorne's *The Marble Faun;* borrowed from Italian *flautista,* from *flauto* flute, from Old Provençal *flaüt;* see FLUTE; for suffix see -IST.

flavor *n.* Probably about 1380 *flavor* aroma, odor (usually pleasing); alteration (influenced by *savor*) of a borrowing from Old French *flaour, flaor, flaur* smell, odor, from Vulgar Latin *flātor* odor (literally, that which blows), from Latin *flātor* blower, from *flāre* to BLOW[2] puff. The sense of taste, savor, is first recorded in Congreve's translation of Juvenal's *Eleventh Satire* (1697) from the fact that taste depends in part on the sense of smell. However, an earlier use in Milton's *Samson Agonistes* (1671) suggests this sense even though seemingly contrasted with "taste." **—v.** 1730-36, to give flavor to, season, in Bailey's *Dictionary;* from the noun. **—flavoring** *n.* 1845, from *flavor,* v. An earlier form existed in Middle English: 1422 *flauryng* perfume; borrowed from Middle French *flaur.*

flaw[1] *n.* fault, defect. Before 1325 *flay* a flake; later *flaw* a flake (probably before 1400), and *flawe* fragment (probably before 1425); probably borrowed from a Scandinavian source (compare Swedish *flaga* flake, Old Icelandic *flaga* slab of stone, Icelandic *flag* spot where turf is cut out, and Old Icelandic *flā* to skin, FLAY). The sense of a defect, fault, is first recorded in 1586, in reference to character, reasoning, etc., and later in reference to material things (1604); probably extended from the original meaning of a fragment. **—v.** 1423, implied in *flaved, flawed,* probably meaning "chipped"; past participle of **flauen* to chip or flake. **—flawless** *adj.* 1648; formed from English *flaw[1],* n. + *-less.*

flaw[2] *n.* sudden gust. 1513, probably borrowed from a Scandinavian source (compare Swedish *flaga* gust of wind; cognate with Middle Low German *vlage* gust, assault, Middle Dutch *vlāghe,* modern Dutch *vlaag* gust, Lithuanian *plàkti* to beat, from Indo-European **plak-* beat (Pok.832).

flax *n.* plant from which linen is made. Before 1325 *flax* flax fibers; earlier in the compound *flexland* field for growing flax (1207, as a surname *Flexland*); developed from Old English *fleax* cloth made of flax, linen (before 899, in Alfred's translation of St. Gregory's *Pastoral Care*). Old English *fleax* is cognate with Old Frisian *flax,* Middle Dutch, modern Dutch, and Middle Low German *vlas,* Old High German *flahs* (modern German *Flachs*), from Proto-Germanic **flaHsan,* and with Greek *plokḗ* a twisting, from Indo-European **plek̑-/plok̑-* (Pok.834). A further possible relationship exists with Old High German *flehtan* (modern German *flechten*) to braid, in that the fiber was prepared by a process of stripping; see PLY[2] fold. **—flaxen** *adj.* About 1450 *flaxen, flexon;* earlier in a surname *Flaxennehed* (1273); formed from English *flax* + *-en[2].*

flay *v.* strip off the skin. Probably about 1300 *fleyen,* in *The Romance of Guy of Warwick;* earlier *flen* (probably about 1225, in *King Horn*) and *flan* (probably before 1200, in Layamon's *Chronicle of Britain*); developed from Old English (before 800) *flēan;* cognate with Old High German *flahan* to skin, Middle Dutch *vlaen,* Old Icelandic *flā* to skin, from Proto-Germanic **flaHanan;* also cognate with Lithuanian *plěšti* to tear, from Indo-European **plēk̑-/plək̑-* (Pok.835). The figurative meaning of scold or criticize severely, is found in Middle English before 1333. The modern spelling *flay* appeared in the late 1300's but was not established until the mid-1800's.

flea *n.* Before 1300 *flei,* developed from Old English (about 700) *flēah;* cognate with Middle Low German and Middle Dutch *vlō* flea (modern Dutch *vlo*), Old High German *flōh* (modern German *Floh*), Old Icelandic *flō;* from Proto-Germanic **flauH-* probably derived from the same source as Old English *flēon* to FLEE. The modern spelling *flea* with *a* was not established until after 1550.

fleck *v.* to spot, streak. About 1378, implied in the past participial form *flekked* spotted, in a version of *Piers Plowman;* probably borrowed from a Scandinavian source (compare Old Icelandic *flekka* to spot, from *flekkr* spot; see the noun). The verb form in Middle English is also analyzed by some as a borrowing from a Scandinavian source that is altered with an addition of English *-ed,* assuming the form of a past participle in English, that is traditionally used with nouns to create such formations as *long-legged,* where there is obviously no verb form as its base. This, of course, is a possibility with *flecked* in view of the great difference in time (about 220 years) between the recording of *flecked* and that of the noun *fleck.* **—n.** 1598, spot, blemish, freckle;

perhaps from the verb in English; or borrowed from Middle Dutch *vlecke* spot; corresponding to Middle Low German *vlecke* spot, blot, Dutch *vlek,* Old High German *flecch, fleccho* (modern German *Fleck* spot, stain, *flecken* to spot, stain), and Old Icelandic *flekkr* spot, from Proto-Germanic **flekk-,* from Indo-European **plik̑-nó-,* root **plēik̑-/plik̑-* (Pok.835).

flection *n.* 1603 *flexion* change, modification; borrowed from Latin *flexiōnem* (nominative *flexiō*) a bending or turning, from *flex-,* past participle stem of *flectere* to bend; see FLEX under FLEXIBLE; for suffix see -ION. The sense of a bending, as of the arm, is first recorded in English in 1615, in a book on anatomy; but it is preceded by the meaning of a bend, curve, or joint (1607). In the late 1700's the spelling was altered to *flection,* partly by influence of *inflection* and partly on analogy with other words such as *affection* and *direction,* and this spelling has been retained in American English.

fledgling *n.* 1846, young bird; formed from *fledge* + *-ling.* The sense of an inexperienced person, is first recorded in 1856. **—fledge** *v.* acquire feathers. 1566, from Middle English *flegge* winged, ready to fly (probably before 1300); developed from Old English *-flycge,* as in *unflycge* unfledged; cognate with Middle Low German and Middle Dutch *vlugge* ready to fly, quick (modern Dutch *vlug* quick), Old High German *flucki* (modern German *flügge* ready to fly, from Middle Low German), from Proto-Germanic **fluȝȝja-;* derived from the same Germanic source as Old English *flēogan* to FLY² move through the air; for the development in the English spelling see EDGE.

flee *v.* Probably before 1200 *flien, fleien,* in Layamon's *Chronicle of Britain;* developed from Old English (about 825) *flēon* take flight, run away; cognate with Old Frisian *fliā* to flee, Old Saxon *fliohan,* Middle Dutch *vlīen* (later Middle Dutch and modern Dutch *vlieden*), Old High German *fliohan* (modern German *fliehen*), Old Icelandic *flȳja,* and Gothic *thliuhan,* from Proto-Germanic **fleuHanan;* probably related to Old English *flēogan* to FLY move through the air. This relationship was questioned at one time on the assumption that Gothic *thliuhan* retains the original initial sound of the inherited Germanic word, but scholars now regard the Gothic initial *thl-* as an alteration of Germanic *fl-.*

The modern form of the past tense and past participle of this verb is *fled* which became established in the 1400's, because, after about 1250, a weak past tense *fledde* and past participle *fled* or *fledd* developed (perhaps by influence of Scandinavian past-tense forms such as Swedish *flydde* and Danish *flyede,* corresponding to Old Icelandic past tense *flȳdha*) displacing the Old English forms of the strong verb *flēon* with its past tense *flēah,* and past participle *flogen.*

fleece *n.* sheep's wool. About 1380 *flees,* in Chaucer's translation of Boethius' *De Consolatione Philosophiae;* developed from Old English (before 1000) *flēos, flīes, flȳs;* cognate with Middle Low German *vlūs* fleece, Middle Dutch and modern Dutch *vlies,* Middle High German *vlius* (modern German *Vlies* fleece, *Flaus, Flausch* thick woolen material or coat), cognate with Latin *plūma* (pre-Latin **plusmā*) feather, down, from Indo-European **pleus-/plūs-/plus-* (Pok.838). The German forms with *v-* (as opposed to *f-*) show the probable influence of Dutch orthography *(vlies)* and the popular etymological association of the word with Latin *vellus* fleece. **—v.** 1537, shear (the wool) from a sheep; (hence, figuratively) to obtain by unfair means; from the noun. **—fleecy** *adj.* 1567, formed from English *fleece,* n. + *-y¹.*

fleet¹ *n.* group of ships. Before 1147 *flete,* developed from Old English (before 1000) *flēot* ship, floating vessel, from *flēotan* to float; cognate with Old Frisian *fliāta* to float, Old Saxon *fliotan,* Middle Dutch and modern Dutch *vlieten* to flow, Old High German *fliozan* to flow, float (modern German *fliessen* to flow), Old Icelandic *fljōta* to flow, float; also cognate with Lettish *pludēt* to float, from Indo-European **pleud-/plud-,* root **pleu-/plou-/plu-* (Pok.837); related to Old English *flōwan* to FLOW; see also FLOAT. The meaning of a group of armed ships, a naval force, is recorded early in Middle English (before 1200); later a wider sense of a number of ships or boats sailing together, is recorded in the late 1600's, and a transferred sense, originally applied to a troop of armed men or an army, is first recorded probably before 1400, in *The Wars of Alexander,* establishing a usage that later led to such applications as *a fleet of trucks.*

fleet² *adj.* swift, rapid. Before 1529 *flete,* in Skelton's writings; possibly a shortened form of earlier unrecorded *fleeting,* adj., flying, moving swiftly, from *fleet,* v., fly, move swiftly; *or* borrowed directly from a Scandinavian source (compare Old Icelandic *fljōtr* swift, related to *fljōta* to flow, float; see FLEET¹). **—fleeting** *adj.* 1563, passing swiftly, soon gone; from *fleet,* v. to drift, probably before 1200, in Layamon's *Chronicle of Britain;* later, to fly, move swiftly (probably about 1200, in *The Ormulum*); developed from Old English *flēotan* to float, swim (about 725, in *Beowulf*), corresponding to Old Frisian *fliāta* to flow, Old Saxon *fliotan,* Middle Dutch and modern Dutch *vlieten,* Old High German *fliozan* to float, flow (modern German *fliessen* to flow), Old Icelandic *fljōta* (Swedish *flyta,* Norwegian *flyte, fliota,* Danish *flyde*); compare FLEET¹.

Fleming *n.* a native of Flanders. Probably before 1150 *flameng;* also found in Old English *Flæming;* borrowed from Old Frisian *Fleming;* corresponding to, and perhaps also borrowed from, Middle Dutch *Vlāming,* and cognate with Old Icelandic *Flæmingr* which was probably borrowed from Old Frisian.

Flemish *adj.* of Flanders, the people living there, or their language. Before 1325 *flemmysshe,* probably borrowed from Old Frisian *Flemsche;* corresponding to, and perhaps also borrowed from Middle Dutch *Vlāmisch;* cognate with Middle Low German *Vlamish, Vlamesh.* It is also possible that in some instances English *Flemish* was formed from earlier English *Flem(ing)* + *-ish¹.* **—n.** the language of the Flemings. Before 1325, possibly from the adjective.

flesh *n.* Probably before 1200 *flesch,* in *Ancrene Riwle;* developed from Old English (before 800) *flǣsc.* The Old English form is cognate with Old Frisian and Old Saxon *flēsk* flesh, Middle Low German *vlēs,* Dutch *vlees,* Old High German *fleisk* (modern German *Fleisch*), and is possibly related to Old Icelandic *flesk* swine's flesh, bacon through Old English *flǣc,* though this form is considered an inaccurate or dialectal spelling by the OED. The Germanic cognates derive from Indo-European **plaik̑-/plēik̑-* to tear (Pok.835). **—v.** Probably about 1425 *fleschen* to produce new tissue; earlier found in the past participle *flesshide* provided with flesh (1422); from the noun. Later, the verb meant to reward (a hound or hawk) with flesh of the game killed to excite its eagerness in the chase and, as an extension of that meaning, to initiate in or inure (sol diers) to bloodshed or warfare; both senses recorded in Palsgrave's *Lesclarcissement* (1530). **—fleshy** *adj.* 1369, in Chaucer's *Dethe of Blaunche;* formed from Middle English *flesch* + *-y*[1].

fleur-de-lis (flėr'dəlē') *n.* design used in heraldry. Before 1325 *flour de lis* royal emblem of France (literally, lily flower); borrowed from Old French *flour-de-lis* (*flour* FLOWER and *de* of, and *lis* lilies, from Latin *lilium* LILY). The current spelling is first recorded in the 1800's, from modern French.

flexible *adj.* easily bent. About 1412; borrowed from Middle French *flexible,* or directly from Latin *flexibilis* that may be bent, pliant, from *flexus,* past participle of *flectere* to bend; of uncertain origin; for suffix see -IBLE. **—flex** *v.* to bend. Before 1521, possibly a back formation from *flexible,* after Latin *flex-,* past participle stem of *flectere.*

flibbertigibbet *n.* flighty, chattering person. Before 1450 *flepergebet, flypyrgebet* chatterer, probably imitative of the sound of meaningless chatter.

The current spelling is first recorded in Shakespeare's *King Lear* (1605), as the name of one of the fiends enumerated by Tom o' Bedlam. In the sense of an impish or flighty person, the word was popularized as the nickname of a character in Scott's novel *Kenilworth* (1821).

flick *n.* quick, light blow. 1591 *flicke;* probably imitative of the sound; but it is found in the earlier phrase *not worth a flykke* worthless, trivial (about 1445, in Bokenham's *Legends of Holy Women*). —v. 1816, in Peacock's *Headlong Hall;* from the noun.

flicker[1] *v.* shine with a wavering light. Probably before 1200 *flikeren* behave frivolously, trifle, in *Ancrene Riwle;* later *flekeren* waver, vacillate (about 1300); developed from Old English (about 1000) *flicorian* to flutter, flap so as to beat quickly and lightly; cognate with Low German *flickern* and modern Dutch *flikkeren,* and perhaps related to Old English *flacor* flying, fluttering. Old English *flacor* is cognate with Middle Dutch *flackeren* to flap, flutter, Middle High German *vlackern* to flicker (modern German *flackern*), and Old Icelandic *flakka* to flicker, *flǫkra* to flutter. Cognates outside Germanic include Greek *plēgnýnai* to beat, and Latin *plangere* to beat, from Indo-European **plāg-/plag-* (Pok.832).

The sense of shine or burn with an unsteady light is first recorded in Shakespeare's *King Lear* (1605), but did not come into common use until the 1800's.

—n. 1857, a flickering, in Hughes' *Tom Brown's School Days;* from the verb.

flicker[2] *n.* woodpecker of North America. 1808, American English, possibly from the habit of flitting to and fro among trees, especially while feeding, thus showing briefly its white spots of plumage on the wings and suggesting wavering light.

flight[1] *n.* act or manner of flying. Before 1225 *fliht,* developed from Old English (before 900) *flyht* a flying, flight, from Proto-Germanic **fluHtiz;* related to Old English *flēogan* to FLY[2]. The spelling *flight* is first recorded in Chaucer's *Canterbury Tales* (about 1385); for the development of the modern spelling see FIGHT. **—flighty** *adj.* 1552, swift; later, fickle or frivolous (1768-74, in an early volume of a work of metaphysics); formed from English *flight* + *-y*[1]. **—flightiness** *n.* 1748, in Richardson's *Clarissa;* formed from English *flighty* + *-ness.*

flight[2] *n.* act of fleeing. Probably before 1200 *fluht,* in *Ancrene Riwle;* later *fliht* (about 1200, in *The Ormulum*), but not found in Old English, though probably existing as **flyht,* suggested by corresponding forms in Old Frisian *flecht* act of fleeing, Old Saxon *fluht,* Dutch *vlucht,* Old High German *fluht* (modern German *Flucht*), Old Icelandic *flōtti,* and Gothic *thlauhs;* derived from the Germanic source of Old English *flēon* to FLEE.

flimsy *adj.* light and thin. 1702, of uncertain origin (perhaps an imitative formation by metathesis of *i* and *l,* suggested by *film* gauzy covering on the surface of something, with the ending patterned on *clumsy, lousy, tricksy,* and similar adjectives).

flinch *v.* 1579, draw back, turn aside, in Lyly's *Euphues;* probably borrowed from Old French *flenchir, flainchir* to bend, from Frankish **hlankjan;* compare (Middle) High German *lenken* to bend, turn; see LANK. The meaning of draw back or shrink from pain, wince, is first recorded before 1677.

fling *v.* Probably before 1300 *flingen* to dash, rush; also to be swung, thrown, or shot forth; both senses in *Kyng Alisaunder;* probably borrowed from a Scandinavian source (compare Old Icelandic *flengja* to beat, thrash, fling, related to *flā* to FLAY). **—n.** 1550, especially in the phrase *have a fling at* an attempt or attack on; from the verb; but it is found earlier in the phrase *maken a flyng* start to do something (1325). The sense of time of doing as one pleases, as in to *have one's fling,* is first recorded in 1827.

flint *n.* 1157-63, as a surname in pipe rolls of account from Lancashire; developed from Old English (about 700) *flint* flint or rock; cognate with Old High German *flins* flint, rock, Middle Dutch *vlint,* Old Icelandic *fletta* (in compounds) slate, slab, and Swedish *flinta* stone splinter, from Indo-European **plind-* (root **plei-/pli-*), Pok.1000; related to SPLIT and SPLINTER. **—flintstone** *n.* (before 1325) **—flinty** *adj.* 1536, in Bishop Hugh Latimer's correspondence with Cromwell; formed from English *flint* + *-y*[1].

flip[1] *v.* toss or move with a snap of a finger and thumb. 1594, in Lyly's plays; earlier, as an element in *flip-flop* (1529, in Skelton's *Elinor Rummyng*); possibly imitative of the sound, but also probably imitative of the form *fillip* to toss (1450) and possibly even a contraction of it; compare FILLIP. The slang meaning of get excited, go wild about something, is first recorded in 1950 in American English. **—n.** 1692, quick blow or stroke, in Locke's *Toleration;* from the verb, and possibly modeled after *fillip,* v. **—flipper** *n.* 1822, limb for swimming; formed from English *flip,* v. + *-er*[1].

flip[2] *n.* a hot drink usually containing beer and sugar. 1695, in Congreve's *Love for Love;* in the sense of a whipped-up mixture, noun use of *flip*[1], v.

flip[3] *adj.* shortened form of FLIPPANT.

flippant *adj.* 1605, fluent or talkative; perhaps formed from *flip*[1] move nimbly + *-ant,* on analogy of adjectives such as *rampant.* The sense of disrespectful or impertinent, is first recorded in 1677. **—flippancy** *n.* 1746, in Walpole's letters; formed from English *flippant* + *-cy.*

flirt *v.* 1553, to turn up one's nose, sneer at; later, to rap or flick, as with the fingers (1563-87, in an edition of John Foxe's *Book of Martyrs*); of uncertain origin (possibly of imitative origin; compare FLIP[1], FLICK, and FLIT; or possibly related to Old English *fleardian* to trifle, play the fool, *fleard* a trifle, deception; borrowed perhaps from Old Icelandic *flærth* deceit; and also possibly related to East Frisian *flirt* a flick or light blow, and *flirtje* a giddy girl).

The meaning of play at courtship (in Garrick's Prologue to Sheridan's *School for Scandal,* 1777), presumably evolved from the earlier sense of flit from one object to another (1578).

—n. 1549, stroke of wit, sneer or jibe, in Coverdale's writings; probably from the verb, though the verb is first recorded slightly later than the noun. The meaning of a person who flirts, is first recorded before 1732, in John Gay's poetry. **—flirtation** *n.* 1718, in Cibber's plays; formed from English *flirt* + *-ation.* **—flirtatious** *adj.* 1834, formed from English *flirtation* + *-ous.*

flit *v.* Before 1200 *flutten* convey, move, take (in southwestern dialect); later *flytten* change, vary (1369, in Chaucer's *Book of the Duchesse*); and *flittynge* passing, transitory (probably before 1387, in a version of *Piers Plowman*); of uncertain origin, perhaps borrowed from a Scandinavian source (compare Old Icelandic *flytja* carry away or out, help; related to *fljōta* to flow, float; see FLEET[1] group of ships). **—n.** a flitting; flutter. 1835, from the verb; earlier *flitting,* n., act of changing (before 1400). **—flitter** *v.* to flutter. Probably before 1400 *fleteren,* in *Morte Arthur;* formed from *flit,* v. + *-er*[4].

flitch *n.* side of a hog salted and cured. Probably about 1200 *fliche,* developed from Old English (before 700) *flicce* side of any animal; cognate with Middle Low German *vlicke* flitch, Old Icelandic *flikki* flitch; related to Old Icelandic *flīk* a rag, from Indo-European **plēiĝ-/plīĝ-* tear (Pok.835).

flivver *n. Slang.* cheap car, especially the Model T Ford. 1910, American English, of unknown origin.

float *v.* Probably before 1200 *floten,* in Layamon's *Chronicle of Britain;* developed from Late Old English *flotian* (1031, in the *Anglo-Saxon Chronicle*); cognate with Middle Dutch *vlōten* to float, and Old Icelandic *flota,* from Proto-Germanic **flutōjanan;* from the same Germanic source as Old English *flēotan* to flow, float; see FLEET[1]. Also, the influence of Old French *floter* (modern French *flotter*), of Frankish origin, is by no means to be ignored. **—n.** Before 1121 *flote* state of floating, later, fleet of ships, in a version of Layamon's *Chronicle of Britain* (about 1300); developed from a fusion of Old English nouns: *flot* body of water, and *flota* ship or fleet; both forms are cognate with Old High German *flōz* fleet, raft, stream (modern German *Floss* raft), Middle Low German and Middle Dutch *vlote* stream, raft (modern Dutch *vlot* raft), and Old Icelandic *floti* stream, fleet; from the same Germanic source as Old English *flēotan* to flow, float. The sense of a raft or other objects that float, is first recorded in 1322.

flock[1] (flok) *n.* group of animals or persons. Probably before 1200 *floc,* in Layamon's *Chronicle of Britain;* developed from Old English *flocc* group of persons (894, in the *Anglo-Saxon Chronicle*); cognate with Middle Low German *vlocke* crowd, flock (of sheep), and Old Icelandic *flokkr* crowd, troop, of unknown origin. **—v.** About 1300 *flocken* gather in a group or crowd, congregate; from the noun.

flock[2] *n.* tuft of wool. About 1250 *flockes,* in *The Owl and the Nightingale;* probably borrowed from Old French *floc,* from Latin *floccus* (pre-Latin **flōcos*); cognate with Old High German *blaha* coarse linen, Old Swedish *bla,* early Danish *blaa* flax or hemp fiber, and Old Icelandic *blæja* bedsheet, from Indo-European **bhlok-/bhlōk-* (Pok.161). Alternatively, *flock*[2] may be an inherited word, cognate with Middle Dutch and Middle Low German *vlocke* (modern Dutch *vlok*), Old High German *floccho* down, flock (modern German *Flocke*), from Indo-European **pluknón-,* root **pleuk-/plouk-/pluk-* (Pok.837). These words, in turn, are cognate with Latvian *plauki* snowflakes, Lithuanian *plaũkas* fibers, tufts of wool, and *plùksna* feather.

floe *n.* sheet of floating ice. 1817, probably borrowed from Norwegian *flo* layer, slab, from Old Icelandic *flō* layer, related to *flak* loosened or torn piece; see FLAKE.

flog *v.* to whip. 1676, a slang term, perhaps originally school slang and therefore a shortened and altered form of Latin *flagellāre* FLAGELLATE, from student exposure to that language.

flood *n.* 1125 *flod* inundation; developed from Old English *flōd* a flowing of water, flood (about 725, in *Beowulf*); cognate with Old Frisian and Old Saxon *flōd* flood, Middle Dutch *vloet* (modern Dutch *vloed*), Old High German *fluot* (modern German *Flut*), Old Icelandic *flōdh,* and Gothic *flōdus,* from Proto-Germanic **flōđús* from the same Germanic source as Old English *flōwan* to FLOW. For development of the vowel see BLOOD. **—v.** 1663, from the noun. **—floodgate** *n.* (about 1440) **—floodlight** *v.* (1923); *n.* (1924). **—flood plain** (1873, in American English)

floor *n.* Before 1200 *flor,* developed from Old English *flōr* floor (about 725, in *Beowulf*); cognate with Middle Dutch and modern Dutch *vloer* floor, Middle Low German *vlōr* floorboard, meadow, Old High German *vluor* field, plain (modern German *Flur*), Old Icelandic *flōrr* floor of a cow stall, from Proto-Germanic **flōruz* ; and outside Germanic cognate with Old Irish *lār* ground, floor, Welsh *llawr,* Breton *leur,* Latin *plānus* level, Old Prussian *plonis* threshing floor, and Latvian *plāns* barn floor; see PLAIN. **—v.** Probably 1440 *flooren* furnish with a floor; earlier, implied in the gerund *florynge* act of making a floor (1387, in Trevisa's translation of Higden's *Polychronicon*); from the noun. The meaning of puzzle or confound, is first recorded in Coleridge's *Table Talk* (1830). The spelling *floor, floore* is not recorded before about 1390, and did not become fully established until the mid-1600's.

flop *v.* move loosely or heavily. 1602, in Marsten's *Antonio and Mellida;* probably variant of FLAP, and according to the OED the vowel change indicates a duller or heavier sound. The sense of fall or drop down heavily, is first recorded in Marryat's *Mr. Midshipman Easy* (1836), and that of the informal figurative use of collapse or fail, in Wodehouse's *Damsel in Distress* (1919). The slang meaning of to sleep, was originally American English (1907, in Jack London's *Road*). **—n.** 1823, the action of flopping; from the verb. The informal figurative use of a failure, collapse, breakdown, is found in Farmer and Henley's *Slang and Its Analogues* (1893). **—flophouse** *n.* cheap rooming house. 1923, American English, formed from *flop* place to sleep on, bed (1910) + *house.* **—floppy** *adj.* 1858, in George Eliot's *Amos Barton;* formed from English *flop,* v. + *-y*[1].

flora (flôr′ə) *n.* plants of a particular region or time. 1777, New Latin *flora,* from Latin *Flōra* name of a Roman goddess of flowers, from *flōs* (genitive *flōris*) flower; see BLOOM. *Flora* is recorded earlier in the title of S. Paulli's *Flora Danica* (1647), and was popularized in the natural sciences after Linnaeus used it in the title of his work *Flora Suecica* Swedish Flora (1745). **—floral** *adj.* of a flower or flowers. 1753, borrowed, possibly by influence of earlier French *floral,* from Latin *flōrālis* of flora or flowers, from *Flōra* a Roman goddess.

florescence (flôres′əns) *n.* a blossoming. 1793, borrowed from New Latin *florescentia,* from Latin *flōrēscentem* (nominative *flōrēscēns*) blooming, present participle of *flōrēscere,* an inceptive form expressing the beginning of the action of *flōrēre* to blossom, FLOURISH; for suffix see -ENCE.

floret *n.* small flower in a flower head. Probably before 1400 *flourette,* in Chaucer's translation of *Roman de la Rose;* borrowed from Old French *florete,* diminutive of *flor* flower; later, *floret* (1671), re-formed in English from Latin *flōris* (genitive of *flōs* flower) + English *-et.*

florid *adj.* ruddy, flowery. 1642, bright or blooming; borrowed through French *floride* flourishing, and directly from Latin *flōridus* flowery, blooming, from *flōs* (genitive *flōris*) flower; see BLOOM. The meaning of ruddy, is first recorded in Jeremy Taylor's works, in 1650.

florin (flôr′ən) *n.* British silver coin. About 1303 *floren* Florentine coin marked with a lily (literally, flower), in Mannyng's *Handlyng Synne;* borrowed from Old French *florin,* adapted from Italian *fiorino,* from *fiore* flower, from Latin *flōrem* (nominative *flōs*) flower; see BLOOM.

florist *n.* 1623, formed in English from *flor-*, stem of Latin genitive *flōris* (nominative *flōs* flower) + English *-ist.*

floss *n.* silk thread. 1759, found in *floss-silk* and *flosh-silk,* probably a partial translation of French *soie floche,* from Old French *soye floche* (*soye* silk + *floche* tuft of wool, from *floc* FLOCK²). An earlier form exists in Middle English, in the surname *Flosmonger* (1314, possibly a dealer in down or tufted wool, perhaps with specific reference to FLEECE, which raises the question of *floss* being a possible borrowing from a Dutch, Scandinavian, or Low German word cognate with English FLEECE: Dutch *vlos* floss, Danish *flos,* Middle Low German *vlūs* fleece.

flotation *n.* act of floating. 1806 *floatation,* from *float,* v. + *-ation.* The current spelling appeared about 1850, probably by influence of French *flottaison* (see FLOTSAM), which was used in technical terms translated into English, such as *ligne de flottaison* line of flotation.

flotilla (flōtil′ə) *n.* small fleet. 1711, borrowed from Spanish *flotilla,* diminutive of *flota* fleet, from *flotar* to float, from Germanic forms of *float,* n. and v. (Dutch, noun: *vlot* raft, *vloot* fleet, and verb: *vlotten* float; Old High German, noun: *floz* raft, and verb: *flozzan* float; modern German, noun: *Floss* raft; verb: *flössen* float; Old Icelandic, noun: *floti* raft, fleet, and verb: *flota* float, launch; see FLOAT).

flotsam (flot′səm) *n.* wreckage of a ship or its cargo. 1607 *flotsen,* found in earlier Anglo-French *floteson,* in French and Middle French *flottaison* a floating, from Old French *floter* to float + *-aison,* from Latin *-ātiōn-(em);* formed from Germanic forms of *float,* n. and v. (see FLOTILLA). The spelling *flotsam* is first recorded in 1853, by influence of *jetsam.*

flounce¹ *v.* go with an agitated fling of the body expressing anger or impatience. 1542, to plunge, perhaps borrowed from a Scandinavian source (compare dialectal Swedish *flunsa* to plunge, fall with a splash, Norwegian *flunsa* to hurry). The spelling *flounce* was possibly influenced by *bounce,* especially in its earliest uses. Later *flounce* is recorded in the sense of fling oneself about showing anger or impatience (1761). **—n.** 1583, from the verb.

flounce² *n.* wide ruffle. 1713, in Swift's *Cadenus and Vanessa;* alteration (probably influenced by *flounce¹*) of earlier *frounce* pleat, wrinkle, fold (about 1378, in a version of *Piers Plowman*); borrowed from Old French *fronce* fold, gather, wrinkle, from Frankish **hrunkja* wrinkle (with replacement of Frankish *hr-* by *fr-*; also compare Old High German *runza, runzala* wrinkle, modern German *Runzel,* and Old Icelandic *hrukka*), of unknown origin. **—v.** 1672, to trim, curl, in Wycherley's *Love in a Wood;* later, to trim or adorn with flounces (1611, Addison in *The Spectator*).

flounder¹ *v.* struggle awkwardly. 1592, to stumble; of uncertain origin, perhaps an alteration of FOUNDER, influenced by English *flounder²* a fish, or by Dutch *flodderen* to flop about or flounder in a mire. **—n.** 1867, in a book on fishing, act of floundering; from the verb.

flounder² *n.* a kind of flatfish. 1304-05 *flundr;* later *flounder* (1450); borrowed through Anglo-French *floundre,* Old Norman French *flondre,* apparently from a Scandinavian source (compare Swedish and Norwegian *flundra* flounder, Old Icelandic *flydhra*); related to Middle Low German *flundere, vlundere* flounder (modern German *Flunder*), and also perhaps to Middle High German *vluoder,* cognate with Latin *planta* sole of the foot, from Indo-European **pla-n-t-/pl n t*, root **plat-/plōt-* (Pok.833).

flour *n.* fine, powdery meal of wheat or other grain. Probably about 1225 *flur,* in *King Horn.* This was a special use of *flur* flower, in the sense of flower being the finest part of meal (compare *flour of huete,* literally, flower of wheat, 1340, in *Ayenbite of Inwyt,* and French *fleur de farine* fine wheaten flour). The spelling *flower* for this word was used as late as 1809, and even Johnson's *Dictionary* (1755) does not recognize the spelling *flour,* but after about 1830 the modern spelling *flour* seems to be the accepted form. **—floury** *adj.* 1591, formed from English *flour* + *-y¹.*

flourish *v.* grow or develop with vigor. Probably before 1300 *florisen* to blossom, flower; later *florishen* (about 1303), and *flourishen* (probably about 1350); borrowed from Old French *floriss-*, stem of *florir,* from Vulgar Latin **flōrīre,* corresponding to Latin *flōrēre* to bloom, blossom, flower, flourish, from *flōs* (genitive *flōris*) a flower; see BLOOM; for suffix see -ISH². **—n.** Before 1500, a blossom; later, bloom, vigor, prosperity (1597); gradually developing from Middle English **flourishing** *n.* the season of blooming; decoration, embellishment (about 1303) and, differentiating then into various meanings extending the notion of embellishment, such as the sense of a graceful brandishing of a weapon (1552), a fanfare of horns, trumpets, etc. (1594, in Shakespeare's *Richard III*), and florid expression, literary embellishment (1603).

flout *v.* treat with scorn, mock, scoff. 1551, in a translation of Sir Thomas More's *Utopia,* apparently a special use of *flowten* to play the flute (about 1410); see FLUTE, v. Similar developments of sense are found in the verbs *hoot* and *whistle,* as in *whistle off* drive off (the stage, etc.).

flow *v.* Old English *flōwan* (before 830; earlier *flēow* past tense, probably about 750); cognate with Middle Low German *vlōien* to flow, Middle Dutch *vloyen* (modern Dutch *vloeijen*), Old High German *flouwen* to wash, rinse, and Old Icelandic *flōa* to flow, flood. Outside Germanic Old English *flōwan* is also cognate with Old Latin *plovere* to rain, Greek *plōtós* floating, *pleîn* to swim, sail, Lithuanian *pláuti* to wash, rinse, Old Slavic *pluti* to flow, navigate, Armenian *luanam* to wash, Sanskrit *plávate* he swims, hovers, flies, Tocharian A, Tocharian B *plu-* to fly, hover, and Tocharian B *plewe* ship, from Indo-European **pleu-/plou-/ plōu-/ plu-* (Pok.835). **—n.** Before 1420 *flowe* act of flowing; high tide, in Lydgate's *Troy Book;* from the verb.

flower *n.* Probably before 1200 *flur* blossom of a plant, in *Ancrene Riwle;* borrowed from Old French *flur, flour, flor,* from Latin *flōrem* (nominative *flōs*) flower; see BLOOM, also FLOUR. The modern spelling *flower* began to appear probably before 1349 in the form *flowre,* and became so deeply entrenched that the spelling *flour* for milled grain, was not completely accepted as a differentiated form until the 1830's; see BOWER for shift in spelling. **—v.** Probably before 1200 *fluren* to blossom, flourish, in *Ancrene Riwle;* probably from Middle English *flur,* n., flower. **—flowery** *adj.* 1369 *floury,* in Chaucer's *Book of the Duchesse;* formed from Middle English *flour, flur* flower + *-y*[1].

flu *n.* influenza. 1839 *flue,* in Southey's Letters; a shortening of INFLUENZA. The current spelling is first recorded in 1893.

flub *v. Informal.* to botch, bungle. 1924, American English, in Percy Marks' *The Plastic Age.* The origin is unknown but it may have been influenced by earlier verbs with similar meanings, such as *fluff* and *flunk,* and possibly in some as yet undetected way with *flubdub* bombastic language (1888), though the semantic barrier is hard to overcome. **—n.** something badly performed. 1952, in John Steinbeck's *East of Eden;* from the verb.

fluctuate *v.* to waver. 1634, possibly developed from earlier English *fluctuate,* adj., wavering; borrowed from Latin *flūctuātum,* past participle of *flūctuāre,* from *flūctus* (genitive *flūctūs*) wave, from past participle of *fluere* to flow; see FLUENT. **—fluctuation** *n.* About 1450, borrowed through Middle French *fluctuation,* or directly from Latin *fluctuātiōnem* (nominative *fluctuātiō*), from *flūctuāre;* for suffix see -ATION.

flue *n.* passage for smoke in a chimney. 1582 *flew;* of uncertain origin; possibly with the more generalized meaning of passage or channel (as the OED suggests) connecting it with earlier use, meaning "a special cavity of a shell" (1562) and "a mouthpiece of a hunting horn" (1410), both meanings suggesting comparison with Middle English *flouen,* v., flow, blow steadily (recorded before 1150, and found in Old English *flōwan*), and with Old French *fluie* stream.

fluent *adj.* flowing. 1589, borrowed from Latin *fluentem* (nominative *fluēns*), present participle of *fluere* to flow, from Indo-European **bhleugw-,* root **bhleu-/ bhlu-* (Pok.158); cognate with Greek *phlýein* boil over, overflow, and Old Slavic *blĭvati* to spit, vomit; for suffix see -ENT. **—fluency** *n.* 1623, abundance; later, a smooth and easy flow (1636); possibly borrowed from Late Latin *fluentia* flowing, flow, from Latin *fluentem,* present participle of *fluere* to flow; *or* formed from English *fluent* + *-cy,* perhaps in part, suggested by, and replacing, earlier English *fluence* fluency (1607).

fluff *n.* light, downy stuff. 1790, apparently a variant of earlier *floow, flue* woolly substance, down, nap (1589); borrowed perhaps through Flemish *vluwe,* from French *velu* shaggy, hairy, from Latin *vellus* fleece, or perhaps through Vulgar Latin **villūtus,* from Latin *villus* tuft of hair; see VELVET. **—v.** 1872, move or settle down like fluff, in Holmes' *Poet at the Breakfast Table;* from the noun. The slang meaning of make a mistake in speaking or performing, is first recorded in theater slang (1884). **—fluffy** *adj.* 1825; formed from English *fluff,* n. + *-y*[1].

fluid *adj.* flowing. Probably before 1425 *fluide,* in a translation of Chauliac's *Grande Chirurgie;* borrowed possibly through Middle French *fluide,* and directly from Latin *fluidus* fluid, flowing, from *fluere* to flow; see FLUENT. **—n.** 1661, in Robert Boyle's treatise on air; from the adjective. **—fluidity** *n.* 1603, in Florio's translation of Montaigne's *Essays;* borrowed from French *fluidité,* from *fluide* + *-ité* -ity, or perhaps formed from English *fluid* + *-ity.*

fluke[1] *n.* flat end of each arm of an anchor. 1561, origin uncertain (perhaps a special use of *fluke*[3] fish, because of the resemblance of the anchor's shape to the flat shape of the fish). *Fluke,* meaning a whale's flattened tail, is first recorded in 1725.

fluke[2] *n.* lucky chance. 1857, lucky shot in billiards; of uncertain origin (possibly from English dialect *fluke* a guess, though this meaning is not recorded before 1876). **—fluky** *adj.* 1879, formed from English *fluke*[2] + *-y*[1].

fluke[3] *n.* flatfish. Probably before 1400, in *Morte Arthur;* developed from Old English (before 700) *flōc* flatfish; cognate with Old Icelandic *flōki* flatfish, Old Saxon *flaka* sole of foot, Old High German *flah* smooth (modern German *flach*), Latin *plaga* flat surface, region, and perhaps Greek *pélagos* open sea, from Indo-European **pelәg-/plāg-/plәg-* (Pok.831); see PLEASE.

flume *n.* channel for carrying water. Probably before 1200 *flum* stream of water, river, in Layamon's *Chronicle of Britain;* borrowed from Old French *flum,* from Latin *flūmen* river, from *fluere* to flow; see FLUENT.

flummery *n.* pudding made with oatmeal or flour. 1623, borrowed from Welsh *llymru* sour oatmeal boiled and jellied, of unknown origin. The figurative meaning of empty flattery, nonsense, humbug, is first recorded in 1749. The English spelling with *fl-* is an approximation of the pronunciation of Welsh *ll-,* as in the English name *Floyd,* after Welsh *Llwyd.*

flummox *v. Informal.* bewilder. 1837, in Dickens' *Pickwick Papers;* probably of English dialectal origin (compare dialectal *flummox* maul or mangle, *flummocky* slovenly, and *flummock* bewilder, which are thought to be descriptive formations, and suggest comparison with earlier *lummox* a clumsy or stupid person, before 1825; a word which is first recorded in British English dialect collections).

flunk *v. Informal.* fail in schoolwork. 1823, college slang in American English, to back out, give up, fail; origin unknown (traditionally considered to be an alteration of *funk,* in British university slang, to be frightened, shrink from, evade).

flunky or **flunkey** *n.* flattering, fauning person. 1782 footman, liveried servant, in notations on Scottish dia lect; of uncertain origin (traditionally considered a possible alteration of *flanker* person positioned at either flank, but outside of military use this term is not recorded before 1827).

Originally a Scottish term (as in Burns' *Twa Dogs*), *flunky* appeared later in works of Thackeray and Hood, and assumed the meaning of a flatterer or toady, in Thackeray's *The Newcomes* (1855).

fluorescence *n.* light produced by a substance exposed to ultraviolet or X rays. 1852, formed from English *fluor* colored mineral which exhibits a glowing light in ultraviolet light + *-escence.* The term was coined by the British mathematician and physicist G.G. Stokes. **—fluorescent** *adj.* 1853, formed from English *fluor* + *-escent,* a term also coined by Stokes.

fluoride *n.* compound containing fluorine. 1826, formed from English *fluor(ine)* chemical element + *-ide.* **—fluoridate** *v.* 1949, back formation from *fluoridation.* **—fluoridation** *n.* 1949, the addition of fluoride to drinking water; formed from English *fluoride* + *-ation.* An earlier meaning of process by which a mineral absorbs fluorine, is first recorded in 1904.

fluorine *n.* gaseous chemical element. 1813, formed from English *fluor* mineral containing fluorine (New Latin *fluor,* a term applied by earlier scientists to several minerals, from Latin *fluor* a flowing, flow, from *fluere* to flow; see FLUENT) + English *-ine*[2]. The term was introduced by the British chemist Sir Humphry Davy as a name suggested to him by the French physicist André Ampère, who probably knew it from *De re metallica* (1546) by the German mineralogist Georg Agricola. The book was first translated into English by Herbert C. and Lou H. Hoover.

flurry *n.* 1686, in American English, sudden light fall of snow, or rarely hail or rain, accompanied by wind; probably formed from English *flurr* to scatter, fly with whirring noise (1627) + *-y*[3], perhaps of imitative origin; however, there is an earlier verb *flouren* to sprinkle, as with flour, sugar, or spices (before 1399), which may be the source of *flurr,* though there is a gap of over 175 years in the record of the use of these two words.

The sense of a sudden commotion, is first recorded in 1710.

—v. Before 1757, agitate or fluster; from the noun. The sense of fall or shower down, as snow, is first recorded in 1883, in American English.

flush[1] *v.* to rush suddenly, spurt. 1548, rush out, flow copiously; probably related to FLUSH[3] to fly up suddenly, through the shared notion of sudden movement. The sense development appears to have been influenced by *flash,* originally to splash water and to dart or flit, and, less likely, by *flux* (a copious flow). The meaning of cause to rush or flow so as to redden the face, is first recorded in Milton's *Paradise Lost* (1667). **—n.** 1529, rush of water, in Sir Thomas More's *A Dialogue Concerning Heresies;* possibly from the verb and its relationship to FLUSH[3], which would explain the earlier date for the noun *flush*[1]*;* or from earlier *flush,* also spelled *flusche* (1311, in a surname), which also explains the date. This suggests a different relationship (possibly that the verb was at least in part developed from the noun).

flush[2] *adj.* even, level. About 1550, perfect or faultless; later, plentiful, abundantly full or supplied (1603, in Dekker's plays, and 1604, in Shakespeare's *Hamlet*); perhaps an extended use of FLUSH[1] (originally, flow copiously). The meaning of even, level, in the same plane, is first recorded in 1791, in Bentham's writings; perhaps, as suggested in the OED, originally applied to a river running full, and therefore level with its banks, but this connection without supporting quotations seems somewhat strained.

flush[3] *v.* fly up suddenly. About 1250 *flisen, flusen;* later *flusshen* (about 1399); perhaps imitative, though if the relationship to *flash* and its variant *flushe* (see FLUSH[1] and FLASH) can be sustained, then it is possible to infer a connection with Dutch *vlacke* and there find the source of *fl-* which has otherwise been suggested in the OED as coming from an association with *fly* and *flutter.* The difficulty with the vowel *u* is superficially accounted for in the variant of *flash* and in the form *flusshen.*

flush[4] *n.* hand of cards all of one suit. Before 1529, in Skelton's writings; perhaps borrowed from Middle French *flus,* found also in Old French *flux* a flowing, as a run of cards, learned borrowing from Latin *flūxus* FLUX.

fluster *v.* 1604, to excite with drink, in Shakespeare's *Othello;* earlier, implied in *flostryng* agitation or excitement; probably borrowed from a Scandinavian source (compare Icelandic *flaustur* haste, hurry). The meaning of make nervous or become excited, is first recorded in 1613. **—n.** 1710, from the verb.

flute *n.* Before 1325 *floute* the musical instrument; earlier, implied in *flouter* a flutist (1225, as a surname); borrowed from Old French *flaüte, fleüte,* from Old Provençal *flaüt,* of uncertain origin; perhaps an alteration of *flaujol* (in Old French *flajol*) FLAGEOLET with some unknown form, but probably not *lute* as is often suggested, because in particular the lute was a stringed instrument held and played in a different manner that had no suggestion of the flute about it.

The meaning of a channel as one of several on the side of a column, is first recorded in 1660, possibly from the shape of a flute split horizontally.

—v. About 1387-95 *floyten* to play the flute, in Chaucer's *Prologue* to the *Canterbury Tales;* later *flowten* (about 1410), borrowed from Old French *flaüter, fleüter* play the flute, from *flaüte, fleüte,* n. flute. **—fluted** *adj.* 1611, from English *flute,* v. **—fluting** *n.* 1481, action of playing the flute; later, the channels on a column. **—flutist** *n.* 1603, in Florio's translation of Montaigne's *Essays;* probably borrowed from French *flûtiste* and replacing earlier English *flouter* (1225).

flutter *v.* wave back and forth. About 1300 *floteren* be tossed by waves; later, fluctuate, shift (about 1380, in Chaucer's translation of Boethius' *De Consolatione Philosophiae*); developed from Old English (before 1000) *floterian* float to and fro, be tossed by waves, a frequentative form of *flotian* to FLOAT. **—n.** 1641, a fluttering, in Milton's *Animadversions;* from the verb.

flux *n.* a flow. About 1350 *flix* excessive flow (of blood); later *flux,* in a version of *Piers Plowman* (about 1378); borrowed through Old French *flux,* or directly from Latin *flūxus* (genitive *flūxūs*), from past participle of *fluere* to flow; see FLUENT. The meaning of continuous succession of changes, is first recorded in Francis Bacon's *Essays* (1625). **—v.** Probably before 1425 *fluxen* to flow, in a translation of Chauliac's *Grande Chirurgie;* from the noun.

fly[1] *n.* insect. Probably before 1200 *flehe,* in *Ancrene Riwle;* later *flie, flye* (about 1300); developed from Old English (before 800) *flēge, flȳge;* cognate with Old

Saxon *fliega* fly, Middle Dutch *vlieghe* (modern Dutch *vlieg*), Middle Low German *vlēge,* Old High German *flioga* (modern German *Fliege*), from Proto-Germanic **fleuȝ(j)ōn,* and Old Icelandic *fluga.* **—black fly** (probably before 1200) **—housefly** *n.* (before 1425)

fly[2] *v.* move through air with wings. Before 1175 *flyen, fleon;* developed from Old English *flēogan* (about 725, in *Beowulf*); cognate with Old Frisian *fliāga* to fly, Old Saxon *fliogan,* Middle Dutch *vlieghen* (modern Dutch *vliegen*), Old High German *fliogan* (modern German *fliegen*), Old Icelandic *fljūga,* from Proto-Germanic **fleuȝanan,* from Indo-European **pleuk-*, root **pleu-* (Pok.837). **—n.** Before 1450 *flie* flight, flying; developed from Old English *flyge,* from *flēogan,* v. The meaning of something attached by the edge, with the sense of flapping as a wing does, is recorded in the use of a tent flap or *fly* (1810), and the covering for buttons that close an opening on a garment (1844). **—flier** or **flyer** *n.* 1440, thing that flies, in *Promptorium Parvulorum;* earlier *Flier* (1289, as a surname); formed from Middle English *flyen* + *-er*[1]. The meaning of aviator, is first recorded in 1934, but probably developed earlier during World War I. **—flying saucer** unidentified flying object (1947).

foal *n.* young horse or donkey. Before 1200 *fole;* developed from Old English (about 950) *fola;* cognate with Old Frisian *fola* foal, Old Saxon *folo,* Middle Dutch and modern Dutch *veulen,* Old High German *folo* (modern German *Fohlen, Füllen*), Old Icelandic *foli,* and Gothic *fula,* from Proto-Germanic **fulōn.* Outside Germanic, Old English *fola* is also cognate with Latin *pullus* young animal, young fowl, Greek *pôlos* foal, Albanian *pelë* mare, and Armenian *ul* goat, from Indo-European **pō[u]l-/pul-*, root **pōu-/pəu-/pu-* (Pok.842). **—v.** to give birth to a foal. Before 1387 *folen,* in Trevisa's translation of Higden's *Polychronicon;* from the noun.

foam *n.* About 1275 *fom* something unstable; later, saliva (1290), and froth on the seashore (before 1393); developed from Old English (before 700) *fām* foam, froth; cognate with Old High German *feim* foam (from Proto-Germanic **faima-*), Old Prussian *spoayno,* Lithuanian *spáinė* streak of foam, Old Slavic *pěna* foam, Latin *spūma* foam, *pūmex* pumice, and Sanskrit *phéna-s* foam, from Indo-European **(s)phoim-, (s)phoin-* (Pok.1001). **—v.** Probably about 1375 (in northern dialect) *famen* to flow over, flood; later *fomen* to froth at the mouth, slaver (about 1395, in the Wycliffe Bible); developed from Old English *fāmgian* to foam (about 725, in *Exodus*). **—foamy** *adj.* About 1385 *fomy,* in Chaucer's *Canterbury Tales;* developed from Old English (before 1000) *fāmig,* from *fām* foam; for suffix see -Y[1].

fob[1] *n.* piece of leather, ribbon, etc., that hangs from a pocket, and is usually attached to a watch. 1653, small pocket for valuables; of uncertain origin (compare Low German *Fobke* little pocket and dialectal German *Fuppe* pocket; also compare English *fob*[2], v., perhaps related to *fob*[1]).

fob[2] *v.* Probably about 1375 *fobben* cheat or trick, impose upon; from the noun *fobbe* cheat, trickster (also about 1375), or perhaps related to FOP, n. The phrase *fob off* to put off deceitfully, try to satisfy with an excuse or pretense, is first recorded in Shakespeare's *2 Henry IV* (1597).

focus *n.* central point. 1644, point at which sound waves meet; New Latin *focus* central point, from Latin *focus* hearth, fireplace, possibly cognate with Armenian *boç* flame (from **bhok̂-so-*) and *bosor* red; originally fiery, from Indo-European **bhok̂-* to flame (Pok.162). The New Latin use was introduced in a Latin text on astronomy in 1604 by the German astronomer and mathematician Johann Kepler, in reference to the "burning point (at which heat rays meet) of a lens or mirror." The transferred meaning of center of activity or energy, is first recorded in 1796. **—v.** 1775, bring into focus; from the noun. **—focal** *adj.* 1693, in Edmund Halley's writings; formed from English *focus,* n. + *-al*[1].

fodder *n.* food for animals. Probably before 1200 *fodder,* in *Ancrene Riwle;* developed from Old English (about 1000) *fōdor,* related to *fōda* FOOD. Compare UDDER.

foe *n.* Probably before 1200 *fo,* developed from Old English (about 1000) *gefā* adversary in deadly feud, from *fāh, fā* at feud, hostile (about 725, in *Beowulf*), from Proto-Germanic **faiHaz;* cognate with Old High German *fēhan* to hate, *gifēh* hostile, and Gothic *bifaihō* envy. The Old English is also cognate outside Germanic with Old Prussian *pickuls* devil, Lithuanian *piktas* angry, and Sanskrit *píśuna-s* evil, from Indo-European **peik̂-/poik̂-/pik̂-* (Pok.795); see FEUD[1] quarrel, and FICKLE. The Old English prefix *ge-* meaning together, mutually, disappeared in early Middle English, as was the case in many other nouns. The spelling with *e* developed in the late 1300's and early 1400's but did not become established until the early 1600's.

fog *n.* 1544, thick mist; probably borrowed from a Scandinavian source (compare Danish *fog* spray or shower, especially in *sne-fog* snowstorm, Old Icelandic *fok* snow flurry, *fjūk* snowstorm, *fjūka* be driven by the wind). It is difficult for semantic reasons alone to connect this word with Middle English *fogge* tall grass, as is done by some traditional source materials. **—v.** 1599, envelop with or as with fog; from the noun. **—foggy** *adj.* 1544, perhaps formed from English *fog,* n. + *-y*[1], or possibly borrowed directly from a Scandinavian source.

fogy or **fogey** *n.* old-fashioned person. 1780 *foggie* (Scottish), originally applied to an army pensioner or veteran; indeterminately related to earlier *fogram* (noun 1775, adjective 1772). It is remotely possible that *fogy* is an extended noun use of earlier *foggy* mossy, covered with moss (1725), though a similar notion is rejected under *fog,* n.; or that *fogy* is a figurative extension of *foggy,* adj. in reference to the supposed mental state thought to be characteristic of older people.

foible *n.* weak point. Before 1648, weak point of a sword blade; borrowed from French *foible,* n. (now obsolete and replaced by *faible*), from *foible,* adj., weak, from Old French *foible, feble* FEEBLE. The general meaning of a weak point or failing, is first recorded in Dryden's *Marriage-à-la-Mode* (1673).

foil[1] *v.* frustrate or blunt the efforts of; baffle. Probably before 1300 *foilen* to trample down, in *Arthour and Merlin;* later, to spoil a trace or scent by running over it (about 1410); perhaps borrowed from Old French *fouler* trample, from Vulgar Latin **fullāre* to clean cloth, from Latin *fullō* one who cleans cloth, fuller; cognate with Lithuanian *bilděti* knock, rummage, from Indo-European **bheḷd-/bhḷd-* (Pok.124). The meaning of overthrow or defeat is first recorded in 1548, and the sense of baffle, in 1564.

foil[2] *n.* very thin sheet of metal. About 1325 *foyle,* borrowed from Old French *fueille, foille* leaf, from Latin *folia* leaves (taken as a collective feminine singular), plural of *folium* leaf; see FOLIAGE.

foil[3] *n.* light sword with a blunt end, used in fencing. 1594, of uncertain origin (perhaps from *foil*[1] to frustrate or blunt the efforts of, in the sense of a weapon that has been made ineffective).

foist *v.* represent or palm off as genuine. 1545, in Roger Ascham's *Toxophilus,* probably borrowed from dialectal Dutch *vuisten* take in hand, from Middle Dutch, from *vuist* FIST. The earliest use referred to concealment of a false or flat die in the palm of the hand, in order to cheat at dice.

fold[1] *v.* bend over on itself. About 1250 *folden,* in *The Owl and the Nightingale;* developed from Old English, Mercian Dialect *faldan,* in West Saxon *fealdan* (before 899, in Alfred's translation of Boethius' *De Consolatione Philosophiae*). The Old English forms are cognate with Middle Low German *volden* to fold, Middle Dutch *vouden* (modern Dutch *vouwen*), Old High German *faldan* (modern German *falten*), Old Icelandic *falda,* Gothic *falthan,* from Proto-Germanic **falthanan.* Outside Germanic cognates appear in Latin *duplus* twofold, double, Greek *diplóos,* Middle Irish *alt* a joint, Albanian *palë* fold, and Sanskrit *puṭa-s* fold, pocket (earlier **pṛta-s,* from Indo-European **polt-/pl̥t-,* root **pel-/pl-* (Pok.802), and by an extended form of the pre-Germanic base *pl-* in Latin *plicāre* to fold. **—n.** About 1250 *folde;* from the verb. **—folder** *n.* 1552, one who folds, from *fold,* v. + *-er*[1]. The meaning of a folding cover for loose papers, is first recorded in 1911.

fold[2] *n.* pen for animals, especially sheep. Before 1200 *fold;* developed from Old English (before 700) *falæd, fald, falod;* cognate with Old Saxon *faled* pen, enclosure, Middle Low German *vālt* enclosure, dunghill, Middle Dutch *vaelt,* and modern Dutch *vaalt* dunghill, of unknown origin.

-fold a suffix meaning:______times as many, as in *tenfold,* or formed or divided into______parts, as in *manifold.* Old English Northumbrian dialect *-fāld,* in West Saxon *-feald;* cognate with Old Frisian *-fald, -faldech* -fold, Old Saxon *-fald,* Dutch *-voud,* Old High German and modern German *-falt,* Old Icelandic *-faldr,* Gothic *-falths.* Outside of Germanic cognates are found in Latin *-plus* -fold (as in *simplus* single, *duplus* double, *triplus* triple), and Greek *-plóos, -plásios* (from pre-Greek *-plátios*); derived from the same source as Old English *faldan* FOLD[1] bend.

foliage *n.* leaves. 1447 *foylage;* later *foillage, feullage* (1601); borrowed from Middle French *fueillage, foillage,* from Old French *fueille, foille* leaf, from Latin *folia* leaves (taken as a collective feminine singular), plural of *folium* leaf, cognate with Greek *phýllon,* from Indo-European **bhol-/bhel-* (Pok.122); for suffix see -AGE. The modern spelling is first recorded in John Evelyn's writing (1664), in imitation of Latin *folium* leaf which was accompanied by a shift in *i* and *l* that thus disguised the connection with *foil;* see FOIL[2].

foliate *adj.* 1626, beaten into a thin sheet, in Francis Bacon's *Sylva Sylvarum;* later, resembling a leaf (1658); borrowed from Latin *foliātus* leaved, leafy, from *folium* leaf; for suffix see -ATE. **—v.** 1665, to apply silver leaf to; later to beat into leaf or foil (1704, in Newton's *Optics*), and put forth leaves (1775); possibly a back formation from *foliation,* or more likely, from *foliate,* adj. **—foliation** *n.* 1623, the leafing of a plant; borrowed possibly from French *foliation,* or directly from Latin *foliātus;* for suffix see -ATION.

folic acid a constituent of the vitamin B complex. 1941 *folic* (from Latin *folium* leaf + English *-ic;* so named because of its abundance in green leaves, such as those of spinach).

folio *n.* sheet of paper. 1447, borrowed from Late Latin *foliō* leaf or sheet of paper, from Latin *foliō,* ablative of location (usual in page references) of *folium* leaf; see FOLIAGE. The differentiated meaning of a sheet of paper folded once, first recorded in 1582, is a borrowing from Italian *in foglio,* from Latin *foliō.*

folk *n.* Old English *folc* common people, tribe, multitude (about 725, in *Beowulf*); cognate with Old Frisian *folk* people, folk, Old Saxon, Middle Low German, and Middle Dutch *volc* (modern Dutch *volk*), Old High German *folc* (modern German *Volk*), and Old Icelandic *folk* band of warriors, troop, people; from Proto-Germanic **folkan;* also cognate with Albanian *plogu* heap, from Indo-European **pelə-go-,* root **pelə-/plē-* full (Pok.798). **—folksy** *adj.* 1852, in American English, sociable or informal; formed from English *folks,* n.pl. + *-y*[1].

follicle (fol'əkəl) *n.* small sac. Probably before 1425 *follicule,* in a translation of Chauliac's *Grande Chirurgie;* borrowed from Latin *folliculus* little bag, diminutive of *follis* bellows (literally, leather bag for inflating), from Indo-European **bholnis* or **bhl̥nis* (Pok.120).

follow *v.* Probably before 1200 *folwen, follewen,* in Layamon's *Chronicle of Britain;* later *folowen* (about 1340); developed from Old English *folgian* (about 725, in *Beowulf*), related to *fylgan* to follow; cognate with Old Frisian *folgia, fulgia,* Old Saxon *folgon,* Middle Dutch *volghen* (modern Dutch *volgen*), Old High German *folgēn* (modern German *folgen*), and Old Icelandic *fylgja;* from Proto-Germanic **fulȝ-,* of unknown origin. **—follower** *n.* Probably before 1200 *folhere,* in *Ancrene Riwle;* developed from Old English *folgere* (*folgian* + *-ere* -er[1]); cognate with Old Frisian *folgere,* Old High German *folgari* (modern German *Folger*). **—following** *n., adj.* Before 1325 *foluing,* in *Cursor Mundi.*

folly *n.* foolish conduct. Probably before 1200 *folie,* in *Ancrene Riwle,* borrowed from Old French (in *The Song of Roland*), from *fol* FOOL; for suffix see -Y[3].

foment *v.* promote trouble. About 1425 *fomenten* apply hot liquids, borrowed from Middle French *fomenter,* or directly from Late Latin *fōmentāre,* from Latin *fōmentum* warm application, from *fovēre* to warm, cherish, encourage; see DAY. The extended sense of stimulate, instigate (an action or course, especially trouble, rebellion, etc.), is first recorded in Francis Bacon's *Henry VII* (1622), possibly from the same sense as in French.

fond *adj.* About 1340 *fonnyd* foolish, silly; later *fond* (probably about 1375); developed from past tense of *fonnen* to fool, be foolish, perhaps from *fonne* fool (before 1325, in *Cursor Mundi*), of uncertain origin; possibly related to FUN, v. The meaning of foolishly tender, is first recorded in Lyly's *Euphues* (1579), followed by the sense of having strong affection for, found in Shakespeare's *Midsummer Night's Dream* (1590).

fondle *v.* 1694, pamper, in Dryden's *Love Triumphant;* found earlier in the participial form *fondling* (1676); developed as a frequentative form of earlier *fond* dote upon (1530, in Palsgrave's *Lesclarcissement*), a special use of FOND, adj.; for suffix see -LE³. The sense of caress, is first recorded in 1796.

fondue (fondü′) *n.* a baked dish combining melted cheese, eggs, and butter. 1878, a French term first recorded in a cooking dictionary, originally, feminine past participle of *fondre* melt; see FOUND² melt.

font¹ (font) *n.* basin holding water for baptism. Old English (about 1000) *font, fant;* borrowed from Latin *fōns* (genitive *fontis*) fountain, spring (in Medieval Latin *fons baptismalis* baptismal font).

font² *n.* set of type of one size and style. 1578, a casting; borrowed from Middle French *fonte,* from feminine past participle of *fondre* melt; see FOUND² melt.

food *n.* Probably before 1200 *fode,* in *Ancrene Riwle;* later *foode* (before 1387) and *food* (1420); developed from Old English *fōda* (about 1000, in Ælfric's works), from Proto-Germanic **fōđṓn*; related to *fōdor* fodder (from Proto-Germanic **fodrán;* which is cognate with Old High German *fuotar* food, fodder (modern German *Futter*), Old Icelandic *fōdhr* fodder, *fœdha, fœdhi* food, and Gothic *fōdeins* food; see also FEED. Outside Germanic Old English *fōdor* is also cognate with Latin *pābulum* food, fodder, *pānis* bread, *pāscere* to feed, graze, Greek *pateîsthai* to eat and drink, Old Slavic *pasti* feed, drive to pasture, Tocharian A *pās-*, Tocharian B *pāsk-* care for, tend, protect, and Hittite *paḫḫši-* protect, from Indo-European **pā-/pə-* (Pok.787).

fool *n.* Probably about 1200 *fol;* later *fool* (about 1375, in Chaucer's *Canterbury Tales*); borrowed from Old French *fol,* from Latin *follis* bellows, leather bag (in late Vulgar Latin used in the sense of windbag, empty-headed person, fool). **—v.** About 1350 *folen* be foolish, act like a fool; later *fool* make a fool of (1596, in Shakespeare's *1 Henry IV*); borrowed through Anglo-French *foler* to play the fool, from Old French *foler, folier,* from *fol,* n. **—foolhardy** *adj.* Before 1250 *folherdi,* in a version of *Ancrene Riwle;* borrowed from Old French *fol hardi.* **—foolish** *adj.* Before 1325 *foles,* in *Cursor Mundi;* later *foolissh* (1380, in Chaucer's translation of Boethius' *De Consolatione Philosophiae*); formed from Middle English *fol,* n. + *-ish.* **—foolscap** *n.* Before 1700, from *fool's* and *cap,* because this type of paper was originally watermarked with a cap worn by court jesters. **—fool's gold** a mineral (1872, in American English).

foot *n.* About 1125 *fot;* later *foot* (before 1325); developed from Old English *fōt* (about 725, in *Beowulf*), from Proto-Germanic **fōt;* cognate with Old Frisian *fōt* foot, Old Saxon *fōt, fuot,* Dutch *voet,* Old High German *fuoz* (modern German *Fuss*), Old Icelandic *fōtr,* and Gothic *fōtus.* Outside Germanic Old English *fōt* is cognate with Latin *pēs* (genitive *pedis*) foot, Greek *poús* (genitive *podós*), Old Irish *īs* under, below (with loss of *p* and change of *ē* to *ī*), Lithuanian *pėdà* footprint, Armenian *otn* foot, Sanskrit *pā́t* (genitive *padás*), and Tocharian A *pe,* Tocharian B *pai* foot, from Indo-European **ped-/pēd-/pod-/pōd-* (Pok.790).

As a linear measurement *foot* is first recorded in Old English (before 1000). The sense of being at the bottom of something *(at a person's feet)* is also recorded in Old English about 950), and the figurative meaning to be subject to another *(under one's foot)* is found early in Old English (about 825).

—v. Probably before 1400 *footen* move the foot, dance, in Chaucer's translation of *Roman de la Rose;* from *foot,* n. The informal sense of pay (a bill), is first recorded in 1848, perhaps from the earlier meaning of place the sum at the foot of a bill.

—footage *n.* 1892, piecework system to pay miners; later, length (in feet) of motion-picture film (1916); formed from English *foot,* n. + *-age.* **—football** *n.* (1409) **—foothills** *n.pl.* (1850, in American English) **—footing** *n.* 1296, in building; later, position of the feet on the ground (before 1398). **—footman** *n.* (probably before 1300) **—footstep** *n.* (before 1250)

fop *n.* vain person. 1440 *foppe* foolish person, in *Promptorium Parvulorum;* of uncertain origin (compare German *foppen* to cheat, deceive; perhaps related to FOB² to cheat). The sense of one who is foolishly attentive to his appearance, dandy, is first recorded in 1672-76. **—v.** Before 1529, act like a fool; probably from the noun.

for *prep.* Old English *for* for, before, on account of (about 725, in *Beowulf*), from Proto-Germanic **fura;* cognate with Old Frisian and Old Saxon *for,* Middle Dutch *vore* (modern Dutch *voor*), Old High German *fora* before, *furi* for (modern German *für, vor*), Old Icelandic *fyr* for, and Gothic *faúr;* also cognate with Latin *per* through, *prō* before, for, *prae* before, Old Irish *ar* before, Greek *pró* before, ahead, Old Prussian *pro, pra* through, for, Sanskrit *prá* forth, *purā́* before, formerly, and Hittite *parā* on, forth, from Indo-European **per/peri/pro/perā* (Pok.810). The use of *for* and *fore* was gradually differentiated in Middle English from the previous interchangeable use of Old English. **—conj.** About 1123 *for,* abstracted from Old English phrases, such as *for thon the* for the (reason) that, because, since.

for- a prefix meaning away, opposite, as in *forbear, forgo,* or completely, as in *forlorn, forsake.* Old English *for-, fær-;* cognate with Old Frisian and Old Saxon *for-,* Old High German *fra-, fir-, far-,* Dutch and German *ver-,* Gothic *fra-, faír-, faúr-,* Old Icelandic *fon-, fynin-*; related to the root of Old English *for* FOR. This prefix was commonly used in Old English to form verbs and adjectives, and it remained productive, through the Middle English period.

forage *n.* food, especially hay or grain, for animals. Before 1333 *forage,* in Shoreham's poetry; borrowed from Old French *forage, fourage* pillage, forage, from *fuerre* fodder, straw, from Frankish **fōdr* food (compare Middle Low German *vōder,* Old High German *fuotar* fodder, FOOD). The term is also found in Anglo-Latin *foragium, farragium* (about 1273). **—v.** to rove for forage or other supplies, often by plundering. 1417, borrowed from Middle French *fourager* to plunder, collect forage, from *fourage,* n., from Old French. **—forager** *n.* Probably before 1387, something that afflicts, in a version of *Piers Plowman;* borrowed from Old French *forragier, fouragier,* from *forage, fourage,* n.; for suffix see -ER¹.

foray *v.* to raid for plunder. 1375 (Scottish), in John Barbour's *The Bruce;* back formation from earlier *forreyer, forrier* raider, forager (before 1338 *foreri,* in Mannyng's *Chronicle of England*); borrowed from Old French *forrier,* from *forrer* to forage; related to *fuerre* fodder; see FORAGE. **—n.** About 1375 (Scottish), in John Barbour's *The Bruce;* from the verb. The word fell into disuse in the 1600's, but was revived in the 1800's by Scott.

forbear¹ *v.* abstain, refrain. 1137 *forberen* refrain from destroying; developed from Old English *forberan* bear up against, control one's feelings, endure (about 725, in *Beowulf*), formed from *for-* against (related to Old English *for* FOR) + *beran* to BEAR² carry. —**forbearance** *n.* 1576, a refraining from enforcing payment of debt; formed from *forbear¹* + *-ance.* The meaning of refraining from, is not recorded before 1591, in Shakespeare's *1 Henry VI.*

forbear² *n.* 1470, an ancestor, forebear; formed from English *for-, fore-* + *beer (be* + *-er¹)* one who exists.

forbid *v.* Probably about 1175 *forbeden;* later *forbiden* (about 1425, in *Rolls of Parliament*); developed from Old English *forbēodan* (about 725, in *Genesis A*); formed from *for-* against (related to Old English *for* FOR) + *bēodan* to command; see BID. The Old English *forbēodan* is cognate with Old High German *farbiotan,* Middle High German and modern German *verbieten,* Dutch *verbieden,* Old Icelandic *fyrirbjōdha,* and Gothic *faúrbiudan,* which shows the process of formation was not confined to English.

force *n.* Probably before 1300 *fors,* in *Arthour and Merlin;* later *force* (before 1325, in *Cursor Mundi*); borrowed from Old French *force,* from Late Latin *fortia,* from neuter plural of Latin *fortis* strong; see FORT. —**v.** Probably before 1300 *forcen,* in *Arthour and Merlin;* borrowed from Old French *forcier,* from Vulgar Latin **fortiāre,* from Late Latin *fortia* force. —**forceful** *adj.* 1571, formed from English *force* + *-ful.* —**forcible** *adj.* About 1422, borrowed from Middle French *forcible,* from *force* + *-ible.*

forceps *n.* tongs used to hold an object. 1563, borrowed from Latin *forceps* (compound of *formus* hot + the root of *capere* to take, hold; see CAPTIVE and WARM).

ford *n.* a place to cross shallow water. Old English *ford* (before 899, in Alfred's translation of Orosius' *Historiarum Adversus Paganos*), and found in such place names as *Hartford, Oxford.* Old English *ford* is cognate with Old Frisian *forda,* Old Saxon and Low German *ford,* Old High German *furt* (modern German *Furt*), from Proto-Germanic **furđús;* also found in place names such as *Frankfurt,* and Old Icelandic *fjǫrdhr* fiord. Outside Germanic cognates are found in Gaulish *ritu-,* an element in placenames *(Ritumagos,* with characteristic Celtic loss of Indo-European *p* and its vocalic *r̥-* developing into *ri-),* Old Welsh *rit* (modern Welsh *rhyd*), Old Cornish *rid,* Old Breton *rit,* all meaning ford. Other cognates are found in Greek *póros* passage, Latin *portus* port or harbor (though the word for ford in Latin is *vadum*), *porta* gate, door, Avestan *pərətuš* ford, and Sanskrit *píparti, pāráyati* (he) brings across; all derived from Indo-European base **per-/pr̥-/por-/pōr-* pass through (Pok.816). —**v.** to cross shallow water. 1614, in Raleigh's *The History of the World;* from the noun.

fore *adv., prep.* Old English *fore,* prep., before, in front of (about 725, in *Beowulf*); Old English *fore,* adv., before, previously (about 750); cognate with Old Frisian *fora, fara* before, fore, Old Saxon and Old High German *fora* (modern German *vor*), Old Icelandic *fyrir,* and Gothic *faúra;* from the same Germanic source as Old English *for* FOR. —**adj.** Before 1450, forward; later, former, earlier, in Caxton's translation of *The Book of Eneydos* (1490); later, in or at the front, in Dunbar's *Poems* (1500-20); abstracted from compounds such as *forecast, forepart (fore-* + *cast, part).* Since such compounds were sometimes written as two words, the first element came to be treated as an adjective. —**n.** front part. 1636 (in the phrase *to the fore* in the front, ready at hand); from the adjective. —**interj.** (in golf) 1878, probably a contraction of *before.*

fore- a combining form meaning front; in front, as in *foreman, foremast,* or before, beforehand, as in *forewarn, forerunner.* Found in Old English *fore-,* unstressed form of FORE, adv.

forearm¹ *n.* 1741, formed from Middle English *fore-* + *arm¹* limb of the body.

forearm² *v.* 1592, formed from Middle English *fore-* + *arm²* take up weapons.

forecast *v.* 1413, earlier implied in *forecasting* (about 1400); formed from Middle English *fore-* + *casten* contrive. —**n.** About 1422; probably from the verb.

forecastle (fōk′səl after sailors' pronunciation) *n.* 1407 *forcastelle;* earlier, probably Anglo-French *forechasteil* (1338); probably formed from Middle English *fore-* + *castel* fortified tower, after earlier Anglo-French.

foreclose *v.* prevent, exclude. About 1300, borrowed from Old French *forclos,* past participle of *forclore* exclude (*for-* out, from Latin *foris* outside + *clore* to shut, from Latin *claudere;* see FOREIGN and CLOSE² confined). Use of this word was perhaps influenced by association with Old and Middle English *for-,* which often implied exclusion or prohibition. —**foreclosure** *n.* 1728, formed from Middle English *foreclose* + *-ure.*

forefather *n.* Before 1325, in *Cursor Mundi;* formed from Middle English *fore-* + *father.*

forefinger *n.* Before 1425 *forfynkyr,* about 1450 *forefynger.*

forefoot *n.* Before 1375, also *fore foot.*

forefront *n.* Before 1450; formed from Middle English *fore-* + *front,* n.

foreground *n.* 1695, in Dryden's translation of Dufresnoy's *The Art of Painting;* formed from English *fore-* + *ground.*

forehead *n.* Probably before 1200, in *Ancrene Riwle,* found in Old English *for-hēafod, fore-hēafod,* formed from *for-, fore-* + *hēafod* head.

foreign *adj.* About 1250 *ferren;* later *foreyne* (about 1380); borrowed from Old French *forain, forein,* from Late Latin *forānus* on the outside, exterior, but generally found as *forāneus* also with the meaning in noun use of canon not in residence or a peddler, from Latin *foris, forās* outside, literally, out of doors, from a lost noun *fora,* related to *foris* DOOR, and altered from *fura* by influence of *foris.* The spelling with *g* is possibly the result of a confused association with *reign* (more likely with the older spelling *sovereign,* 1377, which also fits the accent pattern better), and is first recorded in 1565, but did not become fully established until the late 1600's. —**foreigner** *n.* 1413 *foreyner;* later *foreigner* (1565) outsider, from Middle English *foreyne* + *-er¹.*

foreknowledge *n.* 1535, in Coverdale's translation of the Bible; formed from English *fore-* + *knowledge,* on the pattern of earlier *foreknowynge,* etc. (about 1380, in Chaucer's translation of Boethius' *De Consolatione Philosophiae*).

foreleg *n.* About 1410 *forlegge;* formed from Middle English *for-, fore-* + *legge* leg.

foreman *n.* 1222 *forman;* formed from Middle English *for-, fore-* + *man.*

foremost *adj.* first, leading. Before 1525 *formoste,* alteration of Middle English *formeste* (probably before 1200, in Layamon's *Chronicle of Britain;* the superlative of *forme* first); developed from Middle English *forme,* adj. first and Old English *fyrmest* earliest, first (about 725, in *Beowulf;* the superlative of *forma*); related to *fruma* beginning. The form in modern English developed by association with *fore-* and *most.*

Old English *forma* is cognate with Old Frisian *forma* first, Old Saxon *formo,* Lithuanian *pìrmas* first, and with Old Saxon and Old High German *fruma* advantage, benefit, Middle Dutch *vrome,* Old Icelandic *frum-* first, and Gothic *fruma* first, from Indo-European **pr̥-mó-* **pre-mó-* (Pok.814).
—adv. 1551 *formoste,* alteration of Middle English *formest* (before 1225); developed from the adjective in Middle English and Old English.

forenoon *n.* About 1425; formed from English *fore-* + *noon.*

forensic (fəren′sik) *adj.* of or belonging to a court of law; judicial. 1659, shortened form of earlier *forensical* (1581), formed in English from Latin *forēns-,* the stem of *forēnsis* of a forum (place of assembly + English *-ical,* or perhaps separately formed in English from *forēns-,* the stem of Latin *forēnsis* + English *-ic.*

foreordain *v.* About 1384 *forordeinen,* in the Wycliffe Bible; formed from Middle English *for-* + *ordeinen* ordain, probably modeled on Latin *praeōrdināre* settle beforehand.

forerunner *n.* Before 1325 *foriner,* in *Cursor Mundi;* formed from Middle English *forærnen* to run ahead, anticipate + *-er*[1], probably modeled on Latin *praecursor* precursor.

foresee *v.* About 1384 *forsen,* developed from Old English *fore-sēon (fore-* + *sēon* to see, see ahead). **—foreseeable** *adj.* 1804, formed from English *foresee* + *-able.*

foresight *n.* About 1325 *forsight,* in *Cursor Mundi;* formed from Middle English *for-, fore-* + *sight,* possibly from *forsen,* probably modeled on Latin *prōvidentia* foresight.

forest *n.* Probably before 1300, in *Kyng Alisaunder* and *Sir Tristrem;* borrowed from Old French *forest,* usually considered a learned borrowing from Late and Medieval Latin *forestem silvam* the outside woods. The phrase has two senses which carry over into Middle English: a large, sparsely inhabited, wooded area; and a wooded area belonging to, or at the disposal of, a king or other high nobleman, often enclosed, and devoted usually to hunting. But the sense is generally taken to refer to the woods lying outside the walls of a park, those that are not fenced in, from Latin *foris* outside (literally, out of doors), from a lost noun **fora,* related to *foris* DOOR, and altered from **fura,* by influence of *foris.* Alternatively, it has been proposed that Old French *forest* was a borrowing from Old High German *forst* forest (originally, fir forest), from Medieval Latin. —**v.** 1818, in Keats' *Endymion;* from the noun. **—forestation** *n.* 1898, formed in American English from *forest* + *-ation.* **—forested** *adj.* 1612, formed from English *forest,* n. + *-ed*[2]. **—forester** *n.* About 1300 *forester;* later *forster, foster* (before 1387, in Trevisa's translation of Higden's *Polychronicon*); borrowed from Old French *forestier,* from *forest;* for suffix see -ER[1]. **—forestry** *n.* 1693 (in Scottish law) the privileges of a royal forest; borrowed from Old French *foresterie,* from *forest;* for suffix see -ERY. The meaning of science of cultivating and managing forests, is first recorded in 1859.

forestall *v.* prevent by acting first. Before 1350 *forstallen* to intercept (goods) before they reach the market, from the earlier noun *forestal* an intercepting or waylaying, ambush (about 1120); developed from Old English *foresteall* (about 1000, in Ælfric's works; a compound of *fore* before + *steall* standing position, STALL[1] place in a stable).

foretell *v.* Before 1325, in *Cursor Mundi;* formed from Middle English *for-, fore-* + *tellen* tell, probably modeled on Latin *prae-dīcere* predict.

forethought *n.* Before 1325 *forthoght,* in *Cursor Mundi;* formed from Middle English *for-, fore-* + *thoght* thought.

forever *adv.* Before 1375 *for ever;* later *forever* (1670).

foreword *n.* 1842, formed from English *fore-* + *word,* perhaps modeled on, or even a loan translation of, German *Vorwort* preface, itself modeled on Latin *praefātiō* preface.

forfeit *n.* thing lost or given up. Before 1376 *forfet* penalty for a crime, in *Piers Plowman;* borrowed from Old French *forfait* crime, originally past participle of *forfaire* transgress (*for-* outside, beyond, from Latin *forīs* outside + *faire* do, from Latin *facere;* see FOREIGN and DO[1] perform). **—v.** About 1350 *forfeten* to transgress or sin; probably borrowed from Old French *forfait,* past participle of *forfaire* transgress. **—forfeiture** *n.* Before 1338 *forfeture,* in Mannyng's *Chronicle of England;* borrowed from Old French *forfaiture,* from *forfait* crime; for suffix see -URE.

forge[1] *n.* place where metal is heated and shaped; smithy. 1279, borrowed from Old French *forge,* earlier *faverge,* from Latin *fabrica* workshop, from *faber* (genitive *fabrī*) workman in hard materials, smith; cognate with Old Slavic *dobrŭ* good, fine, Lithuanian *dabìnti* to adorn, Old English *gedafen* fitting, from Indo-European **dhabh-* (Pok.233). Doublet of FABRIC. **—v.** to make, shape, or form, especially in metal. About 1350 *forgen* make, shape, create; borrowed from Old French *forgier,* from Latin *fabricāre* fabricate, from *fabrica* workshop. The meaning of make a fraudulent imitation, counterfeit, is first recorded in *Cursor Mundi* (before 1325), influenced by Anglo-French *forger* to forge, falsify. **—forgery** *n.* 1583 *forgerye* invention, fiction, a deceit; later, the action of counterfeiting or falsifying, in Shakespeare's *The Rape of Lucrece* (1593); formed from English *forge*[1] + *-ery.*

forge[2] *v.* move forward steadily. 1769; earlier, probably in a figurative use (1611), of uncertain origin; perhaps a transferred use of *forge*[1], with reference to the effect of steadily hammering away at something.

forget *v.* Before 1250 *forgeten,* in *Bestiary;* developed from Old English (about 725) *forgytan* (*for-* away, amiss, opposite + *-gietan* or *-getan* get, as in *begietan* beget; see GET); corresponding to Old Frisian *forjeta* forget, Old Saxon *fargetan,* Dutch *vergeten,* and Old High German *firgezzan* (modern German *vergessen*). According to the OED the sense of the verb that can be abstracted from its parts, is that of miss or lose one's hold or grasp (on the mind).

The Old English form would normally have developed into modern **foryet,* not *forget.* The word has been respelled under the influence of Middle English

geten to get, acquire, from a Scandinavian source (compare Old Icelandic *geta*).
—**forgetful** *adj.* About 1384 *forgetful,* in the Wycliffe Bible; formed from Middle English *forget* + *-ful.*

forgive *v.* 1155 *forgifen;* earlier, implied in *forgifenness* (before 1121); developed from Old English (about 900) *forgiefan* give, grant, forgive (*for-* completely + *giefan* GIVE), corresponding to Old Saxon *fargeban* give, forgive, Dutch *vergeven* forgive, Old High German *firgeban* (modern German *vergeben*), Old Icelandic *fyrirgefa,* and Gothic *fragiban,* to which a parallel exists in Latin *perdōnāre* to give, grant.

As in FORGET, except for an intervention of Scandinavian influence (compare Old Icelandic *gefa*), the Old English form would yield modern **foryive, *foryeve.* It is the velar stop *g* in *give* which was passed on by analogy to *forgive.*
—**forgiveness** *n.* Before 1121 *forgivenesse,* developed from Old English *forgifenness (forgifen + -nesse).*

forgo or **forego** *v.* Probably before 1200 *forgon* do without; give up; developed from Old English (about 950) *forgān* go away, pass over, forgo (*for-* away + *gān* GO); associated with Middle High German *vergān, vergēn* forgo (modern German *vergehen* pass away); to which a parallel exists in Latin *perīre* pass away, perish.

fork *n.* Probably before 1200 *forken,* pl. gallows; later *fork* a forked weapon (probably before 1300), and pitchfork (about 1325); developed from Old English *forca* forked instrument used by torturers (about 1000, in Ælfric's writings); borrowed from Latin *furca* pitchfork, of uncertain origin; however, many of the Germanic languages borrowed the word, including Old Frisian *forke,* Old Saxon *furka,* Middle Dutch *vorke* (modern Dutch *vork*), Old High German *furcha,* Middle High German *furke* (modern German dialect *Forke*), and Old Icelandic *forkr,* generally with the meaning of pitchfork.

Several senses of the English word were influenced by Old North French *forque* fork (from Latin *furca*), including the meaning of instrument for eating, which is first recorded in 1463.
—**v.** Before 1325 *forken* divide into branches, in *Cursor Mundi;* from the noun.

forlorn *adj.* wretched, miserable. 1137 *forloren* disgraced, dishonored; repudiated; later *forlorn* forsaken, abandoned (1535), past participle of *forlesen* be deprived of, lose, abandon (1102); found in Old English *forlēosan* (about 725, in *Beowulf*); from *for-* completely + *-lēosan* to LOSE. The Old English verb corresponds to Old Frisian *forliāsa* lose, Old Saxon *farliosan,* Dutch *verliezen,* Old High German *firliosan* (modern German *verlieren*), and Gothic *fraliusan;* examples of past participles corresponding to Middle English *forloren* include Old High German *furlorn, firloran* (modern German *verloren*) lost, and Dutch *verloren.*

The sense of wretched, miserable, is first recorded in 1582.

form *n.* Probably before 1200 *furme,* in *Ancrene Riwle;* later *forme* (about 1300); borrowed from Old French *forme,* learned borrowing from Latin *fōrma* form, mold, shape, case, manner, sort, kind, of uncertain origin (possibly an alteration, through Etruscan loan translation, of Greek *morphḗ* form, shape). —**v.** About 1300 *formen, fourmen;* borrowed from Old French *former,* from Latin *fōrmāre,* from *fōrma* form, mold, etc.
—**formation** *n.* Before 1398 *formacioun,* in Trevisa's translation of Bartholomew's *De Proprietatibus Rerum;* borrowed through Old French *formation,* or directly from Latin *fōrmātiōnem* (nominative *fōrmātiō*), from *fōrmāre* to form. —**formative** *adj.* 1490, in Caxton's translation of *The Book of Eneydos;* borrowed from Middle French *formatif* (feminine *formative*), from *forme,* n.; for suffix see -ATIVE. —**formless** *adj.* 1591, in Spenser's *Tears of the Muses;* formed from English *form,* n. + *-less.*

-form a combining form meaning having the form of _____, as in *cuneiform,* or having _____ form or forms, as in *multiform.* Borrowed through French *-forme,* or directly from Latin *-fōrmis,* from *fōrma* shape, FORM.

formal *adj.* About 1390 *formal,* in Chaucer's *Canterbury Tales;* borrowed through Old French *formel,* and directly from Latin *fōrmālis,* from *fōrma* FORM; for suffix see -AL[1]. —**n.** 1605, plural, things that are formal; later, formal concept (1903, in philosophy) and formal dress (1941); from the adjective. —**formality** *n.* 1531, literary form, agreement as to form, in Elyot's *The Boke Named the Governour;* borrowed from Middle French *formalité,* from Latin *fōrmālis* formal; for suffix see -ITY. The meaning of convention, something done for the sake of form, is first recorded in Richard Hooker's *Ecclesiastical Polity* (1597). —**formalize** *v.* 1597, in Hooker's *Ecclesiastical Polity;* formed from English *formal* + *-ize.*

formaldehyde *n.* 1872, formed from *form-,* abstracted from *form(ic acid)* + *aldehyde,* New Latin formation abstracted from *al(cohol) dehyd(rogenatum)* dehydrogenized alcohol.

format (fôr′mat) *n.* general arrangement of a book. 1840, borrowed from French *format,* abstracted from Latin *liber formatus* book formed (in a special way); *fōrmātus,* past participle of *fōrmāre* to FORM. —**v.** 1964, from the noun. This verb is used chiefly in connection with computers which lay out the format of printed matter.

former *adj.* Before 1375 *former,* comparative of *forme* first (patterned on *formest* foremost); see FOREMOST. Earlier use appears in a transition text of the *Hatton Gospels* (about 1160) where the use of *former* may be that of a Middle English innovation appearing in an Old English textual environment. The striking significance of *former* is that it assumes the function of a comparative formed on an old superlative (the *m* in *forme* and Old English *forma* is a superlative element as old as Indo-European). —**formerly** *adv.* 1596, in Spenser's *Faerie Queene;* formed from English *former* + *-ly*[1].

Formica (fôrmī′kə) *n.* Trademark of a laminated plastic covering. 1922, American English; perhaps influenced in form by New Latin *Formica* the genus of ants (from Latin *formīca* ant) and in meaning by the resemblance of the ant's hard outer covering to the plastic. See FORMIC ACID. The term was coined by the manufacturers, the Formica Insulation Company.

formic acid colorless irritant used as a reagent. 1791, formed in English by shortening of Latin *formīca* ant + English suffix *-ic* (so called because it was first obtained from red ants). Latin *formīca* is cognate with Old Irish *moirbant,* Greek *mýrmēx,* Old Slavic *mravĭi,* Avestan *maoiri-,* and Sanskrit *vamrá-s* ant, *valmīka-s* anthill; also cognate with earlier Middle English *mire* ant, from Indo-European **morwī-,* with variants **worm-, *morm-,* and **mour-* (Pok.749); see PISMIRE.

In the opinion of the Sanskrit scholar Mayrhofer, the

curious deformations in the shape of this word in various Indo-European languages (Dutch *mire;* Polish *mrówka;* Persian *mōr;* Welsh *myrion,* later *morgrug* ants, Breton *merien,* Crimean Gothic *miera*) can have come about only through attempts at avoiding a taboo.

formidable *adj.* inspiring dread or wonder, awesome. About 1450 *formydable;* borrowed from Middle French *formidable,* learned borrowing from Latin *formīdābilis,* from *formīdāre* to fear, from *formīdō* terror or dread, probably cognate with Greek *mormṓ* bugbear, goblin, from Indo-European **mormo-* (Pok.749); for suffix see -ABLE.

formula *n.* Before 1638, a set form of words used in a ceremony or ritual; borrowed from Latin *fōrmula* form, rule, method, formula (literally, small form), diminutive of *fōrma* FORM; for suffix *-la* see English equivalent -LE[1].

The sense of prescription or recipe, is first recorded in 1706, the mathematical use (as in an *algebraic formula*) in 1796, and that in chemistry (as in *molecular formula*) in 1846. A somewhat disparaging sense of formula, "rule, custom, or convention followed slavishly," was introduced from French by Carlyle in *The French Revolution* (1837).

—formulate *v.* 1860, express in a formula; formed from English *formula* + *-ate,* possibly by influence of earlier French *formuler.* **—formulation** *n.* (1876; formed from English *formulate* + *-ion,* possibly after earlier French *formulation.*

fornication *n.* sexual intercourse between unmarried persons. About 1303 *fornycacyoun,* in Mannyng's *Handlyng Synne;* borrowed from Old French *fornication,* learned borrowing from Late Latin *fornicātiōnem* (nominative *fornicātiō*), from *fornicārī* fornicate, from Latin *fornix* (genitive *fornicis*) arch, vault, brothel, probably from *fornus, furnus* oven of arch or dome shape; see FURNACE. Brothels in ancient Rome were often located in underground basements; also, prostitutes solicited their business under the arches of certain buildings. **—fornicate** *v.* 1552, in Huloet's *Abecedarium Anglico-Latinum;* borrowed from Late Latin *fornicātus,* past participle of *fornicārī* fornicate; for suffix see -ATE[1]. In later instances, *fornicate* may have been a back formation from earlier *fornication.*

forsake *v.* Probably before 1200 *forsaken* decline, refuse, in *Ancrene Riwle,* and cease, abandon, desert, in Layamon's *Chronicle of Britain;* developed from Old English (about 700) *forsacan* decline or refuse an offer (*for-* completely + *sacan* to dispute, deny, refuse, from *sacu* a cause at law; see SAKE[1] cause). **—forsaken** *adj.* About 1250, from the verb.

forsooth *adv. Archaic.* in truth, indeed. Probably before 1200 *forsoth,* in *Ancrene Riwle;* developed from Old English *forsōth* (before 899, in Alfred's translation of Boethius' *De Consolatione Philosophiae*), also found as *for sōth,* from *for* FOR and *sōth* truth, SOOTH.

forswear *v.* renounce or deny an oath. Probably about 1175 *forsweren;* developed from Old English *forswerian* forswear, swear falsely (about 725, in *Beowulf;* compound of *for-* completely + *swerian* to SWEAR), corresponding to Old High German *farswerren, fersweren* (modern German *verschwören*) to forswear, swear falsely, and Old Frisian *forswera;* and parallel to Latin *perjūrāre* to commit perjury, forswear oneself.

forsythia (fôrsith′ēə) *n.* shrub with yellow flowers. 1814, American English; New Latin *Forsythia,* the genus name, in allusion to William *Forsyth,* Scottish horticulturist who brought the shrub from China.

fort *n.* Probably before 1375 *forte* courage, fortitude; later, fortress, stronghold (1435); borrowed from Middle French *fort,* noun use of Old French *fort,* adj., strong, fortified, from Latin *fortis* strong; possibly cognate with Sanskrit *bṛhánt-* high, lofty; see BARROW.

forte[1] (fôrt *or* fôr′tā, see note below) *n.* something one does very well. 1648, strong part of a sword blade; later *fort* strong point of a person's abilities (1682); borrowed from French *fort* strong point, fort, from Middle French *fort* FORT. The final *-e* was added in the 1700's, on analogy with Italian *forte* strong, which is reflected in the variant pronunciation given above and is very popular today.

forte[2] (fôr′tā) *adj. Music.* loud, strong. 1724, borrowing of Italian *forte* loud, strong, from Latin *fortis.*

forth *adv.* forward, onward. Before 1121 *forth;* developed from Old English (before 700) *forth* forward, onward; cognate with Old Frisian and Old Saxon *forth* forward, onward, Dutch *voort,* Middle High German *vort* (modern German *fort*), from Proto-Germanic **furtha-,* Indo-European **pṛto-* (Pok.813); related to Old English *for* FOR and FURTHER. **—forthcoming** *adj.* 1531-32; formed from *forth* + *coming,* after earlier *forthcomen* (about 1250), found in Old English *forthcuman* (before 1000, in a version of *Genesis,* originally attributed to Caedmon). **—forthright** *adj.* About 1290, found in Old English *forthriht* (about 1000, in Ælfric's *Glossary*); formed from *forth* + *riht* right. **—forthwith** *adv.* Before 1325 *forthwit,* in *Cursor Mundi;* earlier *forthwith,* prep. (probably about 1200, in *The Ormulum*); formed from *forth* + *with,* possibly also influenced by earlier *forthmid* (1120, prep. 1114), found in Old English phrase *forth mid.*

fortify *v.* Probably before 1425, increase efficacy (of medicine), in a translation of Chauliac's *Grande Chirurgie;* later, to provide with fortifications (1433); borrowed from Middle French *fortifier,* learned borrowing from Late Latin *fortificāre,* from Latin *fortis* strong; see FORT; for suffix see -FY. **—fortification** *n.* 1429, strengthening; later, defensive earthwork, tower (1435); borrowed from Middle French *fortification,* from Late Latin *fortificātiōnem* (nominative *fortificātiō*), from *fortificāre* fortify; for suffix see -ATION.

fortissimo *adj. Music.* very loud. 1724, borrowing of Italian *fortissimo,* from the absolute superlative of *forte* strong, FORTE[2].

fortitude *n.* moral or physical strength. 1422, possibly borrowed from Middle French *fortitude;* earlier *fortitudo* (about 1390, in Chaucer's *Canterbury Tales,* and before 1175, in early homilies); borrowed from Latin *fortitūdō* strength, from *fortis* strong, brave; see FORT; for suffix see -TUDE.

fortnight *n.* two weeks. About 1300 *fourteniht,* in a late version of Layamon's *Chronicle of Britain;* contraction of Old English (before 1000) *fēowertȳne niht* fourteen nights. It is often referred to as representing the "ancient Germanic method of reckoning by nights," mentioned in Tacitus; however, this method is evinced in Celtic culture by Welsh *wythnos* eightnight (for week) and *pythefnos* fifteen-night (for fortnight, by including the night preceding the first day *and* the night following the last day).

Fortran or **FORTRAN** *n.* computer language for scientific and algebraic computations (developed at IBM). 1956, American English, acronym for *For(mula) Tran(slation).*

fortress *n.* Probably before 1300 *fortress,* in *Kyng Alisaunder;* later, variant *forteresse;* borrowed from Old French *forteresse* strong place, variant of *fortelesse,* from Medieval Latin *fortalitia,* from Latin *fortis* strong; see FORT. The suffix *-ess* here represents a Latin ending *-itia* forming nouns denoting quality or condition and though this suffix is not active in English, it can be found in such words as *duress* and *largess.*

fortuitous *adj.* happening by chance. Before 1652, borrowed from Latin *fortuītus,* from *forte* by chance, ablative case of *fors* (genitive *fortis*) chance; see FORTUNE; for suffix see -OUS.

An earlier form, *fortuit* (recorded about 1380, in Chaucer's translation of Boethius' *De Consolatione Philosophiae*) was borrowed from Old French *fortuit,* from Latin *fortuītus,* but was replaced by *fortuitous,* which became the established form in the 1600's.

fortune *n.* Before 1325 *fortune* chance or luck (personified as a goddess, *Dame Fortune*), in *Cursor Mundi;* borrowed from Old French *fortune,* learned borrowing from Latin *fortūna,* from a lost noun **fortus* (genitive **fortūs*), from *fors* (genitive *fortis*) chance, luck, possibly (as being what is brought) related to *ferre* carry, though not so according to Ernout and Meillet; see BEAR[2] carry. **—fortunate** *adj.* Before 1387 *fortunate,* in Trevisa's translation of Higden's *Polychronicon;* borrowed from Latin *fortūnātus* provided with good fortune (quasi-past participial form); from *fortūna* FORTUNE. As used by Chaucer in the *Canterbury Tales* (1390), the word may have been borrowed initially also from Old French *fortuné* happy, since Chaucer translated from French and was probably aware of the word from that source. **—fortuneteller** *n.* 1590, in Shakespeare's *A Comedy of Errors;* earlier *fortunetelling,* n. (1577); formed from the phrase *tellen fortune* (1413).

forty *adj.* 1124, but not recorded in a Middle English spelling before 1200; developed from Old English *fēowertig* (about 750, in *Genesis A, fēower* four + *-tig* -ty[1], group of ten); cognate with Old Frisian *fiuwertich,* Old Saxon *fiwartig, fiartig, fiortig,* Old High German *fiorzug* (modern German *vierzig*), Old Icelandic *fertugr,* and Gothic *fidwōr tigjus.* **—fortieth** *n., adj.* 1107 *fowertigethe,* developed from Old English (about 1000) *fēowertigotha* (*fēower* four + *-tig* -ty[1] + *-otha* -eth[1]).

forum *n.* Before 1464 *forum* public place, marketplace (specifically in ancient Rome); borrowing of Latin *forum* marketplace, which is apparently related to *forīs, forās* out of doors, outside; see FOREIGN. The transferred sense in English of assembly, or place, for public discussion, is first recorded in 1690.

forward *adj.* Probably before 1200 *forwarde,* in Layamon's *Chronicle of Britain;* developed from Old English (before 900) *foreweard* toward the front (*fore-* + *-weard* -ward). **—adv.** Probably about 1300 *forward;* developed from Old English *forewearde* (about 875, in *Genesis B*), from *foreweard,* adj.; cognate with Dutch *voorwaarts* and modern German *vorwärts.* **—n.** Before 1225 *forward;* developed from Old English *foreweard* the fore or front part (about 1000, in Ælfric's translation of *Deuteronomy*); from the adjective. **—v.** to move forward; advance. 1596, in Shakespeare's *1 Henry IV;* from the adverb.

fosse (fos) *n.* ditch, trench. 1327, in a surname *Fosse* ditch, pit; earlier, in the variant compound place name *Vosepole* a pool in a ditch (1296), and in an Old English reference to the *Fosse* one of the principal Roman roads in Britain (1130-35), so called from the drainage ditch dug on either side of the road; borrowed through Old French *fosse,* and directly from Latin *fossa* ditch, from feminine of *fossus,* past participle of *fodere* to dig; see BED.

fossil *n.* 1619, rock or mineral dug out of the earth; borrowed from French *fossile,* from Latin *fossilis* dug up, from *fossus,* past participle of *fodere* to dig; see BED. **—adj.** 1654, obtained by digging; from the noun. In 1665 the word is recorded as applying specifically to the remains of plants or animals. **—fossilize** *v.* 1794, formed from English *fossil* + *-ize,* perhaps modeled after French *fossiliser.*

foster *v.* About 1125 *fostrien* nourish, bring up, rear (a child); later *fostren* (probably before 1200) in both *Ancrene Riwle* and Layamon's *Chronicle of Britain*); probably to be found in Old English (before 1050) **fōstrian* nourish, foster. The probable Old English verb was formed from *fóstor* food, nourishment, a bringing up; from the same Germanic source as Old English *fōda* FOOD. The figurative sense of encourage, strengthen, is first recorded in a version of *Piers Plowman* (about 1378), preceded by the earlier sense of support, nurture (about 1125). **—adj. 1** related, as if by family ties, as in *foster city.* 1618, from the meaning "in the same family, but not related by birth"; abstracted from various modern English compounds such as *foster father, foster mother,* etc.; found in Old English *fōstor-,* as in *fōstorfæder* (before 800) foster father. Other compounds of the original sense include: *foster child* (Old English *fōstercild*), *foster brother* (Old English *fōsterbrōthor,* before 1000), *foster mother* (*fōstermōdor,* probably before 1000). **2** of or for a foster child or children, as in *foster home* (1886) and *foster parent* (1649).

foul *adj.* About 1250 *foul;* developed from Old English *fūl* dirty, impure, vile, rotten, corrupt (before 800-1000, in various glossaries); cognate with Old Saxon and Old Frisian *fūl* foul, Middle Dutch *vuul* (modern Dutch *vuil*), Old High German *fūl* (modern German *faul* foul, lazy), Old Icelandic *fūll,* and Gothic *fūls.* from Proto-Germanic **fūlaz.* Outside Germanic cognates with Old English *fūl* exist without the *l* suffix in Latin *pūs* pus, *pūtēre* to stink, Greek *pýon* pus, *pýthein* cause to rot, Lithuanian *púti* to rot, Armenian *hu* (with *h-* for Indo-European *p-*) purulent blood, and Sanskrit *pūyati* it stinks, from Indo-European **pū-* (Pok.848).

In Middle English *foul* was the opposite of *fair,* in various meanings; thus *foul play* meant unfair conduct; but later developed the sense of treacherous or violent dealings, as recorded in Shakespeare's *The Tempest* (1610). The sense of *foul* out of play in *foul ball,* is first recorded in 1860, in American English.

—v. Probably before 1200 *fulen* make or become foul, in *Ancrene Riwle;* developed from Old English *fūlian* (about 899, in Alfred's translation of Orosius' *Historiarum Adversus Paganos*), and Old English *fȳlan;* both from *fūl,* adj.

—n. 1304, in a surname *Foule* a muddy place; later, that which is foul, deceitful, ugly (before 1420, in Lydgate's *Troy Book*); developed from Old English *fūl* foulness, impurity, guilt, offense (about 750, in Cynewulf's *Elene*); from the adjective.

found[1] *v.* establish, set up. About 1290 *founden;* borrowed from Old French *fonder,* from Latin *fundāre* to lay the bottom or foundation of something, establish, from *fundus* bottom, foundation; see BOTTOM. **—foundation** *n.* Before 1387 *fundacioun,* in Trevisa's translation of Higden's *Polychronicon;* borrowed from Old French *fondation,* or directly from Latin *fundātiōnem* (nominative *fundātiō*) foundation, from *fundāre* to found. **—founded** *adj.* Before 1325, from the verb. **—founder** *n.* Before 1338, in Mannyng's *Chronicle of England,* borrowed through Anglo-French *fundur,* Old French *fondeor,* from Latin *fundātor.*

found² *v.* cast (metal). Before 1399 *founden, funden* to mix or mingle; later *found* melt, cast (1562); borrowed from Middle French *fondre* pour out, melt, mix together, from Old French *fondre,* from Latin *fundere* melt, cast, pour. The Latin form is cognate with Greek *cheîn* to pour, Sanskrit *juhóti* he pours, sacrifices, Armenian *joyl* poured, Old English *gēotan* to pour (which did not survive into Middle and modern English), Old Saxon *giotan,* Middle Dutch *ghieten* (modern Dutch *gieten*), Old Frisian *jāta, giāta,* Old High German *giozzan* (modern German *giessen*), Old Icelandic *gjōta,* and Gothic *giutan,* from Indo-European *ĝheud-/ĝhud-,* root *ĝheu-* (Pok.447). **—foundry** *n.* 1601, borrowed from French *fonderie, fondrie,* from Middle French, from *fondre* to melt, pour, found.

founder *v.* to stumble. Before 1338 *fondren* knock down, in Mannyng's *Chronicle of England;* later *foundren* to stumble (about 1385, in Chaucer's *Canterbury Tales*); borrowed from Old French *fondrer* fall to the bottom, from *fond* bottom, from Latin *fundus* bottom; see BOTTOM. The earlier sense of sink to the ground (about 1385, in Chaucer's *Canterbury Tales*), was extended to mean to fill with water and sink, and is first recorded in a version of Hakluyt's *Voyages and Discoveries of the English Nation* (1610).

foundling *n.* child found deserted. Probably before 1300 *fundelyng,* in *Kyng Alisaunder;* formed from *funden, founden* found (past participle of *finden* to FIND) + *-ling.*

fount *n.* fountain, source. Before 1449 *funte,* in Lydgate's *Te Deum Laudamus;* later *fount* (1593, in Shakespeare's *Lucrece*); probably a shortening of *fountain,* on analogy with *mount, mountain;* influenced by Middle French *font* fount, from Latin *fontem* (nominative *fōns*) spring; see FOUNTAIN.

fountain *n.* About 1410 *fownteyne* natural spring; borrowed from Old French *fontaine,* from Late Latin *fontāna* a fountain, spring, from Latin, feminine of *fontānus* of a spring, from *fōns* (genitive *fontis*) spring; probably cognate with Sanskrit *dhánvati* it flows or runs, and Tocharian A, Tocharian B *tsän* to flow, from Indo-European **dhen-/dhon-* (Pok.249). The meaning of an artificial jet or stream of water, especially a structure built for such a jet or stream, is first recorded in 1509. The term drinking fountain came into use in the mid-1800's, when such fountains began to appear in public places in England. **—fountainhead** *n.* (1585) **—fountain pen** (1710)

four *adj.* 1122 *fower;* later *fowr* (probably before 1200, in *Ancrene Riwle*) and *four* (about 1280); developed from Old English (about 725) *fēower;* cognate with Old Frisian *fiūwer, fiōwer, fiōr* four, Old Saxon *fiuwar, fiwar, fior,* Dutch *vier,* Old High German *fior* (modern German *vier*), Old Icelandic *fjōrir* (Norwegian and Danish *fire,* Swedish *fyra*), and Gothic *fidwōr.* Outside Germanic cognates appear in Old Irish *cethair, cethir,* Gaulish *petor* in *petorritum* four-wheeled chariot, Old Welsh *petguar* (modern Welsh *pedwar*), Breton *pevar;* Latin *quattuor,* Greek *téssares,* Boeotian Greek *péttares,* Lithuanian *keturì,* Old Slavic *ketyre,* Armenian *čork'*, Persian *čahār,* Sanskrit *catvā́ras,* and Tocharian A *śtwar,* Tocharian B *śtwār, śwār,* from Indo-European **kwetwōr-/kwetur-* (Pok.642).

Minor phonological shifts make it somewhat difficult to derive all forms from a common source: the initial *f* in Germanic implies a pre-Germanic *p* (though *p* in Welsh does not, as it represents *kw*); whereas the words in other languages either imply *kw* or could be from it.

—fourth *adj., n.* About 1200 *ferthe,* in *The Ormulum;* developed from Old English *fēortha;* for suffix see -TH². The later spelling *fourth* (before 1450, in a late edition of Chaucer's *Treatise on the Astrolabe*) was patterned on the development of *four.* **—fourfold** *adj., adv.* About 1300; developed from Old English *fēowerfeald (fēower* four + *-feald* -fold); cognate with Old Frisian *fiuwerfald,* Old High German *fiervalt* (German *vierfalt*), and Gothic *fidurfalths.* **—four-footed** *adj.* Before 1325 *four foted,* in *Cursor Mundi;* developed from Old English *fēowerfōte, -fēte* (*fēower* four + *-fōte* -footed); cognate with Old Frisian *fiuwerfoted,* Old High German *fiorfuozi* (modern German *vierfüssig*). **—fourscore** *adj., n.* About 1290; formed from Middle English *four* + *score* twenty. **—foursquare** *adj.* Before 1325, in *Cursor Mundi;* formed from Middle English *four* + *square.* The sense of firm, unyielding (in the adverb, firmly), is first recorded in 1845-46. **—fourteen** *adj., n.* About 1300; developed from Old English *fēowertēne, fēowertȳne* (*fēower* + *-tēne, -tȳne* -teen, from tēn TEN); cognate with Old Frisian *fiuwertine,* Old High German *fiorzehan* (modern German *vierzehn*), Old Icelandic *fjōntān,* and Gothic *fidwōrtaíhun.*

four-flusher *n. Slang.* pretender, braggart. 1904, American English, from the earlier verb *four-flush* to bluff (1896), from the phrase *four flush* a hand in poker with only four cards of the same suit, instead of the five needed to make a flush (1887); for suffix see -ER¹.

fowl *n.* Before 1200 *fuwel;* developed from Old English *fugel* bird (about 725, in *Beowulf*); cognate with Old Frisian *fugel* bird, Old Saxon *fugal,* Middle Dutch *voghel* (modern Dutch *vogel*), Old High German *fogal* (modern German *Vogel*), Old Icelandic *fugl,* and Gothic *fugls;* apparently related to Old English *flēogan* to FLY², as Proto-Germanic **fuȝlaz* resulted by dissimilation from earlier **fluȝlaz.* The narrower sense of domestic rooster or hen, is first recorded in Sidney's *The Arcadia* (1580).

fox *n.* Old English (before 830) *fox;* cognate with Old Saxon *vohs* fox, Middle Low German, Middle Dutch, and modern Dutch *vos,* Old High German *fuhs* (modern German *Fuchs*), Old Icelandic *fōa* vixen, and Gothic *faúhō.* Outside Germanic *fox* is cognate with Lithuanian *paustìs* animal hair, Russian and Polish *puch* woolly hair, tuft, fluff, and Sanskrit *púccha-s* tail (reference to the tail, hair, etc., as the name for a fox possibly involving some taboo), from Indo-European **puk-/pouk-* (Pok.849). —*v.* to trick by craft. Before 1250, implied in *foxing,* n., a clever deceit, in *Bestiary;* later, to pierce or stab with a sword, said to have the figure of a fox or wolf on the blade (1567). **—foxy** *adj.* 1528, foxlike, crafty or cunning; formed from English *fox* + *-y¹.*

foyer *n.* entrance hall. 1859, lobby, lounge; borrowed

from French *foyer* room for actors to rest when not on stage (literally, fireplace), from Old French *foyer,* from Latin *focārius* in the unattested meaning having to do with the hearth (attested as a kitchen servant), from *focus* hearth, fireplace; see FOCUS.

fracas (frā'kəs) *n.* noisy quarrel. 1727, borrowed from French *fracas,* from Italian *fracasso* an uproar, crash, from *fracassare* to smash, crash, break into pieces; of uncertain origin (perhaps a fusion of Latin *frangere* to break, and *quassāre* to shatter).

fraction *n.* Before 1410 *fraccioun* a breaking or dividing of the heart; later, a breaking, fracture of a bone (probably before 1425, in a translation of Chauliac's *Grande Chirurgie*); borrowed through Anglo-French *fraccioun,* and directly from Late Latin *frāctiōnem* (nominative *frāctiō*) a breaking, especially into pieces, from Latin *frag-,* root of *frangere* to BREAK. Doublet of FRAGMENT. The mathematical sense is first recorded in Chaucer's *Treatise on the Astrolabe* (1391), and a general meaning of something broken off, a fragment, scrap, in Shakespeare's *Troylus and Cressida* (1606).

fractious *adj.* 1725, hard to manage, unruly, in Defoe's *A New Voyage Around the World;* formed from *fraction* (in the obsolete sense of a rupture, brawling, discord) + *-ous,* probably patterned on *captious.*

fracture *n.* breakage. Probably before 1425 *fracture,* in a translation of Chauliac's *Grande Chirurgie;* borrowed from Middle French *fracture,* learned borrowing from Latin *frāctūra* a breach, break, cleft, from *frag-,* root of *frangere* to BREAK; for suffix see -URE. **—v.** 1612, in the past participial form *fractured* broken (bone); from *fracture* + *-ed*[2], probably modeled on earlier French *fracturé.*

fragile *adj.* 1513 *fragyll* morally weak; either a back formation of earlier English *fragility,* influenced by Middle French *fragile;* or a direct borrowing of Middle French *fragile,* learned borrowing from Latin *fragilis* brittle, easily broken, from *frag-,* root of *frangere* to break. The sense of easily broken or delicate, is first recorded in Shakespeare's *Timon of Athens* (1607), with a transferred sense of frail, in 1858. Doublet of FRAIL. **—fragility** *n.* Before 1398, in Trevisa's translation of Bartholomew's *De Proprietatibus Rerum;* borrowed from Old French *fragilité,* from Latin *fragilitātem* (nominative *fragilitās,*) brittleness, from *fragilis* brittle, easily broken, from *frag-,* root of *frangere* to break; for suffix see -ITY. The sense of fragile quality, delicacy, is first recorded in Caxton's *Game and Play of Chess* (1474).

fragment *n.* Probably before 1425 *fragmente,* in a translation of Higden's *Polychronicon;* borrowed from Latin *fragmentum* a fragment or remnant, from *frag-,* root of *frangere* to BREAK; for suffix see -MENT. **—v.** break into fragments. 1818, in Keats' *Endymion;* from the noun. **—fragmentary** *adj.* 1611, in Donne's letters; formed from English *fragment* + *-ary.* According to the OED, not in common use until 1835, after Browning's *Paracelsus.* **—fragmentation** *n.* 1881, formed from English *fragment* + *-ation,* perhaps influenced by, or a direct borrowing of earlier French *fragmentation* (1865).

fragrant *adj.* About 1450 *fragrante;* borrowed from Latin *fragrantem* (nominative *fragrāns*) sweet-smelling, present participle of *fragrāre* emit (a sweet) odor, from a pre-Latin adjective, **fragros* smelling, cognate with Old High German *braccho* (modern German *Bracke*) bloodhound, pointer, from Indo-European **bhrag-* smell (Pok.163); for suffix see -ANT. **—fragrance** *n.* sweet smell. 1667, in Milton's *Paradise Lost;* borrowed through French *fragrance,* or directly from Latin *fragrantia,* from *fragrantem,* present participle; for suffix see -ANCE.

frail *adj.* Probably about 1350 *frele* weak, delicate; borrowed from Old French *frele, fraile,* from Latin *fragilis* easily broken; see FRAGILE. Doublet of FRAGILE. **—frailty** *n.* About 1340 *frelte;* borrowed from Old French *fraileté,* from Latin *fragilitātem* (nominative *fragilitās*), from *fragilis* fragile.

frame *v.* Probably before 1300 *framen* join timber, etc., developed from Old English (about 961) *framian* to profit, be helpful, make progress, from *fram* forward (see FROM), influenced in meaning by Old English *fremman* (before 800), *fremian* (about 1000) help forward, promote, benefit, and perhaps influenced in form and meaning by Old Icelandic *frama* to further, execute. Old English *fremman* is cognate with Old Frisian *fremma* perform, Old Saxon *fremmian* promote, further, and Old Icelandic *fremja* to further, carry out, execute. The meaning of compose, devise, fashion, is recorded probably before 1400. The sense of invent or fabricate a story with evil intent is first recorded in 1514. **—n.** About 1250 *frame* composition or plan, in *The Story of Genesis and Exodus;* earlier, profit, benefit (probably about 1200); from the verb and a Scandinavian source (compare Old Icelandic *frami* advancement). **—frame house** (1777; earlier, *framed house,* 1639; both in American English). **—frame of mind** (1711, Steele in *The Spectator*) **—framework** *n.* (1644, in Milton's *Areopagitica*)

franc *n.* French unit of money. About 1390 *frank,* in Chaucer's *Canterbury Tales;* borrowed from Old French *franc,* apparently from Medieval Latin *Francus* a Frank (see FRANK[1]), from, or in reference to, the phrase *Francorum Rex* King of the Franks, inscribed on gold coins first made during the reign of Jean le Bon, 1350-64. The spelling *franc* is first recorded in English in 1420.

franchise *n.* privilege or right. About 1300 *fraunchise* freedom; borrowed from Old French *franchise* freedom, frankness, from *franch-,* variant stem of *franc* free + *-ise,* as in *bêtise, sottise;* see FRANK[1]. **—v.** Probably before 1387 *fraunchisen* make a person a freeman in a city or town, in a version of *Piers Plowman;* from the noun *fraunchise.*

francium (fran'sēəm) *n.* radioactive metallic element. 1946, New Latin; formed from *Francia,* Latin form of *France* + *-ium* (chemical suffix). The name was coined by the French chemist Marguerite Perey.

Franco- a combining form meaning France or French, as in *Francophile, Francophone,* or French and _____, as in *Franco-German.* Borrowed from Medieval Latin *Francus* Frank; see FRANK[1], adj.

Francophone or **francophone** *n.* French-speaking inhabitant of a bilingual or multilingual country. 1900, French-speaking Canadians; borrowed from French *Francophone* (*Franco-* French, from Medieval Latin *Francus* a Frank + *-phone,* from Greek *phōnḗ* sound, voice; see FRANK[1], adj.).

frangible (fran'jəbəl) *adj.* breakable. Probably before 1425 *frangible,* borrowed from Middle French *frangible,* learned borrowing from Medieval Latin *frangibilis,* from Latin *frangere* to BREAK; for suffix see -IBLE.

franglais or **Franglais** (fränggläʹ) *n.* French containing many English words. 1964, French *Franglais* (blend of *français* French, and *anglais* English). The term *franglais* was popularized in the mid-1960's by René Etiemble, a professor of comparative literature at the Sorbonne. In his book *Parlez-vous Franglais?* he proposed French equivalents for Anglicisms to stop their invasion of the French language.

frank[1] *adj.* outspoken, candid. Probably before 1300 *franc* free, liberal, generous; borrowed from Old French *franc* free, sincere, genuine; also earlier in English, in the surname *Franc* (1182); from *Franc* a freeman, a Frank (member of the Germanic people that conquered Gaul in the 400's and 500's), from Frankish (compare Old High German *Franko* and Old English *Franca* a Frank). The sense of outspoken, candid, is first recorded in English in 1548.

The origin of the ethnic name *Frank* is uncertain. One supposition is that the Franks derived their name from the word for their national weapon, the javelin, represented by Old English *franca* javelin, lance. The notion that the name came from the adjective meaning "free" was already current in the tenth century; but the reverse is true: Old French *Franc,* the name, acquired the meaning "free" because in Frankish Gaul only the dominant Franks possessed full freedom or the status of freemen.

—v. send in the mail free of charge. 1708, from the adjective. **—Frankish** *adj.* of the ancient Franks. 1802, formed from English *Frank* + *-ish.* The noun *Frankish,* meaning the Germanic language of the Franks, is first recorded in 1863, though an earlier formation exists in *Frenkis* (before 1400). Earlier forms *Frankische* (1338, in Mannyng's *Chronicle of England*) and *Frankis* (before 1325, in *Cursor Mundi*), are variant terms for Middle English *Frensh* French, referring to inhabitants of France during the Middle English period, and are probably a blend of *Frenkish* and *Franceis* French. The form *Frencisce* (French) is first recorded about 1070, and found earlier in Old English *frencisc* French.

frank[2] *n.* frankfurter. 1936, American English, shortened form of FRANKFURTER, in a letter of E. E. Cummings.

Frankenstein (frangʹkənstīn) *n.* monster causing the ruin of its creator. 1838, in allusion to Baron *Frankenstein,* a character in Mary Shelley's novel *Frankenstein* (1818). In the novel, Frankenstein's life is ruined by a monster which he created from dead bodies. The name *Frankenstein* was mistakenly taken in popular usage as the name of this monster.

frankfurter *n.* 1894, American English; borrowed from German *Frankfurter,* originally, of Frankfurt; so called because a sausage somewhat like the American hot dog (sometimes referred to as a *frankfurter sausage*) was originally made in Germany and associated with the city of *Frankfurt* am Main.

frankincense (frangʹkinsens) *n.* fragrant resin from certain trees. Before 1398 *fraunkencense,* in Trevisa's translation of Bartholomew's *De Proprietatibus Rerum;* apparently from Old French *frank* genuine or true, and *encens* incense.

frantic *adj.* About 1378 *frantyk* crazed, delirious, frenzied; variant of *frentik* (before 1376); both forms found in versions of *Piers Plowman;* see FRENETIC. The extended sense of very much excited, panicky with worry, wild with grief, etc., is first recorded in 1464.

frappe (frapāʹ) *adj.* iced, cooled. 1848, American English, borrowing of French *frappé,* from past participle of *frapper* to chill, beat, from Old French *fraper* to hit, strike; of unknown origin. **—n.** iced drink. 1922, from the adjective.

fraternal *adj.* brotherly. Perhaps 1421 *fraternal;* borrowed probably from Middle French *fraternel,* and, in some instances, from Medieval Latin *fraternalis,* from Latin *frāternus* brotherly, from *frāter* BROTHER; for suffix see -AL[1]. **—fraternity** *n.* Before 1338 *fraternite* brotherhood, in Mannyng's *Chronicle of England;* borrowed through Old French *fraternité,* and directly from Latin *frāternitātem* (nominative *frāternitās*), from *frāternus* fraternal; for suffix see -ITY. **—fraternize** *v.* 1611, borrowed from French *fraterniser,* from Latin *frāternus* fraternal; for suffix see -IZE.

fratricide[1] *n.* killer of one's own brother or sister. Before 1500 *fratricide,* borrowed through Middle French *fratricide,* and directly from Latin *frātricīda* (*frāter* brother + *-cīda* killer, -CIDE[1]).

fratricide[2] *n.* a killing of one's own brother or sister. 1568 *fratricide,* borrowed through Middle French *fratricide,* and directly from Latin *frātricidium* (*frāter* BROTHER + *-cīdium* a killing, -CIDE[2])

fraud *n.* 1345-46 *fraude* criminal deception, false representation; borrowed from Old French *fraude,* learned borrowing from Latin *fraudem* (nominative *fraus*) deceit, injury, of unknown origin. **—fraudulent** *adj.* Before 1420 *fraudelent,* in Lydgate's *Troy Book;* borrowed from Middle French *fraudulent,* from Latin *fraudulentus* cheating, fraudulent, from *fraudem* (nominative *fraus*) deceit.

fraught *adj.* loaded, filled. Before 1375, loaded or full, past participle of Middle English *fraughten* to load (a ship) with cargo, from earlier noun *fraght* cargo or lading of a ship (1228), variant of *freghte* FREIGHT; also, in part, from Middle Dutch *vrachten, vrechten* to load or furnish with cargo. The figurative use (usually in the phrase *fraught with,* as in *fraught with difficulties*), is first recorded in 1576.

fray[1] *n.* noisy quarrel, fight. About 1350, variant form of AFFRAY.

fray[2] *v.* wear away, become ragged. About 1405, to wear, crush, beat; 1410, to rub, wear off; borrowed from Middle French *frayer,* from Old French *freier,* from Latin *fricāre* to rub; see FRICTION.

frazzle *v.* to fray, wear out, unravel. Before 1825, an East Anglian variant of earlier *fazle* to unravel, fray (1643); from *facelyn* to fray (1440), from *fasylle* fringe or frayed edge, a diminutive formed from Old English *fæs* fringe; cognate with Middle Low German and Middle Dutch *vese* fringe, fiber, chaff, and Old High German *fesa* chaff, *fasa* fringe, fiber (modern German *Faser* fiber, thread, *fasern* to fray, unravel, from Indo-European *pes-/pos-* blow, Pok. 823); for suffix see -LE[1]. **—n.** *Informal.* weary condition. 1865, American English; from the verb.

freak *n.* grotesque person or thing, monstrosity. 1847, in *freaks of nature;* earlier, something very unusual, a fancy (1784, in Cowper's writings); a capricious prank (1724, in John Gay's poetry); capriciousness (1678); and capricious notion, sudden change of mind (1563, but given currency in Spenser's *Faerie Queene,* 1590); of uncertain origin, though many agree the word is probably related to Old English *frīcian* to dance, there is

divergent opinion about its antecedents in Middle English: perhaps *freke* remarkable creature or being, especially an angel, demon, or giant (1375); developed from Old English *freca* bold man, warrior, hero, from *frec* greedy, audacious, bold, though a closer semantic connection is found in *frekynge* capricious behavior, whim (1451), and *frekly* quickly (probably before 1400), eagerly (about 1450), from *frek* quick (before 1500), and eager (before 1325); probably related to Old English *fræc* eager, and to Gothic *-friks* greedy (from Indo-European **preg-/prog-,* Pok.845), as well as to Middle English *frike* eager, vigorous, brisk (1230), from *friken* to move fast or nimbly, from Old English *frician* to dance.
—**v.** 1637, in Milton's *Lycidas,* to streak or fleck whimsically, from the noun sense of whim (compare also *frekynge* capricious behavior, whim, 1451). The slang use *freak out* become excited or become stimulated by drugs, is first recorded in 1965 in American English, from the noun *freak* abnormal or slavish user of drugs (recorded since 1945).

freckle *n.* Before 1400 *fraclis,* pl., light-brown spots on the skin; earlier, implied in *fracled* spotted (about 1380); alteration of *fraknes,* probably from a Scandinavian source (compare Old Icelandic *freknóttr* freckled, Icelandic *frekna* freckle, Swedish *fräknar*), from Indo-European **preg-/prog-* break out (Pok. 996).

free *adj.* Probably before 1200 *fre* (in Layamon's *Chronicle of Britain*); developed from Old English (about 725) *frēo* free; cognate with Old Frisian and Old Saxon *frī* free, Dutch *vrij,* Old High German *frī* (modern German *frei*), Old Icelandic *frjāls,* and Gothic *freis,* from Proto-Germanic **frijaz.* Outside of Germanic, Old English *frēo* is cognate with Welsh *rhydd* free, Greek *prāÿs* gentle, mild, Old Slavic *prijati* I care for, *prijatelĭ* friend, beloved, and Sanskrit *priyá-s* dear, beloved, from Indo-European **prāi-/prəi-/pri-* (Pok. 844). According to the OED the primary sense is dear; the Germanic and Celtic meaning comes from its having been applied to the members of a household connected by familial ties with the head, as opposed to the slaves.—**adv.** 1250, from the adjective. —**v.** Probably before 1200 *frien;* later *fren* (about 1250, in *The Story of Genesis and Exodus*); developed from Old English (725) *frēon, frēogan* to free, love; cognate with Old Frisian *frīa, friaia* make free, Old Saxon *friohan* to court, woo, Middle Low German *vrien* make free (modern German *befreien* to free, *freien* to woo), Old Icelandic *frjā* to love, Gothic *frijōn* to love, and Sanskrit *prīyate* he loves. —**freedom** *n.* Probably before 1200, developed from Old English (about 888) *frēodōm* (*frēo* free + *-dōm* -dom). —**free enterprise** (1890) —**free-for-all** *n.* (1881, American English) —**freehold** *n.* Probably before 1400, modeled after Anglo-French *fraunc tenement,* but earlier *freeholder,* n. 1375, modeled after Anglo-French *fraunc tenaunt.* —**free lance** 1820, often a knight who offered his services, in Scott's *Ivanhoe;* later, anyone who offers his services (1864). —**free-lance** *adj.* (1927); *v.* (1903) —**freeman** *n.* 1196, in a surname, found in Old English *frēoman,* about 1000. —**free speech** 1859, in a letter of George Eliot's, with antecedents found in Middle English *free of speeche,* alluded to about 1290. —**free-style** *adj.* (1950) —**freethinker** *n.* (1692, also *freethinking,* n.) —**free trade** (1606) —**freeway** *n.* (1930, American English) —**free will** (probably before 1200, in *Ancrene Riwle*)

freebie or **freebee** *n. Slang.* something obtained free of charge. 1946, American English slang, from an earlier *freebee, freeby,* adj., free of charge (1942 *free,* adj. + suffix *-bee* -by, formed from *-ie,* variant of *-y*[2], and a paragogic *b* infixed to *free-*).

freebooter *n.* pirate. 1570 *frebetter,* borrowed from Dutch *vrijbuiter,* from *vrijbuiten* to rob, plunder (*vrij* free + *buit* booty, from *buiten* to exchange or plunder, from Middle Dutch *būten,* related to Middle Low German *būte* exchange; see FREE and BOOTY). Doublet of FILIBUSTER.

freeze *v.* About 1325 *fresen;* developed from Old English (before 971) *frēosan* turn to ice; cognate with Middle Low German *vrēsen* to freeze (modern Dutch *vriezen, gifroran* frozen and modern German *frieren* to freeze, *gefroren* frozen), Old High German *friosan* to freeze, Old Icelandic *frjōsa,* from Proto-Germanic **freusanan,* and Gothic *frius* frost, coldness. Outside Germanic cognates are found in Latin *pruīna* hoarfrost, Welsh *rhewi* to freeze, Breton *reviñ* (with Celtic loss of *p*), and Sanskrit *pruṣvā́* drop of water, frost, from Indo-European **preus-/prus-* (Pok.846). The sense of chill or be chilled is first recorded in Gower's *Confessio Amantis* (before 1393), and the figurative sense as with fear, etc. (about 1400). The related sense of become motionless, also is first recorded in Gower, and the extension of fix (motionless) at a definite value or level, or to make non-transactable, as assets, is first recorded in 1922. —**n.** About 1400, from the verb. —**freezer** *n.* 1847, machine for freezing (originally, ice cream). The sense of a refrigerated railroad car, is found in 1905 in American English, and was extended to a refrigerated room in 1924, and that of a chest similar to a refrigerator probably before 1939.

freight *n.* 1228 *fraght* cargo or lading of a ship; later *freghte* the transporting of goods or passengers, passage money (1389), and *freight* (1442, in *Rolls of Parliament*); borrowed from Middle Dutch or Middle Low German *vracht, vrecht,* probably from an unrecorded Old Frisian word (cognate with Old High German *frēht* earnings), ultimately derived from the base of Gothic *fra-* FOR- + *aihts* (from Proto-Germanic **aiHtiz*) property, possession, from *aigan* to possess, have; see OWE. —**v.** Before 1375 *fraughten* to load (a ship) with cargo; later *freghten* (1415) and *freighten* (1449); see FRAUGHT. —**freighter** *n.* 1622, one who loads a ship; formed from English *freight,* n. + *-er*[1]. The meaning of cargo vessel is first recorded in 1836.

French *adj.* Probably before 1200 *Frensch* of France or its inhabitants, in *Ancrene Riwle;* developed from Old English *frencisc,* originally, of the Franks (*Franca* Frank + *-isc* -ish; the suffix producing vowel change in *Franca;* see FRANK[1]); cognate with Old High German *frenkisc, frenqisc.* —**n.** the French language. Probably before 1200 *frensch,* in *Ancrene Riwle;* developed from Old English *frencisc,* from the adjective. —**French bread** (1420-21) —**French Canadian** (1758) —**French dressing** (1900, American English) —**french fries** 1918, American English (earlier *french fried potatoes,* 1894 in O'Henry's *Rolling Stones*). —**French horn** (1742)

frenetic *adj.* frenzied. Before 1376 *frentik* crazed, delirious, frenzied, in *Piers Plowman;* later *frenetik* (about 1385, in Chaucer's *Troilus and Criseyde*); borrowed through Old French *frenetique,* and directly from Latin *phrenēticus* delirious, alteration of Greek *phrenītikós,* from *phrenîtis* inflammation of the brain, frenzy, from *phrḗn* (genitive *phrenós*) mind (originally, diaphragm), cognate with Old Icelandic *grunr* suspicion, from Indo-European *gwhren-/gwhr̥ diaphragm, as seat of the intelligence (Pok.496); for suffix see -IC.

frenzy *n.* Probably before 1396 *frensye* delirium, insanity; contraction of earlier *frenesye* (about 1378, in a version of *Piers Plowman*); borrowed from Old French *frenesie,* from Medieval Latin *phrenesia,* from *phrenesis,* back formation from Latin *phrenēticus* delirious; see FRENETIC. The extended sense of excited state of mind, is first recorded probably before 1400, in *Morte Arthur.* **—v.** 1795, in Southey's *Joan of Arc;* from the noun. **—frenzied** *adj.* (1796)

frequent *adj.* About 1450, ample or profuse; borrowed through Middle French *frequent,* or directly from Latin *frequentem* (nominative *frequēns*) crowded, repeated, from Indo-European *bhrekw-, root *bharekw- to pack in (Pok.110); for suffix see -ENT. The meaning of common, usual, well-known, is first recorded in Elyot's *The Boke Named the Governour* (1531), followed by that of happening at short intervals, often recurring in 1604. **—v.** 1477, visit often; borrowed through French *fréquenter,* or directly from Latin *frequentāre* to do or use often, from *frequentem* frequent. **—frequency** *n.* 1553-87, a crowd; borrowed from Latin *frequentia* a crowd, throng, from *frequentem* frequent. The meaning in physics of the rate of recurrence of a vibration is first recorded in English in 1831; for suffix see -ENCY. **—frequentative** *n.* 1530, in Palsgrave's *Lesclarcissement,* verb which expresses a frequent repetition of an action, borrowed from Latin *frequentātīvus,* from *frequentāre* to do or use often, frequent; for suffix see -ATIVE.

fresco (fres'kō) *n.* a painting with watercolors on damp, fresh plaster. 1598 *in fresco, in frisco,* literally, in fresh (air); borrowed from Italian *fresco* cool, fresh, from a Germanic source (compare Old High German *frisc* FRESH). **—v.** paint in the art of fresco. 1849, from the noun.

fresh *adj.* Probably before 1200 *fersch* unsalted, pure, sweet, eager, in *Ancrene Riwle;* later *fresh* (1288); developed from Old English *fersc* (about 893, in Alfred's translation of Orosius' *Historiarum Adversus Paganos*); cognate with Old Frisian *fersk* fresh, Middle Low German and Middle Dutch *versch* (modern Dutch *vers*), Old High German *frisc* (modern German *frisch*), and probably also cognate with Old Slavic *prěsĭnŭ* fresh, Lithuanian *prěskas* sweet, unleavened, from Indo-European *prois-/pris- (Kluge, *Etymologisches Wörterbuch der deutschen Sprache* (1963), 219). Before the 1300's, the spelling with *fre-* became prevalent, along with the wider meaning of new, novel, recent. These developments were in part influenced by Old French *fres* or *freis,* (feminine) *fresche,* from a Germanic source. **—freshen** *v.* 1697, in William Dampier's *A New Voyage Round the World,* formed from English *fresh* + *-en*[1]. **—freshet** *n.* 1596, fresh water flowing into the sea, from earlier *fresh* flood, stream of fresh water (1538); formed from English *fresh,* adj. + *-et.* **—freshman** *n.* About 1550, novice; formed from English *fresh,* adj. + *man.* The word is first recorded in 1596 in the sense of a student in his first year at Cambridge University.

fret[1] *v.* be peevish, unhappy or worried. 1127 *freten;* developed from Old English *fretan* eat, devour (about 725, in *Beowulf*); cognate with Middle Low German and Middle Dutch *vrēten* devour (modern Dutch *vreten*), Old High German *frezzan* (modern German *fressen*), and Gothic *fra-itan;* all derived from a Germanic compound formed from the base of Gothic *fra-* completely, FOR- + *itan* to EAT. The meaning of eat away, corrode, is first recorded before 1200, in *Ancrene Riwle,* and the transferred sense of irritate or worry, about 1200, in *The Ormulum.* **—n.** Before 1420, in Lydgate's *Troy Book;* probably from the verb, but possibly developed from Old English *frǣt. **—fretful** *adj.* 1593, in Shakespeare's *2 Henry VI;* formed from English *fret*[1] + *-ful.*

fret[2] *n.* ornamental interlaced pattern. About 1386, in Chaucer's *Legend of Good Women;* borrowed from Old French *frete* interlaced work, trellis-work, probably from a Germanic source. **—v.** to adorn. Before 1376, borrowed from Old French *freter* decorate (with interlaced work), from *frete* interlaced work. **—fretwork** *n.* 1601, formed from English *fret*[2], n. + *work.*

fret[3] *n.* About 1500, ridge on a guitar, banjo, etc., to dampen a string; of unknown origin (possibly borrowed from Old French *frete* ring or ferrule; see FRET[2]).

friable (frī'əbəl) *adj.* easily crumbled. 1563, borrowed through Middle French *friable,* or directly from Latin *friābilis* easily crumbled or broken, from *friāre* rub away, crumble into small pieces; related to *fricāre* to rub, cognate with Sanskrit *bhrīṇánti* they injure, from Indo-European *bhrēi-/bhrī-/bhri- (Pok.166); for suffix see -ABLE.

friar *n.* member of a Roman Catholic brotherhood. Probably before 1200 *frere,* in *Ancrene Riwle;* later *fryer* (before 1450), and *friar* (before 1596, in Shakespeare's *The Taming of the Shrew*); borrowed from Old French *frere* brother or friar, from Latin *frāter* BROTHER. The shift in spelling is not accounted for, but seems to have parallels in *briar, brier* and *choir,* and may be a spelling from pronunciation.

fricassee (frik'əsē') *n.* meat stew. 1568, borrowed from Middle French *fricassée,* from *fricasser* mince and cook in sauce; of uncertain origin; possibly a compound of Middle French *frire* to fry + *casser, quasser* break, cut up, from Latin *quassāre* frequentative of *quatere* shake, beat, from Indo-European *kwēt-/kwət- (Pok.632). **—v.** 1657, make a fricassee of; from the noun.

fricative *adj. Phonetics.* pronounced with friction of the breath through a narrow opening of the mouth. 1860, formed from Latin *fricātus* (past participle of *fricāre* to rub) + English *-ive.* **—n.** fricative consonant; spirant. 1863, from the adjective.

friction *n.* 1563, a chafing or rubbing, borrowed probably through Middle French *friction,* or directly from Latin *frictiōnem* (nominative *frictiō*) a rubbing or rubbing down, from *fricāre* to rub; see FRIABLE. The sense of resistance to motion or surfaces that touch is first recorded in 1722, though earlier mention of the principle is alluded to in 1704, in Newton's *Optics.* The figurative extension of a disagreement or clash, is first recorded in Sterne's *Tristram Shandy,* volume III (1761).

Friday *n.* 1148 *Friedai;* earlier *fridæi* (1137); developed from Old English (before 1000) *frīgedæg,* literally, Frigga's day (in allusion to the Germanic goddess of heaven and of love); corresponding to Old Frisian *frīgendei, frīadei* Friday, Middle Low German *vrīdach,* Middle Dutch *vrīdag* (modern Dutch *vrijdag*), Old High German *friatag* (modern German *Freitag*), and Old Icelandic *frjādagr.*

The Germanic compounds are a translation of Late Latin *Veneris diēs* Venus' day (the source of French *vendredi* Friday), which in turn was a translation of Greek *Aphrodítēs hēmérā* Aphrodite's day. The identification of the name of the Germanic goddess with those of the Roman and Greek goddesses of love suggests that the Germanic name (Old English *Frīge-*, Old High German *Frīa-*, etc.) is derived from the same source as Old English *frēogan* to love; see FRIEND.

fridge or **frig** (frij) *n. Informal.* refrigerator. 1926 *frig,* 1935 *fridge,* shortened forms of *refrigerator.* The brand name *Frigidaire,* which appeared in English in 1926, may have been the immediate source of the form *frig. Frigidaire,* though perhaps borrowed from French, was probably also a play on the English words *frigid* and *air.* It is interesting to note that Dauzat says the word in French is a historic term describing the ancient Roman bath, and that the term in French for the refrigerator did not appear until 1932. The historic French *frigidaire* was borrowed from Latin *frigidārium* the cooling-room in an ancient Roman bath, from *frigidus* FRIGID.

friend *n.* Probably about 1175 *frend;* developed from Old English *frēond* (about 725, in *Beowulf*); cognate with Old Frisian *friond, friund* friend, Old Saxon *friund,* Dutch *vriend,* Old High German *friunt* (modern German *Freund*), Old Icelandic *frændi,* and Gothic *frijōnds;* all derived from the present participle of Proto-Germanic **frijōjanan,* represented by Old English *frēon, frēogan* to free, love, and Gothic *frijōn* to love; see FREE, v. The formation of *friend* parallels that of FIEND; the spelling change is also found in FIELD, though the so-called long vowel of Middle and early modern English has shortened by analogy with the short vowel in polysyllabic formations like *friendship.* **—friendship** *n.* Probably before 1200 *frendshipe;* developed from Old English *frēondscipe* (about 725, in *Beowulf*); formed from Old English *frēond* friend + *-scipe* -ship.

frieze (frēz) *n.* horizontal, decorative band around a room or building. 1563, borrowed from Middle French *frise,* originally, a ruff, from Medieval Latin *frisium* embroidered border, variant of *frigium, phrygium,* probably from Latin *Phrygium* Phrygian, Phrygian work, as in the phrase *Phrygiae vestes* (ornate, presumably embroidered, garments), from *Phrygia* (from Greek *Phrygíā*), an ancient country in Asia Minor, known for its decorative costumes, especially of embroidery. The general meaning of any decorative band painted or sculpted, is first recorded in Disraeli's writings, in 1847.

frigate (frig′it) *n.* sailing warship. 1585, borrowed from Middle French *frégate,* from Italian *fregata,* of unknown origin.

fright *n.* About 1250 *frigt,* in *The Story of Genesis and Exodus;* developed from Old English (about 950) *fryhto,* variant of (before 830) *fyrhtu* fear, dread; related to *forht* afraid (from Proto-Germanic **furHtaz*), *fyrhtan* to frighten. The Old English *fyrhtan* and *forht* are cognate with Old Frisian *fruchte* fear, *fruchtia* to fear, Old Saxon *forht, foraht* afraid, *forhta* fear, *forhtian* to fear, Middle Dutch *vrucht, vrocht* fear, *vruchten* to fear, Old High German *forht, foraht* afraid, *forhta* fear (modern German *Furcht* fear), Old High German *furihten, for(a)htan* to fear (modern German *fürchten*), Gothic *faúrhts* afraid, *faúrhtei* fear, *faúrhtjan* to fear. Outside Germanic it is suggested that perhaps cognates exist in Tocharian A *pärsk-, prask-,* and Tocharian B *pärsk-, prāsk-* to fear, Tocharian A *praski* and Tocharian B *prosko, proskye* fear, from Indo-European **porg-/pr̥g-* (Pok.820). For the development of the modern spelling see FIGHT. **—frighten** *v.* 1666, in Pepys' *Diary,* from *fright,* n. + *-en*[1], replacing earlier *fright,* v. (Middle English *figten,* about 1250, developed from Old English *fyrhtan* to frighten). **—frightful** *adj.* About 1250, in *The Story of Genesis and Exodus;* formed from Middle English *frigt* fright + *-ful.*

frigid *adj.* very cold. Probably before 1425; borrowed from Latin *frīgidus* cold, chill, cool, related to *frīgēre* be cold, *frīgus* (genitive *frīgoris*) cold, coldness, frost; cognate with Greek *rhîgos* frost, from Indo-European *srīg-* (Pok.1004). **—frigidity** *n.* Probably before 1425, borrowed from Middle French *frigidité,* from Latin *frīgiditātem* (nominative *frīgiditās*) cold, from *frīgidus* cold.

frijol (frē′hōl) *n., pl.* **frijoles.** kind of kidney bean. 1577, American English, borrowed from Spanish *frijol,* earlier *frisol,* ultimately from Latin *faseolus, phaseolus* kidney bean, diminutive of *phasēlus* kind of bean, from Greek *phásēlos,* perhaps borrowed from Illyrian and cognate with Greek *phakós* lentil and Albanian *bathë* vetch, from Indo-European **bhak̂ā* (Pok.106). The Spanish *frisol* was pronounced as if written *frishol* in Old Spanish, and later written with *j* by influence of Mozarabic pronunciation of /sh/ for /s/ which accounts for the change in spelling that reflects the shifts in pronunciation.

frill *n.* ruffle, fringe. 1591, of uncertain origin, sometimes associated with *frill,* v., shiver with cold, in allusion to the way a hawk or other bird ruffles its feathers when cold; another suggestion has been the analogy with the fatty tissue around the entrails of a butchered animal, such as a pig, which have a ruffled appearance. But dates that are too late, forms that are too far removed, and semantic associations that are somewhat strained stand in the way of a definite chain of borrowing.

The figurative sense of useless ornament, is first recorded in 1893, probably as an extension of earlier sense of ornamented dress or mannered air (before 1845).

—v. 1574, furnish or decorate with a frill, probably borrowed from the same source as the noun.

fringe *n.* border or trimming. 1354 *frenge,* borrowed from Old French *frenge,* from Vulgar Latin **frimbia,* corresponding to Latin *fimbriae,* pl., fibers, threads, fringe; of uncertain origin. For an earlier use of *fringe,* see the verb below. The figurative sense of outer edge or margin (as of society), is first recorded in 1894. The spelling *fringe* is a development in modern English parallel to *hinge* and *singe.* **—v.** 1480, furnish or decorate with a fringe; probably from the noun, and though verbal forms appeared as early as the 1200's, they probably reflect forms of the noun, as in *frenged* (1275) *frenge* + *-ed*[2] and *frengyng* (1437-39) *frenge* + *-yng* -ing[1].

frippery *n.* cheap, showy clothes or ornaments. 1568, old clothes, borrowed from Middle French *friperie* old clothes, an old-clothes shop, from Old French *freperie,* from *frepe, ferpe, felpe* rag, from Late Latin *faluppa* chip, splinter, straw fiber; for suffix see -ERY. The sense of tawdry attire, is first recorded in 1637.

Frisbee *n.* Trademark of a saucer-shaped plastic disk

used for throwing and catching. 1957, American English, from *Frisbie,* in Mrs. Frisbie's pies of the *Frisbie* bakery in Bridgeport, Connecticut. The term was patented in 1959 after commercial rights were purchased from its inventor, Fred Morrison, who based his idea on the lightweight pie tins.

frisk *v.* run about playfully. 1519, probably developed from Middle English *frisk* lively (about 1450); borrowed from Middle French *frisque* lively, brisk, possibly from a Germanic source (compare Old High German *frisc* lively, FRESH). The extended slang meaning of run the hands rapidly over a person's clothing to search for something, is first recorded in 1789. **—n.** 1525, from the verb. **—frisky** *adj.* Probably before 1500, lively or playful; formed from Middle English *frysk,* adj., lively (about 1450) + *-y*[1].

fritter[1] *v.* waste little by little, especially in *fritter away.* 1728, in Pope's *Dunciad,* perhaps from the noun (unrecorded at the time), but also possibly confused with *fritter*[2] a small fried cake (1381), though the association of form and meaning in *fritters* fragments, shreds, and earlier *fitters* fragments, is tempting. **—n.** 1767 *fritters* fragment or shred; possibly an alteration of earlier *fitters* fragments or pieces (1532, in Sir Thomas More's writings), from *fitter* to fragment; of uncertain origin, but probably related to Old French *freture, fraiture* fracture, fragment, from Latin *frāctūra,* from *frangere* to break. *Fritter*[1] was perhaps also influenced in its formation by Old French *friture* fritter[2].

fritter[2] *n.* small fried cake. 1381 *frutur,* before 1399 *frytour;* borrowed from Old French *friture,* from Late Latin *frīctūra* a frying (from Latin *frīgere* to roast, FRY[1] cook + *-tūra,* see -URE).

fritz *n. Informal.* 1903, American English slang, found in *on the fritz* out of order, not working, defective; of unknown origin.

frivolous *adj.* 1459 *fryvolus* of little importance, silly; probably a borrowing of Latin *frīvolus* silly, empty, trifling, diminutive of a lost adjective **frīvos* broken, crumbled, from *friāre* break, rub away, crumble; see FRIABLE; for suffix see -OUS. The borrowing was possibly also influenced by *frivol* a trifle; later also used as an adjective; borrowed from Middle French *frivole,* from Latin *frīvolus.* **—frivolity** *n.* 1796, in Burke's *Letters;* borrowed from French *frivolité,* from *frivole* frivolous, from Latin *frīvolus;* or perhaps formed from English *frivol* + *-ity.*

friz or **frizz** *v.* form into crisp curls. 1660, in Pepys' *Diary;* probably borrowed from French *friser* to curl, perhaps from the stem of *frire* to FRY[1] cook. The spelling and pronunciation of this word have been influenced by *frizzle*[1] to curl. **—n.** 1668, frizzed hair; from the verb.

frizzle[1] *v.* curl (hair). 1565-73, of uncertain origin (perhaps related to Old English *frīs* curly; cognate with Old Frisian *frīsle* lock of hair; or possibly formed in English from Middle French *friser* to curl + English *-le*[1]). **—n.** 1613, crisp curl, from the verb.

frizzle[2] *v.* fry with a sputtering noise. 1839, in Thackeray's *Fatal Boots,* probably imitative, perhaps formed from *fry*[1] with the spelling influenced by *sizzle.* **—n.** a hissing noise. (1894)

fro *adv.* from, back. Before 1325 *fra,* in Northern British dialect; also, about 1325 *fro,* in Midland British dialect; from earlier *fro,* prep. (probably before 1200, but now only in Scottish use); probably borrowed from a Scandinavian source (compare Old Icelandic *frā,* adv., prep., from; see FROM). The term is now somewhat archaic but survives in ordinary speech in the phrase *to and fro* (before 1325, in *Cursor Mundi*).

frock *n.* garment. 1350, robe worn by monks and friars, cowl; borrowed from Old French *froc* a monk's habit, from Frankish (compare Old High German *hroc,* cognate with Old Frisian *hrock,* Old Saxon *hroc*). The sense of a garment with a skirt, worn by woman or child, is first recorded in 1538. **—v.** 1828, provide with or dress in a frock; from the noun.

frog[1] *n.* web-footed, leaping animal like a toad but with smooth skin. Probably before 1200 *frogge;* later *froge* (before 1338), and *frog* (1463), developed from Old English *frogga* (about 1000, in Ælfric's *Glossary*), a diminutive formation related to *frox, forsc, frosc* frog; cognate with Middle Dutch *vorsc* frog (modern Dutch *vors*), Old High German *frosk* (modern German *Frosch*), and Old Icelandic *froskr,* from Proto-Germanic **fruska-z,* a noun (Indo-European **prug-sko-*) built on an *-sk-* present stem of a verb meaning to hop; compare the cognate Russian *prýgat'* to hop, and Old Icelandic *frauki;* frog, from Indo-European **proug-/prug-,* root **preu-* (Pok.845).

Another form existed in Middle English *frude, froud* frog or toad, from Old Icelandic *fraudhr* frog (compare Old Icelandic *fraudh* spittle, slaver; the original notion seeming to have been "the creature squirting out a fluid").

Though origin is uncertain, one explanation of Old English *frogga* considers the word an *-n-* stem with accusative *froggan* (nominative *frogga*), from Proto-Germanic **fruthgan-,* in the accusative *frúthaȝanun* (nominative *frúthaȝō*) from Indo-European **prútokonm̥* (nominative *prút-okō*).

—frogman *n.* man equipped for underwater operations. 1945, formed from English *frog* + *man.*

frog[2] *n.* ornamental fastening for clothing. 1719, in Defoe's *Robinson Crusoe;* of uncertain origin (perhaps from Portuguese *froco,* from Latin *floccus* FLOCK[2] tuft). Originally, the word had the sense of belt loop for carrying a weapon; the sense of ornamental fastening for a coat, is first recorded in 1746.

frolic *v.* play, have fun. 1583, from earlier (1538) adjective, joyful, merry (1538); borrowed from Middle Dutch *vrolyc* (*vro-* glad + *lyc* LIKE). Middle Dutch *vro* is cognate with Old Frisian *frō* happy, glad, Old Saxon *frā, frō, fraho,* Old High German *frō* (modern German *froh* glad, *fröhlich* joyful, merry), Old Icelandic *frār* swift, nimble; also cognate with Sanskrit *právate* he leaps up, *pravá-s* fluttering, flying, from Indo-European **preu-/prou-* to leap (Pok.845). **—n.** 1616, mirth or a prank, in Ben Jonson's *The Devil is an Ass;* from the verb. **—frolicsome** *adj.* 1699, formed from English *frolic,* n., v. + *-some*[1].

from *prep.* Old English (before 800) *from;* earlier *fram* (about 700); related to Old English *fram,* adv., forward, forth, away; cognate with Old Saxon *fram* from, away, forward, Old High German *fram,* Old Icelandic *frā* from, *fram* forward, Gothic *fram* forward, cognate with Greek *prómos* foremost man, from Indo-European **promo-* (Pok.814); see also FRO.

frond *n.* divided leaf of a fern or palm. 1785, earlier cited as a Latin word in an English text (1753, in *Chambers Encyclopaedia*); borrowed from Latin *frōns* (genitive *frondis*) leaf, leafy branch, foliage (applied by Linnaeus in a more specific sense than Latin *folium* leaf), cognate with Old Icelandic *brum* leaf-bud, from Indo-European **bhrem-/bhrom-/bhr̥m-* (Pok.142).

front *n.* About 1300, forehead; borrowed from Old French *front* forehead or brow, from Latin *frontem* (nominative *frōns*) forehead; cognate with Irish *braine* prow (of a ship), leader, edge, Cornish *brenniat,* Latvian *bruôdiņš* ridge; also cognate with Old Icelandic *brandr* projecting part, *brattr* steep, high, from Indo-European **bhren-/bhron-* stand out (Pok.167). The meaning of foremost part, is first recorded in Mannyng's *Chronicle of England* (before 1338). **—v.** 1523, to face; in some instances probably from the noun, and in others borrowed from Middle French *fronter,* from Old French *front* front. **—frontal** *adj.* 1656, in Blount's *Glossographia;* borrowed from French *frontal,* and from New Latin *frontalis,* from Latin *frontem* forehead; for suffix see -AL[1].

frontier *n.* Probably before 1400 *frowntere* front line of an army, in *Morte Arthur;* earlier *frountres* an altar cloth hanging over the edge (1392); borrowed from Old French *fronter, frontier,* from *front* brow; see FRONT. The meaning of border of a country or settled land, is first recorded in 1413. **—frontiersman** *n.* (1813)

frontispiece (frun'tispēs') *n.* picture facing the title page of a book. 1597-98 *frontispice* front of a building; borrowed from Middle French *frontispice,* probably from Italian *frontespizio,* and from Late Latin *frontispicium* facade, originally, a view of the forehead (Latin *frōns,* genitive *frontis,* forehead + *specere* look at). The meaning of a title page of a book, is first recorded in 1607, borrowed from earlier French (1500's), and that of a picture facing the title page, in 1682, also borrowed from French (1757). The original spelling was *frontispice,* but the last syllable was soon assimilated (by folk etymology) to *-piece.*

frost *n.* Old English (about 725) *forst;* also (before 800) *frost* a freezing or becoming frozen, extreme cold; cognate with Old Frisian *frost, forst* frost, Old Saxon *frost,* Middle Dutch and modern Dutch *vorst,* Old High German *frost* (modern German *Frost*), and Old Icelandic *frost* (Norwegian, Swedish, and Danish *frost*), related to Old English *frēosan* to FREEZE. **—v.** 1635, to cover with frost or as if with frost.

Even Middle English had both *frost* and *forst* until sometime before 1475. It is not clear what established the spelling *frost* except that it has been the prevailing form among most of the Germanic languages, and its antecedents are found also in Proto-Germanic **frusta-,* which with the abstract suffix *-t-* and the *u* changing to *o* when *a* follows, represents our spelling *frost* (compare **frus-* with full grade, **freus-,* for *freeze,* which indicates the relationship to *freeze,* Old English *frēosan* and Old Icelandic *frjōsa;* see FREEZE).

—frostbite *v.* usually *frostbitten* 1593; formed from English *frost* + *bite; n.* 1813, from the verb. **—frosted** *adj.* 1645, in reference to white or gray hair; later, covered with sugar or icing (1856, in Emerson's writings); from the verb. **—frosting** *n.* 1617, frost; later white sugar covering or icing (1858); from *frost,* v. **—frosty** *adj.* 1375, in Chaucer's *Anelida and Arcite;* probably developed from Old English *frostig,* which is cognate with Dutch *vorstig* frosty, cold, and Old High German *frostag* (modern German *frostig*).

froth *n.* About 1384, in the Wycliffe Bible; probably borrowed from a Scandinavian source (compare Old Icelandic *frodha, fraudh* froth). The noun is not found in Old English, but the Germanic base **freuth-* appears in Old English *āfrēothan* to froth, probably from Indo-European **preut-/prout-/prut,* extended from root **preu-* to spring up (Pok.845). **—v.** About 1384, in the Wycliffe Bible; from the noun.

frou-frou (frü'frü') *n.* a rustling, as of a dress. 1870, borrowing of French *frou-frou,* possibly imitative of the sound. The figurative sense of fussy details or frills, is first recorded in 1876.

froward *adj.* stubborn, contrary. Probably before 1325 *fraward,* in *Cursor Mundi;* later *froward* (about 1330); formed from English *fro* FRO (shortened form of *from*) + *-ward,* literally, turned away from (the opposite of *toward*). A Middle English variant *frommerd* (probably before 1200, in *Ancrene Riwle*), later *fromward* (before 1300), is found in Old English *fromweard* turned from or away (before 899, in Alfred's translation of Boethius' *De Consolatione Philosophiae*); formed from *from* + *-weard* -ward.

frown *v.* About 1395 *frownen,* in Chaucer's *Canterbury Tales;* borrowed from Old French *froignier* to frown or scowl, related to *frongne* scowling look, probably from Gaulish **frognā,* cognate with Welsh *ffroen* nose.

An earlier competing form existed in Middle English *frouncen* (before 1395, scowl; earlier, wrinkle, before 1325); but it is now obsolete or archaic.

—n. 1581, show of disapproval; earlier *frowne* of the lowering of clouds (before 1420, in Lydgate's *Troy Book*); from the verb. The literal meaning of wrinkling of the brow, is first recorded in Shakespeare's *King Lear* (1605).

frowzy or **frowsy** *adj.* dirty, untidy. 1681, ill-smelling or musty; possibly related to dialectal English *frowsty* smelly; of uncertain origin. The OED suggests comparison with obsolete *frowze* (1563), probably with the meaning of a wig of frizzed hair, in which case, for suffix see -Y[1].

fructify (fruk'təfī) *v.* bear fruit. 1340 *fructifien,* in *Ayenbite of Inwyt;* borrowed from Old French *fructifier,* learned borrowing from Late Latin *frūctificāre* bear fruit, from a lost adjective **frūctificus* fruit-bearing, from Latin *frūctus* fruit + the root of *facere* make; see FRUIT; for suffix see -FY. **—fructification** *n.* 1615, either formed from English *fructify* + *-ation,* modeled on such formations with an intrusive *c* as *identification;* or borrowed from French *fructification,* modeled on Late Latin *frūctificāre* + *-tion.*

fructose (fruk'tōs) *n.* fruit sugar. 1864, formed in English from Latin *frūctus* fruit + English *-ose*[2].

frugal *adj.* avoiding waste, saving. 1598, in Shakespeare's *Merry Wives of Windsor,* possibly a back formation from earlier *frugality;* or borrowed through Middle French *frugal,* from Latin *frūgālis,* from the undeclined adjective *frūgī* economical, useful, proper, originally the dative case of *frūx* fruit, profit, value (chiefly in plural *frūgēs* fruits); related to *frūctus* FRUIT; for suffix see -AL[1]. **—frugality** *n.* 1531, in Sir Thomas Elyot's *The Boke Named the Governour;* borrowed from Middle French *frugalité,* from Latin *frūgālitātem* (nominative *frūgālitās*) economy, thriftiness, from *frūgālis* frugal.

fruit *n.* Probably before 1200 *frut,* in *Ancrene Riwle;* later *fruit* (probably about 1200); borrowed from Old French *fruit,* from Latin *frūctus* (genitive *frūctūs*) fruit, produce, profit, from *frūg-,* stem of *fruī* to use, enjoy; see BROOK² tolerate. The spelling with *i,* after the French, became established in the 1500's. **—v.** About 1378, to bear or come to fruit, in a version of *Piers Plowman;* from the noun. **—fruitcake** *n.* (1848, in American English) **—fruiterer** *n.* 1408, in a surname; formed from Middle English *fruter,* 1237 + *-er*¹. **—fruitful** *adj.* About 1390, in Chaucer's *Canterbury Tales;* formed from Middle English *fruyt* + *-ful.* **—fruitless** *adj.* Before 1400; formed from Middle English *fruyt* + *-less.* **—fruity** *adj.* 1657; formed from English *fruit* + *-y*¹.

fruition *n.* 1413 *fruycion* enjoyment; also *fruicioun* (before 1415, in Wycliffe's *The Lantern of Light*); borrowed through Middle French *fruition,* and directly from Late Latin *fruitiōnem* (nominative *fruitiō*) enjoyment, from Latin *fruī* to use, enjoy; see BROOK² tolerate; for suffix see -TION. The meaning of act or state of bearing of fruit, is first recorded in 1885 (by mistaken association with *fruit*), and the figurative sense of realization or fulfillment, in 1889.

frump *n.* 1553, mocking action, jeer; later, shabby, unstylish woman (1817); of uncertain origin, perhaps a shortening of *frumple* to wrinkle or crumple *(frumplen,* 1440, in *Promptorium Parvulorum);* borrowed from Middle Dutch *verrompelen, ver-* for-, completely + *rompelen* to RUMPLE.

frustrate *v.* to thwart, baffle, disappoint. 1445 *frustraten,* borrowed from Latin *frūstrātus,* past participle of *frūstrārī* to deceive, disappoint, frustrate, from *frūstrā* in vain; related to *fraus* (genitive *fraudis*) FRAUD. **—frustration** *n.* 1461, nullification; later, act of frustrating, disappointment (about 1555); either formed from English *frustrate* + *-ion,* or borrowed, probably through Middle French *frustration,* from Latin *frūstrātiōnem* (nominative *frūstrātiō*), from *frūstrārī;* for suffix see -ATION.

fry¹ *v.* cook in hot fat. About 1300 *frien;* borrowed from Old French *frire,* from Latin *frīgere* to roast or fry; cognate with Greek *phrȳ́gein* to roast or fry, Latvian *bir̃ga* smoke or mist, Persian *birištan* to roast, and Sanskrit *bhr̥jjáti* he roasts, from Indo-European **bhereĝ-/bhr̥ĝ-,* **bhrīĝ-,* **bhrūĝ* (Pok.137), variants which can not constitute one root, but are somehow related. **—n.** 1634, excessive heat; 1639, fried food; from the verb. **—frying pan** (1355)

fry² *n.* young fish. 1293 *fry,* probably borrowed through Anglo-French *frei,* Old French *frai, froi* spawn, from *froier, freier* to rub, spawn (by rubbing the belly on sand); see FRAY² wear away.

*Fry*², children or offspring, is first recorded in Scottish before 1400; by 1577 applied to the young of other creatures, especially those produced in large numbers. The sense of young or insignificant persons as a group, is first recorded before 1577. According to most sources these are unrelated to the meaning of young fish, and are borrowed from Icelandic *frjō, fræ* seed, from Old Icelandic *frjō, fræ;* cognate with Swedish *frö,* Danish, and Norwegian *frø* seed, and Gothic *fraiw* seed, offspring, of unknown origin.

fuchsia (fyü′shə) *n.* shrub with drooping flowers. 1753, New Latin *Fuchsia,* the genus name, in allusion to Leonhard *Fuchs,* a German botanist. The sense of a purplish red color (like that of the flower) is first recorded in 1923.

The pronunciation reflects the spelling, and not the proper name, which is pronounced (füks).

fuddle *v.* confuse, stupefy. 1588, to drink too much, tipple; later, to confuse with or as with drink, make tipsy (about 1600); of uncertain origin (compare Low German *Fuddel,* name given to a dissolute woman, and *fuddeln* work in a slovenly manner as if drunk, in dialect, swindle, from *fuddle* worthless cloth, which is related to Dutch *vodde* rag, tatter). The more common variant of this word is now *befuddle,* a derivative which appeared in 1887.

fuddy-duddy *n. Informal.* fussy, old-fashioned person. 1904, American English, of uncertain origin.

fudge¹ *v.* put together clumsily or dishonestly. Probably 1674, apparently an alteration of earlier *fadge* make suit, fit (1573); of unknown origin. **—n.** made-up story. 1797, from the verb.

fudge² *interj.* nonsense, bosh, bunk. 1766, in Goldsmith's *The Vicar of Wakefield,* perhaps from FUDGE¹. **—n.** nonsense; stuff. 1791, from the interjection.

fudge³ *n.* soft candy. 1896, American English; possibly a special use of FUDGE².

fuel *n.* Probably before 1200 *feoile,* in *Ancrene Riwle;* later *fuell* (before 1398, in Trevisa's translation of Bartholomew's *De Proprietatibus Rerum*); borrowed from Old French *feuaile, fouaille* bundle of firewood, from Gallo-Romance **focālia,* from Latin *focus* hearth; see FOCUS. **—v.** About 1592, in Marlowe's *Massacre at Paris;* from the noun.

fugitive *adj.* About 1380 *fugityf* running away, fleeing, in Chaucer's *House of Fame;* borrowed through Old French *fugitif* (feminine *fugitive*), or directly from Latin *fugitīvus* fleeing (but more often as a noun, a runaway), from *fugi-,* stem of *fugere* run away, flee; cognate with Greek *pheúgein* flee, escape, and Lithuanian *bū́gti* be frightened, *baugìnti* frighten from Indo-European **bheug-/bhoug-/bhug-/bhūg-* flee (Pok. 152); for suffix see -IVE. **—n.** Before 1382 *fugitif,* in the Wycliffe Bible; borrowed from Old French *fugitif;* from the adjective.

fugue (fyüg) *n.* 1597 *fuge* a musical composition based on short themes that are interwoven; borrowed from Italian *fuga,* literally, flight, a learned borrowing from Latin *fuga* act of fleeing, from *fugere* to flee; see FUGITIVE.

The current spelling *fugue,* first recorded in Milton's *Paradise Lost* (1667), was borrowed from French *fugue,* also from Italian *fuga. Fuge* with the meaning of flight, is recorded before 1450, but was borrowed directly from Latin *fuga* and was only an indirect influence on the musical term *fuge* fugue.

-ful a suffix forming adjectives (or nouns) and meaning: **1** having, characterized by, as in *careful, thoughtful;* **2** having a tendency to, as in *harmful;* **3** having the qualities of, as in *masterful;* **4** (forming nouns) enough to fill a ______, as in *mouthful, cupful.* The form is found in Old English *-ful, -full,* a suffix formed on the adjective *full* FULL.

fulcrum (ful′krəm) *n.* prop or support. 1674, borrowed from Latin *fulcrum* bedpost, from *fulcīre* to support; see BALK.

fulfill or fulfil *v.* About 1250 *fulfilen* promise or prophesy, in *The Story of Genesis and Exodus;* also as a variant before 1200; developed from Old English *fullfyllan* fill up, make full (about 1000, in Ælfric's *Grammar*); formed from Old English *full* FULL + *fyllan* to FILL. The sense of carry out, satisfy (a prophecy, promise, commandment, etc.), is recorded probably before 1250, and may be a literal translation of Latin *implēre, adimplēre.* **—fulfillment** or **fulfilment** *n.* 1775, formed from English *fulfill* or *fulfil* + *-ment.*

full *adj.* Old English *full* complete, full (917, in the *Anglo-Saxon Chronicle*); cognate with Old Frisian *full, foll* full, Old Saxon *full,* Dutch *vol,* Old High German *fol* (modern German *voll*), Old Icelandic *fullr,* and Gothic *fulls,* from Proto-Germanic **fullaz,* earlier **fulnaz.* Outside Germanic cognates are found in Latin *plēnus* full, *plēre* to fill, Greek *plḗrēs* full, *plḗthein* to be full, Albanian *plot* full, Old Irish *lān* full, Old Welsh *laun,* Welsh *llawn,* Armenian *li,* Lithuanian *pìlnas,* Old Slavic *plŭnŭ,* and Sanskrit *pūrṇá-s* full, from Indo-European **pl̥nós,* root **pelə-/pl̥ē-* (Pok.798). **—adv.** Old English *full* (before 899, in Alfred's translation of Boethius' *De Consolatione Philosophiae*); from the adjective.

Much of the relationship among the cognates can be obtained from the reconstructed Indo-European form **pl̥nós,* as in Old Welsh and Old Irish, which show the usual Celtic loss of Indo-European *p* that is found independently in Armenian, and also independently in Sanskrit *r* (in *pūrṇá-s*), which represents *l.* The *ll* in the Germanic words is from *-ln-* (compare Lithuanian *pìlnas*) and is a continuation of an Indo-European adjective with the *-n* suffix. More immediately of note is that among the so-called West Germanic languages the *o* (as in Old High German *fol*) is represented by Old English *u.*

—full blast (1839, in American English) **—full dress** (1761) **—full-grown** *adj.* (1667, in Milton's *Paradise Lost*) **—full moon** (before 1000)

fulminate *v.* thunder forth; denounce. Probably before 1425 *fulminaten* to hurl or discharge (a formal condemnation), in a translation of Higden's *Polychronicon;* borrowed, perhaps by influence of Old French *fulminer,* from Latin *fulminātus,* past participle of *fulmināre* hurl lightning, lighten, from *fulmen* (genitive *fulminis*) lightning, which is related to *fulgēre* to shine, flash; see EFFULGENCE. **—fulmination** *n.* 1502, discharge of a formal condemnation, borrowed from Middle French, from Latin *fulminātiōnem* (nominative *fulminātiō*) discharge of lightning, from *fulmināre;* for suffix see -ATION.

fulsome *adj.* About 1250 *fulsum* abundant or full; formed from Middle English *ful* full + *-som* -some[1].

Fulsom plump, well-fed, is recorded by about 1350, but by 1642 the meaning is first recorded in the extended sense of overgrown or overfed. The general sense of offensive to tastes or sensibilities, is recorded as early as 1375 (in Scottish), followed by other pejorative senses including coarse, gross, sickening (about 1410), and later (with specific reference to an excess) offensive to good taste, especially because of excessive flattery, praise, cordiality, attention, or the like (1663). However, since the 1960's *fulsome* has frequently appeared in the favorable senses of very flattering, or complimentary; full or complete, a usage that is remarkable because it represents a return to the original meaning of the word, since the first syllable assumes its original force with the meaning of full or abundant.

fumble *v.* About 1450 *fomellen* grope; later *fumble* grope about awkwardly (perhaps earlier, see FUMBLER, but recorded 1534, in Sir Thomas More's writings); of uncertain origin, possibly from a Scandinavian source, and probably cognate with Low German *fummeln, fommeln* to fumble, grope (modern German *fummeln* fumble, handle awkwardly), Dutch *fommelen* to fumble, tumble, and Old Icelandic *fālma* (Swedish *fumla, famla* to fumble, grope). **—n.** 1647, a fumbling attempt, bungle; from the verb. **—fumbler** *n.* 1519; formed from English *fumble,* v. + *-er*[1]. The *-b-* in *fumble* is probably a development parallel to the change of Middle English *cremelen* to *crumble* and *momelen* to *mumble,* and suggesting a parallel to *chimbley* for *chimney.*

fume *n.* About 1390 *fume* vapor or exhalation as given by the body or producing emotions, dreams, etc., in Chaucer's *Canterbury Tales;* later, smoke or vapor given off, especially by a heated substance (about 1395, also in Chaucer's *Canterbury Tales*); borrowed from Old French *fum* smoke, steam, vapor, from Latin *fūmus* smoke; cognate with Middle Irish *dumacha,* pl., fog, Old Prussian *dumis* smoke, Old Slavic *dymŭ,* and Sanskrit *dhūmá-s* smoke, steam, from Indo-European **dhūmós* (Pok.261). Germanic cognates of Latin *fūmus* appear in Old Saxon *dōmian* to steam, and Old High German *toum* steam, mist, *tunst, tumist* storm, breath; see DUST. **—v.** Before 1400, to fumigate; borrowed from Old French *fumer,* from Latin *fūmāre* to smoke, steam, from *fūmus* smoke. The figurative sense of to exhibit anger is first recorded in Sir Thomas More's *Treatise Upon These Words of Holy Scripture* (1522).

fumigate *v.* to scent or purify with fumes. 1530, in Palsgrave's *Lesclarcissement;* back formation from *fumigation,* possibly by influence of Old French *fumiger* to smoke; and in some instances perhaps borrowed from Latin *fūmigāt-,* past participle stem of *fūmigāre* to smoke (from a lost adjective **fūmigus* smoke-driving, from *fūmus* smoke, fume + the root of *agere* to drive; see AGENT); for suffix see -ATE[1]. **—fumigation** *n.* About 1380, act of generating smoke as part of a ceremony, in Chaucer's *House of Fame;* later, treatment with aromatic fumes (probably about 1439); borrowed through Old French *fumigation,* from Latin *fūmigātiōnem* (nominative *fūmigātiō*), from *fūmigāre* to smoke; for suffix see -ATION.

fun *n.* Before 1325 *fon* a fool, in *Cursor Mundi;* later, a jester or buffoon (probably before 1350); of uncertain origin. The spelling *fun* is offered as a possible dialectal pronunciation of *fon* by the OED; by others rejected as having any connection with *fon.* The form *fun* is first recorded before 1700, with the meaning of a trick, hoax, joke; possibly from the verb, to cheat or cajole; perhaps from a dialectal use of Middle English *fonnen* to fool or be foolish, act foolishly (before 1400); see FOND. The meaning of amusement, is found first in Swift's *Miscellanies in Prose and Verse* (1727), and was stigmatized in Samuel Johnson's *Dictionary* as "a low cant word." **—funnies** *n.pl.* comic strips (1852, American English). **—funny** *adj.* 1756, formed from English *fun,* n. + *-y*[1]. **—funny bone** 1840, from the sensation when the nerve of the elbow is struck.

function *n.* 1533 *funccion* proper work or purpose, in Sir Thomas More's *The Confutation of Barnes;* borrowed through Middle French *fonction,* from Old French *function,* and directly from Latin *fūnctiō* (genitive *fūnctiōnis*) performance, execution, from *fūnctus,* past participle of *fungī* perform, execute, discharge. According to the OED, the use of *function* in mathematics was introduced from the Latin *fūnctiō,* by Leibnitz. **—v.** 1856, from the noun. **—functional** *adj.* 1631, formed from English *function* + *-al*[1]. **—functionary** *n.* one serving a function; official. 1791, in Burke's

Thoughts on French Affairs; formed from English *function,* n. + *-ary,* patterned after French *fonctionnaire* (1770).

fund *n.* 1677 *fund* bottom, foundation, basis; borrowed from French *fond* a bottom, floor, ground, also a merchant's stock or capital, from Latin *fundus* bottom, piece of land; see BOTTOM. The spelling *fund* is a Latinization of earlier *fond, fonds* foundation, groundwork (1664). The meaning of stock or sum of money, is first recorded in English in 1673 from French. **—v.** 1776, provide a fund, in Adam Smith's *Wealth of Nations;* from the noun.

fundament *n.* foundation. 1380, borrowed from Latin *fundāmentum,* from *fundāre* to found; see FOUND[1]. The present form replaced Middle English *fundement, fondement* (recorded about 1300); borrowed from Old French *fondement,* learned borrowing from Latin *fundāmentum.*

fundamental *adj.* About 1443 *fundamental* primary, original, probably formed from English *fundament* + *-al*[1], and modeled on Late Latin *fundāmentālis* of the foundation, from Latin *fundāmentum* foundation; see FUNDAMENT. **—fundamentalist** *n.* person who believes in a literal reading of the Bible. 1922, American English; formed from English *fundamental* + *-ist.* **—fundamentalism** *n.* 1923, American English; formed from English *fundamental* + *-ism.*

funeral *n.* 1437 *funerelles,* pl., funeral rites, in *Proceedings of the Privy Council;* borrowed from Middle French *funérailles,* pl., learned borrowing from Medieval Latin *funeralia,* pl., funeral rites, but originally neuter plural of Late Latin *fūnerālis* having to do with a funeral, from Latin *fūnus* (genitive *fūneris*) funeral, death, corpse, probably cognate with Gothic *diwans* mortal, from Indo-European **dheu-* disappear (Pok.260); for suffix see -AL[1]. As in Middle French, the singular and plural of the English word were used in the same sense until the end of the 1600's; by the mid 1600's, the spelling *funeral* was also fixed. **—adj.** About 1385, in Chaucer's *Canterbury Tales;* borrowed from Late Latin *fūnerālis;* see FUNERAL. **—funereal** (fyü-nir′ēəl) *adj.* gloomy; mournful. 1725, in Pope's translation of Homer's *Odyssey;* borrowed, possibly by influence of Middle French *funerail,* from Latin *fūnereus,* from *fūnus* funeral; for suffix see -AL[1].

fungus *n.* 1527 *fungus* toadstool, mushroom; borrowed from Latin *fungus* mushroom, and replacing earlier *funge* mushroom (before 1398, in Trevisa's translation of Bartholomew's *De Proprietatibus Rerum*); borrowed from Old French **funge, fonge,* from Latin *fungus.* The Latin word may be a borrowing from the same source as Armenian *sunk, sung* mushroom, or, Greek *spóngos* SPONGE. **—fungicide** (fun′jəsīd) *n.* substance that destroys fungi. 1889, American English; formed from English *fungi* (plural of *fungus*) + *-cide*[1]. **—fungous** (fung′gəs) *adj.* Probably 1440, borrowed from Latin *fungōsus,* from *fungus* mushroom.

funk[1] *n. Informal.* fear, panic. 1743, recorded as Oxford University slang and found in Junius' *Etymologicum Anglicanum* (compiled before 1677); possibly borrowed from Flemish *fonck* perturbation, agitation, distress; of unknown origin (compare also Old French *funicle* wild, mad). The expression *in a blue funk* is first recorded in 1861. **—v.** *Informal.* flinch or shrink through fear; avoid; evade. 1737-39, Horace Walpole in a letter written while at Eton; possibly from the noun.

funk[2] *n.* strong smell. 1633, probably borrowed from dialectal French *funkière* smoke, from *funkier,* from Old French *funkier,* variant of *fungier* give off smoke, from Latin *fūmigāre* to smoke; see FUMIGATE. **—v.** annoy with smoke. 1699, probably from the noun, but influenced by dialectal French *funkier;* see the noun. **—funky** *adj.* 1784, strong or bad smelling; formed from English *funk,* n. + *-y*[1]. The word is found in American English dialect in the sense of having a strong musty smell, since before 1906, and was probably first adopted in jazz slang in the title of Buddy Bolden's tune *Funky Butt* (about 1900, recorded in Robert Gold's *Jazz Lexicon,* 1964). The sense of strong, earthy, deeply felt, as applied to jazz music, is first recorded about 1954. In the 1960's the meaning of *funk* was extended in general slang use to that of fine, stylish, excellent.

funnel *n.* 1402-03 *funell,* borrowed from Middle French *fonel,* probably through Provençal *founil, enfounilh* funnel, from Late Latin *fundibulum,* shortened from Latin *īnfundibulum* a funnel or hopper in a mill, from *īnfundere* pour in (*in-* in-[2] + *fundere* pour, FOUND[2]). According to Skeat the word probably came into English through the wine trade with France; the OED says the Latin may have been familiar from use of the term in pharmacy. **—v.** 1594, in Thomas Nashe's *The Unfortunate Traveller;* from the noun.

fur *n.* Probably about 1375 *furre* fur trimming or lining, garment trimmed or lined with fur; earlier, *fur* in the surname *Furhode* (1301, with the meaning of a hood lined or trimmed with fur); probably borrowed from Old French *fourrer, forrer* to line, sheathe, from *fuerre* sheath, covering, from Frankish; compare Old High German *fuotar, fōtar* lining, Middle Low German *vōder* (modern German *Futter),* Old Frisian *fōder* coat lining, Old English *fōder* sheath, case, Old Icelandic *fōdhr* lining, and Gothic *fōdr* sword sheath, from Proto-Germanic **fōđran,* from Indo-European **pōtróm* protection, cover, root **pō-* (Pok.839). An alternate form existed in Middle English *furrūre, forour* (before 1338, in Mannyng's *Chronicle of England*); borrowed from Old French *fourrëure, forrëure.* It also had a verb *furrūren* (probably before 1350). These lengthened forms died out in the late 1400's, and only the short form survives. **—adj.** 1597; from the noun. **—v.** Probably before 1300 *fur,* in *Kyng Alisaunder;* borrowed from Old French *fourrer, forrer,* from *fuerre* sheath, covering; see the noun. **—furrier** *n.* 1296 *furrere;* borrowed probably through Anglo-French, from Old French *forreor,* from *fourrer, forrer* line or trim with fur; for suffix see -IER. **—furry** *adj.* Before 1674, in Milton's writings; formed from English *fur* + *-y*[1].

furbelow (fėr′bəlō) *n.* bit of elaborate trimming. 1706, borrowed from modern Provençal *farbello* fringe, lace (found in French *falbala* flounce, also from Provençal *farbello*); perhaps related to Old French *frepe* rag; see FRIPPERY; but possibly from Late Latin *faluppa* fiber, valueless thing. The English spelling *furbelow* is an alteration by confusion in speech, as if formed of *fur* + *below.*

furbish *v.* brighten by rubbing or scouring. About 1384 *furbushen,* in the Wycliffe Bible; probably a back formation from *furbisher,* ultimately borrowed from Old French *forbiss-,* stem of *forbir, fourbir* to polish, from a Germanic source (compare Old High German *furben* to sweep, clean, Middle High German *fürben* to polish); for suffix see -ISH[2]. **—furbisher** *n.* About 1260, in the surname *Furbisur,* borrowed from Old French *fourbis-*

seur, forbisseur, from *forbiss-;* see FURBISH; for suffix see -ER[1].

furious *adj.* About 1375, in Chaucer's *Anelida and Arcite;* borrowed from Old French *furieus,* learned borrowing from Latin *furiōsus* full of rage, mad, from *furia* rage, passion, FURY; for suffix see -OUS.

furl *v.* 1556, of uncertain origin; possibly borrowed from Middle French *ferler* to furl (1553 or 1606), from Old French *ferlier,* said to be from *fer* firm, from Latin *firmus,* + *lier* to bind, from Latin *ligāre.* The French etymologist, Dauzat, believes this is incorrect and that *ferler* is probably a borrowing from English *furl,* v. Another explanation is that *furl* is a formation in English by alteration of the vowel and contraction of the form *fardle, fardel* bundle, bind, or furl (*n.* before 1325, *v.* 1582), borrowed from Old French *fardel,* diminutive of *farde* burden, sometimes associated with *furdle* (1594).

Analysis of the dates shows borrowing from Middle French *ferler* is suspect and the analysis of the French verb (proposed as *fer* and *lier*) does not fit the usual pattern of borrowing, because *-ier* is a common infinitive ending in Old French, and *lier* to bind, still exists. The forms *fardle, fardel* with the vowel shift to *u* in *furdle* are recorded too late to affect *furl.*

—n. roll, coil, curl. 1643, from the verb.

furlong *n.* measure of distance equal to one eighth of a mile. Probably before 1300 *furlong* developed from Old English (about 900) *furlang,* originally, the length of the furrow in the common field (*furh* FURROW + *lang* LONG[1], adj.).

In the 800's, a *furlong* was equivalent to the Roman *stadium* (one-eighth of a Roman mile). During the reign of Elizabeth I both the Roman and British measures were standardized to equal one-eighth of a statute mile and one side of a ten-acre square.

furlough (fėr′lō), *n.* leave of absence. 1625 *vorloffe,* in Ben Jonson's *The Staple of News;* borrowed from Dutch *verlof,* literally, permission, from Middle Dutch (*ver-* completely, for- + *laf* permission, cognate with Old English *lēaf* permission, LEAVE[2]; the last element is also represented in Old Frisian *orlof, orlef,* and German *Urlaub,* all with the meaning of furlough). The spelling with *gh* developed during the 1600's but did not become fixed until after the 1770's; it represents the *f* of *off,* once pronounced in this word, and even though lost probably before the 1700's as evidenced by the spelling *furlow* (1707), the spelling with *gh* remained. —v. to grant a furlough. 1783, from the noun.

furnace *n.* Probably about 1200 *furneise,* Middle English *furneise,* borrowed from Old French *fornais, fornaise,* from Latin *fornācem* (nominative *fornāx*) an oven, kiln; related to *fornus, furnus* oven, and *formus* WARM.

furnish *v.* 1442 *fournesshen* provide, fit out, equip, in *Proceedings of the Privy Council;* borrowed from Middle French *furniss-,* stem of *furnir, fornir* furnish, accomplish, from Old French, from Vulgar Latin **fornīre,* alteration of **formīre, *fromīre,* from a Germanic source (compare Old High German *frummen* carry out, execute, related to *fruma* advantage, benefit; see FOREMOST); for suffix see -ISH[2]. **—furnishings** *n.pl.* 1605, in Shakespeare's *King Lear,* from *furnish,* v. **—furniture** *n.* 1529, action of fitting out or equipping, in Wolsey's correspondence; borrowed from Middle French *fourniture,* from *fournir, furnir* FURNISH. The meaning of provisions or supplies is first recorded in 1549, and the sense of movable household articles, in 1573.

furor or **furore** *n.* Probably before 1475 *furour* rage, fury; borrowed from Middle French *fureur,* learned borrowing from Latin *furor,* related to *furia* rage, passion, FURY. The form *furore* is first recorded as a borrowing of the Italian, from Latin *furōrem* (nominative *furor*). Its original meaning was that of great enthusiasm for someone or something, a rage, craze, or mania, also found in *furor,* in Swift's *A Discourse Concerning the Mechanical Operation of the Spirit* (1704).

furrow *n.* narrow trench made by a plow. Before 1325 *forow;* earlier *forw* (about 1300) and *furg* (before 1250, in *Bestiary*); developed from Old English (before 800) *furh* furrow; cognate with Old Frisian *furch* furrow, Middle Dutch *vore* (modern Dutch *voor*), Old High German *furuh* (modern German *Furche*), and Old Icelandic *for* furrow, ditch, from Proto-Germanic **furH-.* Outside Germanic cognates are found in Latin *porca* ridge of soil between two furrows, Welsh *rhych* furrow, Old Breton *rec* I plow, Lithuanian *pra-paršas* ditch, and probably Sanskrit *párśāna-s* abyss, gap, gulf, from Indo-European **perk̂-/pork̂-/pr̥k̂-* (Pok.821). **—v.** About 1425 *forwen* to plow; from the noun. The sense of make wrinkles in, is first recorded in Shakespeare's *Richard II* (1593).

further *adv.* Probably before 1200 *further,* in Layamon's *Chronicle of Britain;* developed from Old English (about 1000) *furthor, forthor* to a more advanced point, more forward (corresponding to Old Frisian *further,* Old Saxon *furthor,* Old High German *furdir,* obsolete German *fürder*), a comparative form from the same Germanic source as Old English *forth* FORTH and FORE, FOR: see also AFTER for suffix. **—adj.** 1155 *furthur;* later *further* (before 1387); developed from Old English (about 1000) *furthra,* from *furthor,* adv. **—v.** Probably before 1200 *furthren, furthrien* go forth, proceed, assist, improve; later *furtheren* (about 1303); developed from Old English *fyrthrian* help forward, assist, from *furthor,* adv. and *furthra,* adj. **—furtherance** *n.* About 1435, formed from Middle English *furtheran* + *-aunce* -ance. **—furthermore** *adv.* Probably about 1200 *further more,* in *The Ormulum.*

furtive *adj.* secret, stealthy. 1612, implied in earlier *furtively* (1490, in Caxton's translation of *The Book of Eneydos*); borrowed from French *furtif* (feminine *furtive*), from Latin *fūrtīvus* stolen, hidden, secret, from *fūrtum* theft, robbery, from *fūr* (genitive *fūris*) thief, corresponding to Greek *phṓr* thief (literally, one who carries things away), and related to *phérein* to carry; bring; see BEAR[2] carry. Oddly, the noun *furtiveness* is not recorded until 1896.

fury *n.* About 1385 *furie* rage, agony, madness, in Chaucer's *Troilus and Criseyde;* borrowed through Old French *furie,* from Latin *furia* violent passion, rage, madness; related to *furere* to rage, be mad, probably cognate with Greek *thyîa* a bacchante, from Indo-European **dhus-* (root **dhewes-*), Pok.268. An earlier use referring to one of the three furies of mythology appears in Chaucer's translation of Boethius' *De Consolatione Philosophiae* (about 1380), and with the even earlier use of *furious* (1375, in Chaucer's *Anelida and Arcite*), it is possible to assume that specific dates are of no more consequence than an indication that these words were in Chaucer's vocabulary in the latter part of the 1300's.

fuse[1] *v.* melt together. 1681, probably a back formation from *fusible* or *fusion,* perhaps formed by influence of French *fuser,* from Latin *fūsus.* It is also possible that English *fuse* was borrowed from Middle French *fuser,* from Latin *fūsus,* past participle of *fundere* pour, melt; see FOUND[2] cast metal. **—fusible** *adj.* capable of being fused. About 1395, in Chaucer's *Canterbury Tales;* borrowed from Old French *fusible,* from Medieval Latin *fusibilis,* from Latin *fūs-,* stem of *fundere;* for suffix see -IBLE. **—fusion** *n.* 1555, a melting; borrowed from Middle French *fusion,* from Latin *fūsiōnem* (nominative *fūsiō*), from *fūs-,* stem of *fundere;* for suffix see -SION. The figurative sense of a blending together of different things is first recorded in Adam Smith's *Wealth of Nations* (1776).

fuse[2] or **fuze** *n.* tube, cord, etc., for detonating a bomb or other explosive device. 1644, borrowed from Italian *fuso* spindle (because the tube of explosive material that was originally used was spindle-shaped), from Latin *fūsus* spindle, of uncertain origin. Whether earlier *fusee* a spindle-shaped pulley or wheel of a clock (1622, from French *fusée* spindleful of fiber) influenced the formation of *fuse* is conjectural, but the borrowing of *fuso* may have easily blended with earlier *fusee* to form *fuse* in English. The meaning for the device that breaks an electrical circuit if the current becomes too strong, is first recorded in 1884, and is so named for the tube shape of most early fuses, which is still found in the larger fuses; sometimes erroneously attributed to *fuse*[1] because fuses have an element that melts to break the circuit.

fuselage (fyü'zəläzh) *n.* body of an airplane. 1909, borrowed from French *fuselage,* from *fuselé* spindle-shaped, from Old French **fus* spindle, from Latin *fūsus* spindle.

fusilier or **fusileer** (fyü'zəlir') *n.* 1680 *fusilier* soldier armed with a light musket or fusil; borrowed from French *fusilier,* from *fusil* musket, from Old French *fusil, fuisil, foisil* musket (earlier, steel for a tinderbox), from Vulgar Latin **focīlis (petra*) (stone) producing fire, from Vulgar Latin **focus* fire, from Latin *focus* hearth; see FOCUS; for suffix see -IER.

fusillade (fyüzəlād') *n.* rapid or continuous discharge of many firearms. 1801, borrowed from French *fusillade,* from *fusiller* to shoot, from *fusil* musket; see FUSILIER; for suffix see -ADE. **—v.** attack or shoot down by a fusillade. 1816, in Southey's writings; from the noun.

fuss *n.* 1701, bustle, ado, commotion, in Farquhar's play *Sir Harry Wildair;* perhaps imitative of a bubbling or sputtering sound, expressing commotion or agitation. **—v.** 1792, to make a fuss; from the noun. **—fussy** *adj.* 1831; earlier implied in Byron's use of *fussily* (1817); formed from English *fuss,* n. + *-y*[1].

fustian (fus'chən) *n.* kind of coarse, thick cloth. Probably before 1200 *fustane;* later *fustian* (1380); borrowed from Old French *fustaigne, fustaine,* from Medieval Latin *fustaneum,* probably from Latin *fūstis* staff, stick of wood, probably a loan translation of Greek *xýlina lína* linens of wood (cotton), from *xýlinos* wooden, from *xýlon* wood. Sometimes an alternative source is given as a derivation from *Fostat,* town near Cairo, where this cloth was manufactured. The figurative meaning of thick, inflated, pompous language, is first recorded in Marlowe's *Doctor Faustus* (about 1590). Compare BOMBAST for a similar sense development. **—adj.** 1429-30 *fusteyn* made of fustian; later *fustian* worthless, pretentious (1523, in Skelton's writings); from the noun.

fusty *adj.* having a stale or musty smell. 1491 *fusty* smelling of mold, in Caxton's translation of *Vitae Patrum,* developed from earlier *fust* wine cask (1481-90); borrowed from Old French *fust, fuist* (originally, stick, stave), from Latin *fūstis* staff, stick of wood; of uncertain origin; for suffix see -Y[1].

An earlier term *foist* wooden cask, and its adjective *foyste* musty, smelling of a cask (about 1450) were also borrowed from Old French *fuist, fust.*

futile *adj.* About 1555, borrowed from Middle French *futile* and directly from Latin *fūtilis* vain, worthless, futile (literally, pouring out easily), from the base of *fundere* pour, melt; see FOUND[2] cast metal. **—futility** *n.* 1623, probably formed from English *futile* + *-ity,* modeled on French *futilité,* from Latin *fūtilitātem* (nominative *fūtilitās*), from *fūtilis* futile.

future *adj.* About 1380 *future, futur,* in Chaucer's translation of Boethius' *De Consolatione Philosophiae;* borrowed through Old French *futur* (feminine *future*), and directly from Latin *futūrus* about to be, irregular suppletive future participle to *esse* to be; see BE. **—n.** About 1380, also in Chaucer's translation of Boethius' *De Consolatione Philosophiae,* probably from *future, futur,* adj., the use modeled on Latin *futūra,* neuter plural of *futūrus* about to be. **—futurism** *n.* movement in art originating in Italy. 1909, borrowed from Italian *futurismo* (*futuro* future, from Latin *futūrus* + *-ismo* -ism). The term is said to have been coined by Filippo Marinetti, an Italian poet closely associated with the movement. **—futurology** *n.* forecasting. 1946, formed from English *future* + *-ology,* found in a letter by Aldous Huxley, but the word did not gain much currency until the late 1960's. A similar term *futurist* has been recorded since 1842.

fuzz[1] *n.* fluffy hair or fibers, down. 1674 *fuzze* mass of fine or fluffy particles, from earlier *fusse* (1601, or by shortening of *fusball,* 1597, a puffball that is a kind of fungus which gives off a cloud of tiny spores). It is also possible that *fuzz* is a back formation from earlier *fuzzy.* Though *fuzz* is of uncertain origin, possible cognates exist in Low German *fussig* porous, loose, spongy, and Dutch *voos* spongy. **—fuzzy** *adj.* 1616, spongy or fluffy; of uncertain origin, perhaps from Low German *fussig;* see FUZZ; however, if *fuzz* was formed from earlier *fusse,* then *fuzzy* was probably formed from English *fuzz* + *-y*[1], implied also in earlier *fussiness* (1613). The sense of blurred, indistinct, is first recorded in 1778.

fuzz[2] *n. Slang.* policeman or detective. 1929 *the fuzz* the police, American English, of uncertain origin; perhaps a special application of *fuzz*[1].

-fy a suffix forming verbs and meaning: make or cause to be, as in *simplify;* become, as in *solidify;* bring into a certain state, as in *calcify, horrify.* Adopted from Old French verbs ending in *-fier,* or formed on analogy of such verbs, from Latin *-ficāre* (sometimes as a replacement of *-ficere*), from *-ficus* making, from *facere* to make, DO[1] perform. The usual ending for these verbs in English is *-ify,* the *i* being a stem vowel in the original base word or a representation of it, though the *i* may also be a simple connective added to a consonant stem. The same practice is found in *-fic* (see -FIC), in the corresponding adjectives ending in *-ficent* where the *i* usually appears, and in nouns ending in *-fication* and *-faction.*

G

gab *v.* to chatter, gabble. 1369 *gabben* speak foolishly, talk nonsense, in Chaucer's *Book of the Duchesse;* earlier, scoff, jeer (probably about 1150); borrowed from a Scandinavian source (compare Old Icelandic *gabba* to mock). The meaning of chatter or gabble, is first recorded in Burns' *The Author's Earnest Cry and Prayer* (1786), a usage widespread and well-established in Northern English and Scottish dialects in spite of its absence in written texts between the Middle English period and Burns' use. **—n.** Before 1325 *gab* idle talk; earlier *gabbe* gibe, taunt (probably about 1200); borrowed from a Scandinavian source (compare Old Icelandic *gabb, gabba* mockery).

gabardine *n.* closely woven cloth. 1904, from the earlier sense of dress, covering (1594); variant of GABERDINE.

gabble *v.* talk rapidly. 1577, formed from English *gab,* v. + *-le*[3]. **—n.** rapid talk. 1601, meaningless noises made by animals, especially geese, in Shakespeare's *All's Well that Ends Well;* from the verb.

gaberdine *n.* long, loose outer garment. 1520, borrowed from Spanish *gabardina.* The Spanish scholar Corominas analyzes *gabardina* as a blend of *gabán* overcoat and *tabardina* coarse coat. The *e* in the medial and terminal syllables comes from the Middle French *gaverdine, galverdine,* of uncertain origin.

gable *n.* end of a ridged roof. 1347-48 *gabell;* earlier, in the place name *Mykelgavel* (1338). The two spellings reflect the two sources of this word in English. The form in London and generally in the south of England was *gable,* borrowed through Old French *gable,* probably from a Scandinavian source (compare Old Icelandic *gafl* gable; see CEPHALIC). The form in Scotland and the north of England was *gavel,* probably borrowed directly from Old Icelandic *gafl.* In form and sense the word is probably related to Old English *gafol, geafel* fork, possibly all forms developing from Proto-Germanic **ʒablō,* from Indo-European **ghabhlā* (Pok.409) having the sense of fork, as found in Middle and modern Dutch *gaffel,* and Old High German *gabala* (modern German *Gabel*) fork. Another group of words, including Greek *kephalḗ* head, Gothic *gibla* pinnacle, and Old High German *gebal* head, from Indo-European **ghebhel-* (Pok.423), may have given rise to the sense of *gable* as being the top cross member supporting the end of the ridgepole of a roof. **—v.** build a gable. 1848, from the noun.

gad *v.* move about restlessly. Before 1460 *gadden,* of uncertain origin (according to the OED, probably a back formation from earlier (probably about 1150) *gadling, gadeling* companion, fellow, wanderer and in participial use with the sense of wandering; MED suggests possible association with *gad* a goad for driving cattle; see GADFLY). **—gadabout** *n.* wanderer. 1837, developed from *gad-about,* adj. (1817, in Scott's correspondence); formed from English *gad,* v. + *about.*

gadfly *n.* 1626, fly that bites cattle; probably formed from *gad* goad (1250 metal rod) + *fly*[1] insect. Earlier (1591) *gadfly* is recorded with the meaning of someone who likes to go about, often stopping here and there, or roving idly. This strongly suggests some association with *gad* (move about restlessly) and in turn that *gad* is further associated with the old word *gad* meaning a goad, and borrowed from a Scandinavian source (compare Old Icelandic *gaddr* spike), cognate with Gothic *gazds,* Old High German *gart* (from Proto-Germanic **ʒazđaz*), and Latin *hasta* spear, from Indo-European **ĝhasdho-, *ĝhastā* (Pok.412).

gadget *n.* 1886 *gadjet,* probably a simple phonetic spelling of a term said to be known as early as the 1850's, apparently in the jargon of sailors for a small device, fitting, or piece of mechanism of unknown or perhaps indefinite name. It has been suggested that the term may have been a borrowing of French *gâchette* piece of a mechanism, a diminutive form of *gâche* staple of a lock, wall staple or hook (compare *gizmo* for a similar but later formation). The spelling *gadget* is first recorded in Kipling's *Traffics and Discoveries* (1902).

gadolinium (gad′əlin′ēəm) *n.* metallic chemical element. 1886, New Latin *gadolinium;* formed in allusion to the Finnish chemist Johan *Gadolin* (discoverer, in 1802, of gadolinite, a silicate containing this element) + *-ium* (chemical suffix). The term was coined by its co-discoverer, the Swiss chemist de Marignac.

Gaelic *adj.* 1774, earlier *Cathelik* (1596); formed from *Gael,* Scottish *Gaidheal,* from Old Irish *Góidhel* + *-ic.* **—n.** the Celtic language. 1775, in James Boswell's *The Life of Samuel Johnson;* from the adjective.

gaff *n.* hook for landing fish. Probably before 1325 *gaffe* iron hook; borrowing of Old French *gaffe* boat hook; see GAFFE. The specific meaning of hook on a fishing spear, appears in Blount's *Glossographia* (1656). The use of the slang phrase *the gaff* (as in *stand the gaff, get* or *give the gaff*), with the meaning of severe treatment or criticism, is first recorded in American English, in George Ade's *Artie* (1896). **—v.** land (a fish) with a gaff. 1844, from the noun.

gaffe *n.* blunder. 1909, borrowing of French *gaffe* blunder (originally, boat hook), from Old French *gaffe,* from Old Provençal *gaf,* probably from West Gothic **gafa* hook, from Proto-Germanic **ʒafa* (Meyer-Lübke, *Romanisches Etymologisches Wörterbuch,* No. 3633).

gaffer *n.* old man, old fellow. 1589, apparently contraction of *godfather,* originally used as a title or term of address for an elderly man; the vowel, however, may have been partially influenced by *grand-,* in *grandfather.* In the 1800's the term was applied to a foreman or supervisor of a group of workers, from which several specialized meanings emerged later, such as that of a master glass blower or an electrician in charge of the lighting of a film or television studio set.

gag[1] *v.* choke. About 1440 *gaggen* strangle, suffocate, in *Promptorium Parvulorum;* possibly imitative of the sound made in choking, but perhaps related to Old Icelandic *gaghals* with head thrown back. The sense of stop up (a person's mouth) to prevent speech or outcry, is first recorded in 1509. **—n.** anything used to silence a person. 1553, from the verb. **—gag rule** 1810, a legislative rule restricting debate.

gag[2] *n.* joke. 1805, a made-up story, deception, possibly developed from earlier *gag* (1777) to deceive, take in or ply (a person) with talk, especially in the sense of stuff or fill, GAG[1]. The extended meaning of a joke is first recorded in 1863.

gaga *adj. Slang.* foolish, doting. 1920, in Ford Madox Ford's *Letters;* probably borrowed from French *gaga* senile, foolish, imitative of the mumbling of a person sunk into dotage.

gage[1] *n.* pledge. Probably before 1300 *gage* pledge to fight, in *Kyng Alisaunder;* borrowed from Old French *gage, guage,* from Frankish **wadja-,* related to Gothic *wadi* pledge (from Proto-Germanic **wađja-*), cognate with Latin *vas,* genitive *vadis* a surety, from Indo-European **wadh-* (Pok.1109).

gage[2] *v.* See GAUGE.

gaggle *v.* cackle like a goose. 1350 *gagolen,* possibly imitative, formed from *gag* or *gag-gag,* in imitation of the sound of geese + *-le*[3] (however, compare Old Icelandic *gagl* goose). **—n.** flock of geese. Before 1450 *gagalle* flock of geese; from the verb.

gaiety or **gayety** *n.* 1634 *gaity* merrymaking, lively entertainment; later, quality of being gay (1647); borrowed from French *gaieté,* from Old French, from *gai* GAY; probably influenced by earlier *gay,* Middle English *gai* dressed in a showy manner (probably about 1300), joyous, light-hearted (probably about 1380); for suffix see -TY[2].

gaily *adv.* See GAY.

gain *n.* 1473 *gayne* booty or prey; but implied in earlier *gainage* profit from agriculture (before 1393, in Gower's *Confessio Amantis*); borrowed from Middle French *gain,* from Old French *gaaigne,* from *gaaignier* to gain, (also) cultivate land, from Frankish **waidanjan* (compare Old High German *weidenōn* to hunt, pasture, *weidōn* to hunt, seek food, *weida* pasture, fodder (modern German *Weide* pasture, *weiden* to pasture), which is cognate with Old English *wāth* hunt, *wǣthan* to hunt, wander, and Old Icelandic *veidhr* hunt, *veidha* to hunt, Lithuanian *výti* to hunt, chase, and Sanskrit *véti* pursues, strives, leads); the basic Proto-Germanic noun **warthō* is from Indo-European **woi-tā,* root **wei-* (Pok.1123). —**v.** 1530 *gaine* profit, in Palsgrave's *Lesclarcissement;* borrowed from Middle French *gaigner,* from Old French *gaaignier.*

Gain in the noun and verb replaced or merged with the earlier *gein* advantage, benefit, remedy; and *geinen* be useful; suitable, serve (both recorded probably before 1200); both forms borrowed from a Scandinavian source (compare Old Icelandic *gegn,* adj., ready, serviceable; and *gegna* to suit, he meets).

—gainful *adj.* 1555, implied in earlier *gainfully* (1549); formed from English *gain,* n. + *-ful.*

gainsay *v.* deny, contradict. Before 1338 *geynsayen,* implied in earlier *genseyying* contradiction, literally, a saying against (probably before 1325); formed from *gain-* against (Old English *gegn-, gēan-*) + *say;* see AGAIN.

gait *n.* manner of walking. About 1450 *gait, gate,* derivative use of *gate* a going or walking, departure, journey (probably before 1300), and earlier, way, road, path (probably about 1200); borrowed from a Scandinavian source (compare Old Icelandic *gata* way, road, path); cognate with Old High German *gazza* street (modern German *Gasse*), and Gothic *gatwō,* of unknown origin. The form *gait* was not fully established before the 1750's, *gate* being found in Shakespeare's *Love's Labour's Lost* (1588).

gaiter *n.* covering for the ankle and lower leg. 1775, borrowed from French *guêtre,* from Middle French **guestre* (misspelled *guietre*), probably from Frankish **wrist* instep, cognate with modern German *Rist* instep, and English WRIST.

gala *n.* festive occasion. 1625, festive dress or attire; borrowed from Italian *gala,* and later in some instances from French *gala,* from Old French *gale* merriment, from *galer* make merry, from Gallo-Romance **walāre,* from Frankish **wala,* cognate with Old English *wel,* Gothic *waíla;* see WELL[1]. Related to GALLANT, but also suggesting a connection with Middle English *gale* song, singing, merriment (probably before 1200); borrowed from Old French *gale* merriment. The sense of festive occasion is first recorded in Sheridan's *School for Scandal* (1777). **—adj.** festive. 1762, in Sterne's *Tristram Shandy;* from the noun.

galaxy *n.* About 1380, the Milky Way, in Chaucer's *House of Fame;* borrowed from Late Latin *galaxias* Milky Way, from Greek *galaxíās,* from *gála* (genitive *gálaktos*) milk; cognate with Latin *lac* (genitive *lactis*) milk. Greek *gála* was altered from earlier **gla,* from Indo-European **glakt* (Pok.400). The technical meaning of stars in a system is first recorded in 1848. **—galactic** *adj.* 1839, of the Galaxy (Milky Way); borrowed from Late Latin *galacticus* milky, from Greek *gála* (genitive *gálaktos*) milk; see GALAXY. The sense of pertaining to a galaxy or galaxies in general, is first recorded in 1849.

gale *n.* very strong wind. Before 1547 *gaile* wind; origin uncertain. The OED suggests that *gale* may have originally been an adjective, as in *gale wind,* but is reserved about the term's possible Scandinavian origin (comparing Old Icelandic *galenn* mad, frantic, and Norwegian *galen* furious, bad, often said of the weather, a connection which the editors eschew for phonetic reasons pertaining to rhyme and because of spelling).

galena *n.* metallic gray ore containing lead and sulfur. 1601, in Holland's translation of Pliny's *Natural History;* borrowed from Latin *galēna* a mixture of silver and lead ores, dross from smelting lead; of uncertain origin (possibly from Greek).

gall[1] *n.* bitter liquid secreted by the liver, bile. Probably before 1200 *galle* gall bladder, in *Ancrene Riwle;* later *gall* bile (1373); developed from Old English *galla* bile (Anglian dialect, before 830), *gealla* bile (West Saxon). Old English *galla* is cognate with Old Saxon and Old High German *galla* bile (modern German *Galle*), Middle Dutch *galle* (modern Dutch *gal*), and Old Icelandic *gall,* from Proto-Germanic **ʒallōn-;* outside Germanic cognates are found in Latin *fel* (genitive *fellis*) bile (with dialectal *f-*), Greek *cholḗ, chólos* bile, anger, Lithuanian *tulžis* with reversal of *ž* and *t* (compare their regular order in Latvian *žults* gall), Old Slavic *zlŭčĭ,* and Avestan *zāra-,* from Indo-European **ĝhel-/ĝhol-/ĝhḷ-* (Pok.429). The informal meaning of impudence, boldness, is first recorded in American English in 1882, and developed from the figurative use of embittered spirit, asperity, rancor (recorded in English probably about 1200, possibly emerging by influence of that sense in Latin). **—gall bladder** (1676)

gall² *n.* sore spot caused by rubbing. About 1395 *galle* a sore or tender spot, in Chaucer's *Canterbury Tales;* developed from Old English *gealla* painful swelling (about 1000); borrowed from Latin *galla* GALL³ lump on plant. **—v.** make sore by rubbing. Probably before 1325 *gallen* have sores, be sore; from the noun. The sense of irritate or annoy, is first recorded in 1573, from an earlier meaning of harass in warfare (1548). **—galling** *adj.* 1583, irritating, offensive; from *gall²*, v.

gall³ *n.* lump that forms on injured plants. Before 1398 *galle,* in Trevisa's translation of Bartholomew's *De Proprietatibus Rerum;* borrowed from Old French *galle,* learned borrowing from Latin *galla* oak apple, gallnut, of uncertain origin (perhaps cognate with Greek *ganglíon* swelling, Old Slavic *žily* abscess, ulcer, and Sanskrit *gula-s* ball, sphere), from Indo-European **gel-* (Pok.357).

gallant *adj.* brave, showy. About 1440 *galaunt* stylish, showy, in *Promptorium Parvulorum;* also before 1450, brave, noble in spirit; borrowed from Old French *galant* courteous (earlier, spirited or dashing), from present participle of *galer* make merry, of uncertain origin. In form and meaning the word is probably connected with Middle English *gale* merrymaking, and GALA. **—n.** spirited and stylish man. Probably 1388 *galaunt* dissolute man, rake; later, man of fashion (1448); borrowed from Old French *galant,* n., from Old French *galant,* adj. **—gallantry** *n.* 1606 fashionable people, in Shakespeare's *Troylus and Cressida;* borrowed from French *galanterie,* from Old French *galant,* adj. and n. The meaning of gallant behavior, is first recorded in 1632.

galleon (gal'ēən) *n.* large ship. 1529 *gallion, galion;* borrowing of Old French *galion* galleon, from Spanish *galeón* galleon, an armed merchant ship, formed on *galea* galley, from Medieval Greek *galéa* GALLEY.

gallery *n.* long, narrow room or passage. Probably before 1439 *gallerie* covered walkway or passage, in Lydgate's *Falls of Princes;* borrowed from Middle French *galerie* a long portico, gallery, from Medieval Latin *galeria,* of uncertain origin (perhaps alteration of *galilea, galilaea* church porch, probably from Latin *Galilaea,* from Greek *Galilaiā* Galilee, the northernmost region of Palestine in the time of Christ). Corominas, in a discussion of Spanish *galería,* says that the porch or gallery was likened to Galilee, that is, to an outlying area where outsiders remained, while the choir for the monks was compared with Judea.

The meaning of a building to house works of art, is first recorded in English, in Shakespeare's *1 Henry VI* (1591), and the sense of those people who occupy a gallery, as in a theater, is found in Lovelace's poetry, in 1649.

galley *n.* long, narrow ship having oars and sails. Probably about 1225 *galeie,* in *King Horn;* borrowed from Old French *galie, galee,* probably through Catalan *galea,* from Medieval Greek *galéa,* of uncertain origin. The German scholar Kluge supposed that Greek *galéē* weasel, was transferred to various sea animals, including sharks, and that the term was then transferred to the ship. **—galley slave** (1567)

Gallic *adj.* French. 1672, borrowed from Latin *Gallicus* pertaining to Gaul or the Gauls, from *Gallia* Gaul, and *Gallus* a Gaul. **—Gallicism** *n.* 1656, in Blount's *Glossographia;* borrowing of French *gallicisme* (*gallic* + *-isme* -ism). An adjective form *Gallican* from Latin *Gallicānus,* is recorded in earlier use (probably before 1350), but it is now archaic.

gallinaceous *adj.* belonging to order of birds including domestic poultry. 1783, borrowed, possibly by influence of earlier French *gallinacé,* from Latin *gallīnāceus* of poultry, from *gallīna* hen, from *gallus* rooster; for suffix see -ACEOUS.

gallium (gal'ēəm) *n.* metallic chemical element. 1875, New Latin, probably formed from a play on words by the French chemist Lecoq de Boisbaudran, its discoverer, translating French *le coq* rooster into Latin *gallus* + *-ium* (chemical suffix).

gallivant *v.* go about seeking pleasure. 1819, apparently a humorous alteration of *gallant,* v. (1608, play the gallant, flirt, gad about, from GALLANT, adj.).

Gallo- a combining form meaning Gaul, Gaulish, Gallic, as in *Gallo-Latin, Gallo-Romance;* or France, French, as in *Gallophile.* Borrowed from Latin *Gallo-,* combining form of *Gallus* inhabitant of ancient *Gallia* Gaul.

gallon *n.* a measure for liquids. Probably about 1225 *galun,* in *King Horn;* later *gallon* (1475); borrowed from Old North French *galon* (probably Norman dialect), corresponding to Old French *jalon* liquid measure, related to *jale* bowl and *jaloie* measure of capacity, from Medieval Latin *galleta* bucket or pail, of uncertain origin (perhaps from Gaulish *galla* vessel).

gallop *v.* Before 1425 *galopen,* in *Kyng Alisaunder;* borrowed from Middle French *galoper,* from Old French *galoper,* variant of Old North French *waloper;* see WALLOP. **—n.** 1523 *galoppe;* from the verb. These forms in noun and verb apparently existed along with *walop, wallop* which appears in Scottish use as early as 1375, but by the late 1500's *gallop* had completely replaced the older *walop, wallop.*

gallows *n.* 1400 *gallowes;* earlier *galwes,* plural of *galwe* gallows (about 1300), and in the place name *Galowe* (1228-40); developed from Old English *galga* (probably Mercian, about 725, in *Beowulf*), *gealga* (in West Saxon). The Old English forms are cognate with Old Frisian *galga* gallows, Old Saxon and Old High German *galgo* (modern German *Galgen*), Old Icelandic *galgi* gallows, *gelgja* twig, stick, Gothic *galga* cross (from Proto-Germanic **ʒalʒ-*), and Lithuanian *žalgà* a long, thin pole, from Indo-European **ĝhalgh-* flexible branch, pole (Pok.411).

galore *adv.* in abundance. 1675, borrowed from Irish *go leór,* corresponding to Gaelic *gu leóir* sufficiently, enough (*go,* Gaelic *gu,* usually thought to mean *to,* is a particle prefixed to an adjective to form an adverb and does not have the specific meaning usually ascribed to it).

galosh *n.* Usually **galoshes,** *pl.* rubber overshoes, but originally a wooden shoe or sandal fastened to the foot with thongs of leather, and, according to the OED, probably a general term for a boot or shoe. About 1364-65 *galoches,* pl., a kind of footwear; earlier variant *galeys,* probably *galegs,* pl. (1353); and found in the surname *Galocher* maker or seller of galoshes (1306); probably borrowed from Old French *galoche,* possibly a word derived from Vulgar Latin **galopia,* from **galopus,* from Greek *kālopódion,* diminutive of *kālópous* shoemaker's last (*kâlon* wood + *poús* foot). Greek *kâlon* wood is from earlier **káwalon,* from *kau-,* root of *kaíein* burn, from Indo-European **kēu-/kəu-* (Pok.595).

galumph *v.* move clumsily or noisily, gallop triumphantly. 1872, apparently from a blend of *gallop* and *triumph.* A term coined by Lewis Carroll in the nonsense poem "Jabberwocky" in *Through the Looking-Glass.*

galvanism *n.* electricity produced by chemical action. 1797, borrowed from French *galvanisme* or from Italian *galvanismo,* formed in allusion to the Italian scientist Luigi *Galvani* + *-isme, -ismo* -ism. Galvani's anatomical investigations into the cause of muscle contractions when in contact with metals prompted the discovery of electricity produced by chemical reaction. **—galvanic** *adj.* 1797, formed from English *galvan(ism)* + *-ic,* perhaps modeled on French *galvanique.* **—galvanize** *v.* 1802, either formed from English *galvan(ism)* + *-ize,* or borrowed from French *galvaniser,* from *galvanisme* galvanism. The figurative sense of stimulate or excite as if by an electric current, is first recorded in Charlotte Brontë's *Villette* (1853).

gambit *n.* way of opening a game of chess to gain some advantage. 1656 *gambett,* borrowed from Italian *gambetto,* literally, a tripping up (as a trick in wrestling), from *gamba* leg, from Late Latin *gamba;* see GAMBOL. The current spelling, which appeared in English in 1847, came from French *gambit,* from Spanish *gambito,* from Italian *gambetto. Gambit* in the figurative sense of any opening move to gain some advantage, is first recorded in English in 1855.

gamble *v.* play games of chance for money. 1775, implied in *gambling* playing for high stakes (1726), and *gambler* one who plays for money or who cheats at games (1747). Whether *gamble,* v., is a back formation from either of these earlier forms or an alteration of *gamner, gamener* (1509), from *gamen, gamenen* to play, jest, be merry (probably before 1200, in *Ancrene Riwle*), or a derivative from *gamel* to play games (1594) is an unsolved question. The principal problem lies in explaining the intrusion of *b,* which has been suggested as coming from the homophone *gambol,* v., in the meaning of be playful or sportive (1602, in Shakespeare's *Hamlet*). The dates would allow for the later alteration of *gamner,* etc., and also the development of meaning, but the association seems somewhat strained and coincidental, especially because *gamble,* n. and v. appear so late when *gambol,* n. and v. are recorded in the sense of sportive, and be playful, at least 175 years earlier. **—n.** 1823, risky venture; from the verb. **—gambler** *n.* 1747, of uncertain origin.

gambol (gam′bəl) *n.* a running and jumping about in play. 1596, in Shakespeare's *Merchant of Venice,* alteration (by loss of *d*) in earlier *gambolde* a leap or spring (1530), from *gambad* leap of a horse (1503); borrowed from Middle French *gambade,* possibly through Provençal *gambado, cambado,* and *camba* leg, from Late Latin *gamba, camba* horse's hock or leg, from Greek *kampē* bend, cognate with Lithuanian *kam̃pas* corner; see CAMP[1]. The sense of sportive, playful, referred to under *gamble,* is found in Shakespeare's *2 Henry IV* (1597), and the sense of frolicsome movements, merrymaking, in Shakespeare's *Merchant of Venice* (1596). **—v.** run and jump about in play. 1590, in Shakespeare's *Midsummer Night's Dream,* alteration (probably by influence of noun *gambolde, gambauld*), of earlier *gambade* to leap or spring (1508); borrowed from Middle French *gambader,* from *gambade,* n. The sense of to be sportive or frolicsome, is found in Shakespeare's *Hamlet* (1602).

gambrel *n.* In *gambrel roof* a roof with two slopes on each side (1851), so called from its resemblance to the shape of a *gambrel* a horse's hind leg (1601); earlier, stick to hang slaughtered animals on (1547); borrowed from Old North French (Norman dialect) *gamberel,* from *gambe* leg, from Late Latin *gamba;* see GAMBOL.

game[1] *n.* pastime, amusement. Probably before 1200 *gome* (West Midland dialect, in Layamon's *Chronicle of Britain*) and *game;* developed from Old English *gamen* joy, fun, mirth, amusement (about 725, in *Beowulf*); cognate with Old Frisian *game* joy, glee, Old Saxon, Old High German, and Old Icelandic *gaman* game, sport, merriment, of unknown origin. The meaning of wild animals caught for sport is first recorded about 1300. **—v.** Before 1325 *gamen* to play, be merry, formed from a blend of *gomen* (West Midland dialect, probably before 1200), from the noun; and a shortened form of *gomnen* (also West Midland dialect, probably before 1200), later *gomenen* (probably about 1200); developed from Old English *gamenian* to play, from *gamen* joy. **—adj.** 1725, having the spirit of a game cock; brave, showing fight, spirited; from the noun. **—gaming** *n.* 1501, the playing of games of chance for money, gambling; formed from English *game,* v. + *-ing.* **—gamy** *adj.* spirited, plucky. 1844, in Dickens' *Martin Chuzzlewit;* formed from English *game,* n. + *-y*[1]. The sense of having a strong taste or smell, is first recorded in 1863.

game[2] *adj.* lame, crippled. 1787, in Grose's *A Provincial Glossary,* of uncertain origin (possibly a variant of *gammy,* slang for bad, 1839, though the date is late, the record of slang is often defective).

gamete (gam′ēt) *n. Biology.* mature reproductive cell. 1886, borrowed from New Latin *gameta,* from Greek *gametē* wife, *gamétēs* husband, from *gameîn* marry; see BIGAMY.

gamin (gam′ən) *n.* street urchin. 1840, in Thackeray's *Paris Sketch Book;* borrowed from French *gamin,* perhaps from Berrichon dialect *gamer* to steal. **—gamine** (gamēn′) *n.* female gamin, especially an attractively pert girl. 1899, borrowed from French *gamine.*—*adj.* 1925, in D.H. Lawrence's *St. Mawr;* from the noun.

gamma *n.* third letter of the Greek alphabet. Probably before 1425, in Sir John Maundeville's *Travels;* borrowed from Latin *gamma,* from Greek *gámma,* from a Semitic source (compare Hebrew *gīmel* the third letter of the Hebrew alphabet, literally meaning a camel, originally formed from the hieroglyph of a camel). **—gamma globulin** 1937, any of three (alpha, beta, gamma) serum globulins of the blood that contains many antibodies. **—gamma ray** 1903, originally conceived as the shortest of three wavelengths of radiation given off by radium.

gammon (gam′ən) *n.* Probably before 1425 *gambon* hindquarter of a pig; later *gammon* (1611); borrowed from Old North French *gambon* ham, from *gambe* leg, from Late Latin *gamba* leg; see GAMBOL.

-gamous a combining form producing adjectives and meaning marrying, as in *monogamous;* or joining in reproduction, as in *homogamous.* Borrowed from Greek *-gamos,* from *gámos* marriage; see BIGAMY.

gamut (gam′ət) *n.* Before 1450, lowest tone in a musical scale supposedly devised by Guido d'Arezzo, and consisting of all the recognized notes in medieval music. The word is a contraction of Medieval Latin *gamma ut* from *gamma* the name of a Greek letter and *ut,* later replaced by *do*². In medieval musical notation *gamma* was the name of the lowest note on the stave, and *ut* was the next note to it, one tone higher and the first note in any scale. The names of the notes were taken from the syllables in a Latin hymn to St. John the Baptist, the first line of which is *Ut* queant laxis *re*sonare fibris. The figurative sense of whole scale or range of a thing is first recorded in 1626.

-gamy a combining form producing nouns and meaning marriage, as in *monogamy;* or union in reproduction, as in *heterogamy.* Borrowed from Greek *-gamiā* (as in *monogamiā* monogamy), from *gámos* marriage; see -GAMOUS.

gander *n.* male goose. Before 1250 *gandre,* in *Bestiary;* developed from Old English *gandra* (about 1000, in Ælfric's *Grammar*); cognate with Dutch *gander,* and Middle Low German *ganre,* from Proto-Germanic **ʒánez-,* from Indo-European **ĝhan-es-;* see GOOSE. If the Old English variant *ganra* was an earlier form, and the *d* inserted later, then the Old English *ganra* may be related to *gannet,* and, with a different suffix, to Middle High German *ganzer* (modern German *Ganser, Gänserich*). The slang meaning of a long look is first recorded in 1914 in American English, from the verb. **—v.** *Slang.* to look (by craning the neck as a gander does). 1903, American English; from the earlier noun meaning of a male goose.

gang *n.* 1400 *gang* band or company of men; earlier, a number of things used together, a set (probably 1340); also a going, walking, journey (probably about 1200, in *The Ormulum*), a way, road, path (1199), and a privy (1173, in the surname *Gangishider* privy builder); developed from Old English (before 830) *gong* a going, journey, step, passage. It appears from the disparity of meanings that there are two different sources: group of men and set, directly from Old Icelandic; and a going, journey, way, privy, from Old English, which is cognate with Old Frisian, Old Saxon, Dutch, Old High German *gang* (modern German *Gang*) a going, Old Icelandic *gangr* a going (but also, a group), and Gothic *gagg* a going, from Proto-Germanic **ʒangaz;* also cognate with Lithuanian *žengiù* I step, and Sanskrit *jáñghā* shank, from Indo-European **ĝhengh-/ĝhongh-* (Pok.438). **—v.** *Informal.* form a gang. 1856, from the noun. This new verb is a reintroduction of the verb use in English, which is earlier found in the obsolete *gangen* (probably about 1200, walk or wander from place to place; to be or become, in *The Ormulum*). **—gangster** *n.* member of a gang of criminals. 1896, American English; formed from English *gang,* n. + *-ster.* **—gangway** *n.* passageway. Old English *gangweg* road, passage, thoroughfare (about 1000, in Ælfric's *Glossary*); formed from *gang,* n. + *weg* way. Some sources claim that *gangway* is not continuously in the record of English because it is not found again until 1688.

ganglion (gang′glēən) *n.* group of nerve cells forming a nerve center. 1681, swelling on the sheath of a tendon; borrowing of Greek *ganglíon;* see GALL³ lump. The Greek word was used in the sense of a nerve bundle by Galen, the physician and writer of the 100's A.D., and that meaning is first recorded in English in 1732.

gangrene (gang′grēn) *n.* decay from disease or injury of a part of a living person or animal. Before 1400 *cancrena, cancrene* in Lanfranc's *Science of Surgery;* later *gangrene* (1563); borrowing of Medieval Latin *cancrena,* from Latin *gangraena,* from Greek *gángraina* an eating or gnawing sore, perhaps formed with intensive reduplication from *grân* gnaw, eat; see CRESS. **—v.** produce gangrene in. 1607, in Shakespeare's *Coriolanus;* from the noun. **—gangrenous** *adj.* 1612, formed from English *gangrene,* n. + *-ous.*

gannet (gan′it) *n.* large fish-eating sea bird. About 1450 *ganat;* 1440 *gante,* in *Promptorium Parvulorum;* developed from Old English *ganot* (about 725, in *Beowulf*); cognate with Middle Low German *gante* gander, Dutch *gent,* Old High German *ganazzo,* from Proto-Germanic **ʒanat-,* from Indo-European **ĝhan-əd-* (Pok.412); related to Old English *gōs* GOOSE; see also GANDER.

gantlet *n.* See GAUNTLET.

gantry *n.* bridgelike framework. 1356 *ganter* wooden stand for barrels; borrowed from Old North French *gantier,* Old French *chantier,* from Latin *canthērius* rafter, frame, borrowed from Greek *kanthḗlios* pack ass, from the framework placed on its back, *kanthḗlion* rafter, of unknown origin. The later spelling *gauntre(es),* first in surnames (1415, 1449), was perhaps influenced by *-tre* with the meaning of wooden support.

gap *n.* broken place, opening. Before 1325; earlier in the place name *Grenehougap* (1261, and variant about 1250); borrowed from a Scandinavian source (compare Old Icelandic *gap* chasm, related to *gapa* to GAPE). **—v.** 1847, to notch, make jagged; from the noun. The sense of make a gap, is first recorded in 1893.

gape *v.* open the mouth wide. Before 1250 *gapen,* probably borrowed from a Scandinavian source (compare Old Icelandic *gapa* to open the mouth, gape; cognate with Middle Low German, Middle Dutch and modern Dutch *gapen* to gape, Middle High German and modern German *gaffen* to gape, stare, Old English *ofergapian* neglect, forget), of unknown origin. An earlier form in Middle English *geapen* (probably about 1200) may attest to the existence of Old English **gapian,* as found in *ofergapian.* **—n.** 1535, act of opening the mouth, a yawn; from the verb.

gar *n.* 1765, American English, shortened form of GARFISH.

garage *n.* 1902, borrowing of French *garage* place where a carriage or other vehicle is sheltered, from Middle French *garer* to shelter, from a Germanic source (compare Old High German *warōn* take care, modern German *wahren* watch over, safeguard); see WARY. **—v.** 1906, put into a garage; from the noun.

garb *n.* the way one is dressed. 1591, grace, stylishness, borrowed from Middle French *garbe* graceful outline, from Italian *garbo* grace, elegance, perhaps from Germanic; compare Old High German *garawī, garwī* adornment, GEAR. The meaning of fashion of dress, appeared in 1622 from the earlier general meaning of manner of doing something, style of living (1599, in Shakespeare's *Henry V*). **—v.** clothe, cover. 1836, in Newman's early poetry; from the noun.

garbage *n.* 1422, entrails or waste parts of an animal; of uncertain origin (some relation may exist, as the MED implies, with *garbelage* removal of refuse from spices, and further connection may be possible with Old French *garbage,* variant of *jarbage,* though the recorded sense of a toll on sheaves, is hard to reconcile, unless Old French *garbe* a sheaf has a connection with *garbage* a bundle of sheaves, entrails, similar to that of German *Bündel* the entrails of a fish). The specific meaning of refuse or filth is first recorded in 1583.

garble *v.* confuse, mix up. 1419-20 *garbelen* to inspect and remove refuse from; borrowed through Anglo-French *garbeler* to sift, from Middle French, and from Medieval Latin *garbellare,* from Arabic *gharbala* to sift. The Arabic word is related to *ghirbāl* sieve, perhaps from Late Latin *crībellum,* diminutive of Latin *crībrum* sieve, and related to *cernere* to sift, separate, distinguish; see CERTAIN. Presence of Italian *garbellare* and Spanish *garbillo* further testify to the opinion that this was a widespread term in use among Mediterranean traders and merchants. The sense of confuse, mix up or distort by mutilating or making unfair selection from (a statement, writing, etc.), is first recorded in Locke's *Toleration* (1689-92).

garçon (gȧrsôN′) *n.* boy, waiter. 1788, a French term used in Asa Gray's correspondence, from Old French *garçun, garçion* servant, boy, knave, probably from the accusative of Frankish **wrakjō* exiled warrior, mercenary, with *a* and *r* metathesized to **warkjō;* cognate with Old High German *wreckeo, recko* exile, stranger (modern German *Recke* hero, warrior), and Old English *wrecca* WRETCH, which shows another semantic direction. Proto-Germanic **wrakjōn,* source of the Frankish word, is from Indo-European **wreg-/wrog-* drive, hunt down (Pok.1181).

garden *n.* 1171-83 *gardin,* as part of a surname; borrowed from Old North French *gardin,* from *gart* garden, from Frankish (compare Old High German *garto* garden, modern German *Garten;* related to *gart* enclosure, YARD; cognate with Old Saxon *gard,* Old English *geard,* Old Icelandic *gardhr,* and Gothic *gard-s,* all with the meaning enclosure; the sense of garden is also found in Old Frisian *garda,* Old Saxon *gardo,* and Old High German, see above). **—v.** cultivate a garden. 1577; from the noun. **—gardener** *n.* (1130, as part of a surname in *Cardiner,* later *Gardiner* (1169); borrowed from Old North French **gardinier,* from *gardin* + *-ier* (compare Old High German *gartināri,* modern German *Gärtner*). **—garden gate** (about 1400) **—garden house** (1603, in Shakespeare's *Measure for Measure*) **—garden party** (1869, in Trollope's *Phineas Finn*)

gardenia (gärdēn′yə) *n.* fragrant white flower. 1757, New Latin, formed in allusion to the American physician and naturalist Alexander *Garden.* The term was coined by Linnaeus.

garfish *n.* fish with long, narrow jaws. 1440 *garfysche,* in *Promptorium Parvulorum;* a compound of Old English *gār* spear (with reference to the fish's jaws) + *fisc* FISH; see GARLIC.

gargantuan *adj.* very large. 1596, in Thomas Nashe's *Have With You to Saffron-Walden,* in allusion to *Gargantua* (a large-mouthed, good-natured giant in several novels of French satirist Rabelais); for suffix see -AN. The name is supposed to have appeared in medieval folk tales and been derived from Spanish and Portuguese *garganta* gullet, throat.

gargle *v.* wash or rinse (the throat). 1527 *gargle, gargil;* probably borrowed from Middle French *gargouiller* to gurgle, bubble, and replacing Middle English *gargarisen* (recorded probably before 1425, in an anonymous translation of Chauliac's *Grande Chirurgie*). Middle French *gargouiller* was formed from Old French *gargouille* throat, waterspout, perhaps in turn formed from *garg-,* imitative of sounds made in the throat + **goule,* dialect for mouth, from Latin *gula* throat.

Middle English *gargarisen* was borrowed from Latin *gargarizāre,* from Greek *gargarízein* to gargle, and is related to other words in Middle English pertaining to the throat, such as *gargat* (1130 *Gargate* surname), and *gargage* (about 1450); both meaning throat, and *gargarisme* a gargle (before 1400).

—n. liquid used for gargling. 1657, from the verb.

gargoyle *n.* waterspout on a building in the shape of a grotesque human or animal figure. 1286 *gargurl;* later *gargoille* (1363); borrowed from Old French *gargole, gargouille* throat, waterspout; see GARGLE.

garish *adj.* 1545 *garishe* unpleasantly bright; gaudy; possibly formed from Middle English *gawren* to stare (about 1200), from a Scandinavian source (compare Old Icelandic *gaurr* rough fellow) + *-ish*[1]. The OED cautions that formations of a verb stem with *-ish* are rare, which casts considerable doubt on this etymology.

garland *n.* Probably about 1300 *gerlond;* borrowed from Old French *gerlande, garlande,* perhaps from Frankish **wēron* (compare Middle High German *wieren* adorn, bedeck, which seems a dubious connection). **—v.** Before 1425 *gerlonden;* from the noun.

garlic *n.* About 1150 *garleyc;* later *garlec* (before 1300); developed from Old English *gārlēac* (about 700, in early Mercian glossaries), later *gārlēc* (West Saxon); formed from *gār* spear (with reference to the cloves) + *lēac* LEEK. Old English *gār* is cognate with Old Saxon and Old High German *gēr* spear (modern German *Ger*), Old Icelandic *geirr* (from Proto-Germanic **ʒaizás*), Gaulish *gaiso-,* Greek *chaîos* shepherd's staff, and Sanskrit *héṣas* weapon, from Indo-European **ĝhaisos* (Pok.410). See GORE, also AUGER.

garment *n.* article of clothing. Probably before 1400 *garment,* variant of earlier Middle English *garnement* (probably before 1300, in *Kyng Alisaunder*); borrowed from Old French *garnement,* from *garnir* fit out, provide, adorn; see GARNISH; for suffix see -MENT. **—v.** clothe. Before 1547; from the noun.

garner *v.* gather and store away, collect. Before 1400 (in Scottish) *garner,* from the noun (see below). **—n.** storehouse for grain. Probably before 1200 *gerner,* in *Ancrene Riwle;* later *garner* (before 1325, in *Cursor Mundi*); borrowed from Old French *gernier,* variant of *grenier* storehouse, garret, from Latin *grānārium* granary; see GRANARY.

garnet *n.* hard red mineral. About 1325 *gernet;* later *garnet* (about 1400); borrowed from Old French *grenat* garnet, originally an adjective, of a dark-red color, generally considered a form abstracted as *grenate,* from *pomegrenate* POMEGRANATE. *Garnet,* meaning pomegranate, is recorded in Middle English before 1400 and reference to the color is made as early as 1325.

garnish *v.* Probably about 1380 *garnysen* decorate, adorn; borrowed from Old French *garniss-,* stem of *garnir, guarnir* (older *warnir*) provide, furnish, defend, from a Germanic source (compare Old High German *warnōn* provide, take heed, WARN); for suffix see -ISH[2]. The legal sense of to notify of the attachment of a person's money or property to settle a debt, is first recorded before 1577. The specific meaning of embellish food, is found in Dryden's translation of *Juvenal* (epistles, etc.), in 1693. **—n.** 1393, set of dishes, from the verb. The meaning of things placed on or around food to embellish it, is first recorded in 1673. **—garnishee** *n.* person who holds another's money or property until a settlement is made. 1627, formed from English *garnish,* v. + *-ee.* —*v.* to attach money or property. 1892 from the noun. **—garnishment** *n.* 1550, decoration or adornment; formed from English *garnish,* v. + *-ment.* The legal sense of a notice of attaching money or property, is first recorded in 1585. **—garniture** *n.* 1532, outfit, furniture, equipment; borrowed from Middle French *garniture,* from *garnir* provide, furnish. The sense of decoration or ornament, is first recorded in Dryden's *Maiden Queen* (1667).

garret *n.* space in a house below the roof. Probably about 1300 *garite* watchtower; later extended to attic or loft (1310); borrowed from Old French *garite* watchtower, place of refuge, from *garir* (older *warir*) defend, preserve, keep, from a Germanic source (compare Gothic *warjan* forbid, Old High German *weren,* modern German *wehren* defend, Old English *werian* hold, defend, from Proto-Germanic **warjan*); cognate with Sanskrit *vṛnóti* surrounds, covers, Greek *érysthai* fend off, preserve, from Indo-European **wer-/wor-/wṛ-* (Pok.1160).

garrison *n.* About 1250 *garisoun* treasure, payment; later *garnysons,* pl., body of armed men (1338), and protection, fortress (1410); borrowed from Old French *garison* defense, provisions, from *garir* defend; see GARRET.

The variant Middle English *garnyson* was a separate borrowing from Old French *garnison,* from *garnir* defend; see GARNISH, but its meaning and form were displaced by *garrison* by the 1500's.
—**v.** to station soldiers. 1569, from the noun.

garrote (gərot′) *n.* Spanish method of executing a person by strangulation. 1622, borrowed from Spanish *garrote,* literally, stick for twisting cord, of uncertain origin (possibly from French as evidenced by earlier Old French *garoquier, garochier* to garrote). **—v.** execute by garroting. 1851, from the noun.

garrulous (gar′ələs) *adj.* talking too much. About 1611, in Chapman's translation of the *Iliad;* borrowed from Latin *garrulus* talkative, from *garrīre* to chatter; see CARE; for suffix see -OUS. Possibly also a back formation from *garrulity.* **—garrulity** *n.* 1581 *garrulitie,* borrowed from Middle French *garrulité,* from Latin *garrulitātem* (nominative *garrulitās*), from *garrulus;* for suffix see -ITY.

garter *n.* Before 1325 *garter,* borrowed from Old North French *gartier,* from *garet* bend of the knee, perhaps from Gaulish (compare Welsh *gar, garr* leg, referring to the bone). One of the earliest references in English (about 1353) is to *the Garter* (highest order of English knighthood), according to tradition established by Edward III about 1344. —**v.** fasten with a garter. About 1440 *garteren,* in *Promptorium Parvulorum;* from the noun. **—garter snake** (1769)

gas *n.* 1658, from Dutch *gas,* probably an alteration of Greek *cháos* empty space, CHAOS (since *g* in Dutch represents a sound somewhat like the modern Greek sound transliterated as *ch*). The word was coined by the Flemish physician and chemist Van Helmont (1577-1644), who used it in the sense of an occult principle supposedly present in all bodies. The use may have been suggested by the Swiss-born physician and alchemist Paracelsus (1493-1541) who used Greek *cháos* in the sense of proper element of spirits such as gnomes. The current technical sense of any fluid substance that can expand without limit (as air), is first recorded in 1779. Later, as experiment developed knowledge, meanings were specialized to include a mixture of gases that can be burned for fuel, light, etc. (1794), gas used as an anesthetic (1894), and poison gas used in warfare (1900). **—v.** to poison by gas. 1889, from the noun. **—gaseous** *adj.* 1799, formed from English *gas,* n. + *-eous,* form of *-ous.*

gash *n.* 1548 *gashe,* alteration of earlier *garsshe,* in Palsgrave's *Lesclarcissement* (1530), from Middle English *garce* (probably before 1200, in *Ancrene Riwle*); borrowed from Old French **garse,* from Old North French *garser* to scarify, wound, apparently from Vulgar Latin **charassāre,* from Greek *charássein* engrave; see CHARACTER. **—v.** 1570 *gashe,* alteration of Middle English *garsen* (before 1398, in Trevisa's translation of Bartholomew's *De Proprietatibus Rerum*); borrowed from Old North French *garser* to scarify.

The loss of *r* during Middle and early modern English is characteristic of a sizable group of words, including *bass* (Middle English *barse*), *dace* (Middle English *darse*), *bust* break (Middle English *burst*), etc., in which the final consonant sound or sounds influenced the elimination of the preceding r-sound, and a relaxing of the preceding vowel (as in *gash* for *garce*) or a lengthening of that vowel (as in *dace* for *darse*). Sometimes the lengthening preceded the loss of *r,* and may have even contributed to the process of eliminating the r-sound in the pronunciation, but whatever happened to the vowel, the loss of *r* is first seen before *s* and *sh* as a long definite historical process in English which is reflected in the spelling changes of Middle and early modern English.

gasket *n.* (originally) plaited hemp, etc. used for packing a piston, pipe joint, etc. 1622 *caskette* small rope or plaited coil used to secure a sail, later *gassit* (1626), and *gasket* (1630); of uncertain origin. Italian *gaschetta* has a similar sense, but is not found before the 1800's, which suggests that it was probably formed separately or even borrowed from English. French *garcette,* meaning a small cord or rope, is attested only since 1643 and its form and the earliest English form *caskette* are incongruous. This does not, however, preclude English from having adopted the French form only four years after the word is first recorded in English. *Gasket* meaning a packing to seal metal joints is first recorded in 1829.

gasohol (gas′əhôl) *n.* mixture of gasoline and alcohol, used as fuel for internal-combustion engines. 1974, American English; formed from *gas(oline)* + *(alc)ohol.* First developed in the 1930's and sold in the U.S. Midwest as Agrol, from *agri(cultural) (alco)hol,* the mixture under its new name became a trademark.

gasoline *n.* 1865 *gasolene;* later *gasoline* (1871), American English; formed from *gas* + *-ol* (from Latin *oleum* OIL) + *-ene,* variant of *-ine*[2] (chemical suffix). The shortened form *gas* is first recorded in 1905, and the compound *gas station* in 1932 (earlier, in *gas-filling* station, 1925).

gasp *v.* Before 1393 *gaspen,* in Gower's *Confessio Amantis,* of uncertain origin. **—n.** 1577, from the verb.

It is suggested by most sources that *gasp* is a borrowing from the Scandinavian, perhaps Old Icelandic *geispa* to yawn (Danish *gispe* gasp, Norwegian *giespe* yawn, Swedish *gäspa*). This is hard to establish because the spelling *gasp* is so firmly fixed from its original appearance in English.

gastric *adj.* of or near the stomach. 1656, formed in English from Greek *gastḗr* (genitive *gastrós*) stomach

+ English suffix *-ic*. **—gastric juice** (1730-36, in an edition of Bailey's *Dictionary*)

gastro- or **gastr-** (before vowels) a combining form meaning stomach, as in *gastrovascular, gastroenteritis* (inflammation of the enteric membrane lining the stomach and intestines), *gastrectomy* (surgery or cutting of the stomach). Borrowed from Greek *gastro-*, combining form of *gastḗr* (genitive *gastrós*) stomach, earlier **grastḗr* "the eater," from *grân* to devour; cognate with Sanskrit *grásate* swallows, from Indo-European **gres-/gr̥s-* (Pok.404).

gastronomy *n.* art or science of good eating. 1814, borrowed from French *gastronomie,* from Greek *gastronomíā,* from *gastronómos* one who arranges or prepares food, literally, prepares for the stomach (*gastḗr,* genitive *gastrós* stomach + *-nómos* arranging, regulating), on analogy with words such as *astronomíā* astronomy. Greek *gastronomíā* (or *gastrologíā*) was the title of a Greek poem about gastronomy written by Archestratos, a contemporary of Aristotle. **—gastronomic** *adj.* 1828, borrowed from French *gastronomique,* from *gastronomie* gastronomy.

gastropod (gas′trəpod) *n.* mollusk with a disklike organ for locomotion. 1854, earlier *gasteropod* (1826); borrowed from New Latin *Gasteropoda, Gastropoda,* pl., the name of this class of mollusks (from Greek *gastḗr,* genitive *gastrós* stomach + *poús,* genitive *podós* FOOT; so called from the ventral position of its "foot" or locomotive organ). The class name *Gasteropoda, Gastropoda* was offered by the French naturalist Cuvier. **—adj.** 1836-39, of such mollusks; from the noun.

gastrula (gas′trůlə) *n.* developmental stage in which an embryo is usually saclike. 1877, New Latin *gastrula* (from Greek *gastḗr,* genitive *gastrós* stomach + Latin *-ula,* diminutive suffix). The term was coined by the German biologist Emil Haeckel.

gat *n. Slang.* revolver or pistol. 1904, American English, transferred use of the shortened form *gatling* in *Gatling gun* (1867).

gate *n.* About 1200 *gate,* in *The Ormulum;* developed from Old English *gæt* (about 700), and *geat, get,* pl. *geatu, gatu* (778); cognate with Old Frisian *gat, jet* hole, opening, Old Saxon *gat* eye of a needle, hole, Low German and modern Dutch *gat* gap, hole, breach, and Old Icelandic *gat* opening, passage; from Proto-Germanic**ʒatan,* cognate with Sanskrit *hadati* defecates, Armenian *jet* tail (of animals), Greek *chézein* (perfect *-kéchode*) defecate, from Indo-European* *ĝhed-/ĝhod-* hole; defecate (Pok.423).

The modern form of the word, with *g,* was re-formed through Middle English from the Old English plural; otherwise regular derivation from the singular would have produced **yet* or **yat.*

—gatepost *n.* (1522) **—gateway** *n.* (1707)

-gate a combining form meaning scandal, as in *Koreagate, laborgate* (1973, used chiefly in allusion to the *Watergate* scandal of corruption and cover-up in the Nixon administration).

gather *v.* 1137 *gaderen* come together, accumulate; developed from Old English *gadrian, gædrian* (probably about 750, in *Phoenix* and *Andreas*); cognate with Old Frisian *gaderia* to gather, Frisian *gearjen,* Middle Dutch *gaderen* (modern Dutch *garen*), Middle Low German *gadderen* to gather, Middle High German *gatern* unite; related to Old English *gæd* fellowship, *gada* companion, and *gōd* GOOD. *Gather, together, father, weather,* and similar words, were spelled with a *d* until the 1500's; the change to *th* reflected a change in pronunciation that occurred in most of the English dialects of the 1500's. **—gathering** *n.* 1137 *gadering* a meeting, assembly; developed from Old English *gædering* (1050-1175); from the verb.

Gatling gun early type of machine gun. 1867, American English, in allusion to its inventor R.J. *Gatling,* who, in 1862, patented this gun, which was first used to a limited extent in the American Civil War.

gauche (gōsh) *adj.* awkward, tactless. 1751, in Lord Chesterfield's correspondence; borrowed from French *gauche* left (originally, awkward, awry), from Middle French *gauchir* turn aside, swerve, from Old French *gaucher, gauchier* trample, reel, walk clumsily, from Frankish **walkan* (compare German *walken* to full (cloth); see WALK. **—gaucherie** *n.* awkwardness. 1798, borrowed from French *gauche,* from *gauche* awkward; for suffix compare -ERY.

gaucho (gou′chō) *n.* cowboy in the southern plains of South America. 1824, American Spanish, borrowed from Arawakan *cachu* comrade; or perhaps borrowed from Colombian Spanish *guacho* orphan, from Quechua *wáh̩ča* orphan, poor.

gaudy *adj.* 1583, showy, tastelessly fine; earlier, deceptive, full of trickery (before 1529); formed from English *gaud,* n. (1333 *gaude* deception or trick; later, ornament or rosary bead, 1361; possibly borrowed from Anglo-French *gaudir* be merry, from Latin *gaudēre* rejoice) + *-y*[1]; see JOY.

The noun use of *gaudy* is first recorded with the meaning of rosary (1380); its later meaning of a feast or festival, usually marked by pranks or frivolity (1561), is sometimes found in literature with reference to a feast or commemoration of some college event at Oxford or Cambridge.

gauge or **gage** (gāj) *v.* measure accurately. 1440 *gawgen,* in *Promptorium Parvulorum;* borrowed through Anglo-French *gauge,* from Old North French *gauger,* from *gauge* gauging rod, perhaps from Gallo-Romance *galga,* collective plural of Frankish **galgo* (compare Old High German *galgo* rod, GALLOWS). An earlier use in the phrase *gauge over* tower over something, is recorded before 1400. **—n.** About 1432, standard measure; earlier, in a surname *Gageman* (1332); from Old North French *gauge* gauging rod.

The spelling variants *gauge* and *gage* have existed since the first recorded uses in Middle English, though in American English *gage* is used exclusively in some technical uses and especially in technical uses of the verb.

gaunt *adj.* thin and bony. 1440 *gawnt,* in *Promptorium Parvulorum;* earlier probably a surname, especially in Anglo-French *le Gant* (1247); borrowed from Middle French *gant,* of uncertain origin. Originally, the English etymologist Skeat assigned the word an indeterminate Scandinavian source, comparing Norwegian *gand* thin pole, but this does not fit the early surnames in Middle English, nor account for the shift in pronunciation or spelling.

gauntlet[1] (gônt′lit) *n.* iron or steel glove that was part of a knight's armor. Probably before 1425 *gantelet,* in a translation of Higden's *Polychronicon;* borrowed from Middle French *gantelet,* semi-diminutive of *gant* glove, from Frankish **want,* from Proto-Germanic **wantuz* (compare Old Swedish *vanter* glove, Swedish and Danish *vante* mitten, glove, and Old Icelandic *vǫttr* glove, Norwegian *vott* mitten); for suffix see -LET. Middle Dutch is not considered a source, as *want* mitten was probably borrowed from Old French or another Romance language (Spanish or Portuguese *guante,* Italian *guanto,* etc.) that took the word from Germanic.

The spelling with *u* appears as a variant in Middle English but did not become firmly established until the 1500's.

The phrase *throw down the gauntlet* give a challenge, from the stated medieval custom of throwing down a glove when challenging an opponent, is not recorded in English before 1548.

gauntlet[2] or **gantlet** (gônt′lit) *n.* punishment in which the offender runs between two rows of men who strike him with weapons. 1661, in the phrase *run the gantlet,* alteration of earlier *gantlope* (1646); borrowed from Swedish *gatlopp,* probably by English soldiers who fought along with Swedish military forces during the Thirty Years' War. Swedish *gatlopp* is a compound of Old Swedish *gata* lane and *lopp* course, from Middle Low German *lōp* (cognate with Middle Dutch *lōpen* to run); see GAIT and LOPE. The gradual shift from *gantlope* to *gauntlet* (influenced by *gauntlet*[1]) did not become fixed until the mid-1800's.

gauss (gous), *n. Physics.* unit of magnetic induction. 1882, unit of magnetic field strength (later called an *oersted*); in allusion to the German mathematician Karl *Gauss.* The name was proposed by the British physicist S.P. Thompson.

gauze *n.* 1688 *gawse;* earlier *gais* (1561); borrowed from French *gaze,* possibly through Spanish *gasa,* apparently from Arabic *qazz* raw silk, from Persian *kāz, gāz,* perhaps of Eastern origin (compare Hindi *gazī* thin, coarse cotton cloth). **—gauzy** *adj.* 1774, formed from English *gauze* + *-y*[1].

gavel *n.* small mallet used to signal attention or order. 1805, American English, of unknown origin. **—v.** hammer (with a gavel). 1925, in Dreiser's *American Tragedy,* American English; from the noun.

gavotte or **gavot** (gəvot′) *n.* lively dance somewhat like a minuet but livelier. 1696 *gavote,* borrowing of French *gavotte,* from Provençal *gavoto* mountaineer's dance, from *gavot* an Alpine inhabitant, apparently from *gava* gullet, crop of a bird, probably from pre-Latin **gaba* goiter, throat.

gawk *v.* stare rudely or stupidly. 1785 *gawk,* perhaps an alteration of obsolete *gaw,* Middle English *gowen* to stare (probably about 1200, in *The Ormulum*); borrowed from a Scandinavian source (compare Old Icelandic *gā* to heed). The alteration from *gaw* to *gawk* may have been influenced by *gawk hand* left hand (1703, in reference to the unusual and therefore clumsy look of things done with the left hand). *Gawk hand* is a contraction of dialectal (northern England) *gaulick, gaulish hand,* and whether the *-k* ending of the many other verbs in English such as *talk, walk* and *caulk,* might account for the alteration in spelling is unknown. **—n.** awkward person. 1837, from the verb. **—gawky** *adj.* 1759, perhaps from English *gawk* (in *gawk hand*) + *-y*[1].

gay *adj.* Probably about 1300, splendid or beautiful; earlier, as a surname (1178); borrowed from Old French *gai* gay, merry; perhaps from Frankish (compare Old High German *gāhi* rapid, impetuous, modern German *jäh* hasty, sudden). The meaning of joyous or merry appeared probably about 1380. The slang sense of homosexual is first recorded in 1951, apparently shortened from an earlier compound *gay cat* homosexual boy (about 1935, in underworld and prison slang), but used earlier for a young tramp or hobo, often one attached to an older tramp and usually with a connotation of homosexuality (1897, in American English slang). **—n.** a homosexual. 1971, American English; from *gay,* adj.; re-development of earlier *gay,* n. excellent, gallant, or fair person (probably about 1380; also from the adjective). **—gaiety** *n.* 1634 merrymaking; later cheerfulness, mirth (1647); borrowed from French *gaieté,* from *gai* + *-eté* -ity.**—gaily** *adv.* Before 1375, formed from Middle English *gai* + *-li* -ly[1].

gaze *v.* About 1395 *gazen* to stare, in Chaucer's *Canterbury Tales;* probably borrowed from a Scandinavian source (compare dialectal Swedish *gasa* to stare, gape). **—n.** 1542, something which is stared at; later, a long, steady look (1566); from the verb.

gazebo (gəzē′bō) *n.* summerhouse or turret on the roof of a house, often having six or eight sides and a fine view. 1752, supposedly derived from *gaze,* on the pattern of Latin future tenses in *-bo,* such as *vidēbō* I shall see, *placēbō* I shall please; but the earliest quotation of *gazebo* calls it a Chinese Tower, suggesting an altered form of an Oriental word.

gazelle *n.* small, graceful antelope. 1600, borrowed from French *gazelle,* from Old French *gazel,* from Arabic *ghazāl.*

gazette *n.* newspaper. 1605, borrowed from French *gazette,* from Italian *gazzetta,* from Venetian dialect *gazeta* newspaper (originally a small coin); for suffix see -ETTE. The *gazeta* was first published in Venice in the mid-1500's, and was possibly so called from the price of the paper, but the Romance scholar Corominas says that Italian *gazetta* has the meaning of little magpie and that the term was applied by association. **—v.** announce or name in an official gazette. 1678, in Marvell's writings; from the noun. **—gazetteer** *n.* 1611, journalist, in Donne's poetry; probably from French *gazetier* (earlier *gazettier*), from *gazette* newspaper. The meaning of a geographical index, is found in Echard's *The Gazetteer's or Newsman's Interpreter* (1704).

gear *n.* Probably before 1200 *gære* equipment, arms, apparatus, in Layamon's *Chronicle of Britain* (about 1250); borrowed from a Scandinavian source (compare Old Icelandic *gervi, gǫrvi* apparel, related to *gerr* ready, *gerva* make ready); cognate with Old High German *garawi, garwi* adornment, *garawen* make ready, Old Saxon *garewi* apparel, *gėrwian* make ready. The meaning of mechanical wheels with interlocking teeth in machinery is first recorded in 1523. **—v.** Probably before 1200 *geren* equip oneself for fighting; dress (also in Layamon's *Chronicle of Britain*); probably from the noun. The meaning of to mesh, fit together, be in gear, is first recorded in 1734.

geezer *n. Slang.* odd person, now usually an old man, but earlier chiefly applied to old women. 1885, probably an alteration of Scottish and Northern English dialect *gysar* mummer, masquerader (1488), from Middle English *gysen* to dress (about 1399) developed from earlier *gyse* style, attire, in *Kyng Alisaunder; gise,* in *Arthour and Merlin,* both recorded about 1300 and meaning style, attire; borrowed from Old French *guise* GUISE.

Geiger counter (gī′gər) device which detects radioactivity by counting ionizing particles. 1924, in allusion to its inventor, the German physicist Hans *Geiger,* and earlier *Geiger-Müller counter,* in reference to its co-inventor, W. *Müller.*

geisha (gā′shə) *n.* Japanese girl trained to be a professional entertainer and companion for men. 1887, borrowing of Japanese *geisha,* literally, person accomplished in the social arts (*gei* art, performance + *sha* society).

gel (jel) *n.* jellylike or semisolid material. 1899, shortened form of *gelatin;* perhaps influenced by earlier *jell* (1870) jelly. **—v.** form a gel. 1917, from the noun.

gelatine (jel′ətən) *n.* 1713, jellylike substance; later *gelatin* substance obtained by boiling animal tissues, bones, etc. (1800); in part, borrowed from French *gélatine* clear jellylike substance, fish broth, from Italian *gelatina* (*gelata* jelly, from *gelare* to jell, from Latin *gelāre* freeze, from *gelū* frost; see COLD + *-ina* -ine²), and in part formed from Latin model **gelātinus* jellylike, from **gelāta* jelly, from *gelāre* freeze, with the sense of congeal. **—gelatinous** (jəlat′ənəs) *adj.* 1724, in Bailey's *Dictionary,* formed from English *gelatine* + *-ous* after French *gélatineux,* from *gélatine.*

geld *v.* remove the male glands of an animal. About 1300 *gelden,* borrowed from a Scandinavian source (compare Old Icelandic *gelda* castrate, from *geldr* barren; cognate with Old High German *galt* barren, *galza, gelza* castrated swine, Middle Low German *gelde* barren); cognate with Sanskrit *huḍa-s* wether, from Indo-European **ĝhol-/ĝhl̥-* cut (Pok.434). **—gelding** *n.* castrated animal. Before 1382 *geldynge* a gelded man, in the Wycliffe Bible; earlier, in the surname *Geldyng* (1296); borrowed from a Scandinavian source (compare Old Icelandic *geldingr,* from *gelda* castrate).

gem *n.* Before 1300 *gemme* precious stone; also figuratively, precious thing, and later, bud or sprout (before 1382); borrowed from Old French *gemme,* a learned borrowing from Latin *gemma* precious stone, jewel, bud; cognate with Lithuanian *žémbėti* to bud, and Sanskrit *jámbha-s* tooth, from Indo-European **gembh-* bite (Pok.369). Middle English inherited another form *gymme* (recorded probably before 1200); developed from Old English *gim* (recorded about 750 and pronounced as if *yim*), also borrowed from Latin *gemma,* but this latter Middle English form disappeared in the early 1300's. **—v.** adorn with gems. 1610, from the noun. An earlier meaning "put forth buds" is recorded about 1150, but this was a separate and earlier formation on the Old English *gim,* n. **—gemstone** *n.* (about 1000)

-gen a combining form meaning something that produces or causes, as in *allergen, antigen, collagen, estrogen, nitrogen,* etc. Borrowed from French *-gène,* from Greek *-genḗs* born, from *génos* birth, from Indo-European *ĝénos* (Pok. 375).

gendarme (zhän′därm) *n.* (in France and other, chiefly French-speaking, countries) policeman, usually a soldier charged with maintaining order. About 1550 *gentzdarmes* armed cavalryman; also *gendarme* (1688); borrowed from French *gendarme,* new singular formed from Old French *gens d'armes* men of arms (*gens* men, people, from Latin *gentēs,* plural of *gēns* race; see GENTLE + *d'armes* of arms).

gender *n.* Probably about 1350, grammatical class referring to nouns and pronouns; later, referring to verbs (about 1450). The sense of kind, sort, class of individuals or things, is first recorded in 1378 as *gendre,* in a version of *Piers Plowman;* all borrowed from Old French *genre, gendre,* learned borrowing from the stem of Latin *genus* (genitive *generis*) kind, sort, gender (translating Greek *génos,* so used by Aristotle); see GENUS.

gene (jēn) *n. Biology.* part of a cell that transmits hereditary characteristics. 1911, borrowed from Greek *geneá* generation, race; see KIN. The word was originally introduced as German *Gen* in 1909 by the Danish botanist and geneticist, Wilhelm Johannsen, who also proposed the English form *gene* and suggested the word as a combining form. See also GENOTYPE.

genealogy (jē′nēal′əjē) *n.* Before 1325 *geneologi* account of the descent of a person or family, in *Cursor Mundi;* borrowed through Old French *genealogie,* from Late Latin *geneālogia* tracing of a family, from Greek *geneālogíā* (*geneá* generation, race, descent + *-lógos* student of; see -LOGY). **—genealogical** *adj.* 1577, formed in English from Middle French *généalogique* (from Old French *genealogie* genealogy) + English suffix *-al*¹; replacing earlier *genealogyal* (1447).

general *adj.* Probably before 1200, in *Ancrene Riwle;* borrowed from Old French *general* or directly from Latin *generālis* relating to all, of a whole class, from *genus* (genitive *generis*) stock, kind, GENUS; for suffix see -AL¹.

Apparently the sense of *general* pertaining to all, gained prominence in Latin, and thence probably in Western Europe, as a part of the Aristotelian vocabulary (including *genus* and *species*) which was the result of the new medieval studies of Greek philosophical thought, first of Aristotle and then of other Greek and early Roman philosophers, and of their study of the sciences or natural phenomena.

—n. About 1380, a whole class of things or people, in Chaucer's translation of Boethius' *De Consolatione Philosophiae;* probably from the adjective. The meaning of commander of an army, is first recorded in 1576; borrowed from Middle French *général,* from Italian *generale,* from *generale,* adj., relating to all, general, from Latin *generālis.*

—generality *n.* Probably about 1378 *generalte,* in Wycliffe's writings; borrowed from Latin *generālitātem* (nominative *generālitās*), from *generālis* general; see GENERAL, adj. The later *generalitee* (1425) was borrowed from Middle French *généralité,* from *général* general, see GENERAL, n.; for suffix see -ITY. **—generalization** *n.* 1761, in Adam Smith's writings; formed from English *generalize* + *-ation.* **—generalize** *v.* Before 1751; re-formed from *general,* adj. + *-ize;* earlier *generalisen* (before 1425), probably also formed in English, as the French *généraliser* is not found before 1578. **—generally** *adv.* 1340, in *Ayenbite of Inwyt;* formed from English *general* + *-ly*¹.

generalissimo (jen′ərəlis′əmō) *n.* military commander in chief. 1621, borrowing of Italian *generalissimo,* superlative of *generale* commander of an entire army, general; see GENERAL, n.

generation *n.* Before 1325 *generacion* offspring, descendant, in *Cursor Mundi;* borrowed through Old French *generacion* and directly from Latin *generātiōnem* (nominative *generātiō*), from *generāre* bring forth; see GENERATE; for suffix see -ATION. The sense of a group of descendants of one family or of one period of time, is first recorded also in *Cursor Mundi* (before 1325). **—generate** *v.* 1509, probably a back formation from earlier *generation;* and, in some instances, either developed from English *generate,* adj. (probably before 1425), or borrowed directly from Latin *generātus,* past participle of *generāre* bring forth, beget, produce, create, from *genus* (genitive *generis*) kind, race, GENUS. **—generative** *adj.* Before 1398, in Trevisa's translation of Bartholomew's *De Proprietatibus Rerum;* borrowed from Late Latin *generātīvus,* from Latin *generātus,* past participle of *generāre;* for suffix see -ATIVE. **—generator** *n.* 1646, person or thing that generates, borrowed from Latin *generātor,* from *generāre;* for suffix see -OR². The meaning of a machine that generates, is first recorded in 1794, and a machine that generates electric energy, in 1879.

generic *adj.* 1676, belonging to a kind or class, general; formed in English from Latin *gener-,* stem of *genus* kind + English suffix *-ic.* The noun use is first recorded in English in 1807.

generous *adj.* 1588, of noble birth, magnanimous, in Shakespeare's *Love's Labour's Lost;* borrowed through Middle French *généreux,* or directly from Latin *generōsus* of noble birth, from *genus* (genitive *generis*) race, stock, GENUS; for suffix see -OUS. The sense of bountiful, lavish, liberal, is first recorded in English in 1696, probably from earlier French. The extended meaning of copious, abundant, ample (as in *a generous helping of food*), is found in English in 1615. **—generosity** *n.* Probably before 1425 *generosite* excellence, nobility, in a translation of Higden's *Polychronicon;* borrowed from Latin *generōsitātem* (nominative *generōsitās*), from *generōsus* of noble birth; for suffix see -ITY. The sense of magnanimity, is first recorded in 1623.

genesis (jen′əsis) *n.* Old English (before 1000) *Genesis* first book of Old Testament containing an account of creation; borrowing of Latin *Genesis,* from Greek *génesis* origin, creation, generation, from *gígnesthai* be born; see KIN. The general meaning of origin, creation, inception, beginning, is first recorded in Cawdrey's *A Table Alphabeticall* (1604).

genetic (jənet′ik) *adj.* 1831, pertaining to origin, in Carlyle's Essays: *Early German Literature;* borrowed from Greek *genetikós* genitive, from *génesis* origin; for suffix see -IC. The biological sense of having to do with origin and natural growth is first recorded in Darwin's *On the Origin of Species* (1859). **—geneticist** *n.* 1913, formed from English *genetic* + *-ist.* **—genetics** *n.* 1872, laws of origination; formed from English *genetic* + *-s,* on the pattern of *esthetics,* etc. The sense of the principles or study of heredity and variation was introduced in 1905 by the English naturalist William Bateson.

genial *adj.* 1566, nuptial, generative; later, conducive to growth (1647); borrowed from Latin *geniālis* genial, pleasant, festive (literally, pertaining to marriage rites), from *genius* guardian spirit; see GENIUS; for suffix see -AL¹. The meaning of pleasant, cheerful and friendly, is first recorded in Smollett's *Reproof* (1746). **—geniality** *n.* 1609, festivity; formed from English *genial* + *-ity.* The sense of cheerfulness is first recorded in 1652.

-genic a combining form of adjectives meaning producing or tending to produce, as in *carcinogenic* (producing carcinogens or substances that can cause cancer), *pathogenic;* or well-suited to reproduction or dissemination, as in *photogenic.* Formed from English *-gen* + *-ic.*

genie (jē′nē) *n.* 1655 *geny* guardian spirit; borrowed from French *génie,* learned borrowing from Latin *genius* GENIUS. The extension of meaning to the powerful spirit of Moslem mythology, appeared in Smollett's *Adventures of Roderick Random* (1748) and came into English from French *génie,* used by translators of *The Arabian Nights* to render the Arabic word *jinnī,* pl. *jinn* spirit; see JINN.

genital *adj.* having to do with reproduction or the sex organs. Before 1382 *genytale* pertaining to animal generation, in the Wycliffe Bible; borrowed through Old French *genital,* or directly from Latin *genitālis* pertaining to generation or birth, from a lost noun **geneta* (compare Greek *genetḗ* birth), related to *gignere* beget, produce; see KIN; for suffix see -AL¹. **—n. genitals** *pl.* Before 1393, in Gower's *Confessio Amantis,* formed from English *genital,* adj. + *-s.*

genitive *adj.* case in grammar showing possession, source, or origin; in English, the possessive case. Before 1398 *genityf,* in Trevisa's translation of Bartholomew's *De Proprietatibus Rerum;* borrowed through Old French *genitif* (feminine *genitive*), or directly from Latin *cāsus genitīvus* genitive case (expressing origin), from a lost noun **geneta* birth, related to *gignere* beget, produce, originate; see KIN. Latin *cāsus genitīvus* was a mistranslation of Greek *ptôsis genikḗ* general or generic case (now interpreted as the case of dependence of one noun on another, as in *urbis* in the phrase *nōmen urbis* the name of the city).

genius *n.* Before 1393 *genius* protective, guiding spirit within each person at birth, guardian spirit, in Gower's *Confessio Amantis;* borrowed from Latin *genius* guardian deity or spirit, inclination, wit, talent, from the root of *gignere* beget, produce; see KIN. The old sense of a person's inclination or characteristic disposition, which appears in Sidney's *Apology for Poetry* (1581), developed into the meaning of a person endowed with natural ability or talent, and also the sense of natural ability, quality of mind, in Milton's *Iconoclastes* (1649).

genocide (jen′əsīd) *n.* systematic extermination of a cultural or racial group. 1944, formed in American English, from Greek *génos* race, kind + English *-cide*². The word was coined by the American jurist Raphael Lemkin, in reference to the extermination of Jews under the Nazis in World War II. **—genocidal** *adj.* 1948, formed from English *genocide* + *-al*¹.

genotype (jen′ətīp) *n.* genetic makeup of an organism. 1910, borrowed from German *Genotypus,* from Greek *génos* race, kind + German *Typus* type (from Latin *typus,* from Greek *týpos* form, stamp). The term was coined by Wilhelm Johannsen; see GENE.

genre (zhäN′rə) *n.* kind, sort, style. 1816, borrowed from French *genre,* from Old French; see GENDER. The sense of a style of painting depicting ordinary life, is first recorded in 1849.

genteel *adj.* belonging or suited to polite society. 1599 *gentile* stylish, fashionably elegant, in Ben Jonson's *Cynthia's Revels;* borrowed from Middle French *gentil* nice, graceful, pleasing, from Old French, high-born, noble; see GENTLE. The form *genteel* represents a reborrowing from French. The earlier borrowing of Old French *gentil,* in the 1200's is the source of modern English GENTLE and JAUNTY.

gentian (jen′shən) *n.* plant with funnel-shaped flowers. 1373 *gencyan;* borrowed possibly through Old French *genciane,* and directly from Latin *gentiāna,* said by

Pliny to be used in allusion to *Gentius,* a king of ancient Illyria.

gentile or **Gentile** *n.* person who is not a Jew. Found earliest in a surname (1160), but recorded first in literature before 1382, one who is not a Christian, a pagan, in the Wycliffe Bible; confused in Middle English with *Gentle* one who is not a Jew (probably 1384); both forms borrowed from (ecclesiastical) Late Latin *gentīlis* foreign, heathen, pagan, from Latin *gentīlis* person belonging to the same family, fellow countryman, from *gentīlis,* adj., of the same family or clan, from *gēns* (genitive *gentis*) race, clan; see also GENTLE. The Late Latin *gentīlēs,* from *gentīlis* was used to translate Greek *ethnikós,* referring to *tà éthnē* the nations, and in turn translating Hebrew *ha goyim* the (non-Jewish) nations. **—adj.** not Jewish. Probably about 1380, pagan or heathen; borrowed from Late Latin *gentīlis* foreign, heathen, from Latin, of the same family or clan. The specific meaning of not Jewish, is possibly first recorded about 1400, though the MED cites the same quotation as an instance of the noun.

gentility *n.* 1340, in *Ayenbite of Inwyt;* borrowed from Old French *gentilité,* and directly from Latin *gentīlitās* relationship in the same family or clan, from *gentīlis;* see GENTLE, GENTILE; for suffix see -ITY.

gentle *adj.* Probably before 1200 *gentile* noble, of a good family, in *Ancrene Riwle;* borrowed from Old French *gentil* high-born, noble, from Latin *gentīlis* of the same family or clan, from *gēns* (genitive *gentis*) race, clan, from the root of *gignere* beget; see KIN. *Gentle* in the sense of kind, gracious, etc., is first recorded about 1280. **—gentleman** *n.* Probably before 1200, wellborn man; formed from English *gentle* + *man;* see also GENTILE. The meaning of a well-bred man, is first recorded in *The Proverbs of Alfred* (probably about 1150).

gentry *n.* About 1303 *gentry* nobility of rank or birth, in Mannyng's *Handlyng Synne;* borrowed from Old French *genterie,* or perhaps an alteration of earlier *genterise, gentrice* (recorded before 1225); borrowed from Old French *genterise,* variant of *gentilise, gentillise* noble birth, gentleness, from *gentil;* see GENTLE. **—gentrification** *n.* 1977, formed from English *gentrify,* on the analogy of such pairs as *qualify, qualification.* **—gentrify** *v.* to increase the real-estate value of a neighborhood by converting a poor area into one of more expensive housing. 1973, formed from English *gentry* + *-fy.*

genuflect (jen′yůflekt) *v.* bend the knee in reverence or worship. 1630, back formation from earlier *genuflection,* modeled on Late Latin *genūflectere* (Latin *genū* KNEE + *flectere* to bend; see FLEX). **—genuflection** *n.* Probably about 1425 *genufleccion;* borrowed possibly through Middle French *génuflexion,* and directly from Late Latin *genūflexiōnem* (nominative *genūflexiō*), from stem of *genūflectere* genuflect.

genuine *adj.* 1596, natural, not foreign, native; borrowed from Latin *genuīnus* native, natural (perhaps influenced in stem by *ingenuus* native, freeborn, upright, and in formation by contrasting *adulterīnus* spurious); from the root of *gignere* beget; see KIN. It is appealing to make a connection with Latin *genū* knee, but no semantic connection can be made that will withstand close examination.

genus (jē′nəs) *n., pl.* **genera** (jen′ərə). kind, sort, class. 1551, kind or class of things, in logic; borrowed from Latin *genus* (genitive *generis*) race, stock, kind; cognate with Greek *génos* race, kind, and *gónos* birth, offspring, stock; see KIN. *Genus* as used to classify distinct groups of plants and animals, is first recorded in 1608.

geo- a combining form meaning earth, as in *geography, geocentric* from the earth's center; or geographical, as in *geopolitics.* Borrowed through French and Latin, from Greek *geō-,* combining form (as in *geōmetríā* geometry) of *gê* earth, from earlier **gē-o-.* The Greek word *gê,* Doric *gâ,* is of unknown origin.

geocentric *adj.* 1686, implied earlier in the noun (1667, adherent of the geocentric theory); formed from English *geo-* + *centric.*

geodesy (jēod′əsē) *n.* 1570 *geodesie* surveying; borrowed from New Latin *geodaesia,* from Greek *geōdaisíā* division of the earth (ultimately from *gê* earth, land + *daíein* divide, related to *daíesthai* distribute; see TIDE). *Geodesy* meaning mathematical calculation of large portions of the earth and the whole earth, is first recorded in 1853. **—geodesic** *adj.* 1821, formed from English *geodesy* + *-ic.* **—geodetic** *adj.* 1834, formed from English *geodesy,* on the analogy of such pairs as *heresy, heretic.*

geography *n.* 1542, in Udall's translation of Erasmus' *Apothegms;* borrowed from Latin *geōgraphia,* from Greek *geōgraphíā* description of the earth's surface (*gê* earth, land, ground + *-graphíā* description, from *gráphein* write, mark; see CARVE). In some instances *geography* may also have been borrowed from Middle French *géographie.* **—geographic** *adj.* 1630, a shortened form of earlier *geographical,* possibly, in some instances, borrowed from Middle French *géographique.* **—geographical** *adj.* 1559, from Late Latin *geōgraphicus* (from Greek *geōgraphikós,* from *geōgraphíā* geography) + English *-al*[1].

geology *n.* 1735, study of the earth; borrowed from New Latin *geologia,* from Medieval Latin, study of earthly things, from Greek *gê* earth, land, ground + *-logíā,* from *-lógos* one treating of; see -LOGY.

The specific sense of the study of the earth's crust, was popularized in James Hutton's *Theory of the Earth,* which appeared in 1795, and by works in Italian, which is what may have prompted the French scholar Dauzat to believe the word was created in Italian. **—geological** *adj.* 1795, formed from English *geology* + *-ical.* **—geologist** *n.* 1795, formed from English *geology* + *-ist.*

geometry *n.* About 1330 *geometrie,* borrowed from Old French *géométrie,* from Latin *geōmetria,* from Greek *geōmetríā* measurement of earth or land, geometry (*gê* earth, land, ground + *-metríā,* from *metreîn* to measure, from *métron* MEASURE). **—geometric** *adj.* 1630, shortened form of earlier English *geometrical.* **—geometrical** *adj.* 1392, formed in English from Latin *geōmetricus,* from Greek *geōmetrikós,* from *geōmétrēs* geometrician, land measurer (*gê* earth + *metreîn* to measure) + English suffix *-al*[1].

geotropism *n. Biology.* response by plants to gravity. 1875, borrowed from German *Geotropismus,* from Greek *gê* earth + *tropḗ* a turning (see TROPE) + *-ismós* -ism. The term was coined by the German botanist A.B. Frank.

geranium *n.* plant with clusters of showy flowers. 1548, borrowing of Latin *geranium,* the plant name, from Greek *geránion* the plant name (diminutive of *géranos*

CRANE, so called from the supposed resemblance of the seed pod to the bill of a crane).

gerbil (jėr′bəl) *n.* small rodent often kept as a pet. 1849 *gerbille,* borrowing of French, from New Latin *Gerbillus* the genus name (literally, little jerboa; *gerbo,* variant of *jerboa* JERBOA + *-il* -le[1]).

geriatrics *n.* study of old age and its diseases. 1909; formed in English from Greek *gêras* old age + *iātrikós* of a physician (*iātrós,* related to *iâsthai* heal, treat, of uncertain origin). Greek *gêras* is related to *gérōn* old man; see GERONTOLOGY. The term was coined by the American physician I.L. Nascher. **—geriatric** *adj.* 1926, back formation from *geriatrics.*

germ *n.* About 1450 *germ* bud or sprout, in a Middle English translation of Palladius' *De Re Rustica* (a work on agriculture); later earliest form of a living thing (1644); borrowed from Middle French *germe,* from Old French, from Latin *germen* (genitive *germinis*) sprout or bud; (probably an alteration of **genmen,* exactly cognate with Sanskrit *jánman-* creature, from the same source as *gignere* beget; see KIN). The sense of the seed of a disease is first recorded in 1803; later, with the sense of microbe or microorganism (1871, in the phrase *germ theory*).

german (jėr′mən) *adj.* having the same parents, as in *brothers-german;* related as a child of one's uncle or aunt, as in *cousin-german.* Probably about 1300 *germain,* in *The Romance of Guy of Warwick;* later *german* (before 1387); borrowed from Old French *germain,* from Latin *germānus* of brother and sisters, related to *germen* (genitive *germinis*) sprout or bud; see GERM. Related to GERMANE.

German *n.* Before 1387 *Germayn, German* member of the Germanic tribes, in Trevisa's translation of Higden's *Polychronicon;* later, native of Germany (1530, relating to the Holy Roman Empire); borrowed from Latin *Germānus,* a member of the *Germānī,* a group of peoples or tribes inhabiting central and northern Europe at the beginning of the Christian era, almost all of whom spoke closely related languages. The origin of the Latin name is unknown (it was not used by Germanic peoples who have used *Deutsch,* see DUTCH); it has been suggested that the name was given by the Gauls to their eastern neighbors, particularly a group of Celtic peoples in northeastern Gaul and that afterwards the name was extended to all Germanic peoples, but cognates of suggested Celtic derivations such as Old Irish *gair* neighbor, or Old Irish *gāirm* shout, cry, are wanting in form (vowel quantity is long, where a short vowel is expected; *m* comes from an incompatible cluster, such as *-sm*) and possibly in meaning (though the meaning of neighbor may be relevant, if it is not the same word as *German*).**—adj.** 1552, of Germany or its people, from the noun in English, and probably influenced by Latin *Germānus* of or pertaining to the *Germānī* or to *Germānia* the country of the Germanic peoples. **—Germanic** *adj.* 1633, of Germany or the Germans, formed from English *German,* n. or adj. + *-ic,* and probably influenced by Middle French *germanique,* and Latin *Germānicus,* from *Germānus* German.—*n.* 1892, the language family of the Germanic peoples, replacing the older term *Teutonic.*

germane (jėrmān′) *adj.* closely connected, appropriate, relevant. 1340 *germayn,* in *Ayenbite of Inwyt,* a figurative use (with variant spelling) of GERMAN of the same parents, related.

germanium (jėrmā′nēəm) *n.* metallic chemical element. 1886, New Latin *germanium;* formed from *Germania* Germany, from Latin *Germānia* country of the Germanic peoples + *-ium* (chemical element). The word was coined by the German chemist Clemens Winkler, who discovered it in 1886.

Germano- a combining form meaning of Germany or of the Germans, as in *Germanophile;* or German and _____, as in *Germano-American.* Formed from *German* and the connecting vowel *-o-.*

germicide *n.* substance that kills germs. 1881, formed from English *germ* + connective *-i-* + *-cide*[2]. **—germicidal** *adj.* 1888; formed from English *germicide* + *-al*[1].

germinal *adj.* of or in the earliest stage of development. 1808, borrowed from New Latin *germinalis* in the germ, from Latin *germen* (genitive *germinis*) sprout, bud, GERM; for suffix see -AL[1].

germination *n.* About 1450, in a translation of Palladius' *De Re Rustica* (a work on agriculture); borrowed from Latin *germinātiōnem* (nominative *germinātiō*) sprouting forth, budding, from *germināre* to sprout, put forth shoots, from *germen* (genitive *germinis*); see GERM; for suffix see -ATION. **—germinate** *v.* 1610, probably a back formation from *germination,* replacing earlier *germynen* (recorded probably in 1440, also found in Palladius' work); borrowed through, or by influence of, Middle French *germiner,* from Latin *germināre;* for suffix see -ATE[1].

gerontology *n.* study of aging and old age. 1903, formed in English from Greek *gérōn* (genitive *gérontos*) old man + English *-logy.* Greek *gérōn* (genitive *gérontos*) is exactly cognate with Sanskrit *járant-* frail, old; also cognate with Old English *ceorl* man, German *Kerl* fellow, from Indo-European **ĝer-* to age (Pok.390). See CHURL.

gerrymander (jer′ēman′dər, a spelling pronunciation of later development after loss of association with Elbridge Gerry, pronounced ger′ē) *n.* arrangement of electoral divisions to give one political party an unfair advantage. 1812, American English, formed in allusion to Elbridge *Gerry* + *(sala)mander.* Governor Gerry's party redistricted Massachusetts in 1812 to enable the Antifederalists to retain a majority; consequently Essex County was divided so that one district looked somewhat like a salamander, a figure that was widely caricatured and given the name *Gerrymander.* **—v.** subject (an area, especially an election district) to a gerrymander. 1812, American English, from the noun.

gerund (jer′ənd) *n. Grammar.* English verb form ending in *-ing* and used as a noun. 1513, probably a shortening of earlier *gerundif* (referring to nouns as well as adjectives); influenced in the distinction of applying only to nouns by Late Latin *gerundium,* patterned on *participium* participle, from Old Latin *gerundum* (Classical Latin *gerendum*) to be carried out, the gerund form of *gerere* to bear, carry. **—gerundive** *n. Grammar.* verb form ending in *-ing* and used as an adjective. Before 1425, *gerundif* (referring to both nouns and adjectives); borrowed from Late Latin *gerundīvus modus* mood, from *gerundium* gerund. *—adj.* 1612, of the nature of, or having to do with a gerund; from the noun; for suffix see -IVE.

gest or **geste** (jest) *n. Archaic.* story or romance in verse; heroic deed. Probably before 1225 *geste* entertainment, festivity, in *King Horn;* later, poem or song about heroic deeds (before 1300, in *Arthour and Merlin* and

Kyng Alisaunder); borrowed from Old French *geste* a deed or deeds, learned borrowing from Latin *gesta* deeds; see JEST.

Gestalt (geshtält′) *n. Psychology.* integrated group of acts, experiences, etc., which functions as a whole. 1922, in the compounds *Gestalt-psychologists* and *Gestalt theory;* earlier, as part of a German compound *Gestaltqualität* the quality of a Gestalt, used in a paper on experimental psychology (1909), from Middle High German *gestalt* form, configuration, appearance, abstracted from *ungestalt* deformity, noun use of the adjective *ungestalt* misshapen (*un-* UN- + *gestalt,* obsolete past participle of *stellen* to place, arrange); see STALL[1] place.

The term was employed by the German philosopher von Ehrenfels, and used by Max Wertheimer, Wolfgang Köhler, and Kurt Koffka, who founded the school of Gestalt psychology in Germany about 1910.

Gestapo (gəstä′pō) *n.* secret police in Germany under Hitler, formed in 1933. 1934, borrowing of German *Gestapo,* acronym formed from *Ge(heime) Sta(ats)-po(lizei)* secret state police, formed by the Nazis as a para-military instrument to carry out state political policy.

gestation *n.* 1533, in Elyot's *The Castel of Helth;* borrowed from Latin *gestātiōnem* (nominative *gestātiō*) a carrying, from *gestāre* bear, carry, gestate, a frequentative form of *gerere* to bear, carry, bring forth; for suffix see -ATION. The sense of pregnancy or development of young in the womb, is first recorded in English in 1615. **—gestate** *v.* carry (young) in the uterus from conception to birth. 1866, back formation of earlier *gestation,* perhaps modeled on Latin *gestātus,* past participle of *gestāre;* for suffix see -ATE[1].

gesticulation *n.* a making lively or excited gestures. Probably before 1425, in a translation of Higden's *Polychronicon;* borrowed from Latin *gesticulātiōnem* (nominative *gesticulātiō*), from *gesticulārī* to gesture, mimic, from *gesticulus* a mimicking gesture, diminutive of *gestus* (genitive *gestūs*) gesture, carriage, posture; see GESTURE; for suffix see -ATION. **—gesticulate** *v.* 1601, in Ben Jonson's *The Poetaster;* back formation of earlier *gesticulation,* possibly influenced by French *gesticuler,* but probably modeled on Latin *gesticulātus,* past participle of *gesticulārī;* for suffix see -ATE[1].

gesture *n.* About 1400, bearing or deportment; borrowed from Medieval Latin *gestura* bearing, behavior, from Latin *gestus* (genitive *gestūs*) gesture, carriage, posture, from *ges-,* stem of *gerere* to bear, carry, of uncertain origin. The meaning of movement of the body to emphasize speech, is first recorded in English about 1454. **—v.** 1542, make or use gestures; from the noun.

get *v.* Probably about 1200 *geten* obtained by effort, gain, acquire, in *The Ormulum,* borrowed from a Scandinavian source (compare Old Icelandic *geta* to get, reach).

Even though vestiges of the Old English equivalent form *-gietan* (found in various compounds, such as *begietan* beget, *forgietan* forget, *undergietan* understand) remain in the past participle *gotten,* the verb *get* is a Middle English borrowing, because the Old English form would have had the pronunciation equivalent to *yet* if it had developed from Old English through Middle English to modern English. *Gotten* developed into its present pronunciation by analogy with the development of Middle English *get.* Cognates of the Old English *-gietan* are found in Old Frisian *-jeta,* Old Saxon *-getan,* Middle Dutch *-gheten,* Dutch *-geten,* as in *vergeten* forget, Old High German *-gezzan,* German *-gessen,* as in *vergessen* forget, and Gothic *-gitan;* but further association with Latin *-hendere* in *prehendere* to grasp, seize, *hedera* ivy (as clinging), *praeda* prey, and Greek *chandánein* to hold, contain (Indo-European **ghend-, *ghed-,* Pok.437), is not accepted by all scholars today, and especially the linguists Ernout and Meillet.

gewgaw (gyü′gô often pronounced gē′gô, and sometimes written *geegaw*) *n.* trifle, toy, bauble. Probably before 1200 *giuegaue,* in *Ancrene Riwle;* of uncertain origin (considered today to be a reduplicated form perhaps connected with Old French *gogue* joke, game, from the imitative root *gog-;* the connections with *give* and *giff-gaff,* Middle Dutch *ghiveghave,* are thought to be phonologically inappropriate).

geyser (gī′zər) *n.* spring that sends a column of hot water and steam into the air. 1780, in allusion to Icelandic *Geysir,* the name of a hot spring in the valley of Haukadal, Iceland, from *geysa* to gush, from Old Icelandic *geysa,* from Indo-European **ĝheu-s-* (Pok.448); see FOUND[2] cast (metal).

ghastly *adj.* Before 1325 *gastli,* in *Cursor Mundi;* earlier *gastlich* (probably before 1300); formed from *gast* (past participle of *gasten* to frighten, make horrible; developed from Old English *gǣstan* to frighten) + *-lich* -ly[2]. A single instance of *gǣstlīc* appears in Old English, but the precise meaning is debatable and may be equivalent to spiritual, ghostly or to hospitable (guest-like). The spelling *ghastly* (with *gh-*) appeared in Spenser's *Faerie Queene* (1590), influenced by *ghost,* with which *gastli, ghastly* was often confused, especially in Middle English; see GHOST.**—adv.** 1589, from the adjective.

gherkin (gėr′kən) *n.* small cucumber often used for pickles. 1661 *girkin,* in Pepys' *Diary;* borrowed from Dutch *gurken,* plural of *gurk* cucumber, a shortened form (corresponding to English *cuke*) of *augurk, agurk* cucumber; of uncertain origin; probably from a Slavic source (compare Polish *ogórek* cucumber, Czech *okurka,* Serbian *ugorka,* possibly from Medieval Greek *angoúrion* watermelon, perhaps found in Persian *angūr* grape). The suffix *-kin* was adopted in Dutch *(-ken);* see -KIN. The *h* was added in the 1800's to preserve the so-called hard *g.*

ghetto (get′ō) *n.* 1611, a part of a city to which Jews were restricted, chiefly in Italy; borrowed from Italian *ghetto,* of uncertain origin. Many attempts have been made to explain the source of *ghetto* in Italian: that it was borrowed from Hebrew or Yiddish *get* deed of separation, that it developed from Italian (Venetian) *ghetto,* perhaps special use of *getto* foundry (so called for a section of Venice near a foundry, the site of the first ghetto in that city); that it is from *Egitto,* a borrowing from Latin *Aegyptus* Egypt; or that it is abstracted from Italian *borghetto* small section of a town, diminutive of *borgo* town, village, from Medieval Latin *burgus,* Latin, fortress. Specifically the theories about Italian *getto* (jātō) developing into *ghetto* (getō) and *Egitto* (ājētō) becoming *ghetto* (getō) are difficult to explain.

By 1892, in Zangwill's *Children of the Ghetto,* the word had acquired the meaning of any section inhabited by Jews, and since the early 1900's it has been used to describe similar quarters of minority groups.

ghost *n.* Probably before 1200 *gost, gast* spiritual being; angel, devil, or spirit, in *Ancrene Riwle* and Layamon's *Chronicle of Britain;* developed from Old English (before 800) *gāst* soul, spirit; cognate with Old Frisian *jēst* spirit, Old Saxon *gēst,* Middle Dutch *gheest* (modern Dutch *geest*), Old High German *geist* (modern German *Geist*), Old Icelandic *geiska* in *geiskafullr* full of fright, Gothic *usgaisjan* frighten, and Sanskrit *héḍa-s* wrath, from Indo-European **ĝheis-d-/ĝhois-d-* enraged, aghast, terrified (Pok.427). The spelling *ghost* appeared about 1425 (probably influenced by Middle Dutch *gheest*) but remained rare until the late 1500's.

The meaning of soul or spirit of a dead person, existed in Old English, but the specific sense of apparition or specter, is first recorded in Shakespeare's *Venus and Adonis* (1592), and the transferred sense of a faint image or shadow, slight suggestion (as in *a ghost of a chance*) is found in *Purchas his Pilgrimage* (1613). The artistic *ghost* who does work for another, is first found in the 1880's, as *a sculptor's ghost,* and in 1889, as a speechwriter. The verb use of to act as a ghost (writer) is recorded in 1922, and *ghost writer* in 1927.
—ghost town 1931, earlier used in reference to "deserted mining towns, like the ghosts of their departed prosperity" (1875). **—ghost word** 1886, word that is formed by an error in copying or printing or by misunderstanding of a text, in Skeat's writings.

ghoul (gül) *n.* horrible demon believed to feed on corpses. 1786, borrowed, in a translation of Beckford's Oriental romance *Vathek,* from Arabic *ghūl,* an evil spirit that in Mohammedan countries is believed to rob graves and feed on corpses, from *ghāla* he seized. **—ghoulish** *adj.* Before 1845; formed from English *ghoul* + *-ish.*

GI or **G.I.** (jē'ī') *adj.* of or having to do with American soldiers or the United States Army. 1936, American English, apparently from the phrase *G(overnment) I(ssue),* used to designate equipment and supplies issued to members of the armed forces (such as *G.I. shoes, G.I. trucks*) and applied to anything associated with servicemen (*a GI haircut, a GI bride*); possibly influenced by the earlier abbreviation for Galvanized Iron (1928), used chiefly in the phrase *G.I. can,* referring to such iron garbage cans used at military bases. **—n.** *Informal.* an enlisted soldier; serviceman. 1943, American English, from the adjective.

giant *n.* About 1300 *geant, geaunt* mythical being of superhuman height; borrowed from Old French *geant,* from Vulgar Latin **gagantem* (nominative *gagās*), variant of Latin *gigās* giant, from Greek *gígās* (genitive *gígantos*) one of a race of savage men eventually destroyed by the gods, of uncertain origin. The spelling of the initial syllable was first altered from *ge-* to *gi-* about 1350, after the Latin. First use of the meaning of a human being of unusually or abnormally large stature, is recorded in 1559, though early use in Middle English refers to a man being called, or likened to, a giant. The figurative use, applied to any influence or agency of enormous power, is first recorded in Donne's *Poems* (1631). **—adj.** Before 1425 *geaunt,* as an attributive use of the noun.

gibber (jib'ər) *v.* chatter senselessly, babble. 1604, in Shakespeare's *Hamlet,* probably back formation from *gibberish.* **—n.** senseless chatter. 1832, from the verb. **—gibberish** *n.* senseless chatter, jabber. About 1554 *gibbrish (gibbr-* imitative of the sound of chatter, probably influenced by *jabber* + *-ish*[1], after language names such as *Finnish, Turkish,* and *English).*

gibbet (jib'it) *n.* upright post with a projecting arm, from which the bodies of criminals were hung after execution. Probably before 1200, a gallows; borrowed from Old French *gibet,* diminutive of *gibe* club, perhaps from Frankish **gibb* forked stick (compare German Bavarian dialect *Gippel* forked branch); for suffix see -ET. **—v.** hang on a gibbet. 1597, in Shakespeare's *2 Henry IV;* from the noun.

gibbon *n.* small ape with long arms. 1770, borrowed from French *gibbon,* used by the French naturalist Buffon, who based the name on a word supposedly related by Dupleix, governor general of the French colonies in India.

gibbous (gib'əs) *adj.* curved out, humped. Before 1400; borrowed from Late Latin *gibbōsus* hunchbacked, from Latin *gibbus* hump, hunch, related to *gibber* hunchbacked.

gibe or **jibe** (jīb) *v.* jeer, scoff, sneer. 1567; earlier, implied in *giber* one who gibes (1563); of uncertain origin (perhaps borrowed in the sense of to use horseplay, handle roughly in sport, from Middle French *giber* to handle roughly, shake; also of uncertain origin, but possibly an alteration of Old French *gaber* to mock). **—n.** sneering or sarcastic remark. 1573, from the verb.

giblet (jib'lit) *n.* Usually, **giblets,** *pl.* heart, liver, or gizzard of a fowl. 1440 *gybelet,* in *Promptorium Parvulorum;* earlier *gyblot* unnecessary addition or appendage (about 1303, in Mannyng's *Handlyng Synne*); borrowed from Old French *gibelet* game stew, probably a variant of **giberet,* diminutive of *gibier* game; of unknown origin.

giddy *adj.* dizzy. Probably before 1300 *gidi* unstable or crazy, in *Kyng Alisaunder;* developed from Old English (about 1000) *gidig,* spelling variant of **gydig* insane or mad, possessed by a spirit, probably derived from Proto-Germanic **ʒuđiʒás,* from **ʒuđán* GOD + *-ig* -y[1], found in a similar formation in Old English *ylfig* insane (literally *ylf* elf + *-ig* like, possessed); for a similar sense development, see ENTHUSIASM.

gift *n.* About 1250, thing given or a present, in *The Story of Genesis and Exodus;* earlier, in the proper name *Witegift* (1104); borrowed from a Scandinavian source (compare Old Icelandic *gift,* usually written *gipt* a gift). The Old English *gift* does not seem to have long survived Middle English (probably disappearing shortly after 1110), and is recorded only in the sense of payment for a wife; however, cognates are found in Old Frisian *jeft* gift, Old Saxon *gift,* Middle Dutch *ghifte* (modern Dutch *gift* poison), Middle Low German *gifte* gift, Old High German *gift* (modern German *Mitgift* dowry, and *Gift* poison), and Gothic *-gifts* in *fragifts* espousal, all from the same Germanic source found in Old English *giefan* to GIVE. The meaning of poison, found in modern Dutch and German may be a euphemism, but it is also a specialization of meaning, that is similar to Late Latin *dosis* and Greek *dósis* dose of medicine, drug, whose literal meaning is that of a giving. A specialized meaning in English is that of inspiration, found as early as 1175, and later developing into the sense of natural talent, first recorded in *Cursor Mundi* (before 1325). —**v.** 1500's, principally surviving in *gifted,* past tense, and in the past participle or adjective *gifted* talented; from the noun.

gig[1] *n.* light carriage. 1790, a small rowboat or sailboat on a lightship; 1791, light carriage; perhaps transferred uses referring to their bouncing action, of *ghyg, gigge* spinning top, found in early compounds *gygmylle* (1463) and *whyrlegyg* (1440); possibly borrowed from a Scandinavian source (compare Danish *gig* spinning top, and Old Icelandic *geiga* turn sideways; see JIG[1] dance).

gig[2] *n. Informal.* assignment, job. 1926, (in jazz slang) a single musical engagement, one-night stand, said to be used in this sense by U.S. jazz musicians as early as 1905; of uncertain origin. The transferred sense of a job, is first recorded in 1954.

giga- (gig′ə *or* jig′ə) a combining form meaning one billion, as in *gigabit* (unit of information equal to) one billion bits, *gigacycle, gigahertz,* etc. Borrowed from Greek *gígās* giant; of uncertain origin.

gigantic *adj.* 1612, of a giant or giants, possibly formed by substitution of *-ic* from earlier English *gigantine* (1605); or formed in English either from earlier *gigant* giant (probably before 1425) or from Latin *gigant-*, stem of *gigantem,* from *gigās* giant + English suffix *-ic.* It is also possible that the word in English was borrowed directly from Greek *gigantikós,* from *gígās* (genitive *gígantos*) GIANT, with substitution of the English suffix *-ic.* The range of possibilities in formations with antecedents in English and in other languages, especially where a long literary history of reference exists, makes determination of a word's immediate source difficult to establish. Even the seemingly transferred sense referring to something that greatly exceeds ordinary size, as in Hobbes' *Leviathan* (1651), is not necessarily an extension of the literal sense in English.

giggle *v.* 1509, in Barclay's *The Ship of Fools,* probably of imitative origin, similar to other such words in English with the frequentative suffix *-le*[3], as found in *gaggle, cackle.* —**n.** 1577, from the verb.

gigolo (jig′əlō) *n.* man hired as a dancing partner, escort or lover for a woman. 1922, borrowed from French *gigolo,* possibly from *gigolette* dancing girl, prostitute, or directly from *giguer* to dance; see JIG[1] dance. The word appeared in Middle English *giglot* (probably 1350-75) in reference to villainous men, and earlier as *gigelot,* in reference to women (before 1325); borrowed probably from Old French, which marks the present formation as a reborrowing from French after a period of about 600 years.

Gila monster (hē′lə) large, poisonous lizard of Arizona and New Mexico. 1877, American English, in allusion to the *Gila* River, which runs through its general habitat in Arizona and New Mexico.

gild *v.* cover with a thin layer of gold or similar material; make golden. Probably before 1300 *gilden,* in *Kyng Alisaunder;* developed from Old English *gyldan* (especially in compounds, such as *ofergyldan* cover with gold); cognate with Old Icelandic *gylla* to gild, and Old High German *-gulden* in *ubergulden* cover with gold and derived from Proto-Germanic **ʒulthjanan,* from **ʒulthan* gold, the source of Old English *gold* GOLD.

gill[1] (gil) *n.* organ of breathing in fish, tadpoles, etc. Before 1325 *gille,* probably borrowed from a Scandinavian source (compare Old Icelandic *gjǫlnar* gills, Swedish *gel, geel* gill or jaw, modern Swedish *gäl* gill, Old Danish *-gæln* in *fiske-gæln* fish gill, modern Danish *gjælle* gill, Norwegian *gjelle,* which agree in meaning, but are not so close in form); cognate with Greek *chelýnē* lip, jaw, and Armenian *jełun* gums, from Indo-European **ghelun-* (Pok.436).

gill[2] (jill) *n.* measure for liquids, one fourth of a pint. 1310 *gille;* borrowed from Medieval Latin *gillo, gello* earthenware waterpot, jar for cooling things, and from Old French *gille, gello* a wine measure, probably a learned borrowing from Late Latin *gillō, gellō;* of uncertain origin.

gillie (gil′ē) *n.* Before 1605, attendant on a Scottish Highlands chief, Scottish *geilgie,* from Gaelic *gille* lad, servant, from Old Irish *gilla* young man, lad. The term is found earlier as *cuille,* in Spenser's works on Ireland. The meaning of attendant of a sportsman, is first recorded in 1848, in reference to hunting in the Scottish Highlands.

gillyflower (jil′iflou′ər) *n.* any of various flowers that have a clovelike fragrance. 1551, spelling alteration (by association with *flower*) of earlier *gilofre* clove (before 1300); borrowed from Old French *gilofre, girofle* clove (see CLOVE[1]), ultimately from Greek *karyóphyllon* clove, nut leaf, the dried flower bud of the clove tree (*káryon* nut + *phýllon* leaf; see CAREEN and BLADE). The original meaning of clove carried over in the sense of flower with clovelike fragrance (1380). See CLOVE[1].

gilt *n.* thin layer of gold or similar material applied to the surface of some object. 1432, from *gilt, gilte,* past participle of Middle English *gilden,* v.; see GILD. —**adj.** Probably before 1400 *gilten,* formed as a blend of *gilt,* past participle of Middle English *gilden,* v., and earlier *gilden,* adj. (1070), developed from Old English *gylden,* v.; see GILD.

gimbals (jim′bəlz *or* gim′bəlz) *n.pl.* arrangement for keeping an object horizontal, especially concentric rings that swivel on pivots to keep a ship's compass level. 1780, in earlier use with the meaning of joints or connecting links (1577), alteration (possibly in reference to the bolts that separate the concentric rings) of *gemmels, gemels* a hinge (1536), found in Middle English with the meaning of twins (before 1382), plural of *gemel* twin, borrowing of Old French *gemel* twin, from Latin *gemellus,* diminutive of *geminus* twin.

gimcrack (jim′krak′) *n.* showy, useless trifle. 1618, affected or showy person, fop, of uncertain origin; the MED explains it as a possible altered form of *gibecrake* a kind of ornament (1360; earlier in the surname *Gybecrake,* 1229; perhaps formed in English from Old French *giber* to rattle, shake + Middle English *crak* sharp noise, crack). The current meaning is first found in Thackeray's *Pendennis* (1839).

gimlet (gim′lit) *n.* small handtool with a screw point, for boring holes. 1350 *gymbelette,* as a ship carpenter's tool; later *gymlet* (1475); borrowed from Anglo-French *guimbelet,* perhaps from Middle Dutch *wimmelkijn,* diminutive of *wimmel* auger, drill.

gimmick *n. Slang.* 1926, American English, a gadget or device for performing a trick or deception, perhaps an alteration of *gimcrack.* The sense of a tricky or clever idea, is first recorded in the 1940's. —**gimmickry** *n.* 1952, American English, formed from English *gimmick* + *-ry.* —**gimmicky** *adj.* 1957, American English; formed from English *gimmick* + *-y*[1].

gimp[1] *n.* braidlike trimming. 1664, of uncertain origin; possibly related to or borrowed from Dutch *gimp,* of the same meaning; also found in French *guimpe* wimple or neckerchief (possibly a different word, French *guipure* corresponding more closely in meaning, but not in form).

gimp[2] *n. Slang.* lame person or leg. 1925, American English, a lame leg; perhaps formed by association with *limp.* The extended sense of a clumsy person or one who is not very adroit, is found about 1952.

gin[1] *n.* strong alcoholic drink. 1714, alteration and shortening of *geneva* a spirit flavored in Holland with juice from juniper berries (1706), but of no association with that plant in England. The name is an alteration of earlier Dutch *genever, jenever* juniper, from Old French *genevre,* from Vulgar Latin **jeniperus,* altered from Latin *jūniperus* juniper. Association with *Geneva* the city in Switzerland, is difficult to establish.

gin[2] *n.* machine for separating cotton from its seeds. 1740, American English, from earlier *gin* any ingenious device or contrivance, cleverness or skill, artifice (probably about 1200); borrowed from Old French *gin* machine, device, scheme. By some the word is said to be a shortening of *engine,* but this word is not recorded in English before 1275.

ginger *n.* 1363-64 *gynger;* earlier *gingivre,* in *Ancrene Riwle,* and *gingivere,* in Layamon's *Chronicle of Britain* (both probably before 1200); developed, with influence of Old French *gingibre,* from Old English (about 1000) *gingifer.* Both the Old English and Old French forms were borrowed from Medieval Latin *gingiber,* from Latin *zingiberi,* from Greek *zingíberis,* from Middle Indic, as represented in Pali *siṅgivera,* and rendered in Sanskrit as *śṛṅgavera-m* ginger. The Middle Indic form is a compound of Dravidian elements, as represented by Tamil *iñci* ginger and *vēr* root. According to Hultzsch and Burrow, who worked out the original details of this etymology, the word must have come from sources in Southeast Asia where many of the languages have words for *ginger* that are similar in sound to the Tamil.

Ginger with the figurative meaning of spirit, spunk, temper, is first recorded in a slang expression of American English, in 1843.

—gingerbread *n.* Before 1450 *gyngere brede* a kind of stiff pudding; earlier, preserved ginger (1228); borrowed from Old French *gingembraz, gingembras,* from Medieval Latin **gingibratum, gingebrada,* from *gingiber;* the last syllable being re-formed in Middle English to conform to the sense of *bred* bread. The later sense of a kind of cake, is first recorded after 1570, and its form in particular shapes such as letters or proximate human figures, about 1770.

gingerly *adv.* 1519, elegantly, daintily (chiefly in reference to walking or dancing), of uncertain origin; perhaps formed in English from *ginger-,* as a borrowing from Old French *gensor, genzor* in the specialized sense of pretty, delicate (formally, the comparative of *gent* noble, graceful) + English suffix *-ly*[1]. Extended sense of the word was first recorded to mean with extreme caution, especially in order to avoid making noise or injuring something (1607), and is later recorded in the general sense of cautiously or warily (1647). **—adj.** 1533, dainty, delicate, mincing; probably from the adverb. The sense of very cautious or wary, is recorded in the 1800's, about two hundred years later than the same meaning for the adverb.

gingham (ging′əm) *n.* cotton cloth made from dyed yarns. 1615, borrowed through Dutch *gingang, ginggang,* Dutch traders' rendering of a Malay word transliterated as *ginggang* striped, especially later, in reference to cloth. Compare SEERSUCKER.

gingival (jin′jəvəl) *adj.* of the gums of the mouth. 1669, formed in English from Latin *gingīva* gum + English *-al*[1]. Middle English had the form *gyngyve* the gums or gum, but the form is not recorded after 1425, so that the adjective was probably formed by a reborrowing from Latin *gingīva* gums, cognate with Greek *góngros* excrescence, from Indo-European **geng-/gong- lump* (Pok.379). **—gingivitis** *n.* inflammation of the gums. 1874, New Latin, formed in English from Latin *gingīva* + English suffix *-itis* inflammation.

ginkgo (ging′kō) *n.* large, ornamental tree of China and Japan. 1773, borrowed from a Japanese word transliterated as *ginkō,* from Chinese *yin-hing* (*yin* silver + *hing* apricot).

ginseng (jin′seng) *n.* low plant with a thick, branched root. 1654 *gimsem,* borrowed from Chinese *jên shên* (*jên* man + *shên,* possibly with the meaning of image of man; so called in allusion to the forked shape of the root). By the early 1700's the form had been altered to *ginseng.*

giraffe *n.* 1594 *gyraffa,* borrowed from Italian *giraffa,* from Arabic *zarāfa,* probably from an African language. The spelling of this word in English has varied, depending on which language was the immediate source. The current spelling in English is a borrowing from French *girafe,* but earlier forms, such as *jarraf* and *ziraph* (1600's) were probably taken directly from Arabic. In Middle English the spelling *gerfauntz* (about 1400) came possibly from Middle French *gerfaucz,* from an Egyptian form of Arabic; and *gerfaunt* was probably formed in Middle English from Old French *ger-,* in *gerfaucz* + *-faunt,* abstracted from Middle English *olifaunt* elephant.

gird *v.* Probably before 1200 *gurden,* in *Ancrene Riwle;* developed from Old English *gyrdan* put a belt or girdle around (about 725, in *Beowulf*); cognate with Old Frisian *gerda* to gird, Old Saxon *gurdian,* Old High German *gurten* (modern German *gürten*), Old Icelandic *gyrdha,* and Gothic *bigaírdan,* from Proto-Germanic **ʒurđjanan* and **ʒerđanan,* from Indo-European **gherdh-/ghr̥dh-* (Pok.444). The figurative sense of prepare for action, is first recorded before 1500. **—girder** *n.* main supporting beam. 1611, in Cotgrave's *Dictionary;* formed from English *gird,* v. + *-er*[1].

girdle *n.* Probably about 1200 *girdel,* in *The Ormulum;* before 1200 *gurdel,* in Layamon's *Chronicle of Britain;* developed from Old English (about 1000) *gyrdel* belt, sash, cord, etc., worn around the waist; cognate with Old Frisian *gerdel* girdle, belt, Middle Low German and Dutch *gordel,* Old High German *gurtil* (modern German *Gürtel*), Old Icelandic *gyrdhill,* and related to Old English *gyrdan* to GIRD. The modern sense of a lightweight, elastic corset, is first recorded in 1925 in American English. **—v.** form a girdle around, encircle. 1582, from the noun.

girl *n.* Probably before 1300 *gyrle* child of either sex, young person, in *Kyng Alisaunder;* perhaps related to Old English *gierela* garment. Such forms as appear in Low German *gör, göre* child (modern dialectal German *Göre* girl), Norwegian dialect *gorre,* and Swedish dialect *garre, gurre* a small child, may be cognates or simply accidental, vaguely similar forms.

Girl with the specific meaning of female child, is first

recorded in English before 1375, and with the sense of maidservant, in Pepys' *Diary,* in 1668.

girth *n.* the measure around anything. Probably before 1300 *gerth* belt placed around an animal's belly; earlier, in the compound *Gerthmakere;* borrowed from a Scandinavian source (compare Old Icelandic *gjǫrdh* girdle, belt, hoop, from Proto-Germanic **ʒerdu* which suggests cognates in Middle Dutch *gherde* belt, Middle Low German *gorde,* Old High German *gurt,* Gothic *gaírda* belt and a related form in Old English *gyrdan* to GIRD. The meaning of the measurement around an object, is first recorded in 1664.

gist (jist) *n.* the essential part, main idea. 1769, the basis for a legal action, in Blackstone's *Commentaries on the Laws of England;* earlier *git* (1726, paralleling the development of the word from Old French *gist* to modern French *gît*); borrowed, perhaps through the proverb quoted in Cotgrave's *Dictionary* (1611) *Je scay bien ou gist le lievre* I know well which is the very point of the matter; *gist* being from Old French *gist* in *gist en* it consists in, it lies in (third person singular present indicative of *gésir* to lie), from Latin *jacet* it lies, third person singular present indicative of *jacēre* to lie, related to *jacere* to throw, cognate with Greek *hiénai* throw, from Indo-European **yē-k-/yə-k-,* root **yē-/yə-* (Pok.502). Related to JET[1] stream. Another point of view is that *gist* is a borrowing of Old French *gist* in the sense of abode or lodging, referring to where an argument or point resides. The problem here is that it is difficult to find a link in the record between the Old or Middle French and modern English.

The extended meaning of the essential part or essence of anything is first recorded in English in 1823.

give *v.* About 1200 *gifen* (with initial guttural *g*), in *The Ormulum,* alteration of earlier *yiven, yeven* (before 1131). This change probably took place by influence of Scandinavian forms (compare Old Icelandic *gefa* to give, Swedish *giva,* Old Danish *givæ*), as seen first in early texts of the north of England, where forms with *g* originated. The vowel also fluctuated even in Middle English and there is disparity within texts, perhaps being merely graphic but indicating the range *(giefan, gifan, gyfan, gefan),* and between texts (*Ancrene Riwle:* yiven; *Ayenbite of Inwyt:* yeven). Middle English *yiven, yeven* developed largely from the West Saxon dialect form in Old English *ʒiefan* (usually transcribed *giefan* in this book to show antecedents of the development of *g;* recorded about 725, in *Beowulf*).

The Old English forms are cognate with Old Frisian *jeva* to give, Old Saxon *geƀan,* Middle Dutch *gheven* (modern Dutch *geven*), Old High German *geban* (modern German *geben*), Old Icelandic *gefa,* and Gothic *giban* to give, from Proto-Germanic **ʒeƀanan,* certainly altered by influence of its opposite **nemanan* take, from the original stem **ʒaƀ-,* as in Gothic *gabei* riches, cognate with Old Irish *gabāl* the taking, and Latin *habēre* to have, from Indo-European **ghəbh-,* weak form of **ghēbh-/ghōbh-* (Pok.408).

—give-and-take *n.* (1519) **—giveaway** *n.* (1872, American English) **—given name** (1827, American English, in Cooper's *Red Rover*) **—giver** *n.* (1340)

gizmo *n. Slang.* gadget, contraption. 1943, American English, of uncertain origin. This is the longest-lasting of a group of similar words beginning with *g-,* used in American slang in the 1940's, including *gazinkus, gazunkus, gigamaree, gilhickey, gingambob,* and *ginkus.* All are arbitrary formations probably out of the same linguistic mechanism as *gadget, dingus, thingumbob,* and similar words referring to things whose names are unknown or difficult to remember.

gizzard *n.* Before 1450 *gysour* second stomach of a fowl; earlier *gisser* the liver (1373); borrowed from Old French *giser, guiser* formed by a sound change of dissimilation of Latin *gig-,* in *gigeria, gizeria* (neuter plural) cooked entrails of a fowl; of uncertain origin; perhaps from a Phoenician word (compare Hebrew *gəzārīm* pieces of sacrificed animals); or an Iranian word (compare Persian *jigar* liver). Addition of the final *-d* in the 1500's, to form *gizzard,* came from the influence of words ending in *-ard,* such as *coward, dastard.*

glacé (glasā') *adj.* 1847, having a smooth, lustrous surface; borrowed from French *glacé,* past participle of *glacer* to ice or impart a gloss to, from Latin *glaciāre* to freeze, from *glaciēs* ice; see COLD. The meaning of covered with icing or sugar, is first recorded in English in 1882.

glacial *adj.* of ice or glaciers. 1656, cold, icy, in Blount's *Glossographia;* borrowed probably through French *glacial,* from Latin *glaciālis* icy, frozen, full of ice, from *glaciēs* ice; see COLD; for suffix see -AL[1]. The technical sense meaning relating to a time when the earth was covered with glaciers, is first recorded in 1846.

glacier (glā'shər) *n.* large mass of ice formed from snow on high ground. 1744, borrowed from French *glacier* (earlier, dialectal *glacière*), from Old French *glace* ice, from Vulgar Latin *glacia,* from Latin *glaciēs;* see COLD.

glad *adj.* Probably before 1200 *glad* joyful, merry, mild, gracious, pleased, in Layamon's *Chronicle of Britain;* developed from Old English *glæd* bright, shining, joyous, glad (about 725, in *Beowulf*); cognate with Old Frisian *gled* smooth, Old Saxon *glad-* (in compounds such as *gladmōdi* joyous, happy), Old High German *glat* shining, Middle High German *gelat, glat* shining, smooth, slippery (modern German *glatt* smooth), Middle and modern Dutch *glad* smooth, and Old Icelandic *gladhr* bright, glad, from Proto-Germanic **ʒlađaz;* also cognate with Latin *glaber (glabra, glabrum)* smooth, bald, Lithuanian *glodùs* smooth, and Old Slavic *gladŭkŭ* even, polished, from Indo-European **ghlădh-/ghlədh-* shining, smooth (Pok.431).

The modern sense of pleased or satisfied, also found in Middle English, generally represents a weakening of the original meaning.

—gladden *v.* Before 1400 *gladenen* to rejoice, make glad; formed from earlier *gladen* make glad (probably before 1200; developed from Old English, about 950, *gladian* be glad, make glad) + *-en*[1].

glade *n.* About 1400 *glade* a bright or open space in a wood, a clearing; earlier in the place name *Gledele* (1131-41); probably borrowed from a Scandinavian source (compare Old Icelandic *gladhr* bright); see GLAD. In support of this notion, compare early uses of *glade* suggesting a light, sunny place, though later writers associated it with *shade* or an open area in the woods. In American English the sense of a marshy tract of low ground covered with grass, is first recorded in 1644; since the 1800's such tracts are often called *everglades,* from the *Everglades* region in Florida.

gladiator *n.* slave, captive, or paid fighter who fought in the public shows in ancient Rome. Probably before 1439, in Lydgate's *Falls of Princes;* borrowing of Latin *gladiātor* (literally, swordsman), from *gladius* sword, allegedly from Gaulish **kladyos* (compare Welsh *cleddyf* sword), from Indo-European *kləd-/keləd-/klād- strike, hew (Pok.546). In some later instances the word spelled with *-our* may have been borrowed from Middle French.

gladiolus (glad′ēō′ləs) *n.* kind of iris with spikes of large flowers. About 1000, as Latin *gladiolum;* later, Anglicized as *gladiol* (probably 1440, in a translation of Palladius' *De Re Rustica,* a treatise on agriculture); and perhaps reborrowed (1567) from Latin in the form *gladiolus* wild iris (literally, small sword), diminutive of *gladius* sword (so called by Pliny in reference to the plant's sword-shaped leaves; see GLADIATOR). The variant form *gladiola* probably developed as a misunderstood plural of *gladiolum.*

glamour or **glamor** *n.* 1720, Scottish *glamour* magic, enchantment, spell, in Allan Ramsay's *Poems;* possibly earlier *glamer,* alteration of English GRAMMAR and its Scottish variant *gramarye* occult learning. The meaning of magical beauty or alluring charm, is first recorded in 1840.

Glamour was originally used by Scottish poets, such as Ramsay and Burns in the 1700's, and introduced in general literary use in the 1830's by Scott. One explanation of the special meaning of *glamour* is that it derived in part from the word *grammar,* extended in meaning to learning or scholarship in general (also found in *glomery,* originally in Anglo-French variant *glomerie* of *gramarye*), and like *gramarye* in its extended meaning, was associated with the occult and magic. **—glamorize** *v.* 1936, American English; formed from English *glamor* + *-ize.* **—glamorous** *adj.* 1882, formed from English *glamor* + *-ous.*

glance *v.* 1441 *glawncen* to glide off at a slant as a weapon does, probably variant of earlier *glacen* to graze, strike a glancing blow (about 1300); borrowed from Old French *glacer, glacier* to slip, make slippery, from *glace* ice; see GLACIER. The meaning of look quickly, if not the original sense of the word, was probably further influenced by *glenten* look askance (about 1250), and by Old French *gancir, gaunchir* turn aside, swerve, dodge; see GLINT. Interestingly though, *glance* with the meaning of look quickly is not recorded until 1583. **—n.** 1503, swift movement or impact usually producing a gleam of light, from the verb, probably also influenced by *glente,* n., a glimpse, look, glance (before 1338, found in earlier place name *Glentheim,* about 1115). The meaning of a brief or hurried look is first recorded in 1591.

gland *n.* organ of secretion. 1692, possibly a shortened form of earlier *glandele, glandula,* n. (before 1400, in Lanfranc's *Science of Surgery*); borrowed through Old French *glandule,* or directly from Latin *glandula;* and borrowed from French *glande* gland, tumor, altered form of Old French *glandre* gland, swollen gland in the neck, from Latin *glandula* gland of the throat, tonsil, diminutive of *glāns* (genitive *glandis*) acorn; cognate with Greek *bálanos* and Armenian *kalin,* from Indo-European *gwel-/gwelə-/gwlā- (Pok.472). **—glandular** *adj.* 1740, borrowed from French *glandulaire,* from *glandule* small gland, from Latin *glandula* gland of the throat; for suffix see -AR. This word has largely replaced the earlier adjective *glandulous* (recorded before 1400).

glanders (glan′dərz) *n.* disease of horses and mules, accompanied by fever, swelling under the jaw, and heavy discharge from the nostrils. About 1410 *glaundres;* borrowed from Old French *glandres,* plural of *glandre* GLAND. *Glaundres* swellings about the neck in humans, is recorded in Caxton's version of the *Golden Legend* (1483). Darwin, in the *Descent of Man* (1871) recognized *glanders* as communicable between horses and humans.

glare[1] *v.* give too great brightness and showiness. About 1275 *glaren* to shine with a brilliant light; borrowed perhaps from Middle Dutch or Middle Low German *glaren* to gleam, related to *glas* GLASS. The meaning of to stare fiercely, is first recorded in the general prologue to Chaucer's *Canterbury Tales* (about 1387-95). **—n.** Probably before 1400 *glayre* strong, bright light; later, a fierce look (in Milton's *Paradise Lost,* 1667); from the verb. **—glaring** *adj.* 1387-95, from *glare,* v.; later, conspicuous (1706).

glare[2] *adj.* bright and smooth. 1832, American English *glare,* as a shortened form of *glare ice* ice with a smooth surface, from earlier *glare* frost, icy condition (1567); probably an extended use of *glare*[1], n.; and, in some instances, a confusion with *glair,* n., clear, glistening white of an egg (1296, borrowed from Old French *glaire,* from Gallo-Romance *clāria, from Latin *clārus* clear). **—n.** 1854, American English, sheet of ice; from the adjective.

glass *n.* Probably about 1225 *glas;* earlier *gles* (probably before 1200, in *Ancrene Riwle*); found in Old English (about 750) *glæs;* ultimately derived from Proto-Germanic *ʒlása-n, from the base *ʒla-, variant of *ʒlē- to shine (compare Old Frisian *gles* glass, Old Saxon, Middle Low German, Middle High German, Middle Dutch, and modern Dutch *glas,* modern German *Glas,* Old High German *glas* amber, and Old Icelandic *gler* glass, which is cognate with Old English *glǣr* amber), from Indo-European *ĝhlēs-/ĝhləs- (Pok.432). The meaning of a drinking glass is recorded probably before 1200. **—v.** cover or protect with glass. 1577; earlier, to fit or provide with glass, especially with glass windows (1369, in Chaucer's *Book of the Duchesse*); from the noun. **—glassware** *n.* (1745, in Defoe's writings) **—glassy** *adj.* Before 1398 *glasy,* in Trevisa's translation of Bartholomew's *De Proprietatibus Rerum;* formed from Middle English *glas* glass, n. + *-y*[1].

glaucoma (glôkō′mə) *n.* disease of the eye. 1643 *glaucome,* borrowed from Greek *glaúkōma* cataract, opacity of the crystalline lens, from *glaukós* bluish green, gray; (originally) gleaming, of uncertain origin. First used in English in the sense of cataract, the distinction between cataracts and glaucoma not being established until about 1705.

glaze *v.* 1369 *glasen* to fit or furnish with glass, in Chaucer's *Book of the Duchesse;* from *glas* GLASS, probably influenced by earlier *glazier,* but note the Middle English form *glasen.* The sense of cover with glass or a glassy substance is first recorded before 1400. **—n.** 1784, substance used to make a glossy coating; from the verb. An earlier meaning of window is recorded before 1700. **—glazier** *n.* 1296-97 *glasyer* one who makes or repairs glass; formed from *glas,* n., and *glasen,* v. + *-ier.*

gleam *n.* Probably before 1200 *gleam* beam of light, in *Ancrene Riwle;* developed from Old English *glǣm* brightness, splendor, radiance (about 725, in *Genesis A*), from Proto-Germanic *ʒlaimiz; cognate with Old Frisian *glīa* to glow, Old Saxon *glīmo,* Old High German *gleimo* glowworm, Old Icelandic *gljā* to shine, glitter, cognate with Welsh *gloyw* bright, from Indo-European *ĝhlei-/ĝhloi- (Pok.432). **—v.** flash or beam with light. Probably about 1200 *gleamen,* from *gleam,* n.

glean *v.* gather (grain) left on a field by reapers. About 1330 *glenen* to gather; borrowed from Old French *glener,* from Late Latin *glennāre* make a collection, from Gaulish (compare Old Irish *doglinn* he gathers, or gleans), cognate with Lettish *glendi* look at, from Indo-European **ghlendh-* (Pok.431). **—gleanings** *n.pl.* anything that is gleaned. 1440 *glenynge,* in *Promptorium Parvulorum;* later, in the figurative sense (1576).

glee *n.* Before 1250 *gle,* developed from Old English (about 700) *gliu,* (before 800) *glio;* later *glīw, glēo* entertainment, mirth, jest, from Proto-Germanic **ʒliujan;* cognate with Old Icelandic *glȳ* joy, Greek *chleúē* joke, mockery, and Old Lithuanian *glaudas* amusement, pastime, from Indo-European **ghleu-/ghlou-* be merry (Pok.451). Throughout Old and Middle English *glee* was largely of poetic use and became rare after the 1400's, virtually disappearing in the 1700's. Johnson's *Dictionary* (1755) dismisses it as a word only used in comic writing. Its revival shortly thereafter remains unexplained. **—glee club** 1814, a group of singers organized originally to sing part songs and *glees* (song of three or more parts, 1659, from earlier meaning of music or musical entertainment, probably before 1200, in Layamon's *Chronicle of Britain*).

glen *n.* small, narrow valley. 1489, in Scottish; earlier, in a place name *Glendew;* developed from Gaelic *gleann;* earlier, *glenn* mountain valley; cognate with Old Irish *glenn,* Irish *gleann* and Welsh *glyn* valley, of unknown origin.

glengarry (glengar′ē) *n.* Scottish cap with straight sides and a creased top. 1841, from *Glengarry,* valley in Inverness, a county in Scotland.

glib *adj.* speaking or spoken smoothly and easily. 1598, easy or offhand, as of a procedure; 1599, smooth and slippery, as of a surface; earlier, as an adverb (1594); possibly a shortened form of obsolete *glibbery* slippery. The closeness of the appearance in English of the forms *glib* and *glibbery* and the sudden appearance of a variety of forms derived from them, also of about the same date, suggest that *glib* was a vogue word at the turn of the 16th century (1594-1605), and its novelty may have come as a borrowed word from Low German *glibberig* smooth or slippery, from Middle Low German *glibberich* (*glibber* jelly + *-ich* -y[1]), of unknown origin. The meaning of (language) spoken fluently is first recorded in Marston's *Antonio's Revenge* (1602).

glide *v.* Before 1200 *gliden;* found in Old English *glīdan* move along smoothly and easily (about 725, in *Beowulf*); cognate with Old Frisian *glīda* to glide, Old Saxon *glīdan,* Middle Low German *glīden* (modern Dutch *glijden*), Middle High German *glīten,* Old High German *glītan* (modern German *gleiten*), from Proto-West-Germanic **ʒlīdan,* of unknown origin. **—n.** 1590, from the verb. **—glider** *n.* 1440 *glydare* person or thing that glides, in *Promptorium Parvulorum;* formed from English *glide,* n. + *-er*[1]. The specific sense of an airplane without a motor, appears about 1897.

glimmer *v.* Before 1375 *glimeren* to shine brightly; probably a frequentative form related to Old English *glǣm* brightness; see GLEAM, and cognate with Middle Dutch *glimmen* to glimmer, and Middle High German *glimmern* to glow. The Middle English meaning of shine brightly, died out in the early 1500's, leaving only a weakened meaning of shine faintly (first recorded before 1400, in the sense of have a faint perception). **—n.** a faint, unsteady light. 1590, in Shakespeare's *Comedy of Errors;* from the verb. An earlier and obsolete sense "fire", is recorded in 1567.

glimpse *v.* 1592, to shine faintly, alteration of *glymsen* to glance at (1450); earlier, to glisten (before 1325); developed possibly from Old English **glimsian;* cognate with Middle High German *glimsen* to glimmer, and *glimmern* to glow; see GLIMMER, and possibly from Proto-Germanic **ʒlīm-/ʒlaim-/ʒlim-* (brightness, glimpse); see GLEAM, GLIMMER. The *p* is possibly an intrusion that developed dialectally to facilitate pronunciation; the *s,* that is a vestige of the probable Old English form, may be a verb-formative element of Germanic, found in words such as *glisten* or *glissade.* The current meaning of catch a quick view of, is first recorded in 1779. **—n.** About 1540 *glimse* momentary appearance; from the verb, or more immediately from *glimpsing* imperfect vision (about 1359). The current meaning of a momentary view, passing glance, is first recorded in 1579.

glint *v.* to gleam, flash. 1787, Scottish, shine with flashing light, in Burns' *Holy Fair;* apparently an alteration (by influence of the past participle *glynt,* in this spelling as early as 1400) of earlier *glenten* to gleam, flash, glisten (probably about 1380), to move quickly aside, dodge or flinch (before 1338), and to look askance (about 1250); probably from a Scandinavian source (compare dialectal Swedish *glinta* to slip, shine, and dialectal Norwegian *gletta* to look), from Proto-Germanic **ʒlent-.* Also found in various cognates including late Old High German *glanz* bright, clean (modern German *Glanz* a shine, gleam, *glänzen* to shine, gleam), and Middle Dutch *glansen* to gleam, from Indo-European **ghlend-* (Pok.431).

Glint was popularized in the works of Scottish writers such as Burns in the late 1700's, whence it spread into general English literary use during the 1800's. **—n.** 1826, a gleam, momentary appearance; from the verb.

glissade *n.* 1843, a sliding step in ballet; later, a slide down a slope, especially in ice or snow (1862); borrowed from French *glissade,* from *glisser* to slip or slide, from Dutch *glissen,* from Old Dutch *glissen, glitsen;* cognate with Middle Low German *glischen* (modern German *glitschen*) to slide, formed from Proto-West-Germanic **ʒliđ-* (compare GLIDE) with verb-formative *s;* for suffix see -ADE.

glisten *v.* Probably about 1200 *glistnen* to glitter or gleam; developed from Old English (about 1000) *glisnian,* a form related to *glīsian* glisten, and cognate with Old Frisian *glisia* to glimmer or blink, Middle Low German *glisen, glissen* to glitter, Middle High German *glistern* to sparkle, dialectal Norwegian *glissa* to glitter, and Old Danish *glisse* to shine; related to the source of English GLITTER.**—n.** 1840, from the verb, but more immediately probably from *glistening,* n. (1398), also from the verb.

glitch *n. Slang.* a sudden mishap or malfunction, slip-up. 1962, American English; probably borrowed from Yiddish *glitsh* a slip, from *glitshn* to slip, from German *glitschen,* and related to *gleiten* to glide; see GLIDE.

Though popularized in the jargon of astronauts, *glitch* was used originally by electronics and aerospace engineers in the sense of a sudden irregularity in an electric current or signal. By the late 1960's *glitch* was also used in computer programming, astronomy, and other technical fields.

glitter *v.* About 1380 *gliteren* to flash, sparkle; earlier *glideren* (probably before 1300, in *Arthour and Merlin*); borrowed from a Scandinavian source (compare Old Icelandic *glitra* to glitter, related to *glita* to shine); for suffix see -ER[4]. The Old Icelandic forms are cognate with Old Saxon *glītan,* Middle High German and modern German *glitzern* to glitter, Old High German *glīzzan* to shine, Gothic *glitmunjan* to glitter, and Old English *glitenian* to glitter; also cognate with Greek *chlidḗ* luxury (apparently referring to shining objects), from Indo-European **ghleid-/ghlid-* (Pok.433). **—n.** 1602, in Marston's *Antonio's Revenge;* from the verb. The forms in English that begin with *gl-* and refer to light or flashes of light, such as *gleam, glimmer, glitter,* suggest a phono-symbolic relationship that points to Proto-Germanic forms of **ʒlē-* and **ʒlei-;* see GLEAM.

glitzy *adj. Informal.* glittering, dazzling. 1966, American English; probably formed in English from German *glitz(ern)* to GLITTER + English suffix *-y*[1]. **—glitz** *n. Informal.* glitter. 1978, back formation from *glitzy.*

gloaming *n.* evening twilight, dusk. About 1425 *gloming,* Scottish; developed from Old English (about 1000) *glōmung,* from *glōm* twilight, related to *glōwan* to GLOW; for suffix see -ING[1]. By regular phonetic development Old English *glōmung* would have become *glooming* in modern English; however, the vowel sound was perhaps influenced by *glow,* and, therefore, written as *oa* to preserve the sound associated with *o* in *glow.* The word continued to be used by Scottish writers after falling into disuse in standard English and was reintroduced through their writings in the 1800's.

gloat *n.* 1575, to look with a secret or sidelong glance; perhaps borrowed from a Scandinavian source (compare Old Icelandic *glotta* smile scornfully, Swedish *glutta* to peep, peer), from Indo-European **ghlud-* (Pok.434). Although used by many writers in the 1600's and 1700's, *gloat* was unfamiliar to Johnson when he included it in his *Dictionary* (1755). The meaning of gaze or ponder with pleasure is first recorded in Samuel Richardson's *Clarissa* (1748).

globe *n.* About 1450, anything round like a ball, a sphere; borrowed from Middle French *globe,* learned borrowing from Latin *globus* sphere, and borrowed directly from Latin; see CLIP[2] hold tight. The meaning of the planet Earth, is first recorded in Eden's *A Treatise of the New India* (1553), in which *globe* is also used to mean a sphere with the map of the earth on it. **—global** *adj.* 1676, spherical; formed from English *globe,* n. + *-al*[1]. The meaning of universal, world-wide, is first recorded in 1892. **—globular** *adj.* 1656, borrowed from French *globulaire,* modeled on Latin **globulāris,* as if formed from *globulus;* for suffix see -AR. **—globule** (glob'yül) *n.* 1664, small sphere; borrowed from French *globule,* from Latin *globulus,* diminutive of *globus* globe; for suffix see -ULE. Alternatively, *globule* may be a back formation from *globular.*

glockenspiel (glok'ənspēl') *n.* percussion instrument consisting of small, tuned bells, bars, or tubes mounted in a frame. 1825, a carillon; borrowed from German *Glockenspiel* chimes (literally, bell playing). The current sense is first recorded in Carlyle's *Sartor Resartus* (1833-34).

glom[1] *v. Slang.* grab, snatch, steal. 1907 *glahm,* in Jack London's *The Road,* American English underworld slang, variant of earlier Scottish *glaum* (1715); apparently developed from Gaelic *glam* to handle awkwardly, grab voraciously, devour. The slang phrase *glom on to,* meaning to get hold of or latch on to, is first recorded about 1960 in American English.

glom[2] *v. Slang.* look at, watch. 1945, American English, perhaps a transferred use of GLOM[1]. **—n.** a look, glimpse. 1953, American English; from the verb.

gloom *n.* 1596, in Scottish, sullen look; probably from the verb. The sense of darkness or obscurity, is first recorded in Milton's *On the Morning of Christ's Nativity* (1629), and that of a state of melancholy or depression, appears in 1744. **—v.** About 1300, implied in *glouminge* scowling, frowning; later, *gloumben* (probably about 1380), and *gloumen* look gloomy or sullen (probably before 1400); perhaps borrowed from a Scandinavian source (compare dialectal Norwegian *glome* to stare somberly); probably cognate with Low German *glūm* muddiness, deception. **—gloomy** *adj.* 1588, dark or obscure, in Shakespeare's *Titus Andronicus;* formed from English *gloom,* v. + *-y*[1]. The figurative sense of downcast or depressed, is first recorded in Marlowe's *Edward II* (1590).

gloria (glôr'ēə) *n.* song of praise to God, or its musical setting. Before 1225, borrowing of Medieval Latin *Gloria,* in *Gloria Patri,* name of a Medieval Latin hymn praising God, which begins "Glory be to the Father," from Latin *glōria* glory.

glory *n.* Probably before 1200 *gloirc* splendor (of Christ), praise (to God), in *Ancrene Riwle;* later *glorie* (probably about 1200); borrowed from Old French *gloire, glorie,* learned borrowing from Latin *glōria* great praise or honor, self-praise, vain-glory, of uncertain origin. **—v.** About 1350 *glorien* rejoice; borrowed from Old French *gloriicr,* and directly from Latin *glōriārī,* from *glōria* glory. In some instances, this verb may be a back formation from earlier *glorify.* **—glorify** *v.* 1340 *glorifen;* borrowed from Old French *glorifier,* learned borrowing from Late Latin *glōrificāre,* from Latin *glōria* glory; for suffix see -FY. **—glorious** *adj.* About 1275 *glorius;* borrowed from Old French *glorieus,* from Latin *glōriōsus* full of glory, famous, vainglorious, from *glōria* glory; for suffix see OUS.

gloss[1] *n.* smooth, shiny surface; luster. 1538, in Elyot's works; perhaps borrowed from a Scandinavian source (compare Icelandic *glossi* flame, related to *glossa* to flame); cognate with Middle High German *glosen* to glow, and Dutch (obsolete) *gloos* a glowing, which is a possible alternative source of the English word. The relationship is unknown, except that *gloss* is one of the English words in *gl-* that is also related to *gleam* glow, etc.; see GLISTEN, GLEAM. **—v.** put a smooth shiny surface on. Before 1656, from the noun. The figurative meaning of smooth over or hide is first recorded in 1729, influenced by *gloss*[2], v. **—glossy** *adj.* 1556, formed from English *gloss*[1], n. + *-y*[1].

gloss[2] *n.* explanation, interpretation, comment. 1548, in Udall's translation of Erasmus' works; a reborrowing directly from Latin *glōssa* obsolete or foreign word which needs explanation, from Ionic Greek *glôssa* (Attic *glôtta*) obscure word, language (literally, tongue), from earlier **glōch-ya,* of unknown origin. **—v.** explain, comment. 1579, from the noun. The extended meaning of explain away (often in the phrase *gloss over,* 1764), is first recorded in 1638. *Gloss* replaced earlier *gloze* in both noun and verb (*n.,* about 1300, borrowed from Old French *glose* explanation, and directly from Late Latin *glōssa, glōsa,* from Latin *glōssa; v.,* before 1378 *glosen* interpret, comment, provide with a gloss, borrowed from Old French *gloser* make an explanation, from *glose;* and probably developed in English from the noun in the sense of provide with a gloss, but the earlier sense in Middle English, to flatter or use deceit, about 1300, was most likely borrowed from Old French).

glossary *n.* Probably about 1350 *glosarie;* borrowed from Latin *glōssarium,* from Greek *glōssárion,* contemptuous diminutive of *glōssa* obsolete or foreign word which needs explanation; see GLOSS² explanation; for suffix see -ARY, but compare this specialized use with *-arion* from the Greek *-árion* used as a diminutive showing contempt, found in *Kaisárion* Caesar's son by Cleopatra, a Greek form because Greek was the language of Cleopatra's family, the Ptolemies, who were Greek rulers of Egypt from 323 B.C. to 30 B.C.

glottis (glot'is) *n.* opening at the upper part of the windpipe, between the vocal cords. 1578, New Latin, borrowed from Greek *glōttís* (genitive *glōttídos*), from *glôtta,* Attic dialect variant of *glôssa* tongue; see GLOSS² explanation. **—glottal** *adj.* 1846, formed from English *glottis* + *-al*¹.

glove *n.* Probably before 1200 *glove,* in Layamon's *Chronicle of Britain;* developed from Old English *glōf* covering for the hand (about 725, in *Beowulf*); cognate with Old Icelandic *glōfi* glove; possibly a contraction of a Germanic compound of the collective prefix preserved in Old English *ge-,* and the root of the word preserved in Old Icelandic *lōfi* palm of the hand, Old High German *laffa,* and Gothic *lōfa.* **—v.** cover with or as with a glove. About 1400, from the noun.

glow *v.* Old English *glōwan* shine as if red-hot (about 1000, in Ælfric's writings); cognate with Old Frisian *glēd* glow, blaze, Old Saxon *glōian* to glow, Old High German *gluoen* (modern German *glühen*), and Old Icelandic *glōa* to glow; compare *glare, gloaming,* etc., related to *glow* through the Proto-Germanic base **ʒlō-,* from Indo-European **ĝhlō-/ĝhlə-* (Pok.430). **—n.** About 1450 *glou* glowing heat; from the verb. **—glowworm** *n.* (probably about 1350)

glower *v.* stare angrily, scowl. Probably before 1400 *gloren* to glare, glower; earlier, shine (probably about 1350); perhaps borrowed from a Scandinavian source (compare dialectal Norwegian *glora* to glow, stare, Icelandic *glōra* to gleam, glare). The Middle English *gloren* is cognate with Low German *glōren* to glow, and is directly related through the Proto-Germanic base **ʒlō-* to Old English *glōwan* to GLOW; which influenced its eventual spelling *glower.* **—n.** 1715, from the verb.

glucose (glü'kōs) *n.* kind of sugar occurring in plant and animal tissues. 1840, borrowing of French *glucose,* from Greek *gleûkos* must, sweet wine, related to *glykýs* sweet, from Indo-European **dl̥kú-s* (Pok. 222); see DULCET. The word was coined in 1883 by the French chemist Jean Baptiste Dumas.

glue *n.* 1225 *glu* substance used to stick things together; borrowed from Old French *glu, glus,* from Late Latin *glūs* (genitive *glūtis*) glue; see CLAY. **—v.** stick together with glue. About 1392 *glewen;* earlier *gliwen* (about 1380); borrowed from Old French *gluer,* from *glu,* n. **—gluey** *adj.* Before 1398 *glewy,* in Trevisa's translation of Bartholomew's *De Proprietatibus Rerum;* formed from Middle English *glew* glue + *-y*¹.

glum *adj.* gloomy, sullen. 1547 *glumme,* probably developed from Middle English *gloumen* become dark (about 1300), later *gloumben* look gloomy or sullen (about 1380); see GLOOM, v.

gluon (glü'on) *n.* hypothetical elementary particle that carries the strong force binding quarks together. 1972, American English, formed from *glue* + *-on.*

glut *v.* fill full, feed or satisfy fully. Before 1333, implied in *gloutinge* a feasting to excessive fullness, in Shoreham's poetry; later *glotten* (probably before 1400); probably borrowed from Old French *gloter, glotoiier* to swallow, gulp down, from Latin *gluttīre* swallow, gulp down; see GLUTTON. **—n.** 1579, excessive flow; 1594, excess supply; from the verb.

gluten (glü'tən) *n.* sticky substance that remains in flour when the starch is taken out. 1803, specialization of an earlier meaning, animal albumin or fibrin (1597); borrowed probably through Middle French *gluten,* from Latin *glūten* (genitive *glūtinis*) glue, related to Late Latin *glūs* GLUE. **—glutinous** *adj.* Probably before 1425 *glutinose, glutinous,* in an anonymous translation of Chauliac's *Grande Chirurgie;* borrowed probably by influence of Middle French *glutineux,* from Latin *glūtinōsus,* from *glūten* (genitive *glūtinis*) glue.

glutton *n.* Probably before 1200 *glutun* greedy eater, in *Ancrene Riwle;* borrowed from Old French *gluton, gloton,* and from Latin *gluttōnem,* accusative of *gluttō* glutton, related to or formed from *gluttīre* to swallow, *gula* throat. It is possible that Latin *gluttīre* is cognate with Old Irish *gelim* I swallow, eat up, Armenian *klanem* I swallow, and Russian *glotka* gullet, throat, *glotok* mouthful, gulp, from Indo-European **gel-* (Pok.365). **—gluttonous** *adj.* About 1350 *glotounis;* later *glotonos;* borrowed from Old French *glotonos,* from *gloton* glutton; for suffix see -OUS. **—gluttony** *n.* Probably before 1200 *glutunie,* borrowed from Old French *glutonie,* from *gluton* glutton.

glycerin (glis'ərin) *n.* sweet syrupy liquid obtained from fats and oils. 1838, borrowed from French *glycérine,* formed from Greek *glykerós* sweet (related to *glykýs* sweet) + French *-ine* -ine², chemical suffix. The term was coined by the French chemist Chevreul.

glycogen (glī'kəjən) *n.* carbohydrate stored in the liver and other tissues. 1860, borrowed from French *glycogène,* formed from Greek *glykýs* sweet (see GLUCOSE) + French *-gène* -gen. The term was coined by the French physiologist Claude Bernard.

gnarled *adj.* knotted, twisted. 1603, in Shakespeare's *Measure for Measure,* probably a variant of *knarled,* a probable diminutive of *knar* knot in wood (1382, in Wycliffe's writings; earlier, a rock or stone, before 1250, in *The Owl and the Nightingale*); cognate with Middle High German *knorre* knobby protuberance (modern German *Knorren*), from Indo-European **gner-* (Pok.371). *Gnarled* occurs once in Shakespeare and is not recorded again until the 1800's, first in Leyden and Shelley, and later in Washington Irving, Carlyle, etc. **—gnarl** *v.* to make knotted or twisted. 1814, back formation from *gnarled; n.* a knot or twist. 1824, from the verb or back formation from *gnarled,* paralleling *knarl* (1598).

gnash *v.* 1496, possibly a variant of obsolete *gnasten* (before 1325, in *Cursor Mundi,* but implied earlier in *gnaisting* action of grinding the teeth together, about 1300); perhaps borrowed from a Scandinavian source (compare Old Icelandic *gnastan* a gnashing), of unknown origin. The ending in *-sh* may have been influenced by the similar use of *-ish* with French verb stems to create such a formation as *banish*.

gnat *n.* About 1250 *gnatt,* developed from Old English *gnætt* (before 899, in Alfred's translation of Orosius' *Historiarum Adversus Paganos*); earlier *gneat* (before 830, erroneous spelling by analogy with plural forms). Old English *gnætt* is cognate with Low German *gnatte* gnat, dialectal High German *Gnatze,* from Proto-Germanic **ȝnattaz,* from Indo-European **ghnəd-* (Pok. 436); East Frisian *gnit,* Middle Low German *gnitte* (modern German *Gnitze*), Middle High German *gnaz* scurf; and ultimately related to Old English *gnagan* to GNAW.

gnaw *v.* Before 1200 *gnawen,* developed from Old English (before 1000) *gnagan;* cognate with Old High German *gnagan, nagan* (modern German *nagen*), and Old Icelandic and Swedish *gnaga;* cognate with Lettish *gńēga* one who eats with long teeth, from Indo-European **ghnēgh-/ghnəgh-* (Pok.436). Whether the Old English is cognate with Old Saxon *knagan,* and Middle and modern Dutch *knagen* is conjectural, as they suggest a different Indo-European base.

gneiss (nis) *n. Geology.* rocklike granite with a layered structure. 1757, borrowing of German *Gneiss,* from earlier variants *Geneuss, Knaust,* probably alterations of Middle High German *gneist, gneiste, ganeiste* spark (perhaps because the rock sparkles), from Old High German *gneisto* spark, of unknown origin.

gnome *n.* 1712-14, in Pope's *Rape of the Lock;* borrowed from French *gnome,* from New Latin *gnomus,* possibly with the meaning of earth dweller. The word is often said to have been coined by the Swiss-born alchemist and physician Paracelsus, 1493-1541, perhaps from a Greek form **gēnómos* earth dweller, erroneously improvised from Greek *gnṓmē* thought, opinion, intelligence (because gnomes are described as intelligent); see GNOMIC. It is also possible that the quasi-Greek **gēnómos* was formed on analogy with Greek *thalassonómos* dwelling in the sea, from the alleged inhabitants of the four elements; salamander (fire), sylph (air), undine (water), and gnome (earth).

gnomic *adj.* full of instructive sayings. 1815, borrowed, perhaps through French *gnomique,* from Late Latin *gnōmicus* concerned with maxims or didactic, from Greek *gnōmikós,* from *gnṓmē* thought, opinion, maxim, intelligence, from *gignṓskein* to come to know; see KNOW; for suffix see -IC. It is also possible that *gnomic* is a shortened form of earlier *gnomical* (1603).

gnomon (nō′mon) *n.* rod, pointer, or triangular piece especially on a sundial. 1546, borrowed from Latin *gnōmōn,* from Greek *gnṓmōn* indicator (literally, one who discerns), from *gignṓskein* to come to know; see KNOW.

Gnostic (nos′tik) *n.* believer in a mystical religious doctrine of spiritual knowledge, practiced in early Christian times. 1585-87, borrowed from Late Latin *Gnōsticus,* from Late Greek *Gnōstikós,* noun use of adjective *gnōstikós* knowing, able to discern, from *gnōstós* knowable, (to be) known, from *gignṓskein* to come to know; see KNOW. **—adj.** 1656, relating to knowledge; from the noun. **—Gnosticism** *n.* 1664, formed from English *Gnostic,* n. + *-ism.*

gnotobiotic (nō′tōbīot′ik) *adj. Biology.* free of germs or associated only with known germs. 1949, formed in English from Greek *gnōtós* known (from *gignṓskein* to come to KNOW) + English *biotic* of life, as in *antibiotic.* **—gnotobiotics** *n.* study of gnotobiotic organisms or environments. 1949, formed from *gnotobiotic.*

gnu (nü *or* nyü) *n.* African antelope, wildebeest. 1777 *gnoo,* in George A. Forster's *A Voyage Round the World;* borrowed probably through Dutch *gnoe,* alteration of Hottentot *i-ngu* black hartebeest or white-tailed *gnu,* from Southern Bushman, transcribed as *!nu:* (in which *!* and *:* represent clicks). The spelling *gnu* became established after 1786.

go *v.* Probably before 1200 *gon, gan* to walk, move along; developed from Old English *gān* to go (about 725, in *Beowulf*); cognate with Old Frisian, Old Saxon, and Middle Low German *gān* to go, Middle Dutch *gaen* (modern Dutch *gaan*), Old High German *gān, gēn* (modern German *gehen*), Old Danish and Old Swedish *gā* (modern Danish, Norwegian, and Swedish *gå*), and Crimean Gothic *geen,* from Proto-Germanic *ȝai-/ȝæ-.* Outside Germanic, cognates are found in Greek *-chḗ-* in *kichḗmenai* to reach, and Sanskrit *-hā-* in *jáhāti* he leaves, abandons; all theoretically traceable to the Indo-European base **ĝhē(i)-/ĝhəi-* leave, go (Pok.418).

The Old English verb forms include *gān,* infinitive, *gā, gǣst, gǣth* and *gāth,* present tense, and *gegān,* past participle. For the past tense the word *ēode* (Middle English *yode*) was used, until it was replaced in the 1400's by *went,* the past tense of *wenden* to go; see WENT.

—n. 1727, action of going, gait; also, on the verge of destruction, ready to be lost or destroyed; from the verb. The sense of in a state of motion (as in *on the go*), is first recorded in 1843, and that of a spell of work or other activity (as in *at one go*), is first found in 1825. **—adj.** *Informal.* in perfect order; ready to proceed. 1951, American English (used especially in aerospace engineering jargon); from the verb.

—go-ahead *n.* 1840, implied in earlier *go-aheadism* (1838). **—go-between** *n.* 1598, an intermediary, in Shakespeare's *Merry Wives of Windsor.* **—gocart** *n.* 1676, a litter or sedan chair, which is carried on poles by men, a sense curiously sustaining the Old English meaning of to walk, move along; also found in the sense of an infant's walker. **—go-getter** *n.* 1922, an energetic person (antecedents of this are found in the earlier *goer,* n., about 1378, and in a surname, about 1250). **—going** *n.* Before 1250; *goings,* as in *goings on* (1775, in Johnson's letters, but implied in earlier rules *of goinges,* about 1475), formed from *go,* v. **—goner** *n.* 1850, some one or thing that is doomed; formed from English *gone* + *-er*[1]. The idea is found earlier in the phrase *gone goose* (1830).

goad *n.* Before 1200 *gode* pointed stick for driving cattle, etc.; developed from Old English (about 725) *gād;* cognate with Langobardic *gaida* spear, from Proto-Germanic **ȝaiđō;* probably also cognate with Avestan *zaēna-* weapon, and Sanskrit *hinóti, hínvati* urges on, throws, from Indo-European **ĝhei-/ĝhoi-/ĝhī-* (Pok. 424). The figurative sense of anything which urges on, appeared in 1600. **—v.** 1579, to drive or urge on as if with a goad; from the noun.

goal *n.* 1531, place where a race ends; of uncertain origin. An isolated form *gol* boundary or limit, appears in Shoreham's *Poems* (before 1333), and does not recur in the record before 1531, in Elyot's *The Boke Named the Governour,* becoming very common thereafter. In the 200 years between Shoreham's and Elyot's use the word may have survived only in sports and so was unrecorded in literature. It is suggested that *goal* developed from Old English **gāl* obstacle or barrier, for which indirect evidence is furnished by the apparent derivative *gǣlan* to hinder; or, less likely that *goal* is a borrowing from Old French *gaule* a pole, whose meaning and form are both distant from Middle English *gol* boundary. **—goalie** *n.* 1921, goalkeeper (1658, formed from English *goal* + *-ie,* variant of *-y*[2]).

goat *n.* Before 1200 *got,* in Layamon's *Chronicle of Britain,* and *geat,* in *Ancrene Riwle;* developed from Old English (about 700) *gāt* she-goat; cognate with Old Saxon *gēt* she-goat, Middle Dutch *gheet* (modern Dutch *geit*), Old High German *geiz* (modern German *Geiss*), Old Icelandic *geit* (Norwegian *geit,* Swedish *get,* Danish *ged*), Gothic *gaits* goat, she-goat, from Proto-Germanic **ʒaitaz,* and Latin *haedus* kid, from Indo-European **ghaidos* (Pok.409). In Old English, *gāt* was a specialized term, as the male goat was called *bucca;* see BUCK[1]. In the late 1300's the sexes began to be distinguished through the use of *he-goat* and *she-goat.* **—goatee** *n.* 1844 *goaty;* 1847 *goatee* man's beard resembling that of a he-goat, formed from English *goat* + *-ee,* probably a variant of *-y*[2]. **—goatherd** *n.* (1229, in the surname *Gothirde*) **—goatskin** *n.* (before 1387)

gob[1] *n. Informal.* lump, mass. About 1382, Middle English *gobbe,* in the Wycliffe Bible; borrowed probably from Old French *gobe* mouthful or lump, from Old French *gober* gulp or swallow down, probably from Gaulish **gobbo-* (compare Old Irish *gob* beaklike mouth or face, and Gaelic *gob* beak, mouth), of unknown origin.

gob[2] *n. Slang.* sailor. 1915, American English, probably a shortened form of earlier British nautical slang *gobby* a coastguardsman (1890); said to be derived from dialectal *gob* spit (extended sense of *gob*[1]), from the habit of seamen spitting while telling yarns and chewing tobacco; also from the lump of chewing tobacco itself.

gobbet *n.* lump, mass. 1290, a fragment or piece; borrowed from Old French *gobet* mouthful, piece, diminutive of *gobe* GOB[1]; for suffix see -ET.

gobble[1] *v.* eat fast and greedily. 1601; probably a frequentative form of *gob* from *gobben* to drink something greedily; for suffix see -LE[3].

gobble[2] *v.* make the throaty sound of a turkey. 1680, probably imitative, but perhaps influenced by *gobble*[1] or GARBLE. **—n.** 1781, from the verb. **—gobbler** *n.* 1737, formed from English *gobble,* v. + *-er*[1].

gobbledygook (gob′əldēgůk) *n.* something, such as an idea or writing, that cannot be understood, especially because it is presented in official or bureaucratic jargon. 1944, American English; formed in imitation of the gobbling of the turkey cock ("always gobbledy gobbling and strutting with ludicrous pomposity," by Maury Maverick, American lawyer who coined the term in the *New York Times Magazine* May 21, 1944).

goblet *n.* Probably about 1380 *gobelot, goblot;* borrowed from Old French *gobelet,* diminutive of *gobel* cup, probably from Gallo-Romance **gob* beak or mouth, from Gaulish; see GOB[1].

goblin *n.* Probably before 1320 *gobylyn* mischievous sprite or elf; borrowed possibly from Old French *gobelin,* which was apparently the source of Medieval Latin *Gobelinus,* the name of a spirit that supposedly haunted the French town of *Evreux,* in the 1100's. Though French *gobelin* was not recorded until almost 250 years after appearance of the English term it is probably reasonable to assume the French term was in existence long before it was recorded, as it is a French ghost that is mentioned in the Medieval Latin text of the 1100's, and few people who believed in folk magic spoke Medieval Latin. The German *Kobold* a spirit of the earth, is probably of different origin.

God or **god** *n.* Old English (about 725) *god* Supreme Being, deity; cognate with Old Frisian, Old Saxon, and Dutch *god* Supreme Being, deity, Old High German *got* (modern German *Gott*), Old Icelandic *godh, gudh,* and Gothic *guth,* from Proto-Germanic **ʒuđán.* Outside Germanic some probable cognates are found in Armenian *jaunem* I dedicate or consecrate, Avestan *zavaiti* he invokes, curses, and Sanskrit *hávate* he invokes, which may suggest the Indo-European base *ĝheu-/ĝhu-* (Pok.447) with meanings of invoke, and offer sacrifices or pour, this latter sense further suggesting the semantic development of one to whom libations are poured, one worshiped with libations. The Germanic words for *god* were originally neuter, but after the Germanic tribes adopted Christianity, *God* became a masculine syntactic form. Some confusion exists about the derivation of *God* from *good,* and though the words had the same spelling in Middle English, the only association is in terms such as *Good Friday,* written *god friday,* in which *god* has the meaning of holy, sacred. **—godchild** *n.* (probably before 1200) **—goddamn** *n., v.* (probably before 1398) **—goddaughter** *n.* (about 1250) **—goddess** *n.* (probably before 1350) **godfather** *n.* (before 1200) **—godhead** *n.* (probably before 1200) **—godly** *adj.* (probably 1384) **—godmother** *n.* (about 1273) **—godsend** *n.* (1679 *God's send*) **—godson** *n.* (1205) **—Godspeed** *n.* (1275)

gofer *n. Slang.* worker who runs errands for an office staff or work crew. 1956, American English, alteration by humorous or relaxed pronunciation of *for* in *go for,* so called from the worker being told to *go for* coffee and other refreshments, or for spare parts, etc. There is also a passing allusion to or pun on *gopher* with the sense of a little animal who runs around.

goggle *v.* 1540 *gogle* roll one's eyes; stare with bulging eyes, from *gogelen* to roll about (probably about 1400), also influenced by *gogel-eyed* squint- or one-eyed (about 1384, in the Wycliffe Bible); of uncertain origin. **—n.** 1651, goggling look; earlier, person who goggles (1616); perhaps from the adjective *gogle* in *gogle eye(s),* or from the verb. The plural form *goggles* large eyeglasses usually worn for protection, is first recorded in 1715. The spelling with two *g*'s did not become fixed before 1683.

go-go *adj. Informal.* energetic, lively. 1962, American English, reduplication of *go,* v., move fast, be lively, etc. The once-fashionable vogue word is now an archaism, occasionally appearing as a literary device to recall the 1960's.

goiter or **goitre** (goi′tər) *n.* disease of the thyroid gland. 1625, borrowed from French *goître, goitre,* from a dialect of the Rhône region, from Old French and Old Provençal *goitron* throat, gullet, from Vulgar Latin **gutturiōnem,* from Latin *guttur* throat.

gold *n.* Old English (about 725) *gold* a shiny, bright-yellow precious metal; cognate with Old Frisian and Old Saxon *gold* gold, Middle Dutch *gout* (modern Dutch *goud*), Old High German *gold* (modern German *Gold*), Old Icelandic *goll, gull* (Swedish, Danish *guld,*

Norwegian *gull*), and Gothic *gulth,* from Proto-Germanic **ʒulth-;* apparently related to modern English *yellow,* from Old English *geolu* YELLOW, through the Indo-European root **ĝhel-* yellow, found in *ĝhl̥to-,* (Pok.429). **—adj.** made of gold. Probably before 1200; from the noun. **—golden** *adj.* About 1300, and in the surname *Goldene* (1298); formed from *gold,* n. + *-en*². *Golden* replaced the earlier Middle English form *gilden,* which developed from Old English *gylden;* see GULDEN. **—goldenrod** *n.* (1568) **—goldfinch** *n.* 1229, in the surname *Goldfinch,* developed from Old English *gold-finc* (about 1000). **—goldfish** *n.* (1698; *goldfish bowl,* 1935) **—gold-leaf** (1727) **—goldsmith** *n.* 1255, as a surname; found in Old English *gold-smith* (about 1000).

golf *n.* 1457, Scottish *golf, gouf* the game of golf, played first in Scotland in the 1400's and popularized in England in the 1500's; perhaps alteration of Middle Dutch *colf, colve* stick, club, or bat (modern Dutch *kolf*), used in the Netherlands in a ball game called *kolven;* cognate with Middle Low German *kolve* club or bat, *kolven* ball for striking with a club, Old High German *kolbo* club (modern German *Kolben* club, mallet), and Old Icelandic *kolfr* bolt, rod, blunt arrow, from Proto-Germanic **kulb-,* from Indo-European **glebh-/gl̥bh-* (Pok.359). **—v.** 1800, from the noun.

gonad (gō′nad) *n. Anatomy.* organ in which reproductive cells develop. 1880, from New Latin *gonas* (pl. *gonades*), from Greek *gonḗ* seed, from *gignesthai* be born; see KIN.

gondola *n.* 1549; borrowed from Italian (in Venetian dialect) *gondola;* earlier in English *goundel;* borrowed from Old Italian *gondula,* of uncertain origin (possibly from Italian diminutive of *gonda* a kind of boat, perhaps from Greek *kóndy* drinking cup, of unknown origin). **—gondolier** *n.* person who rows or poles a gondola. 1603, in Florio's translation of Montaigne's *Essays;* borrowed from French, from Italian *gondoliere,* from *gondola* gondola; for suffix see -IER.

gong *n.* About 1600, borrowed from Malay *gǒng* or Javanese *gong,* alleged to be a formation imitative of the sound made by the instrument.

gonorrhea (gon′ərē′ə) *n.* venereal disease. 1549, borrowed, probably through Middle French *gonorrhéa,* from Late Latin *gonorrhoea* involuntary discharge of semen, from Greek *gonórrhoia* (*gónos* seed + *rhoḗ* flow, from *rheîn* to flow); so called from the belief that the discharge of mucus in the disease was a discharge of semen; see KIN and STREAM.

gonzo *adj. Slang.* crazy or wild, eccentric, bizarre. 1972, American English, probably borrowed from Italian *gonzo* simpleton or blockhead, perhaps shortened from *Borgonzone* Burgundian. In the record of written English *gonzo* first appeared in the phrase *gonzo journalism* referring to the personal style of reporting by the writer H.S. Thompson for *Rolling Stone* magazine. Also popularized as the name of a puppet (a Muppet) on the television show *Sesame Street.*

goo *n.* 1911, American English; perhaps a shortened form of *burgoo* thick porridge (1787) or stew (1853), but more likely a back formation from *gooey* (1905, formed from *(bur)goo* + *-ey*).

goober *n. Southern U.S.* the peanut. 1833, American English, of African origin; perhaps Bantu (compare Kikongo and Kimbundu *nguba* peanut).

good *adj.* 1124 *god;* later *good* (about 1250, gradually becoming the established form about 1450); developed from Old English (about 725) *gōd* having the right or desirable quality. Old English *gōd* is cognate with Old Frisian and Old Saxon *gōd* good, Dutch *goed,* Old High German *guot* (modern German *gut*), Old Icelandic *gōdhr,* and Gothic *gōths* or *gōds,* from Proto-Germanic **ʒōđaz.* Outside Germanic cognates are found in Old Slavic *godŭ* the right time, Sanskrit adjective *gádhya-s* to be held fast, what suits one, and Tocharian B *kācc-* to rejoice. *Good* is related to *gather* and *together* with the sense of fit or suitable in the Proto-Germanic base **ʒōđ-,* probably a variant of **ʒađ-* to bring together, unite, from Indo-European **ghedh-/ghodh-/ghōdh-* (Pok.423).

This adjective, as in other Germanic languages, has no regular comparative or superlative forms, their place being supplied by *better* and *best.*

—n. 1102 *god;* developed from Old English *gōd* that which is good (about 725, in *Beowulf*); from the adjective.

The plural form *goods* in the sense of property or possessions, is first recorded about 1280; the singular form in the same sense, is found in Old English about 950.

—good-for-nothing *adj.* (1711, in Swift's works); *n.* (1751) **—good-hearted** *adj.* (about 1425) **—goodly** *adj.* Probably about 1150; developed from Old English *gōdlīc* (about 1000). **—good-natured** *adj.* (1577) **—good turn** (about 1475) **—good will** (Old English, about 725)

good-by or **good-bye** *interj.* 1811 *Good-bye;* earlier *godbwye* (1573-80); a contraction (by confusion of *god* good, and *God* God) of "God be with ye (you)," probably influenced by *good day* and *good night* (probably before 1200, in Layamon's *Chronicle of Britain*).

goody¹ *n.* something very good to eat. 1745, in Swift's writings; formed from *good* + *-y*³. **—adj.** 1830, good in a weak or sentimental way; formed from *good* + *-y*¹. The reduplicated form *goody-goody,* with a similar meaning, appeared in 1871, probably by association with *goody*¹, n. in the sense of a person who makes too much of being good (before 1870, in American English). **—interj.** 1796 *goodee* exclamation of pleasure, formed from *good* + *-ee,* alteration of *-y*¹.

goody² *n.* old woman of humble station. 1559, contracted variant of *goodwife* (about 1250 *gode wif* mistress of a house or other establishment, from *gode* good + *wif* wife).

gooey *adj.* See GOO.

goof *n.* 1916, American English slang, a stupid person or fool; possibly a variant of dialectal English *goff* foolish clown or silly fellow (1869), from earlier *goffe* (1570), probably borrowed from Middle French *goffe* awkward or stupid, of uncertain origin. Alternatively, early modern English *goffe* may have developed from *goffen* to speak in a frivolous manner (about 1175), possibly from Old English *gegāf* buffoonery, and *gaffetung* scoffing, related to modern English *gaff* to jest. The sense of a mistake, blunder, appeared about 1954, probably influenced by the earlier verb with this sense, and probably also by modern English *gaffe* blunder. **—v.** 1932, American English slang, waste time, dawdle, idle, loaf (also in the phrase *goof off,* 1941); 1941, to blunder, make a mistake; from the noun. **—goofy** *adj.* 1921, American English slang, stupid or silly, formed from *goof,* n. + *-y*¹.

googol (gü'gol) *n.* the number 1 followed by 100 zeroes or 10^{100}. 1940, in Kasmer and Newman's *Mathematics and the Imagination,* coined (possibly as a word from children's vocabulary, perhaps with some influence of the comic-strip character Barney *Google*) by the nine-year-old nephew of the American mathematician Edward Kasmer when the child was asked to name such a large number.

goon *n. Slang.* stupid person, thug. 1921, American English *goon* a stupid person, possibly a shortened form of earlier *gooney* stupid person (1896). The meaning of thug hired to disrupt labor disputes, is first recorded in 1938 in American English.

goose *n.* Old English (about 700) *gōs;* cognate with Old Frisian *gōs, gōz* goose, Middle Low German *gōs,* Middle Dutch and modern Dutch *gans,* Old High German *gans* (modern German *Gans*), and Old Icelandic *gās,* from Proto-Germanic **ʒans-.* Old English *gōs* is also cognate with Old Irish *gēiss* swan, Latin *ānser* goose, Greek *chḗn,* Old Prussian *sansy,* Russian *gus',* and Sanskrit *haṅsá-s* goose, swan, from Indo-European **ĝhans-* (Pok.412). The loss of *n* (English, Old Frisian, Middle Low German, and Old Icelandic) is a normal development before *s.* The plural *geese* is from Proto-Germanic **ʒans-iz,* and if the *s* is formative to a base **ʒan-,* then a connection can probably be established with *gannet,* and *gander,* though much debate exists about this. **—gooseberry** *n.* 1530, formed from English *goose* + *berry;* and probably not a loan translation, as sometimes suggested. **—goose flesh** (before 1425) **—gooseneck** *n.* (1688, iron hook; 1827, curved metal pipe) **—goose pimples** (1914) **—goose step** (1806)

gopher *n.* burrowing rodent with large cheek pouches. 1814, American English, of uncertain origin; perhaps an alteration attempting to Anglicize American French (Louisiana) *gaufre* honeycomb, waffle (said to be a general term of reference for many burrowing mammals in allusion to the structure of their burrow), from Old French *gaufre,* from Frankish (compare Middle Dutch *wafel* honeycomb, WAFFLE).

Gordian knot (gôr'dēən) a difficult matter. 1579, in allusion to the knot tied in legend by *Gordius,* king of Phrygia; for suffix see -AN. The one to loosen the knot should rule Asia; instead Alexander the Great *cut the Gordian knot,* which means to solve a difficult problem in a quick, easy, or unexpected way.

gore[1] *n.* blood that is shed, clotted blood. About 1150 *gore;* developed from Old English *gor* dirt, dung (about 725, in *Exodus*), related to *gyre* dung, and cognate with Old High German and Middle Low German *gor* dung, Dutch *goor* dingy, Old Icelandic *gor* cud, slimy matter; of uncertain origin. The meaning of blood is first recorded as thickened or clotted blood, especially that shed in battle (1563, found perhaps in the distinction *blood and gore,* also Dutch *bloed en goor*). **—gory** *adj.* About 1480, Scottish *gorrie* bloody, formed from *gore* + *-y*[1].

gore[2] *v.* to wound with a horn, tusk, etc. Before 1400 *goren,* Scottish *gorren* to pierce, stab; origin uncertain (occasionally attributed as a variant of *gore* spear, from Old English *gār).*

gore[3] *n.* long, triangular piece of cloth made in a skirt, sail, etc. About 1250, a skirt, in *The Owl and the Nightingale;* developed from Old English *gāra* angular point, as of land (before 899 in Alfred's translation of Orosius' *Historiarum Adversus Paganos*); cognate with Old High German *gēro, kēro* (modern German *Gehren, Gehre*), Old Icelandic *geire,* and related to *gār* spear (from its shape); see GARLIC. **—v.** put or make a gore in. 1548, from the noun.

gorge (gôrj) *n.* deep, narrow valley. About 1350, throat; earlier, as a surname (1185); borrowed from Old French *gorge* throat, bosom, from Late Latin *gurga,* variant of *gurges* gullet or throat, jaws, probably from classical Latin *gurges* abyss or whirlpool, related to *gurguliō* gullet, from Indo-European **guer-/guerə-* (Pok.474). The meaning of what has been swallowed is first recorded in Lydgate's *Falls of Princes* (probably before 1439). The transferred sense of throat or narrow opening in reference to a narrow valley or ravine, is found in Gray's *Letters* (1769), possibly influenced by a similar sense in French. **—v.** Probably before 1300, eat greedily, in *Kyng Alisaunder;* from Old French *gorger, gorgier,* from Old French *gorge* throat.

gorgeous *adj.* richly colored, splendid. About 1495, in Skelton's works; borrowed from Middle French *gorgias* elegant, fashionable, fond of jewelry (probably with reference to *gorge* neck), perhaps from Old French *gorge* bosom, throat (also in reference to something being suitable for adorning the neck); see GORGE. The forms *gorgayse, gorges,* and *gorgyas* eventually gave way to the spelling *gorgeouse* (also recorded before 1500), which parallels other words ending in *-eous.*

Gorgon (gôr'gən) *n.* any of three sisters in Greek legend who had snakes for hair and whose look turned the beholder to stone. Before 1398, in Trevisa's translation of Bartholomew's *De Proprietatibus Rerum;* borrowed from Latin *Gorgō* (genitive *Gorgōnis*), from Greek *Gorgṓ,* from *gorgós* terrible, of unknown origin.

gorilla *n.* large ape of Africa. 1847, American English, adopted as the specific name of this ape by T.S. Savage, 1804-1880, American missionary and naturalist, who first described it. Savage borrowed the word from Greek *Górillai,* pl., the name given to a group of wild, hairy creatures by Greek interpreters who translated the account of the Carthaginian navigator Hanno, relating his voyage made along the northwest coast of Africa about 500 B.C.

gorse (gôrs) *n.* furze, a prickly shrub. 1287 *gorste;* earlier *Gors-,* found in the place name *Gorsfen* (1270), *Gorst-* in *Gorstley* (1228); found in Old English *gors* (before 800), *gorst* (about 950); cognate with Old Saxon and Old High German *gersta* barley (modern German *Gerste*), Middle Dutch *gherste* (modern Dutch *gerst*), from Proto-Germanic **ʒurst-/ʒerst-;* also outside Germanic cognate with Latin *hordeum* barley, from Indo-European **ĝhersd-/ĝhr̥sd-* (Pok. 446).

gosh *interj.* exclamation or mild oath. 1757, altered pronunciation and spelling of *God,* originally in the phrase *by gosh,* probably developed from *by gosse,* in Udall's *Ralph Roister Doister* (before 1553).

goshawk (gos'hôk') *n.* powerful, short-winged hawk. Probably before 1300 *goshauk,* developed from Old English *gōshafoc* (about 1000, in Ælfric's *Glossary*); from *gōs* GOOSE + *hafoc* HAWK.

gosling *n.* young goose. About 1350 *goselyng;* earlier, in the surname *Goseling* (about 1275), from Middle English *gos* goose + *-ling;* replacement of earlier *gesling* (recorded probably before 1300); borrowed from a Scandinavian source (compare Old Icelandic *gǣslingr*).

gospel *n.* the teachings of Jesus and the Apostles. Before 1250 *gospel,* in *Ancrene Riwle;* developed from Old English *godspell, gōdspel* good news (about 750, in Cynewulf's *Elene*). The Old English word is a compound of *gōd* good + *spell, spel* story or message, and is probably a translation of Latin *bona adnūntiātiō,* itself a translation of Greek *euangélion* evangel; see GOOD and SPELL² charm. The first element *(gōd)* of the Old English compound *gōdspell* was mistakenly associated with *god* God, and for this reason a short *o* appeared in the Old English variant *godspell,* although regular phonetic development would by Middle English times have produced the same result. The process is also seen in Old High German *gotspel,* Old Saxon *gōdspell,* in which *gotspell* has the same substitution of "God" (for good), though Old High German *guotspellōn* to evangelize, clearly has "good" as the first element.

gossamer *n.* film or thread of cobweb. Probably before 1300 *gossumer,* seemingly formed from *gōs* goose + *sumer, sumor* summer.

The reference is to the threads spun especially in fields of stubble or on bushes and which are seen often floating through the air in the calm, clear weather of late fall. It is unclear whether or not the analogy of these threads is to the downy appearance of gossamer and further to the time of year when geese are in season; thus a name for Indian summer as the season of the goose and cobwebs. Dutch has a similar allusion to summer threads in *zomerdraden,* also German *Sommerfäden,* and Swedish *sommartråd.* The spelling with *a* was established by the late 1600's.

—adj. very light and thin, filmy. 1806-07, from the noun.

gossip *n.* idle talk. Probably before 1300 *gossip* godparent; (also a familiar acquaintance, developed from Old English (1014) *godsibb* person acting as a sponsor at baptism, godparent (*god* God + *sibb* relative; see SIB, SIBLING). In Middle English *gossip* was extended in meaning from a familiar acquaintance to that of a form of address for such an acquaintance (probably before 1300), and was later applied to anyone who engages in familiar or idle talk (1566). Probably by influence of the verb, *gossip* further developed the meaning of idle talk about others, trifling or groundless rumor (1811). **—v.** 1590, to act as a familiar acquaintance, in Shakespeare's *Comedy of Errors;* from the noun. The meaning of talk idly, mostly about other people's affairs, is first recorded in 1627.

gouge *n.* 1350-51, borrowed from Old French *gouge,* from Late Latin *gubia,* alteration of *gulbia* hollow beveled chisel, probably from Gaulish (compare Old Irish *gulban* prickle, sting, *gulba* beak, Welsh *gylf* sharp point, knife, beak); perhaps cognate with Greek *glaphyrós* hollow, from Indo-European **gelebh-/gelbh-/gḷbh-* (Pok.359).**—v.** 1570, cut with a gouge; from the noun. The meaning of dig out, tear out, or force out, or with, or as if with a gouge, is first recorded in Ben Jonson's *The Devil is an Ass* (1616).

goulash (gü'läsh) *n.* stew made of beef or veal and vegetables. 1866, borrowed from Hungarian *gulyás hús* herdsman's meat (in Hungary, a beef or lamb soup with onions and paprika, first apparently made by herdsmen while pasturing).

gourd (gôrd) *n.* hard-shelled fruit of certain vines. About 1303, melon similar to a watermelon, in Mannyng's *Handlyng Synne;* borrowed through Anglo-French *gourde* (Old French *cöorde*), ultimately from Latin *cucurbita,* of uncertain origin (possibly related to *cucumis* CUCUMBER).

gourmand (gu̇r'mənd) *n.* person fond of good eating. 1450 *gourmaunt* glutton; borrowed from Middle French *gourmant, gourmand* glutton (originally, gluttonous), of uncertain origin. Despite their similarity in form, French *gourmand* and *gourmet* seem to be unrelated etymologically, since both the current form and meaning of *gourmet* are modern developments, although both meanings were probably influenced by *gourmand.*

gourmet (gu̇r'mā) *n.* person who is expert in judging and choosing fine foods, wines, etc. 1820, borrowing of French *gourmet,* alteration (probably influenced by Middle French *gourmant* gourmand) of Old French *grommes,* pl., wine tasters, wine merchant's servants, of uncertain origin (perhaps from Old English **grom* man servant).

gout *n.* painful disease of the joints. About 1300 *goute;* earlier *gute* in the compound *gutefeastre* festered gouty swelling (probably before 1200, in *Ancrene Riwle*); borrowed from Old French *gote, goute* gout, drop, from Latin *gutta* a drop (in Medieval Latin, gout), of unknown origin. At one time, the disease was thought to be caused by drops of viscous humors seeping from the blood into the joints. **—gouty** *adj.* Before 1398, in Trevisa's translation of Bartholomew's *De Proprietatibus Rerum;* formed from Middle English *goute* gout + *-y*¹.

govern *v.* Probably about 1280 *governen* to rule, as a country, people, or institution; borrowed from Old French *governer* govern, from Latin *gubernāre* to direct, manage, rule, guide (originally, to steer), from Greek *kybernân* to steer or pilot a ship, direct, probably of non-Indo-European origin. **—governess** *n.* About 1450 *governesse,* a shortened form of earlier *governouresse* woman who rules, (also) a governing or guiding influence (about 1370, in Chaucer's *An A.B.C.;* later, guardian, governess, about 1422); borrowed from Old French *governeresse* (*governeor* governor + *-esse* -ess). **—government** *n.* About 1380, in Chaucer's translation of Boethius' *De Consolatione Philosophiae;* borrowed from Old French *governement (governer* govern + *-ment* -ment*).* **—governor** *n.* Probably before 1300, protector or guide, in *Kyng Alisaunder;* borrowed from Old French *governeor,* and directly from Latin *gubernātōrem* (nominative *gubernātor*) director, ruler, governor, (originally, steersman, pilot), from *gubernāre* to govern; for suffix see -OR². The sense of ruler or lord is first recorded in Mannyng's *Chronicle of England* (before 1338).

gown *n.* loose outer garment. Probably before 1325 *gune* an official's robe; borrowed from Old French *goune, gone,* from Late Latin *gunna* leather garment, skin, hide, of unknown origin. **—v.** dress in a gown. 1422, from the noun.

grab *v.* 1589 *grabbe* seize suddenly or snatch; probably borrowed from Middle Dutch or Middle Low German *grabben* to grab; cognate with Old English *græppian* to seize (which did not survive into Middle English), East Frisian and Low German *grapsen* to grab, snatch (modern German *grapschen*), and Old Icelandic *grāpa;* also cognate with Old Slavic *grabiti* to rob, and Sanskrit (in a past-tense form) *agrabhat* he seized, from Indo-European **ghrebh-/ghrobh-* (Pok.455). **—n.** 1824, a sudden grasp or attempt to seize, in De Quincey's writings; from the verb. **—grabby** *adj.* 1910, greedy; formed from English *grab* + *-y*[1].

grace *n.* Probably before 1200 *grace* God's favor or help, in *Ancrene Riwle;* borrowed from Old French *grace* pleasing quality, favor, good will, thanks, from Latin *grātia* pleasing quality, goodwill, gratitude, from *grātus* pleasing, agreeable. Latin *grātus* is cognate with Sanskrit *gūrtá-s* welcome (*gír,* genitive *girás* praise or song, *gṛṇāti* he praises), possibly developed from an ancient Indo-European religious term, from Indo-European **gwṝtós,* root **gwerə-* (Pok.478). The meaning of goodness, virtue, graciousness, is first recorded about 1330, and that of beauty of form, movement, or manner, pleasing or agreeable quality, charm, in *Ayenbite of Inwyt* (1340). **—v.** Probably before 1200 *gracen* to thank, in *Ancrene Riwle,* borrowed from Old French *gracier,* from *grace* thanks, grace. The meaning of give or add grace to is first recorded in Sidney's *The Arcadia* (before 1586). **—graceful** *n.* (before 1449) **—gracious** *adj.* About 1303 *gracyous* filled with God's grace; later, beautiful, fair (about 1325); borrowed from Old French *gracieus* having grace, pleasing, in favor, from Latin *grātiōsus,* from *grātia* GRACE.

grackle *n.* kind of blackbird. 1772 *gracule,* 1782 *grakle,* Anglicized forms of the New Latin genus name *Gracula,* from Latin *grāculus* jackdaw, a European crow, from Indo-European **grā-k-,* root **grā-* (Pok.384).

gradation *n.* 1538, climax; borrowed from Middle French *gradation* and directly from Latin *gradātiōnem* (nominative *gradātiō*) an ascent by steps, a gradation or climax, from *gradus* step, degree; see GRADE. The sense of gradual change is first recorded in 1549; and one of the steps in a gradual change, in 1599.

grade *n.* 1796, step or stage in a process; borrowed from French *grade* grade or degree, learned borrowing from Latin *gradus* (genitive *gradūs*) step or degree, replacement of Middle English *gree, gre* step or degree in a series; degree in order or rank, in amount or intensity; academic degree; step (probably about 1303); borrowed from Old French *gre, grei* step, from Latin *gradus,* related to *gradī* to walk, step, go; cognate with Gothic *grid* step, and Lithuanian *gridyti* to go, from Indo-European **ghredh-* (Pok.456).

Middle English *gre* is also found in *gres* a step, stair; and in the plural, flight of stairs. Modern English *grade* rapidly replaced *gre* in various meanings, some from English *gre,* some already in Latin *gradus,* including: a degree or position in rank, quality, etc. (1808); a class of things or persons of the same rank or quality (1807); and developed other independent senses, such as a class or division of a school arranged according to the pupils' progress (American English, 1835); a degree or quality accomplished, especially in schoolwork (1889); degree of inclination, gradient (1835); and inclined portion of a road, etc., slope (1883).
—v. 1659, arrange in grades; from the noun.
—grade school (American English, 1902)

gradient *n.* rate at which a road, railroad track, etc., rises. 1835 (as a railroading term); probably from the adjective in English. **—adj.** 1641, (of animals) characterized by walking, ambulant; later, going up or down gradually (1855); borrowed from Latin *gradientem,* present participle of *gradī* to walk, go; probably in its later English meanings influenced by GRADE, n.

gradual *adj.* Probably before 1425, having steps or ridges; later, taking place by degrees (1692, in Locke's writings); borrowed from Medieval Latin *gradualis,* from Latin *gradus* step; see GRADE, n.

graduate *adj.* that is a graduate. Before 1415, in the phrase *graduate man;* borrowed from Medieval Latin *graduatus,* past participle of *graduari* to take a degree, graduate, from Latin *gradus* step, GRADE; for suffix see -ATE[1]. **—v.** 1421, confer a university degree on; probably from the adjective, and in some instances, perhaps borrowed from Medieval Latin *graduatus,* past participle of *graduari.* The sense of receive a university degree, is found in Southey's *Letters* (1807), and reference to completion of a high-school course of study is first recorded in 1882 in American English. The technical use of divide (a scale, etc.) by degrees, appeared probably before 1425. **—n.** person who has graduated. 1459; borrowed from Medieval Latin *graduatus,* past participle of *graduari.* **—graduation** *n.* 1423 *graduacion* act of conferring a university degree; borrowed from Medieval Latin *graduationem* (nominative *graduatio*), from *graduari;* for suffix see -ATION.

graffiti (grəfē′tē) *n.pl.* crude drawings or inscriptions on a wall, fence, etc. 1851, ancient drawings or writings scratched on walls, as those of Pompeii and Rome; borrowing of Italian *graffiti,* plural of *graffito* a scribbling, from *graffio* a scratch or scribble, from *graffiare* to scribble, ultimately from Greek *gráphein* draw, write; see CARVE. The transferred meaning, applied to recently made crude drawings or scribblings, is first recorded in English in 1877.

graft[1] *n.* shoot, bud, etc., inserted into another plant. Probably about 1475 *grafte,* alteration of earlier *graff* (probably about 1387, in a version of *Piers Plowman,* in figurative sense); borrowed from Old French *grafe* graft or stylus, from Latin *graphium* stylus, from Greek *grapheion* stylus, from *gráphein* write. The use of *graft* meaning stylus or writing tool, is an allusion to the similarity in shape between the shoot of a plant that is prepared for grafting, usually with a beveled end or tip, and a stylus which looks like a modern pencil; see CARVE. The addition of *t* was possibly a confusion with a past participial form *graffed.* **—v.** Probably about 1475, implied in *graftyng,* alteration of earlier *graffen* (about 1378, in an earlier version of *Piers Plowman*); possibly from English *graff,* n., but more likely borrowed from Old French *grafier* to graft, from *grafe,* n.

graft[2] *n.* the taking of money dishonestly, especially by bribery. 1865, American English, perhaps from the verb. In 1901 the word was applied to the money so obtained. **—v.** make money by dishonest means. 1859, American English, possibly an extension of *graft*[1], v., in the figurative sense of insert or fix upon something as if by grafting.

graham *adj.* (of crackers, bread, etc.) made from unsifted whole-wheat flour. 1834, American English, in allusion to Sylvester *Graham,* 1794-1851, American dietetic reformer, whose ideas were part of the popular wisdom from the 1830's to the 1850's.

Grail *n.* cup, earlier a dish, supposedly used by Christ at the Last Supper, and into which Joseph of Arimathea received the last drops of blood from Christ's body on the Cross. It served as one of the chief elements of Medieval romance writing and in Arthurian legend was the great object of search by the Knights of the Round Table. Probably before 1300 *greal,* in *Arthour and Merlin;* borrowed from Old French *graal* cup; earlier, flat dish, from Medieval Latin *gradalis* a flat dish or shallow vessel, perhaps through Gallo-Romance **crātālis,* or directly from Latin *crātēr* bowl, from Greek *krātḗr* bowl, especially for mixing wine with water; see CRATER.

grain *n.* About 1202, in the surname *Graindorg;* later *greyn* small, hard particle (about 1300), and seed of plants or flowers (about 1325), seeds as fruit of cereal plant (before 1333); borrowed from Old French *grain, grein,* from Latin *grānum* grain, seed; see CORN[1]. The meaning of granular texture or roughness of surface, is first recorded in Lydgate's *Troy Book* (before 1420), and that of any texture about 1600. The figurative extension of quality, nature, temper, is found in Milton's writings (1641). **—grainy** *adj.* Probably about 1425; formed from Middle English *greyn* grain, n. + *-y*[1].

gram *n.* unit of weight in the metric system. 1797 *gramme,* borrowing of French *gramme,* from Late Latin *gramma* small weight, from Greek *grámma* small weight (originally, something written), from the stem of *gráphein* to draw, write.

-gram[1] a combining form meaning: something drawn or written, message, as in *cablegram, telegram, monogram;* or something recorded, record, as in *cardiogram.* Borrowed from Greek *-gramma,* from *grámma* something written; see GRAM.

-gram[2] a combining form meaning: so many grams, as in *kilogram = one thousand grams;* or so many parts of a gram, as in *centigram = one hundredth of a gram.* Borrowed from Greek *grámma* small weight; something written; see GRAM.

grammar *n.* 1176, as a surname *Gramaire* a grammarian or scholar; later *grammer, gramere* (before 1387, in Trevisa's translation of Higden's *Polychronicon*); borrowed from Old French *grammaire, gramaire* learning, especially Latin learning, philology, an irregular learned borrowing from Latin *grammatica,* from Greek *grammatikḗ téchnē* art of letters, from *grámma* (genitive *grámmatos*) something written, letter, from the stem of *gráphein* to draw or write; see CARVE. The borrowing from Latin *grammatica* into Old French *grammaire* may be, in part, the result of a popular form based on a Medieval Latin pattern that could have been assumed to be **grammaria* and is found in the Old French form *artimaire,* representing Latin *artem magicam* or *mathēmaticam.*

In early English use *grammar* meant only Latin grammar, as Latin was the only language taught grammatically. It was not until the 1600's that the word was extended to the study of English and other languages, and that about that time the spelling with *-ar* became firmly fixed in English.

—grammarian *n.* Probably about 1375, learned man; about 1378, Latin scholar; borrowed from Old French *gramarien,* from *gramaire* grammar. **—grammar school** (1642) **—grammatical** *adj.* 1526, borrowed possibly through Middle French *grammatical,* and directly from Late Latin *grammaticālis* of a scholar, from Latin *grammaticus* grammatical, from Greek *grammatikós* skilled in grammar, from *grámma* something written; see GRAMMAR.

Grammy *n.* annual award for outstanding achievement in phonograph recording. 1964, American English, from *gram(ophone)* + *-my,* as in *Emmy.*

Gramophone *n.* an old trademark for a phonograph. 1887 *gramophone,* American English, possibly an inversion of earlier *phonogram* the record or tracing made by a phonograph (1884). The Gramophone, also known originally as the Victor Talking Machine, was invented in 1887 by Emile Berliner, 1851-1929, an American inventor born in Germany. It was the first phonograph to use a disk recording instead of a cylinder.

grampus *n.* large, fierce dolphin. 1593; earlier *graundepose* (before 1529), alteration of earlier *grapays* (1325), and *graspeys* (1267); borrowed from Anglo-French *grampais,* alteration (influenced by *grand* big) of Old French *graspeis,* from Medieval Latin *craspiscis,* literally, fat fish, from Latin *crassus* thick + *piscis* fish; see CRASS.

granary *n.* place where grain is stored. 1570, borrowed from Latin *grānārium,* from *grānum* grain, see CORN[1]; for suffix see -ARY.

grand *adj.* 1125-30, as a surname *Grand,* but generally found in Middle English *graunt* large, big (before 1399); borrowed, in part through Anglo-French *graund, graunt,* and directly from Old French *grand, grant,* from Latin *grandis* big, great, grand; of uncertain origin. **—n.** *Slang.* thousand dollars. 1921, American English, from the adjective. **—grandchild** *n.* (1587) **—granddaughter** *n.* (1611) **—grandfather** *n.* (1424) **—grand jury** (1495) **—grandmother** *n.* (before 1420; earlier *grandame,* probably about 1200) **—grand piano** (1797) **—grandson** *n.* (1586) **—grandstand** *n.* (1834); *v.* to do something for effect; show off. 1900, American English, abstracted from *grandstand play,* 1893.

grandeur *n.* About 1500, loftiness or height; borrowed from Middle French *grandeur* grandness, greatness, from Old French *grand* great; see GRAND. The extended meaning of majesty, nobility, stateliness, is first recorded in 1669.

grandiloquence (grandil′əkwəns) *n.* the use of lofty or pompous words. 1589, in Puttenham's *The Arte of English Poesie;* borrowed from Latin *grandiloquentia,* from *grandiloquus* using lofty speech (*grandis* big, GRAND + *-loquus* speaking, from *loquī* speak); for suffix see -ENCE. **—grandiloquent** *adj.* 1593, in Nashe's writings; probably a back formation from *grandiloquence.* These words and *grandiloquous* (1592) appear to be vogue words of the 1590's.

grandiose *adj.* grand in an imposing or impressive way. 1840, in Thackeray's *Paris Sketch Book;* borrowed from French *grandiose* impressive, from Italian *grandioso,* from Latin *grandis* big, great; see GRAND; for suffix see -OSE[1].

grange *n.* farm. 1252 *Grange,* as a place name; later *gronge* group of farms (about 1300), and *graunge* small farm (1440); borrowed from Old French *grange,* from Gallo-Romance **grānica* barn or shed in which to keep grain, etc., from Latin *grānum* grain; see CORN[1]. **—granger** *n.* 1173, as a surname *Grangier;* later *graunger* man in charge of a grange (1195); borrowed through Anglo-Fench *graunger,* and directly from Old French *grangier,* from Old French *grange,* n.

granite *n.* hard igneous rock made of grains of other rocks. 1646, borrowed from French *granit(e)* granite, from Italian *granito* granite, (originally) grained, past participle of *granire* to granulate, from *grano* grain, from Latin *grānum* grain; see CORN[1].

granny *n.* 1663, in Dryden's writings, probably a

clipped form of *grannam, grandam,* or *grandmother.* **—granny knot** (about 1860)

granola (grənō′lə) *n.* mixture of dry oats, brown sugar, nuts, raisins, etc. 1970, American English, originally a trademark; probably formed from Italian *grano* grain, wheat, corn + *-ola,* suffix forming nouns.

grant *v.* Probably about 1225, in *King Horn;* borrowed through Anglo-French *graunter,* Old French *granter* (with change of *c* to *g* perhaps by association with *garantir* guarantee) or *craanter,* variant of *creanter* to promise, guarantee, confirm, authorize, from Gallo-Romance **crēdentāre,* from Latin *crēdentem* (nominative *crēdēns*), present participle of *crēdere* to trust; see CREDIT. **—n.** thing granted. Probably before 1200, in *Ancrene Riwle;* borrowed from Old French *grant,* variant of *creant* assurance, promise, pledge.

granulation *n.* 1612, formed in English as if from Late or Medieval Latin **granulationem* (nominative **granulatio*), but actually from Late Latin *grānul(um)* + English suffix *-ation* (in part, probably suggested by earlier *granulous, granulus* granular, before 1398; borrowed from Medieval Latin *granulosus,* from Late Latin *grānulum,* diminutive of Latin *grānum* grain; see CORN[1]; for suffix see -OUS). **—granulate** *v.* 1666, back formation from *granulation.* **—granular** *adj.* 1794, formed in English from Late Latin *grānulum* granule + English suffix *-ar.* **—granule** *n.* small grain. 1652, possibly a back formation from *granulation,* but more likely a borrowing from Late Latin *grānulum,* diminutive of Latin *grānum* grain.

grape *n.* Probably before 1300 *grape* a grape; earlier, in the compound *win-grape* bunch of grapes (about 1250, in *The Story of Genesis and Exodus*); borrowed from Old French *grape* bunch of grapes, from *graper* pick grapes, from Gallo-Romance **crappāre* pick grapes (possibly with a vine hook), from Frankish (compare Old High German *krāpfo* hook, from Indo-European **grēb-,* root **gerēb-,* Pok. 388; related to Old High German *kramph, krampho* bent, crooked; see CRAMP[1] metal bar).

grapefruit *n.* 1814, from *grape* + *fruit;* possibly so called because it grows in clusters like grapes. The late appearance of this word was because the fruit was not known in North America until the 1700's and was not planted in the United States until about 1820, though the fruit was known in France (as *pamplemousse*) and may have been referred to by its French name among the few experimental horticulturists in the United States in the 1700's.

graph[1] *n.* line or diagram showing how one quantity depends on or changes in relation to another. 1878, a shortening from *graphic formula* (1866; earlier *graphical,* as in *graphical method,* in a general sense of any line drawing, 1784, and implied earlier in *graphically,* 1771); see GRAPHIC.

The graph was first used to show relationships of any kind, such as astronomical data, then it was used for geometry, and was later applied generally in mathematics by the English mathematician James Sylvester. **—v.** make a graph of. 1898, from the noun.
—graphic *adj.* Before 1637, drawn with pencil or pen, in Ben Jonson's *Underwoods;* probably a shortened form of earlier English *graphical* (1626); formed in English from Latin *graphicus* picturesque, worthy of being painted, from Greek *graphikós* of or for writing, belonging to painting or drawing, picturesque, from *graphḗ* writing, drawing, from *gráphein* write; see CARVE + *-al*[1]. The meaning of producing by words the effect of a picture, vividly descriptive, lifelike, is first recorded in 1669 (from *graphical,* 1644), and the specialized sense of pertaining to drawing or painting (as in *graphic arts*), in 1756 (from *graphical,* 1610). **—n. graphics,** *pl.* 1889, the use of diagrams or graphs in engineering, etc. The sense of diagrams, patterns, pictures, etc., used in graphic art or design, is first found about 1960.

graph[2] *n. Linguistics.* letter or symbol representing any speech sound. 1933, American English; borrowed from Greek *graphḗ* writing, related to *gráphein* write; see CARVE. The term was coined by the American linguist Leonard Bloomfield. **—grapheme** *n. Linguistics.* letter or symbol representing a phoneme. 1937, American English, formed from *graph*[2] + *-eme* unit of language structure (abstracted from *phoneme, morpheme,* in which *-eme* is borrowed as an element of the French *phonème, morphème,* from Greek *phṓnēma,* etc.). The term was coined by the American phonetician R.H. Stetson.

-graph a combining form meaning: **1** to draw, trace, or record, as in *photograph.* **2** machine that draws, traces, or records, as in *seismograph.* **3a** something drawn or written, as in *autograph, monograph.* **b** drawn or written, as in *lithograph.* Borrowed from French *-graphe,* from Latin *-graphus,* from Greek *-graphos* drawn, written, (also) from Greek *-gráphos* one who draws or writes (as in *gēográphos* geographer, literally, earth describer); both Greek forms from *gráphein* draw, write; see CARVE.

graphite (graf′īt) *n.* soft, black form of carbon, used for lead in pencils, etc. 1796, borrowed from German *Graphit* (from Greek *gráphein* write + German *-it* -ite[1], mineral species); see CARVE. The German word was introduced in 1789 by the German mineralogist Abraham Werner.

-graphy a combining form meaning: **1** process of tracing, describing, writing, or recording, as in *radiography = the process of recording with X rays,* or *cryptography = the process of writing in code.* **2** tracing, writing, designing, description, or recording, as in *choreography = the designing or arranging of a ballet.* Borrowed from Greek *-graphíā,* from *gráphein* draw, write.

grapnel *n.* instrument with one or more hooks for seizing. 1373 *grapenel,* later *grapnell* (1436); diminutive formed on Old French *grapin, grapil* hook, from *grape* hook, from Frankish (compare Old High German *krāpfo* hook); see GRAPE; for suffix see -LE[1].An earlier form *grapel* (1295) was borrowed from Old French *grape* hook, also formed in English with the diminutive *-el* -le[1].

grapple *n.* 1295 *grapell* grappling iron; borrowed from Old French *grapil* hook; see GRAPNEL. The meaning of the action of grappling, is first recorded in Shakespeare's *Twelfth Night* (1601), probably from the verb sense of seize, hold fast. **—v.** 1530, in Palsgrave's *Lesclarcissement,* to seize and hold fast; from the noun, in relation to the action of a grappling iron or hook. The meaning of battle or struggle (with), is first recorded in Shakespeare's *2 Henry VI* (1593). **—grappling iron** (1538)

grasp *v.* About 1350 *graspen* reach for; later, to grope, feel around (before 1382, in the Wycliffe Bible), of uncertain origin, possibly developed by metathesis of *s* and *p* from Old English **grǣpsan* (compare East Frisian and Low German *grapsen* to grab, snatch; see GRAB). The sense of seize and hold fast is first recorded in Sidney's *The Arcadia* (before 1586). **—n.** a seizing and holding fast. 1561, from the verb. **—grasping** *adj.* (before 1382)

grass *n.* Probably about 1150 *gras,* found in Old English *græs, gærs* herb, plant, grass (about 725, in *Genesis A;* earlier in the compound *græsgrœni* grass green); cognate with Old Frisian *gres* grass, Old Saxon and modern Dutch *gras,* Old High German *gras* (modern German *Gras*), Old Icelandic *gras* herb, grass, and Gothic *gras* herb, from Proto-Germanic **ʒrasan,* from Indo-European **ghrə-s,* root *ghrō-* (Pok.454). The slang sense of marijuana (for resemblance of cannabis to grass), is first recorded in 1943 in American English; earlier, often called *weed.* **—grasshopper** *n.* About 1350, earlier *greshoppe* (probably about 1200); found in Old English *gærs-hoppa.* **—grassy** *adj.* Probably 1440, in Palladius' work on agriculture; formed from Middle English *gras* grass + *-y*[1].

grate[1] *n.* framework of iron bars to hold a fire. 1348, a grating of pierced iron plate, especially for a drain; borrowed either from Old French *grate* or from Medieval Latin *grata* lattice, or Italian *grata* grate, gridiron, hurdle, from Vulgar Latin **crāta,* from Latin *crātis* wickerwork, hurdle. Doublet of CRATE. **—v.** About 1450, furnish with a grate; from the noun. **—grating** *n.* 1626, framework of wooden or metal bars; formed from English *grate*[1], v. or n. + *-ing*[1].

grate[2] *v.* make a grinding sound, sound harshly. Before 1399 *graten* to reduce (bread) to crumbs or powder; possibly a back formation from earlier *gratur,* or borrowed from Old French *grater* to scrape, scratch, from Frankish **krattōn* (compare Old High German *chrazzōn,* modern German *kratzen* to scratch; see SCRATCH). The sense of sound harshly is first recorded in Shakespeare's *1 Henry IV* (1596). **—grater** *n.* 1390-91, instrument for scraping; borrowed from Old French *grateor, gratour* (or possibly a lost form **gratoir*), from *grater* to scrape, scratch; for suffix see -ER[1]. **—grating** *adj.* 1563, annoying, irritating; formed from English *grate*[2], v. + *-ing*[2].

grateful *adj.* feeling gratitude, thankful. 1552, formed from obsolete *grate* agreeable (1523; borrowed from Latin *grātus* pleasing) + *-ful.* The OED suggests that the unusual formation with *-ful* may have been influenced by Italian *gradevole* pleasing. See GRACE.

gratify *v.* to please. Before 1400 *gratyfien* to favor; later, to reward or show gratitude (about 1540); borrowed from Latin *grātificārī,* from a lost adjective **grātificus* doing a kindness (*grātus* pleasing + the root of *facere* make, do; see GRACE and DO[1] perform); for suffix see -FY. The meaning of give pleasure to or please is first recorded in 1568. **—gratification** *n.* 1598; borrowed through Middle French *gratification,* or directly from Latin *grātificātiōnem* (nominative *grātificātiō*), from *grātificārī.*

gratis *adv.* 1444, voluntary; later, free of charge (1541); borrowing of Latin *grātīs,* contraction of *grātiīs* out of favor or kindness; (hence) without recompense, free; ablative plural of *grātia* favor; see GRACE. **—adj.** 1659, from the adverb.

gratitude *n.* thankfulness. Before 1447, good will; later, grace or favor (1500-20, in Dunbar's *Poems*); borrowed through Middle French *gratitude,* or directly from Medieval Latin *gratitudo* thankfulness, from Latin *grātus* thankful, pleasing; see GRACE. The meaning of kindly feeling because of favor received, thankfulness, is first recorded in English in 1565.

gratuity *n.* present of money in return for service; tip. 1523, graciousness or favor; later, money for service, tip (1540); borrowed through Middle French *gratuité,* or directly from Medieval Latin *gratuitas* gift, probably from Latin *grātuītus* free, freely given, voluntary, from *grātus* pleasing, thankful; see GRACE. **—gratuitous** *adj.* 1656, borrowed from Latin *grātuītus* free, etc.; see GRATUITY. The sense of without reason, unnecessary or uncalled-for, is first recorded in 1691.

grave[1] *n.* place of burial. About 1250 *grave,* developed from Old English (before 1000) *græf* grave, ditch; cognate with Old Frisian *gref* grave, Old Saxon and modern Dutch *graf,* Old High German *grab* (modern German *Grab*), Old Icelandic *grǫf,* and Gothic *graba;* derived from **ʒrab,* the Proto-Germanic base of Old English *grafan* to dig; see GRAVE[3] carve. The expected form in modern English would be **graff,* but it is thought that Old English *græf* was used so often in the plural *grafu* that the modern English word can be accounted for in that way. **—gravestone** *n.* Before 1399, stone marking a grave; earlier, stone coffin or grave (probably about 1200). **—graveyard** *n.* (1773, in American English)

grave[2] *adj.* important, weighty, momentous. 1541, borrowed from Middle French *grave,* learned borrowing from Latin *gravis* weighty, serious, heavy; cognate with Sanskrit *gurú-s* heavy, grave, Greek *báros* weight, *barýs* heavy, serious, and Gothic *kaúrus* heavy, from Indo-European **gwer-/gwr-ə-,* root **gwer-* (Pok.476). **—n.** 1609, accent mark placed over vowel; from the adjective, by influence of the same sense in French (1548).

grave[3] *v.* engrave, carve. Probably before 1200 *graven* carve, engrave; developed from Old English (before 1000) *grafan* to dig, carve; cognate with Old Frisian *grēva* to dig, carve, Middle Dutch *grāven* to dig (modern Dutch *graven*), Old High German *graban,* Middle High German and modern German *graben,* Old Icelandic *grafa,* and Gothic *graban,* from Proto-Germanic **ʒrabanan;* also cognate with Latvian *grebt* to hollow out, and Old Slavic *pogrebǫ* I bury, from Indo-European **ghrebh-/ghrobh-* (Pok.455). **—graven** *adj.* engraved, carved. 1382, in the Wycliffe Bible, from the past participle of the verb.

gravel *n.* Probably about 1225, sand, in *King Horn;* later, pebbles and rock fragments (before 1333, in Shoreham's *Poems*); borrowed from Old French *gravele* diminutive of *grave* sand or seashore, perhaps from Celtic or a pre-Latin **grava* (compare Welsh *gro* gravel, sand, Old Cornish *grou,* and Middle Breton *grouanenn*); for suffix see -LE[1]. **—v.** lay or cover with gravel. Probably 1440, implied in *gravelled,* in Palladius' work on agriculture; from the noun. **—gravelly** *adj.* Before 1382, formed from English *gravel* + *-ly*[1].

gravitate *v.* move or tend to move by the force of gravity. 1644, exert weight or move downward; adapted from New Latin *gravitatum,* past participle of *gravitare* gravitate, a formation based on Latin *gravitās* weight; see GRAVITY; for suffix see -ATE[1]. The extended use of tend to move toward a certain point, is first recorded in Marvell's *The Rehearsal Transposed* (1673). **—gravitation** *n.* 1644, natural tendency toward some point or object, adapted from New Latin *gravitationem* (nominative *gravitatio*), from *gravitatum,* past participle of *gravitare;* see GRAVITATE.

graviton (grav′ətɔn) *n. Physics.* hypothetical unit of gravitation. 1942, formed from English *gravit(ation)* + *-on* elementary unit or particle.

gravity *n.* force that causes objects to move or tend to move toward the center of the earth. 1509, weighty dignity, deep seriousness, in Barclay's *Ship of Fools,* borrowed through Middle French *gravité,* or directly from Latin *gravitātem* (nominative *gravitās*) weight, heaviness, pressure, from *gravis* heavy; GRAVE². The sense of force that causes objects to have weight, is first recorded in 1641, followed by Boyle's use of *specific gravity* in 1666.

gravure (grəvyůr′) *n.* process by which printing plates are produced with the aid of photography. 1893, shortened form of *photogravure* (1879), borrowing of French *photogravure (photo-,* from Greek *phôs,* genitive *phōtós,* light + *gravure* engraving, from Old French *graver* engrave, chisel out*).*

gravy *n.* juice that comes out of meat in cooking. 1381, sauce or dressing for fish, fowl, etc.; probably a misreading of *u* for *n* in Old French *grané* sauce, stew (originally properly grained or seasoned), from Latin *grānum* grain, seed; see CORN¹. The spelling *gravey* is first recorded before 1399. Though some books postulate a Middle French **gravé,* so far no evidence has been found and the explanation in the OED is still the standard.

gray *adj.* Probably before 1200 *greie,* in *Ancrene Riwle;* developed from Old English *grǣg* (about 725; earlier *grēi* in Mercian dialect about 700); cognate with Old Frisian and Old Saxon *grē* gray, Middle Dutch *grā* (modern Dutch *grauw*), Old High German *grāo* (modern German *grau*), and Old Icelandic *grār,* from Proto-Germanic **ʒrǣwyaz,* from Indo-European **ĝhrē-wo-,* root **ĝher-* (Pok.441). **—n.** Probably about 1200 *grei;* from the adjective. **—v.** Before 1618, become gray; from the adjective. An isolated example is recorded in the Middle English romance *Sir Gawain and the Green Knight* (probably about 1390). **—graybeard** *n.* old man. (1579-80) **—grayling** *n.* freshwater food fish related to the trout. 1326, formed from English *gray,* adj. + *-ling.*

The spelling of *gray, grey* is not fixed except in some compounds such as *greyhound* and *grayling.* The words with analogous pronunciation remaining in current use from Old English are *whey* and *clay;* the latter is common and the former is ever less so and phonetically a more obscure, even ambiguous spelling.

graze¹ *v.* feed on growing grass. Before 1393 *grasen;* developed from Old English (about 1000) *grasian* to graze, from *gras-,* the base of *græs* grass; see GRASS (compare Middle Dutch, Middle High German *grasen* (modern Dutch *grazen* and modern German *grasen*).

graze² *v.* touch lightly in passing. 1604, in Shakespeare's *Othello;* perhaps a transferred use of *graze¹* in the sense of crop grass close to the ground, as first suggested by Skeat.

grease *n.* soft animal fat. About 1300 *grece,* later *gres* (before 1325); borrowed through Anglo-French *grece, gresse,* from Old French *graisse, craisse,* from Vulgar Latin **crassia* fat or grease, from Latin *crassus* thick; see CRASS. **—v.** smear with grease. About 1350 *gresen;* from the noun. **—greasy** *adj.* 1514, formed from English *grease,* n. + *-y¹.*

great *adj.* Probably before 1200 *grete* big in size, important, admirable, excellent, in Layamon's *Chronicle of Britain;* earlier, in a place name *Greteleia* (1130); found in Old English *grēat* big, coarse, stout (before 899, in Alfred's translation of Boethius' *De Consolatione Philosophiae*); cognate with Old Frisian *grāt* large, Old Saxon *grōt,* Middle Dutch and modern Dutch *groot,* Old High German *grōz* (modern German *gross*); perhaps related to Old English *grytta* coarse meal, GRITS. The original vowel gradually shifted in Middle English by influence of the preceding *r*-sound from a so-called long *e* to that of *a* instead of the usual sound represented by long *i.*

Great is first recorded as a general term of approbation with the meaning of splendid or wonderful in American English, in Washington Irving's *Knickerbocker's History of New York* (1809). In modern English *great* has replaced earlier *mickle,* which has also been superseded in some uses by *grand.* A similar development has taken place in other Germanic languages.

—Great Britain (about 1400 *Grete Britaigne*) **—great-grandfather** *n.* (1513) **—great-hearted** *adj.* (about 1395) **—greatly** *adv.* Probably before 1200, formed from *gret* great, adj. + *-li* -ly¹. **—great-grandmother** *n.* (1530) **—greatness** *n.* Probably before 1300; found in Old English **grēatnes, grētnys* (about 1020). **—great-uncle** *n.* (1423)

grebe (grēb) *n.* diving bird like a loon. 1766, borrowed from French *grebe;* of uncertain origin (possibly so called with reference to the crest of some species, found in Breton *krib* a comb, Cornish and Welsh *crib;* cognate with Old Irish *crīch* end, border, furrow, from Indo-European **krēk-wā,* Pok.619).

greedy *adj.* Probably about 1175 *gredi* avaricious, covetous; later, gluttonous or ravenous (before 1200); developed from Old English *grǣdig* greedy, covetous (about 725, in *Beowulf*); cognate with Old Saxon *grādag* greedy, (modern Dutch *gretig*), Old High German *grātag,* Old Icelandic *grādhugr,* and Gothic *grēdags* hungry; possibly from Proto-Germanic **ʒrǣđaʒaz,* from **ʒrǣđu-* hunger or greed, found in Gothic *grēdus* hunger, Old Icelandic *grādhr* greed, hunger, and Old English *grǣd,* recorded in the dative plural *grǣdum* eagerly, from Indo-European **ĝhrē-dh-,* root **ĝher-, ĝherē-* (Pok.440). **—greed** *n.* excessive desire, especially for money. 1609, back formation from *greedy.* **—greedily** *adv.* About 1225 *grediliche,* in *Ancrene Riwle;* developed from Old English (about 1000) *grǣdiglīce;* probably a blend of *grǣdelīce,* from **grǣd* (possibly representing lost form of modern English *greed*) + *-līce* -ly¹; and *grǣdig* greedy + *-līce* -ly¹. The first form appeared once in modern English as *greedly* (before 1546), and is reminiscent of the formation of *heavily.*

green *adj.* About 1150 *grene;* found in Old English (about 1000) *grēne;* earlier *grœni* (about 700); cognate with Old Frisian *grēne* green, Old Saxon *grōni* (modern Dutch *groen*), Old High German *gruoni* (modern German *grün*), and Old Icelandic *grœnn;* related to Old English *grōwan* to grow; see GROW through Proto-Germanic **ʒrōnja-* from the base **ʒrō-* from Indo-European **ghrō-* (Pok.440). **—n.** Probably before 1200 *grene* the color green, in Layamon's *Chronicle of Britain;* about 1200, a field or grassy place, in *Ancrene Riwle;* found in Old English (about 1000) *grēne,* from the adjective. **—v.** to make or become green. Probably about 1200 *grenen;* developed from Old English (before 1000) *grēnian* to grow or cover with green; cognate with Old High German *gruonēn* to become green. **—greenback** *n.* legal tender first issued by the U.S. government during the Civil War. (1862, in American English) **—greenery** *n.* 1797, formed from English *green* + *-ery.* **—greengage** *n.* plum with light-green skin and pulp. 1724, formed from *green* + *gage,* in allusion to William *Gage,* English botanist who introduced this plum into England about 1725. **—greenhorn** *n.* person without experience. 1455 *greene horn* horn of a freshly-slaughtered animal; applied to a recently enlisted soldier (1650) and extended to any inexperienced person (1682). Use of *green* in *greenhorn* corresponds to the sense of new, fresh, recent (about 1150, in freshly-cut herb). **—greenhouse** *n.* (1664) **—greening** *n.* a making or becoming green. Before 1325 *grening,* in *Cursor Mundi;* earlier in a plant name *greningwert* (before 1200). **—greensward** *n.* 1600, formed from English *green* + *sward* grassy place.

greet *v.* 1100 *greten;* found in Old English *grētan* to attack, accost, salute, welcome (about 725, in *Beowulf*); cognate with Old Frisian *grēta* accost, greet, Old Saxon *grōtian,* (modern Dutch *groeten* greet, salute), Old High German *gruozen* accost, attack (modern German *grüssen* greet, salute), and Old Icelandic *grœta* cause to weep. These forms derive from Proto-West-Germanic **ʒrōtjan* to resound, which is the causative form of Old Icelandic *grāta* weep (Swedish *gråta* weep, Danish *græde,* Norwegian *gråte*), Gothic *grētan,* Old English *grǣtan* (Anglian) *grētan* weep, bewail, Old Saxon *grātan* weep, and Middle High German *grāzen* cry out, rage, from Proto-Germanic **ʒrǣtanan,* from Indo-European **ghre-d-,* root **gher-* (Pok.439).; also still found in Scottish and northern English dialects *greet* to cry, weep, and probably in *-gret* of *regret.* **—greeting** *n.* About 1125, found in Old English (about 900) *grēting* salutation, formed from *grētan* greet + *-ing*[1].

gregarious *adj.* living in flocks, herds, or other groups. 1668, borrowed from Latin *gregārius,* from *grex* (genitive *gregis*) flock, herd; cognate with Greet *agreésthai* to gather; from Indo-European **ger-/gere-* (Pok.382). For suffix see -OUS. The transferred sense of inclined to associate with others, sociable (applied to persons), is first recorded in 1789.

gremlin *n.* imaginary creature causing mischief. 1941, originally British Royal Air Force slang for an impish sprite causing malfunction in mechanical parts of aircraft; of uncertain origin (said to have been used as early as 1923, and to have been derived from Old English *gremman* to anger, vex + *-lin* of *goblin.* Unless some former university student of Old English was involved in the formation of this word, the explanation seems improbable. More likely *gremlin* was formed from Irish *gruaimin* bad-tempered little fellow, with the ending of *goblin*).

grenade *n.* small bomb, usually hurled by hand. 1591; earlier, pomegranate (about 1532); borrowed from Middle French *grenade* pomegranate, from Old French *grenate* in *pomegrenate;* see POMEGRANATE; so called because the many seeds of the pomegranate are suggestive of granules of powder inside the grenade and the many small parts a grenade flies into on exploding; also from the bomb's shape. **—grenadier** (gren′ədir′) *n.* 1676, (originally) soldier who threw grenades; borrowing of French *grenadier,* from Middle French *grenade* grenade; for suffix see -IER.

grenadine (gren′ədēn) *n.* syrup made from pomegranate or currant juice. 1896, borrowed from French *sirop de grenadine,* from Middle French *grenade* pomegranate; see GRENADE; for suffix see -INE[2].

greyhound *n.* tall, slender, swift dog. Probably before 1200 *greahunt,* in *Ancrene Riwle;* later *greihund* (about 1220), probably alteration of Old English (about 1000) *grīghund, grīeghund (grīg-, grīeg-* + *hund* dog, HOUND. The alteration of the forms in Old English may have been influenced by a Scandinavian source (compare Old Icelandic *greyhundr,* from *grey* bitch or coward).

grid *n.* framework of parallel iron bars, grating, gridiron. 1839, shortened form of GRIDIRON.

griddle *n.* flat plate of metal or soapstone for cooking pancakes, etc. Probably before 1200 *gridil* gridiron, in *Ancrene Riwle;* later, an iron plate for cooking (probably before 1300); borrowed from Old North French *gredil,* with Old French variants *grail, greil, gril* a grate, grating, alteration of *grille,* from Latin *crātīcula* small griddle, gridiron; see GRILL. **—v.** cook on a griddle. Before 1450 *gredylen,* from the noun. **—griddlecake** *n.* (1783)

gridiron *n.* framework of parallel iron bars or wires. 1349-50 *griderne;* later *gridirne* (probably before 1475), alteration of earlier *gridire* griddle (about 1300), variant of *gridil* GRIDDLE. For the spelling change to *gridiron* see IRON.

grief *n.* Probably before 1200 *gref* pain or torment, in *Ancrene Riwle;* later, sorrow (about 1250); borrowed from Old French *grief, grieve* a grieving, from *grever* cause pain; see GRIEVE. The spelling *grief* was introduced in Chaucer's work about 1390, probably because of his familiarity with French. **—grievance** *n.* Probably before 1300 *grevaunce;* borrowed from Old French *grevance,* from *grever* cause pain; for suffix see -ANCE. **—grieve** *v.* Probably before 1200 *greven* cause pain, in *Ancrene Riwle;* later, to be very sad, lament (before 1325, in *Cursor Mundi*); borrowed from Old French *grever,* from Latin *gravāre* to cause grief, make heavy or burdensome, from *gravis* weighty, GRAVE[2]. **—grievous** *adj.* About 1300 *grevous,* borrowed through Anglo-French *grevous,* Old French *grevos, greveus,* from *gref* grief, from *grever* cause pain; for suffix see -OUS.

griffin or **griffon** *n.* creature in Greek mythology with the head and wings of an eagle and the body of a lion. 1338 *griffon;* earlier, as a surname *Griffin* (1205); borrowed from Old French *grifon,* from *grif,* learned borrowing from Latin *grȳphus,* misspelling of *grȳpus,* variant of *grȳps* (genitive *grȳpos*), from Greek *grȳ́ps* (genitive *grȳpós*).

grill *n.* gridiron. 1685, in a translation of Montaigne's works; borrowed from French *gril,* from Old French *greil;* earlier *grail,* alteration of *graille,* from Latin *crātīcula* gridiron, small griddle, diminutive of *crātis* wickerwork; see CRATE. In most instances, however, *grill,* n. is possibly a shortened form of *grille,* influenced perhaps by *grill,* v., or is directly from the verb in English. **—v.** broil. 1668, borrowed from French *griller,* from *gril,* n.

grille (gril) *n.* openwork metal structure or screen. 1661, borrowed from French *grille* grating, from Old French *greille* gridiron, from Latin *crātīcula* gridiron; doublet of GRIDDLE and GRILL.

grim *adj.* Old English *grimm* fierce, cruel (about 725, in

Beowulf); cognate with Old Frisian, Old Saxon, modern Dutch, Middle High German, and Old High German *grim* (modern German *grimm*), and Old Icelandic *grimmr;* also cognate with Greek *chremetízein* to neigh, and Russian *gremét'* to thunder, from Indo-European **ghrem-* (Pok.458). The *-mm*'s in the Germanic cognates are instances of intensive doubling. The sense of dreary or gloomy is first recorded in Middle English about 1175.

grimace (grim′əs) *n.* twisting of the face. 1651, in Hobbes' *Leviathan;* borrowed from French *grimace,* from Middle French *grimache,* replacing the unfamiliar ending *-uche* from Old French *grimuche,* possibly from Frankish (compare Old Icelandic *grīma* face mask, dragon's head carved on a post, Old Saxon *grīma* mask; see GRIME). **—v.** make a grimace. 1762, in Goldsmith's *Citizen of the World;* borrowed from French *grimacer,* from French *grimace,* n.

grime *n.* 1590, in Shakespeare's *Comedy of Errors,* of uncertain origin; probably from *grim* dirt, filth (about 1300, in *Havelok the Dane*); borrowed from Middle Low German *greme* dirt; cognate with Flemish *grijm,* Middle Dutch *grīme* soot, mask, Old Saxon *grīma* mask, East Frisian *grīme,* Old High German *grīmo,* and Old Icelandic *grīma* mask, dragon's head carved on a post; outside Germanic cognate with Greek *chríein* to smear, anoint, Lithuanian *griẽti* skim off the cream, from Indo-European **ghri-* (Pok. 457). **—v.** cover with grime. Probably about 1475 *grymen;* earlier, in a figurative sense of punish, make unhappy (before 1450); borrowed possibly from Middle Low German **gremen,* from *greme* dirt, n. or from Middle Dutch **grīmen,* from *grīme* soot, mask. Alternatively, if the modern noun derives from the earlier Middle English noun, then the verb may very well come from the noun. This verb is now generally replaced by *begrime* (recorded before 1553). **—grimy** *adj.* covered with grime. 1612, formed from English *grime,* n. + *-y*[1].

grin *v.* Before 1200 *grennien* bare the teeth (as an indication of pain or anger), snarl; found in Old English (before 1000) *grennian* show the teeth, snarl; cognate with Middle Low German *greneken* to smile, Old High German *grennen* to snarl, and Old Icelandic *grenja* to howl; possibly related to Old English *grānian* to GROAN through the influence of association between the Germanic bases *gran-* and *grin-,* which would produce a different series of cognates including Old High German *grīnan* gnash the teeth, grimace, grin (modern German *greinen*); Middle High German *grinnen* gnash the teeth, Middle Dutch *grinsen* to grin (modern German *grinsen*), etc. The sense of bare the teeth in a broad smile, is first recorded before 1500.

The spelling *grin* appears to be a phonetic development of the older *gren,* developed from Middle English *grennen,* though possibly influenced by such forms as Middle Low German *grīnen* twist the mouth, and Old Icelandic *grīna* bare the teeth; see GROAN.
—n. broad smile. 1635-56, in an unfinished work of Abraham Cowley's; from the verb.

grind *v.* crush into bits or into powder. Old English (about 1000) *grindan;* earlier, *forgrindan* destroy by crushing (about 725); cognate with Middle Dutch *grinde* thick sand, scab, scurf (modern Dutch *grind, grint* gravel), Old High German *grint* scab, scurf (modern German *Grind*), Old Icelandic *grandi* sandbar, Gothic *grindafrathjis* downcast, from Proto-Germanic **ʒrindanan.* Cognates are also found in Lithuanian *gréndu, grę́sti* rub, scrub, from Indo-European **ghrendh-;* and with Latin *frendere* to grind, crush, Albanian *gründe* bran, Greek *chóndros* grain (altered form of pre-Greek **chróndros*), from Indo-European **ghrend-* (Pok.459). Related to GROUND. **—n.** act of grinding. About 1175, from the verb. The informal sense of steady, hard work, is first recorded in 1851, in a collection of college student vocabulary.

gringo *n.* foreigner, especially a white American or Englishman (used among Spanish-Americans as an unfriendly term). 1849, American English; borrowed from Mexican Spanish *gringo* foreigner, from Spanish *gringo* foreign, unintelligible talk, gibberish, of uncertain origin (perhaps from *griego* Greek, from Latin *Graecus,* from Greek *Graikós*).

grip *n.* Probably before 1200 *gripe,* developed from a fusion of Old English *gripe* grasp, clutch (about 725, in *Beowulf*) and Old English *gripa* handful, sheaf (about 1000). Old English *gripe* corresponds to Old Frisian *gripe* grasp, clutch, Old High German *grif* (modern German *Griff*), and Old Icelandic *gripr* treasure. Both Old English words derive from Indo-European **ghreib-/ghrib-* (Pok. 457), the root of Old English *grīpan* grasp at, GRIPE. **—v.** take a firm hold on. Before 1375 *grippen;* found in Old English *grippan* (about 950, in *Lindisfarne Gospels*) and corresponding to Middle High German *gripfen* to grip; both from the root of Old English *grīpan* GRIPE.

gripe *v.* to grasp or clutch, pinch. Probably about 1150 *gripen* seize; found in Old English *grīpan* grasp at, lay hold (about 725, in *Beowulf*); cognate with Old Frisian *gripa* to grasp or grip, Old Saxon *gripan* (modern Dutch *grijpen*), Old High German *grīfan* (modern German *greifen*), Old Icelandic *grīpa,* and Gothic *greipan* to grasp, from Proto-Germanic **ʒrīpanan;* also cognate with Lithuanian *griẽbti* grasp at or grip. The figurative sense of complain or grouse is first recorded about 1932 in American English. It probably evolved from the meaning of produce griping pains in the bowels, in use before 1611. **—n.** fast hold, gripping, clutch. About 1385, from the verb. The figurative sense of a complaint is first recorded in James T. Farrell's *Studs Lonigan* (1934, in American English).

grippe (grip) *n.* influenza. 1776, borrowed probably through French *grippe* influenza (originally, seizure), from *gripper* to grasp or hook, from Frankish; compare Old Saxon *grīpan* to grasp, GRIPE. The word entered European languages through German *Russische Chrippe* or *Grippe* Russian grippe, with the epidemic of influenza during the Russian occupation of Prussia in the Seven Years' War (about 1760), and is imitative of Russian *khrip* hoarseness; influenza.

grisly (griz′lē) *adj.* horrible. Before 1300 *grisli,* developed from Late Old English *grislīc* horrible or dreadful *(gris-,* related to *-grīsan* to shudder or fear + *-līc* -ly[2]*);* cognate with Old Frisian *grislik* horrible, Middle Low German *grīsen, gresen* to shudder, *greselik* frightful or horrible (modern German *gruselig*), Middle Dutch *grīsen* to shudder (modern Dutch *griezelen*), Old High German *grīsenlīk* horrible, and probably Middle High German *gris-* in *grisgram* gnashing of teeth (modern German *Gries-* in *Griesgram* peevishness, peevish person), from Indo-European **ghrī-s-/ghri-s-* (Pok.457).

grist *n.* grain to be ground. Old English *grīst* action of grinding, grain to be ground (before 1000 in Ælfric's

Glossary); related to *grindan* to GRIND. —**grist mill** (1602)

gristle (gris′əl) *n.* cartilage. Old English (before 700) gristle, related to *grost* gristle; of unknown origin, but found in cognates in Old Frisian *gristel, grestel* gristle, East Frisian *grössel, grüssel,* Middle Low German *gristel,* and Middle High German *gruschel.*

grit *n.* very fine gravel or sand. About 1250 *gret,* in *The Story of Genesis and Exodus;* earlier *grit-* in the place name *Grittona;* developed from Old English *grēot* sand, dust, earth, gravel (about 725, in *Beowulf*); cognate with Old Frisian *grēt* grit, Old Saxon *griot,* Old High German *grioz* (modern German *Griess*), and Old Icelandic *grjōt* grit, gravel, stone, *grautr* groats, from Proto-Germanic **ʒiutan.* Outside Germanic cognates are found in Latvian *graûds* grain, Lithuanian *graudùs* brittle, *grūdas* grain, and Old Slavic *gruda* clod, from Indo-European **ghrēu-/ghrəu-/ghrū-* (Pok.460). The abnormal development of the vowel into *i* may be from the influence of assimilation of *gryt;* see GRITS. The figurative sense of firmness of character, stamina, spirit, pluck, is first recorded in American English in 1808. —**v.** make a grating sound. 1762, in Goldsmith's *Citizen of the World;* probably a reborrowing from the noun. The earliest occurrence of the noun appears before 1500, as a variant in a manuscript version of Chaucer's *Canterbury Tales.* —**gritty** *adj.* 1598, formed from English *grit,* n. + *-y*[1].

grits *n.pl.* coarsely ground corn, oats, etc., with the husks removed. About 1150 *grutta* bran, coarse meal; developed from Old English (about 700) *grytt,* pl. *grytta,* coarse meal, groats, grits; cognate with Middle Low German *grütte, gorte* grits, groats, Middle Dutch *gorte* (modern Dutch *gort*), Middle High German *grütze,* Old High German *gruzzi* (modern German *Grütze*), from Proto-Germanic **ʒrutja-,* from the same root as GRIT. This word and the preceding *grit* sand, are related in form and meaning and have influenced each other in development. The plural form of *grit* coarsely ground meal, with *-s,* is first recorded in 1579.

grizzled *adj.* grayish, gray. 1390 *griseld,* from earlier *grisell* gray (about 1349, also in a surname *Grissel,* 1319); borrowed from Old French *grisel,* diminutive of *gris* gray, from Frankish (compare Old High German *chrisil, gris* gray). Middle English *grisell* is cognate with Old Frisian and Old Saxon *grīs* gray, Middle Dutch and modern Dutch *grijs,* Middle Low and Middle High German *grīs* old man (modern German *Greis*), from Indo-European **ĝhrī-s-* (Pok.442). The spelling with *-zz-* is first recorded about 1425. —**grizzly** *adj.* 1594, from *grizzle* gray + *-y*[1]. The name *grizzly bear* a large, fierce bear of Western North America, is first recorded in 1793, but is found in the variant *grizzled bear* in 1752, with an earlier reference in 1691, that does not use the name. By 1808, the name was shortened to *grizzly;* all names alluding to its fur with white at the tips, making it look grizzled.

groan *v.* Before 1250 *gronen* to moan, bewail; developed from Old English (probably before 800) *grānian* to groan, murmur; cognate with Middle Low German *grīnen* to twist the mouth in a grumble, growl, snarl, etc., Old High German *grīnan* to laugh or cry (modern German *greinen* to whine), and Old Icelandic *grīna* bare the teeth, from Proto-Germanic **ʒrain-.* Related to GRIN. —**n.** Before 1325 *grane,* in *Cursor Mundi;* later *gron* (about 1390); from the verb. The spelling *groan* with *oa* representing a so-called long *o* sound, began to appear in the late 1500's.

grocer *n.* 1418, wholesale dealer in wine, spices, foods, etc.; earlier, found in a surname *Grocere* (1255), and in the London Company of *Grocers* (founded about 1344); borrowed through Anglo-French *grosser,* in Middle French *grossier* wholesaler, from Medieval Latin *grossarius* grocer (with variant form found in *grocerius* grocery, literally, dealer in quantity), from Late Latin *grossus* coarse (of food), great, gross; see GROSS. The meaning of a merchant or his shop, selling individual items of food probably did not occur before 1578 (though recorded earlier in the OED), and may not even be the meaning until the 1700's, when a distinction with one who sold any items of food was reinforced by *green grocer* (1723). —**grocery** *n.* 1436, goods sold by a grocer (now *groceries,* 1635); earlier, in *The Grocery* Grocers' Hall, in London; formed from English *grocer,* n. + *-y*[3]. The meaning of store that sells food, is first recorded in 1791, in American English.

grog *n.* alcoholic drink diluted with water. 1770 *grogg,* supposedly in allusion to *Old Grog,* nickname of Edward Vernon (1684-1757), British Admiral who wore a cloak of *grogram.* The nickname was said to be applied to the drink when in 1740 Vernon ordered his sailors' rum to be diluted. —**groggy** *adj.* 1770, intoxicated; formed from English *grog* + *-y*[1].

grogram (grog′rəm) *n.* coarse cloth of silk, wool, or combinations of these with mohair. 1562, borrowed from Middle French *gros grain* coarse grain or texture; see GROSGRAIN.

groin *n.* part of the body where the thigh joins the abdomen. 1592, in Shakespeare's *Venus and Adonis,* alteration of earlier *grynde* groin (recorded before 1400). The new form *groin* was probably influenced by *loin* and is also found as Old English *grynde* abyss, related to *grund* bottom, GROUND. In an earlier use in Holinshed's *Chronicles* (1587), the form *groin* appears in the sense of a hollow, depression, deep trench, or excavation, and is also used in that sense in *grynde-* in the place name *Gryndewelle* (1281), evidence which seems to bolster the derivation from Old English *grynde* abyss.

grommet *n.* ring of rope used to hold a sail. 1626 *grummet,* borrowed from obsolete French *gromette* (now *gourmette*) curb of a bridle, from *gourmer* to curb; of uncertain origin. The extended sense of a metal eyelet, especially in a piece of cloth, is first recorded in 1769.

groom *n.* Probably before 1200 *grome* male child, boy, youth, servant, attendant, in *Ancrene Riwle;* earlier, in the surname *Grom;* perhaps developed from Old English **grōma,* related to *grōwan* GROW. The meaning of male servant who attends to horses is first recorded in 1553. As the shortened form of BRIDEGROOM, the word first appears in Shakespeare's *Othello* (1604), but that word element in *bridegroom* (earlier *bridegome*) from Old English *guma* man, is not to be confused with this entry *groom* from *grome* which is a different word. However, it is evident that the Middle English *-gome* in *bridegome* was influenced in its later spelling *bridegroom* by the sense of attendant in *groom.* —**v.** feed and take care of (horses); rub down and brush. 1809, from the noun.

groove *n.* Probably before 1400 *grofe* cave, mine, pit; earlier, in a place name *Grovhall* (1290); probably borrowed either from a Scandinavian source (compare Old

Icelandic *grōf* pit); or from Middle Dutch *groeve* furrow, ditch; cognate with Old High German *gruoba* pit, hole, ditch, mine (modern German *Grube*), Old Icelandic *grōf,* and Gothic *grōba,* from Proto-Germanic **ʒrōƀō.* The related Old English *græf* ditch survives in GRAVE[1]. The sense of long, narrow channel or furrow, is first recorded in 1659.

The phrase *in the groove,* with meaning of first-rate, perfect, or the extended sense of fashionable, is first recorded about 1932 in American English slang, originally in reference to jazz music, from the manner of making or playing phonograph records, i.e., with the needle fitting in the groove of the record. The slang sense of the verb to *groove* and the adjective *groovy* derive from this phrase.
—v. make a groove in. 1686, from the noun. The slang sense of enjoy, get along, be in the groove, feel groovy, is first recorded in the late 1930's in American English. **—groovy** *adj. Slang.* first-rate, excellent. 1937, American English, from *(in the) groove* + *-y*[1].

grope *v.* feel about with the hands. Probably before 1200 *grapen,* in Layamon's *Chronicle of Britain;* later *gropen* (about 1280); developed from Old English *grāpian* to feel or handle (about 725, in *Beowulf*); related to *gripan* grasp at; see GRIPE.

grosbeak *n.* finch with a cone-shaped bill. 1678, formed in English, from French *gros-* + English *beak* as a partial loan translation of French *grosbec,* from Old French *gros* large + *bec* beak. The coincidence of French *gros* and English *gross* no doubt preserved the French form of the first syllable.

grosgrain (grō′grān′) *n.* closely woven silk or rayon cloth with heavy cross threads. 1869, reborrowing of French *gros grain,* as a replacement of the older English term *grogram;* see GROGRAM.

gross *adj.* 1347-50 *grosse* large; borrowed from Old French *gros* big, thick, coarse, from Late Latin *grossus* thick or coarse (of food and mind), but curiously not found as an adjective in Classical Latin; perhaps cognate, though the vocalism is dubious, with Welsh, Cornish and Breton *bras* thick, large, big, bulky, through an Indo-European base **gwretso-* (Pok.485). Both the negative sense of glaring, flagrant, monstrous (1581), and the positive sense of entire, total, whole (as in *gross receipts, gross national product*) developed from the earlier meaning of coarse or heavy (probably before 1425, in a translation of Chauliac's *Grande Chirurgie*).
—n. group of 144, twelve dozen. 1394, borrowed probably through Anglo-French *gros,* from Old French *gros;* see the adjective. The sense of a total of or a profit is first recorded in Spenser's *The Shepheardes Calender* (1579). **—v.** to earn a total of, make a profit. 1884, from the noun.

grotesque *adj.* odd or unnatural in shape, appearance, manner, etc. 1603, originally *Crotesko,* in reference to the cave paintings found in Roman ruins, characterized by fanciful or odd representations of human and animal forms; later *grotesque* bizarre (1687, in Dryden's *The Hind and the Panther*); from the noun. **—n.** 1561, originally *crotescque;* later *grotesque* (1643, in John Evelyn's *Memoirs*) and *Grotesques* (1643); borrowed from Middle French *crotesque,* from Italian *grottesco,* literally, of a cave, from *grotta* GROTTO.

grotto *n.* cave. 1617, borrowed from Italian *grotta,* (with substitution of a terminal *o,* possibly from the spelling *grotto* in various later foreign editions of Dante's *Divine Comedy*), from Vulgar Latin **crupta, *grupta,* from Latin *crypta* vault, cavern, from Greek *kryptḗ.* The spelling *grotto,* said to have been used by Dante, is unattested in the Siebzehner-Vivanti *Dizionario della Divina Comedia.* Connection of *grotto* with earlier English *grot* (1507, borrowed from French *grotte*), is hard to establish, especially as both *grotto* and *grot* have existed in English for about 300 years. See the doublet CRYPT.

grouch *n.* a grumbling, sulky person. 1900, American English, back formation from *grouchy.* **—v.** to grumble. 1916, American English; from the noun. **—grouchy** *adj.* 1895, American English; of uncertain origin (possibly formed from *grutch-* in *grutching,* n., complaint, grumbling + *-y*[1]). **—grouchily** *adv.* 1906, formed from *grouchy* + *-ly*[1].

The derivation of *grouch* as a variant of obsolete *grutch,* v., to complain (probably before 1200) and *grutch,* n., complaint (probably about 1400), is hard to substantiate because *grutch,* v. is not recorded in English after 1719 and *grutch,* n. does not appear after 1687, which leaves a gap of 175 years between the first recorded use of *grouch* and the last recorded use of either the noun or verb of *grutch.* The only connection could be through *grutching,* n., found as late as 1892.

ground *n.* About 1280 *ground,* developed from Old English *grund* bottom, foundation, ground, earth (about 725, in *Beowulf*); cognate with Old Frisian and Old Saxon *grund* ground (modern Dutch *grond*), Old High German *grunt* (modern German *Grund*), and Gothic *grundu-* in *grunduwaddjus* foundation wall, (from Proto-Germanic **ʒrunđús*), and Old Icelandic *grunnr* (from Proto-Germanic **ʒrúnthuz*), from Indo-European **ghr̥-tus,* root **ghren-* (Pok.459). Related to GRIND. **—v.** put on or in the ground. 1265 *grounden* to fortify; earlier *grundien* strike to the ground; probably from the noun in Old English *grund.* **—ground hog** (1656, in American English) **—groundnut** *n.* (1622, in American English) **—ground squirrel** (1688, in American English) **—ground water** (1450) **—groundwork** *n.* (1434, *groundwerk*)

group *n.* 1695, assemblage of figures or objects in a painting or design, in Dryden's translation of Dufresnoy's *The Art of Painting;* borrowed from French *groupe* cluster, group, heap, from Italian *gruppo* group, knot, of uncertain origin; perhaps from Germanic (compare Old Low German **cropp,* more precisely, but of too late a date, Middle Low German *kropp* swelling on a bird's throat; see CROP). The generalized sense of any assemblage, is first recorded in English in Bolingbroke's *Letters on the Spirit of Patriotism* (1736). **—v.** 1718, in Prior's *Solomon;* from the noun. **—groupie** *n. Informal.* teen-age fan or follower of celebrities, especially rock groups. 1967, from (rock) *group* + *-ie,* variant of *-y*[2]. An extended sense of any fan or devotee, is first recorded in 1971, in American English.

grouper *n.* large food fish of warm seas. 1697 *grooper,* borrowed from Portuguese *garupa,* probably of South American Indian origin, perhaps from a Tupi word.

grouse[1] *n.* game bird with feathered legs. Before 1547 *grewes;* earlier *grows* (1531); of unknown origin.

grouse[2] *v.* to grumble, complain. 1887, originally British Army slang, in Rudyard Kipling's *From Sea to Sea;* of uncertain origin (perhaps borrowed from French dialect *groucer,* from Old French *groucier, groucher* to murmur, grumble, also the source of GRUDGE; see GROUCH, v.). **—n.** grumble, complaint. 1918, in Wilfred Owen's *Letters;* from the verb.

grout *n.* thin mortar or plaster. 1638, probably a technical application of the earlier sense of coarse porridge (1587); developed from *grut* ground malt grain (probably before 1150), from Old English (about 835) *grūta,* pl. coarse meal. The Old English form corresponds to Middle Dutch *grūte* coarse meal, malt, yeast, and Middle High German *grūz* grain, sand, Old Icelandic *grútr,* a cognomen (Norwegian *grut* grounds), and is related to Old English *grytta* GRITS. **—v.** fill up or finish with grout. 1838, from the noun.

grove *n.* small wood or orchard. Probably before 1200 *grove,* in Layamon's *Chronicle of Britain;* earlier, in the place name *Holgrove* (1128-35); developed from Old English (889) *grāf,* related to *grǣfa* grove, thicket; of uncertain origin, and not derivable phonetically from *grafan* to digg, so that there remains no Germanic or Indo-European base to which *grove* can be referred.

grovel *v.* 1593, crawl at someone's feet, humble oneself, in Shakespeare's *2 Henry VI,* back formation from earlier *groveling* with the face downward, prostrate (before 1325, in *Cursor Mundi*), from the phrase *on grufe* prone (with the adverbial suffix *-ling*); borrowed from a Scandinavian source (compare Old Icelandic *ā grūfu: ā* on, and *grūfu,* related to *grūfa* grovel).

grow *v.* Probably before 1200 *growen,* in *Ancrene Riwle;* found in Old English *grōwan* (of plants) to flourish, develop, grow bigger (about 725, in *Genesis A*); cognate with Old Frisian *grōia* to grow, Middle Dutch *groeyen, groyen* (modern Dutch *groeien*), Old High German *gruoen,* and Old Icelandic *grōa;* see GRASS and GREEN. The application of this verb to human beings and animals generally, began in Middle English in the 1300's. In Old English the usual word with reference to both plants and animals was *weaxan* to WAX. **—grower** *n.* 1449, formed from Middle English *grow,* v. + *-er*[1]. **—grown-up** *adj.* Before 1393; *n.* 1813, in Jane Austen's *Letters.* **—growth** *n.* 1557, formed from *grow* + *-th,* as in *health, stealth,* etc., perhaps by influence of a Scandinavian source (compare Old Icelandic *grōdhi, grōdhr* growth, from *grōa* to grow).

growl (groul) *v.* Before 1667, developed from *groulen* (of the bowels) to rumble, growl (before 1450, in a version of *Piers Plowman*); earlier *grulen* (before 1425, in Wycliffe's works), and *grolling* rumbling in the bowels (before 1398, in Trevisa's translation of Bartholomew's *De Proprietatibus Rerum*); probably borrowed from Old French *grouler* to rumble, from Frankish (compare German *grollen* to grumble); cognate with Middle High German *grellen* scream with anger, from Indo-European **ghr-el-/ghr-ḷ-* roar angrily (Pok.439). **—n.** a deep, low, angry sound. 1727, in John Gay's *Fables;* from the verb.

grub *v.* to dig. Before 1325 *gruben* dig, root up, in *Cursor Mundi;* probably developed from Old English **grubbian,* and earlier Germanic **grubbjan;* cognate with Middle Dutch *grobben* scrape together, earlier Dutch *grobbelen* to root, feel about for something, Low German *grubbeln,* Old High German *grubilōn* to dig, search (modern German *grübeln* to ponder, brood), and Old Icelandic *gryfja* pit, hole (Norwegian *gruble, gruvle* ponder, brood). If the Old English existed and is from earlier Germanic **grubbjan,* from **grub-* variant of the base **grab-* to dig, then *grub* is related to Old English *grafan* to dig; see GRAVE[3] engrave. The extended meaning of to toil or drudge, is first recorded in 1735. **—n.** larva of an insect. Before 1415; earlier, a dwarfish fellow (probably before 1400), and as the surname *Grubbe* (1176); from *grubben,* v. to dig, root up. The slang sense of food is first recorded in 1659. **—grubby** *adj.* Before 1845, dirty or slovenly; formed from English *grub,* n. + *-y*[1]. An earlier meaning of infested with larvae is found in 1725, and that of stunted, dwarfish, in 1611. **—grubstake** *n.* 1863, supplies of a prospector, provided by one who shares in the profits; *v.* 1879, from the noun.

grudge *v.* Before 1382 *grucgen* to grumble, complain (against), in the Wycliffe Bible; variant of earlier *grucchen* (probably before 1200, in *Ancrene Riwle*); borrowed from Old French *groucher* to murmur or grumble; of unknown origin; related to GROUCH and GROUSE. For the spelling of *grudge* (1461), see DRUDGE. The meaning of give unwillingly, envy, begrudge, is first recorded about 1500. **—n.** 1459, ill will or resentment; from the verb.

gruel (grü′əl) *n.* thin, almost liquid food made by boiling oatmeal, etc., in water or milk. About 1330 *gruel* meal or flour; earlier, as a surname (1199); borrowed from Old French *gruel,* from Gallo-Romance **grūtellum,* from Frankish (compare Middle Dutch *grūte* coarse meal or malt, Middle High German *grūz* grain; see GROUT). **—v.** subject to an exhausting or punishing experience. 1850, from *gruel,* n. in the colloquial phrase *have* or *get one's gruel* receive one's punishment, take one's medicine (1797), probably because gruel was often given to sick or invalid people. The participial adjective *grueling* exhausting or punishing, is first recorded in 1891.

gruesome *adj.* horrible. 1570 *growsome,* from *grow* (variant of *grue* feel horror, shudder, tremble) + *-some*[1]. The verb *grue* developed from Middle English *gruen* (before 1325, in *Cursor Mundi*), which was probably borrowed from Middle Dutch *grūwen* or Middle Low German *gruwen, growen* shudder with fear; cognate with Old High German *ingrūēn* to shudder, Middle High German *grūwen* (modern German *grauen* to fear, feel terror, *Grauen* terror, horror). The spelling *gruesome* did not become established until after 1850; before that the spelling varied between *grewsome* and *growsome,* which may have been influenced by the Dutch cognate *gruwzaam,* and at least on one occasion *(grausome)* by the German cognate *grausam.*

gruff *adj.* 1533, coarse or coarse-grained; borrowed from Middle Dutch or Middle Low German *grof* coarse, thick, large; cognate with Old High German *grob, gerob* gross or coarse (modern German *grob*), a compound of the Germanic prefix **ʒa-* + the adjective stem **Hruƀ-,* cognate with Old English *hrēof* rough, scabby, and Lithuanian *kraupùs,* from Indo-European **kreup-/kroup-/krup-* (Pok.623). The figurative sense of rough, surly, or sour in manner, is first recorded in the derivative form *gruffness* (1690-91), and was used to describe the voice or speech before 1712.

grumble *v.* mutter in discontent, complain. Before 1586, in Sidney's *The Arcadia;* borrowed possibly through Middle French *grommeler* mutter between the teeth, or more likely directly from Middle Dutch *grommelen* murmur, mutter, grunt, from *grommen* to rumble; growl; cognate with Middle Low German *grummen* to grumble, and Old High German *-grummōn* in *umbegrummōn* to gnaw (modern German *grummeln* to rumble, of Low German origin). **—n.** mutter of discontent, complaint. 1623, from the verb.

grump *n.* 1727, in the obsolete phrase *humps and grumps* insults, snubs, surly remarks; later *the grumps* a fit of ill humor (1844), and a person in an ill humor (1900); perhaps an extension of *grum* gloomy, morose, surly (1640); of uncertain origin (compare Danish *grum* cruel). **—grumpy** *adj.* 1778, in Frances Burney's *Evelina;* formed from English *grump* + *-y*[1].

grungy (grun′jē) *adj. Slang.* bad, inferior, or ugly. 1965, American English slang, perhaps a blend of *grubby* and *dingy.***—grunge** *n.* something bad, inferior, or ugly. 1965, American English slang, probably a back formation from *grungy.*

grunion (grun′yən) *n.* small fish of the California coast. 1917 *grunyon,* American English, apparently borrowed from American Spanish *gruñón,* found in Spanish *gruñón* grunting fish, from *gruñir* to grunt, from Latin *grunnīre;* see GRUNT.

grunt *v.* Before 1250 *grunten;* developed from Old English (about 725) *grunnettan,* from *grunian* to grunt, probably an imitative formation, possibly cognate with Old High German *grunnizōn* to grunt (modern German *grunzen*), and even Old Icelandic *krytja* to murmur, *krutr* outcry, shouting, but only parallel with Latin *grunnīre, grundīre* to grunt, and Greek *grýzein* to grunt, *grŷ* a grunt. **—n.** 1553, from the verb.

Gruyère (grüyãr′) *n.* variety of firm, light-yellow cheese. 1802, borrowed from French *Gruyère, crème de Gruyère,* from *la Gruyère,* district in Switzerland, where it is made.

G-string *n.* loincloth, breechcloth. 1878 *gee-string,* American English, loincloth worn by American Indians (originally, the string holding up such a loincloth); formed from *gee* (of uncertain origin) + *string.* The spelling with *G* (1891), is perhaps from some influence of *G string* string of a violin, tuned to G (1831). Reference to a piece of cloth worn by stripteasers is first recorded in Dos Passos' *Big Money* (1936).

guacamole (gwä′kəmō′lā) *n.* spread made with avocado mixed with onions, tomatoes, etc. 1920, borrowed from American Spanish (originally Mexican Spanish) *guacamole,* from Nahuatl *ahuacamolli (ahuacatl* avocado + *molli* sauce*).*

guanine (gwä′nēn) *n.* substance in nucleic acid of cells. 1850, formed from *guano* (from which it was originally isolated) + *-ine*[2] (chemical suffix).

guano (gwä′nō) *n.* manure of sea birds, used for fertilizing. 1604, borrowed from Spanish *guano* dung, especially of sea birds found on islands near Peru, from Quechua *huanu* dung.

guarantee *n.* something given as security, pledge, surety. About 1436 *garant, garrant* a warranty or promise that the title of some property is true; borrowed from Old and Middle French *garant, guarant* warrant, protection, found in Old North French *warant,* from Frankish; see WARRANT.

The later forms *garanté* (1679) and *guarantee* (1710) reflect Old French spellings. The later sense of a pledge given as security is a specialization of meaning that developed in the 1600's, though it did not displace the sense of the act of guaranteeing *(guaranty)* which is found in Burke, R.L. Stevenson, etc., and the two forms are still confused.

—v. About 1410 *garanten* to give a warranty or pledge that something is what it purports to be; borrowed from Middle and Old French *garantir* promise, guarantee, from Frankish; see WARRANT.

guaranty *n.* act or fact of guaranteeing, security, warranty. 1592 *garrantie;* though formed in part by influence of earlier *garant* guarantee, the somewhat artificial differentiation of *guarantee* and *guaranty* comes from the borrowing of *guaranty* through Anglo-French *guarantie,* from Old French *garantie, guarantie,* also from *garant, guarant* warrant, protection, corresponding to Old North French *warant,* from Frankish; see WARRANT. Doublet of WARRANTY.

In English *guaranty* and *warranty* are variant forms that were borrowed by way of Old French and Old North French from Frankish. In Old French, *gu-* (later reduced to *g-*) took the place of Frankish *w-* in **wār-jand-s* that therefore developed in Old French as *guarant* (later *garant*) + *-y*[3] in English. However, in Old North French, the original form with *w-* in Frankish was preserved in *warantie,* which was later borrowed into English as *warranty.* The same process is evident in *guard* and *ward,* and in *guardian* and *warden.*

guard *n.* About 1400 *garde* care, custody, protection; earlier in the surname *Legard* (1275); borrowed from Middle French *garde* guardian, warden, keeper, from *garder* to guard, from Old French *guarder,* from Frankish **wardōn* (compare Old High German *wartēn* to watch); see the doublet WARD; and for a general explanation see GUARANTY. **—v.** 1448 *garden* protect, defend; borrowed from Middle French *garder* to guard. **—guardian** *n.* Probably before 1400 *garden* one who guards or protects; later *gardein* (1417); borrowed through Anglo-French *gardein,* from Old French *gardien, gardian;* earlier *guardenc,* from Frankish **warding-,* corresponding to Old North French *wardein,* from *guarder* to guard. Later Old French forms like *gardien, gardian* show substitution of suffix *-ien, -ian.* Doublet of WARDEN; see also GUARANTY.

guava (gwä′və) *n.* tropical American tree with a yellowish, pear-shaped fruit. 1555, in Richard Eden's translation of Peter Martyr's *Decades of the New World or West India;* borrowed from Spanish *guaya,* variant of *guayaba,* from Arawakan (West Indies) *guayabo* guava.

gubernatorial (gü′bərnətôr′ēəl) *adj.* of or having to do with a governor. 1734, American English; borrowed from Latin *gubernātor* GOVERNOR + English *-ial,* variant of *-al*[1].

gudgeon (guj′ən) *n.* small European freshwater fish. Before 1425 *gojune;* borrowed from Middle French *goujon,* from Old French *gojon,* from Latin *gōbiōnem* (nominative *gōbiō*), alteration of *gōbius,* from Greek *kōbiós* a kind of fish; of uncertain origin.

guerrilla *n.* fighter in an independent group, which harasses an enemy in a war by raiding, ambushing, etc. 1809, in the Duke of Wellington's *Dispatches;* borrowed from Spanish *guerrilla* a body of skirmishers, a skirmishing warfare (literally, little war), diminutive of *guerra* war, from Germanic with substitution of *gu-* for *w-* (compare Old High German *werra* strife, conflict WAR). **—adj.** of or by guerrillas. 1811, in Scott's writings; from the noun.

guess *v.* About 1303 *gessen* suppose, assume, think, guess, in Mannyng's *Handlyng Synne;* borrowed probably from a Scandinavian source (compare Middle Danish *gitse, getze* to guess, Middle Swedish and modern Swedish *gissa,* Icelandic *gizka*), probably from Proto

Germanic *ʒetiskanan, desiderative of *ʒetanan get; or less likely, from Middle Dutch *gessen, gissen, ghissen* (modern Dutch and Frisian *gissen*); cognate with Middle Low German *gissen* to guess. The Scandinavian forms are related to Norwegian *gjeta, getta* to guess, and Old Icelandic *geta* to get, (also) to speak of, guess, which would imply that ultimately *guess* is a derivative of the root of GET.

The modern forms with *gh-* in *ghesse* (before 1586), and later *gu-* in *guess* (1591), are sometimes attributed to Caxton and his early experience as a printer in Bruges.

—n. About 1303 *gesse* supposition, assumption, guess; probably from the verb.

—guesstimate *n.* 1936, American English, originally used by statisticians and population experts, as a blend of *guess* and *estimate.* —*v.* 1942, American English, from the noun. **—guesswork** *n.* (1725)

guest *n.* Probably before 1200 *gest,* in *Ancrene Riwle;* borrowed probably from Old Icelandic *gestr* and replacing Old English *gæst, giest* guest, stranger, enemy (about 725, in *Beowulf*); also found in Anglian *gest,* the Old English forms with *g* pronounced approximating *y-* in *yet.* The Old English forms are cognate with Old Frisian *jest* guest, Old Saxon, Middle Dutch and modern Dutch *gast,* Old High German *gast* (modern German *Gast*), Old Icelandic *gestr,* and Gothic *gasts,* from Proto-Germanic *ʒastiz. Outside Germanic cognates are found through the Indo-European *ghosti-s (Pok.453) in Latin *hostis* stranger, enemy, probably Old Slavic *gostĭ* guest, lord, master. Related to HOST.

guffaw (gufô′) *n.* loud, coarse laughter. 1720, Scottish, in Allan Ramsay's *Poems,* possibly imitative of the sound. **—v.** 1721, Scottish; from the noun.

guide *v.* About 1380 *giden* to lead, direct, conduct; implied in *giding* guiding, guidance, in Chaucer's translation of Boethius' *De Consolatione Philosophiae;* borrowed from Old French *guider,* alteration (by influence of Old Provençal *guidar*) of earlier *guier,* from Gallo-Romance *wītāre, from Frankish *wītan show the way; cognate with Old English *wītan* blame, and Greek *eidénai* to know, from Indo-European *weid- (Pok.1125). The spelling with *u* began to appear in English before 1393 but was not a frequent spelling until the late 1500's. **—n.** Before 1376 *gide* one who leads or guides, in *Piers Plowman;* borrowed from Old French *guide,* from Old Provençal *guida,* from *guidar* to guide, from Frankish. **—guidance** *n.* 1538, formed from English *guide,* v. + *-ance,* replacing earlier *guying* (before 1420, in Lydgate's *Troy Book*); the meaning is found earlier in Chaucer's works (1380), see GUIDE, v. **—guidebook** *n.* (1823, in Byron's *Don Juan*) **—guide-post** *n.* (1774, in Burke's works)

guidon (gī′dən) *n.* flag, streamer, or pennant. 1548, borrowed from Middle French, from Italian *guidone* battle standard, from *guidare* to direct, guide, from Old Provençal *guidar;* see GUIDE. This word is a replacement for earlier *gitoun* a military standard (1393).

guild *n.* society for mutual aid or for some common purpose. Before 1338 *gylde,* in Mannyng's *Chronicle of England;* earlier in the compound *Chapmanegilde* (probably about 1230). This Middle English form developed from earlier *yilde* by influence of Old Icelandic *gildi,* which represents a semantic fusion of Old English *gild, gyld* payment, tribute, compensation, and (infrequently) guild; and of Old English *gegyld* guild, both terms recorded before 1000 and cognate with Flemish *gild* guild, Middle Dutch *gilde,* Old Frisian *geld, jeld* money, Old Saxon *geld* payment, sacrifice, reward, Old High German *gelt* payment, tribute, money (modern German *Geld* money), Old Icelandic *gjáld* payment, tribute, compensation, and Gothic *gild* tax; related to the root of English YIELD. The meaning of tribute or payment is associated with the concept of burial societies and benefit societies that existed even before the Norman Conquest and that were also known in the 1800's in England and the eastern United States. In such guilds there was a dominant religious theme, though some developed into the role of municipal corporations.

The merchant guilds with their protected trading rights in a municipality developed after the Norman Conquest, often assuming the functions of town government. Their Continental antecedents are represented in words occurring in Middle Low German and Middle Dutch *gilde* (modern Dutch *gild* and modern German *Gilde*), and Old Icelandic *gildi.* Such terms also refer to the trade guilds that began to emerge in England largely after 1200, some of which assumed the governmental capacities of the older merchant guilds. The term *guild* replaced the earlier *hanse* (see HANSEATIC), known in English before 1135 in the compound *hanshus* guild hall.

—guildhall *n.* 1262, developed from Old English *gegyld-heall* (about 1000).

guilder *n.* silver coin of trade; Dutch florin. 1467 *gilder;* earlier *gyldern, gyldren* (probably 1458); usually considered a mispronunciation of Middle Dutch *gulden,* literally, golden, from the phrase *gulden florijn* golden florin; cognate with Old Frisian *gelden, golden, gulden,* Old Saxon and Old High German *guldin,* Old Icelandic *gullin,* and Gothic *gultheins;* also related to Old English *gylden* golden, and all derived from the same Germanic source as English GOLD.

guile *n.* crafty deceit. Probably about 1150 *gile;* borrowed from Old French *guile,* from Frankish *wigila trick or ruse (compare Old Frisian *wigila* sorcery, witchcraft; see WITCH). Doublet of WILE; for spelling change in Old French see GUARANTY. **—guileful** *adj.* Probably before 1300 *gilful,* in *Kyng Alisaunder;* formed from Middle English *gile* + *-ful.* **—guileless** *adj.* 1728, re-formed from English *guile,* n. + *-less;* originally *gilles* (1435).

guillotine (gil′ətēn) *n.* machine for beheading people. 1793, borrowing of French *guillotine,* formed in allusion to Joseph *Guillotin,* 1738-1814, French physician, incorrectly regarded as the inventor. When a deputy to the National Assembly (1789), he proposed that capital punishment be by beheading, most quickly and humanely performed by a machine, which was built in 1791 and first used in 1792. **—v.** behead with this machine. 1794, borrowed from French *guillotiner,* from French *guillotine,* n.

guilt *n.* Probably about 1175 *gult;* later *gilt* (probably before 1200); developed from Old English (971) *gylt* crime, sin, fault, fine; of unknown origin. **—guilty** *adj.* Before 1250 *gulti,* developed from Old English (about 1000) *gyltig,* from *gylt* guilt + *-ig* -y[1]. In early Middle English *gult, g* represents the old sound represented by *y* (approximating *y* in *yet*); the spelling with *u* in *guilt* is analogous to that of *u* in *guild,* and is found probably before 1338 in Mannyng's *Handlyng Synne.*

guinea (gin′ē) *n.* former British gold coin or amount equal to 21 shillings. 1664, in John Evelyn's *Diary,* in allusion to *Guinea,* a region along the coast of West Africa (so called because the coins were first minted in 1663 for British trade with Guinea and were made of gold from Guinea).

The word *guinea* is also used as a shortened form of *guinea hen* (1578) and *guinea fowl* (1788), because this domestic fowl was imported from Guinea in the 1500's. The *guinea pig* (1664) was probably so called from being brought to England by the "Guinea-men" who sailed on ships plying between England, Guinea, and South America, to which the animal is native.

guise *n.* style of dress, garb. Probably before 1300 *gise* fashion, style, garb; borrowed from Old French *guise,* from Frankish (compare Old High German *wisa* manner, WISE[2]); for development of the Old French spelling in *gu-,* see GUARANTY.

guitar *n.* stringed musical instrument. 1621 *guittara,* in Ben Jonson's *Gipsies' Metamorphosis;* borrowing of Spanish *guittara;* later, blended with *gittar* (1688), borrowed from French *guitare,* also from Spanish *guitarra;* from Greek *kithárā* cithara, possibly from a Mediterranean language. Also probably associated in meaning with earlier *giterne* a four-stringed guitarlike instrument known in England by 1350, and borrowed from Old French *guiterne.* Doublet of CITHARA and ZITHER.

gulch *n.* deep, narrow ravine, canyon, gully. 1832, American English; perhaps found in obsolete or dialect English *gulch* or *gulsh* (of land) to sink in, (of water) to gush through a narrow passage, from earlier *gulchen* to gush forth (about 1410), and to drink greedily (before 1250), formed by metathesis of *u* and *l* from *glucchen* (probably before 1200, in *Ancrene Riwle*).

gulf *n.* Probably about 1380 *golf* deep cavity or abyss; borrowed from Old French *golfe* a gulf or whirlpool, from Italian *golfo* a gulf or bay, from Late Latin *colfus, colpus,* from Greek *kólpos* bay or gulf (originally, bosom).

If the Greek *kólpos* underwent loss of *-w-* by dissimilation and is derived from the Indo-European base **kwolp-,* then the sense of a half-rounded area or structure is found in cognates of Old English *hwealf* arch or vault, Old Icelandic *hvalf,* Old High German *walbo,* Old Saxon *bihwelbian* to vault over, and Gothic *hwilf-* in *hwilftrjōm,* a dative plural form with the meaning of coffin (made of two hollowed-out tree trunks), from Indo-European **kwelp-/kwolp-* (Pok.630). The meaning of a large body of water is first recorded in Maundeville's *Travels* (about 1400).

—Gulf Stream (1775)

gull *n.* gray-and-white bird. Before 1450, of uncertain origin; possibly from a Brythonic Celtic source (compare Welsh *gŵylan* gull, Cornish *guilan,* and Breton *goelann*).

gullet *n.* 1305, as a surname *Gullet;* later *golet* throat (about 1390, in Chaucer's *Canterbury Tales*); borrowed from Old French *goulet,* diminutive of *goule, gole* throat or neck, from Latin *gula* throat; see GLUTTON, and compare GULLIBLE.

gullible *adj.* easily deceived, credulous. 1825, implied in earlier *gullibility* (1793). *Gullible* is first recorded in Carlyle's *Life of Friedrich Schiller* as an alteration of earlier *gullable* (1818, in Scott's *Rob Roy*). The forms are based on *gull* to dupe + *-able, -ible. Gull* (1550) is of uncertain origin, perhaps from *gull* to swallow (1530), from *golen* to act as if swallowing (about 1425), from *gole, gulle* throat; possibly borrowed from Old French *goule,* from Latin *gula* throat.

gully *n.* narrow gorge. 1538, gullet; later, channel made by running water (1657); possibly a variant of earlier *golet* a water channel (1373); see GULLET. **—v.** erode (land) by forming gullies. 1775, American English; from the noun.

gulp *v.* 1530, to gasp or choke when drinking a large draft of liquid, in Palsgrave's *Lesclarcissement;* borrowed probably from Flemish or Dutch *gulpen* to gush, pour forth, guzzle, swallow; cognate with East Frisian *gulpen* to gush or gulp, and Danish *gulpe, gylpe* to gulp; all may be ultimately of imitative origin.

Isolated uses, *ygulpid* gulped (before 1376) and *goppyng, golping, gluping* (probably about 1395); both in versions of *Piers Plowman,* are found in Middle English, but the sense of swallow eagerly or greedily, guzzle, are not recorded again for almost 150 years, in 1542.

—n. act of gulping. 1568 *goulpe,* probably borrowed from Flemish *gulpe,* from *gulpen* to gulp. The spelling with *u* was established by the late 1500's.

gum[1] *n.* sticky juice obtained from certain trees and plants. Before 1325, in *Cursor Mundi;* later *gumme* (1336); borrowed from Old French *gomme,* learned borrowing from Late Latin *gumma,* corresponding to Latin *gummi, cummi,* from Greek *kómmi* gum; of uncertain origin, possibly from Egyptian *kmj-t.* As a shortened form of *chewing gum, gum* is first recorded in American English, in 1842. **—v.** About 1325 *gummen* treat with gum; from the noun. **—gum arabic** (before 1398) **—gumdrop** *n.* (1860, in American English) **—gummy** *adj.* Before 1398, in Trevisa's translation of Bartholomew's *De Proprietatibus Rerum;* formed from Middle English *gomme* gum, n. + *-y*[1]. **—gum tree** (1676, in American English)

gum[2] *n.* Often **gums,** *pl.* flesh around the teeth. About 1150 *gome;* developed from Old English *gōma* palate (before 830); cognate with Old High German *guomo* and *goumo* palate, gum (modern German *Gaumen*), Old Icelandic *gōmr* gum; probably from the Indo-European base **ĝhēu-/ĝhōu-/ĝhəu-* to yawn (Pok.449), and so related to Greek *cháos* chaos and *chaskein* yawn, gape, with the original sense of open jaw. The specific sense of flesh around the teeth is first recorded before 1325.

gumbo (gum'bō) *n.* the okra plant. 1805, American English, borrowed from American French (Louisiana) *gumbo, gombo;* probably borrowed ultimately from a Central Bantu dialect; compare Mbundu *kingombo* (*ki-,* singular prefix + *ngombo* okra).

gumption *n.* 1719, Scottish, common sense or shrewdness, in Allan Ramsay's *Poems;* of uncertain origin. The word may be connected with Middle English *gome* attention, heed, notice (probably about 1200); borrowed from a Scandinavian source (compare Old Icelandic *gaum, gaumr* heed) and the ending *-tion.* The meaning of initiative or enterprise, was an early secondary sense, recorded about 1812.

gun *n.* Probably before 1300 *gunne* an engine of war that throws rocks, arrows, or other missiles, in *Kyng Alisaunder;* probably a shortened form of the name *Gunilda* (compare Anglo-Latin *Domina Gunilda* Lady Gunilda, the name of a specific engine used to throw missiles), possibly derived from Old Icelandic *Gunnhildr* (*gunnr* + *hildr,* both with the meaning of war battle). Old Icelandic *gunnr* is cognate with Old English *gūth* (Proto-Germanic **ʒunthjō*), and Sanskrit *hatyā́* killing, from Indo-European **gwhen-* (Pok.492). In relation to this term Middle English also has *gonnilde,* n., a cannon (before 1325). **—v.** Before 1622, shoot with a gun; from the noun. **—gunboat** *n.* (1777, in American English) **—gunman** *n.* (1624) **—gunner** *n.* (1345) **—gunpowder** *n.* (1400) **—gunshot** *n.* (probably about 1421) **—gunwale** *n.* (1466)

gung ho very eager, zealous, or enthusiastic. 1959, American English; found earlier in *Gung Ho* (1942, a slang term or motto of Carlson's Raiders, a guerrilla unit operating in the Pacific area in World War II); borrowed from Chinese *kūng hō* work together, cooperate.

gunk *n. Slang.* unpleasantly sticky mess or substance. 1949, American English, in allusion to *Gunk,* a trademark for a liquid soap patented in 1932.

gunny *n.* strong, coarse fabric used for sacks, bags, etc. 1711, Anglo-Indian *goney,* borrowed from Hindi *gōnī,* from Sanskrit *goṇī́* sack. **—gunny sack** 1862, earlier *gunny bag,* (1764). The spelling *gunny* is first recorded in 1727.

guppy *n.* very small, brightly colored fish. 1925, in allusion to J.L. *Guppy,* a clergyman of the 1800's from Trinidad, who supplied the first recorded specimen (1866) to the British Museum.

gurgle *v.* to flow with a bubbling sound. Probably before 1425, implied in *gurgulyng* a gurgling heard in the abdomen, in a translation of Chauliac's *Grande Chirurgie,* and found in the related form *gurgulacioun* (before 1400, in Lanfranc's *Science of Surgery*); probably confined to narrow usage as a medical term, even in its earliest noun use; not in use as a descriptive term of the sound of liquids outside the body before 1596 and not in general use before the 1700's. This phenomenon, in which a term has a long history of specialized use before becoming a part of the general vocabulary, is often found in English, and is especially evident today. Thus, instead of looking for a source in one of the Germanic languages, such as Dutch or Middle Low German *gorgelen* to gargle, and modern German *gurgeln,* the immediate source may be found in Medieval Latin (the medical language of the 1400's) in *gurgulationem* (nominative *gurgulatio*) from **gurgulare* to gurgle. **—n.** Probably before 1425, a gurgling, perhaps from an earlier verb. The meaning of bubbling sound is first recorded in 1757.

guru (gü′rü) *n.* 1800 *gooroo* Hindu spiritual leader or guide, in Wellington's *Dispatches;* later *guru* (1876); borrowed from Hindi *gurū* teacher or priest, from Sanskrit *gurú-s,* n., one to be honored, teacher (originally, adj., weighty, heavy, worthy of honor; see GRAVE[2] weighty). The generalized sense of any influential teacher, guide, or mentor is first recorded in H.G. Wells' *Babes in Darkling Wood* (1940). The transferred sense of an expert or authority is first found in Canadian English, about 1966.

gush *v.* Probably before 1200 *gosshien* make noises in the stomach; later *guschen, gosshen* to rush out suddenly, pour out (probably before 1400, in *Morte Arthur*); probably formed in English perhaps by influence of a Scandinavian form such as Old Icelandic *gusa* to gush, spurt. (However, the OED gives a detailed explanation as to the implausibility of phonetic development from a Scandinavian source.) The transferred sense of act or speak in an overly effusive or sentimental manner is first recorded in 1873. **—n.** rush of water or other liquid from an enclosed place. About 1682; from the verb. **—gusher** *n.* 1864, overly effusive or sentimental person, formed from English *gush,* v. + *-er*[1]. The meaning of an oil well that flows without pumping is first recorded in 1886, in American English.

gusset *n.* triangular piece of material inserted in a garment to give greater strength or more room. Before 1420, flexible material used to fill up space in a suit of armor; borrowed from Middle French *gosset, gousset,* perhaps a diminutive of *gousse* husk, shell, of uncertain origin (perhaps from Italian *guscio* husk, shell, by some scholars thought to be a borrowing from Greek *kýstion* blister, little bladder); see CYST.

gussy *v.* Usually, **gussy up.** dress up smartly or showily. 1952, American English slang, apparently from earlier *Gussy,* name applied to an overdressed person (1940); of uncertain origin (perhaps related to *gussie* an effeminate man, 1901).

gust *n.* sudden, violent rush of wind. 1588, in Shakespeare's *Titus Andronicus;* possibly borrowed from a Scandinavian source (compare Old Icelandic *gustr* gust, Old High German *gussa* flood, Middle Irish *guss* violence, anger, strength, from Indo-European **ĝheus-/ĝhu-s-,* Pok.448). The fact that *gust* appears so late in English, suggests that it was confined to dialect or specialized use, perhaps as a term among sailors, according to the OED. **—gusty** *adj.* 1600, in Hakluyt's *Voyages;* formed from English *gust* + *-y*[1].

gustatory (gus′tətôr′ē) *adj.* of the sense of taste; having to do with tasting. 1684, formed in English possibly from Latin *gustātus,* past participle of *gustāre* to taste + English *-ory;* or from English *gust* organ or sense of taste (about 1450; borrowed from Old French *goust,* or directly from Latin *gustus,* genitive *gustūs* taste, a tasting) + *-atory,* form of *-ory;* see CHOOSE.

gusto (gus′tō) *n.* keen relish, hearty enjoyment. 1629, borrowed from Italian *gusto* taste, from Latin *gustus* (genitive *gustūs*) a tasting, related to *gustāre* to taste.

gut *n.* Probably before 1300 *gutte* intestine; developed from Old English (before 1000) *guttas,* pl., bowels, entrails; cognate with Middle Dutch *gote* gutter, drain (modern Dutch *goot*), Old High German *guz* act of pouring (modern German *Gosse* gutter, drain); related to Old English *gēotan* to pour; see FOUND[2] cast (metal). The figurative plural use *guts,* with the meaning of energy, courage, pluck, is first recorded in Farmer and Henley's *Slang and its Analogues* (1893). The figurative adjective with the meaning of basic or fundamental (as in *gut issue*) and instinctive or emotional (as in *gut reaction*) is first recorded in 1963, probably as a back formation from earlier *gutsy.* **—v.** disembowel. About 1390, from the noun. **—gutsy** *adj. Slang.* full of guts, tough, plucky. 1936, formed from English *guts* courage or pluck + *-y*[1].

gutter *n.* 1280 *goteris* channel along the side of a street to carry off water, in Lydgate's *Troy Book;* earlier in the surname *Gutere* (1269); and the later meanings of trough on eaves *(guttur,* 1333*),* and *gutter* watercourse (about 1340), were borrowed from Old French *gutiere, goutiere,* from *goute* a drop; see GOUT.

guttural *adj.* of the throat. 1594, borrowed through Middle French *guttural,* or perhaps directly from New Latin *gutturalis,* from Latin *guttur* throat, probably altered from *gūtur; cognate with Old English *cēod(a)* bag, pocket, Austrian German *Köderl* double chin, crop, and Hittite *kuttar* neck, underarm, from Indo-European **geut-/gut-/gūt-* (Pok.394). **—n.** sound formed in this way. 1696, from the adjective.

guy[1] *n.* rope, chain, wire, etc., attached to something to steady or secure it. 1623 *guie,* developed from Middle English *gye* a guide (before 1375, found also in *girap* guy rope, 1371); borrowed from Old French *guie* a guide, from *guier* to GUIDE. **—v.** steady or secure with a guy or guys. 1712, from the noun.

guy[2] *n. Informal.* man, fellow. 1847, from earlier *guy* a grotesquely or poorly dressed person (1836); originally, a grotesquely dressed effigy of *Guy* Fawkes (1806; Fawkes, 1570-1606, was leader of the Gunpowder Plot to blow up the British king and Parliament in 1605). The meaning of man or fellow originated in Great Britain but became popular in the United States in the late 1800's; it was first recorded in American English in George Ade's *Artie* (1896).

gymnasium *n.* room or building designed for physical exercises and sports. 1598, borrowed from Latin *gymnasium* school for gymnastics, from Greek *gymnásion,* from *gymnázein* to exercise or train, (literally, to train naked), from *gymnós* naked; see NAKED. The informal shortened form *gym* appeared in 1871 in American English. **—gymnast** *n.* 1594, a back formation from *gymnastic,* though in some instances probably borrowed through Middle French *gymnaste,* from Greek *gymnastḗs* trainer of athletes, from *gymnázein* to exercise, train. **—gymnastic** *adj.* 1574, borrowed through Middle French *gymnastique,* from Latin *gymnasticus,* from Greek *gymnastikós* pertaining to or skilled in bodily exercise, from *gymnázein* to exercise. **—gymnastics** *n.* 1652, from *gymnastic* + *-s,* on the analogy of such pairs of words as *mathematic, mathematics.*

gymnosperm (jim′nəspėrm) *n. Botany.* plant having the seeds exposed, not enclosed in ovaries. 1830, borrowed from French *gymnosperme* and probably from New Latin *gymnospermus* having naked seeds, from Greek *gymnóspermos (gymnós* naked + *spérma* seed; see NAKED and SPERM*).*

gynecology (gī′nəkol′əjē) *n.* study of the functions and diseases of women. 1847, borrowed probably from French *gynécologie,* from Greek *gynaiko-,* combining form of *gynḗ* woman (see QUEEN) + French *-logie* -logy, study of. In this word British pronunciation has superseded the original American pronunciation (jī′nəkol′əjē).

gyp *v. Slang.* to cheat, swindle. 1889, American English, probably a shortening of GYPSY. **—n.** *Slang.* a cheat or swindle. 1889, American English, probably a shortening of GYPSY.

gypsum *n.* mineral used for making plaster of Paris and fertilizer. Before 1384 *gypsus;* later *gipsum* (probably before 1425); borrowed from Latin *gypsum,* from Greek *gýpsos* chalk, from Semitic (compare Arabic *jibs* plaster, gypsum, Akkadian *gaṣṣu* gypsum).

Gypsy *n.* person belonging to a wandering group of people. 1600 *gipsy,* in Shakespeare's *As You Like It,* alteration of earlier *gypcian* (before 1400), shortened form of *Egyptian,* Middle English *egypcien* (before 1325, in *Cursor Mundi*); possibly from the mistaken belief that Gypsies came from Egypt. **—adj.** About 1630, in Donne's *Sermons;* from the noun.

gyrate (jī′rāt) *v.* move in a circle or spiral. 1830, back formation from earlier *gyration;* for suffix see -ATE[1] **—gyration** *n.* 1615, borrowed from French *giration* but modeled on Late Latin *gȳrātum,* past participle of *gȳrāre,* from Latin *gȳrus* circle, from Greek *gŷros,* related to *gȳrós* rounded; cognate with Armenian *kor* curved, bowed, Lithuanian *gur̃nas* hip, Norwegian *kūra* squat, German *kauern* cower, from Indo-European **gow-ero,*gū-ro-,*gur-no-* (Pok.397); for suffix see -ATION.

gyrfalcon or **gerfalcon** (jėr′fôl′kən) *n.* large white falcon of the Arctic. 1209 *girfaucon;* later *gerfauk* (probably about 1300); borrowed from Old French *gerfauc, gerfaucon,* from Germanic.

The FEW states that first element *gyr-, ger-* is Old High German *gir* vulture, also found in Old French *gir,* and that the second element is a reinforcement by Latin *falcō* hawk, to clarify the sense of the word; another explanation is that a possible source lies in Old Icelandic *geirfalki* gyrfalcon, probably formed from *geirr* spear, see GARLIC, + *falki* FALCON; so called from the streaks on the gyrfalcon's white feathers, resembling spearheads. This latter explanation is now considered misleading as development of the Old Icelandic form is thought to have been influenced by the Old French word.

gyro- a combining form meaning ring, circle, spiral, rotation, as in *gyrostatistics* = *statistics dealing with the rotation or circling of solid bodies;* or in some compounds, meaning gyroscope, as in *gyrostabilizer* = *stabilizer of a ship controlled by a gyroscope.* Borrowed from Greek *gȳro-,* combining form of *gŷros* ring, circle; see GYRATE.

gyroscope (jī′rəskōp) *n.* device that defies gravity and magnetism, used especially as an aid in navigation. 1856, borrowed from French *gyroscope,* from Greek *gŷros* circle + *skopós* watcher; so called because Foucault built his device to demonstrate that the earth rotates on its axis. The term was coined by the French physicist Jean Foucault, 1819-1868, who built such a device in 1852.

gyve (jiv) *n.* shackle, fetter. Probably before 1200 *gives,* pl., shackles, fetters, in Layamon's *Chronicle of Britain,* of uncertain origin. **—v.** to shackle. About 1300 *gwiven,* later *given* (before 1382), from *gives* shackles.

H

habeas corpus (hā′bēəs kôr′pəs) 1463 *habeās Corpora* a writ or process requiring a sheriff to provide jurymen; also, 1465 *habeās corpus* writ requiring that a prisoner be brought before a judge or court (to decide whether he is being held lawfully); borrowing, especially in Anglo-French documents (1376), of Latin *habeās corpus* have the body, in the phrase *habeās corpus ad subjiciendum* produce or have the body to be subjected to (examination), which are the opening words of the writ. The phrase in Latin is made up of *habeās,* 2nd person singular present subjunctive of *habēre* have or hold, and *corpus,* literally, body; see HABIT and CORPSE.

Though *habeas corpus* was affirmed by the *Magna Charta* (1215), it did not become a general instrument in English law until passage of the Habeas Corpus Act (1679), formally regulating the right which was acknowledged earlier in the Petition of Right (1640).

haberdasher *n.* 1311, a dealer in small articles of trade such as ribbons, trimmings, thread, pins, and needles; earlier as a surname *Haperdasser* (1280); probably an alteration (with formative *-er*) of Anglo-French *hapertas* small wares, petty merchandise, of unknown origin. The meaning of a dealer in men's wear, is first recorded in 1887 in American English, and probably stems from a development of the more specialized sense of a dealer or maker of hats, caps, etc. (possibly 1491). **—haberdashery** *n.* 1419, the goods and wares sold by a haberdasher; formed from English *haberdasher* + *-y*[3]. The meaning of a shop or establishment of a haberdasher, is first recorded in Scott's writings, in 1813.

habiliment (həbil′əmənt) *n.* dress, attire. Also, **habiliments,** articles of clothing. 1422 *ablement, ablements,* also, 1436 *habilement, habilements* military equipment; borrowed from Middle French *habillement, abillement,* from *abiller* prepare or fit out, originally, reduce a tree to a trunk by stripping off the branches (*a-* to + *bille* stick of wood); see BILLET[2] thick stick.

The early forms without an initial *h-* had senses connected with *able* or *ability.* The meaning of clothing, dress (probably about 1450), as well as the spelling with *h-,* developed by association with French *habit* clothing.

habit *n.* Probably before 1200, dress or clothing, especially of a religious order, in *Ancrene Riwle;* borrowed from Old French *habit, abit,* from Latin *habitus* (genitive *habitūs*) condition, demeanor, appearance, dress, character, behavior, from *habi-,* the stem of *habēre* to have, hold, possess. Latin *habēre* is cognate with Gothic *gabei* wealth, and Old Icelandic *gǣfr* generous, from Indo-European **ghēbh-/ghəbh-* take (Pok.408). The extended meaning of outward form, appearance, and customary practice, all of which existed in Latin *habitus,* are first recorded in Middle English in the 1300's. **—habitual** *adj.* About 1445, borrowed, possibly by influence of Middle French *habituel,* from Medieval Latin *habitualis,* from Latin *habitus* behavior; see HABIT. **—habituate** *v.* to make used (to). 1530, in Palsgrave's *Lesclarcissement;* developed from earlier *habituate,* adj. (probably before 1425); borrowed from Late Latin *habituātus,* past participle of *habituārī* be influenced by some attitude, be in a state of, be characterized by, possibly a passive form of **habituāre* bring into a state, from Latin *habitus* behavior; see HABIT, which probably influenced the form and meaning of the word in English; for suffix see -ATE[1]. It is also probable that Middle French *habituer* to accustom, had some influence on the development of the verb use in English. **—habitué** (həbich′üā′) *n.* person who habitually goes to a place. 1818, borrowing of French *habituíé,* past participle of *habituer* accustom, from Late Latin *habituārī* be influenced by some attitude; see HABITUATE.

habitat (hab′ətat) *n.* place where an animal or plant naturally lives or grows. 1762, used as a technical term in a Latin text on plants in Great Britain; literally, it inhabits, third person singular present indicative of *habitāre* live in, dwell; see HABITATION. In the generalized use of a dwelling place or habitation, the term is first recorded in Lowell's writings, in 1854. **—habitable** *adj.* Before 1393 *habitable;* earlier *abitale* (1388, in Wycliffe's writings); borrowed from Old French *habitable, abitable,* from Latin *habitābilis* that is fit to live in, from *habitāre* live in; for suffix see -ABLE. **—habitation** *n.* place to live in; dwelling. About 1375 *habitacioun* act of living in a place, in Chaucer's *Canterbury Tales;* later, dwelling place (about 1384, in the Wycliffe Bible); borrowed through Old French *habitation* act of dwelling, or directly from Latin *habitātiōnem* (nominative *habitatio*) act of dwelling, from *habitāre* dwell, live in, a frequentative form of *habēre* possess, have, hold.

hacienda (hä′sēen′də *or* ä′sēen′də) *n.* large ranch or estate; country house. 1758, in a translation of a travel book about South America; borrowing of Spanish *hacienda* landed estate, from Latin *facienda* (things) to be done, from *facere* DO[1] perform.

hack[1] *v.* cut roughly or unevenly. Probably before 1200 *hacken,* in *Ancrene Riwle;* developed from Old English *-haccian* in *tōhaccian* hack to pieces; cognate with Old Frisian *hakkia* to chop or hack, Middle Low German and Middle Dutch *hacken* (modern Dutch *hakken*), Old High German *hacchōn* (modern German *hacken*), of unknown origin. The sense of give a short dry cough is not found in the record of English before 1802. The American slang use (especially in the phrase *to hack it*) meaning to cope with, handle, comprehend, is first recorded in the 1950's and is reminiscent of, if not influenced by, other modern phrases, with the sense of get through by slashing, as in some effort, as by *cut the mustard.* **—n.** tool used for cutting up or chopping. Before 1325, in *Cursor Mundi;* from the verb. The sense of a dry cough is first recorded in 1885.

hack[2] *n.* carriage or vehicle for hire. Before 1700, slang term for a person hired to do routine work, common drudge; shortened form of HACKNEY. The meaning of carriage for hire is first recorded in Steele's *Lying Lover* (1704). The sense of a henchman (one who will do anything asked), is recorded before 1848, in American English. **—adj.** Before 1734, from the noun. The phrase *hack writer* is first recorded in 1826, that of *hack owner* in 1867. **—v.** 1745, make commonplace; from the noun. The meaning of employ as a hack writer, is first found in Scott's *Letters* (1813).

hackle[1] *n.* a bird's plumage, an animal's skin. Before 1450 *hakle;* later *hakille* (before 1475); developed from Old English *hacele* cloak or mantle (before 899, in Alfred's translation of Orosius' *Historiarum Adversus Paganos.* The specialized sense of "one of the long, slender feathers on the neck of a rooster, pigeon, etc.," is first found in 1496, but the idiom to *raise one's hackles* as a bird does when angry or disturbed, also, later attributed to the hair on the back of a dog's neck, was only recently derived from *with the hackles up* (1881).

hackle[2] *n.* comb used in dressing flax or hemp. 1485 *hakell,* variant of *hekele;* see HECKLE.

hackney *n.* horse for ordinary riding. Probably about 1300 *hakeney;* earlier in a surname *Hakenesho,* horseshoe for a hackney (1205); probably in allusion to *Hakeneye* a town near London (now *Hackney* a borough of London) reputedly famous at one time for its horses. Early mention is made of hackney ponies being hired out (probably about 1387, in a version of *Piers Plowman*). A transferred meaning developed of one working for hire, hireling, common drudge, is first recorded in 1546, but this sense became obsolete in the 1700's, though not before use as the contemporary shortened form *hack*[2]. The meaning of carriage used for hire (also shortened to *hack*[2]) is found in Pepys' *Diary* (1664). **—v.** 1570, use (a horse) as a hack, for ordinary riding; extended in meaning to "make common by indiscriminate everyday usage, make vulgar, trite, or commonplace (in Shakespeare's *1 Henry IV,* 1596). **—hackneyed** *adj.* (1749, from *hackney,* v.)

hadal (hā′dəl) *adj.* of or inhabiting the very deep part of the ocean. 1964, formed from English *Hades* the nether world + *-al*[1].

haddock *n.* food fish of the North Atlantic. 1307-08 *haddok;* earlier as a surname *Haddok* (1286); of unknown origin. The FEW cites a source in Old Picard (1285) but states that the French word was borrowed from English.

Hades *n.* 1597, borrowed from Greek *Hā́idēs* God of the nether world; of uncertain origin. According to the OED, the word was introduced into English in connection with theological controversy that arose over the fifth article of the Apostles' Creed in reference to Christ after crucifixion in which the Creed states: He descended into hell.

hadron *n. Physics.* any of a class of heavy, strongly interacting elementary particles. 1962, formed in English from Greek *hadrós* thick or heavy + English suffix *-on* elementary particle after the original coinage in Russian as *adron.*

hafnium (haf′nēəm) *n.* metallic chemical element. 1923, New Latin *hafnium (Hafnia* Copenhagen, the Medieval Latin form of *havn* in Danish *København,* where the element was discovered in 1923 + *-ium* suffix of chemical elements*).* The term was coined by its codiscoverers, the Hungarian chemist Georg von Hevesy and the Danish physicist C. Dick Coster.

haft *n.* handle of a weapon or tool. About 1330 *haft,* developed from Old English *hæft* handle, in the compound *hæftmece* hilted sword (about 725, in *Beowulf*); also related to *hæft* fetter or shackle (about 725, in *Christ and Satan*). The Old English form is cognate with Old Saxon *haft* captured, modern Dutch *heft* handle, Old High German *hefti* handle, *haft* fetter (modern German *Heft* handle, *Haft* arrest, confinement), Old Icelandic *hapt* fetter, *hepti* handle (with *-pt-* pronounced as if written *-ft-*), and Gothic *hafts* fastened, secured, related to *hafjan* to raise, carry, HEAVE. **—v.** 1440 *haften* furnish with a haft; from the noun.

hag *n.* very ugly old woman, especially one who is vicious or malicious. Probably before 1200 *hagge,* in *Ancrene Riwle;* probably a shortening of Old English *hægtesse, hegtes* witch, fury, on the assumption that *-tesse, -tes* was a suffix (instead of the second member of an ancient compound of uncertain formation). The Old English forms are cognate with Middle Dutch *haghetisse* witch (modern Dutch *heks*), and Old High German *hagzissa, hagazussa* (modern German *Hexe*). Ultimate derivation of *hag* is uncertain, though the Old English, Middle Dutch, and Old High German forms suggest a possible Germanic compound formed from the root of Old English *haga* HEDGE, which is justified semantically in Old High German *zūnrīta,* Old Icelandic *tūnrīdha* witch, literally, hedge rider. Compare also Gaulish **dūsios* demon, Cornish *dus, diz* devil, and Old Lithuanian *dvāsas* spirit, ghost, cognate with Greek *theós* god, from Indo-European **dhwes-/dhwos-/dhus-* (Pok.269). *Hag* did not become a common word in English before the 1500's, and curiously the same development occurred about the same time in German *Hexe,* which had been a rare word throughout the medieval period.

haggard *adj.* looking worn from pain, fatigue, etc. 1580, wild, unruly, in Lyly's *Euphues and his England,* a figurative use of the earlier meaning, wild or untamed, in reference to hawks (1567); borrowed from Middle French *hagard,* of uncertain origin; sometimes said to refer to an earlier Old French *faulcon hagard* wild falcon, literally, falcon of the woods, from Middle High German *hag* hedge, copse, or woods, with the suffix *-ard,* a theory possibly reinforced by Low German and German *hager* gaunt, haggard, but of uncertain connection. The meaning of looking careworn developed through the sense of the effects of pain, fatigue, or worry on the face, found in Charlotte Brontë's *Villette* (1853) which was a generalized application of the earlier use "a wild or haunted expression in someone's eyes," found in Dryden's translation of Vergil's *Georgics* (1697).

haggle *v.* 1583, to advance with difficulty, but possibly implied in earlier *haggler* one who haggles (1577); later, to hack, mangle, mutilate (1599, in Shakespeare's *Henry V*); apparently a frequentative form with addition of the suffix *-le*[3] to earlier *haggen* to chop (probably about 1325); borrowed from a Scandinavian source (compare Old Icelandic *hǫggva* to hack, HEW). The meaning of dispute about a price or terms of a bargain, is first recorded in 1602 and may have developed from the earlier meaning through the notion of "chopping" or "whittling away" at a price. **—n.** 1858, from the verb **—haggler** *n.* 1577, probably from *haggle,* v. (unrecorded at the time) + *-er*[1].

hagiology (hā′jēol′əjē *or* hag′ēol′əjē) *n.* literature that deals with the saints. 1807, in Southey's *Espriella's Letters;* formed in English from Greek *hágios* holy + English *-logy.* Greek *hágios* is cognate with Sanskrit *yájya-s* to be revered, from Indo-European **yag-* worship (Pok.501).

hahnium (hä'nēəm) *n.* artificial radioactive chemical element. 1970, in allusion to the German radiochemist Otto *Hahn* + *-ium* (suffix of chemical elements).

haiku (hī'kü) *n.* poem, at first of Japanese origin, consisting of 17 syllables and having a jesting nature. 1902, borrowing of Japanese *haiku,* but found earlier in the form of *haikai* (1899).

hail[1] *interj.* greetings! welcome! About 1200, borrowed from a Scandinavian source (compare Old Icelandic *heill* healthy, see WHOLE; but also compare Gothic *hails,* used as a salutation without a verb, and Old English *hāls*). The interjection is a shortening of the Middle English phrases *hail be thou* and *wæs hæil,* in which *hail* functions as an adjective with the meaning of healthy; see WASSAIL and HALE[1] healthy. **—v.** greet, cheer. Probably about 1200, in *The Ormulum;* earlier, to drink a toast (before 1200, in Layamon's *Chronicle of Britain*); from the interjection. **—n.** greetings. 1500, in Dunbar's *Poems;* from the verb and the interjection.

hail[2] *n.* small, round pieces of ice falling from clouds like rain. About 1250 *hail,* in *The Story of Genesis and Exodus,* developed from Old English *hægl* (probably about 750), *hagol* (about 1000). The Old English forms are cognate with Old Frisian *heil* hail, Old Saxon and Old High German *hagal,* Middle Low German *hagel* (modern German *Hagel*), Middle Dutch *haghel* (modern Dutch *hagel*), and Old Icelandic *hagl,* from Proto-Germanic **Haȝlaz;* also outside Germanic exactly cognate with pre-Greek **káchlos,* whence Greek *káchlēx* (genitive *káchlēkos*) pebble, from Indo-European **kaghlos-* (Pok.518). **—v.** fall in hail. About 1300 *hailen;* developed from Old English (about 893) *hagalian,* from *hagol,* n. **—hailstone** *n.* Before 1387; developed from Old English *hagol-stān.*

hair *n.* Probably about 1150 *her;* later *heare* (about 1250, also as *hair* in 1200); developed from Old English *hǣr* (about 1000), *hēr* (about 800). The Old English forms are cognate with Old Frisian *hēr* hair, Old Saxon *hār,* Middle Dutch *haer* (modern Dutch *haar*), Old High German *hār* (modern German *Haar*), and Old Icelandic *hār,* which probably also influenced the Middle English formations *har* (before 1300) and *hor* (about 1300), from Proto-Germanic **Hǣran,* cognate with Lithuanian *šerỹs* bristle, from Indo-European **k̑ēr-/k̑ōr-* (Pok.583).

Middle English *her* and *heare* would have normally produced *hear* or *here* in modern English instead of the form *hair.* The modern English spelling derives from influence of the now obsolete Middle English *haire* hair shirt, cloth made of hair (probably before 1200; also found in *hairster* maker of hair cloth, 1299, and *hayrer,* 1252); borrowed from Old French *haire,* from Frankish **hārja,* but ultimately related to Old English *hǣr* hair. **—hairbreadth** *adj., n.* (about 1450, *heere-brede*) **—haircloth** *n.* (1410) **—hairy** *adj.* Before 1325 *hari,* in *Cursor Mundi;* formed from Middle English *har, her* hair + *-i* -y[1].

hake *n.* sea fish related to the cod. 1280, of uncertain origin; perhaps found in Old English *haca* a hook which is represented in *hacod* a pike (fish); or borrowed from a Scandinavian source; compare Norwegian *hakefisk* male salmon having a hooked projection on the lower jaw during or after mating season, from *hake* hook (compare Old Icelandic *haki* HOOK) + *fisk* fish (compare Old Icelandic *fiskr* FISH).

halberd (hal'bərd) *n.* weapon that is both a spear and a battle-ax. 1495 *haubert,* also *halberd* (1497); borrowed from Middle French *hallebarde,* from Old French *alabarde,* from Italian *alabarda,* from Middle High German *halmbarte, helmbarte,* possibly with the meaning of broadaxe with a handle, from *halm, helm* handle (see HELM) + *barte* hatchet, from Old High German *barta,* possibly from *bart* BEARD (the edge of the axe being compared to the beard coming down from the chin). Alternatively, some scholars have suggested that Middle High German *helmbarte* derives from Old High German *helm* HELMET and means "axe for smashing helmets," though this is considered as questionable today as the comparison of the blade of an axe to the beard on the chin.

halcyon (hal'sēən) *adj.* calm, peaceful. 1631 *halcyon,* abstracted from the phrase *halcyon days* fourteen days of calm weather (1601; earlier *Alycon days,* 1578, and *halcyons dayes,* 1545). According to ancient legend, the *halcyon days* occurred during the winter solstice when the *halcyon (Alceoun,* before 1393*),* a mythical bird identified as the kingfisher, was supposed to breed in a nest floating on the sea charming the wind and waves into an especially calm period.

The name *halcyon, alceoun* was borrowed from Latin *halcyōn,* from Greek *halkyṓn,* variant of *alkyṓn* kingfisher; related to Latin *alcēdō* (genitive *alcēdinis*) kingfisher. The Greek variant *halkyṓn* was formed by association with *háls* sea, salt, and *kyôn* conceiving, present participle of *kyeîn* conceive, cognate with Sanskrit *śváyati* gets big, from Indo-European **k̑uw-eyo* (Pok.592).

hale[1] *adj.* strong and well, healthy. Before 1325 *hale* (in Northern dialect of England); developed from Old English (about 725) *hāl* healthy; see HAIL[1] and HEAL. Doublet of WHOLE.

hale[2] *v.* drag, tug, haul. Probably before 1200 *halen,* in Layamon's *Chronicle of Britain;* borrowed from Old French *haler,* from a Germanic source (compare Old High German *halōn, holōn* to fetch, which is cognate with Old Saxon *halōn* to fetch, Old Frisian *halia,* Middle Dutch and modern Dutch *halen* to fetch, draw, haul, and modern German *holen;* Middle English *halen* is probably also related to Old English *-holian* in *geholian* obtain; see HAUL, v.); cognate with Greek *kaleîn* to summon, from Indo-European **kel-, kelē-, kelā-* call (Pok.548).

half *n.* 1123 *half;* found in Old English *half, halb* side, part (about 700, in early Mercian glossaries); later *healf* half (in West Saxon); cognate with Old Frisian *halve* side, Old Saxon *halba,* Middle Dutch and Middle Low German *halve* Old High German *halba,* Middle High German *halbe,* Old Icelandic *halfa,* and Gothic *halba* side, half. According to the OED, the oldest sense in all the languages cited is that of side. **—adj.** 1137 *half;* found in Old English (811) *healf, half;* cognate with Old Frisian, Old Saxon, Middle Dutch, modern Dutch, and Middle Low German *half* half, Old High German and modern German *halb,* Old Icelandic *hālfr,* and Gothic *halbs;* derived from Proto-Germanic **Halbás,* the source of Old English *healf* side, cognate with Sanskrit *kálpate* it fits, from Indo-European **kelp-/kolp-* (Pok.926). **—adv.** Probably before 1200 *half;* found in Old English (944); from the adjective. **—half brother** (before 1338) **—half dollar** (1786, American English)

—**half-hearted** *adj.* (perhaps before 1425) —**half hour** (about 1420) —**half-life** *n.* (1907, in atomic physics) —**half moon** (probably before 1425) —**half sister** (probably before 1200) —**halfway** *adv.* (about 1330) —**half-witted** *adj.* (about 1645) —**halve** *v.* Probably before 1200 *halfen,* in Layamon's *Chronicle of Britain;* from *half,* n.

halibut (hal'əbət) *n.* large flatfish. 1396 *halibut (hali* HOLY + *butte* flatfish, cognate with Low German *hilligbutt, hillebutt,* Middle Low German and Middle Dutch *but* flatfish; also found in modern German *Butte* and *Heilbutt;* perhaps also cognate with *-bot* in French *turbot);* so called from its being eaten especially on holy days. Middle English *butte* flatfish, cognate with Low German *butt* short and fat, is from Proto-Germanic **ƀut-,* from Indo-European **bhud-,* root **bhaud-* (Pok.112).

halite (hal'īt *or* hā'līt) *n.* native rock salt. 1868, borrowed from New Latin *halites,* from Greek *háls* (genitive *halós*) salt + New Latin *-ites* -ite[1] (mineral).

halitosis (hal'ətō'sis) *n.* bad breath. 1874, borrowed from New Latin *halitosis,* from Latin *hālitus* breath (related to *hālāre* to breathe) + New Latin *-osis* -osis.

hall *n.* Probably before 1200 *halle,* in Layamon's *Chronicle of Britain;* developed from Old English *heall* place covered by a roof, spacious roofed residence, temple, etc. (about 725, in *Beowulf*); cognate with Old Saxon *halla* place covered by a roof, Middle Low German and Middle Dutch *halle* (modern Dutch *hal* hall), Old High German *halla* (modern German *Halle* hall), and Old Icelandic *hǫll,* all derived from Proto-Germanic **Hallō-,* and cognate with Old Irish *celim* I conceal, *cuile* cellar, Latin *cella* small room, CELL, Greek *kaliā́* hut, and Sanskrit *śā́lā* hut, hall, from Indo-European **k̂el-/k̂ol-/k̂ēl-* (Pok.553). —**hallway** *n.* (1876)

hallelujah or **halleluiah** (hal'əlü'yə) *interj.* praise ye the Lord! 1535 *halleluya,* in the Psalms of the Coverdale Bible; borrowed from Hebrew *halləlū-yāh* praise Jehovah, probably as a replacement for earlier English *alleluia* (recorded probably before 1200). The Hebrew *halləlū-yāh* derives from *halləlū,* plural imperative of *hallēl* to praise + *yāh,* a shortened form of the name of God (Yahweh) in the Hebrew of the Old Testament. —**n.** 1667, in Milton's *Paradise Lost;* from the interjection.

hallmark *n.* 1721, official stamp indicating a standard of purity in gold and silver articles; formed in allusion to Goldsmiths' *Hall* in London, seat of the Goldsmiths' Company, by whom the standard and stamping were legally regulated + *mark.* The figurative sense of a mark of genuineness or quality, is first recorded in 1864. —**v.** put a hallmark on. 1773, from the noun.

hallow *v.* make holy. Before 1121 *halgod* (past participle); later *halwen* and *halowen* (about 1300); developed from Old English *hālgian* (about 725, in *Genesis A*); related to *hālig* HOLY.

Halloween or **Hallowe'en** *n.* About 1745, Scottish, shortening of *Allhallow-even;* earlier *All hallow eve,* meaning Eve of All Saints, the last night of October (1556). According to the Celtic calendar November 1 began the year and the last evening of October was old-year's night (the night of all witches), which the Christian Church transformed into the Eve of All Saints.

hallucination *n.* perception of an object or sound that is not really present. 1646, borrowed from Latin *alucinātiōnem,* later spelled *hallucinātiōnem* (nominative *hallucinātiō*), from *alucinārī* wander (in the mind), dream, probably from Greek *alýein, halýein* be distraught, be beside oneself; probably related to *alâsthai* wander about; see AMBLE; for suffix see -TION. The Latin word was perhaps influenced in the form of its ending and also semantically by Latin *vāticinārī* to foretell, (also) to rant or rave. —**hallucinate** *v.* 1604, to deceive; 1652, to have illusions, from Latin *alucinātus,* later *hallucinātus,* past participle of *alucinārī;* for suffix see -ATE[1].

halo *n.* ring of light around the sun, moon, etc. 1563, borrowed as Spanish *halon,* later borrowed as French *halo,* or directly as Latin accusative *halō;* all forms from Latin *halōs,* from Greek *hálōs* disk of the sun or moon, and disk around the sun or moon (originally, threshing floor), of unknown origin; the notion of disk possibly derived from the circular path of the oxen on the threshing floor. The sense of a nimbus, or disk of light surrounding the head of a divine or saintly person, is first recorded in 1646. —**v.** surround with a halo. 1801, in Southey's *Thalaba;* from the noun.

halogen (hal'əjən) *n.* any chemical element, such as iodine or chlorine, that combines directly with a metal to form a salt. 1842, borrowing of Swedish *halogen,* from Greek *háls* (genitive *halós*) salt + modern scientific suffix *-gen;* so called because a salt is formed. The term was coined by the Swedish chemist Berzelius.

halt[1] *n.* temporary stop. 1622, earlier *alt, alto* (1591-98); borrowed through French *halte* and earlier Italian *alto,* or directly from German *Halt,* from *halten* to stop or hold, from Old High German *halten* to HOLD. In earliest use *halt* is found in the military phrase *to make halt,* after German *Halt machen.* —**v.** stop for a time. 1656, in Blount's *Glossographia;* from the noun.

halt[2] *adj.* lame. Probably about 1200 *halt;* found in Old English (about 700) *-halt,* in the compound *lemphalt* lame, limping; cognate with Old Frisian, Old Saxon, and Middle Dutch *halt* lame, Old High German *halz,* Old Icelandic *haltr,* and Gothic *halts,* from Proto-Germanic **Haltaz.* Outside Germanic cognates are found in Latin *clādēs* a breaking, destruction, calamity, Greek *klân* to break, *kólos, kolobós* docked, curtailed, Lithuanian *kálti* to beat, forge, and also in Welsh *coll* injury, defect, loss, and Old Irish *coll* loss, injury, detriment, from Indo-European **koldos* broken (Pok.547). —**v.** be in doubt, hesitate, waver. Before 1325 *halten* to limp, in *Cursor Mundi;* later, hesitate, waver (1382, in the Wycliffe Bible); found in Old English (about 830) *haltian* to be lame, to limp, from the adjective.

halter *n.* rope, strap, etc., for leading or tying an animal. Before 1225 *helfter* snare, noose; later *haltre, halter* (about 1300); developed from Old English (before 830) *hælftre, hælfter;* cognate with Old Saxon *haliftra* halter, Middle Low German *halchter,* Middle Dutch *halfter* (modern Dutch *halster*), and Old High German *halftra* (modern German *Halfter*), from Proto-Germanic **Halftra-;* related to HELVE.

halve *v.* See HALF.

halyard (hal'yərd) *n.* rope or tackle used on a ship to raise or lower a sail, yard, flat, etc. 1611, in Cotgrave's *Dictionary,* alteration of earlier *halier* (1373; also found in the surname *Haliere* porter, carrier, 1279), from *halen* to haul, HALE[2]. The spelling was influenced by

YARD[2] in the nautical sense of a long beam used to support a sail.

ham[1] *n.* meat from the upper part of a hog's hind leg. Old English *hamm* hollow or bend of the knee (about 1000, in Ælfric's *Glossary*); cognate with Middle Low German and Middle Dutch *hamme* hollow or bend of the knee, thigh, ham (modern Dutch *ham*), Old High German *hamma,* and Old Icelandic *hǫm,* from Proto-Germanic **Hammō.* Outside Germanic cognates exist in Greek *knḗmē* shinbone, and Old Irish *cnāim* bone, leg, from Indo-European **konəmā* (Pok.613). The meaning of thigh of an animal, especially a hog, used for food, is first recorded probably about 1475.

ham[2] *n. Slang.* performer who overacts, inferior actor or performer. 1882, American English, apparently a shortened form of earlier *hamfatter* (1880), a term of contempt for an actor of low grade, such as a member of a minstrel show, said to be derived from an old minstrel song called "The *Ham-fat* Man."

From the idea of an inexpert or amateurish actor, *ham* was extended in meaning to that of an amateur telegraphist (1919) and an amateur radio operator (1922).

—v. *Slang,* especially in the phrase *ham up* or *ham it up* act like a ham; overact. 1933, from the noun.

hamadryad (ham′ədrī′əd) *n.* wood nymph supposed to live and die with the tree she dwelt in; dryad. About 1385 *amadriades,* pl., in Chaucer's *Canterbury Tales;* borrowed from Latin *Hamadryas* (plural *Hamadryades*), from Greek *Hamadryás,* from *háma* together with (see SAME) + *dryî* (dative of *drŷs*) a tree; see DRYAD.

hamburger *n.* 1908, from earlier (1889, American English) *hamburger steak,* borrowed from German *Hamburger,* originally, of or from the city of Hamburg; perhaps so called because this type of steak may have originated in Germany and was associated with the city and port of Hamburg, from which many immigrants came to the United States.

hamlet *n.* small village. Before 1338 *hamlet, hamelet,* in Mannyng's *Chronicle of England;* borrowed from Old French *hamelet,* diminutive (with *-et*) of *hamel* village, itself a diminutive of *ham* (with *-el* -le[1]); derived from Frankish **haim;* see HOME.

The form *ham* (Old English *hām* home) does not appear in Old or Middle English with the meaning of town, village, except in compounds of place names, such as *Birmingham* and *Nottingham,* in which it refers originally and more specifically to a manor; also, *ham* in this sense should not be confused with Old English *ham, hamm* a meadow, pasture land (often enclosed).

hammer *n.* About 1125 *hamer;* found in Old English *hamor* (about 725, in *Beowulf*); cognate with Old Saxon *hamur* hammer, Middle Dutch and modern Dutch *hamer,* Old High German *hamar* (modern German *Hammer*), and Old Icelandic *hamarr* hammer, stone, crag, from Proto-Germanic **Hamur,* from Indo-European **k̂amr̥* (Walde-Pokorny I 29,30). Outside Germanic cognates are found in Greek *ákmōn* (genitive *ákmonos*) anvil, Lithuanian *ãšmens,* pl., cutting edges, *akmuõ* (genitive *akmeñs*) stone, Old Slavic *kamy,* Russian *kamen'* stone, and Sanskrit *áśman-* stone, related to *áśri-s* EDGE. These latter cognates, primarily with the sense of stone and the Old Icelandic sense of stone or crag, suggest that *hammer* may have originally meant a stone implement. **—v.** drive, work, or hit with a hammer. Probably about 1390, from the noun.

hammock *n.* hanging bed. 1657 *hamock,* alteration of earlier *hamaca* (1555); borrowing of Spanish *hamaca,* from Arawakan language of Haiti in which the word apparently referred to fish nets. The ending *-ock* was possibly influenced by the diminutive suffix *-ock,* as in *hillock.*

hamper[1] *v.* hold back, hinder. Before 1375 *hampren* to surround, imprison, confine; later, to pack in a container; of uncertain origin, possibly from *hamper*[2], n.

hamper[2] *n.* large basket. 1316-17 *hampyr* container for documents, goblets or other utensils; or for foodstuff; contraction of Anglo-French *hanaper* (1314) with change of *-n'p* to *-mp-,* as in *ampersand* from *and per se and* (also found in Anglo-Latin *hanepario,* 1292). The term was borrowed from Old French *hanepier* case for holding a large goblet or cup, from *hanap* goblet, from Frankish (compare Old Saxon *hnapp* cup, bowl, basin, Middle Low German, Middle Dutch, and modern Dutch *nap,* Old High German *hnapf,* modern German *Napf,* Old Icelandic *hnappr,* and Old English *hnæpp*, of unknown origin).

hamster *n.* small rodent with large cheek pouches. 1607, borrowed from German *Hamster,* from Middle High German *hamastra* hamster (possibly also in Old High German *hamastro* but found only in the sense of weevil, also in Old Saxon *hamstra*), probably from Old Slavic *chomĕstorŭ* hamster, in which *-storŭ* corresponds to Lithuanian *stãras* hamster.

hamstring *v.* to cripple, disable. 1641, to disable as if by cutting the hamstrings of, in Milton's writings; from earlier noun *hamstring* tendon at the back of the knee (1565; formed from *ham*[1] bend of the knee + *string*).

hand *n.* Old English (before 830) *hond;* earlier *hand-* in the compound *handful* (about 700); cognate with Old Frisian *hand, hond* hand, Old Saxon and Dutch *hand,* Old High German *hant* (modern German *Hand*), Old Icelandic *hǫnd,* and Gothic *handus,* from Proto-Germanic **Handuz;* (no cognates are found outside Germanic). It should be noted that these words also meant "the hand and the arm" and sometimes "the arm." **—adj.** Before 1000, of, for, by, or in the hand; from the noun. **—v.** Probably before 1400 *handen* take charge of, in *Morte Arthur;* later, seize (probably about 1400); from the noun. **—handball** *n.* (probably before 1400) **—handbell** *n.* (before 1000, in Old English) **—handbook** *n.* (before 900, in Old English) **—handcart** *n.* (1640, as two words, in American English) **—handcuff** *n.* (1645, on sleeves; 1695 shackles, both in American English) **—handful** *n.* (about 830, in Old English) **—handgrip** *n.* (about 725, in *Beowulf*) **—handmaiden** *n.* (about 1303) **—handout** *n.* (1882, in American English) **—handsaw** *n.* (1399) **—hand towel** (about 1350) **—handwork** *n.* (before 1000, in Old English) **—handwriting** *n.* (1421) **—handy** *adj.* 1535, performed by hand, manual; formed from English *hand* + *-y*[1], but the form is found earlier in the surname *Handibody* dexterous (1312), and in an extended form *hondiwerc* (about 1200, from Old English *hand-geweorc*). The meaning of conveniently accessible, is first recorded in 1650. **—handyman** *n.* (1872)

handicap *n.* contest in which the better contestants are given certain disadvantages, or the poorer ones certain advantages. Probably before 1653, from the phrase *hand in cap,* referring to an old wagering game in which forfeit money was deposited in a cap. Reference to horse racing appeared in *Handy-Cap Match* (1754) and then to any race or contest in 1875. The general sense of encumbrance or disability, is first recorded in 1890. **—v.** 1649, to draw or gain as in a wagering game; from the same source as the noun. The meaning of give a handicap to, equalize chances of competitors, is first recorded in 1852, and the transferred sense of put at a disadvantage, disable, cripple, in 1864. **—handicapped** *adj.* disabled or crippled. 1915, from the past participle of *handicap,* v.

handicraft *n.* About 1300, alteration (possibly influenced by *handiwork*) of *hændecraft* (probably before 1200); found in Old English (before 975) *handcræft* (*hand* + *cræft* craft).

handiwork *n.* About 1200 *hand-iwerc* work done with hands; developed from Old English (probably about 725) *handgeweorc* handwork *(hand* + *geweorc,* collective form of *weorc* WORK).

handkerchief *n.* 1530, formed from English *hand* + *kerchief* and parallel in usage to *handkercher* (about 1532), which remained in use through the 1860's.

handle *n.* Old English (before 800) *handle,* from *hand* + *-le* expressing the sense of an appliance or tool as found in *thimble.* **—v.** Old English (about 1000) *handlian* to touch or feel, or move with the hands, manipulate, manage; cognate with Old Frisian *handelia* to handle, Old High German *hantalōn* to handle, touch, manage (modern German *handeln,* and modern Dutch *handelen* to treat, handle, trade), and Old Icelandic *họndla* lay hold of, handle; from Old English *hand* + *-lian* -le[3]. **—handlebar** *n.* (1887, two words) **—handler** *n.* (before 1398)

handsome *adj.* Probably before 1400 *handsom* easy to handle, ready at hand, in *Morte Arthur;* formed from English *hand* + *-some*[1]. An early sense of *handsome* handy, convenient, suitable (1530), was extended to mean of fair size or amount, fair, considerable (1577), and was further extended to that of having a fine form or figure, well-proportioned, good-looking (1590, in Spenser's *Faerie Queene*). The meaning of generous or magnanimous, as in *a handsome donation,* is first recorded in 1660 and is an extension of the sense of "of fair size, considerable."

hang *v.* 1137 *hongen;* developed by fusion of: 1) Old English (about 1000) *hōn* (with past tense *heng*) suspend, and 2) Old English (about 1000) *hangian, hongian* (with past tense *hangode, hongode*) be suspended; also probably by influence of a Scandinavian source (compare Old Icelandic *hengja* suspend, and *hanga* be suspended, hang). Old English *hangian* corresponds to Old Frisian *hangia* be suspended or hang, Old Saxon *hangōn,* Middle Dutch and modern Dutch *hangen,* Old High German *hangēn* (modern German *hangen, hängen*), and Old Icelandic *hanga,* from Proto-Germanic **Hang-*. Old English *hōn* corresponds to Old Frisian *hūa* suspend or hang, Old Saxon *hāhan,* Middle Low German *hān,* Middle Dutch *haen,* Old High German and Gothic *hāhan,* from Proto-Germanic **HanH,* cognate with Sanskrit *śáñkate* hesitates, and Latin *cūnctārī* to delay (contracted from **concitārī*), from Indo-European **k̂onk-* (Pok.614). The Old English form with *a* never died out as a variant (it is found from the 1100's on) and finally prevailed as the current spelling after 1550's, except in the north of Britain.

The distinction between *hanged* and *hung* is one of historical grammar, being established at least by the time of Shakespeare. In the 1500's speakers in northern England adopted *hung* as the form of the past participle completing the inflections as *hing, hang, hung.* This became standard English in the 1600's, but with a new past participle *hung* that gradually replaced *hanged,* which was retained only in law by judges pronouncing capital sentences and in general expressions extending from legal use, such as *be hanged* (in *I'll be hanged if I'll go,* etc.).

—n. 1473-74, a sling to support a workman; later, a curtain for a bed (before 1500); from the verb. The general sense of the way cloth, etc., hangs, is first recorded before 1797.

—hangman *n.* (1345; earlier in the surname *Hangeman,* 1253) **—hangnail** *n.* (1678, earlier *agnail* a corn on the foot, about 950) **—hangout** *n.* (1895) **—hangover** *n.* (1894)

hangar *n.* shed for aircraft. 1852, a covered shed for carriages, in Thackeray's *History of Henry Esmond;* borrowed from French *hangar,* from Middle French *hanghart,* perhaps alteration of Middle Dutch **hamgaerd* enclosure near a house; of uncertain origin. The extended sense of covered shed for airplanes is first recorded in 1902.

hank *n.* coil, loop. 1294-95, probably borrowed from a Scandinavian source (compare Old Icelandic *họnk, hanki* hasp, clasp, hank; cognate with Middle Low German *hank* handle, and Old High German *henken, hengen* to cause to hang, related to *hangēn* HANG).

hanker *v.* crave or yearn. 1601, to linger or hang around with longing or expectation; borrowed probably from Flemish *hankeren,* related to Dutch *hunkeren* to hanker; of uncertain origin (perhaps a frequentative or intensive form of *hangen* to hang, related to Middle Dutch *hangen* to hang).

hanky-panky *n. Informal.* trickery, mischief, foolishness. 1841, British slang, in *Punch;* possibly a variant of *hoky-poky* deception or fraud (1847); altered from HOCUS-POCUS.

Hanseatic *adj.* 1614, of or pertaining to the *Hanseatic League* (medieval political and commercial association of North German towns); borrowed from Medieval Latin *Hanseaticus,* from *hansa* hanse, from Middle Low German *hanse,* from Old High German *hansa* military troop, band, company; cognate with Gothic *hansa* multitude, and Old English *hōs* band, company, of unknown origin. The term *hanse* merchant guild is found in English before 1135 in the compound *hanshus* guild hall, as a borrowing through Old French from Medieval Latin.

hansom *n.* two-wheeled cab drawn by one horse. 1847, in allusion to J.A. *Hansom,* English architect who designed such cabs.

haphazard *n.* 1575, implied in earlier nonce use *haphazarder* (1573); formed from earlier English *hap* chance or luck (probably before 1200, in Layamon's *Chronicle of Britain;* borrowed from a Scandinavian source (compare Old Icelandic *happ* chance, good luck) + *hazard* risk, danger, peril. Old Icelandic *happ,* from Proto-Germanic **Hapan,* is cognate with Old Slavic *kobĭ* destiny, protecting spirit, and Czech *koba* success, from Indo-European **kob-* (Pok.610).

happen *v.* Probably about 1380 *happenen* to come to pass, occur; originally, occur by *hap* or chance in the verb *happen* (about 1303, from *hap,* n., chance, fortune, luck; see HAPHAZARD; and possibly Old English *hæppan*). **—happening** *n.* 1551, occurrence; earlier, chance, luck (before 1450); formed from English *happen* + *-ing*[1]. **—happenstance** *n.* chance occurrence. 1897, American English, formed from *happen(ing)* + *(circum)stance.* **—happenstantial** *adj.* occurring by chance. 1958, American English; formed from *happenstance* + *-ial,* on the pattern of *circumstantial.*

happy *adj.* About 1380, fortunate or lucky, in Chaucer's *House of Fame;* formed from English *hap* chance or fortune + *-y*[1]. The sense of very glad, is first recorded in Chaucer's *Canterbury Tales* (about 1390). **—happiness** *n.* 1530, in Palsgrave's *Lesclarcissement,* formed from English *happy* + *-ness.*

hara-kiri (har'əkir'ē) *n.* suicide by ripping open the abdomen with a knife. 1856 *hari-kari,* borrowed from Japanese *hara-kiri (hara* belly + *kiri* cutting).

harangue *n.* noisy speech. Before 1450, Scottish *arang;* borrowed from Middle French *harangue,* from Old Provençal, probably from Italian *aringare* to harangue, from *aringo* public square, from Gothic **hriggs,* possibly in Germanic **hari-hring* army ring, circular gathering (compare Old High German *hring* circle of spectators, RING). *Harangue* came into general English use from Scottish writers after 1600. **—v.** address in a harangue. 1660, from French *haranguer,* from Middle French *harangue,* n.

harass (həras') *v.* torment, trouble by repeated attacks. Before 1618, to lay waste or devastate, in Raleigh's writings; borrowed from French *harasser* tire out, vex; of uncertain origin (possibly from Old French *harer* set a dog on, and perhaps blended with Old French *harier* to harry, draw, drag). The meaning of trouble by repeated attacks, is found in Bacon's *History of the Reign of King Henry VII* (1622). **—harassment** *n.* 1753, formed from English *harass* + *-ment.*

harbinger *n.* forerunner. About 1471 *herbengar* one sent ahead to arrange lodgings for an army, etc., alteration of earlier *herberger* provider of shelter, innkeeper (before 1200), later *herbergour* one who goes ahead to seek lodging, a purveyor (1384-85); borrowed from Old French *herbergeor,* from *herbergier* provide lodging, from *herberge* lodging or shelter, from Frankish; compare Old High German *heriberga* army shelter, lodging (*heri* army + *berga* shelter, related to *bergan* to shelter); see HARBOR; for suffix see -ER[1]. **—v.** announce beforehand. 1646, from the noun.

harbor *n.* About 1125 *herbyrge* refuge, lodgings; later *herberwe* harbor for ships (probably before 1200, in Layamon's *Chronicle of Britain*), and *harber* (probably about 1475); probably developed from Old English **herebeorg* (*here* army, host (see HARRY) + *beorg* refuge, shelter, related to *beorgan* save, preserve); possibly borrowed from, or at least modeled on late Old Icelandic *herbergi;* also cognate with Old Saxon and Old High German *heriberga* (modern German *Herberge*), Old Frisian *herberge,* Middle Low German *herberge,* and Middle Dutch *herberghe* (modern Dutch *herberg*). The final element (*-beorg, -berge,* etc.) in all of these Germanic forms is related to Gothic *baírgan* protect, from Indo-European **bherĝh-* (Pok.145). **—v.** About 1125 *herebyregen* to shelter; later *herborwen* (before 1200); from the noun.

The spelling change to *har-* in *harbor* is found as early as 1311 and was evident in the 1400's following similar changes as found in *bark* and *marsh.* The weakening to *-bor* began in the late 1300's.

hard *adj.* 1126 *hard,* developed from Old English *heard* not yielding or soft, solid, firm (about 725, in *Beowulf*); cognate with Old Frisian *herd* hard, Old Saxon *hard,* Middle Low German *hard, harde,* Middle Dutch *hart, hard* (modern Dutch *hard*), Old High German and modern German *hart,* Old Icelandic *hardhr,* and Gothic *hardus;* all derived from Proto-Germanic **Harđús,* from Indo-European **kartús,* root **kar-* (Pok.531). **—adv.** Probably before 1200 *harde;* earlier *herde* (about 1175); developed from Old English (about 725) *hearde;* from the adjective. **—hard-boiled** *adj.* tough, rough. 1886, American English, in Mark Twain's speeches. **—harden** *v.* Probably about 1200 *hardnen* make hard, formed from English *hard* + *-nen (-enen)* -en[1]. **—hard hat** helmet (probably about 1380) **—hardheaded** *adj.* (1583, stubborn; 1779, practical, shrewd) **—hard-hearted** *adj.* (probably before 1200) **—hardly** *adv.* (probably before 1200, found in Old English *heardlice*) **—hardship** *n.* (probably before 1200) **—hardware** *n.* (1440)

hardy *adj.* robust. Probably before 1200, bold or daring, especially in battle, in *Ancrene Riwle;* earlier, in a surname *Stonhardi* (1194); probably influenced by English *hard,* adj., but essentially a borrowing of Old French *hardi,* from past participle of *hardir* to harden, be or make bold, from Frankish (compare Gothic *gahardjan* make hard, Old High German *herten* harden, modern German *härten*, Old Icelandic *herdha,* Middle Dutch and modern Dutch *harden,* Old Saxon *herdian,* Old Frisian *herda,* and Old English *hierdan* to make or become hard; derived from West Germanic **hardjan* to make hard), found in Old English *heard* HARD. The meaning of strong, vigorous, robust, is first recorded before 1398. **—hardihood** *n.* (1634, in Milton's *Comus*)

hare *n.* gnawing animal much like a rabbit. Probably about 1200 *hare;* earlier, in a place name *Haredena* (before 1154); found in Old English (about 700) *hara* hare; cognate with Old Frisian *hasa* hare, Middle Dutch *haese* (modern Dutch *haas*), Middle Low German *hase,* Old High German *haso* hare (modern German *Hase* hare), and Old Icelandic *heri* hare. Old High German *haso* developed from Proto-Germanic **Hásan-, Hazán-,* cognate with Sanskrit *śaśá-s* (from **śasá-s*), and Latin *cānus* hoary (from **casnos*), from Indo-European **k̑as-* gray (Pok.533), **—harebrained** *adj.* 1548, formed from English *hare* + *brain* + *-ed*[2].

Hare Krishna (hä're krish'nə) member of a sect devoted to the Hindu god Krishna. 1972, American English, from *Hare Krishna* a chant or mantra used by the sect (1968); borrowed from Hindi *hare Krishnā* O Lord Krishna.

harem *n.* part of a Moslem house where the women live. 1634 *haram,* borrowed from Arabic *ḥaram* women's quarters (literally, something forbidden or kept safe), from the root of *ḥarama* he guarded, forbade. The form *harem,* which is first recorded in 1718, is a borrowing of Turkish *harem,* from Arabic *ḥarīm,* a variant form of *ḥaram.* The meaning of occupants of a harem, the wives, concubines, etc., is first recorded in Cowper's *The Task* (1781).

hark *v.* listen. About 1200 *harkien, harken,* probably developed from Old English **hercian, heorcian* (see HEARKEN); cognate with Old Frisian *harkia, herkia* listen, Middle Low German and Middle Dutch *horken,*

Old High German *hōrechen* (modern German *horchen*); of unknown origin. **—harken** *v.* See HEARKEN.

harlequin (har′lәkin *or* har′lәkwin) *n.* character in comedy and pantomime who is usually masked and has a costume of varied colors (often alternating squares of black and white). 1590 *Harlicken,* in Nashe's *An Almond for a Parrot;* borrowed from Middle French *harlequin* (probably equivalent to Italian *arlecchino*), variant of *Herlequin, Hellequin,* as in Old French *maisnie Hellequin* leader of demons who ride through the air on horses, probably corresponding to Old English *Herla cyning* king Herla, a mythical character sometimes identified with the Germanic god Woden.

In FEW the Old French *hellequin* is said to be a borrowing from Middle English **Herleking,* and Italian *arlecchino* is also attributed to the same source. If that is so the forms would suggest more than a passing correspondence to Old English.

—adj. 1779, characteristic of a harlequin or his dress; from the noun.

harlot *n.* prostitute. Probably before 1200 *hearlot* vagabond or itinerant jester, in *Ancrene Riwle;* later *harlotte* prostitute (probably before 1425); borrowed from Old French *herlot, arlot* vagabond or tramp; of uncertain origin, possibly (in later use) from Catalan with the meaning of "pimp." Early uses in Middle English applied to men.

harm *n.* Probably before 1200 *harm,* in Layamon's *Chronicle of Britain;* earlier, in the surname *Harm* (1176); found in Old English *hearm* hurt, evil, grief, pain, insult (about 725, in *Beowulf*); cognate with Old Frisian *herm* insult or pain, Old Saxon *harm,* Old High German *harm, haram* (modern German *Harm*) grief or harm, and Old Icelandic *harmr* grief; all developed from Proto-Germanic **Harmaz,* and perhaps cognate with Old Slavic *sramŭ* shame, Avestan *fšarәma-* embarrassment or shame, and Middle Persian *šarm* shame, from Indo-European **k̑ormos* (Pok.615). **—v.** About 1225 *harmen;* found in Old English *hearmian* to hurt (about 1000, in Ælfric's writings); from *hearm,* n. **—harmful** *adj.* 1340, in *Ayenbite of Inwyt;* formed from Middle English *harm* + *-ful.* **—harmless** *adj.* About 1280; formed from Middle English *harm* + *-les* -less.

harmonic *adj.* having to do with harmony. 1570, perhaps a back formation from earlier *armonicall* (before 1500), influenced by, and in some instances borrowed from, Middle French *harmonique,* from Latin *harmonicus,* from Greek *harmonikós* harmonic or musical, from *harmoníā* HARMONY; for suffix see -IC. **—n. 1 harmonics.** 1709, theory or system of musical sounds, formed in English on the model of *physics,* etc. **2** overtone. 1777, shortening of *harmonic tone.* **—harmonica** *n.* mouth organ. 1873, American English, alteration of earlier *armonica* glass harmonica (1762, coined by Benjamin Franklin who refined the older concept of musical glasses and introduced them to America; borrowing of Latin *harmonica,* feminine of *harmonicus* harmonic). The later spelling with *h-* was influenced by *harmonic.*

harmony *n.* About 1380 *armonye* concord of sounds, music, melody, in Chaucer's *Parlement of Foules;* borrowed from Old French *armonie, harmonie,* from Latin *harmonia,* from Greek *harmoníā* joining, joint, agreement, concord of sounds; related to *harmós* joint; see ARM[1] limb; for suffix see -Y[3]. The meaning of a combination of notes to form chords, is first recorded in Trevisa's translation of Bartholomew's *De Proprietatibus Rerum* (before 1398), and that of agreement, accord, in Usk's *The Testament of Love* (about 1385). **—harmonious** *adj.* 1549, borrowed from Middle French *harmonieux,* from Old French *harmonie* harmony; for suffix see -OUS. **—harmonize** *v.* 1483, to play or sing in harmony; later, to be in harmony with (1629); borrowed from Middle French *harmoniser,* from Old French *harmonie* harmony; for suffix see -IZE.

harness *n.* Probably before 1300 *harnais, herneys* harness, gear, military equipment; earlier, as a surname *Herneys* (1275); borrowed from Old French *harneis,* perhaps from a Scandinavian source; compare Old Icelandic **hernest* provisions for an army, from *herr* army (see HARRY) + *nest* provisions, cognate with Old English *nest* provisions, related to *nesan* be saved or preserved. Old English *nesan* is cognate with Sanskrit *násate* (he) approaches, Greek *neîsthai* to come home, and *nóstos* homecoming, from Indo-European **nes-/nos-* (Pok.766). **—v.** put harness on. Probably before 1300 *herneysen,* from Old French *harneschier* to arm or equip, from the noun in Old French.

harp *n.* Probably before 1200 *harpe,* in Layamon's *Chronicle of Britain;* found in Old English (about 725) *hearpe;* cognate with Old Saxon *harpa* instrument of fortune, Middle Low German and Middle Dutch *harpe* harp (modern Dutch *harp*), German dialect *harpfe* device for drying corn, Old High German *harpha* harp (modern German *Harfe*), and Old Icelandic *harpa* harp, large sieve for corn (modern Icelandic *harpa* press together, pinch); all derived from Proto-Germanic **harpōn-,* from Indo-European **kerb-/korb-* (Pok.948). Through Gothic **harpō* it is possible to trace the development of Late Latin *harpa,* Italian *arpa, arpe,* Spanish *arpa,* and French *harpe.* **—v.** Probably before 1200 *harpien;* found in Old English *hearpian* to play a harp; possibly, in part, from Old French *harper,* from Germanic; but more likely immediately from Germanic; compare Middle and modern Dutch *harpen,* Middle High German *harpfen* (modern German *harfen*). The later sense of to talk much, or too much about, usually in the phrase *harp on,* is first recorded in 1562.

—harpsichord *n.* musical instrument in which the strings are plucked by quills fitted to a keyboard action resembling that of a piano. 1611, in Cotgrave's *Dictionary,* alteration of obsolete French *harpechorde (harpe* harp + *-chorde,* from Latin *chorda* string; see CORD*).*

harpoon *n.* 1625 *harpon* barbed dart or spear; earlier, implied in *harponier* (1613, in *Purchas his Pilgrimage*); borrowed from French *harpon* (also *harpin* boat hook), from Old French *harpon* cramp iron or clamp, from *harper* to grapple, grasp, possibly from a Germanic source (compare Icelandic *harpa* to press something together, pinch), or from Latin *harpa-* hook, in *harpagónem* grappling hook, from Greek **harpagṓn,* from *harpágē* grappling hook, related to *hárpē* sickle; for suffix see -OON. The spelling *harpoon* (1694) may have been influenced by Dutch *harpoen,* from Middle Dutch, from Old French *harpon.*

The *harpoon* with a rope tied to it and traditionally used in whaling, is not recorded before 1694, and replaces the older term *harping iron* (1442).

—v. strike with a harpoon. 1774; from the noun.

Harpy *n.* monster in Greek legend having women's heads and birds' bodies, wings, and claws. About 1375 *Arpie,* in Chaucer's *Canterbury Tales;* borrowed from

Latin *Harpyia,* from Greek *Hárpyia,* pl., snatchers, probably related to *harpázein* to snatch. The figurative meaning of a rapacious, plundering, or grasping person, spelled *arpie,* is first recorded in Lydgate's *Aesop's Fables* (about 1400).

harquebus (här'kwəbəs) *n.* early portable matchlock gun preceding the musket. 1562; earlier *arkbusshe* (1532); borrowed from Middle French *harquebuse, arquebuse,* from Italian *archibuso, arcobuso,* alteration of Middle Dutch *hakebus (hake* hook + *bus* gun, from Late Latin *buxis* container, BOX[1]); so called because the gun had a hook to fasten it to a support. Alteration of the Middle Dutch word when borrowed into Italian must have been from association in Italian with the fact that the harquebus replaced the crossbow, as evidenced in the elements of the compound *arco* bow + *buso* hole (or pierced), with reference to the gun's barrel.

harrier *n.* small hound used to hunt hares. 1542, developed from *hayrer* a small hunting dog (1408; also *eirer* about 1410); possibly borrowed from Middle French *errier* wanderer.

harrow *n.* heavy frame with iron teeth or upright disks used in farming. About 1300 *harewe;* later *harow* (1377-78); developed from Old English **hearwa,* which would possibly be cognate with Old Icelandic *herfi* harrow, Old Swedish *harf* (Swedish and Danish *harv*). **—v.** draw a harrow over land, etc. Before 1325 *harven,* in *Cursor Mundi,* from the noun.

The participial adjective *harrowing* extremely distressing or painful, is first recorded in Scott's *The Lady of the Lake* (1810), from a now archaic sense of wound, pain, distress, found in Shakespeare's *Hamlet* (1602).

harry *v.* raid and rob with violence, ravage. Probably before 1200 *herigan, herien,* developed from Old English (about 893) *hergian;* cognate with Old Frisian *urheria* lay waste, ravage, plunder, Old Saxon and Old High German *heriōn,* Middle High German *hergen, hern* destroy by war (modern German *verheeren* lay waste, devastate), and Old Icelandic *herja* lay waste, plunder; all derived from Proto-Germanic **Harjaz* an armed force, which is found in Old English *here* army, host, multitude, Old Frisian *here,* Old Saxon and Old High German *heri* (modern German *Heer*), Old Icelandic *herr,* and Gothic *harjis,* and itself derives from Indo-European **koro-, *koryo-* war (Pok.615).

harsh *adj.* 1533 *harrish* bitter or astringent, probably variant of earlier *harske* rough, coarse, sour (probably before 1400, in *Morte Arthur,* but implied earlier in *harskly,* about 1300); borrowed from a Scandinavian source (compare Danish and Norwegian *harsk* rancid or rank, older Swedish *härsk,* now *härsken;* cognate with Middle Low German and modern German *harsch* harsh, related to *harst* a rake; see CARD[2] tool). An adverb use *harsk* loudly or fiercely, appeared earlier in *Cursor Mundi* (before 1325), paralleled by *harskly* roughly, rudely, severely (about 1300).

hart *n.* male deer, stag. Before 1250 *hert,* in *Bestiary;* later *hart* (1410); developed from Old English *heorot, heort* (about 725, in *Beowulf*); cognate with Old Frisian *hert* stag, deer, Old Saxon *hirot,* Middle Dutch and modern Dutch *hert,* Old High German *hiruz, hirz* (modern German *Hirsch*), and Old Icelandic *hjǫrtr* (Norwegian, Swedish and Danish *hjort*); all from Proto-Germanic **Herut-* horned, which without the formative *-t-* is recognizable in Greek *kéras* horn, and other cognates through the Indo-European base **k̑erəw-* (Pok.576), including Greek *keraós* horned, Latin *cervus* stag or deer, Welsh *carw,* Cornish *carow,* Old Prussian *sirwis* roe deer, Old Slavic *srŭna.*

hartebeest (här'təbēst') *n.* large, swift African antelope. 1786, borrowed from Afrikaans *hartebeest* deer or hart beast, from Dutch *hartebeest,* variant of *hertebeest (hert* hart + *beest* beast, from Middle Dutch *beest,* from Old French *beste* BEAST). In modern Afrikaans the word is spelled *hartbees.*

harum-scarum *adv.* recklessly, rashly. 1674-91, in an edition of a glossary, sometimes also written as *hare 'em, scare 'em;* possibly compounded from earlier *hare* harry, worry, harass + *scare,* with *'um, 'em,* reduced form of older *hem* them (before 1121, Old English *heom*). **—adj.** reckless, rash. 1751, in Smollett's *The Adventures of Peregrine Pickle;* from the adverb. **—n.** reckless person. 1784, from the adjective.

harvest *n.* Before 1250 *hervest* time for reaping and gathering in crops, in *Bestiary;* earlier *herfest* season of autumn (1105); developed from Old English *hærfest* autumn (probably about 750, in *Phoenix*). The Old English word is cognate with Old Frisian *herfst* autumn, Old Saxon *hervist,* Middle Low German *hervest,* Middle Dutch and modern Dutch *herfst,* Old High German *herbist* (modern German *Herbst*), and Old Icelandic *haust;* all probably derived from Proto-Germanic **Harƀi-s,* possibly representing an Indo-European formation **korp-is-tó-s* in reference to the month "most fit for picking," and therefore a possible superlative adjective which would explain the appearance of the suffix form *-st-,* also found in *-est, -ist.* Outside Germanic cognates are found in Latin *carpere* to pluck or gather, Greek *karpós* fruit, Lithuanian *kir̃pti* to cut with scissors, Old Slavic *črěpŭ* broken fragment, Middle Irish *corrán* sickle, Sanskrit *kṛpāṇa-s* sword, and perhaps Hittite *karpinaš* tree, from Indo-European **kerp-/korp-/kr̥p-* (Pok.944). **—v.** About 1400 *hervesten* reap and gather in (grain); from the noun. **—harvest home** (1573) **—harvest moon** (1706, in Isaac Watts' *Horae Lyricae*) **—harvesttime** *n.* (before 1387, found in Old English *hærfest-tīma*)

hash[1] *n.* mixture of cooked meat, potatoes, etc. 1662-63 in Pepys' *Diary,* from the verb. *Hash* is a replacement of earlier *hache* (about 1330), also *hachey, hachy;* borrowed perhaps from Old French *haché,* from *hacher* to hack. **—v.** chop into small pieces. 1657, borrowed from French *hacher* to hack, chop, from Old French *hache* axe; see HATCHET.

hash[2] *n.* hashish. 1959, American English; shortened form of *hashish,* in Norman Mailer's *Advertisements for Myself.*

hashish (hash'ēsh) *n.* narcotic drug derived from the hemp plant. 1598, borrowed from Arabic *ḥashīsh* powdered hemp (literally, dry herb), from *ḥashsha* it was dry; see ASSASSIN.

hasp *n.* Before 1200 *hespe* fastening for a door, window, trunk, etc.; later *haspe* (probably before 1300, in *Arthour and Merlin*); developed by alteration in a metathesis of *s* and *p* from Old English *hæpse* (about 1000, in Ælfric's *Grammar*); cognate with Middle Low German *hespe, haspe* hasp or hinge, Middle Dutch *hespe,* Old High German *haspa* (modern German *Haspe*), and Old Icelandic *hespa.* The early Middle English *hespe* was probably formed by influence of Old Icelandic *hespa,* though contact with other Germanic languages could have influenced the same change in spelling. According to the Germanist Kluge, Old English *hæpse* is probably cognate with Latin *capsa* container, from *capere;* see CAPTIVE.

hassle *n.* struggle, trouble. 1945, American English, perhaps from Southern dialect *hassle* to pant, breathe noisily (1928); of unknown origin. **—v.** to trouble, annoy, harass. 1951, from the noun.

hassock *n.* 1440 *hassok* clump of coarse grass, in *Promptorium Parvulorum;* earlier, possibly meaning mound or hillock, in the place name *Hassok* (about 1150); developed from Old English (986) *hassuc* clump of grass, coarse grass; of uncertain origin. The meaning of thick cushion (often stuffed with straw), is first recorded in 1516.

haste *n.* Probably about 1225 *haste* hurry or speed, in *King Horn;* borrowed from Old French *haste,* from Frankish (compare adjectives in Old High German *heist, heisti* vehement, violent, which is cognate with Old Frisian *hāste* violent, Old English *hǣste* violent, vehement, impetuous, and the noun *hǣst* violence, neither of which survived into Middle English); also related to Gothic *haifsts* strife, from Proto-Germanic **Haifstiz,* cognate with Sanskrit *śíbham* quickly, from Indo-European **k̑ēibh-/k̑əibh-/k̑ībh-* (Pok.542).

Though cognates that are near forms are found in some Germanic languages, they had a different meaning, and it was the borrowing of Old French *haste* that yields the sense of hurry or speed in Germanic languages: Old Frisian *hāst* haste, Middle Dutch *haeste, haest* (modern Dutch *haast*), and Middle Low German *hast* (modern German *Hast*) haste.
—hasten *v.* 1565-73, in an edition of an early Modern English thesaurus; formed from English *haste* + -EN[1].
—hasty *adj.* Probably about 1280 *hasti;* formed from Middle English *haste,* n. + *-i* -y[1]; and borrowed from Old French *hasti, hastif,* from Old French *haste* haste + *-if* -ive. The two forms *hasti* and *hastif* had simultaneous use in Middle English (both also produced derivative forms in *-ly* and *-ness*), but the native English form replaced *hastif* by the 1500's.

hat *n.* Old English (before 800) *hæt* hat or head covering; cognate with Frisian *hat, hatt* hat or hood, Old Icelandic *hattr, hǫttr* cowl. These forms derive from Proto-Germanic **Hattuz* hood or cowl (earlier **Hađnús),* from Indo-European **kadh-* (Pok.516); see HOOD[1].
—v. provide with a hat. Before 1425, from the noun.
—hatter *n.* 1212, formed from Middle English *hat* + *-er*[1].

hatch[1] *v.* bring forth from an egg or eggs. Before 1250 *hachen,* of uncertain origin (developed probably from Old English **hæccan, *heccan*); compare Middle High German and modern German *hecken* to hatch or breed, also Swedish *häcka,* Danish *hække* to hatch. Middle English *hachen* developed into the spelling *hatch* in the 1500's as a reflection of the pronunciation.
—n. act of hatching. 1597, in Shakespeare's *2 Henry IV;* from the verb. **—hatchery** *n.* 1880, formed from English *hatch*[1], v. + *-ery.*

hatch[2] *n.* opening in a ship's deck. About 1250 *hacche;* later *hatche* half door, small door, gate, wicket; developed from Old English (1015) *hæc* (genitive *hæcce*); cognate with Middle Low German *heck* fence, Middle Dutch *hecke* hatch, grating (modern Dutch *hek* fence), from Proto-Germanic *Hak-;* of unknown origin. The meaning of plank for a ship's deck, from which the sense "opening in a ship's deck" developed, is first recorded in Anglo-Latin in 1233-34, and in Middle English *hacchenayl* (1294-96).

hatch[3] *v.* draw, cut, or engrave fine parallel lines on. 1389, implied in *hachying* the carving or engraving of parallel lines for ornament; borrowed from Old French *hacher* chop or hatch, from *hache* axe; see HATCHET. For spelling change see HATCH[1].

hatchet *n.* 1307 *hachet;* earlier as a surname (1166); borrowed from Old French *hachette* hatchet, diminutive of *hache* axe or hatchet, possibly from Frankish **hāppja* (compare Old High German *hāppa* sickle, scythe) from Proto-Germanic **Hǣƀjō,* from Indo-European **kēp-* cut (Pok.932); for suffix see -ET.

hate *v.* About 1175 *haten,* developed from Old English *hatian* (before 899, in Alfred's translation of St. Gregory's *Pastoral Care*); cognate with Old Frisian *hatia* to hate, Old Saxon *haton,* Dutch *haten,* Old High German *hazzōn* (modern German *hassen*), Old Icelandic *hata,* and Gothic *hatjan, hatan;* derived from Proto-Germanic **Hatōjanan,* from the Indo-European base **kād-, *kəd-* (Pok.517), found in Greek *kêdos* sorrow.
—n. About 1175 *hate,* developed with *a* by influence of *hate,* v., from Old English *hete* hatred, spite (about 725, in *Beowulf*); cognate with Old Frisian *hat* hatred, Old Saxon *heti,* Middle Dutch *hate* (modern Dutch *haat*), Old High German *haz* (modern German *Hass*), Old Icelandic *hatr,* and Gothic *hatis* hate or anger, from Proto-Germanic **Hatis-,* Indo-European **kədes-.*
—hateful *adj.* About 1380; formed from English *hate,* n. + *-ful.* **—hater** *n.* Before 1382; formed from English *hate,* v. + *-er*[1]. **—hatred** *n.* Before 1200 *hatrede,* from *hate,* n. + *-rede,* from Old English *rǣden* state or condition; see KINDRED.

hauberk (hô'bėrk) *n.* long coat of mail. Probably before 1300, in *Sir Tristrem;* earlier as a surname *Hauberge* (1230); borrowed from Old French *hauberg, hauberc* (earlier *halberc*), from Frankish (compare Old High German *halsbërg,* literally, neck cover; cognate with Old Icelandic *halsbjǫrg*). The Old English *healsbeorg* (from *heals* neck + *beorgan* protect) did not survive into Middle English; see COLLAR and HARBOR.

haughty *adj.* 1530 *hawty* high in one's own estimation; too proud, in Palsgrave's *Lesclarcissement;* earlier *hawte* noble, excellent (probably before 1400); borrowed from Old French *haut* high, from Latin *altus* (with initial *h-* by influence of Frankish *hōh;* see OLD).

The form *haute* was changed in the late 1500's to *haught* after words like *caught, taught,* etc., and then assumed the suffix *-y* on the model of word pairs such as *might, mighty* and *weight, weighty.*

haul *v.* About 1300 *haulen* to pull or drag, transport, carry, variant spelling of *halen* (probably before 1200); see HALE[2] drag. The spelling with *u* represents a development of Middle English pronunciation that departed from *halen* before the 1500's and is paralleled in *crawl, small,* etc. **—n.** 1670, act of hauling; from the verb. The figurative sense of something gathered or gained, is first recorded in John Adams' correspondence, in 1776.

haunch *n.* part of the body around the hip; the hip. Before 1250 *haunche;* earlier *hanche* (probably before 1200, in *Ancrene Riwle*); borrowed from Old French *hanche,* from Frankish **hanka;* cognate with Middle Dutch *hanke, henke* hip, Middle High German *hanke* hip, shank, and Old High German *hinkan* to limp, from

Proto-Germanic **Hink-/Hank-,* from Indo-European **keng-/kong-* (Pok.930); see SHANK.

haunt *v.* go often to, visit frequently. Probably about 1200 *hanten* practice habitually; later *haunten* (before 1250), and in the sense of visit frequently (probably before 1300); borrowed from Old French *hanter* to frequent, resort to, be familiar with (originally, of a spirit coming back to the house he had lived in); probably from Old Icelandic *heimta* bring home, from Proto-Germanic **Haimatjanan,* from **Haimaz* HOME.

The meaning of intrude upon or reappear frequently, especially in the application to imaginary beings, ghosts, etc., as in the phrase *be haunted,* is first found in Shakespeare's *Midsummer Night's Dream* (1590) and *Richard II* (1593).

—**n.** Often, **haunts.** place often visited. Probably before 1300, in *Kyng Alisaunder,* developed from the verb, and as a borrowing from Old French *hant* frequentation, intimacy, acquaintance.

have *v.* 1100 *haven,* developed from Old English *habban* to own, possess (about 725, in *Beowulf*); cognate with Old Frisian *hebba* to have, Old Saxon *hebbjan,* Middle Low German *hebben,* Middle Dutch and modern Dutch *hebben,* Old High German *habēn* (modern German *haben*), Old Icelandic *hafa,* and Gothic *haban,* from the same Proto-Germanic root **Haf-* to take, take hold of, that is found in HEAVE. In all Germanic languages this verb also assumed the function of an auxiliary to mark tense. (Note that English *have* is unrelated to Latin *habēre,* in spite of the resemblance in form and sense.) In Old English, this verb had *-bb-* (from Proto-Germanic *ƀj*) in all parts of the present tense, except the second person singular *hafast, hæfst,* and the third person singular *hafath, hæfth.* In Middle English the forms of Old English in *f* and *v* gradually lost these medial consonants so that *hæſst, hæſth, hæfde* became *hast, hath,* and thence *has, had* and the Old English *-bb-* was supplanted by *-v- (have),* by gradual levelling, on analogy with other parts of the verb. The past participle *had* developed from Old English *gehæfd.*

haven *n.* harbor or port. Probably before 1200, developed from Old English *hæfen* (1031, in the *Anglo-Saxon Chronicle*); borrowed from Old Icelandic *hǫfn,* from Proto-Germanic **Hafnaz,* cognate with Old Irish *cūan* bend, bay, from Indo-European **kopnos* (Pedersen, *Vergleichende Grammatik der keltischen Sprachen* I 94). The figurative sense of refuge is first recorded in Middle English, probably about 1200.

haversack *n.* bag used by soldiers and hikers to carry food. 1749 *havresack,* in Smollett's translation of *Gil Blas;* borrowed from French *havresac,* from obsolete German *Habersack* oat bag, originally a bag in which cavalry carried oats for their horses *(haber* oats, now dialectal, from Old High German *habaro* + *sack* bag, from Old High German *sac* SACK[1]*).* Old High German *habaro* seems to be related to Proto-Germanic **Háfraz* he-goat (compare Old Icelandic *hafr* buck), as "buck's corn" (being raised only as feed), cognate with Latin *caper* he-goat, from Indo-European **kápros* (Pok.529).

havoc *n.* very great destruction or injury. 1419 *havoke,* borrowed from Anglo-French *havok* (in *crier havok* cry havoc, as a signal to soldiers to seize plunder), from Old French *havot* plundering or devastation (in *crier havot*), from a Germanic source (compare Middle Dutch *havot* grain measure, and perhaps plunder; also Old High German *heffen* to raise, HEAVE). The general sense of devastation, is first recorded in 1480. —**v.** devastate. 1577, from the noun.

haw *n.* red berry of the hawthorn. About 1250 *hawe,* developed from Old English (before 1000) *haga* fruit of the hawthorn bush, *hagathorn* HAWTHORN; probably the same word as Old English *haga* enclosure, HEDGE.

hawk[1] *n.* bird of prey. Probably before 1200 *havek;* later *hauk* (probably before 1300, in *Sir Tristrem*); developed from Old English *hafoc* (West Saxon); earlier *heafuc* (before 830), and *-habuc, -hebuc* (about 700); cognate with Old Frisian *havek* hawk, Old Saxon *haƀuc,* Middle Dutch *havic, havec* (modern Dutch *havik*), Old High German *habuh,* Middle High German *habech* (modern German *Habicht*), Old Icelandic *haukr* (Norwegian *hauk,* Swedish *hök,* and Danish *høg*); all derived from Proto-Germanic **haƀukaz,* cognate with Russian *kobec,* and Polish *kobuz* hawk or kite (Pok.528).

The current use of the figurative meaning of a person who favors a warlike or military policy, especially against the Soviet Union, appears in 1962, in American English, probably as a shortened form of *warhawk* or *war hawk,* a term probably coined by Thomas Jefferson, and applied to one who favored war with France during the XYZ Affair of 1798 and later to one advocating war against England in 1811.

hawk[2] *v.* offer goods for sale by calling out on the street. 1390, implied in *hauking* peddling, especially from house to house, *hauker* street peddler (1409); borrowed from Middle Low German *höker,* from *höken* to peddle, carry on the back, squat; cognate with Middle Dutch *hoken, hoeken* to peddle, carry on the back, squat, Middle High German *hūchen* to squat, crouch (modern German *hocken*), and Old Icelandic *hūka* to crouch, *hoka, hokra* to crawl, from Proto-Germanic **Huk-/Hūk-,* from Indo-European **keug-/kug-* crouch (Pok.589). The spelling *hawk* developed sometime before 1425.

hawk[3] *v.* clear the throat noisily. 1581, in Mulcaster's *Positions. . .necessarie for the Training up of Children;* of uncertain origin; possibly imitative of the sound. —**n.** 1604, from the verb.

hawse (hôz) *n.* part of a ship's bow. 1336-37 *hals;* earlier, neck (1137); developed from Old English *hals, heals* prow of a ship, neck; cognate with Old Icelandic *hals* hawse, (literally, neck); see COLLAR. The form *hawse* is a phonetic respelling of the late 1500's, paralleling *crawl, small;* see also HAUL.

hawser (hô′zər) *n.* large rope or small cable. 1294 *ausor,* 1295 *haucer;* borrowed from Anglo-French *haucer,* from Old French *haucier* to hoist or raise; found also in Old French *halcier,* from Vulgar Latin **altiāre,* alteration of Late Latin *altāre* make high, from *altus* high; see OLD. English *hawser* is associated with *hawse* and the hauling of boats, and therefore with the suffix *-er*[1].

hawthorn *n.* thorny shrub or tree that produces haws. Probably about 1300 *hawethorn;* earlier, in the place name *Hauthorn* (about 1220); developed from Old English *hagathorn* (about 950), *hæguthorn, heagothorn* (about 700), a Germanic compound found in Old Dutch *haginthorn,* Middle Dutch *hagedorn* (modern Dutch *haagdoorn*), Middle High German *hagendorn, hagedorn,* and Old Icelandic *hagthorn* (Swedish *hagtorn*).

hay *n.* Before 1200 *hei;* later *hai* (before 1325, in *Cursor Mundi*); developed from Old English, Anglian *hēg* grass cut or mown for fodder (before 830); later, West

Saxon *hīeg, hīg;* cognate with Old Frisian *hā, hē* hay, Old Saxon *hōi,* Middle Dutch *hoy* (modern Dutch *hooi*), Old High German *hewi* (modern German *Heu*), Old Icelandic *hey* (Norwegian *høy, høye,* Danish *hø,* Swedish *hö*), and Gothic *hawi;* all derived from Proto-Germanic *Haujan, adjective used as a noun, meaning that which can be mowed, from **Hauw-,* found also in Old English *hēaw-* of *hēawan* to HEW. **—haycock** *n.* (1296) **—hay fever** (1829) **—hayrick** *n.* (probably before 1300) **—haystack** *n.* (1440)

haywire *adj.* 1905, American English, *hay wire outfit,* a contemptuous term among loggers for poorly equipped or inefficient logging equipment, repaired with the soft wire for binding bales of hay. The sense of out of order, tangled or wrong, in reference to the springy and uncontrollable nature of haywire, was first recorded in American English in the phrase *go haywire* (1929). The extended sense of crazy or mad, is found in John O'Hara's *Appointment in Samarra* (1934).

hazard *n.* risk, danger. About 1300 *hasard* game of chance played with dice; earlier as a surname *Hasard* (1167); borrowed from Old French *hasard,* possibly through Spanish *azar* an unfortunate card or throw at dice, also the game of chance, from Arabic *az-zahr* the die (*az-* a form of the definite article *al-* by assimilation to the *z* of the following word). The extended meaning of chance of loss or harm, risk, danger, is first recorded in 1548. **—v.** take a risk, venture. 1530, in Palsgrave's *Lesclarcissement;* from the noun. **—hazardous** *adj.* 1580, venturesome, in Sidney's *Arcadia;* later, risky, perilous (1618); borrowed from Middle French *hasardeux,* from Old French *hasard* hazard.

haze[1] *n.* small amount of mist, smoke, etc., in the air. 1706, probably a back formation from *hazy* misty; with antecedents found also in earlier English dialect *haze* to drizzle, be foggy (1674-91). The sense of slight confusion, vagueness, is first recorded before 1797, in Burke's writings. **—hazy** *adj.* 1625 *hawsey,* (also *heysey, haizy, hazy*); of uncertain origin.

haze[2] *v.* force (a fellow student) to do unnecessary or ridiculous tasks. 1850, American English, extended use of an earlier nautical sense of punish by keeping at unpleasant and unnecessary hard work, in Dana's *Two Years Before the Mast* (1840); perhaps developed from earlier *haze, hawze* terrify, frighten, confound (1678); borrowed from Middle French *haser* irritate, annoy; of uncertain origin.

hazel *n.* small tree with edible nuts. Old English *hæsl* (about 700); cognate with Middle Low German and Middle Dutch *hasel* hazel (modern Dutch *hazelaar*), Old High German *hasal* (modern German *Hasel*), and Old Icelandic *hasl* (Norwegian, Danish, and Swedish *hassel*); all derived from Proto-Germanic **Hasalaz,* from Indo-European **kosolos* (Pok.616), cognate with Latin *corulus* hazel (by change of *s* to *r*), Old Irish and Welsh *coll* (by development of *sl* to *ll*), and Old Lithuanian *kasulas* hunting spear (made from hazel wood).

he *pron.* Old English (about 725) *hē,* masculine singular pronoun of the third person representing original **His, Hiz* of the demonstrative Proto-Germanic base **Hi-* this, which supplied not only the pronoun forms *him, his, her,* but also the adverbs *here, hence,* and *hither.* Though these forms existed in Old English in both the masculine and feminine forms, during the early Middle English period the feminine forms of *he* began to fall into disuse and were replaced in part by forms from other stems (see SHE, THEY). The *h,* aspirate, is suppressed in British English after accented syllables and this same process has led to *it* for original *hit.*

Old English *hē* is cognate with Old Frisian and Old Saxon *hē, hī* he, Middle Dutch *hi* (modern Dutch *hij*), Old High German *hē* (rare), Old Icelandic *hann* he, and Gothic *himma* (dative case), *hina* (accusative case) this, this person or thing.

Cognates from the Indo-European base **k̂ei-/k̂i-* this (Pok.609), corresponding to Proto-Germanic **Hi-,* include Old Irish *cē* here, on this side, Latin *cis, citrā* on this side, Greek *(e)keî* there, Old Slavic *sĭ* this, Lithuanian *šis,* and Hittite *ki* this.

—n. a male. Old English (about 950) *hē,* from the pronoun.

head *n.* About 1150 *hed;* earlier *hevod* (1123); developed from Old English *hēafod* top of the body (about 725); chief person, leader, ruler (about 897); cognate with Old Frisian *hāved, hāfd* head, chief, Old Saxon *hōƀid,* Middle Dutch *hōvet* (modern Dutch *hoofd*), Old High German *houbit* (modern German *Haupt*), Old Icelandic *hǫfudh,* and Gothic *haubith.* In the Germanic words an unresolved problem of phonology arises in that some words, such as English *head* and German *Haupt* imply an original form in *-au-* represented by Proto-Germanic **Hauƀuđan;* whereas others such as Old Icelandic *hǫfudh* imply *-a -,* as is the case in the cognate Latin *caput* head, from Indo-European **kaput* (Pok.529). The spelling *head* does not appear in the record of English before 1420, and represents an original long vowel.

—adj. at the head. Probably before 1200 *heved* and *heaved,* in *Ancrene Riwle;* later *hed* (before 1393); from the noun. **—v.** About 1230 *heden* provide with a head; later *heafden;* from the noun. The meanings of be at the head, lead (probably about 1200) and of direct the head, face (probably before 1200, in Layamon's *Chronicle of Britain*), developed from Old English *hēdan* in the 1600's.

—headache *n.* (about 1000, in Old English) **—headland** *n.* Probably about 1475, promontory; earlier, boundary at the end of a ploughed field, in Old English, 956. **—headlong** *adv.* (before 1382); *adj.* (about 1550) **—headman** *n.* (about 1000, in Old English) **—headmaster** *n.* (1576) **—headquarters** *n.* (1647) **—headstrong** *adj.* (before 1398) **—headwaters** *n.pl.* (1535 *heade waters*) **—headway** *n.* (about 1300, main road; 1748, motion forward) **—heady** *adj.* (before 1382)

-head *suffix.* See -HOOD.

heal *v.* Probably before 1200 *healen, helen;* developed from Old English *hǣlan* make whole, sound, and well (about 725, in *Genesis A*); cognate with Old Frisian *hēla* to heal, Old Saxon *hēlian,* modern Dutch *heelen,* Old High German *heilan* (modern German *heilen*), Old Icelandic *heila,* and Gothic *hailjan;* derived from Proto-Germanic **Hailaz,* also the source of Old English *hāl* healthy, WHOLE. **—health** *n.* Probably before 1200 *helthe;* later *helth* (about 1450) and *health* (probably before 1425); developed from Old English (about 1000) *hǣlth* a being whole, sound, or well, from *hāl* WHOLE; for suffix see -TH. **—healthful** *adj.* About 1384; formed from Middle English *helth* + *-ful.* **—healthy** *adj.* 1552; formed from English *health* + *-y*[1].

heap *n.* Probably before 1200 *hep;* developed from Old English (about 725) *hēap* pile, great number, multitude; cognate with Old Frisian *hāp* heap, Old Saxon *hōp,* modern Dutch *hoop,* Old and Middle High German *houf,* and Old Icelandic *hōpr;* derived from Proto-Germanic **Haupaz,* Indo-European **kou-b-* (Pok.589), and related to Old English *hēah* HIGH. —**v.** Probably before 1200 *heapen;* later *hepen* (about 1300); developed from Old English (about 900) *hēapian* form into a heap; corresponding to Old High German *houfōn* to heap; derived from the same Germanic base as Old English *hēap,* n. The spelling with *ea* began to appear in modern English after 1520.

hear *v.* 1127 *heren;* developed from Old English, Anglian *hēran* (before 800); later West Saxon *hīeran, hȳran;* cognate with Old Frisian *hēra, hōra* hear, Old Saxon *hōrian,* modern Dutch *horen,* Old High German *hōran* (modern German *hören*), Old Icelandic *heyra,* and Gothic *hausjan;* derived from Proto-Germanic **Hauzjanan,* from Indo-European **kou-s-,* whence Greek *akoúein* hear (from earlier stem **hakouhye-, *sa-kousye-,* with the prefix **sa-* together, from Indo-European **sm̥-,* the whole compound conveying as much force or as little as the like-formed Gothic *ga-hausjan* hear). Outside Germanic the Old English is possibly cognate with Latin *cavēre* (earlier **covēre*) be on one's guard, beware, Greek *koeîn* to notice, hear, Latvian *kavēt* hesitate, delay, Old Slavic *čuti* perceive, notice, and Sanskrit *kaví-s* wise, clever, from the shorter Indo-European root **keu-/kou-* (Pok.587). The spelling *hear* (differentiated from *here,* etc.) began to appear occasionally even before 1200, but was not fully established until after the mid-1500's. —**hearer** *n.* (1340) —**hearsay** *n.* (probably 1438)

hearken or **harken** (här′kən) *v.* listen. Probably before 1200 *hercnien,* in *Ancrene Riwle, hercnen, harcnen,* in Layamon's *Chronicle of Britain;* developed from Old English (about 1000) *heorcnian,* itself a modification of **he(o)rcian* HARK; for suffix see -EN[1].

hearse *n.* vehicle for carrying a dead person. Probably before 1300 *hers* flat framework somewhat like a harrow for candles and decorations, hung or placed over a coffin; borrowed from Old French *herce* harrow, and from Medieval Latin *hercia,* from Latin *hirpicem* (nominative *hirpex,* in Classical Latin *irpex*) harrow, from Oscan *hirpus* wolf, in allusion to the resemblance of a harrow's teeth to those of a wolf. Oscan *hirpus* is cognate with Latin *hircus* he-goat, from Indo-European **ĝherkwos* (Pok.445). The current meaning of a vehicle for carrying a body, is first recorded in 1650. The development of the spelling *hearse* for *hers* parallels that of HEART.

heart *n.* Probably about 1175 *herte,* developed from Old English (about 725) *heorte;* cognate with Old Frisian *herte, hirte* heart, Old Saxon *herta,* Middle Dutch *herte, harte* (modern Dutch *hart*), Old High German *herza* (modern German *Herz*), Old Icelandic *hjarta* (Swedish *hjärta,* Danish and Norwegian *hjerte*), and Gothic *haírtō;* derived from Proto-Germanic **Hertan-,* from Indo-European **k̑erd-/k̑r̥d-/k̑red-,* root **k̑ered-* (Pok.579). This produced cognates outside Germanic in Old Irish *cride* heart, Welsh *craidd* center, heart, Latin *cor* (genitive *cordis*) heart, Greek *kardíā,* Lithuanian *širdìs,* Old Slavic *srĭdĭce,* Russian *sérdtse,* and Hittite *kardi* (dative), *kardiyaš* (genitive) heart, wish. The spelling in *-ea-* in *heart* developed in the 1500's by analogy of pronunciation with *stream, heat,* etc. (replacing the earlier normal development *hart*), but while the pronunciation represented by *ea* changed, the spelling was retained. —**heartache** *n.* (about 1000, in Old English) —**heartburn** *n.* (about 1250) —**hearten** *v.* give heart to, encourage. 1526, formed from English *heart* + *-en*[1]. —**heartfelt** *adj.* (1734, in Pope's *Essay on Man*) —**heartless** *adj.* (before 1382) —**heartsick** *adj.* (about 1390) —**hearty** *adj.* warm and friendly. Before 1375 *herty* courageous or zealous; formed from English *heart* + *-y*[1]. The meaning of vehement, vigorous, is first recorded before 1661; *n.* a hearty fellow (especially in *my hearty,* a term said to be used of old among shipmates). 1839, in Marryat's writings; from *hearty,* adj.

hearth *n.* floor of a fireplace. About 1350 *herthe;* earlier, in compound *huerthselver* tax on households, literally, hearth silver (1189); developed from Old English (about 725) *heorth;* cognate with Old Frisian and Old Saxon *herth* hearth, Middle Dutch *hert* (modern Dutch *haard*), and Old High German *herd* (modern German *Herd*), derived from West Germanic **Herthaz,* cognate with Gothic *haúri* coal and Old Icelandic *hyrr* fire. Outside Germanic cognates are found in Lithuanian *kar̃štis* heat, Latvian *kar̃sts* hot, Old Slavic *kuriti (sę)* to smoke, and Sanskrit *kūḍayati* (he) singes, from Indo-European **ker(ə)-/kor-/ker-, kr̥̄-* (Pok.571). For the spelling in *-ea-* see HEART.

heat *n.* Probably about 1175 *hete;* developed from Old English (about 725) *hǣtu, hǣto;* cognate with Old Frisian *hēte* heat, Middle Dutch *hēte, heete,* and Old High German *heizi,* derived from Proto-Germanic **Haitin-,* formed from **Haitaz,* the source of Old English *hāt* HOT. Also cognate by different vowel grade in Proto-Germanic **Hitjō* with Old Saxon *hittia,* modern Dutch *hitte,* Old High German *hizza* (modern German *Hitze*), Old Icelandic *hita,* and Gothic *heitō* fever, from Indo-European **kāid-/kəid-/kīd-/kid-* (Pok.519). —**v.** Probably before 1200 *heaten* make hot, inflame, inspire, in *Ancrene Riwle;* developed from Old English (about 700) *hǣtan;* cognate with German and Old High German *heizen* to heat, and Old Icelandic *heita;* derived from Proto-Germanic **aitjanan.*

heath *n.* About 1330 *heth* open wasteland, especially such land with heather growing on it; developed from Old English *hǣth* tract of wasteland; earlier, the plant heather (about 700); and from Old Icelandic *heidhr* field. Old English *hǣth* is cognate with Old Saxon *hētha* wasteland, heather, Middle Dutch and modern Dutch *heide,* Middle Low German *heed* heather, *heie* heath, Middle High German *heide* wasteland, heather (modern German *Heide*), and Gothic *haithi,* from Proto-Germanic **Haithjō,* Indo-European **kait-yā,* derived from **kaito-* woods (Pok.521).

heathen *adj.* Before 1121 *hethen* not Christian or Jewish, pagan; developed from Old English (about 725) *hǣthen* and Old Icelandic *heidhinn.* The Old English form is cognate with Old Frisian *hēthen* heathen, Old Saxon *hēthin,* Middle Dutch and modern Dutch *heiden,* Old High German *heidan,* adj., *heidano,* n. (modern German *Heide,* masculine, *Heidin,* feminine), and Gothic *haithnō* Gentile or heathen woman. Historically the word has been assumed to come from Gothic as used by Ulfilas, Bishop of the Goths and translator of the Bible into Gothic, and to be a derivative of Gothic *haithi* with the sense of "dwelling on the heath," but no record of this meaning exists. Nevertheless, such a word would probably have stood as a loose translation of Latin *pāgānus* civilian rustic, and non-Christian, non-Jewish, PAGAN. If, however, *heathen* was developed by influence of Armenian on Ulfilas, then formation in Gothic may be from Armenian *het'anos* heathen, from

Greek *éthnos* nation, and pl. nations, heathens. Such an explanation is said to satisfy Old High German *heidan* and the Old English, with the addition of the suffix *-en,* if the stem vowel is assumed to be patterned on that of *heath.* **—n.** 1128 *hethen,* Old English (about 725) *hǣthen;* from the adjective. **—heathenish** *adj.* 1535, in the Coverdale Bible; formed from *heathen* + *-ish,* a re-formation in English, found also in Old English *hǣthenisc* (before 899, in Alfred's translation of Orosius' *Historiarum Adversus Paganos*).

heather *n.* low, evergreen shrub. 1725, in the compound *heather-bell,* spelling alteration (influenced by *heath*) of earlier *hathir* (1335) and in the place name *Faghadre* (1600-35); found in Old English **hæddre;* of unknown origin.

heave *v.* lift with force or effort. Probably before 1200 *heven;* developed from Old English *hebban* (about 725, in *Beowulf*); cognate with Old Saxon *hebbian* to raise, lift, Dutch *heffen,* Old High German *heffen* (modern German *heben*), Old Icelandic *hefja,* and Gothic *hafjan;* derived from Proto-Germanic **Hafjanan,* from the base **Haf-* (when originally accented), **Haƀ-* (when originally unaccented) to take, take hold of (as found in HEFT). Outside of Germanic, cognates are found in Latin *capere* to take, Albanian *kap* I grasp, seize, Greek *káptein* gulp down, *kṓpē* handle, (possibly in Celtic: Middle Irish *cachtaim* I take prisoner, Old Irish *cacht* female slave, Welsh *caeth* captive, slave), and in Latvian *kàmpt* to seize, from Indo-European **kəp-,* root **kēp-/kōp-* (Pok. 527). The spelling with *-ea-* is a development of the 1500's and coincided, for the most part, with the levelling of similarly formed verbs in English to the spelling *v.* **—n.** act or fact of heaving. Before 1571, from the verb.

heaven *n.* About 1150 *heven;* developed from Old English (about 1000) *heofon* the place where God dwells; earlier, the sky, firmament (about 725, in *Beowulf*); cognate with Old Saxon *heƀan* sky, heaven, Middle Low German *heven* sky, Old Icelandic *himinn* sky, heaven, Gothic *himins,* and, perhaps by dissimilation, with an *-l* suffix, Old Frisian *himel, himul* sky, heaven, Old Saxon *himil,* Middle Dutch and modern Dutch *hemel,* and Old High German *himil* (modern German *Himmel*), from Proto-Germanic **Hemina-.*

It appears that in Old Icelandic *himinn,* the medial *-m-* became *f (v)* when immediately before *-n-* in the declension, as seen in the genitive plural *hifna* and dative plural *hifnum* of *himinn.* In Old English *heofon* the *-v-* spread throughout all of the forms.

The Germanic cognates, apparently referring to a covering or canopy formed by the sky, may be traceable to the Indo-European **kem-* to cover (Pok.556). **—heavenward** *adv., adj.* (about 1250)

heavy *adj.* 1124 *hevi* weighty, grave; developed from Old English *hefig* (about 725); cognate with Old Saxon *heƀīg* heavy, Middle Dutch *hevich* (modern Dutch *hevig* violent, heavy), Old High German *hebīg* heavy, and Old Icelandic *hǫfugr;* derived from Proto-Germanic **Haƀīȝás* from **Hafjanan,* and thereby related to Old English *hebban* to HEAVE; for suffix see -Y[1]. **—n.** About 1250 *hevie* something heavy, heaviness; from the adjective. The sense of having greater atomic weight than another isotope, as in *heavy hydrogen,* is first recorded in 1933. The informal meaning of villain in a play is first recorded as a theatrical usage in 1880; from the sense of serious, sober, dramatic, tragic, as in *heavy villain* (1858).

Hebrew *adj.* of the Jews of Biblical times or their language. About 1250 *Ebru,* in *The Story of Genesis and Exodus;* later *Hebru* (before 1325, in *Cursor Mundi*); borrowed from Old French *Ebreu, Ebrieu,* learned borrowing from Latin *Hebraeus,* from Greek *Hebraîos,* from Aramaic *'ebhrai,* corresponding to Hebrew *'ibhrī* an Israelite, (literally, one from the other side, in reference to the river Euphrates, from *'ēbher* region on the other or opposite side). **—n.** Probably before 1200 *Ebrew* the Hebrew language, in *Ancrene Riwle;* later *Hebrew* a Jew of Biblical times, an Israelite (before 1382, in the Wycliffe Bible); borrowed from Old French *Ebreu, Hebrieu,* from Latin *Hebraeus,* adj. As the word gained wider currency during the Middle Ages, it was regarded as, and often reborrowed from, Classical Latin *Hebraeus,* thereby establishing the spelling with *H-.* **—Hebraic** *adj.* About 1380, in Chaucer's *House of Fame;* borrowed from Old French *hebraïque,* and directly from Late Latin *Hebrāicus* from Greek *Hebrāikós,* from *Hebrai-,* found in *Hebraîos;* HEBREW; for suffix see -IC.

hecatomb (hek'ətüm) *n.* great sacrifice or slaughter. Before 1592, in reference to the sacrifice of 100 oxen among the ancient Greeks and Romans, found in Latin *hecatombē,* from Greek *hekatómbē* (*hekatón* HUNDRED + *-bē,* from the stem of *boûs* ox, COW[1]). The transferred sense of sacrifice or slaughter of many victims, is first recorded in 1598, and the generalized meaning of a large number or quantity (as in *hecatombs of broken hearts* — Shelley, 1821), was first recorded in 1646.

heckle *v.* harass and annoy by asking many bothersome questions. 1808, in Jamieson's *Dictionary of the Scottish Language* (and *Supplement,* 1825); perhaps earlier found in noun use in Burns' writings, 1788; both verb and noun being respectively transferred uses of *hekelen* to comb (flax or hemp) with a hackle (1325), and *hekele* a comb for flax or hemp, hackle (before 1425); borrowed from Middle Dutch *hekelen* comb flax or hemp with a hackle; also, to prickle or irritate; and Middle Dutch *hekele* hackle, from Proto-Germanic **Hakilō.***—heckler** *n.* 1885, one who harasses with questions or remarks; developing parallel to *heckle,* v., from the earlier sense of one who dresses flax or hemp (1440).

hectare (hek'tār) *n.* measure of area equal to 100 ares. 1810, borrowing of French *hectare,* formed from Greek *hekatón* HUNDRED + French *are* ARE[2] measure.

hectic *adj.* Before 1398 *etik* feverish, consumptive, in Trevisa's translation of Bartholomew's *De Proprietatibus Rerum;* borrowed from Old French *etique,* from Late Latin *hecticus,* from Greek *hektikós* continuous, habitual, consumptive (of a disease), from *héxis* habit, from *échein* (earlier stem **heche-*) have, hold, keep on, continue; see SCHEME; for suffix see -IC. The current spelling (influenced by Late Latin *hecticus*) dates from the 1500's. The sense of feverishly exciting or full of disorganized activity, is first recorded in Kipling's *Traffics and Discoveries* (1904).

hecto- a combining form meaning a hundred, as in *hectoliter, hectometer.* Borrowed from French *hecto-,* alteration of Greek *hekatón* a HUNDRED.

hector *v.* 1660 *Hector* to act in a bragging, bullying manner; also, intimidate by bluster, bully (1664 *hector,* in Pepys' *Diary*); from *Hector,* n. bragging, bullying person (1655). The name was originally applied to gangs of disorderly young men on the streets of London in the mid-1600's; used in allusion to *Hector* (Greek *Héktōr*), the Trojan hero of the *Iliad,* who behaved in a swaggering, belligerent way by challenging any Greek to combat.

hedge *n.* row of bushes planted as a fence. About 1250 *hegge,* in *The Owl and the Nightingale;* earlier in the surname *Hegge* (1188); developed from Old English (785) *hecg;* cognate with Middle Dutch *hegge* hedge (modern Dutch *heg*), Old High German *heggia, heckia,* Middle High German *hegge, hecke* (modern German *Hecke*), and Old Icelandic *heggr* bird cherry (a type of cherry tree). Through the root of Proto-Germanic **Hazjō,* these forms are related to Old English *haga* enclosure, hedge, HAW (about 725, in *Beowulf*); and to Old Saxon *hago,* Middle Low German and Middle Dutch *hage* (modern Dutch *haag*) hedge, Old High German and Middle High German *hac, hages* enclosure, hedge (modern German *Hag* grove), and Old Icelandic *hagi* pasture. This group of forms is traceable to the Indo-European base **kagh-* (Pok. 518), and through it to Gaulish *caii,* pl., enclosure, grating, Old Breton *caiou,* pl., defense, fortification, Welsh *cae* hedge, fence, Cornish *kē* hedge, and possibly Latin *caulae* railing or lattice barrier. The figurative sense of any means of protection or defense, is first recorded in *Ayenbite of Inwyt* (1340). **—v.** surround with a hedge or fence. About 1384, in the Wycliffe Bible; from the noun. The sense of dodge or evade, is first recorded in Shakespeare's *Merry Wives of Windsor* (1598), and that of insure oneself against loss, as on a bet, in 1672.

The spelling *hedge* was formed in the 1500's by analogy with *edge, bridge,* etc.

—hedgehog *n.* (about 1450) **—hedgerow** *n.* (940, Old English *heggerǣw*)

hedonism (hē'dənizəm) *n.* doctrine or belief that pleasure or happiness is the chief good. 1856, probably formed from Greek *hēdonḗ* pleasure (related to *hēdýs* SWEET) + English *-ism;* but perhaps also influenced by earlier borrowing from Greek in English *hedonic* of or having to do with the Cyrenaic school of philosophy that deals with the ethics of pleasure (1656). **—hedonist** *n.* one who regards pleasure as the chief good. 1822, in De Quincey's *Confessions of an English Opium-Eater,* formed in English from from Greek *hēdonḗ* pleasure + English *-ist,* but see HEDONISM for earlier influence in English.

heed *v.* Probably before 1200 *heden;* found in Old English *hēdan* to take care, attend (about 725, in *Beowulf*); cognate with Old Frisian *hōda* protect, guard, tend, Old Saxon *hōdian,* Middle Dutch and modern Dutch *hoeden,* Old High German *huotan* (modern German *hüten*), from West Germanic **hōdjan.* These forms are derivatives of the source of Old Frisian *hōde, hūde* protection, guard, Old High German *huota* (modern German *Hut* care, keeping, protection), and probably Old English *hōd* HOOD[1]. **—n.** careful attention. Probably before 1300 *hede,* in *Arthour and Merlin;* from the verb. **—heedful** *adj.* 1548, formed from English *heed* + *-ful.* **—heedless** *adj.* 1579, in Spenser's *The Shepheardes Calender;* formed from English *heed* + *-less.*

heehaw *n.* 1815, probably imitative of the sound made by a donkey; later, a loud laugh (1843, in Thackeray's writings); *v.* 1821, perhaps from the noun, or formed independently.

heel[1] *n.* back part of the foot. Probably before 1200 *hele,* in *Ancrene Riwle;* developed from Old English (about 800) *hēla;* cognate with Old Frisian *hēla* heel, Middle Dutch *hiele* (modern Dutch *hiel*), and Old Icelandic *hǣll;* related to Old English *hōh* heel, HOCK. The meaning of part of a stocking or shoe that covers the heel of the foot, is first recorded in Holinshed's *Chronicles* (1577-87). **—v.** 1605, furnish with a heel; from the noun. The meaning of follow at the heels of, follow closely, is first recorded about 1889 or possibly earlier. **—heeled** *adj.* provided with money (usually in *well-heeled*). 1880, American English, developed from the earlier slang sense of furnished with a gun, armed (1866, in Mark Twain's *Letters*), from the original meaning of furnished with a heel or heel-like projection (1562); formed from English *heel,* n. + *-ed*[2].

heel[2] *v.* lean over to one side, tilt. About 1575, alteration of earlier *hield* to lean, slope (1559), in Middle English *helden, halden* fall, bend, lean (probably before 1200); developed from Old English *hyldan* incline (about 725, in *Beowulf*); cognate with Old Saxon *heldian* to incline, Middle Low German and Middle Dutch *helden* (modern Dutch *hellen*), Old High German *hald* inclined, *helden* to bow (modern German *Halde* slope), and Old Icelandic *hallr* inclined, from Proto-Germanic **Helthjanan;* cognate with Lithuanian *šalis* side, region, from Indo-European **k̂el-/k̂ol-* (Pok. 552). The form *heel* probably arose from the misinterpretation of *-d* in *hield* as a past tense suffix. **—n.** 1760, from the verb.

heel[3] *n.* contemptible person. 1914, American English (underworld slang), an incompetent or worthless criminal (probably a special use of *heel*[1] a person that is the lowest or hindmost in position). The generalized meaning of a contemptible, untrustworthy person, is first recorded in Farrell's *Studs Lonigan* (1932).

heft *n.* weight, heaviness. About 1445, developed from *heave,* v., apparently on the analogy of pairs such as *weave, weft, thieve, theft,* etc., and probably further influenced by *heft,* obsolete variant of *heaved,* past participle. **—v.** lift or heave. Before 1661; from the noun. **—hefty** *adj.* heavy or weighty. 1867, formed from English *heft,* n. + *-y*[1].

hegemony (hijem'ənē) *n.* political domination. 1567, borrowed from Greek *hēgemoníā* leadership, from *hēgemṓn* leader, from *hēgeîsthai* to lead; see SEEK; for suffix see -Y[3]. **—hegemonism** *n.* 1965, variant of *hegemony* in the special sense of a policy of political domination, patterned on *imperialism;* for suffix see -ISM.

hegira (hijī'rə) *n.* exodus, departure, flight. 1757, in Horace Walpole's *Letters;* transferred sense of earlier *Hegira* the flight of Mohammed from Mecca to Medina in 622 (1590); borrowed from Medieval Latin *hegira,* from Arabic *hijrah* flight, from the root of *hajara* he fled.

heifer *n.* young cow that has not had a calf. Probably about 1200 *heifre,* developed from Old English *hēahfore* (about 900); of uncertain origin (possibly a compound of *hēah* HIGH and an irregular form of *fearr* bull, but difficulties of form and meaning are unresolved).

height *n.* About 1230 *hihthe* quality of being high, in a version of *Ancrene Riwle;* later *heght, hight* (before 1325, in *Cursor Mundi*); developed from Old English *hiehthu, hēhthu* highest part or point, summit (before 900, in Cynewulf's *Elene*); cognate with Middle Dutch *hogede, hoochte* height (modern Dutch *hoogte*), Middle Low German *hogede,* Old High German *hōhida,* Old Icelandic *hædh,* and Gothic *hauhitha;* derived from *hauh-* high, and the root of Old English *hēah* HIGH + *-itha* -TH. The form of the suffix has varied from *heighth* to *height,* since the 1200's, but by analogy with words such as *drought,* it has stabilized, dropping the terminal *-h* in most use since the late 1800's. The form of the vowel comes directly from the Old English, Anglian *hēhthu;* for the spelling with *-gh-* see FIGHT. **—heighten** *v.* About 1450 *heightenen* to honor or raise to high position; formed from English *height* + *-en*[1] + *-en*[2].

heinous (hā'nəs) *adj.* extremely offensive, atrocious. About 1385 *heynous,* in Chaucer's *Troilus and Criseyde;* borrowed from Old French *haïneus,* from *haïne* hatred, from *haïr* to hate, from Frankish (compare Old Saxon *hatōn* to HATE); for suffix see -OUS.

heir (ãr) *n.* person who inherits property, etc. Probably about 1225 *heir, aire;* borrowed through Anglo-French *heir, aire,* from Old French *hoir,* from Latin *hērēs* (genitive *hērēdis*) heir, heiress. The root *hēr-* of Latin *hērēs* is cognate with Sanskrit *hāni-s* lack, *jáhāti* leaves, Gothic *gaidw* lack, want, need, Old Frisian *gād,* Old Saxon *gēdea,* and possibly Old High German *geisini* poverty, necessity. Furthermore the Latin *hērēd-* represents an ancient compound with the meaning of receiving what is left, the first part being Indo-European **ĝhēro-* left (Pok. 419), whence Greek *chêros* bereaved (feminine *chḗrā* widow), and the second part being Indo-European **ē-d-,* the reduced form of **ē-dō-* receive, whence Sanskrit *ā-dā-* receive. **—heiress** *n.* 1659, formed from English *heir* + *-ess,* possibly by influence of Middle French *hoiresse.* **—heirloom** *n.* possession handed down from generation to generation. 1424-25 *heyrlome;* earlier *ayre lome* (1421); formed from *heir, aire* + *loom* implement or tool.

heist (hīst) *v.* rob, steal. 1927, implied in *heister* shoplifter or thief, American English slang; probably a spelling alteration of *hoist* to lift or shoplift (in older British slang meaning to lift another on one's back to help him break into a house through the window, as implied in *hoister,* 1708; see HOIST). The alteration in spelling may have been from a dialectal pronunciation. **—n.** *Slang.* robbery, holdup. 1930, American English slang; from the verb.

heli-[1] a form of *helio-* before vowels, as in *helianthus* (New Latin, sunflower).

heli-[2] a combining form abstracted from *helicopter,* as in *heliborne = borne or carried by helicopter* (1966), *heliport = airport for helicopters* (1948).

helical *adj.* See HELIX.

helicopter *n.* aircraft with horizontal propellers. 1887, borrowed from French *hélicoptère* (from Greek *hélix,* genitive *hélikos* spiral + *pterón* wing).

helio- a combining form meaning sun, as in *heliocentric = having or representing the sun as its center.* Borrowed from Greek *hēlio-,* combining form of *hḗlios* sun; see SOLAR.

heliocentric (hē'lēəsen'trik) *adj.* viewed or measured from the sun's center. 1685, formed in English from Greek *hḗlios* sun (see SOLAR) + English *centric* on or at the center (about 1590); borrowed from Greek *kentrikós,* from *kéntron* CENTER.

heliotrope (hē'lēətrōp) *n.* plant which turns its flowers and leaves to the sun. Before 1626 *heliotrope,* in Francis Bacon's *Works,* borrowed from French *héliotrope,* from Latin; earlier in English (about 1000 to 1600), applied especially to the sunflower and marigold, also borrowed from Latin *hēliotropium,* from Greek *hēliotrópion* (*hḗlios* sun + *trópos* turn).

heliport *n.* airport for helicopters. 1948, American English; formed from *heli(copter)* + *(air)port.*

helium *n.* inert gaseous chemical element. 1868, New Latin; formed from Greek *hḗlios* sun (see SOLAR) + New Latin *-ium* (chemical suffix). The term was coined by the English astronomer Lockyer, who inferred existence of helium in the sun's atmosphere from observation of the solar spectrum.

helix *n.* a spiral in the form of a screw thread or watch spring. 1563, borrowing of Latin *helix* spiral, from Greek *hélix* (genitive *hélikos*), related to *eileîn* to turn, twist, roll, *eilýein* enfold; see VOLUME. **—helical** *adj.* spiral. 1613, formed in English from *helic-,* stem of Latin *helix* + English suffix *-al.*

hell *n.* Before 1121 *helle;* found in Old English (about 725) *hel, helle* nether world of the dead, infernal regions, Hades; possibly borrowed, in part, from Old Icelandic *Hel* goddess of death and the underworld, as a transfer of a pagan concept to Christian theology and its vocabulary. Germanic cognates exist in Old Frisian *helle, hille* hell, Old Saxon *hellja,* Middle Dutch *helle* (modern Dutch *hel*), Old High German *hella* (modern German *Hölle*), and Gothic *halja;* derived from Proto-Germanic **Halja* one who covers up or hides something, from **Hel-, Həl-, Hul-* to hide, conceal; also found in Old English *helian* to hide, conceal (now *hele* and chiefly relegated to a gardening term with the sense of cover roots, seeds, etc., with earth); see CONCEAL.

hellebore (hel'əbôr) *n.* plant of the crowfoot family. 1373 *elebyr, elebur;* borrowed from Old French *ellebre, ellebore,* from Latin; also Middle English (about 1150) *elleborum;* borrowed directly from Latin *elleborus, helleborus,* from Greek *elléboros, helléboros,* of uncertain origin (perhaps with the original meaning of eaten by fawns, from *ellós, hellós* fawn, and *borā́* food). The modern spelling dates from the 1500's by a series of analogous spelling changes.

Hellenic *adj.* of the Greeks or Greece. 1644, in Milton's *Areopagitica;* borrowed from Greek *Hellēnikós,* from *Héllēn* a Greek (originally, a legendary king of Thessaly and the *Héllēnes,* supposedly ancestors of the Greeks, first mentioned in Homer, but in historical times applied by the Greeks to themselves); for suffix see -IC. **—Hellenism** *n.* 1609, an idiom or expression peculiar to Greek; possibly borrowed from French *hellénisme* (in a book title), and directly from Greek *Hellēnismós* imitation of the Greeks, use of a pure Greek idiom, from *Hellēnízein* make Greek, speak Greek, from *Héllēn* a Greek. The usual meaning of the culture and ideals of ancient Greece, is first recorded in George Grote's *Plato and the Other Companions of Socrates* (1865), and was popularized by Matthew Arnold in his *Culture and Anarchy* (1869). **—Hellenistic** *adj.* 1706, of or pertaining to Greece or the Greek language or art, especially after the time of Alexander; formed from English *Hellenist* one who affected Greek ways or language + *-ic.*

hellion (hel'yən) *n.* mischievous, troublesome person. 1846, American English; probably an alteration (by association with *hell*) of earlier Scottish and Northern

English dialect *hallion* worthless fellow or scamp (1786, in Burns' *Address to the Deil*); of uncertain origin.

hello *interj.* 1883, alteration of earlier *hallo* (1840 in Dickens' *Barnaby Rudge*), itself an alteration of *holla, hollo* a shout to attract attention (1588), a natural, native English formation, used to attract attention of someone, perhaps from the earlier English exclamation *holla!* stop! cease!; said to be borrowed from Middle French *holà* (*ho,* exclamation to attract attention + *là* there); or perhaps influenced by German *hallo, holla,* used to attract attention. The more probable explanation is that *hello, hallo, holla* and *hollo* are all natural formations in English and that they are parallel to natural formations in German, French, and other, if not all, languages.

helm *n.* handle or wheel by which a ship is steered; tiller. Before 1338 *helme,* in Mannyng's *Chronicle of England;* found in Old English (before 830) *helma;* cognate with Old High German *helmo* tiller, and Middle High German *helm, halm, halme* handle (modern German *Helm* tiller, axe handle), from Proto-Germanic **Helman-/Halman-,* of uncertain origin. The figurative sense of position of guidance or control, is recorded in Old English about 888 and does not appear again until Skelton's use (before 1529). —**v.** steer. 1603, in Shakespeare's *Measure for Measure;* from the noun. —**helmsman** *n.* 1622, formed from English *helm* + *man.*

helmet *n.* About 1450 *helmet, helmete;* borrowed from Middle French *helmet,* diminutive of *helme* helmet, from Frankish (compare Old High German *helm* helmet, modern German *Helm,* Old Frisian, Old Saxon, Middle Dutch, and modern Dutch *helm,* Old Icelandic *hjalmr,* and Gothic *hilms*), from Proto-Germanic **Helmaz,* cognate with Sanskrit *śárman-* cover, protection, from Indo-European **k̑el-* hide (Pok. 553); for suffix see -ET. Curiously the Old English *helm* head covering, helmet (from about 725 to its obsolete or poetic use today) apparently did not assume the diminutive suffix *-et* and the word *helmet* was borrowed as a term in its own right to replace *helm* which the record does not indicate ever became an active term in the standard vocabulary of English.

helminth (hel′minth) *n.* intestinal worm. 1852, borrowed, probably through French *helminthe,* from Greek *hélmins* (genitive *hélminthos*) worm, especially an intestinal worm; related to *eulḗ* worm, and *eileîn* to turn, twist; see HELIX.

helot (hē′lət) *n.* slave or serf in ancient Sparta. 1579, borrowed from Greek *Heilōtes,* plural of *Heílōs,* popularly associated with *Hélos,* a Laconian town whose inhabitants were enslaved by Sparta, but perhaps related to Greek *halônai* be captured, by popular etymology. Greek *halônai,* cognate with Latin *vellere* to tear away, and Gothic *wilwan* rob, is from Indo-European **wel-* tear (Pok. 1144).

help *v.* Before 1200 *helpen,* found in Old English (about 725) *helpan;* cognate with Old Frisian *helpa* to help, Old Saxon *helpan,* Middle Low German, Middle Dutch, and modern Dutch *helpen,* Old High German *helfan* (modern German *helfen*), Old Icelandic *hjálpa,* and Gothic *hilpan,* from Proto-Germanic **Helpanan,* from Indo-European **k̑elb-* (Pok. 554).—**n.** Old English *help, helpe* (about 725, in *Beowulf*); cognate with Old Frisian *helpe* help, Old Saxon *helpa,* Middle Dutch and Middle Low German *helpe,* Old High German *helfa, hilfa* (modern German *Hilfe*), and Old Icelandic *hjalp;* from the stem of Old English *helpan* to help. —**helper** *n.* About 1340, formed from Middle English *helpen* + *-er*[1]. —**helpful** *adj.* About 1384, formed from Middle English *help* + *-ful.* —**helping** *n.* (probably before 1200, from *help,* v.) —**helpless** *adj.* About 1200, formed from Middle English *help* + *-less.*

helter-skelter *adv.* in disordered haste, pell-mell. 1593, in Nashe's correspondence; apparently an expression imitative of the hurried clatter of running feet. It resembles *hurry-scurry* in form, and while *helter* has no explanation other than its suggestive sound and rhyme with *skelter,* the final element is probably based on *skelte* to hasten, scatter hurriedly, though its recorded use is confined to the 1300's and one instance about 1400, which raises a question of continuity about the intervening 200 years.

The adjective meaning of disorderly or confused, is first recorded in 1785; the noun, about 1713.

helve *n.* handle of an ax, hammer, etc. Probably about 1200 *helfe,* in *The Ormulum;* developed from Old English *helfe, hielfe* (before 899, in Alfred's translation of St. Gregory's *Pastoral Care*); cognate with Old Saxon *helvi* helve, Middle Dutch *helf,* and Old High German *halb;* related to HALTER.

hem[1] *n.* border or edge on a garment. Old English *hem* a border (about 1000, in Ælfric's *Glossary*); cognate with Old Frisian *hemma* to hinder, modern German *hemmen,* and Old Icelandic *hemja* hem in, curb, from Proto-Germanic **Hamjanan,* cognate with Lettish *kams* mass, lump, from Indo-European **kem-/kom-* press together (Pok. 555).—**v.** About 1340 (implied in *hemming*) and thus *hemmen* provide with a border (about 1386); from the noun. The phrase *hem in* with the meaning of shut in or confine, is first recorded in 1538.

hem[2] *interj.* a sound like clearing the throat. 1526, in Skelton's *Magnificence;* probably from the verb. —**v.** make this sound. Before 1470, implied in *hemynge,* in Malory's writings; probably imitative of the sound of clearing the throat. The expression *hem and haw* to hesitate, is first recorded in 1786; *haw,* as an imitative word denoting hesitation, is first recorded in 1632.

hem- a form of *hema-* and *hemo-* before vowels, as in *hemagglutination.*

hema- a combining form meaning blood, as in *hemachrome = chroma or red coloring matter of the blood.* Borrowed from Greek *haîma* blood; variant form of HEMO-.

hematite (hem′ətīt *or* hē′mətīt) *n.* reddish-brown iron ore. Before 1398 *emachite,* in Trevisa's translation of Bartholomew's *De Proprietatibus Rerum;* later *haematites* (1543); borrowed probably from Old French *hematite,* from Latin *haematītēs,* from Greek *haimatítēs* bloodlike, from *haîma* (genitive *haímatos*) blood; see HEMO-.

hemato- (also *hemat-* before vowels), a combining form meaning blood, as in *hematology = study of blood, hematogenesis = formation of blood.* Borrowed from Greek *haimato-,* combining form from *haîma* (genitive *haímatos*) blood; see HEMO-.

hemi- a prefix meaning half, as in *hemisphere.* Borrowed from Greek *hēmi-;* cognate with Latin *sēmi-* SEMI-.

hemipterous (himip′tərəs) *adj.* belonging to a large

group of insects. 1816, possibly formed in English from French *hémiptère,* or directly from New Latin *Hemiptera* order of insects (from Greek *hēmi-* half + *pterón* wing, FEATHER) + English suffix *-ous;* so called with reference to the insects' wing structure.

hemisphere *n.* half of a sphere or globe. About 1385 *hemysperie,* in Chaucer's *Troilus and Criseyde;* later re-formed as *hemispere, emispere, hemisphere* (1532), by influence of Middle French *emispere, emisphere;* all forms ultimately borrowed from Latin *hēmisphaerium,* from Greek *hēmisphaírion* (*hēmi-* half, hemi- + *sphaîra* SPHERE). **—hemispheric** *adj.* 1585, formed from English *hemisphere* + *-ic.* **—hemispherical** *adj.* 1624, formed either from English *hemispheric* + *-al*[1] or from *hemisphere* + *-ical.*

hemistich *n.* half a line of verse. 1575, borrowed possibly through Middle French *hémistiche,* from Latin *hēmistichium,* from Greek *hēmistíchion* (*hēmi-* half + *stíchos* row, line of verse; see STAIR).

hemlock *n.* poisonous plant. Before 1325 *hemeloc;* earlier in the place name *Humbelochclaile* (before 1200); developed from Old English *hemlic* (about 1000); earlier *hymlice, hymblice* (about 700); perhaps related to *hymele* the hop plant, and corresponding to Old Icelandic *humli* and Old Slavic *chŭmelĭ* the hop plant; all perhaps related to, or even derived from, a Finno-Ugric word represented by Finnish *humala* and Vogul *qumlix* hop plant. **—v.** poison with hemlock. 1846, in Thackeray's *Cornhill to Cairo;* from the noun.

hemo- a combining form meaning blood, as in *hemoglobin = globin (globulin or protein) of the blood, hemorrhage = discharge or flow of blood.* Borrowed possibly through Old French *hemo-,* and Latin *haemo-* from Greek *haimo-,* from *haîma* blood; of unknown origin.

hemoglobin (hē′məglō′bən) *n.* the protein matter of the blood. 1862, shortened form of earlier *hematoglobulin* (1845), from *hemato-,* from Greek *haímatos* (genitive of *haîma* blood; see HEMO-) + *globulin* a protein, from Latin *globulus* GLOBULE + English *-in,* variant of *-ine*[2].

hemophilia (hem′əfil′ēə) *n.* inherited condition in which the blood does not clot normally. 1854, New Latin *haemophilia,* from Greek *haîma* blood (see HEMO-) + *philíā* affection (medically, a tendency), from *phileîn* to love, related to *phílos* loving; see PHILO-. The term was coined by the German physician Schönlein in 1828. **—hemophiliac** *adj.* 1896, formed from *hemophilia* + *-ac,* adjective suffix, from Greek *-akós; n.* 1897, from the adjective. Both the adjective and noun in English may have been modeled on the earlier French *hémophilique,* adj. (1880), n. (1884).

hemorrhage (hem′ərij) *n.* Probably before 1425 *emorogie,* in Chauliac's *Grande Chirurgie;* later re-formed as *hemorrhage* (1671), borrowed through French *hémorrhagie;* both the Middle English and French forms borrowed from Latin *haemorrhagia,* from Greek *haimorrhagíā* (*haîma* blood; see HEMO- + *rhagḗ* a breaking, from *rhēgnýnai* to break, burst), cognate with Lithuanian *rěžti* cut, strike, from Indo-European **wrēĝ-/wrəĝ* (Pok. 1181).

hemorrhoids (hem′əroidz) *n.pl.* painful swellings near the anus. Before 1398 *emeroides,* in Trevisa's translation of Bartholomew's *De Proprietatibus Rerum;* borrowed from Old French *emorroïdes, hemorroïdes,* learned borrowing from Latin *haemorrhoidae,* from Greek *haimorrhoïdes,* plural of *haimorrhoís,* (*haîma* blood, see HEMO- + *rhóos* a stream, a flowing, from *rheîn* to flow; see STREAM).

hemp *n.* Asiatic plant whose fibers are made into heavy string, rope, etc. About 1300 *hemp,* in *Havelok the Dane;* developed from Old English (before 1000) *hænep;* cognate with Old Saxon *hanap* hemp, Middle Dutch and modern Dutch *hennep,* Old High German *hanaf* (modern German *Hanf*), and Old Icelandic *hampr;* all probably borrowed very early from the same source as Greek *kánnabis* hemp, Albanian *kanep,* Lithuanian *kanapḗs,* Old Slavic *konopljá,* Armenian *kanap',* Persian *kanab,* and Sumerian *kunibu.* It is sometimes claimed that the word is from Scythian on the basis of Herodotus' statement that the Scythians grew hemp or cannabis and distributed it.

hen *n.* Old English *hen* (about 950, in *Lindisfarne Gospel*); earlier, in the compound *edisc-hen* quail (about 700); cognate with Old Frisian *henn* hen, Middle Low German and Middle Dutch *henne* (modern Dutch *hen*), and Old High German *henna* (modern German *Henne*), related to Old English *hana* rooster (modern German *Hahn*); Old English *hen(n),* and its Germanic cognates, are from Proto-West Germanic **Han(e)nī,* cognate with Latin *canere* sing, Greek *ēi-kanós* singing early, from Indo-European **kan-* (Pok. 525).**—henhouse** *n.* (1665, in American English) **—henpecked** *adj.* dominated by one's wife. Before 1680, in Samuel Butler's *Remains,* in allusion to habit of hens in a flock that establish an order of dominance by pecking those below them in social structure. **—henpeck** *v.* 1688, back formation from *henpecked.*

hence *adv.* Probably about 1225 *hennes* away from here, away, in *King Horn;* formed from *henne* away, hence + *-s* adverb ending; developed from Old English *heonan;* cognate with Old Saxon *hinan, hinana* from here, away, Middle Dutch *henen, hin* (modern Dutch *heen*), Old High German *hinnan, hinana, hina* (modern German *hinnen, hin*), from Proto-West-Germanic **Hin-,* from Indo-European **k̑i-* this (Pok. 609); related to Old English *hēr* HERE. The spelling in *-ce* (recorded before 1460) is a spelling device to indicate the sound denoted by earlier *-s* (in *-es*), as in *twice* and *pence.* The extended meaning of from this (fact or circumstance), as a result of this, from these premises, therefore, is first recorded in 1586. **—henceforth** *adv.* (before 1375; earlier *henne forth,* probably about 1200) **—henceforward** *adv.* (probably about 1300; also *henne forward*)

henchman *n.* trusted attendant or follower. 1463-64 *henshman;* earlier *hengsman* high-ranking servant (originally, a groom); formed from Old English *hengest* horse, stallion, gelding + *man* man; cognate with Old Frisian *hengst, hanxt* horse, Middle Dutch *henxt* (modern Dutch *hengst*), Old High German *hengist* stallion, gelding (modern German *Hengst* stallion), from Proto-Germanic **Hanȝistás* best at springing; and Old Icelandic *hestr* (Swedish *häst* horse, Danish and Norwegian *hest*), from Proto-Germanic **HánHistaz,* both from Indo-European **k̑ənk-istos* (superlative), root **kāk-/k̑ək-* to spring (Pok. 522).

Henchman in the sense of personal attendant of a Highland chief, is first recorded in Edward Burt's *Letters from a Gentleman in the North of Scotland* (about 1730). The letters were edited by Scott, who used the word in several of his works, including in *The Lady of the Lake* (1810). The meaning of obedient or unscrupulous follower is found in 1839.

henequen or **henequin** (hen′əkin) *n.* yellow fiber from the leaves of an agave of Yucatán. 1880, American English; borrowed from Spanish *henequén, jeniquén,* from the Maya (Yucatán) native name.

henge (henj) *n.* prehistoric circular structure of stone or wood. 1932, in Kendrick and Hawkes' *Archaeology in England,* abstracted from *Stonehenge,* the prehistoric stone circle in southern England, on the Salisbury Plain.

The name *Stonehenge* appeared about 1130 as *Stanenge,* later *Stanhenge* (1205); the element *henge* is probably derived from the verb *hang,* meaning "that which is hanging or supported in the air," in reference to the horizontal stones resting on pillars found at Stonehenge; these stones have been called *henges* in Yorkshire since at least the early 1700's.

henna (hen′ə) *n.* dark, reddish-orange dye used on the hair. 1600, small thorny tree from whose leaves a dye is made; later, the dye itself; borrowed from the Arabic name for the plant *ḥinnā'.* **—hennaed** *adj.* dyed with henna. 1924, formed from English *henna* + *-ed*[2].

hep *adj. Slang.* informed, up-to-date, stylish. 1908, American English; variant of HIP[3].

hepatic *adj.* of or having to do with the liver. Before 1398 *epatike;* borrowed perhaps through Old French *hepatique,* and directly from Latin *hēpaticus* of or belonging to the liver, from Greek *hēpatikós,* from *hêpar* (genitive *hḗpatos,* earlier **hḗpn̥tos*) liver, cognate with Sanskrit *yákr̥t* (genitive *yaknás*), and Latin *jecur* (genitive *jecinoris*), from Indo-European **yékwr̥(t)/ yḗkwr̥(t)* (genitive **yekwnés*) (Pok. 504); for suffix see -IC.

hepatica *n.* low plant with delicate flowers, liverwort. Probably before 1425 *epatica;* later *hepatica;* borrowed from Medieval Latin *hepatica,* from feminine of Latin *hēpaticus* HEPATIC; so called from the plant's liver-shaped leaves.

hepatitis (hep′ətī′tis) *n.* inflammation of the liver. 1727, New Latin *hepatitis,* from Greek *hḗpatos* (genitive of *hêpar* liver) + New Latin *-itis* inflammation.

hepta- (also *hept-* before vowels). a combining form meaning seven, as in *heptagon = figure with seven angles, heptatonic = having seven tones* (as a musical scale does). Borrowed from Greek *heptá* seven; cognate with Latin *septum* SEVEN.

heptagon *n.* plane figure having seven angles and seven sides. 1570, borrowed probably from Middle French *heptagon,* from Greek *heptágōnon* (*heptá* seven + *gōníā* angle; see KNEE).

her *pron., adj.* Before 1225 *here;* developed from Old English (before 830) *hire, hiere* (third person singular feminine) dative and genitive forms of *hēo, hīo* she, feminine forms of *hē* HE. Old English *hire, hiere* are cognates of Old Frisian *hiri* her, and Middle Dutch *hare* (modern Dutch *haar*). These forms are parallel or analogous to Old Saxon *iru* her, Old High German *iru, iro* (modern German *ihr*), and Gothic *izai* (dative singular), *izē, izō* (genitive plural).—**hers** *pron.* (before 1325)

herald *n.* messenger, forerunner. Probably about 1300 *heraud* officer who is an expert in arms, armorial bearings, and tournaments, in *The Romance of Guy of Warwick,* also as a surname *Haroud* (1204); later *herald* (before 1393, in Gower's *Confessio Amantis*); borrowed through Anglo-French *heraud, herald* from Old French *heraut, hiraut, herault, heralt,* from Frankish **hariwald* commander of an army. The Frankish appears to be a compound whose elements are represented in Old High German *heri* army and *waltan* to command, rule; see HARRY and WIELD. Other forms that support this are found in the Germanic proper names *Chariovalda,* a Batavian chief mentioned by Tacitus, Old Saxon *Hariolt,* and Old Icelandic *Haraldr.*

The meaning "messenger or envoy" is first recorded in a version of *Piers Plowman* (about 1378), developing from the earlier sense of an officer of a tournament who introduced knights, etc.

—v. to proclaim, announce, or introduce. 1380 *herauden,* in Chaucer's *House of Fame;* later *harrold* (1605, in Shakespeare's *Macbeth*); from the noun, by influence of Middle French *herauder, hirauder* to herald, from *heraut, hiraut,* n.

—heraldic *adj.* of or pertaining to heraldry. 1772, borrowed from French *héraldique,* from Medieval Latin *heraldus* (from Germanic); for suffix see -IC. **—heraldry** *n.* Before 1393 *heraldie,* in Gower's *Confessio Amantis;* later, heralds collectively (before 1500) and the art or science of arms and armorial bearings (1572); borrowed from Old French *hiraudie,* from *hiraut,* n.; for suffix see -RY, -Y[3].

herb (ėrb) *n.* Probably before 1300 *erbe, herbe;* borrowed from Old French *erbe,* and from Latin *herba* grass, herb; of uncertain origin.

Although the spelling with *h-* is recorded in Middle English (influenced by the Latin form), the *h-* was not pronounced in *herb* until the 1800's, and is still not the preferred pronunciation in the United States, except in *herbicide* and possibly *herbaceous.*

—herbaceous *adj.* 1646, borrowed from Latin *herbāceus* grassy, from *herba* grass; for suffix see -ACEOUS. **—herbicide** *n.* 1899, American English, originally a trademark, formed from *herb* + *-icide,* as in *fungicide.*

herbivorous *adj.* feeding on grass or other plants. 1661, borrowing of New Latin *herbivorus* herb-eating, from Latin *herba* herb + *vorāre* devour, swallow; for suffix see -OUS.

herculean *adj.* 1596, in Nashe's *Have With You to Saffron-Walden;* formed from *Hercules* + *-an.*

herd *n.* Before 1225 *hurde* (in dialect of Southwestern England, and earlier in the place name *Herdewich,* 1185); later, in general use, *herde* (before 1325, in *Cursor Mundi*); developed from Old English (before 1000) *heord;* cognate with Old High German *herta* herd (and, through Low German, with modern German *Herde*), Old Icelandic *hjǫrdh* (Danish and Swedish *hjord*), and Gothic *haírda;* all derived from Proto-Germanic **Herđō,* from Indo European **k̑erdhā* (Pok. 579). Outside Germanic, through the Indo-European base, cognates are found in Middle Welsh *cordd* troop, family, Greek *kórthys* heap, Lithuanian *kerdžius* shepherd, Avestan *sarədha-* sort or species, and Sanskrit *śárdha-s* herd or troop. **—v.** join or flock together. Probably before 1387 *herdeyen,* in a version of *Piers Plowman;* later, *herden* (about 1400); from the noun. **—herder** *n.* 1327, as a surname for a herdsman; formed from English *herd,* v. + *-er*[1]. **—herdsman** *n.* Probably before 1200 *herdman,* in *Ancrene Riwle,* found in Old English *heordman, hyrdeman* (about 1000). The form with *s* (*herdsman*) appeared by 1603 on the model of *craftsman, kinsman.*

here *adv.* Probably about 1200 *here,* in *The Ormulum;* earlier *her* (1101), found in Old English *hēr* in this place where one puts himself (about 725, in *Beowulf*); cognate with Old Frisian *hīr* here, Old Saxon *hēr, hīr,* Middle Dutch and modern Dutch *hier,* Old High German *hiar* (modern German *hier*), Old Icelandic and Gothic *hēr* (Swedish *här,* Norwegian and Danish *her*); all belonging to the Proto-Germanic base **Hi-,* which is the source of English HE. **—n.** 1605, in Shakespeare's *King Lear,* from the adverb. **—hereabouts** *adv.* 1592, in Shakespeare's *Romeo and Juliet;* earlier *hereabout,* before 1300. **—hereafter** *adv.* Old English *hēræfter* (about 900, in Alfred's translation of Bede's *Ecclesiastical History*); *n.* (1546). **—hereby** *adv.* (about 1250, in *The Story of Genesis and Exodus*) **—herein** *adv.* Old English *herinne* (about 1000). **—heretofore** *adv.* (about 1200) **—herewith** *adv.* Late Old English *hēr-with* (1017-23).

heredity *n.* About 1540, inheritance; either a back formation from *hereditary* or a borrowing through Middle French *hérédité,* from Latin *hērēditās* condition of being an heir, from *hērēs* (genitive *hērēdis*) HEIR; for suffix see -ITY. The meaning of an inheritable quality or character, is first recorded in 1784 in a quotation of General Lafayette; the biological meaning of inheritable traits, is found in Herbert Spencer's *The Principles of Biology* (1863). **—hereditary** *adj.* Probably before 1425 *hereditarie,* in an anonymous translation of Chauliac's *Grande Chirurgie;* borrowed from Latin *hērēditārius,* from *hērēditās* heredity.

heresy *n.* belief different from the accepted belief of a church, sect, etc. Probably before 1200 *heresie,* in *Ancrene Riwle;* borrowed from Old French *heresie, eresie,* alteration of Latin *haeresis* heresy, school of thought, from Greek *haíresis* a taking or choosing, from *haireîn* take, seize, *haireîsthai* choose; of uncertain origin. **—heretic** *n.* 1340 *heretike,* in *Ayenbite of Inwyt;* borrowed from Old French *heretique, eretique* heretic, from Latin *haereticus,* from Greek *hairetikós* able to choose, from *haireîsthai* to choose; for suffix see -IC. **—heretical** *adj.* Before 1425, borrowed from Middle French *heretical* and Medieval Latin *haereticalis,* from Latin *haereticus;* see HERETIC; for suffix see -AL[1].

heritage *n.* what is or may be inherited, legacy. Probably before 1200 *eritage* spiritual inheritance or bequest, in *Ancrene Riwle;* later *heritage* (before 1225); borrowed from Old French *eritage, heritage,* from *heriter* inherit, from Late Latin *hērēditāre,* ultimately from Latin *hērēs* (genitive *hērēdis*) HEIR. **—heritable** *adj.* About 1375, borrowed from Old French *heritable,* from *heriter;* see HERITAGE; for suffix see -ABLE.

hermaphrodite (hėrmaf′rədīt) *n.* animal or plant having the reproductive organs of both sexes. Probably about 1408 *hermofrodyte,* in Lydgate's writings; earlier *hermofrodita* (before 1387, in Trevisa's translation of Higden's *Polychronicon*); borrowed from Medieval Latin *hermofroditus,* from Latin *hermaphrodītus,* from Greek *Hermaphróditos* Hermaphroditus, son of Hermes (Mercury) and Aphrodite (Venus), who was united with the body of the nymph Salmacis, combining male and female characteristics.

The word was known in Old French *hermaphrodite* in the 1200's, but the Middle English spelling with *-mo-* rather than *-ma-* would indicate the original borrowing into English was from Medieval Latin, not French, as would also the ending *-a.*

hermetic *adj.* tightly sealed, airtight. Before 1637 *hermetticke* pertaining to magic or alchemy, in Ben Jonson's *Underwoods,* back formation from earlier *hermetical* (1605); borrowed from New Latin *hermeticus* + English *-al*[1]. *Hermeticus* is an adjective adapted from Greek *Hermês trìs mégistos* Hermes Trismegistus (literally, Hermes thrice greatest). This name was given by the Neoplatonists, mystics, and alchemists to the Egyptian god Thoth, who was identified with the Greek god Hermes, of science and arts, and who supposedly invented the process of making a glass tube airtight by using a secret seal.

hermit *n.* 1196 *heremite* religious recluse; earlier in the place name *Bechermet* (about 1130); borrowed from Old French *heremite, hermite* (influenced by Medieval Latin *heremita*), from Late Latin *erēmīta,* from Greek *erēmī́tēs,* literally, person of the desert, from *erēmíā* desert, solitude, from *erêmos* uninhabited. Latin *erêmos* is cognate with Sanskrit *ṛté* except, without, Lithuanian *ìrti* loosen, separate, and Old Slavic *oriti* loosen, break up, destroy, from Indo-European **er-, erə-* loose, not close together, to part (Pok. 332). **—hermitage** *n.* home of a hermit. About 1300 *ermitage;* earlier in the place name *Le Hermitage* (about 1280); borrowed from Old French *hermitage, ermitage,* from *heremite, hermite* hermit.

hernia *n.* About 1390 *hirnia,* in Chaucer's *Canterbury Tales;* borrowed from Latin *hernia* a rupture, related to *hīra* intestine; see CORD. The spelling with *e,* after the Latin, was introduced in the 1600's.

hero *n.* 1555 *heroes,* pl., men of superhuman strength, courage, or ability; borrowed from Latin *hērōēs,* plural of *hērōs,* from Greek *hḗrōs* (plural *hḗrōes*); see CONSERVE. The sense of the chief male character in a play, poem, motion picture, story, etc., is first recorded in Dryden's works, in 1697.

The earliest English forms of the noun were the plural *heroes* and the singular *heros,* corresponding to the Latin. A variant singular *heroe* was replaced by *hero* in the 1600's, but the plural *heroes* is retained accidentally, and not so much after the Latin form as it is parallel to other English nouns ending in *-o* (compare *tomatoes, tobaccoes, mangoes,* etc.). The earliest citation in the OED (before 1387, in Trevisa's translation of Higden's *Polychronicon*) is now considered a scribal error for *hers;* however, when compared to the early dates of the derivatives *heroical* and *heroycus* and with Old French use (recorded as early as 1361), one is not so sure that *hero* has not slipped through the recording process in English.

—heroic *adj.* 1549, back formation from: 1) earlier *heroycus,* adj. (1410), borrowing of Latin *hērōicus;* 2) earlier *heroical,* adj. (probably before 1425), borrowed from Latin *hērōicus,* from Greek *hērōïkós,* from *hḗrōs* hero; for suffix see -IC. **—heroine** *n.* Before 1659 *heroina* demi-goddess; borrowed through French *héroïne,* and directly from Latin *hērōina, hērōinē,* from Greek *hērōī́nē,* feminine of *hḗrōs* hero. **—heroism** *n.* 1717, borrowed from French *héroïsme,* from *héros* hero (from Latin *hērōs*); for suffix see -ISM. **—hero worship** (1774)

heroin *n.* narcotic drug prepared from morphine. 1898, borrowed from German *Heroin,* a former trademark for this drug, registered in the 1890's by Friedrich Bayer and Company in Germany. Shortly before its registration as a substitute for morphine, clinical trials were conducted at the Second University Hospital of Berlin. The published report on fifty patients suffering from lung disease indicated that the drug was effective against coughs and that the patients felt comfortable and drowsy with no disagreeable side effects.

The origin of the drug's name has not been explained, and there is no evidence so far to indicate, as has been suggested, that it derives from Greek *hḗrōs* HERO, supposedly because of the inflated or euphoric feeling which the drug produces.

heron *n.* wading bird. 1353 *heron;* earlier *heyrun* (1302), *hayroun* (about 1300), and in the surname *Hayrun* (1124-30); borrowed from Old French *hairon, heron,* from Frankish (compare Old High German *heigaro, reigaro* heron, Middle High German *heiger, reiger,* modern German *Reiher*). The German forms correspond to Middle Dutch *reigher,* modern Dutch *reiger,* Old Icelandic *hegri,* Swedish *häger,* and Danish *hejre,* and also to Old English *hrāgra* heron, a form which did not survive into Middle English. As proved by the exactly cognate Old English *hrāgra,* the two Old High German forms are dissimilated variants of **hreigaro,* from Proto-Germanic **Hraiȝrán-,* from Indo-European **kroikro-* root **krik-* (Pok. 570), found in Old Slavic *krikŭ* a screaming, Welsh *cryg* hoarse, and *cregyr* heron.

herpes (hėr′pēz) *n.* virus disease of the skin or mucous membrane. Before 1398 *herpes* skin disease, in Trevisa's translation of Bartholomew's *De Proprietatibus Rerum;* borrowing of Latin *herpēs* a spreading skin eruption, from Greek *hérpēs* the disease shingles (literally, a creeping), from *hérpein* to creep.

herpetology (hėr′pətol′əjē) *n.* branch of zoology dealing with reptiles. 1824, probably borrowed from French *herpétologie,* from Greek *herpetón* creeping thing, reptile, from *hérpein* to creep; see SERPENT; for suffix see -LOGY.

herring *n.* 1130 *hareng;* later *heryng* (before 1300), developed from Old English, Anglian *hēring* (about 700, in the early Mercian glossaries), West Saxon *hǣring* (about 1000); cognate with Old Frisian *hēreng* herring, Old Saxon *hering,* Middle Low German *herink,* Middle Dutch *herinc* (modern Dutch *haring*), and Old High German *hārinc, hering* (modern German *Hering*). The etymology of this West Germanic word is uncertain. A possible explanation refers to the color (as animals were often so named) and that from that the name is related to Old English *hār* gray, HOAR; another explanation refers to the large schools in which the fish is found and that from that the name is related to Old High German *heri* host, multitude. **—herringbone** *n.* 1652, the bone of a herring; *adj.* 1659.

hesitate *v.* Probably before 1622, implied in *hesitating* slow, failing to act promptly; either a back formation from *hesitation;* or borrowed, perhaps by influence of French *hésiter,* from Latin *haesitātum,* past participle of *haesitāre* stick fast, stammer in speech, be undecided, a frequentative form of *haerēre* stick, cling, cognate with Lithuanian *gaĩšti* delay, linger, from Indo-European *ghais-* (Pok. 410); for suffix see -ATE[1]. **—hesitant** *adj.* 1647, probably a back formation from earlier *hesitancy.* **—hesitancy** *n.* 1617, borrowed from Latin *haesitantia* action of stammering, from *haesitantem* (nominative *haesitāns*), present participle of *haesitāre;* for suffix see -Y[3]. **—hesitation** *n.* Before 1400 *hesitacyoun;* borrowed from Old French *hesitation,* or directly from Latin *haesitātiōnem* (nominative *haesitātiō*), from *haesitāre;* for suffix see -ATION.

hetero- a combining form meaning another, other, different, as in *heterosexual = of or having to do with different sexes.* Borrowed from Greek *héteros* one or the other of two by assimilation from earlier *háteros,* from Indo-European **sm̥-teros,* contrastive adjective to **sem-* one (Pok. 902).

heterodox *adj.* not orthodox. 1637, 1650; earlier as a noun (1619); borrowed from Greek *heteródoxos* (*héteros* the other + *dóxā* opinion; see DOXOLOGY). **—heterodoxy** *n.* 1652, an unorthodox opinion; borrowed from Greek *heterodoxíā* error of opinion, from *heteródoxos* heterodox.

heterogeneous (het′ərəjē′nēəs) *adj.* different in kind, unlike. 1624, borrowed from Medieval Latin *heterogeneus,* from Greek *heterogenḗs* (*héteros* different + *génos* kind, gender, race, stock, see KIN); for suffix see -OUS. *Heterogeneous* gradually replaced earlier *heterogeneal* (1605), formed from English *heterogene* (1541, borrowed from Greek *heterogenḗs* of different kinds) + *-al*[1]. **—heterogeneity** *n.* 1641, probably formed from English *heterogene* + *-ity.*

heuristic (hyůris′tik) *adj.* serving to find out or discover, stimulating investigation. 1821, in Coleridge's *Letters;* borrowed as if from Greek **heuristikós* of or having to do with discovery (erroneous form of *heuretikós* inventive), apparently influenced by Greek *heurískein* to find, find out, discover, cognate with Old Irish *fūar* I have found, from Indo-European **uer-* (Pok. 1160). **—n.** science of using heuristic methods. 1860, from the adjective. The plural form *heuristics* heuristic methods or their study is first recorded in 1959.

hew *v.* cut with an ax, sword, etc. Probably before 1200 *hewen,* in Layamon's *Chronicle of Britain;* developed from Old English *hēawan* (before 900), earlier *geheawan* (about 725, in *Beowulf*); cognate with Old Frisian *hawa, howa* to hew, Old Saxon *hauwan,* Middle Dutch *hauwen, houwen* (modern Dutch *houwen*), Old High German *houwan* (modern German *hauen*), Old Icelandic *hǫggva* (Swedish *hugga,* Norwegian *hogge,* Danish *hugge*); all derived from Proto-Germanic **Hawwanan,* cognate with Lithuanian *káuti* beat, forge, Latin *caudex* tree trunk, and *incūdere* hollow out by hammering, from Indo-European **kāu-/kəu-* (Pok. 535).

The phrase *hew to* to hold fast to, stick to, adhere, developed in American English from the expression *hew to the line* to stick to a course (literally, to cut evenly with an axe), first recorded in 1891.

hex *v.* practice witchcraft (on), bewitch. 1830, American English, found in Pennsylvania German *hex* (in German *hexen* to hex, related to *Hexe* witch); see HAG. **—n.** 1856 (a witch), 1909 (magic spell), American English, found in Pennsylvania German *hex* (in German *Hexe* witch).

hexa- (also *hex-* before vowels). a combining form meaning six, as in *hexagon = figure having six angles, hexameter = having six feet or measures* (as a line of poetry does). Borrowed from Greek *hexa-* combining form of *héx* six; see SIX.

hexagon *n.* plane figure having six angles and six sides. 1570, borrowed, perhaps through Middle French *hexagone,* from Greek *hexágōnon* (*héx* SIX + *gōníā* angle). **—hexagonal** *adj.* 1571 *hexagonall,* formed from English *hexagon* + *-al*[1].

hexameter (heksam′ətər) *adj.* consisting of six metrical feet in poetry. 1546, borrowed probably through Middle French *hexamètre* from Latin *hexameter,* from Greek *hexámetros* (*héx* SIX + *métron* meter,

MEASURE). **—n.** line of poetry having six metrical feet. 1579, probably from the adjective.

hey *interj.* Probably about 1200 *hei,* possibly an imitative formation.

heyday (hā'dā') *n.* stage or period of greatest strength, vigor, prosperity, etc.; flush; full bloom. About 1590 *hayday* a state of exaltation or excitement, in Moore's writings; probably alteration of earlier (1526) *heyda,* an exclamation of playfulness, gaiety, surprise, etc. (1526); apparently an extended form of Middle English *hei, hey,* interj.; see HI. The sense of flush, stage of greatest vigor, etc., is first recorded in Smollett's *The Adventures of Peregrine Pickle* (1751); in this use the second element *(day)* is associated with *day* (period from morning to evening), and *heyday* was taken to mean the most flourishing or exalted time.

hi (hī) *interj.* informal greeting. 1862, American English, originally an exclamation used to attract attention (probably before 1500), variant of Middle English *hei* HEY.

hiatus (hīā'təs) *n.* empty space, gap. 1563, borrowing of Latin *hiātus* (genitive *hiātūs*) gap, from *hiāre* to gape, stand open; see YAWN.

hibachi (hibä'chē) *n.* charcoal brazier for heating or cooking. 1863, borrowed from Japanese *hibachi,* literally, fire pot, a compound of *hi* fire, and *hachi* bowl or pot, with a shift from *h* to *b* in the second element, such as is found in *Nippon, Nihon.*

hibernate *v.* spend the winter in sleep or in an inactive condition. Before 1802, in Erasmus Darwin's writings; probably a back formation from *hibernation,* possibly by influence of French *hiberner,* from Latin *hībernāre;* see HIBERNATION. **—hibernation** *n.* 1664, in John Evelyn's *Kalendarium Hortense;* borrowed from Latin *hībernātiōnem* (nominative *hībernātiō*) the action of passing the winter, especially in some suitable place, from *hībernāre* to winter; for suffix see -ATION. The verb in Latin developed from *hībernus* of winter, wintry, and is related to *hiems* winter, cognate with Greek *cheimṓn* winter, Old Prussian *semo,* Old Slavic *zima,* Armenian *jiun* snow, Sanskrit *hemantá-s* winter, and Hittite *gimmanz* winter. Latin *hībernus* derived from the Indo-European **ĝheimrinos* wintry, a form which yielded *-br -* and thence *-ber -* in Latin to give *hībern-;* however, this is almost the only example of such a process in Latin according to the Latin scholar Kieckers. The Indo-European root is **ĝhei-/ĝhi-* (Pok.425).

hibiscus (həbis'kəs) *n.* plant or tree with large flowers. 1706, borrowed from Latin *hibiscum,* later *hibiscus* marshmallow (a plant), perhaps from Gaulish. (Greek *ibískos* is probably from Latin.)

hiccup or **hiccough** *n.* 1580 *hickop,* variant of earlier *hicket* (1540), and *hyckock* (1538), words considered imitative of the sound of hiccuping, and parallel with French *hoquet* hiccup, Walloon (French dialect) *hikéte,* Middle Dutch *hick,* Danish *hikke,* and Swedish *hicka,* among others. The modern spelling *hiccup* is first recorded in 1788, its variant *hiccough* in 1626, in Bacon's *Sylva Sylvarum,* by mistaken association with the word *cough;* however, this change in spelling did not affect the pronunciation hik'up. **—v.** 1580 *hickop,* probably from the noun.

hick *n. Informal.* awkward, unsophisticated, provincial person. 1565, from *Hick;* earlier *Hikke* (1376, in *Piers Plowman*); a former nickname of *Richard.*

hickory *n.* North American tree with edible nuts. 1671, American English; borrowed from Algonquian (perhaps Powhatan), a shortening of *pockerchicory* (about 1618), *pohickery* (1653), and other similar words for a species of walnut. The hickory's tough, heavy wood was used to make switches and walking sticks, hence the word was used to mean a switch (1824) and a cane or walking stick (1748). Because of the resilience he displayed in the War of 1812, Andrew Jackson was nicknamed "Old Hickory" by his soldiers.

hidden *adj.* concealed, secret, occult. Before 1547, from a late past participle of *hide*[1]. The noun *hiddenesse* is first recorded about 1384.

hide[1] *v.* conceal. About 1121 *hiden,* developed from Old English *hȳdan* (before 899, in Alfred's translation of St. Gregory's *Pastoral Care);* cognate with Old Frisian *hēda* conceal, Middle Dutch and Middle Low German *hūden,* from Proto-Germanic **Hūdjanan,* from Indo-European **keudh-, *kudh-* cover (Pok.952), seen in Greek *keúthein* to conceal, Sanskrit *kuhara-m* cave, and Welsh *cudd* hidden.

hide[2] *n.* skin of an animal. About 1150 *hide, hid* skin of an animal or human; found in Old English *hȳd* (891, in the *Anglo-Saxon Chronicle*); cognate with Old Frisian *hēd* skin, Old Saxon *hūd,* Middle Dutch *huut* (modern Dutch *huid*), Old High German *hūt* (modern German *Haut*), and Old Icelandic *hūdh,* from Proto-Germanic **Hūđis,* Indo-European **kūtís,* root **keut-/kut-* (Pok.952); also cognate with Welsh *cwd* scrotum, Latin *cutis* skin, Greek *kýtos* hollow container, and Old Prussian *keuto* shell, husk; also with initial *s,* as seen in Greek *skŷtos* skin, leather; related to Old English *hȳdan* to HIDE[1]. **—v.** *Informal.* beat, thrash. 1757, to flay; 1825, to thrash; from the noun. **—hide-and-seek** *n.* 1672, in Dryden's *Marriage-à-la-Mode;* replacing earlier *All hid* (1588, in Shakespeare's *Love's Labour's Lost*). **—hidebound** *adj.* 1559, in reference to cattle having skin sticking closely to the back and ribs as a result of emaciation; later, of people, attitudes, etc., that are restricted or narrow and often bigoted (1603). **—hide-out** *n.* (1885, in American English)

hideous *adj.* very ugly, frightful. About 1303 *hydus,* in Mannyng's *Handlyng Synne;* later *hidous* (before 1333); borrowed through Anglo-French *hidous,* from Old French *hideus, hidos,* (earlier) *hisdos,* from *hide, hisde* horror or fear, perhaps from Germanic. The ending *-eous* appeared before 1400, patterned on words such as *courteous.*

hie (hī) *v.* hasten, go quickly. Probably before 1200 *hihin,* in *Ancrene Riwle;* later *hien* (before 1250); developed from Old English *hīgian* strive, hasten (before 899, in Alfred's translation of Boethius' *De Consolatione Philosophiae*), from Proto-Germanic **Hīʒ-;* cognate with Russian *sigat'* to leap, and Sanskrit *śīghrá-s* quick, from Indo-European **k̑eigh-/k̑īgh-* (Pok.542).

hierarchy (hī'ərär'kē) *n.* Probably about 1343 *ierarchi, ierarchie* ranked division of angels, borrowed from Old French *ierarchie, jerarchie,* learned borrowing from Medieval Latin *hierarchia,* from Greek *hierarchíā* rule of a high priest, from *hierárchēs* high priest, leader of sacred rites (*tà hierá* the sacred rites, neuter plural of *hierós* sacred + *árchein* to lead, rule; see IRE and ARCH-).

The sense of ranked organization of persons or things, is first recorded in Milton's *Doctrine and Discipline of Divorce* (1643), and seems, by popular confusion of sound with *higher*, to have also been associated semantically with *higher* to explain the sense of ranks; however, this is not a unique phenomenon in English, and other more detailed explanation is necessary. The form with initial *h-* appeared before 1450 and became common in the 1500's, in imitation of the Latin. **—hierarchic** *adj.* 1681, belonging to the hierarchy of angels, back formation from *hierarchical* (in a variant edition, 1471), formed from English *hierarchy* + *-ical*, possibly by influence of Old French *hierarchique* on the model of Medieval Latin *hierarchicus*, from *hierarchia* hierarchy.

hieratic (hī′ərat′ik) *adj.* of the priestly caste, priestly. 1669, borrowed possibly from French *hiératique*, from Latin *hierāticus*, from Greek *hierātikós*, from *hierāteíā* priesthood, from *hierâsthai* be a priest, from *hiereús* priest, from *hierós* sacred; for suffix see -IC.

hieroglyphic (hī′ərəglif′ik) *adj.* of or written in a system using pictures to represent words or sounds. 1585, borrowed, perhaps through Middle French *hiéroglyphique*, from Late Latin *hieroglyphicus*, from Greek *hieroglyphikós* (*hierós* sacred + *glyphḗ* carving, from *glýphein* carve; see IRE and CLEAVE[1] to split); for suffix see -IC. An earlier *hieroglyphical* is found in Mulcaster's writings (1581); this does not preclude the borrowing of *hieroglyphic* from French. **—n.** 1596, probably from the adjective. **—hieroglyph** *n.* 1598, a shortened form of *hieroglyphic*, n., possibly influenced by or, in some instances, borrowed from Middle French *hiéroglyphe* (1576). These were all terms born out of the European fascination with Egyptian hieroglyphic writing that reached a flurry of excitement after Napoleon's troops unearthed the Rosetta stone in 1799.

hifalutin *adj.* See *highfalutin* under HIGH.

hi-fi (hī′fī′) *n., adj. Informal.* high-fidelity, in recorded sound reproduction. 1950, American English, from *hi(gh) fi(delity)*, with a change of stress in *-fi* to so-called long *i* replacing the muted vowel (ə, in fə del′ə tē).

higgledy-piggledy *adv., adj.* 1598 *higledi-pigledie* without any order, in confusion, probably formed in relation to *pig* and its various connotations of messy, disorganized, etc. and perhaps to the confusion of the barnyard and the way in which pigs huddle together when herded.

high *adj.* About 1303 *hygh*, in Mannyng's *Handlyng Synne;* later *high* (before 1325, in *Cursor Mundi*), and *heigh* (about 1375); developed from Old English, in Anglian *hēh* of great height, lofty, tall (about 825), in West Saxon *hēah;* cognate with Old Frisian *hāch* high, tall, Old Saxon *hōh*, Middle Dutch *hooch* (modern Dutch *hoog*), Old High German *hōh* (modern German *hoch*), Old Icelandic *hār* (Swedish *hög*, Norwegian *høy*, *høg*, and Danish *høi*), and Gothic *hauhs;* derived from Proto-Germanic **HauHaz*, cognate with Gothic *hiuhma* heap, Lithuanian *kaũkas* a swelling, and Sanskrit *kuca-s* female breast, from Indo-European **keuk-/kouk-/kuk-* (Pok.589).

In the 1300's the Middle English forms reflect the change of the Old English vowel to so-called long *i*, similar to the change in *die* and *eye*, and by the middle to late 1300's the final guttural sound, represented by *gh*, was dying away, though the spelling with *-gh* remained.

The biological meaning of developed or advanced (as in *the higher plants, the higher apes*) is first recorded in 1848. The meaning of euphoric or exhilarated from the use of alcohol or a narcotic drug or drugs is found in American English, in 1932.

—adv. at or to a high point, place, etc. About 1303 *hygh*, in Mannyng's *Handlyng Synne;* later *heygh* (1397, in *Rolls of Parliament*); developed from Old English (about 1000) *hēage;* from *hēah, hēh*, adj.

—n. Before 1325 *high* high point, top, in *Cursor Mundi* (implied earlier in *hihste* superlative form, 1101); developed from Old English *hēh, hēah*, adj. Various and mostly technical meanings of the noun developed in American English: area of high barometric pressure (1878); high gear in an automobile (1921); highest point, price, temperature, etc., record (1926); high school, as in *Dorchester High* (1928); state of euphoria induced by a narcotic drug (1953). **—highball** *n.* alcoholic drink served in a tall glass. 1898, American English, possibly in allusion to *high ball* signal for a railroad train to proceed (1832); or from *high ball* a game of chance (1881). **—high chair** (1848) **—highfalutin** or **hifalutin** (hī′fəlü′tən) *adj.* pretentious. (1839, American English; of unknown origin). **—high fidelity** (1934) **—high jinks** or **hijinks** *n.pl. Informal.* boisterous merrymaking. 1842, extension of Scottish name for games played at drinking parties, from *high* + Scottish *jinks*, plural of *jink* quick turn, dodge. **—highland** *n.* Before 1000, Old English *heahlond*. **—highlight** *v.* 1934, American English; *n.* (1658). **—highly** *adv.* About 900, Old English *hēalīce*. **—high-minded** *adj.* (1503) **—highness** *n.* Before 899, Old English *hēanes*. **—high school** Before 1475, school for advanced learning, possibly in reference to the type of school founded in Edinburgh (1519, as the principal grammar school) to teach the higher branches of school learning, and expanded in the mid-1800's to general public education in Scotland. First use of the term is recorded in American English, in 1824, referring to the earlier English models. **—high sea** (about 1380) **—hightail** *v.* to leave quickly. 1925, American English. **—high-tech** *n.* style or design based on utilitarian, industrial equipment and materials. 1978, formed from *high-(style) tech(nology)*. A term coined by Joan Kron and Suzanne Slesin, American interior decorators. **—high tide** Before 1000, Old English *heahtide*. **—high time** (about 1390) **—highway** *n.* (probably before 1200)

hight (hīt) *adj. Archaic.* named, called. Before 1300, past participle of *highten* be called, in *Cursor Mundi*. The Middle English term arose out of confusion of two verbs from which the past participle of one assumed the present tense stem forms of the other, and the active and passive verbs with the meaning of to call and to be called also blended in form but not in sense; thus there was a fusion of Old English *hātte* (present and past tense of *hātan* be called or named); and of *heht* (past tense of *hātan* to command, promise, call). Cognates are found in Old Frisian *hēta* command, call, name, Old Saxon *hētan*, Middle Dutch and modern Dutch *heeten*, Old High German *heizzan* (modern German *heissen*), in Old Icelandic *heita* named, be named, promise, and Gothic *haitan* to command, call, call by name, from Proto-Germanic **Haitanan*, from Indo-European **kəi-d-* (root **kēi-/kī-/ki-* (Pok.538), found in Latin *ciēre* rouge, summon, and Greek *kīneîn* set in motion.

hijack (hī′jak) *v.* 1923, American English, to rob (a bootlegger, smuggler, etc.) in transit; apparently a back formation and alteration of *highjacker* (also 1923), perhaps from *high(way)* + *jacker* one who holds up. In the 1960's usage extended to *hijack* to mean "seize (an aircraft) in flight for blackmail, escape, etc."; also found in *skyjack* (1968); in the 1970's extended further to mean "take over any form of public transportation with its passengers."

hike *v.* 1809, English dialect *hyke, heik* to walk vigorously, tramp or march; of uncertain origin. The informal sense of raise with a jerk, pull up (as in *hike up one's pants*), is first recorded about 1873 in American English, followed by the extended sense of raise (wages, prices, etc.) in 1904, also in American English. **—n.** 1865 *heik* a tramp or march, from the verb. The meaning of a raise in wages, prices, etc., is first found in 1931 in American English; from the verb. **—hiker** *n.* (1913)

hilarity (həlăr′ətē) *n.* great mirth, noisy gaiety. Probably 1440 *hillarite,* borrowed through Middle French *hilarité,* or directly from Latin *hilaritās* (genitive *hilaritātis*) cheerfulness, gaiety, from *hilaris, hilarus* cheerful, gay, from Greek *hilarós,* related to *hílaos* gracious, kindly; see SILLY; for suffix see -ITY. **—hilarious** *adj.* 1823, in Scott's writings; formed in English from Latin *hilaris* cheerful, gay + English suffix *-ous.*

hill *n.* Probably about 1175 *hulle,* in dialect of Southwest and Midland England; later *hil* (probably about 1200, in *The Ormulum*); found in Old English *hyll* (about 1000, in Ælfric's writings), derived from Proto-Germanic **Hulnis;* cognate with Old Frisian *holla* head, Frisian *hel* hill, Middle Dutch *hille,* Low German *hull* hill, and Old Saxon *holm,* Old Icelandic *holmr* island (Danish *holm* and Swedish *holme* islet). Outside Germanic cognates are found in Middle Irish *coll* head, leader, Latin *collis* hill, *celsus* high, lofty, great, *culmen* top, summit, Greek *kolōnós* hill, and Lithuanian *kálnas* hill, mountain, from Indo-European **kel-,* **kol-,* **kḷ-* stand out (Pok.544). **—hillbilly** *n.* unsophisticated person from a backwoods or mountain region. 1900, American English, originally *Hill Billie* or *Billy; adj.* 1924, of or relating to country music. **—hillock** *n.* Before 1382 *hilloc* small hill, in the Wycliffe Bible; earlier, as a surname *Hilloc* (1205); formed from English *hill* + *-oc,* diminutive suffix. **—hillside** *n.* (before 1387) **—hilltop** *n.* (1408)

hilt *n.* handle of a sword, dagger, etc. Old English *hilt* (about 725, in *Beowulf*), from Proto-Germanic **Heltiz;* cognate with Old Saxon *hilta* hilt, *helta* handle of an oar, Middle Dutch *helt, hilt,* Middle Low German *hilte,* Old High German *helza,* Middle High German *helze,* and Old Icelandic *hjalt.* Outside of Germanic, the word is cognate with Welsh *cleddyf* sword, Breton *klézé,* from Indo-European **keləd-* (Pok.546); see HALT[2] lame.

him *pron.* Old English *him,* dative of *hē* HE (before 855, in the *Anglo-Saxon Chronicle*); cognate with Gothic *himma* this (dative).

Him originally was the dative masculine and neuter of *hē,* and *hine* was the masculine accusative form of *hē.* During the 1100's to the 1300's *him* replaced the accusative *hine* but the neuter dative was retained as *hit, it.*

hind[1] *adj.* back, rear. 1454 *hynde;* earlier *hint* (probably about 1300) and in the compound *hindeward,* in *Arthour and Merlin* (probably before 1300); a shortened form of Middle English *bihenden* (probably about 1175); developed from Old English *behindan,* adv. and prep., back, behind (about 725, in a version of *Exodus*); and possibly also influenced by Old English *hinder,* adv., back, rear. These forms are probably cognate with Old High German *hintana,* adv., *hintar,* prep., *hintaro,* adj., hind, behind (modern German *hinten, hinter, hintere*), Old Frisian *hindera* behind, Old Icelandic *hindri* later, farther, *hinztr* latest, last, and Gothic *hindana,* adv., *hindar,* prep., behind, beyond. While the root is obscure, Old English *hinder* and Gothic *hindər,* from Proto-Germanic **Hinđerán,* almost certainly embody the Indo-European contrastive suffix *-teros,* as in Greek *próteros* in front. **—hindmost** *adj.* 1375 *henmast,* in Barbour's *The Bruce.*

hind[2] *n.* female deer. Old English (before 970) *hind,* cognate with Middle Dutch and modern Dutch *hinde* hind, Old High German *hinta* (modern German *Hinde*), and Old Icelandic *hind,* from Proto-Germanic **Hindṓ,* Indo-European **ḱemtí-* (Pok.556). Outside Germanic cognates exist in Greek *kemás* young deer, Lithuanian dialect *šmùlas* and Sanskrit *śáma-s* hornless, and perhaps Russian *komólyj* hornless, which derive from the Indo-European base **ḱem-* hornless, and contrasting with *ḱerəw-* horn; see HART.

hinder[1] (hin′dər) *v.* keep back, impede, prevent. About 1385 *hyndre* to impede, keep back, prevent, in Chaucer's *Canterbury Tales;* earlier *hindren* to cause harm or injury (probably before 1200); developed from Old English (about 1000) *hindrian;* cognate with Middle Low German, Middle Dutch, and modern Dutch *hinderen* to hinder, and Old High German *hintarōn* (modern German *hindern*), from Proto-Germanic **Hinderōjanan;* the verb was formed from the adverb (as in Old English *hinder*) meaning back.

hinder[2] (hin′dər) *adj.* hind, back, rear. About 1300 *hindore,* probably from Old English *hinder,* adv., possibly the comparative of HIND[1] back. **—hindermost** *adj.* 1398 *hyndermest,* in Trevisa's translation of Bartholomew's *De Proprietatibus Rerum.*

hindrance *n.* 1436 *hinderaunce* damage, disadvantage, detriment; formed from *hindren, hindre* to harm, damage, obstruct, HINDER + *-aunce* -ance. The meaning of obstruction or hindering is first recorded in 1526.

hinge *n.* 1356 *heyngge* joint on which a door or gate moves, hinge; later *henge* (about 1380, in *Sir Ferumbras*); cognate with Middle Dutch *henghe, henghene* hook, handle, and Middle Low German *henge* hinge; related to HANG. **—v.** attach by or as by hinges. 1607 *hindge* to bend, in Shakespeare's *Timon of Athens;* later, to attach or hang as with a hinge, in Goldsmith's *Essays* (1758-65); from the noun. The figurative sense of to hang and turn on, depend, is first recorded in 1719.

The spelling change from *e* to *i* is a regular shift before *ng;* the pronunciation, as if *-dg-* in *edge,* is a natural development found in the ending *-ge* as in *singe.*

hint *n.* 1604 *hint* a slight sign or indication; an occasion, opportunity, in Shakespeare's *Othello;* probably developed from *hinten* to tell, inform (before 1400); earlier, to catch, seize, grasp (probably before 1300), and *henten* to catch (probably before 1200); developed from Old English (before 1000) *hentan* to seize, from Proto-Germanic **Hantjanan,* from Indo-European **kend-/kond-.* The Old English seems related to Old Frisian *henda, handa* to catch, seize, Old Icelandic *henda* to grasp, and Gothic *-hinthan* in *frahinthan* seize, capture, but the consonants of these forms are different; see HUNT. **—v.** give a hint. 1648; from the noun.

hinterland *n.* back country. 1890, borrowed from German *Hinterland* (*hinter* behind; see HIND[1] back, + *Land* land).

hip[1] *n.* joint formed by the upper thighbone and pelvis; haunch. 1369 *hippe,* in Chaucer's *Book of the Duchesse;* earlier in the combination *hipes-banes* hipbones (about 1150); developed from Old English (before 800) *hype,* from Proto-Germanic **Hupiz;* cognate with Middle Dutch *hōpe, hēpe* hip (modern Dutch *heup*), Old High German *huf* (modern German *Hüfte*), and Gothic *hups.* Cognates outside Germanic include Greek *kýbos* cube, a hollow above the hips of cattle, and Latin *cubitum* elbow, *cubāre* lie down, from Indo-European **keub-/kub-* a curve of the body (Pok.589).

hip[2] *n.* seed pod of a rose bush. About 1415 *hipe,* in Chaucer's *Canterbury Tales;* earlier *hepe* (probably before 1300, in *Kyng Alisaunder*); developed from Old English (about 800) *hēope, hīope.* Old English *hēope* derived from the same root as Old Saxon *hiopo* bramble, thornbush, Old High German *hiafo, hiufa, hiefa,* Middle High German *hiefe,* and Dutch *joop* hip, Norwegian *hjupe,* Danish *hyben,* from Proto-Germanic **Hiup-,* cognate with Old Prussian *kaāubri* thorn, from Indo-European **k̂eub-/k̂oub-* (Pok.595). The irregular shift from the so-called long *e* to modern English short *i* is possibly the result of change in stress in the numerous compounds of this word from Old and Middle English, like *hip-bramble, hip-tree.*

hip[3] *adj.* informed, up-to-date (in archaic slang). 1904, American English; of unknown origin. **—v.** inform, keep up-to-date. 1920, in Fitzgerald's *This Side of Paradise;* from the adjective.

hippie *n.* social dropout, especially of the 1960's, characterized by dress in unconventional clothes, long hair, etc. About 1965, American English, extended use of earlier *hippie* (1953), a disparaging term for a *hipster* person who is hip or keenly aware of what is new or stylish (1941), (*hip*[3] + *-ster* and later *hip*[3] + *-ie*).

hippodrome *n.* oval track for races. 1585, borrowed from French *hippodrome,* and directly from Latin *hippodromos* race course, from Greek *hippódromos* (*híppos* horse + *drómos* course). Greek *híppos* (earlier **íppos,* as in *Álk-ippos*) is cognate with Sanskrit *áśva-s,* Latin *equus,* from Indo-European **ék̂wos* (Pok.301). Greek *drómos* is cognate with Sanskrit *drámati* runs about, from Indo-European **drem-/drom-* (Pok.204).

hippopotamus *n.* 1563 *hippopotame;* later *hippopotamus* (1600), replacing earlier *ypotame* (probably before 1300, in *Kyng Alisaunder*); borrowed from Late Latin *hippopotamus,* from Greek *hippopótamos* riverhorse, an irregular compound of *híppos* horse + *potamós* river (literally, falling or tumbling, as of a brook), related to *pétesthai* to fly; see FEATHER. The earlier forms *ypotame, ypotamus* were borrowed in English through Old French *ypotame,* from Medieval Latin *ypotamus,* itself an alteration of Latin *hippotamus.* The modern spelling is an imitation of the Latin.

hire *v.* Probably before 1300 *hiren,* in *Arthour and Merlin;* earlier *huren* (probably before 1200, in *Ancrene Riwle*); developed from Old English (about 1000) *hȳrian* pay for service, employ for wages, engage, probably from Old English *hȳr,* n., hire; cognate with Old Frisian *hēra* to hire, rent, Middle Low German *hūren* (modern German *heuern* hire, engage), and Middle Dutch *hūren* (modern Dutch *huren*). **—n.** Probably about 1250 *hire,* in *The Story of Genesis and Exodus;* earlier *hure* (probably before 1200, in *Ancrene Riwle*); developed from Old English (about 1000) *hȳr* payment for service, wages; cognate with Old Frisian *hēre* lease, rent, wages, Old Saxon *hūra,* Middle Low German *hūre* (modern Low German *hüre* and German *Heuer* wages, pay, hire), and Middle Dutch *hūre* (modern Dutch *huur*); and probably represented in Proto-Germanic **Hūrja-.* **—hired man** About 1175, a hired servant; found in Old English *hīred-man,* originally a household servant, from *hired* household; later associated with the past participle of *hire* employ for wages. **—hireling** *n.* 1459 *hirlyng;* found in Old English *hyrling* (about 1000); from *hȳr* + *-ling*[1].

hirsute *adj.* hairy. 1621, in Burton's *Anatomy of Melancholy;* borrowed from Latin *hirsūtus* rough, shaggy, originally, having bristles, formed from a lost noun **hirsus* bristle, from Indo-European **ĝherkwsus,* root **ĝher-* (Pok.445), related to *hirtus* shaggy, and possibly to *horrēre* to bristle with fear.

his *pron., adj.* of him, belonging to him. Old English (before 725) *his,* genitive of *hē* HE, from Proto-Germanic **Hisa,* from Indo-European **k̂i-* (Pok.609).

Hispanic *adj.* Spanish or Spanish-speaking. 1889, American English; probably shortened from earlier *Hispanical* of Spain or its people (1584, formed in English from Latin *Hispānicus* Spanish, from *Hispānia* Spain + English suffix *-ical*). **—n.** Spanish-speaking person of Latin-American origin or descent. 1972, American English; from the adjective.

Hispano- a combining form meaning Spanish, as in *Hispano-American.* Borrowed from Spanish *Hispano* Spanish, from Latin *Hispānus.*

hiss *v.* make a sound like *ss.* About 1384 *hissen,* implied in *hissyng,* in the Wycliffe Bible; of imitative origin. **—n.** 1513, from the verb.

histo- (also *hist-* before vowels). a combining form meaning tissue, as in *histology* = *study of tissue.* Borrowed from Greek *histo-* combining form of *histós* loom, web, originally a STAND, formed from *hístasthai* to take a stand, from Indo-European **si-stə-,* root **stā-/stə-/sth-* (Pok.1004).

histology *n.* study of the structure of tissues of animals and plants. 1847, borrowed from French *histologie,* from Greek *histós* web, formed from *hístasthai* to STAND; for suffix see -LOGY.

history *n.* Before 1393 *histoire* story, legend, biography, in Gower's *Confessio Amantis;* borrowed from Old French *histoire, estoire, estorie,* and borrowed from Latin *historia* narrative, account, tale, story, from Greek *historíā* a learning or knowing by inquiry, history, record, narrative, from *historeîn* inquire, from *hístōr* wise man, judge, earlier **ístōr,* from Indo-European **wid-tōr,* root **weid-/woid-/wid-* see (Pok.1125); related to *ideîn* to see, *eidénai* to know; see WIT[2]; for suffix see -Y[3]. Doublet of STORY[1]. The meaning of a formal record of past events is probably first recorded about 1451, and the spelling *historie* (about 1425). **—historian** *n.* Probably before 1439, in Lydgate's *Falls of Princes;* borrowed from Middle French *historien,* from Latin *historia;* for suffix see -IAN, -AN. **—historic** *adj.* 1669, probably a back formation from *historical,* possibly influenced by French *historique.* **—historical** *adj.* Probably before 1425 *historicalle,* in a translation of Higden's *Polychronicon;* formed in English from Latin *historicus,* from Greek *historikós,* from *historíā* history + English suffix *-al*[1] or *-ical.* **—historically** *adv.* (1550)

histrionic *adj.* having to do with actors or acting. 1648 *histrionick* theatrical, hypocritical, deceitful, in Beaumont's *Psyche;* either formed from English *histrion* actor (about 1566) + *-ic,* or borrowed from Late Latin *histriōnicus,* from Latin *histriō* (genitive *histriōnis*) actor, probably from Etruscan *hister;* for suffix see -IC. The meaning of having to do with actors or acting is first recorded in 1759. **—n. histrionics** *pl.* play-acting, theatrics, pretense. 1864, from *histrionic,* adj.

hit *v.* Probably before 1200 *hitten* get at with a blow, to strike, knock, in Layamon's *Chronicle of Britain;* developed from Late Old English (before 1075) *hyttan* come upon, meet with; borrowed from a Scandinavian source (compare Old Icelandic *hitta* to light upon, meet with, Swedish *hitta* to find, Norwegian and Danish *hitte* to hit, find), from Proto-Germanic **Hitjanan,* cognate with Welsh *cwyddo* to fall, *di-gwydd* to happen, from Indo-European **keid-/kid-* fall (Pok.542). **—n.** 1598, a blow, stroke; found earlier in the figurative sense of a rebuke (before 1475); from the verb. The use of *hit* in sports is first found in 1810-11, originally in cricket. The meaning of a successful venture or popular success, especially in reference to a play, song, person, etc., is first recorded also in 1811.

hitch *v.* move or pull with a jerk. 1440 *hytchen* move with a jerk, in *Promptorium Parvulorum;* earlier *hetchyn* (before 1400), probably developed from *icchen* to move, stir (about 1200, in *The Ormulum*). The origin of these words is uncertain, especially because there is a notable lack of cognates in related languages. The meaning of become fastened by a hook, is first recorded in 1578; however, connection to the original sense is not clear. The meaning of get a free ride is first found in 1931, in American English. **—n.** jerky movement. 1664, a limp or hobble; 1674, abrupt movement; from the verb. The figurative meaning of impediment or obstruction is first recorded in Walpole's *Letters* (1748). **—hitchhike** *v.* travel by getting free rides. 1923, American English (*hitch,* v., n., the hitching of a sled to a moving vehicle, 1880 + *hike,* v.). —*n.* 1940, in Agatha Christie's *Buckle my Shoe;* from the verb. **—hitchhiker** *n.* (1927)

hither *adv.* to this place, here. Before 1382 *hyther,* in the Wycliffe Bible; earlier *hider* (1100); found in Old English *hider* (about 725, in an early glossary, from Proto-Germanic **Hiđerán*); cognate with Old Icelandic *hedhra* here or hither, and Gothic *hidrē,* also cognate with Latin *citrō* hither, and *citrā* on this side, from Indo-European **k̂iteros,* contrastive adjective to **k̂i-* this (Pok.609). The phrase *hither and thither* is recorded in Old English (about 725). The change of spelling from *d* to TH, is parallel to that in FATHER. **—hitherto** *adv.* Before 1382 *hytherto,* in the Wycliffe Bible; earlier *hiderto* (probably before 1200; formed from *hider,* adv. + *to,* prep).

hive *n.* 1127 *hive,* developed from Old English *hȳf* (about 725, in an early glossary), from Proto-Germanic **Hūfiz;* probably cognate with Old Icelandic *hūfr* ship's hull, Latin *cūpa* tub, cask, Greek *kýpellon* cup, and Sanskrit *kū́pa-s* cave, hole, from Indo-European **keu-p-,* root **keu-* (Pok.591). **—v.** Before 1400, to make a nest (of bees); from the noun.

hives *n.* itchy condition of the skin with raised patches of red. About 1500 *hyvis,* of uncertain origin.

hoagie (hō′gē) *n.* large sandwich made from a long roll split in half; hero sandwich. 1945, American English, originally in Philadelphia, alteration of earlier *hoggie, hoggy* (about 1936); from *hog* + *-ie, -y,* diminutive suffix; of uncertain origin.

hoard *n.* About 1125 *hord* things saved and stored; developed from Old English *hord* valuable stock or store (about 725, in *Beowulf*); cognate with Old Saxon *hord* treasure, hidden or inmost place, Old High German *hort* (modern German *Hort*), Old Icelandic *hodd,* and Gothic *huzd,* from Proto-Germanic **Huzđan,* from Indo-European **kusdho-,* root **keus-/kus-* (Pok.953). **—v.** Probably about 1200 *horden* to save and store away, in *The Ormulum;* developed from Old English (about 1000) *hordian;* from *hord,* n.

hoarse *adj.* sounding rough and deep. 1369 *hors,* in Chaucer's *Book of the Duchesse;* earlier *hos* (about 1250), developed from Old English (about 1000) *hās;* cognate with Old Frisian *hās,* Old Saxon and Middle Low German *hēs,* modern Dutch *heesch,* Old High German *heis,* from Proto-Germanic **Haisa-;* coexisting, at all times, with this was a longer Proto-Germanic stem **Haisra-,* which is the source of modern German *heiser;* from a metathesized stem **Hairsa-* came Middle English *hors,* Middle Dutch *heersch,* and Old Icelandic *hāss* (from pre-Norse **hairsa-*); all from Indo-European **kəis-* (root **kāi-/kəi-/kī-*) (Pok.519).

hoary *adj.* 1530 *hoory,* in Palsgrave's *Lesclarcissement;* formed from English *hoar,* adj., gray with age; grayish-white + *-y*[1]. Probably before 1300 *hore;* developed from Old English *hār* gray, venerable, old (about 725, in *Beowulf*); cognate with Old Saxon and Old High German *hēr* old (modern German *hehr* august, stately), and Old Icelandic *hārr* gray, from Proto-Germanic **Hairaz;* cognate with Old Slavic *sěrŭ* gray, from Indo-European **k̂oiros* (Pok.540). **—hoarfrost** *n.* (about 1300 *hore-forst*)

hoax *v.* play a mischievous trick on. 1796, in Grose's *Classical Dictionary of the Vulgar Tongue;* probably an alteration of earlier *hocus* conjurer, juggler (1640), or *hocus* to hoax (1675), a shortening of *hocus-pocus.* **—n.** 1808; from the verb.

hob *n.* 1674 *hob* shelf at the back or side of a fireplace; alteration of earlier *hub* (1600), *hubbe* (1511); of unknown origin. The meaning of rounded peg or pin, as in *hobnail,* is first recorded in 1589; it may also be a different word.

hobble *v.* walk awkwardly, limp. Probably before 1300 *hoblen* to rock in a boat, to bob; later *hobelen* to limp (before 1376, in *Piers Plowman*); probably cognate with Dutch *hobbelen* to rock back and forth, toss up and down. The transitive meaning of tie the legs of an animal to prevent it from kicking, straying, etc., is first recorded in 1831, probably an alteration of earlier *hopple* (1586), and probably cognate with Flemish *hoppelen* to rock, jump, related to Dutch *hobbelen.* The figurative sense of hamper, hinder, is first recorded in 1870. **—n.** awkward walk, limp. 1727, in Swift's *Gulliver's Travels;* from the verb. The meaning of something that hobbles, a fetter (*hobbles,* pl.), is first recorded in 1831, probably an alteration of earlier *hopple* (before 1825); from the verb.

hobby *n.* Before 1420 *hoby* small horse, pony, in Lydgate's *Troy Book;* earlier *hobyn* (1298); of uncertain origin. *Hobby horse* a toy or mock horse is first recorded in 1557, and the transferred sense of favorite pastime or avocation, in 1676.

hobgoblin *n.* goblin. 1530 *hobgoblyng,* in Palsgrave's *Lesclarcissement,* a compound of *hob* elf (about 1460, from earlier *hobbe,* 1307, and the surname *Hobbe,* 1230; a variant of *Rob* for *Robert* or *Robin* in reference to *Robin Goodfellow,* elf in Germanic folklore) + *goblin.*

hobnob *v.* associate intimately. 1831, extended sense of earlier *hob-nob* drink together (1828), and in the adverb phrase, to drink, *hob or nob* or *hob and nob* to toast each other by turns (1756). The phrase *hob, nob* give or take, is found in Shakespeare's *Twelfth Night* (1601), and developed from *hab nab, hab or nab* have or have not (about 1550).

hobo *n.* person who wanders about, living by doing odd jobs. 1889, American English, of uncertain origin; (the earliest citations capitalize the word and refer to it as the tramp's name for himself). Compare dialectal English *hawbuck* clumsy fellow, lout, country bumpkin (1805) and *hawbaw* clumsy or coarse fellow, lout (1857), which may be forerunners of *hobo.*

hock[1] *n.* joint in the hind leg of a horse, cow, etc. About 1410 *hokke;* earlier in the compound *hokschyne* ankle or back of the knee (probably about 1395), apparently altered (under influence of *shin*) from Old English *hōh-sinu* Achilles' tendon, possibly a variant of *howghe* (about 1350), *ho* (about 1300); developed from Old English *hōh* heel; *hōh-sinu* is cognate with Old Frisian *hōsene* hamstring, Achilles' tendon, Old Icelandic *hāsin,* and Old High German *hahsa* hock (modern German *Hachse*). Old English *hōh* (from Proto-Germanic **HanHa-*) is cognate with Lithuanian *kenklė̃* the bend of the knee, and Sanskrit *kañkāla-s* skeleton, from Indo-European **kenk-/konk-* (Pok.566).

hock[2] *n.* kind of white Rhine wine. Before 1625, shortened form of *Hockamore* (1673), alteration of a borrowing of German *Hochheimer,* from *Hochheim,* town in Germany, where this wine is made.

hock[3] *n.* pawn, debt. 1859, American English slang, *in hock* in pawn, in debt, in a losing position at cards; possibly borrowed from Dutch *hok* jail, pen, doghouse. —v. 1878, American English slang, to pawn; from the noun.

hock[4] *n.* Obsolete name for several plants, now preserved only in *hollyhock.* Before 1398 *hocke, hokke,* found in Old English *hocc* (before 800, in an early glossary); of uncertain origin.

hockey *n.* game played with curved sticks and a puck. 1527, of uncertain origin (perhaps originally connected with Middle French *hoquet* shepherd's staff, crook, diminutive of Old French *hoc* hook, from Frankish; compare Middle Low German *hōk* corner, edge; see HOOK; however, in the United States the stick was at first known as *hawky*). The original game (now called *field hockey*) was played with eleven on each team. The game of ice hockey (with six on each team) became known in the 1850's. The term *ice hockey* appeared in 1883.

hocus-pocus *n.* formula used in performing magic tricks. 1632; earlier *Hocas Pocas,* name of any magician or juggler (1624); perhaps originally sham Latin used by magicians in performing their tricks; very likely a perversion of the phrase from the Mass *Hoc est corpus meum* This is my body. The extended meaning of trickery or deception is first recorded in 1774.

hod *n.* trough or tray with a long handle, used for carrying bricks, mortar, etc. 1573, perhaps borrowed from Middle Dutch *hodde* basket, from Proto-Germanic **Huđ-,* from Indo-European **kudh-,* root **keudh-* cover (Pok.952); or an alteration of Middle English (before 1300) *hot, hott* pannier, basket, borrowed from Old French *hotte,* apparently from Frankish (compare dialectal German *Hotte* basket, Middle High German *hotze* cradle).

hodgepodge *n.* About 1390 *hochepot* disorderly mixture or jumble, in Chaucer's *Canterbury Tales;* earlier *ochepot* kind of stew, haphazard mixture (1381) and *hochepot* as a legal term in Anglo-French with the meaning of the collecting of property in a common pot (about 1290). This word was a borrowing of Old French *hochepot* stew or soup, a compound of *hocher* to shake, from Germanic (compare Low German *hotten* to balance or rock, Middle High German *hotzen* and modern Dutch *hotsen* to shake) and *pot* pot, also from Germanic (compare Middle Low German *pot, put* POT). The altered and reduplicated form *hotchpotch* is found in 1549, though an earlier form *hoche poche* (1415) is recorded as a manuscript variant in Chaucer's *Canterbury Tales;* and the current spelling followed in 1579.

hoe *n.* 1375 *howis* tool used to loosen soil and cut weeds, in Barbour's *The Bruce;* earlier *houwe* a mattock or pickax (1363); borrowed from Old French *houe,* from Frankish (compare Old High German *houwa* hoe, modern German *Haue;* related to *houwan* to HEW). —v. use a hoe. 1450 *howwen,* probably from the noun, though perhaps in some instances borrowed from Middle French *houer,* from *houe,* n. —**hoecake** *n.* a kind of sweetened bread made of corn meal. 1745, in American English; originally such bread baked perhaps on the broad blade of a field hoe. —**hoedown** *n.* a noisy, lively dance. 1841 (though obliquely referred to as early as 1807, in Washington Irving's *Salmagundi*); possibly developed from the name of a dance among American Blacks, in exaggerated imitation of steps used in hoeing in a field.

hog *n.* Probably before 1300 *hog,* in *Kyng Alisaunder;* earlier, in the surname *Hog* (1174-80); found in Late Old English *hogg* young pig, also applied to young sheep and horses after passing their first year. It is doubtful that the word came from Celtic, though some sources cite a comparison with Welsh *hwch* sow, Cornish *hoch,* and Breton *houc'h, hoc'h* hog. The figurative sense of a gluttonous, coarse, self-indulgent person, is first recorded as *hogg* in Wycliffe's writings, about 1400. —v. *Slang.* take greedily or selfishly. 1884, American English, in Mark Twain's *Huckleberry Finn;* from the noun.

hogan *n.* dwelling used by the Navaho Indians. 1871, American English; borrowed from Athapaskan (Navaho) *hōghan* dwelling, house.

hoi polloi (hoi′ pəloi′) the masses. 1837 *oi polloi,* in James Fenimore Cooper's *Europe;* borrowed from Greek *hoi polloí,* pl., the many (people). Dryden used the phrase in 1668 but wrote the words in Greek, as did Byron in 1821-22; both, curiously preceded the phrase with *the,* though *hoi* means the, and both writers had some familiarity with Greek.

hoist *v.* 1548 *hoihst,* alteration of earlier *hoise* (1509), perhaps a variant of Middle English *hysse,* a nautical term (1490, in Caxton's translation of *The Book of Eneydos*), probably borrowed from Middle Dutch *hyssen* to hoist, related to Low German *hissen,* and Old Icelandic *hissa upp* raise; of unknown origin. —**n.** a hoisting, lift. 1654 *hoyst;* from the verb.

hoity-toity *adj.* inclined to assume affected manners; haughty. 1690 *hoighty toighty* frolicsome, romping, giddy, flighty, in Dryden's *Amphitryon;* possibly an alteration and reduplication of earlier dialectal *hoyting* acting the hoyden, romping about clumsily (1594); perhaps a further alteration from, or related to, HOYDEN. An earlier noun use is recorded in 1668.

The sense of haughty is recorded in the late 1800's.

hokum *n.* humbug, bunk. 1917, originally American English theatrical slang, probably formed after *bunkum,* possibly by influence of *hocus-pocus.* —**hoke** *v.* Often, **hoke up.** falsify, contrive, fake. 1935, originally American English theatrical slang with the meaning of make sentimental, melodramatic, etc., by exaggerated acting; probably a shortened form of HOKUM. —**hokey** *adj.* characterized by hokum; contrived; falsified. 1945, American English slang, formed from *hoke* + *-y*[1].

hol- a form of *holo-* before vowels, as in *holistic.*

hold[1] *v.* take and keep. Probably about 1175 *holden;* developed from Old English, in Anglian *haldan* (before 855), and in West Saxon *healdan;* cognate with Old Frisian *halda* to hold, Old Saxon *haldan,* Middle Low German *halden* (modern Dutch *houden*), Old High German *haltan* (modern German *halten*), Old Icelandic *halda,* and Gothic *haldan* to keep, tend, watch over (cattle), which is considered to be the original sense in the Germanic languages, later developing the sense of "have," from Proto-Germanic **Halđanan;* cognate with Sanskrit *kaláyati* (he) impels, and Greek *késllein* to drive (a boat onto shore), from Indo-European **kel-/kol-* (Pok.548). Old English *heorde healdan,* "to keep flocks," and Old High German *hirta haltente* "keeping flocks" show this development of a pastoral vocabulary from "to keep animals" to the sense of "to hold."

The Anglian form is the source of *hold,* while the Old English past tense *heold* yielded *held,* and the Middle English and early modern English past participle *holden* gave way to the new form *held* in the 1500's.

—**n.** possession, keeping. About 1330 *hold;* earlier *hald* (before 1325, in *Cursor Mundi*), and *hold* a place of refuge, haven (probably before 1200, in Layamon's *Chronicle of Britain*); developed from Old English (1042) *hald, heald* that which holds or is held, from the verbs *haldan, healdan* to hold.

—**holder** *n.* About 1260; formed from English *hold,* v. + *-er*[1]. —**holding** *n.* Probably before 1200; formed from English *hold,* v. + *-ing*[1]. —**holdup** *n.* **1** a stoppage. 1837, in American English. **2** the act of stopping by force and robbing. 1878, in American English.

hold[2] *n.* interior space for cargo below the deck of a ship. 1591 *hold,* in Raleigh's writings, alteration of earlier *hole* (1440, by influence of *hold*[1], n. and *holl* (1333-52), both with the meaning of hold of a ship, and developed in part from Old English *hol* HOLE. Middle English *holl* in the sense of hold of a ship was probably also influenced by Middle Dutch *hol* hold of a ship, and probably replaced by differentiation of meaning earlier *hul,* which had meant both the hold and the hull of a ship (before 1400), developed from Old English *hulu* shell, husk.

hole *n.* Probably before 1200 *hole,* in *Ancrene Riwle;* developed from Old English (about 700) *hol* hole, hollow place; cognate with Old Frisian and Old Saxon *hol* hollow, Middle Dutch and modern Dutch *hol,* Old High German *hol* (modern German *hohl*), and Old Icelandic *holr,* from Proto-Germanic **Hulaz,* cognate with Sanskrit *kulyā́* channel, Greek *kaulós* stem, and Latin *caulis* stalk, from Indo-European **kaul-/kul-* hollow (Pok.537). —**v.** make holes in. Probably before 1300 *holen,* in *Kyng Alisaunder;* earlier *holien* (probably before 1200, in *Ancrene Riwle*); developed from Old English (about 1000) *holian,* from *hol,* n.

-holic variant form of -AHOLIC, as in *carboholic (carbohydrate + -holic), chocoholic (chocolate + -holic), colaholic,* etc.

holiday *n.* 1500's *holiday,* replacing earlier *haliday* (recorded probably before 1200, in *Ancrene Riwle*); developed from Old English *hāligdæg* (about 950, in *Lindisfarne Gospels*), a compound of *hālig* HOLY + *dæg* DAY.

Old English had a concurrent open compound *hālig dæg,* found later in Middle English *holy day* which developed in the late 1300's and became modern English *holiday,* meaning both a religious festival and a day of recreation. This eventually replaced the earlier form *haliday* but finally, by the 1500's, left two forms *holiday* and *holy day,* distinct in appearance, if not in meaning.

holiness *n.* Probably before 1200 *holinesse,* variant (influenced by *holi* holy) of *halinesse* (also probably before 1200, in Layamon's *Chronicle of Britain*); developed from Old English *hālignis* (before 830, in the *Vespasian Psalter*), from *hālig* HOLY + *-nes* -ness.

holistic *adj.* 1926, from *holism* theory that the tendency in nature is to produce whole organisms from small units; on the analogy of such pairs of words as *optimism, optimistic.* The terms *holism* and *holistic* were coined in English by the South African soldier and politician Jan Christiaan Smuts, from Greek *hólos* whole + English suffix *-ism.*

holler *v.* to shout, complain. 1699, American English, variant spelling and pronunciation of *hollo* (1542), from or related to the earlier *holla,* interj. (1523); see HELLO. —**n.** a shout, complaint. 1896, in George Ade's *Artie,* American English, from earlier dialectal English *hollar* (1825), *holler* (1886) a cry to attract attention, variant of *holla,* in Shakespeare's *Venus and Adonis* (1592), from *holla,* interj.

hollow *adj.* About 1330 *holwe;* earlier *holeh* (before 1300); developed from the Old English noun *holh* hollow place, hole, obscurely related to *hol* HOLE. The adjective use in Middle English of the Old English noun developed through the influence of Old English *hol* hollow, adj.; see HOLE. —**n.** hollow place, hole. About 1550; also, low land, valley, basin (1553); from the adjective in modern English, but found in Old English (about 897) *holh.* The noun is not recorded in Middle English. —**v.** make hollow. Before 1400 *holowen,* from the adjective.

The spelling *hollow* begins to appear in Middle English in the late 1300's in early forms *holoug, holowe, holowh.*

holly *n.* tree or shrub with bright-red berries. 1440 *holy,* in *Promptorium Parvulorum;* earlier *holin* (before 1200 in *Ancrene Riwle*); developed from Old English *Holegn* (about 958, in the place name), *holen* (about 1000); cognate with Old Saxon *hulis* holly, Middle Dutch *huls,* Dutch *hulst,* Old High German *huls* (modern German *Hulst*), from Proto-Germanic **Huli-,* from Indo-European **kel-/kol-* to prick (Pok.545).

hollyhock *n.* tall flowering plant of the mallow family. Before 1300 *holihoc* (*holi* HOLY + *hokke* mallow; see HOCK⁴, n.).

holmium *n.* metallic chemical element. 1879, New Latin, from *(Stock)holm,* Sweden, where it was first found + *-ium* (suffix of chemical elements). The term was coined by the Swedish chemist Per Cleve, who discovered the element.

holo- a combining form meaning whole, entire, totally, as in *holocaust, hologram.* Borrowed through French and Latin, from Greek *holo-* combining form of *hólos* whole, entire, complete, earlier **holwos,* cognate with Sanskrit *sárva-s* all, from Indo-European **solwos* (Pok.979).

holocaust *n.* great destruction. 1671 *holocaust* massacre or destruction, in Milton's *Samson Agonistes;* earlier, burnt offering or sacrifice (about 1250, in *The Story of Genesis and Exodus*); borrowed, possibly through, certainly by influence of, Old French *holocauste,* from Latin *holocaustum,* from Greek *holókauston,* neuter of *holókaustos* burned whole (*hólos* whole + *kaustós,* verbal adjective of *kaíein* to burn). Greek *kaustós* is cognate with Lithuanian *kulěti* (of grain) become burnt or blighted, from Indo-European **kēu-/kəu-/kū-* (Pok.595). The phrase *the Holocaust* the Nazi destruction of European Jewry in World War II, is first recorded in 1965.

hologram (hol′əgram) *n.* three-dimensional image formed by using light from a laser. 1949, formed in English from Greek *hólos* whole (three-dimensional) + English combining form *-gram.* **—holography** (həlog′rəfē) *n.* method of using laser light to produce holograms. 1964, from *hologram,* on the analogy of other pairs of words such as *telegraphy, telegram; cardiography, cardiogram.*

holograph (hol′əgraf) *n.* will or other document written wholly in the handwriting of the person in whose name it appears. 1623, borrowed from Late Latin *holographus* written wholly in one's own hand, from Greek *hológraphos* (*hólos* whole + *-graphos* written, from *gráphein* to write).

holster *n.* leather case for a pistol originally attached to a saddle. 1663, in Butler's *Hudibras;* possibly found in *hulster* place of concealment, retreat (1310, only in place names); developed from Old English *heolster,* earlier *helustr* concealment, hiding place; compare later Dutch *holster* or Swedish *hölster,* Danish and Norwegian *hylster* case, sheath; cognate with Icelandic *hulstr* sheath, Middle High German *hulst* cover, Old High German *hulsa* pod or hull (modern German *Hülse* pod), and Gothic *hulistr* veil, from Proto-Germanic **Helus-, *Hulis-,* from Indo-European **k̂el-* hide (Pok.553).

holy *adj.* Probably before 1200 *holi; hali,* in *Ancrene Riwle;* developed from Old English (about 725) *hālig* holy; cognate with Old Frisian *hēlich* holy, Old Saxon *hēlag,* Middle Dutch *hēlich* (modern Dutch *heilig*), Old High German *heilag* (modern German *heilig*), Old Icelandic *heilagr,* and Gothic *hailags,* from Proto-Germanic **Hailaȝás.*

The primary meaning of the word may have been "that must be preserved whole or intact, that cannot be transgressed or violated," which would support its relationship to Old English *hāl* whole; see WHOLE.

hom- a form of *homo-* before vowels, as in *homorganic = produced by the same vocal organ.*

homage (om′ij) *n.* respect, reverence. Probably before 1300 *homage* allegiance or respect for one's feudal lord, in *Kyng Alisaunder;* earlier, a body of vassals owing allegiance (probably about 1225, in *King Horn*); borrowed from Old French *homage,* probably formed in Old French from *homme,* earlier *omne,* from Latin *hominem* (nominative *homō*) man + Old French *-age,* see HUMAN; for suffix see -AGE. The often-quoted source of Old French *homage* is Medieval Latin *hominaticum* state of being a vassal, but there is no mention of this form in FEW, and the Medieval Latin form was probably borrowed from Old French.

hombre (ôm′brā) *n. Southwestern U.S.* a man. 1846, borrowing of Spanish *hombre* man, from Old Spanish *omne,* from Latin *hominem* (nominative *homō*); see HUMAN.

home *n.* Probably before 1200 *hom* dwelling, house, village, in Layamon's *Chronicle of Britain;* developed from Old English (about 725) *hām* dwelling, house, estate or village; cognate with Old Frisian *hām* home or village, Old Saxon *hēm,* Middle Dutch and modern Dutch *heem* home, Old High German *heim* (modern German *Heim*), Old Icelandic *heimr* residence, world (Swedish *hem,* Norwegian *heim,* and Danish *hjem*), and Gothic *haims* village, from Proto-Germanic **Haim-.* Outside Germanic cognates exist in Greek *kṓmē* village, Old Irish *cōim, cōem* dear, beloved, Old Prussian *seimins* household, servants, and Old Slavic *sěmĭja* household, servants, slaves; from Indo-European **k̂oi-m,* root **k̂ei-* lie down (Pok.539). **—adv.** Probably about 1225 *hom;* earlier *ham* (1100); developed from Old English *hām,* accusative form of *hām,* n. **—adj.** 1552; from the noun. **—v.** 1765, go home; from the noun. **—home base** (1856, in American English) **—homecoming** *n.* About 1385 *homcomyng,* in Chaucer's *Troilus and Criseyde.* **—home economics** (1926, in American English) **—homelike** *adj.* (1817, in Coleridge's *Biographia Literaria*) **—homemade** *adj.* (before 1659, in Cleveland's poetry) **—homestead** *n.* 972, Old English *hamstede; v.* 1872, American English. **—homeward** *adj.* About 1250 *homward,* in *The Story of Genesis and Exodus;* from Old English *hām weard* (855); *adv.* (before 1200). **—homework** *n.* Before 1683, lessons (1889). **—homey** *adj.* 1856, formed from English *home,* n. + *-y*¹.

homely *adj.* Probably about 1378 *homely* of or belonging to a home or household, domestic, in Wycliffe's writings; earlier, in Northern dialect, as a comparative form *hamlyer* more intimate, more friendly (1348); from *hom* home + *-li* -ly² (adjective suffix). The meaning of plain, unadorned, simple (about 1380, in Wycliffe's writings) probably developed from the association of home with relaxed and plain practices of everyday living at home. Extension of this meaning to that of having a plain, commonplace, or even unattractive appearance, evolved probably before 1400. **—homeliness** *n.* Before 1340 *hamlynes,* from *hamely,* adj. + *-nes* -ness.

homeopathy (hō′mēop′əthē) *n.* treatment of disease to produce effects similar to those of the disease. 1826, borrowed from German *Homöopathie,* in the Late Latin *homoeopathīa,* from Greek *homoiopátheia,* formed from *hómoios* like + *-pátheia* effect, from *páthos* suffering; compare Greek *homoiopátheia* sympathy, likeness of feeling or condition. The German word was coined in 1796 by the German physician Samuel Hahnemann, who developed this method of treatment.

homicide[1] (hom′əsīd) *n.* the killing of one human being by another. About 1230, in *Ancrene Riwle;* borrowed from Old French *homicide,* learned borrowing from Latin *homicīdium,* with pre-Latin stem *homo- for *hominis* (genitive of *homō* man) + *-cīdium* act of killing, from *caedere* cut (down), kill; see HUMAN and EXCISE[2] to cut.

homicide[2] (hom′əsīd) *n.* person who kills a human being. About 1375 *homycide,* in Chaucer's *Canterbury Tales;* borrowed from Old French *homicide,* learned borrowing from Latin *homicīda,* with pre-Latin stem *homo for *hominis* (genitive of *homō* man) + *-cīda* killer; see HOMICIDE[1].

homiletic *adj.* of or having to do with sermons or the art of preaching. 1644 *homilitick;* borrowed from Late Latin *homīlēticus,* from Greek *homīlētikós* of conversation, affable, from *homīleîn* associate with, from *hómīlos* a crowd, throng. **—n.** Also, **homiletics.** art of composing and preaching sermons. 1830; from the adjective.

homily *n.* sermon, usually on some part of the Bible. Before 1387 *omelye,* in Trevisa's translation of Higden's *Polychronicon;* borrowed from Old French *omelie,* learned borrowing from Late Latin *homīlia* a homily, sermon, from Greek *homīlíā* conversation, discourse (in New Testament Greek, a homily, sermon), from *hómīlos* a crowd or throng, of uncertain origin; for suffix see -Y[3]. The spelling with *h* appeared in English in the 1500's through the influence of Late Latin *homīlia.*

hominid *n.* animal in family of primates that includes man; manlike animal. 1889, borrowed from New Latin *Hominidae* the family name, from Latin *homō* (genitive *hominis*) man; see HUMAN; for suffix see -ID[1]. **—adj.** 1916, from the noun.

hominy *n.* corn hulled and coarsely ground or crushed. 1629, American English, probably abstracted from *rockahominy,* borrowed from Algonquian (Powhatan) *rokēhamĕn* parched corn.

homo[1] *n.* 1597, man or human being, in Shakespeare's *2 Henry IV,* borrowing of Latin *homō* man; see HUMAN.

homo[2] *n.* colloquial shortening of *homosexual,* attested since 1929 (in M. Lief's *Hangover*).

homo- a combining form meaning same, as in *homonym, homosexual.* Borrowed from Greek *homo-,* combining form of *homós* SAME.

homogeneous (hō′məjē′nēəs) *adj.* of the same kind, similar. 1641, in Milton's *Reason of Church Government;* borrowed from Medieval Latin *homogeneus,* from Greek *homogenḗs* of the same kind (*homós* + *génos* kind, gender, race, stock); for suffix see -OUS. *Homogeneous* gradually replaced earlier *homogeneal* (1603), formed from *homogene* (1607, borrowed perhaps through Middle French *homogène,* from Greek *homogenḗs* of the same kind) + *-al*[1]. **—homogeneity** *n.* 1625, probably formed from English *homogene* + *-ity.* **—homogenize** *v.* 1886, make similar; formed from English *homogencous* + *-ize.* The meaning "render (milk) uniform in consistency" appeared in 1904.

homograph *n.* 1810, method of signaling; later, word having the same spelling as another, but a different origin and meaning (1873); probably formed from English *homo-* + *-graph,* modeled on Greek *homógraphos* (*homós* + *graphḗ* writing, from *gráphein* write). The later meaning of a word having the same spelling as another, may have been a separate formation, after French *homographe* (1839), but probably still with a consciousness of the Greek form.

homologous (hōmol′əgəs) *adj.* corresponding in position, value, etc. 1660, borrowed, possibly by influence of French *homologue,* from Greek *homólogos* (*homós* + *lógos* relation, reasoning, computation, related to *légein* reckon, select, speak); see LOGIC; for suffix see -OUS.

homonym *n.* word having the same pronunciation as another, but a different meaning. 1697, borrowed perhaps through French *homonyme,* and directly from Latin *homōnymum,* from Greek *homṓnymon,* from neuter of *homṓnymos* having the same name (*homós* + *ónyma,* dialectal form of *ónoma* NAME).

homophone *n.* letter or symbol representing the same sound as another. 1843, probably formed from English *homo-* + *-phone,* modeled on Greek *homóphōnon,* from neuter of *homóphōnos* having the same sound (*homós* same + *phōnḗ* sound; see EUPHONY); however, it is possible that the English form is a borrowing from French *homophone.* An earlier adjective use is recorded in 1623 and later in 1880. **—homophony** *n.* 1776, borrowed, perhaps by influence of French *homophonie,* from Greek *homophōníā* unison, from *homóphōnos* having the same sound; for suffix see -Y[3].

homopterous (hōmop′tərəs) *adj.* belonging to a group of insects including the aphids and cicadas. 1826, borrowed from Greek *homópteros* (*homós* same + *pterón* wing; see FEATHER).

Homo sapiens (hō′mō sā′pēənz) man, human being. 1802, New Latin, from Latin *homō sapiēns,* literally, man or human being having wisdom (*homō* man, and *sapiēns,* present participle of *sapere* be wise; see SAGE[1]).

homosexual *adj.* showing sexual feelings for one of the same sex. 1892, formed from English *homo-* + *sexual.* **—n.** homosexual person. 1912; from the adjective, possibly by influence of earlier noun use in French (1907).

homunculus (hōmung′kyələs) *n.* little man, manikin. 1656, borrowed from Latin *homunculus,* diminutive of *homō* (genitive *hominis*) man or human being; see HUMAN + diminutive ending *-culus,* source of English *-cle.*

honcho *n.* chief, headman, boss. 1955, American English slang, officer in charge, originally U.S. Army use in Japan and Korea (1947-53); borrowed from Japanese *hanchō* group leader (*han* corps, squad + *chō* head, chief, headman). **—v.** to lead, direct, head. 1955, American English slang, to direct a military detail or operation; from the noun.

hone *n.* fine-grained whetstone on which to sharpen cutting tools. 1440 *hoone* whetstone, in *Promptorium Parvulorum;* earlier, in the place name *Sutton atte hone* in reference to a stone, especially one used as a boundary marker; developed from Old English (939) *hān* stone or rock; cognate with Old Icelandic *hein* whetstone (Danish *hen*), from Proto-Germanic **Hainō.* In languages outside Germanic, cognates are found in Latin *cōs* (genitive *cōtis*) whetstone, Greek *kônos* cone,

Persian *san* whetstone, and Sanskrit *śāṇa-s* whetstone, from Indo-European **k̂ō(i)-/k̂ə(i)-* sharpen (Pok.541). **—v.** sharpen on a hone, sharpen. 1826 (implied in *honer*), in Carlyle's *Early Letters,* from the noun.

honest *adj.* Probably before 1300 *honest* respectable or honorable, in *Kyng Alisaunder;* borrowed from Old French *honeste,* learned borrowing from Latin *honestus* honorable, decent, respected, from *honōs* HONOR. The meaning of truthful, fair, and upright, is first recorded in *Cursor Mundi* (before 1325). **—honesty** *n.* Before 1338 *honeste* honor, in Mannyng's *Chronicle of England;* later, honorable character or behavior (about 1386, in Chaucer's *Legend of Good Women*); borrowed from Old French *honesté,* from Latin *honestātem* (nominative *honestās*) honor or honesty, shortened form of earlier **honestitās,* from *honestus* honorable.

honey *n.* Probably about 1200 *honi;* earlier *huni* (about 1150); developed from Old English *hunig* (before 830, in the *Vespasian Psalter*); earlier in the compound *hunigsūge* honeysuckle (about 700, in an early Mercian glossary); cognate with Old Frisian *hunig* honey, Old Saxon *honeg,* Middle Dutch *honich* (modern Dutch *honig*), Middle Low German *honnich,* Low German *honnig,* Old High German *honag* (modern German *Honig*), and Old Icelandic *hunang* (Swedish *honung,* Danish and Norwegian *honning*), from Proto-Germanic **Hunaʒá-.* Outside the Germanic languages, cognates are found in Latin *canicae* bran, Greek *knēkós* (Doric *knākós*) yellowish, Old Prussian *cucan* brown, and Sanskrit *kāñcaná-m* gold, from Indo-European **kenəkó-/kn̥kó-, kn̥konó-* (Pok.564). **—v.** sweeten with or as with honey. Probably about 1350, implied in the past participle *honied;* from the noun. **—honeycomb** *n.* Before 1050, Old English *hunigcamb* (*hunig* honey + *camb* comb). **—honeyed** *adj.* About 1374 *honyede* sweetened, full of honey, in Chaucer's translation of Boethius' *De Consolatione Philosophiae;* later *honyd* sweet, sweet-sounding (1435); from *honey,* v. **—honeymoon** *n.* 1546 *hony moone,* the initial period of a marriage (said to be an ironic reference to the moon as sweetness, no sooner full than it begins to wane). The transferred sense of a period of good relations, is first found about 1580, and the meaning of a trip taken by a newlywedded couple, in 1801. **—v.** 1821, from the noun. **—honeysuckle** *n.* About 700, Old English *hunigsūge* (*hunig* honey + *sūge* from *sūgan, sūcan* to suck).

honk *n.* cry of the wild goose. 1854, in Thoreau's *Walden,* American English, of imitative origin. **—v.** 1854, make such a sound. The transferred sense of make such a sound on a horn, especially an automobile horn, is first recorded in 1895, in American English.

honor *n.* Probably before 1300 *honour,* in *Sir Tristrem;* earlier *onur* (probably before 1200); borrowed through Anglo-French *honour, onour,* Old French *honor, onor,* from Latin *honōrem* (nominative *honōs,* later *honor*); of uncertain origin.

The form *honor* was adopted in the United States through the influence of Noah Webster.
—v. About 1250 *honuren;* borrowed from Old French *honorer,* from Latin *honōrāre,* from Latin *honor,* n. **—honorable** *adj.* Before 1338 *honorable,* in Mannyng's *Chronicle of England;* earlier, in the surname *Honurable* (1256); borrowed from Old French *honorable,* from Latin *honōrābilis,* from *honōrāre* to honor; for suffix see -ABLE. **—honorary** *adj.* 1614, perhaps formed from English *honor* + *-ary* after Latin *honōrārius.* Possibly also influenced by French *honoraire.* **—honorific** *adj.* conferring honor. 1650 *honorifique,* borrowed from French *honorifique,* and directly from Latin *honōrificus,* from *honōrem* (nominative *honōs)* honor + the root of *facere* DO[1]. **—n.** 1879; from the adjective.

hood[1] *n.* covering for the head and neck. Probably before 1200 *hod,* in Layamon's *Chronicle of Britain;* earlier in the surname *Hode* (1181); developed from Old English (about 700) *hōd;* cognate with Old Frisian *hōd* hood, *hōde* protection, Old Saxon *hōd* hood, Middle Dutch *hoet* (modern Dutch *hoed* hat), Old High German *huot* hat, *huota* protection (modern German *Hut* hat, protection), Old Icelandic *hǫttr, hattr* hat, hood, from Proto-Germanic **Hōđaz,* from Indo-European **kādh-,* root **kadh-* (Pok.516). The modern spelling with *oo* began to appear in the early 1400's and represents a so-called long vowel, no longer associated with this spelling.

In American English, *hood* cover of an automobile, engine, was first recorded in Faulkner's *Sartoris* (1929). **—v.** cover with a hood. Probably before 1200 *hoden,* in Layamon's *Chronicle of Britain;* from the noun. **—hooded** *adj.* About 1440 *hodyd,* in *Promptorium Parvulorum,* from *hood,* v. **—hoodwink** *v.* 1562, cover the eyes with a hood, blindfold, formed from English *hood*[1] + *wink,* v. The figurative meaning of mislead, deceive, is first recorded in 1610, from the earlier sense of conceal (before 1600, in Richard Hooker's *Ecclesiastical Polity*).

hood[2] *n.* gangster or gunman. 1930, American English slang, shortened form of HOODLUM, with some relation to *hood*[1] by folk etymology.

-hood a suffix meaning state or condition of being, as in *boyhood, likelihood;* character of, as in *sainthood;* group of, as in *priesthood;* instance of, as in *falsehood.* Middle English *-hode, -hade;* developed from Old English *-hād,* from *hād* condition, position; cognate with suffixes in Old Frisian and Old Saxon *-hēd* -hood, Old High German and modern German *-heit,* and with words in Old Saxon *hēd* condition, dignity, Old High German *heit* rank, condition, Old Icelandic *heidhr* honor, dignity, and Gothic *haidus* manner, way, from Proto-Germanic **Haiđús,* cognate with Sanskrit *ketú-s* brightness, shape, form, from Indo-European **kəi-tú-s,* root **kāi-* (Pok.916). As a suffix *-hood* has generally replaced the earlier English *-head* (from Old English *-hād*) except in *godhead* and *maidenhead.*

hoodlum *n.* 1871, American English, a young street rowdy or loafer; later, a young delinquent or criminal, gangster (1877); of uncertain origin. The word originated in San Francisco in 1871 and by about 1877 had spread elsewhere in the United States. Among various etymologies that have been proposed, the one most commonly advanced is that *hoodlum* was borrowed from dialectal German (Bavarian) *Huddellump* ragamuffin.

hoof *n.* Before 1200 *hof;* developed from Old English (about 1000) *hōf;* cognate with Old Frisian and Old Saxon *hōf* hoof, Old High German *huof* (modern German *Huf*), Middle Dutch and modern Dutch *hoef,* and Old Icelandic *hōfr* (Swedish, Danish, and Norwegian *hov*), from Proto-Germanic **Hṓfaz,* cognate with Sanskrit *śaphá-s,* from Indo-European **k̂ophó-/k̂ṓpho-* (Pok.530). For the shift in spelling see HOOD[1]. **—v.** to walk, especially in *to hoof it.* 1641, to walk; from the noun. The meaning of to dance, originated in American English and is first recorded in 1925. **—hoofbeat** *n.* 1847, American English, in Longfellow's *Evangeline.*

—hoofer *n.* a dancer. 1923, American English; formed from *hoof* + *-er*[1].

hook *n.* Probably about 1200 *hok;* earlier, in the surname *Hoc* (1166) and *Hoke* (1167); developed from Old English (before 700) *-hōc,* in the compound *wēodhōc* weed hook; corresponding to Old Frisian *hōk* corner, edge, Middle Low German *hōk,* Middle Dutch *hoec* (modern Dutch *hoek*); and perhaps related to Old English *haca* bolt, Old Saxon *haco* hook, Middle Dutch *hake* (modern Dutch *haak*), Old High German *hāko* (modern German *Haken*), and Old Icelandic *haka* chin, from Proto-Germanic **Hōkaz, *Hakan-, Hǣkan-,* cognate with Russian *kógot'* claw, from Indo-European **keg-/kog-/kēg-/kōg-* (Pok.537). The modern spelling is first recorded about 1440, in *Promptorium Parvulorum,* and parallels *hoof;* see HOOF. **—v.** fasten with a hook or hooks. Before 1399 *hoken* to catch with a hook; earlier, furnish with a hook or hooks (probably before 1300), and *hōked,* past participle, curved like a hook, crooked (probably about 1150); developed from Old English (about 1000), past participle *hōced* crooked.

The figurative meaning of to attach as with a hook is first recorded in Shakespeare's *2 Henry IV* (1597). **—hooked** *adj.* addicted, especially to drugs. 1925, from English *hook,* v. **—hooker** *n.* one that catches with or as with a hook. 1567, thief or pickpocket, formed from English *hook,* v. + *-er*[1]. The meaning of a prostitute appeared in 1845 in American English, cited in N.E. Eliason's *Tarheel Talk* (1956).

hooky or **hookey** *n.* **play hooky.** stay away from school without permission. 1848, American English, probably from the slang phrase *hook it* to make off, run away, originally depart, proceed (before 1400).

hooligan *n.* young street tough, hoodlum. 1898, of uncertain origin, first appearing in British newspaper police-court reports. It has been suggested that the word came from the Irish surname *Hooligan,* possibly in allusion to a music-hall song of the 1890's about the doings of a rowdy Irish family in which the name Hooligan figures. Alternatively, the word has been explained as an alteration of the phrase *Hooley gang* or *Hooley's gang.* The word was adopted in Russian as *khuligan* and gained wide currency as a general term of opprobrium for scofflaws, criminals, political dissenters, etc. **—hooliganism** *n.* 1898, formed from English *hooligan* + *-ism.*

hoop *n.* band or ring of metal, wood, etc. About 1175 *hop;* probably developed from Old English **hōp,* which would be cognate with Old Frisian *hōp* ring, hoop, and Middle Dutch and modern Dutch *hoep,* from Proto-Germanic **Hōpa-,* cognate with Lithuanian *kabẽ* hook, from Indo-European **kab-/kāb-* (Pok.918). **—v.** fasten with a hoop or hoops. 1440 *hoopen,* in *Promptorium Parvulorum;* from the noun.

hoopla *n.* excitement or sensational publicity. 1877 *hoop la,* in American English; earlier *houp-la* exclamation accompanying a quick movement (1870); of uncertain origin (perhaps borrowed from French *houp-là* upsy-daisy).

hoosier (hü'zhər) *n.* nickname for a native or inhabitant of Indiana. 1826, American English, of uncertain origin. According to Jacob P. Dunn (in *Indiana and Indianians,* 1919), the word may be related to the dialectal English (Cumberland) word *hoozer,* meaning anything unusually large.

hoot *v.* 1611 *hoot* to call out or shout in disapproval or scorn, in Shakespeare's *A Winter's Tale;* an alteration of *houten* to shout, call out (before 1325), *hūten* to call by shouting, shout at in derision (probably about 1200); perhaps of imitative origin, representing a sound like the cry of owls or the tooting of a horn or pipe. The meaning of drive a person off or from the stage by shouts and sounds of disapproval is first recorded in *Piers Plowman* (probably about 1378). The first recorded use of *hoot* to represent the cry of some birds, especially the owl, is probably about 1450. **—n.** Before 1450 *houte* a shout or outcry; later, a shout of disapproval (1612); from the verb. The meaning of the cry or call of an owl is first recorded in 1795.

hop[1] *v.* spring, or move by springing, on one foot. Probably about 1200 *hoppen;* developed from Old English (about 1000) *hoppian* to spring, dance, corresponding to Old Icelandic *hoppa,* modern Dutch *hoppen,* and Middle High German *hopfen,* from Proto-Germanic **Hupnṓjanan,* from Indo-European **keub-/kub-* (Pok.589); cognate also with Middle Low German *huppen* to hop, modern Dutch *huppelen,* Middle High German and modern German *hüpfen,* this last from **Hupjanan,* from the same root. **—n.** a hopping, spring. 1508, in Dunbar's *The Goldyn Targe;* from the verb.

hop[2] *n.* vine having flower clusters. About 1440 *hoppe* ripened cones of hop plant used to flavor malt drinks (usually *hops*), in *Promptorium Parvulorum;* borrowing of Middle Dutch *hoppe;* cognate with Old Saxon *-hoppo* in *feldhoppo* hop, Middle Low German *hoppe,* Old High German *hopfo* (modern German *Hopfen*), from Proto-Germanic **Hup-nán-,* cognate with Latin *cūpa* cask, from Indo-European **keup-/kup-* (Pok.591). **—v.** 1572, to flavor with hops; from the noun.

hope *v.* Probably before 1200 *hopen,* in Layamon's *Chronicle of Britain;* developed from Old English (971) *hopian* wish and expect, look forward to something; cognate with Old Frisian *hopia* to hope, Middle Low German, Middle Dutch, and modern Dutch *hopen,* Middle High German and modern German *hoffen;* of unknown origin. **—n.** Probably before 1200 *hope;* found in Old English (about 1000) *hopa* expectation, trust, hope; cognate with Old Frisian, Middle Low German, and Middle Dutch *hope* (modern Dutch *hoop*), and Middle High German *hoffe;* all derived from the same Germanic source as Old English *hopian* to hope. **—hopeful** *adj.* Probably before 1200, in *Ancrene Riwle;* formed from Middle English *hope* + *-ful.* **—hopeless** *adj.* 1566, formed from English *hope* + *-less.*

hopper *n.* **1** container having a narrow opening at the bottom. 1277 *hoper* hopper of a mill. **2** person or animal that hops. About 1250 *oppere,* later in *gras-hoppere* grasshopper, in *The Story of Genesis and Exodus;* earlier, in the surname, perhaps of a dancer (1203); perhaps developed from Old English **hoppere* a dancer (possibly found in the feminine *hoppestre*); also probably influenced by *-hoppe* in *gærs-hoppe* (Middle English *gras-hoppere*). Exactly how the two senses are related is a matter of conjecture, though the juggling of grain in a mill hopper is surely suggestive of the movement of hopping.

hopscotch *n.* 1801, earlier *hop-scot* (1789); formed from English *hop*[1] + *scotch* score, from the scoring or scratching of lines in the dirt to make the boxes for the game.

horde *n.* crowd, swarm. 1555 *horda* tribe of Tartar o

Asiatic nomads, in Eden's translation of Peter Martyr's *Decades of the New World or West India,* probably borrowed (or introduced) at various times from Spanish, and possibly from Polish *horda* (reflecting the original spelling of record in English); also from French *horde* (the modern English spelling). All of these languages, including modern German with *Horde* (earlier *Horda*) borrowed the word from Western Turkic (compare Tartar *urda* horde, Turkish *ordu* camp, army). The *h* is a spelling device arbitrarily added in the European languages. **—v.** gather in a horde. 1821, in Byron's *Sardanapalus;* from the noun.

horehound *n.* plant with woolly, whitish leaves. 1373 *horehound;* earlier *horhune* (probably about 1200); developed from Old English (about 1000) *hārhūne* (*hār* HOAR + *hūne* name of a plant). The original Middle English spelling was probably altered to *horehound* by association with "hound" as in the earlier plant name *hound's tongue* (Old English *hundes tunge*).

horizon *n.* line where the earth and sky seem to meet. About 1385 *orisonte,* in Chaucer's *Troilus and Criseyde;* also *orisoun* (probably before 1387, in Trevisa's translation of Higden's *Polychronicon*); borrowed from Old French *orizonte, orizon,* learned borrowing from Latin *horizontem* (nominative *horizōn*), from Greek *horízōn kýklos* bounding circle, from present participle of *horízein* divide or separate, from *hóros* limit, boundary; of unknown origin. In the 1600's the spelling with *h* was adopted in imitation of the Latin form. **—horizontal** *adj.* 1555, relating to or near the horizon, in Eden's translation of Peter Martyr's *Decades of the New World or West India;* later, parallel to the horizon (1638); borrowed from French *horizontal,* from Latin *horizontem* horizon; for suffix see -AL[1].

hormone *n.* substance of the body that influences the activity of some organ, as adrenalin and insulin. 1905, formed in English from Greek *hormôn* setting in motion, with the assimilation of the chemical suffix *-one* into the Greek verbal ending *-ôn.* Greek *hormôn* is the present participle of *hormân* impel, from *hormḗ* impulse, onset, probably related *ornýnai* to rouse, and Latin *orīrī* arise, from Indo-European **er-/or-,* according to H. Frisk, *Griechisches etymologisches Wörterbuch,* II 420. English *hormone* was coined by the British physiologist, E.H. Starling, co-discoverer in 1902 of the intestinal hormone secretin.

horn *n.* Old English *horn* wind instrument (about 830, in the *Vespasian Psalter*), horn of an animal (about 725, in *Beowulf*); cognate with Old Frisian and Old Saxon *horn,* modern Dutch *hoorn,* Old High German *horn* (modern German *Horn*), Old Icelandic *horn,* and Gothic *haúrn;* derived from Proto-Germanic **Hórna-.* This Germanic base is cognate with Breton *karneg* horned, Gaulish *karnon* horn, trumpet, Latin *cornū,* Greek *kéras* horn, and Sanskrit *śŕṅga-m* horn, from Indo-European **k̂er-/k̂or-/k̂r̥-* (Pok.574). **—horned** *adj.* 1393, from *horn,* v. **—hornpipe** *n.* About 1400 *hornepype* musical instrument; later, a dance associated with sailors (about 1485); formed from Middle English *horne* + *pype* pipe.

hornet *n.* Before 1398 *harnet* large wasp, in Trevisa's translation of Bartholomew's *De Proprietatibus Rerum;* earlier, a beetle (1387, in Trevisa's translation of Higden's *Polychronicon*); developed from Old English *hyrnet, hyrnetu;* earlier *hirnitu, hurnitu* (before 800); cognate with Old Saxon *hornut* hornet, Middle Dutch *horsel* (modern Dutch *horzel*), and Old High German *hornaz* (modern German *Hornisse*). The Germanic forms are probably derived from the base **Hurz-,* from Indo-European **k̂r̥s-* (Pok.576), found also in Latin *crābrō,* Old Prussian *sirsilis,* Old Slavic *srŭšenĭ,* and Lithuanian *širšė* wasp. The current spelling *hornet* appeared about 1500, probably by association with *horn,* and by the assumption of *-et* as a suffix.

horology (hôrol'əjē) *n.* science of measuring time. 1819, probably formed from Greek *hṓrā* hour + English *-logy,* but also perhaps, in part, modeled on earlier English *horology* a clock or clock dial (1509; borrowed from Latin *hōrologium* device for telling the hour). It is also possible that *horology* was influenced in its formation by the older English term *horologe* clock, sundial, hourglass, etc., found as early as 1266 in the surname *Orloge,* and later in common vocabulary *orloge* (probably before 1375); borrowed from Old French *orloge* (later *horloge* and *oriloge*), learned borrowing from Latin *hōrologium,* from Greek *hōrológion,* from a lost adjective **hōrológos* hour-counting, from *hṓrā* HOUR + *légein* to count; see LEGEND.

The English spelling with *h* and with an intervening *o* between *r* and *l* are from an imitation of the Latin form.

horoscope *n.* relative position of the planets at the hour of a person's birth, regarded as influence on one's life. 1568, borrowed from Middle French *horoscope,* learned borrowing from Latin *hōroscopus,* from Greek *hōroskópos* (*hṓrā* HOUR + *-skópos* watching; see SCOPE).

Earlier recorded use of *horoscope* is in the Latin form *horoscopus* (about 1050), or as a variant spelling with a Latin inflectional ending, *oruscupum,* in a later edition of Chaucer's *Treatise on the Astrolabe* (about 1400).

horrendous *adj.* horrible. 1659, borrowed from Latin *horrendus* to be shuddered at, from *horrēre* to bristle with fear, shudder; see HORROR. An earlier occurrence is found without the English suffix *-ous* in Middle English *horrend* (probably 1440).

horrible *adj.* causing horror, terrible. Probably before 1300 *orible,* in *Arthour and Merlin;* later *horrible* (about 1375, in Chaucer's *Canterbury Tales*); borrowed from Old French *horrible,* learned borrowing from Latin *horribilis,* from *horrēre* to bristle with fear, shudder; see HORROR; for suffix see -IBLE.

horrid *adj.* 1590 *horrid* bristling, in Spenser's *Faerie Queene;* later, terrible or dreadful (1601, in Shakespeare's *Twelfth Night*); developed from *horred* bristling (1410, past participle of *horren* to bristle, tremble, quake); borrowed from Latin *horrēre* to bristle with fear, shudder; see HORROR. The later spelling *horrid* may have been influenced by Latin *horridus* bristling, terrible, from *horrēre* to bristle.

The weakened sense of unpleasant or offensive (as in *horrid weather*), is first recorded in 1666, though parallel adverbial use is recorded as early as 1615, interestingly in the Middle English spelling *horred.*

horror *n.* a shivering, shaking fear. Before 1325 *horer;* later *orrour* (before 1382); borrowed from Old French *orror, horreur,* and directly from Latin *horror,* from *horrēre* to bristle with fear; cognate with Sanskrit *hárṣate* he shudders, from Indo-European **ĝhers-/ĝhr̥s-* become stiff (Pok.445). Again, the spelling with *h* was a replacement in imitation of the Latin form.

hors d'oeuvre (or' dėrv') relish or light food served

before the regular meal. 1742, in Pope's *The Dunciad;* earlier, used as an adverb (1714, Addison in *The Spectator*); borrowed from French *hors d'œuvre,* literally, apart from the main work, annex *(hors* outside, from Latin *forīs* outside; *de* from; *œuvre* work, from Latin *opera* work; see OPERA*)*.

horse *n.* About 1200 *horse;* earlier *hors* (before 1121); developed from Old English *hors* (about 725, in *Beowulf*); earlier in the compound *horsthegn* horse servant or groom (about 700); cognate with Old Frisian *hors* horse, Old Saxon *hros,* Middle Low German *ros, ors,* Middle Dutch *ors* (modern Dutch *ros* steed), Old High German *hros* horse (modern German, in literary use, *Ross* horse, steed), and Old Icelandic *hross* horse, from Proto-Germanic **Húrsa-,* cognate with Latin *currere* run, Gaulish *carros* wagon, and Greek *epí-kouros* running to help, from Indo-European **k̑ers-/k̑ors-/k̑r̥s-* (Pok.583). **—v.** provide with a horse or horses. About 1330 *horsen,* developed from Old English (1013) *horsian,* from *hors,* n. The sense of make fun of, play jokes on, is first recorded in 1901. **—horseback** *n.* (especially *on horseback;* before 1393, in Gower's *Confessio Amantis*) **—horsefly** *n.* (before 1382, in Wycliffe's writings) **—horsehide** *n.* (before 1325 *hors hide,* in *Cursor Mundi*) **—horselaugh** *n.* (1713, in Steele's writings) **—horseman** *n.* (probably before 1200 *horsman*) **—horseplay** *n.* (1589) **—horsepower** *n.* (1806 *horse power,* in American English; later, as a mechanical unit, 1823) **—horse sense** (1870, in American English **—horseshoe** *n.* (before 1387; as a proper name, 1221)

hortatory (hôr′tətôr′ē) *adj.* giving advice, exhorting. 1586, borrowed, possibly through Middle French *hortatoire,* and directly from Late Latin *hortātōrius* encouraging, cheering, from *hortātus,* past participle of Latin *hortārī* exhort, encourage, an intensive form of *horīrī* urge; see YEARN; for suffix see -ORY.

horticulture *n.* science of growing flowers, fruits, vegetables, etc. 1678, formed in English from Latin *hortus* garden + English *culture;* probably patterned on *agriculture.* Latin *hortus,* cognate with Greek *chórtos* enclosed place, farmyard, and Irish *gort* crop, is from Indo-European **ĝhortos,* root **ĝher-* encompass (Pok.442). **—horticulturist** *n.* 1818, formed from English *horticulture* + *-ist.*

hosanna (hōzan′ə) *interj.* Before 1325, shout of praise to the Lord, in *Cursor Mundi;* developed from Old English *osanna* (before 1050, in the *West Saxon Gospels*); borrowed from Medieval Latin *osanna,* from Late Latin *hōsanna,* from Greek *hōsanná,* from Hebrew *hōsha'nā,* probably a shortened form of *hōshī'āh-nnā* save, we pray; in Rabbinical Hebrew the word was used as a noun to refer to the willow branches used on the holiday of Tabernacles. **—n.** a shout of "hosanna." 1641, in Milton's *Reason of Church Government;* from the interjection.

The spelling *hosanna* (with the initial *h*) was adopted in the 1500's in imitation of the Latin, Greek, and Hebrew.

hose *n.* stockings, flexible rubber tube. Probably before 1200 *hose,* in Layamon's *Chronicle of Britain;* developed from Late Old English (before 1100) *hosa* covering for the leg; cognate with Old Saxon, Old High German, and Old Icelandic *hosa* leg covering (modern German *Hose* trousers), and Middle Dutch *hose* leggings, waterspout, from Proto-Germanic **Húsan-,* from Indo-European **kus-,* root **keus-* cover, hide (Pok.953). The meaning of a flexible rubber tube to carry liquid is first recorded in 1339 (too early to be influenced by Dutch *hoos* water pipe or spout, about 1600). **—v.** Before 1300, furnish with a leg covering, from *hosen,* n. The meaning of water with a hose is first recorded in 1889. **—hosier** (hō′zhər) *n.* 1381 *hosyere;* earlier, in the surname *Hosier* (1195); formed from English *hose,* n. + *-ier.* **—hosiery** *n.* 1789, business of a hosier; 1790, stockings; formed from English *hosier* + *-y*[3].

hospice (hos′pis) *n.* 1818, a rest house for travelers; borrowed from French *hospice,* learned borrowing from Latin *hospitium* guest house, hospitality, from *hospes* (genitive *hospitis*) guest, HOST[1].

In the 1890's the meaning of a rest house was extended to that of a home for the destitute or the sick. *Hospice,* with the new meaning of an institution for the care of the terminally ill, appeared in Great Britain in the 1970's and in the United States in 1976.

hospitable (hospit′əbəl) *adj.* showing hospitality. 1570, borrowed from Middle French *hospitable,* with a change of suffix from older *hospital* hospitable, as if from Medieval Latin **hospitabilis,* from Latin *hospitārī* be a guest, from *hospes* (genitive *hospitis*) guest; see HOST[1]; for suffix see -ABLE.

hospital *n.* About 1300 *hospital;* earlier, in the place name *Ospitol* (1242-43); borrowed from Old French *hospital,* learned borrowing from Medieval Latin *hospitale* guesthouse, inn, neuter form of Latin *hospitālis* of a guest or host, hospitable, from *hospes* (genitive *hospitis*) guest, HOST[1]; for suffix see -AL[1]. Doublet of HOSTEL and HOTEL.

Originally *hospital* meant guest house and shelter for the needy; later it developed the meaning of an institution for sick people (1549).

—hospitalize *v.* 1901, formed from English *hospital* + *-ize,* possibly after earlier French *hospitaliser.*

hospitality *n.* friendly treatment of guests or strangers. About 1384 *hospitalite,* in the Wycliffe Bible; earlier, in Scottish, *hospitalyte;* borrowed from Old French *hospitalité,* learned borrowing from Latin *hospitālitātem* (nominative *hospitālitās*) friendliness to guests, from *hospes* (genitive *hospitis*) guest, HOST[1].

host[1] *n.* person who receives another as his guest. About 1250 *oste;* also, in the surname *Host* (1254); borrowed from Old French *oste, hoste* guest, host, from Latin *hospitem* guest, host, nominative *hospes,* altered (on the pattern *mīlitem: mīles*) from **hospos,* cognate with Old Bulgarian *gospodĭ* lord, from Indo-European **ghosti-pot-s* in charge of the stranger, from **ghostis* (compare Latin *hostis* stranger) + **pótis* master (compare Latin *potis* able, and Sanskrit *páti-s* master); see GUEST. **—v.** Probably 1421 *osten;* later *hosten* (about 1450); from the noun. **—hostess** *n.* About 1300 *hostesse;* borrowed from Old French *hostesse,* from *hoste* host; for suffix see -ESS.

host[2] *n.* large number, multitude. 1265 *host* multitude of armed men; borrowed from Old French *ost, oost, host,* from Medieval Latin *hostis* army, warlike expedition, from Latin *hostis* enemy, stranger; see GUEST. The generalized meaning of a large number is first recorded in *Purchas his Pilgrimage* (1613).

Host *n.* bread or wafer regarded as the body of Christ. About 1303 *oste,* in Mannyng's *Handlyng Synne;* later *hoste* (about 1340); borrowed probably directly from Latin *hostia* sacrifice, the animal sacrificed; of unknown origin (possibly related to *hostīre* requite).

hostage *n.* person given or held as security that a prom ise or agreement will be kept. About 1300 *hostage,* in Layamon's *Chronicle of Britain;* earlier *ostage* (in *Kyng Alisaunder*); borrowed from Old French *ostage, hostage* person given as security or hostage (apparently originally, a lodger held by a landlord as security), from *oste, hoste* guest, host; for suffix see -AGE. The modern sense of a person seized by a political group, criminal, etc., to obtain money, safe passage, or achieve a political goal, is first recorded in the 1970's.

hostel *n.* lodging place. About 1250 *hostel, ostel;* earlier, in the surname *Ostel* (1232); borrowed from Old French *hostel,* from Medieval Latin *hospitale* inn, large house; see HOSPITAL. Doublet of HOSPITAL. **—hostelry** *n.* Before 1387-95 *hostelrye* inn, guesthouse, in Chaucer's *Canterbury Tales;* earlier, in the surname *Ostelrye* (1315); borrowed from Old French *hostelerie,* from *hostel* hostel; for suffix see -RY.

hostile *adj.* 1594, in Shakespeare's *Richard III,* borrowed through Middle French *hostile* of or belonging to an enemy, or directly from Latin *hostīlis,* from *hostis* enemy; see GUEST. **—hostility** *n.* Probably before 1425 *hostilite;* borrowed through Middle French *hostilité* enmity, or directly from Late Latin *hostīlitātem* (nominative *hostīlitās*) enmity, from *hostīlis* hostile; for suffix see -ITY.

hostler *n.* person who cares for horses at an inn or stable. Before 1376 *hostiler,* in *Piers Plowman;* earlier, innkeeper (1350); borrowed through Anglo-French *hostiler,* Old French *hostelier* (from Old French *hostel* inn + *-ier* -ier), and from Medieval Latin *hostilarius, hostellarius* the monk who entertained guests at a monastery, specialized form of *hospitalarius* one who entertains guests, from *hospitale* inn; see HOSPITAL.

hot *adj.* Probably before 1200 *hote;* earlier *hate* (about 1150); developed from Old English (971) *hāt* hot, fervent, spirited, fierce; cognate with Old Frisian and Old Saxon *hēt* hot, Middle Dutch and modern Dutch *heet,* Old High German *heiz* (modern German *heiss*), Old Icelandic *heitr* (Swedish and Norwegian *het,* Danish *hed*), Gothic *heitō* fever, and Lithuanian *kaĩsti* to get hot. Related to HEAT. The so-called short *o* in *hot* began to appear in the 1550's, possibly by influence of the "short-o" sound found in the comparative *hotter* in Middle English. Several of the derivative senses of *hot* have appeared in American English, most notably the sense of exciting, remarkable, very good, in Stephen Crane's *Red Badge of Courage* (1895), and that of something stolen, obtained illegally, in 1925. **—hotbed** *n.* 1626, bed of earth for forcing growing plants; 1768, place where anything develops rapidly. **—hot cake** (1683, in American English) **—hot dog** (1900, in American English) **—hotfoot** *v.* to move swiftly. 1896, in American English, probably from the adverb; *adv.* Before 1300, swiftly. **—hot rod** 1945, in American English, automobile with the engine modified for faster starts and higher speeds. **—hot water** trouble (1537).

hotel *n.* 1765, in Smollett's *Travels Through France and Italy;* earlier, a student residence at a university (1748); borrowed from French *hôtel,* from Old French *hostel* a lodging, from Medieval Latin *hospitale* inn; see HOSTEL. Doublet of HOSPITAL. **—hotelier** (hō′təlir′) *n.* hotelkeeper. 1905, borrowing of French *hôtelier,* from Old French *hostelier,* from *hostel* inn; for suffix see -IER.

hound *n.* About 1250 *hound;* earlier *hund* (1127); developed from Old English *hund* dog (about 725, in *Beowulf*); cognate with Old Frisian and Old Saxon *hund* dog, modern Dutch *hond,* Old High German *hunt* (modern German *Hund*), Old Icelandic *hundr,* and Gothic *hunds;* all derived from Proto-Germanic *Hunđas.* Further cognates are Old Irish *cū* dog, Welsh *ci,* pl. *cwn,* Latin *canis,* Greek *kýōn* (genitive *kynós*), Lithuanian *šuõ,* Armenian *šun,* Persian *sag,* Sanskrit *śvā́* (genitive *śúnas*), Avestan *spā,* Tocharian A and Tocharian B *ku,* from Indo-European (nominative) **k̂(ú)wō(n),* (genitive **k̂unós* (Pok. 633).

The original meaning of dog was narrowed in Middle English, before 1127, to refer to a dog used for hunting. **—v.** 1528, to hunt with hounds; from the noun. Figurative senses of this meaning developed in urge on, incite, first recorded in 1570, and in pursue unrelentingly, found in Bacon's *Of the Advancement of Learning* (1605).

hour *n.* Before 1338 *houre,* in Mannyng's *Chronicle of England;* earlier *our* (before 1300), *ure* (probably before 1200, in *Ancrene Riwle*); borrowed from Old French *hore, ore, ure,* from Latin *hōra* hour, time, season, from Greek *hṓrā;* see YEAR. According to the OED, the *h* is purely a spelling convention, and though it appears in French, Spanish, and English, it has not represented an actual sound in this form since Roman times. **—hourglass** *n.* (about 1515 *our glasse*)

house (hous) *n.* About 1250 *house;* earlier *huse* (before 1121); developed from Old English *hūs* dwelling, shelter, house (about 725, in *Beowulf*); cognate with Old Frisian and Old Saxon *hūs* house, Middle Dutch *huus* (modern Dutch *huis*), Old High German *hūs* (modern German *Haus*), Old Icelandic *hūs,* and Gothic *-hūs* in *gudhūs* temple, from Proto-Germanic **Hūsan,* related to Old English *hosa* stocking, pod, from Indo-European **keu-/ku-/kewə-/kū-* cover, wrap around (Pok.953). —v. (houz) About 1300 *housen* receive into a house, give shelter; earlier *husen* (about 1125); developed from Old English (about 1000) *hūsian,* from *hūs,* n. **—housebroken** *adj.* trained to defecate and urinate outside, as a pet dog or cat is (1900). **—housefly** *n.* (before 1450) **—household** *n., adj.* (probably about 1380) **—House of Commons** (1621, James I in *Lettre to the Speaker;* from earlier *commons* the people, about 1330) **—House of Representatives** (1692, American English, in reference to the legislature of the Colony of Massachusetts) **—housewarming** *n.* (about 1150, possibly fuel for heating a house; later, celebration, 1577) **—housewife** *n.* (probably before 1200)

housing[1] (hou′zing) *n.* About 1350 *housinge* buildings or houses collectively, shelter, dwelling, lodging; earlier *husing* (before 1325, in *Cursor Mundi*); derived from Middle English *huse, hous* + *-ing*[1]. It is interesting to note that *house,* n. is recorded as early as 1250, but there is no record of that spelling in this noun use *(housing)* before 1350.

housing[2] (hou′zing) *n.* 1782, ornamental covering for a horse, American English, in John Adams' *Diary;* from earlier *housings, pl.,* a covering or trappings, especially of cloth; derived from Middle English *houce* (1312-13), *house* (about 1475) a covering for the back and flanks of a horse; borrowed from Old French *houce* (modern French *housse*), from Medieval Latin *hultia* (earlier **hulftia),* from Frankish **Hulftī;* compare Middle Dutch *hulfte* pocket for bow and arrow, and Middle High German *hulft* covering. By the time of Adams' use, the sense of covering for a horse may have merged sufficiently with *housing*[1] to be the same word as that used for any case or enclosure for a machine or part, which is first recorded in 1882.

hovel *n.* house that is small and crude. 1358 *hovel* a roofed passage or vent for smoke; later, a little cottage, hut (1440, in *Promptorium Parvulorum*), and a shed for animals (1425); of uncertain origin. **—v.** lodge in a hovel. 1583, from the noun.

hover *v.* About 1400 *hoveren,* in Lydgate's *Troy Book;* a frequentative form of earlier *hoven* hover, tarry, linger (1250, in *Bestiary*); of uncertain origin; for suffix see -ER[4]. **—n.** act of hovering. 1513 *hovir;* from the verb.

how *adv.* Probably before 1200 *hou* as an adverb, in Layamon's *Chronicle of Britain;* later *how* in what way (probably before 1300); developed from Old English *hū* (about 725, in a version of *Exodus*); cognate with Old Frisian *hū, hō* how, Old Saxon *hwuo, hwō,* Middle Dutch and modern Dutch *hoe,* and Old High German *hwuo,* from Proto-Germanic **Hwō-*, cognate with Latin *quō whither,* and Greek *pō* somehow, from Indo-European **kwō* (Pok.644) A parallel formation is represented by Middle Dutch *hū* how, Old High German *hwio* (modern German *wie*), and Gothic *hwaiwa.* All forms are related to Old English *hwā* WHO.

In the numerous interrogatives reflecting Indo-European **kw-*, most retain the *w* (in some instances the *h* and the *w*); but *who* and *how* lose the *w* in pronunciation, retaining only the *h* (from Indo-European **k-*).

—however *conj., adv.* 1392 *how euere* no matter how, to what extent; and *how ever* in whatever manner (before 1400); later, in any case (1591, in Shakespeare's *Two Gentlemen of Verona*); formed from Middle English *how,* adv. + *ever,* adv.

howitzer (hou'itsər) *n.* short cannon. 1695 *hauwitzer;* also *howitz* (1687); borrowed from Dutch *houwitser,* or directly from German *Haubitze;* earlier *Haubnitze* from early modern German *haufnitz* a catapult, from Czech *houfnice;* introduced during the Hussite wars.

howl *v.* Probably before 1300 *houlen,* in *Kyng Alisaunder;* earlier *hulen* (before 1250, in *Bestiary*); probably of imitative origin, and parallel with Middle Dutch *hūlen* to howl (modern Dutch *huilen*), and Middle High German *hiulen, hiuweln* to howl like an owl (modern German *heulen*), possibly connected with Old High German *hūwila* owl. **—n.** 1599, in Shakespeare's *Henry V;* from the verb. **—howler** *n.* 1840, animal that howls; formed from English *howl,* v. + *-er*[1]. The sense of a severe storm with much wind is first recorded in 1872, and that of a glaring blunder, ridiculous mistake, in 1890.

hoyden *n.* boisterous girl, tomboy. 1593, rude, boorish fellow, in Nashe's *Four Letters Confuted;* perhaps borrowed from Dutch *heiden* rustic, uncultivated man, from Middle Dutch *heiden* HEATHEN. The meaning of *hoyden* as a rude, boisterous female, is first recorded in 1676; the attributive or adjective use in 1728, and the derivative *hoydenish* in 1780.

hub *n.* central part of a wheel. 1649, probably a word earlier confined to wheelwrights' vocabulary and perhaps developing from an unrecorded early sense of *hub* (1600), *hubbe* (1511) the hob of a fireplace, originally, mass, lump; or from the sense of peg or pin (1589); of unknown origin. Until the 1800's the record shows *hub* as a dialectal word, becoming generally known in connection with bicycles. The figurative meaning of any center of interest, activity, importance, etc., is first recorded by Oliver Wendell Holmes in *The Autocrat of the Breakfast-table* (1858).

hubbub *n.* uproar. 1555 *whobub* confused noise, hue and cry; of uncertain origin (sometimes referred to as an Irish outcry, which would suggest it represents an interjection of Celtic origin such as Gaelic *ub! ub! ubub!* an expression of aversion or contempt, or Irish *abu!* an ancient war cry).

hubris (hyü'bris) *n.* insolent pride, arrogance. 1884, possibly a back formation from earlier *hubristic,* or a borrowing from Greek *hýbris* wanton violence, insolence, outrage; of unknown origin. **—hubristic** *adj.* full of hubris. 1831, borrowed from Greek *hybristikós* insolent, wanton, from *hybrízein* to insult, act outrageously, from *hýbris* wanton violence, insolence.

huckleberry *n.* small dark berry. 1670 *huckelberry,* American English, probably an alteration of Middle English *hurtilbery* whortleberry (1452-54, a compound of *hurtil-*, probably diminutive of Old English *horte* whortleberry + *bery* berry).

huckster *n.* Probably about 1200 *hucster* peddler, petty merchant, in *The Ormulum;* probably developed from Old English (compare *hukken* to sell or peddle, recorded since 1181 in personal names; and *hucking,* probably before 1300, in *Arthour and Merlin;* cognate with Middle Dutch *hokester* peddler, from *hoken* to peddle, HAWK[2] sell). The derogatory sense of a person willing to profit in a petty way is first recorded in 1553, and the sense in American English of a person in the advertising industry, in 1946. **—v.** peddle, haggle. 1592, from the noun. **—hucksterism** *n.* practices of a huckster. 1951, American English, formed from *huckster,* n. + *-ism.*

huddle *v.* 1579, crowd close; earlier, as an adverb *hudle* confusedly (1564, in Coverdale's writings); probably related to *hoderen* heap together or huddle (about 1300), and cognate with Low German *hudern* to cover or shelter, Middle Low German *hūden* to cover up, HIDE[1]. **—n.** crowded mass or heap. 1586; apparently from the verb. An earlier sense of a miserly, old person is recorded in 1579, but has only the barest relationship with the general sense of this word.

hue[1] *n.* color. Probably before 1200 *hewe;* later *heu* (about 1250); developed from Old English *hīw* color, form, appearance, beauty (before 899, in Alfred's works); earlier *hīow, hēow* (before 830, in the *Vespasian Psalter*), *hīo* (before 800), and *hēo* (about 750, in Cynewulf's *Elene*). The Old English forms are cognate with Old Icelandic *hȳ* down or complexion (Swedish and Norwegian dialect *hy* complexion), and Gothic *hiwi* form or appearance, from Proto-Germanic **Hiwjan,* from Indo-European **k̑iwyom* color, root **k̑ei-/k̑oi-/k̑i-* (Pok.540). As the pronunciation changed in Middle English, so did the spelling from early *hewe* to later *heu* (1250) and thence to the form *hwe* (probably by 1420) to *hue* (about 1450), but this latter spelling was not fully established until the late 1600's, possibly influenced by the French spelling seen in HUE[2].

hue[2] *n.* a shouting. Probably before 1200 *hiue* outcry, clamor, trumpet, blast, in Layamon's *Chronicle of Britain;* later *hue* (probably about 1380); borrowed from Old French *hue, hu* outcry, noise, war cry, hunting cry; probably of imitative origin.

The phrase *hue and cry* appeared in 1246 as an Anglo-French legal term with the meaning of outcry calling for the pursuit of a felon, and was extended to the general sense of cry of alarm or outcry by 1584.

huff *v.* 1583, to puff or blow; earlier, as an interjection *huf* (about 1450); apparently a word imitative of the sound of blowing or of a blast of air. The extended sense of to puff or swell with indignation, to storm, bluster, is first recorded in 1598, in Ben Jonson's *Every Man in His Humour* and Florio's *A World of Words.* —**n.** 1599, a gust or sudden swell of anger or arrogance; from the verb. —**huffy** *adj.* 1677, blustering; 1680, arrogant, ready to take offense, in Bunyan's *Life and Death of Mr. Badman;* from *huff,* n. + *-y[1].*

hug *v.* 1567 *hugge* to embrace in Drant's translation of Horace's *Art of Poetry;* of uncertain origin (perhaps from a Scandinavian source; compare Old Icelandic *hugga* to comfort). —**n.** 1617, a hold in wrestling; from the verb. The meaning of an embrace is first recorded in 1659.

huge *adj.* Probably about 1150 *huge* extremely large; borrowed apparently as a shortened form of Old French *ahuge* extremely large; of unknown origin.

Huguenot (hyü'gənot) *n.* French Protestant of the 1500's to 1800's. 1565, borrowed from Middle French *huguenot,* the name used in the early 1520's for the Genevan partisans who opposed the Duke of Savoy. The name *Huguenot,* earlier *eiguenot,* was probably an alteration of Swiss German *Eidgenoss* confederate (modern German *Eidgenosse*), from Middle High German *eitgenōze (eit* OATH + *genōze* comrade, from Old High German *ginōzo,* related to *niozan* use, enjoy*).* The Middle French *Huguenot* was re-formed from *eiguenot* probably by association with the name *Hugues* Besançon, leader of the Genevan partisans.

hula (hü'lə) or **hula-hula** *n.* native Hawaiian dance. About 1835, borrowed from Hawaiian *hula* or *hulahula,* a reduplication of *hula.* —v. to dance the hula. 1952, American English; from the noun.

hulk *n.* 1338 *hulk* a trading ship, warship; developed from Old English (about 1050) *hulc* light, fast ship; probably borrowed from Old Dutch *hulke* and from Medieval Latin *hulcus,* from Greek *holkás* merchant ship, from *hélkein* to drag or draw, related to *holkós* furrow. The Greek word is cognate with Latin *sulcus* furrow, and Old English *sulh* furrow, from Indo-European **selk-/solk-/sl̥k-* (Pok.901)

The meaning of a big, clumsy person, is found in *Morte Arthur* (probably before 1400, and probably first recorded as a surname *Hulkebon,* 1316), and that of the body of an old or worn-out ship appears in Dryden's *An Evening's Love* (1671).

—**v.** About 1793, to lounge about; later, loom bulkily (1880); from the noun.

—**hulking** *adj.* big, clumsy. 1698, formed from English *hulk,* n. + *-ing[1].*

hull[1] *n.* outer covering of a seed. Before 1398 *hulle,* in Trevisa's translation of Bartholomew's *De Proprietatibus Rerum;* earlier *hoyle* (1373); developed from Old English (about 1000) *hulu;* from Proto-Germanic **Hulús,* from Indo-European **k̂elú-s,* root **k̂el-/k̂ol-/k̂ēl-/k̂l̥-* (Pok.553); cognate with Old High German *hulla* covering (modern German *Hülle* covering, hull), and with Old High German *hulsa* husk, pod (modern German *Hülse*) and Dutch *huls* hull, these latter formed with the *-s* suffix. —**v.** remove the hull or hulls from. Probably before 1425 *hullen;* earlier *holen* (before 1338, in Mannyng's *Chronicle of England*); from the noun.

hull[2] *n.* body or frame of a ship. 1571, of uncertain origin (perhaps an extended use of *hull[1]*). It is also suggested that this word is the same as Middle English *hoole* a ship's keel or hull (about 1440, in *Promptorium Parvulorum*), probably from the same source as HOLD[2] (interior of a ship).

hullabaloo *n.* 1762 *hollo-ballo* uproar, in Smollett's *Adventures of Sir Launcelot Greaves,* appearing at first chiefly in Scottish and Northern English sources; possibly a rhyming reduplication of the interjection *hollo, holla* (see HELLO).

hum *v.* About 1385 *hommen* make a murmuring sound to cover up embarrassment, in Chaucer's *Troilus and Criseyde;* later *hummen* to buzz, drone (probably 1440, in *Promptorium Parvulorum*); probably of imitative origin and parallel to Middle High German *hummen* and Dutch *hommelen* to hum.

The meaning of sing with closed lips, is first recorded in 1640. In American English, the sense of to be busy and active (1884, in Mark Twain's *Huckleberry Finn*) developed from the earlier meaning of giving forth an indistinct sound by the blending of many voices (1726). —**n.** 1469, murmuring sound to cover up embarrassment or hesitation; from the verb. The first reference to an indistinct sound or murmur is found in Shakespeare's *Henry V* (1599), and to a singing with closed lips in Ben Jonson's *New Inn* (1630).

human *adj.* Probably about 1450 *humaigne, humayne* of or belonging to man; borrowed from Middle French *humain,* learned borrowing from Latin *hūmānus,* probably related to *homō* (genitive *hominis*) man, human being, from Old Latin *hemō* (accusative *hemōnem*), cognate with Oscan **homō(n).* Latin *homō* is cognate with Old English *guma* man (which did not survive into Middle English except in the form *bridegome* bridegroom, from Old English *brȳdguma*), Old High German *gomo,* Old Icelandic *gumi,* and Gothic *guma,* from Proto-Germanic **ʒuman-,* also cognate with Old Lithuanian *žmuõ* (plural *žmónės*), Old Prussian *smoy,* and Tocharian B *śaumo,* from Indo-European **ĝhemō(n)/ĝhomō(n)/ĝhemon-/ĝhmō(n)* earthling (compare Latin *humus* earth) (Pok.415). —**n.** man, human being. Before 1533, from the adjective.

humane *adj.* kind, merciful. Probably about 1450 *humaigne* of or belonging to man; later *humayne* having qualities befitting human beings, gentle, friendly, courteous (about 1500); variant of HUMAN.

In the early 1700's, this word became restricted in use to the meaning kind, merciful. See the note under HUMAN. For about 250 years *human* and *humane* shared the meaning "of or belonging to man," but in the 1700's the meanings differentiated with the spellings and the separate pronunciations so that *human* with its stress on the first syllable, retained the original sense and *humane* with its stress on the last syllable, became restricted to the sense of merciful, kind. The process of a differentiation of meaning, however, was gradual, beginning about 1500.

humanism *n.* The first appearance of this word was in Coleridge, quoted in Southey's *Omniana* (1812) with reference to the belief in the mere humanity of Christ, possibly as a borrowing of French *humanisme* (1763). However, *humanism* has been used in association with several systems of philosophical thought or action. In the sense of the Renaissance revival of interest in the classics, *humanism* appeared in 1832, patterned on the earlier (1589) *humanist,* meaning a classical scholar, borrowed from Middle French *humaniste,* from Latin *hūmānus* HUMAN. *Humanism,* as a pragmatic system of thought, was introduced in 1903 by C.S. Schiller, an English philosopher who wrote in 1907, "Humanism . . .is merely the perception that the philosophic problem concerns human beings striving to comprehend a world of human experience by the resources of human minds." **—humanistic** *adj.* (1845) **—humanize** *v.* (1603) **—humankind** *n.* (about 1645, patterned after *mankind*) **—humanly** *adv.* 1613 *humanely,* in *Purchas his Pilgrimage;* formed from English *human,* adj. + *-ly*[1].

humanity *n.* About 1384 *humanite* kindness, graciousness, in the Wycliffe Bible; borrowed from Old French *humanité,* from Latin *hūmānitātem* (nominative *hūmānitās*) human nature, humanity, from *hūmānus* HUMAN; for suffix see -ITY. The meaning of mankind or the human race, is first recorded as *humanyte* (about 1450). **—humanitarian** *n.* 1819, one who affirms the humanity of Christ; formed from English *humanity* + *-arian,* as in *unitarian, trinitarian.* The meaning of one who devotes himself to human welfare, a philanthropist, is first recorded in 1844 and was originally disparaging, connoting one who goes to excess in his humane principles.

humble *adj.* About 1275 *umble* modest, not proud; later *humble* (about 1375, in Chaucer's *Canterbury Tales*); borrowed from Old French *umble, humble,* earlier *humele,* learned borrowing from Latin *humilis* lowly, humble, from *humus* earth; see HUMUS. The introduction of *b* in Old French is typical of the vowel loss between *m* and *l* in a borrowed word such as *humble* or *semblable.* **—v.** make humble. About 1380; from the adjective.

humblebee *n.* Before 1475 *humbulbe* bumblebee, a compound of *humbul-* (cognate with Middle Low German *hummelbe* humblebee, and Middle Dutch *hommelbij,* related to *hommelen* to HUM) + *bee.* The formation in Middle English was probably influenced by earlier *humble* to hum or buzz (before 1384, in Chaucer's *House of Fame*).

humble pie The word *umbles,* recorded in English since about 1450, was itself a variant of *numbles* (1333-34, in *Ancrene Riwle*), and earlier *noubles* (probably before 1300), which was borrowed from Old French *nombles, numbles* loin or fillet, apparently an alteration of **lumbles* (by agglutination of the indefinite article), from Latin *lumbulus,* diminutive of *lumbus* LOIN.

The expression *eat humble pie,* meaning to be forced to do something very disagreeable or humiliating, appeared in 1830 and was clearly influenced in meaning by the adjective *humble.* The term *humble pie,* however, existed earlier (before 1648) as a spelling variant of *umble pie* (1663, in Pepys' *Diary*) and meant a pie made from the *umbles* or edible inner parts of a deer or other animal and considered a food of inferiors. Hence the expression arose as a fusion of *umble pie* and *humble,* adj.

humbug *n.* fraud, sham. 1751, a slang word among students meaning a hoax, jest, trick, or deception; of unknown origin. The word came into vogue in England about 1750 among fashionable people, but its origin was lost before it attracted attention. The meaning of a person who practices deception, a fraud, is first recorded in 1804. **—v.** to practice humbug on, to trick. 1751, from the noun.

humdinger *n.* superlative person or thing. 1905, American English slang; possibly from *hum* a murmur of approbation + *dinger,* American English dialect or slang, something superlative (1809, from *ding* to beat, surpass, excel, 1724; from Middle English *dingen* to beat + *-er*[1]).

humdrum *adj.* 1553, monotonous; dull, varied reduplication of HUM, v., to make a continuous sound, possibly with the second element influenced by *drum.*

humerus (hyü′mərəs) *n. Anatomy.* long bone in the upper part of the forelimb or arm. 1706, in Kersey's edition of Phillips' *Dictionary;* originally, shoulder (1392); borrowed from Latin *umerus* (misspelled *humerus*) shoulder; cognate with Greek *ômos* shoulder, Armenian *us,* Sanskrit *áṁsa-s,* Tocharian A *es,* and Tocharian B *āntse;* also cognate with Gothic *ams* shoulder, from Indo-European **ómesos, ómsos, ṓmsos* (Pok.778).

humid *adj.* moist, damp. Before 1400 *humide,* in Lanfranc's *Science of Surgery;* borrowed through Old French *humide, umide,* or directly from Latin *ūmidus* (with variant *hūmidus,* by influence of *humus* earth), from *ūmēre* be moist; see HUMOR. **—humidify** *v.* 1885; formed from English *humid* + *-fy.* **—humidity** *n.* 1392 *humidite;* borrowed from Old French *humidité,* from Latin *hūmiditātem* (nominative *hūmiditās*), from *hūmidus* humid; for suffix see -ITY. **—humidor** *n.* place where cigars or tobacco are kept moist. 1903, formed from English *humid* + *-or*[2], patterned on *cuspidor.*

humiliate *v.* 1533-34, probably a back formation from *humiliation,* after Latin *humiliāre,* from *humilis* HUMBLE; for suffix see -ATE[1]. **—humiliation** *n.* About 1390 *humyliacioun,* in Chaucer's *Canterbury Tales;* borrowed from Old French *humiliation,* from Late Latin *humiliātiōnem* (nominative *humiliātiō*), from Latin *humiliāre;* for suffix see -ATION. **—humility** *n.* Probably before 1300 *humilite;* borrowed from Old French *humilité, umilité,* from Latin *humilitātem* (nominative *humilitās*), from *humilis* humble; for suffix see -ITY.

hummock (hum′ək) *n.* small hill, hillock. 1608; earlier *hoommocke* (1555), *hammock* (1556); originally a nautical term with the meaning of conical hillock on the seacoast. The first element is of uncertain origin; the second element *-ock* is a diminutive suffix.

humongous (hyümung′gəs) *adj.* extremely large or great, tremendous. 1976, American English slang, apparently a fanciful coinage from *huge* and *monstrous.*

humor *n.* 1340 *humour* moisture, body fluid; borrowed from Old French *humor, umor,* learned borrowing from Latin *ūmor* (also *hūmor* by fancied connection with *humus* earth) body fluid, related to *ūmēre* be wet, moist, and with *ūvēscere* become wet; cognate with Greek *hygrós* wet, Sanskrit *ukṣáti* he sprinkles; also cognate with Old Icelandic *vǫkr* damp. Latin *ūmor* and *ūmēre* are probably built on a lost adjective **ūmus,* from **ūgw-smos,* from Indo-European **wegw-/wogw-/ugw-/ūgw-/ukws-* (Pok.1118).

In Middle English, *humor* referred to any liquid or moisture, and specifically to one of the four body fluids (blood, phlegm, choler, and melancholy or black bile), the relative proportions of which were thought to determine mental disposition. The meaning of mood, state of mind, which developed from this earlier sense, is first recorded in 1525. The sense of a funny or amusing quality, jocularity, is found in 1682, and developed

probably by way of whim, caprice, recorded in 1565 (a meaning according to OED, that was ridiculed by Shakespeare and Ben Jonson).
—v. give in to the whims of (a person); indulge. 1588, in Shakespeare's *Love's Labour's Lost;* from the noun. **—humorist** *n.* 1596, a whimsical person; 1599, a comical person or wag; probably formed from English *humor* + *-ist,* after Middle French *humoriste.* **—humorous** *adj.* Probably before 1425, relating to the body humors; borrowed from Middle French *humoreux* damp, from Old French *humor, umor* body fluid. The meaning of funny (formed from English *humor,* n. + *-ous*) is first recorded in Addison's *Remarks on Italy* (1705).

hump *n.* 1709, found earlier in the compound *hump-backed* (1681); taking the place of earlier *crump* (recorded in Old English before 800) and corresponding in form to Dutch *homp* lump, Middle Low German *hump* bump, Norwegian *hump* bump, hump, lump, from Proto-Germanic **Hump-;* cognate with Sanskrit *kumba-s* thick end of a bone, Greek *kýmbos* cup, and Old Irish *comm* vessel, from Indo-European **kumb-* (Pok.592). **—v.** 1835, American English slang, exert (oneself) in great effort; from the noun. The meaning of raise into a hump is first recorded in 1840.

humus (hyü′məs) *n.* soil formed from decayed leaves and other vegetable matter. 1796, borrowed probably from French *humus* and directly from Latin *humus* earth, soil (very likely a back formation from *humī* on the ground); cognate with Greek *chamaí* on the ground, and Old Prussian *semmai* down, from Indo-European **ĝhem-/ĝhom-* (Pok.414).

hunch *v.* raise or bend into a hump. Probably before 1500, to push, thrust, shove; of unknown origin.

The meaning of raise or bend into a hump, arch (one's back), is first recorded in Dryden and Lee's *Oedipus* (1678); the same meaning, however, is found in the compound *hunchbacked* as early as 1598, in Shakespeare's *Richard III.* Though the first element in this compound may have been a noun, meaning a hump, rather than the verb, its early appearance suggests that the two meanings, "to push and "a hump" perhaps do not belong to the same word (compare, for example, *bunchbacked* 1519, meaning the same as *hunchbacked*).
—n. 1630, a push, thrust, shove; from the verb. The meaning of a hump, protuberance, is found in 1804, unless the first element in *hunchbacked* (1598) is this noun. The literal sense of push or thrust, gave rise in American English to the figurative sense of a hint or tip, which is first recorded in 1849, followed by the extended meaning of a feeling that something will happen, a premonition or presentiment (1904).
—hunchback *n.* person with a hunched back. 1712, back formation from *hunchbacked.*

hundred *n.* In Old English (about 950) *hundred,* a compound meaning "the count of 100," formed from *hund* 100 + *-red* count, reckoning, and corresponding to Old Frisian *hundred, hunderd,* Old Saxon *hunderod,* Middle Dutch and modern Dutch *honderd,* Old High German *hundert,* modern German *Hundert,* (from Proto-West-Germanic **Húndrađ*), and Old Icelandic *hundradh* one hundred twenty, equivalent to English *great hundred.*

Cognates of *hund,* the common Old English word for 100, are found throughout the Indo-European languages: in Old Saxon *hund,* Old High German *hunt,* and Gothic *hunda, pl,* from Proto-Germanic **Hunđán;* also in Latin *centum,* Greek *hekatón,* Old Irish *cēt,* Welsh *cant,* Old Slavic *sŭto,* Lithuanian *šim̃tas,* Avestan *satəm,* Sanskrit *śatám,* from Indo-European **k̂m̥tóm* (Pok.192); also Tocharian A *känt* and Tocharian B *känte;* all basically meaning "ten times ten" or "ten tenths," and traceable to the Indo-European base **dék̂m̥* plus a dental suffix; see TEN and CENT. Cognates of Old English *-red* appear in Old Icelandic *-rædhr* (in *ni-rædhr* 90) and Gothic *-rathjan* to count or reckon; related to *rathjō* reckoning, number, and Latin *ratiō* calculation; see REASON.
—hundredth *adj.* Before 1325, in *Cursor Mundi;* formed from Middle English *hundred* + *-th²,* possibly by influence of Old Icelandic *hundrædhr* in confusion with Old English variants *hundrath, hundreth* hundred.

hunger *n.* Old English *hungor* pain caused by lack of food, hunger (about 725, in *Genesis A*); cognate with Old Frisian *hunger* hunger, Old Saxon *hungar* (modern Dutch *honger*), Old High German *hungar* (modern German *Hunger*), Old Icelandic *hungr,* from Proto-Germanic **Hunȝrús,* and Gothic *hūhrus* (with loss of *ng* before *h*), from Proto-Germanic **HúnHruz;* also cognate with Lithuanian *keñkti* to pain, and Greek *kénkei* he is hungry, from Indo-European **kenk-/kn̥k-* (Pok.565). **—v.** feel hunger. About 1250 *hungren;* earlier *hungeren* (probably before 1200, in *Ancrene Riwle*); developed from Old English (before 830) *hyngrian, hyngran;* cognate with Old Frisian *hungera* to hunger, Old Saxon *gihungrian,* Middle Low German and Middle Dutch *hungeren* (modern Dutch *hongeren*), Old High German *hungaren* (modern German *hungern*), Old Icelandic *hungra,* and Gothic *huggrjan* (in which *gg* represents *ng*). **—hungry** *adj.* About 1150 *hungri,* developed from Old English (about 950) *hungrig (hunger* hunger + *-ig* -y¹*).*

hunk *n.* Before 1813, possibly borrowed from Flemish *hunke,* which is perhaps related to Dutch *homp* lump, HUMP.

hunker *v.* to squat, crouch. 1720, Scottish, possibly from a Scandinavian source (compare Old Icelandic *hūka* to crouch, *hoka, hokra* to crawl; see HAWK² peddle). The phrase *hunker down* to keep down or away from the center of action, to withdraw or settle back, was originally a southwestern U.S. dialectal use popularized about 1965 by President Lyndon B. Johnson. **—n. hunkers,** *pl.* haunches. 1785, in Burns' *Jolly Beggars;* derived from *hunker.*

hunky-dory *adj.* 1866, American English slang, all right, satisfactory, fine; perhaps an irregular reduplication of *hunkey* all right, satisfactory (1861), from earlier *hunk* in a safe position, all right (1847), adjective use of dialectal (New York) noun *hunk* goal or home (in children's games). *Hunk* was borrowed from Dutch *honk* goal or home, from Middle Dutch *honc* place of refuge or hiding place, probably originally Frisian (compare West Frisian *honcke, honck* house, place of refuge, abode, East Frisian *hunk* corner, nook, retreat; also home, in a game).

hunt *v.* 1127 *hunten;* developed from Old English (about 1000) *huntian* chase wild animals and game; related to *hentan* to seize; see HINT. **—n.** Before 1131, one who hunts; later, act of hunting (about 1375); from the verb. **—hunter** *n.* About 1250 *huntere,* in *The Story of Genesis and Exodus;* earlier, in the place name *Huntercumba* (about 1183); formed from English *hunt,* v.

+ *-er*[1]. *Hunter* replaced earlier *hunte* (1127), developed from Old English (before 900) *hunta.*

hurdle *n.* Probably before 1300 *hirdle* frame or lattice, in *Kyng Alisaunder;* later *hurdel* (1356); developed from Old English (about 725) *hyrdel* frame of intertwined twigs (used as a temporary barrier), diminutive of *hyrd* door; cognate with Old Saxon *hurth* plaiting or netting (modern Dutch *horde* wickerwork), Old High German *hurd* (modern German *Hürde* hurdle), Old Icelandic *hurdh* door, and Gothic *haúrds,* all of these from Proto-Germanic **Hurđís,* exactly cognate with Latin *crātis* wickerwork, hurdle, from Indo-European **kr̥tís* (Pok.584). The meaning of a barrier to jump over in a race is first recorded in 1833, and the figurative sense of an obstacle, difficulty, in 1924. **—v.** 1598, to construct like a hurdle, in Florio's *A World of Words;* from the noun. The meaning of jump over is first recorded in American English, in George Ade's *Artie* (1896).

hurdy-gurdy *n.* 1749, a guitar-like instrument having strings and keys as stops, played by cranking a handle; perhaps imitative of the sound produced, but more likely influenced by earlier *hirdy-girdy* uproar, confusion (about 1500). The meaning of a musical instrument played by turning a handle, barrel organ, is first recorded in Thackeray's *English Humorists of the Eighteenth Century* (1851).

hurl *v.* Probably before 1200 *hurlen* to rush violently, in *Ancrene Riwle;* later, to knock or throw forcibly (about 1300); of uncertain origin, but similar in form to Low German *hurreln* to throw or dash, and East Frisian *hurreln* to roar or bluster. **—n.** forcible or violent throw. 1530 *hurle* forcible throw, in Palsgrave's *Lesclarcissement;* from the verb. The word is recorded in Middle English (probably about 1380) in the sense of rushing water.

hurly-burly *n.* commotion, tumult. 1539, alteration of the earlier phrase *hurling and burling* (about 1530), a varied reduplication of *hurling* commotion, tumult (about 1387), the gerund of *hurl.* Compare HULLABALOO.

hurrah *n.* shout of cheer. 1686 *hurra;* later *hurray* (1694); *hurrah* (1841, in Macaulay's *Essays*); alteration of (and later substitute for) HUZZA. The forms *hurrah, hurray* are parallel to modern German *Hurra,* Danish and Swedish *hurra,* modern Dutch *hoera,* and similar shouts. **—interj.** 1716 *whurra,* in Addison's *The Drummer;* later *hurrea* (1773, in Goldsmith's *She Stoops to Conquer*); *hurray* (1855, in Thackeray's *The Rose and the Ring*); *hurrah* (1845). **—v.** to shout "hurrah." 1798 *hurray;* later *hurrah* (1868); from the noun and interjection.

hurricane *n.* 1555 *furacane* violent tropical cyclone, in Eden's *Decades of the New World or West India;* borrowed from Spanish *huracán,* from Arawakan (West Indies) *hurakán.* The earliest forms, such as *furacane, haurachana,* and *uracan,* are alterations of Spanish *huracán* and of Portuguese *furacão.* The present spelling was established by 1688, some say perhaps influenced by *hurry,* in the sense of agitation, commotion.

Kluge cites Mayan *hunraken* one leg, in reference to the handle of the Big Dipper, the constellation that is most prominent during the hurricane season. This possibility is, however, difficult to accept.

hurry *v.* 1590, to move or act quickly, in Shakespeare's *Comedy of Errors;* probably associated with *hurren* to vibrate rapidly, buzz (before 1398, in Trevisa's translation of Bartholomew's *De Proprietatibus Rerum*), Middle High German *hurren* to whir, move fast, Icelandic *hurra* to hum, and Norwegian *hurre* to whirl, from Proto-Germanic **Hurzá-,* probably cognate with Latin *currere* and Gaulish *carros* wagon, from Indo-European **k̑r̥s-,* root **k̑ers-* run (Pok.583).**—n.** 1600, commotion, agitation, in Holland's translation of Livy's *Ab Urbe Condita Libri;* possibly from the verb. The meaning of quick movement or action is first recorded in Dryden's translation of *Saint-Evremond's Miscellaneous Essays* (1692). **—hurried** *adj.* 1667, in Milton's *Paradise Lost;* from *hurry,* v.

hurt *v.* Probably before 1200 *hurten* to damage, harm, knock or dash against, in *Ancrene Riwle;* probably borrowed from Old French *hurter* to ram, strike, collide, perhaps from Frankish (compare Middle High German *hurten* run at, collide). **—n.** Probably before 1200 *hurt* wound, malady, in *Ancrene Riwle;* probably from the verb.

hurtle *v.* Before 1338 *hurtlen,* in Mannyng's *Chronicle of England;* earlier, as the gerund *hurtlinge* (about 1225, in a version of *Ancrene Riwle*); probably a frequentative form of *hurten* to knock or dash against, damage, HURT; for suffix see -LE[3].

husband *n.* Probably before 1200 *husbonde,* in Layamon's *Chronicle of Britain;* later *houssebonde* master of the house, male spouse, married man; developed from Old English (before 1050) *hūsbonda;* probably borrowed from a Scandinavian source (compare Old Icelandic *hūsbōndi* master of the house, a compound of *hūs* HOUSE and *bōndi* householder, dweller; see BONDAGE). **—v.** manage thriftily. Probably before 1430 *housbonden;* later *husbonden* (1440, in *Promptorium Parvulorum*); from *husbonde, housbonde* husband, n. **—husbandman** *n.* (about 1330 *husbondemen*) **—husbandry** *n.* About 1300 *housebondrie* management of a household, housekeeping, skillful management; later *husbondrie* (about 1390, in *Piers Plowman*); formed from *husbonde, housbonde* husband + *-rie* -ry.

The meaning of the occupation of farming is first recorded in Wycliffe's writings (about 1380).

hush *v.* 1546, make or become silent or quiet, probably a back formation from *huscht,* adj., quiet, silent (about 1405); earlier *huisht* (about 1385, in Usk's *The Testament of Love*), and *hust* (about 1380, in Chaucer's translation of Boethius' *De Consolatione Philosophiae*); probably of imitative origin. **—interj.** 1604, silence! quiet!, probably a back formation from *whist, whisht* be quiet! silence! (about 1382, in the Wycliffe Bible); earlier *hust* (about 1390, in Chaucer's *Canterbury Tales*); either of imitative origin or possibly from the verb. **—n.** silence, quiet. 1689, from the verb. **—hush-hush** *adj. Informal.* secret, confidential. 1916, reduplication of *hush,* interj.

husk *n.* dry outer covering of certain seeds or fruits. About 1400 *husk,* in Maundeville's *Travels;* earlier *huske* the foreskin (1392); perhaps borrowed from Middle Dutch *huuskyn* little house, core of a fruit, case, diminutive of *huus* HOUSE; other possibilities are also found in an association with various forms for HULL, but historical evidence is wanting. **—v.** remove the husks from. 1562, from the noun.

husky[1] *adj.* **1** hoarse. 1552, of, like, or having husks; formed from English *husk* + *-y*[1]. The meaning of dry in the throat or hoarse is recorded before 1722, from the earlier meaning of dry as a husk, without natural moisture (1599).

2 tough and strong, stout, sturdy (like a corn husk). 1869, American English, in Harriet Beecher Stowe's *Oldtown Folks.* An earlier noun with the meaning of a strong or stout person is recorded in 1864.

husky[2] *n.* Eskimo dog. 1830 *Hosky* an Eskimo, Canadian English, shortened from a variant form of the name *Eskimo,* such as the earlier *Ehuskemay* (1743); see ESKIMO. *Husky,* with the meaning of an Eskimo dog, appeared in the 1800's and is recorded as *huski* (1852), and *huskie* (1872), originally as an attributive and chiefly in the phrase *husky dog.*

hussar (hu̇zär′) *n.* European light-armed cavalry soldier. 1532, borrowed perhaps through German *husar* (or in some Medieval Latin documents *huzarone, hussarone,* and found in English *usaron, ussaron*), from Hungarian *huszár* light horseman, (originally, freebooter); from Old Serbian *husar,* variant of *kursar* pirate, from Italian *corsaro* CORSAIR.

hussy (hus′ē) *n.* bad-mannered or impudent girl; low, immoral woman. 1530, mistress of a household, housewife; alteration (by shortening of the vowel and probably a loss of *w*) of Middle English *housewif;* earlier *husewif* (probably before 1200, in *Ancrene Riwle*), a compound of *huse, hous* HOUSE and WIFE; however, perhaps the formation is simply a clipping of *-wife* with the shortening of the vowel in *huse-, hous-* and an addition of the diminutive suffix *-y*[2]. In some rural areas the original meaning of housewife gradually changed to mean "any woman or girl," and by 1650 *hussy* was applied to a country woman or girl, especially one who shows casual or improper behavior, usually with an adjective, such as *bold hussy, naughty hussy;* by the 1800's *hussy* had acquired a generally derogatory, but sometimes jocular meaning.

hustings *n.pl. or sing.* Probably before 1200 *husting* a council or an assembly, in Layamon's *Chronicle of Britain;* developed from Old English *hūsting* meeting, court, tribunal, 1012, in the *Anglo-Saxon Chronicle;* borrowed from a Scandinavian source (compare Old Icelandic *hūsthing* council, a compound of *hūs* house and *thing* assembly); so called because such a meeting was held among the members of a group or "household" of a nobleman or other leader. The shift from *th* to *t* probably represents a weakening of the stress on the second syllable *(thing)* that must have taken place before the word was borrowed into Old English.

The plural form *hustings* assembly or court, in the same sense as the singular, is first recorded in 1463, and gradually became the usual form of the word. The meaning of a temporary platform from which speeches are made in a political campaign, is first recorded in 1719.

hustle *v.* to hurry. 1684, to shake to and fro; borrowed from Dutch *hutselen* or *husseln* to shake, a frequentative form of *hutsen,* variant of *hotsen* to shake; for suffix see -LE[3]. The meaning of push roughly, shove, is first recorded in Smollett's *The Adventures of Peregrine Pickle* (1751). The sense of hurry or move quickly is found in 1812, and that of to obtain in a hurried, rough, or illegal manner, developed in American English (1840). Also developed from the earlier notion of pushing and hurrying, is the sense of sell goods aggressively (1887). **—n.** 1715, a shaking together; later, a jostling (1803); from the verb. The meaning of illegal business activity, racket, swindle, is first recorded in 1963, in American English. **—hustler** *n.* (1825)

hut *n.* 1658, borrowed from French *hutte* cottage, from Old French, from either Middle High German *hütte* cottage or hut, or from Old High German *hutta* roughly built temporary dwelling, from Proto-Germanic **Hudjan-;* probably from the same Germanic source as Old English *hȳdan* to conceal and ultimately that of Old English *hūs* house.

hutch *n.* pen for rabbits, etc. About 1200 *hucche* chest or coffer; borrowed from Old French *huche,* (also) *huge,* from Medieval Latin *hutica* chest, of uncertain origin (perhaps from Germanic; compare Old High German *hutta* HUT). The meaning of a pen for animals, is found before 1398 and that of a hut or small cabin, in 1607. The later sense of a piece of furniture, especially a cupboard for food or dishes, is first recorded in 1671.

huzza (həzä′) *n.* shout of cheer, hurrah. 1665, in John Evelyn's *Diary,* variant of earlier *hussa* (1573), mentioned by many writers of the 1600's and 1700's supposedly as a sailor's cheer or salute, and therefore possibly an alteration of earlier *hissa* a cry also said to be used by sailors in pulling or hauling (about 1500). The term is possibly related to *heise* (1513), *hysse* (1490) to raise aloft or hoist, variants of *hoise;* see HOIST.

hyacinth (hī′əsinth) *n.* plant of the lily family. 1553, precious stone of a blue color, in Eden's translation of *A Treatise of the New India;* later, flowering plant (1578, replacing earlier *iacinct, jacinct* jacinth, recorded probably about 1200); borrowed from Latin *hyacinthus,* from Greek *hyákinthos* a purple or deep-red flower, but explained in mythology to have sprung from the blood of the slain youth *Hyacinthus.* The Greek word is probably borrowed from some non-Indo-European language of the Mediterranean area, from which also was borrowed Latin *vaccinium,* a certain dark-flowered plant.

hybrid *n.* offspring of two animals or plants of different species, varieties, etc. 1601, in Holland's translation of Pliny's *Natural History,* borrowed originally from Latin *hybrida,* variant of *ibrida* mongrel, (specifically) offspring of a tame sow and a wild boar, of uncertain origin, but probably from Greek *hybrída,* accusative of a lost noun *hybrís* mongrel. It is probable that the English *hybrid* was also borrowed in some instances from French *hybride,* also from Latin *hybrida.* **—adj.** bred from two different species, varieties, etc. Before 1716; from the noun. **—hybridize** *v.* 1845, formed from English *hybrid* + *-ize.* **—hybridization** *n.* 1851, formed from English *hybridize* + *-ation.*

hydr- a form of *hydro-* before vowels, as in *hydrate, hydraulic.*

hydra (hī′drə) *n.* freshwater polyp with stinging tentacles. 1835-36, New Latin *Hydra,* the genus name of this polyp, from Latin *Hydra, hydra* mythical many-headed water serpent whose heads grew back as fast as they were cut off until it was finally killed by Hercules, from Greek *Hýdrā,* from *hýdōr* (genitive *hýdatos*) WATER.

The genus *Hydra* was given this name by Linnaeus in 1756 in allusion to the fact that polyps of this genus can regenerate parts of their bodies just as the mythical hydra grew back its heads.

As the name of the mythical water serpent, *hydra* is first recorded in English as *idre* (about 1380, in Chaucer's *Book of the Duchesse*); this form was borrowed through Old French *hydre* from Latin *hydra* and the word did not appear as *hydra* until 1596, in Spenser's *Faerie Queene.* The figurative meaning of a many-sided problem, hindrance, etc., is first recorded in 1494, as *idre.*

hydrangea (hīdrān′jə) *n.* shrub with clusters of small flowers. 1753, New Latin *Hydrangea* a compound of Greek *hydr-,* stem coexisting with *hýdōr* (genitive *hýdatos*) WATER and *angeîon* vessel or capsule, from *ángos* vessel; so called because of the shrub's vessel-shaped seed capsule. Greek *ángos* is probably borrowed from some non-Indo-European language of the Mediterranean area.

hydrant *n.* street fixture from which water may be drawn. 1806; formed in American English from Greek *hydr-,* stem coexisting with *hýdōr* water + English *-ant,* as if from the present participle of a Latin verb.

hydrate *n.* compound produced when certain substances unite with water. 1802, borrowed from French *hydrate,* from Greek *hydr-,* stem coexisting with *hýdōr* (genitive *hýdatos*) WATER. The term was coined by the French chemist J.L. Proust. **—v. 1** combine with water to form a hydrate. 1850, from the noun. **2** to combine with water to restore moisture to (a food product, etc). 1947, an extension of def. 1.

hydraulic *adj.* having to do with water in motion. 1656, in Blount's *Glossographia,* borrowed probably from Middle French *hydraulique,* from Latin *hydraulicus,* from Greek *hydraulikós,* from *hýdraulis* water organ *(hydr-,* stem coexisting with *hýdōr,* genitive *hýdatos*, WATER + *aulós* musical instrument, hollow tube; see ALVEOLUS).

Hydraulic is first recorded as a noun with the meaning of a hydraulic organ (an ancient musical instrument using the pressure of water to compress the air, a translation of Greek *hydraulikòn órganon*), in Sir Francis Bacon's *Sylva Sylvarum* (1626).

—hydraulics *n.* the study in physics of the properties and motion of liquids, especially liquids under pressure. 1671, in Boyle's writings; formed from English *hydraulic* + *-s* on analogy with *mathematics,* etc.

hydro- a combining form meaning: **1** water, as in *hydrometer, hydroplane.* **2** containing hydrogen, as in *hydrocarbon,* containing hydrogen and carbon. Borrowed from Greek *hydro-,* combining form of *hýdōr* WATER.

hydrocarbon *n.* 1826, chemical compound of hydrogen and carbon, such as methane, in writings of Faraday. Formed from English *hydro-* + *carbon.*

hydroelectric *adj.* 1827, of or pertaining to electricity from a battery that uses chemical reaction; later, electricity produced by water power (1851).

hydrofoil *n.* 1959, a boat with fins to raise it out of the water at high speeds; earlier, a fin or plane to reduce friction in water or some other liquid (1920); see FOIL.

hydrogen *n.* gaseous chemical element. 1791, in Erasmus Darwin's *Botanic Garden;* borrowed from French *hydrogène,* from Greek *hydr-,* stem coexisting with *hýdōr* (genitive *hýdatos*) WATER + French *-gène* -gen (something that produces), from Greek *-genḗs;* see GENUS. The compound was formed in allusion to the combining of hydrogen with oxygen to produce water. French *hydrogène* was introduced in 1787 by the French chemist Lavoisier, though the element was isolated in 1766 by the English chemist Henry Cavendish. **—hydrogenate** *v.* 1809, combine with hydrogen, formed from English *hydrogen* + *-ate¹.* **—hydrogen bomb** (1947).

hydrolysis (hidrol′əsis) *n.* chemical decomposition by water. 1880; earlier, implied in *hydrolytic* (1875); formed in English from *hydro-* + Greek *lýsis* a loosening or dissolution, from *lýein* to loosen, dissolve; see LOSE.

hydrophobia *n.* rabies. 1392 *ydroforbia,* erroneous spelling in the borrowing from Late Latin *hydrophobia,* from Greek *hydrophobíā,* from *hydrophóbos* dreading water *(hydr-,* stem coexisting with *hýdōr* water + *phóbos* dread; fear; see -PHOBIA). The form in Middle English was temporarily replaced by a borrowing of French *hydrophobie* (1601), which disappeared or was made to conform with the modern English borrowing from Latin by 1621.

hydroplane *n.* 1904, American English, motorboat that glides on the surface of water; formed from English *hydro-* + *-plane,* as in *airplane* (early 1900's *aeroplane*). —*v.* to travel in a hydroplane. 1909, from the noun. The verb meaning of to skid out of control in an automobile on a wet road because the tires ride on a plane of a thin layer of water, is first recorded in 1962.

hydroponics (hī′drəpon′iks) *n.* the growing of plants without soil by the use of water containing necessary nutrients. 1937, formed from English *hydro-* + *-ponics* (from Greek *poneîn* to labor, toil, from *pónos* labor + English *-ics*). Greek *pónos* is related to *pénesthai* be poor, work hard, strain, cognate with Lithuanian *pìnti* plait, weave, from Indo-European **pen-/pon-/pn̥-* (Pok.988). This horticultural method was developed in 1929 by William Gericke, a plant physiologist at the University of California; the word was coined by his colleague, W.A. Setchell.

hydrozoan *n.* any animal in a class of invertebrate water animals. 1869, in Thomas Huxley's writings; formed in English from New Latin *Hydrozoa* + English suffix *-an.* The class name *Hydrozoa* (coined in 1843 by the English zoologist Owen), is from Greek *hydr-,* stem coexisting with *hýdōr* (genitive *hýdatos*) WATER and *zôion* animal, related to *zōḗ* life, from Indo-European **gwyōwā́* (Pok.468); see BIO- and ZOO-.

hyena *n.* wolflike, flesh-eating mammal. 1340 *hyane,* in *Ayenbite of Inwyt;* later *hiena* (before 1398) in Trevisa's translation of Bartholomew's *De Proprietatibus Rerum;* borrowed from Old French *hiene, hyene,* and directly from Latin *hyaena,* from Greek *hýaina,* from *hȳ́s* pig; see SOW² pig. The hyena was possibly so named from its bristly back, vaguely similar to that of a pig.

hygiene (hī′jēn) *n.* rules or science of maintaining health. 1671, borrowed from French *hygiène,* from New Latin *ars hygieina* the healthful art, translation of Greek *hygieinḗ téchnē,* from *hygíeia* health, from *hygiḗs* healthy (literally, living well), from Indo-European **su-gwiyés,* from **su-* well, **gwyē-* live (Pok.468). **—hygienic** *adj.* 1833, probably borrowed from French *hygiénique,* from *hygiène* hygiene.

hygro- a combining form meaning wet, moist, moisture, as in *hygrometer, hygroscope.* Borrowed from Greek *hygro-,* combining form of *hygrós* wet, moist, fluid; see HUMOR.

hymeneal (hī′mənē′əl) *adj.* pertaining to marriage.

1600 *hymniall,* in Marston's *Antonio's Revenge;* formed in English from Latin *hymenaeus,* from Greek *hyménaios* belonging to wedlock; wedding, wedding song (from *Hymḗn,* Greek god of marriage) + English suffix *-al*[1]. **—hymen** *n.* 1615, borrowed from French *hymen,* and directly from Late Latin *hymēn,* from Greek *hymḗn* (genitive *hyménos*) virginal membrane; cognate with Sanskrit *syū́man* band, strap, suture, Latin *suere* SEW, from Indo-European **syū-/sīw-* (Pok.915).

hymenopterous (hī′mənop′tərəs) *adj.* belonging to a group of insects including ants, bees, and wasps. 1813, but implied as existing much earlier in a customary formation in scientific vocabulary, from *Hymenoptera* (1773); found in New Latin *hymenopterus,* and in Greek *hymenópteros (hymḗn,* genitive *hyménos,* membrane + *pterón* wing*)*, see FEATHER; for suffix see -OUS. The word is descriptive of the transparent, membranous wings of these insects.

hymn *n.* 1613, a song of praise to God, in *Purchas his Pilgrimage,* an alteration in spelling (by influence of Latin *hymnus*) of Middle English *ymne* (probably before 1200, in *Ancrene Riwle*). These forms were in part borrowed from Old French *ymne* (from Medieval Latin *ymnus,* from Latin *hymnus*), and also developed from Old English *ymen, hymen* (before 830, in the *Vespasian Psalter;* borrowed from Latin *hymnus* song of praise, from Greek *hýmnos* song or ode in praise of gods or heroes; earlier wedding hymn; possibly formed on *Hymēn* Greek god of marriage). Greek *hýmnos* was used in the Septuagint to render various Hebrew words meaning a song of praise to God, and is found in the Latin Vulgate and in Christian writers from Augustine onward.

The earliest evidence of a pronunciation without the final *-n* is apparently found in Middle English *hym* (before 1425). However, the final *-n* is retained in *hymnal* and *hymnody.*

—v. praise or honor with a hymn. 1667, in Milton's *Paradise Lost;* from the noun.

—hymnal *n.* book of hymns. Probably before 1500 *hymnale,* borrowed from Medieval Latin *hymnale, imnale,* from *ymnus* hymn; for suffix see -AL[1]. **—hymnbook** *n.* About 900 *ymenbec,* in Alfred's translation of Bede's *Ecclesiastical History;* later *hymn-book* (1779, in the Preface to Wesley's *Hymns*); re-formed from modern English *hymn* + *book.*

hyp- a form of the prefix *hypo-* before vowels, as in *hypabyssal* (below the abyssal plain, in geology).

hype[1] (hīp) *n.* excessive or misleading publicity, promotion, or advertising. 1967, American English slang, probably in part developed from *hyperbole* by back formation; and in part from underworld slang, a swindle by overcharging or short-changing (1926); apparently a back formation from earlier *hyper* a short-change confidence man (1914), probably from *hyper-* over, to excess; see HYPER-. **—v.** 1967, American English slang, to use hype; publicize, promote, or advertise excessively or deceptively; earlier, to deceive, trick, or con (about 1945); and in underworld slang, to swindle by overcharging or short-changing (1926); apparently from the noun.

hype[2] (hīp) *v. Slang.* Usually, **hype up,** stimulate, stir up, excite. 1938, American English (drug addicts' slang), stimulate or excite by or as if by the injection of a narcotic drug; from earlier *hype* a hypodermic injection or needle (1920's; a drug addict), short for HYPODERMIC.

hyper- a prefix meaning over, above, beyond, exceedingly, to excess, as in *hyperacidity, hypersensitive, hypertension.* Borrowed from Greek *hyper-,* from *hypér,* adv. and prep., beyond, overly, OVER.

hyperbola (hīpėr′bələ) *n. Geometry.* conic section. 1668, New Latin *hyperbola,* from Greek *hyperbolḗ* extravagance *(hyper-* beyond + *bol-,* nominal stem of *bállein* to throw); so called from a geometric function of a cone such that any cross section of the cone from the base is at an angle greater than the angle of the sloping sides of the cone.

hyperbole (hīpėr′bəlē) *n.* exaggeration for effect. Probably before 1425 *iperbole,* in the Wycliffe Bible; later *hyperbole* (1579, in Sir Thomas More's writings); borrowing of Latin *hyperbolē* (possibly by influence of Middle French *hyperbole*), from Greek *hyperbolḗ* exaggeration or extravagance; see HYPERBOLA. **—hyperbolic** *adj.* 1646, formed from English *hyperbole* + *-ic,* and possibly also borrowed through French *hyperbolique* from Late Latin *hyperbolicus,* from Greek *hyperbolikós,* from *hyperbolḗ* hyperbole.

hyperglycemia (hī′pərglisē′mēə) *n.* an abnormally high amount of sugar in the blood. New Latin *hyperglycemia (hyper-* over + *glycemia* presence or level of sugar in the blood, from Greek *glykýs* sweet + New Latin *-aemia,* from Greek *haîma,* genitive *haímatos,* blood*)*.

hyperon (hī′pəron) *n.* elementary particle with a mass greater than that of a proton or neutron. 1953, formed from *hyper-* over + *on* elementary particle, as in *proton, neutron.*

hyphen *n.* mark (-) used to connect two words or parts of a word. About 1620, borrowed from Late Latin *hyphen,* from Greek *hyphén* hyphen (mark joining two syllables or words and probably indicating that two notes were to be held or blended together in music, similar to the tie). Greek *hyphén* is formed from *hyp'* (reduced form of *hypó*) under, and *hén,* neuter of *heîs* one; see SAME. **—v.** 1814, from the noun. **—hyphenation** *n.* 1886, formed from English *hyphen,* v. + *-ation.* **—hyphenate** *v.* 1892, possibly a back formation from *hyphenation* and a formation of English *hyphen,* n. + *-ate.*

hypno- (also *hypn-* before vowels). a combining form meaning sleep, as in *hypnology;* or hypnotism, as in *hypnotherapy.* Borrowed from Greek *hypno-* combining form of *hýpnos* sleep; see SOMNOLENT.

hypnosis *n.* condition resembling sleep but more active, induced by suggestions of a hypnotizer. 1882; earlier, inducement of sleep (1876); New Latin *hypnosis,* formed from Greek *hýpnos* sleep + *-ōsis* condition.

hypnotic *adj.* of hypnosis or hypnotism. 1625, inducing sleep, borrowed from French *hypnotique* inclined to sleep, soporific, learned borrowing from Late Latin *hypnōticus,* from Greek *hypnōtikós* inclined to sleep, putting to sleep, sleepy, adjective to **hýpnōsis* a putting to sleep, from *hypnoûn* put to sleep; from *hýpnos* sleep; see SOMNOLENT. The meaning "of hypnosis or hypnotism" is first recorded in English in 1843. **—n.** drug that produces sleep, sedative. 1681; from the adjective. **—hypnotism** *n.* process of hypnotizing or inducing hypnosis. 1843, from English *hypnot(ic)* + *-ism;* coined by James Braid, a British medical writer who investigated hypnotism. He introduced the term *neuro-hypnotism* in 1842 to mean "nervous sleep"; shortened to *hypnotism* in 1843. **—hypnotist** *n.* 1843, formed from English *hypnot(ism)* + *-ist.* **—hypnotize** *v.* put into a hypnotic state, mesmerize. 1843, formed from English *hypnot(ic)* + *-ize.*

hypo- a prefix meaning: **1** under, beneath, below, less than, slightly, or somewhat, as in *hypodermic, hyposensitive, hypotension.* **2** *Chemistry.* indicating amount of oxidation less than that of a compound without the prefix, as in *hypochlorous* acid, which is less oxidized than chlorous acid. Borrowed from Greek *hypo-,* from *hypó,* prep. and adv., under; see UP.

hypochondria (hī'pəkon'drēə) *n.* imaginary illness. 1839, illness without a specific cause; earlier, depression or melancholy without a real cause (1668, in Dryden's *An Evening's Love*); used as a singular form of the earlier plural *hypochondria* (1563; earlier *ypocandria,* 1373) upper region of the abdomen; borrowed from Late Latin *hypochondria* the abdomen, from Greek (neuter plural) *hypochóndria (hypo-* under + *chóndros* cartilage of the breastbone) with loss of *r* in the first syllable by dissimilation from pre-Greek **chrondros,* cognate with Latin *frendere* crunch, gnash, from Indo-European **ghrend-/ghrond-* (Pok.459). The plural sense arose from the belief that the viscera of the *hypochondria* were the seat of melancholy and "the vapors," low spirits, headaches and the like.

Formation of *hypochondria* with the meaning of an imaginary illness, was also influenced by *hypochondriasis,* of the same meaning (1766).

—hypochondriac *n.* 1639, person affected with melancholy; probably a shortened form of earlier *hypochondriacal-* (1611, in Burton's *Anatomy of Melancholy*), and in some instances borrowed from French *hypochondriaque,* originally as an adjective with the sense of affected with melancholy, from Greek *hypochondriakós* of the abdomen, from *hypochóndria* abdomen. The meaning of a person suffering from imaginary illness is first recorded in 1888.

hypocrisy *n.* Probably before 1200 *ypocresie* false appearance of goodness, virtue; pretense, especially in religious matters, in *Ancrene Riwle;* borrowed from Old French *ypocrisie,* learned borrowing from Late Latin *hypocrisis,* from Greek *hypókrisis* acting on the stage, pretense, dissimulation, from *hypokrī́nesthai* play a part *(hypo-* under + *krī́nein* to sift, judge, decide; see CERTAIN*).* The refashioned spelling with *h,* to conform to the Latin and Greek, was adopted in English (as in French) in the 1500's. **—hypocrite** *n.* Probably before 1200 *ypocrite* a person who pretends to virtue, goodness, religious belief, in *Ancrene Riwle;* borrowed from Old French *ypocrite,* learned borrowing from Late (Ecclesiastical) Latin *hypocrita* hypocrite, from Greek *hypokritḗs* actor on the stage, pretender, hypocrite, from *hypokrī́nesthai;* see HYPOCRISY. **—hypocritical** *adj.* 1561, formed from English *hypocrite* + *-ical.*

hypodermic *adj.* under the skin. 1863, formed in English from New Latin *hypoderma (hypo-* under + Greek *dérma* skin*)* + English suffix *-ic;* see DERMA. **—n.** 1875, hypodermic treatment; later, hypodermic syringe or injection (1893); from the adjective.

hypoglycemia (hī'pōglīsē'mēə) *n.* an abnormally low amount of sugar in the blood. New Latin *hypoglycemia (hypo-* under + *glycemia* presence or level of sugar in the blood, from Greek *glykýs* sweet + New Latin *-aemia,* from Greek *haîma,* genitive *haímatos,* blood.

hypotenuse (hīpot'ənüs) *n. Geometry.* side of a right-angled triangle opposite the right angle. 1571 *hypothenusa,* a long-popular but erroneous spelling borrowed possibly from Middle French *hypothenuse, ypothenuse,* from Late Latin *hypotēnūsa,* from Greek *hypoteínousa* stretching under, subtending (the right angle), feminine present participle of *hypoteínein (hypo-* under + *teínein* to stretch; see TEND[1] incline). The spelling *hypotenuse* is not recorded before 1834.

hypothalamus (hī'pəthal'əməs) *n.* the part of the brain under the thalamus, controlling temperature, the pituitary gland, etc. 1896, New Latin, from *hypo-* under + *thalamus* part of the brain where a nerve emerges. The term was coined by the German anatomist W. His, at the suggestion of a colleague Waldeyer-Hartz.

hypothesis (hīpoth'əsis) *n.* theory. 1596, particular case of a general thesis or proposition; borrowed, possibly by influence of Middle French *hypothese,* from Late Latin *hypothesis,* from Greek *hypóthesis* foundation, base, basis of an argument, supposition *(hypo-* under + *thésis* a placing, proposition; see THESIS). The meaning of a supposition, theory, especially in the sciences, is curiously not recorded before 1646. **—hypothesize** *v.* 1738; formed from English *hypothesis* + *-ize.* **—hypothetical** *adj.* 1615; formed in English from Greek *hypothetikós* supposed, hypothetical + English suffix *-ical.*

hyssop (his'əp) *n.* fragrant plant of the mint family. Before 1300 *ysope;* earlier in Biblical use, a plant of Palestine (about 1200); developed (by influence of Latin *hyssōpus, hyssōpum*) from Old English *ȳsōpe* (before 830, in the *Vespasian Psalter*); learned borrowing from Irish Latin *hysōpus,* from Greek *hýssōpos, hýssōpon,* from a Semitic source (compare Ethiopic *'ozub* hyssop, Hebrew *'ēzōbh,* and Syriac *zūfā*).

hysterectomy (his'tərek'təmē) *n.* removal of the uterus or a portion of it. 1886, formed in English from Greek *hystérā* uterus + English combining form *-ectomy.*

hysteria (hister'ēə) *n.* fit of emotional outburst, imaginary illness, and even real disability. 1801, New Latin, formed as an abstract noun to English *hysteric,* adj., of or characterized by hysterical fits and convulsions (1657); borrowed from Middle French *hystérique,* from Latin *hystericus* of or belonging to the womb, from Greek *hysterikós,* from *hystérā* womb; originally associated with disturbance of the uterus and its functions. Greek *hystérā* probably meant originally protruding, exactly cognate with the feminine of Sanskrit *últara-s* upper, outer, contrastive adjective to *ud* OUT, and related to *udára-m* belly, cognate with Latin *uterus* belly, womb; see UTERUS. **—hysterical** *adj.* unnaturally excited or emotional. 1615, characteristic of hysteria; formed in English from Latin *hystericus* of the womb + English suffix *-al*[1]. **—hysterics** *n.pl.* hysterical fits. 1727, in Swift's *To a Very Young Lady;* formed from English *hysteric,* adj. + *-s,* plural suffix.

I

I *pron.* 1137 *i;* later *I* (about 1250, in *The Story of Genesis and Exodus*); developed from the unstressed form of Old English (about 725) *ic* singular pronoun of the first person (nominative case). Modern and Middle English *I* developed from earlier *i* in the stressed position. *I* came to be written with a capital letter thereby making it a distinct word and avoiding misreading handwritten manuscripts. In the northern and midland dialects of England the capitalized form *I* appeared about 1250. In the south of England, where Old English *ic* early shifted in pronunciation to *ich* (by palatalization), the form *I* did not become established until the 1700's (although it appears sporadically before that time).

Old English *ic* corresponds to Old Frisian, Middle Dutch, and modern Dutch *ik,* Old High German *ih* (modern German *ich*), Old Icelandic *ek* (Danish *jeg,* Norwegian *eg/jeq,* Swedish *jag*), and Gothic *ik,* from Proto-Germanic **ekan;* and outside Germanic to Latin *ego* I, Greek *egṓ,* Old Prussian *es,* Old Slavic *azŭ,* Armenian *es,* Avestan *azəm,* Old Persian *adam,* Sanskrit *ahám,* Tocharian *ñuk,* and Hittite *uk,* from Indo-European **eĝom, eĝō* (Pok.291).

-ial a variant form of the suffix *-al*[1], as in *adverbial, exponential, microbial, residential.*

iambic *adj.* 1586, consisting of a metrical foot in poetry with an unaccented syllable followed by an accented one; earlier, using iambic meter (1581, in Sidney's *Apology for Poetry*); borrowed from Latin *iambicus,* from Greek *iambikós,* from *iambos* a metrical foot of an unaccented and an accented syllable, lampoon (so called perhaps because it was first used in satiric verse); without question a word of non-Indo-European origin.

-ian a variant form of the suffix *-an,* as in *comedian, egalitarian, Bostonian;* borrowed from Latin in which it was attached to the root of common or proper nouns and developed into *-ian* (Latin *-iānus*) with a word having a vocalic stem ending in *-i-,* as in *Aemili-* + *-ānus* = *Aemiliānus.* See also -AN. In Middle English the form is more frequently *-ien,* in words borrowed from Old French.

-iana a variant form of the suffix *-ana,* as in *Jacksoniana.* See also -ANA.

ibex (ī'beks) *n.* wild goat of Europe, Asia, or Africa. 1607, borrowed from Latin *ibex* (genitive *ibicis*), from a pre-Latin Alpine language (compare CHAMOIS). This word came into more prominence in English as the Alpine areas and mountain climbing began to attract British attention.

ibid. in the same place; in the same book, chapter, passage, etc. 1663, in Boyle's writings; abbreviation of Latin *ibīdem* in the same place (*ibī* there + demonstrative suffix *-dem*).

ibis (ī'bis) *n.* long-legged wading bird. 1382 *ybyn* (singular), in the Wycliffe Bible; later *ibes* (plural, about 1400); borrowed from Latin *ībis,* from Greek *îbis* (genitive *íbios*), from Egyptian *hab* a sacred bird of Egypt.

-ible a suffix forming adjectives from verbs, and meaning "that can be _____ed, able to be _____ed," as in *collectible, reducible, perfectible.* Middle English, borrowed from Old French *-ible* and directly from Latin *-ibilis, -ibilis,* variants of the suffix *-bilis* forming adjectives from verbs with infinitives in *-ēre, -ere,* and *-īre;* see -ABLE for a discussion of these suffixes.

-ic a suffix forming adjectives from nouns, and meaning: **1** of or having to do with, as in *atmospheric, Icelandic.* **2** having the nature of, as in *heroic.* **3** constituting or being, as in *bombastic.* **4** containing or made up of, as in *metallic.* **5** made by or caused by, as in *volcanic.* **6** like, like that of, characteristic of, as in *meteoric.* **7** an art or system of thought, as in *stoic, logic, music.* **8** in chemical terms *-ic* indicates the presence of an element in a compound or ion that is of a higher valence than indicated by the suffix *-ous,* as in *boric* or *ferric.* Many words ending in *-ic* have two or more of the meanings in definitions 1 to 6, as *bombastic* = *constituting or being bombast,* and *containing or made up of bombast,* or *metallic* which has the meaning of almost all the definitions given above. Middle English, borrowed through French *-ique,* and directly from Latin *-icus,* from Greek *-ikós.*

-ical a suffix forming adjectives meaning roughly the same thing as *-ic* in most instances. **1** *-ic,* as in *historical, grammatical, cosmological.* **2** *-ic,* specialized or differentiated in meaning, as in *economical.* **3** sometimes with the sense of *-al*[1] added to nouns ending in *-ic* or *-ics,* as in *musical* = *music,* n. + *-al*[1], or *statistical* = *statistic* (*s*), n. + *-al*[1]. Middle English, borrowed from Late Latin *-icālis* (Latin *-icus* -ic + *-ālis* -al[1]).

-ically a suffix forming adverbs from adjectives in *-ical* by simple addition of the suffix *-ly*[1], and from adjectives in *-ic* by addition of *-ally,* as in *historically* and *poetically* which are adverbs corresponding to either *historic* or *historical,* and to either *poetic* or *poetical.* Though sometimes heard as *artisticly* and *alphabeticly,* in writing English uses the forms *artistically* and *alphabetically.* The sole exception is *publicly.*

ice *n.* Before 1225 *is;* later *yce* (about 1395, in the Wycliffe Bible); found in Old English *īs* ice (about 725, in *Beowulf*); cognate with Old Frisian, Old Saxon, Middle Low German, and Old High German *īs* ice (modern German *Eis*), Dutch *ijs,* and Old Icelandic *īss,* from Proto-Germanic **īsa-,* cognate with Avestan *isu-* icy, from Indo-European **eis-/is-* (Pok.301). —**v.** Probably before 1400 *ysen* to cover with ice; from the noun. —**ice-cold** *adj.* (before 1000, in Old English *iscalde*) —**ice cream** (1744, earlier *iced cream,* 1688) —**ice skate** 1662 *skeates,* in Pepys' *Diary;* earlier as Holland *schates* (1648). —**ice-skate** *v.* (1696) Though *ice skate* was used as a noun and verb in the latter part of the 1600's, *skate,* n. and v. was the usual term until the invention of roller skates in 1760 made differentiation necessary, and especially even more so with the spreading popularity of an improved roller skate in the United States after 1863. —**icing** *n.* 1769, confection put on pastry. —**icy**

adj. About 1500; formed from English *ice,* n. + *-y*[1]. This adjective is found as Old English *īsig* (about 725, in *Beowulf*), but was formed anew in Middle English. The figurative sense of without warm feeling is first recorded in Shakespeare's *Richard III* (1594).

iceberg *n.* 1774, borrowed as a partial loan translation from Dutch *ijsberg,* literally, ice mountain (*ijs* ICE + *berg* mountain; see BARROW[2] mound of earth). The word occurs in several cognate languages, as in modern German *Eisberg,* Swedish and Norwegian *isberg,* and Danish *isbjerg.*

The figurative sense of anything that is only partly visible or known, is first recorded in 1957; the phrase *tip of the iceberg,* in the sense of a small or superficial part of something, is found in 1963.

ichneumon (iknü′mən) *n.* small, weasellike animal of Egypt. 1572, borrowed from Latin *ichneumōn,* from Greek *ichneúmōn,* literally, searcher, perhaps as for crocodile's eggs, from *ichneúein* hunt after or track, from *íchnos* a track; of uncertain origin, perhaps related to *oíchesthai* to have gone, be off and away, cognate with Armenian *ēǰ* descent, and Lithuanian *eigà* a walk, a course, from Indo-European **eigh-/oigh-/igh-* (Pok.296). The word has been also applied since 1658 to a parasitic insect related to the bees and wasps and commonly called *ichneumon fly.* The name was originally used by Aristotle for a kind of small wasp that hunts for spiders, and Linnaeus applied it to the parasitic flies.

ichthyology (ik′thēol′əjē) *n.* branch of zoology dealing with fishes. 1646, formed from Greek *ichthŷs* fish (cognate with Lithuanian *žuvìs* fish, Old Prussian *suckis,* and Armenian *tsukn*) + English *-ology.* These Greek, Baltic, and Armenian cognates descend from Indo-European **ĝhđū-/ĝhđuw-* or **ĝhyū-* (Pok.416).

ichthyosaur (ik′thēəsôr) *n.* extinct fishlike marine reptile. 1830, in Sir Charles Lyell's *Principles of Geology,* borrowed from New Latin *ichthyosaurus* (from Greek *ichthŷs* fish + *saûros* lizard).

icicle *n.* pointed, hanging stick of ice. Before 1325 *hyysykil;* later *isykle* (*is* ice + *ikel* icicle); developed from Old English (before 1000) *gicel* (compare Old English *cylegicel* cold icicle, probably about 750, in *Andreas* and *Phoenix*), from Proto-Germanic **jekilaz.* The Old English form is cognate with Old High German *ihilla* icicle, Old Icelandic *jǫkull* icicle, glacier, *jaki* piece of ice; also cognate with Middle Irish *aig* and *Welsh iâ* ice, *iaën* piece of ice, glacier, Old Cornish *iey* ice, and perhaps with Hittite *ekunaš* cold, chilly, from Indo-European **yeg-* ice, (Pok.503).

icky *adj.* 1935, American English, overly sweet, cloying, sickening, in slang originally among jazz musicians, but found earlier in *icky-boo* sickly, nauseated, in general slang use; of unknown origin. The sense of nasty, unpleasant, disgusting, is first recorded about 1938.

icon or **ikon** (ī′kon) *n.* in the Eastern Church, a sacred picture or image. 1572, borrowed from Late Latin *icōn,* from Greek *eikṓn* (genitive *eikónos*), Cypriote accusative *weikóna,* likeness, image, portrait, related to *eikénai* be like, look like, of unknown origin.

iconoclast (īkon′əklast) *n.* 1641, earlier in a Scottish variant *Jconoclastæ* (1596, where *J* stands for *I,* especially in Scottish literature) persons who break or destroy religious figurines and images, in reference to those in the Eastern Church of the 700's and 800's who opposed the use of images in religious worship and whose followers raged in mobs that destroyed such religious objects. In the 1500's and 1600's the term was applied to Protestants, especially in the Netherlands, who similarly opposed the use of images in churches and destroyed much of value. The term was borrowed through French *iconoclaste,* and directly from Medieval Latin *iconoclastes,* from Late Greek *eikonoklástēs* (*eikṓn,* genitive *eikónos* image + *klas-,* a past tense stem of *klân* to break; see ICON), cognate with Latin *calamitās* damage, and *clādēs* disaster, from Indo-European **kelə-/klā-* (Pok.545).

The extended sense of one who attacks cherished beliefs and institutions on the grounds that they are wrong or foolish, is first recorded in Elizabeth Barrett Browning's *Some Account of the Greek Christian Poets* (1842).

—iconoclasm *n.* 1797, destruction of images; formed from *iconoclast,* on the pattern of *enthusiast, enthusiasm.* The extended sense of an attack on cherished beliefs or institutions, is first recorded in Froude's *History of England* (1858). **—iconoclastic** *adj.* 1640; formed from English *iconoclast* + *-ic.*

-ics a suffix meaning: facts, principles, science, as in *optics, aesthetics, metaphysics, genetics;* or method, practice, art, as in *athletics, gymnastics, politics, ceramics.* Originally *-ics* was the plural of nouns ending in *-ic* (as *arithmetic*), formed from Latin *-ica,* feminine singular or neuter plural suffix, from Greek *-iká,* neuter plural suffix meaning matters relating to or having to do with something.

id *n. Psychoanalysis.* the primitive instinctual drive in the unconscious. 1924 (in a translation of Freud's collected papers by J. Riviere and others); borrowed from Latin *id* it, as a translation of German *es* IT. German *es* was used by Freud as a noun in *Das Ich und das Es* The I and the It (1923); translated into English as *The Ego and the Id,* similarly used by the German psychiatrist G. W. Groddeck, in *Das Buch vom Es* The Book of the It (1923), in which Groddeck followed Nietzsche's example of using the word *es* to denote impersonal or instinctual forces in nature. Compare EGO.

-id[1] a suffix with a variety of applications most of which identify members of a group or class, especially in scientific and technical terminology: **1a** in botany, a member of an order with the New Latin name in *-idaceae,* as in *amaryllid.* **b** in zoology, a member of a class with New Latin name *-ida,* as in *arachnid* (*Arachnida*), or of a family, New Latin name *-idae,* as in *araneid* (*Araneidae*). **c** a complex structure in biology, as in *capsid, plasmid.* **2** other uses include: **a** in astronomy, the naming of meteor showers, as in *Leonid, Perseid,* and variable stars, as in *Cepheid.* **b** the naming of dynastic lines, as in *Achaemenid, Seleucid.*

English *-id* in its various uses was borrowed, sometimes through French *-ide* and directly from Latin *-idēs,* a masculine patronymic suffix borrowed from Greek *-idēs,* or from Latin *-is* (genitive *-idis*), borrowed from Greek *-is* (genitive *-idos*) a feminine patronymic suffix.

-id[2] a variant of the suffix *-ide,* now little used and virtually replaced by *-ide.*

-ide a suffix used to form names of simple compounds of an element with another element or radical, as in *amide, chloride, sulfide.* Abstracted as *-ide* from *oxide,* the first compound classified in this way.

idea *n.* Before 1398 *ydea* (in Platonic philosophy) general or ideal form, type, or model, in Trevisa's translation of Bartholomew's *De Proprietatibus Rerum;* borrowed from Latin *idea* idea, archetype, from Greek *idéā* look, semblance, form, kind, ideal prototype, from *ideîn* to see (earlier *idéein, idéen*); see WIT[2] know. While the form in Middle English was borrowed from Latin, the Middle and Old French word *idee* must have been known in medieval England and was probably an influence in the borrowing.

The meaning of something imagined or fancied is first recorded in Shakespeare's *Love's Labour's Lost* (1588), that of a mental image recalled from memory, in 1589, and the more general sense of mental image (1612). The familiar sense of any result of mental activity or understanding, is found about 1645.

ideal *adj.* 1410 *ydeall* pertaining to the divine or general type or model of a thing; later, imaginary (1611); perfect (1613); borrowed from Late Latin *ideālis* existing in idea, from Latin *idea* IDEA. **—n.** 1796, a standard of perfection; from the adjective, probably by influence of French *idéal,* n. **—idealism** *n.* 1796, belief that reality is made up of ideas only; formed from English *ideal* + *-ism,* after French *idéalisme,* from *idéal* ideal. The meaning of practice of idealizing or representing things in an ideal form is first recorded in 1829. **—idealist** *n.* 1701, formed from English *ideal* + *-ist,* after French *idéaliste.* **—idealistic** *adj.* 1829, in Carlyle's writings; formed from English *idealist* + *-ic.* **—idealize** *v.* 1786, probably formed from English *ideal,* adj. + *-ize.*

identical *adj.* 1620, expressing an identity (in logic); borrowed from Medieval Latin *identicus* the same, from Late Latin *identitās* IDENTITY. The sense of being the same or very similar, is first recorded before 1633.

The form in Modern English replaced earlier *idemptical* same, identical (recorded about 1475); borrowed from Medieval Latin *idemptitas* identity, from Latin *idem* the same.

identify *v.* 1644, regard as the same; borrowed from French *identifier,* from *identité* identity; for suffix see -FY. The meaning of recognize as being a particular person or thing, is first recorded in 1769. **—identifiable** *adj.* 1804, formed from English *identify* + *-able.* **—identification** *n.* 1644, borrowed from French *identification,* probably from *identifier,* on the pattern of such pairs as *ratifier* to ratify, *ratification;* for suffix see -ATION.

identity *n.* 1603, sameness or oneness; borrowed from Middle French *identité,* learned borrowing from Late Latin *identitātem* (nominative *identitās*) sameness, from *ident-,* combining form of Latin *idem* (neuter) same (related to *id* it), extracted from the adverb *identidem* over and over again, from *idem et idem*; for suffix see -TY. *Identity* in modern English replaced the form *idemptitie* (1570), from earlier Medieval Latin *idemptitas.*

The formation out of Late Latin *ident-* was probably constructed from *idem* because a need was felt to convey "sameness" as a parallel form with *similitās* which expresses the sense of "likeness," but overlaps with *identitās* in the sense of "oneness"; also because there was a need to translate Greek *tāutótēs* sameness.

ideology *n.* 1796, the science of ideas; later, unpractical theorizing, visionary speculation (1813, in John Adams' writings mentioning the usage introduced into French by Napoleon Bonaparte); borrowed from French *idéologie* the study or science of ideas, from *idéo-* of ideas, from Greek *idéā* IDEA; for suffix see -LOGY. The meaning of set of ideas, doctrines, or beliefs, is first recorded in English in 1909. **—ideological** *adj.* 1797, probably formed from English *ideology* + *-ical.* **—ideologist** *n.* 1798, borrowed from French *idéologiste,* from *idéologie;* for suffix see -IST.

ides (īdz) *n. pl.* in the ancient Roman calendar, the 15th day of March, May, July, and October, and the 13th day of the other months. Before 1338, in Mannyng's *Chronicle of England;* earlier in the Latin form *idus* (1124); borrowed from Old French *ides,* and directly from Latin *īdūs* (plural), spelled *eidus* in Old Latin times, probably from Etruscan.

idiolect (id′ēəlekt) *n. Linguistics.* the language of an individual; personal dialect. 1948, American English, formed in English from Greek *ídios* one's own + English (*dia*)*lect.* The word was coined by the American linguist Bernard Bloch.

idiom *n.* 1588, form of speech of a people or country, own language or tongue; borrowed through Middle French *idiome,* or directly from Late Latin *idiōma* a peculiarity in language, from Greek *idíōma* peculiarity or peculiar phraseology, ultimately from *ídios* one's own. The meaning of a phrase or expression peculiar to a language, was introduced in Donne's *Sermons* (1628). **—idiomatic** *adj.* 1712, characteristic of a particular language, in Addison's writings in *The Spectator;* borrowed from Late Greek *idiōmatikós* peculiar or characteristic, from Greek *idíōma* (genitive *idiṓmatos*) peculiarity.

idiosyncrasy (id′ēəsing′krəsē) *n.* personal peculiarity. 1604, peculiarity of physical constitution, 1665, personal peculiarity; borrowed, probably in part, from French *idiosyncrasie,* and, in part, from Greek *idiosynkrāsíā* (*ídios* one's own + *sýnkrāsis* temperament, formed from *sýn-* together and *krâsis* (earlier **krātis*) a mixing, from *krā-,* stem of *kerannýnai* to mix) **—idiosyncratic** *adj.* Before 1779, formed from English *idiosyncrasy* (*-crasy* taking the formative *-crat*) + *-ic,* modeled on Greek *synkrātikós.*

idiot *n.* Before 1325 *idiot* feeble-minded person, fool, in *Cursor Mundi;* later (also) *ydiote* a simple, uneducated person (about 1378, in *Piers Plowman*); borrowed from Old French *idiote* uneducated or ignorant person, from Latin *idiōta* ordinary person, layman, (in Late Latin, uneducated or ignorant person), from Greek *idiṓtēs* layman, ignoramus (originally, private person or individual, as opposed to the state), person without professional skill or knowledge, from *ídios* one's own, earlier **whédios* (compare Argolic *whediéstās* private individual), from Indo-European **swediyos,* based on **swe* oneself (Pok.882); see IDIOM. **—idiocy** *n.* Before 1529, in Skelton's writings; formed from *idiot,* on the model of Greek *idiṓtēs,* and the pattern of pairs of words such as *prophet, prophecy.* **—idiotic** *adj.* 1713, borrowed from Latin *idiōticus* of an ordinary person (in Late Latin, uneducated, ignorant), from Greek *idiōtikós* private, unprofessional, unskilled, from *idiṓtēs* layman, ignoramus, person without professional skill or knowledge.

idle *adj.* Old English *īdel* empty, void, useless, idle (about 725, in *Beowulf*); cognate with Old Frisian *īdel* empty, worthless, vain, Old Saxon *īdal,* Old High German *ītal* (modern German *eitel* bare, mere, pure, vain), Middle Dutch *idel* (modern Dutch *ijdel*) vain, of unknown origin.**—v.** Before 1460, make vain or worthless;

from the adjective. The meaning of spend or waste (time) is first found in 1652. The reference to a motor, in the sense of run slowly and evenly in neutral, is first recorded in 1916. **—idler** *n.* 1534, formed from English *idle,* v. + *-er*[1]. **—idly** *adv.* (about 830, in Old English *idellice*)

idol *n.* About 1250 *idele,* in *The Story of Genesis and Exodus;* later *ydol* (about 1340); borrowed from Old French *idole,* (earlier) *idele,* learned borrowing from Late Latin *īdōlum* image or form, from Greek *eídōlon* image, phantom, fancy, from *eîdos* form, cognate with Sanskrit *védas* possession, and Welsh *gŵydd* presence, from Indo-European **weidos* (Pok.1127); related to *ideîn* to see, and *eidénai* know. The figurative sense of anything that is idolized is first recorded in 1562. **—idolize** *v.* venerate, adore. 1598, formed from English *idol* + *-ize.*

It is interesting to note the difference in spelling of *idol* in Middle English as *idele* and *idolatry* as *ydolatrie,* though both words are first recorded in an edition of *The Story of Genesis and Exodus* (1250). Apparently the spelling *idele* was influenced much earlier by the early spelling in Old French *idele.*

idolatry (īdol′ətrē) *n.* worship of idols. About 1250 *ydolatrie;* borrowed from Old French *idolatrie,* learned borrowing with contraction in the form from Late Latin *īdōlolatrīa,* from Greek *eidōlolatreíā* (*eídōlon* image + *latreíā* worship, service; related to *látron* pay, wages; of unknown origin); for suffix see -TRY. **—idolater** *n.* About 1415 *ydolatre;* earlier *ydolatrer* (about 1384, in the Wycliffe Bible); borrowed from Old French *idolatre,* learned borrowing with contraction in the form from Late Latin *īdōlolatrēs,* from Greek *eidōlolátrēs* (*eídōlon* image + *-látrēs,* from *latreíā* worship, service); for suffix see -ER[1]. The spelling *idolater* is first recorded in a later edition of Chaucer's *Canterbury Tales* (about 1425). All of the later spellings replaced earlier *ydolastre,* borrowed from Old French about 1375. **—idolatrous** *adj.* 1550, formed from English *idolater* + *-ous.*

idyl or **idyll** (ī′dəl) *n.* description of a simple and charming scene. 1601, picturesque pastoral poem, in Holland's translation of Pliny's *Natural History;* borrowed from Latin *īdyllium,* from Greek *eidýllion* short descriptive poem, diminutive of *eîdos* form; see IDOL. The word was probably also borrowed into English from Middle French *idylle.* **—idyllic** *adj.* 1856, in Harriet Beecher Stowe's writings; formed in American English from *idyll* + *-ic.*

-ie a suffix meaning little, as in *dearie;* also used to show kind feeling or intimacy, as in *auntie;* variant of -Y[2]. The suffix is found in Middle English *-ie* and *-i.*

-ier a suffix meaning person occupied or concerned with, as in *financier, cashier, hosier.* Middle English, in part borrowed from Old French *-ier.*

The suffix varies with *-yer,* most older formations from Old French became *-er* in Anglo-French, as in *butler* and *draper;* other formations such as *lawyer* and *clothier* have early coexisting forms, *lawer* and *clother.* Some words which look as if they belong to this group, such as *carrier, courtier,* and *quarrier* are actually formations in *-er,* the *-i-* belonging to the English or French verb stem.

In later words with *-ier,* in which the form represents French and Old French *-ier,* some words have taken the place of earlier forms in *-er;* others occur with the spelling *-eer* which is now an active suffix in English, producing words such as *auctioneer.*

if *conj.* Before 1250 *if,* developed from Old English *gif* (about 725, in *Beowulf*); cognate with Old Frisian *jef, jof* if, Middle Low German *jof,* Old Saxon *of,* Old High German *oba* (modern German *ob*) if, whether, Old Danish *of,* and Gothic *jabái* if, probably coming down from Proto-Germanic **ja-ƀa,* cognate with Sanskrit *yádi* if, from Indo-European **yo-di* "in the case in which," a locative expression from the stem of the relative **yos, yā, yod,* from which derived Greek *hós, hé, hó* who, which (Pok.283). Collaterally with the preceding early Germanic conjunctions there were also Old High German *ibu* whether, Old Frisian *ef,* Old Saxon *ef,* Old Icelandic *ef,* the Gothic interrogative particle *ibái,* and Gothic *ibái* (*iba*) lest, in order that...not, probably coming from Proto-Germanic **e-ƀa,* from the Indo-European demonstrative stem *e-* (from whose locative **ei* "in this case" derives Greek *ei* if) (Pok.284). Both the *yo-* and the *e-* stems have picked up in Proto-Germanic a particle of emphasis *-ƀa,* probably from Indo-European **bhō* (Pok.113). And there must have been confusion of **jaƀa* and **eƀa* in the early Germanic languages.**—n.** condition, supposition. 1513, in Sir Thomas More's *History of King Richard III;* from the conjunction. **—iffy** *adj. Informal.* questionable; doubtful. 1937, American English; formed from *if* + *-y*[1].

igloo *n.* dome-shaped hut of ice blocks built by Eskimos. 1824, Canadian English; borrowing of an Eskimo word for "house or dwelling"; compare Greenlandic *igdlo* house.

igneous (ig′nēəs) *adj.* of or pertaining to fire. 1664, fiery; 1665; produced by fire; borrowed from Latin *igneus,* from *ignis* fire; cognate with Lithuanian *ugnìs,* Old Slavic *ognĭ,* and Sanskrit *agní-s,* all meaning fire, from Indo-European **egnís/ognís* (Pok.293); for suffix see -OUS.

It is also possible that this word was in some instances borrowed from Middle French *igné,* as English has many adjectives in *-eous* corresponding to French *-é,* one of the more prominent being *instantaneous* (French *instantané*).

ignite *v.* set on fire. 1666, in part, apparently developed from *ignite,* adj., intensely heated (probably before 1425), borrowed from Latin *ignītus;* and, in part, borrowed directly from Latin *ignītus,* past participle of *ignīre* set afire, from *ignis* fire; see IGNEOUS. **—ignition** *n.* 1612, act of heating; borrowed from French *ignition,* from Medieval or New Latin *ignitionem* (nominative *ignitio*) from Latin *ignīre;* for suffix see -TION. The later specific meaning of means of producing a spark in an internal-combustion engine is first recorded in 1906.

ignoble *adj.* mean, base. 1447 *ygnoble* of low birth; borrowed from Middle French *ignoble,* learned borrowing from Latin *ignōbilis* (*i-,* variant of *in-* not + Classical Latin *nōbilis* noble, influenced by Old Latin *gnōbilis*). In Latin the development of the pronunciation of *ignō-* in *ignōbilis* was first (inggnō-), then (ingnō-), and later by spelling pronunciation (ignō-); see NOBLE.

ignominy (ig′nəmin′ē) *n.* public shame and disgrace; dishonor. 1540, back formation from *ignominious,* probably influenced by Middle French *ignominie,* and Latin *ignōminia;* see IGNOMINIOUS. **—ignominious** (ig′nəmin′ēəs) *adj.* Probably before 1425 *ignominiose,* in a translation of Higden's *Polychronicon;* borrowed through Middle French *ignominieux,* or directly from Latin *ignōminiōsus,* from *ignōminia* loss of (good) name (*i-,* variant of *in-* not + *nōmen,* genitive *nōminis* name, influenced by Old Latin *gnōscere* come to know).

ignoramus *n.* ignorant person. Before 1616, from earlier (before 1577) *ignoramus,* a legal term borrowed from New Latin, from Latin *ignōrāmus* we do not know, first person plural present indicative of *ignōrāre* not to know; see IGNORE.

Ignoramus was first used in English as a legal term referring to an endorsement made by a grand jury when it considered the evidence insufficient. The meaning "ignorant person" comes from the title of a play (1615) by George Ruggle, intended to expose the ignorance of lawyers. In the play *Ignoramus* is the name of a lawyer.

ignore *v.* 1801, pay no attention to; earlier, be ignorant of (1611, in Cotgrave's *Dictionary*); probably a dictionary word borrowed from French *ignorer,* but surely influenced in its borrowing by earlier English *ignorance* and *ignorant.* French *ignorer* was borrowed from Latin *ignōrāre* not to know, misunderstand, disregard, from *ignārus* not knowing, ignorant, unaware (*i-* not, variant of *in-*[1] + Old Latin *gnārus* aware, acquainted with, from Indo-European **ĝn̥rós* (Pok.378); related to *gnōscere,* Classical Latin *nōscere* come to KNOW); the form of the Latin verb was influenced by *ignōtus* unknown. **—ignorance** *n.* Probably before 1200, in *Ancrene Riwle;* borrowed from Old French *ignorance,* from Latin *ignōrantia,* from *ignōrantem* (nominative *ignōrāns*), present participle of *ignōrāre* not to know; for suffix see -ANCE. **—ignorant** *adj.* About 1380 *ignoraunt,* in Chaucer's translation of Boethius' *De Consolatione Philosophiae;* borrowed from Old French *ignorant,* from Latin *ignōrantem* (nominative *ignorans*), present participle of *ignōrāre;* for suffix see -ANT.

iguana (igwä′nə) *n.* large climbing lizard. 1555, in Eden's translation of *Decades of the New World or West India,* borrowing of Spanish *iguana,* from Arawakan *iguana* or *iwana.*

ikebana (ik′əbä′nə) *n.* Japanese art of flower arrangement. 1901, borrowing of Japanese *ikebana* (*ikeru* arrange + *hana* (*bana*) flower).

ikon *n.* See ICON.

il-[1] a form of the prefix *in-*[1], meaning not, opposite of, found before *l,* as in *illegal, illegitimate, illegible, illiterate.* In words from Latin the form developed from the assimilation of *n* to the following consonant (*l*).

il-[2] a form of the prefix *in-*[2], meaning in, within, found before *l,* as in *illuminate.* In words from Latin the form developed from the assimilation of *n* to the following consonant (*l*). The prefix is also less frequently found in borrowings from Old French with *il-.*

ileum (il′ēəm) *n. Anatomy.* lowest part of the small intestine. 1682, New Latin, from Latin *īlia* groin, flank. The modern English borrowing of the New Latin form replaced the earlier Middle English *ylioun* (1392), borrowed from Medieval Latin *ileon,* from Greek *eileón,* a form of *eileós* intestinal obstruction; erroneously blended with Latin *īlia* groin, flank. **—ileitis** (il′ēī′tis) inflammation of the ileum. 1855, formed from English *ileum* + *-itis.*

ilium (il′ēəm) *n. Anatomy.* upper portion of the hipbone. 1706, in Phillips' *Dictionary,* New Latin, from Latin *īlia* groin, flank; probably influenced by earlier English *iliac.* **—iliac** (il′ēak) *adj.* of the ilium. 1541, probably formed from Latin *īlia* + *-acus,* from Greek *-akós,* adjective suffix. The modern English borrowing from Latin replaced earlier Middle English *yliaca* of the ilium (recorded before 1398), found only in the phrase *yliaca passioun,* from Late Latin *passiō īliaca.*

ilk *n.* class, kind, sort. 1117 *ylce* (pronoun used as a noun); later *ilke* (probably before 1200, in *Ancrene Riwle*); developed from Old English *ilca* same (*n.,* about 725, in *Beowulf*); also same, identical, aforementioned (*adj.,* about 750, in *Ancrene Riwle*). The Old English *ilca* was probably formed from the particle *ī-,* represented in Sanskrit *ī-dŕś-* such (literally, of that look, and Greek *ekeinos-ī* that there (Pok.285) + *-līc,* root of Old English *gelīc* LIKE[1].

The meanings of the Old English word survive in a now archaic adjective with the meaning of same, and also in the phrase *of that ilk* of the same place or name (1536), and of the same kind or sort (1790, sometimes also found as *this ilk* or *that ilk*).

ill *adj.* Probably about 1150 *ille* morally evil, malicious; borrowed from a Scandinavian source (compare Old Icelandic *illr* ill, bad, of uncertain origin). The meaning of incompetent or deficient, is first recorded in *Cursor Mundi* (before 1325); and that of sick or diseased, before 1460. **—adv.** Probably about 1150 *ille* harshly or bitterly; from the adjective. **—n.** About 1250, evil or wicked people, in *The Owl and the Nightingale.* **—ill-fated** *adj.* (1710, in Pope's writings). **—ill-gotten** *adj.* (before 1425) **—ill-mannered** *adj.* (1422) **—illness** *n.* (before 1500) **—ill-tempered** *adj.* (1601, in Shakespeare's *Julius Caesar*) **—ill will** (before 1325)

illegal *adj.* 1626, borrowed through French *illégal,* or directly from Medieval Latin *illegalis* (Latin *il-* not, variant of *in-*[1] before *l* + *lēgālis* LEGAL). **—illegality** *n.* (1639)

illegible *adj.* 1640; earlier *inlegeable* (1615).

illegitimate *adj.* 1536, formed from English *il-* + *legitimate,* adj., modeled on Latin *illēgitimus* not legitimate, and replacing earlier *illegitime.*

illicit *adj.* unlawful, forbidden. Before 1652, borrowed from French *illicite,* learned borrowing from Latin *illicitus* (*il-* not, variant of *in-*[1] before *l* + *licitus* lawful, LICIT).

illiterate *adj.* Probably before 1425, in a translation of Higden's *Polychronicon;* borrowed from Latin *illīterātus, illitterātus* unlettered (*il-*[1] not, variant of *in-*[1] before *l* + *līterātus, litterātus* furnished with letters); for suffix see -ATE[1]. **—n.** 1628; from the adjective. **—illiteracy** *n.* 1660, formed from *illiterate* + *-cy.*

illuminate *v.* light up. Probably before 1425 *illuminaten,* in a translation of Higden's *Polychronicon;* probably a back formation from *illumination* (Middle English *illuminacion*); for suffix see -ATE[1].

This later Middle English form gradually replaced earlier *enlumyen* enlighten (1370) and became the usual spelling for the later meaning of decorate (a letter, word, page, etc.) with gold, silver, and brilliant colors or designs (recorded probably before 1439). While the later back formation *illuminate* is ultimately a Latinate form, Middle English *enlumynen* was borrowed from Old French *enluminer,* from Late Latin *inlūmināre,* variant of Latin *illūmināre.*

—illumination *n.* Before 1396 *illuminacion* enlightenment; borrowed through Old French *illumination,* and directly from Latin *illūminātiōnem* (nominative *illūminātiō*), from *illūmināre* (*il-*[2] in, variant of *in-*[2] before *l* + *lūmen,* genitive *lūminis* light); for suffix see -ATION. Alternatively, it is possible that *illumination* was formed in Middle English from *illumine* + *-acion.* The meaning of lighting up, is first recorded in 1563. **—illumine** *v.* Probably 1348 *illumynen* enlighten spiritually, borrowed from Old French *illuminer,* learned borrowing from Latin *illūmināre* illuminate.

illusion *n.* appearance which is not real. About 1350 *illusioun* mockery; later, deceptive appearance (about 1380, in Chaucer's *House of Fame*); borrowed from Old French *illusion* a mocking, learned borrowing from Latin *illūsiōnem* (nominative *illūsiō*) a mocking, jesting, irony, from *illūdere* mock at (*il-*[2] at, variant of *in-*[2] before *l* + *lūdere* to play; see LUDICROUS); for suffix see -ION. **—illusive** *adj.* 1679; formed from English *illus* (*ion*) + *-ive.* **—illusory** *adj.* Before 1631, in Donne's *Selections;* borrowed perhaps through French *illusoire,* or directly from Late Latin *illūsōrius* of a mocking character, ironical, from Latin *illūdere;* for suffix see -ORY.

illustrate (il'əstrāt *or* ilus'trāt) *v.* make clear by pictures, examples, etc. 1526, light up, shed light on; back formation from *illustration;* for suffix see -ATE[1]. The meaning of make clear by examples, is first recorded in 1612, and that of provide with pictures that explain or decorate, in 1638. **—illustration** *n.* About 1375; borrowed through Old French *illustration,* and directly from Latin *illūstrātiōnem* (nominative *illūstrātiō*) vivid representation (in writing), from *illūstrāre* light up, clear up, elucidate, embellish, distinguish (*il-*[2] in, variant of *in-*[2] before *l* + *lūstrāre* make bright, illuminate; see LUSTER); for suffix see -ATION. **—illustrative** *adj.* 1643; formed from English *illustrate* + *-ive.* **—illustrator** *n.* 1598, formed by influence of Middle French *illustrateur,* from English *illustrate* + *-or*[2], modeled on Late Latin *illūstrātor* one who enlightens, from Latin *illūstrāre.* The sense of one who draws pictures, especially for a book or magazine, is first recorded in 1689.

illustrious *adj.* very famous; outstanding. About 1566, borrowed from Latin *illūstris* bright, lustrous, distinguished, famous, from *illūstrāre* embellish, distinguish, make famous or renowned; see ILLUSTRATE; for suffix see -OUS. The modern English form replaced earlier *illustre* (recorded before 1460); borrowed from Middle French *illustre* illustrious, from Latin *illūstris* illustrious.

im-[1] a form of the prefix *in-*[1], meaning not, opposite of, before *b, m,* and *p,* as in *imbalance, immoral, impossible.* Formed in Latin by assimilation of *n* to a following consonant.

im-[2] a form of the prefix *in-*[2], meaning in, within, before *b, m,* and *p,* as in *imbibe, immure, impart.* Formed in Latin by assimilation of *n* to a following consonant.

image *n.* likeness, representation, picture. Probably about 1200 *ymage* statue, effigy; borrowing of Old French *image,* from Latin *imāgō* (genitive *imāginis*) copy, likeness, statue, picture, thought, idea, semblance, appearance, shadow; related to *imitārī* copy, IMITATE.

Various meanings already known in Latin began to appear gradually in English, especially that of a mental picture or impression, an idea, conception (about 1380, in Chaucer's translation of Boethius' *De Consolatione Philosophiae*), and from that sense the later meaning of an impression or conception that a person, institution, product, etc., presents to the public, as in the phrase *public image* (in Chesterton's *All Things Considered,* 1908). However, this later sense did not gain widespread use until the early 1950's when it was popularized in the United States in such phrases as *image building* and *corporate image.*

—imagery *n.* About 1350 *ymagerie* carved figures; borrowing of Old French *imagerie,* from *image* image, from Latin *imāgō;* for suffix see -ERY. The meaning of ornate description or representation of images, as in poetry, is first recorded in Puttenham's *The Arte of English Poesie* (1589). **—imagism** *n.* movement in poetry originating about 1909 and emphasizing the use of concrete imagery. 1913 *Imagism,* in *Poetry* magazine, American English; borrowing of French *Imagisme* (1912, in Ezra Pound's *Letters*), from *image;* for suffix see -ISM. **—imagist** *n.* 1914 *Imagist,* American English; borrowing of French *Imagiste* (1912, in Ezra Pound's *Letters*), from *image;* for suffix see -IST.

imagine *v.* About 1340 *ymagynen* form an image of, picture in one's mind; borrowed from Old French *imaginer,* learned borrowing from Latin *imāginārī* to picture oneself, imagine (also in Latin *imāgināre* to form an image of, represent, fashion), from *imāgō* (genitive *imāginis*) IMAGE. The meaning of think, suppose, believe, fancy, is first recorded about 1380. **—imaginable** *adj.* About 1380 *ymaginable,* in Chaucer's translation of Boethius' *De Consolatione Philosophiae;* borrowed probably from Old French *imaginable,* and directly from Late Latin *imāginābilis,* from Latin *imāginārī* imagine. **—imaginary** *adj.* About 1395 *ymaginaire,* in the Wycliffe Bible; borrowed from Latin *imāginārius,* from *imāginārī* imagine; for suffix see -ARY. **—imagination** *n.* 1340 *ymaginacion;* borrowed from Old French *imagination,* learned borrowing from Latin *imāginātiōnem* (nominative *imāginātiō*) imagination, probably from *imāginārī* imagine; for suffix see -ATION. Some scholars regard *imāginātiō* as a translation of Greek *phantasía* phantasy. **—imaginative** *adj.* About 1380 *ymaginatyf,* in Chaucer's translation of Boethius' *De Consolatione Philosophiae;* borrowed from Old French *imaginatif,* and directly from Medieval Latin *imaginativus,* from Latin *imāginārī;* for suffix see -ATIVE.

imbecile *n.* 1802, feeble-minded person, developed from earlier adjective *imbecille* weak or feeble, especially in reference to the body (1549); borrowed from Middle French *imbecile, imbécille,* learned borrowing from Latin *imbēcillus* weak or feeble; of unknown origin. While *imbecile* was surely borrowed from Middle French, it is also probable that in some instances it is a back formation from earlier *imbecility.* **—imbecility** *n.* Probably before 1425 *imbecillite* physical weakness, in an anonymous translation of Chauliac's *Grande Chirurgie;* borrowing of Middle French *imbécillité,* and, in some instances, probably borrowed directly from Latin *imbēcillitātem* (nominative *imbēcillitās*) weakness, feebleness, from *imbēcillus* weak; for suffix see -ITY. The sense of mental weakness is not recorded in English before 1624.

In *imbecile* the spelling with one *l* was surely influenced by the Middle French and the form *-ile* in English; this form in English also affected the later spelling of *imbecility* with one *l.*

imbibe *v.* drink, drink in. About 1395 *embiben* absorb (fluid), in Chaucer's *Canterbury Tales;* borrowed from

Old French *embiber* to soak into, and possibly directly from Latin *imbibere* absorb, drink in, inhale (*im-* in, variant of *in-*[2] before *b* + *bibere* to drink, related to *pōtāre* to drink; see POTION). The spelling with *im-* is recorded in English probably before 1425, but did not become widespread until the 1500's.

imbrication *n.* an overlapping, as of tiles, or a pattern that looks like this. 1650, borrowing of French *imbrication,* as if from Latin **imbricātiōnem* (nominative **imbricātiō*), from *imbricāre* to cover with tiles, from *imbrex* (genitive *imbricis*) curved roof tile used to lead off rain, from *imber* (genitive *imbris*) rain, cognate with Sanskrit *abhrá-s* rainy weather, from Indo-European **m̥bhrós;* also with Sanskrit *ámbhas* water, and Greek *ómbros* rain, from Indo-European **embh-/ombh-/m̥bh-* (Pok.316). —**imbricate** *v.* 1784, either developed from the earlier adjective *imbricate* (1656), or as a back formation from *imbrication;* for suffix see -ATE[1].

imbroglio (imbrōl′yō) *n.* 1750, confused heap; 1818, complicated or difficult situation; borrowing of Italian *imbroglio,* from *imbrogliare* confuse or tangle (*im-* in, variant of *in-*[2] before *b* + *brogliare* embroil, probably from Middle French *brouiller* confuse); see BROIL turmoil.

imbrue (imbrü′) *v.* wet or stain, especially with blood. About 1410 *embrowen;* later *inbrowen* (about 1475); borrowed from Middle French *embreuver,* (earlier) *embrever* moisten or soak, alteration (by metathesis of *r* and *v*) of *embevrer,* from Vulgar Latin **imbiberāre* (*im-* from Latin *im-* in, variant of *in-*[2] before *b* + *biberāre* give to drink, from *biber* a drink, from Latin *bibere* to drink; see IMBIBE). The spelling *imbrue* appeared in the 1500's, probably influenced by the Latinate suffix form *im-*.

imbue (imbyü′) *v.* Probably before 1425, as a past participle of *imbute, enbeued* initiated in, absorbed in; probably, in part, borrowed from Middle French *imbu, imbue* steeped in, full of, a form remade, under the influence of Latin *imbūtus* (past participle of *imbuere* moisten, stain), from earlier *embu,* past participle of *emboire,* from Latin *imbibere* drink in, soak in. Also as a verb in English with the meaning of fill, inspire (1555), borrowed in part from Latin *imbuere* moisten, tinge, stain, taint, of unknown origin.

imitate *v.* 1534, in Sir Thomas More's *Treatise Upon the Passion of Christ;* back formation from *imitation* or *imitator;* for suffix see -ATE[1]. —**imitation** *n.* Before 1400 *ymytacyoun;* borrowed from Old French *imitacion,* from Latin *imitātiōnem* (nominative *imitātiō*) imitation, from *imitārī* to copy, portray, imitate, probably cognate with *aemulus* a rival, striving to be like or to excel, from Indo-European **ai-m-/i-m-* (Pok.10); related to *imāgō* IMAGE. —**imitative** *adj.* 1584, probably formed from English *imitate* + *-ive,* perhaps modeled on Middle French *imitatif.* —**imitator** *n.* 1523; probably a back formation from *imitation;* for suffix see -OR[2].

immaculate *adj.* without a spot or stain, absolutely clean or pure. 1441, borrowed from Latin *immaculātus* (*im-* not, variant of *in-*[1] before *m* + *maculātus* spotted, defiled, past participle of *maculāre* to spot, from *macula* spot, blemish, probably from Indo-European **smə-tlā́,* root **smē-* (Pok.966), represented by Greek *smên* to smear); for suffix see -ATE[1]. The term *Immaculate Conception* is first recorded in 1687, borrowed from Middle French *immaculée conception,* (earlier) *conception immaculée* (1497).

immaterial *adj.* 1410 *inmateriall* not material, spiritual; learned borrowing from Medieval Latin *immaterialis,* from Late Latin *immāteriālis* (*im-* not, variant of *in-*[1] before *m* + Late Latin *māteriālis* MATERIAL).

An extended sense of having little substance, flimsy, is found in Shakespeare's *Troylus and Cressida* (1606). The sense of unimportant, of no consequence, is first recorded in 1698, but fifty years later Johnson was commenting, "This sense has crept into the conversation and writings of barbarians; but ought to be utterly rejected," not realizing perhaps that *material* in the sense of important, had been in use at least since 1529.

immature *adj.* 1548, untimely, premature, usually in reference to death; possibly a back formation from *immaturity,* but more likely borrowed from Latin *immātūrus* untimely or unripe (*im-* not, variant of *in-*[1] before *m* + *mātūrus* MATURE). The meaning of unripe, in reference to fruit, is first recorded in 1599, and that of not full-grown or developed, in 1641. —**immaturity** *n.* About 1540, untimeliness; borrowed from Latin *immātūritātem* (nominative *immātūritās*) unripeness, from *immātūrus* unripe; for suffix see -ITY. The meaning of lack of maturity, is first recorded in 1606.

immediate *adj.* 1392 *immediat* intervening, interposed; later *immediate* absolute, conclusive (1410), and *immediate* existing with nothing between, direct (probably before 1425, in an anonymous translation of Chauliac's *Grande Chirurgie*); borrowed from Old French *immediat,* and Medieval Latin *immediatus,* from Late Latin *immediātus* (*im-* not, variant of *in-*[1] before *m* + *mediātus,* past participle of *mediāre* to halve; later, be in the middle, from Latin *medius* middle; see MID); for suffix see -ATE[1].

With reference to time, the meaning of coming at once, done without delay, is found in 1568 and in an earlier adverbial form in 1420; the sense of current, is first recorded in Francis Bacon's *Of the Advancement of Learning* (1605).

—**immediacy** *n.* 1605, in Shakespeare's *King Lear,* formed from English *immediate* + *-cy.* —**immediately** *adv.* Before 1400, from *immediate,* adj.

immemorial *adj.* very old. 1602, probably borrowed from French *immémorial* old beyond memory or record (*im-* not, from Latin *im-*, variant of *in-*[1] before *m* + French *mémorial* of memory, MEMORIAL).

immense *adj.* About 1426 *immens,* borrowed from Middle French *immense,* learned borrowing from Latin *immēnsus* immeasurable, boundless (*im-* not, variant of *in-*[1] before *m* + *mēnsus,* past participle of *mētīrī* to MEASURE). —**immensity** *n.* Probably 1440 *immensite,* borrowed from Middle French *immensité,* from Latin *immēnsitātem* (nominative *immēnsitās*) unmeasurableness, from *immēnsus* immense; for suffix see -ITY.

immerse *v.* 1605, in Francis Bacon's *Of the Advancement of Learning;* earlier found in the participial form *immersed* stuck, imbedded (probably before 1425, in an anonymous translation of Chauliac's *Grande Chirurgie*); borrowed from Latin *immersus,* past participle of *immergere* to plunge in, dip into (*im-* in, variant of *in-*[2] before *m* + *mergere* to plunge, dip; see MERGE). —**immersion** *n.* Before 1500 *inmersionne,* borrowed from French *immersion* and directly from Late Latin *immersiōnem, inmersiōnem* (nominative *immersiō, inmersiō*), from Latin *immergere;* for suffix see -SION.

immigrate *v.* come into a foreign country or region to live. 1623, in Cockeram's *Dictionary;* borrowed from

Latin *immigrātum,* past participle of *immigrāre* to remove, go into, move in (*im-* into, variant of *in-²* before *m* + *migrāre* to move, MIGRATE); for suffix see -ATE¹. **—immigrant** *n.* 1792, borrowed probably from French *immigrant,* from Latin *immigrantem* (nominative *immigrāns*), present participle of *immigrāre* immigrate; for suffix see -ANT. It is also possible that *immigrant* was in some instances formed from English *immigr(ate)* + *-ant.* **—immigration** *n.* 1658, in Phillips' *Dictionary;* formed from English *immigrate* + *-ion.*

imminent *adj.* likely to happen soon, impending. 1436 *ymynent;* borrowed from Middle French *imminent,* and directly from Latin *imminentem* (nominative *imminēns*), present participle of *imminēre* to overhang, impend, be near (*im-* in, variant of *in-²* before *m* + *-minēre* to hang, jut; related to *mōns,* genitive *montis,* hill, MOUNT²); for suffix see -ENT. **—imminence** *n.* 1606, in Shakespeare's *Troylus and Cressida;* probably formed from English *immin (ent)* + *-ence;* possibly also influenced by Late Latin *imminentia,* from Latin *imminentem* (nominative *imminēns*), present participle of *imminēre.*

immobile *adj.* Before 1349 *inmobill* not moving, motionless; borrowed from Old French *immobile,* learned borrowing from Latin *immōbilis* (*im-* not, variant of *in-¹* before *m* + *mōbilis* MOBILE). **—immobility** *n.* Probably before 1425 *immobilite;* borrowed from French *immobilité,* from Late Latin *immōbilitātem* (nominative *immōbilitās*), from Latin *immōbilis* immobile; for suffix see -ITY. **—immobilization** *n.* 1882, formed from English *immobilize* + *-ation.* **—immobilize** *v.* 1871, formed from English *immobile* + *-ize,* possibly by influence of French *immobiliser,* from Old French *immobile* immobile.

immoderate *adj.* excessive. Before 1398, in Trevisa's translation of Bartholomew's *De Proprietatibus Rerum;* borrowed from Latin *immoderātus* unrestrained, excessive (*im-* not, variant of *in-¹* before *m* + *moderātus* restrained, MODERATE); for suffix see -ATE¹.

immolate *v.* kill or offer as a sacrifice. 1548, developed from *immolate* sacrificed, past participle used as an adjective (1534, in Sir Thomas More's *Treatise Upon the Passion of Christ*); borrowed from Latin *immolātus,* past participle of *immolāre* to sacrifice, originally, to sprinkle with sacrificial meal (*im-* upon, variant of *in-²* before *m* + *mola* sacrificial meal; related to *molere* to grind; see MEAL² grain); for suffix see -ATE¹. Alternatively, *immolate* may be a back formation from *immolation.* **—immolation** *n.* Probably about 1425 *immolacion,* borrowed, perhaps from Middle French *immolation,* or directly from Latin *immolātiōnem* (nominative *immolātiō*), from *immolāre.*

immorality *n.* About 1566; formed from English *im-¹* + *morality.* **—immoral** *adj.* 1660, back formation from *immorality.*

immortal *adj.* About 1380, in Chaucer's *Parlement of Foules,* borrowed, probably by influence of Old French *immortel,* from Latin *immortālis* living forever, deathless; (also, as plural noun) the gods (*im-* not, variant of *in-¹* before *m* + *mortālis* dying, MORTAL); for suffix see -AL¹. **—n.** 1600's, from the adjective. Alternatively, *immortal* may be a back formation from *immortality.* **—immortality** *n.* About 1340 *immortalite,* borrowed from Old French *immortalité,* learned borrowing from Latin, and borrowed directly from Latin *immortālitātem* (nominative *immortālitās*) deathlessness, from *immortālis* immortal; for suffix see -ITY. **—immortalize** *v.* About 1566, formed from English *immortal* + *-ize,* perhaps by influence of Middle French *immortaliser.*

immovable *adj.* About 1385 *inmovable;* 1380 *inmoeueable;* possibly a back formation from *inmoeueablete, immoevablete* (1380); or formed from Middle English *im-¹* + *moevable, mevable;* for suffix see -ABLE.

immunity *n.* About 1384 *ynmunite* exemption from taxation, service, laws, etc., freedom from prosecution, in the Wycliffe Bible; borrowed probably from Old French *immunité,* and directly from Latin *immūnitātem* (nominative *immūnitās*) exemption from performing public service or charges, from *immūnis* exempt from a service or charge, exempt, free (*im-* not, variant of *in-¹* before *m* + *mūnis* performing services; see COMMON); for suffix see -ITY. The medical sense of protection from disease (1879), was borrowed from French *immunité.* **—immune** *adj.* Probably 1440, free, exempt; back formation from *immunity;* probably in some instances also borrowed from Latin *immūnis* having immunity. The medical sense of protected from disease (1881), was formed in English by influence of French *immun,* and earlier English *immunity,* as a back formation paralleling the one in Middle English. **—immunization** *n.* 1893, formed from English *immunize* + *-ation.* **—immunize** *v.* 1892; formed from English *immune* + *-ize.*

immuno- a combining form made from *immune,* and meaning immunity or immunization, as in *immunobiology, immunogenic.*

immure *v.* imprison, confine. 1583; borrowed possibly through Middle French *emmurer,* or directly from Medieval Latin *immurare* (Latin *im-* in, variant of *in-²* before *m* + *mūrus* wall; see MURAL). The meaning of imprison, is first recorded in Shakespeare's *Love's Labour's Lost* (1588).

immutable *adj.* Probably before 1422, borrowed from Old French *immutable,* and directly from Latin *immūtābilis* unchangeable (*im-,* variant of *in-¹* before *m* + *mūtābilis* changeable; see MUTABLE).

imp *n.* Probably before 1200 *impe* seedling; developed from Old English *impa* young shoot, graft (before 899, in Alfred's translation of St. Gregory's *Pastoral Care*), from *impian* to graft; borrowed from a Germanic source (compare Old High German *impfōn* to graft), from Vulgar Latin **imputus,* variant of Late Latin *impotus* implanted or engrafted, from Greek *émphytos,* verbal adjective of *emphýein* implant (*em-* in, variant of *en-²* before *p* + *phýein* to plant); see -PHYTE.

Middle English *impe* a child or offspring, especially of a noble family (1377) developed from the earlier horticultural sense, and thence acquired the more sinister meanings of child of the devil (1526), and of little devil (1584), which was weakened in meaning to mischievous child (1642).

—impish *adj.* 1652, formed from English *imp* + *-ish.*

impact *v.* 1601, to press closely or firmly into something (usually in the form *impacted*), in Holland's translation of Pliny's *Natural History;* developed from earlier *impact,* past participle and adjective (1563), borrowed from Latin *impāctus,* past participle of *impingere* to push into, strike against; see IMPINGE. The meaning of strike against something with force, is first recorded in 1916, and the figurative sense of have a forceful effect on, in 1935. **—n.** 1781, collision; from the verb. The figurative sense of forceful impression, was introduced in Coleridge's *Biographia Literaria* (1817). The specific meaning of impression that a person or thing makes on another is found in 1946.

impair *v.* make worse; damage. About 1380 *enpeyren;* 1390 *empeyren;* in part borrowed from Old French *empeirier, empeirer,* from Vulgar Latin **impejōrāre* make worse (Latin *im-* in, variant of *in-*[2] before *p* + Late Latin *pejōrāre* make worse; see PEJORATIVE). The Middle English forms are possibly also, in part, a back formation from *emparement,* modified in spelling by influence of the Old French *empeirier.* **—impairment** *n.* 1340 *emparement,* in *Ayenbite of Inwyt;* borrowed from Old French *empeirement,* from *empeirier, empeirer* impair; for suffix see -MENT. The modern spelling is first recorded in 1611 and influenced the spelling *impair,* both forms in Modern English modeled on the Latin form.

impala (impä'lə) *n.* swift African antelope. 1875, borrowed from Zulu *im-pala,* related to Setswana *phala* and Swahili *p'aa* gazelle (contrasted with the usual but erroneous form *paa* roof).

impale *v.* pierce through with anything pointed. 1530, enclose with pales or stakes, fence in, in Palsgrave's *Lesclarcissement;* borrowed from Medieval Latin *impalare* (Latin *im-* in, variant of *in-*[2] before *p* + *pālus* stake, POLE[1]). The variant *empale* (1553) was borrowed from Middle French *empaler* (*em-* in, variant of *en-*[1] before *p* + *pal,* learned borrowing from Latin *pālus* stake). The meaning of pierce with a pointed stake, is first recorded in *Purchas his Pilgrimage* (1613).

impart *v.* give a share in, give. Probably before 1430 *inparten;* later *imparten* (about 1471); borrowed from Middle French *impartir,* learned borrowing from Late Latin *impartīre,* from Latin *impertīre* share in or divide with (*im-* in, variant of *in-*[2] before *p* + *partīre* to divide, PART).

impartial *adj.* 1593, in Shakespeare's *Richard II,* formed from English *im-*[2], variant of *in-*[2] before *m* + *partial;* see PARTIAL.

impasse (im'pas) *n.* position from which there is no escape; deadlock. 1851, borrowed from French *impasse* impassable road, blind alley, impasse (*im-* not, from Latin *im-,* variant of *in-*[1] before *p* + Middle French *passe* a passing, from *passer* to PASS[1]).

impassion *v.* 1591 *empassion,* in Spenser's *Daphnaïda;* 1593 *impassion,* in Nashe's *Christ's Tears Over Jerusalem;* borrowed from Italian *impassionare* (Latin *im-* in, variant of *in-*[2] before *p* + Italian *passione* passion, from Latin *passiōnem,* nominative *passiō* PASSION); for suffix see -SION. **—impassioned** *adj.* 1603, in Ben Jonson's *Sejanus,* from the verb. **—impassive** *adj.* 1667, in Milton's *Paradise Lost;* formed from *im-*[2], variant of *in-*[2] before *p* + *passive.*

impatience *n.* Probably before 1200 *impatience,* in *Ancrene Riwle;* also *impacience* (1340); borrowed from Old French *impacience,* and directly from Latin *impatientia* (*im-,* variant of *in-*[2] before *p* + *patientia;* see PATIENCE). **—impatient** *adj.* About 1378 *impacient,* in a version of *Piers Plowman;* borrowed from Old French *impacient, impatient,* from Latin *impatientem* (*im-*, variant of *in-*[2] before *p* + *patientem,* nominative *patiēns* suffering; see PATIENT). The formation in English was probably influenced by earlier *impatience.*

impeach *v.* accuse, call in question. Probably 1383 *empechen* accuse or hinder, in Wycliffe's writing; borrowed through Anglo-French *empecher,* from Old French *empëechier* hinder, from Late Latin *impedicāre* to fetter (Latin *im-* on, variant of *in-*[2] before *p* + *pedica* shackle, from *pēs,* genitive *pedis,* FOOT). The specific meaning of accuse a public officer of misconduct, is first recorded in 1568. The spelling *impeach* replaced the original spelling with *em-* in the 1500's through influence of the Latin form. **—impeachment** *n.* Before 1387 *enpechement* accusation or charge, in Trevisa's translation of Higden's *Polychronicon;* borrowed from Old French *empechement,* from *empëechier* hinder. Apparently, in its sense of accusation, *impeachment* was associated with Medieval Latin *impetitionem* (nominative *impetitio*) an attack or accusation, from Latin *impetere;* but this has no connection etymologically with Late Latin *impedicāre.* The modern spelling appeared in the 1500's, simultaneously with a change in the form of the verb.

impeccable *adj.* 1531, not capable of sin, in Latimer's works; later, faultless (1620); borrowed probably through Middle French *impeccable,* from Latin *impeccābilis* (*im-* not, variant of *in-*[1] before *p* + *peccāre* to sin; of uncertain origin, perhaps found in a possible earlier meaning to stumble, formed from a lost adjective **pedcos* having a defect in one's foot, from *pēs,* genitive *pedis,* foot; contrast Latin *mancus* having a useless hand, from pre-Latin **mancos,* from *manus* hand).

impecunious *adj.* penniless, poor. 1596, in Nashe's *Have With You to Saffron-Walden;* formed in English from *im-*[1] not, variant of *in-*[1] before *p* + Latin *pecūniōsus* rich, from *pecūnia* money, property, see FEE; for suffix see -OUS.

impede *v.* hinder, obstruct. 1605, in Shakespeare's *Macbeth;* probably a back formation from *impediment,* influenced by Latin *impedīre* to impede, and in some instances probably borrowed from the Latin. **—impediment** *n.* Before 1400 *impedyment* something which hinders or prevents, obstacle, difficulty; borrowed from Latin *impedīmentum* hindrance, from *impedīre* impede, literally, to shackle the feet (*im-* on, variant of *in-*[2] before *p* + *pēs,* genitive *pedis,* FOOT). **—impedimenta** (imped'əmen'tə) *n.pl.* things that impede progress. 1600, in Holland's translation of Livy's *Roman History;* borrowed from Latin *impedīmenta* baggage, plural of *impedīmentum* impediment; probably influenced in its borrowing into English by earlier existence of *impediment.*

impel *v.* cause to move; drive forward. Probably before 1425 *impellen,* borrowed from Latin *impellere* (*im-* on, variant of *in-*[2] before *p* + *pellere* to push, drive; see PULSE[1] beat). **—impeller** *n.* 1685, in Boyle's writings, formed from English *impel* + *-er*[1].

impend *v.* be about to fall or happen. 1599, hang threateningly, be about to fall or happen; either a back formation from *impendent* (before 1592), *or* a borrowing from Latin *impendēre* (*im-* on, over, variant of *in-*[2] before *p* + *pendēre* hang; see PENDANT).

impenetrable *adj.* 1447; borrowed through Middle French *impénétrable,* from Latin *impenetrābilis* (*im-* not, variant of *in-*[1] before *p* + *penetrābilis* PENETRABLE).

imperative *n.* command. About 1450 *imperatyf* the imperative mood in grammar; later, something imperative (1606); borrowed from Old French *imperatif,* and from Late Latin *imperātīvus* commanded, found in Latin *imperāt-,* past participle stem of *imperāre* to command, to requisition (grain, for example), from *in-*[2] before *p* + *parāre* to get, prepare, related to *parere* beget, bear, cognate with Lithuanian *perêti* to hatch, from Indo-European **per-* bring forth (Pok.818); for suffix see -IVE. **—adj.** 1530, in Palsgrave's *Lesclarcissement,* expressing a command or request; from the noun. The sense of not to be avoided, urgent, is first recorded in Byron's *Don Juan* (1823).

imperfect *adj.* About 1378 *imparfit,* borrowed from Old French *imparfait,* from Latin *imperfectus* unfinished, incomplete (*im-* not, variant of *in-*[1] before *p* + *perfectus* PERFECT). By the mid-1500's the form borrowed from Old French was replaced by a new formation modeled on the Latin and influenced by the spelling of *imperfection* in English. **—imperfection** *n.* 1390 *imperfeccioun,* in Chaucer's *Canterbury Tales;* borrowed from Old French *imperfection,* or directly from Late Latin *imperfectiōnem* (nominative *imperfectiō*), from *imperfectus,* see IMPERFECT); for suffix see -TION.

imperial *adj.* of or pertaining to an empire or its ruler. About 1380, in Chaucer's translation of Boethius' *De Consolatione Philosophiae;* borrowed from Old French *imperial, emperial,* learned borrowings from Latin *imperiālis* of the empire or emperor, from *imperium* empire, from *imperāre* to command, see EMPIRE; for suffix see -AL[1]. **—n.** 1476 *impereal* a type of cloth (as in *cloth imperial*); later *imperiall* soldier of the imperial troops (about 1524); from the adjective. **—imperialism** *n.* 1858, rule by an emperor; formed from English *imperial* + *-ism,* modeled on French *impérialisme* (1836). The meaning of policy of extending the rule of one country over another is first recorded in Joseph Chamberlain's letters (before 1878). **—imperialist** *n.* 1603, adherent of the Emperor; later, advocate of imperialism (1899); either formed from English *imperial* + *-ist,* modeled on French *impérialiste* (1525), or borrowed directly from French. **—imperialistic** *adj.* 1879, formed from English *imperialist* + *-ic.*

imperious *adj.* haughty, domineering. 1541, implied in earlier *imperiously;* borrowed, possibly by influence of Middle French *imperieux* (feminine *imperieuse*), from Latin *imperiōsus* commanding, from *imperium* empire; see IMPERIAL.

impersonal *adj.* 1520, formed from English *im-*[1] not, variant of *in-*[1] before *p* + *personal,* modeled on Late Latin *impersōnālis.*

impersonate *v.* 1624, to represent in bodily form, personify, formed from English *im-*[2] + *person* + *-ate*[1]. The meaning of act the part of, pretend to be, is first recorded in 1715, probably influenced by the earlier verb *personate* (1613), with the same meaning; formed from English *person* + *-ate*[1]. **—impersonation** *n.* 1800, personification; 1825, an acting the part of a character; formed from English *impersonate* + *-ion.* **—impersonator** *n.* 1853, formed from English *impersonate* + *-or*[2].

impertinent *adj.* About 1395 *inpartinent* irrelevant, not to the point, in Chaucer's *Canterbury Tales;* later *impertinent* (before 1422); borrowed through Old French *impertinent,* or directly from Late Latin *impertinentem* (nominative *impertinēns*) not belonging (from Latin *im-* not, variant of *in-*[1] before *p* + *pertinēns* PERTINENT). The meaning of inappropriate, out of place, is first recorded before 1415, and that of meddling beyond one's province, intrusive, rudely bold, in 1681, probably from French (used by Molière in the sense of presumptuous). **—impertinence** *n.* 1603, something inappropriate, in Holland's translation of Plutarch's *Moralia;* borrowing of French *impertinence,* from Medieval Latin *impertinentia,* from Late Latin *impertinentem* not belonging; see IMPERTINENT. The meaning of rude boldness, is first recorded in Steele's writing in the *Spectator* (1712), probably from the French.

imperturbable *adj.* Before 1500, borrowed through Middle French *imperturbable,* and Medieval Latin *imperturbabilis* that cannot be disturbed (from Latin *im-* not, variant of *in-*[1] before *p* + **perturbābilis* PERTURBABLE).

impervious (impėr′vēəs) *adj.* 1650, not letting things through; not penetrable or permeable; borrowed from Latin *impervius* (*im-* not, variant of *in-*[1] before *p* + *pervius* letting things through, PERVIOUS); for suffix see -OUS.

impetigo (im′pətī′gō) *n.* infectious skin disease. Before 1398, in Trevisa's translation of Bartholomew's *De Proprietatibus Rerum;* borrowing of Latin *impetīgō* skin eruption, from *impetere* to attack; see IMPETUS.

impetus *n.* 1641 *impetus* driving force; momentum; earlier *impetous* rapid movement (probably before 1425); borrowed from Latin *impetus,* related to *impetere* to attack (*im-* at, variant of *in-*[2] before *p* + *petere* aim for, rush at); see PETITION. **—impetuous** *adj.* acting hastily or rashly. Before 1398 *inpetuous,* in Trevisa's translation of Bartholomew's *De Proprietatibus Rerum;* later *impetuous* (probably before 1425); borrowed from Late Latin *impetuōsus,* from Latin *impetus* impetus; for suffix see -OUS.

impinge *v.* 1535, to thrust upon or fasten forcibly; borrowed from Latin *impingere* drive into, strike against (*im-* on, variant of *in-*[2] before *p* + *pangere* to fix, fasten; see PACT). The meaning of infringe or encroach upon, is first recorded about 1738.

implacable *adj.* Probably before 1425, in a translation of Higden's *Polychronicon;* borrowed from French *implacable,* from Latin *implācābilis* unappeasable (*im-* not, variant of *in-*[1] before *p* + *plācābilis* PLACABLE).

implant *v.* Probably before 1425, found in *implanted;* formed from English *im-*[1] not, variant of *in-*[1] before *p* + *planted;* patterned on Medieval Latin *implantatus,* past participle of *implantare* to install or invest, literally to insert or graft to (*im-,* variant of *in-*[1] before *p* + *plantare* to PLANT). **—implantation** *n.* 1578, formed from English *implant* + *-ation,* possibly after Middle French *implantation.*

implausible *adj.* 1602, formed from English *im-*[1], variant of *in-*[1] before *p* + *plausible.*

implement *n.* 1445, supplementary payment; borrowed, probably by influence of Old French *emplement* act of filling, from Late Latin *implēmentum* a filling up, as with provisions or stock for a house, from Latin *implēre* to fill (*im-* in, variant of *in-*[2] before *p* + *plēre* to fill; see FULL). The meaning of tool, instrument, utensil, is first recorded in 1538 in the plural sense of equipment needed to do some kind of work, and in the singular sense of such a tool, in 1628. Both senses derive from the meaning of things which serve to supplement or complete a household, needed articles to do some kind of work or perform some duty or function, etc. (first recorded in 1505). **—v.** 1806, to fulfill, complete, carry out; originally chiefly of Scottish use; from the noun in Scottish law with sense of fulfillment or full performance (1754). **—implementation** *n.* an implementing or fulfillment. 1926, formed from English *implement,* v. + *-ation.*

implicate *v.* show to be connected; involve. 1600, involve as a consequence or inference; developed from earlier *implicate,* adj., involved as a complicating factor, connected (probably before 1425); borrowed from Latin *implicātus,* past participle of *implicāre* involve, entangle, connect closely (*im-* in, variant of *in-*[2] before *p* + *plicāre* to fold, abstracted from *implicāre, explicāre,* etc., for pre-Latin **plecāre* see PLY[2] fold); for suffix see -ATE[1]. The meaning of involve (in a charge or crime), is first recorded in Ann Radcliffe's *The Italian* (1797). Doublet of IMPLY. **—implication** *n.* Probably before 1425 *implicacion* complication, action of entangling; later, something implied (about 1555); borrowed from Latin *implicātiōnem* (nominative *implicātiō*) entwining or entangling, from *implicāre,* see IMPLICATE; for suffix see -ATION.

implicit *adj.* implied. 1599, borrowed probably through Middle French *implicite,* and directly from Latin *implicitus,* variant of *implicātus,* past participle of *implicāre* involve, IMPLICATE.

implore *v.* beg earnestly for. 1500-20, in William Dunbar's *Poems,* borrowed through Middle French *implorer,* or directly from Latin *implōrāre* call for help, beseech, originally, invoke with weeping (*im-* toward, variant of *in-*[2] before *p* + *plōrāre* to weep, cry out).

imply *v.* About 1380 *emplien* to enfold, involve, entangle, in Chaucer's translation of Boethius' *De Consolatione Philosophiae;* later *implien* (about 1400); borrowed from Old French *emplier,* from Latin *implicāre* involve, entangle, connect closely; see IMPLICATE. The extended meaning of involve as a necessary consequence or logical inference (as in *friendship implies trust*), is first recorded about 1400 and that of express indirectly, insinuate, hint at, in 1581. Doublet of IMPLY, IMPLICATE, and EMPLOY.

impolite *adj.* 1612, in Drayton's *Poly-Olbion;* borrowed from Latin *impolītus* unpolished, rough, unrefined (*im-* not, variant of *in-*[1] before *p* + *polītus* polished, POLITE).

import (impôrt′) *v.* bring in from a foreign country. Probably before 1425 *importen* convey information, express; borrowed from Latin *importāre* bring in, convey (*im-* in, variant of *in-*[2] before *p* + *portāre* carry; see PORT[4] bearing). The meaning of bring in from an external source, is first recorded in Skelton's *The Boke of Phyllyp Sparowe* (1508); the application of bring in from a foreign country, is found in 1548 and was influenced by Middle French *importer* (1382). The meaning of imply, signify, mean, is first recorded in Sir Thomas More's writings (1529), and was probably borrowed from Medieval Latin *importare,* with the same meaning. **—n.** (im′pôrt) 1588, importance or consequence, in Shakespeare's *Love's Labour's Lost;* from the verb in the archaic sense of be of consequence or importance, a usage borrowed from Middle French *importer,* from Medieval Latin *importare,* from Latin *importāre* to convey or import. The meaning of that which is imported, a commodity imported from abroad, is first recorded in Child's *A New Discourse of Trade* (1690).

important *adj.* having much import or significance. 1444 *importante,* borrowed from Medieval Latin *importantem* (nominative *importans*), present participle of *importare* be significant in, from Latin *importāre* bring in, see IMPORT; for suffix see -ANT. **—importance** *n.* 1508, in Wolsey's correspondence to Henry VII; borrowing of Middle French *importance,* probably learned borrowing from Medieval Latin *importantia,* from *importantem,* present participle of *importare* be significant in.

importune (im′pôrtün′) *v.* ask urgently or repeatedly, trouble with demands. 1530, in Palsgrave's *Lesclarcissement;* perhaps a back formation from *importunity,* or developed from *importune,* adj. (probably before 1400); and apparently in some instances borrowed from Middle French *importuner,* from *importun* persistent, learned borrowing from Latin *importūnus* unfit; see IMPORTUNITY. **—importunate** *adj.* 1529, asking or urging repeatedly, persistent, in Sir Thomas More's writings; probably formed in English by influence of Latin *importūnus* unfit; for suffix see -ATE[1]. **—importunity** *n.* About 1425 *importunyte* persistence; later *importunitie* (before 1500); borrowed from Middle French *importunité,* from Latin *importūnitātem* (nominative *importūnitās*) unsuitableness, from *importūnus* unfit, troublesome, originally having no harbor (*im-* without, variant of *in-*[1] before *p* + *portus* harbor, PORT[1]); for suffix see -ITY.

impose *v.* put (a burden, tax, punishment, etc.) on. About 1380 *imposen* put an obligation on, in Chaucer's translation of Boethius' *De Consolatione Philosophiae;* borrowed from Old French *imposer* (*im-* on, from Latin *im-,* variant of *in-*[2] before *p* + Old French *poser* put, place; see POSE). The meaning of lay (a tax or other burden) on, inflict, is first recorded in 1581, probably from the meaning in Latin. **—imposing** *adj.* 1651, exacting; 1786, impressive because of appearance or manner; formed from English *impose,* v. + *-ing,* modeled on French *imposant.* **—imposition** *n.* About 1380 *imposicioun* tax or duty, in Chaucer's translation of Boethius' *De Consolatione Philosophiae;* borrowed through Old French *imposition* from Latin *impositiōnem* (nominative *impositiō*), from *impōnere* to place upon, see IMPOST; for suffix see -TION. The meaning of an act or instance of imposing on someone, is first recorded in 1632.

impossible *adj.* Before 1325 *impossibile* unbelievable, in *Cursor Mundi;* borrowed from Old French *impossible,* from Latin *impossibilis* not possible (*im-,* variant of *in-*[1] before *p* + *possibilis* POSSIBLE). **—impossibility** *n.* About 1385, formed from English *impossible* + *-ity,* after Old French *impossibilité.* **—impossibly** *adv.* About 1410, formed from English *impossible,* adj. + *-ly*[1].

impost *n.* tax or duty, especially on goods brought into a country. 1568, borrowed probably from written Middle French *impost* (not pronounced with *s* after 1300), from Medieval Latin *impostum,* from neuter of Latin *impostus,* contracted from *impositus,* past participle of *impōnere* to place upon, impose upon (*im-* on, variant of *in-*[2] before *p* + *pōnere* to place, set; see POSITION). **—v.** fix duties on. 1884, American English; from the noun.

impostor *n.* 1586 *impostur* deceiver or swindler; later *impostor* person who assumes a false name or character, in Captain Smith's *The Generall Historie of Virginia* (1624); developed from English *imposture* by confusion with Middle French *imposteur,* learned borrowing from Latin *impostor,* from *impostus,* contracted from *impositus,* past participle of *impōnere* place upon, impose upon, deceive; see IMPOST. **—imposture** *n.* 1537, deception or fraud; borrowed from Middle French *imposture,* from Latin *impostūra,* from *impostus,* contracted from *impositus,* past participle of *impōnere.*

impotent *adj.* Before 1393, physically weak, in Gower's *Confessio Amantis;* borrowed from Old French *impotent* powerless, learned borrowing from Latin *impotentem* lacking control, powerless (*im-* not, variant of *in-*[1] before *p* + *potentem,* nominative *potēns* POTENT). The meaning of sexually powerless, sterile (of a male), is first recorded in Lydgate's writings (before 1444). **—impotence** *n.* About 1412 *impotence* physical weakness; earlier, poverty (probably 1406); borrowed from Middle French *impotence,* learned borrowing from Latin *impotentia* lack of control or power, from *impotentem* (nominative *impotēns*) impotent; for suffix see -ENCE. The meaning of absence of sexual power, male sterility, is first recorded probably before 1450. **—impotency** *n.* 1450; formed from English *impotence* + *-y*[1].

impound *v.* 1434 *inpounden* to shut up in a pen or pound; formed from English *im-*[2] in + *pound*[3] enclosed place. The extended meaning of put in custody of the law, seize or hold by legal means, is first recorded in 1651.

impoverish *v.* make poor. Before 1420 *empoverischen* make poor, in Lydgate's *Troy Book;* later *enpoverisshen* (1435, in *Rolls of Parliament*); borrowed from Old French *empoveriss-,* stem of *empoverir* (*em-* cause to be, variant of *en-*[1] before *p* + *povre* POOR); for suffix see -ISH[2]. The spelling of *impoverish* in imitation of the Latin, is recorded in Middle English before 1443.

impracticable *adj.* 1653, impassable, as of a road, in Cromwell's *Speeches;* later, not practicable (before 1677); formed from English *im-*[1] + *practicable.*

impractical *adj.* 1865, in John Stuart Mill's writings; formed from English *im-*[1] not + *practical.*

imprecation *n.* 1448, a curse, action of invoking evil; later, an invocation (1585); borrowed through Middle French *imprecation,* or directly from Latin *imprecātiōnem* (genitive *imprecātiō*), from *imprecārī* invoke, pray for (*im-* on, variant of *in-*[2] before *p* + *precārī* to PRAY); for suffix see -ATION. **—imprecate** *v.* 1613 *imprecate* call down (curses, evil, etc.), in *Purchas his Pilgrimage,* probably a back formation from *imprecation.*

imprecise *adj.* 1805, formed from English *im-*[1] not + *precise.* **—imprecision** *n.* 1803, formed from English *im-*[1] + *precision.*

impregnable *adj.* that cannot be overcome; unconquerable. 1440 *impregnable,* alteration of earlier *imprenable* (probably before 1439); borrowed from Middle French *imprenable* (Old French *im-* not, from Latin, variant of *in-*[1] before *p* + Old French *prenable* assailable, vulnerable, from the stem of *prendre* to take or grasp, from Latin *prēndere,* contracted from *prehendere* to grasp or seize, see GET); for suffix see -ABLE. The change in form from *imprenable* to *impregnable* was probably influenced by forms such as English *pregnant* and Late Latin *impraegnāre;* though OED supposed the spelling with *g* was also influenced by use of *g* as a spelling device, similar to that in *reign;* however in such a case the *g* did not represent a sound as it does in *pregnant.*

impregnate *v.* 1646 *impregnate* make pregnant, fertilize; earlier, to fill, inspire (1605); back formation from *impregnation;* and, in some instances, probably developed from *impregnate,* adj.; borrowed from Late Latin *impraegnātus,* past participle of *impraegnāre;* for suffix see -ATE[1]. The modern form *impregnate* is a replacement of earlier *impregnen* (probably before 1425, in a translation of Chauliac's *Grande Chirurgie*); borrowed from Late Latin *impraegnāre.* **—impregnation** *n.* Before 1398 *impregnacioun* the action of making or becoming pregnant; borrowed perhaps through Old French *impregnation,* or directly from Late Latin *impraegnātiōnem* (nominative *impraegnātiō*) fertilization, saturation, inspiration, from *impraegnāre* (*im-* in, variant of *in-*[2] before *p* + *praegnāre* make pregnant, from Latin *praegnās* PREGNANT); for suffix see -TION.

impresario (im′presä′rēō) *n.* 1746, organizer or manager of an opera, concert, or theatrical company, in Walpole's *Letters;* borrowed from Italian *impresario,* from *impresa* undertaking, from feminine of *impreso,* past participle of *imprendere* undertake, from Vulgar Latin *imprēndere,* from Latin *im-* on, variant of *in-*[2] before *p* + *prehendere* to grasp, see GET.

impress[1] (impres′) *v.* Probably about 1370 *enpressen* make a permanent image in something; later *impressen* have a strong effect on, fix in the mind or heart (about 1385, in Chaucer's *Troilus and Criseyde*); borrowed from Latin *impressus,* past participle of *imprimere* press into or upon, stamp (*im-* in, variant of *in-*[2] before *p* + *premere* to PRESS[1] squeeze). English *impress* was influenced in its sense development by Old French *empresser* to press, crowd upon, crush, print; see IMPRESSION. **—n.** (im′pres) impression, mark, stamp. 1590, from the verb. **—impression** *n.* About 1380, in Chaucer's *House of Fame,* image produced on the mind, imprint; borrowed from Old French *impression* a pressing, crushing, or having a strong effect on the mind, learned borrowing from Latin *impressiōnem* (nominative *impressiō*) assault, emphasis, mental impression, from *imprimere;* see IMPRESS[1]. **—impressionable** *adj.* 1836, formed from English *impression* + *-able,* probably after French *impressionable,* from *impressioner.* **—impressionism** *n.* 1839, formed from English *impress*[1] + *-ion* + -ism; later, theory or style of painting developed in France (1882); re-formed in English by influence of earlier *impressionist* (1876), after French *impressionisme,* from *impressioniste* impressionist. **—impressionist** *n.* painter in the style of impressionism. 1876, in Henry James' *Parisian Sketches;* borrowed from French *impressioniste,* coined in 1874 from *impression* impression + *-iste* -ist by Louis Leroy, a French critic, with reference to a painting by Claude Monet entitled *Impression, Soleil Levant* (Impression, Sunrise) which was exhibited in Paris in 1874. Leroy used the term derisively, suggesting that Monet was giving merely his own subjective impression of the scene. **—impressive** *adj.* 1573, capable of being impressed, in Nashe's *Christ's Tears Over Jerusalem;* later, making a deep impression (1775); formed from English *impress*[1] + *-ive.*

impress[2] *v.* 1596, force (men) to serve in the armed forces, in Shakespeare's *1 Henry IV;* formed from English *im-*[2] in + *press*[2] force; probably influenced by earlier *imprest* lend or advance a soldier's pay (1565); borrowed from Italian *imprestare* (*im-* in, from Latin, variant of *in-*[2] before *p* + Italian *prestare* to lend, from Latin *praestāre* lend, present, furnish, make available, formed from the adverb *praestō* at hand, from the pre-Latin phrase *prai hestōd, prai* before + ablative case of a lost noun **hestos* which is cognate with Sanskrit *hásta-s* hand, from Indo-European **ĝhéstos,* Pok.447).

imprimatur (im′primā′tər) *n.* official license to print or publish a book, etc. 1640, New Latin *imprimatur* let it be printed (3rd person singular present subjunctive passive of *imprimere* to print), from Latin *imprimere* to mark or engrave, see IMPRESS[1]. The figurative sense of sanction or approval, is first recorded in Marvell's *The Rehearsal Transposed* (1672).

imprint (imprint′) *v.* About 1380 *emprienten, enprienten* to impress on or fix in the mind, memory, etc., in Chaucer's translation of Boethius' *De Consolatione Philosophiae;* borrowed from Old French *empreinter* to stamp or engrave, from *empreint,* past participle of *empreindre* to press on, impress, imprint, from Latin *imprimere* to mark, IMPRESS[1]. The original spelling in the verb with *em-* was altered to *imprinten* (by 1448) to conform to the Latin spelling. **—n.** (im′print) Before 1449 *enpreent* something imprinted; borrowed from Old French *empreinte,* from the feminine past participle of *empreindre* to print. The original spelling of the noun was surely altered in late Middle English to conform to the Latin spelling, but it is not recorded as *imprint* before 1526.

imprison *v.* About 1300 *enprisonen;* borrowed from Old French *emprisoner* imprison (*em-, en-* in + *prison* PRISON). **—imprisonment** *n.* 1386 *emprisonement;* probably borrowed from Old French *emprisonnement,* in 1433, in the *Rolls of Parliament,* from *emprisoner* + *-ment.* The spelling with *im-* is first recorded in 1437.

improbable *adj.* 1598, in Florio's *A World of Words;* probably formed from English *im-*[1] not, variant of *in-*[1] before *p* + *probable,* possibly after Italian *improbabile.*

impromptu (impromp′tü) *adv., adj.* without previous thought or preparation. 1669 *adv.;* 1764 *adj.;* borrowing of French *impromptu,* from the Latin phrase *in prōmptū* in readiness; *prōmptū,* ablative of *prōmptus* readiness, the action of making available, from *prōmere* to bring out (pre-Latin *prō-* forth + *emere* take, cognate with Lithuanian *im̃ti* to take, from Indo-European **em-/m̥-,* Pok.310).

improper *adj.* Before 1393, implied in *improprelich,* adv., improperly; later *impropir* not belonging to the thing under consideration, unsuitable, irregular, incorrect; borrowed from Old French *impropre,* from Latin *improprius* (*im-* not, variant of *in-*[1] before *p* + *proprius* one's own, particular, PROPER).

improve *v.* 1473 *improwen* to turn (land) to profit, enclose and cultivate (wasteland) and make it more valuable, borrowed in part through Anglo-French *emprouwer, emprover* turn to profit (from Old French *em-* make, variant of *en-*[1] before *p* + *prou* profit, from Late Latin *prōde* profitable; see PROUD). The word was also taken into English through Anglo-Latin *improwiāre,* and the spelling with *v* is very rare before the 1600's when it displaced the forms with *w.* It was no doubt influenced by earlier words in English with *-prove,* especially where this formation replaced spellings in *-proue.*

The meaning of utilize or employ to advantage, is first recorded before 1529 and developed, as did *improvement,* from the sense of turning a profit on land. The more specialized sense of make better, is found in 1617.

—improvement *n.* 1449 *enprowment* management of something for profit; later, good or profitable use (about 1611); borrowed from Anglo-French *emprowement,* from *emprouwer* turn to profit. The meaning of betterment or amelioration, is first recorded in 1647 as a specialization of meaning of improving land for better uses (1549, a meaning found in Anglo-French, 1302).

improvidence *n.* About 1450, borrowed from Late Latin *imprōvidentia* (*im-* not, variant of *in-*[1] before *p* + *prōvidentia* foresight, PROVIDENCE).

improvise *v.* compose or utter without preparation. 1826, in Benjamin Disraeli's *Vivian Grey;* back formation from *improvisation,* and probably borrowed from French *improviser;* see IMPROVISATION. **—improvisation** *n.* 1786, borrowed from French *improvisation,* from *improviser* compose or say extemporaneously, from Italian *improvvisare,* from *improvviso* unforeseen or unprepared, learned borrowing from Latin *imprōvīsus* (*im-* not, variant of *in-*[1] before *p* + *prōvīsus* foreseen, past participle of *prōvidēre* foresee, PROVIDE); for suffix see -ATION.

imprudent *adj.* About 1390, in Chaucer's *Canterbury Tales;* borrowed from Latin *imprūdentis,* nominative *imprūdēns* unforesighted (*im-* not, variant of *in-*[1] before *p* + *prūdentis,* nominative *prūdēns* foresighted, contracted form of *prōvidentis,* present participle of *prōvidēre* provide; see PRUDENT); for suffix see -ENT.

impudent *adj.* About 1390, lacking modesty, shameless, in Chaucer's *Canterbury Tales;* borrowed from Latin *impudentis,* nominative *impudēns* (*im-* not, variant of *in-*[1] before *p* + *pudentis,* nominative *pudēns,* present participle of *pudēre* to cause shame; of uncertain origin). **—impudence** *n.* About 1390, shamelessness, in Chaucer's *Canterbury Tales;* borrowed from Latin *impudentia,* from *impudentis* (nominative *impudēns*); see IMPUDENT.

impugn (impyün′) *v.* call in question, attack by words or arguments. About 1378 *inpugnen;* 1382 *impugnen;* borrowed from Old French *impugner,* from Latin *impugnāre* to assault or attack (*im-* toward, variant of *in-*[2] before *p* + *pugnāre* to fight; see PUGNACIOUS).

impulse *n.* sudden, driving force or influence. 1647, probably a back formation from *impulsive,* modeled on Latin *impulsus,* from past participle of *impellere* IMPEL. **—impulsive** *adj.* Probably before 1425 *impulsif* of medicine that has the effect of reducing swelling or humors; later, impelling, driving to action (about 1555); borrowed probably from Middle French *impulsif,* and Medieval Latin *impulsivus,* from Latin *impulsus,* past participle of *impellere* IMPEL. The meaning of acting on impulse, easily moved, is first recorded in 1847.

impunity *n.* freedom from punishment, injury, etc. 1532, in Sir Thomas More's *The Confutation of Tyndale's Answer;* borrowed through Middle French *impunité,* and directly from Latin *impūnitātem* (nominative *impūnitās*) omission of punishment, from *impūnis* unpunished (*im-* not, variant of *in-*[1] before *p* + *poena* punishment; see PAIN); for suffix see -ITY.

impure *adj.* Probably 1440, in some instances; probably borrowed from Middle French *impur, impure,* from Latin *impūrus* (*im-* not, variant of *in-*[1] before *p* + *pūrus* pure); and probably also formed from Middle English *im-*[1] not + *pure.* **—impurity** *n.* Before 1500, formed from Middle English *impure* + *-ity,* perhaps after Middle French *impurité.*

impute *v.* charge (a fault, etc.) to a person; blame. About 1375 *inputen;* later *imputen* (probably before 1425, in a translation of Higden's *Polychronicon*); borrowed through Old French *emputer,* and directly from Latin *imputāre* (*im-* in, against, variant of *in-*² before *p* + *putāre* reckon, think; see PUTATIVE). **—imputation** *n.* 1545, formed in English from *impute* + *-ation,* on the model of Middle French *imputation* and Late Latin *imputātiōnem* (nominative *imputātiō*), from Latin *imputāre* impute.

in *prep.* Old English (before 700) *in* in. The Old English forms *in* in, and *inne* in, within, merged in later Middle English under the simple form *in,* and a similar development took place in the adverbial use of *in* and *inne.*

Cognates with Old English are found in Old Frisian, Old Saxon, and modern Dutch *in* in, Old High German and modern German *in,* Old Icelandic *ī,* and Gothic *in;* cognates outside Germanic are found in Old Irish *in-,* Old Welsh and Old Breton *en, in* (modern Welsh *yn,* modern Breton *e, en*), Cornish *yn,* Latin *in,* Greek *en* in, Albanian *inj* up to, until, Old Prussian *en* in, and Tocharian B *in-,* from Indo-European **en* (Pok.311).

In Old English and early Middle English the prepositional use of *in* was often interchangeable with *on,* which was used generally in Old English where *in* now appears; in later Middle English a distinction was restored.

—adv. Old English *in* (about 725, in *Beowulf*); from the preposition.

—adj. 1599, that is in, internal; from the adverb. The meaning of having power or influence (as in *the in party*) is first recorded in 1817; the sense of exclusive (as in *the in-group*) in 1907, and the extended sense of in style, fashionable, chic (as in *the in thing*) about 1960.

—n. Before 1670, *ins and outs* turns and twists; from the adverb. The meaning of influence with or introduction to someone with power (as in *have an in with*) is first recorded in 1929 in American English.

in-¹ a prefix meaning not, opposite of, without, the absence of, as in *inaccessible, inexpensive, inability, inattention.* Also found in the form *il-* before words beginning with *l; im-* before words beginning with *b, m, p; ir-* before words beginning with *r.* Borrowed from Latin *in-* not; cognate with Sanskrit and Greek *a-* not, and Old English *un-* not; see UN-.

in-² a prefix meaning in, into, on, upon, as in *incase* = *(put) into a case,* and *intrust* = *(give) in trust.* Borrowed from Latin *in-,* related to *in,* prep.; see IN. Also found in the form *il-* before words beginning with *l; im-* before words beginning with *b, m, p; ir-* before words beginning with *r.*

English words having the prefix *in-*² come from two sources. Some were borrowed directly from Latin *in-;* others were borrowed from Old French *en-* (regular phonetic development from Latin *in-*), but were later made over to conform to the Latin. Of this latter group, some English words retained the original *en-;* see EN-¹.

In also has the function of strengthening the meaning of a base form, as in *inweave* = *weave together,* also of changing an intransitive verb to transitive, generally with little alteration of meaning, as in *inearth,* v.t., to bury, and *earth,* v.i., hide; *indwell,* v.t., to inhabit, and *dwell,* v.i., to inhabit.

in-³ a prefix meaning in, within, into, toward, as in *indoors, inland.* Found in Middle English *in-* and Old English *in-;* from the adverb *in.*

in-⁴ a combining form meaning within (something), as in *in-house* (with the specialized meaning of *house* company or organization), *in-country.* These forms with *in-* developed from use in corresponding prepositional phrases, such as *in-depth interview,* meaning an *interview in depth.*

in-⁵ a combining form meaning exclusive, as in *in-group, in-joke.*

-in¹ a combining form of the adverb *in,* formed from a verb + *-in* meaning: **1** a public protest or demonstration, originally in which a group of blacks enter a public place restricted to whites and remain for a long period of time, as in *sit-in* (1960), *wade-in, teach-in.* The early form *sit-in* was probably influenced by *sit-down,* as in *sit-down strike* and *to engage in a sit-down.* **2** any kind of gathering, especially for socializing, as in *sing-in.*

-in² a chemical suffix usually denoting: **1** neutral substances such as fats and proteins, as in *olein, casein.* **2** an antibiotic substance, as in *penicillin, streptomycin.* **3** a vitamin, as in *niacin.* **4** a hormone, as in *insulin.* Variant form of *-ine*².

inaccessible *adj.* Probably before 1425; formed from Middle English *in-*¹ not + *accessible,* after Latin.

inaccurate *adj.* 1669, implied in *inaccurately;* formed from English *in-*¹ not + *accurate;* see ACCURATE.

inactive *adj.* 1725, in Pope's translation of Homer's *Odyssey;* formed from English *in-*¹ not + *active.*

inadequate *adj.* 1675, in Boyle's writings; formed from English *in-*¹ not + *adequate.*

inadvertence *n.* About 1440, borrowed from Middle French *inadvertance.* **—inadvertent** *adj.* 1653, formed from English *inadvertence,* with substitution of suffix *-ent.*

inane (inān′) *adj.* silly, senseless. 1662, empty or void; probably a back formation from *inanity,* modeled on Latin *inānis* empty, of unknown origin. The meaning of empty-headed or silly, is first recorded in Shelley's *The Cenci* (1819). **—inanity** (inan′ətē) *n.* 1603, emptiness, hollowness, in Florio's *A World of Words;* later, silliness (1753); borrowed through French *inanité,* or directly from Latin *inānitātem* (nominative *inānitās*) emptiness, from *inānis* empty; for suffix see -ITY.

A similar development is found in *vain* and *vanity* where the noun is recorded earlier than the adjective. It is also probable that *inanity* was influenced in its borrowing, if not its formation in English, by earlier *inanition* (Middle English *inanision,* 1392; borrowed from Old French *inanicion* or directly from Latin *inānītiōnem,* nominative *inānītiō* emptiness, from Latin *inānīre* to empty, from *inānis* empty).

inanimate *adj.* Probably before 1425, borrowed from Late Latin *inanimātus* lifeless, from Latin *in-* not + *animātus* ANIMATE.

inaugurate *v.* install, dedicate, or establish formally. 1606, a back formation from *inauguration,* and probably developed from earlier *inaugurate,* participial adjective, in Holland's translation of Livy's *Roman History* (1600); borrowed from Latin *inaugurātus,* past participle of *inaugurāre* take omens from the flight of birds, consecrate or install when such omens or auguries are favorable (*in-* on, in + *augurāre* to act as an augur, predict, from *augur* fortuneteller, AUGUR); for suffix see -ATE[1]. —**inauguration** *n.* 1569, borrowed through French *inauguration* installation, consecration, and directly from Latin *inaugurātiōnem* (nominative *inaugurātiō*) consecration or installment under good auspices or omens, from *inaugurāre;* for suffix see -ATION. —**inaugural** *adj.* 1689, possibly a back formation from *inaugurate* + *-al*[1], or borrowed from French *inaugural,* from *inaugurer* to inaugurate (learned borrowing from Latin *inaugurāre*); for suffix see -AL[1]. —*n.* inaugural speech. 1832, American English, from the adjective.

inborn *adj.* Probably before 1350, found in Old English *inboren* native to a place, from *in-* within + *boren* brought forth; see BORN.

incandescent *adj.* 1794, glowing with heat; borrowed through French *incandescent,* or directly from Latin *incandēscentem* (nominative *incandēscēns*), present participle of *incandēscere* become warm, glow, kindle (*in-* within + *candēscere* begin to glow, become white; see CANDESCENT); for suffix see -ENT. The meaning of light produced by incandescence, is first recorded in 1848.

incantation *n.* set of words spoken as a magic charm or to cast a magic spell. Before 1393 *incantacioun,* in Gower's *Confessio Amantis;* borrowed from Old French *incantation,* learned borrowing from Latin *incantātiōnem* (nominative *incantātiō*) art or act of enchanting, from *incantāre* bewitch or charm (literally, chant a magic formula against), see ENCHANT; for suffix see -ATION.

incapable *adj.* 1594, in Shakespeare's *Richard III;* borrowing of Middle French *incapable,* from Medieval Latin *incapabilis* (*in-* not + *capabilis* CAPABLE).

incapacitate *v.* 1657, in Cromwell's speeches; formed from English *incapacity* (1611, borrowed from French *incapacité*) + -ATE[1].

incarcerate *v.* imprison. 1560, probably a back formation from earlier *incarceration,* and, in some instances developed from *incarcerate,* adj. 1528, imprisoned, borrowed from Medieval Latin *incarceratus,* past participle of *incarcerare* imprison (Latin *in-* in + *carcer* enclosed place, prison; of uncertain origin); for suffix see -ATE[1]. —**incarceration** *n.* 1536, imprisonment; borrowed from Old French *incarceration,* from Medieval Latin *incarcerationem* (nominative *incarceratio*), from *incarcerare;* for suffix see -ATION.

incarnate (inkär′nit *or* inkär′nāt) *adj.* embodied in flesh. 1395 *incarnat,* in Wycliffe's writings; borrowed from Late Latin *incarnātus,* past participle of *incarnāre* to make flesh (Latin *in-* in + *carō,* genitive *carnis* flesh; see CARNAL); for suffix see -ATE[1]. —**v.** make incarnate; embody. 1533, embody; later, put into definite form, realize, actualize (1591); probably developed from the adjective, except in instances where it may be a back formation from *incarnation.* —**incarnation n.** About 1300 *incarnacion* embodiment of God in the person of Christ; borrowed from Old French *incarnation,* learned borrowing from Late Latin *incarnātiōnem* (nominative *incarnātiō*), from *incarnāre.* The meaning of a thing that represents some quality or idea, is first recorded in Shelley's *Adonais* (1821).

incendiary *adj.* setting on fire. Before 1460 *incendiary;* probably from the noun. The figurative sense of deliberately stirring up strife or unrest, is first recorded in 1614. —**n.** person who maliciously sets fire. 1402 *incendiarie,* in Trevisa's writings; borrowed from Latin *incendiārius,* n., one who sets afire, from *incendium* fire, from *incendere* set on fire (*in-* in + **candere* to light; see CANDLE).

incense[1] (in′sens) *n.* substance giving off a sweet smell when burned. About 1280 *encens;* borrowed from Old French *encens,* from Late Latin *incēnsus* (genitive *incēnsūs*) burnt incense, from Latin *incendere* set on fire (*in-* in + **candere* to light; see CANDLE). The spelling *in-cense* appeared about 1450, influenced by the Latin form.

incense[2] (insens′) *v.* make very angry. About 1410 *encensen* set afire, kindle the passion; later, to enrage (1494); borrowed from Middle French *incenser,* from Late Latin *incēnsāre,* a frequentative form of Latin *incendere* set on fire; see INCENSE[1]. The spelling *incensen,* influenced by the Latin, is recorded as early as 1477.

incentive *n.* motive, stimulus. Probably before 1425 *incentiue,* in a translation of Higden's *Polychronicon;* borrowed from Late Latin *incentīvum,* noun use of the neuter of Latin adjective *incentīvus* setting the tune (in Late Latin, inciting), from *incen-,* stem of *incinere* strike up, blow into an instrument (*in-* in, into + *canere* sing; see CHANT); for suffix see -IVE. —**adj.** inciting, encouraging. 1603, in Holland's translation of Plutarch's *Moralia;* borrowed from Latin *incentīvus* setting the tune; also, in some instances, probably from the noun in English.

inception *n.* Probably before 1425 *incepcion,* in a translation of Higden's *Polychronicon;* borrowed, perhaps through Middle French *incepcion,* and directly from Latin *inceptiōnem* (nominative *inceptiō*), from *incep-,* stem of *incipere* begin, literally, take in hand (*in-* in, on + *-cipere,* combining form of *capere* take, seize; see CAPTIVE); for suffix see -TION.

incessant *adj.* 1461 *incessaunte* never stopping; borrowed from Old French *incessant,* from Late Latin *incessantem* (nominative *incessāns*), from Latin *in-* not + *cessantem* (nominative *cessāns*), present participle of *cessāre* CEASE; for suffix see -ANT.

incest *n.* Probably before 1200, in *Ancrene Riwle;* borrowed, perhaps from Old French *inceste,* and directly from Latin *incestum* unchastity, lewdness, incest, noun use of neuter adjective, from *incestus* unchaste or impure (*in-* not + *castus* pure; see CASTE). —**incestuous** *adj.* 1532, in Sir Thomas More's *The Confutation of Tyndale's Answer;* borrowed, perhaps by influence of Middle French *incestueux,* from Late Latin *incestuōsus,* from *incestus* (genitive *incestus*) incest; for suffix see -OUS.

inch *n.* Probably before 1200 *unche* measure of length, 1/12 of a foot, in Layamon's *Chronicle of Britain;* later *inch* (about 1300, in *Havelok the Dane*); developed from Old English (about 1000) *ynce,* borrowed from Latin *uncia,* originally, a twelfth part, from pre-Latin **oinicia,* from the root of *ūnus* ONE. Doublet of OUNCE[1] unit of weight. —**v.** move by inches; move little by little. 1599, from the noun.

inchoate (inkō′it) *adj.* just begun, in an early stage, undeveloped. 1534, possibly a back formation from *inchoation* commencement (1530, in Palsgrave's *Lesclarcissement;* borrowed from Middle French *inchoation,* and earlier in Middle English, elements or elementary knowledge, probably before 1400; borrowed directly from Late Latin *inchoātiōnem,* nominative *inchoātiō,* from Latin *inchoāre,* wrongly altered from *incohāre* to begin, start out; originally, to hitch up (a wagon or plough), from *in-* on + *cohum* strap by which a shaft or plough was fastened to the oxen's yoke, from Indo- European **koghom* (Pok.518).). In some instances, *inchoate* may also have been borrowed directly from Latin *inchoātus,* past participle of *inchoāre* to begin; for suffix see -ATE[1].

incident *n.* happening, event. Before 1420 *incydent,* in Lydgate's *Troy Book;* borrowed from Middle French *incident,* from Old French *incident,* adj., and possibly directly from Latin *incidentem* (nominative *incidēns*), past participle of *incidere* happen or befall (*in-* on + *-cidere,* combining form of *cadere* to fall; see CADENCE); for suffix see -ENT. **—adj.** liable to happen, belonging. Probably before 1425, either from the noun in English; or, more likely, borrowed from Middle French *incident,* adj., from Old French *incident,* and possibly directly from Latin *incidentem,* present participle of *incidere.* **—incidence** *n.* Probably before 1437; either formed from Middle English *incident* + *-ence,* or borrowed from Middle French *incidence,* from *incident,* see INCIDENT; for suffix see -ENCE. **—incidental** *adj.* 1616, likely to happen; formed from English *incident,* n. + *-al*[1], and probably also borrowed from French *incidental.* The meaning of not primary, casual or occasional, is first recorded in Milton's *Of Education* (1644); *n.* 1707, casual or occasional circumstances, events, expenses; from the adjective.

incinerate *v.* burn to ashes. 1555, in Eden's translation of Peter Martyr's *Decades of the New World or West India;* developed from *incinerate,* adj., reduced to ashes; borrowed, perhaps by influence of Middle French *incinérer,* from Medieval Latin *incineratus,* past participle of *incinerare* (Latin *in-* into + *cinis,* genitive *cineris* ashes; cognate with Greek *kónis* ashes or dust), from Indo-European **kénis/kónis* (Pok.559); for suffix see -ATE[1]. It is also possible that *incinerate* is, in some instances, a back formation from *incineration.* **—incineration** *n.* Before 1529, in Skelton's writings; borrowed from Middle French *incineration,* from Medieval Latin *incinerationem* (nominative *incineratio*), from *incinerare;* for suffix see -ATION. **—incinerator** *n.* 1883, device for burning substances to ashes; formed from English *incinerate* + *-or*[2].

incipient *adj.* just beginning; in an early stage. 1669; possibly developed from earlier *incipient,* n. (1589); borrowed from Latin *incipientem* (nominative *incipiēns*), present participle of *incipere* begin, take up (*in-* on + *-cipere,* combining form of *capere* take; see CAPTIVE); for suffix see -ENT.

incision *n.* 1392 *inscicioun* (found in various early manuscripts and in Lanfranc, Chauliac, etc.); formed in Middle English from a blend of Old French *incision* or Latin *incīsiōnem* (nominative *incīsiō*) a cutting into, division, and Latin *scissiōnem* (nominative *scissiō*) a cutting, tearing, division, from *scindere* to split, tear, cognate with Sanskrit *chindánti* they cut off, and Greek *schízein* to split, from Indo-European **skeid-/skid-* (Pok.920); also recorded as *incision* (probably before 1422), reborrowed from Middle French *incision* or Latin *incīsiōnem* (nominative *incīsiō*), from *incīdere* to cut into (*in-* into + *-cīdere,* combining form of *caedere* to cut, EXCISE[2]); for suffix see -SION.

The recorded use of *incision* suggests that as an early technical term in medicine the spelling *inscisioun* was confused with Latin *scissiōnem* and blended with Old French *incision,* but that when the word was later adopted into the common vocabulary, the French *incision* was adopted, gradually replacing the earlier Middle English *inscicioun.*
—incisive *adj.* Probably before 1425 *inscissive* cutting, piercing; probably formed in Middle English on the model or earlier *inscicioun* + *-ive* after Middle French *incisif* (feminine *incisive*); also recorded as *incisive* (1528), reborrowed from Middle French *incisif* and probably from Medieval Latin *incisivus,* from Latin *incīdere;* for suffix see -IVE.

The figurative sense of mentally acute, keen, trenchant, is first recorded in 1850 as a French word in an English text, but as early as 1854 *incisive* appears as an English word in Emerson's writings.
—incise *v.* 1541, back formation, probably from *incised,* adj. (re-formed by influence of the modern spellings *incision, incisive*) from earlier *inscised,* adj., cut, slit (before 1425, formed in English with *-ed*[2] on a borrowing of Latin *incīsus,* past participle of *incīdere,* influenced by Latin *scissus,* past participle of *scindere* to divide, cut, tear). It is also probable that English *incise* was later, in part, borrowed from Middle French *inciser,* from Old French *enciser,* from Vulgar Latin **incisāre,* a frequentative form of *incīdere* to cut into. **—incisor** *n.* 1672, tooth adapted for cutting, New Latin *incisor* cutter, from Latin *incīdere;* for suffix see -OR[2]. It is also possible that *incisor* was formed from English *incise* + *-or*[2].

incite *v.* move to action, urge on. 1447 *encyten;* borrowed from Middle French *enciter,* from Latin *incitāre* (*in-* on + *citāre* move, excite; see CITE).

inclement *adj.* 1667, in Milton's *Paradise Lost;* either a back formation from *inclemency* (1559, borrowed from Middle French *inclémence,* from Latin *inclēmentia,* from *inclēmēns*); *or* borrowed from French *inclément* and directly from Latin *inclēmentem* (nominative *inclēmēns*) harsh, unmerciful (*in-* not + *clēmentem* mild, placid); see CLEMENCY; for suffix see -ENT.

incline (inklīn′) *v.* Before 1325 *enclinen* be favorable, be willing, in *Cursor Mundi;* later *enclynen* to slope, slant (about 1380, in Chaucer's translation of Boethius' *De Consolatione Philosophiae*); borrowed from Old French *encliner,* from Latin *inclīnāre* (*in-* in + *clīnāre* to bend; see LEAN[1] slant). The spelling *incline* was influenced by the Latin form, and is found in Lydgate's *Troy Book* (before 1420). **—n.** (in′klīn) 1600, mental tendency; later, slant or slope (1846); from the verb. The noun is recorded in Middle English in an isolated instance as *enclin* inclination of the head or body, a bow (probably before 1400); borrowed from Old French *enclin* a bow. **—inclined** *adj.* About 1384 *enclyned,* in Chaucer's *House of Fame;* formed from English *incline* + *-ed*[1]. **—inclination** *n.* About 1395 *inclinacioun* natural disposition, in Chaucer's *Canterbury Tales;* borrowed from Old French *inclination,* from Latin *inclīnātiōnem* (nominative *inclīnātiō*) leaning, bending, from *inclīnāre* to incline.

include *v.* 1402 *includen* to conceal or hide; later, to comprise or contain (before 1420, in Lydgate's *Troy Book*); borrowed from Latin *inclūdere* (*in-* in + *claudere* to shut, CLOSE[1]). **—inclusion** *n.* 1600, probably formed from English *include* + *-sion,* on the model of Latin *inclūsiōnem* (nominative *inclūsiō*) a shutting up, from *inclūdere* include. It is also possible that inclusion was borrowed from French *inclusion.* **—inclusive** *adj.* 1594, in Shakespeare's *Richard III,* probably re-formed from English *include* + *-ive,* on the model of Medieval Latin *inclusivus,* from Latin *inclūdere. Inclusive* is recorded earlier as an adverb meaning inclusively (1443); borrowed from Medieval Latin *inclusivus.*

incognito (in'kognē'tō) *adj., adv.* with one's name, character and rank, etc., concealed. 1649, both adj. and adv. senses, in John Evelyn's writings; probably borrowed through French *incognito* (by virtue of the pronunciation of *g,* not heard in Italian) from Italian *incognito,* from Latin *incognitus* unknown (*in-* not + *cognitus,* past participle of *cognōscere* to get to know; see COGNIZANCE).

incoherence *n.* 1611, lack of consistency in thought or language, in Florio's *World of Words;* later, lack of connection of subjects (1665, in Boyle's writings); formed from English *in-* + *coherence,* after Italian *incoerenza.* —**incoherent** *adj.* 1626, in Donne's *Sermons;* formed from English *in-* + *coherent,* after earlier *incoherence.*

income *n.* Before 1325, advent, arrival, coming in, in *Cursor Mundi;* earlier *incomen* come in, enter (about 1125); developed from Old English *incuman* (before 971) and *incuma* (about 950, in Northumbrian dialect), from *in,* adv. + *cuman* COME. The meaning of that which comes in through business, labor, etc., proceeds, revenue, is first recorded in 1601. An *income tax* on such proceeds was first enacted and recorded in Great Britain in 1799.

incommodious *adj.* 1551, formed from English *in-*[1] not + *commodious,* in a translation of Latin *incommodus,* in Sir Thomas More's *Utopia.*

incommunicado (in'kəmyü'nəkä'dō) *adj.* deprived of communication with others. 1844, American English; borrowing of Spanish *incomunicado,* from past participle of *incomunicar* deprive of communication (*in-* not + *comunicar* communicate, from Latin *commūnicāre* to share, impart, make common, from *commūnis* COMMON).

incomparable *adj.* 1410, implied in *incomparably;* borrowed through Old French *incomparable* from Latin *incomparābilis* that cannot be equaled (*in-* not + *comparābilis* COMPARABLE).

incompatible *adj.* 1459; borrowed through Old French *incompatible* from Medieval Latin *incompatibilis* (*in-* not + *compatibilis* COMPATIBLE).

incomplete *adj.* Probably 1384, in Wycliffe's writings; borrowed from Old French *incomplette,* and directly from Latin *incomplētus* (*in-* not + *complētus* COMPLETE).

inconsiderate *adj.* About 1475, formed from English *in-*[1] not + *considerate,* possibly after Latin *incōnsīderātus.*

inconsolable *adj.* Before 1500, borrowed from Latin *incōnsōlābilis* (*in-* not + *cōnsōlābilis* CONSOLABLE).

inconvenience *n.* Probably about 1400, inconsistency; later, disadvantage or trouble (1653, in Walton's *The Compleat Angler*); borrowed from Old French *inconvenience,* from Late Latin *inconvenientia* inconsistency (Latin in- + *convenientia* CONSISTENCY). —**inconvenient** *adj.* About 1392, borrowed from Old French *inconvenient,* from Latin *inconvenientem* (nominative *inconveniēns*), from *in-* not + *convenientem* (nominative *conveniēns*) CONVENIENT.

incorporate (inkôr'pərāt) *v.* Before 1398 *incorporaten* combine into one body, include, in Trevisa's translation of Bartholomew's *De Proprietatibus Rerum;* borrowed from Late Latin *incorporātus,* past participle of *incorporāre* unite into one body (Latin *in-* into + *corpus* (genitive *corporis*) body; see CORPSE); for suffix see -ATE[1]. The meaning of establish as a legal corporation is first recorded in the *Rolls of Parliament* (1461). —**incorporation** *n.* 1398, the joining of two or more things, in Trevisa's translation of Bartholomew's *De Proprietatibus Rerum;* borrowed from Late Latin *incorporātiōnem* (nominative *incorporātiō*) uniting, incorporating, from *incorporāre* to incorporate.

incorrect *adj.* Probably before 1425; borrowed from Latin *incorrēctus* uncorrected, unimproved (*in-* not + *corrēctus* CORRECT).

increase (inkrēs') *v.* Before 1333 *encressen* make greater in size or numbers; later *yncreasen* (probably before 1438); borrowed through Anglo-French *encress-,* variant of Old French *encreiss-,* stem of *encreistre,* from Latin *incrēscere* to increase (*in-* in + *crēscere* grow; see CRESCENT). The spelling *increase* was influenced by the Latin form and became the established form in the late 1800's. —**n.** (in'krēs) About 1380 *encrees* a gain in size or numbers; growth, in Chaucer's *Canterbury Tales;* from the verb in Middle English.

increment (ing'krəmənt) *n.* increase, growth. About 1425, borrowed from Latin *incrēmentum* growth, increase, from *incrē-,* stem of *incrēscere* to INCREASE; for suffix see -MENT.

incriminate *v.* accuse of a crime, show to be guilty. 1730-36, in Bailey's *Dictionarium Britannicum,* either a back formation from *incrimination;* or borrowed from Late Latin *incrīminātus,* past participle of *incrīmināre* (Latin *in-* against + *crīmen,* genitive *crīminis* judicial decision, verdict, offense; see CRIME); for suffix see -ATE[1]. —**incrimination** *n.* 1651, formed in English from Late Latin *incrīmināt-,* past participle stem of *incrīmināre* + English *-ion.*

incubate (ing'kyəbāt) *v.* 1641, brood upon; later, to sit on eggs to hatch them (1721, in Bailey's *Dictionary*); borrowed from Latin *incubātus,* past participle of *incubāre* to lie on, hatch (*in-* on + *cubāre* lie; see CUBICLE); for suffix see -ATE[1]. —**incubation** *n.* 1614, in Raleigh's *The History of the World;* borrowed from Latin *incubātiōnem* (nominative *incubātiō*), from *incubāre;* for suffix see -ATION. —**incubator** *n.* 1857, apparatus for hatching birds; formed from English *incubate* + *-or*[2].

incubus (ing'kyəbəs) *n.* Probably about 1350, demon descending on sleeping persons, in Layamon's *Chronicle of Britain;* borrowing of Late Latin *incubus* nightmare, remade from Latin *incubō* (genitive *incubōnis*) (popularly considered a demon lying on the sleeper), from Latin *incubāre* to lie on, INCUBATE.

inculcate (inkul'kāt) *v.* impress by repetition, teach persistently. 1550, in Coverdale's writings; borrowed from Latin *inculcātus,* past participle of *inculcāre* force upon, stamp in (*in-* in + *calcāre* to tread, press in; see CAULK); for suffix see -ATE[1]. —**inculcation** *n.* 1553, borrowed from Latin *inculcātiōnem* (nominative *inculcātiō*), from *inculcāre.*

incumbent *n.* person holding an office. About 1410, person holding a church position, in a version of Chaucer's *Canterbury Tales;* borrowed from Medieval Latin *incumbentem* (nominative *incumbēns*) hold a church position, present participle of *incumbere* to obtain or possess, from Latin *incumbere* recline on, lean or press upon, apply oneself to (*in-* on + *-cumbere* lie down, related to *cubāre* lie; see CUBICLE; for suffix see -ENT. The generalized meaning of any officeholder is first recorded in Marvell's *Rehearsal Transposed* (1672). **—adj.** falling upon as a duty or obligation. 1548, bending one's energies to some work, busy; probably from the noun; perhaps in some instances borrowed from Latin *incumbentem* (nominative *incumbēns*). The meaning of resting upon one as a duty is first recorded in 1567. **—incumbency** *n.* Before 1608, obligation, in Donne's *Letters;* later, term of office (about 1656); formed from English *incumbent* + *-cy.*

incunabula (in'kyùnab'yələ) *n.pl.* earliest stages or first traces of anything; beginnings. 1824, in De Quincey's writings; borrowed from Latin *incūnābula,* neuter plural, swaddling clothes, cradle, (hence) childhood, origin, beginning (*in-* in + *cūnābula* cradle, origin, from *cūnae* cradle; see CEMETERY). The meaning of books produced in the infancy of printing, specifically those printed before 1500, is first recorded in English in 1861, in reference to *Incunabula Typographiae,* the title of the first list of books printed before 1500, published by Cornelius van Beughem, in Amsterdam (1688).

incur *v.* run or fall into (something unpleasant). Probably about 1400 *incurren,* in Wycliffe's writings; borrowed from Middle French *encourir* (also found in Anglo-French *encurir*), from Latin *incurrere* run into, towards, or against (*in-* upon + *currere* to run; see CURRENT). **—incursion** *n.* invasion, raid, sudden attack. Probably before 1425 *incursion,* in a translation of Higden's *Polychronicon;* borrowed through Middle French *incursion,* or directly from Latin *incursiōnem* (nominative *incursiō*) a running against, from *incurrere* INCUR.

incus (ing'kəs) *n.* the middle bone of a chain of three small bones in the middle ear. 1669, borrowed from Latin *incūs* (genitive *incūdis*) anvil, from *incūdere* to forge (on an anvil), fabricate (*in-* in, on + *cūdere* to beat, strike, abstracted from *incūdere, excūdere,* etc., for earlier **caudere;* see HEW); so called because the bone resembles an anvil.

indecent *adj.* 1563-87, unbecoming or unseemly, in an edition of Foxe's *Book of Martyrs;* borrowed through Middle French *indécent,* or directly from Latin *indecentem* (nominative *indecēns*), from *in-* not + *decentem, decēns* fitting or seemly, DECENT; for suffix see -ENT. Some scholars consider Latin *indecēns* a loan translation of Greek *aprepḗs* unseemly or improper. The extended meaning of highly offensive to propriety, morally repugnant, obscene, is first recorded in 1613. **—indecency** *n.* 1589, unseemliness; borrowed perhaps by influence of Middle French *indécence,* from Latin *indecentia,* from *indecentem* (nominative *indecēns*) unseemly; for suffix see -ENCY.

indecorous *adj.* not suitable, improper, unseemly. 1680, borrowed from Latin *indecōrus* (*in-* not + *decōrus* proper, seemly; see DECORUM; for suffix see -OUS.

indeed *adv.* Before 1338 *in dede* in fact, in truth, really, truly, in Mannyng's *Chronicle of England* (*in* + *dede* action, deed, probably about 1175; developed from Old English *dǣd* DEED). *Indeed* was commonly written as two words until about 1600, and still survives in the emphatic *in actual deed.* **—interj.** 1598, as an interrogative with the sense of "really? is that so?", in Shakespeare's *Merry Wives of Windsor;* later, as an expression of surprise, contempt, etc. (1834).

indefatigable *adj.* tireless. 1586, borrowed from Middle French *indéfatigable,* from Latin *indēfatīgābilis* that cannot be tired out (*in-* not + *dēfatīgāre* tire out, from *dē-* out, down + *fatīgāre* to tire; see FATIGUE); for suffix see -ABLE.

indefinite *adj.* Probably about 1425, implied in *indefinitely,* formed from Middle English *in-*[1] not + *definite,* modeled on Latin *indēfinītē, indēfinītus.*

indelible *adj.* that cannot be erased or removed. 1529, in Sir Thomas More's writings; borrowed from Latin *indēlēbilis* (*in-* not + *dēlēbilis* able to be destroyed, from *dēlēre* destroy, blot out; see DELETE); for suffix see -IBLE. The spelling *indelible* was influenced by other words ending with the English suffix *-ible.*

indemnity *n.* payment for or security against damage or loss. 1444 *indempnite* payment for loss; borrowed from Middle French *indempnité, indemnité,* learned borrowing from Late Latin *indemnitātem* (nominative *indemnitās*) security for damage, from Latin *indemnis* unhurt, undamaged (*in-* not + *damnum* damage; see DAMN); for suffix see -ITY. **—indemnify** *v.* to secure against damage or loss. 1611 *indamnifie,* in Cotgrave's *Dictionary;* probably formed in English from French *indemniser* (also found in Cotgrave) + English *-fy.*

indent (indent') *v.* Probably before 1400 *endenten* to notch or dent, in *Morte Arthur;* later *indenten* (about 1400-25); borrowed from Old French *endenter,* from Late Latin *indentāre* to crunch (Latin *in-* in + *dēns,* genitive *dentis* TOOTH). The meaning of set back from the margin on a printed page, is first recorded in 1676. **—n.** (in'dent) 1596, deep recess or notch, in Shakespeare's *1 Henry IV;* from the verb. An earlier sense of written agreement or indenture is first recorded in 1451. **—indentation** *n.* Before 1728, formed from English *indent,* v. + *-ation.* **—indenture** *n.* written agreement. Probably before 1335 *endenture* contract for services, formal agreement; later *indenture* (1440, in *Promptorium Parvulorum*); borrowed through Anglo-French *endenture,* from Old French *endenteüre* indentation, from *endenter* to notch; see INDENT. In some instances the term was probably borrowed into English through Anglo-Latin *indentūra,* perhaps from the Old French; for suffix see -URE.

An *indenture* was written in identical versions on a single sheet which was then cut apart along a zigzag or notched line. By matching the notched edges of two copies, it was possible to prove the genuineness of a document.

—v. 1658, to contract; later, bind by contract (1676); from the noun in English.

independent *adj.* 1611, formed from English *in-*[1] not + *dependent,* probably by influence of Italian *independente* (in Florio's *A World of Words*) and possibly by influence of French *independant;* for suffix see -ENT. **—independence** *n.* 1640, formed from English *independ(ent)* + *-ence; or* as a back formation from *independency* (1611 *independencie,* in Florio's *A World of Words*); for suffix see -ENCY. The word may also be, in part, borrowed from French *independance* (1630).

indeterminate *adj.* About 1391, in Chaucer's *Treatise on the Astrolabe;* borrowed from Latin *indēterminātus* undefined or unlimited *(in-* not + *dēterminātus* defined or limited*);* for suffix see -ATE[1].

index *n.* Before 1398 *index* forefinger (used for point ing), in Trevisa's translation of Bartholomew's *De Proprietatibus Rerum;* borrowed from Latin *index* (genitive *indicis*) forefinger, pointer, sign, list, catalogue, literally, anything which points out, from *indicāre* point out, INDICATE.

The meaning of an alphabetical list of the contents of a book, is first recorded in 1580, a borrowing from such Latin phrases as *Index Nominum* Index of Names, *Index Verborum* Index of Words, often used as headings in English books of that period.

During the 1800's *index* was first used in various sciences in the sense of an indicator, a number or formula indicating some property, form, ratio, etc., of the thing in question; for example *refractive index* in optics (1871), *cephalic index* in craniometry (1866, in Huxley). In economics, *price index* is first recorded in 1886, *cost-of-living index* in the *Commonwealth of Australia Labour Bulletin* in 1913.

—v. 1720, provide with an index; from the noun. The meaning of point out or indicate, is first recorded in Burns' poetry (1788), and that of to adjust to what is indicated; especially to adjust income, interest rates, etc., to changes in the value of money by means of an index, is found in 1972 (this latter sense perhaps from *indexation*).

—indexation *n.* adjustment of wages, rates of interest, etc., to changes in the value of money by means of a cost-of-living or similar index. 1960, formed from English *index,* n. (as in *price index*) + *-ation.*

Indian *n.* Probably before 1300 *Indien* person born or living in India, or the East Indies, in *Kyng Alisaunder;* borrowed from Old French *Indien,* from Medieval Latin *Indianus,* from Latin *India,* from Greek *Indíā* the region of the Indus river; later, the region beyond the Indus river, from *Indós* the Indus river, from Old Persian *Hindu* Indian province of Sind (cognate with Sanskrit *síndhu-s* river, the river Indus); for suffix see -AN. The name *India, Indea* was also known in Old English (before 899, in Alfred's works); borrowed directly from Latin. In Modern English *Indian* has been used at least since 1602 in reference to the original inhabitants the European colonists and explorers found in America. **—adj.** About 1566 *Indian* of or having to do with India or the East Indies; from the noun. In modern English *Indian,* adj., has been recorded since 1608 (*Indian towne*) and was also used by DeSoto (found in a translation, 1544) to refer to the American Indian.

indication *n.* Probably before 1425 *indicacion* a sign, suggestion, in an anonymous translation of Chauliac's *Grande Chirurgie;* borrowed from Latin *indicātiōnem* (nominative *indicātiō*) valuation, from *indicāre* point out, show (*in-* in + *dicāre* proclaim; see DICTION); for suffix see -ATION. The more general sense of a sign or something that indicates, is first recorded in Bacon's *Sylva Sylvarum* (1626). **—indicative** *adj., n.* About 1450 *indicatyf* a verb form in grammar which indicates an actual state or an objective fact; borrowed from Old French *indicatif* (feminine *indicative*), from Late Latin *indicātīvus,* from Latin *indicāre;* for suffix see -IVE. The general sense of pointing out or being a sign of, is first recorded in 1624. **—indicate** *v.* 1651, back formation from *indication,* n. **—indicator** *n.* 1666; formed from English *indicate* + *-or*², modeled on Late Latin *indicātor* one that points out, from Latin *indicāre.*

indict (indīt′) *v.* Before 1626 *indict* charge with an offense or crime, in Bacon's *Elements of the Common Laws;* earlier *indyten* (about 1440, in *Promptorium Parvulorum*); *endyten* (about 1303, in Mannyng's *Handlyng Synne*); borrowed through Anglo-French *enditer* indict, from Old French *enditer, enditier* to dictate or inform; see INDITE.

The alteration of spelling in *indict* reflects the influence of Medieval Latin *indictare* to indict and, in English, its apparent restricted use to the legal sense. Despite the Latinized spelling, the pronunciation reflects the earlier forms of the word.

—indictment *n.* 1594 *indictment,* in Shakespeare's *Richard III;* a spelling alteration by influence of Medieval Latin *indictare,* or earlier *indytement* (1440, in *Promptorium Parvulorum*); *endytement* (about 1303, in Mannyng's *Handlyng Synne*); borrowed through Anglo-French *enditement,* from *enditer* INDICT.

indifferent *adj.* 1380 (implied in *indifferently*), not tending to prefer one to another, unbiased, impartial, neutral, in Chaucer's translation of Boethius' *De Consolatione Philosophiae;* borrowed through Old French *indifferent,* or directly from Latin *indifferentem* (nominative *indifferēns*) not differing, making no difference, not particular (*in-* not + *differentem, differēns,* present participle of *differre* set apart, DIFFER); for suffix see -ENT.

The extended meaning of unconcerned, unmoved, apathetic, is first recorded in 1519. The meaning of neither good nor bad, average (1532) later became a euphemism for not particularly good, poor, inferior, as in an *indifferent writer* (1638).

—indifference *n.* About 1445, impartiality; perhaps a learned borrowing from Middle French *indifférence,* or directly from Latin *indifferentia* lack of difference, equivalence, from *indifferentem* making no difference; see INDIFFERENT. It is also possible that *indifference* was, in some instances, formed from English *indifferent* + *-ence.*

indigenous (indij′ənəs) *adj.* originating in the region or country where found; native. 1646; formed in English from Latin *indigena,* adj. and n., (one) born in a country, native (*indu* in, within + *gen-,* root of *gignere* beget) + English suffix *-ous.*

indigent (in′dəjənt) *adj.* poor, needy. Probably before 1400, in Chaucer's translation of *Roman de la Rose;* borrowed from Old French *indigent,* learned borrowing from Latin *indigentem* (nominative *indigēns*), present participle of *indigēre* to need (*indu* in, within + *egēre* be in need, want, cognate with Old Icelandic *ekla* a lack, from Indo-European **eg-,* Pok.290); for suffix see -ENT. It is possible *indigent* is a back formation from *indigence.* **—indigence** *n.* About 1385 *indigence* lack, lack of; borrowed from Old French *indigence,* learned borrowing from Latin *indigentia,* from *indigentem;* see INDIGENT.

indigestion *n.* 1392, borrowed, possibly through Old French *indigestion,* or directly from Late Latin *indīgestiōnem* (nominative *indīgestiō*), from *in-* not + *dīgestiōnem, dīgestiō* DIGESTION.

indignation *n.* righteous anger. Probably before 1200 *indignatio* disdain, contempt, in *Ancrene Riwle;* later *indignacioun* anger at something unworthy or wrongful (about 1350); borrowed through Old French *indignation,* or directly borrowed from Latin *indignātiōnem* (nominative *indignātiō*), from *indignārī* regard as unworthy, be angry or displeased at, from *indignus* unworthy (*in-* not + *dignus* worthy; see INDIGNITY); for suffix see -ATION. **—indignant** *adj.* 1590, in Spenser's *Faerie Queene,* probably a back formation from *indig-*

nation with suffix *-ant,* modeled on Latin *indignantem* (nominative *indignāns*), present participle of *indignārī* be angry or displeased at. The sense of anger at something unworthy or wrongful, is first recorded about 1350, in the form *indignacioun,* borrowed from Old French *indignation,* from Latin *indignātiōnem;* see above. **—indignity** *n.* unworthy treatment, insult, affront. 1584 *indignitie;* probably borrowed from Middle French *indignité,* from Latin *indignitātem* (nominative *indignitās*), from *indignus* unworthy (*in-* not + *dignus* worthy; see DIGNITY). It is also possible that in some instances the word was formed from English *in-*[1] + *dignity.* The spelling was regularized to *-ity* by the 1750's.

indigo (in'dəgō) *n.* blue dyestuff. 1555 *endego;* later *indigo* (1598) and *indico* (before 1599). The variety of forms is attributable to the variety of immediate source: *indico* from Spanish; *endego* from Portuguese; *indigo* from Dutch by influence of Portuguese, and also directly from Portuguese. The forms all were ultimately borrowed from Latin *indicum,* from Greek *indikón,* literally, Indian substance, from neuter of *indikós* Indian, from *Indós* the Indus river; see INDIAN, from Old Persian *Hindu* Indian province of Sind (cognate with Sanskrit *síndhu-s* river, the river Indus).

Indigo, indico, and *endigo* apparently coexisted from the 1500's until the mid-1600's when *indigo* became the more generally used term. *Indigo* (and variants) replaced Middle English *ynde* indigo pigment (1296), borrowed from Old French *inde,* from Latin *indicum.* **—adj.** deep violet-blue. 1856, from the noun.

indirect *adj.* Probably before 1387, in a version of *Piers Plowman;* probably borrowed from Old French *indirect,* from Late Latin *indīrēctus* not direct (Latin *in-* not + *dīrēctus* direct).

indiscretion *n.* About 1340 *indescrecyone* imprudence; probably borrowed from Old French *indiscretion,* learned borrowing from Latin *indiscrētiōnem* (nominative *indiscrētiō*), from *in-* not + *discrētiōnem, discrētiō* DISCRETION. It is also possible that *indiscretion* was formed from English *in-*[1] not + *discretion.*

indisposed *adj.* Before 1400, formed from English *in-*[1] not + *disposed.*

indite (indīt') *v.* put in words or writing; compose. About 1303 *endyten,* in Mannyng's *Handlyng Synne;* borrowed from Old French *enditer* dictate, inform, compose, from Vulgar Latin ***indictāre*** (formed from Latin *in-* in + *dictāre* declare or compose in words, DICTATE). The variant Middle English spelling *indyten* (1440, in *Promptorium Parvulorum*) was influenced by the Latin prefix *in-. Indite* and *indict* came into English with distinct, but related meanings: a formal accusation was contained in a written legal document. Originally both words also had the same spelling, but *indite* retained a Latin prefix and French root, while *indict* became a thoroughly Latinized form.

indium (in'dēəm) *n.* metallic chemical element. 1864, New Latin, an alteration of Latin *indicum* INDIGO with *-ium,* chemical suffix; so called from the blue lines in its spectrum. The term was coined in 1863 by its codiscoverers, the German chemists Richter and Reich.

individual *adj.* single, separate. 1605 *individuall* peculiar to one person, in Bacon's *Of the Advancement of Learning;* borrowed probably from Middle French *individual,* and directly from Medieval Latin *individualis,* from Latin *indīviduus* indivisible or inseparable (*in-* not + *dīviduus* divisible, from *dīvidere* DIVIDE); for suffix see -AL[1]. An isolated example is recorded in Middle English *indyuyduall* indivisible, single (about 1425). **—n.** 1605, single thing; later, single person (1626); from the adjective. **—individualism** *n.* 1827, pursuit of one's own ends or ideas; formed from English *individual* + *-ism;* also borrowed from French *individualisme,* in a translation of De Tocqueville's *Democracy in America;* the French word is from Medieval Latin *individualis* individual. **—individualist** *n.* 1840 one who practices individualism, in Gladstone's *Church Principles Considered in their Results;* formed from English *individual* + *-ist;* also possibly borrowed from French *individualiste,* from Medieval Latin *individualis* individual. **—individuality** *n.* 1614, in Selden's *Titles of Honor,* individual character, formed from English *individual* + *-ity.*

indivisible *adj.* Before 1425, in Wycliffe's sermons; borrowed from Middle French *indivisible,* and directly from Late Latin *indīvīsibilis* (*in-* not + *dīvīsibilis* DIVISIBLE).

Indo- a combining form meaning India or Indian, as in *Indo-Aryan;* also meaning India and ______, or Indian and ______, as in *Indo-European.* Borrowed from *Indo-,* combining form of Greek *Indós* Indian.

indoctrinate *v.* teach a doctrine, belief, or principle to. 1626, teach or instruct; probably reformed to the pattern of English verbs in *-ate* from earlier *indoctrine* teach or instruct (1509), found in Middle English *endoctrinen* (probably about 1450); borrowed from Middle French *endoctriner* (Old French *en-* put in + *doctrine* DOCTRINE); for suffix see -ATE[1]. **—indoctrination** *n.* 1646, formed from English *indoctrinate* + *-ion.*

Indo-European *adj.* 1814, referring to a particular group of languages spoken in India, Western Asia, and Europe (compare an earlier name *Aryan*). The term, at one time or another vying for prominence with *Aryan* and *Indo-Germanic,* has become the standard form in language study, and is of German origin, as used by early scholars, such as Klaproth, Meyer, and Bopp. Borrowed probably from German *indoeuropäisch,* translated as *indo-européen* in French, and *Indo-European* in English. It is interesting to note that at the time the letter *I* was being compiled for the OED (1899-1901) by Murray, he felt that under the prominence of German studies in linguistics *Indo-Germanic* was probably more in use than *Indo-European.*

indolent (in'dələnt) *adj.* avoiding trouble or work, lazy. 1710, in Steele's writings in the *Tatler,* and 1711, in Addison's writings in *The Spectator;* borrowed from French *indolent,* from Middle French, insensitive or callous, from Late Latin *indolentem* (nominative *indolēns*) insensitive to pain (Latin *in-* not + *dolentem,* nominative *dolēns* grieving, present participle of *dolēre* suffer pain; see DOLOR); for suffix see -ENT. The Latin *indolentem, indolēns* past feeling pain, was coined by Jerome to render Greek *apēlgēkṓs* (found in *Ephesians*).

An earlier use of *indolent,* in the medical sense of causing no pain, painless, is first recorded in Boyle's writings (1663); borrowed directly from Late Latin *indolentem.*

—indolence *n.* laziness. 1710, in Steele's writings in the *Tatler;* borrowed from French *indolence,* from Middle French, ease of living, from Latin *indolentia* freedom from pain, insensibility (*in-* not + *dolentem,* present participle); for suffix see -ENCE.

indomitable *adj.* unconquerable. 1634, that cannot be tamed; borrowed from Late Latin *indomitābilis* untamable, from *in-* not + **domitābilis* tamable, from Latin *domitāre* to tame, frequentative form of *domāre* to tame; see DAUNT). *Indomitable* replaced the earlier form *indomable* untamable (before 1500); borrowed probably from Old French *indomable,* and directly from Latin *indomābilis* (*in-* not + *domābilis* tamable, from *domāre* to tame); for both forms see suffix -ABLE. The extended meaning of unconquerable or unyielding is first recorded in Scott's *The Fair Maid of Perth* (1828).

indoors *adv.* 1799, in Washington's writings, used as an adjective, from the earlier phrase *within doors* (1581).

indubitable *adj.* not to be doubted. 1624, implied in *indubitably;* borrowed from French *indubitable,* or directly from Latin *indubitābilis* (*in-* not + *dubitābilis* doubtful, from *dubitāre* hesitate, waver, DOUBT); for suffix see -ABLE. An isolated example of *indubitable* is recorded in Middle English *indubitabyll* (about 1461); also borrowed from Latin *indubitābilis.*

induce *v.* About 1385 *enducen* lead on, persuade, in Usk's *The Testament of Love;* later *inducen* (1402, possibly influenced by Middle French *inducer*); borrowed from Latin *indūcere* lead into, introduce to, persuade (*in-* in + *dūcere* to lead; see TOW[1] pull). **—inducement** *n.* 1594, in Shakespeare's *Richard III;* formed from English *induce* + *-ment.*

induct *v.* Probably about 1378 *inducten* introduce into a church office, in Wycliffe's writings; borrowed from Latin *inductus,* past participle of *indūcere* lead into; see INDUCE. The generalized sense of introduce into office, install, is first recorded in 1548. The figurative meaning of introduce to knowledge, or the like, initiate, is found in Holland's translation of Plutarch's *Moralia* (1603). A more recent use of bring into the armed forces, enroll for military service, was first recorded in American English (1934).

—induction *n.* Before 1398 *induccioun* introduction to the grace of God, in Trevisa's translation of Bartholomew's *De Proprietatibus Rerum;* later, formal introduction into a church office (about 1400); borrowed through Old French *inducion* introduction, induction, or directly from Latin *inductiōnem* (nominative *inductiō*) introduction, also, a method of reasoning from the particular to the general, from *induc-,* stem of *indūcere* lead into; for suffix see -TION. The meaning of a conclusion in logic reached by inductive reasoning is recorded in Middle English (probably before 1425). In this sense, the Latin word is a translation of Greek *epagōgḗ* (Aristotle). The scientific meaning of a process by which an object having magnetic or electrical properties produces similar properties in a nearby object is first recorded in 1801. A more recent use of enrollment in the armed forces is first recorded in American English (1934). **—inductive** *adj.* Probably before 1425, leading on or inducing; borrowed through Old French *inductif* (feminine *inductive*) inducing, or directly from Late Latin *inductīvus* relating to an assumption, from Latin *induc-,* stem of *indūcere;* for suffix see -IVE. The meaning of reasoning in logic by induction is first recorded in 1764. The scientific meaning relating to electrical or magnetic properties of induction is first recorded in Faraday's writings, in 1832.

indulge *v.* 1638, yield to the wishes of; humor; probably, in part, a back formation from *indulgent, indulgence;* and, in part, borrowed from Latin *indulgēre* be kind, yield, bestow (a favor), concede, allow; of uncertain origin. **—indulgence** *n.* Before 1376 *indulgence* in the Roman Catholic Church, a freeing from temporal punishment for sin, in *Piers Plowman;* later, mercy or leniency (before 1382, in the Wycliffe Bible); borrowed through Old French *indulgence,* or directly from Latin *indulgentia* indulgence, complaisance, fondness, remission, from *indulgentem* (nominative *indulgēns*), present participle of *indulgēre* indulge; for suffix see -ENCE. **—indulgent** *adj.* 1509, probably a back formation from *indulgence,* and possibly in some instances borrowed from Latin *indulgentem* (nominative *indulgēns*), present participle of *indulgēre;* for suffix see -ENT.

industry *n.* About 1477 *industrie* cleverness, skill, application of skill, in Caxton's translation of *History of Jason;* later, diligence, industriousness, effort (1531, in Elyot's *The Boke Named the Governour*); borrowed from Old French *industrie,* learned borrowing from Latin *industria* diligence, earlier **industruia,* formed from early Latin *indostruus* diligent (*indu* in, within + the stem of *struere* to build; see INDIGENT and STRUCTURE); for suffix see -Y[3].

The meaning of a particular form or branch of a skill applied to trade or manufacture, is first recorded about 1566, and that of systematic work or continual employment in useful work, appears in Shakespeare's *Cymbeline* (1611).

—industrial *adj.* 1590 *industriall* resulting from labor; probably originally formed in English from Latin *industria* diligence + English *-al[1].* No recorded use of *industrial* appears after the 1600's, until the word was probably reintroduced (1774) as a new borrowing from French *industriel* (*industrie* industry, from Latin *industria* diligence + *-el* -al[1]). **—industrialize** *v.* 1882, formed in English from *industrial* + *-ize,* on the model of French *industrialiser* (1842). **—industrious** *adj.* 1523, implied in earlier *industriously* skillful, clever; borrowed possibly through Middle French *industrieux,* and directly from Late Latin *industriōsus* diligent, from Latin *industria* diligence; see INDUSTRY. The meaning of diligent or hardworking, is first recorded in Spenser's *Muiopotmos* (1591).

-ine[1] a suffix forming adjectives from nouns, and meaning of, like, like that of, characteristic of, having the nature of, being, as in *crystalline, elephantine.* Borrowed through French *-ine,* feminine form of *-in,* or directly from Latin *-inus, -īnus* of, belonging to, like; cognate with Greek *-inos, -īnos,* Sanskrit *-ina-s.* Related to -EN[2].

-ine[2] a suffix forming nouns, and used in the names of chemical elements, as in *chlorine, fluorine,* and in the names of basic substances, as in *cocaine, amine.* Borrowed from French *-ine* (from Latin *-īna*), or directly from Latin *-īna,* feminine suffix of abstract nouns. The variant suffix *-in,* as in *dextrin,* usually denotes neutral substances, such as fats, glycosides, and proteins.

inebriate (inē′brēāt) *v.* make drunk, intoxicate. 1497, developed from earlier *inebriate,* adj., intoxicated, drunk (1447); borrowed from Latin *inēbriātus,* past participle of *inēbriāre* (*in-* + *ēbriāre* make drunk, from *ēbrius* drunk, of uncertain origin); for suffix see -ATE[1]. **—n.** habitual drunkard, intoxicated person. 1794-96; from the verb. **—inebriation** *n.* 1526, exhilaration; later, intoxication (1646, though this seems a defect in the record); formed from English *inebriate* + *-ation.*

ineffable *adj.* not to be expressed in words. Before 1398 *ineffabile* unexpressible, in Trevisa's translation of Bartholomew's *De Proprietatibus Rerum;* borrowed through Old French *ineffable* unspeakable, or directly from Latin *ineffābilis* unutterable (*in-* not + *effābilis* speakable, from *effārī* utter, *ef-* out, variant of *ex-* before *f* + *fārī* speak); see FATE; for suffix see -ABLE.

ineffectual *adj.* Before 1425; probably formed from Middle English *in-* not + *effectualle,* possibly after Medieval Latin **ineffectualis* or a corresponding form in Old French.

inefficient *adj.* 1750, in Lord Chesterfield's letters (also in his letters *inefficiency,* 1749); formed from English *in-*[1] not + *efficient.*

inept *adj.* inappropriate, absurd, clumsy. 1603, without aptitude, in Florio's translation of Montaigne's *Essays;* 1604, absurd, foolish; borrowed from French *inepte,* from Latin *ineptus* (*in-* not + *aptus* APT). **—ineptitude** *n.* 1615, borrowed possibly from now obsolete French *ineptitude,* from Latin *ineptitūdō,* from *ineptus* unsuitable, absurd. It is also possible that the word was, at least in some instances, formed from English *inept* + connective *i* + *-tude,* on the model of *plenitude,* etc.

inequality *n.* Probably before 1425, borrowed perhaps from Old French *inequalité,* learned borrowing from Medieval Latin, and directly from Medieval Latin *inaequalitas,* from Latin *inaequālis* unequal (*in-* not + *aequālis* EQUAL).

inert *adj.* having no power to move or act, lifeless. 1647 *inert* inactive, in Henry A. More's *The Immortality of the Soul;* borrowed from French *inerte,* and directly from Latin *inertem* (nominative *iners*) unskilled, inactive, motionless, inert (*in-* without + *ars,* genitive *artis* skill, ART).

inertia (inėr′shə) *n.* tendency of matter to continue in its existing state. 1713, New Latin, a specialized use of Latin *inertia* unskillfulness or inactivity, from *iners* (genitive *inertis*) unskilled or inactive, INERT. The term as a form in New Latin was introduced into physics by the German astronomer and mathematician Kepler, in his studies of planetary motion; it is also recorded in Newton's *Principia* (1687). Early examples show *inertia* used as Latin *inertia,* or as *vis inertiae* until the early 1700's. The meaning of inactivity, sloth, apathy, is first recorded in De Quincey's *Confessions of an English Opium-Eater* (1822-56).

inestimable *adj.* About 1380 *inestimable* that cannot be computed, in Chaucer's translation of Boethius' *De Consolatione Philosophiae;* borrowed through Old French *inestimable,* or directly from Latin *inaestimābilis* (*in-* not + *aestimābilis* ESTIMABLE).

inevitable *adj.* About 1443, borrowed from Latin *inēvītābilis* unavoidable; from *in-* not + *ēvītābilis* avoidable, from *ēvītāre* to avoid, from *ē-* out, variant of *ex-* + *vītāre* shun (originally, go out of the way), from a lost adjective **vītus,* cognate with Sanskrit *vīta-s* gone away, disappeared, from Indo-European **wītós,* contracted from **wi-* apart + **itós* gone, verbal adjective to *ei-/i-* to go (Pok. 295).

inexhaustible *adj.* Before 1631 *inexhaustible* that cannot be consumed or spent, in Donne's writings; borrowed from Old French *inexhaustible* not exhaustible; it is also possible that the term was formed in English from *in-*[1] not + *exhaustible.*

inexorable (inek′sərəbəl) *adj.* relentless, unyielding. 1553, perhaps borrowed from Middle French *inexorable,* and directly from Latin *inexōrābilis* (*in-* not + *exōrābilis* easily entreated or moved, from *exōrāre* to prevail upon, pray earnestly, from *ex-* out + *ōrāre* pray, recite; see ORATION); for suffix see -ABLE.

infallible *adj.* Before 1420, in Lydgate's *Troy Book;* borrowed from Medieval Latin *infallibilis* (*in-* not + *fallibilis* FALLIBLE).

infamous (in′fəməs) *adj.* About 1378 *infamis* wicked, notorious, in a version of *Piers Plowman;* borrowed possibly by influence of Old French *infameux,* from Medieval Latin *infamosus,* with the meaning influenced by Latin *īnfāmis* of ill fame (*in-* not, without + *fāma* reputation; see FAME); for suffix see -OUS. The Medieval Latin *infamosus* was formed on Latin *in-* not + *fāmōsus* celebrated, FAMOUS. **—infamy** *n.* Probably before 1425, in a translation of Higden's *Polychronicon;* borrowed from Middle French *infamie,* learned borrowing from Latin, and directly from Latin *īnfāmia,* from *īnfāmis* of ill fame.

infant *n.* About 1384 *infaunt* baby or young child, in the Wycliffe Bible; borrowed from Old French *enfant,* or directly from Latin *īnfantem* (nominative *īnfāns*), noun use of adjective with the meaning of not able to speak, young (*in-* not + *fantem, fāns,* present participle of *fārī* speak; see BAN[1] forbid); for suffix see -ANT. **—adj.** About 1586, from the noun. **—infancy** *n.* Before 1398 *infancia* infancy, in Trevisa's translation of Bartholomew's *De Proprietatibus Rerum;* later *enfaunce* (probably before 1400), and *infancy* (probably before 1425); borrowed through Anglo-French *enfaunce,* or directly from Latin *īnfantia* babyhood, inability to speak, from *īnfantem* (nominative *īnfāns*) infant; see INFANT; for suffix see -CY. **—infantile** *adj.* 1443, of an infant or infancy, in an early stage; borrowed from Latin *īnfantīlis,* from *īnfantem* (nominative *īnfāns*) infant. The meaning of childish is first recorded in 1772.

infanticide *n.* killing of a baby. 1656, in Blount's *Glossographia;* borrowed probably through French *infanticide,* and directly from Late Latin *īnfanticīdium,* from Latin *īnfantem* INFANT; for suffix see -CIDE[2] killing.

infantry *n.* soldiers who fight on foot. 1579, borrowed from French *infanterie,* from older Italian and Spanish *infanteria* foot soldiers, from *infante* foot soldier, originally, a youth, from Latin *īnfantem* INFANT.

infatuate (infach′ủāt) *v.* inspire with a foolish or extreme passion. 1533, to make foolish; later, to inspire with a foolish or extreme passion (1567); developed from earlier *infatuate,* adj. (1471); borrowed from Latin *īnfatuātus,* past participle of *īnfatuāre* make a fool of or infatuate (*in-* in + *fatuus* foolish; see BAT[1] stick); for suffix see -ATE[1]. **—infatuation** *n.* foolish or extreme passion. 1649, formed from English *infatuate* + *-ion,* and in some instances perhaps borrowed from French *infatuation,* from Late Latin *īnfatuātiōnem* (nominative *īnfatuātiō*), from Latin *īnfatuāre;* for suffix see -TION.

infect *v.* A blend of two words in Middle English, both with the meaning corrupt, contaminate, afflict with disease: *infecten,* probably about 1378, in Wycliffe's writings; borrowed from Latin *infectus,* past participle of *inficere* to taint, spoil, stain, literally, put in (*in-* in + *facere* perform, DO[1]); and *enfecten,* about 1380, in Chaucer's translation of Boethius' *De Consolatione Philosophiae;* borrowed from Old French *enfait, infaict,* past participle forms of *infaire,* from Latin *in-* in + *facere* perform, DO[1]. Middle English also had a past participle form *enfect* (about 1380), and *enfeit* (probably about 1400), corresponding to the Old French *enfait.*

Originally *infect* meant to communicate or transmit a disease by the agency of the atmosphere or water. After the discovery of microorganisms *infect* came to mean to communicate germs or viruses that cause disease. The figurative sense of affect or influence with some feeling or quality, is first recorded in Shakespeare's *King John* (1595), and that of engender a belief, especially a heretical opinion, is recorded somewhat earlier, in Caxton's version of the *Golden Legend* (1483).

—infection *n.* 1392 *infeccioun* disease transmitted by air or water; also, any kind of disease; borrowed through Old French *infection,* and directly from Late Latin *īnfectiōnem* (nominative *īnfectiō*), from Latin *īnfect-*, stem of *īnficere;* for suffix see -TION. **—infectious** *adj.* 1542, communicating disease, infecting with disease; formed from English *infection* + *-ous.* The figurative sense of something spreading from one to another, catching or contagious, is first recorded in Beaumont and Fletcher's *The Maid's Tragedy* (before 1611).

infer *v.* find out by reasoning, conclude. 1526 *enferre* bring in, bring forward; borrowed, perhaps in part by influence of Middle French *inférer,* from Latin *īnferre* bring about, bring into, cause, introduce *(in-* in + *ferre* carry, BEAR²*).* The meaning of draw as a conclusion, is first recorded in Sir Thomas More's *A Dialogue Concerning Heresies* (1529). **—inference** *n.* 1594, a conclusion drawn from facts or statements, in Hooker's *Ecclesiastical Polity;* borrowed from Medieval Latin *inferentia,* from Latin *īnferentem* (nominative *īnferēns*), present participle of *īnferre* infer; for suffix see -ENCE. **—inferential** *adj.* 1657, formed in English from Medieval Latin *inferentia* inference + English *-al.*¹

inferior *adj.* lower in position or rank. Probably before 1425, situated below, in a translation of Higden's *Polychronicon;* later, lower in rank or importance (1531); borrowed from Latin *īnferior* lower, a comparative form of *īnferus,* adj., that is below or beneath; cognate with Sanskrit *ádhara-s* lower, and Gothic *undar, undarō* UNDER. **—n.** Before 1425, person who is lower in rank or station; subordinate, also in a translation by Higden; from the adjective. **—inferiority** *n.* 1599 *inferioritie* in Minsheu's *Spanish Dictionary;* borrowed probably through Middle French *infériorité* (also found in Italian *inferiorità* and Spanish *inferioridad*) and directly from Medieval Latin *inferioritatem* (nominative *inferioritas*), from Latin *īnferior;* for suffix see -ITY.

infernal *adj.* About 1385 *infernal* of hell, in Chaucer's *Canterbury Tales;* borrowed from Old French *infernal,* from Late Latin *īnfernālis* belonging to the lower regions, from *īnfernus* hell, literally, the lower world, noun use of Latin *īnfernus* situated below, of the lower regions, lower, related to *īnfernus* below; see UNDER. The extended meaning of like that of hell, hellish, as in *infernal heat,* is first recorded in 1562. *Infernal,* with the sense of diabolical or devilish, as in an *infernal falseness,* is found in Lydgate's *Falls of Princes* (probably before 1439).

inferno (infėr′nō) *n.* 1834, hell; a place of torment; borrowed from Italian *inferno* hell, from Late Latin *īnfernus* hell; see INFERNAL. The use of *inferno* is probably with conscious allusion to Dante's *Divine Comedy,* Part I, *Inferno,* where Vergil leads Dante through the nine circles of hell.

infest *v.* Probably before 1425 *infesten* give pain, distress, hurt, in Chauliac's *Grande Chirurgie;* later, harass, annoy, trouble (1533); borrowed from Middle French *infester,* learned borrowing from Latin *īnfestāre* to attack, from *īnfestus* hostile, dangerous; originally, inexorable, cognate element for element with Greek *áthes-tos* (of the Furies) inexorable, not to be entreated, related to *théssasthai* to entreat, single-action infinitive to *potheîn* yearn for, pray for, from Indo-European **n̥-gwhedh-tos,* root **gwhedh-/gwhodh-* (Pok.488), represented in Old Irish *guidiu* I pray (with first plural of the *s-* subjunctive *gessam*), and Welsh *gweddi* pray.

The meaning of trouble with hostile attacks, visit persistently or in large numbers, especially for purposes of destruction or plunder, is first recorded in 1602.

—infestation *n.* Probably before 1425 *infestacion;* borrowed from Old French *infestation,* from Late Latin *īnfestātiōnem* (nominative *īnfestātiō*) a molesting, troubling, from Latin *īnfestāre* to attack; for suffix see -ATION.

infidel *n.* 1470-85, a non-Christian, especially a Mohammedan, in Malory's *Morte d'Arthur;* later, a person who does not believe in religion (1526, in Tyndale's writings); borrowed from Middle French *infidèle,* learned borrowing from Latin *īnfidēlis* disloyal or unfaithful, later, unbelieving (*in-* not + *fidēlis* faithful; see FIDELITY). **—adj.** Before 1470 *infidel* unbelieving, heathen; borrowed from Middle French *infidèle,* adj. and n. **—infidelity** *n.* Before 1400 *infidelite* lack of faith, in Wycliffe's writings; borrowed from Middle French *infidélité,* from Latin *īnfidēlitātem* (nominative *īnfidēlitās*) unfaithfulness, from *īnfidēlis* unfaithful. The meaning of disloyalty to a person is first recorded in 1529.

infinite *adj.* About 1380 *infinit,* in Chaucer's translation of Boethius' *De Consolatione Philosophiae;* borrowed probably from Old French *infinit,* learned borrowing from Latin, also borrowed directly from Latin *īnfīnītus* (*in-* not + *fīnītus* bounded, FINITE). **—n.** that which is infinite. 1563, from the adjective. **—infinity** *n.* About 1378 *infinite* something unlimited, infinite time, in a version of *Piers Plowman;* about 1380, boundlessness, infinite quality, in Chaucer's translation of Boethius' *De Consolatione Philosophiae;* borrowed from Old French *infinité,* from Latin *īnfīnitātem* (nominative *īnfīnitās*) boundlessness, endlessness, from *in-* not + *fīnis* end.

infinitesimal *adj.* 1710, smaller than any mathematical fraction or magnitude, infinitely small; possibly developed from the noun (1655); but more likely formed in English from New Latin *infinitesimus* an infinitely small part or quantity (originally, adjective nth in rank, from Latin *īnfīnītus* INFINITE + *-ēsimus,* as in *centēsimus* hundredth, CENTESIMAL) + English *-al*¹. The meaning in the common vocabulary of too small to be measured, extremely minute, is first recorded in 1722.

infinitive *n.* form of a verb not limited by person and number. 1530, in Palsgrave's *Lesclarcissement,* borrowed, perhaps by influence of Middle French *infinitif,* from Late Latin *īnfīnītīvus* unlimited, indefinite; also, the infinitive form of a verb, from Latin *īnfīnītus* INFINITE; for suffix see -IVE. It is also possible that the noun appeared earlier from the adjective. **—adj.** of or formed with the infinitive. 1450 *infinityf,* in *Battlefield Grammar;* borrowed through Middle French *infinitif,* or directly from Late Latin *īnfīnītīvus* unlimited, indefinite.

infirm *adj.* About 1380 *infirme* (of things) not firm or strong, weak, in Chaucer's translation of Boethius' *De Consolatione Philosophiae;* borrowed, possibly through Old French *infirme,* from Latin *īnfirmus* (*in-* not + *firmus* FIRM[1]). The meaning of not strong or healthy, feeble, sick, in reference to people, is first recorded about 1425. **—infirmity** *n.* Probably about 1350 *enfermete* an instance of disease; later *infirmite* inability or weakness (before 1382, in the Wycliffe Bible); borrowed from Old French *enfermeté* and from Latin *īnfirmitātem* (nominative *īnfirmitās*), from *īnfirmus* infirm; for suffix see -ITY.

infirmary *n.* hospital or sick quarters in a school or other institution. 1451 *infirmarie;* borrowed from Medieval Latin *infirmarium, infirmaria* an infirmary or hospital, from Latin *īnfirmus* INFIRM; for suffix see -ARY. In the 1700's *infirmary* was the common name in Great Britain for a public hospital. This usage has been retained in some names, e.g. the Royal Infirmary in Liverpool and Edinburgh, the New York Eye and Ear Infirmary.

infix (infiks′) *v.* fix in, drive in, insert, implant. 1502, probably a back formation from *infixed,* adj., stuck in, wedged in (probably before 1425); borrowed from Latin *īnfixus,* past participle of *īnfīgere* to imprint or fasten in, from *in-* in + *fīgere* fasten, FIX. The grammatical meaning of insert (a formative element) in the body of a word, is first recorded in Max Müller's *Stratification of Languages* (1868). **—n.** (in′fiks) *Grammar.* formative element inserted in the body of a word. 1881; from the verb.

inflame *v.* excite, make more violent. About 1340 *enflaumen* kindle, make ardent, set on fire; later *inflamen* (probably before 1425, in a translation of Higden's *Polychronicon*); borrowed from Old French *enflamer,* from Latin *īnflammāre* (*in-* in + *flamma* FLAME).

inflammation *n.* Probably before 1425 *inflammacioun* condition of the body marked by excessive heat, swelling, and redness, in a translation of Chauliac's *Grande Chirurgie;* borrowed, possibly through Middle French *inflammation,* from Latin *īnflammātiōnem* (nominative *īnflammātiō*), from *īnflammāre* INFLAME; for suffix see -ATION. The meaning of act of inflaming the mind or emotions is first recorded in Shakespeare's *2 Henry IV* (1597). **—inflammable** *adj.* Probably before 1425, liable to inflammation; borrowed, possibly through Middle French *inflammable,* from Medieval Latin *inflammabilis,* from Latin *īnflammāre* inflame; for suffix see -ABLE. The literal meaning of easily set on fire, is first recorded in 1605. *Inflammable* in this sense has been largely replaced in commercial usage by *flammable* because the prefix *in-* (meaning in) was often erroneously taken as a negative, thereby meaning "not flammable."

inflate *v.* Probably before 1425 *inflaten* cause to swell, in a translation of Chauliac's *Grande Chirurgie;* developed from *inflate,* adj. (probably about 1350); borrowed from Latin *īnflātus,* past participle of *īnflāre* blow into, fill by blowing, puff up (*in-* into + *flāre* to BLOW[2]); for suffix see -ATE[1]. It is also likely that, in some instances, *inflate* is a back formation from *inflation.* The economic sense in the verb of increase (prices or currency), is first recorded in Emerson's *The Young American* (1844). **—inflation** *n.* About 1340 *inflacioun* a swollen state; borrowed from Latin *īnflātiōnem* (nominative *īnflātiō*) a blowing up or into, from *īnflāre* INFLATE. The meaning of increase in prices or currency is first recorded in 1838, in a speech by the American politician and diplomat Daniel Dewey Barnard. **—inflationary** *adj.* 1920, of or involving monetary inflation; formed from English *inflation* + *-ary.*

inflect *v.* About 1425 *inflecten* bend downward, curve; borrowed from Latin *īnflectere* to bend in, change, alter, modulate (*in-* in + *flectere* to bend; see FLEX). The meaning of vary a word's form to show grammatical relationship is found in 1668; and that of modulate the voice, in 1828 in American English, as a back formation from the earlier *inflection* in this meaning pertaining to the voice. **—inflection** *n.* Probably before 1425 *inflexion* action of bending; later *inflection* (1597); borrowed, probably through Middle French *inflexion,* and directly from Latin *īnflexiōnem,* nominative *īnflexiō* (in Late Latin *īnflectiōnem,* nominative *īnflectiō*), from *īnflectere* inflect. The meaning of modulation of the voice, is first recorded before 1600, and the grammatical meaning of variation in the form of a word to show differences in case, gender, etc., in 1668.

inflexible *adj.* Probably before 1425, borrowed probably through Middle French *inflexible,* and directly from Latin *īnflexibilis* (*in-* not + *flexibilis* FLEXIBLE).

inflict *v.* 1566, possibly developed from *inflict,* adj. (1526); borrowed from Latin *īnflīctus,* past participle of *īnflīgere* (*in-* on, against + *flīgere* to dash, strike; see CONFLICT). Alternatively, *inflict,* v. may be a back formation from *infliction.* **—infliction** *n.* 1534, in Sir Thomas More's *The Confutation of Tyndale's Answer;* borrowed from Late Latin *īnflīctiōnem* (nominative *īnflīctiō*) a striking against, from Latin *īnflīgere;* for suffix see -TION.

inflorescence *n.* 1760, arrangement of flowers on a plant; later, flowering process (1800); borrowed from New Latin *inflorescentia* (coined by Linnaeus), from Late Latin *īnflōrēscentem* (nominative *īnflōrēscēns*) flowering, present participle of *īnflōrēscere* come into flower; see FLORESCENCE; for suffix see -ENCE.

influence *n.* About 1385, a flowing or streaming from the stars of an ethereal fluid acting upon the character and destiny of people, in Chaucer's *Troilus and Criseyde;* borrowed from Old French *influence* emanation from the stars, learned borrowing from Medieval Latin *influentia* a flowing in, from Latin *īnfluentem* (nominative *īnfluēns*), present participle of *īnfluere* to flow into (*in-* in + *fluere* to flow; see FLUENT); for suffix see -ENCE.

The original astrological meaning gradually evolved into the meaning of power of persons to act on others, is first recorded in Shakespeare's *Love's Labour's Lost* (1588).

—v. have power over. 1658, in a speech by Cromwell; from the noun.

—influential *adj.* 1570, having astral influence; later, having power, effective (1655); formed in English from Medieval Latin *influentia* influence + English *-al*[1], or possibly from earlier *influent* (probably before 1439, flowing; 1449, abundant, influential; borrowed from Middle French *influent,* from Latin *īnfluentem, īnfluēns* flowing) + English *-ial.*

influenza (in′flüen′zə) *n.* acute contagious disease; flu. 1743, borrowed during an outbreak of this disease that spread over Europe at the time, from Italian *influenza* influenza or epidemic; originally, visitation, influence (of the stars); learned borrowing from Medieval Latin *influentia;* see INFLUENCE. The use in Italian to refer to particular flulike diseases with specific symptoms, such as scarlet fever (*influenza di febbre scarlattina*) is known as early as 1504.

influx *n.* a flowing in, steady flow. 1626, in Francis Bacon's *Sylva Sylvarum,* formed from English *in-*² in + Latin *flūxus* a flowing, FLUX.

inform *v.* Probably before 1425 *informen,* variant of earlier *enformen, enfourmen* to mold, train, educate, or instruct (probably before 1325); borrowed from Old French *enformer, enfourmer,* learned borrowing from Latin *īnfōrmāre* to shape, form, train, instruct, educate (*in-* into + *fōrma* FORM). The current meaning of provide with facts or news, to report, tell, is first recorded in 1384, as a development in English from the French and Latin meaning of impart instruction to, instruct or teach. **—informant** *n.* one who gives information. 1693, borrowed from Latin *īnfōrmantem* (nominative *īnfōrmāns*), present participle of *īnfōrmāre* to instruct; for suffix see -ANT. **—information** *n.* Before 1387 *informacioun* instruction, direction, teaching, in Trevisa's translation of Higden's *Polychronicon,* variant of earlier *enformacioun* (about 1380, in Chaucer's translation of Boethius' *De Consolatione Philosophiae*); borrowed from Old French *enformacion,* learned borrowing from Medieval Latin *informationem,* from Latin *īnfōrmātiōnem* (nominative *īnfōrmātiō*) outline, concept, form of an idea, from *īnfōrmāre* to shape, form; for suffix see -ATION. **—informative** *adj.* Before 1398 *informative,* in Trevisa's translation of Bartholomew's *De Proprietatibus Rerum;* borrowed from Medieval Latin *informativus,* from Latin *īnfōrmāt-,* past participle stem of *īnfōrmāre* to shape, form; for suffix see -IVE. **—informer** *n.* Probably before 1425, variant of earlier *enfourmer* (about 1385); from the verb in English + *-er*¹, and borrowed from Old French *enformeor,* from the verb in Old French; for suffix see -ER¹.

informal *adj.* Before 1460, formed from English *in-*¹ not + *formal.*

infra- a prefix meaning below, beneath, beyond, as in *infrastructure, infrared, infrasonic.* Borrowed from Medieval Latin *infra-,* from Latin *īnfrā* below, UNDER.

infraction *n.* 1461, a breaking of a law, obligation, right, etc., violation, in *Rolls of Parliament;* borrowed from Middle French *infraction,* and directly from Latin *īnfrāctiōnem* (nominative nfrīāiēāō) a breaking, from *īnfrag-,* stem of *īnfringere* INFRINGE.

infra dig (in′frə dig′) *Informal.* undignified. 1824, in Scott's *Redgauntlet,* informal abbreviation of Latin *īnfrā dignitātem* beneath (one's) dignity.

infringe *v.* About 1467 *enfrangen* violate a law, formed in English from *en-,* variant of *in-* + Latin *frangere.* The later form *infringe* (1553) was influenced by, or perhaps borrowed from Latin *īnfringere* to damage, break (*in-* in + *frangere* to BREAK). The meaning of encroach upon, is first recorded in English in 1760-72. **—infringement** *n.* 1593, contradiction or refutation; later, violation (1628), and encroachment or intrusion (1673); formed from English *infringe* + *-ment.*

infuriate *v.* make furious; enrage. 1667, in Milton's *Paradise Lost;* borrowed from Medieval Latin *infuriatus,* past participle of *infuriare* (Latin *in-* into + *furia* FURY); for suffix see -ATE¹.

infuse *v.* Probably before 1425, pour (a liquid) into something; borrowed through Middle French *infuser,* or directly from Latin *īnfūsus,* past participle of *īnfundere* (*in-* in + *fundere* pour, spread; see FOUND² cast metal). The figurative sense of instill, inspire, implant, is first recorded in 1526. **—infusion** *n.* Before 1400, something poured in; later, the steeping of a substance in water (1573); borrowed through Middle French, or directly from Latin *īnfūsiōnem* (nominative *īnfūsiō*), from *īnfūd-,* stem of *infundere;* for suffix see -SION.

-ing¹ a suffix meaning action, result, product, materials, etc., of verbs, as in *thinking, painting.* Middle English *-ing,* earlier *-ung;* developed from Old English *-ing, -ung;* cognate with Old Frisian *-inge, -unge,* Old Saxon *-unga,* Middle Low German *-inge* (modern Dutch *-ing*), Old High German *-unga* (modern German *-ung*), and Old Icelandic *-ing, -ung.* The earliest function of this suffix in Old English was to form nouns from corresponding verbs, as in *asking, feeding,* and to denote completed action or habit, as in *blētsing* blessing, occasionally with a plural, as in later *tidings;* there were also concrete nouns such as *bedding, offrung* offering. Later, words ending in *-ing* were formed from nouns without a corresponding verb, as in *rail, railing, evening, morning.*

The form also developed a particular noun use with verbal functions that are qualified by adverbs rather than adjectives, as in *practicing regularly,* and that govern objects as a verb does, as in *writing letters.* It is peculiar to English and is unknown in Middle and Old English. Other functions that are productive in English include *-ing* as the ending of a second element in a compound, such as *on-going, far-reaching, childbearing, uprising, handwriting,* or with an adjective function in *carving knife, laughingstock, meetinghouse.*

-ing² a suffix forming the present participle of verbs, as in *walking, seeing, loving.* Middle English, alteration of *-ind, -end;* developed from Old English *-ende,* the inherited form cognate with Gothic *-and-s,* Latin *-ent-,* Greek *-ont-,* and Sanskrit *-ant-, -at-.*

ingenious *adj.* Probably before 1425, intelligent or talented; borrowed from Middle French *ingénieux* and replacing earlier *enginous* (recorded before 1393; borrowed from Old French *engignos*), learned borrowing from Latin *ingeniōsus,* from *ingenium* inborn qualities or talent; see the doublet ENGINE; for suffix see -OUS. The meaning of showing skill or inventiveness, clever at contriving things, is first recorded in 1548. **—ingenuity** *n.* 1599, in Ben Jonson's *Every Man Out of His Humor,* intelligence or talent; borrowed possibly from Middle French *ingénuité,* and directly from Latin *ingenuitātem* (nominative *ingenuitās*) frankness, from *ingenuus* of noble character (in Cicero, frank), originally, freeborn; see INGENUOUS; for suffix see -ITY. The meaning of skill in contriving or inventing, cleverness, is first recorded in 1649 and was influenced by *ingenious.*

ingenue or **ingénue** (an′zhənü) *n.* simple, innocent girl or young woman. 1848, in Thackeray's *Vanity Fair;* borrowing of French *ingénue,* from *ingénue,* adj., ingenuous, artless, simple, learned borrowing from Latin *ingenua* (masculine *ingenuus*) frank, modest; see INGENUOUS.

ingenuous *adj.* 1598, implied in *ingenuously,* frank or candid; borrowed from Latin *ingenuus* with the virtues of freeborn people, of noble character, frank; originally, native, freeborn (*in-* in + *gen-,* root of *gignere* beget, produce, generate; see KIN); for suffix see -OUS. The extended sense of innocently frank and open, artless, guileless, is first recorded in 1673.

ingest *v.* 1620, take (food, etc.) into the body; also, to put in, push in (1617); borrowed from Latin *ingestus,* past participle of *ingerere* put or push in, carry in (*in-* in + *gerere* carry; of uncertain origin). **—ingestion** *n.* 1620, borrowed from Late Latin *ingestiōnem* (nominative *ingestiō*) a pouring in, from Latin *inges-,* stem of *ingerere;* for suffix see -TION.

inglenook *n.* nook or corner beside the fireplace. Before 1774, in Robert Fergusson's *Poems,* Scottish, a compound of *ingle* (1509, from Gaelic *aingeal* fire, light, sunshine, from Indo-European *angelo-, root *ang-, Pok.779) + *nook.*

ingot *n.* About 1395, mold in which metal is cast, in Chaucer's *Canterbury Tales;* probably formed from *in-* in + Old English *goten,* past participle of *gēotan* to pour; see FOUND² cast metal. The form in English corresponds to German *Einguss* ingot mold, which may have been formed independently. The French *lingot* is usually thought to be derived from English, though some question of chronology of sense may exist.

After Chaucer, two additional examples are found in Middle English in the sense of a mold in which metal is cast. *Ingot* reappeared in 1583 in the sense of mass of cast metal.

ingrate *n.* ungrateful person. 1672, developed from Middle English *ingrat,* adj., ungrateful (probably before 1387, in a version of *Piers Plowman*); borrowed from Old French *ingrat* not grateful, learned borrowing from Latin *ingrātus* (*in-* not + *grātus* thankful, pleasing; see GRACE); for suffix see -ATE¹.

ingratiate *v.* bring (oneself) into favor. 1622, in Bacon's *Henry VII;* possibly borrowed through Italian *ingratiare, ingraziare,* developed from the phrase *in grazia* into favor, from Latin *in grātiam,* from *grātus* pleasing, thankful; see GRACE; for suffix see -ATE¹.

ingredient *n.* one of the parts of a mixture. Probably before 1425; borrowed from Latin *ingredientem* nominative *ingrediēns*), present participle of *ingredī* go in, enter (*in-* in + *gradī* to step, go; see GRADE); for suffix see -ENT.

ingress *n.* a going in, entrance. Probably 1440, means of going in, entrance; borrowed from Latin *ingressus* entrance, from *ingred-,* stem of *ingredī* enter; see INGREDIENT.

inhabit *v.* live in. About 1350 *inhabiten, enhabiten;* borrowed from Old French *enhabiter* dwell or dwell in, learned borrowing from Latin *inhabitāre* dwell in (*in-* in + *habitāre* dwell, a frequentative form of *habēre* hold, have; see HABIT). **—inhabitable** *adj.* that can be lived in. 1601, formed from English *inhabit* + *-able;* an earlier form of *inhabitable* not habitable, is found before 1398, formed from *in-* not + *habitable,* but died out after 1742. Loss of the earlier term left a need for the later formation *uninhabitable.* **—inhabitant** *n.* 1425 *inhabitantes, pl.,* probably formed from English *inhabit* + *-ant.* Only the plural form appeared in Middle English; the singular is rarely found until the late 1500's.

inhale *v.* breathe in. 1725, in Pope's translation of Homer's *Odyssey;* probably a back formation from *inhalation,* after Latin *inhālāre* breathe upon (*in-* upon, in + *hālāre* breathe, of uncertain origin). The meaning in English developed from the contrasting verb *exhale.* **—inhalation** *n.* 1623, in Cockeram's *Dictionary,* formed in English from Latin *inhālāre* + English *-ation,* on the analogy of *exhalation.*

inherent *adj.* 1578, fixed or situated in; 1588, intrinsic or essential; borrowed probably from Middle French *inhérent,* and directly from Latin *inhaerentem* (nominative *inhaerēns*), present participle of *inhaerēre* be closely connected with, adhere to (*in-* in + *haerēre* to stick; see HESITATE); for suffix see -ENT.

inherit *v.* About 1350 *inheriten, enheriten* receive as an heir, make (someone) heir; borrowed from Old French *enheriter* make heir, appoint as an heir, learned borrowing from Late Latin *inhērēditāre* (*in-* in + *hērēditāre,* from Latin *hērēs,* genitive *hērēdis,* HEIR). **—inheritance** *n.* Before 1393 *inheritance, enheritaunce,* in Gower's *Confessio Amantis;* borrowed from Old French *enheritaunce,* from *enheriter* to inherit. **—inheritor** *n.* Probably before 1430 *inheriter, enheritour;* probably formed in English or Anglo-French after Middle French (*enheritier,* from *en-* + *heriter.*

inhibit *v.* Probably before 1425, to forbid; later, to hinder or restrain (1535); apparently a back formation from *inhibition,* and also borrowed from Latin *inhibitus,* past participle of *inhibēre.* **—inhibition** *n.* Before 1387 *inhibicioun* formal prohibition, in Trevisa's translation of Higden's *Polychronicon;* borrowed from Old French *inibicion,* learned borrowing from Latin *inhibitiōnem* (nominative *inhibitiō*), from *inhibi-,* stem of *inhibēre* hold in, restrain, hinder (*in-* in + *habēre* hold; see HABIT); for suffix see -TION. The meaning of restraint or hindering is first recorded in English in 1621, but the specific sense of idea, emotion, or other inner force holding back one's impulses, is not found until 1916, in a translation of Freud's *Wit and its Relation to the Unconscious.* **—inhibitor** *n.* 1868, one who inhibits; 1914, substance which hinders a chemical reaction; formed from English *inhibit* + *-or*².

inhuman *adj.* 1461 *inhumayne* cruel; borrowed from Middle French *inhumain,* learned borrowing from Latin *inhūmānus* (*in-* not + *hūmānus* HUMAN). **—inhumanity** *n.* About 1477, borrowed from Middle French *inhumanité,* learned borrowing from Latin *inhūmānitātem* (nominative *inhūmānitās*) inhuman conduct, barbarity, from *inhūmānus* inhuman.

inimical *adj.* unfriendly, hostile. 1643, borrowed from Late Latin *inimīcālis,* from Latin *inimīcus* unfriendly, ENEMY (*in-* not + *amīcus* friendly, friend); for suffix see -AL¹.

iniquity *n.* very great injustice. Probably before 1300 *inequite,* in *Arthour and Merlin;* borrowed from Old French *iniquité,* learned borrowing from Latin *inīquitātem* (nominative *inīquitās*) unequalness, injustice, from *iniquus* wicked, unjust, unequal, uneven (*in-* not + *aequus* just, EQUAL); for suffix see -ITY. **—iniquitous** *adj.* 1726, in Swift's *Gulliver's Travels,* formed from English *iniquity* + *-ous.*

initial *adj.* 1526, borrowed from Latin *initiālis,* from *initium* beginning, from a lost noun **ines* (genitive *initis*) an entrant, from *inīre* go into, enter upon, begin (*in-* in + *īre* go; see EXIT); for suffix see -AL¹. **—n.** first letter of a word or name. 1627, from the adjective. **—v.** mark or sign with initials. 1864, in American English; from the noun.

initiate *v.* 1603, introduce into some knowledge or practice, induct, in Holland's translation of Plutarch's *Moralia;* 1604, begin, set going, in Cawdrey's *A Table*

Alphabeticall; borrowed from Latin *initiātus,* past participle of *initiāre* begin, originate, from *initium* beginning, see INITIAL; for suffix see -ATE[1]. In some instances *initiate* may also be a back formation from *initiation.* **—n.** person who is introduced into some knowledge or practice. 1811, in Coleridge's *Essays;* from the verb. An earlier sense probably with the meaning of something initiated, is recorded in 1603. **—initiation** *n.* 1583, formal admission to a position or group; later, action of starting, beginning (1641); borrowed probably from Middle French *initiation,* and directly from Latin *initiātiōnem* (nominative *initiātiō*) participation in secret rites, from *initiāre;* for suffix see -ATION. **—initiative** *n.* 1793, the first step in an undertaking or process; probably borrowed from French *initiative,* formed from *initier* + *-ive.*

inject *v.* force (liquid) into. 1601, in Holland's translation of Pliny's *Natural History,* borrowed from Latin *injectus,* past participle of *inicere* throw in or on (*in-* in + *-icere, -jicere,* combining forms of *jacere* to throw; see JET[1] stream). In some instances also probably a back formation from *injection.* **—injection** *n.* Probably before 1425 *injeccioun* action of forcing a liquid into a passage or cavity, borrowed probably from Middle French *injection,* and directly from Latin *injectiōnem* (nominative *injectiō*) a throwing in, injection, from *injec-,* stem of *inicere,* see INJECT; for suffix see -TION.

injunction *n.* command, order. Probably about 1425 *injunccion,* borrowed from Late Latin *injūnctiōnem* (nominative *injūnctiō*) a command, from Latin *injūnc-,* stem of *injungere* inflict, impose, charge, ENJOIN; for suffix see -TION. Formation of *injunction* in English was probably also influenced by Middle French *injonction.* The specific meaning of a court order to do or refrain from doing something, is first recorded in 1533-34.

injury *n.* About 1384 *injurie,* in the Wycliffe Bible; borrowed through Anglo-French *injurie,* from Latin *injūria* wrong, hurt, injury, noun use of the feminine of *injūrius, injūrus* wrongful, unjust, injurious (*in-* not + *jūs,* genitive *jūris* right, law, justice; see JUST); for suffix see -Y[3]. **—injure** *v.* About 1450 *injuren* to treat unjustly; borrowed from Middle French *injuriier, injurier* to harm, offend, from Latin *injūriāre,* from *injūria;* see INJURY. It is also possible that in some instances *injure* is a back formation from *injury.* The meaning of to harm or damage, is found in 1586. **—injurious** *adj.* About 1425 *injuryos* abusive, borrowed from Middle French *injurios,* and directly from Latin *injūriōsus,* from *injūria* hurt, injury; for suffix see -OUS. Also possibly formed from Middle English *injurie* + *-os, -ous.*

injustice *n.* Before 1393, unjust action, wrong, in Gower's *Confessio Amantis;* borrowed from Old French *injustice,* learned borrowing from Latin *injūstitia,* from *injūstus* unjust; earlier, lack of a tribune, absence of justice (*in-* not + *jūstus* JUST).

ink *n.* About 1250 *enke;* later *inke* (before 1349); borrowed from Old French *enque,* from Late Latin *encautum,* from Greek **énkauton* (used alongside *énkauston*) the reddish ink used by the Greek and Roman emperors for their signatures; originally a neuter adjective, burnt in, prepared by heat, from the stem of *enkaíein* to burn in (*en-* in + *kaíen* to burn; see CAUSTIC). **—v.** put ink on, mark or stain with ink. 1562, from the noun, possibly after Middle French *encrer* to ink.

inkhorn *n.* 1378, formed from Middle English *inke* + *horn.* **—inkhorn term** (1543)

inkling *n.* slight suggestion, vague notion, hint. 1513, in Sir Thomas More's *History of King Richard III,* apparently from gerund of *inclen* utter in an undertone (about 1350), related to Old English *inca* doubt, suspicion; of unknown origin.

in-law *n. Informal.* person related by marriage. 1894, abstracted from *father-in-law, mother-in-law,* etc. The earliest of these phrases appears to have been *brother-in-law* (probably before 1300), which was coined to indicate that the relationship is not by nature but with respect to the Canon Law, with reference to the degrees of affinity within which marriage is prohibited.

inlet *n.* narrow opening through which water runs into the land. 1570-76, entrance, that which lets in (*in-,* adv. + *let,* v., corresponding to the verb phrase *let in*); earlier *inlate* permission to enter (about 1300), from *inlaten,* variant of *inleten* to let in (probably about 1250).

inmate *n.* 1589, person living with others in a house, especially as a lodger or tenant (*in,* adj., that is inside + *mate*[1] companion). The specific application to someone confined in a public institution did not appear until 1834 (*an inmate of a lunatic asylum*).

inmost *adj.* 1535, alteration of *inmest* (before 1398); developed from Old English *innemest* (before 899, in Alfred's translation of St. Gregory's *Pastoral Care*) and superlative of *inne,* adv., inside, within. The superlative element *-mest* in Old English was mistakenly associated with *most;* compare *foremost.*

inn *n.* 1123 *inne* temporary dwelling or lodging; developed from Old English *inn* lodging, dwelling, house (about 1000, in Ælfric's writings), probably from *inne,* adv., inside, within; see INMOST. The form in Old English is cognate with Old Icelandic *inni* dwelling. In Middle English, probably before 1200, the term is recorded with the meaning of a public house for eating and/or lodging and by the 1430's had also acquired the meaning of a residence hall for university students, especially law students. **—innkeeper** *n.* (about 1449)

innards *n.pl.* internal parts of the body, entrails, viscera. 1825, dialectal variant of *inwards,* found in *inwardes* the organs or inner parts of the body (before 1398, in Trevisa's translation of Bartholomew's *De Proprietatibus Rerum*), and *inward* (probably before 1300), from *inward,* adj.; for suffix see -WARD.

innate *adj.* natural, inborn. About 1412, in Hoccleve's *Regement of Princes;* borrowed from Latin *innātus* (*in-* in + *nātus,* past participle of *nāscī* be born, Old Latin *gnāscī;* see NATIVE); for suffix see -ATE[1].

inner *adj.* farther in, inside. Probably before 1200 *inre,* in *Ancrene Riwle;* developed from Old English *innera, inra* (before 900, in Alfred's translation of Bede's *Ecclesiastical History*). Old English *innera, inra* are comparative forms of *inne,* adv., inside, within, see INMOST; and cognate with Old Frisian *inra* inner, Old High German *innaro, innere* (modern German *innere, innerer*), Old Icelandic *innri, idhri* (Swedish *inre,* Norwegian and Danish *indre*); for suffix see -ER[2].

inning *n.* Probably 1407 *ynnynge* act of getting in, harvesting; later *innyng* act of taking in, reclaiming of marsh land (about 1530); developed from Old English *innung* a taking in or a putting in (before 899 in Alfred's translation of Boethius' *De Consolatione Philoso-*

phiae), gerund of *innian* get within, put or bring in, from *in, inn,* adv., IN; for suffix see -ING[1]. The meaning of a turn of one side or team in a game, chance to play, is first recorded as *innings* in 1738, with reference to that portion of the game of cricket played by either side while "in" or at the bat. The extended sense of an opportunity to do something, to act, being in a position to act, having one's innings, is first recorded in Dickens' *Pickwick Papers* (1836).

innocent *adj.* 1340, not guilty, in a version of *Ayenbite of Inwyt;* later, simple, artless, naive (about 1385, in Chaucer's *Troilus and Criseyde*); borrowed from Old French *innocent,* learned borrowing from Latin *innocentem* (nominative *innocēns*) not guilty, harmless, blameless (*in-* not + *nocentem,* nominative *nocēns,* present participle of *nocēre* to harm; see NOXIOUS); for suffix see -ENT. **—n.** About 1200, guiltless person; later, simple or naive person (about 1230, in *Ancrene Riwle*); borrowed from Old French *innocent,* adj. and n.
—innocence *n.* 1340 *innocence* guiltlessness, in a version of *Ayenbite of Inwyt;* later, simplicity or lack of cunning (about 1385, in Chaucer's *Troilus and Criseyde*); borrowed from Old French *innocence,* learned borrowing from Latin *innocentia* harmlessness, blamelessness, from *innocentem* (nominative *innocēns*), present participle; for suffix see -ENCE.

innocuous (inok′yùəs) *adj.* 1598, harmless, formed in English from Latin *innocuus* (*in-* not + *nocuus* hurtful, from *nocēre* to harm; see NOXIOUS) + English *-ous.*

innovate *v.* 1548, introduce as new, bring in something new; borrowed probably from Middle French *innover,* and directly from Latin *innovātus,* past participle of *innovāre* to renew or change (*in-* + *novus* NEW); for suffix see -ATE[1].

Innovate is recorded earlier as a noun meaning something made to replace something else (1474, borrowed from Latin *innovātus*).
—innovation *n.* 1548, a change or new way of doing things; earlier *innovacyon* restoration, renewal (1440); borrowed probably from Middle French *innovation,* and directly from Latin *innovātiōnem* (nominative *innovātiō*) a renewing, alteration, innovation, from *innovāre;* for suffix see -ATION. **—innovator** *n.* 1598, possibly formed from English *innovate* + *-or*[2], after Italian *innovatore,* also found in Middle French *innovateur.*

innuendo (in′yùen′dō) *n.* indirect hint or reference. 1678, borrowed from Latin *innuendō* by intimating, meaning, pointing to (literally, by giving a nod to), ablative case of the gerund of *innuere* to mean, signify, nod to (*in-* in, toward + *nuere* to nod).

This word appeared originally in English in 1564 as a formula used especially in legal documents to introduce a parenthetical clarification. In this particular use, *innuendo* meant "namely, that is to say." Subsequently, *innuendo* came to refer to the clarification itself, hence, "any indirect reference, hint, or suggestion."

innumerable *adj.* About 1350 *innumerable* very great, numerous, countless, in *Ayenbite of Inwyt;* borrowed from Latin *innumerābilis* (*in-* not + *numerābilis* capable of being counted, from *numerāre* to count, from *numerus* NUMBER); for suffix see -ABLE.

Two variant forms *innoumbrable, innoumberabill* developed in English in the 1400's; borrowed from Old French *innombrable,* from the Latin; but even though its spelling by the 1500's (*innumberable*) conformed to English *number,* it was displaced in the later 1500's by *innumerable.*

inoculate *v.* infect with germs that will cause a very mild form of a disease so that thereafter the individual will not get that disease. Probably 1440 *inoculate* insert a bud into (a plant); borrowed from Latin *inoculātus,* past participle of *inoculāre* graft in, implant (*in-* in + *oculus* bud, EYE); for suffix see -ATE[1]. The meaning of implant the germs of a disease to produce immunity, is first recorded in English in 1722, as a back formation of *inoculation.* The figurative sense of to imbue, is first found in Washington Irving's *Tales of a Traveller* (1824). **—inoculation** *n.* Probably 1440 *inoculacioun* insertion of a plant bud into another plant, grafting by budding; borrowed from Latin *inoculātiōnem* (nominative *inoculātiō*) a grafting in, budding, from *inoculāre;* for suffix see -ATION. The meaning of a process of inoculating to prevent disease, is first recorded in English in 1714, with reference to the introduction of the smallpox virus to induce an immunity to smallpox (a technique first observed by Western Europeans in Constantinople, but known earlier in India and China). Later reference is recorded as *vaccine inoculation* (1799), shortened to *vaccination* (1800).

inoperative *adj.* Before 1631, in Donne's writings; formed from English *in-*[1] not + *operative.*

inordinate *adj.* Probably 1348, not kept within orderly limits, immoderate, excessive; borrowed from Latin *inōrdinātus* disordered or irregular (*in-* not + *ōrdinātus,* past participle of *ōrdināre* to set in order, arrange; see ORDAIN); for suffix see -ATE[1].

inquest *n.* legal inquiry, especially before a jury. About 1300 *enqueste, anqueste* formal inquiry into a matter of public interest; borrowed from Old French *enqueste* inquiry, from Vulgar Latin **inquaesita* thing inquired into, alteration (influenced by **inquaerere* inquire) of Latin *inquisita,* feminine past participle of *inquīrere* INQUIRE. The spelling *inquest* is first recorded about 1475, but was not established until the 1700's.

inquire *v.* About 1300 *enqueren;* later *inqueren* (before 1398) and *enquiren* (probably before 1425); borrowed from Old French *enquerre,* from Vulgar Latin **inquaerere,* alteration (influenced by Latin *quaerere* ask) of Latin *inquīrere* (*in-* into + *quaerere* ask, seek; see QUERY). The spelling *inquire* was influenced by the Latin form. **—inquiry** *n.* 1426 *enquere, enqueri, enquery,* from *enqueren* inquire + *-y -y*[3]. In the 1500's the spelling was changed to *inquiry* by influence of the verb.

inquisition *n.* 1384 *inquisicioun* interrogation, questioning, in the Wycliffe Bible; borrowed from Old French *inquisition, inquisicion,* from Latin *inquīsītiōnem* (nominative *inquīsītiō*) a searching into, examination, legal examination, from *inquīrere* INQUIRE; for suffix see -TION.

The specific meaning of a judicial investigation or inquiry, is first recorded before 1387, and that of a thorough investigation, a searching inquiry, before 1439. Reference to *The Inquisition,* ecclesiastical court appointed by the Roman Catholic Church in the 1200's to suppress heresy, is not found in English before 1502 when the Spanish Inquisition, 1478-83, became notorious for its activities against accused heretics.
—inquisitive *adj.* About 1390 *inquisityf* disposed to asking questions, eager to know, curious, in Chaucer's

Canterbury Tales; borrowed from Old French *inquisitif,* from Late Latin *inquīsītīvus,* from Latin *inquīsītus,* past participle of *inquīrere;* for suffix see -IVE. **—inquisitor** *n.* 1402 *inquisitour* one who inquires or investigates; borrowed from Latin *inquīsītor* searcher, examiner, from *inquīsītus,* past participle of *inquīrere;* for suffix see -OR². *Inquisitor* in the sense of an officer of the Inquisition, is first recorded in 1545.

insane *adj.* 1560, not of sound mind, mentally ill; borrowed from Latin *īnsānus* (*in-* not + *sānus* healthy, sound in body or in mind, SANE). **—insanity** *n.* 1590, unsoundness of mind, mental illness; possibly formed in English from *insane* + *-ity,* modeled on Latin *insānitās* unsoundness, unhealthiness, disease (*in-* not + *sānitās* health, soundness of body or of mind, sanity).

insatiable *adj.* About 1412 *insaciable,* in Hoccleve's *Regement of Princes;* borrowing of Old French *insaciable,* from Latin *insatiābilis* (*in-* not + *satiāre* SATIATE); for suffix see -ABLE.

inscription *n.* Before 1382 *inscripcioun* introductory statement indicating authorship or contents of a book, heading, title, in the Wycliffe Bible; borrowed from Latin *īnscrīptiōnem* (nominative *īnscrīptiō*), from *īnscrībere* inscribe; for suffix see -TION. The meaning of something inscribed, is first recorded in English in 1538. **—inscribe** *v.* 1552, replacement of earlier *inscriven* (1382, borrowed from Old French *inscrire* and from Latin). The later form in modern English was borrowed directly from Latin *īnscrībere* write in or upon (*in-*² on + *scrībere* write; see SCRIBE).

inscrutable *adj.* that cannot be understood; mysterious or obscure. Before 1500, borrowed, perhaps through Middle French *inscrutable,* from Late Latin *īnscrūtābilis* (Latin *in-* not + *scrūtārī* examine, ransack; see SCRUTINY); for suffix see -ABLE.

insect *n.* 1601, in Holland's translation of Pliny's *Natural History,* borrowed, possibly by influence of French *insecte,* from Latin *īnsectum* animal with a notched or divided body (literally, cut into), from neuter past participle of *īnsecāre* cut into, cut up (*in-*² into + *secāre* to cut; see SECTION). The word is part of the international scientific vocabulary, and is therefore cognate with Dutch, Swedish, and Danish *insekt,* German *Insekt,* French *insecte,* Spanish and Portuguese *insecto,* and Italian *insetto.* The reference to notched or divided in the Latin word for insect is to the segmented division of an insect's body; it is a loan translation of Greek *éntomon* insect. See ENTOMOLOGY. **—insecticide** *n.* 1865 (attributive use), formed from English *insect* + *-cide*².

inseminate *v.* 1623, to sow or implant, in Cockeram's *Dictionary;* borrowed from Latin *īnsēminātus,* past participle of *īnsēmināre* (*in-*² in, into + *sēmināre* to plant, propagate, beget, from *sēmen,* genitive *sēminis* seed, SEMEN); for suffix see -ATE¹. The meaning of introduce semen into, impregnate with semen, is first recorded in 1923, as a back formation from *insemination,* in the context of animal breeding by artificial insemination. **—insemination** *n.* 1658, action of sowing or implanting of seed, in Phillips' *Dictionary;* formed from English *inseminate* + *-ion.* The meaning of introduction or injection of semen, is first recorded in Thomas Tanner's *On the Signs and Diseases of Pregnancy* (1860).

insensible *adj.* About 1380, that cannot be perceived by bodily senses, in Wycliffe's writings; borrowed from Old French *insensible,* and directly from Latin *īnsēnsibilis* (*in-* not + *sēnsibilis* SENSIBLE). The application to mental processes is first recorded in English about 1475.

inseparable *adj.* Probably 1348, borrowed from Latin *īnsēparābilis* that cannot be separated (*in-* not + *sēparābilis* SEPARABLE).

insert (insėrt′) *v.* put in, set in. 1529, in Sir Thomas More's *Supplycacyon of Soulys,* developed from *insert* (recorded before 1400), past participle of *inseren;* borrowed from Latin *īnserere* put in (*in-*² + *serere* join together; see SERIES). **—n.** (in′sėrt) something set in or inserted. 1893, from the verb. **—insertion** *n.* 1578, place or manner of attachment of an organ, muscle, etc.; borrowed, probably through Middle French *insertion,* from Late Latin *īnsertiōnem* (nominative *īnsertiō*), from Latin *īnserere.* The general sense of act of putting in is first recorded in 1598, in Florio's *A World of Words.*

inside *n.* 1392 *ynneside* interior of the body; later, inner side (1504); originally in Middle English, a compound of *inne,* adv., and *side;* later, considered as a compound of *in,* adv., and *side.* The later form of *inside* and its opposite, *outside,* appeared about the same time. **—adj.** (in′sīd′) inner, internal. 1611, in Shakespeare's *Winter's Tale;* from the noun. **—prep.** (in′sīd′) on the inside of, within. 1791, from the noun. **—adv.** (in′sīd′) on or to the inside. 1803, Lord Nelson cited in *Dispatches;* from the noun. The phrase *inside out* is first recorded before 1600. **—insider** *n.* 1846, American English, a book carried in an inside coat pocket; 1848, someone who is a member of a group; formed from English *inside* + *-er*¹.

insidious *adj.* crafty, tricky, treacherous. 1545, borrowed, perhaps by influence of Middle French *insidieux,* from Latin *insidiōsus* cunning or deceitful, from *īnsidiae, pl.,* ambush, plot, snare, from *īnsidēre* sit on, settle on, occupy (*in-*² in + *sedēre* SIT); for suffix see -OUS.

insight *n.* Probably before 1200 *insiht* inner sight, discernment, understanding, in Layamon's *Chronicle of Britain;* a compound of *in,* adv. and *siht* SIGHT. The meaning of glimpse or view beneath the surface, faculty or power of understanding the inner nature or character of something, is first recorded in Sidney's *Apology for Poetry* (1581). Application of this meaning was extended in the early 1900's, in psychological studies of behavior and learning, to that of the sudden perception of a solution to a problem (as seen especially in animals), a usage first recorded in R.M. Yerkes' *Mental Life of Monkeys and Apes* (1916).

insignia *n.pl.* emblems, badges, etc. 1648, borrowed from Latin *īnsignia,* neuter plural of *īnsigne* badge, mark (*in-* on + *signum* mark, SIGN). The earlier form *ensigne* (probably before 1400) became differentiated in meaning after *insignia* was introduced and today usually has the sense of a flag or pennant that stands as an emblem or identification of some military group, private club, etc. Doublet of ENSIGN. The singular form *insigne* appeared in English in 1774, at the same time as *insignia* began to be used as a singular, with *insignias* as its plural.

insinuate *v.* 1529, introduce, convey, or instill (an idea) indirectly, in Sir Thomas More's *A Dialogue Concerning Heresies;* borrowed from Latin *īnsinuātus,* past participle of *īnsinuāre* bring in by windings and curvings, wind one's way into, insinuate (*in-* in + *sinus,* genitive *sinūs,* a curve, winding; see SINUS); for suffix see -ATE[1]. —**insinuation** *n.* 1526, subtle instilling of an idea; 1532, subtle suggestion, implication, hint; borrowed, possibly through Middle French *insinuation,* from Latin *īnsinuātiōnem* (nominative *īnsinuātiō*) an insinuating one's way into something or into someone's favor, from *īnsinuāre;* for suffix see -ATION.

insipid *adj.* 1620, without taste; borrowed, probably through French *insipide,* from Late Latin *insipidus* (Latin *in-* not + *sapidus* tasty, from *sapere* have a taste, be wise; see SAPIENT). The figurative extension of uninteresting or dull, is first recorded in John Evelyn's *Diary* (1649), probably borrowed from Medieval Latin *insipidus* dull, from Late Latin *insipidus* tasteless.

insist *v.* 1586, persevere, persist in a course of action; probably a back formation from *insistence,* modeled on Latin *insistere* persist, dwell upon, stand upon (*in-* on + *sistere* take a stand, from *stāre* to STAND). —**insistence** *n.* 1436, formed in Middle English, in some instances from Middle French *insister,* and in some instances directly from Latin *insistere* + English suffix *-ence.* —**insistent** *adj.* 1624, probably a back formation from *insistence* with the suffix *-ent;* modeled, possibly by influence of Middle French *insistant,* on Latin *insistentem* (nominative *insistēns*), present participle of *insistere* stand upon.

insolent *adj.* About 1390, arrogant or haughty, in Chaucer's *Canterbury Tales;* borrowed from Latin *īnsolentem* (nominative *īnsolēns*) arrogant, immoderate, unusual (*in-* not + *solentem,* present participle of *solēre* be accustomed, possibly related to *sodālis* close companion, and *suēscere* become used to; see CUSTOM); for suffix see -ENT. —**insolence** *n.* About 1390, arrogance or haughtiness, in Chaucer's *Canterbury Tales;* borrowed from Latin *īnsolentia* arrogance, excess, unusualness, from *īnsolentem* (nominative *īnsolēns*) arrogant, immoderate, unusual.

insoluble *adj.* About 1384 *insolible* that cannot be dissolved, undone, or loosened, in the Wycliffe Bible; probably before 1387, that cannot be solved, explained, or resolved, in a version of *Piers Plowman;* borrowed from Latin *īnsolūbilis* that cannot be loosened (*in-* not + *solūbilis* SOLUBLE). The Latinate spelling was adopted in English in the early 1500's.

insomnia *n.* inability to sleep. 1758, borrowing of Latin *īnsomnia* (*in-* not + *somnus* sleep; see SOMNOLENT). An Anglicized form *insomnie* appeared in Cockeram's *Dictionary* (1623), probably borrowed from French *insomnie* (1555). Cognates are found in Spanish *insomnio,* Portuguese *insomnia,* and Italian *insonnio,* suggesting that this is a term of the vocabulary of international science. —**insomniac** *n.* 1908; formed from English *insomnia* + *-ac* (from Latin *-acus,* from Greek *-akós*), as in *maniac.*

insouciant (insü′sēənt) *adj.* carefree. 1829, in Scott's *Anne of Geierstein;* borrowing of French *insouciant* (*in-* not + *souciant,* present participle of Old French *soucier* to trouble or care, from Latin *sollicitāre* to agitate or disturb; see SOLICIT); for suffix see -ANT. —**insouciance** *n.* 1799, borrowing of French *insouciance,* from French *insouciant;* for suffix see -ANCE.

inspect *v.* 1623, in Cockeram's *Dictionary* as *inspected;* borrowed from Latin *īnspectus,* past participle of *īnspicere;* see INSPECTION. It is also probable that *inspect* appears somewhat earlier in English, in some instances as a back formation from *inspection,* and/or *inspector.* —**inspection** *n.* Before 1393 *inspeccioun, inspectioun* close examination, in Gower's *Confessio Amantis;* borrowed from Old French *inspection,* from Latin *īnspectiōnem* (nominative *īnspectiō*), from *īnspec-,* stem of *īnspicere* look into, inspect, examine (*in-* into + *specere* to look; see SPY); for suffix see -TION. —**inspector** *n.* 1602, possibly formed from earlier (and unrecorded) English *inspect* + *-or*[2], perhaps modeled on French *inspecteur;* also, probably borrowed from Latin *īnspector* (*īnspec-,* stem of *īnspicere* + *-tor*). The meaning of a police officer, usually ranking below a superintendent, is first recorded in 1840.

inspire *v.* About 1340 *inspiren, enspiren* awaken by divine influence, fill with a thought or feeling; possibly a back formation from *inspiration,* perhaps modeled on Old French *enspirer,* or Latin *īnspīrāre;* and in some instances a borrowing from Old French *enspirer, inspirer,* from Latin *īnspīrāre* inspire, inflame, blow into (*in-* in + *spīrāre* breathe; see SPIRIT). —**inspiration** *n.* About 1303 *inspiracioun, enspiracioun* imparting of spiritual knowledge, divine guidance or influence; borrowed from Old French *inspiration,* and directly from Late Latin *inspīrātiōnem* (nominative *inspīrātiō*), from Latin *īnspīrāre* inspire; for suffix see -ATION. The more general sense of animating action or influence, is first recorded in Hobbes' *Leviathan* (1651).

install *v.* About 1422, to place in office (originally, by seating in an official stall); borrowed from Middle French *installer,* or directly from Medieval Latin *installare* (Latin *in-* in + Medieval Latin *stallum* stall, from Germanic; compare Old High German *stal* standing place, STALL[1]). The meaning of establish in position for service, is first recorded in 1867, borrowed from French *installer,* from Medieval Latin *installare.* —**installation** *n.* 1464 *installacion;* borrowed from Middle French *installation,* and directly from Medieval Latin *installationem* (nominative *installatio*), from *installare* install; for suffix see -ATION. It is also probable that, in some later instances, *installation* was formed from English *install* + *-ation.*

installment[1] *n.* act of installing, establishment. 1589, formed from English *install* + *-ment.*

installment[2] *n.* part of a sum of money or of a debt to be paid at certain stated times. 1732, alteration of earlier (1577-87) *estallment* arrangement for payment of a debt by installments; probably formed in English from Old French *estaler* to fix, place (from *estal* position, from Germanic; compare Old High German *stal* place, STALL[1]) + English *-ment.* The alteration in spelling to *installment* is found in the verb *install* to pay by installments (1679), and was perhaps influenced by *install,* v., to put in place.

instance *n.* About 1380, the present time, present circumstances, in Chaucer's translation of Boethius' *De Consolatione Philosophiae;* later, example or case (probably before 1425); borrowed from Old French *instance* eagerness, anxiety, solicitation, reply to the contrary, from Medieval Latin *instantia* presence, urgency, objection, instance to the contrary, from Latin *īnstantia* presence, earnestness, urgency, from *īnstantem* (nominative *īnstāns*) urgent, see INSTANT; for suffix see -ANCE. —**v.** 1425, to urge or entreat; borrowed from Middle French *instancier* to plead, from the noun in French. The later sense of to cite an instance (1601) developed from the noun in English.

instant *n.* Before 1398, particular moment, in Trevisa's translation of Bartholomew's *De Proprietatibus Rerum;* borrowed probably from Old French *instant,* and directly from Medieval Latin *instantem* (nominative *instans*), from Latin *īnstantem* present, pressing, urgent, present participle of *īnstāre* to be present, be at hand, urge, stand near (*in-* in + *stāre* to STAND); for suffix see -ANT. **—adj.** immediate, without delay. About 1443, developed from the noun in English, and probably, in part borrowed from Old French *instant* imminent, learned borrowing from Latin *instantem* (nominative *īnstāns*) present, pressing, urgent. **—instantaneous** *adj.* 1644, implied in *instantaneously;* formed in English as if from Latin **īnstantāneus,* modeled on Latin *mōmentāneus* momentary, from *mōmentum* movement; for suffix see -OUS.

instead *adv.* Probably before 1200 *i stude,* early dialect form, in *Ancrene Riwle;* later (about 1300) found in *in stede* (*of*) in place (of), in lieu (of), a phrasal combination of *in,* prep., and *stede* STEAD.

The solid compound *instede* is first recorded before 1387, in Trevisa's translation of Higden's *Polychronicon,* but it did not become the established form until about 1640 (with spellings of *insteed, insteede,* and finally *instead,* about 1650) and after that time was separated only when written with a possessive, as *in his stead, in Mary's stead.* The use of *instead* without a following *of* (as in *let me go instead*) is first found in Milton's *Paradise Lost* (1667).

instep *n.* the upper surface of the human foot between the toes and the ankle. About 1450 *instep;* of uncertain origin, perhaps from *in-* in + *step* mistakenly substituted for obsolete *stepe* steep, in the sense of a declivity or slope, a noun use earlier than the record now shows of *steep,* adj. (about 725). The early variant form *stepe* of modern *steep* would tend to support this point. Later spellings of *instep* include *instoppe, instup,* which suggest a connection with *stoop* either in the sense of a bow or a downward slope; and these senses occur simultaneously with the variant spellings cited above.

instigate *v.* urge on, stir up. 1542, probably a back formation from *instigation;* also, in some instances, possibly borrowed from Latin *īnstīgātus,* past participle of *īnstīgāre;* for suffix see -ATE[1]. **—instigation** *n.* Before 1410 *instigacioun,* borrowed through Middle French *instigation,* or directly from Latin *īnstīgātiōnem* (nominative *īnstīgātiō*) an urging or incitement, from *īnstīgāre* urge on, set on, incite (*in-* in, on + **stīgāre* to prick, urge, cognate with Greek *stízein,* earlier **stigye-* to prick, and Gothic *stiks* a point, from Indo-European **steig-/stig-,* Pok.1016); for suffix see -ATION. **—instigator** *n.* 1598 *instigater;* formed from English *instigate* + *-er*[1], later replaced by *-or*[2], after Latin *īnstīgātor.*

instill or **instil** *v.* put in little by little, impart gradually. Probably before 1425 *instillen,* in a translation of Chauliac's *Grande Chirurgie;* borrowed from Latin *īnstīllāre* put in by drops (*in-* in + *stīlla* a drop; see DISTILL).

instinct (in′stingkt) *n.* natural feeling, knowledge, or power. Before 1420, incitement or impulse, in Lydgate's *Troy Book;* later, natural impulse, intuitive knowledge (about 1454); borrowed from Latin *īnstīnctus,* from past participle of *īnstinguere* incite or impel; related to *īnstīgāre* INSTIGATE. **—adj.** (instingkt′) 1538, innate; probably from the noun, but in some instances possibly borrowed from Latin *īnstīnctus,* past participle; see the noun. The sense of impelled or excited is first recorded in Milton's *Paradise Lost* (1667), and also appears in Pope and Swift. A misunderstanding of this use led to the meaning of filled or charged with something, appearing in 1797-1803. **—instinctive** *adj.* 1610, implied in *instinctively;* formed from English *instinct,* n. + *-ive.*

institute *v.* set up, establish, begin. About 1330, establish in an office, appoint; later, set up, start, found (probably before 1425); borrowed from Latin *īnstitūtus,* past participle of *īnstituere* set up (*in-* in + *statuere* establish; see STATUTE). **—n.** organization or society. Before 1520, purpose, design; later, something instituted (1546); borrowed, perhaps through Middle French *institut,* from Latin *īnstitūtum* design or precept, noun use of the neuter past participle of *īnstituere* establish. The meaning of organization or society for some special purpose, such as the promotion of science or art, is first recorded in 1829; borrowed from French *institut,* originally, in *Institut National des Sciences et des Arts,* created in 1795 to replace the old academies suppressed during the Revolution. **—institution** *n.* Before 1400 *institucioun* act of establishing; 1410, a set of established laws; borrowed from Old French *institution,* from Latin *īnstitūtiōnem* (nominative *īnstitūtiō*) arrangement, custom, principles of instruction, from *īnstituere* set up, establish. The meaning of a public establishment, organization, or association instituted for a social purpose, is first recorded in 1707. **—institutional** *adj.* 1617, formed from English *institution* + *-al*[1]. **—institutionalize** *v.* 1865, convert into an institution; later, confine to an institution (1905).

instruct *v.* Probably before 1425 *instructen* tell, inform, in a translation of Higden's *Polychronicon;* later, teach (1447); probably in some instances a back formation from *instruction,* and a borrowing of Latin *īnstrūctus,* past participle of *īnstruere* arrange, furnish with information, teach (*in-* on + *struere* to pile, build; see STRUCTURE). **—instruction** *n.* Probably about 1400 *instruccioun* information, knowledge, lesson, teaching; borrowed from Old French *instruction,* from Latin *īnstrūctiōnem* (nominative *īnstrūctiō*), from *īnstruere,* see INSTRUCT; for suffix see -TION. **—instructive** *adj.* 1611, probably formed from English *instruct* + *-ive,* after French *instructif* (feminine *instructive*). **—instructor** *n.* Before 1464 *instructour* one who instructs, teacher; borrowed through Old French *instructeur* from Latin *īnstrūctor* preparer, from *īnstrūctus,* past participle of *īnstruere;* for suffix see -OR[2].

instrument *n.* About 1300, musical instrument; later, device or implement (probably before 1325); borrowed from Old French *instrument,* and from Latin *īnstrūmentum* a tool, apparatus, furniture, dress, document, from *īnstruere* arrange, furnish, INSTRUCT. **—instrumental** *adj.* Before 1398, serving as a means to an end, in Trevisa's translation of Bartholomew's *De Proprietatibus Rerum;* borrowed from Old French *instrumental,* from *instrument* instrument, from Latin *īnstrūmentum;* for suffix see -AL[1]. The meaning in music of played or written for instruments is first recorded in 1509. **—instrumentalist** *n.* 1823, formed from English *instrumental* + *-ist.* **—instrumentation** *n.* 1845, arrangement of music for instruments; probably borrowed from French *instrumentation,* from *instrument* instrument; for suffix see -ATION.

insubordinate *adj.* 1849, back formation from *insubordination* (1790, in Burke's writings); formed from

English *in-*[1] not + *subordination,* perhaps after French *insubordination.*

insufferable *adj.* Probably before 1425; borrowed perhaps through Middle French *insouffrable,* from Medieval Latin *insufferabilis* (*in-* not + *sufferabilis* SUFFERABLE). It is also possible that in some instances *insufferable* was formed from English *in-*[1] not + *sufferable* (1303).

insufficient *adj.* 1392, borrowed from Old French *insufficient,* and directly from Latin *īnsufficientem* (nominative *īnsufficiēns*) not sufficient (*in-* not + *sufficientem,* nominative *sufficiēns* SUFFICIENT).

insular *adj.* isolated. 1611, of an island, in Cotgrave's *Dictionary;* borrowed by influence of French *insulaire,* from Late Latin *īnsulāris,* from Latin *īnsula* island, see ISLE; for suffix see -AR. The form in modern English replaced earlier *insulan* living on an island (before 1444); borrowed from Latin *īnsulānus,* from *īnsula* island. The figurative sense of isolated, narrow, prejudiced, is first recorded in Johnson's *Journey to the Western Islands of Scotland* (1775), probably as a back formation of *insularity* (1755, in Walpole's writings).

insulate *v.* isolate. 1538, make into an island; later, to isolate (1785, from earlier *insulated,* 1727); of uncertain formation, probably originally formed from Latin *īnsula* island (of unknown origin) + English *-ate*[1]; later, probably developed from *insulate,* adj., detached, isolated (1712, borrowed from Latin *insulātus* made like an island, from **insulāre* make like an island; for suffix see -ATE[1]). It is also probable that in some instances later use of *insulate,* v., in the 1700's was a back formation from *insulation.* The meaning of keep from losing or transferring electricity, sound, heat, etc., is first recorded in 1742. Doublet of ISOLATE. **—insulation** *n.* 1767, formed from English *insulate* + *-ion.* **—insulator** *n.* 1801, formed from English *insulate* + *-or*[2].

insulin *n.* hormone that enables the body to use sugar and other carbohydrates. 1922, formed in English from Latin *īnsula* island + English *-in*[2] chemical suffix; so called because this hormone is secreted by the *islets of Langerhans* in the pancreas.

The French word *insuline* for the then hypothetical hormone was proposed in 1909 by a French physiologist J. de Meyer; the Canadian discoverers Banting, Best, and Macleod, proposed the name *insulin* independently.

insult (insult′) *v.* 1570-76, to exult or brag insolently or scornfully, probably borrowed from Middle French *insulter,* learned borrowing from Latin *īnsultāre* to assail or insult, a frequentative form of *īnsilīre* leap at or upon (*in-* on, at + *salīre* to leap; see SALLY). The sense of assail offensively, treat with scorn or abuse, offend, is first recorded in 1620. **—n.** (in′sult) insulting speech or action. 1603, in Holland's translation of Plutarch's *Moralia,* assault or attack; later, insulting behavior (1671, in Milton's *Paradise Regained*); borrowed through French *insulte,* or directly from Late Latin *īnsultus* (genitive *īnsultūs*) a scoffing, reviling, insult, from *īnsul-,* stem of Latin *īnsilīre* leap at (*in-* on, at + *salīre* to leap).

insuperable *adj.* Before 1349, invincible; borrowed from Latin *insuperābilis* (*in-* not + *superābilis* that may be overcome, from *superāre* overcome or surmount, from *superus* one or that which is above, from *super* OVER). The meaning of impassable, insurmountable, is first recorded in 1657.

insure *v.* About 1412 *insuren* to give or exact a pledge, to assure, variant of earlier *ensuren;* borrowed from Old French *enseürer;* see ENSURE. *Insure* was formerly used in all the senses of *ensure;* the specific meaning of make safe or assure against loss or damage by payment of premiums, is first recorded in 1635. **—insurance** *n.* 1651, act or system of insuring life or property; formed from English *insure* + *-ance.*

insurgent *n.* rebel. 1765, borrowed from Latin *īnsurgentem* (nominative *insurgēns*), present participle of *insurgere* rise up (*in-* against + *surgere* to rise; see SURGE); for suffix see -ENT. **—adj.** rebelling, rebellious. 1814, in Scott's *Waverley;* from the noun. **—insurgence** *n.* 1847, formed from *insurgent,* after such pairs as *emergent, emergence,* or as a back formation from *insurgency,* on the model of French *insurgence;* for suffix see -ENCE. **—insurgency** *n.* 1803, formed from *insurgent,* after such pairs as *agent, agency.*

insurrection *n.* uprising, revolt. Probably before 1425 *insurreccion,* in a translation of Higden's *Polychronicon;* borrowed from Middle French *insurrection,* learned borrowing from Late Latin *īnsurrēctiōnem* (nominative *īnsurrēctiō*) a rising up, from Latin *īnsurreg-,* stem of *īnsurgere* to rise up; see INSURGENT; for suffix see -TION.

intact *adj.* with no part missing. Before 1500, unimpaired, whole, untouched; borrowed possibly through Middle French *intact,* and directly from Latin *intāctus* (*in-* not + *tāctus,* past participle of *tangere* to touch; see TANGENT).

intaglio (intal′yō *or* intäl′yō) *n.* process of engraving by making cuts in a surface. 1644, in John Evelyn's *Diary;* borrowing of Italian *intaglio* carving or engraving, from *intagliare* engrave (*in-* into + *tagliare* to cut, from Late Latin *tāliāre;* see TAILOR).

intangible *adj.* 1640, borrowed probably from French *intangible,* from Medieval Latin *intangibilis* (*in-* not + *tangibilis* TANGIBLE).

integer *n.* whole number. 1571, borrowed from Latin *integer* whole or entire (earlier **entagros*); literally, intact or untouched (*in-* not + *tag-,* the root of *tangere* to touch; see TANGENT). Doublet of ENTIRE.

integral *adj.* essential, intrinsic. 1471, implied in *integrallie,* adv., necessary to make something complete; borrowed probably through Middle French *intégral,* from Medieval Latin *integralis* forming a whole or making complete, from Latin *integer* whole; see INTEGER; for suffix see -AL[1]. The sense in mathematics of relating to integers, not fractional, is first recorded in 1658. **—n.** a whole, a whole number. 1620, something undivided; from the adjective.

integrate *v.* 1638, make complete or constitute; developed from *integrate,* adj., intact, unblemished (about 1450); borrowed from Latin *integrātus,* past participle of *integrāre* make whole, from *integer* whole, see INTEGER; for suffix see -ATE[1] The meaning of combine into a whole, is first recorded in 1802. The specific sense of end the segregation of (blacks), desegregate, is first recorded in 1948 in American English and was probably a back formation from *integration.* **—integration** *n.* 1620, act or process of integrating; borrowed probably from French *intégration,* and directly from Latin *integrātiōnem* (nominative *integrātiō*) renewal or restoration to wholeness, from *integrāre.* The meaning of a bringing of blacks into white society on an equal basis, desegregation, is first recorded in 1940, in the context of South Africa.

integrity *n.* Before 1400 *integrite* soundness, unimpaired or uncorrupted condition; borrowed from Old French *integrité,* learned borrowing from Latin *integritātem* (nominative *integritās*) chastity, soundness, wholeness, from *integer* whole; see INTEGER; for suffix see -ITY. The sense of honesty or uprightness is first recorded in 1548.

integument (integ′yůmənt) *n.* About 1611, in Chapman's translation of the *Iliad,* covering or coating; borrowed from French *intégument,* and directly from Latin *integumentum,* from *integere* to cover, enclose (*in-* on + *tegere* to cover; see THATCH); for suffix see -MENT. The more specific sense of natural covering of an animal or plant is first found in John Evelyn's *Sylva* (1664).

intellect *n.* About 1380, understanding, in Chaucer's *Canterbury Tales;* borrowed from Old French *intellecte,* and directly from Latin *intellēctus* (genitive *intellēctūs*) discernment or understanding, from *intelleg-* (by assimilation of *g* to *c* before *t*), stem of *intelligere* to understand, discern; see INTELLIGENT. **—intellectual** *adj.* Before 1398, of the intellect, in Trevisa's translation of Bartholomew's *De Proprietatibus Rerum;* borrowed from Old French *intellectuel,* and directly from Late Latin *intellēctuālis* pertaining to the understanding, from Latin *intellēctus* intellect. The meaning of having intelligence, inclined to pursuits which exercise the mind, is first found in Byron's *Don Juan* (1819). *—n.* 1599, the intellect, mind; later, intellectual person (1652); from the adjective.

intelligent *adj.* 1509, probably a back formation from *intelligence* modeled on Latin *intelligentem;* see INTELLIGENCE; for suffix see -ENT. **—intelligence** *n.* About 1380, in Chaucer's translation of Boethius' *De Consolatione Philosophiae;* borrowed from Old French *intelligence,* from Latin *intelligentia* understanding, from *intelligentem* (nominative *intelligēns*) discerning, intelligent, present participle of *intelligere;* earlier *intellegere* understand, perceive, discern (*inter-* between + *legere* choose, pick out, read; see LEGEND); for suffix see -ENCE. The sense of information or news, is first recorded before 1475. **—intelligence test** (1914) **—IQ** intelligence quotient (1922) **—intelligentsia** (intel′əjent′sēə) *n.pl.* the intellectuals. 1907 *intelligenzia* borrowed from Russian *intelligentsiya,* possibly from French *intelligentsia,* from Latin *intelligentia* INTELLIGENCE. The present spelling is first recorded in 1914. **—intelligible** *adj.* Before 1382, able to understand, in the Wycliffe Bible; borrowed from Old French *intelligible,* and directly from Latin *intelligibilis,* from *intelligere* understand; see INTELLIGENT. The sense of capable of being understood, comprehensible, is first recorded in 1509.

intend *v.* About 1300 *entenden* direct one's attention to; later *intenden* (about 1425); borrowed from Old French *intendre, entendre,* from Latin *intendere* intend, turn one's attention, strain (*in-* toward + *tendere* to stretch; see TEND). The meaning of have as a purpose, plan, is first recorded in Chaucer's *Troilus and Criseyde* (about 1385).

intense *adj.* Probably before 1425, very strong or acute; borrowed from Middle French *intense,* learned borrowing from Latin *intēnsus* stretched, strained, tight, intense; originally, past participle of *intendere* to stretch out, strain; see INTEND.

According to the OED *intense* and *intent*[2] are more complete differentiations of form and sense development that was already evident in Latin, wherein the two forms of the past participle *intēnsus* and *intentus* of the verb *intendere* had developed restrictions of meanings: *intēnsus* was confined to the meaning of stretched, strained in a physical sense, while *intentus* was extended in sense to that of mentally or nervously stretched, intent, eager, attentive.
—intensify *v.* 1817, make intense, in Coleridge's *Biographia Literaria;* formed from English *intense* + *-ify,* variant of *-fy.* **—intensity** *n.* 1665, extreme strength, force or energy, in Boyle's writings; formed from English *intense* + *-ity.* The sense of extreme depth of feeling is first recorded in Southey's *Life of John Bunyan* (1830). **—intensive** *adj.* About 1450, intense, vehement; probably borrowed from Middle French *intensif* (feminine *intensive*), from Medieval Latin *intensivus,* from Latin *intēnsus* forceful; for suffix see -IVE. *—n.* something that intensifies, as a word or prefix. 1813, in William Taylor's English *Synonyms Discriminated;* from the adjective.

intent[1] *n.* purpose, intention. Probably before 1200 *entent, entente,* in *Ancrene Riwle;* formed in English from a fusion of Old French *entent* intention, application, and *entente* intention, thought, desire, purpose; both forms being learned borrowings from Latin: *entent* from Late Latin *intentus* attention, intention; and *entente* from Vulgar Latin **intenta,* n., a stretching out, a straining, an intending; both forms from the past participle *intentus* (feminine *intenta*) of *intendere* stretch out, lean toward, strain; see INTEND.

The form *entent* appeared more frequently than *entente,* which disappeared toward the end of the Middle English period. The current spelling became established by about 1550.
—intention *n.* About 1380 *entencioun* desire or feeling, in Chaucer's translation of Boethius' *De Consolatione Philosophiae;* later, purpose, aim (about 1390); borrowed from Old French *entention, intention,* from Latin *intentiōnem* (nominative *intentiō*) purpose, effort, straining, from *intendere;* for suffix see -TION. The form *intencioun* is first recorded before 1387, *intention* about 1400. **—intentional** *adj.* 1530, in Palsgrave's *Lesclarcissement;* borrowed from Middle French *intentionnel,* from Medieval Latin *intentionalis,* from Latin *intentiōnem* (nominative *intentiō*) purpose or effort; for suffix see -AL[1]. In later instances *intentional* was probably formed from English *intention* + *-al*[1].

intent[2] *adj.* very attentive. 1606, earnestly engaged, eager; 1610, very attentive; borrowed from Latin *intentus* attentive, eager, strained, past participle of *intendere* to strain, stretch; see INTEND. See note under INTENSE.

inter (intėr′) *v.* bury. 1303 *interen, enteren,* in Mannyng's *Handlyng Synne;* borrowed from Old French *enterrer,* learned borrowing from Medieval Latin *interrare* put in the earth, bury (Latin *in-* in + *terra* earth; see TERRAIN). **—interment** *n.* burial. Probably before 1300 *interment, enterement,* in *Arthour and Merlin;* borrowed from Old French *enterrement,* from *enterrer* inter.

inter- a prefix meaning: together, one with the other, as in *intercommunicate, intermixture;* between, among, as in *interpose.*

Though abstracted from the many compounds in which it entered English and by way of which English *inter-* was treated as a borrowing from Latin *inter-* (from Latin *inter,* prep., adv., among, between, during), the form *inter-* was not generally considered a living prefix in English until the 1400's. During the later period of Middle English many words borrowed in the Old and Middle French forms *entre-, enter-* began to be consciously respelled with Latin *inter-* (though vestiges of the older French borrowings are found in *entertain* and *enterprise*).

On this pattern of the earlier borrowed compounds many new compounds have been formed in English, such as *intermural,* and in Middle English, such as *interlard,* or have been readily borrowed into English (both in whole *interview* and in part *view*). The living prefix *inter-* is now freely added to almost any element in English to create such formations as *interisland, interdependence, intertidal, interact, interbreed.*

The Latin *inter* is cognate with Sanskrit *antár* between, Avestan *antarə,* Old Irish *eter, etir, etar,* from Indo-European **enter,* **n̥ter* (Pok.313).

interbreed *v.* 1859, in Darwin's *On the Origin of Species;* formed from English *inter-* + *breed.*

intercalary (intėr'kəler'ē) *adj.* 1614, inserted in a calendar at intervals, in Raleigh's *The History of the World;* borrowed from Latin *intercalārius* of or for insertion, or *intercalāris* an inserted day, from *intercalāre* proclaim insertion in the calendar of a day or month (*inter-* between + *calāre* proclaim; see LOW² to moo); for suffix see -ARY. In the Jewish, Greek, and Roman calendars, extra days or months had to be inserted chiefly to adapt the lunar to the solar reckoning of time. After the introduction of the Julian calendar in 46 B.C. an intercalated day (then a second February 24, now February 29) was required only once in four years.

intercede *v.* 1578, intervene, come between; later, plead in another's behalf (1606); possibly in part a back formation from *intercession,* modeled on Latin *intercēdere,* and in part borrowed directly from Latin *intercēdere* intervene, go between (*inter-* between + *cēdere* go; see CEDE). —**intercession** *n.* Probably before 1430 *intercession* the act of interceding; later, an interceding prayer (1500-20, in Dunbar's *Poems*); borrowed from Latin *intercessiōnem* (nominative *intercessiō*) intervention; from *intercēdere* intervene; for suffix see -SION.

intercept *v.* 1391 *intercepten* to cut off or mark off (a segment of a line), in Chaucer's *Treatise on the Astrolabe;* later, take or seize on the way between two points (about 1540); borrowed from Latin *interceptus,* past participle of *intercipere* take or seize between, intercept (*inter-* between + *-cipere,* combining form of *capere* to catch, take; see CAPTIVE). —**interception** *n.* Probably before 1425 *intercepcioun* interruption of the flow of body fluids, later, act of intercepting (1599, in Shakespeare's *Henry V*); borrowed from Latin *interceptiōnem* (nominative *interceptiō*) a taking away, from *intercep-,* stem of *intercipere;* for suffix see -TION. In some instances *interception* may have been formed from English *intercept,* v. + *-tion.*

For more than a century, both noun and verb appear to have been confined to technical use.

interchange *v.* About 1374 *enterchaungeden* (past plural) to exchange, give and receive; borrowed from Old French *entre-changier* to change, disguise (*entre-* inter- + *changier, changer* to change). —**n.** 1548, act of exchanging, giving and receiving; from the verb.

intercom *n.* telephone or radio apparatus for communication within or between offices, vehicles, etc. 1940, shortened form of *intercommunication system* (1911).

intercourse *n.* 1449 *entercourse* trade or traffic in goods, commercial dealings, in *Proceedings of the Privy Council;* later, social communication between individuals (1547-64); borrowed from Middle French *entrecours,* from Old French, learned borrowing from Latin *intercursus* a running between or intervention, from the stem of the past participle of *intercurrere* to run between (*inter-* between + *currere* to run; see CURRENT). By the 1700's the Latin form with *i* became the established form. The meaning of sexual relations is first recorded in Malthus' *An Essay on the Principle of Population* (1798).

interdict (in'tərdikt') *v.* prohibit formally. Probably before 1425 *enterditen* to prohibit or forbid, in a translation of Higden's *Polychronicon,* earlier *entrediten* to cut off from the Church (about 1300); borrowed from Old French *entredit,* past participle of *entredire* forbid by decree, from Latin *interdīcere* interpose by speech, prohibit (*inter-* between + *dīcere* speak; see DICTION). The Latinate spelling with *inter-* is first recorded between 1423 and 1450, as a past participle; see INTER-. —**n.** (in'tərdikt) formal prohibition. Before 1464 *interdict;* earlier *entredit* a decree of exclusion from the Church (about 1300); borrowed from Old French *entredit,* from Latin *interdictum* prohibition; noun use of neuter past participle of *interdīcere;* for spelling see INTER-. —**interdiction** *n.* act of interdicting. 1464 *enterdiccioun;* borrowed from Latin *interdictiōnem* (nominative *interdictiō*), from *interdic-,* stem of *interdīcere* prohibit; for spelling see INTER-; for suffix see -TION. The military sense of interrupt by aerial bombing is first recorded in 1944.

interest *n.* Probably about 1425 *interest* concern, right, claim; borrowed from Latin *interest* it is of importance, it makes a difference, it concerns or matters, form of the third person singular present of *interesse* to concern, be of importance (*inter-* between + *esse* be; see IS).

Interest is a replacement of *interesse, intresse* concern, interest in anything (about 1390, in Chaucer's *Fortune*); later, legal concern, title, or claim (1422); borrowed from Anglo-French *interesse,* from Medieval Latin *interesse* compensation for loss, compensatory payment, interest in money lent; noun use of Latin *interesse* to concern, be of importance.

The earliest occurrences of *interest* were in reference to legal and financial uses. The prominent meanings of *interest,* most of which occurred earlier with the spelling *interesse,* are advantageous relation, as in *an interest in a country's welfare,* found in 1450; the meaning of good, profit, benefit, as in *the interests of a family,* is first recorded in 1459, and the related sense of a thing in which one has a share or concern, as in *an interest in a business,* probably about 1425. *Interest* with the meaning of compensation for loss appeared about 1575, and of money paid for the use of money (1545).

—**v.** 1608, to cause to have a concern, to involve; from the noun, replacing earlier *interesse* (1570), also from the noun.

—**interested** *adj.* 1665, in Pepys' *Correspondence;* formed from English *interest,* v. + *-ed²*. —**interesting** *adj.* 1711, important; later, of interest (1768); formed from English *interest,* v. + *-ing*[2].

interface *n.* 1882 (found earlier in *interfacial,* 1837); formed from English *inter-* + *face* a surface. **—v.** 1967, to come into interaction with; implied earlier in *interfacing* (1964); from the noun.

interfere *v.* 1440 *entyferyn* to intermingle or mix, in *Promptorium Parvulorum;* 1449 *enterferen* to meddle, mix in the affairs of others; borrowed from Middle French *enterferer, enterferir* to strike each other (*entre-* between + *ferir* to strike, from Latin *ferīre* to knock, strike, related to *forāre* to bore, cognate with Greek *pháranx* ravine, Old English *borian* bore, Old High German *berjan* strike, from Indo-European **bher-/bhor-* cut, cleave, Pok.133).The Latinate spelling *interfere* is first recorded in 1451. **—interference** *n.* 1783, act or fact of interfering, in Burke's *Report on Affairs of India;* formed from English *interfere* + *-ence.*

interferon (in′tərfir′on) *n.* protein produced by cells in response to viral infection, and having the property of inhibiting the growth of viruses. 1957, formed from English *interfere,* v. + *-on* chemical suffix; so called by its codiscoverers, the Scots virologist Alick Isaacs and the Swiss microbiologist Jean Lindemann, because it inhibits or interferes with replication of viruses.

interim (in′tərim) *n.* 1548 *Interim* temporary arrangement between German Protestants and the Roman Catholic Church to meet to settle doctrinal differences; later, the time between or meantime, in an edition of Foxe's *Book of Martyrs;* borrowing of Latin *interim,* adv., in the meantime; originally, in the midst of that (*inter* between, INTER- + *im,* ancient adverb from the stem of the pronoun *is* this, that). **—adj.** for the meantime; temporary. 1604, intervening; from the noun in English and a borrowing from Latin *interim,* adv.

interior *adj.* 1490, on the inside, inner, in Caxton's translation of *The Book of Eneydos;* borrowed through Middle French *intérieur,* and directly from Latin *interior* inner, a contrastive adjective of *inter* within (opposite to *exterior*); see INTER-. **—n.** 1796, inland part, in Burke's writings; later, the inside (1828); from the adjective.

interject *v.* 1578, come between; probably a back formation from *interjection,* modeled on Latin *intericere* to throw or cast between. The meaning of introduce abruptly, insert, interpose, is first recorded in 1588. **—interjection** *n.* Probably before 1430 *interjeccioun* exclamation or outcry, in Lydgate's writings; borrowed from Middle French *interjection,* from Latin *interjectiōnem* (nominative *interjectiō*) a throwing or placing between, an interjection in grammar, from *interjec-,* stem of *intericere* (*inter-* between + *-icere,* combining form of *jacere* to throw); for suffix see -TION. The grammatical meaning of a part of speech that is an exclamation, is first recorded in English in Palsgrave's *Lesclarcissement* (1530), from the same meaning in Latin.

interlace *v.* About 1380 *entrelace* to tangle or confuse in thinking, in Chaucer's translation of Boethius' *De Consolatione Philosophiae;* borrowed from Old French *entrelacier* lace together, involve (*entre-* inter- + *lacier* to LACE); for spelling see INTER-.

interlard *v.* give variety to, mix, intersperse. Probably before 1425 *enterlarden* mix with alternate layers of fat; borrowed from Middle French *entrelarder* (*entre-* between + *larder* to lard, from Old French *lard* bacon fat, LARD); for spelling see INTER-. The figurative sense of diversify with something intermixed or interjected, is first recorded in an edition of Foxe's *Book of Martyrs* (1563-87). The Latinized spelling is first recorded in 1555.

interlinear *adj.* About 1378 *enterlinarie,* in a version of *Piers Plowman;* borrowed from Medieval Latin *interlinearis* (*inter-* between + *linea* LINE); for suffix see -AR. The variant *interlineal* (1526) was borrowed from Middle French *interlineal.*

interlocutor (in′tərlok′yətər) *n.* 1514, person who takes part in a conversation or dialogue; formed in English as if from Latin **interlocūtor,* from *interlocū-,* stem of *interloquī* interrupt + *-tor;* for suffix see -OR[2]. **—interlocutory** *adj.* 1597, occurring in dialogue, in Richard Hooker's *Ecclesiastical Polity;* formed as if from Latin **interlocūtōrius,* from *interlocū-,* stem of *interloquī* interrupt + *-tory;* for suffix see -ORY. The specific meaning in law of "made during a lawsuit, not final," is first recorded in 1590.

interloper *n.* intruder. About 1590 *enterloper* an unauthorized trader, one who trespasses on the rights of chartered trading companies; later *interloper* (1603-27), probably formed in English from *inter-, enter-* between + *-loper,* as in *landloper* a vagabond, renegade, adventurer (before 1580); borrowed from Middle Dutch *landlōper* (*land* land + *lōper* runner, rover, from *lōpen* to run; see LEAP). The general meaning of intruder, is first recorded in 1632.

interlude *n.* interval. About 1303 *enterlude* a short, humorous play introduced between parts of a long medieval mystery play, in Mannyng's *Handlyng Synne;* later *interlude* (1375, in Scottish); borrowed from Medieval Latin *interludium* (from Latin *inter-* between + *lūdus* a play; see LUDICROUS). The meaning of an interval in the course of an action or event, is first recorded in an article by Johnson in *The Rambler* (1751). The more specific sense of an instrumental piece played between the parts of a hymn or church service, is recorded in 1838.

intermediate *adj.* Probably before 1425 *intermediate* being or occurring between, intervening, in a translation of Higden's *Polychronicon;* borrowed through French *intermédiat,* or directly from Medieval Latin *intermediatus,* from Late Latin *intermedium* place coming between (from Latin *inter-* between + *medius* in the middle; see MIDDLE); for suffix see -ATE[1]. **—n.** something in between. 1650, from the adjective.

intermezzo (in′tərmet′sō) *n.* short dramatic or musical piece between the acts of a play or a longer musical work. 1771, borrowing of Italian *intermezzo,* from Late Latin *intermedium* place coming between; see INTERMEDIATE.

intermission *n.* Before 1415 *intermissioun* a stopping for a time, temporary pause or cessation, interruption, in Wycliffe's writings; borrowed from Latin *intermissiōnem* (nominative *intermissiō*) a breaking off, interruption, from *intermittere* to leave off; see INTERMITTENT; for suffix see -SION.

intermittent *adj.* occurring at intervals. 1603, in Holland's translation of Plutarch's *Moralia;* possibly formed in English from *intermit* (1563-87; borrowed from Latin *intermittere*) + *-ent,* modeled on Latin *intermittentem;* or borrowed directly from Latin *intermittentem* (nominative *intermittēns*), present participle of *intermittere* to leave off (*inter-* between + *mittere* let go, send; see MISSION); for suffix see -ENT.

intern[1] (intèrn′) *v.* 1866, confine within a place; borrowed from French *interner* send to the interior, confine, from Middle French *interne* inner or internal, learned borrowing from Latin *internus* within, INTERNAL. **—internee** *n.* 1918, one who is interned; formed from English *intern*[1] + *-ee.* **—internment** *n.* 1870, act of interning; formed from English *intern*[1] + *-ment,* probably on the model of French *internement.*

intern[2] or **interne** (in′tèrn) *n.* doctor working and training in a hospital after completing medical school. 1879, American English; borrowed from French *interne* assistant doctor working in absence of the attending doctor; literally, inmate, resident within a school, etc., from Middle French *interne* internal; see INTERN[1]. **—v.** serve as an intern in a hospital. 1933, American English; from the noun.

internal *adj.* Probably before 1425 *internalle* (of a sea) extending toward the interior of a continent, in a translation of Higden's *Polychronicon;* later, pertaining to the mind or soul, subjective (1509); borrowed from Middle French *internel,* or directly from Medieval Latin *internalis,* from Latin *internus* within, expanded from pre-Latin **interos,* from *inter,* see INTER-; for suffix see -AL[1]. The meaning of on the inside, inner, is first recorded in English in Spenser's *Faerie Queene* (1590). **—internalize** *v.* 1884, in American English, to give an inward or subjective character to; specifically, to adopt (an idea, custom, mannerism) in one's personality (1942, but found earlier in *internalized,* 1932); formed from English *internal* + *-ize.* **—internal revenue** (1796, in American English)

international *adj.* 1780, in Jeremy Bentham's *Principles of Morals and Legislation;* formed from English *inter-* + *national,* originally replacing the sense "of nations" in the "law of nations."

internecine (in′tərnē′sən) *adj.* destructive to both sides. 1663, deadly, destructive, in Samuel Butler's *Hudibras;* borrowed from Latin *internecīnus,* variant of *internecīvus* murderous or destructive, from *internecāre* kill or destroy (*inter-* each other, as in *inter sē* + *necāre* kill; see NOXIOUS); for suffix see -INE[1]. Butler's use of *internecine* is generally considered as misinterpreted in Johnson's *Dictionary* (1755), where the word is defined as "mutually destructive," the so-called error attributed to an association of *inter-* with words such as *interchange,* in which it carries the meaning of mutual. However, Johnson's interpretation of *internecine* is close to that of the French linguistic scholar Meillet, who interprets the word as carrying the sense of reciprocity.

interplanetary *adj.* Before 1691, in Boyle's writings; formed from English *inter-* + *planetary.*

interpolate *v.* insert between, interpose. 1612, to alter by adding new matter; apparently reborrowed from Latin *interpolātus,* past participle of *interpolāre* alter, freshen up, falsify (*inter-* up + *-polāre,* related to *polīre* to smoothe, POLISH); for suffix see -ATE[1].

The meaning of to insert, introduce between, is first recorded in Bentham's writings (1802-12).

A form of the verb existed in Middle English medical terminology *interpolen* to cease temporarily, interrupt (probably before 1425); borrowed from Medieval Latin and Latin *interpolāre,* but disappears from the record of English probably before 1449.

—interpolation *n.* 1612, the action of inserting, interpolating; borrowed, possibly through French *interpolation,* from Latin *interpolātiōnem* (nominative *interpolātiō*), from *interpolāre;* for suffix see -ATION.

interpose *v.* put between, insert. 1599, borrowed from Middle French *interposer,* which supplanted Latin *interpōnere;* see INTER- and POSE[1]; also see POSTPONE. **—interposition** *n.* 1392; borrowed from Old French *interposicion,* and directly from Latin *interpositiōnem* (nominative *interpositiō*), formed on the stem of *interpositus,* past participle of Latin *interpōnere* put between; for suffix see -TION.

interpret *v.* About 1384 *interpreten* explain the meaning of, in a version of the Wycliffe Bible; possibly a back formation from *interpretation,* and a borrowing through Old French *interpreter,* and directly from Latin *interpretārī* explain, expound, understand. **—interpretation** *n.* Probably about 1350 *interpretacioun,* in the Wycliffe Bible; borrowed through Old French *interpretation,* and directly from Latin *interpretātiōnem* (nominative *interpretātiō*), from *interpretārī* interpret, from *interpretem* (nominative *interpres*) interpreter, translator, agent, mediator (*inter-* between + *-pretem,* possibly related to *pretium* PRICE); for suffix see -ATION. **—interpreter** *n.* About 1384 *interpretour;* possibly formed from English *interpret* + *-our,* variant of *-or*[2]; or borrowed through Old French *interpreteur, entrepreteur,* from Late Latin *interpretātōr,* from Latin *interpretārī* interpret. The Latin form *interpretātōr* existed in English *interpretator* from some time before 1425 until at least 1621.

interregnum (in′tərreg′nəm) *n.* time between the end of one ruler's reign and the beginning of the next one. 1579-80, temporary rule, in North's translation of Plutarch's *Lives;* later, interval between reigns (1590); borrowing of Latin *interrēgnum,* from the phrase *inter rēgna* between reigns (plural of *rēgnum* REIGN).

interrogate *v.* 1483, question thoroughly, in Caxton's translation of Cato's writings; probably a back formation of *interrogation,* and in some instances borrowed from Latin *interrogātus,* past participle of *interrogāre;* for suffix see -ATE[1]. **—interrogation** *n.* About 1390 *interrogacion* a question, in Chaucer's *Canterbury Tales;* later, act of interrogating (1551); borrowed through Old French *interrogation,* or directly from Latin *interrogātiōnem* (nominative *interrogātiō*) a question or questioning, from *interrogāre* (*inter-* between + *rogāre* ask, question; see RIGHT); for suffix see -ATION. **—interrogative** *adj.* Before 1500, (in grammar) used in asking a question; borrowed from Late Latin *interrogātīvus* of or pertaining to a question, from Latin *interrogātus,* past participle of *interrogāre;* for suffix see -IVE.

interrupt *v.* Probably before 1400, interfere with rights, in Wycliffe's writings; later, break into a speech or tale (about 1412); probably borrowed from Latin *interruptus,* past participle of *interrumpere* break apart, break off (*inter-* between + *rumpere* to break, RUPTURE). It is also possible in some instances that *interrupt* is a back formation from *interruption.* **—n.** interruption of a computer program. 1957, from the verb. **—interruption** *n.* Before 1393 *interrupcion* a break, in Gower's *Confessio Amantis;* borrowed, possibly through Old French *interruption,* and directly from Latin *interruptiōnem* (nominative *interruptiō*), from *interrup-,* stem of *interrumpere;* for suffix see -TION.

intersect *v.* 1615, cut or divide by passing through or crossing; probably a back formation from *intersection,* after Latin *intersectus,* past participle of *intersecāre* intersect. **—intersection** *n.* 1559, an intersecting or crossing, place where things intersect or cross; borrowed, probably through Middle French *intersection,* and directly from Latin *intersectiōnem* (nominative *intersectiō*), from *intersec-,* stem of *intersecāre* intersect, cut asunder (*inter-* between + *secāre* to cut; see SECTION); for suffix see -TION. The sense, originally in American English, of a place where streets cross, is first recorded in Hawthorne's writings, in 1858. An earlier form of the word existed in Middle English *intersectacioun* intersection (before 1420, in Lydgate's *Troy Book*).

intersperse *v.* 1566, vary with things scattered or mingled at intervals; borrowed from Latin *interspersus* scattered, past participle of *interspergere* (*inter-* between + *spargere* to scatter; see SPARSE).

interstice (intėr'stis) *n.* small or narrow space, chink. Probably before 1425 *interstice* intervening space (between stars), in a translation of Higden's *Polychronicon;* later, narrow intervening space (1603, in Holland's translation of Plutarch's *Moralia*); borrowed from French *interstice,* from Latin *interstitium,* as if from the past participle stem of *intersistere* to pause (*inter-* between + *sistere* come to stand, from *stāre* to STAND). **—interstitial** *adj.* 1646, formed from English *interstice* + *-al*[1].

interval *n.* time or space between. Before 1325, *intervalle, enterwal,* in *Cursor Mundi;* borrowed from Old French *intervalle, entreval,* from Latin *intervallum,* originally, space between palisades or ramparts (*inter-* between + *vallum* rampart; see WALL).

intervene *v.* 1588, come between, prevent, hinder; a back formation from *intervention,* modeled on Latin *intervenīre* (*inter-* between + *venīre* COME). **—intervention** *n.* About 1425 *intervencioun* intercession, especially by prayer; borrowed, perhaps through Middle French *intervention,* or directly from Late Latin *interventiōnem* (nominative *interventiō*) an interposing, giving security, from Latin *interven-,* stem of *intervenīre* intervene; for suffix see -TION.

interview *n.* 1514 *enterview* meeting of persons face to face for a special purpose; borrowed from Middle French *entrevue,* from *s'entrevoir* to see each other (*entre-* between, from Latin *inter-* + Old French *voir* to see, from *veoir* to VIEW); for spelling see INTER-. **—v.** have an interview with; meet and talk with. 1869, from the noun.

intestate (intes'tāt) *adj.* About 1378, not having made a will, in a version of *Piers Plowman;* borrowed, perhaps through Old French *intestat,* and directly from Latin *intestātus* (*in-* not + *testātus,* past participle of *testārī* make a will, bear witness; see TESTAMENT); for suffix see -ATE[1]. **—n.** person who has died without making a will. 1658, from the adjective.

intestine *n.* part of the alimentary canal that extends from the stomach to the anus. Probably before 1425 *intestine* (but found as plural in Chauliac's *Grande Chirurgie*); borrowed through Middle French *intestin,* or directly from Latin *intestīna,* neuter plural of *intestīnus,* adj., internal, probably altered (by influence of *clandestīnus* hidden) from earlier **intustīnos,* from *intus* within (cognate with Greek *entós* within, *en* IN). **—intestinal** *adj.* Probably before 1425 *intestinale* of the intestines, in Chauliac's *Grande Chirurgie;* probably borrowed from Medieval Latin *intestinalis,* from Latin *intestīnum,* neuter of *intestīnus,* adj. It is also possible that *intestinal* was formed in English from *intestine* + *-al*[1] during the translation of Chauliac.

intimate[1] (in'tәmit) *adj.* very familiar. 1632, deep-seated, most inward; borrowed from Late Latin *intimātus,* past participle of *intimāre* make known, announce, notify, impress deeply upon, from Latin *intimus* inmost; (as noun) close friend, superlative of *in* IN; for suffix see -ATE[1]. The meaning of closely acquainted, is first recorded in English in 1635, from the Latin sense. An earlier form *intime* very familiar, intimate (before 1618), was borrowed from Middle French *intime,* learned borrowing from Latin *intimus.* **—n.** person with whom one is intimate. 1659, from the adjective. **—intimacy** *n.* 1641, formed from English *intimate* + *-acy.*

intimate[2] (in'tәmāt) *v.* suggest indirectly, hint. 1538, to communicate or notify; later, suggest indirectly (1590, in Spenser's *Faerie Queene*); probably a back formation from *intimation,* modeled on Late Latin *intimātus,* past participle of *intimāre* make known or announce; see INTIMATE[1]; for suffix see -ATE[1]. **—intimation** *n.* 1442-43 (Scottish) *intimacion* act of making known; later, suggestion or hint (1531, in Elyot's *The Boke Named the Governour*); borrowed from Middle French *intimation,* from Late Latin *intimātiōnem* (nominative *intimātiō*) an announcement, from *intimāre* make known, announce; for suffix see -ATION.

intimidate *v.* 1646, frighten; borrowed from Medieval Latin *intimidatus,* past participle of *intimidare* (Latin *in-* in + *timidus* fearful, TIMID); for suffix see -ATE[1]. **—intimidation** *n.* 1658, in Phillips' *Dictionary,* probably formed from English *intimidate* + *-ion,* on the model of French *intimidation.*

into *prep.* Old English *intō,* before 900, in Alfred's translation of St. Gregory's *Pastoral Care;* originally the two words *in,* adv. and *tō* to, prep., as in the similar collocations *out to, up to, off to, on to,* in which the adverb expresses the general direction of motion, and the preposition indicates a particular point or place. The collocation arose in Old English as use of case endings weakened, so that the sense "to the interior of some place" could no longer be expressed by the preposition *in* followed by the accusative case of a word. The informal collocation *be into* be very involved or interested in, be an enthusiast or devotee of (as in *He is into astrology*), is first recorded about 1969 in American English, probably as a development of such earlier phrases as *get into* and *go into* in reference to some occupation or field of activity (about 1712).

intolerable *adj.* 1392 *intollerable;* borrowed from Old French *intolerable,* and directly from Latin *intolerābilis* (*in-* not + *tolerābilis* TOLERABLE).

intone *v.* 1385 *entunen;* later *entonen* (before 1446); borrowed from Old French *entoner* sing, chant, from Medieval Latin *intonare* sing according to tone, from Latin *in-* in + *tonus* TONE. The Latinate spelling *intone* is first recorded in 1555. **—intonation** *n.* 1620, opening phrase of a plainsong melody; formed from English *intone,* v. + *-ation,* and in some instances perhaps borrowed through French *intonation,* from Medieval Latin *intonationem* (nominative *intonatio*) sounding, intoning, from *intonare* intone; for suffix see -ATION.

The meaning of modulation of the voice, is first recorded in 1791.

intoxicate *v.* About 1450 *intoxicate* to poison; later, make drunk (1598); developed from *intoxicat,* adj., filled with poison; borrowed from Medieval Latin *intoxicatus,* past participle of *intoxicare;* see INTOXICATION; for suffix see -ATE[1]. It is also probable that *intoxicate* is, in some instances a back formation from *intoxication.* The figurative sense of exhilarate, is first recorded in 1591, from the earlier adjective sense of stupefied or exhilarated (about 1500). **—intoxication** *n.* Probably about 1408 *intoxigacion* poisoning, in Lydgate's *Reson and Sensuallyte;* later, drunkenness (1646); borrowed from Medieval Latin *intoxicationem* (nominative *intoxicatio*) poisoning, from *intoxicare* to poison (Latin *in-* in + *toxicum* poison; see TOXIC); for suffix see -ATION.

intra- a prefix meaning within, inside, on the inside, as in *intravenous = inside of or within a vein or veins, intradisciplinary = within a certain discipline, of a particular field of study.* Borrowed from Late Latin *intrā-,* from Latin *intrā,* adv., prep., inside of or within, related to *inter* between; see INTER-. Use of *intra-* is largely a product of modern times, occurring in words of common and technical vocabulary, where once it was generally a term of science and the academic world. While some words are borrowings from Medieval and even Late Latin, few if any come from Classical Latin.

intractable *adj.* Before 1500, rough, stormy; an extension of docile, not manageable, not easily treated or dealt with; borrowed from Latin *intractābilis* (*in-* not + *tractābilis* TRACTABLE).

intramural *adj.* 1846, formed in English from *intra-* + Latin *mūr(us)* wall + English *-al*[1]; compare *extramural,* a similar formation in English (1854).

intransigent *adj.* unwilling to agree or compromise. 1881, borrowed from French *intransigeant,* from Spanish *los intransigentes,* a name for various extreme political parties (*in-* not + *transigente* compromising, from Latin *trānsigentem,* nominative *trānsigēns,* present participle of *trānsigere* come to an agreement, accomplish, TRANSACT); for suffix see -ENT. **—n.** intransigent person. 1879, borrowed from French *intransigeant,* adj. and n. **—intransigence** *n.* 1882, borrowed from French *intransigeance,* from *intransigeant,* adj.; for suffix see -ENCE.

intransitive *adj.* 1612 *intransitive* in grammar, not transitive; borrowed from Late Latin *intrānsitīvus* not passing over (Latin *in-* not + *trānsire* to pass over). Though the concept of transitive and intransitive was known long before its application to English verbs, it was not applied in English until the 1500's when rules of Latin grammar were first used extensively to analyze the English language, largely as a teaching device.

intravenous (in′trəvē′nəs) *adj.* within a vein or the veins. 1847-49, formed in English from *intra-* + Latin *vēnōsus,* from *vēna* VEIN; for suffix see -OUS **—n.** intravenous injection. 1960, from the adjective.

intrepid *adj.* fearless. 1697, in Dryden's translation of Vergil's *Aeneid;* borrowed through French *intrépide,* and directly from Latin *intrepidus* (*in-* not + *trepidus* alarmed; see TREPIDATION).

intricate *adj.* Probably before 1425 *intricate* entangled, complicated; borrowed from Latin *intrīcātus,* past participle of *intrīcāre* entangle (*in-* in + *trīcae,* pl., perplexities, hindrances; of unknown origin); for suffix see -ATE[1]. It is also possible that *intricate* was, in some instances, borrowed through Old French *entriqué,* Old Provençal *intricat,* from Latin.

The first recorded use in Chauliac's *Grande Chirurgie,* a technical term meaning physically entangled; the general use of something perplexing, complicated, is recorded in 1579.

—intricacy *n.* 1602, formed from English *intricate* + *-cy.*

intrigue (in′trēg) *n.* 1647, secret scheming or plotting, in Clarendon's *History of the Rebellion and Civil Wars in England;* probably from the verb. **—v.** (intrēg′) 1612, deceive or perplex; later, carry on plots (before 1714); borrowed from French *intriguer* to puzzle, plot, from Italian *intrigare* to plot or meddle, from Latin *intrīcāre* entangle; see INTRICATE. The form *intrigue* in modern English replaced earlier *entriken* (recorded before 1393, in Gower's *Confessio Amantis*), which disappears from the record before 1500. The extended meaning of arouse the interest or curiosity of, is first recorded in 1894.

intrinsic *adj.* essential, inherent. 1490 *intrinsique* inner, in Caxton's translation of *The Book of Eneydos;* later, essential (1642); borrowed from Middle French *intrinsèque* inner, learned borrowing from Medieval Latin *intrinsecus* interior or internal, from Latin *intrīnsecus,* adv., inwardly (Old Latin **intrim* coming from inside, related to Latin *inter* among, between + Latin *secus* alongside, following, related to *sequī* to follow; see SEQUEL); for suffix see -IC.

intro- a prefix meaning inward, internally, within, as in *introduce, introvert.* Borrowed from Latin *intrō-,* from *intrō* inward, within, into, in, from pre-Latin **interos,* from *inter* between; see INTER-.

introduce *v.* Probably before 1425 *introducen* bring into being; possibly a back formation from *introduction,* modeled on Latin *intrōdūcere* originate, institute, bring in (*intrō-* inward, related to *inter-* INTER- + *dūcere* to lead; see TOW[1] to pull). The meaning of bring into notice or knowledge, is first recorded in 1559, and bring into personal acquaintance, in 1659. **—introduction** *n.* About 1395 *introduccioun* a preliminary action or step, in Chaucer's *Canterbury Tales;* borrowed from Old French *introduction,* and directly from Latin *intrōductiōnem* (nominative *intrōductiō*) a leading in, introduction, from *intrōduc-,* stem of *intrōdūcere* introduce; for suffix see -TION. The meaning of a preliminary statement is first recorded in Lydgate's *Falls of Princes* (probably before 1439). **—introductory** *adj.* Before 1400, borrowed from Old French *introductoire,* and directly from Late Latin *intrōductōrius,* from *intrōductor,* from *intrōdūcere;* for suffix see -ORY.

introspection *n.* examination of one's own thoughts and feelings. Before 1677, borrowed from Latin *intrōspectus,* past participle of *intrōspicere* look into, observe closely (*intrō-* inward; related to *inter-* INTER- + *specere* to look at; see SPY); for suffix see -ION. **—introspective** *adj.* given to introspection. 1820, in Southey's *Letters;* formed from Latin *intrōspectus;* for suffix see -IVE.

introvert (in′trəvėrt′) *v.* turn (one's thoughts, etc.) upon oneself. 1669, formed as if from Latin **intrōvertere (intrō-* inward; related to *inter-* INTER- + *vertere* to turn; see VERTEX). **—n.** (in′trəvėrt) inwardly-turned person; person who is withdrawn or reserved. 1918, in

Jung's writings in English; borrowed from German *Introvert,* coined by the Swiss psychologist Jung, from Latin *intro-* inward + Latin *vertere* to turn. Compare EXTROVERT. —**introverted** *adj.* 1781 (of the mind or thought) directed inwards; later (1915) in psychology applied as a translation of Jung's term in German *introvertiert;* coined by Jung from *intro-* (from Latin *intrō-*) inward + *-vertiert* turned, from Latin *vertere* to turn; for suffix see -ED².

intrude *v.* About 1422, thrust oneself in; come unasked and unwanted; back formation from *intrusion,* modeled on Latin, and, in some instances, a borrowing from Latin *intrūdere* (*in-* in + *trūdere* to thrust, push; see THREAT). —**intruder** *n.* 1534, formed from English *intrude* + *-er*¹. —**intrusion** *n.* About 1385 *intrusioun* usurpation or trespass; borrowed from Old French *intrusion,* from Medieval Latin *intrusionem* (nominative *intrusio*) a thrusting in, from Latin *intrūs-*, stem of *intrūdere* intrude; for suffix see -ION. —**intrusive** *adj.* 1402, formed from English *intrus(ion)* + *-ive;* probably also formed in English from Latin *intrūs-*, stem of *intrūdere* + English suffix *-ive.*

intuition *n.* About 1450 *intuicioun* spiritual perception, insight, immediate knowledge; borrowed through Middle French *intuition,* from Late Latin *intuitiōnem* (nominative *intuitiō*) a looking at, consideration, from Latin *intuērī* look at, consider, contemplate (*in-* at, on + *tuērī* to look, watch over; see TUITION); for suffix *-ition* see -ATION. The meaning of perception without reasoning, is first recorded before 1600. —**intuitive** *adj.* 1594, perceived immediately, in Richard Hooker's *Ecclesiastical Polity;* borrowed, possibly through Middle French *intuitif* (feminine *intuitive*), from Medieval Latin *intuitivus,* from Latin *intuitus,* past participle of *intuērī;* for suffix see -IVE. It is also possible that *intuitive* was formed from English *intuit(ion)* + *-ive.*

inundate (in'undāt) *v.* overflow, flood. 1623, in Cockeram's *Dictionary;* back formation from *inundation,* perhaps after Latin *inundāre* to overflow; for suffix see -ATE¹. —**inundation** *n.* Probably before 1425 *inundacioun* flood; borrowed, perhaps by influence of Middle French *inondation,* from Latin *inundātiōnem* (nominative *inundātiō*) an overflowing, from *inundāre* to overflow (*in-* onto + *undāre* to flow, from *unda* wave; see UNDULATE); for suffix see -ATION.

inure (inyůr') *v.* toughen or harden, accustom. About 1489 *enuren* to accustom by use or practice, in Caxton's translation of *The Four Sons of Aymon;* formed from Middle English *en-*¹ + earlier *ure* work, practice, exercise, use (about 1420); probably borrowed from Old French *uevre, œuvre* work, from Latin *opera;* see OPERA. The Latinized spelling with *in-* is first recorded in 1519.

It is probable that *inure,* v., was influenced in its formation by earlier *inure,* adj., customary (probably about 1451), developed from the Middle English phrase *in ure* in or according to work or practice.

invade *v.* enter with force or as an enemy. 1491, borrowed from Middle French *invader* to invade, and directly from Latin *invādere* go into, fall upon, attack, invade (*in-* in, into + *vādere* go, walk; see WADE). —**invasion** *n.* Probably before 1439 *invasioun* assault or attack, in Lydgate's *Falls of Princes;* borrowed from Middle French *invasion,* learned borrowing from Late Latin *invāsiōnem* (nominative *invāsiō*) an attack, invasion, from Latin *invāsus,* past participle of *invādere* INVADE.

The specialized meaning of hostile inroad into a country or territory, is first recorded in *Proceedings of the Privy Council* (1441), and from it developed the figurative use "a harmful incursion of any kind (as of disease, doubt, etc.)" about 1566.

invalid¹ (inval'id) *adj.* not valid; without force or effect; worthless. 1635, borrowed from Latin *invalidus* not strong, infirm, weak, inadequate (*in-* not + *validus* strong; see VALID). —**invalidate** *v.* make invalid. 1649, formed from English *invalid* + *-ate*¹, *probably by influence of French invalider.*

invalid² (in'vəlid) *n.* sick, weak person not able to get about. 1707, disabled soldier; 1709, sickly person; noun uses of the earlier adjective with the meaning of weak or disabled from illness or injury (1642); see INVALID¹. This noun was derived as a specialized sense of *invalid*¹, perhaps through, certainly influenced by, French *invalide,* as its later use reflects the French pronunciation, which was picked up by Webster (1828). Its formation in English, however, is established by the early pronouncing dictionaries, such as Bailey's (1727), which gave it the pronunciation of inval'id. —**v.** make an invalid. 1787, Nelson quoted in Nicolas' *Dispatches and Letters;* from the noun.

invaluable *adj.* beyond valuation, priceless. 1576, formed from English *in-* not, beyond + *value* + *-able.*

invariable *adj.* Before 1410, borrowed from Middle French *invariable,* and directly from Medieval Latin *invariabilis* (from *in-* not + *variabilis* VARIABLE).

invective *n.* violent attack in words, abusive language. 1523, in Skelton's *The Garland of Laurel;* developed from *invectif,* adj., denunciation, abusive (probably before 1439, in Lydgate's *Falls of Princes*); borrowed through Middle French *invectif* (feminine *invective*), and directly from Late Latin *invectivus* abusive, from Latin *invectus,* past participle of *invehī* to attack with words; see INVEIGH; for suffix see -IVE.

inveigh (invā') *v.* make a violent attack in words. 1529, in Sir Thomas More's *A Dialogue Concerning Heresies;* borrowed from Latin *invehī* to attack with words; originally, to carry oneself against, a passive verb form of *invehere* bring in, carry in (*in-* against + *vehere* carry; see WEIGH). An earlier meaning of introduce, carry in, is first recorded in 1486. The spelling with *-veigh* is first recorded in the mid-1500's and is parallel to early spellings of *convey* (*conveigh,* Middle English *conveien,* from Anglo-French *conveier*).

inveigle (invā'gəl *or* invē'gəl) *v.* lead by trickery, entice, allure. 1494, beguile, deceive, cajole, alteration of Middle French *aveugler* delude, make blind, from *aveugle* blind, from Vulgar Latin **aboculus* without sight, blind (Latin *ab-* without, away + *oculus* EYE); for suffix see -LE³. It is also possible that the form in Middle French was influenced by Old French *enveogler* to blind and thence by way of Anglo-French *envegler,* the form was further felt in *envegled* (about 1540) and *inuegelyd* (1494). The presence of *in-* is generally accounted for by analogy with *enbraid, abraid,* etc., but this development seems to have taken place much earlier and in Old French.

invent *v.* About 1475, to find, discover; back formation probably from *invention,* after Latin *inventus,* past participle of *invenīre;* see INVENTION.

The meaning of make up or think up, is first recorded in the Coverdale Bible (1535), and that of to create or produce by original thought, in 1538.

—**invention** *n.* About 1400 *invencioun* scheme or plan, in Wycliffe's writings; borrowed from Middle French *invencion,* learned borrowing from Latin *inventiōnem* (nominative *inventiō*) a finding, discovery, from *inven-,* stem of *invenīre* devise, discover, find, come upon (*in-* in, on + *venīre* COME); for suffix see -TION. The extended meaning of a made-up story, is first recorded in Dunbar's *Poems* (1500-20), and that of an original device or method, in Elyot's *The Boke Named the Governour* (1531). —**inventive** *adj.* Before 1420 *inventif,* in Lydgate's *Troy Book;* borrowed from Middle French *inventif* (feminine *inventive*), from Latin *inventus,* past participle of *invenīre;* for suffix see -IVE. —**inventor** *n.* 1509, formed possibly by influence of Middle French *inventeur,* from English *invent* + *-or*[2], on the model of Latin *inventor,* from *invenīre;* for suffix see -OR[2].

inventory *n.* detailed list of articles with their estimated value. 1415 *inventari* a detailed list of goods; borrowed from Middle French *inventaire,* from Late Latin *inventārium* list of what is found, inventory, from Latin *inventus,* past participle of *invenīre* find, come upon; see INVENT; for suffix see -ARY, -ORY.

The spelling with *-ory* is first recorded probably before 1425 and appears to be a separate borrowing from Medieval Latin *inventorium* (also found in Old French *inventore,* Middle French *inventoire*), a variant of the form in Late Latin.

—**v.** make a detailed list of. 1601, in Shakespeare's *Twelfth Night;* from the noun.

inverse (invėrs′ *or* in′vėrs) *adj.* reversed, inverted. Probably 1440, turned upside down, inverted; borrowed from Latin *inversus,* past participle of *invertere* INVERT. The mathematical use of opposite in nature or effect, is first recorded in 1660. —**n.** inverted condition. 1681; from the adjective. —**inversion** *n.* 1551, reversal of position, order, or relation; borrowed, perhaps through Middle French *inversion,* from Latin *inversiōnem* (nominative *inversiō*), from *invertere;* for suffix see -SION.

invert (invėrt′) *v.* turn in an opposite direction. 1533, in Sir Thomas More's writings; borrowed, in part perhaps by influence of Middle French *invertir,* from Latin *invertere* turn upside down, turn about, transpose (*in-* in, on + *vertere* to turn; see VERTEX). —**n.** (in′vėrt) person or thing that is inverted. 1838, from the verb.

invertebrate *adj., n.* 1826, probably suggested by Lamarck's use of *invertébrés* (1809) or earlier by Cuvier (1805); formed in English from New Latin *invertebratus* (from Latin *in-* not + *vertebra* joint) + English suffix *-ate*[1].

invest *v.* 1533-34, to clothe in the insignia of an office, install in an office or rank; borrowed from Latin *investīre* to clothe, cover, surround (*in-* in, into + *vestīre* to dress, clothe, VEST). The figurative meaning of clothe or endow with attributes, qualities, etc., is first recorded in Shakespeare's *Othello* (1604).

The meaning of use (money) to buy something, such as stocks or property, that is expected to produce profit, income, or both, lay out, was originally found in letters and journals of the years 1613-16 dealing with the East Indian trade. The term was apparently borrowed from Italian *investire,* probably with the idea of giving one's capital a new form, from Latin *investīre* to clothe, cover. Italian financial use of *investire* probably passed through the British-owned Levant or Turkey Company (established between 1581 and 1592) to the East India Company's use, from which it came into general currency in English during the 1700's.

—**investiture** *n.* formal investing of a person with an office or rank. Before 1387, in Trevisa's translation of Higden's *Polychronicon;* borrowed from Medieval Latin *investitura,* from Latin *investīre* to clothe + *-tūra* -ture; for suffix see -URE. —**investment** *n.* 1597, vestments, robes, in Shakespeare's *2 Henry IV;* formed from English *invest,* v. + *-ment.* The meaning of the investing of money or capital is first recorded in 1615, with reference to the purchase of Indian goods in the East India trade. —**investor** *n.* 1586, formed from English *invest* + *-or*[2]. The sense of one who makes a financial investment is not recorded before 1862.

investigate *v.* search into, examine closely. About 1510, probably a back formation from *investigation,* after Latin *investīgātus,* past participle of *investīgāre* search into, investigate (*in-* in, on + *vestīgāre* to track, trace, from *vestīgium* footstep, track, VESTIGE); for suffix see -ATE[1]. —**investigation** *n.* Apparently before 1425 *investigacioun,* in a translation of Higden's *Polychronicon;* borrowed from Middle French *investigation,* from Latin *investīgātiōnem* (nominative *investīgātiō*) a searching into, from *investīgāre;* for suffix see -ATION. —**investigator** *n.* 1552, formed, probably by influence of Middle French *investigateur,* from English *investigate* + *-or*[2], after Latin *investīgātor.*

inveterate *adj.* 1392 *inveterat* (of a disease) chronic; borrowed from Latin *inveterātus* inveterate, of long standing, chronic, from past participle of *inveterāre* allow to, become old (*in-* in, into + *vetus,* genitive *veteris* old; see VETERAN); for suffix see -ATE[1]. The specific reference to a confirmed feeling, practice, or habit, is first found in Shakespeare's *Richard II* (1593).

invidious *adj.* likely to arouse ill will or resentment. 1606, in Holland's translation of Suetonius' *History of Twelve Caesars;* borrowed from Latin *invidiōsus* envious, from *invidia* ill will, ENVY; for suffix see -OUS.

invigorate *v.* give vigor to, fill with life and energy. 1646, probably an extended form of English *invigor* to encourage, invigorate (1611, *envigor*) with the suffix *-ate*[1]. The earlier English *envigor* was borrowed from French *envigorer,* from Old French *envigourer* (*en-* in + *vigueur* VIGOR).

invincible *adj.* not to be overcome, unconquerable. Before 1420, in Lydgate's *Troy Book;* borrowed, possibly through Middle French *invincible,* from Latin *invincibilis* (*in-* not + *vincibilis* conquerable, VINCIBLE).

inviolable *adj.* About 1443, borrowed from Middle French *inviolable,* from Latin *inviolābilis* (*in-* not + *violābilis* VIOLABLE).

invisible *adj.* About 1340, that cannot be seen, invisible by nature; borrowed from Old French *invisible* not visible, from Latin *invīsibilis* (*in-* not + *vīsibilis* VISIBLE); for suffix see -IBLE. The extended meaning of too small to be seen (as in *invisible pores*) is first recorded in Hooke's *Micrographia* (1665).

invite (invīt′) *v.* 1533, in Sir Thomas More's writings; probably a back formation from *invitation,* and in some instances borrowed from Middle French *inviter,* learned borrowing from Latin *invītāre* invite, treat, entertain; originally, be pleasant toward (*in-* toward + a lost adjective **vītus* pleasant; cognate with Sanskrit *vītá-s* loved, pleasing, past participle of *véti* desires eagerly), cognate with Greek *híesthai* to rush, from Indo-European **wei-/weyə-/wī-* (Pok.1123). —**n.** (in′vīt) *In-*

formal. invitation. 1659, from the verb. **—invitation** *n.* About 1445 *ynvytacioun;* borrowed from Latin *invītātiōnem* (nominative *invītātiō*), from *invītāre* invite; for suffix see -ATION.

invoice *n.* list of goods sent to a purchaser showing prices, amounts, etc.; bill. 1560, spelling alteration of Middle French *envois* (in Old French also a nominative singular of *envoi*), plural of *envoi* sending, dispatch of goods, from *envoyer* to send; see ENVOY² messenger. **—v.** make an invoice of; enter on an invoice. 1698, from the noun.

invoke *v.* call on in prayer, appeal to for help or protection. Before 1449 *envoken* to summon; borrowed from Middle French *envoquer, invoquer,* learned borrowing from Latin *invocāre* call upon, implore (*in-* upon + *vocāre* to call, related to *vōx,* genitive *vōcis* VOICE). **—invocation** *n.* an invoking or calling upon God, a deity, etc. in prayer. About 1380 *invocacion,* in Chaucer's *House of Fame;* borrowed from Old French *invocation, invocacion,* learned borrowing from Latin *invocātiōnem* (nominative *invocātiō*), from *invocāre* INVOKE.

involuntary *adj.* About 1454, borrowed, possibly by influence of Middle French *involontaire,* from Latin *involuntārius* unwilling (*in-* not + *voluntārius* VOLUNTARY).

involve *v.* Before 1382, envelop, surround, in the Wycliffe Bible; borrowed, possibly through Old Provençal *envolver,* but more likely directly from Latin *involvere* entangle, envelop, roll into (*in-* in + *volvere* to roll; see VOLUME). The meaning of take in or include, is first recorded in Francis Bacon's *Of the Advancement of Learning* (1605). **—involvement** *n.* 1630, an enveloping structure; later, state of being involved (1706); formed from English *involve* + *-ment.*

invulnerable *adj.* 1595, in Shakespeare's *King John;* borrowed, probably through Middle French *invulnerable,* from Latin *invulnerābilis* (*in-* not + *vulnerābilis* VULNERABLE).

inward *adj.* placed within; internal. Probably about 1200 *in-ward;* developed from Old English *innanweard, inneweard* (about 725, in *Beowulf*); *innan* within, *inne* in + *-weard* -ward. The Old English forms are cognate with Old Icelandic *innanverdhr,* adj., inward, Old High German *inwart,* and Middle Dutch *inwaert, inwert.* **—adv.** toward the inside. Probably about 1200; developed from Old English *inweard* within, in, towards the inside (about 950, in *Lindisfarne Gospels; in* in + *-weard* -ward). The Old English form is cognate with Old High German *inwert,* adv., and Middle Dutch *inwaert, inwert,* adv.

iodine (ī′ədīn) *n.* nonmetallic chemical element in the form of bluish-black crystals. 1814, formed in English from French *iode* iodine + English *-ine²* (suffix of chemical elements). The word was patterned after *chlorine* and *fluorine* by the English chemist Sir Humphry Davy. French *iode* was coined in 1812 by the French chemist Gay-Lussac, from Greek *ioeidḗs* violet-colored (a compound of *íon* violet and *eîdos* appearance), from the violet color of the vapor given off when the iodine crystals are heated. Greek *íon* (earlier **wíon,* found in the plural as *wía*) is from the same non-Indo-European language family as Latin *viola* VIOLET. Iodine was discovered in 1811 by another French chemist Bernard Courtois. **—iodized** *adj.* 1841, formed from *iod-* + *-ized, -ize.*

ion (ī′ən *or* ī′on) *n.* atom or atoms having a negative or positive electric charge. 1834, borrowing of Greek *ión,* neuter present participle of *iénai* go (see EXIT); so called because ions move toward the electrode of opposite charge. The term was proposed by the English physicist and chemist Michael Faraday. **—ionize** *v.* 1898, formed from English *ion* + *-ize.*

-ion a suffix forming nouns and meaning: act or state of _____ing, as in *attraction;* condition or state of being _____ed, as in *adoption;* result of _____ing, as in *abbreviation;* thing that _____s, as in *connection.* English *-ion* was borrowed from Latin *-iōnem* (nominative *-iō*) a suffix forming nouns of condition and action, as in *communion,* from Latin *commūniōnem* (nominative *commūniō*) sharing in common. See also -ATION.

Often *-ion* is a spelling replacement of Middle English *-ioun,* borrowed from Old French *-iun, -ion,* from Latin *-iōnem,* and forms words modeled on derivatives from Latin and French (*rebel, rebellion, commune, communion*), but for some there is no underlying verb form (*onion, union*).

ionosphere (īon′əsfir) *n.* region of the atmosphere containing many ions. 1926, formed from English *ion* + connective *-o-* + *-sphere,* as in *stratosphere, troposphere.* The term was coined by the Scottish electronics engineer R.A. Watson-Watt, who helped develop radar.

iota (īō′tə) *n.* 1636, very small part, bit, jot; later, figurative use of *iota* the ninth and smallest letter of the Greek alphabet (1607); borrowed from Latin *iōta,* from Greek *iôta;* see JOT.

-ious a suffix formed of *-i-* + *-ous,* meaning characterized by, or full of, and representing French *-ieux,* Latin *-iōsus;* see -OUS. The suffix *-ious* is found in English *pernicious* from Latin *perniciōsus;* English *odious* from Latin *odiōsus;* it is also found in adjectives that have a corresponding noun ending in *-iō, -iōn-* such as English *ambitious* from Latin *ambitiōsus* (English *ambition* from Latin *ambitiōnem, ambitiō*). In English pairs have been freely extended to *infectious, infection; rebellious, rebellion; cautious, caution.* See *-ous* for the practice in English of adding *-ous* to other Latin forms whose stem ends in *-i-* (*vari-* + *-ous*) and therefore may be confused with *-ious;* also confused with *-itious* in Latin *-īcius* (*advent-* + *-īcius*) to form English *adventitious.*

ipecac (ip′əkak) *n.* medicine used as an emetic or purgative. 1710, American English, abbreviation of *ipecacuanha* (1682); borrowed from Portuguese, from Tupi (Brazil) *ipecacuana* a medicinal plant.

ir-¹ a form of the prefix *in-¹*, meaning not, opposite of, before *r,* as in *irrational, irregular.* In words borrowed from Latin or imitating such borrowing, *ir-* is the result of assimilation of *n* to the following consonant (*r*).

ir-² a form of the prefix *in-²*, meaning in, within, before *r,* as in *irradiate, irrigate.* In words borrowed from Latin or imitating such borrowing, *ir-* is the result of assimilation of *n* to the following consonant (*r*).

irascible (iras′əbəl) *adj.* Before 1398, one of the parts of the soul dealing with irrational nature, such as the power to hate and reject evil, in Trevisa's translation of Bartholomew's *De Proprietatibus Rerum;* noun use of the adjective; later, easily made angry, irritable (1530, in Palsgrave's *Lesclarcissement*); borrowed from Middle French *irascible,* learned borrowing from Late Latin, also borrowed directly from Late Latin *īrāscibilis,* from *īrāscī* grow angry, from *īra* anger, IRE; for suffix see -IBLE.

irate (ī'rāt) *adj.* angry. 1838, borrowed from Latin *īrātus,* past participle of *īrāscī* grow angry, from *īra* anger, IRE; for suffix see -ATE[1].

ire *n.* Probably before 1300 *ire* anger; wrath, in *Kyng Alisaunder;* borrowed from Old French *ire, yre,* from Latin *ira* anger, wrath, rage.

irenic (īren'ik) *adj.* tending to or promoting peace. 1864 *irenic,* shortened form of earlier *irenical;* formed from Greek *eirēnikós,* from *eirḗnē* peace + English *-al*[1]. **—irenology** (ī'rənol'əjē) *n.* the study of peace, especially as part of international relations. 1974; formed from *iren(ic)* + *-ology,* on the pattern of *polemic, polemology* the study of war (1938).

iridescent *adj.* displaying changing colors. 1796, formed in English from Latin *īris* (genitive *īridis*) rainbow, IRIS + English suffix *-escent.* **—iridescence** *n.* 1804, probably formed from English *iridescent* by replacement of the suffix *-escent* with *-escence.*

iridium (īrid'ēəm) *n.* metallic chemical element. 1804, New Latin, from Latin *īris* (genitive *īridis*) IRIS + New Latin *-ium* (suffix of chemical elements); so called by the English chemist Smithson Tennant from the iridescence of the element in solution.

iris *n.* 1373, plant with brightly colored flowers, used as a medicine; later, colored part of the eye (probably before 1425); borrowed from Latin *īris* iris of the eye, iris plant, rainbow; from Greek *îris* (genitive *îridos*) a kind of lily, iris of the eye; originally, name of the female messenger of the gods who appeared as the rainbow.

Irish *adj., n.* About 1205 *Īrisce* of or native to Ireland, an Irishman, in Layamon's *Chronicle of Britain;* developed from *Īr-,* stem of Old English *Īras* inhabitants of Ireland + *-isc* -ish. The Old English form was borrowed from a Scandinavian source (compare Old Icelandic *Īrar,* from Old Irish *Ēriu* Erin). There is also evidence of some influence of Old French *irais, irois* angry and *Irais, Irois* Irish.

irk *v.* irritate, annoy. About 1330 *irken* be weary of, disgusted with; of uncertain origin. The meaning of to trouble, weary, disturb, annoy, is first recorded about 1425. **—irksome** *adj.* Probably about 1425 *irksome* unpleasant, troublesome, formed from Middle English *irken* irk + *-som* -some[1].

iron *n.* 1137 *iren,* found in Old English *īren* the metal, (also) any iron weapon (before 830, in the *Vespasian Psalter*); earlier *īsaern* (about 700); borrowed from the same source as Old Frisian *īsern* iron, Old Saxon *īsarn,* Middle Low German *īsern,* Middle Dutch and modern Dutch *ijzer,* Old High German *īsarn* (modern German *Eisen*), Old Icelandic *īsarn, jarn,* Gothic *eisarn,* Gaulish *Isarno-* in place names, Old Irish *iarn,* and Welsh *haearn.*

It has been conjectured that the Proto-Germanic **īsarnan* was borrowed from Venetic-Illyrian **eisarnon* rather than from Proto-Celtic *Isarno-* with its initial short *i-* (Pok.300). The Hallstatt iron finds are earlier than the Celtic, although the Celts were iron workers from at least 1000 B.C. Attempts have been made to connect the word with the sense of heavenly, divine in an effort to show that the earliest source of iron was from meteorites and the word in Northern and Western European languages may have come from areas where the Italic languages were spoken or from adjacent terrain, citing Etruscan *aisar* god (*aisuna* divine), Volscian *esaristrôm* sacrifice, Umbrian *esono-* divine, etc., and possible parallels in Hittite and Egyptian for association of iron with divine.

Iron with the specific meaning of an implement to press or smooth cloth, is first recorded in 1613. The term *iron curtain,* referring to the ideological and political barrier separating the Soviet Union and its allies from non-Communist nations, was first used about 1920 but did not become well known until Winston Churchill used it in a speech at Westminster College, in Fulton, Missouri (1946). In the general sense of an impassable barrier or obstacle, *iron curtain* was recorded as early as 1819, in a figurative use of the theatrical term for a curtain made of iron that could be lowered to separate the audience from the stage in case of a theater fire (1794).

—v. Before 1400 *irenen* to make of iron; later, to furnish, cover, or arm with iron (1408); from the noun *īren* iron. The meaning of press or smooth cloth with an iron is first recorded before 1680.

—adj. Before 1200 *irene,* found in Old English *īren* and *isern* (about 725, in *Beowulf*).

irony *n.* 1502, dissimulation or pretense, especially in reference to the pretense of ignorance practiced by Socrates to confute an adversary (Socratic irony); borrowed probably in some instances through Middle French *ironie,* and, in part, directly from Latin *īrōnīa,* from Greek *eirōneíā,* from *eírōn* dissembler, perhaps related to *eírein* speak (as if saying it without meaning it); see WORD. The figurative sense of contradictory outcome of events as if in mockery of what is expected, is first recorded in 1649. **—ironic** *adj.* 1630, in Ben Jonson's *The New Inn,* feigning ignorance; probably developed by influence of Middle French *ironique* as a shortened form of *ironical* (1576); formed in English from Late Latin *īrōnicus,* from Greek *eirōnikós,* from *eirōneíā* dissimulation + English suffix *-al*[1].

irradiate *v.* shine upon, illuminate. 1603, to direct rays of light upon; developed from *irradiate,* adj., illuminated (before 1475); borrowed from Latin *irradiātus,* past participle of *irradiāre* shine forth (*ir-* in, on, variant of *in-* before *r* + *radiāre* to shine, RADIATE); for suffix see -ATE[1]. The modern meaning of subject to the action of radiation, such as X rays, is first recorded in 1901.

irrational *adj.* Before 1398 *irracional* quantity in mathematics that cannot be expressed as an integer, in Trevisa's translation of Bartholomew's *De Proprietatibus Rerum;* borrowed from Latin *irratiōnālis* not rational (*ir-* not + *ratiōnālis* RATIONAL). The sense of unreasonable, absurd, is first recorded in 1641.

irregular *adj.* About 1390 *irreguler* not conforming to the rule of the church, in Chaucer's *Canterbury Tales;* borrowed from Old French *irreguler,* from Late Latin *irrēgulāris* (from Latin *ir-* not + *rēgulāris* pertaining to rules, REGULAR).

irreparable *adj.* 1412, borrowed from Old French *irreparable,* and directly from Latin *irreparābilis* (*ir-* not + *reparābilis* REPARABLE).

irreverence *n.* Before 1349, borrowed from Old French *irreverence,* and directly from Latin *irreverentia,* from *irreverentem* (nominative *irreverēns*) not reverent (*ir-* not + *reverēns* REVERENT); for suffix see -ENCE.

irrevocable *adj.* About 1384, in the Wycliffe Bible; borrowed from Old French *irrevocable,* and directly from

Latin *irrevocābilis* (*ir-* not + *revocābilis* that can be called back).

irrigate *v.* supply (land) with water by using ditches. 1615, to wet; developed from *irrigat,* adj., watered, flooded (before 1449, in Lydgate's writings); borrowed from Latin *irrigātus,* past participle of *irrigāre* lead water to, refresh (*ir-* in, variant of *in-*[2] before *r* + *rigāre* to water or moisten, of uncertain origin; probably cognate with Gothic *rign,* German *Regen,* and English *rain*); for suffix see -ATE[1]. The meaning of supply (land) with water is first recorded in Cockeram's *Dictionary* (1623). **—irrigation** *n.* 1612, possibly formed from English *irrigat* + *-ion;* or borrowed, perhaps through Middle French *irrigation,* from Latin *irrigātiōnem* (nominative *irrigātiō*) a watering, from *irrigāre* lead to water. *Irrigation* was originally used in the medical sense of application of a continuous stream of fluid to a body cavity. The reference to supplying water to land is first found in Francis Bacon's *Sylva Sylvarum* (1626).

irritate *v.* 1531, stimulate to action, rouse, incite, in Elyot's *The Boke Named the Governour;* probably borrowed from Latin *irrītātus,* past participle of *irrītāre* excite, provoke, probably the intensive of a lost **ir-rīre,* cognate with Greek *orínein* rouse to anger, from Indo-European **erei-, reiə-/rī-* (Pok.330); for suffix see -ATE[1]. It is also possible that *irritate* is a back formation from *irritation,* but the Middle English meaning which is used in medicine does not appear in modern English before 1674. The meaning of annoy, make impatient or angry, is first recorded in Florio's *A World of Words* (1598). **—irritable** *adj.* 1662, borrowed, perhaps through French *irritable,* and directly from Latin *irrītābilis,* from *irrītāre* irritate. **—irritation** *n.* 1425 *irritacion* stimulation of a sore to excessive sensitivity, in Chauliac's *Grande Chirurgie;* later, excitement to activity, stimulation (1589); borrowed through Middle French *irritation, irritacion,* or directly from Latin *irrītātiōnem* (nominative *irrītātiō*), from *irrītāre* excite, provoke. The meaning of annoyance or vexation is first recorded in 1703.

irruption *n.* a breaking or bursting in, violent invasion. 1577, borrowed probably through Middle French *irruption,* or directly from Latin *irruptiōnem* (nominative *irruptiō*), from *irrup-,* stem of *irrumpere* break in (*ir-* in, variant of *in-* before *r* + *rumpere* to break, RUPTURE); for suffix see -TION.

is *v.* the third person singular present form of the verb *be;* found in Old English (before 725) *is;* developed from an earlier Germanic stem *es-,* whose form existed only in the present tense in Old English. Until the 1500's *is* rhymed with *sis* thereby retaining its association with the earlier Germanic stem.

Old English *is* is cognate with Old Frisian, Old Saxon, and Dutch *is,* Old High German and German *ist,* Old Icelandic *es,* (later) *er,* and Gothic *ist.* Cognates are also found in Latin *est* is (third person singular of *esse* to be), Old Irish *is* is, Greek *estí* (third person singular of *eînai* to be), Venetic *est,* Old Lithuanian *èsti* is, Old Slavic *jestŭ,* Sanskrit *ásti,* Armenian *ê,* Tocharian B *ste,* and Hittite *ešzi,* from Indo-European **ésti* (Pok.341). Compare AM, ARE, BE.

is- a form of *iso-* before vowels in some compounds, as in *isacoustic.*

-ise a spelling variant of the suffix -IZE, especially in British usage.

-ish[1] a suffix forming adjectives from other adjectives and from nouns, and meaning: **1** somewhat ______, as in *oldish, sweetish.* **2** like a ______, as in *childish.* **3** like that of a ______, as in *girlish.* **4** of or having to do with ______, as in *English.* **5a** tending to ______, as in *bookish.* **b** inclined to be a ______, as in *thievish.* **6** near, but usually somewhat past ______, as in *fortyish.* Middle English *-ish, -issh, -isch,* developed from Old English *-isć;* cognate with Old Frisian and Old Saxon *-isc,* Dutch *-isch,* Old High German *-isc,* German *-isch,* Old Icelandic *-iskr,* and Gothic *-isks,* from Proto-Germanic **-iskaz;* also cognate with Greek *-ískos,* a diminutive suffix of nouns.

The semantic notions about *-ish* denoting bad or objectionable qualities as in *apish, clownish,* etc., cannot be sustained. It is interesting to note, however, the implication in the OED that *-ish* was enjoying a vogue period at the time (the work for letter *I* was written by Murray in the late 1890's).

-ish[2] Though not a living suffix for verbs in the borrowing process of modern English, *-ish* occurs in many common verbs of the language today: *abolish, banish, cherish, demolish, establish, finish, impoverish, nourish, polish, relinquish, tarnish, varnish,* etc. These words came into Middle English from Middle and Old French verbs ending in *-ir* (e.g. Old French *banir* was the source of English *banish*) and were originally written *-is, -iss, -ise, -isse* with the Middle English verb ending *-en,* and paralleled the Old French stem ending *-iss-* of French verbs ending in *-ir.* The Old French stem ending *-iss-* originated in Latin *-isc-* as a part of verbs ending in *-ire* and *-ēre.* Gradually during the 1400's, the Middle English endings were modified to *-isshe,* and then to *-ish,* which appeared in the latter 1500's and 1600's.

A few verbs in English did not complete this final step in the process of spelling change and remain in a form close to the Middle English: *advertise, chastise, amortize, rejoice.*

Another group of English verbs look as if they follow the processes described above but do not have the requisite forms in Old French and were simply influenced in their formation by those words: *admonish, astonish, diminish, famish, lavish, publish, relish,* etc.

isinglass (ī′zənglas′) *n.* gelatin obtained from the air bladders of certain fishes. 1660 *isinglasse;* earlier *Isom glas* (1545); presumed alteration of Middle Dutch *huysenblas* sturgeon bladder; occasioned by the similarity in appearance between glass and gelatin.

Islam (is′ləm *or* i släm′) *n.* 1818, religion of the Moslems, in Shelley's *The Revolt of Islam;* earlier, an orthodox Moslem (1613); borrowed from Arabic *islām,* literally, resignation, surrender, submission (to the will of God), from the root of *aslama* he resigned or surrendered, related to *salima* he was safe, and *salām* peace, SALAAM. **—Islamic** *adj.* 1791, formed from English *Islam* + *-ic,* after French *islamique.*

island *n.* 1598, in Hakluyt's *Voyages;* alteration of earlier *isle land* (1546), *ile land* (1494), *yland* (apparently before 1300); developed from Old English *īgland* island (before 899, in Alfred's translation of Boethius' *De Consolatione Philosophiae*). The Old English term is cognate with Old Frisian *eiland* island, and Old Icelandic *eyland,* and is formed from *īeg, īg* island + *land* LAND. Old English *īg* is cognate with Old Frisian *ey* island, Old High German *ouwa* island, damp meadow (German *Aue*), and Old Icelandic *ey* island, from Proto-

Germanic *aujō̆, earlier *aȝwjō̆, built on *áHwō water, cognate with Latin *aqua;* see AQUATIC.

The more common forms in Middle English were *yland, iland,* but gradually, by association with the nearly synonymous but etymologically unrelated *isle,* the spelling of the first part of the word was modified until the current spelling became established by the late 1600's.

isle *n.* Probably about 1225 *ile* island; borrowed from Old French *ile,* earlier *isle,* from Latin *īnsula,* of uncertain origin. The spelling of *isle* (with *s*), is first recorded in 1470, but is rare in English until the late 1500's. Middle French, in the 1400's, had restored the Old French spelling with *s,* and the English spelling was influenced by this earlier form.

ism (iz′əm) *n.* distinctive doctrine, theory, system, or practice. 1680, noun use of the suffix -ISM, found in words such as *Puritanism, Quakerism, Calvinism,* and (since the 1920's) *Communism, Capitalism, Socialism,* etc.

-ism a suffix forming nouns and meaning: **1** act or practice of ______, as in *baptism.* **2** quality or condition of being a ______, as in *heroism, paganism.* **3** illustration or instance of being ______, as in *witticism.* **4** an unhealthy condition caused by ______, as in *alcoholism.* **5** doctrine, theory, system, or practice of ______, as in *Darwinism.* Borrowed through French *-isme* or directly from Latin *-ismus, -isma,* from Greek *-ismós, -isma,* a suffix forming nouns of action from verbs in *-ízein* -ize. Compare -IST. Forms of the suffix were active in both Greek and Latin, and many words containing this suffix and later French terms were borrowed directly into English. The suffix in English became very active from the 1500's on.

iso- a combining form meaning equal, alike, as in *isometric, isotope, isosceles.* Borrowed from Greek *iso-,* from *ísos* equal (Arcadian, Cretan, Boeotian *wiswos*), of uncertain origin. Also *is-* before vowels in some compounds.

isobar (ī′səbär) *n.* line on a weather map connecting places having the same average atmospheric pressure. 1864, borrowed from Greek *isobarḗs* of equal weight (*ísos* equal + *báros* weight, from *barýs* heavy; see GRAVE[2] weighty).

isogloss (ī′səglôs) *n.* line on a dialect map separating areas that differ in the use of a word, pronunciation, or other feature of language. 1925, in Otto Jespersen's *Mankind, Nation, and Individual,* borrowed from German *Isogloss,* from Greek *ísos* equal + *glôssa* language, obscure word; see GLOSS[2] explanation. The term was coined in German (1892) by August Bielenstein, German clergyman and student of Latvian culture.

isolate *v.* 1807, to place apart, separate from others; back formation from earlier *isolated* placed apart, solitary (1763), formed in English from French *isolé* isolated + English suffix *-ate[1]* (*-ated*). French *isolé* was derived from Italian *isolato,* from Latin *īnsulātus* made into an island, from *īnsula* island. Doublet of INSULATE. **—isolation** *n.* 1833, probably in part formed from English *isolate,* v. + *-ion* and borrowed from French *isolation,* from *isoler* to isolate, from *isolé* isolated; for suffix see -ATION. **—isolationist** *n.* person advocating a policy of political or national isolation. 1899, American English, formed from *isolation* + *-ist.* **—isolationism** *n.* (1922)

isomer *n. Chemistry.* one of a group of substances composed of the same elements in the same proportions but differing in properties. 1866, back formation, probably by influence of French *isomère,* from *isomeric* (1838; formed in English from Greek *isomerḗs* (*ísos* equal + *méros* part or share) + English suffix *-ic*). Greek *méros* is related to *meíresthai* receive as one's portion, cognate with Latin *merēre* earn and *merērī* deserve, from Indo-European *smer-* (Pok.969). This was one of a large group of new scientific terms coined on the Continent during the great surge of work done there in the sciences in the 1800's. Both French and German were the vehicles by which the new findings were made known generally and so *isomeric* was patterned after German *isomerisch* isomeric, even though the term was coined by the Swedish chemist Berzelius from Greek *isomerḗs* composed of equal parts + German *-isch* -ic.

isometric *adj.* 1840, a method of using perspective in drawing to obtain equal inclination of the principal axes; formed in English from Greek *isómetros* of equal measure (*ísos* equal + *métron* MEASURE) + English suffix *-ic.*

Later use in physiology with the meaning of denoting muscular tension produced against resistance, became a recent vogue term in English, though the meaning has been recorded in English since 1891 as a borrowing of *isometrisch* in a sense coined in 1882 by the German physiologist Adolf Fick.

—isometrics *n.pl.* exercises in which muscles are tensed by pressing against an unyielding object. 1962, American English, formed from *isometric* + *-s,* on the analogy of *gymnastic, gymnastics.*

isosceles (īsos′əlēz) *adj. Geometry.* having two equal sides. 1551 *Isosceles,* used as a rendering of Greek *isoskelḗs* with equal sides (*ísos* equal + *skélos* leg; see CYLINDER). Also found in Late Latin *isoscelēs* which was probably the model for first uses in English.

isotope (ī′sətōp) *n.* any of two or more forms of a chemical element that have the same chemical properties and the same atomic number, but different atomic weights. 1913, formed in English from *iso-* same or equal + Greek *tópos* place; so called because the various forms of a particular chemical element occupy the same position in the periodic table. The term was coined by the English chemist Frederick Soddy.

issue *n.* Probably before 1300 *issue* exit, a place of exit, a going or flowing out, in *Kyng Alisaunder;* borrowed from Old French *issue,* earlier *eissue* (from Gallo-Romance **exūta*), from feminine past participle of *issir,* earlier *eissir* to go out, from Latin *exīre* (*ex-* out + *īre* go; see EXIT).

The meaning of descendants, offspring, progeny, is first recorded in *Piers Plowman* (about 1378) and was probably adopted from Old French; that of outcome of an action, event, result, appeared in the Wycliffe Bible (about 1380), and the common meaning of a matter or point to be decided, is recorded before 1439.

—v. Before 1338 *issuen* to come or go out, in Mannyng's *Chronicle of England;* borrowed from Old French *issu,* past participle of *issir* to go out.

—issuance *n.* 1865, American English; formed from English *issue* + *-ance.*

-ist a suffix forming nouns and meaning: **1** person who does or makes, as in *theorist, tourist.* **2** an expert in an art or science, as in *botanist.* **3** person who plays a musical instrument, as in *organist.* **4** person connected with as in *artist.* Borrowed through French *-iste,* or directly from Latin *-ista,* from Greek *-istḗs,* noun suffix for verbs in *-ízein.*

The suffix *-ist* is related to *-ism* in meaning and form, but its development in English centers about meaning, where after the extension of its use by the early Christian writers for ecclesiastical and scriptural terms, its extension became so wide that its use, if not its meaning, approaches the suffix *-er* for agent nouns. Where *-ist* at one time indicated probably presence of a verb in *-ize,* the case can no longer be made.

isthmus (is′məs) *n.* narrow strip of land, having water on either side, connecting two larger bodies of land. 1555, borrowed from Latin *isthmus,* from Greek *isthmós* isthmus, strip of land, narrow passage, of uncertain origin.

it *pron.* 1128 *it;* earlier *hit* (1104); developed from Old English *hit* (about 725, in *Beowulf, Genesis A,* etc.), neuter nominative and accusative of the third person singular (originally used as the substitute for any neuter noun). It was this relatively unspecialized use in Old English that gave rise to a Middle English use of *it,* with the meaning of a thing or animal spoken about (before 1325).

The spelling *hit* or *hyt* survived in standard literary English to the end of the Middle English period and nearly to the end of the 1500's, but only as an occasional usage beside the increasingly frequent *it.* Even Old English *hit* appears occasionally without its *h* in Late Old English, and the *it*-form is rather frequent in vernacular legal documents of this period.

The *h* in Old English *hit* and in its cognates, Old Frisian and Middle Dutch *hit* (modern Dutch *het*), was probably due to the influence of the Proto-Germanic demonstrative base *Hi-* this, represented by Old English and Old Frisian *hē* HE. Other cognates of *it* are Old Saxon and Middle Low German *it,* Low German *et,* Gothic *is* he, (neuter) *ita* it, Old High German *ër* he, it, *ëz* it (modern German *er* he, *es* it), and Old Icelandic *es* this. Outside Germanic cognates include Latin *is* he, that, (neuter) *id* it, Old Irish *ē* he, *ed* it, Lithuanian *jìs* he, and Sanskrit *ayám* he, *iyám* she, *idám* it. In the very latest introduction to Indo-European linguistics, that of Oswald Szemerényi, in 1980, the nominative case forms of this Indo-European pronoun are reconstructed as **is* he, *ī* she, *id* it.

italic *adj.* of or in type whose letters slant to the right. 1571, italic handwriting; later, italic type (1612); borrowed, possibly by influence of Middle French *Italique, Ytalique,* from Latin *Italicus* Italian, of Italy, from Greek *Italikós,* from *Italíā* Italy, originally a region of southwest Italy (Oscan *Víteliú*), land of the *Italoí,* very possibly a boastful self-characterization as the "young steers," cognate with Greek *étalon, ételon* yearling, *étos* year; see WETHER.; so called because this style of letter was introduced in 1501 by Aldus Manutius, an Italian printer of Venice. **—n.** 1676 *italics* italic letters; from the adjective.**—italicize** *v.* print in italics. 1795, formed from English *italic* + *-ize.*

Italo- a combining form made from Italy or Italian and meaning of Italy or the Italians, as in *Italophile,* and sometimes meaning Italian and ______, as in *Italo-American.*

itch *n.* tickly, prickling feeling in the skin. Before 1400 *icche, yicche;* developed from Old English (before 800) *gicce,* from *giccan* to itch; cognate with Middle Dutch *joken* to itch (modern Dutch *jeuken*) and Old High German *jucchen* (modern German *jucken*). The figurative sense of a restless desire or hankering after something, is first recorded in Sir Thomas More's writings (1532). **—v.** have an itch. 1440 *ichen;* earlier *icchen, yicchen* (about 1390); developed from Old English (about 1000) *giccan,* of unknown origin.

-ite[1] a suffix meaning: **1** person or thing associated with, inhabitant of ______, as in *Canaanite, Jerseyite, laborite.* **2** follower of ______, as in *Trotskyite.* **3** mineral or fossil, as in *hematite, trilobite.* **4** organic chemical compound, explosive, or commercial product, as in *dynamite, cordite, lucite.* **5** segment of a body, as in *dendrite.* Borrowed through French *-ite,* or directly from Latin *-īta, -ītēs,* from Greek *-ī́tēs, -îtis* pertaining to, connected with, member of. The frequent use of this suffix in Greek to indicate ethnic and local connection, as in *Abderite, Sybarite* was extended to use in the Greek version of the Old Testament where the suffix was used to render Hebrew names, as in *Israelite, Levite.* Later writers used it in much the same style as the Greeks, as in *Jacobite,* and some Greek terms were borrowed directly into Latin and into Medieval Latin from which the suffix came into French and English.

-ite[2] a suffix meaning salt of, as in *phosphite, sulfite, nitrite.* Borrowed from French *-ite,* deliberate alteration of *-ate*[2] from Latin *-ātus* -ATE[2].

item *n.* 1578, separate thing or article; earlier, statement, suggestion, hint (1561); developed from *item,* adv., moreover, in addition (before 1398, in Trevisa's translation of Bartholomew's *De Proprietatibus Rerum*); borrowed, probably by influence of Old French *item,* from Latin *item* likewise, just so, probably related to *ita* thus, and *id* IT.

The Middle English adverb *item* was used before each article in a list, such as an inventory or bill and to introduce a new statement or fact, which later gave rise to the noun use with the meanings of a separate thing, individual article or a statement.

—itemize *v.* 1864, formed from English *item* + *-ize,* replacing the earlier verb *item* (1601).

iterate *v.* 1533, repeat, in Tyndale's *Supper of the Lord;* developed from *iterate,* adj., done repeatedly (probably before 1425); borrowed from Latin *iterātus,* past participle of *iterāre* do again, repeat, from *iterum* again; neuter of a lost adjective cognate with Sanskrit *ítara-s* another, the other; related to Latin *ita* thus, and *id* IT; for suffix see -ATE[1]. It is also possible that, in some instances, *iterate* is a back formation from *iteration* (before 1425). **—iterative** *adj.* 1490, involving repetition, in Caxton's translation of *The Book of Eneydos;* borrowed from Middle French *itératif* (feminine *itérative*), from Late Latin *iterātīvus* serving to repeat, from Latin *iterāre;* for suffix see -IVE. The grammatical meaning of denoting repetition of action, frequentative, is first recorded in 1827.

itinerant (ītin′ərənt) *adj.* traveling from place to place. 1570-76, traveling on a circuit (as a judge or preacher); borrowed from Late Latin *itinerantem,* present participle of *itinerārī* to travel, from Latin *iter* (genitive *itineris*) journey, from *īre* go; see EXIT; for suffix see -ANT. **—n.** itinerant person. 1641, from the adjective. **—intinerary** *n.* Probably before 1425, course of travel, route, in a translation of Higden's *Polychronicon;* borrowed, perhaps through Middle French *itineraire,* from Late Latin *itinerārium* account of a journey, from noun use of neuter of *itinerārius,* adj., of a journey, from Latin (genitive) *itineris* journey; for suffix see -ARY. The meaning of a plan or scheme of travel, outline of a proposed trip, is first recorded in 1856, from the idea of using someone else's previous account as a guide for one's own travels.

-itious a suffix in a few adjectives borrowed (directly or through French) from Latin, where they were formed by addition of a compound suffix *-īcius* (*-īc* + *-ius*) to a participial stem, as seen in English *adventitious, fictitious, surreptitious,* or to a noun stem, as in *cementitious.* A variant spelling *-ītius* occurred in Late Latin, and *-itious* became the regular spelling in English; this suffix has also produced a few adjectives formed on the same model, such as *adscititious.*

In another group of words in *-itious,* such as *ambitious* and *superstitious,* the *-it-* is part of the verbal stem and *-ious* is from Latin *-iōsus;* see -IOUS.

-itis a suffix meaning inflammation of; inflammatory disease of, as in *appendicitis, bronchitis, tonsillitis, bursitis.* Borrowed from New Latin *-itis,* from Greek *-îtis,* feminine of the adjective suffix *-ītēs* of or pertaining to, used to qualify the feminine noun *nósos* disease, as in *arthrîtis nósos* disease of the joints. Some words with *-itis,* such as *arthritis,* are not coinages from New Latin or other compounds of foreign or native elements, but are among the original group of borrowings from which *-itis* was abstracted in English.

-ity a suffix forming nouns from adjectives and meaning condition or quality of being ____, as in *absurdity, brutality, cordiality, activity, hostility, sincerity.* Middle English *-ite,* borrowed through Old French *-ité,* or directly from Latin *-itātem* (nominative *-itās,* formed from *-i-,* as a connective or thematic vowel + *-tās* -TY[2]).

-ium a suffix of chemical elements or radicals, as in *ammonium, curium, sodium.* Borrowed from New Latin, from Latin *-ium,* a neuter suffix.

-ive a suffix forming adjectives from verbs and meaning: of or pertaining to, as in *interrogative, inductive;* tending to, likely to, as in *active, appreciative.* Middle English, borrowed occasionally through Old French *-if* (feminine *-ive*) but usually directly from Latin *-īvus.*

The majority of English words incorporating this suffix end in *-sive, -tive,* and *-ative* (see -ATIVE). A few add *-ive* directly to the verb stem, especially where the stem ends in *s, c,* or *t,* as in *abusive, conducive, adaptive.* Another small group also adds this suffix to nouns, as in *massive.* There is also a special group in which the Old French ending *-if* was lost in borrowing or by development in Middle English, resulting in *-y,* as in *hasty* and *tardy.*

ivory *n.* hard white substance composing the tusks of elephants, walruses, etc. 1263, earlier, as a surname (1181); borrowed through Anglo-French *ivorie,* from Old North French *ivurie,* from Latin *eboreus* of ivory, from *ebur* (genitive *eboris*) ivory, probably borrowed from a Hamitic source; compare Egyptian *āb, ābu* elephant, ivory, Coptic *ebou, ebu,* which is probably from the same source as Hebrew *(shen-)habbīm* (tooth of the) elephant, ivory. **—adj.** made of ivory. About 1330; from the noun.

The phrase *ivory tower,* meaning a condition of seclusion or withdrawal from the realities of life, is first recorded in English as a translation of the French *tour d'ivoire* (1911), coined by the French critic and poet Charles A. Sainte-Beuve. The English phrase was then used as a loan translation from the French by Henry James in his novel *The Ivory Tower* (1916) and popularized by Hart Crane, Ezra Pound, H.G. Wells, Aldous Huxley, and others.

ivy *n.* climbing plant. Probably about 1200 *ivi;* developed from Old English (about 700) *īfig, ifegn;* probably related to Middle Low German *iflōf* ivy, and Old High German *ebahewi, ebah* (modern German *Efeu*), of unknown origin.

-ization a suffix meaning the act of ____izing or the condition of being ____ized, as in *naturalization, Americanization;* formed from *-ize* + *-ation.* Originally *-ization,* when added to proper names *(Americanization,* etc.), meant "act or process of making or becoming (American, etc.)" in form or character. Use of the suffix in the sense of a transfer of authority to native citizens became prominent between the World Wars when the British adopted a policy of *Indianization,* increasing the number of native Indians elected to the legislature of India. This usage began to spread in the 1950's with the coining of *Egyptianization* (a synonym for "nationalization of foreign holdings") and *Nigerianization.* During the early 1970's *Vietnamization* was a widely used political term for transferring the conduct of the Vietnam war to the Vietnamese and withdrawing American forces from Indochina. See also -IZE.

-ize a suffix added to adjectives and nouns to form verbs and meaning: **1** make ____, as in *legalize, apologize.* **2** become ____, as in *crystallize.* **3** engage in or use ____, as in *criticize.* **4** treat or combine with ____, as in *oxidize.* **5** other meanings, as in *memorize, colonize.* Borrowed through French *-iser,* or directly from Latin *-izāre,* or from Greek *-ízein.*

American usage favors *-ize,* whereas British usage often employs *-ise.* However, many verbs that happen to end in *-ise* (of some other origin) such as *devise, exercise,* and *surmise,* do not have the variant *-ize.*

The suffix *-ize* is now often used to form transitive verbs in the sense of transfer (establishments, institutions, or authority) to members of an ethnic or national group. Verbs such as *Algerianize, Vietnamize,* etc., with this meaning are derived by back formation from nouns in -IZATION.

J

jab *v.* thrust with something pointed; poke. 1825-80, in an edition of Jamieson's *Dictionary of the Scottish Language,* a Scottish variant of *job* to strike, pierce, thrust; found in Middle English *jobben* to jab, thrust, peck (before 1500, in a version of *Promptorium Parvulorum*); of uncertain origin. **—n.** sharp thrust or poke. 1825-80; from the verb.

jabber *v.* to chatter. About 1405 *jablen;* later *javeren* (about 1440), *jaberen* (1499); of imitative origin. The spelling *jabber* is first recorded in 1655. **—n.** chatter. 1727, in Swift's *Gulliver's Travels,* from the verb.

jabberwocky (jab′ərwok′ē) *n.* meaningless talk or writing; gibberish. 1953, in Henry Miller's *Plexus,* probably in direct allusion to *Jabberwocky,* title of Lewis Carroll's nonsense poem in *Through the Looking-Glass* (1871), but influenced in meaning by *jabber,* v., n. It is also possible that this noun use is in part from the earlier adjective.

The Scottish writer John Buchan used *Jabberwock* in the sense of gibberish, in *Watcher by Threshold* (1902) and this form sometimes occurs, though in Carroll's poem *Jabberwock* is the name of an imaginary monster with flaming eyes.

—adj. meaningless, senseless, nonsensical. 1939, in allusion to *Jabberwocky,* title of Lewis Carroll's poem. The term was used earlier in the attributive sense of topsy-turvy (1908) since in *Through the Looking-Glass* Alice finds the poem written in reverse, from right to left, to be read by being held up to a mirror.

jack *n.* tool or machine for lifting weights. 1391 *jakke* a mechanical device; developed from earlier *Jacke, Jakke* a surname (1285); later, as a first name; also, any common fellow (about 1390, in Chaucer's *Canterbury Tales*); probably from *Jacque, Jacques,* borrowed from Old French *Jaques,* from Late Latin *Jacobus,* from Latin *Jacōbus,* from Greek *Iakṓb,* from Hebrew *Ya'akōbh.* **—v.** 1873, in the phrase *jack up* abandon, give up; later, hoist with a jack (1885), and in American English, to increase prices, etc. (1904); all from the noun. **—jackass** *n.* (1727) **—jack-in-the-box** *n.* (1555) **—jackknife** *n.* (1711); *v.* (1806). **—jack-o'-lantern** *n.* (1663) **—jackpot** *n.* (1881) **—jack rabbit** (1863)

jackal *n.* wild dog of Asia and Africa. 1603, borrowed from Turkish *çakal,* from Persian *shaghāl,* from Sanskrit *śṛgālá-s.*

The *j* in English is probably in part a phonetic misinterpretation of the initial sound in Turkish and Arabic (approximating the sound of *ch* in *chain*). Any association with the name *Jack* is not recorded until at least sixty years after *jackal* (recorded as *jackalles*) appears in English.

jacket *n.* short coat. 1451 *jaket,* borrowed from Middle French *jaquet,* diminutive of Old French *jaque* a kind of tunic, from *jacques* a nickname given to the French peasant in the 1300's, from *Jacques* Jacob, James; so called because the peasants wore this type of garment; for suffix see -ET.

The German etymologist Kluge traces *jacket* from Old French *jaque (de mailles)* short tight-fitting coat; originally, coat of mail, from Spanish *jaco,* from Arabic *šakk* breastplate.

The extended sense of outer cover or case, is first recorded in 1815, and that of a paper cover of a book, in 1894.

—v. put a jacket on. 1861; from the noun.

jade[1] *n.* hard gemstone. 1721-41, in an edition of *Chambers Cyclopaedia;* earlier *iada* (1598); borrowed from French *le jade;* earlier *l'ejade,* from Spanish *piedra de (la) ijada* stone of colic, pain in the side (because jade was thought to cure this), from Vulgar Latin **īliāta,* from Latin *īlia,* pl., flanks, groin; see ILEUM.

jade[2] *n.* inferior or worn-out horse. About 1390 *iade* cart horse, hack, in Chaucer's *Canterbury Tales,* perhaps a variant of *yaid, yald* whore; literally, mare; borrowed perhaps through Anglo-French **jaud,* from a Scandinavian source (compare Old Icelandic *jalda* mare, apparently borrowed from a Finno-Ugric word represented by Mordvin *äl'd'ä* mare). **—v.** to weary, tire, make or become dull, languid, etc. 1606, in Shakespeare's *Antony and Cleopatra;* from the noun.

jag[1] *v.* cut or tear unevenly. 1373 *jaggid* jagged, from *jaggen* to notch or nick; of uncertain origin. **—n.** Before 1400, a slash or tear in a garment, of uncertain origin. The MED refers to a possible Old French **jagaye* as a variant of *zagaye* spearhead, from *assagaie, azagaia* lance or javelin, from Arabic *az-zagaye.* However, *assagaie* is not attested in French before 1546, so that unless the record is defective, there is no chronological connection possible.

jag[2] *n.* period of unrestrained activity, spell. 1597, a load, as of hay or wood; of unknown origin. The extended sense of a load of drink, drinking spree, was originally a dialectal use first recorded in 1678. The transferred meaning of a period of unrestrained activity (as in *a crying jag*) appeared first in American English, in Jack London's *The Valley of the Moon* (1913).

jaguar *n.* large animal of the Americas much like a leopard. 1604, borrowed from Portuguese *jaguar,* from Tupi (Brazil) *jaguara* and Guarani *yaguará.* The OED says this was a name for all carnivorous animals in Tupi-Guarani (later including dogs), and that the specific name for the jaguar is *jaguareté* (*-ete* being an augmentative rendered as "true," therefore true carnivore).

jai alai (hī əlī′) game played with a hard ball and a basketlike racket strapped to the arm. 1910, borrowed from Spanish *jai alai,* from Basque *jai alai* (*jai* festival, and *alai* merry).

jail *n.* prison. Developed from two concurrent forms in Middle English: 1) *gaiol, gaole* (probably before 1300); borrowed from Old North French and Anglo-French *gaiole, gayolle, gaole;* and 2) *jaiole, jaile* (before 1325, in *Cursor Mundi*); borrowed from Old French *jaiole, jaole, geole.* All the French forms had the meaning of cage or prison and were borrowed from Vulgar Latin

**gavióla,* from Latin **cavéola,* diminutive of *cavea* coop, CAGE.

The current spelling *jail* is first recorded in Milton's *Samson Agonistes* (1674); the now current British spelling *gaol* (a former spelling in Middle English and in old law books) begins to be recorded again in 1689.
—v. put in jail. 1604, from the noun. **—jailer** or **jailor** *n.* Developed, as was *jail,* from concurrent forms in Middle English: 1) *gaioler, gaoler* (1163, as a surname); borrowed from Old North French or Anglo-French *gaolier, gaioler;* and 2) *jaioler, jailere* (1316, as a surname); borrowed from Old French *jaiolier, jeolier.* All the French forms were apparently based on the various Old French forms for *jail* + the suffix *-er, -ere* (only occasionally *-or,* in surnames), some probably modeled on Medieval Latin *gaolarius* jailer.

jalopy *n. Informal.* old or battered automobile. 1920, American English *jaloppi,* in Hostetter and Beesley's *It's a Racket!;* of unknown origin. John Steinbeck spelled the word as *gillopy* in his novel *In Dubious Battle* (1936), but by 1938 *jalopy* was the frequent spelling.

jalousie (jal'əsē) *n.* shade or shutter with horizontal slats. 1766, in the Duchess of Northumberland's *Diary;* borrowed from French *jalousie,* from Middle French, wooden latticework through which one can see without being seen; literally, jealousy, from Old French; see JEALOUSY.

jam¹ *v.* press tightly, squeeze. 1706, to stick or catch, become wedged; of unknown origin, perhaps imitative, but how it is imitative and of what, is uncertain. The meaning of press tightly or squeeze, as between two surfaces, is first recorded in Defoe's *Robinson Crusoe* (1719). **—n.** mass of people or things crowded together. 1806-07, from the verb. The figurative sense of a difficulty or tight spot, is first recorded in 1914 in American English.

The term *jam session* an improvised performance by a jazz group or band, is first found in 1933 in American English, apparently derived from the earlier use of *jam* in the sense of a short, freely improvised jazz passage performed by the whole band (1929), as distinguished from a *break,* which is such a performance (during a break or pause) by a single musician.

jam² *n.* preserve made of fruit boiled with sugar until thick. 1730-36, in an edition of Bailey's *Dictionarium Britannicum;* probably a special use of *jam¹,* in the sense of bruise or crush (the fruit) by pressure.

jamb *n.* upright piece forming the side of a doorway, window, etc. 1334 *jaumbe,* borrowed from Old French *jambe* joint for a window or doorway; originally, leg, from Late Latin *gamba, camba* leg or (horse's) hock; see GAMBOL.

jambalaya (jam'bəlī'ə) *n.* dish of rice cooked together with shrimp, ham, turkey, etc. 1872, American English, borrowed from Louisiana French *jambalaya,* from Provençal *jambalaia* stew composed of rice and fowl.

jamboree *n.* large gathering. 1868, American English, a noisy party or spree; perhaps coined from *jam¹,* on the pattern of *shivaree.*

However, a complicating factor arises from a seemingly unrelated but earlier use of the word, found in both the DAE and DA (1864), which relates to the card game euchre and the playing of a lone hand or jambone. (It allowed the player additional points and "to go on a jamboree," the earliest use, might have been an allusion to this, but no satisfactory evidence exists.)

jangle *v.* sound harshly. About 1300, to chatter or gossip; borrowed from Old French *jangler* to chatter, perhaps from a Germanic source (compare Middle Dutch *jangelen* to whine, modern Dutch *jengelen,* and dialectal German *jangeln* speak with a whine). The meaning of make a harsh or discordant noise, is first recorded in 1494. In at least some instances the word may be from the noun. **—n.** harsh sound. About 1280, gossip or idle talk; borrowed from Old French *jangle,* from *jangler* to chatter. The meaning of discordant sound is first recorded in 1795.

janitor *n.* building superintendent. 1584, an usher; later, doorkeeper (about 1630); borrowed from Latin *jānitor* doorkeeper, from *jānua* door, from *jānus* arched passageway; for suffix see -OR². The meaning of caretaker of a building is first recorded in 1708.

January *n.* first month. 1391 *Januarie,* in Chaucer's *Treatise on the Astrolabe,* a Latinization of earlier *Jenever* (about 1300) and *Genever* (probably before 1300); borrowed from Old North French *Jenever, Genever,* learned borrowings from Latin *Jānuārius* first month of the ancient Roman year (the month dedicated to *Janus,* the Roman God of gates and doors, and of beginnings and endings, from *jānus* arched passageway).

jar¹ *n.* deep container. 1421 (possibly) *jarre* liquid measure smaller than a barrel; borrowed probably from Middle French *jarre* (1449), from Provençal *jarra,* and also through Spanish *jarra* and Medieval Latin *jarra,* from Arabic *jarrah* earthen water vessel.

jar² *v.* to shake or rattle. 1526, make a harsh, grating sound, in Skelton's writings; later, cause to vibrate or shake (1568); probably in some way imitative but not necessarily a part of its origin. The meaning of have a harsh or unpleasant effect on is first recorded in 1538. **—n.** a shake; rattle. 1546, discord, dissension; later, a harsh, grating sound (1553); probably in part from the verb, and possibly, in part of imitative origin.

jargon *n.* language or terminology of a special group. About 1350 *jargoun* unintelligible talk or chattering; borrowed from Old French *jargon,* probably of imitative origin like the French *gargoter* make noise with the throat, and probably related to Latin *garrīre* to chatter, babble. The meaning of talk containing a mixture of languages is first recorded in 1643, and that of an unfamiliar language or terminology of a special group, in Hobbes' *Leviathan* (1651). **—jargoneer** *n.* user of jargon. 1913, in Arthur Quiller-Couch's *On the Art of Writing;* formed from English *jargon* + *-eer.*

jasmine or **jasmin** (jaz'mən *or* jas'mən) *n.* shrub or vine with clusters of fragrant flowers. 1578 *jasmine;* borrowed from French *jasmin,* in Middle French *jassemin, jessemin,* from Arabic *yāsamīn,* from Persian *yāsmīn.*

The earlier *jessamine* (1562) was borrowed from the older Middle French *jassemin.*

jasper *n.* colored quartz. Probably about 1300, borrowed through Anglo-French *jaspre,* from Continental Old French *jaspe,* from Latin *iaspidem* (nominative *iaspis*), from Greek *íaspis* jasper, from a Semitic source (compare Hebrew *yāshpeh,* Arabic *yashb,* and Akkadian *ashpū,* all meaning jasper).

jaundice *n.* disease that causes distorted vision and yellowness of the skin, eyes, etc. About 1303 *jaunes,* in

Mannyng's *Handlyng Synne;* later *jandis* (1373), and *jaundys* (before 1387); borrowed from Old French *jaunisse, jaunice* yellowness, from *jaune;* earlier *jalne* yellow, from Latin *galbinus* greenish-yellow; of uncertain origin. The *d* appears early in the spelling of this word and represents a sound analogous to the *d* added in the Middle English period in *astound* and *thunder.*

The figurative meaning of state of feeling in which views are colored or judgment is distorted is first recorded in 1629.
—v. cause jaundice in. 1791 (figurative use); from the noun.

jaunt *n.* short journey or excursion. 1678, extended sense of the earlier meaning of a fatiguing or tiresome journey (1592, in Shakespeare's *Romeo and Juliet*); the meaning of a short journey or excursion was probably influenced by that earlier sense in the verb. **—v.** take a jaunt. 1647, extended sense of the earlier meaning of trot or trudge about (1575), and tire a horse by riding him back and forth (1570); of unknown origin.

jaunty *adj.* sprightly, carefree. 1662, stylish or elegant; later, carefree (1672); borrowed from French *gentil* nice or pleasing, from Old French *gentil* noble; see GENTLE. The form *jaunty* (earlier *janty, jantee*) represents a reborrowing from French, reflecting the French pronunciation of *gentil* (zhäNtē′). Compare the earlier borrowings GENTILE, GENTEEL, and GENTLE.

java (jä′və *or* jav′ə) *n. Slang.* coffee. 1926, American English slang, from *Java* drink prepared from coffee grown in Java (1850).

javelin *n.* light spear thrown by hand. About 1475 *gavelong;* borrowed from Middle French *javeline,* diminutive of Old French *javelot,* from Old Provençal *javelina,* possibly from a Celtic source (compare Old Irish *gabul* fork, and Welsh *gaflach* feathered lance). An earlier form *javelot* (about 1440), was borrowed directly from Middle French *javelot,* from Old French.

jaw *n.* About 1380 *jowe, iowe,* in Chaucer's *House of Fame;* before 1387 *jawe,* in Trevisa's translation of Higden's *Polychronicon;* perhaps borrowed from Old French *joue* cheek (cognate with Provençal *gauto* and Italian *gota*). The Old French *joue* probably derives from pre-Latin (perhaps Gaulish) *gábuta* cheek. **—v.** *Slang.* to scold; gossip. 1748, to gossip, in Smollett's *Adventures of Roderick Random;* later, to scold (1810); from the noun. An earlier meaning "use the jaws" is recorded in 1612. **—jawbone** *n.* (about 1489)

jay *n.* noisy European bird with patches of blue feathers on a background of black and gray feathers. Probably before 1300 *jai,* in *Kyng Alisaunder;* borrowed from Old French *jay,* in Old North French *gai, gay,* perhaps from Late Latin *gaius,* from Latin *Gāius,* a proper name, following the practice of giving birds proper names (as *robin, martin,* etc.). The word is also applied to the American *blue jay,* a bird of a different species, found in *blew Jawe* (1709), *blue jay* (1808).

The term *jaywalker* is first recorded in American English in 1917, from an earlier use of *jay* in the figurative sense of a bold, impudent, thoughtless or stupid person. The verb *jaywalk* is a back formation of *jaywalker* and is found as early as 1919 in American English.

jazz *n.* 1913, American English, a kind of ragtime dance, perhaps related to earlier *jasm* energy, drive (1860); apparently of African origin (compare Tshiluba *jaja* cause to dance, Mandingo *jasi* and Wolof *yees* step out of character, become unlike oneself, Temne *yas* be extremely lively or energetic). The source of *jazz* in English is not known, and the connection with *jasm* cannot be fully demonstrated, but the form, sense, and chronology suggest that a relationship may exist, though in words of dialect and slang origin it is often very difficult to assign a definite origin or even to trace a series of possible steps to a nebulous origin. References to a connection with sex and sexual intercourse do not appear before the 1920's. See also "The Earliest Citation of Jazz," by David Shulman, *Comments On Etymology,* 16, 5-6 (Dec. 1986).

By 1922 *jazz* was applied to the music used in the original dance as well as to other forms of music originating among American blacks.

The meaning of energy, excitement, pep, is first recorded in 1913, again perhaps influenced by the earlier *jasm.* The sense of meaningless talk, nonsense, rubbish, appeared in 1918, in American English college slang.
—v. 1917, speed or liven up; 1918, play jazz; probably from the noun. **—jazzy** *adj.* 1919, formed from English *jazz* + *-y*[1].

jealous *adj.* Apparently before 1200 *gelus* distrustful of the faithfulness of a spouse or lover, in *Ancrene Riwle;* later *jelus* (before 1325, in *Cursor Mundi*); borrowed from Old French *jelous,* from Old Provençal, and from Old French *gelos,* from Vulgar Latin **zēlōsus,* from Latin *zēlus* jealousy, ZEAL; for suffix see -OUS. **—jealousy** *n.* Apparently before 1200 *gelusie,* in *Ancrene Riwle;* borrowed from Old French *jelousie, jalousie,* from *jelous,* from Old Provençal, and from Old French *gelos* jealous; for suffix see -Y[3].

jeans *n.pl.* trousers made of strong twilled cloth. 1843, derived from the singular *jean* strong twilled cotton cloth (1567), from the earlier adjective *jene* Genoese, of Genoa (1436; about 1466 spelled *Geane*); borrowed from Middle French *Genes* Genoa, city in northwestern Italy; so called because such cloth was made there.

jeep *n.* small general-purpose automobile. 1941, American English, probably coined from the initials *G.P.,* abbreviation of *General Purpose,* the U.S. Army designation for this type of car. The term may have been influenced by the name "Eugene the Jeep," a versatile cartoon character and his cry of "Jeep," introduced in the comic strip "Thimble Theater," (the forerunner of Popeye) by cartoonist Elzie C. Segar in 1936 and used briefly as the name of a commercial motor vehicle in 1937. It has also been claimed that the term is a reduction of "Jeepers creepers!" the exclamation of Major General George Lynch, chief of infantry of the U.S. Army, on the occasion of his first ride in the prototype of the vehicle at Fort Myer, Virginia, in 1939, and adopted at the time by Charles H. Payne, the designer of the vehicle.

jeepers (jē′pərz) *interj.* exclamation of surprise or mild oath. 1929, American English, euphemism for *Jesus;* perhaps an altered or extended form of earlier *Gee, Geez, Geeze,* also spelled *Jeez, Jeeze* (1923). The more intensive variant, *jeepers creepers,* first recorded in 1937 in American English, is a euphemism for *Jesus Christ.*

jeer *v.* 1553 *gyr* (implied in *gyrer*); 1577-87 *geer* call out in derision, mock or scoff; of uncertain origin, perhaps, by alteration of pronunciation from Dutch *gieren* to cry or roar (sometimes with laughter), from Middle Dutch *ghieren* to cry or grunt; *or* perhaps, by alteration of pronunciation and form, from Middle Dutch *scheer-*

en, scheren to trifle, jest, jeer. The OED also suggests that *jeer* may have originated in an ironical use of *cheer,* but says the evidence is wanting. **—n.** act of jeering. 1625, in Ben Jonson's *The Staple of Newes;* from the verb.

Jehovah (jihō′və) *n.* name of God in the Old Testament. 1530 *Iehoua,* in the Tyndale Bible; borrowing of New Latin. The New Latin form *Iehoua* was an erroneous transliteration of the Hebrew divine name *YHWH* (the "tetragrammaton") using the vowel points of Hebrew *ădhōnāi* my lord; these vowel points have been originally added to *YHWH* by the Hebrew scribes as a direction to the reader to substitute *ădhōnāi* for the "ineffable name" (i.e., too sacred for utterance) and not as the vowels of the tetragrammaton itself, which in the Jewish religion is unpronounceable, though scholars often represent and pronounce it as *Yahweh.* The name is generally assumed to be a formation on the Hebrew verb *hāwāh* to be, exist.

jejune (jijün′) *adj.* dull, insipid, flat. 1615 (implied in *jejunely*); borrowed from Latin *jejūnus* unproductive or meager; literally, hungry, fasting; of uncertain origin; related to DINE.

A meaning "dry, arid" existed in Old French *jejune,* but it would be surprising indeed if the English word of the 1600's came from Old French after an interval of about four centuries.

jell *v.* become jelly, congeal. 1869, in Alcott's *Little Women,* American English; probably a back formation from *jelly.* The figurative sense of crystallize, take definite shape, is first recorded in 1908.

An earlier form existed in Middle English *gelen* to congeal (before 1398, in Trevisa's translation of Bartholomew's *De Proprietatibus Rerum*); borrowed from Old French *geler,* and directly from Latin *gelāre* to freeze, but the form disappears in English by the 1500's.

jelly *n.* gelatinous substance. 1381 *gelee, gely,* borrowed from Old French *gelée* jelly or frost, from the feminine past participle of *geler* to congeal, from Latin *gelāre* to freeze, from *gelū* frost; see COLD. **—v.** become jelly. 1601, in Holland's translation of Pliny's *Natural History;* from the noun. **—jellybean** *n.* (1905, American English) **—jellyfish** *n.* (1707)

jenny *n.* early type of spinning machine. 1783 *Spinning Jenny,* from *Jenny,* diminutive of the name *Jane.* See JACK for another example of a name used to designate machines.

jeopardy *n.* Probably before 1300 *juperti* a trick, stratagem; later *jeupardy* a chess problem (1369, in Chaucer's *Book of the Duchesse*); borrowed from Old French *jeu parti* an even or divided game (*jeu* game, from Latin *jocus* pastime or JOKE, and *parti,* past participle of *partir* to divide, PART). The meaning of danger or risk is first recorded in Chaucer's *Troilus and Criseyde* (1385) with the spelling *jupartie;* a form of the modern spelling as *jeopardie,* is recorded in 1474. **—jeopardize** *v.* 1646, formed from English *jeopardy* + *-ize.*

jerboa (jərbō′ə) *n.* small mouselike mammal. 1662 *jerbuah,* probably a phonetic transcription of Arabic *yarbū';* later, replaced by *gerbo,* perhaps borrowed through French *gerbo,* or directly from New Latin *jerboa,* from Arabic *yarbū'.*

jerk[1] *v.* pull or twist suddenly. 1550, to lash, strike with a whip, in Coverdale's writings; of uncertain origin, possibly imitative or otherwise suggestive of the sound or action of the blow. The meaning of pull or twist suddenly is first recorded in Nashe's *An Almond for a Parrot.* **—n.** sudden sharp pull or twist. 1555, a stroke with a whip, a lash; later, sudden sharp pull or twist (1575); of uncertain origin.

jerk[2] *v.* preserve (meat) by cutting it into long thin slices and drying it in the sun. 1707, American English; borrowed from American Spanish *charquear,* from *charquí* jerked meat, from Quechua (Peru) *ch'arki.* **—n.** jerked meat. 1799, American English; from the verb. **—jerky** *n.* jerked meat. 1850, American English; borrowed from American Spanish *charquí.*

jerk[3] *n. Slang.* stupid, dull, or ineffectual person. 1935, American English slang, in A.J. Pollock's *Underworld Speaks;* perhaps from earlier *jerk,* adj., insignificant, inferior (1890's, as in *a jerk town,* short for *jerkwater,* 1897, in reference to a steam train or branch line that serves small towns where a locomotive had to jerk water from streams or a water tower to fill its tender).

jerkin *n.* 1519, of unknown origin. By some authorities related to Dutch *jurk* a frock, which is too distant in meaning and form (Dutch *j* = English *y*). It is interesting to note the Middle English had the form *jerin* cloth tunic (probably before 1400), but this too is defective.

jerry-built *adj.* built cheaply of poor materials. 1869, English dialectal use, from *jerry* bad, defective, apparently a pejorative application of *Jerry,* nickname of the names *Jeremy* and *Jeremiah,* used earlier in various slang formations such as *jerrymumble* (1721) to shake or tumble about, *Jerry Sneak* (1764) a mean, sneaking fellow, and *jerry* (1851-61) or *jerry-shop* (1873) a cheap beer house.

jersey *n.* close-fitting knitted garment. 1836-48, extended sense of the earlier reference to knitted cloth or worsted from the isle of *Jersey* (1583). The term *Jersey* as the name of a breed of cattle also was in allusion to the Channel isle of Jersey, and is first recorded in 1842.

jest *n.* Before 1548, a taunt or jeer; later, joke or witticism (1551); probably influenced by the verb as part of its development from Middle English *geste* satirical utterance, lampoon (before 1387); earlier, poem or song about heroic deeds (probably before 1300, in *Arthour and Merlin*) and entertainment or amusement (probably about 1225, in *King Horn*). Middle English *geste* was borrowed from Old French *geste* action, exploit, romance in verse; learned borrowing from Latin *gesta* deeds, from neuter plural of *gestus,* past participle of *gerere* to carry, behave, act, perform; of uncertain origin. **—v.** to joke, 1526, to taunt or jeer; later, to joke (1553); developed from Middle English *gesten* recite a tale (about 1390, in Chaucer's *Canterbury Tales*); from *geste,* n. **—jester** *n.* About 1510, developed from Middle English *gestour* a minstrel (before 1338, in Mannyng's *Chronicle of England*); from *gesten* recite a tale + *-er*[1].

jet[1] *n.* stream of water, steam, etc. sent with force. 1696, borrowed from French *jet,* from Old French *jet,* from *jeter* to throw, thrust, from Late Latin *jectāre,* abstracted from *dējectāre, prōjectāre,* etc., for Latin *jactāre* toss about, a frequentative form of *jacere* to throw, cast.

Jet is first recorded as an airplane driven by jet propulsion in 1944.

—v. gush out. 1692, borrowed from Middle French

jeter to throw or thrust, from Old French. An earlier but unrelated sense of encroach upon, project, is recorded in Shakespeare's *Titus Andronicus* (1588). The meaning of travel by jet plane is found in 1949 in American English.

jet² *n.* hard black mineral, glossy when polished. 1351 *gete;* later *jeet* (about 1390); borrowed from Anglo-French *geet,* corresponding to Continental Old French *jaiet,* from Latin *gagātēs,* from Greek *gagátēs líthos* stone of Gagai, a town and river in Lycia, in southwest Asia Minor. **—adj.** made of jet. 1444, attributive use of the noun.

jetsam (jet′səm) *n.* goods thrown overboard to lighten a ship. 1570 *jottsome;* later *jetson* (1591) and *jetsam* (1678); developed by alteration (most notably in loss of the medial vowel) from Middle English *jetteson* a throwing of goods overboard to lighten a ship, a jettisoning (1425, in *Rolls of Parliament*); see JETTISON. The term is now most closely associated with *flotsam,* but originally *jetsam* (1678) probably served as the model for the later spelling *flotsam* (1853).

jettison (jet′əsən *or* jet′əzən) *v.* throw (goods) overboard to lighten a ship, aircraft, etc. 1848, developed from *jetteson* the act of throwing goods overboard, especially to lighten a ship in distress (1425, in *Rolls of Parliament*); borrowed through Anglo-French *getteson,* from Old French *getaison,* from Vulgar Latin **jectātiōnem* (nominative **jectātiō*) act of throwing, from Late Latin *jectāre* toss about; see JET¹ stream. The modern spelling of the verb was influenced by the form of the noun *jettison,* which before 1848 had undergone a series of reductions from *getteson, jetteson* to *jetson* (confused with *jetsam*), and was deliberately respelled as *jettison* in the noun to avoid the former confusion with *jetsam.*

jetty *n.* breakwater. 1418 *juteye* overhang, projecting part; later *getti* a breakwater (before 1420), and *jettie* (1432); borrowed from Old French *jetee, geté* a jetty, something thrown up as a breakwater, from feminine past participle of *jeter* to throw; see JET¹ stream.

Jew *n.* Probably before 1200 *giw,* in *Ancrene Riwle;* later *Jeu* (1241, as a surname), *iew* (about 1250); borrowed through Anglo-French *geu, jwe,* and directly from Old French *giu, juiu;* earlier *juieu, jueu,* from Latin *Jūdaeum* (nominative *Jūdaeus*), from Greek *Ioudaîos,* from Aramaic *yĕhūdhāi,* corresponding to Hebrew *yĕhūdhī* (literally, of the kingdom of Judah), from *yĕhūdhāh* Judah, name of the fourth son of Jacob, the tribe descended from him, and the ancient kingdom in southern Palestine peopled by this tribe and that of Benjamin, with Jerusalem as its capital.

The Old English equivalent of this word was *Iudēas* the Jews, an early borrowing (related to Old High German *judeo, judo* Jew, modern German *Jude,* and Old Saxon *judeo, judheo*) from Latin *Jūdaeus.*

—Jewish *adj.* Before 1546, formed from English *Jew* + *-ish.* The Old English equivalent was *Iudēisć,* from *Iudēas* Jews, *Iudēa* Judea + *-isć* -ish. **—Jewry** *n.* Probably before 1200 *giwerie* the Jewish people or their religion, in *Ancrene Riwle;* later *iurie* (1340, in *Ayenbite of Inwyt*), and *iewry* (probably about 1375); borrowed through Anglo-French *jeuerie, gyuerie,* from Old French *juerie,* from *juieu, juiu;* earlier *jueu* Jew + *-erie* -ery.

jewel *n.* precious stone; gem. Probably before 1300 *jeuel* valuable object or treasure, in *Kyng Alisaunder;* later *juel* precious stone (before 1325, in *Cursor Mundi*), and *jewel* (about 1390); borrowed, probably through Anglo-French *juel, jeual,* and from Old French *juel, jouel* ornament or jewel, from Medieval Latin *jocale,* from Latin *jocus* pastime or sport, see JOKE. **—v.** set or adorn with jewels. 1601, in Ben Jonson's *The Poetaster;* from the noun. **—jeweler** *n.* 1340 *Jueler,* as a surname; borrowed through Anglo-French *juellour,* from Old French *joelier, juelier,* from *juel* jewel. **—jewelry** *n.* Probably about 1380 *juelrye* precious ornaments; borrowed from Old French *juelerie,* from *juel* jewel.

jib *n. Nautical.* triangular sail in front of the foremast. 1661 *gibb,* of uncertain origin (perhaps related to *gibbet,* with reference to the sail's suspension from the masthead). **—v.** 1691, to pull (a sail or yard) from one side of a vessel to the other.

jibe¹ *v.* shift (a sail or boom) from one side of a ship to the other when sailing before the wind. 1693 *gybe,* borrowed from Dutch *gijben, gijpen,* apparently related to *gijk, giek* boom or spar of a sailship. The later form *jibe* (1856) was probably influenced in its spelling by *jib.* The shift in pronunciation is unaccounted for.

jibe² *v.* be in harmony, agree, fit. 1813 *gibe,* of uncertain origin; perhaps originally a figurative use of *jibe*¹.

jibe³ *n.* See GIBE (jeer).

jiffy *adj. Informal.* moment, instant. 1785, a very short space of time (used as if it were an actual unit of measured time, as in "six jiffies"), in Rudolph Raspe's *Baron Munchausen's Travels;* perhaps spontaneously coined by the author. The phrase *in a jiffy* was first recorded (with the spelling *jelfy*) in Grose's *Classical Dictionary of the Vulgar Tongue* (1796).

jig¹ *v.* dance a jig 1588, sing or play the tune of a lively dance, in Shakespeare's *Love's Labour's Lost;* possibly borrowed from Middle French *giguer* to dance, and respelled in English by influence of earlier *jig,* n. The relation of the verb in Middle French to *gigue* fiddle is paralleled in Middle English by *gige* fiddle (before 1450) borrowed from Middle French, from Old High German *gíga* fiddle, cognate with Old Icelandic *geiga* turn aside. The borrowing with similar sense in both Middle French and Middle English may give support to the suggestion that the noun sense of the dance also came from the French, or even that the verb is derived from the noun in English. **—n.** lively dance. About 1560, of uncertain origin.

jig² *n.* device used to lure fishes. 1858, of uncertain origin, perhaps from *jig*¹, v., in the sense of jerk, move up and down.

jigger *n.* small flea; chigoe. 1781, alteration of CHIGGER.

jiggle *v.* shake or jerk slightly. 1836, formed from *jig*¹, v., with the frequentative suffix *-le.* **—n.** slight shake or jerk. 1888, from the verb.

jihad (jihäd′) *n.* religious war of Moslems against unbelievers; holy war. 1869, borrowing of Arabic *jihād,* literally, struggle, contest, effort. A transferred sense of any war or crusade for or against some doctrine, etc., is first recorded in 1880.

jilt *v.* cast off (a lover). 1673, be false or faithless, jilt or discard for another, in Dryden's *Marriage-à-la-Mode;* apparently developed from *jilt,* n., a loose, unchaste woman, harlot (1672, in Wycherley's *Love in a Wood*). Wycherley's use was perhaps a contraction of earlier *jelot* (about 1550), *gillot* (1557) of the same meaning, and a diminutive form of *gille* a familiar or contemptuous term for a woman or girl (before 1425), originally a shortened form of the female name *Gillian,* French *Juliane,* Latin *Jūliāna,* feminine of *Jūliānus* Julian, a Roman proper name.

Jim Crow segregation of blacks; racial discrimination. 1842, American English, in *Jim Crow car* segregated railroad car for blacks, from earlier *Jim Crow,* a derogatory name for a black man (1838). Originally *Jim Crow* (1835) was the name of a black minstrel character in a popular song and dance act performed by Thomas Dartmouth Rice, 1808-1860, an American entertainer known as "the Father of American Minstrelsy," and later by other performers made up as this character. The song on which the performance was based appeared in 1828 with the title *Jim Crow* and contained the refrain "My name's Jim Crow, Weel about, and turn about, And do jis so." The word *crow* was used earlier (1823, in James Fenimore Cooper's *The Pioneers*) as a derogatory term for a black man. **—Jim Crowism** 1837, American English, racial segregation and discrimination, formed from *Jim Crow,* derogatory name for a black man + *-ism.*

jimmy *n.* short crowbar. 1848 *jimmey,* dialectal variant of earlier *jemmy* crowbar much used by burglars (1811), apparently a special use of *Jimmy* or *Jemmy,* familiar forms of the proper name *James.* Compare JACK in meaning. **—v.** force open with or as with a jimmy. 1893; from the noun.

jimson or **Jimson weed** coarse, bad-smelling weed with poisonous, narcotic leaves. 1812, American English, shortening and alteration of earlier *Jamestown-weed* (1687), from *Jamestown,* Virginia, where it was first found.

jingle *v.* make a sound like that of coins or keys striking together. About 1387-95 *ginglen,* in Chaucer's *Prologue* to the *Canterbury Tales;* of imitative origin.

OED says that there appears to be no original association with *jangle,* which is recorded by 1300 as chatter, but does not appear before 1490 in the sense of discordant sound; perhaps this later sense of *jangle* was influenced by *jingle.*

—n. jingling sound. 1599, in Ben Jonson's *Every Man Out of His Humor;* from the verb.

jingo[1] *interj.* **by jingo,** exclamation or mild oath, used chiefly for emphasis. 1694 *by jingo,* in Motteux's translation of Rabelais' works (where the French has *par Dieu* by God); apparently a euphemism for *by Jesus,* influenced by earlier *jingo* a magician's call for the appearance of something (1670, contrasting with *presto*), usually in the phrase *high jingo* or *hey jingo;* of uncertain origin.

jingo[2] *n.* one who advocates a belligerent foreign policy; militant nationalist or chauvinist. 1897, Lord Salisbury in *The Times* of London, from the earlier nickname *Jingo* (1878), in reference to one who supported Disraeli's policy of sending a British fleet into Turkish waters to resist the advance of Russia in 1878; developed from the refrain *by Jingo* in a nationalistic music hall song ("We don't want to fight, But, by Jingo! if we do. . .") which became the "theme song" of those ready to fight Russia; see JINGO[1].

jinn *n.pl.* spirits in Moslem mythology that can appear in human or animal form. 1822 *ginns,* misunderstood as a plural of *ginn,* in Byron's *Don Juan;* earlier *dgen* (1684, considered as a singular form borrowed from obsolete French *dgen,* from Arabic *jinn*). Use of *ginn* and *jinn* in English was probably a direct reborrowing from Arabic *jinn* spirits in Moslem mythology, plural of *jinnī* spirit.

The use of *jinn* as a plural is first recorded in English in 1841; previous uses considered *jinn* singular. The spelling with *j* (in *jin*) does not appear in recorded English before 1838.

Early use of the term was in the form *genie,* which was borrowed through French *génie,* used by early translators of *The Arabian Nights* to render *jinnī,* singular of *jinn.*

jinrikisha or **jinricksha** (jinrik′shô) *n.* small, two-wheeled carriage pulled by one or more men. 1874, borrowed from Japanese *jinrikisha* (*jin* man + *riki* power + *sha* cart, carriage).

It is possible the carriage is the invention of a Baptist missionary named Goble in 1869, who is said to have devised the vehicle for his wife who suffered from arthritis, and the first commercial operation of such vehicles was apparently sanctioned in Tokyo that same year.

jinx *n. Informal.* person or thing that brings bad luck. 1911, American English, from earlier *jyng* a charm or spell (before 1643; originally a bird, the wryneck, used in witchcraft); borrowed from Latin *iynx* the wryneck, from Greek *íynx* (genitive *íyngos*). **—v.** bring bad luck to. 1917, American English; from the noun.

jitney (jit′nē) *n.* car or small bus for carrying passengers over a regular route. 1914, American English, from earlier slang *jitney* a nickel (spelled *gitney* in 1903), of uncertain origin. The vehicle was apparently so called because the original jitney buses charged a fare of five cents.

jitterbug *n.* fast, twisting and twirling dance for couples, mainly to boogie-woogie and swing music. 1939, American English; probably developed from earlier *jitterbug* a swing music enthusiast (1937), from *Jitter bug,* title of a song (1934) by Cab Calloway and others in which "jitter bug" refers to one who drinks liquor habitually and "has the jitters ev'ry morn." **—v.** dance the jitterbug. 1938, American English, from the same source as the noun.

jitters *n.pl. Informal.* extreme nervousness. 1929, American English, in Preston Sturges' play *Strictly Dishonorable;* perhaps developed as an alteration of dialectal English *chitter,* v. and n., tremble or shiver, from Middle English *chiteren* to twitter, chatter (probably before 1200, in *Ancrene Riwle*); usually considered of imitative origin. **—jitter** *v. Informal.* act nervously, shake or rattle. 1931, in A.M. Mackenzie's *Cypress in Moonlight,* possibly developed from *jitters,* or directly from *chitter;* see JITTERS. **—jittery** *adj. Informal.* extremely nervous; jumpy. 1931, American English, in Hart Crane's *Letters;* formed from *jitter(s)* + *-y*[1].

jive *v. Slang.* mislead, deceive, fool. 1928, American English, in the title of a record by Louis "Satchmo" Armstrong; originally Black English use, probably of African origin (compare Wolof *jev, jeu* talk about someone absent, especially in a disparaging manner). **—n.** misleading, deceptive, or pretentious talk. 1928, American English; from the same source as the verb.

By the late 1930's *jive* was also the name of a type of fast, lively jazz music and dance, as well as the name of the slang used by blacks in New York City, especially black jazz musicians.

job *n.* 1557 *jobbe of worke* piece of work or task; perhaps a variant form of *gobbe* GOB[1] a mass or lump (about 1382, in the Wycliffe Bible).

The Middle English *jubbe* and its variant *jobbe,* especially in the citation from *Destruction of Troy* (about 1400), refer to a container, specifically a jar or vase.

By the early 1600's (before 1627, in Thomas Middleton's *The Mayor of Quinborough*) *job* itself had come to mean a piece of work, and this meaning was extended to that of a piece of work or transaction done for pay or profit (1660, in Pepys' *Diary*), and later anything one has to do, any business or affair (1694). The meaning of work done for pay, paid position, employment, is first recorded in 1858 in American English.

jock *n. Slang.* athlete, especially at a school or college. 1963, American English, short for *jockstrap* athletic male, slang use of *jock-strap* an elastic undergarment worn to support the male genital organs in sports, a compound of *jock,* a slang word for the genital organs (1790), of uncertain origin, and *strap.*

jockey *n.* Before 1529, boy or fellow, in Skelton's *Against the Scottes;* originally, a Scottish proper name, diminutive of *Jock,* Scottish variant of *Jack.* The meaning of a person who rides horses in races is first recorded in 1670. **—v.** 1708, maneuver so as to get advantage, trick, outwit; from the noun in the extended sense of crafty bargainer or horse trader (1683). The meaning of ride (a horse) in a race is first recorded in 1767.

jocose *adj.* jesting, humorous, playful. 1673; earlier in *jocosity* (1646); borrowed from Latin *jocōsus* full of jesting, joking, from *jocus* pastime, sport, JOKE.

jocular *adj.* funny, comic, joking. 1626, in Ben Jonson's *The Fortunate Isles and their Union;* borrowed from Latin *joculāris* funny, comic, from *joculus,* diminutive of *jocus* JOKE. A similar form but unrelated use, existed in Middle English *joculer* a jester or minstrel (probably before 1425); borrowed probably through Old French *joculer,* from Medieval Latin *jocularis.*

jocund (jok′ənd *or* jō′kənd) *adj.* cheerful, merry. About 1380, in Chaucer's *Rosemounde,* borrowed from Old French *jocond,* learned borrowing from Latin *jōcundus,* later variant (influenced by Latin *jocus* JOKE) of *jūcundus* pleasant; originally, helpful, from *juvāre* to please, benefit, help; of uncertain origin.

jodhpurs (jod′pərz) *n.pl.* breeches for horseback riding. 1913 *Jodpores,* abstracted from earlier *Jodhpur riding-breeches* (1899), in allusion to *Jodhpur,* a former state in northwestern India.

jog[1] *v.* shake with a push or jerk. 1548, shake or move with a jerk; later, in figurative use of stir up by hint or reminder (1601); perhaps alteration of Middle English *shoggen* to shake, jolt, move with a jerk (about 1395); of uncertain origin (perhaps cognate with Middle Dutch *schocken* to shake; see SHOCK[1] jolt). The meaning of walk or ride with a jolting pace, to trot, is first recorded in 1565, and was later extended to running, as found in Stevenson's *Kidnapped* (1866). **—n.** shake, push, or nudge. 1611, act of jogging; later, a shake, push (1635); from the verb. **—jogger** *n.* one that jogs. Before 1700; formed from English *jog,* v. + *-er*[1].

jog[2] *n.* part that sticks out or in. 1845, American English, variant of *jag*[1], in the (1519) sense of a sharp or pointed projection (1519, found earlier in Middle English *jagge* ornamental points on the edge of a garment, probably 1409).

joggle *v.* shake slightly. 1513, shake to and fro; probably formed from *jog*[1] + *-le*[3]. If the formation is based on *jog*[1], there is some question of time in the record of English, for *jog*[1] appears later than *joggle,* which suggests some possible connection by alteration of pronunciation with Middle English *goglen* to shake (probably about 1400). **—n.** slight shake. 1727, in Bailey's *Dictionary,* from the verb.

join *v.* Probably before 1300 *joinen,* in *Arthour and Merlin;* earlier, implied in the surname *Joinur* (1195-1215); borrowed from Old French *joindre, juindre* (also found in the stem forms *joign-, join-*), from Latin *jungere* to join, yoke; related to *jugum* YOKE. **—joiner** *n.* About 1195-1215, in the surname *Joinur;* borrowed from Old French *joigneor,* through the stem *joign-,* from *joindre.*

joint *n.* place at which two things or parts are joined; connection. About 1300, place where bones come together; borrowed from Old French *joint* (past participle of *joindre* JOIN), from Latin *jūnctus,* past participle of *jungere* JOIN.

The slang meaning of any place, building, or establishment, is first recorded in 1877, originally in the sense of a place where people join or get together (earliest references being to a place where swindlers and burglars congregated). The specific meaning of jail or prison is first found in William Burroughs' *Junkie* (1953), but is probably much older.

—adj. joined together. 1424, borrowed from Middle French *joint,* from past participle of *joindre* join.

joist *n.* one of the parallel timbers which support the boards of a floor or ceiling. Before 1325 *giste;* borrowed from Old French *giste* beam, noun use of the feminine past participle of *gesir* to lie, from Latin *jacēre* to lie, rest; related to *jacere* to throw; see JET[1] stream. **—v.** provide with or lay across joists. 1439, from the noun.

The phonetic development of the sound represented by *oi* from *i* preceded the sound of *oi* in *boil* from *bile* and is not yet accounted for, but similar changes are found in *hoist* and *foist.*

joke *n.* something funny or amusing. 1670, borrowed from Latin *jocus* joke, sport, pastime. **—v.** make a joke. 1670, borrowed from Latin *jocārī* to jest, joke, from *jocus* joke, cognate with Old High German *jehan* say, speak, and Middle Welsh *ieith* (modern Welsh *iaith*) language, from Indo-European **yek-/yok-* speak (Pok.503). **—joker** *n.* 1729, one who jokes; later, the odd face card in a pack of playing cards (1885); formed from English *joke* + *-er*[1].

jolly *adj.* Probably before 1300 *jolif* merry, in *Arthour and Merlin;* about 1303 *joly* amorous, in Mannyng's *Handlyng Synne;* borrowed from Old French *joli, jolif* festive, merry, amorous, well-dressed, pretty; perhaps from a Scandinavian source (compare Old Icelandic *jōl* a winter feast, YULE).

The phonetic development and historical connection between the Old French and Scandinavian involved enough difficulty so that Murray in the OED, and Skeat in his Etymological Dictionary both mention an alternative possible borrowing of Old French *joli* from Latin, perhaps from **gaudīvus,* from *gaudēre* to rejoice, and so *gaudia* JOY (citing a shift from *d* to *l* as in Latin *cicāda* to French *cigale* cicada). But this is not a satisfactory solution either, though more plausible semantically.

The early loss of *f* in *jolif* is analogous to that in *tardy* and *hasty.*

—**adv.** *Especially British Informal.* extremely, very. 1549; from the adjective. —**v.** flatter (a person) to make him feel good or agreeable. 1890, American English; from the adjective. Earlier use as a verb is recorded in Middle English *jolifen* be cheerful or cheering (about 1385 *joleyvinge* making cheerful, cheering), but is not connected with the use in American English. —**jollity** *n.* Before 1325 *jolite* merrymaking, festivity, in *Cursor Mundi;* borrowed from Old French *jolité,* from *joli* jolly.

jolt *v.* to jar, shock, jerk. 1599, perhaps alteration of *jollen* to knock or batter (before 1450; earlier to stagger, about 1410). The alteration of *jollen* to *jolt* is usually explained by association with dialectal *jot* to jog or bump (1530) and with reference to *jolt-head* clumsy, stupid person (1533) as a possible influence of form, but unexplained in semantic connection, except as conjectured to refer to halting or jerking movement. —**n.** 1599, a knock against something; probably from the verb. The meaning of a jarring shock or jerk is first recorded in 1632.

Jones *n.* The expression *keep up with the Joneses,* meaning to strive not to be outdone by one's neighbors or associates, is first recorded in 1913 in American English. It was coined by the American cartoonist Arthur R. Momand as the title of a comic strip, *Keeping up with the Joneses,* which he drew under the by-line "Pop" from 1913 to 1941.

The slang term *the Jones,* meaning a drug habit or addiction, especially a large one, appeared in American English in 1968, though it was recorded in a narcotic addict glossary by David W. Maurer between 1952 and 1972. The origin of the term may be connected to the use of *Jones* in Black English as a familiar greeting, derived from the common family name.

jonquil (jong'kwəl) *n.* plant with long slender leaves. 1664 *junquill,* borrowed from French *jonquille,* from Spanish *junquillo,* diminutive of *junco* rush, reed, from Latin *juncus* rush (in reference to the rushlike leaves), (earlier **jūncus*), from **joinikos,* cognate with Middle Irish *āin* rush and Old Icelandic *einir* juniper, from Indo-European **yoini-* (Pok.513). See also JUNIPER.

josh *v. Informal.* to joke, banter, ridicule. 1845 *Josh,* American English, perhaps from the name *Josh,* short for *Joshua,* but the connection is obscure. In the late 1800's it was thought that this word derived from *Josh* Billings, pen name of Henry Wheeler Shaw, 1818-1885, a popular American humorist; however, his work did not attract wide notice until 1860, long after *josh* had come into common use.

joss *n.* Chinese idol. 1711, from a Chinese Pidgin English form of Javanese *dejos,* from Portuguese *deus* god, from Latin *deus;* see DEITY. The term *joss stick,* meaning a stick of fragrant paste burned (originally by the Chinese) as incense, is first recorded in 1883.

jostle *v.* strike, or push against, elbow roughly. 1678 *jostle,* alteration of earlier *justle* (1580) and *iustle* (1546); formed from Middle English *jousten, justen* to JOUST + suffix *-le*[3]. —**n.** a jostling, push, knock. 1607 *justle* struggle or joust; 1611, push or knock; from the verb.

jot *n.* little bit. 1526 *iott* (pronounced as one syllable), in the Tyndale Bible; earlier *ioote* something of no value or importance (before 1500); borrowed from Latin *jōta, iōta,* from Greek *iôta* iota, the ninth and smallest letter in the Greek alphabet, from Phoenician (compare Hebrew *yōd* the tenth letter of the Hebrew alphabet). See IOTA. —**v.** write briefly or in haste. 1721, originally Scottish, in Allan Ramsay's *Poems,* popularized by Scott and other writers.

joual (zhwäl) *n.* dialect or patois of Canadian French. 1962, borrowed from Canadian French, from *joual,* rendition of the joual pronunciation of French *cheval* horse.

joule (jül) *n. Physics.* unit of work or energy, equal to ten million ergs. 1882, in allusion to James P. *Joule,* 1818-1889, the British physicist noted for his research on the mechanical equivalent of heat.

jounce *v.* bounce, bump, jolt. 1440, implied in *jouncinge* jolting movement, in *Promptorium Parvulorum;* possibly an alteration (influenced by *jog* and *jump*) of *bounce.* —**n.** 1787, from the verb.

journal *n.* daily record. 1355-56, book containing the form of church service in the day hours of worship; borrowed through Anglo-French *jurnal, jurnale* a day, a day's work, and directly from Old French *journal,* originally adjective, daily, from Late Latin *diurnālis* daily, DIURNAL.

The meaning of a daily record of public transactions, is first recorded in 1565, and that of a daily personal record, diary, in 1610. The meaning of daily newspaper, and by extension that of any periodical publication appeared in Pope's *The Dunciad* (1728), borrowed from French *journal.* Doublet of DIURNAL.

—**journalism** *n.* 1833, borrowed from French *journalisme,* from French *journal* journal. —**journalist** *n.* 1693, formed from English *journal* + *-ist.*

journey *n.* travel or trip. Apparently before 1200 *jurnee* passage through life, in *Ancrene Riwle* (figurative use); borrowed from Old French *journée, jurnee, jornee* day's work or travel, from Vulgar Latin **diurnāta* events of a day, from *diurnum* day, noun use of neuter of Latin *diurnus* of one day, from *diēs* day; see DEITY. —**v.** take a trip; travel. Before 1338 *journeyen,* in Mannyng's *Chronicle of England;* borrowed from Old French *journoier,* from *journée* day's work or travel. —**journeyman** *n.* 1414 *journeman* workman qualified in his trade; formed from English *journey* + *man.*

joust *v.* Apparently about 1300 *justen;* later *jousten* (about 1378, in a version of *Piers Plowman*); borrowed from Old French *joster, jouster, juster,* from Vulgar Latin **juxtāre* be next to, from Latin *juxtā* beside, near; related to *jungere* to JOIN. An earlier sense of join or ally oneself, is first recorded in *The Story of Genesis and Exodus* (about 1250). —**n.** Probably before 1300 (usually in the plural) *justes,* in *Kyng Alisaunder;* about 1300 (also in the plural) *joustes;* borrowed from Old French *joustes, justes,* from *jouster, juster* to joust.

jovial *adj.* 1590, under the influence of the planet Jupiter, in Spenser's *Faerie Queene;* borrowed through Middle French *jovial,* and directly from Latin *Joviālis* of Jupiter, from *Jovius,* from *Jovis* (genitive of *Juppiter*) Jupiter, Roman god of the sky; see DEITY. The meaning of good-humored and merry derives from the belief that those born under the sign of the planet Jupiter are of a cheerful disposition. —**joviality** *n.* 1626, formed from English *jovial* + *-ity,* possibly by influence of French *jovialité.*

jowl[1] *n.* jaw, especially the underjaw. 1577 *jole,* in the phrase *cheek by jowl,* alteration (possibly by association with JOWL[2]) of Middle English *chawl* (probably about 1380); earlier *chavel* (before 1250); developed from

Old English (about 750) *ceafl.* The Old English form is cognate with Old Saxon *kaflos,* pl., jaws, Middle High German *kiver, kivel* jowl (modern German *Kiefer*), from Proto-Germanic **kaflaz, kefraz, keflaz,* cognate with Avestan *zafar-* mouth, and Old Irish *gop* beak, mouth, from Indo-European **ĝep(h)-/ĝop(h)-* (Pok. 382).

The forms with *j* in *jowl*[1] and *jowl*[2] began to appear in the late 1500's, but the shift from *ch-* to *j-* is not satisfactorily accounted for. Both forms in *j* were preceded by another word in Middle English *jol* head (1371, found in *jolrap* head rope, as for a cow) which may have been the precursor of both *jowl*[1] and *jowl*[2].

jowl[2] *n.* fold of flesh hanging from the jaw. 1591 *joule,* alteration of Middle English *cholle* (probably about 1300); perhaps related to Old English *ceole* throat, cognate with Old High German *kela* throat, Proto-Germanic **kelōn-,* and cognate with Latin *gula* throat and Old Irish *gelid* devours, from Indo-European **gel-* to swallow (Pok.365); see note at JOWL[1].

joy *n.* Probably before 1200 *joie* gladness, delight, joy, in *Ancrene Riwle;* borrowed from Old French *joie,* from Latin *gaudia,* plural of *gaudium* joy, from *gaudēre* rejoice. The Latin verb *gaudēre* is related to Greek *gētheîn* to rejoice, *gaûros* proud, Lithuanian *džiaugiúos* I rejoice (with reversal of initial and medial consonants), Tocharian A *kāwas* request, wish, and Tocharian B *kāw-* to desire, from Indo-European **gāu-/gəu-,* and **gāw-edh-* rejoice (Pok.353).—**joyful** *adj.* About 1250 *joiful;* formed from Middle English *joie* + *-ful.* —**joyous** *adj.* Probably before 1300 *joious,* in *Arthour and Merlin;* borrowed through Anglo-French *joyous,* from Old French *joios,* from *joie* joy; for suffix see -OUS. —**joy ride** American English (1908); **joy-ride** *v.* (1910)

jubilant *adj.* rejoicing, exulting. 1667, in Milton's *Paradise Lost;* probably borrowed from Latin *jūbilantem* (nominative *jūbilāns*), present participle of *jūbilāre* to shout for joy, related to *jūbilum* wild shout. Cognates are found in Middle High German *jū, jūch* shout of joy, *jūchezen* to shout with joy (modern German *jauchzen*), and Middle Low German *jōlen* to rejoice, jubilate, from Indo-European **yū* (exclamation of joy) (Pok.514). —**jubilate** *v.* rejoice, exult. Before 1641, probably a back formation from *jubilation;* for suffix see -ATE[1]. —**jubilation** *n.* Probably before 1375 *jubylacion;* borrowed through Old French *jubilacion* and from Latin *jūbilātiōnem* (nominative *jūbilātiō*), from *jūbilāre;* for suffix see -ATION.

jubilee *n.* fiftieth anniversary. Before 1382, in the Wycliffe Bible; borrowed from Old French *jubilé,* from Late Latin *jūbilaeus* the jubilee year; originally, of the *jubilee,* alteration (by association with Latin *jūbilāre* to shout with joy; see JUBILANT) of Greek *iōbēlaîos,* from *iṓbēlos,* from Hebrew *yōbhēl* a shout of joy; originally, trumpet or ram's horn.

The original reference of *jubilee* was the year of emancipation of slaves and restoration of lands to be celebrated according to the Bible (Leviticus 25) every fiftieth year. The jubilee was proclaimed by the sound of a ram's horn on the Day of Atonement.

The transferred sense of a time or season of rejoicing, is first recorded about 1450. It was influenced by Latin *jūbilāre* JUBILATE or English *jubilation.* In the late 1800's *jubilee* was extended in meaning to any anniversary, such as a silver jubilee (25th anniversary) and diamond jubilee (60th or 75th anniversary).

Judaism *n.* Before 1400 *Iudaisme* religion of the Jews; borrowed, probably through Old French *Judaïsme,* and directly from Late Latin *Jūdāismus,* from Greek *Ioudāïsmós,* from *Ioudaîos* JEW; for suffix see -ISM. —**Judaic** *adj.* of Jews or Judaism. 1611, borrowed probably through Middle French *judaïque,* and directly from Latin *Jūdāicus,* from Greek *Ioudāïkós,* from *Ioudaîos* Jew; for suffix see -IC. In some instances *Judaic* was probably a shortened form of earlier *Judaical* (1464).

judge *n.* About 1303 *juge,* in Mannyng's *Handlyng Synne;* possibly from the verb in English, and borrowed from Old French *juge,* from Latin *jūdicem* (nominative *jūdex*), a compound of *jūs* right or law, and the root of *dīcere* say; see JUST and DICTION. The general meaning of one who decides a question, an expert or umpire, is first recorded in Chaucer's translation of Boethius' *De Consolatione Philosophiae.* The meaning of umpire in a contest, is also found in Chaucer's writings, in the *Canterbury Tales* (about 1385). —**v.** act as judge; interpret the law. Probably before 1200 *jugen, juggen* form an opinion or estimate about, interpret, decide, judge, in *Ancrene Riwle;* borrowed through Anglo-French *juger,* from Old French *jugier* to judge, from Latin *jūdicāre,* from *jūdicem* judge.

The spelling with *-dg-* is not found in English before 1469 and was not established until the 1500's, and follows the spelling pattern representing the sound changes in late Middle English as found in *-gg-* to *-dge;* see note at DRUDGE.

—**judgment** *n.* Before 1250 *jugement, juggement* capacity for making decisions, act of judging, decision, in a version of *Ancrene Riwle;* borrowed from Old French *jugement,* from *jugier* to judge.

judicatory (jü′dəkətôr′ē) *adj.* of or having to do with judgment or justice. 1603, in Florio's translation of Montaigne's *Essays;* borrowed from French *judicatoire,* from Late Latin *jūdicātōrius* judicial, from Latin *jūdicāre* to JUDGE; for suffix see -ORY.

judicial *adj.* of or having to do with courts, judges, or justice. Before 1382, in the Wycliffe Bible; borrowed from Latin *jūdiciālis* of or belonging to a court of justice, from *jūdicium* judgment or decision, from *jūdicem* (nominative *jūdex*) JUDGE; for suffix see -IAL.

judiciary *adj.* 1604, forming a judgment, especially in reference to astrology, discerning; 1611, relating to the courts or the administration of justice; reborrowed, perhaps through French *judiciare,* from Latin *jūdiciārius* of or belonging to a court of justice, from *jūdicium* judgment. An earlier use of *judiciary,* adj. (borrowed directly from Latin), is found in the Wycliffe text *The Lantern of Light* (before 1415), but the word does not appear again in the record of English for almost 200 years. —**n.** 1802, branch of government that administers justice; earlier, art of divination (1587); borrowed from Medieval Latin *judiciarius* judge, justice, from Latin *jūdiciārius;* see the adjective above.

judicious *adj.* showing good judgment, wise, sensible. 1598; borrowed from Middle French *judicieux* (feminine *judicieuse*), from Latin *jūdicium* judgment, from *jūdicem* (nominative *jūdex*) JUDGE; for suffix see -IOUS.

judo (jü′dō) *n.* modern form of jujitsu developed in 1882 by Jigoro Kano, a Japanese sportsman. 1889, borrowing of Japanese *jūdō* (*jū* softness, gentleness; see JUJITSU, + *dō* way, art, from Chinese *tao* way).

jug *n.* container for liquids. Before 1477 *jugge,* variant of *jubbe,* in a version of Chaucer's *Canterbury Tales,* of uncertain origin (sometimes proposed as a use of the proper name *Jug,* a familiar alteration of the female name *Judith* or of *Joan,* used formerly as a common noun in addressing a maidservant, sweetheart, or mistress). The slang sense of prison or jail is first recorded in 1815-16 but is now archaic.

jugate (jü′gāt) *adj.* placed side by side; joined, as two busts or heads on a coin. 1887, borrowed from Latin *jugātus,* past participle of *jugāre* join together, from *jugum* YOKE; for suffix see -ATE[1]. **—n.** button showing two heads, as of a Presidential candidate and his running mate. 1974, American English; from the adjective.

juggernaut (jug′ərnôt) *n.* 1865, relentless, crushing force or object, Longfellow quoted in a biography (published 1891). A figurative use of earlier *Juggernaut* a huge cart or wagon bearing an image of the Hindu god Krishna (1814). The cart was drawn annually in a procession at Puri (also known as Jagannath or Juggernaut), a city of Orissa in eastern India; it is said that formerly many devotees allowed themselves to be crushed under the wheels of the cart as a sacrifice to the god.

Juggernaut, meaning the cart, was an altered form and extended sense of earlier *Jaggarnat* a title of Krishna (1638); borrowed from Hindi *Jagannāth,* literally, lord of the world, from Sanskrit *Jagannātha-s* (*jágat* world; literally, moving + *nāthá-s* lord, master). Sanskrit *jágat* is neuter singular participle of a lost verb **jágāti* goes, coexisting with *jígāti* goes, cognate with Greek *bibâs* (genitive *bibántos*) striding, from Indo-European **gwā-/gwə-* (Pok.463). Sanskrit *nāthá-s* lord, patron, protector is related to *nāthá-m* refuge, help, but is of unknown origin.

British English *juggernaut* has been used since the 1940's to refer to any very large and heavy vehicle, especially a truck.

juggle *v.* About 1378 *jogelen* entertain by clowning or performing tricks, in a version of *Piers Plowman;* probably, in part a back formation from *juggler,* and also a borrowing from Old French *jogler,* from Latin *joculārī* to joke, from *joculus,* diminutive of *jocus* JOKE. The figurative meaning of play tricks, deceive, is first recorded about 1400, followed by that of change by trickery, about 1590. **—juggler** *n.* Probably before 1200 *juglur* an entertainer, in *Ancrene Riwle;* developed from Late Old English *gēogelere* magician, conjuror (before 1100); borrowed through Anglo-French *jugelur, jogelour,* from Old French (accusative) *jogleor,* from Latin *joculātōrem* (nominative *joculātor*) joker, from *joculārī* to joke; for suffix see -OR[2].

jugular (jug′yələr) *adj.* of the neck or throat. 1597, borrowed, perhaps through Middle French *jugulaire,* and directly from New Latin *jugularis,* from Latin *jugulum* collarbone, throat, neck, diminutive formation of *jugum* yoke; related to *jungere* to JOIN. **—n.** jugular vein. 1615, from the adjective.

juice *n.* About 1300 *jus;* borrowed from Old French *jus,* from Latin *jūs* broth, sauce, juice; cognate with Sanskrit *yū́s* broth, Old Prussian *juse* meat broth, Old Slavic *jucha* broth or soup, Old Icelandic *ostr* cheese, and perhaps with Greek *zȳ́mē* leaven, and *zymós* broth, soup, from Indo-European **yōus-/yōs-/yūs-* (Pok.507). The spelling *juyse* is first recorded probably before 1425, followed by *juyce* (*iuyce*) in 1533, and *juice* (*iuice*) in 1553. **—juicy** *adj.* Before 1420 *jousy* full of juice, in Lydgate's *Troy Book;* from *jus* juice. The informal figurative meaning of full of interest, lively, is first recorded in Darwin's letters (1838).

jujitsu (jüjit′sü) *n.* Japanese method of fighting without weapons. 1875 *jiu-jitsu,* from Japanese *jūjutsu* (*jū* softness, gentleness, from Chinese *jou* soft, gentle + *jutsu* art, science, from Chinese *shu, shut*).

jujube (jü′jüb) *n.* Before 1400, datelike fruit of an Asiatic tree; borrowed through Middle French *jujube,* or directly from Medieval Latin *jujuba,* from the plural of Vulgar Latin **zizupum,* from Latin *zizyphum* the jujube tree, from Greek *zízyphon,* from Persian *zayzafūn.* The meaning of a small tablet of gummy candy (flavored with the datelike jujube fruit) is first recorded in 1835 and is generally pronounced jü′jü bē′.

jukebox *n.* coin-operated record-playing machine. 1937, American English, a compound of *juke* (1935) cheap roadside inn or brothel + *box;* so called from the use of jukeboxes in small inexpensive restaurants and bars sometimes called "juke joints." The word *juke* was probably borrowed from Gullah *juke, joog* disorderly, wicked, from a West African language (compare Bambara *dzugu* wicked, Wolof *dzug* to live wickedly).

julep (jü′ləp) *n.* Before 1400, syrup, sweet drink in which medicine was given; borrowed from: 1) Old French *julep,* from Spanish *julepe;* and 2) Medieval Latin *julapium;* both the Spanish and Medieval Latin from Arabic *julab,* from Persian *gulāb* rose water (*gul* rose + *āb* water, from Old Persian *āpi-,* cognate with Sanskrit *ā́pas,* pl., water, from Indo-European **ap-/āp-* (Pok.51)). The meaning of alcoholic drink flavored with mint, blackberry, etc., is first recorded in 1787 in American English.

July *n.* Before 1121 *Julie;* later *Juyl* (before 1393); borrowed through Anglo-French *Julie,* from Old French *Jule, Juil,* from Latin *Jūlius,* from the name of Gaius *Jūlius* Caesar, the Roman general and statesman, born in this month, then called *Quintīlis* (fifth month, March at the time of Caesar's birth being the first month). The modern pronunciation of *July,* with the stress on the last syllable, is of relatively recent origin and remains unexplained. As late as the mid-1700's *July* was pronounced jü′lī and is so heard in much of the southern United States, in accordance with the accentuation of the name Julius from which the word derives.

jumble *v.* Before 1529, in Skelton's *Speke Parrot,* to move about in disorder and confusion, perhaps a coinage on the pattern of *stumble, tumble, fumble,* etc. The meaning of mix, muddle, or confuse, is first recorded in 1542.

An earlier form *jumbeled* made double (about 1460) is probably a separate form related to *gemelled* paired or doubled but without any seeming connection to *jumble.*

—n. confused mixture. 1661, from the verb.

jumbo *n.* big, clumsy person, animal, or thing. 1883, American English, from the name of *Jumbo,* a huge elephant (12 feet tall, and 6 ½ tons) purchased in 1882 from the London Zoological Gardens by the American showman P.T. Barnum. The name was probably taken from the earlier English slang term *Jumbo* a clumsy or unwieldy fellow, recorded in 1823 in John Badcock's *A Dictionary of Turf;* possibly abstracted from *Mumbo-Jumbo* grotesque bogy or idol (1738); see MUMBO-JUMBO. **—adj.** very big. 1897, American English; from the noun.

jump *v.* Before 1460 *jumpen* (probably with the meaning of walk quickly or jump); probably borrowed from the Gallo-Romance dialects of southwestern France during the English occupation of that region (compare *jumbá* to rock, balance, swing; *yumpá* to rock; also surviving in Sardinian *iumpare* to jump). The word *jump* may also have acquired an onomatopoeic flavor which was instrumental in its borrowing into English. If *jump* is of imitative origin, parallel forms may be found in Middle High German and Low German *gumpen* to jump or hop, and possibly Swedish *guppa* to jump. —**n.** act of jumping. 1552, in Huloet's *Abecedarium Anglico-Latinum;* from the verb. —**jumper**[1] *n.* 1611, person or thing that jumps; formed from English *jump,* v. + *-er*[1]. —**jumpy** *adj.* 1869, moving by jumps; 1879, nervous, easily frightened; formed from English *jump,* n. + *-y*[1].

jumper[2] *n.* loose jacket. 1853, apparently derived from earlier *jump* short coat (1653), also kind of woman's under bodice (1666); of uncertain origin; perhaps developed from a nasalized form of *jupe* (about 1300), borrowed from Old French *juppe* woman's jacket or bodice, from Old Provençal *jupa,* from Spanish *aljuba* and Italian *giubba,* from Arabic *jubba* long open coat. From the evidence available the borrowing of *jumper* in this sense from French has phonetic difficulties and is semantically questionable, as *jupe* is found in modern English with the meaning of loose jacket (1837), woman's bodice (1859), and woman's shirt (1886). The application of *jumper* to a sleeveless dress worn over a blouse is first recorded in 1939 in American English.

junco (jungʹkō) *n.* small North American finch. 1706, in Phillips' *Dictionary;* borrowed from Spanish *junco* rush or reed, as in *junco ave* a bird of the Indies, with a very long, narrow tail, and *rabo de junco* a bird of New Guinea (literally, reed tail); see JONQUIL.

junction *n.* 1711, a joining, union, combination, Addison in *The Spectator;* borrowed, perhaps by influence of French *jonction,* from Latin *jūnctiōnem* (nominative *jūnctiō*), from *jungere* to JOIN; for suffix see -TION. The general sense of a place of joining, especially where railroad lines or highways meet, is first recorded in 1841, and was apparently derived from former proper names of canals and railways, such as *Grand Junction Canal* and *South Western Junction Railway.*

juncture *n.* Before 1382, a joining, joint, in the Wycliffe Bible; borrowed from Latin *jūnctūra,* from *jungere* to JOIN; for suffix see -URE. The meaning of a point of time, especially one made critical by a concurrence of events, is first recorded in 1656.

June *n.* 1110 *Junie;* later *June* (probably before 1300, in *Arthour and Merlin;* developed from Old English (about 1050) *Junius;* borrowed from Latin *Jūnius,* probably a variant of *Jūnōnius,* sacred to the goddess *Jūnō.* The Middle English form *Juyn* (recorded before 1387) was borrowed from Old French *Juin,* from Latin *Jūnius.*

jungle *n.* wild land. 1776, borrowed from Hindi *jaṅgal* desert, forest, wasteland, from Middle Indic **jaṅgala-s* desert or dry ground, from Sanskrit *jāṅgala-s* arid or sparingly grown with trees and plants. The Sanskrit is perhaps cognate with Lithuanian *žāgaras* dry branch. The figurative meaning of a wild, tangled mass (as in *a jungle of red tape*), is first recorded in 1850, in Carlyle's *Latter-day Pamphlets.* The sense of a place where the law of the jungle prevails, place of ruthless competition, violence, or disorder, is first found in American English, in Upton Sinclair's *The Jungle* (1906). —**jungle gum** (1923, in American English as a trademark)

junior *adj.* 1296 *Junior* the younger (in a Latin context); later, in a list of names (1311-1423) and in an English context (1448); borrowed from Latin *jūnior* (from pre-Latin *juveniōs*), comparative of *juvenis* YOUNG. The meaning of youthful, is first recorded in English in 1606, and that referring to lower standing or rank, in 1766, but *junior* as in *Junior Class,* in a school or college, is first recorded in 1720, in American English. —**n.** younger person. 1526, from the adjective.

juniper *n.* evergreen shrub or tree. About 1390; earlier, a desert shrub of Biblical times (before 1382, in the Wycliffe Bible); borrowed from Latin *jūniperus,* of uncertain origin. The first element *jūni-* is perhaps related to *juncus* reed, rush; see JONQUIL.

junk[1] *n.* old or discarded objects of little or no value. 1338 *junke, jonke* an old cable or rope (a nautical use), document in N.H. Nicolas' *A History of the Royal Navy;* of uncertain origin (possibly the same word as *junke, jonke* rush, a plant with hollow stems used for mats, baskets, etc.; borrowed from Old French *jonc, junc* rush, reed, from Latin *juncus;* see JONQUIL).

The original nautical meaning of *junk* was extended to any piece of old cable or rope material cut up and used to make fenders, gaskets, etc., in Pepys' *Diary* (1666). Later the meaning was extended in American English to old refuse articles from boats and ships, such as sold in marine stores (1842), which produced such related compounds as *junk dealer* (1866) and *junkman* (1872), both originally meaning a dealer in marine stores. The meaning of old, secondhand, or discarded articles of any kind, is not recorded until about 1880. Other more recent compounds in American English include *junk jewelry* cheap costume jewelry (1939), *junk mail* circulars, advertisements, etc. sent by mail (1954), *junk food* ready-made or quickly prepared food sold in vending machines, fast-food establishments (1973), and *junk bond* a high-risk noncorporate bond (1976).

—**v.** 1803, to cut off in lumps; later, to scrap (1916); from the noun. —**junkie** *n.* 1923, American English slang, a drug addict; formed from English *junk*[1] narcotic drug + *-ie.* —**junky** *adj.* worthless; trashy. 1946, in George Orwell's *Essays;* formed from English *junk*[1] + *-y*[1].

junk[2] *n.* Chinese sailing ship. 1613, in *Purchas his Pilgrimage;* borrowed from Dutch *jonk,* or directly from Portuguese *junco,* from Malay *jong, ajong,* probably from Javanese *jong.*

Junker or **junker** (yůngʹkər) *n.* member of the formerly privileged class in Prussia. 1554, borrowing of German *Junker,* from Old High German *junchērro,* literally, young lord, a compound of *junc* YOUNG + *hērro* lord or master, from *hēriro* (possibly in imitation of Latin *senior* older), comparative of *hēr* old; see HOAR.

junket *n.* 1382 *ionkett, iunket* a basket made of rushes, in the Wycliffe Bible; probably borrowed from Medieval Latin *juncata* rush basket, basket to carry fish, also perhaps in Old North French *jonquette, *jonquet, *jonket* rush basket, perhaps from *jonc* a rush, from Latin *juncus* rush; see JONQUIL. The word in English probably did not derive from *jonc, jonk* a basket because it is not recorded in English until about 1400.

The sense of a food made of curdled milk or cream,

possibly originally served or eaten from a rush basket, is first recorded in English about 1450. While the sense is found in Norman dialect, it was probably also borrowed into English from Italian *giuncata* creamed curds served on a rush mat, from *giunco* a rush, from Latin *juncus* rush.

The meaning of a feast or banquet is first recorded in Middle English before 1500, but is found earlier in the form *jonkrey* (1443), *junkery* (1449); borrowed from Old French *jonceroi;* the shift in form is obscure. The sense of a pleasure trip is first recorded in 1814 and is an extension of the sense of a feast or banquet, as found in a compound like *junket basket* for picnic basket (1825).

junta (jun′tə *or* hu̇n′tə) *n.* political or military group in power, especially after a revolution. 1623, Spanish council for deliberation or administration; borrowed from Spanish *junta* council, borrowed from Medieval Latin *juncta* joint, from Latin *jūncta,* feminine past participle of *jungere* to JOIN. The meaning of a political or military group in power is first recorded in Swift's *Some Free Thoughts Upon the Present State of Affairs* (1714).

junto (jun′tō) *n.* faction, clique, cabal. 1641, alteration of *junta,* probably by confusion with Spanish nouns ending in *-o* owing to the vagueness of final unstressed vowels in English, as in *cargo,* from Spanish *carga,* and *bravado,* from Spanish *bravada.*

juridical (ju̇rid′əkəl) *adj.* having to do with the administration of justice. 1584, formed in English from Latin *jūridicus* (*jūs* right or law, genitive *jūris* + *dīcere* say or speak) + English suffix *-al*[1].

It is possible *juridical* was influenced in its formation by Middle French *juridique* in the same process as English *typical* from French *typique,* and *hypothetical* from *hypothétique.*

jurisdiction *n.* right or power of administering law or justice. Before 1325 *jurediction, jurediccioun* legal power, authority, in *Cursor Mundi;* later *jurisdiccioun* (about 1390); borrowed from Old French *juridiction, jurediction,* learned borrowing from Latin *jūrisdictiōnem* (nominative *jūrisdictiō*), a compound of *jūs* (genitive *jūris*) right, law + *dictiōnem* (nominative *dictiō*) a saying.

The appearance of medial *s* in later Middle English *jurisdiccioun* comes from the influence of the spelling in Latin.

jurisprudence *n.* science or philosophy of law. 1628, in Sir Edward Coke's writings; borrowed, probably in some instances through French *jurisprudence,* and directly from Late Latin *jūrisprūdentia* the science of law, a compound of *jūris* right or law (genitive of *jūs*) + *prūdentia* knowledge, from *prūdentem* PRUDENT.

jurist *n.* expert in law. 1481, in Caxton's translation of *The Mirror of the World;* borrowed from Middle French *juriste,* learned borrowing from Medieval Latin *jurista,* from Latin *jūs* (genitive *jūris*) law; see JUST; for suffix see -IST.

jury[1] *n.* group of persons selected to hear evidence in a law court. 1398, in compound *jurybook;* probably before 1400 *jure* group of men in England sworn to deliver a verdict; later *jurie* (1436); borrowed through Anglo-French *juree,* Old French *jurée* oath or inquest, from *jurer* to swear, from Latin *jūrāre* to swear, from *jūs* (genitive *jūris*) law; see JUST; for suffix see -Y[4]. The word is found earlier in Latin texts in England from 1188. **—juror** *n.* member of a jury. 1301 *jurour;* borrowed through Anglo-French *jurour,* Old French *jureor,* from Latin *jūrātōrem* (nominative *jūrātor*) swearer, from *jūrāre* to swear; for suffix see -OR[2].

jury[2] *adj. Nautical.* for temporary use on a ship; makeshift. 1616, in *jurymast;* probably borrowed ultimately from Old French *ajurie* help or relief, from Latin *adjūtāre* to AID; for suffix see -ERY.

just *adj.* right, fair. Before 1375, having correct fit, as of clothes or armor; later, fair or righteous (about 1380, in Chaucer's translation of Boethius' *De Consolatione Philosophiae*); borrowed from Old French *juste,* learned borrowing from Latin *jūstus* (Old Latin *jovestos) upright or equitable, from jūs* (genitive *jūris*) right or law, from original **yéwos,* but of unknown origin. **—adv.** exactly, barely, only. Probably before 1400, in *Morte Arthur;* from the adjective.

justice *n.* 1140, quality of being fair, just; borrowed from Old French *justise, justice,* learned borrowing from Latin *jūstitia* righteousness, equity, from *jūstus* upright, JUST.

justify *v.* About 1378 *justifien* govern; rule, have charge, in a version of *Piers Plowman;* before 1382 *justefien* prove to be just or right, clear of blame or guilt, in the Wycliffe Bible; borrowed from Old French *justifier,* learned borrowing from Latin *jūstificāre* act justly toward, do justice to, make just, justify, from *jūstificus* dealing justly, righteous (*jūstus* JUST + the root of *facere* to DO[1] perform); for suffix see -FY. **—justification** *n.* About 1384 *justificacion* act of justifying, correction, rectification, in a version of the Wycliffe Bible; borrowed through Old French *justification,* and directly from Late Latin *jūstificātiōnem* (nominative *jūstificātiō*), from *jūstificāre* justify; for suffix see -ATION.

jut *v.* About 1450 *jutteyen* stick out, project; later *jutt* (1565-73). **—n.** projection. 1786, in Burns' *Brigs of Ayr;* from the verb (but compare earlier *jutei,* variant of Middle English *gete,* n., a projection, jetty, overhang).

jute (jüt) *n.* strong fiber used for making coarse sacks, burlap, rope, etc. 1746, borrowed from Bengali *jhuṭo, jhōṭo,* from Sanskrit *jūṭa-s* twisted hair, mat of hair, probably of Dravidian origin (compare Telugu *juṭṭu* tuft of hair).

juvenile (jü′vənəl) *adj.* young, youthful, childish. 1625, in Francis Bacon's *Essays;* borrowed through French *juvénile,* and directly from Latin *juvenīlis* of or belonging to youth, from *juvenis* young person (usually one between age 21 and 40), from *juvenis* YOUNG. **—n.** young person. 1733, from the adjective. **—juvenile delinquency** (1816)

juxtapose (juk′stəpōz′) *v.* put close together, place side by side. 1851, borrowed from French *juxtaposer,* a compound formed from Latin *juxtā* beside, near + Old French *poser* to place; see JOUST and POSE. **—juxtaposition** *n.* 1665 *juxta-position,* in some instances probably a borrowing of French *juxtaposition* (1664), formed from Latin *juxtā* near + French *position,* from Old French; see POSITION; but also formed in English from Latin *juxtā* near + English *position.*

K

Kabuki or **kabuki** (kəbü′kē) *n.* traditional Japanese drama, using highly stylized singing and dancing. 1899, borrowing of Japanese *kabuki* art of song and dance (*ka* song + *bu* dance + *ki* art).

kaffeeklatsch (kä′fäkläch′) *n.* informal gathering at which coffee is served. 1903, borrowing of German *Kaffeeklatsch* coffee party (*Kaffee* coffee + *Klatsch* party, chatter, gossip, from *klatschen* to gossip, chatter; of imitative origin).

Kaiser or **kaiser** (kī′zər) *n.* title of the former emperors of Germany and Austria. 1858, in Carlyle's *History of Friedrich II (Frederick the Great);* borrowing of German *Kaiser,* from Old High German *keisar* emperor, an early borrowing from Latin *Caesar* CAESAR. Similar borrowings are found in Old Saxon *kēsur, kēsar* emperor, Old Frisian *keisar, keiser,* Old English *cāsere,* Old Icelandic *keisari,* and Gothic *káisar.* However, the Gothic form abstracted from *káisara-gild* tribute money, is possibly borrowed from Greek since Latin *ae* ordinarily became *ē* in loanwords in Gothic. In the sense of a Roman emperor, a Caesar, or an emperor, ruler, the forms *keiser* and *kaiser* appeared in Middle English (probably before 1200), apparently as a borrowing of Middle High German *keisar,* and eventually replacing Middle English *kaser* (recorded about 1200) which developed from Old English *cāsere.*

kale *n.* cabbage with loose leaves. Before 1300 *kale;* earlier *cawul* (probably about 1200), eventually becoming a variant (Scots) form of COLE.

kaleidoscope (kəlī′dəskōp) *n.* 1817, formed in English from Greek *kal-,* the root of *kalós* beautiful + *eido-,* the stem of *eîdos* shape + English *-scope.* Greek *kalós* (Boeotian *kalwos*), cognate with Sanskrit *kalyā́ṇa-s* beautiful, is from Indo-European **kal-* (Pok.524). Greek *eîdos* shape, look is related to *ideîn* see; see WIT. The term was coined by its inventor, the Scottish physicist Sir David Brewster, 1781-1868. The figurative meaning of a constantly changing pattern is first recorded in Byron's *Don Juan* (1819).

kamikaze (kä′məkä′zē) *n.* Japanese suicide pilot or his aircraft, in World War II. 1945, American English, borrowing of Japanese *kamikaze* suicide corps; literally, divine or providential wind (*kami* god, providence, divine + *kaze* wind). *Kamikaze* was originally a name given in Japanese lore to a typhoon which in August 1281 saved Japan from invading Mongols by destroying their navy. **—adj.** extremely reckless. 1955, American English (originally applied by American occupational forces to taxi drivers in Japan); from the noun.

kangaroo *n.* mammal of Australia and New Guinea. 1770 *kangooroo, kanguru,* in Captain James Cook's and Joseph Banks' *Journals.* The term is recorded by both men as the native name of the animal among the aborigines at Endeavour River (now Cooktown), in northeastern Queensland, Australia. However, since the name is in dispute according to some sources in the OED, there is no definite explanation for its existence before the time of Cook and Banks, some even saying that though *kangaroo* may have been a localism, it also may have been a mistranscription of a local name.

The term *kangaroo court,* meaning an unauthorized or illegal court, originated in American English and was first recorded in Philip Paxton's *A Stray Yankee in Texas* (1853), where it refers to an irregularly conducted court which was also called a "mustang" court.

kaolin or **kaoline** (kā′əlin) *n.* fine white clay, used in making porcelain. 1727-41, in an edition of *Chambers Cyclopaedia;* borrowing of French *kaolin,* in allusion to *Kao-ling,* transliteration of the name of a mountain in China (*kao* high + *ling* mountain, hill) near which this material was originally obtained.

kapok (kā′pok) *n.* silky fibers around the seeds of a tropical tree. 1858; earlier *capoc* (1750); borrowed from Malay *kapok.*

kaput or **kaputt** (kəpüt′) *adj. Informal.* finished, dead, done for, broken (of a device or machine). 1895, borrowing of German *kaputt,* probably abstracted from the earlier phrase *capot machen,* a partial translation by false interpretation of *faire* in the French *faire capot* be defeated, from its use in the game of piquet where the phrase refers to losing all the tricks in a game; ultimately from *capot* cover or bonnet, from Middle French *cape* cloak, CAPE[1].

karat *n.* See CARAT.

karate (kərä′tē) *n.* Japanese method of fighting without weapons by striking vulnerable parts of the opponent's body. 1955, borrowing in transliteration from Japanese *karate,* literally, empty hand or bare hand (*kara* empty + *te* hand).

karyotype (kar′ēōtīp) *n. Biology.* the typical character or makeup of a cell nucleus. 1929, American English; probably borrowed from French *caryotype* (*caryo-* cell nucleus, from Greek *káryon* nut or kernel + *type,* from Late Latin *typus* form, character, type). According to the OEDS the word was apparently originally proposed by the Russian biologist G.A. Lewitsky in 1924, but the first recorded use in English is in an American technical journal in 1929.

katydid (kā′tidid) *n.* large green grasshopper. 1784, American English, formed in imitation of the sound made by the male when it rubs its front wings together. The sound was described in 1751 in John Bartram's *Observations* (a record of his travels from Pennsylvania to Lake Ontario) as *catedidist.*

katzenjammer (kät′sənyä′mər) *n. Informal.* headache, nausea, etc. following drunkenness; hangover. 1849, American English; borrowed from German *Katzenjammer,* literally, cats' wailing (*Katzen,* plural of *Katze* cat and *Jammer* a wailing, distress, from Old High German *jāmar,* cognate with Old Saxon *jāmar,* and Old English *geōmor* lamentable, from Proto-Germanic **jǣmeraz,* of unknown origin). The figurative meaning of a bad reaction, depression, distress, is first recorded in 1897. The meaning of uproar, clamor, discord (1922), was probably influenced by the *Katzenjammer Kids,* a comic strip which appeared from 1897 in the *New York Journal,* drawn by the American cartoonist Rudolph Dirks.

kayak (kī′ak) *n.* Eskimo canoe. 1757 *kajak,* borrowed, possibly through Danish which may have had the first written form of the word (after Denmark exercised sovereignty over Greenland in 1721), from Eskimo (as spoken in Greenland) *kajakka,* literally, small boat of skins. Earlier reference is made to such boats without use of the name in Hakluyt's *Voyages* (1576). About 1936 *kayak* began to appear in the sense of a canoe similar to the Eskimo kayak, as the boat was used for sport and recreation. **—v.** 1875, from the noun.

kayo (kā′ō′) *v. Slang.* knock out. 1923, American English, spelling for the pronunciation of *K.O.,* abbreviation of *knock out* (in boxing). **—n.** a knockout in boxing. 1933, American English, spelling for the pronunciation of *K.O.,* abbreviation of *knockout* (in boxing), probably influenced by the verb use.

kazoo (kəzü′) *n.* tubelike instrument for humming or singing into. 1884, American English, possibly alteration of earlier *bazoo* trumpet (1877); see BAZOOKA.

kea (kā′ə *or* kē′ə) *n.* large parrot of New Zealand. 1862, borrowed from Maori *kea,* perhaps imitative of the parrot's cry.

keel *n.* main timber or metal piece that extends the length of the bottom of a ship or boat. 1338 *kelle;* later *kele* (1410); borrowed probably from a Scandinavian source (compare Old Icelandic *kjǫlr* keel, Norwegian *kjøl,* Danish *køl,* Swedish *köl*). The Scandinavian forms are cognate with Middle Low German *kil, kel* keel (modern German *Kiel*), Middle Dutch and modern Dutch *kiel,* from Proto-Germanic **keluz,* related to Old High German *kéla* throat, beak of a ship, from Indo-European **gel-* swallow (Pok.365) **—v.** turn up the keel of, turn over, capsize, primarily in the phrase *keel over.* 1828, American English; from the noun.

keelson or **kelson** (kel′sən *or* kēl′sən) *n.* timbers or metal plates fastened along the top of a ship's keel to strengthen it. 1627 *keelson,* in Captain John Smith's *The Seaman's Grammar;* alteration (influenced by *keel*) of earlier *kelsine* (about 1611, in Chapman's translation of Homer's *Iliad*), and *kilson* (before 1618, in Sir Walter Raleigh's *Royal Navy*), from Middle English *kelsyng* (1402), earlier *kelswyne* (1347-50), and *kelswayn* (1296); probably borrowed from a Scandinavian source (compare Swedish *kölsvin* keelson, Danish and Norwegian *kjølsvin,* all derived from the root of Old Icelandic *kjǫlr* KEEL) + *swīn* SWINE, used for a timber, from Proto-Germanic **swīnaz,* from Indo-European **swīnos* (Pok.1038).

keen[1] *adj.* sharp, acute. Probably before 1200 *kene, kenne* bold, brave, daring, sharp-pointed, trenchant, wise, in Layamon's *Chronicle of Britain;* developed from Old English (before 725) *cēne* bold, brave, clever, wise. Old English *cēne* is cognate with Middle Dutch *coene* bold, daring (modern Dutch *koen*), Old High German *kuoni* (modern German *kühn*), Old Icelandic *kœnn* wise, clever, able; related to *kan* know, from Proto-Germanic **kan-/kōn-,* Indo-European **ĝon-/ĝōn-* (Pok.378); see CAN[1] be able to, and KEN.

The informal sense of wonderful, perfect, is first recorded in 1914 in American English.

keen[2] *v.* to wail or lament. 1811, implied in *keener* one who keens; borrowed from Irish *caoinim* I weep, wail, lament, from Old Irish *coínim, caínim.* **—n.** wailing lament for the dead. 1830, borrowed from Irish *caoine,* from *caoinim* I weep, wail, lament.

keep *v.* 1127 *kepen* watch for, observe, retain, hold, take, keep; developed from Old English (about 1000) *cēpan* (from Proto-Germanic **kōpjanan*), possibly related to *capian* to look. Old English *capian* is cognate with Old Saxon *capen* in *upcapen* stand out, be visible, Middle Low German *kapen* to gape, Old High German *kapfēn* to look, and Old Icelandic *kōpa* to stare, gape, from Proto-Germanic **kap-/kōp,* Indo-European **ĝab-/ĝāb-* watch, look out for (Pok.349).

In the OED, Murray states, "The word probably belonged primarily to the vulgar and nonliterary stratum of the language; but it comes up suddenly into literary use about 1000, and that in many senses, indicating considerable previous development." Murray felt the original sense may have been "to lay hold" in the literal sense and so extended figuratively to "keep an eye on, watch," citing its use to render Latin *observāre* to watch, take note of, and Latin *servāre* to watch, observe. He states further that there is an underlying semantic relation between *keep* and *hold,* and further with *have* explaining that the same senses have alternated in use among these words.

—n. About 1250 *kep* care or heed in watching, concern, charge; from *kepen* to keep. The meaning of food required to keep a person or animal, sustenance, support, is recorded before 1825. The historical sense of a central tower or stronghold of a medieval castle is found in Sidney's *Arcadia* (before 1586). **—keeper** *n.* 1279, in the surname *Kepere;* from *keep,* v. + *-er*[1].

keg *n.* 1632, variant of earlier *kag* (1452); borrowed from a Scandinavian source (compare Old Icelandic *kaggi* keg, cask, Swedish *kagge,* Norwegian *kagg, kagge*); origin uncertain.

kelp *n.* large brown seaweed. 1663, dialectal variation of earlier *kilpe* (1601); developed from *culp* or *culpe* (before 1387, in Trevisa's translation of Higden's *Polychronicon*); of unknown origin.

kempt *adj.* neat, trim, well-groomed. Probably about 1378 *kempt* well-combed, neat, in Wycliffe's *Works;* from past participle of *kemben* to comb; developed from Old English *cemban* (about 1000, in Ælfric's *Grammar*). Old English *cemban* is cognate with Old Saxon *kembian, kemmian* to comb, Middle Dutch *kemmen,* Old High German *kemben, chempen* (modern German *kämmen*), Old Icelandic *kemba,* and Danish *kæmme;* all forms derived from the Proto-Germanic **kambjan,* from *kamb-* COMB, *n.* Though *kemben* was largely displaced by *comb,* v., and *kemb* appears infrequently after the 1400's, its use has been stimulated lately as a quaint back formation from *unkempt.*

ken *v. Scottish.* to know, recognize, or understand. Probably before 1200 *kennen,* in Layamon's *Chronicle of Britain;* developed from Old English *cennan* make known, declare, acknowledge (about 725, in *Beowulf*). Introduction of the sense of know (in distinction to make known) found in Old English *cunnan to* to know, was probably influenced by Old Icelandic *kenna* to know, which is cognate with Old Frisian *kanna, kenna* to know, Old Saxon *kennian,* Middle Dutch and modern Dutch *kennen,* Old High German *chennan, kennen,* Middle High German and modern German *kennen,* and Gothic *kannjan* make known, from Indo-European **ĝon-* (Pok.378); see KEEN. **—n.** 1545, distance one can see, especially at sea; earlier found in *kenning* sight or view (probably before 1400), and *kennan* to know, recognize, catch sight of, see. *Ken,* in the sense of mental perception or recognition, is first recorded about 1560, *kenning* in the same sense, before 1325, in *Cursor Mundi.*

kennel *n.* 1301 *kenil,* 1302 *kennel;* borrowed probably from dialectal Old French **kenil,* from Old French *chenil,* from Vulgar Latin **canīle,* from Latin *canis* dog; see HOUND. **—v.** put or keep in a kennel. 1552, to lie in a kennel; from the noun. The meaning of put or keep in a kennel is first recorded in Shakespeare's *Venus and Adonis* (1592).

keratin (ker′ətin) *n.* complex protein, the chief component of horn, nails, etc. 1847-49, formed in English from Greek *kéras* (genitive *kératos*) HORN + English *-in*[2] (chemical suffix).

kerchief *n.* cloth for covering the head. 1223 *kovrechief;* later in the syncopated form *curchef* (before 1325, in *Cursor Mundi*) and *kerchef* (before 1387); borrowed through Anglo-French *courchief,* and directly from Old French *couvrechief* a kerchief; literally, cover-head (*couvrir, covrir* to COVER + *chief* head; see CHIEF). The compounds *neckerchief (neck + kerchief)* and *handkerchief* appeared in close succession, 1384 and 1530, respectively.

kernel *n.* Probably before 1200 *curnel* kernel of grain; later, any seed (about 1300), and with the spelling *kernel* (1381); developed from Old English *cyrnel* (about 1000 in Ælfric's *Homilies*), formed from *corn* seed, grain + *-el* (diminutive suffix); see CORN.

kerosene or **kerosine** *n.* 1852, Canadian English; formed from Greek *kērós* wax + English *-ene* (suffix used in names of pure hydrocarbons). Reference to the Greek word for wax comes from the fact that kerosene contains paraffin in some stages of preparation (in British English kerosene is called *paraffin oil*). Its other name *coal oil* is associated with its original distillation from albertite (a bituminous mineral resembling coal) by the Canadian physician and geologist Abraham Gesner, 1797-1864, who discovered the process about 1846 and patented it in 1854.

The spelling *kerosine,* first recorded in 1864, was adopted in 1925 by the American Society for Testing Materials on the analogy of *gasoline* and to restrict the suffix *-ene* to pure hydrocarbons.

kestrel (kes′trəl) *n.* small European falcon. 1602, variant of earlier *castrell* (before 1500 with development of *t* between *s* and *r*); borrowed probably from Middle French *cresserelle, cresselle, quercelle,* apparently related to *crecerelle, crecelle* rattle, from Gallo-Romance **crepicella,* from Latin *crepitācillum* small rattle, diminutive of *crepitāculum* rattle, from *crepitāre* to crackle, rattle.

ketch *n.* fore-and-aft-rigged sailing ship. 1655, in Cromwell's *Letters,* variant of earlier *catch* (1443-46), *cacche* (1422), and *cache* (1371-72), probably from Middle English *cacchen* to capture, ensnare, chase; see CATCH. For sense development compare YACHT.

ketchup *n.* sauce made from tomatoes, etc. 1711, borrowed from Malay *kĕchap,* perhaps by influence of earlier *catchup.* Compare the variants *catchup* and *catsup* at CATCHUP.

kettle *n.* 1338 *ketil, ketel;* developed from Old English *cetil* (before 700, in Mercian dialect); borrowed probably directly from Latin *catillus* small bowl, dish, or plate, diminutive of *catīnus* bowl, dish, pot; perhaps cognate with Greek *kotýlē* small vessel, cup. If the word was borrowed from Latin, it was an early borrowing also found in Old Saxon and Middle Dutch *ketel,* Old High German *kezzil* (modern German *Kessel*), Old Icelandic *ketill* and Gothic *katilē,* pl. **—kettledrum** *n.* 1542, in the sense of one who plays the kettledrum.

kewpie (kyü′pē) *n.* trademark for a type of chubby doll with a topknot of hair. 1913, American English; *Kewpie,* an altered and diminutive form of *Cupid.* The name was coined according to their American illustrator "because they look like little Cupids" (Rose C. O'Neill, in *Ladies' Home Journal,* Dec. 18, 1909).

key[1] *n.* small metal piece that operates a lock. Before 1200 *kei, keie;* developed from Old English (before 725) *cǣg;* cognate with Old Frisian *kēi, kāi,* and perhaps with Middle Low German *keie, keige* lance, spear, of unknown origin. The figurative meaning of something that unlocks and discloses, solution or explanation, is found in Old English (about 897, in Alfred's translation of St. Gregory's *Pastoral Care*).

The musical sense of a scale or system of tones probably appeared much earlier, as found in the meaning of a note, a tone (before 1450), but the sense of a scale is not recorded before its use in Shakespeare's *Midsummer Night's Dream* (1590). Originally, it may have been a translation of Latin *clāvis* (or French *clef*), after the solmization system of Guido d'Arezzo, in which *clāvis* meant a note or tone, especially the keynote or tonic.

—v. 1577, to lock with a key; from the noun. The musical sense of regulate the pitch of, tune, is first recorded in 1636 and from it came the figurative sense of raise to a high pitch or intensity, stimulate, excite, make tense or nervous, in the phrase *key up* (1888, usually in the past participle *keyed up*). Another figurative meaning of provide with a key or explanation, fit or adjust, is found in 1947 in American English. **—adj.** controlling, very important, essential. 1913, in E.C. Bentley's *Trent's Last Case;* from the attributive use of the noun in such phrases as *key cipher* (1605, meaning "solution cipher") and *key book* (1826).

The standard pronunciation of *key* until the end of the 1600's was (kā), as is normal for words ending in *-ǣg* in Old English, for example *clǣg* clay, *grǣg* gray. The modern pronunciation (kē) is apparently of northern or Scottish origin; such spellings as *kee* are found in northern and Scottish manuscripts of the 1400's.

—keyboard *n.* (1819) **—keyhole** *n.* (about 1592) **—keynote** *n.* (1762) **—keystone** *n.* (before 1637, in Ben Jonson's writings)

key[2] *n.* low island, reef. 1697, borrowed from Spanish *cayo,* from Taino *cayo* or *caya* small island. Both the spelling in English and the borrowing from Spanish were influenced by an association with earlier *key* wharf (about 1200 from Old French *cai, kai*).

khaki (kak′ē) *n.* 1857, the color khaki or a fabric of this color; borrowed from Urdu *khākī,* literally, dusty, from *khāk* dust, from Persian.

Khaki was introduced first in uniforms of a British cavalry force in India (the Guide Corps, 1846). Thereafter it became the standard color for field uniforms in the British army and other armies. In the United States *khakis* came to mean a uniform made of khaki fabric (first recorded in 1936).

—**adj.** dull yellowish-brown; dust-colored. 1863, borrowed from Urdu *khākī.*

khan (kän) *n.* title of a ruler among Tartar or Mongol tribes, or of the emperor of China during the Middle Ages. About 1400 *caan,* in Sir John Maundeville's *Travels;* borrowed through Middle French *chan, can* and Medieval Latin *Caanus* from Turkic *khān* lord, prince (in Turkish, *han*), and Mongolian *qā'ān.* The spelling *khan* is first recorded in Gibbon's *The Decline and Fall of the Roman Empire* (1788).

khedive (kədēv′) *n.* Turkish ruler of Egypt between 1867 and 1914. 1867, borrowed through French *khédive,* from Turkish *hidiv* viceroy (of Egypt), from Persian *khidiv* ruler, prince. An earlier form *Quiteve* is recorded in 1625, but the term does not appear again for almost 150 years.

kibbutz (kibüts′) *n.* communal farm or settlement in Israel. 1931, borrowed from modern Hebrew *qibbūṣ,* from Hebrew, a gathering together, from the root of *qibbēṣ* he gathered together. —**kibbutznik** *n.* member of a kibbutz. 1949, in Arthur Koestler's *Promise and Fulfilment;* borrowing of Yiddish *kibutsnik* (*kibuts* kibbutz + *-nik* personal suffix, -NIK).

kibitz (kib′its) *v. Slang.* look on as an outsider and offer unwanted advice, especially in games. 1927, American English; borrowed from Yiddish *kibitsen,* from German *kiebitzen* to look on at cards, to kibitz; originally in thieves' cant, to visit, from *Kiebitz* the European pewit (a shore bird), meddler; later, onlooker at cards, from Middle High German *gībitz, giwiz* pewit, of imitative origin. —**kibitzer** *n. Slang.* onlooker at cards, etc.; meddler. 1927, borrowed from Yiddish *kibitser,* from *kibitsen* to kibitz.

kibosh (kī′bosh) *n. Slang.* **put the kibosh on,** dispose of finally; finish off; do in. 1836 *kye-bosk,* in Dickens' *Sketches by Boz;* of unknown origin.

In 1856 the word appeared in *Punch* with the spelling *cibosh.* The present spelling is first recorded in *The Slang Dictionary* (1869), defined as nonsense, stuff, humbug, a meaning influenced by *bosh* (1850). The form *kye-bosk* is Dickens' representation of a Cockney variant of *kibosh.*

kick *v.* About 1384 *kiken* strike out with the foot, in the Wycliffe Bible in the phrase *kiken ayens the pricke* kick against the pricks, with the sense of show disobedience or defiance to one's own hurt; borrowed perhaps from a Scandinavian source (compare Old Icelandic *kikna* bend backwards, sink at the knees, Norwegian *keike* bend backwards, wrangle; the sense of kick backwards, perhaps appearing in Middle English and thereby making a possible semantic connection). According to the OED the often cited Welsh form *cicio* is derived from English. The spelling with *-ck* appears in the mid-1500's. —**n.** 1530, in Palsgrave's *Lesclarcissement,* a knock or blow with the foot; from the verb.

kid[1] *n.* young goat. Probably before 1200 *kide,* in *The Ormulum;* borrowed from a Scandinavian source (compare Old Icelandic *kidh* young goat, Swedish, Danish, Norwegian *kid,* and Shetland *kidi*). The Scandinavian forms are cognate with Middle High German and East Frisian *kitze* young goat, Old High German *kizzī* (modern German *Kitz, Kitze*). The forms are possibly ultimately imitative of the cry of young goats and sheep.

The extended meaning of a child, especially a young child, is first recorded as slang usage in Massinger, Middleton, and Rowley's comedy *The Old Law* (1599); it became established in informal use by 1841.

—**adj.** *Informal.* younger. 1895 (in *kid brother*), American English, from the earlier attributive use of the noun, as in *kid fox* young fox (1599, in Shakespeare's *Much Ado About Nothing*). The extended meaning of suitable for children, simple, etc. (as in *kid stuff*), is first recorded in 1929.

kid[2] *v. Informal.* tease playfully, talk jokingly. 1811, in thieves' slang, to coax, wheedle, hoax, or humbug; probably from *kid*[1] in the sense of treat as a child; amuse. The meaning of joke with, tease playfully, is first recorded in 1839.

kidnap *v.* 1682, probably a compound of *kid*[1] child and *nap* snatch away, an earlier (1673) variant of *nab.* It is also possible that *kidnap* is, at least in some instances, a back formation from *kidnapper.*

By 1682, the date of earliest recorded use, *kidnap* was already established, strongly suggesting that it was an older term originating among those who practiced kidnapping. Originally, *kidnap* referred to stealing children or carrying off others in order to provide servants or laborers in the American colonies. Such white servants were called *kids* among the colonists before 1724 and into the 1800's.

—**kidnapper** *n.* 1678, in Phillips' *Dictionary;* formed from *kid*[1] child + *nap* snatch away + *-er*[1].

kidney *n.* Before 1325 *kidenere;* later *kydeneye* (1392); of uncertain origin, but perhaps developed from an unrecorded Old English compound **cydenēore*: the first element of the compound being represented by dialectal English *kid* a pod (related to Old English *cod* a bag, in the form **cyde, *cydde* belly), from Proto-Germanic **kuđjás,* Indo-European **gut-* (Pok.394); the second element of the compound being Old English **nēora,* found in Middle English *nere* kidney (before 1325). Middle English *nere* is cognate with Middle Dutch *niere* kidney (modern Dutch *nier*), Old High German *nioro, niero* (modern German *Niere*), Old Icelandic *nȳra* (Danish *nyre,* and Swedish *njure*), from Proto-Germanic **neuran-,* earlier **neȝwhran-;* also cognate with Greek *nephrós* kidney, and Oscan-Umbrian *nefrōnēs* (Praeneste) and *nebrundinēs* (Lanuvium), from Indo-European **negwhrós* (Pok.319). The modern spelling *kidney* developed from Middle English *kideneye* (1392), apparently an alteration of earlier *kidenere,* by association with *ey, ei* EGG (from the resemblance of the kidney's shape to an egg).

kill[1] *v.* put to death. Probably before 1200 *cullen* to strike or hit, in Layamon's *Chronicle of Britain* and in *Ancrene Riwle;* later, put to death, slay (about 1300); perhaps developed from Old English **cyllan,* related to *cwellan* to kill; see QUELL. The OED disputes the possible Old English formation on semantic grounds, as there is at least a gap of 200 years between the recording of the meaning in Middle English and its possible existence in Old English. —**n.** 1852, act of killing; 1878, animal killed; from the verb. An isolated example is recorded in the sense of stroke or blow (probably before 1200). —**killer** *n.* 1288, in the surname *Kyller.* —**killjoy** *n.* (1776)

kill[2] *n.* stream, creek. 1669, American English; earlier, used as the name of a strait (1639); borrowed from Dutch *kil,* from Middle Dutch *kille* riverbed, channel; cognate with East Frisian *kille* watercourse, of uncertain origin.

Kill is used in areas originally settled by the Dutch,

especially in place names, such as *Schuylkill,* literally, hidden stream.

killdeer *n.* small wading bird that has a loud, shrill cry. 1731 *kildeer,* American English; probably imitative of the bird's call.

kiln (kiln *or* kil) *n.* furnace or oven. Before 1325 *kilne;* developed from Old English (before 800) *cyln, cylen,* borrowed from Latin *culīna* kitchen, cooking stove; see CULINARY. **—v.** burn, bake, or dry in a kiln. 1715, from the noun.

kilo (kē'lō *or* kil'ō) *n.* 1870, short for KILOGRAM.

kilo- a prefix meaning one thousand, as in *kilogram, kilometer, kilowatt.* Borrowed from French *kilo-,* arbitrary alteration of *khilioi,* French transliteration of Greek *chī́lioi* (Aeolic *chéllioi*) a thousand; cognate with Sanskrit *sahásra-m* a thousand, Avestan *hazaŋrem,* and Persian *hazār,* from Indo-European **ĝhéslo-,* of uncertain origin (Pok.446).

This prefix was introduced into French in 1795, when the metric system was officially adopted by France. The words *kilogramme* kilogram, and *kilomètre* kilometer, were introduced in French at the same time.

kilogram *n.* 1000 grams. 1797 *kilogramme,* borrowing of French *kilogramme* (*kilo-* 1000 + *gramme* GRAM).

kilometer *n.* 1000 meters. 1810, borrowing of French *kilomètre* (*kilo-* 1000 + *mètre* METER² unit of measure).

kiloton *n.* measure of explosive power equal to that of 1000 tons of TNT. 1950, formed from English *kilo-* 1000 + *ton* (of explosive energy).

kilowatt *n.* measure of electric power equal to 1000 watts. 1884, formed from English *kilo-* 1000 + *watt* measure of electricity.

Kilroy *n.* a mythical character of graffito, developed by U.S. servicemen during World War II. 1945, especially in the phrase *Kilroy was here,* variously explained as: 1) the name of Sergeant Francis J. *Kilroy,* Jr. of the U.S. Army Air Transport Command, whose friend or friends kept writing Kilroy's name wherever they went; or 2) the name of James J. *Kilroy,* an inspector of war matériels who wrote his name on equipment he inspected.

kilt *n.* a heavily pleated skirt worn by men in the Scottish Highlands; originally, that part of Highland dress that hung below the belt. 1746, from the earlier verb *kilt* to tuck up (the skirts), gird up (1513); developed from Middle English *kilten* to tuck up (about 1340); borrowed from a Scandinavian source (compare Danish *kilte (op)* to tuck up, Swedish dialect *kilta* to swathe, Old Icelandic *kjalta* fold made by gathering up a dress, *kilting* billowing fold of a dress, and Old Swedish *kilta* lap), of unknown origin.

kilter *n.* good condition, order (especially in the phrase *out of kilter*). Before 1657, in Bradford's *History of Plymouth Plantation;* variant of earlier *kelter* (1643); of unknown origin.

kimono (kəmō'nə) *n.* loose outer garment fastened with a sash, generally reaching to the floor and having wide sleeves. 1886, borrowed from Japanese *kimono* (*ki* wear + *mono* thing).

kin *n.* family or relatives. Probably about 1200 *kinn, kin* race, people, family, descendants, sex, in *The Ormulum;* earlier, in the surname *Kinne* (1180), and as found in *cinnes men* (1129); developed from Old English (before 725) *cyn* family, race, kind, nature; cognate with Old Frisian *kenn* kin, Old Saxon *kunni,* Middle Dutch and modern Dutch *kunne* sex or gender, Old High German *chunni* kin or race, *kind* child (modern German *Kind*), Old Icelandic *kyn* family or race, and Gothic *kuni,* from Proto-Germanic **kunján.* Outside Germanic cognates are found in Welsh *geni* be born, Latin *genus* race, stock, kind, *gignere* beget or produce, Greek *geneá* birth, *gónos* offspring, stock, seed, birth, *génos* race or kind, *gígnesthai* be born, Lithuanian *gentìs* relative, kinsman, Old Slavic *zętĭ* son-in-law, Armenian *cin* birth, Avestan *zīzənti* they bear, and Sanskrit *jánati* he begets, *jánas* kin, from Indo-European **ĝen-/ĝon-* (Pok.373). **—kinsfolk** *n.* 1459 *kynsefolk,* formed from English *kin* + *folk.* **—kinship** *n.* 1833, in Elizabeth Barrett Browning's *Prometheus Bound;* formed from English *kin* + *-ship.* **—kinsman** *n.* 1129 *cinnes man,* later *kinnessmann* (about 1200); formed from English *kin* + *man.* **—kinswoman** *n.* 1330; formed from English *kin* + *woman.*

-kin a suffix meaning little, as in *lambkin, pipkin.* Middle English *-kin,* probably borrowed from Middle Dutch *-kijn* and *-ken;* cognate with Old Saxon *-kīn* diminutive suffix, Middle Low German *-kīn,* Old High German *-chīn* (modern German *-chen*).

This suffix appeared in English probably originally in proper names (*Melekin,* 1181); it was also added to common nouns in late Middle English. Some words with *-kin* were borrowed from Dutch or Flemish, such as *bodkin* and *catkin;* others were formed in English, but the diminutive meaning is often no longer perceived, as in *napkin* (fundamentally, *nap, nape* cloth and *-kin, -kyn* diminutive; thus, little cloth).

kind¹ *adj.* friendly, doing good rather than harm. About 1250 *kind, kinde* natural, native, related by kinship; later, benevolent, kind (about 1325, in *Cursor Mundi*); developed from Old English *gecynde* natural, native, innate (about 725, in *Beowulf*) originally, with the feelings that relatives have, from Proto-Germanic **ʒakundjaz,* from *gecynd, cynd* nature, KIND². **—kindhearted** *adj.* (1535) **—kindly** *adj.* Before 1325 *kyndli,* in *Cursor Mundi;* earlier *kuindeliche* (before 1275); developed from Old English *cyndelīc* (before 899, in Alfred's translation of Boethius' *De Consolatione Philosophiae*), formed from *cynd* nature + *-līc* -ly; *adv.* Before 1325 *kindli,* in *Cursor Mundi;* earlier *kinde-like* (about 1250); developed from Old English *gecyndelīce,* formed from *gecynde* kind² + *-līc* -ly²

kind² *n.* class, sort, variety. Probably about 1200 *kinde* nature, character, type, class, in *The Ormulum;* developed from Old English *gecynd, cynd* kind, nature, race (before 899 in Alfred's translation of Boethius' *De Consolatione Philosophiae*); related to *cynn* family, KIN, and developed from Proto-Germanic **(ʒa-)kunđís,* cognate with Sanskrit *jātí-s* birth, Latin *nātiō* tribe, from Indo-European **ĝn̥tís,* root **ĝenə-/ĝn̥-* (Pok.374).

kindergarten *n.* 1852, borrowed from German *Kindergarten,* literally, children's garden (*Kinder* children, plural of *Kind* child + *Garten* GARDEN); from Proto-Germanic **kínthan,* Indo-European **ĝéntom* (Pok. 374). The German word *Kindergarten* was coined in 1840 by the German educator Friedrich Fröbel, 1782-1852, who opened the first such school in 1837 at Blankenburg, Thuringia. Subsequently a kindergarten was established in England in 1850 by Johannes Ronge, a German Roman Catholic priest who was a political refugee.

kindle *v.* set on fire, light. Probably about 1200 *kindelen, kindlen,* in *The Ormulum;* borrowed probably from a Scandinavian source (compare Old Icelandic *kynda* kindle, *kyndill* a candle, torch, Old Swedish *quindla* kindle; cognate with Middle High German *künten, künden* kindle, and Old High German *cuntisal* a burning, fire), of unknown origin; for suffix see -LE[3]. —**kindling** *n.* material for lighting a fire (1513).

kindred *n.* family or relatives; kin. Probably before 1200 *kinrede, kinreden;* formed from *kin* KIN + *-rede, -reden,* from Old English *rǣden* condition or rule, related to *rǣdan* to advise, rule, explain, READ.

The present spelling is infrequently recorded in Middle English, in which it was probably influenced by *kinde* KIND[2] class, sort; but the modern *kindred,* that became common in the 1600's, is probably the result of phonetic intrusion of *d* between *n* and *r,* as in *thunder.* —**adj.** related. 1530, in Palsgrave's *Lesclarcissement;* from the noun.

kinesthetic *adj.* having to do with sensations of movement in muscles, joints, and tendons. 1880 *kinaesthetic;* formed in English from New Latin *kinaesthesis* (compound formed from Greek *kīneîn* to move and *aísthēsis* sensation) + *-ic,* on the pattern of *aesthetic, prosthetic, synthetic.*

kinetic *adj.* of motion. 1864, borrowed from Greek *kīnētikós* moving, from *kīneîn* to move, set in motion; see CITE; for suffix see -IC. —**kinetic energy** (1870)

king *n.* Before 1121 *king* chief ruler, monarch; developed from Old English (before 725) *cyning,* also later contracted to *cyng;* cognate with Old Frisian *kening, kining* king, Old Saxon *kuning,* Middle Dutch *coninc* (modern Dutch *koning*), Old High German *kuning, kunig* (modern German *König*), Old Icelandic *konungr, kongr,* Old Danish *kunung, konung* (modern Danish and Norwegian *konge,* and Swedish *konung, kung*). It is possible that in Old English the form for *king* is derived from Old English *cynn* family, race, KIN + the noun suffix *-ing* one belonging to or descended from (the literal meaning of *king* then being descendant or scion of the race). Another view is that Old English *cyning* derived from Proto-Germanic **kuningaz* one who descended from noble birth, as found in Finnish *kuningas* king, Lithuanian *kuningas* lord, priest. —**kingdom** *n.* About 1250, developed from Old English (about 725) *cyningdōm* (*cyning* king + *-dōm* -dom).

kinin (kī′nən) *n.* substance that causes dilation of blood vessels and contraction of smooth muscles. 1954, apparently abstracted from *bradykinin* (1949, formed in English from Greek *bradýs* slow + *kin-,* abstracted from Greek *kīnētikós* KINETIC + English *-in,* chemical suffix). In botany, *kinin* has been recorded since 1956 as the name of a substance that promotes cell division and regulates growth in plants; also called *cytokinin,* i.e. cellular kinin (since 1965).

kink *n.* twist or curl in thread, rope, hair, etc. 1678, in Phillips' *Dictionary,* originally a nautical term; borrowed from Dutch *kink* twist in a rope. The Dutch form is cognate with Middle Low German *kinke* kink, and Old Icelandic *kikna* bend at the knees. The figurative sense of odd notion or mental twist is first recorded in American English, in Thomas Jefferson's *Letters* (1803). The meaning of imperfection or difficulty, is found in 1868. —**v.** form a kink, make kinks in. 1697, from the noun. —**kinky** *adj.* 1844, American English, twisted or curly; formed from English *kink* + *-y*[1]. The figurative meaning of morally twisted or perverted is first recorded in 1959, occurring as an extension of the sense eccentric or crotchety (1859).

kinkajou (king′kəjü) *n.* mammal which resembles a raccoon. 1796 *kincajou;* borrowed through French *quincajou,* from Tupi-Guarani (a native linguistic stock of central South America).

kiosk (kē′osk) *n.* small building, usually with one or more sides open, used as a newsstand, bandstand, telephone booth, etc. 1625, borrowed from French *kiosque,* from Turkish *köşk* pavilion, palace, from Persian *gōše* corner.

kipper *n.* herring, salmon, etc., that has been salted and dried or smoked. 1326 *kipre, kypre* cured fish; developed from Old English (before 1000) *cypera* male salmon, probably related to *coper* reddish-brown metal, COPPER[1], with reference to the color of the fish. —**v.** 1773, from the noun.

kirk *n. Scottish.* church. Apparently about 1200 *kirke,* in *The Ormulum;* borrowed probably from a Scandinavian source (compare Old Icelandic *kirkja* church, Norwegian and Danish *kirke,* Swedish *kyrka;* see CHURCH). The term is often cited as an example of dialect in Northern England and Scotland.

kismet (kiz′met) *n.* fate, destiny. 1834, borrowed from Turkish *kısmet,* from Arabic *qisma, qismat* portion, lot, fate, from the root of *qasama* he divided.

kiss *v.* About 1175 *cussen* (in Southwestern Dialect of England); about 1250 *kissen* (in Midland Dialect of England); developed from Old English (about 750) *cyssan* to kiss. The Old English is cognate with Old Frisian *kessa* to kiss, Old Saxon *kussian,* Middle Dutch *cussen* (modern Dutch *kussen*), Old High German *kussen* (modern German *küssen,* probably from the noun), Old Icelandic and Swedish *kyssa,* Norwegian and Danish *kysse;* all derived from Proto-Germanic **kussjan,* from **kuss-,* the root of Old English *coss* kiss, Old Frisian *kos,* Old Saxon *kus,* Middle Dutch *cus, cuss,* Dutch *kus,* Old High German *kus, kuss* (modern German *Kuss*), and Old Icelandic *koss;* compare also Greek *kýs(s)ai* to kiss. This is an ancient onomatopoeic word (Pok.626).—**n.** Probably before 1400 *kiss,* alteration (by association with *kissen,* v.) of earlier *coss* (probably before 1200); found in Old English *coss* kiss (about 950).

kit *n.* 1275, in compound *kittewritt* kitwright or maker of kits (wooden tubs or buckets); later *kytt, kyt* (1362); borrowed probably from Middle Dutch *kitte* jug, tankard, wooden container; of uncertain origin. The meaning of soldier's supplies carried in a knapsack is first recorded in 1785; the more general sense of a collection of necessary supplies or equipment is found in 1833. The informal sense of lot or collection appeared in Grose's *Classical Dictionary of the Vulgar Tongue* (1785). A more recent meaning of parts of an article to be assembled by the buyer was known in the 1930's.

For the phrase *kit and caboodle* see CABOODLE. —**v.** *Especially British.* to equip or supply. 1919, from the noun.

kitchen *n.* Probably before 1200 *kuchene* room where food is cooked, in Layamon's *Chronicle of Britain* and in *Ancrene Riwle;* later *kichene* (about 1300); developed from Old English (about 1000) *cycene;* borrowed probably from Vulgar Latin **cocina,* variant of Latin *coquīna* kitchen, from feminine of *coquīnus* of cooks, from *coquus* cook, from *coquere* to COOK.

While it is probable that Old English borrowed from Vulgar Latin, it is also likely that at least some of the Germanic languages borrowed a common West Germanic form **kokina,* though the Old High German *chuhhina* shows the word was borrowed before the High German consonant shift. In turn a Common Germanic form would have provided the source for Middle Low German *kokene* kitchen, Middle Dutch *cokene* (modern Dutch *keuken*), and Old High German *chuhhina* (modern German *Küche*).
—kitchenette *n.* small kitchen. 1910, American English; formed from *kitchen* + *-ette.*

kite *n.* Probably before 1325 *kite* kind of hawk with long, pointed wings and a notched or forked tail; earlier *kete* (probably before 1300, in *Kyng Alisaunder*); developed from Old English *cȳta* (before 800). Old English *cȳta* is cognate with Middle High German *kūze* owl (modern German *Kauz*), probably both named from the cries they make, and Middle Low German *kūten* to chatter (modern German *Köter* cur or dog). The common meaning of a toy, often in the shape of a diamond, flown in the air by means of a long string, is first recorded in Samuel Butler's *Hudibras* (1664), and was so called in allusion to the way a hawk (or kite) hovers in the air.

The commercial slang meaning of a fictitious check, bill of exchange, etc., is first recorded in 1805 in the phrase *to fly a kite,* meaning to raise money or credit by issuing commercial paper on insufficient or nonexistent funds.
—v. fly like a kite, move very fast. 1863, from the noun. The commercial slang meaning of to issue bogus commercial paper is first recorded in 1839 in American English.

kith *n.* friends and relatives. Probably before 1200 *cuththe* one's native land, countrymen, neighbors, friends; developed from Old English *cȳthth, cȳththu* native country, home, from *cūth* known, past participle of *cunnan* to know. Old English *cȳththu* is cognate with Old High German *chundida,* from Proto-Germanic **kunthithō,* the collective (in *-ithō,* from Indo-European *-itā)* of those known to one, * *kúnthaz,* whence Old English *cūth;* see CAN[1] be able to; see COUTH. The spelling *kith* is first recorded about 1300. The phrase *kith and kin* (originally with the meaning of country and kinsmen) is found about 1230.

kitten *n.* About 1378 *kitoun,* in *Piers Plowman;* probably borrowed from an Anglo-French variant of Old French *chitoun, cheton,* from *chat* cat, from Late Latin *cattus* CAT. **—kittenish** *adj.* 1754, formed from English *kitten* + *-ish.*

kittiwake (kit'iwāk) *n.* kind of sea gull. 1684; earlier *cattiwake* (1661); perhaps imitative of the bird's call.

kitty[1] *n.* kitten. 1719, formed from English *kitt(en)* + *-y*[2] (diminutive suffix), perhaps by influence of *kitty* a girl or young woman (1500-20, in Dunbar's poetry), and a pet form of the name *Catherine.*

kitty[2] *n.* pool or fund of money. 1887, money pooled by players in a card game to defray expenses, probably formed from English *kit* a container or a collection of necessary supplies (1833) + *-y*[2] (diminutive suffix). The generalized meaning of any pool or fund of money appeared in American English in Josiah Flynt's *The Rise of Ruderick Clowd* (1903).

kiwi (kē'wē) *n.* bird of New Zealand that cannot fly, apteryx. 1835, in William Yate's *Account of New Zealand,* borrowed from Maori *kiwi,* of imitative origin.

Kiwi was used in 1918 as a nickname for a New Zealander.**—kiwi fruit** an edible fruit exported by New Zealand, where it is grown on a vine, originally imported from China. The name is first recorded in American English in 1966, but probably originated in New Zealand, where it was known as *Chinese gooseberry* (1925).

kleptomania *n.* abnormal impulse to steal. 1830, borrowed from New Latin *kleptomania,* formed from Greek *kléptēs* thief (from *kléptein* to steal) + *maníā* madness, MANIA. Greek *kléptein* is cognate with Latin *clepere* to steal and Gothic *hlifan* to steal and *hliftus* thief, from Indo-European *k̂lep-* (Pok.604).

klieg light (klēg) bright, hot arc light used in taking motion pictures. 1929 *Klieg,* earlier *Kleig* (1923), American English, in allusion to Anton and John *Kliegl* who pioneered in developing lighting equipment for the theater and motion pictures.

klutz (kluts) *n.* 1967 (but known before 1965, as in *klutzy,* etc.), American English; borrowed from Yiddish *klots* clumsy, awkward person; literally, block or lump, from Middle High German *kloz, klotzes* lump or ball (modern German *Klotz* boor, lout, clod, blockhead); see CLOT. **—klutzy** *adj.* awkward and clumsy. 1965, American English; formed from *klutz* + *-y*[1].

knack *n.* 1369 *knakke* deception, stratagem, trick, in Chaucer's *Book of the Duchesse;* of uncertain origin, though the term is suggestive of German *knacken* to solve a puzzle or problem, to crack, etc.; probably an onomatopoeic word. The meaning of a special skill or aptitude is first recorded in 1581, in Mulcaster's *Position. . .necessarie for the Training up of Children* (dealing with the training of children).

knapsack (nap'sak') *n.* bag for carrying clothes, equipment, etc., on the back. 1603, in Drayton's *The Barons' Wars;* borrowed from Low German *Knapsack* (probably from *knappen* to eat, crunch, probably an onomatopoeic word + *Sack* bag, from Middle Low German *sak* SACK[1]; compare modern Dutch *knapzak*).

knave (nāv) *n.* rogue, rascal. Probably before 1200 *cnave* rogue, rascal, boy, in Layamon's *Chronicle of Britain;* later *knave* (probably about 1225, in *King Horn*); developed from Old English (about 1000) *cnafa* boy, male servant; cognate with Old High German *knabo* boy (modern German *Knabe*). The word is not found outside West Germanic and is probably not Indo-European. **—knavery** *n.* 1528, in Tyndale's *Obedience of a Christian Man;* formed from English *knave* + *-ery.* **—knavish** *adj.* About 1390, in *Canterbury Tales;* formed from English *knave* + *-ish.*

knead *v.* mix (dough, clay, etc.) by pressing and squeezing. About 1150 *cneden;* later *kneden* (probably before 1300); developed from Old English *cnedan* (about 950, in *Lindisfarne Gospels*); cognate with Old Saxon *knedan* to knead, Middle Dutch *cneden* (modern Dutch *kneden*), Old High German *knetan* (modern German *kneten*), Old Icelandic *knodha* to knead (from Proto-Germanic **kneđanan, *knuđanan*), *knǫttr* ball, sphere, *knatti* rounded mountaintop; also cognate with Old Slavic *gnesti* to press, and Old Prussian *gnode* trough for kneading bread, from Indo-European **gnet-/gnōt-* (Pok.371).

The change in spelling from *e* to *ea* occurred during the 1500's and reflects the change in pronunciation that took place in the transition during the later Middle English and early modern English periods.

knee *n.* Probably before 1300 *knee, kne;* developed from Old English (about 725) *cnēo, cnēow;* cognate with Old Saxon *kneo, knio* knee, Old Frisian *kni, knē,* Middle Dutch *cnie* (modern Dutch *knie*), Old High German *kneo* (modern German *Knie*), Old Icelandic *knē,* and Gothic *kniu,* from Proto-Germanic **knewan.* Outside Germanic cognates are found in Latin *genū* knee, Greek *góny,* Armenian *cunr,* Sanskrit *jā́nu,* Tocharian A *kanweṃ* (dual) knees, Tocharian B *kenīne,* and Hittite *genu* knee, from Indo-European **ĝenu-/ĝonu-/ĝōnu-/ĝneu-* (Pok. 381). **—v.** Before 1225 *knewen* bend the knee, kneel; developed from Old English (about 1000) *cnēowian,* from *cnēo(w)* knee. The meaning of strike or touch with the knee is first recorded in 1892. **—kneecap** *n.* 1660, a covering or protection for the knee; later, flat bone at the front of the knee (1869); replacing *knee pan (knee panne,* 1392*).* **—knee-deep** *adj.* (before 1400 *kne-depe*) **—knee-high** *adj.* (1743, American English) **—knee-jerk** *adj.* 1951, American English, without thought, automatic; predictable; from *knee jerk* a reflex action of the body (1876).

kneel *v.* go down on one's knee or knees. Probably before 1200 *cnelen, cneolen,* in Layamon's *Chronicle of Britain* and in *Ancrene Riwle;* later *knelen* (probably before 1300); developed from Old English (apparently before 1000) *cnēowlian,* from *cnēow* KNEE. Old English *cnēowlian* is cognate with Middle Low German *knēlen* kneel and Middle Dutch *cnielen* (modern Dutch *knielen*). The formative *-l* is probably of frequentative force.

knell *v.* ring (a bell) slowly. About 1350 *knellen,* variant of *knullen* to knell, (also) to beat, knock (probably before 1325, in Southwest Midland dialect of England) and later *knyllen* (probably before 1400, in East Midland dialect of England); developed from Old English *cnyllan* to knell (about 950, in *Lindisfarne Gospels*). The Old English is cognate with Middle High German *erknellen* to toll, *knüllen* to beat, and Old Icelandic *knylla* to beat, thrash, of unknown origin. **—n.** sound of a bell rung slowly. Before 1325 *knel,* variant of *knyl,* found in Old English (about 961) *cyll* sound of a bell, from *cnyllan* to knell.

knickers *n.pl.* short, loose-fitting trousers gathered at the knees. 1881, shortened from earlier *knickerbockers* (1859). These trousers are said to be so called for their resemblance to the knee breeches of the Dutchmen in Cruikshank's illustrations to *History of New York* (1809), a book penned by Washington Irving under the name Diedrich *Knickerbocker,* in allusion to Irving's friend Herman Knickerbocker, of Schaghticoke, near Albany, New York.

The name *Knickerbocker* also came to be popularly applied in American English by 1831 to any New Yorker, especially one descended from the original Dutch settlers.

knickknack *n.* pleasing trifle, ornament, trinket. 1682, from earlier *knickknack* a petty trick, artifice (1618), varied reduplication of KNACK in the original sense of stratagem, trick.

knife *n.* About 1300 *knif;* developed from Late Old English *cnīf* (before 1100); borrowed from a Scandinavian source (compare Old Icelandic *knífr,* Norwegian, Swedish, and Danish *kniv*). Old English *cnīf* is cognate with Middle Low German *knīf* knife (modern German *Knief, Kneif* pocket knife), Middle Dutch *cnijf,* and obsolete Dutch *knijf* knife from Proto-Germanic **knībaz,* cognate with Lithuanian *gnýbti* to pinch, from Indo-European **gneibh-* (Pok.370), Middle Low German *knīpen* to nip, pinch (modern German *kneifen* and modern Dutch *knijpen*). **—v.** cut or stab with a knife. About 1865, from the noun.

knight *n.* a man raised to an honorable military rank in the Middle Ages. Probably before 1150 *kniht* youth, attendant, military servant, knight; later *Knight* (1241, as a surname); developed from Old English (before 725) *cniht* boy, youth, servant, (rarely) soldier; earlier *cēapcneht* a purchased youth, a young slave (about 700, in earliest Latin-English glossaries). The Old English forms *cniht* and *-cneht* are cognate with Old Frisian *knecht, kniucht* boy, youth, servant, soldier, Old Saxon *kneht,* Middle Dutch and modern Dutch *Knecht* manservant, footman, and Old High German *kneht* boy, youth, page (modern German *Knecht* manservant, serf, slave), of unknown origin. For shift in spelling see note at FIGHT. **—v.** raise to the rank of knight. Probably 1225 *knighten,* in *King Horn;* from *knight,* n. **—knight-errant** *n.* Probably about 1390 *knygt erraunt,* in *Sir Gawain and the Green Knight.* **—knighthood** *n.* Probably about 1225 *knigthod,* in *King Horn;* formed from Old English *knigt* + *-hod* -hood, but also found in Old English *cnihthād* period between childhood and manhood.

knit *v.* About 1150 *cniten;* later *knutten* (probably before 1200), and *knytten* (about 1300); developed from Old English *cnyttan* to tie with a knot, bind, fasten (about 1000, in Ælfric's *Grammar*). Old English *cnyttan* is cognate with Middle Low German *knutten* knit, fasten, Middle High German *knützen* to press, and Old Icelandic *knytja* bind together; related to *knūtr* KNOT.

The figurative sense of join closely together, is first recorded in Chaucer's *Canterbury Tales* (about 1375). The ordinary meaning of make cloth by looping yarn together, is first recorded in Palsgrave's *Lesclarcissement* (1530).

knob *n.* rounded lump. 1373 *knobe;* later *nobbe* (before 1398); cognate with Old Frisian *knopp, knapp* knob, Middle Low German *knobbe* knob, gnarl, bud, Middle Dutch *cnoppe* (modern Dutch *knop*), Old High German *knopf* (modern German *Knopf* button), Norwegian *knubb* block of wood, Old Icelandic *knýfill* short horn, and possibly outside Germanic with Old Irish *gnobh* gnarl, and Lithuanian *gniáubti* surround, embrace, from Indo-European **gnubh-/gnēubh-* (Pok. 371). **—knobby** *adj.* 1543; earlier used in referring to blood, in the sense of full of blood; formed from English *knob* + *-y*[1].

knock *v.* Probably before 1300 *knoken* to strike or hit, in *Arthour and Merlin;* developed from Old English (about 1000) *cnocian* and *cnucian,* possibly of imitative origin. **—n.** About 1333-52 *knoke,* from *knoken* to knock. **—knockabout** *adj.* 1876, Australian English, a handyman; later, noisy or boisterous (1885). **—knocker** *n.* Before 1382, in the Wycliffe Bible; formed from Middle English *knoken* + *-er*[1]. **—knockout** *n.* (1887, in boxing)

knoll *n.* small rounded hill, mound. Probably about 1250 *knol;* earlier as a surname *Knolle* (1203); developed from Old English *cnoll* hilltop, small hill, before 899, in Alfred's translation of Boethius' *De Consolatione Philosophiae.* Old English *cnoll* is cognate with

Middle High German *knolle* clod, lump, tuber (modern German *Knolle,* modern Dutch *knol* tuber, turnip), Old Icelandic *knollr* mountaintop, Norwegian *knoll* tuber, and Swedish *knöl* bump, knot, knoll, of unknown origin.

knot *n.* Probably about 1200 *cnotte;* later *knotte* (about 1300); developed from Old English (about 1000) *cnotta;* cognate with Old Frisian *knotta* knot, Middle Low German *knutte* knot, knob, Dutch *knot* knot, and Middle High German *knotze* a knotty excrescence, from Proto-Germanic **knuttán-* earlier **knuđnán-,* from Indo-European **gneut-/gnut-* (Pok.372). The spelling *cnot* was known by 1154 in place names, such as *Cnotlinid* and that of *knotte* before 1200, in *Thorneknotte.* **—v.** tie or twine together in a knot. Probably 1440 *knotten;* developed from *cnotted* having knots, full of knots; adjective (1137), from *cnotte,* n. + *-ed*². **—knothole** *n.* (1726) **—knotty** *adj.* Probably about 1200 *cnotti, knotti* puzzling, intricate, difficult (figurative use); formed from English *knot,* n. + *-y*¹.

know *v.* Probably before 1200 *cnowen;* later *knowen* (probably about 1225); developed from Old English *cnāwan,* past tense *cnēow* (about 725, in *Beowulf*). The Old English forms are cognate with Old High German *chnāan,* as in *bichnāan, irchnāan* to know, recognize, and Old Icelandic *knā* I can, from Proto-Germanic ** knǣanan.* Outside Germanic cognates are found in Old Latin *gnōscere,* Latin *nōscere* to come to know, Albanian *njoh* I know, Greek *gignṓskein* to come to know, Lithuanian *žinóti,* and Old Slavic *znati* to know, Old Irish *gninim* in *itar-gninim* I know, Armenian *caneay* I knew, Sanskrit *jānā́ti* he knows, and Tocharian A, Tocharian B *knā-* to know, recognize, from Indo-European **ĝnē-/ĝnō* (Pok.376). These cognates derive from the Indo-European root **ĝen-/ĝon-/ĝn̥-,* which is found in *can-* and *ken-* and give rise to numerous words from Latin and Greek that are represented in English by *cognition, ignore, denote, note, notion, nominal, gnostic,* etc. **—n. in the know,** *Informal.* having inside information. 1883, from earlier *know* fact of knowing, knowledge (1592); from the verb. **—knowable** *adj.* (about 1445, implied in *unknowable*) **—know-how** *n.* (1838, American English) **—knowledge** *n.* Before 1121 *cnawlece* acknowledgement; later *knowlych* (1303, in Mannyng's *Handlyng Synne*), *knoweleche* (about 1330), and *knowlege* (probably before 1400, in Chaucer's translation of *Roman de la Rose*); formed from *knowen* + *-lych, -leche, -lege* noun suffixes serving some of the functions of *-ness,* as found in forms with a variant ending, such as in *godleich, godlec* goodness, kindness.

The spelling *knowledge* is found as early as 1471; see EDGE or LEDGE.

knuckle *n.* Probably 1388 *knokel* finger joint; earlier *knokil* first; cognate with Old Frisian and Middle Low German *knokel* knuckle, Middle Dutch *knökel* (modern Dutch *kneukel*), Middle High German *knöchel* (modern German *Knöchel*). All forms cited are diminutives probably derived from the same Germanic root as Middle Low German *knoke* bone, Middle High German *knoche* (modern German *Knochen*), Dutch *knook, knok* bone, knuckle, from Proto-Germanic **knuk-,* from Indo-European **gnuĝ-* (Pok.372); for suffix see -LE¹. **—v.** 1740, put the knuckles on the ground in playing marbles (in the phrase *knuckle down*); from the noun. The extended meaning of to apply oneself earnestly or vigorously to (in the phrase *knuckle down to*) is first recorded in 1864 in American English. The figurative meaning of give in, submit, acknowledge oneself beaten (in the phrase *knuckle under*) is first recorded in 1740.

knurl (nėrl) *n.* knot, knob. 1608, probably a diminutive of earlier *knur* knot (1545); developed from Middle English *knor* hard excrescence, swelling (probably about 1400); cognate with Middle Low German *knorre* hard swelling, knot, Middle Dutch *knorre* (modern Dutch *knor*), Middle High German *knorre* (modern German *Knorren*), and Old High German *chniurig* knotty, rough, rigid, from Proto-Germanic **knw-,* from Indo-European **gner-* (Pok.371). **—knurled** *adj.* 1611; formed from English *knurl* + *-ed*².

koala (kōä'lə) *n.* furry bearlike animal of Australia. 1808, borrowed from the aboriginal name of the animal, recorded at various times and in various places in Australia as *koola, kūlla,* and *kūlā.*

kohl (kōl) *n.* powder used originally in the Orient to darken eyelids and lashes, usually consisting of powdered antimony. 1799 *kohhel,* borrowed from Arabic *koḥ'l, kuḥl* metallic powder, especially antimony. See also ALCOHOL and ANTIMONY.

kohlrabi (kōl'rä'bē) *n.* vegetable with a stem shaped like a turnip. 1807, borrowing of German *Kohlrabi,* alteration of Italian *cavoli rape,* plural of *cavolo rapa* kohlrabi (*cavolo* cabbage, from Latin *caulis* cabbage, stalk of a plant and *rapa* turnip, from Latin *rāpa,* see RAPE² plant). Latin *caulis* is cognate with Greek *kaulós* stem, from Indo-European **kaul-/kul-* (Pok.537). The alteration of Italian *cavoli, cavolo* to *kohl-* occurred through translation of "cabbage" from Italian to German.

koine (koi'nā *or* koi'nē) *n.* standard language or dialect of a region in which different languages or dialects exist. 1926, extended sense of earlier *Koine* the Greek language commonly used during the Hellenistic period (a modified Attic dialect, found in the Septuagint and the New Testament); borrowed from Greek *koinḗ* in *hē koinḕ diálektos* the common dialect, from *koinḗ,* feminine singular of *koinós* common, earlier **komyós,* cognate with Latin *cum* with (and prefix *com-*), from Indo-European adverb **kom* near, along (Pok.612).

kola or **cola** (kō'lə) *n.* bitter brownish nut of an African tree, used to give flavor to soft drinks. 1830, variant of earlier *cola* (1795); of African origin (compare Temne *kola,* Mandingo *kolo*).

kolkhoz (kolkoz') *n.* collective farm in the Soviet Union. 1921, borrowing of Russian *kolkhóz,* acronym formed from *kol(lektívnoe) khoz(yáistvo)* collective economy. **—kolkhoznik** *n.* member of a kolkhoz. 1955, borrowing of Russian *kolkhóznik;* formed from *kolkhóz* + *-nik* personal suffix, -NIK.

kook (kük) *n. Slang.* odd, cranky, or crazy person. 1959, American English; possibly a shortened and altered form of CUCKOO. **—kooky** *adj. Slang.* odd, cranky, or crazy. 1959, American English; formed from English *kook* + *-y*¹.

kopeck or **kopek** (kō'pek) *n.* Russian coin. 1698 *copec,* 1716 *copeck,* borrowed from Russian *kopéika,* diminutive of *kop'yé* lance, spear; so called because kopecks minted from 1535 to 1719 bore a figure of Czar Ivan IV with a lance in his hand.

Koran (kōran') *n.* sacred book of the Moslems. 1625 *Core,* 1735 *Koran;* borrowed from Arabic *qor'ān, qur-*

'ān a reading, recitation, book, from the root of *qara'a* he read, recited.

kosher *adj.* right or fit according to Jewish law. 1851, borrowing of Yiddish *kosher,* from Hebrew *kāshēr* fit, proper, lawful. The informal meaning of legitimate, correct, proper, was first recorded in Farmer and Henley's *Slang and Its Analogues* (1896, though perhaps earlier as this extended sense has been known in German student slang since 1737). **—v.** prepare (food) according to Jewish law. 1892 in Zangwill's *Children of the Ghetto;* from the noun (influenced by Yiddish *kashern* make kosher, from Hebrew *kāshēr*).

kowtow (kou'tou') *n.* act of slavish submission. 1804 *koo-too* Chinese custom of touching the ground with the forehead to show respect or submission, borrowing of Chinese *k'o-t'ou,* literally, knock the head. The meaning of an act of slavish submission is first recorded in 1834. The current spelling is found in 1864. **—v.** show slavish submission to, fawn, truckle. 1826, in Benjamin Disraeli's *Vivian Grey;* from the noun.

Kremlin *n.* citadel of Moscow, the seat of the Soviet government. 1662 *Cremelena,* borrowed from Old Russian *kremlĭnŭ;* later *Kremelin* (1796), borrowed from earlier German *Kremelin* (now *Kreml* after modern Russian *kreml'*). The Old Russian *kremlĭnŭ,* adj., derived from *kremlĭ* citadel, fortress, related to *króma* slice, *kremén'* flint.

The spelling *Kremlin* (without second medial *e*) appeared in 1833, probably influenced by French *Kremlin.* The application of the name to the Soviet government, is first recorded in H. G. Wells' *The Shape of Things to Come* (1933).

—Kremlinology *n.* study of the Soviet government and its policies. 1958, formed from English *Kremlin* + *-ology* study of, variant of *-logy.*

krill *n.* small shrimplike crustacean. 1907, borrowed from Norwegian *kril* small fry of fish.

Kriss Kringle (kris' kring'gəl) Santa Claus. 1830, American English; borrowed from dialectal German *Christkindl* Christmas gift (1792); literally, little Christ child, diminutive of *Christkind* Christ child; see KINDERGARTEN.

krypton (krip'ton) *n.* inert gaseous element. 1898, borrowing of Greek *kryptón,* neuter of *kryptós* hidden; see CRYPT; so called from its being a rare gas, forming a minute part of the atmosphere. The term was coined by its discoverers, the British chemists Sir William Ramsay, 1852-1916, and M.W. Travers.

kudos (kü'dos) *n.* praise, accolade. 1831 (implied earlier in *kudos'd* praised, used by Southey in 1799); borrowed from Greek *kŷdos* glory, fame, renown, cognate with *koeîn* notice, hear, Sanskrit *kavi-s* wise, and Latin *cavēre* watch out for, from Indo-European * *keu-/kowə-/kū-* (Pok.587).

Kudos was originally a singular noun in English, as it was in Greek, but because of the final *-s* it came to be construed as a plural, which led to the appearance in 1941 of the singular form *kudo,* derived by back formation from *kudos.*

Ku Klux Klan (kü' kluks' klan') secret society of militant white supremacists that arose in the southern United States after the Civil War. 1867 *Kuklux Klan,* American English; formed in English supposedly from alteration of Greek *kýklos* circle + English *clan.*

kulak (küläk' *or* kü'läk) *n.* well-to-do Russian peasant farmer or trader. 1886, borrowing of Russian *kulák,* literally, fist, (figuratively) rich peasant, from Turkic *kulak* fist (*kol* hand + diminutive suffix *-ak*). After the Russian revolution *kulak* referred to peasant farmers who were generally landowners opposed to Soviet collectivization.

kumiss (kü'mis) *n.* fermented mare's or camel's milk. 1607, borrowed from Russian *kumys,* from Turkic *kumyz, kymys;* related to *kymmak* to mix.

kumquat (kum'kwot) *n.* yellow fruit somewhat like a small orange. 1699 *camquit,* from Chinese (Cantonese) *kamkwat* (*kam* golden + *kwat* orange). The current spelling is first recorded in 1870.

kung fu (kung' fü') Chinese method of fighting without weapons, similar to karate. 1966, borrowing of dialectal Chinese *kung fu,* literally, boxing method.

L

la *n.* sixth note of the musical scale. Before 1300, borrowed, probably through Italian, from Medieval Latin *la,* from the initial syllable of Latin *labii* of the lip, the word sung to this note in the Hymn for St. John the Baptist's day; see GAMUT.

laager (lä′gər) *n.* camp or encampment, especially one protected by a circle of wagons. 1850 *lager,* in R.G. Cumming's *Hunter's Life in South Africa;* borrowed from earlier Afrikaans *lager,* probably from German *Lager* camp, bed, couch, LAIR. Compare STALAG.

In modern Afrikaans the word is *laer,* corresponding to modern Dutch *leger.* The spelling *laager* (probably influenced by Afrikaans and Dutch *laag* layer) appeared in English in 1881. The transferred military sense of any defensive position protected by a circle of armored vehicles, is first recorded in 1941.

—v. encamp in a laager. 1879, from the noun.

lab *n. Informal.* 1895, short for LABORATORY.

label *n.* Probably about 1300 *lable* narrow band with pendants on a coat of arms, in *Sir Bevis of Hamtoun;* borrowed from Old French *label* ribbon, fillet, fringe, possibly from Frankish (compare Old High German *lappa* flap; see LAP[1] part of a garment). The meaning of a strip of material attached to a document to hold an appended seal is first recorded in Wycliffe's writings before 1400; the more generalized meaning of a tag or sticker is found as early as 1679. **—v.** put or write a label on. 1601, in Shakespeare's *Twelfth Night;* from the noun.

labial *adj.* of the lips. 1594, borrowed from Medieval Latin *labialis* having to do with the lips, from Latin *labium* LIP. **—n.** *Phonetics.* sound made by nearly closing or rounding the lips. 1668, from the adjective.

labile (lā′bəl) *adj.* changeable, unstable. 1447 *labyl* (of the mind) wandering, forgetful; borrowed from Middle French *labile,* or directly from Latin *lābilis* slipping, fleeting, transient, from *lābī* to slip, glide, fall; see LAP[1] flap. The meaning of unstable appeared in Florio's translation of Montaigne's *Essays* (1603). **—lability** *n.* changeableness, instability. 1646, formed from English *labile* + *-ity.*

labium (lā′bēəm) *n. Biology.* lip or liplike part. 1597 (plural *labia*); borrowing of Latin *labium* LIP.

labor *n.* Before 1325 *labour* task, project; later, exertion, toil, work (before 1375); borrowed from Old French *labour,* learned borrowing from Latin *labor* toil, pain, possibly related to *lābī* to slip, glide, fall; see LAP[1]. The spelling *labor* is found in Middle English as early as 1377. The sense of physical exertions of childbirth, was introduced from Latin in Spenser's *Epithalamion* (1595). **—v.** to work, toil. Before 1376 *labouren;* also *laboren* (1387, in a version of *Piers Plowman*); borrowed from Old French *labourer, laborer,* learned borrowing from Latin *labōrāre* to work, toil, suffer, be in distress, from *labor* toil, pain. **—labored** *adj.* (1579, in Spenser's *The Shepheardes Calender*) **—laborer** *n.* (probably before 1350) **—laborious** *adj.* Before 1393, diligent or industrious, in Gower's *Confessio Amantis;* later, requiring hard work, burdensome (about 1415, in Chaucer's *Canterbury Tales*); borrowed through Old French *laborieux,* and directly from Latin *labōriōsus* full of labor, toilsome, from *labor* toil, pain; for suffix see -IOUS. **—labor-saving** *adj.* (about 1776, in Adam Smith's writings) **—labor union** (1866, American English)

laboratory *n.* 1605, borrowed from Medieval Latin *laboratorium* a place for labor or work, from Latin *labōrāre* to work, LABOR; for suffix see -ORY.

labyrinth (lab′ərinth) *n.* maze. 1548, in the figurative sense of a confusing, complicated state of affairs; earlier *laberynthe* maze (1408) and *laboryntus* (about 1380, in Chaucer's *House of Fame*); both forms in allusion to the labyrinth of Greek mythology built to contain the Minotaur; borrowed from Latin *labyrinthus,* from Greek *labýrinthos,* a word of the pre-Greek culture designating a structure that was Egyptian, Cretan, or of Asia Minor. Some have compared the Greek word to Lydian (an Anatolian language related to Hittite) *lábrys,* meaning a double-edged axe, symbol of royal power; hence a labyrinth may have been a royal structure or palace. **—labyrinthine** *adj.* 1747, formed from English *labyrinth* + *-ine*[1].

lac (lak) *n.* resinous substance deposited on trees by certain insects. 1618, perhaps borrowed from Middle French *lacce,* but found also in Middle English as *lacca* (probably about 1425, in a translation of Chauliac's *Grande Chirurgie*); borrowed from Hindi *lākh,* from Sanskrit *lākṣā́,* perhaps originally so called from the color of salmon (Indo-European **lak̂sos,* Pok.653). Related to LACQUER and LAKE[2]. See also SHELLAC.

lace *n.* Before 1325 *lace* cord for tying, in *Cursor Mundi;* also *laas* (before 1382, in the Wycliffe Bible), developed from earlier *laz* (about 1230, in *Ancrene Riwle*); borrowed from Old French *las, laz* a net, noose, string, from Latin *laqueus,* a trapping and hunting term meaning noose, snare; from Indo-European **lək-w-,* root **lēk-* a sprig or string (Pok. 673). Doublet of LASSO.

The sense of a net of thread in an ornamental pattern is first recorded in English in 1555. The earlier sense of a thread or cord for tying is now retained chiefly in reference to shoe or boot laces and string or cord to draw clothing together.

—v. Probably before 1200 *lacen* fasten with a lace, in *Ancrene Riwle;* borrowed from Old French *lacier,* from Latin *laqueāre* ensnare, from *laqueus* noose or snare. Though the verb appears in the record of English slightly before the noun, it is assumed that both noun and verb were probably simultaneous borrowings from Old French, though it is curious that the spelling with *c* in the verb was so late in appearing in the noun. **—lacy** *adj.* 1804, formed from English *lace* + *-y*[1].

lacerate *v.* tear roughly, mangle. Probably before 1425 *laceraten,* in a translation of Chauliac's *Grande Chirurgie;* borrowed from Latin *lacerātus,* past participle of *lacerāre* tear to pieces, mangle, from *lacer* torn, mangled, of uncertain origin; for suffix see -ATE[1]. —**laceration** *n.* 1597, borrowed perhaps through Middle French *lacération,* from Latin *lacerātiōnem* (nominative *lacerātiō*), from *lacerāre* lacerate; for suffix see -ATION.

laches (lach'iz) *n. Law.* negligence in the performance of a duty. Before 1376 *laches, lachesse* laziness, negligence, in a version of *Piers Plowman;* borrowed through Anglo-French *lachesse,* Old French *laschesse,* from *lasche* lax, lazy, from *laschier* let go, loosen; see LUSH[1], adj. The specific legal sense of negligence in performing a duty is first recorded in English in 1574. A transferred sense of inexcusable negligence is found in Disraeli's *Coningsby* (1844).

lachrymal or **lacrimal** (lak'rəməl) *adj.* of or producing tears. Probably before 1425 *lacrimal,* in a translation of Chauliac's *Grande Chirurgie;* borrowed from Medieval Latin *lacrimalis,* from Latin *lacrima* tear (earlier *lacruma*), Old Latin *dacruma* TEAR[1], n.; for suffix see -AL[1]. It is also probable that *lachrymal* was borrowed, in some instances, through Middle French *lachrymal, lacrymal,* the spelling *ch* arising from the practice of substituting it for *c* before *r* in Latin words, such as in *anchor.*

lachrymose (lak'rəmōs) *adj.* tearful, mournful. 1661, tearlike; later, tearful, sorrowful (1727, in Bailey's *Dictionary*); borrowed from Latin *lacrimōsus* tearful, doleful, from *lacrima* tear, see LACHRYMAL; for suffix see -OSE[1].

lack *n.* shortage, need. Before 1300 *lac, lakke;* later *lak* (about 1300); perhaps developed from an Old English **lac;* cognate with Middle Low German *lak* lack, fault, slack, loose, Old Frisian *lek* disadvantage, damage, *lakia* to oppose, dispute, and Old Icelandic *lakr* lacking, from Proto-Germanic **laka-;* possibly also cognate with Latin *laxus* loose, LAX, and Greek *lagarós* slack, loose, thin, and *lḗgein* leave off, cease, from Indo-European **(s)lēg-/(s)ləg-* (Pok. 959). If the word did not exist in Old English, it was probably borrowed from Middle Dutch *lac* deficiency, fault, which may have reinforced the Middle English form regardless of the existence of an Old English **lac.* —**v.** to want, need. Before 1225 *lacen;* later *laken* (about 1250), and *lacken* (about 1325); probably from the noun. —**lackluster** *adj.* dull and drab. 1600, in Shakespeare's *As You Like It,* formed from English *lack,* v. + *luster.*

lackadaisical (lak'ədā'zəkəl) *adj.* languid, lethargic, listless. 1768, affectedly languishing, in Sterne's *Sentimental Journey through France and Italy;* formed from English *lackadaisy,* interj., alas, alack (1748, in Smollett's works) + suffix *-ical. Lackadaisy* is an alteration of the earlier *lack-a-day* (1695, in Congreve's *Love for Love*), a shortened and altered form of the phrase *alack the day,* first found in Shakespeare's *Romeo and Juliet* (1592). It has been suggested that perhaps the shift in meaning to that of languid or lethargic was influenced by words such as *lax* and *lassitude.*

lackey *n.* male servant, footman. 1529, borrowed from Middle French *laquais,* of uncertain origin. Middle French *laquais* was probably borrowed from Old Provençal *lacai,* which must have come from *lecai* glutton, covetous, from *lecar* to lick. The later Spanish *lacayo, alacayo* mercenary, according to the scholar Corominas, probably derived from Basque *alakairu, alokairu, alokari* salary, wages, income, from Latin *locārium* rent, payment, and also possibly from Basque *lekaio* lackey, popular musician who plays for money, also from Latin *locārium.*

The figurative sense of servile follower, toady, appeared in English in 1588.

—**v.** serve as a lackey. 1568, from the noun.

laconic (ləkon'ik) *adj.* using few words, concise. 1583, of or pertaining to Laconia or its inhabitants; 1589, in the Laconian manner, brief, concise; a shortened form of earlier *laconical* (1576), and possibly influenced by Middle French *laconique.* Both the English and French forms were borrowed, probably through Latin *Lacōnicus* Laconian, from Greek *Lakōnikós,* from *Lákōn* a Laconian (person from the ancient district of Laconia in southern Greece whose capital was Sparta); for suffix see -IC.

Reference to the brevity of speech thought characteristic of Laconians appears in the record of English as early as 1570 in the form *Laconism* the habit or practice of imitating the Laconians in brevity of speech.

lacquer *n.* kind of varnish. 1673 *lacker,* in Marvell's *The Rehearsal Transposed;* borrowed from obsolete French *lacre* a kind of sealing wax, from Portuguese *lacre,* from *lacca* resinous substance, lac, from Arabic *lakk,* from Persian *lak,* from Sanskrit *lākṣā́;* see LAC. The spelling *lacquer,* appearing as *laquer* (1697), and both influenced by French *laque* lake[2] (a deep-red coloring matter), is first recorded in the verb (1688). An earlier meaning of *lacquer,* in the sense of dye obtained from lac, is recorded in Hakluyt's *Voyages* (1579). Related to LAC, LAKE[2], and SHELLAC. —**v.** to coat with lacquer. 1687 *lackered,* participial adjective; 1688 *lacquer;* from the noun.

lacrosse (ləkrôs') *n.* game played with a ball and long-handled rackets. 1718, in American English; borrowed from Canadian French *la crosse* the game of lacrosse; originally, the racket used in the game; literally, the hooked stick, the crosier.

lact- a form of *lacto-* before vowels, as in *lactiferous.*

lactation *n.* 1668, act of suckling a baby; later, secretion of milk (1857); borrowed perhaps through French *lactation,* from Late Latin *lactātiōnem* (nominative *lactātiō*), from Latin *lactāre* suckle, from *lac* (genitive *lactis*) milk; for suffix see -ATION. —**lactate** *v.* to secrete milk. 1889, probably a back formation from *lactation;* for suffix see -ATE[1].

lacteal (lak'tēəl) *adj.* of or like milk, milky. 1658, in Phillips' *Dictionary,* formed in English as if borrowed from Latin *lacteus,* from *lac* (genitive *lactis*) milk, see GALAXY; for suffix see -AL[1].

lactic *adj.* of or from milk. 1790 *lactic acid* an acid obtained from sour milk; borrowed from French *lactique,* formed from Latin *lactis* (genitive of *lac* milk) + French *-ique* -ic.

lacto- a combining form meaning milk, as in *lactoglobulin,* or lactic acid, as in *lactobacillus.* Borrowed from Latin *lac* (genitive *lactis*) milk; see GALAXY.

lactose *n.* milk sugar. 1858, formed in English from Latin *lactis* (genitive of *lac* milk) + English suffix *-ose*[2].

lacuna (ləkyü'nə) *n.* empty space, gap, blank. 1663, borrowed from Latin *lacūna* hole or pit, from *lacus* (genitive *lacūs*) pond, LAKE[1]. Doublet of LAGOON.

lad *n.* Probably before 1300 *ladde* foot soldier, in *Kyng Alisaunder;* later, young male servant, man of low social position, vagabond (about 1300, in *Havelok the Dane*); and boy or youth (before 1338, in Mannyng's *Chronicle* *of England*); possibly borrowed from a Scandinavian source (compare Danish and Norwegian *askeladd,* literally, ash lad, referring to the youngest son in a folk tale who pokes in the ashes, and Norwegian *tusseladd* pale, insignificant-looking person, weakling; literally, fairy lad.

In Old English *Ladda* is found as a surname, also in early Middle English *Laddedale* Ladde's dale (about 1160), but whether the Old English form is identical with the Middle English form is unknown.

—laddie *n.* young lad, lad. 1546, formed from English *lad* + *-ie.*

ladder *n.* About 1175 *læddre;* later *laddere* (probably before 1300); developed from Old English *hlǣder* (971). The Old English form is cognate with Old Frisian *hlēdere, hlādder* ladder, Middle Dutch *lēder* (modern Dutch *leer,* also *ladder,* from Frisian), Middle Low German *ledder,* Old High German *leitara* (modern German *Leiter*), and dialectal Danish *lejre* ladder, from Proto-Germanic **Hlaiđr-*. Outside Germanic cognates are found in Old Lithuanian *šlitė* ladder, Greek *klîmax* (genitive *klīmakos*) ladder, *klī́nein* to incline, and Sanskrit *śráyate* leans on, from Indo-European **k̑lei-/k̑loi-/k̑li-/k̑lī-* (Pok.601). Compare UDDER.

lade *v.* to load. Probably about 1200 *laden* to draw water, in *The Ormulum;* later, to load (about 1250); developed from Old English *hladan* to load, heap, draw water (about 725, in *Beowulf*). The Old English form is cognate with Old Frisian *hlada* to load, Old Saxon *hladan,* Middle Dutch and modern Dutch *laden,* and Old Icelandic *hladha,* from Proto-Germanic **Hlađ-;* also with Old High German *hladan, ladan* (modern German *laden*), and Gothic *afhlathan,* from Proto-Germanic **Hláth-,* from Indo-European **klə-t-,* root **kla-* lay out, pile up (Pok.599). **—laden** *adj.* burdened, loaded. 1595, from *laden,* past participle of *lade* to load.

ladle *n.* About 1300 *ladel,* developed from Old English (before 1000) *hlædel,* from *hladan* to load, LADE; the suffix *-le* expresses the sense of an appliance or tool, as in *thimble.* The Old English *hlædel* is ultimately from Proto-Germanic **Hlađlás.* **—v.** dip out. About 1532, from the noun.

lady *n.* Before 1121 *læfdige* female ruler; later *lavedi, levedi* (about 1300), and *ladi* (probably about 1350); developed from Old English *hlǣfdīe* mistress of a household, wife of a lord; literally, one who kneads a loaf or loaves (before 830); earlier *hlǣfdige* (about 750, in Cynewulf's *Elene*), a compound of *hlāf* bread, LOAF[1] + *-dige,* related to *dǣge* breadmaker, maker of dough, from *dāg* DOUGH. **—ladies' man** (1784, in Cowper's *Tirocinium*) **—ladies' room** (1880) **—ladybird** *n.* 1592, sweetheart, in Shakespeare's *Romeo and Juliet;* 1704, a ladybug. **—ladybug** *n.* (1699) **—ladylike** *adj.* (1586) **—ladyship** *n.* Probably before 1200 *læfdischipe;* later *ladyschip* (probably about 1380); formed from Middle English *læfdige, lavedi, ladi* lady + *-schip(e)* -ship.

lag *v.* 1530 move too slowly, fall behind, in Palsgrave's *Lesclarcissement;* developed from earlier *lag,* n. the last or hindmost person (1514), found in the Middle English compound *lag-mon* last man (probably about 1390, in *Sir Gawain and the Green Knight*). The Middle English form was possibly borrowed from a Scandinavian source (compare Norwegian dialect *lagga* go slowly). **—n.** a lagging or falling behind. 1837, from the verb. **—laggard** *adj.* lagging, falling behind. 1702, in Nicholas Rowe's *Tamerlane;* formed from English *lag,* v. + *-ard;* *n.* laggard person. 1808, in Scott's *Marmion;* from the adjective.

lager (lä′gər) *n.* stored beer. 1855, American English, short for *lager beer* (1854), half translation of German *Lagerbier* (*Lager* storehouse, bed, LAIR + *Bier* BEER).

lagniappe or **lagnappe** (lan′yap) *n.* small gift given to a customer with a purchase. 1849, American English; borrowed from Louisiana French or directly from Haitian Creole *lagniappe,* from American Spanish *la ñapa,* or *la yapa* the gift; *ñapa, yapa,* from Quechua *yapa* something given into the bargain, an extra.

lagoon *n.* 1612 *laguna,* later *Lagune* (1673), both forms in reference to Italian places, especially around Venice; borrowed through French *lagune,* and directly from Italian *laguna* pond, lake, from Latin *lacūna* pond, hole, from *lacus* (genitive *lacūs*) pond, LAKE[1]; for suffixal ending see -OON. Doublet of LACUNA. The spelling *lagoon* is first recorded in 1750, in American English, and its use was probably influenced by Spanish *laguna.*

lair *n.* About 1410 *leire* place where an animal takes shelter, from earlier *leir* bed, couch (probably before 1200); developed from Old English *leger* act or place of lying down (about 725, in *Beowulf*). The Old English *leger* is cognate with Old Frisian *leger* situation, Old Saxon *legar* bed, Middle Dutch *lēgher, lēghere* act or place of lying down (modern Dutch *leger* bed, camp), Old High German *legar* bed, a lying down (modern German *Lager* bed, lair, camp, storehouse), Old Icelandic *legr* grave, nuptials (as a lying down together), from Proto-Germanic **leʒran,* and Gothic *ligrs* bed, related to Old English *licgan* to repose, LIE[2]. Outside Germanic cognates are found in Latin *lectus* and Greek *léchos* bed, from Indo-European **legh-* lie (Pok.658).

laird (lārd) *n. Scottish.* landowner. Before 1325, northern Middle English *lavered;* later, Scottish *lard* (about 1450), northern variants of *lord, loverd* LORD.

laissez faire (les′āfār′) absence of regulation and interference by government. 1825, borrowing of French *laissez faire* let do (as one pleases), the slogan of French economists of the 1700's who opposed government regulation of trade and industry (*laissez,* imperative form of *laisser* to let, from Latin *laxare* to slacken, from *laxus* slack or lax, and *faire* to do, from Latin *facere* to do).

laity (lā′ətē) *n.* the lay or ordinary class of people. Before 1415 *laite,* in Wycliffe's *The Lantern of Light,* formed in Middle English from *lay*[2] + *-ity.*

lake[1] *n.* body of water surrounded by land. Before 1121 *lac;* later *lake* (probably before 1300, in *Cursor Mundi*), in part developed from Old English *lacu* body of water (944, in original charter of King Edmund I), and in part borrowed from Old French *lac.* Both Old English *lacu* and Old French *lac* were borrowed from Latin *lacus* (genitive *lacūs*) pond or lake, a word cognate with Old Irish *loch* lake, Greek *lákkos* pond, cistern, pit, and Old Slavic *loky,* from Indo-European **laku-* (Pok.653). Cognates in Germanic are found in Old Icelandic *lǫgr* sea, water, Old Saxon *lagu,* and Old English *lagu,* from Proto-Germanic **laʒús.*

lake[2] *n.* deep-red or purplish-red coloring matter obtained from lac. 1616, probably borrowed through French *laque,* from Old Provençal *laca,* from Arabic *lakk;* see LACQUER.

lam *n. Slang.* on the run, hurried escape, as in *take it on the lam* or *on the lam.* 1897, from the verb meaning of run away; of unknown origin, sometimes compared with *lam* to beat (1589 in *lamback* and 1637 in LAMBASTE), but no apparent connection can be established semantically with the current sense of *lam* hurried escape.

lama (lä′mə) *n.* Buddhist priest or monk in Tibet and Mongolia. 1654, borrowed from Tibetan *blama* (with unsounded *b*). —**lamasery** (lä′məser′ē) *n.* monastery of lamas. 1867, borrowed from French *lamaserie* (*lama,* from Tibetan *blama* + *-serie,* probably from Persian *sarāī* inn, as found in the irregular formation of earlier French *caravanserai* (1686).

lamb *n.* Old English (about 858) *lamb;* earlier *lomb* (about 725; also found in Middle English before 1200). The Old English forms are cognate with Old Frisian *lamb* lamb, Old Saxon *lamb,* Middle Low German *lam,* Middle Dutch and modern Dutch *lam,* Old High German *lamb* (modern German *Lamm*), Old Icelandic *lamb* (Swedish *lamm,* Danish *lam*), and Gothic *lamb,* from Proto-Germanic **lambaz,* without cognates outside Germanic. —**v.** give birth to a lamb. 1611, in Cotgrave's *Dictionary;* from the noun. —**lambkin** *n.* 1579, little lamb, in Spenser's *The Shepheardes Calender;* later, young or dear person, in Shakespeare's *2 Henry IV* (1597); formed from English *lamb* + *-kin.* As a surname, *Lambkin* appeared in Middle English as early as 1257. —**lambskin** *n.* (before 1400, in Lanfranc's *Science of Surgery*).

lambaste (lambāst′) *v. Informal.* to beat, thrash. 1637, probably formed from English *lam* (1596, probably borrowed from a Scandinavian source; compare Icelandic *lama* bruise, and Old Icelandic *lemja* to beat, lame) + BASTE³ to thrash. The figurative meaning of scold or denounce, appeared in 1886.

lambda (lam′də) *n.* eleventh letter of the Greek alphabet. About 1400, in Maundeville's *Travels,* borrowing of Greek *lámbda,* from a Semitic source (compare Hebrew *lāmedh* the twelfth letter of the Hebrew alphabet, probably originally meaning ox-goad and formed from the hieroglyph of such an instrument). Mostly appearing in English in scientific usage, *lambda* is found in such terms as *lambda point* (physics, 1932), *lambda hyperon* (nuclear physics, 1954), *lambda virus* (genetics, 1965), and as the symbol for a millionth of a liter (chemistry, 1934).

lambent *adj.* moving lightly over a surface, flickering, shimmering. 1647, borrowed from Latin *lambentem* (nominative *lambēns*), present participle of *lambere* to lick, see LAP³; for suffix see -ENT. The sense of shining with a soft, clear light, is first recorded in Pope's *Elvira to Abelard* (1717), and that of playing lightly and brilliantly over a subject, in 1871.

lame *adj.* About 1175 *lame;* developed from Old English (about 750) *lama;* cognate with Old Frisian *lam, lom* lame, Old Saxon *lamo,* Middle Dutch and modern Dutch *lam,* Old High German *lam* (modern German *lahm*), Old Icelandic *lami,* modern Scandinavian *lam* from Proto-Germanic **lamōn.* Outside Germanic cognates are found in Middle Irish *lem* foolish, insipid, Lithuanian *lìmti* break down, Old Slavic *lomiti* to break, Russian *lom* fragments, and possibly also in Greek *nōlemés* without pause, unceasingly, from Indo-European **lem-/lom-/lm̥-* break; soft (Pok.674). —**v.** make lame, cripple. About 1300 *lamen* to injure, wound, disable, in *Havelok the Dane;* from the adjective. The sense of to disable in the foot or leg, to cripple, is first recorded in 1460. —**lame duck** 1761, disabled person or thing, in Walpole's letters; later, in American English, a public official who has been defeated for reelection and is serving the last part of his term, in *Congressional Globe* (1863).

lamé (lamā′) *n.* rich fabric made of metal threads, especially ones of gold or silver. 1922, borrowing of French *lamé* a fabric, type of thread; literally, laminated, from *lame* metal leaf, from Latin *lāmina* LAMINA.

lamella (ləmel′ə) *n.* thin plate, scale, or layer, especially of flesh or bone. 1678, borrowing of Latin *lāmella,* diminutive of *lāmina* thin plate, LAMINA.

lament *v.* express grief, mourn. Before 1450 *lementen* to regret, be sorry for; later *lament* express grief (1530, in Palsgrave's *Lesclarcissement*); borrowed from Middle French *lamenter* to moan, bewail, and probably directly from Latin *lāmentārī,* from *lāmentum* a wailing, related to *lātrāre* to bark or cry, and cognate with Lithuanian *lóti* to bark, and Greek *lêros* chatter, from Indo-European **lā-* a crying sound (Pok. 650). It is also possible that in some instances *lament* is a back formation from earlier *lamentation.* —**n.** 1591, in Shakespeare's *1 Henry VI;* borrowing of Middle French *lament,* and probably borrowed directly from Latin *lāmentum.* Also possibly a noun use of the verb in English. —**lamentable** *adj.* Before 1420, in Lydgate's *Troy Book;* borrowing of Middle French *lamentable,* and borrowed directly from Latin *lāmentābilis,* from *lāmentārī* to lament; for suffix see -ABLE. —**lamentation** *n.* Before 1382 *lamentacioun,* in the Wycliffe Bible, borrowing of Old French *lamentation,* and borrowed directly from Latin *lāmentātiōnem* (nominative *lāmentātiō*), from *lāmentārī* to lament; for suffix see -ATION. The earliest recorded use in Middle English is in reference to the *Lamentations* of Jeremiah.

lamina (lam′ənə) *n.* thin plate, scale, or layer. 1656, in Blount's *Glossographia;* borrowing of Latin *lāmina* thin piece of metal or wood, plate, leaf, layer; of uncertain origin. —**laminate** *v.* 1665, to beat or roll into a succession of bonded plates or layers; formed from English *lamina* + *-ate*¹. *Laminated* is first recorded in 1931, and *laminated plastic* in 1938. —**lamination** *n.* 1676, formed from English *laminate* + *-ion.*

lamp *n.* About 1200 *lampe* oil lamp, light; borrowing of Old French *lampe,* from Latin *lampas,* from Greek *lampás* torch, lamp, beacon, meteor, light, from *lámpein* to shine; cognate with Old Irish *lassair* flame, Old Prussian *lopis* flame, Lithuanian *lópė* light, Hittite *lap-* to glow, be hot, and in Germanic with Old Icelandic *leiptr* lightning, from Indo-European **lā(i)p-/ləip-/ləp-* shine, burn (Pok.652). —**lamplight** *n.* (probably about 1380) —**lamppost** *n.* (1790)

lampoon *n.* piece of satirical writing, speech, etc. intended to ridicule or mock. 1645, in John Evelyn's *Memoirs;* borrowed from French *lampon,* of uncertain origin; possibly from *lamponner,* see the verb. It has also been suggested that the word in French may derive from *lampons* let us drink (a popular refrain of satirical drinking songs of the 1600's), from *lamper* to drink or guzzle, a nasalized form of *laper* to lap, of imitative origin. —**v.** ridicule or mock in a lampoon. Before 1657, in Lovelace's *Poems,* either from the noun in English, or borrowed from French *lamponner* scoff or jeer at, from Middle French *lamponner* (used by the French chronicler Brantôme).

lamprey *n.* eel-like water animal with a large, round

mouth. About 1300 *laumprei,* in *Havelok the Dane;* earlier as a surname *Lampre* (1199); borrowed from Old French *lampreie,* from Medieval Latin *lampreda.* The Medieval Latin word may be an alteration (influenced by Latin *lambere* to lick) of Late Latin *naupreda, nauprida* lamprey, perhaps a Gaulish borrowing; or it may have an uncertain relationship to Late Latin *lampetra* lamprey; literally, lick rock, from Latin *lambere* to lick + *petra* (from Greek *pétrā*) rock, as is traditionally explained in reference to their habit of attaching themselves to rocks by their suckerlike mouths. Doublet of LIMPET.

lanai (lənī′) *n.* porch, veranda. Before 1869, borrowing of Hawaiian *lānai* shed, shelter, booth, porch. An earlier spelling, *ranai,* is recorded in 1823 and 1826.

lance *n.* Probably before 1300 *launce* horseman's spear, in *Arthour and Merlin;* earlier as surname *Lance* (1198-99); borrowed from Old French *lance,* from Latin *lancea* light spear, possibly of Celtic origin. **—v.** pierce with a lance. Probably about 1300 *launcen* to throw, thrust, pierce, in *The Romance of Guy of Warwick;* later *lancen* (before 1338, in Mannyng's *Chronicle of England*); borrowed from Old French *lancier,* from Late Latin *lanceāre* wield a lance, pierce with a lance, from Latin *lancea* spear. Doublet of LAUNCH[1] throw forward. **—lancer** *n.* 1590, in Marlowe's *Tamburlane the Great;* formed from English *lance* + *-er*[1].

lancet *n.* small, sharp-pointed surgical knife. 1392 *launcet,* later *lancet* (probably before 1425); borrowed from Old French *lancette* small lance, diminutive of *lance* LANCE; for suffix see -ET.

land *n.* Old English *land, lond* (about 725, in *Beowulf*); cognate with Old Frisian *land, lond* land, Old Saxon *land,* Middle Dutch and modern Dutch *land,* Old High German *lant* (modern German *Land*), Old Icelandic, modern Scandinavian, and Gothic *land,* from Proto-Germanic **landan.* Outside Germanic cognates are found in Old Irish *land* open space or area, Middle Welsh *llan* enclosure, yard, French *lande* moor, heath (from Gaulish **landā*), Old Prussian *lindan* (accusative) valley, Old Slavic *lędina* heath, desert, Byelorussian *lyada* cleared land, and Czech (*lada, lado* fallow land, from Indo-European **lendh-/londh-* (Pok.675).—**v.** Probably about 1225 *londen* bring to land, set ashore, in *King Horn;* later *landen* (probably before 1400, in *Morte Arthur*); from the noun.

The meaning of arrive at a place or position (as in *Fortune landed him in France* or *to land in bankruptcy*) is first recorded in Jeremy Taylor's works, in 1649, and the more specific sense of to alight on the ground after a leap, etc., is found in 1693. The informal sense of get or obtain (as in *to land a job*) is first recorded in 1854, developed from the earlier meaning, in angling, of bring (a fish) to land, to catch, net (1613).

—landed *adj.* owning land. About 1440 *londid,* in *Promptorium Parvulorum;* formed from Middle English *lond* land + *-ed*[2], possibly by influence of earlier Old English *gelandod* landed, past participle of **landian* to have land. **—landfall** *n.* (1627, in Captain John Smith's *The Seaman's Grammar*) **—landing** *n.* Before 1420, disembarkation, in Lydgate's *Troy Book;* later, a landing place (about 1450). **—landlady** *n.* (before 1536, in Tyndale's writings) **—landlord** *n.* 1275, as a surname; formed from Middle English *land* + *lord.* **—landlubber** *n.* Before 1700; formed from English *land* + *lubber.* **—landmark** *n.* About 1400 *londes mark* boundary; formed from Middle English *londes,* genitive of *lond* land + *mark.* **—landowner** *n.* (before 1733) **—landslide** *n.* 1838, American English; the figurative sense of an overwhelming electoral victory is first recorded in 1888, in the *New York Times.* **—landsman** *n.* Probably before 1200 *londesman;* formed from Middle English *londes,* genitive of *lond* land + *man.* **—landward** *adv., adj.* (probably about 1450).

landau (lan′dô) *n.* four-wheeled carriage with a top made in two parts that can be folded back. 1743, from *Landau,* a town in Germany, where this vehicle was first made. The word was applied in English before 1934 to an automobile with a top similar to that of the carriage.

landscape *n.* 1603, a picture of natural inland scenery; borrowed from Dutch *landschap,* from Middle Dutch *landscap* region (*land* LAND + *-scap* -SHIP). The borrowing of Middle Dutch *landscap* is a replacement and cognate of Old English *landscipe* region (though no such term appears in the record of Middle English). The Middle Dutch is also a cognate of Old Saxon *landscepi,* Old High German *lantscaf* (modern German *Landschaft*), and Old Icelandic *landskapr.* The general sense of inland natural scenery appeared in 1606, followed by that of a view of inland scenery, in Milton's *L'Allegro* (1632). **—v.** arrange or embellish to form a landscape. 1927, from the noun. An earlier meaning of represent as a landscape, depict, appeared in Browning's *The Ring and the Book* (1868).

lane *n.* Probably about 1300 *lane,* in *Sir Bevis of Hamtoun;* earlier, as a surname (1176); found in Old English (971) *lane, lanu* narrow, hedged-in road or way; cognate with Old Frisian *lane, lone* lane, Middle Dutch *lāne* (modern Dutch *laan*), and Old Icelandic *lǫn* oblong hayrick, row of houses; of unknown origin.

lang syne, or **langsyne** (lang′zīn′) *adv. Scottish.* long since, long ago. 1500-20, in William Dunbar's *Poems,* a compound of *lang* long and *syne* since, Scottish variants of Middle English *lang* LONG and *sin,* contraction of *sithen, sithens* SINCE. **—n.** time long ago. 1788, in *Auld Lang Syne,* a song written by Robert Burns.

language *n.* About 1280 *langage* what is said, talk; later *language* (about 1330); borrowed from Old French *langage,* from *langue* tongue, language, from Latin *lingua* TONGUE; for suffix see -AGE. The sense of speech of a nation, tongue, is first found in Middle English about 1300. The form with *u* developed in English through Anglo-French, from assimilation with French *langue* in Middle English.

languid (lang′gwid) *adj.* drooping, weak, languishing. 1597, borrowed from Middle French *languide,* learned borrowing from Latin, and borrowed directly from Latin *languidus* faint, listless, from *languēre* be weak or faint; see LAX[1] loose.

languish (lang′gwish) *v.* become weak or weary, lose energy, droop. Before 1325 *languishen* fail in strength, weaken, in *Cursor Mundi;* borrowed from Old French *languiss-,* stem of *languir* be listless, from Vulgar Latin **languīre,* from Latin *languēre* be weak or faint, see LAX[1] loose; for suffix see -ISH[2]. The extended sense of grow dull, slack, or less intense is first recorded in Bacon's *Sylva Sylvarum* (1626).

languor (lang′gər) *n.* lack of energy, weakness, weariness. Probably before 1300 *langour* sickness or misery, in *Sir Tristrem;* later *languor* (about 1350); borrowed from Old French *languor, langour,* from Latin *languor* faintness, feebleness, lassitude, from *languēre* be weak or faint, see LAX[1] loose; for suffix see -OR[1]. The sense of lack of energy, feebleness, was first recorded in English in Blount's *Glossographia* (1656). **—languorous** *adj.* About 1475; borrowed from Middle French *languereous,* from Old French *languoreux,* from *languor;* for suffix see -OUS.

lank *adj.* long and thin, slender, lean. Probably about 1150 *lonke;* later, in a surname *Lank* (1294); developed from Old English (before 1000) *hlanc,* from Proto-Germanic **Hlankaz.* Old English *hlanc* is cognate with Old High German *hlanca* loin, side, flank, Middle High German *lenken* to bend (modern German *lenken* to guide), and Old Icelandic *hlykkr* bend, noose, loop, from Indo-European **kleng-/klong-* bend (Pok. 603). **—lanky** *adj.* 1670, (of hair) straight and flat; later, awkwardly tall and thin (1818); formed from English *lank* + *-y*[1].

lanolin *n.* fat or grease obtained from wool. 1885, borrowed from German *Lanolin,* from Latin *lāna* WOOL + *oleum* OIL + *-īna* -in[2] (chemical suffix). The term was coined by a German physician, Oscar Liebreich.

lantern *n.* About 1250 *lanterne* lamp or lantern; borrowed from Old French *lanterne,* from Latin *lanterna,* from Greek *lamptḗr,* from *lámpein* to shine; see LAMP. The ending *-erna* in Latin *lanterna* (patterned after *lucerna* lamp) may suggest an Etruscan intermediate form or influence of such a form. The architectural meaning of an upright structure on a roof or dome (probably so called from its resemblance to a lantern) is first recorded about 1406.

lanthanum (lan′thənəm) *n.* metallic chemical element. 1841, New Latin, from Greek *lantháneìn* to lie hidden, escape notice; so called because the element was found concealed in oxide of cerium. The term was coined in 1839 by Carl Gustaf Mosander, a Swedish chemist who discovered the element.

lanyard or **laniard** *n.* short rope or cord used on ships to fasten rigging. 1626, in Captain John Smith's writings, perhaps an alteration of Middle English *lainer* thong for fastening parts of armor or clothing (about 1330); later *lanioure* (1425); borrowed from Old French *laniere, lasniere,* from *lasne* strap, thong. Old French *lasne* was apparently an alteration (influenced by *las* LACE) of **nasle* lace, represented by dialectal French (Walloon) *nale* ribbon, from Frankish (compare Old High German and Old Saxon *nestila* lace, strap, band, modern German *Nestel* ribbon, tape, Old Frisian *nestla* lace, band, Middle Dutch and modern Dutch *nestel,* from Proto-Germanic **nastila-,* earlier **nat-st-ila-;* related to Middle Dutch *nette* NET[1] fabric). The later appearance (1626) may have been a reborrowing from French rather than an alteration of Middle English *lanier.* The new form *lanyard* differs greatly from the Middle English and the Middle English form disappears from the record from 1500 to 1626. The spelling of English *lanyard* was influenced by YARD[2] a long beam used to support a sail. Compare HALYARD. *Lanyard* in the sense of a short strap or thong to hold a whistle, knife, etc. is first recorded in 1864.

lap[1] *n.* front part from the waist to the knees of a person sitting down. Probably before 1300 *lappe* lower part of a shirt, in *The Romance of Guy of Warwick;* also, front part from the waist to the knees of a person sitting down; developed from Old English *læppa* skirt or flap on a garment, lappet (before 899, in Alfred's translation of St. Gregory's *Pastoral Care*). The Old English form is cognate with Old Frisian *lappa* flap, Old Saxon *lappo* end, rag, Middle Dutch *lappe* (modern Dutch *lap* rag, patch), Old High German *lappa* flap (modern German *Lappen* rag, cloth), and Old Icelandic *leppr,* from Proto-Germanic **lapp-* (earlier **lapn-*). Outside Germanic possible cognates are also found in Latin *lābī* to slip, glide, fall, and Greek *lobós* pad, flap, from Indo-European **lab-/lob-/lāb-* (Pok. 655).

The figurative sense of a place where anything rests or is cared for (as in *the lap of luxury*) is first recorded in Elyot's *The Boke Named the Governour* (1531). **—lapboard** *n.* (1840, American English) **—lap dog** (1645) **—lapful** *n.* (1611)

lap[2] *v.* to lay (things) together, one partly over another. Probably before 1325 *lappen* to coil, fold, wrap, from *lappe* flap, LAP[1]. The sense of overlap is first recorded in 1607, in Markham's writings. **—n.** 1673, something coiled or wrapped up; from the verb. The meaning of one of the number of turns around the track required to complete the course is first recorded in 1861 (though the verb sense is found as early as 1841 in American English).

lap[3] *v.* lick or lift up with the tongue. Before 1325 *lapen* to drink by lapping; developed from Old English (about 1000) *lapian,* from Proto-Germanic **lapōjanan.* In the Germanic languages Old English *lapian* is cognate with Old High German *laffan* to lick, Old Swedish *lapa* and Icelandic *lepja* to lap, Old Saxon *lepil* spoon, Middle Low German *lepel,* Middle Dutch *lēpel* (modern Dutch *lepel*), and Old High German *leffil* (modern German *Löffel*). Outside Germanic cognates are found in Albanian *lap* I lap water, Latin *lambere* to lick, Greek *láptein* to lap (with *lélaphe* he has lapped), and *laphýssein* to swallow, gulp down, and Armenian *lap'el* to lick, from Indo-European **lab-, *laph-* (Pok.651). The meaning of move with a lapping sound, splash gently, is first recorded in Scott's *Peveril of the Peak* (1823). **—n.** 1567, something lapped; from the verb. The meaning of act of lapping, a lick, smack, or taste, is first recorded in 1820 (though a single instance of a figurative use is found in a version of *Piers Plowman* in 1393).

lapel *n.* part of the front of a coat folded back. 1789, implied earlier in *lapelled* (1751, in Smollett's *The Adventures of Peregrine Pickle*); formed from English LAP[1] flap on a garment + *-el,* diminutive suffix (ultimately from Latin *-ellus, -ella*). Compare LAPPET.

lapidary (lap′əder′ē) *n.* About 1380 *lapidarie* treatise on precious stones, in Chaucer's *House of Fame;* also, before 1382, person who cuts, polishes, or engraves precious stones, in the Wycliffe Bible; borrowed, probably through Old French *lapidaire,* from Latin *lapidārius* stonecutter; originally, adjective, of or working with stone, from *lapis* (genitive *lapidis*) stone, probably cognate with Greek *lépas* bare rock, from Indo-European **lep-* (Pok.678).; for suffix see -ARY.

lapis lazuli (lap′is laz′yəlē) deep-blue, opaque, semiprecious stone. Before 1425, in Trevisa's translation of Bartholomew's *De Proprietatibus Rerum;* borrowed, probably through Old French *lapis lazuli,* from Medieval Latin, a compound of Latin *lapis* stone and Medieval Latin *lazuli,* genitive of *lazulum* lapis lazuli, from Arabic *lāzuward* azure, from Persian *lājward;* compare AZURE.

lappet (lap′it) *n.* small flap, loose fold. Probably about 1425 *lappette* lobe of the lungs or the liver, in a translation of Chauliac's *Grande Chirurgie;* later, flap or fold

(1573); formed from Middle English *lappe* (modern English *lap*) lap[1], flap on a garment + *-et,* diminutive suffix.

lapse *n.* slip of the memory, the tongue, the pen, etc.; slight mistake. 1440 *laps* an elapsing of time; later *lapse* moral transgression, sin (before 1500), and slight mistake (before 1526); borrowed from Middle French *laps* lapse, from Latin *lāpsus* a slipping and falling, flight (of time), a falling into error, from *lābī* to slip, glide, fall; see LAP[1] front part. The legal sense of ending of a right or privilege because of neglect is first recorded about 1447. **—v.** Probably before 1425 *lapsen* (of a humor) to deviate from the normal, in a translation of Chauliac's *Grande Chirurgie;* later, (of time) to go by, pass (about 1443); borrowed from Latin *lāpsāre* lose one's footing, slip, related to *lāpsus* a slipping and falling. The meaning of fall into error, heresy, etc. is first recorded in English in Shakespeare's *Cymbeline* (1611).

As the first recorded meaning of the noun in English refers to time (1440), and the verb sense referring to time also occurs about the same time (1443), it is not very likely that the noun in English developed from the verb, though the verb appears earlier in the record of English.

lapwing *n.* kind of crested plover, pewit. About 1350 *lapwynge,* alteration by folk etymology, which connected the word with *lap*[3], v. and *wing,* n., of Old English (about 1050) *hlēapewince* (*hlēapan* to LEAP + *-wince* totter, waver, related to *wincian* to WINK); so called from the irregular, flapping manner of the bird's flight.

larboard (lar′bərd) *n.* side of a ship to the left of a person looking from the stern toward the bow; port. Perhaps before 1583 *lerbord, larborde,* alteration of Middle English (probably about 1380) *ladde-borde* the loading side (*laden* to load, LADE + *bord* ship's side, BOARD). The alteration of *ladde-borde* to *larborde* and later *larboard* was influenced by *starboard.* **—adj.** on the port side of a ship. 1495, from the noun.

larceny *n.* theft. Before 1475, in John Fortescue's *On the Governance of the Kingdom of England;* borrowed through Anglo-French *larcin* with addition of the English suffix *-y*[3], signifying a condition, from Old French *larrecin* theft, from Latin *latrōcinium* robbery, from *latrō* (genitive *latrōnis*) hireling, mercenary, bandit, from a lost Hellenistic **látrōn* mercenary, formed from Greek *látron* pay, hire, wages; cognate with Sanskrit *rātí-s* willing, generous, from Indo-European **lē (i)-/lə-* provide, furnish (Pok.665). **—larcenous** *adj.* 1742, in Fielding's *Joseph Andrews;* formed from English *larcen(y)* + *-ous.*

larch *n.* tree of the pine family. 1548, in *larch tree;* borrowed from German *Lärche,* from Middle High German *larche, lerche,* from Latin *larix* (genitive *laricis*), possibly from an Indo-European language spoken in prehistoric times in the Alps, since the larch was native to Alpine regions.

lard *n.* fat of pigs and hogs. 1231, as an English word in a Latin context; borrowed from Old French *larde* bacon fat, and directly from Latin *lārdum, lāridum* lard, possibly cognate with Greek *lārīnós* fattened, both words being contractions of derivatives of an Indo-European noun **láyos* bacon, fat (root *lai,* Pok.652). **—v.** insert strips of bacon or salt pork in (meat) before cooking. Before 1338 *larden,* in Mannyng's *Chronicle of England;* borrowed from Old French *larder,* from *larde* bacon fat. The figurative sense of intersperse or garnish (speech or writing), interlard, is first recorded in 1549.

larder *n.* pantry. About 1300, a supply of meat; later, a place for storing meat (1380); borrowed through Anglo-French *larder* a place for meats, corresponding to Old French *lardier* a tub for meats, from Medieval Latin *lardarium* a room for meats, from Latin *lārdum* LARD.

large *adj.* Probably before 1200, abundant, ample, roomy, in *Ancrene Riwle;* also, liberal or generous, lavish; borrowing of Old French *large,* from Latin *lārgus* abundant, copious, of uncertain origin, but possibly related to *lārdum* LARD. The sense of wide in range, extensive, is first recorded before 1325, in *Cursor Mundi;* the general meaning of big, huge, is found in Chaucer's *Canterbury Tales* (about 1385). **—large intestine** (1869) **—largely** *adv.* Probably before 1200 *largeliche;* formed from Middle English *large* + *-liche* -ly[1]. **—large-scale** *adj.* (1887) **—largish** *adj.* (1787)

largess or **largesse** (lärjes′ *or* lär′jis) *n.* generous giving. Probably before 1200, quality of being generous; also, liberal bestowal of gifts, in *Ancrene Riwle;* borrowed from Old French *largesse* a bounty, from *large* LARGE.

largo (lär′gō) *adj. Music.* very slow and dignified, stately. 1683, in notes to a work by Henry Purcell; borrowing of Italian *largo,* literally, wide or broad; from Latin *lārgus* abundant. **—n.** very slow, stately passage or piece of music. 1724, from the adjective in English; also possibly borrowed from Italian *largo,* from the adjective in Italian.

lariat (lar′ēət) *n.* lasso. 1832, American English; borrowed from Spanish *la reata* the rope (*la* the, feminine of *el* + *reata* rope, from *reatar* tie again, *re-* again + *atar* to tie, from Latin *aptāre* to join, from *aptus* joined; see APT).

lark[1] *n.* small songbird. About 1275, as a surname *Larke;* earlier, in the place name *Lauerkesfeld* (1184-85), and *laverche* (probably about 1200); developed from Old English *lāwerce* (about 700); cognate with Frisian *liurk* lark, Old Saxon *lēwerka,* Middle Low German and Middle Dutch *lēwerke* (modern Dutch *leeuwerik*), Old High German *lērihha* (modern German *Lerche*), Old Icelandic *lævirki,* Swedish *lärka,* Danish and Norwegian *lerke,* from Proto-Germanic **laiw(a)rikōn.* The designation is widespread in Germanic but further connections are lacking. **—larkspur** *n.* (1578)

lark[2] *v.* to frolic, sport, play tricks. 1813, possibly a shortened form of *skylark, skylarking* to participate in rough play, originally among sailors, and especially carried on in the rigging of a ship (1809). The verb *lark* was probably also influenced by its earlier noun use. **—n.** 1811, possibly a shortened form of *skylark,* as in *skylarking,* vbl. n.

The meanings of *lark* and *skylark* appear in the record of English about the same time so that one deduction is as likely as another, but it is possible that *lark* was reinforced by northern British English *lake,* a dialect form of the verb meaning to play or sport, developed from *leyken, laiken* to engage in sport or play (probably before 1200, in *The Ormulum*); borrowed from a Scandinavian source (compare Old Icelandic *leika* to play, Swedish *leka,* Danish *lege*); cognate with Middle High German *leichen* to hop, Gothic *laikan* to hop, dance, spring, and Old English *lācan* to swing, play, fight, from Proto-Germanic **laikanan;* cognate also with Old Irish *loíg* calf, and Sanskrit *réjate* hops, from Indo-European **leig-/loig-* (Pok.667).

A similar development is found in the noun *lake,* developed from *leyk, laik* amusement, fun (probably about 1200, in *The Ormulum*); probably borrowed from a Scandinavian source. The correspondence of both the noun and verb meanings of *lake* and *lark* add some force to the suggestion of a connection between the two words.

The OED explains the connection with *lake* (found also as *lairk*) through the shift in pronunciation with an intrusive *r* -sound common to southern British English.

larrup (lar′əp) *v. Informal.* beat, thrash. 1823, originally dialectal; perhaps borrowed from Dutch *larpen* (pronounced lar′əpən) to slap, thrash, box the ears, from *larp* rod, whip, of unknown origin.

larva (lär′və) *n., pl.* **larvae** (lär′vē). *Zoology.* insect in the early immature stage, grub. 1768, New Latin, special use of Latin *lārva,* earlier *lārua* ghost, mask; related to *Lār* (plural *Larēs*) tutelary god or spirit, probably of Etruscan origin.

The word was applied to the immature form of the insect by Linnaeus, because it masked or was a ghost of the adult form (called by Linnaeus an *imago*).

The earliest recorded use of *larva* in English was in the sense of a ghost or specter (1651); also borrowed from Latin *lārva.*

—larval *adj.* 1848, of a larva or grub; borrowed from New Latin *larvalis,* from Latin *lārvālis* of larvae or ghosts, from *lārva* ghost; for suffix see -AL[1]. The earlier sense from Latin is recorded in English in 1656.

laryngeal (lərin′jēəl) *adj.* of the larynx. 1795, formed in English from New Latin *laryngeus* (from Greek *lárynx,* genitive *láryngos*) + English *-al*[1]. **—laryngitis** *n.* inflammation of the larynx. 1822-34, New Latin; formed from Greek *lárynx* (genitive *láryngos*) + *-itis* inflammation.

larynx (lar′ingks) *n.* cavity at the upper end of the windpipe. 1578, borrowed through Middle French *larynx,* from New Latin, from Greek *lárynx* genitive *láryngos*) the upper windpipe, probably altered from *laimós* throat, under the influence of *phárynx* throat, windpipe. The only known relative of Greek *laimós* throat, gullet, is *laîtma* the gulf of the sea, the deep.

lasagna or **lasagne** (ləzän′yə) *n.* dish of wide, flat noodles baked with cheese, tomato sauce, etc. 1846, borrowing of Italian *lasagna,* sing., or *lasagne,* pl., from Vulgar Latin **lasania,* from Latin *lasanum* cooking pot, from Greek *lásanon,* singular of *lásana* trivet or stand for a pot.

lascar (las′kər) *n.* native sailor of the East Indies. 1625, in Purchas' *Pilgrims;* borrowed from Portuguese *lachar* (erroneously *laschar*), probably from Hindi *lashkarī* soldier, native sailor, from *lashkar* army, camp, from Persian *laskar,* from Arabic *al-'askar* the army.

lascivious (ləsiv′ēəs) *adj.* lustful, lecherous. About 1450, perhaps borrowed through Middle French *lascivieux,* from Late Latin *lascīviōsus,* from Latin *lascīvia* lewdness or playfulness, from *lascīvus* lewd or playful, see LUST; for suffix see -OUS.

laser *n.* device which generates and amplifies light waves of a pure color in a narrow and extremely intense beam of light. 1960, acronym formed from *l(ight*) *a(mplification by*) *s(timulated*) *e(mission of*) *r(adiation*), on the pattern of the earlier (1955) MASER. **—lase** *v.* to function or operate as a laser. 1962, back formation from LASER.

lash[1] *n.* part of a whip that is not the handle. Probably before 1300 *las* a blow or stroke, in *Arthour and Merlin;* later *lashe* flexible part of a whip (about 1380, in Chaucer's *Parlement of Foules*), possibly of imitative origin. **—v.** Probably before 1300 *laisen* to strike out, throw, or move violently, in *Arthour and Merlin;* later *lasschen* to whip or flog (before 1398, in Trevisa's translation of Bartholomew's *De Proprietatibus Rerum*); possibly of imitative origin, as the noun.

lash[2] *v.* bind with a rope or cord. 1624, in Captain John Smith's *The General Historie of Virginia;* developed from *lasschyn* to lace a garment (1440, in *Promptorium Parvulorum*); probably borrowed from Middle French *lachier,* from Old French *lacier* to LACE. **—lashing** *n.* cord used for binding (1669).

lass *n.* About 1300 *lasce,* later *las, lasse* (about 1390); possibly borrowed from a Scandinavian source (compare Old Icelandic *lǫskr* idle, weak, Old Swedish *løsk kona* unmarried woman, literally, one without a fixed dwelling); cognate with West Frisian *lask* light, thin, and dialectal German *lasch* slack or weak. **—lassie** *n.* 1725, formed from English *lass* + *-ie.*

lassitude *n.* lack of energy, weakness, weariness. Probably before 1425, in a translation of Chauliac's *Grande Chirurgie;* borrowed from Middle French *lassitude,* from Latin *lassitūdō* faintness or weariness, from *lassus* faint, tired, weary, see LET[1] to allow; for suffix see -TUDE.

lasso (las′ō *or* lasü′) *n.* long rope with a running noose at one end; lariat. 1819, American English; borrowed from Spanish *lazo,* from Latin *laqueum,* accusative of *laqueus* noose, snare; see the doublet LACE. **—v.** catch with a lasso. 1831, American English. A single instance of the verb is found earlier in a travel book on Argentina (1807), but since its wider continuous appearance does not occur until the 1830's, it is probable that the verb use is from the noun.

last[1] *adj., adv.* coming at the end. Probably before 1200 *leaste,* in *Ancrene Riwle;* also *laste, latste* (probably about 1200, in *The Ormulum*); developed from the contraction of Old English *latost* (from Proto-Germanic **latast-*) and Old English, *lætest* (from Proto-Germanic **latist-*), found before 899, in Alfred's translation of Boethius' *De Consolatione Philosophiae.* The Old English forms are superlatives of *læt,* adj. and *late,* adv. (see LATE) and correspond to Middle Dutch *laetst* last (modern Dutch *laatst*), Old High German *lazzost, lezzist* (modern German *letzt*), and Old Icelandic *latastr* slowest.

Though modern English *latest* is similar in form to Old English *lætest,* the superlative *latest* is a formation from Middle English *late* + *-est* (probably before 1200) and is not a resultant of the Old English form.

—n. one that is last. Probably before 1200 *laste,* in Layamon's *Chronicle of Britain;* from the adjective.

—last-ditch *adj.* 1951, back formation from earlier *last-ditcher* one who fights to the last ditch (1909). **—last hurrah** 1956, American English, from *The Last Hurrah,* a novel by Edwin O'Connor, 1918-68, American novelist. **—lastly** *adv.* About 1375, formed from Middle English *laste* last + *-ly*[1]. **—last straw** (1848, in Dickens' *Dombey and Son*) **—last word** (1563)

last[2] *v.* go on, hold out, endure. 1122 *læsten;* later *lasten* (1137); developed from Old English *lǣstan* to continue, endure (possibly about 750, in Cynewulf's *Christ*); earlier, accomplish, carry out (about 725, in *Beowulf*). Old English *lǣstan* is cognate with Old Frisian *lāsta, lesta* to fulfill, Old Saxon *lēstian* to perform, Old High German and modern German *leisten* to perform, carry out, and Gothic *laistjan* to follow, from Proto-Germanic **laistjanan;* all derived from the same Germanic source as Old English *lāst* track, footprint; see LAST[3]. —**lasting** *adj.* Before 1333 (replacing earlier *lestind*); from the present participle of *last*[2] endure; for suffix see -ING[2].

last[3] *n.* shoemaker's block shaped like a foot. Before 1300 *leste;* later *laste* (1395); developed from Old English *lǣste* (about 1000, in Ælfric's *Glossary*), from earlier *lāst* track, footprint, trace (about 725, in *Beowulf*). The Old English forms are cognate with Middle Dutch and modern Dutch *leest* form, model, last, Old High German *leist* (modern German *Leisten* last), Old Icelandic *leistr* trouser leg, sock, and Gothic *laists* footprint, from Proto-Germanic **laistaz,* cognate with Latin *līra* furrow, from Indo-European **leis-/lois-* (Pok.671). —**v.** form (shoes) on a last. 1880, from the noun.

latch *v.* Probably before 1200 *lecchen* catch, ensnare, in *Ancrene Riwle;* later *lacchen* (about 1250), and *latchen* (before 1338); developed from Old English *læccan* to grasp or seize (about 950, in *Lindisfarne Gospels*), from Proto-Germanic **lakkjanan* (with stem **lakk-* from earlier **lagn-*), cognate with Greek *lázesthai* grasp (from earlier **lagwje-*) and *labeîn* seize, from Indo-European **(s)lagw-* (Pok.958). The sense of fasten with a latch (from the noun) is first recorded in *Promptorium Parvulorum* (1440). —**n.** a catch for fastening a door, etc. 1296-97 *lacche* (English word in Latin context); later *latche* (about 1350); from *lacchen* to catch. —**latchkey** *n.* (1825) —**latchstring** *n.* (1791)

late *adj.* Probably before 1200 *let* slow or sluggish; later *lat, late* tardy, remiss (about 1225); developed from Old English *læt* late, slow, sluggish (about 725, in *Beowulf*); cognate with Old Frisian *let* late, Old Saxon *lat* lazy, Middle Low German *lat,* Middle Dutch *laet* (modern Dutch *laat* late), Old High German *laz* slow (modern German *lass* indolent, weary), Old Icelandic *latr* sluggish, lazy (Swedish, Norwegian *lat,* Danish *lad*), Gothic *lats,* from Proto-Germanic **latás,* Indo-European **lədós,* and related to Old English *lǣtan* to allow, LET[1]. —**adv.** Probably before 1200 *late;* found in Old English *late* (about 750, in Cynewulf's *Juliana*); from *læt,* adj. —**latecomer** *n.* (1869) —**lately** *adv.* About 1340 *latly,* formed from Middle English *lat* late + *-ly*[1].

lateen (latēn′) *adj. Nautical.* having a triangular sail held up by a long yard on a short mast. 1727-41, in *Chambers Cyclopædia;* borrowed from French *latine* in *voile latine* Latin sail; so called from its use in the Mediterranean. An earlier form *latten* (1540) with the same sense is cited by Weekley in his *Etymological Dictionary of Modern English.*

latent *adj.* present but not active, hidden. 1459, concealed or secret; borrowed through Middle French *latent,* and directly from Latin *latentem* (nominative *latēns*), present participle of *latēre* to lie hidden, cognate with Greek *latheîn, lanthánein* escape notice, from Indo-European **lā (i)-/lə-, lā-dh-/lə-dh-* Pok.651); for suffix see -ENT. The specialized meaning "(of a disease) dormant," is first recorded in 1684. —**latency** *n.* Before 1638; formed from English *latent* + *-cy.*

lateral *adj.* of or at the side. Probably before 1425 *laterale,* in a translation of Chauliac's *Grande Chirurgie;* borrowed through Middle French *latéral,* and directly from Latin *laterālis* belonging to the side, from *latus* (genitive *lateris*) side; of uncertain origin. —**n.** lateral part or outgrowth. 1635, from the adjective.

latex (lā′teks) *n.* milky liquid found in various plants. 1662, body fluid; borrowed from Latin *latex* (genitive *laticis*) liquid, fluid, probably from Greek *látax* (genitive *látagos*) drops of wine in the bottom of a cup, dregs; cognate with Old Icelandic *lethja* loam, and Middle Irish *laith* a liquid, from Indo-European **lat-* wet (Pok.654). The sense of a milky liquid from plants is first recorded in 1835, and from that the word's application to an emulsion of synthetic rubber is found in 1937.

lath *n.* thin, narrow strip of wood formerly used to make a support for plaster or to make a lattice. 1281-82 *lathe* (English word in Latin context); later *laththe* (before 1393); probably developed from Old English **læththe,* variant of *lætt* lath; cognate with Old Saxon *latta* lath, Middle Dutch *latte* (modern Dutch *lat*), and Old High German *latta* (modern German *Latte*), apparently from Proto-Germanic **laththō,* whose double *th* is otherwise unexampled. The relation of the Germanic types is obscure. Other cognates are found in Celtic: Old Irish *slat* rod, switch, Welsh *llath* rod, wand, yard, and Breton *laz,* from Proto-Celtic **slattā.* The view of W.W. Skeat is still perhaps the best: that the Middle English form was influenced by Welsh *llath* (with *ei lath* for *his rod*). The Indo-European root would be **(s)lat-.* —**v.** cover or line with laths. 1439, from the noun.

lathe (lāᴛʜ) *n.* machine for turning and shaping wood, metal, etc. 1310, device used by coopers, perhaps a turning lathe; probably borrowed from a Scandinavian source (compare Danish *-lad* stand, supporting framework, as in *drejelad* turning lathe, *savelad* saw bench, *væverlad* loom, and Old Icelandic *hladh* layered pile or pile regularly built up as from the shavings of a lathe, related to *hladha* to load, LADE). The first particular reference to a turning lathe is found in Cotgrave's *Dictionary* (1611).

lather *n.* 1583, probably redeveloped in modern English from the Middle English verb. A noun is found in Old English (about 1000) *lēathor* washing soda, lather; cognate with Old Icelandic *laudhr* foam, washing soda, from Proto-Germanic **laúthran,* Greek *loutrón* (earlier *loetrón*) bath, and ultimately with Latin *lavere* to wash, from Indo-European **lou-, lowə-* (Pok.692). No developing form is recorded in Middle English, which strongly suggests that the noun is the result of a functional shift of the verb. —**v.** About 1450 *latheren* to wash or soak clothes, alteration of earlier *litheren, letheren* be bathed in, be covered with foam, sweat, etc. (probably about 1200); developed from Old English *lēthran, lȳthran* to cover with lather (about 950, in *Lindisfarne Gospels*); cognate with Old Icelandic *leydhra* to clean, wash.

Latin *n.* About 1275 *latyn,* possibly from the adjective, and rarely found in Old English *latin* (about 950, in *Lindisfarne Gospels*); borrowed from Latin *Latīnum.* The Old English form in general use was *lǣden* (before 899, in Alfred's translation of St. Gregory's *Pastoral Care*), also found in Middle English, and altered from earlier **læden,* from Vulgar Latin **Ladīnum,* a variant of Latin *Latīnum,* having arisen from a confusion with *lēden, lȳden, lēoden* language. The OED says the confusion originated with the compound *bōc-lēden* book language, which was formed by popular etymology as a synonym for *lǣden.* **—adj.** About 1391 *Latin,* in the *Prologue* to Chaucer's *Treatise on the Astrolabe,* found in Old English *latin* (about 950, in *Lindisfarne Gospels*); borrowing of Latin *Latīnus* belonging to Latium, the part of Italy that included Rome.

Latino (latēʹnō) *n., adj.* Latin American. 1946, American English; borrowing of American Spanish *Latino,* shortened form of Spanish *Latinoamericano* Latin-American, (person) of or from Latin America.

latitude *n.* distance north or south of the equator. About 1390, breadth, width, geographical latitude, in Chaucer's *Canterbury Tales;* borrowed through Old French *latitude,* and directly from Latin *lātitūdō* breadth, width, extent, size, from *lātus* wide, earlier **stlātos,* cognate with Old Slavic *po-stĭlati* to spread out, from Indo-European **stelə-, stl̥tós* (Pok.1018); for suffix see -TUDE.

The figurative sense of an allowable degree or range of variation is first recorded probably before 1425; that of freedom from narrow restrictions, permitted variety of action or opinion, is found in Bacon's *Of the Advancement of Learning* (1605).

—latitudinal *adj.* 1392 *latitudinel* relating to breadth or width; later *latitudinal* (probably before 1425); borrowed from Old French *latitudinel* and from Medieval Latin *latitudinalis,* from Latin *lātitūdinis,* genitive of *lātitūdō* latitude; for suffix see -AL[1]. Reference to geographical latitude is first recorded in 1778.

latrine *n.* toilet in a camp, barracks, etc.; privy. 1297 *laterin* a privy, probably borrowed from Latin *lātrīna,* contraction of *lavātrīna* washbasin, washroom (*lavāre* to wash, LAVE + *-trīna* suffix added to a verb stem and denoting a workplace). The word disappeared from the record of English and is not found again until 1642 as a new borrowing from French (usually in the plural form *latrines*), learned borrowing from Latin *lātrīna.*

latter *adj.* About 1175 *lator, later;* later *lattre,* adj. and adv., less early, at a later time (probably about 1200); developed from Old English *lætra, lator* slower (about 1000). The Old English forms are the comparatives of Old English *læt* LATE, and correspond to Old Frisian *letora* latter, Middle High German *lazzer* slower, and Old Icelandic *latari.* The meaning of second of two is first recorded in 1555.

Though modern English *later* is similar in form to Old English *lætra,* the comparative *later* is a formation in early modern English (1559 adj., 1548 adv.) from *late* + *-er*[2], and is not a resultant of the Old English form.

lattice *n.* 1304 *lattis;* later *latyce* (probably about 1450); borrowed from Old French *latte* lath, from Frankish (compare Old High German *latta* LATH). **—v.** furnish with a lattice or latticework. 1427-28 *latisen;* from the noun.

laud *v.* to praise. About 1378 *lauden,* in a version of *Piers Plowman;* borrowed from Old French *lauder* and from Latin *laudāre* to praise, from *laus* (genitive *laudis*) praise, fame, glory, from Indo-European **ləu-d-.* The Latin *laus* is probably cognate with Old English *lēoth* song, poem, hymn, Middle Dutch *liet* (modern Dutch *lied*), Old High German *liod* (modern German *Lied* song), Old Icelandic *ljōdh* strophe, stanza, from Proto-Germanic **leuthan,* Indo-European **lēu-t-,* root **lēu-/ləu-* a sound or cry (Pok.683). **—n.** praise. About 1375 *laude* praise or fame, in Chaucer's *Canterbury Tales;* borrowed from Old French *laude,* learned borrowing from Latin *laudem,* and probably borrowed directly from Latin *laudem* (nominative *laus*) praise, glory, fame.

The plural form *lauds* a morning church service with psalms of praise to God (one of the canonical hours) is first recorded as *laudes,* in *Ayenbite of Inwyt* (1340); borrowed through Old French *laudes* and directly from Medieval Latin, from Latin *laudēs,* plural of *laus* praise, glory, fame.

It is also possible that this plural use of the noun was the immediate source of the generalized sense of "praise," as found above in Chaucer's *Canterbury Tales,* and that the noun, in some instances, influenced the development of the verb in Middle English.

—laudable *adj.* praiseworthy. Probably before 1425, borrowed from Old French *laudable,* and from Latin *laudābilis* praiseworthy, from *laudāre* to praise; for suffix see -ABLE. **—laudatory** *adj.* expressing praise. 1555, borrowed from Middle French *laudatoire,* and directly from Late Latin *laudātōrius* of praise, from Latin *laudātor* praiser, from *laudāre* to praise; for suffix see -ORY.

laudanum (lôʹdənəm) *n.* solution of opium in alcohol. 1602-3, borrowed through Middle French *laudanum,* and directly from New Latin *laudanum,* a word used by Paracelsus as the name for an expensive concoction used as a medicine which was supposed to contain opium. The origin of the word is uncertain, though it may have been confused with *ladanum,* borrowed from Latin *lādanum* a gum resin, from Greek *lā́danon, lḗdanon,* probably of Semitic origin.

laugh *v.* Probably before 1200 *lahhen,* in *Ancrene Riwle;* later *laughen* (about 1375, in Chaucer's *Anelida and Arcite*); developed from Old English *hlæhhan* (before 830, in the *Vespasian Psalter*); earlier *hlihhan* (before 725, in *Genesis A*); cognate with Old Frisian *hlakkia* to laugh, Old Saxon *hlahhian,* Middle Dutch and modern Dutch *lachen,* Old High German *hlahhan, lahhēn* (modern German *lachen*), Old Icelandic *hlǣja* (Swedish, Danish, and Norwegian *le*), and Gothic *hlahjan,* from Proto-Germanic **HlaHjanan,* cognate with Greek *klṓssein* cluck, from Indo-European **klōk-/klək-* (Pok.600), probably ultimately of imitative origin.

The original sound, as represented by *gh* in *laugh, cough, rough,* etc., was like that of Scottish *loch* or German *ach.* As the pronunciation shifted to the sound of *f* in *off,* the spelling of some words also changed to reflect this process, as in *dwarf, draft* (for *draught*), etc.; but some spellings remained fixed.

The meaning of a cause of laughter, joke, is first recorded in 1895, in George Bernard Shaw's writings.

—n. 1690, act of laughing, laughter; later, instance of laughing (as in *a hearty laugh;* 1713, in Steele's writings); from the verb.

—laughable *adj.* 1596, in Shakespeare's *Merchant of Venice;* formed from English *laugh,* v. + *-able.* **—laughingstock** *n.* (1533) **—laughter** *n.* Probably before 1200 *lahtre,* in *Ancrene Riwle;* later *laughter* (about 1385, in Chaucer's *Troilus and Criseyde*); developed from Old English *hleahtor* (about 725, in *Beowulf*). Old English *hleahtor* corresponds to Old High German *lahtar* laughter (modern German *Gelächter*), Old Icelandic *hlātr,* and Danish, Norwegian *latter,* from Proto-Germanic **HlaHtraz,* and is derived from the same Germanic source as Old English *hlihhan, hlæhhan* to laugh.

launch[1] *v.* throw forward, propel. Probably before 130 *launchen* to leap, spring, rush, in *Kyng Alisaunder;* later, to throw, hurl, as a weapon (about 1330); borrowed from Old North French *lancher, lanchier,* corresponding to Old French *lancer, lancier* to fling, throw, from Late Latin *lanceāre* wield a lance, pierce with a lance, from Latin *lancea* light spear, LANCE.

The sense of put into the water, set afloat, is first recorded probably before 1400, in *Morte Arthur;* the meaning was extended to apply to any vehicle, such as a rocket, by 1873. The figurative sense of start, set going, set out (as in *to launch an enterprise*), is recorded in 1602. Doublet of LANCE, v.

—n. act of launching. 1440 *launche* a leap or bound, in *Promptorium Parvulorum;* from the verb. The application to that of launching a vessel is first recorded in a letter of Scott to Southey in 1814. **—launching pad** (1951)

launch[2] *n.* small, open motorboat. 1697, largest boat carried by a warship; borrowed from Spanish and Portuguese *lancha* barge or launch, apparently from Malay *lanchāran,* from *lanchār* quick, agile. The English spelling was probably influenced by *launch*[1]. The sense of a small boat (later a motorboat) used for transporting passengers from a large ship or as a pleasure craft, is first recorded in 1865.

launder *v.* 1664, in Samuel Butler's *Hudibras;* from the noun *launder* one who washes, especially linen (1440), contraction of earlier *lavender* (about 1325), also found as a surname *Lavendre* (1227); borrowed from Old French *lavandier* male washer, *lavandiere* female washer, laundress, from Medieval Latin *lavandaria* a washer, from Latin *lavanda* (things) to be washed, from *lavāre* to wash, LAVE; for suffix see -ER[1]. The modern specialized meaning "(of money) make seem legitimate, lawfully gained, or acceptable," is first recorded in 1970, from the idea of "cleansing" illegally obtained ("dirty") money. **—laundress** *n.* 1550, in Coverdale's writings; formed from English *launder* + *-ess.* **—laundry** *n.* Before 1450 *lawndre* act of washing; earlier *lavendrye* place for washing (about 1378, in a version of *Piers Plowman*); borrowed from Old French *lavanderie,* from *lavandier, lavandiere* washer; for suffix see -RY.

launderette *n.* = laundromat. 1949, American English, formed from English *launder,* v. + *-ette.*

laundromat (lôn′drəmat) *n.* self-service laundry. 1943 *Laundromat,* American English (a trademark by the Westinghouse Electric Company for an automatic washing machine); formed from English *laundr(y)* + *-o-* + *-mat,* as in *automat.*

laureate *adj.* crowned with a laurel wreath as a mark of honor. About 1375, in Chaucer's *Canterbury Tales;* borrowed from Latin *laureātus,* from *laurea* laurel crown, laurel tree, from feminine of *laureus* of laurel, from *laurus* LAUREL; for suffix see -ATE[3].

The term *poet laureate* is first found in Lydgate's works in 1429, though *laureat poete* is to be found in Chaucer's *Canterbury Tales.* The first poet laureate of England in the modern sense of a poet who receives a stipend from the royal household was Ben Jonson, but the title seems to have been first given officially to his successor, Sir William Davenant, who was appointed in 1638.

—n. poet laureate. Before 1529, in Skelton's *Calliope;* from the adjective.

laurel *n.* small evergreen tree. 1373 *laureol,* and before 1375 *lorel;* later *laurel* (about 1415); borrowed from Latin *laureola* small laurel branch, from *laurus* laurel tree, thought to be somehow from the same (apparently Mediterranean) source as Greek *dáphnē* laurel (with dialectal variants *daúchnā* and *dauchmós*).

lava (lä′və) *n.* molten rock from a volcano. 1750, borrowing of Italian *lava,* from dialectal Italian (Neapolitan or Calabrian) *lava,* of uncertain origin (by traditional etymology, from Latin *lavāre* to wash, originally in Italian said to be from a rivulet caused by sudden downpour of rain, found in Florio, 1611). Italian etymologists derive the word from Latin *lābēs* a fall, from *lābī* to fall; see LAP[1], n. Kluge-Götze, however, consider it to be a pre-Indo-European word for "stone," similar to German *Lawine* avalanche.

lavaliere, lavalier or **lavalliere** (lav′əlir′) *n.* ornament hanging from a chain around the neck. 1873 *Lavalliere* a style of hat; later *La Valiere* a style of necktie, borrowed from French *lavallière* necktie with a large loose knot, in allusion to the Duchesse de *La Vallière* (Françoise Louise de La Baume Le Blanc, 1644-1710, mistress of Louis XIV of France). The meaning of a small microphone hung around the neck is first recorded in 1960 in American English.

lavatory *n.* washroom. Before 1382 *lavatorie, lavatory* washbasin, in the Wycliffe Bible; borrowed from Latin *lavātōrium* place for washing, from *lavāre* to wash, LAVE; for suffix see -ORY. The meaning of a washroom is first recorded in English in Blount's *Glossographia* (1656). *Lavatory* as a euphemism for bathroom or toilet is found in 1845.

lave *v. Archaic.* to wash, bathe. Probably before 1200 *laven* to wash, bathe; formed in part by: 1) development from Old English *gelafian* wash by pouring, pour, as water, etc. (about 725, in *Beowulf*); possibly an early borrowing from Latin *lavāre, lavere* to wash, and corresponding to Old Saxon *laƀon,* Middle Dutch *laven,* and Old High German *labōn* (possibly only accidentally similar in form because the continental Germanic words, especially the Old High German, mean refresh, and only at an early stage, if ever, meant to wash); and 2) by probable influence in form and meaning of Old French *laver* to wash, from Latin *lavāre,* and perhaps reinforced by Latin *lavāre* itself, which is cognate with Greek *loúein* to wash, Old Irish *lūaith* ashes (as a cleansing agent), and Armenian *loganam* I bathe, from Indo-European **lou-/lowə-* (Pok.692).

lavender *n.* plant with pale-purple flowers. 1373 *lavandyr,* borrowed through Anglo-French *lavendre,* from Medieval Latin *lavendula, livendula* lavender, perhaps derived from Latin *līvidus* bluish, LIVID; probably later associated with French *lavande* and Italian *lavanda* lavender, from *lavanda* a washing (so called because of its use in washing or its use to perfume distilled water) from *lavare,* from Latin *lavāre,* from the plant's use as a bath perfume. (The connection with washing is not accepted by Bradley in the OED.) **—adj.** pale-purple. 1840, from the noun.

lavish *adj.* giving or spending without stint; prodigal. 1469 *laves* outpouring, unrestrained, profuse, prodigal; later *lavas* (1485); possibly developed as an adjective use of earlier *lavas,* n., profusion, extravagant outpouring (not recorded before 1483, in Caxton's *The Golden Legend*); borrowed from Middle French *lavasse, lavache* torrent (of rain), deluge, from *laver* to wash, from Latin *lavāre* LAVE; for suffix see -ISH[1]. It is also possible that *lauessh existed as a parallel form, implied in *laues-shenes* lavishness (about 1477). **—v.** give or spend without stint. 1542, in Udall's translation of Erasmus' *Apothegms;* from the adjective.

law *n.* Probably about 1200 *lawe;* developed from Old English (before 1000) *lagu;* borrowed from a Scandinavian source (compare Old Icelandic *lǫg* law, collective plural of *lag* layer, measure, stroke; literally, something laid down or fixed). The Scandinavian forms correspond to *-lag* in Old Saxon *gilag* decree, fate, *orlag* fate, war, and Old High German *urlag* fate, from Proto-Germanic **laȝan,* Indo-European **loghom,* root **legh-* to lie (Pok.658). The semantic development from "something laid down" to "decree, law" is not unique to English but is also found in German *Gesetz* law, from *setzen* to set down, and outside Germanic in Latin and Greek.

The concept of international law, or the *law of nations* is first recorded in English before 1548, as widespread trade, general commerce, and closer contact among the nations of Europe necessitated the function of envoys, ambassadors and other representatives of government. Paralleling the function of such representatives in the Roman Empire, the men of affairs made recourse to Latin *jus gentium,* which was already embodied in part in the concept of the *law of nature,* first alluded to in English about 1225, from Latin *lex naturae, lex naturalis, jus naturale,* in Cicero, Seneca, and other Roman jurists, but ultimately derived from Aristotle. This system of legal concepts was also developed out of Old Testament law, first found in Old English in Ælfric's commentaries (about 1000).

—lawbreaker *n.* (1440 *lawe brekare,* in *Promptorium Parvulorum*) **—lawful** *adj.* About 1300, in a later version of Layamon's *Chronicle of Britain;* as a surname (1230); formed from Middle English *lawe* + *-ful,* possibly influenced by Old Icelandic *lǫgfullr* lawful. **—lawgiver** *n.* Before 1382, in the Wycliffe Bible; formed from Middle English *lawe* + *giver,* possibly influenced by Old Icelandic *lǫg-gjafari,* Danish *lovgiver* lawgiver. **—lawless** *adj.* Before 1268; formed from Middle English *lawe* + *-less.* **—lawmaker** *n.* (about 1475) **—lawman** *n.* 1535, a lawyer; later, law-enforcement officer (1865); in Middle English and late Old English, a magistrate of a borough or town (1130-35, in Anglo-Latin *lagamannus,* probably before 1200 as a surname); possibly influenced in its formation by Old Icelandic *lǫgmann.* **—lawsuit** *n.* 1624; formed from English *law* + *suit.*

lawn[1] *n.* grassy ground. 1548 *laune* glade, open space between woods; developed from *launde* (probably before 1300, in *Arthour and Merlin*); borrowed from Old French *lande* heath, moor, from Gaulish (compare Breton *lann* heath, and Old Irish *land* open space; see LAND). The meaning of grassy ground, kept mown, is first recorded in 1733. **—lawn mower** (1869) **—lawn tennis** (1874)

lawn[2] *n.* thin, sheer linen or cotton cloth. 1416 *lawnd* (possibly by confusion with the spelling *launde* glade, open ground), and *lawn* (1423); probably from *Laon* a city in France, long a center of linen manufacture.

lawrencium (lôren′sēəm) *n.* radioactive chemical element. 1961, a New Latin formation based on the name of Ernest O. *Lawrence* (an American physicist, 1901-1958, who founded the laboratory where this element was discovered) + *-ium,* chemical suffix.

lawyer *n.* Probably 1383 *lawiere* one skilled in the law, in Wycliffe's writings (but found earlier in the surname *Lawyer,* 1336); formed from Middle English *lawe* LAW + *-iere* -ier. The spelling with *y* is first recorded in 1611.

lax[1] *adj.* loose, slack. 1373 *lax* loose or open; later, not strict, careless, negligent (about 1450); borrowed from Latin *laxus* wide, loose, open, from Indo-European *(s)ləg-so-s,* root *(s)lēg-* as in Greek *lḗgein* leave off (Pok.959); related to Latin *languēre* be weak, feeble, faint. **—laxity** *n.* looseness, slackness. 1528, borrowed from Middle French *laxité,* learned borrowing from Latin *laxitātem* (nominative *laxitās*), from *laxus* loose, LAX[1]; for suffix see -ITY.

lax[2] *n.* salmon. Before 1200 *lex,* also in the place name *Lexemer* (1187); later *lax* (about 1300), in *Havelok the Dane*); developed from Old English *leax, læx* (before 800); cognate with Old Saxon, Middle High German, and Old High German *lahs* salmon (modern German *Lachs*), and Old Icelandic, Swedish *lax,* Norwegian and Danish *laks,* from Proto-Germanic **laHs-.* Outside Germanic also cognate with Lithuanian *lãšis* salmon, Russian *losós,* and Tocharian B *laks* fish, from Indo-European **lā̆ksos* (Pok.653). Related to LOX[1] smoked salmon.

laxative *n.* medicine that makes the bowels move. 1373 *laxatife,* borrowed as a noun use from Old French *laxatif,* adj., learned borrowing from Medieval Latin *laxativus* loosening, from Latin *laxāre* loosen, from *laxus* loose, LAX[1]; for suffix see -IVE. The spelling *laxative* is first recorded probably before 1425. **—adj.** making the bowels move. 1373 *laxatife* having freely moving bowels, not constipated; later, making the bowels move (before 1387); borrowed from Old French *laxatif.*

lay[1] *v.* put or set down. About 1150 *leyen, leggen;* developed from Old English *lecgan* put down (before 725, in *Genesis A*); cognate with Old Frisian *lega, leia* to cause to lie, lay, Old Saxon *leggian,* Middle Dutch *legghen* (modern Dutch *leggen*), Old High German and modern German *legen,* Old Icelandic *leggja* (Swedish *lägga,* Danish *lægge, Norwegian legge*), and Gothic *lagjan,* from Proto-Germanic **laȝjanan,* causative of LIE[2], from Indo-European **legh-/logh-* (Pok.658). **—n.** 1558, act of laying a tax; from the verb. The meaning of way in which a thing is laid or lies (as in *the lay of the land*) is first recorded in 1819.

lay[2] *adj.* of ordinary people; not of the clergy or a profession. About 1303 *lai* secular, in Mannyng's *Handlyng Synne;* later *lay* unlearned, uneducated (before 1338), and nonclerical (before 1438); borrowed from Old French *lai,* from Late Latin *lāicus,* from Greek *lāïkós* of the people, from *lāós* (earlier *lāwós*) people, of unknown origin.**—layman** *n.* man outside the clergy or a profession. Probably about 1425, in a translation of Higden's *Polychronicon;* formed from Middle English *lay*[2] + *man.* **—laywoman** *n.* woman outside the clergy or a profession. 1529, in Sir Thomas More's writings; formed from English *lay*[2] + *woman.*

lay[3] *n.* short poem to be sung. Before 1250 *lai* a song or lyric; later *lay* short poem to be sung (probably before 1300, in *Kyng Alisaunder*); borrowed from Old French *lai,* of uncertain origin; possibly from a Celtic source (compare Irish *laid* song, poem); this is rejected in the OED by Bradley, who favors a Germanic connection, citing Old High German and Middle High German *leich* play, melody, song, and Old Icelandic *lag* tune, but Bloch and Wartburg look to a Celtic origin

layer *n.* Before 1382 *leyer* one who lays stones for a building, a mason, in the Wycliffe Bible; earlier *legger* (1282); formed from *leggen,* variant of *leien* to lay[1] + *-er.* The sense of something that is laid, thickness of matter laid over a surface, stratum, course, bed, is first recorded in 1615. **—layer cake** (1881)

layette (lāet′) *n.* set of clothes, bedding, etc., for a newborn baby. 1839, borrowing of French *layette,* from Middle French *layette* chest of drawers, from *laie* drawer or box, from Middle Dutch *laeye;* cognate with Middle High German *lade* box (modern German *Lade* container, box, chest), from Proto-Germanic **Hlathō;* see LADE; for suffix see -ETTE.

lazar (laz′ər *or* lā′zər) *n.* diseased person, especially a leper. Probably about 1300 *lazer,* in *Amis and Amiloun;* also in the surname *Lazur* (1280); borrowed from Medieval Latin *lazarus* leper, from Late Latin *Lazarus,* name of the beggar full of sores described in the New Testament (Luke 16:20).

lazaretto (laz′əret′ō) *n.* hospital for people with contagious diseases. 1549, borrowing of Italian *lazzaretto,* a blend of *lazzaro* leper (from Medieval Latin *lazarus* LAZAR) and dialectal (Venice) *nazareto,* from Santa Maria di *Nazaret* (St. Mary of Nazareth), the name of a hospital in Venice.

lazy *adj.* 1549 *laysy* disliking work, idle, slothful; origin uncertain, possibly borrowed from Middle Low German *lasich* weak, feeble, tired; cognate with Middle High German *erleswen* grow weak, Old Icelandic *lasinn* weak, slack, limp, Gothic *lasiws* weak; also cognate with Bulgarian *loš* bad, wicked, and Tocharian A *ljäsk-* softness, weakness. The spelling with *z* is first recorded in Shakespeare's *Midsummer Night's Dream* (1590). The transferred sense of sluggish, dull, slow-moving (as in *a lazy mist, a lazy hour*), appeared before 1568, in Roger Ascham's *The Schoolmaster.*

It is tempting to construct a development through possible forms such as **lase* to Middle English *laches, lachesse* soft, wanton, lazy (probably about 1425) and *lach, lache* slack, negligent (probably about 1422); loose, open (probably about 1300); and thence to Old French *lasche, lache;* however, the lack of phonological connection and the persistent appearance of the older forms in late Middle English, leave such a connection wanting.

—v. be lazy, laze. 1612; from the adjective.

—n. act of lazing, idleness. 1862; from the verb.

—laze *v.* be lazy, idle. About 1588, in Robert Greene's *The Comicall History of Alphonsus, King of Arragon;* back formation from LAZY. **—lazily** *adv.* (1587) **—laziness** *n.* (1580) **—lazybones** *n.* lazy person (1592).

-le[1] a suffix forming nouns found in the names of tools and utensils, as in *handle, thimble, kettle,* and in the names of articles worn to accomplish a purpose, as in *bridle, girdle.* In words such as *bundle* the purpose of *-le* and its relationship to the base form is unclear.

The suffix had also a diminutive sense in Old English, which is found in words such as *nozzle* and *bramble,* but this has lost its force in modern English (compare use as a frequentative form in Middle English and modern English *-le*[3]).

Modern English *-le* developed from Middle English *-el, -ele,* and is also found in Middle English *-le,* all of which developed from or are found in Old English noun suffixes *-el, -ela, -ele, -le, -l.* The Old English forms are cognate with Old Frisian *-le,* Old Saxon and Old High German *-al, -la* (modern German *-el*), Old Icelandic *-al, -ill* and Gothic *-ils.*

A number of words that have the appearance of belonging to this group are the same in form only by influence of the similarity in pronunciation. Among such words, usually borrowed from Old French are: *battle, bottle, castle, cattle, mantle,* though *riddle,* by confusion of *s* as a sign of the plural in Old English *-els,* is in a separate category. The borrowings from Old French *-el,* as in *castle,* derive from Latin *-ellum* a diminutive suffix, or as in *cattle* from Latin *-āle* neuter singular; in *battle* the Old French form *-aille* is the neuter plural of Latin *-ālis,* in *bottle* the Old French form *-eille* derives from the Latin diminutive suffix *-icula.*

-le[2] a suffix forming adjectives with the meaning of liable (to do something) or apt (to be something), as in *fickle* and *brittle,* and usually having no obvious significance as a particle because the root forms from Middle and Old English are no longer recognizable.

Modern English *-le* developed from Middle English *-el, -ele,* and is also found in Middle English *-le,* all of which developed from Old English adjective suffixes *-ol, -ul, -el.* The Old English forms are cognate with Old Frisian *-ol, -el,* Old Saxon and Old High German *-al, -il,* and Gothic *-ils, -uls.*

-le[3] a suffix forming verbs expressing repeated action or movement (frequentative) as in *sparkle, wriggle, paddle, bubble* and earlier sometimes apparently having a diminutive sense. A few modern examples exist from Old English, including *nestle, twinkle,* and *wrestle,* but most such words are of Middle and modern English formation, such as the imitative words *babble, crackle, giggle,* and *mumble.*

Modern English *-le* developed from Middle English *-elen, -len,* both of which developed from Old English *-lian;* cognate with Old Frisian *-lia,* Old Saxon and Old High German *-lōn,* and Old Icelandic *-la.*

This suffix is equivalent in sense to *-er*[4], as in *clatter, jabber, putter.*

lea *n.* open ground, grassy field, meadow. About 1230 *lehe,* in *Ancrene Riwle;* later *leie* (before 1250); developed from Old English (about 779) *-lēah* meadow, clearing, untilled land; earlier *-lǣch* (before 735, in Bede's *Death Song*). The form is recorded in Old English only in place names such as *Pægralǣch, Godmundeslēah,* and is cognate with Old Frisian *lāch* meadow, Old Saxon *lōh* woods, Old High German *lōh* grove, and Old Icelandic *-lō* (Norwegian *lo*) clearing or meadow, from Proto-Germanic **lauHaz.* Outside Germanic cognates appear in Latin *lūcus* grove, Lithuanian *laũkas* field, Sanskrit *loká-s* open space, from Indo-European **loukos,* root **leuk-* (Pok.687); see LIGHT[1], n.

After the Old English period, the word is chiefly found in poetical or rhetorical use. The spelling *lea* appeared before 1541.

leach *v.* to run (liquid) through slowly; filter. 1796, probably developed from the noun. The traditional source is Old English *leccan* to moisten, but that seems doubtful as there is a hiatus of either 700 or 900 years (depending on whether a citation of use in Shakespeare's *Midsummer Night's Dream* is accepted) between the recorded appearance in Old English (before 830, in the *Vespasian Psalter*) and the appearance in early modern English; further there is no account of semantic development between the sense in Old

English and that in modern English if development through the noun is ignored.

The use of *leach* with reference to the action of rain on soil is first recorded in 1839.

—n. perforated container for use in leaching. 1673; earlier *leche* in *lechecomb* a tub for soaking (1397), and *leche* a solution obtained from leaching (before 1475); probably developed from *lech, leche* muddy ditch or stream (1389, and as a surname, about 1100); developed from Old English **læc, *lec, *læce, *lece,* from *leccan* to moisten; see LEAK.

The meaning of act or process of leaching, derived from the verb and was first recorded in 1828, in Webster's *Dictionary.*

lead[1] (lēd) *v.* show the way, guide. 1125 *leden,* developed from Old English (before 725) *lǣdan* cause to go with one, lead. The Old English word is cognate with Old Frisian *lēda* to lead, Old Saxon *lēdian,* Middle Dutch and modern Dutch *leiden,* Old High German and modern German *leiten,* and Old Icelandic *leidha,* from Proto-Germanic **laiđjanan;* causatives derived from the same Germanic source as Old English *līthan* to go, Old Saxon *līthan,* Old High German *līdan,* Old Icelandic *līdha,* and Gothic *-leithan,* from Proto-Germanic **līthanan;* all cognate with Avestan *raēth-* (or *-raēth*) to die, as in *para-raēth* pass beyond, pass away (euphemism for die), and Greek *loítē* tomb, and Tocharian A *lit-* to go away, from Indo-European **leit(h)-/loit(h)-/lit(h)-* go, go away, die (Pok.672). **—n.** Before 1325 *lede* leading, guidance, in *Cursor Mundi,* from the verb. The meaning of the place in front, place of a leader, is first recorded in 1570. Related to LODE, LOAD. **—leader** *n.* About 1300 *ledere,* formed from Middle English *leden* to lead + *-er*[1]. **—leadership** *n.* 1834, formed from English *leader* + *-ship.*

lead[2] (led) *n.* bluish-gray metal. Probably before 1200 *laed,* in Layamon's *Chronicle of Britain;* later *led* (before 1300); developed from Old English *lēad* (about 750, in Cynewulf's *Juliana*); cognate with Old Frisian *lād* lead, Middle Dutch and modern Dutch *lood,* Middle High German *lōt* (modern German *Lot* plummet), from Proto-Germanic **laudan.* The art of using this metal and its name were borrowed by the Germanic peoples from the Celts; compare Irish *luaidhe* lead, from Proto-Celtic **loudiā,* Indo-European **plou-d-,* root **pleu-d-* to flow (Pok.837). The sense of a piece of graphite used in pencils is first recorded in 1840. **—v.** 1390 *leden* to cover with lead (but found earlier in past participial use *leadet* weighted with lead, probably before 1200, in *Ancrene Riwle*); from the noun.

leaf *n.* Before 1225 *lef, leaf;* developed from Old English (before 725) *lēaf* leaf of a plant, page of a book; cognate with Old Frisian *lāf* leaf of a plant, Old Saxon *lōf,* modern Dutch *loof,* Old High German *loub* (modern German *Laub* foliage), Old Icelandic *lauf* leaf (Danish, Norwegian *løv,* Swedish *löv*), and Gothic *laufs* (attested in the nominative plural masculine form *laubōs*), from Proto-Germanic **lauƀan,* cognate with Old Irish *lub-gort* garden, and Latin *liber* book (earlier **luber* inner bark), from Indo-European **loubh-/lubh-* (Pok.690). **—v.** put forth leaves. 1611, in Cotgrave's *Dictionary;* from the noun. Compare earlier LEAVE[3]. **—leaflet** *n.* 1787, separate blade of a compound leaf; later, flier, handbill (1867); formed from English *leaf* + *-let.* **—leafy** *adj.* 1552, formed from English *leaf* + *-y*[1].

league[1] *n.* association, pact. 1561, formed from: 1) *liege* a pact, agreement (1418); borrowed from Middle French *ligue,* from Italian *liga,* variant of *lega,* and 2) probably in its later spelling *league* directly by influence of Italian *lega,* from *legare* to tie or bind, from Latin *ligāre* to bind; see LIGAMENT. **—v.** associate in a league; form a league. 1611, in Cotgrave's *Dictionary;* from the noun.

league[2] *n.* measure of distance, usually about 3 miles. Before 1387 *lege,* in Trevisa's translation of Higden's *Polychronicon;* borrowed from Provençal *lega* or Old French *legue,* and directly from Late Latin *leuga, leuca,* from Gaulish.

leak *v.* Before 1398 *lyken* lose liquid, in Trevisa's translation of Bartholomew's *De Proprietatibus Rerum;* later *leken* to run off or leak away (probably 1440); probably borrowed from Middle Dutch *leken* to drip or leak. Middle Dutch *leken* is cognate with Old Icelandic *leka* to drip or leak, Middle High German *lechen* to crack from drought, become leaky (modern German *lecken* to leak), and Old English *leccan* to moisten. Outside Germanic the word is cognate with Old Irish *legaim* I melt, dissolve, Welsh *llaith* damp, moist, Breton *leiz* damp, and Armenian *lič* swamp, bog, from Indo-European **leg-/lēg-* (Pok.657). The figurative sense of allow disclosure of (secret information), is first recorded in 1859. **—n.** 1487 *leke* hole causing a leak; probably from the verb in English, and as a borrowing from Middle Dutch *lec, lek,* related to *leken* to drip. The sense of an act of leaking is first recorded in 1828, in Webster's *Dictionary.* The figurative sense of a deliberate disclosure (of secret information) is attested since 1950. **—leakage** *n.* 1490, formed from English *leak* + *-age.*

lean[1] *v.* to slant, incline, bend. Probably before 1200 *lenen, leonen, leonien;* developed from Old English *hleonian* to lean or recline (about 725, in *Beowulf*). Old English *hleonian* is cognate with Old Frisian *lena* to lean, Old Saxon *hlinōn,* Middle Dutch *lēnen* (modern Dutch *leunen*), and Old High German *hlinēn* (modern German *lehnen*), Danish *læne,* and Norwegian *lene.* Cognates outside Germanic are found in Old Irish *clōin* crooked, Latin *clīnāre* to bend, Greek *klī́nein* to cause to lean, Lithuanian *šlíeti* to lean on, Russian *sloĭ* layer, Armenian *learn* mountain slope, and Sanskrit *śráyati* he lays (something) against, from Indo-European **ḱlei-/ḱloi-/ḱli-* (Pok.601). **—n.** 1610, a support; later, act of leaning, inclination (1776); from the verb.

lean[2] *adj.* not fat, thin, slender. Probably before 1200 *læne,* in Layamon's *Chronicle of Britain;* later *lene* (before 1250); developed from Old English (about 1000) *hlǣne,* perhaps from *hlǣnan* cause to lean or bend, from Proto-Germanic **Hlainjanan,* Indo-European **ḱloi-n-,* as in Lettish *slains* where one sinks in; related to Old English *hleonian* LEAN[1]. **—n.** Probably before 1200 *læne* lean people or animals; later *lene* lean meat (about 1450); from the adjective.

leap *v.* Probably before 1200 *lepen,* in Layamon's *Chronicle of Britain;* developed from Old English *hlēapan* to jump, run, leap (about 725, in *Beowulf*). Old English *hlēapan* is cognate with Old Frisian *hlāpa* to run, Old Saxon *hlōpan,* Middle Dutch *lōpen* (modern Dutch *lopen*), Old High German *hlouffan* (modern German *laufen*), Old Icelandic and modern Icelandic *hlaupa* to run, leap, and Gothic *ushlaupan* to jump up, from Proto-Germanic **Hlaupanan.* No cognate relationship outside Germanic has been established. **—n.** Probably before 1200 *lupe;* later *lep, leap* (in place names, 1219 and 1291); developed from Old English

-*hlēp* in *clif-hlēp* cliff leap (before 800, in *Corpus Glossary*); compare West Saxon *hlȳp* (before 900), from Proto-Germanic **Hlaupiz;* related to *hlēapan* to leap. **—leapfrog** *n.* 1599, in Shakespeare's *Henry V; v.* 1872, from the noun. **—leap year** Before 1387 *lepe yere,* in Trevisa's translation of Higden's *Polychronicon.*

learn *v.* Probably before 1200 *leornen;* later *lernen* (probably about 1200); developed from Old English (before 725) *leornian* to get knowledge, be cultivated. Old English *leornian* is cognate with Old Frisian *lernia, lirnia* to learn, Old Saxon *līnōn* (with *-īn-* representing earlier *-izn-,* from *-isn-*), Old High German *lernēn, lirnēn, lernōn,* and Middle High German *lernen* learn, teach (modern German *lernen* learn), originally to follow along a track, from Proto-Germanic **liznōjanan.* Outside Germanic the word is cognate with Latin *līra* ridge between furrows, from Indo-European **leisa,* root **leis-/lois-/lis-* (Pok.671). Related to LORE. **—learned** *adj.* About 1303 *lerned* educated or trained, in Mannyng's *Handlyng Synne,* from past participle of *lernen* learn; for suffix see -ED². **—learning** *n.* About 1380 *lerning,* in Chaucer's *Canterbury Tales;* developed from Old English (before 900) *leornung,* from *leornian* learn; for suffix see -ING¹.

lease *n.* contract for the right to use property by paying rent. About 1384 *lese;* later *lees* (1426); borrowed through Anglo-French *les,* from *lesser* to let or let go, from Old French *laissier, lessier,* from Latin *laxāre* loosen, from *laxus* loose, LAX¹. **—v.** to take possession by a lease. Before 1475 *lesen,* from the noun.

leash *n.* strap or chain for restraining an animal. Probably before 1300 *les, lasse,* in *Arthour and Merlin;* later *leshe* (1356-57); borrowed from Old French *laisse, lesse,* from *laissier* loosen, from Latin *laxāre,* from *laxus* loose, LAX¹. **—v.** to attach by a leash. 1599, in Shakespeare's *Henry V;* from the noun.

least *adj.* less than any other, smallest. Probably before 1200, in *Ancrene Riwle;* developed from Old English (before 950) *lǣst;* earlier *lǣsest* smallest, superlative of *lǣs* smaller, LESS (about 725, in *Beowulf*). Old English *lǣsest* developed from Proto-Germanic **laisistaz*). **—n.** About 1125, least important person; later, smallest thing (probably before 1200); developed from Old English *lǣst;* from the adjective. **—adv.** to the least extent or degree. Probably before 1200, in *Ancrene Riwle;* from the adjective.

leather *n.* Old English (about 700) *lether* hide, skin, leather (found only in compounds, such as *letherwyrhta* leather worker, *gewaldlether* rein, bridle). The Old English word element is cognate with Old Frisian *lether* leather, Old Saxon *lethar,* Middle Low German *leder,* Middle Dutch and modern Dutch *leder,* Old High German *ledar* (modern German *Leder*), and Old Icelandic *ledhr* (Danish *læder,* Swedish *läder,* Norwegian *lær),* from Proto-Germanic **lethran,* Indo-European **letro-* (Pok.681). The only other cognates are in Celtic; Old Irish *lethar* leather, Welsh *lledr,* Middle Breton *lezr,* Breton *ler.* These forms may represent a western Indo-European word, though there could have been borrowing between the Germanic and Celtic forms. The phonology permits either cognates or loans. **—adj.** Before 1333 *lether,* from the noun. **—v.** 1564-65, to cover with leather; from the noun. **—leathery** *adj.* 1552, formed from English *leather* + *-y*¹.

leave¹ *v.* go away. 1127 *leaven* leave alone; later, go away (probably before 1200, in *Ancrene Riwle* and Layamon's *Chronicle of Britain*); developed from Old English *lǣfan* to leave, remain, bequeath (about 725, in *Beowulf*). Old English *lǣfan* is cognate with Old Frisian *lēva* leave over, Old Saxon *farlēƀian,* Middle Low German *lēven,* Old High German *leiban,* Old Icelandic *leifa* leave behind, and Gothic *bilaibjan,* from Proto-Germanic **laiƀjanan;* causatives derived from the same Germanic source as Old English *belīfan* to remain, and Old High German *bilīban* (modern German *bleiben*), from Proto-Germanic **-leiƀanan,* related to the root of LIVE¹.

leave² *n.* permission, consent. 1129 *leve;* developed from Old English *lēafe* (before 900, in Alfred's translation of St. Gregory's *Pastoral Care*). Old English *lēafe* is the dative and accusative form of *lēaf* permission (from Proto-Germanic **lauƀō*), related to *ālȳfan* allow, permit, and cognate with Old High German *irlouben* allow (modern German *erlauben*), Gothic *uslaubjan* from Proto-Germanic **uz-lauƀjanan*), and Old Icelandic *leyfa* allow, permit, *leyfi* permission; also cognate with Old High German *urloub* leave, furlough (modern German *Urlaub*), Old Frisian *orlof,* and Old Saxon *orlōf.* Related to LOVE, BELIEVE, and FURLOUGH.

leave³ *v.* come into leaf, put forth leaves. About 1250 *leaven,* in *Genesis and Exodus;* developed from LEAF.

leaven *n.* substance, such as yeast, that will cause fermentation and raise dough. 1340 *levain,* in *Ayenbite of Inwyt;* later *leven* (probably before 1425) and *leaven* (1471); borrowed from Old French *levain,* from Latin *levāmen* alleviation, mitigation (literally, a lifting), from *levāre* to raise; see LEVER. **—v.** raise with a leaven; make (dough) light or lighter. Before 1400 *levainen,* in a translation of Lanfranc's *Science of Surgery;* from the noun.

lecher *n.* lewd person. Probably before 1200 *lecchur,* in *Ancrene Riwle;* later, in compounds *lecher-* (1280), and the usual spelling *lechour* (from about 1300 to the 1600's); borrowed from Old French *lechëor* licker, from *lechier* to lick, from Frankish (compare Old High German *leckōn* to LICK). **—lecherous** *adj.* About 1300, probably formed from Middle English *lecher-* and *lecherie* lechery + *-ous;* but compare rare Old French *lecheros,* from *lechëor* licker as a possible alternative source. **—lechery** *n.* Probably before 1200 *leccherie,* in *Ancrene Riwle; lecherie* (probably about 1200); borrowed from Old French *lecherie,* from *lechier* to lick; for suffix see -Y³.

lecithin *n.* fatty substance found in plant or animal tissues. 1923, borrowed from French *lécithine* (Greek *lékithos* egg yolk + French *-ine* -INE² chemical suffix).

lectern *n.* reading desk or stand. Before 1425 *lectryne;* also *lectorne* (1440); alterations (influenced by Medieval Latin *lectrinum* lectern) of earlier *lettorne* (about 1390), *letrune* (before 1425); borrowed from Old French *letrin, leitrun.* The Old French forms were adaptations of Medieval Latin *lectrinum* and Late Latin *lectrum* lectern, from Latin *legere* to read; see LEGEND.

lecture *n.* Probably before 1300, literature, written works, in *Kyng Alisaunder;* later, reading, learning from books (probably before 1387, in a version of *Piers Plowman*), and *lectour* reading aloud (about 1443); borrowed through Old French *lecture,* and directly from Medieval Latin *lectura* a reading, lecture, from Latin *legere* to read, see LEGEND; for suffix see -URE.

The sense of a planned talk or discourse, especially

one given to a class, is first recorded in 1536, probably borrowed from Middle French (1498). The sense of a reprimand or scolding is found in Shakespeare's *As You Like It* (1600).
—v. give a lecture. About 1590, from the noun. The sense of reprimand or scold is first recorded in 1706. **—lecturer** *n.* 1583; formed from English *lecture* + *-er*[1].

ledge *n.* narrow shelf. 1272-73 *legge* crossbar on a door; later *ledge* (1452); perhaps formed from *leggen* to place, LAY[1]. For a note on spelling see DRUDGE. The sense of a narrow shelf appeared in 1558.

ledger *n.* 1481, book that lies in a permanent place, especially a large copy of a breviary; probably from *leggen* to place, LAY[1] (perhaps in imitation of Dutch *ligger, legger* one that lies down, a book kept for reference); for suffix see -ER[1]. The sense of a book of accounts is first recorded in 1588, as a shortened form of *ledger-book* a book containing records, book of accounts (1553).

lee *n.* shelter, sheltered side. Probably about 1200 *leohe;* later *le* (before 1325, in *Cursor Mundi*); developed from Old English (before 725) *hlēo* shelter, protection. Old English *hlēo* is cognate with Old Frisian *hlī* shelter, protection, Old Saxon *hleo,* Middle Low German *lē,* modern Dutch *lij* lee side, Old Icelandic *hlē* lee side, shelter (Swedish *lä,* Danish *læ,* Norwegian *le*), also *hlȳ* warmth, and modern German *Lee* lee. The Germanic forms are cognate with Sanskrit *śarád-* autumn, Lithuanian *šilti;* become warm, and Latin *calēre* be hot, from Indo-European **k̂el-/k̂l̥-, k̂l-eu-* (Pok.551). The specialized sense of the sheltered side (of a ship, etc.) appeared in Middle English probably about 1400.
—adj. sheltered from the wind. 1513; from the noun. **—leeward** (lē′wərd; *Nautical* lü′ərd) *adj.* 1666, situated away from the wind; formed from English *lee* + *-ward.* An earlier and obsolete sense of the adjective was "that makes much leeway" (applied to a ship); it appeared before 1618, in Raleigh's writings. The adverb use is first recorded in 1785. **—leeway** *n.* 1669, sideways drift of a ship (away from the wind); formed from English *lee* + *way.* The figurative sense of extra space is first recorded in Scott's *Journal* (1827).

leech[1] *n.* bloodsucking worm. Probably about 1150 *leche;* developed from Old English *lǣce* (before 900), Kentish *lȳce* bloodsucking worm; cognate with Middle Dutch *lieke* leech, of unknown origin. The form and sense in Middle English were transferred to *leche* physician, LEECH[2], by early folk-etymology; however, the meaning of physician eventually became obsolete, leaving only the adopted sense of a bloodsucking worm. The figurative sense of a person who is a parasite, is first recorded in 1784.

leech[2] *n. Archaic.* physician. Probably before 1200 *leche,* developed from Old English (about 900) *lǣce;* cognate with Old Frisian *lētza* physician, Old Saxon *lāki,* Old High German *lāhhi,* Old Icelandic *læknir* (Swedish *läka* to heal, *läkare* physician, Danish *læge,* Norwegian *lege* (to heal, physician), and Gothic *lēkeis* physician, from Proto-Germanic **lǣkjaz* one who counsels, cognate with Greek *légein* say, and Latin *legere* read, from Indo-European **leg-* gather, pick (Pok. 658).

leek *n.* onionlike vegetable. Before 1300 *lek,* developed from Old English: Mercian (about 700) *lǣc, -lēc* (in compound *gārlēc* garlic), West Saxon (about 1000) *lēac* leek, onion, garlic; both Old English forms are cognate with Old Saxon *lōk* leek, Middle Dutch *looc* (modern Dutch *look*), Old High German *louh* (modern German *Lauch*), and Old Icelandic *laukr* (Swedish *lök,* Danish *løg,* Norwegian *løk, lauk*), from Proto-Germanic **lauka-;* related to Old English *locc* curl of hair, LOCK[2].

leer *v.* give a sly, sidelong look. 1530, in Palsgrave's *Lesclarcissement,* probably developed from (obsolete) *leer* cheek, face, countenance; in turn developed from Middle English *ler* (probably before 1300); earlier *leor* (probably before 1200). The Middle English forms developed from Old English (about 700) *hlēor,* originally, area near the ear, from Proto-Germanic **Hleuzás,* cognate with Old Slavic *sluchŭ* hearing, from Indo-European **k̂leu-so-s* (Pok.607). Old English *hlēor* is also cognate with Old Saxon *hleor* cheek, Middle Dutch *liere,* Middle Low German *ler,* and Old Icelandic *hlȳr.*
—n. 1598, in Shakespeare's *Merry Wives of Windsor;* from the verb. **—leery** *adj.* 1718, alert, wide-awake; formed from archaic English *leer* adj., looking slyly + *-y*[1]. The sense of wary, doubtful, suspicious, appeared in American English in George Ade's *Artie* (1896).

lees *n.pl.* dregs, sediment. About 1380 *lies,* in Chaucer's *House of Fame;* borrowed from Old French *lies,* plural of *lie* sediment, probably from Celtic (compare Old Irish *lige* bed, cognate with Old English *licgan* to recline, LIE[2]).

left *adj.* Probably before 1200 *lift, luft, leoft,* in Layamon's *Chronicle of Britain;* later *left* (Kentish dialect, before 1333 and northern British dialects before 1325); developed from Old English *lyft-* weak (not recorded in Kentish dialect of Old English); cognate with Middle Low German *lucht* and Middle Dutch *lucht, luft* left, from Indo-European **lup-t-,* root **(s)leup-/(s)lup-* (Pok.964). The Old English sense of "weak" (as in *lyftādl* lameness, paralysis) apparently arises ultimately from the fact that the left hand is generally the weaker of the two hands. **—adv.** on or to the left side. Before 1325, in *Cursor Mundi;* from the adjective. **—n.** left side or hand. Probably about 1200 *luft,* later *left* (before 1325); from the adjective. *Left,* in the sense of the members of a legislative body assigned to the left side of the chamber is first recorded in Carlyle's *The French Revolution* (1837), probably a loan translation of French *la gauche* (1791).

According to the OED, "This use originated in the French National Assembly of 1789, in which the nobles as a body took the position of honour on the President's right, and the Third Estate [persons not of the nobility or clergy] sat on his left. The significance of these positions, which was at first ceremonial, soon became political," and the left side of a legislative chamber was assigned by custom to those holding political views considered liberal in the 19th century. In the 20th century *Left* is more broadly applied to include members associated with socialism and communism.
—leftist *n.* 1924 *Leftist* person with liberal or radical political ideas; formed from English *Left,* n. + *-ist;* perhaps modeled after French *gauchiste.* **—left field** (1857, American English) **—leftover** *n.* (1891); *adj.* (1897) **—left wing** (1884, in William James' *Will to Believe*) **—left winger** (1891) **—lefty** *n.* left-handed person (1886); left winger in politics (1935).

leg *n.* Probably before 1300, in *Kyng Alisaunder;* borrowed from a Scandinavian source (compare Old Icelandic *leggr* leg, bone, Norwegian *legg,* Danish *læg,* and Swedish *lägg*), from Proto-Germanic **laȝjaz.* The

Scandinavian forms are cognate with Old English *līra* fleshy part of the body, Greek *láx,* adv., with the heel or foot, *laktízein* to kick with the foot, and possibly with Sanskrit *ṛkṣálā* foot joint of a hoofed animal, from Indo-European **lek-/lok-/lk-* (Pok.673). **—leggings** *n.pl.* (1751) **—leggy** *adj.* (1787)

legacy *n.* money or other property left by a will. About 1384, function or office of a deputy or legate, in the Wycliffe Bible; borrowed from Old French *legacie,* from Medieval Latin *legatia,* from Latin *lēgāre* appoint by a last will, bequeath, send as a LEGATE; for suffix see -ACY. The sense of property left by a will appeared in Scottish about 1460. **—legatee** *n.* one to whom a legacy is left. 1679-88, formed from English *legate,* v. (1546, borrowed from Latin *lēgātus,* past participle of *lēgāre* bequeath) + *-ee.*

legal *adj.* 1447, in Bokenham's *Legends of Holy Women;* borrowed from Middle French *légal,* learned borrowing from Latin *lēgālis* legal, from *lēx* (genitive *lēgis*) law, possibly related to *legere* to gather, see LEGEND; for suffix see -AL[1]. Doublet of LOYAL. **—legality** *n.* 1459 *legalite;* borrowed from Medieval Latin *legalitas,* from Latin *lēgālis* legal; for suffix see -ITY. **—legalization** *n.* 1805, formed from English *legalize* + *-ation.* **—legalize** *v.* Before 1716, formed from English *legal* + *-ize.* **—legally** *adv.* (1561) **—legal aid** (1890) **—legal tender** (1740)

legate (leg′it) *n.* ambassador, representative. Before 1121, a representative of the Pope; borrowed through Old French *legat,* and directly from Latin *lēgātus,* originally, provided with a commission, past participle of *lēgāre* send as a deputy, send with a commission, bequeath, from *lēx* (genitive *lēgis*) contract, law, see LEGAL; for suffix see -ATE[3]. **—legatee** *n.* See under LEGACY. **—legation** *n.* Before 1400 *legacyoun* diplomatic mission; borrowed through Old French *legation,* and directly from Latin *lēgātiōnem* (nominative *lēgātiō*), from *lēgāre* send as a deputy, see LEGATE; for suffix see -ATION.

legato (ligä′tō) *adj. Music.* smooth and connected, without breaks between successive tones. 1811, borrowed from Italian *legato* bound, past participle of *legare* to bind, from Latin *ligāre* to bind; see LIGAMENT.

legend *n.* Probably before 1325, story of the life of a saint; borrowed from Old French *legende,* learned borrowing from Medieval Latin, or borrowed directly from Medieval Latin *legenda* legend, story; originally, (things) to be read (on certain days in church, etc.), from Latin, neuter plural gerundive of *legere* to read, gather, select. Latin *legere* is cognate with Greek *légein* to speak, tell, say, gather, choose, *lógos* word, speech, account, reason.

The extended sense of a nonhistorical or mythical story is first recorded in 1386. The sense of a writing or inscription (from French but ultimately derived from the Medieval Latin meaning of "things to be read") is first recorded in Cotgrave's *Dictionary* (1611). **—legendary** *adj.* 1563-87 *legendarie* of the nature of a legend, celebrated in legend; possibly through French; but more likely borrowed directly from Medieval Latin *legendarius,* from *legenda* (things) to be read; for suffix see -ARY.

legerdemain (lej′ərdəmān′) *n.* sleight of hand, conjuring tricks. Probably about 1430 *legerdemeyn;* borrowed from Middle French *léger de main* quick of hand (*léger* light, from Vulgar Latin **leviārius,* from Latin *levis* LIGHT[2] not heavy; *de* of, from, from Latin *dē* from; and *main* hand, from Latin *manus;* see MANUAL).

legible *adj.* Probably before 1440; borrowed from Late Latin *legibilis* that can be read, from Latin *legere* to read, see LEGEND; for suffix see -IBLE. **—legibility** *n.* 1679, formed from English *legible* + *-ity.* **—legibly** *adv.* 1586, formed from English *legible* + *-ly*[1].

legion *n.* body of soldiers, army. Probably before 1200 *legiun* Roman legion, in Layamon's *Chronicle of Britain;* later *legioun* (about 1280); borrowed from Old French *legion, legiun,* learned borrowing from Latin *legiōnem* (nominative *legiō*) a body of soldiers in the Roman army, from *legere* to choose, gather (as for an army), see LEGEND; for suffix see -ION.

The sense of a very large number is first recorded in English about 1378, in a version of *Piers Plowman.* It comes from the Biblical reference in Mark 5:9: "My name is Legion, for we are many." The military legion suggests a host or great number, as the ancient Roman legion consisting of between three and six thousand soldiers.

—legionary *adj.* 1408, belonging to a legion, borrowed from Latin *legiōnārius,* from *legiōnem* (nominative *legiō*); for suffix see -ARY.—*n.* member of a legion. 1598, from the adjective, or borrowed from Middle French *légionnaire* (1495, and found once in Old French, 1265). **—legionnaire** (lē′jənâr′) *n.* member of a legion, 1818, in Shelley's *Letters,* borrowed from French *légionnaire,* from Old French *legion* legion.

legislator *n.* 1605, borrowed, probably from French *législateur,* and directly from Latin *lēgis lātor* proposer of a law; *lēgis,* genitive of *lex* law (see LEGAL); *lātor* proposer, a form serving as agent noun of *ferre* to carry, BEAR[2]; for suffix see -OR[2]. **—legislate** *v.* 1805, back formation from *legislator, legislation;* for suffix see -ATE[1]. **—legislation** *n.* Before 1655, probably borrowed from French *législation,* learned borrowing of Late Latin *lēgislātiōnem* (nominative *lēgislātiō*) enactment of a law or laws, from Latin *lēgis* (genitive of *lēx* law) + *lātiō* a bringing, a form serving as abstract noun of *ferre* to carry, bring, BEAR[2]; for suffix see -TION. It is also possible that in some instances *legislation* was formed after English *legisla(tor)* + *-tion;* compare LEGISLATIVE. **—legislative** *adj.* About 1641, formed (probably through influence of French *législatif*) from English *legislat(or)* + *-ive.* **—legislature** *n.* Before 1676, legislative body, formed from English *legislat(or)* + *-ure.*

legitimate *adj.* rightful, lawful. Before 1464 *legitimat* lawfully begotten; later, lawful (1638); borrowed from past participle of Middle French *legitimer* (from Medieval Latin *legitimare*) and directly from Medieval Latin *legitimatus,* past participle of *legitimare* make lawful, from Latin *lēgitimus* lawful; originally, in line with the law, from *lēx* (genitive *lēgis*) law; see LEGAL; for suffix see -ATE[3]. **—legitimacy** *n.* 1691, formed from English *legitimate,* adj. + *-cy.* **—legitimize** *v.* 1848, formed in English from Latin *lēgitimus* lawful + English *-ize.*

legume (leg′yüm) *n.* plant having a number of seeds in a pod, such as beans, peas, etc. 1676, borrowing of French *légume,* learned borrowing from Latin *legūmen,* of uncertain origin.

According to the ancient Roman scholar Varro, *legūmen* derives from *legere* to gather, in allusion to the fact that the plant's fruit may be gathered by hand. Ernout and Meillet suggest that the word is of non-

Indo-European origin, but provided with a Latin ending.

—leguminous *adj.* 1656, in Blount's *Glossographia,* probably borrowed from French *légumineux,* from Latin *legūmen* (genitive *legūminis*) + French *-eux* -ous. *Leguminous* also appeared in Middle English (probably before 1425, in a translation of Chauliac's *Grande Chirurgie*) in the sense of "containing meal made from the seeds of legumes."

lei (lā) *n.* garland of flowers, shells, etc. 1843, in J. Jarves' *History of the Hawaiian or Sandwich Islands;* borrowed from Hawaiian, in which the word means any ornament worn about the neck or around the head, usually one given as a symbol of affection.

leisure *n.* Probably before 1300 *leiser* time free from work or duties, in *Kyng Alisaunder;* borrowed from Old French *leisir* permission, leisure, from *leisir,* v., be permitted, from Latin *licēre* be permitted; see LICENSE. The spelling *leisure* appeared in English in the 1500's and was used by Shakespeare. It was probably influenced in form by words ending in *-ure,* such as *measure.* **—leisurely** *adv.* (1486); *adj.* (1604)

leitmotif or **leitmotiv** (līt′mōtēf′) *n.* recurring musical theme associated with a particular person, situation, etc. 1876, borrowing of German *Leitmotiv,* literally, leading motive (*leiten* to guide, LEAD[1] + *Motiv* motive, from French *motif* MOTIF*).* The extended sense of any recurring theme, as in a novel or a conversation, is first recorded in Havelock Ellis' writings, in 1896.

lemma (lem′ə) *n.* theme, subject, glossed word. 1570, subsidiary proposition in mathematics; later, heading or theme (1601, in Ben Jonson's *The Poetaster*); borrowing of Latin *lēmma* a theme, from Greek *lêmma* anything received or taken, see DILEMMA. The sense of a word or phrase glossed (as in a glossary) appeared in 1896. **—lemmatize** *v.* group together all inflected or various forms of a word. 1967, formed from English *lemmata,* pl. (from Greek *lḗmmata,* plural of *lêmma*) + *-ize.* **—lemmatization** *n.* (1967)

lemming *n.* small, mouselike arctic animal. 1713, borrowing of Norwegian *lemming, lemende,* related to Old Icelandic *lōmundr, læmingi, læmingr* lemming, of uncertain origin (possibly the barker; cognate with Latin *latrare,* Old Slavic *lajati,* Lithuanian *lōti* to bark).

lemon *n.* About 1400 *lymon,* in Maundeville's *Travels;* borrowed from Old French *limon* (probably influenced by Old Provençal *limon,* or Italian *limone*), from Arabic *līmūn,* from Persian *līmū* (*n*). The shift in spelling to *e* that was a natural development in late Middle English and early modern English did not occur until the mid-1600's in *lemon.* The slang sense of a worthless person or thing is first recorded in 1906 in American English. **—lemonade** *n.* 1663, borrowed from French *limonade,* from Old French *limon* lemon; for suffix see -ADE.

lemur (lē′mər) *n.* animal somewhat like a monkey. 1795, New Latin *lemures,* a name given by Linnaeus from Latin *lemurēs,* pl., specters, ghosts; so called because of the animal's nocturnal habits and ghostlike appearance. Latin *lemurēs* is of uncertain origin, perhaps cognate with Greek *lamyrós* greedy, gluttonous, or with *lámia* monster.

lend *v.* Probably about 1375 *lenden,* alteration of earlier *lenen* (probably before 1200, in Layamon's *Chronicle of Britain*); developed from Old English (before 725 *lǣnan* to lend, from *lǣn* LOAN.

According to the OED, the substitution of *lend-* for *len-,* which began early in Middle English, was due to the influence of the past tense *lende* and to association with many words in *-end,* such as *bend, rend, send, wend.*

length *n.* 1122 *lengthe;* developed from Old English (about 893) *lengthu;* cognate with Old Frisian *lengethe* length, Middle Low German and Middle Dutch *lengede,* and Old Icelandic *lengd,* from Proto-Germanic **langíthō;* derived from the Germanic root that was the source of Old English *lang* LONG[1], adj. **—lengthen** *v.* About 1450 *lenthenen,* formed from Middle English *lengthe* length + *-enen* -en[1]. **—lengthwise** *adv.* (about 1580); *adj.* (1871) **—lengthy** *adj.* 1689, American English; formed from *length*+ *-y*[1].

lenient *adj.* 1652, softening, soothing, relaxing; borrowed from Middle French *lenient,* from Latin *lēnientem* (nominative *lēniēns*), present participle of *lēnīre* soften, from *lēnis* mild; for suffix see -ENT. The Latin *lēnis* was probably an altered form (under the influence of *sēgnis* sluggish or *mollis* soft) of earlier **lēnos,* cognate with Lithuanian *lĕnas* quiet, tame, slow, Greek *lēdeîn* be tired, and Gothic *lētan* permit, from Indo-European **lē(i)*- leave, relax (Pok.666).

The sense of mild, gentle, merciful is first recorded in English in 1787, probably influenced by the meaning of *lenity* mildness, gentleness. **—lenience** *n.* 1796, formed from English *lenient* + *-ence.* **—leniency** *n.* 1780, formed from English *lenient* + *-cy.*

While *lenient, lenience,* etc. are not always exact synonyms for *lenitive, lenity,* etc., the former group of words has generally replaced the words in English developed around *lenity,* except in ecology and phonetics where *lenis, lenitic,* and *lenition* have developed specialized meanings.

lenity (len′ətē) *n.* mildness, gentleness, mercifulness. 1548 *lenitie,* borrowed from Middle French *lénité,* learned borrowing from Latin *lēnitātem* (nominative *lēnitās*), from *lēnis* mild, see LENIENT; for suffix see -ITY. In Middle English (probably before 1425, in a translation of Chauliac's *Grande Chirurgie*) the word was used in medicine with form *lenite* and the sense of "softness." The figurative use of 1548 was probably a reborrowing of the Middle French word.

lens *n.* 1693, New Latin *lens* a shaped piece of glass for focusing rays of light, from Latin *lēns* (genitive *lentis*) LENTIL (in reference to its seeds which have a double-convex shape similar to an optical lens).

Lent *n.* the forty days before Easter. Before 1387 *lente,* in Trevisa's translation of Higden's *Polychronicon,* a shortened form of earlier *lenten* spring, lent (1123); developed from Old English (about 700) *lencten* spring. The Old English form is cognate with Old Saxon and Middle Dutch *lentin* spring (modern Dutch *lente*), and Old High German *lengizin, lenzin, lenzo* (modern German, poetic *Lenz*), all probably derived from a Proto-Germanic compound **langa-tīnaz,* made up of the root that was the source of Old English *lang* LONG[1] and that of Gothic *-teins* (in *sinteins* daily), cognate with Lithuanian *dienà* day, Old Slavic *dĭnĭ,* Sanskrit *dína-m,* and Latin *diēs* (see DEITY). The probable reference is to the lengthening of the days as characterizing the season of spring. Only in English did the ecclesiastical meaning of Lent develop; among the other Germanic languages the meaning remained confined to spring.

lenticular (lentik′yələr) *adj.* having the form of a lens.

Probably before 1425, shaped like a lentil, in a translation of Chauliac's *Grande Chirurgie;* borrowed from Middle French *lenticulaire,* and from Latin *lenticulāris* having the shape of a lentil, from *lenticula* LENTIL; for suffix see -AR.

lentil *n.* a plant whose pods contain seeds shaped like a double-convex lens. About 1250, in *Genesis and Exodus;* borrowed from Old French *lentille,* from Vulgar Latin **lentīcula,* from Latin *lenticula,* diminutive of *lēns* (genitive *lentis*) lentil, possibly from the same unknown source as Old High German *linsīn* (modern German *Linse*), and Old Slavic *lęšta,* both meaning lentil.

lento (len′tō) *adj., adv. Music.* slow, slowly. 1724, borrowing of Italian *lento* slow, from Latin *lentus* slow, lasting, flexible; see LITHE.

l'envoi or **l'envoy** (len′voi) *n.* short concluding passage; postscript, especially to a book or poem. Probably before 1439 *lenvoie,* in Lydgate's *Falls of Princes;* borrowed from Middle French *l'envoy* dedication, postscript; literally, the message (*l',* contraction of *le* the; *envoy* message; see ENVOY[2] a separate borrowing, but a parallel form, found about 1380, in Chaucer's writings).

leonine (lē′ənīn) *adj.* of or like a lion. About 1375, in Chaucer's *Canterbury Tales;* borrowed from Old French *leonin,* from Latin *leōnīnus* belonging to a lion, from *leō* (genitive *leōnis*) LION; for suffix see -INE[1].

leopard *n.* Probably before 1300 *leuparz, lipard;* borrowed from Old French *leupart, leupard, lipard,* learned borrowing from Late Latin *leopardus,* from Greek *leópardos* (*léōn* LION + *párdos* male panther, PARD[1]; the leopard originally being thought a hybrid animal). The spelling *leopard* appeared in Middle English about 1330, apparently borrowed from Late Latin.

The English pronunciation (lep′ərd) reflects that of Old French *leupart, leupard.* The modern French *léopard* has been refashioned on the basis of Latin and is pronounced (lāôpär′).

leotard (lē′ətärd) *n.* tight-fitting one-piece garment. 1920, in allusion to Jules *Léotard,* 1830-1870, a French trapeze artist who performed in Paris and London wearing such a garment.

leper *n.* Before 1398 *lepre* person who has leprosy, in Trevisa's translation of Bartholomew's *De Proprietatibus Rerum,* perhaps developed from *leprous* or, more likely from attributive use of earlier *lepre* leprosy (about 1250, in *Genesis and Exodus*), borrowed from: 1) Old French *liepre, lepre* leprosy, learned borrowing from Late Latin *lepra,* and 2) probably directly from Late Latin *lepra* (in Latin, only *leprae,* pl.), from Greek *léprā* leprosy, formed from the feminine of *leprós,* adj., scaly, from *lépos* a scale, which is related to *lépein* to peel, *lopós* a peel, cognate with Lithuanian *lāpas* leaf, from Indo-European **lep-/lop-* (Pok.678). **—leprosy** *n.* 1535, in the Coverdale Bible; developed from earlier *lepruse* (probably before 1450), from *leprus,* variant of LEPROUS; for suffix see -Y[3]. Middle English *lepruse* replaced the earlier *lepre* leprosy (about 1250); see LEPER. **—leprous** *adj.* Probably before 1200 *leprus* in *Ancrene Riwle;* later *leprous* (about 1280); borrowed from Old French *lepros* and Late Latin *leprōsus,* from *lepra* leprosy, see LEPER; for suffix see -OUS.

lepidopterous (lep′ədop′tərəs) *adj.* belonging to the order of insects with scaly wings, including butterflies and moths. 1797, formed in English from New Latin *Lepidoptera,* pl., the order name (Greek *lepís,* genitive *lepídos*, fish scale, related to *lépein* to peel; see LEPER + *pterón* wing, FEATHER) + English *-ous.*

leprechaun (lep′rəkon) *n.* in Irish folklore, a sprite or goblin resembling a little old man. 1604 *lubrican;* borrowed from Irish *lupracān,* alteration of Old Irish *luchorpān* (*lu* little + *corpān,* diminutive of *corp* body, from Latin *corpus;* see CORPSE). The spelling *leprechaun* appeared in 1860. The Irish word has several variant forms, the one closest to *leprechaun* being *leipreachān.*

lepton *n. Physics.* any of a class of light, weakly interacting elementary particles. 1948, any elementary particle of small mass, formed in English from Greek *leptós* small, thin, delicate; literally, peeled (related to *lépein* to peel; see LEPER) + English suffix *-on.* The current meaning appeared about 1969 to distinguish the group of leptons from hadrons.

lesbian *adj.* 1601 *Lesbian* of or relating to the Greek island of Lesbos (in the northeastern Aegean sea); later *Lesbian* of or relating to homosexual relations between women (1890); borrowed from Latin *Lesbius* of Lesbos, from Greek *Lésbios,* from *Lésbos* Lesbos. The second (and now common) meaning developed because of the reputed homosexuality of Sappho, the Greek lyric woman poet of Lesbos. The lower-case form *lesbian* is first recorded in the 1960's, though certain derived forms, such as *lesbie* have been recorded in lower-case since the 1920's. **—n.** homosexual woman. 1925 *Lesbian,* in Aldous Huxley's *Letters;* from the adjective. **—lesbianism** *n.* female homosexuality. 1870 *Lesbianism,* formed from English *Lesbian* of Lesbos + *ism.*

lese-majesty (lēz′maj′əstē) *n.* crime against the sovereign power, treason. 1536, borrowing of Middle French *lèse-majesté,* learned borrowing from Latin *crīmen laesae majestātis* charge of insulted sovereignty (*laesa,* feminine past participle of *laedere* to damage, see LESION; *majestātis,* genitive of *majestās* MAJESTY). The form in Latin appears about one hundred years earlier in Lydgate's *Falls of Princes* (probably before 1439).

lesion (lē′zhən) *n.* injury, damage. Probably before 1425 *lesioun* bodily injury, in a translation of Chauliac's *Grande Chirurgie;* borrowed from Middle French *lesion,* from Latin *laesiōnem* (nominative *laesiō*) injury, from *laedere* to strike, hurt, damage, of uncertain origin; for suffix see -SION. **—v.** cause a lesion in. 1972, from the noun.

less *adj.* About 1125 *læsse* the younger or smaller (in importance); later *lesse, lasse* (about 1150). The forms in Middle English developed from a fusion of Old English *lǣs,* adv. (before 725), and *lǣssa,* adj. (about 725, in *Beowulf*) comparative of *lǣs* (from Proto-Germanic **laisiz*), which is cognate with Old Frisian and Old Saxon *lēs* less, Middle High German, Middle Low German, and Middle Dutch *līse* soft or gentle, modern German *leise* soft, gentle, slight. Outside Germanic the word is cognate with Lithuanian *líesas* thin, and Greek *liarós* mild or gentle, *loîsthos* last, from Indo-European **leis-/lois-/lis-* (Pok.662). **—adv.** Probably about 1175 *lesse, lasse,* developed from Old English *lǣs.* **—n.** Probably about 1175 *lesse,* developed from a fusion of Old English *lǣsse* (about 1000, from *lǣssa,* adj.) and *lǣs* (about 725, in *Beowulf,* from the adv.). **—lessen** *v.* Probably about 1380 *lesnen* make less; later *lessenen* (probably before 1400), from earlier *lessen* (probably about

1200), formed from *lesse,* adj. + *-en*[1]. **—lesser** *adj.* (as in *the lesser evil*). About 1225, comparative of *less,* formed from Middle English *lesse* + *-er*[2]. *—adv.* less. 1594, in Shakespeare's *Richard III,* now generally archaic except, since about 1960, in *lesser-known* (for *less well-known*), formed by analogy with *better-known.*

-less a suffix meaning without a ____, that has no ____, as in *childless, homeless;* that does not ____, as in *tireless;* that cannot be ____ed, as in *countless.* Middle English *-lesse,* developed from Old English *-lēas,* from *lēas* free from, without. The Old English forms are cognate with Old Saxon *lōs* loose, Middle Dutch and modern Dutch *los,* Old High German *lōs* (modern German *los, lose*), Old Icelandic *lauss,* and Gothic *laus* empty, from Proto-Germanic **lausaz,* Indo-European **lou-so-s* (Pok.682).

lesson *n.* something learned. Probably before 1200 *lesceun,* in *Ancrene Riwle;* later *lessoun* (about 1300); borrowed from Old French *leçon,* from Latin *lēctiōnem* (nominative *lēctiō*) a reading, from *legere* read; see LEGEND.

The earliest recorded meaning of *lesson* in Middle English was a portion from the Bible or other sacred writing read aloud to the congregation. This was followed by the meanings of something designed to be read or listened to (probably before 1300) and something set to be learned by a student, a lesson for formal study (before 1300).

lest *conj.* for fear that. Probably before 1200 *leste,* in Layamon's *Chronicle of Britain,* contraction of the phrase *les te* less that, developed from Old English (about 1000) *thӯ lǣs the* whereby less that (*thӯ,* instrumental case of *thæt* THAT; *lǣs* LESS; *the,* relative particle, Old English *thē, the,* a worn-down form of Proto-Germanic demonstrative stem **tha-*).

let[1] *v.* allow, permit. 1106 *leten,* developed from Old English (before 725) *lǣtan, lētan* to allow, let, let go, rent. The Old English forms are cognate with Old Frisian *lēta* to let, Old Saxon *lātan,* Middle Dutch, modern Dutch, and Middle Low German *laten,* Old High German *lāzzan* (modern German *lassen*), Old Icelandic *lāta,* and Gothic *lētan,* from Proto-Germanic **lǣtanan.* Cognates outside Germanic are found in Latin *lassus* weary, Albanian *l'oth* I tire, and Lithuanian *léisti* to let, from Indo-European **lēid-/lēd-/ləd-* (Pok. 666).

The shortening of the vowel from Old English *lǣtan* and *lētan* (which through the Proto-Germanic root **lǣt-* developed from **lēd-* and is related to **lat-* the Proto-Germanic root of English *late*) has not been accounted for.

let[2] *v. Archaic.* prevent, hinder. Before 1121 *lætten;* later *letten* (probably before 1200); developed from Old English *lettan* hinder or delay (before 889, in Alfred's translation of Boethius' *De Consolatione Philosophiae*). Old English *lettan* is cognate with Old Saxon *lettian* to hinder, Middle Dutch *letten,* Old High German *lezzen* to delay or hurt (modern German *verletzen* to hurt), Old Icelandic *letja* hold back, and Gothic *latjan,* from Proto-Germanic **latjanan;* all derived from the Proto-Germanic root that was the source of Old English *læt* LATE. **—n.** prevention, hindrance. Probably before 1200 *lette;* from the verb. The sense of interference with the ball in tennis and similar games is first recorded in 1871, though now many amateurs at tennis in America call a let ball, a net ball.

-let a suffix meaning: little, as in *booklet, leaflet;* thing worn as a band on, as in *anklet.* Middle English *-let;* borrowed from Old French *-elet,* a compound formed of *-el* (from Latin *-ellus,* diminutive suffix, or *-āle,* neuter of *-ālis* -AL[1]) + *-et* -ET. *The suffix -let* was not common in English before the 1700's.

lethal *adj.* causing death, deadly. 1583, borrowed from Late Latin *lēthālis,* an alteration with *th* of Latin *lētālis,* from *lētum* death, of uncertain origin (perhaps from an Indo-European **lē-to-m* a slackening, root **lēi-,* Pok. 666); or with Etruscan connection (compare Etruscan *leine* he is dead, *Leinth* goddess of the underworld); for suffix see -AL[1]. The development of the Late Latin form with *th* came by association with Latin *Lēthē,* name in classical mythology for a river in Hades, the waters of which when drunk caused forgetfulness of the past. The Romans borrowed *Lēthē* from Greek *lḗthē* forgetfulness, along with the mythology associated with *Lḗthēs hýdōr* the name of the river in Greek mythology (literally, water of Lethe). **—lethality** *n.* 1656, formed from English *lethal* + *-ity.*

lethargy *n.* drowsy dullness, sluggishness. 1373 *litarge,* also *litargie* (about 1380), and *letargye* (about 1410); borrowed from Old French *litargie, letargie,* or directly from Medieval Latin *litargia,* from Late Latin *lēthārgia,* from Greek *lēthārgíā,* from *lḗthārgos* forgetful; originally, inactive through forgetfulness (*lḗthē* forgetfulness, related to *lanthánein* escape notice + *ārgós* idle, from *a-* without + *érgon* WORK); for suffix see -Y[3]. The spelling *lethargy* (with *th*) is first recorded about 1593, influenced by the Latin and Greek forms. **—lethargic** *adj.* Before 1398 *litargik,* in Trevisa's translation of Bartholomew's *De Proprietatibus Rerum;* borrowed from Old French *litargique, lethargique,* from Latin *lēthārgicus,* from Greek *lēthārgikós,* from *lēthārgíā* lethargy; for suffix see -IC.

The difference in the Old French forms *litargie, letargie* for the noun and *lethargique* (*litargique* a one-time occurrence) for the adjective demonstrates the vagaries of tracing forms. Surely with only 25 years between the recording of the noun and the adjective in Middle English, both forms (in *-it-* and *-eth-* must have existed side-by-side in Old French, though the record is incomplete on this point.

letter *n.* Probably about 1150 *lettre* knowledge of reading and writing, book learning; later alphabetic sign, written message (probably before 1200, in *Ancrene Riwle*); borrowing of Old French *lettre,* from Latin *littera,* earlier *lītera* (spelled *leitera*) letter of the alphabet, *litterae,* pl., epistle, written documents, literature, probably related to *linere* smear, rub out; see LINIMENT. It has been suggested (especially by Hesychius, who was notorious for his improved words and assertions) that Latin *littera* was borrowed (through Etruscan) from Greek *diphthérā* tablet, since the Latin alphabet was adopted from the Greek. However, this theory has everything against it: the development of *l* from *d* (in spite of such examples as *Odysseus; Ulixes*) and the earlier Latin *-eit-* for expected *-ipt-.*
—v. 1668, mark with letters; from the noun.
—letterhead *n.* (before 1887) **—letter-perfect** *adj.* (1845)

lettuce *n.* About 1300 *letuse;* borrowed from Old French *laituës,* plural of *laituë,* from Latin *lactūca* lettuce, from *lac* (genitive *lactis*) milk; so called from the milky juice of the plant; see GALAXY. The slang sense of paper money (from the green color) was first recorded in 1929 in American English.

leuco- or **leuko-** a combining form meaning white, colorless, or slightly colored, as in *leucocyte, leukemia.* Also spelled **leuc-** or **leuk-** before vowels. Borrowed from Latin *leuco-,* from Greek *leuko-,* combining form of *leukós* clear, white; see LIGHT[1] radiant energy.

leucocyte *n.* white blood cell. 1870 (probably influenced by French *leucocyte* and German *Leukocyt*); formed from English *leuco-* + *-cyte.*

leukemia *n.* disease characterized by a large excess of white blood cells. 1855; formed in English from *leuk-* white + *-emia* blood, after earlier German *Leukämie* (1848). Another form *leucocythæmia* occurred earlier (1852), but disappeared from the record of English in the early 1900's.

Levantine (ləvan′tən) *adj.* of or belonging to the Levant, the countries of the eastern part of the Mediterranean. 1649, formed from Middle English *levant* the Levant (1497) + *-ine*[1]. Middle English *levant* was a borrowing of Middle French *levant* the Levant, the East, the Orient, from *levant,* present participle of *lever* to rise, from Latin *levāre* to raise, from *levis* LIGHT[2] in weight; so called because of the Levant's position relative to the rising sun. The capitalized form *Levant* is first recorded in English in 1558. Attributive use of *Levant* is recorded as early as 1503-04 in English. **—n.** 1706, native of the Levant; from the adjective. The special use of *levantine* (lower-case) in the sense of a sturdy twilled silk cloth is first recorded in English in 1831 as a borrowing from French, from Middle French *levant* in reference to the Levant, where this kind of cloth was originally made and exported.

levee[1] (lev′ē) *n.* bank built to keep a river from overflowing. 1719 *levée* a French word used in a description of New Orleans, in Justin Winsor's *Narrative and Critical History of America;* originally, feminine past participle of *lever* to raise, from Old French, from Latin *levāre,* from *levis* LIGHT[2] in weight. The sense of a landing place for boats, dock, was first recorded in 1813, in American English.

levee[2] (lev′ē) *n.* reception. 1672, in Dryden's *Marriage-à-la-Mode;* borrowed from French *lever* a rising from bed, reception held while rising, noun use of the verb *lever* to rise, raise; see LEVEE[1]. French kings used to hold levees in the morning while they were getting up and dressing.

level *n.* 1340, device for showing whether a surface is horizontal, flat, or even, in *Ayenbite of Inwyt;* borrowed from Old French *livel,* from Vulgar Latin ***lībellum,* from Latin *lībella* a balance, level, diminutive of *lībra* balance, scale, unit of weight; of uncertain origin.

The sense of a horizontal condition or position (as in *the level of the lake*) appeared in Middle English probably before 1400. The figurative sense of a position or standard on a certain scale, degree of something (as in *level of intellect*) is found in 1609.

—v. About 1450, to make even or level; from the noun. **—adj.** 1431, having an even surface, horizontal, flat; from the noun. **—level-headed** *adj.* (1879)

lever *n.* About 1300 *levour* bar used for prying or dislodging something; later *lever* (1408); borrowed from Old French *levier* a lifter or lever (Old French *leveor* with a different suffix is also sometimes cited), from *lever* to raise, from Latin *levāre* to raise, from *levis* LIGHT[2] in weight; for suffix see -ER[1]. **—v.** move with a lever. 1856; from the noun. **—leverage** *n.* 1724, action of a lever; formed from English *lever,* n. + *-age.* The figurative sense of advantage for accomplishing a purpose, power, influence, appeared in 1858, in Gladstone's writings.

leviathan (ləvī′əthən) *n.* Before 1382, a huge sea animal in the Bible; also, the Devil, in the Wycliffe Bible; borrowed from Late Latin *leviathan,* from Hebrew *livyāthān* dragon, serpent, huge animal of the sea, probably from the root of *lāvāh* he twisted, wound. The figurative sense of a great and powerful person or thing is first recorded in 1607.

Levi's (lē′vīz) *n.pl.* trademark for heavy blue denim trousers; blue jeans. 1926, American English, from the name of *Levi* Strauss and Company, the original American manufacturer of such trousers. The forms *Levis* (1926) and *levis* (1944) are frequent alterations of the trademark form.

levitate *v.* rise or cause to rise in the air. 1673, in Andrew Marvell's *The Rehearsal Transposed;* formed in English from Latin *levitās* lightness (see LEVITY) + English *-ate*[1], patterned on earlier *gravitate.* It is also possible that *levitate* is a back formation from *levitation.* **—levitation** *n.* 1668, in Henry More's *Divine Dialogues,* formed in English from Latin *levitās* lightness + English *-ation,* patterned on earlier *gravitation.*

levity *n.* lack of seriousness, frivolity. 1564, borrowed from Latin *levitās* (genitive *levitātis*) lightness, frivolity, from *levis* LIGHT[2] in weight; for suffix see -ITY.

levo- (lev′ə-) a combining form in chemistry and physics meaning toward the left, as in *levorotatory* (turning the plane of polarized light to the left), or meaning levorotatory, as in *levoglucose.* Borrowed from French *lévo-,* from Latin *laevus* left, cognate with Greek *laiós* and Old Slavic *lěvŭ,* from Indo-European ***laiwós* (Pok. 652).

levy *n.* imposition or collection of a tax, etc. 1416 *leve* act of raising taxes, etc.; borrowed through Anglo-French *leve,* from Old French *levée* act of raising, levy, from feminine past participle of Old French *lever* to raise; see LEVER. The term is found in Anglo-French context as early as 1227. **—v.** impose or collect (a tax, etc.). 1436-37 *leveyen;* from the noun.

lewd *adj.* Before 1121 *lewed* nonclerical, lay, uneducated; developed from Old English *lǣwede* (before 899, in Alfred's translation of Bede's *Ecclesiastical History*); of uncertain origin. The sense of wicked, unchaste, lustful, is recorded probably about 1378 in Wycliffe's treatise *De Officio Pastorale.*

lexeme (lek′sēm) *n. Linguistics.* minimal meaningful element in the vocabulary of a language. 1940, in Whorf's *Language, Thought, and Reality;* formed in English from Greek *léxis* word + English *-eme,* as in *morpheme, phoneme;* see LEXICON.

lexicographer (lek′səkog′rəfər) *n.* compiler of dictionaries. 1658, formed in English from French *lexicographe* lexicographer (1578) + English suffix *-er*[1]. The French word was borrowed from Greek *lexikográphos* (*lexikón* wordbook, LEXICON + *gráphein* to write; see CARVE). It is also possible that *lexicographer* was formed from English *lexicon* + *-grapher,* on the pattern of *geographer.* **—lexicography** *n.* compilation of dictionaries. 1680, formed from English *lexicon* + *-graphy,* or from *lexicographer,* on the pattern of such pairs as *geographer, geography.*

lexicology *n.* study of words. 1828, borrowed from French *lexicologie,* from Greek *lexikón* wordbook + French *-logie* -logy.

lexicon (lek'səkon) *n.* wordbook, dictionary. 1603, borrowed probably through Middle French *lexicon* from Greek *lexikòn* (*biblíon*) wordbook, from neuter of *lexikós* pertaining to words, from *léxis* word, from *légein* say; see LEGEND. The sense of vocabulary of a language or subject is first recorded in 1647. **—lexical** *adj.* of words or vocabulary. 1836, formed from English *lexicon* + *-al*[1].

liable *adj.* 1450, bound by law, legally subject; probably formed with the English ending *-able* from Old French *lier* to bind, from Latin *ligāre;* see LIGAMENT. The sense of likely to suffer from (something unpleasant) is first recorded in 1593; that of subject to the possibility, likely, in 1682. **—liability** *n.* 1794-1809; formed from English *liable* + *-ity.*

liaison (lē'əzon *or* lēā'zon) *n.* Before 1648, act of thickening a sauce; borrowed from French *liaison* a union, entanglement, a binding together, from Latin *ligātiōnem* (nominative *ligātiō*) a binding, from *ligāre* to bind; see LIGAMENT; for suffix see -SION. The sense of a close relation or connection between persons or groups is first recorded in 1809, followed by that of an illicit connection or intimacy between a man and a woman, in Byron's *Don Juan* (1821). **—liaise** (lēāz') *v.* form a liaison. 1928 (military use); back formation from *liaison.*

liar *n.* before 1225 *liar, lier;* developed from Old English *lēgere* (about 950, in the gloss of the *Lindisfarne Gospels*); later *lēogere* (before 1023, in *Wulfstan*); from Anglian *lēgan,* and West Saxon *lēogan* be untruthful, LIE[1].

The form in *-ar* is a common variant of *-er*[1] found in northern dialect forms of England in such words as *syngar* singer, and in such modern words as *beggar, pedlar,* probably in imitation of the refashioned forms such as *scholar* for *scoler* and *pillar* for *piler.*

lib or **Lib** *n.* 1970, American English, shortened form of *liberation* (originally in *Women's Lib,* short for *Women's Liberation*). **—libber** *n. Informal.* one who favors a liberation cause. 1971, American English, formed from *lib* + *-er*[1].

libation *n.* a pouring out of wine, etc., as an offering to a god. About 1384 *libacioun,* in the Wycliffe Bible; borrowed from Latin *lībātiōnem* (nominative *lībātiō*), from *lībāre* pour out (an offering), earlier **loibāye-,* formed from a lost **loibā,* cognate with Greek *loibḗ* libation, related to *leíbein* to pour, from Indo-European **leibh-/loibh-* (Walde-Pokorny II,393); for suffix see -ATION. The sense of any liquid poured out to be drunk is first recorded in 1751.

libel *n.* About 1300, formal written statement; later, little book (about 1382, in the Wycliffe Bible); borrowed through Old French *libel, libelle* and directly from Latin *libellus* a little book, pamphlet, note, petition, lampoon, diminutive of *liber* book; see LIBRARY.

The meaning of a plaintiff's statement of charges is first recorded in *Ayenbite of Inwyt* (1340); this usage evolved into the sense of any published or written statement that is likely to harm the reputation of a person, as first recorded in 1521.

—v. write or print a libel about. 1570, from the noun. **—libelous** *adj.* 1619, formed from English *libel,* n. + *-ous.*

liberal *adj.* Probably before 1350, befitting free men, noble, generous; borrowed from Old French *liberal,* learned borrowing from Latin *līberālis* noble, generous, from *līber* free; for suffix see -AL[1]. Cognates of Latin *līber* are found in Greek *eleútheros* free (originally) belonging to the people, of genuine tribal stock, Old High German *liut* people (modern German *Leute*), Old English *lēod,* Russian *ljudi* people, from Indo-European **leudh-* to grow (Pok.684).

The term *liberal arts,* referring originally to the seven arts (the *trivium* and *quadrivium*) that were considered "worthy of or befitting free men" in the Middle Ages, appeared in Middle English before 1398 (in Trevisa's translation of Bartholomew's *De Proprietatibus Rerum*) and was a translation of Medieval Latin *artes liberales.* The sense of free from prejudice, tolerant, is first recorded in Gibbon's *Decline and Fall of the Roman Empire* (1776-88), followed by the political sense of favoring constitutional change and legal reforms in 1801. The latter was probably borrowed into English from French *libéral,* attested in 1750 with the sense of favorable to individual political freedoms.

—n. 1820, member of a liberal political party; later, person who holds liberal views, especially in theology (1887); from the adjective.

—liberalism *n.* 1819, formed from English *liberal,* adj. + *-ism.* **—liberality** *n.* Probably about 1350 *liberalite* generosity; borrowed from Old French *liberalité,* from Latin *līberālitātem* (nominative *līberālitās*), from *līberālis* liberal; for suffix see -ITY. **—liberalization** *n.* 1835, in De Quincey's writings; formed from English *liberalize* + *-ation.* **—liberalize** *v.* 1774, in Burke's writings; formed from English *liberal* + *-ize.*

liberate *v.* set free. 1623, in Cockeram's *Dictionary;* borrowed from Latin *līberātus,* past participle of *līberāre,* from *līber* free, see LIBERAL; for suffix see -ATE[1]. In some instances, *liberate* is probably a back formation from earlier *liberation.* **—liberation** *n.* Probably before 1425 *liberacion,* in a translation of Higden's *Polychronicon;* borrowed (perhaps in some instances through Middle French *libération*) and directly from Latin *līberātiōnem* (nominative *līberātiō*), from *līberāre* set free; for suffix see -ATION. **—liberator** *n.* 1650, formed from English *liberate* + *-or*[2].

liberationist *n.* person advocating freedom from social biases or restrictions. 1970, American English, abstracted from *Women's Liberationist;* formed from English *liberation* + *-ist.*

An earlier use of this term (1869) was restricted to a member of the "Liberation Society" of Great Britain, which advocated disestablishment (withdrawal of state support from the established church). The current form is a redevelopment in English.

libertarian *n.* 1789, one who holds the doctrine of free will; later, person advocating liberty in thought and conduct (1878); formed from English *liberty* + *-arian,* as in *Unitarian.*

libertine *n.* dissolute or licentious person. About 1384, emancipated slave, freedman, in the Wycliffe Bible; borrowed from Latin *lībertīnus* member of the class of freedmen, from *lībertus* one's freedman, from *līber* free, see LIBERAL; for suffix see -INE[1]. The sense of a freethinker is first recorded in an edition of Foxe's *Book of Martyrs* (1563-83), evidently influenced by the word *liberty,* and the sense of a dissolute or licentious person is found in 1593. **—adj.** 1577, freethinking; later, dissolute, in Bacon's *Of the Advancement of Learning* (1605); from the noun.

liberty *n.* About 1375 *libertee,* in Chaucer's *Canterbury Tales;* borrowed from Old French *liberté* freedom, learned borrowing from Latin *lībertātem* (nominative *lībertās*), from *līber* free, see LIBERAL; for suffix see -TY².

libido (ləbē′dō) *n.* sexual desire or instinct. 1909, in A.A. Brill's translation of Freud's *Selected Papers on Hysteria;* borrowed from Latin *libīdō* desire or lust, from *libēre* be pleasing, please; see LOVE. **—libidinal,** *adj.* of the libido. 1922, formed from English *libido* + *-al*¹. **—libidinous** *adj.* lustful. 1447, borrowed probably through Middle French *libidineux* (feminine *libidineuse*), from Latin *libīdinōsus,* from *libīdō* (genitive *libīdinis*) desire or lust; for suffix see -OUS.

library *n.* About 1380 *librarye* place containing books, in Chaucer's translation of Boethius' *De Consolatione Philosophiae;* later *librarie* collection of books, in the Wycliffe Bible (before 1382); borrowed through Anglo-French *librarie,* from Old French *librairie* collection of books, and directly from Latin *librārium* chest for books, from *liber* (genitive *librī*) book, paper, parchment, inner bark of a tree (used in early times for writing), earlier **luber,* from Indo-European **lubhros;* see LEAF.

The Romance languages now use the word to mean bookstore, derived from that sense in Late Latin, as formed in French *librairie,* Italian *libreria,* Spanish *librería,* Portuguese *livraria,* etc.; *library* in the English sense is rendered *bibliothèque* in French, etc.

—librarian *n.* 1670, scribe; later, custodian of a library (1713, in Steele's writings); formed from English *library* + *-an.*

libretto (ləbret′ō) *n.* words of an opera or other long musical composition. 1740, in Richardson's *Pamela;* borrowing of Italian *libretto,* diminutive of *libro* book, from Latin *liber* (genitive *librī*); see LIBRARY. **—librettist** *n.* 1862, probably borrowed from French *librettiste* (1846), from *libretto* (from Italian) + *-iste* -ist.

license *n.* Before 1376 *licence* permission given by law to do something, in *Piers Plowman;* borrowed from Old French *licence,* learned borrowing from Latin *licentia,* from *licentum* (nominative *licēns*), present participle of *licēre* be allowed, be lawful, cognate with Oscan *likítud* let it be allowed, and with Lettish *līkt* to come to terms (of sale), from Indo-European **leik-/lik-* (Pok.669). **—v.** give a license to, permit by law. Probably before 1400 *licencen;* from the noun. **—licensee** *n.* 1868, formed from English *license* + *-ee.*

licentious (līsen′shəs) *adj.* lawless, immoral. 1535, lawless; later, lewd or lustful (1555); borrowed from Latin *licentiōsus* full of license, unrestrained, from *licentia* LICENSE; for suffix see -OUS.

The later meaning "lewd" may have come from Middle French *licencieux* (1537), appearing in a translation of Castiglione's *Il Cortegiano* (The Courtier).

An earlier example of *licentious* is found in Middle English about 1425 in the sense of freely, with permission (adjective used as an adverb).

lichen (lī′kən) *n.* organism consisting of a fungus and alga growing together. 1601, liverwort (formerly included in the same group with the lichens), in Holland's translation of Pliny's *Natural History;* borrowed from Latin *līchēn,* from Greek *leichḗn,* (originally) what eats around itself, probably from *leíchein* to LICK. The current meaning of *lichen* is first recorded in 1715.

licit *adj.* lawful, permitted. 1483, in Caxton's translation of Cato's writings; borrowed from Middle French *licite,* learned borrowing from Latin *licitus* lawful; and borrowed directly from Latin *licitus,* from *licēre* be allowed, be lawful; see LICENSE.

lick *v.* Probably about 1200 *licken;* developed from Old English *liccian* (830, in the *Vespasian Psalter*). Old English *liccian* is cognate with Old Saxon *likkōn* to lick, modern Dutch *likken,* Old High German *leckōn* (modern German *lecken*), Old Icelandic *sleikja,* and Gothic *bilaigōn;* cognates are also found outside Germanic in Latin *lingere* to lick, *ligurrīre* to lick, lick up, Old Irish *ligim* I lick, Greek *leíchein* to lick, Lithuanian *liẽšti,* Old Slavic *lizati,* Armenian *lizum* I lick, and Vedic Sanskrit *léḍhi, réḍhi* (he) licks, Classical Sanskrit *lihati,* from Indo-European *(s)*leiĝh-/loiĝh-/lēiĝh-/(s)liĝh-* (Pok.668).

The sense of beat or thrash is first recorded in 1535; the extended sense of overcome or defeat is found in 1800.

—n. stroke of the tongue over something. 1603, from the verb. **—licking** *n.* a beating or thrashing (1756).

lickety-split *adv. Informal.* at full speed. 1859, in Bartlett's *Dictionary of Americanisms;* American English, formed from earlier (1817) *lickitie* very fast (irregular formation from *lick,* n., used dialectally in the sense of "fast") + *split,* n. *Lickety-split* was one of a group of formations that included *lickety cut* (1831), *lickety-click* (1847), and *lickety-switch* (1858).

licorice (lik′əris *or* lik′ərish) *n.* sweet, gummy extract of a root, used as flavoring. Probably before 1200 *licoriz,* in Layamon's *Chronicle of Britain;* borrowed through Anglo-French *lycorys,* Old French *licorice, licorece,* from Late Latin *liquiritia,* alteration of Latin *glycyrrhiza,* from Greek *glykýrrhiza,* a compound of *glykýs* sweet + *rhíza* root. The development of Late Latin *liquiritia* was in part influenced by Latin *liquēre* become fluid, in reference to the process of treating the root to obtain its extract.

lid *n.* Before 1250 *lid* eyelid, in *Bestiary;* later, covering or cover (about 1300); developed from Old English (about 1000) *hlid* lid, cover, opening, gate. Old English *hlid* is cognate with Old Frisian *hlid* lid, Middle Low German *lit,* Middle Dutch *lit* (modern Dutch *lid*), Old High German *lit, hlit* (modern German *Lid* and *Augenlid* eyelid), Old Icelandic *hlidh* gate, from Proto-Germanic **Hliđán,* cognate with Sanskrit *śritá-m,* neuter of *śritá-s* leaning, lying, and Greek *klī́nein* lean, from Indo-European **k̑lei-/k̑li-* (Pok.601).

lie¹ *v.* speak falsely. Probably about 1175 *lien;* later *ligen* (probably before 1200) and *legen* (before 1250); developed from Old English *lēgan, līgan* (before 830, in the *Vespasian Psalter*), and earlier *lēogan* (before 725). The Old English forms are cognate with Old Frisian *liāga* to lie, Old Saxon *liogan,* Middle Dutch *lieghen* (modern Dutch *liegen*), Old High German *liogan* (modern German *lügen*), Old Icelandic *ljūga* (Swedish *ljuga,* Danish *lyve*), and Gothic *liugan,* from Proto-Germanic **leuʒanan;* also cognate outside Germanic with Old Slavic *lŭgati* to lie, and Lithuanian *lūgóti* to request, from Indo-European **leugh-/lugh-* (Pok.686). **—n.** false statement. About 1175 *lyge;* later *lye* (about 1385); developed from Old English (about 900) *lyge* lie; cognate with Old High German *lugī* (modern German *Lüge*), and Old Icelandic *lygi,* from Proto-Germanic **luzīn,* from the root **luz-/leuz-* that is the source of Old English *lēogan* to lie.

lie² *v.* rest horizontally. 1137 *lien;* later *liggen* (probably before 1200); developed from Old English *licgan* to lie (about 725, in *Beowulf*); cognate with Old Frisian *liga, lidzia* to lie, Old Saxon *liggian,* Middle Dutch *ligghen,* modern Dutch *liggen,* (from Proto-Germanic **lezjanan),* Old High German *ligen* (modern German *liegen*), Old Icelandic *liggja* (Swedish *ligga,* Danish and Norwegian *ligge*), and Gothic *ligan.* Outside Germanic cognates are found in Gaulish *legasit* he put, laid, Old Irish *lige* bed, grave, *laigid* lies, Latin *lectus* bed, Greek *léchos* bed, *léchesthai* lie down, Old Slavic *ležati* to lie, Tocharian A *lake* and Tocharian B *leke* bed, and Hittite *lagari* he lies, from Indo-European **legh-/logh-* (Pok.658).

Middle English *liggen* represents a regular phonetic development from Old English *licgan.* The form *lien,* from which modern English *lie* developed, was a new formation based upon Old English *lig-,* stem of the second and third person singular.

—n. way in which something lies. 1697, from the verb.

lieder (lē′dər) *n.pl.* of **lied,** used principally in reference to German songs of Schubert and Schumann. 1852, borrowed from German *Lieder,* plural of *Lied* song; see LAUD.

lief (lēf) *adv.* About 1300 *leve,* adv., willingly, gladly; later *lef* (before 1376, in *Piers Plowman*); from the adjective *leve, leove* dear, beloved (before 1121); developed from Old English *lēof* dear, beloved (about 725, in *Beowulf*). The Old English adjective is cognate with Old Frisian *liāf* dear, Old Saxon *liof,* Middle Dutch and modern Dutch *lief,* Old High German *liob* (modern German *lieb*), Old Icelandic *ljūfr,* and Gothic *liufs;* related to Old English *lufu* LOVE. Compare LIVELONG.

liege (lēj) *adj.* entitled to feudal allegiance and service. Probably before 1300 *liege,* in *Kyng Alisaunder,* also *lige* (about 1300); later *lege* (probably about 1390); borrowed through Anglo-French *lege,* and directly from Old French *liege, lige,* from Late Latin *laeticus* cultivated by serfs, from *laetus* serf, probably from a Germanic source (compare Old English *lǣt* half-freedman, serf, Old Frisian *lēt,* Old High German *lāz,* Middle Low German *lāt,* and Gothic *fra-lēts* forgiveness; all probably derived from the Proto-Germanic root that is the source of Gothic *lētan* and Old English *lǣtan* to allow, LET[1]). **—n.** lord entitled to feudal allegiance. Probably about 1375 *lige* vassal, in Chaucer's *Canterbury Tales;* and *lege* feudal lord (about 1380); from the adjective.

lien (lēn) *n.* legal claim on the property of another for payment of a debt. 1531, borrowing of Middle French *lien* a band or tie, from Latin *ligāmen* bond, from *ligāre* to bind; see LIGAMENT.

lieu (lü) *n.* place, stead. 1534 *in (the) lieu of* in place of, instead of (possibly also about 1300, in a single use recorded in OED); borrowed from Middle French *lieu* place, Old French *leu,* from Latin *locum* (nominative *locus*) place; see LOCATE.

lieutenant (lüten′ənt; *British* leften′ənt) *n.* About 1378 *lieutenant,* civil or military officer who acts for a superior, in a version of *Piers Plowman,* and *leeftenaunt* one who acts for another (before 1387, in Trevisa's translation of Higden's *Polychronicon*); borrowed from Old French *luetenant* substitute; literally, placeholder (*lieu* place, LIEU + *tenant,* present participle of *tenir* to hold, from Latin *tenēre;* see TENANT). The origin of the British pronunciation, represented before 1387 in such spellings as *leeftenaunt,* remains uncertain.

life *n.* Before 1121 *life,* in *Peterborough Chronicle;* developed from Old English *life,* dative of *līf* (about 725, in *Beowulf*); cognate with Old Frisian *līf* life, person, body, Old Saxon *līf* life, person, Middle Dutch and modern Dutch *lijf* body, Old High German *līb* life (modern German *Leib* body), and Old Icelandic *līf* life (Swedish *lif,* Danish and Norwegian *liv* life, body), from Proto-Germanic **lība-;* related to Old English *lifian, libban* to have life, LIVE[1]. **—lifeblood** *n.* (1590, in Spenser's *Faerie Queene*) **—lifeboat** *n.* (1801) **—lifeguard** *n.* (1896, American English) **—life insurance** (about 1809, American English) **—lifeless** *adj.* Before 1200 *lifleas;* developed from Old English *līflēas* (*līf* life + *-lēas* -less). **—lifelong** *adj.* (1855; earlier, 1757, as a substitute for *livelong*) **—lifetime** *n.* (before 1250 *lif time*) **—lifework** *n.* (1871)

lift *v.* Probably about 1200 *liften,* in *The Ormulum;* borrowed from a Scandinavian source (compare Old Icelandic *lypta* to raise). Old Icelandic *lypta* is cognate with Middle Low German *lüchten* to raise, lift, Middle Dutch *luchten* (modern Dutch *lichten*), Middle High German *lüften,* from Proto-Germanic **luftjanan;* all derived from the Proto-Germanic root that is the source of Old English *lyft* heaven, air; see LOFT **—n.** act of lifting. 1485, in Malory's *Morte d'Arthur;* from the verb.

The figurative sense of act of helping, helping hand is first recorded in 1633, and that of help given by offering a ride in a vehicle, in Swift's *Journal to Stella* (1712). *Lift* meaning an elevator (now only in British usage) is found in 1851 in the specific sense of a dumbwaiter and in 1861 as a passenger elevator.

—liftoff *n.* takeoff of a rocket or aircraft. (1956, in Dr. Woodford Heflin's *The U.S. Air Force Dictionary,* American English).

ligament *n.* 1392, band of strong tissues; borrowed from Latin *ligāmentum* band, tie, ligature, from *ligāre* to bind, tie; for suffix see -MENT. Latin *ligāre* is cognate with Middle Low German *līk* band, Middle High German *geleich,* joint, limb, Albanian *lith* I bind, and Ukrainian *nalýhaty* to bridle, fetter, from Indo-European **leiĝ-/liĝ-, also *leig-/lig-* (Pok.668).

ligature (lig′əchůr *or* lig′əchər) *n.* anything used to bind or tie up. Before 1400, in a translation of Lanfranc's *Science of Surgery,* borrowed through Old French *ligature,* and directly from Late Latin *ligātūra,* from Latin *ligāre* to bind, see LIGAMENT; for suffix see -URE.

The sense in music of a method indicating notes to be sung to one syllable is first recorded in 1597. The sense of two or more letters joined in writing and printing is first recorded in 1693, possibly taken from French (1680).

—v. bind or tie up with a ligature. 1716-20; from the noun.

light[1] *n.* radiant energy. About 1175 *liht;* later *light* (before 1325, in *Genesis and Exodus,* and 1317, as a surname); developed from Old English *lēht* (before 830, in the *Vespasian Psalter*); earlier *lēoht* (about 725, in *Beowulf*). The Old English forms are cognate with Old Frisian *liacht* light, Old Saxon *lioht,* Middle Dutch and modern Dutch *licht,* Old High German *lioht* (modern German *Licht*), Old Icelandic *ljōs,* and Gothic *liuhath.* The word is represented outside Germanic by Old Irish *luchair* luster, Latin *lūx* (genitive *lūcis*) light, *lūcēre* to shine, Greek *leukós* white or light, Lithuanian *laũkas* pale, Old Slavic *luča* ray or beam, Armenian *lois* light, Sanskrit *rócate* (it) shines, Tocharian A and Tocharian B *luk-,* and Hittite *luk-, lukk-* to shine, from Indo-European **leuk-/louk-/luk-* (Pok.687).

By the early 1300's *gh* was beginning to appear as a variant and then a substitute for Old English *h* in the middle of such words as *light,* also formerly written *liȝt* in early Middle English, owing in particular to influence of the French scribes who were familiar with Anglo-French.

—adj. having light, bright. 1122 *liht;* later *light* (before 1325, in *Cursor Mundi*); developed from Old English (before 830) *lēht* bright, shining. Old English *lēht* is cognate with Old Frisian *liacht* bright, Old Saxon *lioht,* Middle Dutch and modern Dutch *licht,* Old High German *lioht* (modern German *licht*); related to Old English *lēoht,* n. **—v.** give light, shine. Probably before 1160 *lihten;* later *lighten* (before 1325, in *Cursor Mundi*); developed from Old English *līhtan* (about 1000, in Ælfric's *Grammar*), *lȳhtan* (before 1000), *līehtan.* The Old English forms are cognate with Old Saxon *liuhtian* give light, light up, Middle Dutch and modern Dutch *lichten,* Old High German *liuhten* (modern German *leuchten*), Old Icelandic *lýsa,* and Gothic *liuhtjan,* from Proto-Germanic **leuHtjanan,* from **leuHtan* light, the source of Old English *lēoht,* n.

—lighthouse *n.* (1662) **—light-year** *n.* (1888)

light[2] *adj.* not heavy. Before 1150 *liht;* later *light* (about 1300); developed from Old English *lēoht* (before 899, in Alfred's translation of Orosius' *Historiarum Adversus Paganos*); later *līht* (about 950, in *Lindisfarne Gospels*). The Old English forms are cognate with Old Frisian *licht* not heavy, light, Old Saxon *līht,* Middle Dutch and modern Dutch *licht,* Old High German *līhti* (modern German *leicht*), Old Icelandic *lēttr* (Danish *let,* Norwegian *lett,* Swedish *lätt*), and Gothic *leihts,* from Proto-Germanic **linHtaz.* Outside Germanic cognates are found in Latin *levis* light, Greek *elachýs* small, Old Irish *laigiu* smaller, Lithuanian *leñgvas* light, Old Slavic *lĭgŭkŭ,* and Sanskrit *laghú-s* light, quick, from Indo-European **legwh-ú-s, legwh-, lengwh-, lengwh-to-* (Pok.660).

It is interesting to note how many extended and transformed senses of *light* existed in Old English (among them are: lightly constructed, as in *a light cart;* of little force, gentle, as in *a light touch;* easily digested, as in *light food;* of little alcoholic content, as in *light beer;* trivial, slight, as in *light regard;* nimble, swift, as in *light of foot;* easy to bear, as in *a light punishment;* easy to perform, as in *light housework;* easily shaken off, as in *light sleep*).

—adv. Probably about 1150 *lihte,* later *light* (before 1325); developed from Old English (about 900) *lēohte, līhte;* from the adjective.

—light-headed *adj.* About 1537; from earlier *lighthead,* n., in Middle English *ligthede* (1340, in *Ayenbite of Inwyt*). **—light-hearted** *adj.* (probably before 1400) **—lightweight** *n.* (1773); *adj.* (1809)

light[3] *v.* come down to the ground, alight. About 1175 *lihten* descend, dismount, lighten a load; later *lighten* (before 1325, in *Cursor Mundi*); developed from Old English (about 900) *līhtan,* from *līht, lēoht* not heavy. The Old English verb is cognate with Old Frisian *līchta* to lighten a load, Middle Dutch *lichten,* Old High German *līhten,* and Old Icelandic *létta* (Danish and Norwegian *lette,* Swedish *lätta*), from Proto-Germanic **linHtjanan,* from **linHtaz* LIGHT[2].

The sense of come or arrive by chance is first recorded about 1470. The slang phrase *light out* with the meaning of leave suddenly is first recorded in American English, in Mark Twain's *Letters From Hawaii* (1866). Another American slang use, *light into* with the meaning of attack, is found in 1889.

lighten[1] *v.* make or grow light, brighten. Before 1325 *lightenen,* about 1340 *lightnen* make clear, illuminate, brighten; developed from *light* bright, LIGHT[1].

lighten[2] *v.* take weight off. Probably about 1350 *lihtnen* make lighter, make more cheerful; later *lightenen* (probably about 1380), from *light* not heavy, LIGHT[2]; compare LIGHT[3], v.

lighter[1] *n.* thing or person that starts something burning. 1553, person who lights or kindles something; formed in English from *light*[1] make bright + *-er*[1]. The sense of an instrument for lighting is first recorded in 1851; the first reference to a cigarette lighter is found in 1895.

lighter[2] *n.* flat-bottomed barge. 1372-74, perhaps formed in English from *light*[3] in the sense of lighten a load + *-er*[1]. Alternatively, *lighter* was perhaps borrowed from Dutch *lichter,* from Middle Dutch *lichten* to lighten a load; see LIGHT[3] alight. **—v.** carry (goods) in such a barge. 1840; from the noun.

lightning *n.* discharge of electricity in the sky. About 1280, formed from Middle English *lightnen* make light, brighten + *-ing*[1]; see LIGHTEN[1]. **—lightning bug** firefly. (1778, American English) **—lightning rod** (1789, American English)

lights *n.pl.* lungs, especially of animals. Probably before 1300 *lightes,* in *Sir Tristrem,* earlier *lihte* (before 1200, in a version of *Body and Soul*), from *liht* LIGHT[2] not heavy; so called because the lungs were distinguished from other internal parts of the body by their lightness.

ligneous (lig′nēəs) *adj.* of or like wood; woody. 1626, in Bacon's *Sylva Sylvarum;* borrowed (perhaps through French *ligneux,* feminine *ligneuse*) from Latin *ligneus* wooden, of wood, from *lignum* wood, from *legere* to gather, see LEGEND; for suffix see -OUS.

lignite (lig′nīt) *n.* a dark-brown coal, often having the texture of the wood. 1808, borrowed from French *lignite,* from Latin *lignum* wood; for suffix see -ITE[1].

lignum vitae (lig′nəm vī′tē) kind of extremely heavy and hard wood. 1594, New Latin *lignum vitae,* literally, wood of life; supposedly so called from the fact that resin obtained from the wood was formerly thought to have great medicinal value.

like[1] *adj.* similar. About 1200 *iliche, ilik;* later *like* (about 1225); developed as an abbreviated form of Old English *gelīc* like, similar (about 725, in *Beowulf*). The Old English *gelīc* is cognate with Old Frisian *gelīk* like, Old Saxon *gilīk,* Middle Dutch *ghelijc* (modern Dutch *gelijk*), Old High German *gilīh* (modern German *gleich*), Old Icelandic *glíkr, líkr* (Norwegian and Swedish *lik,* Danish *lig*), and Gothic *galeiks,* all derived from a Proto-Germanic compound **ȝalíkaz* having the same form, made up of the prefix that was the source of Old English *ge-* with, together (see ENOUGH), and the word that was the source of Old English *līc* body. Old English *līc* is cognate with Old Frisian and Old Saxon *līk* body, Middle Dutch *lijc* corpse (modern Dutch *lijk*), Old High German *līh* (modern German *Leiche* corpse), Old Icelandic *lík* body, form, corpse (Norwegian and Swedish *lik,* Danish *lig*), and Gothic *leik* body, flesh, corpse, from Proto-Germanic **līkan,* cognate with Lithuanian *lýg* alike, from Indo-European **līg-* form, shape (Pok.667). Compare -LY[2]. **—prep.** similar to. Apparently about 1200 *lic,* in *The Ormulum;* later *like* (before

1250); from the adjective. **—adv.** *Informal.* probably. Before 1325, in the same manner as, in *Cursor Mundi;* from the adjective. **—conj.** *Informal.* as if; as. Probably about 1380; from the adverb. **—n.** match, counterpart, equal. Probably before 1200 *liche;* later *like* (before 1393); from the adjective. **—likeness** *n.* About 1175 *licnesse;* later *liknesse* an analogy, something similar (about 1250); appearance, guise, shape (probably before 1300); developed from Old English *gelīcness,* from *gelīc* like, similar + *-ness.* **—likewise** *adv.* About 1443, from the phrase *in lik wise* in a similar manner.

like² *v.* be pleased with. Probably about 1150 *liken* to please; later, be pleased, find agreeable (probably before 1200); developed from Old English *līcian* to please (before 899, in Alfred's translation of Boethius' *De Consolatione Philosophiae*). Old English *līcian* is cognate with Old Frisian *līkia* to please, Old Saxon *līkōn* (from Proto-Germanic **likójanan*), Old High German *līhhēn,* Old Icelandic *līka,* and Gothic *leikan;* derived from the Proto-Germanic root that was the source of Old English *gelīc* similar, LIKE¹. **—n. likes,** 1851, likings, preferences; earlier *like, likes* pleasure or will (before 1325, in *Cursor Mundi*); from the verb. **—likable** *adj.* 1882, in Stevenson's *Familiar Studies;* variant of *likeable.* **—likeable** *adj.* 1730, in Gay's writings; formed from English *like* + *-able.* **—liking** *n.* Probably before 1200 *licung, liking;* developed from Old English *līcung,* from *līcian* to please + *-ung* -ing¹.

-like a suffix forming adjectives from nouns and meaning: like, resembling, as in *daisylike, wolflike;* characteristic of, as in *childlike, workmanlike;* suited to, as in *businesslike.* Late Middle English, abstracted from LIKE¹, adj.

-like is a living suffix, freely added to nouns to form adjectives and sometimes rather inelegantly added to adjectives to form quasi-adverbs meaning "like one that is ____, so as to appear ____," as in a *used-up-like* appearance, or to keep *friendly-like.*

likely *adj.* probable. Before 1325 *licly,* in *Cursor Mundi;* later *likly* (about 1385); developed from late Old English *gelīclīc;* perhaps borrowed from a Scandinavian source (compare Old Icelandic *līkligr, glīkligr* likely, formed from *līkr, glīkr* similar, LIKE¹ + *-ligr* -ly², adjective suffix). **—adv.** probably. Apparently about 1378 *licly;* later *likly* (probably before 1400); from the adjective. **—likelihood** *n.* 1390 *liklyhede;* later *liklyhode* (1427); formed from Middle English *likly* likely + *-hede, -hode* hood.

liken *v.* compare. 1280 *liknen,* formed from Middle English *like* similar, like¹ + *-nen* -en¹.

lilac (lī′lək *or* lī′lak) *n.* shrub with clusters of pinkish-purple or white flowers. 1625 *lelacke tree,* in Bacon's *Essays;* later *lilac* (1658); borrowed from obsolete French *lilac* (now *lilas*), from Persian *līlak,* variant of *nīlak* bluish, from *nīl* indigo, from Sanskrit *nīla-s* dark blue, of unknown origin. **—adj.** pale pinkish-purple. 1801, from the noun.

lilt *v.* sing or play in a light, tripping manner. Apparently about 1380 (West Midland dialect) *lulten* to sound an alarm; of uncertain origin. The East Midland form *lilten* is not recorded, but the compound *lilting-horn* indicates that the verb existed. The sense of sing in a light, tripping manner is first recorded in Robert Burns' *Ordination* (1786). **—n.** lively song or tune. 1728, lively song, in Ramsey's *Poems;* from the verb. The sense of rhythmical swing or cadence is first recorded in Carlyle's *On Heroes, Hero Worship, and the Heroic in History* (1840).

lily *n.* About 1150 *lilie;* developed from Old English (971) *lilie;* borrowed from Latin *līlia,* plural of *līlium* a lily, from the same (non-Indo-European) source as Greek *leírion* lily. A corresponding designation of the lily is found in Coptic *hrēri, hlēli,* from Egyptian *ḥrr-t.* **—adj.** Before 1533, like a white lily, pure, lovely; later, pallid or colorless in Shakespeare's *Midsummer Night's Dream* (1590); from the noun.

lima bean (lī′mə) 1756; according to a quotation from a book on natural history in Cassidy's *Dictionary of Jamaican English,* the plant was cultivated as an importation to local agriculture, and is therefore associated with *Lima* (lē′mə), Peru, through which it was first introduced.

limb¹ *n.* leg, arm, wing, or branch. 1547 *limb,* alteration (with added *b* as in *thumb*) of early modern English *lim, lymme, lym,* etc., found in Middle English *lim* (1125, in *Peterborough Chronicle*), and Old English *lim* limb, part of the body, joint, main branch of a tree (about 725, in *Beowulf*); cognate with Old Icelandic *limr, lim* limb, branch (Swedish, Norwegian, and Danish *lem* limb, member of the body), from Proto-Germanic *limu-,* perhaps cognate with Greek *leimṓn* meadow; originally, a hollow, and Latin *līmes* embankment between fields, from Indo-European **(e)lei-/(e)li-* bend (Pok. 309). The informal expression *out on a limb,* with the meaning of in a vulnerable or dangerous position, is first recorded in 1897. **—v.** dismember. 1674, from the noun.

While the loss of final *-b* in the pronunciation of many words, such as *comb, dumb, lamb,* is part of natural development, the *-b* in words such as *limb* and *thumb* is unhistorical and began to appear at the end of the 1500's. The terminal *-b* has no etymological significance as it does in Old English *dumb.* It is probable that the spelling with *-b* developed by influence of *limb²* either by design or confusion.

limb² *n.* 1392, graduated edge of a quadrant or other astronomical instrument; borrowed from Old French *limbe* and directly from Latin *limbus* border, edge, fringe, the zodiac; see LIMP¹, v. The meaning of the edge of the disk of a celestial body is first recorded before 1677.

limber¹ *adj.* bending easily, flexible. 1565, of uncertain origin. The origin has been ascribed to a possible derivation from *limb¹,* in allusion to the relatively easy movement of boughs of a tree; another suggestion makes a connection with *limber²,* in allusion to the flexible movement of the shafts of a cart (this ignores the difference in date and form: *limber²* is not recorded with *-b* until more than fifty years after the appearance of *limber¹*); still another suggestion points to *limp²,* adj., (this, too, ignores the time of appearance in the record of English by 140 years and does not account for the shift in form and pronunciation from *p* to *b*). **—v.** make or become limber. 1748, in Richardson's *Clarissa;* from the adjective.

limber² *n.* detachable front part of the carriage of a field gun. 1628, alteration of Middle English *lymer* (1454), *lymour* (1430), from earlier *lymon* shaft of a cart (about 1400); borrowed from Old French *limon* shaft of a carriage or cart, of uncertain origin; (perhaps from a

Germanic source; compare Old Icelandic *limr, lim* LIMB[1]; but possibly, according to Bloch-Wartburg and Dauzat, from a Celtic source). —**v.** attach the limber. 1843, from the noun.

limbo[1] (lim′bō) *n.* place for people and things forgotten, cast aside, out of date, etc. About 1378, region on the border of hell, in a version of *Piers Plowman;* borrowed from Latin *(in) limbō* (on) the edge, ablative case of *limbus* edge, border; see LIMP[1], v. The figurative sense of a place for people and things forgotten is first recorded in Milton's *Works* (1642).

limbo[2] (lim′bō) *n.* dance in which performers bend backwards to pass under a low horizontal stick without touching it. 1956, probably a shortening and alteration (in Trinidad and Barbados) of Jamaican English *calimbe* a dance performed on a pair of horizontal sticks raised from the ground (1924); probably of African origin (compare West African Gũ *kalimo* a slave, possibly a slave dance; *kalimo* may also be the source of *calinda* an Afro-American dance, once known especially in the southern United States, and first recorded in American English in 1763).

Limburger *n.* soft white cheese with a strong smell. About 1870; earlier *Limburg cheese* (1817); borrowed from Dutch *Limburger* of or from *Limburg,* a province in northeastern Belgium, where the cheese is made.

lime[1] *n.* white substance made up of calcium oxide, obtained by burning shells, bones, etc. About 1150 *lim* lime; developed from Old English (about 700) *līm* sticky substance, birdlime, glue. Old English *līm* is cognate with Old Saxon *līm* birdlime, glue, Middle Dutch *līm* (modern Dutch *lijm*), Old High German *līm* (modern German *Leim*), and Old Icelandic *līm* (Danish, Norwegian, and Swedish *lim*), from Proto-Germanic **leimaz.* Outside Germanic cognates are found in Latin *līmus* mud, dirt, from Indo-European **loimos,* root **lei-* (Pok. 662), Albanian *leth* wet clay, and Old Prussian *layso* earth, clay. Related to LOAM. See also SLIME. —**v.** Probably before 1200 *limen* to cement, in *Ancrene Riwle;* developed from Old English *gelīman* (before 800, in *Corpus Glossary*). The Old English verb is cognate with Old High German *līmen* to cement, and Old Icelandic *līma;* derived from the Germanic root that is the source of Old English *līm,* n. The meaning of put lime on is first recorded in 1649. —**limestone** *n.* Before 1398, in Trevisa's translation of Higden's *Polychronicon.*

lime[2] *n.* greenish-yellow fruit. 1638, borrowed from Spanish *lima,* from Arabic *līma* citrus fruit, probably a back formation from *līmūn* lemon, from Persian. Related to LEMON.

lime[3] *n.* linden tree. 1625, in Bacon's *Essays,* variant of earlier *line* (about 1510); developed from Middle English *lynde* (about 1325), found in Old English *lind* LINDEN.

limelight *n.* 1826, an intense white light produced by directing an oxyhydrogen flame against a block of lime enclosed in a lamp. This type of light was much used in the 1800's in theaters to light scenes and actors and thereby call attention to them. The figurative sense of center of public attention or interest is first recorded in 1877. —**v.** to illuminate by or as if by limelight. 1909, from the noun.

limerick *n.* kind of nonsense verse of five lines. 1896, in A.V. Beardsley's *Letters,* in allusion to *Limerick,* a county and city in Ireland. There is no evidence to support the explanation that the verse was named after the custom at parties of presenting extemporaneous nonsense verses, each followed by the refrain "will you come up to Limerick?"

limey (lī′mē) *n. Slang.* an Englishman or Briton, especially a sailor. 1918, American English, applied also to a British ship, possibly from the earlier Australian slang name for an English immigrant (1888). *Limey* is first recorded as an Australian shortening for *lime-juicer* (1859), so called from the use of lime juice on British naval ships (introduced by the Navy in 1795) to prevent scurvy among sailors. *Lime-juicer* is first recorded in American English in the 1880's in the sense of a British sailor or ship, and *limey* may have been an independent formation in American English, possibly unrecorded from the War of 1812, when American sailors had their first close contact with British ships as impressed members of British men-of-war.

limit *n.* Probably 1384, a legal limitation on power or authority, in Wycliffe's writings; later, a geographical boundary (probably before 1400); borrowed from Old French *limite* a boundary, learned borrowing from Latin *līmitem* (accusative of *līmes*) a boundary, embankment between fields, border, related to *līmen* threshold, and perhaps to *līmus* sidelong; see LIMB[1], n. The general sense of a point where something ends, as in *a limit to one's patience,* is first recorded in English in 1413. —**v.** About 1390, prescribe, fix, in Chaucer's *Canterbury Tales;* also, set a limit to (before 1398, in Trevisa's translation of Bartholomew's *De Proprietatibus Rerum*); borrowed from Old French *limiter,* from Latin *līmitāre* bound, limit, fix, determine, from *līmes* boundary. —**limitation** *n.* About 1395 *limitacioun* district allotted for begging, in Chaucer's *Canterbury Tales;* later, an assigned limit or bound (probably before 1430); borrowed through Old French *limitacion,* and directly from Latin *līmitātiōnem* (nominative *līmitātiō*), from *līmitāre* to limit; for suffix see -ATION. —**limited** *adj.* Before 1460; developed from *limit,* v. —**limited monarchy** (1648) —**limitless** *adj.* (1581).

limn (lim) *v.* paint (a picture). About 1420 *lemynen;* also *limnen* to illuminate a manuscript (before 1425); both forms are variants of earlier *luminen* (before 1398, in Trevisa's translation of Bartholomew's *De Proprietatibus Rerum*); borrowed from Old French *luminer,* from Latin *lūmināre* illuminate, burnish, from *lūmen* (genitive *lūminis*) radiant energy, LIGHT[1]. The sense of paint a picture, portray, depict, is first recorded in English in Shakespeare's *Venus and Adonis* (1592).

The Middle English forms spelled with *-i-* and *-e-* are probably the result of analogy with earlier Middle English *limnour, liminur,* and *lemner,* all meaning an illumination of manuscripts and borrowed from Anglo-French *lymnour.*

limnology *n.* study of lakes and other bodies of fresh water. 1893, formed in English from Greek *límnē* lake, marsh + English *-o-* + *-logy.* Greek *límnē* is probably related to *leimṓn* meadow; originally, a hollow, and *limḗn* harbor (as a protected bay), from Indo-European **(e)lei-/(e)li-* bend (Pok. 309).

limo (lim′ō) *n. Informal.* limousine. 1968, American English, shortened form of *limousine.*

limousine (lim′əzēn′ *or* lim′əzēn) *n.* large automobile with a separate compartment for the driver. In early models the passenger compartment was enclosed and the driver's seat had no roof over it. 1902, borrowing of French *limousine* (about 1900), earlier a cloak of wool or goat's hair used by cart drivers or wagoners (since 1836), from the name *Limousin,* a region in central France, earlier an adjective referring to the capital, Limoges. According to the FEW (V, p.347), the automobile was so called from a comparison of the cart driver's protective cloak to the closed compartment of the automobile. Curiously, the FEW editors do not regard as probable that the name for the automobile derived from 18th-century dialectal French (Saintonge) *limousine,* meaning a style of carriage or coach.

limp[1] *v.* walk lamely. 1570, of uncertain origin; not found in Middle or Old English, but possibly related to Middle English *lympen* to fall short, as of the truth (probably before 1400); perhaps best taken as short for *lympe hault* (as recorded in Palsgrave's *Lesclarcissement,* 1530), from Old English *lempheult, læmpihalt* halting, lame, limping (about 700); see HALT[2]. The Old English forms are cognate with Middle High German *limpfen* to limp, *lampen* hang down; also outside Germanic cognate with Sanskrit *lámbate* (it) hangs down, *lamba-s* hanging down, and Latin *limbus* border, fringe, from Indo-European **lemb-/lomb-* (Pok. 656). Others have based the probable development of *limp*[1] on *limp*[2] (lacking firmness), which does not seem right, if only for the disparity in the dates. **—n.** 1818, in Todd's edition of Johnson's *Dictionary;* from the verb.

limp[2] *adj.* lacking stiffness or firmness. 1706, in Kersey's edition of Phillips' *Dictionary,* of uncertain origin, but probably related to LIMP[1].

limpet *n.* small shellfish. 1312-13 *lempet,* developed from Old English (about 1050) *lempedu;* borrowed from Medieval Latin *lampreda* limpet; see the doublet LAMPREY. The spelling *limpet* appeared in 1602.

limpid *adj.* clear, transparent. 1613, in Cawdrey's *A Table Alphabeticall of English Words;* borrowed through French *limpide,* and directly from Latin *limpidus,* of uncertain origin. **—limpidity** *n.* 1656, possibly formed in English from *limpid* + *-ity,* after Late Latin *limpiditās* clarity, from Latin *limpidus* clear, or after French *limpidité.*

linchpin *n.* 1376-77 *linspin,* formed from earlier (before 1333) *lins* linchpin + *pin.* Middle English *lins* developed from Old English *lynis* (before 809, in *The Epinal Glossary*); cognate with Old Saxon *lunisa* linchpin, Middle Dutch *lunse* (modern Dutch *luns*), late Middle High German *luns, lunse* (modern German *Lünse*), from Proto-Germanic **lunísō,* cognate with Sanskrit *āṇí-s* linchpin (earlier **ālní-s*), Welsh *olwyn* wheel, and Armenian *oɫn* shoulder, from Indo-European **olen, ōlni-, oleinā, l-uni-,* root **el-/elei-* bend (Pok. 307).

linden *n.* shade tree. 1577, noun use of *linden,* adj., made of wood of the linden tree; Middle English (probably before 1300, in *Sir Tristrem*) and Old English (before 1000), from earlier *lind* linden (about 700). Old English *lind* is cognate with Old Saxon *linda,* Middle Dutch and modern Dutch *linde,* Old High German *linta* (modern German *Linde*), and Old Icelandic *lind,* from Proto-Germanic **lindṓ,* cognate with Sanskrit *latā* a creeper, Latin *lentus* pliant, from Indo-European **lent-/l̥nt-* (Pok. 677). Related to LIME[3].

Lindy or **lindy** (lin′dē) *n.* dance similar to the jitterbug. 1931 *Lindy Hop,* American English, in allusion to *Lindy,* popular nickname of Charles *Lindbergh,* 1902-1974, the American aviator who in 1927 made the first solo nonstop "hop" across the Atlantic ocean. **—v.** to dance the Lindy. 1932 *Lindy hop,* as verb in American English, from *Lindy Hop,* as a noun.

line[1] *n.* long thin mark. By 1425, most of the ordinary senses of *line* in modern English had been recorded in Middle English and any sense division between the Old and Middle English forms had been completely coalesced in a fusion of: 1) Old English *līne* rope, row (before 900, in *Solomon and Saturn*), and 2) Middle English *line, ligne* cord or rope, line (probably about 1225, in *King Horn*), borrowed through Old French *ligne.* Both Old and Middle English forms were ultimately borrowed from Latin *līnea* linen thread, string, line, from the phrase *līnea restis* linen cord, from *līneus,* adj., of linen, from *līnum* flax, LINEN. **—v.** mark with lines. Before 1398 *linen* to tie with a cord, in Trevisa's translation of Bartholomew's *De Proprietatibus Rerum;* from the noun. The sense of mark or mark off with lines probably appeared before 1460. **—liner**[1] *n.* Probably about 1400, an official in Scotland who supervises land boundary records; later, a ship (1829) or airplane (1905, in Kipling's writings) belonging to a transportation system; formed from English *line*[1], n. and v. + *-er*[1]. The meaning of cosmetic marker to highlight features of the face, especially the eyes, is first recorded in 1926.

line[2] *v.* put a layer inside of. About 1387-95 *linen,* in Chaucer's *Prologue* to the *Canterbury Tales;* developed from Old English (about 700) *līn* linen cloth, LINEN. **—liner**[2] *n.* 1611, person who lines or fits a lining to something; later, something that serves as a lining or as a piece between two parts (1869), and the lining of a garment (1947); formed from English *line*[2] + *-er*[1]. It is possible that this word was known as early as 1454 in the form *lineur* which may have meant linen underwear.

lineage (lin′ēij) *n.* descent in a direct line from an ancestor. 1697, in Dryden's translation of *The Works of Virgil,* spelling alteration (influenced by *line*[1]) of Middle English *linage* (probably before 1300, in *Arthour and Merlin*); borrowed from Old French *lignage,* from *ligne* LINE[1]; for suffix see -AGE.

lineal *adj.* in the direct line of descent. Before 1398, linear, in Trevisa's translation of Bartholomew's *De Proprietatibus Rerum;* borrowed through Anglo-French *lineale,* Old French *lineal,* and Late Latin *līneālis;* both from Latin *līnea* LINE[1]; for suffix see -AL[1]. Compare LINEAR. The sense of in the direct line of descent is first recorded in Lydgate's *Troy Book* (before 1420).

lineament (lin′ēəmənt) *n.* part or feature (of the face). Probably before 1425 *liniament* part or feature, with attention to its outline, in Trevisa's translation of Higden's *Polychronicon;* borrowed from Latin *līneāmentum* line, feature, from *līneāre* reduce to a straight line, from *līnea* string, LINE[1]; for suffix see -MENT.

linear *adj.* of or in a line or lines. 1642, in Henry A. More's *A Platonical Song of the Soul;* borrowed, perhaps through French *linéaire,* from Latin *līneāris* belonging to a line, from *līnea* string, LINE[1]; for suffix see -AR.

Linear and *lineal* are of the same Latin origin: in Latin *līneāris* the original suffix *-ālis* was dissimilated to *-āris,* but in Late Latin, this rule was no longer productive and the formation or re-formation in *-ālis* remained unchanged.

linen *n.* cloth made from flax. Probably before 1325, a garment made of linen, from earlier *linnen,* adj., made of flax, made of linen (probably before 1200, in *Ancrene Riwle* and in Layamon's *Chronicle of Britain*); developed from Old English (about 700) *līnin,* adj., made of flax, from *līn* flax, linen thread or cloth. Old English *līn* was probably an early borrowing (along with Old Saxon, Old High German, and Old Icelandic *līn* flax, and Gothic *lein* linen cloth) from Latin *līnum* flax, linen; probably borrowed from the same (non-Indo-European) source as Greek *línon* flax. Alternatively, it is possible that the Germanic words are cognates, rather than borrowings, of Latin *linum* (from Indo-European **lino-/līno-,* Pok. 691).

ling *n.* food fish of northern Europe and Greenland. 1228 *lenge;* later *ling* (1340); cognate with early modern Dutch *lenghe, linghe* and modern Dutch *leng* ling, Middle Low German *lange* ling (modern German *Leng*), Old Icelandic *langa* (Norwegian *lange*); probably derived from the Proto-Germanic root that is the source of Old English *lang* LONG[1], adj.

-ling a suffix forming nouns and meaning: little, unimportant, as in *lordling, duckling;* one that is _____, as in *underling;* one belonging to, as in *earthling.* Middle English and Old English *-ling;* cognate with Old High German and modern German *-ling,* Old Icelandic *-lingr,* and Gothic *-lings;* probably formed from the Germanic suffixes *-el* -LE[1] + *-ing[1].*

linger *v.* Before 1325 *lengeren* reside, dwell, in *Cursor Mundi,* frequentative form of *lengen* prolong, lengthen (before 1225); developed from Old English *lengan* prolong, lengthen (about 725, in a translation of the book of *Daniel*). Old English *lengan* is cognate with Old Frisian *lendza* lengthen, Middle Dutch and modern Dutch *lengen,* Old High German *lengan* lengthen, draw out, and Old Icelandic *lengja,* from Proto-Germanic **langijanan;* derived from the Proto-Germanic root that is the source of Old English *lang* LONG[1], adj. The meaning of stay on or go slowly, as if unwilling to leave, is first recorded in Palsgrave's *Lesclarcissement* (1530).

lingerie (län'zhərē' *or* län'jərā') *n.* women's underwear. 1835, borrowing of French *lingerie* things made of linen, from Old French *linge* linen, from Latin *līneus,* adj., of linen, from *līnum* flax, LINEN.

lingo *n.* language regarded as strange or peculiar; slang or jargon. 1660, possibly borrowed from Provençal *lingo, lengo* language or tongue, from Old Provençal *lenga,* from Latin *lingua* TONGUE. Apparently *lingo* is a word of the 1700's (OED's first citation, dated 1660, is found in a record not published until 1858, at which time *lingo* may have been inserted). Whether *lingo* came perhaps through Marseilles, where Provençal was in use, and thence into English is questionable. The older theory that *lingo* is an alteration of Latin *lingua* (a few quotes use an Anglicized form *linguo*) is not without its merits. It is then just a step away from Italian *lingua franca.*

lingua franca (ling'gwə frang'kə) trade or communication language used by people of diverse speech. 1678, in Dryden's *Limberham;* borrowed from Italian *lingua franca,* literally, Frankish language. The original lingua franca, spoken especially in the Levant, was a hybrid language of some French, Spanish, Greek, Arabic, and Turkish, but consisting largely of Italian words with reduced inflections. "Frankish" probably meant European to the Arabs and other users of the original lingua franca.

lingual *adj.* of the tongue. 1650, probably borrowed directly from Medieval Latin *lingualis,* from Latin *lingua* TONGUE; for suffix see -AL[1].

In Middle English (before 1400, in Lanfranc's *Science of Surgery*), *lingual* and *linguale* were used as nouns meaning a tongue-shaped surgical instrument for cauterization.

linguine (linggwē'nē) *n.* kind of flat tongue-shaped pasta. 1948, borrowing of Italian *linguine,* plural of *linguina* little tongue, diminutive of *lingua* tongue, from Latin *lingua* TONGUE.

linguist *n.* 1588, person skilled in languages, formed in English from Latin *lingua* language, TONGUE + English *-ist.* The sense of a student of language is first recorded in 1641. **—linguistic** *adj.* 1856, having to do with the study of languages; formed from English *linguist* + *-ic,* and probably in some instances borrowed from French *linguistique* (1833). **—linguistics** *n.* 1847, American English, the study or science of languages; formed from English *linguist* + *-ics,* on the patterns of *physics, mathematics,* etc. An earlier singular noun form, *linguistic* (1837) was apparently borrowed from German *Linguistik,* which was also the source of French *linguistique* (1826).

liniment *n.* Probably before 1425, an ointment, salve, in a translation of Chauliac's *Grande Chirurgie;* borrowed from Late Latin *linīmentum* a soft ointment, from Latin *linīre,* earlier *linere* to daub, smear, cognate with Greek *alínein* to anoint, from Indo-European **lei-/li-* (Pok. 662); for suffix see -MENT.

lining *n.* material with which garments are lined. 1378, formed from Middle English *linen* to LINE[2] + *-ing[1].*

link *n.* one ring or loop of a chain. Before 1415 *lynke* section of a rope or cord, in Wycliffe's *The Lantern of Light;* later, link of a chain (about 1443); probably borrowed from a Scandinavian source (compare Old Swedish *lænker* chain or link, modern Swedish *länk,* Norwegian *lenke,* Danish *lænke*); from Proto-Germanic **Hlankijaz;* cognate with Old English *hlencan,* pl., armor, Middle High German *gelenke* flexible parts of the body (modern German *Gelenk* joint or link), *lenken* to bend; see LANK. **—v.** join as a link does, unite or connect. About 1385 *linken* to bind or fasten, in Usk's *The Testament of Love;* probably from the noun, although recorded some thirty years earlier, which suggests a defect in the record of this word. **—linkage** *n.* 1874, formed from English *link,* v. + *-age.*

links *n.pl.* golf course. 1728, from Scottish and Northumbrian *links* sandy, rolling ground, usually covered with turf, and found near the seashore (1702); developed from Old English (931) *hlinc* rising ground, ridge (plural *hlincas*), possibly cognate with Old High German *hlanca* side, flank; see LANK.

linnet (lin'it) *n.* small songbird. About 1530, borrowed from Middle French *linette,* from *lin* flax, from Latin *līnum* LINEN; so called because flaxseed forms much of the bird's diet. Compare German *Leinfink* linnet (*Lein* flax + *Fink* finch).

linoleum (lənō'lēəm) *n.* floor covering. 1878, a compound of Latin *līnum* flax, LINEN + *oleum* OIL. The word was coined in 1860 and used in a patent (1863) by

Frederick Walton, an English inventor, as the name of a preparation of solidified linseed oil used to coat canvas for making floor coverings.

linseed *n.* seed of flax. About 1150 *linsed;* developed from Old English (about 1000) *līnsǣd* flaxseed (*līn* flax, LINEN + *sǣd* SEED).

linsey-woolsey (lin′zēwu̇l′zē) *n.* Probably about 1475 *linsy wolsy* fabric made of linen and wool or cotton and wool (*lynen, linen* LINEN + *wolle, wulle* WOOL, with rhyming endings).

lint *n.* 1392 *linet* fleecy material, obtained by scraping linen; also *lint* (before 1400); borrowed from Middle French *linette* grain of flax, diminutive of *lin* flax, from Latin *līnum* flax, LINEN. The sense of bits of thread or fluff is first recorded in Cotgrave's *Dictionary* (1611). **—linty** *adj.* 1607, formed from English *lint* + *-y*[1].

lintel *n.* horizontal beam or stone over a door, window, etc. 1315, borrowed from Old French *lintel* threshold, of uncertain origin; probably alteration of *lintier,* from Vulgar Latin **līmitāris* threshold, from Latin *līmitāris,* adj., that is on the border, from *līmes* (genitive *līmitis*) border or boundary, LIMIT; the Vulgar Latin meaning "threshold" was influenced by Latin *līmen* (genitive *līminis*) threshold.

The traditional etymology traces the borrowing of Old French *lintel* from Vulgar Latin **līntellus* headpiece of a door or window, altered form of **līmitellus,* diminutive of Latin *līmes* (genitive *līmitis*) border or boundary, confused with *līmen* threshold.

In the first version of the Wycliffe Bible, it should be noted that what was later written as *threisfold* was originally *ouerthreswold,* which may help to explain the confusion surrounding *lintel* and how it got from the sense of a doorsill to that of the top of a door or window. Interestingly, this confusion over *threshold* persisted, though it was rare, at least until 1834.

lion *n.* About 1175 *leon;* later *lyon* (about 1200), and *lioun* (probably before 1300); borrowed from Old French *lion* and Latin *leōnem* (nominative *leō*), from Greek *léōn* (genitive *léontos*), of unknown origin (a Semitic source, compare Hebrew *lābī'* and Akkadian *labbu* lion, would seem unlikely).

The form *lēo,* recorded in Old English (before 830) as a variant of Anglian *lēa,* was a borrowing directly from Latin *leō.* The Latin word was the source for all Germanic forms, as found in Old Frisian *lawa,* Old Saxon *leo,* Middle Dutch *leuwe* (modern Dutch *leeuw*), Old High German *lēwo, louwo,* Middle High German *lewe, louwe* (modern German *Löwe, Leu*), and Old Icelandic *leōn, liōn.* Outside Germanic cognates are found in Lithuanian *lëvas,* Old Slavic *lĭvŭ,* Russian *levŭ,* Polish *lew;* all derived from Latin, but borrowed through Old High German.

—lionize *v.* treat (a person) as very important. 1809, Scott quoted in Lockhart's *Memoirs of the Life of Sir Walter Scott;* formed from English *lion* + *-ize,* from the idea of treating one as a lion, such animals being great attractions in Europe in the early 1800's.

lip *n.* Before 1200 *lippe,* in a version of *Body and the Soul;* developed from Old English *lippa* (about 1000, in Ælfric's *Glossary*); cognate with Old Frisian *lippa* lip, Middle High German and Middle Dutch *lippe* (modern Dutch *lip*), Old High German *lefs,* dialectal High German *Lefze,* modern German *Lippe* (from Low German), Swedish *läpp,* Norwegian *leppe,* from Proto-Germanic **lepjōn*; probably also cognate with Latin *labium, labrum* lip, from Indo-European **leb-* (Pok. 655). The slang sense of saucy talk, impudence appeared in 1821, probably from the earlier (1579) phrase *move the lip* to utter even the slightest word (against someone). **—v.** 1604, to kiss, in Shakespeare's *Othello;* later, to touch with the lips (1826); from the noun. **—adj.** merely from the lips, not heartfelt, superficial, insincere. 1558 *lip gospeller,* from the noun. The phrase *lip service* is first recorded in 1644. **—lip-read** *v.* 1892, back formation from *lip-reading,* n. (1874). **—lipstick** *n.* (1880).

lipid *n.* any of the group of organic compounds including the fats, oils, waxes, and sterols. 1925 *lipide,* borrowed from French (coined in 1923 by the French biochemist Gabriel Bertrand, 1867-1962) from Greek *lípos* fat + French *-ide* (chemical suffix). Greek *lípos* is cognate with Sanskrit *limpáti* (he)smears, and Lithuanian *lìpti* to paste, from Indo-European **leip-/lip-* (Pok. 670). The spelling *lipid* (first recorded in 1927) was perhaps formed independently in English from Greek *lípos* + *-id,* variant of *-ide.*

liquefy (lik′wəfī) *v.* change into a liquid. Probably before 1425 *liquefien,* in a translation of Chauliac's *Grande Chirurgie;* borrowed from Old French *liquefier,* learned borrowing from Latin *liquefacere* make liquid, melt (*liquēre* be fluid + *facere* make; see LIQUID and DO[1] perform); for suffix see -FY. **—liquefaction** *n.* About 1425 *liquefaccion* act of liquefying; borrowed from Middle French *liquéfaction* (in Old French, 1314, *liquefacion*), from Late Latin *liquefactiōnem* (nominative *liquefactiō*), from Latin *liquefacere* liquefy; for suffix see -TION.

liqueur (likėr′ or likyu̇r′) *n.* sweet, highly flavored alcoholic liquor. 1729, in Pope's *The Dunciad;* borrowed from French *liqueur,* from Old French *licour* liquid; see LIQOUR.

liquid *adj.* Before 1384, in the Wycliffe Bible; borrowed from Old French *liquide,* from Latin *liquidus* fluid, liquid, moist, from *liquēre* be fluid, related to *līquī* to melt, flow, *lixa* water, lye, and cognate with Old Irish *fliuch* moist, Welsh *gwlyb,* Breton *gleb,* and Welsh *gwlith* dew, all from Indo-European **wleikw-/wlikw-* (Walde-Pokorny II, 397). Of the various figurative senses that are recorded in English, the application to sound with the meaning of clear, flowing, is found in Ben Jonson's writings before 1637, and that pertaining to finance as of assets, securities, etc. is not found before 1879, though the verb form, *liquidate,* as applied to finance, is recorded as early as 1575. **—n.** 1530 *liquid* the sound of *l* or *r,* liquid consonant, in Palsgrave's *Lesclarcissement;* borrowed from Middle French *liquide,* from Latin *liquidae (litterae)* the letters *l, m, n, r,* a translation of Greek *hygrá (stoicheîa),* applied to these letters either on account of their flowing sound as compared with other consonants or perhaps because they were thought to have an indeterminate or unstable character as between consonant and vowel.

The now common meaning of a liquid substance is not recorded before 1708; from the adjective.

liquidate *v.* About 1575, make clear or ascertain the amount (of a debt, etc.); borrowed, perhaps through influence of Middle French *liquider,* from Late Latin *liquidātus,* past participle of *liquidāre* to melt, make liquid or clear, clarify, from Latin *liquidus* LIQUID; for suffix see -ATE[1].

The sense of clear away (a debt) is first recorded in Johnson's *Dictionary* (1755). The sense of settle the accounts of (a business, etc.) by distributing the assets is first recorded in English in 1870, and is also found in Italian, which has prompted the suggestion that the meaning is a borrowing from that language. A more recent meaning of eliminate, wipe out, kill (1924), was possibly a loan translation from Russian *likvidirovat'*. **—liquidation** *n.* About 1575, act of liquidating assets, etc.; borrowed from Middle French *liquidation* (*liquider* liquidate + *-ation* -ation). **—liquidity** *n.* 1620, quality of being liquid; borrowed from French *liquidité*, learned borrowing from Latin *liquiditātem* (nominative *liquiditās*) fluidity, from *liquidus* liquid; for suffix see -ITY.

liquor (lik'ər) *n.* alcoholic drink. Probably before 1200 *licur* a liquid, in *Ancrene Riwle;* later *liquour* (before 1398); borrowed from Old French *licour, likeur,* learned borrowing from Latin *liquor* liquid, liquidity, from *liquēre* be fluid; see LIQUID. Related to LIQUEUR. The sense of any drink, especially wine is first recorded in *Arthour and Merlin* (probably before 1300).

liquorice *n.* = licorice.

lira (lir'ə) *n.* unit of money in Italy, Turkey, etc. 1617, borrowing of Italian *lira,* from Old Provençal *liura,* from Latin *lībra* pound (unit of weight, 12 ounces); see LITER.

lisle (līl) *n.* fine, hard-twisted linen or cotton thread. 1851, borrowing of French *Lisle,* earlier spelling of *Lille,* a city in northern France, the capital of French Flanders, where this thread was originally made.

lisp *v.* use a sound represented by *th* instead of *s* as in *sing* and *z* as in *zap* in speaking. Before 1225 *wlispin;* later *lyspyn* (about 1440); developed from Old English (before 1100) *-wlyspian,* as in *āwlyspian,* from *wlisp,* adj., lisping; probably of imitative origin and similar in formation to Middle Low German *wlispen* to lisp, Low German *lispen,* Middle Dutch and modern Dutch *lispen,* Old High German *lispen* (modern German *lispeln*), Swedish *läspa,* Norwegian *lespe,* and Danish *læspe.* **—n.** act, habit, or sound of lisping. Before 1625, from the verb.

lissome (lis'əm) *adj.* lithe, limber. Before 1800, variant of earlier *lithesome* (1768-74); formed from English *lithe* + *-some*[1].

list[1] *n.* series of names, numbers, words, etc. 1602, in Shakespeare's *Hamlet;* borrowed from French *liste,* from Old French *liste* border, band, row, group, from Italian *lista,* from a Germanic source (compare Old High German *līsta* strip, border, LIST[2]). **—v.** make a list of, enter in a list. 1614, in Raleigh's *The History of the World;* from the noun.

It is interesting to note that the meaning of *list*[1] (series, row, strip of items) is a Romance development and that in Common Germanic (as represented by Old High German *lista* strip, border) there existed the source of Old French *liste* border, and Old English *liste* border, but the sense of a list of names, etc., came from French, and not by way of Middle English from the already existing Old English form.

list[2] *n.* border or edge of cloth. Probably about 1280 *liste;* found in Old English (about 700) *līste* border. Old English *līste* is cognate with Middle Low German *līste* border or edge, Middle Dutch *lijste* (modern Dutch *lijst*), Old High German *līsta* (modern German *Leiste*), Old Icelandic *lista* (Norwegian and Swedish *list,* Danish *liste*), from Proto-Germanic **līstōn.* Outside Germanic a cognate exists in Albanian *leth* border, edge, from Indo-European **leizd-/loizd-* (Pok. 672). **—v.** to border or edge. Probably before 1300 *listen,* from the noun.

list[3] *v.* (of a ship) to lean or incline to one side, tilt. 1880, variant of earlier *lust* (1626, in writings of Captain John Smith); of uncertain origin (sometimes referred to Middle English *lysten* LIST[4], as an extended use of "be inclined to," but while the form *lust* in early modern English fits cognates of *list*[4], the development of the spelling in English is at odds with *list*[4]). **—n.** a leaning over, inclination, tilt. 1793, variant of earlier *lust* (1633); from the verb.

list[4] *v. Archaic.* to please, desire. About 1150 *lysten* to please, desire, wish, like; later *listen* (probably before 1200); developed from Old English *lystan* to desire (before 899, in Alfred's translation of Boethius' *De Consolatione Philosophiae*). Old English *lystan* is cognate with Old Saxon *lustian* to desire or wish, modern Dutch *lusten* to like, fancy, Old High German *lusten* to desire or wish (modern German *lüsten*), and Old Icelandic *lysta,* from Proto-Germanic **lustijanan;* all derived from the Proto-Germanic root that is the source of Old English *lust* desire; see LUST. **—n.** *Archaic.* desire, longing, inclination. Probably before 1200 *liste,* in Layamon's *Chronicle of Britain;* from *listen,* v. See LISTLESS.

list[5] *v. Archaic.* listen. About 1175 *lysten,* later *listen* (probably before 1200); developed from Old English *hlystan* hear, hearken, LISTEN (before 899, in Alfred's translation of St Gregory's *Pastoral Care*). Old English *hlystan* was formed from *hlyst* hearing (from Proto-Germanic **Hlustiz*), cognate with Sanskrit *śruṣti-s* obedience, from Indo-European **k̂lustis,* stem **k̂lu-s-* (Pok. 606).

listen (lis'ən) *v.* Probably about 1150 *lusnen* pay attention, try to hear; later *lustnen* (probably before 1200), and *listnen* (before 1250). The Middle English forms with *t* are spelling alterations (by association with *listen* to try to hear, LIST[5]) of Old English *hlysnan* to listen (before 800), corresponding to Middle High German *lüsenen,* from Proto-Germanic **Hlusinōjanan,* and related to *hlystan* to hear, listen, and *hlyst* hearing. The Old English forms are cognate with Old Icelandic *hlusta* to hear, listen, *hlust* hearing, ear, Old Saxon *hlust* hearing, ear, Old High German *lūstrēn* to listen, *hlosēn* to listen, attend. Outside Germanic cognates are found in Old Irish *cluas* ear, Welsh *clust* ("hearer") ear, Old Slavic *slyšati* to hear, and Sanskrit *śroṣantu* they are to obey, from Indo-European **k̂leu-s-/k̂lou-s-/k̂lu-s-/k̂lū-s-* (Pok. 606), related to *śṛṇóti* (he) hears; see LOUD. **—n.** act of listening. 1788, American English; from the verb. **—listenable** *adj.* (1920)

listless *adj.* indifferent, languid. 1440 *listles,* in *Promptorium Parvulorum;* formed from Middle English *liste* desire, LIST[4] + *-less.* Compare German *lustlos* listless (same formation of cognate elements).

lists *n.pl.* place where knights fought in tournaments. About 1385 *listes,* in Chaucer's *Canterbury Tales;* a blend of *list*[2] border, and Old French *lisse* place of combat, from Germanic (compare Old High German *līsta* border, edge, LIST[2]).

litany *n.* series of prayers with alternate responses. Probably before 1200 *letanie,* in *Ancrene Riwle;* borrowed from Old French *letanie* and Medieval Latin *letania,* both from Late Latin *litanīa,* from Greek *litaneía* litany, an entreating, from *litḗ* prayer, entreaty, of uncertain origin.

The generalized sense of a repeated series (as in a

litany of curses) is recorded before 1822, in Shelley's *Studies of Epipsychidion,* probably borrowed from French *litanie* in the sense of a monotonous enumeration, found in French since 1671. Earlier (1500's) Middle French *letanie* also meant a long enumeration (FEW V, p.375a). The spelling *litany* appeared in English in 1679, influenced by the Late Latin and Greek forms.

-lite a combining form meaning stone or rock, used especially in many rocks and minerals, as in the names of *chrysolite, aerolite* (meteorite made up of stone). Borrowed from French *lite* or *-lithe,* from Greek *líthos* stone, of unknown origin.

liter (lē′tər) *n.* metric measure of capacity. 1797 *litre,* borrowing of French *litre* (1793), from *litron,* an obsolete French measure of capacity, from Medieval Latin *litra,* from Greek *lī́trā* pound (unit of weight, 12 ounces), apparently from the same source (probably Sicilian Italic **līthrā)* as Latin *lībra* pound (12 ounces), balance, pair of scales.

literal *adj.* Before 1397, not figurative or allegorical, in the Wycliffe Bible; also before 1398, pertaining to letters of the alphabet, in Trevisa's translation of Bartholomew's *De Proprietatibus Rerum;* borrowed from Old French *literal* and from Late Latin *līterālis, litterālis* of or belonging to letters or writing, from Latin *lītera, littera* LETTER; for suffix see -AL[1]. The sense of in the exact words of the original, as in *a literal translation,* is first recorded in 1599. **—literally** *adv.* (before 1500)

literary *adj.* 1646, pertaining to letters of the alphabet; later, pertaining to literature (1737); borrowed from French *littéraire,* from Latin *litterārius, līterārius* belonging to letters or learning, from *littera, lītera* LETTER; for suffix see -ARY.

The OED notes that the word does not appear in Johnson's *Dictionary* (1755), in spite of his wide acquaintance with and active participation in the literary activities of his day. The word, however, is entered as a cross reference to an article under *literary criticism,* in *Chambers Cyclopaedia* (1737).

literate *adj.* Probably before 1425 *litterate* able to read and write, educated, in a translation of Higden's *Polychronicon;* borrowed from Latin *litterātus, līterātus* lettered, learned, formed in imitation of Greek *grammatikós* (see GRAMMATICAL) from Latin *littera, lītera* LETTER; for suffix see -ATE[1]. **—literacy** *n.* 1883, formed from English *literate* + *-cy,* in contrast to earlier *illiteracy* (1660).

literati (lit′ərä′tē) *n.pl.* scholarly or literary people. 1621, in Burton's *Anatomy of Melancholy;* borrowed from Latin *līterātī, litterātī,* plural of *līterātus, litterātus* lettered, LITERATE.

The singular form *literatus* one of the literati is first recorded in English in 1704 and was used by Lamb, De Quincey, and others. Also in 1704 the synonym *literato* was borrowed from earlier Italian (today spelled *letterato*) as the singular of *literati,* from Latin *līterātus,* and this form was used by Steele, Cowper, and others.

literatim (lit′ərā′tim) *adv.* exactly as written. 1643, borrowed from Medieval Latin *literatim, litteratim* letter for letter, from Latin *lītera, littera* LETTER. Compare SERIATIM, VERBATIM.

literature *n.* Probably before 1425 *litterature* knowledge from books, book learning, in a translation of Higden's *Polychronicon;* borrowed through Middle French *littérature,* and directly from Latin *līterātūra, litterātūra* writing, from *lītera, littera* LETTER; for suffix see -URE.

The meaning of a body of writings of a period or of a country, emerged relatively late both in English and French; in French the usage is first attested in 1782, and in English in 1812, in Sir Humphry Davy's *Elements of Chemical Philosophy.* The sense of a bibliography or list of works published on a given subject is first recorded in French in 1758 and in English in 1860.

lith- a form of **litho-** before a vowel, as in *lithic* consisting of stone or rock (1797).

-lith a combining form meaning stone or rock, as in *megalith, monolith.* Borrowed, through New Latin *-lithus* or French *-lithe,* from Greek *líthos* stone, of unknown origin.

lithe (līᴛʜ) *adj.* About 1150, gentle, smooth, pleasant; found in Old English *līthe* soft, mild, gentle (about 725, in *Beowulf*). Old English *līthe* is cognate with Old Saxon *līthi* soft, mild, gentle, Old High German *lindi* (modern German *lind*), and Norwegian *linn,* from Proto-Germanic **linthijaz;* also cognate with Latin *lentus* supple, slow, Welsh *llathr* smooth, bright, and Sanskrit *latā* climbing plant, vine, from Indo-European **lent-/l̥nt-* (Pok. 677). The Old English and Old Saxon forms show a characteristic loss of *n* before *th.* In Welsh and Sanskrit the *a* can be from vocalic *n̥.* The sense of supple, bending easily, is first recorded in Middle English about 1300.

lithium *n.* metallic chemical element. 1818, New Latin, from Greek *líthos* stone + New Latin *-ium* (suffix of chemical elements); so called from the mineral or "stone" origin of this alkali metal, as distinguished from two previously known alkalis of vegetable origin. Lithium was discovered in 1817 by the Swedish chemist Johann Arfvedson, 1792-1841.

litho- a combining form meaning stone or rock, as in *lithography, lithosphere.* Also spelled *lith-* before vowels. Borrowed from Greek *litho-,* from *líthos* stone, of unknown origin.

lithography *n.* art of printing from a flat stone or metal plate. 1813, borrowed from German *Lithographie* (*litho-* stone + *-graphie* -graphy). The German word was first used about 1804 by associates of Alois Senefelder, 1771-1834, German cartographer and playwright, who invented the process in 1798.

In the obsolete sense of a description of stones or rocks, *lithography* appeared in English as early as 1708, borrowed from New Latin *lithographia.*

—lithograph *n.* 1839, print made by lithography; back formation from *lithography; v.* 1825, to print by lithography; back formation from *lithography.*

lithosphere *n.* solid portion of the earth. 1887, formed from English *litho-* + *sphere.*

litigate *v.* engage in a lawsuit. 1615, borrowed, perhaps through influence of Middle French *litigier,* from Latin *lītigātus,* past participle of *lītigāre,* from a lost adjective **lītigus* carrying on a lawsuit (*līs,* genitive *lītis,* lawsuit + the root of *agere* to drive, conduct, see AGENT); for suffix see -ATE[1]. Latin *līs* is from Old Latin *stlīs, slīs,* of uncertain origin. **—litigant** *n.* 1659, from (1638) adj., engaged in a lawsuit; borrowed from French *litigant,* learned borrowing from Latin *lītigantem* (nominative *lītigāns*), present participle of *lītigāre* litigate; for suffix see -ANT. **—litigation** *n.* 1567, disputation; 1647, act of carrying on a lawsuit; borrowed from Middle French *litigation,* learned borrowing of Late Latin *lītigātiōnem* (nominative *lītigātiō*), from Latin *lītigāre* litigate; for suffix see -ATION. In this instance *litigate* was probably not a back formation from earlier *litigation* because the sense of *litigation* a carrying on of a lawsuit was later (1647) than the first recorded use of the verb (1615).

litigious (lətij′əs) *adj.* About 1384, quarrelsome, in the Wycliffe Bible; later, engaged in litigation (about 1450); borrowed from Latin *lītigiōsus* contentious or quarrelsome, from *lītigium* dispute, strife, from a lost adjective **lītigus* carrying on a lawsuit, see LITIGATE; for suffix see -IOUS.

litmus (lit′məs) *n.* coloring matter that turns red in acid solution and blue in alkaline solution. 1324-25 *litemose,* borrowed from a Scandinavian source; compare Old Norwegian *litmosi* (*lita* to dye + *mosi* moss), Swedish *letmossa.* The earliest Middle English form is *lykemose* (1320), borrowed from Middle Dutch *lijkmoes,* variant of *lēcmoes* (*lēken* to drip, LEAK + *mos* MOSS); so called because this dye is obtained from various lichens.

The spelling *litmus* was probably reinforced by obsolete English *lit* to dye or stain, borrowed from Old Icelandic *lita,* from *litr* color, dye, cognate with Old English *wlite* brightness, beauty, and Gothic *wlits* face, from Proto-Germanic **wlitiz,* from Indo-European **wleid-/wlid-* look, appearance (Pok. 1136). The phrase *litmus test* with the figurative meaning of a decisive or acid test (1957), derives from the use of paper treated with litmus as a chemical indicator (*litmus paper,* 1803, in writings of Sir Humphry Davy).

litotes (lī′tətēz) *n.* figure of speech that makes an assertion by denying its opposite, as "that was no short speech." 1657, borrowing of Greek *lītótēs,* from *lītós* small, plain, simple, related to *leîos* smooth from Indo-European **lei-* (Pok. 662); see LIME[1] white substance.

litter *n.* Probably before 1300 *liter* portable bed, in *Arthour and Merlin;* later *litter* (1410); borrowed through Anglo-French *litere,* Old French *litiere,* alteration of expected **leitiere* (by influence of *lit* bed), from Medieval Latin *lectaria,* from Latin *lectus* bed, couch; see LIE[2] recline; for suffix see -ER[1]. It is also probable that Middle English *liter* was influenced in formation by Anglo-Latin *litera,* alteration of Medieval Latin *lectaria.*

The sense of straw used for bedding is first recorded about 1410. The meaning of the offspring of an animal at one birth is first recorded in *Promptorium Parvulorum* (1440). The common meaning of odds and ends, things scattered about, rubbish, debris, is first recorded in Swift's *Lady's Dressing-room* (1730), probably from the verb.

—**v.** Before 1398 *literen* provide with bedding, in Trevisa's translation of Bartholomew's *De Proprietatibus Rerum;* from the noun. The meaning of scatter things about is first recorded in Swift's *Cadenus and Vanessa* (1713).

little *adj.* 1106 *litel;* earlier *litle* (1066), both forms in *Peterborough Chronicle;* developed from Old English *lȳtel* (about 725, in *Beowulf*), related to *lȳt* little or few (from Proto-Germanic **lūti*). Old English *lȳtel* is cognate with Old Saxon *luttil* little, Middle Dutch and modern Dutch *luttel,* Old High German *luzzil,* dialectal German *lützel* (the meaning "little" coming from earlier "depressed, reduced"), Old Icelandic *lūta* to stoop, and Gothic *lutōn* to cheat, mislead, from West Proto-Germanic **lūtila-, *luttila-* (compare Latin *Jūpiter/Juppiter*), from **lūt-,* from Indo-European **leud-* depress, reduce (Pok. 684), represented by Welsh *lludded* weariness, Lithuanian *liūsti* to be sad, and Russian *ludít′* deceive.

A cognate, synonymous and phonetically similar Proto-Germanic form, **lītila-,* from Indo-European **lei-* weaken, slender is found as Gothic *leitils* small, little, Old Icelandic *lītell* (Swedish and Norwegian *liten,* Danish *liden*), Old Frisian *lītik,* and Middle Dutch *lītel.* In some of the British dialects that are characterized by a large Scandinavian element in the vocabulary, the vowel of *little* is mostly long, the pronunciation being (lā′tl) or the like. This seems to suggest influence from Old Icelandic *lītell.*

—**adv.** slightly. Before 1125 *litel,* developed from Old English (about 1000) *lȳtel;* from the adjective.

—**n.** small amount or degree. Before 1121 *litel,* developed from Old English (about 1000) *lȳtel;* from the adjective.

littoral (lit′ərəl) *adj.* of a shore. 1656, in Blount's *Glossographia;* borrowed from Latin *littorālis, lītorālis* of or belonging to the seashore, from *lītus* (genitive *lītoris*) shore; from Indo-European **lei-/lēi-/lī-* (Pok. 664); for suffix see -AL[1]. —**n.** region along the shore. 1828, borrowed from Italian *littorale,* originally adj., of the seashore, from Latin *littorālis, lītorālis.* The first recorded use of French *littoral,* n., is also 1828, making the borrowing from Italian most likely, since Italian *littorale* was used in 1728, and the earlier form *litorale* before 1498. In 1815, the Duke of Wellington used Italian *littorale* in one of his dispatches.

liturgy (lit′ərjē) *n.* form of public worship. 1560, borrowed through Middle French *liturgie,* or directly from Late Latin *lītūrgia* public service, public worship, from Greek *leitourgíā,* from *leitourgós* one who performs a public ceremony or service (*leito-,* earlier *lēito-* public, from *lāós* people; see LAY[2] + *-ergos* that works, from *érgon* WORK); for suffix see -Y[3]. —**liturgical** *adj.* 1641, in Milton's *Animadversions;* formed in English from Late Latin *lītūrgicus* (from Greek *leitourgikós,* from *leitourgiā* liturgy) + English *-al[1].*

live[1] (liv) *v.* have life, exist. Before 1121 *lifen;* later *liven* (probably before 1160), both forms in *Peterborough Chronicle;* developed from Old English *lifian, libban* (about 725, in *Beowulf*). Old English *lifian* (Anglian) and *libban* (West Saxon) are cognate with Old Frisian *libba* to live, Old Saxon *libbian,* Middle Dutch *lēven* (modern Dutch *leven*), Old High German *lebēn* (modern German *leben*), Old Icelandic *lifa* (Swedish *lefva,* Danish and Norwegian *leve*), and Gothic *liban;* all from the Proto-Germanic stem **libǣ,* from the root **lib-* to remain, continue (from Indo-European **lei-bh-/li-bh-,* Pok. 670), whence English LIFE. —**livable, liveable** *adj.* 1611, likely to live; later, conducive to living (in Pepys' *Diary,* 1664); and suitable for living in (in Jane Austen's *Mansfield Park,* 1814); formed from English *live[1]* + *-able.* The modern spelling *livable* was first recorded in 1865. —**living** *n.* About 1350, fact, state, or manner of being alive; formed from Middle English *liven* to live + *-ing[1].* —*adj.* Before 1375, having life, being alive; alteration of earlier *liviend* (probably before 1200), developed from Old English *lifiende,* present participle of *lifian* to live; for suffix see -ING[2]. —**living room** (1825) —**living wage** (1888)

live[2] (līv) *adj.* alive. 1542, having life; later, burning, glowing (1611); variant of ALIVE. The meaning "heard or seen at the time of occurrence, not recorded" (as *a live broadcast, a live performance*) is found first in 1934 in British English. —**livestock** *n.* domestic animals. (1742 *live stock,* American English) **—live wire** 1890, connected to a source of electricity; later, in figurative sense of energetic, dynamic person (1903).

livelihood *n.* 1611, in the King James Bible; alteration of *livelode* means of keeping alive, by association with *livelihood* liveliness. The older Middle English form *livelode* (probably before 1325) took the form *livelihood* (1566, from *lyvelyhed,* before 1475, a compound of *lyvely* living + *-hed* -head). The Middle English forms *liflode, livelode* developed from Old English (about 1000) *līflād* course of life, a compound of *līf* LIFE + *lād* way, course; see LOAD.

livelong (liv′lông′) *adj.* whole, entire. About 1410 *live long (day), leve longe (day),* in Lovelich's *History of the Holy Grail;* formed from Middle English *leve, lef* dear (see LIEF) + LONG[1]. Compare the corresponding use in German *die liebe lange Nacht* (literally) the dear long night.

lively *adj.* 1377 *liflich* active, energetic; later *lyvely* (probably before 1400); developed from Old English (before 1000) *līflīc* living, existing (*līf* LIFE + *-līc* -ly[2]).

liven *v.* 1884 *liven up;* formed from English *life* + *-en[1],* under the influence (or as an abstracted form) of the earlier *enliven* (1633) from *en-[1]* + *life* + *-en[1].*

liver *n.* organ that secretes bile. About 1150 *liver,* in compound *liver-sar* pain or disease of the liver; developed from Old English *lifer* (before 899, in Alfred's translation of Boethius' *De Consolatione Philosophiae*). Old English *lifer* is cognate with Old Frisian *livere,* Middle Low German and Middle Dutch *lēver* (modern Dutch *lever*), Old High German *lebara* (modern German *Leber*), and Old Icelandic *lifr,* genitive and plural *lifrar* (Swedish *lefver,* Danish and Norwegian *lever*), from Proto-Germanic **librṓ* fattened up, an adjective left after the loss (partly perhaps for reasons of taboo) of the original noun for liver; cognate with Greek *lipar̄á,* feminine of *liparós* fat (compare Italian *fégato* liver from Vulgar Latin **jecur ficatum* liver stuffed with figs), and Greek *lípos* fat; see LIPID.

liverwort *n.* mosslike plant. Before 1325 *liverewort,* developed from Old English (before 1100) *liferwyrt* (*lifer* LIVER + *wyrt* WORT[1]); loan translation of Medieval Latin *hepatica* HEPATICA; so called from the plant's liver-shaped leaves.

liverwurst (liv′ərwėrst′) *n.* liver sausage. 1869, American English, half translation of German *Leberwurst* liver sausage (*Leber* LIVER + *Wurst* sausage).

livery *n.* Probably about 1300 *liveray* allowance of food and drink; later *livere* servants' rations, and *lyvery* delivery of merchandise (probably about 1400); borrowed from Old French *livrée,* from feminine past participle of *livrer* dispense, from Latin *līberāre* LIBERATE; for suffix see -Y[4].

The sense of distinctive clothing given to servants is found in Middle English about 1380, and in Old French since the late 1200's. The sense of allowance or provender for horses is first recorded before 1440, and the meaning of a stable where horses are cared for or hired out, as in *livery stable,* is recorded by 1705.

livid *adj.* having a dull-bluish or grayish color. Probably before 1425 *livide,* in a translation of Chauliac's *Grande Chirurgie;* borrowed from Middle French *livide* and Latin *līvidus,* from *līvēre* be bluish. Latin *līvēre* (formed from a lost adjective **līvos,* Indo-European **līwos,* Pok. 965) is cognate with Old Irish *lī* color, Welsh *lliw,* Old Slavic *sliva* plum, and Old English *slā, slāh* SLOE. The modern extended sense of angry, as if livid with rage, is first recorded in 1912.

living *n.* See under LIVE[1].

lizard *n.* About 1378 *lusarde* any reptile, such as a crocodile or serpent, in a version of *Piers Plowman;* also, before 1382 *lisard* a lizard; borrowed through Anglo-French *lusard,* Old French *lesard* (feminine *laisarde*), from Latin *lacertus,* (feminine *lacerta*) lizard, of unknown origin.

llama (lä′mə) *n.* animal of South America somewhat like a camel. 1600, in Hakluyt's *Voyages and Discoveries of the English Nations;* borrowing of Spanish *llama,* from Quechua (Peru) *llama.*

llano (la′nō) *n.* broad treeless plain. 1613, in *Purchas his Pilgrimage;* borrowing of Spanish *llano,* from Latin *plānum,* neuter of *plānus* level; see PLAIN.

lo (lō) *interj.* look! see! behold! Before 1121 *la;* later *lo* (probably before 1200); a fusion of Old English *lā,* an exclamation indicating surprise, grief, or joy (about 725, in *Beowulf*), and of Middle English *lok* look! imperative of *loken* to LOOK.

load *n.* Before 1250 *lode* burden or load, in a version of *Ancrene Riwle,* earlier *lade* course, way (probably about 1200); found in Old English *lād* way, course, carrying (about 725, in *Beowulf*), from Proto-Germanic **laiđṓ;* related to *lǣdan* to guide, LEAD[1]; influenced in meaning by Middle English *laden* to load, LADE. Also compare LODE for differentiation of meaning.

The spelling *load* appeared in the 1500's. The slang idiom *get a load of,* meaning take notice of, is first recorded in American English, in Damon Runyon's writings (1929).

—v. put a load in or on. Before 1470 *loden,* from *lode,* n.

loaf[1] *n.* bread baked as one piece. About 1280 *lof,* developed from Old English (before 725) *hlāf* bread or loaf; cognate with Old Frisian *hlēf* loaf, Old High German *hleib, hlaiba* (modern German *Laib*), Old Icelandic *hleifr* (Swedish *lev*, Norwegian *leiv*), and Gothic *hlaifs,* from Proto-Germanic **Hlaiƀaz.*

Whether the sense of "bread" or that of "loaf" is the earlier is uncertain, as the ultimate etymology is obscure. Some sources suggest a connection with Old English *hlīfian* rise, or be raised high, with reference to the rising of leavened bread. Outside Germanic several words are possibly in some way connected with Germanic sources: Old Slavic *khlěbŭ* (Russian *khleb*) bread, Lithuanian *klêpas,* Latvian *klaips,* Finnish *leipä,* Estonian *leib.*

loaf[2] *v.* spend time idly. 1835, American English; back formation from *loafer* an idler or vagabond (1830), variant of *land-loafer* (1836, earlier *land loper,* 1795); partial loan translation of earlier German *Landläufer* vagabond or tramp (*Land* LAND + *Läufer* runner, from *laufen* to run; see LEAP). The word *loafer* in the sense of a slip-on shoe for casual wear was originally a trademark, *Loafer* (1939, registered by the firm of Fortnum and Mason in London).

loam *n.* rich, fertile earth. Before 1325 *lam* moistened clay; later *lom* (about 1350); developed from Old English (probably about 700) *lām* clay, mud, mire, earth (from Proto-Germanic **laimaz*). Old English *lām* is cognate with Old Saxon *lēmo,* Middle Dutch and modern Dutch *leem,* Old High German *leime* (modern

German *Lehm*), and related to Old English *līm* glue; see LIME[1] white substance. **—v.** cover or fill with loam. 1600, from the noun.

loan *n.* About 1175 *lan;* later *loan* (before 1250); borrowed from a Scandinavian source (compare Old Icelandic *lān,* related to *ljā* to lend). Through Middle English *lan* is cognate with Old English *lǣn* loan, the Old English form did not survive into Middle English, but its verb is found in modern English *lend.* Other Germanic cognates are found in Old Frisian *lēn,* Old Saxon *lēhen* loan, Middle Dutch and modern Dutch *leen,* Old High German *lēhan* loan, *līhan* borrow, lend (modern German *leihen* lend, *Lehn, Lehen* fief), and Gothic *leihwan* to lend. Old Icelandic *lān* (Danish, Norwegian, and Swedish *lån) is from Proto-Germanic *laiHwniz, -az-,* cognate with Sanskrit *réknas* inheritance, from Indo-European **loikwnes-, -os.* Outside Germanic, cognates are Sanskrit *rinákti* leaves behind, Greek *leípein* leave, Latin *(re)linquere,* and Lithuanian *lìkti,* from Indo-European *leikw-/likw-* (Pok. 669). **—v.** 1542-43 (perhaps before 1200, in Layamon's *Chronicle of Britain*); from the noun.

loath (lōth) *adj.* unwilling, reluctant. About 1280 *loth;* earlier *lath* (probably before 1200); developed from Old English (about 700) *lāth* hostile, loathsome, injurious. Old English *lāth* is cognate with Old Frisian and Old Saxon *lēth* loathsome, Old High German *leid* (modern German *Leid* sorrow, harm), Middle Dutch *leet* (modern Dutch *leed*), and Old Icelandic *leidhr* loathsome (Swedish and Danish *led,* Norwegian *lei*), from Proto-Germanic **laithaz.* Outside Germanic probable cognates are found in Old Irish *liuss* horror, disgust, and Greek *aleitēs* offender, sinner, *alitainein* offend, transgress, from Indo-European **leit-/loit-/lit-* abhor; transgress (Pok. 672). **—loathsome** *adj.* Before 1400 *laithsum* foul, detestable, in a version of *Cursor Mundi;* later *lothsom* fearsome, terrifying (before 1420); formed from Middle English *lath, loth* loath + *-sum, -som,* -some[1].

loathe (lōᴛʜ) *v.* abhor, hate. About 1300 *lothen* be hateful or distasteful; also, about 1303, to hate, dislike; developed from Old English *lāthian* to hate (before 899, in Alfred's translation of Orosius' *Historiarum Adversus Paganos*), from *lāth* hostile, LOATH. Old English *lāthian* is cognate with Old Saxon *lēthon* and Old Icelandic *leidha,* from Proto-Germanic **laithōjanan.*

lob *v.* 1847, possibly developed from an amalgam of earlier meanings: to move heavily or clumsily (1819), to cause to hang heavily (1599, in Shakespeare's *Henry V*); perhaps associated with *lobbe, lob,* n., country bumpkin (1533, used as an adjective meaning rustic, loutish, clumsy, 1508), from earlier *lobi* a lazy lout (before 1376, in *Piers Plowman,* and found as a surname *Lobb,* 1291); probably developed from Old English (unrecorded). **—n.** a lobbed ball. 1875, from the verb.

lobar (lō′bər) *adj.* of a lobe or lobes, especially of the lung. 1856, formed from English *lobe* + *-ar.*

lobate (lō′bāt) *adj.* having a lobe or the form of a lobe. 1760, borrowed from New Latin *lobatus,* from Late Latin *lobus* LOBE; for suffix see -ATE[1].

lobby *n.* 1593, entrance hall, passageway, in Shakespeare's *2 Henry VI;* earlier, cloister or covered walk (1533); borrowed from Medieval Latin *lobia* covered walk, from a Germanic source (compare Old High German *louba* hall, roof, modern German *Laube* covered way, bower, arcade); see the doublets LODGE, LOGE, LOGGIA.

The meaning of persons who try to influence legislators is first recorded in 1808 in American English, from the lobbyists' custom of gathering in the lobby outside a legislative chamber. Such a lobby originally (1640) referred to the one in the British House of Commons, and was called *the Lobby,* serving chiefly for interviews between members and persons not belonging to the House.

—v. try to influence legislators; try to get (a bill) passed by lobbying. Before 1848, American English; from the noun.

—lobbyist *n.* person who lobbies. 1863, American English, formed from *lobby,* v. + *-ist.*

lobe *n.* rounded projecting part, as of a leaf, the lungs, the brain, etc. Probably before 1425, in a translation of Chauliac's *Grande Chirurgie;* borrowed from Middle French *lobe,* learned borrowing from Late Latin *lobus* hull, husk, pod, and directly from Medieval Latin *lobus,* from Late Latin *lobus,* from Greek *lobós* lobe, vegetable pod. Greek *lobós* is cognate with Latin *labāre* totter, and Old English *læppa* lap, from Indo-European **lob-/leb-* (Pok. 655).

lobelia (lōbēl′yə) *n.* plant with showy flowers. 1739, New Latin, in allusion to Matthias de *Lobel,* 1538-1616, Flemish botanist.

loblolly pine (lob′lol′ē) pine tree that grows in swampy soils. 1760, American English, probably a special use as "mud or bog" of earlier English (1597) *loblolly* thick gruel or stew (dialectal English *lob* to bubble up + *lolly* broth, stew).

lobo (lō′bō) *n.* large gray wolf, timber wolf. 1854, American English; borrowed from Spanish *lobo* wolf, from Latin *lupum,* accusative of *lupus* WOLF.

lobotomy (lōbot′əmē) *n.* surgical incision into a lobe of the brain for the purpose of treating mental disorders. 1936, formed from English *lobe* + connective *-o-* + *-tomy* surgical incision.

lobster *n.* Before 1311-12 *lopister;* later *lobster* (1390); developed from Old English (before 1000) *lopystre,* probably from *loppe* spider, variant of *lobbe.* Old English *lobbe* is cognate with Middle Low German *lobbe, lubbe* thick, hanging lip, and Old Icelandic *lubba* large cod (fish), from Indo-European **lubh-,* root **leubh-* hang down loosely (Pok. 965).

According to the OED, Old English *lopystre* may have been an alteration of Latin *lōcusta* lobster, LOCUST, with the ending *-stre* by assimilation of the Latin to Old English feminine agent nouns (see -STER). However, substitution of *p* for the Latin *c* is obscure.

local *adj.* 1392, borrowed possibly through Old French *local,* and directly from Late Latin *locālis,* from *locus* place, see LOCATE; for suffix see -AL[1]. **—n.** 1824, local inhabitant; later, train, bus, etc., that makes all or most stops (1879); from the adjective. **—localism** *n.* (1823, local idiom, custom, etc.) **—localization** *n.* (1816) **—localize** *v.* 1792, make local in character, in Mary Wollstonecraft's *Vindication of the Rights of Woman.*

locale (lōkal′) *n.* place, especially with reference to events connected with it. 1772 *local;* later *locale* (1816); borrowed from French *local;* noun use of *local,* adj., from Old French; see LOCAL. The spelling with *e* is probably based on *morale.*

locality *n.* 1628, the fact of having a place or location;

borrowed from French *localité,* from Late Latin *locālitātem* (nominative *locālitās*), from *locālis* belonging to a place, LOCAL; for suffix see -ITY. The sense of a place or site, especially a geographical place or location, is first recorded in 1830, in Lyell's *Principles of Geology,* probably taken from French, in which *localité* meant a place (1590), and part of a region (1799).

locate *v.* 1739, mark the limits of (a place); borrowed from Latin *locātus,* past participle of *locāre* to place, from *locus* a place, from Old Latin *stlocus,* of uncertain origin; for suffix see -ATE[1]. The meaning of fix or establish in a place is first recorded in 1807. The meaning of find the exact place or locality of is first recorded in American English, in Bret Harte's *Flip* (1882). **—location** *n.* 1592, (in civil and Scots law) act of leasing for hire; borrowed from Middle French *location,* learned borrowing of Latin *locātiōnem* (nominative *locātiō*) a placing, leasing, from *locāre* hire out, lease, (originally) to place; for suffix see -ATION. The general sense of position or place is first recorded in English in 1597.

locative (lok′ətiv) *adj. Grammar.* indicating place or place in which. 1841; earlier, pertaining to location (1816); borrowed from New Latin *locativus,* from Latin *locātus,* past participle of *locāre* to place, LOCATE; for suffix see -IVE. **—n.** the locative case. 1859, from the adjective.

loch (lok *or* loH) *n. Scottish.* lake. 1375 *lauch,* in Barbour's *The Bruce;* borrowed from Gaelic *loch,* from Old Irish *loch* body of water, LAKE[1].

lock[1] *n.* means of fastening doors, boxes, etc. About 1250 *lok;* developed from Old English *loc* (about 750, in Cynewulf's *Elene,* from Proto-Germanic **lukan*), related to *lūcan* to lock or close. Old English *lūcan* is cognate with Old Frisian *lūka* to close, Old Saxon *lūkan,* Old High German *lūhhan* to close (from Proto-Germanic **lūkanan*), *loh* hole, opening (modern German *Loch*), Old Icelandic *lok, loka* fastening, lock, *lūka* to close, and Gothic *galūkan* to close, *usluk* opening. Possible cognates outside Germanic are Greek *lýgos* a withe, and Lithuanian *lùgnas* supple, pliable (on the assumption that a lock was a fastening made by bending two branches until they met), from Indo-European **leug-/ lug-/ lūg-* bend (Pok. 685). —**v.** fasten with a lock. About 1300 *lokken;* from the noun. **—locker** *n.* 1313 *loker* a means of locking; later, locked receptacle (1388); formed from Middle English *lokken,* v., to lock + *-er[1]*. **—lockjaw** *n.* (1803) **—locksmith** (1440, earlier in a surname, 1226).

lock[2] *n.* tress of hair. Probably before 1200, in Layamon's *Chronicle of Britain;* developed from Old English (about 700) *locc;* cognate with Old Frisian and Old Saxon *lok* lock, Middle Dutch *loc, locke* (modern Dutch *lok*), Old High German *loc* (modern German *Locke*), and Old Icelandic *lokkr,* from Proto-Germanic **lukkás,* from Indo-European **lugnós,* represented by Latin *luctārī* dislocate, *luxus* dislocated, sprained, Greek *lygízein* to twist or bend, *lýgos* flexible twig, and Lithuanian *lùgnas* supple, pliable; see LOCK[1].

locket *n.* small ornamental case usually worn on a necklace. 1679, ornamental case (with hinged cover); developed from Middle English *loket* crossbar, fastener (1354-55); borrowed from Old French *loquet* latch, diminutive of Old French *loc,* from Frankish (compare Old Icelandic *lok* fastening, LOCK[1]).

loco (lō′kō) *n.* weed of the western United States that affects the brains of horses, sheep, etc., that eat it. 1844, American English, borrowed from Spanish *loco,* adj., insane, of uncertain origin. According to Corominas, Spanish *loco* may have been borrowed from Arabic *lāuqa, lāuq,* feminine and adjective forms of *'ālwaq* fool, crazy person. **—adj.** *Informal.* crazy. 1887, American English; borrowed from Spanish *loco.*

locomotion *n.* a moving from place to place. 1646, in Sir Thomas Browne's *Pseudodoxia Epidemica;* formed in English from Latin *locō* from a place (ablative of *locus* place, LOCUS) + *mōtiōnem* (nominative *mōtiō*) MOTION.

locomotive *adj.* 1612, of or pertaining to locomotion; borrowed from French *locomotif* (feminine *locomotive*), from Latin *locō* from a place (ablative of *locus* place, LOCUS) + Late Latin *mōtīvus* moving, impelling, MOTIVE; for suffix see -IVE. *Locomotive,* adj., was applied to a railroad engine in 1815 and to a vehicle in 1825. **—n.** railroad engine. 1829, from the adjective.

locus (lō′kəs) *n.* place. 1715, borrowing of Latin *locus;* see LOCATE. The specific sense in mathematics of a curve or other figure that contains all the points that satisfy a given condition is first recorded in *Chambers Cyclopaedia* (1727-51).

locust[1] *n.* kind of grasshopper that migrates in great swarms, destroying crops. Before 1325, in *Cursor Mundi;* borrowed from Old French *locuste,* and directly from Latin *lōcusta* locust, lobster, possibly cognate with Lithuanian *lě̃kti* to fly from Indo-European **lek-* to bend, wriggle (Pok. 673).

The two senses of the Latin, locust and lobster, are paralleled in Greek *kárabos,* meaning beetle and crayfish, and Latin *lacerta,* meaning lizard and a fish (Spanish mackerel).

locust[2] *n.* any of various trees. 1615, fruit of the carob tree, probably so called from a supposed resemblance of the carob pod to the locust (insect). The Greek word *akrís,* meaning a locust or grasshopper, was commonly applied in the Levant to the carob pod because of this supposed resemblance; and from very early times it has been believed by many that the "locusts" eaten by John the Baptist (see Mark 1:6 and Matthew 3:4) were these pods. The connection with John the Baptist is also seen in the German name *Johannisbrot* and the English name *St. John's bread* for the fruit of the carob tree.

In 1623 the word was used in the phrase *locust tree* for the carob tree, and by 1640 *locust* was applied to various other trees.

locution *n.* style of speech. Probably before 1425 *locucion,* in a translation of Higden's *Polychronicon;* borrowed through Middle French *locution,* and directly from Latin *locūtiōnem* (nominative *locūtiō*) a speaking, from *loquī* speak, see LOQUACITY; for suffix see -TION.

lode *n.* vein of metal ore. 1602, vein of metal ore; earlier, watercourse, channel (1572); developed from Middle English *lode, lade* course, carrying, LOAD.

The form *lode* was the original Middle English spelling of *load;* however, the two forms became differentiated in sense during the 1500's.

—lodestar *n.* star that shows the way, such as the North Star. About 1385 *lodesterre,* in Chaucer's *Canterbury Tales,* formed from *lode* course, carrying, LOAD + *sterre* STAR. **—lodestone** *n.* kind of iron oxide that has magnetic properties. About 1515, literally, way-stone; formed from Middle English *lode* course, way, carrying

+ *stone;* so called from the early use of this stone as a magnet in guiding mariners.

lodge *n.* 1231 *lhoge* siege tower; later *logge* small, often temporary shelter (1290); and *lodge* (probably before 1400); borrowed from Old French *loge* arbor, covered walk, from Frankish **laubja* (compare Old High German *louba* hall, roof, modern German *Laube* covered way, bower, arcade; cognate with Old Icelandic *lopt* upper story, LOFT). Doublet of LOGE, LOGGIA, LOBBY.

The sense of a local branch of any of various societies appeared in 1686, especially in reference to a branch of the Freemasons, having developed from an early sense of Middle English *logge* as the workshop in which a group of masons worked (1348).

—v. live in a place for a time. Probably before 1200 *loggen,* in *Ancrene Riwle;* later *lodgen* (before 1470); borrowed from Old French *logier,* from *loge* covered walk.

—lodger *n.* Before 1325 *loger* tent dweller, in *Cursor Mundi;* earlier, as a surname *Loggere* (1208-12); formed from Middle English *loggen* to lodge + *-er*[1]. The sense of *lodger* as one who lives in a rented room or rooms is first found in Shakespeare's *The Taming of the Shrew* (1596) and *Henry V* (1599). **—lodgment, lodgement** *n.* 1598 *lodgement* place for lodging; *lodgment* the action of placing or depositing (1702); formed from English *lodge,* v. + *-ment.*

loess (lō'is *or* lœs) *n.* yellowish-brown loam. 1833, borrowed from German *Löss,* from Swiss German *lösch,* adj., loose, related to German *los* loose; see -LESS. The word was coined in 1823 by the German mineralogist and geologist Karl C. von Leonhard, 1779-1862, who evidently regarded the *-sch* of Swiss German *lösch* as dialectal and altered it to *-s (-ss).* However, he also gave *Lösch* as a variant form of the noun.

loft *n.* Before 1225, upper room, sky; developed from Old English (before 1000) *loft* air; borrowed from a Scandinavian source; compare Old Icelandic *lopt* air, sky, upper story (*-pt-* pronounced as *-ft-*), Swedish, Norwegian, and Danish *loft.* The Scandinavian forms are cognate with Old English *lyft* air, Old Saxon *luft,* Middle Dutch and modern Dutch *lucht,* Old High German *luft* (modern German *Luft*), and Gothic *luftus;* all from Proto-Germanic **luftuz,* apparently originally meaning roof, perhaps at first of LEAVES, related to the source of English LIFT. **—v.** hit (a ball) high up. 1518, to store (goods) in a loft; from the noun. The sense of hit (a ball) high into the air is first recorded in 1857. **—lofty** *adj.* About 1426 *lofte* of high rank, noble; earlier, as a surname *Lofty* (1332); formed from Middle English *loft* (in *on loft* on high, ALOFT) + *-y*[1]. The sense of elevated in style and sentiment, sublime, appeared in 1565, while that of extending to a great height, of imposing altitude, first occurs in 1590, in Spenser's *Faerie Queene.*

log *n.* Before 1398 *logge,* in Trevisa's translation of Bartholomew's *De Proprietatibus Rerum;* earlier, as a surname *Log* (about 1210); of uncertain origin.

The OED rejects the possibility that Middle English *logge* was a borrowing of Old Icelandic *lāg* felled tree, which would yield **low* in modern English. As for its being an adoption from a later stage of Scandinavian (Norwegian *låg,* Swedish dialect *låga*) due to Norwegian timber trade, the OED considers the conjecture plausible but open to strong objection on phonological grounds.

The sense of a wooden float to measure a ship's speed is first recorded in 1574; hence *logbook,* a journal for recording the progress of a ship (before 1679). The shortened form *log* is found in 1825.

—v. 1699, cut into logs; from the noun. The sense of to record in a log is first recorded in 1823; that of travel (a distance) or attain (a speed) as noted in a log, is found in 1883.

loganberry *n.* large, purplish-red fruit. 1893, American English, in allusion to James H. *Logan,* 1841-1928, an American horticulturist and jurist, who developed it + *berry.*

logarithm (lôg'əriᴛʜəm) *n. Mathematics.* the power to which a fixed number (usually 10) must be raised in order to produce a given number. 1615-16, borrowed from New Latin *logarithmus* (coined in 1614 by the Scottish mathematician John Napier, 1550-1617); a compound of Greek *lógos* proportion, ratio, word (from *légein* speak; see LEGEND) + *arithmós* number; see ARITHMETIC.

loge (lōzh *or* lōj) *n.* box in a theater; forward section of the balcony in a theater. 1749, booth stall; 1768, box in a theater; borrowed from French *loge,* from Old French *loge* covered walk; see the doublets LODGE and LOGGIA.

loggerhead *n.* stupid person, blockhead. 1588, in Shakespeare's *Love's Labour's Lost;* probably formed from dialectal English *logger* heavy block of wood (*log* + *-er*[1]) + *head.* The phrase *at loggerheads,* with the meaning of in disagreement, is first recorded in 1831, probably from the earlier *loggerhead* thick-headed iron instrument (1687).

loggia (loj'ēə) *n.* gallery or arcade open to the air on at least one side. 1742, borrowing of Italian *loggia,* from Old French *loge* covered walk, from Frankish (compare Old High German *louba* hall roof); see the doublets LODGE and LOBBY.

logic *n.* Before 1378 *logyk* system of reasoning, in a version of *Piers Plowman;* borrowed from Old French *logique,* learned borrowing from Latin *logica,* from Greek *logikḕ téchnē* reasoning art, from *lógos* reason, idea, word, from *légein* speak; see LEGEND. The meaning of use of argument, reasoning, is first recorded in 1601 and that of reason, sound sense in 1682. The sense of a system or principles underlying the nonarithmetical operations in a computer is first recorded in 1950. **—logical** *adj.* Probably before 1425, based on logic or reason, in a translation of Chauliac's *Grande Chirurgie;* later, capable of reasoning correctly (1664, in Pepys' *Diary*); borrowed from Medieval Latin *logicalis,* from Late Latin *logica* logic; for suffix see -AL[1]. **—logician** *n.* Before 1382 *logicien,* in the Wycliffe Bible; borrowed from Old French *logicien,* from *logique* logic + *-ien* -ian.

logistic *adj.* 1628, pertaining to reasoning, logical; later, pertaining to reckoning or calculation (1706) and pertaining to a logarithmic curve (1727); borrowed from Medieval Latin *logisticus,* from Greek *logistikós* skilled in calculating, from *logízesthai* to reckon, to reason, from *lógos* reckoning, account, reason; see LOGIC; for suffix see -IC. The modern sense of connected with or having to do with logistics is first recorded in 1934.

logistics *n.* the planning and carrying out of military or other complex movement, evacuation, supply, etc. 1879, borrowed from French *logistique* logistics, from Middle French *logistique,* formed (by influence of *logistique* pertaining to calculation) from *logis* lodging, from Old French (1308) *logeïs* (earlier **logeïz*) shelter for an army, encampment (with *-eïz,* suffix from Vulgar Latin *-ātīcius*), from *loge;* see LODGE; for suffix see -ICS.

logo *n.* trademark or other figure frequently associated with an enterprise. 1937, probably shortened form of *logogram* sign or character representing a word (1840, in Pitman's *Manual of Phonography*); formed in English from Greek *lógos* word (see LOGIC) + English *-gram¹.*

Alternatively, *logo* may be a shortened form of *logotype* (before 1816) type containing a word, or two or more letters, cast in one piece; formed in English from Greek *lógos* word + English *type.*

logrolling *n.* a giving of political aid in return for a like favor. 1812, American English, a transferred use of the earlier meaning in American English, "a gathering of neighbors to assist one of them in rolling and burning logs that hinder him in his farming or other work" (before 1792). **—logroll** *v.* engage in political logrolling. 1835, in Davy Crockett's *Tour to the North and Down East,* American English; back formation from *logrolling.*

logy (lō′gē) *adj.* heavy, sluggish, or dull. 1848, American English; perhaps borrowed from Dutch *log* heavy, dull; cognate with Middle Low German *luggich* sleepy, sluggish. The American English *logy* may be a variant of British English *loggy* (1847), which also had the meaning of heavy, sluggish in movement, and by its form and pronunciation is more easily identifiable with *log* than is the American English form *logy* with its so-called long *o* pronunciation.

-logy a combining form meaning: study or science of, as in *biology;* speech, expression, or discussion, as in *eulogy, tautology;* collection, as in *anthology.* Borrowed through French *-logie* or Latin *-logia,* and directly from Greek *-logíā,* in part from *lógos* speech, word, discourse, but generally from *-lógos* one who deals with or treats of (a certain subject, e.g. *astrológos* astronomer); both Greek forms from *légein* speak (of); see LEGEND. See also -OLOGY.

loin *n.* Often **loins,** *pl.* part of the body between the ribs and the hipbones. Before 1325 *loyne;* borrowed from eastern Old French *loigne,* from Vulgar Latin **lumbea,* shortened form of **lumbea carō* meat of the loin, from Latin *lumbus* loin, from Indo-European **londhwos.* The Latin word is cognate with Old High German *lentī, lentīn* kidneys, loins (modern German *Lende* loin, *Lenden* loins), Old Saxon *lendin* loins, Middle Dutch *lendine* (modern Dutch *lende* loin), Old English *lendenu* loins, Old Frisian *lendenum* loins (from Proto-Germanic **landwīn-,* Indo-European **londhwīn-,* root *lendh-* loin, kidney, Pok. 675), Old Icelandic *lend* loin (Norwegian *lend,* Swedish *länd* and Danish *lænd*); and outside Germanic with Old Slavic *lędvĭję* loins, and Russian *lyádveya* thigh, haunch. Related to LUMBAGO, LUMBAR.

This borrowing from Old French replaced the native Middle English *lende* (plural *lendes*), from Old English *lendenu,* pl., loins (see above). *Lendes* became obsolete before 1550.

The poetic phrase *gird (up) one's loins,* meaning to prepare for strenuous action or exertion, derives from the biblical use (Proverbs 31:17), where the act of binding one's loincloth symbolized preparedness.
—loincloth *n.* (1859)

loiter *v.* About 1425 *loitren,* borrowed from Middle Dutch *loteren* be loose or erratic, shake, totter, from which modern Dutch *leuteren,* meaning to loiter, developed. The Middle Dutch word is probably cognate with Old English *lūtian* be concealed, lurk, Middle Low German and late Middle High German *lūschen* (modern German *lauschen* listen from a concealed place, eavesdrop), Old High German *luzēn* lurk, and Gothic *lutōn* mislead; see LITTLE. The diphthong *oi* approximates the pronunciation of the Dutch word.

loll *v.* Before 1376 *lollen* to lounge idly, hang loosely, in *Piers Plowman;* possibly of an imitative origin similar to that of Middle Dutch *lollen* to doze, sleep, mumble; later, to droop, hang loosely; see LULL.

lollapaloosa (lol′əpəlü′zə) *n. Slang.* very remarkable person or thing. 1904 *lallapalootza,* American English, in H. McHugh's *I'm from Missouri;* later *lollapaloosa* (1909); of uncertain origin; sometimes suggested as a fanciful extension of LULU¹.

Lollard (lol′ərd) *n.* one of the followers of John Wycliffe, who advocated certain religious, political, and economic reforms. 1395, borrowed from Middle Dutch *lollaerd* member of any of various religious groups of the early 1300's in Holland; literally, mumbler or mutterer, so called contemptuously by their critics, who regarded them as heretics pretending to be pious and humble, from *lollen* to mumble or doze; see LOLL.

lollipop or **lollypop** *n.* 1784 *lolly-pops* sweetmeats, candy, perhaps formed from earlier (1611) *loll* to dangle the tongue, LOLL + *pop¹* stroke, slap. The present usage, of a piece of hard candy on a stick, is first recorded in the 1920's.

lollygag *v. Slang.* to fool around, dawdle, dally. 1862 *lallygag* a fooling around; 1868 *lolly-gag* to fool around, hug, kiss, and caress; American English, perhaps formed from dialectal English *lolly* tongue (see LOLLIPOP) + *gag²* deceive or trick.

lone *adj.* alone. About 1378, in a version of *Piers Plowman;* shortened form of *alone,* by mistaken division of *al one, alone* all by oneself, as *a lone* (see ALONE) or possibly through loss of weakly stressed *a-* in *al one, alone.* **—lonely** *adj.* 1607, in Shakespeare's *Coriolanus;* formed from English *lone* + *-ly¹.* **—loneliness** (before 1586) **—lonesome** *adj.* 1647, in Henry A More's *A Platonical Song of the Soul;* formed from English *lone* + *-some¹.*

long¹ *adj.* that measures much from end to end. About 1175 *long;* also *lang* (in earlier manuscripts and in Northern British dialects); found in Old English (before 725) *lang, long.* The Old English forms are cognate with Old Frisian and Old Saxon *lang* long, Middle Dutch *lanc* (modern Dutch *lang*), Old High German and modern German *lang,* Old Icelandic *langr* (Danish and Norwegian *lang,* Swedish *lång*), and Gothic *laggs,* from Proto-Germanic **langa-,* a development of Indo-European **(d)longho-,* found in Latin *longus* long, and Middle Persian *drang* (Pok.197).
—adv. throughout the whole length of. About 1175 *longe;* found in Old English *lange, longe* (about 725, in *Beowulf*); from the adjective. The informal expression of parting *so long,* meaning good-by, farewell, is first recorded in 1865. Its origin is uncertain, but it is felt as meaning "(it will seem so long) until we meet again." Though sometimes suggested as an alteration of *salaam,* the connection is impossible to make from available data.

—n. long time. Apparently about 1200; from the adjective.

—longboat *n.* (1451) **—longbow** *n.* (1386) **—long distance** (1884 *long distance telephoning,* in *Whitaker's Almanack.*) **—longhand** *n.* handwriting. 1666, in Pepys' *Diary.* **—long house** North American Indian communal dwelling. 1643, American English. **—longish** *adj.* (1611, in Cotgrave's *Dictionary*) **—long johns** long, warm underwear (1943). **—long-lived** *adj.* (before 1400, in a version of *Cursor Mundi,* a possessive compound formed from the phrase *long life,* not from the verb to *live*). **—long-playing** *adj.* (1912 *long-playing needle;* 1929 *long-playing record*) **—long-range** *adj.* (1854) **—long run** (1627 *at the long run;* 1768 *in the long run*) **—long shot** (1867) **—long-standing** *adj.* (1814, in Jane Austen's *Mansfield Park*) **—long-suffering** *n.* 1526, in Tyndale's translation of the New Testament; *adj.* 1535, in the Coverdale Bible. **—long-winded** *adj.* (1589)

long[2] *v.* wish very much, yearn. Probably before 1200 *longen,* in Layamon's *Chronicle of Britain;* developed from Old English (about 875) *langian,* from Proto-Germanic **langōjanan.* The Old English form is cognate with Old Saxon *langōn* to long, Middle Low German *langen* to reach, hand, Middle Dutch *langhen* (modern Dutch *aanlangen*), Old High German *langēn* to long (modern German *verlangen* ask, desire, demand), and Old Icelandic *langa* to long; derived from the Proto-Germanic root that is also the source of Old English *lang* LONG[1].

"Impersonal" expressions in Old High German *mich (be)langēt* and Middle Dutch *mī langhet* have a basic sense of "It's (taking) too long for me," from which "I'm longing" follows. This is similar to the sense of *so long* under LONG[1] *adv.* **—longing** *n.* Before 1250 *longinge* a yearning desire, formed from Middle English *longen* yearn + *-inge* -ing[1].

longevity (lonjev′ətē) *n.* long life. 1615, borrowed from Late Latin *longaevitās,* from Latin *longaevus* long-lived (*longus* LONG[1], adj. + *aevum* lifetime, AGE); for suffix see -ITY.

longitude (lon′jətüd) *n.* distance east or west on the earth's surface. 1391, in Chaucer's *Treatise on the Astrolabe;* borrowed through Old French *longitude,* and directly from Latin *longitūdō* length, from *longus* LONG[1], adj.; for suffix see -TUDE. **—longitudinal** *adj.* 1392 *longitudinel;* later *longitudinal* (probably before 1425); borrowed from Old French *longitudinel* and Medieval Latin *longitudinalis,* from Latin *longitūdō* (genitive *longitūdinis*) longitude; for suffix see -AL[1].

longshoreman *n.* man who loads and unloads ships. 1811, formed from *long shore, longshore* along the shore + *man. Longshore* is a shortening of *alongshore* (1779, *along* + *shore*).

look *v.* Before 1121 *locon,* in *Peterborough Chronicle;* later *loken* (about 1200); developed from Old English *lōcian* see, gaze, look, spy (before 899, in Alfred's translation of St. Gregory's *Pastoral Care*). Old English *lōcian* is cognate with Old Saxon *lōkon* see, look, spy, Middle Dutch *loeken,* Old High German *luogēn* look out (modern German *lugen* look, peep), of unknown origin. The modern spelling *look* began to appear in the early 1400's, but is recorded as early as about 1350. **—n.** Probably before 1200 *loke* act of looking, glance; from the verb. **—look-alike** *n.* (1947, American English) **—looker-on** *n.* onlooker; spectator (1539). **—looking glass** (1526) **—lookout** *n.* watchman, scout (1699).

loom[1] *n.* machine for weaving cloth. Probably before 1200 *lome* tool, implement, in *Ancrene Riwle;* later, a loom for weaving (1380); developed from Old English *gelōma* utensil, tool (before 800, in *Corpus Glossary*); formed from *ge-* perfective prefix (see ENOUGH) + *-lōma,* as in *andlōman,* pl., apparatus, furniture, of unknown origin. The modern spelling *loom* appears as early as 1440, in *Promptorium Parvulorum.*

loom[2] *v.* appear indistinctly. 1591, applied to a ship; perhaps borrowed from a Scandinavian source (compare dialectal Swedish *loma* move slowly; see LUMBER[2], v.).

loon[1] *n.* large diving bird. 1634, in William Wood's *New England's Prospect;* borrowed from a Scandinavian source (compare Norwegian *lom* loon, Old Icelandic *lōmr*); see LAMENT. The phrase *crazy as a loon* is first recorded in 1845, and is often referred to the bird's wild cry, but it seems equally plausible to refer to LOON[2], *n.,* especially in other common phrases, such as "drunk as a loon," and the sense may also have been influenced by *lunatic,* n. *Loon* in the sense of a crazy person is found in 1885, probably influenced by *loony* (also *luny*) and *lunatic.*

loon[2] *n.* worthless or stupid person, rogue, scamp, idler. Probably about 1450 *lowen* worthless person, rascal, of uncertain origin (compare early modern Dutch *loen* stupid person).

loony *adj. Slang,* crazy. 1872, in Bret Harte's *An Heiress of Red Dog,* American English; generally considered to have developed by shortening and alteration from LUNATIC, but also probably influenced by *loon*[1], and by *lunatic* also found with the spelling *luny.* The humorous reference to an insane asylum in the phrase *loony bin,* was introduced in Wodehouse's *My Man Jeeves* (1919). **—n.** crazy person. 1884, from the adjective.

loop *n.* Probably about 1390 *loupe,* in *Sir Gawain and the Green Knight;* borrowed probably from a Celtic source (compare Gaelic *lub* bend, Irish *lúbaim*). However, the form of the Middle English word suggests that the Celtic word has been reshaped by blending with a borrowing from Scandinavian (compare Old Icelandic *hlaup* a leap, run, *hlaupa* to LEAP). **—v.** make a loop of. Probably before 1400 *loupen,* from *loupe,* n., loop.

loophole *n.* 1464 *lopehole* small opening for ventilation; later *loop hole* small opening to look through, shoot through, or admit light and air (1591). The word is formed after Middle English *loupe* opening in a wall (1386); possibly cognate with Middle Dutch *lūpen, glūpen* to lie in wait, watch, peer (modern Dutch *luipen, gluipen* to spy, sneak). The Medieval Latin *loupa* (attested since 1388) was apparently borrowed from Middle English.

The common figurative meaning of an outlet or means of escape is first recorded in Andrew Marvell's *Correspondence* (1663-64).

loose *adj.* Probably before 1200 *lowse* not firmly attached, in *Ancrene Riwle;* later *los* (before 1300), and *loos* (about 1350); borrowed from a Scandinavian source (compare Old Icelandic *lauss* loose; see -LESS). **—v.** set free, let go. Probably before 1200 *lowsen;* later *loosen* (about 1325); from the adjective. **—loose-jointed** *adj.* (1859) **—loose-leaf** *adj.* (1902) **—loose-tongued** *adj.* (1647) **—loosen** *v.* make loose. Before 1382 *losnen;* later *lousnen* (probably before 1425); formed from Middle English *los, loos* loose + *-nen* -en[1].

loot *n.* spoils, plunder, booty, 1788, Anglo-Indian *loot,* borrowed from Hindi *lūṭ,* probably from Sanskrit *lóta-m, lótra-m* booty, stolen property, alteration (through Prakrit) of *loptra-m* booty, from *lumpáti* he breaks; cognate with Latin *rumpere* break, from Indo-European **reup-/roup-/rup-* (Pok.870). **—v.** plunder, rob. 1842, from the noun.

lop[1] *v.* cut off. 1519, developed from Middle English *loppe,* n., the smaller branches and twigs trimmed from trees (1355–56); of uncertain origin, but related to *lopped* (1458), participial adj., trimmed; found earlier in the place name *Loppedthorn* (1287).

lop[2] *v.* hang loosely or limply, droop. 1578, probably variant of LAP (as *flop* is of *flap*) and closely related in meaning to LOB to droop (1599) and perhaps in form, as in *flab, flap* in which *flab, flabby* are variants of *flap, flappy.* **—lopsided** *adj.* 1711 *lapsided* (of a ship) disproportionately heavy on one side, unevenly balanced; formed from English *lop*[2] + *-sided* (1400's), as in *two-sided, many-sided;* on the pattern of *lop-eared* (1687, *lap-eared*). The spelling *lopsided* is first recorded in 1820, the spelling *lop eared* in 1692.

lope *v.* About 1300 *loupen* to jump or leap, in *Havelok the Dane;* later *lopen* (before 1376, in *Piers Plowman*); borrowed from a Scandinavian source (compare Old Icelandic *hlaupa* to run, LEAP). The sense of run with a long, easy stride is first recorded before 1825. **—n.** Before 1393 *lope* a jump or leap, in Gower's *Confessio Amantis;* from the verb. The sense of a long, easy stride is first recorded in 1846.

loquacious (lōkwā′shəs) *adj.* talkative. 1667, in Milton's *Paradise Lost;* probably a back formation from English *loquacity* + *-ous,* though theoretically formed in English from the stem of Latin *loquāx* (genitive *loquācis*) talkative + English *-ous.* **—loquacity** (lōkwas′ətē) *n.* talkativeness. Probably before 1200 *loquacite,* in *Ancrene Riwle;* borrowed from Latin *loquācitātem* (nominative *loquācitās*) talkativeness, from *loquāx* (genitive *loquācis*) talkative, from *loquī* to speak, talk, of uncertain origin; for suffix see -ITY. Related to ELOQUENT and LOCUTION.

loran (lor′an) *n.* device using radio signals by which a navigator can determine his geographical position regardless of weather conditions. 1943, American English, acronym formed from *lo(ng) ra(nge) n(avigation);* originally abbreviated as *LRN* (1942).

lord *n.* owner, ruler, or master. Before 1121 *laverd,* in *Peterborough Chronicle;* later *loverd, lord* (about 1250); developed from Old English *hlāford* master of a household, ruler, superior (about 725, in *Beowulf*); literally, one who guards a loaf or loaves (*hlāf* bread, LOAF[1] + *weard* keeper, guardian, WARD); compare LADY. **—v.** to rule, domineer. About 1340 *lorden,* in Richard Rolle's *The Psalter;* from the noun. **—lordly** *adj.* Before 1225 *loverdlich;* later *lordlich* (before 1376) and *lordli* (about 1395); formed from Middle English *loverd, lord* lord + *-lich, -li* -ly[2].—*adv.* About 1350, from the adjective. **—lordship** *n.* About 1300 *louerdsipe;* later *lordschipe* (about 1350); developed from Old English *hlāfordscipe* rule or dominion of a lord (before 899, in Alfred's translation of St. Gregory's *Pastoral Care*), from *hlāford* lord + *-scipe* -ship.

lore *n.* About 1300, developed from Old English (before 725) *lār* learning, teaching, knowledge, doctrine; cognate with Old Frisian *lāre* doctrine, teaching, Old Saxon *lēra,* Middle Dutch *lēre* (modern Dutch *leer*), Old High German *lēra* (modern German *Lehre*), from Proto-Germanic **laizṓ;* related are Gothic *laisjan* to teach, Old High German *lērran, lēren,* Old Saxon *lērian,* Old English *lǣran,* from Proto-Germanic **laizijanan;* all related to the Proto-Germanic source of Old English *leornian* to LEARN.

lorn *adj. Archaic.* forsaken, forlorn. Probably about 1300, developed from Old English *-loren,* past participle of *-lēosan* to LOSE; related to FORLORN.

lorry *n.* 1838, long, flat wagon; possibly from dialectal English *lurry* to pull, lug, of unknown origin. The current meaning in British English of a large truck for transporting goods appeared in the early 1900's.

lose *v.* 1120 *losen* be lost, perish, in *Peterborough Chronicle;* later, be deprived of, lose (probably before 1200); developed from Old English (before 725) *losian* be lost, perish, from *los* destruction, loss, related to Old English *forlēosan* to lose. Old English *forlēosan* is cognate with Old Frisian *forliāsa* to lose, Old Saxon *farliosan,* Middle Dutch *verliesen* (modern Dutch *verliezen*), Old High German *firliosan* (modern German *verlieren*), and Gothic *fraliusan,* from Proto-Germanic **fra-leusanan,* Indo-European **pro-leu-s-*. Cognates outside Germanic include Latin *luere* release from debt, expiate, Greek *lýein* untie, set free, dissolve, Albanian *laj* I pay a debt, Sanskrit *lunā́ti* he cuts off, Tocharian A *lo,* Tocharian B *lau* removes, divides, and Hittite *luzzi* compulsory labor, load, from Indo-European **leu-/lu-, lēu-/ləu-* cut off, separate (Pok. 681).

The expected modern English pronunciation representing Middle English *losen* and Old English *losian* would be (lōz), but the standard modern English pronunciation of *lose* (lüz) is probably the result of influence of *loose,* which in some contexts (as in *to loose one's hold*) closely approaches the meaning of *lose.*

loss *n.* a losing or being lost. Probably before 1200 *los* death, destruction, in Layamon's *Chronicle of Britain;* later, a losing, loss (before 1338, in Mannyng's *Chronicle of England*); found in Old English *los* loss, destruction (before 899, in Alfred's translation of St. Gregory's *Pastoral Care*), and possibly influenced by Old Icelandic *los* looseness, breaking up, from Proto-Germanic **lusan;* see LOSE.

To account for the modern form, as the corresponding noun to the verb *lose,* it is conjectured that the Old and Middle English form would normally have become *lose* (lōz) in modern English, but that it was probably reshaped by analogy with *lost,* past participle of *losen* to lose. However, it is probable that the final *-s* of Old English would retain the sound represented by *s* in *sat* (as in the noun *house* from *hūs*), and the so-called short *o* of Old English would not become the long *o* in a closed syllable.

lot *n.* About 1300, in a version of Layamon's *Chronicle of Britain;* later, portion, share (probably before 1350); developed from Old English *hlot* in compound *huonhlotum,* adv., by little portions, minutely (before 800, in *Corpus Glossary*). The Old English form *hlot,* abstracted from the compound above, and from Proto-Germanic **Hlutan,* is cognate with Old Frisian *hlot* lot, Old Saxon *hlōt,* Middle Low German *lot,* Middle Dutch and modern Dutch *lot,* Old High German *hluz, hlōz* (modern German *Los*), Old Icelandic *hlutr* (Danish *lod,* Swedish *lott,* and Norwegian *lodd, lott*), and Gothic *hlauts.* The primary Germanic sense is unknown. The Germanic forms are cognate with Greek (Doric) *klā̂is.* (genitive *klāîdos*) bar, key, from Indo-European **klāw-*

id-; Germanic forms point to Indo-European **klēu-d-/ kləu-d-/klu-d-* (Pok. 604).

The sense of a plot or portion of land is first recorded in 1633. This was followed in 1725 by the generalized sense of a number of persons or things, group, collection, set (as in *a bad lot, a large lot of ore*), which by 1812 evolved into the informal sense of a great many, a good deal, often used in the plural *(a lot of people, lots of money).*

Lothario (lōthä′rēō) *n.* fashionable libertine or rake. 1756, from the name of the principal male character ("that Haughty, Gallant, Gay Lothario") who seduces Calista, the fair penitent, in Nicholas Rowe's play *The Fair Penitent* (1703). The name had been previously used for a somewhat similar character in William Davenant's play *The Cruel Brother* (1630). The character in Rowe's play was the model for the libertine Robert Lovelace in Samuel Richardson's novel *Clarissa Harlowe* (1747-48).

lotion *n.* Before 1400 *loscion,* in Lanfranc's *Science of Surgery;* borrowed through Old French *lotion,* from Latin *lōtiōnem* (nominative *lōtiō*) a washing, from *lōtus,* popular form of *lautus,* past participle of *lavere* to wash; later, *lavātus,* past participle of *lavāre* to wash, LAVE; for suffix see -TION.

The spelling *lotion,* after the French and Latin, appeared in English in 1549.

lottery *n.* scheme for distributing prizes by lot or chance. 1567, borrowed from Middle French *loterie,* from Middle Dutch *loterje,* from *lot* share, LOT; for suffix see -ERY.

lotto *n.* game played by drawing numbered disks from a bag or box and covering the corresponding numbers on cards. 1778 *loto,* borrowed through French *loto,* and directly from Italian *lotto* lotto, lot, from Old French *lot* lot, from Frankish (compare Old Frisian and Old English *hlot* LOT).

lotus *n.* water lily. 1540-41, in Elyot's *The Image of Governance;* borrowed from Latin *lōtus,* from Greek *lōtós,* the name of several plants, perhaps from a Semitic source (compare Hebrew *lōṭ* myrrh).

loud *adj.* About 1175 *lude;* later *loud* (probably before 1300); developed from Old English (before 725) *hlūd* making noise, sonorous. Old English *hlūd* is cognate with Old Frisian and Old Saxon *hlūd* loud, Middle Dutch *luut* (modern Dutch *luid*), Old High German *hlūt, lūt* (modern German *laut*) from Proto Germanic **Hlūđás,* Old Icelandic *hljōdh* silence, hearing, and Gothic *hliuma* hearing. Cognates outside Germanic include Old Irish *cloth* glory, fame, Latin *cluēre* be called, be spoken of, Greek *klytós* famous, celebrated, Lithuanian *šlovẽ* splendor, Old Slavic *sluti* be called, Armenian *lu* known, Sanskrit *śṛnóti* (he) hears, and Tocharian A and Tocharian B *klā̆w-* make known, from Indo-European **k̂leu-/k̂lu-, k̂lewə-/k̂lū-* (Pok. 605). **—adv.** Probably before 1200 *lude;* later *loude* (about 1300); developed from Old English (about 750) *hlūde,* from Proto-Germanic **Hlūđaí.* Old English *hlūde* is cognate with Old Saxon *hlūdo,* Middle Dutch *luut* (modern Dutch *luid*), Old High German *hlūto, lūto* (modern German *laut*).

—loudmouth *n.* 1934, in John O'Hara's *Appointment in Samarra,* American English; *adj.,* 1668, probably back formation from *loudmouthed.* **—loudmouthed** *adj.* (1628) **—loud-speaker** *n.* (1884)

lounge (lounj) *v.* loll about, move about lazily. 1508, Scottish, of uncertain origin, but possibly borrowed from French: compare French *s'allonger (paresseusement)* to lounge about, to stretch out, to lie at full length, Middle French and Old French *alongir, longuir, eslongier,* with the same meaning; all from Old French *alongier* lengthen, *long, lonc* long, from Latin *longus* LONG[1], adj. **—n.** 1775, place for lounging, in Sheridan's *The Rivals;* from the verb. The meaning of a comfortable drawing room or parlor is first recorded in 1881, and that of a sofa or couch for reclining, in 1830 in American English.

lour *v.* See LOWER.

louse (lous) *n.* Before 1300 *lowse;* developed from Old English (about 700) *lūs;* cognate with Middle Low German *lūs* louse, Middle Dutch *luus* (modern Dutch *luis*), Old High German *lūs* (modern German *Laus*), and Old Icelandic *lūs* (Swedish, Danish, and Norwegian *lus,* modern Icelandic *lús*), from Proto-Germanic **lūs,* Indo-European **lūs* (Pok.692). Cognates outside Germanic are only found in the Celtic languages: Welsh *llau* lice (collective), *lleuen* louse, Cornish *lowen,* and Breton *louen.*

The plural form *lice* was known in primitive Old English before the end of the 600's *(lyse, lyse)* and is the result of adjustment of the vowel in *louse* to a more forward position, caused by the following vowel sound represented by *i* in Proto-Germanic **lūsiz,* altered from Indo-European **luwes* lice. This is a regular process of mutation in Old English.

—v. Before 1387, to remove lice from, in Trevisa's translation of Higden's *Polychronicon;* from the noun. **—louse up** *Slang.* spoil, mess up. 1934, in John O'Hara's *Appointment in Samarra,* American English, apparently from the earlier (1931) meaning of infest with lice. **—lousy** (lou′zē) *adj.* Probably about 1350 *lowsy* infested with lice; formed from Middle English *lowse* louse + *-y*[1]. The figurative sense of worthless, inferior, contemptible, is first recorded in Chaucer's *Canterbury Tales* (1395). The slang sense of being well supplied, full of (as in *The town is lousy with tourists*) is found in American English 1843), as an obvious extension of the concrete meaning.

The figurative sense of *lousy* is not an exclusive innovation in English; it is found in German *lausig,* French *pouilleux,* Spanish *piojoso,* etc.

lout *n.* awkward, stupid fellow, boor. Before 1548, generally considered to be developed from Middle English (probably before 1300) *louten,* v., bow down, from Old English (before 900) *lūtan* bow low, earlier *forthlūtan* (before 830, in the *Vespasian Psalter*). Old English *lūtan* is cognate with Old Icelandic *lūtr* bend down, stooping, *lūta* to stoop; see LITTLE. **—loutish** *adj.* boorish. Before 1553; formed from English *lout* + *-ish*[1].

louver (lü′vər) *n.* Before 1325 *lover* chimney, skylight; later *luver* (1367-68); borrowed from Old French *lover, lovier* and Medieval Latin *lovarium, luvarium;* both the Old French and Medieval Latin forms are perhaps from Germanic (compare Old High German *louba* upper room, roof; see LOBBY).

The sense of overlapping strips in a window, etc., to keep out rain is first recorded in 1555, and earlier in *louerboord* (1448-49) and *louerstringes* cords to adjust louverboards (1356-57). The spelling with *ou* did not begin to appear before the mid-1600's.

love *n.* About 1200 *luve;* later *love* (probably before 1300); developed from Old English (before 725) *lufu* love. Old English *lufu* is cognate with Old Frisian *luve* love, Old Saxon *luva,* Old High German *luba,* and Gothic *-lubō,* from Proto-Germanic **luƀō.* A different grade, **leuƀa-* and its derivatives, produced Middle Dutch and modern Dutch *liefde,* and Old High German *liubi, liuba* (modern German *Liebe*). Outside Germanic the word is represented by such cognates as Latin *lubēre, libēre* to please, Lithuanian *liaupsė̃* song of praise, Old Slavic *l'uby* love, *l'ubŭ* beloved, dear, and Sanskrit *lúbhyati* (he) desires, from Indo-European **leubh-/lubh-* (Pok. 683). Related to LEAVE² permission. See also LIBIDO.

In Germanic, as in Celtic, the old Indo-European word for love (seen in Sanskrit *prīyate,* Old Slavic *prijati*) assumed the meaning "free" (see FREE); hence another word (meaning "desire") took its place.

—v. Before 1121 *luven;* later *loven* (probably before 1300); developed from Old English (before 725) *lufian;* cognate with Old High German *lubōn* to love (modern German *lieben*) from Proto-Germanic **luƀōjanan.*

—lovable or **loveable** *adj.* About 1422 *lovable,* about 1426 *loveable;* formed from Middle English *love* + *-able.* **—lovebird** *n.* 1595, in Lyly's *Woman in the Moon;* so called from the affection this bird seems to show its mate. **—loveless** *adj.* About 1330 *loveles* without love; earlier, as surname *Loveles* (1237); formed from Middle English *love* + *-les* -less. **—lovelorn** *adj.* forsaken by one's love. 1634, in Milton's *Comus;* formed from English *love* + LORN bereft of, lost. **—lovely** *adj.* Probably before 1200 *luvelich,* before 1375 *loveli* lovely, loving; developed from Old English (about 1000) *luflīc* (from *lufu* love + *-līc* -ly²).—*n.* probably about 1390 *loveli* beautiful woman or lovely person; from the adjective. **—lover** *n.* About 1250, one who loves as a friend; later, one who loves a thing, an action, etc. (about 1350), and one who loves sexually (about 1380); formed from Middle English *love* + *-er¹.* **—lovesick** *adj.* (before 1450) **—loving-kindness** *n.* (1535, in the Coverdale Bible)

low¹ *adj.* not high. About 1175 *lah;* later *low* (about 1280); borrowed from a Scandinavian source (compare Old Icelandic *lāgr* low, Swedish *låg,* Danish *lav,* Norwegian *lav, låg,* from Proto-Germanic **lǣ3az*). The Scandinavian words are cognate with Old Frisian and Middle Low German *lēch* low, Middle Dutch *lage* (modern Dutch *laag* low), Middle High German *læge* flat, and dialectal German *läg* flat. Cognates outside Germanic are found only in the Baltic and Slavic families, as shown by Lithuanian *lė̃kštas* flat, Old Slavic *lěsti* to creep, crawl, from Indo-European **lēĝh-/ləĝh-* (Pok. 660), perhaps related to *lešti* lie down, *ležati* to lie; see LIE². **—n.** that which is low. About 1300, from the adjective. **—adv.** near the floor, base, or ground. Probably before 1200 *lahe;* later *lowe* (before 1250); from the adjective.

low² *v.* make the sound of a cow, moo. Before 1300 *lowen,* developed from Old English (before 1000) *hlōwan;* cognate with Middle Low German *lōien* to low, Middle Dutch *loeyen, loyen* (modern Dutch *loeien*), Old Low Franconian *luon, luogin,* and Old High German *hluoen,* from Proto-Germanic **Hlō-,* from Indo-European **klā-,* represented outside Germanic by Latin *clāmāre* cry out, call, proclaim, *calāre* to call, call out, Greek *kaleîn* to call, Latvian *kal'uôt* to chatter, Lithuanian *kalbà* language, Old Slavic *klakolŭ* bell, Sanskrit *uṣākala-s* dawn-caller, cock, Old Irish *cailech* cock, and perhaps Hittite *kallesuwanzi* to invite, entice, from Indo-European **kel-/kol-/kelē-/kelā-/klā-* (Pok. 548). **—n.** sound a cow makes; mooing. 1549, from the verb.

lower (lou'ər) or **lour** (lour) *v.* look dark and threatening. Probably about 1225 *luren* to frown or scowl; later *louren* (probably before 1300); either developed from Old English **lūran* or borrowed from Middle Low German or Middle Dutch. The probable Old English form would be cognate with Middle Low German *lūren* lie in wait, Middle Dutch and modern Dutch *loeren,* Middle High German *lūren* (modern German *lauern*), and dialectal Norwegian and Swedish *lurka* move slowly, creep forward.

The word's form and meaning is reminiscent of Latin *luscus* one-eyed, *lusciōsus* dim-sighted, and also suggests a number of words starting with *gl-,* for example English *glower* and Low German *gluren.*

lox¹ *n.* kind of smoked salmon. About 1930-34, American English; borrowed from Yiddish *laks,* from Middle High German *lahs* salmon, LAX².

lox² *n.* 1923 LOX, acronym formed from *L(iquid) Ox(ygen).* The lower-case spelling is first recorded in 1946.

loyal *adj.* 1531, faithful, especially in allegiance to a ruler or country, in Elyot's *The Boke Named the Governour;* borrowed from Middle French *loyal* faithful, from Old French *loial, leial,* from Latin *lēgālis* legal, from *lēx* (genitive *lēgis*) law; for suffix see -AL¹. See the doublet LEGAL. Modern English *loyal* replaced Middle English *lel* (recorded probably before 1300); later *leal* (about 1350); borrowed from Old French *leal, leial,* from Latin *lēgālis* legal. **—loyalty** *n.* Probably before 1400, borrowed from Old French *loialté,* from *loial* loyal. During the 1500's *loyalty* replaced earlier *leaute* (1265, borrowed from Old French *leauté,* from *leal*); for suffix see -TY².

lozenge (loz'inj) *n.* figure shaped like a diamond; rhombus. 1320 *losonge;* 1330 *lozenge;* borrowed from Old French *losenge* windowpane, small square cake of herbs, etc., or other things with a quadrilateral shape, from pre-Roman, perhaps Iberian **lausa* flat stone (the source of Old Provençal *lauza,* Catalan *llosa,* Spanish *losa,* Portuguese *lousa*), found also in Latin *lausiae lapidēs* stone chips.

The editors of FEW (V, 43, p.211) maintain that **lausa* is a Gaulish word, which perhaps came from a pre-Celtic language.

The sense of small tablet of medicine or candy (originally of a diamond or square shape) is first recorded in Palsgrave's *Lesclarcissement* (1530).

LSD chemical that produces hallucinations. 1950, borrowing of German *LSD,* abbreviation of *L(yserg)-s(äure)-d(iäthylamid)* lysergic acid diethylamide (1944), a chemical compound that is a derivative of an acid obtained from the fungus that causes the plant disease ergot, which is theorized to be the source (through wheat flour and thence bread) of much of the abnormal behavior that initiated the New England witch trials of the 1690's. The name *lysergic acid* was formed in 1934 in English from *(hydro)lys(is)* + *erg(ot)* + *-ic* + *acid.*

luau (lü'ou) *n.* 1853, feast generally held outdoors; earlier, baked dish of young taro tops (1843); borrowed from Hawaiian *lū'au* (literally) young taro tops (so called because taro tops were served at an outdoor feast).

lubber *n.* big, clumsy fellow. About 1390 *lobre;* later *lobur* (before 1475); developed from or related to earlier *lobi* a lazy lout (before 1376); see LOB. Compare LANDLUBBER.

lubricate *v.* 1623, in Cockeram's *Dictionary;* borrowed from Latin *lūbricātus,* past participle of *lūbricāre* make slippery or smooth, from *lūbricus* slippery, see SLEEVE; for suffix see -ATE¹. Modern English *lubricate* gradually replaced earlier Middle English *lubrifien* (recorded probably before 1425, and borrowed from Medieval Latin *lubrificare*), which in a modern English spelling *lubrify* became obsolete after 1866. **—lubricant** *adj.* 1822-34, lubricating; borrowed from Latin *lūbricantem* (nominative *lūbricāns*), present participle of *lūbricāre* to lubricate; for suffix see -ANT.—*n.* substance used to lubricate machinery. 1828, from the adjective. **—lubrication** *n.* 1803, formed from English *lubricate* + *-ion.*

lucent *adj.* shining, luminous. 1449, borrowed from Latin *lūcentem* (nominative *lūcēns*), present participle of *lūcēre* to shine; see LIGHT¹ radiant energy; for suffix see -ENT.

lucid *adj.* clear. 1591, bright or shining, in Spenser's *Mother Hubbard's Tale;* borrowed through Middle French *lucide,* and directly from Latin *lūcidus* light, bright, clear; related to *lūcēre* to shine; see LIGHT¹ radiant energy. The sense of easy to follow or understand is first recorded in 1786. **—lucidity** *n.* 1656, brightness, in Blount's *Glossographia;* later, intellectual clearness (1851); borrowed from French *lucidité,* learned borrowing from Late Latin *lūciditās,* from Latin *lūcidus* bright; for suffix see -ITY.

Lucifer *n.* Satan. Old English *Lucifer* Satan; also, the morning star (probably about 725, in *Christ and Satan);* borrowed from Latin *lūcifer* the morning star; literally, light-bringing (*lūx,* genitive *lūcis* LIGHT¹ + *ferre* carry, BEAR²). Compare the derivation of PHOSPHORUS.

This name for Satan comes from the Biblical passage (translated from the Vulgate) "How art thou fallen from heaven, O Lucifer, son of the morning!" (Isaiah 14:12). Early Christian biblical commentators interpreted this name (a rendering of Hebrew *hēlēl*) allegorically as referring to the archangel hurled from heaven for his wickedness. The actual reference is to the king of Babylon, who was compared to the morning star.

luck *n.* Before 1500 *lucke, luk* good fortune; possibly a back formation from earlier *lukky,* but more likely borrowed from Middle Dutch *luc,* shortened form of *gheluc, ghelucke* happiness, good fortune, luck (modern Dutch *geluk*); cognate with Middle Low German *lucke* luck, Middle High German *gelücke,* and modern German *Glück* happiness, good fortune, success, luck. Perhaps the word came into English as a gambling term, the Low German dialects, according to the OED, being frequently a source of such terms in the 1400's and 1500's. Old Frisian *lukk* happiness, good fortune, late Old Icelandic *lukka,* Danish and Norwegian *lykke,* and Swedish *lycka* were all borrowed from the same source as English *luck.* The ultimate etymology of the word is unknown.

The citation from a late version of *Promptorium Parvulorum* (before 1475) is thought to be a probable error for *lucre* gain or profit.

—luckily *adv.* (1530) **—luckless** *adj.* (1563) **—lucky** *adj.* About 1450 *lukky;* probably formed from Middle English *luk* luck + *-y¹.*

lucrative *adj.* profitable. About 1412 *lucratif,* in Hoccleve's *Regement of Princes;* borrowed from Old French *lucratif* (feminine *lucrative*), and directly from Latin *lucrātīvus,* from *lucrārī* to gain, from *lucrum* gain or profit, see LUCRE; for suffix see -IVE.

lucre (lü′kər) *n.* money considered as a bad influence. About 1390 *lucre* illicit gain, in Chaucer's *Canterbury Tales;* also, monetary gain, profit (before 1393); borrowed from Latin *lucrum* gain or profit, with dissimilation of *l* (in *tl*) or *r* (in *cr*) from earlier **lutlom.* The Latin word is probably cognate with Old Irish *lōg, lūag* reward or price, Greek *leíā* (earlier **lāwíā*) booty, Old Slavic *lovŭ* hunt, booty, and Gothic *laun,* Old English *lēan* payment, from Indo-European **lāu-/ləu-/lu-* (Pok. 655).

lucubration (lükyəbrā′shən) *n.* laborious study. 1595 *lucubrations,* borrowed from Middle French *lucubrations,* fem. pl., learned borrowing from Latin *lūcubrātiōnem* (nominative *lūcubrātiō*), from *lūcubrāre* work late at night by lamplight, formed from a lost noun **lūcubrum,* earlier **leukosrom,* related to *lūcēre* to shine, see LIGHT¹ radiant energy; for suffix see -ATION.

The Middle French word has been replaced in modern French by *élucubrations,* which today has the pejorative meaning of wild imaginings, but in the 1500's had the sense of work done by staying awake at night.

The sense of a literary work or ideas showing signs of careful elaboration appeared in 1611, in Coryat's *Crudities;* by 1892 this sense was used derisively or playfully, suggesting pedantic or overelaborate ideas.

luddite or **Luddite** (lud′īt) *n.* 1811, person strongly opposed to increased mechanization, in allusion to the *Luddites,* one of the organized groups of English workmen who between 1811 and 1816 went about destroying manufacturing machinery in the midlands and north of England for fear that the use of machinery would put them out of work. Their name supposedly derives from Ned *Ludd* (an unstable worker who destroyed stocking frames in a Leicestershire village about 1779) + *-ite¹.*

The word has been used since 1811 generally in historical reference to the Luddites, but by 1961 it had taken on contemporary application in reference to use of automation and computers.

ludic *adj.* playful. 1940 (use in psychology), formed in English from Latin *lūdus* sport, game, play (from *lūdere* to play, see LUDICROUS) + English suffix *-ic.*

ludicrous *adj.* 1619, intended for play or pastime, sportive; borrowed from Latin *lūdicrus,* from *lūdicrum* source of amusement, joke, from *lūdere* to play; for suffix see -OUS. Latin *lūdere* is cognate with Greek *loídoros* abusive or insulting, and *lízein* to play (found only in glosses), from Indo-European **leid-/loid-/lid-* play, jest (Pok. 666). The current sense of causing derisive laughter, ridiculous, is first recorded in English in 1782, in Frances Burney's *Cecilia.*

luff *n.* a turning the bow of a ship toward the wind. Probably before 1200 *lof* a spar holding out and down the windward tack of a square sail, in *Ancrene Riwle* and Layamon's *Chronicle of Britain;* later *loef* (1294-95) and *lufe* (probably before 1400, in *Morte Arthur*); borrowed through Old French *lof* probably an implement or device for adjusting a sail; perhaps originally, an oar to assist in steering; or borrowed directly from Middle Dutch *loef* probably the windward side of a ship. The Middle Dutch word is cognate with Middle Low German *lōf* side of a ship toward the wind, and perhaps with Old Icelandic *lōfi* palm of the hand; see GLOVE.

The sense of the windward side of a ship appeared

about 1380 in Middle English and that of a turning the bow toward the wind before 1400.
—**v.** turn the bow of a ship toward the wind. Before 1393 *loven,* in Gower's *Confessio Amantis,* from *lof,* n., luff.

lug[1] *v.* pull with effort, drag. Probably about 1380 *luggen* move heavily; later *loggen* pull, drag forcibly (about 1390); borrowed from a Scandinavian source (compare Swedish *lugga* to pull by the hair, *lugg* forelock or nap of cloth, Norwegian *lugge* to pull by the hair, *lugg* tuft of hair). —**n.** act of pulling, hauling, or dragging. 1545, something heavy; later, act of lugging (before 1616, in Beaumont and Fletcher's *The Nice Valour*); from the verb.

lug[2] *n.* projecting part used to hold or grip something. 1624, handle of a pitcher, etc.; developed from Middle English (1495) *lugge,* Scottish, earflap of a cap, ear; perhaps borrowed from a Scandinavian source (compare Swedish *lugg* forelock); see LUG[1] to drag. The modern sense, as represented by *lug* in *lug bolt* is first recorded in 1794.

luge (lüzh) *n.* small coasting sled, used especially in Switzerland. 1905, borrowing of French *luge,* from dialectal French (Savoy and Switzerland), from Medieval Latin *sludia,* perhaps from a Gaulish word of the same root as English SLED and SLIDE.

luggage *n.* baggage. 1596, in Nashe's *Have With You to Saffron-Walden;* formed from English *lug*[1] to drag + *-age.*

lugger *n.* boat rigged with lugsails. 1757, probably formed from English *lug(sail)* + *-er*[1]. The OED compares the term to Dutch *logger,* perhaps from Middle Dutch *loggen, luggen* to fish with a dragnet. However, in Bense's *Dictionary of the Low-Dutch Element in the English Vocabulary* the connection is not accepted, as the author claims that modern Dutch *logger* was borrowed from French *lougre,* which was probably borrowed from English *lugger,* since the Dutch word appears later than either the English or French word.

lugsail *n.* four-cornered sail. 1677, formed probably from English *lug*[1] + *sail.*

lugubrious (ləgü'brēəs) *adj.* sad, mournful, 1601, formed in English from French *lugubre,* or directly from Latin *lūgubris* mournful, mourning (from *lūgēre* mourn) + English suffix *-ous.* Latin *lūgēre* (earlier **lūgosris*) is cognate with Greek *lygrós* mournful or sad, Lithuanian *lúžti* (v.i.), *láužti* (v.t.) to break, Armenian *lucanem* I break open, and Sanskrit *rujáti* (he) breaks, tortures, from Indo-European **leuĝ-/louĝ-/luĝ-* break (Pok. 686). The semantic connection between "break" and "mourn" appears in Lithuanian *širdis lúžta* the heart breaks.

lugworm *n.* large marine worm used for bait. 1802, formed from earlier English *lug* lugworm (1602) + *worm.* The origin of *lug* in this sense is uncertain; perhaps it is connected with *lug* something heavy and clumsy (1545, in reference to its appearance and movement); compare also Low German *lug* and Dutch *log* slow or heavy.

lukewarm *adj.* neither hot nor cold. 1373 *lwke warm;* later *leuke-warm, luke-warm* (probably before 1425), a compound of *leuk, luke,* adj., lukewarm or tepid + *warm.* Note also, about 1450, *lew warm,* from Old English *hlēowe* (adverb) warm. The source of Middle English *leuk, luke* (probably before 1200, in Layamon's *Chronicle of Britain*), if related to *-hlēow* warm, *hlēo* shelter or LEE, remains obscure, though it is cognate with Low German *lūk* tepid, modern Dutch *leuk,* East Frisian *lūk, luke* tepid, weak.

lull *v.* Before 1325 *lullen* hush to sleep; possibly of imitative origin; similar forms are found in Swedish *lulla,* Danish and Norwegian *lulle* lull, Middle Dutch *lollen* to doze, mumble (modern Dutch *lullen* to prattle), Middle Low German *lollen* (modern German *lullen*) to lull, Lithuanian *leliúoti* to rock, and Sanskrit *lólati* (he) moves to and fro, from Indo-European **lul-/lel-* (Pok. 650). —**n.** period of brief calm. 1719, something which lulls; from the verb.

lullaby *n.* 1588, song sung to children to soothe them to rest; developed from earlier *lulley by* a soothing refrain to pacify infants (about 1560); formed from Middle English *lollai* (probably before 1325; later *lullay,* 1372; from *lullen* to LULL) + *-by,* as in *good-by.*

lulu[1] *n. Slang.* remarkable person or thing. 1886 *lu-lu,* American English, alteration (probably by association with *Lulu,* nickname of *Louise*) of earlier *looly* (1857), in the phrase of admiration *looliest looly of the loolies.* Since the 1940's and the further popularization of the word in the cartoon "Little Lulu" of Saturday Evening Post fame, *lulu* has been used chiefly ironically, as in *That mistake was a real lulu.*

lulu[2] *n. Slang.* allowance paid to a legislator in lieu of expenses. 1953, American English, a reduplication (probably influenced by *lulu*[1]) of LIEU.

lumbago (lumbā'gō) *n.* pain in the muscles of the back and in the loins. 1693 (possibly earlier, implied by *lumbaginous,* 1620); borrowing of Late Latin *lumbāgō* disease or weakness of the loins or lumbar region of the lower back, from Latin *lumbus* LOIN.

lumbar *adj.* of the loin or loins. 1656, in Blount's *Glossographia;* borrowed from New Latin *lumbaris* (also found as neuter *lumbāre* in Late Latin, used as a noun with the meaning of loincloth), from Latin *lumbus* LOIN; for suffix see -AR. —**n.** lumbar vertebra, artery, nerve, etc. 1858, in Gray's *Anatomy;* from the adjective.

lumber[1] *n.* timber or logs cut into boards. Probably 1662, American English, specialized meaning of the earlier sense of disused articles of furniture or the like, heavy, useless objects that take up room inconveniently (1552); probably a noun use of LUMBER[2], v. —**lumberjack** *n.* one who cuts down trees for lumber. 1831, Canadian English. —**lumberman** *n.* (before 1817, American English) —**lumberyard** *n.* (1786, American English)

lumber[2] *v.* move heavily or clumsily. 1530, in Palsgrave's *Lesclarcissement;* developed from Middle English *lomeren* move slowly or haltingly (probably about 1380 *lomerande,* present participle); perhaps borrowed from a Scandinavian source (compare dialectal Swedish *loma* move slowly and haltingly, related to Old Icelandic *lami* LAME).

lumen (lü'mən) *n. Physics.* unit of light. 1898, borrowed from French *lumen,* from Latin *lūmen* light, opening; see LUMINOUS. The word in French was coined by the French physicist André Blondel, 1863-1938.

luminary *n.* sun, moon, or other celestial body that reflects or gives off light. Before 1449 *luminary* source of light, lamp; later *luminarye* (before 1475); borrowed from Middle French *luminarie, luminaire* lamp, light from Late Latin *lūmināre* that which gives light, light-giver; formed from Latin *lūmen* (genitive *lūminis*) light, see LUMINOUS + *-āris* (specialized neuter use of adjective suffix); for suffix see -ARY. The figurative sense of a famous or notable person, celebrity, is first recorded in 1692.

luminescence (lü′mənes′əns) *n.* emission of light occurring at a low temperature. 1896, possibly a back formation from *luminescent,* or perhaps an independent formation in English from Latin *lūminis* (genitive of *lūmen* light; see LUMINOUS) + English *-escence.* **—luminescent** *adj.* 1889, formed in English from Latin *lūminis* (genitive of *lūmen* light) + English *-escent.*

luminous *adj.* full of light, shining. Probably before 1425 *luminose,* in a translation of Higden's *Polychronicon;* later *luminouse* (1471); borrowed, perhaps by influence of Middle French *lumineux,* from Latin *lūminōsus* shining, from *lūmen* (genitive *lūminis*) light, opening, related to *lūcēre* to shine, see LIGHT[1] radiant energy; for suffix see -OUS. **—luminosity** *n.* 1634, either borrowed from French *luminosité,* from Latin *lūminōsus* luminous + French *-ité* -ity; or formed from English *luminous* + *-ity,* perhaps by influence of French *luminosité.*

lummox *n. Informal.* awkward, stupid person. Before 1825, English dialect (East Anglia), apparently related to dialectal *lummock* to move heavily or clumsily, of uncertain origin; but compare German *Lümmel* lout, from an archaic (now dialectal) adjective *lumm* limp, flabby, Middle High German *lüeme* flabby, soft, mild. The natural phonetic modification from *-ock* to *-ocks,* written *-ox* was probably influenced by association with *ox* as a heavy-moving and somewhat dull beast of burden.

lump[1] *n.* solid mass. Before 1325 *lumpe;* possibly borrowed from Dutch (compare early modern Dutch *lompe* mass, chunk, piece; related to Dutch *lomp* rag, tatter). The Dutch forms are cognate with German *Lumpen* rag, and Middle High German *lumpe* rag, *lampen* hang down; see LIMP[1], v. **—v.** put together. 1624; from the noun. **—adj.** in a lump. Before 1700; probably from the noun. **—lumpish** *adj.* 1528, stupidly dull, sluggish; later, heavy and clumsy in appearance, movement, etc. (about 1555); formed from English *lump*[1] + *-ish*[1]. **—lumpy** *adj.* 1707, full of lumps; 1708, having a heavy and clumsy appearance; formed from English *lump*[1] + *-y*[1].

lump[2] *v. Informal.* put up with, endure. 1791 (in the expression "As you like it, you may lump it"), American English, apparently extended sense of earlier meaning, to look sulky or disagreeable, dislike (1577); of uncertain origin.

lumpectomy (lumpek′təmē) *n.* surgical removal of a cancerous tumor from the breast. 1972, American English, formed from English *lump*[1] + *-ectomy,* as in *mastectomy.*

lumpenproletariat (lüm′pənprō′letãr′ēət) *n.* section of the proletariat that lacks class-consciousness. 1924, in H. Kuhn's translation of Marx's *Class Struggles in France;* borrowing of German *Lumpenproletariat,* coined in 1850 by Karl Marx from *Lumpen(volk)* rabble (from *Lumpen* rag) + *Proletariat* proletariat; see LUMP[1] mass.

lunacy *n.* insanity. 1541, formed from English *luna(tic)* + *-cy.* The sense of extreme folly is first recorded in 1588.

lunar *adj.* Probably before 1425 *lunare, lunar* crescent-shaped, in a translation of Chauliac's *Grande Chirurgie;* borrowed through Old French *lunaire,* or directly from Latin *lūnāris* of the moon, from *lūna* moon; for suffix see -AR. Latin *lūna,* earlier **leucsnā* or **loucsnā* is cognate with Middle Irish *lūan* moon or light, Old Prussian *lauxnos,* pl., stars, Old Slavic *luna* moon, Avestan *raoxšna-* shining, and Armenian *lusin* moon, *lois* LIGHT[1] radiant energy. The modern sense "of or belonging to the moon" is first recorded in Bacon's *Sylva Sylvarum* (1626).

lunate *adj.* crescent-shaped. 1777, borrowed from Latin *lūnātus* crescent-shaped, from *lūna* moon, see LUNAR; for suffix see -ATE[1].

lunatic *adj.* insane. About 1300 *lunatyke,* borrowed from Old French *lunatique* insane, from Latin *lūnāticus* moon-struck, epileptic, from *lūna* moon, see LUNAR; so called because it was originally thought that recurrent attacks of insanity were brought about by the varying phases of the moon; for suffix see -IC. The phrase *lunatic fringe* is first recorded in American English in Theodore Roosevelt's writings (1913). **—n.** insane person. About 1378 *lunatik,* in *Piers Plowman;* probably from the adjective.

lunch *n.* 1829, shortened form of LUNCHEON. **—v.** eat lunch. 1823, in Isaac D'Israeli's *Curiosities of Literature;* from the noun, though of preceding date. **—lunchroom** *n.* (1830, American English) **—lunchtime** *n.* (1859, in George Eliot's *Letters*)

luncheon *n.* 1580 *luncheon* a thick piece, hunk; later, a light meal (*lunching,* before 1652, and *luncheon,* 1706). The semantic development was probably influenced by north English *lunch* hunk of bread or cheese; the morphological development may have been by alteration of dialectal *nuncheon* light meal, developed from Middle English *nonechenche, nonschench* (1342), a compound of *none* NOON + *schench* drink, from Old English *scenc,* from *scencan* pour out. Old English *scencan* is cognate with Old Frisian *skenka* pour out, Old Saxon *skenkian,* Middle Dutch *scencen* (modern Dutch *schenken*), and Old High German *skenken* (modern German *einschenken*), from Proto-Germanic **skankjanan* draw off (liquor), formed from **skankōn* shinbone, SHANK (in Old English *scanca*), "a hollow bone. . and hence a pipe, a pipe thrust into a cask to tap it" (W.W. Skeat). **—luncheonette** *n.* 1924. American English; formed from *luncheon* + *-ette.*

lung *n.* Probably before 1300 *lunge,* in *Kyng Alisaunder;* developed from Old English *lungen,* pl. (about 1000, in Ælfric's *Glossary*). The Old English form is cognate with Old Frisian *lungen* lung, Old Saxon *lunga,* Middle Low German *lunge,* Middle Dutch *longe* (modern Dutch *long*), Old High German *lungun* (modern German *Lunge*), and Old Icelandic *lunga* (Danish and Norwegian *lunge,* Swedish *lunga*), from Proto-Germanic **lungw-.* Outside Germanic the word is cognate with Russian *lëgkoie* lung, Armenian *lanjk'* breast, from Indo-European **lengwh-/lṇgwh-* (Pok. 660) light (not heavy), the source of Russian *lëgkiĭ* light, Sanskrit *laghú-s* LIGHT[2]. The lungs were so called because of their lightness; see LIGHTS.

lunge *v.* 1735, shortened form of earlier *allonge* to thrust (1668); borrowed from French *allonger* to extend, thrust, from Old French *alongier* to lengthen, make long (*à-* to, from Latin *ad-* + Old French *long,* from Latin *longus* LONG[1], adj.). **—n.** sudden forward movement; thrust. 1748, in Smollett's *Adventures of Roderick Random;* probably from the verb *lunge;* or shortened form of earlier *allonge* (1731, in Bailey's *Dictionary*); from the English verb *allonge.*

lunk *n.* slow-witted person. 1867, American English, shortened form of earlier *lunkhead* (1852, possibly alteration of *lump*[1] solid mass + *head*).

lupine[1] (lü'pən) *n.* plant of the same family as peas and beans. 1373 *lupyne;* borrowed from Old French *lupin* or directly from Latin *lupīnus, lupīnum* a lupine (plant), from *lupīnus* of or belonging to the wolf, LUPINE[2]. The association with wolf is unknown, but is perhaps in allusion to the plant's quality of destroying or exhausting the land it grows on.

lupine[2] (lü'pin) *adj.* wolflike, fierce. 1660, borrowed from earlier French *lupine,* learned borrowing from Latin *lupīnus* of or belonging to the wolf, from Latin *lupus* WOLF; for suffix see -INE[1].

lurch[1] *n.* sudden leaning or roll to one side. 1819, in Byron's *Don Juan;* originally a nautical term, of unknown origin. It has been suggested that *lurch* was abstracted from *lee lurches* which is a variant of *lee larches* a sudden jerky roll of a ship to the leeward. The OED contends that if the original term is *lee larches* it may represent an altered pronunciation of *lee latch* in reference to keeping a ship from going leeward off her course (found in the command *'look to the lee latch', 'have a care of the lee latch'*). **—v.** lean suddenly to one side. 1833; from the noun.

lurch[2] *n.* 1584, predicament or discomfiture; later found in the phrase *leave in the lurch* (1596); probably back formation from Middle English (about 1330) *lurching* a complete victory in *lorche* a game similar to backgammon (about 1450); perhaps related to *lorchen* to skulk (before 1450) and *lurken* (about 1300), *lorken* (before 1375) to lie hidden, lie in ambush, move stealthily, LURK.

lure *n.* About 1386, attraction, enticement, in Chaucer's *Canterbury Tales,* earlier *bringen to lure* bring under control (about 1300); borrowed through Anglo-French *lure,* Old French *loirre* device used to recall hawks, lure, from Frankish (compare Middle High German *luoder* and Middle Low German *lōder* lure, bait, from Proto-Germanic **lōthran,* in modern German *Luder,* related to Old High German *ladōn* to call, invite, German *einladen* invite). Old High German *ladōn* is cognate with Old Saxon and Old English *lathian* to call or invite, Old Frisian *lathia,* Middle Dutch *laden,* Old Icelandic *ladha,* and Gothic *lathōn,* from Indo-European **lē-t-/lō-t-/lə-t-* wish (Pok. 665). **—v.** About 1378 *luren,* in a version of *Piers Plowman;* from the noun.

lurid *adj.* 1656, lighted up with a red or fiery glare, in Blount's *Glossographia;* borrowed from Latin *lūridus* pale yellow, ghastly, of uncertain origin. The figurative sense of terrible, ghastly, sensational, is first recorded in English in Charles Kingsley's *Alton Locke, Tailor and Poet* (1850).

lurk *v.* stay about without arousing attention, sneak, prowl. About 1300 *lurken* to hide or lie hidden, perhaps developed from Old English **lyrcan, *lyrcean, *lorcian,* or borrowed from a Scandinavian source (compare dialectal Norwegian and Swedish *lurka* move slowly, creep forward); see LOWER.

luscious *adj.* Before 1400 *licius* delicious; later *lucius* (about 1450); perhaps an altered back formation from DELICIOUS.

lush[1] *adj.* tender and juicy, growing thick and green. 1440 *lusch* lax or soft, in *Promptorium Parvulorum;* probably an alteration of earlier *lasche* loose or weak (1440), earlier *lacche* (before 1300, in *Kyng Alisaunder*) and in a surname *Lacheman* (1212); borrowed from Old French *lasche* soft, succulent (as young shoots), from *laschier* loosen, from Late Latin *laxicāre* become shaky, related to Latin *laxāre* loosen, from *laxus* loose, LAX[1]. The sense of succulent and luxuriant in growth is first recorded in Shakespeare's *The Tempest* (1610).

lush[2] *n. Slang.* drunkard. 1890, person who drinks too much, in Jacob Riis' *How the Other Half Lives;* earlier, liquor (1790); perhaps a humorous use of LUSH[1], in the sense of watery or juicy.

The meaning of drunkard was probably influenced by earlier *lushington* a drunkard (1840) and *lush* in this sense may even be considered a back formation from *lushington,* though other use (v., indulge in drink, 1811) and various derivatives and applications of *lush* (*lushy* drunk, 1811; *lushing* action of drinking, 1829; *lush ken* alehouse, 1790) must surely have contributed to the modern current meaning.

lust *n.* strong desire. Old English (before 725) *lust* desire, pleasure; cognate with Old Frisian and Old Saxon *lust* desire, Middle Dutch and modern Dutch *lust,* Old High German *lust* (modern German *Lust*), Old Icelandic *losti* (Middle Swedish *luste, loste,* Danish *lyst,* possibly borrowed from Low German), and Gothic *lustus,* from Proto-Germanic **lustús.* Cognates outside Germanic are found in Old Irish *lainn* greedy, Latin *lascīvus* wanton, Greek *lilaíesthai* to desire, Lithuanian *lokšnùs* tender, loving, Russian *lásyĭ* fond of (sweets), and perhaps Sanskrit *láṣati* (he) desires, from Indo-European **las-/les-* be greedy, wanton (Pok. 654).

The sense of physical desire, bodily appetite, appeared in Old English before 1000, and that of sexual desire, passion, is first recorded about 1000.

—v. About 1175 *lusten* to desire, from the noun.

—lustful *adj.* Old English (before 900) *lustfull* having a strong or excessive desire (*lust* + *-full* -ful). The meaning of sensuous is first recorded in *Ayenbite of Inwyt* (about 1340).

luster *n.* bright shine. About 1522 *lustre,* in Sir Thomas More's *Treatise Upon These Words of Holy Scripture;* borrowed from Middle French *lustre,* from Italian *lustro* splendor, brilliancy, luster, from *lustrare* illuminate, from Latin *lūstrāre* spread light over, brighten, related to *lūcēre* shine; see LIGHT[1] radiant energy. The figurative sense of fame, glory, brilliance, is first recorded in English about 1555. **—v.** put a luster or gloss on. 1582, in Stanyhurst's translation of Vergil's *Aeneid;* borrowed from Latin *lūstrāre* brighten, or verb use of English *luster,* n. **—lustrous** *adj.* 1601, in Shakespeare's *All's Well That Ends Well;* formed from English *lustre* + *-ous.*

lustral *adj.* of or used in ceremonial purification. 1533, borrowed from Middle French *lustral,* and directly from Latin *lūstrālis,* from *lūstrum,* a quinquennial ceremony of purification; of uncertain origin, but possibly related to *lūstrāre* spread light over, brighten; see LUSTER; for suffix see -AL[1].

lusty *adj.* healthy, vigorous. Probably about 1200 *lusty* merry, cheerful, lively; later, healthy, strong, vigorous (about 1387-95, in Chaucer's *Prologue* to the *Canterbury Tales*); formed from Middle English *lust* vigor, energy, disposition, happiness (in Old English, desire, pleasure; see LUST) + *-y*[1] (adjective suffix), perhaps by influence of Middle Dutch *lustich* merry, cheerful. Middle Dutch *lustich* and probably Middle English *lusty* are cognate with Middle High German *lustic* (modern German *lustig* merry), and Old Icelandic *lostigr* willing.

lute *n.* stringed musical instrument. 1295, borrowed from Old French *lut, leüt,* from Old Provençal *laüt,* from Arabic *al-'ūd* the oud (Arabian lute), formed from *al* the + *'ud* oud; literally, wood.

lutein (lü'tēin) *n.* yellow pigment obtained from egg yolks and certain hormones. 1869, formed in English from Latin *lūteum* egg yolk (from neuter of *lūteus* yellow, from *lūtum* yellow weed) + English *-in*[2].

lutetium (lütē'shēəm) *n.* metallic chemical element. 1911, New Latin, from Latin *Lutetia* Paris (the name of an ancient town on the site of modern Paris) + New Latin *-ium* (chemical suffix). The word was coined in 1907 by the French chemist Georges Urbain, 1872-1938.

lutz (lu̇tz) *n.* jump in figure skating. 1938, probably alteration of the name of Gustave *Lussi,* 20th-century Swiss figure skater, who invented the jump.

lux (luks) *n.* unit of illumination. 1889, borrowed from Latin *lūx* LIGHT[1] radiant energy.

luxuriant *adj.* growing thick and green. About 1540, prolific, producing abundantly; borrowed possibly from Middle French *luxuriant* (used specifically of vegetation), or directly from Latin *luxuriantem* (nominative *luxuriāns*), present participle of *luxuriāre* have to excess, grow profusely, LUXURIATE; for suffix see -ANT. The sense of growing abundantly, lush, is first recorded in 1661. **—luxuriance** *n.* 1728-46, formed from English *luxuriant;* for suffix see -ANCE.

luxuriate *v.* indulge in luxury. 1621, in Burton's *Anatomy of Melancholy;* borrowed perhaps by influence of French *luxurier* indulge in lustful pursuits, from Latin *luxuriātum,* past participle of *luxuriāre* indulge or have to excess, from *luxuria* excess, LUXURY; for suffix see -ATE[1].

luxury *n.* comforts of life beyond what is really necessary. 1340 *luxurie* lust, lasciviousness, in *Ayenbite of Inwyt,* borrowed from Old French *luxurie,* from Latin *luxuria* excess, luxury, from *luxus* (genitive *luxūs*) excess, extravagance, magnificence, related to *luxus,* adj., dislocated, and *luctārī* dislocate, sprain; see LOCK[2] tress; for suffix see -Y[3].

The sense of indulgence in what is choice or costly is first recorded in 1633, and that of something giving comfort or pleasure but not really necessary in 1780 in Bentham's writings, and possibly in 1704 in Addison's writings.

—luxurious *adj.* Probably before 1300 *luxsorius* lustful, lascivious, in *Arthour and Merlin;* borrowing of Anglo-French *luxurious,* Old French *luxurios,* from Latin *luxuriōsus,* from *luxuria* luxury; for suffix see -OUS. The sense of given to luxury, self-indulgent, is first recorded in 1606.

-ly[1] a suffix forming adverbs, chiefly from adjectives, and meaning: **1** in a _____ manner, as in *cheerfully, warmly.* **2** in _____ ways or respects, as in *financially.* **3** to a _____ degree, as in *greatly.* **4** in, to, or from a _____ direction, as in *northwardly.* **5** in the _____ place, as in *thirdly.* **6** at a _____ time, as in *recently.* Middle English *-ly, -li* (the common form by the 1400's), shortening (influenced by Scandinavian *-liga*) of earlier *-liche, -like,* developed from Old English *-līce* (derived from the adjective suffix *-līc* -LY[2]).

In Old English most adverbs were formed on an adjective in *-lic* (except for *bealdlīce* boldly, *swētlīce* sweetly, and a few others formed directly on the simple adjective), but as the sound represented by -e in *-liche* and *-like* was gradually lost in Middle English, it became the practice to attach *-ly, -li* to an adjective without the intervening adjective suffix, though some are still found into the 1600's, such as *earlily, lovelily,* but are now considered ungraceful, except for an occasional use of *friendlily.* A curious formation also exists in *partly* which is formed of a noun + *-ly.*

Other adjectives that form adverbs in *-ly* undergo contraction. This group ending in *-le* (double, simple) includes *doubly, simply,* and though some are found in an uncontracted form as late as the 1600's, the process of contraction was already established in the 1300's. Another form of contraction (but only graphically) is the loss of *l* in words that end in *-ll,* such as *full,* which becomes *ful-* + *-ly* when written.

-ly[2] a suffix forming adjectives and meaning: **1** like a _____, as in *ghostly.* **2** like that of a _____, as in *brotherly.* **3** suited to a _____, as in *womanly.* **4** of each or every _____, as in *daily.* **5** that is a _____, as in *heavenly.* Middle English *-ly, -li* (the universal form by the 1400's, but found commonly in the 1300's), shortening (influenced by Scandinavian *-lig-*) of earlier *-lich, -lik;* developed from Old English *-līc;* cognate with Old Frisian and Old Saxon *-līk* -ly, Middle Dutch *-lijc,* Old High German *-līh, -lih* (modern German *-lich*), Old Icelandic *-ligr,* and Gothic *-leiks;* derived from the Proto-Germanic root that is the source of Old English *līc* body; see LIKE[1] similar. See also the etymologies of SUCH, WHICH.

The process of shortening forms was a characteristic of Old and Middle English, but the reduction of *-līc* to *-li* was particularly accelerated by frequency of use of the suffix which as a consequence lost its secondary accent and thereby had a shortening of the vowel and loss of the final consonantal sound.

The suffix is one of widest use in English, and in it and all other Germanic languages is applied to nouns and adjectives with the sense of having the qualities of. Other senses in Germanic include that of having to do with, of or pertaining to. Curiously, this sense in English has not been sustained in *-ly,* and words such as *manly* are no longer used to mean "belonging to human beings," instead being replaced by *human.*

lyceum (līsē'əm *or* lī'sēəm) *n.* lecture hall. 1579-80, in North's translation of Plutarch's *Lives;* borrowing of Latin *Lycēum,* a grove near Athens, where Aristotle taught, from Greek *Lýkeion,* from neuter of *Lýkeios* "Wolf-slayer," an epithet of Apollo, whose temple was near the Lyceum. Compare the etymology of ACADEMY.

lye *n.* strong alkaline solution. Before 1300 *leihe;* later *lie* (before 1400); developed from Old English (about 700) *lǣg, lēag;* cognate with Middle Dutch *lōghe* lye (modern Dutch *loog*), Old High German *louga* (modern German *Lauge*), Old Icelandic *laug* bath, hot spring, from Proto-Germanic **lauʒṓ,* Indo-European **lou-k-ā́,* the latter found in Gaulish *lautro* bath, Old

Irish *loathar* basin, Middle Breton *louazr* trough, and Armenian *loganam* I wash, bathe; see LAVE.

lymph *n.* 1725, nearly colorless liquid in the tissues of the body; earlier, water (before 1630); borrowed from French *lymphe* and New Latin *lympha,* both from Latin *lympha* water, clear water, variant of *lumpae* waters, borrowed from Greek *nýmphē* goddess of a spring, NYMPH.
—**lymphatic** *adj.* 1649, of the lymph, in Evelyn's *Memoirs;* borrowed from French *lymphatique* and from Medieval Latin *lymphaticus* of water, from Latin *lympha* water; for suffix see -IC. —**lymph gland** (1856-58) —**lymphocyte** (lim′fəsīt) *n.* cell found in lymph. 1890, formed from English *lympho-,* combining form of *lymph* + *-cyte* cell. —**lymphoid** *adj.* resembling lymph. 1867, formed from English *lymph* + *-oid.* —**lymphoma** *n.* tumor of the lymphatic tissue. 1873, New Latin, formed from *lympha* lymph + *-oma.*

lynch *v.* put to death without a lawful trial. 1835 *Lynch,* American English; also, *lynch* (1839), to punish an accused person without a lawful trial; shortened form of earlier *Lynch law* practice of punishing an accused person without a lawful trial (1811, in allusion to William *Lynch,* 1742-1820, of Virginia, who in 1780 with his neighbors established a vigilance committee to maintain order and punish criminals in their community).

Originally the term chiefly implied forms of punishment such as whipping, tarring and feathering, or the like, but since the late 1800's, it has meant only to inflict sentence of death without a lawful trial.

lynx *n.* wildcat of the Northern Hemisphere. 1340, in *Ayenbite of Inwyt;* borrowing of Latin *lynx,* from Greek *lýnx.* The Greek word is cognate with Lithuanian *lūšis* lynx, Old Prussian *luysis,* Armenian *lusanunk',* pl., lynxes. Germanic cognates exist in Old High German *luhs* lynx (modern German *Luchs*), Middle Dutch and modern Dutch *los,* Old Saxon *lohs,* and Old English *lox* lynx (the word apparently did not survive into Middle English). These words are cognate with Sanskrit *rúśant-* white, light, related to *rócate* (it) shines, from Indo-European **leuḱ-/luḱ-* beside **leuk-/luk-* (Pok. 690); see LIGHT[1] radiant energy. The lynx probably derives its name from its shining eyes.

lyonnaise (lī′ənāz′) *adj.* fried with pieces of onion. 1846, from French *lyonnaise* (as used in *à la mode lyonnaise* in the manner of Lyons), feminine of *lyonnais* of or from *Lyon,* city in southeastern France.

lyre (līr) *n.* ancient stringed musical instrument somewhat like a small harp. Probably before 1200 *lire,* in Layamon's *Chronicle of Britain;* borrowed through Old French *lire, lyre,* and directly from Latin *lyra,* from Greek *lýrā;* of uncertain origin.

lyric *adj.* characterized by expression of feeling. 1589, in Puttenham's *The Art of English Poesie;* borrowed through Middle French *lyrique,* and directly from Latin *lyricus* of or for the lyre, from Greek *lyrikós,* from *lýrā* LYRE; for suffix see -IC.
—**n.** 1581, short poem expressing personal emotion; borrowed through Middle French *lyrique,* from Latin *lyricum* a lyric poem, from neuter of *lyricus,* adj. The sense of words for a song is first recorded in 1876, now used chiefly in the plural, *lyrics,* from its original sense of verses in lyric meter.
—**lyrical** *adj.* 1581, of lyric poetry, in Sidney's *Apology for Poetry;* formed from English *lyric,* n. + *-al*[1]. —**lyricism** *n.* lyric character or style. 1760, formed from English *lyric* + *-ism.* —**lyricist** *n.* writer of lyrics. 1881, formed from English *lyric* + *-ist.*

lyse (līs) *v.* bring about the dissolution of cells, bacteria, etc. 1922, back formation from LYSIS.

lysis (lī′sis) *n.* dissolution of cells, bacteria, etc. 1902, borrowed from Latin *lysis,* from Greek *lýsis* dissolution, from *lýein* untie; see LOSE.

lysozyme (lī′səszīm) *n.* enzymelike substance capable of destroying certain bacteria. 1922, a compound of Greek *lýsis* dissolution, LYSIS and English *(en)zyme.*

M

macabre *adj.* 1833, in *The Dance of Macabre;* earlier *the dance of Machabray* (1598, in John Stow's *Survey of London*), and *The Daunce of Machabree* (probably about 1430, in Lydgate's translation of an Old French poem *Danse Macabré,* of which it has been suggested that Lydgate mistook *Macabré* as the name of the French author). However, Lydgate's use of the form *Machabree* suggests a connection with *Maccabee* and also a familiarity with the Middle French *danse Macabré* which was probably a translation of Medieval Latin *chorea Macchabeorum,* literally, the dance of the Maccabees (leaders of the revolt of the Jews against Syria, about 166 B.C.).

The allegorical representation of Death leading mankind in a dance to the grave is first found in English literary and artistic works (Stow's *Survey* and especially Holbein's "Dance of Death") perhaps as an allusion to the vivid description of the martyrdom of the Maccabees in the Apocryphal books of the Maccabees, especially II Maccabees 7. From this representation characterizing the gruesome descriptions of the *danse macabre* modern English abstracted the sense of gruesome, horrible (1889), probably by influence of French *macabre* gruesome (1842).

macadam (məkad′əm) *n.* kind of paving material or pavement. 1824, in allusion to its inventor, John L. *McAdam,* 1756-1836, a Scottish civil engineer. Compare the related entry TARMAC. **—macadamize** *v.* 1826, formed from English *macadam* + *-ize.*

macaque (məkäk′) *n.* kind of monkey of Asia and Africa (genus *Macacus*). 1840, borrowing of French *macaque,* from Portuguese *macaco* monkey, from a Bantu word used in the Congo (probably Angola) and brought by the Portuguese to Brazil; *ma-* is a Bantu prefix.

Originally *macaque* was applied to some Brazilian species of monkey (1698). The later meaning of a monkey of the genus *Macacus* came from the French naturalist Cuvier, 1769-1832, and was introduced into English in 1840 in a translation of Cuvier's *Animal Kingdom* (1817).

macaroni *n.* **1** kind of pasta in the form of hollow tubes. 1599, in Ben Jonson's *Cynthia's Revels;* borrowed from southern Italian dialect *maccaroni* (Italian *maccheroni*) macaroni, originally a mixture of flour, cheese, and butter, plural of *maccarone;* possibly from *maccare* bruise, batter, crush; and perhaps ultimately from Late Greek *makaríā* a barley broth, of uncertain origin.

2 fop, dandy. 1764, in Walpole's *Letters,* in allusion to members of the *Macaroni Club,* who affected French and Italian fashion in dress, mannerisms, and food (macaroni was considered an exotic dish in England at the time). An earlier use by Addison in an issue of *The Spectator* (1711) in the sense of blockhead, fool, is probably not connected with this sense of fop, dandy.

macaronic *adj.* 1611, mixed or jumbled; later, denoting a burlesque form of verse with a mixture of native and foreign words, usually Latin words with words from another language, or with non-Latin words that are given Latin endings (1638); borrowed from New Latin *macaronicus,* from dialectal Italian *maccarone* MACARONI. The word was popularized by the satiric Mantuan poet Teofilo Folengo, 1491-1544, in his poem *Liber Macaronicus* (1517), in which he explains that the poem's coarse, rustic mixture of words is comparable to macaroni, hence "macaronic verse." An earlier use in Italian is found in Tifi degli Odasi's *Carmen Macaronicum* (before 1488).

macaroon *n.* small sweet cookie. 1611, borrowed from French *macaron,* from dialectal Italian *maccarone,* singular of *maccaroni* MACARONI; for ending see -OON. The French meaning was apparently an invention of Rabelais, who introduced the word in 1552.

macaw (məkô′) *n.* kind of large parrot. 1668, borrowed from Portuguese *macau,* from a Brazilian name (perhaps from Tupi *macavuana*).

mace[1] *n.* medieval weapon of war, formed of a club, often with a spiked head. Probably before 1300, in *Arthour and Merlin;* earlier as a surname (1229); borrowed from Old French *mace* a club, scepter, from Vulgar Latin **mattea,* from Latin *mateola* (in Late Latin also *matteola*) a kind of mallet. The Latin *mateola* is cognate with Sanskrit *matyá-m* harrow, and Old High German *medela* plow, from Indo-European **mat-* pick-ax, mattock (Pok.700). Related to MATTOCK.

mace[2] *n.* spice made from nutmegs. Probably before 1300, in *Kyng Alisaunder;* back formation as a new singular form from earlier *maces* (1234), and *macis* (1381); borrowed from Old French *mace, macis,* mistaken to be a plural form; or borrowed directly from Medieval Latin *macis.* The Medieval Latin form was apparently a scribal error for Latin *macir* a red spicy bark from India, from Greek *mákir* a fragrant resin of a species of ailanthus, of unknown origin.

Mace *n.* trademark of a tear gas spray. 1966, American English, acronym for the chemical compound *M(ethylchloroform) (chloro)ace(tophenone);* originally patented as *Chemical Mace,* probably in allusion to *mace*[1] the weapon. Also spelled **mace**[3]. **—v.** Usually spelled **mace.** to attack or disable with Mace. 1967, American English; from the noun.

macerate (mas′ərāt) *v.* soften by soaking for some time. 1547, cause to waste away, in Andrew Boorde's *Breviary of Health;* either developed from earlier *macerate* wasted, weakened (1540), from Latin *mācerātus;* borrowed, perhaps through influence of Middle French *macérer,* from Latin *mācerātus,* past participle of *mācerāre* soften, related to *māceria* garden wall (originally of kneaded clay), cognate with Lettish *màkt* to press, worry, from Indo-European **māk-* knead, squeeze (Pok. 698); for suffix see -ATE[1]. Alternatively *macerate* may be, in some instances, a back formation from earlier *maceration* (1491); borrowed from Latin *mācerātiōnem* (nominative *mācerātiō*), from *mācerāre;*

for suffix see -ATION. The meaning of soften by soaking is first recorded in 1563.

machete (məshet'ē) *n.* large heavy knife. 1832, American English, borrowing of Spanish *machete,* probably diminutive of *macho* sledge hammer, alteration of *mazo* club, probably dialectal variant of *maza* mallet, from Vulgar Latin **mattea* war club, MACE[1].

Machiavellian (mak'ēəvel'ēən) *adj.* 1579 (earlier as a noun, 1568; and in the form *Machiavel* one who acts on the principles of Machiavelli, 1570); from *Machiavellian,* n., or formed from *Machiavelli,* 1469-1527, Florentine statesman who advised rulers to place advantage above morality, + *-an, -ian.*

machicolation (məchik'əlā'shən) *n.* opening in the floor of a projecting gallery or parapet of a castle or other fortified structure through which missiles, hot liquid, etc., might be thrown upon attackers. 1788, in Grose's *Military Antiquities;* borrowed from Medieval Latin *machicolationem* (nominative *machicolatio*) from *machicolare* furnish with openings; for suffix see -ATION. Medieval Latin *machicolare* is a Latinization of Old French *machicouler,* ultimately from Old Provençal *machacol* machicolation, a southern dialect variant of **macacol;* literally, neck crusher (*macar* to crush, from Vulgar Latin **maccāre* crush + *col* neck, from Latin *collum;* see COLLAR).

This family of words (*machicolate, machicolate, machicoulis*) seems to have come into use only in the late 1700's; even *machicoulis,* a borrowing from French *mâchecoulis* (from Medieval Latin *machicoulis,* curiously identical with the form in English, which suggests an earlier unrecorded direct borrowing) is not recorded before 1779. However, a connection may be found in the earlier recorded past participle *machekolud* machicolated, having openings in a parapet (1408, a variant form of *machecolled,* from *machecole,* probably borrowed from Old French *machecoller,* and directly from Medieval Latin *machecollare* provide with machicolation).

machination *n.* Before 1475 *machynacion* intrigue, fraud, trick; borrowed through Old French *machinacioun,* and directly from Latin *māchinātiōnem* (nominative *māchinātiō*) device, contrivance, machination, from *māchinārī* contrive, plot, from *māchina* MACHINE; for suffix see -ATION.

machine *n.* 1549, any structure or contrivance; borrowed from Middle French *machine* device, contrivance, learned borrowing from Latin *māchina,* from Greek *māchanā́,* Doric variant of *mēchanḗ* device, means; related to *mêchos* means, expedient; see MAY. The usual sense today of an apparatus for applying mechanical power to do work, is first recorded in 1673. An earlier noun form is found in *machinament* (1413, borrowed from Latin *māchināmentum,* from *māchinārī* to contrive, plot) and is attested as late as 1727 in Bailey's *Dictionary,* but became obsolete thereafter. **—v.** make with a machine. 1878, from the noun. An earlier form is found in *machynen* decide a course of action, contrive, plot (probably about 1450) borrowed from Old French *machiner,* and directly from Latin *māchinārī* to contrive, plot. **—machine gun** (1870, American English) **—machine-gun** *v.* (1915) **—machinery** *n.* 1687, devices for creating stage effects, formed from English *machine* + *-ery.* **—machinist** *n.* 1706, an engineer; later, person who works a machine (1879); borrowed from French *machiniste,* from *machine* + *-iste* -ist, and formed in English from *machine* + *-ist.*

machismo (mächēs'mō) *n.* masculine drive, virility. 1948, American English; borrowed through American Spanish *machismo,* from Spanish *macho* male, MACHO.

macho (mä'chō) *n. adj.* (virile) male. 1928, American English; borrowed from Spanish *macho,* literally, male, from Latin *masculus* MASCULINE. Corominas rejects derivation of the Spanish form from Portuguese *macho,* saying the often-cited Spanish *maslo* is only a variant of native *macho.*

mackerel *n.* kind of saltwater fish. About 1300 *makerel;* earlier, as a surname (1183); borrowed from Old French *makerel, maquerel;* of uncertain origin. Though apparently the same word as Old French *maquerel* pimp or procurer, from a Germanic source (compare Middle Dutch *makelaer* broker) and in spite of the many attempts to make a semantic connection between the two (especially because the sense "pimp" is also found in Middle English for this word, probably before 1430), it is difficult to accept such theories.

mackinaw (mak'ənô) *n.* a word with the original form *Mackinac* found in various combinations: *Mackinac blanket* made of heavy woolen cloth (1822), later *Mackinaw* (1836); *Mackinaw boat* (1833), earlier *Mackina* (1812); *Mackinaw jacket* short coat made of heavy woolen cloth (1906), earlier *mackinaw* (1902); American and Canadian English, from earlier *Mackinac* name of a trading post on the site of what is now Mackinaw City, Michigan; borrowed from Canadian French *michili-mackinac,* from Algonquian (Ojibwa) *mitchi makinâk* large turtle.

mackintosh (mak'əntosh) *n.* waterproof raincoat. 1836, in allusion to Charles *Macintosh,* 1766-1843, inventor of a waterproofing process.

macro- a combining form meaning large or long, especially in scientific and technical terms, such as *macrocephalic* having an abnormally large head and in some general terms with the sense of on a large scale, from early use in *macrocosm.* Borrowed through Middle and Old French and from Medieval Latin, from Greek *makro-,* combining form of *makrós* large, long; see MEAGER. Compare MEGA-.

macrocosm (mak'rəkozəm) *n.* the universe. 1600; borrowed from French *macrocosme,* learned borrowing from Medieval Latin *macrocosmus,* and borrowed directly from Medieval Latin, a compound of Greek *makrós* large, long (see MEAGER) + *kósmos* COSMOS, probably formed in distinction to *microcosm.* The Medieval Latin *macrocosmus* is found in a translation of Higden's *Polychronicon* (about 1400), and as English *macrocosm* in Lydgate's *Reson and Sensuallyte* (probably before 1408).

macron (mā'kron) *n.* horizontal line placed over a vowel to show that it is pronounced as a so-called long vowel. 1851, borrowed from Greek *makrón,* neuter of *makrós* long; see MEAGER.

mad *adj.* About 1275 *madde* crazy, angry; later *mad* (about 1300); developed from Old English (before 1000) *gemǣdde,* pl.; earlier *gemǣded* rendered insane (before 800), past participle of **gemǣdan* make mad, from *gemād* mad. Old English *gemād* is cognate with Old Saxon *gimēd* foolish, Old High German *gimeit* foolish, vain, and Gothic *gamaidans* (accusative plural) crippled (from Proto-Germanic **ʒa-maiđaz,* compound of *ʒa-* perfective prefix + **maiđás*), corresponding to Old Icelandic *meida* to hurt. Possible cognates outside Germanic are Latvian *màitât* to spoil, destroy, Latin *mūtāre* to change, and Sanskrit *méthati* (he) comes to blows, from Indo-European **meit(h)-/moit(h)-* (Pok.715). **—madcap** *adj.* wildly impulsive, reckless. (1588, in Shakespeare's *Love's Labour's Lost*) **—madden** *v.* 1735, in Pope's *Prologue to Satires;* formed from English *mad* + *-en*[1]. During the 1700's *madden* replaced earlier *mad* v., developed from Middle English *madden* to drive mad (about 1395), to become insane (probably about 1380), from earlier *medden* (before 1325); from *mad,* adj. **—maddening** *adj.* annoying, irritating. Before 1743, from *madden,* v. **—madding** *adj.* acting as if mad, frenzied. 1579, in Spenser's *The Shepheardes Calender,* from *mad,* v. + *-ing*[2]. **—madhouse** *n.* (1687) **—madman** *n.* (about 1330) **—madness** *n.* (before 1398) **—madwoman** *n.* (before 1438)

madam (mad′əm) *n.* polite title for a lady. Probably before 1300 *madame,* borrowed from Old French *ma dame* my lady (*ma* my, from Latin *mea; dame* lady, from Late Latin *domna,* from Latin *domina* mistress of the house, from *domus* house; see DOME). The sense of a woman who is a prostitute or who runs a brothel, is first recorded in 1719.

madame (mad′əm *or* French mȧdȧm′) *n.* French title for a married woman. 1599, in Shakespeare's *Henry V;* see MADAM.

madder *n.* plant whose root is used to make dye. Probably before 1300 *madere;* later *madder* (1347-48); in part developed from Old English (about 1000) *mædere* plant used for making dyes; and in part borrowed from a Scandinavian source (compare Old Icelandic *madhra*). The Old English and Old Icelandic forms and Old High German *matara* (from Proto-Germanic **mađr-*), are cognate with Old Slavic **modrŭ* blue (represented, for example, by Czech *modrý*), from Indo-European **modhro-* or **madhro-* (Pok.747).

Madeira *n.* a fine sherry wine. 1584 *Madera,* shortened form of *Madeira* or *Madeira wine,* in allusion to the island of *Madeira,* from Portuguese *madeira* wood, from Latin *māteria* wood, matter; see MATTER.

mademoiselle (mad′əməzel′) *n.* French title for an unmarried woman. 1642, in Milton's *Works;* see DAMSEL. An isolated example of this word is recorded in Middle English, probably about 1450, in *The Book of the Knight of La Tour-Landry.*

Madonna (mədon′ə) *n.* 1644, in Evelyn's *Diary,* in reference to a wall painting of the Virgin Mary; earlier, Italian form of address for a lady (1584); Mary; borrowing of Italian *madonna (ma* my, weakly stressed variant of *mia,* from Latin *mea* + *donna* lady, from Late Latin *domna,* from Latin *domina* mistress of the house, from *domus* house; see DOME).

madras (mad′rəs) *n.* 1882 *Madras-net muslin* closely woven cotton cloth, and earlier *Madras handkerchief* brightly-colored handkerchief of silk and cotton (1833); in allusion to the former state of *Madras* (now Tamil Nadu) in southeastern India, and its capital *Madras,* where this type of cloth was exported.

madrigal (mad′rəgəl) *n.* 1588 *madrigales* short lyrical poem, song with parts for several voices; borrowing of Italian *madrigale,* probably from dialectal Italian (Venice) *madregal, maregal* simple, ingenuous, from Late Latin *mātrīcālis* invented, original, of or from the womb, from *mātrīx* (genitive *mātrīcis*) womb; see MATRIX.

Connection with Italian *mandra* herd, flock, from Latin *mandra* stall, herd, from Greek *mándra* a fold, enclosed space, though traditionally cited is difficult to maintain both in sense and form.

maelstrom (māl′strəm) *n.* great or violent whirlpool of water. 1701 *Maelstrom,* whirlpool near the Lofoten Islands off the northwestern coast of Norway (recorded in English in 1682 as *Male Stream,* and about 1560 as *Malestrand*); borrowed from Danish *Malstrøm,* from earlier Dutch *Maelstrom* (now *Maalstroom,* a compound of *malen,* see MEAL[2] to grind + *stroom* STREAM).

The generalized sense of any great or violent whirlpool was popularized by Poe's *A Descent into the Maelstrom* (about 1841), which describes the ordeal of two Norwegian fishermen drawn into a maelstrom during a violent storm.

The figurative sense of a violent confusion of ideas, conditions, etc., is first recorded in English in Carlyle's *Sartor Resartus* (1831).

maenad (mē′nad) *n.* woman attendant of Bacchus. 1579, in Spenser's *The Shepheardes Calender;* borrowed from Latin *maenas* (genitive *maenadis*) from Greek *mainás* (genitive *mainádos*) priestess of Bacchus; literally, madwoman, from *maínesthai* to rage, go mad; see MANIA.

maestro (mīs′trō) *n.* master of an art, especially a great musician or composer. 1724, borrowing of Italian *maestro* master, from Latin *magistrum,* accusative of *magister* MASTER.

Mae West (mā′ west′) inflatable vest worn as a life preserver. 1940, American English, named after *Mae West,* 1892-1980, an American actress; so called from a whimsical comparison of the inflated vest to her celebrated bust size.

Mafia (mä′fēə) *n.* secret society of criminals, according to the DAE, introduced into the US about 1860. 1875, borrowing of Italian *Mafia* secret society of criminals in Sicily, from dialectal Italian (Sicily) *mafia* boldness, bravado, probably from Arabic *maḥjaṣ* aggressive boasting, bragging.

The transferred sense of any exclusive set or clique (as in *the academic Mafia,* the *Labor Party Mafia*) is first recorded about 1967. **—Mafioso** (mä′fēō′sō) *n., pl.* **-si** (-sē). member of the Mafia. 1875, borrowing of Italian *mafioso,* from *Mafia* Mafia.

magazine *n.* 1583 *magosine;* also 1589 *magasin* warehouse, depot, store; borrowed from Middle French *magasin,* from Italian *magazzino,* from Arabic *makhāzin,* plural of *makhzan* storehouse, from *khazana* to store up.

The spelling *magazine* is first recorded in English in 1599, and appeared in 1639 in the title of a book (in the sense of a storehouse of information on a particular subject). Its first use in the title of a periodical is recorded in 1731, though first reference to the sense of a periodic publication is found in Pope's *The Dunciad* (1742).

The sense of a storehouse specifically for ammunition, gunpowder, etc., appears in Spenser's *View of Ireland* (1596), and that of chamber for bullets or cartridges, in 1744.

magenta (məjen′tə) *n.* purplish-red dye. 1860, named in allusion to the Battle of *Magenta,* Italy, 1859, because the dye was discovered in that year. **—adj.** purplish-red. 1875; from the noun.

maggot *n.* insect in the wormlike stage. Probably before 1475 *magat,* and *magot* (before 1500); perhaps related to earlier *mathek* maggot (about 1225), and *maddokk* earthworm, maggot (before 1400); possibly developed from Old English *matha* maggot, grub, with a Proto-Germanic suffix in *-k-*, as represented in Middle English suffix *-ok*, as in *hillock, bullock.*

The Middle English *mathek* corresponds to Old Icelandic *madhkr* maggot and Middle Low German *medeke;* Old English *matha* is cognate with Gothic *matha,* Old Saxon *matho,* Old High German *mado* (modern German *Made*), Middle Dutch and modern Dutch *made,* all meaning maggot, from Proto-Germanic **mathōn,* cognate with Armenian *mat'il* louse, from Indo-European **math-* or **moth-* gnawing or biting vermin (Pok.700).

Magi (mā'jī *or* maj'ī) *n.pl.* the Three Wise Men who followed the star to Bethlehem and brought gifts to the infant Jesus. Probably about 1200 *magy* men skilled in magic and astrology, in *The Ormulum;* later *mages* (before 1350); borrowing of Latin *magī,* plural of *magus,* from Greek *mágos,* either: one of the Magi or Magians (a Median tribe); or one of the members of the Persian learned and priestly caste who were in charge of sacred rites, interpretation of dreams, etc., though also portrayed as pagan kings in the Bible, in a tradition as old as the second century; see MAGIC.

magic *n.* About 1380 *magik,* in Chaucer's *House of Fame;* borrowed from Old French *magique,* from Latin *magicē* sorcery, magic, from Greek *magikḗ,* from feminine of *magikós* magical (presumably used to modify *tekhnḗ* art), from *mágos* one of the members of the learned and priestly caste who were in charge of sacred rites, interpretation of dreams, etc., from Old Persian *maguš* a member of a priestly caste, said by ancient historians to have been originally a Median tribe. **—adj.** Before 1393 *magique,* in Gower's *Confessio Amantis;* borrowed from Old French *magique,* from Latin *magicus,* from Greek *magikós* magical; see MAGIC. **—magical** *adj.* 1555, formed from English *magic,* n. + *-al*[1]. **—magician** *n.* About 1375 *magicien* sorcerer, in Chaucer's *Canterbury Tales;* borrowed from Old French *magicien,* from *magique* magic.

magisterial (maj'əstir'ēəl) *adj.* invested with or assuming authority, authoritative, imperious. 1632, borrowed from Late Latin *magisteriālis* of or pertaining to the office of magistrate, director, teacher; of or pertaining to teaching, from *magisterius* having the authority of a magistrate, director, teacher, magisterial, from Latin *magister* MASTER; for suffix see -AL[1].

Old French *magisterial* is recorded about 1260 (FEW VI, part 1, p. 43a), but since the English form is first recorded almost 400 years later, it is very unlikely that the French word served as the source of *magisterial.*

magistrate (maj'əstrāt) *n.* public official with the power to administer the law. About 1380, *magistrat* office of a magistrate, in Chaucer's translation of Boethius' *De Consolatione Philosophiae;* 1384, a civil official, magistrate, in the Wycliffe Bible; borrowed, perhaps through Old French *magistrat,* from Latin *magistrātus* (genitive *magistrātūs*) a magistrate; originally, magisterial rank or office, from *magistrāre* serve as a magistrate, from *magister* chief, director, MASTER; for suffix see -ATE[3].

magma (mag'mə) *n.* molten material beneath the earth's crust. Probably 1440, sediment or dregs; borrowed from Latin *magma* dregs of an ointment, from Greek *mágma* an ointment; related to *mássein* to knead, mold; see MINGLE. The meaning of molten material beneath the earth's crust, is first recorded in 1865. **—magmatic** *adj.* of or pertaining to magma. 1890, in the *Century Dictionary;* formed in English from Latin *magma* (genitive *magmatis*) + English *-ic.*

magnanimous *adj.* noble, generous. 1584, possibly a back formation from *magnanimity* + *-ous;* or more likely borrowed (probably by influence of *magnanimity*) from Latin *magnanimus* high-minded (*magnus* great, see MUCH + *animus* mind, soul, spirit, see ANIMAL); for suffix see -OUS.

Latin *magnanimus* is probably a loan translation of Greek *megalópsȳchos* high-souled, generous, or *megáthȳmos* great-hearted. **—magnanimity** *n.* 1340 *magnanimite* high-mindedness, in *Ayenbite of Inwyt;* borrowed from Old French *magnanimité,* learned borrowing from Latin *magnanimitātem* (nominative *magnanimitās*) greatness of soul or loftiness of mind, from *magnanimus* having a great soul or lofty mind, high-minded; for suffix see -ITY.

magnate *n.* important or powerful person. Probably before 1439 *magnates,* pl., in Lydgate's *Falls of Princes;* borrowed from Late Latin *magnātēs,* plural of *magnās* (genitive *magnātis*) great person, nobleman, from Latin *magnus* great; see MUCH.

Possibly the word was borrowed in Middle English through Church Latin. In Ecclesiasticus 33:18 (the Apocrypha) the Latin reads: *Audite me, magnates* (Hear me, O ye great men).

magnesia (magnē'zhə) *n.* magnesium oxide, a white tasteless powder, used as a laxative. About 1395 *magnasia* mineral ingredient of the philosophers' stone, in Chaucer's *Canterbury Tales;* borrowed from Medieval Latin *magnesia,* from Greek *(hē) Magnēsíā (líthos)* the lodestone; literally, the Magnesian stone, from *Magnēsíā* Magnesia, a region in Thessaly. The meaning of magnesium oxide appeared in chemistry in the 1800's.

magnesium (magnē'zēəm *or* magnē'zhəm) *n.* silver-white metallic chemical element. 1812, New Latin, from Medieval Latin *magnesia* MAGNESIA + New Latin *-ium* (chemical suffix). The word was coined by the English chemist Sir Humphry Davy, 1778-1829. Earlier Davy had used *magnesium* to refer to manganese in 1808.

magnet *n.* piece of iron, steel, lodestone, etc., that attracts iron or steel. Before 1398 *magnes, magnas* piece of lodestone, in Trevisa's translation of Bartholomew's *De Proprietatibus Rerum;* later *magnet* (1429, in Lydgate's writings); borrowed from Latin *magnētem,* accusative of *magnēs* lodestone, from Greek *Mágnēs líthos, Magnêtis líthos* Magnesian stone, from *Magnēsíā* Magnesia, a region in Thessaly. The figurative sense of something or someone that attracts, is first recorded in 1655 in Vaughan's *Silex Scintillans.* **—magnetic** *adj.* 1634, of or acting like a magnet; borrowed through French *magnétique,* and directly from Late Latin *magnēticus,* from Latin *magnēs* (genitive *magnētis*) magnet; for suffix see -IC. Curiously the figurative sense of having powers of attraction, very attractive is first recorded in Ben Jonson's *The Magnetick Lady* (1632). This pre-dating of the figurative sense, either of a borrowing or a native term, is not unusual in English, nor is it peculiar to English. **—magnetism** *n.* 1616, the properties of a magnet; borrowed from New Latin *magnetismus,* from Latin *magnēs* (genitive *magnētis* MAGNET + *-ismus* -ism. The figurative sense of attractive power or influence, allure, charm, is first recorded in 1655, in Vaughan's poetry, see MAGNET. **—magnetization** *n.* 1801, formed from English *magnetize* +

-ation. **—magnetize** *v.* 1787, formed from English *magnet,* n. + *-ize.*

magneto (magnē'tō) *n.* small machine, using permanent magnets to produce an electric field. 1882, shortened form of *magnetoelectric,* in *magnetoelectric machine.* The adjective *magnetoelectric* characterized by electricity produced by magnets (1831), was formed from *magneto-* + *electric* by the English physicist and chemist Michael Faraday.

magneto- a combining form meaning magnetic, magnets, or magnetism, as in *magnetometer* (instrument for measuring magnetic strength), *magnetoelectric* (see *magneto*), and *magnetochemistry* (the relation between magnetism and chemistry). Formed in English from *magnetic,* but also representing the combining form of Latin *magnēs* (genitive *magnētis*) lodestone, MAGNET.

magnificence *n.* 1340, high-mindedness, fortitude; in *Ayenbite of Inwyt;* later, grandeur, glory, in Chaucer's *Canterbury Tales;* borrowed from Old French *magnificence* splendor, nobility, grandeur, learned borrowing from Latin *magnificentia,* from the comparative and superlative stem *magnificent-* of *magnificus* noble, eminent, splendid (*magnus* great, see MUCH + the root of *facere* to make, DO[1]); for suffix see -ENCE. **—magnificent** *adj.* Before 1460, splendid, exalted, glorious; probably as a back formation from *magnificence;* and a borrowing from Middle French *magnificent,* from *magnificence;* for suffix see -ENT.

magnify *v.* About 1380, *magnyfying,* in Chaucer's *House of Fame,* gerund of *magnifien* glorify, praise, make greater (before 1382, in the Wycliffe Bible), borrowed from Old French *magnifier,* learned borrowing from Latin *magnificāre* esteem greatly, extol from *magnificus* splendid; see MAGNIFICENCE: for suffix see -FY.

The meaning of increase the apparent size of an object artificially, as with the lens of a telescope or microscope, appeared in Boyle's writings in 1665. Though what is now considered the figurative sense existed in Middle English, its specific application to representing or enlarging upon a person's character or actions, or to making things greater than they are, is first recorded in 1759. **—magnification** *n.* Probably before 1425 *magnificacioun* enlargement, in a translation of Chauliac's *Grande Chirurgie;* borrowed from Middle French *magnification,* from Old French, act of magnifying, glorification, praise, from Late Latin *magnificātiōnem* (nominative *magnificātiō*), from Latin *magnificāre* esteem greatly; for suffix see -ATION.

magniloquence (magnil'əkwəns) *n.* high-flown, lofty style of speaking or writing. 1623, in Cockeram's *Dictionary;* borrowed from Latin *magniloquentia* lofty style of language (*magnus* great, see MUCH + *loquentem* (nominative *loquēns*) speaking, present participle of *loquī* speak, see LOQUACIOUS); for suffix see -ENCE. **—magniloquent** *adj.* 1656, in Blount's *Glossographia,* back formation from *magniloquence* and probably borrowed directly from Latin *magniloquentia;* for suffix see -ENT.

magnitude *n.* size. Before 1400, grandeur, magnificence; later, size, extent (before 1425); borrowed, probably through Old French *magnitude,* and directly from Latin *magnitūdō* greatness, bulk, size, from *magnus* great; see MUCH; for suffix see -TUDE.

magnolia *n.* tree with large white, pink, or purplish flowers. 1748, American English adoption of New Latin *Magnolia* the genus name (coined by Linnaeus, from *Magnolius,* the Latinate name of Pierre *Magnol,* 1638-1715, a French botanist).

magnum (mag'nəm) *n.* bottle that holds two quarts of alcoholic liquor. 1788, in Robert Burns' *Prose Works,* borrowing of Latin *magnum,* neuter of *magnus* great; see MUCH.

magnum opus (mag'nəm ō'pəs) great work of literature or art. 1704, in Swift's *A Tale of a Tub,* borrowing of Latin *magnum opus* great work (*magnum* great, neuter of *magnus,* see MUCH; *opus* work, see OPUS).

magpie *n.* chattering bird. 1605, a compound of *Mag,* nickname for *Margaret,* and *pie*[2] magpie. The nickname *Mag* was long used in various proverbial phrases referring to idle chattering, such as Middle English *magge tales* tall tales, nonsense, trifles (before 1410). **—adj.** having characteristics attributed to the magpie, such as chattering and hoarding. 1808, from the noun.

maharaja or **maharajah** (mä'hərä'jə) *n.* former ruling prince in India. 1698 *mau raja,* in John Fryer's *A New Account of East India and Persia;* borrowed from Sanskrit *mahārājá-s* (*mahā-* great, see MUCH + *rā́jan-* RAJAH).

mahatma (məhät'mə) *n.* wise and holy person in India. 1855, borrowed from Sanskrit *mahātmā,* nominative of *mahātman-,* literally, great-souled (*mahā-* great, see MUCH + *ātmán-* soul, breath; cognate with Old English *ǣthm,* Old High German *ātum* breath (modern German *Atem*), from Indo-European **ēt-mén-,* Pok.345). Compare the etymology of MAGNANIMOUS for the striking parallel in Latin. As a title, *Mahatma* has been associated since the 1920's with the name of the Hindu nationalist leader Mohandas Karamchand Gandhi (better known as Mahatma Gandhi), 1869-1948, who led the struggle to free India from British rule. The common people of India began to call him Mahatma after Gandhi had led several successful nonviolent campaigns against the colonial government.

mah-jongg or **mah-jong** (mä'jong') *n.* Chinese game played with 144 dominolike pieces. 1922, borrowed from dialectal Chinese (Shanghai) *ma chiang* the name of the game; literally, hemp birds, sparrows; so called from a design on the game pieces.

mahogany *n.* hard reddish-brown wood, much used for furniture. 1671 *mohogeney,* borrowed from obsolete Spanish *mahogani,* perhaps from the native name in Maya (Honduras). **—adj.** made of mahogany. 1730, from the noun.

maid *n.* Probably before 1200 *maide* young woman, female servant, in Layamon's *Chronicle of Britain,* shortened form of MAIDEN.

The coincidence of form and use found in English *maid* and German *Maid,* which survives in German as a poetical word, and *Maidenschule* a training school in agriculture and domestic science, is striking and may in part be an example of Sapir's concept of "drift."

maiden *n.* About 1200 *maiden, mæden,* in *Vices and Virtues;* developed from Old English (about 950) *mǣden,* (before 971) *mægden,* diminutive of *mægth, mægeth* maid. Old English *mægden* is cognate with Old High German *magatīn,* from Proto-Germanic **maʒađinan;* and Old English *mægeth* is cognate with Old Frisian *maged, megith* maiden, Old Saxon *magath,* Middle Dutch *maghet* (modern Dutch *maagd*), Old

High German *magad* (modern German *Magd*), and Gothic *magaths* virgin, from Proto-Germanic **maȝađis* young womanhood, related to **maȝuz,* whence Gothic *magus* boy and Old Icelandic *mǫgr* son. Cognates outside Germanic are found in Old Irish *maug, mug* slave, perhaps *macc* son, Albanian *makth* young hare, Latvian *mač* small, and perhaps Avestan *magava-* unmarried, from Indo-European **magho-, maghu-* boy; **maghotís* young womanhood. **—adj.** Probably about 1300, virgin, unmarried; from the noun. The figurative sense of new, fresh, first (as in *maiden voyage, maiden speech*) is first recorded in 1555. **—maidenhood** *n.* About 1200 *maidenhad* virginity, in *Vices and Virtues;* developed from Old English *mægdenhād* (about 750, in Cynewulf's *Christ*), from *mægden* maiden + *-hād* -hood. **—maidenly** *adj.* Before 1450; formed from Middle English *maiden* + *-ly²*. **—maiden name** (1689, in Sewall's *Diary,* American English) **—maid of honor** (about 1586) **—maid servant** *n.* (before 1382, in the Wycliffe Bible).

mail¹ *n.* letters, parcels, etc., sent by post. Probably before 1200 *male* traveling bag, in Layamon's *Chronicle of Britain;* later *mayll* (before 1460); borrowed from Old French *male* wallet, bag, from Frankish (compare Old High German *malha, malaha* wallet, bag; cognate with Middle Dutch *māle* bag, modern Dutch *maal* mailbag, mail). The sense of a bag of letters, is first recorded in 1654. **—v.** send by mail. 1828-32, American English; from the noun. **—mailbox** *n.* (1810) **—mail carrier** (1790, American English) **—mailman** *n.* (1881) **—mail order** (1867, American English).

mail² *n.* armor made of metal rings or small loops of chain. Probably before 1300 *maile* mail, link of mail; later *mayl* (before 1400); borrowed from Old French *maille* link of mail, a mesh of a net, from Latin *macula* a mesh in a net; originally, spot, blemish; of uncertain origin (perhaps from Indo-European **smə-tlā,* root **smē-/smə-,* whence Greek *smên* to smear; Pok.966). Compare IMMACULATE.

maim *v.* to cripple, disable. About 1300 *maymen;* later *maheimen* (about 1415); borrowed from Old French *mahaignier,* possibly from a Germanic source; compare Gothic *gamaidans* (accusative plural) crippled, and Old Icelandic *meidha* to hurt; see MAD. Related to MAYHEM.

main *adj.* Probably before 1200, *mæin* outstanding because of size, most important, in Layamon's *Chronicle of Britain;* later *main* (1303); developed from Middle English *main,* n.; and from Old English *mægan-* in compounds (about 725, in *Beowulf*), from *mægen* power, strength, force. Old Icelandic *megenn* strong, powerful, was also probably instrumental in the formation of the adjective in Old English, and would, with Icelandic *magn, megin* strength, be cognates of the Old English along with Old High German and Old Saxon *magan, megin;* see MAY. **—n.** Probably before 1200 *maine* power, strength, force, in Layamon's *Chronicle of Britain;* developed from Old English *mægen.* The phrase *with might and main* (before 1425) derives from this meaning of power or force.

Main in the sense of the principal part, essential point (1595) is derived from the adjective; the phrase *in the main,* with the meaning of for the most part, is found before 1628. The meaning of principal channel in a utility system is recorded in 1727, abstracted from the earlier phrase *main drain* (1707-12). **—mainland** *n.* (probably before 1400) **—mainmast** *n.* (1485) **—mainsail** *n.* (1466) **—mainspring** *n.* (1591) **—mainstay** *n.* (1485; figurative use, 1787) **—mainstream** *n.* (1667; figurative use, 1831).

maintain *v.* Probably about 1300, Middle English *mayntenen, meintenen* keep, keep up; borrowed through Anglo-French *meintenir,* Old French *maintenir, meintenir* keep, maintain, from Latin *manū tenēre* hold in the hand (*manū,* ablative of *manus* hand, see MANUAL; *tenēre* to hold, see TENANT). **—maintenance** *n.* Before 1333, Middle English *mentenaunce* action of wrongfully aiding and abetting litigation, in Shoreham's *Poems;* later *mayntenaunce* support, backing (about 1378, in a version of *Piers Plowman*); borrowed through Anglo-French *mayntenaunce,* Old French *maintenance* act of maintaining, from *maintenir* maintain. The meaning of financial provision, upkeep, is first recorded about 1383 in Wycliffe's writings.

maître d'hôtel (me′trə dōtel′), now reduced to **maître d'** (mā′trə dē′, mā′tər dē′). headwaiter. Before 1953, in American English; developed from *maître d'hôtel* headwaiter (1907), hotel manager (1891), butler or steward (1540); borrowing of Middle French *maître d'hôtel,* literally, master of the house (*maître,* from Old French *maistre* MASTER; *hôtel,* from Old French *hostel,* see HOTEL).

maize *n.* corn, especially Indian corn, as distinguished from British usage; any grain, especially wheat. 1555, in Eden's translation of *Decades of the New World or West India;* borrowed from Spanish *maíz;* earlier *mahiz, mahis, mayz,* from Arawakan (Haiti) *mahiz.*

majesty *n.* About 1300 *majeste, mageste* dignity, magnificence, especially of God; borrowed from Old French *majesté* grandeur, nobility, from Latin *majestātem* (nominative *majestās*) greatness, dignity, from the stem of *major,* comparative of *magnus* great; see MUCH. **—majestic** *adj.* grand, dignified, stately. 1601, in Shakespeare's *Julius Caesar;* formed from English *majesty* + *-ic.*

major *adj.* Probably before 1300 *maiour* great, greater (initially used in names, as in *Inde maiour* Greater India); borrowed from Latin *major,* irregular comparative of *magnus* large, great; see MUCH. Doublet of MAYOR. The meaning in music, referring to chromatic tones, is first recorded in English in 1694. **—n.** army officer. 1579, borrowed from Middle French *major* (as in *sergent-major* sergeant-major), from Medieval Latin *major* chief officer, magnate, superior person, from Latin *major* an elder, adult, noun use of the adjective, greater, superior. **—v. major in** take as a major subject of study, especially in a college or university. 1924, American English; from the noun, in the earlier sense of a subject of specialization (1890).

major-domo (mā′jərdō′mō) *n.* butler or steward. 1589, in Puttenham's *The Arte of English Poesie;* borrowed from Spanish *mayordomo* or Italian *maggiordomo,* both from Medieval Latin *major domūs* chief of the household (*major* chief, from Latin *major* greater; *domūs,* genitive of *domus* house; see MAJOR and DOME).

majority *n.* the larger number, greater part. 1552, condition of being greater, in Latimer's *Sermons;* borrowed from Middle French *majorité,* from Medieval Latin *majoritatem,* from Latin *major,* adj., MAJOR. The sense of the greater number or part (as in *the majority of voters*) is first recorded in 1691. An earlier sense, the state of being of full age (as in *to attain majority at 21*), is found in 1565.

make *v.* Before 1121 *macen* put together, build, form later *maken* (1137); developed from Old English (before 901) *macian;* probably borrowed from Old Saxon *makōn,* from Old High German *mahhōn, machōn.* The Old High German forms are cognate with Old Frisian *makia* to make, build, and Middle Dutch and modern Dutch *maken,* from Proto-Germanic **makōjanan,* cognate with Greek *magênai* to be kneaded, be molded, *mageús* baker, and Old Slavic *mazati* anoint, from Indo-European **maĝ-* to knead, press (Pok.696).

—**n.** way in which a thing is made. Probably about 1300 *make* design, construction; from the verb.

—**make-believe** *n.* pretense. (1811); *adj.* pretended; imaginary. (1824) —**maker** *n.* 1340, the Creator; later, a writer or composer (about 1350), and a manufacturer or builder (1391); formed from Middle English *maken* make + *-er*[1]. —**makeshift** *adj.* 1683, serving as a temporary and inferior substitute; earlier, shifty, roguish (1592, from the noun).—*n.* 1802-12, temporary substitute; earlier, shifty person, rogue (1565). The word derives from the phrase *to make shift* to *to make a shift* to try all means (about 1460); to manage to do (1504); to do one's best with, put up with (1577). —**makeup** *n.* composition, constitution. (1821). The meaning of cosmetics is first recorded in 1886, from the earlier sense of an appearance of face, dress, etc., assumed by an actor to impersonate a character (1858).

mal- a combining form meaning: **1** bad or badly, as in *malfunction, malodorous.* **2** poor or poorly, as in *malnutrition, maltreat.* **3** abnormal or abnormally, as in *malabsorption, malformed.* **4** wrongly or unfairly, as in *malapportion.* **5** wrong or unfair, as in *malpractice.* Borrowed from Old French *mal-, male-,* and Latin *male-,* prefixes formed on Latin *malus,* adj., bad (see SMALL), and *male,* adv., badly. —**maladjustment** *n.* (1833) —**maladroit** *adj.* clumsy. 1685, borrowed from French (*mal-* badly + *adroit*). —**malcontent** *adj.* 1586, borrowed from Middle French (*mal-* poorly + *content*). —*n.* discontented person. 1581, from the adjective (even though attested a few years earlier). —**malformation** *n.* (1800) —**malformed** *adj.* (1817) —**malfunction** *v.* (1928); *n.* (1941) —**malnutrition** (1862) —**malodorous** *adj.* (1850, in writings of Carlyle) —**malpractice** *n.* (1671) —**maltreat** *v.* 1708, borrowed from French *maltraiter* treat badly, abuse (*mal-* badly + *traiter* to treat). —**maltreatment** *n.* (1721).

malachite (mal′əkīt) *n.* green mineral, used for ornamental articles. Before 1398 *melochites,* in Trevisa's translation of Bartholomew's *De Proprietatibus Rerum;* later *molochites* (before 1500); borrowed from Old French *melochite,* learned borrowing from Latin *molochitis;* and borrowed directly from Latin *molochitis,* from Greek *molochîtis líthos* mallow stone, from *molóchē, maláchē* MALLOW: perhaps so called from the similarity in color between the mineral and the leaves of the mallow plant. The modern spelling is first recorded in Blount's *Glossographia* (1656).

malady *n.* sickness. About 1275 *maladie,* borrowed from Old French *maladie* sickness, illness, disease, from *malade* ill, from Latin *male habitus* doing poorly, feeling unwell; literally, ill-conditioned (*male,* adv., badly; *habitus,* past participle of *habēre* have, hold).

malaise (malāz′) *n.* vague bodily discomfort, uneasy or disturbed condition. Before 1300 *maleise* pain, suffering; also *malayse* distress, sorrow, in *Kyng Alisaunder;* borrowed from Old French *malaise* (*mal* bad + *aise* EASE).

malamute or **malemute** (mä′ləmyüt) *n.* large, strong dog of Alaska, used for pulling sleds. 1898, earlier *maglemut* (1874), from the name of an Alaskan Eskimo tribe that developed this breed of dog.

malapropism (mal′əpropiz′əm) *n.* ridiculous misuse of words. 1849, in Charlotte Brontë's *Shirley;* formed from earlier *malaprop* a malapropism (1823) + *-ism.* The forms *malaprop* and *malapropism* are an allusion to Mrs. *Malaprop,* a character in Sheridan's play *The Rivals* (1775), noted for her ridiculous misuse of words. Sheridan coined her name by back formation from MALAPROPOS.

malapropos (mal′aprəpō′) *adv.* in an inappropriate or awkward manner; at the wrong time or place. 1668, in Dryden's *Essay on Dramatic Poesy;* borrowed from French *mal à propos* badly for the purpose, inappropriate (*mal* badly; *à propos* appropriately, to the purpose, from *proposer* PROPOSE).

malaria (məlãr′ēə) *n.* disease accompanied by fever and chills, transmitted by the bite of infected anopheles mosquitoes. 1740, in Walpole's *Letters;* borrowing of Italian *malaria,* from *mala aria* bad air (*mala* bad, feminine of *malo,* from Latin *malus; aria* air, from Vulgar Latin **arja* AIR). The disease was formerly thought to be caused by bad air in swampy areas. —**malarial** *adj.* 1847, formed from English *malaria* + *-al*[1].

malarkey or **malarky** (məlär′kē) *n. Slang.* nonsense, baloney. 1929 *malaky,* in J.P. McEvoy's *Hollywood Girl,* American English; of unknown origin.

male *n.* 1373, borrowed from Old French *male, masle, mascle,* from Latin *masculus* masculine, male, diminutive of *mās* (genitive *maris*) male person or animal, male; of uncertain origin. —**adj.** About 1378, in a version of *Piers Plowman;* borrowed from Old French *male,* adj. and n. The sense in mechanics of a part designed to fit inside a corresponding part to make a connection (as in *a male plug*), is first recorded in Boyle's writings, in 1669.

malediction *n.* a speaking evil of or to a person; curse. 1447 *malediccyoun;* borrowed through Old French *maledicion, maledition,* from Latin *maledictiōnem* (nominative *maledictiō*) the action of speaking evil of; slander (in Late Latin, a curse), from *maledīcere* to speak badly or evil of, slander (*male* badly + *dīcere* to say); for suffix see -TION.

malefactor *n.* criminal, evildoer. Before 1438, borrowing of Latin *malefactor,* from *malefacere* to do evil (*male* badly + *facere* to perform, DO[1]); for suffix see -OR[2].

malevolence (məlev′əlens) *n.* ill will, spite. About 1454 *malivolence;* later *malevolence* (1464); borrowed from Middle French *malivolence,* and from Latin *malivolentia, malevolentia,* from *malivolentem, malevolentem* (nominative *malivolēns, malevolēns*) malevolent (*male* badly + *volentem,* nominative *volēns,* present participle of *velle* to wish; see WILL[1] wish); for suffix see -ENCE. —**malevolent** *adj.* showing ill will, spiteful. 1509, in Barclay's *Ship of Fools;* borrowed from Middle French *malivolent,* and from Latin *malivolentem, malevolentem;* for suffix see -ENT. It is also possible that *malevolent* is a back formation from earlier *malevolence.*

malfeasance (malfē′zəns) *n.* wrongdoing or misconduct

by a public official. 1696; borrowed from French *malfaisance* wrongdoing *mal-* badly + *faisant,* present participle of *faire* to do, from Latin *facere* to perform, DO[1]); for suffix see -ANCE. *Malfeasance,* originally a legal term, but now also of general application for any wrongdoing (recorded since 1856, in Emerson's writings) has largely replaced the older *maleficence* a general term for evil or wrongdoing (1598, borrowed, probably through Middle French *maleficence,* from Latin *maleficentia,* from *maleficus* wicked, *male* badly; *facere* perform).

malice *n.* active ill will, spite. About 1300, borrowed from Old French *malice* ill will, spite, learned borrowing from Latin *malitia* badness, ill will, spite, from *malus* bad. It is probable that the borrowing of *malice* was influenced by the earlier use of *malicious.* **—malicious** *adj.* About 1225 *malicius,* in *Ancrene Riwle;* later *malicious* (probably before 1300, in *Kyng Alisaunder*); borrowed from Old French *malicios* showing ill will, spiteful, from Latin *malitiōsus* full of malice, from *malitia* badness, malice; for suffix see -OUS.

malign (məlīn′) *adj.* evil, injurious. Before 1333 *maligne,* in Shoreham's *Poems;* borrowed from Old French *malign* having an evil nature, learned borrowing from Latin *malignus* evilly-disposed, bad-natured (*male* badly + *-gnus* born, from *gignere* to bear, beget; see KIN). **—v.** speak evil of, slander. Before 1420 *malignen,* in Lydgate's *Troy Book;* borrowed from Middle French *malignier* to plot, deceive, pervert, and from Late Latin *malignāre* injure maliciously, from Latin *malignus* evil, bad-natured. The late date of the verb use suggests that it may derive from the adjective in English, and that at the least the adjective influenced the verb use. **—malignancy** *n.* 1601, in Shakespeare's *Twelfth Night,* malignant quality or character; formed from *malignant* + *-cy;* for suffix see also -ANCY. The medical sense of a malignant growth or tumor, is first recorded in 1685. **—malignant** (məlig′nənt) *adj.* very evil. 1542-45, disaffected, malcontent; borrowed from Middle French *malignant* deceitful, and Late Latin *malignantem* (nominative *malignāns*) acting from malice, present participle of *malignāre* injure maliciously, see MALIGN; for suffix see -ANT.

The medical use with the meaning of severe, virulent, is first recorded in 1568. The general sense of having an evil influence, is first found in Shakespeare's *1 Henry VI* (1591).

—malignity *n.* About 1390 *malignite* ill will, spite, malice; borrowed from Old French *malignité,* learned borrowing from Latin *malignitātem* (nominative *malignitās*), from *malignus* evil; for suffix see -ITY.

malinger (məling′gər) *v.* pretend to be sick in order to escape work or duty; shirk. 1820 (implied earlier in the once slang term *malingeror,* n. 1785), probably an unrecorded slang term as a verb; borrowed from French *malingrer* to suffer; perhaps also, pretend to be ill, from *malingre* ailing, sickly, possibly a blend of Old French *mingre* sickly or miserable, and *malade* ill. Old French *mingre* is itself a blend of *maigre* MEAGER and *haingre* sick, haggard, possibly from a Germanic source (compare Middle High German and modern German *hager* thin).**—malingerer** *n.* (1843)

mall *n.* public walk or promenade. 1737, from *The Mall,* broad promenade in St. James's Park, London (1674); formerly an alley used in *pall-mall,* a game in which a ball was hit with a mallet (*mall,* now *maul*) through a ring at the end of an alley. The name of the game, literally "ball-mallet," was borrowed into English from obsolete French *pallemaille,* from Italian *pallamaglio* (*palla* ball + *maglio* mallet).

The word *mall* (now *maul*) with the meaning of mallet or hammer, a shortened form of *pall-mall* (1568), is first recorded in English in 1662. *Mall* was reinforced in English by French *mail,* from Old French *mail, maul,* from Latin *malleus* MALLET.

mallard *n.* kind of wild duck. Probably before 1300 *maulard,* in *Arthour and Merlin;* later *mallard* (1348); borrowed from Old French *malart,* and from Medieval Latin *mallardus,* also from Old French *malart,* apparently from *male, masle, mascle,* from Latin *masculus;* see MALE. The original meaning was probably "male of the wild duck."

malleable (mal′ēəbəl) *adj.* capable of being hammered or pressed into various shapes. About 1395 *malliable,* in Chaucer's *Canterbury Tales;* later *malleable* (1413); borrowed from Old French *malleable,* and directly from Medieval Latin *malleabilis,* from *malleare* to beat with a hammer, from Latin *malleus* hammer; see MALLET: for suffix see -ABLE. The figurative sense of adaptable, yielding, is first recorded in English in 1612. **—malleability** *n.* 1690, in Locke's *Essay Concerning Human Understanding;* formed from English *malleable* + *-ity.*

mallet *n.* wooden hammer. 1392 *maylet;* earlier in surname *Malet* (1159); also *mallet* (1406); borrowed from Old French *maillet, mallot* wooden hammer, diminutive of *mail,* from Latin *malleus* hammer, related to *molere* to grind; see MEAL[2] ground grain.

mallow *n.* kind of ornamental plant. Before 1325 *malue;* later *malowe* (1392); possibly developed from Old English (about 1000) *malwe, mealwe,* from Latin *malva,* but more likely borrowed from Old French *malve, mauve,* from Latin *malva,* and directly from Latin *malva,* from the same (Mediterranean) source as Greek *maláchē, molóchē* mallow. Doublet of MAUVE.

malmsey (mäm′zē) *n.* kind of strong sweet wine. 1407 *malmesey;* later *malmsey* (probably before 1475); borrowed, perhaps through Provençal **malmesie,* or Middle Dutch *malemesye,* from Medieval Latin *malmasia,* alteration of Medieval Greek *Monembasía* Monemvasia, town in southeastern Peloponnesus that was an important center for production of wine in the Middle Ages.

A variant name in English *malvoisie* (1828, in Scott's *The Fair Maid of Perth*); earlier *malveisyn* (1361) was borrowed from Old French *malvesie,* and directly from Medieval Latin *malvesia,* also an alteration of Medieval Greek *Monembasía;* see above. Another variant in English *malvasia* (1839) was borrowed from Italian *malvasia* which may also have been the immediate source for Old French *malvesia.* The word is further complicated by the fact that a variety of wine of Madeira is also called *malmsey* and first appears as *malmsey madeira* (1723).

malt *n.* barley or other grain used in brewing alcoholic liquors. Old English (about 700, in Anglian dialect) *malt;* later (about 950, in West Saxon) *mealt.* The Old English forms are cognate with Old Saxon *malt* malt, Middle Dutch and modern Dutch *mout,* Old High German *malz* (modern German *Malz*), and Old Icelandic (also Norwegian, Swedish, and Danish) *malt,* from Proto-Germanic **maltaz;* derived from the Germanic root that is the source of Old English *meltan* to MELT.

—**v.** change into malt. 1440 *malten,* in *Promptorium Parvulorum;* earlier, the gerund *malting* (1298-1300); from the noun.

mamba (mam′bə) *n.* long, slender snake of Central and South Africa. 1862, borrowing of Zulu *(i)mamba,* or Swahili *mamba.*

mambo (mäm′bō) *n.* ballroom dance of Caribbean origin. 1948, American English; borrowed from Cuban Spanish *mambo* probably from Haitian Creole *mambo, mambu* voodoo priestess, of African origin (compare Yoruba *mambo* to talk).

mameluke (mam′əlük) *n.* slave in Moslem countries. 1600, in Hakluyt's *Voyages;* earlier *Mamoluke* a member of a military body, originally consisting of Caucasian slaves (1511; they seized the Egyptian throne in 1254 and ruled until 1517). The name was borrowed through Middle French *mameluk;* earlier *mamelos,* and directly from Arabic *mamlūk* purchased slave, from past participle of *malaka* he possessed.

mamma[1] or **mama** (mä′mə) *n.* mother. 1579 *mamma,* in Lyly's *Euphues;* later *mama* (1727); ultimately probably of imitative origin, representing sounds made by infants. However, the word is found in many European languages and must have been transmitted over time, perhaps going back to an Indo-European base **mammā* (Pok.694), found in Irish, Cornish, Breton, and Welsh *mam,* Latin *mamma* mother, breast, Greek *mámmē* mother, breast, Lithuanian *mamà* mother, Russian *máma,* and Armenian *mam* grandmother. The late appearance of the English word is not surprising as many common children's words are not found nor would they be expected, in the early written records of language. It is further probably inaccurate to describe any such word as "borrowed" from another language.

mamma[2] (mam′ə) *n., pl.* **mammae** (mam′ē). milk-giving gland in female mammals. 1693, borrowed from Latin *mamma* breast, mother.

mammal *n.* vertebrate animal that gives milk to its young. 1826, in J.M. Good's *The Book of Nature;* borrowed from New Latin *Mammalia* the class of mammals (coined by Linnaeus), from neuter plural of Late Latin *mammālis* of the breast, from Latin *mamma* breast, see MAMMA[1] mother; for suffix see -AL[1]. —**mammalian** (məmā′lēən) *n.* one of the class of mammals. 1835, formed in English from New Latin *Mammalia* + English *-an.—adj.* of the mammals. 1851, from the noun.

mammary (mam′ərē) *adj.* of the mammae or breasts. 1682, borrowed from French *mammaire* (formed from Latin *mamma* breast, mother + French *-aire* -ary; see MAMMA[1] mother). —**mammary gland** (1831)

Mammon or **mammon** (mam′ən) *n.* riches thought of as an evil. About 1390 *Mammona,* in a version of *Piers Plowman;* also *Mammon* (about 1400); borrowed from Late Latin *mammōna,* from Greek *mamōnâs,* from Aramaic *māmōnā, māmōn* riches, gain. The Aramaic word occurred in the Greek text of the New Testament (Matthew 6:24) passage: "Ye cannot serve God and mammon." It is also found in Luke 16:9. Medieval writers used the word as the proper name of the devil of covetousness; this personification appears in Middle English and was revived by Milton in *Paradise Lost* (1667). The word does not occur in the New Testament translation in the Wycliffe Bible (which substitutes *richessis*), but it was used in the Tyndale Bible and other subsequent translations.

mammoth *n.* very large, extinct kind of elephant. 1706, borrowed from earlier Russian *mammot',* now *mámont,* probably from Ostyak, a Finno-Ugric language (compare Finnish *maa* earth, so called because of the mammoth's once supposed habit of burrowing in the earth). —**adj.** huge, gigantic. 1802, American English; from the noun, in allusion to the mammoth's enormous size.

mammy *n.* mother. 1523, in Skelton's *The Garland of Laurel;* a diminutive formed from earlier *mam* (probably before 1500) + *-y*[2]. *Mam* is probably from children's speech and ultimately from the same source as English MAMMA[1].

man *n.* Old English (before 725) *man, mann, mon* (pl. *men, menn*) human being, person; later, adult male (about 1000). The Old English forms are cognate with Old Frisian *monn* human being, man, Old Saxon *man,* Middle Dutch and modern Dutch *man,* Old High German *man,* sing. and pl. (modern German *Mann,* pl. *Männer*), Old Icelandic *madhr* (*-dhr* from *-nr,* pl. *menn*), Swedish *man,* Danish *mand,* from Proto-Germanic **manwaz.* In addition, Old English had *manna,* cognate with Gothic *manna* (earlier **mana*), from Proto-Germanic **manōn.* Cognates are found outside Germanic in Old Slavic *mǫži* man, Russian *muzh* man, husband, Avestan *Manus-* (in names); and Sanskrit *mánu-s* human being, man, from Indo-European **manus* or **monus* (Pok.700). If the form was **monus,* some have ascribed a meaning of "the thinking creature" or "the creature that remembers" which gives the impression of being overly sophisticated, but supports comparison with Old English *hē man* he thinks. Indo-European **monus* is from the base **men-/mon-* (Pok.726).

In all the Germanic languages, the word originally had the twofold sense "human being" and "adult male human being." Later, with the exception of English, the sense "human being," was mainly assumed by a derivative (German *Mensch,* Swedish *människa,* Dutch *mens,* etc.). The primary sense of Old English *man* was "human being." The words *wer* and *wīf* (meaning man and woman) were used to distinguish the sexes; see VIRILE, WIFE, and WOMAN. By the late 1200's Middle English *were* (Old English *wer*) began to disappear, and was replaced by *man* in the sense "adult, male human being."

—**v.** Probably before 1300 *mannen* supply (a ship, etc.) with men; from the noun. The sense of take charge, manage, is first recorded in Mannyng's *Chronicle of England* (1338), and that of behave like a man, act with courage, is found in *Kyng Alisaunder* (about 1400). —**manful** *adj.* Before 1393 *manfull* bold, resolute, in Gower's *Confessio Amantis,* formed from Middle English *man* + *-full* -ful. —**manhandle** *v.* Probably 1458 *manhandelen* to wield (a tool); later, to attack (an enemy); formed from Middle English *man* + *hondlen* manage. A later revival of the form (1865) with the sense of handle roughly, may have developed from dialect *managle* to mangle, that was soon misinterpreted by general speakers as *manhandle* in the literal sense of the elements of the compound. —**manhole** *n.* (1793) —**manhood** *n.* Before 1250 *manhede* human condition, nature, or form, in *Bestiary;* later, manliness (before 1300); also *manhode* bravery (before 1333); formed from Middle English *man* + *-hede, -hode* -hood. —**mankind** *n.* Before 1225 *man-kende* (influenced by earlier *mankenne, mannkinn*); later *mankinde* (about 1300, *man* + *kinde* sort, KIND[2]). *Mankind* replaced earlier *mankenne, mannkinn* (both recorded before 1200); developed from Old English *mancynn* human race (about 725, in *Beowulf*); formed from *man* MAN + *cynn* KIN. **—manly** *adj.* Probably before 1200 *monliche* human, in *Ancrene Riwle;* later *manlich* masculine (about 1300); also *manly* brave, bold, noble (before 1375); formed from Middle English *mon, man* man + *-lich, -ly,* -ly[2].—*adv.* Probably before 1200 *monliche* bravely, boldly, in Layamon's *Chronicle of Britain;* developed from Old English *manlīce* (about 725, in *Beowulf*); formed from *man* + *-līce* -ly[1]. **—man-made** *adj.* (before 1718) **—man-of-war** *n.* About 1437, a soldier; later, a warship (1484). **—manpower** *n.* (1862, in Herbert Spencer's *First Principles*). **—manslaughter** *n.* Before 1325 *mans-slaghter,* in *Cursor Mundi;* later *manslaghter* killing of a human being, homicide (probably about 1375); formed from Middle English *man* + *slaghter* slaughter. This form replaced the earlier *monslaht* (before 1225); developed from Old English (Anglian, before 1000) *mannslæht,* (West Saxon, before 899) *mannslieht;* formed from *mann* man + *slæht, slieht* act of killing, SLAUGHTER. **—menfolk** *n.pl.* (1802 *menfolk;* 1886 *menfolks*).

manacle *n.* handcuff. About 1340 *manykil;* later *manacle* (about 1395); borrowed from Old French *manicle,* from Latin *manicula* handle, little hand, diminutive of *manicae* long sleeves of a tunic, manacles, from *manus* hand; see MANUAL. **—v.** put manacles on. 1307 *manklen;* later *manaclen* (1422); from the noun.

manage *v.* 1561 *manege* to handle or direct (a horse); probably borrowed from Italian *maneggiare,* from Vulgar Latin **manizāre,* from Latin *manus* hand; see MANUAL. The English word was influenced in meaning by French *manège* horsemanship, MANÈGE, and by French *ménager* to use carefully, to husband, from *ménage* household, MENAGE. The original spelling *manege* was altered by 1570 to *manage* through the influence of the suffix *-age.* The extended sense of administer or direct the affairs of (a household, business, etc.), is first recorded in 1609, but is found earlier in the specific sense of conduct or carry on an undertaking, such as a war, as early as 1579. **—manageable** *adj.* 1598, in Florio's *A World of Words;* formed from English *manage* + *-able.* **—management** *n.* 1598, act or manner of managing, in Florio's *A World of Words;* formed from English *manage* + *-ment.* The collective sense of a group of persons who manage a business or institution, is first recorded in 1739. **—manager** *n.* 1588, one who manages (something), in Shakespeare's *Love's Labour's Lost;* later, one who manages a business establishment or a public institution (1705, in Addison's writings). **—managerial** *adj.* (1767)

mañana (mänyä'nä) *n., adv.* tomorrow, some time. 1845, borrowing of Spanish *mañana* tomorrow; originally, in the morning, early, from Vulgar Latin **māneāna* early, from Latin *māne* morning, in the morning, in a good time, locative of *mānis* good (compare *mānus* good); see MATURE.

manatee (man'ətē') *n.* a large sea mammal, sea cow. 1555, in Eden's translation of Peter Martyr's *Decades of the New World or West India;* borrowed from Spanish *manatí,* from Carib *manati* breast, udder.

mandamus (mandā'məs) *n.* written order from a higher court to a lower court directing that a certain act be done. 1535, borrowing of Latin *mandāmus* we order, first person plural present indicative of *mandāre* to order, MANDATE. A single instance of use appears in a French context in the *Rolls of Parliament* for the year 1378.

mandarin (man'dərin) *n.* Chinese official of high rank. 1589 *mandelines,* an erroneous transcription in a translation of Mendoza's *Historie of the great and mightie Kingdome of China,* borrowed from Spanish *mandarín,* from Portuguese *mandarim;* later *mandorijn* (1598, in a translation of *J.H. van Linschoten his discours of voyages into the Easte and West Indies*); borrowed from Dutch *mandorijn,* now *mandarijn,* probably from Portuguese *mandarim,* from Malay *mantrī.* The Malay word is found in Hindi *mantrī* councilor, minister of state, from Sanskrit *mantrí,* nominative of *mantrín-* advisor, from *mántra-s* advice, counsel; related to *mányate* (he) thinks; see MIND. The transferred sense of person important in political or intellectual circles, is first recorded in 1907. The sense of the chief dialect of Chinese (usually capitalized), is first recorded in 1604.

mandate *n.* command, order. 1552, borrowed through Middle French *mandat,* and directly from Latin *mandātum,* noun use of neuter past participle of *mandāre* to order, commit to one's charge (probably from *manus* hand, see MANUAL + *dare* to give, with transfer to the *-āre* conjugation, see DATE[1] time); for suffix see -ATE[1]. **—v.** give a mandate to. 1623, in Cockeram's *Dictionary;* from the noun. **—mandatory** *adj.* 1576, borrowed from Late Latin *mandātōrius* of or belonging to one who commands, analyzed as either from Latin *mandātor* + *-y* or as *mandāt-,* participle stem of *mandāre* to order; for suffix see -ORY.

mandible (man'dəbəl) *n.* jaw, especially the lower jaw. 1392, borrowed from Old French *mandible,* and directly from Late Latin *mandibula,* from Latin *mandere* to chew, cognate with Greek *máthyiai* jaws, from Indo-European **madh-, mandh-* chew (Hjalmar Frisk, *Griechisches etymologisches Wörterbuch,* II 180).

mandolin (man'dəlin) *n.* stringed musical instrument. 1707, borrowed from French *mandoline,* from Italian *mandolino,* diminutive of *mandola, mandora* a larger kind of mandolin, alteration of Late Latin *pandūra* three-stringed lute, from Greek *pandoûra,* possibly of Oriental origin.

mandrake *n.* plant with a very short stem and a thick root, used in medicine. About 1325 *mondrake;* later *mandrake* (1373); alteration of earlier *mandragora* (about 1150); borrowed from Medieval Latin *mandragora,* from Latin *mandragorās,* from Greek *mandragórās,* of unknown origin.

The alteration of *mandragora* to *mandrake* is the result of a Middle English writers' equating the *-drago-* of *mandragora* with the *drago-* of *dragoun* dragon, and this with the rather common noun *drake,* also with the meaning of dragon. Association of the form of the root of this plant to that of the human form, and the fabled shriek the plant is supposed to utter when pulled from the ground (all to explain the element *man* of *mandrake*), is often cited.

mandrill (man'drəl) *n.* large, fierce baboon. 1744, either formed from English *man* + *drill*[3] baboon, or from an African language, with misdivision of the form into recognizable English components. French *mandrill* (1751) and Spanish *mandril* (1817) were apparently borrowed from English.

mane *n.* Probably before 1300, in *Kyng Alisaunder;* developed from Old English (before 800) *manu* mane, related to *mene* necklace. Old English *manu* is cognate with Old Frisian *mana* mane, Middle Dutch *mane* mane, Old High German *mana* mane (modern German *Mähne*), and Old Icelandic *mǫn* mane (Swedish, Norwegian, and Danish *man*), from Proto-Germanic **manō.* Old English *mene* necklace, collar is cognate with Old Saxon *menē,* Old Icelandic *men,* from Proto-Germanic **maniz.* Cognates outside Germanic are found in Middle Irish *mong* mane, Welsh *mwng,* Latin *monīle* necklace, Old Slavic *monisto,* Avestan *manaothrī* neck, nape of the neck, and Sanskrit *mányā* nape of the neck, from Indo-European **mon-, monī* (Pok.747).

manège or **manege** (mənezh′ *or* mənāzh′) *n.* art of training or riding horses; horsemanship. 1644, in Evelyn's *Diary;* borrowing of French *manège,* from Italian *maneggio,* from *maneggiare* to handle, MANAGE. An earlier English form *manage* (1577-87), used in a similar sense, represents a borrowing directly from Italian *maneggio.*

maneuver *n.* 1758 *manœuvre;* later *maneuver* (1778); borrowing of French *manœuvre* manipulation, maneuver, from Old French *maneuvre* manual labor, from Medieval Latin *manuopera,* from *manuoperare* to work with the hands, from Latin *manū operārī;* see the doublet MANURE. **—v.** 1777, in John Adams' *Familiar Letters;* borrowed from French *manœuvrer,* from Old French *manouvrer* to work with the hands, from Medieval Latin *manuoperare.* **—maneuverability** *n.* 1923, formed from English *maneuverable* + *-ity.* **—maneuverable** *adj.* 1921, formed from English *maneuver* + *-able.*

manganese (mang′gənēs *or* mang′gənēz) *n.* grayish-white metallic chemical element. 1676, oxide or ore of manganese, in Coles' *Dictionary;* borrowing of French *manganèse,* from Italian *manganese,* alteration of Medieval Latin *magnesia;* see MAGNESIA. *Manganese* was first used to refer to the metal itself in 1783.

mange (mānj) *n.* skin disease of animals. Before 1425, *manjewe;* borrowed from Middle French *manjüe, mangeue* the itch, from *manju-,* accented stem of Old French *mangier* to eat, from Latin *mandūcāre* to chew, eat, from *mandūcus* glutton, from *mandere* to chew; see MANDIBLE. **—mangy** *adj.* shabby and dirty, squalid. Before 1529, in Skelton's *Works;* formed from English *mange* + *-y*[1]. The literal sense of having mange, is not recorded until about 1540.

manger *n.* box or trough for horses or cows to eat from. Before 1333 *manyour,* in Shoreham's *Poems;* also *manger* (before 1338, in Mannyng's *Chronicle of England*); borrowed from Old French *mangeoire,* from *mangier* to eat + *-oire* (common suffix for implements and receptacles); see MANGE. Although various standard sources derive Old French *mangeoire* from Vulgar Latin **mandūcātōria,* it is probably not necessary to postulate a Latin form, since the Latin words for "manger" are *alveus, praesēpe, falisca.* Furthermore, Italian *mangiatoia* manger did not come directly from a Vulgar Latin form, since Italian *mangiare* to eat, is derived from Old French *mangier* (the native Italian forms *manucare, manicare* coming from Latin *mandūcāre*).

mangle[1] *v.* cut or tear roughly. Probably before 1400 *manglen* to mutilate, borrowed through Anglo-French *mangler,* frequentative forms of Old French *mangoner* cut to pieces; of uncertain origin (sometimes connected with Old French *mahaignier* to maim). The sense of spoil, ruin, is first recorded in 1533, in Sir Thomas More's writings.

mangle[2] *n.* machine with rollers for pressing and smoothing sheets and other flatwork. 1774, borrowed from Dutch *mangel,* from Middle Dutch *mange,* from Late Latin *manganum* contrivance, mechanism, from Greek *mánganon* machine for defending fortifications, contrivance, means of enchanting, related to *manganeúein* deceive. The Greek machine for defending a fortification by hurling stones, is found in Middle English *mangonel* (1265) and the general sense of a machine using stones, is found in modern English *mangle*[2] which used stones to roll and press linen and cotton to give a luster after washing. **—v.** make smooth in a mangle. 1775, from the noun, or borrowed from Dutch *mangelen,* from *mangel,* n.

mango (mang′gō) *n.* juicy, slightly tart fruit. 1681, earlier *mangas* (1582); borrowed from Portuguese *manga,* from Malay *mangga,* from Tamil *mānkāy.*

mangrove *n.* tropical tree. 1613 *mangrow* (probably influenced in formation by *grow*); borrowed from Spanish *mangle,* earlier *mangue,* probably from Carib or Arawakan. The current spelling appeared in 1697, influenced by *grove.*

mania (mā′nēə) *n.* About 1385 *manye* derangement, frenzy, in Chaucer's *Canterbury Tales;* also *mania* (before 1398, in Trevisa's translation of Bartholomew's *De Proprietatibus Rerum*); borrowed from Late Latin *mania* insanity, madness, from Greek *maníā* madness, related to *maínesthai* to rage, go mad, also related to *ménos* passion, spirit; see MIND. The sense of unusual or unreasonable fondness, rage, craze, is first recorded in Evelyn's *Correspondence* (1689).

Since the 1500's *mania* has been used as a final element in compounds to express the general sense of a certain kind or state of madness, after some Greek compounds such as *erōtomaníā* love madness, *hippomaníā* craze for horses, etc. Some of the compounds in *-mania* that were formed as medical New Latin and adopted in English were *nymphomania* (1775), *kleptomania* (1830), and *megalomania* (1890). Since the 1700's it has become fairly common to invent new words, often for the nonce, with this ending. Examples are *Anglomania* (1787) a craze for things English, *tulipomania* (1710) a craze for tulips, *decalcomania* (1864) a craze for decals, and more recently *Beatlemania* (1963) a craze for the Beatles, a rock music group.

—maniac *adj.* affected with mania, mad, insane. 1604 *maniacque,* in Cawdrey's *A Table Alphabeticall of English Words;* borrowed from French *maniaque,* from Late Latin *maniacus,* from Greek *maniakós,* from *maníā* madness. A revival of a Latinate spelling, found in the present-day *maniac,* is first recorded in English in 1727.—*n.* person affected with mania, madman. Before 1763, in Shenstone's *Elegies;* from the adjective. **—maniacal** (mənī′əkəl) *adj.* 1678, affected with mania; formed from English *maniac,* n. + *-al*[1]. **—manic** *adj.* of or affected with mania. 1902, borrowed from Greek *manikós* mad, from *maníā* madness; for suffix see -IC.

manicure *n.* 1880, a manicurist; later, care of the fingernails and hands (1887); borrowing of French *manicure,* variant of *manucure,* a compound formed from Latin *manus* hand + *cūra* care. In 1877 both *manicure* and *manucure* appeared in French, but today only *manucure* survives in French. **—v.** to care for the fingernails and hands. 1889; from the noun. —**manicurist** *n.* 1889, American English; formed from English *manicure* + *-ist.*

manifest *adj.* plain, clear, evident. About 1380, in Chaucer's translation of Boethius' *De Consolatione Philosophiae;* borrowed through Old French *manifeste,* or directly from Latin *manifestus, manufestus* caught in the act, plainly apprehensible, from *manus* hand, see MANUAL + *-festus* (able to be) seized, perhaps from earlier **ferstos,* cognate with Lesbian Greek *thérsos* courage and Sanskrit *dharṣáyati* overpowers, from Indo-European **dhers-* attack (Pok.259). —**v.** show plainly, reveal. About 1380 *manyfesten;* also in Chaucer's translation of Boethius; from the adjective by influence of Latin *manifestāre* to make plain, from *manifestus* palpable. —**n.** 1561, indication, manifestation; borrowed from Middle French *manifeste,* from *manifester* to manifest, from Latin *manifestāre* to make plain. The sense of a list of a ship's cargo, is first recorded in 1706. —**manifestation** *n.* Probably before 1425 *manyfestacioun,* borrowed through Middle French *manifestation,* learned borrowing from Late Latin; and borrowed directly from Late Latin *manifestātiōnem* (nominative *manifestātiō*), from Latin *manifestāre* to manifest; for suffix see -ATION. It is also possible that in some instances *manifestation* was a formation in English of *manifest,* v. + *-ation.*

manifesto (man′əfes′tō) *n.* 1644, proof of evidence; also 1647, proclamation; borrowing of Italian *manifesto* a manifestation, indication, public declaration, from Latin *manifestus* MANIFEST.

manifold *adj.* of many kinds, many and various. Before 1200 *monifold,* in *Body and Soul;* later *manyfold,* (about 1300, in Layamon's *Chronicle of Britain*); developed from Old English *monigfald* (Anglian form, before 830, in the *Vespasian Psalter*); earlier *manigfeald* (West Saxon form, about 750 in Cynewulf's *Christ II; manig* MANY + *-feald* -FOLD*).*

The Old English compound has corresponding forms in Old Frisian *manichfald,* Old Saxon *managfald,* Old High German *manacfalt,* Old Icelandic *margfaldr,* and Gothic *managfalths,* all possibly formed in imitation or translation of Latin *multiplex;* see MULTIPLY.

—**n.** About 1250 *monie volde* variety, great number, in *The Owl and the Nightingale;* later *manyfolde* (about 1303, in Mannyng's *Handlyng Synne*); from the adjective. The modern common meaning of pipe with several openings, is first recorded before 1884.

—**v.** make many copies of. 1767, make manifold, multiply; later, make many copies of (1865); a new formation from the adjective. An older verb which existed in English before 1500 developed as Middle English *manifolden* to increase, multiply (about 1350), from earlier *monifalden* (probably before 1200, in *Ancrene Riwle*), which in turn developed from Old English *gemonigfaldian* augment, multiply (before 830, in the *Vespasian Psalter*); from the adjective.

manikin (man′əkin) *n.* jointed model or figure of a person, used by artists, tailors, etc. 1570 *manneken* artist's manikin; borrowing of Dutch *manneken,* literally, little man, diminutive of *man* MAN. Compare MANNEQUIN. The literal sense of little man, dwarf, pygmy, is first recorded in Shakespeare's *Twelfth Night* (1601).

manipulate *v.* handle or treat skillfully. 1827, in Faraday's *Chemical Manipulation,* back formation from MANIPULATION; for suffix see -ATE[1]. The sense of manage by clever use of influence, especially to one's own advantage, is first recorded in Carlyle's biography of Frederick the Great, in 1864. —**manipulation** *n.* 1727-41, method of digging ore, in *Chambers Cyclopaedia;* later, method of handling chemical apparatus or preparing material in experimentation (1796), and the skillful handling of any object (1826); borrowed from French *manipulation,* in part as if from New Latin **manipulationem* (nominative **manipulatio*), from **manipulare;* and in part a formation in French from *manipule* handful measure in pharmacy, learned borrowing from Latin *manipulus* handful, sheaf (*manus* hand + the root of *plēre* to fill) + *-ation* -ation. The sense of clever use of influence especially to one's own advantage, or of unfair changes in books of account or other records to one's own advantage, is first recorded in 1828. —**manipulative** *adj.* 1836, formed from English *manipulate* + *-ive.* —**manipulator** *n.* 1851, formed from English *manipulate* + *-or*[2], probably on the model of French *manipulateur* (1783).

manna *n.* food miraculously supplied to the Israelites in the wilderness. Old English *manna* (before 899, in Alfred's translation of St. Gregory's *Pastoral Care*); borrowed from Late Latin *manna,* from Greek *mánna,* from Hebrew *mān.* The extended sense of something that is supplied unexpectedly, is first recorded in 1593.

mannequin (man′əkin) *n.* 1730-36 *manequine* jointed figure used by artists, manikin; borrowed from French *mannequin,* from Dutch *manneken* MANIKIN. The extended sense of a model, usually a woman, employed to wear and display new clothes is first recorded in 1902. In French the word refers to female models (attested since 1830) despite the etymological meaning "little man."

manner *n.* Probably before 1200 *manere* way of acting, kind, sort, in *Ancrene Riwle;* borrowed through Anglo-French *manere,* Old French *maniere* way or mode of handling, from feminine of *manier,* adj., handmade, skillful, from Vulgar Latin **manārius,* from Latin *manuārius* belonging to the hand, from *manus* hand; see MANUAL. —**mannered** *adj.* About 1378 *manered* having manners of a certain kind, in a version of *Piers Plowman;* formed from *manere* manner + *-ed*[2]. —**mannerism** *n.* 1803, excessive or affected adherence to a distinctive manner or style, especially in art and literature, formed from English *manner* + *-ism.* The sense of habitual peculiarity of action, expression, etc. characteristic of a person is first recorded in Coleridge's *Literary Remains* (1819). —**mannerly** *adj.* Probably about 1390 *manerly* well-mannered, in *Sir Gawain and the Green Knight;* formed from Middle English *manere* manner + *-ly*[2]. —*adv.* Probably 1350-75 *manerlich* properly, becomingly, formed from Middle English *manere* manner + *-lich* -ly[1]. It is interesting to note that while the adverb form remained more prominent in Middle English, the adjective form for *mannerly* in perhaps less than 20 years twice assumed the modern *-ly* ending.

manor *n.* landed estate. About 1300 *maner,* borrowed through Anglo-French *maner,* Old French *manoir;* earlier *maneir,* noun use of *maneir* to dwell, from Latin *manēre* to stay, abide; see MANSION. —**manorial** *adj.* 1785, formed from English *manor* + *-ial.*

manqué (mäNkā′) *adj.* defective or abortive, unfulfilled. 1773, in Horace Walpole's *Letters;* generally still considered a French word, *manqué* is from past participle of *manquer* to lack, fail, from Italian *mancare,* from *manco* lacking, from Latin *mancus* afflicted with a defect of the hand, maimed, infirm, perhaps from *manus* hand.

mansard (man′särd) *n.* roof with two slopes on each side. 1734, borrowing of French *mansarde,* formed in allusion to François *Mansard,* 1598-1666, a French architect who revived the use of such roofs after they had been used about a hundred years before by the Renaissance architect Pierre Lescot.

manse *n.* minister's house, parsonage. 1534; earlier manor house (1490); borrowed from Medieval Latin *mansa* a dwelling, noun use of feminine past participle of Latin *manēre* to stay, abide; see MANSION.

-manship a combining form meaning the art or skill of being, doing, or using (something) to one's own advantage, as in *growthmanship, quotemanship, lifemanship, one-upmanship.* 1950, abstracted from *gamesmanship* (1947) the skill of winning games by various gambits and ploys; coined by the 20th-century English writer Stephen Potter, on the model of *craftsmanship, sportsmanship,* etc., which were formed in the 1600's and 1700's from *craftsman, sportsman,* etc. + *-ship.*

mansion *n.* About 1340 *mansyon* abode, act of dwelling; also, a house; borrowed from Old French *mansion,* and directly from Latin *mānsiōnem* (nominative *mānsiō*), from *manēre* to stay, abide; for suffix see -SION. Latin *manēre* is cognate with Greek *ménein* to remain, *monḗ* a staying, and Armenian *mnam* I remain, await, from Indo-European **men-/mon-/mn-* (Pok.729). The meaning of manor house is first recorded before 1512; that of stately residence is found in 1807.

mantel *n.* 1489, moveable shelter used by soldiers besieging a fortress; a spelling variant of MANTLE. *Mantel,* meaning a piece of timber or stone supporting the masonry above a fireplace, is first recorded in 1519 as a shortened form of Middle English *mantiltre* manteltree, mantel (1451-52). **—mantelpiece** *n.* (1686)

mantilla (mantil′ə *or* mantē′yə) *n.* veil or scarf covering the hair. 1717, borrowing of Spanish *mantilla,* diminutive of *manta* kerchief, from *manto* cloak, from Late Latin *mantus,* probably a back formation from Latin *mantellum* MANTLE.

mantis (man′tis) *n.* insect that holds its forelegs doubled up as if praying; praying mantis. 1658, New Latin *Mantis* the genus name, from Greek *mántis,* literally, prophet, from *maínesthai* be inspired, go mad, related to *ménos* passion, spirit; see MIND.

mantle *n.* loose cloak, cape. Probably before 1200 *mentel;* also about 1200 *mantel, mantle;* borrowed through Old French *mantel,* and directly from Latin *mantellum;* also influenced by Old English *mentel* cloak (before 899, in Alfred's translation of St. Gregory's *Pastoral Care*); borrowed from Latin *mantellum,* perhaps from a Celtic source. **—v.** cover with a mantle. Probably about 1225 *mantelen,* in a version of *Ancrene Riwle,* from *mantel,* n. and, in some instances, borrowed from Old French *manteler.*

mantra (man′trə) *n.* (in Hinduism and Buddhism) prayer or invocation. 1808, passage from a sacred text (used as a prayer); borrowed from Sanskrit *mántra-s* sacred message or text, charm, spell, counsel; related to *mányate* thinks; see MIND. The sense of a sacred name or special word used for meditation is first recorded in English in 1956.

manual *adj.* of or done with the hands. Probably 1406 *manuel;* later *manual* (about 1450); borrowed through Middle French *manüel,* or directly from Latin *manuālis* of or belonging to the hand, from *manus* hand; for suffix see -AL[1]. Latin *manus* (from Indo-European **mənús*) is cognate with Old English, Old Frisian, and Old Icelandic *mund* hand, Old High German *munt* (from Proto-Germanic **munđṓ,* Indo-European **mn̥tā́* hand, Pok.740)., modern German *Vormund* guardian, and possibly Gothic *manwus* ready, prepared. **—n.** handbook. 1432 *manwel* service book used by a priest; also *manual* (1447); borrowed from Old French *manuel,* and directly from Late Latin *manuāle* the case or cover of a book, handbook, service book, from neuter of Latin *manuālis,* adj., manual.

manufacture *n.* act or process of making articles by hand or by machine. 1567, something made by hand; borrowed from Middle French *manufacture* (1511), possibly from Italian *manifattura* or, more likely, Spanish *manufactura,* but generally considered a compound formed independently from Latin *manus* hand + *factūra* a working, formation (*fact-,* participial stem of *facere* to perform, DO[1]); for suffix see -URE. The sense of act or process of manufacturing is first recorded in Bacon's *Henry VII* (1622). **—v.** make by hand or by machine. 1683, in Thomas Tryon's *The Way to Health;* from the noun, or possibly borrowed from French *manufacturer,* from Middle French *manufacture,* n.

manumission *n.* act of freeing from slavery. Probably before 1400 *manumissioun;* borrowed from Latin *manūmissiōnem* (nominative *manūmissiō*) the freeing of a slave, from *manūmittere* to set free, from *manū mittere* release from control (*manū,* ablative of *manus* hand, power of a master; *mittere* let go, release, of uncertain origin; for suffix see -SION.

manure *v.* Probably before 1400 *manouren, maynoyren* to cultivate or manage land; borrowed through Anglo-French *meynoverer, meinourer,* Old French *manovrer, manouvrer* to work with the hands, from Medieval Latin *manuoperāre,* from Latin *manū operārī* (*manū,* ablative of *manus* hand; *operārī* to work, OPERATE). Doublet of MANEUVER. The meaning of put on the soil as fertilizer is first recorded in 1599 (implied earlier in sense of spread like manure, 1592); probably from the noun. **—n.** dung, etc., spread over or mixed with soil to fertilize it. 1549; from the verb.

manuscript *n.* book or paper written by hand or with a typewriter. 1600, borrowed from Medieval Latin *manuscriptum* document written by hand, from Latin *manū scrīptus* written by hand (*manū,* ablative of *manus* hand; *scrīptus,* past participle of *scrībere* to write). Since Latin already had the form *chīrographum* for a manuscript, the form in Medieval Latin may be a loan translation of Greek *cheirógraphon.*

many *adj.* 1137 *mani;* later *monie* (about 1175); developed from Old English *monig, manig* (about 725, in *Beowulf*). These Old English forms are cognate with Old Frisian *manich* many, Old Saxon *manag,* Old High German *manag* (modern German *manch* many a), Old Icelandic *margr* many, Old Swedish *manger* (Swedish *mången,* Danish *mangen*), and Gothic *manags,* from Proto-Germanic **manaȝaz,* Indo-European **monoghos;* on the other hand, the Old English forms *mænig, menig* are cognate with Old Frisian *menich,* Middle Dutch *mēnich* (modern Dutch *menig*), and Old High German *menig,* from Proto-Germanic **maniȝaz,* Indo-European **moneghos.*

—n. great number. 1137 *mani;* later *monie* (probably before 1200); from Proto-Germanic **manaȝīn-,* from which cognates are found in Gothic *managei* multitude, crowd, Old High German *managī, menigī* large number, plurality (modern German *Menge* multitude), and Old English *menigu, mengu.* Outside Germanic the word is cognate with Old Irish *menicc* frequent, Old Slavic *mŭnogŭ* much, from Indo-European **menegh-/monogh-/monegh-/menogh-* (Pok.730).

map *n.* 1527 *mappe;* probably in part abstracted from *mappemound* (1393, in Gower's *Confessio Amantis*); earlier *mapemounde* (about 1380, in Chaucer's *Rosemounde*); and in part borrowed from Middle French *mappe,* from Old French *mape* (abstracted from Old French *mapemond, mappemond;* earlier *mappe del monde*), and from Medieval Latin *mappa* map (abstracted from earlier *mappa mundi* map of the world), from Latin *mappa* napkin, cloth (on which maps were once drawn), from Carthaginian or Phoenician (compare Hebrew *mĕnaphā* fan). **—v.** make a map of. 1586, from the noun.

maple *n.* Probably before 1300 *mapel;* earlier, in a place name *Maplescanyse* (1211-12); developed from Old English *mapul-,* as in *mapultrēo* maple tree (774); earlier, in *mapuldur* (about 700). Old English *mapul-* is cognate with Old Saxon *mapul-* in *mapulder,* and Middle Low German *mapel-* in *mapeldorn.*

mar *v.* spoil the beauty of, disfigure, deface. Probably before 1200 *meren* kill, defeat, in Layamon's *Chronicle of Britain;* also *merren* harm, ruin (probably about 1200); later *marren* (before 1250); developed from Old English *merran* to waste, spoil (about 950, in Anglian dialect); *mierran* (before 900, in West Saxon). The Old English forms are cognate with Old Frisian *meria* hinder, Old Saxon *merrian,* Middle Low German *merren, marren,* Old High German *marren, merren* hurt, harm, hinder, and Gothic *marzjan* offend, hinder, cause to stumble, from Proto-Germanic **marzjanan.* According to some scholars, Proto-Germanic **marzja-* is formally equivalent to Sanskrit *marṣaya-,* causative stem of *mṛ́ṣyate* (he) forgets (Indo-European ** mer-s-,* Pok. 737), and is thus possibly cognate with Lithuanian *miršti* forget, and Armenian *moṙanam* I forget.

marabou or **marabout** (mar′əbü) *n.* kind of large stork. 1823, tuft or plume; 1826, large stork or heron; borrowed from French *marabout,* originally, Mohammedan hermit, from Portuguese *marabuto,* from Arabic *murābiṭ* hermit; possibly facetiously applied to the bird because it appears meditative, or because of its solitary habits.

maraschino (mar′əskē′nō *or* mar′əshē′nō) *n.* liqueur made from a bitter black cherry. 1791-93, borrowed from Italian *maraschino,* from *marasca* bitter black cherry, shortened form of *amarasca,* from *amaro* bitter, from Latin *amārus* sour, cognate with Sanskrit *amlá-s* sour, *āmá-s* raw, Greek *ōmó-s* raw, Old Irish *om* raw, from Indo-European **om-/em-/ōm-* (Pok.777). The name *maraschino cherry,* for a cherry preserved in a sweet syrup, is first recorded in 1905 in American English.

marasmus (məraz′məs) *n.* a wasting away of the body, especially due to malnutrition or old age, rather than disease. 1656, New Latin *marasmus,* from Greek *marasmós* a wasting, withering, decay, from *maraínein* put out, quench, weaken, wither, cause to waste away; see MORTAR[2] pounding bowl. An isolated example of *maras* wasting away of the body, is recorded about 1450 (probably as an abbreviated form of *marasmus,* borrowed from Medieval Latin, or directly from Greek.

marathon (mar′əthon) *n.* foot race of 26 miles, 385 yards. 1896 (found in earlier *Marathonian,* 1767), in allusion to *Marathon,* a plain in Greece about 25 miles from Athens, where the Athenians defeated the Persians in the battle of Marathon (490 B.C.). The foot race was introduced in 1896 with the revival of the Olympic Games, to commemorate the unknown runner who carried the news of the victory to Athens.

Since the turn of the century *marathon* has also been applied to any competition requiring endurance, as in *dance marathon* (1928). This usage gave rise to the modern combining form -ATHON or -THON. Figuratively *marathon* has also appeared (since about 1915) in the sense of any event or activity that lasts a long time, as in *a 24-hour marathon legislative session, a marathon love affair.*

maraud *v.* go about in search of plunder, make raids on (a place) for booty. 1711, in Addison's writings in *The Spectator;* borrowed from French *marauder,* from Middle French *maraud* rascal (probably as a prowler, but originally, tomcat), of uncertain origin (sometimes conjectured as from *marau* meow, an imitative word, in reference to tomcat; others compare German *marodieren* to maraud, etc). **—n.** raid for booty. 1837, in Washington Irving's *Adventures of Captain Bonneville;* from the verb.

marble *n.* Before 1200 *marbra;* later *marbre* (about 1300), and *marble* (before 1338, in Mannyng's *Chronicle of England;* a form thought to have developed by dissimilation of the second *r* in *marbre* to *l);* borrowed from Old French *marbre,* from Latin *marmor,* from Greek *mármaros* marble, gleaming stone; probably originally with the sense of what is breakable, and related to *márnantai* they fight; originally, they crush each other, related to *marasmós* a wasting away, cognate with Sanskrit *mūrṇá-s* crushed, and Latin *mortārium* mortar, from Indo-European **mer-, merə-/mr̥̄-* (Pok.735). **—adj.** made of marble. Probably about 1375, from the noun. **—v.** to color in imitation of the patterns in marble. 1683, from the noun. **—marble cake** (1882, in American English). **—marbles** *n.pl.* 1709, children's game played with small glass, clay, or (originally) marble balls about ½ inch to one inch in diameter. The marble (ball) was recorded in 1694-95. Since marbles is an ancient game played among Egyptian and Roman children and probably known in one form or another since the time marble was first quarried, it is curious that *marbles* shows up so late in the record of English.

march[1] *v.* walk in time and with steps of the same length, as soldiers do. About 1410 *marchen;* borrowed from Middle French *marcher* to march or walk, from Old French *marchier* to trample, stride, march; probably from Frankish (compare Old High German *marchōn* to mark out, delimit, MARK[1], v.).

Another view is that Old French *marchier* developed from a Gallo-Romance verb **marcāre* to hammer, beat or mark time, from Latin *marcus* hammer, perhaps a back formation from *marculus* small hammer, and related to *malleus* hammer; see MALLET.

—n. act of marching. About 1572, rhythmic drumbeat to accompany marching; borrowed from Middle French *marche,* from *marcher* to march. The meaning of act of marching is first recorded in 1590.

march[2] *n.* land along the border of a country; frontier. About 1300; earlier *marche* (probably before 1300, in

Arthour and Merlin), and in a surname (1207); borrowed from Old French *marche* boundary, frontier, borderland; from Frankish (compare Old High German *marca, marha* boundary, MARK[1], n.). The Old French form is related to MARQUIS.

The borrowing *marche,* from Old French, replaced and coalesced with Old English *mearc* boundary, mark, limit of space or time.

In Great Britain the plural, *the Marches,* refers to the portions of England bordering on Scotland and on Wales; this is the earliest recorded usage of the word in English.

—v. to border on. Probably before 1300, in *Arthour and Merlin;* borrowed from Old French *marchier* to have a common border, bound, from *marche* boundary.

March *n.* third month. Probably about 1200 *march,* in *The Ormulum;* also *marz* (about 1300, in *Havelok the Dane*); borrowed through Anglo-French *march, marche,* Old French *march,* dialect variant of *marz, mars,* from Latin *Mārtius mēnsis* month of Mars, the Roman god of war, from *Mārs* (genitive *Mārtis*) Mars; earlier *Māvors* (genitive *Māvortis*). In the ancient Roman calendar that preceded the Julian calendar, March was the first month and originally began at the vernal equinox.

marchioness (mär′shənis) *n.* woman who is the wife of a marquis, or holds such a title in her own right. Before 1600 (perhaps much earlier, as the form *marchiun* marquis is recorded probably before 1350); borrowed from Medieval Latin *marchionissa,* from *marchio* (genitive *marchionis*) marquis; literally, ruler of a border area, from *marca* borderland, MARCH[2]; for suffix see -ESS.

Mardi gras (mär′dē grä′) last day before Lent, often celebrated with festivities; Shrove Tuesday. 1699, in Martin Lister's *Journey to Paris,* borrowing of French *mardi gras,* literally, fat Tuesday (*mardi* Tuesday, from Latin *Mārtis diem* day of the planet Mars; *gras* fat, from Latin *crassus* thick; see CRASS). The festival was named "fat Tuesday" because it is marked by excessive eating and festivities, before the fasting season of Lent.

mare[1] (mãr) *n.* female horse. Before 1250 *mare* a riding horse, mare; also *mere* (about 1250), alteration (probably influenced by some form of Old English *merh, mearh* horse) of Old English (Mercian) *mēre,* (before 900, in West Saxon) *mȳre,* from **mīere* mare. The Old English forms are cognate with Old Frisian *merrie* mare, Old Saxon *meriha,* Middle Dutch and modern Dutch *merrie,* Old High German *marha, mariha* (modern German *Mähre* mare, jade), and Old Icelandic *merr* mare, *marr* steed (Swedish *märr,* Norwegian *merr,* and Danish *mær* mare), from Proto-Germanic **marHjōn;* compare Old High German *marah* horse, and Old Icelandic *marr,* from Proto-Germanic **marHaz.* Outside Germanic cognates are found in Irish *marc* and Welsh *march* horse, from Indo-European **markos* (Pok.700).

mare[2] (mär′ē *or* mãr′ē) *n., pl.* **maria** (mär′ēə *or* mãr′ēə). *Astronomy.* broad dark area of the moon or of another planet. 1860, New Latin *Mare* in the names of lunar or Martian "seas" such as *Mare Tranquillitatis* (Sea of Tranquility) and *Mare Australe* (Southern Sea), from Latin *mare* sea; see MARINE. The word was first applied by Galileo to the dark areas of the moon.

margarine *n.* substitute for butter consisting mainly of vegetable fat; oleomargarine. 1873, borrowed from French *margarine* (in *oléo-margarine,* 1854), from *margarique* margaric acid; literally, pearly (in reference to the acid's pearly luster), from Greek *margarítēs* pearl. The name was given to fatty acids by the French chemist Chevreul, 1786-1889. See MARGUERITE.

The pronunciation with *g* in *gin* (mär′jə rin) is an English development (since French has the sound represented by *g* in *get*), probably from the influence of words like *margin* and such alternations in pronunciations as those of *Margaret* and *Margie.*

margin *n.* edge, border. Probably before 1350 *margine;* borrowed from Latin *margō* (genitive *marginis*) edge. **—v.** 1607, enter (notes) in the margin; from the noun. The meaning of provide with a margin or border is first recorded in English in 1715. **—marginal** *adj.* 1576, written or printed in the margin; borrowed from Middle French *marginal* and Medieval Latin *marginalis,* from Latin *margō–* (genitive *marginis*) margin; see MARK[1]; for suffix see -AL[1]. The meaning of that which is on the margin or close to the limit of value, usefulness, etc., of minor effect or importance, is first recorded in English in 1887.

margrave (mär′grāv) *n.* title of certain German princes. 1551 *marcgrave,* in Robinson's translation of Sir Thomas More's *Utopia,* borrowed from Middle Dutch *marcgrāve* count of a border area (corresponding to modern Dutch *markgraaf,* Middle Low German *Markgrēve,* Old High German *Marcgrāvo,* and modern German *Markgraf*), a compound of *marc* boundary, MARK[1] + *grāve* count, Dutch *graaf,* cognate with Old High German *grāvo, grāvio* count (modern German *Graf*), Middle Low German *grāve, grēve,* and Old Frisian *grēva,* of unknown origin.

marguerite (mär′gəret′) *n.* kind of daisy with white petals and a yellow center. 1866, in John Lindley and Thomas Moore's *Treasury of Botany;* borrowing of French *marguerite,* from Old French *margarite* daisy, pearl, from Latin *margarīta* pearl, from Greek *margarítēs* pearl, from Middle Persian *marvārīt.*

marigold *n.* plant of the aster family with yellow, orange, or reddish-brown flowers. 1373 *marygolde,* in an old handbook of plants; later *marigold* (about 1425); a compound of *Mary* (probably genitive, in reference to the Virgin) and *gold.* See note under MARRY[2].

marijuana or **marihuana** (mar′əwä′nə) *n.* the hemp plant, or a preparation of its leaves and flowers smoked for its narcotic effect. 1918 *marajuana,* American English, alteration (probably influenced by the Spanish proper name *María Juana* Mary Jane) of earlier *mariguan* (1894); borrowed from Mexican Spanish *mariguana, marihuana* (a restored variant spelling in English, first recorded in 1907); of uncertain origin.

marimba (mərim′bə) *n.* musical instrument somewhat like a xylophone. 1704, in John Churchill's *Collection of Voyages and Travels,* a translation of Merolla's *Voyage to the Congo;* borrowed from an African language, probably Bantu (compare Kimbundu and Swahili *marimba* xylophonelike instrument, Tshiluba *madimba*).

marina (mərē′nə) *n.* dock, usually with service facilities for small boats. 1805, a promenade by the sea, in Washington Irving's *Life and Letters;* a dock where moorings are available (1935); borrowed from Spanish or Italian *marina* shore, coast, from feminine of *marino* of the sea, from Latin *marīnus* MARINE.

marinade (mar′ənād′) *n.* spiced vinegar, wine, etc., for pickling meat or fish. 1704, borrowed from French *marinade,* from *mariner* to pickle, MARINATE; for suffix see -ADE.

marinate (mar′ənāt) *v.* steep in brine, vinegar, etc. About 1645, formed in English from French *mariner* to pickle in (sea) brine, from Old French *marin,* adj., of the sea, from Latin *marīnus* MARINE + English suffix -ATE[1].

marine *adj.* of the sea. Probably 1440 *maryne,* in prose translation of Palladius' *De Re Rustica;* borrowed from Middle French *marin* (feminine *marine*), from Old French *marin,* learned borrowing from Latin *marīnus* (feminine *marīna*) of the sea, from *mare* (genitive *maris*) sea. Latin *mare* is cognate with Gothic *marei* sea, Old Icelandic *marr,* Old High German *meri* (modern German *Meer*), Middle Dutch *mēre* (modern Dutch *meer*), Old Saxon *meri,* Old Frisian *mere,* and Old English *mere* sea, lake, pool, pond (which did not survive into Middle English), from Proto-Germanic **mari.* The Latin form is also cognate with Old Irish *muir* sea, Lithuanian *mãrės* (plural), and Old Slavic *morje* sea, from Indo-European **mori/mōri* (Pok.748). **—n.** shipping, fleet. 1669; later, a soldier who serves aboard a ship (1672, possibly from earlier *mariner,* 1642); borrowing of French *marine,* from Old French *marine,* adj. This is a new and separate borrowing from French, having no connection with an earlier borrowing found before 1375 with the meaning of seacoast, or area or promenade by the sea (surviving in 1703, and later in MARINA), and earlier in names such as *Willemo de la Marine* (1279). **—mariner** *n.* About 1250, sailor, seaman; earlier as a surname *Marinier* (1197); borrowed through Anglo-French *mariner,* Old French *marinier,* from *marin* of the sea, MARINE; for suffix see -ER[1].

marionette (mar′ēənet′) *n.* small doll moved by strings or the hands. About 1620, borrowed from French *marionnette,* from *Marion,* diminutive of *Marie* Mary; for suffix see -ETTE. *Marion* was a common name for female characters in Old French plays, such as the *Jeu de Robin et Marion.*

marital *adj.* of marriage. 1603, in Florio's translation of Montaigne's *Essays;* borrowed from French *marital, maritale,* and directly from Latin *marītālis* of or belonging to married people, from *marītus* married man, husband; see MARRY[1], v.; for suffix see -AL[1]. An isolated example of this word is recorded in Middle English before 1500, with French plural in *-s.*

maritime *adj.* of or near the sea. 1550, intended for service at sea; borrowed through Middle French *maritime,* and directly from Latin *maritimus* of the sea, from *mare* (genitive *maris*) sea; see MARINE. The Latin ending *-timus* was originally a superlative suffix (as in Latin *optimus,* superlative of *bonus* good) denoting close association.

marjoram (mär′jərəm) *n.* fragrant plant of the same family as mint. 1373 *magiron,* in a handbook of plants; later *majorane* (before 1393), and *margerum* (about 1550); borrowed from Old French *majorane,* from Medieval Latin *maiorana;* of uncertain origin.

mark[1] *n.* trace, impression. Apparently before 1200 *mearke, merke, marke* boundary, border, track, trace, imprint, mark, in *Ancrene Riwle,* and in Layamon's *Chronicle of Britain;* later *mark* (about 1303, in Mannyng's *Handlyng Synne*); in part, developed from Old English *mearc* boundary, sign, limit (701, in West Saxon) and *merc* a mark, as in the compound *merciseren* branding iron (about 700, in Mercian); also, in part, borrowed from a Scandinavian source (compare Old Icelandic *mǫrk* border area). The Old English and Old Icelandic forms are cognate with Old Frisian *merke* boundary, sign, Old Saxon *marka* boundary, Middle Dutch *marc, marke* (modern Dutch *mark*), Middle Low German *mark* district, Old High German *marca, marha* boundary, district (modern German *Mark*), and Gothic *marka* boundary, from Proto-Germanic **markō.* Outside Germanic cognates are found in Latin *margō* edge, border, Old Irish *mruig* border area, Welsh *bro* region, district (with *br* for *mr,* a regular development), and Persian *marz* tract of land, boundary, from Indo-European **morĝ-/merĝ-/mroĝ-,* root **mereĝ-* (Pok.738).
—v. Probably before 1200 *mearken,* in *Ancrene Riwle;* also *merken, marken* (probably about 1200); in part, developed from Old English *mearcian* to trace out boundaries (about 888, in West Saxon) and *merciga* (about 950, in Anglian); also, in part, borrowed from a Scandinavian source (compare Old Icelandic *marka, merkja* to mark). The Old English and Old Icelandic forms are cognate with Old Frisian *merkia* to mark, Old Saxon *markon,* Middle Dutch and modern Dutch *merken,* and Old High German *marchōn, markōn* delimit, plan, *merken, merchen* to mark, note, observe (modern German *merken*), from Proto-Germanic **markōjanan;* derived from the Proto-Germanic root that is the source of Old English *mearc* boundary, sign.
—marker *n.* 1486, formed from Middle English *mark* + *-er*[1]. Apparently a form *mearcere* existed in Old English as a gloss for Latin *notārius* clerk, secretary, but the word was not found again until late Middle English.
—marksman *n.* (1660; earlier, 1577, *markman*) **—marksmanship** *n.* (1859) **—markswoman** *n.* (1802)

mark[2] *n.* unit of money of Germany, first issued as a silver coin in 1875 (a sense not found in English before 1883). Probably before 1200 *mark* unit of weight or of money, in Layamon's *Chronicle of Britain;* developed from Old English (about 960) *marc* unit of weight (about eight ounces); earlier, in the compound *healfmarc* (886, in Alfred's treaty with the Danish chief Guthrum); probably borrowed from a Scandinavian source (compare Old Icelandic *mǫrk* unit of weight, Swedish, Danish, and Norwegian *mark*). The Old English form is cognate with Middle High German *mark, marke* unit of weight, about half a pound (modern German *Mark* monetary unit), Middle Dutch *marc* unit of weight, and Old Frisian *merk.* Old French *marc* and Medieval Latin *marca, merca,* although themselves loans from the Germanic languages, may have affected the development of the word in Middle English. Essentially *mark*[2] is a derivative of *mark*[1] in that the meaning sign or imprint was a feature of the weight (bar) or coin.

market *n.* gathering of people for buying and selling. Before 1121 *markete;* also *market* (1124); borrowing of Old North French *market,* variant of Old French *marchiet;* later *marchié,* from Latin *mercātus* (genitive *mercātūs*) trading, trade, market, from *mercārī* to trade, deal in, from *merx* (genitive *mercis*) wares, merchandise. Related to MART, MERCHANT, MERCANTILE.
—v. buy or sell in a market. 1635, from the noun.
—black market (1931) **—Common Market** (1954) **—marketability** *n.* 1877; formed from English *marketable* + *-ity.* **—marketable** *adj.* 1600, in Shakespeare's *As You Like It;* formed from English *market* + *-able.*
—marketeer *n.* one who sells in a market. 1832, American English, formed from *market* + *-eer.* **—marketer** *n.*

1787, American English; formed from *market* + *-er*[1]. **—marketplace** *n.* (1389) **—market price** (about 1440) **—market research** (1926, American English)

marl *n.* soil containing clay. 1358 *marle;* earlier in a surname *Marleward* (1265); borrowed from Old French *marle,* and probably directly from Medieval Latin *marla, margila,* from Latin *marga,* said by Pliny to have come from Gaulish. The word is not found, however, in the modern Celtic languages except as a loanword: Breton *merl* from French, and Welsh *marl* and Irish and Gaelic *marla* from English. The modern French word is *marne.*

marlin (mär′lən) *n.* large sea fish related to the swordfish. 1917, American English, shortened form of *marlinspike* a marlinespike (iron spike used by sailors to separate strands of rope; so called from the resemblance of the marlin's pointed snout to the shape of a marlinespike, see MARLINE).

marline (mär′lən) *n. Nautical.* small cord wound around the ends of a rope to keep it from fraying. 1417 *merlyn;* later *marlyne* (1485); borrowed from Middle Dutch *marlijn,* variant (influenced by *lijn* line) of *marling* small cord, from *marlen* to fasten or secure (a sail) with a marline, probably a frequentative form of Middle Dutch *māren, mēren* to tie, MOOR[1], v. **—marlinespike** *n.* 1626, originally *marling spike,* from *merlyng iren* a pointed iron tool used by sailors to separate strands of rope, especially for splicing (1485, also compare *marlyne* of the same date); formed originally from *merlyng, marling* after Middle Dutch *marling* (with later substitution of *marline-*); see MARLINE.

marmalade *n.* preserve made of oranges or other fruit. 1524, borrowed from Middle French *marmelade, marmellade,* from Portuguese *marmelada,* from *marmelo* quince (formed by dissimilation of the first *l* in the Latin *melimēlum* to *r*) in borrowing from Latin *melimēlum* a kind of sweet apple, from Greek *melímēlon* (*méli* honey + *mêlon* apple).

marmoreal (märmôr′ēəl) *adj.* of marble. 1798, like marble, cold, smooth, in Landor's *Gebir;* formed in English from Latin *marmoreus* of marble (from *marmor* MARBLE) + English -AL[1], possibly by influence of earlier *marmorean* (1656, also formed in English from Latin *marmoreus* + English -AN).

marmoset (mär′məzet) *n.* very small monkey. Before 1398 *marmusette* a kind of small monkey, in Trevisa's translation of Bartholomew's *De Proprietatibus Rerum;* borrowed from Old French *marmouset* grotesque figurine, perhaps variant of *marmot* monkey, little child, from *marmonner, marmouser* to mumble; probably of imitative origin.

marmot (mär′mət) *n.* rodent related to the squirrels. 1607, borrowed from French *marmotte,* perhaps related to *marmotter, marmonner* to mumble; probably of imitative origin. Alternatively, French *marmotte* may be an altered form (by influence of *marmot* monkey; see MARMOSET) of **mormont,* from Latin *mūrem montis* mountain mouse, the source also of Lombard and Romansh *murmont,* and Old High German *murmunto, murmuntīn* marmot.

maroon[1] *n., adj.* very dark brownish-red. 1594, a kind of chestnut, in a translation of a French book on general topics; later, a chestnut color (1791, in a book on dyeing); borrowed from French *marron* chestnut, from the French dialect of Lyons, from a pre-Roman (perhaps Ligurian) word; for ending see -OON.

maroon[2] *v.* put (a person) ashore in a desolate place and leave there. 1697, be lost in the wilds, in Dampier's *A New Voyage Round the World;* from earlier *maron,* n., a fugitive black slave living in the mountains and forests of the West Indies and Dutch Guiana, now Surinam (1666, but earlier found as Symeron, 1626). This noun was originally borrowed, perhaps once, from Spanish *cimarron* wild, untamed, and later borrowed from French *marron,* a shortening of American Spanish *cimarrón* runaway person or animal; originally an adjective meaning wild, untamed, with the literal sense of living high in the mountains; probably derived from Spanish *cima* summit, top, from Latin *cȳma* sprout; see CYME. The English suffix *-roon, -oon,* as in *octoroon,* is an extended form of the noun suffix in French *-on* and Spanish *-ón,* often used in a derogatory manner.

The sense of put ashore on a desolate island or coast, is first recorded in 1724 as *marooning,* gerund.

marque (märk) *n.* official permission to capture enemy merchant ships, especially in the phrase *letters of marque.* 1419 *merque, marque,* in *Proceedings of the Privy Council;* earlier *mark* (1353, in *Rolls of Parliament*); borrowed through Anglo-French *mark* from Old Provençal *marca* reprisal, from *marcar* seize as a pledge, mark, from Germanic (compare Old High German *marchōn, markōn* delimit, MARK[1], v.). Used from the 1400's to the 1800's (abolished among European nations by 1856), this term is found in the U.S. Constitution, "The Congress shall have power . . . to declare war, grant letters of marque and reprisal . . ." (Art. I, Sec. 8).

marquee (märkē′) *n.* rooflike shelter over an entrance. 1690, large tent, back formation (mistaken as a plural) from French *marquise* linen tent placed over an officer's tent to distinguish it from others; originally, marchioness; see MARQUISE. The meaning of a canopy over the entrance of a hotel, theater, etc., is first recorded in 1934 in American English, as a borrowing of French *marquise* glass canopy (1867).

marquess *n.* See **marquis.**

marquis (mär′kwis *or* märkē′) or **marquess** (mär′kwis) *n.* nobleman ranking below a duke and above an earl or count. Probably about 1300 *marchis,* in *The Romance of Guy of Warwick;* later *markys* (about 1395) and *marques* (1444); borrowed from Old French *marquis, marchis,* literally, ruler of a border area; compare Old French *marche* frontier, MARCH[2]. Old French *marquis, marchis* is cognate with Provençal *marques,* from Gallo-Romance **markēnsis,* from Frankish **marka.*

marquise (märkēz′) *n.* 1894, a marchioness; earlier, a ring with gems set in an oval shape (1885); borrowed from French *marquise,* feminine of *marquis* (from Old French) MARQUIS.

marriage *n.* About 1300 *mariage;* borrowing of Old French *mariage,* from *marier* to MARRY; for suffix see -AGE. **—marriageable** *adj.* About 1555; formed from English *marriage* + *-able.*

marrow *n.* soft tissue in bone. About 1340 *mergh;* later *marwe* (before 1387) and *marowe* (before 1398); developed from Old English (before 1000) *mearg* marrow; earlier *merg* (before 800) and *mærh* (about 700). The Old English forms are cognate with Old Frisian *merg* marrow, Old Saxon *marg,* Middle Dutch *merch* (modern Dutch *merg*), Old High German *marg, marag* (modern German *Mark*), and Old Icelandic *mergr*

(Swedish *merg,* Danish *marv*), from Proto-Germanic **mazga-*. Cognates outside Germanic are found in Old Prussian *musgeno* marrow, Old Slavic *mozgŭ* brain, Russian *mozg* marrow, Sanskrit *majján-, majjā́,* and Tocharian A *mäśśunt* marrow, from Indo-European **mosgh-* (Pok.750). In the Germanic forms, the sound represented by *-r-* is a substitution for the sound represented by *-s-* (with the intermediate development of *-z-*) in Indo-European.

marry[1] *v.* join as husband and wife. About 1300 *marien* to give in marriage; borrowed from Old French *marier,* from Latin *marītāre* wed, marry, from *marītus* married man or husband; of uncertain origin (very possibly a quasi-participle with the meaning of provided with a **marī,* a young woman). Cognates of Latin are found in Sanskrit *márya-s* man, young man, suitor, Greek *meîrax* boy or girl, Lithuanian *marti* bride, *mergà* girl, Latvian *mārša* brother's wife, Old Prussian *mergo* girl, and Welsh *merch* daughter, woman, from Indo-European **meryo-, meri-/mori-* (Pok.738). **—married** *adj.* joined in marriage. Before 1376 *maried,* in *Piers Plowman;* developed from past participle of *marien* to marry; *n.* Usually **marrieds,** *pl.* (1890). **—married couple** (before 1817, in Jane Austen's *Persuasion*)

marry[2] *interj. Archaic.* exclamation showing surprise, indignation, etc. Before 1375 *Marie,* from the name of (the Virgin) *Mary.* When the sense of (the Virgin) *Mary* has been forgotten (as here and in *marigold*), the spelling is altered severing the connection.

marsh *n.* soft wet land, swamp. About 1250 *mersh,* in *The Owl and the Nightingale;* later *marsh* (probably about 1450); developed from Old English (about 700) *mersc, merisc.* The Old English forms are cognate with Old Frisian and Old Saxon *mersk* marsh, Middle Low German *mersch, marsch* (modern German *Marsch* fen, marsh, bog), and Middle Dutch *mersch, marsch;* derived from Proto-Germanic **mariskō.* **—adj.** swampy, marshy. Before 1121, in the phrase *mersc lande* marshland; from the noun. **—marshland** *n.* 1121 *mersc lande,* found in Old English *mersclond.* **—marshy** *adj.* Before 1382 *mershi,* in the Wycliffe Bible; formed from *mersh* marsh + *-i -y*[1].

marshal *n.* officer of various kinds. 1258 *mareschal* high officer of a royal court; earlier as a surname *Marshal* (1218); borrowed from Old French *mareschal, marescal,* originally, stable officer, horse tender, groom, from Frankish (compare Old High German *marahscalc* groom, corresponding to modern German *Marschall* marshal, Middle Low German *marschalk* groom, Middle Dutch *maerschalc,* and modern Dutch *maarschalk* marshal).

Sense development in Old French is similar to Old High German in which *marahscalc* is a compound of *marah* horse + *scalc* servant, cognate with Old English *scealc* servant, Old Saxon and Old Frisian *scalc,* and Gothic *skalks,* originally perhaps a jumper, errand boy, related to Middle High German *schel* jumping, *schelch* he-goat, from Indo-European **sḱel-/sḱol-* jump (Pok.929). Compare CONSTABLE for a similar sense development.

—v. arrange in proper order. About 1450 *marchalen* arrange in order, tend horses; from the noun.

marshmallow *n.* soft, white, spongy confection. Before 1400 *marshmalue* kind of mallow plant which grows near salt marshes, found in a glossary of botanical terms for medicine; developed from Old English (about 1000) *mersc-mealwe* (*mersc* MARSH + *mealwe* MALLOW). *Marshmallow* became the name of the confection (1884) since it was originally made from the root of the marsh mallow plant.

marsupial *adj.* having a pouch for carrying the young. 1696, in Phillips' *Dictionary;* formed in English from New Latin *marsupium* + English *-al*[1]. *Marsupium* is found in Late Latin *marsūpium* pouch or purse, from Latin *marsuppium, marsīpium,* from Greek *marsíppion,* diminutive of *mársippos, mársyppos* pouch, perhaps from Iranian (compare Avestan *maršū-* abdomen). **—n.** marsupial animal. 1835, from the adjective.

mart *n.* market. 1436, market or fair; borrowed from Middle Dutch *marct,* or colloquial *mart;* borrowing of Latin *mercātus* trade, MARKET. Similar borrowing from Latin *mercātus* appear in Old High German *markāt, merkāt,* Old Saxon *markat,* Old Frisian *merked,* and Old Icelandic *markadhr.*

marten *n.* animal like a weasel. Probably about 1250 *martre* the animal or its fur; later *martrin* (before 1300) and *marten* (1437); borrowing in part from Old French *martrine,* noun use of feminine *martrin* of or pertaining to the marten, from *martre, marte* marten; and, in part from Medieval Latin *martrina, martina;* both the Old French and Medieval Latin forms are from Germanic (compare Old Saxon *marthrīn,* adj., of or pertaining to marten, Old High German *mardar* marten, modern German *Marder,* Middle Dutch *maerter,* modern Dutch *marter,* Old Icelandic *mǫrdhr,* Old Frisian *merth,* and Old English *mearth,* which did not survive into Middle English; all of the Germanic forms from Proto-Germanic **marthuz,* of unknown origin).

martial (mär′shəl) *adj.* of or suitable for war. About 1385 *marcial,* in Chaucer's *Troilus and Criseyde;* later *martial* (before 1475); borrowed from Latin *Mārtiālis* of Mars or war, from *Mārs* (genitive *Mārtis*) Mars, the Roman god of war. The term *martial law,* meaning military rule over civilians, is first recorded in Sir Thomas More's *Debellacyon of Salem and Bizance* (1533). *Martial arts,* referring to the Oriental arts of fighting, especially in self-defense, is first found in 1933, in an official English-language guide to Japan. The term is reminiscent of earlier *martial sports* (1568) or *exercises* (before 1586).

Martian *adj.* of the planet Mars. About 1395 *marcien* subject to influence of the planet Mars, in Chaucer's *Canterbury Tales;* later *Martian* of or pertaining to war (1591), and of or pertaining to the month of March (1623); in present-day English *Martian* of the planet Mars (1880); formed from Latin *Mārtius* pertaining to Mars (from *Mārs,* genitive *Mārtis* Mars) + English *-an.* The term is also found in French *martien,* adj. (1530), and this may have influenced its revival in English in the late 1500's. **—n.** a supposed inhabitant of Mars. 1892, from the adjective.

martin *n.* kind of swallow with a short beak and forked tail. 1589; earlier Scottish *martoune* (about 1450); probably borrowed from Middle French *martin,* from *Martin,* a proper name. The bird is perhaps specifically named after Saint *Martin,* bishop of Tours (about 371), whose festival of *Martinmas* is celebrated on November 11, at about the same time as the bird's migration or during St. Martin's summer (in French, *l'été de la Saint Martin*), the period of Indian summer around Martinmas.

It is, however, interesting to note that *martin* replaced earlier *martnet* (1440), *martynet* (1513), variant names probably for the European martin or swift; borrowed from Middle French *martinet* and from Medieval Latin *martineta,* diminutive forms of *Martin,* the proper name.

martinet (mär′tənet′ *or* mär′tənet) *n.* person who enforces very strict discipline. 1779 *Martinet* a military or naval officer who is a strict disciplinarian, developed from earlier *Martinet* a system of drill (1676); it was reputedly invented by Colonel Jean *Martinet,* a French general and drill master of the 1600's who instituted his system during the reign of Louis XIV.

Although named after a Frenchman, this sense of *martinet* is first found in English and not in French. In French *martinet* refers to cat-o'-nine-tails, the use or invention of which has been attributed to a Colonel *Martinet* of the 1600's, possibly the same person after whom English *martinet* was named.

martingale *n.* strap of a horse's harness. 1589, borrowed from Middle French *martingale,* originally, a style of fastening trousers, perhaps from Provençal *martegalo,* feminine of *martegal* inhabitant of *Martigues,* a small town near Marseilles, France. Alternatively, it has been suggested that Middle French *martingale* was an alteration of Spanish *almártaga* a check, rein, from a Spanish-Arabic word derived from Arabic *rāta'* to shackle, fetter. This latter, at least, has the virtue of coherent semantic development, if somewhat dubious development of form.

martini (märtē′nē) *n.* cocktail made with gin or vodka and dry vermouth. 1894, American English, in allusion to *Martini* and Rossi, an Italian company that manufactures vermouth. Earlier use of the term (1870) referred to a make of rifle.

martyr (mär′tər) *n.* person tortured or killed for holding a principle or belief. Old English *martyr* (before 899, probably in Alfred's translation of Bede's *Ecclesiastical History*); borrowed from Late Latin *martyr,* from Greek *mártyr,* late form of *mártys* (genitive *mártyros*) martyr, witness, probably related to *mérmēra* care, trouble, *mermaírein* be anxious or thoughtful; see MEMORY. In Middle English the term was reinforced by borrowing (probably before 1200, in Layamon's *Chronicle of Britain*) from Old French *martir,* from Late Latin *martyr.*
—**v.** put (a person) to death or torture for holding a principle or belief. Probably before 1200 *martren,* in Layamon's *Chronicle of Britain;* later *martiren* (about 1200, in *Vices and Virtues*); developed from Old English *gemartyrian* (before 899, in Alfred's translation of Bede's *Ecclesiastical History*), and *gemartrian* (before 899, in Alfred's translation of Orosius' *Historiarum Adversus Paganos*); from *martyr,* n. In Middle English, the verb was also reinforced by borrowing from Old French *martirier, martirer,* and Medieval Latin *martyriare.* In both noun and verb the spelling with *-y-* was used in an attempt to preserve the Latin form.
—**martyrdom** *n.* sufferings and death of a martyr. About 1175, Middle English *martirdom,* developed from Old English *martyrdōm* (before 899, in Alfred's translation of Bede's *Ecclesiastical History*); formed from Old English *martyr,* n. + *-dōm* -dom. —**martyrology** *n.* 1599 (possibly before 1475, in a version of Higden's *Polychronicon*) list of martyrs; borrowed from Medieval Latin *martyrologium,* from Late Greek *martyrológion* (Greek *mártyr* martyr + *lógos* account). *Martyrology* replaced Middle English *martiloge* (recorded before 1387); borrowed from Medieval Latin *martilogium,* alteration of *martyrologium.*

marvel *n.* Probably before 1300 *merveile, mervayle* something wonderful, in *Kyng Alisaunder;* later *marveyle* (probably before 1400); borrowed from Old French *merveille* a wonder, from Vulgar Latin **miribilia,* alteration of Latin *mīrābilia* wonderful things, from neuter plural of *mīrābilis* strange or wonderful, from *mīrārī* to wonder at, from *mīrus* wonderful; see MIRACLE. —**v.** Probably before 1300 *mervelyen* be filled with wonder, in *Kyng Alisaunder;* later *marvaylen* (1439, in Lydgate's writings); borrowed from Old French *merveillier* to wonder, from *merveille,* n. —**marvelous** *adj.* Probably before 1300 *merveillouse* causing wonder, in *Kyng Alisaunder;* borrowed from Old French *merveillos,* from *merveille* marvel; for suffix see -OUS.

Marxism (märk′sizəm) *n.* the theories of Karl Marx. 1897 (implied earlier in *Marxist,* 1886); probably borrowed from French *marxisme,* from Karl *Marx,* 1818-1883, German political theorist + *-isme* -ism.

marzipan (mär′zəpan) *n.* ground almonds and sugar, molded into various forms. 1901, borrowing of German *Marzipan,* from Italian *marzapane. Marzipan* replaced earlier *marchpayne* (1494); borrowed from Middle French *marcepain,* also from Italian *marzapane.* The Italian word also means a candy box; earlier, especially in Medieval Latin, a small box, perhaps containing items paid as a tax; and a medieval coin bearing the image of a seated Christ, at one time conjectured to be a borrowing from Arabic *mauṭabān* seated king.

mascara (maskar′ə) *n.* cosmetic for the eyelashes and eyebrows. 1890 *mascaro,* in the *Century Dictionary;* probably an alteration of Spanish *máscara* soot, stain, mask, from the same source as Italian *maschera* MASK. The spelling *mascara* is first recorded in English in 1922.

mascot *n.* animal, person, or thing supposed to bring good luck. 1881, borrowed from French *mascotte* sorcerer's charm, good luck piece, from Provençal *mascoto* sorcery, fetish, from *masco* witch, from Old Provençal *masca,* from Medieval Latin *masca* mask, specter, nightmare; of uncertain origin. French *mascotte* was first used by the novelist Émile Zola in 1867 and popularized in *La Mascotte* (1880), an operetta by the French composer Edmond Audran. Related to MASK.

masculine *adj.* Probably about 1350 *masculyn* masculine in grammatical gender; later, of men, male (about 1380, in Chaucer's translation of Boethius' *De Consolatione Philosophiae*); borrowed from Old French *masculin,* and directly from Latin *masculinus* male, masculine, of the masculine grammatical gender, from *masculus,* diminutive of *mās* (genitive *maris*) male person, male, of uncertain origin. —**n.** *Grammar.* masculine gender. About 1450 *masculin,* in *Battlefield Grammar;* from the adjective. —**masculinity** *n.* 1748, borrowed from French *masculinité* (*masculin* masculine + *-ité* -ity).

maser (mā′zər) *n.* device which amplifies or generates electromagnetic waves. 1955, acronym formed from *m(icrowave) a(mplification by) s(timulated) e(mission of) r(adiation).* Compare LASER.

mash[1] *n.* soft mixture. 1305 *mas-* in *masfat* vat used to hold mash (wort) in making beer or ale; later *massh-* in *masshfat* (1335); developed from Old English (about

1000) *mǣsc-* in *mǣsc-wyrt* mash-wort). The Old English element *mǣsc-* is cognate with Middle High German *meisch* crushed grapes, infused malt for beer (modern German *Maisch*), from Proto-Germanic **maisk-*, earlier **maiH-sk-*, Indo-European **moiḱ-;* see MIX. The general meaning of soft mixture, is first recorded in Florio's *A World of Words* (1598). **—v.** press or beat into a soft mass. About 1250 *meshen* to reduce to a pulp, in *The Owl and the Nightingale;* developed from Old English **mǣscan, mǣscan* to make pulp; from *mǣsc-*, see the noun.

mash² *v. Slang.* make amorous advances, flirt. 1879 (but said to be in theatrical parlance as early as 1860), American English, probably a figurative use of *mash¹*, v., either in the sense of press or force (one's attentions) on someone, or in the sense of reduce someone's emotions to a soft mass or mash. Alternatively, *mash²* could be a back formation from *masher*, with the same sense development. **—masher** *n. Slang.* man who makes advances to women. 1875, American English, probably formed from *mash¹* (in the sense of press or force one's attentions on someone, or reduce someone's emotions to a soft mass or mash) + *-er¹*.

mask *n.* 1534, borrowed from Middle French *masque* covering to hide or protect the face, through Italian *maschera,* and perhaps also directly from Medieval Latin *masca* mask, specter, nightmare, of uncertain origin, possibly shortened from Arabic *maskhara* buffoon, from *sakhira* to ridicule. A striking parallel to Medieval Latin *masca* is Latin *lārva,* also meaning ghost, specter, mask. **—v.** cover (the face) with a mask. 1560, take part in a masquerade; later, to disguise (1579); either from the noun or borrowed from Middle French *masquer* (1550), from *masque,* n.

masochism (mas′əkizəm) *n.* abnormal pleasure derived from pain. 1893, in Dunglison's *Medical Dictionary;* borrowed from German *Masochismus,* from the name of Leopold von Sacher-*Masoch,* 1836-1895, an Austrian novelist who described this abnormality in his works + *-ismus* -ism. German *Masochismus* was coined in 1883 by the German neurologist Richard von Krafft-Ebing, 1840-1902. **—masochist** *n.* person who derives pleasure from pain. 1895, in a translation of Max Nordau's *Degeneration;* borrowed from German *Masochist,* from Sacher-*Masoch* + *-ist.* **—masochistic** *adj.* 1904, in G.S. Hall's *Adolescence;* probably formed from English *masochist* + *-ic,* after German *masochistisch.*

mason *n.* Probably before 1200 *machun* worker who builds with stone or brick, in Layamon's *Chronicle of Britain;* later *masoun* (probably before 1300, in *Arthour and Merlin*); borrowed from Old French *masson, maçon, machon,* from Frankish (compare Old High German *steinmezzo* stone mason, modern German *Steinmetz* mason, related to *mahhōn* to MAKE). *Mason* is also found as a surname *Macun* (1125-30).

The form *fre mason* freemason, is first recorded in Wycliffe's writings, probably in 1383. Originally a freemason was a member of a class of skilled stone masons in the 1300's and later, who traveled from place to place and formed a society using secret signs and passwords; in modern times, this became a secret society for the purpose of mutual aid and fellowship. **—masonry** *n.* part of a building built by a mason. Probably about 1375, borrowed from Old French *maçonerie,* from *maçon* mason, and influenced in form by Middle English *masoun* mason; for suffix see -RY. The meaning of freemasonry is first recorded in 1435.

masque (mask) *n.* masquerade, masked ball. 1514 *maske,* borrowed from Middle French *masque;* see MASK. Originally this was the same word as *mask,* but the French spelling is now retained to distinguish the special meaning of a form of amateur dramatic entertainment, popular especially among the English nobility in the 1500's and 1600's, a sense first recorded in 1562, or a play written for such entertainment (1605, in Ben Jonson's *The Queenes of Masque*).

masquerade *n.* 1597 *mascarado,* in imitation of Italian, using French *mascarade* with a supposed Italian ending *-o;* and also *mascarad* (1613); borrowed from French *mascarade* party or dance at which masks and fancy costumes are worn, from Italian *mascarata,* variant of *mascherata* masquerade, from *maschera* MASK. **—v.** appear in disguise. 1654, to disguise as at a masquerade; from the noun.

mass¹ *n.* lump, heap. Before 1382 *masse,* in the Wycliffe Bible; borrowed from Old French *masse* lump, learned borrowing from Latin, and borrowed directly from Latin *massa* kneaded dough, lump, from Greek *mâza* barley bread, related to *mássein* to knead; see MINGLE. The phrase *the masses,* meaning the common people, appeared in 1837, probably borrowed from French *les masses* (late 1700's, 1826 as a political term). **—adj.** involving many people or the public. 1733 *mass meeting,* American English; from the noun. The term *mass media* appeared in 1923 as a technical term in advertising; *mass audience* appeared in 1938 in American English. The meaning of on a large scale (as in *mass production*) appeared in 1920. **—v.** form into a mass. 1563; from the noun. An isolated example is recorded earlier in Middle English *ymaced,* ppl. (about 1380).

Mass or **mass²** *n.* central service of worship in the Roman Catholic Church; eucharist. Before 1121 *messe;* also *masse* (1135), both forms recorded in *Peterborough Chronicle;* developed from Old English *mæsse* (before 901); earlier *messe* (before 810); borrowed as alteration of Vulgar Latin **messa* dismissal; also, the name of the religious service, from Late Latin *missa* dismissal; probably also, the name of the religious service, from Latin *missa* dismissal, feminine past participle of *mittere* to let go, send (see MISSION); probably so called from the concluding words of the Mass *Ite, missa est,* meaning "Go, it (the prayer) has been sent." The phrase in Latin has also been interpreted to mean: Go, it is the dismissal, or Go, dismissed, and thought to have been used at that point of the Mass when those learning the catechism but not yet confirmed in the Church were dismissed and the communion service followed; however, originally the phrase may have referred to dismissal of the congregation at the end of the Mass, probably with the sense first given above.

massacre *n.* 1586, borrowed from Middle French *massacre, maçacre* wholesale slaughter, carnage, related to Old French *macrecre, macecle* a shambles, slaughterhouse, butchery, of uncertain origin (compare Latin *macellum* provisions store, butcher shop). **—v.** to slaughter in large numbers. 1581, borrowed from Middle French *massacrer* to slaughter, from *massacre* massacre, n.

massage (məsäzh′) *n.* a rubbing and kneading of the muscles and joints. 1876, borrowed from French *massage* friction or kneading, from *masser* to massage, from Arabic *massa* to touch, feel, handle. **—v.** give a massage to. 1887, from the noun.

masseur (masœr′) *n.* man whose work is massaging people. 1876, borrowing of French *masseur,* from *masser* to MASSAGE. **—masseuse** (masœz′) *n.* 1876, borrowing of French *masseuse,* feminine of MASSEUR.

massive *adj.* big and heavy. Probably about 1408, *massiffe;* later *massif* (before 1420), both forms in Lydgate's writings; borrowed from Middle French *massif* (feminine *massive*) bulky, massive, from Old French *masse* lump, MASS[1]; for suffix see -IVE.

mast[1] *n.* long upright pole on a ship to support the sails and rigging. Probably before 1200 *mast,* in Layamon's *Chronicle of Britain;* developed from Old English *mæst* (about 725, in *Beowulf*). Old English *mæst* is cognate with Middle Dutch and modern Dutch *mast* mast or pole, Middle Low German *mast,* and Old High German *mast* (modern German *Mast*), from Proto-Germanic **mastaz,* Indo-European **masdos* (Pok.701); and outside Germanic cognate with Latin *mālus* mast. Latin *mālus* may have been influenced by *pālus* stake, paling, pole. **—masthead** *n.* 1748, top of a ship's mast; later, in American English, the part of a periodical that gives the title, address, etc. (1838).

mast[2] *n.* acorns, chestnuts, beechnuts, etc., that have fallen to the ground especially when used as food for swine. About 1380 *mast,* in Chaucer's *The Former Age;* earlier *maste* a feeding ground for swine (about 1300); developed from Old English (825) *mæst;* cognate with Middle Dutch and modern Dutch *mast* food, mast, Old High German *mast* (modern German *Mast*), from Proto-Germanic **mastaz,* cognate with Sanskrit *médas* fat, marrow, earlier **mazdas,* from Indo-European **maddos;* related to Old English *mete* food; see MEAT.

mastectomy (mastek′təmē) *n.* surgical removal of a woman's breast, as when cancerous. 1923, formed in English from Greek *mastós* breast + English *-ectomy* surgical removal. Greek *mastós* is apparently related to *madân* be moist, and *madarós* wet, from Indo-European **mad-tó-s* (Pok.694).

master *n.* Probably about 1150 *maister, master* person in authority, person holding a teaching degree; a fusion of 1) Old English (about 1000) *mægester,* borrowed from Latin *magister* chief, head, director, teacher, and 2) Old French *maistre, mastre, meister,* from Latin *magister,* contrastive adjective formed from *magis,* adv., more, comparative of *magnus* great; see MUCH. Latin *magister,* originally, the more important person, was formed in contrast with *minister,* originally, the less important person, servant, formed from *minus* less. **—adj.** being master, of a master. Before 1225 *meister, maister;* from the noun.

—v. become master of. Probably before 1200 *meistren* to overcome, defeat, in *Ancrene Riwle;* later *maistren* (before 1300); from the noun, and also borrowed from Old French *maistrier,* from *maistre,* n., master. The meaning of make oneself master of, become expert in, is first recorded in English in 1740.

—masterful *adj.* Probably about 1380 *maisterful;* formed from *maister* master + *-ful.* **—masterly** *adv.* Probably about 1395, in a version of *Piers Plowman;* formed from English *master* + *-ly[1]*; *adj.* 1531-32, formed from English *master* + *-ly[2]*. **—mastermind** *n.* (1720); *v.* be the mastermind behind (a scheme, etc.). 1941, American English; from the noun. **—master of ceremonies** (1662 *Master of the Ceremonies;* 1888 *Master of Ceremonies*) **—masterpiece** *n.* 1605 *masterpiece,* in Ben Jonson's *Volpone;* formed as an Anglicization of earlier *maisterstik* (1579), probably a borrowing from, or loan translation of, Dutch *meesterstuk* or perhaps German *Meisterstück* work by which a craftsman gained from his guild the rank of master. **—masterstroke** *n.* 1679, in Dryden's *Troilus and Cressida;* formed from English *master* + *stroke,* possibly by influence, or loan translation of German *Meisterstreich.* **—masterwork** *n.* About 1606; formed from English *master* + *work,* possibly by influence, or loan translation of German *Meisterwerk.* **—mastery** *n.* Probably before 1200, Middle English *meistrie,* in *Ancrene Riwle;* later *masterie* (before 1250); borrowed from Old French *maistrie,* from *maistre,* n., master.

mastic *n.* yellowish resin used in making varnish, chewing gum, and formerly as an astringent in medicine. 1373 *mastik,* in a handbook on plants; borrowed from Old French *mastic,* and directly from Late Latin *mastichum, masticha,* naturalized forms of Latin *mastichē,* from Greek *mastíchē,* related to *masâsthai* to chew (see MOUTH). The association with chew results from the ancient use of mastic as a form of chewing gum.

masticate *v.* chew. 1649, probably a back formation from earlier *mastication;* for suffix see -ATE[1]. **—mastication** *n.* Probably before 1425 *masticacioun,* in a translation of Chauliac's *Grande Chirurgie;* borrowed from Old French *mastication,* and directly from Late Latin *masticātiōnem* (nominative *masticātiō*), from *masticāre* chew, probably from Greek *mastichân* gnash the teeth; related to *mástax* mouth, jaws, and *masâsthai* chew; see MOUTH; for suffix see -ATION. In Latin it is also plausible that *masticāre* may have been formed from Latin *mastichē* with the meaning of chew mastic (i.e. treat as one treats mastic) + *āre.*

mastiff *n.* large, strong working dog. Before 1338 *mastif,* in Mannyng's *Chronicle of England;* irregular borrowing from Old French *mastin,* from Vulgar Latin **mānsuētīnus* domesticated, from Latin *mānsuētus* tame, gentle (*manus* hand + *suētus,* past participle of *suēscere* become used to). The ending of *mastiff* was influenced in Middle English by Old French *mestif* mongrel, from Late Latin *misticius, mixticius* mingled, from Latin *mixtus,* past participle of *miscēre* to MIX. The dialect forms in British English (especially *mastis*) from Provençal *mastis* were probably constructed on the Old French pattern of *baillis: baillif; mastis* thus being the nominative of Old French *mastin* and later *mastif.*

mastodon (mas′tədon) *n.* 1813, extinct animal much like an elephant; borrowed from French *mastodonte* (used by Cuvier in 1806), from New Latin *Mastodon* the genus name, formed from Greek *mastós* breast + *odṓn* (genitive *odóntos*) tooth; so called from the nipplelike projections on the mastodon's teeth.

mastoid (mas′toid) *adj.* of or having to do with the projection of bone behind the ear. 1732, borrowed from Greek *mastoeidḗs* resembling a breast (*mastós* breast + *eîdos* form). **—n.** 1800, conical or nipple-shaped projection of bone; from the adjective.

masturbation *n.* manual stimulation of the genitals. 1766, in A. Hume's *Onanism;* borrowed from French *masturbation* (1570 in Montaigne) and probably directly from New Latin *masturbationem* (nominative *masturbatio*), from Latin *māsturbārī,* alteration, probably by influence of *turbāre* to stir up, of earlier **man-stuprāre* (*manus* hand + *stuprāre* defile), which would reinforce the connection of form with the earlier form in English *mastupration,* 1621, in Burton's *Anatomy of*

Melancholy; for suffix see -ATION. **—masturbate** *v.* engage in masturbation. 1857, back formation from *masturbation;* for suffix see -ATE[1].

mat[1] *n.* piece of coarse fabric made of woven rushes, fiber, straw, etc., and used as a rug. Probably before 1200 *matte,* in *Ancrene Riwle;* later *mat;* developed from Old English *matte* (before 800, in *Corpus Glossary*); borrowed from Late Latin *matta,* probably from Phoenician (compare Hebrew *mittāh* bed, couch, from *nāṭāh* he spread out). **—v.** 1549, cover with mats; also tangle thickly together (1577); from the noun. An isolated example is recorded earlier in Middle English *matten* make mats (before 1425).

mat[2], **matt,** or **matte** *adj.* not shiny, dull. Before 1648 *matte,* probably developed from the verb in English, and in part borrowed from French *mat* dull, from the verb. **—v.** give a dull finish to. 1602, borrowed from French *mater,* from *mat* dull, from Old French *mat* beaten down, withered, probably from Latin *mattus* maudlin or sodden with drink (probably a dialectal or colloquial form of **maditus* soaked, drenched, from *madēre* be wet or sodden, be drenched with wine, be drunk, cognate with Greek *madarós* wet, from Indo-European **mad-,* Pok.694). **—n.** backing for a picture. 1845, borrowed from French *mat* a dull surface or finish, from the adjective.

matador (mat′ədôr) *n.* chief bullfighter. 1681, in Dryden's *The Spanish Friar;* borrowing of Spanish *matador,* literally, killer, from *matar* to kill or wound, probably from Vulgar Latin **mattāre* beat down, dominate, afflict, wound; possibly from **mattus* stupid, brutish, from Latin *mattus* drunk; see MAT[2] dull.

Mata Hari (mä′tə hä′rē) woman spy, especially one who seduces men to obtain military secrets. 1936, in Evelyn Waugh's *Waugh in Abyssinia,* in allusion to *Mata Hari,* professional name of Gertrud Margarete Zelle, 1876-1917, a Dutch dancer who lived in France and spied for the Germans during World War I. As an exponent of Indonesian dancing, she took the name Mata Hari from the Indonesian words *mata* eye and *hari* day; compare DAISY for an English compound of the same meaning.

match[1] *n.* stick with an easily combustible head for striking up a fire. About 1378 *macche* wick of a candle or lamp, in a version of *Piers Plowman;* later *mecche* (before 1400) and *matche* (probably about 1450); borrowed from Old French *meiche* wick of a candle, cognate with Old Provençal *meca,* of uncertain origin (probably from Gallo-Romance **micca, *mycca,* perhaps a blend of Latin *myxa,* from Greek *mýxa* lamp wick, mucus, and Latin *muccus, mūcus* MUCUS*);* the semantic connection (going back to antiquity) is that the spout of a lamp resembles a nostril, and the wick is suggestive of mucus. The modern meaning of *match,* a stick tipped with a substance ignited by friction, is first recorded in 1831, as a modernized substitute for the old match, a piece of cord, cloth, paper, etc., dipped in sulphur and ignited by a spark from a tinder box (1530, in Palsgrave's *Lesclarcissement*). **—matchbook** *n.* (about 1945) **—matchbox** *n.* (1850, American English) **—matchstick** *n.* (1791)

match[2] *n.* an equal. Probably about 1200 *macche* one's spouse, mate, in *The Ormulum;* later, one's equal (about 1300); developed from Old English (about 1000) *mæcca,* from *gemæcca* companion, mate, wife (before 971, from Proto-Germanic **ʒamakjōn*); earlier *gemecca* companion (before 810). Old English *gemecca* is cognate with Old Saxon *gimaco* fellow, equal, Old High German *gimahho* (from Proto-Germanic **ʒamakōn*), and Old Icelandic *maki* companion, mate; see MAKE.

The meaning of contest, competitive game is first recorded in 1545, from an earlier sense of matching of adversaries (probably before 1400). The sense of a marriage union (especially in the phrase *to make a match*) is found in 1575-85.

—v. be a match for. About 1353 *machen,* from the noun.

—matchless *adj.* without an equal, peerless (1530, in Palsgrave's *Lesclarcissement*); formed from English *match* + *-less.* **—matchmaker** *n.* one who brings about a match or marriage. Before 1639, formed from English *match* + *maker.*

mate[1] *n.* one of a pair. Probably about 1350, fellow; also companion (about 1380); borrowed from Middle Low German *māte, gemate* one eating at the same table, messmate (modern German *Maat* mate); cognate with Old High German *gimazzo* messmate from Proto-Germanic **ʒa-matōn* having food (**matiz*) together (**ʒa-*). See MEAT. **—v.** join in a pair. 1509, to equal, rival; later, to join in marriage (1589); and to associate, couple, pair (1593, in Shakespeare's *Venus and Adonis*); from the noun.

mate[2] *v.* to defeat in chess, checkmate. Probably before 1300 *maten,* in *Sir Tristrem;* earlier, to overcome, defeat, damage (probably about 1200, in *Ancrene Riwle*); borrowed from Old French *mater,* from *mat,* n., checkmate, in *eschecmat;* see CHECKMATE. **—n.** the move in chess that ends the game. Probably before 1300 *mat,* in *Arthour and Merlin;* borrowed from Old French *mat;* see the verb above.

maté or **mate**[3] (mä′tā *or* mat′ā) *n.* kind of tea made from the dried leaves of a South American holly. 1758, the tea, but implied earlier in cup holding the drink (1717); borrowed from Spanish *mate,* from Quechua (Peru) *mati* calabash dish. The form *maté* (1826) was borrowed from French, from Spanish *mate.*

material *n.* About 1380, thing made of matter, substance, in Chaucer's translation of Boethius' *De Consolatione Philosophiae;* from the adjective. Doublet of MATERIEL. **—adj.** About 1340 *materiel* of matter, physical, concrete, earthly; later *material* (about 1390); borrowed through Old French *materiel, material,* and directly from Late Latin *māteriālis* of or belonging to matter, from Latin *māteria* matter; see MATTER; for suffix see -AL[1]. **—materialism** *n.* 1748, belief that all action, thought, and feeling is made up of material things; borrowed from French *matérialisme* or from New Latin *materialismus,* from Late Latin *māteriālis* of matter; for suffix see -ISM. It is also likely that in some instances *materialism* is a formation in English based on earlier *materialist.* The meaning of devotion to material objects and needs, is first recorded in Hawthorne's *The Snow Image* (1851). **—materialist** *n.* 1668, borrowed from French *matérialiste* or from New Latin *materialista,* from Late Latin *māteriālis* + *-ista* -ist. It is also likely that in some instances *materialist* is a formation in English from *material* + *-ist.* **—materialistic** *adj.* 1845; formed from English *materialist* + *-ic.* **—materialize** *v.* give material form to. 1710, Addison, in *The Tatler,* formed from English *material,* adj. + *-ize.* **—materialization** *n.* 1843; formed from English *materialize* + *-ation.*

materiel or **matériel** (mətir′ēel′) *n.* equipment, supplies. 1827; earlier, the mechanical part of an art, such as style, technique, etc. (1814); borrowing of French *matériel* material, from Old French *materiel,* adj., learned borrowing from Late Latin *māteriālis* of matter, from *māteria* substance, MATTER. Doublet of MATERIAL.

maternal *adj.* motherly. 1481, in Caxton's *The Mirror of the World,* borrowing of Middle French *maternel,* learned borrowing from Vulgar Latin **māternālis,* derived (probably on the model of Latin *mātrōnālis* of or befitting a matron) from Latin *māternus* maternal, from *māter* MOTHER; for suffix see -AL[1].

maternity *n.* condition of being a mother; motherhood. 1611, in Cotgrave's *Dictionary;* borrowing of French *maternité,* learned borrowing from Medieval Latin *maternitatem* (nominative *maternitas*), from Latin *māternus* MATERNAL; for suffix see -ITY.

mathematics *n.* science of numbers. 1581 *mathematikes,* plural of Middle English *methametik* (before 1387, in Trevisa's translation of Higden's *Polychronicon*), borrowed from Latin *mathēmatica;* and *mathematique* (before 1393, in Gower's *Confessio Amantis*); borrowed from Old French *mathematique,* from Latin *mathēmatica.* Latin *mathēmatica* was borrowed from Greek *mathēmatikḕ téchnē* mathematical science, feminine singular of *mathēmatikós* relating to mathematics, from *máthēma* (genitive *mathḗmatos*) learning, knowledge, mathematical knowledge; related to *manthánein* to learn. This Greek word is cognate with Lithuanian *mañdras, mandrùs* awake, alert, Old Slavic *mǫdru* wise, Gothic *mundōn* pay mind to; and in Germanic with Old Icelandic *munda* strive for, Old High German *muntar* eager, awake (modern German *munter* awake, alert). All these Greek, Baltic, Slavic, and Germanic forms are thought to derive ultimately from different grades of an Indo-European compound **men(s)-dhē-* (Pok.730), with the meaning of direct the mind (toward), found in Sanskrit *medhā́* wisdom, intelligence, and Avestan *mazdā* memory (from proto-Indo-Iranian **mn̥s-dhā́*), the two elements representing the Indo-European bases that are the ultimate sources of English MIND and English DO[1] respectively.
—mathematical *adj.* Probably before 1425 *mathematicalle,* in a translation of Higden's *Polychronicon;* borrowed from Medieval Latin *mathematicalis,* from Latin *mathēmaticus* (from Greek *mathēmatikós*) + *-ālis* -al[1]. **—mathematician** *n.* Probably before 1425 *mathematicioun,* in a translation of Higden's *Polychronicon;* borrowed from Middle French *mathematicien,* from *mathematique* mathematical, from Latin *mathēmaticus;* for suffix see -IAN.

-matic a combining form abstracted from *automatic,* and used in allusion to the sense of automatic, often with a connective vowel, such as *-a-* or *-o-*, as in *Adjustomatic, Instamatic.*

matinee or **matinée** (mat'ənā') *n.* dramatic or musical performance held in the afternoon. 1848, as a French term in *matinée musicale,* in Thackeray's *Vanity Fair;* French *matinée,* from *matin* morning (i.e. daytime), from Old French *matines;* see MATINS. **—adj.** of a matinee. 1895 *matinée actor,* from the noun. The term *matinee idol* handsome actor who attracts large audiences of women, presumably as women were once thought of as "free" in the afternoons, is first recorded in 1902.

matins *n.pl.* first of the seven canonical hours in the breviary. About 1250, church service held in the morning; borrowed from Old French *matines,* from Late Latin *mātūtīnās* (accusative) morning prayers, originally *mātūtīnās vigiliās* morning watches, from Latin *mātūtīnus* of or in the morning, associated with *Mātūta* a dawn goddess.

matri- a combining form borrowed from Latin *mātri-*, as found in such forms as *mātricīda* matricide and *matrimōnium* matrimony, from *māter* (genitive *mātris*) MOTHER, used especially in the social sciences to coin terms describing relationships or kinship with the mother or the female line, as in *matricentric* mother-centered (1956), *matrilineal* (1904), *matrilocal* located in the home of the wife's family (1906). Contrasted with PATRI-.

matriarch *n.* mother who is the head of a family or tribe. 1606, formed from English *matri-* + *-arch,* abstracted from *patriarch;* see PATRIARCH. **—matriarchal** *adj.* of a matriarch. 1863, in Jowett's writings; formed from English *matriarch* + *-al*[1], patterned after *patriarchal.* **—matriarchy** *n.* matriarchal social organization. 1885, formed from English *matriarch* + *-y*[3], patterned after *patriarchy.*

matricide[1] *n.* person who kills his mother. 1638, borrowed perhaps through French *matricide* mother killer, from Latin *mātricīda,* from *māter* MOTHER + *-cīda* -cide[1], killer.

matricide[2] *n.* act of killing one's own mother. 1594, borrowed perhaps through French *matricide* mother killing, from Latin *mātricīdium,* from *māter* MOTHER + *-cīdium* -cide[2], a killing.

matriculate *v.* enroll as a student in a college or university. 1579; earlier, to place a name on an official list (1577); either developed from English *matriculate,* adj., registered, enrolled (1487), borrowed from Medieval Latin **matriculatus,* past participle of **matriculare;* or borrowed directly from Medieval Latin **matriculare* (possibly through influence of Middle French *emmatriculer* enroll) from Late Latin *mātrīcula* a public register, diminutive of *mātrix* (genitive *mātrīcis*) list, roll, sources, womb, from Latin *mātrīx* breeding animal, MATRIX; for suffix see -ATE[1].

The Late Latin meaning (also found in Latin) of *mātrīx* as list or roll is understandable only as a loan translation of Greek *mḗtrā* register, lot (compare Sanskrit *mā́trā* measure, *mímāti* he measures, and Latin *mētīrī* to measure, from Indo-European **mē-*, Pok.703) as if that were the same word as Greek *mḗtrā* womb. **—matriculation** *n.* 1588, formed from English *matriculate* + *-ion.*

matrimony *n.* marriage. About 1300 *matirmoyne,* also *matrymony* (about 1303, in Mannyng's *Handlyng Synne*); borrowed from Old French *matrimoine* (learned borrowing from Latin *mātrimōnium*) and borrowed directly from Latin *mātrimōnium* wedlock, marriage; literally, establishment of a mother in a household, derived (probably on the model of *patrimōnium* patrimony) from *māter* (genitive *mātris*) MOTHER + *-monia* suffix signifying action, state, condition. **—matrimonial** *adj.* of or having to do with marriage. 1449 *matrimonyal;* borrowed from Middle French *matrimonial* (from Latin) and borrowed directly from Latin *mātrimōniālis,* from *mātrimōnium* matrimony; for suffix see -AL[1].

matrix (mā'triks *or* mat'riks) *n.* that which gives origin or form to something enclosed within it, such as a mold for a casting. Probably before 1425; earlier *matrice* womb (1373); borrowed from Old French *matrice,* from Latin *mātrīx,* and directly from Late Latin *mātrīx* (genitive *mātrīcis*) womb, from Latin, breeding animal, derived (on the model of *generātrīx* one who brings forth, mother, and *nūtrīx* foster mother, nurse, from *māter* (genitive *mātris*) MOTHER.

The meaning of a place or medium in which something is produced or developed, is first recorded in 1555.

—v. arrange or organize in a matrix. 1951 (implied in *matrixing*); from the noun.

matron *n.* wife or widow. Before 1393 *matrone* married woman, in Gower's *Confessio Amantis;* borrowing of Old French *matrone* (learned borrowing from Latin *mātrōna*), and borrowed directly from Latin *mātrōna* married woman, from *māter* (genitive *mātris*) MOTHER. The meaning of a woman who has some charge of, or manages a hospital, school, prison, or other public institution, is first recorded in 1557. **—matronly** *adj.* 1656, formed from English *matron* + *-ly*[2]. **—matron of honor** (1903, American English)

matt or **matte** (mat) *adj., n.* see MAT[2].

matter *n.* Probably before 1200 *materie* substance, concern, subject, as of discussion, in *Ancrene Riwle;* later *mater* (before 1325, in *Cursor Mundi*); borrowed from Old French *matere, matiere,* and directly from Latin *māteria* substance from which something is made, timber, stock and shoots of a plant, growing layer in trees, from *māter* origin, source, MOTHER. —v. be of importance. 1581; from the noun. An earlier meaning of form or discharge pus, is found in Palsgrave's *Lesclarcissement* (1530). **—matter-of-fact** *adj.* 1712, in writings of Steele; from the earlier phrase *matter of fact* (1581). **—matter-of-factly** *adv.* (1873) **—matter-of-factness** *n.* (1816)

mattock (mat′ək) *n.* tool like a pickax with a broad blade for cutting roots and loosening soil. About 1303 *mattok,* in Mannyng's *Handlyng Synne;* developed from Old English (about 700) *mættoc;* probably borrowed from Vulgar Latin **matteūca* club, related to Latin *mateola* kind of mallet; see MACE[1] war club.

mattress *n.* About 1300 *materas;* later *materace* (1388); borrowed from Old French *materas,* from Italian *materasso,* and from Medieval Latin *matracium, materacium,* both Italian and Medieval Latin forms from Arabic *al-maṭraḥ* the cushion; literally, thing thrown down, from *ṭaraḥa* he threw (down).

maturate *v.* discharge pus, ripen. 1541, probably a back formation from the earlier *maturation,* perhaps by influence of Middle French *maturer* ripen; for suffix see -ATE[1]. It is also possible that the verb developed from *maturate,* adj., matured, (of an abscess) brought to a head (probably about 1425); borrowed from Latin *mātūrātum* ripened, past participle of *mātūrāre* to ripen; see MATURATION.

The old sense of mature, develop (1622) that was once obsolete is now experiencing a revival in the social sciences.

—maturation *n.* process of growing and developing. 1392 *maturacioun* formation of pus; borrowed from Middle French *maturation,* and directly from Latin *mātūrātiōnem* (nominative *mātūrātiō*) a hastening, from *mātūrāre* to ripen, from *mātūrus* ripe; for suffix see -ATION. The extended sense of the process of growing and developing is first recorded in English in 1616, though as applied to the making of wine, it is recorded as early as 1605.

mature *adj.* Probably 1440, ripe, full-grown, in a translation of Palladius' *De Re Rustica;* later, well-considered, careful (1454, in *Rolls of Parliament*); borrowed through Middle French *mature,* and directly from Latin *mātūrus* ripe, timely, early. —v. 1392 *maturen* ripen, bring to a head; borrowed from Latin *mātūrāre* to ripen, from *mātūrus* ripe. The meaning of come or bring to maturity or full development is first recorded in Bacon's *Sylva Sylvarum* (1626). **—maturity** *n.* Probably before 1430 *maturyte,* in Lydgate's writings; borrowed through Middle French *maturité,* and directly from Latin *mātūritātem* (nominative *mātūritās*) ripeness, from *mātūrus* ripe; for suffix see -ITY.

matzo or **matzoh** (mat′sə) *n.* thin piece of unleavened bread, such as eaten by Jews during Passover. 1846, borrowed from Yiddish *matse,* from Hebrew *maṣṣāh* unleavened bread; literally, that which is drained out (of juice).

maudlin *adj.* 1607, tearful; later, sentimental in a weak or emotional way (before 1631, in Donne's *Letters*); developed from Middle English *Maudelen* (probably before 1325), *Maudelayne* (about 1386), *Magdalene* (about 1390), all forms of Magdalene (the woman from whom Jesus cast out seven devils, Luke 8:2, commonly supposed to be the repentant sinner forgiven by Jesus, Luke 7:37); borrowed from Old French *Madelaine,* and directly from Latin *Magdalēnē,* from Greek *Magdalēnḗ* of *Magdala,* a town on the Sea of Galilee. The figurative meaning developed in allusion to the paintings in which Mary Magdalene was often represented as weeping in repentance.

The Middle English spelling of the name of Magdalene approximates the pronunciation (môd′lən), which is still current for the names of Magdalen College, Oxford, and Magdalene College, Cambridge.

maul *n.* very heavy hammer or mallet. 1545, spelling alteration of Middle English *malle* (before 1400); earlier *mealle* (probably about 1200) and, in the surname *Maulmanger* seller of mauls (1205); borrowed from Old French *mail* MALLET. —v. beat and pull about, handle roughly. 1593, spelling alteration of Middle English *mallen* to strike with a maul (probably about 1350); earlier *meallen* (probably about 1200); generally considered to be from the noun. The meaning of knock about, handle roughly is first recorded about 1610.

maunder *v.* 1621, to grumble, mutter, or growl, in Burton's *Anatomy of Melancholy;* of uncertain origin, perhaps imitative. The meaning of move in an aimless or confused manner, is first recorded about 1746. The extended sense of talk in a rambling, foolish manner is first recorded in Carlyle's *Sartor Resartus* (1831).

Maundy Thursday (môn′dē) the Thursday before Easter. 1440, developed from *maunde* the Last Supper, also the ceremony of washing the feet on Maundy Thursday; borrowed from Old French *mandé,* from Latin *mandātum* command, commandment, in reference to the first word of the church service for this day, from the passage in John 13:34, "A new commandment (*mandātum novum*) I give unto you, that ye love one another," spoken by Jesus to the Apostles after washing their feet at the Last Supper.

mausoleum (mô′səlē′əm) *n.* large, magnificent tomb. 1600, in Holland's translation of Livy's *Roman History,* from earlier reference to *Mausoleum* (probably about

1425, name of the magnificent tomb built at Halicarnassus, in Asia Minor); borrowed from Latin *Mausōlēum,* from Greek *Mausōleîon,* from *Maússōllos* Mausolus, king of an ancient region of southwest Asia Minor. This tomb was considered one of the Seven Wonders of the ancient world.

mauve (mōv) *n., adj.* delicate, pale purple. 1859, borrowing of French *mauve,* from Old French *mauve* mallow, from Latin *malva,* from the same (Mediterranean) source as Greek *maláchē, molóchē* mallow; so called from the color of the mallow plant. Doublet of MALLOW.

maven or **mavin** (mā′vən) *n. Informal.* expert, connoisseur. 1965, American English, borrowed from Yiddish *meyvn,* from Hebrew *mēbhin,* literally, one who understands, from the root *bin* to understand.

maverick *n.* calf or other animal not marked with an owner's brand. 1867, American English, unbranded calf, in allusion to Samuel *Maverick,* 1803-1870, a Texas cattle owner who did not brand the calves of one of his herds. The transferred meaning of individualist, unconventional person, is first recorded in 1886; later, a politician who refuses to affiliate or who breaks with a regular political party (1900).

maw (mô) *n.* mouth, throat, gullet, or stomach. Probably before 1300 *mawe* stomach; earlier *mahe* (probably before 1200, in *Ancrene Riwle*); developed from Old English *maga* (before 800, in *Corpus Glossary*). Old English *maga* is cognate with Old Frisian *maga* stomach, Middle Dutch *maghe* (modern Dutch *maag*), Old High German *mago* (modern German *Magen*), and Old Icelandic *magi,* from Proto-Germanic **maʒṓn,* cognate with Lithuanian *mãkas,* Lettish *maks* bag, Old Slavic *mošĭna,* and Welsh *megin* bellows, from Indo-European **mak-* skin bag, leather bag (Pok.698).

mawkish (môk′ish) *adj.* sickening, nauseating. 1668, inclined to sickness, without appetite, in Dryden's *Works;* formed from dialectal *mawk* maggot + *-ish*[1]. *Mawk* is found in Middle English *mawke* (recorded before 1425); borrowed from a Scandinavian source (compare Old Icelandic *madhkr* MAGGOT). The meaning of sickening or nauseating is first recorded before 1697, and the figurative sense of sickly sentimental or weakly emotional, is found in 1702.

maxilla (maksil′ə) *n.* jaw or jawbone. 1676, borrowed from Latin *maxilla* upper jaw, diminutive of *māla* cheekbone, jaw; of uncertain origin. The word was apparently lost for 250 years after its earlier appearance in Middle English *maxille* (1425, in a translation of Chauliac's *Grande Chirurgie*); borrowed from Middle French, from Latin *maxilla.* **—maxillary** (mak′səler′ē) *adj.* of the jaw or jawbone. 1626, in Bacon's *Sylva Sylvarum;* formed in English from Latin *maxilla* jaw + English *-ary* or borrowed from French *maxillaire,* from Latin *maxilla* jaw + *-aire* -ary.

maxim *n.* Probably before 1430 *maxime* proverb, adage, in Lydgate's writings; borrowed from Middle French *maxime,* learned borrowing from Late Latin *maxima,* usually cited in *maxima prōpositiō* axiom; literally, greatest premise, feminine of *maximus* greatest; see MAXIMUM.

maximum *n.* the largest or highest amount. 1740, borrowed through French *maximum,* and directly from Latin *maximum,* neuter of *maximus* greatest, superlative of *magnus* great or large; see MUCH. **—adj.** largest or highest possible. 1834, from the noun. **—maximize** *v.* increase to the highest possible degree. 1802, in Bentham's writings; formed from English *maximum* + *-ize.*

may *v.* be able to. Before 1200 *mai, may* have power, may (first and third person singular present indicative for the infinitive *mouen,* with the past tense *mighte, moghte*); developed from Old English (perhaps 650) *mæg* (infinitive *magan,* past tense *meahte, mihte*). The Old English forms are cognate with Old Frisian *mei* have power, may (infinitive *muga,* past tense *machte*), Old Saxon *mag* (infinitive *mugan,* past tense *mahte*), Middle Dutch *mach* (infinitive *moghen,* past tense *mohte;* modern Dutch *mag,* infinitive *mogen,* past tense *mocht*), Old High German *mag* (infinitive *magan,* past tense *mahta;* modern German *mag,* infinitive *mögen,* past tense *mochte*), Old Icelandic *mā* (*mega,* past tense *mātte;* Norwegian, Danish, Swedish *må,* past tense *måtte*), and Gothic *mag* (infinitive *magan,* past tense *mahte*). The Proto-Germanic root **mag-* (infinitive **maʒanan*) corresponds to Indo-European **magh-* power, might, ability, be able, as represented in Old Slavic *mogǫ* I can, Greek *mêchos* means, *mēchanḗ* (Doric *māchanā́*) means, machine, Armenian *marthankh* (from **magh-thra-*) means, and Sanskrit *maghá-m* power, wealth, from Indo-European **magh-/māgh-* (Pok.695). Related to MIGHT.

May *n.* fifth month. 1110 *Mai;* borrowed from Old French *mai,* and directly from Latin *Majus, Maius mēnsis* month of May, possibly related to *Maja, Maia,* an earth goddess whose name is probably cognate with Latin *magnus* great, with reference either to her stature or her furthering growth of crops. Latin *Maia,* earlier **Magja,* is cognate with Sanskrit *mahī́* the Great One, the Ancient One, the earth, related to *mahā-* great, and Greek *mégas,* from Indo-European **meĝ-, meĝhā-/meĝhə-* (Pok.708). **—May Day** 1438, the first day of May (the traditional beginning of summer was celebrated throughout Europe. Also associated with rights of workmen, especially since 1517, when apprentices in London rose against foreigners who had privileges giving them an advantage in trade; later, associated with demonstrations of Socialist support, 1890). **—mayflower** *n.* 1626, a flower that blooms in May (traditionally, any of several varieties; also alluded to earlier, in a figurative sense, 1576). **—Mayfly** or **mayfly** *n.* (1651-53) **—Maypole** or **maypole** *n.* (1554)

maybe *adv.* perhaps. Before 1400 *may be,* in a version of *Cursor Mundi;* a variant form of the phrase *(it) may be;* also corresponding to archaic *mayhap* (1444 *may happe,* in *The Paston Letters;* a variant form of the phrase *(it) may hap* it may happen; see HAPHAZARD, HAPPEN).

Mayday or **mayday** (mā′dā′) *n.* the international radiotelephone call for help. 1927, adapted from the pronunciation of French *m'aider,* a shortening of *venez m'aider* come help me! Compare SOS.

mayhem (mā′hem *or* mā′həm) *n.* crime of intentionally maiming a person. Probably before 1300 *maym* a mutilation, injury, in *Kyng Alisaunder;* later *maheym* (about 1405); borrowed through Anglo-French *mahaim, maihem,* Old French *mahaigne* injury, related to *mahaignier* to MAIM, from Vulgar Latin **mahanāre,* of unknown origin. The figurative sense of any excessive violence, damage, or disorder, is first recorded in 1868.

mayonnaise (mā′ənāz′) *n.* kind of salad dressing. 1841, in Thackeray's *Essays,* borrowing of French *mayon-*

naise, mahonnaise (1807), probably named in allusion to *Mahon,* a seaport on the island of Minorca, captured by the Duc de Richelieu in 1756, whose chef is said to have introduced the *Mahonnaise* in commemoration of his employer's victory.

mayor (mā′ər *or* mãr) *n.* About 1300 *mer,* in an old chronicle; later *maire* (about 1378, in a version of *Piers Plowman*), but also found as a surname *Mair* (1242); borrowed from Old French *maire, major* head of a city or town government; originally, greater or superior, adj., from Latin *maior, major,* comparative of *magnus* great; see MUCH. Doublet of MAJOR. **—mayoralty** *n.* 1386, borrowed from Old French *mairalte,* from *maire* + *-alte* as in *principalte,* and re-formed in English as *-alty.*

maze *n.* About 1300 *mase* delusion, deception, bewilderment; later *maze* (about 1385, in Chaucer's *Troilus and Criseyde*); developed from *amasen* AMAZE. The meaning of a network of paths, labyrinth, is first recorded in Chaucer's *Legend of Good Women* (about 1386).

mazuma (məzü′mə) *n. Slang.* money, cash. 1904 *mazume,* in G.V. Hobart's *Jim Hickey,* American English; borrowed from Yiddish *mazume* cash, dialectal variant of *mezumen,* from *bimzumen* in cash, from Medieval Hebrew *bimĕzūmān* in fixed currency, from Mishnaic Hebrew *mĕzumān, mĕzūmmān* fixed, appointed, ultimately from Hebrew *zĕmān* appointed time.

mazurka or **mazourka** (məzėr′kə) *n.* lively Polish dance. 1818, borrowed probably from Russian *mazúrka,* from Polish *mazurek* dance of the *mazur,* inhabitant of *Mazowsze* (Mazovia), ancient region in central Poland; in Russian the accusative in the Polish expression *tańczyć* (to dance) *mazurka* was reinterpreted as a feminine form with the suffix *-ka,* hence the form *mazúrka.* Even Chopin's famous pieces (dating from 1825) were known under the Russian name which was the popularized form for the dance in Western Europe.

McCarthyism *n.* policy of hunting out and persecuting suspected subversives, especially Communists. 1950, American English, in allusion to Joseph R. *McCarthy,* 1908-1957, Republican United States senator (1947-57) from Wisconsin + *-ism.* McCarthy charged the Department of State with harboring Communists, and made numerous allegations of Communist activity, especially in the government.

McCoy *n.* **the real McCoy,** *Informal.* the genuine article, the real thing. 1922, American English, alteration of the earlier Scottish phrase *the real Mackay* (used by Stevenson in a letter dated 1883); of uncertain origin.

Several derivations have been proposed: 1) from *Mackay,* a Scotch whiskey distilled by A. and M. Mackay of Glasgow; a citation (1908) refers to liquor as "the clear McCoy"; 2) from, or influenced by, Kid *McCoy,* a former welterweight boxing champion (1898-1900); 3) from the northern branch of the Scots clan *Mackay,* whose chief, Lord Reay, in rivalry with other branches, was referred to as "the *Reay* Mackay," said to be later altered to "the *real* Mackay" or the genuine article.

me *pron.* Old English *mē* dative, and *mē, mec* accusative case of *I* (about 650); cognate with Old Frisian *mi* me (accusative), *mi, mir* (dative), Old Saxon *mī* (dative and accusative), Middle Dutch *mī,* modern Dutch *mij,* Old High German *mih* (accusative), *mir* (dative), modern German *mich, mir,* Old Icelandic *mik* (accusative), *mēr* (dative), Gothic *mik* (accusative), *mis* (dative), from Proto-Germanic accusative **meke,* dative **mes.* Cognates outside Germanic include Old Irish *mē* me, Welsh *mi,* Latin *mē,* Greek *me, emé, emé-ge,* Old Slavic *mę,* Sanskrit *mā,* and Hittite *amug,* from Indo-European accusative **me/mē, *me-ge* (**ge* meaning at least) (Pok.702).

mead[1] (mēd) *n. Archaic.* meadow. Probably about 1150 *mede;* developed from Old English (before 901) *mǣd,* from Proto-Germanic **mǣdwṓ,* Indo-European **mētwā́* mowed land; earlier *mede* in *Medeshamsted,* Old English name of Peterborough (about 737, in Bede's *Ecclesiastical History*); see MEADOW.

mead[2] (mēd) *n.* alcoholic drink of fermented honey and water. About 1150 *mede;* developed from Old English *medu* mead (about 725, in *Beowulf*). Old English *medu* is cognate with Old Frisian *mede* mead, Middle Low German and Middle Dutch *mēde* (modern Dutch *mede, mee*), Old High German *metu* (modern German *Met*), and Old Icelandic *mjǫdhr* (Swedish *mjöd,* Danish, Norwegian *mjød*), all from Proto-Germanic **međuz,* corresponding to Indo-European **médhu,* represented by Old Irish *mid* mead (genitive *medo*), Welsh *medd,* Lithuanian *medùs* honey, Old Slavic *medŭ,* Greek *méthy* wine, and Sanskrit *mádhu* honey, mead, sweet food or drink.

meadow *n.* piece of grassy land. Probably before 1200 *medewe,* in Layamon's *Chronicle of Britain;* later *medwe* (about 1300) and *medow* (before 1338, in Mannyng's *Chronicle of England*); developed from Old English *mǣdwe* (777, in the *Anglo-Saxon Chronicle*), from Proto-Germanic **mǣđwōn,* accusative, Indo-European **mētwā́m* mowed land, root *mē-* (Pok.703). Old English *mǣdwe* is the oblique case of *mǣd* meadow, cognate with Old Frisian *mēde* meadow, Middle Low German and Middle Dutch *māde,* Middle High German *mate, matte,* modern German (poetic or dialectal) *Matte,* and Old Swedish *math;* related through, but not derived from, Old English *mǣth* a mowing or crop of hay, *māwan* to cut down, MOW[1]. The spelling *meadow* is a partial revival of the Old English, first recorded in Shakespeare's plays. **—meadowland** *n.* 1653, later variant of *meadow ground* (1523, *medowe ground*). **—meadowlark** *n.* (1611)

meager *adj.* poor, scanty. About 1378 *megre,* in *Piers Plowman;* earlier, in a surname (1179); borrowed from Old French *megre,* variant of (half-learned) *maigre,* from Latin *macrum,* accusative of *macer* thin. The Latin word is cognate with Greek *makrós* long, tall, *mêkos* (Doric *mâkos*) length, Avestan *mas-* long, Hittite *maklantes,* pl., thin, from Indo-European **māk̂-/mək̂-* long and thin (Pok.699). Germanic cognates, from Proto-Germanic **maȝrás,* include Old Icelandic *magr* thin (Swedish, Norwegian, and Danish *mager*), Old High German *magar* (modern German *mager*), Middle Dutch *māgher* (modern Dutch *mager*), Middle Low German *māger,* and Old English *mæger.* The spelling *meager* is first recorded in Spenser's *Mother Hubbard's Tale* (1591).

meal[1] *n.* food served. Probably before 1200 *mele, mel,* in Layamon's *Chronicle of Britain* and in *Ancrene Riwle;* developed from Old English (before 725) *mǣl* appointed time, mealtime, meal. Old English *mǣl* is cognate with Old Frisian *mēl* time, Middle Low German *māl* appointed time, Middle Dutch *mael* time, meal (modern Dutch *maal*), Old High German *māl* (modern German *Mahl* meal, *Mal* time), Old Icelandic *māl* measure, time, meal (Swedish, Norwegian, Danish *mål* mark, measure, meal), Gothic *mēl* time (pl. *mēla* marks, writing), from Proto-Germanic **mǣla-;* probably related to Old English *mǣth* MEASURE. Semantic parallels are found in German *Mahlzeit* meal, which contains two words for "time," Welsh *pryd* meal; also, time, and Breton *pred* moment, measure (in music), meal.

meal[2] *n.* ground grain. About 1150 *melewe;* later *mele* (probably about 1200, in *The Ormulum*); developed from Old English *melu* (before 899, in Alfred's translation of Boethius' *De Consolatione Philosophiae*). Old English *melu,* from Proto-Germanic **melwan,* is cognate with Old Frisian *mele* meal, Old Saxon *melo,* Middle Dutch *mele* (modern Dutch *meel*), Old High German *melo* (modern German *Mehl*), Old Icelandic *mjǫl* meal (Swedish *mjöl,* Danish *mel*), Old Saxon, Old High German, and Gothic *malan* to grind (modern German *mahlen*), and Middle Dutch and modern Dutch *malen* to grind. Outside Germanic cognates are found in Old Irish *melim* I grind, Welsh *blawd* (with *bl* from *ml*) flour, meal, Albanian *mjel* meal, Greek *mýlē* mill, Latin *molere* to grind, Lithuanian *málti,* Old Slavic *mlěti,* Armenian *malim* I crush, Sanskrit *mṛṇā́ti* (he) bruises, grinds, Tocharian A *malywët* you press, Tocharian B *melye* they tread on, and Hittite *mallai* (he) bruises, grinds, from Indo-European **mel-/mol-, melā-/melə-/mī-* (Pok.716). **—mealy** *adj.* like meal; powdery. 1533, in Elyot's *The Castel of Helth;* formed from English *meal* + *-y*[1]. **—mealy-mouthed** *adj.* About 1572, unwilling to tell the truth in plain words.

mean[1] *v.* have a purpose, intend. About 1175, Middle English *menen;* later *meanen* (probably before 1200, in Layamon's *Chronicle of Britain* and in *Ancrene Riwle*); developed from Old English *mǣnan* mean, tell, say (about 725, in *Beowulf*). Old English *mǣnan* is cognate with Old Frisian *mēna* signify or mean, Old Saxon *mēnian* intend or make known, Middle Dutch *mēnen* mean or think (modern Dutch *menen*), and Old High German *meinen* have in mind (modern German *meinen* hold an opinion, mean), from Proto-Germanic **mainijanan.* Outside Germanic cognates are found in Old Irish *mian* wish or desire, and Old Slavic *měniti* to mention, think, take to be, from Indo-European **mei-n-/moi-n-* (Pok.714). **—meaning** *n.* Before 1387 *mening* sense or interpretation; from *menen* to mean + *-ing*[1]. Compare German *Meinung* opinion, Dutch *mening.* **—meaningful** *adj.* (1852) **—meaningless** *adj.* (1797, in a letter of Lamb's to Coleridge)

mean[2] *adj.* low in quality or grade, inferior. Probably before 1200 *mene* shared by all, common; later, inferior, poor (before 1325, in *Cursor Mundi*); developed from Old English *gemǣne* common. Old English *gemǣne* is cognate with Old Frisian *mēne* common, Old Saxon *gimēni,* Middle Low German *gemeine,* Middle Dutch *ghemēne* (modern Dutch *gemeen*), Old High German *gimeini* (modern German *gemein*), and Gothic *gamains,* from Proto-Germanic **ʒa-mainiz* possessed jointly, corresponding to Indo-European **moinis* in Latin *commūnis* common, also cognate with *mūnus* office, duty, service, present, Old Irish *mōin, māin* costliness, Lithuanian *maĩnas* barter, exchange, Old Slavic *měna* change, and Sanskrit *mayate* he exchanges, from Indo-European **mei-/moi-* (Pok.710).

The sense development of inferior, of low grade, was probably influenced by confusion over the shared form *mene* in Middle English of the two adjectives *mean*[2] and *mean*[3]. The extended sense of small-minded, ill-natured, nasty, vile, is first recorded in 1665; it developed from the earlier sense of petty, unimportant (1585). The informal use of remarkably good, clever, etc. (as in *plays a mean trumpet*), is first recorded in 1920 in American English, a development from earlier use in the phrase *no mean* ______ not inferior or inconsiderable (1596, in Shakespeare's *Merchant of Venice*). This also illustrates the Middle English confusion of *mean*[2] and *mean*[3], for the definition given above for *no mean* ______ could surely be rewritten as "not average, or intermediate," as in *New York is no mean city.*

mean[3] *adj.* halfway between two extremes, intermediate. 1340 *men,* in *Ayenbite of Inwyt;* later *mene* (about 1375, in Chaucer's *Anelida and Arcite*); borrowed probably through Anglo-French (found in pl. *meines*), Old French *meien,* variant of *moien,* from Latin *mediānus* of or that is in the middle, from *medius* MIDDLE. Doublet of MEDIAN. The meaning of only tolerable, mediocre, in a disparaging sense, may be found in the earliest recorded use of the word from *Ayenbite* (1340), but is more generally thought to be found later in Malory's works (before 1470); but all cited uses are easily confused with *mean*[2], as is referred to there. **—n.** something halfway or intermediate. Probably about 1300 *mene* intermediate tone, intermediate state, intermediary agent or tool, instrument or course of action, means of attainment; borrowed from Old French *meien, moien* from *meien,* adj.

The plural form *means* (Middle English *menes*) a course of action, method, way, is first recorded in Chaucer's *Canterbury Tales* (about 1390), and is found in phrases such as *by all means* (1472-73) and *by means of* (before 1460). The meaning of wealth or resources (as in *a man of means*), corresponding to French *moyens* and German *Mittel,* is first recorded in Shakespeare's *Measure for Measure* (1603). The mathematical sense of an intermediate or average value or quantity (such as the *arithmetic mean*), corresponding to French *moyenne,* is found before 1500, derived from the earlier adjective sense, as in *mean diameter* (about 1391, in Chaucer's *Treatise on the Astrolabe*). **—meantime** *n.* (1340 *mene-time,* in *Ayenbite of Inwyt*); *adv.* (before 1382, in the Wycliffe Bible) **—meanwhile** *n.* (before 1375 *mene while*); *adv.* (before 1382, in the Wycliffe Bible)

meander *n.* winding course. 1576, confusing ways, intricacies; later, a winding course (of a river, 1599), or (extended to anything, 1631); borrowed from Latin *meander* a winding course, in allusion to Greek *Maíandros,* name of a winding river in southwestern Asia Minor. **—v.** follow a winding course. About 1612, in writings of William Drummond; from the noun.

measles *n.* Before 1325 *maseles* measles or pustules, plural of *masel;* perhaps borrowed from Middle Dutch *masel* blemish, or Middle Low German *masele;* cognate with Old High German *masala* blood blister (modern German *Masern* measles), from Proto-Germanic **mas-,* of unknown origin. The Middle English variants *mesels* (before 1398), *meseles* (about 1450), which are the source of the current spelling, were probably influenced by earlier *mesel* leprous (about 1280); borrowed from Old French *mesel,* from Latin *misellus* wretched, unfortunate, diminutive of *miser* wretched; see MISER.

measly (mēz′lē) *adj.* 1687, affected with measles; formed from English *measles* + *-y*[1]. The meaning of poor, meager, contemptible, is first recorded in 1864, originally in British slang.

measure *v.* Before 1325 *mesuren* to control, govern, regulate, in *Cursor Mundi;* later, to find the extent, size, etc., of (about 1380, in Chaucer's translation of Boethius' *De Consolatione Philosophiae*); borrowed from Old French *mesurer,* from Late Latin *mēnsūrāre* to measure, from Latin *mēnsūra* a measuring, a thing to measure by, from *mētīrī* to measure; for suffix see -URE. Latin *mētīrī* is cognate with Greek *métron* measure or meter, Albanian *matë* measure, Lithuanian *mētas* year, time, measure, Sanskrit *mā́ti* (he) measures, Tocharian A *me-,* Tocharian B *mai-* to measure, and Old English *mǣth* measure, which did not survive into Middle English, from Indo-European **mē-/mə-* (Pok.703). It is also probable that to some extent the development of the verb in Middle English was influenced by the earlier use of the noun in Middle English.

—n. Probably before 1200 *mesure,* in *Trinity Homilies;* borrowed from Old French *mesure,* from Latin *mēnsūra* a measuring, a thing to measure by; see the verb above.

—measurable *adj.* Probably before 1300, moderate, not excessive, in *Kyng Alisaunder;* later, that can be measured (about 1340); borrowed from Old French, from *mesure* measure + *-able.* **—measurably** *adv.* Probably about 1378, sufficiently, duly; later, moderately, slightly (before 1400). The sense of to an amount or degree that can be measured, is first recorded in Ruskin's *The Ethics of the Dust* (1866). **—measured** *adj.* About 1390, deliberate and restrained; from *measure,* v. The sense of uniform, regular, is recorded before 1400, and that of rhythmical is found in 1581, in Sydney's works, perhaps a development of the earlier sense of proportioned (before 1400). **—measurement** *n.* 1751, formed from English *measure,* n. + *-ment.*

meat *n.* About 1125 *mete* food, meal (as in *meat and drink*); later, animal flesh (about 1250, in *The Story of Genesis and Exodus*); developed from Old English (before 725) *mete* food, item of food. Old English *mete* is cognate with Old Frisian *mete* food, Old Saxon *meti,* Old High German *maz,* Old Icelandic *matr* (Swedish and Norwegian *mat,* Danish *mad*), and Gothic *mats* food, from Proto-Germanic **matiz,* cognate with Latin *madēre* be wet, from Indo-European **mad-* (Pok.694). Some evidence for the spelling *meat* begins to appear about 1450.

Mecca or **mecca** (mek′ə) *n.* place or goal which many aspire to reach. 1850, in George H. Boker's *Anne Boleyn,* an allusion to *Mecca* the sacred city of Islam where Mohammed was born and to which Moslems go on pilgrimages, from Arabic *Mekkah,* variant of *Makkah.*

mechanic *n.* worker skilled with tools. 1562, borrowed through Middle French *mechanique, mecanique,* n. and adj.; and directly from Latin *mēchanicus,* n. and adj., from Greek *mēchanikós,* n., an engineer, and adj., pertaining to machines or contrivances, inventive, from *mēchanḗ* MACHINE*;* for suffix see -IC. An adjective use also existed in Middle English before 1393. **—mechanical** *adj.* of or having to do with machinery. Probably before 1425 *mechanicalle,* in a translation of Higden's *Polychronicon;* formed from English *mechanic,* adj. (earlier *mechanique,* before 1393; borrowed from Old French *mecanique* and Latin *mēchanicus*) + suffix *-al*[1]. **—mechanics** *n.* (1648) **—mechanism** *n.* machine or its working parts. 1662, borrowed from Late Latin *mēchanisma* piece of construction, alteration of Greek *mēchánēma,* from *mēchanâsthai* devise, from *mēchanḗ* machine; for suffix see -ISM. **—mechanistic** *adj.* 1884; formed from English *mechanist* (1606) a mechanic + *-ic.* **—mechanization** *n.* 1839; formed from English *mechanize* + *-ation.* **—mechanize** *v.* 1678; formed from English *mechanic* + *-ize.*

medal *n.* piece of metal with an inscription, given as an award. Before 1586, metal disk used as a charm, in Sidney's writings; borrowed from Middle French *médaille,* from Italian *medaglia* medal; originally, a coin worth half a denarius, from Vulgar Latin **medālia,* a form postulated on the probable dissimilation of *iā . . . ia* in Late Latin *mediālia* little halves, neuter plural of *mediālis* of the middle, medial; see MEDIAL.

The traditional etymology traced a connection with Greek *métallon* metal and Latin *metallum* metal, through a Vulgar Latin **metallea* medal, but when the sense of the coin is introduced and the form of the Latin words in *d* and *t* is weighed, the evidence shifts in favor of the present explanation.

medallion (mədal′yən) *n.* large medal. 1658, borrowed from French *médaillon,* from Italian *medaglione* large medal, augmentative of *medaglia;* see MEDAL.

meddle *v.* interfere. About 1300 *medlen* to mix, mingle; also, to interfere (before 1338); earlier *melen* (before 1300); borrowed from Old North French *medler, *mesdler;* standard Old French *mesler,* later *meller,* from Vulgar Latin **misculāre,* from Latin *miscēre* to MIX. Related to MELEE. **—meddler** *n.* Before 1450, one who interferes; earlier, a practitioner, as of law (about 1395); formed from Middle English *medlen* + *-er*[1]. **—meddlesome** *adj.* 1615, formed from English *meddle* + *-some.* **—meddling** *n.* (before 1375); *adj.* (about 1384)

media (mē′dēə) *n.pl.* the forms of communication, such as the press, television, or radio, used to carry advertising, news, and other information to large numbers of people; mass media. 1927 (used as a singular), American English; perhaps abstracted from *mass media,* originally, a technical use in advertising (1923). The form *media* is the plural of *medium* in the sense of intermediate agency, means, vehicle, or channel, which is first found in Bacon's *Of the Advancement o[f] Learning* (1605); the plural *media* is first recorded in this sense in Cornelius Felton's *Greece, Ancient an[d] Modern* (1866).

medial *adj.* in the middle. 1570, mean or average; bor rowed from Late Latin *mediālis* of the middle, fro[m] Latin *medius* MIDDLE; for suffix see -AL[1].

median *adj.* middle. 1592, middle (vein, nerve, etc.) borrowed through Middle French *médian,* or directl[y] from Latin *mediānus* of the middle, from *medius* MID DLE. An earlier use restricted to medicine, is found i[n] Middle English *mediana* a vein of the arm (1392); bo[r] rowing of Medieval Latin *mediana* median vein. —[n.] middle number of a series. 1541, a median part (i[n] anatomy); borrowed from Latin *mediānus,* adj. Th[e] sense in mathematics of the middle number of a serie[s] is first recorded in 1902; that of a strip of grassy are[a,] an embankment, etc., between directions of traffic o[n] highways, is first recorded in 1954.

mediate (mē′dēāt) *v.* be a go-between. 1542, divide in[to] two equal parts; later, to settle a dispute by interveni[ng]

(1568); either a back formation from earlier *mediation,* or developed from the earlier adjective. *Mediate* replaced Middle English *medien* to halve (probably about 1425); borrowed from Late Latin *mediārī*. **—adj.** (mē′dēit) connected, but not directly. Probably before 1425, intermediate, in a translation of Higden's *Polychronicon;* borrowed from Late Latin *mediātus,* past participle of *mediārī* to be or divide in the middle, intervene, from Latin *medius* MIDDLE; for suffix see -ATE[1]. The meaning of acting through an intermediate agency, is first recorded before 1456. **—mediation** *n.* action of mediating. Before 1387 *mediacioun,* in a translation of Higden's *Polychronicon;* borrowed through Old French *mediacion,* and directly from Late Latin *mediātiōnem* (nominative *mediātiō*), from *mediārī* intervene, mediate, from Latin *medius* MIDDLE; for suffix see -ATION. **—mediator** *n.* About 1350 *mediatur;* later *mediatour* (before 1387); borrowed from Late Latin *mediātōr* one who mediates, from *mediārī* intervene, mediate; for suffix see -OR[2].

medic *n.* 1659, medical student, physician; borrowed from Latin *medicus* physician; see MEDICAL. The meaning of serviceman in a military medical corps, is first recorded in 1925, in reference to the British Royal Army Medical Corps.

medical *adj.* 1646, in Sir Thomas Browne's *Pseudodoxia Epidemica;* borrowed from French *médical,* from Medieval Latin *medicalis,* from Latin *medicus,* n., physician, and adj., healing, from *medērī* to heal; originally, know the best course for; for suffix see -AL[1]. Latin *medērī* is related to *modus* measure and cognate with Greek *médesthai* be mindful, *mḗdesthai* plan, Avestan *vī-mad-* healer, physician, Welsh *meddwl* mind, and Old English *metan* to measure, from Indo-European *med-/mod-/mēd- measure (Pok.705, 706).

Medicare or **medicare** (med′əkār) *n.* government program of medical care for the elderly. 1957, American English; formed from a blend of English *medical* and *care.*

medicate *v.* treat with medicine. 1623, in Cockeram's *Dictionary,* probably a back formation from *medication,* possibly influenced by Latin *medicātus,* past participle of *medicāre, medicārī* medicate, heal, cure; see MEDICATION; for suffix see -ATE[1]. **—medication** *n.* Probably before 1425 *medicacioun* medical treatment, in a translation of Chauliac's *Grande Chirurgie;* borrowed through Middle French *médication,* and directly from Latin *medicātiōnem* (nominative *medicātio*), from *medicāre, medicārī* medicate, heal, cure, from *medicus* healing; see MEDICAL; for suffix see -ATION.

medicine *n.* Probably before 1200 *medecine, medicine* medicinal substance, art of healing, in *Ancrene Riwle;* borrowed from Old French *medicine, medecine,* learned borrowing from Latin *medicīna,* and borrowed directly from Latin *medicīna* (originally *ars medicīna* the medical art), from feminine of *medicīnus,* adj., of a doctor, from *medicus* a physician; see MEDICAL. **—medicinal** *adj.* About 1384, in the Wycliffe Bible; borrowed from Old French *medicinal,* and directly from Latin *medicīnālis* of or pertaining to medicine, from *medicīna* medicine; for suffix see -AL[1]. **—medicine man** (1801, American English)

medieval (mē′dēē′vəl) *adj.* of or belonging to the Middle Ages (the period between the Classical culture of ancient Greece and Rome and the height of the European Enlightenment; a purely subjective term reflecting the point of view of 19th century Europe). 1827 *mediæval,* formed in English from Latin *medi(um)* middle + *aev(um)* age + English *-al*[1].

mediocre *adj.* average, ordinary. 1586, in general borrowed from Middle French *médiocre,* learned borrowing from Latin *mediocris* of middling or moderate quality; originally, halfway up a mountain (*medius* middle + *ocris* jagged mountain). It is also probable that in some instances *mediocre* was a back formation from earlier *mediocrity.* **—mediocrity** *n.* mediocre quality. Probably before 1425 *mediocrite* moderate or intermediate state or condition, in a translation of Chauliac's *Grande Chirurgie;* borrowed from Middle French *médiocrité,* learned borrowing from Latin, and borrowed directly from Latin *mediocritātem* (nominative *mediocritās*) a middling state or condition, from *mediocris* mediocre. The specific sense of mediocre quality, average, especially with a disparaging connotation, is first recorded in 1588.

meditate *v.* ponder, muse, reflect. 1560, probably a back formation from earlier *meditation,* possibly by influence of Middle French *méditer;* for suffix see -ATE[1]. **—meditation** *n.* quiet thought, reflection. Probably before 1200 *meditatium,* in *Ancrene Riwle;* later *meditacioun* (about 1390); borrowed from Old French *meditation,* and directly from Latin *meditātiōnem* (nominative *meditātiō*), from *meditārī* to meditate, cognate with Greek *médesthai* be mindful, *mḗdesthai* take thought, plan, and Welsh *meddwl* mind, from Indo-European *med-/mēd- measure (Pok.705); for suffix see -ATION. **—meditative** *adj.* 1656, perhaps from the earlier noun (1612), but more likely formed from English *meditate* + *-ive,* patterned after Late Latin *meditātīvus,* from Latin *meditārī* to meditate.

Mediterranean *adj., n.* About 1400; borrowed from Late Latin *Mediterrāneum* in *Mediterrāneum mare* Mediterranean Sea, from Latin *mediterrāneus* midland or inland, with the sense originally of the sea in the middle of the earth (formed from Latin *medius* middle + *terra* land or earth); for suffix see -AN.

medium *n.* middle condition. 1584, something lying in the middle, borrowing of Latin *medium,* from neuter of *medius,* adj., MIDDLE.

The meaning of substance through which something is conveyed, is first recorded in 1595; the extended sense of a person who conveys messages from the spirits of dead people is found in 1853, and was first used by the Swedish philosopher and mystic Emanuel Swedenborg. The technical sense of a liquid with which pigments are mixed in paint, is first recorded in 1854. The meaning of enveloping substance, environment, is first recorded in 1865 as a specialized use of any substance through which forces act (1595), also found in the specific application to commerce in *medium of exchange* (1740). See MEDIA.

—adj. having a middle position or quality. 1670, from the noun.

medley *n.* mixture of things. Before 1400 *mele,* in a translation of Lanfranc's *Science of Surgery;* later *medle* (1440) and *medley* (1438); borrowed from Old French *mellee, medlee;* earlier *mesdlee, meslee, from Gallo-Romance *misculāta, from Vulgar Latin *misculāre to mix; see MEDDLE. Related to MELEE. An earlier meaning of a battle, war (probably in the sense of a confused fight), is found in *Arthour and Merlin* (probably before 1300), and a later generalized sense of a brawl, is recorded in *Ayenbite of Inwyt* (1340). **—adj.**

mixed. About 1303 *medel,* in Mannyng's *Handlyng Synne;* later *medle* (about 1350); from the noun.

medulla (midul'ə) *n. Anatomy.* inner substance of an organ; marrow. 1392, borrowing of Latin *medulla* marrow, of uncertain origin.

medusa (mədü'sə) *n.* jellyfish. 1758, New Latin *Medusa* the genus name, from Latin *Medūsa* Medusa (legendary monster with snakes for hair), from Greek *Médousa;* the genus name was coined by Linnaeus, in allusion to Medusa's hair and the resemblance of the feelers of some jellyfish. As the name of the legendary monster, *Meduse* is found in Middle English (before 1393, in Gower's *Confessio Amantis*) and *Medusa* in 1594.

meed *n. Archaic.* reward, prize. Before 1150 *mede* recompense or reward; developed from Old English *mēd* reward, pay (about 725, in *Beowulf*); cognate with Old Saxon *mēda* reward or recompense, Middle Dutch *miede,* Old High German *mēta,* later *miata, mieta* reward, payment (modern German *Miete* rent, hire), from Proto-Germanic **mizdṓ* (with loss of the *-z-* in West Germanic dialect regions, and compensatory lengthening of the vowel). An Anglian form *meord, meard* is not satisfactorily explained, but with its *-r-* represents the expected Old English form as a cognate of Gothic *mizdō.*

Cognates of the Proto-Germanic form are Sanskrit *mīḍhá-m* prize, reward, Avestan *mižda-,* Greek *misthós* wages, pay, Old Slavic *mĭzda,* from Indo-European **misdhó-* (Pok. 746).

meek *adj.* Probably before 1200 *mēok* gentle, humble, in *Ancrene Riwle;* later *mēc* (probably about 1200, in *The Ormulum*); borrowed from a Scandinavian source (compare Old Icelandic *mjūkr* soft, pliant, gentle, from Proto-Germanic **meukaz;* see MUCUS).

meerschaum (mir'shəm) *n.* light, claylike mineral used to make tobacco pipes. 1784, borrowing of German *Meerschaum,* literally, sea foam; said to be a translation of Persian *kef-i-daryā* foam of the sea, in allusion to the lightness and white color of the mineral that was supposed to be reminiscent of froth in the sea or surf.

meet[1] *v.* come face to face with. Probably before 1200 *meten,* in Layamon's *Chronicle of Britain;* developed from Old English *mētan* (about 725, in *Beowulf*), related to *gemōt* meeting. Old English *mētan* (from Proto-Germanic **mōtijanan*) and *gemōt* are cognate with Old Frisian *mēta* to meet, Old Saxon *mōtian* to meet, *mōt* meeting, Middle Dutch *ghemoete* (modern Dutch *tegemoet*), Old High German *muoz* meeting, Old Icelandic *mœta* to meet (Swedish *möta, Norwegian møte,* and Danish *møde*), *mōt* meeting, and Gothic *gamōtjan* to meet. Outside Germanic a cognate is found in Armenian *matčim* I approach, from Indo-European **mōd-* (or *mād-*) / *məd-* (Pok. 746). Related to MOOT. **—n.** a meeting, gathering. 1831-34, meeting of hounds and men in preparation for a hunt; from the verb. **—meeting** *n.* Probably before 1300 *meting,* in *Kyng Alisaunder;* developed from gerund of *meten* to meet. In Old English the form was *gemēting* a meeting, assembly, association, society; developed from gerund of *gemētan* to find, come upon, meet with.

meet[2] *adj.* proper, fitting. Probably about 1300 *mete;* developed from Old English (about 961) *gemǣte* suitable; cognate with Old High German *gamāzi, gemāze* suitable, acceptable (modern German *gemäss* appropriate), from Proto-Germanic **ʒa-mǣtjaz,* built either on the noun represented by Old High German *māza* manner, Middle Dutch *māte* measure (modern Dutch *maat*), from Proto-Germanic **mǣtō;* or on the noun represented by Middle High German *maz* measure, way (modern German *Mass*), Old Icelandic *māt* valuation or measure, Gothic *usmēt* way of life, from Proto-Germanic **mǣtan;* see METE[1] allot.

meg- or **mega-** a combining form used especially to form scientific terms and meaning: **1** large or great, as in *megaspore, megadose, megohm.* **2** one million, as in *megacycle, megaton.* Borrowed from Greek *mégas* great; see MUCH. Words formed with *meg-, mega-* often have contrasting terms formed with *micr-, micro-* and sometimes also synonyms formed with *macr-, macro-.* Except for a scattering of words such as *megacosm* (1617 = *macrocosm*), most terms formed with *mega-* are products of the 1800's and early 1900's.

megalith (meg'əlith) *n.* stone of great size. 1853, back formation from *megalithic,* after the pattern *mega-* large + *-lith* stone. **—megalithic** *adj.* of or marked by megaliths. 1839, formed from English *mega-* large + *-lith* (borrowed from Greek *lithos*) stone + *-ic.*

As part of the international vocabulary of archaeology, *megalith* is found in German, the Scandinavian languages, French, and so forth.

megalomania *n.* insanity marked by delusions of grandeur. 1890, borrowed from French *mégalomanie,* formed from Greek *mégas* (genitive *megálou*) great + *maníā* madness, MANIA.

megalopolis (meg'əlop'əlis) *n.* city of great size. 1832, in Webster's *Dictionary;* formed in English from Greek *mégas* (genitive *megálou*) great + *pólis* city; see POLITICS. Curiously, the Greeks had already coined this word and applied it to Athens, Syracuse, and Alexandria.

megaphone *n.* funnel-shaped horn to amplify the voice. 1878, American English, formed from *mega-* great + *-phone* sound.

megaton (meg'ətun') *n.* measure of explosive power equal to that of one million tons of TNT (used especially in reference to nuclear bombs). 1952, formed from English *mega-* one million + *ton* (of explosive energy).

megillah (məgil'ə) *n. Slang.* long story or account. 1957, American English, especially in the phrase *the whole megillah;* borrowing through Yiddish *megile* of Hebrew *megīllah* scroll or roll, in allusion to the scroll of the Book of Esther, which is unrolled and read in the synagogue during the festival of Purim.

In the technical sense of one of the five books of the Old Testament (Song of Songs, Ruth, Lamentations, Ecclesiastes, and Esther) read in the synagogue on certain Jewish festivals, the word *Megillah* is first recorded in English in 1650, in Edmund Chilmead's translation of Leon of Modena's *History of the Rites of the Jews* written in Italian.

meiosis (mīō'sis) *n. Biology.* process by which the number of chromosomes in reproductive cells is reduced to half the original number; reduction division. 1905 New Latin *meiosis,* borrowing of Greek *meíōsis* a lessening, from *meioûn* lessen, from *meíōn* less; see MINOR.

melancholy (mel'ənkol'ē) *n.* About 1303 *malyncoli* mental disorder characterized by depression, in Mannyng's *Handlyng Synne;* later *melancolie* (before 1398 in Trevisa's translation of Bartholomew's *De Proprietatibus Rerum*); borrowed from Old French *melancolie, malencolie,* learned borrowing from Lat

Latin, and borrowed directly from Late Latin *melancholia*, from Greek *melancholíā* sadness, (excess of) black bile (*mélās*, genitive *mélanos* black + *cholḗ* bile; see MELANIN and CHOLERA). In medieval times melancholy was thought to be caused by an excess of black bile, a secretion of the spleen in a condition associated with jaundice.

The Old French variant *malencolie* was formed by false association with *mal* sickness (from Latin *malum* an evil).

—adj. 1392 *malancolie* mixed with or caused by black bile, gloomy or sad of temperament; later *melancolie* (probably before 1425); from the noun. (Note that as late as the end of the 1300's the form was still influenced by its early association with *mal.*)

—melancholic *adj.* About 1385 *malencolyk*, in Chaucer's *Canterbury Tales;* formed from Middle English *malencoly* (earlier *malyncoly*) melancholy + *-ic.*

mélange (mālänzh') *n.* mixture, medley. 1653, borrowing of Middle French *mélange,* from Gallo-Romance **miscellānea* (neuter plural of Latin *miscellāneus* mixed). The stem of French *mélange* was probably influenced by the related *mêler* to mix, from Old French *mesler,* from Vulgar Latin **misculāre* to mix, formed from Latin *miscēre* MIX. For the development of Gallo-Romance *-ānea* to Middle French *-ange* (instead of the expected *-a(i)gne*), compare *estrange* strange, from Latin *extrāneus.* Related to MELEE, MEDDLE, and MEDLEY.

melanin (mel'ənin) *n.* black pigment in the skin, hair, and eyes of human beings and many animals. 1843, formed in English (probably by influence of earlier *melanoma* blackish tumor, 1840), from Greek *mélās* (genitive *mélanos*) black + English suffix *-in*[2]. Greek *mélās* is cognate with Lithuanian *mēlas, mėlynas* blue, Latvian *męlns* black, Russian *malína* raspberry, and Sanskrit *mála-m* dirt, filth, from Indo-European **mel-/melə-* dark (Pok.720).

Melba toast (mel'bə) kind of very crisp, thin toast. 1925, named after Dame Nellie *Melba,* 1861-1931 (stage name of Helen Mitchell, Australian opera star who adopted the stage name Nellie Melba in allusion to her native city of *Melbourne*).

Peach Melba, an ice-cream dessert, was a translation (in 1909) of French *Pêche Melba,* created and named about 1907 in Melba's honor by the chef Escoffier.

meld[1] *v.* announce and show (cards for a score) in rummy, canasta, pinochle, etc. 1897, borrowed from German *melden* announce (Old High German *meldōn*); cognate with Middle Dutch and modern Dutch *melden* announce, Old Saxon *meldon,* and Old English *meldian,* from Proto-Germanic **meldōjanan,* cognate with Armenian *malt'em* I beg, and Hittite *maldi* he prays, from Indo-European **meldh-* to address ritual words to the deity (Pok. 722).

An earlier form, developed from Old English *meldian* (probably about 750), appears in Middle English *melden* accuse, call to account (about 1300); later, reveal, show (probably before 1325), but this form apparently did not survive into Modern English and reappeared in the late 1800's as a borrowing from German, especially with the popularity of pinochle among German immigrants.

—n. card or group of cards to be melded. 1897; from the verb.

meld[2] *v.* to merge, blend. 1939, American English, probably verb use of *melled* mingled or blended, past participle of dialectal English *mell* to mingle or blend, from Middle English *mellen* (about 1380), variant of *medlen;* borrowed from Old French *meller, medler,* variants of *mesler* to mix or mingle; see MEDDLE. **—n.** a blend. 1974, from the verb.

melee or **mêlée** (mā'lā) *n.* confused fight. Before 1648, borrowing of French *mêlée,* from Old French *meslee* confused fight, mixture, from feminine past participle of *mesler* to mix; see MEDDLE. Related to MEDLEY. The word is found in Middle English *mele* mixture (before 1400); earlier *melle* war or battle (before 1325, in *Cursor Mundi*), and *medle, medlay* (probably before 1300); borrowed from Old French *medlee, mellee,* variants of *meslee.* Apparently the Middle English word did not survive into modern English, and so the present-day form is a reborrowing from modern French.

meliorate (mēl'yərāt) *v.* improve. Before 1552, in John Leland's *The Itinerary,* perhaps borrowed by influence of Middle French *meliorer,* from Late Latin *meliōrātus,* past participle of *meliōrāre* improve, but more likely a back formation from earlier *melioration;* for suffix see -ATE[1]. **—meliorative** (mēl'yərā'tiv) *adj.* 1808, formed from English *meliorate* + *-ive.* **—melioration** *n.* Before 1400 *melioracioun* improvement; borrowed from Late Latin *meliōrātiōnem* (nominative *meliōrātiō*), from Latin *meliōrāre* improve, from *melior* better (comparative of *bonus* good); see MULTI-; for suffix see -ATION.

mellifluous (məlif'lüəs) *adj.* sweetly or smoothly flowing. Probably before 1425, in a translation of Higden's *Polychronicon;* borrowed from Late Latin *mellifluus* (Latin *mel,* genitive *mellis,* honey + *-fluus* flowing, from *fluere* to flow; see FLUENT); for suffix see -OUS. Latin *mel* is cognate with Greek *méli,* genitive *mélitos,* Old Irish *mil,* Welsh *mel,* and Gothic *milith,* from Indo-European **meli-t* (Pok. 723).

—mellifluent *adj.* mellifluous. 1601, borrowed probably from Middle French *mellifluent,* learned borrowing from Late Latin, and directly from Late Latin *mellifluentem* (nominative *mellifluēns*), a compound of Latin *mel* (genitive *mellis*) honey + *fluentem* (nominative *fluēns*), present participle of *fluere* to flow; for suffix see -ENT.

mellow *adj.* ripe, soft, rich. 1440 *melwe,* in *Promptorium Parvulorum;* of unknown origin (possibly an attributive use of *melowe,* variant of *mele* ground grain, MEAL[2]; its meaning possibly influenced by Middle English *merow* soft or tender, Old English *mearu,* cognate with Old High German *marawi, muruwi,* modern German *mürbe*). —v. make or become mellow. 1572; from the adjective.

melodeon (məlō'dēən) *n.* small reed organ. 1847, American English, variant of *melodion,* borrowing of German *Melodion,* from *Melodie* melody, from Old French *melodie;* see MELODY.

melodrama (mel'ədrä'mə) *n.* sensational drama. 1809, romantic stage play with music, in Southey's *Letters;* earlier *melodrame* (1802); borrowing of French *mélodrame* (Greek *mélos* song, MELODY + French *-drame,* Greek *drâma* DRAMA). **—melodramatic** *adj.* 1816, substitution of *dramatic* for *drama* in *melodrama,* on the analogy of *drama, dramatic.*

melody *n.* Probably before 1300 *melodie* sweet music, tunefulness, in *Kyng Alisaunder;* borrowed from Old French *melodie,* learned borrowing from Late Latin, and borrowed directly from Late Latin *melōdia,* from

Greek *melōidíā* singing, chanting, a tune to which lyric poetry is set (*mélos* song + *ōidḗ* song, ODE); for suffix see -Y[3]. **—melodic** *adj.* 1823, formed from English *melody* + *-ic,* after French *mélodique,* from Late Latin *melōdicus,* from Greek *melōidikós,* from *melōidíā* melody. **—melodious** *adj.* tuneful. About 1385, in Chaucer's *Troilus and Criseyde;* borrowed from Old French *melodïos,* from *melodie* melody; for suffix see -OUS.

melon *n.* large juicy fruit. About 1395 *meloun,* also *melon* (before 1398); borrowed from Old French *melon,* and directly from Medieval Latin *melonem,* shortened form of Latin *mēlopepōnem* a kind of pumpkin, from Greek *mēlopépōn* (*mêlon* apple, perhaps from a Mediterranean language + *pépōn* a kind of gourd, a noun use of *pépōn* ripe; see PUMPKIN). It is also possible that in some instances the Medieval Latin *melonem* may have been borrowed directly from Greek *mêlon,* interpreted as an augmentative meaning "applelike fruit."

melt *v.* to change from solid to liquid. Probably about 1150 *melten,* a fusion of Old English *meltan* become liquid (about 725, in *Beowulf*), from Proto-Germanic **meltanan,* and of Old English *gemæltan* make liquid (before 830, Anglian), *gemyltan* (West Saxon), from Proto-Germanic **ʒa-maltjanan.* The Old English forms are cognate with Old Icelandic *melta* to digest, melt, and Gothic *gamalteins* dissolution. Cognates outside Germanic include Greek *méldein* to soften by boiling, Latin *mollis* soft, mild, and Sanskrit *mṛdú-s* soft, tender, from Indo-European **meld-/mold-/mḷd-* (Pok. 718). Related to SMELT and MILD. **—n.** 1854, melted substance; from the verb. **—melting point** (1842) **—melting pot** 1420-21; later, in a figurative sense, in Israel Zangwill's play *The Melting Pot,* 1908.

member *n.* Probably 1280 *membre* part of the body; later, person belonging to a group (before 1338); borrowed from Old French *membre,* from Latin *membrum* limb, member of the body, part. Latin *membrum* (earlier **mēmsrom*) is cognate with Old Irish *mír* piece, bit, Greek *mērós* thigh, Albanian *mish* flesh, Old Prussian *mensā,* Old Slavic *męso,* Armenian *mis,* Sanskrit *māṁsá-s,* Tocharian B *misa,* pl., flesh, and Gothic *mimz* flesh, from Indo-European **mēmso-, mē(m)s-ro-* flesh (Pok. 725) **—membership** *n.* 1647, formed from English *member* + *-ship.*

membrane *n.* 1519, parchment; later, thin layer of tissue (1615); borrowed from Latin *membrāna* parchment, skin, tissue covering part of the body, from *membrum* limb, member of the body, part, member. The later sense in English of a thin layer of tissue, may have been borrowed from French *membrane;* surely the sense was reinforced by the French word, which was a learned borrowing from Latin. **—membranous** *adj.* of or like a membrane. 1597, borrowed from Middle French *membraneux,* from *membrane* membrane, from Latin *membrāna;* for suffix see -OUS.

memento *n.* keepsake, souvenir. Before 1376, in *Piers Plowman;* borrowing of Latin *mementō* remember, imperative of *meminisse* to remember, related to *mēns* MIND.

Memento was first used in English to refer to either of two prayers beginning "Memento" in the canon of the Mass, in which the living and the dead are commemorated. The meaning of an object serving to remind or warn, is first recorded in 1580, and from it developed the meaning of a keepsake, first found in 1768.

memo *n.* 1889, shortened form of MEMORANDUM.

memoir (mem′wär *or* mem′wôr) *n.* biography. 1427 *memoire* written record, variant form of *memorie* memory, written record; borrowed through Anglo-French *memorie,* Old French *memoire,* learned borrowing from Latin *memoria* MEMORY. The plural form *memoirs* appeared in 1659 in the sense of a personal record of events, and in 1673, in the sense of an autobiographical record, in Evelyn's *Diary.*

memorabilia (mem′ərəbil′ēə) *n.pl.* things or events worth remembering. 1806-07, borrowing of Latin *memorābilia,* neuter plural of *memorābilis* worthy of being remembered or noted; see MEMORABLE.

memorable *adj.* 1436 *memorable;* borrowed from Middle French *mémorable,* learned borrowing from Latin *memorābilis* worthy of being remembered or noted, from *memorāre* to bring to mind, mention, remind, from *memor* mindful, remembering, see MEMORY; for suffix see -ABLE.

memorandum *n.* short written statement for future use. Probably 1435, borrowed from Latin *memorandum* (thing) to be remembered, especially as a notation in manuscripts, neuter singular of *memorandus,* gerundive of *memorāre* to bring to mind, mention, remind; see MEMORABLE.

In Middle English, the word *memorandum* was placed at the head of a note as a memory aid; it was later used to refer to the note itself (1542-43). The usual plural until the 1800's was *memorandums;* the plural *memoranda,* in imitation of Latin, is first recorded in English in 1813.

memorial *n.* reminder of some event or person. Before 1382, commemorative act, faculty of memory, in the Wycliffe Bible; borrowed from Old French *memorial,* learned borrowing from Late Latin, and borrowed directly from Late Latin *memoriāle,* from neuter of Latin *memoriālis,* adj., of or belonging to memory, from *memoria* MEMORY; for suffix see -AL[2]. **—adj.** helping to remember, commemorative. About 1375, in Chaucer's *Anelida and Arcite,* borrowed from Latin *memoriālis* of or belonging to memory. **—memorialize** *v.* (1798)

memory *n.* About 1250 *memorie* remembrance, renown; later, faculty of remembering (about 1380, in Chaucer's *Canterbury Tales*); borrowed through Anglo-French *memorie,* Old French *memoire,* learned borrowing from Latin, and directly from Latin *memoria,* from *memor* mindful, remembering. Latin *memor* is cognate with Greek *mérmēra* care, trouble, *mermaírein* be anxious or thoughtful, Old Lithuanian *merěti* to care for, and Sanskrit *smarati* (he) remembers. Germanic cognates include Middle Dutch *mimeren* to muse, brood (modern Dutch *mijmeren*) and Old English *gemimor* known, *mimorian* remember, which did not survive into Middle English, from Indo-European **(s)mer-/(s)mor-/(s)mṛ-* (Pok. 969).

The meaning of a device in a computer in which information is stored, is first recorded in 1946.

—memorize *v.* 1591, to commemorate in writing, in Spenser's *Ruines of Time;* formed from English *memory* + *-ize.* The meaning of commit to memory, is first recorded in 1838 in American English. **—memorization** *n.* 1886-87; formed from English *memorize* + *-ation*

menace *n.* About 1303 *manas,* in Mannyng's *Handlyng Synne;* later *manace* (before 1325); borrowed from Ol

French *menace, manace* threat, from Vulgar Latin **minācia,* singular of Latin *mināciae,* from *mināx* (genitive *minācis*) threatening, from *minārī* threaten, jut, project, from *minae* threats, projecting points; see MOUNT² hill. —**v.** Probably before 1300 *manacen,* in *Kyng Alisaunder;* borrowed from Old French *menacer, manacer* threaten, from Vulgar Latin **mināciāre,* from **mināci̇a* menace.

ménage or **menage** (mānäzh′) *n.* household. 1698, management of a household, domestic establishment, borrowing of French *ménage,* from Old French *menage, menaige, manaige* household, family dwelling, from Vulgar Latin **mānsiōnāticum* household, from Latin *mānsiōnem* dwelling, MANSION.

Ménage or *menage* is a reborrowing in modern English of a word that appeared in Middle English in the sense of members of a household (probably before 1300, in *Kyng Alisaunder*); borrowed from Old French *menage* household; the Middle English word became obsolete before 1500.

menagerie (mənaj′ərē *or* mənazh′ərē) *n.* collection of wild animals kept in cages for exhibition. 1712 *menagery,* borrowed from French *ménagerie* housing for domestic animals; literally, management of a household, from Old French *menage* MÉNAGE. Except for the single instance of the Anglicized spelling with *-y* the French spelling and an approximation of the French pronunciation have prevailed in English.

mend *v.* to repair. Probably before 1200 *menden* repair; later, make right, remove a fault (probably before 1300), shortened variant form of *amenden* amend; see AMEND. —**n.** place that has been mended. Before 1325 *mende* (usually *mendes,* pl.) recompense, reparation, remedy, in *Cursor Mundi;* from the verb. The phrase *on the mend,* in the sense of improving or recovering, is first recorded in 1802 in conversations of Coleridge.

mendacious (mendā′shəs) *adj.* untruthful, lying. 1616, borrowed probably from Middle French *mendacieux,* from Latin *mendācium* a lie, from *mendāx* (genitive *mendācis*) lying, deceitful, from *menda* fault, carelessness in writing; see MENDICANT; for suffix see -IOUS. —**mendacity** *n.* 1646, borrowed probably from French *mendacité,* learned borrowing from Late Latin, and directly from Late Latin *mendācitās,* from Latin *mendāx* lying; for suffix see -ITY. It is also probable that in some instances *mendacity* was formed in English from earlier *mendac(ious)* + *-ity.*

mendelevium (men′dəlē′vēəm) *n.* artificial chemical element. 1955, New Latin, in allusion to Dmitri Ivanovich *Mendeleev,* 1834-1907, Russian chemist + *-ium* (chemical suffix). The term was coined by A. Ghiorso and co-discoverers.

mendicant *n.* beggar. 1395 *mendicaunt,* in Wycliffe's writings; borrowed from Latin *mendīcantem* (nominative *mendīcāns*), present participle of *mendīcāre* to beg, from *mendīcus* beggar, physically handicapped person (especially such a person who resorts to begging), from *menda* fault, physical defect, possibly cognate with Sanskrit *mindā́* physical defect (probably altered from **mandā́* by influence of *nindā́* injury, reviling), and with Old Irish *mind* sign, mark, and Welsh *man geni* birth-mark, from Indo-European **mendā́/mn̥dā́* (Pok. 729); for suffix see -ANT. Compare MENDACIOUS. —**adj.** begging. 1470, borrowed from Latin *mendīcantem,* present participle.

menhaden (menhā′dən) *n.* common sea fish, pogy. 1643, in Roger Williams' *A Key into the Language of America,* American English, from Algonquian (probably Narragansett) *munnawhateaûg* herringlike fish, once the most abundant fish on the eastern coast of the United States; literally, they fertilize; so called because these fish (menhaden, alewife, and herring) were used by the Indians as fertilizer.

menial (mē′nēəl) *adj.* belonging to or suited to a servant, lowly, humble. Before 1387 *meynal* belonging to the household, domestic, in Trevisa's translation of Higden's *Polychronicon;* later *meynyal* (1433); borrowed through Anglo-French *meignial,* from *meignée, meiné,* Old French *maisniée* household, from Vulgar Latin ** mānsiōnāta,* from Latin *mānsiōnem* dwelling, MANSION; for suffix see -IAL. The meaning of lowly, humble, suited to a servant, is first recorded in 1673. —**n.** servant who does the lowliest or humblest tasks. Before 1387 *meynyal* domestic servant, in Trevisa's translation of Higden's *Polychronicon;* probably from the adjective.

meninges (mənin′jēz) *n.pl. Anatomy.* the three membranes that surround the brain and spinal cord. 1616, borrowing of Middle French *meninges* (1532, in Rabelais); learned borrowing, probably through Late Latin *mēninga,* from Greek *mē̂ninx* (genitive *mḗningos*) membrane, especially of the brain; see MEMBER. —**meningitis** (men′injī′tis) *n.* inflammation of the meninges. 1828, New Latin, formed from *mening(es)* + *-itis.*

meniscus (mənis′kəs) *n.* 1693, a lens convex on one side and concave on the other, in Edmund Halley's writings; New Latin *meniscus,* from Greek *mēnískos* a crescent, diminutive of *mḗnē* MOON. The meaning in physics of the curved surface of a column of liquid is first recorded in English in John Playfair's *Natural Philosophy* (1812-16).

menopause *n.* cessation of menstruation. 1872, borrowed from French *ménopause,* formed from Greek *mḗn* (genitive *mēnós*) month + connective *-o-* + *paûsis* cessation, pause.

mensch (mench) *n. Slang.* respected person, decent human being. 1953, borrowed through Yiddish *mentsh,* literally, a person or human being, from Middle High German *mensch, mensche,* from Old High German *mennisco,* from Proto-Germanic **manniskōn;* cognate with Middle Dutch *mensce* human being (modern Dutch *mens*), Old Saxon *mennisco,* and Old Frisian *männska;* derived from the Germanic root that was the source of Old High German *man* human being, MAN.

menses (men′sēz) *n.pl.* menstruation. 1597, borrowing of Latin *mēnsēs,* plural of *mēnsis* month; see MOON.

Menshevik (men′shəvik) *n.* member of the less radical wing of the Russian Social Democratic Party, opposed to the Bolsheviks from 1903 to 1917. 1917, borrowed from Russian *men′shevík* (*men′she* lesser, a comparative form to *malo* little + *-evik* suffix meaning "one that is"). The Mensheviks were so called (by Lenin) from the fact that they held a temporary minority within the party. Compare BOLSHEVIK.

menstrual (men′strůəl) *adj.* of or having to do with menstruation. Before 1398, in Trevisa's translation of Bartholomew's *De Proprietatibus Rerum;* borrowed through Old French *menstruel,* or directly from Latin *mēnstruālis* monthly, of or having monthly courses, from *mēnstruus* of menstruation, monthly, from *mēnsis* month, see MOON; for suffix see -AL¹.

menstruate *v.* to discharge blood from the uterus, normally at intervals of four weeks. 1800, probably a back formation from earlier *menstruation;* for suffix see -ATE[1]. The form appeared as an adjective as early as 1384, in the Wycliffe Bible, borrowed from Late Latin *mēnstruāta,* past participle of *mēnstruāre* menstruate, but did not survive into modern English. **—menstruation** *n.* act or period of menstruating. 1776-84, probably borrowed from French *menstruation,* and formed directly in English from Late Latin *mēnstruāre* menstruate, from Latin *mēnstrua* the menses, neuter plural of *mēnstruus* of menstruation, monthly, from *mēnsis* month, see MOON + English suffix *-ation.*

mensuration (men′shərā′shən) *n.* act or process of measuring. 1571, borrowed from Middle French *mensuration,* learned borrowing from Late Latin, and directly from Late Latin *mēnsūrātiōnem* (nominative *mēnsūrātiō*), from *mēnsūrāre* to MEASURE; for suffix see -ATION.

-ment a suffix forming nouns, especially from the verbs, and meaning act or process of ______ing, as in *enjoyment;* condition of being ______ed, as in *amazement;* product or result of ______ing, as in *pavement;* means or instrument that ______s, as in *inducement.* Middle English, borrowed from Old French *-ment,* from Latin *-mentum.* In the Middle English period *-ment* occurred mainly in words borrowed from Old French or through Anglo-French; these words either represented Latin nouns ending in *-mentum* or were formed in French on the analogy of Latin forms by the addition of *-ment* to verb stems. Since in most cases the French verb was borrowed by English along with the noun in *-ment* derived from the verb, the suffix came to be treated as English and in the 1500's was freely added to English verb stems, producing such common words as *atonement, amazement, betterment,* and *bewilderment.*

mental *adj.* of the mind. About 1422, borrowed from Middle French *mental,* learned borrowing from Late Latin *mentālis* of the mind, from Latin *mēns* (genitive *mentis*) MIND; for suffix see -AL[1]. **—mental age** (1912) **—mentality** *n.* mental capacity. 1691, formed from English *mental* + *-ity.* The sense of outlook (as in *a childish mentality*), is first recorded in 1895.

menthol *n.* substance obtained from oil of peppermint, used in medicine, as flavoring, etc. 1876, borrowing of German *Menthol,* from Latin *mentha* MINT[1] (herb) + German *-ol,* from Latin *oleum* OIL. The term was coined in 1861 by the German chemist Friedrich Oppenheim, 1833-1877. **—mentholated** *adj.* containing or treated with menthol. 1933, formed from English *menthol* + *-ate[1]* + *-ed[2].*

mention *n.* About 1300 *mencion* act of commemorating by speech or writing; borrowed from Old French *mencion,* learned borrowing from Latin *mentiōnem* (nominative *mentiō*) a calling to mind, a speaking, mention, from the root *men-* of Old Latin *minīscī* to think, related to *mēns* (genitive *mentis*) MIND; for suffix see -TION. **—v.** 1530, in Palsgrave's *Lesclarcissement,* borrowed from Middle French *mentionner,* from Old French *mention,* n.

mentor *n.* wise and trusted adviser. 1750, in Lord Chesterfield's *Letters to his Son;* borrowed in allusion to Greek *Méntōr,* the name of a friend and adviser to Odysseus, in Homer's *Odyssey.* The name may ultimately mean "adviser," having the form of an agent noun related to Greek *ménos* intent, purpose, spirit, passion; see MIND. In its current meaning *mentor* was popularized by the prominence of Mentor as an adviser to *Télémaque,* in a didactic novel of that name by the French writer and prelate Fénelon, published in 1699.

menu (men′yü) *n.* 1837, detailed list of what is served at a meal; borrowing of French *menu,* from Middle French *menu,* adj., small or detailed, from Latin *minūtus* small; see the doublet MINUTE[2] small. The transferred sense of any detailed list, is first recorded in English in 1889. A sole instance of an earlier borrowing of *menu* as a shortened form of *menu peuple* common people, is recorded in 1658.

meow *n., interj.* 1873, sound made by a cat; earlier *miaow* (1634 *miau,* a spelling in imitation of the sound a cat makes, probably influenced in form by French *miaou*). **—v.** 1894, make the characteristic sound of a cat; earlier *meaw* (1632).

mercantile (mėr′kəntil) *adj.* of merchants or trade; commercial. 1642, in James Howell's *Instructions for Foreign Travel;* borrowed from French *mercantile,* from Italian *mercantile,* from Medieval Latin *mercantilis* of a merchant or trade, or from Italian *mercante* merchant, from Latin *mercantem* (nominative *mercāns*) a merchant; also, trading, present participle of *mercārī* to trade; see MARKET.

mercenary *n.* soldier serving for pay in a foreign army. About 1387-95 *mercenarie* hireling, person working for money only, in Chaucer's *Canterbury Tales;* borrowed perhaps through Old French *mercenaire,* and directly from Latin *mercēnnārius,* n., one who does anything for pay, from a lost noun **mercēdō* (genitive **mercēdinis*) pay, from *mercēs* (genitive *mercēdis*) pay, reward, wages, see MERCY; for suffix see -ARY.

The meaning of soldier serving for pay in a foreign army, is probably first recorded in a translation of Froissart's *Chronique de France, d'Angleterre* (etc.), in 1523-25.

—adj. working for money only. 1532 *mercennary,* in Sir Thomas More's *Works;* from the noun in English, and probably borrowed in part from Latin *mercēnnārius* doing anything for pay; also, as a noun.

mercer *n.* dealer in cloth. Probably before 1200, in *Ancrene Riwle;* earlier, as a surname (1168); borrowed from Old French *mercier* trader, dealer in small wares, from *merz* merchandise, from Latin *merx* (genitive *mercis*) merchandise, see MARKET; for suffix see -ER[1].

merchandise *n.* Before 1250 *marchaundise* act of trading, wares; later *merchaundise* (probably before 1387); borrowed through Anglo-French *marchaundise,* Old French *marcheandise,* from *marchaunt, marchaund* MERCHANT + *-ise;* for suffix see -ISE. The question as to why there was a *-d-* in Old French *marcheandise* (for expected **marcheantise*) or in French *marchand,* feminine *marchande,* or the verb *marchander* to bargain (for expected **marchanter*) seems not to have been raised. The same problem arises with Middle French *brigand* brigand (and *brigandage*) from Italian *brigante.* **—v.** buy and sell, trade. About 1384 *marchaundisen,* in the Wycliffe Bible; from the noun.

merchant *n.* Probably about 1200 *marchaunt;* later, in the surname *Merchaunt* (1332); borrowed through Anglo-French *marchaunt,* Old French *marchëant,* from Vulgar Latin **mercātantem* (nominative **mercātāns*) a buyer, present participle of **mercātāre,* a frequentative form of Latin *mercārī* to trade, see MARKET; fo suffix see -ANT. **—adj.** trading, pertaining to trade. Probably before 1400 *marchant;* from the noun, and probably influenced by Old French *marchëant,* adj. **—merchantman** *n.* 1449, merchant. The meaning of a commercial ship is first recorded in 1627, in Captain John Smith's *The Seaman's Grammar.* **—merchant marine** (1855, American English)

mercury *n.* About 1150 *mercuris* the Roman god; later, the planet (probably before 1300, in *Kyng Alisaunder*), and *mercurie* silver-white metal, quicksilver (about 1395, in Chaucer's *Canterbury Tales*); borrowing of Medieval Latin *mercurius,* from Latin *Mercurius* Mercury, the Roman god. **—mercurial** *adj.* 1647, sprightly, volatile, quick; originally, having the qualities of one born under the planet Mercury (1593); developed from Middle English *Mercurial* of or relating to Mercury (before 1393, in Gower's *Confessio Amantis*); borrowed from Latin *mercuriālis* of Mercury (the god or planet), from *Mercurius,* see MERCURY; for suffix see -AL[1]. **—mercuric** *adj.* 1828-32; formed from English *mercury* + *-ic.*

mercy *n.* Probably before 1200 *mearci,* in *Ancrene Riwle;* later *merci* (probably about 1200); borrowed from Old French *merci* reward, gift, kindness, mercy; earlier *mercit,* from Latin *mercēdem* reward, wages, from *merx* (genitive *mercis*) wares, merchandise; see MARKET. **—merciful** *adj.* About 1340, in *Ayenbite of Inwyt;* formed from Middle English *merci* + *-ful.* **—merciless** *adj.* Probably about 1380 *mercyles;* formed from Middle English *merci (mercy)* + *-les* -less.

mere[1] *adj.* nothing more than, only, bare. About 1390, pure or unmixed; borrowed from Old French *mere, mier* pure, entire, and directly from Latin *merus* unmixed, pure, bare, mere, probably originally clear, bright, cognate with Old English *mare* silver-weed, Sanskrit *máríci-s* ray of light, and Greek *marmaírein* glisten, sparkle, from Indo-European **mer-/mor-* glisten, sparkle (Pok. 733).

The meaning now associated with *mere,* "nothing more than," (as in *the merest scratch*), is first recorded in 1581. At the same time, however, another and conflicting sense existed, "nothing less than, absolute, sheer, downright," (as in *of mere malice*), is first recorded about 1443 and in wide use for over 300 years (Bacon, Shakespeare in *Othello,* Defoe in *Robinson Crusoe,* and Smollett in *Gil Blas*). By the latter half of the 1700's this older meaning began to disappear and is no longer found, except in a few vestiges such as *mere folly.* It is interesting to note that both senses also existed in Latin.

—merely *adv.* nothing more, simply, only. About 1449, formed from Middle English *mere*[1] + *-ly*[1]. The now obsolete meaning "absolutely, quite, utterly" (corresponding with that of the adjective), is first recorded about 1445 in the form *mere,* and later in the form *merely* in 1546, as used by Shakespeare in *Hamlet* ("things rank and gross in nature possess it merely").

mere[2] *n.* lake, pond. Old English (before 700) *mere* sea, lake, pool, pond; cognate with Old Saxon *meri* a lake, Old Frisian *mar* sea, ditch, Middle Dutch *mare, maer* (modern Dutch *meer*) sea, pool, Old High German *mari, meri* (modern German *Meer*) sea, Old Icelandic *marr,* from Proto-Germanic **mari,* and Gothic *marei* lake, from Proto-Germanic **marīn;* also cognate outside Germanic with Latin *mare* sea; Old Slavic *morje,* Russian *more,* Old Prussian *mary,* Lithuanian *mārė,* Old Irish *muir,* and Welsh, Cornish, Breton *mor,* from Indo-European **mori/meri/mōri* (Pok. 748).

meretricious (mer'ətrish'əs) *adj.* attractive in a cheap, gaudy way; alluring by false charms. Before 1626, characteristic of a prostitute, in Bacon's *The New Atlantis;* borrowed from Latin *meretrīcius* of or pertaining to prostitutes, from *meretrīx* (genitive *meretrīcis*) prostitute, from *merēre, merērī* to earn, gain, see MERIT; for suffix see -OUS.

merganser (mərgan'sər) *n.* large, fish-eating duck. 1752, in John Hill's *A History of Animals,* New Latin (from Latin *mergus* waterfowl, diver, from *mergere* to dip, immerse + *ānser* goose).

merge *v.* 1636, to plunge or immerse in an activity, environment; later, be absorbed or swallowed up in something else (1726); borrowed from Latin *mergere* to dip, immerse. Latin *mergere* is cognate with Lithuanian *mazgóti* to wash, and Sanskrit *májjati* (he) dives, submerges, from Indo-European **mesg-* dive under (Pok. 745). **—merger** *n.* act of merging. 1728, absorption of an estate, etc., in another; formed from English *merge* + *-er*[1]. The meaning of combination of one business firm with another is first recorded in 1889 in American English.

meridian *n.* circle on the earth's surface passing through the North and South Poles. Probably about 1350 *meridien* middle, noon; later *meridian* (probably 1397); borrowed from Old French *meridien,* from Latin, and directly from Latin *meridiānus* of noon, southern, from *merīdiēs* noon, south, from *merīdiē* at noon, formed by dissimilation of *r* for *d* in the pre-Latin form **mediei diē* (the locative form of *medius* mid, see MIDDLE + *diēs* day, see DEITY); for suffix see -IAN.

Meridian in the sense of a circle of the earth passing through the poles, is first recorded in Chaucer's *Treatise on the Astrolabe* (1391); this meaning developed from the fact that the sun crosses the meridian at noon, hence *meridian circle* or *line* (literally, midday circle or line) or simply the *meridian.*

meringue (mərang') *n.* mixture of egg whites beaten stiff and sweetened. 1706, in Kersey's edition of Phillips' *Dictionary;* borrowed from French *meringue,* of unknown origin.

merino (mərē'nō) *n.* sheep with long, fine wool. 1781, in a travel book on Spain; borrowing of Spanish *merino* describing a breed of sheep pastured in the mountains in summer and the lowlands in winter, and therefore sometimes said to imply the sense of roving from pasture to pasture; possibly an alteration (influenced by *merino* inspector of cattle pastures and sheep paths) of Arabic *Merīni* the Beni-Merin, a famous Berber family of sheep farmers in northwestern Africa, whose sheep were imported into Spain in the 1300's and 1400's to improve local breeds.

Spanish *merino* in the sense of inspector of sheep paths and cattle pastures (also judicial officer) was borrowed from Medieval Latin *majorinus,* as used in Spain to mean head of a village, overseer, from Latin *majōrinus,* adj., of the greater kind, from *major* greater, MAJOR.

meristem (mer'əstem) *n. Botany.* undifferentiated tissue of the younger parts of plants. 1874, formed from Greek *meristós* divisible or divided (from *merízein* to divide, from *méros* part; see MERIT + the ending *-em,* as in German *Phloem* phloem and *Xylem* xylem).

merit *n.* goodness, worth, value. Probably before 1200, in *Ancrene Riwle;* borrowed from Old French *merite,* learned borrowing from Latin, and directly from Latin *meritum,* neuter of *meritus,* past participle of *merēre, merērī* to earn, deserve, acquire, gain. Latin *merēre, merērī* are cognate with Greek *méros* part, *móros* fate, and *émmore* he got his share, from Indo-European **(s)mer-/(s)mor-* give (one) his due, his portion, his lot (Pok. 970). —**v.** deserve. 1484, in Caxton's translation of *Fables of Aesop;* borrowed from Middle French *meriter,* from *merite,* n. —**meritorious** *adj.* Probably before 1425, in a translation of Higden's *Polychronicon;* borrowed, perhaps by influence of Old French *meritoire,* from Latin *meritōrius* serving to earn money, from *meritus,* past participle of *merēre, merērī;* for suffix see -ORY, and -OUS.

merle or **merl** (mérl) *n.* European blackbird. 1483, in Caxton's version of the *Golden Legend;* borrowing of Middle French *merle,* from Latin *merula* blackbird, possibly from earlier **mesolā* and cognate with Old High German *amsala* blackbird (modern German *Amsel*), and Old English *ōsle* blackbird, OUZEL.

mermaid *n.* maiden in fairy tales having the form of a fish from the waist down. About 1350 *meremayde;* later *mermayde* (about 1390); formed from Middle English *mere²* sea, lake + *maide* maid.

merry *adj.* Before 1200 *murie* mirthful, joyous, pleasing; later *mirie* (about 1250), and *mery, meri* (probably before 1300; as a surname *Merilord,* about 1273); developed from Old English *myrige* pleasing, agreeable (before 899, in Alfred's translation of Boethius' *De Consolatione Philosophiae*). Old English *myrige* (from Proto-Germanic **murʒijaz*) is cognate with Old High German *murg, murgi* short, and Gothic *gamaúrgjan* shorten. Cognates outside Germanic include Greek *brachýs,* Latin *brevis,* Avestan *mərəzu-,* and Sogdian *murzak,* all meaning short, from Indo-European **mreĝhu-/mr̥ĝhu-* short (Pok. 750).

The transition from what was the original Proto-Germanic and Indo-European sense "short" to the Old English sense "pleasant" may have occurred through the intervention of a lost Old English verb meaning "to shorten," and hence "to shorten time, to cheer"; compare Old Icelandic *skemta* to shorten time, amuse oneself, derived from *skammr* short, and modern German *Kurzweil* amusement; literally, short while, and *Langweile* boredom; literally, long while.

—**merriment** *n.* 1576, comic performance, jest; later, merrymaking, mirth, fun (1588, in Shakespeare's *Love's Labour's Lost*); formed from English *merry* + *-ment.* —**merry-andrew** *n.* clown. 1673 *Merry-Andrew,* in writings of Dryden; the reason for the name *Andrew* in this word is uncertain. —**merry-go-round** *n.* carousel (1729). —**merrymaking** *n.* festivity (1714).

mes- a combining form, the form of *meso-* before vowels, as in *mesencephalon* (the midbrain), *meson.*

mesa (mā'sə) *n.* small, high plateau with steep sides. 1759, in a translation of a book on the natural history of Spanish colonial California, American English; borrowing of Spanish *mesa,* literally, table, from Latin *mēnsa* table, of uncertain origin.

mescal (meskal') *n.* any of a species of *Agave,* especially a small cactus whose buttonlike tops are used as a stimulant; peyote. 1702, American English, borrowing of Mexican Spanish *mescal,* from Nahuatl *mexcalli* fermented drink made from the desert plant maguey (*metl* maguey and *ixcalli* stew). —**mescaline** (mes'kəlēn) *n.* stimulant contained in the buttonlike tops of the mescal. 1896, formed from English *mescal* + *-ine²*.

mesentery (mes'ənter'ē) *n. Anatomy.* membrane that enfolds and supports an internal organ. Probably before 1425 *mesentarie,* in a translation of Chauliac's *Grande Chirurgie;* borrowed from Medieval Latin *mesenterium,* from Greek *mesentérion* (*mésos* middle + *énteron* intestine, cognate with Sanskrit *ántara-s* inner, Latin *interior,* and Old High German *untar* among, from Indo-European **enter/n̥ter* between, among, Pok. 313).

mesh *n.* About 1395 *mesche* mesh of a net, in the Wycliffe Bible; also found as *mask, maske* (1343; 1440, in *Promptorium Parvulorum,* etc.); developed from Old English (probably about 1050) *max* net (a form showing metathesis of the sounds represented by *sk* to *ks*); earlier *mæscre* (probably about 950), from **masc, *mæsc,* from Proto-Germanic **mask-.* The Old English forms are cognate with Middle Dutch *maessce* (early modern Dutch *maesche,* later *maas*) mesh, from Proto-Germanic **mǣsk-* Old Icelandic *mǫskvi,* Old Saxon *masca,* and Old High German *masca* (modern German *Masche*) mesh, net. A cognate outside Germanic is found in Lithuanian *mãzgas* knot, *mègsti* to knit, from Indo-European **mesg-/mosg-/mēsg-* (Pok. 746).

—**v.** catch or be caught in a net. 1532, to entangle, enmesh, in Sir Thomas More's *Works;* from the noun. The literal meaning of catch in the meshes of a net, is first recorded before 1547, and the technical use in reference to the teeth of a wheel or gear in machinery, is found in Knight's *Practical Dictionary of Mechanics* (1875).

mesmerism (mez'mesrizəm) *n.* hypnotism. 1802, borrowing of French *mesmérisme,* formed in allusion to the Austrian physician Friedrich or Franz *Mesmer,* 1734-1815 + *-isme* -ism. Mesmer developed the theory of animal magnetism, according to which a mysterious body fluid allows a person to have a powerful "magnetic" or hypnotic influence over another person. —**mesmerize** *v.* hypnotize. 1829, formed from English *mesmerism* + *-ize.*

meso- a combining form meaning middle, halfway, midway, intermediate, used in scientific terms of modern formation, such as *mesoderm, mesomorph, mesosphere.* Borrowed from Greek *meso-,* combining form of *mésos* MIDDLE. Many words in *meso-* have related forms in *pro-,* meaning anterior, *proto-,* meaning first, and *meta-,* meaning behind or after. Also *mes-* before vowels.

mesoderm (mes'ədérm) *n.* the middle layer of cells in an embryo. 1873, borrowing of German *Mesoderm* and French *mésoderme* (from *meso-* middle + *-derm, -derme;* from Greek *dérma* skin).

meson (mes'on *or* mez'on) *n.* unstable elementary particle with a mass between that of the electron and the proton. 1939, alteration of earlier *mesotron* (1938, from *meso-* midway + *-tron,* as in *electron*). The alteration to *meson* was due to the influence of the suffix *-on,* as in *proton, phonon, photon,* and possibly by an earlier French *méson,* about 1935.

mesosphere *n.* area of the atmosphere about 20 to 50 miles above the earth's surface where most ozone is created. 1950, formed from English *meso-* + *-sphere,* as specifically used in reference to *atmosphere.*

mesquite (meskēt') *n.* tree or shrub common in the

southwestern United States and Mexico. 1759, in a translation of a book on the natural history of Spanish colonial California, American English; borrowing of Mexican Spanish *mezquite,* from Nahuatl *mizquitl.*

mess *n.* Probably before 1300 *mes* portion of food, prepared dish; in *Arthour and Merlin;* later, group of people who dine together (about 1410, in compound *mes-men,* and 1470 *messe,* in Malory's *Morte d'Arthur*); borrowed from Old French *mes* portion of food, a prepared dish, a course at dinner, from Late Latin *missus* (genitive *missūs*) course at dinner; literally, placing or putting (as if on the table), from *mittere* to put or place, from Latin *mittere* to send, let go; see MISSION.

In the 1400's *mess* meant any prepared dish, especially to a liquid or pulpy food, such as broth, porridge, etc. The expression *mess of pottage* (in connection to the Biblical story of Esau's sale of his birthright) is found in Middle English (about 1452) as *mese of potage.* Pope used *mess* in 1738 in the sense of a kind of liquid or mixed food for an animal, a usage that led to the contemptuous use of a concoction, jumble, mixed mass (recorded in Webster's *Dictionary,* 1828). The figurative sense of a state of confusion or muddle (as *to get into a mess* or *to make a mess of*), is first recorded in 1834, and later that of a dirty or untidy condition in 1851.

—v. 1381 *messen* serve food; from the noun. The sense of make untidy or dirty, is first recorded in 1853.

—mess kit cooking utensils for a soldier or camper (before 1877). **—messmate** *n.* companion at meals (1746). **—messy** *adj.* dirty or untidy. 1843, in Mrs. Carlyle's *Letters;* formed from English *mess,* n. + *-y[1].*

message *n.* Probably about 1300 *message* words sent from one to another; probably a back formation from earlier *messager,* and in part a borrowing of Old French *message,* from Medieval Latin *missaticum,* from Latin *missus,* past participle of *mittere* to send; see MISSION. **—messenger** *n.* Probably before 1200 *messager,* in *Ancrene Riwle;* later *messanger* (probably before 1300, in *Arthour and Merlin*); borrowed from Old French *messagier;* from *message,* n., message; for suffix see -ER[1].

In late Middle English the *n* was phonetically inserted before *-ger* in *messager* as in some other words, such as *harbinger, passenger, scavenger* (a phenomenon for which no satisfactory explanation has been given, though it exists in other words such as English *nightingale,* contrasting with such forms as German *Nachtigall*).

Messiah (məsī'ə) *n.* expected deliverer or savior; Lord's anointed. 1560, in the Geneva Bible, alteration of Middle English *Messyass* (probably about 1200, in *The Ormulum*); later *Messie* (about 1300); borrowed from Old French *Messie,* from Late Latin, and directly from Late Latin *Messīās,* from Greek *Messíās,* from Aramaic *mĕshīḥā* and Hebrew *māshīaḥ* anointed (of the Lord), from *māshaḥ* anoint. The Hebrew word was applied in the prophetic writings of the Old Testament to a promised deliverer of the Jewish nation, and later in the New Testament (John 1:41, 4:25) to Jesus as the fulfilment of that promise. In the Septuagint, Hebrew *māshīaḥ* was translated as *chrīstós* Christ.

According to the OED the form *Messiah* was invented by the translators of the Geneva Bible to give a more Hebraic appearance to the name in place of the Grecized *Messīās.*

—Messianic (mes'ēan'ik) *adj.* of or having to do with the Messiah. Before 1834, in Coleridge's *Literary Remains;* borrowed from New Latin *Messianicus,* from Late Latin *Messīās* Messiah; for suffix see -IC.

mestizo (mestē'zō) *n.* person of mixed descent. About 1588, borrowing of Spanish *mestizo* of mixed European and Amerindian parentage, from the meaning "mixed," from Late Latin *mixtīcius* mixed, mongrel, from Latin *mixtus,* past participle of *miscēre* to MIX.

met- a combining form, the form of *meta-* before vowels, as in *metencephalon, metonymy.*

meta- a prefix meaning: **1** between, among, as in *metacarpus* (bones between the fingers and the carpus or wrist). **2a** over or across, in the sense of change of place or state, as in *metathesis* (transposition of sounds, syllables, or letters), *metamorphosis.* **b** reciprocal, as in *metacenter.* **3a** behind, after, as in *metathorax* (posterior segment of insect's thorax). **b** later, more advanced, as in *metazoan* (animals of more than one cell). **4** beyond, transcending, as in *metalinguistics.* **5** similar in chemical composition to, as in *metaphosphate.* Borrowed from Greek *meta-,* from *metá,* preposition meaning with, after, between; cognate wtih Old English *mid, mith* with (as in Middle English *midwif* MIDWIFE), Old Frisian *mith,* Old Saxon *mid, midi* (Dutch *met, mede*), Old High German *mit, miti* (modern German *mit*), Old Icelandic *medh,* and Gothic *mith,* from Proto-Germanic **míthi* or **midi,* Indo-European **mé-ti* or **me-ti* (Pok. 702).

metabolism (mətab'əlizəm) *n.* process by which the body turns food into energy and living tissue. 1878, formed from English *metabol(ic)* + *-ism* and borrowed from French *métabolisme,* formed from Greek *metabolḗ* change (see METABOLIC) + *-isme* -ism. **—metabolic** (met'əbol'ik) *adj.* 1743, involving change, in Henry Fielding's *Works;* borrowed from Greek *metabolikós* changeable, from *metabolḗ* change, from *metabállein* to change (*meta-* over + *bállein* to throw; see BALL[2] dancing party); for suffix see -IC. The sense of pertaining to metabolism (1845) was borrowed from French in a translation of a book on physiology. **—metabolite** (mətab'əlīt) *n.* substance produced by metabolism. 1884, formed from English *metabolism* + *-ite[1].*

metal *n.* About 1250, in *The Story of Genesis and Exodus;* borrowing of Old French *metal,* learned borrowing from Latin *metallum* metal, mine, quarry, substance obtained by mining, from Greek *métallon* metal, ore; originally, mine, quarry, pit or cave where minerals are sought, probably a back formation from *metalleúein* to mine, to quarry, a technical term borrowed from a language unknown. **—adj.** made of metal. About 1477; (earlier in attributive use *metal ore,* etc., before 1382); from the noun. **—metallic** *adj.* of or like a metal. Probably before 1425, in a translation of Chauliac's *Grande Chirurgie;* borrowed from Latin *metallicus,* from Greek *metallikós* of or concerning mines or metal; for suffix see -IC. **—metalliferous** (met'əlif'ərəs) *adj.* containing or yielding metal. 1656, in Blount's *Glossographia,* formed in English from Latin *metallifer* (*metallum* metal + *-fer* carrying, productive, from *ferre* to carry) + English suffix *-ous.* **—mettallurgy** (met'əlėr'jē) *n.* science or art dealing with metals. 1704, borrowed through French *métallurgie,* or directly from New Latin *metallurgia,* from Greek *metallourgós* worker in metal (*métallon* metal + *-orgós,* earlier **-worgós,* from *érgon* work); for suffix see -Y[3]. **—metallurgical** *adj.* 1812, formed from English *metallurgy* +

-ical. **—metallurgist** *n.* 1670, borrowed from French *métallurgiste,* formed from *métallurgie* metallurgy + *-iste* -ist. **—metalwork** *n.* (before 1850) **—metalworking** *n.* (1882)

metamorphosis (met′əmôr′fəsis) *n.* change of form. 1533, in Sir Thomas More's *Debellacyon of Salem and Bizance,* borrowed perhaps through Latin *metamorphōsis,* from Greek *metamórphōsis* a transforming, from *metamorphoûn* to transform (*meta-* change + *morphḗ* form); see MORPHOLOGY. An earlier Anglicized form *Metamorphoseos,* in allusion to the Roman poet Ovid's work, is found in Chaucer's *Canterbury Tales* (about 1390). It is also mentioned in Gower, Lydgate, etc. **—metamorphic** *adj.* 1816, exhibiting metamorphosis; formed, perhaps by influence of French *métamorphique,* from English *metamorphos(is)* + *-ic.* The geological sense of altered by heat and pressure appeared in 1833, in Sir Charles Lyell's *Principles of Geology.* **—metamorphose** *v.* to change in form. 1576, borrowed from Middle French *métamorphoser,* from *métamorphose* metamorphosis, perhaps through Latin *metamorphōsis,* from Greek *metamórphōsis.*

metaphor *n.* implied comparison between two different things. About 1477 *methaphor,* borrowed from Middle French *métaphore,* from Latin or Greek, and directly from Latin *metaphora* or from Greek *metaphorá* a transfer, especially to one word of the sense of another, from *metaphérein* transfer, carry over (*meta-* over, across + *phérein* to carry, BEAR[2]). **—metaphorical** *adj.* Before 1555, formed from English *metaphor* + *-ical.*

metaphysics *n.* branch of philosophy concerned with the explanation of reality and knowledge. 1569, plural of Middle English *methaphisik* (about 1449); earlier *methaphesik* (before 1387, in Trevisa's translation of Higden's *Polychronicon*); borrowed from Medieval Latin *metaphysica,* neuter plural, from Medieval Greek *(tà) metaphysiká,* from Greek *tà metà tà physiká* the (works) after the Physics, the title given to a collection of Aristotle's writings by the editor Andronicus of Rhodes, with reference to the fact that the treatises on metaphysics were placed after the treatises on physics. For suffix see -ICS. **—metaphysical** *adj.* of metaphysics, highly abstract. Probably before 1425 *metaphisicalle,* in a translation of Higden's *Polychronicon;* formed from Middle English *methaphesik* + *-al*[1], and probably borrowed from Medieval Latin *metaphysicalis.*

metastasis (mətas′təsis) *n.* 1586, New Latin *metastasis* transition from one subject to another (a term in rhetoric), from Late Latin *metastasis* transition, from Greek *metástasis* transference, removal, change, from *methistánai* to remove, change (*meta-* over, across + *histánai* to place, cause to stand). The sense of a transfer of pain, or disease from one organ or part of the body to another, especially such a transfer of cancerous cells, is first recorded in Boyle's writings in 1663. **—metastasize** *v.* undergo metastasis. 1907, formed from English *metastasis* + *-ize.*

metathesis (məthath′əsis) *n.* transposition or interchange, as of sounds, syllables, or letters. 1608, transposition of words; later, transposition of letters (1660); borrowed from Late Latin *metathesis* transposition of words, from Greek *metáthesis* transposition, from *metatithénai* to transpose (*meta-* over, across, change of place + *tithénai* to set, put).

mete[1] *v.* allot, distribute. About 1175 *meten* to measure; later, to allot, apportion (before 1225); developed from Old English *metan* to measure (about 725 in *Beowulf*). Old English *metan* is cognate with Olc Frisian *meta* to measure, Old Saxon *metan,* Middle Dutch *mēten* (modern Dutch *meten*), Old High German *mezzan* (modern German *messen*), Old Icelandic *meta* to value, estimate, measure (Swedish *mäta* tc measure), and Gothic *mitan* to measure, from Proto-Germanic **metanan.* Cognates outside Germanic include Old Irish *med* scale, balance, *midiur* I judge Latin *meditārī* to think or reflect upon, consider, Greek *médesthai* be mindful of, *médimnos* bushel, and Armenian *mit* thought, from Indo-European *med-* measure (Pok. 705). Related to MEET[2] proper.

The word is now literary in use, except in the phrase *mete out* which is first recorded in the Coverdale Bible (1535).

mete[2] *n.* 1402, goal; later, boundary (about 1440); borrowed from Old French *mete, mette,* from Latin, and directly from Latin *mēta* boundary mark, limit, goal perhaps cognate with Sanskrit *mēthís* pillar, post and Lithuanian *miẽtas* stake, from Indo-European **mei-t-, mēi-t-* (Pok. 709).

meteor (mē′tēər) *n.* Probably 1471 *Metheours* atmospheric phenomena (as the spelling of the title o Aristotle's *Meteorologica*); borrowed from Middle French *météore,* and directly from Medieval Latin *meteora,* from Greek *tà metéōra* the celestial phenomena, plural of *metéōron* celestial phenomenon literally, thing high up, neuter of *metéōros* high up raised above the ground, earlier *metḗoros* (*meta-* over beyond + *-aoros* lifted, related to *aeírein* to lift up raise, of uncertain origin).

The modern spelling *meteor* is first recorded in English in Fleming's *A Panoply of Epistles* (1576). The specific meaning of falling or shooting star, is first recorded in a figurative sense in Shakespeare's *Comedy of Errors* (1590), in a literal sense in Shakespeare's *Richard II* (1593).
—meteoric *adj.* Before 1631, in Donne's *Letters,* elevated, lofty; formed from English *meteor* + *-ic.* The meaning of pertaining to or of meteors is first recorded in 1812, in Sir Humphry Davy's writings, and later in the figurative sense of swift or dazzling, in 1836 **—meteorite** (mē′tēərit) *n.* meteor that has fallen on earth. 1834, in the writings of the American physicis and astronomer Denison Olmsted; formed from English *meteor* + *-ite*[1].

meteorology (mē′tēərol′əjē) *n.* science dealing with the atmosphere and weather. 1620 borrowed througl French *météorologie,* and directly from Greek *meteōrologíā* treatise on celestial phenomena, from *metéōron* celestial phenomenon, see METEOR + *-logí* treatment of; -logy.

The earlier appearance of the derivative *meteorological* suggests a defect in the record of English fo *meteorology* (recorded 50 years later, especially as the form in French is recorded from 1547.)
—meteorological *adj.* 1570, formed in English from Middle French *météorologique* or Greek *meteōrologikós* + English suffix *-al*[1]*;* for suffix see -ICAL **—meteorologist** *n.* 1621, in Burton's *Anatomy of Melancholy;* formed in English from Greek *meteōrológo* one who deals with celestial phenomena + English suffix *-ist.* Other terms were in existence at the time including *meteorologician* (1580) and *meteorologian* (1614).

meter[1] *n.* measured rhythm in poetry or verse. Old English *mēter* (before 899, probably in Alfred's translation of Bede's *Ecclesiastical History*); borrowed from Latin *metrum,* from Greek *métron* meter, MEASURE, cognate with Prākrit *metta-m,* from Sanskrit **mitra-m,* the corresponding Greek word having been altered from expected **mátron* by influence of *mĕ́trā* register (compare Sanskrit *mā́trā* measure), from Indo-European **mē-/mə-* (Pok. 703). As the word disappears from the record of English for almost 300 years (reappearing first in Mannyng's *Chronicle of England,* before 1338), it is possible that use in Middle English was a reborrowing of Old French *metre* with the additional meaning of metrical scheme or composition, verse, poetry, learned borrowing from Latin *metrum* poetic measure or meter.

meter[2] *n.* unit of length in the metric system. 1797 *metre,* borrowed from French *mètre,* learned borrowing from Greek *métron* MEASURE. The term was officially adopted by the National Assembly of France in 1795-96, during the Revolution, after their request of the French Academy of Sciences to develop a system of weights and measurement, which was based on a proposal for a decimal system of measure originated in 1670 by a French clergyman, Gabriel Mouton.

meter[3] *n.* mechanical device for measuring. 1830, probably abstracted from *gas-meter* (1815), but also found in earlier use (1790) in a translation of Lavoisier's works describing a *gazometer* a device to give a measured flow of oxygen in chemical experiments. The word in English was probably much influenced by the combining form *-mètre* in French and was also probably, in part, an extended use of earlier *meter* person who measures (about 1384), and as a surname (1307); formed from *meten* to measure, METE[1] + *-er*[1]. —v. to measure with a meter. 1884, from the noun. An earlier verb use is found in *metren* to measure in metrical feet of poetry (before 1425), but does not formally belong to *meter*[3].

-meter a combining form meaning a device or instrument for measuring something, in actual use commonly *-ometer,* as in *speedometer, barometer, hygrometer, pedometer,* and in some later formations *-imeter,* as in *gravimeter, calorimeter.* Borrowed from French *-mètre,* from Greek *métron* MEASURE. In some later formations *-meter* is attached to modern words without any attempt to parallel the form of the first element to that of a Greek or Latin combining form, as in *voltameter, ammeter.*

methadone (meth′ədōn) *n.* synthetic narcotic used to relieve pain and treat heroin addiction. 1947, from *(di)meth(yl)a(mino) d(iphenyl)-heptan)one,* the chemical name of the drug.

methane (meth′ān) *n.* gaseous hydrocarbon commercially important as fuel. 1868, formed from English *meth(yl)* + *-ane* (chemical suffix).

methinks *v. Archaic.* it seems to me. Before 1200 *me thinketh;* later *me thinkes* (before 1375); developed from Old English *mē thyncth* it seems to me (before 899, in Alfred's translation of Boethius' *De Consolatione Philosophiae*); formed from *mē,* dative of *I* (see ME) and *thyncth,* third person singular of *thyncan* to seem, parallel to German *mich* (or *mir*) *dünkt,* third person singular of *dünken* to seem, from Proto-Germanic **thunkjanan.*

In Old English, the word *thyncan* to seem, and the closely related *thencan* to THINK, were kept distinct; but in Middle English, because Old English *thync-* and *thenc-* developed into Middle English *think-,* the two words became confused and finally coalesced.

method *n.* Probably before 1425, recommended medical procedure, in a translation of Chauliac's *Grande Chirurgie;* borrowed from Latin *methodus* way of teaching or proceeding, from Greek *méthodos,* originally, pursuit, following after (*meta-* after + *hodós* a traveling road, way; see CEDE). The extended sense of any special procedure or way of doing things, is first recorded in English in 1586.

The name *Methodist* was originally applied to a member of a religious society of Protestants founded at Oxford in 1729 by John and Charles Wesley, whose object was the promotion of piety and morality. The precise origin of the name is obscure though reference is made as early as 1692 to *methodists* in terms of religious practices. (In the sense of one who practices or follows a particular method, the word is first recorded in 1593.) The term *Methodism* appeared in 1739, in John Wesley's writings.

—methodic *adj.* 1541, probably borrowed through Middle French *méthodique,* and directly from Latin *methodicus,* from Greek *methodikós.* **—methodical** *adj.* done according to a method. 1570, formed in English from Late Latin *methodicus* (from Greek *methodikós,* from *méthodos* method) + English *-al*[1]. **—methodology** *n.* 1800, formed from English *method* + connective *-o-* + *-logy.*

methyl (meth′əl) *n. Chemistry.* univalent hydrocarbon radical. 1844, borrowed from French *méthyle,* back formation from *méthylène* METHYLENE; for suffix see -YL.

methylene *n.* hydrocarbon radical derived from methane. 1835, borrowed from French *méthylène,* from Greek *méthy* wine + *hýlē* wood or substance; for suffix see -ENE.

meticulous *adj.* **1** *Obsolete.* fearful or timid (1535); borrowed from Latin *meticulōsus* fearful or timid (*metus* fear, of uncertain origin + *-iculōsus,* a suffixal ending patterned after *perīculōsus* perilous), of which the more common variant *metūculōsus* is an alteration due to *metus* (genitive *metūs*) fear, a fear with good reason as opposed to *timor* an unreasonable fear; for suffix see -OUS.

2 extremely careful about small details (1827); borrowed by influence of French *méticuleux,* from Latin *metīculōsus,* see def. 1, with the sense of timorously fussy about details.

métier (mātyā′) *n.* kind of work for which one shows special abilities. 1792, in Charlotte Smith's *Desmond;* borrowing of French *métier* trade, profession, from Old French *mestier,* from Gallo-Romance **misterium,* contraction (influenced by the form of Latin *mystērium* religious service) of Latin *ministerium* office, service, from *minister* servant; see MINISTER.

metonymy (məton′əmē) *n.* figure of speech using one word or name to suggest another, as "Whitehall" for "the British government or its policies." 1562, borrowed, perhaps through French *métonymie,* and directly from Late Latin *metōnymia,* from Greek *metōnymíā,* literally, a change of name (*meta-* change + *ónyma* dialectal form of *ónoma* NAME); for suffix see -Y[3]. An earlier form *metonomian* is recorded in 1547.

metric *adj.* of the meter or metric system. 1864, probably in part borrowed from French *métrique,* from *mètre* METER[2] unit of length; for suffix see -IC; and also formed by reduction of earlier English *metrical* (1797) of or having to do with the meter or metric system. **—metricate** *v.* convert to the metric system. 1965, probably a back formation from *metrication.* The form *metricate* replaced earlier *metricize* (1873). **—metrication** *n.* 1965, formed from English *metric* + *-ation.* **—metric system** (1864)

metrical *adj.* pertaining to poetic meter. Probably before 1425, borrowed from Latin *metricus* metrical, from Greek *metrikós,* from *métron* poetic meter, MEASURE. For suffix see -ICAL.

metronome *n.* clocklike device for marking rhythm for musicians. 1815, formed in English from Greek *métron* MEASURE + *-nómos* regulating, verbal adjective of *némein* to regulate (see NIMBLE).

metropolis (mətrop′əlis) *n.* large or important city. 1535, the see of a metropolitan bishop; later, the mother city or parent state of a Greek colony (before 1568, in Ascham's *The Schoolmaster*); borrowed from Late Latin *mētropolis* mother city, from Greek *mētrópolis* (*mḗtēr* MOTHER + *pólis* city).

The sense of a large or chief city appeared in Middle English (about 1386) in the form *metropol,* borrowed from Late Latin *mētropolis,* Modern English *metropolis* is first recorded in this sense, in Marlowe's *Tamburlane the Great* (1590).

—metropolitan *n.* a chief bishop. Probably before 1350, borrowed from Late Latin *mētropolītānus,* from Greek *mētropolítēs* resident of a city, chief bishop, from *mētrópolis* chief city; for suffix see -AN; *adj.* of a metropolis. Probably before 1425, pertaining to a chief bishop of a church province, in a translation of Higden's *Polychronicon;* probably from the noun, in part by influence of Late Latin *mētropolītānus* of a metropolis.

-metry a combining form meaning the process or art of measuring, as in *geometry, optometry.* Borrowed from Greek *-metriā,* from *metreîn* to measure, from *métron* MEASURE.

mettle *n.* disposition, spirit, courage. 1581, spirit or courage; also, quality of disposition or temperament (1584); figurative use of *metal,* as the material of which a person is made. *Mettle* was originally an indiscriminately used variant spelling of *metal,* later formally differentiated (1706, in Kersey's revision of Phillips' *Dictionary*) in the figurative senses cited above. **—mettlesome** *adj.* spirited or courageous. 1662, formed from English *mettle* + *-some[1].*

mew[1] *v.* make the characteristic sound of a cat. Before 1325 *mewen;* of imitative origin. **—n., interj.** 1596, in Shakespeare's *1 Henry IV;* of imitative origin.

mew[2] *n.* sea gull. Before 1200 *meau;* later *mewe* (about 1450); developed from Old English (about 700) *mǣw;* cognate with Frisian *meau, mieu* sea gull, Old Saxon *mēw,* Middle Low German *mēwe* (modern German *Möwe*), Middle Dutch *mēwe* (modern Dutch *meeuw*), from Proto-Germanic **maizwís,* and cognate with Old High German *mēh* and Old Icelandic *mār,* from Proto-Germanic **maiHwaz,*

The French word *mouette* sea gull, was borrowed from a Germanic source. According to the OED, the word comes down from an Indo-European **moikw-;* but in the opinion of Friedrich Kluge (*Etymologisches Wörterbuch der deutschen Sprache*) the word was perhaps originally imitative of the bird's cry in Proto-Germanic.

mew[3] *n.* a cage. Before 1375 *meuwe* a hiding place, place of confinement; later, cage for hawks, especially while molting (about 1395); borrowed from Old French *mue,* from *muer* to molt, from Latin *mūtāre* to change, MUTATE; see also MOLT. **—v.** to cage or coop up. About 1450; later, to hide, conceal (1577-87).

mewl *v.* cry like a baby, whimper. 1600, in Shakespeare's *As You Like It,* perhaps borrowed from French *mouiller (les yeux)* to cry, literally, to wet (the eyes), from Vulgar Latin **molliāre* to make bland, make soggy, from Latin *mollis* soft, mild; see MELT.

mews (myüz) *n.pl.* group of stables or garages built around a court or alley. Before 1631, in Donne's *Satires,* developed from Middle English (1387) *Mewes*name of the royal stables at Charing Cross in London (1387, so called because they were built on the site where the royal hawks were formerly caged at molting time), from plural of *mewe;* see MEW[3].

Mexican *n.* 1604, borrowed from Spanish *Mexicano,* from *Mexico* + *-an.* **—adj.** (1696).

mezzanine (mez′enēn) *n.* 1715, low story between two higher stories of a building; borrowing of French *mezzanine,* from Italian *mezzanino,* from *mezzano* middle, from Latin *mediānus* of the middle, from *medius* MIDDLE. The extended sense of the lowest balcony in a theater, is first recorded in 1927, in American English.

mezzo (met′sō *or* mez′ō) *adj., adv. Music.* middle, intermediate, moderate or moderately (as in *mezzo forte* moderately loud). 1811, borrowing of Italian *mezzo,* from Latin *medius* MIDDLE. **—n.** voice intermediate between soprano and contralto. 1832, shortened form of earlier *mezzo-soprano* (1753); borrowed from Italian *mezzosoprano* (*mezzo* half + *soprano* SOPRANO).

mi (mē) *n.* third note of the musical scale. Before 1450, borrowed from Medieval Latin *mi,* from the initial syllable of Latin *mīra* wonders (wondrous things), the word sung to this note in the Hymn for St. John the Baptist's day; see GAMUT. Latin *mīra* developed from *mīrus,* adj., wonderful; see MIRACLE.

miasma (mīaz′mə) *n.* noxious vapors arising from rotting organic matter. 1665, New Latin *miasma,* from Greek *míasma* stain, pollution, related to *miaínein* to pollute; see MOLE[1] spot.

miaw *n., interj., v.* variant of MEOW.

mica (mī′kə) *n.* mineral that divides into thin, partly transparent layers. 1706, in Kersey's revision of Phillips' *Dictionary;* New Latin *mica,* special use (perhaps influenced by Latin *micāre* to flash, glitter) of Latin *mīca* grain or crumb, cognate with Greek *mīkrós* small; see MICRO-.

Mickey Finn or **mickey finn,** *Slang.* drugged alcoholic drink. 1928, American English, from an Irish proper name, of uncertain reference. The shortened form *Mickey* appeared in 1938.

Mickey Mouse 1935 (as a noun), something or someone, that is unnecessary, unimportant, trivial, etc.; developed as an allusion to the childish appeal of simplicity and triviality of *Mickey Mouse,* an American cartoon character invented by Walt Disney, before 1928. 1936 (as an adjective) worthless, unnecessary, unimportant, in Orwell's writings; from the noun.

mickle *adj., adv., n. Scottish and Northern English Dia-*

lect. much. Probably about 1175 *muchel;* later *michel* and *mikel* (probably about 1200); developed from Old English *micel* (before 725), *mycel* (before 900), from Proto-Germanic **mekilaz;* see MUCH.

micro- a combining form used chiefly to form scientific terms and meaning: **1** small, very small, as in *microorganism, microcomputer.* **2** one millionth of, as in *microfarad.* **3** that magnifies or amplifies, as in *microscope, microphone.* Borrowed from Greek *mīkro-*, from *mīkrós, smīkrós* small, short; cognate with Latin *mīca* a grain or crumb, Old Icelandic *smār* (earlier **smāha*) small, and Old High German *smāhi* little, slight, from Indo-European **smē(i)k-/smīk-* (Pok. 966). Compare MACRO-.

microbe *n.* microscopic organism, germ. 1881, borrowing of French *microbe,* formed as if from Greek *mīkrós* small + *bíos* life. The word was coined in 1878 by the French physician and surgeon Charles E. Sédillot, 1804-1883. **—microbial** *adj.* of microbes. 1887, formed from English *microbe* + *-ial.*

microbiology *n.* study of microscopic organisms. 1888, formed from English *micro-* + *biology.* **—microbiological** *adj.* (1897) **—microbiologist** *n.* 1885, formed from English *micro-* + *biologist.*

microcosm *n.* little world, universe in miniature. Probably before 1430 *mycrocosme,* in Lydgate's translation of De Guileville's *Pilgrimage of the Life of Man;* borrowed from Middle French *microcosme,* from Medieval Latin *microcosmus* (found in Boethius' *De Consolatione Philosophiae*), from Greek *mīkròs kósmos* little world. Earlier in Middle English *microcosmos* man thought of as an epitome of the universe, is found in *The Ormulum* (probably about 1200) as a direct borrowing from Medieval Latin *microcosmus.* The meaning of universe in miniature, as applied to a community or group of people, is first recorded in 1562.

microfilm *n.* film for very small photographs of printed matter. 1927, formed from English *micro-* small + *film.* **—v.** to record on microfilm. 1940, from the noun.

micron (mī'kron) n. one millionth of a meter. 1885, borrowing of French *micron* (1880), from Greek *mīkrón,* neuter of *mīkrós* small; see MICRO-.

microorganism *n. Biology.* microscopic organism. 1880, formed from English *micro-* small + *organism.*

microphone (mī'krəfōn) *n.* instrument for amplifying or transmitting sounds. 1683, ear trumpet to intensify small sounds for the hard-of-hearing; formed from English *micro-* small + *-phone* sound. In 1878 *microphone* was applied to a telephone transmitter, and later to use in radio broadcasting and motion-picture recording, before 1929.

microscope *n.* instrument for magnifying minute things. 1656, borrowed from New Latin *microscopium* (about 1628, from *micro-* small + Greek *-skópion* means of viewing, from *skopeîn* look at; see SPY). **—microscopic** *adj.* that cannot be seen without a microscope, extremely small. 1732, like a microscope, in Pope's *Essay on Man;* formed, perhaps by influence of French *microscopique,* from English *microscope* + *-ic.* The sense of extremely small, is first recorded before 1770. **—microscopy** *n.* use of a microscope. 1664-65, in Pepys' *Diary,* formed from English *microscope* + *-y³*.

microwave *n.* very short radio wave. 1931, formed from English *micro-* small + *wave,* n.

mid *adj.* in the middle of. Old English (before 725) *mid;* cognate with Old Frisian *midde* mid or middle, Old Saxon *middi,* Old High German *mitti,* Old Icelandic *midhr,* and Gothic *midjis,* from Proto-Germanic **međjaz,* corresponding to Indo-European **medhyos,* found in Middle Irish *mide* middle, Sanskrit *mádhya-s,* and Latin *medius* MIDDLE.

The Old English form was rare except in inflected forms, as *midde, middes, midre, midne,* etc. In modern English its most common use is as the prefix *mid-*.

mid- a prefix meaning middle point or part of, as in *midday, midnight, midcontinent;* of, in, or near the middle of, as in *midsummer.* Middle English, developed from *mid,* adj., in the middle of.

midday *n.* 1135 *mid dæi;* later *middei* (probably before 1200, in *Ancrene Riwle*), and *midday* (about 1275); found in Old English (about 1000) *middæg;* earlier *midne dæg* (971); cognate with Old High German *mittitag, mitter tag* (modern German *Mittag*), Middle Dutch and Middle Low German *middach* (modern Dutch *middag*), and Old Icelandic *midhdagr* (Swedish, Norwegian, and Danish *middag*). **—adj.** Before 1325, in *Cursor Mundi;* from the noun.

middle *adj.* Probably before 1200 *midle,* in *Ancrene Riwle;* developed from Old English (785) *middel;* cognate with Old Frisian *middel* middle, Old Saxon *middil,* Middle Dutch and modern Dutch *middel,* Old High German *mittil* (modern German *mittel*), from Proto-West-Germanic **middila,* formed from **middi,* from Proto-Germanic **međjaz* MID; and cognate with Old Icelandic *medhal* among, between (Swedish *medel* Danish and Norwegian *middle* center). Cognates outside Germanic include Old Irish *immedōn* in middle, Latin *medius* middle, Greek *mésos* (earlier *méthyos*), Armenian *mēj,* Old Slavic *meždu* between, Old Russian *meži* between, Russian *mezhá* boundary, hedge (between two fields), Avestan *maithya-,* and Sanskrit *mádhya-s* middle, from Indo-European **medhyos* (Pok. 706).

—n. Probably before 1200 *midle,* in Layamon's *Chronicle of Britain;* developed from Old English (about 750) *middel,* from the adjective.

—middle age period between youth and old age. About 1378 *myddel age;* in a version of *Piers Plowman.* **—middle-aged** *adj.* (1608) **—Middle Ages** period of history intermediate between ancient and modern times (1722). In earlier usage, the *Middle Ages* were usually considered to extend from about A.D. 500 to about 1500, but now the term is often used to refer to a period extending roughly from A.D. 1000 to 1500. **—middle class** social class between the wealthy and the poor (1766). **—middleman** *n.* 1795, trader who buys goods from a producer and sells them to a retailer or consumer; earlier, one who takes a middle course (1741), and soldier in a middle rank of a formation (1616).

middling *adj.* medium in size, quality, grade, etc. 1456, Scottish *mydlyn;* probably formed from English *mid,* adj. + *-ling¹*. **—adv.** *Informal or Dialect.* moderately, fairly. 1719, in Defoe's *Robinson Crusoe;* from the adjective.

middy *n. Informal.* midshipman. 1818, shortened and altered form of *midshipman* low-ranking naval officer (1685); formed from English *midship* middle part of a ship (1555) + *man;* for suffix see -Y². *Middy* in the sense of loose blouse like that of a sailor's, is first recorded in 1911.

midge *n.* tiny insect, gnat. About 1340 *mydge;* developed from Old English (about 700) *mygg, mycg, mycge.* The Old English forms are cognate with Old Saxon *muggia* midge, Middle Dutch *mugghe* (modern Dutch *mug*), Middle Low German *mügge,* Old High German *mucka* (modern German *Mücke*), from Proto-Germanic **muʒjōn,* from Indo-European **mukyṓn* or **mughyōn,* and cognate with Old Icelandic *mȳ.* Cognates outside Germanic include Latin *musca* fly, Albanian *müzë,* Greek *myîa* (earlier **musya*), Old Prussian *muso,* Old Slavic *mucha,* Lithuanian *musė̃,* Latvian *músa,* and Armenian *mun* gnat, from Indo-European **mus-* (Pok. 752).

midget *n.* 1884, very small person exhibited as a curiosity; earlier, dialectal *midget* anything very small, mite (1865); formed from English *midge* + *-et* (diminutive suffix).

midland *adj.* Before 1447 *mydlonde* located or living in the Midlands of England; later *mid land,* in *mid land sea* the Mediterranean Sea (1579), and *midland* inland (1601); formed from Middle English *mid* + *lond* land. **—n.** 1555 *mydlande* the interior part of a country.

midnight *n.* Probably before 1200 *mid-niht,* in Layamon's *Chronicle of Britain;* later *midnigt* (probably before 1300, in *Kyng Alisaunder* and in *Arthour and Merlin*), and *mydnyght* (about 1385, in Chaucer's *Canterbury Tales*); found in Old English *mid-niht, midde neaht* (before 899, in Alfred's translation of Bede's *Ecclesiastical History*). The Old English forms are cognate with Old High German *mittinaht,* Middle Dutch *midnacht,* and through the Old English combination *midde niht,* inflected in the dative case as *middre niht* corresponding to modern Dutch *middernacht* and German *Mitternacht.*

midriff *n.* wall separating the chest cavity from the abdomen, diaphragm. Before 1333 *midrif;* developed from Old English (about 1000) *midhrif* (*mid* MID + *hrif* belly, abdomen; cognate with Old High German *(h)ref* body, abdomen, womb, from Proto-Germanic **Hrefiz;* and outside Germanic with Sanskrit *kṛpā́* shape, beautiful appearance, and Latin *corpus* body, from Indo-European **krep-/kṛp-,* Pok. 620).

midst *n.* the middle, center. Before 1325 *middes,* in *Cursor Mundi;* formed from Middle English and Old English *mid* MID + adverbial genitive *-s* or *-es;* the ending was changed to *-st* in the 1400's by association with superlatives in *-st* and *-est* (compare *amongst* and *against*); alternatively the final *-t* may have been added to the ending *-s* or *-es* for phonetic or articulatory reasons (compare *betwixt*). **—adv.** in the middle place. 1667, in Milton's *Paradise Lost,* from the noun, especially in the adjective use. The adverb also occurs in Middle English in the form *myddys* (1432). **—prep.** in the midst of, amid. 1591, in Shakespeare's *1 Henry VI;* commonly considered a shortened form of *amidst.* The preposition also occurs in Middle English as *myddis* (probably before 1400, and in that form was separate from *amidde,* 1200, and *amyddes,* 1391).

midsummer *n.* 1101 *midde sumeran;* later *midsumer* (1131), and *Midsummer* in a place name (1269); found in Old English *mid-sumor* (about 1050), *middum sumere* (before 899, in Alfred's translation of Bede's *Ecclesiastical History*), formed from Old English *mid* + *sumor,* but also found in Old Icelandic *midhsumar,* Middle Dutch *midsomer* (modern Dutch *midzomer*).

midway *n.* Probably before 1200 *mid wei,* in *Ancrene Riwle;* later *midwai* (about 1225); found in Old English *mid-weg* (before 899, in Alfred's translation of St. Gregory's *Pastoral Care*). **—adj.** 1050 (but published in 1500) *midway;* from the noun. **—adv.** Probably before 1200 *mid wei,* in *Ancrene Riwle;* from the noun.

midwife *n.* woman who helps women in childbirth. Probably before 1300 *midwif,* in *Arthour and Merlin* (*mid* with + *wif* woman; see WIFE). The forms with *med-* may derive from influence of Latin *medius* mediator or *med-* in words such as *mediate.*

midwinter *n.* About 1000, Old English *midwinter;* earlier *midde wintre* (827); corresponding to Old Frisian *midwinter,* Middle Dutch *midwinter, middewinter,* Middle High German *mittewinter* (modern German *Mittwinter*), Old Icelandic *midhr vetr.* **—adj.** 1135, from the noun.

mien (mēn) *n.* bearing, demeanor. 1513, probably a shortened form of Middle English *demean* bearing or demeanor (about 1450, from DEMEAN[2] behave); influenced by Middle French *mine* appearance or expression of the face, perhaps from Breton *min* muzzle, beak, related to Welsh *min* lip, edge, Old Irish *mēn* mouth.

miff *n.* peevish fit, petty quarrel. 1623, perhaps imitative of an exclamation of disgust. **—v.** offend, be offended. 1797, from the noun.

might[1] *v.* past tense of *may.* About 1387-95 *myghte,* developed from Old English *mihte, meahte* (before 899, in Alfred's translation of Bede's *Ecclesiastical History*); earlier *mæhte* (before 830); see MAY.

might[2] *n.* great strength, power. Before 1325 *might,* developed from Old English (before 900) *miht;* earlier *mæht* (before 830), and *mæct* (before 700). The Old English forms are cognate with Old Frisian *macht* might, Old Saxon *maht,* Middle Dutch and modern Dutch *macht,* Old High German *maht* (modern German *Macht*), Gothic *mahts,* from Proto-Germanic **maHtís,* and Old Icelandic *máttr,* from Proto-Germanic **maHtuz.* **—mighty** *adj.* About 1380 *mighti;* developed from Old English *mihtig* (before 899, in Alfred's translation of Bede's *Ecclesiastical History*); earlier *mæhtig* (before 830), from *miht, mæht* might + *-ig* -y[1] see MAY.

migraine (mīʹgrān) *n.* severe headache. 1373 *migrane,* later *mygrayne* (before 1425); borrowed from Old French *migraigne, migraine,* from Late Latin *hēmicrānia* pain on one side of the head, headache, from Greek *hēmikrāníā* (*hēmi-* half + *krānion* skull, CRANIUM).

The variant Middle English forms *mygreyme* (1440), *mygrem* (probably about 1450) gave rise to modern English *megrim* (pronounced mēʹgrim), used chiefly in the figurative senses of a whim, fancy (1593) and (in the plural) low spirits, the blues (1633). The form *migraine* was reinforced by a borrowing from modern French in the 1700's.

migrant *adj.* 1672, borrowed from Latin *migrantem* (nominative *migrāns*), present participle of *migrāre* to move from one place to another; for suffix see -ANT.

migrate *v.* 1697, back formation from *migration;* for suffix see -ATE[1]. **—migration** *n.* 1611, in Cotgrave's *Dictionary;* borrowed through French *migration,* or directly from Latin *migrātiōnem* (nominative *migrātiō*), from *migrāre* to move from one place to another, remove, depart, formed from a lost adjective **migwrós* moving, cognate with Greek *ameíbein* to change, and *amoibḗ* change, from Indo-European **meigw-/moigw-/migw-* (Pok. 713); for suffix see -ATION. **—migratory** *adj.* 1753, formed from English *migrate* + *-ory.*

mikado or **Mikado** (məkä′dō) *n.* 1727, Anglicized transcription of Japanese characters for the former title of the emperor of Japan. It is rendered in English as *mikado* (*mi* honorable + *kado* gate, portal). The literal meaning of *mikado* resembles the title of the former Turkish government or its ruler, the *Sublime Porte,* as well as the Egyptian royal title *Pharaoh,* which means literally "great house."

mike *n.* 1927, shortened and altered form of MICROPHONE. **—v.** 1957, from the noun.

mil *n.* unit of length. 1721 (in *per mil* per thousand, corresponding to *per cent*); borrowed from Latin *mīlle* a thousand; see MILE. The meaning of a unit of length equal to 0.001 of an inch, is first recorded in 1891.

milady or **miladi** (milā′dē) *n.* my lady. 1839, borrowing of French *milady,* a term of address corresponding to English *my lady.* Compare MILORD.

milch (milch) *adj.* giving milk. About 1250 *milche* giving milk, milky, in *The Story of Genesis and Exodus;* developed from Old English word element *-milce* a milking (as found in *thrimilce* the month of May, referring to the time in which cows could be milked three times a day). The Old English form is cognate with Old High German *melch* giving milk (modern German *melk*), Old Icelandic *mjólkr;* and related to Old English *meoluc,* from Proto-Germanic **meluk-,* and Old English *milc* milk, from Proto-West-Germanic **melik-,* altered from **meluk-;* see MILK.

mild *adj.* Old English (before 725) *milde* gentle, merciful, clement; cognate with Old Frisian *milde* mild, Old Saxon *mildi,* Middle Dutch *milde* (modern Dutch *mild*), Old High German *milti* (probably modern German *milde*), Old Icelandic *mildr* (Norwegian, Swedish, and Danish *mild*), and Gothic *-mildeis, -mild-s* in compounds such as *mildítha* kindness (from Proto-Germanic **melđijaz*). Cognates outside Germanic include Greek *malthakós* soft, and Sanskrit *márdhati* he leaves behind, neglects, from Indo-European **mel-dh-* (Pok. 719). Related to MELT.

mildew *n.* About 1225 *mildeu* honeydew, nectar; later, kind of fungus, in reference to the sticky, honeylike appearance of some mildew (1340, in a Latin context); developed from Old English (before 1000) *mildēaw, meledēaw.* The Old English forms are cognate with Old Saxon *milidou* honeydew, and Old High German *militou,* and all forms are derived from a Proto-Germanic compound of the root represented in Gothic *milith* honey (see MELLIFLUOUS) and that found in Old English *dēaw* DEW. The Old English variant *meledēaw* was probably influenced by Old English *melu* ground grain, MEAL². French *mildiou* and Spanish *mildiú* are borrowings from English. **—v.** cover or become covered with mildew. 1552, (implied in *mildewed*); from the noun.

mile *n.* Before 1121 *mile,* developed from Old English (before 800) *mīl;* borrowed from Latin *mīlia, mīllia* thousands (as in *mīlia passuum* thousands of Roman paces), plural of *mīlle* a thousand (as in *mīlle passūs* a thousand paces). The Latin form *mīlle* is of uncertain origin; *passuum* is the genitive plural of *passus* step; see PACE¹. At one time most European countries used the Roman mile or some variation of it; many languages also borrowed the word from Latin, as found in Middle Dutch *mīle,* Old High German *mīla,* Old French *mille, mile,* Italian *miglio,* Portuguese *milha,* and Spanish *milla,* and through English, Old Icelandic *mīla* (Norwegian, Swedish, and Danish *mil*).

The ancient Roman *mile* was equal to one thousand double paces (one step with each foot or about 4,860 feet), a distance about 400 feet shorter than a statute mile.

—mileage *n.* 1754, allowance paid to members of a governing body or convocation of delegates for traveling expenses at so much a mile, in Franklin's writings; formed from English *mile* + *-age.* The meaning of distance in miles, is first recorded in 1861 (preceded by figurative use, 1860).

milieu (mēlyœ′) *n.* surroundings, environment. 1877, a French word used in J.A. Symond's *Renaissance in Italy;* a compound of *mi* middle (from Latin *medium*) + *lieu* place (from Latin *locum,* accusative of *locus*).

militant *adj.* aggressive, warlike. Before 1415 *militant* engaged in warfare; borrowed from Middle French *militant,* learned borrowing from Latin, and borrowed directly from Latin *mīlitantem* (nominative *mīlitāns*), present participle of *mīlitāre* serve as a soldier, see MILITATE; for suffix see -ANT. **—n.** militant person. 1610, from the adjective. **—militancy** *n.* 1648, formed from English *militant* + *-cy.*

military *adj.* 1460, borrowed from Latin *mīlitāris* of soldiers or war, warlike, from *mīles* (genitive *mīlitis*) soldier, Old Latin *meiles,* perhaps from Etruscan; for suffix see -Y¹. **—n.** 1736, an officer; later, the army, soldiers (1757); from the adjective. **—militarism** *n.* 1864, formed from English *military* + *-ism* by influence of French *militarisme.* **—militarist** *n.* 1601, in Shakespeare's *All's Well That Ends Well;* formed from English *military* + *-ist.* **—militaristic** *adj.* 1905, formed from English *militarist* + *-ic.* **—militarization** *n.* 1881, formed from English *militarize* + *-ation,* perhaps by influence of French *militarisation.* **—militarize** *v.* 1880, formed from English *military* + *-ize,* perhaps by influence of French *militariser.*

militate (mil′ətāt) *v.* have or exert force. 1625, serve as a soldier, borrowed from Latin *mīlitātum,* past participle of *mīlitāre* serve as a soldier, from *mīles* (genitive *mīlitis*) soldier, see MILITARY; for suffix see -ATE¹. The extended sense of exert force, operate (against), is first recorded in 1642.

militia (məlish′ə) *n.* army of citizens. 1590, military system, military force; borrowing of Latin *mīlitia* military service, warfare, from *mīles* (genitive *mīlitis*) soldier; see MILITARY. The specific sense of citizen army is first recorded in 1696, in Phillip's *Dictionary,* and may have been taken from French *milice* troops of the bourgeois (from Latin *mīlitia*). **—militiaman** *n.* member of a militia. 1780, American English, in writings of Hamilton.

milk *n.* About 1150 *mylc;* later *milk* (about 1300); developed from Old English, in West Saxon *meoluc* (before 899, in Alfred's translation of Bede's *Ecclesiastical History*), and in Anglian *milc,* both related to *melcan* to milk. Cognates are found in Old Frisian *melok* milk, Old Saxon *miluk,* Middle Dutch *melc* (modern Dutch *melk*) milk, Old High German *miluh* (modern German *Milch*) milk, Old Icelandic *mjólkr* milk (Swedish *mjölk,* Norwegian *melk, mjølk,* Danish *melk*) and Gothic *miluks* milk, from Proto-Germanic **meluk-,* from Indo-European **meləĝ-.* Cognates of Old English *melcan* to milk, Old High German *melchan,* Proto-Germanic

**melkanan* exist outside Germanic in Latin *mulgēre* to milk, Middle Irish *melg* milk, Greek *amélgein* to milk, Old Slavic *mlěsti,* Sanskrit *mā́rṣṭi* (he) wipes or rubs, Tocharian A *mālklune* a milking, *malke* milk, and Tocharian B *malk-wer* milk; from Indo-European **melĝ-/molĝ-/mēlĝ-, meləg-* (Pok. 722).

—**v.** About 1300 *milken;* developed from Old English (971) *meolcian,* (about 1000) *milcian,* from the noun; also merged with *melcan.*

—**milk chocolate** (1723) —**milk fat** (1901) —**milkmaid** *n.* (1552) —**milkman** *n.* (1589) —**milk shake** (1889, American English) —**milksop** *n.* unmanly fellow. About 1390, in Chaucer's *Canterbury Tales;* formed from Middle English *milk* +*sop* piece of food soaked in a liquid. —**milkweed** *n.* plant with milky juice (1598). —**milky** *adj.* About 1380, in Chaucer's *House of Fame;* formed from Middle English *milk* + *-y[1]*. —**Milky Way** About 1380, in Chaucer's *House of Fame,* loan translation of Latin *via lactea.*

mill[1] *n.* machine for grinding grain into flour or meal. Probably before 1200 *mulne* building with machinery for grinding grain, in *Ancrene Riwle;* later *mylne* (before 1225), and *mille* (about 1390, in Chaucer's *Canterbury Tales*); developed from Old English (about 961) *mylen* mill. The Old English word is an early borrowing from Late Latin *molīna, molīnum* mill, originally feminine and neuter of *molīnus* pertaining to a mill, from Latin *mola* mill, millstone, related to *molere* to grind; see MEAL[2] ground grain. The Late Latin *molīna* was also borrowed into Old Frisian *mole* mill, Old Saxon *mulin,* Old High German *mulī, mulin* and Old Icelandic *mylna.*

The meaning of a machine for grinding grain is probably recorded before 1425; the wider sense of a building or machinery for manufacturing something (as a textile mill), is first recorded in 1417-18.

—**v.** 1552, pass (cloth) through a mill; later, grind (grain) into flour (1570); from the noun. The meaning of move or mass in a circle (as in *to mill about,* originally applied to cattle), is first recorded in American English in 1888, in Theodore Roosevelt's writings.

—**miller** *n.* Before 1376 *myllere, in Piers Plowman;* earlier as a surname *Mulner* (1230); formed from Middle English *mille* and *mulne* mill + *-ere* -er[1]. —**millpond** *n.* (1371) —**millstone** *n.* Before 1225; earlier as a surname *Mileston* (1205).

mill[2] *n.* 1/10 of a cent. 1791, American English, shortened form of Latin *millēsimum* one thousandth, from *mīlle* a thousand; see MILE. It was so called from being one thousandth of a dollar.

millennium *n.* period of a thousand years. Before 1638, New Latin *millennium,* a compound of Latin *mille* thousand + *annus* year, patterned on Latin *biennium* two-year period, and *triennium* three-year period.

Millennium was first used in English to refer to the period of one thousand years during which, according to one interpretation of Revelation 20:1-5, Christ is expected to reign on earth. The general meaning of a period of a thousand years is first recorded before 1711. The figurative meaning of a period of great happiness and benign government appears in the writings of Byron (1820).

—**millennial** *adj.* of a thousand years. 1664, pertaining to the prophesied millennium; formed from English *millenni(um)* + *-al[1]*. The general sense of pertaining to a thousand years, is first recorded in 1807.

millet (mil′it) *n.* kind of small cereal grain. Probably before 1425 *milet,* in Sir John Maundeville's *Travels;* borrowed from Middle French *millet,* diminutive of *mil* millet, from Latin *milium.* Latin *milium* is cognate with Greek *melínē* millet. An earlier form *myle* is first recorded before 1382, in the Wycliffe Bible; developed from Old English *mil,* from Latin *milium.*

milli- a combining form meaning one thousandth, as in *millimeter, millisecond.* Borrowed from French *milli-,* and directly from Latin *mīlli-,* from *mīlle* a thousand; see MILE. —**milligram, milliliter** *n.* 1810, borrowed from French. —**millimeter** *n.* 1807, borrowed from French.

milliner *n.* person who makes, trims, or sells women's hats. 1530 *myllenor* dealer in fancy goods and apparel, especially of the kind associated with those imported from Milan, probably special use of earlier *Milener* native or inhabitant of Milan, possibly considered as stylish or fashionable in dress and also associated with the straw work in hats manufactured there (1449); formed in English from *Milan,* city in northern Italy famous for its straw work + *-er[1]*. The modern sense of one who makes or sells women's hats, is first recorded perhaps as early as 1742, and in earlier references possibly in the 1530's. —**millinery** *n.* 1679-88, articles made or sold by milliners; formed from English *milliner* + *-y[3]*.

million *n.* a thousand thousands. Before 1376 *mylion,* in *Piers Plowman,* also *milioun;* borrowed from Old French *millon, million* (with later restoration of the French spelling), probably from Italian *milione,* earlier *millione,* augmentative form of *mille* thousand, from Latin *mīlle;* see MILE. —**adj.** 1694, from the noun. —**millionaire** *n.* 1826, in Benjamin Disraeli's *Vivian Grey;* borrowed from French *millionnaire* (*million* million + *-aire* -ary). —**millionth** *adj., n.* 1673, formed from English *million* + *-th[2]*.

millipede (mil′əpēd) *n.* small, wormlike arthropod with two pairs of legs on each segment. 1601, in Holland's translation of Pliny's *Natural History;* borrowed from Latin *mīlipeda* kind of crawling insect (*mille* thousand + *pēs* (genitive *pedis*) FOOT, possibly a loan translation of Greek *chīliópous.* The spelling with double *l* was influenced by Latin *mīlle* thousand, or French *mille* thousand, *mille-pieds* millipede.

milord (milôrd′) *n.* my lord. 1596, Scottish; later in general use (1758); borrowed from French *milord,* a term of address corresponding to English *my lord.* Compare MILADY.

milquetoast or **Milquetoast** (milk′tōst′) *n.* extremely timid person. 1938, American English, in allusion to Caspar *Milquetoast* (cartoon character in *The Timid Soul,* created by H.T. Webster, 1885-1952). The name was a humorous formation of *milk toast.* Compare MILKSOP (under MILK).

milt *n.* sperm cells of fishes with the fluid containing them. 1483 *milte,* in Caxton's version of the *Golden Legend;* probably developed from *mylte* spleen (considered as source of milt in fish or frogs, before 1398, or as a spermatic member, 1392), possibly influenced in sense by Middle Dutch *milte* milt, spleen, but found in Old English *milte* spleen. The Old English form is cognate with Old High German *milzi* (modern German *Milz*) and Old Icelandic *milti* (Swedish *mjelte,* Danish *milt*) spleen, from Proto-Germanic **meltijōn,* from Indo-European **meld-* soft (Pok. 718); see MELT.

mime *n.* mimic, jester, pantomimist. 1616, in Ben Jonson's *Epigrams;* borrowed from French *mime,* and directly from Latin *mīmus,* from Greek *mîmos* imitator or actor, of unknown origin, but the source of *mīmeîsthai* to imitate. It is probable that *mime* was borrowed by influence of an earlier sense of *mimic,* adj., acting as a mime (1598), and n., a mime (1590). **—v.** act as a mime; mimic. 1616 (implied in *miming,* in Ben Jonson's *Epigrams*); from the noun.

mimetic (mimet′ik) *n.* imitative. 1637, borrowed from Greek *mīmētikós* imitative, from *mīmeîsthai* to imitate, see MIME; for suffix see -IC.

mimic *adj.* 1598, borrowed from Latin *mīmicus,* from Greek *mīmikós* of or pertaining to mimes, from *mîmos* MIME; for suffix see -IC. Occasional later borrowing from French *mimique* is also recorded. It is further possible that in some instances the adjective in English was a development from the noun. **—n.** person or thing that mimics. 1590, in Shakespeare's *Midsummer Night's Dream;* borrowed from Latin *mimicus,* adj. **—v.** imitate. 1687, in Dryden's *The Hind and the Panther;* from the noun. **—mimicry** *n.* act or practice of mimicking. 1687, formed from English *mimic,* n. + *-ry.*

mimosa (mimō′sə *or* mimō′zə) *n.* kind of tropical tree, shrub, or plant. 1751, New Latin *Mimosa* the genus name, in John Hill's *A History of Plants;* formed from Latin *mimus* mime + *-ōsa,* adjective suffix, feminine of *-ōsus* -ose[1]; so called because some species of this plant seem to mimic animal reactions by folding their leaves at the slightest touch (hence also called *sensitive plants*).

minaret (min′əret′) *n.* tower of a mosque. 1682, borrowed from French *minaret,* probably from Turkish *minare* a minaret, from Arabic *manārah, manārat* a lamp, lighthouse, minaret, related to *manār* candlestick, lighthouse, tower, a derivative of *nar* fire.

mince *v.* chop up into very small pieces. 1381, borrowed from Old French *mincier* make into small pieces, from Vulgar Latin **minūtiāre* make small, from Late Latin *minūtiae* small bits, from Latin *minūtus* small, MINUTE[2]. **—mincemeat** *n.* 1747, meat chopped fine, alteration of earlier *minced meat* (1578). **—mince pie** pie containing mincemeat (1600). **—mincing** *adj.* affectedly dainty (1530).

mind *n.* About 1175 *mynd;* later *minde* (probably before 1200); developed from Old English (before 725) *gemynd* memory; thinking. The Old English is cognate with Old High German *gimunt* memory, Gothic *gamunds,* (from Proto-Germanic **ʒa-mundis*), Old High German *minna* love, Old Saxon *minnea,* and Old Frisian and Middle Dutch *minne,* developed from the stem of the word for remembrance found in Old Icelandic *minni* and Gothic *gaminthi,* Proto-Germanic **ʒa-menthijan.* Cognates outside Germanic include Old Irish *domoiniur* I believe or think, Latin *mēns* mind, Greek *ménos* intent, purpose, spirit, passion, *mimnéskesthai* to recall, *mnâsthai* remember, Lithuanian *miñti* remember, Old Slavic *mĭněti* to think, Armenian *imanam* I understand, Sanskrit *mánas* mind or sense, *mányate* (he) thinks, Tocharian A *mnu* thinking, Tocharian B *mañu* request, wish, and Hittite *memmāi* he says, mentions, from Indo-European **men-/mon-/mn̥-,* **mnā-/mnə-,* **menēi-* (Pok. 726). **—v.** Probably before 1350 *minden* remember, remind, notice, turn one's attention to; from the noun. The meaning of care or object is first recorded in Shakespeare's *Pericles* (1608). **—mindful** *adj.* (about 1340) **—mindless** *adj.* (before 1400)

mine[1] *pron.* belonging to me. 1100 *mine,* developed from Old English *mīn* mine, my (about 725, in *Beowulf*); cognate with Old Frisian and Old Saxon *mīn,* Middle Dutch and modern Dutch *mijn,* Old High German *mīn* (modern German *mein*), Old Icelandic *mīnn* (Norwegian, Swedish, and Danish *min*), and Gothic *meins,* all derived from Proto-Germanic **mīnaz,* an adjective formed from the old genitive (Gothic *meina* of me, Old English mīn) of the pronoun.

mine[2] *n.* pit dug in the earth to extract minerals. About 1303 *myne,* in Mannyng's *Handlyng Synne;* borrowed from Old French *mine,* either from the verb in Old French or possibly through Gallo-Romance **mīna,* from Celtic (compare Welsh *mwyn* ore, mine, and Irish *mein* ore, mine, from Proto-Celtic **meini-*). **—v.** dig a mine, get from a mine. Probably before 1300 *minen,* borrowed from Old French *miner,* possibly from *mine,* n. **—miner** *n.* About 1303 *mynur* one who mines for metals; earlier, one who undermines fortifications or tunnels into towns in military operations (before 1300), and as a surname *Miner* (1212).

mineral *n.* Probably before 1425, a substance obtained by mining; earlier, a variety of the philosophers' stone (before 1393, in Gower's *Confessio Amantis*); borrowed from Medieval Latin *minerale* something mined, from neuter of *mineralis* pertaining to mines, from *minera* mine, from Old French *miniere* mine, from *mine* MINE[2]; for suffix see -AL[1]. The meaning of an ore of a metal, is first recorded before 1449. **—adj.** of minerals. Probably before 1425, borrowed from Medieval Latin *mineralis.* **—mineralogical** *adj.* 1791; formed from English *mineralogy* + *-ical.* **—mineralogist** *n.* 1646, formed probably from English *mineral* + *-logy* + *-ist;* or if *mineralogy* existed in English before 1690, formed from English *mineralogy* + *-ist.* **—mineralogy** *n.* science of minerals. 1690, in Boyle's *Works;* formed from English *mineral,* n. + *-logy;* or perhaps borrowed from French *minéralogie* (1649). **—mineral water** (1562)

mingle *v.* to mix. Before 1475 *menglen,* a frequentative form (showing repeated action) of earlier *myngen* to mix (about 1348), and *mengen* (about 1150); developed from Old English (before 800) *mengan,* related to AMONG. Old English *mengan* is cognate with Old Frisian *mendza* to mix, Old Saxon *mengian,* Middle Dutch *menghen* (modern Dutch *mengen*), Old High German and modern German *mengen,* from Proto-Germanic **mangijanan.* Cognates outside Germanic include Albanian *mekem* I make moist, Greek *mássein* to knead, Lithuanian *minkyti,* Old Slavic mękŭkŭ soft, and Sanskrit *mácate, mañcate* (he) crushes, deceives, from Indo-European **menək-,* **menk-/monk-/mn̥k-* (Pok. 730).

mini (min′ē) *adj.* very small or short, little, tiny. 1963, in part a shortened form of *miniature,* and in part developed as an isolated word from the prefix *mini-* (as in *minicab*); see MINI-. **—n.** 1962, a very small car, shortened form of *minicab* (1960); later, very short skirt (1966); see MINI-.

mini- a combining form meaning miniature or minor, as in *minicomputer, minicrisis, minicourse, minisurvey;* very short, as in *miniskirt, minidress.* Abstracted from *miniature,* but also influenced by *minimum.* The form *mini-* was popularized in Great Britain with the appearance of the *Mini Minor* (produced in 1960 by the British Motor Corporation). Appearance of the *minicab* a small taxicab (1960), furthered the use of *mini-,* though the form is recorded occasionally before the

1960's, as in *Minipiano* (1934), *Minicamera* (1936), *Minicar* (1948), *mini-bomb* (1956), *mini-bus* (1958), and *mini-sub* (1959, a small submarine).

miniature *n.* Before 1586, thing represented on a small scale, in Sidney's *The Arcadia;* borrowed from Italian *miniatura* manuscript illumination or small picture, from past participle of *miniare* to illuminate a manuscript, from Latin *miniāre* to paint red, from *minium* red lead, perhaps of Iberian origin.

Because illuminated pictures in medieval manuscripts were of small size, *miniature* developed the sense of small picture or reduced image, influenced by association with Latin *min-* expressing smallness in *minor* less, *minimus* least, and *minūtus* small; see MINUTE[2].
—adj. 1714, in Gay's poetry; from the noun.
—miniaturization *n.* (1947) **—miniaturize** *v.* reduce to a very small size. 1946, formed from English *miniature,* adj. + *-ize.*

minim (min′əm) *n.* smallest liquid measure. Probably before 1475 *mynym* half note (in music), in *Promptorium Parvulorum;* borrowed from Latin *minimus* smallest; see MINIMUM. The meaning of smallest liquid measure, is first recorded in 1809.

minimum *n.* 1663, portion so small that it is indivisible; borrowed from Latin *minimum* smallest (thing), neuter of *minimus* (earlier *minumus*) smallest, superlative to *minor* smaller (see MINOR, MINUS).

The meaning of least possible amount attainable, allowable, etc., is first recorded in 1676.
—adj. 1810, in Bentham's *The Elements of the Art of Packing;* from the noun.
—minimal *adj.* 1666, formed in English from Latin *minimus* smallest + English *-al*[1]. **—minimize** *v.* 1802, in Bentham's *Principles of Judicial Procedure;* formed in English from Latin *minimus* smallest + English *-ize.*

minion (min′yən) *n.* servant or follower. 1500-20, beloved or favorite person, in William Dunbar's *Poems;* also, servile dependent (1501); borrowed from Middle French *mignon,* n., a favorite, darling, and adj., dainty, pleasing, favorite, from Old French *mignot,* perhaps from Celtic (compare Old Irish *mīn* tender, soft); or sometimes derived from Old High German *minnja, minna* love, memory.

minister *n.* About 1300 *ministre* agent or clergyman; later, servant (about 1325); borrowed from Old French *ministre* servant, learned borrowing from Latin *minister* (genitive *ministrī*) servant, attendant, priest's assistant, from *minus* less; hence inferior, subordinate; patterned after *magister* MASTER. In Medieval and Late Latin *minister* had the ecclesiastical meaning of a priest, which was adopted directly into Middle English.
—v. be of service. Before 1338 *ministren* to serve, supply, administer, perform religious rites, in Mannyng's *Chronicle of England;* borrowed from Old French *ministrer,* from Latin *ministrāre* to serve, from *minister,* n., servant.**—ministerial** *adj.* having to do with a minister. 1561, borrowed through Middle French *ministériel,* or directly from Late Latin *ministeriālis* of a minister, from Latin *ministerium* ministry, from *minister* minister; for suffix see -IAL.

ministrant *adj.* that ministers, ministering. 1667, in Milton's *Paradise Lost;* borrowed from Latin *ministrantem* (nominative *ministrāns*), present participle of *ministrāre* to serve, from *minister* servant, see MINISTER; for suffix see -ANT. **—n.** person who ministers. 1818, in Keats' *Endymion;* from the adjective. **—ministration** *n.* service. About 1340 *mynystracyon,* in Richard Rolle's *The Psalter;* borrowed through Old French *ministration* or directly from Latin *ministrātiōnem* (nominative *ministrātiō*), from *ministrāre;* for suffix see -ATION.

ministry *n.* office, duties, or time of service of a minister. About 1200 *menstre* service in religious matters; later *mynisterie* (about 1384); borrowed perhaps from Old French *ministere,* and directly from Latin *ministerium* office or service, from *minister* servant, see MINISTER; for suffix see -RY.

mink *n.* 1431 *mynke* mink fur; possibly borrowed from a Scandinavian source (compare Danish and Norwegian *mink* and Swedish *mink* the European species of mink). In English *mink* was the name of the fur before it was applied to the animal. As the name of an animal, *mink* is first recorded in 1624, in Captain John Smith's *The Generall Historie of Virginia.*

minnow *n.* tiny freshwater fish. Before 1425 *menew,* probably related to Old English *myne,* earlier **mynwe* minnow. Old English *myne* is cognate with Middle Low German *möne* a kind of fish, modern Dutch *meun,* and Old High German *muniwa* (modern German *Münne*), from Proto-Germanic *muniwōn,* whose structure is baffling but which seems cognate with Greek *manós* (earlier **manwós*) scanty, infrequent, Armenian *manr,* genitive *manu* small, thin, Old Irish *menb* small, and Middle Welsh *di-fanw* insignificant, from Indo-European **menwo-/menwó-* (Pok.728).

The Middle English forms may have been influenced by Old French *menu* small, from Latin *minūtus* small, MINUTE[2].

minor *adj.* About 1410, lesser (used to designate smaller plant species and lesser religious orders); earlier, as part of surnames (1212); borrowed from Latin *minor* lesser, formed as masculine/feminine (on the pattern of *maior: maius* greater) to *minus,* though in early Italic times *minus* was not a neuter or even a comparative at all, but a *u*-stem adjective meaning small (compare Greek *miny-* short), from which was formed *minuere* to lessen. Latin *minuere* is cognate with Cornish *minow* to lessen, Greek *meíōn* less, Old Slavic *mĭnĭji* smaller, Sanskrit *minā́ti* (he) lessens, and Tocharian B *maiwe* little, young, from Indo-European **mei-/mi-* (Pok. 711). Germanic cognates include Gothic *minniza* smaller, Old Icelandic *minni* smaller, Old High German *minniro* (modern German *minder*), Middle Dutch and modern Dutch *minder,* Old Saxon *minniro,* and Old Frisian *minnera,* from Proto-Germanic **minwizōn.*

The general sense of less important, not significant, is first recorded in Ben Jonson's writings (1623).
—n. Probably before 1400, minor premise of a syllogism in logic; borrowed from Medieval Latin *minor,* from Latin *minor,* adj.; later, person under legal age (1612); from the adjective in English, probably also influenced by the sense in *minority* (1547).
—v. minor in take as a minor subject of study. 1934, American English; verb use of *minor,* n., in the earlier sense of a minor subject of study (1890).
—minority *n.* 1533, condition of being smaller, in Sir Thomas More's *Answer to the Poisoned Book;* borrowed from Middle French *minorité,* or directly from Medieval Latin *minoritatem* (nominative *minoritas*) from Latin *minor* lesser; for suffix see -ITY. The meaning of condition of being under legal age is first recorded in 1547. The meaning of a smaller number or part

(as in *a minority of the citizens*), is first found in 1736. **—minor league** (1889)

minster *n.* church of a monastery. 1127 *minstre* monastery, church of a monastery; developed from Old English (probably about 750) *mynster,* from Vulgar Latin **monisterium,* altered from Late Latin *monastērium* MONASTERY.

minstrel *n.* singer or musician. Probably before 1300 *minstrel, minestral, menestral;* earlier *menestral* a servant (probably before 1200); borrowed from Old French *menestrel* entertainer or servant, from Late Latin *ministeriālis* imperial officer, from *ministeriālis,* adj., ministerial, from Latin *ministerium* MINISTRY. **—minstrelsy** *n.* art or practice of a minstrel. Probably before 1300 *minstralsie,* borrowed through Anglo-French *menestralsie,* from Old French *menestrel* minstrel.

mint¹ *n.* sweet-smelling plant used for flavoring. Old English (before 800) *minte,* borrowed from Latin *menta, mentha* mint, from the same (unknown) source as Greek *mínthē.* Other early Germanic borrowings from the Latin include Old Saxon *minta* mint, Middle Dutch *mente, minte,* and Old High German *minza.*

mint² *n.* place where money is coined. 1423 *mynt* coin, money, place where money is coined, earlier (before 1200) *munet* coin, money; developed from Old English (about 700) *mynit* coin, an early borrowing (like Old Frisian *menote, munte* coin, Old Saxon *munita,* Middle Dutch *munte,* and Old High German *munizza*), from Latin *monēta* mint; see MONEY. **—v.** to coin (money). 1546, in Langley's *Works,* from the noun. **—adj.** in perfect condition, as a freshly minted coin (1902).

minuend (min'yůend) *n.* number from which another is to be subtracted. 1706, borrowed from Latin *minuendus* to be made smaller, in *minuendus numerus* number to be made smaller, gerundive form of *minuere* to lessen; see MINOR.

minuet (min'yůet') *n.* slow, stately dance. 1673, in Dryden's *Marriage-à-la-Mode;* borrowing of French *menuet,* from Old French *menuet,* adj., small, delicate, from *menu* small, from Latin *minūtus* small, MINUTE² (so called from the small steps taken in the dance); for suffix see -ET. The spelling of the English word may have been influenced by Italian *minuetto,* from French *menuet.*

minus *prep.* less, subtracted from. 1481-90 *mynus,* borrowed from Latin *minus* less, neuter of *minor* smaller, MINOR.

The sense in English of subtracted from, probably originated in the commercial language of the Middle Ages, as it did not exist in Latin of any period. According to the OED, the Latin words *plus* and *minus* were perhaps first used by German merchants next to a number to indicate an excess or deficiency in weight or measure. Earlier use is recorded in Italian in philosophical works judging the results of experiments (1202, Leonardo of Pisa). The extended sense of short of, without, is first recorded in 1840.

—adj. less than. 1789, from the preposition.

—n. a sign (−) of subtraction. 1654, from the preposition.

—minus sign (1889)

minuscule (min'əskyül) *adj.* extremely small. 1893, American English, an extended sense of the earlier meaning of small letter, not capital (1727-41); borrowing of French *minuscule,* learned borrowing from Latin, and possibly borrowed directly from Latin *minuscula* in *minuscula littera* slightly smaller letter, feminine of *minusculus* rather less, diminutive of *minus* less, MINUS.

minute¹ (min'it) *n.* time span of 60 seconds. About 1378, one sixtieth of an hour or degree, in a version of *Piers Plowman;* borrowed from Old French *minut,* or directly from Medieval Latin *minuta* minute (shortened form of *pars minuta prima* first minute part), short note, from Latin *minūta,* feminine of *minūtus* small, MINUTE².

The meaning of a rough draft, memorandum, is first recorded in *Proceedings of the Privy Council* (1443); the plural *minutes,* in the sense of a record of proceedings, developed from it about 1710.

—minute hand (1726, in Swift's *Gulliver's Travels*) **—minuteman** *n.* militiaman who can be ready at very short notice (1774, American English) **—minute steak** (1934)

minute² (mīnüt' *or* mīnyüt') *adj.* very small, 1472, in *Rolls of Parliament,* borrowed from Latin *minūtus* small, past participle of *minuere* lessen; see MINOR. Doublet of MENU.

minutiae (minü'shēē) *n.pl.* very small matters, trifling details. 1751, borrowing of Late Latin *minūtiae* trifles, plural of Latin *minūtia* smallness, from *minūtus* small, MINUTE².

minx (mingks) *n.* 1542 *mynx* a pet dog, of uncertain origin; later, a pert girl, hussy (1592), perhaps a shortened form of earlier *minikins* a playful or endearing term for a girl or woman (before 1550); borrowed from Middle Dutch *minnekijn* darling, beloved (*minne* love + *-kijn* -kin, diminutive suffix).

miracle *n.* 1137, in *Peterborough Chronicle;* borrowing of Old French *miracle,* from Latin *mīrāculum* object of wonder (in church Latin, a marvelous event by the intervention of God), from *mīrārī* to wonder at, from *mīrus* wonderful, earlier **smeiros,* cognate with Sanskrit *smáyate* he smiles, *smaya-s* surprise, astonishment, from Indo-European **smei-/smi-* part the lips, be amazed, smile (Pok. 967). **—miraculous** *adj.* 1447, borrowed through Middle French *miraculeux,* or directly from Medieval Latin *miraculosus,* from Latin *mīrāculum* miracle; for suffix see -OUS. The word is implied earlier in the adverb *myraculosly* (before 1410).

mirage (mərázh') *n.* misleading appearance. 1812, in Southey's *Moral and Political Essays;* borrowing of French *mirage,* from *mirer* look at, *se mirer* look at oneself in a mirror, be reflected, from Latin *mīrāre,* variant of *mīrārī* to wonder at, see MIRACLE; for suffix see -AGE.

mire *n.* soft deep mud. 1219, in the compound *mirepit* muddy hole; later *muir* a swampy or boggy place (1300), and *myre* (before 1338); borrowed from a Scandinavian source (compare Old Icelandic *mýrr* bog, swamp, cognate with Old English *mos* bog; see MOSS). **—v.** get stuck in mire. Probably about 1400, (figurative use) to involve in difficulties; from the noun. The literal sense of plunge into a swampy place, is not recorded until 1559.

mirror *n.* About 1250 *mirour;* borrowed from Old French *mireor* a reflecting glass, *mirouer,* from *mirer* look at, from Latin *mīrāre,* variant of *mīrārī* to wonder at, admire; see MIRACLE. **—v.** reflect as a mirror does. 1820, in Keats' *Lamia;* from the noun. The verb also appeared in Middle English *mirouren* to be a model of conduct for (probably 1410); also from the noun.

mirth *n.* merry fun, laughter. Probably about 1300 *mirthe* a source of joy (in East Midland British dialect); earlier *murhthe* (probably about 1150); developed from Old English *myrgth* joy or pleasure (before 899, in Alfred's translation of Boethius' *De Consolatione Philosophiae*); related to *myrge* pleasing, agreeable (see MERRY); for suffix see -TH[1]. **—mirthful** *adj.* (before 1325, in *Cursor Mundi*) **—mirthless** *adj.* (about 1380 *myrtheles,* in Chaucer's *Parlement of Foules*)

mis- a prefix meaning bad or badly, as in *misgovernment, misbehave;* wrong or wrongly, as in *mispronunciation, misapply.* The prefix *mis-* represents two separate developments: 1) In native words, Old English *mis-;* cognate with Old Frisian, Old Saxon, Middle Dutch, and modern Dutch *mis-,* Old High German *missa-, missi-* (modern German *miss-*), Old Icelandic *mis-,* Gothic *missa-,* from Proto-Germanic **missa-,* stem of an ancient past participle, Indo-European **mittós,* of root *mei-t(h)-/moit(h)-,* and related to Old English *missan* fail to hit, MISS[1]; 2) In borrowed words, Middle English *mis-, mes-;* borrowed from Old French *mes-,* from Frankish (compare Old High German *missa-, missi-* mis-).

In Old English and Middle English manuscripts forms with *mis-* are written sometimes as two words, sometimes as one word, but not hyphenated. From the 1500's onward, the forms are regularly printed as one word, with or without the hyphen, which gradually appeared less frequently and is now used chiefly in new formations or in words such as *mis-say,* where omission of the hyphen would disguise the word's identity.

In early Middle English the use of *mis-* was greatly extended by combining freely with words of native and of foreign origin alike. Many of the new formations were probably suggested by French forms with *mes-* so that a word such as *misjudge* probably originated in part as a native formation and also as a borrowing of Old French *mesjuger.*

misadventure *n.* mishap. Probably before 1300 *misaventour,* in *Arthour and Merlin;* borrowed from Old French *mesaventure,* from *mesavenir* to turn out badly (*mes-* mis- + *avenir* to happen); and perhaps formed from Middle English *mis-* + *aventure* (before 1200); see ADVENTURE.

misanthrope (mis′ənthrōp) *n.* hater of men or mankind. 1563, borrowing of Greek *mīsánthrōpos;* later *misanthrop* (1683); borrowed through Middle French *misanthrope* (1552, in Rabelais), or directly from Greek *mīsánthrōpos* hating mankind (*mīseîn* to hate, of unknown origin + *ánthrōpos* man). **—misanthropic** *adj.* 1762, formed from English *misanthrope* + *-ic,* or more likely as a shortened form of earlier *misanthropical* (1621). **—misanthropy** *n.* hatred of men or mankind. 1656, in Blount's *Glossographia;* borrowed from French *misanthropie,* from Greek *mīsanthrōpiā,* from *mīsánthrōpos* hating mankind; for suffix see -Y[3].

misbehave *v.* 1451, implied in *misbehaving;* formed from Middle English *mis-* + *behave.* **—misbehavior** *n.* (1486)

miscarry *v.* About 1300 *miscaryen* go astray; later, come to harm (about 1340); formed from Middle English *mis-* + *caryen* carry. The meaning of deliver a baby before it can live, is first recorded in 1527. The meaning of fail is found in Shakespeare's *Coriolanus* (1607). **—miscarriage** *n.* 1614, failure; formed from English *mis-* + *carriage.* The meaning of birth of a baby before it can live is first recorded in 1662.

miscegenation (misej′ənā′shən) *n.* interbreeding between different races. 1864, formed in American English from Latin *miscēre* to MIX + *genus* race, GENUS + English *-ation.*

Miscegenation was probably coined by an American journalist, D.G. Croly, in *Miscegenation: the Theory of the Blending of the Races, Applied to the American White Man and Negro* (1864; see *American Speech,* Vol. xxiv, No. 4).

miscellaneous *adj.* of a mixed character, kind, or nature. 1637, borrowed from Latin *miscellāneus,* from *miscellus* mixed, diminutive of a lost adjective **misculus* (compare Vulgar Latin **misculāre,* whence Old French *mesler*), from *miscēre* to MIX; for suffix see -OUS. **—miscellany** *n.* miscellaneous collection. 1615, collection of literary compositions, probably borrowed from French *miscellanées,* feminine plural, from Latin *miscellānea,* from neuter plural of *miscellāneus* miscellaneous. The form *miscellany* is parallel to earlier *Miscellanea* (1571), which was never accepted except in reference to literary composition.

mischief *n.* Probably before 1300 *mischef* misfortune, harm, injury, in *Arthour and Merlin;* borrowed from Old French *meschief,* from *meschever* come or bring to grief (*mes-* badly + *chever* happen, come to an end, from Vulgar Latin **capāre,* from **capum* head, end, from Latin *caput* HEAD). The meaning of playful behavior causing annoyance, is first recorded in Cowper's *Tirocinium* (1784); probably influenced by the early adjective use of this sense. **—mischievous** *adj.* Before 1350 *myschevous* miserable, calamitous, formed from Middle English *mischef* misfortune + *-ous.* The meaning of disposed to playful, annoying behavior, is first recorded in Wycherley's *The Plain-Dealer* (1676), but is preceded by the sense of causing trouble, harmful, in reference to things, events, or actions (probably before 1400).

miscible *adj.* capable of being mixed. 1570, borrowed from Medieval Latin *miscibilis* mixable, from Latin *miscēre* to MIX; for suffix see -IBLE.

misconstrue *v.* About 1385 *mysconstruwen,* in Chaucer's *Troilus and Criseyde;* formed from Middle English *mys-* mis- + *construwen* construe.

miscreant *adj.* villainous, base. Probably before 1300 *miscreaunt* unbelieving, heathen, in *Arthour and Merlin;* borrowing of Old French *mescreant* (*mes-* wrongly + *creant,* present participle of *creire* believe, from Latin *crēdere;* see CREDIT); for suffix see -ANT. The meaning of villainous is first recorded in 1593. **—n.** villain. Probably 1383 *myscreaunt* unbeliever, infidel, in Wycliffe's writings; from the adjective. The meaning of villain is first recorded in Spenser's *Faerie Queene* (1590).

misdemeanor (mis′dimē′nər) *n.* criminal act less serious than a felony. 1487, formed from Middle English *mis-* wrong + *demenure* demeanor.

miser *n.* 1542, wretch, wretched, in Udall's translation of Erasmus' *Apothegms;* borrowing of Latin *miser* unhappy, wretched, related to *maestus* sad, and *maerēre* to grieve, from Indo-European **mais-/mis-* (Walde-Hofmann, *Lateinisches Etymologisches Wörterbuch II,*8). The meaning of a person who hoards money, avaricious person, is first recorded about 1560. **—miserly** *adj.* 1593, formed from English *miser* + *-ly*[2].

miserable (miz′ərəbəl) *adj.* About 1412, very unhappy, wretched; borrowing of Old French *miserable,* and borrowed directly from Latin *miserābilis* pitiable, lamentable, from *miserārī* to pity, lament, from *miser* wretched; for suffix see -ABLE. **—misery** *n.* About 1375 *miserie* miserable state of mind, in Chaucer's *Canterbury Tales;* borrowed from Old French *miserie,* learned borrowing from Latin *miseria* wretchedness, from *miser* wretched; for suffix see -Y[3].

misfeasance (misfē′zəns) *n. Law.* wrongful performance of a lawful act. 1596, in Bacon's *The Elements of Common Laws;* borrowed from Middle French *mesfaisance,* from *mesfaisant,* present participle of Old French *mesfaire* to misdo (*mes-* wrongly + *faire* do, from Latin *facere* to perform, DO[1]); for suffix see -ANCE.

misgiving *n.* feeling of doubt. 1601, in Shakespeare's *Julius Caesar;* formed from earlier *misgive* to cause to feel doubt (1513, in writings of Sir Thomas More) + *-ing*[1]. The verb *misgive* is formed from English *mis-* + *give,* in the archaic sense of suggest, incline, as in "Therefore, do as thy mind giveth thee" in Scott's *Ivanhoe.*

mishap *n.* unlucky incident. Before 1250, bad luck, in *Ancrene Riwle;* formed from Middle English *mis-* mis- + *hap* luck (see HAPHAZARD).

mishmash *n.* confused mixture, hodgepodge, jumble. About 1475 *mysse-masche;* probably imitative reduplication of *mash*[1] soft mixture, possibly influenced by Middle English *mis-* prefix meaning bad (see MIS-) and parallel to such later terms as *mixty-maxty* (adj 1786, n. 1824, a reduplication of *mixt* mixed). Compare German *Mischmasch* mishmash, from reduplication of *mischen* to mix. The current spelling appeared in 1585.

misnomer *n.* 1455 *misnoumer* mistake in naming, in *Rolls of Parliament;* borrowed from Middle French *mesnomer* to misname *mes-* wrongly + *nommer* to name, from Latin *nōmināre* NOMINATE); for suffix see -ER[3]. The sense of a wrong name or designation, is first recorded in 1657.

misogamy (misog′əmē) *n.* hatred of marriage. 1656, in Blount's *Glossographia;* borrowed from New Latin *misogamia,* formed from Greek *mîsos* hatred (of unknown origin) + *gámos* marriage (see BIGAMY); for suffix see -GAMY and -Y[3].

misogyny (misoj′ənē) *n.* hatred of women. 1656, in Blount's *Glossographia;* borrowed from Greek *mīsogyníā,* from *mīsogýnēs* woman hater (*mîsos* hatred, of unknown origin + *gynḗ* woman; see QUEEN); for suffix see -Y[3]. It is also possible that in some instances *misogyny* is a back formation in English from earlier *misogynist.* **—misogynist** *n.* hater of women. 1620, formed in English from Greek *mīsogýnēs* woman hater + English *-ist.*

misprision (misprizh′ən) *n.* wrongful action or omission. 1425, in *Rolls of Parliament;* borrowed through Anglo-French *misprision,* Old French *mesprison,* from *mespris,* past participle of *mesprendre* to mistake or act wrongly (*mes-* wrongly + *prendre* take, from Latin *prēndere,* contracted from *prehendere* seize; see GET); for suffix see -ION.

miss[1] *v.* fail to hit, attain, etc. Probably before 1200 *missen* fail to obtain, in *Ancrene Riwle;* discover to be absent, lack, in Layamon's *Chronicle of Britain;* developed from Old English *missan* fail to hit (about 725, in *Beowulf*) and probably from Old Icelandic *missa* to miss or lack. The Old English and Old Icelandic forms are cognate with Old Frisian *missa* to miss, Middle Low German, Middle Dutch and modern Dutch *missen,* Old High German *missan* (modern German *missen*), from Proto-Germanic **missijanan,* formed from a noun **missan* (whence Old English *miss* loss), neuter of an ancient past participle, Indo-European **mittós,* related to Gothic *maidjan* to change, falsify. Cognates outside Germanic include Latin *mūtāre* to change, Latvian *mituôt* to exchange, Old Slavic *mitě* alternately, and Sanskrit *méthati* he alternates, engages in alternation, from Indo-European **mei-t(h)-/moi-t(h)-/mi-t(h)-* (Pok. 715). **—n.** Probably about 1175 *misse* loss, lack; probably developed from Old English *missan* and from Old Icelandic *missa* to miss; later, wrong, wicked (about 1200, in *Ancrene Riwle,* from the prefix *mis-*); from the verb. The meaning of a failure to hit, is first recorded in 1555 (an earlier form *misyengen* to miss the mark with an arrow, is recorded about 1250). **—missing** *adj.* 1530, absent; formed from English *miss*[1] + *-ing*[2]. Earlier as a noun with the meaning of absence (before 1325, in *Cursor Mundi*); formed from Middle English *missen* miss[1] + *-ing* -ing[1].

miss[2] *n.* girl, young woman. 1645, prostitute or concubine, in Evelyn's *Diary,* shortened form of MISTRESS. The meaning of young unmarried woman, girl, is first recorded as a capitalized title before a name in Pepys' *Diary* (1666-67), and as a term of address in Dryden's *Works* (1667).

missal *n.* book of the Mass. Probably before 1300 *messel,* in *Arthour and Merlin;* later *missale* (before 1400); borrowed from Old French *messel* and directly from Medieval Latin *missale,* from Late Latin *missa* MASS.

missile *n.* 1656, in Blount's *Glossographia;* borrowed from French *missile,* and directly from Latin *missile* weapon that can be thrown, from neuter of *missilis,* adj., capable of being thrown, from *missus,* past participle of *mittere* to send; see MISSION. The meaning of a self-propelled rocket or bomb, is first recorded in 1738, in *Chambers Cyclopaedia* (2nd edition). **—adj.** capable of being thrown, hurled, or shot. 1611, borrowed from Latin *missilis;* see the noun. **—missilery** or **missilry** *n.* science dealing with missiles and rockets. 1880, missiles collectively; formed from English *missile,* n. + *-ry.*

mission *n.* 1598, a sending or being sent on some special work; errand; borrowed from Middle French *mission,* and directly from Latin *missiōnem* (nominative *missiō*) act of sending, from *mittere* to send, of uncertain origin; for suffix see -SION. The extended sense of a body of persons sent to a foreign country to establish relations (*diplomatic mission*) or for the conversion of non-Christians (*religious mission*) is first recorded in 1622 and 1626 in Bacon's *Works,* and that of a headquarters of a mission, in the *Annual Register* (1769). **—missionary** *n.* person sent on a religious mission. 1656, in Blount's *Glossographia,* from the earlier adjective, sent on a mission (1644); borrowed from New Latin *missionarius* pertaining to a mission, from Latin *missiōnem* (nominative *missiō*) mission; for suffix see -ARY.

missive *n.* written message, letter. 1501, from the earlier adjective, sent by a superior authority (1444, in *Proceedings of the Privy Council*); borrowed from Medieval Latin *missivus* for sending, sent, from Latin *mis-*

sus, past participle of *mittere* to send, see MISSION; for suffix see -IVE.

mist *n.* Old English *mist* dimness, mist (875, in a version of *Genesis*); earlier, in compounds *misthleothu* misty cliffs, *wælmist* the mist of death (about 725); cognate with Middle Low German, Middle Dutch, and modern Dutch *mist* mist, modern Icelandic *mistur,* Norwegian *mist,* and Swedish *mist,* from Proto-Germanic **miHstaz.* Cognates outside Germanic include Greek *omíchlē* cloud or mist, Lithuanian *miglà* mist, Old Slavic *mĭgla,* Armenian *mēg,* and Sanskrit *míh-* mist, *meghá-s* cloud, from Indo-European **meigh-/moigh-/migh-* (Pok. 712). **—v.** come down in mist. Before 1300 *misten;* developed from Old English (about 1000) *mistian* to grow dim, mist, from *mist,* n. **—misty** *adj.* About 1325 *mysty;* developed from Old English *mistig* (about 725, in *Beowulf*); formed from *mist* mist + *-ig* -y[1].

mistake *v.* Before 1338 *mistaken* to transgress (in Mannyng's *Chronicle of England*); later, misunderstand (before 1393); borrowed from a Scandinavian source; compare Old Icelandic *mistaka* take by mistake, miscarry (*mis-* wrongly + *taka* TAKE). **—n.** error or blunder. 1638, from the verb.

mister *n.* man's title of courtesy; Mr. 1447-48 as abbreviated form *Mr.;* later unaccented variant of MASTER (1551). **—v.** *Informal.* address as "mister." 1742, in Fielding's *History of the Adventures of Joseph Andrews;* from the noun.

mistletoe (mis′əltō) *n.* plant with small, waxy, white berries and yellow flowers. Probably about 1125 *misteltа;* later *mistelto* (probably before 1425); developed from Old English (about 1000) *mistiltān* (*mistel* mistletoe + *tān* twig).

Old English *mistel* (about 700) is cognate with Old Saxon *mistil* mistletoe, Old High German *mistil* (modern German *Mistel*), modern Dutch *mistel,* and Old Icelandic *mistilteinn* (Swedish *mistel,* Norwegian *misteltein,* and Danish *mistelten*) mistletoe, from Proto-Germanic **miHstilaz,* diminutive of **miHstuz,* represented in Gothic *maíhstus* dung, Old High German *mist* (the seeds being carried in the dung of birds). Proto-Germanic **miHstuz* would be cognate with Sanskrit *méhati* urinates, Greek *omeíchein* to urinate, Latin *meiere,* and Old English *mīgan,* from Indo-European **meiĝh-* urinate (Pok. 713).

Old English *tān* (mistaken for the plural of *tā* toe) is cognate with Old Frisian and Old Saxon *tēn* twig, Middle Dutch and modern Dutch *teen,* Old High German *zein,* Old Icelandic *teinn,* and Gothic *tains,* from Proto-Germanic **tainaz,* with no known cognates.

mistral (mis′trəl) *n.* cold, dry, northerly wind. 1604, borrowing of French *mistral* from Provençal *mistral,* n., literally, the dominant wind, from *mistral,* adj., dominant, from Latin *magistrālis* dominant, from *magister* MASTER; for suffix see -AL[1].

mistress *n.* Probably before 1300 *maistresse* woman at the head of a household, in *Sir Tristrem;* borrowing of Old French *maistresse,* feminine of *maistre* MASTER. In Middle English *mistress* had a variety of senses: woman at the head of a household, ruler or queen, goddess or tutelary spirit; beloved woman, woman who is a leader or example, schoolmistress or governess, an expert in a skill, woman notorious for some action, and a polite form of address. The pejorative sense of a woman who illicitly takes the place of a wife is first attested in 1601.

mite[1] *n.* tiny animal. 1373 *myte;* developed from Old English (about 1000) *mīte;* cognate with Middle Dutch *mite* mite (modern Dutch *mijt*), Middle Low German *mite,* and Old High German *mīza* mite, from Proto-Germanic **mītōn* "the cutter," cognate with Gothic *maitan* to cut and Old High German *meizil* (modern German *Meissel*) chisel, from Indo-European **mēi-/məi-/mī-* cut (Pok. 697).

mite[2] *n.* Before 1375, little bit or jot; borrowed from Middle Dutch or Middle Low German *mite* tiny animal, MITE[1].

miter *n.* tall folded cap worn by bishops. About 1303 *mytyr,* in Mannyng's *Handlyng Synne;* later *mitre* (probably about 1350); borrowed from Old French *mitre,* from Latin, and directly from Latin *mitra,* from Greek *mítrā* headband or turban, of uncertain origin. Use of *miter* as the name for a bishop's formal headdress was derived from Latin *mitra* in the Vulgate and Greek *mítrā* in the Septuagint for the ceremonial headdress of the high priest, in Hebrew called *miṣnepheth.* **—v.** bestow a miter on; make a bishop. Probably about 1308 *mytren;* from the noun.

mitigate *v.* make or become mild. Probably before 1425, relieve pain, abate, in a translation of Chauliac's *Grande Chirurgie;* borrowed from Latin *mītigātus,* past participle of *mītigāre* make mild or gentle, from a lost adjective **mītigus* making mild, formed from *mītis* gentle, soft + *-igus,* from the root of *agere* do, make, act; see AGENT; for suffix see -ATE[1].

In some instances Middle English *mitigate* is probably a back formation from earlier Middle English *mytygacioun* mitigation, or from the past participle *mitigate.*

—mitigation *n.* action or process of mitigating. Before 1376 *mytygacioun,* in *Piers Plowman;* borrowed probably from Old French *mitigation,* and directly from Latin *mītigātiōnem* (nominative *mītigātiō*) soothing, from *mītigāre;* for suffix see -ATION.

mitosis (mītō′sis) *n. Biology.* cell division. 1887, New Latin; formed from Greek *mítos* warp thread (of unknown origin) + New Latin *-osis* act or process; so called because the chromatin of the cell nucleus appears as long threads in the first stage of mitosis.

mitt *n.* long glove without fingers. 1765, shortened form of MITTEN. The baseball meaning of a glove with a big pad over the palm and fingers is an American usage, first found in a Sears Catalogue of 1902.

mitten *n.* kind of winter glove. About 1390 *miteyn,* in Chaucer's *Canterbury Tales;* earlier in a surname *Mytayn* (1248), and *mytten* (probably 1440); borrowed from Old French *mitaine* mitten, half-glove, from Old French *mite* mitten, of uncertain origin; and borrowed possibly from Medieval Latin *mitta,* perhaps from Middle High German *mittemo,* Old High German *mittamo* middle, midmost in the sense of half-glove.

mix *v.* 1538, in Elyot's *Dictionary;* developed as a back formation from earlier *myxte* mixed (probably before 1425); borrowed through Anglo-French *mixte,* learned borrowing from Latin *mixtus,* past participle of *miscēre* to mix, which was borrowed early by certain Germanic languages (compare Old English *miscian* and Old High German *miskan*). Latin *miscēre* is cognate with Old Irish *mescaim* I mix, Greek *mísgein, meignýnai* to mix Lithuanian *miẽšti,* Old Slavic *měšiti,* and Sanskrit *miśrá-s* mixed, from Indo-European **meik̂-/mik̂-* (Pok 714). **—n.** a mixing, mixture. About 1586; from the verb. **—mixer** 1611, person who mixes. The meaning o a sociable person is first recorded in 1896, and that of a social gathering, in 1916, both in American English. The meaning of a machine for mixing is first recorded in 1876, with specific reference to a kitchen appliance for mixing, in 1931. **—mixture** *n.* action or fact of mixing. Probably before 1425, borrowed from Middle French *misture, mixture,* and directly from Latin *mixtūra,* from *mixtus,* past participle. **—mix-up** *n.* confusion (1898).

mizzen (miz′ən) *n. Nautical.* fore-and-aft sail. 1413-20 *mesan;* later *myson* (1466-67); borrowed from Middle French *misaine* foresail, foremast, alteration (influenced by Italian *mezzana* mizzen) of Old French *migenne,* from Catalan *mitjana,* from Latin *mediānus* of the middle, MEDIAN. Italian *mezzana* is a noun use of *mezzana* middle, from Latin *mediānus.* **—mizzenmast** *n.* 1413-20 *mesan mast* mast aft of the mainmast.

mnemonic (nimon′ik) *adj.* aiding the memory. 1753, in *Chambers Cyclopaedia;* either a back formation from earlier *mnemonics;* or borrowed from Greek *mnēmonikós* of or pertaining to memory, from *mnḗmōn* (genitive *mnḗmonos*) remembering, mindful, from *mnâsthai* remember, see MIND; for suffix see -IC. **—mnemonics** *n.* art or method of improving the memory. 1721, in Bailey's *Dictionary,* borrowed from New Latin *mnemonica,* from Greek *mnēmoniká,* neuter plural of *mnēmonikós* mnemonic; for suffix see -ICS.

moan *n.* long, low sound of suffering. Probably before 1200 *man* complaint, lamentation, in *Ancrene Riwle;* later *mon, mone* (before 1250); developed from Old English **mān* complaint (from Proto-Germanic **main-*), related to *mǣnan* complain, moan (also, tell, intend; whence obsolete English *mean*¹ complain). The meaning of sound of suffering is first recorded in Milton's *Sonnets* (1673). **—v.** make moans. About 1250 *monen* to lament, mourn, in *The Story of Genesis and Exodus;* developed from *mon* lamentation. The meaning of make a mournful sound is first recorded in 1724 (implied in *moaning*).

moat *n.* 1300 *mote* mound or embankment, later, ditch surrounding a castle (before 1376, in *Piers Plowman*); borrowed from Old French *mote* or Medieval Latin *mota* mound, fortified height; of uncertain origin.

mob *n.* large crowd. 1688, disorderly crowd or rabble, shortened form of earlier *mobile* (pronounced mob′ilē) the common people, the populace, rabble (1676); borrowed from Latin *mōbile vulgus* fickle common people; *mōbile,* neuter of *mōbilis* fickle, movable, MOBILE. **—v.** to mill around in curiosity, anger, etc. 1709, from the noun. **—mobster** *n.* gangster. 1917, formed in American English from *mob,* n. + *-ster.*

mobile (mō′bəl) *adj.* movable, easy to move. 1490, in Caxton's translation of *The Book of Eneydos;* borrowing of Middle French *mobile,* learned borrowing from Latin *mōbilis* movable, shortened form of **movibilis,* from *movēre* to MOVE. **—n.** Probably before 1430, outermost sphere of the universe, in Lydgate's writings; borrowed from Latin *mōbilis.* 1549, a prime mover (in philosophical works); later, a body in motion (before 1676); borrowed from Middle French *mobile* and reborrowed from Latin *mōbilis.* The later meaning of a mobile construction or sculpture (mō′bēl), is first recorded in English in 1949; from the adjective in English, influenced by Alexander Calder's work referred to as *mobile sculpture* (1936). **—mobility** *n.* ability or readiness to move or be moved. Probably before 1425 *mobilitee* capacity for motion, in a translation of Chauliac's *Grande Chirurgie;* borrowed from Middle French *mobilité,* from Latin *mōbilitātem* (nominative *mōbilitās*) capacity to move, from *mōbilis* mobile; for suffix see -ITY.

mobilize *v.* 1838, put into circulation; borrowed from French *mobiliser,* from *mobile* movable, MOBILE; for suffix see -IZE. The meaning of call (troops) into active service, is first recorded in 1853. The figurative sense of put (forces, energy, resources) into active service, is found in 1871. **—mobilization** *n.* act of mobilizing. 1799, a putting into circulation; borrowed from French *mobilisation,* from *mobiliser* mobilize; for suffix see -IZATION. The meaning of act or process of mobilizing an army, is first recorded in 1866.

moccasin *n.* soft leather shoe or sandal. 1612, in Captain John Smith's *A Map of Virginia,* American English, borrowed from Algonquian, probably of a Virginia tribe (compare Powhatan *mäkäsĭn* shoe, Ojibwa *makisin*). The French word *moccasin* was borrowed from English.

mocha (mō′kə) *n.* choice variety of coffee, originally imported from southwestern Arabia. 1773, in allusion to *Mocha,* a seaport in Southern Yemen, at the mouth of the Red Sea, from which mocha was originally exported. The meaning of a mixture of coffee and chocolate, used as a flavoring in cakes, etc., is first recorded in 1892.

mock *v.* laugh at, make fun of. Probably before 1430 *mokken* to deceive, in Lydgate's writings; later *mocken* to make fun of (probably about 1450); borrowed from Middle French *mocquer,* from Old French, of uncertain origin (sometimes said to represent a Vulgar Latin **muccāre* to wipe the nose, possibly reflected in modern French *se moquer,* perhaps with an original sense of a derisive gesture; Skeat and others have suggested a comparison with Germanic forms, such as Middle Dutch *mocken* to mumble, Middle Low German *mucken* to mumble, grumble; perhaps ultimately of imitative origin). **—adj.** not real, copying, sham, imitation. 1548, adjective use of earlier *mokke,* n., act of mocking, jest, trick (about 1425); from the verb. **—mockery** *n.* a making fun, ridicule. Probably before 1430 *mokerye,* in Lydgate's writings; borrowed from Middle French *moquerie,* from Old French, from *mocquer* to mock; for suffix see -ERY. **—mockingbird** *n.* (1676)

mod *adj.* 1965, very up-to-date and fashionable; adjective use of earlier *Mod,* n., one of a group of British teen-agers of the 1960's affecting extreme neatness of appearance and a foppish liking for very fine or stylish clothes (1960); shortened form of *modern.*

modal (mō′dəl) *adj.* of or having to do with mode, manner, or form, as contrasted with substance. 1569, (in logic) involving the affirmation of possibility, impossibility, etc.; borrowed from Middle French *modal,* and directly from Medieval Latin *modalis* of or pertaining to a mode, from Latin *modus* measure, manner, MODE. The meaning of pertaining to mode or form, is first recorded in 1625; the sense in grammar first appears in John Horne Tooke's *The Diversions of Purley* (1798). **—modality** *n.* Before 1617, quality of being modal; borrowed from French *modalité,* or directly from Medieval Latin *modalitatem* (nominative *modalitas*) a being modal, from *modalis* modal, see MODAL; for suffix see

-ITY. The meaning of a particular mode, method, or procedure, is first recorded in 1957.

mode[1] *n.* manner. About 1380 *moedes,* pl., melodies, songs, in Chaucer's translation of Boethius' *De Consolatione Philosophiae;* later *mode* grammatical mood; MOOD[2] (about 1450); borrowed from Latin *modus* measure, rhythm, song, manner; related to *meditārī* to think or reflect upon, consider; see METE[1] allot. The meaning of manner in which a thing is done, is first recorded in 1667.

mode[2] *n.* current fashion, style, or custom. About 1645; borrowed from French *mode,* learned borrowing from Latin *modus* manner, MODE[1]. **—modish** *adj.* fashionable or stylish. 1660, formed from English *mode*[2] + *-ish.*

model *n.* 1575, a representation made to scale; borrowed from Middle French *modèle,* from Italian *modello* a model, mold, from Vulgar Latin **modellus,* diminutive of Latin *modulus* measure, standard, diminutive of *modus* manner, measure, MODE[1]. The meaning of a thing or person to be imitated is first recorded in 1639 but this sense is suggested in the earlier sense of a person or thing that is the likeness of another, in Shakespeare's *Richard II* (1593). The meaning of a person or thing serving as a pattern for artists is first recorded in 1691. Later senses include fashion model (1904), automobile model (1900), and mathematical or scientific model (1913). **—v.** to shape or fashion. 1604, to present as in a model; borrowed from French *modeler,* or developed from the noun in English. **—adj.** serving as a model (as in *a model student*). 1844, from the noun.

modem (mō′dem) *n.* device used in telecommunications to convert digital signals to analog form and vice versa. 1961, formed from *mo(dulator)* + *dem(odulator).*

moderate (mod′ərit) *adj.* 1392 *moderat,* borrowed from Latin *moderātus,* past participle of *moderārī* to regulate, from a pre-Latin stem **medes-* (compare *modestus* MODEST); for suffix see -ATE[1]. **—v.** (mod′ərāt) make less extreme. Probably before 1425 *moderaten,* in a translation of Higden's *Polychronicon;* probably from *moderate,* adj., by influence of Latin *moderātus,* past participle. The meaning of regulate or preside over (a debate, etc.), is first recorded in 1577. **—n.** (mod′ərit) person who holds moderate opinions. 1794, in Burke's *Letters;* from the adjective. **—moderation** *n.* Probably before 1425 *moderacioun* quality of being moderate, in a translation of Chauliac's *Grande Chirurgie;* borrowed from Middle French *modération,* from Latin *moderātiōnem* (nominative *moderātiō*), from *moderārī;* for suffix see -ATION. **—moderator** *n.* Before 1398 *moderatour,* in Trevisa's translation of Bartholomew's *De Proprietatibus Rerum;* borrowed from Latin *moderātor,* from *moderārī;* for suffix see -OR[2]. The sense of one who presides over a debate, etc., is first recorded in 1573.

modern *adj.* 1500-20, now existing, extant, in Dunbar's *Poems;* later of the present and recent times (1585); borrowed from Middle French *moderne,* and directly from Late Latin *modernus,* (probably patterned on *hodiernus* of today) from Latin *modo* just now, in a (certain) manner, from *modō,* ablative case of *modus* manner, MODE[1]. **—n.** person of modern times. 1585, from the adjective. **—modernism** *n.* modern attitude or methods. 1737, in Swift's *Letters,* formed from English *modern,* adj. + *-ism.* The use of *modernism* as a cover term for the movement or style away from classical or traditional modes in art, architecture, literature, etc. is first recorded in 1929.**—modernist** *n.* 1588, person of modern times (compare *modern,* n.); later, person holding modern views (1704, in Swift's *Tale of a Tub*); formed from English *modern* + -ist. **—modernistic** *adj.* 1909, formed from English *modernist* + *-ic.* **—modernity** *n.* 1627, probably formed from English *modern* + *-ity.* **—modernization** *n.* 1770, formed from English *modernize* + *-ation.* **—modernize** *v.* 1748, in Walpole's *Letters;* formed from English *modern* + *-ize.*

modest *adj.* 1565, in an early thesaurus; probably a back formation from *modesty,* and in some instances possibly borrowed from Middle French *modeste,* or directly from Latin *modestus* modest, moderate, in due measure, from a pre-Latin stem **medes-*; related to *modus* measure, manner, MODE[1]. **—modesty** *n.* 1531, moderation, in Elyot's *The Boke Named the Governour;* also, the quality of being modest (1553); borrowed from Middle French *modestie,* or directly from Latin *modestia* moderation, from *modestus* moderate; for suffix see -Y[3].

modicum (mod′əkəm) *n.* small or moderate quantity. About 1470 (Scottish), borrowing of Latin *modicum,* neuter of *modicus* moderate, from *modus* measure, manner, MODE[1].

modify *v.* About 1385 *modifyen* to alter, amend, in Chaucer's *Canterbury Tales;* borrowed from Old French *modifier,* learned borrowing from Latin *modificāre* to limit, restrain, from a lost adjective **modificus* regulating, forming according to rule (*modus* measure, manner, MODE[1] + the root of *facere* to make, perform, DO[1]); for suffix see -FY. **—modification** *n.* 1502, a bringing into a particular mode; borrowed from Middle French *modification,* learned borrowing from Latin, and borrowed directly from Latin *modificātiōnem* (nominative *modificātiō*) a measuring, from *modificāre* to limit, restrain; for suffix see -ATION. The meaning of a partial alteration is first recorded in Burke's writings (1774).

modular (moj′ələr) *adj.* 1798, (in mathematics) of or involving a number (called a *modulus*) by which two given numbers can be divided to leave the same remainders; borrowed from New Latin *modularis,* from *modulus* small measure; see MODULE; for suffix see -AR. The meaning of having to do with modules or interchangeable units, is first recorded in 1936. **—modularity** *n.* use of modules in construction or design. 1937, formed from English *modular* + *-ity.* **—modularize** *v.* make modular, build with modules. 1959, formed from English *modular* + *-ize.*

modulate *v.* regulate, adjust, vary. 1615, probably a back formation from earlier *modulation,* perhaps influenced in formation by Latin *modulātus,* past participle of *modulārī* regulate, measure rhythmically. **—modulation** *n.* act or process of modulating. Before 1398 *modulacioun* act of making music, air or melody, in Trevisa's translation of Bartholomew's *De Proprietatibus Rerum;* borrowed from Old French *modulation,* or directly from Latin *modulātiōnem* (nominative *modulātiō*) rhythmical measure, singing and playing, melody, from *modulārī;* for suffix see -ATION.

module (moj′ül) *n.* 1586, scale or allotted measure; later, standard for measuring (before 1628); borrowed through Middle French *module,* or directly from Latin *modulus* small measure, diminutive of *modus* measure, manner, MODE[1]; for suffix see -ULE. Doublet of MOLD[1] hollow shape. The meaning of any standardized or interchangeable part or unit, is first recorded in reference to electronics and mechanics (1955), and later in aeronautics, especially in reference to spacecraft (1961). Use of *module* in computer programming is found in 1963.

mogul[1] (mō′gul) *n.* prominent or powerful person. 1678, in Dryden's *The Kind Keeper,* from earlier *Mogul* Mongol, as conqueror of India (1588); borrowed from Persian and Arabic *mughal, mughul,* alteration of *Mongol* member of an Asiatic people now inhabiting Mongolia and certain parts of China and Siberia.

mogul[2] (mō′gəl) *n.* moundlike elevation on a ski slope. 1961, probably borrowed from a Scandinavian source (compare dialectal Norwegian *muge, mugje,* feminine *muga* a heap or mound); the form suggests influence of English *mogul*[1].

mohair (mō′hãr) *n.* cloth made from the hair of the Angora goat. 1619, alteration (by association with *hair*) of earlier *mocayare* (1570); borrowed from Middle French *mocayart,* and from obsolete Italian *mocaiarro,* both from Arabic *mukhayyar* cloth of goat hair; literally, selected or choice, from *khayyara* he chose.

moiety (moi′ətē) *n.* 1444 *moyte* one of two equal parts, half; borrowed from Middle French *moitié,* from Old French *meitiet,* from Late Latin *medietātem* (nominative *medietās*) half (in Latin, the middle; coined by Cicero to translate Greek *mesótēs*), from *medius* MIDDLE; for suffix see -TY. The meaning of a part, share, or portion, is first recorded in Shakespeare's *The Rape of Lucrece* (1593) and *1 Henry IV* (1596).

moil *v.* work hard, drudge. Probably about 1400 *moillen* moisten; borrowed from Old French *moillier* moisten, paddle in mud, from Medieval Latin *molliare* soften by wetting, from Latin *mollīre* soften, from *mollis* soft; see MELT. The meaning of work hard is first recorded in Latimer's sermons in 1548-49, probably developed from the original sense make or get dirty, perhaps in part by influence of *toil,* as in *toil and moil.* **—n.** hard work, drudgery. 1612, from the verb.

moire (mwär *or* môrā′) *n.* fabric with a watered or wavelike appearance. 1660, in Pepys' *Diary,* watered mohair, later, watered silk; borrowing of French *moire* fabric having a wavelike appearance, especially watered mohair; earlier *mouaire,* probably alteration of English MOHAIR.

moiré (mwärā′ *or* môrā′) *n.* = moire. 1818, clouded or wavelike appearance, such as that of watered silk; borrowed from French *moiré* watered, from past participle of *moirer* give a watered look to, from *moire,* probably alteration of *mohair;* see MOIRE. **—adj.** having a wavelike pattern, watered. 1823, from the noun.

moist *adj.* 1373, borrowed from Old French *moiste* damp, alteration (influenced by Latin *musteus* juicy from *mustum* fresh, MUST[2]) of Vulgar Latin **mucidus* moldy, altered from Latin *mūcidus* slimy, moldy, musty, from *mūcus* slime, MUCUS. **—moisten** *v.* 1580 (implied in *moistened* in Sidney's translation of the *Psalms*); formed from English *moist* + *-en*[1]; but earlier in Middle English *moisten* (about 1325), formed from the adjective and as a borrowing from Old French *moistir* and *enmoistir.* Apparently the Middle English verb, which would have developed into the form *moist* in modern English, was replaced after 1500 with a new formation based on the adjective. **—moisture** *n.* About 1350 *moysture* (in figurative sense of inspiration); borrowed from Old French *moisture, moistour,* from *moiste* moist; for suffix see -URE. **—moisturize** *v.* 1945, in H.L. Mencken's *The American Language;* formed in American English, from *moisture* + *-ize.*

mol *n.* See **mole**[4].

molar[1] *n.* tooth for grinding. About 1350, borrowed from Latin *molāris dēns* grinding tooth, from *mola* millstone, MILL[1] machine for grinding; for suffix see -AR. **—adj.** adapted for grinding. 1626, in Bacon's *Sylva Sylvarum;* from the noun.

molar[2] *adj.* of or having to do with one mole or gram molecule of a substance. 1902, formed from English MOLE[4] + *-ar.*

molasses *n.* kind of sweet syrup obtained in making sugar from sugar cane. 1582 *melasus,* borrowed from Portuguese *melaço,* from Late Latin *mellāceum* new wine, MUST[2], from Latin *mel* (genitive *mellis*) honey; see MELLIFLUOUS. The spelling with *o* is recorded as early as 1588, in the form *molassos,* but is unaccounted for.

mold[1] *n.* hollow shape for casting. Probably before 1200 *molde* fashion, form, nature, character, in *Ancrene Riwle;* later *mold* pattern on which something is made, form in which metal is shaped in *Sir Tristrem;* borrowed from Old French *molde, molle* mold, measure, from Latin *modulus* measure, model, diminutive of *modus* manner, MODE[1]. Doublet of MODULE. **—v.** to form or shape. About 1350 *moldon* to form, knead (dough) into shape; from the noun. **—molding** *n.* 1327, kneading, shaping. The meaning of architectural ornamentation, is first recorded in 1643.

mold[2] *n.* fungus growth. Before 1400 *molde,* in *Cursor Mundi;* probably developed from *mouled, moulde,* past participle of *moulen* to grow moldy (about 1390; earlier *muhelin,* before 1200, in *Ancrene Riwle*). The Middle English forms are cognate with Old Icelandic *mygla* (Swedish *mögla,* Danish *mugle*) grow moldy; possibly related to *mugga* drizzle; see MUGGY. **—v.** become covered with mold. Probably before 1500 *moulden;* from the noun. **—moldy** *adj.* covered with mold. 1570, formed from English *mold,* n. + *-y*[1]. Earlier (before 1398) *mowly,* formed from Middle English *moulen* grow moldy + *-y*[1].

mold[3] *n.* loose earth. Old English (before 725) *molde* earth, soil, dust; cognate with Old Frisian *molde* earth, soil, Middle Dutch *moude,* Old High German *molta,* Old Icelandic *mold* (Swedish *mull,* Norwegian *mold*), and Gothic *mulda,* from Proto-Germanic **muldṓ,* Indo-European **ml̥-tā;* see MEAL[2] ground grain. **—moldboard** *n.* curved metal part of a plow that turns earth. 1508, formed from English *mold*[3] + *board,* n.; replacing earlier *moldebredd* (1343); formed from Middle English *molde* mold[3] + *bredd* board.

molder *v.* turn into dust, crumble. 1531, in Elyot's *The Boke Named the Governour;* probably a frequentative form of *mold*[3] loose earth.

mole[1] *n.* congenital spot on the skin. 1373 *moyle* stain, in an early book on medicinal plants; later *mole* spot on the skin (before 1398, in Trevisa's translation of Bartholomew's *De Proprietatibus Rerum*); developed from Old English *māl* spot, mark, mole (about 1000, in Ælfric's *Glossary*). Old English *māl* is cognate with Old

High German *meil* spot or mark (modern German *Mal*), and Gothic *mail* wrinkle, from Proto-Germanic **mailan,* cognate with Greek *miarós* defiled, and *miaínein* to stain (formations that probably sprang from a lost noun **miar,* genitive **mianos* a stain), from Indo-European **mai-* (or *moi-*)/*mi-* (Pok. 697).

mole[2] *n.* small burrowing mammal. 1362 *mol;* later *molle, molde* (about 1400), probably related to Old English *molde* earth, soil; see MOLD[3] loose earth. Corresponding forms are found in Old Frisian *moll* mole, Middle Low German *mol, mul,* Middle Dutch and modern Dutch *mol.* A synonym is found in earlier Middle English *moldewarpe* mole; literally, earth thrower (before 1325). The transferred sense of an intelligence agent who becomes entrenched in legitimate activities before spying, is first recorded in 1976, and popularized by John Le Carré, British novelist. **—molehill** *n.* (about 1450)

mole[3] *n.* massive pier or breakwater. Before 1548, borrowed from Middle French *môle* breakwater, from Italian *molo,* from Medieval Greek *môlos* from Latin *mōlēs* mass, massive structure, barrier; also difficulty, trouble. The Latin and Medieval Greek forms are related to Greek *môlos* effort, *mólis* barely, scarcely (whose short *-o-* is probably due to influence from *mógis* with difficulty), cognate with Old High German *muoan* (modern German *mühen*) take pains *or* trouble, from Indo-European **mō-* (Pok. 746).

mole[4] or **mol** *n.* molecular weight of a substance expressed in grams; gram molecule. 1902, borrowed from German *Mol,* shortened form of *Molekül,* from French *molécule,* from New Latin *molecula* MOLECULE.

molecule *n.* smallest particle into which a substance can be divided without chemical change. 1794, borrowed from French *molécule* (1674), from New Latin *molecula* a molecule, diminutive of Latin *mōlēs* mass, barrier, MOLE[3]. Use of the New Latin *molecula* is recorded in English contexts as early as 1678 and in translation in 1800, all with the Latinate plural *-æ.* **—molecular** *adj.* having to do with molecules. 1823, in Henry J. Brooke's *Familiar Introduction to Crystallography;* formed in English (perhaps through influence of French *moléculaire*) from New Latin *molecula* molecule + English *-ar.*

molest *v.* About 1385 *molesten,* in Chaucer's *Troilus and Criseyde;* borrowed from Old French *molester,* from Latin, and directly from Latin *molestāre* to disturb, trouble, annoy, from *molestus* troublesome, related to *mōlēs* trouble or barrier; see MOLE[3]. **—molestation** *n.* act of molesting. Probably about 1400 *molestacioun,* borrowed from Old French *molestation* from *molester* molest, and directly from Medieval Latin *molestationem* (nominative *molestatio*), from Latin *molestāre* to disturb; for suffix see -ATION. It is also possible in some instances that *molestation* was formed from Middle English *molesten* + *-acioun* -ation.

moll *n. Slang.* female companion of a criminal or vagrant. 1567, as a feminine personal name; later, a prostitute (1604), and a female companion of a thief (1823); developed as a shortened form of *Molly,* informal variant of *Mary.*

mollify *v.* soften, appease. 1392 *mollifien* to soften; borrowed from Old French *mollifier,* or directly from Late Latin *mollificāre* make soft, mollify, from *mollificus* softening (Latin *mollis* soft + the root of *facere* make, perform, DO[1]); for suffix see -FY. **—mollification** *n.* act of mollifying or softening. About 1395 *mollificacioun,* in Chaucer's *Canterbury Tales;* borrowed from Old French *mollification,* learned borrowing from Medieval Latin *mollificationem* (nominative *mollificatio*), from Late Latin *mollificāre* soften, mollify; for suffix see -ATION.

mollusk *n.* shellfish. 1783 *mollusque,* borrowing of French *mollusque,* learned borrowing from New Latin *Mollusca,* name of an order in biological classification, from Latin *mollusca,* neuter plural of *molluscus* thin-shelled, from *mollis* soft; see MELT. New Latin *Mollusca* was originally the name applied by Linnaeus in 1758 to an order of generally soft-bodied invertebrates including echinoderms, annelids, and mollusks without shells; shell-bearing mollusks were added to the order by later naturalists. The current use of the term *Mollusca* for a phylum consisting largely of shellfish was first proposed by Cuvier in 1788-1800. The spelling *mollusk* is first recorded in English in 1839.

mollycoddle (mol′ēkod′lə) *n.* boy or man accustomed to being coddled and pampered. 1849, in Thackeray's *Pendennis* (*Molly* effeminate man, milksop, from *Molly,* proper name + *coddle*). **—v.** to coddle, pamper. 1870, in Dickens' *The Mystery of Edwin Drood;* from the noun.

molt *v.* shed feathers, skin, etc., before new growth. 1591, alteration of Middle English *mouten* (before 1400); developed from Old English *-mūtian* (as in *bemūtian* to exchange), from Latin *mūtāre* to change; see MUTABLE.

The modern spelling with *-l-* developed on the analogy of words like *assault* and *fault,* in which the *l* was originally inserted only for purposes of attaining supposedly correct spelling.

—n. act or time of molting. 1815, from the verb.

molten (mōl′tən) *adj.* melted. About 1150 *moltan* dissolved by water; later *molten* made liquid by heat (about 1300), from past participle of *melten* to MELT.

molybdenum (məlib′dənəm) *n.* silver-white metallic chemical element. 1816, New Latin, alteration of earlier *molybdena* any of several ores of lead (1693), from Latin *molybdaena,* from Greek *molýbdaina,* from *mólybdos* lead, of uncertain origin, possibly Iberian.

mom *n.* 1894, American English, shortened form of earlier *momma* (1884), alteration of MAMMA[1]. **—mommy** *n.* 1902, American English, alteration of earlier MAMMY. British has similar formations in *mum* (1823) and *mummy* (1839).

moment *n.* About 1380, in Chaucer's translation of Boethius' *De Consolatione Philosophiae;* borrowed from Old French *moment,* or directly from Latin *mōmentum* movement, movement of time, instant, moving power, consequence, importance, contraction of **movimentum,* from *movēre* to MOVE; for suffix see -MENT. Doublet of MOMENTUM. **—momentarily** *adv.* 1654-66, for a moment; formed from English *momentary* + *-ly*[1]. The meaning of at any moment, is first recorded in 1928, in American English. **—momentary** *adj.* lasting only a moment, fleeting. About 1460 *momentare,* in Lydgate's writings; borrowed from Latin *mōmentārius,* from *mōmentum* moment; for suffix see -ARY. **—momentous** *adj.* very important, of great consequence. 1656, formed from English *moment* importance + *-ous.* An earlier meaning of having momentum, is first recorded in 1652.

momentum *n.* force with which a body moves. 1699, borrowing of Latin *mōmentum* movement, moving power; see the doublet MOMENT.

mon- a form of *mono-* before a vowel, as in *monaural, monism, monomial, monoxide.*

monarch *n.* king, queen, emperor, or similar ruler. Probably before 1439 *monarke,* in Lydgate's *Falls of Princes;* later *monarcha* (before 1449; borrowed from Middle French *monarque,* or directly from Late Latin *monarcha,* from Greek *monárchēs, mónarchos* (*mónos* alone, single + *árchein* to rule). **—monarchical** *adj.* of a monarch. 1576, formed from English *monarch* + *-ical.* **—monarchist** *n.* advocate of monarchy. 1647, formed from English *monarch* + *-ist.* **—monarchy** *n.* government by a monarch. Probably before 1350 *monarchie;* borrowed from Old French, from Late Latin *monarchia,* from Greek *monarchíā* absolute rule, from *monárchēs, mónarchos* monarch; for suffix see -Y[3].

monastery *n.* About 1400 *monasterye;* borrowed from Old French *monastere,* and directly from Late Latin *monastērium,* from Late Greek *monastḗrion* a monastery, from Greek *monázein* to live alone (from *mónos* alone; see MONK) + *-tḗrion* place for (doing something). Doublet of MINSTER.

monastic *adj.* About 1449 *monastik;* borrowed from Middle French *monastique,* or directly from Late Latin *monasticus,* from Late Greek *monastikós* solitary, pertaining to a monk, from Greek *monázein* to live alone, from *mónos* alone, single, see MONK; for suffix see -IC. The form was earlier *monastical* (1402); borrowed from Medieval Latin *monasticalis,* from Late Latin *monasticus;* for suffix see -ICAL. **—n.** monk. 1632, from the adjective. **—monasticism** *n.* system or condition of living a monastic life. 1795, formed from English *monastic* + *-ism.*

Monday *n.* Probably before 1200 *monedæi,* in Layamon's *Chronicle of Britain;* developed from Old English (about 1000) *mōnandæg, mōndæg,* literally, day of the moon (*mōnan,* genitive of *mōna* MOON + *dæg* DAY). The Old English forms correspond to Old Frisian *mōnadei* Monday, Middle Low German and Middle Dutch *mānendach* (modern Dutch *Maandag*), Old High German *mānetag* (modern German *Montag*), and Old Icelandic *mānadagr* (Swedish *måndag,* Danish, and Norwegian *manadag*).

The Germanic compounds are a translation of Latin *lūnae diēs* day of the moon (the source of French *lundi* Monday), which in turn is a translation of Greek *selḗnēs hēmérā.*

monetary *adj.* of money or currency. 1802-12, in Bentham's writings; borrowed, perhaps through influence of French *monétaire,* from Late Latin *mōnētārius* pertaining to money; originally, of the mint, from Latin *monēta* mint, coinage; see MONEY; for suffix see -ARY. **—monetarism** *n.* theory or policy of a monetarist. 1969, American English, from *monetarist,* on the analogy of such pairs as *capitalist, capitalism;* for suffix see -ISM. **—monetarist** *n.* advocate of tighter control of a country's money supply. 1963, formed from English *monetary* + *-ist.* Earlier, found as adjective, meaning "of a monetary character or on a monetary basis" (1914).

money *n.* About 1250 *moonay;* later *mone* (about 1300), and *moneie* (before 1325); borrowed from Old French *moneie,* from Latin *monēta* mint, coinage, from *Monēta* a cult title of the goddess Juno in whose temple at Rome money was coined; hence any place used as a mint. Doublet of MINT[2]. The Latin form *Monēta* as a proper name may have developed from an Etruscan family name. **—moneyed** *adj.* having money. 1457 *monyed;* formed from the past participle of earlier *monien* to supply with money (1450), from *moneie* money. **—moneylender** *n.* (about 1780) **—money manager** (1571) **—money order** (1802) **—monies** *n.pl.* About 1300 *mones* coins. The meaning of sums of money is first recorded in Francis Bacon's *Essays* (1625).

monger *n.* dealer in some particular article. Before 1200 *mangare;* later *mongere* (1274); developed from Old English (before 975) *mangere,* from Latin *mangō* (genitive *mangōnis*) trader, dealer, borrowed from a Greek word related to *mánganon* contrivance, means of enchanting; see MANGLE[2] machine; for suffix see -ER[1].

The combining form *-monger* (as in *fishmonger, newsmonger*) is found in Middle English, as early as 1193 (*haymonger*); from the 1500's on it was often used in a pejorative sense.

—v. to deal or traffic in. 1928, in the figurative sense of spread (gossip or other evil); from the noun.

mongoose *n.* ferretlike animal. 1698, borrowed from an Indic language (compare Marathi *mangūs* mongoose), apparently ultimately from Dravidian (compare Telugu *mangisu* mongoose, Kanarese *mungisi*).

mongrel *n.* animal or plant of mixed breed. About 1460, heraldic term for a kind of dog, probably one of mixed breed, developed from earlier *mong* mixture (probably before 1200), and *mange* (about 1175); developed from Old English (about 700) *gemang, gemong* mingling; see AMONG; for suffix compare PICKEREL. **—adj.** of mixed breed, race, origin, etc. 1576, in Abraham Fleming's translation of Johannes Caius' *Of English Dogs;* from the noun.

monition *n.* admonition, warning. About 1400 *monicioun,* borrowed from Old French *monition,* learned borrowing from Latin, and borrowed directly from Latin *monitiōnem* (nominative *monitiō*) warning, reminding, from *monēre* to warn; see MONITOR. For suffix see -TION.

monitor *n.* 1546, borrowing of Latin *monitor* one who reminds, admonishes, or checks, from *monēre* admonish, warn, advise, related to *meminī* I remember, I am mindful of, and *mēns* MIND; for suffix see -OR[2]. **—v.** 1818, in Keats' *Endymion,* to guide; from the noun. The meaning of check the quality of (a radio transmission, etc.), is first recorded in 1924, and is found in the extended meaning of listen to radio or telephone messages and report on them, in 1939. **—monitory** *adj.* admonishing, warning. 1586 *monitorie,* developed from earlier noun *monytorie* letter of admonition (1437); borrowed from Medieval Latin *monitoria* admonition, from Latin *monitōrius* admonishing, from *monēre* admonish; for suffix see -ORY.

monk *n.* Before 1121 *munec,* in *Peterborough Chronicle;* later *munk* (probably before 1220, in Layamon's *Chronicle of Britain*), and *monk* (before 1300); developed from Old English *munuc* (before 899, in Alfred's translation of Bede's *Ecclesiastical History*); borrowed from Late Latin *monachus* monk; originally, a religious hermit, from Late Greek *monachós* monk, from Greek, adj., individual or solitary, from *mónos* (earlier **mónwos*) alone, single. Greek *mónos* is related to *manós* (earlier **manwós*) thin, sparse, loose, infrequent, cognate with Armenian *manr* (genitive *manu* small, thin),

Old Irish *menb* small, and Middle Welsh *di-fanw* insignificant, from Indo-European **menwo-/monwo-/menwó-* (Pok. 728).

monkey *n.* 1530, in Palsgrave's *Lesclarcissement,* possibly borrowed from Middle Low German *Moneke* (a term conceivably introduced by itinerate German entertainers), perhaps developed as an allusion to *Moneke,* son of Martin the Ape in the medieval beast epic *Reynard the Fox;* or perhaps borrowed directly from Italian *monna* or Spanish *mona* monkey + *-key,* a probable diminutive form, of uncertain origin. **—v.** *Informal.* 1859, to mimic; later, to fool, play (1881); from the noun. **—monkey business** 1883, American English slang, trickery, foolishness. **—monkeyshines** *n.pl.* 1829, American English slang, antics, pranks. **—monkey wrench** (1858)

mono- a combining form meaning one, sole, single, occurring in a number of words adopted from existing Greek compounds, such as *monogamy, monogram, monologue, monopoly,* but also commonly used to form words in English, mostly of a technical or scientific character, such as *monosyllable, monopetalous,* and often combined (instead of *uni-*) with a Latin element, as in *monocellular.* Borrowed from Greek *mono-,* from *mónos* single, alone; see MONK.

monochrome (mon′əkrōm) *n.* painting, drawing, print, etc., in a single color. 1662, in Evelyn's *Sculptura;* borrowed from Medieval Latin *monochroma,* from Greek *monóchrōmos* of a single color (*mono-* single + *chrôma,* genitive *chrômatos,* color, complexion, skin, see CHROMATIC). **—adj.** monochromatic. 1849, in Ruskin's *Seven Lamps of Architecture;* from the noun. **—monochromatic** *adj.* having or done in a single color. 1822, formed in English from Latin *monochrōmatos* of a single color, from Greek *monochrṓmatos* (*mono-* single + *chrôma,* genitive *chrṓmatos,* color) + English *-ic.*

monocle (mon′əkəl) *n.* eyeglass for one eye. 1886 (earlier entered in an English language trade dictionary as a French term, 1858); borrowing of French *monocle,* learned borrowing from Late Latin *monoculus* one-eyed (*mono-* one, single, from Greek + *oculus* EYE).

monody (mon′ədē) *n.* mournful song. 1623, in Cockeram's *Dictionary;* borrowed from Late Latin *monōdia* a solo, from Greek *monōidíā,* from *monōidós* singing alone (*mono-* alone + *ōidḗ* song, ODE).

monogamy (mənog′əmē) *n.* condition of being married to only one person at a time. 1612, borrowed from French *monogamie,* learned borrowing from Late Latin *monogamia,* from Greek *monogamíā,* from *monógamos* marrying only once (*mono-* single, one + *gámos* marriage; see BIGAMY); for suffix see -GAMY. **—monogamous** *adj.* practicing monogamy. 1770, borrowed from Late Latin *monogamus,* from Greek *monógamos;* for suffix see -OUS.

monogram *n.* person's initials, especially as combined in a particular design. 1696, in Phillips' *Dictionary,* borrowed through French *monogramme,* or directly from Late Latin *monogramma,* from Late Greek *monógrammon* a character of several letters in one design, from neuter of *monógrammos,* adj., consisting of a single letter (*mono-* one, single + *grámma* letter, something written; see GRAM). **—v.** decorate with a monogram. 1939, from the noun.

monograph *n.* treatise on a particular subject. 1821, treatise on a single species, genus, etc., in natural history; formed from English *mono-* single + *graph* something written, and eventually replacing earlier *monography* (1773), formed from English *mono-* + *-graphy.* The general sense of a treatise on a single subject (in any field), is first recorded in 1880.

monolith *n.* single large block of stone. 1848, but implied in earlier *monolithic* (1825), *monolithal* (1830), and found as *monolithoi,* a transcription from Greek in an English context (1827); borrowed from French *monolithe,* learned borrowing from Latin *monolithus,* adj., consisting of a single stone, from Greek *monólithos* (*mono-* single + *líthos* stone). The figurative sense of a rigid or unyielding political state, party, or organization, is first recorded in W.H. Auden's *Another Time* (1940), perhaps suggested by the earlier use of this sense in *monolithic.* **—monolithic** *adj.* 1825, consisting of a monolith, probably formed in English from French *monolithe* + English *-ic,* or from an earlier English **monolith + ic.* The figurative sense of like a monolith, massive, and unyielding, is first recorded in D.H. Lawrence's *England, My England* (1920).

monologue *n.* long speech, especially one given by an actor out of a group. 1668, a dramatic soliloquy, in Dryden's *An Essay of Dramatic Poesy;* borrowing of French *monologue,* from Late Greek *monólogos* speaking alone (*mono-* alone, single + *lógos* speech, word; see LOGIC). The general sense of a long speech or harangue, is first recorded in 1859.

monomania *n.* obsession with a single idea. 1823, New Latin (*mono-* single + *mania*). Originally a term of medical psychology, it entered popular usage by 1834.

monomer (mon′əmər) *n.* single molecule that can combine with others to form a polymer. 1914, formed from English *mono-* one, single + suffixal *-mer,* as in *polymer.*

monomial (mōnō′mēəl) *n.* expression consisting of a single term or name. 1706, in Phillips' *Dictionary;* formed from English *mon-* single + *-omial,* abstracted by a false division of *binomial* as if from *bin-* (as in *binary, binocular,* and Latin *bīnī* two at a time) + *-omial.* **—adj.** consisting of a single term or name. 1801, from the noun.

mononucleosis (mon′ənü′klēō′sis) *n.* abnormal increase of mononuclear white cells in the blood. 1920, formed in English from *mononuclear* having one nucleus (1886, *mono-* one + *nuclear*) + New Latin *-osis* abnormal condition.

monophonic (mon′əfon′ik) *adj.* having to do with sound transmission or reproduction by means of a single channel. 1958, formed in American English from *mono-* single + *phonic.* The word was used earlier in music (before 1885) in the sense of having one part or melody predominating.

monoplane *n.* 1907, formed in American English from *mono-* single + *(aero)plane.*

monopoly *n.* exclusive control of a commodity or service. 1534, in Sir Thomas More's *Works;* borrowed from Latin *monopōlium,* from Greek *monopṓlion* right of exclusive sale (*mono-* single + *pōleîn* to sell). Greek *pōleîn* to sell is related to *empolḗ* merchandise, purchase, profit, from a lost verb **empélesthai* to engage in, a compound of *pélesthai* come to be, originally move (oneself), cognate with Sanskrit *cárati* moves, and Latin *colere* attend to, from Indo-European **kwel-/kwol-/kwōl-* (Pok. 639).

As a board game of buying and selling real estate,

Monopoly appeared as a trademark in 1935, in American English.

—monopolistic *adj.* 1883, American English; formed from earlier English *monopolist* (1601) + *-ic.* **—monopolize** *v.* get exclusive control of. 1611, in Cotgrave's *Dictionary;* formed from English *monopoly* + *-ize.*

monotheism (mon′əthēiz′əm) *n.* doctrine or belief that there is only one God. 1660, in Henry More's *An Explanation of the Grand Mystery of Godliness;* formed from English *mono-* single + *the-* god (variant of *theo-*; see THEOLOGY) + *-ism.* **—monotheist** *n.* 1680, in Henry More's *Apocalypsis Apocalypseos,* derived from English *monotheism,* on the pattern of such pairs as *atheism, atheist.* **—monotheistic** *adj.* (1846, Archbishop Trench)

monotony (mənot′ənē) *n.* tiresome sameness, tedium. 1706, in Pope's *Letters;* borrowed, perhaps through French *monotonie* (1671), from Greek *monotoníā,* from *monótonos* monotonous, of one tone (*mono-* one + *tónos* TONE).**—monotone** *n.* sameness of tone, style, etc. 1644, borrowed from Greek *monótonos* monotonous. **—monotonous** *adj.* dull, tedious. 1778, in Thomas Warton's *The History of English Poetry;* borrowed from Greek *monótonos;* for suffix see -OUS.

monoxide *n.* oxide containing one oxygen atom in each molecule. 1869, formed from English *mon-* one + *oxide.*

Monseigneur or **monseigneur** (monsēn′yər) *n.* 1610, French title of honor equivalent to my lord (*mon* my + *seigneur* lord); see SENIOR.

monsieur (məsyėr′) *n.* 1500-20, in William Dunbar's *Poems,* French word for Mr. or sir, from Middle French, from Old French *monsieur;* earlier, *mon sieur* my lord (*mon* my and *sieur* lord, from Gallo-Romance **sejōrem,* unaccented variant, used before the name of the person addressed, from Latin *seniōrem,* accusative of *senior* elder, SENIOR).

Monsignor or **monsignor** (monsēn′yər) *n.* 1670, title given to certain dignitaries in the Roman Catholic Church; borrowed from Italian *monsignore,* formed after French *monseigneur* MONSEIGNEUR with Italian *signore* lord).

monsoon *n.* seasonal wind of the Indian Ocean and southern Asia. 1584, in a version of Hakluyt's *Voyages;* borrowed through early modern Dutch *monssoen,* from Portuguese *monção,* from Arabic *mawsim* appropriate season (for a voyage, pilgrimage, etc.), from *wasama* he marked.

monster *n.* Before 1325 *monstre* abnormal or malformed animal, in *Cursor Mundi;* borrowed from Old French *monstre,* learned borrowing from Latin, and borrowed directly from Latin *mōnstrum* monster, monstrosity, omen, portent, sign; perhaps related (as from earlier **monistrom*) to *monēre* to warn; see MONITOR. Related to DEMONSTRATE. **—monstrosity** *n.* 1402 *monstruosite;* later *monstrosity* (1555); borrowed, probably from Middle French *monstruosité,* from Medieval Latin *monstruositas,* from Latin *mōnstruōsus* monstrous; for suffix see -ITY.**—monstrous** *adj.* About 1380 *monstruous* unnatural, hideous, in Chaucer's translation of Boethius' *De Consolatione Philosophiae;* later *monstrous* (probably before 1430); borrowed from Old French *monstruos,* learned borrowing from Latin, and borrowed directly from Latin *mōnstruōsus,* from *mōnstrum;* for suffix see -OUS. The meaning of huge, enormous, is first recorded in Dunbar's *Poems* (1500-20), and that of the figurative sense of outrageously wrong or absurd, in 1573-80.

montage (montäzh′) *n.* combination of several film shots to make a composite picture. 1929, in Montagu's translation of Pudovkin's *On Film Technique;* borrowing of French *montage* a mounting, from Old French *monter* to go up, MOUNT[1]

month *n.* Before 1110 *monthe,* in *Peterborough Chronicle;* also *moneth* (probably before 1200 and thence through the 1600's); developed from Old English (probably about 750) *mōnath.* Old English *mōnath* is cognate with Old Frisian *mōnath* month, Old Saxon *mānoth,* Middle Dutch *mānet* modern Dutch *maand*), Old High German *mānōd* (modern German *Monat*), Old Icelandic *mānadhr* (Swedish *månad,* Norwegian and Danish *måned*), and Gothic *mēnōths;* from Proto-Germanic **mǣnṓth-,* cognate with Lithuanian *mẽnuo,* from Indo-European **mēnṓt* (Pok. 732). Proto-Germanic *mǣnṓth-* is related to *mǣnōn-* moon, developing out of the calculation of a month's duration from full moon to full moon; however, the calculation of the traditional month was in some early systems displaced by periods of a fixed number of days, usually one-twelfth of a year, and having no relation to phases of the moon, but with intercalary days occurring in alternate months or in various specific months. **—monthly** *adv.* (1533-34), *adj.* (1572); formed from English *month* + *-ly* [1] (adv.) and *-ly*[2] (adj.).

monument *n.* building, pillar, statue, etc., erected in memory of a person or event. About 1280, tomb or memorial; borrowed, perhaps through Old French *monument,* and directly from Latin *monumentum* monument, something that reminds, from *monēre* to remind, warn, see MONITOR; for suffix see -MENT. **—monumental** *adj.* of or like a monument. 1604, in Shakespeare's *Othello;* formed from English *monument* + *-al*[1].

moo *v.* make the sound of a cow, low. 1549, of imitative origin. **—n.** sound made by a cow. 1789, from the verb,

mooch *v.* 1440 *mychyn* to pilfer, steal; later *mowchen* (before 1460); borrowed from Old French *muchier, mucier* to hide, conceal, of uncertain origin. It is also possible that *mooch* developed from Middle English *mucchen* to hoard, be stingy (1303, in Mannyng's *Handlyng Synne*); probably originally, keep coins in one's nightcap, from *mucche* nightcap; borrowed from Middle Dutch *muste* cap or nightcap; ultimately from Medieval Latin *almucia,* of uncertain origin.

The meaning of sponge off others is first recorded in 1857, probably from the sense of loaf, sneak (1851).

mood[1] *n.* state of mind or feeling. Probably about 1150 *mod* mind, heart as governing thoughts; later *mood* (about 1250); developed from Old English *mōd* mind, heart, spirit, courage (about 725, in *Beowulf*). Old English *mōd* is cognate with Old Frisian and Old Saxon *mōd* mind or thought, Middle Dutch *moet* mood or emotion (modern Dutch *moed* courage or spirit), Old High German *muot* (modern German *Mut*), Old Icelandic *mōdhr* anger or grief (Swedish and Danish *mod,*Norwegian *mot* courage), and Gothic *mōths* anger or courage from Proto-Germanic **mōđá-,* from Indo-European **mō-tó-,* extension of root **mō/mə-* desire strongly (Pok. 704). **—moody** *adj.* Before 1200 *modi* brave, proud, high-spirited, in Layamon's *Chronicle of Britain;* developed from Old English *mōdig* (about 725, in *Beowulf*), from *mōd* spirit, courage + *-ig* -y[1]. The meaning of often having gloomy moods is first recorded in Shakespeare's *The Rape of Lucrece* (1593).

mood[2] *n. Grammar.* form of a verb that shows whether the act or state is thought of as a fact, a command, etc. 1573, alteration (influenced by *mood*[1]) of Middle English *mode* form of a verb (about 1450, in *Battlefield Grammar*); borrowed from Old French *mode,* and directly from Latin *modus;* see MODE[1] manner.

moola or **moolah** (mü'lə) *n. Slang.* money. 1939 *moola,* American English, in O'Hara's *Pal Joey;* of unknown origin.

moon *n.* Before 1135 *mone;* later *moone* (about 1380, in Chaucer's *Canterbury Tales*); developed from Old English *mōna* (before 725, in the book of *Daniel*). Old English *mōna* is cognate with Old Frisian *mōna* moon, Old Saxon *māno,* Middle Dutch *māne* (modern Dutch *maan*), Old High German *māno* (modern German *Mond*), Old Icelandic *māni* (Swedish, Danish, and Norwegian *måne*), and Gothic *mena,* from Proto-Germanic **mǣnōn.* Cognate words for *moon* and *month* are found in all branches of Indo-European, including, outside Germanic, Latin *mēnsis* month, Greek *mḗnē* moon, *mḗn* (genitive *mēnós*) month, Old Irish *mī-* month, Welsh *mis,* Albanian *muai,* Lithuanian *mė̃nuo, mė̃nesis* moon, month, Latvian *mēness* moon, Old Slavic *měsęcĭ* moon, month, Armenian *amis* month, Sanskrit *mā́s, mā́sa-s* moon, month, and Tocharian A *mañ,* Tocharian B *meñe* month, from Indo-European **mēnṓt* (genitive **mēneses*), *mēnes-, mēns-, mēs-, mēn-* (Pok. 731).
—**v.** 1601, expose to moonlight; later, pass (time) idly (1836), and move listlessly (1848); from the noun.
—**moonbeam** *n.* (1590, in Shakespeare's *Midsummer Night's Dream*) —**moonless** *adj.* (1508, in Dunbar's poetry) —**moonlight** *n.* About 1300 *Mone lith;* later as a surname *Monelight* (1337); formed from *mone* moon + *lith* light.—*v.* hold a second job, usually at night. 1957, American English, back formation from *moonlighter* one who holds a second job, especially at night (1954), or *moonlighting* practice of a moonlighter (1955). —**moonshine** *n.* 1500, moonlight; later, smuggled or illicit alcoholic liquor (1785); and in American English, illicitly distilled whiskey (1875). —**moonstruck** *adj.* 1674, mentally affected or deranged, in Milton's *Paradise Lost.* The sense is associated with the supposed influence of the moon. Compare LUNATIC. —**moony** *adj.* Before 1586, of or belonging to the moon, in Sidney's *The Arcadia;* formed from English *moon* + *-y.* The meaning of inclined to moon, dreamy, is first recorded in Thackeray's *Book of Snobs* (1848).

moor[1] *v.* put or keep (a ship, etc,) in place. Probably before 1200 *moren* to take root; later, to fix or fasten (about 1380), and to secure a ship (probably before 1497); probably related to Old English *mǣrels* mooring rope, and possibly **mǣran* to moor, which would correspond with Middle Dutch *māren, mēren* to tie up, moor (modern Dutch *meren*), Old High German *marawen* to join, Low German *vermoren* to moor, and Old Frisian *mere* strap. —**mooring** *n.* 1420 *moring* process of making a ship secure, from gerund of *moren* to moor. —**moorings** *n.pl.* 1774, place where a ship is moored.

moor[2] *n.* open land. 1150 *mor-,* in compound *morsecge* sedge from a marsh; later *mor* wasteland or marshland (probably before 1200, in Layamon's *Chronicle of Britain*); developed from Old English *mōr* (about 725, in *Beowulf*). Old English *mōr* is cognate with Old Saxon *moer* swamp, Middle Low German *mōr* (modern German *Moor*), Middle Dutch *moer,* Old High German *muor* swamp or sea, from Proto-Germanic **mōra-,* from Indo-European **mōro-* standing water (Pok. 748). Related to MERE[2] lake. —**moorland** *n.* About 1250 *more-lond* marshland, in *The Story of Genesis and Exodus;* earlier, in surnames and place names *Morlandes* (1179), *Murlund* (1231), *Morlaunde* (1257).

Moor *n.* member of a Moslem people of mixed Arab and Berber stock living in northwestern Africa. Before 1393 *More,* in Gower's *Confessio Amantis;* borrowed from Old French *More;* later *Maure,* or directly from Medieval Latin *Mōrus,* from Latin *Maurus,* from Greek *Maûros* inhabitant of *Mauritania,* an ancient country in North Africa.

From the Middle Ages through the 1600's, Moors were commonly supposed to be black or very dark in color, and hence the word is often found as a substitute for "Negro" (see Shakespeare's *Merchant of Venice*). In *Othello,* however, reference to "the Moor of Venice" is complicated by Othello's association with the *Mori* family, whose coat of arms bore a mulberry tree (in Italian *moro*).

moose *n.* animal like a large deer. 1613, American English; borrowed probably from Algonquian (compare Narragansett *moos,* apparently from *moosu* he strips off, in reference to the habit of stripping the bark of young trees as food).

moot *n.* assembly. Before 1121 *mot,* in *Peterborough Chronicle;* developed from Old English (probably about 750) *gemōt* meeting (to discuss judicial and political affairs); from Proto-Germanic **(ʒa-)mōtan,* cognate with Old Saxon and Old Icelandic *mōt* meeting, Old High German *muoz;* see MEET[1], v. The modern spelling with *-oo-* is found before 1475.

The meaning of a discussion of a hypothetical case by law students is first recorded in 1531.
—**adj.** that can be argued, debatable, doubtful. Before 1650 *moot point,* from earlier attributive use of the noun, as in *moot case* hypothetical case used in a law-student discussion (1577-87).

mop *n.* 1496 *mappe* bundle of yarn, cloth, or wool for cleaning or spreading pitch on a ship's planking; borrowed through dialectal French (Walloon) *mappe* napkin, or directly from Latin *mappa* napkin; see MAP. The spelling *mop* is first recorded in 1665; however, if it is possibly implied in *moppet* rag doll, it is found in *moppe* (1440). —**v.** wash or wipe up, clean with a mop. 1709 *mop up;* from the noun.

mope *v.* to be dull, silent, and sad. 1568, implied in *moping* wandering aimlessly; later, be sad or spiritless (about 1590); perhaps of imitative origin, as found in Low German *mopen* to sulk, and Dutch *moppen* to grumble or grouse, from Indo-European **mu-b-,* extended from root **mu-* speak indistinctly (Pok. 752). —**n.** listless person. 1693, from the verb.

moped (mō'ped) *n.* heavily built motorized bicycle. 1956, in I. Dunlop's *Going to Britain;* borrowing of Swedish *moped,* acronym formed from *mo(tor)* + *ped(al).*

moppet *n.* child. 1601, formed from Middle English *moppe* little child, baby, doll (1440, in *Promptorium Parvulorum*) + *-et,* diminutive suffix. Middle English *moppe* also with the meaning of simpleton or fool (about 1330), is perhaps cognate with Low German *mop, mops* simpleton, pugnosed dog, Dutch *mop, mops* pugnosed dog.

moraine (mərān′) *n.* mass of rocks, dirt, etc., deposited at the side or end of a glacier. 1789, in William Coxe's *Travels in Switzerland;* borrowing of French *moraine,* from dialectal French (Savoy) *morêna* mound of earth, from Provençal *morre* snout, muzzle, from Vulgar Latin **murrum* round object, of uncertain origin.

moral (môr′əl) *adj.* ethical, virtuous. About 1340, in Richard Rolle's *The Psalter;* borrowed from Old French *moral,* learned borrowing from Latin, and borrowed directly from Latin *mōrālis* of morals or manners, from *mōs* (genitive *mōris*) one's disposition, humor, custom, in plural *mōrēs* customs, manners, morals, cognate with Old English *mōd* spirit, courage, MOOD, from Indo-European **mō-/mə-* desire strongly (Pok. 704); for suffix see -AL[1].

It is said that Latin *mōrālis* was formed by Cicero as a rendering of Greek *ēthikós* ethical. The word has passed into the modern Romance and Germanic languages, as found in French, Spanish, Portuguese *moral,* Italian *morale;* German *moralisch,* Dutch *moraal,* Scandinavian *moral,* etc.

—n. lesson, moral teaching. Before 1500, from the adjective. The plural form *morals* with the meaning of moral habits or conduct, is first recorded in John Fletcher's *The Captain* (about 1613).

—moralist *n.* 1621; formed from English *moral* + *-ist.* **—moralistic** *adj.* 1865; formed from English *moralist* + *-ic.* **—morality** *n.* the right or wrong of an action. About 1375 *moralitee* instruction in morals, moral doctrine, in Chaucer's *Canterbury Tales;* borrowed from Old French *moralité,* and from Late Latin *mōrālitātem* (nominative *mōrālitās*) manner, characteristic, character, from Latin *mōrālis* of morals or manners, moral. **—moralize** *v.* interpret morally. Probably before 1400 *moralizen;* borrowed from Old French *moraliser,* from *moral* moral, and borrowed directly from Medieval Latin *moralizare,* from Latin *mōrālis;* for suffix see -IZE.

morale (məral′) *n* mental condition in regard to confidence, enthusiasm, etc. 1752, moral principles or practice, in Chesterfield's *Letters to his Son;* borrowed from French *morale* morality or good conduct, from feminine of Old French *moral* MORAL.

The meaning of mental condition in regard to confidence, enthusiasm, etc. (especially of military troops), is first recorded in 1831, and derived from French *morale* morality or good conduct, by confusion with *moral* mental or moral condition, from Old French *moral,* adj.

morass *n.* swamp. 1655, in Thomas Fuller's *History of the University of Cambridge;* reborrowing from Dutch *moeras* marsh or fen, alteration (influenced by Middle Dutch *moer* MOOR[2]) of Middle Dutch *maras, marasch,* from Old French *marais* marsh, and Old Provençal *maresc,* from Frankish; possibly representing West Germanic **marisk-,* from Proto-Germanic **mariskaz* like a lake, like the sea, from **mari* sea, Indo-European **mori* (Pok. 748). West Germanic **marisk-* is the form from which also developed Medieval Latin *mariscus,* and now obsolete English *marish* marsh.

Modern English *morass* replaced earlier *mareis* marshland, swamp (recorded before 1338, in Mannyng's *Chronicle of England,* and earlier as a proper name, 1130, 1189); borrowed from Old French *marais, mareis.*

The figurative sense of difficult or confused state of affairs is first recorded in 1867.

moratorium (môr′ətôr′ēəm) *n.* 1875, legal authorization to delay payments, New Latin *moratorium,* from neuter of Late Latin *morātōrius* tending to delay, from Latin *morārī* to delay, from *mora* pause, delay; originally, a standing there thinking, cognate with Old Irish *mar(a)im* I stay, Breton *mar* doubt, Sanskrit *smárati* remembers, thinks of, and Latin *memor* mindful, from Indo-European **(s)mer-/(s)mor-* (Pok. 969). The general sense of temporary cessation of action, is first recorded in 1932.

morbid *adj.* 1656, of disease, diseased, in Henry More's *Enthusiasmus Triumphatus;* borrowed perhaps through French *morbide,* or more likely, directly from Latin *morbidus,* from *morbus* disease, of uncertain origin.

The meaning of unhealthy, not wholesome, in reference to mental conditions, ideas, etc., is first recorded in 1834, but is implied earlier in *morbidness* (as in *morbidness of mind,* 1681).

—morbidity *n.* morbid condition or quality. 1721, in Bailey's *Dictionary;* formed from English *morbid* + *-ity.*

mordant *adj.* biting, cutting, sarcastic. 1474 *mordent,* in Caxton's *Game and Play of Chess;* borrowed from Middle French *mordant,* present participle of *mordre* to bite, from Vulgar Latin **mordere,* from Latin *mordēre* to bite or sting. Latin *mordēre* is cognate with Greek *smerdnós* fearful, Old English *smeart* painful, and Old High German *smerzan* (modern German *schmerzen* to pain, hurt), from Indo-European **smerd-/smord-* (Pok. 737). **—n.** acidic substance that fixes colors in dyeing. 1791, borrowed from French *mordant,* from Middle French *mordant,* present participle. A related noun *mordaunt* hooked clasp, is found in Middle English about 1400.

more *adj.* About 1125 *mare;* later *more* (before 1250); developed from Old English (before 725) *māra* greater or more, used as the comparative of *micel* great, MUCH, and related to *mā* more (adv. and adj.).

Old English *māra* and *mā* (originally adverbs) are cognate with Old Frisian *māra* more, adj. and *mā, mē* more, adv.; Old Saxon *mēro,* adj. and *mēr,* adv.; Middle Dutch *mēre,* adj. and *mee,* adv. (modern Dutch *meer*); Old High German *mēro,* adj. and *mēr,* adv. (modern German *mehr*); Old Icelandic *meiri,* adj. and *meir,* adv. (Norwegian, Swedish, and Danish *mer*); and Gothic *maiza,* adj. and *mais,* adv. —the adjective from Proto-Germanic **maizōn,* —the adverb from **mais* which are cognate with Old Irish *māu* more, Welsh *mwy,* and perhaps Oscan *mais,* adv., more, and Old Prussian *muisieson,* adv., more; from Indo-European comparative **mēyes/mēis, məyes/məis,* root **mē-/mō-/mə-* great (Pok. 704).

—adv. to a greater extend or number. Before 1129 *mare;* later *more* (about 1250); developed from Old English (about 1000) *māre,* from neuter of *māra,* adj. **—n.** a greater number, amount, etc. 1128 *mare;* later *more* (about 1250); developed from late Old English (before 1100) *māre,* from neuter of *māra,* adj.

mores (môr′āz) *n.pl.* traditional rules or customs of a society or group. 1907, in W.G. Sumner's *Folkways;* borrowing of Latin *mōrēs* customs, manners, morals; see MORAL.

morganatic (môr′gənat′ik) *adj.* relating to marriage between a man of high social rank and a woman of lower rank with an agreement that neither she nor their children will have any claim to his title or property. 1727-41, in *Chambers Cyclopaedia;* borrowed through French *morganatique,* or directly from New Latin *morganaticus* of the morning, from the Medieval Latin phrase *matrimonium ad morganaticam* morganatic marriage; literally, marriage of the morning, in which the word *morganaticam* probably derives from Old High German **morgangeba* (found in *morganegiba,* used by St. Gregory of Tours in the 500's A.D.), in Middle High German *morgengābe* morning gift, gift of the bridegroom to the bride on the morning after the wedding (corresponding to Old English *morgengifu* morning gift). The gift is traditionally the wife's only share in her husband's possessions.

morgue *n.* place in which bodies are kept until identified. 1821, borrowed from French *Morgue,* building in Paris used as a morgue where bodies were exposed for identification; originally, place in a Paris prison where new prisoners were viewed for establishing their identification among keepers (probably the same word as French *morgue* haughtiness; originally, a sad expression, solemn or sour look, from Old French *morguer* look at solemnly, from Vulgar Latin **murricāre* to make a face, pout, from **murrum* muzzle, snout, of imitative origin.

moribund (môr′əbund) *adj.* dying. 1721, in Bailey's *Dictionary;* borrowed from French *moribund,* learned borrowing from Latin *moribundus* dying, subject to death, from *morī* to die; see MURDER.

Mormon *n.* member of the Church of Jesus Christ of Latter-day Saints, founded by Joseph Smith. 1830, American English, in allusion to *Mormon,* an ancient prophet and author of the Book of Mormon, last leader of the Nephites (one of certain ancient peoples in America). The Book of Mormon was published in 1830 by Joseph Smith.

morn *n.* morning. About 1175 *maregen;* later *morewen, morn* (about 1250); developed from Old English *margen,* dative *mārne* (in Mercian, before 830, in the *Vespasian Psalter*); earlier *morgen,* dative *morgne* (about 725, in *Beowulf,* though found only in a late West Saxon copy, about 1000).

The Old English forms *margen* (from Proto-Germanic **marȝanaz*), and *morgen* (Proto-Germanic **murȝanaz*) are cognate with Old Frisian *morgen, mergen* (Proto-Germanic **marȝinaz*) morning, Old Saxon *morgan,* Middle Dutch *morghen* (modern Dutch *morgen*), Old High German *morgan* (modern German *Morgen*), Old Icelandic *morginn, morgunn* (Swedish *morgon,* Norwegian and Danish *morgen*), and Gothic *maúrgins* (from Proto-Germanic **murȝinaz*), of unknown origin.

morning *n.* About 1250 *morning, morewening,* in *The Owl and the Nightingale;* later *morning* (about 1330); formed from Middle English *morn, morewen* MORN + *-ing*[1]; on the same pattern as *evening.* **—adj.** of or in the morning. 1535, in the Coverdale Bible; from the noun. **—morning-glory** *n.* (1814, American English) **—morning star** 1535 *morning starre;* earlier *morwnstere* (1440); probably developed from Old English *morgensteorra* (before 899, in Alfred's translation of Boethius' *De Consolatione Philosophiae*).

morocco (mərok′ō) *n.* fine leather made from goatskin. 1727-41, in *Chambers Cyclopaedia;* in allusion to *Morocco,* country in northwestern Africa, where it was first made.

moron *n.* person of low intelligence. 1910, American English; borrowing of Greek (Attic) *môron,* neuter of *môros,* general Greek *mōrós* foolish or dull, of uncertain origin.

Moron was originally a technical term adopted by the American Association for the Study of the Feebleminded and defined as an adult having a mental age of eight to twelve years. The informal meaning of a stupid person, is first recorded in W.R. Inge's writings (1922). **—moronic** *adj.* of or like a moron. 1926, American English; formed from *moron* + *-ic.*

morose *adj.* gloomy, sullen. 1565, in an early thesaurus; borrowed from Latin *mōrōsus* morose, peevish, fastidious, from *mōs* (genitive *mōris*) habit or custom; see MORAL; for suffix see -OSE[1].

morpheme (môr′fēm) *n. Linguistics.* smallest meaningful grammatical unit in a language. 1925, in P. Radin's translation of Joseph Vendryès' *Le Langage;* borrowing of French *morphème,* from Greek *morphḗ* form; patterned on French *phonème* phoneme.

In an earlier citation the OED Supplement shows the term *morpheme* is used (on the model of *phoneme*) in the now obsolete sense of any meaningful element in a language, such as a suffix, prefix, inflection, part of speech, or stress pattern (R.J. Lloyd, in *Neueren Sprachen*).

morphine *n.* drug made from opium. 1828, borrowing of French *morphine* or German *Morphin,* in allusion to Latin *Morpheus* the Roman god of dreams; so called from the drug's sleep-inducing properties; for suffix see -INE[2]. *Morpheus* is a proper name meaning literally "fashioner or molder," coined by Ovid from Greek *morphḗ* form or shape, in reference to the forms seen in dreams. *Morphine* replaced the earlier New Latin *morphia* (1818), also formed from Latin *Morpheus.*

morphology *n.* branch of biology that deals with the forms and structure of animals and plants. 1830, borrowed from German *Morphologie* (said to be coined by Goethe); formed from Greek *morphḗ* form + German *-logie* -logy. Greek *morphḗ* may have originally had the meaning of a shimmering variegated exterior, corresponding to a lost verb **mérphein,* cognate with Lithuanian *márgas* variegated, beautiful, and *mirgěti* to shine in a variegated play of colors, from Indo-European **mergwh-/morgwh-/mr̥gwh-,* Hjalmar Frisk, *Griechisches etymologisches Wörterbuch* II 257.

The meaning of a branch of linguistics that deals with structure of words and their formation, is first recorded in 1869, but is implied in earlier *morphological* (1860).

morris dance old English folk dance performed chiefly on May Day, by dancers in costume often representing characters from legend. 1458 *moreys daunce;* earlier *morys* Moorish (1434); borrowed from Old French *morois,* earlier *moreis* MOOR.

morrow *n.* the following day or time. About 1250 *morewe;* later *morwe* (about 1300); shortened variant of *morewen* morrow, MORN.

Morse (môrs) *adj.* of or designating the Morse telegraph or the code or a system using it. 1858, in allusion to Samuel F.B. *Morse,* 1791-1872, inventor of the electric telegraph (1837) and a code for using it, otherwise known as *Morse code* (1867).

morsel *n.* About 1280, borrowing of Old French *morsel* small bite, diminutive of *mors* a bite, from Latin *morsus* (genitive *morsūs*) act of biting or bite, from *mordēre* to bite; see MORDANT.

mortal *adj.* About 1370, causing death, deadly; also, grievous; later, subject to death (about 1380); all found in Chaucer's writings; borrowed from Old French *mortal, mortel* destined to die, and directly from Latin *mortālis* subject to death, from *mors* (genitive *mortis*) death, see MURDER; for suffix see -AL[1]. **—n.** 1526, mortal thing or substance, in the Tyndale Bible; from the adjective. **—mortality** *n.* About 1400 *mortalite,* in Gower's *In Praise of Peace;* borrowed from Old French *mortalité,* learned borrowing from Latin *mortālitātem* (nominative *mortālitās*) state of being mortal, from *mortālis* mortal; for suffix see -ITY.

mortar[1] *n.* mixture of lime or cement, sand, and water. About 1250 *morter* cement; later *mortar* (1367); borrowed from Old French *mortier,* from Latin *mortārium;* see MORTAR[2]. **—mortarboard** *n.* 1854, academic cap, resembling a square mason's board for carrying mortar (1876, though surely the mason's tool is much earlier). The *mortarboard,* formerly known as *mortar cap* (1686, and *morter* 1604), probably developed from the French *mortier* a cap once worn by high French officials.

mortar[2] *n.* bowl in which substances are pounded or ground, usually with a pestle. About 1150 *morter;* later *mortar* (1381); in part developed from Old English (about 1000) *mortere,* and in part borrowed through Old French *mortier;* both the Old English and Old French forms from Latin *mortārium* bowl for mixing or pounding, and the material prepared in it; formed from an original past participle **mr̥tós* pounded up, cognate with Greek *maraínein* extinguish, wear away, from Indo-European **mer-/mr̥-* (Pok. 736).

mortar[3] *n.* short cannon for shooting missiles or artillery shells at a high angle. 1558, found in *morter piece;* borrowed from Middle French *mortier* short cannon, from Old French, bowl for mixing or pounding, from Latin *mortārium;* see MORTAR[2].

mortgage *n.* pledge of property as security for a debt. Before 1393 *morgage* a pledge, in Gower's *Confessio Amantis;* also, a pledge of property (about 1400); borrowed from Old French *morgage* and *mort gaige,* literally, dead pledge (*mort* dead + *gage* pledge, GAGE[1]; so called because the debt becomes void or "dead" when the pledge was redeemed). Old French *mort* derived from Vulgar Latin **mortus* dead, from Latin *mortuus,* past participle of *morī* to die. **—v.** to pledge (property) as security. 1530, in Palsgrave's *Lesclarcissement;* from the noun. The *t* was introduced in the words in English during the 1500's and 1600's by writers aware of the Latin origins. **—mortgagee** *n.* person to whom property is mortgaged. 1584, formed from English *mortgage* + *-ee.* **—mortgagor** *n.* person who mortgages his property. 1584, formed from English *mortgage* + *-or*[2].

mortician (môrtish′ən) *n.* undertaker, funeral director. 1895, American English; formed from *mort(uary)* + *-ician* (as in *physician*), in an advertisement in the *Columbus* (Ohio) *Dispatch.*

mortify *v.* Before 1382 *mortefien* to kill, in the Wycliffe Bible; later *mortifien* to subdue (bodily desires) by abstinence; borrowed from Old French *mortifier* from Late Latin *mortificāre* cause death, from *mortificus* producing death (Latin *mors,* genitive *mortis,* death + the root of *facere* to make, perform, DO[1]). The meaning of wound (a person's feelings), humiliate, is first recorded in 1691, but is implied earlier in *mortification* (1645). **—mortification** *n.* About 1390 *mortificacioun* suppression of bodily desires, in Chaucer's *Canterbury Tales;* borrowed from Old French *mortification,* learned borrowing from Late Latin, and borrowed directly from Late Latin *mortificātiōnem* (nominative *mortificātiō*) a killing, destruction, from *mortificāre* to kill; for suffix see -ATION. The meaning of humiliation is first recorded in English, in Evelyn's *Diary* (1645).

mortise (môr′tis) *n.* hole in one piece of wood cut to receive a projection from another piece. About 1390 *morteys;* later *mortaise* (before 1450); borrowed from Old French *mortaise,* possibly from Arabic *murtazz* fastened, past participle of *razza* cut a mortise in. **—v.** fasten securely. Before 1450 *morteysen;* from the noun.

mortuary *n.* Probably 1383 *mortuarie* gift to a parish priest from the estate of a deceased parishioner, in Wycliffe's writings; earlier, in a Latin context (1330); borrowed through Anglo-French *mortuarie,* Old French *mortuaire,* from Medieval Latin, and borrowed directly from Medieval Latin *mortuarium,* from neuter of *mortuarius* pertaining to the dead, from Latin *mortuus,* past participle of *morī* to die; see MURDER; for suffix see -ARY. The meaning of a place where bodies are kept until burial is first recorded in 1865. **—adj.** of death or burial. 1514, from the noun.

mosaic *n.* small pieces of stone, glass, etc., inlaid to form a picture or design. Probably before 1400 *musycke* process of making a mosaic; borrowed from Old French *musaique, mosaïque* mosaic work, from Italian *musaico, mosaico,* from Medieval Latin *musaicum* mosaic work, work of the Muses, neuter of *musaicus* of the Muses, from Latin *Mūsa* MUSE; so called from the decorative mosaics of medieval grottoes dedicated to the Muses. Late Greek *mouseîon* mosaic work, and Late Latin *mūsivum* mosaic work, influenced the formation of Medieval Latin *musaicum.*

The meaning of a piece of mosaic work, a design in mosaic, is first recorded in 1699, but is earlier implied in figurative use, in Marvell's writings (before 1678). **—adj.** formed by or resembling mosaic. 1585, from the noun.

Mosaic (mōzā′ik) *adj.* of or having to do with Moses or the laws attributed to him in the Bible. 1662, borrowed, perhaps through French *Mosaïque* (Calvin, 1542), or directly from New Latin *Mosaicus,* from Latin *Mōsēs* Moses, from Greek *Mōsês,* from Hebrew *Mōsheh;* for suffix see -IC.

mosey (mō′zē) *v. Slang.* to move along or away slowly. 1829, American English, of uncertain origin (perhaps a shortening and alteration of Spanish *vamos* let's go, compare the later VAMOOSE, but more in keeping phonetically as an alteration abstracted from dialectal English *mose about* go about in a dull, stupid manner.

Moslem or **Muslim** *n.* believer in the religion based on the teachings of Mohammed and the Koran. 1615, borrowed as *muslim,* a transliteration from Arabic, a believer in the Mohammedan faith; literally, one who professes submission or submits (to the faith), from the root of *aslama* he resigned; see ISLAM. Related to SALAAM. **—adj.** 1777, from the noun.

mosque *n.* Moslem place of worship. 1717, in Lady Montagu's *Letters,* alteration of earlier *muskee, moskee,* borrowed from Middle French *mosquée,* from

Italian *moschea,* an alteration of *moscheta,* from Spanish *mezquita,* from *masjid,* a transliteration from Arabic, from *sajada* he worshiped. The earlier Middle English forms *moseak* and *moseache* (probably before 1425), are of obscure development, but may reflect simple metathesis of the Middle French *mosquée.*

mosquito *n.* About 1583, borrowed from Spanish *mosquito* little gnat, diminutive of *mosca* fly, from Latin *musca;* see MIDGE. **—mosquito net** (1745)

moss *n.* small plants that grow close together on the ground, rocks, trees, etc. Probably about 1125 *mose;* later *mosse* (1350-51); in part developed from Old English (975) *mos* bog, related to *mēos* moss; and in part, borrowed from: 1) a Scandinavian source (compare Old Icelandic *mosi* moss, bog) and 2) Medieval Latin *mossa* moss, from a Germanic source (compare Old High German *mos* moss, bog). Old English *mos* from Proto-Germanic **musan* is cognate with Middle Low German *mos* moss, Middle Dutch and modern Dutch *mos,* Old High German *mios, mos* moss (modern German *Moos* moss), and Old Icelandic *mosi* moss, bog (Danish and Norwegian *mose,* Swedish *mossa*). Cognates outside Germanic are found in Latin *muscus* moss, Lithuanian *mūsaĩ,* pl., scum on sour milk, mold, mildew, Old Slavic *mŭchŭ* moss, and probably with Armenian *mamur* moss, from Indo-European **meus-/mus-/mūs-* (Pok. 742).

most *adj.* Probably about 1175 *mest;* later *moste, most* (before 1250); developed from Old English (about 950) *māst* greatest number, amount, or extent; earlier *mǣst* (before 725). The Old English forms are cognate with Old Frisian *māst* most, Old Saxon *mēst,* Middle Dutch and modern Dutch *meest,* Old High German and modern German *meist,* Old Icelandic *mestr* (Norwegian, Swedish, and Danish *mest*), and Gothic *maists;* from Proto-Germanic **maistaz,* Indo-European **məistos;* corresponding to a superlative form derived from the Germanic root that is the source of Old English *mā, māra* MORE. **—adv.** in or to the greatest extent or degree. Probably about 1200 *mest;* later *most* (about 1250); developed from Old English (about 893) *māst, mǣst;* from the adjective.

-most a suffix forming superlatives of adjectives and adverbs, and meaning greatest in amount, degree, or number, as in *foremost, inmost, topmost.* Middle English, alteration (influenced by *most*) of *-mest;* found in Old English *-mest,* a so-called double superlative formed from *-mo, -ma* + *-est* superlative suffixes.

mot (mō) n. clever or witty remark. 1586, saying or motto; borrowing of Middle French *mot* word or saying, from Late Latin *muttum* grunt or word; see the doublet MOTTO. The meaning of a witty saying is first recorded in 1813, but in a context in which it was considered a foreign word. The synonymous phrase *bon mot,* literally, good saying, was borrowed in 1735 from French.

mote *n.* speck. About 1300 *mote, mot,* in *Arthour and Merlin;* developed from Old English (about 1000) *mot;* cognate with Middle Dutch *mot* sand or dust (modern Dutch *mot* peat dust), and Frisian *mot,* of unknown origin.

motel *n.* hotel for motorists. 1925, American English, a blend of *motor* and *hotel.* The term *motor hotel* appears in the same citation in which *motel* is first found, in the magazine *Hotel Monthly.*

moth *n.* small winged insect. About 1225 *mohthe;* later *mothe* (1373), *moght* (1386), *motthe* (about 1390), and *mouthe* (about 1400); developed from Old English (about 1000 *moththe,* and *mohthe* (about 950, in the *Lindisfarne Gospels*). The Old English forms are perhaps cognate with Middle Low German and Middle Dutch *motte, mutte* moth (modern Dutch *mot*), Middle High German *motte* (modern German *Motte*), and Old Icelandic *motti;* or perhaps they are related to Old English *matha* MAGGOT, or to Old English *mycg* MIDGE.

The Old English forms with *h* do not clearly correspond to other Germanic or Old English forms, which may indicate that two or more originally different words are involved.

—mothball *n.* 1906, American English, in O. Henry's writings; formed from *moth* + *ball* (of camphor or naphthalene).—*v.* 1943, to place in mothballs; later to store away, in reference to military equipment, such as a ship or airplane (1949).

mother[1] *n.* female parent. About 1125 *moder;* later *mother* (probably before 1425); developed from Old English (before 725) *mōdor.* A classic word of Indo-European etymology like *brother, father,* etc., the cognates of *mother* have appeared in a wide variety of languages, including the Germanic group of Old Frisian *mōder* mother, Old Saxon *mōdar,* Middle Dutch and modern Dutch *moeder,* Old High German *muoter* (modern German *Mutter*), and Old Icelandic *mōdhir* (Swedish, Danish, Norwegian *moder, mor*), from Proto-Germanic **mōđér.* Outside Germanic cognates appear in Celtic with Gaulish *Matrebo* (dative) to the mothers, and Old Irish *māthir* mother; in Italic with Latin *māter* mother, Oscan *Maatreís* (genitive) and Umbrian *mātrer;* in Hellenic with Greek *mḗtēr,* Doric *mā́tēr;* in Balto-Slavic with Lithuanian *mótė* wife, *mótyna* mother, Latvian *mâte* mother, Old Slavic *mati,* and Russian *mat';* in Armenian *mair* mother, in Indo-Iranian with Sanskrit *mātár-* and Avestan *mātar-;* and Tocharian A *mācar,* Tocharian B *mācer,* from Indo-European **mātḗr-.*

As with *father,* the spelling *-ther* (-ŦHER) for Middle English *-der* dates from the beginning of the 1500's, though the pronunciation with (ŦH) probably existed earlier.

—adj. that is a mother. Probably about 1200 *moder;* from the noun.

—v. 1542, attribute the maternity of to (a woman); 1548, be the mother of; from the noun. The meaning of take care of is first recorded in 1863.

—mother country (1587) **—motherhood** *n.* (before 1333 *moderhede;* later *moderhode,* 1459) **—mother-in-law** *n.* (before 1382) **—motherland** *n.* (1711) **—motherless** *adj.* (probably before 1200 *moderles,* Old English *mōdorlēas*) **—motherly** *adj.* About 1220 *moderliche,* Old English (about 1000) *mōdorlīc; adv., moderly,* about 1433; from the adjective. **—mother-of-pearl** *n.* (before 1510) **—mother's milk** (1500-20) **—mother tongue** (probably about 1378, in Wycliffe's writings).

mother[2] *n.* stringy, sticky substance found in vinegar. 1538, dregs or scum, in Elyot's *Dictionary;* probably a special use of MOTHER[1]. This etymology seems to be supported by the parallel French phrase *mère de vinaigre* and the German *Essigmutter.* Remoter semantic support is seen in English *matter* in the sense of pus, discharge, from Latin *māteria* itself a derivative of *māter* mother. It is also possible that this word was influenced by, if not borrowed from, Middle Dutch *modder* mud or mire; cognate with Middle Low Ger man *modder* mold, decay, sludge, and *mudde* thick mud (in ditches); see MUD). The meaning of a sticky substance formed in vinegar, is first recorded in Holland's translation of Pliny's *Natural History* (1601).

motif (mōtēf′) *n.* principal idea or feature, theme. 1848, borrowing of French *motif* dominant idea, theme, motive, from Old French, see MOTIVE.

motile (mō′təl) *adj.* able to move by itself. 1864, back formation from *motility.* **—motility** *n.* ability to move (as a characteristic of organisms). 1835-36, borrowed from French *motilité* (1827), from Latin *mōt-* (past participle stem of *movēre* MOVE) + *-ilité,* as in *mobilité* mobility.

motion *n.* movement. About 1385 *mocioun* suggestion, proposal, in Chaucer's *Troilus and Criseyde;* later, process of moving (before 1398, in Trevisa's translation of Bartholomew's *De Proprietatibus Rerum*); borrowed from Old French *motion,* learned borrowing from Latin *mōtiōnem* (nominative *mōtiō*) a moving, an emotion, from *movēre* to MOVE; for suffix see -TION. **—v.** make a movement. 1476, to request, petition, propose; from the noun. The meaning of make a movement (as in *motion for silence*) is first recorded in 1747. **—motionless** *adj.* (1599, in Shakespeare's *Henry V*) **—motion picture** (1896, American English; compare *moving picture* under MOVE) **—motion sickness** (1942, American English)

motivate *v.* provide with a motive or incentive. 1863, formed from English *motive,* n. + *-ate* [1], perhaps after French *motiver;* compare also German *motivieren.* **—motivation** *n.* 1873, formed from English *motivate* + *-ion.*

motive *n.* Before 1376 *motif* something moved or brought forward as an argument or assertion in *Piers Plowman;* later, motive or reason for acting (before 1439); and *motive* (before 1443); borrowed from Old French *motif,* n., from *motif* (feminine *motive*), adj., moving, learned borrowing from Medieval Latin, and borrowed directly from Medieval Latin *motivus* moving, impelling, from Latin *mōtus,* past participle of *movēre* to MOVE. **—adj.** that makes something move. 1392 *motif, motive;* borrowed from Old French *motif,* adj., and directly from Medieval Latin *motivus,* adj.

motley *adj.* made up of different things or kinds. About 1380 *motley* variegated; possibly borrowed through Anglo-French *motteley,* from Old English *mot* speck, MOTE. **—n.** mixture of things that are different. 1371 *motle* cloth of more than one color; later *motley* (1394); from the same source as the adjective.

moto-cross (mō′tōkrôs′) *n.* cross-country motorcycle race. 1951, borrowed from French *moto-cross* (*moto* motorcycle shortened form of *motocyclette* + *cross,* shortened form of *cross-country,* borrowed from English); French has similar words, such as *motoculture* for motorized or mechanized agriculture.

motor *n.* thing that imparts motion. 1447 *motour* controller or prime mover, in reference to God; borrowed from Latin *mōtor* mover, from *movēre* to MOVE; for suffix see -OR[2]. The meaning of an agent or force that produces mechanical motion is first recorded in 1664, and that of a machine that supplies motive power in 1856 in Emerson's writings. **—adj.** 1824, causing motion; from the noun. **—v.** 1896, take in an automobile; 1897, travel by automobile; from the noun, and as a shortened form of *motor car,* used as a noun. **—motorboat** *n.* (1902) **—motorcade** *n.* procession of automobiles. 1913, American English, in the *Arizona Republican;* formed from *motor* automobile + *-cade,* as in *cavalcade;* for suffix see -ADE. **—motorcar** *n.* (1895) **—motorcycle** *n.* (1896); *v.* ride a motorcycle (1902). **—motorcyclist** *n.* (1902) **—motorist** *n.* (1846) **—motorize** *v.* furnish with a motor. 1913, American English; formed from English *motor* + *-ize.* **—motorman** *n.* 1890, American English, driver of a motor vehicle; later, driver of a street car, or engineer of an electric train (1908). **—motor scooter** (1919)

mottle *v.* to mark with spots or streaks of different colors. 1676, implied in *mottled,* adj.; probably back formation from *motley,* adj., but found in earlier *motleyd,* adj., clothed in *motley.* **—n.** mottled coloring or pattern. 1676, probably back formation from *motley,* adj.

motto *n.* 1589, legend attached to a heraldic design, in Robert Greene's *The Spanish Masquerado;* borrowed from Italian *motto* a saying or motto, from Late Latin *muttum* grunt or word, from Latin *muttīre* to MUTTER. Doublet of MOT.

mound *v.* to heap up. 1515, to fence in; later, to enclose with an embankment (1600, probably from the noun); of uncertain origin. The meaning of heap up is first recorded in George Meredith's *The Ordeal of Richard Feverel* (1859). **—n.** 1551, fence or hedge; probably from the verb. The sense of an embankment was probably influenced by association with MOUNT[2] and from that meaning of *mound* developed the later sense of a heap of earth or stones, first recorded in Pope's translation of Homer's *Odyssey* (1726).

mount[1] *v.* go up, ascend. Probably before 1300, borrowed from Old French *monter,* from Vulgar Latin **montāre,* from Latin *mōns* (genitive *montis*) mountain, MOUNT[2]. The meaning of to set or place in position is first recorded in 1539. 1739, something on which a thing is mounted, a support; later, a horse for riding (1856); from the verb.

mount[2] *n.* high hill, mountain. Before 1300 *mount;* in part borrowed through Anglo-French *mount,* Old French *mont* mountain; and in part developed from Old English (probably about 750 *munt* mountain; both Old French and Old English borrowed from Latin *mōns* (genitive *montis*) mountain; related to *minae* projecting points, threats, and *mentum* chin. Cognates of Latin are found in Welsh *mynydd* mountain, Cornish *meneth,* Breton *menez,* Avestan *mati-* promontory, and Old Icelandic *mœ̄na* to project, *mœ̄nir* ridgepole, from Indo-European **men-/mon-/mn̥-* tower up, project (Pok. 726).

mountain *n.* Probably before 1200 *montaine, mountayne,* in Layamon's *Chronicle of Britain;* also *mounteyne* (about 1384); borrowed from Old French *montaigne* mountain, from Vulgar Latin **montānea* mountain or mountain region, from feminine of **montāneus* of a mountain, mountainous, from Latin *montānus* mountainous, from *mōns* (genitive *montis*) mountain, MOUNT[2]. **—adj.** of mountains. 1373, from the noun. **—mountaineer** *n.* native of mountains. 1610, in Shakespeare's *The Tempest,* formed from English *mountain* + *-eer; v.* be a mountain climber. 1802, in Southey's *Letters;* from the noun. **—mountainous** *adj.* of or characterized by mountains. About 1384 *mounteynous,* in the Wycliffe Bible; formed from *mounteyne* mountain + *-ous;* perhaps by influence of Old French *montagneux* (1265, feminine *montagneuse*). **—mountain range** (1831, but also found in *range of* *mountains,* 1705) **—mountainside** *n.* (about 1350) **—mountaintop** *n.* (1593, in Shakespeare's *2 Henry VI*)

mountebank (moun′təbangk) *n.* charlatan, quack. 1577, peddler of quack medicine who is traditionally thought of as standing on a wagon or platform to appeal to his audience with stories, tricks, juggling, etc.; borrowed from Italian *montambanco, montimbanco,* contracted form of *monta in banco* mountebank; literally, mount on bench (*monta,* imperative of *montare* to mount and *banco,* variant of *banca* bench or BANK², place for keeping money). The extended sense of charlatan, quack is first recorded in Nashe's *Works* (1589). **—v.** 1607, to trick or beguile like a mountebank, in Shakespeare's *Coriolanus;* from the noun.

mourn *v.* grieve. Probably before 1200 *mornen,* in Layamon's *Chronicle of Britain,* and *murnen,* in *Ancrene Riwle;* later *mournen* (about 1250), developed from Old English (before 725) *murnan* to mourn; also, be anxious, be careful. Old English *murnan* is cognate with Old Saxon *mornian* to mourn, Old High German *mornēn,* Old Icelandic *morna,* and Gothic *maúrnan,* from Proto-Germanic **murnanan;* outside Germanic, cognate with Latin *memor* mindful; see MEMORY. **—mourner** *n.* About 1395 *mournere,* in the Wycliffe Bible, formed from Middle English *mournen* mourn + *-ere* -er¹. **—mournful** *adj.* Probably before 1450 *mornyful,* formed from Middle English *morne,* n., mourning, grief (probably before 1300) + *-ful* -ful. The noun *morne* developed from the verb *mornen.*

mouse (mous) *n.* About 1325 *mous;* earlier, in surname *Mous* (about 1280), and *Muse* (1154-63); developed from Old English (before 700) *mūs;* cognate with Old Frisian and Old Saxon *mūs* mouse, Middle Dutch *muus* (modern Dutch *muis*), Old High German *mūs* (modern German *Maus*), and Old Icelandic *mūs* (Swedish, Danish, and Norwegian *mus*), from Proto-Germanic **mūs,* Indo-European **mūs.* Outside Germanic the word is cognate with Latin *mūs* mouse, Albanian *mï,* Greek *mŷs,* Old Slavic *myšĭ,* Armenian *mukn,* and Sanskrit *mū́s.* See also MUSCLE. The plural *mice* is found in Middle English *myse* (1373), earlier *myys* (about 1303); developed from the Old English plural (before 900) *mȳs* (compare Old High German *mūsi, miuse,* Old Icelandic *mȳss).* **—v.** (mouz) hunt for mice. Probably about 1150 *musen;* later *mowsyn* (1440); from the noun. The meaning of prowl like a mouse, search for, is first recorded in 1575. **—mousetrap** *n.* (about 1475); *v.* to entrap or deceive. 1607, implied in *mousetrapped;* from the noun. **—mousy** *adj.* 1812, quiet as a mouse; formed from English *mouse* + *-y*¹. The meaning of resembling or suggesting a mouse in appearance or behavior is first recorded in 1859.

moussaka (müsä′kə) *n.* baked dish of ground meat with eggplant or zucchini. 1941, in H.D. Harrison's *Soul of Yugoslavia;* borrowed through Serbo-Croatian from Turkish *musakka,* from Arabic *musakk'a.* The Arabic word is also the source of modern Greek *mousakás,* Bulgarian *musaka,* and Romanian *musaca.*

mousse (müs) *n.* rich pudding made with whipped egg whites. 1892, borrowing of French *mousse,* from Old French, froth, scum, from Late Latin *mulsa* mead, from Latin *mulsum* honey wine, mead, from neuter of *mulsus* mixed with honey, related to *mel* honey; see MELLIFLUOUS. The sense of a preparation used as a hairdressing is first recorded in the 1970's.

moustache *n.* See **mustache.**

mouth *n.* About 1250 *mouthe;* developed from Old English *mūth* (before 830, in the *Vespasian Psalter*). Old English *mūth* is cognate with Old Frisian and Old Saxon *mūth* mouth, Middle Dutch and modern Dutch *mond,* Old High German *mund* (modern German *Mund*), Old Icelandic *mudhr, munnr* (Swedish *mun,* Danish *mund,* Norwegian *munn*), and Gothic *munths,* from Proto-Germanic **munthaz.* Outside Germanic cognates are found in Welsh *mant* jawbone, and Latin *mentum* chin, from Indo-European **mn̥to-,* root **men-/mon-/mn-* standout, project (Pok. 726). The loss of the n-sound in the Old English, Old Frisian, and Old Saxon forms represents a normal development in which a nasal sound is lost before a fricative such as *th.* The semantic connection between mouth and stomach can be seen in Greek *stóma* mouth, *stómachos* throat, stomach. **—v.** (mouᴛʜ) speak, pronounce, talk. Before 1325, *muthen,* in *Cursor Mundi;* later *mouthen* (about 1378); from the noun. **—mouthful** *n.* (probably before 1425) **—mouth organ** (before 1668) **—mouthpiece** *n.* (1683)

move *v.* About 1275 *moven;* also *meven* (about 1300); borrowed through Anglo-French *movir,* Old French *movoir, moevre,* from Latin *movēre* move. The Latin *movēre* is probably cognate with Greek *ameúsasthai* surpass, *amŷnein* ward off, Lithuanian *máuti* strip off, and Sanskrit *kā́ma-mūta-s* moved by love, from Indo-European **meu-, mewə/mū-* push forward (Pok. 743). **—n.** 1656, the right or the time to move in a game; from the verb. The meaning of an act of moving is first recorded in Disraeli's *Vivian Grey* (1827). **—movable** or **moveable** *adj.* About 1380 *moevable* causing motion; also *mevable* capable of movement (before 1382); formed from Middle English *moven, meven* move + *-able.* **—movement** *n.* About 1380 *moevement,* in Chaucer's translation of Boethius' *De Consolatione Philosophiae;* also *mevement* (1422); borrowed from Old French *movement, mouvement,* from *movoir* to move; and formed from Middle English *meven,* v. + *-ment.* **—moving picture** 1709, picture in which objects appear to move; later, a cinematographic picture or film, in Queen Victoria's journals (1896). Compare *motion picture* under MOTION.

movie *n.* motion picture. 1912 (but apparently referred to in the reports of social workers as early as 1908, *American Speech,* Vol. I, p. 357), American English, shortened and altered form of *moving picture* (1896); for suffix see -IE. *The movies* in the sense of a motion-picture show is first recorded in 1914. **—adj.** of or in motion pictures. 1913 *movie actor,* attributive use of the noun. **—moviedom** *n.* the motion-picture industry (1916). **—moviegoer** *n.* (1923)

mow¹ (mō) *v.* cut down. Probably about 1150 *mowen* cut down (grass); later, destroy at a sweep (before 1400); developed from Old English *māwan* (before 899, in Alfred's translation of Bede's *Ecclesiastical History* and in *Orosius*). Old English *māwan* is cognate with Middle Low German *meien, meigen* to mow, Middle Dutch *maeyen* (modern Dutch *maaien*), and Old High German *māen* (modern German *mähen*), from Proto-Germanic **mǣanan* (or **mǣwanan*), cognate with Greek *amân* to mow, *ámētos* reaping, from Indo-European **mē-/mə-* (Pok. 703); see AFTERMATH. **—mower** *n.* Before 1325 *mouwer,* formed from Middle English *mouen* + *-er* ¹; but found earlier as a surname *Mawere* formed from Old English *māwan.*

mow² (mou) *n.* place where hay is stored; stack of hay

Probably before 1300, stack of hay or grain; developed from Old English (about 1000) *mūga, mūwa* a heap; earlier *mūha* (before 800, in *Corpus Glossary*). The Old English forms from Proto-Germanic **mūʒōn,* are cognate with Old Icelandic *mūgi, mūgr* crowd or heap (dialectal Norwegian *muge* heap or pile, dialectal Swedish *moa* to crowd together), Middle High German *mocke* lump, and Greek *mýkōn* heap, from Indo-European **muk-/mūk-* (Pok. 752).

moxie (mok′sē) *n. Archaic Slang.* courage, nerve, energy, initiative. 1930, Damon Runyon in *Collier's,* in allusion to earlier *Moxie,* a trademark for a bitter-tasting nonalcoholic drink that originated as a patent medicine about 1876. It contained cinchona alkaloids, sugar, caramel, and flavoring, and was widely advertised as a drink "that will build up your nerve."

mozzarella (moz′ərel′ə) *n.* mild Italian cheese. 1911, borrowing of Italian *mozzarella,* diminutive of *mozza* kind of cheese made from buffalo's milk.

Mr. (mis′tər), *pl.* **Messrs.** 1447-48, abbreviated form of *maister* master. The plural in English is a borrowing and abbreviated form of French *messieurs,* plural of *monsieur.*

Mrs. (mis′iz), *pl.* **Mmes.** 1615, abbreviated form of *mistress.* The plural in English is a borrowing and abbreviated form of French *mesdames,* plural of *madame.*

Ms. (miz), *pl.* **Mses.** or **Ms.'s** (miz′ēz). title put in front of a woman's surname instead of *Miss* or *Mrs.* 1949, in Mario Pei's *The Story of Language,* American English; considered as a blend of *Miss* and *Mrs.* The pronunciation (miz) was probably reinforced by the adoption of the pronunciation prevailing in some Southern American dialects for both *Miss* and *Mrs.*

much *adj.* Probably before 1200 *muche,* in Layamon's *Chronicle of Britain;* also *miche* (about 1200), shortened forms of *muchel, michel* much; developed from Old English (before 725) *micel* great in amount or extent. Old English *micel* is cognate with Old Saxon *mikil* great or large, Middle Low German *michel,* Old High German *mihhil,* Old Icelandic *mikill* (Swedish *mycken,* Danish *meget,* Norwegian *my(kj)e*), and Gothic *mikils,* from Proto-Germainc **mekilaz.* Cognates outside Germanic include Latin *magnus* great or large, Middle Irish *mag-, maige,* Albanian *math, madhi,* Greek *mégas* (genitive *megálou*), Armenian *mec,* Sanskrit *mahā-, mahánt-,* Tocharian A *mak,* Tocharian B *makā,* and Hittite *mekkiš* great, much, many, from Indo-European **meĝ(h)-/meg-* (Pok. 708).

The shortening of Middle English *muchel, michel* to *muche, miche* (with loss of *-l*) is probably parallel to that of *wench* in Middle English *wenche,* from *wenchel,* where the sound represented by *ch* possibly influenced the loss of the sound represented by the terminal *-l.* The shortening may also have been influenced by the process found in *lut* from longer *lutel* (see LITTLE).

—adv. Probably about 1200 *muche;* later *miche* (before 1382), from *muchel,* adj.

—n. Probably before 1200 *muche,* in *Ancrene Riwle;* later *miche* (before 1382), from *muchel,* adj.

mucilage (myü′səlij) *n.* 1392 *mussillage* gummy substance; also *muscillage* (before 1400); borrowed from Medieval Latin *muscilago, mucilago,* from Late Latin *mūcillāgō* musty or moldy juice, from Latin *mūcēre* be moldy or musty, from *mūcus* MUCUS. The specific sense of a gummy substance used as an adhesive is first recorded in 1859 in American English. **—mucilaginous** *adj.* sticky, gummy. Probably before 1425, borrowed from Medieval Latin *muscilaginosus,* from Late Latin *mūcilāginōsus,* from *mūcillāgō* mucilage; for suffix see -OUS.

muck *n.* About 1250 *muc* filth, manure; later *muk* (probably before 1325); probably borrowed from a Scandinavian source (compare Old Icelandic *myki, mykr* cow dung; see MUCUS). **—v.** make dirty; soil. About 1375 (Scottish) *mukken* to remove manure, clean out; later, to fertilize, spread manure (before 1400); from *muk,* n. The transferred sense of make dirty, is first recorded in Lamb's *Letters* (1832). The idiom *muck about* (or *around*) go about aimlessly, be busy or tamper with without accomplishing much, is first recorded in 1856.

muckluck or **mukluk** (muk′luk) *n.* fur-lined sealskin boot worn by Eskimos. 1868, sealskin, in American English; later, sealskin boot (1898, in Canadian English); both uses borrowed from Eskimo *maklak* large seal, sealskin boot. Since the 1960's *muckluck* or *mukluk* has acquired the meaning of canvas boots and also slipper socks.

muckraker *n.* person who exposes corruption. 1906, American English; formed from *muckrake* + *-er*[1]. *Muckrake* is found earlier as a person who seeks to find scandal, especially in a troubled situation (1872, in allusion to a figurative use in Bunyan's *Pilgrim's Progress,* 1684, in which a man with the muckrake pursues worldly gain at expense of celestial things by continuing to rake filth from the floor and not looking up to see a celestial crown offered to him in return for the muckrake he is using).

Theodore Roosevelt used Bunyan's metaphor in a speech in 1906, also possibly conscious of the meaning of *muckrake,* to describe persons who seek to expose corruption, in the passage "the men with the muckrakes are often indispensable to the well-being of society; but only if they know when to stop raking the muck." The American journalist Lincoln Steffens, 1866-1936, who had previously published muckraking articles, contributed to the wide currency of the term *muckraker,* as did others, such as Ida Tarbell and Upton Sinclair.

—muckrake *v.* expose corruption. 1910, American English; back formation from *muckraker,* perhaps influenced by earlier noun use of *muckrake* (1872).

mucus (myü′kəs) *n.* slimy substance that moistens the linings of the body. 1661, replacing earlier *muscilage, mussillage* (1392), and borrowed from Latin *mūcus, muccus* slime, mucus, mold, related to *ēmungere* sneeze out, blow one's nose, and *mūcēre* be moldy or musty. Latin *mūcus, muccus* is cognate with Welsh *mign* swamp, Greek *mýxa* mucus, Latvian *mukls* swampy, Sanskrit *muñcáti* (he) releases. Germanic cognates include Middle Low German *muik* soft, Old Icelandic *myki, mykr* cow dung, *mjūkr* soft, and Gothic *muka-* gentle, from Indo-European **meug-/mug-, meuk-/muk-* (Pok. 744). **—mucous** (myü′kəs) *adj.* of or like mucus. 1646, replacing *muscilaginous;* borrowed from Latin *mūcōsus* slimy, moldy, from *mūcus* mucus; for suffix see -OUS.

mud *n.* Probably about 1380 *mudde;* later *mode* (before 1400); probably borrowed from Middle Low German *mudde* and Middle Dutch *modde* thick mud; cognate with Middle High German *mot* bog, peat, Swedish *modd* mud, mire, from Proto-Germanic **muđ-*, cognate with Irish *mothar* bog, and Armenian *mut'* darkness, mist, from Indo-European **mut-* (Pok. 742). **—muddy** *adj.* of or like mud. 1410, morally impure; formed from English *mud* + *-y*[1]. The meaning of having much mud is recorded earlier in the place name *Modyputte* muddy pit (1330). The figurative sense of obscure, vague, confused, is first recorded in the Preface to the King James (Authorized Version) of the Bible (1611).

muddle *v.* bring into disorder or confusion. 1596, to mottle or obscure colors, stir up sediment in Nashe's *Have With You to Saffron-Walden;* perhaps a frequentative form of MUD. Alternatively, *muddle* may have been borrowed from early modern Dutch *moddelen* to make water muddy, a frequentative form of *modden* make muddy, from *modde* mud. The figurative sense of make confused is first recorded in 1687. **—n.** disorder, confusion. 1818, in Todd's revision of Johnson's *Dictionary;* from the verb. **—muddleheaded** *adj.* (1759, in Sterne's *Tristram Shandy*)

muezzin (myüez'ən) *n.* crier who calls Moslems to prayer, 1585, borrowed as a transliteration from Arabic dialectal pronunciation of *mu'azzin* the one who proclaims (*mu-*, formative prefix + *'azzana* inform, from *'azana* hear, from *'uzn* ear; the sound represented by *z* is pronounced like *th* in English *this,* but in widespread dialectal pronunciation, as in Turkey, and Iran, pronounced with the sound represented by *z* in English).

muff[1] *n.* covering for keeping both hands warm. 1599, in Ben Jonson's *Cynthia's Revels;* borrowed from Dutch *mof* a muff, from French *moufle* mitten, from Old French *moufle* thick glove, from Medieval Latin *muffula* a muff; of uncertain origin.

muff[2] *v.* to bungle, fail to catch (a ball). 1841 (implied in *muffing*), from earlier *muff* awkward person (1837), perhaps from *muff*[1], in the sense of "one who keeps his hands in a muff."

muffin *n.* small, round cake. 1703, originally dialectal; possibly borrowed from Low German *muffen,* plural of *muffe* small cake, from Middle Low German.

muffle *v.* Probably before 1425 *muffelen* to cover up, conceal; perhaps borrowed from Middle French *mofler* to stuff, from Old French *mofle, moufle* thick glove, *mitten,* MUFF[1] (compare Old French *enmouflé* wrapped up). The meaning of wrap in something to soften the sound is first recorded in 1761. **—n.** muffled sound. 1570, thing that muffles; from the verb. The meaning of a muffled sound is first recorded in Stevenson's *Strange Case of Dr. Jekyll and Mr. Hyde* (1886). **—muffler** *n.* 1535-36, a covering for the face and neck; formed from English *muffle,* v. + *-er*[1]. The meaning of something to deaden sound is first recorded in 1856; the specific reference to an automobile muffler is first found in 1895.

mufti[1] (muf'tē) *n.* Moslem judge or jurist. 1586 *muphtie* official head of the state religion in Turkey; also, Moslem official who assists a judge; borrowed from Arabic as a transliteration *muftī* judge, active participle of *aftā* to give, conjugated form of *fatā* he gave a (legal) decision. The spelling *mufti* is first recorded in English in 1695.

mufti[2] (muf'tē) *n.* ordinary clothes, not a uniform. 1816, perhaps a special use of *mufti*[1], in reference to the informal clothing worn by off-duty officials, as suggested by the costume formerly traditional to the stage role of a mufti, consisting of dressing gown, cap, and slippers.

mug *n.* heavy drinking cup. 1570, bowl, pot, jug; perhaps borrowed from a Scandinavian source (compare Swedish *mugg* mug, jug, Norwegian *mugge* pitcher). The slang sense of a person's face is first recorded in 1708, possibly alluding to drinking mugs commonly made in the shape of a grotesque human face. The extended sense of a picture or photograph of a person's face, especially for police records, is first recorded in 1887, in American English. **—v.** attack. 1818, (in boxing slang) to strike the face; from the noun sense of face. The meaning of hit, beat up, attack, is first recorded in 1846, and the extended sense of attack with the intention of robbing, in 1864. The slang sense of exaggerate one's facial expressions is found in Dickens' *Little Dorrit* (1855), and the meaning of make a picture or photograph of a person's face, especially for police records appears in 1899, in American English. **—mugger** *n.* one who commits robbery with violence. 1865, formed from English *mug* to attack and rob (1864) + *-er*[1].

muggy *adj.* warm and humid. 1731, in Bailey's *Dictionary,* probably developed from Middle English *mugen* to drizzle (probably about 1390, in *Sir Gawain and the Green Knight*); borrowed from a Scandinavian source (compare Norwegian *mugg* drizzle, mildew, mold, Old Icelandic *mugga* drizzle, mist, related to *mjūkr* soft; see MUCUS); for suffix see -Y[1].

mugwump (mug'wump') *n. Archaic.* an independent in politics. 1832, a jocular term for an important person, American English; borrowed from Algonquian (Natick) transcribed as *mugquomp* great man, a word used by the English missionary John Eliot in his translation of the Bible into that Indian language (1633).

In 1884 *mugwump* was applied to a Republican who refused to support the party candidate, James G. Blaine, for President; hence, the extended sense of a self-important person who stays aloof from party politics.

mulatto (məlat'ō) *n.* person having one white and one black parent. 1595, borrowed from Spanish and Portuguese *mulato,* literally, young mule, from *mulo* mule, from Latin *mūlus* (feminine *mūla*) MULE[1]; so called possibly in allusion to the hybrid origin of a mule.

mulberry *n.* tree that yields a berrylike fruit. Before 1300 *murberie;* later *mulbery* (about 1350); in part developed from Old English *mōrberie,* and in part borrowed from Middle High German *mūl-beri,* alteration of *mūr-beri.* Both English and German forms were formed from Latin *mōrum* mulberry, blackberry (from Greek *móron* mulberry) + either Old English *berie* or Old High German *beri* BERRY. The appearance of *-l-* in Middle English *mulberry* may be by dissimilation of the first *r* to *l* in *murberie.* Greek *móron* mulberry, blackberry is from Indo-European *moro-* blackberry (Pok. 749).

mulch *n.* mixture of wet straw, leaves, loose earth, etc. 1657, probably a noun use of Middle English *molsh* soft, moist (probably 1440), variant of earlier *melsche, melissche* (before 1398); developed from Old English *melsc, milisc* mellow, sweet; see MELLIFLUOUS.**—v.** cover with mulch. 1802, from the noun.

mulct (mulkt) *v.* punish by a fine. 1611, in Ben Jonson's *Catiline;* borrowed from French and Middle French *mulcter* to fine or punish, learned borrowing from Latin *mulctāre,* false archaism for *multāre* punish o fine, from *multa* penalty or fine, related to Oscan *moltam* (accusative) and Umbrian *mutu* penalty or fine, of uncertain origin. The modern English *mulct* replaced earlier *multen* to fine (in use probably before 1425); borrowed from Latin *multāre*. The figurative sense of deprive or divest of by cunning or deceit, defraud, is first recorded in 1748.

mule[1] *n.* offspring of a donkey and horse. About 1150 *mule,* in part developed from Old English *mūl* (before 830, in the *Vespasian Psalter*), and in part borrowed from Old French *mul* (feminine *mule*); both from Latin *mūlus* (feminine *mūla*) a mule. The Latin *mūlus* was probably borrowed from a Mediterranean language and related to the source of Phocian Greek *mychlós* male donkey, and Albanian *mušk* mule. **—muleteer** *n.* driver of mules. 1540-41, in Elyot's *The Image of Governance;* borrowed from Middle French *muletier,* from *mulet,* diminutive of Old French *mul* MULE[1]; for suffix see -EER. **—mulish** *adj.* intractable, stubborn. 1751, in Smollett's *The Adventures of Peregrine Pickle;* formed from English *mule*[1] + *-ish*[1].

mule[2] *n.* loose slipper. 1562, borrowed from Middle French, from Latin (*calceus*) *mulleus* red high-soled shoe (worn by Roman patricians). Latin *mulleus,* earlier **mulneyos* is cognate with Greek *mélās* black, Sanskrit *maliná-s* dark gray, and Lithuanian *mul̃vas* reddish, from Indo-European **mel-/ml̥-* dark (Pok. 720). It is interesting to note that though the form of borrowing is similar, the semantics are disparate.

mull[1] *v.* work over mentally, ponder. 1873, American English; perhaps a figurative use developed from Middle English *mullyn* grind to powder, pulverize (1440), from earlier *molle* dust, ashes, rubbish (before 1400; *mul,* about 1303, in Mannyng's *Handlyng Synne*); probably borrowed from Middle Dutch *mul* grit, loose earth; cognate with Middle Low German *mul* (modern German *Müll*) dust, and Old Icelandic *mylja* to crush, related to *mylna* MILL[2] machine for grinding grain.

mull[2] *v.* make (wine, beer, etc.) into a sweetened and spiced hot drink. 1607, implied in *mulled,* past participle of *mull;* perhaps borrowed from obsolete Dutch *mol* a kind of white, sweet beer, related to Flemish *molle* a kind of beer.

mullah (mul′ə) *n.* Moslem religious teacher or scholar. 1613, in *Purchas his Pilgrimage;* borrowed from Turkish *molla,* in Persian and Hindu *mullā,* from a transcription of Arabic *mawlā* master.

mullein or **mullen** (mul′ən) *n.* kind of weed. 1373 *molay, moleyne;* borrowed through Anglo-French *moleine,* perhaps from Old French *mol* soft, from Latin *mollis,* see MELT. Some sources refer the Anglo-French *moleine* to a Gaulish word for yellow, in reference to the flower of this weed, but the FEW does not accept such a connection.

mullet *n.* kind of edible fish, 1440 *molett,* in *Promptorium Parvulorum;* earlier, in Anglo-French context, 1393; borrowed from Old French *mulet* and directly from Medieval Latin *mulettus,* from Latin *mullus* red mullet, from Greek *mýllos* a marine fish. The spelling with *u* is recorded in Middle English *mulett* before 1500.

mulligatawny (mul′əgətô′nē) *n.* soup flavored with curry. 1784, borrowed from Tamil *miḷagutaṇṇi,* literally, pepper water (*miḷagu* pepper + *taṇṇīr* cool water, itself a compound of *taṇ* cool + *ṇīr* water).

mullion (mul′yən) *n.* vertical bar between window panes, wall panels, etc. 1567, alteration by metathesis of *n* and *l* in Middle English *moyniel* (1330-32); later *moniel* (1379-80), *munell* (1426-27); borrowed from Anglo-French *moinel,* noun use of *moienel, meienel,* adj., middle, from Old French *meien* intermediate, MEAN[3]. From the 1500's to the middle 1800's existence of the variant *munnion* shows a long-standing uncertainty about form.

multi- a combining form meaning: **1** many or several, as in *multicolored* (1845), *multilingual* (1838). **2** many times, as in *multimillionaire* (1858). Middle English; borrowed from Latin *multi-,* from *multus* much or many; related to *melior* better, and cognate with Greek *mála* greatly, very, *mâllon* more, and Lettish *milns* very much, from Indo-European **mel-/ml̥-* strong, great (Pok.720).

multifarious *adj.* having many different parts, elements, forms, etc. 1593, in Nashe's *Christ's Tears Over Jerusalem,* reborrowing of Latin *multifārius* manifold, from *multifāriam* in many places or parts (*multi-* many + *-fāriam* parts, as in *bifāriam* in two parts, in two ways); for suffix see -OUS. Compare OMNIFARIOUS.

The second element of the Latin compound is now often given as a base form *fās,* originally, utterance, expression, cognate with *fārī* to tell and *fābula* story. The *-s* of *fās,* once between vowels would become *r,* but semantic development of this analysis poses problems.

Earlier and separate borrowings in Middle English from Latin include the forms *multipharie,* adj., in Lydgate's *Tale of Two Merchants* (before 1449); borrowed from Latin *multifārius,* adj., and *multiphary,* adv. (1436); borrowed from Late Latin *multifāriē,* probably also from Latin *multifārius,* adj.

multiple *adj.* 1647, involving many parts, elements, etc., manifold; borrowing of French *multiple,* from Late Latin *multiplus* manifold (Latin *multi-* many + *-plus* -FOLD). **—n.** number that contains another number (a certain number of times without a remainder). 1685, from the adjective.

multiplicand (mul′təpləkand′) *n.* number to be multiplied by another. 1594, borrowed from Middle French *multiplicande,* learned borrowing from Latin *multiplicandus,* gerundive of *multiplicāre* MULTIPLY.

Multiplicand replaced the earlier *multipliant,* found in *The Art of Numbering* (before 1500); borrowed from Old French *moltipliant,* past participle of *moltepliier,* from Latin *multiplicāre.*

multiply *v.* Probably about 1150 *multeplier* to cause to increase; later *multiplyen* to perform the arithmetical operation of multiplication (before 1398, in Trevisa's translation of *De Proprietatibus Rerum*); borrowed from Old French *multiplier,* from Latin *multiplicāre* to increase or multiply, from *multiplex* (genitive *multiplicis*) having many folds, many times as great in number (*multi-* many + *-plex,* related to *plicāre* to fold; see PLY[2] fold).

—multiplication *n.* Probably about 1350 *multyplicatione;* later *multiplicacioun* (about 1380); borrowed from Old French *multiplication,* from Latin *multiplicātiōnem* (nominative *multiplicātiō*), from *multiplicāre* multiply; for suffix see -ATION. **—multiplicity** *n.* About 1454 *multiplicite;* borrowed from Middle French *multiplicité,* from Late Latin *multiplicitās* manifoldness, from Latin *multiplex* manifold (*multus* many + *-plex* -fold, from *plicāre* fold); for suffix see -ITY.

multitude *n.* a great many, crowd. About 1340, in Richard Rolle's *The Psalter;* borrowed from Old French *multitude,* learned borrowing from Latin, and borrowed directly from Latin *multitūdō* (genitive *multitūdinis*) a great number, crowd, from *multus* much, many; see MULTI-; for suffix see -TUDE. **—multitudinous** *adj.* very numerous. 1629, in Donne's *Sermons;* formed in English from Latin *multitūdin-* (in *multitūdinis,* genitive of *multitūdō*) multitude + English suffix *-ous.*

mum *adj.* silent, saying nothing. 1521, developed from Middle English *mum,* n., inarticulate sound made with closed lips (about 1405); earlier *mom* (before 1376, in *Piers Plowman*); of imitative origin. **—interj.** hush! silence! 1568, probably from the adjective. The expression *mum's the word,* with the meaning of be silent, is first recorded before 1704. The form *mum,* interj., cited in OED is in reference to the character *mum* in *mum and soth-segger* (about 1399), who believes in hiding unpleasant truths, and is not an interjection.

mumble *v.* About 1325 *momelen* (meaning uncertain, perhaps, to talk with one's mouth full); later, to speak indistinctly (about 1350); probably of imitative origin, similar to Middle Dutch *mommelen* to mumble, modern German *mummeln,* Swedish *mumla,* and Danish *mumle.* **—n.** a mumbling. 1902, from the verb.

mumbo jumbo, foolish or meaningless incantation, talk, or writing. 1896, in Farmer and Henley's *Slang and Its Analogues,* from earlier *Mumbo-Jumbo* grotesque bogy or idol supposedly worshiped in Africa (1738); a borrowing perhaps from Mandingo *mama* ancestor + *dyumbo* pompom-wearer.

mummer *n.* person who wears a mask, fancy costume, or disguise for fun. About 1405 *mummer* one who conceals the truth in silence; later, actor in a pantomime (1429); probably a fusion of: 1) borrowing from Middle French *momeur* mummer, from *momer* mask oneself, from *momon* mask, perhaps of imitative origin; and 2) development in Middle English *mommen* to mutter, be silent (about 1390), from or related to *mum,* adj.; for suffix see -ER¹. **—mummery** *n.* performance of mummers. 1530, in Palsgrave's *Lesclarcissement;* probably formed in English from *mummer* + *-y*³ after Middle French *momerie* masquerade, from *momer* mask oneself. The transferred meaning of silly show or ceremony, is first recorded in 1549,

mummy *n.* body embalmed to preserve from decay. 1392 *mummie* medicinal preparation made from bone or tissue of mummies; borrowed from Medieval Latin *mumia,* from Arabic, transcribed as *mūmiyāh* embalmed body from Persian *mūmiyā* asphalt, from *mūm* wax. The meaning of embalmed body is first recorded in 1615. **—mummification** *n.* process of mummifying. 1800, formed from English *mummify,* after such pairs as *sanctify, sanctification;* for suffix see -FICATION. **—mummify** *v.* make into a mummy. 1628, formed from English *mummy* + *-fy.*

mumps *n.pl.* contagious viral disease. 1598, in Florio's *A World of Words,* from the plural of obsolete *mump* a grimace (1592), of uncertain origin, but probably connected with the sense of grimace because the disease causes swelling of the face, and perhaps further with *mum* because the accompanying soreness of the throat makes speaking difficult.

munch *v.* chew steadily. Before 1325 *mocchen* to eat greedily, chew audibly; later *mucchen* (about 1385); perhaps of imitative origin, but possibly influenced in later forms by *mangen* to eat (before 1376; later *maungen,* about 1385); borrowed from Old French *mangier,* from Latin *mandūcāre* to chew; see MANGER. **—n.** something to eat. Before 1816, from the verb. **—munchies** *n.pl.* 1959, American English, food or snack; formed from *munch,* n. + *-ie,* diminutive suffix, + *-s.*

mundane *adj.* worldly. Probably about 1451 *mondeyne* of this world, earthly; borrowed from Middle French *mondain,* learned borrowing from Latin *mundānus* belonging to the world, from Latin *mundus* universe, world; possibly identical with *mundus* adorned, elegant, or ornament, decoration, of uncertain origin (compare Greek *kósmos* ornament, COSMOS); for suffix see -ANE.

municipal *adj.* About 1540, of or having to do with the affairs of a state; later, of a city or town (1600); borrowed from Middle French *municipal,* learned borrowing from Latin, and borrowed directly from Latin *mūnicipālis* of or belonging to a citizen or a free town, from *mūniceps* (genitive *mūnicipis*) citizen, inhabitant of a town having self-government (*mūnus* office, duty + *-ceps,* related to *capere* assume, take, see CAPTIVE); for suffix see -AL¹. **—municipality** *n.* city, town, etc., having local self-government. 1790, borrowed from French *municipalité,* from Middle French *municipal* municipal; for suffix see -ITY.

munificence *n.* very great generosity. About 1425 *munyficence,* borrowed from Middle French *munificence,* learned borrowing from Latin *mūnificentia,* from the comparative stem *mūnificent-* of *mūnificus* generous (*mūnus,* genitive *mūneris,* gift or service, duty, office + *-ficus,* related to *facere* perform, DO¹); for suffix see -ENCE. Latin *mūneris* is cognate with Lithuanian *maĩnas* exchange, and Sanskrit *ni-mayate* changes, from Indo-European **mei-/moi-* exchange, service (Pok. 710). **—munificent** *adj.* 1583, in Hakluyt's *Voyages,* from *munificence,* patterned on *magnificence, magnificent;* for suffix see -ENT.

munition *n.* military supplies. 1448 *municion* a right or privilege by document; later *monysyon* provision (before 1533); borrowed from Middle French *municion* fortification, and directly from Latin *mūnītiōnem* (nominative *mūnītiō*) a defending, fortification, from *mūnīre* to fortify, from *moenia* defensive walls; related to *mūrus* wall; see MURAL; for suffix see -TION. The plural form *munitions* military supplies, especially ammunition, is first recorded before 1533. **—adj.** having to do with military supplies. 1569, from the noun. **—v.** provide with military supplies. 1578-79, from the noun.

muon (myü'on) *n.* elementary particle having a mass about 207 times that of the electron. 1953, shortened form of earlier *mu-meson;* (1952), formed in English from Greek *mu* twelfth letter of the Greek alphabet (μ), used as an arbitrary designation in a series + English *meson.*

mural *adj.* of or on a wall. Probably before 1439, in Lydgate's *Falls of Princes;* borrowed from Latin *mūrālis* of a wall, from *mūrus* wall; for suffix see -AL¹. Latin *mūrus* is probably from Old Latin *moerus, moirus,* related to *moenia* defensive walls, which is cognate with Sanskrit *minóti* fortifies, founds, builds, Old Icelandic *mǣri* in *landamǣri* borderland, Middle Dutch *mēre* stake, and Old English *mǣre, gemǣre* boundary, from Proto-Germanic **ʒa-mairja-,* from Indo-European **mei-/moi-/mi-* fortify, strengthen (Pok. 709). **—n.** pic ture painted on a wall. 1921, shortened form of *mural painting,* from *mural,* adj.

murder *n.* Probably before 1200 *morthre,* in *Ancrene Riwle;* later *murthre* (before 1250), and *murdre* (before 1300); developed from Old English *morthor* secret killing of a person, unlawful killing (about 725, in *Beowulf*); cognate with Gothic *maúrthr* murder, from Proto-Germanic **murthran.* A synonymous word from the same root as the source of Old English *morthor* is found in all the Germanic languages except Gothic: Old Frisian and Old Saxon *morth* murder, Middle Dutch *moort* (modern Dutch *moord*), Old High German *mord* (modern German *Mord*), and Old Icelandic *mordh,* from Proto-Germanic **murtha-.* Outside Germanic cognates are found in Latin *mors* (genitive *mortis*) death, *morī* to die, Old Irish *marb* dead, Greek *brotós* mortal, Lithuanian *mir̃ti* to die, Old Slavic *mrěti,* Armenian *meṙanim* I die, Sanskrit *mara-s, māra-s* death, *mṛtá-s* dead, *mriyáte* (he) dies, and Hittite *merta* he died, from Indo-European **mer-/mor-/mr̥-* to die (Pok. 735).

The spelling with *d* in Middle English *murdre,* probably developed from the influence of Anglo-French *murdre,* from Old French *mordre,* and Medieval Latin *murdrum,* from Germanic.
—**v.** to kill unlawfully. Probably before 1200 *murthren,* in Layamon's *Chronicle of Britain,* and *Ancrene Riwle;* later *murdren* (before 1300); from the noun. The spelling *murdren* developed from Anglo-French and Old French *murdrir* to murder, from *murdre,* n.
—murderer *n.* 1340, in *Ayenbyte of Inwyt;* developed from earlier *murtherer* (before 1325, in *Cursor Mundi*); probably in part borrowed from Old French *mordrere, murdëour* and Medieval Latin *murdrarius,* and in part developed from Old English *myrthra.* **—murderess** *n.* 1588, formed from English *murder* + *-ess.* **—murderous** *adj.* 1535, in the Coverdale Bible; formed from English *murder* + *-ous.*

murk *n.* darkness, gloom. About 1303 *myrke,* in Mannyng's *Handlyng Synne;* probably borrowed from a Scandinavian source (compare Old Icelandic *myrkr* darkness, from *myrkr* dark; cognate with Old English *mirce, mierce* dark, and Old Saxon *mirki*). The spelling *murk* is first recorded in Shakespeare's *All's Well That Ends Well* (1601). **—murky** *adj.* 1340 *mirky;* later *murky* (1605 in Shakespeare's *Macbeth*), formed from Middle English *myrk* + *-y*[1].

murmur *n.* About 1380 *murmure* continuous noise, grumbling, in Chaucer's *House of Fame;* borrowed from Old French *murmure* and directly from Latin *murmur* a humming, muttering, roaring, rushing, probably of imitative origin. Similar formations are found in Greek *mormýrein* to roar, boil, Lithuanian *murménti, murmlénti* to murmur, Armenian *mrmram, mrmrim* I murmur, Sanskrit *marmara-s* murmuring, rustling, Old High German *murmurōn, murmulōn* to murmur, and German *murmeln.* These are reduplicated forms of an imitative root, perhaps in Indo-European (represented by Old Icelandic *murra* to murmur, Middle Low German *murren,* Middle Dutch and modern Dutch *morren,* and Old English *murcian* to complain, grieve) which would explain the strong resemblance between the different forms. —**v.** Before 1325 *murmuren,* in *Cursor Mundi;* borrowed from Old French *murmurer* and directly from Latin *murmurāre,* from *murmur,* n.

murrain (mėr′ən) *n.* infectious disease of cattle. 1303 *moreyne* plague, pestilence, death, in Mannyng's *Handlyng Synne;* later, *morayne* (before 1400); borrowed from Old French *morine,* and directly from Medieval Latin *morina* plague, from Latin *morī* to die; see MURDER. The specific sense of a disease of cattle is first recorded in 1421.

muscatel (mus′kətel′) *n.* strong, sweet wine made from muscat grapes. 1535, in the Coverdale Bible, variant form of Middle English *muskadell* (probably before 1400, in *Morte Arthur*); borrowed from Medieval Latin *muscatellum, muscadellum,* probably from Provençal *muscat* with the fragrance of musk, musky, from *musc* musk, from Late Latin *muscus* musk; see **MUSK**.

muscle *n.* 1392 *mucell;* later *muscle* (probably before 1425); borrowed from Latin *mūsculus* a muscle; literally, little mouse, diminutive of *mūs* MOUSE; so called from the resemblance between some muscles and the shape of a mouse; also, sometimes referred to the rippling motion of a muscle and that of a mouse. The same sense development is found in Greek *mŷs,* meaning both mouse and muscle, and German *Maus,* meaning mouse and ball of the thumb. —**v.** *Informal.* use muscles or strength; move with force. 1913, from the noun. **—muscular** *adj.* of or having muscles. 1681, formed in English from Latin *mūsculus* muscle + English *-ar.*

muse *v.* think, meditate. 1340 *musen,* in *Ayenbite of Inwyt;* borrowed from Old French *muser* to ponder or loiter, literally, stay with one's nose in the air, from *muse* muzzle, from Gallo-Romance **mūsa* snout, of uncertain origin.

At one time thought to be related to Italian *musare* to stare about, idle, loiter; or the Old French *muser* was considered to be derived from a lost noun **mus* muzzle, from Vulgar Latin **mūsus* (compare Medieval Latin *musus* snout); but FEW (VI, p.275) now confirms the existence of Old French *muse.*

Muse *n.* one of the nine Greek goddesses of the arts and sciences. About 1380, in Chaucer's *House of Fame;* borrowed from Old French *Muse,* and directly from Latin *Mūsa,* from Greek *Moûsa* (Aeolic *Moísa,* Doric *Môsa,* Spartan *Môha*), from earlier **montya,* of unknown origin.

museum *n.* 1615, in reference to the university building erected by Ptolemy in Alexandria; later, a study (about 1645); borrowing of Latin *Mūsēum* library or study, from Greek *Mouseîon* place of study, library or museum; originally, a seat or shrine of the Muses, from *Moûsa* MUSE. Early generalized use of *museum* in English was in the sense of a library, study, or place of learning (until 1973 the *British Museum* included an active library). The meaning of a building where objects of art, science, etc. are displayed, is first recorded in reference to the *Ashmolean Museum* in Oxford, England (opened 1683).

mush[1] *n.* corn meal boiled in water. 1671, American English, variant of *mash*[1] soft mixture. The meaning of a soft and pulpy mass, is first recorded in 1824. **—mushy** *adj.* 1839, formed from English *mush*[1] + *-y*[1]. The figurative sense of weakly sentimental is first recorded in 1870.

mush[2] *v.* travel through snow, usually with a dog sled. 1862 *mouche,* American English, perhaps from the command *mush on!;* possibly an alteration of French *marchons!* let us advance, imperative of *marcher* to MARCH[1]. The spelling *mush* is first recorded in Canadian English in 1897. —**n.** a journey through snow, usually with a dog sled. 1910, in Robert Service's *The Trail of '98;* from the verb.

mushroom *n.* 1440 *muscheron,* in *Promptorium Parvulorum;* later *musseroun* (about 1450); borrowed through Anglo-French *musherun,* Old French *moisseron,* from Medieval Latin *mussirionem* type of mushroom, of uncertain origin. **—adj.** of or like a mushroom. 1599, in Ben Jonson's *Every Man Out of His Humour;* from the noun. **—v.** 1893 (of bullets) become flattened at one end; from the noun. The meaning of grow very fast is first recorded in 1903 in American English. The spelling *mushroom* is first recorded in English in 1563, but is not fully established until the 1700's.

music *n.* About 1250 *musike,* in *The Story of Genesis and Exodus;* borrowed from Old French *musique,* learned borrowing from Latin and borrowed directly from Latin *mūsica,* from Greek *mousikḗ téchnē* art of the Muses, from *Moûsa* MUSE; for suffix see -IC. The spelling *music,* often attributed to Noah Webster, was already in use by Wordsworth, Gray, Johnson, and others before its appearance in Webster's dictionaries (1806-1829), and is first recorded in 1633. **—musical** *adj.* Probably about 1421 in Lydgate's writings; borrowed from Middle French *musical,* and directly from Medieval Latin *musicalis,* from Latin *mūsica* music; for suffix see -AL[1].—*n.* About 1500, musical instrument; later, musical performance (1579, in Spenser's *The Shepheardes Calender*); from *music,* n. The meaning of a play or motion picture in which music is the essential part is first recorded in 1938; a shortened form of *musical comedy* (1765). **—music box** (1773, in Goldsmith's *She Stoops to Conquer*) **—music hall** (1842, in Dickens' *American Notes*) **—musician** *n.* About 1380 *musicyen,* in Chaucer's translation of Boethius' *De Consolatione Philosophiae;* borrowed from Old French *musicien,* from *musique* music; for suffix see -IAN. **—musicology** *n.* 1909, probably formed from English *music* + *-ology,* after French *musicologie.*

musicale (myü'zəkal') n. social gathering to enjoy music. 1872, American English; borrowed from French *musicale,* shortened form of *soirée musicale* musical evening (party), recorded in an English context in 1846. An earlier appearance of the meaning as the English form *musical,* n., is recorded in Isaac D'Israeli's writings, in 1823.

musk *n.* substance with a strong odor, obtained from a gland of an Asiatic deer. 1394 *musk;* borrowed from Old French *musc,* learned borrowing from Late Latin, and borrowed directly from Late Latin *muscus,* from Late Greek *móschos,* from Persian, transliterated as *mushk,* from Sanskrit *muṣká-s* testicle, formed from the ancient oblique-case form **mus-* of *mū́s* MOUSE. **—musky** *adj.* of or like musk. About 1610, formed from English *musk* + *-y*[1].

muskellunge (mus'kəlunj) *n.* large freshwater fish. 1789 *masquenongez,* American English; borrowed from Canadian French *masquinongé,* a transcription of Algonquian (Ojibwa) *mâskinonjē,* literally, big fish. Many different spellings of this word have been recorded, including *muskinunge* (1798), *maskinonge* (1891), and *muskellunge* (1884).

musket *n.* old type of gun used before rifles were invented. About 1587, borrowed from Middle French *mousquette,* from Italian *moschetto* crossbow, arquebus; originally, a kind of hawk that looks as if speckled with flies, diminutive of *mosca* fly, from Latin *musca,* see MIDGE; for suffix see -ET.

Old guns were often named after animals, especially birds of prey; for example *falcon* and *falconet* (1496, 1559, light cannons), *basilisk* (1577, a large cannon), *serpentine* (about 1450, ship's gun).

The word appears in such a context in English as the name of the sparrow hawk, before 1398, in Trevisa's translation of Bartholomew's *De Proprietatibus Rerum.*

—musketeer *n.* soldier armed with a musket. 1590, in Marlowe's *Tamburlane the Great;* re-formed later from English *musket* + *-eer;* but originally borrowed from Middle French *mousquetaire,* from *mousquette* musket; for suffix see -EER. **—musketry** *n.* muskets. 1646, re-formed later from English *musket* + *-ry,* but originally borrowed from French *mousqueterie,* from Middle French *mousquet* musket; for suffix see -RY.

muskrat (mus'krat') *n.* water animal somewhat like a rat, and having a musky smell. 1607 (erroneous *muskat*); later *muskrat* (1688), American English, alteration (by association with *musk* and *rat*) of earlier *musquash;* a transcription of Algonquian (probably Powhatan) *muscascus,* literally, it is red; so called because of the animal's color.

muslin (muz'lən) *n.* fine cotton cloth. 1609 *Muslina* a kind of linen cloth, said to be brought to Aleppo from *Musola,* later *Muzlin* (1682); borrowed from French *mousseline,* from Italian *mussolina,* from *Mussolo* Mosul, a city in northern Iraq where muslin was formerly made and also used as a name for the cloth; from Arabic transcribed as *Mawṣil.* **—adj.** made of muslin. 1684, from the noun.

muss *v.* put into disorder, rumple. 1837, American English; possibly a variant of *mess,* in the sense of a disturbance or row; but more likely an extension in meaning of earlier *muss* a scramble or scrambling (1591, of uncertain origin). **—mussy** *adj.* 1859, American English, formed from *muss,* v. + *-y*[1].

mussel *n.* saltwater mollusk. 1298-99 *moscle;* 1307 *muscle,* also *muskel* (1307); developed from Old English (before 1000) *muscle, musle;* earlier *muscel* (before 850); borrowed from Vulgar Latin **muscula,* from Latin *mūsculus* mussel, (also) MUSCLE. Other early Germanic borrowings from Vulgar Latin **muscula* include Old Saxon and Old High German *muscula* mussel, Middle Low German *muschele,* and Middle Dutch *musscele.*

The spelling *mussel,* differentiated from *muscle,* is first recorded in Shakespeare's *The Tempest* (1610), but was not fully established before the 1870's.

must[1] *v.* have to. Before 1131 *moste* (past tense of *moten*); later *muste* (about 1250, in *The Story of Genesis and Exodus*); developed from Old English *mōste* (about 725, in *Beowulf*), past tense of *mōtan* have to, be obliged to, be able to. Old English *mōtan* is cognate with Old Frisian *mōta* have to, Old Saxon *mōtan,* Middle Dutch and modern Dutch *moeten,* Old High German *muozan* (modern German *müssen*), from Proto-Germanic **mōtanan* and Gothic *gamōtan* to have room; derived from the Proto-Germanic root that is the source of Old English *metan* to measure; see METE[1] allot. **—n.** necessity, obligation. 1892, American English, from the verb. **—adj.** *Informal.* necessary, obligatory, 1912, American English, from the noun.

must[2] *n.* new wine. Old English *must* (before 899, in

Alfred's translation of Boethius' *De Consolatione Philosophiae*); borrowed from Latin *vīnum mustum* fresh wine, neuter of *mustus* fresh or new, of uncertain origin.

must[3] *n.* musty condition, mold. 1602, perhaps back formation from MUSTY.

must[4] *n.* 1878, dangerous excitement or frenzy, as that of a male elephant at certain periods; noun use of earlier *must,* adj. (1871); borrowed from Hindi, transcribed as *mast* intoxicated, in rut, from Persian.

mustache or **moustache** (mus'tash) *n.* 1585, borrowed from French *moustache,* from Italian *mostaccio, mostacchio,* from Medieval Greek *moustákion,* diminutive of Doric Greek *mýstax* (genitive *mýstakos*) upper lip, mustache, alteration (under influence of *mýllon* lip) of *mástax* jaws, mouth. Greek *mástax* (genitive *mástakos*), related to *máthyiai* jaws and *masâsthai* to chew is cognate with Irish *méadal* stomach, intestines, from Indo-European **menth-/mn̥th-* chew (Pok. 732).

The meaning is recorded earlier in English *mustachio,* n. (1551) as a borrowing directly from Italian *mostacchio* mustache, but the form is now found in the plural *mustachios* and suggests a large mustache. The pronunciation with *sh* instead of the expected Italian *ch* [k] is probably a late development that results from influence of *mustache.*

mustang *n.* small wild horse of the North American plains. 1808, American English; borrowed from Mexican Spanish *mestengo* animal that strays, from earlier Spanish *mestengo* wild, stray, ownerless; literally, of the *mesta,* from *mesta* association of graziers who divided strays or unclaimed animals, from Latin *mixta* mixed, feminine past participle of *miscēre* to MIX.

mustard *n.* seasoning made from the hot, sharp-tasting seeds of the mustard plant. 1289 *mostard;* later *mustard* (1391); borrowed from Old French *mostarde, mustarde,* from *moust* must, from Latin *mustum* MUST[2] new wine (so called because mustard was originally prepared by adding must or new wine to ground mustard seeds).

muster *v.* gather together, collect. Before 1325 *musteren* to display, reveal, appear, be present, in *Cursor Mundi;* later *moustren* (before 1420) and *musteryn* (1440) to assemble, in reference to troops; borrowed from Old French *mostrer,* from Latin *mōnstrāre* to show, from *mōnstrum* omen, sign; see MONSTER. **—n.** assembly, collection. About 1378 *moustre* and *mustre* (before 1425) display, collection; also *mostre* (about 1400) and *moustre* (before 1420) assembling of troops for review; borrowed from Old French *mostre,* from *mostrer,* v. The expression *pass muster* to be inspected and approved, is first recorded in 1575, as *pass the muster.*

musth *n.* See MUST[4]. The spelling *musth* was first used by Kipling in *Departmental Ditties* (1886), either to give the word a foreign or exotic appearance or to distinguish it from other words spelled *must,* e.g. *must*[1], *must*[2], etc.

musty (mus'tē) *adj.* having a smell or taste suggesting mold. 1530, in Palsgrave's *Lesclarcissement,* perhaps a variant of earlier *moisty* moist or damp, new, in reference to ale (about 1390, in Chaucer's *Canterbury Tales*); formed from English *moist* + *-y*[1].

mutable *adj.* liable to change. About 1380, in Chaucer's translation of Boethius' *De Consolatione Philosophiae;* borrowed, possibly by influence of Old Provençal *mutable,* from Latin *mūtābilis* changeable, from *mūtāre* to change; see MISS[1], v.; for suffix see -ABLE. **—mutability** *n.* About 1380 *mutabilite,* in Chaucer's translation of Boethius above; borrowed from Old French *mutabilité,* and directly from Latin *mūtābilitātem* (nominative *mūtābilitās*), from *mūtābilis* mutable; for suffix see -ITY.

mutagen (myü'təjən) *n.* agent that induces mutation in an organism. 1946, formed in English from Latin *mūtāre* to change (see MISS[1], v.) + English *-gen* thing that produces.

mutant (myü'tənt) *n.* new genetic character resulting from mutation. 1901, borrowed from Latin *mūtantem* (nominative *mūtāns*) changing, present participle of *mūtāre* to change; see MISS[1], v. **—adj.** 1903, from the noun.

mutation *n.* change, alteration. About 1380 *mutacion* act or process of changing, in Chaucer's translation of Boethius' *De Consolatione Philosophiae;* borrowed from Old French *mutacion,* and directly from Latin *mūtātiōnem* (nominative *mūtātiō*) a changing, from *mūtāre* to change; see MISS[1], v.; for suffix see -ATION.

The specific application in biology to the kind of change which results in new genetic characteristics or a new species, is first recorded in 1894 in American English.

—mutate *v.* to change, undergo or produce mutation. 1818, to change; later, to undergo genetic mutation (1913); probably a back formation from *mutation,* though the earlier use in 1818 may be a borrowing from Latin *mūtātus,* past participle of *mūtāre* to change.

mute *adj.* About 1385 *muwet, mewet* silent, speechless, in Chaucer's *Troilus and Criseyde;* later *muet* (about 1408); borrowed from Old French *muet,* diminutive of *mut* and *mu,* and directly from Latin *mūtus* silent, dumb. Latin *mūtus* is cognate with Greek *mȳkós, mȳ̂tēs* mute, Armenian *munǰ,* and Sanskrit *mū́ka-s* mute, from Indo-European **mu-, mū-* imitation of a dull sound made with tight-pressed lips (Pok. 751). **—n.** person who cannot speak. About 1378 *mute,* in a version of *Piers Plowman;* from the adjective. **—v.** put a device on a musical instrument to soften the sound. 1883, from the adjective.

mutilate *v.* cut, tear, or break off a limb, etc., maim, mangle. 1534, in Sir Thomas More's *Works;* probably, in part, developed from *mutilate,* adj., mutilated (1532), borrowed from Latin *mutilātus;* and in part, borrowed directly from Latin *mutilātus,* past participle of *mutilāre* to cut or lop off, from *mutilus* maimed, from Indo-European **mutos* curtailed (Pok. 753); for suffix see -ATE[1]. **—mutilation** *n.* 1525, act of disabling or wounding in a limb; borrowed perhaps from Middle French *mutilation,* and directly from Late Latin *mutilātiōnem* (nominative *mutilātiō*), from Latin *mutilāre;* for suffix see -ATION.

mutiny *n.* 1567, discord or contention; later, open rebellion (1579), formed from obsolete English *mutine* to revolt + *-y*[3]. Early modern English *mutine* was borrowed from Middle French *mutiner* to revolt, from *mutin, meutin* rebellious, from *meute, muete* a revolt, movement, from Vulgar Latin **movita* a military rising or revolt, from feminine past participle of *movēre* to MOVE. For a parallel to this formation compare Vulgar Latin **fallita* lack (whence French *faute*) from Latin *fallere*, or Vulgar Latin **perdita* (whence French *perte* loss) from Latin *perdere*. **—v.** take part in a mutiny, rebel. 1584, from the noun. **—mutineer** *n.* person who takes part in a mutiny. 1610, in Shakespeare's *The Tempest;* borrowed from French *mutinier*, from Middle French *mutin* rebellious. The term finally replaced earlier *mutine* (1581, in this sense), also found in Shakespeare's *King John* (1595). **—mutinous** *adj.* 1578, either formed from English *mutin* mutiny (1560) + *-ous;* or borrowed from Middle French *mutineus*, from *mutin* mutiny, for suffix see -OUS.

mutt (mut) *n.* 1901, American English, a stupid or foolish person; later, a dog, especially a mongrel (1906). The meaning of a stupid person is probably a shortened form of *muttonhead* (1803, a compound of *mutton* + *head*); the sense of a mongrel dog, may have been derived from the meaning of a stupid person, or it may be of independent derivation.

mutter *v.* Before 1333 *moteren* to mumble; later *muttren* (probably before 1450); borrowed from Latin *muttīre* to mutter. The Latin word is probably cognate with Old High German *mutilōn* to murmur, and Old Icelandic *mudhla*. **—n.** act of muttering. 1634, in Milton's *Comus;* from the verb.

mutton *n.* meat from a sheep. Probably before 1300 *motoun*, in *Kyng Alisaunder;* later *mutton* (about 1450); borrowed from Old French *moton, mouton* ram, wether, sheep, and from Medieval Latin *multonem*, from Gallo-Romance **multōnem* ram, probably from the accusative of Gaulish **multō* (compare Old Irish *molt* wether, Middle Breton *mout*, and Welsh *mollt*).

mutual *adj.* reciprocal. 1539, attributed to Cromwell, in Merriman's *Life and Letters of Thomas Cromwell;* borrowed from Middle French *mutuel*, from Latin *mūtuus* reciprocal; related to *mūtāre* to change, exchange; see MISS[1], v. **—mutual fund** (1950, American English)

muumuu or **mumu** (mü'mü') *n.* long, loose-fitting cotton dress, originally worn by Polynesian women. 1923, borrowed from Hawaiian *mu'u mu'u*, literally, cut off, shortened (so called because the yoke was formerly left off the garment and often the sleeves were short).

muzhik or **muzjik** (müzhik' or mü'zhik) *n.* Russian peasant. 1568, borrowed from Russian *múzhik*, diminutive of *muzh* MAN. Russian peasants were referred to as little men, because they were deemed minors under ancient Russian law. Several variant forms have been recorded for this word in English; the spelling *muzhik* appeared in 1877.

muzzle *n.* About 1385 *mosel* a halter for an animal, in Chaucer's *Canterbury Tales;* later, snout (about 1410), and *musel* (probably before 1421); borrowed from Old French *musel*, from *muse* muzzle, from Gallo-Romance **mūsa* snout, of unknown origin.

The extended meaning of an end of a firearm from which the shot is discharged, is first recorded in 1566. **—v.** put a muzzle on. Probably before 1430 *moselyn*, in Lydgate's writings; later *musellen* (before 1450); from the noun. The figurative sense of force to keep quiet, is first recorded in Shakespeare's *A Winter's Tale* (1611) and *Henry VIII* (1613).

my *adj.* Probably about 1200 *mī* belonging to me, in Lydgate's *Chronicle of Britain;* variant form before consonants of *mīn* MINE[1]. **—interj.** *Informal.* exclamation of surprise. 1825, probably a shortened form of *my God!*

my- the form of *myo-* before a vowel, as in *myalgia* a muscular pain.

mycelium (mīsē'lēəm) *n.* main part of a fungus. 1836, New Latin, from Greek *mýkēs* mushroom, fungus (see MYCOLOGY) + New Latin *-lium*, perhaps as found in *epithelium*.

mycology (mīkol'əjē) *n.* branch of botany that deals with fungi. 1836, borrowed from New Latin *mycologia* study of fungi, from Greek *mýkēs* fungus + connective *-o-* + *-logiā* -logy.

myna or **mynah** (mī'nə) n. Asiatic bird that mimics human speech. 1769, borrowed from Hindi *mainā*. Some dictionaries derive Hindi *mainā* from Sanskrit *madana-s* love or passion, with numerous special senses, one of which is "bird," found only in lexicons, a fact that makes any connection with the Hindi name for the myna somewhat doubtful.

myo- a combining form meaning muscle, as in *myocardium* the heart muscle, *myoneural* having to do with muscle and nerve. Borrowed from Greek *myo-*, combining form of *mŷs*, genitive *myós* mouse, muscle. Greek *mŷs* is cognate with MOUSE, and Latin *mūs*, diminutive *mūsculus* mouse, MUSCLE.

myopia (mīō'pēə) *n.* near-sightedness. 1727-52, in *Chambers Cyclopaedia*, New Latin, from Late Greek *mȳōpiā* near-sightedness, from *mȳ́ōps* near-sighted (*myein* to shut + *ṓps*, genitive *ōpós* EYE). **—myopic** *adj.* near-sighted. 1800, formed from English *myopia* + *-ic*.

myriad (mir'ēəd) *n.* very great number. 1555 *myriade* ten thousand; borrowed from Middle French *myriade*, from Late Latin *mȳrias* (genitive *mȳriadis*) ten thousand, from Greek *mȳriás* (genitive *mȳriádos*) ten thousand, from *mȳríos* innumerable, countless, of unknown origin.

The figurative sense of countless numbers, multitudes, is also first recorded in 1555. **—adj.** innumerable, countless. Before 1800, in Coleridge's *Hymn to Earth;* from the noun.

myrrh (mėr) *n.* fragrant substance. About 1150 *mirra;* developed from Old English *myrre* (before 830, in the *Vespasian Psalter*); borrowed from Latin *myrrha*, from Greek *mýrrha*, from a Semitic source (compare Akkadian *murrû* myrrh, Hebrew *mōr*, and Arabic *murr*). The Old English *myrre* was an early borrowing from Latin, similar to Old Saxon *myrra*, Middle Dutch *myrre*, Old High German *myrra*, and Old Icelandic *mirra*.

myrtle *n.* evergreen shrub or vine. 1392, Middle English *mirtille* fruit of the myrtle, borrowed from Old French *mirtile*, from Medieval Latin *myrtilus*, diminutive of Latin *myrtus* myrtle tree, from Greek *mýrtos*, from the same (Semitic) source as Greek *mýrrha* MYRRH.

mystery[1] *n.* secret, secrecy. Before 1333 *mysterye* secret or hidden thing, religious doctrine beyond human understanding; borrowed from Latin *mystērium*, from Greek *mystḗrion* secret rite, secret doctrine, from *mýstēs* one who has been initiated, from *mȳ́ein* to shut the eyes (because only those already initiated were permitted to witness secret rites), earlier **mȳ́he-*, from **mȳse-*, from Indo-European **mu-s-/mū-s-* (Pok. 752). The sense of a detective or crime story is first recorded in English in 1908, in writings of Chesterton. **—mysterious** *adj.* 1616, probably borrowed from French *mys-*

térieux, from *mystère* mystery, from Latin *mystērium;* for suffix see -OUS.

mystery[2] *n. Archaic.* craft, trade. About 1390 *mysterye* ministry, service, in Chaucer's *Canterbury Tales;* later *mystrie* an art, handicraft (before 1400); borrowed from Medieval Latin *misterium,* alteration of Latin *ministerium* office, MINISTRY. The form in Medieval Latin was shortened by influence of Latin *mystērium* MYSTERY[1].

The *mystery plays,* medieval religious plays based on the Bible, were so named because they were often performed by members of craft guilds.

mystic *adj.* occult, secret, arcane. Before 1382 *mistyke* spiritually symbolic, in the Wycliffe Bible; borrowed from Old French *mistique,* and directly from Latin *mysticus,* from Greek *mystikós* secret, mystic, from *mýstēs* one who has been initiated; see MYSTERY[1] secret. The meaning of pertaining to occult practices, is first recorded in 1615. **—n.** person who believes in mystic things. 1679, in William Penn's writings; from the adjective. An earlier sense of symbolic meaning or interpretation, is recorded in Middle English before 1333. **—mystical** *adj.* About 1471 *mystical* enigmatic, obscure, symbolic; formed from English *mystic,* adj. and n. + *-ical.* The meaning of having a spiritual significance or value, is first recorded in Sir Thomas More's *Supplycacyon of Soulys* (1529). **—mysticism** *n.* beliefs of mystics. 1736 formed from English *mystic,* adj. and n. + *-ism.*

mystify *v.* bewilder, perplex. 1814, in Hazlitt's *Political Essays;* borrowed from French *mystifier* (*mystique* mystic, from Latin *mysticus* mystic + *-fier* -fy). **—mystification** *n.* 1815, borrowing of French *mystification,* from *mystifier* mystify; for suffix see -FICATION.

mystique (mistēk′) *n.* atmosphere of mystery about someone or something; mystic quality or air. 1891, borrowing of French *mystique,* n., a mystic; from the adjective, from Latin *mysticus* MYSTIC.

myth *n.* legend or story. 1830, in part borrowed, perhaps through French *mythe* (1818), and directly from New Latin *mythus,* from Greek *mŷthos* speech, thought, story, myth, of unknown origin; and in part probably a back formation from earlier *mythology* and perhaps *mythical.*

The earlier form *mythus,* though used by Coleridge in 1825, and later by Carlyle, Trench, and Thackeray, never became established in English but gave way to the popular *myth.*

—mythical *adj.* of myth, like a myth. 1678, formed in English from Late Latin *mȳthicus* legendary, from Greek *mȳthikós,* from *mŷthos* myth + English suffix -AL[1]. **—mythological** *adj.* 1614, in Sir Walter Raleigh's *The History of the World,* formed from English *mythology* + *-ical.* The less common variant, *mythologic* is first recorded in Samuel Butler's *Hudibras* (1664); probably a shortened form of *mythological.* **—mythology** *n.* body of myths. Before 1420 *methologie* the exposition or interpretation of myths, in Lydgate's *Troy Book,* later *mythologie* (about 1450); borrowed through Middle French *mythologie,* and directly from Late Latin *mȳthologia,* from Greek *mȳthologiā* legendary lore, from *mŷthos* myth; for suffix see -LOGY. The meaning of a body of myths, is first recorded in Gibbon's *Decline and Fall of the Roman Empire* (1781).

N

nab *v.* catch or seize suddenly. 1686, variant of earlier *nap* (1673), as in *kidnap;* possibly borrowed from a Scandinavian source (compare Norwegian *nappe* to catch, snatch, Swedish *nappa,* and Danish *nappe* to pinch, pull). A suggestion of the Scandinavian form is found in earlier Middle English *napand* grasping, greedy (before 1460), which shows much earlier use than is generally a part of the record of English.

nabob (nā′bob) *n.* native ruler in India under the Mogul empire. 1612, Anglo-Indian, borrowed from Hindi *nabāb,* from Arabic *nuwwāb,* plural of *nā'ib* deputy. The transferred meaning of a person of great wealth is first recorded in Walpole's *Letters* (1764).

nacre (nā′kər) *n.* mother-of-pearl. 1598, mollusk yielding mother-of-pearl, in Florio's *A World of Words;* borrowed from Middle French, from earlier Italian *naccaro,* borrowed from Arabic *naqqāra* small drum. The semantic transition from "drum" to "mollusk" has not been explained. As an alternative source Corominas suggests the related Arabic word *nāqūr* hunting horn, which the mollusk resembles in shape. The extended meaning of mother-of-pearl is first recorded in 1718.

nadir (nā′dər) *n.* point in the heavens opposite the zenith. 1391, in Chaucer's *Treatise on the Astrolabe;* borrowed from Medieval Latin (and possibly Old French) *nadir,* from Arabic *naẓīr* opposite to (the zenith). The figurative meaning of lowest point is first recorded in Walpole's *Letters* (1793).

nag[1] *v.* irritate or annoy by peevish complaints. 1825, to gnaw or nibble; 1828, annoy or irritate; perhaps borrowed from a Scandinavian source (compare Old Icelandic *nagga* to complain, groan, grumble, Icelandic *nagg* grumbling, dialectal Norwegian and Swedish *nagga* to gnaw, nibble, irritate).

nag[2] *n.* horse, especially an old or inferior horse. Probably before 1400 *nagge* small riding horse or pony, of uncertain origin (corresponding to Dutch *negge* small horse, perhaps related to Middle Dutch *nijgen, nighen* to NEIGH). The meaning of *nag* was extended as a generalized term of abuse by 1598, and probably from that developed the sense of an old or inferior horse, curiously not recorded until 1934, except in the form *naggy* (before 1800).

naiad (nā′ad *or* nī′ad) *n.* nymph guarding a stream or spring. Before 1393, in Gower's *Confessio Amantis;* borrowed from Latin *nāïas* (genitive *nāïadis*), from Greek *Nāïás* (genitive *Nāïádos*), from a lost noun **nāwā,* related to Homeric *náei* it flows, cognate with Sanskrit *snāuti* trickles, and Middle Irish *snāu, snō* stream, from Indo-European **snāu-/snəu-,* extended form of root **snā-/snə-* (Pok.971).

nail *n.* Probably before 1200 *nail,* in Layamon's *Chronicle of Britain;* probably about 1200 *neil,* in *Ancrene Riwle;* developed from Old English *-negl* metal peg, found in the compound *scōhnegl* shoe nail, before 800; earlier *nægel* fingernail, toenail (before 725). The Old English forms are cognate with Old Frisian *neil* nail, Old Saxon *nagal,* Middle Dutch *nāghel* (modern Dutch *nagel*), Old High German *nagal* (modern German *Nagel*), and Old Icelandic *nagl* fingernail (Swedish *nagel,* Danish *negl*), from Proto-Germanic **naʒlaz.* Cognates outside Germanic include Latin *unguis* fingernail, toenail, claw, Old Irish *ingen,* Old Welsh *eguin,* Welsh *ewin,* Cornish *ewyn,* Greek *ónyx* (genitive *ónychos*), Lithuanian *nãgas,* Old Slavic *nogŭtĭ,* and Sanskrit *nakhá-s,* from Indo-European **onogh-/ongh-/nogh-/n̥gh-* (Pok.780). In the development of meaning, that of a metal spike or pin derives from the animal claw or nail, so that the distinction in meaning had already been made before the word appeared in Old English, and both senses are recorded, for instance, in the *Corpus Glossary.* **—v.** fasten with a nail or nails. Probably before 1200 *neilen, nailen;* developed from Old English *næglian* (about 950, in the *Lindisfarne Gospels*). The Old English form is cognate with Old Saxon *neglian* to nail, Old High German *negilen,* Old Icelandic *negla* (Swedish *nagla,* Danish *nagle*), and Gothic *ganagljan,* from Proto-Germanic **ʒa-naʒlijanan.* The informal sense of secure by prompt action, catch, seize, is first recorded in 1760.

The wide variety of forms among the Indo-European cognates suggests to some scholars that forms in some languages, such as Sanskrit and Greek, underwent alterations by "popular" formation (for instance, that instead of the expected *gh* in Sanskrit, *kh* appears, and that while *y* and *ch* in Greek are ambiguous, as for example in that *ch* may come from either *kh* or *gh,* they may also be "popular" alterations; omission of *n̥* in Celtic, and the absence of a prothetic vowel in Germanic also suggest alteration). Perhaps some diversity is also the result of taboo, in which superstition, particularly that in relation to nail cuttings, and the ancient admonition to bury them in order to keep a part of oneself out of the hands of one's enemies, was extended to not talking about them except by indirection or in other terms.

naive (näēv′) *adj.* artless. 1654, borrowing of French *naïve,* feminine of *naïf,* from Old French *naïf* native or natural, from Latin *nātīvus* native, rustic. See the doublet NATIVE. **—naiveté** (näēv′tā′) *n.* quality of being naive. 1673, in Dryden's *Marriage-à-la-Mode,* borrowing of French *naïveté,* from Old French *naiveté* native disposition, from *naïv-* native or natural + *-eté* -ity.

naked *adj.* Probably before 1200 *naked,* in Layamon's *Chronicle of Britain;* developed from Old English *nacod* (about 725, in *Beowulf*); cognate with Old Frisian *naked* naked, Middle Dutch *nāket* (modern Dutch *naakt*), Old High German *nackot, nackat* (modern German *nackt*), Gothic *nagaths,* from Proto-Germanic **nakwađaz,* and Old Icelandic *nǫkkvidhr,* from Proto-Germanic **nakweđaz.* Cognates outside Germanic include Latin *nūdus* naked, Old Irish *nocht,* Welsh *noeth,* Greek *gymnós* (transposed from earlier **nugmós*), Lithuanian *núogas,* Old Slavic *nagŭ,* Sanskrit *nagná-s,* and Hittite *nekumanza,* from Indo-European **nog-wodhos, *nogw-tó-s, *nogw-nós, *nōgwos, *nogwos* (Pok.769).

Though *naked* has the appearance of a past participle in English (and a later verb, now obsolete, did develop by back formation in Middle English), and though corresponding or equivalent forms of *naked* occur in Germanic as early as Gothic, no verb appears in the earliest records.

namby-pamby *adj.* weakly simple or sentimental, insipid. 1745, from the earlier nickname *Namby Pamby,* rhyming alteration in allusion to the name of *Ambrose Philips,* 1674-1749, an English poet. The nickname *Namby Pamby* is first recorded in 1726, as the title of a farce by the English poet Henry Carey, about 1690-1743, which ridiculed Philips' verses addressed to infants. In 1733 *Namby Pamby* was used by Pope in *The Dunciad,* a satirical poem in which he ridiculed poets and writers like Philips.

—n. Before 1764, namby-pamby writing; later, a namby-pamby person (1885); from the adjective.

name *n.* About 1125 *name,* developed from Old English *nama* (about 725, in *Beowulf*); also *noma, nama* (before 725, in *Genesis A*). The Old English forms are cognate with Old Frisian *nama* name, Old Saxon *namo,* Middle Dutch *nāme* (modern Dutch *naam*), Old High German *namo* (modern German *Name*), Old Icelandic *nafn* (Swedish *namn,* Danish *navn*), and Gothic *namō,* from Proto-Germanic **namōn.* Cognates outside Germanic include Latin *nōmen* name, Old Irish *ainm,* Old Welsh *anu,* Greek *ónoma,* (Aeolic or Doric) *ónyma,* Old Prussian *emnes, emmens,* Old Slavic *imę,* Armenian *anun,* Sanskrit *nā́man-,* Tocharian A *ñem,* Tocharian B *ñom,* and Hittite *lāman* (with dissimilation of *n* to *l*). The variety of forms among the cognates suggests that a prothetic vowel was added before an original root form; from Indo-European **en (o)mn̥-/(o)nomn̥/nōmn̥* (Pok.321). **—v.** give a name to. About 1200 *namen;* developed from Old English (about 1000) *namian;* from the noun. **—nameless** *adj.* About 1380, unidentified; also, without reputation, in Chaucer's translation of Boethius' *De Consolatione Philosophiae;* formed from Middle English *name* + *-les* -less.

—namely *adv.* Probably before 1200, chiefly or especially; also, that is to say; formed from Middle English *name* + *liche* -ly[1]. **—namesake** *n.* one having the same name as another, one named after another. 1646, probably from the earlier phrase *for (one's) name-sake* for (one's) name's sake (1599).

nannofossil (nan′ōfos′əl) *n.* very small or microscopic fossil, as that of a bacterial colony. 1963, formed from English *nanno-* very small (see NANO-) + *fossil.*

nanny (nan′ē) *n. Especially British.* children's nurse. 1795, found earlier with reference to women in *nanny-house* a brothel (before 1700); probably from the name *Nanny,* a nickname of *Anne.*

nanny goat female goat. 1788, from the female name *Nanny,* a nickname of *Anne.* Compare *billy goat.*

nano- or **nanno-** a combining form meaning: **1** one billionth, as in *nanoequivalent, nanosecond, nanometer.* **2** very small, dwarf, as in *nanoplankton, nannofossil.* Borrowed from Greek *nânos, nánnos* dwarf, of unknown origin.

nanosecond (nan′əsek′ənd) *n.* billionth of a second. 1959, formed from English *nano-* + *second*[2], n.

nap[1] *v.* take a short sleep. Probably before 1200 *nappen;* developed from Old English (before 900), *hnappian* to doze, sleep lightly; earlier *hneappian* (before 830, in the *Vespasian Psalter*). The Old English forms are cognate with Old High German *hnaffezan* to nap (modern German dialect *nafzen*), and Norwegian *napp* nap, of unknown origin. **—n.** short sleep. About 1353 *nappe,* from the verb.

nap[2] *n.* surface of cloth. 1440 *noppe,* in *Promptorium Parvulorum;* borrowed from Middle Dutch *noppe* nap, tuft of wool. Middle Dutch *noppe* is cognate with Middle Low German *noppe* tuft of wool, Old Swedish *niupa* to pinch, Gothic *dishniupan* to tear, and Old English *hnoppian* to pluck, *āhnēopan* pluck off. The spelling *nap* appeared in 1589, perhaps influenced by Middle French *nape* tablecloth, from Old French (see NAPKIN).

napalm (nā′päm) *n.* thickened or jellied gasoline, used in incendiary bombs and flamethrowers. 1942, formed from English *na(phthenic)* + *palm(itic)* acids; so called because the aluminum salts of these acids are used in the manufacture of the chemical that thickens gasoline. **—v.** to attack with napalm. 1950, American English; from the noun.

nape *n.* back of the neck. Probably before 1300, in *Kyng Alisaunder,* of uncertain origin (perhaps related to Old French *hanap* a goblet, with reference to the concavity at the base of the skull; but earlier thought to be a variant of *knap* a knot or protuberance (before 1398). However, the date is significantly later for the knot or knob than the specific application to the nape of the neck; the spelling with *n-,* rather than *kn-* or *cn-,* is exceedingly rare and relatively late; and there are no recorded *kn-* spellings of *nape.*

naphtha (nap′thə) *n.* volatile liquid used as fuel and cleaning fluid. 1572, borrowing of Latin *naphtha,* from Greek *náphtha,* originally, an inflammable liquid issuing from the earth, from Iranian (compare Avestan *napta-* moist, and Persian *naft* naphtha). The word is also recorded in Middle English (about 1384), in the Wycliffe Bible, as *napte,* but was borrowed through Old French *napte,* from Latin *naphtha;* however, this form did not survive in English.

napkin *n.* 1384-85 *napkin, napekin;* formed in Middle English from Old French *nape* tablecloth (from Latin *mappa* napkin; see MAP) + Middle English *-kin* -kin (diminutive suffix).

napoleon *n.* an oblong pastry of rich cream filling in layers of flaky crust, usually served in strips. 1896, shortened form of earlier *Napoleon Cake* (1892, named after *Napoléon* I, Emperor of France, 1804-15).

narc (närk) or **narco** (när′kō) *n. Slang.* federal narcotics agent. 1960 *narco,* 1967 *narc,* both American English, shortened form of *narcotics agent.*

Narco appeared earlier in American English as a shortened form of *narcotics hospital* (1955) and of *narcotics addict* (1958).

narcissism (när′sisizəm) *n.* excessive love or admiration of oneself. 1905, in Havelock Ellis' *Studies in the Psychology of Sex;* borrowed from German *Narzissmus* (coined in 1899), from *Narziss* Narcissus, the beautiful youth in Greek mythology who fell in love with his own reflection in a spring and was changed into the plant narcissus (which grows beside springs); for suffix see -ISM.

An isolated use of *Narcissism* by Coleridge in a letter

dated January 15, 1822 is cited in the OED Supplement.
—narcissist *n., adj.* (person) characterized by narcissism. 1930, in Bertrand Russell's *The Conquest of Happiness;* formed from English *narcissism* + *-ist.*
—narcissistic *adj.* of or having to do with narcissism. 1916, formed from English *narcissism* on the analogy of such pairs as *egotism, egotistic* and *optimism, optimistic;* for suffix see -IC.

narcissus *n.* kind of flowering plant. 1548, in William Turner's *The Names of Herbs;* borrowed from Latin *narcissus,* from Greek *nárkissos,* probably from a pre-Greek Aegean word, but associated by folk etymology (from the plant's sedative effect) with Greek *nárkē* numbness; see NARCOTIC.

narcolepsy (när′kəlep′sē) *n.* disorder characterized by uncontrollable spells of sleepiness. 1880, borrowed from French *narcolepsie,* formed in French from Greek *nárkē* numbness + *lêpsis* seizure. **—narcoleptic** *adj.* affected by narcolepsy. 1904, borrowed from French *narcoleptique,* from *narcolepsie,* on the pattern of *épilepsie* epilepsy, *épileptique* epileptic.

narcosis (närkō′sis) *n.* insensible state caused by narcotics, narcotic stupor. 1693, New Latin *narcosis;* formed from Greek *nárkōsis,* from *narkoûn* to benumb; see NARCOTIC; for suffix see -OSIS. An earlier form appeared in Middle English *narcosite* narcosity, in a translation of Chauliac's *Grande Chirurgie* (probably before 1425), but remains unrecorded after that time.

narcotic *n.* drug that produces a dull, insensible, painless condition. About 1385 *narcotik,* in Chaucer's *Canterbury Tales;* borrowed through Old French *narcotique,* n., from *narcotique,* adj., and directly from Medieval Latin *narcoticum,* from Greek *narkōtikós* making stiff or numb, narcotic, from *narkoûn* to benumb or make unconscious, from *nárkē* numbness, cramp; for suffix see -IC. Greek *nárkē* is cognate with Armenian *nergev* thin, and Old Icelandic *snara* noose, SNARE[1].

In 1926 and thereafter, especially in the United States, the meaning of *narcotic* was extended to include any sedative, stimulant, or other type of drug that causes addiction and is legally controlled or prohibited.
—adj. having the properties and effects of a narcotic. 1601, in Holland's translation of Pliny's *Natural History;* borrowed through French *narcotique,* or possibly German *narkotisch* (1525, in Paracelsus), and directly from Medieval Latin *narcoticus, narcoticum.*

narrate *v.* relate, recount. 1656, probably a back formation from *narration,* possibly influenced in formation by Latin *narrātus,* past participle of *narrāre;* for suffix see -ATE[1]. **—narration** *n.* act of narrating. Probably before 1425 *narracioun,* in Trevisa's translation of Higden's *Polychronicon;* borrowed from Old French *narration* and directly from Latin *narrātiōnem* (nominative *narrātiō*), a relating, narrative, from *narrāre* relate, recount, explain, from a possible pre-Latin word **gnārāre,* related to Old Latin *gnārus* knowing, skilled (also found in IGNORE); further related to *gnōscere, nōscere* KNOW; for suffix see -ATION.

narrative *adj.* that narrates or recounts. About 1450 *narratyf;* borrowed from Middle French *narratif,* from Late Latin *narrātīvus* suited to narration, from Latin *narrāre* NARRATE; for suffix see -ATIVE. The modern spelling is first recorded in Bacon's *Of the Advancement of Learning* (1605). It is also probable that in some instances *narrative* was formed from English *narrate* + *-ive.* **—n.** story or account, tale. 1561 (in Scottish law) that part of a deed or document which contains a statement of the relevant or essential facts; 1566-67, an account or narration; probably from the adjective, and in some instances borrowed from Middle French *narrative,* originally feminine of *narratif,* adj.

narrow *adj.* 1137 *nareu,* in *Peterborough Chronicle;* later *narwe* (probably before 1200, in *Ancrene Riwle*), *narow* (before 1400); developed from Old English *nearu* (about 725, in *Beowulf*). Old English *nearu* is cognate with Old Saxon *naru* narrow, Dutch *naar,* Old High German *narwa* (modern German *Narbe*) scar, from Proto-Germanic **narwaz;* also cognate with modern German *Nehrung* narrow strip of land. spit, and perhaps with Old Icelandic *snœ̄ri* twisted rope, and Gothic *snōrjō* basket.
—n. narrows, narrow part of a river, strait, valley, etc. Probably before 1200 *nearewe* narrow part, place or thing, in *Ancrene Riwle;* later *narwe* (probably about 1300); from the adjective. The specific meaning "narrow part of a river, etc." is first recorded in 1633 (singular form); the plural *narrows* in 1743.
—v. make or become narrower. Before 1338 *narwen,* in Mannyng's *Chronicle of England;* developed from Old English (before 1000) *nearwian,* from *nearu,* adj.
—narrow-minded *adj.* prejudiced. 1625, in Ben Jonson's *The Staple of News.*

narwhal (när′hwəl) *n.* kind of arctic whale. 1658 *Narh whale;* later *Narwhale* (1747); alteration (by association with English *whale*) of Danish and Norwegian *narhval* or Swedish *narval,* related to Icelandic *náhvalur,* from Old Icelandic *nāhvalr* (*nār* corpse + *hval* WHALE; it is said to be so called from the resemblance of the whale's whitish color to that of a corpse). Even though the *r* in *nār* is a sign of inflection (the genitive is *nās*), the form does not suit the Danish and Norwegian.

nary (nãr′ē) *adj.* not, no, never a. 1746, American English, alteration and further contraction of *ne'er a,* a shortened form of *never a.* An earlier form of *ne'er a* is recorded in Middle English *ner a* (about 1325, in *King Horn*).

nasal *adj.* of or from the nose. 1656, in Blount's *Glossographia;* probably borrowed from French *nasal;* formed from Latin *nāsus* nose + French *-al* -al[1]; or adopted from a surviving Medieval Latin *nasalis,* from Latin *nāsus* NOSE; for suffix see -AL[1].

The word may also have survived in English medical or other technical terminology from Middle English *nasale* (probably before 1425, in a translation of Chauliac's *Grande Chirurgie*); borrowed from Medieval Latin *nasalis.*
—n. nasal sound. 1669, from the adjective. The word appears in Middle English with the meaning "nose-piece on a helmet" (probably about 1300, in *The Romance of Guy of Warwick*), and was borrowed from Middle French *nasal, nasel,* from Old French *nes* nose, from Latin *nāsus,* but this meaning probably remained separate, and the sense of a nasal sound was created from Blount's use of the adjective.

nascent (nā′sənt) *adj.* coming into existence. Before 1624, borrowed, perhaps by influence of earlier French *naissant,* from Latin *nāscentem* (nominative *nāscēns*), present participle of *nāscī* be born; see NATIVE; for suffix see -ENT.

nasturtium (nəstėr′shəm) *n.* kind of flowering plant.

About 1150 *nasturcium;* borrowed from Latin *nasturcium, nasturtium;* perhaps a compound, by popular etymology in reference to the plant's somewhat pungent smell, of *nāsus* NOSE + *torquēre* to twist (see TORTURE).

The earliest use of this word referred to a plant of the mustard family, such as the watercress. The ordinary current meaning of plant with showy flowers and sharp-tasting leaves and seeds is first recorded in 1704.

nasty *adj.* About 1390 *nasti* disgustingly dirty, foul, probably an alteration of Old French *nastre* bad, strange, shortened from earlier *villenastre* infamous, bad, ignoble, formed from *vilein* VILLAIN + *-astre* pejorative suffix (from Latin *-aster;* compare POETASTER); for suffix see -Y[1].

It is also possible that *nasty* was reinforced by a borrowing from a Scandinavian source (compare the stem **nasc-* possibly occurring in Swedish dialect *naskug* dirty, nasty. See R. de Gorog's *Etymology of Nasty,* in *American Speech,* 51, p. 276-78.

natal *adj.* of one's birth. About 1385 *natal,* in Chaucer's *Troilus and Criseyde;* borrowed from Latin *nātālis* pertaining to birth or origin, from *nātus,* past participle of *nāscī* be born; see NATIVE; for suffix see -AL[1]. Doublet of NOEL.

natant *adj.* swimming, floating. 1707, borrowed from Latin *natantem* (nominative *natāna), present participle of natāre* to float, swim, related to *nāre* to swim, and cognate with Homeric Greek *náei* it flows; see NAIAD; for suffix see -ANT. **—natatorial** *adj.* having to do with swimming. 1816, formed in English from Latin *natātōrius* (from *natātor* swimmer, from *natāre* to swim) + English *-al*[1].

nation *n.* Probably before 1300 *nacioun* a country under one government, group of people of common descent, in *Kyng Alisaunder;* borrowed from Old French *nation,* and directly from Latin *nātiōnem* (nominative *nātiō*) nation, stock, race; also, birth, from *nāscī* be born; see NATIVE; for suffix see -TION. **—national** *adj.* 1597, borrowed from Middle French *national,* from Old French *nation* nation; for suffix see -AL[1]. It is also probable that in some instances *national* was formed from English *nation* + *al*[1]. The noun meaning "citizen of a nation" is first recorded in 1904. **—national debt** (1784, American English) **—National Guard** reserve militia of a state in the U.S. 1793, member of a French national militia; later, member of a state militia in the U.S. (1847). The current meaning of a state militia is first recorded in 1857. **—nationalism** *n.* 1836, doctrine of divine election of nations; later, devotion to one's own nation (1844); formed from English *national* + *-ism;* and, in some instances possibly borrowed from French *nationalisme* (*national* + *-isme* -ism). **—nationalist** *n.* 1715, formed from English *national* + *-ist.* **—nationality** *n.* 1691, national quality or character; later, condition of membership in a particular nation (1828); formed from English *national* + *-ity,* and in some instances possibly borrowed from French *nationalité* (*national* + *-ité* -ity). **—national park** (1868, American English) **—nationwide** *adj.* (1915)

native *adj.* About 1385 *natif* innate, natural, belonging to a person because of his birth, in Chaucer's *Troilus and Criseyde;* later *native* born in bondage (probably before 1425); borrowed from Old French *natif* (feminine *native*), learned borrowing from Latin, and borrowed directly from Latin *nātīvus* innate, produced by birth, natural, from *nāscī, gnāscī* be born, related to *gignere* beget; see KIN; for suffix see -IVE. Doublet of NAIVE. **—n.** About 1460 *natife* person born in bondage, from the adjective. In some instances the noun was probably borrowed from Medieval Latin *nativus,* noun use of Latin *nātīvus* innate. The meaning of a person born in a certain place is first recorded in 1535, in the Coverdale Bible; the meaning "person who lives in a place, as opposed to visitors and foreigners" is found in 1603.

nativity *n.* Probably before 1200 *nativite* the birth of Christ, in relation to a church festival; later *nativitie* (about 1400); borrowed from Old French *nativité* birth, from Late Latin *nātīvitātem* (nominative *nātīvitās*) birth, from Latin *nātīvus* born, NATIVE; for suffix see -ITY. The word also appears somewhat earlier (1105, in *Peterborough Chronicle*) as *nativiteth,* borrowed from Old French *nativited,* from Late Latin *nātīvitātem* (nominative *nātīvitās*).

NATO (nā′tō) *n.* North Atlantic Treaty Organization. 1950, American English, acronym formed from the initials of *N*orth *A*tlantic *T*reaty *O*rganization, established in 1949.

natter (nat′ər) *v.* to grumble, fret. 1829, northern, English dialect, variant of earlier *gnatter* to chatter, talk fretfully, grumble (1806-07); earlier, to gnaw or nibble away (1747); of uncertain origin; for suffix see -ER[4]. **—n.** idle or peevish chatter. 1866, northern English dialect; from the verb.

natty (nat′ē) *adj.* neatly smart in dress or appearance. 1785, perhaps alteration of earlier *nettie* neat, natty (1573), from Middle English *net* pure, fine, elegant (see NET[2]) + *-ie* -Y[1].

natural *adj.* produced by nature, not artificial. About 1250, in *Exodus and Genesis;* borrowed from Old French *naturel, natural,* and directly from Latin *nātūralis,* from *nātūra* NATURE; for suffix see -AL[1]. **—n.** one that is natural. Before 1325 *naturel* a natural ability or capacity; later, a native of a place or country (1509, perhaps as a new formation); both uses from the adjective. The informal meaning of a person with a natural gift or talent for something is first recorded in 1925 in American English. **—natural gas** combustible gas, usually methane (1825, in Canadian English). **—natural history** 1587, account of natural phenomena; later, study of animals, plants, minerals, and other things in nature (1662). **—naturalism** *n.* Before 1641, action arising from natural instincts; later, close adherence to nature or reality in art and literature (before 1850, in Dante Gabriel Rossetti's writings); formed from English *natural* + *-ism.* **—naturalist** *n.* 1587, one who studies natural rather than spiritual things; formed from English *natural* + *-ist.* The meaning of a student of natural history is first recorded in 1600, and that of an artist who practices or advocates naturalism in 1784. **—naturalize** *v.* admit (a foreigner) to the rights of a native citizen or subject. 1559, implied in *naturalized;* formed from English *natural* + *-ize,* and perhaps, in some instances, borrowed from Middle French *naturaliser,* from Old French *natural, naturel* natural + *-iser* -ize. **—natural law** (probably about 1425) **—natural resources** (1870) **—natural science** (before 1393)

nature *n.* About 1275, bodily processes, restorative powers of the body; later, innate character or disposition (about 1380), and inherent creative power or impulse (about 1385); borrowed from Old French *nature,* and directly from Latin *nātūra* birth, character, from *nāscī* be born; see NATIVE.

The meaning of the material world, the features and products of the earth is first recorded in 1662. The use of *nature* in the sense used in *human nature* is found in 1526.

naught or **nought** (nôt) *pron.* nothing. 1123 *naht;* 1175 *noht;* later *noght* (before 1325, in *Cursor Mundi*), *nought* (about 1385), *naught* (about 1390); developed from Old English *nōwiht,* n. (literally) no thing (about 830, in the *Vespasian Psalter*), a compound of *nā, nō* NO + *wiht* thing, creature, being (see WIGHT). Similar compounds appear in other Germanic languages, such as Old Saxon *neowith* nothing, Old High German *niwiht, neowiht* (modern German *nicht* not, *nichts* nothing), and Gothic *ni waíhts* nothing. **—n.** zero, nothing. Before 1325 *noght;* later *nawght* (about 1380); developed from Old English *nōwiht* (before 830, in the *Vespasian Psalter*). **—adj.** unworthy, worthless. Probably about 1200 *nawt* unacceptable; later *naght* unworthy (1402); developed from Old English (before 900) *nāwiht, nōwiht;* from the noun and pronoun. **—adv.** *Archaic.* in no way. Before 1121 *naht* not, not at all, in no way, in *Peterborough Chronicle;* later *noht* (1140); developed from Old English *nōwiht, nōwht* (before 830, in the *Vespasian Psalter*).

naughty *adj.* bad, not obedient. About 1378 *naughty* needy, having nothing, in a version of *Piers Plowman;* also *noghty* evil, immoral (1380); formed from Middle English *noght* nothing, evil, NAUGHT + *-y* -Y[1]. The meaning of not obedient is first recorded before 1633, but the milder sense of somewhat improper is recorded earlier in 1536.

nausea *n.* the feeling of being about to vomit. Probably before 1425, in a translation of Chauliac's *Grande Chirurgie;* borrowed from Latin *nausea* seasickness, from Ionic Greek *nausíē* seasickness, nausea, disgust (compare Attic Greek *nautíā*), from *naútēs* sailor, from *naûs* ship; see NAVY. Doublet of NOISE. **—nauseate** *v.* 1640, to feel nausea; later, to cause nausea (1654); formed from English *nausea* + *-ate*[1], after Latin *nauseāre* to be seasick, from *nausea;* for suffix see -ATE[1]. **—nauseous** *adj.* 1604, inclined to nausea, in Cawdrey's *A Table Alphabeticall;* later, causing nausea (1612); probably formed from English *nausea* + *-ous,* after Latin *nauseōsus,* from *nausea;* for suffix see -OUS. An extension of the older sense "inclined to nausea" is found in the meaning "feeling nausea, nauseated," which is first recorded in the 1950's in American English.

nautical *adj.* of ships, sailors, or navigation. 1552, borrowed, perhaps by influence of Middle French *nautique,* from Latin *nauticus* pertaining to ships or sailors, from Greek *nautikós,* from *naútēs* sailor, from *naûs* ship; see NAVY; for suffix see -ICAL. **—nautical mile** unit of distance equal to about one minute of longitude. 1834; earlier, *maritime mile* (1632).

nautilus (nô′tələs) *n.* kind of mollusk. 1601, in Holland's translation of Pliny's *Natural History;* borrowed from Latin *nautilus* a kind of marine snail, from Greek *nautílos,* originally, sailor, from *naútes* sailor, from *naûs* ship; see NAVY.

naval *adj.* Probably before 1425 *nauall* pertaining to a ship or ships, of a ship, in a translation of Chauliac's *Grande Chirurgie,* referring particularly to a distillation of ship's tar used in surgery; later *naval* of a navy (probably before 1439, in Lydgate's *Falls of Princes*); borrowed perhaps from Old French *naval,* and directly from Latin *nāvālis* pertaining to a ship or ships, from *nāvis* ship; see NAVY.

nave[1] *n.* long, narrow main part of a church. 1673, borrowed from Medieval Latin *navis* nave of a church, from Latin *nāvis* ship; see NAVY. The semantic connection between a ship and a church where the congregation sits or stands is traditionally said to be an allusion to the Christian church as a ship exposed to buffeting of the sea (but surely this borders on the resemblance of the long, narrow hall to the hull of a ship).

nave[2] *n.* hub of a wheel. Before 1325, developed from Old English *nafu, nafa* (before 899, in Alfred's translation of Boethius' *De Consolatione Philosophiae*); cognate with Middle Dutch *nave, naef* hub (modern Dutch *naaf*), Old High German *naba, napa* (modern German *Nabe*), Old Icelandic *nǫf* (Swedish *naf,* Danish *nav*), from Proto-Germanic **naƀō.* Cognates outside Germanic include Latvian *naba* navel, Old Prussian *nabis,* and Sanskrit *nábhya-m* hub, and *nā́bhi-s* hub, NAVEL.

navel *n.* umbilical knot on the abdomen. Probably about 1200 *navele;* developed from Old English (before 900) *nafela;* earlier *nabula* (before 800). The Old English forms are cognate with Old Frisian *navla* navel, Middle Low German and Middle Dutch *nāvel* (modern Dutch *navel*), Old High German *nabalo* (modern German *Nabel*), Old Icelandic *nafli* (Swedish and Danish *navle*), from Proto-Germanic **naƀalan.* Cognates outside Germanic include Old Prussian *nabis,* Greek *omphalós,* Latin *umbilīcus,* and Sanskrit *nā́bhi-s* navel, hub of a wheel, from Indo-European **nobh-/nōbh-/onbh-,* often with *l*-suffixes (Pok.314). **—navel orange** (1846, American English)

navigate *v.* 1588, probably a back formation from *navigation,* and in part, borrowed from Latin *nāvigātus,* past participle of *nāvigāre;* for suffix see -ATE[1]. **—navigable** *adj.* 1464, borrowed from Old French *navigable,* and probably directly from Latin *nāvigābilis* pertaining to sailing or sailing over, from *nāvigāre.* **—navigation** *n.* 1533, borrowed through French *navigation,* or directly from Latin *nāvigātiōnem* (nominative *nāvigātiō*), from *nāvigāre* to sail, sail over, go by sea, sail or steer a ship, from a lost adjective **nāvigus* steering or driving the ship, from *nāvis* ship (see NAVY) + the root of *agere* to drive; see AGENT; for suffix see -ATION. **—navigator** *n.* 1590, borrowed from Latin *nāvigātor* a sailor, from *nāvigāre;* for suffix see -OR[2].

navvy *n. Especially British.* a laborer on an artificial waterway, such as a canal, or on a railway. 1832-34, in De Quincey's writings; an altered and abbreviated form of earlier *navigator* a laborer employed in excavating a canal or artificial waterway (1775).

navy *n.* Before 1338 *navy,* in Mannyng's *Chronicle of England;* borrowed from Old French *navie* fleet or ship, from Latin *nāvigia,* plural of *nāvigium* vessel, boat, from *nāvis* ship. Latin *nāvis* is cognate with Greek *naûs* ship, Old Irish *nāu,* Armenian *nav,* and Sanskrit *nāú-s,* from Indo-European **nāus-* (Pok.755). **—navy bean** (1856, American English) **—navy blue** 1840; so called because it was the color of the British naval uniform.

nay *adv. Archaic.* no. Before 1325 *nai,* in *Cursor Mundi;* borrowed from a Scandinavian source (compare Old Icelandic *nei,* a compound of *ne* not + *ei* ever, AY[1]).

—n. no; a denial or refusal. Probably before 1300 *nay,* from the same source as the adverb.

Nazi (nät′sē) *n.* follower or supporter of Adolf Hitler and his policies. 1930, borrowing of German *Nazi,* a shortened and altered form of *Nationalsozialist* (pronounced nätsēonälzōtsēälist) National Socialist, a member or supporter of the *Nationalsozialistische Deutsche Arbeiter-Partei* National Socialist German Workers' Party, led by Hitler from 1920 and in power in Germany from 1933 to 1945.

According to Ernst Schwarz, in *Kurze deutsche Wortgeschichte* (1967), the name *Nazi* was based on the pattern of earlier German *Sozi,* short for *Sozialist* socialist.

—adj. of the Nazis. 1930, from the noun.

—Nazism *n.* doctrines and practices of the Nazis. 1934, formed from English *Nazi* + *-ism,* perhaps by influence of earlier French *Nazisme* (1930).

Neanderthal (nēan′dərthôl) *adj.* having to do with an extinct population of humans of the early Stone Age. 1861, borrowed from German *Neanderthal, Neandertal* Neander valley, a gorge near Düsseldorf, western Germany, where the first fossils of these humans were identified in 1856.

The figurative sense of resembling a Stone Age man or cave man (in attitude, appearance, etc.) is first recorded in 1928.

—n. Neanderthal man. 1923, in Alfred L. Kroeber's *Anthropology;* from the adjective.

neap (nēp) *adj.* of the lowest level of high tide. 1479 *neep;* developed from Old English (about 725) *nēp-,* as in *nēpflōd* neap flood; of unknown origin. **—n.** a neap tide. 1584, from the adjective.

near *adv.* Probably before 1200 *neor* close by, near, in Layamon's *Chronicle of Britain;* later *ner* (about 1250); developed from Old English *nēar* closer, nearer (about 725, in *Beowulf*), comparative of *nēah, nēh* NIGH. Cognate comparatives of Old English *nēar* include Old Frisian *niār* nearer, Old Saxon and Old High German *nāhōr,* Middle Dutch *naer,* modern German *näher,* Old Icelandic *nǣr,* and Gothic *nēhwis.*

Near meant originally "nearer" and was the comparative form of *nigh.* However, in Middle English *near* came to be used as a positive form, from which the new comparative *nearer* developed in the 1500's. The change from the comparative to the positive form may have been influenced by the Old Icelandic comparative *nǣr,* in such phrases as *ganga nǣr* go nearer (to), *standa nǣr* stand nearer (to), in which "nearer" can also be translated as "near."

—adj. close by. About 1300 *ner;* from the adverb.

—v. draw near, approach. 1513, from the adverb or adjective.

neat[1] *adj.* spruce, tidy. 1542, free of impurities, in Udall's *Works;* 1546, trim or smart, especially in dress; 1549, well-conceived or proportioned; later, tidy (1577); borrowed from Anglo-French *neit,* Old French *net* clear, pure, from Latin *nitidus* gleaming, from *nitēre* to shine. Latin *nitēre* is cognate with Middle Irish *nīam* radiance, beauty, Old Irish *nōib* holy, Old Persian *naiba-* and Persian *nēw* beautiful, good, from Indo-European **nei-/noi-/ni-, neyə-/nī-* be excited, beautiful; gleam (Pok.760).

The informal sense of very good, pleasant, attractive, is first recorded in 1934 in American English, in James T. Farrell's *Calico Shoes.*

neat[2] *n.pl. or sing. Obsolete.* cattle, oxen (found now in occasional use of *neat's-foot oil,* 1579). Probably before 1200 *net, nete;* developed from Old English (before 830) *nēat;* cognate with Old Frisian *nāt* cattle, Old Saxon *nōt,* Old High German *nōz,* and Old Icelandic *naut,* from Proto-Germanic **nautan,* related to Old English *nēotan* enjoy, Old High German *niozan* (modern German *geniessen* enjoy); cognate with Lithuanian *naudà* use, profit, from Indo-European **neud-/noud-* (Pok.768).

nebula (neb′yələ) *n.* cloudy cluster of stars or of gases and dust particles. Before 1449 *nebule* cloud or mist, borrowed from Latin *nebula* cloud or mist; 1661, film covering the eye, a reborrowing of Latin *nebula;* cognate with Greek *nephélē, néphos* cloud, Old Slavic *nebo* sky, Sanskrit *nábhas* fog, cloud mass, sky, and Hittite *nepis* sky. Germanic cognates (from Proto-Germanic **neƀlaz*) include Old Icelandic *njōl* night, Old High German *nebul* fog (modern German *Nebel*), Middle Dutch *nēvel* (modern Dutch *nevel*), Old Saxon *neƀal,* Old Frisian *nevil,* from Indo-European **nebh-* (Pok.315).

The astronomical meaning of a cloudy cluster of stars, gases, etc. was first recorded in 1727-38, in *Chambers Cyclopaedia.*

—nebular *adj.* having to do with a nebula or nebulae. 1837 *nebular hypothesis* the theory that the solar system developed from a nebula; later, consisting of or relating to a nebula (1856); from the noun; for suffix see -AR. **—nebulous** *adj.* Probably before 1425, cloudy or foggy, in a translation of Chauliac's *Grande Chirurgie;* borrowed from Latin *nebulōsus* cloudy, misty, foggy, from *nebula* mist; see NEBULA; for suffix see -OUS. The figurative sense of vague or indistinct, is first recorded in Carlyle's *Sartor Resartus* (1831). A variant *nebulose* is recorded as early as 1440, but has never achieved wide use.

necessary *adj.* About 1380, *necessarie* needed, required, essential, in Chaucer's translation of Boethius' *De Consolatione Philosophiae;* borrowed, perhaps in some instances through Old French *necessaire,* and directly from Latin *necessārius,* from *necesse* unavoidable, indispensable, necessary; originally, no backing away (*ne-* not; see NO + pre-Latin **cessis* withdrawal, an abstract noun to *cēdere* withdraw; see CEDE); for suffix see -ARY. **—n.** necessary thing. About 1340 (plural *necessaris* needs); borrowed from Latin *necessāria,* from neuter plural of *necessārius,* adj. The singular form *necessarie* is first recorded probably before 1425. **—necessitate** *v.* make necessary, require. 1628, borrowed perhaps by influence of French *nécessiter,* from Medieval Latin *necessitatus,* past participle of *necessitare* to compel, from Latin *necessitātem* (nominative *necessitās*) necessity, *necesse* necessary; replacing earlier Middle English *necesseden, necessen* (1380, in Chaucer's translation of Boethius' *De Consolatione Philosophiae*); borrowed from Late Latin *necessārī* to be made necessary, from Latin *necessārius,* adj.; for suffix see -ATE[1]. **—necessity** *n.* need. About 1380 *necessite,* in Chaucer's translation of Boethius' *De Consolatione Philosophiae;* borrowed from Old French *necessité,* learned borrowing from Latin *necessitātem* (nominative *necessitās*) compulsion, need for attention, from *necesse* necessary; for suffix see -ITY.

neck *n.* Probably about 1225 *nekke;* later *necke* (about 1250); developed from Old English *hnecca* neck, back of the neck (before 899, in Alfred's translation of St.

Gregory's *Pastoral Care*). Old English *hnecca* is cognate with Old Frisian *hnekka* neck, back of the neck, Middle Low German and Middle Dutch *necke* (modern Dutch *nek*), from Proto-Germanic **Hnekkōn,* earlier **kneknốn;* also cognate with Old High German *hnac* neck (modern German *Nacken* neck, *Genick* nape), and Old Icelandic *hnakki, hnakkr* neck, nape (Danish *nakke,* Swedish *nacke*), from Indo-European **knek-/knok-*. Cognates outside Germanic include Old Irish *cnocc* hill, Welsh *cnwch* joint, protuberance, Old Breton *cnoch,* and Tocharian A *k'ñuk* back of the neck, from Indo-European *kneuk-/knuk-* (Pok. 558, 559).
—v. *Slang.* hug, caress. 1825, originally northern English dialect, to clasp around the neck, fondle; from the noun.
—neckerchief *n.* About 1384, *neckercheuys,* in the Wycliffe Bible; later *nekkyrchefe* (1483); formed from Middle English *nekke* neck + *koverchief* kerchief. **—necklace** *n.* About 1590, formed from English *neck* + *lace* cord, string. **—neckline** *n.* 1672, narrow part of a bastion; 1904, line around the neck where a garment ends. **—necktie** *n.* 1838, formed from English *neck* + *tie* ornamental knot or bow, necktie.

necrology (nekrol'əjē) *n.* list of persons who have died. 1727-38, in *Chambers Cyclopaedia;* borrowed from New Latin *necrologia,* from Greek *nekrós* dead body + Latin *-logia* -logy. Greek *nekrós* is cognate with Sanskrit *náśyati* (he) disappears, perishes. Latin *nex* (genitive *necis*) violent death, *perniciēs* destruction, *nocēre* to harm; from Indo-European **neḱ-/noḱ-/n̥ḱ-* (Pok.762).

necromancy (nek'rəman'sē) *n.* foretelling of the future by communicating with the dead. 1550, alteration of Middle English *nigromaunce* (probably before 1300, in *Kyng Alisaunder*); also about 1303 *nygromauncy;* borrowed from Old French *nigramancie, nigremance,* and directly from Medieval Latin *nigromantia,* from Late Latin *necromantīa* divination from an exhumed corpse, from Greek *nekromanteíā* (*nekrós* dead body + *manteíā* divination, oracle, from *manteúesthai* to prophesy, from *mántis* prophet; see MANTIS); for suffix see *-Y*[3].

The Middle English, Old French, and Medieval Latin spelling (*nigro-*) developed from association with Latin *niger* black, necromancy being the black art. The modern spelling was an attempt to "correct" the spelling by returning to Late Latin *necromantīa.*

necrosis (nekrō'sis) *n.* death or decay of body tissues. 1665, borrowed probably from Greek *nékrōsis,* from *nekroûn* make dead, from *nekrós* dead body; see NECROLOGY.

nectar *n.* 1555, borrowing of Latin *nectar* the drink of the gods in mythology, from Greek *néktar,* of uncertain origin (often taken to be a compound, formed from *nek-* death + *-tar* overcoming, and similar in its meaning to *ambrosia*).

The transferred sense of any delicious wine or other drink is first recorded in 1583, and specific application to the sweet liquid found in many flowers, in 1609.

nectarine (nek'tərēn) *n.* a variety of peach with no down on its skin. 1664, earlier *nectrine* (1657), and *nectarya* (1616), noun use of earlier *nectarine,* adj., of or like nectar (1611 in Cotgrave's *Dictionary*); formed from English *nectar* + *-ine*[1].

nee or **née** (nā) *adj.* originally named (at one time usually placed before a woman's maiden name). 1758, in Lady Montagu's *Letters;* borrowed from French *née* born, from Latin *nāta,* feminine past participle of *nāscī* be born; see NATIVE.

need *n.* Probably about 1200 *nede* want, necessity, in *The Ormulum;* developed from Old English *nīed* necessity, compulsion, want (before 901, West Saxon), earlier *nēd* (probably about 750, Mercian, in *Andreas*). The Old English forms are cognate with Old Frisian *nēd* need, want, Old Saxon *nōd,* Middle Dutch and modern Dutch *nood,* Old High German *nōt* (modern German *Not*), Old Icelandic *naudhr* (Norwegian *naud/nød,* Danish *nød,* Swedish *nöd*), and Gothic *nauths* (genitive *naudais*), from Proto-Germanic **nauđís,* Indo-European **nəutís.* Cognates outside Germanic include Old Irish *nūne* famine, Welsh *newyn,* and Old Slavic *naviti* to weary, tire, from Indo-European **nāu-/nəu-* (Pok.756). **—v.** Probably about 1200 *neden,* in *The Ormulum;* developed from Old English (about 960) *nēodian* be necessary, from *nēd* need. **—needs** *adv.* because of necessity. 1131 *nedes,* from *nede;* found in Old English *nēde, nēd.* **—needy** *adj.* Before 1225 *nedy* needing or wanting things, poor; formed from Middle English *nede* need + *-y* -y[1].

needle *n.* Probably about 1200 *nedle* instrument used for sewing; developed from Old English *naethlae, nethle, nedlæ* (about 700, in the earliest Anglo-Latin glossaries). Though the Old English forms do not show the reversed *d* and *l* by metathesis found in some Germanic forms, they are nonetheless cognate with Old Frisian *nēdle, nēlde* needle, Old Saxon *nāthla,* Middle Dutch *naelde* (modern Dutch *naald*), Old High German *nādala, nālda* (modern German *Nadel*), Old Icelandic *nāl* (Swedish, Danish, and Norwegian *nål*), and Gothic *nēthla.* All of these forms are derived from the Proto-Germanic **næthlō,* from the base **nē-* to sew, which appears in Middle Low German *neien* to sew, Middle Dutch *naeyen* (modern Dutch *naaien*), and Old High German *nājan* (modern German *nähen*). Cognates outside Germanic include Old Irish *snāthat* needle, Old Cornish *notuid,* Welsh *nodwydd,* Middle Breton *nadoez,* Latin *nēre* to spin, Greek *neîn,* Latvian *snāt,* Russian *nít'* thread, and Sanskrit *snā́yu-s* sinew, from Indo-European **(s)nē-/(s)nō-* (Pok.973). **—v.** Before 1715, to sew or pierce with or as with a needle, from the noun. The figurative meaning of provoke to anger, goad, or incite is first recorded in 1881, probably developed from the earlier sense of haggle in making a bargain (1812). **—needlework** *n.* Before 1382, in the Wycliffe Bible.

nefarious *adj.* very wicked, villainous. 1604, in Cawdrey's *A Table Alphabeticall;* borrowed from Latin *nefārius* wicked, abominable, from *nefās* crime, wrong, impiety, something not according to divine law (*ne-* not + *fās* right, lawful, divine decree, related to *fārī* speak; see BAN[1] forbid); for suffix see -OUS.

negate *v.* deny, nullify. 1623, recorded by Cockeram in his *Dictionary;* probably a back formation from *negation;* and possibly, borrowed from Latin *negātus,* past participle of *negāre* deny, say no, from Old Latin *neg-,* variant of *nec* not (as in *nec-opīnāns* unsuspecting), related to *nē* not, NO; for suffix see -ATE[1].

According to the record in the OED *negate* was not in common use until the late 1800's, which suggests that its appearance was probably the result of several separate formations in English.
—negation *n.* act of negating; denial. Probably before 1425 *negacioun* denial, borrowed from Old French

negacion, and directly from Latin *negātiōnem* (nominative *negātiō*) denial, from *negāre;* for suffix see -ATION. —**negative** *adj.* not positive, implying negation. Probably about 1400 *negatyff;* later *negative* (about 1445); probably borrowed through Old French *negatif* (feminine *negative*), or directly from Latin *negātīvus,* from *negāre;* for suffix see -ATIVE. It is also possible that the adjective, in some instances, is from the noun. —*n.* Probably about 1383, negative command, prohibition, in Wycliffe's writings; later, absence, opposite (about 1385); borrowed through Old French *negatif,* n. and adj., or directly from Latin *negātīvus.* The meaning of a photographic film image in which the lights and shadows are reversed is first recorded in 1853. —*adv. Informal.* no. 1955, in American English; originally used for clarity in radio communication.

neglect *v.* disregard, slight. 1529, in Sir Thomas More's *A Dialogue Concerning Heresies;* borrowed from Latin *neglēctus,* past participle of *neglegere,* variant of *neclegere* (Old Latin *nec* not + *legere* pick up, select; see LEGEND).

The word also occurs in Middle English as a verbal adjective *neglecte* ignored, neglected (probably before 1425, in a translation of Chauliac's *Grande Chirurgie*); borrowed from Middle French *neglect,* or directly from Latin *neglēctus.* However, this form disappeared after 1724, being gradually replaced by *neglected* (1600, in Shakespeare's *As You Like It*).
—**n.** act of neglecting. 1588, in Shakespeare's *Love's Labour's Lost;* from the verb.

negligee (negʹləzhāʹ) *n.* woman's loose dressing gown. 1756, a kind of loose, informal gown worn by women in the 1700's; borrowing of French *négligée,* from feminine past participle of *négliger* to neglect, from Latin *neglegere* to NEGLECT.

The modern use of this word is a revival of the 18th-century term; the meaning of a woman's loose dressing gown, usually lightweight and often trimmed with lace, etc., is first recorded in 1930.

negligence *n.* About 1340 *necgligens;* later *negligence* (1351, borrowed from Old French *negligence*), and *necligence* (about 1386, borrowed from Latin *neclegentia*). Latin *neclegentia, neglegentia* carelessness, heedlessness, are from *neglegentem* (nominative *neglegēns*), present participle of *neglegere* to NEGLECT; for suffix see -ENCE. —**negligent** *adj.* Before 1382 *necgligent,* in the Wycliffe Bible; also *necligent* (probably 1383, borrowed from Latin *neclegentem,* nominative *neclegēns, neglegēns*), and *negligent* (probably before 1400, in Chaucer's translation of *Roman de la Rose;* borrowed from Old French *negligent*). Latin *neclegēns, neglegēns* are forms of the present participle of *neglegere* to NEGLECT; for suffix see -ENT.

negligible *adj.* that can be disregarded, trifling, unimportant. 1829, in Sir John F.W. Herschel's *Essays,* formed from English *neglig(ence*) or *negli(gent*) + *-ible.* French *négligeable,* earlier *négligible* (1834), is probably a borrowing from English.

negotiate *v.* 1599, in Shakespeare's *Much Ado About Nothing;* probably a back formation from *negotiation;* for suffix see -ATE[1]. —**negotiable** *adj.* 1758, legally transferable or assignable; later, that can be talked over (1794, in Burke's *Letters*); probably borrowed from earlier French *négociable* (1675), but perhaps also formed from English *negotiate* + *-able.* —**negotiation** *n.* act of negotiating. 1425 *negociacion* a dealing with people; borrowing of Old French *negociacion,* or borrowed directly from Latin *negōtiātiōnem* (nominative *negōtiātiō*), from *negōtiārī* carry on business, from *negōtium* business (*neg-* not, variant of Old Latin *nec* not + Latin *ōtium* ease, leisure), of uncertain origin; for suffix see -ATION. Latin *negōtium* is possibly a loan translation of Greek *ascholíā* occupation, business (*a-* not; A-[4] + *scholḗ* leisure; see SCHOOL). Since the Middle English use appears only once, and no new form appears for over 150 years, it is also possible that English *negotiation* (1579) is a reborrowing from Latin, or perhaps from Middle French.

Negro *n.* 1555, black-skinned person from Africa or of African descent, in Eden's translation of Peter Martyr's *Decades of the New World or West India;* borrowed from Spanish or Portuguese *negro* black, Negro, from Latin *niger* black, of uncertain origin. —**adj.** 1594, of or characteristic of Negroes, black-skinned; from the noun.

neigh *v.* make the characteristic sound of a horse. Probably before 1300 *nayghen,* in *Kyng Alisaunder;* later *neighen* (before 1382, in the Wycliffe Bible); developed from Old English *hnǣgan* (about 1000, in Ælfric's *Grammar*); probably of imitative origin, and similar to Middle Dutch *nijgen, nighen* to neigh, Middle High German *nēgen,* and Old Icelandic *gneggja.* —**n.** sound of neighing. 1513, from the verb.

neighbor *n.* 1117 *nehhebure,* in *Peterborough Chronicle;* later *neighebore* (about 1390); developed from Old English, West Saxon *nēahgebūr* nearby dweller (before 899, in Alfred's translation of St. Gregory's *Pastoral Care*), and Anglian *nēhebūr* (about 950). Old English *nēahgebūr* is a compound of *nēah* near, NIGH + *gebūr* dweller, and corresponds to Middle Dutch *nāghebuur, nābuur* neighbor (modern Dutch *nabuur*), Old Saxon *nābūr,* Old High German *nāhgibur,* Middle High German *nāchbūr* (modern German *Nachbar* and surnames *Nachgebauer, Nachbauer*), and Old Icelandic *nābūi* (Danish and Norwegian *nabo*); Old English *gebūr* is related to *būr* dwelling; see BOWER. —**v.** live or be near (to). Before 1586, in Sidney's *The Arcadia;* from the noun. —**neighborhood** *n.* Probably before 1425 *neighboreheed, neighborhood* friendly relations between neighbors; formed from Middle English *neighebore* neighbor + *-hode* -hood. The meaning of vicinity or environs is first recorded in 1577. The phrase *in the neighborhood of* somewhere about, approximately, is first recorded in 1854 in American English.

neither *conj.* About 1150 *næther* not either; later, *neither* (about 1200); developed from Old English *nāwther* (before 899, in Alfred's translation of Boethius' *De Consolatione Philosophiae*), contraction of *nāhwæther* not of two (*nā* NO + *hwæther* which of two; see WHETHER). A similar formation appears in Old High German *neweder* neither (*nē-* not + *hwedar* which of two). The spelling *neither* was patterned on *either,* because in very late Old English or very early Middle English, the diphthong of Old English *ǣghwæther, ǣgther* (Middle English *either,* pron. and conj.) replaced the original diphthong of Old English *nāwther* (Middle English *neither*). —**pron.** not either. About 1250 *neither,* developed from Old English *nāwther,* pron. and conj. —**adj.** not either. Probably before 1350 *nethys;* later *neither* (about 1400); probably from the pronoun.

nematode (nemʹətōd) *adj.* belonging to a class of worms including the roundworm, hookworm, and pinworm. 1861, borrowed from New Latin *Nematoda* the class or phylum name, from the stem of Greek *nêma* (genitive *nḗmatos*) thread, related to *neîn* to spin; see NEEDLE + *-ode,* a suffixal ending with the sense of something in the nature of (whatever is expressed in the first element). **—n.** nematode worm. 1865, from the adjective.

Nemesis or **nemesis** (nem′əsis) *n.* just punishment, retribution. 1597 *Nemesis,* in Bacon's *Essays;* in allusion to *Nemesis* the Greek goddess of retribution or vengeance (1576); borrowed from Greek *Némesis,* related to *némein* distribute, allot; see NIMBLE. The meaning of any agent of retribution, one who avenges or punishes, is first recorded in Shakespeare's *1 Henry VI* (1591).

neo- a combining form meaning new, recent, as in *neoclassical, neocolonialism.* Borrowed from Greek *neo-,* combining form of *néos* NEW.

neodymium (nē′ədim′ēəm) *n.* metallic chemical element. 1885, New Latin; formed from *neo-* new + (*di*)-*dymium;* so called because the supposed element didymium was found to consist of two elements, neodymium and praseodymium; for suffix see -IUM. The term was coined by its discoverer, the Austrian chemist Carl A. von Welsbach.

neolithic or **Neolithic** (nē′əlith′ik) *adj.* of or belonging to the latest part of the Stone Age. 1865, in Sir John Lubbock's *Prehistoric Times;* formed from English *neo-* new + *-lith* stone + *-ic.*

neologism (nēol′əjizəm) *n.* 1800, the use of new words; 1803, a new word or expression; borrowed from French *néologisme* (*néo-* neo-, new + *log-,* from Greek *lógos* word + French *-isme* -ism). It is also possible that *neologism* was formed in English from *neolog-,* found in such earlier formations as *neological* (1754), *neologist* (1785), and *neology* (1797).

neon *n.* gaseous chemical element. 1898, New Latin; borrowed from Greek *néon,* neuter of *néos* NEW. The term was coined by its codiscoverers, the Scottish chemist Sir William Ramsay and the English chemist Morris W. Travers.

neonatology (nē′ənātol′əjē) *n.* branch of medicine concerned with newborn babies. 1960, in A.J. Schaffer's *Diseases of the Newborn;* formed from English *neonate* (1932, from English *neo-* new, and Latin *nātus* born) + *-ology.*

neophyte (nē′əfīt) *n.* beginner, novice. Before 1400 *neophite* a new convert, novice; borrowed from Late Latin *neophytus,* from Greek *neóphytos,* literally, newly planted (*néos* NEW + *-phytos* planted, from *phýein* cause to grow, beget, plant; see BE). The meaning of a beginner is first recorded in Ben Jonson's *Every Man Out of His Humour* (1599).

nephew *n.* Before 1250 *neweu* kinsman; later *neveu* nephew, grandson (about 1300), and *nephew* (probably before 1400); borrowed from Old French *neveu* grandson, descendant, from Latin *nepōtem* (nominative *nepōs*) sister's son, grandson, descendant. Latin *nepōs* is cognate with Old Lithuanian *nepotis, nepuotis* nephew, Old Persian and Avestan *napāt-* grandson, descendant, and Sanskrit *nápāt,* from Indo-European **népōt-s* (Pok.764). Germanic cognates include Old English *nefa* nephew, grandson, Old Icelandic *nefi* nephew, relative, Old High German *nevo* (modern German *Neffe*) nephew, Middle Dutch *nēve* (modern Dutch *neef*), Old Saxon *nebo,* and Old Frisian *neva,* from Proto-Germanic **néfōn.* The word was originally pronounced with a sound represented by *v* as it still is in British English (nev′yü). The native word *neve* nephew (developed from Old English *nefa*) is attested throughout the Middle English period and is last recorded about 1540.

nephritis (nifrī′tis) *n.* inflammation of the kidneys. 1580, borrowed from Late Latin *nephrītis,* from Greek *nephrîtis,* from *nephrós* kidney (see KIDNEY) + *-îtis* inflammation. An earlier form is found in Middle English *nefresis* (before 1398); borrowed from Medieval Latin *nefresis,* from Late Latin *nephrītis.*

nepotism *n.* favoritism shown toward relatives. 1662, privileges of a pope's nephew; borrowed from French *népotisme,* from early modern Italian *nepotismo,* from *nepote* nephew, learned borrowing from Latin *nepōtem* (nominative *nepōs*) grandson, NEPHEW.

In early use (attested in English from 1670) *nepotism* referred to the practice of popes and other church dignitaries of showing special favor to nephews or other relatives in conferring offices.

neptunium (neptü′nēəm) *n.* radioactive metallic chemical element. 1941, New Latin; formed from *Neptune* the planet (from Latin *Neptūnus* god of the sea) + *-ium* (chemical suffix); so called because neptunium followed uranium in the periodic table of the elements just as the planet Neptune follows Uranus in the solar system. The term may have been coined by its codiscoverer, the American physicist Edwin M. McMillan.

nerd (nėrd) *n. Slang.* foolish or ineffectual person. 1965 (but in oral use before 1955), American English, originally hot-rod and surfing slang, probably an alteration of earlier slang *nert* stupid or crazy person (1940's), itself an alteration of NUT.

nerve *n.* About 1385 *nerf* sinew, tendon, in Chaucer's *Troilus and Criseyde;* later *nerve* a nerve (before 1400, in Lanfranc's *Science of Surgery*); borrowed from Old French *nerf* sinew, tendon, nerve, and directly from both Medieval Latin *nervus* nerve and Latin *nervus* sinew, tendon. Latin *nervus,* with metathesis *rv* for *ur* of a pre-Latin **neuros,* is cognate with Greek *neûron* sinew or tendon; later, nerve, Armenian *neard* sinew or fiber, Sanskrit *snā́van-* sinew or band, Avestan *snāvarə* sinew, and Tocharian B *ṣñaura* sinews or nerves. All these are re-formations of an original Indo-European noun **snḗwr̥(t),* genitive **snḗwenos* (Pok.977).

The figurative sense of strength, vigor (from the original meaning of sinew) is first recorded in 1605, though the plural *nerves* is recorded earlier in Shakespeare's *Measure for Measure* (1603). The sense of courage or boldness is first recorded in Irving's *Knickerbocker's History of New York* (1809), and that of impudence or cheek in 1887.

—v. arouse strength or courage in. Before 1749, give strength or vigor to; later, fill with courage, embolden, in Scott's *The Lady of the Lake* (1810); from the noun. **—nerve cell** (1858) **—nerve fiber** (1877) **—nervous** *adj.* 1392, of or related to the nerves, containing nerves or sinews; borrowed from Latin *nervōsus* sinewy, from *nervus* sinew; see NERVE; for suffix see -OUS. The meaning of suffering from a disorder of the nerves is first recorded in 1734, and that of restless, agitated, excitable in 1740. **—nervous system** (1740) **—nervy** *adj.* 1607, vigorous, sinewy, in Shakespeare's *Coriolanus;* formed from English *nerve* + *-y*[1]. The informal meaning of cool, confident or impudent, is first recorded in American English, in George Ade's *Artie* (1896).

-ness a suffix forming nouns meaning: **1** quality, state, or condition of being, as in *blackness, preparedness.* **2** action or behavior, as in *carefulness.* **3** an instance of being or involving some quality or condition, as in *kindness = an instance of being kind.* Middle English *-ness, -nes,* developed from Old English *-ness, -nes, -nyss, -nys;* cognate with Old Frisian *-nesse, -nisse,* Old Saxon *-nesse, -nissi, -nussi,* Middle Dutch *-nisse, -nesse* (modern Dutch *-nis*), and Old High German *-nissa, -nassī, -nussī* (modern German *-nis*).

The initial *n* in the suffix was originally part of the stem of the preceding word as found in Gothic where the suffix is *-assus,* as in *ibnassus* evenness (*ibn* even + *-assus* -ness) and *ufarassus* abundantness, excessiveness (*ufar* over + *-assus* -ness). The *-assus* suffix is the resultant of Indo-European **-ad-tu-s,* the first element of which is the same as the *-at-* in Gothic *-atjan,* Old English *-ettan,* and the *-ad-* in Greek *-ázein,* in verbs like Gothic *lauhatjan* to lighten, Greek *gymnázein* to exercise.

nest *n.* Old English *nest* bird's nest, snug retreat (probably about 750, in *Phoenix*); cognate with Middle Low German *nest* bird's nest, Middle Dutch and modern Dutch *nest,* and Old High German *nest* (modern German *Nest*), from Proto-Germanic **nistaz.* Cognates outside Germanic include Latin *nīdus* bird's nest, dwelling, Middle Irish *net,* Welsh *nyth,* Lithuanian *lìzdas,* Old Slavic *gnězdo,* Armenian *nist* position, seat, residence, and Sanskrit *nīḍá-s* resting place, bed; all ultimately from Indo-European **nizdos* (**ni-* down + **-zd-, *sed-* sit + ending **-os;* Pok.887). **—v.** build or have a nest. Probably before 1200 *næstien,* in Layamon's *Chronicle of Britain;* later *nesten* (probably before 1300); from the noun; replacement of Old English (before 830) *nistan;* cognate with Middle Dutch, Old High German, and modern German *nisten* to nest, from Proto-Germanic **nistjanan.* **—nest egg** Before 1325, egg left in a nest to induce a hen to continue laying eggs there. The meaning of a sum of money kept in reserve is first recorded before 1700.

nestle *v.* About 1300 *nestlen* build a nest, settle, in a version of Layamon's *Chronicle of Britain;* developed from Old English (about 1025) *nestlian* build a nest, from *nest* NEST. Old English *nestlian* is cognate with Middle Dutch, modern Dutch, and Middle Low German *nestelen* to build a nest.

The meaning of settle comfortably or snugly is first recorded in 1687, and that of press or lie close, as if in a nest, about 1696, in Prior's poetry.

nestling *n.* bird too young to leave the nest. About 1399, probably formed from English *nest* + *-ling* (compare Dutch *nesteling* nestling, German *Nestling*).

net[1] *n.* open fabric, mesh. Old English (before 830) *net;* cognate with Old Saxon *netti* net, Middle Dutch and modern Dutch *net,* Old High German *nezzi* (modern German *Netz*), Old Icelandic *net* (Danish *net,* Norwegian *nett,* Swedish *nät*), Gothic *nati,* from Proto-Germanic **natjan,* related to **nōt-* whence Old Icelandic *nōt* trawling net. Cognates outside Germanic include Latin *nōdus* knot, and Old Irish *nascim* I bind, *naidm* act of tying, contract, from Indo-European **ned-/nod-/nōd-*(Pok.758). —**v.** catch in a net. Before 1425 *netten;* from the noun. **—network** *n.* 1560, netlike structure. The meaning of a complex collection or system is first recorded in 1839, and that of a broadcasting system consisting of many stations, possibly in 1914.

net[2] *adj.* remaining after deductions. Probably before 1300 *net* worthy, pure, fine, elegant, in *Arthour and Merlin;* borrowed from Old French *net* clean, pure, bright; see NEAT[1] spruce.

The meaning of free from, or not subject to, any deduction, remaining after deductions is first recorded in 1418, probably borrowed from Italian *netto* remaining after deductions, from Latin *nitidus* gleaming (see NEAT[1]).

—v. to gain as a net sum or clear profit. 1758, in John Adams' *Diary;* from the adjective.

—n. net gain or profit. 1910, from the adjective.

nether *adj.* lower. About 1200 *nether;* developed from Old English (before 971) *neothra,* earlier *niotherra* (before 830); from earlier *nither, niothor* (adv.) down, downwards (about 725, in *Beowulf*). The Old English forms are cognate with Old Frisian *nithera* (adj.), *nither* (adv.) down, downwards, Old Saxon *nitheri* (adj.), *nithar* (adv.), Middle Dutch *nēder* (adv.), modern Dutch *neder, neer,* Old High German *nidari, nidaro* (adj.), *nidar* (adv.), modern German *nieder* (adj. and adv.), and Old Icelandic *nedhri, nedharri* (adj.), *nidhr* (adv.), from Proto-Germanic **nitheraz.* A cognate outside Germanic is found in Sanskrit *nitarā́m* downwards. All forms are from an Indo-European comparative **niteros* whose positive form is represented by Sanskrit *ní* down, Old English *niowol* headlong, and Greek *neióthen* from the bottom, from Indo-European **nei-/ni-* (Pok.312).

nettle *n.* kind of plant that stings when touched. Before 1200 *netle;* later *nettle* (before 1300); developed from Old English (before 800) *netele;* cognate with Old Saxon *netela* nettle, Middle Dutch *nētel* (modern Dutch *netel*), Old High German *nezzila* (modern German *Nessel*), and Norwegian *nesle, netle,* from Proto-Germanic **natilōn,* diminutive of **natōn,* the source of Old High German *nazza* nettle. Cognates outside Germanic include Middle Irish *nenaid* nettle, and Greek *adíkē* stinging nettle, from earlier **n̥d-ikā,* from Indo-European **ned-/nod-/n̥d-* twist together, fasten (Pok.759). **—v.** sting the mind, irritate. provoke. Probably before 1400 *netlen* irritate, provoke, sting with nettles; from the noun.

neur- the form of *neuro-* before vowels, as in *neural, neuritis.*

neural (nůr′əl) *adj.* of a nerve, nerve cell, or nervous system. 1839-47, formed from English *neur-* + *-al*[1].

neuralgia (nůral′jə) *n.* pain along a nerve. 1822-34, New Latin *neuralgia,* formed from Greek *neûron* NERVE + *álgos* pain; see ANALGESIC.

neurasthenia (nůr′əsthē′nēə) *n.* nervous exhaustion or weakness. 1856, New Latin *neurasthenia,* formed from Greek *neûron* NERVE + *asthéneia* weakness, from *asthenḗs* weak (*a-* without + *sthénos* strength, of unknown origin).

neuritis (nůrī′tis) *n.* inflammation of a nerve or nerves. 1840, formed from English *neur-* + *-itis.*

neuro- a combining form meaning nerve, nerve tissue, or nervous system, as in *neurology, neurobiology, neuromuscular.* Borrowed from Greek *neuro-,* combining form of *neûron* NERVE.

neurology (nůrol′əjē) *n.* study of the nervous system. 1681 *neurologie,* borrowed from New Latin *neurologia,* from *neuro-* nerve + *-logia* -logy. **—neurologist** *n.* 1832, formed from English *neurology* + *-ist.*

neuron (nůr′on) *n.* nerve cell. 1891, borrowed from

German *Neuron,* from Greek *neûron* sinew, cord, (later) NERVE. The term was coined by the German anatomist Waldeyer-Hartz.

neuropterous (nůrop′tərəs) *adj.* belonging to an order of insects having delicate, finely veined wings. 1802, borrowed from New Latin *Neuroptera* the order name, formed from Greek *neûron* vein, tendon, NERVE + *pterón* wing, FEATHER; for suffix see -OUS.

neurosis (nůrō′sis) *n.* mental or emotional disorder. 1776-84, disorder or disease of the nervous system; New Latin *neurosis,* formed from Greek *neûron* NERVE + New Latin *-osis* abnormal condition (see -OSIS).

The meaning of a psychic or mental disorder is first recorded in Thomas Huxley's *Works* (1871), where it was distinguished from psychosis.

neurotic *adj.* 1775, acting upon the nerves; later affected by neurosis (1887); formed in English from Greek *neûron* nerve + English *-otic,* as in *hypnotic, erotic,* etc. **—n.** neurotic person. 1896, from the adjective; earlier, a drug having an effect on the nervous system (1661).

neuter *adj. Grammar.* neither masculine nor feminine. Before 1398 *neutir, newtre,* in Trevisa's translation of Bartholomew's *De Proprietatibus Rerum;* borrowed through Old French *neutre,* or directly from Latin *neuter* (*ne-* not, NO + *uter* either; see WHETHER), probably a loan translation of Greek *oudéteros* neither, neuter. **—n.** *Grammar.* neuter word or form. About 1450 *neutre,* in *Battlefield Grammar;* from the adjective. **—v.** castrate. 1903, from the noun or adjective.

neutral *adj.* 1471 *neuteral* compound of contrasting elements; borrowed through Middle French *neutral,* or directly from Latin *neutrālis* of neuter gender, from *neuter* NEUTER; for suffix see -AL[1].

The meaning of on neither side in a quarrel or war is first recorded in English in 1549, probably adopted from Medieval Latin. The sense in chemistry of having neither acid nor alkaline properties, is first recorded in Boyle's writings, in 1661; and that in electricity of neither positive nor negative in charge, in 1837.

—n. neutral person or country. About 1449, probably from the adjective, though because of a gap in the record the noun appears earlier. The meaning as it applies to the gears of an automobile is first recorded in 1912.

—neutrality *n.* condition of being neutral. About 1475, neutral position or middle ground; borrowed from Middle French *neutralité,* or directly from Medieval Latin *neutralitatem* (nominative *neutralitas*) a neutral condition, from Latin *neutrālis* of neuter gender, neutral; for suffix see -ITY. **—neutralization** *n.* 1808, in Sir Humphry Davy's writings; formed from English *neutralize* + *-ation.* **—neutralize** *v.* Before 1665, remain neutral; (but implied in earlier *neutralizer* 1628); 1759, make neutral; borrowed from French *neutraliser,* from *neutre* neuter, from Latin *neuter;* for suffix see -IZE.

neutrino (nütrē′nō) *n.* elementary particle with no electric charge and little or no mass. 1934, borrowed from Italian *neutrino,* formed from *neutrone* neutron + *-ino* (diminutive suffix). The term was coined in 1933 by the Italian physicist Enrico Fermi.

neutron (nü′tron) *n.* elementary particle that is neutral electrically and has about the same mass as a proton. 1921, from English *neutr(al)* + *-on,* as in *electron, proton.* The term was coined by the British physicist Ernest Rutherford, though it remained a hypothetical particle until its discovery in 1932 by the British physicist James Chadwick.

The term was probably also coined independently for other meanings, such as "hydrogen atom" or "one proton and one electron," used in 1921 by the American chemist W.D. Harkins. Much earlier (1899) it was used to mean "combination of a normal electron and a hypothetical positive electron."

never *adv.* not ever. 1137 *nevre,* in *Peterborough Chronicle;* later *never* (probably about 1150); developed from Old English (before 725) *nǣfre,* a compound of *ne* not, NO + *ǣfre* EVER. **—nevermore** *adv.* (1123, in *Peterborough Chronicle*) **—nevertheless** *adv.* (before 1325, in *Cursor Mundi*)

new *adj.* Probably about 1200 *new,* in *The Ormulum;* developed from Old English *nēowe, nīowe* (before 830, in the *Vespasian Psalter*); earlier *nīwe* (about 725, in *Beowulf*). The Old English forms are cognate with Old Frisian *nīe, nī* new, Old Saxon *niuwi,* Middle Dutch *nieuwe, nūwe, nīe* (modern Dutch *nieuw*), Old High German *niuwi* (modern German *neu*), Old Icelandic *nýr* (Swedish and Danish *ny*), and Gothic *niujis;* from Proto-Germanic **newjaz.* Cognates outside Germanic include Old Irish *nūe* new, Welsh *newydd,* Latin *novus,* Greek *néos,* Lithuanian *naũjas,* Old Slavic *novŭ,* Armenian *nor,* Sanskrit *náva-s, návya-s,* Tocharian A *ñu,* Tocharian B *ñune,* and Hittite *nēwa-,* from the Indo-European base **newo-,* related to Indo-European **nu, nū* NOW; *thus, new* may be a formation meaning "nowish," or *now* in the sense of "newish" may show an ablaut variant of *new: *neu-/nu-/nū-* (Pok.770). **—adv.** newly, recently. About 1307 *newe* recently; earlier *nywe* again, anew (about 1280); developed from Old English *nīwe* recently (before 971, in the *Blickling Homilies*), from the Old English adjective. **—newborn** *adj.* recently born (before 1325, in *Cursor Mundi*); *n.* newborn baby (1929), earlier *the new-born* newborn babies in general (1768). **—newcomer** *n.* (about 1450) **—New Deal** President Franklin D. Roosevelt's domestic policies. 1932, American English, in a speech by Franklin D. Roosevelt. **—newly** *adv.* Before 1325 *newli,* in *Cursor Mundi;* developed from Old English *nīwlice* (before 899, in Alfred's translation of Orosius' *Historiarum Adversus Paganos,* from *nīwe,* adj. + *liche*). **—newlywed** *n.* (1918) **—new moon** the moon when its dark side is facing the earth (Old English, about 1000). **—New Testament** the later part of the Bible, which contains an account of the life and teachings of Christ (before 1398, in Trevisa's translation of Bartholomew's *De Proprietatibus Rerum*). **—New World** the Americas (1555). **—New Year** (probably about 1200, in *New Yeress Dayy,* in *The Ormulum*)

newel (nü′əl *or* nyü′əl) *n.* post that supports the steps of a stairway. 1362 *nowell,* borrowed from Old French *novel, noel* knob, newel, from Vulgar Latin **nōdellus* little knot, diminutive of Latin *nōdulus,* itself diminutive of *nōdus* knot; see NET[1] mesh.

newfangled *adj.* lately come into fashion, of a new kind. Possibly before 1470 *newfanglyd* very fond of novelty; from earlier *neufangel* (about 1250), formed from Middle English *new* NEW + *-fangel* (a form occurring only in this compound), from the root of Old English *fōn* to capture (see FANG). *Newfangled* in the sense of lately come into fashion, novel, is first recorded before 1533, probably from the earlier sense of recent (probably about 1475).

news *n.* Before 1382 *newes* new things, in the Wycliffe

Bible; plural of earlier *new, newe* new thing (about 1200, in *Ancrene Riwle*); from *new,* adj., NEW. The meaning of tidings is first recorded in Middle English probably before 1437. **—newspaper** *n.* (1670) **—newsstand** *n.* (1871, American English)

newspeak *n.* language in which the words are distorted for purposes of propaganda, deception, etc. 1950, from *Newspeak* an artificial ideological language in the novel *Nineteen Eighty-Four* (1949), by the British author George Orwell; formed from English *new,* adj. + *speak,* v.

A noun combining form *-speak,* abstracted from *newspeak,* became a vogue word element in the 1970's in the sense of "typical language, jargon, or vocabulary of," producing such terms as *artspeak, sportsspeak, computerspeak, videospeak.*

newt (nüt *or* nyüt) *n.* salamander. Before 1425 *newte,* from the mistaken division of *an ewte* as *a newte. Ewte* is a variant of Middle English *evete* EFT. Compare APRON, NICKNAME, and UMPIRE for other examples of misdivision.

newton *n.* unit of force in physics. 1904, named after the English mathematician and physicist Isaac *Newton,* 1642-1727.

next *adj.* Probably before 1200 *neste, nexte* nearest or closest, in *Ancrene Riwle;* developed from Old English *nīehsta, nȳhsta* (about 725, West Saxon, in *Beowulf), nēhst-* (about 725, in the book of *Daniel), nēsta* (before 830, Anglian, in the *Vespasian Psalter*); superlative forms of West Saxon *nēah,* Anglian *nēh* near; see NIGH; see -EST. Cognate superlatives include Old Frisian *nēst* nearest, Old Saxon *nāhist,* Middle Dutch *naest* (modern Dutch *naast*), Old High German *nāhost, nāhisto* (modern German *nächst*), and Old Icelandic *næstr* (Danish *næst,* Norwegian *nest,* Swedish *näst*). **—adv.** Probably before 1200 *nest* most recently, just, in *Ancrene Riwle,* and *nexte,* in the nearest position, soonest, last, in Layamon's *Chronicle of Britain;* developed from Old English (before 900) *nēhst, nīehst* nearest, next, last; superlative forms of *nēah, nēh* NIGH; and reinforced in Middle English by development from the Middle English adjective. **—prep.** Probably before 1200 *nest* nearest to; later *next* (probably before 1300); developed from Old English (before 900) *nēhst, nīehst,* from the adverb, and reinforced in Middle English by development from the Middle English adverb. **—next door** 1542, very close, in Udall's translation of Erasmus' *Apothegms;* from the earlier meaning of the door of the nearest house (about 1485). The meaning of in or at the next house appears in adverbial use in 1579, in Lyly's *Euphues,* and in adjectival use in 1749, in Fielding's *Tom Jones.*

nexus (nek'səs) *n.* connection, link. 1663, in Boyle's *Works;* borrowing of Latin *nexus* (genitive *nexūs*), from *nectere* to bind; see CONNECT.

niacin (nī'əsin) *n.* nicotinic acid, a vitamin that prevents pellagra. 1942, American English; formed from *ni* (*cotinic*) *ac*(*id*) + *-in*². *Niacin* was coined, principally as a commercialism, to replace the term *nicotinic acid* as an ingredient of enriched bread, because anti-tobacco groups warned consumers that using enriched bread would create nicotine addiction and foster cigarette smoking.

nib *n.* point of a pen. 1585, beak or bill; originally Scottish variant of *neb* (about 700, in Old English); cognate with Middle Low German *nebbe* beak, Middle Dutch and modern Dutch *nebbe,* and Old Icelandic *nef,* Danish *næb,* Swedish *näbb,* Norwegian *nebb,* from Proto-Germanic **nabjan;* and probably also cognate with Middle Low German *snāvel* beak, Middle Dutch *snāvel* (modern Dutch *snavel*), Old High German *snabul* (modern German *Schnabel*) beak, and Old Frisian *snavel* mouth, probably cognate with Lithuanian *snãpas* beak. The meaning of point of a pen appeared in 1611.

nibble *v.* eat with quick, small bites. 1500-20, in Dunbar's *Poems,* from *nebyllen* to peck at, nibble at (before 1460); perhaps borrowed from Low German *nibbeln* or *knibbeln* to nibble, gnaw. Low German *nibbeln* is cognate with Middle Dutch *cnibbelen* (modern Dutch *knibbelen*) to haggle, squabble. The spelling with *e* was influenced by rhyme. **—n.** 1658, act of nibbling; later, small bite (1838); from the verb.

nice *adj.* Probably before 1300 *nyce* foolish or ignorant, in *Kyng Alisaunder;* borrowed from Old French *nice* silly, from Latin *nescius* ignorant (*ne-* not; see NO + *scire* know; see SCIENCE).

Although the earliest meaning of *nice* in English was "foolish or ignorant," several other senses occur in Middle English, including: timid (before 1300), fussy or fastidious (probably about 1380), dainty (about 1405), extravagant (1395), and lascivious (before 1338). The extended meanings "precise, exact, careful, punctilious" are first recorded in the 1500's. The current popular meaning of agreeable or delightful, is found in 1769, and that of kind or thoughtful in 1830.

nicety *n.* 1369 *nicete* foolishness, in Chaucer's *Book of the Duchesse;* borrowed from Old French *niceté* (*nice* silly + *-ité* -ity). The meaning of minute distinction, subtle point (usually plural in form), is first recorded in 1589, and that of precision or accuracy in 1660.

niche *n.* recess or hollow in a wall. 1611, in Cotgrave's *Dictionary,* borrowing of French *niche,* borrowed into Old French from Italian *nicchia* niche, nook (in writings of Dante), from *nicchio* seashell, probably from Latin *mītulus* mussel, of unknown origin (the change from *m* to *n* has not been fully explained).

The figurative meaning of a place or position for which a person is suited is first recorded in Swift's *To a Lady* (1726). The ecological meaning of a place of an organism or species within a community is first recorded in 1927.

nick *n.* small cut, notch, groove. Probably before 1450 *nik;* of uncertain origin, but possibly related to Middle English *nokke* NOCK or influenced by Middle French *niche* niche.

The figurative expression *in the nick of time,* meaning "just at the right moment," is first recorded in 1643. **—v.** to make a nick or nicks in. 1523, score by making a nick on a tally; from the noun.

nickel *n.* metallic chemical element. 1755, borrowing of Swedish *nickel,* shortened form of *kopparnickel* the copper-colored ore from which nickel was first obtained. Swedish *kopparnickel* was a half-translation of German *Kupfernickel,* literally, copper demon (*Kupfer* COPPER¹ + *Nickel* demon, goblin, rascal; originally, nickname of *Nikolaus* Nicholas). The ore was called "copper demon" because it resembled copper but yielded none; compare the etymology of COBALT. The name of the element was coined in 1754 by its discoverer, the Swedish mineralogist and chemist Baron Axel Fredrik Cronstedt.

The meaning of a coin made partly of nickel appeared in 1857 in American English, originally in reference to a one-cent piece. The meaning of a five-cent piece appeared in 1881, also in American English.

nickelodeon (nik′əlō′dēən) *n.* a former type of motion-picture theater to which the price of admission was five cents. 1888, American English, a blend of *nickel* (the coin) and *-odeon,* as found in *Melodeon* music hall (1840, an early use of *-odeon* for earlier *-odium; odeon* a music hall, not being recorded as a free form before 1912, but ultimately from Greek *ōideîon* building for musical performances, from *ōidḗ* song; see ODE). In 1938 *nickelodeon* was also applied to a jukebox that played a record for a nickel.

nickname *n.* additional or substitute name. 1440 *neke name,* in *Promptorium Parvulorum;* from *a neke name* the mistaken division of original *an eke name,* literally, an additional name; compare APRON and NEWT for similar misdivisions. Middle English *eke* addition or increase, developed from Old English (894) *ēaca* an increase, related to *ēacian* to increase, EKE.

The extended meaning of a familiar form of a given name (as Hank for Henry or Meg for Margaret) appeared in 1605.

—**v.** give a nickname to. 1536, to misname; later, give a nickname to (1567-69); from the noun.

nicotine (nik′ətēn) *n.* poison contained in tobacco leaves. 1819 *nicotin;* later *nicotine* (1839); borrowing of French *nicotine,* from New Latin *Nicotiana* the tobacco plant, from the name of Jean *Nicot,* about 1530-1600, French ambassador to Portugal who introduced tobacco into France about 1560; for suffix see -INE[2]. —**nicotinic** *adj.* of or derived from nicotine. 1873, shortened from *nicotinic acid* an acid formed when nicotine is oxidized, found as a vitamin in many foods; formed from *nicotine* + *-ic* + *acid,* as a loan translation of German *Nikotinsäure.* See NIACIN.

nictitate (nik′tətāt) *v.* 1822-34 to wink, in *nictitating membrane* inner eyelid (1713); borrowed from Medieval Latin *nictitatus,* past participle of *nictitare,* frequentative form of Latin *nictāre* wink, blink; for suffix see -ATE[1]. An earlier *nictate* (1691, borrowed from Latin *nictāre*) is now again sometimes heard in place of *nictitate* in the phrase *nictating membrane.*

niece *n.* About 1300 *nece;* borrowed from Old French *niece;* earlier *niepce,* from Latin *neptia,* from *neptis* granddaughter, niece (cognate with Sanskrit *naptī́-s* granddaughter), related to *nepōs* grandson, NEPHEW. In the 1500's the borrowed word *niece* replaced the native Middle English *nifte* niece; developed from Old English *nift* (from Proto-Germanic **nettiz*), related to *nefa* NEPHEW.

nifty *adj.* attractive, stylish, smart. 1868, American English, in Bret Harte's *Poems;* perhaps a shortened and altered form of *magnificent;* for suffix see -Y[1].

niggard *n.* stingy person. About 1384 *nygard,* in the Wycliffe Bible; possibly from earlier *nig* stingy (about 1300); borrowed from a Scandinavian source (compare Old Icelandic *hnøggr* stingy, from Proto-Germanic **Hnauwjaz*); for suffix see -ARD. Old Icelandic *hnøggr* is cognate with Old English *hnēaw* stingy, niggardly, which did not survive in Middle English, and with Middle High German *nouwe* careful, exact (modern German *genau*), Middle Low German *nouwe* small, tight, narrow, and Middle Dutch *nauwe* (modern Dutch *nauw*), from Proto-Germanic **Hnawaz,* Indo-European **knowos,* root **kneu-* to scrape (Pok.562). Both *nig* and *nigon* a niggard or miser, existed in Middle English, but are now obsolete. —**adj.** stingy. Probably before 1400 *nygard,* in Chaucer's translation of *Roman de la Rose;* from the noun. —**niggardly** *adj.* 1561, formed from English *niggard,* n. + *-ly*[2].

niggle *v.* do things in a trifling way. 1619, in Beaumont and Fletcher's *The Little French Lawyer;* possibly borrowed from a Scandinavian source (compare dialectal Norwegian *nigla* be busy with trifles, perhaps related to the source of English NIGGARD).

The meaning of criticize, nag, annoy, is first recorded in 1886, and earlier in the specific sense of complain of trifles from ill temper or bad humor (1844).

The participial adjective *niggling* is first recorded in Nashe's *Lenten Stuffe* (1599), and may imply a verb form before 1619.

nigh *adv., adj.* near. Probably before 1200 *nih,* in Layamon's *Chronicle of Britain;* later *neigh* (before 1325, in *Cursor Mundi*); *nygh* (1369); developed from Old English, West Saxon *nēah,* (about 725, in *Beowulf*), and Anglian *nēh* (about 830, in the *Vespasian Psalter*), of which the comparative form was *nēar* NEAR, and the superlative form was *nēhst* NEXT. Phonetic changes obscured the relationship of the comparative and the superlative forms to the positive form *nigh* (1391), so that a new comparative and superlative, *nigher* and *nighest,* began to develop in the late 1300's and were in general use by the mid 1500's. See NEIGHBOR.

Cognates of Old English *nēah, nēh* include Old Frisian *nei, nī* nigh, Middle Dutch *na, nae* (modern Dutch *na*), Old Saxon and Old High German *nāh* (modern German *nah*), Old Icelandic *nā-* (in combinations like *nā-būi* neighbor), and Gothic *nēhw, nēhwa,* of unknown origin.

night *n.* Before 1250 *nigt;* later *night* (about 1300); developed from Old English *niht* (about 725, in *Beowulf*). Old English *niht* shows replacement of the vowel of older West Saxon *neaht,* Anglian *næht,* by that of oblique cases (genitive *nihte,* dative *niht*). Cognates of Old English *neaht, næht* include Old Frisian, Middle Dutch, and modern Dutch *nacht* night, Old Saxon and Old High German *naht* (modern German *Nacht*), Old Icelandic *nātt, nōtt* (Norwegian and Swedish *natt,* Danish *nat*), and Gothic *nahts.* Cognates outside Germanic are numerous, and include Latin *nox* (genitive *noctis*) night, Greek *nýx* (genitive *nyktós*), Albanian *natë,* Old Irish *innocht* tonight, Welsh *trannoeth* overnight, tomorrow, Welsh and Cornish *nos* night, Breton *noz,* Sanskrit *nák* (accusative *náktam*), Old Prussian *naktin* (accusative), Lithuanian *naktìs,* Latvian *nakts,* Old Slavic *nošti* night, Tocharian A *nktim* (for *naktim*) at night, Tocharian B *nekcīye* in the evening, and Hittite *nekuz* nightfall, evening, *nekuzi* night falls, from the Indo-European base **nekw-/nokw-,* with the suffix *t, ti* (Pok.762). For development of the spelling with *-ght,* see FIGHT.

—**nightcap** *n.* 1378, a cap worn in bed; 1818, drink taken before going to bed. —**nightfall** *n.* (1700) —**nightgown** *n.* (before 1456, perhaps before 1400) —**nightlong** *adv.* About 1000, through the night. —*adj.* 1850, in Tennyson's *In Memoriam.* —**nightly** *adj.* Probably before 1400 *nyghtly;* developed from Old English *nihtlec* (before 899, in Alfred's translation of St. Gregory's *Pastoral Care*), formed from Old English *niht* night + *-līc* -ly[2]. —*adv.* 1440-41 *nyghtly* (Middle English *night* + *-ly* -ly[1]). —**nighttime** *n.* (before 1393, in

Gower's *Confessio Amantis*) **—nightwatch** *n.* (about 1000)

nightingale *n.* small European songbird. About 1250 *niȝtingale,* in *The Owl and the Nightingale,* later *nyghtyngale* (about 1380); alteration of *nyhtegale* (1300, but probably before 1250); developed from Old English (about 700) *næctigalæ.* Cognates of Old English include Old Saxon and Old High German *nahtagala, nahtigala* (modern German *Nachtigall*), and Middle Dutch *nachtegāle, nachtegael* (modern Dutch *nachtegaal*), all developed from Proto-Germanic **naht-* night + **galōn* to sing, related to Old English *giellan* YELL. The appearance of the medial *-n-* has no etymological significance.

nightmare *n.* About 1300 *niȝt-mare* an evil female spirit afflicting sleepers with a feeling of suffocation; later *nytmare* (about 1350), and *nyghte mare* (1440) a compound of Middle English *niȝt* night + *mare* goblin that causes nightmares by sitting on the chest of a sleeper, incubus. Middle English *mare,* found in Old English *mare* (about 1000), developed from *mera, maere* (before 700), and these forms are cognate with Middle Dutch *mare, maer* incubus, Old High German *mara,* Middle High German *mar, mare* (dialectal modern German *Mahr* nightmare), and Old Icelandic *mara* incubus (Swedish *mara* nightmare, Danish and Norwegian *mare* incubus, nightmare), from Proto-Germanic **marōn,* Indo-European **morā* (Pok.736).

The meaning of a feeling of suffocation during sleep is first recorded in the 1500's, and that of a bad dream producing such a feeling in the 1600's. The modern sense of any bad or frightening dream is first recorded probably in Carlyle's writings, in 1829, and his use of the figurative sense of a very distressing experience, in 1831.

nihilism (nē'əlizəm) *n.* complete rejection of established beliefs. Before 1817, borrowed from German *Nihilismus,* formed from Latin *nihil* nothing, NIL + German *-ismus* -ism. The term was coined in 1799 by the German philosopher F.H. Jacobi.

Nihilism as the term for the movement in Russia in the 1800's advocating skepticism and rejection of authority appeared in 1868; it was originally popularized by Turgenev in *Fathers and Sons* (1862).

—nihilist *n.* 1836-37, borrowed from French *nihiliste,* formed from Latin *nihil* nothing + French *-iste* -ist. **—nihilistic** *adj.* 1857, in Max Müller's *Chips from a German Workshop;* formed from English *nihilist* + *-ic.*

-nik a suffix freely used in recent years in American slang to designate a person associated with or characterized by a thing or expression, usually with a jocular or derisive intent, as in *beatnik, folknik* (folk-song devotee), *no-goodnik, peacenik.* Borrowed from Yiddish *-nik,* as in *nudnik* a bore (a Yiddish word borrowed in American slang), from Russian *-nik,* a common personal suffix, as in *kolkhoznik* member of a kolkhoz. The extended use of *-nik* in English was stimulated by sudden acquaintance in 1957 with *sputnik,* meaning in Russian simply a satellite but in English meaning specifically a Russian artificial satellite.

nil *n.* nothing. 1833, borrowed from Latin *nīl,* contraction of *nihil, nihilum* nothing (*ne-* not; see NO + *hīlum* small thing, trifle, of unknown origin).

nimble *adj.* Before 1325 *nemel,* in *Cursor Mundi;* later *nymyl* (before 1440), and *nymbyll* (1496); developed probably from Old English (about 1000) *nǣmel* quick to grasp, related to *niman* to take and from Old English (before 1000) *numol,* from the participial stem *num-* of *niman;* for suffix see -LE². Old English *niman* is cognate with Old Frisian *nima* to take, Old Saxon *niman,* Old High German *neman* (modern German *nehmen*), Old Icelandic *nema,* and Gothic *niman,* from Proto-Germanic **nemanan.* Cognates outside Germanic are found in Greek *némein* deal out, distribute, manage, pasture, *nomós* pasture, district, *nómos* custom, law, Latin *numerus* number, Lithuanian *núoma* interest, lease, and Avestan *nəmah-* loan, from Indo-European **nem-/nom-/nēm-/nōm-* (Pok.763). The *b* in *nimble* is analogous to the *b* in BRAMBLE.

nimbus (nim'bəs) *n.* halo. 1616, bright cloud surrounding a god, in Ben Jonson's *Works;* borrowing of Latin *nimbus* cloud, perhaps related to *nebula* cloud, mist; see NEBULA.

The meaning of a halo is first recorded in 1727-38, in *Chambers Cyclopaedia.* The meteorological sense of a kind of rain cloud is first recorded in 1803.

nincompoop (nin'kəmpüp) *n.* fool, simpleton. 1706, in Phillips' *Dictionary;* alteration (probably influenced by *ninny*) of earlier *nicompoop,* in Wycherley's *The Plain-Dealer* (before 1676); of uncertain origin. Johnson's suggestion that *nincompoop* may have been derived from *non compos* (1628) one who is not in his right mind (short for Latin *non compos mentis*) does not agree with the early forms *nicompoop, nickumpoop.*

nine *adj.* Probably before 1200 *nihene,* in *Ancrene Riwle;* later *niene* (before 1250), *nine* (before 1300); developed from Old English (about 840) *nigen.* Old English *nigen* is cognate with Old Frisian *nigun, niugun* nine, Old Saxon *nigun,* Middle Dutch *nēghen* (modern Dutch *negen*), Old High German *niun* (modern German *neun*), Old Icelandic *nīu* (Swedish *nio,* Danish and Norwegian *ni*), and Gothic *niun,* from Proto-Germanic **niwun.* Cognates outside Germanic include Latin *novem* nine, Albanian *nëndï,* Old Irish *nōi,* Greek *ennéa,* Lithuanian *devynì,* Old Slavic *devęti,* Armenian *inn,* Sanskrit *náva,* and Tocharian A, Tocharian B *ñu,* from Indo-European *(*e*)*newn̥* (Pok.318).

The Indo-European source, **e-newen*/**newn̥*/ **enwn* may be related to **newo-* NEW, on the supposition that nine is the beginning of the third group of four numbers in a number system based on four, which may explain such things as the dual form of the word for EIGHT.

—nineteen *adj.* About 1300 *nintene,* later *nynetene* (before 1338); developed from Old English (before 1000) *nigontēne* (*nigon* nine + *-tēne* -teen, from *tēn* TEN). **—ninety** *adj.* About 1250 *nigenti;* later *ninty* (about 1300); developed from Old English (about 1000) *nigontig* (*nigon* nine + *-tig* group of ten, -TY¹). **—ninth** *adj.* About 1300 *nynthe;* developed from Old English *nigonthe* (*nigon* nine + *-tha* -TH²); for suffix see FIFTH and -TH.

ninny *n.* fool, simpleton. 1593, perhaps derived from a misdivision and shortening of *an inno* (*cent*) as *a ninny;* for suffix see -Y².

niobium (nīō'bēəm) *n.* metallic chemical element. 1845, New Latin *niobium,* from Latin *Niobē* (from Greek *Nióbē* Niobe, daughter of Tantalus) + New Latin *-ium* (chemical suffix); so called because niobium occurs in nature with the element tantalum. The term was coined in 1844 by its discoverer, the German chemist Heinrich Rose.

nip[1] *v.* to pinch, bite suddenly. Probably before 1387 *nyppen,* in a version of *Piers Plowman;* probably borrowed from Middle Low German *nīpen* to nip. Middle Low German *nīpen* is cognate with Middle Dutch *nīpen* to pinch (modern Dutch *nijpen*), and Old Icelandic *hnippa* to prod. Cognates outside Germanic include Greek *knī́ps* a type of insect, and *skniptein* to nip, from Indo-European **knip-/knīp* (Pok.562). **—n.** pinch, sudden bite. 1551, in Thomas Cranmer's *Works;* from the verb. The noun use is recorded earlier in the figurative sense of a sharp saying or comment (1549). **—nippy** *adj.* biting; sharp. 1575, formed from English *nip*[1], v. + *-y*[1].

nip[2] *n.* small drink, especially of alcoholic liquor. 1796, in Grose's *Classical Dictionary of the Vulgar Tongue,* a shortened form of earlier *nipperkin* small measure of spirits (1671), possibly of Dutch or Low German origin. The meaning may also have been influenced or reinforced by the sense of a fragment or bit such as may be pinched off of something (1606, perhaps mistakenly associated with *nip*[1]). **—v.** 1887, to take small drinks of alcoholic liquor; from the noun.

nipple *n.* projection on the breast or udder, teat. 1538, in Elyot's *Dictionary;* alteration of earlier *neble* (1530, in Palsgrave's *Lesclarcissement*), probably diminutive of NEB. The transferred sense of mouthpiece of a nursing bottle is first recorded in 1875.

nirvana or **Nirvana** (nirvä′nə) *n.* (in Buddhism and Hinduism) the extinction of all desires and attainment of perfect bliss. 1836, borrowing of Sanskrit *nirvāṇa-s* (mistakenly transcribed as *nirvana*) a blowing out or becoming extinguished, extinction, disappearance (*nis-, nir-* out + *vā́ti* it blows; see WIND[1], n.).

nit *n.* egg of a louse or similar insect, very young insect. About 1350 *nete;* later *nit* (1373); developed from Old English (about 700) *hnitu.* Old English *hnitu* is cognate with Middle Low German and Middle Dutch *nete* nit (modern Dutch *neet*), and Old High German *hniz,* (modern German *Nisse*), from Proto-Germanic **Hnitō.* Cognates outside Germanic include Middle Irish *sned* nit, Welsh (plural) *nedd,* Breton *nez,* Greek *konís* (genitive *konídos*), Albanian *thëní* louse, and Armenian *anic,* from Indo-European **k̂nid-* (Pok.608). **—nit-pick** *v.* 1962, search for petty faults; back formation from earlier *nitpicker* (1951).

niter (nī′tər) *n.* potassium nitrate, saltpeter. About 1400 *nitre* sodium carbonate, in a translation of Lanfranc's *Science of Surgery;* borrowing of Old French *nitre,* learned borrowing from Latin *nitrum,* from Greek *nítron,* from Egyptian *ntr.* The meaning "saltpeter" appeared in the 1600's. **—nitrate** *n.* salt or ester of nitric acid. 1794, borrowed from French *nitrate,* from *nitre;* for suffix see *-ate*[2]; and probably in some instances formed from English *nitr* (*ic*) + *-ate*[2]. **—nitric** *adj.* of or derived from niter. 1794, borrowed from French *nitrique,* from Old French *nitre* niter; for suffix see -IC; and in some instances formed from English *niter* + *-ic.* **—nitrous** *adj.* having the nature of niter. 1601, in Holland's translation of Pliny's *Natural History;* reborrowed, perhaps through influence of French *nitreux,* from Latin *nitrōsus,* from *nitrum* niter; for suffix see -OUS. An earlier form *nitrose* is found in Middle English, probably before 1425, in a translation of Chauliac's *Grande Chirurgie;* borrowed from Latin *nitrōsus.*

nitrogen *n.* gaseous chemical element. 1794, borrowing of French *nitrogène,* formed from Greek *nítron* NITER + French *-gène* -gen, producing; the French word elements literally translate as "niter-producing," because nitrogen was discovered in the analysis of nitric acid. The term was coined in 1790 by the French chemist J.A. Chaptal, though the gas had been first produced from air by the Scottish physician Daniel Rutherford in 1772 and named "mephitic air."

nitroglycerin or **nitroglycerine** (nī′trəglis′ərin) *n.* explosive liquid made by treating glycerin with nitric and sulfuric acids. 1857, in W.A. Miller's *Elements of Chemistry,* formed from English *nitro-,* combining form for nitric acid + *glycerin.*

nitty-gritty *n. Slang.* the essential part; the core or basics. 1961 *knitty-gritty,* in John A. Williams' *Night Song;* American English (said to be originally used chiefly by black jazz musicians), of uncertain origin (perhaps ultimately connected with *nit*[1] egg of the louse, and *grits* finely ground corn; for a history of the word see "The Real Nitty-Gritty" by W.R. Higginbotham, with an appendix by John Algeo, in *American Speech* 49, 1-2, 1974, pp. 90-101). **—adj.** *Slang.* basic, essential. 1966, American English, from the noun.

nitwit *n. Informal.* stupid person. 1922, American English, probably formed from earlier slang *nit* nothing (1895, from dialectal German or Yiddish *nit,* from Middle High German; see NIX[1] nothing) + *wit;* perhaps influenced in meaning by *nit*[1] insect.

nix[1] *n. Slang.* nothing, none. 1789, probably a borrowing of German *nix,* dialectal variant of *nichts* nothing, from Middle High German *nihtes,* from genitive of *niht, nit* nothing, from Old High German *niwiht* (*ni, ne* NO + *wiht* thing, creature, WIGHT); compare NAUGHT. **—adv.** *Slang.* no, not possibly. 1909, American English; from the noun. **—v.** *Slang.* cancel, refuse. 1903, American English; from the noun.

nix[2] *n.* water fairy in German legends. 1833, in Thomas Keightley's *The Fairy Mythology;* borrowing of German *Nix,* from Old High German *nihhus* water spirit, water monster. Old High German *nihhus* is cognate with Middle Dutch *nicor* (modern Dutch *nikker*) malevolent water spirit, Old Icelandic *nykr* water goblin, hippopotamus, and Old English *nicor* monster, water spirit, hippopotamus. **—nixie** *n.* female water fairy in German legends. 1816, in Scott's *The Antiquary;* borrowed from German *Nixe* (Old High German *nihhussa*), feminine of *Nix.*

no *adv.* About 1150 *no;* developed from Old English (before 725) *nā* never, no (*ne* not, no, + *ā* ever; see AGE). Old English *ne* is cognate with Old Frisian, Old Saxon, and Old High German *ne, ni* not, Old Icelandic *ne, nē,* and Gothic *ni,* from Proto-Germanic **ne.* Cognates outside Germanic are found in Old Irish *ni, nī* not, Latin *ne-, nē,* Greek *nē-,* Lithuanian and Old Slavic *ne,* Sanskrit *ná,* and Hittite *natta* not, no, from Indo-European **ne/nē* (Pok.756). Compounds similar to Old English *nā* are found in Old Frisian *nā, nō* never, no, Old Saxon and Old High German *neo, nio* (modern German *nie*) never, Old Icelandic *nei* no. **—adj.** not any. Before 1131 *no,* variant of Middle English *non,* developed from Old English *nān,* adj.; see NONE. As an adjective, the form *no* was originally used only before consonants. **—n.** word used to deny, refuse, or disagree. Probably before 1300, in *Arthour and Merlin,* and *Kyng Alisaunder,* from the adverb; later 1588, in Shakespeare's *Love's Labour's Lost;* readapted from the adverb. **—nowhere** *adv.* Probably before 1200 *nowher,* in *Ancrene Riwle;* developed from Old English *nāhwǣr* (971), *nōhwǣr* (before 1050). —*n.* 1831, in Carlyle's *Sartor Resartus.* **—nowise** *adv.* About 1400 *no-wyse;* formed from Middle English *no,* adj. + *wise*[2], n.

No or **Noh** (nō) *n.* Japanese classical drama. 1871, borrowed from Japanese as the transliteration of *nō, noh,* literally, talent, faculty, ability, accomplishment.

nobelium (nōbē′lēəm) *n.* radioactive chemical element. 1957, New Latin *nobelium,* formed from the name *Nobel* + *-ium* (chemical suffix); coined in reference to both Swedish chemist and engineer Alfred *Nobel,* 1833-1896, and to the *Nobel Institute for Physics,* where work on the element was done.

nobility *n.* Probably about 1350 *nobelte* honor, majesty; later *nobilite* noble birth, rank, or character, also people of the noble class (before 1387, in Trevisa's translation of Higden's *Polychronicon*); borrowed from Old French *nobilité,* learned borrowing from Latin, and borrowed directly from Latin *nōbilitātem* (nominative *nōbilitās*), from *nōbilis* well-known, prominent, NOBLE; for suffix see -ITY.

noble *adj.* high and great by birth, rank, or title. Probably before 1200 *noble,* in *Ancrene Riwle;* borrowed from Old French *noble,* learned borrowing from Latin *nōbilis;* earlier *gnōbilis* renowned, well known, noble, related to *nōscere, gnōscere* to come to KNOW.

The extended sense of worthy of honor or respect is first recorded probably before 1300, in *Kyng Alisaunder.*

—n. person of noble rank. About 1300, from the adjective.

—noble gas inert gas (1902). **—nobleman** *n.* Probably before 1200 *noble man* man of noble birth, in *Ancrene Riwle;* later, *nobleman* (about 1300).

nobody *pron.* About 1303 *nobody* no person, no one, in Mannyng's *Handlyng Synne* (*no,* adj., not any + *bodi* body).

nock *n.* notch on the end of a bow or arrow for the bowstring. Before 1398 *nokke,* in Trevisa's translation of Bartholomew's *De Proprietatibus Rerum;* probably related to Old English *hnocc* penis, from Proto-Germanic **Hnukk-,* earlier **Hnukn′-.* Old English *hnocc* is cognate with Middle Dutch *nocke* projection, point, tip (early modern Dutch *nocke* nock, modern Dutch *nok* yardarm), Low German *nock* tip of a sail, and Old Icelandic *hnykill* knot, swelling (Swedish *nock* pin, peg, Norwegian *nokke* and Icelandic *hnjúkr* peak), from Indo-European **knug-,* root **kneug-* (Pok.559).

nocturnal *adj.* of or in the night. 1485, in Caxton's translation of *Life of Saint Wenefryde;* borrowed from Middle French *nocturnal,* or directly from Late Latin *nocturnālis,* from Latin *nocturnus* belonging to the night, from *nox* (genitive *noctis*) NIGHT; for suffix see -AL[1].

nocturne (nok′tėrn) *n.* dreamy or pensive musical piece. 1862, in Thomas A. Trollope's *Marietta,* borrowed from French *nocturne,* noun use of Old French *nocturne* nocturnal, learned borrowing from Latin nocturnus NOCTURNAL.

The term *nocturne* was coined about 1814 by the Irish composer John Field, 1782-1837, who lived most of his professional life in Russia and wrote nocturnes to which those of Chopin are said to owe much in form and spirit. Though Chopin's works popularized the term, Field's coinage is a case of a word created by an English-speaking person away from his native country.

Nocturne also appears in Middle English, probably before 1200, in *Ancrene Riwle,* with the meaning of a group of Psalms used in the nocturnes (a division of the office of matins, consisting of selected Psalms), borrowed from Medieval Latin *nocturna,* from Latin *nocturnus;* see NOCTURNAL.

nod *v.* About 1390 *nodden* nod the head in drunkenness, sleepiness, gloominess, etc., in Chaucer's *Canterbury Tales;* later, make a quick bow of the head in salutation, assent, etc. (1440, implied in the gerund *noddynge,* in *Promptorium Parvulorum*); of unknown origin, but perhaps cognate with Old High German *hnotōn* to shake, (from Proto-Germanic **Hnuđōjanan*), Middle High German *notten* move about, and Old Icelandic *hnjōdha* to push, hit, rivet, from Indo-European **kneudh-/knudh-* (Pok.563). **—n.** a quick bow of the head, especially in salutation or assent. 1440, from the verb.

noddle *n.* Probably before 1425 *nodel, nodle, nodulle* the back of the head; perhaps borrowed from Latin *nōdulus* small knot (see NODULE). The informal meaning of *noddle* "the head as the seat of the mind or thought" is first recorded in 1579.

node *n.* Probably before 1425, a knot or lump in the flesh, in a translation of Chauliac's *Grande Chirurgie;* later, complication, entanglement; borrowed from Latin *nōdus* knot; see NET[1] mesh. The meaning of point of intersection is first recorded in 1665. **—nodal** *adj.* of a node. 1831, in writings of Faraday; formed from English *node* + *-al*[1].

nodule *n.* small knot or knob. Probably before 1425, a knot or lump in the flesh, in a translation of Chauliac's *Grande Chirurgie;* later, small lump of some mineral (1695, in John Woodward's *An Essay towards a Natural History of the Earth*); borrowed from Latin *nōdulus* small knot, diminutive of *nōdus* knot; see NET[1] mesh.

The word is also recorded earlier in Middle English in the form *nodulum* a type of surgical instrument, in a translation of Lanfranc's *Science of Surgery* (before 1400).

Noël (nōel′) *n.* Probably about 1390 *Nowel* feast of Christmas, in *Sir Gawain and the Green Knight;* about 1395, cry of joy at the birth of Christ, especially in carols of the Annunciation and Nativity, in Chaucer's *Canterbury Tales;* earlier, in the surname *Noel* (1130); borrowed from Old French *noel* the Christmas season, variant of earlier *nael,* from Latin *nātālis* natal, in reference especially to the natal day of Christ, from *nātus,* past participle of *nāscī* be born; see NATIVE. Doublet of NATAL. A later meaning of a Christmas carol is first recorded in 1811, borrowed separately from modern French *noël,* from Old French *noel.*

noggin *n.* 1630, a small cup or mug; later, a small drink of liquor (1693); of unknown origin. Connection with *nog* a kind of strong ale (now chiefly in the compound *eggnog*) is possible but doubtful, since *nog* is first recorded in 1693 as a dialectal (East Anglian) term.

The informal meaning of the head, transferred from the original sense of a mug or cup, is first recorded in 1866, in American English.

noise *n.* Probably before 1200 *noise* sound of a musical instrument, in *Ancrene Riwle;* later *nowse* loud speech, outcry (about 1225), and *noyse* loud or unpleasant sound (about 1300); borrowed from Old French *noise* uproar or brawl, possibly from Gallo-Romance *nausea* annoyance, discomfort, from Latin *nausea* NAUSEA.

Though the tracing of the Old French to Gallo-Romance is now recorded in most sources, it is difficult to accept the disparity of both sense and form, which makes it tempting to suggest that *noise* may be related to the obsolete English *noisance,* a variant of *nuisance;* however, such a relationship is not sustainable if the record of Middle English is accurate, for *noisance* and its related words do not appear until at least 100 years after *noise* and in most instances almost 200 years. Even establishing a relationship with *annoy* or with *noi* (shortened form of *anoi*) is out of place in view of the lapse of time. **—v.** About 1380, *noysen* to praise, in Chaucer's translation of Boethius' *De Consolatione Philosophiae;* later *noisen* make noise (before 1393); from the noun; and, in some instances, borrowed from Old French *noisier* to quarrel noisily. **—noisy** *adj.* 1693, in Dryden's translation of *Juvenal;* formed from English *noise,* n. + *-y*[1], and gradually replacing *noiseful* (also used by Dryden), first recorded before 1382.

noisome (noi′səm) *adj.* offensive, disgusting. Before 1382 *noȝesum* harmful, troublesome, in the Wycliffe Bible; later *noyesom, noysom* (probably before 1425); formed from Middle English *noye* harm, misfortune (shortened form of *anoi* annoyance, from Old French, from *anoier* ANNOY + *-som* -some[1].

nomad *n.* 1555 *Nomades,* in reference to wandering groups in Arabia; later *Nomad* member of a tribe that wanders, especially in search of pasture (1587); borrowed possibly from Middle French *nomade,* and directly from Latin *Nomas* (genitive *Nomadis*), from Greek *nomás* (genitive *nomádos*) roaming, roving, grazing, related to *nomós* pasture, *némein* to pasture; see NIMBLE.

The general sense of one who lives a roaming life, wanderer, is first recorded in Carlyle's *Past and Present* (1843), with the lower-case spelling *nomad.*
—adj. like a nomad, wandering. 1798, from the noun. **—nomadic** *adj.* wandering. 1818, in Todd's revision of Johnson's *Dictionary;* probably borrowed from Greek *nomadikós* pastoral, from *nomás* (genitive *nomádos*) nomad; for suffix see -IC; and, in some instances, probably formed from English *nomad* + *-ic.*

nom de plume (nom′dəplüm′) pen name. 1823, in De Quincey's *Works;* apparently formed in English from French, from *nom* name; *de* of; *plume* pen. The French *nom de guerre* for a pseudonym, literally, war name, is first recorded in English in Dryden's comedy *The Kind Keeper* (1678). The coinage of *nom de plume,* perhaps patterned on earlier French *homme de plume* writer, may have been prompted by the feeling that *nom de guerre* was an inappropriate term for a literary pseudonym.

nomenclature (nō′mənklā′chər) *n.* set or system of names or terms. 1610, name; later, set of names (1664); borrowed from French *nomenclature,* or directly from Latin *nōmenclātūra,* from *nōmenclātor* namer (*nōmen* NAME + *-clātor* caller, from *calāre* call out; see LOW[2] moo); for suffix see -URE. The specific meaning of terminology of a particular art or science is first recorded in 1789, in Jefferson's *Writings.*

nominal *adj.* being so in name only. Before 1500 *nominalle* of nouns; later, of names (1620); borrowed from Latin *nōminālis* pertaining to a name or names, from *nōmen* (genitive *nōminis*) NAME; for suffix see -AL[1]. The meaning of being so in name only, not real or actual is first recorded in 1624.

nominate *v.* 1545, to name; later, to name as a candidate for office (1560); probably, in part, a back formation from *nomination,* and perhaps, in part, from *nominate* named, called (about 1450), past participle; borrowed from Latin *nōminātus,* past participle of *nōmināre* to name, from *nōmen* (genitive *nōminis*) NAME; for suffix see -ATE[1]. **—nomination** *n.* About 1412 *nominacioun* mention of a name, in Hoccleve's *Regement of Princes;* later *nomination* act of naming as a candidate (1430); borrowed from Middle French *nomination,* and directly from Latin *nōminātiōnem* (nominative *nōminātiō*), from *nōmināre* to name; for suffix see -ATION. **—nominative** *adj. Grammar.* showing the subject of a verb. Before 1387 *nominatyf,* in Trevisa's translation of Higden's *Polychronicon;* borrowed from Old French *nominatif,* learned borrowing from Latin *nōminātīvus,* from *nōmināre* to name; for suffix see -ATIVE. **—nominee** *n.* 1664, person named for something; later, person named as a candidate for office (1688); formed from English *nomin(ate*) + *-ee.*

non- a prefix meaning: **1** not or lack of, as in *nonalcoholic, nonaggression, nonswimmer, non-European.* **2** not real, sham, pretended, as in *nonart, nonbook, nonevent. Non-* is found in Middle English probably before 1200 with the meaning "not," in such formations as *non-kinnes* (*none cunnes*) no kind of, and is found in closed compounds, such as *noun-certeyn* (about 1350); developed from Middle English *non,* adj., from Old English *nān,* and borrowed through Anglo-French *noun-,* Old French *non-;* both from Latin *nōn-,* from *nōn* not, not a, from unaccented Old Latin *noenum, ne oinom* not one (*ne* not, and *oinom,* neuter of *oinos* one); compare NONE.

nonage (non′ij *or* nō′nij) *n.* condition of being a minor. 1400 *noun age;* later *nonage* (1439); borrowed through Anglo-French *nounage,* Old French *nonaage* (*non-* not + *aage* AGE).

nonagenarian (non′əjənãr′ēən) *n.* person who is between 90 and 100 years old. 1804, formed in English from Latin *nōnāgēnārius* containing ninety (in Late Latin, n., a person ninety years old), from *nōnāgēnī* ninety each, *nōnāgintā* ninety, from *nōnus* ninth; see NOON + English suffix *-ian.* **—adj.** between 90 and 100 years old. 1893, from the noun.

nonagon (non′əgon) *n.* plane figure having nine angles and nine sides. 1688, formed irregularly in English from Latin *nōnus* ninth + English *-agon,* as in *pentagon, hexagon.*

nonce *n.* particular purpose or occasion, especially in the phrase *for the nonce.* Probably before 1200 *for the nones,* alteration by a mistaken division of *for then anes* for the one, in reference to a particular purpose or occasion (*for* for; *then,* dative singular neuter of *the* the; *anes,* alteration (with adverbial *-s*[3]) of *ane,* dative singular neuter of *an* ONE. For various misdivisions see NEWT and APRON. **—adj.** (of a word) coined for a particular purpose or occasion. 1884, from the noun.

nonchalant (non′shəlänt′) *adj.* coolly unconcerned, indifferent. 1813, in Byron's *Letters and Journals;* earlier, as two words *non chalant* (before 1734); borrowed from French *nonchalant,* from present participle of *nonchaloir* be indifferent to, have no concern for (*non-* not + *chaloir* have concern for, care for, be warm, from Latin *calēre* be warm, be roused); for suffix see -ANT. It is probable that the borrowing of *nonchalant* was influenced by the earlier appearance in English of *non-*

chalance. **—nonchalance** *n.* cool unconcern, indifference. 1678, borrowed from French *nonchalance,* from *nonchalant* nonchalant; for suffix see -ANCE.

nonconformity *n.* 1618, refusal to conform to the doctrines of the Church of England, in Donne's *Sermons;* formed from English *non-* + *conformity.* The general sense of a refusal to conform to a rule or practice is first recorded in 1682. **—nonconformist** *n.* (1619)

nondescript *adj.* 1683, (of a species) not yet described; formed from English *non-* + Latin *dēscrīptus,* past participle of *dēscrībere* DESCRIBE. The meaning of not easily described or classified is first recorded in 1806-07. **—n.** nondescript person or thing. 1693, a species not yet described; from the adjective. The meaning of a nondescript person or thing is first recorded in 1811, in Southey's writings.

none *pron.* Probably about 1150 *non;* later *none* (probably before 1200); developed from Old English (probably about 750) *nān* not one, not any (*ne* not; see NO + *ān* ONE: compare NON-). **—adv.** not at all, not. Before 1200 *non;* later *none* (about 1300); from the pronoun.

nones or **Nones** (nōnz) *n.pl.* service for the fifth of the seven canonical hours. 1709 *nones;* found also in Middle English *nones* (probably before 1430), plural of *none* the fifth canonical hour, originally fixed for the ninth hour after sunrise, or about 3 P.M. (before 1225), and earlier *non* the office of nones (probably before 1200, in *Ancrene Riwle*). The two forms are also recorded in the sense of midday: *non,* probably before 1200, in Layamon's *Chronicle of Britain,* and *nones,* about 1378, in a version of *Piers Plowman;* see NOON.

nonpareil (non′pərel′) *adj.* having no equal, peerless. About 1450 *nounparalle,* borrowed from Middle French *nonpareil* (*non-* not + *pareil* equal, from Vulgar Latin **pariculus,* diminutive of Latin *pār,* genitive *paris* equal; see PAIR). **—n.** person or thing having no equal. 1593, from the adjective. The meaning of a kind of candy in the form of or covered with colored sugar pellets, is first recorded in 1697.

nonplus (nonplus′) *n.* 1582, a condition in which no more can be said or done, a state of perplexity; borrowed from Latin *nōn plūs* no more, no further. **—v.** perplex or puzzle completely. 1591, from the noun.

nonresidence *n.* Probably about 1378 *noun residense,* in Wycliffe's writings; later *non residence* (1425); probably borrowed from Medieval Latin *non-residentia* (*non-* + *residentia,* see RESIDENCE). It is also probable that *nonresidence* was formed in English. **—nonresident** *n.* 1425; formed from English *non-* + *resident.*

nonsense. *n.* 1614, in Ben Jonson's *Bartholomew Fair;* formed, perhaps by influence of French *nonsens,* from English *non-* + *sense.* **—nonsensical** *adj.* absurd, foolish. 1655, formed from English *nonsense* + *-ical.*

non sequitur (nonsek′wətər) inference or conclusion that does not follow from the premises. 1564, borrowing of Latin *nōn sequitur* it does not follow. A single instance of the phrase is recorded probably before 1450 in reference to clothing, perhaps with the meaning of an open collar or an attachable collar.

noodle[1] *n.* ribbonlike dough. 1779; borrowed from German *Nudel,* of uncertain origin.

noodle[2] *n.* simpleton, fool. 1753, perhaps alteration of NODDLE. The slang meaning of the head is first recorded in 1914, in Jackson and Hellyer's *Vocabulary of Criminal Slang.*

noodle[3] *v.* to improvise by playing casually on a musical instrument. 1937, from the noun. **—n.** a trill or improvisation on a musical instrument. 1926, probably in allusion to *noodle*[1] from the suppleness of noodles in the reference to "fancy figures in saxophone, such as triple trills [that] often crowd out the melody" (Paul Whiteman, *Jazz*).

nook *n.* Probably about 1300 *noke* recess, corner, angle; later *nok* (probably about 1380); perhaps borrowed from a Scandinavian source (compare dialectal Norwegian *nok* hook, bent figure).

The adjective *nooked* having (so many) corners or angles, is found as *noked* earlier in Middle English than the noun, probably before 1200, in Layamon's *Chronicle of Britain;* for suffix see -ED[2].

noon *n.* 1140 *non* midday, 12 o'clock in the daytime, in *Peterborough Chronicle;* later *none* (probably before 1200); developed from Old English *nōn* the canonical hour of nones, or 3 P.M. (about 725, in *Beowulf*). Old English *nōn* was borrowed (as was Old Icelandic *nōn* and Dutch *noen*) from Latin *nōna hōra* ninth hour (of daylight by Roman reckoning, or about 3 P.M.); *nōna,* feminine singular of *nōnus* ninth, related to *novem* NINE.

The meaning of Middle English *non, none* shifted from 3 P.M. to 12 o'clock when the time of church prayers changed from the ninth to the sixth hour; thereafter the word began to be used with the meaning of midday. The spelling *noon* first appears about 1280, but did not become the established spelling until after the mid-1500's.

noose *n.* loop with a slip knot. About 1450 *nose;* probably borrowed from Old Provençal *nous* knot, from Latin *nōdus* knot; see NET[1] mesh. **—v.** Probably about 1600, fasten as by a noose; later, tie a noose (1814, in Scott's *The Lord of the Isles*); from the noun. The spelling *noose* is first recorded about 1600.

nope *adv. Informal.* no. 1888, American English, spelling representation of an emphatic form of *no,* adv., the letter *p* probably representing a sound of the closing of the lips after pronouncing the vowel. Compare YEP.

nor *conj.* About 1250, contraction of unaccented Middle English *nauther, nouther* NEITHER; compare Old Frisian *nander, nor* neither; or sometimes said to be from *ne,* adv., and *or,* conj.

Nordic *adj.* of the Germanic people of northern Europe, Scandinavian. 1898, borrowed probably from French *nordique,* from *nord* north, from Old French *north,* from Old English *north* NORTH; for suffix see -IC. It is also possible that the term in French and English was at least influenced by German *Nordisch,* from early modern High German *nortisch* (1534).

The meaning in sports "of or designating ski competition involving cross-country and ski-jumping events" is first recorded in 1954, probably by association of such competition with its origins in Scandinavia. Compare ALPINE.

—n. a northern European, Scandinavian. 1901, from the adjective.

norm *n.* standard, type, model. 1821, in Coleridge's *Writings;* reborrowed from French *norme,* from Old French, from Latin *norma* carpenter's square, rule, pattern, of uncertain origin. Modern English also had an earlier form *norme* (1635) which was a borrowing of French *norme;* and the Latinate *norma* (before 1676).

normal *adj.* Before 1500, typical, common (of a verb),

in the Middle English translation of Donatus' *Ars grammatica;* borrowed from Late Latin *normālis* in conformity with rule, normal, from Latin, made according to a carpenter's square, from *norma* carpenter's square, rule, NORM. The general sense in English of usual, regular (also in Late Latin), must surely have been in use before its first appearance in the record in 1828. **—normalcy** *n.* 1857, mathematical condition of being at right angles; later, general condition of being normal or usual (1893); formed from English *normal* + *-cy.* The word was popularized by President Warren G. Harding, who used it in his first message to Congress in 1920. **—normality** *n.* Before 1849, in Poe's *Works;* probably formed from English *normal* + *-ity,* perhaps by influence of earlier French *normalité* (1834). **—normalize** *v.* 1865, formed from English *normal* + *-ize.*

normative *adj.* establishing a norm. 1880, probably borrowed from French *normatif* (feminine *normative*), from Latin *norma* rule, NORM; for suffix see -ATIVE.

Norse *n.* people of ancient Scandinavia, especially Norwegians or a Norwegian. 1598, probably borrowed from earlier modern Dutch *Noorsch,* adj., Norwegian (now *Noors*), from *noordsch* (now *noords*) northern, from *noord* NORTH; also perhaps in some instances borrowed from modern Danish or Norwegian *norsk* (reminiscent of Shakespeare's use of *Dansker* for "Dane").

A parallel form *Northman* has existed in English since the time of Alfred (before 899) and has had a discontinuous history, appearing in the record of Old English until about 1000 and then reappearing in 1605. During the Middle English period the form was altered to *northern man,* appearing before 1200.

—adj. of ancient Scandinavia, its people, or their language. 1768, in Thomas Gray's *Odes;* from the noun.

north *adv.* Old English *north* (about 725, in *Beowulf*); cognate with Old Frisian and Old Saxon *north* north, Middle Low German *nort,* Middle Dutch *nort, noort* (modern Dutch *noord*), Old High German and modern German *nord,* and Old Icelandic *nordhr* (Norwegian and Swedish *nord*), from Proto-Germanic **nurthra-.* Cognates outside Germanic are found in Oscan *nertrak* left, Umbrian *nertru,* and Greek *nérteros* nether, infernal, from Indo-European **ner-teros/nŕ̥-tros* (Pok.765).

The Oscan and Umbrian cognates make it clear that the source of the words for "north" originally meant "to the left," which would hold true for worshippers praying toward the rising sun.

The word for *north* in the Romance languages came ultimately from English: French *Nord* was a borrowing of Old English *North,* and Spanish *Norte* and Italian *Nord* were borrowed from French.

—adj. 1131, in *Peterborough Chronicle;* found in Old English *north-* (about 725, in *Beowulf*), from *north,* adv.

—n. Probably before 1200, in Layamon's *Chronicle of Britain;* from the adverb.

—northerly *adj.* 1551, situated toward the north; from *north,* adj., on the pattern of *easterly;* for suffix see -LY[2]. *—adv.* 1596, in a northern position or direction; for suffix see -LY[1]. **—northern** *adj.* Probably before 1200, in Layamon's *Chronicle of Britain;* developed from Old English (about 890) *northerne* (*north* north + *-erne,* suffix denoting direction); cognate with Old High German *nordrōni* northern, and Old Icelandic *norrœnn, nordhrœnn* Nordic. **—northward** *adv.* About 1300, developed from Old English (about 1016) *northweard* (*north* north + *-weard* -ward).

nose *n.* About 1150 *nose;* developed from Old English *nosu* (before 899, in Alfred's translation of St. Gregory's *Pastoral Care*). Old English *nosu* (from Proto-Germanic **nusuz*) is cognate with Old Frisian *nose* nose, Middle Dutch *nōse* (modern Dutch *neus*), and Middle Low German *noster* nostril (modern German *Nüster*); and *nosu* is probably related to a similar Old English form, *nasu* nose (from Proto-Germanic **nasuz*), whose cognates include Middle Low German *nāse* nose, Middle Dutch *nāse,* Old High German *nasa* (modern German *Nase*), Old Icelandic *nǫs.* Cognates of Old English *nasu* outside Germanic include Latin *nāsus* nose, Old Prussian *nozy,* Lithuanian *nósis,* Old Slavic *nosŭ,* and Sanskrit (dual) *nā́sā,* from Indo-European **nas-/nās-/nes-* (Pok.755). **—v.** 1577-87, perceive the smell of (something); later, pry or search (1648); from the noun. **—nosebleed** *n.* bleeding from the nose. 1848, American English, formed from *nose* + *bleed.* The word also appeared earlier as *noseblede* a plant, the common milfoil or yarrow (before 1400), formed from Middle English *nose* + *bleden* bleed. **—nose dive** swift downward plunge by an aircraft (1912); **nose-dive** *v.* take a nose dive (1915). **—nosegay** *n.* About 1420 in Lydgate's writings; formed from English *nose* + *gay.*

nosh *v. Slang.* to nibble or snack. 1957, borrowed from Yiddish *nashn* nibble, from Middle High German *naschen,* from Old High German *hnascōn, nascōn* to nibble, from Proto-Germanic **Hnaskwōjanan;* cognate with Gothic *hnaskwus* soft, tender, from Indo-European **knostwus,* root **kenes-* rub (Pok.561). **—n.** *Slang.* a nibble or snack. 1965, American English, borrowed from Yiddish *nash,* from *nashn,* v. In British English the noun *nosh* had two earlier meanings, neither of which exists in Yiddish: "restaurant or snack bar" (1917), and "food or meal" (1963), the more usual sense in Great Britain. **—noshery** *n. Slang.* restaurant, snack bar. 1963, American English (*nosh* v. + *-ery,* as in *eatery*). Oral evidence indicates that *nosheries* existed in England and the United States in the 1950's.

nostalgia *n.* 1770, severe homesickness, New Latin *nostalgia* and New Greek *nostalgía,* both formed from Greek *nóstos* homecoming + *álgos* pain, grief, distress; see ANALGESIC. Greek *nóstos* is related to *neîsthai* to come, go, go back, which is cognate with Sanskrit *násate* (he) approaches, from Indo-European **nes-/nos-* (Pok.766).

The transferred sense of wistful yearning for a past or earlier time, is first recorded in D.H. Lawrence's *The Lost Girl* (1920).

—nostalgic *adj.* 1806, caused by nostalgia; later, affected with nostalgia (1869, in Oliver Wendell Holmes' *Cinders from Ashes*); formed from English *nostalg(ia* + *-ic.*

nostril *n.* Before 1387 *nostrille,* in Trevisa's translation of Higden's *Polychronicon;* developed from Old English (about 1000) *nosthyrl* (*nosu* nose + *thyrel* hole; see NOSE and THRILL). An earlier formation is found in Middle English probably about 1200, from *nase, nese, nose* nose + *thril* hole.

nostrum (nos′trəm) *n.* 1602, patent medicine; borrowed from Latin *nostrum remedium* our remedy; so called because it was presumably prepared by the person recommending it. Latin *nostrum* is the neuter form of *noster* our, ours, from *nōs* we; see US. The extended meaning of special or favorite remedy, cure-all, panacea, is first recorded in Fielding's *Tom Jones* (1749).

nosy or **nosey** *adj. Informal.* prying, inquisitive. 162

having a prominent nose; later, inquisitive (1882); formed from English *nose,* n. + *-y*[1]. An independent formation appeared earlier in Middle English *nasee* having a big nose (actually an ironic use in reference to one who has no nose or a mutilated nose), in Mannyng's *Chronicle of England* (before 1338), borrowed through Anglo-French, from Old French *nasé,* ultimately from Latin *nāsus* NOSE.

not *adv.* About 1250 *not;* later *nat* (1303); unstressed variants of *noht, naht* not, in no way, NAUGHT.

notable *adj.* About 1340 *notabile, notabil* worthy of notice, in Rolle's *The Psalter;* later *notable* (about 1390, in Chaucer's *Canterbury Tales*); borrowed from Old French *notable* and directly from Latin *notābilis* noteworthy, extraordinary, from *notāre* to NOTE; for suffix see -ABLE. **—n.** notable person. About 1447, probably from the adjective in English, but also found in Middle French *notable* important person in a town (1355). The superlative *notablest* appeared as a noun in 1442.

notary (nō′tərē) *n.* person authorized to certify legal documents. About 1303 *notarye* secretary, in Mannyng's *Handlyng Synne;* later, notary or clerk; borrowed probably through Old French *notarie,* and directly from Latin *notārius* shorthand writer, clerk, secretary, from *nota* shorthand character, letter, mark, NOTE; for suffix see -ARY. **—notarize** *v.* certify (a legal document). 1935, American English, formed from *notary* + *-ize.*

notation *n.* 1570, etymological explanation of a word; later, note or annotation (1584); borrowed through Middle French *notation,* and directly from Latin *notātiōnem* (nominative *notātiō*) a marking, notation, designation of and etymological explanation, from *notāre* to NOTE; for suffix see -ATION. The meaning of representation of numbers, quantities, or other values by symbols or signs, is first recorded in Phillips' *Dictionary* (1706).

notch *n.* V-shaped nick or cut. 1577, probably alteration (by a misdivision of *an otch* as *a notch*) of Middle French *oche* notch, from Old French *ochier, oschier* to notch; of uncertain origin.

A Middle English verb *ochen* to cut or slash, corresponding to the noun form **och* or **otch,* is recorded in *Morte Arthur* (probably before 1400) and was borrowed from Old French *ochier, oschier.*
—v. make a notch or notches in. 1597, cut (hair) unevenly; later, make notches in (1600); from the noun.

note *n.* Probably before 1300 *note* musical note, in *Sir Tristrem;* also, mark or sign (about 1380, in Chaucer's translation of Boethius' *De Consolatione Philosophiae*); borrowed from Old French *note,* learned borrowing from Latin, and borrowed directly from Latin *nota* a mark, sign, letter, note, very possibly an alteration of Old Latin **gnata* (Indo-European **gnətā́*) under the influence of *gnōscere* to recognize (Latin *nōscere* come to know), from Indo-European **gnō-* (Pok.376); see KNOW. The meaning of a record of the gist or substance of something, is first recorded probably before 1400, and that of a short letter, in Shakespeare's *Richard III* (1594). The meaning of a bank note is found in 1696. It is also possible that in some instances, the noun developed from the earlier verb use. **—v.** Probably before 1200 *noten* to take mental note of, in *Ancrene Riwle;* later, to record in writing (before 1325); borrowed from Old French *noter* to notice, from Latin *notāre* to mark, remark on, note, from *nota* a note. **—notebook** *n.* (1579) **—noted** *adj.* celebrated, famous. Probably about 1380, formed from Middle English *noten* note + *-ed* -ed[1]. **—note paper** (1849) **—noteworthy** *adj.* 1552, formed from English *note,* n. + *-worthy* as a combining form of WORTHY.

nothing *n.* Probably about 1175 *nathing;* later *nothing* not any thing (probably before 1200); found in Old English (about 1000) *nāthing, nān thing* (*nān* not one, see NONE + *thing* THING). The sense of an insignificant thing, trifle, is first recorded in Shakespeare's *All's Well That Ends Well* (1601). **—adv.** not at all, in no way. Probably before 1200 *nathing,* in Layamon's *Chronicle of Britain;* later *nothing* (about 1250); from the noun. **—adj.** 1961, insignificant, worthless; from the noun.

notice *n.* About 1412 *notise;* acquaintance; also 1415 *notice* knowledge, information; both spellings in Hoccleve's *Works;* borrowed from Middle French *notice,* learned borrowing from Latin, and directly from Latin *nōtitia* a being known, fame, knowledge, from *nōtus* known, past participle of *nōscere* come to KNOW.

The phrase *take notice,* in the sense of give attention, is first found in Shakespeare's *Venus and Adonis* (1592). **—v.** About 1410 *notisen* notify, proclaim; probably from the noun (although recorded slightly earlier). The meaning "take notice of, observe, perceive" is first recorded in 1757. According to the record of English the verb was apparently not in common use until the 1700's.
—noticeable *adj.* easily noticed. 1796, formed from English *notice* + *-able.*

notify *n.* About 1385 *notifien* take notice of, observe; also, about 1390, inform or indicate; both senses in Chaucer's *Works;* borrowed from Old French *notifier* make known, from Latin *nōtificāre* make known, from a lost adjective **nōtificus* making known, from *nōtus* known, see NOTICE + the root of *facere* make, DO[1]; for suffix see -FY. It is also possible that Chaucer formed *notify* in English from *notification.* **—notification** *n.* About 1380 *notificacioun,* in Chaucer's translation of Boethius' *De Consolatione Philosophiae;* borrowed from Old French *notification,* from Medieval Latin *notificationem* (nominative *notificatio*), from Latin *nōtificāre* make known, notify; for suffix see -ATION.

notion *n.* Before 1398 *nocioun* concept, conception, in Trevisa's translation of Bartholomew's *De Proprietatibus Rerum;* later *nocien* inclination, desire (1450); borrowed from Latin *nōtiōnem* (nominative *nōtiō*) concept, from *nōscere* come to KNOW; for suffix see -TION. The sense of belief or opinion is first recorded in 1603, in Holland's translation of Plutarch's *Moralia.* **—notional** *adj.* theoretical, imaginary. 1597, formed from English *notion* + *-al*[1]. The word is also recorded once in Middle English *nocional* (before 1398, in Trevisa's translation of Bartholomew's *De Proprietatibus Rerum;* borrowed from Medieval Latin *notionalis,* from Latin *nōtiōnem* (nominative *nōtiō*) concept.

notorious *adj.* well-known because of something bad. 1548-49, in *The Book of Common Prayer;* borrowed from Medieval Latin *notorius* well-known, commonly known, from Latin *nōtus* known, past participle of *nōscere* come to KNOW; for suffix see -OUS. **—notoriety** *n.* fact or condition of being notorious. 1592, borrowed through Middle French *notoriété,* or directly from Medieval Latin *notorietatem* (nominative *notorietas*) condition of being well-known, from *notorius* well-known; for suffix see -TY[2].

notwithstanding *prep.* Probably about 1378 *not-withstandinge* not prevented by, in spite of, in Wycliffe's writings; (*not* + *withstanding,* present participle of *withstand* prevent, oppose, stand against; loan translation of Medieval Latin *non obstante* being no hindrance, not standing in the way). **—adv.** nevertheless. 1425 *notwithstondyng,* in *Rolls of Parliament;* from the preposition. **—conj.** although. Before 1420, in Lydgate's *Troy Book;* from the preposition.

nougat (nü′gət) *n.* kind of soft candy containing nuts. 1827, borrowing of French *nougat,* from Provençal *nougat* cake made with almonds, from Old Provençal *nogat,* from *noga, nuga* nut, from Vulgar Latin **nuca,* from Latin *nux* (genitive *nucis*) NUT.

nought (nôt) *pron., n., adj., adv.* See NAUGHT.

noun *n.* Before 1398, in Trevisa's translation of Bartholomew's *De Proprietatibus Rerum;* borrowed through Anglo-French *noun* name, noun, Old French *nom, non,* from Latin *nōmen* name, noun; see NAME.

In older grammars a distinction was made between noun substantives and noun adjectives, as in *whiteness, white.*

nourish *v.* Probably before 1300 *norisshen* to bring up (a young person), to raise, in *Kyng Alisaunder;* also about 1300 *norischen* to feed; borrowed from Old French *norriss-* (found in *norrissement*), stem of *norrir, nurrir,* from Vulgar Latin **nutrīre,* from Latin *nūtrīre* to feed, nurse, foster, support, preserve; for suffix see -ISH[2]. Latin *nūtrīre* derives from earlier **snūtrī,* **sneutrī* letting milk flow; cognate with Sanskrit *snāuti* (she) drips, lets milk flow, from Indo-European **sneu-/snāu-* (Pok.972).**—nourishment** *n.* Probably before 1300 *norisement* nurture, fostering, in *Arthour and Merlin;* later *nurshement* fuel (before 1382, in the Wycliffe Bible) and *norisshement* food, sustenance (1413); borrowed from Old French *norrissement,* from *norriss-,* stem of *norrir* nourish; for suffix see -MENT.

nouveau riche (nüvō′ rēsh′) newly rich person. 1813, borrowed as a French phrase, literally, new rich (*nouveau* new, from Old French *novel* NOVEL[1]; *riche* rich, from Old French *riche* rich, powerful; see RICH).

nova (nō′və) *n. Astronomy.* star that suddenly glows brightly, then gradually fades to its normal brightness. 1877, New Latin, from Latin *nova,* feminine singular of *novus* NEW, used with *stēlla* star (a Latin feminine noun). The original use of *nova* in English was to denote a new star or nebula not previously recorded. The current meaning is first recorded in 1927.

novel[1] *adj.* of a new kind, strange. About 1450 *novel* new, young; later *novell* recent, strange (before 1500); borrowed from Middle French *novel* new, fresh, recent, from Old French, learned borrowing from Latin *novellus* new, young, recent, diminutive of *novus* NEW. The word is also recorded earlier as part of a legal phrase (1405) and as a noun meaning "new shoot" (about 1400). **—novelty** *n.* About 1384 *novelte* newness, innovation, in the Wycliffe Bible; borrowed from Old French *noveleté* newness, from *novel* new; for suffix see -TY[2].

novel[2] *n.* long work of fiction. 1566, one of the tales or short stories in a collection; later, long work of fiction (1639); borrowed from Italian *novella* short story or novel, tale, news, from Latin *novella* new things, neuter plural or feminine of *novellus* NOVEL[1]. **—novelette** *n.* 1814, short novel; formed from English *novel*[2] + *-ette.* **—novelist** *n.* writer of novels. 1728, formed, probably by influence of Italian *novellista,* from English *novel*[2] + *-ist.* The word is also recorded earlier, in the sense of innovator; formed from English *novel*[1] + *-ist.* **—novella** (nōvel′ə) *n.* 1902, short or compact novel, William Dean Howells in *Literature and Life;* borrowed from Italian *novella;* see NOVEL[2].

November *n.* Probably about 1200 *novembre,* borrowed from Old French *novembre,* learned borrowing from Latin, and borrowed directly from Latin *November,* from *novem* NINE, this being the ninth month of the ancient Roman calendar (which began with March); see DECEMBER. The earlier Old English name was *Blōtmōnath* the month of sacrifice (so called because during this month the early Saxons made provision for winter and offered in sacrifice many of the animals they then butchered).

novena (nōvē′nə) *n.* series of nine days of prayers or services in the Roman Catholic Church. 1853, borrowing of Medieval Latin *novena,* feminine of Latin *novēnus* ninefold, from *novem* NINE.

novice *n.* beginner. 1340 *novice, novis* beginner, probationer in a religious order, in *Ayenbite of Inwyt;* borrowed from Old French *novice, novisse,* learned borrowing from Medieval Latin *novicius,* noun use of Latin *novīcius* (of a slave) newly imported, (of any person) recently entered into some condition, inexperienced, from *novus* NEW. **—novitiate** (nōvish′ēit) *n.* period of religious preparation. 1600, borrowed from French *noviciat,* from Medieval Latin *noviciatus,* from *novicius* novice; for suffix see -ATE[1].

novocaine or **novocain** (nō′vəkān) *n.* a compound used as a local anesthetic. 1905, originally a trademark; formed in English from Latin *novus* new + English *-caine,* abstracted from *cocaine.* The drug was introduced as an anesthetic by a German firm in 1905 to be a substitute for cocaine.

now *adv.* Probably before 1200 *nou,* in Layamon's *Chronicle of Britain;* later *now* (about 1250); developed from Old English (before 725) *nū;* cognate with Old Frisian and Old Saxon *nū* now, Middle Dutch *nū* (modern Dutch *nu*), Old High German *nū, nu* (modern German *nun*), Old Icelandic *nū* (Swedish *nu*), and Gothic *nu.* Outside Germanic cognates are found in Latin *nunc* now, Greek *ny, nŷn,* Lithuanian *nù, nūnaĩ,* Old Slavic *nyně,* Sanskrit *nū́, nú,* Tocharian A *nu* but, then, Tocharian B *no,* and Hittite *nu* then, and, but; all from Indo-European **nu/nū* (Pok.770). See also NEW. **—conj.** since. About 1250 *nou, now;* developed from Old English (before 725) *nū;* from the adverb. **—adj.** stylish, up-to-date. About 1385 *now* current; from the adverb. The slang meaning of stylish appeared in 1963. **—n.** the present, this time. Probably before 1300 *now,* in *Kyng Alisaunder;* from the adverb.

nowadays *adv.* at present, in these times. Before 1376 *nowadayes,* in *Piers Plowman,* (*now* NOW + *adayes* during the day, in the daytime; originally *a dayes,* an adverbial phrase formed from *a* on + *dayes,* genitive of *dai, day* DAY).

noxious (nok′shəs) *adj.* very harmful, poisonous. Before 1500 *noxius,* borrowing of Latin *noxius* hurtful, injurious; later *noxious* (1612); re-borrowed from Latin *noxius,* from *noxa* hurt, damage, related to *nocēre* to hurt and *nex* violent death, slaughter, see NECROLOGY; for suffix see -IOUS.

nozzle *n.* Before 1450 *noselle* socket on a candlestick, diminutive of *nose* NOSE; for suffix see -LE[1]. The cur rent meaning "small spout" is first recorded in 1683, and the current spelling in 1741.

nth (enth) *adj.* last in the series 1, 2, 3, 4. . .n; being of the indefinitely large or small amount denoted by *n.* 1852 *to the nth* to the utmost, figurative use of the mathematical term for indicating an indefinite number; probably a loan translation of French *nième,* formed from the letter *n,* abbreviation for *nombre* number + *-ième* -th².

nuance (nüäns′) *n.* shade of expression, meaning, feeling, etc. 1781, in Walpole's *Letters;* borrowed from French *nuance,* slight difference, shade of color, from *nuer* to shade, from *nue* cloud, from Gallo-Romance **nūba,* from Latin *nūbēs,* related to *obnūbere* to veil, and cognate with Avestan *snaoδa-* clouds, and Welsh *nudd* mist, fog, from Indo-European **sneudh-/snoudh-* (Pok.978); for suffix see -ANCE. **—v.** give nuances to. 1897, from the noun.

nub *n.* knob, protuberance. 1594, husk of silk; later, knob, lump (1727); variant of dialectal *knub* (1570), probably variant of KNOB. The figurative meaning of a point or gist of anything is first recorded in 1834, in American English. **—nubby** *adj.* 1876, formed in American English from *nub* + *-y*¹.

nubbin *n.* small lump or piece. 1692, American English, stunted ear of corn, diminutive of NUB. The transferred sense of a small piece is first recorded in 1857, also in American English.

nubile (nü′bəl) *adj.* (of a girl) old enough to be married. Before 1642, borrowed from French *nubile,* or directly from Latin *nūbilis* marriageable, from *nūbere* take as a husband; see NUPTIAL.

nuclear *adj.* 1846, of or like the nucleus of a cell, formed from English *nucleus* + *-ar,* probably by influence of French *nucléaire.*

The use of *nuclear* in physics with reference to an atomic nucleus or nuclei is first recorded in 1914. The term *nuclear physics* is found in 1933, *nuclear fission* in 1939, *nuclear energy* in 1941, *nuclear power* and *nuclear bomb* in 1945, *nuclear weapon* in 1948, and *nuclear war* in 1954.

—n. nuclear weapon. 1962, elliptical use of the adjective; later applied to a nuclear-powered submarine (1969).

nucleic acid genetic substance present in the nuclei of cells. 1892, probably a translation of German *Nukleinsäure* (*Nuklein* substance obtained from cell nuclei + *Säure* acid). The word *nucleic* was formed from English *nucleus* + *-ic.*

nucleo- a combining form meaning nucleus, as in *nucleoplasm,* or nucleic acid, as in *nucleoprotein.* Adapted from New Latin *nucleus* nucleus, from Latin *nucleus* kernel.

nucleon (nü′klēon) *n.* nuclear particle, especially a proton or neutron. 1923, a proton; formed from *nucle-,* abstracted from *nucleus,* + *-on,* as in *electron.* The meaning of any nuclear particle was first recorded from 1939. **—nucleonics** *n.* science or study of nucleons. 1945, a blend of *nucleon* and *-onics,* probably abstracted from *electronics;* for suffix see -ICS.

nucleus *n.* center, kernel, or core of a thing. 1708, part of the head of a comet; later, central part, core (1762); re-borrowed from Latin *nucleus, nuculeus* kernel, formed from *nucula* little nut, diminutive of *nux* (genitive *nucis*) NUT. The word also appeared in Middle English as *nucle* kernel, in a translation of Chauliac's *Grande Chirurgie* (probably before 1425); borrowed from Latin *nucleus.*

The first recorded reference to the nucleus of a cell is found in 1831. The meaning in physics, "part of an atom," is first recorded in 1844; however, the modern sense of a positively charged central part of an atom was introduced by the British physicist Ernest Rutherford in 1912, a year after he presented his model of atomic structure.

nude *adj.* naked. 1531, (in law) unsupported, not formally attested; later, mere, plain, simple (1551); borrowed from Latin *nūdus* NAKED. The meaning "unclothed, uncovered" is recorded in Cotgrave's *Dictionary* (1611), and in Blount's *Glossographia* (1656), although apparently it was not in common use before the 1800's. Various applications of the sense of Latin *nūdus* are found earlier in Middle English *nudate,* adj., naked, exposed (probably before 1425) and *nude,* adv., plainly or openly (1447-48). **—n.** naked figure in painting, sculpture, or photography. 1708, loan translation of French *nu,* from Latin *nūdus* naked. **—nudism** *n.* practice of going naked. 1929, American English, borrowed from French *nudisme* (Latin *nūdus* naked + French *-isme* -ism). **Nudist** appeared at the same time, borrowed from French *nudiste* or formed from English *nude, nud* (*ism*) + *-ist.* **—nudity** *n.* nakedness. 1611, in Cotgrave's *Dictionary,* borrowed from French *nudité,* or directly from Late Latin *nūditātem* (nominative *nūditās*), from Latin *nūdus* nude; for suffix see -ITY.

nudge (nuj) *v.* push slightly, jog with the elbow. 1675, in Hobbes' translation of Homer's *Odyssey;* perhaps borrowed from a Scandinavian source (compare Norwegian *nugge* and *nyggje* to jostle, rub, Icelandic *nugga* to rub, massage, and Swedish *gnaga* to nibble, GNAW). **—n.** slight push or jog. 1836, in Marryat's *Mr. Midshipman Easy;* from the verb.

nudnik or nudnick (nu̇d′nik) *n. Slang.* tiresome, annoying person. 1927, American English, in a film title "Nudnik of the North"; borrowing of Yiddish *nudnik,* from *nudne* boring, *nudyen, nudzhen* to bore, pester (from Russian *núdnyĭ* boring, *nudá* boredom, related to Old Slavic *nužda* NEED) + *-nik,* personal suffix.

nugatory (nü′gətôr′ē) *adj.* worthless, invalid. 1603, worthless, in Holland's translation of Plutarch's *Moralia;* also 1605, invalid; borrowed from Latin *nūgātōrius* worthless, futile, from *nūgātor* (genitive *nūgātōris*) jester, trifler, from *nūgārī* to trifle, from *nūgae* (genitive *nūgārum*) trifles, of uncertain origin.

nugget *n.* lump. 1852, lump of native gold, perhaps from dialectal *nug* lump, of uncertain origin.

nuisance *n.* annoyance, trouble. About 1400 *nusaunce* injury, trouble; later, *nuysance* general annoyance or inconvenience (1412); borrowed through Anglo-French *nusaunce,* from Old French *nuisance, noisance* (formed after Medieval Latin *nocentia* an injury, hurt), from Old French *nuis-,* stem of *nuire* to harm, from Vulgar Latin **nocere,* corresponding to Latin *nōcere* to hurt; see NOXIOUS; for suffix see -ANCE.

nuke (nük) *n. Slang.* nuclear weapon. 1959, American English, shortened and altered form of *nuclear* (weapon, device, etc.). —**v.** *Slang.* to attack with nuclear weapons. 1967, American English; from the noun.

null *adj.* void, invalid. 1563-67, borrowed through Middle French *nul,* and directly from Latin *nūllus* not any, none (*ne-* not, no + *ūllus* any, diminutive of *ūnus* ONE).

nullify *v.* make null, render void. 1595, borrowed from Late Latin *nūllificāre* to make nothing, from a lost adjective **nūllificus* making null (from Latin *nūllus* not any; see NULL + the root of *facere* make, DO[1]); for suffix see -FY. **—nullification** *n.* 1798, American English, action taken by a state to nullify a federal law, in Jefferson's *Writings;* borrowed from Late Latin *nūllificātiōnem* (nominative *nūllificātiō*) a making as nothing, from *nūllificāre* to make nothing, nullify; for suffix see -ATION. An earlier meaning "reduction to nothing" is found in Donne's *Sermons* (1630). **—nullity** *n.* 1570, invalidity; later, nothingness (1589); borrowed from Middle French *nullité,* from Medieval Latin *nullitatem* (nominative *nullitas*), from Latin *nūllus* not any (see NULL); for suffix see -ITY.

numb *adj.* Before 1400 *nomme* deprived of motion or feeling, paralyzed, in a version of *Cursor Mundi;* later *nomyn* (1440) and *nome* (before 1460); from the past participle of *nimen* to take, seize, developed from Old English *niman;* see NIMBLE. A similar semantic development is found in German *benommen* dazed, stupefied, from the past participle of *benehmen* take, take away (*be-* be- + *nehmen* take; see NIMBLE).

The spellings *num, numme* began to appear in the mid-1500's, and though the form *numb* (with *b* added to conform to such spellings as *comb, limb,* and *dumb*) is recorded as early as 1642, it did not become established till the 1700's; Spenser, Shakespeare, Bacon, and Milton spelled it usually *numme.* The old spelling *num* is still retained in the compound *numskull.*

—v. make numb. 1553 (as past participle *nummed*); from the adjective.

number *n.* Probably before 1300 *noumbre* sum, total, or aggregate, amount, number, in *Arthour and Merlin;* later *numbre* (about 1300) and *number* (about 1475); borrowed through Anglo-French *noumbre,* Old French *nombre,* and directly from Latin *numerus* a number, quantity. Latin *numerus,* earlier **nomesos,* is cognate with Greek *némein* distribute, manage, *nómos* custom, law, Lithuanian *núoma* interest, lease, and Avestan *nəmah-* loan, from Indo-European **nem-/nom-/nōm-* (Pok.763). **—v.** Probably before 1300 *noumbren* to count, ascertain the number of, in *Kyng Alisaunder;* later *numberen* (about 1425); borrowed from Old French *nombrer, numbrer,* from Latin *numerāre,* from *numerus* a number.

numeral *adj.* Before 1398, of or expressing a number, in Trevisa's translation of Bartholomew's *De Proprietatibus Rerum;* borrowed from Late Latin *numerālis* of or belonging to a number, from Latin *numerus* NUMBER; for suffix see -AL[1]. **—n.** 1530, in Palsgrave's *Lesclarcissement,* word expressing a number; later, figure standing for a number (1686); from the adjective.

numerate *v.* to number or enumerate. 1721, in Bailey's *Dictionary,* developed from earlier *numerate* numbered, counted (probably before 1425, in a translation of Higden's *Polychronicon*); borrowed from Latin *numerātus,* past participle of *numerāre* to NUMBER; for suffix see -ATE[1]. **—numerator** *n.* number above the line in a fraction, which shows how many parts are taken. 1575, borrowed, perhaps by influence of Middle French *numérateur,* from Late Latin *numerātor* counter, numberer, from Latin *numerāre* to number, count; for suffix see -OR[2].

numerical *adj.* 1628, of a number or numbers, in Thomas Spencer's *The Art of Logic;* formed in English, perhaps by influence of French *numérique,* from Latin *numerus* NUMBER + English *-ical.* An earlier use with the meaning of individual or identical is recorded in Burton's *The Anatomy of Melancholy* (1621).

numerous *adj.* Probably before 1425, in a translation of Higden's *Polychronicon;* borrowed from Latin *numerōsus,* from *numerus* NUMBER: for suffix see -OUS.

numinous (nü′mənəs) *adj.* spiritual, holy, divine. 1647, formed in English from Latin *nūmen* (genitive *nūminis*) divine power + English suffix *-ous.* Latin *nūmen* meant originally a nod (of assent by a god), from Indo-European **neumn̥,* parallel to Greek *neûma,* from Indo-European **neu-s-mn̥* (Pok.767).

numismatics (nü′mizmat′iks) *n.* study of coins and medals. 1829-32, from earlier *numismatic,* adj., of coins (1792), borrowed from French *numismatique,* from Late Latin *numisma* (genitive *numismatis*) coin, currency; for suffix see -ICS. Late Latin *numisma,* a variant of *nomisma,* was influenced in development of meaning by Latin *nummus* coin, money, from Greek *nómimos* customary, legal; but the Late Latin form *nomisma* derives from Greek *nómisma* current coin, usage, anything approved by usage, from *nomízein* have in use, from *nómos* custom; see NIMBLE. **—numismatist** (nümiz′mətist) *n.* student of coins, coin collector. 1799, formed in English from Late Latin *numisma* (genitive *numismatis*) coin, currency + English *-ist.*

numskull or **numbskull** *n.* 1717, the head, in Prior's *Poems;* later, blockhead, in Swift's writings (1724); formed from English *num,* NUMB + *skull.*

nun *n.* Probably before 1200 *nunne,* in *Ancrene Riwle;* later *nonne* (about 1300) and *nun* (before 1450); found in Old English *nunne* (before 899, in Alfred's translation of Bede's *Ecclesiastical History*); borrowed from Late Latin *nonna* nun, tutor (feminine of *nonnus* monk), originally a term of address to elderly persons, possibly from children's speech, reminiscent of English *nana* and its variants. Compare Albanian *nanë* mother, nurse, northern Welsh *nain* grandmother, Greek *nánnē* maternal aunt, *nínnē* grandmother, Bulgarian *neni* the older one, Russian *nyanya* child's guardian, and Sanskrit *nanā́* mother.

In Middle English and through the 1500's the form *nonne* was common, borrowed from Old French *nonne,* from Latin *nonna.*

—nunnery *n.* Probably about 1280 *nonnerie* nunhood; also *nunnerie* convent of nuns (before 1300); formed from Middle English *nonne, nunne* nun + *-erie* -ery.

nuncio (nun′tsēō) *n.* ambassador from the pope to a government. 1528, borrowing of Italian *nuncio, nunzio,* from Latin *nūntius* messenger, of unknown origin.

nuptial *adj.* of marriage or weddings. 1490 *nupcyalle,* ir Caxton's translation of *The Book of Eneydos;* borrowe from Middle French *nuptial,* or directly from Latir *nuptiālis* pertaining to marriage, from *nuptiae* wed ding, from *nupta,* feminine past participle of *nūbere* take as a husband. Latin *nūbere* is possibly cognat with Greek *nýmphē* bride, nymph. **—n. nuptials,** *p.* wedding. About 1555, from the adjective.

nurse *n.* Before 1382 *nurse* foster parent, tutor, in th Wycliffe Bible; contraction of earlier *nurrice* we nurse, woman or man who takes care of a young chil (probably before 1200, in *Ancrene Riwle*), also *nuric norice* (about 1250); borrowed from Old French *no rice, nurice,* from Vulgar Latin **nutrīcia,* from La Latin **nūtrīcia* nurse, governess, tutoress, from Lati feminine of *nūtrīcius* that suckles, nourishes, from *nūtrīx* (genitive *nūtrīcis*) wet nurse, from *nūtrīre* to suckle, NOURISH. The meaning of a person who takes care of the sick is first recorded in English in Shakespeare's *Comedy of Errors* (1590). **—v.** 1526 *nourse* to bring up (a child), in the Tyndale Bible; later *nurse* to suckle (1535); alteration of Middle English *nurshen* nourish (before 1382), *norischen* (probably before 1300); see NOURISH. The figurative meaning of foster, promote the growth of, is first recorded before 1542. The extended meaning of wait on, take care of (a sick person), is first recorded in Swift's *Letters* (1736).

nursery *n.* Probably about 1300 *noricerie* room set apart for young children with their nurse; later *norserye* (before 1400); borrowed from Old French *nourricerie* (though recorded in Old French somewhat later), formed from Old French *norrice, nurice* nurse + *-erie* -ery. The spelling *nursery* does not appear before the 1580's. The meaning of a place or piece of ground where young plants and trees are raised, is first recorded in 1565. **—nursery rhyme** (1832) **—nursery school** (1835)

nurture *n.* rearing, bringing up. Probably before 1300 *norture,* in *Kyng Alisaunder;* later *nurture* (about 1330), and earlier as surname, *Nurtur* (1289); borrowed from Old French *norture, nurture,* partially a learned development adapted from Late Latin *nūtrītūra* a nursing, suckling, from Latin *nūtrīre* to nourish, suckle; see NOURISH; for suffix see -URE. **—v.** to rear, bring up, foster. Probably before 1400, implied in past participle *nurtrid;* later *norturen* (about 1410); from the noun.

nut *n.* Probably about 1125 *nute,* developed from Old English (about 700) *hnutu;* cognate with Middle Low German and Middle Dutch *not* nut (modern Dutch *noot*), Old High German *nuz, hnuz* (modern German *Nuss*), and Old Icelandic *hnot* (Norwegian *nøtt,* Swedish *nöt*), from Proto-Germanic **Hnut-*, Indo-European **knu-d-*. Cognates outside Germanic are found in Middle Irish *cnū* nut, Welsh *cnau* nuts (singular *cneuen*), Breton *kraoñ* (with *kr-* for *kn-*), and Latin *nux* (genitive *nucis*) nut, from Indo-European **kneu-/knou-/knu-* (Pok.558). The word is found only in Celtic, Germanic, and Italic languages, which constitute the westernmost Indo-European languages.

The meaning of a small piece of metal with a threaded hole to attach to a bolt, is first recorded in 1611. The meaning of a crazy person or crank is first recorded in 1903, in American English, probably by influence of such expressions as *nut* a disparaging word for a person (1887), *off one's nut* drunk, insane (1860), and the adjectives *nuts* and *nutty.*

—nuts *adj. Slang.* crazy. 1846, from earlier *be nutts upon* be very fond of or enthusiastic about (1785), possibly from earlier *nuts,* n.pl., any source of pleasure (1617). **—nutty** *adj.* Probably about 1421 *notty* nutlike, formed from Middle English *nute, note* nut + *-y* -y[1]. The meaning of crazy is first recorded in 1898, probably by influence of *nuts* crazy.

nutmeg *n.* hard, spicy seed used for flavoring food. Probably before 1300 *notemuge,* in *Kyng Alisaunder;* later *notemege, nutmuge* (about 1450); alteration and partial translation of Old North French or Anglo-French **noiz mugue,* Old French *nois muguete,* alteration of *nois muscade* nut smelling like musk (*nois* nut, from Latin *nux,* accusative *nucem,* nut, *muscade, muscat* musky, from Provençal *muscat;* see MUSCATEL).

It is also probable that the formation in English was influenced by, or in some instances a loan translation and alteration of Medieval Latin *nux maga, nux mugata,* variant forms of *nux muscata, nux muscade.*

nutrient *adj.* nourishing. 1650, borrowed from Latin *nūtrientem* (nominative *nūtriēns*), present participle of *nūtrīre* NOURISH; for suffix see -ENT. **—n.** nourishing substance. 1828-32; from the adjective.

nutrition *n.* act or process of nourishing. Probably before 1425 *nutricioun, nutricion,* in a translation of Chauliac's *Grande Chirurgie;* borrowed through Old French *nutrition,* and directly from Latin *nūtrītiōnem* (nominative *nūtrītiō*) a nourishing, from *nūtrīre* nourish, suckle; see NOURISH; for suffix see -TION. **—nutritionist** *n.* expert in nutrition. 1926, formed from English *nutrition* + *-ist.* **—nutritious** *adj.* nourishing. 1665, borrowed from Latin *nūtrīcius,* from *nūtrīx* (genitive *nūtrīcis*) a nurse, from *nūtrīre* nourish; for suffix see -OUS. **—nutritive** *adj.* 1392 *nutritif, nutritive* of nutrition, giving nourishment; borrowed from Old French *nutritif* (feminine *nutritive*), and directly from Late Latin *nūtrītīvus,* from Latin *nūtrīre* nourish; for suffix see -IVE.

nux vomica (nuks vom′əkə) medicine containing strychnine. 1578, medical use of a Medieval Latin phrase, literally, vomiting nut (Latin *nux* nut, and Medieval Latin *vomica* vomiting, irregularly derived from Latin *vomere* to vomit). The word is also recorded in Middle English, in Trevisa's translation of Bartholomew's *De Proprietatibus Rerum* (before 1398) as *nux vomyta,* from Latin *vomita,* feminine past participle of *vomere.*

nuzzle *v.* Probably about 1425 *noselen* to bend down, grovel, bring the nose towards the ground; probably a back formation from earlier *noselyng* on the nose, prostrate, formed from Middle English *nose* + *-ling.*

The meaning of burrow with the nose is first recorded in Palsgrave's *Lesclarcissement* (1530), and that of poke with the nose is found in Shakespeare's *Venus and Adonis* (1592). Another meaning, to lie snug, appeared in 1597 as a figurative use, influenced by *nestle.*

nylon *n.* synthetic plastic substance. 1938, American English, coined by the Du Pont Company as a generic term. According to Du Pont the word is an arbitrary formation of *nyl-* + English *-on,* as in *rayon* and *cotton.*

nymph *n.* nature goddess in classical mythology. About 1385 *nymphe,* in Chaucer's *Canterbury Tales* and *Troilus and Criseyde;* also *nimphe* (before 1393); borrowed from Old French *nimphe,* and directly from Latin *nympha* nymph, bride, from Greek *nýmphē;* see NUPTIAL.

The transferred sense of a young woman, girl, maiden is first recorded in 1584, probably by influence of similar meanings of Greek *nýmphē.* The meaning in biology of an insect in the larval stage is found as early as 1577, probably adapted from the meaning "young bee or wasp" of Greek *nýmphē,* found in writings of Aristotle.

nymphomania *n.* abnormal sexual desire in a woman. 1775, in E.S. Wilmot's translation of de Bienville's *Nymphomania,* New Latin; formed from Greek *nýmphē* nymph + *maníā* madness, mania. The word is found earlier in French *nymphomanie* (1732). **—nymphomaniac** *n.* one who is affected with nymphomania. 1867, from English *nymphomania,* on the pattern of *mania, maniac.*

O

o or **O** *interj.* See **oh.**

-o- a connecting vowel used to join parts of a compound, as in ethnic and language names such as *Anglo-Saxon, Franco-American, Indo-European,* and *Gallo-Romance;* in scientific terms, such as *pneumogastric, occipitofrontal, oceanography, odontology,* and *lobotomy;* and in various new and nonce formations, such as *mobocracy* (*mob* + *-o-* + *-cracy*), *speedometer* (*speed* + *-o-* + *-meter*), *industrio-political, seriocomic, meritocracy, insectology, laundromat,* etc. Formed on the analogy of Greek compounds, in which the combining stem usually ended in *-o,* seen in such words of Greek origin as *acropolis, democracy, mythology* and in similar adaptations and imitations in Latin.

Because it often appears before *-logy,* this form with a connective is often considered to be *-ology* or at least a variant form of *-logy.* The same analysis is made of *-cracy, -meter,* etc., producing such combinations as *plutocracy* and *galvanometer.*

oaf *n.* stupid or deformed person. 1625 *oph,* earlier *auf* or *aulf* (1621), but also *oaf-* in *oafish* (1610); borrowed from a Scandinavian source (compare Old Icelandic *ālfr* silly person; see ELF). The original sense of this word in English was "stupid or ugly child left by elves in place of a child carried off by them," from which developed the meaning "stupid or deformed person." The spelling *oaf* appeared in 1638.

oak *n.* Before 1200 *oc,* later *ok, ooc* (about 1250); developed from Old English (about 700) *āc* oak tree; cognate with Old Frisian and Old Saxon *ēk* oak tree, Middle Dutch *eike* (modern Dutch *eik*), Old High German *eih* (modern German *Eiche*), and Old Icelandic *eik* (Swedish *ek,* Norwegian *eik, ek,* Danish *eeg*), from Proto-Germanic **aiks.* Outside Germanic, Old English *āc* is perhaps cognate with Greek *aigílōps* type of oak, and possibly with Latin *aesculus* a type of oak, from Indo-European **aig-* (Pok. 13). The spelling *oak* began to appear in the 1570's. **—adj.** made of oak. Probably before 1300 *ok, oc,* from the noun. **—oaken** *adj.* made of oak wood. 1393 *oken,* formed from Middle English *ok* oak + *-en*[2].

oakum (ō'kəm) *n.* loose fiber obtained by taking apart old ropes. 1422-23 *okam, okom,* developed from Old English (about 1000) *ācumba* flax fibers separated by combing (*ā-* out + *cemban* to comb, from *camb* a COMB). Old English *ācumba* is cognate with Old High German *āchambi,* Middle High German *akambe,* from Proto-Germanic **us-kambōn* (with *us-* out, from Indo-European **ud-s-,* Pok. 1104).

oar *n.* Before 1300 *or, ore* pole for rowing, developed from Old English *ār* (897, in the *Anglo-Saxon Chronicle*); cognate with Old Icelandic *ār* oar (Swedish *åra,* and Danish *åre*), from Proto-Germanic **airō,* cognate with Sanskrit *iṣā́* shaft, and Greek *oíāx* helm, tiller, from Indo-European **eis-/ois-/īs-, *oier-* (Pok. 298). The spelling *oar* began to appear in the 1580's. —v. to row. 1610, in Shakespeare's *The Tempest;* from the noun. An isolated example of the verb is recorded in Middle English *oren* (about 1410). **—oarlock** *n.* 1350 *orlok,* formed from Middle English *or* oar + *lok* lock[1]. **—oarsman** *n.* (1701, American English; earlier *oarman* 1608)

oasis (ōā'sis) *n.* fertile place in the desert. 1616 *Oasis* fertile area in the Libyan desert; borrowed from French *oasis,* and directly from Late Latin *oasis,* from Greek *Óasis,* probably from Hamitic (compare Coptic *wahe, ouahe* dwelling place, oasis, from Egyptian *wh'-t* kettle-shaped depression). The general meaning of any fertile place in the middle of a desert (written in lowercase), appeared in English between 1800 and 1816.

oat *n.* Before 1250 *ote* (plural *otes, oten*) the cereal plant or its grain, in a version of *Ancrene Riwle;* developed from Old English (about 1000) *āte* grain of the oat plant (plural *ātan*), of unknown origin. The common Germanic name of this cereal is **Haƀran-,* appearing in Middle English as *haver* (probably borrowed from Scandinavian) and not found in Old English. The spelling with *oa-* began to appear in the 1560's. **—oaten** *adj.* consisting of oats or oatmeal. 1381 *oten,* formed from Middle English *ote* oat + *-en*[2]. **—oatmeal** *n.* 1393 *otemele,* formed from Middle English *ote* oat + *mele* meal[2].

oath *n.* About 1300 *oth* solemn promise or affirmation, act of swearing, in *Havelok the Dane;* later, profane oath, curse (probably about 1350); developed from Old English *āth* (about 725, in *Beowulf*). Old English *āth* is cognate with Old Frisian and Old Saxon *ēth* oath, Middle Dutch *eet* (modern Dutch *eed*), Old High German *eid,* Middle High German *eit, eid* (modern German *Eid*), Old Icelandic *eidhr* (Swedish, Norwegian, and Danish *ed*), and Gothic *aiths,* from Proto-Germanic **aithaz.* Outside Germanic the word may be cognate with Old Irish *ōeth* oath and Welsh *an-udon* perjury (*an-* negative prefix + *ud-,* from Brythonic **oit* oath + *-un* suffix), apparently cognate with Greek *oîtos* fate, doom, from Indo-European **oitos* (Pok. 295). The spelling with *oa-* began to appear in the late 1580's.

ob- a prefix meaning: **1** against, hindering, as in *obliterate, obdurate;* **2** toward, to, by, as in *obtrude, obvert;* **3** on, over, as in *obtuse, obduct;* **4** down, away, as in *obese, obituary.* Borrowed from Latin *ob-* from *ob,* prep., against, toward, before; see EPI-. In combination with verbs and their derivatives, the *b* is assimilated to certain consonants, becoming *oc-* before *c,* as in *occupy; of-* before *f,* as in *offend;* and *op-* before *p,* as in *oppress.*

In scientific terms formed in New Latin and in English, *ob-* is prefixed to adjectives in the sense "inversely" or "in the opposite direction," as in *obcordate* inversely cordate (as in an *obcordate leaf*), *obovate, obtriangular,* etc. Apparently this use of the prefix derives from the *ob-* of the New Latin adverb *obverse* obversely.

obbligato (ob'ləgä'tō) *adj. Music.* indispensable, not to be omitted. 1794, borrowing of Italian *obbligato,* literally, obliged, obligatory, from Latin *obligātus,* past participle of *obligāre* OBLIGATE. Earlier use with the spelling *obligato* is recorded in 1724.

In this century musical passages marked *obbligato* are often considered optional, so that the term has by indirection assumed an almost opposite sense.

—**n.** obbligato accompaniment. 1845, in Edward Holmes' *The Life of Mozart;* from the adjective.

obduct *v. Geology.* push (one crustal plate of the earth) on top of another. 1971, borrowed from Latin *obductus,* past participle of *obdūcere* cover over (*ob-* over + *dūcere* to lead; see TOW[1] pull).

Obduct in the general sense of cover over is first recorded in English in 1623, but became obsolete by 1646.

—**obduction** *n.* 1971, process of obducting; probably formed in English from *obduct* + *-ion* (also found in Latin *obductiōnem,* nominative *obductiō,* a covering, from *obdūcere* cover over). *Obduction* in the general sense of a covering, or an enveloping, is recorded in 1578, but it too became obsolete, in this case by 1656.

obdurate (ob'dərit) *adj.* stubborn, unyielding. About 1450, in *Jacob's Well;* borrowed from Latin *obdūrātus,* past participle of *obdūrāre* harden (*ob-* against + *dūrāre* harden; see ENDURE); for suffix see -ATE[1]. —**obduracy** *n.* stubbornness. 1597, in Shakespeare's *2 Henry IV;* formed from English *obdurate* + *-cy.*

obedient *adj.* willing to obey. Probably before 1200, in *Ancrene Riwle;* borrowed from Old French *obedient,* learned borrowing from Latin *oboedientem* (nominative *oboediēns*), present participle of *oboedīre* OBEY; for suffix see -ENT. —**obedience** *n.* Probably before 1200, borrowed from Old French *obedience,* learned borrowing from Latin *oboedientia* (nominative *oboediēns*), present participle of *oboedīre;* for suffix see -ENCE.

obeisance (ōbā'səns) *n.* bow of respect or submission. Before 1382 *obeisaunce* obedience, deference, respectful bow, in the Wycliffe Bible; borrowed from Old French *obeissance* obedience, from *obeissant,* present participle of *obëir* obey, from Latin *oboedīre* OBEY; for suffix see -ANCE.

obelisk *n.* tapering shaft of stone. 1569 *obelisk,* borrowed probably from Middle French *obélisque,* and directly from Latin *obeliscus* obelisk, small spit, from Greek *obelískos,* diminutive of *obelós* a spit, pointed pillar, of uncertain origin.

obese *adj.* very fat. 1651, probably a back formation from earlier *obesity,* but in some instances also probably borrowed from Latin *obēsus* fat, that has eaten itself fat, stout, from past participle of **obedere* devour (*ob-* away + *edere* EAT). —**obesity** *n.* excessive fatness. 1611 *obesitie,* in Cotgrave's *Dictionary,* borrowed from French *obésité,* or directly from Latin *obēsitās,* from *obēsus* obese; for suffix see -ITY.

obey *v.* Probably before 1300 *obeyen,* in *Kyng Alisaunder;* borrowed from Old French *obëir,* from Latin *oboedīre* give ear, pay attention to, obey (*ob-* to + *audīre* listen, hear; see AUDIBLE).

obfuscate (ob'fuskāt) *v.* darken, obscure, confuse. 1536, possibly, in some instances developed from earlier *obfuscate,* adj. (1531) and, in part, borrowed from Latin *obfuscātus,* past participle of *obfuscāre* (*ob-* over + *fuscāre* darken, from *fuscus* dark; see DUSK); for suffix see -ATE[1]. —**obfuscation** *n.* 1608, probably, in some instances, formed from English *obfuscate* + *-tion,* and in part, borrowed from Latin *obfuscātiōnem* (nominative *obfuscātiō*), from *obfuscāre* obfuscate; for suffix see -ATION.

obi (ō'bē) *n.* long, broad sash worn about the waist with a Japanese kimono. 1878, in Lady Brassey's *A Voyage in the Sunbeam;* borrowing of Japanese *obi* belt.

obit (ōbit') *n.* obituary. 1459, record of the date of death, an extension of earlier (before 1382, in the Wycliffe Bible) *obyte,* probably before 1400 *obit* death, day of death (recorded as *obit* before 1400, and *obyte* before 1382, in the Wycliffe Bible); borrowed from Old French *obit,* or directly from Latin *obitus* death; see OBITUARY.

Although *obit* has been in use since the Middle English period, in modern informal usage it is popularly regarded as a clipped form of *obituary.*

obituary (ōbich'üer'ē) *n.* notice of death. 1706, in Kersey's edition of Phillips' *Dictionary;* borrowed, perhaps through influence of French *obituaire,* from Medieval Latin *obituarius,* from Latin *obitus* (genitive *obitūs*) a going to meet, encounter, death, from stem *obi-* of *obīre* go to meet, as in *mortem obīre* meet death (*ob-* against + *īre* go; see EXIT); for suffix see -ARY. Compare OBIT.

object (ob'jikt *or* ob'jekt) *n.* Before 1398 *obiect* tangible thing, in Trevisa's translation of Bartholomew's *De Proprietatibus Rerum;* borrowed from Old French *object,* and directly from Medieval Latin *objectum* thing put before (the mind or sight), neuter of Latin *objectus,* past participle of *obicere* to present, oppose, cast in the way of (*ob-* against + *-icere,* combining form of *jacere* to throw; see JET[1] stream).

The meaning of a thing aimed at, purpose, end, goal, is first recorded probably before 1425. The grammatical sense of a word, etc., toward which the action of a verb is directed (especially in *direct object*) is found in English before 1729.

—**v.** (əbjekt') oppose. Probably about 1400 *obiecten,* in Wycliffe's writings; borrowed from Old French *objecter, objeter,* and directly from Latin *objectāre* to cite as grounds for disapproval or condemnation, frequentative form of *obicere* to oppose, object.

objection *n.* Before 1387 *objectioun,* in Trevisa's translation of Higden's *Polychronicon,* borrowed from Old French *objection,* and directly from Medieval Latin *obiectionem* (nominative *obiectio*), from Latin *obicere* to oppose, OBJECT. —**objectionable** *adj.* 1781, in Cowper's *Works;* formed from English *objection* + *-able.*

objective *adj.* 1620, formed in English from *object* + *-ive,* patterned on Medieval Latin *objectivus,* from *objectum* OBJECT.

The meaning of existing outside the mind, real is first recorded in 1647; the meaning "dealing with outward things, impersonal, unbiased" is found in 1855, probably influenced by German *objektiv.*

—**n.** 1738, something objective to the mind, or the power to make anything intelligible (now obsolete). The modern use of a microscope or telescope lens closest to the object, developed from the adjective, but was earlier known as an *object glass* (1738). The meaning "goal or aim" is first recorded in English in 1881, probably influenced by, or a shortened form of, *objective point,* as a military term (1864), and also probably reinforced by French *objectif* (1869).

—**objectivity** *n.* 1803, formed from English *objective* + *-ity.*

objurgate (ob′jərgāt *or* əbjėr′gāt) *v.* rebuke vehemently. 1616, in Bullokar's *An English Expositor;* probably a back formation from earlier *objurgation,* but also, in some instances, probably borrowed from Latin *objūrgātus,* past participle of *objūrgāre* to chide, rebuke (*ob-* against + *jūrgāre,* Old Latin *jūrigāre* scold, blame, quarrel, sue at law; formed from a lost adjective **jūrigus* proceeding by right, embodying the phrase *jūre agere,* from *jūre,* ablative of *jūs* right, and *agere* proceed, act; see JUST and AGENT); for suffix see -ATE[1]. **—objurgation** *n.* sharp or severe rebuke. Before 1500, borrowed from French *objurgation,* and directly from Latin *objūrgātiōnem* (nominative *objūrgātiō*), from *objūrgāre* objurgate; for suffix see -ATION.

oblate[1] (ob′lāt *or* oblāt′) *adj.* flattened at the poles. 1705, New Latin *oblatus* stretched, carried toward; fashioned from Latin *ob-* and *lātus,* as abstracted from Latin *prōlātus* lengthened out (*lātus,* past participle of *ferre* bring).

oblate[2] (ob′lāt *or* oblāt′) *n.* person offered or devoted to the service of a monastery. 1864, in *The Complete Works of St. John of the Cross* (edited by the Oblate Fathers. . .); borrowed from Medieval Latin *oblatus,* noun use of Latin *oblātus,* a form serving as past participle of Latin *offerre* to OFFER; for suffix see -ATE[3]. Though oblate groups were founded in Italy as early as 1433, it was not until the first half of the 1800's that several groups were established in English-speaking countries, thus accounting for the late introduction of the term in English.

oblation *n.* an offering to God or a god. Before 1400 *oblacyoun;* borrowed from Old French *oblacion,* or directly from Late Latin *oblātiōnem* (nominative *oblātiō*) an offering, presenting, gift, from Latin *oblātus,* a form serving as past participle of *offerre* bring to, present, OFFER; for suffix see -ATION.

obligate *v.* 1541, to pledge as security; later, bind morally or legally (1668); developed from Middle English *obligate,* adj., bound, obliged (probably before 1425, in a translation of Higden's *Polychronicon*); borrowed from Latin *obligātus,* past participle of *obligāre* (*ob-* to + *ligāre* to bind; see LIGAMENT); for suffix see -ATE[1]. It is also possible that in some instances *obligate,* v., was a back formation from earlier *obligation.* **—obligation** *n.* About 1300 *obligacion* binding pledge; borrowed from Old French *obligacion,* and directly from Latin *obligātiōnem* (nominative *obligātiō*) a bond, pledge, from *obligāre* to bind, oblige; for suffix see -ATION. **—obligatory** *adj.* compulsory. About 1400 *obligatorie* creating an obligation; borrowed from Old French *obligatoire,* and directly from Late Latin *obligātōrius* binding, from Latin *obligāre* to bind, oblige; for suffix see -ORY.

oblige *v.* Probably about 1280 *oblegen* bind by a promise, contract, duty, etc.; also *obligen* (about 1300); borrowed from Old French *obligier,* learned borrowing from Latin *obligāre* OBLIGATE. **—obliging** *adj.* helpful, accommodating. 1632, from the present participle of English *oblige;* for suffix see -ING[2].

oblique (əblēk′) *adj.* slanting. Probably before 1425 *oblique, oblike* slanting; figurative, indirect, in a translation of Chauliac's *Grande Chirurgie* and Higden's *Polychronicon;* borrowed from Middle French *oblique,* and directly from Latin *oblīquus* (*ob-* against + root *līqu-, lic-* to bend, as in *līquis* oblique, *licinus* bent upward), from Indo-European **lei-/li-* bend (Pok. 309).

obliterate *v.* blot out, destroy. 1600, borrowed from Latin *oblīterātus, oblitterātus,* past participle of *oblīterāre, oblitterāre* cause to disappear, efface (*ob-* against + *lītera, littera* letter), abstracted from the phrase *ob līterās scrībere* write across letters, strike out letters; for suffix see -ATE[1]. The borrowing from Latin may have been influenced by, or in some instances taken from, earlier Middle French *oblitérer,* from Latin *oblīterāre.* **—obliteration** *n.* 1658, in Phillips' *Dictionary,* probably formed from English *obliterate* + *-ion,* on the pattern of Latin *oblīterātiōnem, oblitterātiōnem* (nominative *oblīterātiō, oblitterātiō*), from *oblīterāre, oblitterāre* obliterate.

oblivion *n.* condition of being entirely forgotten. Before 1393, in Gower's *Confessio Amantis;* borrowed from Old French *oblivion,* and from Latin *oblīviōnem* (nominative *oblīviō*) forgetfulness, from *oblīvīscī* forget; originally, even out, smooth over (*ob-* over + the root of *lēvis* smooth; see LIME[1] white substance); for suffix see -ION. **—oblivious** *adj.* not mindful, forgetful. About 1450 *oblyvyous,* borrowed from Latin *oblīviōsus* forgetful, from *oblīviō* oblivion; for suffix see -OUS.

oblong *adj.* longer than broad, elongated. Probably before 1425, in a translation of Chauliac's *Grande Chirurgie,* borrowed from Latin *oblongus* somewhat long (*ob-* perhaps in the sense of to or toward but also functioning as an intensive + *longus* LONG[1], adj.). **—n.** oblong figure. Before 1608, from the adjective.

obloquy (ob′ləkwē) *n.* public reproach, abuse, blame. Before 1438 *obloquie;* borrowed from Medieval Latin *obloquium* abusive contradiction, from Latin *obloqui* interpose remarks, interrupt (*ob-* against + *loqui* speak; see LOQUACIOUS).

obnoxious *adj.* 1581, subject to authority; later, subject to something harmful (1597); borrowed from Latin *obnoxiōsus,* from *obnoxius* subject, liable, exposed to harm or danger (*ob-* to, toward + *noxa* hurt, harm, punishment; see NOXIOUS); for suffix see -OUS. The meaning "offensive or hateful" is first recorded in English in 1675, influenced by the earlier *noxious.*

oboe *n.* woodwind musical instrument. 1794 (but included earlier in an explanation of foreign terms in music, 1724); borrowing of Italian *oboe,* from Middle French *hautbois* (found as *hautboy, hautboiz,* in English, 1575) a compound of *haut* high (see HAUGHTY + *bois* wood (from Gallo-Romance **boscī,* plural to **boscum* from Frankish **busk;* compare German *Busch* BUSH); so called from the instrument's high notes and wooden construction.

obscene *adj.* 1593, disgusting, foul, loathsome, repulsive, in Shakespeare's *Richard II;* borrowed from Middle French *obscène,* learned borrowing from Latin *obscēnus* offensive, especially to modesty; originally a term of the augurs' vocabulary, meaning of ill omen boding ill; of uncertain origin. As explained by Walde Hofmann, Latin *obscēnus* is a back formation from **obscēnāre* to bring filth upon, from *ob-s-* onto + **cēnum* filth (compare the urbanized Latin form *caenum* filth), originally probably a rural form of earlier **coinom* (pre-Latin **quoinom*), cognate with Latin *inquināre* bring stain upon, befoul, from Indo-European **k̑wei-/k̑woi-/*k̑wi-* (Pok. 628). Ernout-Meillet dispute connection with Latin *caenum* and maintain that the etymology of *obscēnus* is unknown.

The meaning "offensive to modesty or decency indecent, lewd," is first recorded in English in 1598.

—obscenity *n.* obscene language or behavior. 1608, borrowed from French *obscenité,* from Latin *obscēnitātem* (nominative *obscēnitās*) moral impurity, from *obscēnus* offensive, obscene; for suffix see -ITY.

obscure *adj.* Probably before 1400, borrowed from Old French *obscur, oscur* dark, dim, not clear, and directly from Latin *obscūrus* covered over, dark, obscure (*ob-* over + *-scūrus* covered).

The Latin form *-scūrus,* from the root *scu-* is cognate with Old Frisian *skūre* shelter, shed, Middle Dutch *schuur,* Old High German *scūr,* Old Icelandic *skūr* covering or skin of an almond, Latvian *skura* husk, pod, *skaût* to embrace, and Greek *skŷtos* HIDE[2] skin. **—v.** to darken, dim. Probably before 1425 *obscuren,* from the adjective. **—obscurant** *n.* one who obscures. 1799, borrowed by influence of French *obscurant* and German *Obskurant,* from Latin *obscūrantem* (nominative *obscūrāns*), present participle of *obscūrāre* to obscure, from *obscūrus* obscure. *—adj.* that obscures. 1878, from the noun. **—obscurantism** *n.* opposition to progress and the spread of knowledge. 1834, borrowed from French *obscurantisme,* from *obscurant* + *-isme* -ism. **—obscurity** *n.* About 1477 *obscuryte* dimness, condition of being imperfectly comprehended or known, in Caxton's *The Game and Play of Chess;* borrowed from Middle French *obscurité,* variant of Old French *oscurté,* from Latin *obscūritātem* (nominative *obscūritās*), from *obscūrus* obscure; for suffix see -ITY. The meaning "condition of being unknown (not famous)" is first recorded in 1619.

obsequies (ob'səkwēz) *n.pl.* funeral rites. About 1385, in Chaucer's *Canterbury Tales;* borrowed from Old French *obseques* funeral rites, plural of *obseque* funeral, or directly from Medieval Latin *obsequiae* funeral rites, probably a blend in form and meaning of Latin *exequiae* funeral rites, and *obsequia,* plural of *obsequium* dutiful service; see OBSEQUIOUS. Latin *exequiae* is derived from *exsequī* follow out to the cemetery, follow in a funeral procession (*ex-* out + *sequī* follow; see SEQUEL).

obsequious (əbsē'kwēəs) *adj.* servile, fawning. About 1475 *obsequyouse* compliant, obedient (but implied earlier in *obsequyousnesse,* 1447); borrowed, perhaps through influence of Middle French *obséquieux,* from Latin *obsequiōsus* compliant, obedient, from *obsequium* compliance, dutiful service (*ob-* after + *sequī* follow; see SEQUEL); for suffix see -OUS. The meaning of unduly compliant or servile, fawning, cringing, is first recorded in Marston's *History of Antonio and Mellida* (1599).

observance *n.* act of keeping customs or laws. About 1250 *observaunce* precept, rule, custom, in a version of *Ancrene Riwle;* borrowed from Old French *observance,* or directly from Latin *observantia* act of keeping customs or laws, regard, attention, from *observantem* (nominative *observāns*), present participle of *observāre* OBSERVE; for suffix see -ANCE. **—observant** *adj.* 1602, quick to notice, in Shakespeare's *Hamlet;* also 1608, careful in observing (a law or custom); probably formed from English *observe-* + *-ant,* after *observance,* modeled on the pattern of *importance, important,* and reinforced by Latin *observantem* (nominative *observāns),* present participle of *observāre.*

observation *n.* Before 1382 *observacioun* act of keeping customs or laws, performance of religious rites, in the Wycliffe Bible; later, act of seeing and noting (1557, in the *Geneva Bible*); borrowed from Old French *observation,* learned borrowing from Latin; and borrowed directly from Latin *observātiōnem* (nominative *observātiō*), from *observāre* OBSERVE; for suffix see -ATION.

observatory *n.* place where astronomical observations are made. 1676, in Evelyn's *Diary;* borrowed from French *observatoire,* from *observer,* from Old French *observer* to OBSERVE; for suffix see -ORY.

observe *v.* About 1390 *observen* follow in practice, keep to, in Chaucer's *Canterbury Tales;* borrowed from Old French *observer,* from Latin *observāre* watch over, look to, attend to, guard (*ob-* over + *servāre* to watch, keep; see CONSERVE).

The meaning "see and note omens" appeared in 1391, but the generalized sense "watch, perceive, notice" was not in common use until the mid 1500's. **—observable** *adj.* 1608, formed from English *observe* + *-able.* **—observer** *n.* 1555, formed from English *observe* + *-er*[1]. The meaning of one who watches or takes notice is first recorded in Mulcaster's writings, in 1581.

obsess *v.* 1503, besiege; later, beset, haunt, harass, trouble (1531); borrowed from Latin *obsessus,* past participle of *obsidēre* besiege, occupy; literally, sit opposite to (*ob-* against + *sedēre* SIT). It is also possible that English *beset* (Old English *besettan*) and its cognates may have been borrowed from a German loan translation of Latin *obsidēre.* **—obsession** *n.* a being obsessed. 1513, act of besieging; later, a being beset or haunted, in Ben Jonson's *Volpone* (1605); also, persistent influence or idea (1680); borrowed from Middle French and modern French *obsession,* learned borrowing from Latin *obsessiōnem* (nominative *obsessiō*), from *obsess-,* past participle stem of *obsidēre* besiege; for suffix see -ION. **—obsessive** *adj.* causing obsession. 1911, formed from English *obsess* + *-ive.*

obsidian (obsid'ēən) *n.* glassy rock formed when lava cools. 1656, in Blount's *Glossographia,* borrowed possibly from earlier French *obsidiane* (1600), and directly from Latin *obsidiānus,* misreading of *obsiānus lapis* stone of *Obsius,* name of a Roman alleged by Pliny to have found this or a similar rock in Ethiopia.

obsolescent *adj.* passing out of use. 1755, in Johnson's *Dictionary,* borrowed from Latin *obsolēscentem* (nominative *obsolēscēns*), present participle of *obsolēscere* fall into disuse; see OBSOLETE; for suffix see -ESCENT. **—obsolescence** *n.* a passing out of use. Before 1828, in Webster's *Dictionary,* formed from English *obsolescent,* on analogy of *evanescent, evanescence,* etc.; for suffix see -ESCENCE.

obsolete *adj.* no longer in use. 1579, in Spenser's *The Shepheardes Calender;* borrowed from Latin *obsolētus,* past participle of *obsolēscere* fall into disuse (probably *ob-* away + **-solēscere,* formed on *solēre* to be used to, be accustomed; see INSOLENT). **—v.** make or become obsolete. 1640, from the adjective, or perhaps borrowed from Latin *obsolēt-,* past participle stem of *obsolēscere* fall into disuse.

obstacle *n.* About 1340 *obstakil,* in Rolle's *The Psalter;* later *obstacle* (about 1385, in Chaucer's *Canterbury Tales*); borrowed from Old French *ostacle, obstacle* hindrance, or directly from Latin *obstāculum,* from *obstāre* stand opposite to, block, hinder (*ob-* against + *stāre* to STAND); for suffix see -CLE.

obstetrics *n.* branch of medicine dealing with childbirth. 1819, midwifery; formed from earlier English *obstetric* + *-s* (plural suffix), after Latin *obstetrīcia* (neuter plural) midwifery, from *obstetrīx* (genitive *obstetrīcis*) midwife; literally, one who stands opposite to (the woman giving birth), from *obstāre* stand opposite to; see OBSTACLE; for suffix see -ICS. —**obstetric** *adj.* of obstetrics. 1742, of a midwife or midwifery, in Pope's *The Dunciad;* borrowed from Latin *obstetrīcius* pertaining to a midwife, from *obstetrīx* midwife; for suffix see -IC. —**obstetrician** *n.* physician specializing in obstetrics. 1828, in Webster's *Dictionary;* formed from Latin *obstetrīcia* midwifery + English suffix *-an,* on the pattern of *physician.*

obstinate *adj.* stubborn. Probably 1387 *obstinat;* borrowed from Latin *obstinātus,* past participle of *obstināre* persist, stand stubbornly (*ob-* by + *-stināre,* earlier **-stanāre,* related to *stāre* to STAND); for suffix see -ATE[1]. —**obstinacy** *n.* stubbornness. Before 1393 *obstinacie,* in Gower's *Confessio Amantis;* borrowed from Medieval Latin *obstinacia, obstinatia,* from Latin *obstinātus,* past participle; for suffix see -ACY.

obstreperous (əbstrep′ərəs) *adj.* noisy, boisterous. About 1600, borrowed from Latin *obstreperus* clamorous, from *obstrepere* make a noise against, drown with noise, oppose noisily (*ob-* against + *strepere* make a noise, of imitative origin); for suffix see -OUS.

obstruct *v.* 1611, block or close up, in Cotgrave's *Dictionary;* probably a back formation of earlier *obstruction.* The figurative sense of hinder is first recorded in English in 1647, probably to correspond to the same sense in earlier *obstruction* (1601). —**obstruction** *n.* 1533, fact of blocking a passage, in Sir Thomas More's *The Apology Made By Him;* borrowed from Latin *obstrūctiōnem* (nominative *obstrūctiō*), from *obstrūct-,* past participle stem of *obstruere* obstruct, build against, block up, hinder (*ob-* against + *struere* to pile, build; see STRUCTURE); for suffix see -ION. —**obstructionism** (1879) —**obstructionist** (1846) —**obstructive** (1611, in Cotgrave's *Dictionary*)

obtain *v.* About 1412 *opteenen* get or acquire, in Hoccleve's *Regement of Princes;* later *obteenen* (about 1422), and *obteynen* (probably before 1425); borrowed from Middle French *optenir, obtenir,* or directly from Latin *optinēre, obtinēre* hold, keep, get, acquire (*ob-* to + *tenēre* to hold; see TENANT). —**obtainable** *adj.* 1617, formed from English *obtain* + *-able.*

obtrude *v.* put forward unasked and unwanted, force. About 1555, borrowed from Latin *obtrūdere* thrust into, press upon (*ob-* toward + *trūdere* to thrust; see THREAT). —**obtrusion** *n.* 1579, borrowed from Latin *obtrūsiōnem* (nominative *obtrūsiō*), from *obtrūdere* obtrude; for suffix see -SION.—**obtrusive** *adj.* intrusive. 1667, in Milton's *Paradise Lost;* formed in English from Latin *obtrūs-,* past participle stem of *obtrūdere* obtrude + English suffix *-ive.*

obtuse *adj.* not sharp or acute, blunt. Probably before 1425, in a translation of Chauliac's *Grande Chirurgie;* later, in a figurative sense of stupid (1509), borrowed from Middle French *obtus* (feminine *obtuse*), learned borrowing from Latin *obtūsus* blunted, dull, past participle of *obtundere* to beat against, blunt, dull (*ob-* against + *tundere* to beat; see STUDY).

obverse (ob′vėrs) *adj.* Before 1656, turned toward the observer, frontal; borrowed from Latin *obversus,* past participle of *obvertere* to turn toward or against (*ob-* toward + *vertere* to turn; see VERTEX). The technical sense of narrower at the base or point of attachment than at the apex or top, is first recorded in 1826. The transferred sense of being a counterpart to something else is found in 1875. —**n.** side of a coin, medal, etc., that has the principal design. 1658, from the adjective.

obviate *v.* meet and dispose of, remove. 1598, borrowed from Late Latin *obviātus,* past participle of *obviāre* act contrary to, go against, from Latin *obvius* that is in the way or path, that moves against, see OBVIOUS; for suffix see -ATE[1].

obvious *adj.* 1586, frequently met with or found; borrowed from Latin *obvius* that is in the way or path, presenting itself readily, commonplace, from *obviam,* adv., in the way, towards (*ob* against + *viam,* accusative of *via* way; see VIA); for suffix see -OUS. The meaning of plainly clear, perfectly evident, is first recorded in English in 1635.

oc- a form of the prefix *ob-* before *c* in words of Latin origin, as in *occupy.* The form is due to assimilation of *b* to the following consonant (*c*).

ocarina (ok′ərē′nə) *n.* wind musical instrument. 1877, borrowing of Italian *ocarina,* diminutive of *oca* goose (so called from its shape), from Vulgar Latin **avica,* back formation from Latin *avicula* small bird, diminutive of *avis* bird; see AVIARY.

occasion *n.* Before 1382 *occasyoun, occasion* opportunity, favorable juncture, reason, cause, in the Wycliffe Bible; borrowed through Old French *occasion,* or directly from Latin *occāsiōnem* (nominative *occāsiō*) opportunity, fit time, favorable moment, from *occāsum,* past participle of *occidere* fall down, go down (*oc-* down, away, variant of *ob-* before *c* + *cadere* to fall; see CADENCE); for suffix see -SION.

The meaning of a particular time or event is first recorded in 1568.

—**v.** to cause. About 1445 *occasionen;* from the noun. —**occasional** *adj.* happening now and then. Before 1398 *occasyonal,* in Trevisa's translation of Bartholomew's *De Proprietatibus Rerum;* formed from Middle English *occasyoun, occasion* + *-al*[1], possibly by influence of Late Latin *occāsiōnāliter* as occasion arises, occasionally.

Occident *n.* countries in Europe and America; the West. About 1375, part of the sky or the world in which the sun sets, the West, in Chaucer's *Canterbury Tales,* borrowed from Old French *occident,* or directly from Latin *occidentem* (nominative *occidēns*) the part of the sky in which the sun sets; originally, *adj.,* setting, present participle of *occidere* fall down, go down; see OCCASION; for suffix see -ENT. Compare ORIENT. —**Occidental** *adj.* About 1400, westerly or western, in Chaucer's *Treatise on the Astrolabe;* later, of the western countries (1553); borrowed from Old French *occidental,* or directly from Latin *occidentālis* of the West, from *occidentem,* present participle; for suffix see -AL[1].

occiput (ok′səpət) *n. Anatomy.* back part of the head or skull. Before 1398, in Trevisa's translation of Bartholomew's *De Proprietatibus Rerum;* later, occipital bone (1578); borrowed from Latin *occiput* (*oc-* against, behind, variant of *ob-* before *c* + *caput* HEAD). —**occipital** *adj.* of the occiput. 1541, borrowed from Middle French *occipital,* from Medieval Latin *occipitalis,* from Latin *occiput* (genitive *occipitis*) occiput; for suffix see -AL[1].

occlude (əklüd′) *v.* stop up (a passage, pores, etc.). 1597, borrowed from Latin *occlūdere* shut up, close up (*oc-* against, up, variant of *ob-* before *c* + *claudere* to shut, CLOSE[1]). —**occlusion** *n.* About 1645, borrowed from

Latin *occlūsiōnem,* from *occlūdere* occlude; for suffix see -SION.

occult (əkult′) *adj.* secret, mysterious. 1533, concealed, kept secret; later, beyond ordinary knowledge (1545); possibly from the verb in English, but probably also borrowed from Middle French *occulte,* and directly from Latin *occultus* hidden, past participle of *occulere* cover over, conceal (*oc-* over, variant of *ob-* before *c* + *-culere,* related to *cēlāre* to hide; see CELL). **—v.** hide from view, cover, conceal. Before 1500 *occulten* (in figurative use); probably a back formation from earlier *occultation,* and possibly in some instances borrowed from Latin *occultāre,* frequentative form of *occulere* cover over. **—occultation** *n.* concealment. Probably before 1425 *occultacion,* in a translation of Higden's *Polychronicon;* borrowed from Latin *occultātiōnem* (nominative *occultātiō*), from *occultāre* hide, conceal, frequentative form of *occulere* cover over; for suffix see -ATION. The astronomical sense "concealment of one heavenly body by another" is first recorded in 1551.

occupant *n.* 1596, one who takes possession of something having no owner, in Bacon's *The Elements of Common Laws;* probably borrowed from Middle French *occupant,* learned borrowing from Latin *occupantem* (nominative *occupāns*), present participle of *occupāre* OCCUPY; for suffix see -ANT. It is also possible that *occupant* was separately formed in English as a direct borrowing from Latin *occupantem* (nominative *occupāns*). This would account for Bacon's use of both *occupant* and *occupancy,* the appearance of the latter seeming to be simultaneous with *occupant.*

The meaning of occupier or resident is first recorded in English in 1622.

—occupancy *n.* 1596, in Bacon's *The Elements of Common Laws,* condition of being an occupant; probably formed from English *occupan(t)* + *-cy.*

occupation *n.* Before 1325 *occupacioun* act of holding or possessing lands or goods; later, business, employment (probably 1348); borrowed from Old French *occupacion,* from Latin *occupātiōnem* (nominative *occupātiō*) a taking possession, business, employment, from *occupāre* OCCUPY; for suffix see -ATION. **—occupational** *adj.* 1850, in Hawthorne's *American Notebooks;* formed from English *occupation* + *-al*[1].

occupy *v.* Before 1325 *occupien* keep busy; later, take possession of, hold (before 1382, in the Wycliffe Bible), irregular borrowing from Old French *occuper,* or directly from Latin *occupāre* take over, seize, possess, occupy (*oc-* over, variant of *ob-* before *c* + **-capāre,* intensive form of *capere* to grasp, seize; see CAPTIVE).

The final *-ien* in Middle English (which developed into *-y* in modern English), found also in inflections (*occupied*) and derivatives (*occupier,* etc.) at their earliest appearance, cannot be explained from the Old French *occuper, occupant, occupe,* etc. or from Latin *occupāre* and its derivatives. It is possible that the change took place in Anglo-French (which has *occupiours* for *occupiers*) but this may be itself a borrowing from English. Old French did have a noun *occupier* he who occupies, but this would have been too remote to influence the English verb.

Generally in books on the development of English, a notation appears about the relative disappearance of *occupy,* v. from the record in the 1600's and 1700's. The cause is attributed to the obsolete sense of have sexual relations with (first recorded probably before 1425, in a translation of Higden's *Polychronicon*). As contemporary writers have objected to our present-day use of *screw* and *suck,* v., and *gay,* adj. and n., Shakespeare laments: These villains will make the word as odious as the word occupy, which was an excellent good word before it was ill sorted—*2 Henry IV.*

occur *v.* 1527, meet with, encounter; also, happen (1538); borrowed, perhaps through influence of Middle French *occorrer, occurrir* happen unexpectedly, from Latin *occurrere* run to meet, run against, befall, present itself, occur (*oc-* against, toward, variant of *ob-* before *c* + *currere* to run; see CURRENT). **—occurrence** *n.* 1539, in Thomas Cromwell's *Letters,* probably borrowed from Middle French *occurrence* unexpected happening, from *occurrir* happen unexpectedly; for suffix see -ENCE.

ocean *n.* About 1300 *occean* the main or great sea; borrowed from Old French *ocëan, occean,* learned borrowing from Latin *ōceanus,* from Greek *ōkeanós* the great stream or river supposed to surround the disk of the earth, and personified as *Ōkeanós* the god of the ocean, son of Uranus and Gaea, and husband of Tethys. **—oceanic** *adj.* 1656 *oceanick,* in Blount's *Glossographia;* probably borrowed from French *océanique,* from *océan* ocean + *-ique* -ic.

oceanography *n.* science of the oceans and seas. 1859, formed from English *ocean* + *-o-* + *-graphy.* French *océanographie* occurred in Middle French in 1584 but was rare before 1876. It may have been the model for the English word.

ocelot (os′əlot) *n.* spotted wildcat. 1775, borrowing of French *ocelot,* from Nahuatl *ocelotl* jaguar. The word was introduced into French by the French naturalist Georges L.L. de Buffon, 1707-88.

ocher or **ochre** (ō′kər) *n.* earth mixture used as pigment. 1296 *ocre;* later *ocra* (before 1398); borrowing of Old French *ocre* and Late Latin *ōcra;* both from Latin *ōchra,* from Greek *ṓchrā,* from *ōchrós* pale yellow, of uncertain origin. The respelling *ocher, ochre* in imitation of Latin, was first recorded in 1601. The meaning of a pale brownish yellow, the color of ocher, is first recorded about 1440.

-ock a suffix forming diminutives, as in *bullock, hillock,* etc. Middle English *-ok* developed from Old English *-oc, -uc.*

o'clock About 1720, contraction of earlier *of the clock* (1647), from Middle English *of the clokke* (1389).

oct- or **octa-** variants of OCTO-, as in *octet, octagon.* Borrowed from Greek *okt-, okta-,* from *oktṓ* EIGHT.

octagon (ok′təgon) *n.* plane figure having eight angles. 1660, borrowed from Latin *octagōnos,* from Greek *oktágōnos* (*okta-* eight + *gōníā* angle, related to *gony* KNEE). An earlier form *octogon* (1656, in Blount's *Glossographia*) was borrowed from French *octogone.* **—octagonal** (oktag′ənəl) *adj.* 1812-16, formed from English *octagon* + *-al*[1].

octane (ok′tān) *n.* hydrocarbon in petroleum. 1872, in Henry Watts' *Dictionary of Chemistry;* formed from English *oct-* eight (variant of *octo-* before vowels) + *-ane,* as in *methane.* The reference to eight in *octane* pertains to the number of carbon atoms (C_8) in the hydrocarbon.

octave (ok′tiv) *n.* Probably before 1425 (plural) *octaves* period of eight days after a festival, the eighth day of this period, in a translation of Higden's *Polychronicon;*

borrowed from Middle French *octave,* or directly from Medieval Latin *octava,* from Latin *octāva diēs* eighth day, feminine of *octāvus* eighth, from *octō* EIGHT. An earlier Middle English form, *utaves* (before 1325), came by way of Anglo-French from Old French *oitieve,* from Latin *octāva.*

The meaning in music of eighth note above or below a given tone, interval of eight degrees of the diatonic scale is first recorded in Blount's *Glossographia* (1656), borrowed perhaps from French, where it occurs in 1534. *Octave* in this sense replaced the earlier English *eighth,* n., found in Middle English before 1450 as *eyghte.*

octavo (oktā′vō *or* oktä′vō) *n.* page size in which each leaf is one eighth of a whole sheet of paper. 1582, borrowed from Medieval Latin *in octavo* in an eighth, ablative of Latin *octāvus* eighth, from *octō* EIGHT.

octet or **octette** *n.* musical composition for eight voices or instruments. 1880 *octet,* in Grove's *Dictionary of Music and Musicians;* formed from English *oct-* eight (variant of *octo-* before vowels) + *-et,* patterned on *duet, quartet,* etc. The form *octet* was an adaptation of Italian *ottetto; octette* is a variant influenced by the suffix *-ette.*

octo- a combining form of Latin *octō* and sometimes of Greek *oktṓ* EIGHT, as in *octopus* and *octosyllable.* Also, *oct-* before vowels. The Greek form is more frequently *okta-* octa-.

October *n.* tenth month. Old English (about 1050) *october;* borrowed from Latin *Octōber,* from *octō* EIGHT, this being originally the eighth month of the ancient Roman calendar (which began with March); for the origin of the ending *-ber* see DECEMBER. The Julian calendar (46 B.C.) changed October to the tenth month.

A Middle English form (about 1150) *Octobre* (borrowed from Old French *Octobre,* from Latin *Octōbrem,* accusative of *Octōber*) was replaced in the 1500's by the current Latinized form.

octogenarian (ok′təjənâr′ēən) *n.* person between 80 and 90 years old. 1815, in *Paris Chit-Chat,* formed with the English ending *-an* from French *octogénaire* aged eighty, learned borrowing from Latin *octōgēnārius* containing eighty, from *octōgēnī* eighty each, from *octō* EIGHT. **—adj.** between 80 and 90 years old. 1818, in Byron's *Childe Harold's Pilgrimage;* from the noun.

octopus *n.* sea mollusk with eight arms. 1758, New Latin *Octopus* the genus name, from Greek *oktṓpous* eight-footed (*oktṓ* EIGHT + *poús* FOOT).

The figurative application of *octopus* to any organized power with far-reaching influence, especially when harmful or destructive, appeared in 1878 in American English; the usage was popularized by Frank Norris' novel of social commentary about the railroads *The Octopus* (1901).

ocular *adj.* having to do with the eye. About 1575, borrowed from Late Latin *oculāris* of the eyes, from Latin *oculus* EYE; for suffix see -AR. The borrowing was perhaps influenced by the existence of Middle French *oculaire,* from Late Latin *oculāris.* **—n.** eyepiece of a telescope, microscope, etc. 1835, in John Lindley's *An Introduction to Botany;* from the adjective. The humorous meaning "eye" appeared in 1825. An isolated occurrence of the plural *ocularies* occurs in Middle English (probably before 1425) with the meaning "spectacles," borrowed from Medieval Latin *ocularium,* from Late Latin *oculāris* ocular. **—oculist** *n.* eye doctor; ophthalmologist or optometrist. 1615, borrowed from French *oculiste,* formed from Latin *oculus* eye + French *-iste* -ist.

OD (ō′dē′) *n. Slang.* overdose of a narcotic; drug addict who has taken an overdose. 1960, American English, from the abbreviation of *overdose.* The word *overdose,* originally applied to an excessive portion of any substance (such as honey), is first recorded in Locke's *Essay Concerning Human Understanding* (1700). **—v.** *Slang.* become sick or die from an overdose of a narcotic. 1969, American English, from the noun.

odd *adj.* About 1280 *odde* left over, single, unique; borrowed from a Scandinavian source (compare Old Icelandic *oddi* third or odd number; earlier, triangle, angle, point of land, found also in the genitive form *odda* in such compounds as *oddatala* odd number, and *oddamadhr* third or odd man, the notion deriving from the three sides of a triangle). Old Icelandic *oddi* is related to *oddr* point of a weapon, and cognate with Old High German *ort* angle, point (modern German *Ort* place), Middle Dutch *ort* point, edge (modern Dutch *oord* place), Old Saxon and Old Frisian *ord* point or tip (also found in Old English *ord,* which did not survive), from Proto-Germanic **uzdaz* pointed upwards, from Indo-European **ud-dh-o-s,* from **ud-* up, out + **dhē-/dhō-/dhə-/dh-* set, place (Pok. 237).

The sense of peculiar or strange is first recorded in Shakespeare's *Love's Labour's Lost* (1588).

—oddity *n.* peculiarity, strangeness. 1713, in Steele's writings in *The Guardian;* formed from English *odd* + *-ity.* **—oddments** *n.pl.* odds and ends. 1796, formed from English *odd* + *-ments,* plural of *-ment.* **—odds** *n.pl.* 1500-20, odd things, in Dunbar's *Poems;* formed from English *odd,* adj. (taken as a noun) + *-s*[1], plural suffix. The meaning of amount of difference appeared in 1548, and that of difference favoring one of two contending parties in 1574. **—oddball** *n.* very eccentric person. 1948, American English, a compound of *odd,* adj. + *ball*[1], n., patterned on *screwball.*

ode *n.* lyric poem. 1588, in Shakespeare's *Love's Labour's Lost;* borrowed from Middle French *ode,* learned borrowing from Late Latin *ōdē* lyric song, from Greek *ōidḗ,* Attic contraction of *aoidḗ,* from *aeídein* sing; probably by dissimilation from earlier **a-we-wd-éen,* related to *audḗ* voice, tone, sound. The Greek words are cognate with Lithuanian *vadìnti* to call, name, Sanskrit *vádati* he speaks, sings, *uditá-s* spoken, and Tocharian A, Tocharian B *wätk-* to command, from Indo-European **(a)wed-/(a)wod-/ud-* (Pok. 76).

odious *adj.* hateful, offensive. Before 1382 *odyous,* in the Wycliffe Bible; borrowed from Old French *odieus,* or directly from Latin *odiōsus* hateful, from *odium* hatred, ODIUM; for suffix see -OUS.

odium (ō′dēəm) *n.* hatred. 1602, in William Warner's *Albions England;* borrowed from Latin *odium* ill-will, hatred, offense, related to *ōdī* I hate (infinitive *ōdisse*). Latin *ōdisse* is cognate with Greek *odýssasthai* to be angry at, to hate, Armenian *ateam* I hate, Old English *atol* dire, hostile and Hittite *hatukis* terrible, from Indo-European **od-* (Pok. 773).

odometer (ōdom′ətər) *n.* device for measuring distance traveled by a vehicle. 1791, in Jefferson's writings, American English; borrowed from French *odomètre,* from Greek *hodómetron* (*hodós* way, see CEDE + *métron* MEASURE).

odontology (ōdontol′əjē) *n.* branch of anatomy dealing

with the teeth. 1819, borrowed from French *odontologie,* formed from Greek *odont-* (stem form of Ionic *odṓn* TOOTH) + French connective *-o-* + *-logie* -logy, study of.

odor *n.* Before 1300 *odur,* in *The Land of Cokaygne;* also, probably before 1300 *odour,* in *Kyng Alisaunder;* later *odor* (before 1325, in *Cursor Mundi*); borrowed from Old French *odor, odur,* and directly from Latin *odor* smell, scent, related to *olēre* to smell of, emit a smell, earlier **odēre.* The Latin words are cognate with Greek *ózein* to smell, *odmḗ, osmḗ* odor, Lithuanian *úosti* to smell, Armenian *hot* odor, and possibly with Swedish and Norwegian *os* odor, from Indo-European **od-/ōd-* to smell (Pok. 772). **—odoriferous** *adj.* giving forth an odor. Probably before 1475, formed in English from Latin *odōrifer* odoriferous (*odor* odor + *-fer* bearing, from *ferre* to BEAR[2] carry) + English suffix *-ous.* **—odorless** *adj.* Before 1849, in Poe's writings, American English; formed from *odor* + *-less.* **—odorous** *adj.* fragrant. Probably before 1425, in a translation of Chauliac's *Grande Chirurgie;* borrowed from Medieval Latin *odorosus,* from Latin *odōrus* having a smell, from *odor* smell; for suffix see -OUS.

of *prep.* 1100 *of* of, from, in *Peterborough Chronicle;* later *off* (about 1250); developed from Old English (about 700) *of,* unstressed form of *æf,* prep. and adv., away or away from; cognate with Old Frisian *of, af,* prep. and adv., from, Old Saxon *af,* Middle Dutch and modern Dutch *af* off, Old High German *aba* away, away from (modern German *ab* off, from), Old Icelandic and Gothic *af,* from Proto-Germanic **aƀa,* corresponding outside Germanic to Latin *ab* from, Greek *apó* away from, Sanskrit *ápa,* and Hittite *appa* afterwards, again, from Indo-European **apo* (Pok. 53). Related to OFF and AB-[1].

of- a form of the prefix *ob-* before *f* in words of Latin origin, as in *offer.* The form is due to assimilation of *b* to the following consonant (*f*).

off *adv.* Before 1121 *of* off, of, in *Peterborough Chronicle;* later *offe* (probably before 1200); developed from Old English (before 971) *of,* adv., away; see OF.

Off was originally the same word as *of.* In the 1100's, however, it began to appear as *off, offe,* a variant spelling which gradually came to be used as the emphatic form, that is, as the adverb, while *of* was retained in the weakened senses, in which the preposition is usually without stress and becomes (əv).

—prep. 1100 *of* away from; developed from Old English (before 855) *of.* The meaning "not on" is first recorded in 1688.

—adj. 1666, farther; later, not at work (1826); from the adverb.

—offbeat *adj.* 1927, of an unaccented beat in music; later, (figurative) unusual, unconventional (1938), American English. **—off-color** *adj.* 1860, defective in color; later (figurative) improper, risqué (1875). **—offhand** *adv.* (1694); *adj.* (1708) **—offish** *adj.* aloof or reserved; standoffish. 1834, formed from English *off,* adv. + *-ish*[1]. **—offset** *n.* (before 1555); *v.* (1792) **—offshoot** *n.* (1710, Addison) **—offshore** *adv.* (1720, Defoe); *adj.* (1845, Darwin) **—offstage** *adv., adj.* (1922) **—off-the-cuff** *adj.* not prepared, extemporaneous, impromptu. 1948, from earlier American English adverbial phrase *off the cuff* on the spur of the moment, extemporaneously, as if reading or reciting off some notes jotted down on a shirt cuff (1938). **—off-the-record** *adj.* (1933, American English)

offal (ôf′əl *or* of′əl) *n.* waste, garbage, refuse. Before 1398 *offall,* in Trevisa's translation of Bartholomew's *De Proprietatibus Rerum;* a blended compound of *off* + *fall,* n., in the sense of "that which falls off or away (from the butcher's block)." Compare German *Abfall* and Dutch *avfal,* similar formations with the same meaning as *offal.*

offend *v.* Probably 1350-75 *offendien* sin against, displease, do wrong; later *offenden* (about 1378); borrowed from Old French *ofendre,* and directly from Latin *offendere* strike against, stumble, commit a fault, displease (*of-* against, variant of *ob-* before *f* + *-fendere* to strike; see DEFEND). **—offender** *n.* 1472-75, lawbreaker, criminal, in *Rolls of Parliament;* in part formed from Middle English *offenden* offend + *-er*[1], and in part an alteration of earlier *offendour* (about 1412, in Hoccleve's *Regement of Princes*); probably borrowed from Anglo-French.

offense *n.* wrongdoing, crime, sin. Probably 1350-75 *offens;* later *offence* (about 1380); borrowed from Old French *ofense* injury, wrong, annoyance, and directly from Latin *offēnsa* an offense, injury, from feminine past participle of *offendere* OFFEND. **—offensive** *adj.* giving offense. 1547-64, used for attack; later, annoying or insulting (1576); borrowed through Middle French *offensif* (feminine *offensive*), and directly from Medieval Latin *offensivus,* from past participle stem of Latin *offendere* offend for suffix see -IVE. —*n.* attack, assault. 1720, position or attitude of attack; from the adjective.

offer *v.* Before 1121 *offren* to present as a sacrifice, bestow in worship, in *Peterborough Chronicle:* later *offeren* (before 1325, in *Cursor Mundi*); developed from Old English *ofrian* (before 830, in *The Vespasian Psalter*); borrowed from Late Latin *offerre* present in worship or devotion, from Latin *offerre* present, bestow, bring before (*of-,* variant of *ob-* before *f* + *-ferre* bring, carry, BEAR[2]). Other early borrowings in Germanic of Late Latin *offerre* include Old Frisian *offria* present as a sacrifice, Old Saxon *offrōn,* Middle Dutch *offeren,* and Old Icelandic *offra.*

The general sense of present or proffer is first recorded in Middle English before 1420 and was reinforced by Old French *offrir,* from Latin *offerre.*

Despite the similarity in form and meaning of Middle English *offeren* and Middle High German and German *opfern* (from Old High German *opfarōn*), the two words are not related. Old High German *opfarōn,* (older form *opparōn*), was borrowed from Latin *operārī,* which besides the basic meaning "to work, labor, OPERATE" had the sense of "to perform sacred rites, honor or worship by bringing sacrifices."

—n. 1433 *offre,* borrowed from Old French *ofre, offre,* from *offrir* to offer, from Latin *offerre.*

offertory (ôf′ərtôr′ē) *n.* collection of offerings at a religious service. About 1350 *offertori* verses sung or chanted during the offertory; borrowed from Medieval Latin *offertorium* place where offerings were brought, from Latin *offerre* to OFFER; for suffix see -ORY.

The meaning of the part of a religious service at which bread and wine are offered to God, is first recorded in 1539; the extended sense of a collection of money at a religious service is first found in 1862.

office *n.* About 1250 *offiz* official post or employment, in *The Story of Genesis and Exodus;* later *office* duty, function, service (probably before 1300, in *Arthour and Merlin*); borrowed from Old French *office,* or directly from Latin *officium* service, duty, function, business, alteration of *opo-fakyom (*opus* work, see OPERATE + *facere* perform, DO[1]).

The ordinary meaning of a place for conducting business is first recorded in Middle English about 1395, in Chaucer's *Canterbury Tales.*

officer *n.* Before 1338, person holding a public, church, or government office, in Mannyng's *Chronicle of England;* later, agent, minister (1384, in Wycliffe's writings); borrowed from Old French *officier,* learned borrowing from Medieval Latin *officiarius* an officer, from Latin *officium* service, OFFICE; for suffix see -ER[1]. The meaning of a person who commands others in the armed forces is first recorded about 1565, but military use of the term extends from about 1378 when the term referred to a soldier or military retainer. **—v.** 1670, from the noun.

official *n.* About 1330, church officer, earlier, in surname (1252); borrowing of Old French *official,* learned borrowing of Latin, and borrowed directly from Latin *officiālis* attendant to a magistrate, public official, noun use of *officiālis,* adj., of or belonging to duty, service, or office, from *officium* duty, service, OFFICE; for suffix see -AL[1].

The meaning of a person in charge of some public work or duty (as a *government* or *municipal official*), is first recorded in 1555.

—adj. 1392, performing a service (for the body); borrowed from Old French *official,* and directly from Latin *officiālis.* The meaning of pertaining to an office or post is first recorded in Shakespeare's *Coriolanus* (1607).

officiate *v.* perform the duties of an official or clergyman. 1631, perform (a religious service); later, perform the duties of a church official (1641); borrowed from Medieval Latin *officiatum,* from past participle of *officiare* perform religious services, from Latin *officium* service, OFFICE; for suffix see -ATE[1].

officinal (əfis′ənəl) *adj.* kept in stock by druggists; medicinal. About 1720, borrowed from French *officinal,* learned borrowing from New Latin *officinalis,* literally, of or belonging in an *officina* storeroom for medicines and necessaries, from Latin *officina* workshop, contraction of *opificīna,* from *opifex* (genitive *opificis*) worker, maker, doer (*opus* work, see OPERATE + *-fex, -ficis* one that does, from *facere* DO[1] perform); for suffix see -AL[1].

officious (əfish′əs) *adj.* minding other people's business, fond of meddling. 1565, eager to please, obliging, dutiful, in Stapleton's translation of Bede's *History of the Church of England;* borrowed, perhaps by influence of Middle French *officieux,* from Latin *officiōsus* dutiful, from *officium* duty, service, OFFICE; for suffix see -OUS.

The pejorative meaning of excessively eager to offer services or of taking another's business on oneself, meddlesome, is first recorded in William Warner's *Albions England* (1602).

offing *n.* **in the offing** in the making, impending. 1779, in the distant future, from earlier nautical term *offing* the more distant part of the sea as seen from the shore (1627, in Captain John Smith's *The Seaman's Grammar*); formed from English *off,* adv. + *-ing*[1]. The modern sense of impending, on hand, likely to happen soon, is first found in Dreiser's *The Titan* (1914).

offspring *n.* Old English (about 949) *ofspring* children or young collectively, descendants, progeny; literally, those who spring off someone (*of* OFF + *springan* to SPRING). The singular use, as in *an offspring* a child, is first recorded in 1712, in Steele's writings. The spelling with *off-* appeared probably before 1425 but did not become established until the 1600's.

oft *adv.* often (now usually hyphenated in adjective compounds, as in *oft-told, oft-repeated*). Probably about 1175 *ofte,* developed from Old English (before 725) *oft;* cognate with Old Frisian *ofta* oft, Old Saxon *oft, ofto,* Old High German *ofto* (modern German *oft*), Old Icelandic *opt* (modern Icelandic *oft,* Swedish *ofta,* Danish and Norwegian *ofte*), and Gothic *ufta.*

In early Middle English the Old English form *oft* was extended to *ofte* (apparently in imitation of adverbs in *-e*). In the 1500's, with the sound represented by final *-e* becoming lost, *oft* gradually displaced *ofte,* which occurs however as a spelling variant until about 1580.

often (ôf′ən) *adv.* About 1250 *often,* in *The Story of Genesis and Exodus,* extended from *ofte* OFT, probably by influence of Middle English *selden* seldom (Old English *seldan*).

ogle (ō′gəl) *v.* look at with desire, make eyes at. 1682-87, in Thomas Shadwell's *The Lancashire Witches,* probably borrowed from Low German *oeglen,* frequentative form of *oegen* look at, from *oege* eye; cognate with Middle Dutch *ōghe* EYE. **—n.** ogling look. 1711, Addison in *The Spectator;* earlier, an eye (before 1700); from the verb. **—ogler** *n.* (1692)

ogre (ō′gər) *n.* hideous giant in folklore and fairy tales. 1786 (but earlier found as *Hogre,* in a translation of the *Arabian Nights,* 1713); borrowed from French *ogre* (first used by Charles Perrault in his collection of fairy tales, 1697), perhaps from Old French *orc, from Latin *Orcus* Hades, god of the infernal regions. Another suggestion, found in the OED, is that Perrault may have formed *ogre* on an Italian dialect *ogro, alteration of *orgo, variant of Italian *orco* demon, monster, from Latin *Orcus* Hades.

oh or **Oh** *interj.* expression of surprise, pain, appeal, joy, etc. Before 1548 *Oh,* spelling alteration of Middle English *O, o* (probably before 1200); borrowed from Old French *ô, oh* and Latin *ō, ōh,* interj., found also in Greek as *ô, ṓ.* Gothic had such a form but it was probably borrowed from Greek.

The respelling of Middle English *O* to modern English *oh* was possibly influenced by the Latin *ōh,* interj., variant of *ō.* In Old English, Latin *ō* was rendered by *lā* or *ēalā.*

—n. the interjection as a name for itself. 1534 *oh!,* in Sir Thomas More's writings; from the interjection.

ohm (ōm) *n.* unit of electrical resistance. 1867, alteration of earlier *ohma* (1861), in allusion to the German physicist Georg S. *Ohm,* who originated the theory of electric circuits, in 1827.

-oholic a combining form meaning one having an addiction or avid devotion to a thing or a practice; abstracted from *alcoholic;* so spelled in random examples (*bloodoholic, cokeoholic, jogoholic*) but almost entirely replaced by the spelling -AHOLIC.

-oid a suffix meaning: like, like that of, as in *Mongoloid, ameboid;* thing like a ______, as *spheroid, opioid.* Borrowed from New Latin *-oïdes,* contraction of Greek *-oeidḗs* (*-o-,* stem vowel + *-eidḗs* in the form of, from *eîdos* form, related to *ideîn* to see, and *eidénai* to know; see WIT[2] know).

oil *n.* Probably before 1200 *eoile, eoli* olive oil, in *An-*

crene Riwle; later *oille* (probably about 1225), and *olie* (about 1250); borrowed from Anglo-French *olie* and Old French *oile, oille,* and directly from Latin *oleum* oil, olive oil, from Greek **élaiwon* (dialectal variant of *élaion*), from **elaíwā* OLIVE. The Middle English form displaced Old English *ele,* earlier *œle;* cognate with Old High German *oli,* from Latin *oleum.*

The general meaning of any fatty or greasy substance (extracted from animals, vegetables, and parts of plants) is first recorded about 1303, in Mannyng's *Handlyng Synne.* The specific sense of a mineral oil, especially petroleum, is first recorded in 1526. The Americanism *to strike oil,* meaning to find oil by boring a hole in the earth, is found in 1862, and the informal figurative sense of hit upon a source of quick profit or wealth is first recorded in 1875, in *Punch.* Figurative senses of oil appear as early as 1200, in reference to fuel generating light for a lamp, and about 1340, in reference to something that soothes.

—v. Before 1425 *oylen* apply oil to, consecrate with oil, anoint; from the noun.

—oily *adj.* 1528, of or like oil; formed from *oil,* n. + *-y*[1]. An isolated earlier example is found in Middle English *oylei* (1392), from *oile* oil + *-i -y*[1]. The meaning of smeared or covered with oil, greasy, fat, is first recorded in Shakespeare's *1 Henry IV* (1597), and the figurative sense of excessively smooth, unctuous, slippery, in 1598. **—oilcloth** *n.* (1697) **—oilskin** *n.* (1816)

ointment *n.* About 1280 *oynement;* later *oignement* (about 1300); borrowed from Old French *oignement, oingnement,* from Vulgar Latin **unguimentum,* variant of Latin *unguentum* UNGUENT.

The spelling *ointment* (1392) developed by association of *oynement* with the earlier verb *ointen* to anoint (1375; borrowed from Old French *oint,* past participle of *oindre,* from Latin *unguere;* see UNGUENT) and with *anointen, enointen* to ANOINT.

O.K. or **OK** *adj., adv.* all right, satisfactory, correct. 1839, American English, originally an abbreviation of *oll korrect,* representing a spelling alteration of "all correct." This abbreviation was one of many similar ones (such as *K.G.,* standing for "no go" as if spelled *know go*) that arose during a vogue for using abbreviations in the summers of 1838 and 1839 in Boston and New York City. The abbreviation was further popularized and gained national currency in 1840 as the election slogan of the "O.K. Club," a Democratic club of New York City formed in 1840 by supporters of Martin Van Buren, in allusion to his nickname "Old Kinderhook," Van Buren having been born at the village of Kinderhook, near Albany, New York. For a detailed history of *O.K.,* see Allen Walker Read's series of articles in *American Speech* 38:1, 2 (1963), and 39:1, 2, 4, (1964). **—n.** endorsement, approval. 1841, American English; from the adjective. **—v.** endorse, approve. 1888, American English; from the noun.

The form *okay,* representing the pronunciation of *O.K.,* appeared in 1929 in American English, replacing the earlier spelling *okeh* (1919, in Mencken's *The American Language*).

okra (ō′krə) *n.* plant used in soups and as a vegetable. 1679 *ocra,* later *okra* (1696); borrowed from a West African language (compare Akan *ṇkrūmā* okra); see also GUMBO.

-ol[1] a suffix meaning: **1** containing, derived from, or like alcohol, as in *phenol.* **2** phenol, or phenol derivative, as in *thymol* (phenol obtained from oil of thyme). Abstracted from *(alcoh)ol.*

-ol[2] a variant form of the suffix -OLE, as in *cholesterol.*

old *adj.* Probably before 1200 *old, olde;* developed from Old English (before 725), found in Anglian *ald* and West Saxon *eald.* The Old English forms are cognate with Old Frisian and Old Saxon *ald* old, Middle Dutch *out* (modern Dutch *oud*), Old High German and modern German *alt,* and Crimean Gothic *alt* old, from Proto-Germanic **alđás,* originally a past participle formation from the verb stem **al-* found in Old Icelandic *ala* to nourish, bring up, Old English *alan,* and Gothic *alan* grow, nourish; Gothic *altheis* old is from Proto-Germanic **althijaz.* These Germanic forms are cognate with Latin *alere* nourish, *almus* fostering, nourishing, *alēscere* grow, increase, *altus* high, originally full-grown, grown up; Old Irish *alim* I nourish, *altru* foster/father, Old Cornish *altrou* stepfather, Middle Welsh *alltraw* godfather; Greek *aldḗskein* grow, *ánaltos* insatiable, Sanskrit *ṛdhnóti* (he) thrives, and Tocharian A *ālym-* life, spirit, from Indo-European **al-* to grow, make grow, nourish, with extensions **al-d-, al-dh-/ḷ-dh-* (Pok. 26) Related to ALDERMAN, ELDER[1].

—n. time long ago. Before 1393, in Gower's *Confessio Amantis;* from the adjective. An earlier noun sense, "old person," is found about 1250 as *olde,* from earlier (before 1150) *ealde* (before 1150), from the Old English adjective.

—olden *adj.* of old. Before 1400, in *Cursor Mundi,* formed from Middle English *old, olde* + *-en*[2]. **—Old English** About 1303 *olde Englys* archaic or obsolete English, earlier *ald Englis* (probably about 1200). The technical sense of English before 1100, Anglo-Saxon, was introduced by Henry Sweet in 1871. **—old-fashioned** *adj.* (1653, in Walton's *The Compleat Angler*) **—oldish** *adj.* somewhat old. (1668-69, in Pepys' *Diary*) **—old maid** (1530, in Palsgrave's *Lesclarcissement*) **—oldster** *n.* 1818, experienced midshipman; later, elderly person, in Dickens' *Dombey and Son* (1848); formed from English *old* + *-ster,* after *youngster.* **—Old Testament** (about 1350 *olde testament,* in *Midland Prose Psalter*) **—old-time** *adj.* (1824 *old-times;* 1870 *old-time,* in Mark Twain's writings) **—old-timer** *n.* (1866, American English) **—old wives' tale** Before 1680, in Samuel Butler's *Remains;* earlier *olde wyves fable* (1526, in Tyndale's translation of the New Testament). **—old-world** *adj.* (1712, of bygone years; later, of the Eastern Hemisphere, 1844).

-ole a chemical suffix denoting: **1** containing a five-part ring, as in *pyrrole* (liquid compound obtained mostly from coal tar). **2** belonging to the ethers, as in *anisole* (compound used in perfumes). Abstracted from Latin *oleum* OIL.

oleaginous (ō′lēaj′ənəs) *adj.* oily. 1634, borrowed from French *oléagineux,* from Latin *oleāginus* of the olive, from *olea* olive, alteration (influenced by *oleum* oil) of *olīva* OLIVE; for suffix see -OUS. An isolated example of this word is found in Middle English (probably before 1425) *oliaginose,* borrowed directly from the Latin *oleāginus.*

oleander (ō′lēan′dər) *n.* poisonous evergreen shrub. 1548, borrowed from Medieval Latin *oleander,* perhaps by influence of Middle French *oléandre.* The Middle French and Medieval Latin word is probably an alteration of Late Latin *lorandrum,* recorded as a further alteration of Latin *rhododendron* RHODODENDRON by influence of Latin *laurea* laurel tree or branch, from the resemblance of its leaves to those of the laurel (a semantic association supported by French *laurier rose,* meaning oleander). The initial *olea-* suggests the influence of Latin *olea* olive; see OLEAGINOUS.

olefin (ō′ləfin) *n.* one of a series of hydrocarbons. 1860 *olefine;* later *olefin* (1923); formed in English from French *gaz oléfiant* oil-forming gas (*olé-,* from Latin *oleum* oil + *-fiant,* present participle of *-fier* -fy) + English *-in*[2], or *-ine*[2] (chemical suffix).

olein (ō′lēən) *n.* ester of oleic acid and glycerin. 1838, borrowing of French *oléine,* from *olé-* (from Latin *oleum* oil) + *-ine* -ine[2] (chemical suffix), patterned after *glycerin.* The word was coined by the French chemist who discovered it, M.E. Chevreul, 1786-1889.

oleomargarine (ō′lēōmär′jərin) *n.* margarine. 1873, American English; borrowed from French *oléo-margarine* (*oléine* olein + *margarine*), so called because it was regarded as a chemical combination of olein and margarine, by the French chemist Berthelot.

olfactory (olfak′tərē) *adj.* of smell. 1658, in Phillips' *Dictionary;* borrowed from Latin *olfactōrius,* from *olfact-,* past participle stem of *olfacere* to get a smell of, sniff, (*olēre* give off a smell of, see ODOR + *facere* make, DO[1]); for suffix see -ORY.

oligarchy (ol′əgär′kē) *n.* form of government in which a few people have the ruling power. 1577 *oligarchie;* borrowed through Middle French *oligarchie,* from Greek *oligarchíā* government by the few (*olígoi* few + *árchein* to rule; see ARCH). Greek *olígoi* is related to *loigós* ruin, destruction, which is cognate with Albanian *lig* thin, Old Prussian *licuts* few, and Armenian *ałkʻat* meager, from Indo-European **(o)leig-/(o)loig-/(o)lig-,*(o)leik-/(o)lik-* (Pok. 667).

An earlier example of this word is found in Middle English (before 1500) *oligracie;* borrowed from Old French *olygrachie,* variant of *oligarchie* oligarchy.

—oligarch *n.* one of the rulers in an oligarchy. Before 1610 *olygarche;* later *oligarch* (1821, Byron); borrowed through Middle French *olygarche;* later *oligarque,* from Greek *oligárchēs* an oligarch (*olígoi* few + *árchein* to rule). **—oligarchic** or **oligarchical** *adj.* Before 1649 *oligarchic,* 1586 *oligarchical;* borrowed perhaps through New Latin *oligarchicus* or French *oligarchique,* from Greek *oligarchikós,* from *oligárchēs* oligarch; for suffix see -IC or -ICAL.

oligopoly (ol′əgop′əlē) *n.* condition in which a few producers supply a commodity or service. 1895, borrowed from Medieval Latin *oligopolium,* from Greek *oligoi* few + *-pōlium,* from Latin *monopōlium* MONOPOLY.

olive *n.* Probably before 1200, borrowed from Old French *olive,* or directly from Latin *olīva,* from Greek **elaíwā,* dialectal variant of *elaíā* olive tree, olive, probably borrowed from the same (Aegean, perhaps Cretan) source as Armenian *ewł* oil. **—adj.** yellowish-green. 1657, from the noun. **—olive branch** Before 1325, branch of an olive tree, in *Cursor Mundi;* later (figurative) a token of peace or good will (before 1338, in Mannyng's *Chronicle of England*). **—olive oil** 1774, replacing earlier *oil of olive,* from Middle English *oyle of olyve* (1381).

ology (ol′əjē) *n. Informal.* any science or branch of knowledge. 1811, abstracted from words considered by popular etymology to end with -OLOGY.

-ology a combining form meaning study or science of, originally used in jocular nonce words such as *insectology* (1803), *commonsensology* (1805), but now treated as a variant of -LOGY, with connective *-o-* as in *sexology, terminology.* 1803, abstracted from such words as *geology, mythology, philology,* in which the *-o-* is considered a connective, though in many instances it belonged to the preceding element as a stem-final or thematic vowel.

Olympiad (ōlim′pēad) *n.* 1614, a celebration of the Olympic Games, back formation from Middle English *Olympiades,* pl. (before 1490, in sense of celebration of the Olympic Games; probably before 1422, in sense of a period of four years between the Olympic Games); borrowed from Middle French *olimpiade,* from Latin *Olympiadem* (nominative *Olympias*), from Greek *Olympiás,* from *Olympia* (Greek *Olympíā*) site of the Olympic Games. The form *Olympias* (from Latin) appears in Middle English before 1387, in Trevisa's translation of Higden's *Polychronicon.*

Olympic Games Before 1610, the contests held every fourth year by the ancient Greeks; replacing the earlier *Olympian Games* (1593, in Shakespeare's *3 Henry VI*), in reference to *Olympia* (Greek *Olympíā*), town in ancient Greece where the contests were held. The modern Olympic Games were revived at Athens in 1896.

-oma a suffix meaning a growth or tumor, as in *carcinoma, lymphoma, melanoma, sarcoma.* New Latin, borrowed from Greek *-ōma* (genitive *-ṓmatos*), a suffix of some nouns taken from verbs in *-óein, -oûn.*

ombudsman (om′budzmən) *n.* official who investigates grievances of citizens against the government. 1959, borrowing of Swedish *ombudsman,* literally, commission man or commissioner, corresponding to Old Icelandic *umbothsmadhr* (*umboth* commission, from *um-* around and *bjōdha* to offer, see BID + *madhr* MAN).

The office of ombudsman originated in Sweden in 1809 and was introduced into other countries, including Finland, New Zealand, Great Britain, and the United States during the 1950's and 1960's.

omega (ōmeg′ə *or* ōmā′gə) *n.* last letter of the Greek alphabet. About 1400, borrowed from Medieval Greek *ō̂méga* big o (although the name was Classical, not Medieval; so called because the vowel was long in ancient Greek. Compare OMICRON.

omelet or **omelette** *n.* pancake of eggs. 1611, in Cotgrave's *Dictionary;* borrowing of French *omelette;* earlier *amelette,* alteration of *alemette,* from *alemelle* blade of a knife or sword, probably from the misdivision of *la lemelle,* from Latin *lāmella* small, thin plate (see LAMELLA); so called from the omelet's flattened shape; for suffix see -ETTE.

omen (ō′mən) *n.* sign of what is to happen, augur, presage. 1582, in Stanyhurst's translation of Vergil's *Aeneid;* borrowing of Latin *ōmen,* of unknown origin.

omicron (ō′məkron) *n.* 15th letter of the Greek alphabet. About 1400, borrowed from Medieval Greek *ò micrón* small o (although the name was Classical, not Medieval); so called because the vowel was short in ancient Greek. Compare OMEGA.

ominous *adj.* of bad omen, threatening. 1589, in William Warner's *Albions England;* borrowed from Latin *ōminōsus* full of foreboding, from *ōmen* (genitive *ōminis*) foreboding, OMEN; for suffix see -OUS.

omission *n.* Probably 1348 *omission* neglect of duty, lack of action; borrowed from Late Latin *omissiōnem* (nominative *omissiō*) an omitting, from Latin *omiss-*

past participle stem of *omittere* OMIT; for suffix see -ION. The meaning of an omitting or leaving out is first recorded in English in 1555.

omit *v.* Probably about 1422 *ommitten,* in Hoccleve's *Works;* also *omitten* (probably before 1425, in a translation of Higden's *Polychronicon*); borrowed from Latin *omittere* lay aside, disregard, let go. Latin *omittere* was formed from *om-* by, variant of *ob-* before *m* + *mittere* let go, send (see MISSION), but with the ensuing double *m* of earlier **ommittere,* it was simplified (as a form of dissimilation) before the following double *t.*

omni- a combining form meaning all, completely, as in *omnipresent, omnirange, omnidirectional, omnifocal.* Borrowed from Latin *omni-,* combining form of *omnis* all, perhaps related to *ops* wealth; see OPULENT.

omnibus *n.* bus. 1829, borrowed from French (*voiture*) *omnibus* common (conveyance), from Latin *omnibus* for all, dative plural of *omnis* all; see OMNI. **—adj.** including many things at once. 1842, American English; from the noun.

omnifarious (om'nəfãr'ēəs) *adj.* of all forms, varieties, or kinds. 1653, in Henry A. More's *Antidote Against Atheism;* borrowed from Late Latin *omnifārius* of all sorts, from Latin *omnifāriam* on all places or parts (*omni-* all + *-fāriam* parts, as in *bifāriam* in two parts, in two ways); for suffix see -OUS. Compare MULTIFARIOUS.

omnipotent (omnip'ətənt) *adj.* all-powerful, almighty. Probably before 1300, in the *Romance of Guy of Warwick;* borrowed from Old French *omnipotent, omnipotente,* or directly from Latin *omnipotentem* (nominative *omnipotēns*) *omni-* all + *potēns* powerful, POTENT.

In Middle English *omnipotent* was applied only to God. The general sense, applied to anything, is first recorded in Shakespeare's *The Merry Wives of Windsor* (1598).

—n. the Omnipotent God. 1601, from the adjective.

—omnipotence *n.* complete power. Before 1460 *omnipotens,* borrowed from Middle French *omnipotence,* learned borrowing from Late Latin *omnipotentia,* from Latin *omnipotentem* omnipotent; for suffix see -ENCE.

omniscience (omnish'əns) *n.* complete or infinite knowledge. 1612, borrowed from Medieval Latin *omniscientia* (Latin *omni-* all + *scientia* knowledge; see SCIENCE). **—omniscient** *adj.* knowing everything. 1604, in Cawdrey's *A Table Alphabeticall;* borrowed from New Latin *omniscientem* (nominative *omnisciens*), from Medieval Latin *omniscientia* omniscience.

omnium-gatherum (om'nēəm gaᴛʜ'ərəm) *n.* miscellaneous collection. 1530, a mock-Latin compound formed from Latin *omnium* of all (genitive plural of *omnis* all; see OMNI-) + *gatherum,* a Latinization coined from English *gather.* This form replaced Middle English (probably before 1430 *omnegadrium,* last attested as *omne-gatherum* in 1819.

omnivorous (omniv'ərəs) *adj.* eating every kind of food. 1656, in Blount's *Glossographia,* borrowing of Latin *omnivorous* (*omni-* all + *-vorus,* from *vorāre* devour, swallow; see VORACIOUS); for suffix see -OUS.

on *prep., adv.* Old English (before 800) *on,* unstressed variant of earlier (about 700) *an* in, on, into; cognate with Old Frisian and Old Saxon *an* on, Middle Dutch *āne, aen* (modern Dutch *aan*), Old High German *ana* (modern German *an*), Old Icelandic *ā,* and Gothic *ana.* Outside Germanic cognates are found in Umbrian *an-*in, Greek *aná* on, upon, up, Lithuanian *anóte, anót* in conformity with, according to, and Avestan *ana* over, from Indo-European **an, anō* (Pok. 39).

In Old English as a variant of *an* the word had a wider function than it does in modern English and took on much of the function of present-day *in.*

—oncoming *adj.* (1844) **—ongoing** *adj.* (1877; earlier noun, 1825, *ongoings* doings, goings-on) **—onlooker** *n.* (1606) **—onrush** *n.* (1844)

-on a suffix meaning: **1** elementary particle, as in neutron. **2** unit particle of energy, as in *photon, fermion.* **3** unit of genetic material, as in *codon, operon.* Abstracted from *(i)on, (electr)on, (prot)on,* etc.

onager (on'əjər) *n.* wild donkey of Asia. About 1340 *onagir,* in Rolle's *The Psalter;* borrowed from Latin *onager,* from Greek *ónagros,* from *ónos ágrios* wild donkey (*ónos* donkey, from the same source as Latin *asinus* ASS; *ágrios* wild, living in the fields, related to *agrós* field; see ACRE).

onanism (ō'nənizəm) *n.* masturbation. 1727-41, in *Chambers Cyclopaedia;* formed in allusion to *Onan* (Genesis 38:9, who spilled his semen on the ground rather than impregnate his deceased brother's wife) + *-ism.* **—onanistic** *adj.* (1892)

once *adv.* About 1250 *ones* one time, on one occasion, in *The Story of Genesis and Exodus;* earlier *anes* (1131, in *Peterborough Chronicle*); formed from *on, ane* ONE + *-es,* genitive singular ending, used adverbially. This form replaced the Old English *ǣne,* adv., and finally displaced the Middle and early modern English *enes* at about 1500.

As *ones* gradually lost a pronunciation in two syllables in the late Middle English and with its final *-s* which represents a voiceless sound of *s* in *sit* (not the expected sound of *s* in *bones*) the word began to be respelled with *-ce,* as in *hence, pence, ice, mice,* to reflect such spelling conventions for this pronunciation. The development of the pronunciation with *w* (wuns) parallels ONE.

—n. About 1300 *ones* one time, single occasion; earlier *anes* (probably before 1200); from the adverb.

—conj. Probably about 1300 *ones* when once, if once, once that; from the adverb.

—adj. that once was; former. 1691, from the noun.

—once-over *n.* short inspection. (1915, American English)

onco- a combining form meaning tumor, as in *oncology, oncogenesis.* New Latin adaptation of Greek *ónkos* mass or bulk, related to *enenkeîn* carry, which is cognate with Sanskrit *ān-anś-a* I have attained, *náśati* (he) reaches, Lithuanian *nešù* I carry, Gothic *ga-nah* it suffices, and Latin *nactus sum* I have obtained, from Indo-European **enek̂-/nek̂-/nok̂-/enk̂-/onk̂-* (Pok. 316).

oncogene (ong'kəjēn') *n.* tumor-producing gene. 1969, formed from English *onco-* tumor + *gene;* influenced in formation by *oncogenic* tumor-producing. **—oncogenesis** (ong'kəjen'əsis) *n.* formation or generation of tumors. 1932, in Dorland and Miller's *Medical Dictionary;* formed from English *onco-* tumor + *genesis.* **—oncogenic** *adj.* tumor-producing. 1949, in *New Gould Medical Dictionary,* formed from English *onco-* tumor + *-genic.*

oncology (ongkol'əjē) *n.* branch of medicine dealing with tumors. 1857, formed from English *onco-* tumor + *-logy* science or study of.

oncornavirus (ongkôr′nəvī′rəs) *n.* tumor-producing virus that contains ribonucleic acid. 1970, formed from English *onco-* tumor + *RNA* (ribonucleic acid) + *virus.*

one *adj., pron.* About 1200 *one,* in *Vices and Virtues,* earlier *on* (probably about 1150), developed from Old English (before 725) *ān,* adj., pron., and n. (earlier in compounds, such as, *ānmōd* of one mind, resolute, about 700). Old English *ān* is cognate with Old Frisian *ān* one, Old Saxon *ēn,* Middle Dutch and modern Dutch *een,* Old High German and modern German *ein,* Old Icelandic *einn* (Danish, Norwegian, and Swedish *en*), and Gothic *ains,* from Proto-Germanic **ainaz,* from Indo-European **oinos,* found in Latin *ūnus* one (from Old Latin *oinos*), Old Irish *ōen,* Greek *oínē* ace (in dice), Old Prussian *ains* one, Lithuanian *víenas,* Old Slavic *inŭ,* Avestan *aēva-* (from Indo-European *oi-wo-*), and Sanskrit *éka-s* (from Indo-European *oi-ko-s*). Observe that **oi-no-s* (Pok. 286), **oi-wo-s,* and **oi-ko-s* are all extensions of an original root **oi-.* **—n.** Probably about 1175 *one;* later *on* (probably before 1200) the number one, developed from Old English *ān.*

The now standard pronunciation (wun) developed in the Middle English period from *ôn, oon,* which by the 1400's had evolved (through *ōn, uon, uön, won, wun*) an initial sound represented by *w* in southwestern and western England. This pronunciation appears only occasionally in the spelling and is first referred to by a scholar in 1701; earlier grammarians give to *one* the sound that it had in *alone, atone, only* and the following suffix -ONE. The same development occurred with the word *once.* See also AN.

—oneness *n.* (1594) **—oneself** *pron.* (1621) **—one-sided** *adj.* (1813, American English) **—one-time** *adj.* (1850) **—one-way** *adj.* (1824)

-one a suffix used in names of chemicals to denote certain compounds containing oxygen, as in *acetone, cortisone.* Adapted from Greek *-ōnē,* a feminine suffix.

onerous (on′ərəs) *adj.* burdensome, oppressive. 1395, in Wycliffe's writings; borrowed from Old French *(h)onereus, onereux,* and directly from Latin *onerōsus,* from *onus* (genitive *oneris*) burden, ONUS; for suffix see -OUS.

onion *n.* 1130 *ungeon;* later *oinoin* (1225), *unyon* (1356-57), and *onyon* (1381); borrowed from Old French *oignon,* and directly from Latin *uniōnem* (nominative *uniō*) a kind of onion; also, a pearl; of uncertain origin.

only *adj.* Probably before 1200 *anlich,* in *Vices and Virtues;* later *onelik* (before 1338, in Mannyng's *Chronicle of England*), and *only* (about 1386, in Chaucer's *Legend of Good Women*); developed from Old English *ǣnlīc, ānlīc* only, unique, solitary (about 725, in *Beowulf*); formed from *ān* ONE + *-līc* -ly². **—adv.** merely, just. About 1250 *on-like,* in *The Story of Genesis and Exodus;* later *onliche* (about 1280), and *only* (about 1303, in Mannyng's *Handlyng Synne*); from the adjective. **—conj.** except that, but. About 1384, in the Wycliffe Bible; from the adjective.

onomastic (on′əmas′tik) *adj.* of a name or names, 1716 *onomastick,* borrowed from French *onomastique,* from Greek *onomastikós* of or belonging to naming, from *onomázein* to name, from *ónoma* NAME; for suffix see -IC. **—onomastics** *n.* study of names. 1936, formed from *onomast(ic)* + *-ics,* as in *gymnastics, physics.* An earlier form is recorded as *onomastic,* n. (1930, in T.S. Eliot's translation of St. John Perse's *Anabase*).

onomatopoeia (on′əmat′əpē′ə) *n.* coinage or formation of a word in imitation of a sound. 1577, in Henry Peacham's (the elder) *The Garden of Eloquence;* borrowing of Latin *onomatopoeia* the coining of words, from Greek *onomatopoiíā* the making of a name or word, from *onomatopoiós* (*ónoma,* genitive *onómatos* word, NAME + *poieîn* compose, make; see POET). **—onomatopoeic** *adj.* imitative of sound. 1860, in Frederic W. Farrar's *Essay On the Origin of Language;* borrowed from French *onomatopéique* (*onomatopée* onomatopoeia, from Latin *onomatopoeia* + *-ique* -ic), and probably formed in English directly from Greek *onomatopoiós* + English *-ic.*

onset *n.* 1535, a setting on (an enemy), attack, assault; later, a starting up, beginning (1561); formed from English *on* + *set,* n.

onslaught (on′slôt′) *n.* vigorous attack. Before 1625 *anslaight,* in John Fletcher's *Monsieur Thomas;* borrowed from Dutch *aanslag* attack, from Middle Dutch *aenslach* (*aen* ON + *slach* blow, related to *slaen* SLAY).

The spellings *anslaight, onslaught* (1654) were probably influenced by the obsolete English noun *slaught,* meaning slaughter, going back to Old English *sleaht* SLAUGHTER.

onto *prep.* 1581 *on to* to a position on (as in *he stepped on to the stage*); formed from English *on,* adv. + *to,* prep. The closed-compound form *onto* is first recorded in Keats' *Otho the Great* (1819).

ontogeny (ontoj′ənē) *n. Biology.* development of an individual organism. 1872, formed in English from Greek *ṓn* (genitive *óntos*) being, present participle of *eînai* to be; see IS + *-géneia* origin, from *-genḗs* born; see -GEN.

ontology (ontol′əjē) *n. Philosophy.* study of being. 1721, in Bailey's *Dictionary;* borrowed from French *ontologie,* from New Latin *ontologia,* from Greek *ṓn* (genitive *óntos*) being; see ONTOGENY + *-logíā* -logy. In an etymological sense, from its structure *ontology* would be expected to be merely the study of a being or of beings; the study of being would be expected to have been called **ousiology,* from Greek *ousíā* being, existence.

onus (ō′nəs) *n.* burden, responsibility. About 1640, borrowed from Latin *onus* (genitive *oneris*) load or burden; cognate with Sanskrit *ánas* cart, and possibly with Greek *aníā* (Aeolic *oníā*) grief, from Indo-European **onos* burden (Pok. 321). Related to EXONERATE, ONEROUS.

onyx (on′iks) *n.* semiprecious variety of quartz. About 1250 *oneche,* later *onix* (before 1300); borrowed through Old French *oniche, onix,* or directly from Latin *onyx* (genitive *onychis*), from Greek *ónyx* (genitive *ónychos*) claw, fingernail, onyx (see NAIL); so called from the resemblance of this mineral to the color of a fingernail.

Other forms existed in Middle English but for the most part disappeared in early modern English; *onichine* (before 1382, in the Wycliffe Bible; borrowed from Old French *onichinon,* and directly from Latin *onychina, onychinus*), and *onicle* (about 1250, borrowed from Old French *onicle,* and directly from Medieval Latin *onychulus*).

oocyte (ō′əsīt) *n. Biology.* ovum in the stage that precedes maturation. 1895, formed from English *oo-* (combining form of Greek *ōión* EGG¹) + *-cyte.*

oodles (ū′dəlz) *n.pl.* large quantity or number. 1869 American English, of uncertain origin.

-oon The form *-oon* is an English suffixal type used

especially from the 1500's to the 1700's to add emphasis to English borrowings of French nouns ending in *-on* stressed on the final syllable, and of Italian nouns in *-one,* such as *balloon, bassoon, buffoon, cartoon, doubloon, macaroon.* The form may have been influenced by apparently similar French use in *pantaloon* and perhaps *dragoon* for the gun carried by dragoons. It probably also influenced the present-day spelling *baboon,* and perhaps even Japanese *tycoon,* and is found in English formations as *spittoon.* By imitation, *-oon* may also have been broadened in its general application to include the spellings of *lagoon, typhoon,* etc., just as it does *pontoon* and *harpoon.*

ooze[1] *n.* slow flow. 1340 *wose* juice, flowing liquid, in *Ayenbite of Inwyt;* developed from Old English (about 1000) *wōs* juice; cognate with Middle Low German *wōs* froth, juice, from Proto-Germanic **wōsan,* related to Old High German *wasal* rain, (modern German *Wasen* turf), Sanskrit *vásā* fat, from Indo-European **wes-/wos-/wōs-* wet (Pok. 1171).

The modern spelling *ooze,* without the initial *w,* came from a dialectal alteration first recorded in the late 1500's. The meaning of act of oozing, slow flow is first recorded in 1718; the noun in this sense was derived from *ooze,* v.

—v. flow slowly, exude. Before 1387 *wosen,* in Trevisa's translation of Higden's *Polychronicon;* from *worse* flowing liquid.

—oozy[1] *adj.* exuding moisture. 1714 (but implied in earlier *ooziness,* 1684); formed from English *ooze*[1] + *-y*[1].

ooze[2] *n.* soft mud or slime. 1340 *wose,* in *Ayenbite of Inwyt;* earlier *waise* (before 1338, in Mannyng's *Chronicle of England*); developed from Old English (before 800) *wāse* mud, mire; cognate with Old Frisian *wāse* slime, mud, Old Icelandic *veisa* slime, stagnant pool, from Proto-Germanic **waisōn,* and Latin *vīrus* poison; see VIRUS.

The modern spelling *ooze,* without the initial *w,* is first recorded in the mid-1500's and was influenced by *ooze*[1].

—oozy[2] *adj.* of or like soft mud or slime. Before 1398 *wosie;* formed from Middle English *wose* ooze[2] + *-ie* -y[1].

op- a form of the prefix *ob-* before *p* in words from Latin, such as *opponent* (Latin *oppōnentem,* nominative *oppōnēns*). The form is due to the assimilation of *b* to the following consonant (*p*).

opacity (ōpas′ətē) *n.* a being opaque. 1560, darkness or obscurity of meaning; borrowed from French *opacité,* learned borrowing from Latin *opācitātem* (nominative *opācitās*) shadiness, shade, from *opācus* shaded, shady, dark, OPAQUE. **—opacify** *v.* make or become opaque. 1940, probably borrowed from French *opacifier,* from *opacité* opacity + *-fier* -fy.

opal (ō′pəl) *n.* kind of silica valued as a gem. 1598 *opale,* in Florio's *A World of Words;* borrowed through French *opale, opalle,* learned borrowing from Latin *opalus,* supposedly from Greek *opállios,* possibly from Sanskrit *úpala-s* gem, opal. The Latin form *opalus* is recorded in Middle English texts before 1398. **—opalescence** *n.* play of colors like that of an opal. 1805-17; formed from English *opal* + *-escence.* **—opalescent** *adj.* having opalescence. 1813; formed from English *opal* + *-escent.*

opaque (ōpāk′) *adj.* not transparent. Probably 1440 *opake;* borrowed from Latin *opācus* shaded, shady, dark; of uncertain origin. The current English spelling (established in the 1800's) was influenced by French *opaque,* a learned borrowing from the Latin.

op art form of abstract art involving optical effects and illusions. 1964, American English, shortened form of *optical art* (1964), on the analogy of POP ART.

Op-Ed *n.* newspaper page of views and commentary opposite the editorial page. 1970, American English; shortened form of *Op(posite) Ed(itorial page).*

open *adj.* Old English *open* not closed down, raised up, open (about 725, in *Beowulf*); cognate with Old Frisian *epen, open* open, Old Saxon *opan,* Middle Dutch *ōpen* (modern Dutch *open*), Old High German *offan* (modern German *offen*), and Old Icelandic *opinn* (Swedish *öppen,* Norwegian *åpen,* Danish *åben*); not recorded in Gothic; from Proto-Germanic **upana-/upina-,* and related to *up.*

—v. make open. Probably before 1200 *openen;* developed from Old English (before 725) *openian;* cognate with Old Frisian *epenia* to open, Old Saxon *opanōn,* Middle Dutch and modern Dutch *openen,* Old High German *offanōn* (modern German *öffnen*), and Old Icelandic *opna;* derived from the Germanic source of Old English *open,* adj.

—open air (1420) **—open-air** *adj.* (1830) **—open-and-shut** *adj.* straightforward. (1841, American English) **—open book** something readily known or understood (1853). **—open door** admission to a country for purposes of commerce. (1856, American English) **—open-door** *adj.* (1898) **—open-end** *adj.* (1908), **open-ended** *adj.* (1825) **—opener** *n.* (1440) **—open-eyed** *adj.* (1601) **—open-face** *adj.* (1906), **open-faced** *adj.* (1610) **—open-handed** *adj.* (1601) **—open-hearted** *adj.* (1611) **—open house** hospitality. (1530) **—open letter** published letter of protest, etc. (1878) **—open-minded** *adj.* (1828, Carlyle) **—open-mouthed** *adj.* (about 1532) **—open season** period when hunting, etc. is allowed. (1896) **—open sesame** any marvelous means of reaching a goal. Before 1837, figurative use of *Open Sesame* (1793, in the *Arabian Nights*), the magic words by which the door of the robbers' cave flew open in the tale of *Ali Baba and the Forty Thieves.* **—open shop** workplace employing union and nonunion personnel (1904, but implied earlier in *open,* adj., 1896). **—openwork** *n.* ornamental work that shows openings. (1598, in Florio's *A World of Words*)

opera *n.* 1644, drama that is mostly sung, in Evelyn's *Diary;* borrowing of Italian *opera,* literally, a work, from Latin *opera* work, effort; related to *opus* (genitive *operis*) a work; see OPERATE.

The term *soap opera,* originally referring disparagingly to daytime radio drama sponsored by soap manufacturers, appeared in 1939 in American English. *Horse opera,* in the sense of a circus show featuring horses, is an Americanism attested since 1863; the modern sense of a western or cowboy movie appeared in American English about 1941. **—opera glass** (1738) or **glasses** (1862) **—opera hat** (1810) **—opera house** (1720) **—operatic** *adj.* of or like opera. 1749, irregularly derived from *opera,* apparently on the analogy of *drama, dramatic.* **—operetta** *n.* light opera. 1770, borrowed from Italian, diminutive of *opera.*

operable *adj.* that may be done, practicable. 1646, formed from English *operate* + *-able.* The sense of capable of being treated by a surgical operation (as in *an operable tumor*) appeared in 1904.

operand (op′ərənd) *n.* number or symbol to be operated on. 1886, borrowed from Latin *operandum,* neuter gerundive of *operārī* to work, OPERATE.

operant (op′ərənt) *adj.* that operates or works, effective. 1602, in Shakespeare's *Hamlet;* borrowed from Latin *operantem* (nominative *operāns*), present participle of *operārī* to work, OPERATE; for suffix see -ANT. The meaning in psychology "of or involving spontaneous behavior that produces a reinforcing effect" was coined in 1937 by the American psychologist B.F. Skinner to distinguish such behavior from one that is *respondent* or due to a stimulus. **—n.** one that operates. 1700, from the adjective.

operate *v.* 1606, in Shakespeare's *Troylus and Cressida,* probably a back formation from earlier *operation,* and, in part, borrowed from, or a least reinforced by, Latin *operātus,* past participle of *operārī* to work, labor (in Late Latin, to have effect, be active, cause), from *opera* work, effort, related to *opus* (genitive *operis*) a work; cognate with Sanskrit *ápas* work, *ápnas* possession, work, and *ā́pas* work, religious action, from Indo-European **op-/ōp-* work, produce, wealth (Pok. 780). Cognates in Germanic include Old English *efnan* carry out, perform, Old Icelandic *efna* carry out, execute, perform, from Proto-Germanic **aƀnijanan;* Old High German *uoben* put to work, exercise, practice (modern German *üben* to practice), and Old Saxon *ōƀian* celebrate, from Proto-Germanic **ōƀijanan.*

The meaning of perform a surgical operation is first recorded in 1799, perhaps influenced by French *opérer* (from Latin *operārī),* attested in this sense in 1690. **—operation** *n.* 1391 *operacioun* action, performance, working, in Chaucer's *Treatise on the Astrolabe;* borrowed from Old French *operacion,* and directly from Latin *operātiōnem* (nominative *operātiō*), from *operārī* to work; for suffix see -ATION. The meaning of a surgical procedure performed on the body is first recorded in a translation of Chauliac's *Grande Chirurgie* (probably before 1425). **—operational** *adj.* (1922) **—operative** *adj.* operating. Probably before 1425, borrowed from Middle French *operatif,* and directly from Late Latin *operātīvus* creative, formative, from Latin *operāt-,* past participle stem of *operārī* to work, operate; for suffix see -IVE. —*n.* 1809-10, worker, operator; noun use of *operative,* adj. The meaning "private detective" is first recorded in American English in 1905, probably introduced by the Pinkerton Detective Agency. In the 1930's *operative* was also applied to a secret agent or spy. **—operator** *n.* 1611, in Cotgrave's *Dictionary;* borrowed from Late Latin *operātor* worker, producer, from Latin *operārī* to work, OPERATE; for suffix see -OR².

operon (op′əron) *n.* unit of coordinated genetic activity in the chromosome. 1961, borrowing of French *opéron,* from *-opér(ateur)* operator, in the sense of the genetic segment that regulates the structural genes in an operon + *-on* (genetic unit). French *opéron* was coined in 1960 by the French molecular biologists François Jacob and Jacques Monod.

ophthalmia (ofthal′mēə) *n.* acute inflammation of the membrane around the eye. Before 1398 *obtalmia,* in Trevisa's translation of Bartholomew's *De Proprietatibus Rerum;* later *obtalmie* (probably before 1425); borrowing of Medieval Latin *obtalmia,* and Old French *obtalmie,* from Late Latin *opthalmia,* or directly from Greek *ophthalmíā* region of the eyes, from *ophthalmós* eye; originally, the seeing; related to *ṓps* EYE. Greek *ophthalmós* was derived from a lost verb **ophthállesthai* built on a noun **óphthallos,* a variant of Boeotian *óktallos* eye, most closely cognate with Sanskrit *ákṣi* eye, from Indo-European **okwth-* (Pok. 776). The Latin spelling began to appear at the end of the 1500's. **—ophthalmic** *adj.* of the eye, ocular, optic. 1727-41, in *Chambers Cyclopaedia;* formed from English *ophthalm(ia)* + *-ic,* in imitation of Greek *ophthalmikós* of the eye. The earlier Middle English *obtalmic* (probably before 1425) had the restricted meaning of affected with *ophthalmia;* borrowed from Medieval Latin *obtalmicus.* **—ophthalmology** *n.* branch of medicine dealing with the eyes. 1842 (but implied earlier in *ophthalmologist,* 1834); formed in English from Greek *ophthalmós* eye + English *-ology.*

opiate *adj.* 1543, of or containing opium, narcotic, borrowed from Medieval Latin *opiatus,* from Latin *opium* OPIUM; for suffix see -ATE¹. The figurative meaning of inducing drowsiness or inaction, dulling the feelings, is first recorded before 1626. **—n.** drug containing opium or one having the narcotic effects of opium or its derivatives. 1603, in Ben Jonson's *Sejanus;* from the adjective. A single example is recorded in a translation of Chauliac's *Grande Chirurgie* (probably before 1425), borrowed from Medieval Latin *opiatus.* The figurative meaning of anything that quiets pain or dulls the feelings is first recorded in Milton's *Animadversions* (1641).

opine *v.* express an opinion. About 1450 *opynen;* borrowed from Middle French *opiner,* learned borrowing from Latin, and borrowed directly from Latin *opīnārī* have an opinion, suppose, think, judge, perhaps related to *optāre* to desire, choose; see OPTION.

opinion *n.* Before 1325, in *Cursor Mundi;* borrowed from Old French *opinion* what one thinks, supposition, judgment, belief, learned borrowing from Latin, and borrowed directly from Latin *opīniōnem* (nominative *opīniō*), related to *opīnārī* think, judge, suppose, OPINE; for suffix see -ION. **—opinionated** *adj.* obstinate in one's opinions; dogmatic. 1601, formed from earlier *opinionate,* adj. (1553, based on opinion, supposed; later, dogmatic, 1576, from *opinion* + *-ate*¹) + *-ed*².

opium (ō′pēəm) *n.* narcotic made from the juice of poppy. 1392, borrowed from Latin *opium,* from Greek *ópion* poppy juice, poppy, diminutive of *opós* vegetable juice (Ionic dialectal variant of Attic **hopós*); cognate with Old Slavic *sokŭ,* from Indo-European **sokwós* (compare Lithuanian *svekas* from **swekwos,* and Lettish *svakas* from **swokwos*) (Pok. 1044).

opossum (əpos′əm) *n.* small mammal. 1610 *apossoun,* American English; borrowed from Algonquian (Powhatan) *âpäsûm* white animal. See also POSSUM.

The replacement of the original spelling with *a* by *o* is found in other words of American Indian origin, for example *tobacco* (from earlier *tabaco*).

opponent *n.* adversary, antagonist. 1588, probably from the adjective. **—adj.** opposing. 1647, borrowed from Latin *oppōnentem* (nominative *oppōnēns*), present participle of *oppōnere* oppose, object to, set against (*op-* against, variant of *ob-* before *p* + *pōnere* to put, set, place; see POSITION); for suffix see -ENT.

opportune *adj.* favorable, suitable. Probably about 1408, in Lydgate's *Reson and Sensuallyte;* borrowed from Old French *opportun* (feminine *opportune*) timely, learned borrowing from Latin, and borrowed directly from Latin *opportūnus* favorable, from the phrase *ob portum veniēns* coming toward a port, in reference to the wind (*ob-* toward; see OB-, and *portum,* accusative of *portus,* genitive *portūs* harbor, PORT[1]). **—opportunism** *n.* practice of using every opportunity to one's advantage. 1870; probably formed in English from *opportune* + *-ism,* by influence of Italian *opportunismo,* from *opportuno* opportune (from Latin *opportūnus*) + *-ismo* -ism. The term was originally used in Italian politics, and later also in French politics (*opportunisme,* about 1869, which may also have influenced the formation in English, and it is possible that English borrowed the French term directly). **—opportunist** *n.* 1881, borrowed from French *opportuniste* (applied in 1877 to the French statesman Léon Gambetta), from *opportunisme* (from Italian *opportunismo*) + *-iste* -ist. **—opportunistic** *adj.* (1892) **—opportunity** *n.* favorable time. About 1380 *oportunyte* good fortune, in Chaucer's translation of Boethius' *De Consolatione Philosophiae;* also, before 1387 *opportunite* fitness, competency, favorable time, chance, occasion, in Trevisa's translation of Bartholomew's *De Proprietatibus Rerum;* borrowed from Old French *opportunité,* and directly from Latin *opportūnitātem* (nominative *opportūnitās*) fitness, suitableness, favorable time, from *opportūnus* opportune; for suffix see -ITY.

oppose *v.* About 1380 *opposen* confront with objections or hard questions, in Chaucer's *Canterbury Tales;* borrowed from Old French *opposer,* a blend of Old French *poser* to place, lay down, POSE and Latin *oppōnere* oppose, object to, set against; see OPPONENT. The meaning of try to hinder, resist, struggle against, is first recorded in Shakespeare's *1 Henry IV* (1596). **—opposable** *adj.* 1667, formed from English *oppose* + *-able.* The application of this word to a digit, especially the thumb, is first found in 1833.

opposite *adj.* placed or lying against. 1391 *opposyt,* in Chaucer's *Treatise on the Astrolabe;* borrowed from Old French *oposite,* learned borrowing from Latin *oppositus,* past participle of *oppōnere* set against; see OPPONENT.

The meaning of contrary in nature, diametrically different, is first recorded in Lyly's *Euphues and his England* (1580).
—n. thing or person that is opposite. About 1385 *oposit,* in Chaucer's *Canterbury Tales;* borrowed from Old French *oposite,* n., from *oposite,* adj.
—prep. over against, across. 1758, in Goldsmith's *The Memoirs of a Protestant,* from the adjective, probably by omission of *to* in the phrase *opposite to.*
—adv. in the opposite position or direction. 1817, in Shelley's *Prince Athanase;* from the adjective.

opposition *n.* About 1395 *opposicioun* the position of two heavenly bodies exactly opposite to each other, in Chaucer's *Canterbury Tales;* borrowed from Old French *oposicion, opposition,* or directly from Medieval Latin *oppositionem* (nominative *oppositio*), from Latin *oppositiōnem* (nominative *oppositiō*) act of opposing, from *opposit-,* past participle stem of *oppōnere* set against; see OPPONENT; for suffix see -ION.

The meaning of contrast or contradistinction is first recorded in 1581, and that of contrary or hostile action, antagonism, in Shakespeare's *Love's Labour's Lost* (1588). The meaning of a political party opposed to the party in power (usually spelled *Opposition*) is found in 1704.

oppress *v.* About 1380 *oppressen* lie heavy on, weigh down, burden, in Chaucer's *Canterbury Tales;* borrowed from Old French *oppresser,* from Medieval Latin *oppressare,* frequentative of Latin *opprimere* press against, push down, crush, overwhelm (*op-* against, variant of *ob-* before *p* + *premere* to PRESS[1] push). It is also possible that in some instances *oppress* is a back formation from earlier *oppression.*

The meaning of trample down, burden unjustly, tyrannize over, is first recorded in the Wycliffe Bible (1382).
—oppression *n.* a burdening, tyranny. 1334, borrowed from Old French *opression, oppression,* from Latin *oppressiōnem* (nominative *oppressiō*), from *oppress-,* past participle stem of *opprimere;* for suffix see -ION. **—oppressive** *adj.* burdensome, tyrannical. 1627-77, probably formed from English *oppress* + *-ive,* after French *oppressif* (feminine *oppressive*). **—oppressor** *n.* About 1400 *oppresser* one who oppresses, tyrant, also *oppressour* (1422); borrowed from Old French *oppresseur,* from Latin *oppressor,* from *opprimere* oppress; for suffix see -OR[2].

opprobrium (əprō′brēəm) *n.* scorn, abuse, infamy. 1656, reborrowing of Latin *opprobrium,* as a replacement of Middle English *opprobry* (probably before 1425, in a translation of Higden's *Polychronicon*), earlier borrowed from Latin *opprobrium,* from *opprobrāre* to reproach, taunt (*op-* against, variant of *ob-* before *p* + *probrum* reproach, infamy, shameful act). **—opprobrious** *adj.* expressing scorn or abuse, infamous. Before 1387, in Trevisa's translation of Higden's *Polychronicon;* borrowed through Old French *opprobrieux,* and directly from Late Latin *opprobriōsus,* from Latin *opprobrium* opprobrium; for suffix see -OUS.

opt *v.* choose or decide. 1877, borrowed from French *opter* to choose, learned borrowing from Latin *optāre* choose, desire; see OPTION. The phrase *opt out,* meaning to choose to back out of or not do (something), is first recorded in 1922.

optic *adj.* of the eye or sight, visual. Probably before 1425 *optik, obtic,* in a translation of Chauliac's *Grande Chirurgie;* borrowed from Middle French *obtique,* and directly from Medieval Latin *opticus* of sight or seeing, from Greek *optikós* of or having to do with sight, from *optós* seen, visible, from *op-,* root of *ópsesthai* be going to see, related to *óps* EYE; for suffix see -IC. **—optical** *adj.* 1570, formed from English *optic* + *-al*[1], perhaps after Middle French *optique* or Medieval Latin *opticus* optic. **—optician** *n.* 1687, person who studies or is an expert in optics; later, maker of optical instruments (1737); formed in English from *optic(s)* + *-ian* (as in *physician*), after French *opticien,* from Medieval Latin *optica* optics; for suffix see -IAN. The meaning of a maker or seller of eyeglasses is first recorded in 1892 in American English. **—optics** *n.* branch of physics dealing with light. 1579 *optikes* the science of light (as the medium of sight), a plural of *optik, optick,* adj., used as a noun in place of Medieval Latin *optica* optics, neuter plural, borrowed from Greek *tà optiká* optical matters, optics (used by Aristotle, Ptolemy, etc.), from neuter plural of *optikós* optic; for suffix see -ICS.

optimism *n.* tendency to look on the favorable side of things. 1782 *Optimism;* earlier *Optimisme* (1759) name given to the doctrine that the actual world is the best of all possible worlds (found in Leibnitz's work on theology, *Théodicée,* 1710). The word in English was originally a borrowing of French *optimisme* (1737), from New Latin *optimum* (as used by Leibnitz to mean the greatest good), from Latin *optimus* the best; see OPTIMUM; for suffix se -ISM.

Leibnitz used *optimum* (presumably on the model of *maximum* and *minimum*), but as his theories of unity of substance were discussed by the Jesuits in France (1737), their name of *optimisme* became the standard term, which gained wide currency in Voltaire's attack upon Leibnitz's doctrine in *Candide ou l'Optimisme* (1759).

The general meaning of a disposition to look for the best or on the bright side of things is first recorded in English in Shelley's *Essays* (1819).

—optimist *n.* 1766, formed from English *optim(ism)* + *-ist,* after French *optimiste.* **—optimistic** *adj.* of or given to optimism. 1848, formed from English *optimist* + *-ic,* in Matthew Arnold's *To A Republican Friend.*

optimize *v.* **1** act as an optimist. 1844, back formation from English *optimist,* in Gladstone's *Gleanings of Past Years.* **2** make the best or most of, make optimal. 1857, formed in English from Latin *optimum* + English suffix *-ize.*

optimum *n.* the best or most favorable for the purpose. 1879, borrowing of Latin *optimum,* neuter singular of *optimus* best, probably related to *ops* power, resources; see OPULENT. **—adj.** optimal. 1886, from the noun. **—optimal** *adj.* best, most favorable. 1890, formed from English *optimum,* n. + *-al*[1].

option *n.* 1604, act of choosing, in Cawdrey's *A Table Alphabeticall;* borrowed from French *option,* learned borrowing from Latin *optiōnem* (nominative *optiō*) choice, free choice, related to *optāre* to desire, choose. Latin *optāre* is cognate with Umbrian *upetu* let him choose, Greek *epiópsesthai* be going to choose, and perhaps with Tocharian A *opyāc,* Tocharian B *epyac* understanding, from Indo-European **op-* to choose (Pok. 781); for suffix see -TION.

The meaning of opportunity or freedom of choice is first recorded in 1633, and the commercial sense of the right to buy or sell something at a certain price within a certain time, is first recorded in 1755.

—optional *adj.* 1765, leaving something to choice; formed from English *option* + *-al*[1]. The meaning of being a matter of choice, that is left to one's option, is first recorded in 1792.

optometry *n.* measurement of visual powers; occupation of testing eyes and fitting them with glasses. 1886, formed from English *optometer* (1737) + *-ry,* on the pattern of such pairs as *audiometer, audiometry; spectrometer, spectrometry;* probably influenced by French *optométrie,* from *opto-* sight, from Greek *optós* seen, visible; see OPTIC; for combining form see -METRY. **—optometrist** *n.* 1903, American English; formed from *optometry* + *-ist.*

opulent *adj.* wealthy. 1601, probably, in part, a back formation from earlier *opulence,* and, in part, borrowed from Middle French *opulent,* learned borrowing from Latin *opulentus* wealthy; see OPULENCE. **—opulence** *n.* wealth. About 1510, borrowed from Middle French *opulence,* learned borrowing from Latin *opulentia,* from *opulentus* wealthy, from *ops* wealth, power, resources. Latin *ops* is cognate with Greek *ómpnē* food, and Sanskrit *ápnas* possession or property; see OPERATE.

opus (ō′pəs) *n.* work or composition. 1809, in Southey's *Letters;* borrowing of Latin *opus* work, effort; see OPERATE.

The term *magnum opus* great work or masterpiece, used especially in reference to a large or important literary work, is first recorded in English in Swift's *A Tale of A Tub* (1704) as *opus magnum.* In 1791 Boswell wrote, "*My magnum opus,* the 'Life of Dr. Johnson' . . .is to be published on Monday, 16th May."

or[1] *conj.* Probably about 1200 *or,* in *The Ormulum;* a fusion of the reduced form (analogous to *e'er* from *ever*) of: 1) *other,* conj. (probably before 1200); developed from Old English (before 1050) *other* or, from *oththe, oththa;* earlier *eththa* (probably before 725); and 2) *outher* (before 1121); developed from Old English (before 901) *āhwæther, āther,* pron.; originally the same as *either,* probably by association in such phrases of alternative condition as *either. . .or* (Old English *āther. . .oththe*), and *whether. . .or* (Old English *hawæther. . .oththe*). The Old English forms *oththe, oththa* are cognate with Old High German *odo, odar;* earlier *eddo* (modern German *oder*), Old Icelandic *edha* and Gothic *áiththau.*

Kluge states that the initial *o* in the Germanic forms is a peculiarity, also citing Old Saxon *eththo,* and states that the Gothic *áiththau* is an ancient compound containing as its first element Gothic *ith* but, which is cognate with Greek *éti* still, yet, Latin *et* and, also, and Sanskrit *áti* beyond, part, from Indo-European *éti* (Pok. 344).

The ending *-r* appeared in late Old English as well as in Old High German *odar.* Kluge regards the *-r* as added through the influence of *aber* but, and *weder* neither. Perhaps words like *either, neither,* and *whether* (all of which have to do with two-way oppositions) provided the *-r* in English.

or[2] *adv., prep., conj.* before, variant of Middle English *er;* see ERE.

-or[1] a suffix meaning action or condition, especially in words from Latin, as in *error, horror, demeanor, behavior.* Middle English *-or, -our,* borrowed from Old French *-eor, -eur,* from Latin *-or,* abstract noun suffix.

-or[2] a suffix meaning person or thing that does (something) as in *conqueror, vendor, donor, actor, accelerator, orator.* Middle English *-or, -our,* borrowed through Anglo-French *-our, -ur,* and from Old French *-eor, -eur,* from Latin *-ātōrem* (nominative *-ātor*) and other combinations of stem vowel and agent suffix *-tor.* In some cases, *-or* was acquired as part of *-tor* in words borrowed directly from Latin *-ātor* (stem *-ā-* + *-tor*) or adapted from French *-eur* in *-teur* in learned borrowings from Latin. The suffix is often found attached to verbs in *-ate*[1], as in *demonstrator, illustrator, generator,* etc., or to verbs in *-it,* as in *depositor, auditor,* or *-t,* as in *instructor, corrector,* etc. Occasionally it appears in the form *-sor,* as in *confessor.*

oracle (ôr′əkəl) *n.* divine revelation; place where divine secrets are revealed. About 1380, in Chaucer's *House of Fame;* borrowed from Old French *oracle,* learned borrowing from Latin, and borrowed directly from Latin *ōrāculum,* from *ōrāre* pray, plead; see ORATION. **—oracular** (ôrek′yələr) *adj.* of or like an oracle. 1631, formed in English from Latin *ōrāculum* oracle + English *-ar.*

oracy (ôr′əsē) *n.* competence in speech or oral skills 1965, formed from English *or(al)* + *-acy,* on the pattern of *literacy.*

oral *adj.* 1625, done with the mouth (but implied earlier in *orally,* 1608); perhaps later reinforced in English by French *oral,* but borrowed from Late Latin *ōrālis,* from Latin *ōs* (genitive *ōris*) mouth; for suffix see -AL[1]. Latin *ōs* is cognate with Sanskrit *ā́s,* Hittite *ais,* and Middle Irish *ā* (genitive, singular), all meaning mouth, as well as with Old Icelandic *ōss* mouth of a river, from Proto-Germanic **ōsaz,* ultimately from Indo-European **ō(u)s* (Pok. 784).

The meaning of spoken or verbal is first recorded in 1628.

—n. 1876, American English, shortened form of *oral examination.*

orange *n.* Probably about 1380 *orenge* an orange (fruit); earlier, as a surname (1296); *orange* (before 1425); borrowed from Old French *orenge,* in *pome dorange* and in Medieval Latin *pomum de orenge;* alteration of Arabic *nāranj,* from Persian *nārang,* from Sanskrit *nārāngá-s* orange tree, possibly from Dravidian (Tamil).

Loss of initial *n-* in early Old French was probably by absorption into the indefinite article in *une *narange* an orange; contrast Spanish *naranja* which retained the *n-.* The shift in spelling from *arange* to *orenge* may have been influenced by Old French *or* gold, in allusion to the color of the fruit, and perhaps by the name *Orange* town in southern France through which oranges were shipped north, though it does not account for retaining the medial *e.*

The meaning of reddish-yellow color is recorded in English before 1600.

—adj. of the color of an orange. 1542, from the noun (originally an attributive use, as in *orange hue,* but by 1620 used as an adjective, as in *orange velvet*).

—orangeade *n.* 1706, in Kersey's addition of Phillips' *Dictionary;* formed from English *orange* + *-ade,* after *lemonade.*

orangutan (ōrang'ūtan') *n.* large ape of Borneo and Sumatra. 1699 *Orang-Outang,* borrowed from Dutch *orang-outang* (1631), from Malay *orang utan,* literally, man of the woods (*orang* person, man + *utan, hutan* woods, forest, jungle).

orate *v.* make an oration. About 1600, to pray; probably borrowed from Latin *ōrātus,* past participle of *ōrāre* pray, plead, speak before a court or assembly; see ORATION; for suffix see -ATE[1].

The meaning "make a formal speech" appeared in 1669. In the United States *orate* came into common use about 1860 as a back formation from *oration* and then chiefly as a humorous or sarcastic term with the sense of hold forth, speechify.

oration *n.* Probably before 1375 *oracion* prayer; borrowed from Late Latin *ōrātiōnem* (nominative *ōrātiō*), from Latin *ōrāre* pray, plead, speak before a court or assembly; for suffix see -ATION. Latin *ōrāre* is cognate with Attic Greek *ará,* Ionic *ārḗ* prayer (from earlier **arwā́*), Russian *orát'* to shout, cry, and probably with Sanskrit *ā́ryati* (he) praises, from Indo-European **ōr-/ər-* (Pok. 781). Doublet of ORISON.

The meaning of formal speech or discourse is first recorded in English in William Atkynson's translation of Thomas à Kempis' *Imitation of Christ* (1502). In French this sense is recorded in the late 1400's.

orator *n.* About 1380 *oratour* spokesman or advocate, in Chaucer's translation of Boethius' *De Consolatione Philosophiae;* borrowing through Anglo-French *oratour,* variant of Old French *orateur,* learned borrowing from Latin *ōrātor* speaker, from *ōrāre* speak before a court or assembly, plead; see ORATION; for suffix see -OR[2].

The spelling *orator* appeared in the 1500's in imitation of the Latin form.

oratorio (ôr'ətôr'ēō) *n.* extended musical composition, usually based on a religious theme. 1727-38, in *Chambers Cyclopaedia;* borrowing of Italian *oratorio,* originally, place of prayer, and specifically the oratory of St. Philip Neri in Rome, where musical services based on older mystery plays were presented in the 1500's, from Late Latin *ōrātōrium* place of prayer, from neuter of Latin *ōrātōrius* of or for praying or pleading, from *ōrāre* pray, plead, speak before a court or assembly; see ORATION.

oratory[1] (ôr'ətôr'ē) *n.* formal public speaking. Before 1586, in Sidney's *The Arcadia;* borrowed from Latin *ars ōrātōria* oratorical art, feminine of *ōrātōrius* of speaking or pleading, from *ōrāre* speak before a court or assembly, plead; see ORATION; for suffix see -ORY.

Sidney's use of *oratory* was figurative; in the literal sense, the first recorded use of the meaning "the delivery of orations or speeches, the exercise of eloquence" is found in Shakespeare's *Titus Andronicus* (1588). The earliest occurrence of the meaning "art of oratory, rhetoric" is also in Shakespeare's writing: in *The Rape of Lucrece* (1593).

—oratorical *adj.* characteristic of oratory. 1634, formed from English *orator* or *oratory* + *-ical.*

oratory[2] (ôr'ətôr'ē) *n.* small chapel set aside for prayer. Probably before 1325 *oratorie;* borrowed from Old French *oratorie, oratoire,* and directly from Late Latin *ōrātōrium* place of prayer; see ORATORIO.

orb *n.* About 1449 *orbe* orbit of a celestial body (possibly influenced by earlier *orbicular,* 1440); later, circular formation of soldiers (before 1460); borrowing of Middle French *orbe,* learned borrowing from Latin, and borrowed directly from Latin *orbis* circle, disk, ring, of unknown origin, though probably related to *orbita* wheel track, rut, course, ORBIT. The meaning of sphere or globe, is first recorded in 1526. **—v.** form into an orb. 1600, from the noun.

orbicular (ôrbik'yələr) *adj.* circular, spherical. Probably 1440 *orbiculer,* borrowed from Middle French *orbiculaire,* or directly from Late Latin *orbiculāris,* from Latin *orbiculus* small orb, diminutive of *orbis* ORB.

orbit *n.* 1392 *orbita* eye socket; borrowing of Medieval Latin *orbita;* also, probably before 1425 *orbite;* borrowing of Old French *orbite;* both the Old French and Medieval Latin forms from Latin *orbita* wheel track, course, orbit, cognate with Umbrian *urfeta* wheel-shaped object; see ORB.

The meaning in astronomy of a path or course of a celestial body, especially the curved path of a planet or comet around the sun, or of a satellite around its primary, or of one star around another, was borrowed from Latin in 1696; the application of this meaning to an artificial earth satellite is first recorded in 1951. The meaning in physics of a curved path of an electron about the nucleus of an atom, is first recorded in 1891. The figurative sense of a sphere or activity or influence, is found in Sterne's *Tristram Shandy* (1759).

—v. travel around in an orbit. 1946, from the noun.

—orbital *adj.* 1541, of the eye socket; formed from English *orbit* + *-al*[1], probably after New Latin *orbitalis,* from Medieval Latin *orbita* eye socket, orbit. The sense in astronomy "of or in the orbit of a celestial body" is found in 1839. **—orbiter** *n.* something that orbits, especially a spacecraft intended only for orbiting and not landing. 1954, American English (originally military use), formed from *orbit,* v. + *-er*[1].

orchard *n.* Probably before 1200 *orchard,* in *Ancrene Riwle;* developed from Old English *orceard* fruit garden (about 1000, in Ælfric's *Grammar*); alteration of earlier *ortgeard* orchard, garden (before 899, in Alfred's translation of St. Gregory's *Pastoral Care*). Old English *ortgeard* is perhaps a reduced form of *wortgeard, wyrtgeard* (*wort, wyrt* vegetable, plant, root + *geard* garden, YARD[1]), or as a compound corresponding to Gothic *aúrti-gards,* the Old English *ortgeard* may be formed (like the Gothic) from the root of Gothic *aúrtja* farmer, and Old English *geard.*

The Middle English spelling *orchard* (with *h*) may have a connection by folk etymology with the Latin *hortus* garden, but the association seems distant and the *h* out of place.

orchestra *n.* 1606, in Holland's translation of Suetonius' *History of the Caesars;* borrowed from Latin *orchēstra* place where the senate sat in a theater, from Greek *orchḗstrā* space where the chorus of dancers performed in the ancient Greek theater, from *orcheîsthai* to dance, intensive form of *érchesthai* to go, come. The Greek word is probably cognate with Sanskrit *ṛghāyáti* (he) rages, raves, and perhaps related to Greek *ornýnai* to stir up; rouse; see RISE.

The meaning of a group of musicians performing at a concert, opera, etc., is first recorded in 1720, in John Gay's correspondence; the meaning of a part of a theater or auditorium in front of the stage is found in Sterne's *Sentimental Journey* (1768).

—orchestral *adj.* 1811, formed from English *orchestra* + *-al*[1]. **—orchestrate** *v.* compose or arrange for an orchestra. 1880, back formation from earlier *orchestration;* for suffix see -ATE[1]. The figurative sense of arrange or combine harmoniously is first recorded in 1883. **—orchestration** *n.* 1864, borrowing of French *orchestration,* from *orchestrer* orchestrate + *-ation* -ation. The figurative sense is first recorded in 1888.

orchid *n.* 1845, borrowed from New Latin *Orchideae, Orchidaceae* the plant's family name, assigned by Linnaeus in 1751, from *orchid-,* erroneously assumed as the stem of Latin *orchis* a kind of orchid, from Greek *órchis* (genitive *órcheōs*) orchid, testicle, cognate with Armenian *orjik'* testicles, Albanian *herdhë* testicle, Middle Irish *uirgge,* and Avestan (dual) *ərəzi,* from Indo-European **orĝhi-/ṛĝhi-* (Pok. 782); so called from the shape of the plant's root. **—adj.** light-purple. 1923, from the noun, in association with the color of the early cultivated orchids.

ordain *v.* About 1250 *ordeynen* assign, decree, appoint, arrange; borrowed from Old French *ordener,* with the stems *ordein-, ordeign-,* and borrowed directly from Latin *ōrdināre* put in order, arrange, dispose, appoint, from *ōrdō* (genitive *ōrdinis*) ORDER.

The meaning of to appoint or admit to a ministerial or priestly function in the church, is first recorded in Middle English about 1300, and was borrowed from Late Latin *ōrdināre,* from Latin, to appoint, arrange.

ordeal *n.* About 1385 *ordal* a method of trial in which an accused person is subjected to a dangerous physical test in the belief that God would not let an innocent person come to harm, in Chaucer's *Troilus and Criseyde;* later *ordel* right of jurisdiction over trials by ordeal (1403); developed from Old English (about 915) *ordēl, ordāl,* literally, judgment or verdict. The Old English forms are cognate with Old Frisian *ordēl, urdēl* judgment or verdict, Old Saxon *urdēli,* Middle Dutch and modern Dutch *oordeel,* and Old High German *urteili, urteil* (modern German *Urteil);* all derived from Proto-Germanic **uzdailijan,* represented in Old English *ādǣlan* to deal out, allot in shares, DEAL.

The spelling *ordeal,* first recorded in 1605, was influenced by *deal.* The meaning of a severe test, trying experience, is an extension of the original meaning and is first recorded in 1658, in Cleveland's writings.

order *n.* Probably before 1200 *ordre* rank, class, sequence, methodical arrangement, in *Ancrene Riwle;* borrowed from Old French *ordre, orde,* from *ordene,* learned borrowing from Latin *ōrdinem* (nominative *ōrdō*) row, rank, series, regular arrangement, of unknown origin.

The meaning of act of ordering, regulation, command, mandate, is first recorded before 1548, but the sense of a decree, rule, etc., is found in general use about 1350, and in specific application to religious rule probably before 1200, in *Ancrene Riwle.*

—v. Probably about 1200 *ordren* arrange, ordain; from the noun. The meaning of command, direct, is first recorded before 1550.

—orderly *adj.* arranged in order. Before 1577, formed from English *order* + *-ly*[1], but earlier found as an adverb (about 1477). The meaning of well-behaved, keeping order, is first recorded in Shakespeare's *Merry Wives of Windsor* (1598). **—n.** 1800, military attendant who carries out orders; from the adjective, perhaps by influence of French *ordonnance* orderly. The meaning of an attendant in a military or other hospital, is first recorded in 1809.

ordinal *adj.* showing order or position in a series. About 1410 *ordinel* orderly, proper, regular; later *ordynal* (before 1425); borrowed from Old French *ordinel,* and directly from Late Latin *ōrdinālis* showing order, from Latin *ōrdō* (genitive *ōrdinis*) row, series, ORDER; for suffix see -AL[1]. The meaning of showing order in a series is first recorded in English in 1599. **—n.** ordinal number. 1591, from the adjective.

ordinance *n.* rule or law. Probably before 1300 *ordinaunce* decree, orderly arrangement, regulation, in *Arthour and Merlin;* borrowed from Old French *ordenance,* or directly from Medieval Latin *ordinantia,* from Latin *ōrdinantem* (nominative *ōrdināns*), present participle of *ōrdināre* put in order, regulate, rule, ORDAIN; for suffix see -ANCE.

The meaning of military supplies is first recorded about 1390, in Chaucer's *Canterbury Tales,* developed from the earlier senses of preparation for war (1330), military procedure (1303). Compare ORDNANCE.

ordinary *adj.* Before 1402 *ordenarye* having authority by ecclesiastical office, in reference to a parish priest; later *ordinarie* orderly, regular, usual (probably before 1425, in a translation of Chauliac's *Grande Chirurgie*); borrowed from Old French *ordinarie, ordenaire,* and directly from Latin *ōrdinārius* according to the usual order, customary, regular, usual, from *ōrdō* (genitive *ōrdinis*) order; see ORDER; for suffix see -ARY.

ordination *n.* Before 1400 *ordynacyone* divine decree; later *ordinacioun* a putting in order, the ordaining of an archbishop (probably before 1425); borrowed from Middle French *ordinacion,* or directly from Late Latin and Latin *ōrdinātionem* (nominative *ōrdinātiō*) a setting in order, ordinance, from *ōrdināre* arrange, ORDAIN; for suffix see -ATION.

ordnance *n.* cannon, artillery. Before 1548, shortened variant of *ordinaunce* military supplies (about 1390, in Chaucer's *Canterbury Tales*); see ORDINANCE.

ordure (ôr′jər) *n.* filth, excrement. About 1380, in Chaucer's translation of Boethius' *De Consolatione Philosophiae;* borrowed from Old French *ordure,* from *ord* filthy, from Latin *horridus* dreadful, HORRID; for suffix see -URE.

ore *n.* mineral containing metal. Probably before 1200 *or,* in *Ancrene Riwle;* developed in part from Old English *ōra* ore or unworked metal, and in part from Old English *ār* brass, copper, bronze. Old English *ōra* is related to *ēar* earth, and cognate with Low German *ūr* iron-containing ore, modern Dutch *oer,* and Old Icelandic *aurr* gravel. Old English *ār* is cognate with Old Saxon and Old High German *ēr* bronze (modern German *ehern* brazen), Old Icelandic *eir* bronze or copper, and Gothic *aiz* bronze, from Proto-Germanic **ajiz-.* Cognates outside Germanic include Latin *aes* bronze or copper, Sanskrit *áyas* iron or metal, and Avestan *ayah-* iron or metal, from Indo-European **ayos,* stem *ayes-* metal (copper or bronze) (Pok. 15).

Although Old English *ār* began to be identified in meaning with Old English *ōra* as early as the 1100's, the forms descended from both (*or, oar, ore,* from *ār; oor, oure, ure* from *ōra*) continued to develop side by side until the 1600's, when the forms from *ōra* became obsolete or assimilated with those from *ār.* Thus modern *ore* appears to derive its meaning from Old English *ōra,* but its form from Old English *ār* brass, copper, bronze, which may have been extended to the sense "metal" and hence to "ore."

oregano (əreg′ənō) *n.* aromatic herb, a species of marjoram. 1771, borrowing of Spanish *orégano* wild marjoram, from Latin *orīganum,* from Greek *oríganon.* The term has largely displaced the earlier *origanum* (about 1150), *organy* (1545), *organum* (before 1450), *origan* (about 1150), all names for wild marjoram, and ultimately from the Greek *oríganon,* a word of Mediterranean origin.

oreo (ôr′ēō *or* ō′rēō) *n. Slang.* black person who thinks or acts like a white person (used contemptuously). 1969, American English, figurative use of *Oreo,* a trademark for a kind of dark chocolate cookie with a white vanilla cream filling.

organ *n.* Probably before 1300 *orgne* a kind of stringed or wind musical instrument, in *Kyng Alisaunder;* later *organ* (before 1325, in *Cursor Mundi*); also, functional part of the body, organ (1392); developed from a fusion of Old English (about 1000) *organe* musical instrument, and of Old French *orgene, organe* musical instrument; both Old English and Old French forms are borrowed from Latin *organa,* neuter plural of *organum,* from Greek *órganon* implement, tool, musical instrument, organ of sense, organ of the body; related to *érgon* WORK. It is also evident that, in some instances, the term was reborrowed directly from Latin in Middle English.

The specific meaning of a pipe organ is first recorded in English in Mannyng's *Chronicle of England* (before 1338). The meaning "instrument, means of action or operation, tool," is first recorded probably before 1425. The modern sense of a means or medium of communication or of expression of opinion is found in 1788.

—organ grinder (1806-07) **—organist** *n.* one who plays the pipe organ. 1591, probably formed from English *organ* + *-ist* by influence of Middle French *organiste* or Medieval Latin *organista.* The term replaced Middle English *organister* (recorded probably before 1300), *Organistre* (recorded as a surname, 1309); borrowed from Old French *organistre,* alteration of Medieval Latin *organista.*

organdy or **organdie** (ôr′gəndē) *n.* fine, thin muslin. 1835, borrowed from French *organdi,* perhaps an alteration of *Organzi,* medieval form of *Urgench,* a city in Uzbekistan in central Asia, where this kind of fabric was produced. Compare ORGANZA.

organelle (ôr′gənel′) *n. Biology.* any specialized part of a cell. 1924, borrowed from New Latin *organella,* diminutive from Medieval Latin *organum* organ of the body, from Latin *organum* organ, instrument; see ORGAN.

organic *adj.* Before 1400 *organik* having special properties or functions, in reference to parts of the body, in Lanfranc's *Science of Surgery;* borrowed from Old French *organique, organice,* and directly from Medieval Latin *organicus;* later, serving as an organ or instrument (1517); reborrowed from Latin *organicus,* from Greek *organikós,* from *órganon* instrument, ORGAN; for suffix see -IC.

The meaning "of the bodily organs, structural" (as in *an organic disease*) does not again appear in the record of English before 1706, and may be another reborrowing from Latin. The sense "having organs or derived from organized living beings" (as in *organic matter*), is first recorded in 1778. The extended sense in chemistry "of or pertaining to compounds containing carbon (and existing naturally in plant and animal bodies)" is first attested in Faraday's *Chemical Manipulation* (1827). The general meaning "belonging to or inherent in the organization of a person or thing, constitutional, fundamental," is first found in 1796.

organism *n.* 1664, organic structure, organization, in Evelyn's *Sylva;* probably formed on English *organize* + English suffix *-ism,* on the model of such pairs as *symbolize, symbolism* and *evangelize, evangelism.* The meaning of an organized or organic system (as in *society as an organism*) is first recorded in 1768-74; the meaning of a living body made up of organs or specialized parts, individual animal or plant, is first recorded in 1842.

Since French *organisme* is first attested in 1729 and did not become current until the 1800's and Spanish and Italian *organismo* were borrowed from English in the 1800's, it appears that the word was probably first formed in English.

organize *v.* 1413 *organysen* give structure to, provide with organs, borrowed through Middle French *organiser,* and directly from Medieval Latin *organizare,* from Latin *organum* instrument; see ORGAN; for suffix see -IZE.

The general meaning of systematize, form into a coordinated whole, is first recorded in 1632.

—organization *n.* Probably before 1425 *organizacioun* bodily structure or composition, in a translation of Chauliac's *Grande Chirurgie;* borrowed from Middle French *organisation,* and directly from Medieval Latin *organizationem* (nominative *organizatio*), from *organizare* organize; for suffix see -ATION. The meaning of condition or manner of being organized is first recorded in Burke's *Reflections on the Revolution in France* (1790), and that of the action of organizing parts into a systematic whole, in 1816. The concrete meaning of an organized body, system, establishment, etc., is first recorded in Herbert Spencer's *The Study of Sociology* (1873).

organza (ôrgan′zə) *n.* kind of sheer dress fabric resembling organdy. 1820, probably alteration of the name *Organzi;* see ORGANDY.

orgasm *n.* 1684, excitement or violent action in an organ or part; borrowed through French *orgasme* or New Latin *orgasmus,* from Greek *orgasmós* excitement, swelling, from *orgân* be in heat, become ripe for; literally, to swell, be excited; related to *orgḗ* impulse, excitement, anger. Greek *orgḗ* is cognate with Old Irish *ferc* anger, and Sanskrit *ūrjā́* nourishment, vigor, from Indo-European **werĝ-/worĝ-* swell with sap (Pok. 1169).

The sense of climax of sexual excitement during coitus is first recorded in 1802. The figurative extension of paroxysm of excitement or rage is found before 1763. **—v.** experience orgasm. 1973, from the noun. **—orgasmic** *adj.* of or involving orgasm. 1935, formed from English *orgasm* + *-ic.*

orgy (ôr′jē) *n.* wild revel. 1589 *orgies,* pl., secret rites in the worship of certain Greek and Roman gods, especially those of Dionysus or Bacchus, celebrated with wild dancing, drinking, etc.; borrowed from Middle French *orgies,* learned borrowing from Latin *orgia,* and borrowed directly from Greek *órgia,* pl., secret rites; related to *érgon* WORK.

The singular form *orgy* is first recorded in English in 1665 but remained comparatively rare except in the generalized meaning of wild, dissolute, or drunken revel, debauchery, which is first recorded in 1703. The figurative sense of wild excess (as in *an orgy of blood*) is first found in 1883. **—orgiastic** *adj.* of or characterized by orgies. 1698, borrowed from Greek *orgiastikós,* from *orgiastḗs* one who celebrates orgies, from *orgiázein* to celebrate orgies, from *órgia* orgies; for suffix see -IC.

oriel (ôr′ēəl *or* ōr′ēəl *n.* bay window projecting from the outer face of a wall. 1360, porch, corridor, balcony, bay window; earlier, a room containing an *oriel* (1236); borrowed from Old French *oriol,* and perhaps from Medieval Latin *oriolum,* both of uncertain origin, though the Medieval Latin form may be a borrowing from Old French.

Orient *n.* About 1375 *Orient, orient* the part of the sky or the world in which the sun rises, the East, in Chaucer's *Canterbury Tales;* borrowed from Old French *orient,* or directly from Latin *orientem* (nominative *oriēns*) the part of the sky in which the sun rises; originally adjective, (of heavenly bodies) rising, from present participle of *orīrī* to RISE; for suffix see -ENT. Compare OCCIDENT. **—v. orient,** take the bearings of. 1727-41, to place or arrange facing the east, in *Chambers Cyclopaedia;* borrowed from French *orienter,* from *orient* east (from Old French). The extended meaning of determine the bearings of, is first recorded in English in 1842, and that of adjust, correct, or bring into proper relations, in 1850. **—Oriental** *adj.* of or belonging to the Orient. About 1386, in Chaucer's *Legend of Good Women;* borrowed from Old French *oriental,* and directly from Latin *orientālis* of the East, from *orientem* the East; for suffix see -AL[1]. **—orientation** *n.* the act or fact of orienting. 1839, placing or arrangement of a building, etc., to face the east or any other specified direction; possibly borrowed from French *orientation* (*orienter* to orient + *-ation* -ation), but more likely formed from English *orient* + *-ation,* by influence of French. The meaning "determination of one's bearings or relative position," in both the literal and figurative sense, is first recorded in English in 1868-70.

orifice *n.* opening, hole, mouth. Probably before 1425, the opening of a wound, in a translation of Chauliac's *Grande Chirurgie;* borrowed from Middle French *orifice,* learned borrowing from Late Latin, and borrowed directly from Latin *ōrificium* (*ōs,* genitive *ōris* mouth, opening; see ORAL, + *facere* make DO[1]).

oriflamme (ôr′əflam) *n.* bright banner or other symbol serving as a rallying point. 1600 *auriflambe,* figurative use of *oriflamble* the red banner of St. Denis given by abbots of St. Denis to early French kings on setting out to war (probably about 1451); borrowed from Middle French and Old French *oriflambe, oriflamble,* from Medieval Latin *aurea flamma,* literally, golden flame (*aurea,* feminine of Latin *aureus* golden, and *flamma,* from Latin, FLAME).

The form *oriflamme* is first recorded in English in Macaulay's *Essays* (1824), in imitation of French *oriflamme* banner or standard, from Old French *oriflambe.*

origami (ôr′əgä′mē) *n.* Japanese art of folding paper to make decorative objects. 1956, from Japanese *origami* (*ori* fold + *kami* paper). The word has been known in Japanese since the late 1600's.

origin *n.* Probably before 1400 *origyne* fact of arising from some ancestor, ancestry, derivation; borrowed possibly from Old French **origine* (compare Middle French *origine*), and directly from Latin *orīginem* (nominative *orīgō*) beginning, source, birth, from *orīrī* to RISE.

The meaning of that from which anything arises, starting point, source, is first recorded in English in 1604. **—original** *adj.* Before 1325 *origenal* first in time, earliest, borrowed from Old French *original,* and directly from Latin *orīginālis,* from *orīginem* (nominative *orīgō*) origin; for suffix see -AL[1]. The extended meaning of new, fresh, novel, is first recorded in English in Joseph Warton's *Essay on the Genius and Writings of Pope* (1756-82). —*n.* About 1350, original sin; later, an original text (about 1386, in Chaucer's *Legend of Good Women*); borrowed from Medieval Latin *originale.* **—originality** *n.* 1742, in Walpole's *Letters;* formed from English *original* + *-ity,* probably after French *originalité.* **—original sin** About 1390, in Chaucer's *Canterbury Tales,* with the early sense of inherited, specifically from Adam. **—originate** *v.* arise, come or bring into existence, initiate. 1657-83, give rise to, in Evelyn's *History of Religion;* probably a back formation from earlier *origination* origin or derivation (1614, in Seldon's *Titles of Honor*); probably borrowed from Middle French *origination,* from Latin *orīginātiōnem* (nominative *orīginātiō*) in the specific sense of derivation of words, from **orīgināre* originate, from *originem* (nominative *orīgō*) origin; for suffix see -ATION. **—originator** *n.* 1818, formed from English *originate* + *-or*[2] on the pattern of *creator* and *administrator.*

oriole (ôr′ēōl) *n.* bird with yellow or orange and black feathers. 1776, borrowed from earlier French *oriol* (now *loriot,* from *l'oriot*), from Old French, from Latin *aureolus* golden; see AUREOLE. *Oriole* probably replaced a native English word, such as *woodwall,* which became obsolete in the 1600's.

orison (ôr′əzən) *n. Archaic.* prayer. Probably before 1200 *ureisun,* in *Ancrene Riwle;* borrowed through Anglo-French *ureisen,* Old French *oreison,* from Late Latin *ōrātiōnem* (nominative *ōrātiō*) prayer, from Latin *ōrāre* pray, plead, speak before a court or assembly; see the doublet ORATION.

ormolu (ôr′məlü) *n.* alloy of copper and zinc. 1765, in Walpole's *Letters;* borrowed from French *or moulu,* literally, ground gold (*or* gold, from Latin *aurum,* and *moulu* ground up, past participle of *moudre* to grind, from Latin *molere;* see MEAL² ground grain).

ornament *n.* Probably before 1200 *urnement* useful accessory, decoration, embellishment, in *Ancrene Riwle;* later *ournement* (1340, in *Ayenbite of Inwyt*), and *ornament* (probably before 1350); borrowed from probable Anglo-French *urnement,* Old French *ornement,* learned borrowing from Latin *ōrnāmentum* equipment, trappings, embellishment, from *ōrnāre* equip, adorn; see ORNATE; for suffix see -MENT. **—v.** adorn, decorate. 1720, in Pope's translation of Homer's *Iliad,* from the noun. *Ornament* is a replacement in modern English for earlier *ournen* to adorn, ornament (recorded before 1382, in the Wycliffe Bible); borrowed from Old French *orner,* from Latin *ornāre.* **—ornamental** *adj.* decorative. 1646, formed from English *ornament* + *-al*¹, and, probably in some instances, borrowed from Latin *ōrnāmentalis,* from *ōrnamentum.* **—ornamentation** *n.* 1851, decorations, ornaments; formed from English *ornament,* v. + *-ation.* The meaning of act of ornamenting is first recorded in English in 1860, in J.S. Mill's writings.

ornate *adj.* Before 1400, seemly, decorous; later, adorned, ornamented (about 1412); borrowed from Latin *ōrnātus,* past participle of *ōrnāre* adorn, fit out, contracted from earlier **ōrdināre,* formed from the stem *ōrdin-* of *ōrdō* ORDER (later re-formed in Latin *ōrdināre;* see ORDAIN); for suffix see -ATE¹.

ornery *adj. Informal.* mean, low, vile. 1816, American English, dialectal contraction of ORDINARY.

ornithology (ôr′nəthol′əjē) *n.* study of birds. 1678, borrowed from New Latin *ornithologia* (1599), from Greek *órnīs* (genitive *órnīthos*) bird, also *órneon;* for suffix see -LOGY. Greek *órnīs* and *órneon* are extensions of an ancient stem **orn-,* cognate with Old High German *aro, arn* (modern German *Aar* eagle), Old English *earn* eagle, Old Slavic *orĭlŭ,* Welsh *eryr,* and Hittite *haras* (genitive *haranas*), from Indo-European **er-/or-* eagle; big bird (Pok. 325).

orotund (ôr′ətund) *adj.* strong, full, rich, and clear in voice or speech, resonant. 1792-99, alteration of Latin *ōre rotundō* in well-rounded phrases (from Horace's *Ars Poetica*); literally, with round mouth (*ōre,* ablative of *ōs* mouth; see ORAL; *rotundō,* ablative of *rotundus* ROUND). The alteration of Latin *ōre rotundō* by haplology of *-re* in *ōre,* adjacent to *ro-* of *rotundō,* is a type of omission familiar in the borrowing process of English. **—orotundity** *n.* a being orotund, orotund expression. 1909, in *Century Dictionary* (Supplement), replacing the earlier *ororotundity* (1831), a blend of *orotund* and *rotundity;* for suffix see -ITY.

orphan *n.* Probably before 1300, in *Kyng Alisaunder;* borrowed from Late Latin *orphanus* parentless child, from Greek *orphanós* deprived, orphaned. The Greek word is cognate with Latin *orbus* deprived or orphaned, Old Irish *orbe* inheritance, Old Slavic *rabŭ* slave, Armenian *orb* orphan, and Sanskrit *árbha-s* small, weak, from Indo-European **orbhos* (Pok. 781). Germanic cognates (from Proto-Germanic **arƀijan*) include Gothic *arbi* inheritance, Old Icelandic *arfi,* Old High German *erbi* (modern German *Erbe*), Old Saxon *erƀi,* Old Frisian *erve,* and Old English (West Saxon) *ierfe* and (Anglian) *erfe,* which did not survive into modern English. **—adj.** having no parent. 1483, in Caxton's *Golden Legend;* from the noun. **—v.** make an orphan of. 1814, in Southey's *Roderick;* from the noun. **—orphanage** *n.* 1538, guardianship of orphans; later, condition of being an orphan (1579-80); formed from English *orphan* + *-age.* The meaning of an institution or home for orphans is first recorded in 1865, though the concept was known in *orphan asylum* as early as 1811, and *orphan house* (before 1711).

orris (ôr′is) *n.* fragrant rootstock of a kind of iris. 1545, probably an alteration of Middle English *yreos* (before 1400); and *yrrios* (1392); borrowed from Medieval Latin *yreos,* derivative of alteration of Latin *īris* IRIS. **—orrisroot** *n.* (1598, in Florio's *A World of Words*)

ortho- a combining form meaning: **1** straight or upright, as in *orthodontics, orthopterous.* **2** correct or proper, as in *orthography, orthopedics.* Borrowed through Middle French and Latin *ortho-,* from Greek *ortho-,* stem of *orthós* straight, right, true, correct, earlier **worthwós,* cognate with Sanskrit *ūrdhvá-s* erected, high (altered from **ūrdhá-s* by influence of *ṛṣvá-s* high), related to *várdhati* (it) grows, increases, from Indo-European **werdh-/wordh-* (Pok. 1167).

orthoclase (ôr′thəklās) *n.* common or potash feldspar, used in making glass, ceramics, etc. 1849, borrowed from German *Orthoklas* (formed from Greek *ortho-* straight + *klásis* cleavage, from *klân* to break; see CLONE; so called from its crystals having two cleavages at right angles to each other). The word was coined in 1823 by the German mineralogist August Breithaupt, 1791-1873.

orthodontics (ôr′thədon′tiks) *n.* branch of dentistry that deals with straightening and adjusting teeth. 1909, formed in English from New Latin *orthodontia* (1849 *ortho-* straight + Greek *odṓn,* genitive *odóntos* TOOTH) + *-ics,* as in *orthopedics.* **—orthodontist** *n.* specialist in orthodontics. 1903, formed in English from New Latin *orthodontia* orthodontics + English *-ist.*

orthodox *adj.* generally accepted, especially in religion. About 1454 *ortodox,* and 1456 *orthodoxe;* borrowed from Middle French *orthodoxe,* and directly from Late Latin *orthodoxus,* from Greek *orthódoxos* having the right opinion (*ortho-* straight, right, true + *dóxa* opinion, praise; see DOXOLOGY).

Orthodox as the specific name of the Eastern Church (originally used to distinguish it from various doctrinal divisions within the Church), is first recorded in 1772. As the name of the Jewish group adhering strictly to rabbinical law and tradition, *Orthodox* is first recorded in 1904, from earlier *orthodox* strictly observant (1853). **—orthodoxy** *n.* orthodox practice or belief. 1630, borrowed from French *orthodoxie,* learned borrowing from Late Latin, and borrowed directly from Late Latin *orthodoxia,* from Greek *orthodoxíā* right opinion (*ortho-* straight, right, true + *dóxa* opinion); for suffix see -Y³.

orthography (ôrthog′rəfē) *n.* correct, accepted, or customary spelling. 1530 *orthographie,* in Palsgrave's *Lesclarcissement,* alteration of *ortographie* (before 1460); borrowed from Middle French *orthographie,* learned borrowing from Latin *orthographia,* from Greek *orthographiā* (*ortho-* straight, correct + root of *gráphein* to write; see CARVE). **—orthographic** or **orthographical** *adj.* of or pertaining to orthography. 1589 *orthographical,* from *orthography* + *-ical;* 1868 *orthographic,* shortened form of *orthographical.*

orthopedic (ôr′thəpē′dik) *adj.* of or having to do with the correction of deformities of bones and joints, especially in children. 1840, borrowed from French *orthopédique,* from *orthopédie* (coined in 1741) orthopedic surgery (*ortho-* straight, correct + *-pédie,* from Greek *paideíā* rearing of children, from *paîs,* genitive *paidós* child, see FEW); for suffix see -IC. **—orthopedics** *n.* orthopedic surgery. 1853, formed from English *orthopedic* + *-s*[1], as in *-ics.*

orthopterous (ôrthop′tərəs) *adj. Zoology.* belonging to the order of insects including crickets, grasshoppers, cockroaches, etc. 1826, formed from English *ortho-* straight + Greek *pterón* wing; see FEATHER; so called from their usually straight and narrow forewings.

orthosis (ôrthō′sis) *n.* artificial support, such as a brace. 1958, New Latin *orthosis,* from Greek *órthōsis* a making straight, from *orthoûn* set straight, from *orthós* straight; see ORTHO-. **—orthotic** *adj.* of or pertaining to an orthosis. 1955, from New Latin *orthosis,* on the analogy of *prosthesis, prosthetic.*

-ory a suffix forming adjectives and nouns and meaning: **1** of or having to do with, as in *illusory.* **2** characterized by, as in *compulsory.* **3** serving to, as in *preparatory.* **4** tending to or inclined to, as in *contradictory, conciliatory.* **5** place or establishment for, as in *depository, conservatory.* Middle English *-orie,* borrowed from Old North French *-ory, -orie,* Old French *-oir, -oire,* from Latin *-ōrius, -ōria, -ōrium.* French *-oire* and English *-ory* became the conventional endings in words borrowed or adapted from Latin with suffix *-tōrius* or *-sōrius* (stem form following the past participle in *-tus* or *-sus*), formed from the Latin agent suffix *-tor, -sor* and adjective suffix *-ius;* the neuter in *-tōrium, -sōrium* furnished nouns such as *dormītōrium* dormitory.

oryx (ôr′iks) *n.* kind of African antelope. Before 1382 *orix,* in the Wycliffe Bible; borrowed from Latin *oryx,* from Greek *óryx* (genitive *órygos*) antelope with pointed horns; a borrowed word.

In Biblical Latin and Greek, this word referred to a wild ox, but in Middle English the animal is variously identified as a kind of wild goat, or a creature similar to a dormouse.

os- a form of the prefix *ob-* in some cases before *c* and *t* in words of Latin origin, as in *ostentation.* The form developed from the loss of *b* (or *p*) from a prehistoric lengthened variant *obs-* (or *ops-*); compare *abs-,* which survives as a lengthened variant of *ab-* (as in *abstract*).

Oscar *n.* statuette awarded since 1928 for the best work in motion pictures. 1936, American English, supposedly adopted from the remark, "He reminds me of my Uncle Oscar," made in 1931 by the secretary of the Academy of Motion Picture Arts and Sciences when she saw one of the statuettes; her uncle was *Oscar* Pierce, an American wheat and fruit grower.

oscillate *v.* swing to and fro like a pendulum. 1726, probably a back formation of earlier *oscillation,* and perhaps in some instances borrowed from Latin *ōscillātum,* past participle of *ōscillāre* to swing, rock, from *ōscillum* a swing, of uncertain origin; for suffix see -ATE[1]. **—oscillation** *n.* 1658, action of oscillating, in Phillips' *Dictionary;* borrowed probably through French *oscillation,* learned borrowing from Latin *ōscillātiōnem* (nominative *ōscillātiō*), from *ōscillāre* to swing; for suffix see -ATION. **—oscillator** *n.* 1835, in writings of De Quincey; formed from English *oscillate* + *-or*[2].

osculate (os′kyəlāt) *v.* to kiss. 1656, in Blount's *Glossographia,* borrowed from Latin *ōsculātus,* past participle of *ōsculārī* to kiss, from *ōsculum* kiss; literally, little mouth, pretty mouth, diminutive of *ōs* mouth, see ORAL; for suffix see -ATE[1]. **—osculation** *n.* 1658, in Phillips' *Dictionary,* act of kissing; probably formed from English *osculate* + *-ation,* perhaps by influence of French *osculation,* learned borrowing from Latin *ōsculātiōnem* (nominative *ōsculātiō*), from *ōsculārī* to kiss.

-ose[1] a suffix meaning: **1** full of, having much or many, as in *verbose, comatose.* **2** inclined to, fond of, as in *jocose.* Borrowed from Latin *-ōsus.* Related to *-ous.* Also a frequent variant of *-ous* in Middle English.

-ose[2] a suffix used to form chemical terms, especially names of sugars and other carbohydrates, as in *cellulose, fructose, lactose, glucose.* Borrowed from French *-ose,* abstracted from *glucose* GLUCOSE.

osier (ō′zhər) *n.* kind of willow tree. Probably before 1300 *hosyer* willow twig, switch of osier, in *Kyng Alisaunder;* later, an osier (1392); borrowed from Old French *osier, osiere,* and directly from Medieval Latin *osera, osiera* willow, of uncertain origin. It is also possible that the Middle English word developed from Old English *oser* (recorded in a manuscript of the later 1100's); borrowed from Medieval Latin. **—adj.** made of osiers. 1578, from the noun.

-osis a suffix meaning: **1** act or process of, or state or condition of, as in *osmosis, hypnosis.* **2** abnormal condition, as in *neurosis, thrombosis.* Borrowed from Latin *-osis,* and directly from Greek *-ōsis;* formed from the addition of the common verbal abstract suffix *-sis* to *-o-* (in a stem ending, usually in denominative verbs in *-ó-ein,* contracted *-oûn,* as in *sklḗrōsis* hardening, from *sklēró-ein, sklēroûn* harden, from *sklērós* hard; infrequently from the addition of *-sis* directly to the noun or adjective stem, as in *thrómbōsis* clotting, from *thrómbos* a clot).

osmium (oz′mēəm) *n.* metallic chemical element. 1804, New Latin, from Greek *osmḗ* smell, ODOR + New Latin *-ium* (suffix of chemical elements); so called from the strong odor of one of the oxides of osmium. The term was coined by the English chemist Smithson Tennant, 1761-1815, who discovered this element in 1803.

osmosis (ozmō′sis *or* osmō′sis) *n.* tendency of two fluids separated by something porous to go through it and become mixed. 1867, Latinized form of earlier *osmose* (1854), shortened form of earlier *endosmosis* (1836-39), probably formed on *endosmose* inward passage of a fluid through a porous septum (1829); borrowed from French, from *endo-* inward + Greek *ōsmós* a thrusting or pushing, from *ōtheîn* to push, thrust, related to *éthōn* damaging or ripping up, cognate with Sanskrit *vádhet* he would slay, from Indo-European **wedh-/wōdh-* (Pok. 1115). **—osmotic** *adj.* of or involving osmosis. 1854, shortened form of earlier *endosmotic* of or involving endosmosis; formed on the pattern of *neurosis, neurotic, sclerosis, sclerotic,* etc.

osprey (os′prē) *n.* large hawk. Before 1475 *ospray;* earlier *hospray* (about 1450); borrowed from Anglo-French *ospriet* (found as a surname, 1198), from Medieval Latin *avis prede* bird of prey, from Latin *avis praedae;* see AVIARY and PREY.

osseous (os′ēəs) *adj.* bony. Probably before 1425 *ossous, ossuous,* in a translation of Chauliac's *Grande Chirurgie;* borrowed from Medieval Latin *ossous,* from Latin *osseus;* later, re-formed in English (1682), perhaps by influence of French *osseux,* from Latin *osseus* bony, from *os* (genitive *ossis*) bone, earlier **ost;* for suffix see -OUS. Latin *osseus* is cognate with Greek *ostéon* bone, Albanian *asht, ashtë,* Sanskrit *ásthi,* and Hittite *hastăi,* from Indo-European **ost(h)-, óst(h)i, ost(h)éyom* (Pok. 783).

ossifrage (os′əfrij) *n.* large bird of prey. 1601, in Holland's translation of Pliny's *Natural History;* borrowed from Latin *ossifraga* sea eagle, osprey, feminine of *ossifragus,* literally, bone-breaker, from *ossifragus,* adj., bone-breaking (*os,* genitive *ossis* bone; see OSSEOUS + *-fragus* breaking, from the root of *frangere* to BREAK); probably so called either from the bird's great strength or from its alleged habit of dropping bones from a great height in order to break them.

ossify *v.* change into bone. 1713, probably a back formation of earlier *ossification,* perhaps modeled on French *ossifier,* from Latin *ossis* (genitive of *os* bone; see OSSEOUS); for suffix see -FY. **—ossification** *n.* formation of bone. 1697, possibly formed from English *ossific* becoming or making bone (1676) + *-ation.*

ossuary (os′yu̇erē *or* osh′yu̇erē) *n.* vault or urn for the bones of the dead. 1658, borrowed from Late Latin *ossuārium* receptacle for bones of the dead, charnel house, from neuter of Latin *ossuārius* of bones, from *ossua* bones (perhaps formed on the model of *artua* limbs), from *os* (genitive *ossis*) bone, see OSSEOUS; for suffix see -ARY (def. 1).

ostensible *adj.* 1762-71, capable of being shown, presentable, in Walpole's writings; borrowed from French *ostensible,* from Latin *ostēnsus,* past participle of *ostendere* to show; see OSTENTATION; for suffix see -IBLE.

The meaning of declared as genuine, apparent, pretended, professed, is first recorded in 1771.

ostensive *adj.* directly demonstrative. 1605, in Sir Francis Bacon's *Of the Advancement of Learning;* borrowed from Late Latin *ostēnsivus* showing, from Latin *ostēnsus,* past participle of *ostendere* to show, see OSTENTATION; for suffix see -IVE.

ostentation *n.* 1436 *ostentacione* portent, foreshadowing; later *ostentacioun* a showing off (before 1475); borrowed from Old French *ostentacion,* and directly from Latin *ostentātiōnem* (nominative *ostentātiō*) a showing or vain display, from *ostentāre* to display, frequentative form of *ostendere* to show, stretch toward (*os-* toward, variant of *ob-* before *t* + *tendere* to stretch; see TEND); for suffix see -ATION. **—ostentatious** *adj.* showy, pretentious. 1658 (implied in *ostentatiousness*); formed from English *ostentation* + *-ous.* This word displaced *ostentative* (1600), *ostentatory* (1657), *ostentive* (1599), and *ostentous* (1624).

osteology (os′tēol′əjē) *n.* branch of anatomy that deals with bones. 1670 *osteologie,* borrowed from French *ostéologie,* from New Latin *osteologia,* from Greek *ostéon* bone (see OSSEOUS); for suffix see -LOGY.

osteopathy (os′thēop′əthē) *n.* treatment of disease chiefly by manipulating the bones and muscles. 1891, said to be formed in American English from Greek *ostéon* bone; see OSSEOUS + English *-pathy* treatment of disease, but also probably influenced by earlier *osteopathy* disease of the bones (1857). **—osteopath** *n.* one who practices osteopathy. 1897, American English; back formation from *osteopathy.*

ostomy (os′təmē) *n.* operation in which an artificial opening is made in the body. 1957, American English, abstracted from *colostomy* (artificial opening into the colon), *ileostomy* (artificial opening into the ileum), and similar terms for surgical procedures, ultimately from New Latin *stoma* opening, orifice, from Greek *stóma* mouth; see STOMACH.

ostracize (os′trəsīz) *v.* banish. 1649, in Marvell's *Works;* formed on English *ostracism* + *-ize,* after Greek *ostrakízein* banish by ostracism, expel by voting with potsherds, from *óstrakon* tile, potsherd, from an ancient stem **ostr-* (found in *óstreion* oyster), related to *ostéon* bone; see OSSEOUS. **—ostracism** *n.* banishment. 1588, method of temporary banishment in ancient Greece, determined by popular ballot, cast by potsherds or tiles; borrowed, possibly through Middle French *ostracisme,* and directly from Greek *ostrakismós,* from *ostrakízein* to ostracize; for suffix see -ISM. The transferred and figurative meaning of banishment by general consent, exclusion from society, favors, etc., is first recorded before 1631, in John Donne's *Works.*

ostrich *n.* About 1225 *ostrice;* later *ostriche* (probably about 1350); borrowed from Old French *ostrice, ostrusce,* and Medieval Latin *ostrica, ostrigius;* both the Old French and Medieval Latin from Vulgar Latin **avis strūthiō* (*avis* bird, from Latin; *strūthiō* ostrich, from Late Latin, from Greek *strouthíōn* ostrich, from *strouthòs megálē* great sparrow).

other *adj., pron.* Old English *ōther* the second, other (before 899, in Alfred's translation of Boethius' *De Consolatione Philosophiae* and of Orosius); cognate with Old Frisian *ōther* the second, other, Old Saxon *āthar, ōthar,* Middle Dutch and modern Dutch *ander,* Old High German *andar* (modern German *ander*), Old Icelandic *annarr,* and Gothic *anthar,* from Proto-Germanic **antheraz.* Cognates outside Germanic include Old Prussian *antars* other, Lithuanian *añtras,* and Sanskrit *ántara-s,* all from the Indo-European adverb *an* there, on the other side (found in Sanskrit *anyá-s* other) + the comparative suffix **-teros* (Pok. 37).

The sense of the ordinal number "second" in Germanic was replaced in most Germanic languages to avoid ambiguity (*second* in English, *zweiter* in German, etc.). The Old English, Old Saxon, and Old Frisian forms show a normal loss of *n* before fricatives.

—adv. otherwise, differently. Before 1121, from the pronoun.

—otherwise *adv.* Old English *on ōthre wīsan* (before 899, in Alfred's translation of Boethius' *De Consolatione Philosophiae*). **—other world** 1884, as an adjective in Tennyson's writings; found earlier, probably as a separate formation in Middle English in *on* or *of other world* not of this world, different from normal (about 1300). **—otherworldy** *adj.* 1873 (but implied earlier in *otherworldliness,* before 1834, in Coleridge's writings).

otiose (ō′shēōs *or* ō′tēōs) *adj.* 1794, ineffective, futile; later, at leisure, inactive or lazy (1850), and superfluous or useless (1866); reborrowed from Latin *ōtiōsus* having leisure or ease, not busy, from *ōtium* leisure, of uncertain origin.

An earlier form is found in English *otious* at ease, idle

(1614); probably borrowed from Latin *ōtiōsus,* but possibly a back formation from earlier *otiosity* (1483 *ociosyte,* in Caxton's translation of Cato's writings); borrowed from Middle French *ociosité,* from Old French *ocios,* from Latin *ōtiōsus;* for suffix see -ITY.

otolaryngology (ō′təlar′inggol′əjē) *n.* branch of medicine dealing with the ears, nose, and throat. 1897, formed in English from *oto-* (combining form of Greek *oûs,* genitive *ōtós* EAR[1]) + *laryngology* branch of medicine dealing with the larynx (1842). Greek *oûs* shows shortening of the original long diphthong of Indo-European **ōus,* whose genitive in Greek became **ōusn̥tos,* later **owatos,* contracted to *ōtós.*

otter *n.* Before 1300 *oter,* developed from Old English (before 700) *otr, oter, otor;* cognate with Middle Low German, Middle Dutch and modern Dutch *otter* otter, Old High German *ottar* (modern German *Otter*), and Old Icelandic *otr* (modern Icelandic *otur,* Norwegian *oter,* Danish *odder,* Swedish *utter*), from Proto-Germanic **utraz,* from Indo-European **udros,* found in Greek *hýdros* water snake, and in Sanskrit *udrá-s* water animal, related to *udaká-m* (genitive *udnás*) WATER.

Ottoman (ot′əmən) *adj.* of or belonging to the former Turkish empire. 1603, borrowing of French *Ottoman,* from Italian *Ottomano,* from Arabic *'uthmāni* of or belonging to *'Uthman* Othman, *Osman,* 1259-1326, founder of the Ottoman dynasty and empire. Earlier use is recorded in the noun form *Othomann* (1585). **—ottoman** *n.* low cushioned seat without a back or arms. 1806, borrowed from French *ottomane,* from *Ottomane,* feminine of *Ottoman* Ottoman, Turkish; probably so called to suggest the Oriental style of the seat.

ought[1] *v.* have as a duty, be obliged. Before 1225 *ahten, aghten, aughten, oughten* be bound to, owe; earlier *ahte, aghte, aughte, oughte* owned, possessed, owed (before 1121), past tense of *aghen, oughen, ouen, owen* to OWE; developed from Old English (about 950) *āhte,* past tense of *āgan* to own, possess, OWE.

Ought is an auxiliary verb that now has a present tense meaning but was originally confined to the past tense of *owe* expressing duty or obligation of any kind. In the past tense usually formed in a dependent clause modern use is shown in *The judge did not think the defendant ought to be kept in prison,* or *You ought to have known.* In the present tense modern use is found in *The precedent ought to be followed,* or *You ought to do it.*

ought[2] *n.* naught, zero. 1844, in Dickens' *Martin Chuzzlewit,* alteration (possibly by mistaken division of *a nought* as *an ought*) of *nought,* variant of NAUGHT; perhaps reinforced in use by the figure 0 (zero), assumed to be the initial letter of *ought,* as in *oughts and crosses* (tick-tack-toe). The meaning was probably also influenced by *aught* anything.

Ouija (wē′jē′) *n.* trademark for a board with letters and symbols used at spiritualistic meetings and in games. 1891, American English, coined from a combination of French *oui* yes and German *ja* yes.

ounce[1] *n.* unit of weight. Before 1338 *unce* 1/12 of a pound in troy weight, in Mannyng's *Chronicle of England;* later *ounce* (before 1382, in the Wycliffe Bible); borrowing of Old French *unce,* from Latin *uncia* one twelfth part (of a pound, foot, etc.), developed through numerous changes from earlier **oinicīā,* built on **oinos,* which itself developed into Latin *ūnus* ONE. Doublet of INCH.

The Middle English forms borrowed from Old French replaced earlier *untsa, yntsa* (1150), developed from Old English *yndse, ynse* (before 899, in Alfred's translation of Orosius); earlier *ynce;* borrowed from Latin *uncia.*

ounce[2] *n.* carnivorous wild cat. Probably before 1300 *unce,* in *Kyng Alisaunder;* later, also Scottish *once* (about 1470); borrowed from Old French *once,* alteration of *lonce* (with *l* mistaken as the definite article in *lonce*), from Vulgar Latin **luncea,* from Latin *lynx* LYNX.

our *adj.* Probably before 1200 *oure,* in Layamon's *Chronicle of Britain;* later *our* (probably before 1300); developed from Old English *ūre* of us (about 725, in *Beowulf*), used as the genitive of *wē* we. Old English *ūre* is a variant of *ūser, ūsser* our; cognate with Old Frisian *ūse* our, Old Saxon *ūsa,* Middle Dutch *onse* (modern Dutch *onze*), Old High German *unsēr* (modern German *unser*), Old Icelandic *vārr,* and Gothic *unsar;* derived from the Proto-Germanic source of Old English *ūs* US.

Old English *ūser* is from earlier **unser,* with loss of the nasal sound represented by *n* before fricative *s,* a development shared with Old Saxon and Old Frisian. The later appearance of a sound represented by *r* developed as a replacement of the sound represented by *z* between vowels.

—ours *pron.* About 1303 *ours,* in Mannyng's *Handlyng Synne* (also found as *urs,* before 1325, in *Cursor Mundi;* and *oures,* about 1390, in Chaucer's *Canterbury Tales;* and *ouren, ourn,* before 1382, in the Wycliffe Bible); all from the adjective.

-ous a suffix forming adjectives from nouns and meaning: **1** having, having much, full of, as in *joyous, famous.* **2** characterized by, as in *zealous.* **3** having the nature of, as in *murderous.* **4** of or having to do with, as in *monogamous.* **5** like, as in *thunderous.* **6** committing or practicing, as in *bigamous.* **7** inclined to, as in *blasphemous.* **8** in chemical terms *-ous* indicates the presence of an element in a compound or ion that is of a lower valence than indicated by the suffix *-ic,* as in *ferrous* or *stannous.* Middle English, borrowed from Old French *-ous, -os, -eus, -eux,* and directly from Latin *-ōsus.* Related to -OSE[1]. See also -IOUS.

This suffix is also often used to represent the Latin adjective ending, *-us,* as in Latin *omnivorus* omnivorous, or the Greek adjective ending, *-os,* as in Greek *anṓnymos* anonymous.

oust *v.* 1420 *ousten* (in law) to put out of possession, dispossess; borrowed through Anglo-French *ouster,* Old French *oster* put out of place, keep off, remove, avert, from Latin *obstāre* stand opposite to, block, hinder (*ob-* against + *stāre* to STAND). Related to OBSTACLE.

The meaning of eject or expel from any place or position, force out, dismiss, is first recorded in Pepys' *Diary* (1668).

—ouster *n.* an ousting, dismissal, expulsion. 1531, (in law) ejection from a freehold or other possession; noun use of Anglo-French *ouster* to oust.

out *adv.* Probably before 1200 *out* away, from, forth, in Layamon's *Chronicle of Britain;* developed from Old English (before 725) *ūt;* cognate with Old Frisian, Old Saxon and Middle Low German *ūt* out, Middle Dutch *uut* (modern Dutch *uit*), Old High German *ūz* (modern German *aus*), Old Icelandic *ūt* (Swedish and Norwegian *ut,* Danish *ud*), and Gothic *ūt.* Cognates outside

Germanic include Latin *usque* without interruption, and Sanskrit *út-, úd-* up, out, with comparative *últara-s,* cognate with Greek *hýsteros* later, from Indo-European **ud-* (and **ud-s*), *ūd-* (Pok. 1103).

The sports sense (originally used in cricket) of no longer in the game, not in play, is first recorded in 1609. The meaning of no longer in vogue, out of fashion, is first found in Pepys' *Diary* (1660).

—adj. Probably before 1200 *ut* outside, outlying, in *Ancrene Riwle;* later *oute* (about 1280); from the adverb.

—prep. About 1250 *out* of, away from; from the adverb.

—n. 1622, a being out of something; from the adverb. The meaning in baseball of the act of putting out a player is first recorded in 1860 in American English. The informal meaning of a way out, defense, excuse, alibi, is also first recorded in American English, in Ring Lardner's *The Real Dope* (1919).

out- a prefix that has a range of uses with meanings which in part parallel the meanings of *out* as a separate word, especially: adverbially with verbal nouns, as in *outburst, outcry, outgrowth,* and with participial adjectives, as in *outgoing, outflung,* or with adjectives, as in *outbound;* less often with the finite verb as in *outcrop, outpour;* adjectivally with nouns, as in *outbuilding, outfield, outpatient,* sometimes yielding an adjectival or adverbial compound, as in *outboard;* prepositionally, as in *outdate, outdoor, outlaw.* In addition, *out-* as a prefix frequently forms transitive verbs meaning to do longer or more than, as in *outlive, outsleep,* or to surpass, to do better than, as in *outdistance, outguess, outgeneral.* For etymology, see OUT.

—outboard *adj.* outside of a ship or boat. (1823) **—outcome** *n.* effect, result. (1788) **—outdo** *v.* exceed, excel. (1607, in Shakespeare's *Coriolanus*) **—outdoor** *adj.* (1748, in Richardson's *Clarissa*) **—outdoors** *adv.* (1817); *n.* (1844, American English) **—outfield** *n.* (1851, in cricket; 1868, in baseball) **—outfit** *n.* (1769, act of fitting out; 1787, equipment; 1852, a set of clothes); *v.* to equip (1847). **—outflow** *n.* (before 1800) **—outgo** *n.* (about 1640) **—outgrowth** *n.* (1837) **—outhouse** *n.* (before 1325, a shed; 1819, American English, a privy) **—outlandish** *adj.* About 1300 *outlandisse* foreign, alien; developed from Old English (about 1000) *ūtlendisc,* from *ūtland* foreign land. The extended sense of unfamiliar, strange, odd, bizarre, is first recorded in 1596. **—outlay** *n.* expenditure. (1798) **—outlet** *n.* 1600, but found in Middle English (about 1250) in the sense of a river mouth. **—outline** *n.* (1662); *v.* to draw in outline (about 1790) **—outlook** *n.* (1667, a place to watch from; 1742, a mental view or survey) **—out-of-date** *adj.* (1628) **—outpost** *n.* (1757, American English in letters of Washington) **—output** *n.* (1858) **—outrigger** *n.* (1748) **—outright** *adv.* completely, entirely (about 1300); *adj.* direct, downright (1532). **—outset** *n.* start, beginning. (1759) **—outstanding** *adj.* 1611, in Cotgrave's *Dictionary,* projecting, protruding; prominent, eminent (1830).

outage (ou'tij) *n.* period of interrupted service, as of electric power or gas. 1903, American English; formed from *out,* adv. + *-age,* on the model of *shortage.*

outer *adj.* on the outside. About 1380 *outter,* in Chaucer's *Canterbury Tales;* later *outer* (1385, in Chaucer's *Troilus and Criseyde*), a new comparative formed from *out* + *-er*[2] (by analogy with *inner*) in place of the earlier *utter* (before 1325), and *uttre* (probably before 1200); developed from Old English *ūterra, ūtera,* comparative of *ūt* OUT. The new comparative was formed when Middle English *uttre, utter* ceased to show relationship to *out* and developed (before 1400) the meaning of complete or total, resulting in English UTTER[1], adj. **—outer space** (1901, in H.G. Wells' *The First Men in the Moon*)

outlaw *n.* About 1300 *outlawe;* developed from Old English *ūtlaga* (about 1000, in Ælfric's *Grammar*); borrowed from a Scandinavian source (compare Old Icelandic *ūtlagi* outlaw, from *ūtlagr,* adj., outlawed, banished) **—v.** declare unlawful. About 1300 *outlawen;* developed from Old English *ūtlagian,* from *ūtlaga,* n. **—outlawry** *n.* condition of being declared an outlaw. About 1395 *outlawerie,* in the Wycliffe Bible, alteration (influenced by *outlawe*) of Anglo-Latin *utlagaria* and Anglo-French *utlagarie,* both from Old English *ūtlaga* outlaw; for suffix see -RY.

outrage *n.* Probably before 1300, violent behavior, excess, extravagance, in *Kyng Alisaunder;* borrowing of French *outrage* (*outre* beyond, from Latin *uitrā* + *-age* -age). Present-day use of *outrage* is popularly associated with *rage,* as if the word were formed from *out* + *rage.* **—outrageous** *adj.* About 1300 *utrageous* violent, unrestrained, excessive; later *outrageous* (about 1390, in Chaucer's *Canterbury Tales*); borrowed from Old French *outrageus,* from *outrage* outrage; for suffix see -OUS.

outside *n.* 1505, outer side (*out,* adv. + *side*). **—adj.** outer, external. 1634, from the noun. **—prep.** on the outside of, external to. 1826, from the noun. **—adv.** on or to the outside. 1813, from the noun. The phrase *outside of,* meaning with the exception of (as in *outside of art he has no interests*), is first recorded in 1859 as an Americanism. **—outsider** *n.* 1800, in Jane Austen's *Letters.*

outward *adj.* turned toward the outside. Probably before 1200 *utward,* in *Ancrene Riwle;* later *outward* (before 1382, in the Wycliffe Bible); developed from Old English *ūteweard* (893, in the *Anglo-Saxon Chronicle*); earlier *ūtanweard* (before 725, a compound of *ute, ūtan* outside, from outside, from *ūt* OUT + *-weard* -ward). **—adv.** toward the outside. Probably before 1200 *utward,* in *Ancrene Riwle;* later *outward* (about 1300); developed from Old English (about 950) *ūtaword;* from the adjective.

ouzel or **ousel** (ü'zəl) *n.* kind of European thrush. Before 1325 *osel;* developed from Old English (about 700) *ōsle* blackbird, corresponding to Old High German *amusla, ams(a)la* blackbird (modern German *Amsel*) from Proto-West-Germanic **amuslōn;* ultimate origin unknown. The Old English form *ōsle* shows typical loss of the nasal *m* before fricative *s.*

oval *adj.* egg-shaped. 1577, in John Dee's *A True and Faithful Relation of What Passed Between. . .J.D. and Some Spirits;* borrowed from Middle French *ovale,* or directly from Medieval Latin *ovalis* of or pertaining to an egg, from Latin *ōvum* EGG[1]; for suffix see -AL[1]. **—n.** oval figure or object. 1570, in John Dee's *Preface* to a text on geometry; borrowed from Middle French *ovalle,* n., oval figure or *ovale,* adj., egg-shaped; both from Medieval Latin *ovalis* egg-shaped, oval.

ovary *n.* female organ in which eggs are produced. 1658, borrowed from New Latin *ovarium* ovary (in Medieval Latin *ovaria* the ovary of a bird), from Latin *ōvum* EGG[1], for suffix see -ARY.

The corresponding meaning in botany of the part of

a flowering plant in which the ovules or young seeds are produced, is first recorded in 1744.

ovate *adj.* egg-shaped. 1775, borrowed from Latin *ōvātus,* from *ōvum* EGG[1]; for suffix see -ATE[1].

ovation *n.* enthusiastic public welcome or approval. 1533, in Bellenden's translation of Livy's *Roman History;* borrowed possibly from Middle French *ovation,* learned borrowing from Latin, and borrowed directly from Latin *ovātiōnem* (nominative *ovātiō)* a triumph, rejoicing, from *ovāre* exult, rejoice, triumph; for suffix see -ATION. Latin *ovāre* is cognate with Greek *euázein* utter a cry of joy in honor of Dionysus, *euaí, euoî* a cry of joy, from Indo-European **eu* (a cry of joy) (Pok. 347).

oven *n.* Before 1200 *oven;* developed from Old English *ofen* furnace, oven (about 725, in a translation of *Daniel*). Old English *ofen* is cognate with Old Frisian, Middle Low German, Middle Dutch, and modern Dutch *oven* oven, Old High German *ovan* (modern German *Ofen* stove), Old Icelandic *ofn,* and Gothic **aúhns* (accusative *aúhn*), from Proto-Germanic **úHnaz,* a simplification of **úHwnaz.* Cognates outside Germanic include Latin *ōlla* (from Old Latin *aulla,* from earlier **auxlā*) pot, Greek *ipnós* oven (dissimilated from **upnós*), and Sanskrit *ukhá-s* pot, from Indo-European **auk(h)w-/uk(h)w-* (Pok. 88).

over *prep., adv.* 1135 *over* above, upon, throughout, across, beyond; developed from Old English (before 725) *ofer;* cognate with Old Frisian *over, uver* (prep. and adv.) over, Old Saxon *oƀar, uƀar,* Middle Low German, Middle Dutch, and modern Dutch *over,* Old High German *ubar,* prep., *ubiri,* adv. (modern German *über,* prep. and adv.), Old Icelandic *yfir* (Danish and Norwegian *over,* Swedish *över*), and Gothic *ufar,* prep., from Proto-Germanic **uƀeri.* Cognates outside Germanic include Latin *super* (prep. and adv.) over (by misdivision of **ex-uper* over and above, as **ec-super*), Greek *hypér,* Old Irish *for,* prep., and Sanskrit *upári* (prep. and adv.) over, from Indo-European **upéri* (Pok. 1105); related to *úpa* towards, at, under; see UP. **—adv.** Probably before 1200 *over* above, across, completely, in *Ancrene Riwle;* developed from Old English (before 899) *ofer.* **—adj.** Probably before 1200 *over, uvere* upper, higher, outer, in *Ancrene Riwle;* developed from Old English (before 899) *uferra,* comparative of *ofer,* adv.

over- a prefix meaning: **1** above, as in *overhead.* **2** higher in rank, as in *overlord.* **3** across, as in *overseas.* **4** too much, too, as in *overcrowded, overburden.* **5** above normal, as in *oversize, overtime.* **6** outer, as in *overcoat.* Middle English, developed from Old English *ofer-* (as in *ofercuman* overcome, *oferdōn* overdo, *ofermicel* overmuch), from *ofer,* prep. and adv. Old English *ofer-* (like its cognates Gothic *ufar-,* Old High German *ubar-,* and Old Icelandic *yfir-*) was used in combination with verbs, nouns, adjectives, adverbs, and derivatives of phrases.

—overall *adj.* (1876); *n.* usually *overalls* (1776, American English) **—overcase** *adj.* (about 1300, of weather) **—overdo** *v.* (about 1000, Old English *oferdōn*) **—overflow** *v.* (before 899, Old English *oferflōwan*) **—overgrown** *adj.* Before 1398, from *overgrouen; v.* probably about 1390. **—overlay** *v.* (before 1325) **—overlook** *v.* (1369, in Chaucer) **—overlord** *n.* (probably about 1200) **—overnight** *adv.* (about 1303) **—overrate** *v.* (1589, implied in *overrated*) **—override** *v.* (probably before 1300) **—overrun** *v.* (about 1250); *adj.* (before 1349) **—overseas** *adv., adj.* (1583, from earlier *oversea,* 1104) **—oversee** *v.* (before 899, Old English *oferseōn*) **—overseer** *n.* (before 1382) **—overshadow** *v.* (about 725, Old English *ofersceadwian*) **—oversight** *n.* (before 1325) **—overspread** *v.* (probably before 1200) **—overtake** *v.* (about 1225) **—overthrow** *v.* (probably before 1300) **—overtime** *n.* (1536, but also found as a form in *overtymely* prematurely, about 1303) **—overturn** *v.* (probably before 1200)

overage (ō'vərij) *n.* surplus, excess. 1945, in Mencken's *The American Language,* American English; formed from English *over,* adv. + *-age,* on the model (and as the opposite) of *shortage.*

overboard *adv.* from a ship or boat into the water. Old English (about 1000) *ofor bord; ofer, ofor* over; *bord* the side of a ship (compare STARBOARD). The expression *go overboard,* meaning "to behave immoderately" or "to go too far," appeared in 1931.

overcome *v.* Old English *ofer-cuman* (about 725, in *Beowulf*); also, to reach, overtake (before 800, in *Corpus Glossary*); formed from *ofer-* over + *cuman* come.

overt (ōvėrt') *adj.* open, evident. About 1330 *overt* unfastened, open, evident, uncovered; borrowed from Old French *overt,* past participle of *ovrir* to open, from regional Vulgar Latin **ōperīre,* alteration of Latin *aperīre* to open, uncover; see WEIR.

The Vulgar Latin pronunciation with initial *ō-* was influenced by Latin *cōperīre* to cover up, contracted from *cooperīre;* see COVER.

The contrasting terms *overt* and *covert* have both been in use since the early 1300's and have perhaps reinforced each other.

overture *n.* 1249-50 *overture* opening, aperture; later, proposal, offer, opening of negotiations (1427); borrowed from Old French *overture* opening, proposal, from Vulgar Latin **ōpertūra,* alteration (compare OVERT) of Latin *apertūra* opening, from *aperīre* to open, uncover; see WEIR; for suffix see -URE. The musical sense of an opening or introductory orchestral piece, is first recorded in English in 1667, in Davenant and Dryden's adaptation of Shakespeare's *The Tempest.* Doublet of APERTURE.

overweening *adj.* conceited, presumptuous. Before 1338 *overwenyng,* present participle of earlier *overwenen* be conceited, presume (about 1303); formed from Middle English *over-* + *wenen* expect, think, WEEN; for suffix see -ING[2].

overwhelm *v.* Before 1338 *overwhelmen* overthrow, overturn; formed from Middle English *over-* + *whelmen* to turn upside down; see WHELM. The figurative meaning of overcome completely in mind or feeling is first recorded in the Coverdale Bible (1535).

oviduct (ō'vədukt) *n.* tube through which the egg passes from the ovary. 1757, borrowed from New Latin *oviductus* (*ovi-,* combining form of Latin *ōvum* EGG[1] + *ductus,* genitive *ductūs,* a leading; see DUCT).

oviparous (ōvip'ərəs) *adj.* producing eggs, like birds and most fishes. 1646, borrowed from Latin *ōviparus* that produces eggs (*ōvum* EGG[1] + *-parus,* from *parere* bring forth; see PARENT); for suffix see -OUS.

ovipositor (ō'vəpoz'etər) *n.* organ in certain insects by which eggs are deposited. 1818, formed from English *ovi-* (combining form of Latin *ōvum* EGG[1]) + Latin *positor* builder; originally, one who places, from *pōnere* to put, place; see POSITION; for suffix see -OR[2].

ovoid (ō'void) *adj.* egg-shaped. 1828, borrowed from

French *ovoïde* (from Latin *ōvum* EGG[1] + French *-oïde* -oid).

ovulation *n.* production of ovules or ova. 1848, formed in English from New Latin *ovulum* OVULE + English *-ation.* **—ovulate** *v.* produce ovules or ova. 1888, back formation from *ovulation;* for suffix see -ATE[1].

ovule (ō′vyül) *n.* 1830, the part of a plant that develops into a seed; borrowed from French *ovule,* and directly from New Latin *ovulum,* literally, small ovum, diminutive of Latin *ōvum* EGG[1]; for suffix see -ULE. The zoological and physiological meaning of a small or unfertilized ovum, is first recorded in English in 1857.

ovum (ō′vəm) *n., pl.* **ova** (ō′və). female germ cell, egg. 1706, in Kersey's edition of Phillips' *Dictionary;* borrowing of Latin *ōvum* EGG[1].

owe *v.* Probably about 1200 *aghen* to possess, have, own, have to pay, have an obligation to; later *owen* (about 1250); developed from Old English (before 725) *āgan* (past tense *āhte*). Old English *āgan* is cognate with Old Frisian *āga* possess, have, Old Saxon *ēgan,* Old High German *eigan,* Old Icelandic *eiga,* and Gothic *aigan,* from Proto-Germanic **aiʒanan.* A cognate outside Germanic is found in Sanskrit *íśe* he possesses, owns (contraction of a reduplicated form, originally **i-iś-ai*), from Indo-European **oiḱ-/iḱ-* (not **ēik-,* as in Pok. 298).

In the 1400's a new past tense *owed* replaced the earlier *oughte* (Old English *āhte*), which became English OUGHT[1] (an auxiliary verb that, like *can, may,* and *shall,* now has a present or future tense that was originally a past tense, usually expressed in a dependent perfect infinitive, as *You ought to have known* = you should have known).

owl *n.* Probably before 1300 oule, in *Sir Tristrem;* later *owle* (about 1385, in Chaucer's *Canterbury Tales*); developed from Old English (before 800) *ūle;* cognate with Middle Low German and Middle Dutch *ūle* owl (modern Dutch *uil*), Old High German *ūwila* (modern German *Eule*), and Old Icelandic *ugla,* all derived from a word imitative of the owl's characteristic sound.

own[1] *adj.* of or belonging to oneself or itself. Probably about 1150 *owen;* later *oune* (about 1300), and *owne* (probably before 1325); developed from Old English (before 725) *āgen.* Old English *āgen* is cognate with Old Frisian *ēgen* own, Old Saxon *ēgan,* Middle Dutch *eighen* (modern Dutch *eigen*), Old High German *eigan* (modern German *eigen*), and Old Icelandic *eiginn;* all derived from Proto-Germanic **aiʒanás,* past participle of **aiʒanan* to possess, the source of Old English *āgan* to have, own, OWE.

own[2] *v.* have as one's own, possess. 1607, in Shakespeare's *Coriolanus;* formed in part from OWN[1], adj., and in part a back formation from *owner,* earlier *owener* (1399), *oghener* (1340), formed from *ahnien, ohnen* take possession of, appropriate + *-er*[1]. Middle English *ahnien* (probably before 1200, in Layamon's *Chronicle of Britain*) developed from Old English *geāgnian* (about 725, in a version of *Genesis*); its cognates include Middle Dutch *eigenen, egenen* take or put in possession of, appropriate, own, Old High German *eiginēn* (modern German *eignen*), and Old Icelandic *eigna;* related to *eiginn* OWN[1].

Though the original Middle English and Old English verb dropped from use about 1300, it was restored indirectly through back formation from the derivative *owner,* when the verb *owe* in its original sense "possess" was becoming obsolescent.
—ownership *n.* 1583, formed from English *owner* + *-ship.*

ox *n.* Probably before 1200 *oxe* (plural *oxen*), in *Ancrene Riwle* and Layamon's *Chronicle of Britain;* developed from Old English *oxa* (plural *oxan*), before 830, in the *Vespasian Psalter.* The Old English forms are cognate with Old Frisian *oxa* ox, Old Saxon *ohso,* Middle Dutch *osse* (modern Dutch *os*), Old High German *ohso* (modern German *Ochse*), Old Icelandic *oxi, uxi,* and Gothic *aúhsa,* from Proto-Germanic **uHsōn.* Cognates outside Germanic include Welsh *ych* ox, Cornish *ohan* oxen, Breton *oc'hen,* Middle Irish *oss* deer, Irish *os* deer, fawn, Tocharian B *okso* bull, and Sanskrit *ukṣā́* bull, ox, from Indo-European **ukwsṓn* (stem **ukwsén-*) (Pok. 1118). **—oxblood** *n.* deep-red color. (1705) **—oxbow** *n.* (before 1325) **—oxcart** *n.* (1749) **—oxtail** *n.* Old English *oxan tægl,* in the *Laws of Ine.* (693)

oxalic acid (oksal′ik) poisonous organic acid. 1791, borrowed from French *acide oxalique,* from Latin *oxalis* sorrel[2] (plant with sour leaves), in which the acid is found, from Greek *oxalís,* from *oxýs* sour, sharp; see OXYGEN; for suffix see -IC.

oxford *n.* kind of low shoe laced over the instep. About 1890, short for earlier *Oxford shoes* (1847), and *Oxford-cut shoes* (in 1721), from the name of the university town of *Oxford,* England.

oxide *n.* compound of oxygen and another element or radical. 1790, borrowing of French *oxide* (now *oxyde*), formed from French *ox(ygène)* oxygen + *(ac)ide* acid. The term was coined in 1787 by the French chemists Morveau and Lavoisier. **—oxidation** *n.* an oxidizing or being oxidized. 1791, borrowing of French *oxidation* (now *oxydation*), from *oxider* oxidize, from *oxide* oxide; for suffix see -ATION. **—oxidize** *v.* combine with oxygen, make into an oxide. 1802 (implied in *oxidizable*); formed from English *oxide* + *-ize.*

Oxonian *n.* inhabitant of Oxford, England, member or graduate of Oxford University. About 1540, formed in English from Medieval Latin *Oxonia* + English *-an.* Medieval Latin *Oxonia* is a Latinized form of Middle English *Oxforde* Oxford (probably about 1475); earlier *Ocsenford* (about 1190); developed from Old English (912) *Oxnaford,* literally, ford of oxen. **—adj.** of or belonging to Oxford University or to Oxford, England. 1644, from the noun.

oxygen *n.* gaseous chemical element. 1790, borrowed from French *oxygène,* formed in French from Greek *oxýs* acid, sharp (related to *akḗ* point; see EDGE) + French *-gène* something that produces (see -GEN). The French word was intended to mean literally "acidifying principle, acid-producer," because oxygen was considered to be the essential element in the formation of acids. The term was coined in 1786 by the French chemists Morveau and Lavoisier though the element was earlier isolated by Priestley in 1774. **—oxygenate** *v.* treat or combine with oxygen. 1790, borrowed from French *oxygéner,* from *oxygène* oxygen; for suffix see -ATE[1]. The term was coined by the French chemists Morveau and Lavoisier in 1787.

oxymoron (ok′simôr′on) *n.* figure of speech using words of contradictory meaning, as *a wise fool, cold fire.* 1657, borrowing of Greek *oxýmōron,* noun use of the neuter of *oxýmōros,* adj., pointedly foolish (*oxýs* sharp + *mōrós* stupid); see OXYGEN and MORON. **—oxymoronic** *adj.* like an oxymoron, contradictory. 1965, formed from English *oxymoron* + *-ic.* The adverb *oxymoronically* appeared earlier, in Max Beerbohm's *Around Theatres* (1924).

oyez or **oyes** (ō'yes *or* ō'yez) *interj.* hear! attend! a cry uttered by a court crier. About 1425 *oyes;* borrowed from Anglo-French *oyez* hear ye!, Old French *oiez* from the Latin subjunctive *audiātis*), plural imperative of *oïr,* Anglo-French *oier* to hear, from Latin *audīre;* see AUDIBLE.

oyster *n.* 1321, in the compound *oystermonger;* earlier in the place name *Oystregate* (1259); borrowed from Old French *oistre,* from Latin *ostrea* oyster, from the plural of *ostreum* oyster, from Greek *óstreon,* related to *óstrakon* hard shell, and *ostéon* bone (see OSSEOUS).

ozone (ō'zōn) *n.* form of oxygen produced by electricity and present in the air. 1840, borrowed from German *Ozon,* from Greek *ózon,* neuter present participle of *ózein* to smell; see ODOR (so called from its pungent odor). The term was coined in 1840 by its discoverer, the German chemist C.F. Schönbein.

P

pabulum (pab′yələm) *n.* food, nourishment. 1678, borrowed from Latin *pābulum* fodder; see FOOD. The figurative meaning of intellectual or spiritual nourishment, food for thought, is first recorded in Sterne's *Tristram Shandy* (1765).

It is a curiosity that a commercial word derived from *pabulum* should furnish a figurative sense opposite to that of *pabulum.* The breakfast cereal *Pablum,* patented in 1932, was a bland food designed for infants, its name based on association with the sense of nourishment in *pabulum;* but its trademark protection was formed in the unique spelling without the first *u.* However, contrary to the manufacturer's intention, what was notable about the cereal was its blandness, which in turn gave rise to the general sense of something bland, watered-down, or having the consistency of pap or mush (before 1960).

pace *n.* rate, speed, About 1280 *pas* way of life, course of action; perhaps later, speed or gate (probably before 1300), and *pace* a step or a pace (probably 1348); borrowed from Old French *pas,* and directly from Latin *passus* (genitive *passūs*) a step, from *pandere* to stretch, spread out; see EXPAND. **—v.** 1513, walk with regular steps, from the noun.

pachyderm (pak′ədėrm) *n.* thick-skinned mammal, such as the elephant or hippopotamus. 1838, borrowed from French *pachyderme* (introduced by the French naturalist Cuvier in 1797), from Greek *pachýdermos* thick-skinned (*pachýs* thick + *dérma* skin; see DERMA). Greek *pachýs* is cognate with Sanskrit *bahú-s* dense, numerous (comparative *báṅhīyān*), Latin *pinguis* fat (altered from **finguis* by influence of *opīmus* plump, rich), Hittite *panku-* whole, and Old Icelandic *bingr* heap, from Indo-European **bhenĝh-/bhn̥ĝh-* stout (Pok.127).

pacific *adj.* making peace, peaceful. Before 1548 *pacifique,* borrowing of Middle French *pacifique,* learned borrowing from Latin *pācificus* peaceful, peace-making, from *pāx* (genitive *pācis*) PEACE + the root of *facere* make, perform DO[1]; for suffix see -FIC.

The spelling *pacific* (lower case) is first recorded in Milton's *Paradise Lost* (1667, but is implied earlier in *pacificable,* 1621), after the Latin form. The word in the form *pacifick* (1660), and earlier *Pacificum* (1555) for the name *Pacific Ocean* was borrowed from Medieval Latin *Pacificum* (from neuter of Latin *pācificus* pacific); so called by Magellan because at the time of his voyage he found it relatively free of violent storms.

An early example of adjective use appears in Middle English *pacificall* peace-loving (1464), probably borrowed from Medieval Latin *pacificalis,* or formed from English *pacific* + *-al*[1]. Though use of the word is rare today, it is still recorded in English dictionaries, as found in the writings of Meredith (*pacifical*) and Carlyle (*pacifically*).

—pacification *n.* 1437, in *Proceedings of the Privy Council;* borrowing of Middle French *pacification* act of making peaceful, from Latin *pācificātiōnem* (nominative *pācificātiō*), from *pācificāre* PACIFY; for suffix see -ATION. The military meaning "elimination of enemy activity in an area by removal of the inhabitants and often destruction of buildings, food supplies, etc." (widely regarded as a euphemism for wanton destruction) is first recorded in 1946, in the writings of the British author George Orwell.

pacifism *n.* opposition to war. 1902, borrowed from French *pacifisme,* from *pacifique* pacific + *-isme* -ism. **—pacifist** *n.* 1906, borrowed from French *pacifiste,* from *pacifisme* + *-iste* -ist.

pacify *v.* make calm, quiet down. Before 1475 *pacifien,* possibly, in some instances, a back formation from earlier *pacification,* but more likely borrowed from Middle French *pacifier,* from Old French, make peace, learned borrowing from Latin *pācificāre* to make peace, pacify, from *pācificus* PACIFIC; for suffix see -FY. **—pacifier** *n.* person or thing that pacifies. 1533, in Sir Thomas More's *The Apology Made by Him;* formed from English *pacify* + *-er*[1]. A common meaning of a nipple-shaped device for a baby to suck on (in order to keep it quiet) is first recorded in 1904 in American English.

pack[1] *n.* bundle. Probably before 1200 *packe,* in *Ancrene Riwle,* and 1228 *pak;* earlier, in a surname *Pakbyndere* (1191); possibly borrowed from Middle Dutch *pac, pack* bundle, Middle Low German *pak,* or early Middle Flemish *pac* (compare also Old Icelandic *pakki*), of unknown origin.

The meaning of a number of animals kept or hunting together is first recorded before 1450, and that of a set of playing cards, about 1597.

—v. put together in a bundle. About 1378 *packen,* in a version of *Piers Plowman;* later *packen* (probably before 1387); from the noun, possibly influenced by Anglo-French *empaker,* Medieval Latin *paccare,* Middle Dutch *packen,* all with the meaning to pack. **—packer** *n.* (1351, earlier in a surname *Pakkere,* 1254). **—pack horse** (probably before 1500) **—pack rat** kind of rat that collects objects. 1885, American English, in the writings of Theodore Roosevelt.

pack[2] *v.* arrange unfairly, conspire or plot. Before 1529, in Skelton's writings; of uncertain origin (sometimes said to be a possible alteration of earlier *pact,* n., enter into a pact, 1535; verb use of *pact;* however, this sense is recorded later than the appearance of *pack*).

It is interesting to note that not only is the chronology out of order, but that the semantic connection is not established except in the sense of cheating in shuffling playing cards and in plotting to arrange a vote of a decision-making body, such as a jury.

package *n.* 1611, the packing of goods, in Cotgrave's *Dictionary;* later, bundle or parcel (1722); formed from English *pack,* v. + *-age.* **—v.** put in a package. 1928, from the noun. **—adj.** 1952 *package deal* an offer or transaction agreed to as a unit, from the noun.

packet *n.* Probably before 1450 *pekette* a small package; earlier as a surname *Paket;* probably formed from Middle English *pak* bundle + *-et, -ette* diminutive suffix, perhaps modeled on Anglo-French *pacquet* (also found in Palsgrave's *Lesclarcissement,* 1530). The editors of the OED and FEW are of the opinion that French *pacquet* derives from Middle English, while the MED shows that the word in Middle English was a borrowing from Old French *pacquet,* from Germanic **pak,* which others relate to Middle Dutch *pak.*

pact *n.* 1429, in the *Rolls of Parliament;* borrowing of Middle French *pacte* agreement, treaty, compact, learned borrowing from Latin, and borrowed directly from Latin *pactum,* from neuter past participle of *pacīscī* to covenant or agree, related to *pangere* to fix, fasten. Latin *pangere* is cognate with Greek *pēgnýnai* to fix, fasten, Russian *paz* joint, Sanskrit *pā́śa-s* noose, cord, and Gothic *fāhan* to catch, from Indo-European **paḱ-/pāḱ-, *paĝ-/pāĝ-,* perhaps diverging from a set of present-tense forms **páĝmi* I fasten, **páḱ-si* you fasten, **páḱ-ti* fastens.

pad[1] *n.* thick, cushionlike mass. 1554, bundle of straw or the like to lie on; of unknown origin. The meaning of something soft, like a cushion, recorded before 1700, probably developed from the earlier sense of a soft, stuffed saddle (1570), and from both of these meanings developed the slang sense of bed (1718).

The extended meaning of a writing or drawing pad of paper is first recorded in Dickens' *Our Mutual Friend* (1865), and that of a cushioned part of an animal's foot (1836-39). The technical use of a rocket launching pad is first recorded in 1949, and that of a telephone or calculator keyboard in 1967.

—**v.** to fill out, stuff. 1827, from the noun. The figurative sense of to add words to fill space is first recorded in Macaulay's *Essays* (1831). The sense of expand (an expense account or other record) by false entries is found in 1913 in Canadian English.

pad[2] *v.* to walk, tramp, trudge. 1553, possibly borrowed from Middle Dutch *paden* walk along a path, make a path (cognate with Low German *padjen* to pad, and East Frisian *padden*), from *pad, pat* PATH (also found in Middle English *pæd* path).

The meaning of walk or trot with dull-sounding steps is first recorded in English in 1871.

paddle[1] *n.* short oar. 1407 *padell* spadelike implement with a handle; borrowed from Medieval Latin *padela, padula,* of uncertain origin, but compare Latin *patella* pan, plate (diminutive of *patina*); see PATEN.

The extended meaning "a short spade-shaped oar," used freely without an oarlock as by the American Indians in canoeing, is first recorded in Captain John Smith's *Works* (1624). The sense was extended to various paddle-shaped instruments used in a variety of trades by 1662. The meaning in zoology of a flipper or similar limb, as of a whale or penguin, is first recorded from 1835. A meaning in sports of a small flat racket first occurs in the term *paddle tennis* in 1925, in American English.

—**v.** propel with a paddle. 1677, from the noun. The meaning of beat with a paddle, spank, is first recorded before 1846 in American English.

—**paddle wheel** wheel with paddles for propelling a boat (1685).

paddle[2] *v.* move about in water with the hands and feet, or with flippers or the limbs, as animals do. 1530, in Palsgrave's *Lesclarcissement;* of uncertain origin, but probably cognate with Low German *paddeln* tramp about, from *padjen* to tramp, PAD[2]; for suffix see -LE[3].

paddock *n.* small enclosed field. 1622 *paddok,* variant of Middle English *parrock* (found as a place name, 1253) and *parrok* (1283); developed from Old English (about 700) *pearroc, pearuc* enclosed space, fence. The Old English forms are probably cognate with Middle Low German *perk, park* paddock, Middle Dutch *parc, parric,* and Old High German *pfarrih, pferrih* enclosed space, from Proto-Germanic **parrukaz,* probably formed from Iberian **parra* (compare Spanish *parra* trellis). However, it has also been suggested that Old English *pearroc* was borrowed from early Medieval Latin *parricus.*

The meaning "pen at a race track, where horses are saddled" is first recorded in 1862.

paddy *n.* 1623, rice in the husk (but found earlier with the spelling *batte,* 1598); borrowed from Malay *pādi* rice. The meaning of rice field is first found in the open compound *paddy field* (1762) and later in the shortened form *paddy* in 1948.

padlock *n.* detachable lock that hangs from a hasp. 1478-79 *padlokke,* from *pad* (of uncertain meaning) + *lokke, lok* lock. —**v.** fasten with a padlock. 1645, in Milton's *Colasterion,* from the noun.

padre (pä′drā) *n.* priest or other Christian clergyman. 1584, in Hakluyt's *Voyages;* borrowing of Italian, Spanish, or Portuguese *padre,* from Latin *patrem* (nominative *pater*) FATHER.

The British in India used *padre* to refer to a minister or priest of any church, which suggests a borrowing from Portuguese; later, British soldiers and sailors applied the term in the 1890's to a military chaplain.

paean (pē′ən) *n.* 1592, a hymn or chant of deliverance in ancient Greece; later, song of praise, joy or triumph (1599); borrowing of Latin *paeān,* from Greek *paiā́n* hymn to Apollo, from *Paiā́n,* a name of Apollo.

pagan *n.* Probably before 1400 *paygan* heathen, in *Morte Arthur;* later *pagan* (probably before 1425, in a translation of Higden's *Polychronicon*); borrowed from Late Latin *pāgānus* pagan, from Latin, villager, rustic, civilian, from *pāgus* rural district, originally one limited by markers; related to *pangere* to fix, fasten; see PACT.

The meaning "heathen" of Late Latin *pāgānus* may derive from the Latin meaning "villager," since ancient idol worship lingered on in rural areas after Christianity had been generally accepted in the towns and cities of the Roman Empire. Alternatively, it may derive from the Latin meaning "civilian," as opposed to the *mīlitēs Christī* soldiers of Christ, Christians.

—**adj.** 1422, borrowed from Late Latin *pāgānus,* adj.; and probably from the noun in English.

—**paganism** *n.* pagan beliefs and practices. 1433, formed from Middle English *pagan* + *-ism.* —**paganize** *v.* make or become pagan. 1615, probably formed from English *pagan* + *-ize,* by influence of French *paganiser.*

page[1] *n.* side of a sheet of paper. 1589, in Nashe's *Works;* borrowed from Middle French *page,* reduced form of Old French *pagine, pagene,* learned borrowing from Latin *pāgina;* related to *pangere* to fasten; see PACT.

The later form *page* replaced earlier Middle English *pagyn* page, leaf of a book (before 1398), *pagine* a document or writings (before 1250), and *pagne* (probably

before 1200); borrowed from Old French *pagine, pagene,* and directly from Latin *pāgina.*
—**v.** number the pages of. 1628, from the noun.

page[2] *n.* boy servant, errand boy. Probably before 1300, youth preparing to be a knight, in *Kyng Alisaunder;* later, a boy servant (about 1300); borrowing of Old French *page,* possibly from Italian *paggio,* Medieval Latin *pagius* servant, perhaps ultimately from Greek *paidíon* boy, lad, diminutive of *paîs* (genitive *paidós*) child. The sense from Greek is attractive, but the phonetic development is difficult to account for. —**v.** 1596, wait on, attend, or follow like a page, from the noun. The meaning of try to find (a person) by having his name called out is first recorded in 1904 in American English.

pageant *n.* elaborate spectacle, procession in costume. 1386-87 *pagyn* a play in a cycle of mystery plays (in an Anglo-French context); also 1392-93 *pagent* a wheeled platform as a stage for a mystery play (in an Anglo-Latin context, with the addition of *-t,* as in *ancient*); borrowed from Medieval Latin *pagina,* from Latin *pāgina* PAGE[1] (of a book). The spelling *pageant* is first recorded probably in 1443.

The chronology of sense and form in Middle English is not altogether fixed, and simultaneous forms with different meanings probably existed, so that sense development perhaps came through both "a play in a cycle of mystery plays," possibly developed from the meaning of a manuscript page of a play, and from the other meaning "a moveable platform," which can be related to the ultimate source: Latin *pangere* to fasten. The meaning "showy parade, elaborate spectacle" appeared in Southey's *Madoc* (1805).

—**pageantry** *n.* 1608, pageants collectively, in Shakespeare's *Pericles;* later, splendid show, pomp (1651); formed from English *pageant* + *-ry.*

paginate *v.* mark the number of pages of, page. 1884, probably a back formation from earlier *pagination;* for suffix see -ATE[1]. —**pagination** *n.* act or process of paginating. 1841, in Isaac D'Israeli's *Amenities of Literature;* probably borrowed from French *pagination* (from Latin *pāgina* page + French *-ation*).

pagoda (pəgō′də) *n.* Oriental temple. 1634, in Sir Thomas Herbert's *Works;* earlier *pagode* (1582); borrowing of Portuguese *pagode,* perhaps from Tamil *pagavadi,* from Sanskrit *bhágavatī* goddess, feminine of *bhágavant-* blessed, from *bhága-s* good fortune, related to *bhájate* receives as his share, enjoys, and Greek *phageîn* to eat, from Indo-European **bhag-* apportion (Pok.107).

pail *n.* 1336-37 *payle* container, kitchen utensil; later, bucket or pail (1352-53); probably borrowed from Old French *päielle, päele* warming pan, liquid measure, bath, possibly from Latin *patella* small pan or dish, diminutive of *patina* broad shallow pan; see PATEN, or perhaps from Medieval Latin *pagella* a measure, a diminutive from Latin *pāgina,* originally, something fixed.

Since Old English *pægel* wine vessel, gill (about 1000) is three centuries removed from the Middle English, no connection probably exists.

pain *n.* About 1280 *peyne* pain, punishment, penalty; also *pain, paine* (probably before 1300, in *Arthour and Merlin*); borrowed from Old French *peine,* from Latin *poena* punishment, penalty, from Greek *poinḗ,* related to *tínein* to pay, and *tīmḗ* price, esteem. Greek *tīmḗ* is cognate with Sanskrit *cáyate* he avenges, punishes, and Avestan *kaēnā-* punishment, from Indo-European **kwei-/kwoi-/kwi-* (Pok.636). Doublet of PINE[2] (to yearn).

The plural form *pains,* in the sense "great care or effort" is first recorded in 1528, in Tyndale's *Works.*
—**v.** Probably about 1300 *peynen* to exert, strain, strive, in *The Romance of Guy of Warwick;* later, to punish (before 1375), and to cause pain (about 1375); borrowed from Old French *peinir,* variant of *pener,* from *peine* pain. Also, in some instances the verb is from the noun in Middle English.
—**painful** *adj.* Before 1349 *peynful,* in Richard Rolle's *Meditations on the Passion;* formed from Middle English *peine* pain + *-ful.* —**painless** *adj.* 1447 *peynlesse;* formed from Middle English *peine* pain + *-lesse* -less. —**painstaking** *adj.* 1696, formed from English *pains,* pl., great care + *taking.* An earlier noun phrase *paynes taking* is recorded in 1556.

paint *v.* Probably before 1200, implied in *peintunge* a painting, in *Ancrene Riwle;* later *peinten* to paint, decorate (about 1250), and *painten* (before 1325); borrowed from Old French *peintier, pointier,* from *peint, point,* past participles of *peindre, poindre* to paint, from Latin *pingere* to paint. Latin *pingere* is cognate with Greek *poikílos* variegated, Lithuanian *piẽšti* to paint or write, Old Slavic *pěgŭ* variegated, Sanskrit *piṅkte* he paints, and Tocharian A *pik-, pek-* to write, Tocharian B *pink-, paik-* to write. Germanic cognates include Gothic *-faihs* colored, Old Icelandic *fā* to paint, Old High German and Old Saxon *fēh* variegated, and Old English *fāh* colored, from Indo-European **peig-/pig-, *peiḱ/poiḱ-/piḱ-* to scratch, to color (Pok.794).
—**n.** 1290-91 *peinte* in *peinteselde* paint shop, and *peyntmaker* a maker of paints, one who mixes paints (1454-55); from the verb. The meaning of coloring matter for the face or body, cosmetic, is first recorded in Dryden's letters (1660). —**paintbrush** *n.* (1827)

painter[1] *n.* one who paints. 1220, in the surname *Peintur,* and 1240 *Paintur;* later *peyntur* (1313); borrowed from Old French *peintour,* from Vulgar Latin **pinctor,* alteration (influenced by Latin *pingere* to paint) of Latin *pictor,* from *pingere* to PAINT; for suffix see -ER[1].

painter[2] *n.* rope for tying a boat. 1336-37 *peyntour;* probably borrowed from Old French *pentoir, penteur* cordage for hanging, from *pendre* to hang, from Vulgar Latin **pendere,* from Latin *pendēre;* see PENDANT.

painter[3] *n.* panther or cougar. 1764, American English; alteration of Middle English *panter* PANTHER.

pair *n.* About 1250 *peire;* later *pair* (before 1325, in *Cursor Mundi*); borrowed from Old French *paire, peire,* and directly from Latin *paria* equals, neuter plural of *pār* (genitive *paris*) a pair, counterpart, equal; noun use of *pār,* adj., equal, of unknown origin. —**v.** 1603, be a match for; also 1607, arrange in a pair; from the noun.

paisley or **Paisley** (pāz′lē) *n.* cloth with an elaborate and colorful pattern. 1834, in allusion to *Paisley,* town in southwestern Scotland, where such cloth was originally made. —**adj.** made of paisley. 1900, from the noun.

pajamas *n.pl.* 1800 *pai jamahs* loose trousers tied around the waist, worn by Moslems and adopted by Europeans, especially for night wear; later *pajamas* (1845); alteration with *-s,* as in *trousers;* borrowed from Hindi *pājāma, pāijāma,* probably from Persian *pā-*

ëjāmah, literally, leg clothing (*pāë* leg + *jāmah* clothing).

In the late 1800's *pajamas* (spelled in British English *pyjamas*) was extended in meaning by British manufacturers to a sleeping suit of loose trousers and jacket, which became the prevailing usage.

pal *n.* comrade, chum. 1681-82 *pall,* borrowed from Romany (of England) *pal* brother, comrade; variant of Romany (of continental Europe, especially Turkey) *pral, plal, phral,* probably from Sanskrit *bhrātā* BROTHER. The *l* remains unaccounted for. **—v.** associate as pals. 1879, from the noun.

palace *n.* Probably about 1225 *palais;* later *palace* (about 1475); borrowing of Old French *palais, pales,* and borrowed directly from Medieval Latin *palacium* a palace, also borrowed directly from Latin *palātium,* from *Palātium* the Palatine Hill in Rome, in reference to the house of Augustus Caesar that was situated there, and to the splendid residence later built there by Nero; this usage was also transferred to other imperial and royal residences.

paladin (pal′ədin) *n.* knightly defender. 1592, one of the twelve knights in attendance on Charlemagne, in Samuel Daniel's *Poems;* borrowing of Middle French *paladin* a warrior, from Italian *paladino,* learned borrowing from Medieval Latin *palatinus* or from Latin *palātīnus* palace official, noun use of *Palātīnus* of the palace (see PALATINE).

The figurative meaning of a knightly defender or hero, champion (of a cause) is first recorded in English, in Gibbon's *Decline and Fall of the Roman Empire* (1788), possibly from the French.

palanquin or **palankeen** (pal′ənkēn′) *n.* covered litter carried by poles. 1588, borrowed through Italian *palanchino,* and later probably directly from Portuguese *palanquim,* from Malay and Javanese *palangki,* ultimately from Sanskrit *palyañka-s, paryañka-s* couch, bed, litter (*pari* around + *áñcati* it bends, curves, related to *añká-s* a bend, hook, ANGLE[1]).

palate *n.* roof of the mouth. 1382 *palet* roof of the mouth, in the Wycliffe Bible; later *palate* sense of taste (before 1398); borrowed from Old French *palat, palet, palé,* and directly from Latin *palātum* roof of the mouth, of uncertain origin. **—palatable** *adj.* agreeable to the taste. 1669, formed from English *palate* + *-able.* **—palatal** *adj.* of or having to do with the palate. 1828-32, in Webster's *Dictionary;* borrowing of French *palatal,* from Latin *palātum* palate; for suffix see -AL[1]. It is also possible that in some instances *palatal* was formed from English *palate* + *-al*[1].

palatial *adj.* like a palace, magnificent. 1754, borrowed from French *palatial,* and perhaps formed in English from Latin *palātium* PALACE + English suffix *-al*[1].

palatine (pal′ətīn) *adj.* having royal rights in a lord's own territory. 1436, in *Countee Palentyne* or *Palantyne* in reference to a county governed by an independent lord, in *Rolls of Parliament;* later *County Palatine* (1461); borrowed from Old French *palatin, palantien,* and directly from Medieval Latin and Latin *palātīnus* of the palace, from *palātium* PALACE; for suffix see -INE[1]. **—palatinate** *n.* territory under the rule of a count palatine. About 1580, specifically, a state of the Holy Roman Empire; formed from English *palatine* + *-ate*[1].

palaver (pəlav′ər) *n.* parley or conference. Probably before 1735, borrowed from Portuguese *palavra* word, speech, talk, alteration (by metathesis of *r* and *l*) from Late Latin *parabola* speech, discourse, from Latin *parabola* comparison; see the doublets PARABLE, PARABOLA, and PAROLE. The meaning "unnecessary or idle words, mere talk" is first recorded in Smollett's *Adventures of Roderick Random* (1748). **—v.** to talk. 1733, from the noun, despite the earlier date, as there is no verb use in Portuguese. According to the OED *palaver* was at first confined to nautical slang, picked up by English sailors from Portuguese traders along the African coast.

pale[1] *adj.* without much color, wan. Before 1325, in *Cursor Mundi;* earlier in a surname *Pail* (1225, perhaps confused with Old French *paile,* 1100's); borrowed from Old French *pale, paile,* a book word from Latin *pallidus* pale, pallid, wan, from *pallēre* be pale; see FALLOW[2], adj. Doublet of PALLID. **—v.** About 1380 *palen* make pale, turn pale, in Chaucer's translation of Boethius' *De Consolatione Philosophiae;* probably borrowed from Old French *paleir, palir,* from *pale,* adj., and possibly also from the adjective in English.

pale[2] *n.* stake or picket, as of a fence. Before 1200 *pal,* later *pale* (before 1338, in Mannyng's *Chronicle of England*); borrowed from Old French *pal, pel,* learned borrowing from Latin, and borrowed directly from Latin *pālus* stake (earlier **pacslos*), related to *pangere* to fix or fasten; see PACT. Doublet of POLE[1] stake.

The extended meanings of an enclosed area, district within bounds, limits, bounds, boundary, are first recorded in English before 1400.

—v. enclose with pales. Before 1338, in Mannyng's *Chronicle of England;* borrowed from Old French *paler,* from *pal,* n., and borrowed directly from Latin *pālāre* support with stakes, from *pālus,* n.

—paling *n.* About 1390, decorating with stripes, in Chaucer's *Canterbury Tales;* later, enclosing with a fence (1469); from *pale,* v. The sense of a *pale* in a fence is first recorded in Ainsworth's *Rookwood* (1834).

paleo- a combining form meaning old, ancient, especially in scientific terms referring to early, prehistoric, primitive phenomena, as in *paleolithic, paleontology.* Borrowed from Greek *palaio-,* combining form of *palaiós* old, ancient, from *pálai* long ago, far back, related to *têle* far, cognate with Sanskrit *caramá-s* farthest out, from Indo-European **kwel-/kwēl-* (Pok.640).

paleography (pā′lēog′rəfē) *n.* ancient writing. 1822, formed from English *paleo-* + *-graphy,* after French *paléographie.*

paleolithic or **Paleolithic** (pā′lēəlith′ik) *adj.* of or belonging to the earlier part of the Stone Age. 1865, in Sir John Lubbock's *Prehistoric Times;* formed from English *paleo-* + *-lith* stone + *-ic.*

paleontology (pā′lēontol′əjē) *n.* study of fossils. 1838, in Sir Charles Lyell's *The Elements of Geology;* probably borrowed from French *paléontologie,* formed in French from *paléo-* + Greek *ṓn* (genitive *óntos*) being; see ONTOGENY + French *-logie* -logy; patterned on *ontologie* ontology. **—paleontologist** *n.* 1871, formed from English *paleontology* + *-ist.*

palette *n.* painter's board to lay and mix colors on. 1622, borrowing of French *palette,* from Old French *palete* small shovel or blade, diminutive of *pale* shovel, oar blade, from Latin *pāla* spade, shoulder blade, perhaps related to *pālus* stake, PALE[2]; for suffix see -ETTE.

palfrey (pôl′frē) *n.* gentle riding horse. Probably before 1200 *palefrei,* and *palfrey* (probably before 1300, in

Kyng Alisaunder); earlier, as a surname *Pallefrei* (1166); borrowing of Old French *palefrei,* and borrowed directly from Medieval Latin *palafredus,* a word formed by dissimilation of *r* to *l* in Late Latin *paraverēdus* post horse for outlying districts, originally extra horse (from Greek *pará* beside, secondary; see PARA-[1] + Latin *verēdus* light horse, from Gaulish **woreidos,* with *wo-* from Indo-European **upo* under). German *Pferd* horse is also ultimately a borrowing from Late Latin *paraverēdus.*

palindrome (pal'indrōm) *n.* word, verse, sentence or numeral which reads the same backward or forward. About 1629, in Ben Jonson's *Underwoods;* borrowed from Greek *palíndromos* a recurrence, literally, a running back (*pálin* again, back, related to *pólos* axis, see WHEEL, + *drómos* a running; see DROMEDARY).

palisade *n.* fence of stakes. 1600, in Holland's translation of Livy's *Roman History;* borrowed from French *palissade* a palisade, from Provençal *palissada,* from *palissa* a stake or paling, from Gallo-Romance **pālīcea,* from Latin *pālus* stake, PALE[2].

The military meaning "a strong pointed wooden stake set with others in a row for defense" is first recorded in Dryden's *Aeneid* (1697). *Palisades* in the sense of a line of high steep cliffs appeared in 1827 in American English (originally as the name of the cliffs on the west bank of the Hudson River in New Jersey).
—v. fence in with a palisade. 1632, from the noun.

pall[1] *n.* heavy cloth spread over a coffin, hearse, or tomb. Probably before 1200 *palle, pal* a fine cloth or a covering for an altar, seat, or bed, in Layamon's *Chronicle of Britain;* later, a shroud for a corpse or a heavy cloth for a coffin (about 1400); developed from Old English *pæll* rich cloth, cloak, altar cloth (before 899, in Alfred's translation of Bede's *Ecclesiastical History*); borrowed from Latin *pallium* cloak, covering, related to *palla* robe, cloak, of uncertain origin.

The transferred sense of something that covers as a mantle or cloak does is first recorded before 1500, and the figurative extension of a dark, gloomy covering or mood (as in a *pall of despair*) is found in 1742.
—v. cover with or as with a pall. Probably before 1400 *palen,* in *Morte Arthur;* later *pallen* (probably before 1430); from the noun.
—pallbearer *n.* 1707 *pall bearer* one who holds the corners of the pall at a funeral; formed from English *pall*[1], n. + *bearer.* By the early 1900's the function of *pallbearers* became the carrying of the coffin.

pall[2] *v.* become distasteful or very tiresome. Probably before 1325 *pallen* become faint or grow feeble, possibly a shortened form of *appallen* to dismay, fill with horror or disgust; see APPALL.

The figurative meaning of make or become tasteless, tiresome, or insipid, is first recorded in Dryden's *Palamon and Arcite* (1700), and was popularized by Addison and Steele in the early 1700's.

palladium[1] (pəlā'dēəm) *n.* important safeguard, protecting institution. 1600, in Holland's translation of Livy's *Roman History;* figurative use of earlier *Palladium* the sacred image of the Greek goddess *Pallas* Athena (1585), and *Palladion* (about 1385, in Chaucer's *Troilus and Criseyde*); borrowing of Latin *Palladium,* and Greek *Palládion,* neuter of *Palládios* of Pallas, from *Pallás* (genitive *Palládos*) Pallas Athena, the goddess of wisdom, industries, arts, and sciences, which was in the citadel of Troy and on which the safety of the city was supposed to depend.

palladium[2] (pəlā'dēəm) *n.* metallic chemical element. 1803, New Latin, from *Pallas,* an asteroid discovered in 1802 and named after *Pallas* Athena, the Greek goddess of wisdom, industries, arts, and sciences, from Greek *Pallás* (genitive *Palládos*); for suffix see -IUM. The word was coined by its discoverer, the English chemist William H. Wollaston. Compare CERIUM for a similar coinage.

pallet[1] *n.* bed of straw. 1370 *palet;* later *paillet* (about 1385, in Chaucer's *Troilus and Criseyde*); borrowed through Anglo-French *paillet, paillete* straw, bundle of straw, Old French *paillete* chaff, from *paille* straw, from Latin *palea* chaff, cognate with Greek *pálē* fine meal, and Sanskrit *pálala-m* ground sesamum, from Indo-European **pel-* (Pok.802).

pallet[2] *n.* flat blade. Probably before 1425 *palet* flat instrument for depressing the tongue, in a translation of Chauliac's *Grande Chirurgie;* borrowed from Old French *palete* small shovel or blade, diminutive of *pale* shovel, from Latin *pāla* (earlier **pacslā*) spade, related to *pālus* stake, PALE[2].

palliate (pal'ēāt) *v.* alleviate, mitigate. Probably before 1425 *palliaten* to alleviate the symptoms of a disease, in a translation of Chauliac's *Grande Chirurgie;* borrowed from Medieval Latin *palliatus,* from Late Latin, past participle of *palliāre* cover with a cloak, conceal, from Latin *pallium* cloak; see PALL[1] cloth; for suffix see -ATE[1].

The meaning of extenuate or excuse is first recorded in 1459.
—palliative *adj.* 1425 *palliatif;* borrowed perhaps from Medieval Latin *palliativus* under a cloak, covert, perhaps a Latinization of Old French *palliatif,* or directly from Middle French *palliatif,* both forms from Late Latin *palliātus,* past participle of *palliāre* cover with a cloak, conceal; for suffix see -IVE. *—n.* medicine or other substance that alleviates pain. 1724, in Swift's *Works;* from the adjective.

pallid *adj.* pale. 1590, in Spenser's *Faerie Queene;* borrowed from Latin *pallidus* pale, from *pallēre* be pale; see PALE[1].

pallor *n.* paleness. About 1400 *pallour;* borrowed from Old French *palor,* and directly from Latin *pallor,* from *pallēre* to pale; for suffix see -OR[1].

palm[1] *n.* inside of the hand. Probably before 1300 *palme,* in *Kyng Alisaunder;* later *paume* (about 1300); borrowing of Old French *palme, paume,* from Latin *palma* palm of the hand. Latin *palma* is cognate with Greek *palámē* palm of the hand, Old Irish *lām* hand, Welsh *llaw,* Sanskrit *pāṇí-s* hand, Old High German *folma,* and Old English *folm* palm of the hand, which survives in English *fumble,* from Indo-European **pl̥mā/peləmā* flat hand (root **pelə-/plā-,* Pok.805).
—v. conceal in the hand. 1673, from the noun. The extended sense of pass off fraudulently is first recorded in 1679.

palm[2] *n.* tree of warm climates. Before 1200 *palm;* reborrowed through Old French *palme, paume* from Latin *palma;* and developed from Old English (before 830); borrowed from Latin *palma* palm tree, palm of the hand (see PALM[1]); so called from the shape of the tree's leaves.

palmate *adj.* shaped like a hand. 1760, in James Lee's *An Introduction to Botany;* borrowed, perhaps by influence of French *palmé,* from Latin *palmātus* marked with the palm of the hand, from Latin *palma* PALM[1] (of the hand); for suffix see -ATE[1].

palmetto (palmet′ō) *n.* kind of palm with fan-shaped leaves. 1583 *palmito,* borrowing of Spanish *palmito* a dwarf fan palm tree, diminutive of *palma* palm tree, from Latin *palma* PALM[2].

The variant form *palmeto* is first recorded in Captain John Smith's *The Generall Historie of Virginia* (1624), and *palmetto* (probably influenced by the Italian diminutive suffix *-etto*) in 1727.

palmistry *n.* the reading of a person's fortune from the palm of his hand. About 1450 *palmestrie;* formed from *palme* PALM[1] (of the hand) + the ending *-estrie,* of uncertain origin (probably a blend of *-ster,* from Middle English *-estre,* an occupational suffix, as in *webster, tapster,* from Middle English *webbestre* weaver, *tappestre* bartender, and of the suffix *-rie, -erie,* as in Middle English *archerie* archery). The spelling of the suffix changed gradually to *-istry,* so that *palmistry* now looks misleadingly like a derivative of the modern *palmist.* **—palmist** *n.* one who practices palmistry. 1886, probably a back formation from *palmistry.*

palomino (pal′əmē′nō) *n.* cream-colored horse with light mane and tail. 1914, American English, borrowing of American Spanish *palomino* cream-colored horse, from Spanish *palomino* young dove, perhaps from Italian *palombino* dove-colored, from Latin *palumbīnus* of wood pigeons, from *palumba* ringdove, wood pigeon; the horse was so called because of its dovelike coloring.

palooka (pəlü′kə) *n. Slang.* inferior or average boxer. 1925, American English, of uncertain origin; its coinage was ascribed to Jack Conway, an American journalist who died in 1928. The sense of a big, strong, but stupid or awkward person, possibly derives from the name of Joe *Palooka,* a brawny but rather naive and awkward boxing champion of the world, who is the hero of a popular comic strip (by the American cartoonist Ham Fisher).

palpable *adj.* About 1380, plain, evident, obvious, in Chaucer's *House of Fame;* borrowed from Old French *palpable,* and directly from Late Latin *palpābilis* that may be touched or felt, from Latin *palpāre* touch gently, stroke; see FEEL; for suffix see -ABLE.

The literal meaning "capable of being touched, tangible" is first recorded after the appearance of the figurative sense, in a version of *Piers Plowman* (1387).

palpate *v.* examine by the sense of touch. 1849-52, probably a back formation from *palpation,* perhaps by influence of Latin *palpātus,* past participle of *palpāre* touch gently, stroke, see FEEL; for suffix see -ATE[1]. **—palpation** *n.* act of touching. 1483 *palpacion,* in Caxton's version of the *Golden Legend;* borrowed possibly through Middle French *palpation,* from Latin *palpātiōnem* (nominative *palpātiō*) stroking, flattery, from *palpāre* touch gently.

palpitate *v.* beat very rapidly. 1623, in Cockeram's *Dictionary;* borrowed from Latin *palpitātum,* past participle of *palpitāre* to throb or flutter, a frequentative form of *palpāre* touch gently, stroke, see FEEL; for suffix see -ATE[1]. In some instances *palpitate* is also probably a back formation from earlier *palpitation.* **—palpitation** *n.* Probably before 1425 *palpitacioun,* in a translation of Chauliac's *Grande Chirurgie;* borrowed probably through Middle French *palpitation,* learned borrowing from Latin *palpitātiōnem* (nominative *palpitātiō*), from *palpitāre* throb or flutter; for suffix see -ATION.

palsy *n.* paralysis, usually associated with muscular tremors. About 1300 *palasie;* later *palsie* (before 1325); borrowed through Anglo-French *parlesie,* Old French *paralisie,* learned borrowing from Latin *paralysis* PARALYSIS. Though a form with *r* (as in *parlesie*) existed in Middle English it appears to be well differentiated from the forms without *r* by the end of the 1400's; so while the *r* disappeared in some of the borrowings from Old and Middle French, much of the distinction of form continued to be carried out in Middle English itself. **—v.** paralyze. 1615, in Chapman's translation of Homer's *Odyssey;* from the noun.

palter (pôl′tər) *v.* talk or act insincerely, trifle deceitfully. 1601, in Shakespeare's *Julius Caesar;* of uncertain origin.

Palter was perhaps popularized by Shakespeare, who used it in *Troylus and Cressida, Macbeth,* and *Antony and Cleopatra,* though examples preceding Shakespeare have been recorded: in John Bale's *A Comedy Concerning Three Laws* (1538), spelled *paulter* with the meaning of speak indistinctly, mumble, babble; in William Harrison's *The Description of England* (1577), with the meaning of shift or alter (in position); and in Robert Greene's *Perimedes the Blacksmith* (1588), with the meaning of jumble or patch up (a composition). The form of *palter* is that of a frequentative in *-er* (see -ER[4]), but no underlying verb *to palt* with a corresponding meaning has been found, and no adequate connection with *paltry* has been established.

paltry (pôl′trē) *adj.* trifling, petty, mean. 1570, probably attributive use of earlier *paltry* trash, worthless thing (1556); associated with dialectal *palt, pelt* trash, dirty rag, waste (1567). English *palt* is cognate with Middle Low German and East Frisian *palte* rag, Middle Dutch *palt* broken or torn fragment, Danish *pjalt,* and Swedish *palta* rag; for suffix see -RY.

Alternatively, it has been suggested that *paltry,* adj., was borrowed directly from Low German or East Frisian *paltrig* ragged, torn, derived from *palte* rag, which would account for the gap in time of dating the dialectal form *palt, pelt* (1567) and the association with *paltry* (1556).

pampas (pam′pəz) *n.pl.* treeless plains of South America. 1704, borrowing of Spanish *pampas,* plural of *pampa,* from Quechua (Peru) *pampa* a plain.

pamper *v.* About 1390 *pampren* indulge, especially with food; later *pamperen;* probably borrowed from Middle Dutch (compare Flemish *pamperen* cram with food, overindulge, pamper, and dialectal German *pampen* to cram).

pamphlet *n.* booklet in paper covers. About 1385 *pamflet,* in Usk's *The Testament of Love;* borrowed from Anglo-Latin *panfletus, pamfletus,* probably a generalized use of *Pamphilet,* popular name of "Pamphilus, seu de Amore" (Pamphilus, or About Love, a short Latin love poem of the 1100's), from Greek *pámphilos* loved by all (*pan-* all + *phílos* loving, dear; see -PHILE); for suffix see -ET.

The specific application of *pamphlet* to a brief work dealing with some question of current interest (about which the writer wishes to appeal to the public) is first recorded in Gabriel Harvey's *Works* (1592), and was soon adopted by Chapman, Milton and others. **—pamphleteer** *n.* writer of pamphlets. 1642, formed from English *pamphlet* + *-eer.* —*v.* write or issue pamphlets. 1715, from the noun.

pan[1] *n.* dish for cooking. About 1150 *panna;* later *panne* (probably before 1300) and *pan* (1404); developed from Old English *panne* (before 899, in Alfred's translation of St. Gregory's *Pastoral Care*); earlier *ponne* (before 800, Mercian dialect), and *-ponne, -panne* (about 700, in compounds such as *fyrponne, fyrpanne* fire pan). Old English *panne, ponne* was inherited from West Germanic **panna* (compare Old Frisian *panne* pan, Old Saxon *panna,* Old Icelandic *panna,* Old Low German *panna* and Old High German *phanna*), probably an early borrowing from Vulgar Latin **patna,* from Latin *patina* shallow pan, dish (see PATEN). —**v.** 1839 *pan out* wash (gravel) in a pan to separate the gold, American English; from the noun. The figurative sense of yield results, turn out (as in *let's see how things pan out*) is first recorded in 1868, also in American English. The extended informal sense of to *pan* criticize severely, is another Americanism which is first recorded in 1911. —**pancake** *n.* Before 1400 *pankakus,* a Latinate form; earlier as a surname *Panecak, Panekake* (1283).

pan[2] *v.* to follow a moving object with a camera. 1913, American English; shortened from *panoramic,* especially in the term *panoramic camera* a camera designed to rotate automatically to take a panoramic picture (1878). —**n.** act or process of panning. 1922, from the verb.

pan- a combining form meaning all, whole, all-inclusive, as in *Pan-American, panchromatic, pandemic.* Borrowed from Greek *pan-,* combining form of Greek *pâs* (neuter *pân,* masculine and neuter genitive *pantós*) all, Mycenaean Greek *pāsi-* (= Greek dative plural *pâsi* to all), cognate with Tocharian B *pont-* all (Pok. 593, is utterly wrong in trying to explain Greek *pant-* as from an Indo-European **k̑wā-nt-*).

panacea (pan'əsē'ə) *n.* cure-all. 1548, in Udall's translation of Erasmus' *Upon the New Testament;* borrowed from Latin *panacēa* an all-healing herb, from Greek *panákeia* cure-all, from *panakḗs* all-healing (*pan-* all + *-akēs,* from *ákos* cure), cognate with Old Irish *hicc* healing, and Welsh *iach* healthy, from Indo-European **yĕk-/yək-* to heal (Pok.504).

An earlier use in Middle English (probably about 1425, in Chauliac's *Grande Chirurgie*) refers to the medicinal herb and was a direct borrowing from Latin.

panache (pənash') *n.* ornamental tuft or plume of feathers. 1553 *pinnach,* borrowed from Middle French *pennache,* from Italian *pennaccio,* variant of *pennacchio,* from Late Latin *pinnāculum* small wing, gable, peak; see PINNACLE.

The figurative sense of display, swagger, verve, flamboyance, is first recorded in a translation of Rostand's *Cyrano de Bergerac* (1898, borrowed from French *panache*). The spelling *panache* is first recorded in English in 1819.

pancreas (pan'krēəs) *n.* gland near the stomach that helps digestion. 1578 *panchreas;* later *pancreas* (implied in *pancreatick,* 1665-66); borrowed from Greek *pánkreas* sweetbread, pancreas (*pan-* all + *kréas* flesh; see RAW). —**pancreatic** *adj.* of the pancreas. 1665-66, formed from Greek *pankreat-* (stem of *pánkreas* pancreas) + English *-ic.*

panda *n.* 1835, a raccoonlike mammal of the Himalayas, lesser panda; borrowed from French (introduced by Cuvier in 1824), apparently from one of the names of this animal in Nepal. The first reference in English to the black-and-white bearlike mammal of Tibet and China (the Giant Panda) is found in 1901; it was originally described in China by the French missionary and naturalist Armand David in 1869.

pandemic (pandem'ik) *adj.* affecting all the people, general or universal. 1666, formed in English from Greek *pándēmos* pertaining to all the people (*pan-* all + *dêmos* people; see DEMOCRACY) + English *-ic,* modeled on *epidemic.* —**n.** pandemic disease. 1853, from the adjective.

pandemonium (pan'dəmō'nēəm) *n.* 1779, place of wild uproar, in Swinburne's *Travels Through Spain;* transferred use of New Latin *Pandemonium,* name of the palace built by Satan as the central part of hell (coined in 1667 by Milton in *Paradise Lost,* from Greek *pan-* all + Late Latin *daemonium* evil spirit, from Greek *daimónion* divine power, from *daímōn* lesser god, the power controlling the destiny of individuals, see DEMON); for suffix see -IUM.

The extended meaning of a wild uproar, lawless confusion, is first recorded in Francis Parkman's *Pioneers of France in the New World* (1865).

pander *n.* procurer for a prostitute, pimp. 1598, in Shakespeare's *Merry Wives of Windsor;* spelling alteration (influenced by *-er*[1]) of earlier *pandar* (1530), from Middle English *Pandare* (about 1385, in Chaucer's *Troilus and Criseyde*); borrowed from Latin *Pandarus,* from Greek *Pándaros* a name used by Boccaccio (in the Italian form *Pandaro*) for the man who procured for Troilus the love of Cressida. Though Chaucer's Pandare is depicted as a kind and friendly go-between for the lovers, by Spenser's and Shakespeare's time the character has become debased, just as Cressida had been turned into a wanton, flirtatious creature or common harlot. An isolated example of the more generalized meaning of a provider of pleasure is recorded about 1450. —**v.** act as a pander. 1602, in Shakespeare's *Hamlet,* from the noun. The transferred meaning of to cater or minister to the whims or desires (of another) is recorded in 1603.

pandowdy (pandou'dē) *n.* kind of apple dessert. 1830, American English; perhaps from obsolete dialectal English *pandoulde* custard, formed from English *pan*[1] + *doulde,* related to dialectal English *dowl* mix dough in a hurry.

pane *n.* single sheet of glass. About 1250 *pane* garment, such as a cloak; later, part of a garment (probably before 1300); side of a building, section of wall (about 1380); later, a window glass (1466); borrowed from Old French *pan* piece or panel, from Latin *pannus* a cloth, piece of cloth, garment; see VANE.

panegyric (pan'əjir'ik) *n.* speech or writing in praise of a person or thing. 1620, earlier as attributive noun (1603), possibly from the adjective (a shortened form of earlier *panegyrical,* 1592-93), but also probably influenced by *panegyre* a eulogy (1603), and possibly by French *panégyrique* (1512); borrowed from Latin *panēgyricus,* from Greek *panēgyrikòs (lógos)* (a speech) given in a public assembly, festive, from *panḗgyris* public assembly (*pan-* all + *ágyris* place of assembly, Aeolic form of *agorā́* AGORA); for suffix see -IC.

panel *n.* Before 1325, saddle cloth or pad, piece of cloth, in *Cursor Mundi;* borrowing of Old French *panel* saddle cushion, piece of anything, especially cloth, from Vulgar Latin **pannellus,* diminutive of Latin *pannus* piece of cloth; see VANE.

From the original sense in Latin and Old French of "piece of cloth," Anglo-French developed the legal sense "piece of paper listing jurors, jury list, jury," which is also recorded in Middle English, about 1378, in a version of *Piers Plowman.* The wider sense "list of persons or group selected for a particular purpose" is first found in Shaw's *Too True to Be Good* (1934).

The meaning "part or division" (about 1450) is found in the special application of "distinct part of the surface of a wall, door, etc.," in Shakespeare's *As You Like It* (1600).

—v. 1451 *panellen* put on a jury list; from the noun. The meaning of furnish with panels is first recorded in 1633.

—panelist *n.* person who takes part in a discussion among a number of members of a panel. 1952, American English; formed from *panel,* n. + *-ist.*

pang *n.* 1526, a brief sharp spasm of pain (in the phrase *pang of death*); of uncertain origin. The figurative meaning of a sudden sharp mental pain or anguish (as in the *pangs of love*) is first recorded in 1570. **—v.** About 1502, to pierce or penetrate with sharp physical or mental pain; of uncertain origin, possibly recorded earlier than the noun as a matter of accident.

panhandle *v. Informal.* to beg, especially in the streets. 1903, American English; back formation from earlier *panhandler* beggar (1897, *pan* + *handler*). **—n.** 1851, anything that suggests the form of the handle on a pan, especially a geographical area (1856); American English, formed from *pan* + *handle.*

panic *n.* unreasoning fear. 1627, contagious emotion supposedly induced by Pan; from the adjective. The meaning of unreasoning fear is first recorded in 1708. **—adj.** caused by unreasoning fear. 1603, as found in *panic fear, panic horror;* borrowed from French *panique,* from Greek *Pānikós* of Pan, from *Pā̂n* Greek god said to cause contagious fear in herds and crowds. **—v.** get into a panic. 1827, from the noun. **—panicky** *adj.* characterized by panic. 1869, formed from English *panic,* n. + *-y*[1].

panicle (pan′əkəl) *n. Botany.* compound raceme, loose, diversely branching flower cluster. 1597, borrowed from Latin *pānicula,* diminutive of *pānus* swelling, ear of millet, perhaps earlier **pancnos,* cognate with Polish *pąk* bud, from Indo-European **pank-* to swell (Pok.789); for suffix see -CLE.

pannier (pan′ēər) *n.* basket, especially one of a pair slung across the back of a beast of burden. 1290 *paner* a large basket; about 1300 *panier;* borrowed from Old French *panier, panniere,* from Latin *pānārium* bread basket, from *pānis* bread, earlier **pastnis* (compare the diminutive *pastillus* little loaf or wafer); see FOOD.

panoply (pan′əplē) *n.* 1576, borrowed from Greek *panoplíā* complete suit of armor, from *pan-* all + *hópla,* pl., arms. First recorded use in English was in the figurative sense of complete equipment or array, and the literal meaning of a complete unit of armor is not recorded until 1632, in Ben Jonson's *The Magnetick Lady.* The transferred meaning of any splendid array is first found in Bulwer-Lytton's *Devereux* (1829).

panorama *n.* wide, unbroken view. 1796 *Panorama* a picture of a landscape or other scene presented on a revolving cylindrical surface; formed from English *pan-* all + Greek *hórāma* a view, from *horân* to look, see; see WARY. *Panorama* was coined about 1789 by the Scottish inventor Robert Barker, who created the device. Compare CYCLORAMA, DIORAMA.

The transferred sense of a wide, unbroken view of a surrounding region is first recorded in 1828, and that of a continuously passing scene (as in the *panorama of city life*) in 1836. Curiously the figurative sense of a complete and comprehensive survey (as in *the political panorama, the panorama of science and art*) is found as early as 1801.

—panoramic *adj.* of or like a panorama. 1813, formed from English *panorama* + *-ic.*

pansy *n.* variety of violet. About 1450 *pancy;* later *pensee* (before 1475); borrowed from Middle French *pensée, pense, panse* a pansy; literally, thought, remembrance (consequently, a symbol of remembrance, a souvenir), from feminine past participle of *penser* to think, from Latin *pēnsāre* weigh, consider; see PENSIVE. The spelling *pansy* is first recorded in 1597.

pant *v.* About 1350 *panten* breathe hard and quickly; borrowed perhaps as a shortened form from Old French *pantaisier,* probably from Vulgar Latin **pantasiāre* be oppressed with a nightmare, struggle for breath during a nightmare, from Greek *phantasioûn* have or form images, subject to hallucinations, from *phantasíā* appearance, image, FANTASY. **—n.** short quick breath. 1500-20, in Dunbar's *Poems;* from the verb.

pantaloons *n.* 1661, in Evelyn's writings, a kind of breeches with stockings in the fashion of tights, worn during the English Restoration (1660-88), from an association with *Pantaloun, Pantaloon* (recorded in English from about 1590), a Venetian character in early Italian comedy shown as a lean, foolish old man wearing spectacles, slippers, and tight trousers that were a combination of breeches and stockings. The name of this stage character came into English from Middle French *Pantalon,* from Italian *Pantalone, Pantaleone,* originally the name of San *Pantaleone* Saint Pantaleon, a Roman physician who died a Christian martyr in 305 and was for a time a favorite saint of the Venetians; for ending see -OON.

Pantaloons was later applied to the late 1700's to tight-fitting trousers passing under the shoes, a fashion which began to replace knee breeches. By 1800, especially in the United States, *pantaloons* was applied to any sort of trousers, this use possibly taken independently from French *pantalon.* The modern *pants* is a shortened form of *pantaloons.*

pantheist *n.* believer in the doctrine that God and the universe are the same. 1705, formed from English *pan-* all + *the-* god (variant of *theo-*) + *-ist.* The word was coined by the Irish deist John Toland. **—pantheism** *n.* 1732, borrowed from French *panthéisme* (1712, formed from English *pantheist* + French *-isme* -ism). **—pantheistic** *adj.* 1732, formed from English *pantheist* + *-ic.*

pantheon (pan′thēən) *n.* 1549 *Pantheon,* in Coverdale's works; alteration of earlier *Panteon* (before 1425, temple for all the gods, especially the circular temple built in Rome by Agrippa and completed by Hadrian); borrowed from Greek *Pántheion* (*hierón*) (shrine) of all the gods; *pántheion,* neuter of *pántheios* (*pan-* all + *theîos* of or for the gods, from *theós* god; see THEOLOGY).

The figurative sense of any group of exalted persons

or things (as in *the pantheon of science*) is first recorded in 1596, in Nashe's *Have With You to Saffron-Walden.*

panther *n.* cougar. Before 1250 *panter* leopard; borrowed from Old French *pantere,* learned borrowing from Latin, and borrowed directly from Latin *panthēra,* from Greek *pánthēr,* probably borrowed from a language of Asia Minor.

The spelling *panthere* (from which modern *panther* is formed) is found in Caxton's translation of *Fables of Aesop* (1484); probably borrowed from Latin *panthēra.* In America the name *panther* was given to the cougar or puma (first attested in 1730).

An earlier use of *panther* (1471) in alchemy, suggests a multi-colored or spotted appearance of certain substances.

panties *n.pl.* 1845, American English; pair of drawers or shorts for men, diminutive of PANTS; for suffix see -Y[2]. The specific application to underpants for women or children is first recorded in 1908.

pantograph (pan′təgraf) *n.* instrument for copying plans, drawings, etc., on any scale desired. 1723 *pentograph;* borrowed from French *pentographe, pantographe,* formed from Greek *panto-* all (combining form of *pâs* all; see PAN-) + French *-graphe* -graph.

The meaning of a jointed framework on top of an electric railroad engine to convey electricity from overhead wires is first recorded in 1907.

pantomime *n.* play without words. 1615, a mimic actor, mime; probably influenced in form by French *pantomime,* but also found earlier as *pantomimus,* implied in plural *pantomimi* (1589); borrowing of Latin *pantomīmus* mime, dancer, from Greek *pantómimos* imitator of all (*panto-* all, see PANTOGRAPH + *mîmos* imitator, see MIME).

The meaning of a drama or play performed without words is first recorded before 1735.
—v. express by pantomime. 1768, from the noun.

pantry *n.* 1275, as a surname *Paneterie;* later *pantre* room in which bread and other provisions are kept (before 1325), and *pantrye* (about 1350); borrowed through Anglo-French *panetrie,* from Old French *paneterie* bread room, and directly from Medieval Latin *panataria, penetrie* office or room of a servant who has charge of the food (literally, bread), from Latin *pānis* bread; see FOOD; for suffix see -RY.

pants *n.pl.* single pair of trousers. 1840, American English; formed by shortening of PANTALOONS. **—pant** *n.* single pair of trousers. 1893, American English; back formation from *pants.* **—pantsuit** *n.* woman's suit of trousers and jacket, 1966; earlier *pants suit* (1964).

panzer (pan′zər) *adj.* armored. 1940, borrowed as a shortened form of German *Panzerdivision* armored unit, from *Panzer* tank; literally, armor, from Middle High German *panzier,* from Old French *panciere* armor for the belly, from *pance* belly, from Latin *pantex* (genitive *panticis*) belly; see PAUNCH. **—n.** tank. 1943, from the adjective.

pap *n.* soft food for infants or invalids. Before 1399, borrowed from Old French *papa* watered gruel (also found in Middle Dutch *pappe* pap, Middle Low German *pappe,* Spanish and Portuguese *papa,* and Italian *pappa*); probably also borrowed directly from Medieval Latin *pappa,* from Latin *pappa* word in children's language for food; compare PABULUM, especially for semantic development. It is also possible the word is associated with *pap* a nipple of a woman's breast, found in Middle English *pappe* (probably before 1200); borrowed from Latin *papilla* nipple; see PAPILLA.

The figurative meaning of watered-down or oversimplified ideas is first recorded in 1548.

papacy (pā′pəsē) *n.* position, rank, or authority of a pope. Before 1393 *papacie,* in Gower's *Confessio Amantis;* borrowed from Medieval Latin *papatia* papal office, from Late Latin *pāpa* POPE; for suffix see -CY.

papal (pā′pəl) *adj.* of or having to do with a pope. Before 1393, in Gower's *Confessio Amantis;* borrowed from Old French *papal,* and directly from Medieval Latin *papalis* of the pope, from Late Latin *pāpa* POPE; for suffix see -AL[1].

paparazzo (pä′pərät′sō) *n., pl.* **paparazzi** (pä′pərät′sē). aggressive photographer who pursues celebrities. 1961, American English, borrowing of Italian *paparazzo,* in allusion to the surname of a free-lance photographer in the Italian motion picture *La Dolce Vita* (1959).

papaw (pô′pô) *n.* small tree bearing edible fruit. 1624 *papaw,* American English; unexplained variant of PAPAYA. The word originally referred to the papaya fruit or tree; it was used in 1760 to designate the papaw tree.

papaya (pəpä′yə) *n.* tropical American tree. 1598, the fruit of this tree; later, the tree itself (1613); borrowed from Spanish *papaya,* probably from Arawakan (West Indies) *papaya.* The first recorded English spelling is *papaio;* the current spelling appeared in 1769.

paper *n.* 1364 *paper* writing material; also 1389 *papir;* borrowed through Anglo-French *paper,* from Old French *papier,* learned borrowings from Latin *papӯrus* paper; see PAPYRUS. The meaning of a newspaper is first recorded in English in 1642. **—adj.** of paper. 1592, from the noun. **—v.** 1594, to put down on paper; also 1599, to cover with paper; from the noun. **—paperback** *n.* (1899, in writings of Rudyard Kipling) **—paperboy** *n.* (1876) **—paper money** (1691) **—paperweight** *n.* (1858) **—paperwork** *n.* clerical work. 1917, in writings of Rudyard Kipling; earlier, written work of a student (1889), a literary work (1599), structure made of paper (1587).

papier-mâché (pā′pərməshā′) *n.* paper pulp mixed with some stiffener and molded when moist. 1753, borrowing of French *papier-mâché* (Old French *papier* PAPER + *mâché* compressed or mashed, from past participle of *mâcher,* literally, to chew, from Late Latin *masticāre* MASTICATE).

papilla (pəpil′ə) *n.* 1693, a nipple; later, small, nipple-like projection (1713); borrowing of Latin *papilla* nipple of the breast, diminutive of *papula* swelling, pimple, cognate with Lithuanian *pāpas* nipple, from Indo-European **pap-* to swell (Pok.91).

papoose or **pappoose** (papüs′) *n.* North American Indian baby. 1634, in William Wood's *New England's Prospect,* American English; borrowed from Algonquian (Narragansett) *papoos* child; literally, very young.

paprika (paprē′kə) *n.* seasoning made from a kind of red pepper. 1896, borrowing of Hungarian *paprika,* from Serbo-Croatian *pàpar* pepper, from Latin *piper* PEPPER.

papyrus (pəpī′rəs) *n.* tall water plant from which the ancients made paper. About 1395 *papirus,* in the Wycliffe Bible; borrowed from Latin *papӯrus* the paper plant, paper as a writing material made from it, from Greek *pápӯros* any plant of the paper plant genus; borrowing of a foreign word of unknown origin. Doublet of PAPER.

par *n.* equality, equal level. 1622, equality of value between currencies; later, equality of value or standing, equal footing (1662); borrowed from Latin *pār* equal, (as noun) that which is equal; see PAIR. Doublet of PEER[1].

The extended meaning of average, normal, or usual amount, degree, condition, or quality (found especially in the phrases *on a par, below par, up to par*) is first recorded in Sterne's *Tristram Shandy* (1767). The sense in golf of a score used as a standard for a particular hole or course (representing the number of strokes taken if the hole or course is played well) is first recorded in 1898-1900 and is probably from the sense in finance, in *par value* meaning "value at par"; the informal expression *par for the course* nothing unusual, the expected thing (1946) derives from usage in golf.
—adj. average, normal. 1861, from the noun.

par- the form of *para-*[1] before vowels where the prefix is part of a borrowed word, as in *parenthesis, paresis,* also before *h* in *parhelion,* although in Greek (*parḗlion,* from *hḗlios* the sun) the rough breathing and in Latin (*parēlion*) the *h* was not written; but *para-* keeps its full form in recent compounds such as *para-hydrogen* and *parainfluenza.*

para-[1] a prefix meaning: **1** alongside of, beside, as in *parataxis, parathyroid.* **2** closely related, as in *paraldehyde,* and in the nomenclature of certain benzene derivatives. **3a** resembling, as in *paratyphoid.* **b** supplementary or subsidiary, as in *paramedical, paramilitary.* **c** beyond, as in *parapsychology.* **4a** alteration, change, as in *paramorph, paraphrase.* **b** beside the mark, amiss, wrong, as in *paresthesia, paranoia, paraplegia.* **5** comparison, which was the meaning of the Greek original of *parabola.* Borrowed from Greek *para-* (before vowels *par-*), from the preposition *pará,* which is cognate with English FOR, FORE-, Gothic *faúr, faúra,* Latin *por-, prō,* Sanskrit *purá-s* in front, *purā́* before, formerly, from Indo-European **per-/pr̥-, prō* (root **per* originally referring to carrying over), Pok.810.

para-[2] a combining form meaning protect against (*parasol* a protector against the sun, *parachute* a protector against a fall), or shortened form of parachute, as in *paratroops.* Borrowed from French, from Italian *para-,* stem of *parare* parry, protect against, from Latin *parāre* prepare, related to *parere* bear, beget, cognate with Old High German *far, farro* bullock, Old English *fearr* ox, and Greek *pórtis* heifer, from Indo-European **per-* to bear (Pok.818).

parable *n.* story used to teach some truth or moral lesson, allegory. About 1250 *parabol* a proverb; later, an allegory, comparison (about 1340), and *parable* (before 1382); borrowed from Old French *parable,* learned borrowing from Latin, and borrowed directly from Latin *parabola* comparison, from Greek *parabolḗ* a placing side by side, comparison, analogy, parable (*para-* alongside + *bolḗ* a throwing, casting, related to *bállein* to throw); see BALLISTICS. Doublet of PALAVER, PARABOLA, and PAROLE.

parabola (pərab′ələ) *n. Geometry.* plane curve forming a conic section. 1579, New Latin; from Greek *parabolḗ* parabola, application, parallelism; so called because a parabola is produced by the "application" of a given area to a given straight line. Doublet of PALAVER, PARABLE, and PAROLE.

parachute *n.* 1785, borrowing of French *parachute* (*para-* defense against + *chute* a fall; see CHUTE[1] inclined trough). The word was coined by the pioneer French balloonist Blanchard and came into prominence in 1785 when Blanchard put a dog in a basket attached to a parachute and dropped it from a balloon.
—v. descend by parachute. 1807, from the noun.
—parachutist *n.* 1888, formed from English *parachute* + *-ist.*

parade *n.* 1656, display, show, assembling of troops for inspection or display, in Blount's *Glossographia;* borrowed from French *parade* display, show, military parade, from Middle French *parade* (influenced in meaning by *parer* arrange, prepare, adorn), from the meaning in horsemanship of the act of stopping a horse, borrowed from Spanish *parada* a stopping, from *parar* to stop, place, position, from Latin *parāre* prepare, provide; see PARE; for suffix see -ADE.

The meaning of a march or procession, especially one organized on a grand scale for a particular cause, is first recorded in 1673-74.
—v. 1686 (implied in *parading*), to assemble troops for inspection or display; later, to march in a procession with great display (1748); from the noun. The transferred sense of make a display of one's talents, success, etc., show off, is first recorded in Samuel Richardson's *Grandison* (1754).

paradigm (par′ədīm) *n.* pattern, example. 1483, in Caxton's version of the *Golden Legend;* borrowed from Late Latin *paradīgma* pattern, example, from Greek *parádeigma,* from *paradeiknýnai* show side by side, compare (*para-* side by side, beside + *deiknýnai* to show, point out; see DICTION). **—paradigmatic** (par′ədigmat′ik) *adj.* of or like a paradigm, exemplary. 1662, shortened form of *paradigmatical* (1577); formed in English from Greek *paradeigmatikós* serving as a pattern or example, from *parádeigma* (genitive *paradeígmatos*) pattern, example + *-ical.*

paradise *n.* Before 1200 *paradise, paradis* the Christian heaven, the Garden of Eden, place or condition of bliss; borrowed from Old French *paradis,* learned borrowing from Late Latin, and borrowed directly from Late Latin *paradīsus,* from Greek *parádeisos,* from an Iranian source (compare Avestan *pairidaēza* enclosure or park, a compound of *pairi-* around + *daēza-* wall); see PERI-; *daēza-* is cognate with Greek *toîchos* wall, from Indo-European **dhoiĝhos* mud wall (root **dheiĝh-* to knead), Pok.244.

The Greek word *parádeisos* was first used by Xenophon to describe an enclosed park, orchard, or hunting preserve in Persia; in the Septuagint it was used for the Garden of Eden, and in the New Testament (and thence in the works of various early Christian writers) for the abode of the blessed, heaven, which is the earliest meaning of *paradise* recorded in English.

paradox *n.* 1540, statement contrary to common opinion; borrowed, perhaps through Middle French *paradoxe,* from Latin *paradoxum,* from Greek *parádoxon,* from neuter of *parádoxos* contrary to expectation, incredible (*para-* contrary to + *dóxa* opinion, praise; see DOXOLOGY).

The meaning of a statement that may be true but seems contradictory is first recorded in Robert Crowley's *A Setting Open of the Subtle Sophistry of T. Watson* (1569).
—paradoxical *adj.* having to do with a paradox. 1581

(implied in *paradoxically,* in Sidney's *Apology for Poetry*); formed from English *paradox* + *-ical.*

paraffin *n.* substance like wax, used for making candles, etc. 1838, borrowed from German *Paraffin,* formed from Latin *parum* not very, too little + *affinis* associated with, bordering upon; so called from paraffin's low affinity for other substances. The word was coined in 1830 by the German chemist Karl von Reichenbach. Latin *parum* was originally the neuter (accusative) of *parvus* little, cognate with Greek *paûros* small, scanty and Latin *paucī* FEW.

Apparently *paraffin* is found in Middle French *paraffine* resin, pitch, in the mid-1500's, and in Cotgrave's *Dictionary* (1611) with the sense of "mineral resin." It is also found in the form *parafine* (1552). All of these forms suggest an earlier borrowing of the Latin elements, and an influence on the later form in German.

paragon *n.* model of excellence or perfection. Before 1548; borrowed from Middle French *paragon* a model, from Italian *paragone,* originally, touchstone to test gold, or tell good from bad, from *paragonare* to test on a touchstone, compare, from Greek *parakonân* to sharpen, whet (*para-* on the side + *akónē* whetstone, related to *akḗ* point; see EDGE).

paragraph *n.* Before 1500 *paragraf* distinct part of a composition, chapter, or book (originally marked by a division sign such as ¶ or ⁋), in *Promptorium Parvulorum;* later *paragraph* (1525); borrowed from Middle French *paragraphe,* Old French *paragrafe,* learned borrowing from Medieval Latin, and borrowed directly from Medieval Latin *paragraphus* division sign for a distinct passage or section of a discourse, etc., from Greek *parágraphos* short line or stroke (in the margin) marking a break in sense, from *paragráphein* write by the side (*para-* beside + *gráphein* to write; see CARVE). The forms *paragraf, paragraph* replaced earlier *paraf* paragraph or paragraph mark (recorded about 1395, in Wycliffe's writings), borrowed from Medieval Latin *paraffus, paraphus,* shortened form of *paragraphus.*
—**v.** 1601, to sign or initial; later, write paragraphs about (1764), and divide into paragraphs (1799); from the noun. The verb form *paragraph* replaced earlier *parafen* divide into paragraphs (recorded 1440), from the noun in Middle English.

parakeet *n.* small parrot. 1621 *parakeete,* borrowed from Spanish *periquito,* probably a diminutive of the name *Perico,* itself a diminutive of the name *Pedro* Peter. The word appeared earlier as *parroket* (1581), borrowed from Middle French *paroquet, perroquet,* from Old French, perhaps a diminutive of *Pierre* Peter; compare PARROT. The relationships between Spanish *periquito,* French *perroquet,* and the Italian word *parrocchetto* are unclear.

The English spellings were probably influenced by English *parrot.*

parallax (par′əlaks) *n.* apparent displacement of an object observed. 1594, borrowed from Middle French *parallaxe,* from Greek *parállaxis* change, alternation, mutual inclination of two lines meeting at an angle, from *parallássein* to alter, make things alternate (*para-* beside + *allássein* to change, from *állos* other, another; see ELSE).

parallel *adj.* at a constant distance apart lengthwise, like two rails, 1549, borrowed from Middle French *parallèle,* or directly from Latin *parallēlus,* from Greek *parállēlos,* from *parà allḗlois* beside one another, side by side (*pará* beside and *allḗlois* each other, contraction of the earlier phrase *álloi állois* some to others, from *állos* other; see ELSE).
—**n.** parallel line or surface. 1551, from the adjective. The figurative sense of a counterpart, equal, match, is first recorded in Ben Jonson's *Every Man Out of His Humour* (1599).
—**v.** 1598, bring into comparison; from the adjective. The meaning of be a parallel to, be equal to, match, is first recorded in Shakespeare's *All's Well That Ends Well* (1601), and that of find or provide a match for, in *Troylus and Cressida* (1606).
—**parallel bars** pair of bars used in gymnastics. (1868, in writings of Anthony Trollope) —**parallelism** *n.* 1610, condition of being parallel; formed from English *parallel* + *-ism,* probably modeled on Greek *parallēlismós* a placing side by side; for suffix see -ISM. The meaning of correspondence or analogy is first recorded in 1636.
—**parallelogram** *n.* geometric figure. 1570, borrowed from Middle French *parallélogramme,* learned borrowing from Latin, and borrowed directly from Latin *parallēlogrammum,* from Greek *parallēlógrammon* from neuter of *parallēlógrammos* bounded by parallel lines (*parállēlos* parallel + *grammḗ* line, related to *grámma* letter, something written; see GRAM).

paralysis *n.* lessening or loss of the ability to move or feel. 1525, borrowing of Latin *paralysis,* from Greek *parálysis,* literally, loosening, from *paralýein* loosen from beside, disable, enfeeble (*para-* beside + *lýein* loosen, untie; see LOSE). Doublet of PALSY. —**paralytic** *adj.* of or having paralysis. Probably about 1380 *parlatyk;* later *paralitik* (before 1398); borrowed from Old French *paralitique,* from Latin *paralyticus,* from Greek *paralytikós,* from *parálysis* paralysis; for suffix see -IC.
—**paralyze** *v.* affect with paralysis. 1804, borrowed from French *paralyser,* from Old French *paralisie* paralysis, learned borrowing from Latin *paralysis.* An isolated example of a verbal is recorded in Middle English *paralized,* past participle (probably before 1425).

paramecium (par′əmē′sēəm) *n.* one-celled animal with an oblong body. 1752, New Latin *Paramecium* the genus name, formed from Greek *paramḗkēs* oblong, oval (*para-* on one side, against + *mêkos* length, related to *makrós* long; see MEAGER); for suffix see -IUM.

paramedic[1] (par′əmed′ik) *n.* medical corpsman who parachutes from an aircraft. 1951, American English; formed from *para-*[2] parachute + *medic.*

paramedic[2] (par′əmed′ik) *n.* medical technician or other auxiliary worker in medicine. 1970, back formation from earlier *paramedical,* adj., 1921, related to medicine in an auxiliary capacity (*para-*[1] + *medical*).

parameter *n.* 1656, a constant right line in a conic section, in Hobbes' *Works;* borrowed from New Latin *parametrum,* formed from Greek *para-* beside, subsidiary + *métron* MEASURE.

A general meaning in mathematics "a constant in a particular case that varies in other cases" is recorded since 1852. The transferred meaning (used in scientific contexts) "measurable factor or feature which helps to define a particular system" is first recorded in the 1920's, and from this latter sense developed (partly by influence of *perimeter*) a widely used nontechnical sense of "a boundary, limit, defining or characteristic factor," which began to appear in the 1950's.
—**parametric** *adj.* of, relating to, or in the form of a parameter. 1864, formed from English *parameter* + *-ic.*

paramount *adj.* 1531, above others in rank or order, supreme; borrowed from Anglo-French *paramont, peramont* above, formed from Old French *par* by, from Latin *per* by, through + *amont* up, *a mont* upward; see AMOUNT. The meaning of superior to all others in influence, power, or importance, preeminent, is first recorded in English in 1596, in Sir Francis Bacon's works.

paramour (par′əmůr) *n.* illicit lover. Before 1325, a term of endearment for Christ or the Virgin Mary, in *Cursor Mundi;* later, a general term of endearment equivalent to darling, sweetheart (before 1375), and mistress, concubine, lover (about 1390). In all of these senses Middle English *paramour* was a noun use of the earlier adverbial phrase *par amur* passionately, with very strong love or desire (before 1300); borrowed through Anglo-French *par amour,* from Old French *par amor* by or through love (*par,* from Latin *per* by, through, and *amour,* from Latin *amōrem,* accusative of *amor* love).

paranoia *n.* mental disorder characterized by delusions. 1891, New Latin; earlier *paranœa* (1811); from Greek *paránoia* mental derangement, madness, from *paránoos, paránous* mentally ill, insane (*para-* beside, beyond + *nóos, noûs* mind, of uncertain origin). **—paranoiac** *adj., n.* 1892, formed in English from New Latin *paranoia* + English *-ac,* as in *maniac.* **—paranoid** *adj.* resembling or tending toward paranoia. 1904, formed in English from New Latin *paranoia* + English *-oid.* —*n.* 1922, from the adjective.

parapet *n.* low wall or barrier. 1590, breast-high wall to protect soldiers, in Marlowe's *Tamburlane the Great;* borrowed from Middle French *parapet* a breastwork, from Italian *parapetto* (*para-* defense, protection + *petto* breast, from Latin *pectus;* see PECTORAL). The meaning of a low wall or barrier at the edge of a balcony, roof, etc., is first recorded in Florio's *A World of Words* (1598).

paraphernalia (par′əfənāl′yə) *n.pl.* personal belongings, equipment, apparatus. 1651, personal property which the law allows a woman to keep over and above her dowry; borrowed from Medieval Latin *paraphernalia,* neuter plural of *paraphernalis,* adj., from Late Latin *parapherna* a woman's personal property besides her dowry, from Greek *parápherna,* neuter plural (*para-* beside, supplementary + *phernḗ* dowry, related to *phérein* to carry; see BEAR[2]). The meaning of personal belongings is first recorded in Fielding's *Pasquin* (1736), and that of equipment, apparatus, in 1791.

paraphrase *n.* 1548, expression of a statement in other words; borrowed from Middle French *paraphrase,* learned borrowing from Latin *paraphrasis* a paraphrase, from Greek *paráphrasis,* from *paraphrázein* to tell in other words (*para-* beside, alongside of + *phrázein* to tell, explain; see PHRASE). **—v.** 1606 (in figurative use); 1630, to express in other words; borrowed from French *paraphraser,* from Middle French *paraphrase,* n., paraphrase.

paraplegia (par′əplē′jēə) *n.* paralysis of the lower part of the body. 1657, New Latin, from Ionic Greek *paraplēgíē* paralysis of one side of the body, from *paraplḗssein* strike at the side, *paraplḗssesthai* be stricken on one side, be paralyzed (*para-* beside + *plḗssein* to strike; see PLAINT). The New Latin form may have been modeled on Middle French *paraplégie,* from Greek. **—paraplegic** *adj.* affected with paraplegia. 1822-34, formed from English *paraplegia* + *-ic,* as if borrowed from Ionic Greek *paraplēgikós,* from *paraplēgíē.* —*n.* paraplegic person. 1890, in William James' *Principles of Psychology;* from the adjective.

parasite *n.* 1539, person who lives on others, hanger-on; borrowed from Middle French *parasite,* learned borrowing from Latin *parasītus,* and borrowed directly from Greek *parásitos* person who eats at the table of another, earning meals by flattery, noun use of adjective, in the sense of feeding beside (*para-* beside, alongside of + *sîtos* food, of uncertain origin).

The scientific meaning of an animal or plant that lives on another organism is first recorded in English in *Chambers Cyclopaedia* (1727-41) with reference to plants.

—parasitic *adj.* of or like a parasite. 1627, shortened form of *parasitical* (1577-87); borrowed from Latin *parasīticus,* from Greek *parasītikós,* from *parásītos* parasite; for suffix see -ICAL.

parasol *n.* umbrella to keep off the sun. 1616, anything serving as a defense against the sun's rays; borrowing of French *parasol,* from Italian *parasole* (*para-* para-[2], defense against + *sole* sun, from Latin *sōlem,* nominative *sōl;* see SOLAR). The specific sense of an umbrella-like sunshade is first recorded in 1660.

paratrooper *n.* soldier trained to use a parachute. 1941, American English; formed from *para-*[2] parachute + *trooper.*

parboil *v.* boil till partly cooked. 1381 *parboylen* to boil partially or thoroughly; borrowed from Old French *parboillir, parbolir, parbouillir,* from Medieval Latin, and borrowed directly from Medieval Latin *perbullire* boil thoroughly (Latin *per-* thoroughly + *bullīre* to BOIL[1]). The meaning of boil partially was influenced by mistaken association with Middle English *part.*

parcel *n.* About 1303 *parcelle* part, portion, division, in Mannyng's *Handlyng Synne;* later *parcel* (before 1376, in *Piers Plowman*); borrowing of Old French *parcelle, parcel* a small piece, particle, parcel, from Vulgar Latin **particella,* diminutive of Latin *particula* PARTICLE.

The meaning of a package is first recorded in English in 1465, and is preceded by the sense of bundle, about 1436.

—v. 1584-85, divide into parcels; from the noun.

parch *v.* dry by heating. Before 1338 *parchen* burn, lay waste, in Mannyng's *Chronicle of England;* earlier in a surname *Parchehare* (1246-47); before 1382, to roast or dry, in the Wycliffe Bible; of uncertain origin (possibly from *perchen,* variant of *perishen* perish).

parcheesi or **parchesi** (pärchē′zē) *n.* game somewhat like backgammon. 1800 *pachees,* borrowed from Hindi *pacīsī,* from *pacīs* twenty-five (highest throw of the dice), from the compound of Sanskrit *páñca* FIVE + *viṅśati-s* twenty.

The common spelling was originally *pachisi;* the spelling *parcheesi* became more frequent after 1892.

parchment *n.* About 1250 *parchemyne* skin of sheep, goats, etc., prepared for use as a writing material; earlier, in a surname *Perchamunt* (1200); borrowed from Old French *parchemin, perchemin,* alteration (with *ch* for *g*) of Late Latin *pergamēnum,* from Late Greek *pergamēnón,* formed in allusion to *Pérgamon* Pergamum, the Greek city in ancient western Asia Minor where parchment was supposedly first made. It is also possible that a Gallo-Romance form **particamīnum* developed from a blend of Late Latin *pergamēnum* with Latin *parthica* in *parthica pellis* Parthian leather. The late Middle English *parchement* (1438, with added *t*) was influenced by Medieval Latin *pergamentum* from Late Latin *pergamēnum.*

pard[1] *n. Archaic.* leopard, panther. Probably before 1300 *perde,* in *Kyng Alisaunder;* later *parde* (before 1325, in *Cursor Mundi*); from Old French *parde,* learned borrowing from Latin, and borrowed directly from Latin *pardus,* from Greek *párdos* male panther, from the same source (probably Iranian) as Sanskrit *pṛdāku-s* leopard, tiger, snake, and Persian *palang* panther.

pard[2] *n. Dialect.* partner. 1850, American English; shortened form of earlier *pardener, pardner* (1795), variants of PARTNER.

pardon *v.* 1433 *pardonen* forgive, in *Rolls of Parliament;* borrowed from Old French *pardoner, pardonner* to grant, concede, condone, forgive, and directly from Vulgar Latin **perdōnāre* to give wholeheartedly (from Latin *per-* through, thoroughly + *dōnāre* give, present; see DONATION). **—n.** Probably before 1300 *pardoun* forgiveness; about 1300 *pardon;* borrowed from Old French *pardon,* from *pardoner* to grant, pardon, and directly from Vulgar Latin **perdonum.*

pare *v.* Probably before 1300 *paren* cut, trim, or shave off the outer part of, in *Sir Tristrem;* borrowed from Old French *parer* arrange, prepare, trim, dress, adorn, and directly from Latin *parāre* make ready, prepare; related to *parere* produce, bring forth, give birth to. Latin *parere* is cognate with Greek *póris* calf, Lithuanian *parẽti* to brood, and Sanskrit *pṛthuka-s* calf, young of an animal, from Indo-European **per-* to bear (Pok.818). Doublet of PARRY.

paregoric (par′əgôr′ik) *n.* soothing medicine, used to relieve intestinal upset. 1704, from earlier adjective, soothing (1684); borrowed perhaps through French *parégorique,* from Late Latin *parēgoricus,* from Greek *parēgorikós* soothing or encouraging, from *parēgoreîn* speak soothingly to, from *parḗgoros* consoling (*para-* beside + the root of *agoreúein* speak in public, from *agorā́* marketplace, AGORA); for suffix see -IC.

parenchyma (pəreng′kəmə) *n.* essential tissue in higher plants and animals. 1651, borrowed, perhaps through influence of French *parenchyme,* from Greek *parénchyma* anything poured in, from *parencheîn* pour in beside (*para-* beside + *énchyma* infusion, *en-* in + *chýma* what is poured, from *cheîn* to pour); see FOUND[2] cast. It was formerly supposed that the tissues of organs were poured in by the blood vessels.

parent *n.* Before 1410 *parens,* pl.; borrowed from Latin nominative *parēns;* and later *parent* (1413); earlier as a surname *Parent* (1185); borrowing of Old French *parent;* borrowed from Latin *parentem* father or mother, ancestor, a noun use of earlier past (aorist) active participle of *parere* bring forth, give birth to, produce; see PARE. **—v.** be a parent. 1663, be a parent of, beget; from the noun. The intransitive use of be a parent (often as a verbal noun, *parenting*) is first recorded in the 1950's in American English. **—parentage** *n.* descent from parents. 1490, in Caxton's translation of *The Book of Eneydos;* probably borrowed from Middle French *parentage* (*parent* parent + *-age* -age); also possibly formed from Middle English *parent* + *-age.* **—parental** *adj.* 1623, in Cockeram's *Dictionary;* formed from English *parent* + *-al*[1]. **—parenthood** *n.* 1856, formed from English *parent* + *-hood.*

parenthesis *n.* 1568, explanatory or qualifying comment inserted in a passage; borrowed, perhaps by influence of Middle French *parenthèse,* from Late Latin *parenthesis* addition of a letter or syllable in a word, from Greek *parénthesis* a putting in beside, from *parentithénai* put in beside (*para-* beside + *en-* in + *tithénai* put, place; see DO[1] perform).

The meaning of one or both of the curved marks ( ) used to set off an explanatory or qualifying comment is first recorded in a concrete sense in 1715, but was known earlier by its appearance in transferred use referring to Vulcan's horns (1608).

—parenthesize *v.* insert as or in a parenthesis. 1837, in Southey's *The Doctor;* formed from English *parenthesis* + *-ize.* **—parenthetical** *adj.* of or pertaining to a parenthesis. 1624, from Medieval Greek *parénthetos* interpolated; for suffix see -ICAL.

parfait (pärfā′) *n.* kind of ice cream dessert. 1894, borrowing of French *parfait,* literally, perfect thing, noun use of *parfait,* from Old French *parfait* PERFECT.

pariah (pərī′ə) *n.* outcast. 1613, member of a low caste in southern India, in *Purchas his Pilgrimage;* borrowed from Portuguese *pariá,* or directly from Tamil *paṛaiyar,* plural of *paṛaiyan* drummer (the caste's hereditary duty at festivals), from *paṛai* large festival drum.

The meaning of a person of no caste, an outcaste, is first recorded in English in 1711, and the sense of a social outcast is first recorded in Shelley's *Letters* (1819).

parietal (pərī′ətəl) *adj.* of the wall of the body or of one of its cavities. Probably about 1425, in a translation of Chauliac's *Grande Chirurgie;* borrowed from Late Latin *parietālis* of walls, from Latin *pariēs* (genitive *parietis*) wall, of unknown origin; for suffix see -AL[1]. **—n.** parietal bone, plate, etc. Probably about 1425, in a translation of Chauliac's *Grande Chirurgie;* noun use of Latin *parietālis,* adj.

pari-mutuel (par′imyü′chùəl) *n.* system of betting on races, in which those who bet on the winners divide the bets placed. 1881, borrowing of French *pari-mutuel* mutual wager (*pari* wager, from *parier* to bet, from Latin *pariāre* to square (accounts), settle a debt, from *pār,* genitive *paris* equal; see PAIR + *mutuel* mutual, from Latin *mūtuus* MUTUAL).

parish *n.* About 1300 *paroche* district with its own church and clergyman; also, the members of that district; later *parosshe* (about 1325), and *parish* (about 1330); probably, in part, a back formation of earlier *paroschien, parysshen* inhabitant of a parish, parishioner; and, in part, borrowed from Old French *paroisse, parroche,* learned borrowing from Late Latin *parochia* a diocese, alteration of Late Greek *paroikíā* any ecclesiastical district; also, a diocese or parish, from Greek *paroikíā* a sojourning, from *pároikos* a sojourner; earlier, neighbor, neighboring (*para-* near + *oîkos* a house; see VICINITY); for suffix see -ISH.

According to Bloch-Wartburg, the Late Latin form *parochia* apparently resulted from confusion between Greek *pároikos* sojourner and *párochos* provider of necessaries to officials who were traveling. Greek *párochos* is related to *par-échein* supply, hand over (*para-* from + *échein* hold; see HECTIC).

—parishioner *n.* member of a parish. 1465 *parishioner;* earlier *parysshen* member of a parish (about 1303); earlier *paroschien* (probably before 1200, in *Ancrene Riwle*); formed in Middle English from Old French *paroissien, parrochien* parishioner, from *paroisse, parroche* parish + Middle English *-er*[1].

parity *n.* equality. 1572, equality of rank or status; borrowed from Middle French *parité,* or directly from Late Latin *paritās* equality, from Latin *pār,* adj. (genitive *paris*) equal; see PAIR; for suffix see -ITY.

park *n.* About 1300 *parc, parke* park, enclosed tract of land, game preserve; earlier, in *parkselver* fee paid for the privilege of maintaining a tract of enclosed land (1222); borrowed from Old French *parc,* possibly from West Germanic **parrik* or **parrak* (compare Old High German *pfarrih,* and Old English *pearruc* enclosure; see PADDOCK). **—v.** 1526 (implied in *parking*) enclose in a park; from the noun. The meaning of put (a vehicle) in a certain place is first recorded in 1844, in military use, though it was earlier applied to placement of cannon in 1812. **—parkway** *n.* (1887, American English)

parka (pär′kə) *n.* jacket with a hood. 1813; earlier *parki,* pl. (1780); borrowed from Aleut *parka,* from Russian *párka* a pelt or jacket made from pelt, from Samoyed.

parlance *n.* way of speaking, talk. 1579-80, speech, especially debate, in a version of Plutarch's *Lives;* borrowed perhaps from Anglo-French (according to the OED, used in Anglo-French context in the 1300's), but more likely borrowed from Middle French *parlance,* from Old French *parlaunce, parlance,* from *parler* to speak; see PARLEY. The meaning of a way of speaking, idiom, is first recorded in 1787.

parlay (pär′lā) *v.* risk an original bet and its winnings on another bet. 1828 *paralee,* American English; alteration of earlier *paroli* (1701); borrowed from French, of unknown origin. The meaning of exploit an asset or circumstance to advantage is first recorded in 1942 in American English.

parley (pär′lē) *n.* conference, informal talk. Probably before 1449, conversation or discussion; later, conference to discuss disputed matters (1581); borrowed from Middle French *parlée,* from feminine past participle of Old French *parler* to speak, from Late Latin *parabolāre,* from *parabola* speech or discourse, from Latin *parabola* comparison; see PARABLE. **—v.** discuss terms, especially with an enemy. 1570, to speak; later, discuss terms (1600); from the noun, probably influenced by Middle French *parler* to speak. An earlier form is found in Middle English *parlen* to speak, confer (about 1378, in a version of *Piers Plowman*), but this is probably a separate borrowing from Old French *parler* to speak.

parliament (pär′ləmənt) *n.* Probably before 1300 *parlement* formal council, lawmaking body, in *Arthour and Merlin;* later *parliamente* (about 1400); borrowing of Old French *parlement,* from *parler* to speak; see PARLEY; for suffix see -MENT. The spelling *parliamente, parliament* was probably formed after Medieval Latin *parliamentum,* also found in Anglo-Latin; both forms which may have come from English *parlement,* according to the OED. **—parliamentary** *adj.* of or done by a parliament. 1616, formed from English *parliament* + *-ary.*

parlor *n.* Probably before 1200 *parlur* window through which to make confession or to hold audience with those outside the cloister, in *Ancrene Riwle;* later *parlore* chamber in a monastery (about 1300), *parlour* (1338), and conference chamber, sitting room (about 1378); borrowed from Old French *parlur, parlëur, parlëor,* from *parler* to speak; see PARLEY; for suffix see -OR[1].

The sense of a kind of commercial establishment (such as an *ice cream parlor, a beauty parlor, a funeral parlor*) is first recorded in 1884 in American English. **—adj.** advocating views as if from a safe, comfortable parlor rather than from practical contact or experience (as in *a parlor radical, a parlor Communist*). 1910, from the noun.

—parlor car railroad car with special accommodations for day travel (1868, in American English).

parlous (par′ləs) *adj. Archaic.* risky or awkward to deal with, perilous. Probably about 1400 *parlows; perlous* (1401); variants of PERILOUS; for suffix see -OUS. **—adv.** extremely. 1599, from the adjective.

parochial *adj.* of or in a parish. 1393 *parochiell;* 1400 *parochial;* borrowed from Anglo-French *parochiel,* and from Old French *parochial,* from Late Latin *parochiālis* of a parish, from *parochia* PARISH; for suffix see -AL[1]. The figurative sense of very limited or narrow is first recorded in Emerson's *English Traits* (1856). **—parochialism** *n.* narrowness of interest or view. 1847, formed from English *parochial* + *-ism.*

parody *n.* humorous imitation. 1598, in Ben Jonson's *Every Man in His Humour;* borrowed from Latin *parōdia* parody, from Greek *parōidíā* burlesque poem or song (*para-* beside, parallel to + *ōidḗ* song, ODE); for suffix see -Y[3]. **—v.** make a parody of. Before 1745, in Pope's *Works;* from the noun.

parole (pərōl′) *n.* Before 1616, word of honor given by a prisoner of war not to escape; borrowing of French *parole* word, speech, formal promise, from Late Latin *parabola* speech or discourse, from Latin *parabola* a comparison; see the doublet PARABLE. Doublet also of PALAVER and PARABOLA.

The sense of a system of conditional release of a prisoner before serving a full term is first recorded in 1908. **—v.** 1716, pledge one's word; later, put a prisoner of war or other combatant on parole, in Emerson's *Works* (1853); from the noun.

paroxysm (par′əksizəm) *n.* Probably before 1425 *paroxism* periodic attack of a disease, in a translation of Chauliac's *Grande Chirurgie;* borrowed from Medieval Latin *paroxysmus* irritation, sev͟ere fit of a disease, from Greek *paroxysmós,* from *paroxýnein* to exasperate, irritate, goad (*para-* beyond + *oxýnein* sharpen, make acute, goad, from *oxýs* sharp, pointed; see OXYGEN). The sense of any severe or sudden attack, fit, is first recorded in 1604. **—paroxysmal** *adj.* of, like, or having paroxysms. 1651, formed from English *paroxysm* + *-al*[1].

parquet (pärkā′) *n.* inlaid wooden flooring. 1816, borrowing of French *parquet, parchet* wooden flooring, compartment, enclosed portion of a park, diminutive of Old French *parc* PARK; for suffix see -ET. The noun in English was surely influenced by an earlier verb use. **—v.** furnish with a parquet floor. 1678, in Evelyn's *Diary;* borrowed from French *parqueter,* from *parquet,* n., parquet. **—parquetry** *n.* mosaic of wood. 1842, borrowed from French *parqueterie,* from *parquet,* n., parquet; for suffix see -RY.

parricide[1] (par′əsīd) *n.* person who kills his parent or other near relative. 1554, borrowed from Middle French *parricide,* learned borrowing from Latin *parricīda,* (earlier) *pāricīda* (**pārus* relative + *-cīda* killer). Compare PATRICIDE[1]. Latin **pārus, pāros* is cognate with Greek *pēós* (Doric *pāós*) a relative by marriage from Indo-European **pāsós* (Pok.789).

parricide[2] *n.* the act of killing a parent or near relative

1570, borrowed from Middle French *parricide,* learned borrowing from Latin *parricīdium;* earlier *pāricīdium* (**pārus* relative; see PARRICIDE[1] + *-cīdium* killing). Compare PATRICIDE[2].

parrot *n.* bird with a stout, hooked bill, and often with brightly colored feathers; some parrots are noted for imitating human sounds. About 1525, in Skelton's *Poetical Works;* perhaps borrowed from dialectal Middle French *perrot,* from a variant of the man's name *Pierre* Peter; compare *Perot* or *Pierrot* name in modern French for the house sparrow; see also PARAKEET. **—v.** repeat without understanding. 1596, in Nashe's *Have With You to Saffron-Walden;* from the noun.

parry *v.* 1672, ward off a weapon or blow, in Marvell's *The Rehearsal Transposed;* borrowed from French *parez!* imperative of *parer* ward off, from Italian *parare,* from Latin *parāre* make ready, prepare; see PARE. The figurative sense of evade, avoid, turn aside, is first recorded in 1718. **—n.** act of parrying. 1705, from the verb.

parse *v.* analyze grammatically. Before 1553, probably verb use of Middle English *pars* part of speech (probably before 1300, in *Kyng Alisaunder*); borrowed perhaps through Old French *pars,* plural of *part* part, and directly from Latin *pars* in the school question *Quae pars ōrātiōnis?* What part of speech? See PART.

parsimony (pär′səmō′nē) *n.* frugality; stinginess. Probably before 1425 *parcimony,* in a translation of Higden's *Polychronicon;* borrowed from Latin *parsimōnia* sparingness, frugality, from *pars-,* the stem of *parsī,* perfect tense of *parcere* to spare, save, of uncertain origin, + *-mōnia,* suffix signifying action, state, condition. **—parsimonious** *adj.* frugal, stingy. 1598, probably formed from English *parsimony* + *-ous.*

parsley *n.* garden plant used to flavor food. Before 1300 *persely,* a fusion of Old English (about 1000) *petersilie* and Old French *percil, persil.* The Old French derives from Medieval Latin *petrosilium,* altered from Latin *petroselīnum,* from Greek *petrosélīnon* (*pétros* rock, stone + *sélīnon* celery). The Old English *petersilie* probably came from a West Germanic form (compare Old High German *petarsile,* Middle Dutch *petersilie,* which was borrowed from Medieval Latin *petrosilium).*

parsnip *n.* vegetable of the same family as the carrot. 1533 *parsnepe;* earlier *persenepe* (before 1500); alteration of *pasnepe* (1373); borrowed from Old French *pasnaie,* from Latin *pastināca* parsnip or carrot, a name connected with *pastinum* two-pronged gardening fork, perhaps used in harvesting tubers. In the Middle English form *pasnepe,* the ending was altered to *nepe* turnip, which is found in Old English (Anglian *nēp,* West Saxon *nǣp;* borrowed from Latin *nāpus*) because the parsnip was considered a kind of turnip. Latin *nāpus* turnip is a borrowing from Greek *nâpy* mustard, from some foreign source.

parson *n.* clergyman in charge of a parish. About 1250 *persone;* earlier, in a surname *Persun* (1197); about 1300 *parson;* borrowing of Old French *persone* curate, parson, from Medieval Latin *persona* parson, and borrowed directly from Latin *persōna* PERSON.

According to the OED, ecclesiastical use of Latin *persōna* parson (still a new term as late as 1096) may have been in reference to a clergyman considered as the legal "person" holding the actual property of the church; or a personage, eminent person, or dignitary, especially one figuring merely in the role of the parish clergyman, the actual ministerial duties being discharged by the resident vicar. These senses are also reinforced in *parsonage.*

—parsonage *n.* About 1378 *parsonage* a benefice granted to a parson, in a version of *Piers Plowman;* also *personage,* in Wycliffe's writings; borrowed from Old French *personage, personnage* benefice of a parson (*persone* parson + *-age*), and from Medieval Latin *personagium* parsonage, benefice. The meaning of a house provided for a parson's living or benefice is first recorded in English in 1486.

part *n.* About 1250 *part* division of a whole, portion; borrowed from Old French *part,* from Latin *pars* (genitive *partis*) part. Latin *pars* (from Indo-European **perə-tí-s*) is cognate with Sanskrit *pūrtí-s* present, reward (from Indo-European *pr̥̄-tí-s,* Pok.817), and perhaps Hittite *parsiya-* fraction, part. An Old English *part* part of speech is recorded in Ælfric's *Grammar,* borrowed directly from Latin, but it is considered rare and did not survive. **—v.** Probably before 1200 *parten* to depart, separate oneself, in *Ancrene Riwle;* later to divide into parts, separate (before 1300); borrowed from Old French *partir,* from Latin *partīre,* from *pars* (genitive *partis*) part, n. **—adj.** less than the whole. 1597, in Shakespeare's *2 Henry IV;* from the noun. **—adv.** in some measure or degree, partly. 1513, Sir Thomas More in Grafton's *Chronicles;* from the noun.

partake *v.* 1561, to share or impart; later, to take or have a share (about 1585); back formation from earlier *partaker* sharer, participant (1547); formed from Middle English *part-taker* (probably before 1400), from *part* + *taker* (also found in *part takynge,* about 1384), a translation of Latin *particeps* participant; see PARTICIPATE.

partial *adj.* Before 1398 *parcial* not whole, incomplete, in Trevisa's translation of Bartholomew's *De Proprietatibus Rerum;* borrowing of Old French *parcial,* from Medieval Latin, and borrowed directly from Medieval Latin *partialis* divisible, solitary, partial, from Latin *pars* (genitive *partis*) PART; for suffix see -AL[1]. The spelling *partiall,* as well as the extended meaning of one-sided, biased are recorded in 1425, but the meaning is reflected earlier in *parcyalte* partiality (1421). **—partiality** *n.* a being one-sided or biased. 1421, Middle English *parcyalte;* later *partialte* (1461); borrowed from Middle French *parcialité, parcialté,* from Medieval Latin *partialitatem* (nominative *partialitas*), from *partialis* partial; for suffix see -ITY.

participate *v.* have a share, take part. 1531, in Elyot's *The Boke Named the Governour;* probably a back formation from *participation;* for suffix see -ATE[1]. **—participant** *n.* 1562, from *participant,* adj. (before 1470); borrowed from Middle French *participant,* from Latin *participantem* (nominative *participāns*), present participle of *participāre* participate; for suffix see -ANT. **—participation** *n.* About 1380 *participacioun,* in Chaucer's translation of Boethius' *De Consolatione Philosophiae,* borrowed from Old French *participation,* learned borrowing from Late Latin, and borrowed directly from Late Latin *participātiōnem* (nominative *participātiō*), from Latin *participāre* participate, from *particeps* (genitive *participis*) partaker (*pars,* genitive *partis* part + the root of *capere* to take); for suffix see -ATION.

participle *n.* form of a verb used as an adjective. Before 1397, in the Wycliffe Bible; borrowed from Old French *participle,* variant of *participe,* learned borrowing from

Latin, and borrowed directly from Latin *participium,* literally, a sharing, partaking, from *particeps* partaker; see PARTICIPATE. **—participial** *adj.* of a participle. 1591, borrowed from Middle French *participial,* and directly from Latin *participiālis,* from *participium* participle; for suffix see -AL[1].

particle *n.* Before 1398 *particle* little bit, small unit of matter, in Trevisa's translation of Bartholomew's *De Proprietatibus Rerum;* borrowed from Latin *particula* little bit or part, diminutive of *pars* (genitive *partis*) PART; for suffix see -CLE. **—particle accelerator** device for physics research (1946) **—particle physics** branch of physics dealing with elementary particles of matter (1946)

parti-colored *adj.* varied in color. 1535 *party colored,* in the Coverdale Bible; formed from *party* of different colors, variegated (about 1385, borrowed from Old French *parti* striped, past participle of *partir* to divide, PART) + *colored.*

particular *adj.* Before 1387 *particuler* distinct, partial, in Trevisa's translation of Higden's *Polychronicon;* later, private, personal (1442); borrowed from Old French *particuler,* learned borrowing from Late Latin, and borrowed directly from Late Latin *particulāris* of or concerning a part, from Latin *particula* particle; for suffix see -AR.

The spelling *particular,* after the Latin form, appeared in the 1500's. The extended meaning of precise, exacting, fastidious, is first recorded in the Duke of Wellington's *Dispatches* (1814).

—n. 1392 *particuler* body part; later, individual factor, feature or circumstance (probably before 1425); from the adjective.

—particularity *n.* 1528, detail, particular point; borrowed from Middle French *particularité,* from Late Latin *particulāritātem* (nominative *particulāritās*), from *particulāris* particular; for suffix see -ITY. The meaning of detailed quality, minuteness, is first recorded in 1638, and that of special carefulness, in 1671. **—particularize** *v.* 1588, formed from English *particular* + *-ize,* after Middle French *particulariser,* also formed as in English.

particulate *adj.* consisting of small, separate particles. 1871, formed from Latin *particula* PARTICLE + English *-ate*[1]. **—n.** particulate substance. 1960, from the adjective.

partisan *n.* 1555, one who takes part or sides with another, loyal adherent or supporter; borrowing of Middle French *partisan,* adaptation of dialectal Italian *partezan, partisano,* corresponding to Italian *partigiano* member of a party or faction, a partner, from *parte* part, from Latin *partem* (nominative *pars*) PART; compare the development of *courtesan.*

The meaning of a member of an irregular volunteer military force, a guerrilla, is first recorded in 1692. The name gained popularity during World War II in reference to such guerrilla groups in eastern Europe and the Balkans.

—adj. of or like a partisan. 1708, of or pertaining to guerrillas or to guerrilla warfare; from the noun. The meaning in politics "of or like a partisan in one's strong support of a person, party, or cause, often based on feeling rather than on reasoning," is first recorded in 1842.

partition *n.* About 1400 *partisoun* a logical distinction or division; 1410 *particioun* division into parts, apportionment; borrowed from Old French *particion,* learned borrowing from Latin *partītiōnem* (nominative *partītiō*) division or portion, from *partīre* to PART; for suffix see -TION. The meaning of something that separates is first recorded in 1465-66. **—v.** divide into parts. 1741, in Samuel Richardson's *Pamela;* from the noun.

partitive *n. Grammar.* word or phrase meaning a part of a collective whole. 1530, in Palsgrave's *Lesclarcissement,* from earlier *partitive,* adj. (before 1398, in Trevisa's translation of Bartholomew's *De Proprietatibus Rerum*); also *partytyf* (about 1450, in *Battlefield Grammar*); borrowed from Middle French *partitif,* and directly from Medieval Latin *partitivus,* from Latin *partīre* to PART; for suffix see -IVE.

partner *n.* About 1300 *partiner;* later *partnier* (about 1415), alteration (influenced by *part*) of *parciner* one that shares or has a part with another, sharer (about 1300), and *parcener* (before 1338); borrowed from Old French *parçener, parçonier,* from *parçon* portion or division, from Latin *partītiōnem* (nominative *partītiō*) portion, division; see PARTITION; for suffix see -ER[1]. **—partnership** *n.* 1576, formed from English *partner* + *-ship.*

partridge *n.* kind of game bird. Probably before 1300 *pertris,* in *Arthour and Merlin;* earlier, in a surname *Pertriz* (1176); about 1300 *partrich;* borrowed from Old French *pertris, pertriz, perdriz,* alteration of *perdis* (perhaps by influence of *-tris, -triz* feminine ending, from Latin *-trīx;* see -ESS) from Latin *perdīcem* (nominative *perdix*), from Greek *pérdīx* the Greek partridge, probably related to *pérdesthai* to break wind (so called from the whirring noise of the bird's wings). The alteration of earlier Old French *perdis* to *pertris* suggests influence of the Old French feminine ending *-(t)riz, -(t)ris* (modern French *-rice,* as in *actrice* actress), from Latin *-trix;* see -ESS.

The modern English spelling in *-dge* shows the usual change of final unaccented *-ch* also present in such a formation as *knowledge* from Middle English *cnowleche,* or *cabbage* from *cabache.*

parturient (pärtůr′ēənt) *adj.* bringing forth young. 1592, borrowed from Latin *parturientem* (nominative *parturiēns*), present participle of *parturīre* be in labor, be pregnant, formed from *parere* to bear; see PARTURITION; for suffix see -ENT.

parturition (pär′tůrish′ən) *n.* childbirth. 1646, borrowed from Latin *parturītiōnem* (nominative *parturītiō*) travail, from *parturīre* be in labor, desire to produce or give birth to, from *parere* produce, give birth to; see PARENT; for suffix see -TION.

party *n.* Probably before 1300 *partie* side, end, edge, division, in *Kyng Alisaunder;* also, an opposing force, in *Sir Tristrem;* about 1300, those on one side in a contest, participant, litigant; borrowed from Old French *partie* a part or party, from feminine past participle of *partir* divide; see PART.

The meaning of a gathering for social pleasure is first recorded in 1716, and that of a group doing something together in 1773; both borrowed from French *partie,* from Old French *partie.*

—v. Before 1639, to side with (now obsolete); later, to give or attend a party, have a good time (1922, in E.E. Cummings' *Letters*); from the noun.

parvenu (pär′vənü) *n.* one who has risen to a higher place than he is fit for, upstart. 1802, borrowing of

French *parvenu,* noun use of past participle of *parvenir* to arrive, from Latin *pervenīre* (*per-* through + *venīre* to COME). **—adj.** like or characteristic of a parvenu. 1828, in writings of John Stuart Mill; from the noun.

parvovirus (pär′vōvī′rəs) *n.* very small virus that affects various animals, especially dogs. 1965, formed from Latin *parvus* small (related to *paucī* few) + English *virus.*

paschal (pas′kəl) *adj.* of or having to do with Passover or Easter. Probably before 1425 *paschalle,* in a translation of Higden's *Polychronicon;* borrowed from Late Latin *paschālis;* later *pascal* (1442), borrowing of Middle French *pascal,* from Late Latin *paschālis,* from *pascha* Passover or Easter, from Greek *páscha* Passover, from Aramaic *pasḥā* pass over, emphatic form corresponding to Hebrew *pesaḥ,* from *pāsaḥ* to pass over; see PASSOVER; for suffix see -AL[1]. Middle English *paschalle* was probably also influenced in its formation by the earlier *Pasche* Easter (1122, in *Peterborough Chronicle*); borrowed from Old French *pasche* and Latin *pascha.* The spelling with *ch* became the established form in the 1600's.

pasha (pä′shə) *n.* former Turkish title of rank. 1646, borrowed from Turkish *paşa,* perhaps a variant of *başa,* from *baş* head, chief. The form with *b* was apparently the earlier, being the one first adopted in western languages, for example *bashaw* in English (1534) and in German *Bascha* before *Pascha.*

pass[1] *v.* move past, go by. Probably before 1200 *passen* to die, in *Ancrene Riwle;* also, to surpass (probably about 1200); later, proceed, go past, through or beyond (probably before 1300, in *Kyng Alisaunder* and *Arthour and Merlin*); borrowed from Old French *passer,* from Vulgar Latin **passāre* to step, walk, pass, from Latin *passus* (genitive *passūs*) step, PACE[1]. **—n.** act of passing, passage. About 1300 *pas* a journey, later *pase* (before 1400); also *passe* a going, passing, departure (probably before 1400); borrowed from Old French *pas,* from *passer* to pass, and directly from Latin *passus* a step; originally, a stretch, related to *passum,* past participle of *pandere* spread out; see EXPAND. Several senses of the noun are derived from English *pass,* v. The meaning of a written permission to leave or enter a place is first recorded in 1647, extended from the sense of permission or authorization to pass, in Spenser's *Prosopopoia* (1591). **—passable** *adj.* (1413, that can be passed; 1489, that can pass muster, tolerable) **—passkey** *n.* (about 1817) **—password** *n.* (about 1817)

pass[2] *n.* narrow path, especially through mountains. Probably before 1300 *pas* road, path, passageway, in *Arthour and Merlin;* later, a narrow strait (before 1350), and narrow and difficult path (before 1393, in Gower's *Confessio Amantis*); also *passe* road, path (about 1378, in a version of *Piers Plowman*); borrowed from Old French *pas* step, track, from Latin *passus* (genitive *passūs*) step, PACE[1].

passage *n.* Probably about 1225 *passage* a road, pathway, in *King Horn;* later, act or means of passing (about 1300); borrowed from Old French *passage,* from *passer* to go by, PASS[1], from Latin *passus* step; for suffix see -AGE. The specific meaning of a corridor or hall in a building is first recorded in English in Coryat's *Crudities* (1611). **—passageway** *n.* (1649, American English)

passé (pasā′) *adj.* past, out-of-date. 1775, past one's prime, a French word used in Madame d'Arblay's *The Early Diary of Frances Burney;* from Old French *passé,* past participle of *passer* to go by, PASS[1]. The sense of past or out-of-date is first recorded in English in 1886.

passel (pas′əl) *n. Informal.* group, pack. 1835, in A.B. Longstreet's *Georgia Scenes,* American English variant of PARCEL.

passenger *n.* 1337 *passajour* passenger ferry; also before 1338 *passager* traveler, in Mannyng's *Chronicle of England;* borrowed from Old French *passagëor,* noun use of *passagier, passager,* adj., passing, fleeting, traveling, from *passage* PASSAGE.

In late Middle English the sound represented by *n* was added before *-ger* in *passager* forming the more familiar form *passynger* (probably 1421), and as is also found in *harbinger* and *scavenger* (compare MESSENGER).

The meaning of a traveler in a vehicle or vessel is first recorded in English in Guylford's *Pilgrimage* (1511).

passerine (pas′ərin) *adj.* of or belonging to the perching birds. 1776, borrowed from Latin *passerīnus* of a sparrow, from *passer* sparrow, of uncertain origin; for suffix see -INE[1]. **—n.** perching bird. 1842, from the adjective.

passion *n.* Probably before 1200 *passiun* suffering or affliction, in *Ancrene Riwle;* later *passioun* (about 1280); borrowed from Old French *passïon,* learned borrowing from Late Latin, and borrowed directly from Late Latin *passiōnem* (nominative *passiō*) suffering, enduring, from *pass-,* stem of Latin *patī* to suffer, endure; see PATIENT; for suffix see -ION.

According to the OED Latin *passiō* was chiefly a word of Christian theology, referring especially to the sufferings of Christ, and was also the earliest meaning of Old French *passïon* and Middle English *passium, passioun.* The extended sense of a strong emotion or desire is first recorded before 1250, but that of a strong sexual love or emotion is not recorded until 1588, in Shakespeare's *Titus Andronicus.* The generalized meaning of a strong liking, enthusiasm (as in *a passion for horses*) is first recorded in 1638.

—passionate *adj.* Before 1420 *passionat* angry, furious, in Lydgate's *Troy Book;* also probably before 1425 *passionate* emotional; borrowed from Medieval Latin *passionatus* affected with passion, from Latin *passiō* (genitive *passiōnis*) passion; for suffix see -ATE[1]. **—passion play** (1870)

passive *adj.* About 1385 *passive* producing upset, in relation to disease, in Usk's *The Testament of Love;* later, not active, capable of being acted upon (1398, in Trevisa's translation of Bartholomew's *De Proprietatibus Rerum*); borrowed from Latin *passīvus;* also *passif* having a passive verb form in grammar (1397, in *Prologue* to the Wycliffe Bible), borrowed from Old French *passif,* from Latin *passīvus* capable of feeling or suffering, from *pass-,* stem of *patī* to suffer; see PATIENT; for suffix see -IVE. **—passivity** *n.* quality or condition of being passive. 1659, in Henry A. More's *The Immortality of the Soul;* formed in English from Latin *passīvus* passive + English *-ity.*

Passover *n.* Jewish holiday commemorating the freeing of the Israelites from slavery in Egypt. 1530, in the Tyndale Bible; formed from the verbal phrase *pass over,* a translation of Hebrew *pesaḥ* (see PASCHAL), in reference to the Biblical account, in Exodus 12:23,27, of the Lord "passing over" the houses of the Israelites in Egypt when He killed the first-born of the Egyptians.

Modern English *Passover* replaced Middle English

pasche (1122, in *Peterborough Chronicle*), and *paske* (probably about 1200, in *The Ormulum*); borrowed from Old French *pasche, pasque,* from Latin *pascha,* a translation of Hebrew *pesaḥ.*

passport *n.* Probably about 1500 *pase-porte* authorization to pass through a port or to leave or enter a country; borrowed from Middle French *passeport* (*passe,* imperative of Old French *passer* to pass, go by + *port* harbor, port, passage).

past *adj.* Before 1325 *past* gone by, ended, over, in *Cursor Mundi;* later *passed* (about 1380, in Chaucer's translation of Boethius' *De Consolatione Philosophiae*); from past participle of *passen* go by; see PASS[1]. The derivation corresponds to similar words in other languages, such as French *passé* and Italian *passato.* The meaning in grammar of indicating time gone by, or former action or state, is first recorded in Palsgrave's *Lesclarcissement* (1530). **—n.** the time gone by. Before 1500 *passid,* from the adjective.

pasta (päs′tä) *n.* any of various dough mixtures, such as noodles, macaroni, or spaghetti. 1874, an Italian word used in a book about Rome, from Late Latin *pasta* pastry cake; see PASTE[1].

paste[1] *n.* doughlike mixture. About 1303, moistened flour, dough, in Mannyng's *Handlyng Synne;* earlier, in a surname *Paste* (1166); borrowing of Old French *paste,* and directly from Late Latin *pasta* pastry cake, paste, from Greek *pastá* barley porridge (probably originally a salted mess of food), from neuter plural of *pastós,* adj., sprinkled, salted, from *pássein* to sprinkle (earlier **patye-*), cognate with Latin *quatiō* I shake, *quatere* to shake, from Indo-European **kwēt-/kwət-* (Pok.632).

The meaning of a mixture used as glue is first recorded in English in *Promptorium Parvulorum* (1440). **—v.** 1561-62, to stick with paste; earlier *pasten* to make a paste of something (probably before 1425); from the noun. **—pasteboard** *n.* (1548-49) **—pasty** *adj.* 1659, like or resembling paste, made of paste; possibly later, of pale complexion (1864); formed from English *paste*[1] + *-y*[1].

paste[2] *v. Slang.* hit hard, beat, thrash. 1846, probably alteration of BASTE[3] beat.

pastel *n.* 1662, dry paste of ground pigments used in making crayons; also, a colored crayon, in Evelyn's writings; borrowed from French *pastel* a colored crayon, from Italian *pastello* a pastel, literally, material reduced to a paste, from Late Latin *pastellus* dye obtained from the woad plant, diminutive form of *pasta* PASTE[1]; so called because the plant's leaves were made into a paste in producing the dye.

The meaning of a drawing made with pastel crayons is first recorded in Thackeray's *The Newcomes* (1855); the meaning of a pale or light color, especially of dress material is first recorded in 1899.
—adj. of a pale or light color. 1884, from the noun.

pastern *n.* part of a horse's foot between the fetlock and the hoof. 1284 *pastron* shackle or fetter attached to the pastern of a grazing horse; later, the pastern of a horse (before 1450); borrowed from Old French *pasturon,* diminutive of *pasture* pastern, tether, shackle for a horse on pasture, altered from **pastoire* (compare Italian *pastoia* tether), from Vulgar Latin **pāstōria,* noun use of the feminine of Latin *pāstōrius* of herdsmen, from *pāstor* shepherd, PASTOR. The shift in spelling to *pastern* (with metathesis of *r* and the originally following vowel) occurred in the 1500's.

pasteurize *v.* heat (milk, etc.) to destroy harmful bacteria. 1881, borrowed from French *pasteuriser,* formed in allusion to the name of the French chemist and bacteriologist Louis *Pasteur,* 1822-1895, who invented the process of using heat to destroy harmful bacteria or stop fermentation; for suffix see -IZE. **—pasteurization** *n.* 1885, formed from English *pasteurize* + *-ation.*

pastiche (pastēsh′) *n.* artistic, musical, or literary work made up of portions of various works. 1878, in Swinburne's *Poems and Ballads;* borrowing of French *pastiche,* from Italian *pasticcio* an invitation, medley; also, pastry cake, from Vulgar Latin **pastīcium* composed of paste, from Late Latin *pasta* paste, pastry cake; see PASTE[1]. **—v.** to form a pastiche. 1957, from the noun.

pastille (pastēl′) *n.* flavored or medicated lozenge. Before 1648, borrowing of French *pastille,* from Spanish *pastilla* perfume pellet, and from Italian *pastillo,* both forms from Latin *pastillus* little loaf or wafer, round lozenge, diminutive of *pānis* bread (earlier **pastnis*); see FOOD.

Another meaning "small roll of aromatic paste burned as a disinfectant or incense" appeared in 1658.

pastime *n.* About 1489 *passe tyme* recreation or diversion, in Caxton's translation of *Blanchardyn and Eglantine;* replacement of Middle English *pastaunce* (before 1500); formed in English after Middle French *passetemps, passetamps, passetans* (*passer* to pass + *temps* time).

pastor *n.* Before 1376 *pastour* shepherd, in *Piers Plowman;* earlier, in a surname *Pastur* (1242); also *pastor* spiritual guide, shepherd of souls, pastor, bishop (1387, in Trevisa's translation of Higden's *Polychronicon*); borrowed from Old French *pastur, pastor* herdsman, shepherd, and directly from Latin *pāstōrem* (nominative *pāstor*) shepherd, from *pāscere* to feed, lead to pasture, graze; see FOOD; for suffix see -OR[2]. **—pastoral** *adj.* of shepherds or country life. Probably before 1425 *pastoralle,* in a translation of Higden's *Polychronicon;* borrowed from Old French *pastoral,* learned borrowing from Latin *pāstōrālis,* from *pāstor* shepherd; for suffix see -AL[1].

pastrami (pəsträ′mē) *n.* well-seasoned smoked beef. 1940, in Groucho Marx's letters, American English, borrowed from Yiddish *pastrame,* from Rumanian *pastrámă,* probably from modern Greek *pastṓnō* I salt, from Classical Greek *pastós* sprinkled with salt, salted, from *pássein* to sprinkle; see PASTE[1]. The English spelling in *-mi* was probably influenced by *salami.* Compare also *salami* for semantic development.

It has also been suggested that the Rumanian word came from dialectal Turkish *pastırma,* variant of *basdırma* dried meat, from *basmak* to press.

pastry *n.* 1442 *pastre;* 1449 *pastree, pastry-* (as in *pastre bowrde*) food made of paste or dough, formed from Middle English *paste*[1] + *-re, -ry;* probably influenced by Old French *pastaierie* pastry, from *pastoier* pastry cook, from *paste* PASTE[1], and in some instances probably borrowed from Medieval Latin *pasteria* pastry from Latin *pasta* PASTE[1].

pasture *n.* Probably before 1300 Anglo-Latin *pastura* land on which animals graze, in *Kyng Alisaunder;* also in a place name *Oxpasture* (before 1300); borrowed from Old French *pasture* grass eaten by cattle, and directly from Late Latin *pāstūra* a feeding, grazing from Latin *pāst-*, past participle stem of *pāscere* to feed, graze; see FOOD; for suffix see -URE. —**v.** put (cattle, etc.) out to pasture. Before 1393 *pasturen* to graze, forage, in Gower's *Confessio Amantis;* also, as the gerund *pasturyng* (about 1390); borrowed from Old French *pasturer,* from *pasture,* n., and directly from Medieval Latin *pasturare,* from Late Latin *pāstūra* pasture. —**pasturage** *n.* Before 1533, piece of grazing land, pasture; borrowed from Middle French *pasturage,* from *pasturer* to pasture; for suffix see -AGE.

pasty *n.* pie filled with meat, game, fish, etc. Before 1300 *pastei;* earlier, as a surname *Pastey* (1269); probably before 1400 *pasty;* borrowed from Old French *paste,* earlier *pastée,* from Gallo-Romance **pastāta* meat dish wrapped in pastry.

pat[1] *n.* light stroke or tap. About 1400, a blow, stroke; perhaps imitative of the sound made by patting. The meaning of a light stroke or tap with the hand is first recorded about 1804. An earlier meaning of that which is formed by patting, small mass (as of butter), is first recorded in 1754. The OED suggests that the noun may have been re-formed from the verb in the 1600's. —**v.** 1567, to strike, hit, throw; from the noun. The meaning of tap or strike lightly, is first recorded in Byron's *Phoebe* (1714, though found in an earlier use by Dryden in 1668).

pat[2] *adv.* aptly, readily, promptly. 1578, perhaps a special use of *pat*[1], in the sense of hitting the mark, being successful in one's object or aim, and thus "opportunely" so as to be ready for any occasion. —**adj.** apt. 1638, from the adverb.

patch *n.* Before 1382 *patche* piece of cloth, etc.; 1384 *pacche* piece of material used to mend a hole or tear, in the Wycliffe Bible; perhaps a variant of *pece, pieche* PIECE. —**v.** put patches on, mend. 1447 *pacchen,* from the noun. —**patchwork** *n.* (before 1692) —**patchy** *adj.* 1798, formed from English *patch,* n. + *-y*[1].

pate (pāt) *n.* the head. Before 1325; earlier, as a surname *Pate* (1197); of uncertain origin (perhaps borrowed as a shortened form of Old French *patene* or Medieval Latin *patena, patina* pan, dish; compare PATEN). The transferred meaning of brains, intellect, is first recorded in Shakespeare's *The Tempest* (1610).

pâté (pätā′) *n.* paste of finely chopped meat, liver, etc. 1706, in Kersey's edition of Phillips' *Dictionary;* borrowing of French *pâté,* from Old French *paste;* earlier *pastée,* from *paste* PASTE[1].

patella (pətel′ə) *n.* kneecap. 1671, structure in the form of a shallow pan; later, kneecap (1693); borrowed from Latin *patella* pan, kneecap, diminutive of *patina* pan; see PATEN.

paten (pat′ən) *n.* plate used for the bread at the Eucharist or Mass. About 1300 *pateyn,* in *Havelok the Dane;* later *paten* (probably about 1350); borrowed from Old French *patene,* learned borrowing from Medieval Latin, and borrowed directly from Medieval Latin *patena, patina,* from Latin, pan or dish, from Greek *patánē* flat dish, probably assimilated from **petánā,* related to *petannýnai* spread out; see FATHOM.

patent *n.* Before 1376 *patent* a papal indulgence, pardon, in *Piers Plowman;* later *patente* a document granting a right, title, property, etc., in the general prologue to Chaucer's *Canterbury Tales* (about 1387-95); shortened from *lettre patent;* borrowed from Old French *patente,* adj., in *lettre patente* open letter; see adjective. Though the noun appears before the adjective in the record of English, this is probably only a matter of accident.

The extended and now ordinary sense "license to make or sell an article to the exclusion of others, a government grant protecting someone's right to an invention, etc.," is first recorded about 1588, though as early as 1378 the sense of a license is recorded, also in a version of *Piers Plowman.* Used attributively, the noun appeared in the term *patent leather* (made by a process formerly patented) in 1829 in American English. *Patent medicine* (a proprietary medicine) is first attested in 1770, also in American English.

—**adj.** Before 1387 *patent,* in *lettre patent* letter granting a right, title, etc., literally, open letter or document, in Trevisa's translation of Higden's *Polychronicon;* borrowed from Old French *lettres patentes;* also, in Medieval Latin *(litterae) patentes,* both from Latin *patentem* (nominative *patēns*) open, lying open, present participle of *patēre* lie open, be open (see FATHOM); for suffix see -ENT. The idea of lie flat and open is said to be significant because the original documents were written on open sheets of parchment, not closed or folded. The extended sense "wide open or unconfined" is first recorded before 1398, and the current meaning "open to view, clear, plain, evident, manifest" (as in *a patent fact or situation, a patent lie or insult*) is attested by 1508. The meaning "protected or covered by a patent" (as in *a patent right*) is found as early as 1707. —**v.** 1675, to obtain a patent right to land, American English; from the adjective. The sense "to obtain a patent for (an invention)" is first recorded in 1822 (or is perhaps implied in earlier *patentee,* in the sense of one who has patented some new device, 1691). —**patentee** *n.* 1442, one who holds property by letters patent; formed from Middle English *patente* patent + *-ee.* The sense of a patent holder for a new device is cited under the verb.

paternal *adj.* fatherly. About 1433 *paternall;* borrowed from Old French *paternal* of a father, and perhaps directly from Medieval Latin *paternalis,* from Latin *paternus* of a father, from *pater* FATHER; for suffix see -AL[1].

The meaning of related through a father or on the father's side, is first recorded in 1611, though the meaning is found in the adverb *paternally* by 1603.

—**paternalism** *n.* paternal management. 1881, American English; formed from *paternal* + *ism.* —**paternalistic** *adj.* Before 1890, from English *paternalism,* formed after such pairs as *material, materialistic.*

paternity *n.* fatherhood. Before 1449 *peternytee,* in Lydgate's writings; earlier *paternyte* used as a term of address to a bishop; borrowed from Middle French *paternité,* learned borrowing from Late Latin *paternitātem* (nominative *paternitās*) fatherly care, fatherhood, from Latin *paternus* of a father, from *pater* FATHER; for suffix see -ITY.

The meaning of paternal origin or descent (as in *a child's paternity*) is first recorded in Gladstone's *Juventus Mundi* (1868).

paternoster (pā′tərnos′tər) *n.* the Lord's Prayer, especially in Latin. Old English (before 900) *Pater Noster,* borrowing from Latin *pater noster* our father (from the first two words of the Lord's Prayer in Latin, *pater* FATHER and *noster* our, ours, from *nōs* we; see US).

The later form *paternoster* is first recorded about 1175, and the later meaning of a rosary or set of rosary beads, is found about 1250. From this sense in English, German, and other languages meanings developed that were various applications especially to tools (such as a water wheel, fishing line, etc.) that resembled a rosary.

path *n.* Old English *path* (about 725, in a version of *Exodus,* spelled with *a* instead of expected *æ*, by analogy with plural *pathas*); also *pæth* in compound *ānpæth* narrow path, literally, one-by-one path (about 725, in *Beowulf*); cognate with Old Frisian *path* path, Middle Low German and Middle Dutch *pat, pad* (modern Dutch *pad*), and Old High German *phad, pfad* (modern German *Pfad*).

This word has a unique history in that the Proto-Germanic ancestor (**patha-*) was borrowed relatively late, in the course of the wanderings of the Germanic people, from an Iranian language (compare Avestan *pathō,* genitive of *pantå,* cognate with Sanskrit *pathás,* genitive of *pánthās*); cognate also with Greek *pátos* path, Latin *pōns* (genitive *pontis*) bridge, and Greek *póntos* sea (originally, a way from one land to another), from Indo-European **pent-/pont-* go; arrive at (Pok. 808).

—**pathway** *n.* (before 1536)

-path a combining form associated with *-pathy:* **1** one suffering from the disorder named, as in *psychopath.* **2** a practitioner of the medical system named, as in *osteopath.* The first meaning is adapted from Greek *-pathḗs* feeling, suffering; the second is a back formation from *-pathy.*

pathetic *adj.* 1598 *pathetique* moving, stirring, affecting, in Marston's *The Scourge of Villainy;* shortened form of earlier *pathetical* (1573); borrowed from Middle French *pathétique,* from Late Latin *pathēticus,* from Greek *pathētikós* sensitive, from *pathētós* liable to suffer, from *path-,* stem of *páschein* to suffer; see PATHOS; for suffix see -IC.

Both the spelling *pathetic* and the meaning of arousing pity, pitiful are first recorded in 1737, in Pope's writings.

pathogen (path′ǝjǝn) *n.* microorganism or other agent that produces disease. 1880, back formation from *pathogenic.* —**pathogenic** (path′ǝjen′ik) *adj.* producing disease. 1852, borrowed from French *pathogénique,* from Greek *páthos* disease + French *-génique* -genic, producing.

pathology *n.* study of diseases. 1611, in Cotgrave's *Dictionary,* borrowed from French *pathologie,* from New Latin *pathologia* (from Greek *páthos* suffering; see PATHOS + *-logíā* -logy). —**pathological** *adj.* (1688, in Boyle's writings)

pathos (pā′thos) *n.* quality that arouses pity or sadness. 1668, in Dryden's *Essays;* borrowed from Greek *páthos* suffering, feeling, emotion, related to *páschein* to suffer, and *pénthos* grief or sorrow. The Greek forms are cognate with Old Irish *cēssaim, cēssim* I suffer, Lithuanian *kęsti* and Latvian *ciest* to suffer, from Indo-European **kwenth-/kwn̥th-* (Pok.641).

-pathy a combining form meaning: **1** feeling, suffering, emotion, as in *sympathy, antipathy.* **2** disorder, disease, as in *neuropathy, psychopathy.* **3** a system of treatment of disease, as in *homeopathy, osteopathy.* Borrowed from Greek *-pátheia* act or quality of suffering, feeling, from *patheîn* feel, suffer, from *páthos* suffering, feeling; see PATHOS.

patient *adj.* About 1350 *pacient* enduring calmly, bearing (pain, etc.); later, *patient* (before 1400); probably influenced in development by earlier *patience,* but also borrowed from Old French *pacient,* adj., learned borrowing from Latin, and later borrowed directly from Latin *patientem* (nominative *patiēns*), present participle of *patī* to suffer or endure, possibly formed from a lost adjective **patos* hurt, damaged (an Indo-European participle **pǝtós*); for suffix see -ENT. The Latin verb is perhaps cognate with Greek *pêma* suffering, and Sanskrit *pāmán-* kind of skin disease, from Indo-European **pē-/pǝ-* harm (Pok.792). —**n.** About 1385 *pacyent* suffering or sick person under medical treatment, in Chaucer's *Troilus and Criseyde;* later *patient* (about 1400); borrowed from Old French *pacïent,* n. —**patience** *n.* Probably before 1200 *patience* calm endurance, in *Ancrene Riwle;* also later *pacience* (before 1250); borrowed from Old French *patience, pacience,* and directly from Latin *patientia,* from *patiēns,* present participle; for suffix see -ENCE.

patina (pat′ǝnǝ) *n.* film or coloring on the surface of old bronze, wood, etc. 1748, in Walpole's *Letters,* borrowing of Italian *patina,* perhaps from Latin *patina* dish, pan (see PATEN); so called from the incrustation on ancient dishes. The figurative sense of a refinement in manners or a degree of social and cultural sophistication, is first recorded in 1933, in Harold Nicolson's *Diary.*

patio (pat′ēō *or* pä′tēō) *n.* 1828, in Washington Irving's *Life and Letters,* American English; borrowed from Spanish *patio* inner court or yard open to the sky, probably from Old Provençal *patu, pati* untilled land, place for communal pasture, from Latin *pactum* agreement, PACT. The sense of a paved terrace next to a building is first recorded in Schulberg's *What Makes Sammy Run?* (1941).

patois (pat′wä) *n.* local dialect. 1643, in Sir Thomas Browne's *Religio Medici;* borrowing of French *patois* a native or local speech in a particular area, from Old French *patoier* handle clumsily, from *pate* paw, from Vulgar Latin **patta,* perhaps of imitative origin.

patri- a combining form used especially in the social sciences to coin terms describing relationships or kinships with the father or the paternal line, as in *patricentric* father-centered (1949), *patrilineal* (1904), *patrilocal* located in the home of the husband's family (1906). Borrowed from Latin *patri-,* abstracted from such forms as *patrimōnium* patrimony, from *pater* (genitive *patris*) father; contrasted with MATRI-.

patrial *adj.* of one's fatherland or native country. 1629, borrowed from French *patrial* (now obsolete), from Latin *patria* fatherland, from *pater* FATHER; for suffix see -AL¹. A new meaning of having the status of a native or naturalized citizen is first recorded in 1971 in Great Britain. —**n.** *British.* person having the status of a native or naturalized citizen. 1971, probably from the adjective.

patriarch *n.* father who is the head of a family or tribe. Probably before 1200 *patriarche* one of the Old Testament fathers, in *Ancrene Riwle;* later *patriark* high-ranking bishop (about 1300); borrowed from Old French *patriarche,* and directly from Late Latin *patriarcha,* from Greek *patriárchēs* (*patriá* family, clan, from *patḗr* FATHER + *árchein* to rule; see ARCH-). —**patriarchal** *adj.* of a patriarch. About 1450 *patriarcal* of an ecclesiastical patriarch; formed from Middle English *patriarche* + *-al*¹, and borrowed from Late

Latin *patriarchālis,* from *patriarcha* patriarch; for suffix see -AL[1]. **—patriarchy** *n.* 1561, the see of an ecclesiastical patriarch; later, patriarchal form of social organization (1632, in William Lithgow's *Travels*); borrowed from Late Greek *patriarchíā* the office of a patriarch, from Greek *patriárchēs* patriarch; for suffix see -Y[3].

patrician *n.* member of the nobility of ancient Rome. Probably before 1425 *patricion,* in a translation of Higden's *Polychronicon;* borrowed through Middle French *patricien,* from Latin *patricius* noble, of the senators, from *patrēs* Roman senators, fathers, plural of *pater* FATHER; for suffix see -AN. The Latin *patrēs* was a shortening of *patrēs cōnscrīpti,* a usual title of address of the senate of ancient Rome.

The sense of any person of noble birth or high social rank is first recorded in English in 1631, probably from the earlier use in reference to a hereditary nobleman of some Italian city-states, such as Genoa and Venice (1611), and of Germany (1617), or perhaps from the same meaning in adjective use.

—adj. of the patricians. 1615, noble, aristocratic; from the noun.

patricide[1] *n.* person who kills his father. 1593, borrowed probably through Middle French *patricide,* from Medieval Latin *patricida,* from Latin *pater* FATHER + *-cīda* -cide[1], killer. Medieval Latin *patricida* replaced the classical Latin *parricīda* parricide[1] as a more specific word for a father killer.

patricide[2] *n.* act of killing one's own father. 1625, borrowed from Late Latin *patricīdium,* from Latin *pater* FATHER + *-cīdium* -cide[2], a killing. Late Latin *patricīdium* replaced the classical Latin *parricīdium* parricide[2] as a more specific word for the killing of one's father.

patrimony *n.* property inherited from one's father or ancestors. 1340 *patremoyne* the property of the Church, the spiritual legacy of Christ to the Church, in *Ayenbite of Inwyt;* later *patrimoyne* inherited property (probably about 1384), and *patrimony* (probably before 1425, in a translation of Higden's *Polychronicon*), borrowed from Old French *patrimoine,* learned borrowing from Latin, and later borrowed directly from Latin *patrimōnium* a paternal estate or inheritance (*pater,* genitive *patris* FATHER + *-mōnium* suffix signifying action, state, condition); compare MATRIMONY. **—patrimonial** *adj.* of patrimony, hereditary. 1530, in Palsgrave's *Lesclarcissement;* borrowed from Middle French *patrimonial,* and directly from Late Latin *patrimōniālis,* from Latin *patrimōnium* patrimony; for suffix see -AL[1].

patriot *n.* 1596, fellow countryman; also 1605, person who loyally supports his country, in Ben Jonson's *Volpone;* borrowed from French *patriote,* and directly from Late Latin *patriōta,* from Greek *patriṓtēs* fellow countryman, from *patriá* fatherland, from *patḗr* (genitive *patrós*) FATHER, with the ending *-ṓtēs* expressing a state or condition as of one's origin. **—patriotic** *adj.* 1653, of one's country, in a translation of the works of Rabelais; borrowed from French *patriotique,* from Latin; later, loyally supporting one's country (1757), perhaps a shortened form of *patriotical* (1691), but more likely borrowed from Late Latin *patriōticus,* from Greek *patriōtikós* pertaining to descent or race, or to a fellow countryman, from *patriṓtēs* fellow countryman; for suffix see -IC. **—patriotism** *n.* 1726, in Bailey's *Dictionary,* formed from English *patriot* + *-ism.* French *patriotisme* is not attested before 1750 and may have been formed independently in French or borrowed from English.

patrol *n.* 1664, act of going about on watch to guard a garrison, camp, or (later) a city, against intrusion or disorder, in Butler's *Hudibras;* borrowed from French *patrouille* a night watch of soldiers, from *patrouiller* go the rounds to watch or guard, originally, paddle in mud, paw about in water, from Old French *patouiller,* variant of *patouiller, patoiller* paddle or dabble in water, probably from *pate* paw or foot, from Vulgar Latin **patta,* perhaps imitative of the sound made by a paw. It has also been suggested that Old French *pate* may have developed from Frankish, by comparison with German *Patsche* an instrument for striking the hand, *patsch* in *patsch-fuss* a web foot, *patzen* to strike, pat.

The semantic connection between moving about in water or mud and the military sense of move about on watch possibly developed as a descriptive term of the action of patrolling, that is tramping about in mire and muck. The meaning of a soldier or group of soldiers that go about on patrol is first recorded in English in 1670.

—v. 1691, possibly, in part, from the verb in English, and, in part, borrowed from French *patrouiller.* **—patrol car** (1931) **—patrolman** *n.* 1867, American English, one who patrols; later, a policeman patrolling a district (1879).

patron *n.* About 1300 *patron, patroun* benefactor, bestower of a church living or benefice; borrowed from Old French *patron,* learned borrowing from Medieval Latin, and borrowed directly from Medieval Latin *patronus* patron saint, bestower of a church living, lord or master, model or pattern to be followed, from Latin *patrōnus* defender, protector, advocate, from *pater* (genitive *patris*) FATHER. Doublet of PATROON.

The meaning of one who supports or frequents a store, shop, etc., a regular customer, is first recorded in Ben Jonson's *Volpone* (1605).

—patronage *n.* 1395, right to bestow a church living, in Wycliffe's writings; borrowed from Old French *patronage,* from *patron* patron, and borrowed directly from Medieval Latin *patronagium* advowson (right in England to select a person to be appointed to a vacant church), from *patronus;* for suffix see -AGE. The meaning of support from a patron is first recorded in 1553, and the extended sense of power to give jobs or favors in 1769. The meaning of regular business given by customers is first recorded in 1804. **—patronize** *v.* 1589, act as a patron toward; borrowed from Middle French *patroniser,* from Medieval Latin *patronizare,* from Latin *patrōnus* patron; for suffix see -IZE. The meaning of treat in a condescending way is first recorded in 1797, and that of give regular business to in 1801.

patronymic (pat′rənim′ik) *n.* name derived from that of a father or ancestor. 1612, borrowed from Late Latin *patrōnymicum,* from neuter of *patrōnymicus* derived from a father's name, from Greek *patrōnymikós* pertaining to one's father's name, from *patrṓnymos* named from the father (*patḗr,* genitive *patrós* FATHER + *ónyma* NAME).

patroon (pətrün′) *n.* landowner with certain privileges under the former Dutch governments of New York and New Jersey. 1744, American English; borrowing of Dutch *patroon,* from French *patron* master or patron, from Old French; see the doublet PATRON; for ending see -OON.

patsy (pat′sē) *n. Slang.* person who is an easy object of ridicule, deception, etc., dupe. 1903, American English, of uncertain origin (sometimes suggested as a possible alteration of Italian *pazzo* madman, or dialectal southern Italian *paccio* fool).

patter[1] *v.* make quick taps. 1611, in Cotgrave's *Dictionary,* frequentative form of PAT[1], v.; for suffix see -ER[4]. **—n.** sound of quick taps. 1844, from the verb.

patter[2] *v.* talk rapidly and easily. Probably about 1395 *patren* to patter, (especially) to mumble prayers rapidly, in a version of *Piers Plowman;* also *pateren* (about 1400); developed from earlier *pater* (probably about 1300); shortened form of PATERNOSTER, in reference apparently to the rapid, mechanical way in which the Lord's Prayer and others were repeated in church services. **—n.** 1758, jargon or lingo; later, rapid and easy talk (1858); from the verb.

pattern *n.* 1324 *patron* outline, plan, model or pattern; later, model of behavior or appearance (before 1420); borrowed from Old French *patron,* learned borrowing from Medieval Latin, and borrowed directly from Medieval Latin *patronus* PATRON. The extended meaning of decorative or artistic design, as for china, carpets, wallpaper, etc., is first recorded in English in 1582.

The transfer of sense from "patron" to "model, pattern" developed from the idea of a patron as a model to be imitated; in fact, *pattern* was originally used to denote a human model. *Pattern* and *patron* were generally differentiated in form and sense in the 1700's. **—v.** 1581, to design, plan, in Sidney's *Apology for Poetry;* later, make according to a pattern (1599, in Ben Jonson's *Cynthia's Revels*); from the noun.

patty *n.* small flat cake of chopped food, etc. 1694, in *patti-pan* something baked in a small pan, small pasty or pâté; borrowed from French *pâté* PÂTÉ.

paucity (pô′sətē) *n.* fewness, scantiness. 1392 *paucete* paucity or thinness; later *paucite* (probably before 1425); borrowed from Old French *paucité,* and directly from Latin *paucitātem* (nominative *paucitās*), from *paucus* little; see FEW; for suffix see -ITY.

paunch *n.* 1373 *pawnce* belly or abdomen; earlier in a surname *Panzeuot* (1186); also *paunche* (about 1378); borrowed from Old French *pance, panche,* from Latin *panticem* (nominative *pantex*) belly, bowels, possibly related to *pānus* swelling (earlier **pancnos*), from Indo-European **pank-* to swell (Pok.789). **—paunchy** *adj.* big-bellied. 1598, in Florio's *A World of Words;* formed from English *paunch* + *-y*[1].

pauper *n.* 1516, impoverished person, beggar; borrowing of Latin *pauper* poor, from pre-Latin **pavo-pars* getting little (*pau-,* root of *paucus* little; and *parere* get, produce); see the doublet POOR.

The use of *pauper* in English originated in the Latin legal phrase *in fōrmā pauperis* in the form or character of a pauper (that is, allowed on account of poverty to sue or defend in a law court without paying legal fees).

pause *n.* About 1426, a short stop or rest; borrowed from Middle French *pause,* learned borrowing from Latin, and borrowed directly from Latin *pausa* a halt, stop, cessation, from Greek *paûsis,* from *paúein* to stop or cease, of unknown origin.

The phrase *to give pause,* meaning to cause to stop or hesitate, is first recorded in Shakespeare's *Hamlet* (1602).

—v. 1440 *pawson* make a pause, stop, hold back, in *Promptorium Parvulorum;* also *pausen* (about 1450); adopted in part from the noun, and in part borrowed from Middle French *pauser,* from Late Latin *pausāre* to stop, cease, from Latin *pausa* a stop, pause.

pave *v.* About 1325 *paven* cover (a street, room, etc.) with stones, tiles, or other material; borrowed from Old French *paver,* from Latin *pavīre* to beat, tread down, of uncertain origin. It is also possible that in some instances *pave,* v., is a back formation from earlier *pavement.*

The figurative meaning of make smooth or easy, prepare (as in *pave the way*) is first recorded before 1585. **—pavement** *n.* About 1250, paved surface of a street, etc.; borrowed from Old French *pavement, paviment,* and directly from Latin *pavīmentum* beaten floor, from *pavīre* to beat; for suffix see -MENT.

pavilion *n.* light building, usually one somewhat open. Probably before 1200 *pavilun* large, elaborate tent or booth; later *paviloun* (probably before 1300); borrowed from Old French *paveillon, pavilloun, pavilun,* from Latin *pāpiliōnem* (nominative *pāpiliō*) butterfly, tent (so called from the resemblance of a tent to a butterfly with outstretched wings). Latin *pāpiliō* is cognate with Old Prussian *penpalo* quail, and Lithuanian *píepala* quail. These are intensive, reduplicated forms from the Indo-European root **pel-/pol-* (Pok.801) found in Greek *pállein* to shake, swing. Cognates are also found in Germanic in Old Icelandic *fīfrildi* butterfly, Old High German *vīvaltra* (modern German *Falter*), Middle Dutch *vīveltre,* Dutch *vijfwouter,* Old Saxon *fifoldara,* and Old English *fīfealde* butterfly (which did not survive), from Proto-Germanic **fifalđrōn* **—v.** shelter in a pavilion. Probably before 1300 *paveillounen* to shelter in tents, in *Kyng Alisaunder;* from the noun.

paw *n.* Probably before 1300 *powe* foot of an animal having claws, in *Arthour and Merlin;* later *pawe* (before 1350); borrowed from Old French *powe, poe,* from Gallo-Romance **pauta,* the source of Provençal *pauta* paw, Catalan *pota,* Galician *po(u)ta.* The Gallo-Romance word is usually referred to a pre-Celtic form that was also the source of Middle Low German *pōte* paw (modern German *Pfote*), and Middle Dutch *pote* (modern Dutch *poot*).

Paw meaning the hand is first recorded before 1450 in the sense of a forceful or brutal hand, and in the humorous sense of a clumsy or awkward hand, in Chapman's comedy *All Fools* (1605).

—v. 1604, use the hands roughly, awkwardly, or rudely; from the noun. The meaning of strike or scrape with the paws or feet, first occurs in 1611, in the King James Bible. An isolated instance of this verb is found in Middle English *pawen,* probably meaning touch or strike something with the paw (probably 1404).

pawl *n.* bar to prevent movement backward or to impart motion. 1626, bar to prevent the capstan of a ship from turning back, in Captain John Smith's works; probably borrowed from Dutch *pal* pawl, or French *pal* stake, of uncertain origin (usually compared with Latin *pālus* stake).

pawn[1] *n.* something left as security. 1496 *paun,* borrowed from Middle French *pan, pant* pledge or security, from a Frankish word cognate with Old Frisian *pand* pledge or security, Old Saxon and Middle Dutch *pant,* and Old High German *pfant* (modern German *Pfand*), of unknown origin. **—v.** leave (something) as security. 1567, from the noun. **—pawnbroker** *n.* (1687) **—pawnshop** *n.* (1849)

pawn[2] *n.* chess piece of lowest value. About 1369 *poun,* in Chaucer's *Book of the Duchesse;* later *paun* (about 1400), and *pawne* (1474, in Caxton's *The Game and Play of Chess*); borrowed through Anglo-French *poun,* Old French *pëon, päon, pon,* from Medieval Latin *pedonem* foot soldier, from Late Latin *pedōnem* flat-footed person, from Latin *pēs* (genitive *pedis*) FOOT. Doublet of PEON.

pay *v.* Probably before 1200 *paien* to please, satisfy, put money down, in *Ancrene Riwle;* later, recompense, requite, appease (probably before 1300); borrowed from Old French *paiier,* from Latin *pācāre* to appease, pacify or satisfy, especially a creditor, from *pāx* (genitive *pācis*) PEACE.

The meaning in Latin of pacify or satisfy developed through Medieval Latin into that of pay a creditor, and so to pay, generally, in the Romance languages (Old French *paiier,* Provençal, Spanish, Portuguese *pagar,* Italian *pagare,* etc.). In some of these languages the verb still has both senses; but in French and in English the sense of satisfy or please has become obsolete.

—n. About 1300 *pay* satisfaction, liking, reward, deserts; later, payment, compensation, wages (probably about 1380); borrowed from Old French *paie,* from *paiier* to pay.

—paycheck *n.* (1904, American English, in O. Henry's writings) **—payday** *n.* (1529) **—payee** *n.* person to whom money is to be paid. 1758, formed from English *pay,* v. + *-ee.* **—payload** *n.* Before 1930, the part of an aircraft's load from which revenue comes; 1936, the cargo of an aircraft or rocket. **—payment** *n.* Probably about 1375 *payement* a paying or the amount paid; borrowed from Old French *paiement* (*paiier* to pay + *-ment* -ment). **—payoff** *n.* (1905) **—payroll** *n.* (1740)

pea *n.* 1380 *pease;* earlier *pese* pea, *pesen,* pl. (about 1200); developed from Old English (West Saxon, about 1000) *pise* pea, *pisan,* pl., earlier *piose* pea, *piosan* and *pisan,* pl. (before 800, in *Corpus Glossary,* Mercian dialect; also later Mercian **peose, *peosan,* pl.); borrowed from Late Latin *pisa,* variant of Latin *pisum* pea, from Greek *píson, písos,* of unknown origin.

Pea was a new singular form evolved from the earlier collective or singular noun *pease* (now largely archaic) the pea plant or a single pea, derived from the mistaken notion that *pease, peaes,* or *peas* (normally collective nouns similar to *wheat* or *corn*) were plurals formed by adding the suffix *-es* or *-s.* Earlier the plural form *peaes* is recorded in Beaumont and Fletcher's *A King and No King* (1611). Compare CHERRY for a similar formation.

—peanut *n.* 1807, American English, formed from *pea* + *nut,* in Washington Irving's *Salmagundi;* earlier called *ground nut* or *ground pea* (1769). **—peanut brittle** (1903) **—peanut butter** (1903) **—peanut gallery** (1897)

peace *n.* Probably before 1140 *pais,* in *Peterborough Chronicle;* later *pes* (probably about 1200), and *peace* (1358); borrowed from Old French *pais, peis, pes,* from Latin *pācem* (nominative *pāx*) treaty of peace, tranquility, absence of war; related to *pacīscī* to covenant or agree; see PACT. Though the spelling *peace* is recorded in the mid-1300's, it was not the established form until the 1500's reflecting the shift in vowel pronunciation from so-called long *a* to a long *e.*

The meaning of silence or quiet is first recorded in about 1250. **—peaceable** *adj.* Before 1338 *pesyble,* formed from Middle English *pes* peace + *-ible;* also borrowed from Old French *paisible, peisible* (Old French *pais-, peis-* + *-ible*). In the 1500's the word was altered in spelling (and pronunciation) to conform to *peace* and to words ending in *-able.* **—peaceful** *adj.* Before 1325 *paisful,* in *Cursor Mundi;* formed from Middle English *pais* peace + *-ful.* **—peacemaker** *n.* (before 1415) **—peace pipe** (1760, American English) **—peacetime** *n.* (1551, in a translation of Sir Thomas More's *Utopia*)

peach *n.* juicy fruit. Before 1400 *peche* peach, peach tree; earlier, as a surname *Pecche* (1184-85); borrowed from Old French *peche, pesche, peske,* and directly from Medieval Latin *pesca,* from Late Latin *pessica,* variant of *persica* peach, peach tree (compare *dossum,* variant of *dorsum* back), from Latin *Persicum mālum* Persian apple, from Greek *Persikòn mâlon,* from *Persís* Persia. **—peachy** *adj.* 1509, like a peach in color, etc., formed from English *peach* + *-y*[1]. The slang sense of fine, marvelous, wonderful, is first recorded in 1926.

peacock *n.* Probably about 1200 *pococ* the male of a peafowl pheasant; earlier, as a surname *Paucoc* (1194); probably before 1400 *pacok;* formed from Middle English *pō* peacock + *coc* COCK[1] male bird, and from *pa* + *cok;* developed from Old English *pāwa* peafowl. Also found in *pecok* (probably before 1300), formed after Old English *pēa* peafowl (before 1000) + *cok* COCK[1] male bird. Old English *pēa, pāwa* are borrowed from Latin *pāvō* peafowl, of uncertain origin, and are related to Old Saxon *pāo* peafowl, Middle Low German *pāwe,* Middle Dutch *paeu, pau,* Old High German *pfāwo,* and Old Icelandic *pāi.*

pea jacket short, double-breasted coat of thick woolen cloth. 1721 *Pee-Jacket,* American English, borrowed by loan translation from North Frisian *pijekkat,* from Dutch *pijjekker* (*pij* coarse woolen cloth + *jekker* jacket). The word *pee* was known in English from the late 1400's as a coat of coarse, thick wool, but is now found only as remnant in the altered spelling *pea* of *pea jacket.*

peak *n.* 1530, pointed or projecting part, in Palsgrave's *Lesclarcissement;* variant of PIKE[2] sharp point.

The meaning of a pointed top of a mountain is first recorded in 1634 paralleling the Middle English use of PIKE[2] in the sense of a mountain (probably 1400). The figurative sense of highest point or summit is first recorded in 1784, in Cowper's works.

—v. 1577, rise to a peak; from the noun. The figurative sense of reach the highest point is not recorded until 1958.

peaked (pē′kid) *adj.* sickly, thin. 1835-40, from past participle of earlier *peak* look sickly or thin (1605, in Shakespeare's *Macbeth,* in the expression *peak and pine*); of uncertain origin.

peal *n.* loud ringing of bells. Probably about 1350 *pel, pele* summons to church by bell, generally considered a shortened form of *apel, appel* APPEAL.

The meaning of loud ringing of bells is first recorded in 1511, and that of a loud, long sound in 1535, in the Coverdale Bible.

—v. to sound out in a peal. 1632, in Milton's *Il Penseroso;* from the noun.

pear *n.* Probably before 1300 *pere,* in *Kyng Alisaunder;* later *peare* (before 1470); developed from Old English *pere, peru* (about 1000, in Ælfric's *Grammar*); borrowed from Vulgar Latin **pira,* feminine singular use of Latin *pira,* plural of *pirum* pear (earlier **pisom*), a word borrowed from the same source (probably a

Mediterranean language) as Greek *ápion* pear, *ápios* pear tree. Old English *pere* is cognate with Middle Dutch *pēre* pear and Old High German *pira, bira,* also borrowed from Vulgar Latin **pira* which developed into the common Romance words for pear: Italian, Spanish, and Portuguese *pera,* French *poire.*

pearl *n.* Before 1349 *perle;* earlier as a surname *Perle* (about 1258); before 1400 *pearl;* borrowed from Old French *perle,* and Medieval Latin *perla;* both from Vulgar Latin **pernula,* diminutive from Latin *perna* ham, ham-shaped mollusk (sometimes yielding pearls), cognate with Sanskrit *pā̆rṣṇi-s* heel, Greek *ptérnē* heel, Gothic *faírzna,* and Old English *fiersn* heel, from Indo-European **pērsnā,* **pērsnis* (Pok.823). **—pearly** *adj.* Before 1450 *perly* round and shiny like a pearl, in reference to dew; formed from Middle English *perle* pearl + *-y*[1].

peasant *n.* About 1410 *passant* countryman, rustic; later *paissaunt* (probably about 1451); borrowed through Anglo-French *paisant,* Old French *païsant,* alteration with *-ant* of earlier *païsenc,* formed from *païs, pays* country or region, with the Frankish suffix *-enc, -inc* -ing. Old French *païs* is from Vulgar Latin **pāgēnsis* territory of the district, from Late Latin *pāgēnsis* inhabitant of the district or canton, from Latin *pāgus* country or rural district; see PAGAN. **—peasantry** *n.* Before 1553, peasants collectively; formed from English *peasant* + *-ry.*

peat *n.* kind of heavy turf. 1333 *pete* (found in Anglo-Latin in 1278 as *peta*); earlier in a place name *Petepottes* (about 1200); probably borrowed from Celtic **pett-* (compare Cornish *peyth,* Welsh *peth* quantity, part, thing, Old Irish *pet* and Breton *pez* PIECE).

peavey (pē′vē) *n.* lumberer's lever with a sharp spike at the end. About 1870, American English, said to be named after a John *Peavey,* blacksmith at Bolivar, Allegheny County, New York, who was supposed to have invented the tool.

pebble *n.* About 1300 *puble* small smooth stone; later *pobbel, pibbil* (before 1382); developed from Old English (about 1000) *papol-, popel-,* found in the compound *papolstān, popelstān* pebblestone, found also in English place names *Poppleford, Papplewick,* etc. The word is of unknown origin. **—v.** 1605, to pelt with pebbles; later, to pave with pebbles (1835); from the noun. The technical sense of prepare (leather) so that it has a grained surface, is first recorded in 1875.

pecan (pikän′) *n.* oblong nut of a kind of hickory. 1773 *paccan* the pecan tree or a related hickory, American English; borrowed from Algonquian (compare Cree *pakan* hard-shelled nut). Both the spelling *pecan* and the use of the word for the nut of the pecan tree are first recorded in 1822.

peccadillo (pek′ədil′ō) *n.* slight sin or fault. 1591, borrowed from Spanish *pecadillo,* diminutive of *pecado* a sin, from Latin *peccātum* a sin, from neuter past participle of *peccāre* to make a mistake, sin, of uncertain origin.

peccary (pek′ərē) *n.* kind of wild pig. 1613 *pockiero,* in Robert Harcourt's *A Voyage to Guiana;* borrowed from Carib (Guiana or Venezuela) *pakira, paquira.* The spelling *peccary* is first recorded in Dampier's *A New Voyage Round the World* (1697).

peck[1] *v.* strike and pick with the beak. Probably before 1300 *pechen* (apparently a misspelling); later *pekken* (about 1330; figurative use in the phrase *pekken mod* to become angry or enraged); possible variant of *picken* to PICK[1], V.; perhaps, in part, borrowed from Middle Low German *pekken* to peck with the beak.

The literal meaning "(of a bird) to strike with the beak" is first recorded before 1382, in the Wycliffe Bible.

—n. 1591, a mark made by pecking; from the verb. An earlier meaning of food is recorded in 1567; originally thieves' argot and still a slang term in Great Britain. The informal meaning of a quick kiss is found in 1893.

peck[2] *n.* unit of dry measure. About 1280 *pek,* in an Anglo-Latin context; later *peck* a dry measure (generally ¼ bushel), container holding a peck (1296); of unknown origin. The occasional reference to Medieval Latin *pecca, peccum,* and to Old French *pek,* all with the same meaning, are untenable as the Medieval Latin and the Old French were borrowings from English. The figurative meaning of a great deal (as in *a peck of troubles*) is first recorded about 1535.

pectin (pek′tən) *n.* substance in fruits that makes fruit jelly stiff. 1838, borrowed from French *pectine,* from (*acide*) *pectique* pectic (acid), a constituent of fruit jellies. *Pectique* is the French form of Greek *pēktikós* curdling or congealing, from *pēktós* curdled or congealed, from *pēgnýnai* to make stiff or solid; see PACT. The term *pectine* was probably coined by the French chemist N.L. Vauquelin, 1763-1829.

pectoral *adj.* of, in, or on the breast or chest. 1576, good for diseases of the chest; 1578, of or on the chest; probably borrowed from Middle French *pectoral,* learned borrowing from Latin *pectorālis* pertaining to the breast, from *pectus* (genitive *pectoris*) breast, chest; for suffix see -AL[1]. It is also possible that the adjective in English is in part from the noun. **—n.** 1422 *pectorall* ornament worn on the breast, in Lydgate's writings; borrowing of Middle French *pectoral,* learned borrowing from Latin, and borrowed directly from Latin *pectorāle* breastplate, noun use of neuter of *pectorālis,* adj.

peculate (pek′yəlāt) *v.* embezzle. 1749, rob; 1802, embezzle; probably a back formation from earlier *peculation;* for suffix see -ATE[1]. **—peculation** *n.* embezzlement. 1658, in Phillips' *Dictionary;* borrowed from Late Latin *pecūlātiōnem* (nominative *pecūlātiō*) from Latin *pecūlārī* defraud by embezzlement, from a lost adjective **pecūlis* as one's own; see PECULIAR; for suffix see -ATION.

peculiar *adj.* About 1449, belonging exclusively to a person, special; borrowed from Latin *pecūliāris* of one's own (property), from *pecūlium* money or property managed as one's own, from a lost adjective **pecūlis* as one's own, from *pecū* cattle, flock (representing what is one's own); related to *pecus* cattle; see FEE; for suffix see -AR.

The extended meaning of unusual or strange is first recorded in 1608.

—peculiarity *n.* 1610, exclusive possession; formed from English *peculiar* + *-ity.* The meaning of a distinguishing feature, special characteristic, is first recorded in 1646, and that of singularity, uncommonness, oddity, in 1777, in Boswell's *The Life of Samuel Johnson.*

pecuniary (pikyü′nēer′ē) *adj.* of or in the form of money. 1502, borrowed, perhaps through influence of Middle French *pecuniaire,* from Latin *pecūniārius* pertaining to money, from *pecūnia* money, property, wealth, from *pecū* cattle, flock (representing property), related to *pecus* cattle; see FEE; for suffix see -ARY.

pedagogue (ped′əgog) *n.* teacher. Before 1387 *pedagoge* teacher of children, in Trevisa's translation of Higden's *Polychronicon;* borrowed from Old French *pedagogue, pedagogien,* from Latin *paedagōgus* a slave who took children to and from school and generally supervised them; later, a teacher, from Greek *paidagōgós* (*paîs,* genitive *paidós* child; see FEW + *agōgós* leader, from *ágein* to lead; see AGENT). **—pedagogical** (ped′əgoj′əkəl) *adj.* of teaching. 1619, formed in English from French *pédagogique* + English *-al*[1], or from English *pedagogue* + *-ical,* modeled on Greek *paidagōgikós* pedagogic, from *paidagōgós* teacher. **—pedagogy** (ped′əgō′jē) *n.* teaching. 1583, instruction, discipline, training; borrowed from Middle French *pédagogie,* from Greek *paidagōgíā* education, from *paidagōgós* teacher; for suffix see -Y[3].

pedal *n.* 1611, lever (on an organ) worked by the foot, in Cotgrave's *Dictionary;* borrowed from French *pédale,* from Italian *pedale* treadle or pedal, from Late Latin *pedāle* (thing) of the foot, from neuter of Latin *pedālis* of the foot (in size or shape), from *pēs* (genitive *pedis*) FOOT. **—v.** 1866, to work a pedal; from the noun.

pedant *n.* 1588, a teacher or tutor, in Shakespeare's *Love's Labour's Lost;* borrowed from Middle French *pédant,* from Italian, or borrowed directly from Italian *pedante* teacher, schoolmaster, pedant. The meaning of a person who displays or emphasizes minor points of learning in an unnecessary or tiresome way, is first recorded in Nashe's *Have With You to Saffron-Walden* (1596).

The origin of Italian *pedante* is uncertain. It is suggested, by Bloch-Wartburg, that *pedante* was formed from the root of Greek *paideúein* to teach, at a period of the early Renaissance when it was still the fashion to pronounce Greek *ai* with the sound represented by *e* in *let.* On the other hand, and according to Corominas, the word had the early meaning of "foot soldier" and was humorously identified with *pedagogo* PEDAGOGUE in allusion to the fact that a teacher of children is always on his feet.

—pedantic *adj.* characteristic of a pedant. About 1600, in Donne's *Works;* formed from English *pedant* + *-ic.* **—pedantry** *n.* pedantic quality. 1612, in Donne's *Progress of the Souls;* formed from English *pedant* + *-ry,* possibly modeled on French *pédanterie* or Italian *pedanteria.*

peddle *v.* 1532, implied in *peddling* going about with small goods for sale; back formation from *peddler.* **—peddler** *n.* 1378 *pedeler* person who goes about with small goods for sale, also *pedlere,* in a version of *Piers Plowman,* and as a surname *Pedelare* (1307); probably alteration of earlier *peoddere, peddere* (probably before 1200, in *Ancrene Riwle*); earlier as a surname *Peddere* (1166); of uncertain origin (sometimes suggested as being from Middle English *pedde* wicker basket, such as might be used by peddlers; but doubtful, since *pedde* is not attested before 1390-91).

pederasty (ped′əras′tē) *n.* 1609 *paederastie* sexual intercourse between a man and a boy; borrowed from French *pédérastie,* or directly from Greek *paiderastíā,* from *paiderastḗs* pederast (*paîs,* genitive *paidós* child; see FEW + *erastḗs* lover, from *erâsthai* to love; see EROTIC). **—pederast** *n.* man who engages in pederasty. 1730-36, in Bailey's *Dictionarium Britannicum;* borrowed from French *pédéraste,* from Greek *paiderastḗs.*

pedestal *n.* 1563, base on which a column or a statue stands; borrowed from Middle French *piedestal,* from Italian *piedistallo* base of a pillar, sill of a door (*piè* foot, from Latin *pedem,* nominative *pēs* FOOT + *di* of, from Latin *dē* from + *stallo* stall, from Germanic; compare Old High German *stal* place, STALL[1]).

The English spelling *pedestal* was influenced by Latin *pedem* foot.

pedestrian *adj.* 1716, (of writing) prosaic, without imagination, dull; formed in English from Latin *pedester* (genitive *pedestris*) plain, prosaic, not elevated, without poetic flights + English suffix *-ian.* Greek also has an equivalent word, *pezós* (earlier **pedyós*), in reference to writing that has the sense of prosaic, plain, commonplace.

The literal meaning in English of on foot, going on foot, having to do with walking, is first recorded in 1791, reflected in Latin *pedester* on foot, that goes or is done on foot, from *pedes* one that goes on foot, from *pēs* (genitive *pedis*) FOOT.

—n. 1793, one who goes on foot, walker; from the adjective.

pediatric *adj.* having to do with the medical care or treatment of children. 1880 *paediatric;* formed in English from Greek *paid-,* stem of *paîs* child; see FEW + *iātrikós* medicinal, medical, from *iātrós* physician, from *iâsthai* to heal, of unknown origin; for suffix see -IC. **—pediatrician** *n.* specialist in pediatric medicine. 1903, formed from English *pediatric* + *-ian.* **—pediatrics** *n.* pediatric medicine. 1884, formed from English *pediatric* + *-s* (plural suffix, as in later *geriatrics*).

pedicab *n.* passenger tricycle with a hooded cab. 1948, formed from Latin *ped-* (stem of *pēs*) FOOT + the English connecting vowel *-i-* + *-cab,* on the model of *taxicab.*

pedicel (ped′əsəl) *n.* small stalk or stalklike part. 1821, borrowed (perhaps through French *pédicelle*) from New Latin *pedicellus* (coined by Linnaeus), diminutive of Latin *pediculus* footstalk, itself diminutive of *pēs* (genitive *pedis*) FOOT.

pedigree *n.* 1410 *pedicru* genealogical chart or table, family tree; later *pe-de-grew* lineage, descent (before 1420, in Lydgate's *Troy Book*); also *peedegree* (1425, in *Rolls of Parliament*); probably borrowed from Anglo-French *pe de gru,* variant of Old French *pied de grue* foot of a crane; so called from the clawlike, three-branched mark used in genealogies to show succession (*pied* foot, from Latin *pedem,* nominative *pēs* FOOT; and *de* of; and *grue* crane, from Vulgar Latin **grūa,* from Latin *gruem,* nominative *grūs* CRANE).

The meaning of ancestry, lineage as applied to animals, is first recorded in 1608.

—pedigreed *adj.* 1818, formed from English *pedigree* + *-ed*[2].

pediment *n.* triangular gablelike part on the front of a building. 1664, alteration of earlier *periment, peremint* (1592); of uncertain origin. According to the OED *periment, peremint* seems "more than likely" to be a workmen's alteration of *pyramid,* in reference to its similarity to a triangular gable.

pedology *n.* study of soils. 1924, probably borrowed from Russian *pedológiya,* from Greek *pédon* ground, earth + *-logíā* -logy, study of. Greek *pédon* is cognate with Sanskrit *padá-m* step, from Indo-European **pedom;* see FOOT.

pedometer *n.* instrument for measuring the distance

traveled on foot. 1723, borrowed from French *pédomètre,* formed from Latin *ped-* (stem of *pēs* FOOT) + the French connecting vowel *-o-* + *-mètre* -meter (device for measuring).

peduncle (pidung'kəl) *n.* stalk, stem. 1753, in *Chambers Cyclopaedia;* borrowed from New Latin *pedunculus* (coined by Linnaeus), diminutive of Latin *pēs* (genitive *pedis*) FOOT; for suffix see -CLE.

peek *v.* About 1385 *piken* look quickly and slyly, in Chaucer's *Troilus and Criseyde,* of uncertain origin. The shift in pronunciation, reflected in the forms *peke* and *peeke,* begins to be recorded in the 1500's.

It is not clear what the relationship is between the Middle English words *keek,* v. and *peek,* v. on the one hand and their connection with early modern English *peep,* v. on the other. It has been suggested that *peek* (*pīken* about 1385) may have been formed by dissimilation of *p* and *k* from *keek* (*kiken* about 1390) and that *keek* or *peek* (both earlier spelled with *i* for *e* or *ee*) may be borrowings from Middle Dutch *kieken, kijken,* variants of *kiken.* On the surface the dates would argue against that contention, but the record is distant and the span of years between forms so short, that since *peek* and *keek* are first recorded in Chaucer's works, there is strong support for the suggestion in Bense's *Dictionary of the Low-Dutch Element in the English Vocabulary* that Chaucer may have heard the word *kīken* "among the Flemings in England or picked it up himself in Flanders." Bense goes on to say that, "we think it very likely that it [*keek*] is a Dutch loan-word and developed along the same lines as its synonym *peek.*"

The early modern English *peep,* v. (about 1460) is perhaps separate from the above considerations, but must be parallel in its development in English complete with the form *peep-bo* (1837), also found in *peek-bo* (1599) and *keek-bo* (1791). The English *peer,* v. (1591) does not seem to be connected to any of the words in the preceding discussion, except by a shared sense of look.

—n. quick, sly look. 1844, from the verb.

peel *v.* Probably before 1200 *pilien, pilewin* to oppress, extort, deprive; also, to remove the rind, shell, etc., in *Ancrene Riwle;* later *pilen* (probably about 1225), and *pelen* (about 1303); probably developed from Old English *pilian* to peel (and reinforced by Old French *pillier*); both borrowed from Latin *pilāre* to strip of hair, from *pilus* hair (see PILE[3] nap). The Middle English form *pelen* was probably further reinforced by Old French *peler* to strip of hair, to skin, also from Latin *pilāre,* with influence of Old French *pel* skin, from Latin *pellis* skin, hide, FELL[3]

The shift in pronunciation reflected in the forms *pele, peel* begins to be recorded in the 1420's and 1450's.

—n. 1583, rind, outer covering; developed from earlier *pill* rind, husk, skin (about 1450), *pile* (about 1300); from *pilen,* v.

peen *n.* part of the head of a hammer opposite to the face. 1683 *pen,* probably borrowed from a Scandinavian source (compare Norwegian *penn* peen, Old Swedish *pæna* beat iron thin with the hammer).

peep[1] *v.* look through a small hole or crack, to glance. Before 1460 *pepen,* perhaps alteration by assimilation of *p* for *k* in *piken* to PEEK, with the accompanying development in the pronunciation of the vowel. **—n.** a look through a hole or crack, peek. 1530, the first appearance (of day), in Palsgrave's *Lesclarcissement;* from the verb. The meaning of a furtive glance is first recorded in Swift's *Traulus* (1730).

peep[2] *v.* make a short, sharp sound. Probably 1420 *pepen* (implied in Lydgate's writings); alteration of earlier *pipen* to peep (about 1250); see PIPE[1]. **—n.** short, sharp sound. Probably before 1437 *pepe;* from *pepen* to peep.

peer[1] *n.* person who is an equal. About 1250 *pere* an equal; earlier as a surname *Pere* (1230); probably before 1300 *per;* also, a nobleman (before 1338); borrowed through Anglo-French *peir,* and directly from Old French *per, pier,* from Latin *pār* equal; see PAIR. Doublet of PAR.

From the point of view of the subject matter of time (activities of State and the governing class) there was no contradictory meaning in an equal and a nobleman. These two meanings already existed side by side in Old French, where *per* was the title of the king's chief vassals since the time of Charlemagne; they were so called because among themselves they were equals (of the same rank).

—peerage *n.* rank of peer (noble), peers, nobility. 1454 *perage,* in *Rolls of Parliament;* formed from Middle English *per* peer + *-age;* probably on the model of Old French *parage.* **—peerless** *adj.* Probably about 1300 *perles* without equal, matchless; formed from Middle English *per* an equal + *-les* -less.

peer[2] *v.* look closely. 1591, probably reborrowed from East Frisian *pīren* to look, of uncertain origin, but influenced, especially in form, by *peren* (1375, later *peeren,* before 1425 and before 1500), shortened form of *aperen* to APPEAR; also found in Middle English *piren* to peer (before 1393, in Gower's *Confessio Amantis;* later *peren,* 1449, and continuing in the record of English through about 1475); originally borrowed from East Frisian *pīren.*

peeve *v.* make peevish. 1908, American English, back formation from PEEVISH. **—n.** complaint, annoyance. 1919 *pet peeve,* in C.H. Darling's *Jargon Book,* American English; from the verb. **—peevish** *adj.* cross, fretful, complaining. Probably before 1387 *peyvesshe* perverse, wayward, capricious, in a version of *Piers Plowman;* later *pevish* (probably before 1425); of uncertain origin (but possibly modeled on Latin *perversus* reversed, distorted, misguided, perverse, past participle of *pervertere* to turn about, PERVERT). The meaning of cross, fretful, is first recorded about 1530.

peewee[1] *n.* See PEWEE.

peewee[2] *adj.* small, tiny. 1877, dialectal English, possibly a varied reduplication of WEE. In American English *peewee* is first recorded in 1930. **—n.** a small marble. 1848, American English, in Bartlett's *Dictionary of Americanisms.* The extended sense of a small child is first recorded in 1894.

peg *n.* 1440 *pegge,* in *Promptorium Parvulorum;* borrowed from Middle Dutch *pegge* peg, of uncertain origin.

The figurative meaning of a step or degree, as in the phrase *to take* (a person) *down a peg,* is first recorded in 1589 (possibly from the interval between successive pegs, as in a ladder).

—v. 1543, insert a peg into; later, fasten with or as if with pegs (1598); from the noun. The meaning in commerce of keep the price of (a commodity) from going up or down is first recorded in 1882.

—pegboard *n.* (1899)

peignoir (pānwär′) *n.* woman's loose or very full dressing gown. 1835, borrowing of French *peignoir,* from Middle French *peignouer* garment worn over the shoulders while combing the hair, from *peigner* to comb, from Latin *pectināre,* from *pecten* (genitive *pectinis*) a comb, related to *pectere* to comb. Latin *pecten* is cognate with Greek *kteís,* genitive *ktenós* comb, earlier **pḱten-,* from Indo-European **peḱ-* pull out wool or hair (Pok.797).

pejorative (pijôr′ətiv) *adj.* tending to make worse, disparaging. Before 1888, probably borrowed from French *péjoratif* (feminine *péjorative*), as if from Late Latin **pejōrātīvus,* from Late Latin *pejōrātus,* past participle of *pejōrāre* make worse, from Latin *pejor* worse (earlier * *pedyōr*), related to *pessimus* worst; see PESSIMISM; for suffix see -ATIVE.

It is also possible that the adjective in English was from the earlier noun or that *pejorative* was formed independently in English from *pejorate* to worsen, deteriorate (1653) + *-ive.*

—n. pejorative word or expression. 1882, in Annandale's edition of Ogilvie's *Imperial Dictionary;* borrowed from French *péjoratif,* n.

pekoe (pē′kō) *n.* kind of black tea. 1712, Addison in *The Spectator;* borrowed from Chinese (Amoy dialect) *pekho,* literally, white down; so called because the leaves are picked young with the "down" still on them.

pelf *n.* money or riches, thought of as bad or degrading. Probably about 1375, stolen goods, property, riches; borrowed through Anglo-French *pelf,* Old French *pelfre* booty, spoils, of unknown origin (compare Medieval Latin *pelfa, pelfra* stolen or forfeited goods, possibly a Latinization of Old French); related to PILFER. The meaning of money or riches, thought of as bad, is first recorded in Dunbar's *Poems* (1500-20).

pelican *n.* large fish-eating water bird. Probably before 1200 *pellican,* in *Ancrene Riwle;* developed from Old English (before 1050) *pellicane;* borrowed from Late Latin *pelecānus,* from Greek *pelekán,* related to *pélekys* ax, from the same source as Sanskrit *paraśú-s* ax; so called from the shape of the bird's bill. The Sanskrit word is apparently from Indo-European **peleḱu-s,* but this must be a borrowed word. Assyrian *pilaqqu* ax, with which Sanskrit *paraśú-s* was long compared, is now known to mean spindle, and therefore to have no relevance.

By 1425 the Middle English spelling was *pelican,* influenced by Old French *pelican,* and Late Latin *pelicānus.*

pelisse (pəlēs′) *n.* coat lined or trimmed with fur. 1718, borrowing of French *pelisse,* from Old French *pelice* a skin of fur, from Late Latin *pellīcia* cloak, from Latin *pellīcius* made of skin, from *pellis* skin, hide; see FELL³.

pellagra (pəlā′grə) *n.* disease caused by improper diet, marked by eruption of skin. 1811, borrowed from Italian *pellagra* (*pelle* skin, from Latin *pellis* skin, hide; see FELL³ + Italian *-agra* painful seizure, from Latin *-agra,* ultimately from Greek *ágrā* hunting, catch, related to *agreîn* to take, seize; cognate with Middle Welsh *aer* battle, slaughter, from Indo-European **aĝrā* a hunt, Pok.6).

pellet *n.* 1372-74 *pelotte* stone or metal ball used as a missile, small ball; earlier as a surname *Pilet* (1235); also *pelet* (about 1380); borrowed from Old French *pelote,* from Vulgar Latin **pilotta,* diminutive of Latin *pila* ball; see PILL. **—v.** 1597, in Shakespeare's *A Lover's Complaint,* to form into pellets; from the noun.

pell-mell *adv.* in a rushing, tumbling mass or crowd. 1579-80, borrowed from Middle French *pele-mele, pelle-melle,* from Old French *pesle mesle,* alteration of *mesle-mesle,* a reduplication of *mesle,* imperative of *mesler, medler* to mix, MEDDLE.

A similar adverb phrase *pelly melly* appears in the Middle English (probably about 1450, and is recorded as late as 1601); borrowed from Middle French *pelle melle.*

—adj. headlong, tumultuous. 1585, from the adverb.

—n. violent disorder or confusion. 1598, from the adverb.

pellucid (pəlü′sid) *adj.* transparent, clear. 1619, borrowed from Latin *pellūcidus, perlūcidus* transparent, from *pellūcēre, perlūcēre* shine through (*per-* through + *lūcēre* to shine; see LIGHT¹ radiant energy).

pelt¹ *v.* throw things at, assail. Probably about 1225 *pelten* to strike, thrust at, in *King Horn;* variant of earlier *pilten* to thrust, push, strike (probably before 1200), *pulten* (before 1225), perhaps developed from Old English **pyltan,* from Medieval Latin **pultiare,* Latin *pultāre* to beat, strike, knock, variant of *pulsāre;* see PULSE¹ beat.

pelt² *n.* skin of an animal before it is tanned. 1303 *pelt,* probably contraction of earlier *pelet* (1298); borrowed from Old French *pelete* foreskin, fine skin, membrane, diminutive of *pel* skin, from Latin *pellis* skin, hide; see FELL³. **—peltry** *n.* pelts, skins, furs. 1436, in the compound *peltreware* furs and skins prepared for sale; later *peltry* (before 1451); borrowed through Anglo-French *pelterie, peletrie,* Old French *peleterie,* from *pelletier* furrier, derived from *pel* skin; for suffix see -RY.

pelvis *n.* 1615, basin-shaped cavity formed by the hipbones and the end of the backbone; borrowing of Latin *pēlvis,* Old Latin *pēluis* basin. The Latin is cognate with Greek *pélla* bowl, pail, cup, and Sanskrit *pālavī* type of pottery; also cognate with Old Icelandic, Old Saxon, and Old English *full* cup, from Indo-European **pel-/pēl-/pḷ-* vessel, also **pēlowi-* (Pok.804). **—pelvic** *adj.* 1830, formed from English *pelvis* + *-ic.*

pemmican (pem′əkən) *n.* dried meat pounded into a paste. 1791 *pimmecon;* later *pemmican* (1824); American English, borrowed from Algonquian (Cree) *pimikan,* from *pimikew* he makes grease, from *pimiy* grease.

pen¹ *n.* instrument for writing. Probably about 1280 *penne* writing instrument; later *pen* quill pen, feather (1373); borrowed from Old French *penne, pene, paine,* and directly from Latin *penna* FEATHER.

The term *pen name* (first recorded in 1864) is a translation of NOM DE PLUME. The word *penknife* (appearing in Middle English before 1425) is so called because these small pocketknives were originally used to sharpen quill pens.

—v. to write. 1490 *pennen,* from *penne* pen.

—penman *n.* (1591, skillful writer) **—penmanship** *n.* (1695) **—pen pal** (1938, American English, replacing earlier *pen friend,* 1933)

pen² *n.* enclosure for animals. Probably about 1380 *penne, pen;* earlier in the place name *Yppelpen* (1172); developed from Old English (957) *pen* enclosure or pen, of uncertain origin. —v. Probably before 1200 *pennen* confine closely, shut in; probably developed from Old English **-pennian* (attested only in the participle *onpennad* unpenned, opened) from *pen* enclosure. Related to PENT. The specific sense of enclose in a pen is first recorded about 1610.

pen[3] *n.* penitentiary. 1884, American English, short for *penitentiary;* form influenced by *pen*[2].

penal *adj.* of or having to do with punishment. 1439, borrowed from Middle French *peinal,* and directly from Medieval Latin *penalis,* from Latin *poenālis* pertaining to punishment, from *poena* punishment; see PAIN; for suffix see -AL[1]. **—penalize** *v.* punish. 1868, formed from English *penal* + *-ize.* **—penalty** *n.* punishment. Probably 1462 *penalté* hardship or difficulty; borrowed from Middle French *penalité,* and directly from Medieval Latin *poenalitatem* (nominative *poenalitas*), from Latin *poenālis* penal; for suffix see -TY[2].

penance *n.* punishment borne to show sorrow for sin. About 1280 *penaunce* penance (as a sacrament of the church), penitence; also *penance* (before 1300); borrowed through Anglo-French *penaunce, penance,* and borrowed directly from the corresponding Old French *penance, penëance, penanche,* from Latin *paenitentia* PENITENCE; for suffix see -ANCE.

penchant *n.* inclination. 1672, in Dryden's *Marriage-à-la-Mode;* borrowing of French *penchant,* from present participle of Old French *pencher* to incline, from Vulgar Latin **pendicāre,* from Latin *pendēre* to hang; see PENDANT; for suffix see -ANT.

pencil *n.* About 1325 *pinsel* artist's paintbrush; *pencel* (about 1385, in Chaucer's *Canterbury Tales*); borrowed from Old French *pincel, peincel* paintbrush, alteration of Vulgar Latin **pēnicellus,* variant of Latin *pēnicillus* paintbrush, pencil, literally, little tail, diminutive of *pēniculus* brush, itself a diminutive of *pēnis* tail, PENIS.

The meaning of a writing implement made of graphite is first recorded in 1612, though *pencil case* for carrying graphite pencils is first recorded in 1552.
—v. About 1532, to draw or sketch with a brush; from the noun. The meaning of write or jot down with a pencil is first recorded in 1760-72.

pendant *n.* hanging ornament. 1323 *pendaunt;* earlier as a surname *Pendant* (1274); borrowed from Anglo-French *pendaunt, pendant* hanging, Old French *pendant,* noun use of present participle of *pendre* to hang; for suffix see -ANT. Old French *pendre* developed from Vulgar Latin **pendere,* from Latin *pendēre* to hang, related to *pendere* cause to hang (on the scales), weigh, value, pay, and *pondus* weight, pound. Latin *pendere* is cognate with Lithuanian *spéndžiu* I lay a snare, Old Lithuanian *spandyti* to stretch, and Old Slavic *pęndĭ* a span, from Indo-European **(s)pen-(d-)/(s)pon-(d-)* pull, stretch (Pok.988).

pendent *adj.* hanging. 1392 *pendaunt* hanging, overhanging; later *pendant* (about 1412); borrowed from Anglo-French *pendaunt,* Old French *pendant* hanging, present participle of *pendre* to hang; see PENDANT; for suffix see -ENT. The spelling *pendent* began to appear in English about 1600, influenced by Latin *pendentem* (nominative *pendēns*), present participle of *pendēre* to hang.

pending *prep.* while waiting for, until. 1642, during, throughout the continuance of, in the process of; formed in English from French *pend-* in *pendant* hanging + English *-ing.* French *pendant* is the present participle of *pendre* to hang or suspend, and both English *pending* and this particular use of French *pendant* are patterned on Latin *pendente* hanging, suspended, not decided (as in *pendente līte* while the suit is pending, during litigation), ablative case of *pendentem* (nominative *pendēns*), present participle of *pendēre* to hang; see PENDANT; compare DURING.

The extended meaning of while awaiting, until (as in *pending the completion of the new building*) is first recorded in Dickens' *Nicholas Nickleby* (1838).

Use of the present participle before the noun (as in French *pendant le procès* and *pending the suit*) gradually caused it to be thought of as a preposition.
—adj. 1797, remaining undecided, awaiting decision or settlement; formed in the process of the preposition, but functioning as an adjective.

pendulous (pen′jələs) *adj.* hanging loosely. About 1605, overhanging; later, hanging loosely (1656); borrowed from Latin *pendulus* hanging down, from *pendēre* to hang; see PENDANT; for suffix see -OUS.

pendulum (pen′jələm) *n.* a weight so hung that it is free to swing to and fro. 1660, in Robert Boyle's *New Experiments Physico-Mechanical,* New Latin *pendulum,* from neuter of Latin *pendulus* hanging down, from *pendēre* to hang; see PENDANT.

The New Latin word is perhaps a Latinization of Italian *pendolo* first used by Galileo in 1637, from *pendolo,* adj., hanging down, from Latin *pendulus.*

penetrate *v.* 1530, in Palsgrave's *Lesclarcissement;* borrowed from Latin *penetrātus,* past participle of *penetrāre* to put or get into, enter into, penetrate; related to *penitus* (earlier **penetos*) inmost, and *penus* innermost part of a temple, store or provision of food; for suffix see -ATE[1]. **—penetration** *n.* 1605, insight, shrewdness, in Bacon's *Of the Advancement of Learning;* borrowed perhaps through French *pénétration,* learned borrowing from Latin, and borrowed directly from Latin *penetrātiōnem* (nominative *penetrātiō*) a penetrating or piercing, from *penetrāre* penetrate; for suffix see -ATION. The literal meaning of act of penetrating is first recorded in 1623, in Cockeram's *Dictionary.* An isolated example is recorded in Middle English *penetracioun* a puncture, penetrating wound (probably before 1425), from Old French *penetracïon,* learned borrowing from Latin *penetrātiō* (accusative *penetrātiōnem*).

penguin *n.* 1578, a name given to the great auk of the seas of Newfoundland, later applied to the birds now called penguins (1588); of unknown origin. Any connection with Welsh is doubtful, as the compound usually suggested (*pen* head and *gwyn* white, referring to the white headland of Newfoundland, where great auks abounded in the 1500's) would yield *penwyn* with automatic loss of *g.* The alternate suggestions of a French source from *pingouin* is not possible, since the French word (1600) is borrowed from English, and Breton *pengouin* is borrowed from French.

penicillin (pen′əsil′in) *n.* antibiotic made from a common mold. 1929, formed in English from New Latin *penicillium* (1867) the common mold from which penicillin was later purified + English *-in*[2]. *Penicillium* is the genus name of the mold, from Latin *pēnicillus* paintbrush; see PENCIL; so called from the resemblance of the penicillium cells to small brushes. The word was coined by the British bacteriologist Sir Alexander Fleming, 1881-1955, who discovered penicillin in 1928.

peninsula *n.* piece of land almost surrounded by water

1538, in John Leland's *The Itinerary;* probably borrowed directly from Latin *paenīnsula* (*paene* almost, of unknown origin + *īnsula* island; see ISLE). **—peninsular** *adj.* 1612, formed, perhaps by influence of French *péninsulaire,* from English *peninsula* + *-ar.*

penis *n.* 1676, borrowed perhaps through French *pénis,* or directly from Latin *pēnis* tail, penis (earlier **pesnis*). The Latin word is cognate with Greek *péos* and Sanskrit *pásas* penis, from Indo-European **pes-/pos-* (Pok.824).

penitence *n.* Probably before 1200, punishment borne to show sorrow for sin, penance, contrition, repentance, in *Ancrene Riwle;* borrowing of Old French *penitence,* learned borrowing from Latin, and borrowed directly from Latin *paenitentia* repentance, from *paenitentem* (nominative *paenitēns*) penitent, present participle of *paenitēre* cause or feel regret, of unknown origin; for suffix see -ENCE. Doublet of PENANCE.
—penitent *adj.* repentant, contrite. 1341 *penytente,* borrowed perhaps from Old French *penitent,* learned borrowing from Latin, and surely directly from Latin *paenitentem* (nominative *paenitēns*) penitent, present participle of *paenitēre* cause or feel regret; see PENITENCE; for suffix see -ENT. *—n.* repentant person. About 1370, in Chaucer's *An A.B.C.;* from the adjective. **—penitential** *adj.* 1508, borrowed from Medieval Latin *penitentialis,* from Latin *paenitentia* penitence + *-ālis* -al[1]. **—penitentiary** *n.* Probably 1421, place of punishment for offenses against the church; borrowed from Medieval Latin *penitentiaria,* from feminine of *penitentiarius,* adj., of punishment or penance, from Latin *paenitentia* penitence; for suffix see -ARY. The meaning of a reformatory prison for criminals, house of correction, is first recorded in 1816, though as an adjective (*penitentiary house, penitentiary system*) the word appeared in 1776, in Bentham's writings.

pennant *n.* flag. 1611, rope hanging from a ship's mast, in Cotgrave's *Dictionary,* probably a blend of *pennon* and *pendant,* in the nautical sense of a suspended rope.

The meaning of a flag on a warship is first recorded in 1698. In the sense of a flag representing a sports league championship, especially in baseball, *pennant* is first recorded in 1880, in American English; by 1915 the word is recorded as applying to the championship itself (as in *to win the pennant*).

pennon (pen′ən) *n.* long, triangular flag; streamer. About 1380 *penoun;* later, *penon* (before 1393, in Gower's *Confessio Amantis*), and *pennon* (probably before 1400); borrowed from Old French *penon, pennon, pignon* feather of an arrow, streamer, from *penne* feather, from Latin *penna* FEATHER.

penny *n.* 1125 *peni* a silver coin equal to 1/12 of a shilling, in *Peterborough Chronicle;* later *peny* (1340, in *Ayenbyte of Inwyt*); *penny* (before 1425); developed from Old English (before 725) *pening, penig* penny; also, a pennyweight; cognate with Old Frisian *panning, penning* coin (of a particular value), Old Saxon *penning,* Middle Dutch *penninc* (modern Dutch *penning*), Old High German *pfenning* (modern German *Pfennig*), Old Icelandic *penningr* (Swedish *penning* piece of money, coin, Danish *penge* money, coin); not recorded in Gothic or found outside Germanic. **—penniless** *adj.* About 1330 *penyles,* formed from Middle English *peni, peny* + *-les* -less. **—pennyweight** *n.* 1373 *peny weyȝte,* from Old English *peneȝa ȝewiht.* **—pennywise** *adj.* (1607, *penny wise*).

penology *n.* branch of criminology dealing with punishment and rehabilitation of criminals and the management of prisons. 1838, formed from English *pen-,* as in *penitentiary,* after Latin *poena* punishment, penalty; see PAIN + English *-ology.*

pensile (pen′səl) *adj.* hanging, pendent. 1603, in Ben Jonson's *Works;* borrowed from Latin *pēnsilis* hanging down, from *pēnsum,* past participle of *pendēre* to hang; see PENDANT.

pension *n.* regular payment to a retired employee. Before 1376 *pencioun* reward, payment out of a benefice, in *Piers Plowman;* also *pensioun* tax (before 1387, in Trevisa's translation of Higden's *Polychronicon*); later *pension* salary (1413); borrowed from Old French *pensïon* payment, rent, learned borrowing from Latin, and borrowed directly from Latin *pēnsiōnem* (nominative *pēnsiō*) payment, rent, from *pendere* pay, weigh; see PENDANT; for suffix see -ION.

The meaning of regular payment in consideration of past services is first recorded in 1529, in Wolsey's correspondence.
—v. give a pension to. 1702, in Addison's *Dialogues Upon the Usefulness of Ancient Medals;* from the noun.
—pensioner *n.* recipient of a pension. 1487, in *Rolls of Parliament;* borrowed from Anglo-French *pensionner,* variant of Old French *pensionnier,* from *pension* pension + *-ier* -er[1].

pensive *adj.* Before 1376 *pensif* thoughtful, contemplative, meditative, in *Piers Plowman;* borrowed from Old French *pensif* (feminine *pensive*), from *penser* to think, from Latin *pēnsāre* weigh, consider, ponder, a frequentative form from *pendere* weigh; see PENDANT; for suffix see -IVE.

pent *adj.* closely confined, shut. Before 1550, variant of *penned,* past participle of *pen*[2] confine closely.

penta- a combining form meaning five, as in *pentagon, Pentateuch;* in chemistry: containing five atoms or other units. Borrowed from Greek *penta-,* combining form of *pénte* five, cognate with English FIVE. Also spelled *pent-* before a vowel, as in *pentoxide.*

pentagon *n.* figure having five angles and five sides. 1570, borrowed from Middle French *pentagone,* or directly from Late Latin *pentagōnum* pentagon, from Greek *pentágōnon,* from neuter of *pentágōnos* five-angled (*pénte* FIVE + *gōníā* angle, related to *góny* KNEE).

The five-sided building in Washington, D.C. that is the headquarters of the United States Department of Defense has been called *the Pentagon* since it was built in 1943. *The Pentagon* is also recorded from about 1951 as an informal name for the Department of Defense and often for the United States military establishment in general.
—pentagonal *adj.* 1570, borrowed from Middle French, from *pentagone* pentagon + *-al* -al[1].

pentameter (pentam′ətər) *adj.* consisting of five metrical feet. 1546, borrowed from Middle French *pentametre,* from Latin *pentameter,* from Greek *pentámetros* (*pénte* FIVE + *métron* meter, MEASURE).
—n. line of poetry having five metrical feet. 1589, probably from the adjective.

Pentateuch (pen′tətük) *n.* the first five books of the Old Testament. About 1405 *Penteteuke,* borrowed from Late Latin *pentateuchus,* from Greek *pentáteuchos* (*pénte* FIVE + *teûchos* book; originally, case for the scrolls, implement, something made, related to *teúchein* to make, produce, of unknown origin).

pentathlon (pentath′lon) *n.* athletic contest consisting of five different events. 1852, in Grote's *History of Greece;* borrowing of Greek *péntāthlon* (*pénte* FIVE + *âthlon,* earlier *áethlon* prize, contest, of uncertain origin).

The ancient Greek *pentathlon* consisted of jumping, sprinting, discus throwing, spear throwing, and wrestling. The *modern pentathlon,* introduced in 1912, consists of horseback riding, fencing, shooting, swimming, and cross-country running.

Pentecost *n.* **1** the Seventh Sunday after Easter (commemorating the descent of the Holy Ghost on the day of the Jewish Pentecost described in Acts 2). Before 1121 *Pentecosten,* in *Peterborough Chronicle.* **2** the Jewish harvest festival of Shavuoth (often translated as the Feast of Weeks) observed at the end of seven weeks or fifty days after Passover. About 1384, in the Wycliffe Bible. Middle English *Pentecost* developed from Old English (about 1000) *Pentecosten,* borrowed from Late Latin *pentēcostē,* from Greek *pentēkostḕ hēmérā* fiftieth day, feminine of *pentēkostós,* from *pentḗkonta* fifty, from *pénte* FIVE.
—Pentecostal *adj.* of or having to do with any of various Protestant groups or sects that stress the gifts of the Holy Ghost, such as speaking in tongues. 1904, formed from English *Pentecost* + *-al*[1]; so called in allusion to the day of the Pentecost described in Acts 2 when "they were all filled with the Holy Ghost, and began to speak with other tongues." **—Pentecostalist** *n.* member of a Pentecostal sect. 1925, American English; formed from *Pentecostal* + *-ist.*

penthouse *n.* 1530, an attached building with a sloping roof; also, an awning, in Palsgrave's *Lesclarcissement;* alteration by folk etymology (through association with Middle French *pente* slope, and English *house*) of earlier Middle English *pentis* a building attached to another and having a sloping roof (1364 *pentys;* earlier *pendize,* about 1300, and in a surname *de la Pentic,* 1232; borrowed through Anglo-French *pentiz,* and directly as a shortened form of Old French *apentis* attached building, appendage, from Medieval Latin *appendicium,* from Latin *appendere* to hang; see APPEND).

From the available citations, it appears that *pentice, pentis* maintained a separate sense of a sloping roof, and that in the 1500's (though less so in the 1600's-1800's) *pentice* was used for the roof itself, while *penthouse* was used in reference to the building with or without the sloping roof. The meaning of an apartment or small house built on the roof of a tall building is first recorded in 1921.

penult (pē′nult *or* pinult′) *n.* the next to the last syllable in a word. 1828, shortening of earlier English *penultima* (1589); borrowed from Latin *paenultima* (as in *paenultima syllaba* next-to-last syllable), feminine adjective (*paene* almost, of unknown origin + *ultimus* last; see ULTIMATE).

penultimate *adj.* next to the last. 1677, formed from earlier *penultima* the next to the last syllable (of a word or verse) + *-ate*[1] on the model of *proximate;* see PENULT.

penumbra (pinum′brə) *n.* partial shade or shadow. 1666, the partial shadow outside the complete shadow during an eclipse; New Latin *penumbra* (Latin *paene* almost, of unknown origin + *umbra* shadow; see UMBRAGE). The term was coined by the German astronomer Kepler in 1604.

The figurative meaning of partial shade or shadow (as in *a penumbra of holiness*) is first recorded in 1801.
—penumbral *adj.* 1768, formed from English *penumbra* + *-al*[1].

penury (pen′yərē) *n.* great poverty. Before 1400 *penurye,* borrowed from Latin *pēnūria* want or need; of unknown origin. **—penurious** (pinůr′ēəs) *adj.* 1596, in a condition of penury, in Spenser's *Faerie Queene;* borrowed from Medieval Latin *penuriosus,* from Latin *pēnūria* penury; for suffix see -OUS. It is also probable that formation of *penurious* in English was influenced by French *penurieux,* Italian *penurioso* and, as a derived form by English *penury.* The meaning of stingy is first recorded in Milton's *C us* (1634).

peon (pē′on) *n.* **1** originally in English, a native foot soldier or footman in India or Ceylon. 1609 *peon,* borrowed from Portuguese *peão,* and 1613 *pion,* borrowing of French *pion;* both Portuguese and French forms from Medieval Latin *pedonem* foot soldier; see the doublet PAWN² chess piece. **2** an unskilled worker or laborer in Spanish America. 1826, American English; borrowing of Mexican Spanish *peón,* from Spanish, day laborer or pedestrian; originally, foot soldier, from Medieval Latin *pedonem* foot soldier. **—peonage** (pē′ənij) *n.* condition or service of a peon, especially one in Spanish America. 1849, American English, formed from *peon* (definition 2) + *-age.*

peony *n.* garden plant with large, showy flowers. 1548, developed from Middle English (about 1380) *pyony;* earlier *peonie* (about 1150); developed from Old English *pēonia* (about 1000, probably a direct borrowing of Latin); borrowed from Old North French *pione,* variant of Old French *pioine, pionie,* learned borrowings from Latin *paeōnia;* and in part borrowed directly from Latin *paeōnia,* from Greek *paiōníā,* perhaps from *Paiṓn* physician of the gods (supposedly because of the plant's use in medicine).

people *n.* About 1280 *people* the masses, populace in general; later *peple* persons (probably before 1300, in *Kyng Alisaunder*); borrowed through Anglo-French *people, peple,* Old French *peupel, pople, poeple, puple,* in part a learned borrowing from Latin *populus* people; see POPULAR. **—v.** fill with people, populate. 1450 *peuplien,* also *peoplen* (about 1450); from Middle French *peupler, popler, popliier,* from Old French *peuple,* n.

pep *n. Informal.* spirit, energy, vim. 1912, American English, shortened from *pepper* (recorded about 1847 in this figurative sense). Compare GINGER for the figurative sense.

The phrase *pep talk* inspiring or exhorting speech is first recorded in 1926; *pep pill* a stimulant drug is first found in American English college slang (1937).
—v. *Informal.* **pep up,** instill spirit or energy in. 1925 from the noun.
—peppy *adj. Informal.* full of pep. 1922, American English, in Sinclair Lewis' *Babbitt;* formed from *pep* + *-y*[1].

pepper *n.* About 1150 *piper;* later *pepir* (probably before 1300), and *peper* (about 1378); developed from Old English (about 1000) *pipor* and probably (Anglian) **peopor;* borrowing of Latin *piper,* from Greek *píper* variant of *péperi,* probably from Middle Indic *pipparī* (compare Sanskrit *pippalī* long pepper), of unknown origin. Old English *pipor* is cognate with other early Germanic borrowings of Latin *piper,* including Old Frisian *piper* pepper, Middle Low German and Middle Dutch *pēper,* Old High German *pfeffar,* and Old Icelandic *piparr.* —**v.** 1581, sprinkle with pepper; from the noun. The transferred sense of sprinkle thickly, dot, is first recorded in 1612, and that of pelt with something, about 1644; the figurative sense of make (writing, speech, etc.) spicy is found in 1835. —**peppermint** *n.* (1696) —**peppery** *adj.* (1699)

pepperoni (pep′ərō′nē) *n.* highly spiced beef and pork sausage. Before 1934, American English, borrowing of Italian *peperoni,* plural of *peperone* pepper, chili, from *pepe* pepper, from Latin *piper;* see PEPPER.

pepsin *n.* enzyme that helps to digest proteins. 1844, borrowed from obsolete German *Pepsine,* (now) *Pepsin,* from Greek *pépsis* digestion; originally, ripening, from *péssein,* later *péptein* soften or ripen; see COOK. The word was coined in 1836 by its discoverer Theodor Schwann, German physiologist, 1810-1882.

peptic *adj.* having to do with or promoting digestion. 1651, borrowed from Latin *pepticus,* from Greek *peptikós* able to digest, from *peptós* cooked or digested, from *péssein,* later *péptein* to COOK; for suffix see -IC.

per *prep.* 1588, by means of; later, for each, for every (1598); borrowed from Latin *per* through, during, by means of, on account of; see FOR.

Several Latin phrases with *per* came into English, especially through Medieval Latin and Middle French, in the distributive sense of to, for every, for each, as in the following:

—**per annum** (pər an′əm) 1601, per year, yearly. —**per capita** (pər kap′ətə) 1682, for each person, (literally) by heads. —**per diem** (pər dē′əm) 1520, per day, for each day. —**per se** (pėr sā′) 1572, by itself, in itself, intrinsically. —**per stirpes** (pər stėr′pēz) 1682, (in law) by stocks or families. See also *per cent* or *percent.*

per- a prefix meaning: **1** through, throughout, thoroughly, utterly, very, as in *perforate, perennial, pervade.* **2** (in chemistry) **a** the maximum or a large amount of, as in *peroxide.* **b** having the indicated element in its highest or a high valence, as in *perchloric acid.* **3** to do away, away entirely, to destruction (the meaning usually deriving from the combination of the prefix and the verb), as in *pervert.* Borrowed from Latin *per-,* from *per,* prep., through, during, by means of, on account of: see FOR.

This prefix appears as *par-* in several Middle English words borrowed from Old French, as in *parfit* perfect, and *parfourmen* perform. Later in Middle English the distinction between *par-* and *per-* disappeared as the result of a shift in pronunciation of *e* before *r* and with alteration of *par-* by influence of the Latin form.

perambulate (pəram′byəlāt) *v.* walk through or about. 1568, borrowed from Latin *perambulāre* (*per-* through + *ambulāre* to walk, AMBLE); for suffix see -ATE[1]. —**perambulator** *n.* 1611, one who perambulates, traveler; borrowed from Medieval Latin *perambulator,* from Latin *perambulāre* traverse, go through; for suffix see -OR[2]. The ordinary meaning of a baby carriage (often informally contracted in British English to *pram*) is first recorded in 1856.

percale (pərkāl′) *n.* smooth closely woven cotton cloth. 1840, in Thackeray's *The Paris Sketch Book;* borrowing of French *percale,* perhaps from Persian *pargālah* rag. An earlier form, *percallas,* appeared in 1621 with reference to a different type of cloth imported from the East Indies.

perceive *v.* Probably before 1300 *percyven* to see or observe, in *Kyng Alisaunder;* also *perceiven* become aware or conscious of (probably about 1300); borrowed through Anglo-French *parceif, parceit,* and **parceivre,* Old French *perçoivre, parcevoir,* from Latin *percipere* take possession of, obtain, gather, grasp with the mind, apprehend (*per-* thoroughly + *capere* to grasp, take; see CAPTIVE).

per cent or **percent** *n.* 1568 *per cent.;* shortened form of New Latin *per centum* by the hundred (compare Italian *per cento*); Latin *per* by, through (see FOR); *centum* HUNDRED. The form in English was perhaps also influenced in some instances by Middle French *pour cent* (for New Latin *pro centum,* like German *Prozent*). —**percentage** *n.* part of each hundred. 1786-90, in Jeremy Bentham's *Works;* formed from English *percent* + *-age.* —**percentile** *n. Statistics.* number of one hundred parts of in order of magnitude. 1885, probably formed from English *percent* + *-ile,* patterned on *quartile.*

perception *n.* Before 1398 *percepcioun* act of perceiving, in Trevisa's translation of Bartholomew's *De Proprietatibus Rerum;* borrowed from Old French *percepcion,* and directly from Latin *perceptiōnem* (nominative *perceptiō*) perception, apprehension, a taking, from *percipere* PERCEIVE; for suffix see -TION. —**perceptive** *adj.* 1656, formed in English from Latin *perceptus,* past participle of *percipere* perceive + English *-ive.*

perch[1] *n.* bar, branch, etc. on which a bird can rest. 1208-09 *perche* a unit of linear measure; earlier as a surname *Perche* (1199); also, a measuring rod, a pole, bar (about 1300), and perch (about 1385, in Chaucer's *Canterbury Tales*); borrowed from Old French *perche,* from Latin *pertica* pole, long staff, measuring rod, of uncertain origin. —**v.** alight and rest, sit. About 1380 *perchen,* in Chaucer's *House of Fame;* borrowed from Old French *perchier,* from *perche,* n.

perch[2] *n.* kind of freshwater fish. Probably before 1300 *perche,* in *Kyng Alisaunder;* borrowed from Old French *perche,* from Latin *perca* perch (fish), from Greek *pérkē,* related to *perknós* dark-colored, cognate with Sanskrit *pṛśni-s* spotted, Old High German *forhana* trout, Welsh *erch* speckled, dusky, from Indo-European **perk̂-/pṛk̂-* spotted (Pok.820).

perchance *adv.* maybe, perhaps. Before 1338 *perchaunce,* in Mannyng's *Chronicle of England;* later *parchance, perchance* (probably before 1350); borrowed from Old French *par cheance,* literally, by chance. Compare Anglo-French *par cheanse* (1341-42).

percolate *v.* drip or drain through small holes or spaces. 1626, in Bacon's *Sylva Sylvarum;* borrowed from Latin *percōlātus,* past participle of *percōlāre* strain through (*per-* through + *cōlāre* to strain; see COLANDER); for suffix see -ATE[1]. In some instances *percolate* may be a back formation from earlier *percolation.* —**percolation** *n.* act of percolating. 1613, in *Purchas his Pilgrimage;* borrowed from Latin *percōlātiōnem* (nominative *percōlātiō*), from *percōlāre* strain through; for suffix see -ATION. —**percolator** *n.* apparatus for percolating a liquid, especially one for straining coffee. 1842, formed from English *percolate* + *-or*[2].

percussion *n.* Probably before 1425, a striking, blow, in a translation of Chauliac's *Grande Chirurgie;* borrowed from Middle French *percussion,* and directly from Latin *percussiōnem* (nominative *percussiō*), from *percutere* to strike (*per-* through + *quatere* to strike, beat, shake; see QUASH[1] crush); for suffix see -SION. The sense of *percussion* in reference to musical instruments is first recorded in English in 1776. **—percussion cap** (1823) **—percussive** *adj.* of percussion. 1793, formed in English from Latin *percussus,* past participle of *percutere* to strike + English *-ive.*

perdition *n.* spiritual destruction, damnation. About 1340 *perdicion* consignment of the soul to hell, damnation; later *perdicioun* destruction of property, complete ruin (before 1382, in the Wycliffe Bible); borrowed from Old French *perdicion,* or directly from Late Latin *perditiōnem* (nominative *perditiō*) ruin, destruction, from Latin *perdere* do away with, destroy, lose (*per-* away entirely, to destruction + *-dare* to put, from the Indo-European base **dhē-/*dhə-;* see DO); for suffix see -TION.

perdure (pərdůr′) *v.* last, endure. Probably before 1475 *perduren;* borrowed from Middle French *perdurer,* or directly from Latin *perdūrāre* last, hold out, endure (*per-* on through, to the end + *dūrāre* to last, harden, ENDURE). It is also possible since *perdure* has been used erratically in English (at one point being absent for about 265 years) that in later instances it is a back formation from earlier *perdurable.* **—perdurable** *adj.* lasting, enduring. About 1380, in Chaucer's translation of Boethius' *De Consolatione Philosophiae;* earlier, implied in *pardurableliche* perdurably (about 1275); borrowed from Old French *pardurable,* from Late Latin *perdūrābilis,* or borrowed directly from Medieval Latin, from Latin *perdūrāre* perdure.

peregrination (per′əgrənā′shən) *n.* Probably about 1425 *peregrinacion* journey; borrowed through Middle French *pérégrination,* or directly from Latin *peregrīnātiōnem* (nominative *peregrīnātiō*) a journey, from *peregrīnārī* to journey or travel abroad, from *peregrīnus* from foreign parts, foreigner; see PILGRIM; for suffix see -ATION. **—peregrinate** *v.* to travel, journey. 1593, in Nashe's *Christ's Tears Over Jerusalem;* borrowed from Latin *peregrīnārī* sojourn or travel abroad.

peregrine (per′əgrin) *n.* 1555, large falcon of wide distribution, shortened from Middle English phrase *faukon peregryn* (about 1395, in Chaucer's *Canterbury Tales*); borrowed from Old French *faulcon pelerin,* and directly from Latin *falcō peregrīnus;* found earlier in English adjective (1530, not native, foreign), borrowed from Middle French *pérégrin* (feminine *pérégrine*), or directly from Latin *peregrīnus* from foreign parts, foreigner; see the doublet PILGRIM; for suffix see -INE[1].

peremptory (pəremp′tərē) *adj.* decisive, final. 1443 *peremptorie* (legal use) absolute, allowing no refusal, in *Proceedings of the Privy Council;* borrowed through Anglo-French *peremptorie,* from Middle French *peremtoire,* and directly from Latin *perēmptōrius* decisive, final, deadly, that puts an end to, from *perēmptor* destroyer, from *perimere* destroy, cut off (*per-* away entirely, to destruction + *emere* to take; see REDEEM); for suffix see -ORY.

perennial *adj.* 1644, remaining green throughout the year, evergreen, in Evelyn's *Diary;* formed in English from Latin *perennis* lasting through the year or years (*per-* through + *annus* year; see ANNUAL) + English *-al*[1].

The botanical meaning "(of plants, roots, etc.) remaining alive through a number of years" is first recorded in 1672-73. The general meaning "lasting a long time, enduring, permanent" appeared in 1750, in Johnson's writings in *The Rambler.*

—n. perennial plant. 1763, from the adjective.

perfect (pėr′fikt) *adj.* About 1300 *parfijt* fully formed, faultless; earlier as a surname *Parfet* (1196); also *parfit* (before 1325); *perfet* (about 1380); *perfect* (probably before 1425); borrowed from Old French *parfit, parfet, perfet,* and directly from Latin *perfectus* completed, past participle of *perficere* accomplish, finish, complete (*per-* completely, to the end + *facere* perform, DO[1]). It is also probable that *perfect* was influenced in its formation by earlier *perfection.* **—v.** (pərfekt′) remove all faults from. Before 1398 *parfiten,* in Trevisa's translation of Bartholomew's *De Proprietatibus Rerum;* from the adjective. **—perfectible** *adj.* 1635, formed from English *perfect,* v. + *-ible,* perhaps influenced in formation by earlier Italian *perfettibile,* in Florio's *Queen Anna's New World of Words* (1611). **—perfection** *n.* faultlessness. Probably before 1200 *perfectiun,* in *Ancrene Riwle;* borrowed from Latin *perfectiōnem* (nominative *perfectiō*); later *perfeccioun* (before 1333); borrowed from Old French *perfeccion,* from Latin *perfectiōnem* (nominative *perfectiō*), from *perficere* accomplish; for suffix see -TION. **—perfectionist** *n.* 1657-83, person who believes that religious or moral perfection may be attained; formed from English *perfection* + *-ist.* The sense of a person who is only satisfied by the highest standards is first recorded in 1934.

perfecta (pərfek′tə) *n.* exacta. 1971, American English, borrowed from American Spanish *perfecta,* shortening of *quiniela perfecta* perfect quiniela, from Spanish *perfecta* + American Spanish *quiniela* a game of chance, a bet in horse racing, formed from Old Spanish *quina* game of dice, from Latin *quīnī* (earlier **quencnoi*) five each; see FIVE.

perfervid (pėrfėr′vid) *adj.* very fervid, glowing, ardent. 1856, borrowed from New Latin *perfervidus;* formed from *per-* throughout + Latin *fervidus* FERVID.

perfidy (pėr′fədē) *n.* treachery. 1592, borrowed from Middle French *perfidie,* from Latin *perfidia* falsehood, treachery, from *perfidus* faithless, from the phrase *per fidem (dēcipere*) (to deceive) through trustingness; *per* through; *fidem* accusative of *fidēs* FAITH; for suffix see -Y[3]. **—perfidious** *adj.* treacherous. 1598, in Florio's *A World of Words;* borrowed from Latin *perfidiōsus,* from *perfidia* falsehood, treachery; for suffix see -OUS.

perforate *v.* 1538, make a hole through, in Elyot's *Dictionary;* possibly a back formation from earlier *perforation,* and also borrowed from Latin *perforāre* bore or pierce through (*per-* through + *forāre* to pierce BORE[1]); for suffix see -ATE[1]. **—perforation** *n.* Probably before 1425 *perforacioun,* in a translation of Chauliac's *Grande Chirurgie;* borrowed from Middle French *perforation,* or directly from Medieval Latin *perforationem* (nominative *perforatio*), from Latin *perforāre* bore through; for suffix see -ATION.

perform *v.* About 1300 *parfourmen* to do, carry out, go through or render; later *performen* (1376, in *Piers Plowman*); borrowed through Anglo-French *perfourmir,* and Old French *parfornir, parforner.* The Anglo

French form is an alteration (influenced by Old French *forme* form) of Old French *parfornir* to do, carry out (*par-* completely, from Latin *per-* per- + *fornir* to provide, FURNISH). The Middle English word also existed in the forms *parformen* and *parfournen;* borrowed directly from Old French *parfornir, parforner.* **—performance** *n.* a performing or thing performed. About 1500, formed from English *perform* + *-ance.* The sense of a public exhibition or entertainment is first recorded in 1709, in an article by Steele in the *Tatler.* **—performer** *n.* 1588-89, formed from English *perform* + *-er*[1]. The specific sense of one who performs in a public exhibition or entertainment is first recorded in 1711, in writings of Steele.

perfume (pėr′fyüm) *n.* 1533, fumes from a burning substance, in Elyot's *The Castel of Helth;* borrowed from Middle French *parfum,* from *parfumer* to scent, from dialectal Italian *perfumare* or Provençal *perfumar* (Latin *per-* through + *fūmāre* to smoke; see FUME). The meaning of a substance having a sweet smell is first recorded in 1542. **—v.** (pərfyüm′) 1538, to fumigate, in Elyot's *Dictionary;* also, give a sweet scent to (1539); borrowed from Middle French *parfumer* to scent.

perfunctory (pərfungk′tərē) *adj.* indifferent, careless, mechanical. 1581 (implied in *perfunctorily*); borrowed from Late Latin *perfūnctōrius* careless, in a superficial manner, negligent; literally, like one who wishes to get through a thing, from *perfungī* discharge, get through (*per-* through + *fungī* perform); for suffix see -ORY.

perfusion *n.* 1574, borrowed from Middle French *perfusion,* and directly from Latin *perfūsiōnem* (nominative *perfūsiō*) a pouring over, from *perfundere* pour out (*per-* throughout + *fundere* pour); for suffix see -SION.

perhaps *adv.* About 1475 *perhappous* (probably *-pons*) possibly; literally, by chances; plural form of earlier *perhap* (before 1464), *parhap* (probably 1350-75); formed from Middle English *per, par* by or through, and *hap* chance.

peri- a prefix used in Greek and quasi-Greek formations, having the meaning: **1** around or surrounding, as in *perimeter = measure (meter) around, periscope = instrument (scope) for looking around, peristalsis = contracting or compressing around.* **2** near, as in *perihelion = near or nearest the sun* (Greek *hḗlios*). Borrowed from Greek *peri-,* from the preposition *perí* around, about, cognate with Sanskrit *pári* around, about, and related to Greek *pró* before, ahead; see FOR.

pericardium (per′əkär′dēəm) *n.* Probably before 1425 *pericardium* membranous sac enclosing the heart, in a translation of Chauliac's *Grande Chirurgie,* from Medieval Latin, from Greek *perikárdion* membrane around the heart, neuter of *perikárdios* around the heart (*peri-* around + *kardíā* HEART). **—pericarditis** (per′əkärdī′tis) *n.* inflammation of the pericardium. 1799, formed from English *pericardium* + *-itis.*

pericarp (per′əkärp) *n. Botany.* walls of a ripened ovary or fruit, seed vessel. 1759, borrowed probably through French *péricarpe,* and from New Latin *pericarpium,* from Greek *perikárpion* pod, husk (*peri-* around + *karpós* fruit; see HARVEST).

perigee (per′əjē) *n.* 1594, point in the orbit of a planet, comet, etc., at its closest distance to the earth or to any other celestial body about which it orbits, in John Davys' *The Seamans Secrets;* borrowed from French *périgée,* learned borrowing from New Latin *perigeum,* and borrowed directly from Late Greek *perígeion,* neuter of *perígeios* near the earth, from *perì gês* (*perí* near + *gês,* genitive of *gê* earth). Compare APOGEE. In the Space Age this term has been extended in its application to space flight and rocket trajectories.

perihelion (per′əhē′lēən) *n.* point of an orbit closest to the sun. 1690, borrowed as a form of New Latin *perihelium* patterned on Greek (with the Greek ending *-on*). The earlier New Latin *perihelium* (1666) was coined by the German astronomer Johann Kepler, writing in Latin in 1596, and was formed from Greek *perí* near + *hēlíon,* genitive of *hḗlios* sun, prompted probably by the pattern of Greek *perígeion* PERIGEE; compare APHELION.

peril *n.* Apparently before 1200, chance of harm, danger, in *Ancrene Riwle;* borrowed from Old French *peril,* from Latin *perīculum* an attempt, risk, danger; see FEAR. **—v.** put in danger. 1567, from the noun. **—perilous** *adj.* About 1300, dangerous, risky; later *perilous* (before 1325); borrowed from Old French *perillous, perilleus,* from Latin *perīculōsus* dangerous, hazardous, from *perīculum* an attempt, risk, danger; for suffix see -OUS.

perimeter (pərim′ətər) *n.* Probably before 1425 *perimetre* outer boundary of a surface or figure; borrowed from Latin *perimetros,* from Greek *perímetros* circumference (*peri-* around + *métron* MEASURE).

perineum (per′ənē′əm) *n.* Probably before 1425 *perineum* area of the body between the thighs, in a translation of Chauliac's *Grande Chirurgie;* borrowed from Medieval Latin *perinaeon,* Late Latin *perinēum,* from Greek *perínaion, perínaios* region of evacuation (*peri-* near + *inân* to carry off by evacuation, of unknown origin).

period *n.* 1413 *pariode* course or extent of time; probably before 1425 *periode;* borrowed from Middle French *periode,* and directly from Medieval Latin *periodus* recurring portion, cycle, from Latin *periodus* a complete sentence; also, the cycle of the four Grecian games, from Greek *períodos* rounded or complete sentence, cycle, orbit, circuit; literally, a going around (*peri-* around + *hodós* a going, way, journey; see CEDE). The meaning of a dot marking the end of a sentence is first recorded in English in 1609, borrowed from Medieval Latin *periodus* (1267), and from earlier use in English referring to a full pause made at the end of a sentence (1587). See note under COMMA. **—adj.** characteristic of a certain period of time. 1905, from the noun. **—periodic** *adj.* occurring at regular intervals. 1642, shortened form of earlier *periodical* (1603); formed in English (possibly by influence of French *périodique*) from Latin *periodicus,* from Greek *periodikós* recurring at stated intervals, from *períodos* cycle, period + *-ical. Periodical* in the sense of a magazine that appears regularly is first recorded in 1798, from the earlier adjective meaning of published at regular intervals (1766; earlier, writing for or connected with such magazines, 1716 in Addison's writings). **—periodicity** *n.* occurrence at regular intervals. 1833, in Sir John Herschel's *Treatise on Astronomy;* borrowed from French *périodicité,* formed in French from Latin *periodicus* + French *-ité* -ity. **—periodic table** table of chemical elements. 1895; so-called because the elements are arranged according to a regular pattern of chemical properties, described earlier by the *periodic law* (1872, the law that the properties of the elements are periodic functions of their atomic weights, proposed by the Russian chemist Dimitri Mendeleev in his *Elements of Chemistry,* 1868, and in work independently done by the German chemist Julius L. Meyer in 1869).

peripatetic (per'əpətet'ik) *n.* Before 1450 *peripatatik* disciple of Aristotle or his teachings; borrowed from Latin *peripatēticus,* n., a disciple of Aristotle, from Greek *peripatētikós* given to walking about (*peri-* around + *pateîn* to walk); for suffix see -IC. The meaning of a person who wanders about is first recorded in 1617, and developed from the reference to Aristotle's custom of walking about, especially while teaching or disputing, because Aristotle taught in the walkways of the Lyceum at Athens. **—adj.** 1566, having to do with Aristotle's philosophy; later, walking about, traveling from place to place (1642, though recorded earlier in the sense of pacing up and down, 1631); from the noun on the model of Greek *peripatētikós.*

periphery (pərif' ərē) *n.* Before 1393 *periferie* layer of atmosphere around the earth; borrowing of Medieval Latin *periferia,* from Late Latin *peripherīa* circumference, from Greek *periphéreia* circumference, part of a circle, outer surface, from *peripherḗs* rounded, *periphérein* carry around, move around (*peri-* around + *phérein* to carry, BEAR[2]). The sense of an outside boundary of a round or rounded surface is first recorded in English in 1571, and that of any boundary or outside margin in 1666. **—peripheral** *adj.* at the outside, external. 1808, formed from English *periphery* + *-al*[1], and generally replacing such formations as *peripherial* (1672-73) and *peripherical* (1690).

periphrasis (pərif' rəsis) *n.* roundabout way of speaking or writing. 1533, in Sir Thomas More's *The Apology Made by Him;* borrowed from Latin *periphrasis* circumlocution, from Greek *períphrasis,* from *periphrázein* speak in a roundabout way (*peri-* around + *phrázein* to express; see PHRASE). **—periphrastic** *adj.* expressed in a roundabout way. 1805, probably borrowed through French *périphrastique,* and directly from Greek *periphrastikós* roundabout, from *periphrázein* speak in a roundabout way; for suffix see -IC. It is also possible that *periphrastic* was formed in English on the model of Greek *periphrastikós.*

periscope *n.* instrument for viewing, used principally to see the surface of the sea from a submarine. 1899, formed from English *peri-* around + *-scope* instrument for viewing.

perish *v.* About 1275 *perissen* die, be destroyed, come to ruin; later *perishen, perischen* (about 1340); borrowed from Old French *periss-,* stem of *perir,* from Latin *perīre* (*per-* away entirely, to destruction + *īre* to go; see EXIT); for suffix see -ISH[2]. **—perishable** *adj.* liable to perish, liable to spoil or decay. Before 1475 *perysabyl;* later *perishable,* in Cotgrave's *Dictionary* (1611); probably borrowed from Middle French *périssable,* and later re-formed from English *perish* + *-able.*

peristalsis (per'əstal'sis) *n.* wavelike contractions in the wall of a hollow organ. 1859, New Latin *peristalsis,* formed after Greek *peristaltikós* contracting around + the ending *-sis,* on the model of English *emphasis, emphatic,* and *paralysis, paralytic.* **—peristaltic** *adj.* of peristalsis. 1655, borrowed from Greek *peristaltikós* contracting around (found in Galen's *Terapeutike*), from *peristéllein* compress, wrap around (*peri-* around + *stéllein* send, put, place; see STALL[1] place); for suffix see -IC.

peristyle (per'əstīl) *n.* 1612, borrowed from French *péristyle* row of columns surrounding a building, learned borrowing from Latin *peristȳlum,* from Greek *perístȳlon,* from neuter of *perístȳlos* surrounded with a colonnade (*peri-* around + *stŷlos* pillar; see STEER[1] to guide).

peritoneum (per'ətənē'əm) *n.* membrane that lines the walls of the abdomen. Probably before 1425 *peritonei,* in a translation of Chauliac's *Grande Chirurgie;* probably about 1425 *perytoneum;* borrowed from Late Latin *peritonaeum,* from Greek *peritónaion* abdominal membrane; literally, part stretched over, neuter of *peritónaios* stretched over, from *perítonos* stretched around (*peri-* around + *teínein* to stretch; see TEND). **—peritonitis** (per'ətənī'tis) *n.* inflammation of the peritoneum. 1776, New Latin, formed from Late Latin *peritonaeum* + New Latin *-itis.*

periwig *n.* wig. 1579, alteration of earlier *perwyke* (1529); borrowed from Middle French *perruque* PERUKE.

periwinkle[1] *n.* evergreen plant with blue flowers. Before 1475 *pervyncle;* earlier, as a surname *Perivencle* (1327); diminutive of earlier *parvink* (probably about 1300); developed from Old English *perwince* (about 1000); borrowed from Late Latin *pervinca,* Latin *vincapervinca,* of uncertain origin.

periwinkle[2] *n.* kind of sea snail. 1530, in Palsgrave's *Lesclarcissement;* alteration of Old English *pīnewincle* (probably influenced by Middle English *pervinkle* periwinkle[1]). Old English *pīnewincle* was formed from *pīne-* (probably borrowed from Latin *pīna* mussel, from Greek *pínē, pîna,* of Mediterranean origin) + *-wincle,* related to *wincel* corner, and cognate with Old Frisian *winkel* corner, Middle Dutch and Dutch *winkel,* Old High German *winkil* (German *Winkel* corner). The sea snail *periwinkle* is not recorded in Middle English.

perjure *v.* make (oneself) guilty of swearing falsely. 1453, implied in the past participle *perjured,* influenced in its formation by earlier Middle English *perjury* but modeled on Middle French *parjurée,* past participle of *parjurer,* learned borrowing from Latin *perjūrāre* swear falsely, break one's oath (*per-* away entirely, to destruction + *jūrāre* to swear; see JURY[1], n.). **—perjury** *n.* act or instance of swearing falsely. Before 1393 *perjurie,* in Gower's *Confessio Amantis;* borrowed through Anglo-French *perjurie,* Old French *parjuré,* from Latin *perjūrium* false oath, from *perjūrāre* swear falsely; for suffix see -Y[3].

perk[1] *v.* raise briskly, act saucily. About 1485, make trim or smart (as a bird trims its plumage), of uncertain origin (possibly developed from earlier *perken* to perch, about 1390; from *perk,* n., probably about 1375, and perhaps borrowed from Old North French *perquer* to perch, from *perque* perch, from Latin *pertica* rod, PERCH[1]).

The meaning of act saucily is first recorded before 1550, and that of raise oneself briskly, before 1591. The phrase *perk up,* meaning to liven or brighten up, become lively, is first recorded before 1656.

—perky *adj.* brisk, saucy. 1855, in Tennyson's poetry, formed from English *perk* + *-y*[1].

perk[2] *n. Informal.* perquisite. 1869, shortened form and spelling alteration of PERQUISITE.

perk[3] *v. Informal.* percolate (coffee). 1934, American English, shortened form and spelling alteration of PERCOLATE.

perm *n.* permanent wave. 1927, shortened from *permanent wave* (1909, special process for putting a wave in the hair that lasts several months). **—v.** give a permanent wave to. 1928, from the noun.

permafrost *n.* permanently frozen ground. 1943, formed from English *perma(nent)* + *frost.* The word was coined by Siemon W. Muller, Russian-born American geologist.

permanent *adj.* Probably before 1425, continuing indefinitely without change, lasting, from a translation of Higden's *Polychronicon;* borrowed from Middle French *permanent,* and directly from Latin *permanentem* (nominative *permanēns*) remaining, present participle of *permanēre* stay to the end (*per-* through + *manēre* stay; see MANSION); for suffix see -ENT. **—n.** lasting wave put in the hair by a special process. 1926, shortened from *permanent wave* (1909). **—permanence** *n.* Probably before 1425; borrowed from Middle French *permanence,* and directly from Medieval Latin *permanentia,* from Latin *permanēns* present participle; for suffix see -ENCE.

permeate *v.* spread through the whole of, pervade. 1656, formed in English, probably by influence of earlier *permeable,* from Latin *permeātus,* past participle of *permeāre* pass through (*per-* through + *meāre* to pass, cognate with Czech *míjeti* pass by, Welsh *myned* to go, and Gaulish *Moenus* River Main, from Indo-European **mei-/moi-/mi-,* Pok.710) + English suffix *-ate*[1]. **—permeable** *adj.* that can be permeated. Probably before 1425, in a translation of Higden's *Polychronicon;* borrowed from Late Latin *permeābilis* passable, from Latin *permeāre* permeate; for suffix see -ABLE.

permission *n.* About 1410, *permissioun* a permitting, consent; borrowed from Middle French *permission,* from Latin *permissiōnem* (nominative *permissiō*), from *permittere* to PERMIT; for suffix see -SION. **—permissible** *adj.* Probably before 1430, in Lydgate's writings; borrowed from Middle French *permissible,* and directly from Medieval Latin *permissibilis* allowable, from Latin *permissus,* past participle of *permittere* to permit; for suffix see -IBLE. **—permissive** *adj.* Probably before 1475, allowed, tolerated; borrowed from Middle French *permissif* (feminine *permissive*), from Old French, from Latin *permittere* to permit; for suffix see -IVE. The sense of allowing or not forbidding is first recorded in English in Shakespeare's *Measure for Measure* (1603).

permit *v.* 1429 *permytten* resign; later allow (about 1475); borrowed perhaps from Middle French *permetre,* and directly from Latin *permittere* give up, allow, let go (*per-* through + *mittere* let go, let loose, send). **—n.** formal, written order. 1714, from the verb.

permutation *n.* Before 1376 *permutacioun* alteration or exchange, in *Piers Plowman;* borrowed from Old French *permutation,* learned borrowing from Latin *permūtātiōnem* (nominative *permūtātiō*), from *permūtāre* change thoroughly, exchange (*per-* thoroughly + *mūtāre* to change, see MISS[1], v.); for suffix see -ATION.

The mathematical meaning of the changing of the order of a set of things, variation of order or arrangement, is first recorded in 1570.

pernicious *adj.* destructive, injurious. Probably before 1425, harmful or fatal, in Chauliac's *Grande Chirurgie;* borrowed from Middle French *pernïcios,* learned borrowing from Latin, and borrowed directly from Latin *perniciōsus* destructive, from *perniciēs* destruction (*per-* completely + *necāre* to kill, from *nex,* genitive *necis* slaughter; see NOXIOUS); for suffix see -IOUS.

pernickety *adj. Informal.* overly fastidious, fussy. 1808-18 *pernickitie,* in Jamieson's *Dictionary of the Scottish Language;* an extended form of Scottish *pernicky,* of uncertain origin (the OED suggests a possible association with *knickknack* and perhaps with a children's alteration of *particular,* neither of which is satisfactory semantically or phonologically); for suffix see -Y[1]. Compare PERSNICKETY.

peroration *n.* last part of an oration or discussion. 1447 *peroracyoun;* borrowed from Latin *perōrātiōnem* (nominative *perōrātiō*) the ending of a speech or argument of a case, from *perōrāre* argue a case to the end, bring a speech to a close, conclude (*per-* to the end, thoroughly + *ōrāre* speak or plead; see ORATION); for suffix see -ATION. **—perorate** *v.* speak at length. 1603, in some instances probably a back formation from *peroration,* and in some instances borrowed from Latin *perōrātum,* past participle of *perōrāre;* for suffix see -ATE[1].

peroxide *n.* oxide containing a large amount of oxygen. 1804, formed from English *per-* maximum or large amount + *oxide.*

perpendicular *adj.* at right angles, vertical. About 1475 *perpendyculere,* adjective use of earlier adverb *perpendiculer* (1391, in Chaucer's *Treatise on the Astrolabe*); borrowed from Old French *perpendiculer,* learned borrowing from Latin *perpendiculāris* vertical, as a plumb line, from *perpendiculum* plumb line, from *perpendere* balance carefully (*per-* thoroughly + *pendere* to weigh; see PENDANT); for suffix see -AR. The spelling with *-ar* is in imitation of the Latin and appears as early as 1555. **—n.** perpendicular line or plane. 1571, from the adjective.

perpetrate *v.* commit (a crime, fraud, trick, etc.). 1547, developed from earlier *perpetrat,* adj., perpetrated, executed, committed (1472-73, in *Rolls of Parliament*); borrowed from Latin *perpetrātus,* past participle of *perpetrāre* execute, perform (*per-* thoroughly + *patrāre* carry out, bring to pass; originally, bring into existence, from *pater* FATHER); for suffix see -ATE[1]. **—perpetrator** *n.* 1570, borrowed from Late Latin *perpetrātor,* from Latin *perpetrāre* perform; for suffix see -OR[2].

perpetual *adj.* eternal. About 1340 *perpetuel;* probably before 1350 *perpetual;* borrowed from Old French *perpetüel,* learned borrowing from Latin, and borrowed directly from Latin *perpetuālis* universal (in Medieval Latin, permanent), from *perpetuus* continuous, constant, universal, from *perpetis,* genitive of *perpes* lasting (*per-* through + root of *petere* to seek, go to, aim at; see FEATHER); for suffix see -AL[1]. **—perpetuate** *v.* make perpetual. 1530, in Palsgrave's *Lesclarcissement;* perhaps a back formation from *perpetuation* or formed from *perpetuate,* adj., made perpetual (1503-04); borrowed from Latin *perpetuātus,* past participle of *perpetuāre* make continuous, from *perpetuus* continuous; for suffix see -ATE[1]. **—perpetuation** *n.* a perpetuating or being perpetuated. 1395 *perpetuacioun;* borrowed from Medieval Latin *perpetuationem* (nominative *perpetuatio*) continuation, from Latin *perpetuāre* perpetuate; for suffix see -ATION. **—perpetuity** *n.* state of being perpetual. About 1380 *per-*

petuyte; borrowed from Old French *perpetüité,* learned borrowing from Latin, and borrowed directly from Latin *perpetuitātem* (nominitive *perpetuitās*) continuity, from *perpetuus* continuous; for suffix see -ITY.

perplex *v.* to puzzle, bewilder. 1595, in Shakespeare's *Life and Death of King John;* probably a back formation from *perplexed, perplexid,* participial adjective, confused (1477), from earlier *perplex,* adj., confused or puzzled (before 1425; in Wycliffe's writings); borrowed from Middle French *perplexe,* and directly from Latin *perplexus* confused or involved (*per-* completely + *plexus* entangled, from past participle of *plectere* to twine or braid; see PLY[2] fold). It is also probable that *perplex,* adj. was influenced in its formation by earlier *perplexity.* **—perplexity** *n.* Probably 1348 *perplexite,* in Rolle's writings; borrowed from Old French *perplexité,* from Late Latin *perplexitātem* (nominative *perplexitās*) obscurity, perplexity, from Latin *perplexus* confused or involved; for suffix see -ITY.

perquisite (pėr′kwəzit) *n.* 1443 *perquysite* property acquired otherwise than by inheritance; borrowed from Medieval Latin *perquisitum* thing gained or profit, from Latin *perquīsītum* thing sought after, from neuter past participle of *perquīrere* to seek, ask for (*per-* thoroughly + *quaerere* to seek; see QUERY).

The extended meaning of any fee or profit received for work besides the regular salary or wages is first recorded in 1565, and that of a gratuity or tip in 1721.

persecute *v.* 1450 *persecuten* pursue in order to harm, torment, oppress; earlier confused with *prosecuten* (probably before 1425, in a translation of Higden's *Polychronicon*); borrowed from Middle French *persécuter* follow after, pursue, torment, start a legal action, back formation from *persécuteur* persecutor, learned borrowing from Late Latin, and borrowed directly from Late Latin *persecūtor* person who follows close after, pursuer, one who starts a legal action, from Latin *persequī* follow after, pursue, start a legal action (*per-* through + *sequī* follow; see SEQUEL). **—persecution** *n.* act of persecuting. About 1340 *persecucioun;* borrowed from Old French *persecucïon, persecution,* learned borrowing from Latin, and borrowed directly from Latin *persecūtiōnem* (nominative *persecūtiō*) a following close after, chase, the start of a legal action, from *persequī* follow after; for suffix see -TION. **—persecutor** *n.* one that persecutes. Probably about 1425 *persecutor;* borrowed from Middle French *persécuteur;* for suffix see -OR[2].

persevere (pėr′səvir′) *v.* About 1380, implied in the gerund of *perseveren* continue steadfastly, persist, in Chaucer's *Canterbury Tales;* borrowed from Old French *perseverer,* learned borrowing from Latin, and borrowed directly from Latin *persevērāre* continue steadfastly, persist, abide by strictly, from *persevērus* very strict or earnest (*per-* as an intensive with the sense of very + *sevērus* strict, earnest; see SEVERE).

This word and its derivative forms were usually pronounced with the primary accent on the second syllable, as in pərsev′ər (spelled *persever*) until the late 1600's, and this stress pattern continues to be evident in modern English *perseverate* and *perseveration.* **—perseverance** *n.* persistence, tenacity. 1340, in *Ayenbite of Inwyt;* borrowed from Old French *perseverance,* and directly from Latin *persevērantia* (nominative *persevērāns*) steadfastness, constancy, persistence, present participle of *persevērāre* persevere; for suffix see -ANCE. **—perseverate** (pərsev′ərāt) *v.* 1915, back formation in English from earlier *perseveration;* for suffix see -ATE[1]. **—perseveration** (pərsev′ərā′shən) *n.* (in psychology) the tendency to continue or repeat an action after the need or stimulus has passed. Before 1415 (and not recorded after 1658), persevering, perseverance; borrowed from Old French *perseveracion,* and directly from Latin *persevērātiōnem* (nominative *persevērātiō*), from *persevērāre;* but later probably re-formed in English from *persevere* + *-ation* (1901).

persiflage (pėr′səflāzh) *n.* light, joking talk. 1757, in Lord Chesterfield's *Letters;* borrowing of French *persiflage,* from *persifler* to banter, formed from Latin *per-,* as an intensive + French *siffler* to whistle, hiss, from Old French, from Latin **sīfilāre,* dialect variant of *sībilāre* to hiss; see SIBILANT; for suffix see -AGE.

persimmon (pərsim′ən) *n.* North American tree with a plumlike fruit. 1612, in Captain John Smith's *A Map of Virginia,* American English; borrowed from Algonquian (Powhatan) *pasimenan* fruit dried artificially, from *pasimeneu* he dries fruit.

Early forms of this word include *putchamin* (1612), *pessemmin* (about 1612) and *posimon* (1670); the current spelling is first recorded in 1705.

persist *v.* continue firmly. 1538, in Elyot's *Dictionary;* borrowed from Middle French *persister,* from Latin *persistere* continue steadfastly (*per-,* as an intensive + *sistere* come to stand, from *stāre* to STAND). **—persistence** *n.* 1546, in John Bale's *Works;* borrowed from Middle French *persistance,* formed from Middle French *persister* persist + *-ance,* variant of *-ence.* **—persistent** *adj.* 1826 (in biology) not falling off, permanent; borrowed from Latin *persistentem* (nominative *persistēns*), present participle of *persistere* persist; for suffix see -ENT. The meaning of tenacious is first recorded in 1830.

persnickety *adj. Informal.* overly fastidious, fussy. 1905, American English; alteration of PERNICKETY.

person *n.* Probably before 1200 *persone* an individual; also, role or character, in *Ancrene Riwle;* borrowed from Old French *persone, persoune* human being; also, parson or priest, and directly from Latin *persōna* human being, individual; originally, character in a drama, actor, mask worn by an actor, possibly borrowed from Etruscan *phersu* mask. **—personable** *adj.* Probably 1435, well-made, attractive, presentable; perhaps formed from Middle English *persone* + *-able,* and borrowed from Middle French *personable,* from Old French *personable, persounable,* from Latin *persōna;* for suffix see -ABLE. **—personage** *n.* person of importance. About 1460, in *Proceedings of the Privy Council,* borrowed from Middle French *personage,* from Old French *personage, persounage* church dignitary; originally, a parsonage or rectory, from Latin *persōna;* for suffix see -AGE.

persona (pərsō′nə) *n.* 1917, (in Jungian psychology) a person's outward or social personality; later, a literary character representing the voice of the author (1958); borrowed from Latin *persōna* PERSON.

By the 1930's the psychological sense of *persona* was generalized to that of outward appearance, façade, image, as in *to create a new persona, a conflict between his private and public persona.*

personal *adj.* Before 1387, of a person, individual, private, in Trevisa's translation of Higden's *Polychron* *con;* borrowed from Old French *personel, personal,* from Latin *persōnālis,* from *persōna* PERSON; for suffix see -AL[1]. **—personality** *n.* Before 1425, quality or fact of being a person, in Wycliffe's writings; borrowed from Middle French *personalité,* and directly from Medieval Latin *personalitatem* (nominative *personalitas*) character, personality, from Latin *persōnālis* personal; for suffix see -ITY. The meaning of a distinctive personal or individual character is first recorded in 1795.

personify *v.* 1727-41, represent as a person, in *Chambers Cyclopaedia;* later, embody or exemplify (1803, in Wellington's *Despatches*); borrowed from French *personnifier,* from Old French *persone, personne* PERSON + *-fier* -FY. **—personification** *n.* 1755, act of personifying, in Johnson's *Dictionary;* from English *personify,* on the pattern of *magnify, magnification, pacify, pacification,* etc.; for suffix see -ATION.

personnel (pėr′sənel′) *n.* persons employed in any work, business, or service. 1857; borrowed from French *personnel* (used as a contrastive term to *matériel* material). In French this is a noun use of *personnel,* adj., personal, from Old French *personel* PERSONAL.

perspective *n.* Before 1387, optics, in Trevisa's translation of Higden's *Polychronicon;* borrowed in some instances perhaps from Old French *perspective,* and directly from Medieval Latin *perspectiva ars* science of optics; *perspectiva,* feminine of *perspectivus* of sight, optical, from Latin *perspect-,* past participle stem of *perspicere* inspect, look through (*per-* through + *specere* look at; see SPY); for suffix see -IVE.

The meaning of the art of picturing objects to give the appearance of distance or depth was possibly borrowed from Middle French and was surely influenced by Italian *prospettiva,* from *prospetto* view, from Latin *prōspectus* PROSPECT. The word in this meaning was first recorded in English in 1598.

The figurative sense of a view of things in which they are in the right relation (as in *a lack of perspective*) is first recorded in Bacon's *Of the Advancement of Learning* (1605). The related meaning of a mental view, outlook, or prospect, is first recorded in Goldsmith's *Citizen of the World* (1762), and that of a way of seeing things, point of view, in *The Education of Henry Adams* (1907).

—adj. Probably before 1425, of sight, optical, especially as pertaining to the study of optics, in a translation of Higden's *Polychronicon;* perhaps from the noun in English, but also borrowed from Medieval Latin *perspectivus.* The meaning of drawn or painted according to perspective is first recorded in English in 1606.

perspicacious *adj.* 1616-61, clear-sighted, in a translation of Persius' *Satires;* formed in English as an adjective to earlier *perspicacity,* perhaps by influence of French *perspicace,* from Latin *perspicāx* (genitive *perspicācis*) sharp-sighted, penetrating, acute, from *perspicere* look through; see PERSPECTIVE; for suffix see -OUS. The meaning of acute, discerning, shrewd, is first recorded in English in 1640. **—perspicacity** *n.* 1548, keen judgment, discernment; borrowed from Middle French *perspicacité,* and directly from Late Latin *perspicācitās* sharp-sightedness, discernment, from Latin *perspicāx* sharp-sighted; for suffix see -ITY.

perspicuous *adj.* 1584 (from a redated manuscript, originally 1477) clear-sighted; borrowed from Latin *perspicuus* transparent, clear, evident, from *perspicere* look through; see PERSPECTIVE; for suffix see -OUS. The meaning of easily understood, clear, lucid, is first recorded in English in 1586, but the sense of lucidity appears in the noun *perspicuity* as early as 1546.

perspire *v.* 1646, to evaporate, exhale; probably a back formation from earlier *perspiration,* and in some instances borrowed from French *perspirer,* from Latin *perspirāre* blow or breathe constantly (*per-* through + *spirāre* to breathe, blow; see SPIRIT).

The meaning "to sweat," developed from *perspiration,* is not recorded in the verb sense before 1725. **—perspiration** *n.* 1611, a breathing out or through, in Cotgrave's *Dictionary;* later, sweating (1626, in Bacon's *Sylva Sylvarum*); borrowed from French *perspiration,* from *perspirer* perspire; for suffix see -ATION.

persuade *v.* 1513, induce (a person) to believe or do something, in Sir Thomas More's *History of King Richard III;* borrowed from Middle French *persuader,* and directly from Latin *persuādēre* (*per-* strongly + *suādēre* to urge, persuade; see SUASION). It is also probable that *persuade* was, in some instances, a back formation of earlier *persuasion,* modeled on the Latin or French verb form. **—persuasion** *n.* a persuading. About 1380, in Chaucer's *House of Fame;* borrowed through Old French *persuasīon,* and directly from Latin *persuāsiōnem* (nominative *persuāsiō*), from *persuādēre* persuade; for suffix see -SION. **—persuasive** *adj.* convincing. 1589, borrowed from Middle French *persuasif* (feminine *persuasive*), from Medieval Latin *persuasivus,* from Latin *persuādēre* persuade; for suffix see -IVE. Like the verb *persuade,* the adjective may have been formed in English from *persuas(ion)* + *-ive* or earlier *persuas(ible)* with substitution of *-ive.* By the late 1600's *persuasive* had replaced earlier *persuasible* (before 1400).

pert *adj.* saucy, bold. About 1250, evident or unconcealed, in *The Story of Genesis and Exodus,* shortened from *apert* open or frank; borrowed from Old French *apert,* learned borrowing from Latin, and borrowed directly from Latin *apertus,* past participle of *aperīre* to open; see APERTURE.

The sense of saucy or bold is first recorded in English in Chaucer's *Canterbury Tales* (about 1390), probably influenced by Old French *espert* EXPERT.

pertain *v.* Before 1325 *portenen* attach legally; later *pertenen, partenen* belong, be connected, associated with (probably before 1350); borrowed from Old French *pertenir, partenir,* and directly from Latin *pertinēre* to reach, stretch, tend (to), relate, concern (*per-* through + *tenēre* to hold; see TENANT).

pertinacious *adj.* very persistent, determined. 1626, formed from English *pertinacy* + *-ous,* from Latin *pertinācia* stubbornness, from *pertināx* (genitive *pertinācis*) very firm, tenacious (*per-* with intensive sense of very + *tenāx* TENACIOUS). **—pertinacity** *n.* persistent or determined quality. 1504, borrowed from Middle French *pertinacité,* formed in Old French from *pertinace* obstinate or pertinacious, from Latin *pertinācem* (nominative *pertināx*) very firm, tenacious + *-ité* -ity. The older form *pertinacy* (recorded about 1390) was gradually replaced by *pertinacity* in the 1700's.

pertinent *adj.* About 1390 suitable, appropriate, in Chaucer's *Canterbury Tales;* also, relevant, pertaining, apt (probably about 1408, in Lydgate's *Reson and Sensuallyte*); borrowed from Old French *partenant,* and directly from Latin *pertinentem* (nominative *pertinēns*) pertaining, present participle of *pertinēre* to relate, concern, PERTAIN; for suffix see -ENT. **—perti-**

nence *n.* 1659, fact of being pertinent; probably formed from English *pertinent* + *-ence* as a noun to the earlier *pertinent.* An older form in English with the sense of something that belongs to or is a part of another larger thing is first recorded in English probably before 1425; borrowed from Old French *pertinence, pertinance,* from *partenant* pertinent; for suffix see -ENCE.

perturb *v.* About 1385 *perturben* disturb greatly, in Chaucer's *Troilus and Criseyde;* probably borrowed from Old French *perturber,* and directly from Latin *perturbāre* confuse, disorder, disturb (*per-* an intensive form with the meaning of thoroughly + *turbāre* disturb, confuse, from *turba* turmoil, crowd; see TURBID). It is also possible, especially as both *perturb* and *perturbation* are found in Chaucer, that his use of *perturb* is a back formation of *perturbation.* **—perturbation** *n.* About 1380 *perturbacion, perturbacioun,* in Chaucer's translation of Boethius' *De Consolatione Philosophiae;* borrowed from Old French *perturbacïon,* and directly from Latin *perturbātiōnem* (nominative *perturbātiō*) confusion, from *perturbāre* perturb; for suffix see -ATION.

peruke (pərük′) *n.* wig. 1548, natural head of hair, in Elyot's *Dictionary;* borrowed from Middle French *perruque,* from Italian *perrucca* head of hair, wig, of uncertain origin; compare PERIWIG. The meaning of false hair, wig is first recorded in 1606, from the original use in *false perruke* (1565-73).

peruse (pərüz′) *v.* 1479 *perusen* examine, go through, use up; formed from Middle English *per-* an intensive form with the meaning of completely or thoroughly + *use* to use. The meaning of read through carefully is first recorded in 1532, in Elyot's writings. Later use in the sense of read through quickly or casually is probably first recorded as early as the 1800's. The etymological make-up of the compound with *-use* is not obvious in this latter sense, but similar formations are found in *peract* perform or accomplish and *understand.* **—perusal** *n.* About 1600, in Shakespeare's *Sonnets;* formed from English *peruse* + *-al*².

pervade *v.* permeate, penetrate. 1653, in Henry A. More's *Antidote Against Atheism;* borrowed from Latin *pervādere* spread or go through (*per-* through + *vādere* go; see WADE). **—pervasive** *adj.* pervading. About 1750, in Shenstone's *Works;* formed in English from Latin *pervāsus* (past participle of *pervādere* pervade) + English *-ive.*

perverse *adj.* contrary. 1369 *pervers,* in Chaucer's *Book of the Duchesse;* borrowed from Old French *pervers, perverse, parvers,* and directly from Latin *perversus* turned away from what is right, contrary, askew, past participle of *pervertere* to corrupt; see PERVERT. **—perversity** *n.* condition of being perverse. 1528, borrowed from Middle French *perversité,* from Latin *perversitātem* (nominative *perversitās*), perverseness from *perversus,* past participle of *pervertere;* for suffix see -ITY.

pervert (pərvėrt′) *v.* to corrupt. About 1380 *perverten* overthrow, lead or turn from what is right, misconstrue, misapply, in Chaucer's translation of Boethius' *De Consolatione Philosophiae;* borrowed from Old French *pervertir, parvertir,* and directly from Latin *pervertere* corrupt, turn the wrong way, turn about (*per-* away, to destruction + *vertere* to turn; see VERTEX). —*n.* (pėr′vėrt) perverted person. 1661, corrupted person, apostate, in Blount's *Glossographia;* from the verb. The meaning of one who practices sexual perversion is first recorded in 1897. **—perversion** *n.* Before 1387, act of perverting, condition of being perverted; borrowed from Old French *perversion,* and directly from Latin *perversiōnem* (nominative *perversiō*) a turning about, from *pervertere* to pervert; for suffix see -SION. The meaning of deviant sexual practice is first recorded in 1892.

pervious *adj.* giving passage or entrance. Before 1614, in Donne's *Works;* borrowed from Latin *pervius* letting things through (*per-* through + *via* road; see VIA); for suffix see -OUS.

pesky *adj. Informal.* troublesome, annoying. 1775, American English, perhaps a dialectal formation from *pest* + *-y*¹.

pessary *n.* 1392 *pessarie* a suppository inserted in an aperture of the body, especially into the vagina; borrowed from Late Latin *pessarium,* from Greek *pessárion* medicated tampon of wool or lint, diminutive of *pessós* pessary; earlier, oval stone used in games; of unknown origin. The meaning of a contraceptive device is first recorded in English in 1886.

pessimism *n.* tendency to look on the unfavorable side of things. 1794, in Coleridge's *Letters;* borrowed from French *pessimisme,* formed from Latin *pessimus* worst; originally, bottom-most + French *-isme* -ism; patterned on French *optimisme* optimism; for suffix see -ISM. Being cognate with Sanskrit *pádyate* falls, Latin *pessimus* is from Indo-European **ped-temos* (perhaps a derivative of the root *ped-* foot, Pok.791). Related to PEJORATIVE. **—pessimist** *n.* 1836, borrowed from French *pessimiste,* from *pessimisme* pessimism, on the pattern of *optimisme, optimiste;* for suffix see -IST. **—pessimistic** *adj.* 1868, formed from English *pessimist* + *-ic.*

pest *n.* 1568, plague or pestilence; borrowed from Middle French *peste,* from Latin *pestis* any deadly contagious disease, plague, pestilence; of unknown origin. Appearance of the form *pest* in English was probably also influenced by earlier *pestilence.* The weakened sense of any noxious, destructive, or troublesome thing or person, nuisance, is first recorded in English in 1609.

pester *v.* About 1536, to obstruct or encumber; probably shortened from Middle French *empestrer, empaistrier* place in an embarrassing situation, from Vulgar Latin **impāstōriāre* to hobble (an animal); formed from Latin *im-* in, variant of *in-*² before *m* + Medieval Latin *pastoria (chorda)* rope to hobble an animal, shackle, noun use of Latin *pāstōria,* feminine of *pāstōrius* of a herdsman, from *pāstor* herdsman, from *pāscere* to graze; see FOOD.

The sense of annoy, trouble, plague, is first recorded in 1586, influenced by *pest.*

pesticide *n.* substance used to kill insects, fungi, and other pests. 1939, formed from English *pest* + connective *-i-* + *-cide*¹, as in *insecticide.*

pestiferous *adj.* bringing disease or infection. Probably before 1449 *pestiferus,* perhaps in Lydgate's writings, probably originally borrowed from Latin *pestiferus* that brings plague or destruction, variant of *pestifer* bringing plague (*pestis* plague; see PEST + *-fer* bearing from *ferre* to carry, BEAR²). The spelling *pestiferous* (1458 or 1523) was probably re-formed in English from Latin *pestifer* + English *-ous,* and perhaps from Latin *pestis* + English *-ferous.*

pestilence *n.* epidemic disease, plague. About 1303 *pestelens,* in Mannyng's *Handlyng Synne;* later *pestilence* (probably about 1350); borrowed from Old French *pestilence,* learned borrowing from Latin, and borrowed directly from Latin *pestilentia* plague, from *pestilentem* (nominative *pestilēns*) pestilent, infected, unwholesome, noxious, from *pestis* any deadly disease, plague; see PEST; for suffix see -ENCE. **—pestilent** *adj.* Before 1398, in Trevisa's translation of Bartholomew's *De Proprietatibus Rerum;* borrowed possibly through Old French *pestilent,* from Late Latin *pestilentus* infected, tending to produce infection, and directly from Latin *pestilentem* (nominative *pestilēns*) infected; for suffix see -ENT.

pestle (pes′təl) *n.* tool for pounding or crushing substances. 1349 *pestell;* earlier *pestel* leg of pig, used for food (1326), and as a surname *Pestel* (about 1280); borrowed from Old French *pestel,* from Latin *pistillum* pounder or pestle, related to *pīnsere* to pound. Latin *pīnsere* is cognate with Greek *ptíssein* to trample, crush, Old Slavic *pĭchati* to pound, and Sanskrit *pináṣṭi* he pounds, crushes, from Indo-European **pis-* (Pok.796). Doublet of PISTIL, **—v.** pound with a pestle. 1413 *pestelen,* borrowed from Middle French *pesteler,* from Old French *pestel,* n.

pet[1] *n.* animal kept as a favorite. 1508, indulged child; later, animal kept as a favorite (1539); originally a Scottish and Northern English dialectal usage; probably associated with *petty,* Middle English *pety* small, but ultimately of unknown origin. **—adj.** treated or kept as a pet. 1584, from the noun. **—v.** treat as a pet. 1629, from the noun. The later sense of to stroke is found in 1818, and the extended meaning of have erotic physical contact with another person is first recorded in 1924, in American English.

pet[2] *n.* fit of peevishness. 1590, in the phrase *take the pet* to take offence, become peevish; of uncertain origin. Use in phrase *in a pet,* is found as early as 1647.

petal *n.* part of a flower that is usually colored. 1726 (but found as *petala* in an English context, 1704); borrowed from New Latin *petalum* a petal (1649), from Greek *pétalon* leaf, thin plate, originally *pétalos* outspread, broad, flat; related to *petannýnai* to spread out; see FATHOM.

petard (pitärd′) *n.* explosive device formerly used in warfare. 1598, in Florio's *A World of Words;* borrowed from French *pétard,* from Middle French *péter* expel intestinal gas, break wind, from Old French *pet* a breaking of wind, from Latin *pēditum,* from neuter past participle of *pēdere* to break wind. Latin *pēdere* is cognate with Greek *bdeîn* and Lithuanian *bezdě́ti* to break wind, from Indo-European **pesd-/psd-* (Pok. 829).

The expression *hoist with* (or *on*) *one's own petard,* meaning (to be) blown up by one's own bomb, beaten with one's own weapon, caught in one's own trap, comes from a passage in Shakespeare's *Hamlet* (1604): "Let it work; For 'tis the sport to have the enginer Hoist with his own petar." The early spelling *petar* was based on the French pronunciation.

peter v. *Informal,* in **peter out,** become exhausted, diminish gradually, give out. 1846, American English (mining slang); earlier **to peter** cease, stop (1812); of uncertain origin.

petiole (pet′ēōl) *n.* slender stalk by which a leaf is attached to the stem. 1753, in *Chambers Cyclopaedia;* borrowed from French *pétiole,* from New Latin *petiolus,* special use by Linnaeus of Latin *petiolus,* misspelling of *peciolus* stalk, stem; literally, little foot, contracted from **pediciolus,* diminutive of *pediculus* foot stalk; see PEDICEL.

petit (pet′ē) *adj. Law.* small, petty, minor. About 1378, in a version of *Piers Plowman;* earlier, as a proper name *Petit* (1086); borrowed from Old French *petit* little or small, probably derived from the Gallo-Romance stem *pitt-* little, related to the stem *pit-, pis-* of Late Latin *pitinnus, pisinnus* small, of uncertain origin. The form in English law has been largely replaced by *petty,* as in *petty jury,* but is retained in such established forms as *petit bourgeois* (1853, Charlotte Brontë), *petit four* (1884), and *petit mal* (1842).

petite (pətēt′) *adj.* little. 1784, but found earlier in French phrases used in English, such as *petite pièce* minor writing of an author (1712); borrowing of French *petite,* feminine of *petit* little, from Old French; see PETIT.

petit four (pet′ē fôr′) small fancy cake or cookie. 1884, borrowing of French *petit four* little oven (*petit* little, from Old French; see PETIT; *four* oven, from Latin *furnus;* related to FURNACE).

petition *n.* formal request. Before 1338 *peticioun, peticion,* in Mannyng's *Chronicle of England;* borrowed from Old French *peticion,* learned borrowing from Latin *petītiō,* and borrowed directly from Latin *petītiōnem* (nominative *petītiō*) a request, solicitation, from *petere* to require, seek; see FEATHER; for suffix see -TION. **—v.** make a petition for. 1607, in Shakespeare's *Coriolanus;* from the noun.

petrel *n.* any of various sea birds. 1703, in Dampier's *A New Voyage Round the World,* but found earlier with the spelling *pitteral* (1676); perhaps a formation in English on analogy with *pickerel* and *cockerel* representing a diminutive form of *Peter* in Latin, such as **Petrellus,* from Late Latin *Petrus* Peter, from Greek *Pétros* Peter; literally, rock.

According to Dampier the name was a diminutive of St. *Peter,* and was given to petrels by seamen in allusion to St. Peter's walking upon the Lake of Gennesaret (Matthew 14:29), because as these birds fly they pat the water with their feet as if they were walking upon it.

Petri dish or **petri dish** (pē′trē) shallow circular glass dish for keeping bacterial cultures. 1892, named after the German bacteriologist Julius *Petri,* 1852-92, who devised such a dish and introduced it in 1887.

petrify *v.* 1594, turn into stone; found in earlier *petrified* hardened, solidified (probably before 1425, in a translation of Chauliac's *Grande Chirurgie*), and borrowed from Middle French *pétrifier;* formed in French (as if a borrowing from Latin **petrificāre* to make or become stone) from Latin *petra* rock, from Greek *pétrā* + Middle French *-fier* -fy. The figurative sense of change as if to stone, benumb, paralyze with fear, horror, or surprise, is first recorded in Goldsmith's *Haunch of Venison* (1771). **—petrification** *n.* 1611, in Cotgrave's *Dictionary;* borrowed from French *pétrification,* from Middle French *pétrifier* petrify, on the model of such pairs as *édifier, édification;* for suffix see -ATION. An isolated occurrence is found in Middle English *petrifaccioun* (probably before 1425, in a translation of Chauliac's *Grande Chirurgie*), formed after Medieval Latin *petrificatio,* which would be a nominative form to Latin **petrificātiōnem.*

petro- a combining form meaning: **1** stone, rock, rocks, as in *petrology.* **2** petroleum, as in *petrochemical.* **3** of or having to do with petroleum production or the industry that has developed around it, as in *petropower, petrodollar.* Borrowed from Greek *petro-,* combining form of *pétrā* rock, of uncertain origin.

petrochemical *n.* chemical obtained from petroleum or natural gas. 1942, formed from English *petro-* petroleum + *chemical.*

petrography *n.* branch of geology that deals with the description and classification of rocks. 1858, formed from English *petro-* rock + *-graphy,* after French *pétrographie.*

petrol *n.* 1895, gasoline; earlier, petroleum (1596); borrowed from Middle French *petrole* petroleum, from Old French, learned borrowing from Medieval Latin *petroleum* PETROLEUM. The later use with the meaning of gasoline was reinforced by modern French *pétrole.*

petrolatum (pet′rəlā′təm) *n.* salve or ointment made from petroleum. 1887, New Latin, the official name in United States pharmacology for petroleum jelly or vaseline, formed from *petroleum* (from Medieval Latin) + *-atum* -ate[1].

petroleum *n.* oily liquid found in the earth. Probably before 1425, in a translation of Chauliac's *Grande Chirurgie;* borrowing of Medieval Latin *petroleum* (from Latin *petra* rock, from Greek *pétrā* + Latin *oleum* OIL).

petrology *n.* science of rocks. 1876, formed from English *petro-* + *-logy.* The earlier spelling *petralogy* (1811) was formed from Greek *pétrā* rock + English *-logy.*

petticoat *n.* skirt worn beneath the dress. Before 1420 *petycote* padded coat worn under armor, in Lydgate's *Troy Book;* later, short coat worn by men (1439), formed from *pety* small, PETTY + *cote* COAT.

By 1464 the word was applied to a garment worn by women and young children, perhaps originally a kind of tunic or chemise but usually a skirt hanging from the waist. The sense of an underskirt is first recorded in Shakespeare's *The Taming of the Shrew* (1596). Shakespeare also used *petticoat* as the typical feminine garment (*3 Henry VI,* 1593) and applied it to the wearer of a petticoat, a female, or the female sex in general (*As You Like It,* 1600), a sense which developed into the adjective use with the meaning of relating to or characteristic of women; womanlike (1660).

pettifogger *n.* lawyer who uses petty, cheating methods. 1564-78, formed from English *petty* + *fogger,* of unknown origin. It is tempting to connect the word *fogger* with the sense of one who obscures or bewilders, but this meaning is not recorded, and does not appear for the verb *fog* until sometime before 1684. The explanation in the OED of *fogger* probably being associated with *Fugger,* the surname of a renowned family of merchants and financiers of Augsburg, in the 1400's and 1500's and thence standing for monopolist, usurer, rich man, does not seem justified on either semantic or phonological grounds.
—pettifog *v.* act as a pettifogger. 1611, in Cotgrave's *Dictionary;* back formation from *pettifogger.* **—pettifoggery** *n.* pettifogging practice; legal chicanery. 1653, in Milton's *Works;* formed from English *pettifogger* + *-y*[3].

petty *adj.* Probably before 1387 *pety* small, minor, in a version of *Piers Plowman;* earlier found in *petti-wacche* petty watch (1372, an old name of coast guards), and in the surname *Petipas* (1191); borrowed from *peti,* variant of Old French *petit* small, PETIT.

petulant (pech′ələnt) *adj.* peevish. 1599, immodest, wanton, saucy, in Marston's *The Scourge of Villainy;* borrowed through Middle French *petulant,* or directly from Latin *petulantem* (nominative *petulāns)* wanton, forward, insolent, from the root of *petere* rush at, seek; see FEATHER. It is also probable that *petulant* was in some instances a back formation formed as an adjective to earlier *petulancy,* n. (1559). The meaning of peevish, irritable is first recorded in English in Johnson's *Dictionary* (1775). **—petulance** *n.* 1610, immodesty, wanton or saucy behavior, in Ben Jonson's *Works;* borrowed from French *pétulance,* from Latin *petulantia,* from *petulantem* (nominative *petulāns*) wanton, insolent. The meaning of peevishness is first recorded in English in Cowper's *The Task* (1784). *Petulance* is a replacement of earlier *petulancy* and in some instances perhaps represents a phonological shortening of *petulancy.*

petunia *n.* plant with funnel-shaped flowers. 1825, New Latin *Petunia* the genus name, from French *petun* tobacco, from Middle French, from Portuguese *petum,* from Guarani (Paraguay) *petȳ* (the *ȳ* represents a nasal sound); so called from its close botanical affinity to the tobacco plant.

pew *n.* Probably before 1387 *puwe* a raised bench in a church, in a version of *Piers Plowman;* later *pewe* (1406); borrowed from Old French *puie, puy* balcony or elevation, from Latin *podia,* plural of *podium* balcony; see PODIUM.

pewee or **peewee** (pē′wē) *n.* kind of small American bird. 1796, American English; its name is imitative of its cry.

pewit (pē′wit) *n.* crested plover, lapwing. Before 1529, in Skelton's *Poetical Works;* its name is imitative of its cry.

pewter *n.* alloy of tin with lead, copper, or other metals. 1310 *peuter;* later *pewter* (1393); borrowed from Old French *peautre, peaultre, peutre* (compare Provençal *peltre* and Italian *peltro*), from Vulgar Latin **peltrum* pewter, of uncertain origin.

peyote (pāō′tē) *n.* 1849, American English, a stimulant drug prepared from mescal, in J.W. Audubon's *Western Journal;* later, the mescal or any one of several other cacti (1885); borrowing of Mexican Spanish *peyote,* from Nahuatl *peyotl.*

pH symbol for the acidity or alkalinity of a solution. 1909, formed from *P,* the initial letter of German *Potenz* potency, power + H, symbol for the hydrogen ion; *pH* denoted the relative concentration of the hydrogen ion in a scale used to express the acidity or alkalinity of a solution. The symbol was coined by the Danish chemist Sören Peter Lauritz Sörensen.

phage (fāj) *n.* kind of virus that destroys various bacteria. 1926, shortened from earlier *bacteriophage* (1921); borrowed from French *bactériophage* (*bactério-,* from New Latin *bacterium* + Greek *phageîn* to eat; cognate with Sanskrit *bhága-s* happiness, fortune, and *bhájate* receives as his portion, enjoys, from Indo-European *bhag-* apportion, Pok.107).

phagocyte (fag′əsīt) *n.* cell capable of absorbing and

destroying waste or harmful material. 1884, borrowed from German (plural) *Phagocyten,* formed in German from Greek *phageîn* to eat + *kýtos* hollow container in allusion to cells of the body; see HIDE[2] animal skin. The word was coined by the Russian bacteriologist Élie Metchnikoff.

-phagous a combining form meaning eating, as in *anthropophagous* man-eating, *saprophagous* living on decaying matter. Adapted from Greek *-phagos,* from *phageîn* to eat.

phalanger (fəlan′jər) *n.* small, tree-climbing marsupial. 1774, in Goldsmith's *Natural History;* New Latin, from Greek *phalángion* venomous spider, spider's web, from *phálangos,* genitive of *phálanx* spider, PHALANX; so called from the resemblance of the phalanger's webbed hind toes to a spider's web.

phalanx (fā′langks) *n.* 1553, an ancient Greek battle formation of infantry fighting in close ranks; borrowing of Latin *phalanx,* or borrowed directly from Greek *phálanx* (genitive *phálangos*) line of battle, finger or toe bone; originally, trunk, log; see BALK.

The figurative sense of a body of people united for a common purpose is first recorded in 1600, and that of a compact body of people, animals, etc. (as in *a dense phalanx of elms*) in Pope's *Essay on Man* (1733). In anatomy, the first recorded meaning was that of a row of finger or toe bones, likened to a battle array (1693), although in current use *phalanx* refers to any one of these bones.

The earlier form in English was *phalange* (before 1460), from Latin *phalangem* (nominative *phalanx*), from Greek *phálanx.*

phallus (fal′əs) *n.* penis. 1613, image of the phallus, symbolizing the generative power in nature, in *Purchas his Pilgrimage;* borrowed from Latin *phallus,* from Greek *phallós* penis, figure of the penis used in the cult of Dionysus; related to *phállē* whale, cognate with Latin *follis* bag, and Old English *bulluc* bullock, from Indo-European **bhel-/bhol-/bhl̥-* blow up, swell up (Pok.120). **—phallic** *adj.* 1789, in Thomas Twining's translation of Aristotle's *Treatise on Poetry;* borrowed from Greek *phallikós,* from *phallós* phallus; for suffix see -IC.

phantasm (fan′tazəm) *n.* unreal fancy. 1614, spelling alteration of earlier *phantasma* (1598) and *fantesme* (before 1250, in a version of *Ancrene Riwle*); later *fantasme* (probably about 1350); borrowed from Old French *fantasme, fantesme, fantosme,* and directly from Latin *phantasma* an apparition, specter, from Greek *phántasma* image, phantom, from *phantázein* make visible, from *phaínein* to show; see FANTASY.

phantasmagoria (fantaz′məgôr′ēə) *n.* shifting scene of real things, illusions, fancies, etc. 1802 *Phantasmagoria,* the name of an exhibition of optical illusions by means of the magic lantern held in London in 1802, alteration (with Latinized ending) of French *phantasmagorie,* formed from Greek *phántasma* image + *agorā́* assembly + French *-ie* -y[3]. The transferred sense of a shifting and changing scene of many elements is first recorded in Hazlitt's *Table-talk* (1822), and the figurative sense of a shifting succession of imaginary figures, as seen in a dream or feverish condition, in Landor's *Imaginary Conversations with Literary Men and Statesmen* (1828).

phantom *n.* ghost. 1590 *phantome,* spelling alteration (influenced by Latin *phantasma*) of earlier *fantom* (about 1340) ghost, unreal fancy; earlier *fantome* (about 1303, in Mannyng's *Handlyng Synne*), and *fantesme* (before 1250, in a version of *Ancrene Riwle*); borrowed from Old French *fantosme, fantesme, fantasme,* from Vulgar Latin **fantauma,* from **fantagma,* alteration of Latin *phantasma* PHANTASM. The *s* in Old French *fantosme,* etc., was not pronounced (compare BLAME) and ultimately resulted in its loss in Middle English.

Pharisee (far′əsē) *n.* member of an ancient Jewish sect characterized by strict observance of the law and claims to superior piety. Probably before 1200 *pharíseu,* in *Ancrene Riwle;* also *farisew* (probably about 1200), and later *faresee* (about 1384, in the Wycliffe Bible); in part developed from Old English (about 897) *fariseus,* and perhaps in part borrowed from Old French *pharise* or directly from Late Latin; both the Old English and Old French forms are learned borrowings from Late Latin *Pharīsaeus,* from Greek *Pharīsaîos,* from Aramaic *pĕrishayyā,* emphatic plural of *pĕrīsh* separated, separatist, corresponding to Hebrew *pārūsh,* from *pārash* he separated.

The transferred meaning of a self-righteous or sanctimonious person is first recorded in 1589 (written as *pharisee*).

—pharisaic *adj.* of or like a pharisee; self-righteous; rigidly formal. Before 1618, borrowed from French *pharisaïque* (1541, in Calvin), or directly from Late Latin *Pharīsāicus,* from Greek *pharīsāikós,* from *pharīsaîos* Pharisee; for suffix see -IC.

pharmaceutical (fär′məsü′təkəl) *adj.* of or pertaining to drugs. 1648, formed in English from Late Latin *pharmaceuticus* of drugs or the art of preparing drugs (from Greek *pharmakeutikós,* from *pharmakeús* preparer of drugs; see PHARMACY) + English *-al*[1]. **—pharmaceutics** *n.* preparation of drugs. 1541 *pharmaceutic;* later with *-s*[1] (1670), from Late Latin *pharmaceuticus* of drugs or the art of preparing drugs; for suffix see -ICS and -S[1].

pharmacology *n.* science of drugs. 1721, in Bailey's *Dictionary;* borrowed from New Latin *pharmacologia* (1683); formed from Greek *phármakon* drug, poison; see PHARMACY + *-logiā* -logy. **—pharmacologist** *n.* Before 1728; formed from English *pharmacology* + *-ist.*

pharmacopoeia or **pharmacopeia** (fär′məkəpē′ə) *n.* book containing a list and description of drugs and medicines. 1621, in Burton's *The Anatomy of Melancholy,* New Latin *pharmacopoeia,* from Greek *pharmakopoiîā* the art of preparing drugs, from *pharmakopoiós,* adj., preparing drugs, from *pharmakopoieîn* prepare drugs, dyes, etc. (*phármakon* drug, poison; see PHARMACY + *poieîn* to make, Doric Greek *poiweîn,* cognate with Sanskrit *cinóti* arranges in layers, heaps up, from Indo-European **kwei-/kwoi-/kwi-,* Pok.637).

pharmacy *n.* About 1385 *fermacie* a drug, the use of drugs, in Chaucer's *Canterbury Tales;* later *farmacie* (probably before 1425); borrowed from Old French *farmacie,* from Medieval Latin *pharmacia,* from Greek *pharmakeíā* the use of drugs or medicines, from *pharmakeús* preparer of drugs, from *phármakon* drug, poison, charm, spell, of uncertain origin; for suffix see -Y[3].

The meaning of the preparation of drugs and medicines is first recorded in English in 1651 (written *pharmacie*); the meaning of a drugstore is found in 1833. **—pharmacist** *n.* 1834, in Bulwer-Lytton's *The Last Days of Pompeii;* formed from English *pharmacy* + *-ist.*

pharynx (far′ingks) *n.* tube that connects the mouth with the esophagus. 1693, New Latin, from Greek *phárynx* (genitive *pháryngos*) pharynx, windpipe, throat. Greek *phárynx* was altered (under influence of *lárynx*) from earlier *pháryx* (genitive *phárygos*) and is related to *pháranx* chasm, cleft, cognate with Latin *frūmen* pharynx, earlier **frug-smen,* from Indo-European **bherug-/bhrug-* (Pok.145). **—pharyngal** *adj.* of or having to do with the pharynx or a speech sound articulated in the pharynx. 1835, formed from New Latin *pharyngem* by the use of the suffix *-al*[1]. **—pharyngeal** *adj.* of or having to do with the pharynx or a speech sound articulated in the pharynx. 1828, formed from New Latin *pharyngeus* with substitution of English *-al*[1] for New Latin *-us.*

phase *n.* one stage, side, or view (of something). 1812, phase of the moon, in Robert Woodhouse's *An Elementary Treatise on Astronomy;* formed as a singular of New Latin *phases,* plural of *phasis,* perhaps in some instances by influence of French *phase* (compare *base,* with plural *bases*). New Latin *phasis* is a borrowing from Greek *phásis* appearance, from *phaínein* to show; see FANTASY.

The general application to one stage or aspect of a thing is first recorded in 1841.

—v. bring into the same phase, adjust. 1938, from the noun. The meaning of carry out by stages is first recorded in 1949.

pheasant *n.* kind of game bird. 1299 *fesaund;* earlier as a surname *Faisant* (1166); borrowed through Anglo-French *fesaunt,* Old French *fesan, faisan, fesant,* from Latin *phāsiānus,* from Greek *phāsiānós* a pheasant; literally, Phasian bird, from *Phâsis,* the river Phasis in Colchis, ancient country in Asia, on the Black Sea, where these birds were said to have been numerous.

The spelling with *ph* (influenced by Latin) appeared before 1393, in Gower's *Confessio Amantis.*

phen- or **pheno-** a combining form indicating a benzene derivative, as in *phenol, phenyl.* Borrowed from French *phén-,* from Greek *phaínein* to bring to light, show (because such early substances were by-products from the making of illuminating gas).

phenol (fē′nol) *n.* chemical substance used as a disinfectant and antiseptic. 1852, formed from English *phen-* + *-ol*[1].

phenomenon *n.* 1625, fact or occurrence, manifestation, in Bacon's *Essays;* borrowed from Latin *phaenomenon,* from Greek *phainómenon* that which appears or is seen, noun use of neuter present participle of *phaínesthai* appear; see FANTASY. The meaning of an exceptional fact, extraordinary occurrence, prodigy, is first recorded in the *Junius Letters* (1771). **—phenomenal** *adj.* 1825, of a phenomenon, in Coleridge's *Aids to Reflection in the Formation of a Manly Character;* formed from English *phenomenon* + *-al*[1]. The meaning of remarkable or extraordinary is first recorded in Rossetti's *Dante and His Circle* (1850).

phenotype (fē′nətīp) *n.* observable make-up of an organism, as distinguished from the genotype. 1911, borrowed from German *Phänotypus,* formed from Greek *phaínein* to show; see FANTASY + German *Typus* type, from Latin *typus.* The term was coined in 1909 by Wilhelm Johannsen; see GENE.

phenyl (fen′əl) *n.* univalent radical formed by removing one hydrogen atom from benzene. 1850, borrowed from French *phényle* (*phène* benzene, from Greek *phaínein* to show + *-yle* -yl).

pheromone (fer′əmōn) *n.* substance secreted by an animal species that causes specific response in other members of the species. 1959, formed from English *phero-,* from Greek *phérein* to carry, BEAR[2] + *(hor)mone.*

phial (fī′əl) *n.* small bottle. Probably about 1380 *fyole;* borrowed from Old French *fiole,* probably from Medieval Latin *phiola,* variant of Latin *phiala,* from Greek *phiálē* broad flat drinking vessel, of uncertain origin. Compare VIAL. The spelling *phial* is found in Middle English before 1398, in borrowings from Latin *phiala.*

phil- form of *philo-,* before vowels and before *h* or *l,* as in *philately, philharmonic, phillumenist.*

-phil form of *-phile,* as in *acidophil, Francophil.*

philander *v.* 1737 (implied in *philandering*), to make love in a trifling manner, play at courtship, flirt; literally, to act the Philander, from earlier English *Philander* a lover (1700, in Congreve's *The Way of the World*), originally the proper name of a lover in stories, drama, and poetry, as in Ariosto's *Orlando Furioso* and Beaumont and Fletcher's *Laws of Candy.* The name *Philander* was borrowed from the Greek adjective *phílandros* loving or fond of men (perhaps misunderstood later as meaning a loving man); formed from *phil-* loving; see PHILO- + *andr-,* stem of *anḗr* man. Greek *anḗr,* cognate with Sanskrit *nar-* man, hero, Latin (Sabine) *Nerō* brave, and Middle Welsh *ner* lord, is from Indo-European **ner-* (Pok.765). **—philanderer** *n.* 1841, a male flirt; formed from English *philander* + *-er*[1].

philanthropy (fəlan′thrəpē) *n.* 1623, love of mankind, benevolence to humanity, in Cockeram's *Dictionary;* earlier *philanthropia* (1608); borrowed perhaps from French *philanthropie,* learned borrowing from Late Latin, also borrowed directly from Late Latin *philanthrōpia,* and in earliest use directly from Greek *philanthrōpíā* humanity, benevolence, generosity, from *philánthrōpos,* adj., loving mankind (*phil-* loving + *ánthrōpos* man, mankind; see ANTHROPOID); for suffix see -Y[3]. The meaning of a philanthropic action or agency, humanitarian act is first recorded in 1884. **—philanthropic** *adj.* of philanthropy. 1789, (implied earlier in *philanthropically,* 1787); borrowed from French *philanthropique,* from Greek *philánthrōpos* loving mankind; for suffix see -IC. **—philanthropist** *n.* person who practices philanthropy. 1730-36, lover of mankind, in Bailey's *Dictionarium Britannicum;* formed from English *philanthropy* + *-ist.*

philately (fəlat′əlē) *n.* the collecting of postage stamps. 1865, borrowed from French *philatélie* (coined in 1864 by the French stamp collector M. Herpin); formed from French *phil-* loving + Greek *atéleia* exemption from tax (because a postage stamp shows prepayment of postal tax), from *atelḗs* free from tax or charge (*a-* without + *télos* tax, charge); for suffix see -Y[3]. Greek *télos* is related to *talássai* (single-act infinitive) to bear, suffer; originally, to lift, raise; cognate with Old Latin *tetulī* I have borne, and Gothic *thulan* suffer, from Indo-European **tel-/tol-* (Pok.1060). **—philatelist** *n.* stamp collector. 1865, borrowed from French *philatelist,* formed from *philatélie* philately + *-iste* -ist.

-phile a combining form meaning loving, admiring, or having a strong affinity for, or someone or something that loves, admires, or has a strong affinity, as in *acidophile, Francophile.* Borrowed through French and

Latin from Greek *-philos,* especially in personal names, *phílos* loving, dear, from *phileîn* to love.

philharmonic *adj.* devoted to music. 1813, borrowed from French *philharmonique,* from Italian *filarmonico,* literally, loving harmony (also said to be found in *Accademia Filarmonica di Verona,* 1500's), from Greek *phílos* loving + *tà harmoniká* theory of harmony or music, from neuter plural of *harmonikós* HARMONIC.

Philharmonic came into English as part of the name of various musical societies, especially the *Philharmonic Society* founded in London in 1813 for the promotion of instrumental music; hence a *Philharmonic* concert (1862) was one given by the Philharmonic Society, and the first *Philharmonic orchestra* (1895) was the Philharmonic Society's orchestra. After the turn of the century many symphony orchestras called themselves *Philharmonic* (e.g. the *Berlin Philharmonic,* the *New York Philharmonic*).

-philia a combining form meaning admiration, fondness, or affinity for, or tendency toward, as in *Anglophilia, hemophilia, necrophilia.* New Latin, from Greek *philíā* affection, from *phílos* loving.

philippic (fəlip′ik) *n.* bitter attack in words. 1592 *Philippique;* borrowing of Middle French *philippique,* learned borrowing from Latin *ōrātiōnēs Philippicae* a series of speeches made by the Roman orator Cicero against Mark Antony in 44 and 43 B.C. Cicero's *ōrātiōnēs Philippicae* were named after the series of speeches made by the Greek orator *Demosthenes* in 351, 344, and 341 B.C. in which he attacked *Philip II* of Macedon, attempting to arouse the Athenians to resist Philip's growing power. Latin *ōrātiōnēs Philippicae* was a translation of Greek *Philippikoì lógoi,* from masculine plural of *Philippikós* of Philip, from *Phílippos* Philip.

philistine (fəlis′tin) *n.* person with commonplace ideas and tastes. 1827 *Philistine,* in Carlyle's *Miscellaneous Essays;* translation of German *Philister* enemy of God's word, a name applied by German university students to townsmen or outsiders, hence, any unenlightened or uncultured person, from Late Latin *Philistaeus* of or from *Philistaea* the land of the Philistines, Philistia, from Greek *Philistíā,* from Hebrew *Pĕlesheth.* An earlier sense of a person regarded as hostile to those in his control is first recorded in English in 1600.

English *Philistine,* in the original sense of one of an ancient people of southwestern Palestine who were enemies of the Israelites, is first recorded before 1325, in *Cursor Mundi* as *philistiens, philistens;* borrowed from Late Latin *Philistīnī,* plural from Greek *Philistînoi,* from Hebrew *Pĕlishtīm* the people of *Pĕlesheth* Philistia.

—adj. characteristic of philistines, uncultured, commonplace, prosaic. 1831, in Carlyle's *Miscellaneous Essays;* from the noun.

philo- a combining form meaning loving or having admiration or fondness for, as in *philology, philosophy.* Borrowed from Greek *philo-,* combining form from *phílos* dear or friend (earliest meaning, one's own, of unknown origin), and *phileîn* to love.

philodendron (fil′əden′drən) *n.* climbing evergreen plant. 1877, New Latin *philodendron* the genus name, from Greek *philódendron,* neuter of *philódendros* loving trees (*philo-* loving + *déndron* tree, because it clings to trees; see DENDRITE).

philology *n.* About 1395 *philologie* the personification of knowledge pertaining to language and literature, in Chaucer's *Canterbury Tales;* also probably 1420, in Lydgate's *Temple of Glass;* borrowed from Latin *philologia.* The later sense of the study of learning and literature, literary scholarship, is first recorded in English in John Selden's *Titles of Honor* (1614); borrowed from French *philologie,* learned borrowing from Latin *philologia* love of learning or literature, literary pursuits, from Greek *philologíā* love of argument, discussion, learning, and literature, from *philólogos* fond of discussion and argument, studious of words, literary (*philo-* loving + *lógos* word, speech; see LEGEND); for suffix see -Y[3]. *Philology* as the study or science of language (now usually *linguistics*) is first recorded in English about 1716 but is alluded to earlier in this narrow sense in such forms as *philologer* a linguistic scholar (1660), *philological* (1659), and *philologue* a linguist (1594). **—philologist** *n.* 1648, literary person, classical scholar; formed from English *philology* + *-ist.* The meaning of a student of language, linguistic scholar, is first recorded in 1716. This term replaced earlier *philologer* and *philologue.*

philosophy *n.* About 1300 *philosofie* knowledge, body of knowledge, learning; later *philosophye* (before 1333); borrowed from Old French *filosofie* and later *philosophie,* learned borrowing from Latin; also borrowed directly from Latin *philosophia,* and directly from Greek *philosophíā* love or pursuit of knowledge, speculation, philosophy (*philo-* loving + *sophíā* knowledge, learning, wisdom, from *sophós* wise, learned, of uncertain origin); for suffix see -Y[3]. **—philosopher** *n.* About 1330 *philosofre* learned man or scholar; later *philosophre* (about 1378); in part borrowed from Old French *filosofe, philosophe,* learned borrowing from Latin; also borrowed directly from Latin *philosophus,* and directly from Greek *philósophos* lover of wisdom, philosopher (*philo-* loving, lover of + *sophíā* knowledge, wisdom); for suffix see -ER[1]; and in part developed from Old English *philosophe* (before 899, in Alfred's translation of Orosius' *Historiarum Adversus Paganos*); borrowed from Latin *philosophus.* **—philosophic** *adj.* About 1475 *philosophik* of philosophy or philosophers; borrowed from Middle French *philosophique,* learned borrowing from Latin; also borrowed directly from Latin *philosophicus,* and directly from Greek *philosophikós,* from *philosophíā* philosophy; for suffix see -IC. **—philosophical** *adj.* About 1385, in Chaucer's *Canterbury Tales,* formed in Middle English from Latin *philosophicus* of philosophers or philosophy + Middle English *-al* -al[1]. **—philosophize** *v.* 1594, think or reason as a philosopher does; formed from English *philosophy* + *-ize.*

philter or **philtre** (fil′tər) *n.* love potion. Probably 1587, borrowing of Middle French *philtre,* learned borrowing from Latin *philtrum,* from Greek *phíltron* love, charm, from *phileîn* to love, from *phílos* loving; for suffix see -ER[1].

phlebitis (flibī′tis) *n.* inflammation of a vein. 1822-34, New Latin, formed from Greek *phléps* (genitive *phlebós*) vein + New Latin *-itis* inflammation. Greek *phléps* is perhaps cognate with Old High German *bolca, bulchunna* bubble, from Indo-European **bhlegw-/ bhl̥gw* (Pok.155).

phlebotomy (flibot′əmē) *n.* opening a vein to let blood. Before 1400 *fleobotomie,* in a translation of Lanfranc's *Science of Surgery;* borrowed from Old French *flebotomie,* learned borrowing from Medieval Latin, and possibly borrowed directly from Medieval Latin *phlebotomia,* from Greek *phlebotomíā* (*phléps,* genitive *phlebós* vein + *-tomíā* a cutting, from *témnein* to cut; see PHLEBITIS and TOME); for suffix see -Y³. Since the 1960's *phlebotomy* has been used as a technical name for the transfusion and collection of blood, as at a blood bank. **—phlebotomist** *n.* 1657, one who practices phlebotomy, a surgeon who bleeds patients; formed from English *phlebotomy* + *-ist.* The meaning of a technician in charge of blood transfusion or collection, as at a hospital or blood bank, is first recorded in 1969.

phlegm (flem) *n.* thick discharge from the nose or throat. 1373 *fleume* cold and moist humor of the body (also, possibly as an error *feme,* about 1250); borrowed from Old French *fleume, flaime,* borrowed from Late Latin *phlegma* one of the four humors of the body, from Greek *phlégma* inflammation, heat, humor caused by heat, from *phlégein* to burn; see EFFULGENT.

The meaning of mucus, thick discharge, is first recorded in late Middle English before 1398. The original spelling *fleume* was replaced in the late 1500's by adaptation of the Latin *phlegma.*

—phlegmatic (flegmat′ik) *adj.* 1340 *fleumatik* abounding in phlegm (one of the four humors of the body), in *Ayenbite of Inwyt;* borrowed from Old French *fleumatique,* from Late Latin *phlegmaticus* full of phlegm, from Greek *phlegmatikós* of or like phlegm, from *phlegma* PHLEGM; for suffix see -IC. The sense of sluggish or indifferent is first recorded in English in 1574; developed because this temperament was formerly supposed to result from an abundance of phlegm in the body. It is interesting to note that the adjective is recorded perhaps before the noun if the reading of 1250 is not accepted.

phloem (flō′əm) *n. Botany.* the bast and associated tissue of a tree, as distinct from the xylem or woody portion. 1875, borrowing of German *Phloem, Phlöem,* from Greek *phlóos* bark, skin; originally, a swelling or growth, from *phleîn* be full of, abound; related to *phlýein* boil over; see FLUENT.

phlox (floks) *n.* plant with clusters of showy flowers. 1706, in Kersey's edition of Phillips' *Dictionary;* borrowing of Latin *phlox,* from Greek *phlóx* (genitive *phlogós*) a kind of plant with a showy flower; literally, flame, related to *phlégein* to burn; see EFFULGENT.

-phobe a combining form meaning one have a certain fear, hatred, or dread, as in *Anglophobe, xenophobe.* Borrowed from French *-phobe,* learned borrowing from Latin *-phobus,* from Greek *-phóbos* fearing, from *phóbos* fear, *phobeîn* to fear.

phobia *n.* excessive or abnormal fear. 1786, New Latin, abstracted from compounds formed with Latin *-phobia* and Greek *-phobíā* -PHOBIA. **—phobic** *adj.* having or characterized by a phobia. 1897, formed from English *phobia* + *-ic.* As a noun, *phobic,* meaning a person having a phobia, is first recorded about 1968.

-phobia a combining form meaning an excessive or abnormal fear of something or someone, as in *acrophobia, agoraphobia, claustrophobia.* Borrowed from Greek *-phobíā,* from *phóbos* fear, *phobeîn* to put to flight, frighten, related to *phébesthai* flee in terror, cognate with Lithuanian *bė̃gti* run, and Hindi *bhāg-* flee, from Indo-European **bhegw-/bhēgw-/bhogw-* (Pok.116).

phoebe (fē′bē) *n.* kind of small American bird, a flycatcher. 1700 *phebe,* American English; its name was formed in imitation of its cry, but later (1839) the spelling was adapted to *Phoebe,* a proper name.

phoenix (fē′niks) *n.* the mythical bird that burns itself and rises from its own ashes. Before 1150 *fenix;* found in Old English (about 750) *fēnix;* borrowed from Medieval Latin *phenix* from Latin *phoenīx,* from Greek *phóinīx* (genitive *phoínīkos*) the mythical bird phoenix; compare Egyptian *bjn;* of unknown origin. The Greek word cannot be associated with the unrelated words *phoinós* red with blood, and *phónos* murder. In the 1500's the original spelling *fenix* was refashioned in English to *phoenix* after the Latin form.

phon- the form of *phono-,* before vowels, as in *phonetic, phonic.*

phone¹ *n. Informal.* telephone. 1884, American English; shortened form of TELEPHONE. **—v.** *Informal.* to telephone. 1889, from the noun.

phone² *n. Phonetics.* speech sound. 1866, borrowed from Greek *phōnḗ* sound or voice; see -PHONE.

-phone a combining form meaning sound or voice, as in *microphone, telephone, xylophone;* or speaking or speaker of, as in *Anglophone, Francophone.* Adapted from Greek *phōnḗ* voice, sound. Greek *phōnḗ* is traditionally presented as related to Doric *phāmí* I say, Attic Greek *phēmí,* Latin *fātur* he says, from Indo-European **bhā-* speak. But there is no other evidence of an ablaut grade **bhō-* to the root **bhā-;* and semantically Greek *phōnḗ* accords better with Old Slavic *zvonŭ* tone, sound. Therefore Hjalmar Frisk, in his *Griechisches etymologisches Wörterbuch* (II, p. 1059) derives it from Indo-European **ĝhwōnā* (root *ĝhwen-/ĝhwon-*), Pok. 490.

phoneme (fō′nēm) *n.* 1894, any speech sound, vowel or consonant; later (specifically in linguistics) smallest contrastive unit of sound in a language (1896); borrowed from French *phonème,* from Greek *phṓnēma* a sound, from *phōneîn* to sound or speak, from *phōnḗ* sound or voice; see -PHONE. **—phonemic** *adj.* of phonemes. 1933, in Leonard Bloomfield's *Language;* formed from English *phoneme* + *-ic.* **—phonemics** *n.* study of phonemes. 1936, William F. Twaddell, in *Language,* formed from English *phoneme* + *-ics.*

phonetic *adj.* of or representing speech sounds. 1826, borrowed from New Latin *phoneticus* (1797), from Greek *phōnētikós* vocal, from *phōnētós* to be spoken, utterable, from *phōneîn* to speak, from *phōnḗ* sound, voice; for suffix see -IC. **—phonetics** *n.* study of speech sounds and pronunciation. 1841, in Robert G. Latham's *The English Language;* formed from English *phonetic* + *-s*¹; for suffix see -ICS.

phonic (fon′ik) *adj.* 1823, of sound, acoustic; later, phonetic (1843); back formation from earlier *phonics.* **—phonics** *n.* 1683-84, the science of sound, acoustics; later, phonetics (1894); formed from English *phon* sound + *-ics.* The current meaning of a method of teaching reading by the association of letters with the speech sounds they represent, is first recorded in E.B. Huey's *Psychology and Pedagogy of Reading* (1908), though this system of analyzing sounds to teach reading is recorded at least as early as 1844.

phono- a combining form meaning sound, as in *phonograph, phonology.* Borrowed from Greek *phōno-,* combining form of *phōnḗ* voice or sound.

phonograph *n.* 1835-40, a written character or symbol representing a speech sound; formed in English from

Greek *phōno-* sound + *-gráphos* writing, writer; later, instrument that reproduces sounds from records (1877, American English; invented in 1877 by Thomas Edison); formed from English *phono-* sound + *-graph* machine that records.

phonology (fōnol′əjē) *n.* study of or the system of the sounds of a language. 1799, formed from English *phono-* sound + *-logy* study of. **—phonological** *adj.* 1818, formed from English *phonology* + *-ical.*

phonon (fō′non) *n. Physics.* particle or quantum of energy in the form of sound or vibration. 1932, formed from English *phon-* sound + *-on* particle or unit, as in *meson,* etc.

phony or **phoney** *adj.* not genuine, fake, sham. 1900 *phoney,* in George Ade's *More Fables,* American English; perhaps an alteration of earlier English slang *fawney* a gilt brass ring used by swindlers (1781), borrowed from Irish *fáinne* ring. **—n.** fake, pretender. 1902 *phony,* American English, probably from the adjective. **—v.** to fake, falsify. 1942, American English; from the adjective.

phosphate *n.* salt or ester of phosphoric acid. 1795, borrowing of French *phosphate,* formed from *phosph(ore)* PHOSPHOROUS + *-ate* -ate².

phosphor (fos′fər) *n.* any substance which gives off light, especially when exposed to X rays, ultraviolet light, etc. 1705, borrowed from New Latin *phosphorus* phosphorus, and reinforced by French *phosphore;* later reinforced by German *Phosphor,* from New Latin *phosphorus* PHOSPHORUS.

An earlier use *Phosphor* (1635-50) is found in reference to the morning star, especially the planet Venus, borrowed from Latin *Phōsphorus,* and Greek *Phōsphóros* Lucifer, the morning star, from earlier adjective.

phosphorescent *adj.* giving out light without burning or by very slow burning. 1766, formed in English from New Latin *phosphorus* + English *-escent.* **—phosphorescence** *n.* a being phosphorescent. 1796, probably used in English as a natural formation of the noun to the adjective *phosphorescent* with substitution of *-ence,* but also found earlier in French *phosphorescence* (before 1788), formed from *phosphore* phosphorus + *-escence* -escence.

phosphorus (fos′fərəs) *n.* solid nonmetallic chemical element. 1645 phosphorescent substance, in Evelyn's *Diary;* New Latin, special use of Latin *phōsphorus* morning star, from Greek *phōsphóros* morning star, torchbearer, formed from *phôs* light (see FANTASY) + *-phóros* bearer, from *phérein* carry, BEAR². An earlier use *Phosphorus* (1629) is found in reference to the morning star; see PHOSPHOR.

The specific reference to the chemical element (one form of which glows in the dark) first occurs in 1680, in Robert Boyle's *Works.* The element was discovered in 1669 by the German alchemist Hennig Brand. **—phosphoric** *adj.* 1784, phosphorescent; probably a shortened form of *phosphorical* (1753); formed from English *phosphorous* + *-ical;* later, containing phosphorus (1791); probably developed in meaning by influence of French *phosphorique,* from New Latin *phosphorus;* for suffix see -IC.

photo *n. Informal.* photograph. 1860, in Queen Victoria's *Letters,* shortened from PHOTOGRAPH. **—v.** 1868, in Dante Gabriel Rossetti's letters.

photo- a combining form meaning light, as in *photoelectric, photograph, photosynthesis;* or a shortened form of photograph, as in *photoengraving, photogenic,* or of photoelectric, in *photocell.* Borrowed from Greek *phōto-,* combining form of *phôs* (genitive *phōtós*) light; see FANTASY. Also formed in compounds such as *photojournalism,* n. (1944) and *photojournalist,* n. (1959).

photogenic *adj.* 1839, produced by the chemical action of light on a sensitized surface, as in *photogenic drawing* (the earlier term for photography); formed from English *photo-* + *-genic* produced by. The word was coined by William Talbot, English inventor (contemporaneously with Daguerre) of photography.

The original sense of this word was replaced by *photographic,* and since 1855 *photogenic* has been used technically to mean "produced or caused by light." In 1928, in American English, *photogenic* was re-formed (from *photo* photograph + *-genic* producing) with the meaning "suitable for photography, photographing very well."

photograph *n.* 1839, formed from English *photo-* light + *-graph* instrument for recording. The terms *photograph, photographic,* and *photography* were introduced by the English astronomer and physicist Sir John Herschel, who contributed much to the science of photography. The OED suggests that the English terms may have been originally abstracted as the obvious elements of *photogenic* and French *héliographie.* **—v.** 1839, from the noun. **—photographer** *n.* 1847, formed from English *photography* + *-er*¹. **—photographic** *adj.* 1839, formed from English *photograph* + *-ic.* **—photography** *n.* 1839, formed from English *photo* + *-graphy.*

photon (fō′ton) *n. Physics.* particle or quantum of light. 1926, formed from English *photo-* light + *-on* particle or unit, as in *proton.*

photosynthesis *n.* process by which plants make carbohydrates using light. 1898, loan translation of German *Photosynthese* (*photo-* light + *synthese* synthesis). **—photosynthesize** *v.* 1921, from *photosynthesis* + *-ize.* **—photosynthetic** *adj.* 1900, from *photosynthesis* + *-ic.*

phrase *n.* 1530, manner of expression, combination of words, idiomatic expression, in Palsgrave's *Lesclarcissement;* borrowed from Latin *phrasis,* from Greek *phrásis* speech, way of speaking, phraseology, from *phrázein* to point out, express, tell, from *phrázesthai* to think upon, consider; possibly related to *phrḗn* (genitive *phrenós*) mind, sense; see FRENETIC. **—v.** Before 1550, to use a phrase or phrases; later, to express in a particular way (1570); from the noun. **—phrasal** *adj.* 1871, in John Earle's *The Philology of the English Tongue;* formed from English *phrase* + *-al*¹. **—phraseology** *n.* selection and arrangement of words. 1558, in the title of a book of phrases, appearing as if from Greek **phraseología,* irregularly formed from Greek *phrásis* way of speaking + *-logíā* -logy, and as a subtitle in New Latin *phraseologia,* irregularly formed from Latin *phrasis* way of speaking + *-logia* -logy. Later *phraseology* appears in the sense of selection and arrangement of words (1664).

phrenetic (frinet′ik) *adj.* frenzied, frenetic. 1558 *phrenetike,* borrowed from Greek *phrenētikós* FRENETIC; for suffix see -IC.

phylactery (fəlak′tərē) *n.* small leather case containing texts from Jewish law, worn during prayer. About 1384 *filaterie,* in the Wycliffe Bible; later *philateri* (probably about 1400); borrowed from Old French *philaterie,* and directly from Medieval Latin *filacterium, philaterium,* alteration of Late Latin *phylactērium* a reliquary or phylactery, from Greek *phylaktḗrion* guardpost, safeguard, preservative, especially an amulet, from *phylaktḗr,* from *phylássein* to guard, ward off, from *phýlax* (genitive *phýlakos*) guard or watchman, of uncertain origin; for suffix see -Y³. The spelling *phylactery* (influenced by the Late Latin form) began to appear in the 1500's.

phylogeny (fīloj′ənē) *n.* origin and development of a species of animal or plant. 1872, in Darwin's *Origin of Species,* borrowed from German *Phylogenie,* formed from Greek *phŷlon* race (see PHYLUM) + *-géneia* origin, from *-genḗs* born; see -GEN; for suffix see -Y³. The word was coined in 1866 by the German biologist Ernst Haeckel.

phylum (fī′ləm) *n.* primary division of a kingdom of living things. 1876, in Lankester's translation of Haeckel's *History of Creation;* New Latin, from Greek *phŷlon* race, stock, related to *phȳlḗ* tribe, clan, and *phýein* bring forth; see BE.

physic (fiz′ik) *n.* medicine, especially one that moves the bowels. About 1300 *fysike* a healing potion, medicine; later, natural science (about 1330; see PHYSICS), and *phisik* (about 1378); borrowed from Old French *phisike, fisique* natural science, art of healing, and directly from Latin *physica,* feminine singular, study of nature, from Greek *physikḗ epistḗmē* knowledge of nature, from *phýsis* nature; see PHYSICS. An isolated use as a proper name *Fisikus* appeared in 1221.

The sense of a medicine that acts as a laxative is first recorded in 1617.

physical *adj.* Probably before 1425 *phisicale* medical, as distinguished from surgical, in a translation of Chauliac's *Grande Chirurgie;* borrowed from Medieval Latin *physicalis* of nature, natural, from Latin *physica* study of nature; see PHYSIC; for suffix see -AL¹. The meaning of according to the laws of nature is first recorded in 1580, and that of pertaining to matter, material in 1597, in Hooker's *Ecclesiastical Polity.* The sense of having to do with the body, bodily, corporeal, is first attested in 1780, in Bentham's writings. **—physical education** (1838) **—physical therapy** (1922).

physician *n.* Probably before 1200 *fisitien* doctor of medicine, in *Ancrene Riwle;* later *phisicien* (1369, in Chaucer's *Book of the Duchesse*); borrowed from Old French *fisicien,* from *fisique* art of healing; see PHYSIC; for suffix see -IAN.

physics *n.* 1589, natural science; later, science that deals with matter and energy (1715); borrowed as a translation of Latin neuter plural *physica* natural science; also formed from earlier English *physic* natural science (about 1330) + *-s*¹. Latin *physica* is from Greek *tà physiká,* literally, the natural things, a name given to Aristotle's treatises on nature, from neuter plural of *physikós* of nature, from *phýsis* nature, from *phýein* bring forth; see BE; for suffix see -ICS. **—physicist** *n.* 1840, in William Whewell's *The Philosophy of the Inductive Sciences;* formed from English *physic(s)* + *-ist.*

physio- a combining form meaning nature, natural, physical, as in *physiography, physiology, physiotherapy.* Borrowed from Greek *physio-,* combining form of *phýsis* nature; see PHYSICS.

physiognomy (fiz′ēog′nəmē *or* fiz′ēon′əmē) *n.* one's features or type of face. Before 1393 *phisonomie* art of judging a person's nature by observing his features, especially of the face, in Gower's *Confessio Amantis;* also, the face or its expression (before 1400); borrowed from Old French *phisionomie,* learned borrowing from Late Latin *physiognōmia,* from Greek *physiognōmíā,* a variant of *physiognōmoníā* the judging of a person's nature by his features (*physio-* nature + *gnṓmōn,* genitive *gnṓmonos* judge, indicator; see GNOMON); for suffix see -Y³. The current English spelling (influenced by the Late Latin form) began to appear in the 1600's.

physiology *n.* study of the functions of living things. 1564, natural science, natural philosophy; borrowed through Middle French *physiologie,* or directly from Latin *physiologia* natural science, study of nature, from Greek *physiologíā* natural science (*physio-* nature + *-logíā* -logy, study of).

The biological meaning of the study of the functions of living things is first recorded in 1615 as a borrowing from New Latin *physiologia,* from Latin.

—physiological *adj.* 1610, of natural science; later, of physiology (1814); formed from Latin *physiologicus* of or belonging to natural science (from Greek *physiologikós,* related to *physiologíā* physiology) + English *-al*¹.

physiotherapy *n.* treatment of diseases and physical disabilities by remedies such as massage or electricity. 1905, formed from English *physio-* physical + *therapy.*

physique (fizēk′) *n.* bodily structure, physical appearance, body. 1826, borrowed from French *physique,* noun use of *physique,* adj., physical, from Latin *physicus* natural, physical, from Greek *physikós,* from *phýsis* nature; see PHYSICS.

-phyte a combining form meaning: **1** plant, planting, growth, as in *epiphyte* plant growing on another, *neophyte* "newly planted" (figuratively, a new convert), *saprophyte* plant living on decaying matter. **2** abnormal growth, as in *osteophyte* bony excrescence. Adapted from Greek *phytón* plant, *phýein* beget, produce, grow; see BE.

phyto- a combining form meaning plant, as in *phytochemistry, phytohormone, phytotoxic.* Borrowed from Greek *phyto-,* combining form of *phytón* plant; see -PHYTE.

pi (pī) *n.* the ratio of the circumference of any circle to its diameter. 1841, as a symbol indicated by the Greek letter π (used earlier in a Latin context, 1748). Borrowing of the name of the Greek letter π, used as an abbreviation of Greek *periphéreia* periphery.

pianissimo (pē′ənis′əmō) *adj., adv. Music.* very soft or softly. 1724, borrowed from Italian, superlative of *piano* soft, PIANO². **—n.** *Music.* passage played very softly. 1883, from the adjective.

piano¹ (pēan′ō) *n.* musical instrument. 1803, borrowing of French *piano* and Italian *piano,* shortened form of PIANOFORTE. **—pianist** *n.* 1839, in Longfellow's writings; borrowed from French *pianiste,* from Italian *pianista,* formed from *piano* piano + *-ista* -ist.

piano² (pēä′nō) *adj., adv. Music.* soft, softly. 1683, borrowed from Italian *piano,* from Late Latin *plānus* smooth, graceful, deliberate, from Latin, level; see PLAIN.

pianoforte (pēan′əfôr′tē) *n.* piano¹, the musical instrument. 1767, borrowing of Italian *pianoforte,* from the earlier phrase *piano e forte* soft and loud (1598, *piano* soft, PIANO²; *e* and, from Latin *et; forte* loud, from Latin *fortis* strong; see FORT).

Italian *pianoforte* derives from the old descriptive name *gravicembalo col piano e forte* harpsichord with soft and loud, so called by its inventor, Bartolommeo Cristofori (about 1710), because it is capable of producing gradations of tone, in contrast with the unvarying tone of the ordinary harpsichord.

pianola (pē′ənō′lə) *n.* piano played automatically, player piano. Before 1896 *Pianola,* American English, trademark of a player piano developed by the American inventor Edwin S. Votey and produced by the Aeolian Company. The name *Pianola* was formed from *piano*¹ + the ending *-ola,* perhaps abstracted from *viola.*

The popularity of the Pianola inspired the coinage of many names in *-ola,* notably (in 1906) the *Victrola,* eventually leading to the use of *-ola* in slang words such as *payola* and *plugola.* (See William Randle's article "Payola" in *American Speech* 36:2, 1961.)

piazza (pēaz′ə *or* pyat′sə) *n.* 1583, public square or marketplace; borrowing of Italian *piazza,* from Latin *platea* courtyard, broad street; see the doublet PLACE. The extended meaning of a colonnade, covered gallery or walk surrounding an open square, is first recorded in English in 1642, and that of a large porch or veranda, in 1724 in American English.

pica (pī′kə) *n.* size of type. 1588, probably borrowed from Medieval Latin *pica* name of a book of rules for determining dates of holy days (supposed to have been printed in pica), probably from Latin *pīca* magpie, PIE²; so called from the color and confused appearance of the old black type on the page which looked pied on the white paper.

picador (pik′ədôr) *n.* horseman at a bullfight who lances the bull. 1797, borrowing of Spanish *picador,* literally, pricker, from *picar* to pierce, from Vulgar Latin **piccāre;* see PIKE¹ spear.

picaresque (pik′əresk′) *adj.* dealing with rogues and their adventures. 1810, borrowed from Spanish *picaresco* roguish, from *pícaro* rogue, possibly from *picar* to pierce, from Vulgar Latin **pīccāre* to pierce; see PIKE¹ spear; for suffix see -ESQUE.

picayune (pik′əyün′) *adj.* small, petty, trifling. 1813, American English, from the noun (*n.* 1804, coin of small value, probably from Louisiana French *picaillon* coin worth 5 cents, from French, a coin of Savoy, from Provençal *picaioun,* derivative of *picaio* money, perhaps related to *pica* to sound, clink, perhaps from Vulgar Latin **piccāre* to pierce; see PIKE¹ spear).

piccalilli (pik′əlil′ē) *n.* relish of East Indian origin made of chopped vegetables. 1769 *piccalillo,* perhaps thought of as a derivative of PICKLE. The spelling *piccalilli* appeared in 1845.

piccolo (pik′əlō) *n.* small, high-pitched flute. 1856 *piccolo flute;* borrowed from French *piccolo,* from Italian *flauto piccolo* small flute; *piccolo* small, perhaps from *picca* point or from Vulgar Latin root **pīkk-* little, perhaps related to **piccāre* to pierce; see PIKE¹ spear.

pick¹ *v.* choose, select. About 1225 *picken* to peck, in *Ancrene Riwle;* about 1300 *piken* to work with a pick, dig; about 1330, to choose, select; probably a fusion of Old English **pīcian* to prick (implied in *pīcung* pricking), and of Old Icelandic *pikka* to prick, peck; both the Old English and Icelandic forms cognate with Middle Dutch *picken* to pick, prick, peck, (modern Dutch *pikken).* The verb in Middle English was later reinforced by Old French *piquer* to stick, pierce; see PIKE¹ spear. **—n.** Before 1450 *pike* a blow with a pointed instrument; later *pik* (1573); and in the meaning of choice, selection (1760-72); from the verb. **—picker** *n.* (1526) **—pickpocket** *n.* 1591, replacing Middle English *pikepurse* (about 1385, in Chaucer's *Canterbury Tales*), from *piken* to pick + *purse.* **—pickup truck** 1948, earlier in *pick-up body* referring to an early modification in style of car construction with a bin instead of a trunk, 1932. **—picky** *adj.* choosy. 1867, formed from English *pick*¹, v. + *-y*¹.

pick² *n.* sharp-pointed tool. Probably before 1200 *pic* pickaxe; later *pikke* sharp tool (1337), variants of PIKE² sharp point.

pickax or **pickaxe** *n.* 1428 *pecaxe,* 1494 *pycax,* alteration (influenced by *axe, ax*) of earlier Middle English *picas* (1256), *picoyc* (1278); borrowed through Anglo-French *piceis,* and from Old French *picois, pecois;* and probably borrowed directly from Medieval Latin *picosa* pick, pickax. Old French *picois* and *pecois* were also, in part, borrowed from Medieval Latin and, in part, formed from Old French *pic* pointed instrument, woodpecker, from Latin *pīcus;* see PIE² magpie.

pickerel *n.* kind of freshwater fish. 1290 *pikerel,* diminutive of PIKE³ fish; earlier as a surname (1200). The suffix *-erel* (also found in *mackerel, doggerel,* etc.) was borrowed from Old French *-erel, -erelle,* and appears sometimes in the form *-rel* as a derogatory suffix, as in *mongrel, scoundrel, wastrel,* etc.

picket *n.* 1690, a pointed stake used in a military punishment; later, used for other military purposes, such as building fences, marking positions in surveying, as a defense against cavalry, etc. (1702); borrowed from French *piquet,* from *piquer* to pierce; see PIKE¹ spear.

The military sense of a body of troops posted at some place to watch for the enemy is first recorded in 1761, probably borrowed from the older French sense of a group of horsemen ready to leave upon a signal (their horses being attached to a picket). The meaning of a group of people stationed by a labor union or the like to deter nonunion members, strikebreakers, customers, etc., from entering a workplace or business establishment, is first recorded in 1867.

—v. 1745, enclose with pointed stakes, from the noun. The meaning of post as a military picket is first recorded in 1775, and that of act as a picket in a labor dispute in 1867.

pickle *n.* Probably before 1400 *pekill* a highly-seasoned sauce served with meat or fowl, in *Morte Arthur;* earlier as a surname *Pikel;* probably borrowed from Middle Dutch *pekel* pickle or brine; cognate with Frisian *pikel,* Middle Low German *pēkel* (modern German *Pökel*).

The meaning of food, especially a vegetable, such as a cucumber, preserved in pickle is first recorded in 1707, and developed from the earlier sense of a salt or acid liquid in which meat, vegetables, etc., are preserved (1502, *pigell*).

The figurative meaning of a disagreeable or sour condition, trouble, difficulty (often in the phrase *in a pickle*), is first recorded in 1562. The usage is common and natural enough to English to be formed therein, but may have been reinforced by Dutch, in which the figurative expressions with the same sense appear, such as *in de pekel zijn* be in a pickle, *iemand in de pekel*

laten (or *zitten*) get someone in a pickle, etc., most of which are common from the 1500's.
—v. preserve in pickle. 1552 (implied in *pickled*), from the noun + *-ed*².

picnic *n.* 1748, a fashionable social gathering in which each participant contributes a share of the provisions, in Lord Chesterfield's *Letters to his Son;* borrowed from French *piquenique* (1692), of uncertain origin; perhaps a rhyming reduplication of French *piquer* to pick, peck, from Old French (see PIKE¹ spear) or possibly a compound of French *piquer* to pick + *nique* worthless thing (in the expression *faire la nique* thumb one's nose), from a Germanic source.

From its earliest use *picnic* occurs only in reference to foreign countries, not appearing as an English institution before 1800, at which time it began to take on the sense of a pleasure trip with a meal in the open air.
—v. 1821, furnish (provisions) by individual contribution; later, go on a picnic (1842, in Tennyson's *Audley Court*); from the noun.

pico- a combining form meaning: **1** one trillionth, used especially in the nomenclature of units in science, as in *picosecond.* **2** very small, as in *picornavirus.* Adapted from Spanish *pico* additional amount, a little over, a small balance; literally, sharp point, beak, peak, from Celtic (compare Gaulish *beccus* BEAK).

picornavirus (pikôr′nəvī′rəs) *n.* virus containing ribonucleic acid. 1962, formed from English *pico-* very small + *RNA* (abbreviation of *ribonucleic acid*) + *virus.*

picosecond (pē′kōsek′ənd) *n.* trillionth (10^{-12}) part of a second. 1966, formed from English *pico-* trillionth + *second.*

pictograph *n.* picture used as a sign or symbol, as in a system of picture writing. 1851, formed from Latin *pictus* painted (past participle of *pingere* to PAINT) + English connective *-o-* (perhaps influenced by *photo-*) + *-graph.*

pictorial *adj.* 1646, pertaining to painting, produced by the painter; formed as if from a Latin form **pictōriālis,* from Latin *pictōrius* of a painter, from Latin *pictor* painter, from *pict-,* past participle stem of *pingere* make pictures, PAINT; for suffix see -AL¹.

This word was not in general use before 1800. The meaning of having to do with or consisting of pictures is first recorded in 1807, that of containing pictures, illustrated, in Disraeli's *Vivian Grey* (1826), and that of picturesque or graphic, in 1829 (in Landor's *Works*).

picture *n.* Before 1420, drawing, painting, act of painting; in Lydgate's *Troy Book;* borrowed from Latin *pictūra,* from *pictus,* past participle of *pingere* make pictures, PAINT; for suffix see -URE.

The meaning of mental image, visualized conception, is first recorded before 1547, and that of the figurative meaning of graphic description, vivid account, in Shakespeare's *Love's Labour's Lost* (1588).
—v. About 1489 *picturen* to paint, draw, depict, in Caxton's *Sonnes of Aymon;* from the noun. The meaning of depict in words is first recorded in 1586, and that of form a picture of in the mind, imagine, in 1738.
—picture book (1847, in Thackeray).

picturesque *adj.* 1703, quaint or interesting enough to be used as the subject of a picture, in Sir Richard Steele's *The Tender Husband;* formed from English *picture* + *-esque,* perhaps patterned on French *pittoresque,* from Italian *pittoresco* pictorial, from *pittore* painter, from Latin *pictōrem,* accusative of *pictor* painter; see PICTORIAL.

piddle *v.* do anything in a trifling or ineffective way. 1545, in Roger Ascham's *Toxophilus,* of uncertain origin; the form of the verb is that of a frequentative (see the suffix -LE³). The participial adjective *piddling,* meaning insignificant, petty, trifling, appeared in 1559.

pidgin (pij′ən) *n.* any language spoken by non-natives with reduced grammatical structure and vocabulary. 1876, in Charles Leland's *Pidgin English Sing-Song,* shortened form of *Pidgin English,* alteration of earlier *pigeon English* the reduced form of English used at seaports in China for communication between Chinese and Europeans (1859), from the Pidgin English form *pigeon, pidgeon* business, from the Chinese pronunciation of English *business.*

The generalized meaning of *pidgin* any simplified language used for communication between foreigners is first recorded in 1921.
—pidginize *v.* change (a language) to a pidgin. 1937, back formation from earlier *pidginization* (1934); formed from *pidgin* + *-ization.*

pie¹ *n.* food enclosed in pastry. 1357-58; earlier in Medieval Latin context (1303) *pie* meat or fish enclosed in a pastry; also found in *Piehus* bakery (1199); perhaps from Medieval Latin *pia* pie, pastry, of uncertain origin. The reference to fruit pie is first recorded perhaps before 1568, the earliest reference specifically to *apple pie* being 1590.

pie² *n.* magpie, a chattering bird. About 1250, in *The Owl and the Nightingale;* probably earlier as a surname *Pie* (1177); borrowed from Old French *pie,* from Latin *pica* magpie, related to *pīcus* woodpecker. Latin *pīcus* is cognate with Umbrian *peico* magpie, Old Prussian *picle* fieldfare (a kind of thrush), and Sanskrit *piká-s* the Indian cuckoo.

piebald (pī′bôld′) *adj.* spotted in two colors, especially white and black. 1589, in the figurative sense of mixed or mongrel; formed from English *pie*² magpie + *bald* spotted or white; so called from the spotted plumage of the magpie. Compare PIED. **—n.** piebald horse. 1765, from the adjective.

piece *n.* Probably before 1200 *pece* part, portion, section, in *Ancrene Riwle;* later *piece* (about 1330); borrowed from Old French *piece, pece,* from Vulgar Latin *pettia, probably from a Gaulish word (compare Welsh *peth* thing, Breton *pez* piece, and Old Irish *cuit* part).
—v. about 1400 *pesen* to patch, repair, join the pieces of; later *pecen* (1440); from *pece, piece,* n.

piecemeal *adv.* piece by piece. About 1300 *pecemele* (*pece* PIECE + *-mele,* obsolete suffix meaning "by small measures," developed from Old English *-mǣlum* from *mǣlum* at a time, dative plural of *mǣl* appointed time, food served, MEAL¹).

pied *adj.* many-colored. 1382 *pyed;* earlier in the surname *Pydecoke* (1310); formed from Middle English *pie*² magpie + *-ed*²; so called from the spotted plumage of the magpie.

Early use of this word is associated with *pyed freres,* the name of an order of friars who wore a habit with a pattern of colors resembling the black and white plumage of the magpie.

pier *n.* structure extending into the water. Before 1125, as the inflected form *peran;* later *pere* (about 1380); borrowed from Medieval Latin *pera,* perhaps a Latinization of Old North French *pire, piere* a break-water, from Vulgar Latin **petricus,* from Latin *petra* rock; see PETRO-.

pierce *v.* Probably before 1300 *percen* to thrust through, stab, prick, puncture, in *Arthour and Merlin* and *Kyng Alisaunder;* earlier in the surname *Percehaie* (1202); borrowed through Anglo-French *perser, piercer,* Old French *percer, percier,* probably from Vulgar Latin **pertūsiāre,* from Latin *pertūsus,* past participle of *pertundere* to thrust or bore through (*per-* through + *tundere* to beat, pound; see STUDY).

piety *n.* About 1325 *piete* mercy, tenderness, pity; earlier as a surname *Piete* (1195); borrowed from Old French *pieté,* learned borrowing from Latin *pietātem* (nominative *pietās*) dutiful conduct, kindness, compassion, pity, from *pīus* dutiful, kind, devout, PIOUS; for suffix see -TY². Related to PITY.

The meaning of reverence for God, devotion to religion is first recorded in 1604, in Cawdrey's *A Table Alphabeticall.*

—pietism *n.* 1697, a movement in Germany to revive personal piety in the Lutheran Church; borrowed from German *Pietismus,* from Latin *pietās* piety + German *-ismus* -ism. The movement was led by Philip Jakob Spener, who instituted religious services to be held in the home and called them *collegia pietatis.* Participants in such devotions were mockingly called *Pietisten,* in English *Pietists* (1697). The extended sense of *pietism* "piety, pious sentiment" (often implying an affectation or pretension of piety) is first recorded in English in 1829.

piezo- a combining form meaning pressure, as in *piezometer, piezoelectricity* (electric polarity induced by pressure). Adapted from Greek *piézein* to press, squeeze, perhaps altered (under the influence of *hézesthai* to sit) from **pízein,* cognate with Sanskrit *pīḍáyati* to press, oppress, from Indo-European **pisd-* (Hjalmar Frisk, *Griechisches etymologisches Wörterbuch,* II 534).

piezometer (pē'əzom'ətər) *n.* instrument for measuring pressure. 1820, formed from English *piezo-* + *-meter.* The word was coined by the American inventor Jacob Perkins, 1766-1849.

piffle *v.* talk or act in a trifling or ineffective way. 1847-78, perhaps alteration of *trifle* (by association with such forms as *piddle*). **—n.** foolish, trifling talk or behavior. 1890, from the verb.

pig *n.* About 1250 *pigge,* in *Ancrene Riwle;* later *pig* (before 1325), and as a surname (1186); probably developed from Old English **picga, *pigga,* found in the compound *pic-bred* acorn, mast, a possible alteration of *pic-brēad,* literally, pig-bread, of uncertain origin.

The offensive slang meaning of *pig* "police officer" is recorded in British underworld slang since about 1812; it was revived in American English slang in the late 1960's.

—v. Probably 1440 *piggen* to bear pigs, farrow; from the noun. The meaning of live in filth like pigs is first recorded in 1675; the phrase *to pig it* is first recorded in 1889. The sense of eat like a pig in *pig out* is not found until the 1970's.

—piggish *adj.* 1792, in Coleridge's letters (implied in *piggishly*), formed from *pig,* n. + *-ish*¹. **—piggy** *n.* 1799, formed from English *pig,* n. + *-y*². **—piggy bank** (1941) **—pig-headed** (1620, in Ben Jonson's writings) **—pig Latin** About 1926, in American English, a low, distorted form of English, in which initial consonants are transposed to the end and followed by *-ay,* as in *amscray* for *scram!* and *igpay atinlay* for *pig Latin.* **—piglet** *n.* 1883, formed from English *pig,* n. + *-let.* **—pigpen** *n.* (1803, American English) **—pigskin** *n.* 1855, leather made from pig's skin; 1894, American English, a football. **—pigsty** *n.* 1591, formed from English *pig,* n. + *sty*¹. **—pigtail** *n.* 1688, tobacco in the form of a thin, twisted roll; later, a braid of hair hanging from the back of the head worn by soldiers and sailors, in the late 1700's, and a girl's pigtail, in Dickens' *Nicholas Nickleby* (1838).

pigeon *n.* 1373 *pichon* dove or pigeon; also *pygeon* (probably before 1422); earlier as a surname *Pigun* (1211); borrowed from Old French *pijon, pyjoun* young dove, probably from Vulgar Latin **pībiōnem,* alteration (by dissimilation of *p* to *b*) of Late Latin *pīpiōnem* squab, young chirping or piping bird, from Latin *pīpiāre* to chirp, related to *pīpāre;* see PIPE. The word was differentiated from Old English *dove,* in Middle English. **—pigeonhole** *n.* 1577, small recess for a pigeon to rest in; later, a boxlike compartment in a desk, etc. (1688). The figurative sense of a category or class is first attested in 1847. **—v.** 1840, to put in a pigeonhole (boxlike compartment); later, to assign to a category or class (1870); from the noun. **—pigeon-toed** *adj.* (1801)

piggyback *adv.* on the back or shoulders. 1838, American English, alteration of dialectal English *pig back* (1783), itself an alteration (by association with *pig*) of earlier *pickback* (1565), also *pick pack* (1591); probably formed from English *pick* (a dialectal variant of *pitch*¹ to throw) + *back* or *pack.* The form *piggyback* was also influenced by *pick-a-back,* a variant of *pickback* which is first recorded in 1694. **—adj.** 1823 *pick-a-back,* in Lamb's *Elia;* 1944 *piggyback,* American English; from the adverb. The technical meaning "of or having to do with the transporting of loaded truck trailers on railroad flatcars" is first recorded in 1953 in American English. **—v.** to carry on the back, transport on railroad flatcars. 1952, American English; from the adverb.

pigment *n.* coloring matter. Before 1398, a spice or red dye, in Trevisa's translation of Bartholomew's *De Proprietatibus Rerum;* re-borrowed, probably by influence of Old French *pigment* spice, balm, from Latin *pigmentum* pigment, paint, from root of *pingere* to color; see PAINT. An earlier form *pyhmentum* a spice, as a plural dative, is found about 1150, possibly also known in Old English, and borrowed from Latin *pigmentum.* Doublet of PIMENTO. **—v.** to color with a pigment. 1900; from the noun. **—pigmentation** *n.* deposit of pigment in tissue. 1866, formed from English *pigment* + *-ation.*

pigmy *n.* See PYGMY.

pike¹ *n.* About 1511, borrowed from Middle French *pique* a spear, pikeman, from *piquer* to pick, prick, pierce, from Old French *pic* sharp point or spike, possibly through Vulgar Latin **pīccus,* ultimately from Germanic (compare Old English *pīc*). The word was also developed in part directly from Old English *pīc* pointed instrument; see PIKE².

pike² *n.* sharp point or spike. Before 1200 *pike,* in *Body and Soul;* developed from Old English *piic, pīc* pointed instrument, pickax (about 725), of uncertain origin; perhaps borrowed from a Celtic source (compare Gaelic *pic* pickax, Irish *pice* pike, pitchfork, Breton *pik* pike, pickax, and Welsh *pig* point, pike, beak, which are all borrowings from an unknown source). See also PICK[2]. Middle English *pike*[2] was confused with *pike*[1] by influence of Old French *pic;* and Middle French *pique* and probably by Middle Dutch *picke, peke.*

pike[3] *n.* freshwater fish. 1314 *pik;* earlier in the place name *Pichmere;* also *pike* (1345); probably a special use of *pike*[2] sharp point, because of the fish's long, slender snout. Compare GARFISH for a similar etymology.

pike[4] *n.* turnpike. 1837, in Dickens' *Pickwick Papers,* shortened form of TURNPIKE.

Dickens used the word in the sense of tollgate; the specific sense of turnpike or highway is first recorded in American English, in Harriet Beecher Stowe's *Uncle Tom's Cabin* (1852).

piker *n. Slang.* person who does things in a small way, miserly person. 1872, American English, probably from earlier *Piker* a poor migrant to California (1860, but originally one from *Pike* County, Missouri).

pilaf (piläf′) or **pilau** (pilô′) *n.* Oriental dish of seasoned rice often boiled with mutton, fowl, etc. 1612 *pilaw,* in a travel book; borrowed from Persian *pilāw,* from Turkish *pilâv.*

The spelling *pilaff* is first found in 1813 in Byron's *The Corsair;* it is probably a borrowing from modern Greek *piláfi,* from Turkish *pilâv.*

pilaster *n.* rectangular partial pillar set against a wall. 1575, borrowed from Middle French *pilastre,* from Italian *pilastro;* formed from *pila* buttress or pile (from Latin *pīla* PILLAR) and Latin *-aster* expressing incomplete resemblance (compare *surdaster* somewhat deaf, *filiaster* stepson).

pile[1] *n.* mass, heap. About 1410 *pyle;* borrowed from Middle French *pile,* and directly from Latin *pīla* stone barrier, PILLAR. It is possible that an earlier use of *pyle* a castle, tower, stronghold (about 1378, in a version of *Piers Plowman*), and now meaning any very large building, belongs to this group of meanings as indicated in the MED; however, the OED equates this sense with *peel* one of the border castles of England and Scotland, which is derived from Old French. **—v.** make into a pile. Probably before 1400 *pilen,* from the noun, and perhaps also borrowed from Medieval Latin *pilare* to pile up, stack.

pile[2] *n.* heavy beam driven into the earth. 1190 *pile* an arrow or dart; later, a timber or stake driven into the ground (before 1338, in Mannyng's *Chronicle of England*); developed from Old English (before 1000) *pīl* stake, shaft, spike, arrow; borrowed from Latin *pīlum* heavy javelin, pestle, related to *pīnsere* to pound; see PESTLE. Old English *pīl* is cognate with Old High German *pfīl* arrow, stake. **—v.** provide with piles. About 1390 *pilen* fasten with nails; later, drive piles into the ground, provide with piles (1432); from the noun, and also probably borrowed from Medieval Latin *pilare* drive in piles.

pile[3] *n.* nap of a fabric. About 1350 *pilus,* pl., feathers or plumage; later *piles* hair; borrowed probably from Middle Dutch *pijl,* and directly from Latin *pilus* hair. Though Latin *pilleus, pilleum* felt cap and Greek *pîlos* felt cap, felt may appear related, they are probably merely culture words from an unknown foreign source.

The meaning of a nap of a fabric is first recorded in English in 1568.

pile[4] *n.* Usually **piles** *pl.* hemorrhoids. Probably before 1425 *pillis, pilez;* borrowed from Medieval Latin *pili* piles, probably from Latin *pila* ball; generally thought to be in reference to the shape of hemorrhoids; see PILL.

pilfer *v.* to steal. Before 1548, in Edward Hall's *Chronicle,* verb use of Middle English *pylfre* spoils or booty (before 1400); later, plundering or despoiling (before 1420, in Lydgate's *Troy Book*); borrowed from Middle French *pelfre* booty or spoils, found in Old French, but of unknown origin; possibly related to PELF. The form *pelfra* booty or spoils, occurs in Anglo-Latin and may have also been a source of Middle English *pylfre.* Though probably not a direct source of the verb in English, Middle French *pelfrer* to rob, must have influenced its formation. **—pilferage** *n.* petty theft. About 1626, formed from English *pilfer* + *-age.*

pilgrim *n.* person who journeys to a holy place as an act of religious devotion. Probably before 1200 *pilegrim, pelegrim,* in *Ancrene Riwle* and Layamon's *Chronicle of Britain;* later *pilgrim* (about 1280); borrowed from Old French *peligrin, pelerin,* from Latin *peregrīnus* foreigner, from foreign parts, from *peregrē* (*per-* beyond + **agrē,* Old Latin ablative case of *ager* field), and *peregrī* abroad, from abroad (*per-* beyond + *agrī,* locative case of *ager* field, see ACRE). Doublet of PEREGRINE.

In the Romance languages (except for Spanish *peregrino*) the Latin *peregrīnus* became *pelegrin(o)* (by dissimilation of the first *r* to *l*) resulting in Old French *peligrin, pelerin.* The final *m,* found also in the Dutch, Frisian, Old Icelandic, and Old High German forms of the word, has been accounted for on the basis of a Germanic masculine name (compare Old High German *Piligrim,* from *bili-* sword + *grim* helmet), which may also explain the appearance of the first *i* in *pilgrim.*

In American history, the name *pilgrim* applies to the English Puritans who founded the colony of Plymouth, Massachusetts in 1620. Their governor, William Bradford, wrote in 1630 of the first settlers as *pilgrims* in the spiritual sense of earthly sojourners, referring to Hebrews 11:13 (". . .they were strangers and pilgrims on earth"). The phrase *Pilgrim Fathers* founders of Plymouth colony is first recorded in 1799 in American English.

—pilgrimage *n.* pilgrim's journey. About 1275 *pelrimage;* later *pilgrimage* (probably before 1300); in part formed from English *pilgrim* + *-age,* and in part borrowed from Old French *pelerinage,* from *pelerin, peligrin* pilgrim; for suffix see -AGE.

pill *n.* Before 1400 *pille* small ball of medicine, in a translation of Lanfranc's *Science of Surgery;* borrowed from Middle Dutch or Middle Low German *pille,* and from Middle French *pile;* all of these forms from Latin *pilula* little ball, pellet, pill, diminutive of *pila* ball, ball of cloth, related to *pilus* hair; see PILE[3] nap.

The figurative sense of something disagreeable that must be "swallowed" or endured is first recorded in 1548; the meaning of an objectionable person or bore is first recorded in Maugham's *Liza of Lambeth* (1897). **—v.** 1736, to dose with pills, in Fielding's *Pasquin;* from the noun. The meaning of form small fuzzy balls on fabrics is first recorded in 1953.

—pillbox *n.* 1730, box for holding pills, American English; 1887, small, round emplacement for housing a machine gun, etc.

pillage *n.* robbery, plunder. Before 1393 *pilage* spoils or booty, in Gower's *Confessio Amantis;* later *pillage* robbery (probably about 1421, in Lydgate's writings); borrowed from Old French *pillage* plunder, from *piller* to plunder, origin uncertain; possibly from *pille,* dialectal variant of *peille* rag, probably from Latin *pilleus* felt cap; see PILE[3] nap; for suffix see -AGE. Alternatively, Old French *piller* may have come from Vulgar Latin **pīliāre* to plunder. **—v.** to rob, plunder. About 1592; from the noun.

pillar *n.* column. Probably before 1200 *pilar* pillar, pcst, in *Ancrene Riwle;* later *piler* (probably about 1200), and *pillar* (1434); borrowed from Old French *piler, pilier, piller,* and directly from Medieval Latin *pilare,* from Latin *pila* pillar, stone barrier (earlier **peilā*), cognate with Oscan *ehpeílatasset* they are erected.

pillory *n.* wooden framework with holes for a person's head and hands, used for punishment. 1275 *pillory;* earlier as a surname *Pillori* (1257-58); borrowed from Old French *pilori, pillori, pelori,* and directly from Medieval Latin *pilloria, pilorium, pellorium* (1190, though some forms probably represent Latinized forms of Old French); of uncertain origin. **—v.** put in a pillory. Probably before 1600; from the noun. The figurative sense of expose to public ridicule or abuse is first recorded in 1699.

pillow *n.* About 1150 *pule;* later *pilowe* (about 1350), and *pillow* (1440); developed from Old English **pulwi, pylu, pyle* (before 899, in Alfred's translation of Orosius' *Historiarum Adversus Paganos*); cognate with Old Saxon *puli, puliui* cushion, pillow, Middle Dutch *pölu, pöluwe* (modern Dutch *peluw* bolster), and Old High German *pfuliwi, pfulwo* cushion (modern German *Pfühl*); all representing West Germanic **pulwi (n),* an early borrowing from Latin *pulvīnus* cushion, pillow, of uncertain origin. In some instances the Middle English word was also borrowed directly from Latin. **—v.** rest on a pillow. 1629, in Milton's *On The Morning of Christ's Nativity;* from the noun. **—pillowcase** *n.* (1724, American English)

pilot *n.* 1530, one who steers a ship, in Palsgrave's *Lesclarcissement;* borrowed from Middle French *pilot, pilote,* from Italian *piloto, pilota;* earlier *pedoto, pedota,* from Medieval Greek **pēdṓtēs,* from Greek *pēdón* steering oar, related to *poús* (genitive *podós*) FOOT. (For the change of *d* to *l* compare Latin *odor: olet* it smells.)

The application of *pilot* to one who steers or controls a balloon, etc., is first recorded in 1848.
—v. act as the pilot, steer. 1649, in the figurative sense of guide, lead; from the noun. The literal meaning of conduct as a pilot is first attested in 1693.
—adj. 1788, of or pertaining to a pilot; from the noun. The adjective meaning of serving as a guide, prototype, or experimental version of some project or undertaking (as in *a pilot study, a pilot program, a pilot film*) is first recorded in 1928.
—pilothouse *n.* (before 1846, American English) **—pilot light** (1890, in *Century Dictionary*)

pimento (pimen'tō) *n.* kind of sweet pepper. 1690 *piemento;* later *pimento* (1718); borrowing of Spanish *pimiento* green or red pepper, also *pimienta* black pepper, from Late Latin *pigmenta,* plural of *pigmentum* vegetable juice (in Medieval Latin, spiced wine), from Latin *pigmentum* pigment; see the doublet PIGMENT.

pimp *n.* 1607, a man who procures for prostitutes, pander, in Thomas Middleton's *Your Five Gallants;* perhaps connected with Middle French *pimper* to dress up elegantly or adorn, present participle *pimpant* alluring in dress, seductive, Old Provençal *pimpar,* variant of *pipar* to dress elegantly, spruce up, from the expressive root *pipp-* to adorn, ornament. **—v.** 1636, to act as a pimp, pander, in Massinger's *The Bashful Lover;* from the noun.

pimpernel *n.* kind of primrose, often scarlet. 1373 *pympirnell,* 1392 *pimpernelle;* borrowed from Old French *piprenelle, pinpernele, pimpernelle,* and directly from Late Latin *pimpinella* a medicinal plant, of unknown origin.

An extended use with the meaning of something or someone very elusive is first recorded in 1953, in allusion to the Scarlet *Pimpernel,* code name of the hero of the adventure novel *The Scarlet Pimpernel* (1905) by the Hungarian-born English author Baroness Orczy, 1865-1947. The meaning developed from the hero's skill in eluding his pursuers and effecting daring rescues of French aristocrats during the Reign of Terror.

pimple *n.* 1373 *pymple* small inflamed swelling; earlier as a surname *Pympél* (1311); of uncertain origin; perhaps related to Old English **piplian* (found in the present participle *pipligende* affected with herpes, having shingles). **—pimply** *adj.* full of pimples. 1748, in Richardson's *Clarissa;* formed from English *pimple* + *-y*[1].

pin *n.* Before 1200 *pin* part of a latch or bolt; later, fastener for clothing (about 1250); developed from Late Old English (before 1100) *pinn;* cognate with Old Saxon *pin* peg, Middle Low German and Middle Dutch *pin, pinne* (modern Dutch *pin*), and Old High German *pfinn* (modern German *Pinne*); late Old Icelandic *pinni* was borrowed from Middle Low German *pinne.* The Germanic forms suggest Proto-Germanic **penn-* jutting point or peak, from Indo-European **bend-n-,* possibly represented in Celtic (through *bn̥d-no-*) by Middle Irish *benn* summit, horn, Welsh and Cornish *ban* peak, point, horn (Pok.96). **—v.** Probably 1350-75 *pynen* to fasten with a pin; also probably about 1375 *pynnen;* from the noun. **—pinball** *n.* game propelling a small ball or marble across a slanted board toward targets. 1911 *pinball game;* 1936 *pinball machine.* **—pincushion** *n.* (1632) **—pinhead** *n.* (1662) **—pinpoint** *n.* (1849); *v.* (1917)

pinafore (pin'əfôr) *n.* apronlike covering over a dress. 1782 *pin-a-fore,* in Frances Burney's *Cecilia;* formed from English *pin,* v. + *afore* on the front (*a-*[1] on + *fore* FORE); so called because it was originally pinned to the dress front.

pincers *n.pl. or sing.* tool for gripping and holding tight. Probably before 1325 *pynsours;* later *pinsers* (1371); borrowed from Old French *pinceure* pincers, from *pincier* to PINCH.

Pincers was applied in 1658 as a zoological term to a pair of organs for grasping or tearing, as those of crustaceans. The term *pincer (s) movement,* a military maneuver to encircle enemy forces, is first recorded in Auden and Isherwood's *Journey to War* (1939).

pinch *v.* About 1230 *pinchen* to pluck, in *Ancrene Riwle;* earlier in a surname *Pincheneio;* also, to be stingy with (probably before 1325), and to pinch, nip, or assail (about 1350); borrowed from Old North French **pinchier* (found in modern Norman dialect *pincher*), variant of Old French *pincier,* of uncertain origin; perhaps from Vulgar Latin **pīnctiāre,* a possible fusion of **pūnctiāre* to pierce (from Latin *pūnctum* POINT) and **piccāre* to pierce; see PIKE[1] spear. **—n.**

1489, time of special stress or need, critical juncture; from the verb. The literal meaning of act of pinching is not recorded before 1591, in Shakespeare's *1 Henry VI.* **—pinchers** *n.pl.* = pincers. (1575) **—pinch hitter** (1912, American English)

pine[1] *n.* kind of evergreen tree. About 1150 *pin;* later *pine* (before 1325, in *Cursor Mundi*); developed from Old English (about 1000, in compounds as *pintreow, pin-beam*) *pīn-,* borrowed from Latin and from Old French *pin,* also from Latin *pīnus.* Latin *pīnus* (earlier **pitsnus*) is cognate with Greek *pítys* pine, Albanian *pishë* fir, and Sanskrit *pítu-dāru-s* fir ("gum-tree"), from Indo-European **pit-/pīt-* (Pok.794). **—pineapple** *n.* Possibly before 1350, in the compound *pine-appeltre,* in reference to *pine appel* cone or fruit of the pine tree. The *pineapple,* a fruit that resembles a pine cone and is harvested from a tropical plant, is first recorded in 1664, but is found earlier as Queen Pine (1661). **—pine cone** (1695, replacing earlier *pine-appel,* 1350, and *pine nut* 1600, found in Old English *pinhnyte,* about 1000).

pine[2] *v.* yearn. About 1125 *pinen* to torture, crucify; later, to torment, punish (1137), and to waste away with hunger, pain, desire, etc., yearn (before 1325); developed from Old English *pīnian* cause to suffer (before 899, in Alfred's translation of Orosius' *Historiarum Adversus Paganos*), from **pīne* pain, torture, punishment, borrowed possibly through Medieval or Vulgar Latin **pēna,* variant from Latin *poena* punishment, penalty, from Greek *poinḗ;* see the doublet PAIN.

The Old English noun **pīne* corresponds to Old Saxon *pīna,* Middle Dutch *pīne* (modern Dutch *pijn* pain), Old High German *pīna* (modern German *Pein*), and Old Icelandic *pīna* (Swedish *pina,* Danish *pine*), all borrowed from Latin. This was one of the words introduced into Germanic with Christianity, and in English it was applied first to the pains of hell. The noun has not been found in Old English however, whereas the verb *pīnian* was common from an early period.

pineal (pin′ēəl) *adj.* of or having to do with a cone-shaped gland in the brain. 1681, borrowed from French *pinéal,* literally, like a pine cone, from Latin *pīnea* pine cone, from *pīnus* PINE[1] tree.

ping-pong *n.* table tennis. 1900 *Ping-Pong,* trademark for table tennis equipment; probably formed of *ping,* n. (1835) and *pong,* n. (1823), imitative of the sound of the celluloid ball hitting the originally parchment-covered paddle and then the table; perhaps modeled after *ding-dong.* **—v.** play ping pong. 1901, from the noun. The figurative sense of move or send something or someone back and forth (as if a ping-pong ball) is first recorded in American English, in 1952.

pinion[1] *n.* last joint of a bird's wing. Probably before 1425 *pinion* wing; borrowed from Middle French *pignon,* perhaps from Old French *penon, pennon* feather of an arrow, from Latin *penna* feather; but it is more likely Middle French *pignon* is from Vulgar Latin **pinniōnem* (nominative **pinniō*), an extended form of Latin *pinna,* variant of *penna* wing; see FEATHER. **—v.** 1558, disable by binding the arms; 1577, bind the wings of; from the noun.

pinion[2] *n.* small gear with teeth that fit into a larger gear. 1659, borrowed from French *pignon,* also found in Middle French, either from: **1** Old French *pignon* crenellation or battlement, from Vulgar Latin **pinniōnem* (nominative **pinniō*), an extended form of Latin *pinna* pinnacle, battlement, float of a waterwheel, variant of *penna* wing, feather, peak; or **2** from *peignon,* from *peigne* comb (in reference to the teeth of a comb or rake), variant of *pigne,* from Latin *pectinem,* (nominative *pecten*) comb or rake. It may be that *pinion*[1] and *pinion*[2] are closely related (perhaps even the same word) if both words are derived through Vulgar Latin from Latin *pinna, penna;* certainly earlier etymologists thought so; however, the possible derivation of *pinion*[2] with the semantic comparison to "comb" would argue against such a supposition.

pink[1] *n.* light red color. 1573, a garden plant of various colors; of uncertain origin.

The figurative meaning of the finest example of excellence, the flower (of some good quality) is first recorded in Shakespeare's *Romeo and Juliet* (1592); from it evolved the meaning of the most perfect condition or degree of something, the height (as *in the pink of health*), first found in 1767.

About 1720 the plant name began to be used attributively in the sense of having the color of the garden pink when pale or light red, of a pale rose color. Curiously, the noun use of this attributive is not recorded until 1828 in Webster's *Dictionary* as that of a color used by painters and later in Worcester's *Dictionary* as that of the usual color of the flower, a light crimson, in 1846.

pink[2] *v.* to prick or pierce with a sharp object. Probably before 1200 *pungen* pierce or stab, in Layamon's *Chronicle of Britain;* later, to punch holes in (about 1325); developed from a possible Old English *pyngan* and borrowed directly from Latin *pungere* to pierce, prick.

The meaning of cut or perforate (cloth, etc.) in an ornamental pattern is first recorded in 1503, and from it developed **pinking scissors** or **shears** (before 1951).

pinkie *n.* the smallest finger. 1808, in Jamieson's *Dictionary of the Scottish Language;* borrowed from Dutch *pinkje,* diminutive from *pink* little finger; of uncertain origin.

pinnace (pin′is) *n.* ship's boat. 1546, borrowed from Middle French *pinace,* from Italian *pinaccia,* or from Spanish *pinaza,* from *pino* pine tree, ship, from Latin *pīnus* PINE[1], also (by metonymy) ship.

pinnacle *n.* Probably about 1300 *pinacle* mountain, peak, promontory, in the *Romance of Guy of Warwick;* later spire, turret (probably 1350-75), and *pynnacle* (probably before 1425); borrowed from Old French *pinacle, pinnacle,* learned borrowing from Late Latin, and borrowed directly from Late Latin *pinnāculum,* diminutive of *pinna* peak; originally, wing, feather, variant of *penna* FEATHER. **—v.** put on a pinnacle. 1656, from the noun.

pinnate (pin′āt) *adj.* like a feather. 1727, in Bailey's *Dictionary,* having leaflets arranged like the vanes of a feather, in reference to a compound leaf; borrowed from Latin *pinnātus* feathered, winged, from *pinna* feather; for suffix see -ATE[1].

pinochle *n.* kind of card game. 1864 *Peanukle, Penuchle;* 1892 *pinochle;* American English, of uncertain origin.

Because the game was popularized among German immigrants, if not developed by them (consider the German verb *melden,* English *meld* used in play of the game), some etymologists consider *pinochle* (and its phonetic spellings *Peanukle, Penuchle*) to be a borrowing of *Binokel,* found in Swiss dialect of German, probably from *binocle,* found in Swiss dialect of French. The French and German words mean spectacles and suggest a formation similar to *bezique* (a game that with elements of skat is the precursor of pinochle) that is sometimes mistakenly associated with French *besicles* spectacles for no apparent reason semantically and very little phonetically.

piñon (pin′yən *or* pēn′yōn) *n.* pine with large, edible seeds. 1831, American English; borrowed from Spanish *piñón* pine nut, a pine bearing edible seed, from *piña* pine cone, from Latin *pīnea,* from *pīnus* PINE[1] tree.

pinscher (pin′chər) *n.* kind of short-haired dog. 1926, borrowing of German *Pinscher,* earlier *Pintscher,* also *Pintsch* or *Pinsch,* probably from English *pinch* (because his ears are usually clipped).

pint *n.* unit of measure, half quart. 1354 *pynte* vessel containing a pint; later, a pint as liquid measure (1378); borrowed from Old French *pinte,* probably from Vulgar Latin **pīncta,* variant of Latin *picta* painted, feminine past participle of *pingere* to PAINT; thought to be so called from the painted mark on a vessel showing the level that indicates this standard measure.

pintle *n.* pin or bolt. 1486 *pyntell;* earlier *pyntul* penis (about 1350); developed from Late Old English (before 1100) *pintel* penis, probably a diminutive formation from a root represented by Old Frisian and Middle Low German *pint* penis; for suffix see -LE[1].

pinto (pin′tō) *n.* spotted or piebald horse. 1860, American English; borrowed from American Spanish *pinto,* literally, painted or spotted, from Spanish *pinto,* from Vulgar Latin **pinctus,* variant of Latin *pictus* painted, past participle of *pingere* to PAINT. **—adj.** 1867, from the noun.

Pinyin (pin′yin′) *n.* system for transliterating modern Chinese into Roman characters. 1963, borrowed from Chinese *pinyin* to combine sounds into syllables, phonetic alphabet, Pinyin (*pīn* put together, piece together + *yīn* sound, tone, pronunciation).

pion (pī′on) *n. Nuclear Physics.* meson having a mass 264-273 times that of an electron. 1951, contraction of earlier *pi-meson* (1947).

pioneer *n.* 1523, foot soldier who prepares the way for an army; borrowed from Middle French *pionnier,* from Old French *peonier* foot soldier, from *peon;* see PAWN[2] chess piece; for suffix see -EER.

The general sense of a person who goes first or does something first is first recorded in Bacon's *Of the Advancement of Learning* (1605).

—v. prepare or open up for others. 1780, from the noun.

pious *adj.* having or showing piety. About 1450 *piouse,* borrowed from Latin *pīus* dutiful, kind, devout; related to PIETY and PITY.

pip[1] *n.* seed of fleshy fruit. 1797, shortened form of *pipin* (before 1325); see PIPPIN.

pip[2] *n.* disease of birds, characterized by the secretion of thick mucus in the mouth and throat. 1373 *pipe;* earlier in the surname *Piphed* (1273); borrowed from Middle Dutch *pip, pippe* pip or mucus, from Vulgar Latin **pippīta, pīpīta,* through **pītwīta* from Latin *pītuita* phlegm; see PITUITARY.

pip[3] *n.* one of the spots on playing cards, dominoes, or dice. 1674, in Charles Cotton's *The Complete Gamester,* alteration of earlier *peep* (1604), of unknown origin.

pipe[1] *n.* Probably before 1200 *pipe* musical wind instrument, in Layamon's *Chronicle of Britain;* later, water pipe, conduit (about 1250); developed from Old English (before 1000) *pīpe* musical wind instrument, tube to convey water, smoke, etc.; borrowed from Vulgar Latin **pīpa* a pipe, from Latin *pīpāre* to chirp or peep, of imitative origin like Oscan *pipātiō* cry of lamentation, weeping, Greek *pîpos, píppos* young bird, Sanskrit *píppakā* kind of bird, and Lithuanian *pỹpti* to pipe, whistle. The Old English form is cognate with Old Frisian *pipe* pipe, Old Saxon *pīpa,* Middle Dutch *pīpe,* Old High German *pfīfa,* and Old Icelandic *pīpa;* all borrowed from Vulgar Latin **pīpa.*

The meaning of a pipe for smoking is first recorded in English in 1594, originally with the defining word, as *pipe of tobacco.*

—v. About 1250 *pipen* make a shrill sound, whistle, peep, in *The Owl and the Nightingale;* later, play a pipe (probably before 1300, as a gerund in *Kyng Alisaunder*); developed from Old English (before 1000) *pīpian,* in part from Old English *pīpe,* n., and in part borrowed from Latin *pīpāre, pīpiāre* to chirp or peep; of imitative origin.

The meaning of convey (water, gas, oil, etc.) through a pipe or pipes is first recorded in 1889; from the noun.

pipe[2] *n.* large container, cask, vat. 1314, as part of the name of a rent or fee paid by a vassal, originally probably kind of customary rental of a cask and armor called "Pipe and Puleyn", and later a large storage container (1348); borrowed from Old French *pipe* a liquid measure, cask for wine, tube, pipe, from Vulgar Latin **pīpa* PIPE[1]. The word was also influenced in its development by earlier Middle English *pipe* PIPE[1].

pipette (pīpet′) *n.* slender pipe or tube for transferring liquids. 1839, borrowing of French *pipette,* from Middle French *pipette* tube, diminutive of Old French *pipe,* from Vulgar Latin **pīpa* PIPE[1]; for suffix see -ETTE.

piping *n.* a narrow band of material for trimming along the edges of clothing. 1858, from *pipe,* v. to trim or ornament with material (1841), special use of *pipe*[1], n. in the sense of tube, referring to the cordage often drawn through piping to give it a rounded edge.

pipit *n.* small songbird. 1768, in Thomas Pennant's *British Zoology,* a coined word (originally spelled *pippit*), imitative of the bird's cry.

pippin *n.* kind of apple. Before 1325 *pipin, pepin* seed of a fleshy fruit, in *Cursor Mundi;* earlier as a surname *Pypin* (1297), also, kind of apple (1432, in Lydgate's writings); borrowed from Old French *pepin,* probably from the root **pipp-,* expressing smallness.

pipsqueak *n. Slang.* insignificant person or object. 1910, formed from English *pip*[3] small spot + *squeak,* n.

piquant (pē′kənt) *adj.* 1521, unpleasantly sharp or biting, Wolsey quoted in State Papers of Henry VIII; borrowing of Middle French *piquant* pricking, stimulating, irritating, from Old French, present participle of *piquer* to prick, sting, pierce, nettle; see PIKE[1] spear.

The meaning of stimulating to the taste, appetizing, is first recorded about 1645, and the figurative sense of stimulating to the mind or interest in 1695.

—piquancy *n.* 1664, pungency, tartness, in Evelyn's *Pomona,* formed from English *piquant* + *-cy.*

pique (pēk) *n.* 1532, ill feeling, personal quarrel, Cromwell quoted in Merriman's *Life and Letters of Thomas Cromwell;* borrowed from Middle French *pique* a prick, sting, irritation, from *piquer* to prick, sting, pierce, nettle, from Old French; see PIKE[1] spear.

The meaning of a feeling of anger at being slighted is first recorded in Nashe's *Four Letters Confuted* (1592). Early forms of this word included *pyke, peake,* and *picke;* the current spelling is first recorded in 1653. **—v.** cause pique in. 1664, borrowed from French *piquer* irritate, excite, prick, from Old French, to prick, pierce, nettle.

piqué (pikā′) *n.* kind of textured cotton fabric. 1852, borrowed from French *piqué,* literally, quilted, past participle of *piquer* to quilt, backstitch, prick; see PIQUE.

piranha (pirän′yə) *n.* small South American fish that attacks large mammals. 1869, in Richard F. Burton's *Explorations of the Highlands of Brazil;* borrowed from Portuguese *piranha,* from Tupi (Brazil) *pira nya,* variant of *pira'ya,* literally, scissors.

pirate *n.* Probably before 1300, in *Kyng Alisaunder;* earlier as a surname *Pyrot* (1254); borrowed from Old French *pirate,* and directly from Latin *pīrāta* sailor (in Medieval Latin *piratus* sea robber, 1328) from Greek *peirātḗs* brigand or pirate; literally, one who attacks, from *peirân* to attack, make a hostile attempt on, try, from *peîra* trial, experience, an attempt, attack; see FEAR.

The transferred meaning of a person who appropriates or reproduces the work or invention of another without right or permission is first recorded in 1701, in Defoe's works.

—v. be a pirate, plunder, rob. 1574, from the noun. The transferred meaning of appropriate or reproduce without right or permission, infringe on the work of another, is first recorded, as in the corresponding noun, in 1701 in Defoe's works.

—piracy *n.* Before 1552, borrowed from Medieval Latin *piratia,* from Medieval Greek **peirāteíā,* from Greek *peirātḗs* PIRATE; for suffix see -CY. **—piratical** *adj.* 1565, obtained by piracy (but implied earlier in *piratically* by piracy, 1549); 1579-80, of or like a pirate; formed in English from Latin *pīrāticus* (from Greek *peirātikós,* from *peirātḗs* pirate) + English *-al*[1].

pirouette (pir′üet′) *n.* a whirling about on the toes. 1706, borrowing of French *pirouette,* from Old French *pirouet* spinning top, whirligig, from the Gallo-Romance root **pir-* peg or plug (represented by dialectal French *pire* large peg, *piron* kind of hinge, *piroc* bud, shoot); for suffix see -ETTE. **—v.** whirl about on the toes. 1822, from the noun in English, influenced by French *pirouetter,* from *pirouette,* n.

piscatorial (pis′kətôr′ēəl) *adj.* of fisherman or fishing. 1828, in Hawthorne's works, from Latin *piscātōrius* of fishermen, pertaining to fishing, from *piscātor* (genitive *piscātōris*) fisher, from *piscārī* to fish, from *piscis* FISH; for suffix see -AL[1]. It is also possible that *piscatorial* was formed in English from *piscatory* + *-ial* on the model of Latin *piscātōrius.* **—piscatory** (pis′kətôr′ē) *adj.* piscatorial. 1633, borrowed from Latin *piscātōrius.*

piss *v. Slang.* urinate. About 1300 *pissen;* borrowed from Old French *pissier* urinate, from Vulgar Latin **pissiāre,* of imitative origin. **—n.** *Slang.* urine. Before 1387 *pisse,* in Trevisa's translation of Higden's *Polychronicon,* from *pissen,* v. **—pismire** *n.* ant. Probably about 1350 *pyssmourre;* earlier as a surname *Pessemere* (1327); also *pissemyre* (about 1395), a compound of *pyss, pisse* urine (so called from the acrid smell of an anthill) + *mire* ant (before 1250). Middle English *mire* was probably borrowed from a Scandinavian source (compare Old Icelandic *maurr* ant, and Old Swedish *myr,* modern Swedish *myra* ant); cognate with Middle Dutch *miere* ant (modern Dutch *mier*), Middle Low German *mīre,* and Crimean Gothic *miera;* for cognates outside Germanic see FORMIC ACID.

pistachio (pista′shēō) *n.* kind of greenish nut. 1598, borrowed from Italian *pistacchio,* learned borrowing from Latin *pistacium* the pistachio nut, from Greek *pistákion,* from *pistákē* the pistachio tree, from an Eastern language (compare Persian *pistā* the pistachio tree).

The earlier form *pistace,* recorded in Middle English about 1440, was borrowed from Middle French *pistace, pistache,* learned borrowing from Latin *pistacium* a pistachio nut.

The Italian pronunciation (pistä′kēō) may have been originally the one adopted by English, but the present pronunciations indicate the influence of modern French *pistache* (pistäsh′) or Spanish *pistacho* (pistä′chō).

pistil (pis′təl) *n.* part of a flower that produces seeds. 1749, borrowing of French *pistil,* learned borrowing from New Latin *pistillum* a pistil (so called from its resemblance to a pestle), from Latin *pistillum* pestle; see the doublet PESTLE.

pistol *n.* About 1570, in Sir Humphrey Gilbert's *Queen Elizabeth's Academy;* borrowed from Middle French *pistole* small, short firearm, from German *Pistole,* from Czech *píš′tala* firearm; originally, pipe, from *pištěti* to squeak or whistle, of imitative origin. An earlier form *pistolet* (1550), borrowed from Middle French *pistolet,* is possibly connected with Italian *pistolese,* in reference to *Pistoia* a town in Tuscany once known for its metal industry and gunsmithing. **—v.** to fire at with a pistol. 1607, from the noun.

piston *n.* disk or short pluglike piece fitting inside a cylinder and moving back and forth to receive or transmit motion. 1704, borrowing of French *piston* (1648, Pascal), from Middle French *piston* pestle for a mortar, from Italian *pistone,* variant of *pestone* large pestle, from *pestare* to pound or beat, from Late Latin *pistāre,* frequentative form of Latin *pīnsere* to pound; see PESTLE.

pit[1] *n.* hole, hollow, depression. About 1175 *putte* water hole, pool, spring; later *put, pit* depression, hole, grave, hell (probably before 1200); developed from Old English (847) *pytt* water hole, pit; cognate with Old Frisian *pet* pit, Old Saxon *putti,* Middle Low German *putte,* Middle Dutch *put, putte* (modern Dutch *put* well, pit), Old High German *pfuzzi, pfuzza* (modern German *Pfütze* puddle, pool); all representing West Germanic **puttjaz,* an early borrowing from Latin *puteus* well, pit, shaft, perhaps from *putāre* to cut, prune; see PUTATIVE. **—v.** 1456 *pitten* cast into a pit, mark with pits, from *pit,* n. The meaning of set (cocks, dogs, wrestlers, etc.) to fight for sport is first recorded in 1760, in reference to the pits where such matches took place. The figurative sense of set to compete, oppose, match, is found in 1777 (Johnson quoted by Boswell). **—pitfall** *n.* Before 1382 *pit falle* a concealed hole in which one may fall and be trapped, in the Wycliffe Bible; earlier *put-falle* (about 1325) unfavorable terrain in which troops may be captured. The figurative sense of any hidden danger or error occurs in Middle English before 1425.

pit[2] *n.* hard seed of a cherry, peach, etc. 1841, American English; borrowing of Dutch *pit* kernel, seed, marrow, from Middle Dutch *pit, pitte* PITH. **—v.** remove pits from (fruit). Before 1930, from the noun.

pitch[1] *v.* to throw, thrust. Probably before 1200 *pihte* (past tense of *pichen, picchen* to thrust or drive something); later, to throw, hurl, cast (about 1380); probably developed from Old English **pīcian* to prick; cognate with Old Icelandic *pikka, pjakka,* Middle Dutch *pikken, pecken,* East Frisian *pikken.*

The meaning of set up, erect, build (as in *pitch a tent*) is first recorded about 1250. The sense of throw a ball in cricket (now *bowl*) is first recorded in 1773, and in baseball, in 1845, in American English.

—n. Before 1500, act of pitching; from the verb. The common meaning of something pitched is first recorded in 1523, that of the degree of slope, sloping part in 1542, and musical pitch, degree of acuteness of tone in 1597.

The sense in sport of the act of pitching a ball was first used in cricket in 1833. The informal meaning of talk used in selling or promoting something is first found in 1876, probably as an extended sense of a stall pitched or set up for the sale of something (1811).

—pitchfork *n.* 1364 *pichforke,* alteration (by influence of *pichen* to thrust, throw) of earlier *pikfork* (1356), *pic-forken* (probably before 1200), from *pik-, pic-,* combining forms of PIKE[2] (Old English *pīc*) or *pikke* PICK[2] + *fork, forken* fork.

pitch[2] *n.* black, sticky substance made from tar or the like. Probably about 1175 *pich;* later *pytche* (before 1382); developed from Old English (about 700) *pic,* from Latin, and borrowed through Anglo-French *piche, piz,* Old French *poiz,* from Latin *pix* (genitive *picis*) pitch; cognate with Greek (Ionic) *píssa,* (Attic) *pítta,* earlier **pikya* pitch, turpentine, fir tree, and Old Slavic *pĭcŭlŭ* pitch, from Indo-European **pik-* (Pok.794). **—v.** cover with pitch. About 1300 *piken, pichen,* developed from Old English (about 1000) *pician,* from *pic,* n. **—pitch-black** *adj.* (1599).

pitcher[1] *n.* 1707, iron bar for making holes in the ground, especially to erect posts, as for a fence; later, a person who pitches hay or sheaves (before 1722), and the baseball player who pitches the ball (1845, in American English).

pitcher[2] *n.* 1208-09 *picher* earthenware jug, metal container, cooking pot; later *pitchere* (probably before 1350); borrowed from Old French *pichier, picher,* alteration of *bichier,* from Medieval Latin *bicarium,* probably from Greek *bîkos* earthen vessel; see BEAKER.

piteous *adj.* Probably before 1300 *pitous* deserving pity; later *pitiuous* full of pity (about 1300), *piteous* (probably before 1425); borrowed through Anglo-French *pitous,* Old French *pitos, piteus,* from Medieval Latin *pietosus* merciful, pitiful, from Latin *pīetās* dutiful conduct, compassion, PIETY.

pith *n.* central, spongy tissue of plant stems. Before 1325 *pith* strength, force, vigor, in *Cursor Mundi;* about 1330 interior tissue, inner portion; developed from Old English *pitha* pith of plants, (figurative) essential part (before 899, in Alfred's translations); cognate with Middle Low German *pedik, peddik* pith, possibly also with Middle Low German *pit, pitte* kernel, pith, and Middle Dutch *pit, pitte* pith, kernel of a nut, from West Germanic **pithan-, piththan-,* of uncertain origin. **—pithy** *adj.* full of substance, meaning, or force. Before 1325 *pithier,* (comparative of *pithi* vigorous, strong), in *Cursor Mundi;* formed from English *pith* + *-y*[1]. The meaning of full of substance, meaning, or force is first recorded in Sir Thomas More's *Supplycacyon of Soulys* (1529).

piton (pē′ton) *n.* iron bar or spike with a ring in one end to which a rope can be secured, used in mountain climbing. 1898, borrowing of French *piton* hook, peak, piton, from Old French, nail, hook, from the Vulgar Latin root **pītt-* point or peak.

pittance *n.* Probably before 1200 *pitance* donation to a religious community, small portion of food, in *Ancrene Riwle,* borrowing of Old French *pitance* portion of food allowed a monk or poor person, pious dole, formed from *pitié* PITY + *-ance* -ance, from Latin *pīetās* PITY; for suffix see -ANCE.

The general meaning of a small amount, portion, or allowance is first recorded in English in 1561.

pituitary (pitü′əter′ē) *adj.* designating a small gland in the brain that regulates many bodily functions. 1615, borrowed from New Latin *pituitarius,* from Latin *pītuītārius* mucous, relating to phlegm, from *pītuīta* phlegm, mucus, cognate with Sanskrit *pítu-dāru-s* fir (gum tree); see PINE[1] tree; for suffix see -ARY.

The name for the gland in the brain was adopted from the Latin word for phlegm or mucus, because it was believed in the 1500's and 1600's that the pituitary gland channeled mucus to the nose.

—n. pituitary gland. 1899, from the adjective. An earlier noun use (recorded in 1845) referred to a mucous membrane of the olfactory organ.

pity *n.* sympathy, compassion. Before 1250 *pite* pity, in a version of *Ancrene Riwle;* earlier as a surname *Pitie* (1195); also, devotion, piety (1340, in *Ayenbite of Inwyt*), and *pitee* (about 1369, in Chaucer's *Book of the Duchesse*); borrowed from Old French *pité, pitié,* from Latin *pīetātem* (nominative *pīetās*) compassion, pity, from Latin, piety; from *pīus* PIOUS. The English words *pity* and *piety* were not completely differentiated in meaning until the 1600's. **—v.** Probably before 1475 *pete* (variant of **pitien* have compassion for), in the *Ludus Coventriae;* borrowed from Old French *piteer, pitier* to feel pity or compassion for; also, probably developed from the noun in English.

—pitiful *adj.* About 1303 *pityful* compassionate (implied in *pytyffully,* in Mannyng's *Handlyng Synne*); later, deserving pity, lamentable (about 1460); formed from Middle English *pite, pitee* pity + *-ful.* The extended sense of exciting pitying contempt, despicable, wretched, is first recorded in 1582. **—pitiless** *adj.* 1410 *piteles* merciless, about 1412 *piteeles;* formed from Middle English *pite, pitee* pity + *-les* -less.

pivot *n.* shaft, pin, or point on which something turns. 1611, in Cotgrave's *Dictionary,* borrowing of French, from Old French *pivot* hinge, pivot, of uncertain origin. Some French scholars believe that Old French *pivot* derived from a word not attested in French but represented by Old Provençal *pua* tooth of a comb (corresponding to Spanish *púa* sharp point, tooth of a comb, and Portuguese *pua*), from an Italic dialectal or pre-Celtic Indo-European **puga* point, peak; found in Latin *pūgiō* dagger, related to *pungere* to prick or pierce, from Indo-European **peuĝ-/puĝ-/pūg-* (Pok.828).

The figurative sense of that on which something turns or hinges, cardinal or central point, is first recorded in English in 1813.
—**v.** 1841, turn as if on a pivot; from the noun in English, influenced by French *pivoter,* from French *pivot,* n. —**pivotal** *adj.* being that on which something turns or hinges, central, cardinal. 1844, formed from English *pivot* + *-al*[1].

pix *n.pl. Informal.* pictures. 1932, American English, spelling alteration of earlier *pics* (1884), plural of *pic,* informal abbreviation of *picture.*

pixel (pik′səl) *n.* one of the photographic elements of a television image. 1969, formed from English *pix* pictures + *el(ement).*

pixie or **pixy** *n.* fairy or elf. About 1630 *pixy* in the compound *pixy-path* bewilderment (path on which one is supposed to be led astray by pixies); later *pixie* in the compound *pixie-led* lost (led astray by pixies); of uncertain origin.

The first use of *pixie* or *pixy* as a single word is recorded in 1746.

pixilated (pik′səlā′tid) *adj. Informal.* slightly crazy, dazed or confused. 1848, American English, formed from *pixie* + *-lated,* as in *elated, titillated,* etc., perhaps by influence of *pixie-led* (1659, attested till 1895).

pizza (pēt′sə) *n.* baked pie covered with cheese, tomato sauce, etc. 1935, borrowing of Italian *pizza,* originally, cake, tart, pie; of uncertain origin (variously explained by such forms as Vulgar Latin **pīts-* point, Latin *pix,* genitive *picis,* pitch, Latin *pīnsere* to pound, beat; but none overcomes the obstacles of form or meaning). —**pizzeria** (pit′sərē′ə) *n.* place where pizzas are made and sold. 1943, in John Steinbeck's *Once There Was War,* although orally attested since the 1930's; American English, probably borrowed from Italian, from *pizza* + *-eria* -ery, or in some instances perhaps formed from English *pizza* + *-eria,* as abstracted from *cafeteria.*

pizzazz or **pizazz** (pəzaz′) *n. Slang.* flair, liveliness, showiness. 1937 *pizazz,* American English, a coined word, probably originally college slang.

pizzicato (pit′səkä′tō) *n., adj.* (music) plucked, played by plucking the strings with the finger. 1845, n.; 1880, adj.; borrowing of Italian *pizzicato,* past participle of *pizzicare* to pluck (strings), pinch, from *pizzare* to prick or sting, from *pizzo* point or edge, from Vulgar Latin **pīts-,* probably of imitative origin.

placard (plak′ərd) *n.* poster. 1481 *plakart* plate of armor; 1482 *placquart* sealed document; later, *placard* (1495); borrowed from Middle French *placard, plackart, placquard* sealed document, plate of armor, from Old French *plaquier* to piece together, stick, plaster, from Middle Dutch *placken* to patch, related to *placke* patch or stain; see PLAQUE; for suffix see -ARD.

The meaning of poster is first recorded in English in 1560, influenced by Middle French, where this sense occurs since the 1400's.
—**v.** (plak′ärd) put placards on or in. 1813, from the noun.

placate (plā′kāt) *v.* soothe or satisfy the anger of. 1678, probably, in part, developed from earlier *placate,* adj., placid (1662); borrowed from Latin *plācātus,* past participle of *plācāre* to calm, soothe, related to *placēre* to PLEASE; for suffix see -ATE[1]. It is also probable that *placate* is, in some instances, a back formation from *placation* (1589), perhaps formed in part through influence of Middle French *plaquer* placate, from Latin. —**placable** (plā′kəbəl) *adj.* Before 1500, pleasing; later, capable of being placated, mild, gentle (1586); borrowed from Middle French *placable,* and directly from Latin *plācābilis,* from *plācāre* to placate; for suffix see -ABLE.

place *n.* Probably before 1200, in *Ancrene Riwle;* borrowed from Old French *place,* and directly from Medieval Latin *placea, placia* place, spot, from Vulgar Latin **plattea,* from Latin *platea* courtyard, broad street, from Greek *plateîa* (*hodós*) broad (way), feminine of *platýs* broad. The Greek word is cognate with Latin *planta* sole of the foot, Lithuanian *platùs* broad, Old Irish *lethan,* Armenian *lain* broad, and Sanskrit *pr̥thú-s* broad, wide, roomy. Derived forms from Latin *platea* include Middle Dutch *plaetse* (modern Dutch *plaats*), Middle High German *platz* (modern German *Platz*), Icelandic *plāz* (Swedish *plats,* Danish *plads,* Norwegian *plass*). Doublet of PLAZA and PIAZZA. The Middle English *place* replaced Old English *stow* and *stede,* but is not generally recorded in place names in Middle English until 1330 and after. —**v.** 1442 *placen* to put or set in a particular place; from the noun. —**place mat** (1951) —**placement** *n.* 1844, a placing or arrangement, formed from English *place,* v. + *-ment.* —**place name** (1868).

placebo (pləsē′bō) *n.* substance or treatment without therapeutic value, given as medicine to satisfy a patient. 1785, in Motherby's *New Medical Dictionary,* New Latin, from Latin *placēbō* I shall please, first person singular future indicative of *placēre* to PLEASE.

Since about 1950 *placebo* has been used in reference to any inactive substance or nontherapeutic treatment used as a control in testing the effectiveness of a drug or therapy. An early use of *placebo* appeared in Middle English, probably before 1200, in *Ancrene Riwle,* as the liturgical name commonly given to the Latin rite of Vespers of the Office for the Dead, from the first word of the first antiphon (Psalm 114:9) used in this rite. The usage was extended to various allusive phrases in Middle English (1340, in *Ayenbite of Inwyt*), such as *to sing or play with placebo* to flatter, act servilely.

placenta (pləsen′tə) *n.* organ by which the fetus is attached to the womb. 1677, ovarian tissue of flowering plants, in Nehemiah Grew's *The Anatomy of Fruits,* New Latin *placenta uterina* uterine cake, from Latin *placenta* flat cake, altered from Greek *plakóenta,* accusative of *plakóeis* flat, later contracted to *plakoûs* (genitive *plakoûntos*) flat cake, flat seed of the mallow, from *pláx* (genitive *plakós*) flat surface; see FLUKE[3] flatfish.

The meaning of the organ by which the fetus is attached to the womb is first recorded in English in 1691.

placer (plas′ər) *n.* place where gold, etc., is washed out of loose sand or gravel. 1842, American English, borrowed from Spanish *placer* deposit, shoal, from Catalan *placer* undersea plain, from *plassa* place, from Medieval Latin *placea, placia* place, spot; see PLACE.

placid *adj.* calm, peaceful. 1626, in Bacon's *Sylva Sylvarum;* probably a back formation from *placidity* and borrowed perhaps through French *placide,* and directly from Latin *placidus* pleasing, gentle, calm, from *placēre* to PLEASE. —**placidity** *n.* 1619 *placiditie,* borrowed from Latin *placiditās* gentleness, calmness, from *placidus;* for suffix see -ITY.

placket *n.* opening or slit in a garment. 1605, in Shakespeare's *King Lear,* of uncertain origin; possibly a variant of PLACARD, in the Middle English *plackert* piece of armor, undergarment (1483).

plagiarism (plā′jərizəm) *n.* literary theft. 1621, formed from earlier English *plagiary* one who wrongfully takes another's words or ideas, literary thief (1601, in Ben Jonson's *The Poetaster*) + *-ism.* English *plagiary* was borrowed (perhaps through influence of earlier French *plagiere*) from Latin *plagiārius* kidnaper, seducer, plunderer, literary thief, from *plagium* kidnaping, from *plaga* snare, net, apparently the same word as *plaga* flat surface, region; see FLUKE³ flatfish **—plagiarist** *n.* 1674, formed from earlier English *plagiary* (in the sense of literary theft) + *-ist.* **—plagiarize** *v.* commit literary theft. 1716, formed from earlier English *plagiary* + *-ize.*

plague *n.* epidemic disease, pestilence. Before 1382 *plage* blow, wound, affliction, in the Wycliffe Bible; later, torment or disease (about 1425), borrowed from Late Latin *plāga* pestilence, from Latin, blow or stroke, probably related to the root *plag-* of *plangere* to strike, beat the breast, lament; see PLAINT. Latin *plāga* was also the source of late Old High German and late Old Icelandic *plāga,* Middle High German and Middle Dutch *plāge,* now represented by modern German *Plage,* modern Dutch *plaage,* and Norwegian *plage.*

The meaning of an epidemic disease that causes many deaths is first recorded in 1548-49, in the *Book of Common Prayer,* where introduction of the spelling *plague* is first found, probably from Middle French *plague* (though FEW considers the occurrence in the 1400's a one-time instance, until its regular appearance after 1574).

—v. afflict with plague. 1481 *plaghen,* in Caxton's translation of *The History of Reynard the Fox;* borrowed from Middle Dutch *plaghen,* from *plaghe* plague, from Late Latin *plāga;* later *plage,* in the Coverdale Bible (1535); from the noun. The figurative sense of torment or trouble of any kind is first recorded in Spenser's *Amoretti* (1594).

plaice *n.* kind of flatfish. 1267 *plays;* later *playce* (about 1300, in *Havelok the Dane*); borrowed from Old French *plaïs,* from Gallo-Romance **platicem,* altered from Late Latin *platessa* flatfish, probably from Greek *platýs* flat or broad; see PLACE.

plaid (plad) *n.* cloth with a pattern of checks or crisscross stripes. 1512, Scottish, from Gaelic *plaide* blanket or mantle; cognate with Irish *plaid, ploid* blanket, quilt, plaid. **—adj.** having a pattern of checks or crisscross stripes. Before 1600, from the noun.

plain *adj.* Probably before 1300 *playne* smooth, flat, straight, in *Kyng Alisaunder;* later *plain* open, clear, pure, simple (before 1325, in *Cursor Mundi*), and sincere, honest (about 1375); also, ordinary, unaffected (about 1386, in Chaucer's *Legend of Good Women*); borrowed from Old French *plain,* from Latin *plānus* flat, even, level. The Latin *plānus* is cognate with Lithuanian *plónas* thin, Latvian *plãns* flat, even, thin, Old Slavic *polje* field, Armenian *hol* earth, land, soil, and Hittite *palhis* broad, from Indo-European **pelə-/plā-* (Pok.805). For Germanic cognates, see FIELD. Doublet of PLANE¹ (level surface), and PLAN. **—adv.** Before 1325 *plain* in a plain manner, in *Cursor Mundi;* from the adjective. **—n.** Probably before 1300 *plain, pleyn, pleine* flat stretch of land, in *Arthour and Merlin;* borrowed from Old French *plain,* from Latin *plānum* level surface, from neuter of *plānus* flat, even, level. **—plain clothes** civilian dress (1822). **—plainclothesman** *n.* detective (1899). **—plain Jane** or **Plain Jane** (1912). **—Plains** *n.pl.* 1755, broad open lands of Midwestern America (but earlier as singular *plain* in reference to the Indians living on the Plains, 1697, and in reference to the area itself, 1684). The word is found earlier with the same meaning in Middle English about 1395. **—plainsman** *n.* inhabitant of Midwestern America (1870). **—plainsong** *n.* vocal music of the church, usually sung without instrumental accompaniment (before 1450).

plaint *n.* Probably before 1200 *pleinte* mourning, lamentation, in *Ancrene Riwle;* later *plainte* complaint; and legal statement of grievance (probably before 1300, in *Arthour and Merlin*); borrowed from Old French *plaint, pleint,* from Latin *plānctus* (genitive *plānctūs*) lamentation, beating, from *plangere* to lament, beat the breast, strike. Latin *plangere* is cognate with Middle Irish *léssaim* I strike violently, Greek *plḗssein* (earlier **plākye-*) to strike, from Indo-European **plag-/plāg-, *plak-/plāk-* (Pok.832). Cognates in Germanic include Old Frisian *flōka,* Old Saxon *flōkan,* Middle Dutch and modern Dutch *vloeken,* Middle Low German *vlōken,* Old High German *fluohhan* to curse (modern German *fluchen*), Old Icelandic *flōkinn* disordered, confused, and Gothic *flōkan* to lament.

plaintiff *n.* person who begins a lawsuit. Before 1400 *playntyf, pleyntyff,* borrowed through Anglo-French *pleintif,* noun use of Old French *plaintif* complaining; see PLAINTIVE.

plaintive *adj.* Before 1393 *pleintif* complaining, lamenting, in Gower's *Confessio Amantis;* later *plaintive* (1434); borrowed from Old French *plaintif* complaining, from *plaint* PLAINT; for suffix see -IVE. The meaning of mournful or sad is first recorded in 1579. Originally *plaintiff* and *plaintive* were the same word in English but the form ending in *-iff* retained its spelling and meaning in legal usage while the adjective use in the common vocabulary was Anglicized.

plait (plāt) *n.* braid. About 1385 *plite* pleat, fold, wrinkle, in Usk's *Testament of Love;* later *pleit* braid (before 1398, in Trevisa's translation of Bartholomew's *De Proprietatibus Rerum*); probably from the verb in English by influence of Anglo-French *pleit,* Old French *pleit* a fold, way of folding, from Latin *-plictus, -plicitus* folded, variant of *plicātus,* neuter past participle of *plicāre* to fold; see PLY² fold, and compare PLEAT. **—v.** to braid. About 1330 *pliten* to join, fasten; later *pleiten* (before 1376, in *Piers Plowman*), and *plaiten* to fold (about 1380), also, to braid or weave (about 1385); though said to be from the noun in English (no early verb is found in French) the dates in the record, and the development in meaning from earlier "fold" to later "braid" in first the verb and then the noun suggests that the verb is truly the original form in English and that if the noun is not from the verb, then both were borrowings into English; but if the dates reflect the development in English then the verb was borrowed from Old French *plier* to fold, variant of *pleiir* from Latin *plicāre* to fold.

plan *n.* 1678, plane perpendicular to the line of vision, in Phillips' *Dictionary;* borrowed from French *plan* plane surface, ground plan, map, from Medieval Latin *planus* level or open (of land), from Latin *plānus* level or flat. French *plan* was probably also a learned borrowing from Latin *plānum* level or flat surface.

The meaning of a drawing of any object, made by

projection upon a flat surface, and the more general sense of a scheme of action, design, method, are first recorded in 1706, in Kersey's edition of Phillips' *Dictionary.*
—v. 1728, in Pope's *Dunciad;* from the noun.

plane[1] *n.* level surface. 1646, borrowed from Latin *plānum* flat or level surface, from neuter of *plānus* flat or level; see the doublet PLAIN. **—adj.** flat, level. 1666, borrowed from Latin *plānus* flat or level. **—v.** soar, glide. 1410 *planen,* in John Walton's translation of Boethius' *De Consolatione Philosophiae;* borrowed from Middle French *planer,* from *plan* plane surface, from Latin *plānum* flat or level surface (so called because a bird when soaring extends its wings in a plane). The meaning of both noun and verb is found in an extended sense in *plane*[2], as a shortening of *aeroplane, airplane,* but originally an element of the compound *airplane.*

plane[2] *n.* airplane. 1908, shortened from AEROPLANE. **—v.** to travel by airplane. 1908, from the noun. The extended sense of *plane*[1], v., though found in this now somewhat archaic use of travel by airplane, probably did not play a part in its development, since verb use of *plane*[1] was too far removed in sense from its use as an element of *airplane.*

plane[3] *n.* tool for smoothing surfaces. 1350, borrowed from Old French *plane,* and perhaps directly from Late Latin *plāna,* from *plānāre* make level (with a cutting tool), from Latin *plānus* level or flat; see PLAIN. **—v.** smooth with a plane. Before 1325 *planen* to gloss over, explain away, in *Cursor Mundi;* later, to smooth, make even; perhaps from the noun, and as a borrowing from Old French *planer,* and directly from Late Latin *plānāre* make level (with a cutting tool). **—planer** *n.* (1413, tool for smoothing; 1596, tool for planing wood)

plane[4] *n.* tall tree with broad leaves. Before 1382, in the Wycliffe Bible; borrowed from Old French *plane* descended (with regular loss of *t* before *n*) from Latin *platanus,* from Greek *plátanos,* earlier called *platánistos* the plane tree of Asia Minor, very possibly of foreign origin, but eventually associated with Greek *platýs* broad (from the shape of its leaf); see PLACE.

planet *n.* Probably before 1300 *planete* a celestial body having an apparent motion of its own among the fixed stars, in *Kyng Alisaunder;* borrowed from Old French *planete,* and borrowed directly from Latin *planēta* (cited usually in the plural *planētae*), from Greek *astéres planêtai* wandering stars, from *planâsthai* to wander, of unknown origin.

The modern scientific meaning in astronomy of a celestial body moving around the sun is first recorded in 1640.
—planetary *adj.* 1593, of or belonging to a planet; probably formed from English *planet* + *-ary,* by influence of Middle French *planétaire,* from Old French *planete* planet + *-aire* -ary.

planetarium (plan′ətãr′ēəm) *n.* 1734, apparatus, especially an orrery, for showing the movement of the planets; New Latin, formed from Late Latin *planēta* PLANET + Latin *-ārium,* neuter of *-ārius* -ary.

The modern sense of *planetarium,* a machine for projecting light that represents stars and planets on a domed surface, is first recorded in 1929. The meaning of the building housing such a machine under a dome is first recorded in 1935, in WPA *New York City Guide.*

planetesimal (plan′ətes′əməl) *n.* minute celestial body. 1903, formed from English *planet* + *-esimal,* abstracted from *infinitesimal.* **—adj.** of or pertaining to the hypothesis that the planets were formed by the accretion of planetesimals. 1904, probably from the noun.

plank *n.* long, flat piece of sawed timber. 1294-95 *plaunke;* earlier as a surname *Plank* (1206); borrowed from Old North French *planke,* variant of Old French *planche,* from Late Latin *planca* board, slab. Late Latin *planca* is thought to be cognate with Greek *pláx* (genitive *plakós*) flat surface; see FLUKE[3] flatfish. **—v.** to cover or furnish with planks. 1432 *planken,* from the noun.

plankton (plangk′tən) *n.* small animal and plant organisms in water. 1891, borrowing of German *Plankton,* from Greek *planktón,* neuter of *planktós* wandering, drifting, from *plázesthai* to wander, roam, drift, from *plázein* (earlier **plangye-*) to drive astray; originally, to strike, knock; see PLAINT. German *Plankton* was coined in 1887 by the German physiologist and marine biologist Viktor Hensen, 1835-1924. **—planktonic** *adj.* 1893, formed in English from *plankton* + *-ic* on the model of German *planktonisch,* from *Plankton* + *-isch* -ic. German *planktonisch* was introduced in 1891 by the German biologist Ernst Haeckel, 1834-1919.

plant *n.* Before 1376 *plante* young plant, sprout, cutting, in *Piers Plowman;* earlier as a surname *Plant* (1301); found in Old English (before 830) *plante;* borrowed from Latin *planta* sprout, slip, cutting, and later reborrowed into Middle English from Old French *plante* and directly from Latin *planta.* Latin *planta* is perhaps derived from **plantāre* to drive in with the feet, push into the ground with the feet, from *planta* sole of the foot. As for the source of Latin *planta* sole of the foot, Ernout and Meillet (*Dictionnaire étymologique de la langue latine*) say that it can be understood only as formed from the present tense of a lost *n*-infix verb of the Indo-European root **pletā-/pletə-* spread out (Pok.833).

The biological sense of any living thing that is not an animal is first recorded in English in 1551, apparently borrowed from Middle French. From the general sense of something planted or fixed developed the meaning of a building or machinery used in carrying out any industrial process, first recorded in 1789. The sense of someone who spies or gathers information for others, as in *the spy was a plant,* is first recorded in 1812.
—v. 1137 *planten* put in the ground to grow, in *The Peterborough Chronicle;* later, to establish, settle, found (probably about 1380); in part developed from Old English (before 830) *plantian* to plant, and in part borrowed from Old French *planter,* both the Old English and Old French forms borrowed from Latin *plantāre* to plant, set, from *planta* sprout.
—planter *n.* (before 1382, one who plants seed, in the Wycliffe Bible; earlier, 1281, as a surname; 1957, container for plants, American English).

plantain[1] *n.* kind of large banana. 1555 *plantan* the bananalike fruit of the plantain tree; 1589 *plantano* the plantain tree, later Anglicized to *plantain* (1604); borrowing of Spanish *plántano, plátano,* learned borrowing from Medieval Latin *plantanus* plane tree, alteration (by association with Latin *planta* plant) of Greek *plátanos* and Latin *platanus* PLANE[4] tree; so called from the broad, flat leaves of the plant. It is also possible, as the OED suggests, that Spanish *plátano* was influenced in form by some native name for this or a similar plant, such as Galibi *palatana* and Carib *balátana.*

plantain[2] *n.* common weed. Before 1300 *plauntein;* later *plantayne* (about 1395); borrowed through Anglo-French *plaunteyne,* and directly from Old French *plantain, plantaine, plaintain,* from Latin *plantāginem* (nominative *plantāgō*) the common weed, from *planta* sole of the foot (so called from its flat leaves); see PLACE.

plantation *n.* Probably before 1425 *plantacion* foundation or source (of nerves extending from the brain), in a translation of Chauliac's *Grande Chirurgie;* later, the act of planting (before 1450); borrowed from Middle French *plantation,* and directly from Latin *plantātiōnem* (nominative *plantātiō*) a planting, from *plantāre* to PLANT; for suffix see -ATION.

The meaning of a large farm or estate on which cotton, tobacco, and other crops are grown is first recorded in Phillips' *Dictionary* (1706).

plantigrade (plan′təgrād) *adj.* walking on the whole sole of the foot. 1831, borrowing of French *plantigrade* (1795), formed from Latin *planta* sole of the foot + *gradus* step. **—n.** plantigrade animal, such as the bear. 1835, from the adjective.

plaque (plak) *n.* ornamental tablet. 1848, in Thackeray's *Vanity Fair;* borrowing of French *plaque,* from Middle French *plaque* metal plate, coin, of uncertain origin (perhaps through Flemish *placke, plak* small coin; originally flat disk or tablet, flat board, or directly from Middle Dutch *placke* disk, patch, stain; cognate with Middle Low German and Middle High German *placke* patch, stain).

The meaning in medicine of a patch of eruption or the like is first recorded in 1876, that of a patch of fibrous tissue on the wall of an artery in 1891, and that of a patch of deposit containing bacteria that adheres to the teeth in 1898.

plash *n.* Probably before 1400 *plashe* a pool of water, puddle, in *Morte Arthur;* earlier as a surname *Pleisse* (1277); developed from Old English *plæsc;* cognate with Middle Dutch and Flemish *plasch* pool, also with Middle Dutch and Middle Low German *plas.* The later meaning of a splash is first recorded in a translation of Vergil's *Aeneid* (1513) and the OED separates this as a different word, probably of imitative origin, but the semantic and phonological similarity is so compelling that this distinction seems somewhat artificial. **—v.** to splash. 1582, in Stanyhurst's translation of Vergil's *Aeneid,* probably from the noun, as used in the earlier translation of the *Aeneid* as cited above.

plasma (plaz′mə) *n.* liquid part of blood or lymph. 1712, form or shape; earlier *plasm, plasme* mold in which something is formed (1620); borrowed from Late Latin *plasma,* from Greek *plásma* something molded or created, from *plássein* to mold; see PLASTER.

The physiological sense of the liquid part of blood or lymph (apparently semantically "from which blood is molded or made") is first recorded in 1845. The sense in physics of a highly ionized gas in which there is a relative balance of positive ions and electrons is first recorded in 1928.

-plast a combining form used in biology to name particles, granules, cells, or other small formations of living matter, as in *bioplast, chromoplast, mesoplast.* Adopted from Greek *plastós* formed, molded; see PLASTER.

plaster *n.* About 1150 *plaster* medicinal application, such as a poultice; developed from Old English (before 1000) *plaster* medicinal application; also 1284 *plastre* cementing material, borrowed from Old French *plastre* cementing material; both the Old English and Old French forms were borrowed from Latin *emplastra, emplastrum* a plaster, from Greek *émplastron,* variant of *émplaston* salve or plaster, from neuter of *émplastos* daubed on (*em-* on + *plastós* molded, from *plássein* (earlier **plathye-*) to mold; originally, to spread thin; cognate with Latin *plānus* level, flat; see PLAIN). **—v.** Before 1325 *plasteren* to daub or cover with plaster, in *Cursor Mundi;* probably from the noun in Middle English; also 1373 *plastren,* borrowed from Old French *plastrir,* from Old French *plastre,* n. **—plasterer** *n.* 1368, earlier in Anglo-French, about 1300; borrowed from Old French *plastrier,* from *plastrir* to plaster. **—plaster of Paris** (1284 *Plastre de Parys*).

plastic *adj.* easily molded or shaped. 1632, molding or giving shape to material, in Ben Jonson's *The Magnetick Lady;* borrowed, perhaps through influence of French *plastique,* from Latin *plasticus,* from Greek *plastikós* able to be molded, pertaining to molding, from *plastós* molded, from *plássein* to form, mold; see PLASTER; for suffix see -IC.

The meaning of easily molded, shaped, or influenced, is first recorded in 1711.

—n. 1905, solid substance that can be molded; from the adjective. The extended meaning of a synthetic product made from oil derivatives (i.e. modern plastic) is first recorded in 1909, in reference to an early product known under the trade name *Bakelite.*

—plasticity *n.* plastic quality. 1782-83, formed from English *plastic,* adj. + *-ity.* **—plastic surgery** (1839), **—plastic surgeon** (1911), both terms perpetuating the now somewhat archaic sense of molding or giving shape to something.

plate *n.* About 1250 *plate* gold or silver coin, in *Genesis and Exodus;* later, flat sheet of metal (about 1300), and metal utensils, shallow dish (1415, but see *platter* 1280); borrowed from Old French *plate,* noun use of *plate,* adj., feminine of *plat* flat, and borrowed directly from Medieval Latin *plata* plate, piece of metal, probably from Vulgar Latin **plattus,* perhaps formed on the model of Greek *platýs* flat, broad; see PLACE.

It is also possible that development of *plate* in Middle English was influenced to some extent by Old English *plætt* buffet or smack, in that the OED definition of flat blow or smack may represent a semantic connection through "flat" with Old French *plat* and thence Middle English *plat* flat (probably before 1300).

—v. to cover with a thin layer of silver, gold, or other metal. About 1380 *platen,* in Chaucer's *House of Fame;* from the noun.

—plate glass (1727-41, in *Chambers Cyclopedia*). **—platelet** *n.* small plate or disk, especially a corpuscular structure of the blood. 1895, formed from English *plate* + *-let* (found earlier in reference to blood platelets as *blood plate,* 1885).

plateau (platō′) *n.* large, high plain. 1796, borrowing of French *plateau* from Old French *platel,* diminutive of *plat* flat surface or thing, noun use of *plat* adj.; see PLATE. The figurative sense of a level, especially one at which something stabilizes for a period of time, is first recorded in 1894. **—v.** reach a peak, level out. 1952, from the noun.

platen (plat′ən) *n.* 1541, flat metal plate, in Robert Copland's *Works;* borrowed from Middle French *platine,* from Old French *plat* flat; see PLATE.

The meaning of a flat metal plate in a printing press is first recorded in 1594, and that of the cylindrical roller against which the paper rests in a typewriter, in 1890.

platform *n.* 1550, plan of action, scheme, design, in the letters of Bishop Gardiner; borrowed from Middle French *plate-forme,* literally, flat form (from Old French *plate* flat, feminine of *plat;* see PLATE + *forme* FORM).

The meaning of a raised level surface from the literal sense "flat form" is first recorded in 1560 with the specific application to the mounting of guns; a generalized sense of any such surface made with planks or boards is found in 1727. A related meaning of a piece of raised flooring from which a speaker addresses an audience is said to have been in use about 1820; but possibly earlier, if the figurative sense of a statement of principles and policies of a political party (1803, in American English) is developed from the literal meaning. However, this sense of a statement of principles was surely influenced in its development by the earlier sense of a set of rules governing church doctrine, found as early as 1648, in American English.

The meaning of a railroad station platform is first recorded in 1838, and that of a railroad car in 1832. **—platform tennis** (1934).

platinum *n.* metallic chemical element. Coined in 1812 by the British chemist Sir Humphry Davy, as an alteration of earlier (1750) *platina* platinum, to conform to the names of other metals ending in *-um,* for example *tantalum.* Earlier *platina* was a borrowing of Spanish *platina,* diminutive of *plata* silver (so called because the element resembles silver), from Vulgar Latin **plattus* flat; see PLATE. Compare ALUMINUM.

platitude *n.* dull or commonplace remark. 1812, flatness, dullness, triteness, especially in relation to use of language; borrowing of French *platitude* flatness, vapidness, from Old French *plat* flat (see PLATE), formed on analogy of *latitude, certitude,* etc.; for suffix see -TUDE.

Platonic *adj.* 1533, of or having to do with the Greek philosopher Plato; later, now usually **platonic,** of or having to do with love free of sensual desire, in Ben Jonson's *The New Inn* (1631). The latter sense is in reference to Plato's writings, specifically his *Symposium.*

platoon *n.* small military unit. 1637, borrowed from French *peloton* platoon, group of persons, from Middle French *peloton,* literally, little ball, diminutive of Old French *pelote* ball; see PELLET; for suffixal ending see -OON.

The sense in sports, originally in football, of a group of players trained to act together especially as a defensive unit, is first recorded in 1941, followed by its application in baseball referring to players who alternate in the same position.

—v. 1706, to fire a volley; later redeveloped in American English with the sense of interchange or alternate (baseball or football players) in the same position (1955), from the noun use in football.

platter *n.* large, shallow dish. About 1280 *platere,* borrowed from Anglo-French *plater,* Old French *plate* PLATE, and from Anglo-Latin *platera,* of uncertain origin.

platypus (plat′əpəs) *n.* duckbill, an egg-laying mammal. 1799, in George Shaw's *The Naturalists' Miscellany,* New Latin, from Greek *platýpous* flat-footed (*platýs* broad, flat; see PLACE + *poús* FOOT).

plaudit (plô′dit) *n.* enthusiastic approval or praise. 1624, shortened from earlier *plaudite* an actor's request for applause (1567); borrowing of Latin *plaudite!* applaud! (the customary appeal for applause made by Roman actors at the end of a play). Latin *plaudite* is 2nd person plural imperative of *plaudere* to clap, applaud, approve, of uncertain origin.

The English form *plaudite* was originally pronounced in three syllables; later, the sound represented by the final *-e* became mute, giving rise to the shortened form *plaudit.*

plausible *adj.* 1541, acceptable, agreeable, pleasing, deserving applause; borrowed from Latin *plausibilis* deserving applause, acceptable, from *plaus-,* past participle stem of *plaudere* to applaud; see PLAUDIT; for suffix see -IBLE.

The meaning of seemingly true or reasonable, as applied to arguments or statements, is first recorded in 1565.

—plausibility *n.* 1596, quality of being agreeable, formed in English from Latin *plausibilis* agreeable, acceptable + English *-ity.* The meaning of seeming worthiness of acceptance, appearance of reasonableness, is first found in 1649, in Milton's writings.

play *n.* Probably before 1200 *plage, ploge, pleige, pleowe, plohe,* variously found in *Ancrene Riwle* and Layamon's *Chronicle of Britain* with meanings of a game or martial sport, activity of children, joke or jesting, revelry; later *play, pleie* (before 1250), and dramatic or theatrical performance (before 1325, in *Cursor Mundi*); developed from Old English (West Saxon) *plega* recreation, exercise, quick movement (about 725, in *Beowulf*), related to *plegian* to exercise, frolic, take part in a game, perform music. Another group of Middle English forms, including *plahe, plawe,* and *plau,* developed from Anglian *plaga* and left no direct descendants in modern English. Old English *plegian* is cognate with Middle Dutch *playen, pleyen* to dance, play, rejoice, and perhaps with *pleghen* attend to, cultivate, practice (modern Dutch *plegen* commit, practice), Old Saxon *plĕgan* vouch for, be responsible for, take charge of, Old Frisian *plega* be accustomed to, tend to, and Old High German *pflĕgan* to tend, attend to, cultivate (modern German *pflegen*), from West Germanic **plegan,* of unknown origin.

The meaning of action, operation, working (as in *the play of fancy*) is found in Shakespeare's *Henry V* (1599), but is probably recognizable before 1200, in Layamon's *Chronicle of Britain* in the phrase *fulle ploge* complete freedom of movement, as is the sense of free action, scope for activity (in *to allow the fullest play*) later found in 1641, in Milton's *Works.*

—v. Probably before 1200 *pleien,* in *Ancrene Riwle* and Layamon's *Chronicle of Britain;* later *plaien* (about 1250); developed from Old English (about 830) *plegian* to play.

—playbill *n.* (1673) **—playboy** *n.* (1829) **—player** *n.* About 1340 *player* reveler, in *Ayenbite of Inwyt;* earlier as a surname *Pleyere* (1275); developed from Old English *plegeri* (about 1000, in Ælfric's *Glossary*); formed from *plegan* + *-er*[1]. **—player piano** (1907) **—playful** *adj.* About 1225 *pleiful,* formed in Middle English from *plei* play + *-ful.* **—playground** *n.* (1780; Middle English *playstude,* about 1251, and in Old English *plægstede;* probably before 1000). **—playhouse** *n.* theater (1599, in Shakespeare's *Henry V*). **—playing card** (1543) **—playmate** *n.* (1642, variant *playfere,* before 1765, from Middle English, probably before

1200; formed from *plage* + *fere* companion) **—playpen** *n.* (1931) **—playroom** *n.* (1819) **—plaything** *n.* (1675) **—playtime** *n.* (1616, in Ben Jonson's writings) **—playwright** *n.* (1687)

plaza (plaz′ə) *n.* public square. 1836, American English, borrowing of Spanish *plaza* square, place, from Latin *platea* courtyard, broad street; see the doublet PLACE.

plea *n.* the noun form of *plead.* About 1250 *plait* strife, contention, complaint, in *The Owl and the Nightingale;* later *plai* lawsuit, court pleading, controversy (about 1300); *ple* (probably about 1350); borrowed through Anglo-French *plai,* and directly from Old French *plait, plet, plai* lawsuit, decision, decree, from Late Latin *placitum* decision, decree, from Latin, opinion, decree; literally, that which pleases, from neuter past participle of *placēre* to PLEASE.

The extended meaning of an appeal, argument, excuse, is first recorded in English before 1550.
—plea bargain (1968); *v.* (1973). **—plea bargaining** agreement to plead guilty to a lesser charge (1963).

plead *v.* the verb form of *plea* (itself found as a verb in English from about 1440. About 1250 *plaiden* make a plea in court, debate legally, argue a case, in *The Owl and the Nightingale;* later *pleden* (about 1387); borrowed through Anglo-French *pleder,* and directly from Old French *pleidier, plaidier,* from Medieval Latin *placitare,* from Late Latin *placitum* PLEA. A variant form, Middle English *plaiten* (before 1325), was borrowed from Old French *plaitier,* altered from *plaidier* by influence of *plait* lawsuit.

The extended meaning of make an earnest appeal, request, beg, implore, is first recorded in *Sir Gawain and the Green Knight* (probably before 1390).

pleasant *adj.* About 1378 *plesaunte* pleasing or agreeable, in a version of *Piers Plowman;* earlier *pleisant* pleased, favorable; also, as a surname *Plesent* (1320); borrowed from Old French *plaisant,* present participle of *plaisir* to PLEASE; for suffix see -ANT. **—pleasantry** *n.* 1655, fun or joking; later pleasant or witty remark (1701); borrowed from French *plaisanterie,* from Old French *plesanterie,* from *plaisant* pleasant; for suffix see -RY.

please *v.* About 1303 *plesen* to satisfy, placate, appease, in Mannyng's *Handlyng Synne;* later, delight (probably about 1380); also *pleasen* (probably before 1400); borrowed from Old French *plesir, plaisir* to please, from Latin *placēre* to be acceptable, be liked or approved.

The intransitive use of to be pleased, to like (as in *I do as I please*) is first recorded in Dunbar's *Poems* (1500-20). The imperative use (now merely a polite addition to requests or commands, as in *Please follow me*) was probably originally a shortening of the earlier phrase *if you please* (1530), as well as the earlier construction *Please to* (1622, as in *Please to take my place*), itself a shortening of *May it please you to,* also found in Shakespeare as *Please you* (1600).
—pleasure *n.* About 1370 *plesure* will, wish, desire, in Chaucer's *Complaint to His Lady;* later *pleasure* (probably before 1425); also, gratification, enjoyment, liking (before 1450); borrowed from Old French *plesir, plaisir* enjoyment, delight, noun use of *plaisir,* v., to please; for suffix see -URE. **—pleasurable** *adj.* 1579, formed from English *pleasure* + *-able.*

pleat (plēt) *n.* flat, usually narrow, fold in cloth. 1581, variant of PLAIT, n.

Although the form *pleat* is not found in print from the late 1600's to the late 1800's, the pronunciation it represents did survive and eventually led to reestablishment of the written form *pleat* in the specific sense of a fold in cloth.
—v. to fold or arrange in pleats. 1570, variant of *plait,* v. Use of the spelling *pleat* for the verb parallels the history of the noun.

plebe (plēb) or **pleb** (pleb) *n.* freshman at a military or naval academy. 1833-34 *plebe;* later *pleb* (1852); American English, probably a shortened form of PLEBEIAN. It is also a remote possibility that *plebe* in its modern sense is an extension of meaning and a revival in form of English *plebe* (1612) the common people; borrowed from French *plèbe,* from Old French *plebe* or perhaps a learned borrowing among students from Latin *plēbem* (nominative *plēbs*); see PLEBEIAN.

plebeian (plibē′ən) *n.* commoner. 1533, commoner of ancient Rome, in a translation of Livy's *Roman History;* possibly borrowed from Middle French *plébéien,* but more likely formed in English from Latin *plēbeius* of the common people, from *plēbēs* (later *plēbs*) the common people + English *-ian.* Latin *plēbēs* (from Indo-European **plēdhwēs*) is cognate with Greek *plēthýs* crowd, throng, related to *plḗthein* be full; see FULL. The general sense of any commoner is first recorded in English before 1586, in Sidney's writings. **—adj.** of plebeians. 1566, from the noun.

plebiscite (pleb′əsīt) *n.* direct vote by the populace on some important issue or question. 1860, borrowed from French *plébiscite,* learned borrowing from Latin *plēbiscitum* a decree or resolution of the people (*plēbis,* genitive of *plēbs* the common people, see PLEBEIAN + *scītum* decree, from neuter past participle of *sciscere* to assent, vote for, approve; originally, inquire of the people, a form of *scīre* to know; see SCIENCE); for suffix see -ITE[1].

The modern meaning of *plebiscite* became familiar in English in connection with the popular ratification of the coup d'état of 1851 in France. An earlier use in the sense of law enacted by a Roman plebeian is first recorded in 1533 in a translation of Livy's *Roman History.*

plectrum (plek′trəm) *n.* piece of ivory, horn, metal, etc., for plucking the strings of a musical instrument. 1626, in Bacon's *Sylva Sylvarum,* borrowing of Latin *plēctrum,* from Greek *plêktron* thing to strike with, from *plēk-,* root of *plḗssein* to strike; see PLAINT.

pledge *n.* 1348 *plegge* a surety, guarantor, bail; earlier as a surname *Plegg* (1284); also *pledge* (before 1463); borrowed from Old French *plege,* probably from Frankish **plegan* to guarantee (compare Old Saxon *plëgan* vouch for; see PLAY); compare PLIGHT[2] pledge.

The meaning of a solemn promise or vow is first recorded in English in 1814.
—v. Probably about 1400 *pleggen* give in pledge, promise; later, become surety for; from the noun in English, and in part borrowed from Old French *plegier* to guarantee, bail, from *plege* pledge.

For an explanation of the spelling *-dge* see EDGE and DRUDGE.

plenary (plen′ərē) *adj.* full, complete. 1517, borrowed from Medieval Latin *plenarius* entire, complete, from Latin *plēnus* FULL. The modern English form *plenary* is a replacement of Middle English *plener* (recorded about 1250); borrowed through Anglo-French *plener,* and from Old French *plenier,* from Medieval Latin *plenarius* entire, complete, from Latin *plēnus* FULL; for suffix see -ARY.

plenipotentiary (plen'əpəten'sheer'ē) *adj.* having or giving full power and authority. About 1645, in James Howell's *Letters;* borrowed from French *plénipotentiaire,* and directly from Medieval Latin *plenipotentiarius,* from Late Latin *plēnipotentem* (nominative *plēnipotēns*) having full power, (from Latin *plēnus* FULL + *potentem* powerful; see POTENT); for suffix see -ARY. **—n.** person having full power or authority. 1656, in Blount's *Glossographia;* from the adjective, influenced by the noun use in French.

plenitude (plen'ətüd) *n.* fullness, plentifulness. Probably before 1425, in a translation of Higden's *Polychronicon,* borrowed from Old French *plenitude,* and directly from Latin *plēnitūdinem* (nominative *plēnitūdo*) abundance, completeness, fullness, from *plēnus* complete, FULL; for suffix see -TUDE.

plenteous (plen'tēəs) *adj.* plentiful. Probably before 1400 *plentiose, plentius,* alteration of *plentiuous* (1300) and *plenteuous* abundant or plentiful (before 1382, in the Wycliffe Bible); borrowed from Old French *plentiveus, plentivous,* fertile or rich, from *plentif* abundant, from *plenté* abundance + *-if* (Latin *-īvus*); see PLENTY; for suffix see -OUS.

plenty *n.* Before 1250 *plente* full supply, abundance, in a version of *Ancrene Riwle;* later *plenty* (1373); borrowed from Old French *plenté,* earlier *plentet,* from Latin *plēnitātem* (nominative *plēnitās*) fullness, from *plēnus* complete, FULL; for suffix see -TY[2]. A now obsolete form *plentith,* (before 1382), *plenteth* (about 1250), existed until the mid to late 1400's; borrowed from Old French *plentet.* **—adj.** Before 1325 *plente* full or abundant, in *Cursor Mundi;* from the noun. **—adv.** *Informal.* quite, fully. 1842, from the adjective. **—plentiful** *adj.* About 1400 *plenteful,* formed from Middle English *plente,* n. + *-ful.*

plenum (plē'nəm) *n.* full assembly. 1678, space completely filled with matter; borrowing of Latin *plēnum* (*spatium*) full (space), neuter of *plēnus* complete, FULL.

The meaning of a full assembly (of legislators) is first recorded in 1772.

pleonasm (plē'ənazəm) *n.* redundancy of expression. 1586, borrowed from Late Latin *pleonasmus,* from Greek *pleonasmós* abundance, exaggeration, (in grammar) redundancy, from *pleonázein* abound, be redundant, from *pléōn, pleíōn* more, comparative of *polýs* much, related to *plḗrēs* FULL. Middle French *pléonasme* (1571) may have influenced the English borrowing. **—pleonastic** *adj.* redundant. 1778, probably a shortened form of earlier *pleonastical* (1653), formed on the pattern of such pairs as *sarcasm, sarcastic,* etc.; for suffix see -IC, -ICAL.

plethora (pleth'ərə) *n.* excessive fullness, too much. 1541, abnormal condition caused by an excess of body fluid; borrowing of Late Latin *plēthōra,* from Greek *plēthṓrā* fullness, from *plḗthein* be full; see FULL.

The general sense of an excessive fullness is first recorded in English in 1700, taken directly from the Greek. English *plethora* may also have been borrowed by influence of Middle French *plethore* (1538), in which the final *e* was still pronounced (ə).

pleura (plůr'ə) *n.* thin membrane covering the lungs. Probably before 1425, in a translation of Chauliac's *Grande Chirurgie;* borrowed from Medieval Latin **pleura,* from Greek *pleurá* side of the body, rib; see PLEURISY.

pleurisy (plůr'əsē) *n.* inflammation of the pleura. Before 1398 *pleuresi,* in Trevisa's translation of Bartholomew's *De Proprietatibus Rerum;* borrowed from Old French *pleuresie,* variant of *pleurisie,* and directly from Medieval Latin *pleurisis* pleurisy, altered from Latin *pleurītis* pain in the side, from Greek *pleurîtis,* from *pleurá* side of the body, rib, of uncertain origin.

Plexiglas (plek'səglas') *n.* trademark for a transparent plastic used in place of glass, originally manufactured in Germany. 1936, American English, alteration of earlier *Plexiglass* (1935, *plexi-,* combining form of New Latin *plexus* intertwined mass, network, PLEXUS + *glass*).

plexus (plek'səs) *n.* network of nerves, blood vessels, etc. 1682, New Latin *plexus,* from past participle of Latin *plectere* to twine, braid, fold; see PLY[2] fold. The formation in New Latin and the English borrowing were probably influenced by the existence of French *plexus* as early as 1560.

pliable *adj.* 1392, easily bent, flexible; borrowing of Old French *pliable* flexible, from *plier* to bend, see PLY[2] fold; for suffix see -ABLE. **—pliability** *n.* 1768, in Sterne's *Sentimental Journey;* formed from *pliable* on the model of such pairs as *durable, durability, plausible, plausibility.*

pliant *adj.* bending easily. Before 1382 *pleaunt* turning about, in the Wycliffe Bible; later *plyant, pliaunt* bending easily, malleable, supple; borrowed from Old French *pliant* bending, present participle of *plier* to bend, see PLY[2] fold; for suffix see -ANT. **—pliancy** *n.* pliant condition or quality. 1711, in Addison's writings; formed from English *pliant* + *-cy.*

plié (plēā') *n.* ballet movement with both knees bent. 1892, borrowing of French *plié,* past participle of *plier* to bend, from Old French; see PLY[2] fold.

pliers *n.pl.* small pincers for bending wire, etc. 1568-69, formed from English *ply*[2], v. + *-ers,* plural of *-er*[1].

plight[1] *n.* solemn promise, pledge. About 1250 *pligt;* later *plyt* (probably about 1380) pledge or promise, usually with great risk to the pledger in default; developed from Old English *pliht* danger, risk (before 830, in the *Vespasian Psalter*). The Old English form is cognate with Old Frisian *plicht* danger, concern, care, Middle Dutch and modern Dutch *plicht* obligation, duty, Old High German *pfliht* (modern German *Pflicht*); all derived from the Proto-Germanic root **pleȝ-,* found in Old English *plēon* to risk the loss of, expose to danger, Old Saxon *plëgan* vouch for, be responsible for, and Old High German *pflëgan* to tend take care of; see PLAY.

The form with *gh* was a spelling alteration mostly of the 1400's and 1500's introduced by similarity in pronunciation, probably on the model of *weight, straight flight;* see FIGHT.

—v. to pledge, promise. Probably before 1200 *plihten* to promise or pledge, swear allegiance, in Layamon's *Chronicle of Britain;* later *plighten* (probably before 1350); developed from Late Old English (before 1016 *pligtan* endanger, from *pliht* danger or risk.

plight[2] *n.* condition or state, usually bad. About 117 *plihte;* later *plight* (before 1275); also *plyt* (probably about 1380) danger, harm, strife, a bad condition; borrowed from Anglo-French *plit, pleit,* Old French *plei ploit* manner of being, condition; originally, way folding; see the doublet PLAIT. The common pronunciation and the common spelling *plyt* (about 1380) is evidence that the sense of a harmful condition (modern English *plight*[2]) was confused with solemn promise or pledge (modern English *plight*[1]) in the converging sense of entangling risk, with ensuing harmful consequences, in the 1400's, as further evidenced by the gradual shift in spelling of both words after 1425 to *plight* (though isolated instances of *plight* are recorded before 1275).

plinth *n.* lower, square part of the base of a column. 1611, in Cotgrave's *Dictionary,* borrowed probably from French *plinthe* (1544), and directly from Latin *plinthus,* from Greek *plínthos* plinth, brick, tile, probably from a pre-Indo-European language of the Aegean region.

plod *v.* walk heavily or slowly. 1562, in a figurative sense of work laboriously, drudge; 1566, in the literal sense of walk heavily or slowly; of uncertain origin; not seemingly connected with Middle English *plodder* a ruffian (probably before 1400), or with *plud, pludde* puddle (about 1300), but rather as the OED speculates "to suggest the dull sound of labouring steps on moderately firm ground." **—n.** act or course of plodding. 1880, from the verb.

plosive (plō′siv) *n., adj. Phonetics.* (of certain consonants) pronounced with a slight, sudden expression of the breath, as the sound represented by *g* in *go.* 1899, shortened form of *explosive.*

plot *n.* Late Old English *plot* (probably before 1100) small area, small piece of ground, patch; of unknown origin.

The extended sense of ground plan, map, chart is first recorded in 1551, that of a plan or scheme in 1587 and specifically a secret plan or conspiracy in 1594, in Shakespeare's *Richard III* (in this latter sense *plot* was probably influenced by the accidental similarity in *complot,* 1577, borrowed from Old French *complot* combined plan, itself of unknown origin). The meaning of a plan or scheme of a play, story, or novel is first recorded in 1649, in Lovelace's *Poems.*

—v. 1588, make a plan or diagram of, in Spenser's *Virgils Gnat;* 1589, lay plans for, contrive; from the noun.

plover (plŏ′vər) *n.* small shore bird. 1304 *pluver;* later *plover* (about 1353); borrowing of Anglo-French *plover,* and borrowed directly from Old French *plovier, pluvier, plevier,* from Vulgar Latin **pluviārius,* perhaps literally, rain bird, from Latin *pluvia* rain; see PLUVIAL.

plow *n.* Probably about 1150 *plowe,* later *plow* (about 1300), and *plough* (before 1325); developed from Late Old English (before 1100) *plōg, plōh* plow, plowland (an Old English measure of land). The Old English word may be a borrowing from a Scandinavian source (compare Old Icelandic *plōgr* plow, Norwegian, Swedish, and Danish *plog*), cognate with Old Frisian *plōch* plow, Old Saxon *plōg,* Middle Low German *plōch,* Middle Dutch *ploech* (modern Dutch *ploeg*), and Old High German *pfluoc* (modern German *Pflug*). The word appeared late in the Germanic languages, and is not found in Gothic, which used *hōha* for this implement. Early Old English used *sulh* (cognate with Latin *sulcus* furrow), and in Old Icelandic, also, the earlier name appears to have been *ardhr.* The ultimate source of *plow* is unknown.

The spelling *plough* has been the accepted spelling in Great Britain since about 1700, while *plow* is the usual form in the United States. In pronunciation, the final guttural sound of *gh* has disappeared in English except in Scotland; in the north of England it is represented by the sound of *f* as in *cough, rough,* etc.

—v. 1374 *pluen;* also *plowen* (before 1400), from *plough, plow,* n. The figurative meaning of go through laboriously or doggedly, plod, is first recorded in 1891. The sense of reinvest in something, as *plow back profits into a business,* is first found in 1930.

—plowboy *n.* (1569) **—plow horse** (1539) **—plowman** *n.* (about 1300) **—plowshare** *n.* Before 1387 *plow schare;* see SHARE[2].

ploy *n.* a move or maneuver to gain an advantage. 1722, pursuit, pastime, game, sport; originally a term of Scottish and Northern English; possibly a shortened form of *employ,* n., in the earlier obsolete meaning of employment, use (1666).

Use of the present meaning was reinforced by the English author Stephen Potter in his book *Lifemanship* (1950).

pluck *v.* Probably about 1300 *ploken;* later *plukken* (before 1376); also *plucken* (about 1384); developed from Old English (before 1000) *pluccian, ploccian* pull off or cull; later, draw or snatch; borrowed from Vulgar Latin **pilūccāre* remove the hair, contracted from earlier **pilūcicāre,* frequentative form of **pilūcāre,* extended from Latin *pilāre* pull out hair, from *pilus* hair; see PILE[3] nap. The Old English forms are cognate with Middle Low German and Middle Dutch *plucken* to pluck, Middle High German *pflücken,* and Old Icelandic *plukka, plokka.* **—n.** act of plucking or pulling. Probably before 1400 *plucke;* also *plukke* (1408), from *plucken, plukken,* v.

The sense of courage, boldness, spirit, originally probably boxing slang, is first recorded in Grose's *Classical Dictionary of the Vulgar Tongue* (1785). It developed from an earlier sense of *pluck* as the heart or other viscera of an animal (1611, perhaps so called because these organs could be removed at one pull or *pluck* during preparation). **—plucky** *adj.* brave, courageous. 1842, formed from English *pluck,* n. + *-y*[1].

plug *n.* 1627, in Captain John Smith's *The Seaman's Grammar;* probably borrowed from Dutch *plug,* from Middle Dutch *plugge* a bung, stopper. The Dutch forms are cognate with Middle Low German *pluck, plugge* plug, Middle High German *pfloc,* and modern German *Pflock.*

The informal meaning of an advertisement, publicity, promotion is first recorded in American English in George Ade's *Girl Proposition* (1902), perhaps from the verb sense of advertise (perhaps known before 1906) or to strive for, work energetically at (about 1865).

—v. stop up or fill with a plug. 1630, from the noun. The slang meaning of stick to it, plod, work steadily or energetically at, is first recorded about 1865. The informal meaning of advertise, publicize, promote, is found in 1906 in American English.

plug-ugly *n.* a tough, rowdy, or roughneck. 1856, *Plug Uglies,* American English, the name of a gang of rowdies active in the 1850's in Philadelphia, New York, and Baltimore. By 1892 (in Hart Crane's *Maggie*) the name was spelled in lower-case as *plug-ugly* and meant any rowdy or ruffian. The origin of the gang's name is obscure; similar gangs of the 1850's were called *Blood Tribes* and *Dead Rabbits.*

plum *n.* About 1150 *plum;* later *plumme* (before 1425, showing shortening of the vowel, as in *thumb*), and *ploume* (about 1450, still found in Scotland and dialect of northern England); developed from Old English *plūme* (about 700), corresponding to Middle Low German *plūme* plum, Middle Dutch *prūme,* and Old High German *pflūmo* plum tree (modern German *Pflaume* plum). These forms with *l,* found only in Germanic, were variants of earlier Middle Low German and Middle Dutch *prūme* (modern Dutch *pruim* plum) and Old High German *pfrūma,* which were early borrowings from Vulgar Latin **prūna,* feminine singular formed from neuter plural of Latin *prūnum* plum, from Greek *proûnon,* later form of *proûmnon,* probably from an unknown source in Asia Minor. Doublet of PRUNE.

The figurative meaning of something very good or desirable is first recorded in English in 1825. The differentiation of *prune* (as a dried plum) and *plum* in English is first formed in Middle English about 1400 in *drie prunes, prune* being borrowed from Old French *prune* a plum, from Vulgar Latin **prūna*.
—plum pudding 1711, the name deriving from early substitution of raisins or currants for dried plums or prunes, common in recipes before 1660, as found in *plum pie* a kind of mince pie.

plumage *n.* feathers of a bird. About 1395, in Chaucer's *Canterbury Tales;* borrowing of Old French *plumage,* from *plume* PLUME; for suffix see -AGE.

plumb *n.* small weight used to find the depth of water or to see if a wall is vertical. Before 1325 *plum,* in *Cursor Mundi;* later *plumbe* (probably about 1400); borrowed from Old French *plom, plomb* sounding lead, and directly from Latin *plumbum* lead, from a word of the Mediterranean region that was also the source of Greek *mólibos, mólybos, mólybdos* lead. **—adj.** vertical. Before 1460 *plom;* from the noun. The meaning of sheer, downright, completely (as in *plumb worn out*), is first recorded in 1748, in Richardson's *Clarissa.* **—adv.** vertically. About 1400 *plum,* in Lydgate's *Troy Book;* from the noun. **—v.** 1392 *plumen* to immerse; later *plumben* to sink like lead (before 1425); from the noun. The meaning of sound with a plumb or plumb line is first recorded before 1568. **—plumb line** (1538)

plumber *n.* one who installs and repairs water pipes and fixtures. 1370 *plumbiner* worker in lead; earlier as a surname *Plumberre* (1102-07); also *plummer* (1399-1400); borrowed from Old French *plomier,* and directly from Latin *plumbārius* worker in lead, from *plumbum* lead, see PLUMB; for suffix see -ER[1]. **—plumbing** *n.* 1450, the act of attaching a weight to a fishing line; from *plumb,* v. + *-ing*[1]. The modern meaning of the water pipes and fixtures of a building is first recorded in 1884, though an earlier sense of the action or work of one who fashions things in lead is found in 1666.

plume *n.* long feather. About 1399, in *Mum and the Sothsegger,* borrowing of Old French *plume,* and borrowed directly from Latin *plūma* feather, down; see FLEECE. **—v.** furnish with plumes. About 1399 *plumen* to strip prey of feathers, in *Mum and the Sothsegger;* later, to furnish or adorn with plumes (probably before 1437, found as participle *plumyt* plumed); borrowed from Old French *plumer* pluck feathers from (a bird), from *plume,* n., plume. The sense of smooth or arrange the feathers, preen, is first recorded in 1702, curiously after the figurative sense of show pride in oneself (1643).

plummet *n.* weight fastened to a line; plumb. About 1384 *plomet,* in the Wycliffe Bible; borrowed from Old French *plomet,* diminutive of *plom, plomb* sounding lead, see PLUMB; for suffix see -ET. **—v.** to plunge, drop. 1626, to fathom, sound (now obsolete); 1933, American English; both uses from the noun.

plump[1] *adj.* rounded out. 1481, blunt, dull, stupid; later, of full and rounded form, implied in *plumpness* (1545); borrowed from Middle Dutch *plomp* (or Middle Low German *plump, plomp*) blunt, thick, massive, stumpy, probably related to *plompen* fall or drop heavily, PLUMP[2]. **—v.** make or become plump. 1533, probably from the adjective, though the verb is recorded somewhat earlier than the adjective, possibly by mere accident of the record.

plump[2] *v.* fall or drop heavily or suddenly. Probably before 1300 *plumten* to plunge abruptly into water, in *Kyng Alisaunder;* later *plumpen* to immerse quickly (perhaps from the noun); borrowed from Middle Dutch *plompen,* or Middle Low German *plumpen,* probably of imitative origin, and related in form with other words in *-ump,* perhaps of imitative origin, such as *bump, thump,* etc. **—n.** *Informal.* sudden plunge, heavy fall. 1596, from the verb; but found also in the earlier form *plumb* a sudden plunge (before 1450). **—adv.** heavily or suddenly. 1594, from the verb. The figurative sense of directly, bluntly is first recorded before 1734. **—adj.** 1611, in Cotgrave's *Dictionary,* descending directly, from the verb. The figurative sense of direct or blunt, as in *a plump denial,* is first recorded in 1789.

plunder *v.* rob by force. 1632, borrowed from modern German *plündern,* from Middle High German *plundern,* from *plunder, blunder* household goods; cognate with Middle Dutch *plunder, plonder* household goods, clothes, Middle Low German *plunder-,* Frisian *plunje, plonje* clothes.

The word is first recorded in English in connection with the Thirty Years' War (1618-1648), when it was much used in Germany, where this war between Protestants and Catholics was mostly fought. For the relationship between household goods, clothes, and spoils or booty, compare ROBE and ROB.
—n. 1643, act of plundering, from the verb. The meaning of goods plundered, booty, spoil, loot, is first recorded in 1647.

plunge *v.* About 1380 *plungen* to immerse, submerge, thrust; borrowed from Old French *plungier, ploncher,* from Vulgar Latin **plumbicāre* to heave a sounding lead, from Latin *plumbum* lead; see PLUMB. **—n.** Probably before 1400, deep pool, place for diving, from *plungen,* v. The meaning of the act of plunging, a dive into water, is first recorded in Addison's writings in *The Spectator* (1711).

plunk *v.* 1805, pluck a stringed instrument; 1808, drop down abruptly; probably of imitative origin. An earlier meaning of croak or cry is recorded in Scottish, probably before 1800. **—n.** act or sound of plunking. 1809, from the verb. An earlier slang meaning of a fortune is first recorded in 1767. **—adv.** with a plunk. 1894, from the verb.

pluperfect (plü'pėr'fikt) *adj. Grammar.* of or designating the past perfect tense. Before 1500 *pluperfyth* shortened from Latin (*tempus praeteritum*) *plū* (*quam*) *perfectum* (past tense) more (than) perfec (*plūs* more; see PLUS and *perfectum,* neuter of *perfec* *tus* PERFECT); translation of Greek (*chrónos*) *hypersyntelikós.*

plural *adj.* About 1378 *plurel,* in *Piers Plowman;* borrowed from Old French *plurel* more than one, from Latin *plūrālis* of or belonging to more than one (also in grammar), from *plūs* (genitive *plūris*) more, see PLUS; for suffix see -AL[1]. **—n.** *Grammar.* form of a word indicating more than one. Before 1398 *plurell,* in Trevisa's translation of Bartholomew's *De Proprietatibus Rerum;* from the adjective. **—pluralism** *n.* 1818, the holding of two or more church benefices at one time, in Bentham's writings; formed from English *plural* + *-ism,* by influence of earlier *plurality.* The meaning in philosophy "the theory that reality is made up of a plurality of things" is first recorded in 1882, in William James' *Letters.* The meaning in sociology "a condition of ethnic or cultural diversity in society" is first recorded in 1933. **—plurality** *n.* Before 1376 *pluralite* the holding of two or more church benefices at one time, in *Piers Plowman;* borrowed from Old French *pluralité* large number, learned borrowing from Late Latin, and probably borrowed directly from Late Latin *plūrālitātem* (nominative *plūrālitās*), from Latin *plūrālis* plural; for suffix see -ITY. The meaning "fact or condition of being plural" is first recorded in Trevisa's translation of Bartholomew's *De Proprietatibus Rerum* (before 1398). The meaning of the greater number or part, majority, is first recorded in Scottish use in 1578, as a borrowing of French *pluralité.*

pluri- a combining form meaning more than one, several or many, multi-, as in *pluricellular* (1895, having several or many cells), *pluridisciplinary* (1970, consisting of several branches of learning). Borrowed from Latin *plūri-,* from *plūs* (genitive *plūris*) more; see PLUS.

pluripotential *adj. Biology.* (of a cell, etc.) capable of developing in various ways. 1925, formed from English *pluri-* several or many + *potential.*

plus *prep.* added to. 1579, borrowing of Latin *plūs* more (comparative of *multus* much). Latin *plūs* (Old Latin *plous*) is from earlier **pleus,* altered (by influence of *minus* less) from **pleos,* originally neuter comparative, from Indo-European **plē-yos* fuller (Pok.800). The English sense of added to did not exist in Latin of any period; it probably originated in the commercial language of the Middle Ages. **—adj.** and more. 1756, from the preposition. **—n.** the plus sign (+). 1654, from the preposition. The transferred sense of something additional or extra, an addition, a gain, an advantage, is first recorded in 1791, in Walpole's *Letters.* **—conj., adv.** *Informal.* in addition; and. 1968, American English, from the preposition used in the position of an obvious connective. **—plus fours** loose or baggy knickers. 1920, a compound of *plus,* adj. + *four,* n. (so called because they were originally four inches longer than ordinary knickers).**—plus sign** (1889, in *Century Dictionary*)

plush *n.* thick, soft fabric. 1594, in Nashe's *The Unfortunate Traveller;* borrowed from Middle French *pluche* shag, plush, contraction of *peluche,* literally, hairy fabric, from Old French *peluchier* to pluck, because the final process in weaving plush is to pluck or cut the loops of the projecting woven fabric; Old French *peluchier* is from Vulgar Latin **pilūccāre* remove the hair; see PLUCK. **—adj.** luxurious, expensive. 1927, from the noun. **—plushy** *adj.* like plush. 1611, in a version of Florio's *New World of Words;* formed from English *plush,* n. + *-y*[1].

plutocracy (plütok′rəsē) *n.* government of the rich. 1652, in Urquhart's works; borrowed from Greek *ploutokratíā,* from *ploûtos* wealth (related to *pleîn* FLOW) + *-kratíā* rule, from *krátos* rule, power, see ARISTOCRACY; for suffix see -CRACY. **—plutocrat** (plü′təkrat) *n.* member of a plutocracy. 1850, in Charles Kingsley's works; formed from English *plutocracy,* on analogy of *aristocracy, aristocrat, bureaucracy, bureaucrat,* etc.

plutonium (plütō′nēəm) *n.* radioactive chemical element. 1942, New Latin, from *Pluto* the planet (from Latin *Plūtō,* genitive *Plūtōnis,* god of the region of the dead, from Greek *Ploútōn,* who was also god of wealth, especially the fertility of the ground, from *ploûtos* wealth; see PLUTOCRACY) + *-ium* (suffix of chemical elements); so called because plutonium followed neptunium in the periodic table of the elements just as the planet Pluto orbits beyond Neptune in the solar system. The term was coined by the American physicists Glenn T. Seaborg and Arthur C. Wahl, who discovered the element in 1940.

pluvial (plü′vēəl) *adj.* of rain, rainy. 1656, in Blount's *Glossographia,* borrowed from French *pluvial,* learned borrowing from Latin *pluviālis* of or pertaining to rain, from (*aqua*) *pluvia* rain (water), from feminine of *pluvius* (earlier **plovius*), adj., rainy, from *plovere* to rain, see FLOW; for suffix see -AL[1]. The earlier English form *pluvious* (probably about 1440) was borrowed from Middle French *pluvieus,* from Latin *pluviōsis,* from *pluvius* rainy; for suffix see -IOUS.

ply[1] *v.* work with, use. Probably about 1380 *plyen* to cover; 1385, to use, apply, employ, work busily at, in Chaucer's *Canterbury Tales;* probably shortened from *aplien* join to; borrowed from Old French *aplier;* see APPLY for relationship to Latin *plicāre* to fold, lay. The extended meaning of work away at (a person), importune, urge, is first recorded in 1587. The specialized sense of travel back and forth regularly between certain places (1803) probably developed from an earlier nautical use of beat against the wind, to tack, work to windward (1556), and that of to steer a course, move onwards (1556).

ply[2] *n.* thickness or fold, layer. 1532, borrowed from Middle French *pli* a fold, from Old French *plier,* formed from the accented stem of *pleier, ployer* to bend or fold. It is probable that the noun in English was also in part influenced in its development by the early verb, if not developed directly from it in some instances.

The term *plywood,* referring to several thin layers of wood bonded together, is first recorded in 1907.

—v. to bend, twist, fold, Probably about 1380 *plyen,* borrowed from Old French *plier,* alteration (influenced by *pli-,* the accented stem) of *pleier, ployer* to bend or fold, from Latin *plicāre* (earlier **plecāre*) to fold, lay, related to *plectere* to twine, braid. Latin *plectere* is cognate with Greek *plékein* to plait, braid, Old Slavic *plesti,* and Sanskrit *praśna-s* plaiting, turban. In the Germanic languages the word is cognate with Gothic *flahta* braid, Old Icelandic *flētta* to plait, braid, Old Saxon and Old High German *flehtan* (modern German *flechten* to braid, from Indo-European **plek̂-/plok̂-* (Pok.834); related to FLAX.

pneumatic (nümat′ik) *adj.* worked by or filled with air. 1659, a shortened form of earlier *pneumatical* (1609), perhaps influenced by Middle French *pneumatique,* and borrowed directly from Latin *pneumaticus* of the wind, belonging to the air, from Greek *pneumatikós* of wind or breath, from *pneûma* wind or breath, from *pneîn* to blow or breathe, from Indo-European **pneu-* (Pok.839); for suffix see -IC, -ICAL. **—n.** *Archaic.* tire containing air. 1890, from the adjective.

Earlier use, as in *pneumatiks* (1656), *pneumatica* (before 1650) also applied to the study of spirits and spiritual beings.

pneumonia (nümōn′yə) *n.* inflammation of the lungs. 1603, in Holland's translation of Plutarch's *Moralia;* New Latin, from Greek *pneumoníā* inflammation of the lungs, from *pneúmōn* (genitive *pneúmonos*) lung, alteration (perhaps by association with *pneîn* to breathe) of *pleúmōn* lung; see PULMONARY.

poach[1] *v.* trespass on. 1528, to push or poke; borrowed from Middle French *pocher* to thrust, poke, from Old French *pochier* poke out, gouge, from Germanic (compare Middle High German *puchen, bochen* to pound, beat, knock, modern German *pochen,* Middle Dutch *bōken* to beat, *pōken* to poke; see POKE[1]).

The meaning of trespass on is first recorded in 1611 in Cotgrave's *Dictionary,* where the exact sense is undetermined but may perhaps be translated as to pocket another man's labor (*pocher le labeur d'autruy*), thence: 1) *pocher* to pocket, from *poche* a pocket, pouch, *or* 2) *pocher* to thrust (see above). The sense of *poach* in order to steal game is not recorded before 1706, though this sense is implied earlier in *poacher* (see below).

—poacher *n.* one who trespasses on another's land to hunt or fish. 1667, formed from English *poach*[1] + *-er*[1].

poach[2] *v.* cook by simmering in a liquid. About 1450 (implied in the past participle *pocched,* pertaining to an egg cooked by breaking it into boiling water, from *pochee* poached egg (before 1399); borrowed from Old French *poché, pochié,* past participle of *pochier,* literally, put into a bag or pocket, from the cooked egg white forming a pocket around the yolk, from *poche* bag, pocket, possibly from Germanic (compare Old English *pocca, pohha* bag, see POKE[2]). The extended sense of cook (fruit, fish, etc.) by simmering in a liquid is first recorded in English before 1693.

pock *n.* pimple, mark, or pit on the skin. About 1280 *pokkes* disease accompanied by pimply sores; later *poke* a pimple or sore (before 1325); developed from Old English (about 1000) *pocc* pustule. The Old English form is cognate with Middle Low German and Middle Dutch *pocke* pock (modern Dutch *pok*), and dialectal German *Pfoche;* it is also related to Old English *pocca, pohha* bag, POKE[2].

The early plural forms *pokkes, pocks* developed into modern English *pox* (1503, curiously also found in a surname *Poxe,* as early as 1271).

—pockmark *n.* (1673) **—pockmarked** *adj.* (1756)

pocket *n.* 1350 *pokete* pocket, bag, sack; earlier as a surname *Poket* (1210); also *pockete* (about 1410); borrowed from Anglo-French *pokete,* diminutive of Old North French *poke, poque* bag, from a Germanic source (compare Old English *pocca, pohha* bag; see POKE[2]). **—v.** put in a pocket. 1589, from the noun. The figurative sense of to appropriate (often dishonestly) is first recorded in English in 1637. **—adj.** of or for a pocket. 1612, from the noun, as in *pocket watch* (1640), *pocket dictionary* (1864). **—pocketbook** *n.* 1617, a small book; 1685, a notebook; 1816, a woman's handbag or purse (originally a booklike case with compartments for papers, banknotes, etc.). **—pocketful** *adj.* (1611, in Cotgrave's *Dictionary*) **—pocketknife** *n.* (1727) **—pocket money** (1632) **—pocket-size** (1909) or **pocket-sized** *adj.* (1907) **—pocket veto** (1842, American English)

pod *n.* seed case. 1688, of uncertain origin (associated with earlier *podware* seed of legumes, seed grain, 1467), and with parallel forms *codware* husked or seeded plants, such as peas (1398) and *cod* husk or covering of seeded plants (about 1150, found in Old English about 1000). The transferred meaning of any container or shell like a pod is first recorded in 1753. **—v.** bear or produce pods. 1734, from the noun.

podgy *adj.* = pudgy. 1846, in Thackeray's writings.

podiatry (pədī′ətrē) *n.* treatment of the feet; chiropody. 1914, formed in English from Greek *pod-* (stem of *poús* FOOT) + *iātreíā* healing, from *iātrós* physician; see PEDIATRIC. **—podiatrist** *n.* 1914, formed from English *podiatry* + *-ist.*

podium (pō′dēəm) *n.* 1789, borrowed perhaps through French *podium* (1765), or directly from Latin *podium* raised platform surrounding the arena in an ancient amphitheater, from Greek *pódion* foot of a vase, diminutive of *poús* (genitive *podós*) FOOT.

Podunk (pō′dungk) *n.* any small, backward, or insignificant town. 1846, American English, originally an Indian place name in Connecticut and Massachusetts (1666), also used attributively for a small group of Indians living around the Podunk River in Connecticut (1656); borrowed from Algonquian (Mohegan or Massachusetts) *Potunk,* perhaps alteration of *ptukohke* neck or corner of land.

poem *n.* 1548, composition in verse, piece of poetry; replacing earlier *poesy* and borrowed from Middle French *poème,* learned borrowing from Latin *poēma* verse, poetry, from Greek *póēma,* early variant of *poíēma* thing made or created, fiction, poetical work, from *poeîn, poieîn* to make or compose; see POET.

poesy (pō′əzē) *n. Archaic.* poetry. About 1378 *poysye,* in a version of *Piers Plowman;* also *poesye* (about 1385); borrowed from Old French *poësie,* learned borrowing from Latin *poēsis* poetry, from Greek *póēsis,* variant of *poíēsis* composition, poetry, from *poieîn* to make or compose; see POET.

poet *n.* Before 1325 *poet* writer of poems, in *Cursor Mundi;* earlier as a surname *Poet* (about 1200); borrowed from Old French *poëte,* learned borrowing from Latin, and borrowed directly from Latin *poēta* poet, author, from Greek *poētḗs,* early variant of *poiētḗs* maker, author, poet, from *poieîn* to make or compose. Greek *poieîn* (Argolic *poiweîn*) is cognate with Old Slavic *činiti* to arrange or order, and Sanskrit *cinóti, cáyati* he gathers, arranges in layers, from Indo-European **kwei-/kwoi-/kwi-* (Pok.637). **—poetess** *n.* 1530, in Tyndale's writings; formed from English *poet* + *-ess.* **—poetic** *adj.* of or like poetry. 1530, in Palsgrave's *Lesclarcissement,* a shortened form of earlier *poetical* (about 1380, in Chaucer's writings); probably formed from Middle English *poet* + *-ical,* later *-ic* perhaps by influence of Old French *pöetique,* and Latin *poēticus,* from Greek *poētikós,* variant of *poiētikós* creative, poetic, from *poiētḗs* maker, author, poet. The extended meaning of showing beautiful or imaginative language or thought is first recorded in English in 1854, though the same meaning is found in the form *poetical* probably before 1439.

The phrase *poetic justice* (for the ideal justice shown often in plays and stories) appeared originally as *poetical justice* in 1679, in Dryden's *Troilus and Cressida.*

The phrase *poetic license* (for the license taken by a writer or artist for the sake of effect) is found first as *license poetical* in 1530, in Palsgrave's *Lesclarcissement.*
—Poets' Corner. a part of Westminster Abbey containing monuments and tombs of many well-known poets. 1765, earlier *poetical Quarter* (1711).

poetaster (pō′itas′tər) *n.* writer of rather poor poetry. 1599, in Ben Jonson's *Cynthia's Revels;* borrowed from New Latin *poetaster,* possibly by influence of Middle French *poetastre,* from Latin *poēta* POET + *-aster,* diminutive or pejorative suffix.

poetry *n.* About 1380 *poetrie* poetry, creative literature, in Chaucer's *House of Fame;* borrowed from Old French *pöeterie, pöetrie,* learned borrowing from Medieval Latin and probably borrowed directly from Medieval Latin *poetria,* from Latin *poēta* POET; for suffix see -RY. The Latin word *poētria* appears in Cicero's writings, but in the sense of poetess, from Greek *poiétria,* feminine of *poiētḗs* maker, author, poet.

pogo *n.* or **pogo stick.** *Archaic.* long pole with a spring, used for jumping about. 1921, a coined word, perhaps from *po(le)* + *go,* v. In 1942 *Pogo* was patented in the United States as a trademark for jumping sticks of this kind. It was revived in the 1950's (probably reinforced by the popular cartoon *Pogo*) as a term for "getting going" in the sense of becoming active, and was found in such phrases as *get on one's pogo stick,* later reduced to *to get on the stick* and *(be) on the stick* (be) active or knowledgeable.

pogrom (pō′grəm) *n.* organized massacre, especially of Jews. 1882, borrowing of Yiddish *pogrom,* from Russian *pogróm* devastation or destruction (*po-* by, through + *grom* thunder, roar, related to *gremét'* to thunder, roar; see GRIM). **—v.** to destroy in a pogrom. 1915, American English; from the noun.

poi *n.* Hawaiian food made from the taro root. 1823 *poe,* borrowing of Hawaiian *poi.* The spelling *poi* replaced *poe* in English in 1833.

poignant (poin′yənt) *adj.* About 1387-95 *poynaunt* pungent, tart, painfully sharp, distressing, in Chaucer's *Canterbury Tales;* borrowed from Old French *poignant,* present participle of *poindre* to prick, from Latin *pungere* to prick; see the doublet PUNGENT; for suffix see -ANT. The sense of painfully sharp or distressing, also in *Canterbury Tales,* appeared about 1390.
—poignancy *n.* Before 1688, sharpness or keenness of words, etc.; formed from English *poignant* + *-cy.* The sense of sharpness or keenness of feelings appeared in the 1700's.

poinsettia (poinset′ēə) *n.* tropical plant with large, scarlet leaves. 1836, New Latin *Poinsettia* genus name of the plant, formed in allusion to Joel R. *Poinsett* (1779-1851, first American minister to Mexico, who is said to have found the plant in Mexico in 1828) + *-ia,* noun ending of plant and animal names formed on personal names in New Latin.

point *n.* Probably before 1200, opportune moment or chance; also, state of being, condition, in *Ancrene Riwle;* later, sharp end of a sword, knife, etc.; also, subject or topic (about 1300); and a small mark, dot, period (about 1353). The borrowing into Middle English is considered to come from two Old French words at two different times: 1) in the older sense of opportunity, moment of chance, *point* was borrowed from Old French *point* prick, a mark, small measure of space or time, from Vulgar Latin **punctum* a puncture, mark on dice, moment, alteration of Latin *pūnctum,* neuter past participle of *pungere* to prick, stab (see PUNGENT); and 2) in the later sense of a sharp end, as of a sword, *point* was borrowed from Old French *pointe* a pricking, sharp end, from Medieval Latin *puncta* sharp point, analogically altered from Latin *pūncta,* feminine past participle of *pungere* to prick.

In Middle English the distinction was lost and the final *-e* disappeared, unlike most other European languages where there is a marked difference in meaning maintained in two different words (compare German *Punkt* and *Spitze*).
—v. About 1300, in the past participle *pointed* having a sharp end; later *pointen* insert the mark of punctuation, punctuate or end (before 1376, in *Piers Plowman*); and to prick, stab (before 1400); borrowed from Old French *pointer,* from 1) Old French *point* prick, mark, and 2) Old French *pointe* a pricking, sharp end. The meaning of aim or direct at is first found in the sense of direct attention or discourse to (probably before 1387, in a version of *Piers Plowman*).
—point-blank *adj.* (1591); *adv.* (1594) **—pointed** *adj.* About 1300, having a sharp point; 1665, cutting, stinging, sharp, in Dryden's writings. **—pointer** *n.* 1500, maker of needlepoint lace; 1574, thing that points; 1717, dog trained to point at game; formed from *point,* n., v. + *-er*[1]. **—pointless** *adj.* About 1330 *pointles* (of a sword) having no sharp point, blunt; 1726, in Pope's translation of Homer's *Odyssey,* without point or force, ineffective, futile. **—point of view** (1727-41, in *Chambers Cyclopaedia*)

poise *n.* 1421 *pois* weight; later, significance (1457); borrowed from Old French *pois, peis* weight, balance, consideration, from Medieval Latin *pesum* weight, from Latin *pēnsum,* noun use of neuter past participle of *pendere* to weigh; see PENDANT. The figurative sense of steadiness, composure, mental balance, is first recorded in English in 1649, in Lovelace's *Poems.* **—v.** to balance. About 1378 *poisen* to weigh, in a version of *Piers Plowman;* borrowed from Old French *pois-,* stressed stem of *peser* to weigh, consider, from Vulgar Latin **pēsāre,* from Latin *pēnsāre* to weigh, compensate, consider, frequentative form of *pendere* to weigh; see PENSIVE. The meaning of hold balanced or carry steadily is first recorded in English in 1598, and that of ready or set (1932, in Faulkner's *Light in August*), now usually in the form of *poised,* adj. (from the verb sense of hover or suspend, hang in suspense, 1847, and hold suspended, 1639; earlier, hold balanced; see above 1598).

poison *n.* Probably about 1200 *poisun* deadly substance, potion made with a deadly drug; borrowed from Old French *poison* a drink, potion, poisonous drink, from Latin *pōtiōnem* (nominative *pōtiō*) a drink, poisonous drink; see the doublet POTION. **—v.** Probably before 1300 *poysonen* to kill or harm by poison, in *Kyng Alisaunder;* in part from the noun in Middle English, and in part borrowed from Old French *poisoner* to give to drink, from *poison,* n. **—poison ivy** (1784) **—poison oak** (1743) **—poisonous** *adj.* containing poison. 1573-80, in John Baret's *Dictionary;* formed from English *poison,* n. + *-ous.* **—poison-pen** *adj.* (1914, American English)

poke[1] *v.* push with something pointed. Probably before 1300 *puken* to poke, nudge, in a version of *The Romance of Guy of Warwick;* later *poken* (before 1325);

of uncertain origin (compare Middle Dutch *pōken* to poke, *poke* dagger, and Middle Low German *pōken* to stick with a knife; suggesting a Proto-Germanic stem **puk-*, preserved in Low German). **—n.** a poking, thrust, push. 1796, in Grose's *Classical Dictionary of the Vulgar Tongue;* from the verb.

poke[2] *n.* bag, sack. 1228, probably borrowed from Old North French *poke, poque* (corresponding to Old French *poche* pocket, POUCH) from a Germanic source (compare Old English *pocca, pohha* bag, pocket, Middle Dutch *poke,* dialectal German *Pfoch,* and Old Icelandic *poki* pouch).

The English word is now chiefly dialectal except in the phrase *a pig in a poke* something unseen or of unknown value.

poke[3] *n.* bonnet with a projecting brim. 1770, brim of a bonnet, from *poke*[1] to push. The meaning of a bonnet with a projecting brim is first recorded before 1845, as a shortened form of earlier *poke bonnet* (1820).

poke[4] *n.* kind of weed used in medicine; pokeweed. 1634, American English, tobacco plant, shortened form of earlier *uppowoc* (1588); borrowed from Algonquian (Virginia) *uppowoc.* In the sense of pokeweed, *poke* has been recorded in American English since 1708; it is a shortened form of earlier *puccoon* (1612); borrowed from Algonquian (Virginia) *puccoon* any plant used for dyeing.

poker[1] *n.* metal rod, especially for poking or stirring a fire. 1534, formed from English *poke*[1], v. + *-er*[1].

poker[2] *n.* kind of card game. 1834, American English, of uncertain origin (sometimes explained as borrowed from German *Poch, Pochspiel* card game similar to poker, from *pochen* to brag, boast; literally, to knock, as used by players who pass in bidding by declaring "Ich poche" I knock, or by rapping on the table—one of the explanations offered by Mencken; another and related connection is made with Middle Low German, Middle Dutch *poken* to brag; also to play; and an alternative suggestion to the borrowing from German is that *poker* was borrowed from French *poque* a kind of card game resembling poker, said to have come ultimately from the Persian *às nàs*). All of these explanations attempt to make a connection of form and meaning, but without documentation they are mere speculation.

pokey[1] *n. Slang.* jail. 1919, perhaps an alteration of earlier American English slang *pogy* or *pogie* poorhouse (1891); of unknown origin.

poky or **pokey**[2] *adj.* acting dull or moving slowly. 1849, confined, shabby; later, slow, dull (1856); formed from English *poke*[1] to push + *-y*[1].

polar *adj.* of or near the poles of the earth. 1551, borrowed from New Latin *polaris* of or pertaining to the poles, from Latin *polus* POLE[2]*;* for suffix see -AR. The figurative sense of opposite in character, like the poles of a magnet, is first recorded in 1832, from the earlier use "of or having to do with a central principle" (1799). **—polar bear** (1781) **—polar cap** (1894) **—polar circle** (1551) **—polarity** *n.* quality of being polar or having magnetic poles. 1646, formed from English *polar* + *-ity.* The figurative sense of possession of two opposite or contrasted principles or tendencies is first recorded in 1862, from the earlier use "possession of qualities or properties of opposite points" (1818). **—polarization** *n.* 1812, from French *polarisation,* formed from *polariser* + *-ation.* **—polarize** *v.* give polarity to, divide into opposing poles. 1811 (in optics), borrowed from French *polariser,* formed from New Latin *polaris* polar + French *-iser* -ize. As used by Faraday and others, said to be formed in English from *polar* + *-ize,* but surely influenced by the earlier and continuous use of *polarize* in optics. The figurative sense of divide into opposing sides or factions appeared in 1949, in Koestler's *Promise and Fulfilment,* from the earlier use of "give arbitrary or special application to" (1860, in Oliver Wendell Holmes' writings).

pole[1] *n.* long, slender piece of wood, etc. Before 1325 *polle;* earlier in a surname *Waghepol* (1218); also, *pole* (1340, in *Ayenbite of Inwyt*); developed from Old English (about 1050) *pāl* stake; borrowed from Latin *pālus* (earlier **pagslos*) stake, related to *pangere* fasten; see PACT. Old English *pāl* is cognate with Old Frisian and Old Saxon *pāl* stake, Middle Dutch *pael,* Old High German *pfāl,* and Old Icelandic *páll.* Doublet of PALE[2] stake. **—v.** 1573, furnish with poles; later, push with a pole (1753); from the noun. **—pole vaulting** sport of vaulting with the aid of a pole. (1877, American English)

pole[2] *n.* either end of the earth's axis. About 1380 *pool,* in Chaucer's translation of Boethius' *De Consolatione Philosophiae;* later *pole* (1391); borrowed perhaps through Old French *pole, pol,* or directly from Latin *polus* end of an axis, the sky, from Greek *pólos* pivot, axis, the sky; see WHEEL. **—polestar** *n.* the North Star, Polaris. (1555)

poleax *n.* 1356-57 *poleax* (more commonly *polax, pollax*) a kind of battle-ax; formed from *pol* head (see POLL) + *ax.* The modern spelling *poleax* was influenced by *pole*[1].

polecat *n.* animal related to the ferret, fitch. 1320 *polcat,* probably formed through Anglo-French *pol, pul,* from Old French *poule, pol* fowl, hen; see PULLET + *cat,* variant of *chat,* reinforced by Middle English *cat;* perhaps so called because it preys on poultry. Another explanation is that the first element *pol-,* later *pul-,* is from Old French *pulent* stinking, because of the polecat's foul odor, and while this seems plausible, the form *pulcat* does not appear in the record of English before 1440.

polemic (pəlem′ik) *n.* argument, dispute, controversy. 1638, in William Drummond's *Works;* borrowed probably from French *polémique,* from Middle French *polemique,* adj., disputatious or controversial; or perhaps, in some instances, directly from Greek *polemikós* warlike, belligerent, from *pólemos* war, related to *pelemízein, pállein* to shake, see FEEL; for suffix see -IC. **—adj.** of argument or dispute, controversial. 1641, borrowed probably from French *polémique,* from Middle French *polemique;* or perhaps, in some instances, directly from Greek *polemikós.*

polemology (pōləmol′əjē) *n.* study of war. 1938, formed in English from Greek *pólemos* war (see POLEMIC) + English *-logy.* **—polemologist** *n.* 1970, formed from English *polemology* + *-ist.*

police *n.* 1716, public order, civil administration, regulation and discipline of a community enforced through Commissioners of Police (1714); found in the earlier and now obsolete sense of civil organization (1530, *police,* not differentiated from earlier use in the form *policie,* probably before 1439, in Lydgate's *Falls of Princes,* and perhaps about 1390, in Chaucer's *Canterbury Tales;* see POLICY[1]). The English form *police* is the modern sense of law enforcement was borrowed from modern French *police,* but in its older sense of civil organization was borrowed from Old French *policie* civil organization; see POLICY[1].

The first recorded use of *police* in specific reference to those concerned with enforcing the law and maintaining public order is found from about 1730 in Scotland.

—v. 1589 (implied in *policing*), keep order in; borrowed from Middle French *policer,* from *police,* n. The sense of keep order in by use of a police force (1841) is probably from later use of the noun in English.

An earlier sense of make policies or improve land is first recorded in 1535, in Scottish. The meaning of make clean and orderly, clean up (a camp, etc.) is first found in American English (1851).

—police dog (1908) **—police force** (1838, in Dickens' writings) **—policeman** *n.* (1801) **—police officer** (1800) **—police station** (1858) **—policewoman** *n.* (1853)

policy[1] *n.* way of management. About 1385 *policye* the art, study or practice of government, in Usk's *The Testament of Love;* also *policie* organized government, civil administration (1390, in Chaucer's *Canterbury Tales*); borrowed from Old French *policie,* learned borrowing from Late Latin *polītia* settled order of government, the State, from Latin *polītia* the State, from Greek *politeíā* state, administration, government, citizenship, from *polī́tēs* citizen, from *pólis* city; cognate with Lithuanian *pilìs* citadel, and Sanskrit accusative *púram* (nominative *pū́r*) citadel, town, from Indo-European **pel-* (root *pel-* heap up) stronghold (Pok.799); for suffix see -Y[3]. Doublet of POLITY. The general meaning of a plan of action, way of management is first recorded probably about 1406.

policy[2] *n.* written agreement about insurance. 1565 *police of assuraunce* insurance policy; borrowed from Middle French *police* contract or bill of lading, from Italian *pòlizza,* from Old Italian *pòliza* written evidence of a transaction, alteration of Medieval Latin *apodissa, apodixa* receipt or security for money, from Greek *apódeixis* proof, publication, declaration (*apo-* off + *deiknýnai* to show; see DICTION); for suffix see -Y[3]. According to the OED, the form development *apódissa, pódissa, pólissa* is supported by Portuguese *apólice* (from Latin *apódīxem*) and the Provençal form *pódiza.*

poliomyelitis (pō'lēōmī'əlī'tis) *n.* infantile paralysis. 1878, New Latin, formed from Greek *poliós* gray (see FALLOW[2]) + *myelós* marrow (probably related to *mŷs* muscle; see MYO- and MOUSE) + New Latin *-itis* inflammation; so called because the disease involves inflammation of the gray matter in the spinal cord, causing paralysis of various muscles; earlier called infantile paralysis, 1843, because it affected chiefly the young. The shortened form *polio* is first recorded in 1931.

polish *v.* Before 1325 *polisen* make smooth and shiny, in *Cursor Mundi;* later *polishen* (probably before 1400); borrowed from Old French *poliss-,* stem of *polir,* from Latin *polīre* to polish, make smooth, of uncertain origin; for suffix see -ISH[2]. The figurative sense of free from coarseness, cleanse, refine, is first recorded about 1340, in an early psalter. **—n.** 1597, absence of coarseness, refinement; from the verb. The literal sense of the act of polishing is first recorded in Newton's *Optics* (1704), and that of a substance used for polishing is first found in 1819.

politburo (pol'ətbyůr'ō) *n.* Communist Party executive committee. 1927, borrowed from Russian *Politbyuro,* shortened form of *Polit(icheskoe) Byuro* Political Bureau.

polite *adj.* Before 1398 *polit* polished, burnished, in Trevisa's translation of Bartholomew's *De Proprietatibus Rerum;* earlier as a surname *Polyte* (1263); borrowed from Latin *polītus* refined, polished, elegant, from past participle of *polīre* to polish.

The figurative meaning of refined, elegant, cultured, is first recorded in English in 1501; the weakened sense of courteous, behaving properly, is first found in Goldsmith's *Citizen of the World* (1762, from the earlier use of civilized, cultivated in respect of art or scholarship, 1629).

politic *adj.* 1427 *pollitique* of or having to do with public affairs, political; also 1436 *politik* prudent, judicious; borrowed from Middle French *politique,* and directly from Latin *polīticus* of or having to do with citizens or the State, civil, civic, from Greek *polītikós* having to do with citizens or the State, from *polī́tēs* citizen, from *pólis* city; see POLICY[1]; for suffix see -IC. **—v.** Now usually **politick.** engage in political activity, campaign. 1917, back formation from *politics* or *political.* **—political** *adj.* 1551, having to do with citizens or government; formed in English probably from Latin *polīticus* political + English *-al*[1], and, perhaps in some instances, from *politic,* adj. + *-al*[1]. **—political science** (1779, in Hume's writings) **—politician** *n.* 1588, shrewd person; 1589, person skilled in politics; formed from English *politic,* adj. + *-ian.* **—politics** *n.* Before 1529, in Skelton's *Poetical Works;* formed from English *politic,* adj. + *-s*[1], and also found in 1450 as *Polettiques* Aristotle's book on the subject of governing and government.

politico (pəlit'əkō) *n.* politician. 1630, borrowed from Italian *politico* or Spanish *político,* noun use of adjective, political, from Latin *polīticus* POLITIC.

polity *n.* government. 1538, civil organization, borrowed from Late Latin *polītia* organized government, civil administration; see the doublet POLICY[1]; for suffix see -TY[2]. The meaning of a particular form of government is first recorded in 1597, and that of a community with a government, in 1650.

polka (pōl'kə) *n.* kind of lively dance of Bohemian origin. 1844, borrowing of French *polka,* from German *Polka,* from Czech *polka,* the dance; literally, Polish woman; also found in Polish *Polka* Polish woman, feminine of *Polak* a Pole. The dance was introduced in Prague in 1831 (in tribute to the unsuccessful Polish rebellion against the Russians in 1830) and quickly spread through Europe and into England. It has also been suggested that Czech *polka* was, at least in part, an alteration of *pulka* half, in reference to the half steps of the original Bohemian peasant dance.

The term *polka dot* (pō'kə), meaning a pattern of dots of uniform size and arrangement, is first recorded in 1884 and was named after the dance, whose popularity in the mid-1800's was such that it was reputedly prefixed as a trade name to many articles of food, clothing, and ornament.

—v. dance a polka. 1846, in Dickens' *Letters;* from the noun.

poll *n.* 1625, collection of votes; extended from earlier counting of heads (1607, in Shakespeare's *Coriolanus*); developed from Middle English (about 1300) *polle* hair of the head; later *pol* person or individual, head (before 1325); borrowed from Middle Low German or Middle Dutch *pol* head, top; probably cognate with Latin *bulla* bubble; see BULL[2] papal decree. The meaning of the action, time, or place of voting, is first recorded in 1832. The extended meaning of a survey of public opinion is first found in 1902. —**v.** 1625, to record the votes of, developed from Middle English *pollen* cut the hair of (probably before 1300, in *Kyng Alisaunder*); from the noun in Middle English. —**pollster** *n.* person who conducts and analyzes public-opinion polls. 1939, American English; formed from *poll,* n. + *-ster.*

pollack (pol′ək) *n.* kind of saltwater food fish, related to the haddock and the cod. Before 1672, alteration of earlier *pollock* (1602), itself an alteration of Scottish *podlok* (1502), of unknown origin.

pollen *n.* 1760, in a botany text book; borrowed from New Latin *pollen* (1751, introduced by Linnaeus), found in Latin *pollen* (genitive *pollinis*) mill dust, fine flour, related to *polenta* peeled barley, and *pulvis* (genitive *pulveris*) dust. These Latin words are cognate with Greek *póltos* porridge, *pálē* fine meal, Lithuanian *pelenaĩ* ashes, and possibly with Sanskrit *palala-m* ground seeds, porridge, dirt, from Indo-European **pel-/pol-* fine meal, dust (Pok.802).

pollinate *v.* carry pollen to the stigma of (a flower). 1875, probably a back formation from English *pollination;* for suffix see -ATE[1]. —**pollination** *n.* 1875, borrowed from obsolete French *pollination* (1812, replaced by later *pollinisation*), from New Latin *pollen* (genitive *pollinis*) + French *-ation;* for suffix see -ATION.

polliwog (pol′ēwog) *n.* frog or toad in the larval stage, tadpole. 1440 *polwygle,* in *Promptorium Parvulorum,* probably a compound of *pol* head (see POLL) + *wiglen* to WIGGLE.

Later spellings include: *polwigge* (1592), *polliwig* (before 1825), and *pollywog* (1835-40). Compare TADPOLE.

pollute *v.* About 1380 *polluten* defile, in Chaucer's translation of Boethius' *De Consolatione Philosophiae;* also, to desecrate, profane, sully (before 1382, in the Wycliffe Bible); back formation from earlier *pollution,* and probably borrowed from Latin *pollūtus,* past participle of *polluere* to soil or defile (*pol-, por-* before + *-luere* smear, related to *lutum* mud). Latin *lutum* is cognate with Albanian (Tosk dialect) *lum* mud, Old Irish *loth* dirt, Greek *lŷma* dirt, and Lithuanian *lutýnas* puddle (of loam), from Indo-European **leu-/lu-,* **lewə-/lū-* (Pok.681).

The meaning of make physically foul or filthy, to dirty, is first recorded in English before 1548, and the extended meaning of contaminate the atmosphere or environment with toxic and other harmful substances, since 1954.

—**pollutant** *n.* a polluting agent or medium. 1892, formed from English *pollute* + *-ant.* —**pollution** *n.* Before 1349 *pollusyone* discharge of semen other than during coition; later *pollucioun* desecration, defilement; borrowed through Old French *pollution,* or directly from Late Latin *pollūtiōnem* (nominative *pollūtiō*) defilement, from Latin *polluere* to soil, defile; for suffix see -ATION. The modern sense of contamination of the atmosphere or environment by toxic and other harmful substances has been recorded sporadically in technical sources since 1877 but came into general use about 1955, especially in the phrase *air pollution.*

Pollyanna *n.* irrepressible optimist. 1921, American English, in allusion to the child heroine of the novels *Pollyanna* (1913) and *Pollyanna Grows Up* (1915) by Eleanor H. Porter, 1868-1920, an American writer of juvenile novels and stories. Pollyanna is noted for her "overwhelming, unquenchable gladness" and her skill at playing her favorite "glad game" of finding a reason to be cheerful and optimistic in the worst situations.

polo *n.* kind of game somewhat like hockey played on horseback with a ball and mallets. 1872, Anglo-Indian *polo,* from Balti (a Tibetan language) *polo* ball, related to Tibetan *pulu* ball. The term *polo shirt* for a close-fitting pullover shirt (originally used by polo players) is first attested in American English, in F. Scott Fitzgerald's *This Side of Paradise* (1920).

polonaise (pol′ənāz′) *n.* 1773, woman's overdress; 1797, stately dance of Polish origin; both borrowings of French *polonaise,* from feminine of *polonais,* adj. Polish, of the Polish, from *Pologne* Poland, from Medieval Latin *Polonia* Poland.

polonium (pəlō′nēəm) *n.* radioactive chemical element. 1898, New Latin *polonium;* formed from Medieval Latin *Polonia* Poland + New Latin *-ium* (suffix of chemical elements). The term was coined by the French physicists Marie Curie and Pierre Curie, who discovered the element in 1898, and named it after Marie Curie's homeland, Poland.

poltergeist (pōl′tərgīst) *n.* noisy spirit or ghost. 1848, borrowing of German *Poltergeist* (*poltern* make noise, rattle, rumble + *Geist* GHOST).

poltroon *n.* wretched coward. Before 1529, in Skelton's *Works;* borrowed from Middle French *poltron* knave, rascal, coward, from Italian *poltrone* a lazy fellow, coward, either from *poltro* a sluggard; originally, bed or couch, or from *poltro,* adj., lazy, slothful; or from Italian *poltrone* colt (perhaps from a colt's habit of skittishness); of uncertain origin; for suffix see -OON.

poly- a combining form meaning: **1** much, many, multi-, as in *polysyllable, polygraph.* **2** in chemistry, **a** one or more units, as in *polyamide;* **b** polymer, polymeric, as in *polyester, polyvinyl.* Borrowed from Greek *poly-* combining form of *polýs* much (plural *polloí* many), related to *plḗres* FULL.

polyandry (pol′ēan′drē) *n.* practice of having more than one husband at the same time. 1780, borrowed from Late Greek *polyandríā* populousness, from *polyándros* having many men or mates (*poly-* much, many + *andr-,* stem of *anḗr* man, husband); see PHILANDER; for suffix see -Y[3].

polyester *n.* polymeric substance made from esters and used for making synthetic fibers, plastics, etc. 1929, formed from English *poly-* + *ester.*

polygamy (pəlig′əmē) *n.* practice of having more than one spouse at the same time. Before 1591, borrowed perhaps through Middle French *polygamie,* and directly from Late Greek *polygamíā* polygamy, from *polýgamos* often married (*poly-* many + *gámos* marriage; see BIGAMY); for suffix see -Y[3]. —**polygamous** *adj.* 1613, in *Purchas his Pilgrimage,* from Late Greek *polýgamos* often married; for suffix see -OUS.

polyglot *n.* person knowing several languages. About 1645, borrowed perhaps through French *polyglotte,* n. and directly from Greek *polýglōttos* speaking many languages (*poly-* many + *glôtta,* Attic variant of *glôssa* language, tongue; see GLOSS[2] explanation). —**adj.** knowing several languages. 1656, in Blount's *Glosso-*

graphia; borrowed perhaps through French *polyglotte,* adj., and directly from Greek *polýglōttos* speaking many languages. It is also possible that the adjective use in English was, at least in part, from the earlier noun.

polygon *n.* plane figure having three or more angles and sides. 1656, in Blount's *Glossographia* (1571 in Latin plural form *polygona*); borrowed probably from French *polygone* (1567), learned borrowing from Latin, and borrowed directly from Latin *polygōnum,* from Greek *polýgōnon* a polygon, from neuter of *polýgōnos* many-angled (*poly-* many + *gōníā* angle, related to *góny* KNEE). **—polygonal** *adj.* 1704, formed from English *polygon* + *-al*[1].

polygraph *n.* 1805, a mechanical device for making two or more copies at the same time of something written or drawn, in Thomas Jefferson's writings; later, an instrument for recording several pulsations of the body (as of an artery, a vein, and the heart) at the same time (1871, and first used as a lie detector in 1921); borrowed from Greek *polygráphos* writing much (*poly-* much + *-gráphos* writing, from *gráphein* write; see CARVE). **—v.** examine with a polygraph. 1969, from the noun.

It is possible that Jefferson's use of the form itself was influenced by earlier French *polygraphe* (1536) and was probably also affected by earlier *polygraphic* (1788, in reference to a method of mechanical copying). Related terms appear earlier, such as *polygraphy* (1593) and *polygrapher* (1588).

polygyny (pəlij′ənē) *n.* practice of having more than one wife at the same time. 1780, formed from Greek *polygýnēs* having many wives (*poly-* many + *gynḗ* woman, wife); form patterned on *bigamy, polygamy.*

polyhedron *n.* solid figure having many faces. 1570, borrowed from Greek *polýedron,* neuter of *polýedros* having many bases or sides (*poly-* many + *hédrā* side, seat, base; see SIT).

polymath (pol′ēmath) *n.* person of much or varied learning. 1621, in Burton's *Anatomy of Melancholy;* borrowed from Greek *polymathḗs* having learned much (*poly-* much, many + root of *manthánein* learn; see MATHEMATICS).

polymer *n.* chemical substance consisting of large molecules formed by the combination of identical simpler molecules, a polymeric compound. 1866, replacing earlier *polymeride* (1857), and probably borrowed from German *Polymere,* from Greek *polymerḗs* having many parts (*poly-* many + *méros* part; see MERIT). The term was introduced in 1830 by the Swedish chemist J.J. Berzelius, 1779-1848, and was probably known much earlier except for a defect in the record of English. **—polymeric** *adj.* consisting of a polymer or polymers. 1833, borrowed from German *polymerisch* (introduced by Berzelius in 1830), formed from Greek *polymerḗs* + German *-isch* -ic. **—polymerize** *v.* form large molecules from identical smaller ones. 1865, probably formed from English *polymer(ic)* + *-ize.* **—polymerization** *n.* 1872, formed from English *polymerize* + *-ation.*

polymorphous (pol′ēmôr′fəs) *adj.* having or passing through many forms, stages, etc. 1785, borrowed from Greek *polýmorphos* multiform, manifold (*poly-* many + *morphḗ* form).

polynomial (pol′ēnō′mēəl) *n.* expression consisting of many terms or names. 1674, formed from English *poly-* + *-nomial,* as in BINOMIAL. **—adj.** consisting of many terms or names. 1704, from the noun.

polyoma (pol′ēō′mə) *n.* virus that produces many tumors. 1958, formed from English *poly-* many + Latinate *-oma* tumor.

polyp *n.* simple form of water animal. Before 1400 *polippe* nasal tumor (having branches like tentacles), in Lanfranc's *Science of Surgery;* 1583, animal with many tentacles or feet; later *polyp* (1602); borrowed from Middle French *polype,* learned borrowing from Latin, and borrowed directly from Latin *pōlypus* cuttlefish, nasal tumor, from Greek (Doric, Aeolic) *pṓlypos,* a Mediterranean word of unknown origin, construed by folk etymology as from *poly-* many + *poús* FOOT. The extended sense of any small tumorlike growth is first recorded in English in 1897.

polyphony (pəlif′ənē) *n.* composition having two or more voices or parts, counterpoint. 1828, a multiplicity of sounds; earlier, in the form *polyphonism* (1713); borrowed from Greek *polyphōníā* variety of sounds, from *polýphōnos* having many sounds or voices (*poly-* many + *phōnḗ* voice or sound; see -PHONE); for suffix see -Y[3]. Later use (perhaps a separate word) meaning "counterpoint" (1864) was influenced by and is perhaps a back formation from *polyphonic.* **—polyphonic** *adj.* contrapuntal. 1782, formed in English from Greek *polýphōnos* having many sounds + English *-ic.*

polytheism (pol′ēthē′izəm) *n.* belief in more than one god. 1613, in *Purchas his Pilgrimage;* borrowed from French *polythéisme,* formed from Greek *polýtheos* of many gods (*poly-* many + *theós* god) + French *-isme* -ism; see THEOLOGY.

polyvinyl (pol′ēvī′nəl) *adj.* of or having to do with polymers derived from vinyl compounds. 1933, formed from English *poly-* + *vinyl.*

pomade (pəmād′) *n.* perfumed ointment for the scalp. 1562, borrowed from Middle French *pommade* an ointment, from Italian *pomata,* from *pomo* apple, from Latin *pōmum* fruit; see POME; so called because the ointment originally contained apple pulp; for suffix see -ADE. **—v.** put pomade on. 1889, from the noun.

pome *n. Botany.* fruit consisting of flesh surrounding a core that contains several seeds, as an apple or pear. 1381 *pomme* meatball; later *pome* ball, fruit of any kind (1392); borrowed from Old French *pome, pomme,* from Vulgar Latin **pōma,* feminine formed from the neuter plural of Latin *pōmum* fruit, of uncertain origin. The word in Middle English was also borrowed directly from Latin *pōmum.*

The modern botanical meaning is first recorded in 1816, in Keith's *A System of Physiological Botany.*

pomegranate (pom′gran′it *or* pom′əgran′it) *n.* kind of reddish-yellow fruit. Probably about 1300 *pomme-garnate;* later *poumgarnet* (about 1330), and *pome granate* (1398); borrowed from Medieval Latin *pomum granatum,* and from Old French *pome grenate* (*pome* apple, fruit; see POME, and *grenate* having grains, learned borrowing from Latin *grānāta,* feminine of *grānātus,* from *grānum* grain; see CORN[1] grain).

pommel (pum′əl *or* pom′əl) *n.* part of a saddle that sticks up at the front. About 1250 *pomel* ornamental knob, round finial; later, knob at end of a sword's hilt (probably before 1300, in *Arthour and Merlin*); borrowed from Old French *pomel,* diminutive of *pom* hilt of a sword; originally masculine variant of *pome* fruit; see POME. The sense of the front peak of a saddle appeared probably about 1450, in *Merlin* (a later version of the Merlin legend, as found also in *Arthour and Mer-*

lin). —**v.** beat, pummel. 1530, in Palsgrave's *Lesclarcissement,* from the noun (in the sense of the knob ending the hilt of a sword, dagger, etc.). The original, or literal, sense of the verb was probably to strike with the pommel of a sword instead of its edge or point.

pomp *n.* stately display. Probably about 1300 *pompe;* borrowing of Old French *pompe,* learned borrowing from Latin, and borrowed directly from Latin *pompa* procession, pomp, from Greek *pompḗ* procession, display; literally, a sending, from the root of *pémpein* to send, of uncertain origin.

pompadour (pom′pədôr) *n.* 1887, American English, a style of brushing men's hair straight up and back from the forehead; also, a woman's style of hair swept up high over the forehead (1899); in allusion to the Marquise de *Pompadour* (Jeanne-Antoinette Poisson, 1721-1764), mistress of Louis XV of France, who wore her hair in an upswept style.

From 1752 until the late 1800's the name of the Marquise de Pompadour was widely used to designate styles of dress, coiffure, furniture, etc., which she popularized.

—**v.** dress (the hair) in a pompadour. 1908, from the noun.

pompano (pom′pənō) *n.* kind of food fish. 1778 *pampano,* American English; borrowed from American Spanish *pámpano* any of various fish, from Spanish, a kind of fish with golden markings; originally a vine tendril or scion, from Latin *pampinus* tendril or leaf of a vine, probably from the same (Mediterranean) source as Greek *ámpelos* vine.

The spelling *pompano* appeared in 1840 in American English. The spelling seems to indicate oral transmission from American Spanish, since the Spanish *a* resembles the *o* in the English pronunciation of *Honduras* (which in Spanish starts with a vowel approaching the vowel in English *own*). Compare English *poplin* from French *papeline.*

pompon *n.* ornamental tuft or ball of feathers, silk, etc. 1748, borrowed from French *pompon,* perhaps from Old French *pompe* POMP.

pompous *adj.* About 1375, self-important, pretentious, inflated, in Chaucer's *Canterbury Tales;* borrowed from Old French *pompeux,* and directly from Late Latin *pompōsus* stately, pompous, from Latin *pompa* POMP; for suffix see -OUS. —**pomposity** *n.* pompous display. Probably before 1425 *pomposite* pomp, solemnity, in a translation of Higden's *Polychronicon;* borrowed from Late Latin *pompōsitās,* from *pompōsus* stately, pompous; for suffix see -ITY. The sense of pompous display, ostentatiousness, appeared in English in 1620, perhaps borrowed from French *pompositė* (1518), learned borrowing from Late Latin *pompōsitās.*

poncho (pon′chō) *n.* large cloak, now often waterproof, with a slit in the middle. 1717, borrowing of American Spanish *poncho* and commonly believed to have come from Araucanian (Chile) *pontho* woolen fabric. Corominas, however, writes that because of the word's early appearance in Castilian Spanish in 1530, it could not have come from Araucanian or any other related language. He suggests instead that it came from the Spanish adjective *poncho,* a variant of *pocho* discolored, faded, because it designates a blanket or shawl without bright colors and without designs. The original sense of *poncho* in Spanish was that of a light blanket or a thick shirt; the sense of a cloak with a slit in the middle, such as those worn by the Indians of Chile, did not appear in Spanish until the 1700's, about the time English borrowed the word from American Spanish.

pond *n.* About 1300 *ponde* artificially enclosed body of water, in *King Horn,* variant of POUND³ enclosed place. The form is found earlier in the compound *pundpani* pond-penny (1248, a levy imposed for the maintenance of ponds). The meaning of a body of still water, sometimes also called a lake, is probably not recorded before about 1350.

ponder *v.* Before 1338 *pundren* to reckon, calculate, in Mannyng's *Chronicle of England;* later *ponderen* to think, presume, suppose (probably about 1378, in Wycliffe's writings); also, appraise, weigh (before 1387); borrowed from Old French *ponderer* to weigh, balance, and directly from Latin *ponderāre* to weigh, from *pondus* (genitive *ponderis*) weight; see PENDANT.

ponderous *adj.* very heavy, weighty. Before 1400, (of a discharge) thick or viscous, in a translation of Lanfranc's *Science of Surgery;* later, heavy or weighty (probably before 1425, in a translation of Chauliac's *Grande Chirurgie*); borrowed perhaps through Old French *pondéreux,* but more likely directly from Latin *ponderōsus* of great weight, from *pondus* (genitive *ponderis*) weight, see PENDANT; for suffix see -OUS. The meaning of heavy in the sense of labored, dull, or tedious, is first recorded before 1704.

pone *n.* corn bread. 1634 *poane;* earlier *ponap, appone* (1612), American English; borrowed from Algonquian (Powhatan) *äpan* something baked, from *äpen* she bakes.

pongee (ponjē′) *n.* kind of soft silk. 1711, transliterated borrowing of Mandarin Chinese *pen-chī* one's own machine (loom).

poniard (pon′yərd) *n.* dagger. 1588, in Shakespeare's *Titus Andronicus;* borrowed from Middle French *poignard,* from Old French *poing* fist, from Latin *pugnus* fist, see PUNGENT; for suffix see -ARD.

pontiff *n.* pope. 1610, high priest; borrowed from French *pontif, pontife,* learned borrowing from Latin *pontifex* (genitive *pontificis*) member of the principal college of priests in ancient Rome, Roman high priest (in Medieval and Late Latin bishop, archbishop), probably formed from *pont-* (stem of *pōns* bridge + *-fex, -ficis,* from *facere* make, DO¹). The Latin *pontifex* probably originally meant "bridgemaker" or "pathmaker" (compare Sanskrit *pánthā-s* path, cognate of Latin *pōns*), referring to the priest's rôle in leading, or the first elements *pont-,* as suggested in the OED, may be ultimately from Oscan *puntis* offering.

Pontiff as a title referring to a pope (a Bishop of Rome) is not recorded in English before 1677; as the noun referring to a pope's office or tenure, *pontificality, pontificalty,* and *pontifate* are found probably before 1425.

pontifical *adj.* Probably about 1425, of or having to do with a high church official; borrowed from Middle French *pontifical,* learned borrowing from Latin, and borrowed directly from Latin *pontificālis* of or belonging to a high priest of Rome, from *pontifex* (genitive *pontificis*) Roman high priest, see PONTIFF; for suffix see -AL¹. The sense of being characteristic of a pontiff, stately, pompous, is first recorded in English in 1589. —**pontificate** *v.* 1818, officiate as a pontiff; borrowed from Medieval Latin *pontificatum,* past participle of *pontificare,* from Latin *pontifex* (genitive *pontificis*)

Roman high priest; for suffix see -ATE[1]. The extended meaning of act the pontiff, behave or speak pompously, is first recorded in English in 1825.

pontoon *n.* flat-bottomed boat. 1676, borrowing of French *pontoon,* from Middle French *ponton,* from Latin *pontōnem* (nominative *pontō*) flat-bottomed boat, from *pōns* (genitive *pontis*) bridge, see FIND; for ending see -OON. The term *pontoon* bridge, meaning a temporary bridge supported by pontoons or other floating structures, is first recorded in 1779. The extended meaning of pontoon in the sense of any floating or buoyant structure is first recorded in 1941.

pony *n.* small horse. 1659 *powny,* Scottish, apparently borrowed from obsolete French *poulenet* little foal, diminutive of Old French *poulain* foal, from Late Latin *pullāmen* (genitive *pullāminis*) young of an animal, from Latin *pullus* young of a horse, etc., young fowl; see FOAL. **—pony express** (1847, American English) **—ponytail** *n.* (1952, American English)

pooch *n. Slang.* dog. 1924, American English, in Ben Hecht's *Cutie;* of unknown origin.

poodle *n.* breed of dog. 1825, in Bulwer-Lytton's *Falkland;* borrowed from German *Pudel,* shortened form of *Pudelhund* water dog (Low German *Pudel* PUDDLE + German *Hund* dog, HOUND; probably so called because it was used to hunt water fowl).

pool[1] *n.* small body of water. Probably before 1200 *pole* lake, pond, in Layamon's *Chronicle of Britain,* later *pol* (probably before 1300), and *pool* (about 1384); developed from Old English *pōl* (before 899, in Alfred's translation of St. Gregory's *Pastoral Care*). Old English *pōl* is cognate with Old Frisian and Middle Low German *pōl* pool, Middle Dutch and modern Dutch *poel,* and Old High German *pfuol* (modern German *Pfuhl*). The meaning of a swimming pool is first found in Aldous Huxley's *Crome Yellow* (1921).

pool[2] *n.* game similar to billiards. 1693, card game with collective stakes by the players; borrowed from French *poule* stakes, booty, plunder; literally, hen, from Old French *poule* hen, young fowl; see PULLET. The meaning of collective stakes in a card game is first recorded in Swift's *Journal to Stella* (1711-12), although it was probably in use before 1693. The meaning of a game similar to billiards, originally played for a pool of money, is first recorded in Thackeray's *Book of Snobs* (1848). The transferred meaning of a common fund of money or things owned or used in common by a group of people (as in *motor pool, typing pool*) is first recorded in 1869 in the attributive use *pool selling.* **—v.** put (things or money) together for common advantage. 1872, from the noun.

poop[1] *n.* deck at the stern of a ship. 1405-10 *poupe,* borrowed from Middle French *poupe* the stern of a ship; earlier *pope,* from Italian *poppa,* from Latin *puppis* poop, stern; of uncertain origin. **—v.** (of a wave) break over the stern of (a ship). 1748, from the noun.

poop[2] *v. Slang.* tire out, become exhausted. 1931, American English, of unknown origin.

poop[3] *n. Slang.* up-to-date or inside information. 1941, American English, originally army slang; etymology unknown.

poor *adj.* Probably before 1200 *poure, pouere,* in *Ancrene Riwle* and Layamon's *Chronicle of Britain;* later *poure, pore* (about 1280) and *poore* (about 1390); borrowed from Old French *poure, povre,* from Latin *pauper* poor, from pre-Latin **pavo-pars* getting little, from *pau-* (root of *paucus* little) and *parere* get, produce; see FEW, PARE. Doublet of PAUPER. **—n.** Probably about 1150 *pouere* poor people as a group; later *poure* (probably about 1200); collective use of the adjective. **—poor box** a box for contribution to the poor. (1621, in Ben Jonson's writings) **—poorhouse** *n.* 1745 *poorshouse,* 1785 *poorhouse,* American English. **—poorish** *adj.* somewhat poor. (1657) **—poorly** *adv.* About 1230 *poureliche* inadequately, badly, insufficiently, formed from Middle English *poure* poor + *-liche* -ly[1]. *—adj.* in a poor state of health; somewhat ill. 1573, probably from the adverb, but possibly formed from English *poor* + *-ly*[2]. **—poor mouth** a claim or complaint of poverty. (1822) **—poor-mouth** *v.* to claim or complain of poverty. (1963, American English)

pop[1] *v.* make a short, quick, explosive sound. 1433 *poppen* to strike, rap, from the noun. The meaning of thrust or put suddenly is first recorded before 1529, and that of move, go, or come suddenly or unexpectedly in 1530. The meaning of make a short, quick, explosive sound is first recorded in 1576. **—n.** About 1400 *poppe, pop* blow or stroke, of imitative origin. The meaning of a short, quick, explosive sound is found in 1591; from the verb. **—adj.** with a pop, suddenly, unexpectedly. 1621, in John Fletcher's *The Pilgrim;* from the verb and noun. **—popcorn** *n.* 1819, American English, a variety of corn; 1855, the white kernels when puffed open as food (implied in *pop-corn men,* but found earlier as *popped corn,* 1850 and 1842). **—popgun** *n.* (1662, in Hobbes' writings) **—popover** *n.* (1876, American English)

pop[2] *adj. Informal.* popular. 1926, American English, shortened from *popular,* originally and chiefly designating songs and music having wide public appeal. The usage may have been influenced by the earlier *pop* (1862, in George Eliot's *Letters*), informal shortening of *popular concert,* often in the plural, as in *Boston Pops Orchestra.* **—pop art** art that uses everyday objects of the popular culture as its subject matter. 1957, shortened form of *popular art* (1898). Compare OP ART.

pop[3] *n. Informal.* father, dad. 1838, American English, shortened and altered form of earlier *papa* (1681, borrowing of French *papa,* from Old French, a children's word similar to Latin *pāpās* tutor, from Greek *pápās,* and to Latin *pappa* infant's word); compare PAP, POPE. The variant form *poppa* is first attested in 1897, in George Bernard Shaw's writings.

pope or **Pope** *n.* supreme head of the Roman Catholic Church. Before 1118 *pape* (implied in *papdom, papedom*); later *pope* (probably before 1200); developed from Old English *pāpa* (before 899, in Alfred's translation of Bede's *Ecclesiastical History*); borrowed from Medieval or Late Latin *pāpa* bishop, archbishop, pope, found in Latin *pāpa* bishop, archbishop, and *pāpās* tutor, from Greek *pápās, páppās* patriarch, bishop; originally, father (the form is the same as Latin *pappa,* a word used by infants; compare PAP).

popinjay *n.* vain and overly talkative person. 1322 *popingaye* parrot, figure or model of a parrot; earlier as a surname *Papejaye* (1270); also *popynjay* (about 1380); borrowed from Old French *papingay, papegai,* from Spanish *papagayo,* from Arabic *babaghā',* from Persian *babghā, babbaghā,* all meaning parrot. The meaning of a vain, talkative person is first recorded in 1528, in allusion to the parrot's gaudy plumage and mechanical repetition of words.

poplar *n.* tree of the willow family. 1356 *popler;* earlier as a place name *Populer* (1346); borrowed from Old French *poplier,* extended from *pouple* poplar, from Latin *pōpulus* poplar, of uncertain origin.

poplin *n.* ribbed fabric used especially in clothing, curtains, etc. 1710, borrowed from French *papeline* cloth of fine silk, probably from Provençal *papalino,* feminine of *papalin* of or belonging to the pope, but in this case especially to the papal seat of Avignon where there was much manufacturing of silk fabric, from Medieval Latin *papalis* PAPAL; apparently so called in English from confusion of the Flemish name *Poperinghe,* a town in Flanders where poplin was also made, with the French word *papeline* cloth of fine silk. Curiously the French word in the spelling *popelin,* meaning poplin, was borrowed from English *poplin.*

poppy *n.* kind of plant with showy flowers. About 1150 *papig;* later *popi* (before 1200); developed from Old English *popig* (about 1000, in Ælfric's *Glossary*) earlier *popæg* (about 700); borrowed probably as an alteration of Vulgar Latin **papāvum,* itself an alteration of Latin *papāver* poppy; of uncertain origin.

poppycock *n. Informal.* nonsense. 1865, American English, probably borrowed from dialectal Dutch *pappekak* (Middle Dutch *pappe* soft food, PAP + *kak* dung, excrement, from *kakken, cacken* to excrete, from Latin *cacāre*). The Latin *cacāre* is cognate with Middle Irish *caccaim* I excrete, Greek *kakkân* to excrete, and Armenian *k'akor* dung, from Indo-European **kakka-* (Pok. 521).

popsicle *n.* flavored ice or ice cream on a stick. 1923 *Popsicle,* a trademark for lollypops and ices on a stick, American English; probably formed from English *(lolly)pops* + *(ic)icle.* The lower-case or generic spelling is first recorded in 1941.

populace *n.* the common people. 1572, borrowed from Middle French *populace,* from Italian *popolaccio* mob or rabble, a pejorative form of *popolo* people, from Latin *populus* people; see POPULAR.

popular *adj.* Probably before 1425 *populer* commonly known, public; borrowed from Middle French *populeir, populaire,* and directly from Latin *populāris* belonging to the people, from *populus* people; perhaps of Etruscan origin (compare Etruscan *puplu,* **pupluna* a town on the coast of Etruria, in Latin *Populōnia*); for suffix see -AR. The meaning of intended for or suited to the general public (as in *popular science*) is first recorded in 1573, and that of liked, beloved, or admired by the people, in 1608. **—popularization** *n.* (1797) **—popularize** *v.* 1593, to cater to popular taste; 1797, make popular (a sense probably borrowed from French *populariser,* 1622); but the word was originally formed from English *popular* + *-ize.* The meaning of present (a scholarly or scientific subject) in a way that is understandable to most people is not recorded before 1836.

populate *v.* inhabit. 1578, in Florio's works; 1574, as a past participial adjective; borrowed from Medieval Latin *populatus,* past participle of *populare* inhabit, from Latin *populus* inhabitants, people; see POPULAR; for suffix see -ATE[1]. **—population** *n.* inhabitants of a place. 1612, in Bacon's *Essays;* borrowed from Late Latin *populātiōnem* (nominative *populātiō*) a people, multitude, from Latin *populus* people; for suffix see -ATION. Old French *populacion* (a learned borrowing from Latin) is recorded in the 1300's, but was rare until used in modern French of the mid-1700's in the form *population,* as a reborrowing from English.

populist *n.* 1892, American English, formed from Latin *populus* people + English *-ist.* In 1892 *populist* referred to a member or supporter of the *Populist Party* or *People's Party,* organized in the United States in 1891 to champion the interests of farmers and workers; after the Democratic Party adopted many of its ideas in 1896, the People's Party dissolved about 1908. The term *populist,* however, continued to be used (especially as an adjective) to describe political views similar to those of the original populists, especially policies that are thought to favor or represent the interests of the common people. **—adj.** 1893, American English, of the People's Party, adjective use of *populist,* n. By the 1920's, *populist* meant "of the common people, representing the views of the masses." **—populism** *n.* 1893 *Populism* the policies of the Populist or People's Party, American English; formed from *populist,* on the pattern of *socialist, socialism,* etc.

populous *adj.* full of people. About 1425 *populous;* 1439 *populus;* borrowed from Latin *populōsus* full of people, populous, from *populus* people; see POPULAR; for suffix see -OUS.

porcelain *n.* very fine earthenware, china. About 1530 *Porseland;* also *Porcelana* (1555), and *porcelain* (1615); in some instances (as *purcelan,* 1585) confused in form with *purslane* an herb (as *purcelane,* before 1400). The sense and form referring to chinaware was borrowed from Middle French *porcelaine,* from Old French *porcelaine, pourcelaine,* and directly from Italian *porcellana* cowrie shell; also, porcelain (so called from the resemblance of chinaware to the surface of cowrie shells). The further extension of sense and form in Italian is found in *porcella* young sow, from Latin (masculine) *porcellus* young pig, diminutive of *porculus* piglet, itself a diminutive of *porcus* pig (see PORK); so called because the curved shape of the cowrie shell was thought to be suggestive of the curve in a pig's back, and because of the added similarity of color between the two.

porch *n.* About 1300 *porche* roofed structure, covered entrance; borrowing of Old French *porche,* from Latin *porticus* (genitive *porticūs*) colonnade, arcade, porch, from *porta* gate; see FORD. Doublet of PORTICO.

porcine (pôr'sīn) *adj.* of pigs or hogs. Probably before 1425, borrowed from Old French *porcin,* and directly from Latin *porcīnus* of a hog, swinish, from *porcus* hog, pig; see PORK.

porcupine *n.* rodent covered with spines or quills. Probably before 1400 *porke despyne,* in *Morte Arthur;* also *porte-pyn* (about 1400); borrowed from Old French *porc-espin* (literally, pig of spines) a compound of Latin *porcus* hog, pig; see PORK + *spīna* thorn, SPINE. The German word for porcupine, *Stachelschwein* (literally, prickle pig), has the same elements in German as Old French *porc-espin* but reversed; according to Kluge-Götze, it is a loan translation of Medieval Latin *porcus spinosus.*

pore[1] *v.* look intently. Probably about 1225 *puren,* in *King Horn;* later *pouren* (probably before 1300); of uncertain origin (perhaps from an Old English **pūrian,* **pȳran,* related to: 1) Old English *spyrian* to investigate, examine; cognate with Old Icelandic *spyrja,* Old High German *spurien,* and Old Frisian *spera,* and 2) Old English *spor* trace, vestige; cognate with Old Icelandic and Old High German *spor,* from Indo-European **sper-* (root **sper-*) kick (Pok.992).

pore² *n.* very small opening in the skin. Before 1387 *poore,* in Trevisa's translation of Higden's *Polychronicon;* also *pore* (before 1398); borrowed from Old French *pore,* learned borrowing from Latin, and borrowed directly from Latin *porus* a pore, from Greek *póros* a pore; literally, passage; see PORT⁴ bearing.

porgy (pôr′gē) *n.* kind of saltwater food fish. 1725 *porgie;* 1734 *porgy,* probably alteration of earlier *porgo* (1616) and *pargo* (1557) the sea bream, a fish related to the porgy; borrowing of Spanish and Portuguese *pargo,* from Latin *phagrum,* accusative of *phager,* from Greek *phágros* sea bream (kind of fish).

pork *n.* meat of a pig or hog. About 1300 *porc;* earlier in the surname *Porkuiller* (1215); also *pork* (before 1398); borrowing of Old French *porc,* and borrowed directly from Latin *porcus* pig, tame swine. The Latin word is cognate with Middle Irish *orc* piglet, Old Prussian *prastian,* Old Slavic *prasę* pig, piglet, and Kurdish *purs* pig; related to FARROW. **—pork barrel** government appropriation that will benefit a particular body of constituents. 1909, the State's financial resources, regarded as a source of distribution, from earlier use with the sense of a source of supply of food (pork) kept in a *pork barrel* (1801). The meaning of *pork* as another name for government appropriation to a constituency is recorded from 1879. **—pork-barrel** *adj.* 1913, from the noun use. **—porker** *n.* pig, especially one fattened for market. (1643) **—porkpie** *n.,* or **porkpie hat** (1860)

porn or **porno** *adj.* 1952 *porno,* 1963 *porn,* American English, shortened form of *pornographic.* **—n.** pornography. 1962 *porn,* 1968 *porno,* shortened form of *pornography.*

pornography *n.* 1857, description of prostitutes or prostitution; 1864, obscene writings or pictures; borrowed from French *pornographie,* from Greek *pornográphos* (one) writing of prostitutes (*pórnē* prostitute + *gráphein* write; see CARVE; for suffix see -Y³). Greek *pórnē* is related to *pernánai* to sell, and *poreúein* to convey, carry, which is cognate with Latin *portāre* to carry; see PORT⁴ bearing. **—pornographic** *adj.* 1880, formed from English *pornography* + *-ic.*

porous *adj.* full of pores. 1392, borrowed probably through Old French *poreux,* from Medieval Latin *porosus,* and borrowed directly from Latin *porus* opening, PORE²; for suffix see -OUS. **—porosity** *n.* porous quality or condition. 1392 *porrosite,* borrowed probably through Old French *porosité,* from Medieval Latin *porositatem* (nominative *porositas*), from *porosus;* for suffix see -ITY.

porphyry (pôr′fərē) *n.* kind of hard, red or purplish rock. About 1450 *porphiri,* in John Capgrave's *A Guide to the Antiquities of Rome,* spelling alteration (influenced by Latin *porphyrītēs*) of Middle English *porfurie* (about 1395, in Chaucer's *Canterbury Tales*); borrowed from Old French *porfire,* from Italian *porfiro,* and borrowed directly into English from Latin *porphyrītēs* a purple precious or semi-precious stone originally quarried in Egypt (mentioned in Pliny's writings as a stone much used in building and for ornamental purposes), from Greek *porphyrítēs,* from *porphýrā* purple, of uncertain origin. See PURPLE. There is some confusion about the use of the words in Italian, and in Latin and Greek, because of the application of the names to various stones, sometimes locally quarried.

porpoise *n.* sea mammal related to the whale. 1309-10 *porpas;* later *porpeys* (1381) and *porpoys* (1391); borrowed from Old French *porpais, porpeis,* literally, pork fish (*porc* PORK + *peis* fish, from Latin *piscis* FISH). The Old French *porpois, porpeis* is probably a loan translation of a Germanic compound (compare Middle Dutch *mēreswijn* porpoise; literally, sea swine, modern German *Meerschwein,* Danish *marsvin,* and modern Icelandic *marsvin*). French *marsouin* porpoise (attested since 1396) was a Scandinavian borrowing. Medieval Latin *porcopiscis* porpoise; literally, pork fish (occurring in 1265) was probably modeled on Old French *porcpais, porcpeis,* since the Latin term for porpoise was *porculus marinus.* See MARINE, SWINE.

porridge *n.* food made of oatmeal or other cereal. About 1532 *porage* soup of meat and vegetables, alteration of POTTAGE. The spelling *porridge* appeared in 1601, in Ben Jonson's *The Poetaster.* The alteration from *pottage* to *porage* was possibly influenced by obsolete English *porray, porrey* a vegetable soup, from Middle English *porreie* (before 1325); borrowed from Old French *poree* leek soup with other vegetables, from *por* leek, from Latin *porrum,* cognate with Greek *práson,* from Indo-European **pr̥som* (Pok.846), very likely borrowed from some Mediterranean language. The meaning of a food made of oatmeal is recorded before 1643.

porringer *n.* small dish for porridge or similar food. 1467 *porrynger;* alteration of Middle English *potynger* small dish for stew (1454); earlier *potager* (1415), from *potage* POTTAGE; for suffix see -ER¹.

port¹ *n.* harbor. Old English *port* harbor or haven (before 899, in Alfred's translation of Orosius' *Historiarum Adversus Paganos*); reinforced in Middle English *port* (1340, and 1102 as a place name) by Old French *port;* both the Old English and Old French forms borrowed from Latin *portus* port; see FORD.

port² *n.* opening in the side of a ship, porthole. About 1300 *porte* port or gate, gateway; earlier as a surname *Port* (1243); also *port* (before 1325); borrowed from Old French *porte* gate, entrance, from Latin *porta* gate, door; see FORD.

port³ *n.* left side of a ship or aircraft when facing the bow or front. 1625-44, in Sir Henry Manwayring's *The Seaman's Dictionary;* probably from PORT¹ harbor, the side of a ship facing the harbor having originally been called *port side.*

port⁴ *n.* bearing, carriage, mien. Probably before 1300 *pourt,* in *The Romance of Guy of Warwick;* later *porte* (about 1378); borrowed from Old French *port,* from *porter* to carry, from Latin *portāre* (earlier **poritāre*). The Latin word is cognate with Albanian *pruva, prura* he brought, led, Greek *poreúein* convey, carry, *póros* passage, Armenian *hordan* go away, and Sanskrit *píparti* he brings over, from Indo-European **per-/por-/pr̥-, *perə-* (Pok.816). **—v.** bring, hold, or carry (a rifle or sword) across and close to the body. 1566, convey or bring; borrowed from French *porter,* from Old French, to carry.

port⁵ *n.* kind of strong, sweet wine. 1691, shortened form of *Oporto* (in Portuguese *O Porto* the Port), city in northwestern Portugal, from which the wine was originally shipped.

portable *adj.* easily carried. Probably before 1425, borrowed from Middle French *portable* that can be carried, and directly from Late Latin *portābilis* that can be carried, from Latin *portāre* to carry; see PORT[4] bearing. **—n.** that which is portable. 1883, from the adjective.

portage (pôr′tij) *n.* the carrying of boats, provisions, or goods overland from one body of water to another. 1423 *portage* act of carrying; borrowing of Old French *portage,* from *porter* to carry, see PORT[4] bearing, for suffix see -AGE. The specific sense of the carrying of boats, etc. from one body of water to another is first recorded in 1698 in American English.

portal *n.* door, gate, or entrance. Probably about 1380 *portale,* borrowed from Old French *portal* gate, and directly from Medieval Latin *portale* city gate, porch, from neuter of *portalis,* adj., of a gate, from Latin *porta* gate; see FORD.

Special application of *portal* is found in anatomical use, first in reference to the valves of the heart (1615), later pertaining to circulation of the blood through the *portal vein* (1845), but *portal* in a medical sense was borrowed directly from the Medieval Latin adjective *portalis* of or pertaining to a gate, though first referred to in Middle English in the noun *porta* (1392, a borrowing directly from Latin *porta* gate).

portcullis (pôrtkul′is) *n.* strong gate or grating of iron that can be raised or lowered. Probably before 1300 *port colice,* in *Arthour and Merlin;* later *portculis* (probably about 1350); borrowed from Old French *porte coleïce* sliding gate (*porte* gate, door, from Latin *porta* gate; see FORD; and *coleïce* sliding or flowing, feminine of *coleïs,* from Vulgar Latin **cōlātīcius* sliding, from Latin *cōlāre* to filter or strain; see COLANDER).

portend *v.* indicate beforehand, presage, foretell. Probably before 1425 *portenden,* in a translation of Higden's *Polychronicon;* borrowed from Latin *portendere* foretell or predict (*por-* forth, forward, related to *per-* through + *tendere* to stretch, extend; see TEND).

portent *n.* warning, sign, omen. 1563-87, in Foxe's *Book of Martyrs;* borrowed from Middle French *portente,* from Latin *portentum* a sign, omen, from neuter of *portentus,* past participle of *portendere* foretell or predict; PORTEND. It is also probable that formation of *portent* in English was influenced by earlier *portentous.* **—portentous** *adj.* ominous, threatening. About 1540 *portentius,* later *portentous* (1553); borrowed possibly through Middle French *portentueux,* and directly from Latin *portentōsus, portentuōsus* monstrous, portentous, from *portentum* portent; for suffix see -OUS.

porter[1] *n.* person employed to carry loads or baggage. Before 1382 *portor,* in the Wycliffe Bible; earlier as a surname *Portur* (1263); also *portour* (probably before 1387); borrowed from Anglo-French *portour, porter,* Old French *portëor,* from Late Latin *portātōrem* one who carries, accusative of *portātor,* from Latin *portāre* to carry; see PORT[4] bearing; for suffix see -ER[1].

porter[2] *n.* doorkeeper, janitor. About 1250; earlier as a surname *Portier* (1183-85); borrowed from Anglo-French *porter, portour,* Old French *portier,* from Late Latin *portārius* gatekeeper, from Latin *porta* gate, see FORD; for suffix see -ER[1].

porter[3] *n.* kind of heavy, dark-brown beer. 1739, shortened from earlier (1727) *porter's ale* (see PORTER[1]).

This is a word around which several folk etymologies have been given to explain the connection with *porter* a carrier of packages, bundles, or produce, and sometimes *porter* a doorman or janitor. Its connections are as obscure as *porterhouse* and its associated terms *porterhouse steak* and *porterhouse ale* (also *porter's ale*). Whether *porter* or *porter's ale* was made at low cost for, and consumed chiefly by, porters as a low and vulgar class of laborers is not known, though that is the thrust of the early quotations, such as found in Swift's writings. Others have referred to the strength of the drink, presumably suitable to men and women engaged in the hard manual labor of a porter. But on the face of it, there is no reason to think that the beverage was the choice of porters, or more suitable to them, than to other artisans (cabmen, for instance).

porterhouse *n.* choice beefsteak. 1800, restaurant or chophouse where porter and other malt liquors are served (*porter*[3] beer + *house*). The meaning of a choice cut of beefsteak is first recorded in American English as *porterhouse steak* (1841), said to be associated with a porterhouse in New York City where this cut of meat was popularized about 1814.

portfolio (pôrtfō′lēō) *n.* briefcase. 1806-07; earlier *port folio* (1796), and *porto folio* (1722); borrowed from Italian *portafoglio* a case for carrying loose papers (*porta,* imperative of *portare* to carry, from Latin *portāre* to carry + *foglio* sheet or leaf, from Latin *folium* leaf; see FOLIAGE).

portico (pôr′təkō) *n.* roof supported by columns, forming a porch or a covered walk. 1605, in Ben Jonson's *Volpone;* borrowing of Italian *portico,* from Latin *porticus* (genitive *porticūs*) colonnade, arcade, porch, from *porta* gate; see FORD. Doublet of PORCH.

portion *n.* Before 1325 *porcion* part or share, in *Cursor Mundi;* also, about 1330 *portion;* borrowed from Old French *porcïon, portion,* learned borrowing from Latin, and borrowed directly from Latin *portiōnem* (nominative *portiō*) share or part, accusative of a noun which was traditionally found only in the phrase *prō portiōne* according to the relation (of parts to each other); see PROPORTION. **—v.** divide into portions. Before 1338 *portionen,* in Mannyng's *Chronicle of England;* borrowed from Old French *porcïoner, portiouner,* from *porcïon, portion,* n.

portly *adj.* stout, corpulent. Before 1475, stately or dignified (*port*[4] bearing + *-ly*[2]). The meaning of stout or corpulent is first recorded in Shakespeare's *The Merry Wives of Windsor* (1598).

portmanteau (pôrtman′tō) *n.* traveling bag with two compartments. 1584, borrowing of Middle French *portemanteau* traveling bag, clothes rack; also, officer who carries a prince's mantle (*porte,* imperative of Old French *porter* to carry + *manteau* cloak, from Latin *mantellum* MANTLE*).* **—adj.** combining or blending two or more different things, but of the same type. 1882 *portmanteau word* a word made up of the blended sounds of two different words; originally applied (as a noun, 1872) by Lewis Carroll to such coinages of his as *slithy* (*lithe* and *slimy*), subsequently extended to anything suggesting a combination of two different things of the same kind.

portrait *n.* 1570, drawing, painting, or carving of any object, in George Buchanan's works; probably, in part, a back formation from *portraiture,* influenced by *portreit, purtrayt* painted, sculptured, past participle of *portraien, purtrayen* portray; and in part borrowed from Middle French *portrait,* from Old French *portret, portraict, purtraict,* noun use of past participle *portrait* of *portraire* to paint, depict; see PORTRAY. The specific and narrowed use of a picture of a person's face is first recorded in English in 1585. **—portraiture** *n.* About 1380 *portreyture* a painting, picture, portrait, in Chaucer's *House of Fame;* also, about 1385, act of portraying; borrowed from Old French *portraiture,* from *portrait* portrait; for suffix see -URE.

portray *v.* depict. About 1250 *purtrayen* to draw, paint, or engrave (a picture, etc.); later *portrayen* (probably about 1300); borrowed from Anglo-French *purtraire* and from Old French *portraire* to draw or paint, portray, represent; literally, trace (a line) or draw forth (*por-* forth, from Latin *prō-* + *traire* trace, draw, from Latin *trahere* to drag, draw; see TRACT[1] extent).

Some sources refer the Old French *portraire* to Latin *prōtrahere* bring into the open, reveal; or to Vulgar Latin **prōtragere* to draw or paint (with the Vulgar Latin element **-tragere* altered from Latin *trahere* to drag by influence of the past participle *tractus,* on the pattern of Latin *agere* and its past participle *āctus*).

Neither explanation is accepted by the FEW, which shows the word to be a separate formation in Old French.

The figurative meaning of picture in words, describe, illustrate is first recorded in Middle English, in Chaucer's *An A.B.C.* (about 1370).
—portrayal *n.* 1847, formed from English *portray* + *-al*[2].

portulaca (pôr′chəlak′ə) *n.* plant of the purslane family. 1373 *portulake;* later *portulaca* (probably about 1450); borrowed from Latin *portulāca* purslane, from *portula,* diminutive of *porta* gate (see FORD); so called from the gatelike covering of the plant's seed capsule.

pose[1] *v.* put in a certain position. About 1378 *posen* suggest, propose, suppose, especially for the sake of argument, in a version of *Piers Plowman;* later, place something, put, place in a certain condition or situation (before 1425, in Wycliffe's writings); borrowed from Old French *poser* put, place, propose, from Vulgar Latin **pausāre* put, place, from Late Latin *pausāre* to halt, rest; see PAUSE.

In Old French (also in Spanish *posar,* Portuguese *pousar,* Italian *posare,* and Provençal *pausar*) the verb acquired the sense of Latin *pōnere* to put, place by confusion with *pos-,* perfect stem of *pōnere* and came to be practically identified with it in use, taking many of its compounds, which coexist in English, such as *compose, dispose, expose, impose,* and *propose,* and derivatives as *component, exponent; composition, imposition, proposition.*
—n. position of the body. 1818, borrowed from French, from Old French *poser* to pose.

pose[2] *v.* to puzzle completely. 1593, in Donne's writings, from earlier sense of question, interrogate (1526, in Tyndale's translation of the New Testament); probably, in part, borrowed from Middle French *poser,* originally, suppose, assume, from Old French *poser;* see POSE[1]; and probably a shortened form of English *appose* to examine closely, question (before 1333) and *oppose* of the same meaning (about 1385).

poseur (pōzœr′) *n.* affected person. 1872, borrowing of French *poseur,* from *poser* affect an attitude or pose, from Old French *poser* to put or place, POSE.

posh *adj. Informal.* elegant, stylish. 1903 *push,* in Wodehouse's writings; later *posh* (1918, in *Punch*); perhaps from British slang *posh* a dandy (1890); earlier money (1830; originally a coin of small value, a halfpenny, possibly borrowed from Romany *posh* half).

The often quoted derivation from the initial letters of *port outward, starboard home,* in reference to the more desirable cooler, and therefore more expensive side, of shipboard accommodations for those traveling down the coast of Africa between England and India, especially on the P&O Lines, is without substance. According to the OED, Supplement 1982, vol. 3, the main objections to this derivation are enumerated by G. Chowdharay-Best in *Mariner's Mirror,* 1971, Jan. 91-2.

posit (poz′it) *v.* lay down or assume as a fact or principle. 1647, put in position; borrowed from Latin *positus,* past participle of *pōnere* put or place; see POSITION. The meaning of lay down or assume as a fact or principle is first recorded in 1697.

position *n.* About 1380 *posicioun* statement of belief, proposition, in Chaucer's translation of Boethius' *De Consolatione Philosophiae;* later, place where a person or thing is, location; borrowed from Old French *posicïon,* and directly from Latin *positiōnem* (nominative *positiō*) act or fact of placing, position, affirmation, from *posit-,* past participle stem of *pōnere* put or place, a contraction of **posinere* (*po-* away, related to Greek *apó* away, from, see AB-[1] + *sinere* set down, let, leave; see SITE); for suffix see -ION. Also see POSE[1] for further explanation of the development of this form in Old French and English. **—v.** 1678, assume a position; later, to put or place (1817); from the noun.

positive *adj.* Before 1325, formally laid down or imposed in reference to a law, etc.; borrowed from Old French *positif* of that which is laid down, learned borrowing from Latin, and borrowed directly from Latin *positīvus* settled by arbitrary appointment or agreement, positive, from *positus,* past participle of *pōnere* put or place; see POSITION; for suffix see -IVE.

The meaning of explicitly laid down, definite, precise (as in *proof positive*) is first recorded in Shakespeare's *The Merry Wives of Windsor* (1598), and that of unqualified, absolute, unconditional (as in *a positive fool, miracle,* etc.) in Shakespeare's *Troylus and Cressida* (1606).

As the opposite of *negative, positive* first appears in a translation of Bartholomew's *De Proprietatibus Rerum* (before 1398), but is not found in most technical uses until somewhat later; in philosophy, practical or empirical (1594); in mathematics, greater than zero (1704); in logic, denoting presence or possession (1725); in electricity (1755); in photography (1840).
—n. positive degree or quantity. 1530, in Palsgrave's *Lesclarcissement;* from the adjective.
—positively *adv.* About 1443, in a definite way, expressly; also, absolutely or extremely (1777, in Sheridan's *School for Scandal*).

positron (poz′ətron) *n.* positive electron. 1933, formed from English *posi(tive),* adj. + *(elec)tron.*

posse (pos′ē) *n.* 1645, armed force or strong band; 1691, body of male citizens who may be summoned by a sheriff to help him; shortened form of earlier *posse comitatus* (1626), literally, the force of the county; borrowed from Medieval Latin (*posse* body of men, power, potentiality, from Latin *posse* have power, be able, see POTENT and *comitatus* of the county, genitive of Late Latin *comitātus* court, palace; see COUNTY).

possess *v.* About 1380 *possessen* to have, hold, or own, in Chaucer's translation of Boethius' *De Consolatione Philosophiae;* probably, in part, a back formation from *possession,* and in part borrowed from Old French *pos-*

sesser possess, from Latin *possess-*, past participle stem of *possidēre* to own or possess (pre-Latin **pot-s* as master; compare *potis* able; see POTENT + *-sidēre,* from *sedēre* to SIT). **—possession** *n.* 1340 *possession,* in *Ayenbite of Inwyt;* borrowed from Old French *possession,* and directly from Latin *possessiōnem* (nominative *possessiō*), from *possess-*, past participle stem of *possidēre* possess; for suffix see -ION. **—possessive** *adj.* About 1450 *possessyf* of the possessive case in grammar (also as a noun); borrowed from Middle French *possessif* (feminine *possessive*), and directly from Latin *possessīvus* possessive (in grammar), from *possess-*, past participle stem of *possidēre* possess; for suffix see -IVE.

possible *adj.* Probably 1350-75 *possybil* that can be or capable of being; also, possible (probably about 1370); borrowed from Old French *possible,* and directly from Latin *possibilis* that can be done, from *posse* be able; see POTENT; for suffix see -IBLE. Latin *possibilis* was coined by scholars in the first century A.D. as a translation of Greek *dynatós* possible. **—possibility** *n.* About 1385 *possibilite,* in Chaucer's *Canterbury Tales* and *Troilus and Criseyde;* borrowed from Old French *possibilité,* and directly from Late Latin *possibilitātem* (nominative *possibilitās*) possibility, from Latin *possibilis* possible; for suffix see -ITY. **—possibly** *adv.* About 1400, formed from English *possible,* adj. + *-ly*[1].

possum *n.* opossum. 1613, American English, shortened form of OPOSSUM. The phrase *play possum* feign, pretend ignorance or illness (in allusion to the opossum's habit of pretending to be dead when threatened or attacked) is first recorded in 1822 in American English.

post[1] *n.* piece of timber, etc. set upright. Old English *post* post, pillar, doorpost (about 1000, in Ælfric's *Lives of Saints*); borrowed from Latin *postis* post (probably originally "projecting," perhaps then from *por-*, variant of *per-* forth + *stāre* to stand). Latin *postis* is cognate with Sanskrit *pr̥ṣṭí-s* rib, *pr̥ṣṭhá-m* back, roof, top, and developed ultimately from Indo-European **pr̥-sth-i-s.* Germanic cognates include Old Saxon and Old High German *first* ridgepole (modern German *First*), Old English *fierst, first,* from Indo-European **per-sth-i-s,* and Middle Low German and Dutch *vorst* ridgepole, from Indo-European **pr̥-sth-ā,* compounds of **stā-stə-/sth-* stand (Pok.1004).

It is probable that *post* was a very early borrowing from Latin and, in spite of its absence from the early record of Old English, it probably came into Old English before the Angles, Saxons, and Jutes left the continent, but continuing use of the word in Middle English (*post,* before 1200) was reinforced by Old French *post* post, pillar, beam.

—v. 1650, fasten (a notice) to a post, etc., in a public place, from the noun. Earlier use is found in the sense of square (timber) before sawing (about 1520), and as *posting* (gerund) in the sense of a post or posts (1295). **—posthole** *n.* (1591)

post[2] *n.* place where one is supposed to be when on duty or in employment. 1598, borrowed from Middle French *poste* place where one is stationed, employment, military post (also a station for post horses), from Italian *posto* post, station, employment, from Medieval or Vulgar Latin **postum* station, from Latin *positum,* neuter past participle of *pōnere* to place or put; see POSITION; see related POST[3] system of mail. The generalized meaning of a job, position, place, is first recorded in English in 1695-96, from the meaning in French and as a transferred use of a military post in English. **—v.** 1683, to station at a post; later, appoint to a post of command (1800); from the noun.

post[3] *n.* system for sending mail. 1506, riders and horses posted at intervals along a route to carry mail or messages in relays; borrowed from Middle French *poste* specifically, station for post horse, from Italian *posta* an establishment for the conveyance of mail, from Medieval or Vulgar Latin **posta* station, fixed place on a road, variant of Latin *posita,* feminine past participle of *pōnere* to place or put; see POSITION; also see related POST[2] place where one is stationed.

The meaning of a system for carrying mail is first recorded in English in Pepys' *Diary* (1663); the meaning of a single delivery of letters is found before 1674. **—v.** 1533, travel with relays of horses; from the noun. The meaning of carry swiftly is first recorded in Shakespeare's *Cymbeline* (1611); and that of send by post, mail is found in 1837.

It is curious that the specific sense of a place where post horses are stationed for carrying mail or messages (1506) and that of the couriers or carriers of mail or messages (1507), should precede the general sense of a place where soldiers or others are stationed (1598); both senses of a fixed place or station being immediately derived from Middle French *poste* and part of the international vocabulary of the time when such systems of mail were being formally established by various governments (see, for instance, German *Post,* 1521). **—postage** *n.* 1590, the sending of mail by post; formed from English *post*[3], n. + *-age.* The meaning of amount charged for sending something by mail is first recorded in 1654. **—postage stamp** (1840, and eventually replacing the aspect of the postmark, 1678, that showed a fee for mailing was "paid" or "unpaid"). **—postal** *adj.* 1843, of or pertaining to the post; borrowed from French *postal,* from Middle French *poste* post[3], n.; for suffix see -AL[1]. **—postcard** *n.* (1870; also *postal card,* 1872) **—posthouse** *n.* (1635, a post office; 1645, an inn) **—postman** *n.* (1529) **—postmark** *n.* (1678) **—postmaster** *n.* (1513) **—post office** (1652; earlier *letter office,* 1635) **—postpaid** *adj.* (1653) **—post road** (1657)

post- a prefix meaning after, afterwards, behind, in both space and time relations; the use of the prefix may be prepositional, as in *postglacial, Postimpressionism, postmeridian,* or adverbial or adjectival, as in *postlude, postpone, postscript.* Borrowed from Latin *post-*, from adverb and preposition *post* behind, after, afterward, earlier **posti,* cognate with Sanskrit *paścā́t* from behind, *paścā́* behind, after, from Indo-European **pos* (Pok.841). **—postgraduate** *n.* (1890); *adj.* (1858) **—postmodern** *adj.* (1949) **—postnasal** *adj.* (1897) **—postoperative** *adj.* (1899, occurring after a surgical operation) **—postpaid** *adj.* (1828) **—postwar** *adj., adv.* (1908)

poster *n.* large printed sheet or notice. 1838, in Dickens' *Nicholas Nickleby;* formed from English *post*[1], v., to fasten (a notice) + *-er*[1].

posterior *adj.* 1534, coming after, later, subsequent, in Sir Thomas More's *Works;* situated behind (1632); borrowed, perhaps in some instances by influence of Middle French *postérieur,* but more likely directly from Latin *posterior* after, later, behind, comparative of *posterus* coming after, subsequent, from *post* after; see POST-.

posterity *n.* generations of the future. Before 1387 *posterite,* in Trevisa's translation of Higden's *Polychronicon;* borrowed from Old French *posterité,* learned borrowing from Latin *posteritātem* (nominative *posteritās*) posterity, from *posterus* coming after, subsequent; (but as *posterī*, n.pl., coming generations, posterity), from *post* after; see POST-; for suffix see -ITY.

postern *n.* back door or gate. Probably before 1300 *posterne,* in *Kyng Alisaunder;* earlier as a surname *Posterne* (1242-43); borrowing of Old French *posterne,* alteration of *posterle,* from Late Latin *posterula* small back door or gate, diminutive from Latin *posterus* that is behind, coming after, subsequent; see POSTERIOR.

posthaste *adv.* very speedily. 1593, in Shakespeare's *Richard II;* developed from the earlier noun, meaning of great speed (1545); usually said to be from an old direction on letters "Haste, *post, haste,*" in which the words are the imperative of *haste,* v. and *post*[3] system for sending mail; subsequently written as a compound of *post*[3] and *haste,* n. **—adj.** speedy. 1604, in Shakespeare's *Othello;* from the adverb.

posthumous (pos′chůməs) *adj.* occurring after death. Before 1464 *posthumus* born after the death of the father; borrowed from Late Latin *posthumus,* alteration of Latin *postumus* last, last-born, born after the father's death, superlative of *posterus* coming after, subsequent; see POSTERIOR; for suffix see -OUS. The alteration in form to Late Latin *posthumus,* literally, after the ground or earth, is supposed to have developed either by: 1) association with Latin *humus* earth, HUMUS, thus forcing the sense of after the father has been put into the ground; or 2) by attribution to Latin *humāre* to bury.

postilion or **postillion** (pōstil′yən) *n.* 1591, guide; later, one who rides a horse to carry mail (1616); borrowed from Middle French *postillon,* from Italian *postiglione* guide, especially for one carrying mail by horseback, forerunner (*posta* mail, see POST[3] + *-iglione,* from Latin *-iliō* compound suffix).

The transferred meaning of one who rides the near horse of a carriage is first recorded in Fletcher and Shirley's *The Night-Walker* (1623-33).

postlude *n.* concluding part, especially of a musical composition. 1851, formed from English *post-* after or later + *(pre)lude.*

postmortem or **post-mortem** *adv., adj.* after death. Before 1734, adv.; 1835-36, adj.; borrowed from Latin *post mortem* (*post* after; see POST-, and *mortem,* accusative of *mors* death; see MURDER). **—n.** autopsy. 1850, shortened form of *post-mortem examination.* The transferred sense of an analysis or dissection of some earlier event, such as the loss of an election is first recorded in 1907. **—v.** perform an autopsy on. 1871, from the noun.

postpone *v.* 1500-20, Scottish, in William Dunbar's *Poems;* borrowed from Latin *postpōnere* put after, neglect, postpone (*post-* after + *pōnere* put, place; see POSITION). **—postponement** *n.* (1818)

postprandial (pōstpran′dēəl) *adj.* after-dinner. 1820, in Coleridge's *Letters;* formed from English *post-* after + Latin *prandium* luncheon, meal (of uncertain origin) + English *-al*[1].

postscript *n.* addition to a letter. 1551; earlier as a Latinate plural *postscripta* (1523, in Wolsey's writings); borrowed from Medieval Latin **postscriptum,* from neuter past participle of Latin *postscrībere* write after (*post-* after + *scrībere* to write; see SCRIBE).

postulant *n.* petitioner or candidate, especially for admission to a religious order. 1759, in Lord Chesterfield's *Letters to his Son;* borrowed from French *postulant* an applicant or candidate, from Latin *postulantem* (nominative *postulāns*), present participle of *postulāre* to ask, require, demand; see POSTULATE; for suffix see -ANT.

postulate (pos′chəlāt) *v.* 1533, to nominate or elect to a church office, ask a church authority to admit (a nominee); either: 1) developed in English from earlier *postulate,* adj., nominated to a bishopric (1433, in *Proceedings of the Privy Council*), borrowed from Medieval Latin *postulatus,* past participle of *postulare* to nominate to a bishopric (see 2 below); or a back formation from earlier *postulation,* in Middle English *postulacioun,* n., petition or request (before 1400); borrowed from Old French *postulacïon* and directly from Latin *postulātiōnem* (nominative *postulātiō*) a request or demanding; or 2) borrowed from Medieval Latin *postulatus,* past participle of *postulare* to nominate to a bishopric, from Latin *postulāre;* for suffix see -ATE[1]. As this was originally an ecclesiastical term in English, it is quite possible that the verb came into use by way of all three routes.

The meaning of assume (a principle, etc.) as a basis of reasoning, take for granted, is first recorded in English in 1646, and was possibly borrowed from the meaning in Medieval Latin.

—n. (pos′chəlit) 1588, a request or demand, replacing earlier *postulation,* in Middle English *postulacioun* (before 1400); and either; 1) developed from the verb in English; or 2) borrowed from Latin *postulātum* thing requested, from neuter past participle of *postulāre* to request or demand, which is probably formed from the lost past participle **posctos* of *poscere* ask urgently or demand, possibly as a frequentative form. Latin *poscere* (earlier **porc-sce-*) is cognate with Old Irish *arco* I ask, Lithuanian *piřsti* woo someone, Armenian *harç* question, Sanskrit *pṛccháti* he asks, and in Germanic with Old High German *forscōn* (modern German *forschen*) ask, seek, from Indo-European **pṛk̑-sk̑e-* (Pok.821). These words are also related to Latin *prex* prayer; see PRAY.

The meaning of a fundamental assumption or condition is first recorded in English in 1646, and was possibly borrowed from the meaning in Medieval Latin.

—postulation, *n.* Before 1400 *postulacioun* petition, request; borrowed from Old French *postulacïon* and directly from Latin *postulātiōnem* (nominative *postulātiō*) a request or demanding, from Latin *postulāre* to request or demand; see POSTULATE, n.; for suffix see -ATION.

posture *n.* position of the body. 1605, position of one thing or person relative to another, in Bacon's *Of the Advancement of Learning;* 1606, position of the body, in Shakespeare's *Antony and Cleopatra;* borrowing of French *posture,* from Italian *postura,* from Latin *positūra* position, from *positus,* past participle of *pōnere* put or place; see POSITION; for suffix see -URE. The figurative meaning of a mental or spiritual attitude is first recorded in 1642. The modern political and military use of an attitude or behavior, stance (as in *America's diplomatic posture*) is first recorded about 1956, developed from the earlier sense of a condition or situation in relation to circumstances (as in *the posture of affairs, a posture of defense*), first recorded also in 1642. **—v.** take a certain posture. Before 1628, found in *posturing;* from *posture,* n. + *-ing*[1].

posy *n.* flower, bouquet. 1533, motto or line of poetry engraved within a ring; variant of POESY. The meaning of a flower or bouquet is first recorded in 1573, and was perhaps so called from the use of flowers to express sentiments such as those engraved on rings.

pot[1] *n.* Probably before 1200 *pot* container or vessel, in *Ancrene Riwle;* developed from Late Old English *pott* and reinforced in Middle English by Old French *pot,* both Old English and Old French forms originating in Vulgar Latin **pottus,* of uncertain origin, though probably not related to Late Latin *pōtus* drinking cup, nor to Latin *pōtus* a drink, drinking. Old English *pott* is cognate with Old Frisian *pott* pot, Middle Low German *pot, put,* and Middle Dutch *pot, pott.* **—v.** 1594 (implied in *potting*), to drink from a pot; later, put in a pot (1616); from the noun. **—potbellied** *adj.* (1657) **—potbelly** *n.* (about 1714, in Pope's writings) **—potboiler** *n.* (1864, worthless literature or art often produced simply to generate income, in Rossetti's letters; earlier, a head of household who can vote in an election, 1826). **—potholder** *n.* (1928; earlier *holder,* in this meaning, 1910) **—pothole** *n.* 1826, deep hole formed in a river. The sense of a hole in a road is first recorded in 1909. **—potluck** *n.* whatever food happens to be on hand for a meal (1592). **—potpie** *n.* (before 1792, in American English) **—pot roast** piece of beef cooked in a pot (1881, American English). **—potshot** *n.* 1858, shot fired at game to get food, without regard to skill or sportsmanship; hence, a quick shot fired from close range, especially in ambush (1860). The figurative sense of a piece of random or opportunistic criticism (as in *take potshots at*) is first recorded in 1926, in American English.

pot[2] *n. Slang.* marijuana. 1938, American English; probably borrowed as a shortened form of Mexican Spanish *potiguaya* marijuana leaves.

potable (pō'təbəl) *adj.* fit for drinking. Probably before 1425, in a translation of Chauliac's *Grande Chirurgie;* borrowed from Old French *potable,* and directly from Late Latin *pōtābilis* drinkable, from Latin *pōtāre* to drink; see IMBIBE; for suffix see -ABLE. **—n.** Usually, **potables.** anything drinkable. 1623, from the adjective.

potash *n.* substance made from wood ashes and used in soap, fertilizers, etc.; impure potassium carbonate. 1751, in John Hill's *A History of the Materia Medica;* from earlier *pot-ashes* (1648); borrowed as a loan translation of obsolete Dutch *potaschen,* plural of *potasch,* literally, pot ash; so called because the substance was originally obtained by leaching wood ashes and evaporating the solution in an iron pot.

potassium *n.* metallic chemical element. 1807, formed from New Latin *potassa* potash; earlier in English *potass* (1799) + *-ium,* chemical suffix; so called because potassium is the basis of potash. The term was coined by the British chemist Sir Humphry Davy, who first separated the chemical element from potash.

potation *n.* act of drinking. Probably about 1425 *potacion* an occasion of drinking; borrowed from Middle French *potacion,* and directly from Latin *pōtātiōnem* (nominative *pōtātiō*) a drinking party, from *pōtāre* to drink; see IMBIBE.

potato *n.* 1565, in Sir John Hawkins' *Voyages;* borrowed from Spanish *patata,* from Carib (of Haiti, perhaps Taino) *batata* sweet potato, probably influenced by or blended directly with Spanish *papa* potato; earlier, from Quechua. If there was any real and clear distinction of form in English between *batata* and *patata,* it was quickly lost in *potato* which has been the common form for sweet potatoes and white potatoes, though the latter was known as *Virginia potato* by false association with Sir Walter Raleigh.

potent *adj.* powerful. Probably about 1425; borrowed from Latin *potentem* (nominative *potēns*) powerful, strong, present participle of a lost Latin verb **potēre* be powerful, be able, from *potis* powerful. Probably by confusion of *potis,* in the phrase *potis esse* be powerful, *potentem* was used as present participle of *posse* have power, be able, which is a contraction of *potis esse* (*potis* powerful, and *esse* to be; see IS); for suffix see -ENT. Latin *potis* is cognate with Sanskrit *páti-s* master, Greek *pósis* husband, and Gothic *brūth-faths* bridegroom, from Indo-European **pótis* (Pok.842). **—potency** *n.* power, force. Before 1450 *potencie;* borrowed from Latin *potentia* power, from *potentem* (nominative *potēns*) potent; for suffix see -CY.

potentate *n.* ruler. Probably about 1400 *potentat,* in Wycliffe's writings; borrowed from Old French *potentat,* and directly from Late Latin *potentātus* a ruler, also political power; both Old French and Late Latin forms from Latin, power, dominion, from *potentem* (nominative *potēns*) powerful; see POTENT; for suffix see -ATE[3].

potential *adj.* possible as opposed to actual. Before 1398 *potencial* potential, latent, in Trevisa's translation of Bartholomew's *De Proprietatibus Rerum;* borrowed probably through Old French *potenciel,* and directly from Late Latin *potentialis* potential, from Latin *potentia* power; see POTENCY; for suffix see -AL[1]. **—n.** something potential, possibility. 1817, in Coleridge's *Biographia Literaria;* from the adjective. An earlier sense of something that gives power is recorded in Blount's *Glossographia* (1656), and in Middle English the sense of a cauterization is found in a translation of Chauliac's *Grande Chirurgie* (probably before 1425). **—potentiality** *n.* 1625, probably formed from English *potential* + *-ity,* but also found in Medieval Latin *potentialitas,* from *potentialis* latent; see POTENTIAL.

potion *n.* drink, especially a drink used as a medicine or poison. Probably before 1300 *pocioun* a medicinal drink, in *Kyng Alisaunder;* borrowed from Old French *pocion,* from Latin *pōtiōnem* (nominative *pōtiō*) potion or a drinking, from *pōtus* drunken, irregular past participle of *pōtāre* to drink; for suffix see -ION. Latin *pōtāre* is cognate with Sanskrit *pāti* (he) drinks, from Indo-European **pō(i)-* to drink (Pok. 840). Doublet of POISON.

potlatch *n.* a ceremony involving the giving of gifts, especially possessions among certain American Indians of the northern Pacific coast. 1845, gift, in Charles Wilkes' *Narrative of the U.S. Exploring Expedition;* American English; borrowed from Chinook jargon, from Wakashan (Nootka) *patshatl* giving, gift. The sense of an occasion on which gifts are distributed is first recorded in Theodore Winthrop's *The Canoe and the Saddle* (before 1861).

potpourri (pō'pùrē') *n.* medley, mixture. 1611, *pot pourri* mixed meats served as a stew, in Cotgrave's *Dictionary;* borrowing of French *pot pourri* stew; literally rotten pot, loan translation of Spanish *olla podrida* as *pot* pot and *pourri,* past participle of *pourrir* to rot, from Latin *putrēscere;* see PUTRESCENT. The meaning of a fragrant mixture of dried flowers and spices is first recorded in English in 1749. The figurative meaning of a literary or musical medley is recorded in 1864, probably from the French.

potsherd *n.* broken piece of earthenware. Before 1325 *potschoord* (*pot* container + *schoord, sherd* SHARD).

pottage *n.* thick soup. Probably before 1200 *potage,* in *Ancrene Riwle;* later *pottage* (probably about 1425); borrowed from Old French *potage, pottage* soup, formed from *pot* pot (from Vulgar Latin **pottus* container; see POT[1]) + *-age* -age. Compare PORRIDGE.

potter[1] *n.* person who makes pottery. Before 1325 *potter,* in *Cursor Mundi;* earlier *pottere* (about 1200); found in Late Old English (before 1100) *pottere,* formed from *pott* container, POT[1] + *-ere* -er[1]. The form in Middle English was reinforced by Anglo-French *potter;* Old French *potier,* and Anglo-Latin *pottarius.* **—potter's field** piece of ground set aside for burial of the poor or friendless (in reference to Matthew 27:7, 1526 in the Tyndale Bible). The name is said to derive from a field where suitable clay was obtained to make pottery. It was later purchased by the high priests of Jerusalem as a burying ground for strangers, criminals, and the poor, with the thirty pieces of silver (blood money) that Judas cast before them after his betrayal of Christ. **—pottery** *n.* 1727-41, manufacture of earthenware, in *Chambers Cyclopaedia;* borrowed from French *poterie,* from Old French *potier* potter, from *pot* POT[1]; for suffix see -Y[3]. An earlier but isolated example of the sense of a potter's workshop is recorded in Middle English about 1483.

potter[2] *v.* keep busy in a rather useless way; putter. 1740, developed from the earlier and now dialectal, meaning of poke again and again (about 1530), probably a frequentative verb form of Middle English *poten* to push, poke (about 1250), from Old English *potian;* see PUT; for suffix see -ER[4]. Compare PUTTER.

pouch *n.* 1299 *puche* a fish trap; earlier as a surname *Poche* (1184); also *pouch* bag (1327); borrowed through Anglo-French *puche* and from Old North French *pouche,* Old French *poche, puche, pouche,* from a Germanic source (compare Old English *pocca, pohha* bag; see POKE[2]). **—v.** put into a pouch. Before 1566, in Richard Edwards' *Damon and Pithias;* from the noun.

poultice *n.* soft, moist mass of mustard, meal, etc., applied to the body as a medicine. 1592 *poultesse,* in Shakespeare's *Romeo and Juliet;* later *poultice* (1611); alteration of Middle English *pultes* (1392); borrowed from Latin *pultēs,* plural of *puls* (genitive *pultis*) porridge; see PULSE[2] food. The late spelling change to *ou* may suggest influence by some now unknown but supposed relationship with *poultry* (Middle English *pultrie*). **—v.** put a poultice on. 1730, from the noun.

poultry *n.* 1345-46 *pultry* market where domestic fowl is sold; later *pultrie* domestic fowl (before 1387, in Trevisa's translation of Higden's *Polychronicon,* and in Chaucer's *Canterbury Tales*); borrowed from Old French *pouletrie* domestic fowl, from *pouletier* dealer in domestic fowl, from *poulet* young fowl; see PULLET; for suffix see -RY and -ERY. **—poulterer** *n.* 1638, developed as an extended form of *poulter* (1576); earlier *pulter* (1247) and *pulleter* (1226); borrowed from Anglo-French *poleter, pulleter,* Old French *poletier, pouletier;* see POULTRY.

pounce *v.* 1686, to seize with the talons, swoop down and seize; developed from Middle English *pownse,* n., the claw or talon of a bird of prey (before 1475); earlier, a tool for making holes or embossing metal (1367); probably borrowed from Old French *poinçon, poinson, ponchon* (see PUNCH[1]), the source of Middle English *ponsone, ponchoun* pointed tool, piercing weapon, dagger; see PUNCHEON[2]. **—n.** act of pouncing, sudden swoop. 1841, in Edward Lane's translation of *The Arabian Nights;* from the verb (and probably recorded earlier as *pownse,* n., noted above under verb).

pound[1] *n.* measure of weight. Before 1121 *punde;* later *pound* (about 1280); developed from Old English (before 810) *pund.* Old English *pund* is derived from the West Germanic stem **punda-* pound (measure of weight), and is cognate with Old Saxon, Old Frisian, Old Icelandic, and Gothic *pund* pound, Old High German *phunt* (modern German *Pfund*), and Middle Dutch *pont* (modern Dutch *pond*). The West Germanic stem **punda-* represents a very early borrowing from Latin *pondō* a pound or pounds; originally in *lībra pondō* a pound by weight, from *pondō,* adv., by weight, ablative of a lost noun **pondos* weight; see PENDANT. It is also possible that some form of Old English *pund* was borrowed earlier from Latin *pondō,* before the arrival of the West Germanic tribes in Britain.

Pound as a unit of money in ancient Britain is recorded in Old English (about 975), and was so called because originally it was a pound weight of silver, which was 12 ounces troy weight. Several measures of pound for various commodities existed in Medieval Europe, and in England some of these were accorded specific names, such as Tower pound and merchant's pound. The pound of 16 ounces (avoirdupois), originally used for bulky material in the 1200's and 1300's, was established as a fixed weight for trade before 1377.

pound[2] *v.* hit hard again and again. Before 1500 *pownden* crush by beating, reduce to a powder; later *pound* (1594); developed by alteration (with added *d*) of Middle English *pounen* grind to a powder, break to pieces (before 1325), developed from Old English (about 1000) *pūnian* pulverize or crush; derived from West Germanic **pūnō-* stem of **pūnōjanan* and so probably cognate with Dutch *puin* rubbish, rubble, of unknown origin.

The meaning of strike with repeated blows, hit hard again and again, in the modern spelling *pound* is first recorded in Dryden's works, in 1700.
—n. act of pounding. 1562, from the verb.

pound[3] *n.* enclosed place in which to keep animals. Probably about 1378, in Wycliffe's *Works;* earlier, as the surname *Pond* (1206), and in compounds, such as the place name *Pandmad* (1198); developed from Old English **pund-,* found only in compounds such as *pund-fald* penfold or pound; related to *pyndan* to dam up or enclose (water); of uncertain origin.

pour *v.* Probably about 1300 *pouren* send forth in a stream; probably borrowed from dialectal Old French (Flanders) *purer* to sift (grain), pour out (water), from Latin *pūrāre* to purify, from *pūrus* PURE. **—n.** 1790, from the verb.

pout *v.* thrust out the lips, as when displeased. Probably before 1325 *pouten,* of uncertain origin; perhaps borrowed from a Scandinavian source (compare Norwegian *pute* fat woman and Swedish dialect *puta* to be puffed out); also found in Frisian (compare East Frisian *püt* bag, swelling, which is related perhaps through a verbal stem **put-* to inflate, found in Old English *ǣlepūte* a small eel-like saltwater fish with inflated parts, and in Middle Dutch *puyt* (modern Dutch *puit*), Flemish *puut* a frog. **—n.** a pouting. 1591, in Nashe's *Works;*

from the verb. **—pouter** *n.* 1809, one who pouts; earlier, a breed of pigeon that has the characteristic of puffing up the breast (1725), formed from English *pout,* v. + *-er*[1].

poverty *n.* Before 1200 *poverte* condition of being poor, in *Ancrene Riwle;* borrowed from Old French *poverté, povreté,* both forms from Latin *paupertātem* (nominative *paupertās*) poverty, from *pauper* POOR; for suffix see -TY[2].

powder *n.* Probably before 1300 *poudre* pulverized substance, dust, in *Arthour and Merlin;* earlier as a surname *Poudre* (1260); also medicinal powder (1340), and gunpowder (about 1380, in *Cursor Mundi*); borrowed from Old French *poudre;* earlier *pouldre,* from Latin *pulvis* (genitive *pulveris*) dust; see POLLEN. **—v.** Before 1300 *pudren* put powder on, season; later *poudren* (probably before 1325), *powderen* (probably about 1380, in *Sir Ferumbras*), and make into powder (before 1400); in some instances from the noun in Middle English, and in part borrowed from Old French *poudrer, pudrer* cover with powder, from *poudre,* n. **—powder horn** (1533) **—powder keg** (1855, American English; later in a figurative sense, 1893). **—powderpuff** *n.* (before 1704) **—powder room** 1627, room for storing gunpowder aboard ship; later, women's lavatory in a hotel, club, etc. (1941; from earlier *powdering room* room for dressing a wig, before 1774, in Robert and James Adam's *Architecture*) **—powdery** *adj.* About 1425, formed from Middle English *poudre, powder* + -Y[1].

power *n.* Probably before 1300 *power,* in *Arthour and Merlin;* also about 1300 *poër, pouer;* borrowed through Anglo-French *poër, pouair, püeir,* and directly from Old French *poeir, pöer, povoir,* noun use of the infinitive in Old French, to be able, from Vulgar Latin **potēre* be powerful, be able, from *potis* powerful; see POTENT. **—v.** to supply with power. 1540, make powerful, strengthen; later, to supply with power (1898); from the noun. **—power broker** (1961, T.H. White, *Making of the President*) **—power failure** (1933) **—powerful** *adj.* Probably before 1400, formed from Middle English *pouer* + *-ful.* **—powerhouse** *n.* (1881) **—powerless** *adj.* Before 1420, formed from Middle English *pouer* + *-les* -less. **—power line** (1894) **—power steering** (1932) **—power tool** (1959)

powwow (pou′wou′) *n.* American Indian ceremony or tribal council. 1624 *Powah* American Indian medicine man; later, ceremony, often accompanied by magic (1648); American English; borrowed from Algonquian (probably Narragansett) *powwow* shaman, medicine man, from a verb meaning "to use divination, to dream." The informal sense of any meeting or conference, parley is first recorded in 1812 in American English. **—v.** hold a powwow, confer. 1642, American English; from the noun.

pox *n.* disease with sores, such as smallpox or chicken pox. 1503, spelling alteration of Middle English *pockes, pokkes,* plural of *pocke* POCK; but found in an isolated use in the surname *Poxe* (1273).

practicable *adj.* 1670, that can be put into practice, formed in English from *practic* put into action or practice (about 1475, from Middle French *practiquer* and Medieval Latin *practicare* to practice, from *practica;* see PRACTICAL) + *-able,* probably formed, in part, by influence of French *praticable,* from *pratiquer* to practice, from Old French *practiquer* to PRACTICE; for suffix see -ABLE. **—practicability** *n.* 1767, formed from English *practicable* + *-ity.*

practical *adj.* Probably before 1425 *practicale* of or having to do with matters of practice, applied, in a translation of Chauliac's *Grande Chirurgie;* in part, borrowed from Medieval Latin *practicalis;* earlier *practicus,* also found in Late Latin *prācticus,* from Greek *prāktikós* and also formed from Middle English *practik,* n. method, practice, use (1392; earlier, applied science before 1387) + *-al*[1]. Middle English *practik,* n., was borrowed from Old French *practique* practice, usage and directly from Medieval Latin *practica* practice familiar or practical knowledge, from Greek *prāktikḗ* practical knowledge, feminine singular of *prāktikós* practical, from *prāktós,* verbal adjective of *prā́ttein* Attic variant of *prā́ssein* to do or act from the root *perā-/prā-* found in *pernánai* export for sale, related to *póros* passage; see PORT[4] bearing; for suffix see -ICAL.

The form *practical* gradually replaced the earlier Middle English adjective form *practik* which was also borrowed from Old French *practique,* adj., from Late Latin *prācticus* active, from Greek *prāktikós* practical.

In a sense the forms parallel modern English *classic,* adj., n. and *classical.*

—practicality *n.* 1828, in J.S. Mill's writings, formed from English *practical* + *-ity.* **—practical joke** (1804) **—practically** *adv.* 1623, in a practical manner; formed from English *practical* + *-ly*[1]. The meaning "almost" is recorded in 1869. **—practical nurse** (1921)

practice *v.* 1392 *practisen* to do, act, or perform, especially habitually; later *practicen* (1477); borrowed from Old French *practiser* to practice, alteration by substituting the common suffix *-iser* of *practiquer,* from Medieval Latin *practicare* do, perform, practice, from Late Latin *prācticus* practical, from Greek *prāktikós;* see PRACTICAL; for suffix see -IZE. **—n.** 1421 *practise;* probably before 1425 *practice;* from the verb in Middle English. The form *practice* finally took the place of the more widely used *practik,* n., but both spellings existed through the 1800's. **—practiced** *adj.* experienced, skilled (1568). **—practitioner** *n.* 1548, extended form of *practisen* to carry on some activity, employ (before 1400); borrowed from Old French *practiser;* see PRACTICE, v.

praetor (prē′tər *or* prē′tôr) *n.* magistrate or judge in ancient Rome. Probably before 1425 *pretor,* in a translation of Higden's *Polychronicon;* perhaps borrowed through Old French *pretor,* from Latin *praetor,* from **prai-itōr* one who goes before, in the early sense of a consul acting as leader of an army (*prae-* before + the root of *īre* to go; see EXIT); for suffix see -OR[2]. Alternatively, Ernout-Meillet suggest that the word may have been an alteration by folk etymology of a borrowing from Etruscan. **—praetorian** *adj.* 1425, of or having to do with a soldier or bodyguard of a Roman commander or emperor, in a translation of Higden's *Polychronicon,* formed from Latin *praetor* + English *-ian,* after Latin *praetōriānus.*

pragmatic *adj.* 1616, busy, interfering, meddlesome, in Ben Jonson's *The Devil is an Ass;* a shortened form of *pragmatical* (1543); borrowed probably through Middle French *pragmatique* (with English *-ical*), from Latin *prāgmaticus* skilled in business or law, from Greek *prāgmatikós* active, businesslike, versed in affairs, from *prâgma* (genitive *prā́gmatos*) civil business deed, act, from *prā́ssein* to do, act, perform; see PRACTICAL; for suffix see -IC. The meaning of concerned with practical results or values is first recorded in the form *pragmatical* (1597) and later as *pragmatic* in 1853. **—pragmatism** *n.* philosophy that stresses practical results. 1898, in William James' *Philosophical Conceptions and Practical Results;* formed from English *pragmat(ic)* + *-ism.* James attributed the coinage of *pragmatism* to the American philosopher Charles S. Peirce, who first outlined the philosophy of pragmatism in 1878, though the French etymologist Dauzat states that German philosophers had used the term *Pragmatismus* in the 1700's. Before the philosophical application, *pragmatism* was used in English in 1863 in the sense of pedantry and in the sense of matter-of-fact treatment, attention to facts, in George Eliot's *Middlemarch* (1872).

prairie *n.* 1691, implied in American English *prairie chicken* a kind of grouse; later, large area of grassland (1734); borrowing of French *prairie;* also found earlier as *prerie* meadow (before 1682); borrowed from Old French *praerie,* from Vulgar Latin **prātāria,* from Latin *prātum* meadow, originally a hollow, related to *prāvus* crooked; probably cognate with Middle Irish *rāth, rāith* earthworks or fortification, and Middle Welsh *bedrawt* grave mound, from Indo-European **prā-* to bend (Pok.843).

An earlier form existed in Middle English *prayere* meadow (probably about 1390), *praer* (about 1300), borrowed from Old French *praerie* (and in its Latinized form in Medieval Latin *praiere,* probably before 1260), but the word disappeared from the record of English quite early so that modern American English *prairie* represents a reborrowing from French. **—prairie dog** kind of burrowing rodent (1774, American English). **—prairie schooner** covered wagon (1841, American English).

praise *v.* Probably before 1200 *preisen* to praise, value, price, prize, in *Ancrene Riwle;* later *praisen* (probably before 1300); borrowed from Old French *preisier,* variant of *prisier* to praise, value; see PRICE. **—n.** Before 1325 *praise, pres,* in *Cursor Mundi;* from the verb in Middle English. **—praiseworthy** *adj.* (about 1450)

praline (prä′lēn *or* prā′lēn) *n.* kind of brown candy with nuts. 1727 *prawlin;* later *praline* (1809); American English, borrowed from French *praline,* from the name of Marshal Duplessis-*Praslin,* 1598-1675, whose cook invented pralines. The *s* in *Praslin* is not pronounced in French. For similar formations of French feminine nouns from proper names compare *guillotine,* after Joseph *Guillotin,* and *Sorbonne,* after Robert de *Sorbon.*

pram *n. British Informal.* baby carriage. 1884, shortened and contracted from PERAMBULATOR; perhaps humorously influenced in its formation by earlier *pram* a flat-bottomed boat (1634; earlier *praam* in compounds, 1548).

prance *v.* to spring about as if dancing. About 1380 *prauncen,* in *Sir Ferumbras;* earlier as a surname *Praunce* (1318); also *prancen* (before 1393); of uncertain origin; sometimes associated with Middle English *pranken,* v., to show off, behave in a showy way (about 1450, from Middle Dutch *pronken* to strut, parade; the OED draws attention to Danish dialectal *prandse, pranse* to go in a stately manner, but the history of these words is unknown. **—n.** act of prancing. 1751, Samuel Johnson, in *The Rambler;* from the verb.

prank[1] *n.* playful trick, practical joke. Before 1529, malicious or mischievous trick, in Skelton's *Against the Scottes;* of uncertain origin. **—prankish** *adj.* 1827, formed from English *prank*[1] + *-ish*[1]. **—prankster** *n.* person who plays pranks. 1927, American English; formed from English *prank*[1] + *-ster.*

prank[2] *v.* dress in a showy way. 1546, from earlier *pranken* behave in a showy way, show off (about 1450); borrowed from Middle Dutch *pronken* to show off, strut, *pronk* show, display, and from Middle Low German *prunken* make a show or display, *prank* pomp, display; cognate with modern German *prangen* to show off, vaunt.

praseodymium (prā′zēōdim′ēəm) *n.* metallic chemical element. 1885, New Latin, formed from Greek *prásios* leek-green (from *práson* leek) + New Latin *(di)dymium* double; so called from the green color of its salts, and because the supposed element didymium was found to consist of two elements, neodymium and praseodymium; for suffix see -IUM. The term was coined by its discoverer, the Austrian chemist Carl A. von Welsbach.

prate *v.* talk idly or foolishly. Probably before 1425 *praten,* borrowed from Middle Dutch *praten* to prate; cognate with Middle Low German *praten* to prate or chat, Swedish *prata,* and Norwegian *prate,* of unknown origin. **—n.** idle or foolish talk. 1579, from the verb.

pratfall *n. Slang.* fall on the buttocks, especially in comedy. 1939, in Noel Coward's *Play Parade;* formed from English slang *prat* buttocks (1567, of unknown origin) + *fall,* n.

prattle *v.* prate, chatter. 1532, in Sir Thomas More's *The Confutation of Tyndale's Answer;* a frequentative form of PRATE, corresponding to Middle Low German *pratelen* to chatter or grumble, frequentative of *praten* to prate; for suffix see -LE[3]. **—n.** idle talk, chatter. 1555, from the verb.

prawn *n.* kind of edible shellfish. 1426 *prayne;* later *prane* (1440); of uncertain origin.

praxis (prak′sis) *n.* practice, especially as contrasted with theory. 1581, in Sir Philip Sidney's *Apology for Poetry;* borrowed from Medieval Latin *praxis* practice, action, from Greek *prâxis* practice, action, doing, acting, from the stem of *prássein* to do or act; see PRACTICAL.

pray *v.* Probably before 1225 *preien* ask earnestly, beg, in *King Horn;* later *praien* pray to a god, saint, etc. (probably before 1300, in *Sir Tristrem*); borrowed from Old French *preier, prier,* from Latin *precārī* ask earnestly, beg, pray, from *prex* (genitive *precis*) prayer, request, entreaty. Latin *prex* is cognate with Lithuanian *prašýti* to demand, request, Sanskrit *prāś-* questioning, *pṛccháti* asks and Tocharian A *prak-,* Tocharian B *prek-* ask, inquire. Germanic cognates include Gothic *fraíhnan* ask, inquire, Old Icelandic *fregna,* Old High German *frāga* question, *frāgēn* (modern German *fragen*) ask, Old Saxon *frāgōn,* and Old Frisian *frēgia,* from Indo-European **prek̑-/prok̑-/prēk̑-/pr̥k̑-* (Pok. 821). **—prayer** *n.* Probably before 1300 *prayer, preier* an earnest request, in *Arthour and Merlin;* also about 1300 *preiere* supplication or prayer; borrowed from Old French *preiere, praiere,* from Medieval Latin *precaria* petition or prayer, from feminine of Latin *precārius,* adj., obtained by begging, given as a favor, from *precārī* ask earnestly, beg, pray. The informal sense of a slim chance (as in, *not to have a prayer of* *winning*) is first recorded in 1941. **—prayerful** *adj.* (1626)

pre- prefix meaning before, beforehand, in front, ahead, in place, rank, or time; its relation in the compound may be prepositional, as in *Precambrian, prenuclear, Pre-Raphaelite,* or adverbial or adjectival, as in *prearrange, precaution, precook, precede.* Borrowed and abstracted from Old French words with *pre-,* also from Medieval Latin *pre-* (or Medieval Latin words with *pre-*) and directly from Latin *prae-,* from *prae* before, adv. and prep., earlier *prai,* cognate with Oscan *prai* and with Greek *paraí* near, by, from Indo-European **prai/perai,* apparently an ancient use in the dative case of a noun **per* (Pok.811).

Use of *pre-* with adverbial force in English has become of such a common and regular practice that it is attached to verbs of almost any origin, not only Latin or Greek, but also native forms such as *prestrike, presift, preload, preheat, preharden.*

Use of *pre-* in a prepositional position is so extensive as to be preferred to *ante-,* probably because of possible confusion with *anti-,* and thus *ante-* is now found only in a remarkably small group of firmly established words, among them *ante-bellum, antecedent, antedate, antediluvian,* and *anteroom.*

The prefix *pre-* is also embedded in many words borrowed from Latin, such as *preach, precinct, precipice, precise, pregnant, premier.* Some words, however, are formations with *pre-* probably by confusion with other prefixes (going back to Middle English) such as *preserve* from *perserven* and *preposen* as a variant of *proposen,* though forms such as *precession* and *procession* may be from confusion among whole words.

In spelling words with *pre-* it used to be thought desirable to make the distinction, that formations in English should be hyphenated, and those that were borrowed should be written solid with no hyphen. This, of course, no longer pertains and the hyphen is found between *pre-* and a proper name, or is generally reserved for emphasis or where two vowels come together, as in *pre-exist* or *pre-eminent* (later often written with a dieresis *preëminent,* but now *preeminent*).

preach *v.* The word was adopted early in Europe from ecclesiastical Latin, as it appears in nearly all of the Germanic and Romance languages. It is found in Old English *predician,* but did not survive into Middle English. Probably before 1200 *preachen* speak publicly on a religious subject, deliver a sermon, in *Ancrene Riwle;* borrowed from Old French *preëcher,* from a possible **predichier* (compare Provençal *predicar*), from Late Latin *praedicāre* to proclaim publicly, announce (in Medieval Latin, preach), found in Latin, proclaim or declare (*prae-* forth, before + *dicāre* proclaim). Doublet of PREDICATE. **—preacher** *n.* Apparently before 1200 *preachur* one who preaches sermons, in *Ancrene Riwle;* borrowed from Old French *preëcheor,* from *preëcher* preach; for suffix see -ER[1]. **—preachment** *n.* Before 1388 *prechement* a preaching or sermon, in Mannyng's *Chronicle of England;* earlier, an annoying or tedious speech (probably about 1300), borrowed from Old French *preëchement* (*preëcher* preach + *-ment* -ment).

preamble *n.* preliminary statement. About 1395, in Chaucer's *Canterbury Tales;* borrowed from Old French *préambule,* learned borrowing from Medieval Latin, and borrowed directly from Medieval Latin *preambulum,* noun use of neuter adjective *preambulum* preliminary, from Late Latin *praeambulus* walking before (Latin *prae-* before + *ambulāre* to walk, AMBLE).

prebend (preb′ənd) *n.* salary of a clergyman connected with a cathedral or collegiate church. 1422 *prebend* clergyman's salary, property or tax that yields this salary, in *Rolls of Parliament;* borrowed from Middle French *prebende,* learned borrowing from Medieval Latin, and borrowed directly from Medieval Latin *prebenda* allowance, subsistence; see PROVENDER.

precarious *adj.* dependent on chance, uncertain. 1646, borrowed from Latin *precārius* obtained by entreaty or begging, given as a favor of another and therefore also with the meaning of uncertain, from *prex* (genitive *precis*) entreaty, prayer; see PRAY; for suffix see -OUS.

precaution *n.* 1603, in Holland's translation of Plutarch's *Moralia,* and in Florio's translation of Montaigne's *Essays;* borrowed from French *précaution,* learned borrowing from Late Latin, and borrowed directly from Late Latin *praecautiōnem* (nominative *praecautiō*) a safeguarding, from Latin *praecavēre* guard against beforehand (*prae-* before + *cavēre* be on one's guard; see HEAR); for suffix see -TION. **—precautionary** *adj.* 1757, advising precaution; formed from English *precaution* + *-ary.* The meaning "of or being a precaution" is first recorded in 1807.

precede *v.* Probably before 1425 *preceden* go or come before; borrowed from Middle French *preceder,* and directly from Latin *praecēdere* (*prae-* before + *cēdere* to go; see CEDE). **—preceding** *adj.* Probably before 1425, in a translation of Higden's *Polychronicon,* present participial adjective, from the verb.

precedent *n.* case that may serve as an example for a later case. 1427 *precydente;* 1433 *precedent,* both forms in *Rolls of Parliament;* earlier *precedent,* adj., preceding (about 1400, in Chaucer's *Treatise on the Astrolabe*); borrowed from Middle French *precedent,* from Latin *praecēdentem* (nominative *praecēdēns*), present participle of *praecēdere* go before; see PRECEDE; for suffix see -ENT. **—precedence** *n.* 1558, a precedent; later, a person or thing that precedes another (1588, in Shakespeare's *Love's Labour's Lost*); probably from *precedent,* on the analogy of *evidence, evident,* etc.; for suffix see -ENCE. The meaning of the fact of preceding another or others, priority is first recorded in English in 1605, and that of a higher position, superiority, preeminence in Phillips' *Dictionary* (1658).

precept *n.* rule of action or behavior. About 1375, in Chaucer's *Canterbury Tales;* borrowed from Old French *precept,* and directly from Latin *praeceptum* maxim, rule, order, from neuter past participle of *praecipere* take beforehand, give rules to, order, advise, anticipate (*prae-* before + *capere* to take; see CAPTIVE). **—preceptor** *n.* teacher, tutor. About 1425, an expert in the art of writing; borrowed from Latin *praeceptor,* from *praecipere* give rules to, order, advise; for suffix see -OR[2].

precession *n.* 1594, the earlier occurrence of the equinoxes in each successive sidereal year; borrowed from Late Latin *praecessiōnem* (nominative *praecessiō*) a coming before, from Latin *praecēdere* PRECEDE; for suffix see -SION. The meaning of the act or fact of going first is first recorded before 1628. The meaning in physics of the slow rotation of the axis of a spinning body analogous to the gyration of the earth's axis in the precession of the equinoxes is first recorded in 1879.

precinct *n.* About 1400 *prasaynt* specific district or area, especially of a city or town; later *precincte* (1447); borrowed from Medieval Latin *precinctum* enclosure, boundary line, from neuter past participle of Latin *praecingere* to gird about, enclose (*prae-* before + *cingere* to gird, surround, encircle; see CINCTURE).

The application of *precinct* to a division of a city for the purpose of police patrol is first recorded in 1882, in American English, originally as a shortening of the earlier phrase *precinct station* police station of a precinct (1864).

precious *adj.* valuable. About 1250 *preciouse;* later *precious* (about 1280); borrowed from Old French *precios, preciouse,* learned borrowing from Latin *pretiōsus* costly or valuable, from *pretium* value; see PRICE; for suffix see -OUS. The extended meaning of fastidious, particular, over-refined is first recorded in Chaucer's *Canterbury Tales* (about 1395) and that of very great, out-and-out, thoroughgoing in 1449, in Lydgate's writings.

precipice (pres′əpis) *n.* very steep cliff. 1598, sudden or headlong fall, in Ben Jonson's *Every Man Out of His Humour;* borrowed from Middle French *précipice,* learned borrowing from Latin *praecipitium* a falling headlong, steep place, from *praeceps* (genitive *praecipitis*) steep, headlong, precipitous (*prae-* forth, before + *caput* HEAD). The meaning of a very steep cliff is first recorded in English in 1632, and that of the figurative sense of perilous situation in 1651.

precipitate (prēsip′ətāt) *v.* hurl headlong, hasten, rush. 1528, hurl headlong; probably a back formation from earlier *precipitation,* in some instances perhaps influenced by Latin *praecipitātus,* past participle of *praecipitāre* hurl headlong, fall, be hasty, from *praeceps* (genitive *praecipitis*) headlong; see PRECIPICE; for suffix see -ATE[1].

The meaning of hasten the beginning of is first recorded in English in 1625. The meaning in chemistry of be deposited from solution as a solid found before 1626 and developed from the same sense (1477) in earlier *precipitation,* also influenced by the earlier noun use of *precipitate* (1563).

—adj. (prēsip′ətit) 1607, hasty or rash; later, very hurried, sudden (1658); borrowed from Latin *praecipitātus,* past participle of *praecipitāre;* see the verb.

—n. (prēsip′ətāt) 1563, substance separated out from a solution as a solid; back formation from *precipitation* in the verbal use of this sense. A later sense of moisture condensed from vapor and deposited in drops (1832) developed from the earlier noun use.

—precipitation *n.* act of precipitating. Before 1475 *precypitacion* act of precipitating or casting down; also, about 1477, separation of a solid from a solution; borrowed possibly from Middle French *précipitation,* and directly from Latin *praecipitātiōnem* (nominative *praecipitātiō*) act or fact of falling headlong, headlong haste, from *praecipitāre* hurl headlong, fall, be hasty; for suffix see -ATION. **—precipitous** *adj.* 1646, abrupt, hasty; later, rushing headlong (1774); probably in part formed from: 1) a shortening or refashioning of earlier *precipitious* (1613, itself formed in English from Latin *praecipitium* precipice + English *-ous*); and 2) English *precipitate* + *-ous,* developing by influence of French, and earlier Middle French *précipiteux,* formed from Latin *praecipitium* PRECIPICE + Middle French *-eux* -ous. The meaning of like a precipice, very steep is first recorded in 1806, replacing the same sense (1635) of earlier *precipitious.*

précis (prā′sē) *n.* abstract, summary. 1760, in Lord Chesterfield's *Letters;* borrowing of French *précis,* noun use of Middle French *précis,* adj., condensed, cut short, PRECISE.

precise *adj.* exact. About 1443; borrowed from Middle French *précis, précise* condensed, cut short, from Medieval Latin, and borrowed directly from Medieval Latin *precisus,* from Latin *praecīsus* abridged, cut off, past participle of *praecīdere* to cut off, abridge, shorten (*prae-* in front + *caedere* to cut; see EXCISE[2] cut). The extended meaning of strictly formal or correct, punctilious, scrupulous is first recorded in Palsgrave's *Lesclarcissement* (1530). **—precision** *n.* 1640, a cutting short; later, exactness (1740); borrowed through French *précision,* or directly from Latin *praecīsiōnem* (nominative *praecīsiō*) a cutting off abruptly, from *praecīdere* to cut off; for suffix see -SION.

preclude *v.* shut out, prevent. 1618; borrowed from Latin *praeclūdere* to close, shut off, impede (*prae-* before, ahead + *claudere* to shut; see CLOSE[1] shut).

precocious *adj.* developed earlier than usual. 1650, formed in English from Latin *praecox* (genitive *praecocis*) maturing early + English *-ous.* Latin *praecox* is from *praecoquere* ripen fully (*prae-* before + *coquere* to ripen; see COOK). **—precocity** *n.* early development. 1640, in James Howell's *Dodona's Grove;* formed in English from Latin *praecox* (genitive *praecocis*) precocious + English *-ity.*

preconceive *v.* 1597, formed from English *pre-* + *conceive.* **—preconception** *n.* (1625)

precursor *n.* forerunner. Probably about 1425 *precursoure;* borrowed from Middle French *precurseur,* and directly from Latin *praecursor* forerunner, advanced guard, from *praecursum,* past participle of *praecurrere* run before (*prae-* before, ahead + *currere* to run; see CURRENT); for suffix see -OR[2].

predaceous or **predacious** (pridā′shəs) *adj.* living by prey, predatory. 1713 *predaceous,* in William Derham's *Physico-Theology;* formed from Latin *praedārī* to plunder, rob; see PREY, + English *-aceous,* as in *cretaceous, herbaceous,* etc. The variant spelling *predacious,* due to confusion with the suffix *-ious* influenced by such words as *voracious* and *ferocious,* is first recorded in 1774.

predation *n.* act or habit of preying on others. Before 1475 *predacion,* borrowed from Latin *praedātiōnem* (nominative *praedātiō*) a plundering, act of taking booty, from *praedārī* to plunder or rob; see PREY; for suffix see -ATION. The sense in animal studies of the effects on a species of such habits by another species is first recorded in 1932.

predatory (pred′ətôr′ē) *adj.* of or inclined to preying or plundering. 1589; borrowed from Latin *praedātōrius* plundering, from *praedātor* plunderer or hunter, from *praedārī* to rob or plunder; see PREY; for suffix see -ORY. **—predator** *n.* one that preys upon others. 1922, in W.M. Wheeler's *Social Life Among the Insects,* developed from earlier *Predatores* (1840), name proposed for a group of insects that prey upon other insects; borrowed from Latin *praedātor;* for suffix see -OR[2].

predecessor *n.* person preceding another in a position or office. Before 1387 *predecessoure, predecessor,* both forms in Trevisa's translation of Higden's *Polychronicon;* borrowed from Old French *predecesseur,* and directly from Late Latin *praedēcessor* (from Latin *prae-* before + *dēcessor* retiring official, from *dēcēdere* go away, die; see DECEASE; for suffix see -OR[2]).

predestine *v.* destine or determine beforehand; foreordain. About 1385 *predestinen,* in Usk's *Testament of Love;* borrowed from Old French *predestiner,* and directly from Late Latin *praedēstināre* appoint or determine beforehand (Latin *prae-* before + *dēstināre* appoint, determine, DESTINE). **—predestinate** *v.* to determine or foreordain by divine decree or purpose. Apparently about 1450, probably in part a back formation from earlier *predestination,* and in part developed from *predestinate,* adj., foreordained by decree or purpose of God (about 1380, in Chaucer's translation of Boethius' *De Consolatione Philosophiae*); borrowed from Late Latin *praedēstinātus,* past participle of *praedēstināre* predestine; for suffix see -ATE[1]. **—predestination** *n.* action of foreordaining. About 1340 *predestinacioun,* borrowed from Old French *predestinacion,* and directly from Late Latin *praedēstinātiōnem* (nominative *praedēstinātiō*) a determining beforehand, from *praedēstināre* predestine; for suffix see -ATION.

predetermine *v.* 1625, in Donne's *Sermons;* formed from English *pre-* + *determine,* after Latin *praedētermināre* (found in St. Augustine's writings). **—predetermination** *n.* 1637, formed from English *predetermine* + *-ation.*

predicament *n.* unpleasant, difficult, or dangerous situation. Before 1425, a category or class; specifically, one of Aristotle's ten categories, in Wycliffe's *Works;* borrowed from Middle French *prédicament,* and directly from Medieval Latin *predicamentum,* from Late Latin *praedicāmentum* quality, category, something predicated, a loan translation of Greek *katēgoríā* CATEGORY, using Latin *praedicāre* declare publicly; see PREDICATE; for suffix see -MENT. The meaning of condition, state, or situation, especially one that is unpleasant or dangerous is first recorded in English in 1586.

predicate (pred′əkāt) *v.* to base (a statement, action, etc.) on something. 1552, in Huloet's *Abecedarium Anglico-Latinum,* borrowed from Latin *praedicātus* past participle of *praedicāre* assert, proclaim, declare publicly (*prae-* forth, before + *dicāre* proclaim; see DICTION); for suffix see -ATE[1]. It is also possible that *predicate* is, in part, a back formation from earlier *predication* a preaching, sermon, exhortation, a statement, especially of belief (before 1325); borrowed from Middle French *predicacion,* and directly from Medieval Latin *predicationem* (nominative *predicatio*), from Latin *praedicātiōnem* (nominative *praedicātiō*), from *praedicāre;* for suffix see -ATION.

The verb in English may also have been influenced in its development by the earlier noun *predicate* that which is said on a subject. The earliest recorded sense in English is that of proclaim, assert, but that may be an accident in the record of English, because the meaning in logic of state or assert (something) about the subject of a proposition, though not recorded before 1570, was known at least from Medieval Latin (1290) in the scholastic community of Europe. The sense of base (a statement, etc.) on something is first recorded in American English, in Thomas Clap's *History of Yale College* (1766). Doublet of PREACH.

—n. (pred′əkit) About 1450, that which is said of the subject in a logical proposition; borrowed from Middle French *predicat,* and directly from Medieval Latin *predicatum* a predicate in logic, from Late Latin *praedicātum,* noun use of neuter past participle of Latin *praedicāre* declare publicly. The meaning in grammar of a word or words expressing something about the subject is first recorded in English before 1638.

—adj. (pred′əkit) belonging to the predicate, in grammar. 1887, from the noun.

predict *v.* foretell, prophesy. 1671, in Milton's *Paradise Regained;* possibly a back formation from earlier *prediction,* and probably borrowed from Latin *praedictus,* past participle of *praedīcere* foretell, advise, give notice of (*prae-* before + *dīcere* to say; see DICTION). **—prediction** *n.* a foretelling, prophecy. 1561, borrowed from Middle French *prédiction,* and directly from Medieval Latin *predictionem* (nominative *predictio*) a prediction, from Latin *praedictiōnem* (nominative *praedictiō*) a saying before, premising, prediction, from *praedīcere* foretell; for suffix see -TION. **—predictability** *n.* 1868, formed from English *predictable* + *-ity.* **—predictable** *adj.* 1857, formed from English *predict* + *-able.*

predilection *n.* a liking, preference. 1742, in David Hume's *Dissertations;* borrowed from French *prédilection,* formed from Medieval Latin *predilect-,* past participle stem of *prediligere* prefer before others (from Latin *prae-* before + *dīligere* choose, love; see DILIGENCE careful effort) + French *-ion.*

predominate *v.* be greater in strength or numbers, prevail. 1597, (in astrology) have ascendancy, exert controlling influence; probably borrowed from Medieval Latin *predominare* (Latin *prae-* before + *domināre* to rule); for suffix see -ATE[1]. The sense of be greater, prevail, is first recorded in 1594. **—predominance** *n.* 1615, (in astrology) ascendancy, controlling influence; formed from English *predominant* + *-ance,* by influence of French *prédominance,* formed as in English from Middle French *prédominant* + *-ance.* The sense of preponderance or prevalence is first recorded in English in 1853. **—predominant** *adj.* 1576, exerting a controlling influence; borrowed from Middle French *prédominant,* formed as if from Medieval Latin *praedominantem* (nominative *praedominans*), present participle of *praedominare* predominate; for suffix see -ANT. The sense of greater, prevailing, is first recorded in English in 1601.

preemie *n. Informal.* premature baby. 1927 *premy,* American English; formed from *prem(ature)* + *-y*[2]; the present spelling with *ee,* influenced by the pronunciation of *premature,* appeared in 1949 as *preemies,* pl., and in 1954 as *preemie.*

preeminence (prēem′ənəns) *n.* distinction; superiority. Probably before 1200 *preminence, pre eminence,* in *Ancrene Riwle;* borrowed probably from Medieval Latin *preeminentia,* from Late Latin *praeēminentia* distinction, superiority, from Latin *praeēminēns,* present participle of *praeēminēre* project forwards, rise above, excel (*prae-* before + *ēminēre* stand out, project; see EMINENT); for suffix see -ENCE. **—preeminent** (prēem′ənənt) *adj.* distinguished, superior. Before 1460 *premynent;* later *preeminent* (1473); borrowed from Medieval Latin *preeminentem* (nominative *preeminens*), from Latin *praeēminentem* (nominative *praeē-*

minēns), present participle of *praeēminēre;* for suffix see -ENT.

preemption *n.* act or right of purchasing before others. 1602, formed in English from *pre-* before + Latin *ēmptiōnem* (nominative *ēmptiō*) buying, from *emere* to buy; originally, take; see REDEEM; for suffix see -TION. Compare PREMIUM. **—preempt** (prēempt′) *v.* seize before others, appropriate. 1850, American English, secure (public land) by preemption; back formation from *preemption.* The meaning of secure before someone else can is first recorded in 1888.

preen *v.* trim, dress up, or decorate oneself; primp. About 1395 *preynen* to trim, preen, in Chaucer's *Canterbury Tales;* later *prenen* (1486); both forms variants of Middle English *proinen* to trim, preen, found as *pruynen* (about 1390), *prunen* (before 1393), and *proynen prouynen* (probably before 1430; gradually formed as a blend of two words borrowed from Old French: 1) *poroindre* anoint before (*por-* before, from Latin *prō-* + *oindre* anoint, from Latin *unguere;* see UNGUENT); and 2) *proöignier, proignier* round off, prune or cut back; see PRUNE², v., clip, trim. Traditionally, the etymology of *preen* has been related through the spelling *preynen* to Middle English *prenen* to stitch, stab (about 1250), from *prene* pin, brooch (before 1200), in allusion to the boring or pricking action of a bird's beak as it preens itself, but the semantic connection is tenuous when compared to the sense of trim and groom under *prune;* also the forms and phonetic development accord more with that of the variants of *prune.*

prefab *adj. Informal.* prefabricated. 1937, American English; shortened from *prefabricate* (1932) to make all standardized parts of, formed from English *pre-* beforehand + *fabricate.* **—n.** *Informal.* prefabricated house, building, etc. 1942, from the adjective.

preface (pref′is) *n.* foreword, introduction. About 1380 *preface* introduction to the Canon of the Mass, in Chaucer's *Canterbury Tales;* borrowed from Old French *preface,* and directly from Medieval Latin *prefatia,* also borrowed from Latin *praefātiō* a saying beforehand, an introduction, preface, from *praefārī* to say beforehand, introduce, preface (*prae-* before + *fārī* speak; see BAN¹ forbid). **—v.** introduce with a preface. 1616, to introduce, precede, herald; from the noun. The meaning of introduce (a book, speech, etc.) with a preface is first recorded in 1691. **—prefatory** (pref′ətôr′ē) *adj.* of or like a preface. 1675, in John Ogilby's *Britannia;* formed in English from Latin *praefāt-,* past participle stem of *praefārī* to say beforehand, preface + English *-ory.*

prefect *n.* chief officer or magistrate. Probably about 1350 *prefecte* a civil or military officer, borrowed from Old French *prefect,* learned borrowing from Latin, and borrowed directly from Latin *praefectus* public overseer, commander, director, civil or military officer, from past participle of *praeficere* to put in front, put in authority over (*prae-* in front, before + the root of *facere* to make, perform, DO¹).

The use of *prefect* in modern reference to an administrative head of a government or one of its departments is first recorded in English in 1540, and especially in reference to France (from modern French *préfet*) and a *prefect of police,* in 1848. The sense of a student monitor in a school is first recorded in reference to English public (American private) schools, in 1865.

—prefecture *n.* office or district of a prefect. Probably before 1439, in Lydgate's *Falls of Princes;* borrowed from Middle French *préfecture,* and directly from Latin *praefectūra* the office of a prefect, from *praefectus* a prefect; for suffix see -URE.

prefer *v.* Before 1393 *preferren* like better, choose rather, promote, advance, in Gower's *Confessio Amantis;* borrowed from Old French *preferer,* learned borrowing from Latin, and borrowed directly from Latin *praeferre* place or set before, advance, prefer (*prae-* before + *ferre* carry, place; see BEAR²). **—preferable** *adj.* more desirable. 1648 (implied in *preferableness*); formed from English *prefer* + *-able,* probably on the model of French *préférable,* formed from parallel elements in French. **—preferably** *adv.* by choice. 1729, formed from English *preferable* + *-ly*¹. **—preference** *n.* 1456 *preferraunce* advancement in position or status, preferment, in the *Paston Letters;* formed in English from English *prefer* + Middle French *-aunce* -ence, on the model of Middle French *preference,* learned borrowing from Medieval Latin *preferentia,* from Latin *praeferēns,* present participle of *praeferre* prefer; for suffix see -ENCE. The meaning of act or attitude of preferring is first recorded in English in Blount's *Glossographia* (1656). **—preferential** *adj.* showing or giving preference. 1849, formed in English from Medieval Latin *preferentia* preference + English *-al*¹. **—preferment** *n.* advancement or promotion. 1443 *preferrement* prior claim or right; later, advancement (1454); formed from Middle English *preferren* prefer + *-ment.*

prefix *n.* affix put at the beginning of a word. 1646, from the verb in English (see below); earlier, New Latin *prefixia* (1614, plural of *praefixum,* noun use of the neuter form of Latin *praefixus,* past participle of *praefigere* fix in front, *prae-* in front, before + *figere* to fix, fasten; see DIKE). **—v.** put before. 1414 *perfixen;* 1415 *prefixen* fix or appoint beforehand; borrowed from Middle French *prefixer* (*pre-* before + *fixer* to fix or place, from Latin *fixus,* past participle of *figere* to fix). The meaning of place in front is first recorded in the Coverdale Bible (1538).

pregnable *adj.* open to attack. About 1540, alteration (probably influenced by English *pregnant*) of Middle English *preignable* (probably before 1440, with *gn* representing a pronunciation usually recorded by *ny,* as in English *poignant*); which superseded earlier Middle English *prenable* (1435), *pernable* (1393, in Gower's *Confessio Amantis*); for suffix see -ABLE.

The later Middle English *preignable* was borrowed from Old French *pregnauble,* with the subjunctive stem *pregn-,* while the earlier Middle English *prenable, pernable* were borrowed perhaps through Anglo-French *pernable,* Old French *prenable,* with the indicative stem *pren-;* all with the meaning of assailable or vulnerable; see IMPREGNABLE.

pregnant *adj.* About 1385, convincing or compelling, in Chaucer's *Troilus and Criseyde;* later, filled with meaning, heavy with significance, weighty (1402), and being with child (probably before 1425, in a translation of Chauliac's *Grande Chirurgie*); borrowed from Latin *praegnantem* (nominative *praegnāns*), variant of *praegnātem* (nominative *praegnās*) before birth, with child (*prae-* before + the root of *gnāscī, nāscī* be born; see NATIVE); for suffix see -ANT. **—pregnancy** *n.* Before 1529, condition of being pregnant (used figuratively), in Skelton's *Works;* later, condition of being with child, gestation, in Florio's *A World of Words* (1598); formed from English *pregnant* + *-cy*.

prehensile (prēhen′səl) *adj.* adapted for grasping or holding on. 1781-85, borrowed from French *préhensile,* from Latin *prehēnsus,* past participle of *prehendere* to grasp or seize (*pre-* before, unaccented variant of *prae-* + *-hendere,* related to *hedera* ivy, in the sense of clinging, and cognate with Greek *chandánein* to hold; see GET). Related to PREY.

prehistoric *adj.* 1851, formed from English *pre-* + *historic,* probably modeled on French *préhistorique.* **—prehistory** *n.* 1871, perhaps a back formation from *prehistoric,* but more likely an independent formation of English *pre-* + *history.*

prejudice *n.* About 1300 *prejudice* in the phrase *in prejudice of* to the detriment of, in contempt of; later, detriment or injury caused by some action or judgment (before 1333) and previous, premature or hasty judgment (about 1395, perhaps also before 1387); borrowed from Old French *prejudice,* and directly from Medieval Latin *prejudicium* injustice, from Latin *praejūdicium* previous judgment, opinion formed in advance (*prae-* before + *jūdicium* judgment, from *jūdex,* genitive *jūdicis* JUDGE). **—v.** 1447 *prejudicen* injure or be detrimental to a right or claim by some action or judgment, in *Rolls of Parliament;* from the noun in Middle English, and in part borrowed from Middle French *prejudicier* to prejudice or be injurious, from Old French *prejudice,* n. prejudice. The meaning of affect or fill with prejudice is first recorded in 1610. **—prejudicial** *adj.* of or causing prejudice, damaging. 1418 *prejudiciel;* later *prejudicial* (1434), borrowed from Middle French *prejudiciel, prejudicial,* and directly from Medieval Latin *prejudicialis* injurious, from Latin *praejūdicium* prejudice; for suffix see -AL[1].

prelate *n.* clergyman of high rank. Probably before 1200 *prelat,* in *Ancrene Riwle* and Layamon's *Chronicle of Britain;* borrowed from Old French *prelat,* and directly from Medieval Latin *prelatus* clergyman of high rank, from Latin *praelātus* one preferred, one given preference; *praelātus* serves as past participle of *praeferre* PREFER; for suffix see -ATE[1]. **—prelacy** *n.* office of a prelate. About 1300, borrowed from Anglo-French *prelacie,* and directly from Medieval Latin *prelatia* office of a prelate, from *prelatus* clergyman of high rank; see PRELATE.

preliminary *adj.* introductory, preparatory. Before 1667, in Jeremy Taylor's *Sermons;* borrowed perhaps in some instances from French *préliminaire* (as in Addison's writings in *The Tatler,* 1709); and directly from New Latin *praeliminaris,* formed from Latin *prae-* before + *līmen* (genitive *līminis*) threshold; see LIMIT; for suffix see -ARY. It is also possible that the adjective use was in part influenced by the earlier noun. **—n.** preliminary step, measure, etc. 1656, often in the plural *preliminaries,* as in Oliver Cromwell's *Letters and Speeches;* borrowed from New Latin *praeliminaris,* n. and adj.

prelude (prel′yüd *or* prē′lüd) *n.* introductory part or piece. 1561, borrowed from Middle French *prélude* set of notes sung or played to test the voice or an instrument, learned borrowing from Medieval Latin *preludium* prelude, preliminary, from Latin *praelūdere* to play beforehand for practice or rehearsal, compose a prelude, to attempt to preface (*prae-* before + *lūdere* to play; see LUDICROUS). The specific sense of piece of music that introduces another piece is first recorded in English in Phillips' *Dictionary* (1658). **—v.** be a prelude to. 1655, in Henry Vaughan's *Silex Scintillans;* borrowed from Latin *praelūdere;* see the noun.

premature *adj.* too early. Probably 1440, borrowed from Latin *praemātūrus* early ripe, as fruit; very early, too early (*prae-* before + *mātūrus* ripe, timely). It is also possible that *premature* was, especially in some later instances, formed from English *pre-* + *mature.*

premeditate *v.* Before 1548, possibly a back formation from *premeditation* or an independent formation of English *pre-* + *meditate.* In some instances *premeditate* may also have been borrowed from Latin *praemeditātus,* past participle of *praemeditārī,* or from the Latin past participle by way of English *premeditate,* adj., deliberate, composed or planned beforehand (though not recorded before 1555). **—premeditation** *n.* Probably before 1425 *premeditacion,* in a translation of Higden's *Polychronicon;* borrowed from Old French *premeditacion,* and directly from Latin *praemeditātiōnem* (nominative *praemeditātiō*) consideration beforehand from *praemeditārī* to consider beforehand (*prae-* before + *meditārī* to consider); for suffix see -ATION.

premier (prē′mēər) *adj.* first in rank, chief. 1448 *prymer* first in time, earliest; earlier as a surname *Primer* (1287); also *primier* first in rank, foremost (before 1471); borrowed from Middle French *premier, primier* first, chief, from Latin *prīmārius* of the first rank, chief. Doublet of PRIMARY. **—n.** prime minister. 1711, shortened from earlier *premier minister,* literally, first minister (1686, in Evelyn's *Diary*).

premiere or **première** (primir′ *or* prəmyãr′) *n.* first public performance. 1889, in Frank Leslie's correspondence; borrowing of French *première* in *première représentation,* from feminine of Old French *premier* first, PREMIER. **—v.** to present publicly for the first time. 1940, in Walter Winchell's column; American English; from the noun.

premise *n.* introductory statement used to draw a conclusion. About 1380 *premisse,* in Chaucer's translation of Boethius' *De Consolatione Philosophiae;* borrowed from Old French *premisse,* learned borrowing from Medieval Latin *premissa (propositio)* (the proposition) put before, from feminine past participle of Latin *praemittere* send or put before (*prae-* before + *mittere* to send; see MISSION). The plural form *premisses,* in the legal sense of things mentioned previously is first recorded in 1429. The more specific legal meaning of property specified at the beginning of a deed is found in 1464; from this developed the meaning of a house or building with its grounds (1730). **—v.** set forth as an introduction or basis for argument. About 1450, implied in *premised,* stated or mentioned previously, aforesaid; from the noun.

premium *n.* reward, prize. 1601, borrowed from Latin *praemium* reward, profit derived from booty, booty (*prae-* before + *emere* to buy; originally, to take; see REDEEM). Compare PREEMPTION. The meaning of an amount of money paid for insurance is first recorded in Blount's *Glossographia* (1656). The idiom *at a premium,* meaning at more than the usual value, above par, in high esteem, is recorded in 1828.

premonition (prē′mənish′ən *or* prem′ənish′ən) *n.* forewarning. 1545, borrowing of Middle French *premonition,* learned borrowing from Late Latin *praemonitiōnem* (nominative *praemonitiō*) a forewarning, from Latin *praemonēre* forewarn (*prae-* before + *monēre* to warn; see MONITOR); for suffix see -TION. The word appears earlier in Middle English *premunicion* a preliminary warning (probably 1456) and *premunition* (1472-73), found in Anglo-French *premunition* and Anglo-Latin *premunitio* warning, premonition, forms resulting from confusion with Latin *praemūnīre* protect in front (*prae-* before, pre- + *mūnīre* fortify; see MUNITION).

prenatal *adj.* 1826 in Southey's writings; formed from English *pre-* + *natal.*

preoccupy *v.* take up all the attention of, engross, absorb. 1567, formed from English *pre-* + *occupy,* possibly as a verb to earlier *preoccupation,* and on the model of Latin *praeoccupāre* seize beforehand (*prae-* before + *occupāre* seize, OCCUPY). **—preoccupied** *adj.* absorbed in thought. 1849, in Charlotte Brontë's *Shirley;* formed from English *preoccupy* + *-ed*[2]. **—preoccupation** *n.* 1552, anticipation; borrowed from Latin *praeoccupātiōnem* (nominative *praeoccupātiō*) a seizing beforehand, anticipation, from *praeoccupāre.* The meaning of the state of being preoccupied, absorption is first recorded in English in 1854, the derivative sense of something that takes precedence of all else is found in 1873.

prep *n. Informal.* 1862, preparation of lessons, shortened form of *preparation;* later *prep* or *prep school* (1895), American English, shortened form of *preparatory school* (1828). **—v.** *Informal.* 1915, to attend preparatory school, American English, from the noun; later, to prepare, train (1927), American English, shortened form of *prepare.* **—preppy** *n. Informal.* student or graduate of a preparatory school. 1962, American English; formed from *prep,* n. + *-y*[2]. *—adj.* of or in the style characteristic of preppies. 1966, from the noun.

prepare *v.* 1466 *preparen* make ready beforehand; borrowed from Middle French *preparer,* from Latin *praeparāre* make ready beforehand (*prae-* before + *parāre* make ready; see PARE). Later Middle English *preparen* replaced earlier *preperaten* (1392) and *preparaten* (about 1395); borrowed directly from Latin *praeparātus* past participle of *praeparāre.* **—preparation** *n.* About 1390 *preparacion;* borrowed from Old French *preparacïon,* and directly from Latin *praeparātiōnem* (nominative *praeparātiō*) a making ready, from *praeparāre* prepare; for suffix see -ATION. **—preparatory** *adj.* 1413, borrowed from Middle French *préparatoire,* and directly from Late Latin *praeparātōrius* preliminary, from Latin *praeparāre* prepare; for suffix see -ORY. **—preparedness** *n.* readiness. 1590, formed from English *prepared,* adj. (1526) + *-ness.*

preponderate *v.* be greater than, outweigh. 1611, borrowed from Latin *praeponderātus,* past participle of *praeponderāre* outweigh (*prae-* before + *ponderāre* to weigh; see PONDER); for suffix see -ATE[1]. **—preponderance** *n.* greater number, weight, or power. 1681, greater weight; formed from English *preponderant* + *-ance.* The sense of greater power is first recorded in 1780, and that of greater number, in 1845. **—preponderant** *adj.* outweighing in influence, power, etc. Before 1450, borrowed from Latin *praeponderantem* (nominative *praeponderāns*), present participle of *praeponderāre* preponderate; for suffix see -ANT.

preposition *n. Grammar.* word showing the relation between other words, such as *in, for, on, from.* Before 1397 *preposicioun,* borrowed from Old French *preposicion,* and directly from Latin *praepositiōnem* (nominative *praepositiō*) a putting before (but in the sense of a preposition *praepositiō* is a loan translation of Greek *próthesis*), from *praepōnere* put before (*prae-* before + *pōnere* put, set, place; see POSITION); for suffix see -TION. **—prepositional** *adj.* of or expressed by a preposition. Before 1831, in Jeremy Bentham's *Works;* formed from English *preposition* + *-al*[1].

prepossess *v.* impress favorably. 1614, to take beforehand; formed from English *pre-* + *possess.* The meaning of fill with a feeling or opinion beforehand is first recorded in 1639, and that of to bias or prejudice, in 1647. The sense of impress favorably at the outset, is recorded in 1849. **—prepossessing** *adj.* attractive. 1642, biasing; formed from English *prepossess* + *-ing*[2]. The sense of attractive is first recorded in 1805.

preposterous *adj.* contrary to reason or common sense, nonsensical, absurd. 1542, in Udall's translation of Erasmus' *Apothegms;* borrowed from Latin *praeposterus* absurd; originally, with the last coming first (*prae-* before + *posterus* subsequent; see POSTERIOR); for suffix see -OUS.

prepuce (prē′pyüs) *n.* foreskin of the penis. About 1400, in Lanfranc's *Science of Surgery;* borrowed from Old French *prepuce,* learned borrowing from Latin *praepūtium* foreskin (possibly formed from *prae-* before + **pūtos* penis), from Indo-European **pu-t-/pū-t-,* extended from the root **pu-/pū-* to swell (Pok.847).

prerequisite *n.* 1633, something required beforehand. **—adj.** 1651, required beforehand. Both uses formed from English *pre-* + *requisite,* n. and adj.

prerogative *n.* right or privilege. Before 1387, in Trevisa's translation of Higden's *Polychronicon;* borrowing of Old French *prerogative,* and directly from Medieval Latin *prerogativa* special right, from Latin *praerogātiva* prerogative, previous choice or election; originally referring to the Roman centuria, a unit of one hundred voters, who by lot voted first and so set the example for those that voted after; from feminine of *praerogātīvus,* adj., chosen to vote first, from *praerogāre* ask before others (*prae-* before + *rogāre* ask; see RIGHT); for suffix see -IVE.

presage (pres′ij) *n.* sign felt as a warning, omen. Before 1393, in Gower's *Confessio Amantis;* borrowed from Latin *praesāgium* a foreboding, presentiment, from *praesāgīre* to feel or perceive beforehand, forebode, from *praesāgus* foreboding, foreshowing (*prae-* before + *sāgus* prophetic, related to *sāgīre* perceive or feel keenly; see SEEK). **—v.** (prisāj′) give warning (of), predict. 1562, borrowed from Middle French *présager,* from *présage* omen, from Latin *praesāgium.*

presbyter (prez′bətər) *n.* elder in the early Christian church. 1597, borrowed from Late Latin *presbyter* presbyter, an elder, from Greek *presbýteros* an elder, also as an adjective with the meaning of older, a comparative form of *présbys* old, as in the noun sense of old man, possibly originally meaning one who leads a herd of cattle (compare PASTOR), from a primitive compound **pres-* before, in advance, related to *páros* before and *pró* before, ahead; see FOR + the root of *boûs, bôs* COW. This compound is also found in Sanskrit *puro-gavá-s* guide; originally, leader of a band. **—Presbyterian** *adj.* of or belonging to a church governed by presbyters. 1641, formed from English *presbytery* a body or assembly of presbyters or elders (1578) + *-an,* and perhaps also, in some instances, from *presbyter* + *-ian.* **—presbytery** *n.* 1466 *presbetory* part of a church reserved for the clergy; later, assembly of presbyters or elders (1578); borrowed from Late Latin *presbyterium* presbytery, from Greek *presbytérion,* from *presbýteros* presbyter; for suffix see -Y³. The term appears earlier in Middle English *prismatorie* (1412), probably an error by confusion with *cris-* in *crismatorie* chrismatory (vessel for holding sacred oil used in baptism).

preschool *adj.* 1924, formed from English *pre-* + *school.* **—n.** 1934, nursery school, or other school for children before kindergarten; from the adjective.

prescience (presh′ēəns) *n.* foreknowledge, foresight. About 1380, in Chaucer's translation of Boethius' *De Consolatione Philosophiae;* borrowed from Old French *prescïence,* learned borrowing from Late Latin, and borrowed directly from Late Latin *praescientia* foreknowledge, from **praescientem* (nominative **praesciēns*), present participle of **praescīre* to know in advance (Latin *prae-* before + *scīre* to know; see SCIENCE); for suffix see -ENCE. **—prescient** *adj.* having prescience. Before 1626, in Bacon's *Works;* borrowed from French *prescient,* learned borrowing from Late Latin, and borrowed directly from Late Latin **praescientem* (nominative **praesciēns*), present participle of **praescīre;* for suffix see -ENT.

prescribe *v.* to order, direct. 1445 *prescriben,* borrowed from Latin *praescrībere* write before or in front, order, direct (*prae-* before + *scrībere* to write; see SCRIBE). The medical meaning of direct in writing the use of (a medicine, remedy, or treatment) is first recorded in English in 1581, probably a back formation from *prescription.* **—prescription** *n.* act of prescribing. Probably 1383 *prescripcion* right to something acquired through long possession or use, in Wycliffe's writings; borrowed from Old French *prescription,* learned borrowing from Latin, and borrowed directly from Latin *praescrīptiōnem* (nominative *praescrīptiō*) a writing before or in front, order, direction, from *praescrībere* PRESCRIBE; for suffix see -TION. The meaning of a written direction given by a doctor for preparing and using a medicine, or more generally for any treatment, etc., is first recorded in English in 1579. **—prescriptive** *adj.* 1748, that prescribes or directs, in Richardson's *Clarissa;* probably formed in English from earlier *prescript* a direction, instruction, order (about 1540, from Latin *praescrīptum* something prescribed, from neuter of *praescrīptus,* past participle of *praescrībere* prescribe) + *-ive.* The meaning of prescribed by custom is first recorded in Johnson's Preface in *Plays of Shakespeare* (1765).

presence *n.* a being present. About 1330 *presens* surrounding space, immediate vicinity; also 1340 *presense* fact or state of being present; borrowed from Old French *presence,* and directly from Latin *praesentia* a being present, from *praesentem* (nominative *praesēns*) PRESENT¹, adj.; for suffix see -ENCE.

present¹ *adj.* being at hand, not absent. About 1303, in Mannyng's *Handlyng Synne;* borrowed from Old French *present,* learned borrowing from Latin, and borrowed directly from Latin *praesentem* (nominative *praesēns*) present, immediate, prompt, from present participle of *praeesse* be before (a person or thing), be at hand, take the lead (*prae-* before + *esse* to be; see IS); for suffix see -ENT. **—n.** present time. Probably before 1300 *present* presence, and in the phrase *in present* in this place, in *Arthour and Merlin;* also probably about 1300, present time; borrowed from Old French *present,* n. and adj. **—presently** *adv.* About 1380, at present, now, in Chaucer's translation of Boethius' *De Consolatione Philosophiae;* formed from Middle English *present,* adj. + *-ly*¹. The sense of immediately is first recorded in Lydgate's *Minor Poems* (about 1430), and that of the weakened sense of in the time that follows shortly, soon, before 1566.

present² (prez′ənt) *n.* thing given, gift. Probably before 1200, in *Ancrene Riwle;* borrowed from Old French *present* in the phrase *en present* (to offer) in or into the presence of, and in *mettre en present* place before, give. Old French *en present* is from Late Latin *in praesentī* face to face, from Latin *in rē praesentī* in the situation in question (*praesentī,* from *praesēns* being there; see PRESENT¹, adj.). **—v.** (prizent′) to give. Probably before 1300 *presenten* to present, give, offer, in *Kyng Alisaunder;* also, bring before, introduce; borrowed from Old French *presenter,* and directly from Latin *praesentāre* place before, exhibit, from *praesentem* (nominative *praesēns*) being at hand, immediate; see PRESENT¹, adj. **—presentable** *adj.* 1451 (in law) liable to a formal charge of wrongdoing, in *The Paston Letters.* The meaning of suitable in appearance, dress, or manner is first recorded in 1827. **—presentation** *n.* Probably 1383 *presentacioun* the action or right of presenting a clergyman to a bishop as a candidate for a benefice; borrowed from Old French *presentacïon,* from Late Latin *praesentātiōnem* (nominative *praesentātiō*) a placing before, an exhibition from Latin *praesentāre* to place before, exhibit, present; for suffix see -ATION. **—present-day** *adj.* current, contemporary (1887). **—presentment** *n.* presentation. About 1303, in Mannyng's *Handlyng Synne;* borrowed from Old French *presentement,* formed from *presenter* to present + *-ment.*

presentiment (prizen′təmənt) *n.* anticipation or foreboding (usually of evil). 1714, borrowing of French *presentiment,* variant of *pressentiment,* from Middle French, from *pressentir* to have foreboding or premonition, from Latin *praesentīre* to sense beforehand, have a feeling of foreboding (*prae-* before + *sentire* perceive or feel; see SENSE); for suffix see -MENT.

preserve *v.* 1392 *preserven* keep from harm, keep alive; borrowed through Anglo-Latin *preservare,* from Late Latin; and borrowed from Old French *preserver,* learned borrowing from Medieval Latin *preservare* keep, preserve; from Late Latin *praeservāre* observe beforehand, preserve (Latin *prae-* before + *servāre* to watch or keep; see CONSERVE). **—n.** 1552 a preservative; later (usually *preserves*), fruit preserved with sugar (1600); from the verb. The meaning of a place where animals or plants are protected is first recorded in 1807. **—preservation** *n.* act of preserving. Probably before 1425 *preservacioun* protection from a disease, in a translation of Chauliac's *Grande Chirurgie;* borrowed from Middle French *preservation,* learned borrowing from Medieval Latin *preservationem* (nominative *preservatio*), from *preservare* to preserve; for suffix see -ATION. **—preservative** *n.* Before 1420 *preservatif* a protection or defense, in Lydgate's *Troy Book;* also, before 1422, a preventive medicine; developed from the earlier adjective *preservative* serving to prevent or protect against disease (before 1398); borrowed from Old French *preservatif* (feminine *preservative*), and directly from Medieval Latin *preservativus,* from *preservare* to preserve. The specific meaning of a chemical substance used to preserve things subject to decomposition, such as perishable foodstuffs, is first recorded in English in 1875. **—preserver** *n.* 1535, formed from English *preserve,* v. + *-er*[1].

preside *v.* act as a head or chief officer, exercise rule or control. 1611, in Cotgrave's *Dictionary;* borrowed from French *présider* preside over, govern, learned borrowing from Latin *praesidēre* stand guard, preside; literally, sit before (*prae-* before, ahead + *sedēre* to SIT).

president *n.* Before 1382 *president* person who presides, chief officer, in the Wycliffe Bible; borrowed from Old French *president,* learned borrowing from Latin, and borrowed directly from Latin *praesidentem* (nominative *praesidēns*) a president or governor, noun use of present participle of *praesidēre* to act as head or chief; see PRESIDE; for suffix see -ENT. The application of *president* to the chief executive officer of a republic is first recorded in American English in 1787, the year in which the Constitution was drafted, and was extended from the earlier use of *president* as the presiding officer at meetings of the Continental Congress (1774), and that of chief officer of an American colony (1608). Other uses of the sense of chief presiding officer include that of head of a college (1448), head of an academy or learned society (1660), head of a commercial establishment (1781). **—presidency** *n.* 1591, in Percival's *Spanish Dictionary;* borrowed from Medieval Latin *praesidentia* office of president, from Latin *praesidentem* (nominative *praesidēns*), present participle of *praesidēre;* for suffix see -CY. **—president-elect** *n.* one who has been elected president, but has not taken office (1825, American English). **—presidential** *adj.* 1603, borrowed from Medieval Latin *presidentialis,* from *praesidentia* office of president; see PRESIDENCY; for suffix see -AL[1].

presidium (prisid′ēəm) *n.* executive or administrative committee. 1924, borrowed from Russian *prezídium,* from Latin *praesidium* means of defense, garrison, guard; literally, one that sits in front of or presides over, from *praesidēre* stand guard; see PRESIDE. The original, and still most common use of *presidium* in English is in reference to the governing body of a Communist country, especially the Soviet Union.

press[1] *v.* to push or thrust against. Before 1325 *pressen* offer, urge, recommend; later, push ahead (1338), crowd (before 1350), exert pressure, torment (about 1380); borrowed from Old French *preser, presser,* and directly from Latin *pressāre* to press, a frequentative form (influenced in formation by *pressus,* past participle) of *premere* to press, hold fast, cover, crowd, compress. It is also quite likely that the verb in English was influenced by the earlier noun. The sense of pressing cloth is implied in *pressour* a device used to press cloth (before 1376). **—n.** Probably before 1200 *prease* society or companionship of people, in *Ancrene Riwle;* later *pres* crowd, multitude (about 1280), *presse* crowding (before 1300), and device for exerting pressure (1373 in *preshous*); borrowed from Old French *presse,* from *presser* to press.

The meaning of pressure of business, urgency, haste, is first recorded before 1393, in Gower's *Confessio Amantis.* The meaning of a machine for printing, printing press is first recorded in 1535, borrowed from Middle French *presse,* from *presser* to press, from Old French. By 1579 *press* was used as an inclusive name for a printing or publishing house, as in the *Clarendon Press,* Oxford, and the *Pitt Press,* Cambridge. Such phrases as *the freedom of the press,* meaning the free use of the printing press, the right to publish freely and without censorship, *a shackled press, to write for the press,* etc., began to appear about 1680, though the idea of free use of the press had been long in the air and was earlier argued in Milton's *Areopagitica* (1644). This use of *press* developed by the late 1700's the general meaning of newspapers, magazines, and periodical literature as a group, as in the *British press, the conservative press, the business press,* etc., a usage that is perhaps fading before the term *media.*
—pressing *adj.* urgent. About 1391, burdensome; formed from English *press*[1] overburden + *-ing*[2]. The sense of urgent is first recorded in 1616.

press[2] *v.* force into service. 1578, alteration (by association with *press*[1], v.) of earlier *prest* engage (recruits) by loan, pay in advance (1513); found in Middle English *prest* loan (1359-60); borrowed from Old French *prest,* from *prester* to lend, from Latin *praestāre* lend, supply, make available, from *praestō,* adv., ready, available; see PRESTO.

pressure *n.* About 1384, distress, anguish, affliction, suffering, in the Wycliffe Bible; borrowed from Old French *pressure, pressur,* learned borrowing from Latin, and borrowed directly from Latin *pressūra* action of pressing, from *pressus,* past participle of *premere* to PRESS[1]; for suffix see -URE. The literal meaning of exertion of continuous force, act of pressing is first recorded in Middle English probably before 1425, and the sense in physics (as *in the pressure of air*) is found in 1660, in Robert Boyle's writings. The figurative meaning of a need for a decisive action, urgency is first recorded in 1812. **—v.** force or urge by exerting pressure. 1939, American English, in Raymond Chandler's writings; from the noun. **—pressure cooker** (1915) **—pressurize** *v.* produce or maintain pressure in. 1938 (implied in *pressurized*); formed from English *pressure,* n. + *-ize.*

prestige (prestēzh′) *n.* reputation, influence, or distinction. 1656, illusion, deception, magic spell, in Blount's *Glossographia;* borrowing of French *prestige* illusion, fascination, learned borrowing from Latin *praestīgia* a delusion, an illusion, but usually found as *praestīgiae,* pl., juggler's or conjurer's tricks, probably alteration of *praestrīgiae,* from *praestringere* to bind, blindfold, dazzle (*prae-* before + *stringere* to tie or bind; see STRAIN[1] stretch).

The transferred sense of blinding or dazzling influence, glamour, distinction is first recorded in English in 1829 (applied to Napoleon in 1815 as a French word in an English context).
—prestigious (prestij′əs) *adj.* having prestige. 1546, deceitful, practicing magic, in John Bale's *The Acts of the English Votaries;* borrowed from Latin *praestīgiōsus* full of tricks, deceitful, from *praestīgiae* juggler's tricks; for suffix see -OUS. The meaning of having reputation or influence or showing distinction is first recorded in English in Joseph Conrad's *Chance* (1913).

presto *adv., adj.* quickly, quick. 1598-99, in Ben Jonson's *Works;* borrowing of Italian *presto,* from Latin *praestus* ready, from *praestō,* adv., ready, available, at hand, contracted from the pre-Latin phrase **prai hestōd* at hand; from **prai* before, earlier form of Latin *prae;* and **hestōd,* ablative case of **hestos* hand, cognate with Sanskrit *hásta-s* hand, Avestan *zasta-,* and Lithuanian *pa-žastẽ* space under the arm, armpit, from Indo-European **ĝhesto-* (Pok.447).

presume *v.* About 1378 *presumen* take for granted, assume overconfidently, in a version of *Piers Plowman;* later, venture, dare (about 1390); borrowed from Old French *presumer,* and directly from Late Latin *praesūmere* take for granted, assume, dare, from Latin, to take before or anticipate (*prae-* before + *sūmere* to take, from pre-Latin **sups-* up + Latin *emere* to take; see REDEEM. The intransitive meaning of be arrogant or presumptuous, behave too boldly or with effrontery is recorded in 1415. —**presumably** *adv.* probably. 1646, with a taking of things for granted; 1846, probably, in Poe's *Works;* formed from English *presumable (presume + -able,* perhaps after French *présumable*) + *-ly*[1]. —**presumption** *n.* Before 1250 *presumpcion* arrogance, thought of as a kind of sinful pride, in *Ancrene Riwle;* later, assumption, supposition (before 1376); borrowed from Old French *presumpcïon,* and directly from Late Latin *praesūmptiōnem* (nominative *praesūmptiō*) confidence, audacity, from Latin, a taking beforehand, anticipation, from *praesūmere* anticipate, take for granted, assume; for suffix see -TION. —**presumptive** *adj.* presumed. About 1443, borrowed from Medieval Latin *presumptivus,* from Late Latin *praesumptīvus,* from *praesūmpt-,* past participle stem of *praesūmere.* —**presumptuous** *adj.* presuming, arrogant. Before 1349, borrowed from Old French *presumptueux,* and directly from Late Latin *praesūmptuōsus,* variant of *praesūmptiōsus* full of boldness, from *praesūmptiōnem* (nominative *praesūmptiō*) boldness, presumption; for suffix see -OUS.

pretend *v.* Probably 1382 *pretenden* to claim, profess to have, in Wycliffe's writings; later, feign or claim falsely (1402); borrowed from Old French *pretendre,* or directly from Latin *praetendere* stretch in front, put forward, allege, pretend (*prae-* before + *tendere* to stretch; see TEND[1] incline). The intransitive meaning of make pretense or make believe, is first recorded in 1526. —**pretender** *n.* 1591, one who intends or purposes; later, one who puts forth a claim (1622), and a claimant to a throne or office (1697), in Dryden's *Works;* formed from English *pretend,* v. + *-er*[1].

pretense (prē′tens) *n.* make-believe, pretending. Before 1420 *pretense, pretence* claim, false show, feigning, in Lydgate's *Troy Book;* borrowed from Middle French *pretensse,* from Late Latin *praetēnsus,* corresponding to Latin *praetentus,* past participle of *praetendere* PRETEND. —**pretension** *n.* act of pretending, assertion of claim, ostentation. About 1443 *pretensioun, pretencioun* signification, sense; later, assertion (about 1449), and purpose, intention (about 1456); borrowed from Late Latin *praetēnsus,* corresponding to Latin *praetentus,* past participle of *praetendere;* for suffix see -SION. The meaning of pretentiousness, ostentation is first recorded in English in 1727.

pretentious (priten′shəs) *adj.* full of pretension, ostentatious. 1845, borrowed from French *prétentieux,* from *prétention* pretension, learned borrowing from Medieval Latin *pretentionem* (nominative *pretentio*) pretention, variant of *pretensionem* (nominative *pretensio*), from Late Latin *praetēnsus* PRETENSE; for suffix see -IOUS.

preterit or **preterite** (pret′ərit) *adj. Grammar.* expressing past time. 1340, bygone or past, in *Ayenbite of Inwyt;* later, (in grammar) expressing past time (before 1397, in Wycliffe's writings); borrowed from Old French *preterit,* and directly from Latin *praeteritum,* as in *tempus praeteritum* time past, gone by (*praeter* beyond, from *prae-* before + *itum,* past participle of *īre* go; see EXIT). —**n.** About 1380, past time, the past, in Chaucer's translation of Boethius' *De Consolatione Philosophiae;* developed from the adjective in English, and probably, in part, borrowed from Old French *preterit,* and directly from Latin *praeteritum,* neuter of *praeteritus.* The meaning in grammar of the past tense is curiously not recorded before 1530, in Palsgrave's *Lesclarcissement.*

preternatural (prē′tərnach′ərəl) *adj.* out of the ordinary course of nature. 1580, borrowed from Medieval Latin *preternaturalis,* from the Latin phrase *praeter nātūram (praeterque fātum)* beyond nature (and beyond fate); *praeter* beyond (from *prae-* before) and *nātūram,* accusative of *nātūra* NATURE; for suffix see -AL[1].

pretext *n.* false reason, excuse. 1513, in Sir Thomas More's *The History of King Richard III;* borrowed from Latin *praetextum* a pretext, originally neuter past participle of *praetexere;* or from *praetextus* (genitive *praetextūs*) outward display, show, from past participle stem of *praetexere* to disguise, cover, display outwardly (*prae-* in front, before + *texere* to weave; see TEXT).

pretty *adj.* Probably before 1400 *praty* manly, gallant, fine; also, about 1405, in the superlative form *pretiest* clever, skillful; and probably before 1410, handsome, attractive, pleasing; developed from Old English (about 1000, West Saxon *prættig,* Mercian **prettig*) cunning, skillful, artful (*prætt, *prett* trick, wile, craft, of unknown origin + *-ig* -y[1]). Old English *prætt* is cognate with Middle Dutch *perte* trick (modern Dutch *pret* sport, fun, pleasure), and Old Icelandic *prettr* trick, deceit. Compare modern Dutch *prettig* pleasant, agreeable.

The sense development in English from that of cunning to pleasing, attractive, has parallels in other adjectives, such as *cunning, fine,* and *nice.*

—**n.** pretty person or thing. 1773, in Goldsmith's *She Stoops to Conquer;* from the adjective.

—**adv.** fairly, rather. 1565, in Cooper's *Thesaurus Linguae Romanae et Britannicae;* from the adjective.

—**prettify** *v.* 1850, formed from English *pretty,* adj. + *-fy.*

pretzel *n.* hard biscuit in the form of a knot or stick. 1856, American English; borrowing of German *Prezel, Pretzel;* also *Brezel, Bretzel,* from Old High German *brezitella* a pretzel, from Medieval Latin **brachitellum* presumably a kind of biscuit baked in the shape of folded arms (compare Italian *bracciatella*), diminutive from Latin *bracchiātus* having branches (resembling arms), from Latin *bracchium* arm (see BRACE); probably so called from the resemblance of a knotted pretzel to a pair of folded arms.

prevail *v.* exist widely. Before 1400 *prevailen* be successful or effective, in a translation of Lanfranc's *Science of Surgery,* later, prove superior, overcome, be victorious; borrowed from Old French *prevaloir,* and directly from Latin *praevalēre* be very able, have greater power (*prae-* before + *valēre* have power, be worth; see VALUE). The spelling in *ai,* according to the MED, "is probably due to analogy with Middle English *availen* and *vailen.*" The meaning of exist widely, predominate is first recorded in English, in Hobbes' translation of Thucydides' *History of the Peloponnesian War* (1628). —**prevailing** *adj.* Before 1586, victorious; later, widely accepted (1685); from *prevail,* v. + *-ing*[2].

prevalent *adj.* widespread. Probably before 1425, very strong or powerful, in a translation of Higden's *Polychronicon;* borrowed from Latin *praevalentem* (nominative *praevalēns*), present participle of *praevalēre* PREVAIL; for suffix see -ENT. The current meaning of widespread is first recorded in English in 1658. **—prevalence** *n.* condition of being widespread. 1592, mastery; later, influence (1631); possibly formed, in part, as a noun to earlier adjective *prevalent;* and in part borrowed from Middle French *prévalence,* from Latin *praevalentia,* from *praevalēns,* present participle; for suffix see -ENCE. The current sense of a condition of being widespread, is first recorded in 1713, in writings of Steele.

prevaricate *v.* lie. 1582, deviate from the right course, go astray; a back formation from earlier *prevarication,* perhaps influenced by Latin *praevāricātus,* past participle of *praevāricārī;* for suffix see -ATE[1]. The meaning of act or speak evasively, equivocate, lie, is first recorded in Donne's *Selections* (before 1631). **—prevarication** *n.* About 1384 *prevaricacioun* transgression, trespass, in the Wycliffe Bible; borrowed from Old French *prevaricacïon,* and directly from Latin *praevāricātiōnem* (nominative *praevāricātiō*) a stepping out of line in duty or behavior, from *praevāricārī* to make a sham accusation, deviate; literally, walk crookedly (*prae-* before + *vāricāre* to straddle, from *vāricus* straddling, from *vārus* bowlegged, crooked, of uncertain origin); for suffix see -ATION. The meaning of deception, evasion, equivocation is first recorded in English before 1655; from the Latin. **—prevaricator** *n.* Before 1400, transgressor of the law; borrowed from Old French *prevaricator,* and directly from Latin *praevāricātor* (*praevāricārī* to deviate + *-tor* -or[2]).

prevent *v.* Probably before 1425, act in anticipation of, in a translation of Higden's *Polychronicon;* borrowed from Latin *praeventus,* past participle of *praevenīre* come before, anticipate, hinder (*prae-* before + *venīre* to COME). The meaning of keep from happening by anticipatory action is first recorded in Elyot's *Dictionary* (1548), and that of hinder in 1663. **—prevention** *n.* 1447 *prevencion* action of stopping, restriction; borrowed from Middle French *prévention,* and directly from Late Latin *praeventiōnem* (nominative *praeventiō*) a going before, anticipation, from Latin *praevenīre* come before; for suffix see -TION. The meaning of an act of preventing is first recorded in 1661. **—preventive** *adj.* 1639, formed from English *prevent* + *-ive.*

preview *v.* 1607, formed from English *pre-* + *view,* v. **—n.** 1855, from the verb.

previous *adj.* coming before. 1625, borrowed from Latin *praevius* going before, leading the way (*prae-* before + *via* road; see VIA); for suffix see -OUS.

prey *n.* animal hunted or seized for food. About 1225 *preie* a company of men, army, in *King Horn;* later *praie* animal hunted or seized for food (about 1250, in *Genesis and Exodus*), and *preye* booty, plunder (probably before 1300); borrowed from Old French *preie* booty, animal taken in the chase, from Latin *praeda* booty, plunder, game hunted or seized; related to *prehendere* to grasp, seize; see PREHENSILE. Latin *praeda* is usually given as a contracted form of **praehedā,* from pre-Latin **prai-hedā* (*prai,* earlier form of *prae* before, in front of + **hedā,* from a root **hed-* to seize, take, GET. **—v.** hunt or kill for food. About 1300 *preien* to pillage, plunder; from the noun in English, and probably borrowed from Old French *preier,* earlier *preder,* from Latin *praedārī* to plunder, rob, from *praeda,* n., booty.

price *n.* Probably before 1200 *pris* value, worth, praise, in *Ancrene Riwle;* later, cost, recompense, prize (about 1250); and in the spelling *price* (before 1382); borrowed from Old French *pris,* from Latin *pretium* reward, prize, value, worth, price. **—v.** 1382, Middle English *prisen* set the price to, value, prize, praise, borrowed from Old French *prisier,* variant of *preisier,* from Late Latin *pretiāre* to prize, from Latin *pretium* reward, prize, value, price; originally, an equivalent standing over against; cognate with Sanskrit *práti* against, Greek *protí* toward, Old Slavic *protivŭ,* Lettish *pret* against, from Indo-European **preti/proti,* and **pretyom* (Pok.815).

Middle English *praise* is said to have developed from Middle English *pris* originally with the senses of value, worth, praise, but the differentiation was probably already in progress in Old French, as shown by the difference in spelling, not only in early Middle English *pris,* n., value, worth, praise, as contrasted with *preisen,* v., to value, praise, price, but also in the distinction made in Old French *pris* (variant of *preis,* n., value, praise), and *preiser,* v., to value, praise. Further differentiation was completed in Middle English as *pris,* n., and *preisen,* v., became distinct, each developing a new noun or verb form for the corresponding differentiated part of speech, so that before 1325 *preisen,* v., had a new noun form *pres, praise,* to correspond to the differentiated *praise,* n., while before 1382 *pris, price,* n., had a new verb form to correspond to the differentiated *price,* n. This gave the two words *price* and *praise* (finally separated in meaning and form) complete paradigms of noun and verb.

The later differentiation of *prize*[1], n., reward and *prize*[3], v., value highly, from *price, prise* became evident in form only in the very late 1500's, when a felt need brought about the introduction of a new form with the spelling *-z-.*
—priceless *adj.* beyond price; extremely valuable. 1593, in Shakespeare's *The Rape of Lucrece;* formed from English *price,* n. + *-less.*

prick *n.* Probably before 1200 *pricke* a point in space, in *Ancrene Riwle;* later, a pricking, sharp pain, goad (probably about 1225); developed from Old English *prica* point, puncture, particle (about 1000, in Ælfric's *Grammar*); cognate with Middle Low German and Middle Dutch *pricke* prick, and modern Dutch *prik.* **—v.** Probably before 1200 *priken* to pierce with a sharp point; also, cause agitation or distress, in *Ancrene Riwle;* developed from Old English *prician* to prick (about 1000, in Ælfric's *Homilies*); cognate with Middle Low German and Middle Dutch *pricken* to prick, modern Dutch *prikken,* and Middle High German *pfrecken;* all derived from Proto-Germanic **prikōjanan* and **prikjanan,* of unknown origin. **—pricker** *n.* (about 1325)

prickle *n.* thorn, spine. About 1303 *prykyl* (figurative) temptation, in Mannyng's *Handlyng Synne;* also *prykel* small, sharp point, goad or spike (before 1338, in Mannyng's *Chronicle of England*); developed from Old English (about 950) *pricel,* variant of *pricels* thing to prick with; cognate with Middle Low German *prēkel* prickle, and Middle Dutch *prikel* (modern Dutch *prikkel*). These words are all apparently derived from the Germanic source of Old English *prician* to PRICK; for suffix see -LE[1] (later meanings were influenced by the frequentative suffix -LE[3]). **—v.** feel a prickly sensation. 1500-20, in William Dunbar's *Poems;* developed in part from *prickle,* n., and probably in part as a diminutive or frequentative from *prick,* v. + -LE[3]. **—prickly** *adj.* 1578, full of prickles, thorny; formed from English *prickle* + *-y*[1]. The figurative sense of irritable or touchy is first recorded about 1862, in Emily Dickinson's *Poems.* The extended meaning of smarting, stinging, or tingling, is first found in 1836.

pride *n.* Probably before 1200 *prude, prute* high opinion of one's worth; also magnificence, glory, honor, in *Ancrene Riwle* and Layamon's *Chronicle of Britain;* about 1200 *pride;* developed from Old English (before 1000) *prȳde,* from *prūd* PROUD. **—v.** Probably about 1150 *pruden* to be proud, pride oneself, in *The Proverbs of Alfred;* later *priden* (about 1340), from the noun in Old English.

priest *n.* Before 1121 *preost,* in *Peterborough Chronicle;* later *prest* (probably before 1200), and *prieste* (about 1200); developed from Old English (695-96) *prēost.* Some etymologists have regarded Old English *prēost* as a shortening of a form represented by Old Frisian *prēstere* priest, Old Saxon *prēstar,* Middle Dutch and modern Dutch *priester,* and Old High German *prēstar* (modern German *Priester*), borrowed (perhaps through Vulgar Latin **prester* priest), from Late Latin *presbyter* presbyter, elder, from Greek *presbýteros* an elder, also as an adjective with the meaning of older, a comparative form of *présbys* old man, possibly originally meaning one who leads a herd of cattle (compare PASTOR), from a primitive compound **pres-* before, in advance, related to *pará* near, alongside of, and *pró* before, ahead; see FOR + the root *boûs, bôs* COW. This would make *priest* a doublet of PRESBYTER. However this derivation does not account for the *ēo* of Old English *prēost,* which is explained in an alternative etymology suggested by the German scholar Kluge. By assuming a correspondence of Old English *prēost* to Old High German *priast, prēst* it is possible to suppose that both the Old English and Old High German forms were borrowed through an intermediate form **prēvost* from Latin *praepositus* person placed in charge, from the past participle of *praepōnere* put in charge, place in front (*prae-* before + *pōnere* put, set; see POSITION). **—priestess** *n.* 1693, formed from English *priest* + *-ess.* **—priesthood** *n.* About 1378 *presthode,* in a version of *Piers Plowman;* developed from Old English *prēosthād* (before 899, in Alfred's translation of Bede's *Ecclesiastical History*); formed from *prēost* priest + *-hād* -hood.

prig *n.* person who is too particular, especially about speech or manners. 1753, in Smollett's *Count Fathom;* earlier, puritanical person (before 1704), and dandy, fop (1676); probably the same word as the old slang terms *prig* thief (1610), and *prig* tinker (1567), originally thieves' cant, of unknown origin. **—priggish** *adj.* overly precise. 1752, formed from English *prig* + *-ish*[1]. The word was used earlier to mean dandyish (1702), and is probably the same word used in the sense of thievish (before 1700).

prim *adj.* precise, neat, proper. 1709, Steele and Swift, in *The Tatler;* related to earlier *prim,* v., to assume a formal, precise, or demure manner (1684), and *prim,* n., a formal, precise, or haughty person (before 1700); perhaps from obsolete French *prim* thin, small, delicate, from Old French *prim* fine, delicate, from Latin *prīmus* first, finest, PRIME[1].

primacy *n.* superiority. About 1384, in the Wycliffe Bible; borrowed from Old French *primacie,* learned borrowing from Medieval Latin, and borrowed directly from Medieval Latin *primatia* office of a church primate, from Late Latin *prīmās* (genitive *prīmātis*) principal, chief, of first rank; see PRIMATE[1] bishop; for suffix see -CY.

prima donna (prē′mə don′ə *or* prim′ə don′ə) principal woman singer in an opera. 1812, in Southey's *Letters;* borrowing of Italian *prima donna* first lady, from Latin *prima,* feminine of *prīmus* first, see PRIME[1], adj.; and *domina* lady, see DAME. The figurative meaning "temperamental, self-important person" is first recorded in Charlotte Brontë's *Works* (1834).

prima facie (prē′mə fā′shēē *or* prē′mə fā′shē) at first view, before investigation. Probably before 1475, in *The Assembly of Gods;* borrowing of Latin *prīmā faciē,* ablative case of *prīma faciēs* first appearance (*prīma,* feminine of *prīmus* first, see PRIME[1], adj.; and *faciēs* form, see FACE).

primal *adj.* of early times, primeval. 1602, in Shakespeare's *Hamlet;* borrowed from Medieval Latin *primalis* primary, from Latin *prīmus* first; see PRIME[1], adj.; for suffix see -AL[1].

primary *adj.* Probably before 1425, in a translation of Chauliac's *Grande Chirurgie;* borrowed from Latin *prīmārius* of the first rank, chief, principal, excellent, from *prīmus* first; see PRIME[1], adj.; for suffix see -ARY. Doublet of PREMIER. **—n.** anything primary. Before 1721, from the adjective. The word *primary* in the meaning of a primary election (a preliminary election at which members of a political party choose candidates for office), is first recorded before 1861 in American English, shortened from earlier *primary election* (1835). **—primary color** any of a group of colors that can be combined to form any other color (1612). **—primary school** (1802).

primate[1] (prī′māt) *n.* superior bishop or archbishop. Probably before 1200 *primat,* in Layamon's *Chronicle of Britain;* borrowed from Old French *primat,* learned borrowing from Medieval Latin, and directly from Medieval Latin *primas* (genitive *primatis*) a church primate, from Late Latin *prīmās* of first rank, chief, principal, from *prīmus* first; see PRIME[1] chief, adj.; for suffix see -ATE[3]. In some early (and unrecorded) instances of the use of *primate* the word may have been extracted from Medieval Latin *archiprimatum* (about 793).

primate[2] *n.* member of the order of mammals that includes monkeys, apes, and humans. 1898, Anglicized singular of New Latin *Primates* the order name, coined by Linnaeus from Latin *prīmātēs,* plural of *prīmās* (genitive *prīmātis*) of first rank, chief; see PRIMATE[1]. Alternatively, the word may have been borrowed from earlier French *primate,* from New Latin *Primates.*

prime[1] *adj.* first in rank, chief. About 1385 *pryme* first in order of time, basic, in Usk's *The Testament of Love* borrowed from Old French *prime,* learned borrowing from Latin, and borrowed directly from Latin *prīmu* first, from pre-Italic **prīs-mos* (Indo-European **pri-is mo-s),* related to Old Latin *prī* before; see PRIOR[1]. The meaning of first in rank or importance, chief, principal is first recorded in Shakespeare's *The Tempest* (1610) and that of first in quality in 1628. **—prime ministe** 1694, head of a parliamentary government; earlier, the chief minister or servant of a sovereign (1655), and an important minister (1647). **—prime number** number divisible only by itself and one (1570). **—prime rate** lending rate banks charge their best customers (1958). **—prime time** peak listening or viewing period for broadcasting (1961).

prime[2] *n.* the best time, best condition. Probably before 1200 *prime* the first daylight canonical hour, in *Ancrene Riwle;* later, beginning of a period, course of events, etc. (1385, in Chaucer's *Canterbury Tales*); developed from Old English (about 961) *prīm;* borrowed from Medieval Latin *prima* the first service, and reinforced by Old French *prime;* both Medieval Latin and Old French forms from Late Latin *prīma,* from Latin *prīma hōra* first hour, in reference to the Roman day (*prīma,* feminine of *prīmus* first, see PRIME[1], adj.; and *hōra* HOUR*).* The meaning of the best or most vigorous stage or state is first recorded in English about 1536.

prime[3] *v.* to fill, charge, load. 1513, in a translation of Vergil's *Aeneid;* probably from PRIME[1], adj. (the usage developing from the fact that priming a pump, gun, etc., is a first step preliminary to the operation of some device). The meaning of cover (a surface) with a first coat of paint, etc., is first recorded in 1609. The figurative sense "furnish (a person) with information" is found in 1791.

primer[1] (prim′ər) *n.* beginner's book. 1378, prayer book, often used to teach children to read; borrowed from Medieval Latin *primarius,* noun use of Latin *prīmārius* of the first; see PRIMARY. The specific editions of such books for reading, marked by the inclusion of a section to teach the ABC's, is, according to the OED, first found in the 1530's; but from earliest times prayer books were used for the purpose of teaching reading.

primer[2] (prī′mər) *n.* 1497, a priming wire to keep the touchhole of a cannon open; formed from English *prime*[3], v. + *-er*[1]. The sense of a base coat of paint or other preparation applied to make the finish coat adhere well, is first recorded in 1688.

primeval (prīmē′vəl) *adj.* of the first ages. 1653, in Urquhart's translation of the works of Rabelais; formed in English from Latin *prīmaevus* early in life (*primus* first; see PRIME[1], adj. + *aevum* AGE*)* + English *-al*[1].

primitive *adj.* 1392 *premetif* of original or primary cause, in reference to disease; later *primitive* of early times (probably before 1425); borrowed from Old French *primitif* (feminine *primitive*), learned borrowing from Latin, and borrowed directly from Latin *prīmitīvus* first or earliest of its kind, from *prīmitus* at first, originally from *prīmus* first; see PRIME[1], adj.; for suffix see -IVE.

The meaning of very simple, crude, uncivilized, is first recorded in Evelyn's *Diary* (1685). By 1847 *primitive* was applied to the paintings of an early period, especially before the Renaissance, probably after French *primitif.*

—n. Before 1400, the first-born, original ancestor, spiritual ancestor; from the adjective. The meaning of a person living in a primitive society is first recorded in 1779. In art, the meaning of a painter of an early period, especially before the Renaissance, is found in 1892, and in the 1930's this usage was extended in American English to any early or modern painter lacking sophistication, a naive painter.

primogenitor *n.* first parent, earliest forefather. 1654, borrowed possibly through French *primogeniteur,* and directly from Late Latin *prīmogenitor* (Latin *prīmus* first, PRIME[1] + *genitor* begetter, from *genit-,* past participle stem of *gignere* beget; see KIN); for suffix see -OR[2]. Late Latin *prīmogenitor* was patterned on *prīmogenitus* first-born; see PRIMOGENITURE.

primogeniture *n.* condition of being first-born; inheritance by the first-born. 1602, borrowed probably through French *primogeniture,* and directly from Medieval Latin *primogenitura,* from Late Latin *prīmogenitus* first-born (Latin *prīmus* first, PRIME[1] + *genitus,* past participle of *gignere* beget; see KIN); for suffix see -URE. Late Latin *prīmo-genitus* rather curiously shows the connecting vowel *-o-* in deliberate imitation of Greek compounds (such as *prōtó-tokos* first-born; compare the Roman cognomen *Ahēno-barbus* "Bronze-beard").

primordial *adj.* existing at the very beginning, original, primeval. Before 1398, in Trevisa's translation of Bartholomew's *De Proprietatibus Rerum;* borrowed from Late Latin *prīmōrdiālis,* from Latin *primōrdium* the beginning (*prīmus* first, see PRIME[1], adj. + the stem of *ōrdīrī* to begin, related to *ōrdō* row or series, ORDER); for suffix see -AL[1].

primp *v.* dress or adorn in a prim manner. 1801, perhaps alteration of earlier *prim* to assume a formal, precise, or demure manner (1684); see PRIM.

primrose *n.* plant with flowers of various colors. 1373 *prymrose;* earlier as a surname *Primerose* (1365-66); borrowed from Old French *primerose,* and directly from Medieval Latin *prima rosa,* literally, first rose (*prīma* first, from Latin *prīma,* feminine of *prīmus,* see PRIME[1], adj.; and *rosa* rose, from Latin, see ROSE). The plant was so called because it comes early in the spring. **—adj.** pale-yellow (color of the common primrose of Europe). 1844, from the noun. The phrase *primrose path* path abounding in primroses, in the figurative sense of a path of pleasure, pleasant or easy way comes from Shakespeare's *Hamlet* (1602).

OED remarks on the obscurity of the name, and in particular on the fact that the primrose is not one of the very first flowers of spring nor is it much like a rose in habit or color, which leads to comparison with other flowers, such as the cowslip, itself showing up later than the primrose; however, comparison of the cowslip and its Latin name *primula vēris* (little firstling of spring) suggests that the conception of "first" is a correct assumption.

prince *n.* Probably before 1200, ruler of a principality, sovereign, chief, leader, great man, in *Ancrene Riwle;* earlier as a surname (1166); borrowing of Old French *prince,* from Latin *princeps* (genitive *principis*) first or principal person, leader, chief; originally, adj., first, chief, leading, original; literally, that takes first (*prīmus* first; see PRIME[1], adj. + *-ceps,* regular development of unaccented **-caps,* from the root of *capere* to take, hold; see CAPTIVE). **—princess** *n.* About 1370 *princesse,* in Chaucer's *An A.B.C.;* formed from English *prince* + *-ess,* and borrowed from Old French *princesse,* feminine of *prince;* for suffix see -ESS.

principal *adj.* About 1300, largest, most important, main, chief; borrowed from Old French *principal,* learned borrowing from Latin, and borrowed directly from Latin *principālis* first in importance, primary, from *princeps* (genitive *principis*) first, chief, leading, original; see PRINCE; for suffix see -AL[1]. **—n.** About 1300, chief, ruler; later, original sum of money on which interest is paid (1430-31); from the adjective in English, also in part influenced by if not borrowed from Old French, where the noun use was developed from the adjective, and Latin, in which the same process of development from the adjective took place. The meaning of chief person in some transaction or function may be recorded as early as 1300. The specific sense of a person in charge of a school is first recorded in 1827, in American English. See note for differentiation of spelling in English at PRINCIPLE.

principality *n.* About 1350 *principalte* government by a prince; later, kingdom, state or country ruled by a prince (probably about 1380); with the spelling *principalite* (about 1385); borrowed from Old French *principalité,* learned borrowing, and borrowed directly from Late Latin *principālitātem* (nominative *principālitās*) the first place, superiority, from Latin *principālis* first in importance, PRINCIPAL; for suffix see -ITY.

principle *n* About 1380 *princieple* law, rule, essential feature, trait, characteristic, basic assumption, in Chaucer's translation of Boethius' *De Consolatione Philosophiae;* also *principlis* origin, source, beginning, in the Wycliffe Bible (about 1382); alteration with *l* of Old French *principe,* learned borrowing from Latin *principium* first part, beginning, origination (plural *principia* first principles, fundamentals, elements), from *princeps* (genitive *principis*) first, chief, original; see PRINCE. The English spelling with *l* apparently developed on the learned analogy of such words as English *participle,* corresponding to Latin *participium.*

The extended meaning of basic rule, in the sense of right action, uprightness, rectitude, is first recorded in 1653, in a speech by Cromwell.

print *n.* About 1300 *prente* mark made by pressing, printed state or form; later *prient* (before 1325), and *prynt* (about 1340); borrowed from Old French *preinte, priente* impression, from feminine of *preint,* past participle of *preindre* to press, alteration (under influence of such verbs as *feindre* pretend) of earlier *prembre,* from Latin *premere* use force, PRESS[1]. Though cited for comparison, Dutch *prent* picture, print, is also borrowed from Old French. —**v.** About 1380 *prynten* to imprint, instill; also before 1382 *preenten* to mark, impress, stamp, and *prenten* (about 1385); from the Middle English noun. The meaning of produce (a book, etc.) by applying inked type to paper is first recorded in 1511, replacing Middle English *emprynten* (before 1474, in Caxton's *The Game and Play of Chess*), variant of *emprienten* IMPRINT. —**printer** *n.* 1504, person whose business is the printing of books, etc.; formed from English *print,* v. + *-er*[1]. —**printing press** (1588, though this sense is known in the word *press,* recorded in 1535)

prior[1] *adj.* preceding, earlier. 1714, borrowing of Latin *prior* former, earlier, superior, a comparative form of Old Latin *prī* before, related to Latin *prae* before; see PRE- and FOR. —**priority** *n.* condition of preceding, precedence. About 1385 *priorite,* borrowed from Old French *priorité,* learned borrowing from Medieval Latin, and borrowed directly from Medieval Latin *prioritatem* (nominative *prioritas*), from Latin *prior* prior; for suffix see -ITY. —**prioritize** *v.* give priority to, establish priorities for. 1972, American English; formed from *priority* + *-ize.*

prior[2] *n.* head of a priory of men. Old English (1093) *prior,* borrowing of Medieval Latin *prior* superior officer, prior, noun use of Latin *prior* superior, PRIOR[1]. The word was reinforced in Middle English (first recorded in 1123) by Old French *priur, prior, prieux,* as found in Middle English forms, such as *priur* (about 1230) and *priour* (about 1330). —**prioress** *n.* head of a priory of women. About 1300, borrowing of Old French *prioresse,* from Medieval Latin, and borrowed directly from Medieval Latin *priorissa,* from *prior* prior; for suffix see -ESS. —**priory** *n.* monastery or convent ranking below an abbey. About 1300 *priorie,* borrowed through Anglo-French *priorie,* from Medieval Latin *prioria,* from *prior* prior; for suffix see -Y[3].

prism *n.* geometric solid, often with three-sided ends. 1570, borrowed from Late Latin *prisma,* from Greek *prísma,* originally, thing sawed off, from *priéin* to saw, related to *prístis* sawfish, cognate with Albanian *prish* break up, spoil, from Indo-European **prīs-* crush (Pok.846). The meaning in optics of a transparent prism is first recorded in English in 1612. —**prismatic** *adj.* of a prism, especially a transparent prism. 1709, in Pope's *An Essay on Criticism,* shortened form of *prismatical* (1654); developed by influence of French *prismatique* (1647, in Pascal), formed from Greek *prîsma* (genitive *prísmatos*) + French *-ique* -ic.

prison *n.* Before 1112 *prisune* confinement; later, place for confinement (probably before 1200); borrowed from Old French *prison, prisoun, prisun* a prison, imprisonment (influenced in vocalism by *pris* taken, seized; see PRIZE[2]), from Latin *prēnsiōnem* (nominative *prēnsiō,* contracted from **prehēnsiō*) a seizing, arrest, from *prehēns-,* past participle stem of *prehendere* seize; see PREHENSILE. —**prisoner** *n.* Probably 1350-75 *prysner* one kept in prison, or one captured in war; later *prisoner* (before 1375); borrowed from Old French *prisonier,* from *prison* prison; for suffix see -ER[1]. After the 1400's *prisoner* replaced earlier *prison* (first recorded probably before 1200, in *Ancrene Riwle*).

prissy *adj. Informal.* too precise and fussy. 1895, in Joel Chandler Harris' *Mr. Rabbit at Home,* American English; perhaps humorous alteration of *precise* with suffix *-y*[1], or a blend of *prim* and *sissy.*

pristine (pris′tēn′) *adj.* as it was in its earliest time or state. 1534, borrowed perhaps from Middle French *pristin* (feminine *pristine*) or directly from Latin *pristinus* former, early, original, primitive, from *prīs-,* related to *prīmus* first; see PRIME[1], adj.; for suffix see -INE[1]. A weakened sense of untouched, not marred, unspoiled, pure, is first recorded in 1899 in the adverbial form *pristinely.*

prithee (priᴛʜ′ē) *interj. Archaic.* I pray thee; I ask you. 1577 *preythe,* contraction of *(I) pray thee.* The spelling *prithy* is recorded in 1728; *prithee* appeared in 1807.

privacy *n.* 1591 *privacie* a private matter, secret; later, condition of being withdrawn from others, seclusion (1598-1601, in Shakespeare's *Troylus and Cressida*); formed from English *private,* adj. + (*-cie*) *-cy.* The meaning of absence or avoidance of publicity or display is first recorded in Shakespeare's *The Merry Wives of Windsor* (about 1600).

private *adj.* Probably 1384 *pryvat* distinctive, set apart in Wycliffe's writings; borrowed from Latin *prīvātus* apart from the public life, deprived of office, belonging to an individual (also as a noun, a private friend or place); originally, past participle of *prīvāre* deprive free, release, from *prīvus* one's own, single, individual from Indo-European **preiwos* (Pok.812), and related to Old Latin *pri-* before in the sense of apart from the rest see PRIOR[1]; for suffix see -ATE[1]. Doublet of PRIVY. **—n.** 1599, a private citizen, in Shakespeare's *Henry V;* from the adjective. The meaning of a common soldier, not an officer, is first recorded in 1775, from the earlier phrase *private soldier* (1579). Other senses in English including that of a secret, private affairs, solitude or privacy, and *privates* in the sense of the genitals, developed from a borrowing (about 1350 to 1400) of Old French *privauté* privacy, a secret, formed as if from Latin **prīvālitās* from *prīvus* private, and were absorbed into the English formation *privity.* **—private detective** (1868, in Trollope's works) **—private enterprise** (1844) **—private school** (1830, American English)

privateer (prī′vətir′) *n.* privately owned armed ship holding a government commission to attack and capture enemy ships. 1664, formed from English *private,* adj. + *-eer,* probably patterned after *volunteer;* originally an informal term for *private man of war* (1646).

privation *n.* lack of comforts or necessities. Before 1398 *privacioun* condition of being deprived, lack, in Trevisa's translation of Bartholomew's *De Proprietatibus Rerum;* borrowed from Old French *privacion,* and directly from Latin *prīvātiōnem* (nominative *prīvātiō*) a taking away, from *prīvāre* deprive; see PRIVATE; for suffix see -ATION. The sense of a want of the comforts or necessities of life is first recorded in 1790.

privet (priv′it) *n.* shrub much used for hedges. 1542, in Elyot's *Dictionary;* of uncertain origin, though by some variously and unsuccessfully connected to the unexplained name *primprint* for privet (first recorded in 1548).

privilege *n.* 1137 *privilegie* a grant, commission, license, in *Peterborough Chronicle;* later *privilege* a distinction, power (probably before 1200, in *Ancrene Riwle*), and a special right, advantage, or favor (1340, in *Ayenbite of Inwyt*); borrowed from Old French *privilege,* learned borrowing from Latin, and borrowed directly from Latin *prīvilēgium* law applying to one individual, (later) privilege, prerogative (*prīvus* individual; see PRIVATE + *lēx,* genitive *lēgis* law; see LEGAL). It is probable that the early borrowing in *Peterborough Chronicle* was directly from Latin *prīvilēgium.* **—v.** Before 1325 *privelegen* grant a privilege to, implied in *priveleginge,* in *Cursor Mundi;* later *pryvylegen* (about 1390); from the noun in Middle English, and borrowed from Old French *privelegier, privilegier,* from the noun in Old French.

privity *n.* Probably before 1200 *privite* privacy, secrecy, in *Ancrene Riwle;* in part probably formed from *prive* special, personal, individual (probably before 1200, in *Ancrene Riwle*) + *-te* -ty; and in part borrowed from Old French *priveté* privacy, secrecy, formed as if from Latin **prīvitās,* from *prīvus* PRIVATE; for suffix see -ITY.

privy (priv′ē) *adj.* private. Probably before 1200 *prive* private, having private knowledge, personal, intimate, in *Ancrene Riwle;* later *pryvy* (1303, in Mannyng's *Handlyng Synne*); borrowed from Old French *privé,* from Latin *prīvātus* private; for suffix see -Y[3]. Doublet of PRIVATE. **—n.** Probably before 1200 *prive* toilet, private place, in *Ancrene Riwle;* later, confidant, intimate (about 1300), and with the spelling *privie* (about 1395); borrowed from Old French *privé,* from *privé,* adj., private. **—Privy Council** About 1300, private affairs, confidential advice, secret plan; later, a secret meeting (about 1383, in Wycliffe's writings), and group of advisors to a king (about 1390, in Chaucer's *Canterbury Tales*).

prize[1] *n.* reward. 1593, in Shakespeare's *3 Henry VI;* spelling alteration with differentiation of meaning of Middle English *pris* prize, value, reward; see PRICE. **—adj.** 1803, worthy of a prize; from the noun.

prize[2] *n.* thing taken or captured. 1596, in Spenser's *Faerie Queene;* spelling alteration with differentiation of meaning of Middle English *prise* (about 1250; see PRICE); borrowed from Old French *prise* a taking hold, grasp, seizure; from *pris* (influenced in vocalism by *pris* I seized, from Vulgar Latin **prēsī*), past participle of *prendre* to seize, take, from Latin *prēndere,* contracted from *prehendere;* see PREHENSILE.

prize[3] *v.* value highly. 1586, spelling alteration of Middle English *prisen* to prize, value (probably about 1380; see PRICE).

prize[4] *n.* lever, leverage. About 1400 *prise* instrument for prying, lever, borrowed from Old French *prise* a taking hold, grasp, seizure; see PRIZE[2]. The extended meaning of leverage is first recorded in 1835. **—v.** raise or move by force, pry. 1686, from the noun.

pro[1] *adv.* for (a proposition, opinion, etc.). 1572, abstracted from earlier *pro & contra* for and against (probably before 1430); borrowing of New Latin *pro et contra;* see PRO-[1]. **—n.** reason or argument for. Probably about 1400, borrowed from Latin *prō* for; see PRO-[1].

pro[2] *n., adj. Informal.* professional. 1866, in a magazine *Sporting Life;* shortened form of *professional,* n. As an adjective, *pro* appeared in 1932, also in sports use.

pro-[1] a prefix meaning forward, to the fore, forth, as in *proclaim, proceed, progress, propel;* beforehand, as in *provide;* taking care of, as in *procure;* in place of, as in *proconsul, pronoun;* and on the side of, favoring, as in *pro-American.* Borrowed from Latin *prō-,* from preposition *prō* on behalf of, in place of, before, FOR; see also PRO-[2].

pro-[2] a prefix meaning before, ahead, in front, earlier than, especially in words borrowed (often through Latin and French) from Greek, as in *prologue, prophet, prophylactic,* but also in words of later formation, as in *procephalic, proseminar, provirus.* Borrowed from Greek *pro-,* from preposition *pró* before, in front of; see FOR. The prefix is also embedded in words such as *problem* and *program* where the formation is not recognizably obvious, nor is the meaning of forward, forth.

The distinction between *pro-*[1] and *pro-*[2] weakened in Middle English, so that most users became unaware of any differences in sound or meaning, but curiously the distinction survives, in modern coinages and in the sense of favoring (as in *pro-union*) a use not known in Latin.

probable *adj.* Before 1387, likely or plausible, in Trevisa's translation of Higden's *Polychronicon;* borrowed from Old French *probable,* from Latin *probābilis* that may be proved, from *probāre* to try or test; see PROVE; for suffix see -ABLE.

The extended meaning of that may be reasonably expected to happen, likely to occur, is probably first recorded in English in Shakespeare's *Antony and Cleopatra* (1606).

—probability *n.* About 1443 *probabilite* the fact of being probable, likelihood; borrowed from Middle French *probabilité,* learned borrowing from Latin *probābilitātem* (nominative *probābilitās*) credibility, probability, from *probābilis* probable; for suffix see -ITY.

probate *n.* the official proving of a will as genuine. Before 1400 *probeyt* proof, evidence; later *probat* the official approval of a will's validity (about 1439); borrowed from Latin *probātum,* neuter of *probātus,* past participle of *probāre* to test, PROVE; for suffix see -ATE[1]. —**v.** 1570, to prove; later, prove the genuineness of a will (1792); from the noun.

probation *n.* About 1412 *probacioun* a testing or proving, in Hoccleve's *Regement of Princes;* borrowed from Middle French *probacion,* and directly from Latin *probātiōnem* (nominative *probātiō*) inspection, examination, from *probāre* to test, PROVE; for suffix see -ATION. The system by which criminals are put on *probation,* under the supervision of a *probation officer,* was introduced in the United States in the 1800's; these terms are first recorded about 1878.

probe *n.* Probably before 1425, instrument for exploring wounds, cavities, etc.; also, an examination, in a translation of Chauliac's *Grande Chirurgie;* borrowed from Medieval Latin *proba* examination, in Late Latin, test or proof, from Latin *probāre* to PROVE.

The meaning of an act of probing is first recorded in English in 1890; from the verb.
—**v.** 1649, search into, explore, investigate, in Lovelace's *Poems;* from the noun.

probity *n.* uprightness, honesty. About 1425 *probyte,* borrowed from Middle French *probité,* from Latin *probitātem* (nominative *probitās*) goodness, uprightness, honesty, from *probus* righteous, proper, worthy, good; see PROVE; for suffix see -ITY.

problem *n.* Before 1382 *probleme* puzzling question, riddle, in the Wycliffe Bible; borrowed from Old French *problème,* learned borrowing from Latin, and borrowed directly from Latin *problēma,* from Greek *próblēma* a problem, question proposed for solution; literally, a thing put forward, from *probállein* propose, put forward or before (*pro-* forward, pro-[2] + *bállein* to throw; see BALL[2] dancing party).

The meaning of a difficulty (in mathematics) to be solved is first recorded in English in 1570, and that of a doubtful or difficult question in 1594, both meanings developing directly from earlier senses of a scholarly or scientific question for investigation (before 1387), and that of a difficulty (1464).
—**problematic** *adj.* 1609, having the nature of a problem; shortened form of *problematical* (1570, of the nature of a problem; later, doubtful or uncertain, 1611); formed in English by influence of Middle French *problématique,* from Late Latin *problēmaticus,* from Greek *problēmatikós* pertaining to a problem, from *próblēma* (genitive *problḗmatos*) problem + English *-ical;* see also the suffix -IC.

proboscis (prōbos′is) *n.* elephant's trunk. 1609, borrowing of Latin *proboscis,* from Greek *proboskís* (genitive *proboskídos*) an elephant's trunk; literally, means for taking in food, from *pro-* forward, pro-[2] + *bóskein* to nourish, feed, *bóskesthai* graze, be fed, related to *botón* grazing animal, *botánē* pasture, and *su-bṓtēs* swineherd, cognate with Lithuanian *gúotas* herd, and *gaujà* flock, from Indo-European *gwō(u)-/gwəu-/gwə- (Pok.483).

Proboscis was applied to certain tubular and flexible parts of the mouth of insects as recorded in 1645 and to similar organs in other invertebrates in 1796, and in vertebrates such as the tapir (1849), and a particular kind of monkey in Borneo (1793). It was first used humorously of the human nose in 1630 by Ben Jonson.

It is interesting to note that the English plural form *proboscides* follows after the pattern of the French singular *proboscide* (1532, used by Rabelais), from Latin *proboscidem* (nominative *proboscis*) proboscis.

procaryote or **prokaryote** (prōkar′ēōt) *n.* cell without a visible nucleus. 1963, borrowed from French *procaryote* (*pro-* before, pro-[2] + *caryote* cell nucleus, from Greek *káryon* nut, kernel; see CAREEN). The forms *procaryote, prokaryote* were influenced by earlier *prokaryotic* (1957), and preceded by *prokaryon* (1957).

procedure *n.* 1611, in Cotgrave's *Dictionary;* borrowing of French *procédure* manner of proceeding, method, from Old French *proceder* to PROCEED; for suffix see -URE. —**procedural** *adj.* 1889, formed from English *procedure* + *-al*[1].

proceed (prōsēd′ *or* prəsēd′) *v.* About 1380 *proceden* spread, continue, come or result from, in Chaucer's *Canterbury Tales,* and a translation of Boethius' *De Consolatione Philosophiae;* borrowed from Old French *proceder,* learned borrowing from Latin, and borrowed directly from Latin *prōcēdere* go forward, advance, go on (*prō-* forward, pro-[1] + *cēdere* go; see CEDE). —**n. proceeds** (prō′sēdz) *pl.* money obtained from a transaction. 1665, in Pepys' *Diary,* plural of earlier *proceed* that which proceeds from something, outcome, profit (1643); from the verb. An earlier meaning of the act or manner or proceeding is first recorded in 1628. —**proceeding** *n.* 1517 *procedyng* action of going forward; later, what is done, action, conduct, often *proceedings,* pl. (1553); from *proceed,* v. + *-ing*[1].

process *n.* Before 1338 *processe* content of a discourse, subject matter, meaning, in Mannyng's *Chronicle of England;* later *proces* proceedings in a legal action (probably about 1350); borrowed from Old French *proces* journey, a going, and directly from Latin *prōcessus* (genitive *prōcessūs*) process, progress, from past participle stem of *prōcēdere* go forward; see PROCEED. The meaning of a set of actions or changes in a special order (as in *the process of making cloth from wool*), is first recorded in English in 1627. —**v.** 1532, start legal action against; borrowed from Middle French *processer* to prosecute, from Old French *proces,* n., process. The meaning of treat or prepare by a special method or process, is first recorded in English in 1884, from the noun. —**processor** *n.* that which processes something. 1909, formed from English *process* + *-or*[2]; found in such formations as *data processor* in 1958, *microprocessor* (a computer processing unit) in 1970, *word processor* about 1974, and *food processor* in 1977. —**process server** 1611, person who serves summonses, subpoenas, etc., in Shakespeare's *A Winter's Tale.*

procession *n.* 1103, act of marching or proceeding, in *Peterborough Chronicle;* borrowed from Old French *procession,* learned borrowing from Late Latin, and borrowed directly from Late Latin *prōcessiōnem* (nominative *prōcessiō*) ceremonial, especially religious procession, from Latin *prōcessiōnem* a marching onwards, from the stem of *prōcessum,* past participle of *prōcēdere* to PROCEED; for suffix see -SION. —**processional** *n.* 1440 *processyonal* book containing hymns, etc., for use in religious processions, in *Promptorium Parvulorum;* borrowed from Medieval Latin *processionale* a processional book, from neuter of *procession* *alis* of a procession, from Late Latin *prōcessiōnem* (nominative *prōcessiō*) ceremonial procession; for suffix see -AL[1]. The meaning of a hymn sung during a procession is first recorded in English in 1884. —*adj.*1611, of or belonging to a procession, in Cotgrave's *Dictionary;* formed from English *procession* + *-al*[1], probably by influence of French *processional* and Medieval Latin *processionalis.*

proclaim *v.* Before 1393 *proclamen* make known publicly, in Gower's *Confessio Amantis;* borrowed perhaps from Old French *proclamer,* and directly from Latin *prōclāmāre* to cry out or call out (*prō-* forth, pro-[1] + *clāmāre* cry out; see LOW[2], v.). The Middle English spelling *proclaymen* (about 1425) was influenced by *claymen* to CLAIM. —**proclamation** *n.* 1386 *proclamacion* act of proclaiming; borrowed from Old French *proclamacion,* and directly from Latin *prōclāmātiōnem* (nominative *prōclāmātiō*) a crying out or calling out, from *prōclāmāre* proclaim; for suffix see -ATION.

proclivity *n.* tendency, inclination. Before 1591, borrowed from Middle French *proclivité,* and directly from Latin *prōclīvitātem* (nominative *prōclīvitās*) a tendency, propensity, from *prōclīvis* prone to; literally, sloping or inclining (*prō-* forward, pro-[1] + *clīvus* a slope, related to *clīnāre* to bend; see LEAN[1] slant); for suffix see -ITY.

proconsul *n.* About 1384, governor or military commander of an ancient Roman province, in the Wycliffe Bible; borrowing of Latin *prōcōnsul,* from the phrase *prō cōnsule* (acting) in place of a consul (*prō* in place of, before, see FOR; and *cōnsule,* ablative case of *cōnsul* CONSUL).

procrastinate *v.* put off until later, delay. 1588, possibly, in part, a back formation from *procrastination* and, in part, borrowed from Latin *prōcrāstinātus,* past participle of *prōcrāstināre* put off till tomorrow, defer (*prō-* forward, pro-[1] + *crāstinus* belonging to tomorrow, from *crās* tomorrow, of uncertain origin); for suffix see -ATE[1]. An earlier verb form *procrastine* (before 1548) was borrowed from Middle French *procrastiner,* but did not survive. —**procrastination** *n.* Before 1548, borrowed probably from Middle French, and directly from Latin *prōcrāstinātiōnem* (nominative *prōcrāstinātiō*) a putting off, from *prōcrāstināre* put off; for suffix see -ATION.

procreate *v.* beget, generate, engender. 1536, developed from earlier *procreate,* adj., begotten, born; borrowed from Latin *prōcreātus,* past participle of *prōcreāre* bring forth (offspring), engender (*prō-* forth, pro-[1] + *creāre* CREATE); for suffix see -ATE[1]. It is also probable that in some instances *procreate,* v., is a back formation from earlier *procreation.* —**procreation** *n.* About 1395 *procreacioun* a begetting, generation, reproduction, in Chaucer's *Canterbury Tales;* borrowed from Old French *procreacion,* and directly from Latin *prōcreātiōnem* (nominative *prōcreātiō*) generation, from *prōcreāre* bring forth; for suffix see -ATION. —**procreative** *adj.* 1634, formed from English *procreate* + *-ive.*

procrustean or **Procrustean** (prōkrus′tēən) *adj.* aiming to produce uniformity or conformity by heavy-handed and arbitrary means. Before 1846, formed in allusion to *Procrustes* (robber in Greek legend who caused his captives to fit the length of his bed by stretching their bodies or cutting short their legs) + English *-an.* The name in Greek is *Prokroústēs,* literally, one who stretches, from *prokroúein* to beat or hammer out, stretch out (*pro-* out + *kroúein* to beat, cognate with Lithuanian *krùšti* pound up, and Old Icelandic *hrosti* mashed malt, from Indo-European **krous-/krus-,* Pok.622).

proctology (proktol′əjē) *n.* branch of medicine dealing with the rectum and anus. 1899, formed from Greek *prōktós* anus + English *-logy.* Greek *prōktós* derives from Indo-European **prōk̂tós,* and is cognate with Armenian *erastank'* buttocks, formed from **erast,* from the Indo-European variant *prək̂tó-* (Pok.846).

proctor *n.* official in a university or school. Probably before 1350 *proketour* defender of a realm; earlier as a surname (1301); also *proctour* agent, steward, officer (probably about 1378, in Wycliffe's writings), and *procutour* agent or legal advocate (about 1405); contraction of *procuratour* PROCURATOR. The meaning of a university official, especially one of two officials in charge of administration, the conferring of degrees, and the examinations leading to degrees, is first recorded in English in 1447, from the earlier English use of *procurator* (1410, from similar use of Latin *procurator,* 1248). —**v.** serve as a proctor. 1676, in Marvell's *Mr. Smirke;* from the noun.

procurator *n.* About 1300 *procuratour* steward, overseer, manager; earlier as a surname (1275); also, financial administrator of a college, church, or abbey (about 1410); borrowed from Old French *procuratour, procurator,* learned borrowing from Latin, and borrowed directly from Latin *prōcūrātor* manager, agent, deputy, administrator, from *prōcūrāre* manage; see PROCURE; for suffix see -OR[2].

procure *v.* Probably before 1300 *procouren, procuren* cause, bring about, recruit, entice, in *Arthour and Merlin;* borrowed from Old French *procurer,* learned borrowing from Late Latin, and borrowed directly from Late Latin *prōcūrāre,* in Latin, manage or take care of (*prō-* in behalf of, pro-[1] + *cūrāre* care for; see CURE, v.).

The meaning of obtain (women) for sexual purposes, act as procurer, is first recorded in Shakespeare's *Measure for Measure* (1603).

—**procurement** *n.* About 1303, the improper use of influence in the making of an appointment or a legal decision, connivance, inducement, in Mannyng's *Handlyng Synne;* later, act of procuring or bringing about (about 1400); borrowed from Old French *procurement,* from *procurer* procure, from Late Latin *prōcūrāre* procure; for suffix see -MENT. —**procurer** *n.* Before 1398 *procurour* an advocate or spokesman, in Gower's *Confessio Amantis;* later, an instigator, promoter, contriver (1451, in *Rolls of Parliament*); borrowed from Old French *procureur, procureor,* from *procurer* + *-eur, -er* and later refashioned from English *procure* + *-er*[1]. The meaning of one who procures women for sexual purposes, pander, is first recorded in 1632.

prod *v.* to poke or jab with something pointed. 1535, in the Coverdale Bible; possibly a variant of *brod* (also perhaps influenced by *poke*); developed from Middle English *brodden* to goad, urge, prod (probably about 1475), from earlier *brode,* n., pointed instrument, goad (before 1425); earlier, a nail (1295), from *brodd* a sprout or shoot (probably about 1200, in *The Ormulum*); borrowed from a Scandinavian source (compare Old Icelandic *broddr* shaft, spike, sprout; see BRAD).

Middle English *brodden* had an earlier meaning to sprout (probably about 1200), but if the verb *prod* developed from Middle English *brodden,* it was from the

meaning found about 1475 which had developed from the noun sense known before 1425.
—n. poke, thrust. 1787, in Grose's *A Provincial Glossary;* from the verb.

prodigal (prod′əgəl) *adj.* spending too much. 1500-20, in William Dunbar's *Poems;* possibly in part a back formation from earlier *prodigality,* and in part borrowed from Middle French *prodigal,* and from Late Latin **prōdigālis* wasteful, from Latin *prōdigus* wasteful, from *prōdigere* drive away, waste (*prōd-,* variant of *prō-* forth, pro-[1] + *agere* to drive; see AGENT); for suffix see -AL[1]. **—n.** prodigal person. 1596, in Shakespeare's *Merchant of Venice,* from the adjective, and replacing earlier *prodige* (recorded before 1470), borrowed from Old French *prodige,* from Latin *prōdigus.* **—prodigality** *n.* quality of being extravagant or prodigal. 1340 *prodigalite,* borrowed from Old French *prodigalité,* and directly from Late Latin *prōdigālitātem* (nominative *prōdigālitās*) wastefulness, from **prōdigālis* (found only in Medieval Latin), from Latin *prōdigus* wasteful; for suffix see -ITY.

prodigy (prod′əjē) *n.* marvel, wonder. Before 1470 *prodige* extraordinary sign, portent, omen; borrowed from Latin *prōdigium* (*prōd-,* variant of *prō-* forth, pro-[1] + *-igium,* of uncertain origin, previous explanations being unconvincing).

The meaning of something out of the ordinary, a marvel or wonder, is first recorded in 1626, and that of a person endowed with exceptional qualities, especially a child of precocious genius, in Evelyn's *Diary* (1658), the latter sense perhaps influenced by the meaning an extraordinary person (1639, in French).
—prodigious (prədij′əs) *adj.* marvelous, astounding. 1552, ominous, portentous, in Huloet's *Abecedarium Anglico-Latinum;* borrowed perhaps from Middle French *prodigieux,* and directly from Latin *prōdigiōsus* marvelous, from *prōdigium* prodigy; for suffix see -OUS. The meaning of marvelous, astounding, is first recorded in English in 1568, and that of very great, huge, in 1601, in Holland's translation of Pliny's *Natural History.*

produce (prədüs′) *v.* Probably before 1425 *producen* extend, proceed, in a translation of Chauliac's *Grande Chirurgie;* borrowed from Latin *prōdūcere* lead or bring forth, draw out (*prō-* forth, pro-[1] + *dūcere* to bring, lead; see TOW[1] pull).

The meaning of bring into existence, give rise to, is first recorded in 1513 (implied in *producer*), that of give birth to, beget, generate, in 1526, and that of yield, furnish, supply, in 1585. The meaning of compose (a work of art or literature) is found in 1638, but may have been known as early as 1585 in the sense of produce or perform a theatrical work.
—n. (prō′düs *or* prod′üs) what is produced, yield. 1695, from the verb.
—producer *n.* 1513, in a translation of Vergil's *Aeneid;* formed from English *produce,* v. + *-er*[1]. The specific meaning of a person who produces a play is first recorded in 1891, and was transferred to one who produces a motion picture (1911), and to one who produces a radio program (1933).

product *n.* About 1450, quantity produced by multiplying numbers; possibly influenced in use by earlier *product,* adj., produced (before 1398), but borrowed from Medieval Latin *productum,* from Latin *prōductum* something produced, noun use of neuter past participle of *prōdūcere* to bring forth, PRODUCE. The meaning of something produced by any action, operation, or work, is recorded in English in 1575.

production *n.* 1410 *produccioun* act of producing; later, product (about 1450); borrowed from Middle French *producïon,* and directly from Medieval Latin *productionem* (nominative *productio*), from Latin *prōductus,* past participle of *prōdūcere* bring forth; see PRODUCE; for suffix see -TION. **—productive** *adj.* 1612, tending to produce, creative, generative; borrowed from French *productif* (feminine *productive*), and directly from Medieval Latin *productivus,* from Latin *prōductus,* past participle of *prōdūcere* bring forth; for suffix see -IVE. **—productivity** *n.* 1809-10, power to produce, in writings of Coleridge; formed from English *productive* + *-ity.* The economic sense of the ratio of output to input is first recorded in 1899.

proem (prō′əm) *n.* introduction, preface. Before 1400 *proheme;* borrowing of Old French *proheme, prōeme,* from Latin *prooemium, prohoemium,* from Greek *prooímion, phroímion* musical prelude, overture, preamble (*pro-* before, pro-[2] + *oímē* song, strain, course of a song, of unknown origin). An earlier form *proemy* is found in Middle English before 1382, in the Wycliffe Bible, and is borrowed directly from Latin *prooemium.*

profane *adj.* not sacred, worldly. About 1450 *prophane,* borrowed from Middle French *profane, prophane,* learned borrowing from Latin, and borrowed directly from Latin *profānus* profane, not consecrated, from the phrase *prō fānō* not admitted into the temple (with the initiates); literally, out in front of the temple (*prō* before, see FOR; and *fānō,* ablative case of *fānum* temple; see FEAST). *Prophane* was the usual spelling in English until the mid 1700's. **—v.** treat (sacred things) with contempt. About 1384 *prophanen,* in the Wycliffe Bible; borrowed possibly from Old French *profaner,* and directly from Latin *profānāre* to desecrate, from *profānus,* adj., profane. **—profanity** *n.* 1607, quality or condition of being profane, profane word or act, borrowed from Late Latin *profānitās* profaneness, from Latin *profānus,* adj., profane; for suffix see -ITY. The synonym *profaneness* was more frequently used until 1800.

profess *v.* declare openly, avow, acknowledge. Before 1333 *professen* to take the vows of a religious order; in part a back formation from earlier *profession,* and probably, in part, borrowed from Old French *profes,* adj., that has taken a religious vow, from Medieval Latin *professus* professed, avowed, found in Latin *professus,* past participle of *profitērī* declare openly, lay claim to (*pro-* forth, pro-[1] + *fatērī* utter, declare, disclose; see CONFESS). The meaning of declare openly, acknowledge (1526) was a direct borrowing of the sense from Latin, and its extended meaning of lay claim to, allege, pretend to, is first recorded in English in Palsgrave's *Lesclarcissement* (1530).

profession *n.* Probably before 1200 *professiun* vow made by a person entering a religious order, in *Ancrene Riwle;* borrowed from Old French *profession,* from Latin *professiōnem* (nominative *professiō*) public declaration, avowal; also, avowed occupation, calling, from *professus,* past participle of *profitērī* declare openly, PROFESS; for suffix see -SION.

The meaning of an occupation requiring professed skill or qualified training is first recorded in English in 1541.
—professional *adj.* 1747-48, of or having to do with a

profession, formed from English *profession* + *-al*¹. An earlier isolated sense of pertaining to a religious order is found about 1420. —*n.* 1811, person who makes a profession of something that others do for pleasure, in Jane Austen's *Letters;* from the adjective. The general meaning of a person engaged in a profession is first recorded in Dickens' *Dombey and Son* (1848). —**professionalism** *n.* professional quality or conduct. 1856, formed from English *professional* + *-ism.*

professor *n.* Before 1387 *professour* teacher of a branch of knowledge, in Trevisa's translation of Higden's *Polychronicon;* borrowed from Old French *professeur,* and directly from Latin *professor* person who professes to be expert in some art or science, teacher of the highest rank, from *profitērī* lay claim to, PROFESS; for suffix see -OR². —**professorial** *adj.* of a professor; characteristic of professors. 1713, in writings of Richard Bentley; formed from English *professor* + *-ial.*

proffer *v.* offer for acceptance. Probably before 1300 *proferen* to offer, deliver, in *Arthour and Merlin;* borrowed through Anglo-French *profrier,* and directly from Old French *poroffrir, profrir* (*por-* forth, from Latin *prō-* pro-¹ + *offrir* to offer, from Latin *offerre* to OFFER). —**n.** an offer made. Before 1375 *profer* a petition, request; 1380, an offer; borrowed through Anglo-French *profre,* from *proffrir* to proffer.

proficient *adj.* skilled, expert. About 1590, in Marlowe's *Doctor Faustus;* possibly, in part, a back formation from *proficiency,* and borrowed perhaps through Old French *proficient,* from Latin *prōficientem* (nominative *prōficiēns*), present participle of *prōficere* accomplish, make progress, profit, be useful (*prō* forward, pro-¹ + the root of *facere* to make, perform, DO¹); for suffix see -ENT. —**proficiency** *n.* 1544, progress toward a high degree of skill, in Coverdale's correspondence; usually said to be formed from English *proficient* + *-cy,* but in view of the later date of *proficient,* probably formed from Latin *prōficientem* (nominative *prōficiēns*), present participle of *prōficere* + English *-cy;* see -ENCY. The meaning of skill, expertness, is first recorded before 1639.

profile *n.* 1656, sideview or outline, especially of a face, in Blount's *Glossographia;* borrowed from Italian *profilo,* from *profilare* to draw in outline; formed from *pro-* forth (from Latin *pro-;* see PRO-¹) + *filare* draw out, spin (from Late Latin *filāre;* see FILE² line).

The extended meaning of a biographical sketch or character description is first recorded in English before 1734. Since the early 1900's *profile* has been used especially in science and technology to mean a diagrammatic representation of data about some natural phenomenon.

—**v.** 1715, draw a profile of; borrowed from Italian *profilare* draw in outline. The meaning of write a biographical or character sketch of was first recorded in 1948, in American English.

profit *n.* 1263 *profit* income, earning, revenue, proceeds; borrowed from Old French *profit* advantage, profit, from Latin *prōfectus* (genitive *prōfectūs*) profit, progress, advance, from past participle of *prōficere* advance, make progress, profit, be useful; see PROFICIENT. —**v.** About 1330, *profiten* to advance, benefit, gain, from the noun in Middle English, and borrowed from Old French *profiter,* from *profit,* n. —**profitable** *adj.* Probably about 1300, yielding profit; borrowed from Old French *profitable,* from *profit,* n., advantage (also found in Anglo-Latin *profitabilis*); for suffix see -ABLE. —**profiteer** *n.* one who makes an unfair profit. 1912, formed from English *profit,* n. + *-eer.* —*v.* be a profiteer. 1916, from the noun (but implied in an earlier perhaps isolated instance of *profiteering,* 1814). The word was made popular during World War I in reference to armament makers, such as the Krupps. —**profit sharing** sharing of profits between employers and employees (1881).

profligate (prof'ləgit) *adj.* given to vice, licentious or immoral. 1647, borrowed from Latin *prōflīgātus* immoral, ruined; also, overthrown (see below), past participle of *prōflīgāre* to cast down, defeat, ruin (*prō-* down, forth, pro-¹ + *-flīgāre,* an intensive form of *flīgere* to strike, dash; see CONFLICT; for suffix see -ATE¹. The word also appears earlier with the now obsolete meaning of overthrown or routed (1535), borrowed also from Latin *prōflīgātus* overthrown, ruined. —**n.** profligate person. 1709, in Swift's *Works;* from the adjective. —**profligacy** *n.* condition of being profligate. 1738, formed from English *profligate* + *-cy.*

profound *adj.* About 1300, characterized by depth of thought and knowledge, very learned; borrowed from Old French *profond* deep, and directly from Latin *profundus* deep, bottomless, vast (*pro-* forth, pro-¹ + *fundus* BOTTOM). The meaning of very deep (as a physical or material quality), of great depth, is first recorded in Middle English about 1408 (implied in adverb *profoundely*). —**profundity** *n.* Probably before 1425 *profundite* bottom or depth of the ocean, in a translation of Higden's *Polychronicon;* borrowed from Old French *profundité,* learned borrowing from Late Latin, and borrowed directly from Late Latin *profunditātem* (nominative *profunditās*) depth, immensity, from Latin *profundus* deep, vast; for suffix see -ITY. The meaning of depth of intellect, insight, source of the mystery of scripture, is first recorded before 1500, from the original use of the adjective, and the meaning of depth (in the physical sense) is found in 1471.

profuse *adj.* very abundant. Probably before 1425, lavish, extravagant, in a translation of Higden's *Polychronicon;* borrowed from Latin *profūsus* poured forth, spread out, profuse, from past participle of *profundere* pour forth, (*pro-* forth, pro-¹ + *fundere* to pour; see FOUND² cast). The meaning of very abundant, bountiful, is first recorded in English before 1610. —**profusion** *n.* great abundance. 1545, lavish and wasteful expenditure; borrowed from Middle French *profusion,* from Latin *profūsiōnem* (nominative *profūsiō*) a pouring out, from *profūsus,* past participle of *profundere* pour forth; for suffix see -SION. The meaning of great abundance is first recorded in English in 1705.

progenitor (prōjen'ətər) *n.* forefather, ancestor. About 1384 *progenitour,* in the Wycliffe Bible; borrowed from Old French *progeniteur,* and directly from Latin *prōgenitor* ancestor, from *prōgenit-,* past participle stem of *prōgignere* beget (*pro-* forth, pro-¹ + *gignere* to produce, beget; see KIN); for suffix see -OR².

progeny (proj'ənē) *n.* offspring, descendants. Before 1325 *progeni,* in *Cursor Mundi;* borrowed from Old French *progenïe,* learned borrowing from Latin, and directly from Latin *prōgeniēs* descent, offspring, from *prōgignere* beget; see PROGENITOR.

prognosis (prognō'sis) *n.* forecast of the probable course of a disease. 1655, borrowed from Late Latin *prognōsis,* from Greek *prógnōsis,* from *progignṓskein* come to know beforehand (*pro-* before, pro-² + *gignṓskein* come to KNOW). The general meaning of prognostication or forecast is first recorded in Kersey's edition of Phillips' *Dictionary* (1706).

prognosticate *v.* predict, forecast. Probably before 1425 *pronosticaten,* in a translation of Chauliac's *Grande Chirurgie;* in part a back formation from earlier Middle English *pronostication,* and in part borrowed from Medieval Latin *prognosticatus, pronosticatus,* past participle of *prognosticare, *pronosticare,* from Latin *prognōstica* signs by which one may know what sort of weather is coming, from the neuter plural of Greek *prognōstikós* foreknowing, from *progignṓskein* come to know beforehand; see PROGNOSIS; for suffix see -ATE[1]. **—prognostication** *n.* 1392 *pronosticacioun* a symptom, something that foretells death; borrowed from Old French *pronosticacïon,* and directly from Medieval Latin *prognosticationem, *pronosticationem* (nominative *prognosticatio, *pronosticatio*), from *prognosticare, *pronosticare* foretell; for suffix see -ATION. The spelling *prognostication* (with *g*) is first recorded in Middle English about 1450 in imitation of the Latin and Greek.

program *n.* 1633, public notice; borrowed from Late Latin *programma* proclamation, edict, from Greek *prógramma* a written public notice, from *prográphein* write publicly (*pro-* forth, pro-[2] + *gráphein* to write; see CARVE).

According to the OED *program* was restricted to Scottish use until the early 1800's, when it was reborrowed from French *programme,* in the sense of a descriptive notice or listing of items or events. The French spelling is now the usual form in British English. The general meaning of a list of pieces to be performed at a musical concert, or playbill for a theatrical event, is first recorded in 1805, and that of any definite plan or scheme of activity, in Carlyle's *The French Revolution* (1837). The meaning of a performance broadcast over the radio is found as early as 1923. The computer use of *program* for a set of coded instructions has been recorded since 1945.

—v. arrange a program. 1896, from the noun. The meaning of work out a set of coded instructions for (a computer) is first recorded in 1945.

—programmatic *adj.* 1896, formed in English from Greek *prógramma* (genitive *prográmmatos*) program + English suffix *-ic.* **—programmer** *n.* 1890, one who draws up a program of events; later, person who programs a computer (1948); formed from English *program,* v. + *-er*[1].

progress (prog′res) *n.* Probably before 1425 *progresse* course or process (of action, events, narrative, etc.), forward movement, in a translation of Higden's *Polychronicon;* borrowed from Latin *prōgressus* (genitive *prōgressūs*), from past participle of *prōgredī* go forward (*prō-* forward, pro-[1] + *gradī* to step, walk; see GRADE).

The meaning of a royal or state journey is first recorded probably about 1450, and that of a military march or expedition before 1460. The figurative sense of advance, growth, development, is first recorded in 1603.

—v. (prəgres′) About 1590, to journey or travel; from the noun. The meaning of proceed or advance is first recorded in Shakespeare's *King John* (1595), and that of the figurative sense of make progress or develop, in Ben Jonson's *The Alchemist* (1610).

—progression *n.* About 1380 *progressioun* action of moving from one state of an operation or development to another, in Chaucer's translation of Boethius' *De Consolatione Philosophiae;* borrowed from Old French *progressïon,* and directly from Latin *prōgressiōnem* (nominative *prōgressiō*) a going forward, from *prōgressus,* past participle of *prōgredī* go forward; for suffix see -ION. **—progressive** *adj.* 1607-12, making progress, in Bacon's *Essays;* borrowed from French *progressif* (feminine *progressive*), formed as if from Latin **prōgressīvus,* from *prōgressus,* past participle of *prōgredī* go forward; for suffix see -IVE. *Progressive* in the sense of favoring or advocating efforts toward progress or reform, especially in political and social matters, is first recorded in 1884, perhaps after earlier use in French (about 1830). The meaning in the field of education, that of aiming to develop the abilities and interests of pupils rather than fitting them to a given curriculum, is first recorded in 1839 but was not widely used until popularized by writers discussing the educational philosophy of the American educator John Dewey and others in the 1920's. *—n.* 1865, one who favors or advocates progress or reforms, especially in political and social matters, from the adjective.

prohibit *v.* Probably before 1425 *prohibiten,* in a translation of Higden's *Polychronicon;* borrowed from Latin *prohibitus,* past participle of *prohibēre* hold back, forbid, prevent (*prō-* away, forth, pro-[1] + *habēre* to hold; see HABIT). It is also possible that *prohibit* is, in some instances, a back formation from *prohibition.* **—prohibition** *n.* About 1385 *prohibicion* act of prohibiting, in Usk's *The Testament of Love;* borrowed from Old French *prohibicïon,* and directly from Latin *prohibitiōnem* (nominative *prohibitiō*) a hindering or forbidding, from *prohibēre* hold back; for suffix see -TION. *Prohibition* in the sense of law or laws against making and selling alcoholic liquors for general use has been recorded since 1851 in American English, though this sense came into widespread use during the period of national prohibition in the U.S. (1920-33) under the Volstead Act. **—prohibitive** *adj.* 1602, that prohibits; borrowed from French *prohibitif* (feminine *prohibitive*), from Late Latin *prohibitīvus,* from Latin *prohibitus,* past participle of *prohibēre* hold back; for suffix see -IVE. The sense of tending to prohibit or prevent the use of something (said of a high tax or price), is first recorded in modern English in 1886, but this sense is a revival of an older use of Middle English "preventive against" (1425, in a translation of Chauliac's *Grande Chirurgie,* borrowed from Medieval Latin *prohibitivus,* from Late Latin).

project (proj′ekt) *n.* Probably before 1400 *projecte* plan, draft, scheme; borrowed from Latin *prōjectum* something thrown forth (in Medieval Latin, a projecting roof), noun use of neuter of *prōjectus,* past participle of *prōicere* stretch out, throw forth (*prō-* forward, pro-[1] + *-icere,* combining form of *jacere* to throw; see JET[1] stream).

The meaning in the field of education of a special assignment carried out by a student or group of students, is first recorded in 1916. The meaning of a group of low-rent apartment buildings first appeared about 1958 in American English, as a shortened form of earlier *housing project* (1930's).

—v. (prəjekt′) About 1477 *projecten* to plan, devise, in Caxton's translation of *The History of Jason;* developed from earlier *project,* adj., extended, inclined, disposed (probably before 1425); borrowed from Latin *prōjectus,* past participle of *prōicere.* The meaning of throw, hurl, shoot, is first recorded in Spenser's *Faerie Queene* (1596), and that of stick out, protrude, in 1718. The meaning of throw or cause light or shadow to fall on a surface (1664), was the basis for the modern meaning of cause (a photographic image or projection of some object) to appear on a screen (1865). The meaning in psychology of transfer (an emotion, sensation, or other subjective state of mind) to an external person or thing, is first recorded in English in 1923.

—projection *n.* 1477 *projeccion* the conversion of a baser metal into gold, in Thomas Norton's *Ordinal of Alchemy;* borrowed from Latin; later, representation on a plane of any spherical surface, especially in constructing maps (1557); borrowed probably from Middle French *projection,* and directly from Latin *prōjectiōnem* (nominative *prōjectiō*) a throwing forward, extension, projection, from past participle of *prōicere* to PROJECT; for suffix see -TION. The sense of an act of projecting is first recorded in 1599. **—projector** *n.* 1596, one who forms a project; formed from English *project,* v. + *-or*[2]. The meaning of an apparatus for projecting an image on a screen is first recorded in 1884.

projectile (prəjek'təl) *n.* object that can be thrown or shot. 1665 *projectil,* borrowed from New Latin *projectilis,* from Latin *prōjectus,* past participle of *prōicere* throw forth; see PROJECT.

proletarian *n.* member of the lowest economic or social class in a community. 1658, formed in English from Latin *prōlētārius* a Roman citizen of the lowest class (under the constitution of Servius Tullius, one too poor to serve the state except by furnishing it with his offspring) + English *-an.* Latin *prōlētārius* derives from *prōlēs* offspring, progeny (*prō-* forth, pro-[1] + *-olēs,* as in *sub-olēs* offspring; related to *alere* nourish; see OLD). **—adj.** of or belonging to the lowest economic or social class. 1663, in Samuel Butler's *Hudibras;* formed in English from Latin *prōlētārius* of or belonging to the lowest class of Roman citizens + English *-an,* and in some instances probably formed in English with *-ian* as an adjective to earlier *proletary* (1579). *Proletarian* in both noun and adjective eventually replaced earlier *proletary,* n. (1579), and adj. (1609). **—proletariat** (prō'lətãr'ēət) *n.* 1853, the lowest economic or social class in a community; borrowed from French *prolétariat,* from Latin *prōlētārius* a Roman citizen of the lowest class + French *-at* -ate[3]. By 1856 *proletariat* was applied specifically to the laboring or working classes of Europe that were characterized as having no reserve of capital but depended on wages for subsistence. The term had been used in German by Marx and Engels in the *Communist Manifesto* (1848) and eventually became associated with the vocabulary of Communism.

proliferation *n.* reproduction, spreading, propagation. 1867, reproduction by budding or division; borrowing of French *prolifération,* from *prolifère* producing offspring (*proli-,* from Latin *prōlēs* offspring; see PROLETARIAN + *-fère,* from Latin *ferre* carry, BEAR[2]); for suffix see -ATION. **—proliferate** *v.* grow or produce by proliferation. 1873, back formation from *proliferation;* for suffix see -ATE[1].

prolific *adj.* productive, fertile. 1650, borrowed from French *prolifique;* from Medieval Latin *prolificus* (from Latin *prōlēs* offspring; see PROLETARIAN + the root of *facere* make) and perhaps in some instances a back formation from *prolification* (before 1393, in Gower's *Confessio Amantis*), borrowed from Medieval Latin *prolificationem* (nominative *prolificatio*), from *prolificare* to fertilize, make prolific; from *prolificus* prolific; see PROLIFERATION; for suffix see -ATION.

prolix (prō'liks) *adj.* lengthy, long-winded, wordy. Before 1420, in Lydgate's *Troy Book;* borrowed through Middle French *prolixe,* and directly from Latin *prōlixus,* literally, poured out (*prō-* forth, pro-[1] + **lix-,* related to *liquēre* to flow, be fluid; see LIQUID). It is also possible that *prolix* is in some instances a back formation from *prolixity.* **—prolixity** *n.* quality of being *prolix.* About 1385 *prolixitee,* in Chaucer's *Troilus and Criseyde;* borrowed from Old French *prolixité,* learned borrowing from Latin *prōlixitātem* (nominative *prōlixitās*), from *prōlixus* prolix; for suffix see -ITY.

prologue *n.* introduction to a play, speech, etc. Before 1325 *prolog,* in *Cursor Mundi;* later *prolog, prologe* (about 1385); borrowed from Old French *prologue, prologe,* learned borrowing from Latin, and borrowed directly from Latin *prologus,* from Greek *prólogos* prologue of a play, speaker of a prologue (*pro-* before, pro-[2] + *lógos* speech, from *légein* speak; see LEGEND). The modern spelling *prologue* is first recorded about 1405 by influence of the French spelling, after the Latin.

prolong *v.* make last longer, extend. Probably about 1408 *prolongen,* in Lydgate's *Reson and Sensuallyte;* probably in part a back formation from *prolongation,* and also borrowed from Middle French *prolonguer,* and directly from Late Latin *prōlongāre* prolong, extend (Latin *prō-* forth, pro-[1] + *longus* LONG[1], adj.). **—prolongation** *n.* a prolonging. 1392 *prolongacioun* extension, length; borrowed from Old French *prolongation,* formed from Late Latin *prōlongāre* prolong, extend + Old French *-ation.* The sense of a lengthening of duration is recorded in Middle English in a translation of Chauliac's *Grande Chirurgie* (probably before 1425).

prom *n. Informal.* dance given by a school. 1894, American English; shortened form of earlier *promenade,* in the same sense (1887).

promenade (prom'ənäd') *n.* a walk for pleasure or display. 1567, borrowing of Middle French *promenade,* from *promener* take for a walk, from Latin *prōmināre* drive (a beast) on (*prō-* forth, forward, pro-[1] + *mināre* drive with shouts; see AMENABLE); for suffix see -ADE. The meaning of a public place for social promenades is first recorded in 1648. The transferred sense of a dance given by a school, prom, is first recorded in 1887 in American English. **—v.** take a promenade, parade. 1588 (implied in *promenading*); from the noun.

promethium (prəmē'thēəm) *n.* radioactive metallic chemical element. 1948, New Latin, formed in allusion to *Prometheus* (from Greek *Promētheús* the Titan in Greek mythology who stole fire from heaven and taught mankind its use) + *-ium,* chemical suffix. *Promethium* was coined by the American chemists J.A. Marinsky, L.E. Glendenin, and C.D. Coryell, who first isolated this element in 1945, and associated that with *Prometheus'* deed because the element was a product of mankind's new-found ability to harness the energy of nuclear fission.

prominent *adj.* Probably 1440 *promynent* projecting or jutting out, in a translation of Palladius' *De Re Rustica;* borrowed from Latin *prōminentem* (nominative *prōminēns*), present participle of *prōminēre* jut or stand our (*prō-* forward, pro-[1] + *-minēre,* related to *mōns* MOUNT[2] hill); for suffix see -ENT. The extended meaning of conspicuous or striking is first recorded in 1759, and that of notable, distinguished, leading, in 1849. **—prominence** *n.* condition of being prominent. 1598, projection or protuberance, in Florio's *A World of Words;* borrowed from obsolete French *prominence,* from Latin *prōminentia* a jutting out, from *prōminentem* (nominative *prōminēns*) prominent; for suffix see -ENCE. The meaning of distinction, notoriety, conspicuousness, is first recorded in 1828.

promiscuous (prəmis′kyüəs) *adj.* confusedly mingled; indiscriminate. 1603, consisting of a disorderly mixture of persons or things; borrowed from Latin *prōmiscuus* mixed (*prō-* forward, pro-[1] + *miscēre* to MIX); for suffix see -OUS. The meaning of confusedly mingled, indiscriminate, is first recorded in Bacon's *Of the Advancement of Learning* (1605); the now common meaning of indiscriminate in sexual relations is first recorded in 1900, probably as a back formation of meaning from its earlier use in *promiscuity.* **—promiscuity** *n.* indiscriminate mingling. Before 1849, in Poe's writings; borrowed from French *promiscuité,* formed in French from Latin *prōmiscuus* promiscuous + French *-ité* -ity. Reference to promiscuous sexual relations is first recorded in 1865.

promise *n.* About 1400, Middle English *promys* a pledge, vow, in a version of Maundeville's *Travels;* borrowed from Latin *prōmissum* a promise, noun use of neuter past participle of *prōmittere* send forth, foretell, promise (*prō-* before, pro-[1] + *mittere* to put, send; see MISSION). A coexisting form *promisse* (before 1410) was borrowed from Old French *promise, promesse,* from Medieval Latin *promissa* a promise, from Latin *prōmissum.* **—v.** Probably before 1400 *promicen* make a promise; later *promysen* (probably before 1425); probably from the noun in Middle English. **—promissory** *adj.* conveying or implying a promise. About 1445 *promissorye;* borrowed from Medieval Latin *promissorius,* from Latin *prōmissor* a promiser, from *prōmittere* send forth, promise; for suffix see -ORY. **—promising** *adj.* likely to turn out well. 1601, in Shakespeare's *All's Well That Ends Well,* from *promise,* v. + *-ing*[2].

promo (prō′mō) *n. Informal.* advertising, publicity, or other promotional presentation. 1962, American English; shortened form of earlier *promotion,* in the same sense (1925).

promontory (prom′əntôr′ē) *n.* point of land which juts out from a coast; headland. 1548, borrowed perhaps from Middle French *promontoire,* and directly from Medieval Latin *promontorium,* alteration (influenced by Latin *mōns* MOUNT[2] hill) of Latin *prōmunturium* mountain ridge, headland, probably related to *prōminēre* jut out; see PROMINENT; for suffix see -ORY.

promote *v.* Before 1387 *promoten* to advance, raise to a higher rank or position, in Trevisa's translation of Higden's *Polychronicon;* borrowed from Old French *promoter,* and directly from Latin *prōmōtus,* past participle of *prōmovēre* move forward, advance (*prō-* forward, pro-[1] + *movēre* to MOVE). The extended meaning of further the growth, development, or progress of anything, is first recorded in Middle English before 1400.

Latin *prōmovēre* was also borrowed into Middle English in *promoven* (probably about 1400) in the sense of encourage someone in a certain course of action, promote; but the word gradually became obsolete in the 1600's and even in its derivative forms, such as *promovent,* is not recorded after 1877.

—promoter *n.* 1384, one who furthers the interests of another, supporter; borrowed from Old French *promoteur, promotor,* and directly from Medieval Latin *promotor,* from Latin *prōmovēre* to PROMOTE. **—promotion** *n.* Before 1400 *promocione* advancement in rank or position; later *promotion* (1429); borrowed from Old French *promocïon,* and directly from Latin *prōmōtiōnem* (nominative *prōmōtiō*) advancement, from *prōmovēre* advance; for suffix see -TION. The meaning of act of furthering or helping forward, furtherance, encouragement, is first recorded about 1412; and the specific use in the sense of a furthering of sales by advertising and publicity, is first recorded in 1925. **—promotional** *adj.* 1922, of promotion; formed from English *promotion* + *-al*[1]. The specific sense of relating to the promotion or advertising of commercial products, is first recorded in 1926.

prompt *adj.* About 1415, ready, prepared, eager; probably in part from the verb in Middle English and in part borrowed from Old French *prompt,* and directly from Latin *prōmptus* visible, at hand, ready, quick, from past participle of *prōmere* bring forth, bring to light (*prō-* forward, pro-[1] + *emere,* originally, take; see REDEEM). Doublet of PRONTO. **—v.** About 1340 *promtten* urge or incite to action; later *prompten* (1440, probably normalized by influence of *prompt,* adj., and Latin *prōmptus*); probably borrowed from Medieval Latin **promptare,* from Latin *prōmptus* prompt. The specific meaning of remind (a speaker, learner, actor) of the words or actions needed is recorded in Middle English in 1428, and that of inspire, give rise to (thought, action, etc.), in 1602. **—prompter** *n.* 1440 *promptator;* later *prompter* (before 1548). The specific sense of one who tells actors what to say when they forget a word or line, is first recorded in Shakespeare's *Othello* (1602).

promulgate (prōmul′gāt) *v.* proclaim formally. 1530, in Palsgrave's *Lesclarcissement;* perhaps, in part, developed from *promulgate,* adj., set forth; borrowed from Latin *prōmulgātus;* and borrowed directly from Latin *prōmulgātus,* past participle of *prōmulgāre* make publicly known, perhaps altered from *prōvulgāre* in the same sense (*prō-* forth, pro-[1] + *vulgāre* make public, publish; see VULGATE); for suffix see -ATE[1]. **—promulgation** *n.* 1604, in Cawdrey's *A Table Alphabeticall;* borrowed from French *promulgation,* learned borrowing from Latin *prōmulgātiōnem* (nominative *prōmulgātiō*) proclamation, publication, from *prōmulgāre* make known, publish; for suffix see -ATION.

prone *adj.* inclined, liable. 1408 *proone* inclined, disposed to, in the Wycliffe Bible; borrowed from Latin *prōnus* bent forward, inclined to, perhaps from a lost adverb **prō-ne* forward, in front, from *prō-* forward, PRO-[1]; for the Latin ending *-nus* compare Latin *īnfernus* situated below (INFERNAL) and *externus* outside (EXTERNAL). The meaning in English of having the front part downward, lying face down, is first recorded in 1578.

prong *n.* pointed end of a fork, antler, etc. Probably about 1425 *prange* pointed instrument; later *pronge* agony, pain (1440); borrowed from Anglo-Latin *pronga* prong, pointed tool; of uncertain origin, perhaps related to Middle Low German *prange* stick, restraining device, *prangen* to press, pinch, Middle Dutch *pranghen* (modern Dutch *prangen*), Middle High German *pfrengen,* and Gothic *anaprangan* oppress, cognate with Lettish *brankti* lying close, from Indo-European *bronk- (Pok.103). **—pronghorn** *n.* hooved mammal of western North America. 1826, American English; shortened form of *prong-horned antelope* (before 1815, American English).

pronominal *adj.* of or having to do with pronouns. 1680, borrowed from Late Latin *prōnōminālis* belonging to a pronoun, from Latin *prōnōmen* (genitive *prōnōminis*) PRONOUN; for suffix see -AL[1].

pronoun *n. Grammar.* word used to take the place of a noun. About 1450, in *Battlefield Grammar;* formed from English *pro-*[1] + *noun,* modeled on Middle French *pronom,* learned borrowing from Latin, and modeled directly on Latin *prōnōmen* (*prō-* in place of, pro-[1] + *nōmen* noun, NAME).

pronounce *v.* Before 1338 *pronuncen* declare, decree, in Mannyng's *Chronicle of England;* later *pronouncen* (about 1350), and utter or articulate, speak (1393); borrowed from Old French *pronuncier, prononcier,* learned borrowing from Latin, and borrowed directly from Latin *prōnūntiāre* to proclaim, announce, publish, pronounce (*prō-* forth, pro-[1] + *nūntiāre* announce, from *nūntius* messenger, of uncertain origin). **—pronounced** *adj.* 1577, spoken; formed from English *pronounce* + *-ed*[2]. The figurative sense of strongly marked, emphatic or decided, is first recorded in *Chambers Cyclopaedia* (1727-41). **—pronouncement** *n.* declaration, assertion. 1593, in Nashe's *Christ's Tears Over Jerusalem;* formed from English *pronounce* + *-ment.* **—pronunciation** *n.* Probably before 1425 *pronunciation* act of pronouncing, speaking, in a translation of Higden's *Polychronicon;* borrowed perhaps by influence of Middle French *prononciation,* from Latin *prōnūntiātiōnem* (nominative *prōnūntiātiō*) act of speaking; also, a proclamation, publication, from *prōnūntiāre* announce; see PRONOUNCE; for suffix see -ATION.

pronto *adv.* quickly, promptly. 1850, American English, borrowing of Spanish *pronto,* perhaps also influenced by earlier use of *pronto* (1740) borrowing of Italian *pronto;* both the Spanish and Italian from Latin *prōmptus,* adj. Doublet of PROMPT.

proof *n.* Probably before 1200 *preove* that which proves a statement, evidence, in *Ancrene Riwle;* later *prove, prōf* (before 1325); borrowed from Anglo-French *prove, preove,* Old French *proeve, prueve,* from Late Latin *proba* a proof, from Latin *probāre* to PROVE. Doublet of PROBE. **—adj.** of tested value against something. 1592, in the phrase *proof against,* in Shakespeare's *Romeo and Juliet;* from the noun, as in the usage *proof of* in the sense of proved or tested power (1456). This sense was extended to use as the second element in such compounds as *bulletproof* (1824), *fireproof* (before 1638), *soundproof* (1884), *waterproof* (1736). **—proofread** *v.* read and mark errors to be corrected. Before 1927, back formation from *proofreader.* **—proofreader** *n.* one who proofreads. 1832, American English; formed from English *proof* trial impression from type, test + *reader* one who reads; for suffix see -ER[1].

prop[1] *n.* support. 1440 *proppe* a stick, rod, pole, beam, or other rigid support, in *Promptorium Parvulorum;* borrowed from Middle Dutch *proppe* vine prop, support, of uncertain origin. **—v.** to support. 1456 *proppen;* from the Middle English noun.

prop[2] *n.* portable object used in a play. 1911, back formation from earlier *props,* pl. (1841), shortened form of earlier *properties,* in the same sense (1578).

prop[3] *n. Informal.* aircraft propeller. 1914, shortened form of *propeller.* Since the 1940's *prop* has often been used to form compounds such as *prop-fan, prop-jet,* and *turboprop,* all referring to the fan-like mechanism attached to aircraft engines.

propaganda *n.* systematic efforts to spread opinions or beliefs. 1718 *Propaganda* committee of cardinals in charge of Catholic missionary activity, founded in 1622 by Pope Gregory XV; borrowing from New Latin *Congregatio de propaganda fide* Congregation for propagating the faith; New Latin *propaganda* is an ablative feminine gerundive construction of Latin *propāgāre* to PROPAGATE. The general meaning of any systematic scheme or concerted efforts to propagate a particular doctrine or practice is first recorded in 1908, developed from the earlier meaning of any association for the propagation of a particular practice or doctrine (1790). **—propagandist** *n.* 1829, a person devoted to the propagation of a particular doctrine or practice, in Southey's *Sir Thomas More;* formed from English *propaganda* + *-ist.* **—propagandize** *v.* 1844, formed from English *propaganda* + *-ize.*

propagate *v.* 1570, multiply by reproduction, cause to breed; back formation from earlier *propagation;* also, perhaps developed from earlier *propagate,* adj. propagated (before 1548), borrowed from Latin *propāgātus,* past participle of *propāgāre* multiply plants by means of layers or slips, breed, enlarge or extend the stock or race of, from *propāgō* (genitive *propāginis*) that which propagates, a layer or slip or a plant, offspring (*pro-* forth, pro-[1] + *pāg-,* root of *pangere* to fix, fasten; see PACT); for suffix see -ATE[1]. The extended meaning of spread, disseminate (as in *propagate a rumor*) is first recorded in 1600. **—propagation** *n.* Probably 1440 *propagacioun* procreation, generation, reproduction; borrowed from Middle French *propagacion,* and directly from Latin *propāgātiōnem* (nominative *propāgātiō*) a propagation or extension from *propāgāre* propagate; for suffix see -ATION. The extended meaning of dissemination, making more widely known, is first recorded in 1588, and that of the transmission of some form of energy, such as motion or light, in 1656.

propel *v.* Probably 1440 *propellen* drive away or expel; borrowed from Latin *prōpellere* push forward (*prō-* forward, pro-[1] + *pellere* to push, drive; see PULSE[1] beat). The meaning of drive forward is recorded in Phillips' *Dictionary* (1658). **—propellant** *n.* thing that propels. 1881, firearm explosive, from earlier *propellant,* adj., that propels a bullet, etc. (1858); formed from English *propel* + *-ant,* as an alteration of earlier *propellent.* The application of this term to the fuel of a rocket or missile is first recorded in 1919, in the writings of the American rocket scientist Robert H. Goddard. **—propellent** *adj.* driving forward. 1644, formed from English *propel* + *-ent,* modeled on Latin *prōpellentem* (nominative *prōpellēns*), present participle of *prōpellere* propel. —*n.* something or someone that propels. 1814, from the adjective. **—propeller** *n.* 1780, mechanical contrivance for propelling machinery or a vehicle such as a ship (1809); formed from English *propel* + *-er*[1]. The meaning of apparatus by which to propel a flying machine (such as by mechanical flapping wings) is first recorded in a British patent (1842). Later a mechanism analogous to a ship's propeller is applied to a toy flying machine (1853).

propensity *n.* natural inclination or bent. 1570, probably formed from obsolete English *propense.* adj., inclined, disposed, prone (1528) + *-ity;* and in some instances perhaps formed as if from Latin **prōpēnsitātem* (nominative **prōpēnsitās*) inclination, from *prōpēns-*, past participle stem of *prōpendēre* incline to, hang forward, weigh over (*prō-* forward, pro-[1] + *pendēre* hang; see PENDANT) + English suffix *-ity.*

proper *adj.* Probably before 1300 *propre* special, commendable, in *Kyng Alisaunder;* also, *proper* one's own (1303), and appropriate or correct (1340); borrowed from Old French *propre,* learned borrowing from Latin, and borrowed directly from Latin *proprius* one's own, particular, special, peculiar; of uncertain origin. The specialized meaning of socially appropriate, decent, respectable, is first recorded in Swift's apology to *A Tale of a Tub* (1704). **—proper fraction** fraction less than 1 (1674). **—proper noun** noun naming a particular person, place, or thing (1889, though the phrase also appears in Middle English as *propur nown,* probably before 1500).

property *n.* About 1303 *properte* nature, quality, attribute, characteristic, in Mannyng's *Handlyng Synne;* later, possession, things owned (before 1325, in *Cursor Mundi*), and probably about 1380 *property;* borrowed from Old French *proprete, propriete,* learned borrowing from Latin, and borrowed directly from Latin *proprietātem* (nominative *proprietās*) special character, propriety, property, from *proprius* one's own, special, PROPER; for suffix see -TY. Latin *proprietās* is a translation (by Cicero) of Greek *idiótēs* peculiar nature, specific character, from *ídios* one's own, personal; see IDIOM.

prophecy *n.* foretelling of future events; prediction. Probably before 1200 *prophecie,* in *Ancrene Riwle;* also *prophesie* (about 1300); borrowed from Old French *prophetie, prophecie, prophesie,* learned borrowing from Late Latin, and borrowed directly from Late Latin *prophētia,* from Greek *prophēteíā* gift of interpreting the will of the gods, from *prophḗtēs* PROPHET; for suffix see -CY. The spelling of the noun (*prophecy*) and the verb (*prophesy*) did not become fully differentiated until after 1700. **—prophesy** *v.* foretell the future. About 1350 *prophecien;* also *prophesien* (about 1384); borrowed from Old French *prophecier, prophesier,* from *prophetie* prophecy. **—prophesier** *n.* 1477, formed from English *prophesy* + *-er*[1].

prophet *n.* Probably before 1200 *prophete* person who speaks for God, person who foretells what will happen, inspired preacher, in *Ancrene Riwle;* borrowed from Old French *prophete, profete,* and directly from Latin *prophēta,* from Greek *prophḗtēs* (Doric *prophā́tās*) an interpreter, spokesman, especially of the will of the gods; also, an inspired person (*pro-* before, pro-[2] + *phā-*, root of *phánai* to speak; see BAN[1] forbid). The transferred sense of an inspired spokesman, proclaimer, or preacher of some principle, cause, or movement, is first recorded in English in 1848. **—prophetic** *adj.* of a prophet or prophecy. Before 1475 *prophetyk,* borrowed from Middle French *prophetique,* and directly from Late Latin *prophēticus,* from Greek *prophētikós* pertaining to a prophet or to a prophecy, from *prophḗtēs* prophet; for suffix see -IC.

prophylactic (prō′fəlak′tik) *adj.* protecting from disease. 1574, borrowed perhaps from Middle French *prophylactique* (1546, in Rabelais), and directly from Greek *prophylaktikós* precautionary, adjective to **prophýlaxis,* from *prophylássein* keep guard before (*pro-* before, pro-[2] + *phylássein,* Ionic variant of *phyláttein* to guard, from *phýlax,* genitive *phýlakos,* a guard, of uncertain origin); for suffix see -IC. **—n.** prophylactic medicine or treatment. 1642, from the adjective. *Prophylactic* in the sense of a condom is first recorded in 1943, originally in the armed forces, where use of these devices was urged upon servicemen as protection against venereal disease; earlier called *preventive* (1822) and *preventative* (1901). **—prophylaxis** (prō′fəlak′sis) *n.* protection from disease. 1842, New Latin, noun formed to Greek *prophylaktikós* PROPHYLACTIC, from Greek *pro-* before, pro-[2] + *phýlaxis* guarding, protection, from *phylássein* to guard.

propinquity (proping′kwətē) *n.* nearness. About 1380 *propinquyte* nearness in relationship, kinship, in Chaucer's translation of Boethius' *De Consolatione Philosophiae;* later, physical proximity (probably before 1425); borrowed from Old French *propinquite,* and directly from Latin *propinquitātem* (nominative *propinquitās*) nearness, vicinity, from *propinquus* near, neighboring, from *prope* near; see APPROXIMATE; for suffix see -ITY.

propitiate (prəpish′ēāt) *v.* appease, conciliate. 1645, probably a back formation from *propitiation,* and in part probably developed from *propitiate,* adj. appeased, conciliated, favorable; borrowed from Latin *propitiātus,* past participle of *propitiāre* render favorable, from *propitius* PROPITIOUS; for suffix see -ATE[1]. **—propitiation** *n.* appeasement, conciliation, atonement. About 1395 *propiciacioun,* in the Wycliffe Bible; borrowed from Late Latin *propitiātiōnem* (nominative *propitiātiō*) an atonement, from Latin *propitiāre* render favorable; for suffix see -ATION.

propitious (prəpish′əs) *adj.* favorable. 1440 *propicius* inclined to grant favor, generous; borrowed from Anglo-French *propiciius, propiciös,* Middle French *propicieux* favorable, gracious, learned borrowing from Latin, and borrowed directly from Latin *propitius* favorable, gracious, kind (*prō-* forward, pro-[1] + *petere* go to; see FEATHER); for suffix see -IOUS. The earlier form was *propice* (about 1350); borrowed from Old French *propice,* from Latin *propitius;* see above. This form gradually disappeared from the record of English in the 1600's.

proponent *n.* person who makes a proposal; advocate. 1588, borrowed from Latin *prōpōnentem* (nominative *prōpōnēns*), present participle of *prōpōnere* put forward, PROPOSE; for suffix see -ENT. It is also probable that in some instances *proponent* was formed in English from *propone,* v. to put forth, propose (1402, from Latin *prōpōnere* put forward) + *-ent.*

proportion *n.* Before 1382 *proporcyon* relation between parts, shape, form, in the Wycliffe Bible; also, comparative relation of things, in size, degree, number, etc. (before 1387, in Trevisa's translation of Higden's *Polychronicon*); borrowed from Old French *proportion,* learned borrowing from Latin, and borrowed directly from Latin *prōportiōnem* (nominative *prōportiō*) comparative relation, analogy, from the earlier phrase *prō portiōne* according to the relation (of the parts to each other), alteration of *prō *partiōne,* ablative case of a lost noun **partiō* division, related to *pars* (genitive *partis*) PART; for suffix see -TION. **—v.** make proportionate, adjust. About 1385 *proporcionen,* from the noun in English, and probably borrowed from Old French *proportionner,* from Old French *proportion,* n., and perhaps from Medieval Latin *proportionare,* formed as a verb to *prōportiōnem* (nominative *prōportiō*). **—proportional** *adj.* in proportion, corresponding. 1392 *proporcional;* borrowed, perhaps by influence of Old French *proporcionnel,* from Late Latin *prōportiōnālis* pertaining to proportion, from Latin *prōportiō* (genitive *prōportiōnis*) proportion; for suffix see -AL[1].**—proportionate** *adj.* adjusted in proportion. Before 1398 *proporcionate* of proper proportion, appropriate, corresponding, in Trevisa's translation of Bartholomew's *De Proprietatibus Rerum;* borrowed from Late Latin *prōportiōnātus* proportioned, from Latin *prōportiō* (genitive *prōportiōnis*) proportion; for suffix see -ATE[1].

propose *v.* 1340 *proposen* to put forward a scheme, form an intention, in *Ayenbite of Inwyt;* later, put forward for consideration (before 1398, in Trevisa's translation of Bartholomew's *De Proprietatibus Rerum*); borrowed from Old French *proposer* (*pro-* forth, pro-[1] + *poser* put, place; see POSE). Old French *proposer* was influenced in its formation by Latin *prōpos-,* perfect stem of *prōpōnere* put forward, PROPOUND; Latin *prōpōnere* is also the source of obsolete English *propone,* which coexisted for a time with *propose,* but is now evident only in such words as *proponent.* **—proposal** *n.* 1653, formed from English *propose* + *-al*[2]. **—proposition** *n.* About 1340 *proposicion* a parable, obscure statement; later, assertion or statement (about 1380, in Chaucer's translation of Boethius' *De Consolatione Philosophiae*); borrowed from Old French *proposition,* learned borrowing from Latin *prōpositiōnem* (nominative *prōpositiō*) a setting forth, purpose, statement, from *prōposit-,* past participle stem of *prōpōnere* put forward; for suffix see -TION. —*v.* propose a plan, etc. to, often an improper one. 1924, American English; from the noun.

propound *v.* put forward an idea, suggestion, etc.; put forward, propose. 1551, alteration of earlier *propowne, propoune* (1537), developed from Middle English *proponen* to put forward, propose, assert (1402); borrowed from Latin *prōpōnere* put forward, declare, propose, intend (*prō-* before, pro-[1] + *pōnere* to put, place; see POSITION). The *d* in *propound* began to appear in the late 1500's, and is similar in its development to the *d* of COMPOUND and EXPOUND.

proprietary *adj.* About 1450 *proprietarye* possessing worldly goods in excess of a cleric's needs; later, held in private ownership (1589); probably from earlier noun (1401 *proprietarie* person interested in worldly goods to the distraction of a devotion to God; later, property owner, 1473); borrowed from Middle French *propriétaire,* and directly from Medieval Latin *proprietarius* owner of property, Late Latin *proprietārius* of a property holder, from Latin *proprietās* ownership, PROPERTY; for suffix see -ARY.

proprietor *n.* owner. 1639, American English, owner, by royal grant, of an American colony; probably alteration of English *proprietary* property owner (1473); see PROPRIETARY; for suffix see -OR[2].

propriety *n.* Probably before 1425 *proprite* quality of being proper, appropriateness, fitness; borrowed from Old French *proprieté, proprete,* learned borrowing from Latin *proprietātem* (nominative *proprietās*) appropriateness, propriety, ownership; see PROPERTY; for suffix see -TY[2].

propulsion *n.* a propelling or being propelled. 1611, act of driving away, expulsion, in Florio's *New World of Words;* formed in English from Latin *prōpuls-,* past participle stem of *prōpellere* to PROPEL + English suffix -ION. The meaning of the act of driving forward or condition of being driven forward, propelling force or effect, is first recorded in 1799.

pro rata (prō rä′tə) in proportion. 1575, borrowing of Latin *prō ratā* (*parte*) according to (the part or portion) figured for each (*prō* for; and *ratā,* ablative case singular of *ratus,* past participle of *rērī* to count, reckon; see REASON).

prorate (prō′rāt′) *v.* distribute or assess proportionally. 1860, American English; from PRO RATA. **—proration** *n.* act of prorating. 1923, formed from English *prorate* + *-ion.*

prorogue (prōrōg′) *v.* 1419 *proroguen* prolong or extend (an agreement, truce, etc.); later, discontinue regular meetings of a legislature or parliament for a time (1455, in *Rolls of Parliament*); borrowed from Middle French *proroguer,* learned borrowing from Latin, and borrowed directly from Latin *prōrogāre* defer, prolong; literally, ask publicly (*prō-* forward, pro-[1] + *rogāre* ask, propose, request; see RIGHT).

prosaic (prōzā′ik) *adj.* like prose, ordinary, not exciting. 1656, of, in, or having to do with prose, in Blount's *Glossographia;* borrowed probably from French *prosaïque,* and directly from Late Latin *prōsāicus* in prose, pertaining to prose from Latin *prōsa* PROSE; for suffix see -IC. It may be that Late Latin *prōsāicus* (contrasting with *lyricus*) was formed on the model of Late Latin *lāicus* of the laity (contrasting with *clēricus* of the clergy).

The meaning of characteristic of prose rather than poetry is first recorded in English in 1746, and the extended sense of ordinary, not exciting, in 1813; both senses probably from earlier use in French.

proscenium (prōsē′nēəm) *n.* part of the stage in front of the curtain, forestage. 1606, the stage of an ancient theater, in Holland's translation of Suetonius' *History of Twelve Caesars;* borrowed from Latin *proscaenium,* from Greek *proskḗnion* the space in front of the scene or scenery where the action took place, the entrance of a tent (*pro-* in front of, pro-[2] + *skēnḗ* stage, tent; see SCENE). The modern theatrical meaning of forestage is first recorded in 1807.

prosciutto (prōshü′tō) *n.* dry-cured and spiced Italian ham. About 1938, borrowing of Italian *prosciutto,* alteration (probably influenced by *prosciugato* dried) of earlier *presciutto* (*pre-* an intensive form + *-sciutto,* from Latin *exsūctus* lacking juice, dried up, from past participle of *exsūgere* suck out, draw out moisture, from *ex-* out + *sūgere* to SUCK).

proscribe *v.* condemn. Probably before 1425 *proscriben* write before, prefix, in a translation of Higden's *Polychronicon;* later *proscribed* excited, past participle (1445); borrowed from Latin *prōscrībere* publish in writing, publish as having forfeited one's property, condemn, outlaw (*prō-* before, pro-[1] + *scrībere* to write; see SCRIBE). The meaning of prohibit as wrong or dangerous is first recorded in English in 1622. **—proscription** *n.* condemnation. About 1380 *proscripcion* exile, banishment, in Chaucer's translation of Boethius' *De Consolatione Philosophiae;* borrowed from Latin *prōscrīptiōnem* (nominative *prōscrīptiō*) public notice, outlawry, from *prōscrīpt-,* past participle stem of *prōscrībere* proscribe; for suffix see -TION. **—proscriptive** *adj.* 1757, formed in English from Latin *prōscrīpt-,* past participle stem of *prōscrībere* proscribe + English suffix *-ive.*

prose *n.* Probably before 1300, a story or narration; later, prose writing, language not arranged in verse or meter (about 1338, in Mannyng's *Chronicle of England*); borrowed from Old French *prose,* learned borrowing from Latin, and borrowed directly from Latin *prōsa* (*ōrātiō*) straight-forward or direct speech with no transpositions or ornamental variations as in verse; *prōsa,* feminine of *prōsus,* earlier *prōrsus* straightforward, direct, a contraction of Old Latin *prōvorsus* (moving) straight ahead (*prō-* forward, pro-[1] + *vorsus* turned, past participle of *vertere* to turn; see VERTEX). **—prosy** *adj.* like prose, matter-of-fact, tiresome. 1837, in Dickens' *Pickwick Papers;* formed from English *prose* + *-y*[1].

prosecute *v.* bring before a court of law. Probably before 1425 *prosecuten* carry out, follow up, pursue, in a translation of Higden's *Polychronicon;* borrowed from Latin *prōsecūtus,* past participle of *prōsequī* follow after, PURSUE. The meaning of bring before a court of law is first recorded in English in 1579. **—prosecution** *n.* 1564, action or effort to get possession of; also 1567, act of following up or pursuing; borrowed from Middle French *prosecution,* and probably directly from Late Latin *prōsecūtiōnem* (nominative *prōsecūtiō*) a following or accompanying, from Latin *prōsecūt-,* past participle stem of *prōsequī* pursue. The meaning of the act of carrying on a lawsuit is first recorded in 1631. **—prosecutor** *n.* 1599, one who carries out some action; borrowing of Medieval Latin *prosecutor,* from Latin *prōsecūt-,* past participle stem of *prōsequi* pursue + *-or* -OR[2]. The meaning of a person who brings a case before a court of law is first recorded in Burton's *Anatomy of Melancholy* (1621), and is earlier found in the term *promoter* (1485, in *Rolls of Parliament*).

proselyte (pros′əlīt) *n.* convert. About 1384 *proselite,* in the Wycliffe Bible; borrowed from Old French *proselite,* from Late Latin *prosēlytus,* from Greek *prosḗlytos* one who has come over to a place, stranger, convert; literally, having arrived (*prós-* to, toward, alteration of *protí;* see PRICE + the root *ely-* of *eleúsesthai* to be going to come, and of *né-ēlys* new-comer, from Indo-European **eleu-/elu-* move, go, come; Pok.306). **—proselytize** (pros′ələtīz) *v.* make converts, convert. 1679, formed from English *proselyte* + *-ize.*

prosody (pros′ədē) *n.* study of poetic meters and versification. Probably before 1475 *prosodye;* borrowed from Latin *prosōdia,* from Greek *prosōidiā́* song sung to music; also, accent, modulation and other features that characterize speech (*prós-* to, toward; see PROSELYTE + *ōidḗ* song, poem, ODE); for suffix see -Y[3].

prospect *n.* Probably before 1425 *prospecte* outlook, view, in a translation of Higden's *Polychronicon;* borrowed from Latin *prōspectus* (genitive *prōspectūs*) view, outlook, from past participle of *prōspicere* look out on, look forward (*prō-* forward, pro-[1] + *specere* look at; see SPY).

The meaning of an extensive view is first recorded in Elyot's *Dictionary* (1538), and that of the act of looking forward, in Shakespeare's *Macbeth* (1605). The meaning of a thing expected or looked forward to is first recorded in 1665, and in its plural form (as in *good prospects for the coming year*) in 1667.

—v. look out for, explore, search. 1841, American English, explore for gold or other minerals; from earlier *prospect,* n., a spot giving prospects of the presence of a mineral deposit (1832). The figurative meaning of search about, look out for something, is first recorded in 1867 in American English. **—prospective** *adj.* probable, expected, future. 1588, affording an extensive view; borrowed from Old French *prospectif* (feminine *prospective*), and directly from Late Latin *prōspectīvus* belonging to or affording a prospect, from Latin *prōspectus,* past participle of *prōspicere* look out on; see PROSPECT; for suffix see -IVE. The meaning of concerned with or relating to the future, effective in the future, is first recorded in 1800, and that of expected, hoped for, future, in 1829, in Southey's writings. **—prospector** *n.* person who explores for gold or other minerals. 1846, American English; from *prospect,* v. + *-or*[2]. **—prospectus** *n.* printed statement describing and advertising something. 1777, in Goldsmith's writings; borrowed from French *prospectus,* and directly from Latin *prōspectus* view, outlook, PROSPECT.

prosper *v.* 1350 *prospern,* borrowed from Old French *prosperer,* learned borrowing from Latin, and borrowed directly from Latin *prosperāre* cause to succeed, from *prosperus* favorable, fortunate, prosperous, perhaps formed from an Old Latin phrase *prō spēre* in accordance with hope (*prō* according to, FOR, + Old Latin *spēre,* ablative singular of *spēs* hope; see SPEED). The disparity between the short *e* of Latin *prosperus* and the long *e* of Latin *spēre, spēs* causes difficulty; hence the relationship between these words may be just a folk etymology. **—prosperity** *n.* Probably before 1200 *prosperite* success, well-being, in *Ancrene Riwle;* borrowed from Old French *prosperité,* and directly from Latin *prosperitātem* (nominative *prosperitās*) good fortune, from *prosperus* fortunate, prosperous; for suffix see -ITY. **—prosperous** *adj.* About 1425, favorable, fortunate; in part probably borrowed from Anglo-Latin *prosperosus,* and Middle French *prospereus,* from Latin *prosperus;* and in part a re-formation in Middle English directly from Latin *prosperus* favorable + English *-ous.*

prostaglandin (pros′təglan′dən) *n.* hormonelike substance found originally in seminal fluid of the prostate gland. 1936, borrowing of German *Prostaglandin* (*Prosta* (*ta*) prostate or English *prost(ate)* + *gland* + *-in,* chemical suffix). The term was coined by the Swedish physiologist Ulf S. von Euler.

Although prostaglandins were first isolated in the 1930's, scientists did not discover their functions and many uses until the late 1960's. It was then that the term came into wide use.

prostate (pros′tāt) *n.* large gland surrounding the male urethra. 1646, borrowed from Middle French *prostate,* and directly from Medieval Latin *prostata,* from Greek *prostátēs* (*adḗn*) prostate (gland), from *prostátes* one standing in front, from *proïstánai* set before (*pro-* before, pro-[2] + *histánai* cause to STAND); so called in allusion to the prostate's position at the base of the bladder.

prosthesis (prosthē′sis) *n.* replacement of a missing part of the body with an artificial one. 1553, addition of a letter or syllable to a word; borrowed from Late Latin, from Greek *prósthesis* addition, from *prostithénai* add to (*prós-* to, toward; see PROSELYTE + *tithénai* to put, place; see DO[1] perform). The meaning of replacement of a missing part of the body with an artificial one is first recorded in Kersey's revision of Phillips' *Dictionary* (1706). **—prosthetic** *adj.* 1837, borrowed from Greek *prosthetikós* of the nature of addition, giving additional power, from *prósthetos* added, verbal adjective of *prostithénai* add to; for suffix see -IC.

prostitute *n.* 1613, woman who has sexual intercourse for payment, in Purchas' *Pilgrimage;* borrowed from Latin *prōstitūta* prostitute, from feminine of *prōstitūtus,* past participle of *prōstituere* to offer for sale, expose publicly to prostitution (*prō-* before, pro-[1] + *statuere* cause to stand, establish; see STATUTE). The figurative meaning of a person who does base things for money is first recorded in English in 1647. **—v.** 1530, to offer oneself or another to prostitution, in Palsgrave's *Lesclarcissement;* borrowed from Latin *prōstitūtus,* past participle of *prōstituere* to expose to prostitution. The figurative meaning of put to an unworthy or base use, to defile or dishonor, is first recorded in Nashe's *Christ's Tears Over Jerusalem* (1593). **—prostitution** *n.* 1533, borrowed from Middle French *prostitution,* and directly from Latin *prōstitūtiōnem* (nominative *prōstitūtiō*), from *prōstituere* to prostitute; for suffix see -TION.

prostrate *v.* lay down flat, cast down. Before 1425 *prostraten* fall down in submission; from the adjective. **—adj.** lying down flat. Probably about 1350 *prostrat,* borrowed from Latin *prōstrātus,* past participle of *prōsternere* strew in front, throw down (*prō-* forth, pro-[1] + *sternere* to spread out; see STREW).

prot- a combining form of *proto-* before vowels, as in *protagonist, protactinium* (except in proper names, such as *Proto-Indo-European*). Borrowed from Greek *prōt-,* variant (before vowels) of *prōto-* first, PROTO-.

protactinium (prō'taktin'ēəm) *n.* radioactive metallic chemical element of the actinide series. 1918 *protoactinium,* formed in English from *proto-* + *actinium,* modeled on German *Protactinium,* and replaced in English by *protactinium* (1919). The name derives from the process of radioactive disintegration of protactinium to form the more stable element ACTINIUM.

protagonist *n.* main character in a play, story, or novel. 1671, in Dryden's *An Evening's Love;* borrowed from Greek *prōtagōnistḗs* actor who plays the chief or first part (*prōt-* first, prot- + *agōnistḗs* actor, competitor, combatant, from *agṓn* contest; see AGONY); for suffix see -IST.

protean (prō'tēən *or* prōtē'ən) *adj.* readily assuming different forms or characters. 1598, in Marston's *The Metamorphosis of Pygmalion's Image;* formed in English from *Prōteús* Greek sea god who could assume many different shapes + English *-an.*

protect *v.* About 1456 *protecten* defend or guard from harm or danger; developed from *protecte,* adj. defended, cared for (probably before 1425); borrowed from Latin *prōtēctus,* past participle of *prōtegere* cover in front, protect (*prō-* in front, pro-[1] + *tegere* to cover; see THATCH). It is also probable that in some instances *protect* is a back formation from earlier *protection,* and perhaps *protector.* **—protection** *n.* About 1350 *proteccioun* act of protecting, shelter, defense; borrowed from Old French *proteccïon, protectïon,* and directly from Latin *prōtēctiōnem* (nominative *prōtēctiō*) a covering over, from *prōtēctus,* past participle of *prōtegere* protect; for suffix see -TION. **—protectionist** *n.* 1844, person who supports high duties on imported goods to favor purchase of lower-cost domestic products; formed from English *protection* + *-ist,* modeled on French *protectionniste.* —*adj.* 1846, supporting or favoring the policy of protectionists; from the noun. **—protectionism** *n.* 1852, the policy of protectionists; formed from English *protection* + *-ism,* modeled on French *protectionnisme.* **—protective** *adj.* 1661, tending to protect, defensive; formed from English *protect* + *-ive.* **—protector** *n.* About 1390 *protectour* one that protects, defender, guardian; borrowed from Old French *protector,* and directly from Latin *prōtēctor,* from *prōtēct-,* past participle stem of *prōtegere* protect; for suffix see -OR[2]. The meaning of head of a kingdom in a sovereign's absence is first recorded in 1426, and that of Lord Protector of the Commonwealth under Oliver, and later Richard, Cromwell, in 1653. **—protectorate** *n.* 1692, office or position of the Protector of the Commonwealth held by Oliver, and later Richard, Cromwell (1653-59); formed from Middle English *protector* (1426) + *-ate*[3]. The meaning of a territory or country under the protection and partial control of another country or countries is first recorded in 1836, in reference to the protectorate of Cracow, Poland, under the stewardship of Austria, Prussia, and Russia. The use derives from earlier reference to protection of Ireland in Burke's correspondence 1795, and in a proclamation of the British government to the inhabitants of one of the Greek islands (1809). Later the term was extended in use to the southeastern part of New Guinea colonized in 1884 by Great Britain, after French *protectorat* (formed from Latin *prōtēctor* + French *-at* -ate[3]).

protégé (prō'təzhā) *n.* person under the care of a patron. 1778, in Sheridan's dramatic writings; borrowing of French *protégé* one who is protected, from past participle of Middle French *protéger* protect, learned borrowing from Latin *prōtegere* PROTECT.

protein (prō'tēn) *n.* complex nitrogen-containing compound essential to living cells. 1844, borrowed from French *protéine,* from Greek *prṓteios* of the first quality, from *prôtos* first; see PROTO-; for suffix see -INE[2].

The French word (coined by the Dutch chemist Gerardus Johannes Mulder) originally referred to a nitrogenous substance thought to be the essential constituent of all animals and plants. The current use of the word (borrowed from German *Proteïn*) dates from 1907.

protest (prō'test) *n.* Probably about 1400, solemn or formal declaration, borrowed from Old French *protest,* from *protester* declare publicly, learned borrowing from Latin, and probably borrowed directly from Latin *prōtestārī* declare publicly, testify, protest (*prō-* forth, before, pro-[1] + *testārī* testify, from *testis* witness; see TESTAMENT). The extended meaning of a statement of declaration of objection, disapproval or dissent, is first recorded in English in 1751, from the verb sense in English. **—v.** (prətest') 1430 *protesten* to vow, in *Proceedings of the Privy Council;* later, declare solemnly or formally (1440); borrowed from Middle French *protester* declare publicly. The extended meaning of object, dissent, or disapprove is first recorded in English in 1608. **—protestation** *n.* 1382, avowal, declaration, assertion; borrowed from Old French *protestacïon,* learned borrowing from Late Latin, and borrowed directly from Late Latin *prōtestātiōnem* (nominative *prōtestātiō*) a declaration or protest, from Latin *prōtestārī* to protest; for suffix see -ATION.

Protestant *n.* 1539, any one of the German princes who protested the decision of the Diet of Speyer (Spires) in 1529, which had denounced the Reformation; the word *protestant* became a general name (especially among the French, Dutch, and Scandinavians) for an adherent of the Reformation in Germany; borrowed perhaps from German *Protestant,* or more likely from French *protestant,* from Latin *prōtestantem* (nominative *prōtestāns*), present participle of *prōtestārī* to PROTEST; for suffix see -ANT.

In the later 1500's the name *Protestant* was eventually taken in Germany and Poland by the Lutherans, while the Swiss and the French used the term *Reformed.* The extended meaning of a member or adherent of any of the Christian churches which broke away from the Roman Catholic Church during the Reformation is first recorded in English in 1553.

—adj. of or belonging to the Protestants. 1539, from the noun.

—Protestantism *n.* 1649, the religious principles and practices of the Protestants, in Milton's *Works;* borrowed from French *protestantisme,* from *protestant* Protestant (from German) + *-isme* -ism.

protist (prō′tist) *n.* one-celled organism. 1889 (earlier implied in *Protistic* 1869); borrowed from New Latin *Protista* a third kingdom (alongside plants and animals) proposed in 1868 by the German biologist Ernst Heinrich Haeckel, from German *Protisten,* from Greek *prṓtistos* the very first, principal, superlative of *prôtos* first; see PROTO-.

proto- a combining form meaning first, with various shades of meaning: source or parent (*Proto-Germanic*), preceding (*protohuman*), earliest form (*protogalaxy*), original or model (*prototype*), basic (*protoplasm*). Borrowed from Greek *prōto-,* combining form of *prôtos* first; earlier **próatos,* related to *pró,* prep., before, forward; see FOR. Also **prot-** (the usual form before vowels).

protocol (prō′təkol *or* prō′təkôl) *n.* 1541 *prothogall;* later, *prothocoll* original draft or record of a document or transaction (1552); borrowed from Middle French *prothocole, protocolle* the draft of a document or register of a transaction, from Medieval Latin *protocollum* the first sheet or flyleaf of a volume, especially with its contents, public register, draft of a document, from Greek *prōtókollon* first sheet (containing date and contents) glued onto a manuscript or papyrus roll and describing the origin of the manuscript (*prôtos* first; see PROTO- + *kólla* glue; see COLLAGE).

The extended meaning of a formal or official record of a proceeding or transaction is first recorded in English in 1880, and that of a procedure used in scientific experiments, in 1887. The meaning of rules of etiquette and procedure to be observed in affairs of state and diplomatic relations is first recorded in 1896, in the context of French diplomacy.

proton *n.* elementary particle carrying one unit of positive electricity. 1920, from Greek *prôton,* neuter of *prôtos* first; see PROTO-; modeled on such words as *electron* and *ion.* The word was coined by the English physicist Ernest Rutherford, and has been attributed to a suggested reference to the English chemist and physician William *Prout,* who hypothesized that hydrogen was a constituent of all the elements. *Proton* was used earlier (in 1893) to designate the primitive cell structure from which an embryonic part develops.

protoplasm *n.* living substance of plant and animal cells. 1848, borrowed from German *Protoplasma,* formed from *proto-* first (from Greek *prōto-;* see PROTO-) + *Plasma* something molded (from Greek *plásma;* see PLASMA). The word was coined in 1846 by the German botanist Hugo von Mohl, or adopted by him from a similar use of the term (in 1839) by the Bohemian physiologist Johannes E. Purkinje.

prototype (prō′tətīp) *n.* the first or primary type of anything. 1603, in Samuel Daniel's writings; borrowed from French *prototype,* from both Late Latin *prōtotypus* original, primitive, and Greek *prōtótypon* a first or primitive form, from neuter of *prōtótypos* original, primitive (*prōto-* first + *týpos* impression; see TYPE). *Prototype* eventually replaced earlier *prototypon* (1596), borrowed directly from Greek *prōtótypon.* **—prototypical** *adj.* 1650, formed from English *prototype* + *-ical.*

Protozoa (prō′təzō′ə) *n.pl.* a kind of protist, that comprises a large group of single-celled organisms. Before 1834, New Latin *Protozoa;* formed from Greek *prôtos* first; see PROTO- + *zôia,* plural of *zôion* animal; see ZOOLOGY. The classification *Protozoa,* when coined by the German paleontologist Georg August Goldfuss, included higher forms of life, such as sponges and corals, but was later restricted to the current sense in 1845. **—protozoan** *n.* member of the phylum Protozoa. 1864, formed from English *Protozoa* + *-an.*

protract *v.* draw out, lengthen in time. Before 1548, probably a back formation from earlier *protraction,* and in part borrowed from Latin *prōtractus,* past participle of *prōtrahere* draw forth, prolong, extend, defer (*prō-* forward, pro-[1] + *trahere* to draw; see TRACT). **—protraction** *n.* About 1458 *protraceioun* the drawing or writing of numbers; later *protraction* prolongation, extension of time (1535); borrowed possibly from Middle French *protraction,* and directly from Late Latin *prōtractiōnem* (nominative *prōtractiō*) a drawing out or lengthening, from Latin *prōtract-,* past participle stem of *prōtrahere* draw forth; for suffix see -TION. **—protractor** *n.* 1611, one who prolongs or extends something; later, an instrument for drawing or measuring angles (1658, in Phillips' *Dictionary*); borrowed from Medieval Latin *protractor,* from Latin *prōtract-,* past participle stem of *prōtrahere* draw forth; for suffix see -OR[2].

protrude *v.* 1620, drive along, thrust forward; borrowed from Latin *prōtrūdere* thrust or push forward (*prō-* forward, pro-[1] + *trūdere* to thrust; see THREAT). The meaning of stick out is first recorded before 1626, in Bacon's writings. **—protrusion** *n.* the action of protruding. 1646, probably borrowed from French *protrusion,* and formed in English as if from Latin **prōtrūsiō,* from *prōtrūs-,* past participle stem of *prōtrūdere* protrude + English suffix -ION. The meaning of something that juts out, a swelling or protuberance, is first recorded in Swift's *A Tale of a Tub* (1704).

protuberant (prōtü′bərənt) *adj.* sticking out, prominent. 1646, borrowed in part from French *protubérant,* and in part directly from Late Latin *prōtūberantem* (nominative *prōtūberāns*) protruding, present participle of *prōtūberāre* to swell or bulge, grow forth (Latin *prō-* forward, pro-[1] + *tūber* lump, swelling, TUBER); for suffix see -ANT. **—protuberance** *n.* 1646, that which is protuberant, a swelling, bump; borrowed from Late Latin *prōtūberantem* (nominative *prōtūberāns*) present participle of *prōtūberāre;* for suffix see -ANCE; also in some instances possibly formed from English *protuber(ant)* + *-ance.*

proud *adj.* Probably about 1150 *prude* noble, excellent splendid; later *prud, prut, prute* haughty, arrogant (probably before 1200); and *proud* (probably before 1300); developed from Old English (about 1000) *prūd* and *prūte.*

The Old English *prūd* was borrowed from Old French *prod, prud* (found in Old French *prud'homme, produme* brave man, *prou de homme* a stalwart of a man, formations in which the first element represents the oblique case *prou* of an adjective *prouz* brave, valiant). Old French *prouz* is cognate with Italian *prode* valiant, from Vulgar Latin **prōdis,* derived from Late Latin *prōde* advantageous, profitable, of use, abstracted from Latin *prōdesse* be useful (*prōd-,* variant before vowels of *prō-* before, pro-[1] + *esse* to be; see IS); compare PROWESS, PRUDE.

The Old English *prūte* (before 1000, with final *-te*) was borrowed from Old French *prouz* (earlier **prouþ-s*) and from Old English *prūte* developed the Old English noun *prȳte* pride; compare Old English *prȳde* PRIDE.

prove *v.* Probably before 1200 *pruven* to try, test, in *Ancrene Riwle;* also *proven* examine, evaluate, demonstrate, prove; borrowed from Old French *prover, pruver,* from Latin *probāre* to test, prove to be worthy, from *probus* worthy, good (*pro-* before, pro-[1] + *-bus,* probably original **probhwos* from the Indo-European base **bhū-;* see BE). **—provable** *adj.* About 1382, worthy of approval, in the Wycliffe Bible; later, that can be proved (probably before 1400, in Chaucer's translation of *Roman de la Rose*); borrowed from Old French *provable (prover* prove + *-able*)

provenance (prov′ənəns) *n.* source, origin. 1785, borrowed from French *provenance* origin, production, from *provenant,* present participle of Middle French *provenir* come forth, arise, originate, learned borrowing from Latin *prōvenīre* come forth, originate (*prō-* forth, pro-[1] + *venīre* COME); for suffix see -ANCE.

provender *n.* food, provisions. About 1300 *provendre* the allowance paid each chapter member of a cathedral; later, food for domestic animals (about 1325), and food or provisions for people (1340, in *Ayenbite of Inwyt*); borrowed through Anglo-French *provendir,* Old French *provendier, provendre,* variant of *provende,* from Gallo-Romance **prōvenda,* altered (through influence of Latin *prōvidēre* supply) from Late Latin *praebenda* allowance, subsistence, from Latin *praebenda* (things) to be furnished, neuter plural gerundive of *praebēre* to furnish, offer (contraction of Old Latin *praehibēre* to hold before, from *prae-* before, pre- + *habēre* to hold; see HABIT).

provenience (prōvē′nēəns) *n.* source, origin. 1881, probably alteration of *provenance,* influenced by Latin *prōvenientem* (nominative *prōveniēns*), present participle of *prōvenīre* originate; see PROVENANCE; for suffix see -ENCE. The word's formation may have been patterned after English *convenience,* and its use promoted among those who in the late 1800's and early 1900's objected to the French form of *provenance.*

proverb *n.* 1303 *proverbe,* in Mannyng's *Handlyng Synne;* borrowed from Old French *proverb,* learned borrowing from Latin, and borrowed directly from Latin *prōverbium* a common saying, proverb; literally, words or saying put forward (*prō-* forth, forward, pro-[1] + *verbum* WORD). **—proverbial** *adj.* Probably before 1425 (implied in adverb *proverbially,* in a translation of Higden's *Polychronicon*); borrowed from Latin *prōverbiālis* pertaining to or characteristic of a proverb, from *prōverbium* proverb. The extended meaning of that has passed into a proverb or into common talk, notorious, well-known, is first recorded in English in 1571.

provide *v.* Probably about 1408 *provyden* make provision for, use foresight in arranging, prepare, in Lydgate's *Reson and Sensuallyte;* borrowed from Latin *prōvidēre* look ahead, prepare in advance, supply (*prō-* ahead, before, pro-[1] + *vidēre* to see; see WIT[2] know). Doublet of PURVEY.

The common meaning of supply or furnish for use is first recorded before 1420, in Lydgate's *Troy Book.* **—provided** *conj.* on the provision or condition (that). About 1460, from the past participle of *providen* provide. **—provider** *n.* 1523, formed from English *provide,* v. + *-er*[1]. **—providing** *conj.* = provided. 1423, from the present participle of *providen* provide.

providence *n.* divine care, help, or guidance. Before 1382 *provydence* care for the future, foresight, provision; also, divine foreknowledge, care, and help, in the Wycliffe Bible; borrowed from Old French *providence,* and directly from Latin *prōvidentia* foresight, precaution, providence, from *prōvidentem* (nominative *prōvidēns*), present participle of *prōvidēre* to PROVIDE; for suffix see -ENCE. Related to PRUDENCE.

The capitalized form *Providence,* applied to God as providing beneficent care or guidance, is first recorded in English in William Warner's *Albions England* (1602), perhaps taken directly from Latin *prōvidentia,* as the sense was known during the period of imperial Rome. **—providential** *adj.* 1614 (implied in *providentially,* adv.) of or proceeding from divine providence; formed from Latin *prōvidentia* providence + English *-al*[1].

provident *adj.* having or showing foresight. Probably about 1408, prudent, careful, in Lydgate's *Reson and Sensuallyte;* borrowed from Latin *prōvidentem* (nominative *prōvidēns*), present participle of *prōvidēre* to foresee, PROVIDE; for suffix see -ENT. Related to PRUDENT. The meaning of thrifty or frugal is first recorded in English in 1596.

province *n.* Before 1338, a country, territory, district, or region, in Mannyng's *Chronicle of England;* borrowing of Old French *province,* learned borrowing from Latin, and borrowed directly from Latin *prōvincia* a territory outside of Italy brought under Roman domination, usually by conquest; also, official duty or charge of a magistrate, governorship of a territory; of uncertain origin, but traditionally analyzed as *prō-* before, in front of + *vincere* to conquer, although this does not account for the earliest known meaning in Latin "lordship, jurisdiction, governorship of a territory."

The meaning of function, responsibility, duty, office, or business of a person, is first recorded in English before 1626, in Bacon's *Works.* **—provincial** *adj.* Before 1378, in a version of *Piers Plowman,* of a province or provinces, (also, as a noun, 1376); borrowed from Old French *provincial,* learned borrowing from Latin, and borrowed directly from Latin *prōvinciālis* pertaining to a province, from *prōvincia* province; for suffix see -AL[1]. The meaning of countrified, lacking refinement or polish, is recorded in Johnson's *Dictionary* (1755).

provirus (prōvī′rəs) *n.* latent form of a virus. 1952, formed from English *prō-*[2] before + *virus.*

provision *n.* Before 1387 *provisioun* appointment to a church office not yet vacant, in Trevisa's translation of Higden's *Polychronicon;* later, foresight, preparation, act of providing or preparing (before 1398, in Trevisa's translation of Bartholomew's *De Proprietatibus Rerum;* borrowed, perhaps through Old French *provision,* from Latin *prōvīsiōnem* (nominative *prōvīsiō*) foresight, precaution, preparation, from *prōvidēre* look ahead, PROVIDE; for suffix see -SION.

The meaning of something provided, stock or store of something, is first recorded in English in 1451; that of a supply of food (usually *provisions,* pl.), in 1610. The legal sense of a clause providing for some particular matter, stipulation, proviso, is found in 1450, in the *Rolls of Parliament.*

—provisional *adj.* 1601, of or belonging to a temporary provision or arrangement, provided for present needs or for the time being, probably formed from English *provision* + *-al*[1], perhaps by influence of Middle French *provisionnal,* from Old French *provision* provision + *-al* -al[1].

proviso (prəvī′zō) *n.* stipulation, provision. 1434, borrowed from Medieval Latin *proviso quod* it being provided that (a phrase often appearing at the beginning of a clause in a legal or formal document), from Latin *prōvīsō* provided, ablative case neuter of *prōvīsus,* past participle of *prōvidēre* PROVIDE. **—provisory** *adj.* 1611, subject to a proviso, conditional, in Cotgrave's *Dictionary;* borrowed through French *provisoire,* or directly from Medieval Latin *provisorius* of or for papal provision, from Latin *prōvīsus,* past participle of *prōvidēre;* for suffix see -ORY.

provocateur (prôvôkàtœr′) *n.* person who provokes trouble or violence. 1922, shortened from earlier *agent provocateur* person hired to provoke trouble, agitator (1877); borrowing of French *agent provocateur; provocateur* one who provokes, is a learned borrowing from Latin *prōvocātor* challenger, from *prōvocāre* PROVOKE.

provocation *n.* Before 1400 *provocacyoun* act of provoking or inciting, incitement, instigation; borrowed from Old French *provocacion,* learned borrowing from Latin, and borrowed directly from Latin *prōvocātiōnem* (nominative *prōvocātiō*) a calling forth, challenge, from *prōvocāre* PROVOKE; for suffix see -TION. **—provocative** *adj.* inciting, stimulating, provoking. About 1443, borrowed from Middle French *provocatif* (feminine *provocative*), and directly from Late Latin *prōvocātīvus* calling forth, from Latin *prōvocāre* PROVOKE; for suffix see -IVE.

provoke *v.* 1392, (in medicine) to induce, stimulate; also, to incite, urge, persuade (before 1400); borrowed from Old French *provoker, provoquer,* learned borrowing from Latin, and borrowed directly from Latin *prōvocāre* to call forth, challenge, appeal, excite (*prō-* forth, pro-[1] + *vocāre* to call; see VOICE).

provost (prov′əst) *n.* head or overseer of an institution. Before 1121 *provost,* developed from Old English (before 900) *profost, prafost,* and reinforced by Old French *provost;* both from Medieval Latin *propositus,* alteration of Latin *praepositus* a chief, prefect; literally, placed in charge of, from past participle of *praepōnere* put before; see PREPOSITION.

prow *n.* bow or front part of a ship or boat. 1555, borrowed from Middle French *proue,* from Genoese *prua,* from Vulgar Latin **prōda* (retained in Italian *proda* shore, bank, but obsolete in the sense of prow of a ship) and the source of Spanish, Portuguese, and Catalan *prod* prow. The Vulgar Latin word **prōda* developed by dissimilation of *r* to *d* in Latin *prōra* prow, from Greek *prôira,* earlier **prṓwarya* or **prṓwerya,* related to *pró* before, forward; see FOR.

prowess (prou′is) *n.* bravery, daring. Probably 1225 *pruesse* an act of bravery, in *King Horn;* later *prouesse* bravery, valor (about 1280), and *prowesse* (about 1300); borrowed from Old French *pröece (pro, prou,* later variants of *prod, prud* brave, valiant + *-ece,* from Latin *-itia*). Old French *prod, prud,* developed from Vulgar Latin **prōdem,* accusative of **prōdis;* see PROUD.

prowl *v.* About 1395 *prollen* go or move about, especially in search of something, in Chaucer's *Canterbury Tales;* of unknown origin.

The meaning of go about stealthily, especially on the lookout for a victim or prey, is first recorded in Sidney's *The Arcadia* (before 1586). According to the OED, change in the original form *proll(en)* to *prowl* occurred during the 1500's, but the pronunciation remained (prōl). After about 1750 the change in spelling was reflected in the pronunciation (proul).

—n. 1803, act of prowling, from the verb.

—prowler *n.* 1519 *proller;* later *prowler* (1557); formed from *proll* (later *prowl*) + *-er*[1].

proximal *adj.* situated near the point of origin or attachment. 1727, situated near; formed in English from Latin *proximus* nearest; see PROXIMITY + English suffix *-al*[1]. The specific sense in anatomy of situated near the point of origin or attachment (of a limb, bone, etc.) is first recorded in 1803.

proximate *adj.* next, nearest. 1597 (implied in *proximately*); borrowed from Latin *proximātum,* past participle of *proximāre* come near, from *proximus* nearest; see PROXIMITY; for suffix see -ATE[1].

proximity *n.* nearness. 1480, in Caxton's translation of Ovid's *Metamorphoses;* borrowed from Middle French *proximité* nearness, from Latin *proximitātem* (nominative *proximitās*) nearness, vicinity, from *proximus* nearest, next, superlative of *prope* near; see APPROXIMATE; for suffix see -ITY.

proxy (prok′sē) *n.* action of a deputy or substitute. Probably before 1425 *proccy* letter containing power of attorney, in a translation of Higden's *Polychronicon;* later *prokecye* stewardship (1440); also *proxi* (1454); contraction of earlier *procracie* an annual payment required to be made to a bishop or other prelate (about 1300); borrowed from Anglo-French *procuracie,* and directly from Medieval Latin *procuratia,* alteration of Latin *prōcūrātiō* care, management, from *prōcūrāre* manage; see PROCURE.

prude *n.* prim or priggish person. 1704, in Cibber's *The Careless Husband;* borrowed from French *prude* excessively prim or demure woman, from Old French *prude, prode, preude* good, virtuous, modest, (found in Old French *preudefemme, prodefemme* virtuous woman, *prou de femme;* formed as a parallel to *prud'homme, produme* brave man); see PROUD.

Originally *prude* was recorded in English as applying only to women, as it did in French (in 1709 Steele defined it as "a Courtly word for Female Hypocrites") but by 1781 it was recorded as applying also to men perhaps after such application to men in use of *pruder* (1745, in Walpole's *Letters*).

—prudery *n.* 1709, Steele, in *The Tatler;* perhaps formed from English *prude* + *-ery,* or borrowed directly from French *pruderie,* from *prude* prude; for suffi see -ERY. **—prudish** *adj.* 1717, in Pope's *Works;* formed from English *prude* + *-ish.*

prudence *n.* 1340, wisdom to see what is virtuous, in *Ayenbite of Inwyt;* earlier as a surname (1203); also foresight, practical wisdom, discretion (probably about 1350); borrowed from Old French *prudence,* learned borrowing from Latin, and borrowed directly from Latin *prūdentia* foresight, sagacity, skill, prudence; contraction of *prōvidentia* foresight; see PROVIDENCE; for suffix see -ENCE. **—prudent** *adj.* 1382, wise, discerning, in the Wycliffe Bible; borrowed from Old French *prudent,* learned borrowing from Latin *prūdentem* (nominative *prūdēns*), contraction of *prōvidentem* having foresight, see PROVIDENT; for suffix see -ENT. **—prudential** *adj.* showing prudence. About 1454 *prudencial,* probably borrowed from Medieval Latin *prudentialis,* from Latin *prūdentia* PRUDENCE; for suffix see -AL[1]. It is also possible that in some instances *prudential* was formed in English from Latin *prūdentia.*

prune[1] *n.* dried plum. 1345-46 *prunne;* earlier in the place name *Prunhill* (1201); also *prune* (before 1398); borrowed from Old French *prune, pronne* plum, from Vulgar Latin **prūna* (feminine singular formed from neuter plural of Latin *prūnum*), and borrowed directly from Latin *prūnum;* see PLUM.

prune[2] *v.* cut out useless parts from, clip, trim. 1547 *proine;* 1575 *prune;* developed from Middle English *proinen,* found as *pruynen* (of a bird) trim the feathers with the beak, preen (about 1390); also *prunen* (before 1393, in Gower's *Confessio Amantis*); borrowed possibly from Old French *proignier, proöignier* cut back, prune, from Gallo-Romance **prō-retundiāre* (*prō-* forth, pro-[1] + **retundiāre* round off, from Vulgar Latin **retundus* rounded, from Latin *rotundus* ROUND. The general sense of trim or cut back useless parts appeared probably before 1430, in Lydgate's translation of De Guileville's *Pilgrimage of the Life of Man.* Related to PREEN.

prurient (průr′ēənt) *adj.* lewd, lustful. 1639, itching; later, having an itching desire or curiosity (1653); borrowed from Latin *prūrientem* (nominative *prūriēns*), present participle of *prūrīre* to itch, long for, be wanton; perhaps related to *prūna* glowing coals, and *pruīna* hoarfrost (see FREEZE), from Indo-European **preus-* to freeze or burn (Pok. 846); for suffix see -ENT.

The meaning of lewd or lustful is first recorded in English in Smollett's *Reproof* (1746) **—prurience** *n.* Before 1688, quality or condition of being prurient; formed from English *prurient,* on the analogy of such pairs as *patient,* and *patience,* etc.

prussic acid poisonous liquid used in making plastics and dyes. 1790, in a translation of Lavoisier's *Elementary Chemistry;* borrowed from French *acide prussique* (*acide* ACID and *prussique* Prussian, in reference to Prussian blue, a blue pigment chemically related to prussic acid); for suffix see -IC.

pry[1] *v.* look inquisitively. 1307 *prien* to peer in, seek for; later, look about, especially inquisitively, of uncertain origin; perhaps developed from Old English (about 1000) *beprīwan* to wink.

pry[2] *v.* raise or move by force. 1823, altered form of PRIZE[4], v., lever.

psalm *n.* sacred song or hymn, especially any of those in the Biblical Book of Psalms. Probably before 1200 *psalme,* in *Ancrene Riwle;* also *salme,* in Layamon's *Chronicle of Britain;* developed from Old English *psalm* (about 1000, in Ælfric's *Glossary*); earlier *salm* (before 830, in the *Vespasian Psalter*). Old English *salm, psalm* were early borrowings from Latin *psalmus,* from Greek *psalmós* song sung to the harp, psalm; originally, performance on a stringed instrument, from *psállein* play on a stringed instrument, pull, pluck, of uncertain origin.

Other early Germanic borrowings from the Latin include Old High German *salm, psalm* psalm, and Old Icelandic *salmr, psalmr,* which also show that initial *p* of the Latin and Greek was often dropped, even as in the variant Middle English spelling *saume* (säm), borrowed from Old French *saume, psaume,* from Latin *psalmus.* In many languages *p* was later restored on the model of Latin and Greek, and in such cases became a spelling pronunciation. English is almost alone in writing *ps* and pronouncing as if only spelled with *s.* (It should also be noted that *l,* though preserved in Old English, was often omitted in Middle English, as well as Old French.) **—psalmist** *n.* author of a psalm or psalms. 1483, in Caxton's translation of Cato's writings; borrowed from Middle French *psalmiste,* and directly from Late Latin *psalmista,* from Greek *psalmistḗs,* from *psalmízein* sing psalms, from Greek *psalmós* psalm; for suffix see -IST. The word replaced in Middle English the earlier *psalmistre* (before 1387, in Trevisa's translation of Higden's *Polychronicon*), borrowed from Old French, variant of *psalmiste.*

Psalter (sôl′tər) *n.* Book of Psalms in the Old Testament. Probably before 1200 *sawter,* in *Ancrene Riwle;* also *salter* (before 1225) and *sauter* (About 1280); later *psauter* (about 1340) and *psalter* (1440); developed from Old English *psaltere* (about 1000); earlier *saltere* (737, in Bede's *Ecclesiastical History*); also reinforced in Middle English by borrowing through Anglo-French from Old French *sautier, psaultier.* Both the Old English and the Old French forms were borrowings from Late Latin *psaltērium* Psalter, from Latin, stringed instrument, PSALTERY. For the form and pronunciation of *Psalter* compare the parallel form *psalm* with its specific note.

psaltery (sôl′tərē *or* sôl′trē) *n.* ancient stringed musical instrument. Probably about 1300 *sautri;* earlier as a surname *Sautre* (1248); also *psautery* (about 1340); borrowed from Old French *sauterie, psalterie,* and directly from Latin *psaltērium* stringed instrument, from Greek *psaltḗrion* stringed instrument, from *psállein* play on a stringed instrument, pull, pluck.

pseud- the spelling of the combining form *pseudo-* before vowels, as in the botanical term *pseudaxis* a false axis or stem, the full form *pseudo-* being sometimes retained, as in *pseudoarchaic.*

pseudo (sü′dō) *adj.* false, sham, pretended. About 1449, and perhaps before 1400, adjective use of the combining form PSEUDO-. **—n.** false person. About 1380, in Wycliffe's writings; borrowed from Medieval Latin *pseudo,* from Greek *pseudo-;* and also developed from noun use of the combining form PSEUDO-.

pseudo- a combining form meaning: **1** false, falsely claimed or pretended, as in *pseudoscience, pseudoliberal.* **2** falsely supposed or appearing, as in *pseudohexagonal.* **3** substitute or replacement, as in *pseudonym.* **4** resembling, related, as in *pseudopod, pseudoscorpion.* Borrowed from Greek *pseudo-,* combining form of *pseûdos* falsehood, fallacy, or *pseudḗs* false, from *pseúdein* to cheat by lies, falsify, deceive, of uncertain origin.

Rare in Middle English, *pseudo-* appears chiefly in borrowings from Latin (as in *pseudoprophet*), but is occasionally found in Middle English formations modeled on Latin words, as for example *pseudofrere* false friar, *pseudoprest* heretical priest.

pseudonym (sü'dənim) *n.* pen name. 1846, in Worcester's *Dictionary,* possibly a dictionary word and thereby a back formation from earlier *pseudonymous,* influenced by, and later actually borrowed from, French *pseudonyme,* from Greek *pseudṓnymon,* neuter of *pseudṓnymos* falsely named (*pseudo-* false + *ónyma,* dialectal form of *ónoma* NAME). —**pseudonymous** *adj.* writing under or bearing a pen name. 1706, in Kersey's edition of Phillips' *Dictionary,* borrowed from Greek *pseudṓnymos* falsely named; for suffix see -OUS.

psilocybin (sī'ləsī'bin) *n.* hallucinogenic substance extracted from a kind of mushroom. 1958, formed in English from New Latin *Psilocybe (mexicana)* the mushroom (Greek *psīlós* bare + *kýbē* head) + English *-in*[2].

psittacosis (sit'əkō'sis) *n.* contagious disease of parrots and other birds. 1897, New Latin, formed from Latin *psittacus* parrot, from Greek *psittakós* (probably of Oriental origin) + New Latin *-osis* abnormal condition, disease.

psoriasis (səri'əsis) *n.* kind of chronic skin disease. 1684, New Latin, formed from Late Latin *psōriāsis* mange or scurvy, from Greek *psōríāsis* a being itchy, from *psōriân* have the itch, from *psṓrā* itch or mange, related to *psên* to rub (stem *psā-*), cognate with Sanskrit *psā́ti* chews, from a stem **(bhs-ā-*, an extension of the Indo-European root **bhes-* to rub away (Pok.145) found in Sanskrit *bábhasti* chews, devours.

psych *v. Informal.* 1917, to psychoanalyze; shortened form of *psychoanalyze* (by influence of *psych,* n., meaning psychology or psychiatry, which appeared in 1895).

The meaning of affect, stimulate, influence, or figure out psychologically, is first recorded about 1957, probably as a shortened form of *psychologize* (1830).

psych- the combing form of *psycho-* before vowels, as in *psychic,* and in *psychiatry.*

psyche (sī'kē) *n.* the soul or mind. 1647, animating spirit, soul, in Henry A. More's *Song of Soul;* borrowing of Latin *psȳchē,* from Greek *psȳchḗ* soul, mind, spirit, breath, life, from *psȳ́chein* to breathe, blow, of uncertain origin.

The specific sense in psychology of the mind as the center of thought, emotions, and behavior, is first recorded in 1910, in Carl G. Jung's writings.

psychedelic (sī'kədel'ik) *adj.* (of a drug) expanding the consciousness and perception. 1957, formed in English from Greek *psȳchḗ* mind; see PSYCHE + *dēloûn* make visible, reveal, from *dêlos* visible, clear + English *-ic.* Greek *dêlos* developed from earlier **déalos,* formed from the root of *déato* he appeared, cognate with Sanskrit *dī́deti* shines, from Indo-European **dei-, deyə-* (Pok.183). The word *psychedelic* was coined in 1956 by Humphry Osmond, a British research scientist, then living in Saskatchewan, Canada. —**n.** psychedelic drug. 1956, from the same source as the adjective.

psychiatry *n.* study and treatment of mental disorders. 1846, in Worcester's *Dictionary;* probably borrowed from French *psychiatrie,* formed from Greek *psȳchḗ* soul, mind, PSYCHE + *iātreíā* healing, cure, from *iātrós* physician; see PEDIATRIC. —**psychiatric** *adj.* 1847, probably borrowed from French *psychiatrique,* formed from *psychiatrie* psychiatry + *-ique* -ic. —**psychiatrist** *n.* 1890, student or professor of psychiatry, formed from English *psychiatry* + *-ist.*

psychic (sī'kik) *adj.* 1871, having to do with forces or influences that cause telepathy, clairvoyance, etc., spiritualistic; borrowed perhaps through French *psychique,* but more likely directly from Greek *psȳchikós* of the soul, spirit, or mind, from *psȳchḗ* soul, mind, PSYCHE; for suffix see -IC. Unlike other forms in *-ic* and *-ical* that share meanings, it is unlikely that *psychic* is a shortened form of *psychical,* as the meaning of *psychic* appears at least eleven years before the same meaning for *psychical.*

The meaning of characterized by sensitivity to psychic forces, specially sensitive to psychic influences (as in *to be psychic, psychic gifts*) is first recorded in English in 1895.

—**n.** a psychic person. 1871, probably from the adjective.

—**psychical** *adj.* 1642, of the soul or mind; formed in English from Greek *psȳchikós* + English *-al*[1]. The meaning of having to do with psychic forces or influences is first recorded in English in 1882.

psycho *adj. Informal.* **1** psychological (as in *a psycho drama*). 1927, in *Variety,* American English, shortened form of *psychological.* **2** psychopathic (as in *a psycho killer*). 1936, in Raymond Chandler's writings, American English, shortened form of *psychopathic.* —**n.** a psychopath. 1942, in Berrey and Van Den Bark's *American Thesaurus of Slang,* American English, shortened form of *psychopath.*

psycho- a combining form meaning: **1** of the mind, mental, as in *psychoanalysis, psychology.* **2** of the brain, as in *psychosurgery;* psychological, as in *psychodrama, psychotherapy.* Borrowed from Greek *psȳcho-,* combining form of *psȳchḗ* soul, mind; see PSYCHE. —**psychodrama** *n.* (1937) —**psychohistory** *n.* (1934) —**psychoneurosis** *n.*(1883) —**psychopathology** *n.*(1847) —**psychosomatic** *adj.* (1863) —**psychotherapy** *n.* (1853)

psychoanalysis *n.* examination of a person's mind to discover the unconscious. 1906, borrowed from German *Psychoanalyse* (*Psycho-* mental, psycho- + *Analyse,* from Greek *análysis* ANALYSIS). The term was coined about 1896 by Sigmund Freud, founder of psychoanalysis. —**psychoanalyst** *n.* person who practices psychoanalysis. 1911, formed from English *psychoanalysis,* on the pattern of such pairs as *analysis, analyst.* —**psychoanalytic** *adj.* 1906, formed from English *psychoanalysis,* on the pattern of such pairs as *analysis, analytic.* —**psychoanalyze** *v.* examine by psychoanalysis. 1911, back formation from earlier *psychoanalysis;* formed on the pattern of such pairs as *analysis, analyze.*

psychology *n.* science of the mind. 1653, study of the human soul; borrowed from New Latin *psychologia,* from Greek *psȳchḗ* soul, PSYCHE + *-logiā* -logy. The meaning of the study of the human mind is first recorded in English in 1748. The New Latin *psychologia* is believed to have been coined in Germany in the 1500's, possibly by the scholar Melanchthon (Philipp Schwarzert); its first appearance in literature is in 1590-97, in the sense of the doctrine or study of the soul, as distinguished from *somatologia* study of bodies or material things. The word's first appearance in English is in a 1653 translation of a discourse by James de Back a Dutch physician. The modern sense of psychology a the study or science of the mind began with the works in 1732-34 of the German philosopher Christian von Wolff, and is first found in English in the works of Heartly in 1748. **—psychological** *adj.* Before 1688, formed from English *psychology* + *-ical.* **—psychologist** *n.* 1727, student of the human soul, in Bailey's *Dictionary;* formed from English *psychology* + *-ist.* The meaning of a student of the human mind is first recorded in 1817, in Coleridge's writings.

—psychologize *v.* 1830, to theorize, speculate, or reason psychologically; formed from English *psychology* + *-ize.* The meaning of influence psychologically is first recorded in 1885.

psychopathic *adj.* having a severe mental disorder, mentally ill. 1847, borrowed from German *psychopathisch,* formed from German *psycho-* of the mind + Greek *páthos* suffering; see PATHOS + German *-isch* -ic. **—psychopath** (sī′kəpath) *n.* psychopathic person. 1885, probably a back formation from English *psychopathic.*

psychosis (sīkō′sis) *n.* severe form of mental disorder or disease. 1847, New Latin, from Greek *psȳchḗ* soul, mind; see PSYCHE + New Latin *-osis* abnormal condition. **—psychotic** *adj.* having a psychosis. 1890, from *psychosis,* on the pattern of *neurosis, neurotic.* *—n.* psychotic person. 1910, from the adjective.

ptarmigan (tär′məgən) *n.* kind of grouse. 1599, borrowed from Gaelic *tarmachan.* Early forms (in Scottish use) include *termigan* and *tormichan;* the form *ptarmigan* is first recorded in English in 1684, said to be influenced by Greek words with *pt-,* newly known and used in zoology at the time and usually referred to Greek *pterón* wing, feather.

pterodactyl (ter′ədak′təl) *n.* extinct flying reptile, now in some question as to its supposed existence. 1830 *pterodactyle,* in Sir Charles Lyell's *Principles of Geology;* borrowed from French *ptérodactyle* (1821), from New Latin *Pterodactylus* the genus name (Greek *pterón* wing; see FEATHER + *dáktylos* finger, toe).

ptomaine or **ptomain** (tō′mān) *n.* substance, often poisonous, produced in decaying matter. 1880, borrowed from Italian *ptomaína* (coined by Francesco Selmi, Italian toxicologist), from Greek *ptôma* corpse; literally, a fall, fallen thing, from the root of *píptein* to fall; see FEATHER. **—ptomaine poisoning** (1893)

pub *n. Especially British.* tavern, inn. 1859, in Hotten's *Dictionary;* shortened form of *public house* (1768, in this sense; earlier, an inn or hostelry for the general public, 1658; originally, any building open to the public, 1574).

puberty *n.* physical beginning of manhood and womanhood. About 1384 *puberte,* in the Wycliffe Bible; borrowed through Old French *puberté,* and directly from Latin *pūbertātem* (nominative *pūbertās*) age of maturity, manhood, from *pūbēs* (genitive *pūberis*) adult, full grown, manly, perhaps related to *puer* boy, see PUERILE; for suffix see -TY².

pubescent *adj.* arriving or arrived at puberty. 1646, in part a back formation from earlier *pubescence,* and in part borrowed from French *pubescent,* and directly from Latin *pūbēscentem* (nominative *pūbēscēns*) reach the age of puberty, present participle of *pūbēscere* arrive at puberty, from *pūbēs* adult, full grown; see PUBERTY; for suffix see -ENT. **—pubescence** *n.* Probably before 1425, in a translation of Chauliac's *Grande Chirurgie;* borrowed from Medieval Latin *pubescentia,* from Latin *pūbēscentem* (nominative *pūbēscēns*), present participle of *pūbēscere;* for suffix see -ENCE.

pubis or **pubes** (pyü′bis) *n.* **1** *pubes* pubic hair; about 1570, borrowing of Latin *pubes;* later, the pubic bone (1872, but also in a plural sense, 1841). **2** *pubis* part of either hipbone that forms the front of the pelvis; 1597, borrowed from Middle French *pubis,* a shortening of New Latin *os pubis* bone of the groin, from Latin, and borrowed directly as a shortening of Latin *os pūbis; os* bone; see OSSEOUS; and *pūbis,* genitive of *pūbēs* genital area, groin, related to *pūbēs* full grown, adult; see PUBERTY. **—pubic** *adj.* 1831, having to do with the pubes (hair appearing on the lower abdomen) or the pubis (area formed by pelvic bones at the front of the lower abdomen); formed from English *pub(is), pub(es)* + *-ic.*

public *adj.* 1394 *pupplik* open to general observation, sight, or knowledge; later *publique* of or concerning the people as a whole (1427), and in the spelling *publik* (1447); borrowed from Old French *public, publique,* and directly from Latin *pūblicus,* alteration (influenced by *pūbēs* adult population, adult) of Old Latin *poplicus* pertaining to the people, from *populus* people, see PUBERTY and POPULAR. The spelling *public* began to appear in the 1600's as a revival of the Latin form and was gradually established as the common spelling in the early 1800's. **—n.** Before 1500 *publike* public view, place open to all persons; from the adjective. The meaning of the community, nation, or state, is first recorded in the King James Bible (1611); and that of the people in general in 1665. **—public-address system** (1923) **—public enemy** (1756) **—public health** (1617) **—public library** (1614) **—public office** (1792, room or rooms set aside for public business; 1844, position held by a public official) **—public opinion** (1781, in Gibbon's *Decline and Fall of the Roman Empire*) **—public relations** (1807, in Thomas Jefferson's writings, American English) **—public school** (1580, endowed private school; 1636, free school maintained by taxes, American English) **—public servant** (1676; *public service,* 1570-76) **—public speaking** (1762, American English) **—public utility** (1903) **—public works** (1676, American English)

publican (pub′lәkən) *n. British.* keeper of a pub. Probably before 1200 *puplicane* tax collector of ancient Rome, in *Ancrene Riwle;* later with spelling *publycan* (about 1303, in Mannyng's *Handlyng Synne*); borrowed from Old French *publicain, publican, pupplican,* from Latin *pūblicānus* a tax collector; originally as an adjective, pertaining to the public revenue, from *pūblicum* public revenue, noun use of *pūblicum,* neuter of *pūblicus* PUBLIC; for suffix see -AN. The meaning of a keeper of an inn or public house is first recorded in Bailey's *Dictionary* (1728).

publication *n.* Before 1387 *publicacioun* action of making publicly known, in Trevisa's translation of Higden's *Polychronicon;* borrowed from Old French *publicacion,* and directly from Latin *pūblicātiōnem* (nominative *pūblicātiō*) a making public, from *pūblicāre* make public; see PUBLISH; for suffix see -ATION. The meaning of issuing or offering to the public a book, map, etc., is first recorded in 1576, and that of a work published, a book or the like produced for public sale, in 1656.

publicist *n.* person skilled in public affairs. 1792, a person learned in public law, in Burke's *Works;* 1795, writer or journalist on current public topics, in Hamilton's writings as recorded in the *Congressional Record;*

borrowed from French *publiciste* (*public* PUBLIC + *-iste* -ist).

publicity *n.* 1791, the condition of being public; borrowed from French *publicité* (*public* PUBLIC + *-ité* -ity).

The meaning of the act or fact of making something publicly known, public notice, advertising, is first recorded in Audubon's *Journal* (1826).
—publicize *v.* give publicity to. 1928, formed from English *public,* adj. or n. + *-ize.*

publish *v.* About 1378 *publisshen,* in a version of *Piers Plowman;* also *publishen* (1387); formed from Middle English *publicen* by replacement with *-ish* -ISH[2], as if from Old French **publiss-,* stem of **publir* (not found in Anglo-French or Old French), but actually formed in imitation of other words in Middle English, such as *accomplish, admonish, banish, blandish,* and *finish.* The original Middle English *publicen* (before 1338) was borrowed from Old French *publier, puplier,* learned borrowing from Latin *pūblicāre* make public, from *pūblicus* PUBLIC.

The meaning of issue (copies of a book, etc.) for sale to the public is first recorded in 1529 in reference to the common meaning associated with movable type, but an earlier reference is found to publishing a book, though the means is obscure (about 1450).
—publisher *n.* About 1453, one who makes something known publicly; later, one who publishes a book, etc. (1654); formed from English *publish* + *-er*[1]. **—publishing** *n.* Probably about 1450, the act of making publicly known; about 1454, the issuing of copies of a book for sale to the public; from gerund of English *publish;* for suffix see -ING.[1].

puck[1] *n.* mischievous fairy in English folklore. Probably before 1300 *puke, pouke* the Devil, Satan; later, evil spirit, goblin (about 1378, in a version of *Piers Plowman*); developed from Old English (before 1000) *pūca;* cognate with Frisian *puk* goblin, Old Icelandic *pūki* devil, and Norwegian *pokker* devil, deuce, of unknown origin.

From the 1500's on, notably in Shakespeare's *Midsummer Night's Dream* (1590), the name *Puck* referred to a mischievous goblin called also Robin Goodfellow and Hobgoblin.
—puckish *adj.* mischievous, impish. 1874, formed from English *puck* + *-ish.*[1].

puck[2] *n.* hard disk used in ice hockey. 1891, from earlier *puck,* v., to hit or strike (1861, perhaps related to *poke*[1] to push).

pucker *v.* 1598, to draw into wrinkles or small folds, in Florio's *A World of Words;* possibly formed from English *pock* (dialectal variant of POKE[2] bag, sack) + *-er*[4] (frequentative suffix), the notion being that of forming small baglike or purselike gatherings. Verbs of this type often shorten or obscure the original vowel; compare *clutter, flutter, putter,* etc. **—n.** a wrinkle. 1741 (figurative) state of agitation, flutter, in Richardson's *Pamela;* from the verb. The literal sense of a wrinkle is first recorded in 1744-50.

pudding *n.* 1287 *puding* animal's stomach or casing stuffed with meat, etc., kind of sausage; earlier as a surname *Pudding* (1176); also *poding* (before 1300); of uncertain origin (perhaps related to Old English *puduc* a wen, with allusion to swelling as the basic meaning of the root; *or* traditionally associated semantically with Old French *bodin, boudin* sausage, from the root **bod-* bloated or swollen; and possibly cognate with Low German *pudderwurst* a thick black pudding, *puddig* thick, bloated). German *Pudding* pudding and Dutch *pudding* were borrowed from English.

The meaning of a soft cooked food resembling custard may be recorded as early as 1670, but the original use referring to food boiled or steamed in a bag or cloth is first recorded in 1544.

puddle *n.* Before 1338 *podel* small pool of water, in Mannyng's *Chronicle of England;* probably a diminutive formed from Old English *pudd* ditch + *-le*[1]; and cognate with Low German *pūdel,* High German dialect *Pfūdel* puddle. **—v.** 1440 *pothelen* to dabble or wallow in a puddle, in *Promptorium Parvulorum,* from *pothel,* a variant, of *podel,* n.

The spelling with *u* began to appear in modern English during the first half of the 1500's.

pudendum (pyüden′dəm) *n.* external genitals, especially of the female. 1634, borrowing of Latin *pudendum,* pl. *pudenda,* literally, thing to be ashamed of, neuter gerundive of *pudēre* make ashamed, fill with shame, of uncertain origin. The Latin plural, *pudenda,* is recorded in Middle English before 1398, in Trevisa's translation of Bartholomew's *De Proprietatibus Rerum,* and an Anglicized singular *pudende* appears before 1425, in a translation of Chauliac's *Grande Chirurgie.*

pudeur (püdœr′) *n.* modesty, especially in regard to sexual matters. 1937, in letters of Wyndham Lewis, borrowing of French *pudeur,* from Latin *pudōrem,* accusative of *pudor* shame, modesty, from *pudēre* make ashamed; see PUDENDUM. The modern term is a revival of obsolete *pudor* modesty, bashfulness (1623; borrowed directly from Latin *pudor* shame).

pudgy *adj.* short and fat or thick. 1836, in Dickens' *Sketches by Boz,* formed from English *pudge* (1808) anything short and thick, of uncertain origin + *-y*[1].

Both *pudgy* and the variant *podgy* were popularized in the works of Thackeray, and are perhaps related to, if not simple variants of, *pudsy* plump (1754, possibly a diminutive and embellished form of *pud* a name in children's language for hand or forepaw, 1654).

pueblo (pweb′lō) *n.* Indian village built of adobe and stone. 1808, American English, borrowing of Spanish *pueblo* village or small town, people, community, from Latin *populum,* accusative of *populus* people; see POPULAR.

puerile (pyü′ərəl) *adj.* childish. 1661, a back formation from earlier *puerility,* probably influenced by, and in some instances borrowed through, French *puéril* (feminine *puérile*), from Latin *puerīlis* childish, boyish, from *puer* child, boy; see FEW. **—puerility** *n.* childishness. About 1475 *puerilite,* borrowed from Middle French *puérilité,* from Latin *puerīlitātem* (nominative *puerīlitās*), from *puerīlis* childish, puerile; for suffix see -ITY.

puerperal (pyüėr′pərəl) *adj.* of or pertaining to childbirth. 1768, borrowed from New Latin *puerperālis,* from Latin *puerpera* bearing a child, from *puer* child, boy; see FEW + *parere* to bear (children), bring forth; see PARENT; for suffix see -AL[1]. It is possible that *puerperal* was formed as a replacement for the awkwardly pronounced *puerperial* (1628); formed in English from *puerpery* (1602) + *-ial.*

puff *v.* Probably before 1200 *puffen* blow with short quick blasts, in *Ancrene Riwle;* developed from Old English (about 1000) *pyffan,* of imitative origin. **—n**

Probably before 1200 *puf, puffe,* short, quick blast, in *Ancrene Riwle;* later, light, airy pastry (before 1399); from the verb in Middle English, and in Old English. The figurative meaning of flattery, inflated praise, is first recorded in 1732, probably developed from the earlier sense of bombast, inflated speech or boast (1567). The meaning of a small round mass, usually of down, to apply powder is found in 1712, perhaps as a shortened form of *powder puff* (before 1704). **—puff adder** (1789) **—puffball** *n.* kind of ball-shaped fungus. (1649) **—puff pastry** (1853) **—puffy** *adj.* 1599, (figurative use) vain, bombastic; formed from English *puff,* n. + *-y*[1]. The meaning of swollen, puffed out, fluffy, is first recorded in 1664.

puffin *n.* sea bird of the arctic regions. 1337 *poffoun;* earlier as a surname *Puffin* (1279); also *poffin* (1345); of uncertain origin. Most suggestions make a connection with *puff,* referring to the "puffy" appearance of the bird. The OED rejects this connection, citing the early spellings in *poff-;* the MED, however, shows a 1369 citation with the spelling *puffon* as well as the spelling *Puffin* as a surname.

pug *n.* small, heavy-bodied dog. 1749 *Pug-dog;* earlier *Pug,* nickname for a monkey or dog (1731, in Bailey's *Dictionary*); extended sense of *pug* monkey (1664), sprite, imp (1616); of uncertain origin. **—pug nose** a short squat or snub nose. 1778; so called from the resemblance to a monkey's or dog's nose.

pugilism (pyü′jəlizəm) *n.* boxing. 1791, formed in English from Latin *pugil* boxer (related to *pugnus* fist; see PUNGENT) + English *-ism.* **—pugilist** *n.* 1700, formed in English from Latin *pugil* boxer + English *-ist.* **—pugilistic** *adj.* 1789, either formed from English *pugilist* (perhaps accidentally later in the record of English) + *-ic,* or from French *pugiliste* (1789) + English *-ic.* Another possibility is that *pugilistic* was formed in English from Latin *pugil* boxer + English *-istic,* as in *antagonistic* (1632), etc. These words, all formed at about the same time, give the impression of being vogue words of the late 1700's, and are probably not formed on English *pugil* boxer (1646) which was, according to the OED, a rare word in English. These words were once popular among sportswriters in the United States but have largely died out except in the formation *pugil stick* used in the military as a substitute for a rifle in training for close combat (1962).

pugnacious (pugnā′shəs) *adj.* quarrelsome. 1642, in Henry More's *A Platonical Song of the Soul;* perhaps a back formation from earlier *pugnacity;* or formed in English as an adjective to *pugnacity,* from Latin *pugnācis* genitive of *pugnāx* combative, from *pugnāre* to fight, from *pugnus* fist; see PUNGENT + English suffix *-ous.* **—pugnacity** *n.* quarrelsomeness. 1605, in Bacon's *Of the Advancement of Learning;* borrowed from Latin *pugnācitās,* from *pugnāx* (genitive *pugnācis*) combative; for suffix see -ITY.

puissant (pyü′əsənt) *adj.* powerful, mighty. 1450 *puissaunt;* either formed in English as an adjective to *puissance;* or borrowed from Middle French *puissant,* from *puiss-,* stem of Old French *poeir* to be able; see POWER; for suffix see -ANT. **—puissance** *n.* About 1410 *pusaunce* power, strength, authority; later *puissance* (1431); borrowed from Middle French *puissance, puisance,* from *puissant* puissant; for suffix see -ANCE.

puke *Informal.*—**v.** to vomit. 1600, in Shakespeare's *As You Like It,* perhaps of imitative origin. **—n.** vomit. 1737, from the verb.

Puke was accepted as standard English from the time of Shakespeare until the middle of the 1800's, but is now generally avoided in careful speech or writing.

pulchritude (pul′krətüd) *n. Archaic or Stilted.* beauty. Probably about 1400, borrowed from Latin *pulchritūdo,* from *pulcher* beautiful, of uncertain origin; for suffix see -TUDE. **—pulchritudinous** *adj. Archaic or Stilted.* beautiful. 1912, American English; formed from Latin *pulchritūdo* (genitive *pulchritūdinis*) + English *-ous.*

pule (pyül) *v.* to whine, wimper. 1534, in Sir Thomas More's *A Dialogue of Comfort Against Tribulation;* perhaps borrowed from Middle French *piauler* chirp, whine; possibly of imitative origin. It is also possible that the Middle French form is only parallel to the English.

pull *v.* About 1300 *pullen* to drag, move by pulling; developed from Old English (about 1000) *pullian* to pluck or draw out; of uncertain origin, perhaps cognate with Frisian *pûlje* to shell (peas, etc.), husk, Middle Low German *pulen* to shell, pluck, tear, Middle Dutch *polen* to peel, strip (modern Dutch *peul* husk, shell), and modern Icelandic *pūla* work hard. **—n.** act or effort of pulling. Before 1338 *pul,* in Mannyng's *Chronicle of England;* earlier, a fishing net (1303), from the verb. The informal figurative sense of personal influence used to one's advantage is first recorded in 1887, in American English. **—pullover** *adj.* 1907 *Pullover Storm Coat;* 1921 *Pull-Over Sweater;* probably from the noun. —*n.* 1875, the felt or silk outer covering over the body of a hat. The sense of a sweater or other garment put on by pulling it over the head is first attested in 1925.

pullet *n.* young hen. Before 1376 *pulettis,* pl., in *Piers Plowman;* earlier as a surname *Pulete* (1297); also *pollettes,* pl. (1412-13); borrowed through Anglo-French *pullet,* Old French *polet, pollet, poulette,* diminutives of *poule* hen, from Vulgar Latin **pulla,* feminine of Latin *pullus* young animal, young fowl; see FOAL; for suffix see -ET.

pulley *n.* wheel with a grooved rim in which a rope can run. 1296 *puly;* later *poley* (1324), and *pullyes* (1468); borrowed from Old French *polie, pulie,* and from Medieval Latin *poliva, puliva;* both probably from Medieval Greek **polídia,* plural of **polídion,* diminutive of Greek *pólos* pivot, axis; see POLE². The spelling *pulley* is first recorded in 1574.

Pullman *n.* railroad car with sleeping accommodations. 1867 *Pullman car,* American English, in allusion to George M. *Pullman,* 1831-1897, American inventor, who designed a railroad passenger car with folding upper and lower berths and patented them in 1864-65.

pulmonary *adj.* of the lungs. 1704, in John Harris' *Lexicon Technicum;* borrowed, perhaps by influence of French *pulmonaire,* from Latin *pulmōnārius* the lungs, from *pulmō* (genitive *pulmōnis*) lung; for suffix see -ARY. Latin *pulmō* (metathesized by reversal of *l* and *u* from **plumō*) is cognate with Greek *pleúmōn* lung, and Sanskrit *klóman-* the right lung (formed by dissimilation of *p . . . m* to *k . . . m*), from Indo-European **pleu-mon-/plu-mon-* lung (Pok. 837), from the root **pleu-* to FLOW, swim (see FLOW), so called from the fact that when the innards of a slaughtered animal are placed in a tub of water, the lungs float, while the heart and liver do not. Compare LIGHTS, PNEUMONIA.

Though the word *pulmonary* is a recent formation in English, a history of other words with Latin *pulmō* exists in English, including *pulmonary* as a noun for the lungwort (1658; earlier *pulmonaria,* 1578); *pulmonic* occurring in or affecting the lungs (1661; earlier *pulmonical,* 1597); and *pulmon* a lung or the lungs (probably before 1425).

pulp *n.* soft part of a fruit or vegetable. Before 1400 *pulpe,* in a translation of Lanfranc's *Science of Surgery;* borrowed from Latin *pulpa* (earlier **pelpā*) animal or plant pulp, pith of wood, of uncertain origin.

The slang meaning of a magazine using paper made of cheap wood pulp, and usually containing sensational material, is first recorded in 1931 in American English. **—v.** reduce to pulp. 1662 (implied in *pulping*), from the noun.
—pulpy *adj.* soft, fleshy. 1591, formed from English *pulp,* n. + *-y*[1].

pulpit *n.* Before 1338 *pulpite,* in Mannyng's *Chronicle of England;* later *pulpit* (about 1395); borrowed from Late Latin *pulpitum,* from Old French *pulpite,* and directly from Latin, scaffold, platform, of uncertain origin.

pulsar (pul′sär) *n.* astronomical source of pulsating radio waves. 1968, formed from English *pulse*[1] or *puls(ation)* + *-ar,* on the analogy of earlier *quasar.*

pulsate *v.* to beat, throb. 1794, in Erasmus Darwin's *Zoonomia;* back formation from earlier *pulsation;* for suffix see -ATE[1]. Doublet of PUSH. **—pulsation** *n.* Probably before 1425 *pulsacioun* throbbing of the blood, beating, in a translation of Chauliac's *Grande Chirurgie;* borrowed probably through Middle French *pulsation,* and directly from Latin *pulsātiōnem* (nominative *pulsātiō*) a beating or striking, from *pulsāre* to beat, strike, or push; for suffix see -ATION.

pulse[1] *n.* beating of the arteries. Before 1338 *pous,* in Mannyng's *Chronicle of England;* later *puls, pulse* (before 1390, in Trevisa's translation of Bartholomew's *De Proprietatibus Rerum*); borrowed from Old French *pous, pulse,* and directly from Latin *pulsus,* (genitive *pulsūs*) from past participle of *pellere* to push, drive. The figurative sense of the throbbing of life, emotion, energy, etc. (as in the phrase *to feel the pulse of public sentiment*) is first recorded about 1540. The extended sense of the rhythmical recurrence of vibrations, etc., as of sound, first occurs in 1657. **—v.** Probably before 1425 *pulsen* to throb, in a translation of Chauliac's *Grande Chirurgie;* 1549, to drive, expel, borrowed from Latin *pulsāre* to beat, strike, push, frequentative form of *pellere* to push.

pulse[2] *n.* peas, beans, and lentils, used as food. 1297 *pols* (in the compound *polscorn*); later *puls* (1388-89); borrowed from Old French *pols, pouls,* and directly from Latin *puls* (genitive *pultis*) porridge, probably, through Etruscan, from Greek *póltos;* see POLLEN.

pulverize *v.* Probably before 1425 *pulverizen,* in a translation of Chauliac's *Grande Chirurgie;* borrowed from Late Latin *pulverizāre* reduce to powder or dust, from Latin *pulvis* (genitive *pulveris*) dust, see POLLEN; for suffix see -IZE.**—pulverization** *n.* 1658, borrowed from French *pulvérisation,* from Middle French *pulveriser* pulverize + *-ation.*

puma (pyü′mə) *n.* cougar. 1777, in William Robertson's *The History of America,* borrowing of Spanish *puma,* from Quechua (Peru) *puma.*

pumice (pum′is) *n.* volcanic glass. 1400 *pomyse;* later *pumyce* (probably about 1475); borrowed through Anglo-French *pomis,* Middle French *ponce,* from Late Latin *pōmex* (genitive *pōmicis*), an adaptation of Oscan **poimex,* variant of Latin *pūmex* pumice; see FOAM. **—v.** smooth or polish with pumice. Before 1425 *pomeysen;* probably about 1425 *pumycen;* from the noun.

pummel *v.* beat or strike repeatedly. 1548 *pumble, poumle,* alteration of POMMEL, v. The spelling *pummel* is first recorded in Beaumont and Fletcher's *Four Plays in One* (1608).

pump[1] *n.* apparatus for forcing liquids, air, etc. in or out of things. 1420 *pomp* ship's pump; 1427 *pumpe;* possibly borrowed from Middle Dutch *pompe* water conduit, pipe, and Middle Low German *pumpe* pump (modern German *Pumpe*), both derived probably from the same source in nautical use. Danish *pumpe,* Swedish *pump,* and French *pompe* were probably borrowings from the Middle Dutch and Middle Low German. **—v.** move (liquids, air, etc.) by a pump. 1508, from the noun.

If an association with *plump* (1300) exists, it is through Low German *plumpe* and the verb *plumpen,* possibly in early reference to the plunging action of the piston, and therefore of an origin imitative of the sound of something hitting water, though some suggestion of an association with Latin *plumbum* lead, *plumbāre* to cast a plumb line has been offered.

pump[2] *n.* shoe without fasteners. 1555, a light, close-fitting, slipperlike shoe; of unknown origin. It is of unknown significance why the thin soles of pumps were usually mentioned in reference to pumps. Early etymologies of this word suggest a connection with pomp, ornament, or show and compare German *Pumpstiefel* large, clumsy boot, but the references are obscure.

pumpernickel *n.* kind of heavy, dark bread. 1839, American English, in Longfellow's *Hyperion;* borrowing of German *Pumpernickel,* from dialectal German of Westphalia; originally an abusive term, a compound of *pumpern* to break wind + *Nickel* goblin, rascal; see NICKEL.

An early example, spelled *Pompernickel,* is recorded in British English in 1756, which suggests that its appearance in American English probably represents a reborrowing from the German, or, less likely, a defect in the record of English.

pumpkin *n.* 1647, in Nathaniel Ward's *The Simple Cobler of Aggawam in America,* alteration (influenced by *-kin*) of earlier *pompone, pumpion* melon or pumpkin (1545); borrowed from Middle French *pompon, pepon,* learned borrowing from Latin *pepōn* melon, from Greek *pépōn,* originally, cooked by the sun, ripe, from *péptein, péssein* to COOK.

The term *pumpkin pie* appeared in 1654 in American English. An informal U.S. spelling is *punkin* (1825).

pun *n.* play on words. 1662, in Dryden's *The Wild Gallant, a Comedy,* of uncertain origin. *Pun* was probably a clipped word, such as *mob,* which came into fashionable slang in the late 1600's. Longer equivalents, found before 1676, were *punnet* and *pundigrion.* While *punnet* may have been a diminutive of *pun,* the form *pundigrion* suggests that *pun* may have been originally shortened from Italian *puntiglio* equivocation, trivial objection, small or fine point; see PUNC-

TILIO. Nothing, however, has been found in the early history of *pun,* or in the English uses of *punctilio,* to confirm the origin of *pun.* **—v.** to make puns. 1670, from the noun. **—punster** *n.* 1700, in Congreve's *The Way of the World;* formed from English *pun,* n. + *-ster.*

punch[1] *v.* to pierce, hit. About 1384 *punchen* to poke or prod, in the Wycliffe Bible; later, to stab, pierce, (1440 in *Promptorium Parvulorum*); borrowed from Old French *ponchonner, poinçonner* to punch, prick, from *ponchon, poinçon* pointed tool, piercing weapon, from Vulgar Latin **punctiōnem* (nominative **punctiō*) pointed tool, from **punctiāre* to pierce, prick, from Latin *pūnct-* past participle stem of *pungere* to prick; see PUNGENT.

The meaning of hit with the fist is first recorded in 1530, in Palsgrave's *Lesclarcissement,* and that of pierce, cut, stamp, emboss, etc., with a tool, in 1423. **—n.** Before 1400 *punche* a stab or thrust; later, a dagger, a tool or instrument for piercing, punching, etc. (1505); probably a variant of *ponchon;* see PUNCHEON[2]. The meaning of a tool or machine for stamping a dye is first recorded in 1628. The meaning of act of punching, quick blow (1580) is probably from the verb.

The informal sense of vigorous force or effectiveness is found in 1911 in American English.

—punch card (1919 *punched card,* 1945 *punch card*) **—punch-drunk** *adj.* dazed from continual punching (as in boxing). 1918, in *Saturday Evening Post,* American English. **—punch line** (1921, in *Variety,* American English)

punch[2] *n.* mixed drink. 1632, of uncertain origin. The English author John Fryer, who traveled in western India in the 1670s's, wrote that the word was borrowed from Hindi or Marathi *pānch* five, from Sanskrit *páñca* (see FIVE), in reference to the number of ingredients in the drink. This etymology has been long disputed on various grounds: that no equivalent meaning is found in the Indian vernaculars, that the Hindi or Marathi form *pānch* should have yielded English *paunch;* that the early pronunciation of *punch* was with the *u* in *put* (u), which could not have represented *pānch;* and that the number of ingredients in the drink does not seem to have been fixed or specified as five at any time. Despite these difficulties, the Indian derivation is widely cited as a possibility, primarily because no better substitute has been proposed so far.

Punch *n.* hooknosed, humpbacked puppet. 1709, Steele, in *The Tatler;* shortened from PUNCHINELLO. *Punch* is the name of a puppet who quarrels violently with his wife Judy in the puppet show *Punch and Judy.* The wife's name is curiously not recorded until the early 1800's.

The phrase *pleased as Punch,* with the meaning of very much pleased, is first recorded in 1813.

In 1841 *Punch* became the title of a humorous weekly journal published in London, of which the puppet is assumed editor.

puncheon[1] *n.* cask for liquor. 1400 *pynson;* later *pownchon* (1419-20) and *ponchon* (1468); borrowed from Middle French *poinchon, poinçon, ponson,* of uncertain origin.

Although the forms in Middle French and English are identical with *puncheon*[2], and the barrel staves of a *puncheon* are reminiscent of "upright slabs of timber", there seems to be little else that provides a connection in the meaning between the two words. The spelling *puncheon* does not appear before 1833, perhaps influenced by the similarity in sound with *luncheon.*

puncheon[2] *n.* slab of timber, short upright piece of wood. 1348 *pounchonn,* 1374 *punchon* short supporting beam, strut; earlier, as a surname *Punchian* (1274); also *ponson, ponchon* pointed tool for piercing, punch (1370); borrowed from Old French *ponchon, poinçon;* see PUNCH[1], v. The extended sense of a slab of timber with a roughly finished face is first recorded in 1725, in American English.

punchinello (pun′chənel′ō) *n.* clown. 1666 *punchinello,* (also) *Polichinello,* borrowed from Italian *Pulcinella* (or Neapolitan dialect *Pollecinella*), diminutive of *pollecena* turkey pullet (the beak of which bears a resemblance to the nose of Pulcinella), from Latin *pullus* young fowl; see FOAL.

Punchinello was originally the name of the principal character in a traditional Italian puppet show, the prototype of *Punch.* The name was applied in 1669 to any person or thing thought to resemble the puppet's characteristic behavior.

punctilio (pungktil′ēō) *n.* detail of honor, conduct, ceremony, etc. 1596 *puntilio* small point or mark; probably borrowed from Italian *puntiglio* small or fine point, trivial objection, from Spanish *puntillo* small point, diminutive of *punto* point, from Latin *pūnctum* prick, POINT. The specific sense of a detail of conduct, a petty formality, is first recorded in English in 1599, but the spelling *punctilio* is not found before 1626, and was at that time influenced by Latin *pūnctum.* **—punctilious** *adj.* very careful and exact. 1634 *puntillious,* probably borrowed from Italian *puntiglioso,* from *puntiglio* fine point; for suffix see -OUS. The spelling *punctilious* is first recorded in 1742 (though an earlier spelling *punctillious* is found in 1653), influenced by English *punctilio* or by Latin *pūnctum.*

punctual *adj.* prompt. Before 1400, having a sharp point, producing small punctures, in a translation of Lanfranc's *Science of Surgery;* borrowed (perhaps through influence of Old French *punctuel*) from Medieval Latin *punctualis,* from Latin *pūnctus* (genitive *pūnctūs*) a pricking, POINT; for suffix see -AL[1]. The meaning of attentive to points or details of conduct is first recorded in 1598 (implied in *punctually*), and the sense of being strictly observant of an appointed time, prompt, in 1675. **—punctuality** *n.* 1620, exactness, precision, apparently formed from English *punctual* + *-ity.* The Medieval Latin *punctualitas* had the literal sense of the condition of being punctured, and the French *punctualité* is not recorded until 1627 (though that is probably not a significant difference of time). The current sense of the fact or habit of being punctual, exact observance of an appointed time, is first recorded in Sheridan's *School for Scandal* (1777).

punctuate *v.* use periods and other marks in sentences. 1818, in Todd's revision of Johnson's *Dictionary,* probably a back formation from the earlier English *punctuation;* for suffix see -ATE[1]. **—punctuation** *n.* Before 1539, insertion of points to mark pauses in a text; borrowed, perhaps through Middle French *punctuation,* and directly from Medieval Latin *punctuationem* (nominative *punctuatio*) a marking with points, from *punctuare* to mark with points or dots, from Latin *pūnctus* a prick; see POINT; for suffix see -ATION. The meaning of insertion of periods and other marks in sentences is first recorded in English in 1661. **—punctuation mark** (1866).

puncture *n.* 1392, small perforation or wound, act of pricking or stinging; borrowed from Late Latin *pūnctūra* a pricking, a puncture, from Latin *pūnctus,* past participle of *pungere* to prick, pierce, see PUNGENT; for suffix see -URE. **—v.** 1699, to prick, pierce, from the noun.

pundit *n.* very learned person. 1672, very learned Hindu, borrowed from Hindi *paṇḍit* a learned man, master, teacher, from Sanskrit *paṇḍitá-s* a learned man, scholar; adj. learned, skilled, of uncertain origin. The transferred meaning of any very learned person or authority is first recorded in English in 1816 (originally in a satirical context). **—punditry** *n.* characteristics of a pundit. 1926, formed from English *pundit* + *-ry.*

pungent *adj.* 1597, (figurative) sharp, keen, acute; borrowed from Latin *pungentem* (nominative *pungēns*), present participle of *pungere* to prick, pierce, sting; related to *pugnus* fist. The Latin *pugnus* is cognate with Greek *pygmḗ* fist and *peukedanós* piercing, bitter, from Indo-European **peuĝ-/puĝ-, *peuk̑-* to prick, stab (Pok.828); for suffix see -ENT. Doublet of POIGNANT.

The meaning of sharply affecting the organs of smell or taste appeared in English in 1668.
—pungency *n.* 1649, sharpness, poignancy, piquancy; formed from English *pungent* + *-cy.*

punish *v.* About 1303 *ponysshen* to inflict divine retribution on, in Mannyng's *Handlyng Synne;* later *punissen* to cause pain, loss, or discomfort to for a fault or offense (1340, in *Ayenbite of Inwyt*), and in the spelling *punishen* (1348); borrowed from Old French *puniss-,* stem of *punir,* from Latin *pūnīre* inflict a penalty on, cause pain for some offense, formed from *poena* penalty, punishment; see PAIN; for suffix see -ISH². **—punishable** *adj.* 1429 *punisshable,* borrowed through Anglo-French *punisable,* from Middle French *punissable,* from Old French *puniss-,* stem of *punir* punish; for suffix see -ABLE. It is also possible that in some instances Middle English *punisshable* was formed from Middle English *punish* + *-able.* **—punishment** *n.* 1385 *punisshment,* in Usk's *Testament of Love,* borrowed through Anglo-French *punisement,* from Old French *punissement,* from *puniss-,* stem of *punir* punish; for suffix see -MENT.

punitive (pyü′nətiv) *adj.* concerned with punishment. 1624, borrowed from French *punitif* (feminine *punitive*), from Medieval Latin *punitivus,* from Latin *pūnīre* PUNISH; for suffix see -IVE.

punk *n.* 1687, rotten wood used as tinder, American English, probably borrowed from Algonquian (Delaware) *ponk,* literally, living ashes.

The extended meaning of slow-burning preparation in the form of sticks, used to light fireworks, is first recorded in 1869, in Thomas Bailey Aldrich's *The Story of A Bad Boy.* A transferred sense of something rotten or worthless, nonsense, rubbish, is also first recorded in 1869, and its figurative use of a worthless person, young hoodlum, is found in 1917 (in E.E. Cummings' *Letters*). This latter use was probably shortened from the earlier underworld slang term *punk kid* a criminal's apprentice (1908). The term *punk rock,* referring to an aggressive, boisterous type of rock music, appeared in 1971, forming a new adjective with the meaning of in the style of ragged clothes and garish makeup worn by punk-rock musicians or their fans.
—adj. 1902, American English, (of wood) rotten, decayed; from the noun. The informal figurative sense of worthless, rotten, inferior, is first recorded in George Ade's *Artie* (1896).

punt¹ *n.* shallow, flat-bottomed boat. 1568, shortened form of earlier *pontebot* punt boat (1500); developed from Old English (about 1000) *punt,* borrowed from Latin *pontō* flat-bottomed boat, PONTOON. The Old English word probably continued into the Middle English period, although there are no recorded examples until the reappearance of the term in early modern English. **—v.** propel (a boat) by pushing with a pole. 1816, from the noun.

punt² *v.* to kick (a football or soccer ball). 1845, perhaps special use of dialectal English *punt* to push, strike, alteration of *bunt,* of uncertain origin. **—n.** a kick. 1845, from the same source as *punt²,* v.

puny (pyü′nē) *adj.* small, weak. Before 1577, subordinate, inferior in rank; borrowed from Middle French *puîné,* from Old French *puisné* born later, younger, (*puis* afterwards, from Vulgar Latin **postius,* from Latin *posteā,* from *post* after + Old French *né* born, from Latin *nātus,* past participle of *nāscī* be born; see POST- and NATIVE). The *-y* is now considered suffixal, but is no more than a representation of *-é* from the French form. The sense of small, weak, insignificant, appeared in Shakespeare's *Richard II* (1593). *Puny* is the original spelling in English, preceding the form *puisne* (pyü′nē) in most senses by some 25 to 50 years. The French form was adopted in English during the 1600's and died out in the 1700's, except for legal use in the 1800's in reference to junior judges of a superior court.

pup *n.* puppy. 1773, young dog, shortened variant form of PUPPY. Extended application to a young seal is first recorded in 1815. An earlier figurative sense of silly, conceited person, is found in 1589, the same year that this sense is found for the form *puppy.* **—pup tent** small, low tent. (1863, American English)

pupa (pyü′pə) *n.* stage between the larva and adult insect. 1773, New Latin, special use of Latin *pūpa* girl, doll, puppet; see PUPIL¹ student. **—pupal** *adj.* (1866, in Darwin's *Origin of Species*) **—pupate** *v.* become a pupa. 1879; formed from New Latin *pupa* + English *-ate¹.* **—pupation** *n.* (1892)

pupil¹ *n.* student. 1384 *pupille* an orphan child, ward, in the Wycliffe Bible; borrowed from Old French *pupille,* and directly from Latin *pūpillus* (feminine *pūpilla*) orphan, ward, minor, diminutives of *pūpus* boy (feminine *pūpa* girl), probably related to *puer* child, boy; see FEW. The meaning of one who is learning or being taught, disciple, student, is first recorded in English in 1563.

pupil² *n.* spot in the iris of the eye. 1392 *pupilla* (as a Latinate form); before 1400 *pupille;* later *pupil* (about 1425); borrowed from Old French *pupille,* and directly from Latin *pūpilla,* originally, little doll, diminutive of *pūpa* girl, doll (see PUPIL¹); so called from the tiny image of oneself that can be seen reflected in the pupils when looking into another person's eyes.

puppet *n.* 1538, doll moved by strings or wires, in Elyot's *Dictionary;* developed from Middle English *poppet, popet* doll (1413; earlier, small person, 1390; wax figure, probably before 1300, in *Kyng Alisaunder,* and as a surname *Pupet,* 1191). The Middle English forms were probably borrowed from Old French (compare Middle French *poupette* little doll, diminutive of Old French *poupée* doll, from Vulgar Latin **puppa,* from Latin *pūpa* girl, doll; see PUPIL[1] student); for suffix see -ET.

The figurative meaning of a person whose actions are manipulated by another is first recorded in English in 1592, and earlier with the spelling *poppet* (1550). **—puppeteer** *n.* 1930, one who manipulates puppets, formed from English *puppet* + *-eer.* **—puppetry** *n.* 1528, action of or representation by puppets; formed from English *puppet* + *-ry.* **—puppet show** (1650; earlier *puppet play,* 1599, and implied in *puppet-playing,* 1552).

puppy *n.* 1486 *popi* woman's small pet dog; of uncertain origin, but on the analogy of a small pet dog being considered a toy, possibly borrowed from Middle French *poupée* doll, toy, from Vulgar Latin **puppa,* from Latin *pūpa* girl, doll; see PUPIL[1] student; for suffix see -Y[1]. The meaning of a young dog, whelp, is first found in Shakespeare's *Two Gentlemen of Verona* (1591); the figurative sense of a vain, impertinent young man, fop, coxcomb, is attested since 1589. **—puppy dog** (1595, in Shakespeare's *King John*) **—puppy love** (1834, American English)

purblind (pėr′blīnd′) *adj.* nearly blind. About 1300 *pur blind* pure (entirely) blind; earlier a near-sighted person (before 1300). A weakened meaning of nearly or partially blind, dim-sighted or blind in one eye, appeared before 1382, and the figurative sense of having imperfect perception, stupid, obtuse, dull, is found in 1533, in Sir Thomas More's writings.

purchase *v.* Probably before 1300 *purchasen, purchacen* acquire, buy; also, bring about, recruit or hire, in *Arthour and Merlin* and *Kyng Alisaunder;* borrowed through Anglo-French *purchaser* go after, pursue, from Old French *porchacier, pourchachier, purchacier* (*pur-* forth, from Latin *prō-* forth, pro-[1] + Old French *chacier* run after, CHASE[1]). **—n.** Probably before 1300 *purchas* booty, spoil, in *Arthour and Merlin* and *Kyng Alisaunder;* also, *porchas* something acquired, a possession (about 1300), and in the spelling *purchace* (before 1338); borrowed through Anglo-French *purchace, purchaz,* from Old French *purchas,* from *purchacier* to purchase. The sense of the act of buying something is first recorded in the King James Bible (1611). The meaning of a firm hold to help move something appeared in 1711, from the verb in the sense of haul in (a rope) with the hands, in effect to gain or acquire one portion after another (1567).

pure *adj.* About 1250 *pur* refined, unmixed, unalloyed; earlier as a surname (1178); also with the spelling *pure* (about 1280); borrowed from Old French *pur, pure,* and directly from Latin *pūrus* clean, clear, unmixed, chaste. Latin *pūrus* is cognate with Middle Irish *ūr* fresh, new, Welsh *ir,* Sanskrit *punā́ti* (he) cleanses, and possibly with Old High German *fowen* to winnow grain, sift, from Indo-European **peu-/pu-, *pewə-/pū-* (Pok.827). **—purebred** *adj.* of pure breed or stock. (1868, American English)

purée (pyu̇rā′) *n.* cooked food pushed through a sieve. 1707, in J. Mortimer's *Whole Art of Husbandry;* borrowing of French *purée,* from past participle of *purer* to strain, cleanse, from Latin *pūrāre* purify, from *pūrus* PURE. **—v.** make into a purée. Before 1934, from the noun.

purgatory *n.* place of spiritual purging. Probably before 1200 *purgatoire,* in *Ancrene Riwle,* later *purgatorie* (before 1250); borrowed from Old French *purgatore, purgatoire* (first used by the Anglo-French poet Marie de France in the late 1100's), and borrowed directly from Medieval Latin *purgatorium,* from Late Latin, means of cleansing, from neuter of *pūrgātōrius,* adj., purging, cleansing, from Latin *pūrgāre* to PURGE; for suffix see -ORY. **—purgatorial** *adj.* Before 1500, formed in English from Medieval Latin *purgatorium* or Late Latin *pūrgātōrius* + English *-al*[1].

purge *v.* About 1300 *puyrgien* to clear of a charge or suspicion of guilt, establish innocence; later *purgen* cleanse, clear, get rid of, purify; borrowed through Anglo-French *purger,* Old French *purgier,* learned borrowing from Latin, and borrowed directly from Latin *pūrgāre* cleanse, purify, Old Latin *pūrigāre,* from a lost adjective **pūrigus* purifying (*pūrus* PURE + the root of *agere* to drive, make; see AGENT).

The medical sense of empty (the bowels) is first recorded about 1390. The meaning of get rid of (any politically undesirable person or people) developed from the meaning in law of wipe out (an offense or sentence), 1681, passing into the sense of *purge* in *Pride's Purge* exclusion of Royalist members of the Long Parliament prior to the English Civil War (first recorded in 1730), and later reinforced in the 1930's in the context of Soviet politics, as a loan translation of Russian *chistit'* to clean, purge.

—n. 1447, an examination in a court of law to clear of a charge or suspicion of guilt; later, a purgative (1563); and act of purging (1598); in all senses probably from the verb in English, though Murray in the OED felt "the act of purging" was borrowed from the French *purge.* The meaning of the act or fact of getting rid of a person who is politically undesirable appeared in H.G. Wells' *The Shape of Things to Come* (1933), in reference to Soviet politics, and while reinforcing the sense known earlier in *Pride's Purge* (1730), by introducing this loan translation of Russian *chístka* cleaning, purge, from *chistit'* to clean, purge, it was not a new sense in present-day English as is sometimes claimed. **—purgation** *n.* act of purging. About 1382 *purgacioun* purification from sin, in the Wycliffe Bible; also, discharge of waste matter (1387); borrowed from Old French *purgacion,* and directly from Latin *pūrgātiōnem* (nominative *pūrgātiō*) a cleansing, *pūrgāre* to purge; for suffix see -ATION. **—purgative** *adj.* purging, laxative. Before 1398 *purgatif,* in Trevisa's translation of Bartholomew's *De Proprietatibus Rerum;* borrowed from Old French *purgatif* (feminine *purgative*), and directly from Late Latin *pūrgātivus,* from Latin *pūrgāre* to purge; for suffix see -IVE. **—n.** purging medicine; a cathartic or laxative. Probably before 1425, in a translation of Chauliac's *Grande Chirurgie;* from the adjective in English, and perhaps in some instances borrowed from Middle French *purgatif.*

purify *v.* Before 1338 *purifien,* in Mannyng's *Chronicle of England;* borrowed from Old French *purifier,* from Latin *pūrificāre,* from a lost adjective **pūrificus* (*pūrus* PURE + the root of *facere* to make, perform, DO[1]); for suffix see -FY. **—purification** *n.* 1350 *purificaciun* Feast of the Purification of the Virgin Mary; borrowed through Old French *purification,* and directly from Latin *pūrificātiōnem* (nominative *pūrificātiō*) a purifying, from *pūrificāre* purify; for suffix see -ATION.

purism *n.* 1803 *purisms,* pl. uses of language that reflect strict observance of purity or "correctness" in language; 1804, strict observance of purity in language, style, etc., in William Mitford's *An Inquiry into the*

Principles of Harmony in Language; borrowed from French *purisme* (*pur* PURE + *-isme* -ism), and, in some later instances, formed from English *pur(e)* + *-ism.* **—purist** *n.* 1706, in Kersey's edition of Phillips' *Dictionary;* formed from English *pur(e)* + *-ist,* and in later instances (such as Chesterfield's *Letters*) borrowed from French *puriste* (*pur* pure + *-iste* -ist).

Puritan *n.* Protestant of the 1500's and 1600's advocating a return to a stricter moral standard and church government, doctrine, and ceremony that was not so closely associated with that of the Roman Catholic practice. 1564 (applied to opponents of the Anglican hierarchy's directives in matters of ritual and vestments; later, those within the Church of England who demanded further reformation in the direction of Presbyterianism, 1571); probably formed from English *purity* + *-an.*

From 1592 on, *Puritan* (as a name for the "Brownists," those who were associated with their chief spokesman Robert Brown) was commonly applied, often in reproach or ridicule, to anyone considered overly strict in religion and morals. By the 1800's, especially in the United States in reference to the Puritans who settled in New England in the early 1600's, the term became historical and lost much of its derogatory connotation (though not in the derivatives *puritanical* and *puritanism*).

—puritanical *adj.* of or like a Puritan; excessively strict in morals or religion. 1607, formed from English *Puritan* + *-ical.* **—puritanism** *n.* 1573, doctrines and principles of the Puritans; later, excessive strictness in morals or religion (1592); formed from English *Puritan* + *-ism.*

purity *n.* Probably before 1200 *purte* quality or condition of being pure, in *Ancrene Riwle;* also as a surname (1198); later *puryte* (about 1380); borrowed from Old French *purté, pureté,* and directly from Late Latin *pūritātem* (nominative *pūritās*) cleanness, pureness, from Latin *pūrus* PURE; for suffix see -ITY. The modern spelling *purity* is first recorded in 1563.

purl[1] *v.* flow with rippling motions and murmuring sound. Before 1586 (implied in *purling*), in Sidney's *Astrophel and Stella;* perhaps borrowed from a Scandinavian source (compare Norwegian *purla* to purl). **—n.** 1650, purling motion or sound; earlier *perle* a surge of water (before 1500); perhaps borrowed from a Scandinavian source (compare Norwegian *purl* purl).

purl[2] *v.* knit with inverted stitches. 1526 *pirl, pyrle* to embroider with metallic thread; related to earlier *pirl* to twist thread (1523), and probably with Middle English *pirlyng* revolving or twisting (1448-49); of uncertain origin.

The specific meaning of knit with inverted stitches is first recorded before 1825.

—n. 1394, bordering, edging, frilling of twisted loops; later, metallic thread used for bordering and embroidering (1535); from the verb. The sense of an inversion of stitches in knitting is first recorded in 1825, curiously in Jamieson's *Etymological Dictionary of the Scottish Language.*

purlieu (pėr′lü) *n.* one's haunt or resort. 1482 *purlewe* piece of land on the border of a forest, perhaps an alteration (influenced by Middle French *lieu* place; see LIEU) of Middle English *porale* royal or official perambulation to determine boundaries of manor, district, or forest (1306); later *purale* (1338); borrowed through Anglo-French *puralé, puralee,* originally, a going through, Old French *poralé,* from *poraler* go through (*por-* forth, from Latin *prō-* forth, pro-[1] + *aler* to go; see ALLEY).

The figurative sense of one's haunt or resort is first recorded in Sir Thomas Browne's *Religio Medici* (1643).

purloin *v.* to steal. 1348 *purloinen* remove, make distant, misappropriate; borrowed through Anglo-French *purloigner, purloiner* remove, and directly from Old French *porloigner* put off (*por-* forth, from Latin *prō-* forth, pro-[1] + Old French *loing, loin* far, from Latin *longē,* from *longus* LONG[1], adj.).

purple *adj.* about 1250 *purpel,* later *purpul* (about 1425, in the Wycliffe Bible), and *purple* (1436); developed from Old English *purpul, purbple* (about 950, in *Lindisfarne Gospels),* from earlier *purpure* purple garment (before 899, in Alfred's translation of Orosius' *Historiarum Adversus Paganos*). The Old English word was borrowed from Latin *purpura* purple-dyed cloth, purple dye, shellfish yielding a purple dye, from Greek *porphýrā,* of uncertain origin. Related to PORPHYRY.

The Old English form *purpul* probably developed by dissimilation of the second *r* to *l,* as found in *marble* (from the original *marbre, marbra*).

—n. About 1390 *purpul, purpel* rich cloth dyed purple; later, *purpil* the color purple (probably before 1439); from the adjective.

—v. make or become purple. Probably before 1400 (implied in the past participle *perpulid*); later *purpullen* (1425, in a translation of Higden's *Polychronicon*); from the adjective.

purport (pėr′pôrt) *n.* main idea, meaning. 1422 *purporte;* borrowed through Anglo-French *purport* contents (Anglo-Latin *purportum,* Old French *purport*) from *purporter* to contain (Old French *porporter* convey, carry); formed from *por-* forth, from Latin *prō-* forth, pro-[1] + Old French *porter* carry; see PORT[4] bearing. **—v.** (pərpôrt′) to claim, mean. 1424 *purporten* to indicate, express, set forth; originally borrowed through Anglo-French *purporter* (Old French *porporter*); formed as in the noun; in later instances perhaps from the noun in English.

purpose *n.* About 1300 *porpos* intention, aim, goal; 1307 *purpos;* later *purpose* (about 1350); borrowed through Anglo-French *purpos* aim, intention, from *purposer* to design, intend; and directly from Old French *porpos* aim, intention, from *porposer* to put forth (*pur-, por-* forth, from Latin *prō-* forth, pro-[1] + Old French *poser* to put, place, POSE, influenced by the perfect stem *prōpos-* of Latin *prōpōnere* put forward, PROPOUND). **—v.** to aim, intend. About 1380 *purposen* to state, set forth, in Chaucer's translation of Boethius' *De Consolatione Philosophiae;* about 1384, to aim, intend; probably from the noun in Middle English, influenced by, or in some instances borrowed through Anglo-French *purposer,* to design, intend, Old French *porposer* intend. **—purposely** *adv.* with intent, on purpose (1590, in Shakespeare's *Comedy of Errors,* gradually replacing earlier *of purpose,* recorded before 1382, in the Wycliffe Bible).

purr *n.* low murmuring sound such as a cat makes. 1601, in Shakespeare's *All's Well That Ends Well;* of imitative origin. **—v.** make a purr. 1620, in Thomas Shelton's translation of Cervantes' *Don Quixote;* of imitative origin.

purse *n.* About 1250 *purse;* earlier *purs* (probably before 1200, in *Ancrene Riwle*); found in Old English (before 1000) *purs* small bag for carrying money, alteration (perhaps influenced by Old English *pusa* bag) of Medieval Latin *bursa* purse, from Late Latin, variant of *byrsa* hide, from Greek *býrsa,* of unknown origin. —v. 1303 *pursen* put in a purse, in Mannyng's *Handlyng Synne;* from the noun in Middle English. The meaning of draw together (as one does the strings of a purse or money bag), press into wrinkles, is first recorded in Shakespeare's *Othello* (1604).

—purser *n.* 1445 *pursere* treasurer, ship's officer in charge of accounts and provisions; earlier as a surname *Pursere* (1272); formed from Middle English *purse,* n. + *-er*[1]. Doublet of BURSAR.

purslane (pėrs′lān) *n.* common trailing herb. Before 1392 *purcelane;* later *purslane* (1440); probably borrowed through Anglo-French *purcelane,* and directly from Old French *porcelaine,* alteration (influenced by confusion in form with *porcelaine* PORCELAIN) of Latin *porcilāca,* variant of *portulāca* purslane; see PORTULACA.

pursue *v.* About 1280 *pursuwien* to harass, torment, persecute; later, to chase, follow, seek after (about 1300), and in the spelling *pursuen* (about 1350); borrowed through Anglo-French *pursuer,* and directly from Old French *poursuïr, porsüir,* variants of *porsivre, porsivir,* from Vulgar Latin **prōsequere,* from Latin *prōsequī* follow after (*prō-* forward, pro-[1] + *sequī* follow; see SEQUEL). **—pursuance** *n.* 1596, in Bacon's writings, probably borrowed from Middle French *poursuiance* act of pursuing or following, from Old French *poursuïr* pursue; for suffix see -ANCE.

—pursuant *adj.* 1691, following; earlier, prosecuting (1542-43); possibly borrowed from Middle French *poursuiant,* present participle of Old French *poursuïr* pursue; but more likely developed from the earlier noun recorded until sometime before 1657, and first found in Gower's *Confessio Amantis* (before 1393) as *poursuiant* one who seeks or aspires; also, a plaintiff; later *pursuant* (1464); borrowed through Anglo-French *pursuant,* present participle of *pursuer,* and directly from Old French *poursuiant,* present participle of *poursuïr* variant of *porsivre, porsivir;* for suffix see -ANT. **—pursuit** *n.* About 1383 *pursuyt* persecution, in Wycliffe's writings; before 1387 act of pursuing; borrowed through Anglo-French *pursuite,* and directly from Old French *poursiuite,* from *poursuire, porsivre* pursue. The meaning of occupation, interest, etc., that one pursues, is first recorded in 1529.

pursy *adj.* short-winded or puffy. 1440 *purcy,* in *Promptorium Parvulorum;* later, in the spelling *pursy* (probably before 1475); alteration of Middle English *pursyf* asthmatic, short-winded; borrowed from Anglo-French *pursif, porsif* (Old French *poussif*), variants of Old French *polsif,* from *poulser* to pant, PUSH. The associated meaning of fat developed in English by 1576.

purulent (pyůr′ələnt) *adj.* containing or resembling pus. Probably before 1425 *purulente* of the coloring of pus, in a translation of Chauliac's *Grande Chirurgie;* borrowed from Middle French *purulent,* and directly from Latin *pūrulentus* full of pus, festering, from *pūs* (genitive *pūris*) pus; see FOUL; for suffix see -ENT.

purvey (pərvā′) *v.* to supply, provide. Probably before 1300 *purvaien, porvaien* to make preparations, prepare, supply, in *Arthour and Merlin* and in the *Romance of Guy of Warwick;* about 1300 in the spelling *purveien, porveien;* borrowed through Anglo-French *purveier, purvëer,* and directly from Old French *porvëer, porvëoir,* from Latin *prōvidēre* provide. Doublet of PROVIDE. **—purveyance** *n.* About 1300 *purveance, porveance* foresight, prudence; later, provisions, supplies (before 1325), and in the spelling *purveyance* (1334); borrowed through Anglo-French *purvëaunce,* and directly from Old French *porvëance,* from *porvëer* provide; for suffix see -ANCE.

purview *n.* scope, extent. 1442 *purveu* provisional clause, proviso, in *Rolls of Parliament;* later *purvewe* provision or scope of a statute; borrowed from Anglo-French phrase *purveu est* it is provided, or *purveu que* provided that (clauses that introduce a statute), from Old French *porveü,* past participle of *porvëer, porvëoir* provide, PURVEY. The extended sense of scope or extent is first recorded in a passage written by James Madison in *The Federalist* (1788). The form *purview* (influenced by *view*) is first recorded before 1677, and a further extension of meaning (influenced by *view*) is found in that of range of vision, outlook, range of experience or thought, which is recorded in 1837.

pus *n.* viscous matter of a sore. 1392, borrowing of Latin *pūs* pus; see FOUL.

push *v.* About 1325 *pushen;* earlier *possen* to shove, thrust, surge, in *King Horn;* borrowed from Old French *pousser;* earlier *poulser,* from Latin *pulsāre* to beat, strike, push, frequentative form of *pellere* to push, drive, beat; see PULSE[1] beat. Doublet of PULSATE. The meaning of try to advance or promote (as in *to push a book)* appeared in 1714. From it developed the sense of to peddle drugs illegally, first recorded in 1938 in American English. **—n.** act of pushing. 1563, from the verb. The informal expression *when push comes to shove,* meaning if worse comes to worst, is first attested in 1958 in American English. **—push button** (1878) **—pushcart** *n.* (1893) **—pusher** *n.* 1591, formed from English *push,* v. + *-er*[1]. The sense of a local dealer in illegal drugs is first recorded in 1935. **—push-over** *n.* (1906) **—pushup** *n.* (1906) **—pushy** *adj.* forward, aggressive. 1936, in Margaret Mitchell's *Gone With the Wind,* American English; formed from *push,* n. or v. + *-y*[1].

pusillanimous (pyü′səlan′əməs) *adj.* cowardly. Before 1425 *pusillanimus,* borrowed from Late Latin *pusillanimus, pusillanimis* having little courage (from Latin *pusillus* little, diminutive of *pullus* young animal; see FOAL + *animus* spirit, courage; see ANIMAL); for suffix see -OUS. Compare MAGNANIMOUS. The English form with *-ous* appeared in 1586.**—pusillanimity** *n.* Before 1393 *pusillamite* timidity, cowardliness, in Gower's *Confessio Amantis;* before 1400 *pusillanimite;* originally borrowed as a contracted form from Old French *pusillanimité,* from Late Latin *pusillanimitātem* (nominative *pusillanimitās*) faint-heartedness, from *pusillanimus, pusillanimis* faint-hearted, timid, pusillanimous; for suffix see -ITY.

puss *n.* cat. Before 1530, a conventional name for a cat; perhaps originally merely a call to attract a cat, common to several Germanic languages (compare Dutch *poes,* Low German *pus, pus-katte,* Norwegian *puse, pus*). **—pussy** *n.* cat. 1726, diminutive of *puss.* **—pussyfoot** *v.* move or act cautiously. 1903, American English, formed from English *pussy* + *foot,* n. **—pussy willow** (1869).

pustule (pus′chül) *n.* pimple containing pus. 1392, borrowed from Old French *pustule,* and directly from Latin *pustula* blister, pimple, also *pussula;* for suffix see

-ULE. The Latin forms are probably cognate with Greek *phȳsallís* a bladder, pustule, and Greek *phȳsân* to blow, *phȳsa* blast, breath, Lithuanian *pūslė̃* bladder, and Sanskrit *pupphusa-, phuphusa-* the lungs, *puṣṇā́ti, pṓṣati* (he) thrives, grows, from the Indo-European root **p(h)u-* imitative of the cheeks when blown out (Pok.848).

put *v.* Probably before 1200 *putten, puten* to thrust, push, move, place, in *Ancrene Riwle* and Layamon's *Chronicle of Britain;* developed from Old English **putian,* implied in *putung* instigation, urging (about 1050); related to Old English *potian* to push (about 1000, in Ælfric's *Homilies*) and to Old English *pȳtan* put out, thrust out (about 1100, in the *Anglo-Saxon Chronicle*). Old English *potian* is cognate with Middle Dutch and Middle Low German *pōten* to plant, Icelandic *pota* to poke, thrust, and Danish *putte* to put, of unknown origin. **—n.** a throw or cast. About 1300 *put,* in *Havelok the Dane;* from the verb in Middle English. The sense in commerce of the option of delivering a certain amount of stock or other securities at a specified price in a certain period of time is first recorded in 1717. **—put-down** *n.* (1962, a slighting or belittling) **—put-on** *n.* (1621 *adj.* feigned or pretended; 1937 *n.* a hoax, ruse)

putative *adj.* supposed, reputed. Probably before 1425, in a translation of Higden's *Polychronicon;* borrowed perhaps through Middle French *putatif* (feminine *putative*), from Latin *putātīvus* supposed, from *putāre* cleanse, trim, prune; also, think, suppose (related to *pūrus* PURE); for suffix see -IVE.

putrescent *adj.* becoming putrid, rotting. 1732, in John Arbuthnot's *Rules of Diet;* back formation from earlier *putrescence,* possibly by influence of French *putrescent,* learned borrowing from Latin *putrēscentem* (nominative *putrēscēns*), present participle of *putrēscere* grow rotten, from *putrēre* be rotten; see PUTRID; for suffix see -ENT. **—putrescence** *n.* process of rotting, decay. 1646, formed as if from Latin **putrēscentia,* from *putrēscentem* (nominative *putrēscēns*), present participle of *putrēscere* grow rotten; for suffix see -ENCE.

putrid *adj.* rotten, foul. Before 1398 *putrida,* a Latinate form; borrowed directly from Latin *putridus;* later *putred* (probably before 1425, in a translation of Chauliac's *Grande Chirurgie*); borrowed from Middle French *putride,* from Latin *putridus,* from *putrēre* be rotten, from *putris* rotten, crumbling; related to *pūtēre* to stink; see FOUL.

putt (put) *v.* strike (a golf ball) gently and carefully. 1743 (implied in *putter*), Scottish, special use of PUT, v., and found in earlier *putting* pushing, shoving, thrusting (before 1398, probably associated with earlier *putting,* now known in *shot putting,* about 1300). **—n.** stroke made by putting. 1743, Scottish; either from the verb or the same source as the verb. **—putting green** (1841, Scottish)

puttee (put′ē *or* putē′) *n.* long strip of cloth wound around the leg from ankle to knee. 1886, borrowed from Hindi *paṭṭī* bandage, strip, from Sanskrit *paṭṭikā,* from *paṭṭa-s* strip of cloth, of uncertain origin. The term was known earlier among the British in India by the spelling pronunciation "patawa", 1875.

putter[1] (put′ər) *v.* keep busy in a rather useless way. 1877, American English, in Louisa May Alcott's *Under Lilacs;* alteration of POTTER[2].

putter[2] (put′ər) *n.* golf club used in putting. 1743; formed from *putt* + *-er*[1]. It is difficult to determine when the differentiation took place between the golfing terminology *putt, putting, putter,* pronounced (put, put′ing, put′ər) and that of the track and field sport of *shot-putting* (pu̇t′ing). The OED makes a differentiation in pronunciation between the *shot-putter* and the *golf putter* in 1909.

putter[3] (pu̇t′ər) *n.* 1820, found in *shot-putter.*

putty (put′ē, in American English; sometimes found as pu̇t′ē, an altered pronunciation, perhaps by confusion in spelling) *n.* 1663, powder used for polishing, in Robert Boyle's *Works;* borrowed from French *potée* a polishing powder; originally, potful, contents of a pot, from Old French *pot* container, see POT[1]. The meaning of a soft mixture of powdered chalk and linseed oil for fixing panes of glass in a window frame or for filling small holes, is first recorded in Phillips' *Dictionary* (1706). **—v.** stop up or cover with putty. 1734, from the noun.

puzzle *v.* About 1595 *pusle* bewilder, confound, possibly a frequentative form of POSE, v. (as *nuzzle* is of *nose*); for suffix see -LE[3].

The meaning of exercise one's mind on a problem, be perplexed, is first recorded in 1605.

—n. 1607–12, puzzled condition, in Bacon's *Essays;* later, a hard problem (1655); from the verb. The sense of dissected pieces of a figure or picture to be put together is first attested about 1815.

—puzzlement *n.* 1822, formed from English *puzzle,* v. + *-ment.* **—puzzler** *n.* thing that puzzles, problem, puzzle. Before 1652, formed from English *puzzle,* v. + *-er.*[1].

pygmy or **pigmy** *n.* very small person. About 1384 *Pigmei* member of an ancient race of dwarfs inhabiting Ethiopia and India, in the Wycliffe Bible; borrowed from Latin *Pygmaeī,* from Greek *Pygmaîoi* a tribe of dwarfs, referred to by Homer and Herodotus, and being placed in various localities, including Ethiopia, India, and Africa; originally, as a plural adjective in the sense of dwarfish ("no taller than a cubit"), from *pygmḗ* cubit, fist; see PUNGENT.

The generalized sense of a very small person is first recorded in English in 1520.

—adj. very small. 1591, from the noun.

pylon (pī′lon) *n.* tall structure. 1850, monumental gateway to an Egyptian temple; borrowed from Greek *pylṓn* gateway, from *pýlē* gate, of unknown origin. The transferred meaning of a supporting structure flanking the entrance to a bridge is first recorded in 1903, and that of a steel tower for carrying high-tension electric lines in 1923, this latter sense developing from the now obsolete meaning of a post or tower for guiding aviators (1909).

pylorus (pīlôr′əs) *n.* opening leading from the stomach into the intestine. 1615, in Helkiah Crooke's *A Description of the Body of Man;* borrowing of Late Latin *pylōrus,* from Greek *pylōrós* lower opening of the stomach; originally **pylāhorós* gatekeeper (*pýlē* gate; see PYLON + *-horós* watcher, related to *horân* to see see WARY). **—pyloric** *adj.* of the pylorus. 1807, formed from English *pylorus* + *-ic.*

pyorrhea (pī′ərē′ə) *n.* disease of the gums. 1811, New Latin; formed from Greek *pýon* pus; see FOUL + *rhoía* a flow, from *rheîn* to flow; see STREAM.

pyr- a combining form of *pyro-* before vowels in derivatives, as in *pyruvic acid.*

pyramid (pir′əmid) *n.* figure or structure with triangular sides meeting in a point. 1549 *Pyramides* (singular and then plural, 1552); borrowed from Latin *pȳramidēs,* plural of *pȳramis* one of the stone pyramids of Egypt or any structure or figure like it, from Greek *pȳramís* (plural *pȳramídes*), apparently alteration by transposition of Egyptian *pimar* pyramid.

The form *piramis* (borrowed from Latin *pȳramis* as a singular form) is recorded in Middle English before 1398, in a translation of Bartholomew's *De Proprietatibus Rerum,* and was used through the 1500's. The modern English form *pyramid,* in imitation of the Latin, gradually became the established spelling in the 1600's.

—v. be or put in the form of a pyramid. 1845, from the noun. The meaning in finance of build up (holdings) by trading stock on margin is first recorded in 1901.

—pyramidal *adj.* of or shaped like a pyramid. Before 1398 *piramydal,* in Trevisa's translation of Bartholomew's *De Proprietatibus Rerum;* borrowed perhaps through Old French *pyramidal,* and directly from Medieval Latin *pyramidalis,* from Latin *pȳramis* (genitive *pȳramidis*) pyramid; for suffix see -AL[1].

pyre (pīr) *n.* pile of wood for burning a dead body. 1658, borrowed from Latin *pyra,* and probably directly from Greek *pyrā́* a hearth, place where a fire is kindled, place of a funeral fire, a funeral pile, from *pŷr* (genitive *pyrós*) FIRE.

pyretic *adj.* of or having to do with fever. 1858, borrowed, perhaps by influence of French *pyrétique,* from New Latin *pyreticus* feverish, from Greek *pyretós* fever, from *pŷr* (genitive *pyrós*) FIRE; for suffix see -IC.

Pyrex (pī′reks) *n.* trade name for a type of glassware that resists breaking when heated. 1915, an invented word formed by association with Greek *pŷr* fire, but said to be from the similar sounding *pie* in reference to dishes made earlier by Corning Glass Works for baking pies + *-ex* an ending also used by the manufacturer for earlier glassware. A letter in the OEDS from the Corning Glass Works claims the *r* was inserted for euphony, but an advertisement used by Corning in 1915 refers to "fire-glass"; so it would seem that the Greek *pŷr* was actually the first element of this word.

pyrite (pī′rīt) *n.* 1868, yellow mineral that glitters so that it suggests gold, fool's gold; also known as iron *pyrites* (1567); from earlier *pirite,* before 1500, and *pe-rides* firestone, before 1398; borrowed from Old French *pirite,* and directly from Latin *pyrītēs* firestone, flint, from Greek *pyrī́tēs líthos* stone of fire, flint, from *pŷr* (genitive *pyrós*) FIRE.

pyro- a combining form meaning: of, having to do with, using, or caused by fire, as in *pyromania;* heat, high temperatures, as in *pyrometer;* formed by heat, as in *pyroacid.* Borrowed through Latin, especially New Latin *pyro-,* from Greek *pyro-,* combining form of *pŷr* (genitive *pyrós*) FIRE.

pyromania *n.* an uncontrollable desire to set fires. 1842, formed from English *pyro-* + *mania.* **—pyromaniac** *n.* person affected by pyromania. 1887, American English, from *pyromania,* on the analogy of *mania, maniac.*

pyrotechnics *n.* the making of fireworks. 1729, formed from earlier English *pyrotechnic,* adj. (1704, of or relating to the use of fire in chemistry, metallurgy, etc.) + the plural suffix *-s*[1]; see -ICS. The adjective *pyrotechnic* is a shortened form of earlier *pyrotechnical* and may also have been borrowed from French *pyrotechnique,* from *pyro-* fire + *technique* technical; see TECHNIQUE. The figurative sense of a brilliant display (as in *orchestral pyrotechnics*) is first recorded in 1901. **—pyrotechnical** *adj.* 1610, formed from English *pyrotechny* (1579, borrowed from French *pyrotechnie,* and formed from English *pyro-* + Greek *téchnē* art, skill) + *-ical.*

Pyrrhic (pir′ik) *adj.* of or denoting a victory won at too great a cost. 1885, formed in allusion to *Pyrrhus,* king of Epirus in Greece, who defeated the Roman armies in 280 B.C., but lost so many men he was unable to attack Rome itself; for suffix see -IC.

pyruvic acid (pīrü′vik) kind of acid important in metabolism. 1838, formed in English from *pyr-* (variant of PYRO- before vowels) of fire + Latin *ūva* grape + English *-ic;* so called because this acid is produced by the distillation of an acid found in grapes.

python (pī′thon) *n.* kind of large snake that kills its prey by crushing. 1836, borrowed probably from French *python,* learned borrowing from Latin *Pȳthōn* the huge serpent killed near Delphi by Apollo, from Greek *Pȳ́thōn,* probably related to *Pȳthṓ,* older name of Delphi.

As the name of the fabled serpent killed by Apollo, *Python* is first recorded in English in 1590.

Q

quack[1] *v.* make the characteristic sound of a duck. 1617, of imitative origin; variant of earlier *quake* (before 1529) and *queken* (before 1333, also found as *quelke* before 1325). The Middle English form *queken* was probably developed from the interjection *quek* sound made by a duck or goose (1342) in spite of the later date, which appears to be a defect in the record of Middle English. Though similar forms are found in Middle Dutch *quacken* make a noise like a duck or goose (modern Dutch *kwaken*) and German *quaken,* it is unlikely that the English word was borrowed, as these similarities of imitative words appear independently in numerous languages. **—n.** 1839, the sound of a duck; from the verb.

quack[2] *n.* impostor, charlatan. 1638, shortened form of QUACKSALVER. **—adj.** of or used by quacks, sham or fake. 1653, in Henry H. More's *An Antidote Against Atheism;* from the noun. **—quackery** *n.* practice of a quack. 1709-11, in a book title; formed from English *quack*[2], n. + *-ery.*

quacksalver *n.* quack doctor. 1579, in Stephen Gosson's *The School of Abuse;* borrowed from Dutch *quacksalver,* literally, a hawker of salve (from Middle Dutch *quacken* to boast of, quack, make a noise like a duck or goose + *salve* SALVE [1], n.); for suffix see -ER[1]. The modern Dutch form is *kwakzalver,* which with Middle Dutch provided German *Quacksalber,* Danish and Norwegian *kvaksalver* and Swedish *kvacksalvare.*

quad[1] *n. Informal.* quadrangle of a college. 1820, (originally Oxford University slang); shortened form of QUADRANGLE.

quad[2] *n. Informal.* quadruplet. 1896, a bicycle with four riders, shortened form of QUADRUPLET. *Quad,* one of four children born at the same time to the same mother, is first recorded in 1951, although this was the earliest meaning of *quadruplet,* first recorded in 1787; and the pattern is found in earlier *quints* (1935, in reference to the Dionne *quintuplets* born in 1934; see also earlier *quintuplet* in this sense, 1899).

quad[3] *n.* unit of energy equal to one quadrillion British thermal units. 1974, shortened form of QUADRILLION.

quad[4] *adj., n.* quadraphonic. 1970, adjective; 1971, noun; shortened form of QUADRAPHONIC.

quadr- the form of *quadri-* before vowels, as in *quadrangle, quadrant.*

quadrangle *n.* Before 1398, plane figure with four angles and four sides, in Trevisa's translation of Bartholomew's *De Proprietatibus Rerum;* borrowed from Old French *quadrangle,* adj., and directly from Late Latin *quadrangulum* a four-sided figure, from neuter of Latin *quadrangulus, quadriangulus,* adj., having four corners (*quadri-* four, quadri- + *angulus* ANGLE). The sense of a four-sided space or court is first recorded in English in Shakespeare's *2 Henry VI* (1593). **—quadrangular** *adj.* 1592, borrowed from Late Latin *quadrangulāris,* from *quadrangulum* quadrangle; for suffix see -AR. An isolated occurrence of the word is recorded in Middle English as *quadrangulere,* in a translation of Chauliac's *Grande Chirurgie* (probably before 1425), also from Late Latin *quadrangulāris.*

quadrant *n.* Before 1398, quarter of a day, in Trevisa's translation of Bartholomew's *De Proprietatibus Rerum;* borrowed from Latin *quadrantem* (nominative *quadrāns*) a fourth, related to *quattuor* FOUR.

The meaning of an instrument with a scale of 90 degrees, used for angular measurements, is first recorded before 1400, and that of a quarter of a circle in 1571.

quadraphonic (kwod'rəfon'ik) *adj.* of or having to do with high-fidelity sound transmission or reproduction over four different channels. 1970, alteration of earlier *quadriphonic* (1969, *quadri-* four + *phonic*).

quadrate (kwod'rət) *adj.* square, rectangular. Before 1398, in Trevisa's translation of Bartholomew's *De Proprietatibus Rerum;* borrowed from Latin *quadrātus* square, from *quadrum* a square, related to *quattuor* FOUR; for suffix see -ATE[1]. **—n.** something square or rectangular. Probably about 1400 *quadrat;* borrowed from Latin *quadrātum* a square, from neuter of *quadrātus,* adj., square. **—quadratic** *adj.* square. 1656, in Blount's *Glossographia;* formed from English *quadrate,* n. + *-ic.* The meaning in algebra of involving the square and no higher power of an unknown quantity is first recorded in 1668.

quadrature (kwod'rəchər) *n.* Before 1460, square formation of troops; borrowed from Middle French *quadrature,* and directly from Latin *quadrātūra,* from *quadrāre* make square, from *quadrum* a square; see QUADRATE; for suffix see -URE. The astronomical meaning of the position of one celestial body relative to another when they are ninety degrees apart is first recorded in 1591, and the sense in mathematics of the finding of a square equal in area to a given surface in 1596.

quadrennial *adj.* 1656 *quadriennial* lasting four years; later, occurring every four years (1701, probably from the noun); originally formed in English from Latin *quadriennium* period of four years (*quadri-* four + *-ennium,* from *annus* year) + English *-al*[1]. The spelling *quadrennial* is first recorded in Bailey's *Dictionary* (1727). **—n.** Before 1646 *quadriennal* event that occurs every four years; formed as if from Latin **quadriennālis,* adj., from *quadriennium* period of four years; for suffix see -AL[1]. The spelling *quadrennial* is first recorded in 1856.

quadri- a combining form meaning four, as in *quadrilateral, quadrivalent.* Also *quadr-* before vowels and *quadru-* before *p.* Borrowed from Latin *quadri-* (fo[r] expected **quatr-*); related to *quattuor* FOUR.

quadrilateral *adj.* having four sides and four angles 1656, formed in English from Latin *quadrilateru[m]* (*quadri-* four + *latus,* genitive *lateris* side; see LATERAL) + English *-al*[1]. **—n.** quadrilateral figure, 1650, either from the adjective (although the noun is recorde[d] slightly earlier), or formed independently of the adjective in English from Latin *quadrilaterus,* adj.

quadrille *n.* 1773, square dance for four couples; earlier, one of four groups of horsemen taking part in a tournament or carousel (1738); borrowing of French *quadrille,* originally, one of four groups of horsemen, from Spanish *cuadrilla,* from *cuadro* square formation (in battle), from Latin *quadrum* a square, related to *quattuor* FOUR. *Quadrille* is also recorded earlier with the meaning of a card game for four people (1726); also borrowed from French, but from a different word in Spanish or Italian.

quadrillion *n.* 1674, (in Great Britain) fourth power of a million; borrowed from French *quadrillion,* formed from *quadri-* four + *(m)illion,* from Old French *million* MILLION. In the United States, Canada, and France, quadrillion is the fifth power of a thousand. Compare BILLION.

quadriplegia (kwod′rəplē′jēə) *n.* paralysis of both arms and both legs. 1921, formed from English *quadri-* four + Greek *plēgḗ* stroke, from the root of *plḗssein* to strike, see PLAINT; for suffix *-ia* compare *poinsettia.* **—quadriplegic** *adj.* afflicted with quadriplegia. 1921, formed as an adjective to English *quadriplegia* with the suffix *-ic.* —*n.* quadriplegic person. 1958, from the adjective.

quadru- the form of *quadri-* before *p,* as in *quadruped, quadruplex.* In Latin, *quadru-* was the older form which survived before *p* when in other words it became *quadri-* by analogy with *tri-* three.

quadruped *n.* four-footed animal. 1640 *quadrupede,* borrowed from French *quadrupède,* from Middle French, and borrowed directly from Latin *quadrupēs* (genitive *quadrupedis)* four-footed, a four-footed animal *(quadru-,* variant of *quadri-* four + *pēs* FOOT). **—adj.** four-footed. 1741, in Isaac Watts' *The Improvement of the Mind;* from the noun.

quadruple (kwodrü′pəl) *adj.* consisting of four parts, fourfold. 1557, from the noun, possibly by influence of Middle French *quadruple* and Latin *quadruplus,* adj., *quadruplum,* n., quadruple. The modern form replaced earlier *quatreble* (see below) in the 1500's. **—v.** multiply by four, increase fourfold. 1375 *quadruplen,* in Barbour's *The Bruce;* borrowed from Latin *quadruplāre* make fourfold, from *quadruplum,* n., quadruple. **—n.** About 1425 *quadriple* a fourfold amount (probably influenced by *triple,* and found as *quatriple* probably before 1425); earlier *quadruple* tooth having a quadruple root (probably before 1425), and *quadruply* (before 1398); borrowed from Old French *quadruple,* variant of *quadruble,* and directly from Latin *quadruplum* (*quadru-*, variant of *quadri-* four + *-plus* -FOLD).

A variant form *quatreble* existed in the verb and adjective (before 1398) and the noun (1429); probably influenced by *treble.* The noun use was recorded as late as 1870 in the meaning of the highest part in contrapuntal singing, but the verb and adjective uses gradually disappeared by the 1500's.

—quadruplet *n.* 1787, one of four children born at one birth; formed from English *quadruple,* adj. + *-et.* The sense of any combination or group of four is first recorded in 1852.

quaff *v.* to drink in large swallows. 1523 *quaft;* later, *quaff* (1555); of uncertain origin (usually suggested as imitative of the sound of drinking deeply). The derivative form *quaffer,* one who drinks deeply, is first recorded in 1520, which implies an earlier *quaff* or perhaps *quaft.* **—n.** deep drink. 1579, from the verb.

quagmire *n.* soft, muddy ground. 1579-80, formed from *quag* bog (variant of earlier *quabbe* a marsh, bog, as a surname 1208-09; developed from Old English **cwabba*) + MIRE. The figurative sense of a difficult situation is first recorded in Sheridan's *Rivals* (1775).

quahog (kwô′hog) *n.* kind of edible American clam. 1753 *quogue,* American English; borrowed from Algonquian (probably Pequot) *p'quaghhaug* hard clam.

quail[1] *n.* kind of game bird. About 1380 *quayle,* in Chaucer's *Parlement of Foules;* earlier as a surname (1327); borrowed from Old French *quaille,* of uncertain origin (variously offered as being from a word recorded as Medieval Latin *quaccula, *quaquila,* or Gallo-Romance **coacula;* or from a Germanic source, for example Old High German *quahtala, wahtala* quail, modern German *Wachtel*).

quail[2] *v.* lose courage, cower. About 1450 *quaylen* to fade, fail, give way; earlier (with substitution of *w* for *qu*) *wailen* to grow sick or feeble (probably before 1425, in a translation of Higden's *Polychronicon*), and *weilynge* having a morbid craving (about 1400, in Wycliffe's writings); probably borrowed from Middle Dutch *quelen, queilen* to suffer, be ill, cognate with Old High German *quelan,* from Proto-Germanic **kwel-* to die. Cognates outside Germanic include Greek *belónē* needle, Lithuanian *gélti* prick, and Armenian *kełem* I torment, from Indo-European **gwel-* prick, pierce (Pok.470).

The sense of lose courage or cower is first recorded in English in 1555. This word disappeared from literary use after 1650 to be revived by Scott in the early 1800's.

quaint *adj.* strange or odd in an interesting, pleasing, or amusing way. Probably before 1200 *cointe* cunning, sly, clever, vain or proud, in *Ancrene Riwle;* later *queynte* wise, clever (about 1280); elaborate, skillfully made (about 1300); with the spelling *quaint* (before 1325); and unusual, strange especially in an interesting or clever way (before 1338, in Mannyng's *Chronicle of England*); borrowed from Old French *cointe, queinte* pretty, clever, knowing, from Latin *cognitus* known, past participle of *cognōscere* get to know, come to know well; see COGNIZANCE. The extended sense of uncommon or old-fashioned but pleasing, is first recorded in Southey's *Joan of Arc* (1795).

The rather remarkable development of senses, which for the most part took place in Old French, is also found to a degree in *couth* and *uncouth;* the development of form, not surprisingly parallels *acquaint.*

quake *v.* Probably before 1200 *cwakien, quakien* to shake or tremble, in Layamon's *Chronicle of Britain;* later *quaken* (about 1250); developed from Old English (about 830) *cwacian,* related to *cweccan* to cause to shake, of unknown origin. **—n.** a shaking, trembling. Before 1325 *quak,* in *Cursor Mundi;* later *quake* (before 1400); from *quaken,* v. The sense of an earthquake is first recorded in 1881, though earlier indirect reference in the form *quake* is found before 1643, and in the verb sense probably about 1200.

Quaker *n.* 1651, member of the Religious Society of Friends, founded by George Fox of England in the 1600's; formed from English *quake,* v. + *-er*[1]. According to Fox's Journals, referred to in the OED, the name was first given to him and to his followers by Justice Bennet at Derby in 1650 "because I bid them, Tremble at the Word of the Lord." It appears, however, that the name was used previously in the 1600's in reference to a foreign sect of women given to fits of shaking in religious fervor; so it is probable that Judge Bennet merely used a term already familiar in those days. **—Quakerism** *n.* 1656, the principles and practices of the Quakers, formed from English *Quaker* + *-ism.*

qualify *v.* 1465 *qualifyen* to make a document legal by specifying time and place of execution, etc., in the *Paston Letters;* later, to limit, modify (1533, in Sir Thomas More's writings); borrowed from Medieval Latin *qualificare* attribute a quality to, from a lost adjective **quālificus* (Latin *quālis* of what sort; see QUALITY + the root of *facere* to make, perform, DO[1]); for suffix see -FY. The sense of make legally capable is first recorded in English in 1583, and that of make oneself fit for a job, etc., before 1588. **—qualification** *n.* 1543-44, modification, limitation; borrowed from Middle French *qualification,* and directly from Medieval Latin *qualificationem* (nominative *qualificatio*), from *qualificare* qualify; for suffix see -ATION. The sense of something that qualifies a person for a job, etc., is first recorded in 1669.

quality *n.* About 1300 *qualite* character, disposition, temperament; later, grade of excellence (before 1396); with the spelling *qualitie* (about 1450); borrowed from Old French *qualité,* learned borrowing from Latin, and borrowed directly from Latin *quālitātem* (nominative *quālitās;* coined by Cicero as a loan translation of Greek *poiótēs*), from *quālis* of what sort, related to *quis* WHO; for suffix see -ITY. **—qualitative** *adj.* Probably before 1425, *qualitatyve* (of a medicine) that produces one of the four primary qualities of heat, cold, moisture, or dryness; borrowed from Medieval Latin *qualitativus.* The word was later revived in English in the sense of concerned with quality or qualities (1607); borrowed from French *qualitatif* (feminine *qualitative*), or reborrowed directly from Medieval or Late Latin *quālitātīvus,* from Latin *quālitās* quality; for suffix see -IVE.

qualm (kwäm) *n.* About 1530, feeling of faintness or sickness; possibly identical with Middle English *qualm* pestilence, plague (probably before 1200); developed from Old English (West Saxon) *cwealm* death, destruction, torment, plague (before 899, in Alfred's translation of Orosius' *Epitome of Universal History,* and corresponding to Anglian *-cwalm* in *ūtcualm* utter destruction, before 800). The Old English forms are cognate with Old Saxon and Old High German *qualm* death, destruction, and related to Old English *cwellan* to kill; see QUELL. The transferred sense of uneasiness, misgiving, doubt, is first recorded before 1555; and that of the disturbance or scruple of conscience in 1649.

quandary (kwon′dərē) *n.* state of perplexity, dilemma. 1579, in Lyly's *Euphues;* of uncertain origin. The word's original stress was quandar′y; the present stress was favored by Johnson and Webster. The word's form suggests that it might have been an alteration of some term of scholastic Latin, specifically an infinitive ending in *-are.*

quantify *v.* determine the quantity of. About 1840, (in logic) make explicit the quantity or extent of; borrowed from Medieval Latin *quantificare,* from a lost adjective **quantificus* (Latin *quantus* how great; see QUANTITY + the root of *facere* make, perform, DO[1]); for suffix see -FY. **—quantification** *n.* action of quantifying. About 1840, probably formed from English *quantify,* on the analogy of *qualify, qualification;* for suffix see -ATION.

quantity *n.* Before 1325 *quantite* amount or extent, in *Cursor Mundi;* later, size, magnitude, dimension (about 1380); borrowed from Old French *quantité,* learned borrowing from Latin, and borrowed directly from Latin *quantitātem* (nominative *quantitās;* coined as a loan translation of Greek *posótes*) relative greatness or extent, from *quantus* how great, related to *quam* how, and *quis* WHO; for suffix see -ITY. **—quantitative** *adj.* 1581, having quantity; later, measurable (1656); borrowed from Medieval Latin *quantitativus,* from Latin *quantitās* quantity; for suffix see -IVE.

quantize *v.* apply the quantum theory or quantum mechanics to, measure (energy) in quanta. 1922, formed from English *quantum* + *-ize.* **—quantization** *n.* 1922, probably formed from English *quantize* + *-ation.*

quantum (kwon′təm) *n., pl.* **quanta.** 1619, sum or quantity, in Purchas' *Microcosmus;* borrowed from Latin *quantum* how much, neuter of *quantus* how great; see QUANTITY. The meaning in physics (originated by Planck and Einstein) of the smallest amount of radiant energy capable of existing independently, is first recorded in 1910. The term *quantum theory,* meaning the theory of energy and matter based on the division of radiant energy into definite *quanta,* is first found in 1912. The related term *quantum mechanics,* meaning the quantum theory as applied to the physical measurement of matter and radiation, is first recorded in 1925. **—adj.** of sudden, spectacular significance or effect, representing a major breakthrough. 1971, abstracted from the earlier *quantum jump* (1955) and *quantum leap* (1970) a sudden, spectacular advance, figurative uses of the terms in physics referring to the sudden jump of an electron, etc., from one energy level to another.

quarantine *n.* 1) 1609, a period of forty days in which a widow had the right to remain in her dead husband's house, especially if the house was to be seized for debt. 2) 1663, period during which a ship suspected of carrying disease is kept in isolation, in Pepys' *Diary;* borrowed from Italian *quarantina,* from *quaranta* forty (perhaps from early use in Venice, where vessels suspected of carrying disease were banned from the port for forty days), from Latin *quadrāgintā* forty, related to *quattuor* FOUR; in form, *quadrāgintā* is an old neuter plural having as its second member the Indo-European stem *(d)k̑m̥to-* TEN; so called from the forty days of the original period of isolation.

The transferred sense of any period, instance, etc., of isolation or seclusion, is first recorded before 1680, preceded by an earlier sense of a period of forty days (1639); both senses developed partly perhaps in allusion to Middle English *quarentyne* the desert in which Christ wandered and fasted for forty days (probably 1458); borrowed from Medieval Latin *quarentina* forty days, and *quarentena* the desert of Christ's fast.
—**v.** put in quarantine. 1804, Washington Irving in *Life and Letters;* from the noun.

quark (kwôrk) *n.* hypothetical nuclear particle smaller than a proton or neutron. 1964, from a line in James Joyce's *Finnegans Wake:* "Three quarks for Muster Mark!" perhaps from German *Quark* curds, rubbish. The word was whimsically adopted by the American physicist Murray Gell-Mann in reference to his original theory that there were three types of quarks from which protons and other elementary particles were composed.

quarrel[1] *n.* angry dispute. 1340 *querele* a dispute, in

Ayenbite of Inwyt; later *quarele* complaint, cause for a dispute (probably about 1375); borrowed from Old French *quarrel, querele,* and directly from Latin *querella,* variant of *querēla* a complaining, complaint, from *querī* to complain, lament, with past participle *questus,* cognate with Sanskrit *śvásati* he pants, from Indo-European **k̂wes-* (Pok.631). **—v.** Before 1393 *querelen* to dispute, in a supplement to Gower's *Confessio Amantis,* from the noun in Middle English. **—quarrelsome** *adj.* 1596, in Shakespeare's *The Taming of The Shrew;* formed from English *quarrel, n.* + *-some*[1]. Though the spelling *quar-* has been the established form from late Middle English times, the spelling *quer-* has remained in *querulous.*

quarrel[2] *n.* a square-headed bolt or arrow used with a crossbow. Before 1250 *quarreus,* pl., in *Ancrene Riwle;* later *quarel* (probably before 1300); borrowed from Old French *quarel,* plural *quarreaus,* from Vulgar Latin **quadrellus,* diminutive of Late Latin *quadrus,* adj., square, related to *quattuor* FOUR. The sense of a square or diamond-shaped pane of glass is first recorded in English in 1447.

quarry[1] *n.* place where stone is dug out for use in building. Before 1382 *quarre,* in the Wycliffe Bible; earlier as a place name (1266); also *quarey* (about 1400); borrowed from Medieval Latin *quareia,* dissimilated (by loss of the second *r*) from earlier *quareria,* a Latinized form based on Old French *quarriere* quarry, from **quarre* cut stone, from Latin *quadrum* a square, related to *quattuor* FOUR; for suffix see -Y[3]; probably so called in reference to the work at a quarry of squaring stones for building. An earlier form existed in Middle English *quarrere* (before 1375, and as a surname, 1166); also found as *quarreris* (before 1382, in the Wycliffe Bible); borrowed from Anglo-French **quarrere,* Old French *quarriere* quarry. **—v.** obtain from a quarry. 1774, in Goldsmith's *A History of the Earth and Animated Nature;* from the noun.

quarry[2] *n.* animal chased in a hunt. Probably before 1300 *quirre* entrails of game given to the dogs as a reward, in *Sir Tristrem;* later *querre* game killed in the chase (probably about 1390, in *Sir Gawain and the Green Knight*), and *quary* (before 1400); borrowed through Anglo-French *quirreie,* and directly from Old French *curee, cuiriee,* alteration (influenced by *cuir* skin, hide, from Latin *corium* hide) of Old French *corée* viscera, entrails, from Vulgar Latin **corāta,* from Latin *cor* HEART. The figurative sense of anything hunted or eagerly pursued is first recorded in 1615.

quart *n.* quarter of a gallon. Probably before 1325 *quarte* a quart container; later *quart* a liquid measure (probably about 1350); borrowed from Old French *quarte* a fourth part, from Latin *quārta,* feminine of *quārtus* fourth, related to *quattuor* FOUR through development from **quatvortos* to **quavortos* to *quārtus.*

quarter *n.* Probably before 1300 *quarter* one fourth, fourth part (of some measure or standard), in *Sir Tristrem;* earlier as a surname (1267); borrowed from Old French *quarter, quartier,* from Latin *quārtārius* a fourth part, from *quārtus* fourth, related to *quattuor* FOUR; see QUART.

The meaning of the fourth part of a year is first recorded in 1389, that of the lunar period, before 1420; the meaning of a quarter of an hour is attested before 1456, but the sense in sports of one of four periods of play in football, hockey, etc., did not become current before 1911. The word was used as one of the four principal divisions of the horizon as early as 1391, and the sense of any region or locality is first recorded probably before 1300, though a particular area of a town (as in *the French quarter*) is not found before 1526. The meaning of dwelling place (found mostly in the plural *quarters*) is first recorded in 1591. A meaning of a coin worth 25 cents or quarter of a dollar is peculiar to American English and is first recorded in 1783. Origin of the meaning of mercy shown to an enemy (as in *to give no quarter,* 1611) may have derived from the earlier military meaning of assigned position, battle station (1549).

—**v.** divide into quarters. About 1353 *quarteren,* from the noun in Middle English.

—adj. consisting of a quarter or quarters. About 1390, in Chaucer's *Canterbury Tales,* from the noun in Middle English.

—quarterback *n.* (1879, American English) **—quarter horse** strong horse bred for racing on quarter-mile tracks (1834, American English). **—quarterly** *adj.* occurring every quarter of a year. 1563, formed from English *quarter,* n. + *-ly*[2]. *—adv.* every quarter of a year. 1418, formed from Middle English *quarter,* n. + *-ly*[1]. *—n.* quarterly publication. 1830, from the adjective. **—quartermaster** *n.* 1415 *quartermaistre* petty naval officer, formed from Middle English *quarter,* n. + *maistre* master. The sense of an army officer in charge of quarters, clothing, etc., is first recorded in 1600; formed from English *quarter* lodging + *master.*

quartet, *n.* composition for four voices or instruments. 1790, Coleridge, *Inside the Coach;* borrowed from French *quartette,* from Italian *quartetto,* diminutive of *quarto* fourth, from Latin *quārtus;* see QUART.

quartile *n.* 1509, (in astrology) aspect of two celestial bodies when their longitudes differ by 90 degrees; probably developed from Middle English *quartile,* adj., of or pertaining to the relative position of two celestial bodies (1450); borrowed from Middle French *quartil,* and directly from Medieval Latin *quartilis* of a quartile, from Latin *quārtus* fourth; see QUART. The statistical meaning of one of four parts of a frequency distribution is first recorded in 1879.

quarto (kwôr′tō) *n.* page size measuring one quarter of a sheet. 1589, borrowed from Medieval Latin *in quarto* in the fourth part of a sheet (also found in Middle English *in quarto,* probably before 1475); *quārtō,* ablative case of Latin *quārtus* fourth; see QUART. **—adj.** having this size. 1633, from the noun.

quartz *n.* kind of very hard mineral. 1756, borrowed from German *Quarz* rock crystal, quartz, from late Middle High German *twarc, quarc, zwarc;* probably borrowed from a West Slavic source (compare Czech *tvrdý,* Polish *twardy* quartz, Old Slavic *tvrŭdŭ* hard). Spelling with *t* is also found in French *quartz* and Dutch *kwarts.*

quasar (kwā′zär) *n.* celestial object that emits powerful light and radio waves. 1964, acronym formed from earlier *quas(i-stell)ar,* as in *quasi-stellar radio source* (1963) or *quasi-stellar object* (1964); so called because the object gives a starlike image on a photographic plate though it is much larger and brighter than any star.

quash[1] *v.* to crush. Before 1387 *quaschen,* in Trevisa's translation of Higden's *Polychronicon;* also *quasshen* (probably before 1425); borrowed from Old French *quasser* to break, smash, from Latin *quassāre* to shatter, frequentative form of *quatere* to shake (past participle *quassus*), cognate with Lithuanian *kutėti* to shake up, and Old High German *scutilōn* (modern German *schütteln*) to shake, from Indo-European **kwēt-/kwōt-/kwət-/kut-/skut-* (Pok.632, 957).

Though not always analyzed as two different words in English, because the differences in meaning are considered literal for *quash*[1] and figurative for *quash*[2], these two words come from distinctly different sources in Latin and Medieval Latin and they maintain a distinction in meaning in Old French, as well, which is of course also evident in English.

quash[2] *v.* make void, annul. Before 1338 *quassen,* in Mannyng's *Chronicle of England;* earlier *cwessen* to suppress, overcome (about 1250); borrowed from Old French *quasser* to annul, and probably directly from Medieval Latin *quassare* bring to naught, make null and void, alteration (influenced by Latin *quassāre* shatter; see QUASH[1]) of *cassare,* from Latin *cassus* empty, void, null, probably related to *carēre* be devoid of, lack, and *castus* pure or chaste; see CASTE.

quasi (kwā′zī *or* kwā′sī) *adv.* seemingly, partly, almost. 1485, as it were, as if, in Caxton's translation of *Paris and Vienne;* borrowed from Middle French *quasi,* and directly from Latin *quasi* as if, as it were, almost, from *quam* how, as + *sī* if; see QUANTITY and SO. **—adj.** seeming. 1643, from the adverb.

quasi- a prefix added to nouns, adjectives, and adverbs, and meaning literally as if, applied to substitutes and replacements that resemble or serve as a designated thing, or that perform a designated function, as in *quasiscience, quasigovernmental, quasi-judicially.* Abstracted from QUASI, adv., adj.

quaternary (kwät′ərnerē) *n.* group of four. About 1450, the number four; borrowed from Latin *quaternārius,* adj., consisting of four each, from *quaternī* four each, from *quater* four times (earlier **quatrus*), related to *quattuor* FOUR; for suffix see -ARY. **—adj.** consisting of four things or parts. 1605, borrowed from Latin *quaternārius* consisting of four each. The sense of fourth in order is first recorded in 1843.

quatrain (kwot′rān) *n.* stanza or poem of four lines. 1585, borrowing of Middle French *quatrain* stanza of four lines, from Old French *quatre* four, from Latin *quattuor* FOUR + *-ain* -AN.

quaver *v.* vibrate, tremble, quiver. Probably before 1425 *quaveren,* probably a frequentative form of earlier *cwavien* to tremble, shake (probably about 1225), of unknown origin; for suffix see -ER[4]. The coexisting form *quaven* (about 1378) may have developed from Old English **cwafian* (compare Middle English *cwavien*). Compare QUAKE. The meaning of use trills or quavers in singing is first recorded in Elyot's *Dictionary* (1538). **—n.** 1570, an eighth note; from the verb. The sense of a trill in singing is first recorded in 1611, probably from the earlier verb use; the sense of a shake or tremble in the voice is first found in Richardson's *Clarissa* (1748).

quay (kē *or* kwā) *n.* landing platform, wharf. 1696, in Phillips' *Dictionary;* variant of earlier *key* (1548); developed from Middle English *keye* (before 1400) *caye* (1306), and as a surname *Keye* (about 1200); borrowed from Old North French *cai, caie,* from Gaulish (compare Welsh *cae* fence, field, HEDGE).

The form *quay* was influenced by French *quai,* of the same meaning, from Old North French *cai, caie.* The original (and still chief) pronunciation of English *quay* is that of *key,* though Swift and Tennyson rhymed the word with *day.*

quean (kwēn) *n.* bold, impudent girl or woman, hussy. Probably before 1200 *quene* a woman, old woman, in Layamon's *Chronicle of Britain;* later, a low-born woman (probably before 1300), and with the spelling *queane* (probably before 1425); developed from Old English (before 1000) *cwene* woman, hussy, prostitute. Old English *cwene* is cognate with Old Saxon *quena* woman, wife, Middle Dutch *quene,* Old High German *quena,* Old Icelandic *kona* (Swedish *kvinna*), and Gothic *qinō,* from Proto-Germanic **kwenōn,* and outside Germanic with Old Irish *ben* woman, Greek *gynḗ,* Albanian *zonjë,* Old Prussian *genna,* Old Slavic *žena,* Armenian *kin,* Sanskrit *-jáni-s* woman, wife, and Tocharian A *śäm,* Tocharian B *śana* woman; all from Indo-European **gwen-* (Pok.473). Old English *cwene* woman, is also related to Old English *cwēn* QUEEN.

queasy *adj.* inclined to nausea, easily upset. About 1450 *kyse* unsettling to the stomach; later *queysy* uncertain, unsettled; possibly from a Scandinavian source (compare Old Icelandic *kveisa* in *idhra-kveisa* bowel pains). In the sense of unsettled and especially with the spelling *coisy* there may be some influence of Anglo-French *queisier,* Old French *coisier* to wound, hurt, make uneasy, apparently of Germanic origin, from the same root as the Scandinavian word cited above.

queen *n.* Probably before 1200 *quene, quen* king's wife, in Layamon's *Chronicle of Britain;* developed from Old English (before 725) *cwēn* queen, woman, wife, earlier *cwǣn.* The Old English forms, from Proto-Germanic **kwǣniz,* Indo-European **gwēnis* (Pok.473), are cognate with Old Saxon *quān* wife, Old Icelandic *kvæn, kvān,* and Gothic *gēns;* and outside Germanic with Sanskrit *-jāni-s* wife, and Avestan *jāni-* in ablaut relationship with Old English *cwene;* compare QUEAN.

queer *adj.* strange, odd. 1508, Scottish, in William Dunbar's *Poems;* probably borrowed from Low German (perhaps Brunswick) *queer* oblique, off-center, related to German *quer* oblique, perverse, odd, from Old High German *twerh* oblique; see THWART. The slang sense of homosexual is first recorded in 1922 in American English. **—v.** *Slang.* to spoil, ruin. 1812, probably from the adjective. An earlier sense of trick, swindle, cheat, is recorded about 1790. **—n.** *Slang.* homosexual. 1935, American English, from the adjective.

quell *v.* put down, subdue. Probably before 1200 *quellen* put to death, kill, destroy, in Layamon's *Chronicle of Britain;* developed from Old English (before 725) *cwellan* to kill; cognate with Old Saxon *quellian* to torture or kill, Middle Dutch *quelen* (modern Dutch *kwellen* harass, torment), Old High German *quellen* to torture, kill (modern German *quälen* to pain, torment), and Old Icelandic *kvelja* to torture, kill (Swedish *qvälja,* Danish *kvæle*), from Proto-Germanic **kwaljanan.* The same Proto-Germanic root **kwel-/kwal-* is the source of Old English *cwelan* to die, *cwalu* death, destruction, and is also found in QUAIL[2]. Other cognates that are more immediately identifiable with English *qualm* (through Old English *cwealm* death, *cwellan* to kill) include Old Saxon *quelan* die, *quāla* death, destruction, Middle Dutch *quelen* suffer, be ill, *qwāle* death (modern Dutch *kwaal* disease, trouble), Old High German *quelan* die, *quāla* death, destruction (modern German *Qual* pain, torment, grief), and Old Icelandic *kvǫl* torment, torture. Indo-European cognates of these Germanic forms include Old Prussian *golis* death *gallintwei* to kill, Lithuanian *gėlà* pain, *gālas* end, death, Old Slavic *želja* sorrow, grief, *žalĭ* pain, and Armenian *kełem* I torture, from Indo-European **gwel-/gwol-/gwēl-/gwōl-* (Pok.470).

The weakened sense of put an end to, suppress, subdue (fear, opposition, etc.), is first recorded probably about 1200 in *The Ormulum*.

quench *v.* Probably about 1175 *quenchen* put out, extinguish; later, put an end to, bring to naught (probably about 1200, in *The Ormulum*); developed from Old English *-cwencan* (as in *ācwencan* to quench, before 899, in Alfred's translation of Orosius' *Epitome of Universal History*). Old English *-cwencan* is a causative form that arose in Old English purely by analogy (as *drencan* drench is the causative of *drincan* drink) to correspond to the strong verb *cwincan* go out, be extinguished (found in *ācwincan*, about 1000, in Ælfric's *Lives of Saints*) and cognate with Old Frisian *quinka* disappear. These later Old English forms are extended by *-ne-* for *-n-* from the old verb root found in Old English *ā-cwīnan* dwindle away, disappear, which is cognate with Sanskrit *jīna-s* old, aged, and *jināti* becomes old, from Indo-European **gwei-/gwi-, *gweyə-/gwī-* (Pok.470).

querulous (kwer′ələs) *adj.* given to complaining, faultfinding. Probably about 1400 *querelouse* having the habit of going to law, litigious; also later *querulose* quarrelsome; borrowed from Old French *querelos*, and directly from Late Latin *querulōsus*, from Latin *querulus* full of complaints, complaining, from *querī* to complain; see QUARREL; for suffix see -OUS.

query *n.* question, inquiry. Before 1635 *quaery*, alteration (influenced by *inquiry*) of earlier *quere, quaere* question (1589); borrowed from Latin *quaere* ask, imperative of *quaerere* to seek, gain, ask, of unknown origin. The spelling *query* is first recorded in 1645. —**v.** 1654, to question, interrogate; 1657, to ask about, inquire; from the noun.

quest *n.* search, hunt. About 1303 *quest* search, official inquiry, in Mannyng's *Handlyng Synne;* borrowed from Old French *queste*, and directly from Medieval Latin *questa* search, inquiry, from Vulgar Latin **questa*, from pre-Latin **quaesta, *quaesita*, feminine of **quaestus, *quaesitus*, original past participle of *quaerere* seek, gain, ask, of unknown origin. —**v.** search or seek for, hunt. About 1350 *questen*, perhaps from the noun in Middle English, and in part borrowed from Old French *quester*, from the noun in Old French.

question *n.* Before 1200 *questiun* a philosophical or theological problem; later *questioun* any problem, matter, or thing asked, also the act of asking (before 1325, in *Cursor Mundi*); borrowed through Anglo-French *questiun*, and directly from Old French *question* legal inquest or subject of inquest, learned borrowing from Latin *quaestiōnem* (nominative *quaestiō*) a seeking, inquiry, investigation, from *quaes-*, root of *quaerere* to ask; see QUERY; for suffix see -TION. —**v.** Before 1470 *questionen*, in Malory's *Morte d'Arthur*, perhaps from the noun in Middle English, and in part borrowed from Middle French *questionner*, from the noun in Middle French. —**question mark** 1869; earlier *question stop* (1862).

questionnaire (kwes′chənār′) *n.* formal list of questions. 1901, borrowing of French *questionnaire*, from *questionner* to question, from Middle French; see QUESTION, V.

The word was preceded in English by isolated instances of *questionary* (1541, a catechism, borrowed from Medieval Latin *questionarium*, and 1887, a list of questions, borrowed from French *questionnaire*).

quetzal (ketsäl′) *n.* kind of bird with brilliant plumage. 1827, borrowing of Mexican Spanish *quetzal;* earlier *quetzale*, from Nahuatl *quetzalli* (brilliant tail feather of the bird called *quetzaltototl* (*quetzal-*, combining form of *quetzalli* + *tototl* bird).

queue (kyü) *n.* 1592, tail of a beast; later, a braid of hair (1748, in Smollet's *Adventures of Roderick Random*); borrowing of French *queue* a tail, from Old French *cue, coue, coe* tail, from Latin *cōda* (dialect variant of *cauda*) tail, of unknown origin; see COWARD. In Middle English the word had the meaning of a band of vellum or parchment (about 1475), and later, a line of dancers (probably before 1500), the latter of which is found as an extended meaning in a line of people, vehicles, etc., in Carlyle's *The French Revolution* (1837). —**v.** 1777, put up (hair) in a braid; later, move, form, or stand in a line (1893); from the noun.

quibble *n.* evasion of a point at issue, equivocation. 1611, play on words, pun; later, equivocation (1670, perhaps from this sense earlier in *quib*, 1656); often considered a diminutive form of earlier *quib* evasion of a point at issue (before 1550); probably borrowed from Latin *quibus* by what (things)? (dative and ablative plural of *quid* what, neuter of *quis* WHO), a word which, according to the OED, was much used in legal jargon and hence associated with legal quibbles; for suffix see -LE[1]. —**v.** Before 1629, to play on words, pun; later, to indulge in quibbles, equivocate (1656); from the noun. Though related to English *quip* by etymology (ultimately a form of Latin *quis* who, from *quī* who, which) *quibble* and *quip* are almost surely independent formations in English, in spite of the fact that from the mid-1600's on (and in dictionaries, such as those of Johnson, Ainsworth, etc.) the two words shared the meaning of equivocation. The evidence for separate borrowing lies not only in the difference in form but also in the original meanings of *quibble* a play on words (1611) and *quip* a sharp or sarcastic remark (1532), and the same evidence pertains even if *quibble* is considered a diminutive form of earlier *quib* (before 1550).

quiche (kēsh) *n.* kind of savory custard baked in a pie shell. 1949, borrowing of French *quiche* (1810), from dialectal German (Alsace-Lorraine) *Küche*, diminutive of German *Kuchen* CAKE.

quick *adj.* Probably about 1175 *quik* alive, lively; also ready to act, swift; later *quick* (before 1325); developed from Old English *cwic* alive (about 725, in *Beowulf*); earlier *cuic-* (as in *cuicbēam* aspen; about 700, in earliest Latin-English glossaries). The Old English forms are cognate with Old Frisian and Old Saxon *quik* alive, Middle Dutch *quic* alive (modern Dutch *kwik* quicksilver, mercury), Old High German *quec* alive (modern German *keck* lively, bold, high-spirited), Old Icelandic *kvikr* alive (Swedish *qvick*, Danish *kvik*, Norwegian *kvikk*), from Proto-Germanic **kwikwaz*, and Gothic *qiwai* (nominative plural). Cognates outside Germanic include Old Irish *biu, beo* living, alive, Welsh *byw*, Latin *vīvus* alive, *vīvere* to live, Greek *bíos* life, course of life, *zōḗ* life, *zôion* animal, Latvian *dzîga* life, *dzîguôt* to live, Lithuanian *gývas* living, alive, Old Slavic *živŭ*, and Sanskrit *jīvá-s*, from Indo-European **gwei-/gwi-, *gwey-ō-/gwy-ō, *gweyə-/gwī-* (Pok.467). —**adv.** quickly. Probably before 1300 *quyk;* from the adjective. —**n.** Probably before 1200 *quike* living persons or things; developed from Old English (before 899) *cwic;* from the adjective. The sense of the tender flesh under a fingernail or toenail is first recorded in 1523, followed by the figurative sense of a tender, sensitive part of one's feelings (as in *cut to the quick*) in 1526. —**quicken** *v.* About 1300 *quikkenen,* formed from Middle English *quick,* adj. + *-en*[1], and gradually replacing earlier *quiken* (recorded probably before 1200), probably developed from Old English *gecwician* (before 830). —**quicklime** *n.* calcium oxide, lime[1]. Probably before 1375 *qwyke lyme;* Middle English *qwyke* living, and *lyme* lime[1]; loan translation of Latin *calx viva.* —**quicksand** *n.* 1300 *Quyksond;* formed from Middle English *quyk* living + *sond* sand. —**quicksilver** *n.* mercury. 1387-95 *quyk silver,* in Chaucer's *Canterbury Tales;* Middle English *quyk* living + *silver* silver. —**quick-tempered** *adj.* easily angered (1830). —**quick-witted** *adj.* having a ready wit, clever (1530).

quid[1] *n.* piece (of tobacco, etc.) to be chewed. 1727, in Bailey's *Dictionary;* from a dialectal variant of Middle English *cudde, cud;* developed from Old English *cudu, cwidu* CUD.

quid[2] *n. British Slang.* one pound sterling. 1688, possibly borrowed from Latin *quid* what (see QUIDDITY), especially as a shortening of the phrase *quid pro quo* one thing in exchange for another, found in English since 1565.

quiddity (kwid′ətē) *n.* 1539, a subtlety or fine point in argument, quibble (alluding to scholastic arguments on the *quidditas* or essence of things); borrowed perhaps from Middle French *quiddité,* and directly from Medieval Latin *quidditas* essence of a thing, that which a thing is; literally, whatness, from Latin *quid* what, neuter of *quis* WHO; for suffix see -ITY. The Medieval Latin sense of the essence of a thing is first recorded in Middle English *quidite* (before 1398, in Trevisa's translation of Bartholomew's *De Proprietatibus Rerum*).

quiescent (kwies′ənt) *adj.* quiet, still. 1646, in Sir Thomas Browne's *Pseudodoxia Epidemica;* borrowed from Latin *quiēscentem* (nominative *quiēscēns*), present participle of *quiēscere* to come to rest, be quiet, from *quiēs* rest, quiet, see WHILE; for suffix see -ENT. —**quiescence** *n.* quietness. Before 1631, in Donne's *Letters;* borrowed from Late Latin *quiēscentia,* from Latin *quiēscēns,* present participle; for suffix see -ENCE.

quiet *n.* Probably before 1300 *quiet* calmness, rest, stillness, in *Arthour and Merlin;* borrowed from Old French *quiete,* and directly from Latin *quiēs* (genitive *quiētis*) rest, quiet; see WHILE. —**adj.** Before 1382 *quyete* at rest, still, in the Wycliffe Bible; about 1384 *quyet;* borrowed through Old French *quiet, quiete,* and directly from Latin *quiētus* resting, peaceful, calm, from past participle of *quiēscere* to come to rest; see QUIESCENT. Doublet of COY and QUIT, adj. —**v.** Before 1398 *quieten* subdue, lessen, make quiet; possibly from the adjective in Middle English, and borrowed from Late Latin *quiētāre* put to rest, calm, from Latin *quiētus* resting. The intransitive sense of become quiet (as in *the wind quieted down*) is first recorded in American English, in Thomas Paine's *The Rights of Man* (1791). —**adv.** quietly. 1573, from the adjective. —**quietude** *n.* calmness, stillness. 1597, borrowed through Middle French *quiétude,* and directly from Late Latin *quiētūdō,* from Latin *quiētus* resting; for suffix see -TUDE.

quietus (kwīē′təs) *n.* discharge or release, final settlement. 1540, discharge or receipt given on payment; shortened form of Middle English phrase *quietus est* (1427-28); borrowing of Medieval Latin *quietus est* (he) is discharged (the original words of the receipt or writ), from Latin *quiētus est* (he) is at rest; see QUIET; adj. The transferred sense of a discharge or release from life, finishing stroke, death, is first found in Shakespeare's *Hamlet* (1602).

quill *n.* hollow stem of a feather. Probably before 1425 *quille,* of uncertain origin, but probably cognate with Middle High German *kil* quill (modern German *Kiel*), and Low German *Quiele.* The meaning of a writing pen made from a quill is first recorded in English in 1552, and that of one of the sharp spines of a porcupine, in Shakespeare's *Hamlet* (1602).

quilt *n.* bedcover. Probably about 1300 *quoilt, quilte* mattress of woven material with a soft lining; borrowed through Anglo-French *quilte, coilte,* Old French *cuilte, coute,* from Latin *culcita* mattress, cushion, of unknown origin. The sense of a thick outer bed covering is first recorded in English in the 1500's. —**v.** 1555, stitch together with a soft lining, line or pad with a quiltlike material; from the noun.

quince *n.* kind of hard, yellowish fruit. Before 1325 *quince,* in the compound *quince tre;* also *coyns,* pl., quince (about 1350); borrowed from Old French *cooin,* from Latin *cotōneum mālum* quince fruit. This Latin term was probably a variant of *cydōnium mālum,* from Greek *kydṓnion mâlon,* apparently a variant of earlier *kodúmālon* apple of Kodu (*kodú-* a Lydian name for the fruit, associated in popular etymology with *Kydōníā* Cydonia, ancient city in Crete).

quinine (kwī′nīn) *n.* drug used against malaria and fevers. 1826, formed in English from Spanish *quina* cinchona bark + English *-ine*[2]; so called because this drug is made from the bark of a cinchona tree. Spanish *quina* is borrowed from Quechua (Peru) *kina.* Earlier references are found in *quinic* (also *kinic* 1814) in the form *quinic acid,* and *quinaquina* (1727), also *China China* (1707).

quinque- a combining form meaning five, as in *quinquevalent* (having a valence of five). Also *quinqu-* before vowels. Borrowed from Latin *quīnque-,* from *quīnque* FIVE.

quinquennial (kwinkwen′ēəl) *adj.* About 1475, *quinqueniale* lasting five years, formed in Middle English from Latin *quīnquennium* period of five years (*quīnque-* five + *-ennium,* from *annus* year) + English *-al*[1]. The sense of occurring every five years is first recorded in 1610. —**n.** 1895, person holding office for five years; later, fifth anniversary (1903); from the adjective.

quinsy (kwin′zē) *n.* tonsillitis with pus. 1373 *quyncie;* about 1450 *quinsy, quinesye;* borrowed from Old French *quinancie,* and through Anglo-Latin *quinancia,* both from Late Latin *cynanchē,* from Greek *kynánchē* dog quinsy; originally, dog's collar (*kýōn,* genitive *kynós* dog; see HOUND + *ánchein* to strangle; see ANGER).

quint *n.* quintuplet. 1935, Canadian English, shortened form of QUINTUPLET. This clipped form was popularized by the press after the birth of the Dionne quintuplets of Canada in 1934. The corresponding British form is *quin* (1935). An earlier use of *quint* group of five people, is recorded in an isolated instance, in Butler's *Hudibras* (1638-78).

quintal (kwin′təl) *n.* weight of 100 pounds, hundredweight. 1401 *quyntowes,* pl.; later *quintale* (about 1436); borrowed from Old French *quintal,* and directly from Medieval Latin *quintale,* from Arabic *qinṭār,* from Late Greek *kentēnárion,* from Latin *centēnārius* consisting of or containing a hundred; see CENTENARY. The Middle English plural *quyntowes* was influenced by the Old French plural *quintaus.*

quintessence (kwintes′əns) *n.* pure essence, purest form. Probably about 1435 *quyntessense* the fifth essence (ether) of ancient and medieval philosophy, in Lydgate's *Minor Poems;* borrowed from Middle French *quinte essence,* learned borrowing from Medieval Latin, and borrowed directly from Medieval Latin *quinta essentia* fifth essence (from Latin *quīnta,* feminine of *quīntus* fifth, related to *quīnque* FIVE; *essentia* ESSENCE). The Medieval Latin phrase is a loan translation of Greek *pémptē ousíā,* the ether of Aristotle, a fifth element (added to water, earth, fire, and air) permeating all things and forming the substance of the heavenly bodies. The sense of pure essence, purest form, is first recorded in English in 1570. **—quintessential** *adj.* of the purest or most perfect kind. 1605, formed from English *quintessence,* on analogy of *essence, essential;* for suffix see -AL[1].

quintet or **quintette** (kwintet′) *n.* group of five musicians, etc. 1811 *quintet,* probably borrowed from Italian *quintetto,* diminutive of *quinto* fifth, from Latin *quīntus,* related to *quīnque* FIVE. The form *quintette,* which is first recorded in English in 1864, was borrowed from French *quintette,* from Italian *quintetto.*

quintillion *n.* 1674, (in Great Britain) fifth power of a million, formed in English from Latin *quīntus* fifth (related to *quīnque* FIVE) + English *(m)illion.* In the United States, Canada, and France, a quintillion is the sixth power of a thousand. Compare BILLION.

quintuple (kwintü′pəl *or* kwin′tüpəl) *adj.* consisting of five parts, fivefold. 1570, borrowed from Middle French *quintuple,* from Latin *quīntus* fifth, after Middle French *quadruple.* **—v.** multiply by five, increase fivefold. 1639, from the adjective, modeled on verb use of earlier *quadruple* (1375), also *double* (probably before 1300), etc. **—n.** fivefold number or amount. 1684, in John Wallis' *A Treatise of Algebra;* from the adjective. **—quintuplet** *n.* 1873, group of five; formed from English *quintuple,* adj. + *-et.* The meaning of one of five children born at one birth is first recorded in 1889.

quip *n.* clever or witty saying. 1532, in Sir Thomas More's *The Confutation of Tindale's Answer,* from earlier *quippy* (1519), perhaps borrowed from Latin *quippe* indeed, really (used sarcastically), from *quid* what, neuter of *quis* WHO; compare note at QUIBBLE. **—v.** make quips. 1579, in Lyly's *Euphues;* from the noun.

quire (kwīr) *n.* 24 or 25 sheets of paper of the same size and type. Probably before 1200 *quaer, cwaer* a book or treatise, in *Ancrene Riwle;* later *quaiers* standard commercial unit for selling paper (1393); also *qwayr* a set of folded pages for a book; originally, a set of four such pages (1438) and *quayer* (1445); borrowed through Anglo-French *quier,* Old French *quaier;* earlier *quaer, caier,* from Vulgar Latin **quaternus,* from Latin *quaternī* four each, from *quater* four times, related to *quattuor* FOUR.

quirk *n.* 1565, verbal trick, quibble, evasion; of uncertain origin. The ordinary sense of a peculiarity or mannerism is first recorded in Shakespeare's *Twelfth Night* (1601). The sense of a sudden twist, turn, or curve, is found in Ben Jonson's *Volpone* (1605). **—v.** 1596, to subject to quirks, in Nashe's *Have With You to Saffron-Walden;* from the noun. The meaning of move with sudden twists is first recorded in 1821. **—quirky** *adj.* full of quirks, twists, or shifts. 1806, formed from English *quirk,* n. + *-y*[1].

quirt *n.* riding whip. 1845, American English, borrowed from American Spanish *cuarta* whip; originally, said to be a whip long enough to reach the guide mule of a team of four, from dialectal Spanish *cuarta* guide mule (also according to Corominas, oxen attached behind a wagon, possibly in groups of four, to reduce speed going downhill), from Spanish *cuarta* a fourth, from Latin *quārta,* feminine of *quārtus* fourth, related to *quattuor* FOUR.

quisling (kwiz′ling) *n.* traitor, collaborator with the enemy. 1940 *Quisling,* in allusion to Vidkun *Quisling,* 1887-1945, a Norwegian politician who was premier of the puppet government during the German occupation of Norway in World War II. The lower-case spelling *quisling* is first recorded in C.S. Lewis' *Christian Behaviour* (1943).

quit *adj.* Probably before 1200 *cwite* free, clear, rid (as of debt or obligation); later *quite, quit* (1275), in *Ancrene Riwle;* borrowed from Old French *quite* free, clear, a learned borrowing from Medieval Latin **quíetus* (with a hyper-correct accent), from Latin *quiētus* free (from war, debts, etc.), calm, resting; see the doublet QUIET, adj. **—v.** Probably before 1200 *cwiten* to pay, settle (a debt or obligation); later *quiten* to release, clear, give up (before 1250); borrowed from Old French *quiter* to free, clear, from the adjective in Old French. The sense of leave, separate, or part from, is first recorded in Middle English about 1390, and that of cease, stop, discontinue, in 1754, though antecedents of this latter sense are found in Middle English usage, in the early 1300's. **—quitclaim** *n.* a relinquishing of right, property, or interest (probably before 1300). **—quits** *adj.* even or equal with another, on even terms. 1478, discharged of a liability, free, clear; from Middle English *quit* rid of debt (probably before 1200), perhaps by influence of Medieval Latin *quittus* free of debt or claim, alteration of Latin *quiētus* free; see QUIET, adj. Such a development would in part parallel *fins* for "time out" or "quits", possibly in schoolyard slang as a borrowing by shortening of Latin *finis;* or perhaps by the same process that produced *times* also for "time out."

quite *adv.* completely, wholly. Probably before 1300 *quite, quit,* in *The Romance of Guy of Warwick;* developed in Middle English as the adverb form to the adjective *quite, quit* free, clear, QUIT.

quiver[1] *v.* to tremble, shake. 1490 *quiveren,* in Caxton's translation of *The Book of Eneydos;* possibly an alteration of *quaveren* to QUAVER; or possibly developed from the earlier Middle English adjective *quyver* active, nimble, quick (before 1398), *cwiver* (before 1250); developed from Old English *cwifer-* (found in *cwiferlīce* actively, quickly), perhaps related to *cwic* alive; see QUICK. **—n.** a quivering. 1715, from the verb.

quiver[2] *n.* case to hold arrows. 1322, borrowed through Anglo-French *quiveir,* Old French *quivre, coivre,* probably from a Germanic source (compare Old High German *kohhari* quiver, modern German *Köcher,* Old Saxon *kokar,* and Old Frisian *koker*). The Germanic word itself was probably borrowed (along with Medieval Latin *cucura* quiver, Medieval Greek *koúkouron,* and Albanian *kukurë* quiver) from **kukur* container, a word said to be from the language of the Huns, who moved out of the area east of the Volga River about 350 A.D. and invaded the Roman Empire in the early 400's.

quixotic (kwiksot′ik) *adj.* extravagantly visionary and impractical. 1815, in John Adams' *Works;* formed from the English borrowing of *Quixote* an extravagantly visionary and impractical person (1786; earlier *Quixot* 1648) + English *-ic.* English use of *Quixot, Quixote* is in allusion to Don *Quixote,* the chivalrous, romantic, and very impractical hero of Cervantes' novel *Don Quixote de la Mancha* (1605). The name *Quixote* is found in Spanish *quixote* armor for the thigh, from Catalan *cuixot,* from *cuixa* thigh, from Latin *coxa* hip.

quiz *v.* to question, interrogate. 1847 *quies;* perhaps borrowed from the Latin phrase *qui es?* who are you? the first question of oral exams in Latin in grammar schools. The spelling *quiz* is first recorded in 1886, but may have appeared earlier, by influence of the spelling of the noun. The specific meaning of examine (a student or class) orally is first recorded before 1889 in American English. **—n.** 1867, American English, an examination of a student or class; from the verb. While the spelling is unusual, it is most difficult to associate *quiz* question, with earlier *quiz* an odd or eccentric person (1782), or any of its derived senses and its verb use of make sport of, ridicule (1796), this latter word of unknown origin.

quizzical *adj.* odd, queer, amusing, whimsical. 1800, formed from earlier *quiz* an odd or eccentric person (1782); of unknown origin, + *-ical.* The sense of sporting, teasing, bantering, questioning (as in *a quizzical smile* or *glance*), is first recorded in 1801.

quoin (koin *or* kwoin) *n.* 1532, external angle of a wall or building; later, wedge-shaped block (1570); variant of COIN.

quoit (kwoit) *n.* iron or rope ring thrown to encircle a peg. 1388 *coytes,* pl., game played by throwing *quoits;* later *cote* a flat stone (1410) and *quoit* a quoit (1477); borrowed from Old French *coite* flat stone, mattress, cushion, variant of *coilte;* see QUILT.

Quonset hut (kwon′sit) trademark for a prefabricated metal building. 1942, American English; named after *Quonset* Point, Naval Air Station, Rhode Island, where this type of structure was first built in 1941.

quorum (kwôr′əm) *n.* number of members that must be present at a meeting. 1426, certain justices of the peace whose presence was necessary to make a court session legal, in *Proceedings of the Privy Council;* borrowing of Latin *quōrum* of whom, genitive plural of *quī* WHO; so used in commissions mentioning certain persons generally and specifying one or more as always to be included, as in the phrase *quorum unum. . .esse volumus* of whom we specify that. . .be one. By 1602 *quorum* was used in English of other bodies or select groups of people. The general sense of a fixed number of members of a group or body whose presence is necessary for transaction of business is first recorded in 1616.

quota *n.* proportional share. 1668, share (of men or supplies) to be contributed by a particular district; borrowed from Medieval Latin *quota,* from Latin *quota pars* how large a part; *quota,* feminine singular of *quotus* which or what number (in a sequence); see QUOTE. The meaning of maximum number (of immigrants or imports) permitted to enter a country within a fixed period is first recorded in 1921 in American English. The term *quota system* was originally (1924) used in reference to immigration quotas; since about 1963 it has been used in the United States to refer to a system to determine the percentage of people of a particular social or ethnic group that must be admitted to an institution or hired by a government agency or business to redress past discrimination.

quotation *n.* 1456, a numbering, number; later, a marginal notation (1532); probably formed from Middle English *quote,* v. + *-ation,* and also borrowed from Medieval Latin *quotationem* (nominative *quotatio*), from *quotare* to number chapters, see QUOTE; for suffix see -ATION. The meaning of an act of citing or quoting is first recorded in 1646, and that of a passage quoted from a book, etc., in 1690. The commercial meaning of an amount stated as a price of stocks or any commodity for sale is first recorded in 1812. **—quotation mark** (1888, American English)

quote *v.* Before 1387 *coten* mark (a book) with numbers or marginal references, in Trevisa's translation of Higden's *Polychronicon;* borrowed from Old French *coter;* later *quoten* (probably before 1425); from Medieval Latin *quotare* to number chapters; both the Old French and Medieval Latin forms derive from Latin *quotus* which or what number (in a sequence), from *quot* how many, related to *quis* WHO. The meaning of cite or refer to passages from (a particular source) is first recorded in 1574, and that of copy out or repeat exactly the words of another, before 1680, in Butler's writings. **—n.** 1600, marginal reference; from the verb. The meaning of a quotation is first recorded in 1885.

quoth *v. Archaic.* said. Probably about 1200, past tense of *quethen* to say (preserved in modern English *bequeath*); developed from Old English (before 725) *cwethan* (past tense *cwæth*) to say, declare. The Old English forms are cognate with Old Frisian *quetha* to say, Old Saxon *quethan* (past tense *quath*), Old High German *quethan, quedan* (past tense *quad*), Old Icelandic *kvedha* (past tense *kvath*), and Gothic *qithan* (past tense *qath*), from Proto-Germanic **kwethanan,* perhaps cognate with Sanskrit *gádati* says, altered (by influence of synonymous *vádati*) from earlier **gátati,* from Indo-European **gwet-* (Pok.480).

quotient (kwō′shənt) *n.* number obtained by dividing one number by another. About 1450 *quocient;* borrowed from Latin *quotiēns* how many times, from *quot* how many, related to *quis* WHO. The Latin adverb *quotiēns* was mistaken in Middle English for a present participle ending in *-ēns,* which produced the late Middle English form *quocient.*

qwerty or **QWERTY** (kwėr′tē) *n. Informal.* the standard typewriter keyboard. 1929, as an attributive use of the acronym formed from *q, w, e, r, t, y,* the first six keys in the upper row of letters on a standard typewriter keyboard. An article about the use and development of *qwerty* appears in *Natural History,* Vol. 96, no. 1 (January 1987).

R

rabbet (rab′it) *n.* a cut or groove made on the edge or surface of a board, stone, etc., to receive the end of another board, stone, etc., shaped to fit into the cut or groove. 1382 *rabet,* in the Wycliffe Bible; borrowed from Old French *rabat, rabbat* a recess in a wall; literally, beating down, from *rabattre* beat down; see REBATE. —**v.** 1440, implied in *rabetynge* the joining together of boards, in *Promptorium Parvulorum;* later, cut a rabbet in (1572); from the noun.

rabbi *n.* Jewish religious leader. Before 1325 *rabi, rabbi* master (used as a term of address), in *Cursor Mundi;* borrowed from Old French *rabi,* and directly from Late Latin *rabbī,* from Greek *rhabbí,* from Hebrew *rabbī* my master (*rabh* master + pronoun suffix *-ī*). An isolated example of *rabbi* occurs before 1050 in the *West Saxon Gospels,* but the meaning of a Jewish religious leader is not found until 1387 in titles of Jewish scholars, in Trevisa's translation of Higden's *Polychronicon.* —**rabbinate** *n.* office of a rabbi, group of rabbis of a particular area or authority. 1702, formed from earlier English *rabbin* rabbi (1531) + *-ate*[3]. English *rabbin* was borrowed through French, probably from Aramaic *rabbīn,* plural of *rab* master. —**rabbinical** *adj.* of a rabbi or rabbis. 1622, formed from earlier English *rabbinic* (1612) + *-al*[1], or from earlier English *rabbin* rabbi (1531) + *-ical. Rabbinic* is borrowed from French *rabbinique* or formed from English *rabbin* + *-ic.*

rabbit *n.* Before 1398 *rabbete,* in Trevisa's translation of Bartholomew's *De Proprietatibus Rerum;* later *rabet* (probably about 1425); borrowed from a dialectal French source (compare modern French dialect *rabbotte* rabbit, rabbit hole, and Walloon *robète,* in form a diminutive), from Flemish or Middle Dutch *robbe* rabbit, dogfish; of uncertain origin. The original reference in English was to the young animal only; the adult was called *cony.*

rabble *n.* mob. About 1389 *rabul* meaningless string of words; also, probably about 1390 *rabel* crowd of people, in *Sir Gawain and the Green Knight;* possibly related to *rablen* speak in a rapid confused manner (before 1410); borrowed from Middle Dutch *rabbelen* to chatter, cognate with Low German *rabbeln* to chatter.

rabid *adj.* About 1611, furious or raging, in a translation of Homer's *Iliad;* borrowed from Latin *rabidus,* from *rabere* be mad, rave; see RAGE. The specific medical sense of affected with rabies, made mad by rabies, is first recorded in 1804.

rabies *n.* virus disease transmitted by the bite of a rabid animal. 1598, in Florio's *World of Words;* borrowed from Latin *rabiēs* madness, rage, fury; related to *rabere* be mad, rave. Doublet of RAGE.

raccoon *n.* small, omnivorous mammal. 1608 *arocoun,* American English; borrowed from Algonquian (Powhatan) *ärähkun,* from *ärähkuněm* he scratches with the hands, so called perhaps from the animal's habit of leaving long scratches on the trees he climbs or in reference to the use of its hands in hunting for shellfish and insects. The sense of the skin or fur of a raccoon is first recorded in 1815 in American English, though coonskin is not found before 1818; however *raccoon skin* is recorded as early as 1624.

race[1] *n.* contest of speed. Probably before 1300 *ras* a charge in a battle, an onslaught, in *Arthour and Merlin;* later, onward movement, act of running, (before 1325, in *Cursor Mundi*); later in the spelling *race* (probably before 1350); borrowed from a Scandinavian source (compare Old Icelandic *rās* running, rush); cognate with Middle Dutch *rāsen,* modern Dutch *razen* to rage, Middle Low German *rās* strong current, and Old English *rǣs* running, rush). The Germanic words derive from Proto-Germanic **rǣs-,* cognate with Greek *erōē* a quick motion, a rush, from Indo-European **rēs-/rōs-,* root **eres* (Pok.336). The meaning of a contest of speed is first recorded in English in 1513, developed from the earlier sense of an act of running. The meaning of a strong current of water is found in Barbour's *The Bruce* (1375, perhaps in part from Old French *ras, raz* strong current of water). —**v.** engage in a race. 1680 (implied in *racing*); from the noun. —**racehorse** *n.* (before 1626) —**racetrack** *n.* (1862, American English)

race[2] *n.* group of people traditionally thought of as connected by common descent or origin. 1520, a class of wine with a characteristic flavor; also, a group of people thought of as a particular set (as in *a new race of poets*); later, a generation (probably 1549), a group of people of common origin (1570); borrowed from Middle French *race;* earlier *rasse* breed, lineage, family, from Italian *razza* race, breed, lineage, of uncertain origin. —**racial** *adj.* 1862, formed from English *race*[2] + *-ial.* —**racism** *n.* belief in the superiority of a particular race. 1936, formed from English *race*[2] + *-ism.* —**racist** *n.* 1932, formed from English *race*[2] + *-ist; adj.* (1938).

raceme (rāsēm′ *or* rəsēm′) *n.* flower cluster having its flowers on nearly equal stalks along a stem. 1785, borrowed from Latin *racēmus* cluster of grapes or berries. Doublet of RAISIN. The form is recorded earlier in Middle English with the meaning of a raisin or currant (probably before 1425), and is found imbedded in earlier terms in modern English such as *racemose* arranged in racemes (1698) and *racemiferous* bearing racemes (1656).

rack[1] *n.* frame with bars. About 1300 *rekke;* 1343-44 *rakke, rekke,* possibly borrowed from Middle Dutch *rec* framework, related to *recken* to stretch out. Middle Dutch *recken* is cognate with Old English *reccan* to stretch out, Old Frisian *reza,* Old Saxon *rekkian,* Old High German *recchen* (modern German *recken*), Old Icelandic *rekja,* and Gothic *ufrakjan,* from Proto-Germanic **rakjanan.* Cognates outside Germanic are found in Greek *orégein* to stretch out, and Latin *regere* direct; see RIGHT.

The meaning of an instrument of torture on which the body is stretched is first recorded probably about

1425, and its figurative sense of agony, great suffering, is found in 1591, anticipated by Middle English *the reccys* the racks, meaning pain in the side (1373).
—v. Probably 1435 *rakken* to stretch on a frame for drying; about 1433, to torture on the rack; from the noun, possibly reinforced by borrowing from Middle Dutch *recken* to stretch out. The sense of torment is first recorded in Shakespeare's *Twelfth Night* (1601).

rack[2] *n. Archaic.* wreck, destruction. 1599, in the phrase *go to rack and ruin* to be destroyed; variant of WRACK.

rack[3] *v.* (of a horse) move with a kind of fast, lively gait. 1530, in Palsgrave's *Lesclarcissement;* of uncertain origin. Palsgrave renders "racking of a horse in his pace" by the French *racquassure,* itself of unknown origin. **—n.** racking gait. 1580, probably from the verb.

rack[4] *n.* broken clouds driven before the wind. Probably about 1380 *rak* rain cloud; earlier, rapid movement, rush (probably before 1300); possibly found in Old English *racu* cloud (of uncertain date), reinforced by a probable Scandinavian source (compare Old Icelandic *rek* jetsam, wreckage, Swedish dialect *rak*). It is also possible that the Middle English noun was formed by influence of Old English *wræc* something driven. **—v.** (of clouds or fog) to be driven before the wind. Probably before 1200, move quickly, rush; possibly found in Old English *racian* hasten.

racket[1] or **racquet** *n.* oval frame strung across with netting and a long handle, used to hit a ball in tennis, etc. About 1385 *raket* game like tennis in which players hit a ball with their palm, in Chaucer's *Troilus and Criseyde;* later *rakket* racket used in tennis, badminton, etc. (1500-20, in William Dunbar's *Poems*); borrowed from Old French *requette, rechete* racket or battledore, palm of the hand (perhaps reinforced by Spanish *raqueta*), from Arabic *rāḥat,* a form of *rāḥa* palm of the hand.

racket[2] *n.* loud noise, loud talk. 1565, of uncertain origin; traditionally said to be of probable imitative origin. The meaning of any dishonest scheme or activity is first recorded in 1812; originally British slang, perhaps from *racket*[1] with the underlying sense of *game* (a scheme, about 1250) and possibly further reinforced by the sense of *rack*[1] in *rack-rent* excessively high or extortionate rent. **—racketeer** *n.* gangster, criminal. 1928, American English; formed from *racket*[2] + *-eer.*

raconteur (rak′ontėr′) *n.* person clever in telling stories. 1828, a French word used in a memoir, from Old French *raconter* relate or recount (*re-* again + *aconter* count up; see ACCOUNT, v.) + French *-eur.*

racy *adj.* 1654, (of wine, fruits, etc.) having the characteristic taste or quality of a race or kind; formed from English *race*[2] a class of wine + *-y*[1]. The extended meaning of having a distinctive quality or vigor, liveliness, piquancy, is first recorded before 1667. The modern sense of so lively as to be improper, suggestive, risqué, is first recorded in 1901. Compare the similar semantic development of German *rassig* (*Rasse* race[2] + *-ig* -y[1]).

rad *n.* unit for measuring absorbed doses of radiation. 1918, unit of a dose of X rays, shortened form of *radiation.* The later meaning, in which a rad is equal to 100 ergs per gram of absorbing material, is first recorded in 1954 and is said to have been formed anew as an acronym from the first letters of *radiation absorbed dose.*

radar *n.* device for detecting position of unseen objects by the reflection of radio waves. 1941, American English; acronym formed from *ra(dio) d(etecting) a(nd) r(anging).*

radial *adj.* of or like a radius or rays. Before 1400, pertaining to a surgical instrument with raylike parts; borrowed from Medieval Latin *radialis,* from Latin *radius* beam of light, RAY[1]; for suffix see -AL[1].

radiant *adj.* About 1450, borrowed perhaps through Middle French *radiant,* but more likely directly from Latin *radiantem* (nominative *radiāns*) shining, present participle of *radiāre* to beam, shine; see RADIATE; for suffix see -ANT. **—radiance** *n.* 1601, in Shakespeare's *All's Well that Ends Well;* formed from English *radiant* + *-ance.*

radiate *v.* Before 1619, to spread in all directions from a center, figurative use of the sense of emit rays of light (1649); back formation from earlier *radiation,* and in part probably reinforced by Latin *radiātum,* past participle of *radiāre* to beam, shine; for suffix see -ATE[1]. The sense of give off in rays (said of light or heat) is first recorded in Locke's *Elements of Natural Philosophy* (1704). **—radiation** *n.* Before 1450, act or process of radiating; later, ray or rays emitted (1570); borrowed from Middle French *radiation,* and earlier directly from Latin *radiātiōnem* (nominative *radiātiō*), from *radiāre* to beam, shine, radiate, from *radius* beam of light; see RAY[1]; for suffix see -ATION. **—radiator** *n.* 1836, thing that radiates; formed from English *radiate* + *-or*[2]. The meaning of a device which radiates heat into a room is first recorded in 1851, and that of a device on an automobile that dissipates heat from the motor, in 1900, in American English.

radical *adj.* going to the root, fundamental. Before 1398, of or in a plant root or in the ground and thereby fundamental to existence; also (of bodily organs or fluids) vital to life, fundamental, in Trevisa's translation of Bartholomew's *De Proprietatibus Rerum;* borrowed from Late Latin *rādīcālis* of or having roots, from Latin *rādīx* (genitive *rādīcis*) ROOT; for suffix see -AL[1]. The sense of inherent or fundamental in a generalized use is first recorded in English in 1562, but was probably used much earlier. The sense of advocating fundamental reform is recorded in 1800, and that of favoring extreme changes or reforms in the 1840's. By the 1920's *radical* had developed the meaning of unconventional or unorthodox in attitude, conception, etc., as in *radical in design, radical art.* **—n.** 1641, root part of a word, from the adjective. The sense of a person advocating fundamental reform is first found in 1802 paralleling the adjective use. In scientific use the meaning of an atom or group of atoms acting as a unit in a chemical reaction is first recorded in 1816 as a direct borrowing from modern French, in which the term was introduced in 1787. **—radical chic** vogue among fashionable people of socializing with radicals. 1970, American English; coined by Tom Wolfe, an American author. **—radicalism** *n.* 1820, formed from English *radical,* adj. or n. + *-ism.* **—radical sign** mathematical sign placed before an expression to show that one of its roots is to be found (1668).

radio *n.* 1903 (in *radio-receiver*) transmission and reception through the atmosphere of voice signals or messages by electromagnetic waves; abstracted from such earlier combinations as *radiophone* (1881, used by Bell in reference to work of Mercadier in producing sound from radiant energy) and *radioconductor* (1898, a device used in early wireless telegraphy), but also traditionally associated with *radiotelegraphy* transmission through the atmosphere of telegraph signals by electromagnetic waves (1898); formed from English *radio-* + *telegraphy* (after the work of Marconi). The meaning of sound broadcasting as a medium of communication (as in *representatives of the press and radio*) is first found in 1922 in American English. **—adj.** of, used in, or transmitted by radio. 1912, from the noun. **—v.** transmit, communicate, or broadcast by radio. 1919, from the noun. **—radio astronomy** branch of astronomy dealing with radio waves received from objects in space (1948) **—radio station** (1912) **—radio telescope** device for receiving radio waves from objects in space. 1948; earlier, in science fiction (1929). **—radio wave** (1916)

radio- a combining form meaning: **1** radiant energy, as in *radiometer* (1875), *radioactive* (1900), *radiotherapy* (1903). **2** radioactive, radiation, as in *radioisotope* (1946), *radiology* (1900). **3** radio, as in *radiobroadcast* (1922), *radiojournalism* (1968). In the sense of radioactive, *radio-* is a combining form in English abstracted from *radiation;* in the sense of radio or electronic it is a combining form of *radio;* formed in part on the model of Latin *radius,* and in part abstracted from earlier combinations in English, such as *radiotelegraphy;* both meanings ultimately adapted from Latin *radius* spoke of a wheel, radius of a circle, beam of light; see RAY[1].

radiosonde (rā′dēōsond′) *n.* airborne radio device for transmitting data on atmospheric temperature, pressure, and humidity. 1937, borrowing of German *Radiosonde* (1931, *Radio-* radio- + *Sonde* depth sounding, probe, from French *sonde,* literally, sounding line, from Old French; see SOUND[3] fathom).

radish *n.* sharp-tasting root of a plant of the mustard family. Before 1200 *redic;* later *redich* (before 1300), and *radisshe* (1373); developed from Old English (about 1000) *rǣdic,* borrowed from Latin *rādix* (genitive *rādīcis*) ROOT. The spelling with *-ish* was perhaps influenced by Old French *radise,* variant of *radice,* from Latin *rādīx* root.

radium (rā′dēəm) *n.* radioactive metallic chemical element. 1899, New Latin, formed from Latin *radius* RAY[1] + New Latin *-ium,* chemical suffix; so called because the element was found to give off radioactive rays. The word was coined in 1898 by the element's discoverers, the French chemists Pierre Curie and Marie Curie.

radius (rā′dēəs) *n.* 1597, staff of a cross, borrowed from Latin *radius* radius, staff, spoke, beam of light. Doublet of RAY[1]. The meaning of a line drawn straight from the center to the outside of a circle or sphere is first recorded in Hobbes' *Six Lessons* (1656).

radon (rā′don) *n.* radioactive gaseous chemical element. 1918, borrowed from German *Radon,* from *Rad(ium)* radium + *-on,* as in the other inert gases *argon, neon, xenon;* so called because this element is formed by the radioactive decay of radium. Radon was discovered in 1900 by the German physicist Friedrich Ernst Dorn.

raff *n.* worthless people, riffraff. 1673, from Middle English *raf* rubbish, scrap, sweepings (1440); earlier, a class or group of people (probably of a lower sort or ilk, before 1338 in Mannyng's *Chronicle of England*); apparently abstracted from the second member of the phrase *rif and raf* every scrap, everyone, the rabble (also 1338); but also found as an independent element with the sense of crude, worthless verse as early as 1330; see RIFFRAFF. Middle English *raf,* also found in Anglo-French *rif et raf,* is probably related to Swedish *rafs* rubbish. **—raffish** *adj.* disreputable, vulgar, rakish. 1801, in Jane Austen's *Letters;* formed from English *raff* + *-ish*[1].

raffia (raf′ēə) *n.* fiber used in making baskets and mats. 1882; earlier *raphia* (1866) and probably *rofia* (1729 *rofeer*); borrowed from Malagasy *rafia.*

raffle *n.* About 1390 *rafle* dice game, in Chaucer's *Canterbury Tales;* borrowed from Old French *rafle* dice game, plundering, stripping; perhaps from a Germanic source (compare Middle Dutch *raffel* dice game, which is possibly cognate with Middle High German and modern German *raffen* to grab, Middle Low German *reppen* to move, Old Frisian *hreppa* to move, and Old Icelandic *hreppa* to reach, get), from Proto-Germanic **Hrap-,* from IndoEuropean **kreb-/krob-* (Pok.949). The meaning of a sale of chances to win an item is first recorded in English in 1766, referring to the various diversions available in the resorts at Bath, England. **—v.** Before 1680, take part in a raffle, in Butler's *Remains;* from the noun.

raft[1] *n.* floating platform. Probably about 1300, beam, rafter; later, floating platform of logs (1497); borrowed from a Scandinavian source (compare Old Icelandic *raptr* log, with *pt* for *ft*); see RAFTER. **—v.** to transport by raft. 1706, from the noun.

raft[2] *n.* large collection, crowd. 1833, variant of earlier *raff* heap, large amount (before 1677); also large crowd (1673); from Middle English *raf,* probably identical with the second member in the phrase *rif and raf* one and all, everyone, every scrap; see RAFF and RIFFRAFF.

rafter *n.* slanting beam of a roof. Before 1200 *refter* a beam or pole; also about 1200, *raftre;* developed from Old English (West Saxon, before 899) *ræftras,* pl. and (Mercian, about 700) *reftras.* The Old English forms are cognate with Middle Low German *rafter, rachter* rafter, and Old Icelandic *raptr* (Swedish and Danish *raft*), related to Old Icelandic *rāfr, rǣfr* roof made with rafters, from Proto-Germanic **rāf-/raf-.* The Germanic forms are cognate with Lithuanian *rĕplinti* to erect, and Old Slavic *rĕpĭjĭ* pole, from Indo-European **rēp-/rəp-* pole, beam (Pok.866).

rag[1] *n.* scrap of cloth. About 1325 *ragge;* borrowed from a Scandinavian source (compare Old Icelandic *rǫgg* shaggy tuft, earlier *raggw-,* and Old Danish *rag;* see RUG). Earlier Old English *raggig* raglike, shaggy, is very late, and was almost surely developed from Scandinavian. **—ragbag** *n.* 1820, motley collection; later, bag for scraps of cloth (1861). **—ragged** *adj.* About 1300 *ragged* rough, shaggy, frayed; formed from *rag*[1] + *-ed*[2], reinforced by borrowing from a Scandinavian source (compare Old Icelandic *raggathr* shaggy, Swedish *raggig* shaggy, rough, Norwegian *raggad*). **—ragtag** *adj.* disreputable, disorderly. 1883, from earlier *ragtag,* n., riffraff or rabble (*rag*[1] scrap of cloth + *tag*[1] hanging piece, usually in *ragtag and bobtail,* 1820). An older form was *tag and rag,* common in the 1500's and 1600's according to the OED.

rag[2] *v. Slang.* to scold. 1739, of uncertain origin. The extended sense of annoy, tease, torment, is first recorded for *rag* in Jamieson's *Etymological Dictionary of the*

Scottish Language (1808, but is already found in the stronger sense of intimidate in the combination *ballarag,* 1807).

rag[3] *n.* style of jazz characterized by syncopation and a regularly accented accompaniment, ragtime. 1895, American English, possibly a shortened form of *ragged;* so called from the apparent rhythmic imbalance or irregularity of the music; also found in such forms as *ragamuffin* used as an attributive in the sense of disorderly. The compound *ragtime* (presumably *rag*[3] + *time*) appeared in 1897 in American English.

raga (rä′gə) *n.* traditional Hindu melodic form. 1788, Sir William Jones, in *Asiatick Researches;* borrowed from Sanskrit *rāga-s* harmony, melody; literally, color or mood, related to *rájyati* it is dyed, from Indo-European **reg-/rēg-,* and Greek *rhézein* to dye, *rhêgos* rug, blanket, from Indo-European **sreg-/srēg-* to dye (Pok.854).

ragamuffin (rag′əmuf ′ən) *n.* ragged fellow, especially a child. 1344 *ragamuffyn,* a personal name; formed from Middle English *raggi,* adj., ragged + Middle Dutch *muffe, moffe* mitten.

rage *n.* Probably before 1300 *rage* violent anger, madness, passion, in *Kyng Alisaunder* and in *Arthour and Merlin;* borrowed from Old French *rage, raige,* from Medieval Latin *rabia,* also Late Latin, from Latin *rabiēs* madness, rage, fury; related to *rabere* be mad, rave, rage. These Latin words are cognate with Sanskrit *rábhas* violence, impetuosity, from Indo-European **rabh-* (Pok.852). Doublet of RABIES. **—v.** About 1250, to play, romp; later, to be furious (before 1325, in *Cursor Mundi*); from the noun.

raglan *n.* loose outer coat with sleeves extending to the collar. 1863, in allusion to Lord *Raglan,* British field marshal in the Crimean War, from the Welsh place name *Raglan, Rhaglan.* **—adj.** with sleeves extending to the collar. 1906, from the noun.

ragout (ragü′) *n.* highly seasoned stew. 1656-57, borrowing of French *ragoût,* from Middle French *ragoûter* awaken the appetite (Old French *re-* back + *à* to + *goût* taste, from Latin *gustum,* nominative *gustus;* see GUSTO).

ragweed *n.* weed whose pollen often causes an allergic reaction. 1790, American English (*rag*[1] + *weed;* so called from the ragged shape of the leaves; applied earlier to another plant, 1658).

raid *n.* About 1425, military expedition on horseback, Scottish and Northern English form of Old English *rād* a riding, cognate with Old Icelandic *reidh* a riding, raid; see ROAD. *Raid* is not recorded after the 1500's except in the obsolete sense of a place near shore where ships may anchor, and as an isolated use of the gerund *raiding.* Later modern use is attributed to revival by Scott in *The Lay of the Last Minstrel* (1805) and *Rob Roy* (1818) with the extended sense of an attack, hostile incursion, foray. **—v.** 1865, take part in a raid; from the noun. The sense of make a raid on (a place, herd of animals, etc.) is first recorded in 1880; but the sense of take part in or make a raid is implied in earlier *raider* (1863) and *raiding* (1785).

rail[1] *n.* bar of wood or metal. Probably about 1300 *raile;* earlier *reyle* the railing of a ship (1294-95); borrowed from Old French *reille, raille,* from Latin *rēgula* straight stick, diminutive form related to *regere* to straighten, guide; see RIGHT. **—v.** provide with rails. About 1385 *railen* fence in with rails, in Chaucer's *Troilus and Criseyde;* from the noun in Middle English. **—railing** *n.* fence made of rails. 1432 *raylynge* rail or framework to support vines; later, specifically, a fence (1440); formed from Middle English *railen* fence in with rails (about 1385), support vines with rails (1387) + *-ing*[1]. The word appeared in the sense of a vine or shoot (before 1382). **—railroad** *n.* (1757), **railway** *n.* (1776) road laid with rails on which wagons with heavy loads are made to run; later, a track for trains pulled by a locomotive; *railroad* (1825) *railway* (1832).

rail[2] *v.* use violent language, complain bitterly. Before 1470 *railen;* borrowed from Middle French *railler* to tease or joke, from Old Provençal *ralhar* to prattle, chat, joke, from Vulgar Latin **ragulāre* to bray, from Late Latin *ragere* to roar; of uncertain origin. Related to RALLY[2] to tease.

rail[3] *n.* kind of small bird. Before 1450 *rale;* later *rayl* (probably about 1475); borrowed from Old French *raale,* related to French *râler* to rattle, of uncertain origin.

raillery *n.* good-humored ridicule. 1653, borrowed from French *raillerie,* from Middle French *railler* to tease; see RAIL[2], v.; for suffix see -ERY.

raiment *n.* clothing. About 1400 *rameunt;* also *rayment* (probably before 1425), shortened form of *arayment* clothing, attire (before 1399); borrowed through Anglo-French *araiement,* Old French *areement* (*arëer* to ARRAY + *-ment* -ment).

rain *n.* 1116 *rein;* later *rain* (before 1325); developed from Old English *regn* rain (before 725, in *Genesis A*) and earlier in compounds, such as *regnwyrm* rainworm or earthworm (about 700, in the earliest Latin-English glossaries) sometimes contracted to *rēn-, rēn.* The Old English forms are cognate with Old Frisian *rein* rain, Old Saxon *regan,* Middle Dutch *reghen* (modern Dutch *regen*), Old High German *regan* (modern German *Regen*), Old Icelandic, modern Danish, Norwegian, and Swedish *regn,* and Gothic *rign,* from Proto-Germanic **reȝna-.*

If one is to include Lithuanian *rõkti* to drizzle, *rõki* drizzling rain, as cognates outside Germanic on the basis of Indo-European **rōk-,* then Proto-Germanic **reȝna-* can only be explained as a syncopated or shortened form from earlier **reȝaná-,* from Indo-European **rekenó-,* root **rek-/rōk-* (Pok.857). A collateral root is found in Indo-European **reĝ–/roĝ–,* underlying Albanian *rrjeth* to flow, drip, Old Icelandic *raki* dampness, and Latin *rigāre* to wet, soak, altered from **regāre* (by influence of the compound *ir-rigāre* to irrigate).

—v. Probably before 1200 *reinen* to rain; developed from Old English (about 950) *regnian,* but usually *rīnan,* a contraction of the commoner *rignan.* The Old English forms are cognate with Middle Dutch *reghenen* to rain (modern Dutch *regenen*), Old High German *reganōn* (modern German *regnen*), Old Icelandic *regna* (Danish and Norwegian *regne,* Swedish *regna*), and Gothic *rignjan;* all derived from the Germanic source of Old English *regn,* n., rain. **—rainbow** *n.* About 1250 *reinbowe,* in *Genesis and Exodus;* developed from Old English *rēnboga* (about 1000, in Ælfric's translation of *Genesis*); formed from *rēn* (older *regn*) rain, n. + *boga* bend, BOW[2] (weapon). **—raincheck** *n.* 1884, ticket for future use, given to the spectators at an outdoor event stopped by rain; American English, formed from *rain,* n. + *check* receipt, token. The figurative expression *take a rain check,* reserve the right to accept an offer at a later, more convenient time, is first recorded in 1959. **—raincoat** *n.* (1830, American English) **—raindrop** *n.* About 1400 *reindrope;* developed from Old English (about 1000) *rēndropa;* formed from *rēn* rain, n. + *dropa* drop. **—rainfall** *n.* 1854, amount of rain that falls in a certain place; also, shower of rain (1848-58); formed from English *rain,* n. + *fall,* n. **—rain forest** (1903, possibly a loan translation of German *Regenwald*) **—rainstorm** *n.* (1816, in writings of Coleridge) **—rainy** *adj.* About 1384 *reyny;* developed from Old English (before 1000) *rēnig;* formed from *rēn* rain + *-ig* -y[1].

raise *v.* Probably about 1200 *reysen* lift up, give rise to, make greater, increase, in *The Ormulum;* later, *raisen* (before 1250); borrowed from a Scandinavian source (compare Old Icelandic *reisa* to raise; see REAR[2], v.). **—n.** About 1500, a levy; later, act of raising (1538); from the verb. The sense of an increase in amount, value, etc., is first recorded in 1728, and the specific sense of an increase in salary is found in 1898 in American English.

raisin *n.* sweet dried grape. Probably before 1300 *reisyn* grape, raisin, in *Kyng Alisaunder;* later *raysyn* (probably about 1425); borrowed through Anglo-French *reisin,* Old French *raisin* grape, raisin, from Vulgar Latin **racīmus,* alteration of Latin *racēmus* cluster of grapes or berries; probably from the same (Mediterranean) source as Greek *rhā́x* (genitive *rhāgós*) grape, berry. Doublet of RACEME.

rajah or **raja** (rä′jə) *n.* ruler or chief in India, Java, Borneo, etc. 1555, in Eden's translation of *Decades of the New World or West India;* borrowed as *rājā,* a transliteration from Hindi, from Sanskrit *rājā,* nominative of *rā́jan-* king; cognate with Latin *rēx* (genitive *rēgis*) king; see REGAL.

rake[1] *n.* tool for gathering leaves, hay, etc. Before 1325 *rake,* developed from Old English *raca* rake (about 1000); earlier *ræce* (before 800).

The Old English forms are cognate with Middle Low German *rake* rake, from Proto-Germanic **rak-,* representing Indo-European **rog-;* and with Old High German *rehho* rake, *rehhan* gather, heap up (modern German *Rechen* rake), Middle Dutch *reke,* Old Icelandic *reka* spade, shovel, and Gothic *rikan* heap up, from Proto-Germanic **rek-,* representing the Indo-European root **reg-/rog-* (Pok.854). Cognates outside Germanic are perhaps found in Old Irish *rogaid* stretches out, and Greek *orégein* to stretch out; see RIGHT.

—v. move with a rake. About 1250 *raken* gather, rake, in *Genesis and Exodus;* borrowed from a Scandinavian source (compare Old Icelandic *raka* to scrape, rake). The meaning of Middle English *raken* was influenced by the noun *rake* rake.

rake[2] *n.* dissolute or immoral person, scoundrel. 1653, in Henry A. More's *An Antidote Against Atheism,* shortened form of earlier *rakehell* (1554 and as an adjective, before 1547), possibly alteration (by association with *rake*[1] and *hell*) of Middle English *rakel,* adj., hasty, rash, headstrong (before 1300); probably from *raken,* v. to go, proceed (compare *rakeden* went hastily, rushed, probably before 1200), of unknown origin.

rake[3] *n.* slant or slope. 1626, sloping cut of a ship's hull from the projecting deck to the keel; perhaps from the verb in spite of the slightly later date. **—v.** 1627, to have a sloping cut to a ship's hull; of uncertain origin (compare Old Swedish *raka* project, reach, Danish *rage* protrude, though these forms have been suggested as borrowings of German *ragen* protrude, jut out).

rakish[1] *adj.* of or like a scoundrel. 1706, formed from English *rake*[2] + *-ish*[1].

rakish[2] *adj.* smart, jaunty, dashing. 1824, in Washington Irving's writings, probably formed from English *rake*[3] + *-ish*[1].

rally[1] *v.* bring together. 1603, in Florio's translation of Montaigne's *Essays;* borrowed from French *rallier,* from Old French *ralier* reassemble, unite again (*re-* again + *alier* unite; see ALLY). The sense of pull together, revive, rouse, is first recorded in Milton's *Paradise Lost* (1667). **—n.** 1651, rapid reunion for renewed effort, from the verb sense of recovery, renewal of strength, is first recorded in Scott's writings in 1826. The extended meaning of a mass meeting to arouse group support is first recorded in 1840 in American English, and that of gathering of automobile enthusiasts, especially for a race, was borrowed about 1930 from French *rallye,* which was borrowed earlier from English *rally*[1], n., about 1911, with the variant spelling *rallye* (borrowed from French about 1949). A specialized meaning of the act of hitting a ball, shuttlecock, etc., a number of times after service, is first recorded in 1878.

rally[2] *v.* to make fun of, tease. 1668, borrowed from French *railler* to rail, reproach, from Middle French; see RAIL[2], v.

ram *n.* Before 1325 *ram, rom* male sheep; earlier in a place name *Ramtune* (1086); also, a pile driver (1256), a battering ram (1408); found in Old English *ramm* male sheep, battering ram (about 1000); earlier *rom* male sheep (before 725). The Old English forms are cognate with Middle Low German, Middle Dutch, modern Dutch, and Old High German *ram* ram, and probably with Old Icelandic *rammr, ramr* sharp, strong, of unknown origin. **—v.** butt against, strike head-on. Probably before 1300 *rammen* to tramp down earth so as to make it hard and firm, in *Arthour and Merlin.* Probably from the noun in Middle English. The meaning of drive down or in by heavy blows is first recorded in 1519, but probably appeared much earlier.

ramada (rəmä′də) *n.* (in western U.S.) an arbor or porch. 1869, American English, borrowed from American-Spanish *ramada* tent, shelter, from Spanish *ramada* an arbor, from *rama* branch, from Vulgar Latin **rāma,* a collective (perhaps formed on the model of Latin *folia* leaves) from Latin *rāmus* branch, probably from earlier **wrādmos,* related to *rādīx* ROOT.

Ramadan (ram′ədän′) *n.* ninth month of the Moslem year, observed as a thirty days' fast from dawn to sunset. 1601, borrowed from Arabic *Ramaḍān,* originally, the hot month, from *ramiḍa* be burnt, scorched. Another form *Ramazan* (1599) was borrowed from Turkish *ramazān,* from Arabic *Ramaḍān.*

ramble *v.* wander about. About 1443 *ramblen,* perhaps a frequentative form of **ramben,* variant of *romen,* v. to walk, go, ROAM (compare variants: *ramedan* past plural, and *rombide* past singular); or perhaps an alteration of *romblen* to ramble (about 1378), also a frequentative form of *romen* to ROAM; for suffix see -LE[3]. **—n.** a walk for pleasure. 1654, from the verb. **—rambler** *n.* 1624, person or thing that rambles; later, any of various climbing roses (1837); formed from English *ramble* + *-er*[1]. **—rambling** *adj.* 1623, wandering or moving about; later straying from one subject to another (1635), extending haphazardly in various directions (about 1702), from the verb.

rambunctious (rambungk′shəs) *adj. Informal.* wild, unruly. 1830 *rumbunctious;* later *rambunctious* (1859); American English, alterations of earlier *rambustious* (1853, possibly influenced by *ram,* v. and *rumbustious* boisterous, turbulent, unruly (1778), the latter an arbitrary re-formation (probably influenced by *rum*[1]) of earlier *robustious* boisterous, robust (before 1548, *robust* + *-ious,* as in *pernicious, rebellious,* etc.). It is also possible that re-formation of the medial syllable from *-bus-* to *-bunc-* was in part influenced by *bumptious,* and that the suffixal ending *-tious* was reinforced by the pattern found in *captious, fractious,* etc.

ramekin or **ramequin** (ram′əkin) *n.* small, separately cooked portion of cheese, with bread crumbs, eggs, etc. 1706, in Kersey's edition of Phillips' *Dictionary;* borrowing of French *ramequin,* perhaps from early modern Dutch *rammeken* toasted bread; or more obscurely from Low German *ramken,* diminutive of *ram* cream, from Middle Low German *rōm, rōme.* The extended meaning of a dish in which ramekins or other small portions of food are baked and served is first recorded in English in 1895.

ramify *v.* divide or spread out into branchlike parts. Probably before 1425 *ramifien* branch out; borrowed from Middle French *ramifier,* from Medieval Latin *ramificare,* from a lost adjective **ramificus* (Latin *rāmus* branch; see RAMADA, + the root of *facere* make, perform); for suffix see -FY. **—ramification** *n.* 1677, branch or offshoot; borrowed from French *ramification,* from Medieval Latin *ramificare* ramify; for suffix see -FICATION. The sense of outgrowth, subdivision, consequence, is first recorded in Johnson's *Dictionary* (1755).

ramp[1] *n.* a sloping way connecting different levels of a building, walkway, road, etc. 1778, borrowed from French *rampe,* from Old French *ramper* to climb; see RAMP[2]. An earlier meaning of difference in level between the supports of an arch is recorded in 1725.

ramp[2] *v.* rush wildly about. Before 1325, especially as present participle *rampand* standing on the hind legs, rearing, in *Cursor Mundi;* later *rampyng* (about 1400), forms of the present participle of *raumpen;* borrowed from Old French *ramper* to creep, climb, from Frankish (compare Middle Low German and Middle Dutch *ramp* cramp, Middle High German *rampf,* and Old High German *rimpfan* to wrinkle; see RUMPLE.). Perhaps related to ROMP. Later use of *ramp,* particularly *raumpand* may have been affected by the coeval *raumpant,* adj., rampant. The meaning of rush wildly about, attack, behave violently, is first recorded about 1390, in Chaucer's *Canterbury Tales,* and the original sense in Old French of creep or crawl along the ground is not found until its use in Gower's *Confessio Amantis* (before 1393).

rampage (ram′pāj) *v.* rush wildly about, behave wildly. 1715, Scottish; probably formed from *ramp*[2] rave, rage (about 1390, in Chaucer's *Canterbury Tales*) + *-age,* on the model of *ramagen* be furious, rage (before 1500, from the adjective *ramage* wild, violent, about 1300). **—n.** (rampāj′) wild action or behavior. 1861, in Dickens' *Great Expectations;* from the noun.

rampant *adj.* growing without any check. Before 1382 *raumpaunt* fierce, ravenous, in the Wycliffe Bible; earlier, rearing or standing on the hind legs (about 1300); borrowed from Old French *rampant,* present participle of *ramper* to creep, climb; see RAMP[2], v. The sense of growing without any check (as in *vines running rampant over the fence*) is first recorded in 1619 and is, in spite of its late appearance, the only use of the French meaning of creep or climb found in English.

rampart *n.* bank of earth built around a fort to help defend it. 1583, borrowing of Middle French *rampart, rempart* (with added *t*), from *remparer* to fortify (*re-* again + *emparer* fortify, from Old Provençal *amparar,* from Vulgar Latin **anteparāre* prepare, from Latin *ante-* before + *parāre* prepare; see PARE).

ramrod *n.* 1757, rod for pushing the charge of a gun in place. **—v.** 1948, to force through, push forward vigorously.

ramshackle *adj.* loose and shaky, rickety. 1830, from earlier *ranshackled* (1675), alteration of *ransackled,* from past participle of obsolete *ransackle* to ransack, frequentative form of RANSACK; for suffix see -LE[3].

ranch *n.* 1808, hut or house in the country; later, farm for raising animals or crops (1831); American English, borrowed through American Spanish *rancho* small farm, group of farm huts, from Spanish *rancho,* originally, group of persons who eat together, from *ranchar, ranchear* to lodge or station, from Old French *ranger* install in a position, from *rang* row or line; see RANK[1], n. **—v.** work on, manage, or own a ranch. 1866, Bret Harte in *Californian;* American English, from the noun. **—rancher** *n.* 1836, owner or worker on a ranch; formed from English *ranch,* n. and v. + *-er*[1] and perhaps influenced by, if not borrowed in part from earlier American Spanish *ranchero* (1827).

rancid *adj.* 1646, borrowed from Latin *rancidus* rank, stinking, offensive, from *rancēre* be spoiled or rotten (found only in *rancēns* present participle); of uncertain origin. **—rancidity** *n.* 1654, formed from English *rancid* + *-ity.*

rancor (rang′kər) *n.* Probably before 1200 *rancor* bitter resentment or ill will, in *Ancrene Riwle;* borrowed from Old French and directly from Late Latin *rancor* rancidness, grudge, bitterness, from Latin *rancēre* be spoiled or rotten; see RANCID; for suffix see -OR[1].

rand *n.* unit of money of the Republic of South Africa. 1961, borrowed from Afrikaans *rand,* from Dutch *rand* field border; so called with reference to The *Rand* (Witwatersrand), a gold-mining district in the Transvaal, northeastern South Africa.

random *adj.* 1655, by chance or with no plan; abstracted from the earlier phrase *at random, at randon* by chance, with no plan; originally, at great speed, without care or control (1565), developed from Middle English *randun* impetuosity, speed, force, violence (about 1300; later *random,* before 1470; also in the phrase *o randon* before 1300, *at randon,* before 1376); borrowed from Old French *randon, randum* rapid rush, disorder, from *randir* to run fast, from Frankish **rant* a running (compare Old High German *rennen* to cause to RUN). For a similar shift of the terminal consonant from *n* to *m* see RANSOM. **—randomize** *v.* make random or haphazard, especially in scientific procedures; use a random selection or sampling. 1926, formed from English *random* + *-ize.*

randy *adj.* 1698, rude, disorderly, loudmouthed; Scottish, probably formed from obsolete English *rand* to rant, rave (1601, variant of RANT) + *-y*[1]. The sense of lewd or lustful is first recorded before 1847, in dialectal English.

range *n.* Before 1325 *range* row, line, act of placing in a row or arranging, in *Cursor Mundi;* borrowed from Old French *range,* variant of *renge* range or rank, from *rangier, ranger* to place in a row, arrange in order, from *rang,* variant of *reng* row or line; see RANK[1].

The meaning of scope or extent is first recorded in English in Bunyan's *Grace Abounding* (1666), and that of an extensive area over which animals range for food, in 1626 in American English.

—v. 1375 *rangen* to place (soldiers, plants, etc.) in a row, arrange in order, in Barbour's *The Bruce;* borrowed from Old French *rangier,* variant of *rengier* to place in a row. The meaning of move over a large area, wander, roam, is first recorded in English about 1477. **—ranger** *n.* 1388, gamekeeper, forest officer; formed from Middle English *range,* v. + *-er*[1]. The meaning of a group of armed men employed to police an area is first recorded in 1670, in American English, and such a group acting as soldiers, is probably first recorded in 1742. **—rangy** *adj.* 1868, (of a horse, etc.) adapted for ranging; later, having a long slender form (1876); formed from English *range,* n. and v. + *-y*[1].

rani or **ranee** (rä′nē) *n.* wife of a rajah. 1698, in John Fryer's *A New Account of East India and Persia;* borrowed from Hindi *rānī,* from Sanskrit *rā́jñī,* feminine of *rā́jan-* RAJAH.

rank[1] *n.* row or line. Before 1325, row, line, series; borrowed from Old French *ranc,* variant of *rang, reng,* from Frankish (compare Old High German *hring* circle, RING). The meaning of a social division or group, usually of high position (as in *people of rank*) is first recorded in English probably about 1430, and that of relative position or status (as *in the first rank*) in Shakespeare's *Macbeth* (1605). **—v.** 1573, arrange in lines, from the noun. The sense of put in order, classify, is first recorded in Shakespeare's *Romeo and Juliet* (1592). **—rank and file** 1598, in reference to soldiers in marching or battle formation; later, common soldiers (1796), and common people (1860, in Mill's writings).

rank[2] *adj.* large and coarse. Probably about 1200 *ranc* proud, determined, in *The Ormulum;* about 1250, strong, violent; also, growing thickly and coarsely; found in Old English (about 1000) *ranc* proud, overbearing, showy; cognate with Middle Dutch *ranc* slender, slim (modern Dutch *rank*), Middle Low German and modern German *rank* long and thin, and Old Icelandic *rakkr* erect, bold, from Proto-Germanic **rankaz,* of unknown origin. The meaning of strongly marked, extreme, is first recorded in English in 1513 (perhaps also found in the earlier sense of excessive, about 1303), and that of having a strong, bad smell, before 1529, in Skelton's *Elinor Rummyng.*

rankle *v.* Probably about 1300 *ranclen* (of a sore) to fester; borrowed from Old French *rancler, räoncler,* from *draoncle* festering sore, learned borrowing from Latin *dracunculus* little snake, diminutive of *dracō* (genitive *dracōnis*) serpent, DRAGON. The figurative sense of continue to give a painful, bitter, or malignant feeling, is first recorded in 1508.

ransack *v.* About 1250 *ransaken* search thoroughly, study, plunder; borrowed from a Scandinavian source (compare Old Icelandic *rannsaka* search the house, especially as a legal term used in looking for stolen goods; *rann* house, cognate with Old English *ærn, ern* place or house, Old Frisian *-ern,* and Gothic *razn* house, from Proto-Germanic **rasnan;* see REST, + *-saka* to search, related to Old Icelandic *sœkja* SEEK).

ransom *n.* Probably before 1200 *rancun* payment made for an offense, fine, in *Ancrene Riwle;* later *raunson* price paid for release of a captive (about 1300), and in the spelling *ransome* (probably before 1425); borrowed from Old French *rançon;* earlier, *räençon* ransom, redemption, from Latin *redēmptiōnem* (nominative *redēmptiō*) a redeeming, especially by ransom; from *redimere* to redeem. Doublet of REDEMPTION. **—v.** Before 1325 *ranscunen* make amends for a wrong; also, redeem, in *Cursor Mundi;* later *raunsonen* pay for release of a captive (about 1378), and in the spelling *ransomen* (before 1387); borrowed from Old French *rançonner;* earlier *räençonner* redeem, from the noun in Old French.

The shift of the terminal consonant from *n* to *m* is also found in such English forms as *random* and *seldom.*

rant *v.* speak wildly, extravagantly, or noisily. 1598, in Shakespeare's *Merry Wives of Windsor;* borrowed from obsolete Dutch *randten, ranten, randen* talk foolishly, rave; of uncertain origin. The forms in obsolete Dutch and in Flemish *randen* were the source of a parallel form *rand* to rave, that appeared briefly in the record of English from 1601, in Ben Jonson's *Poetaster,* to 1714. **—n.** extravagant, violent, or noisy speech. 1649, from the verb.

rap[1] *n.* quick, light blow. About 1300 *rappe,* possibly of imitative origin, but curiously similar in form and meaning to Swedish *rapp* a rap, tap, smart blow, also to Norwegian *rapp* and Danish *rap* which, if their development were known, might suggest a Scandinavian source. The transferred meaning of a rebuke or criticism is first recorded in 1777, in American English, and possibly from this developed the American slang sense of a criminal accusation or charge (1903), and the sense of a punishment or prison sentence (especially in such phrases as *take the rap, beat the rap*) in 1927. **—v.** knock sharply, tap. Probably before 1350 *rappen* to strike, hit; later, to knock at a door (1440), possibly from the noun or of independent imitative origin.

rap[2] *v. Slang.* to talk or converse informally, chat. 1929, in Damon Runyon's writings; later popularized in American English (about 1965), possibly by way of Caribbean English, from the earlier British slang sense of say or utter (1879), originally with the specific meaning of let off (an oath, etc.) sharply, vigorously, or suddenly (1541), an expressive use of RAP[1] knock sharply. **—n.** *Slang.* informal talk or chat. 1898, British English, later popularized in American English, from contemporary use of the verb.

rap[3] *n. Informal.* the least bit. 1724, counterfeit coin used in the 1700's in Ireland for a halfpenny, in Swift's *The Drapier Letters;* of uncertain origin. The figurative sense of the least bit (as in *not to care a rap,* 1834) is from the extended meaning of a coin of the smallest value, or the smallest amount of money, found in Byron's *Don Juan* (1823), in allusion to Swift's use for the counterfeit coin.

rapacious *adj.* seizing by force, plundering. 1651, formed in English probably from *rapacity* with substitution of *-ious* or *-ous,* perhaps further influenced by French *rapace,* from Latin *rapāx* (genitive *rapācis*) grasping, plundering, from *rapere* seize. **—rapacity** *n.* quality of being rapacious. 1543, in Bacon's *Policy of*

War; borrowed from Middle French *rapacité,* learned borrowing from Latin *rapācitātem* (nominative *rapācitās*) greediness, from *rapāx* grasping, rapacious; for suffix see -ITY.

rape[1] *v.* assault sexually. Probably 1387 *rapen* seize prey, take by force; in part developed from the noun in Middle English, and in part a borrowing, perhaps through Anglo-French *raper,* of the learned (legal) Old French *raper* to seize, abduct, and directly from Latin *rapere* seize, carry off, ravish; see RAPID. The sense of abduct (a woman) is recorded in Middle English, in a translation of Higden's *Polychronicon* (probably before 1425), but whether this specifically includes the meaning of ravish is rather fuzzy, since abduction was frequently accompanied or followed by sexual assault. The meaning of rob or plunder is recorded before 1721. **—n.** Before 1325, booty or prey, in *Cursor Mundi;* later, act of seizing, raid, robbery (probably about 1350); borrowed through Anglo-French *rap, rape,* and directly from Latin *rapere* seize. The sense of sexual abduction or assault is recorded in Middle English, probably about 1400. **—rapist** *n.* 1883, American English; formed from *rape*[1], n. + *-ist.*

rape[2] *n.* kind of small plant used for fodder and as a source of lubricating oil. Before 1398 *rape* rape, turnip, borrowed from Old French *rape,* and directly from Latin *rāpa, rāpum* turnip. The Latin forms are cognate with Greek *rhápys, rháphys* turnip, Lithuanian *rópė,* and Old Slavic *rěpa,* from Indo-European **rāp-/rēp-/rəp-* (Pok.852). Germanic cognates include Middle Low German *röve* turnip, Middle Dutch *roeve,* and Old High German *rāba, ruoba* (modern German *Rübe*).

According to the OED confusion has existed from the earliest history of this word as to its application to specific plants, and while an early name for the turnip is directly assignable to Latin, the meaning of the plant used for fodder may have come partly from a Dutch word *raap,* which itself means both turnip and rape.

rapid *adj.* 1634, moving at great speed, swift, very quick; borrowed from French *rapide,* learned borrowing from Latin, and borrowed directly from Latin *rapidus* hasty, snatching, from *rapere* hurry away, carry off, seize, plunder, cognate with Greek *eréptesthai* feed on; originally, to tear away, Lithuanian *ap-rěpti* grasp, seize, and Albanian *rjep* pull away, from Indo-European **rep-* (Pok.865). **—n. rapids** *pl.* part of a river where the water rushes quickly. 1765, formed from English *rapid,* adj. + *-s*[1], by influence of French *rapides,* and in some instances borrowed from the French. **—rapidity** *n.* swiftness, celerity. 1654, borrowed from French *rapidité,* and directly from Latin *rapiditās* swiftness, from *rapidus* rapid; for suffix see -ITY.

rapier (rā′pēər) *n.* light sword. 1553, borrowed from Middle French *rapière* from Old French *espee rapiere* rapier sword, of uncertain origin; perhaps earlier referred to as a *raspiere* a poker or scraper in a derisive sense, and thereby related to *râpe* grater, rasp; see RASP.

rapine (rap′ən) *n.* robbing and carrying off by force. About 1412, borrowed from Middle French *rapine,* learned borrowing from Latin *rapīna* robbery, plunder, from *rapere* seize, carry off, rob; see RAPID. Doublet of RAVINE.

rappel (rapel′) *n.* descent from a cliff or rock face using a doubled rope secured above the climber. 1931, reborrowing of French *rappel,* literally, recall, from Old French *rapel,* from *rapeler* to recall, summon; see REPEAL. An earlier meaning of a drum roll to summon soldiers is first recorded in English in 1848. **—v.** descend a cliff or rock face by the method of rappel. 1957, from the noun.

rapport (rapôr′) *n.* agreement, harmony. 1661, reference, relationship, connection; borrowing of French *rapport,* from *rapporter* bring back; formed in Old French from *re-* again + *apporter* to bring, from Latin *adportāre* (*ad-* to + *portāre* carry; see PORT[4] bearing). The meaning of a relationship of mutual trust (as in hypnotism, therapy, teaching, etc.) is first recorded in English in 1845, and a more general sense of harmonious accord or full communication, is found in 1915.

rapprochement (ràprôshmäN′) *n.* establishment or renewal of friendly relations. 1809, borrowing of French *rapprochement* reunion, reconciliation, from *rapprocher* bring near (Old French *re-* back, again + *aprochier* to APPROACH) + French *-ment* -ment.

rapscallion (rapskal′yən) *n.* rascal, rogue. 1699, alteration of earlier *rascallion* (1649), a fanciful derivative of RASCAL, and probably a parallel term of *rampallion* (1593), possibly formed on *ramp,* n., vulgar, ill-behaved woman (before 1450), and *ramp,* v., to behave in a loose, immodest way (1530).

rapt *adj.* About 1390, carried away in body or spirit, in an ecstatic trance; borrowed from Latin *raptus,* past participle of *rapere* seize, carry off; see RAPID. The extended sense of engrossed or absorbed is first recorded in 1509.

raptorial (raptôr′ēəl) *adj.* adapted for seizing prey. 1825, formed in English from Latin *raptor* robber + English *-ial.* Latin *raptor* is formed from *rapt-,* past participle stem of *rapere* seize (see RAPID) + *-or* -or[2].

rapture *n.* 1600, act of carrying off; borrowed from Middle French *rapture* (now obsolete), formed from *rapt* rape, kidnapping, from Latin *raptus* (genitive *raptūs*) a carrying off, from *rapere* to seize; see RAPID; for suffix see -URE. The sense of spiritual or emotional ecstasy is first recorded in Milton's *On the Morning of Christ's Nativity* (1629). **—rapturous** *adj.* 1678, full of rapture; formed from English *rapture* + *-ous.*

rare[1] *adj.* unusual. 1392 *rere* thin, airy, porous; also *rare* (before 1400); borrowed from Old French *rere, rer, rare* sparse, hard to find, and directly from Latin *rārus* thin, airy, porous, infrequent, unusual, of uncertain origin. The meaning of unusual, uncommon, exceptional, is recorded in Middle English in 1447, and that of unusually good or great, in Shakespeare's *Merchant of Venice* (1596). **—rarity** *n.* Probably before 1425 *rarite* thinness; later, fewness (1560-61), and something rare (1592); borrowed from Middle French *rarité,* and directly from Latin *rāritās* thinness, looseness, fewness, from *rārus* rare; for suffix see -ITY.

rare[2] *adj.* undercooked. 1655 (of eggs) soft-cooked, variant of dialectal *rear,* in Middle English *rere* (1392); developed from Old English (about 1000) *hrēr* lightly cooked; probably related to *hrēran* to stir, move. Old English *hrēran* is cognate with Old Frisian *hrēra* to stir or move, Old Saxon *hrōrian,* Middle Dutch and modern Dutch *roeren,* Old High German *hruoren* (modern German *rühren*), and Old Icelandic *hrœra.* The modern English word is not recorded in reference to the cooking of meat before 1784.

rare[3] *v.* to rise up, rear. 1833, American English, especially in *rare up* (of an animal) to rise up on its hind legs; dialectal variant of REAR[2]. The extended sense of eager to go or start, found in *to be raring to go,* is first recorded in 1909.

rarefy *v.* make or become less dense. Before 1398 *rarefien,* in Trevisa's translation of Bartholomew's *De Proprietatibus Rerum;* borrowed from Old French *rarefier,* learned borrowing from Medieval Latin and borrowed directly from Medieval Latin *rarificare,* altered from Latin. Middle English *rarefien* was also, in part, borrowed from Latin *rārēfacere* make rare (*rārus* RARE[1] + *facere* make, perform, DO[1]); for suffix see -FY. The figurative sense of refine or purify is first recorded in Ben Jonson's *Every Man Out of His Humour* (1599). **—rarefaction** *n.* 1603, in Holland's translation of Plutarch's *Moralia;* borrowed from French *raréfaction,* and directly from Medieval Latin *rarefactionem* (nominative *rarefactio*), from Latin *rārēfact-,* past participle stem of *rārēfacere* rarefy; for suffix see -TION.

rascal *n.* Before 1338 *rascaile* (collective noun) persons of the lowest class, rabble, mob, in Mannyng's *Chronicle of England;* borrowed from Old French *rascaille,* perhaps from *rasque* mud, filth, from Vulgar Latin **rāsicāre* to scrape; see RASH[2].

It has been offered that Old French *rascaille* was influenced in meaning and form by *canaille* rabble (about 1470) and is related to Icelandic *rask* (Norwegian *rask*) fish waste, trash; but this would seem to be more an association of form and meaning rather than chronological development.

The form *rascal* and the singular sense of a person belonging to the rabble are first recorded about 1475, but, curiously, the extended sense of a low, dishonest person, rogue, knave, is recorded about 130 years earlier (before 1338). Since about 1610 *rascal* has also been used in a much weakened sense as a mild term of almost jocular reproof (as in *the lucky rascal, you little rascal*).

—rascality *n.* (before 1577)

rash[1] *adj.* too hasty, careless, reckless. About 1380 *rasch* active, impetuous, unrestrained; earlier as a surname *Rasshe* (1316); perhaps developed from Old English *-ræsc* (found in the compound *līgræsc* lightning, a flash of lightning, before 1050); and possibly in part borrowed from Middle Low German or Middle Dutch *rasch* fast, active. The Middle Low German and Middle Dutch words are cognate with Old High German *rasc* fast, hasty, strong (modern German *rasch* fast, quick, hasty), Old Icelandic *rǫskr* brave, vigorous (Swedish and Danish *rask* quick, swift, nimble), from Proto-Germanic **raskuz,* earlier **rathskuz,* and perhaps also with Old English *ræd, ræth* fast, Old High German *rado, rato* quickly, and Gothic **raths* (comparative *rathizō*) light, easy, cognate with Sanskrit *rátha-s* wagon, Latin *rota* wheel, and Welsh *rhedeg* to run, from Indo-European **ret/rot-* run, roll (Pok.866).

The meaning of too hasty, careless, reckless, is first recorded in Barclay's *Ship of Fools* (1509).

rash[2] *n.* eruption of small red spots on the skin. 1709, Steele, in *The Tatler;* borrowed from obsolete French *rache* a sore, especially on the head, Old French *rache* ringworm, from Vulgar Latin **rāsicāre* to scrape, scratch, from Latin *rāsus* scraped, shaved, past participle of *rādere* to scrape, scratch, shave; see RAT. The figurative sense of a sudden outbreak or proliferation is first recorded in James Hogg's *Winter Evening Tales* (1820).

rasp *v.* make a harsh, grating sound. About 1250 *rospen* to scrape, scratch, or score, especially with a rough instrument, in *Genesis and Exodus;* later *raspen* (probably about 1380); borrowed from Middle Dutch *raspen* and from Old French *rasper* to grate, rasp, from a Germanic source (compare Old High German *raspōn* scrape together, related to *hrespan* to pluck, earlier **hrepsan,* Old Frisian *hrespa* to tear, Old English *gehrespan,* and perhaps Old English *hreppan* to touch, from Indo-European **kreb-/krob-,* Pok.949). For a similar transposition of *s* and *p* see WASP. The sense of utter with a harsh, grating sound is first recorded in 1843. **—n.** rasping sound. 1541, coarse file with point-like teeth; borrowed from Middle French *raspe,* from Old French *rasper* to rasp. The sense of a grating sound is first recorded in English before 1851.

raspberry *n.* 1623, formed in English from earlier *raspis berry* (before 1548); also *raspis* raspberry (about 1532). It is possible that early modern English *raspis* is related to, if not developed from, Middle English *raspise* a sweet, rose-colored wine (before 1475), earlier *rospeys* (1440), and *rayspeys* (before 1450), from Anglo-Latin *vinum raspeys* (compare Old French *raspe* and Medieval Latin *raspecia, raspeium* raspberry, 1290), of uncertain origin. The slang meaning of a derisive sound made with the tongue and lips is first recorded in Barrère and Leland's *A Dictionary of Slang, Jargon and Cant* (1890). This sense is probably an elliptical use of *raspberry tart,* rhyming slang for *fart.*

Rastafari (ras′təfär′ē) *n.* Jamaican cult of black nationalists who worship Haile Selassie, the former Emperor of Ethiopia, as God. 1955, formed in English from *Ras Tafari,* the title and surname of Haile Selassie, 1892-1975 (*Ras,* borrowed from Amharic *rās* chief; literally, head, from Arabic *rā's,* cognate with Hebrew *rō'sh* and Aramaic *rēsh;* and *Tafari,* borrowed from Amharic *təfəri* to be feared). **—Rastafarian** *n.* member of the Rastafari. 1955, formed in English from *Ras Tafari* + *-an.*

raster *n.* pattern of parallel scanning lines, as in the cathode-ray tube on which the image is formed in a television set. 1934, borrowed from German *Raster* screen; earlier, a screen used in photoengraving, from Latin *rāstrum* rake, from *rādere* to scrape or scratch; see RAT.

rat *n.* 1378 *rat,* in a version of *Piers Plowman;* earlier in a place name *Rat* (1185); found in Old English (about 1000) *ræt.* The relationship to each other of the Germanic, Romance, and Celtic words for *rat* is uncertain, but the ultimate source of the words is Indo-European **rəd-,* the weak grade of the root **rēd-/rōd-* to gnaw (Pok.854), as found in Latin *rōdere* gnaw, though it must be borne in mind that this refers only to the complexion of the word, as the animal itself was probably not known in Europe much before 900-1000. Germanic cognates are considered to include Old Saxon *ratta* rat, Middle Low German *rotte,* Middle Dutch *ratte* (modern Dutch *rat*), Old High German *rato* (feminine *ratta*), also *ratza* (modern German *Ratte,* dialectal *Ratz*), Old Icelandic *rottu-,* as element in proper names (Swedish *råtta,* Danish and Norwegian *rotte,* and Icelandic *rotta*). Cognates outside Germanic are perhaps found in the Celtic languages of Welsh *rhathu* to grate, rasp, Irish *radan,* and Breton *raz,* and among the Romance languages in French *rat* (feminine *rate*), Spanish *rata,* Portuguese *rato,* Italian *ratto.*

Old French *raton* (augmentative of *rat*) is also found in Middle English *ratoun* (about 1350); earlier *raton* (before 1325), and as a surname *Ratun* (1275); however, this form fell out of use in the 1500's.

—**v.** 1812, in Southey's *Letters,* to desert one's party or associates, from the earlier sense in the noun of one who deserts his party (1792, in Earl of Malmesbury's *Diaries*); so called from the popular belief that rats leave a house about to fall or a ship about to sink. The slang sense of turn traitor, act as an informer, is first recorded in 1934 in American English, from the earlier noun slang sense of police informer or spy (1902).

—**ratty** *adj.* 1865, full of rats, in George Meredith's *Farina: A Legend of Cologne;* formed from English *rat,* n. + *-y*[1]. The figurative sense of poor in quality, shabby, is first recorded in 1867, in Mark Twain's *Notebooks.*

ratchet *n.* wheel or bar with teeth. 1659 *rochet,* borrowed from French *rochet* bobbin or spindle, from Italian *rocchetto* spool, ratchet, diminutive of *rocca* distaff (stick for holding wool or flax during spinning); see ROCKET; for suffix see -ET. The current form is first recorded in 1721, influenced by the synonymous word *ratch,* perhaps borrowed from German *Rätsche, Ratsche* ratchet.

rate *n.* 1425 *rate* estimated worth or quantity, amount or degree in proportion to something else, in *Rolls of Parliament;* borrowed from Middle French *rate* price or value, and directly from Medieval Latin *rata (pars)* fixed (amount), from Latin *rata* determined, fixed, settled, feminine past participle of *rērī* to reckon, think, judge; see REASON. The meaning of degree of speed or progress is first recorded in 1652. —**v.** 1457-58 *raten* to allot, settle the amount or value of, from *rate,* n. The sense of consider or regard (as in *rated as best of the lot*) is first recorded in 1565. —**ratable** *adj.* 1503, formed from English *rate,* v. + *-able.*

rather *adv.* Probably about 1175 *rather* more readily, more properly, more quickly, sooner; later, instead of (probably before 1200); developed from Old English *hrathor* (about 725, in *Beowulf*) a comparative form of *hrathe, hræthe* quickly (before 725), related to *hræth* quick. Old English *hræth* is cognate with Middle Low German and Middle Dutch *rat* quick, Old High German *hrad, rad,* and Old Icelandic *hradhr,* from Proto-Germanic **Hrathaz,* cognate with Lithuanian *kratýti* to shake, from Indo-European **kret-/krot-* (Pok.620). Use of *rather* as an interjection (as in *Do you wish to go? Rather!*) is first recorded in Dickens' *Sketches by Boz* (1835-36).

ratify *v.* confirm, approve. About 1357 *ratifien,* borrowed from Old French *ratifier,* learned borrowing from Medieval Latin *ratificare* confirm, approve, from a lost adjective **ratificus* making valid (from Latin *ratus* fixed, valid, past participle of *rērī* to reckon, think; see REASON + the root of *facere* make, perform, DO[1]); for suffix see -FY. —**ratification** *n.* About 1435, borrowed through Middle French *ratification,* and directly from Medieval Latin *ratificationem* (nominative *ratificatio*), from *ratificare* ratify; for suffix see -ATION.

ratio *n.* 1636, reason or cause; later, relation between two numbers or quantities (1660); borrowed from Latin *ratiō* (genitive *ratiōnis*) reckoning, calculation, relation, proportion, reason, from *rat-,* past participle stem of *rērī* to reckon, calculate, think. Doublet of RATION and REASON.

ration *n.* 1550, reasoning; later, relation of one number or quantity to another, ratio (1666); and fixed allowance of food, often *rations* (1702-11); borrowed from French *ration* (in the sense of fixed allowance), learned borrowing from Latin, and (in earlier senses) borrowed directly from Latin *ratiōnem* (nominative *ratiō*) reckoning, calculation, proportion. Doublet of RATIO and REASON; for suffix see -TION. —**v.** supply with rations. 1859, from the noun. The extended sense of apportion or distribute in fixed amounts is first recorded in 1870.

rational *adj.* sensible, reasonable. Before 1398 *racional* able to reason, in Trevisa's translation of Bartholomew's *De Proprietatibus Rerum;* borrowed from Old French *racïonel,* and directly from Latin *ratiōnālis* of or belonging to reason, reasonable, from *ratiō* (genitive *ratiōnis*) reckoning, calculation, reason, from *rat-,* past participle stem of *rērī* to reckon, calculate, think; for suffix see -AL[1].

The meaning of able to reason, sensible, reasonable, is first recorded in English about 1450. The meaning in mathematics in reference to any number that can be expressed as a positive or negative whole number or as a ratio between such numbers, especially in the term *rational number,* is first recorded in English in 1570.

—**rationalism** *n.* 1800, use of medical treatments based on reason; formed from English *rational* + *-ism,* and in its later use as a complementary form to earlier *rationalist.* The meaning of the philosophical principle or view that reason is the only basis of knowledge and truth, as is used in theology, is first recorded in English in 1827, and as applied to human knowledge in general, in 1831; perhaps influenced by earlier French *rationalisme* (1803). —**rationalist** *n.* Before 1626, in Bacon's writings; formed from English *rational* + *-ist,* perhaps by influence of French *rationaliste* a physician whose treatment is based on reason. As applied to religious doctrine, *rationalist* is first recorded in English in 1876. —**rationality** *n.* 1628, probably formed from English *rational* + *-ity,* after Latin *ratiōnālitās* reasonableness, from *ratiōnālis* rational. —**rationalize** *v.* 1817, make rational, explain on a rational basis, in Coleridge's *Biographia Literaria;* formed from English *rational* + *-ize.*

rationale (rash′ənal′) *n.* fundamental reason. 1657, statement of reasons or principles; borrowed from Late Latin *ratiōnāle,* noun use of neuter of Latin *ratiōnālis* of or belonging to reason; see RATIONAL. The sense of fundamental reason, rational basis, is first recorded in English in 1688.

ratline or **ratlin** (rat′lin) *n.* 1481-90 *ratling, radelyng* any thin line or rope, of uncertain origin. The specific nautical sense of one of the small ropes that cross the shrouds of a ship is first recorded in Cotgrave's *Dictionary* (1611), but the spelling *ratlin* is not recorded before 1711, and *ratline* not before 1773 (both forms probably influenced by *line*[1], n).

rattan (ratan′) *n.* kind of palm with a very long stem. 1660 *rattoon* switch or stick made from the stem of a rattan, in Pepys' *Diary;* borrowed from Malay *rōtan.* The spelling *rattan* is first recorded in English in 1665, as the name of the palm.

rattle *v.* make a number of short, sharp sounds. Probably before 1300 *ratelen;* possibly borrowed from Middle Dutch *ratelen* to rattle, which is cognate with Middle Low German *rettelen,* and Middle High German *razzeln, razzen* (modern German *rasseln*); probably of imitative origin. The sense in American English of agitate, fluster is first recorded in 1869. —**n.** short, sharp sounds. 1500-20, in William Dunbar's *Poems,* from the verb. The meaning of an instrument that makes a rattling sound is first recorded in 1519. —**rattler** *n.* About 1449, one who talks at great length, usually holding a view that is not acceptable to the hearer; earlier as a surname *Rateler* (1309); formed from Middle English *ratelen,* v. + *-er*[1]. The meaning in American English of a rattlesnake is first recorded in 1827. —**rattlesnake** *n.* (1630) —**rattletrap** *n.* 1766, pl. trifles, odds and ends; later, a rattling, rickety coach (1822), and any shaky, cheaply built thing (1833).

raucous (rô′kəs) *adj.* hoarse, harsh-sounding. 1769, borrowed from Latin *raucus* hoarse, related to *ravus* hoarse; see RUMOR; for suffix see -OUS. The meaning of hoarse was known earlier in Middle English *rauc* (probably before 1425, in a translation of Chauliac's *Grande Chirurgie*).

raunchy *adj. Slang.* coarse, vulgar. 1939, American English, clumsy, careless, sloppy (probably originally in Air Force slang); of unknown origin. The sense of coarse, vulgar, smutty, is first recorded in the 1960's. —**raunch** *n. Slang.* coarseness, vulgarity. 1964, American English; back formation from *raunchy.*

ravage *v.* lay waste, destroy. 1611, in Cotgrave's *Dictionary;* borrowed from French *ravager* lay waste, devastate, from Old French *ravage* destruction, especially by rain and snowfall, from *ravir* to RAVISH; for suffix see -AGE. —**n.** violence, destruction. 1611, in Cotgrave's *Dictionary;* borrowed from French *ravage* havoc, spoil, destruction, from Old French *ravage* destruction.

rave *v.* Before 1325 *reven;* also *raven* talk wildly (probably about 1325); borrowed from Old French *raver, rever,* variants of *resver* to dream, wander, rave; of uncertain origin; see REVERIE. The extended sense of talk with great enthusiasm is first recorded in Locke's *Of the Conduct of the Understanding* (before 1704). —**n.** frenzy, great excitement. 1598, from the verb. The informal sense of a highly favorable review appeared in 1926 in American English. —**raving** *adj.* About 1475, delirious, frenzied, raging; formed from English *rave,* v. + *-ing*[2]. The meaning of remarkable, in the sense of worth raving about, as in *a raving beauty,* is first recorded in Isaac D'Israeli's *Amenities of Literature* (1841).

ravel *v.* 1582, (figurative) to untangle, unwind, unravel; also, to entangle or become tangled or confused (before 1585); borrowed from earlier Dutch *ravelen* (now *rafelen*) to tangle, fray, unweave, from *rafel* frayed thread. Dutch *rafel* is cognate with Old Icelandic *refill* piece of cloth, *rāf, rāfr* spar, roof support, Old High German *rāvo, rāfo* rafter, Middle Low German *rāve,* and Old English *ræftras,* pl.; see RAFTER. Curiously *ravel* and *unravel* have long been synonyms in the sense of disentangle, unwind, and antonyms, in that *ravel* has also carried the meaning of entangle, confuse. The apparent reason for this is that as threads (either literal or figurative) become unwoven, their ends become tangled. However today, the prevailing use is that of fray out, separate into threads. —**n.** 1634, a tangle, complication, in Thomas Jackson's *Works;* from the verb. The meaning of frayed thread is first recorded in 1832.

raven *n.* Probably before 1200 *reaven, reven,* in *Ancrene Riwle;* also *raven* (probably about 1200); developed (with loss of *h-*) from Old English (Mercian dialect) *hræfn* (before 800) and *hrefn* (before 830), *hræfn* (Northumbrian and West Saxon dialects); cognate with Middle Low German and Middle Dutch *rāven* raven (modern Dutch *raaf*), Old High German *hraban* (from Proto-Germanic **Hraƀanás*) and Old Icelandic *hrafn* (Danish *ravn,* Norwegian *ramn*). Old English also had the forms *hræmn, hrem, hremm,* which represent a normal shift from *-fn,* also found in Old High German *hram, ram,* Middle High German *ram, ramm,* and Old Swedish *ramn.* A weak form of the stem is seen in Old High German *rabo* (modern German *Rabe*). It is a matter of conjecture whether cognates exist outside Proto-Germanic **Hraƀanás* and may be found in Latin *crepāre* to grate, rattle and Sanskrit *kŕpate* he wails, from the Indo-European root **krep-/krop-* (Pok.569). —**adj.** deep, glossy black. 1634, in Milton's *Comus;* from the noun.

ravenous (rav′ənəs) *adj.* very hungry. Probably before 1387 *ravenes* devouring with great eagerness, rapacious; later *ravenous* (1402); borrowed from Old French *ravinos, ravineus* rapacious, violent, from *raviner* to seize; originally, fall impetuously or precipitously, from *ravine* violent rush, robbery; see RAVINE; for suffix see -OUS.

ravine (rəvēn′) *n.* 1779 *ravine* deep narrow gorge, especially one eroded by running water; earlier *ravin* (1760-72); borrowed from French *ravin* a gully, hollowed-out place, from Old French *raviner* to hollow out, and from French *ravine* a gully; also a violent rush of water; from Old French *ravine* violent rush, robbery, rapine, from Latin *rapīna* RAPINE.

An earlier word *ravine* booty, plunder (about 1350), and later with the meaning of robbery (about 1380), was borrowed from Old French *ravine* in the sense of a violent rush; but this original borrowing from Old French is not found in the record of English after 1500 which, in effect, makes the appearance of English *ravine* in the 1700's a reborrowing from French.

ravioli (rav′ēō′lē) *n.pl.* small, thin pieces of dough filled with meat, cheese, etc. 1611 *raviol* small meatballs baked in a crust, borrowed from Italian *raviolo;* earlier *raffyolys* (probably about 1425), and *rafyols* (before 1399), borrowed probably from Old French *raviole* or directly from Italian *rafioli.* Though perhaps known in cookery from Middle English times, but only intermittently recorded, it appears that each occurrence may be a separate borrowing, including that from Thackeray in 1841 in *Fraser's Magazine,* which is a direct borrowing of Italian *ravioli, raviuoli,* from plural of dialectal *raviolo, raviuolo,* diminutive of some noun now unknown.

ravish *v.* About 1303 *ravyshen* to carry off by force, rape, in Mannyng's *Handlyng Synne;* also *ravissen* to plunder (about 1300), and transport with emotion (probably before 1300, in *Arthour and Merlin*); borrowed from Old French *raviss-,* stem of *ravir* to seize, take away hastily, from Vulgar Latin **rapīre,* from Latin *rapere* to seize; see RAPID; for suffix see -ISH[2]. —**ravishing** *adj.* About 1340, seizing upon prey, ravenous; later, delightful or enchanting (about 1380, in Chaucer's *Parlement of Foules*); from Middle English present participle of *ravishen.*

raw *adj.* Before 1325 *rau* uncooked, unfinished, crude; developed (with loss of *h-*) from Old English (about 1000) *hrēaw* uncooked, raw; cognate with Old Saxon *hrāo* raw, Middle Low German *rō, rōer,* Middle Dutch *rau* (modern Dutch *rauw*), Old High German *hrao, hrawēr* (modern German *roh*), and Old Icelandic *hrār*

(Norwegian and Swedish *rå,* Danish *raa*); from Proto-Germanic **Hrawaz.* Cognates outside Germanic include Latin *crūdus* uncooked, raw, crude, *cruor* blood, Middle Irish *crū* hard, firm, Middle Welsh *crau* gore, Greek *kréas* meat, Lithuanian *kraũjas* blood, Old Slavic *krŭvĭ,* and Sanskrit *kravís* raw flesh, from Indo-European **kreu-/krou-, *krewə-/krū-/kruw-* (Pok.621).

The sense of tender, sore, or painful, as when the raw flesh is exposed, is first recorded in Middle English about 1390, and that of inexperienced or untrained, probably before 1590. The meaning of damp and chilly (applied to the weather) is found in 1546.

—n. 1823, exposed flesh, in Byron's *Don Juan;* later, sore spot (1825); from the adjective. The phrase *in the raw,* with the meaning of in a natural or crude state, or naked, is first recorded in the 1930's in American English. **—raw-boned** *adj.* (1591, in Shakespeare's *1 Henry VI*) **—rawhide** *n.* (1658) **—raw material** (1796)

ray[1] *n.* beam of light. Probably about 1380, borrowed from Old French *rai* ray, spoke, from Latin *radius* ray, spoke, staff, rod, perhaps from earlier **wradyos,* cognate with Welsh *gwraidd* root, from Indo-European **wrəd* (Pok.1167); possibly related to Latin *rādīx* ROOT. Doublet of RADIUS. **—v.** send forth in rays, radiate. 1598, in Florio's *A World of Words;* from the noun.

ray[2] *n.* variety of fish, related to the sharks. 1323-24, borrowed from Old French *raie,* and directly from Latin *raia,* of uncertain origin.

rayon *n.* fiber or fabric made of cellulose treated with chemicals. 1924, American English; probably borrowed from French *rayon* beam of light, ray, derived from *rai* RAY[1]; so called from its shiny appearance. This fiber was patented in 1884 under the name of *artificial silk.* An earlier use of *rayon* paralleling the French is found in English from 1591, in Spenser's writings, but it is unknown whether the English word had any influence on the present use.

raze *v.* tear down, destroy. Before 1547, in a translation of Vergil's *Aeneid,* alteration of Middle English *racen* to pull or knock down (before 1375); earlier *rasen* to scratch, slash, scrape, erase (before 1349); borrowed from Old French *raser* to scrape, shave, and directly from Medieval Latin *rasare,* frequentative form of Latin *rādere* to scrape, shave, perhaps related to Sanskrit *rádati* gnaws, cuts (Mayrhofer, *Kurzgefasstes etymologisches Wörterbuch des Altindischen,* p. 40).

razor *n.* Probably before 1300 *rasoure* sharp-edged tool, especially for shaving, in *Kyng Alisaunder;* later *razur* (1392); borrowed from Old French *rasor, rasour* a razor, from *raser* to scrape, shave; see RAZE; for suffix see -OR[2].

razz *n.* derision. Before 1919, American English, shortened form and altered spelling of RASPBERRY (derisive sound). **—v.** laugh at, make fun of. 1921, American English; from the noun.

razzle-dazzle *n. Slang.* dazzling glitter, excitement. 1889, American English, varied reduplication of DAZZLE.

razzmatazz (raz′mətaz′) *n. Slang.* razzle-dazzle, fanfare. 1899, American English, in George Ade's *Fables in Slang;* perhaps alteration of RAZZLE-DAZZLE, but more likely a varied reduplication of *jazz* from the word's early association with that form of music.

re[1] (rā) *n.* second note of the musical scale. About 1325, borrowed from Medieval Latin *re,* from the initial syllable of Latin *resonāre* to resound, the word sung to this note in the Hymn for St. John the Baptist's day; see GAMUT.

re[2] (rā *or* rē) *prep.* with reference to. 1707, in Thomas Hearne's *Remarks and Collections;* borrowed from Latin *rē* in the matter of, ablative case of *rēs* matter, thing; see REAL[1], adj.

re- a prefix in modern English generally with the meaning again, anew, once more, as in *reappear, rebuild, reheat, reopen,* or back, as in *repay, recall, react,* that can be added to any English verb, adjective, or noun or to derivatives whether found either as a part of an original borrowing (*reform* = to make better) or as a new emphatic (*re-form* = to form again, take a new shape). Borrowed through Old French, or directly from Latin *re-, red-* again, back, a prefix not found outside Italic. In many borrowings from Latin or Old French, the precise sense of *re-* is not clear, and often secondary meanings develop that further obscure the original sense. In general, however, appearance of Latin and Old French *re-* can be analyzed into various senses that denote: 1) movement back or in reverse, as in *recede, repel;* 2) withdrawal, reversal of an earlier process, as in *retract, reveal;* 3) restoration or renewal, as in *restitution, relegate;* 4) response or opposition, as in *reluctant, repugnant;* 5) repeated or intensified action, as in *revise, resume.* These are not fixed meanings and for the most part *re-* can be glossed only in terms of its function in a particular word as "intensive," "opposite," etc.

In some words borrowed into English from Latin and Old French any sense of *re-* has been so weakened as to be only artificially abstracted in English; some examples include *receive, recommend, reduce, rejoice, religion, remain, repair, report, require.*

reach *v.* Probably before 1200 *reachen,* about 1250 *rechen;* developed from Old English *rǣcan* to extend, hold forth (about 725, in Beowulf); cognate with Old Frisian *rēka, rētsa* to reach, Middle Low German *rēken,* Middle Dutch and modern Dutch *reiken,* Old High German and modern German *reichen* (from Proto-Germanic **raikjanan*), and Old Icelandic *reik* parting of the hair. Cognates outside Germanic include Old Irish *riag* torture, and Lithuanian *ráižytis* stretch oneself repeatedly, from Indo-European **reiĝ-/roiĝ-* (Pok.862). **—n.** 1536, part of a river between bends; earlier, a bay (1526); from the verb. The meaning of extent or distance of reaching is first recorded before 1548, preceded by the figurative sense of power of comprehension, extent of knowledge (1542). The sense of an act of reaching is not recorded before 1570.

react *v.* 1611, implied in *reacting;* formed from English *re-* again, anew + *act,* v.; probably by influence of French *réagir* react, from Middle French; both words from Late Latin *reagere* (past participle *reāctus*), formed from Latin *re-* back + *agere* to do, act; see AGENT. The sense of act chemically is first recorded in English in 1797. **—reactant** *n.* substance that enters into a chemical reaction. 1928, formed from English *react* + *-ant.* **—reaction** *n.* 1611, action in response; formed in English from *re-* again, anew + *action,* n., by influence of obsolete Italian *reattione* and probably French *réaction;* both words from Medieval Latin *reactionem* (nominative *reactio*), from Late Latin *reāct-,* past participle stem of *reagere* react; for suffix see -TION. The sense of chemical action is first recorded in English in 1836.

reactionary *adj.* favoring a return to a previous, usually more conservative state of affairs. 1840, in John Stuart Mill's writings; formed from English *reaction* + *-ary,* on the model of French *réactionnaire,* from *réaction* reaction, from Medieval Latin *reactionem* (nominative *reactio*) REACTION. **—n.** reactionary person. 1858, from the adjective.

reactor *n.* device for reducing a nuclear chain reaction for the release of atomic energy, nuclear reactor. 1890 *reacter* person or animal that reacts, in William James' *The Principles of Psychology;* formed from English *react* + *-er*[1]. The spelling *reactor* is first recorded in 1895; formed from English *react* + *-or*[2]. The meaning of a device in which a controlled nuclear chain reaction is produced is first recorded in the term *nuclear reactor* (1945).

read (rēd) *v.* Probably about 1175 *reden* consider, discern, read (writing); developed from Old English (West Saxon) *rǣdan* to explain, read, rule, advise (before 899), and (Anglian) *rēdan* (compare Mercian *berēdan* to advise falsely, betray, about 700); related to *rǣd, rēd* advice. The sense of advise, counsel, consider or explain something hard to understand is common to various Germanic languages as found in the cognates Old Frisian *rēda* to advise, Old Saxon *rādan,* Middle Low German *raden,* Middle Dutch *rāden* (modern Dutch *raden*), Old High German *rātan* (modern German *raten*), Old Icelandic *radha,* and Gothic *garēdan* to consider. But transfer of this sense to apprehending the meaning of written symbols is apparently unique to English and Old Icelandic *rādha.*

By way of Proto-Germanic **rǣđanan* cognates exist in Old Irish *immrādim* I consider, Old Welsh *amraud* mind, Old Slavic *raditi* to care for, and Sanskrit *rādhnóti, rā́dhyati* he succeeds, accomplishes, makes fit (related to Latin *rērī* calculate, think, consider), from Indo-European **rē-dh-/rō-dh-/rə-dh-* (Pok.59).

—n. *Informal.* act or spell of reading. 1825, in Jamieson's Supplement to the *Etymological Dictionary of the Scottish Language;* from the verb.

—adj. (red) having knowledge gained by reading, informed. 1586, originally past participle of the verb, now considered a separate form in most general dictionaries.

—readability *n.* (1860,Trollope) **—readable** *adj.* (1570) **—reader** *n.* Probably about 1200 *redere,* developed from Old English (about 961) *rǣdere* person who reads aloud to others. **—reading** *n.* Probably before 1200 *redunge* act of reading, skill in reading, in *Ancrene Riwle,* about 1300 *reding;* developed from Old English *rǣding,* from *read,* v. The meaning of interpretation (as in *What is his reading of the situation?*) is first recorded in reference to the interpretation of dreams probably before 1350. *—adj.* used in reading, meant for reading, as in a *reading book* (before 1333).

ready *adj.* Probably before 1200, *rædi,* in Layamon's *Chronicle of Britain;* also *redi* (probably before 1200); formed from Old English *rǣde, gerǣde* ready (before 899, in Alfred's translation of Bede's *Ecclesiastical History*) + Middle English *-i,* shortened from Old English *-ig* -y[1]. Old English *rǣde, gerǣde* is cognate with Old Frisian *rēde* ready, Middle Low German *rēde,* Middle Dutch *gereit, gereet* (modern Dutch *gereed*), Old High German *reiti* (modern German *bereit*), Old Icelandic *greidhr,* Gothic *garaiths* ordered (from Proto-Germanic **ʒa-raiđijaz*), and related to Old English *rīdan* to RIDE. The form with *-y,* as in *redy,* began to appear probably before 1300. **—v.** make ready, prepare. Before 1338 *redyen,* in Mannyng's *Chronicle of England;* earlier, to take aim (probably about 1300), and to direct or guide (before 1225); from *redi,* adj. **—n.** 1688, (slang) ready money, cash, from the adjective. The sense of a condition or position of being ready is first recorded in 1837. **—readily** *adv.* Before 1300 *redily* willingly; later, quickly (as in *answer readily,* before 1375), and easily (as in *readily accessible,* about 1380). **—ready-made** *adj.* (probably before 1425).

reagent (rēā'jənt) *n.* substance used to detect the presence of other substances by the chemical reactions it causes. 1797, formed from English *re-* + *agent* substance that produces a chemical reaction (1756), perhaps vaguely influenced by French *réagir* react.

real[1] *adj.* actual, true. Probably before 1325 *real* having physical existence, actual; later, genuine or authentic (1440); in law, pertaining to property (1444, in *Rolls of Parliament*); borrowed from Old French *rëel, rëal,* from Late Latin *reālis* actual, from Latin *rēs* matter or thing. Latin *rēs* is cognate with Vedic Sanskrit *rayí-s* (genitive *rāyás*) possession, wealth, traditionally assigned to Indo-European **rei-/rēi-* (Pok.860), though Oswald Szemerényi in his *Einführung in die Vergleichende Sprachwissenschaft* (1970) gives the Indo-European noun as **reh-i-s* (genitive **reh-y-os*). The sense in mathematics of either rational or irrational, but not imaginary, is first recorded in *Chambers Encyclopaedia* (1727-41, though implied earlier in *really,* 1706) but the term *real number* is not recorded before 1909. **—adv.** very, extremely. 1658, from the adjective. **—real estate** (1666) **—realism** *n.* thought and action based on reality, in Coleridge's *Biographia Literaria;* formed from English *real*[1], adj. + *-ism,* perhaps after French *réalisme,* and by contrast with earlier *idealism.* **—realist** *n.* 1605, one concerned with things rather than words; formed from English *real*[1] + *-ist,* after French *réaliste.* The meaning of a person devoted to what is real, as opposed to what is fictitious or imaginary, is first recorded in Emerson's writings (1847). **—realistic** *adj.* 1856, representing things as they are, in Emerson's writings. **—reality** *n.* 1550, quality of being real; borrowed from Middle French *réalité,* and directly from Medieval Latin *realitas,* from Late Latin *reālis* real; for suffix see -ITY. The sense of real existence, what is real, is first recorded in English in 1647, and that of really, actually, in fact, found in the phrase *in reality,* in 1679. An earlier word with the meaning of reality is found in Middle English *realte* (1440, in *Promptorium Parvulorum*) and is also borrowed from Middle French and Medieval or Late Latin.

real[2] (rāäl') *n.* former small Spanish silver coin. 1611, in Cotgrave's *Dictionary;* borrowing of Spanish *real,* noun use of *real* regal, from Latin *rēgālis* REGAL. The form *real* from Latin *rēgālis* was also known in Middle and early modern English as an adjective meaning royal or fit for a king, lavish, beautiful, etc. and in Middle English as a noun especially with the meaning of a noble and a gold coin once known as a real of eight or a piece of eight. The term was borrowed immediately, however, from Old French *rëal, rial,* not from Spanish.

realize *v.* 1611, bring into real existence, in Cotgrave's *Dictionary;* borrowed from French *réaliser* make real, from Middle French *real* actual, REAL[1] + *-iser* -ize. The meaning of convert (property) into money is first recorded in 1727-41, and that of obtain as a return or profit in 1753. The sense of understand clearly is first found in 1775. **—realization** *n.* 1611, action of making fact of or becoming real, in Cotgrave's *Dictionary;* borrowed from French *réalisation* a making real, from *réaliser;* for suffix see -ATION.

really *adv.* Before 1400, substantially or in reality with reference to the presence of Christ in the Eucharist; later, in the general sense of actually (probably before 1425); formed from *real*[1] + *-ly*[1].

realm *n.* kingdom. Probably before 1300 *rem,* in *Arthour and Merlin;* borrowed as a reduced form of Old French *rëaume;* also in Middle English *reaume* (about 1300), borrowed directly from Old French *rëaume;* and later in Middle English *realme* (about 1380), borrowed from Old French *rëalme.* Old French *rëaume* is probably formed from *roiaume, reiemme* from Gallo-Romance, while *rëalme* is an alteration (by influence of Old French *reial* regal, from Latin *rēgālis* REGAL*)* of a possible Gallo-Romance **regiminem,* formed as an accusative on Latin *regimen* government, rule, REGIMEN.

The transferred sense of any sphere or area of influence is first recorded in Chaucer's translation of Boethius' *De Consolatione Philosophiae* (about 1380).

Realtor (rē′əltər) *n.* 1916 *realtor* real-estate agent, American English; formed from *realt(y)* + *-or*[2]. The service mark *Realtor* was patented in 1948 by the National Association of Real Estate Boards.

realty *n.* real estate. 1670; earlier, a right, real possession (1618); formed from English *real*[1], adj. + *-ty*[2].

ream[1] *n.* large quantity of paper, usually 500 sheets. 1356 *rem;* borrowed from Old French *rame, reyme,* from Spanish *resma,* from Arabic *rizmah* bundle. The word was introduced into Europe through Spanish by the Moors, who brought the manufacture of cotton paper into Spain. While early use of the term in English was from Old French, a later spelling *rym* (1473-74) shows probable Dutch influence from *riem,* also borrowed from Spanish, probably during the time when the Spanish Hapsburgs controlled Holland. The transferred sense of a large quantity is first recorded in D. H. Lawrence's *Love Poems and Others* (1913).

ream[2] *v.* enlarge a hole. 1815 (implied in *reaming*), probably found in Middle English *remen* (probably before 1300, in *Kyng Alisaunder*), dialectal variant of *rimen* make room, clear (probably about 1150); developed from Old English *rȳman* widen, extend, spread, enlarge (before 725, in *Genesis A*). Old English *rȳmen* is cognate with Old Frisian *rēma* make room, Old Saxon *rūmian,* Middle Dutch *rūmen* (modern Dutch *ruimen*), Old High German *rūmen* (modern German *räumen*), and Old Icelandic *rȳma,* all derived from Proto-Germanic **rūmjanan,* from **rūmaz* spacious; see ROOM. **—reamer** *n.* (1825)

reap *v.* Probably about 1175 *repen* to cut grain, gather, obtain; developed from Old English (before 830) *reopan,* Mercian form of *ripan* to reap. Old English *ripan, *rīpan* is possibly cognate with Middle Low German *repen* remove seeds from flax, Middle Dutch *reipen* to tear, comb flax, and Norwegian *ripe* to score, scratch, and related to Old English *rīpe* RIPE. **—reaper** *n.* Before 1382; earlier as a surname *Reper* (1327); developed from Old English *ripere* (about 1000, though the sense is found earlier in the compound *hripemann,* about 950).

rear[1] *n.* back part. Before 1338 *rere* back part of an army, in Mannyng's *Chronicle of England,* abstracted from earlier *rerewarde* rear guard (probably before 1300); borrowed through Anglo-French *rerewarde,* Old French *rieregarde* (*rere, riere* behind, from Latin *retrō* back, behind, retro- + *garde* GUARD). The spelling *rear* appears about 1557; Shakespeare used both *rere* and *reare.* **—adj.** at or in the back. About 1303 *rere* late, last, in Mannyng's *Handlyng Synne;* later, hindmost (probably before 1325); borrowed from Old French *rere, riere* behind, from Latin *retrō* back, behind.

English *rear* is sometimes considered a shortened form of *arrear,* but Middle English *rere* in *rereward* and in *arere* appear about 1300, which would tend to support the view that originally *rere* was a bound form in English, known only in specialized compounds and was, therefore, abstracted from the military terminology *rereward.*

—rear admiral (1587) **—rearward** *adv., adj.* 1598, from the noun *rearward* hindmost part (before 1450), misconstrued as *rear,* n. + *ward.*

rear[2] *v.* to raise. Probably about 1150 *reren* to bring into being, bring about, cause; later, bring up, lift up (as in *rear a child,* probably before 1200); also, rise on the hind legs (1375); developed from Old English (before 725) *rǣran* to raise; cognate with Old High German *rēren* cause to fall, Old Icelandic *reisa* to raise, and Gothic *urraisjan* lift up, all derived from Proto-Germanic **raizjanan* to raise, from Indo-European **reis-/ rois-* (Pok.331).

reason *n.* Probably before 1200 *reison* cause or motive for an action, explanation, ability to think, in *Ancrene Riwle;* also *resoun* (about 1200); later *reason* (probably before 1400); borrowed through Anglo-French *resoun, raisun,* Old French *reson, raison,* from Latin *ratiōnem* (nominative *ratiō*) reckoning, account, relation, proportion, understanding, motive, cause; related to *rērī* to reckon, think. Latin *rērī* is cognate with Old Frisian *rethe* conversation, account, evidence, Old Saxon *rethia,* Old High German *redia,* Gothic *rathjō* reckoning, number, *-rathjan* to count, reckon, and *gerēdan* to consider; see READ. Doublet of RATIO and RATION.

—v. Before 1325 *resunen* to question, argue, discuss, in *Cursor Mundi;* borrowed from Old French *resoner, raisoner,* from *raison,* n. It is also very likely that Middle English *reason,* v. is in part a development from earlier *reason,* n., influenced by parallel development found in Old French and in Latin.

—reasonable *adj.* Before 1325 *resonabil,* in *Cursor Mundi;* earlier *resonable* (1303, in Mannyng's *Handlyng Synne,* with the rare and esoteric sense of bound by a monastic rule); borrowed from Old French *raisonable,* and directly from Latin *ratiōnābilis,* from *ratiō* reason; for suffix see -ABLE. **—reasonably** *adv.* (about 1378) **—reasoning** *n.* (about 1380, in Chaucer)

rebate *v.* give a partial refund to. Before 1398 *rebaten* to reduce or diminish, in Trevisa's translation of Bartholomew's *De Proprietatibus Rerum;* later, to subtract or deduct (1425, in *Rolls of Parliament*); borrowed from Old French *rabattre, rebattre* beat down, drive back; also, deduct (*re-* repeatedly + *abattre* beat down; see ABATE). The meaning of give or allow a deduction or partial refund to is first recorded in 1523. **—n.** partial refund, discount. 1656, in part probably from the verb in English, and also borrowed from French *rabat* a discount, from Middle French *rabattre, rebattre* beat down.

rebel (reb′əl) *adj.* Probably before 1300, in *Kyng Ali-*

saunder; borrowed from Old French *rebelle,* learned borrowing from Latin, and borrowed directly from Latin *rebellis* insurgent, rebellious, from *rebellāre* to rebel, revolt, wage war again (*re-* opposite, against + *bellāre* wage war, from *bellum* war; earlier *duellum;* see DUEL). Doublet of REVEL.

In Middle English *rebel* was commonly used both as a predicate adjective and as an attributive; since the 1600's it has been used chiefly attributively, as in *a rebel host, a rebel war.*

—n. About 1350, from the adjective, and probably in part borrowed from Old French *rebelle,* n., from *rebelle,* adj.

—v. (ribel′) 1340 *rebelen,* in *Ayenbite of Inwyt;* borrowed from Old French *rebeller,* and directly from Latin *rebellāre* to rebel.

—rebellion *n.* About 1340, borrowed from Old French *rebellion,* and directly from Latin *rebelliōnem* (nominative *rebelliō*) rebellion, renewal of a war, from *rebellis* rebellious; for suffix see -ION. **—rebellious** *adj.* Probably before 1425 *rebellous,* in a translation of Higden's *Polychronicon;* formed in English from Latin *rebellis* rebel + English *-ous,* perhaps by influence of Old French *rebelleux.* The form *rebellious* (probably influenced by *rebellion*) is first recorded in 1462.

rebound *v.* About 1380, to spring, leap; also, return to afflict (before 1382); borrowed from Old French *rebondir, rebundir* leap back, resound (*re-* back + *bondir* leap, bound, or *bundir* resound).

rebuff *v.* to snub. Before 1586, in Sidney's *Arcadia;* borrowed from obsolete French *rebuffer* to check, snub, from Italian *ribuffare, rabbuffare* to check, chide, snub, from *ribuffo, rabbuffo* a snub (*ri-* back, from Latin *re-* + *buffo* a puff, of imitative origin). **—n.** a snub. 1611, borrowed from obsolete French *rebuffe,* from Italian *ribuffo, rabbuffo* a snub.

rebuke *v.* About 1330 *rebouken* chide severely, scold; later *rebuken* (probably before 1350); borrowed through Anglo-French *rebuker,* Old French *rebuchier* (*re-* back + *buschier* to strike, chop wood, from *bûche, busche* wood, firewood; see BUSH). **—n.** Before 1420, shame, disgrace, in Lydgate's *Troy Book;* also, scolding (about 1433); from the verb.

rebus (rē′bəs) *n.* representation of words by pictures. 1605, borrowed through French *rébus,* and directly from Latin *rēbus* by means of objects, ablative case plural of *rēs* thing, object; see REAL[1], adj. The original reference is not altogether clear, but based on early usage in German of *Rebus de Picardie,* and the explanation of the French philologist of the 1600's Gilles Ménage, it may be that *rebus* was first used in *de rebus quae geruntur* of things which are going on, in reference to satirical pieces that the clerics of Picardy composed at the annual carnival, which referred to current topics, follies, etc., in pictures suggesting words, phrases, or syllables of names.

rebut *v.* try to disprove. Probably before 1300 *rebouten* rebuke, assail, in *Arthour and Merlin;* later *rebuten* repel (before 1325, in *Cursor Mundi*); borrowed from Old French *rebuter, rebouter, reboter* (*re-* back + *boter* to thrust, hit, BUTT[3]). The sense of try to disprove, refute, is first recorded in 1817. **—rebuttal** *n.* 1830, act of rebutting; formed from English *rebut* + *-al*[2].

recalcitrant (rikal′sətrənt) *adj.* obstinately disobedient. 1843, in Thackeray's writings; borrowed from French *récalcitrant,* or directly from Latin *recalcitrantem* (nominative *recalcitrāns*), present participle of *recalcitrāre* to kick back (*re-* back + *calcitrāre* to kick, from a lost noun **calcitrus* a kick, from *calx,* genitive *calcis* heel; see CALK[1], v.); for suffix see -ANT. It is also possible that *recalcitrant* was influenced in its use in English by the earlier verb *recalcitrate* (1623, to kick out, and especially in its figurative context of to resist obstinately, in Sterne's *Tristram Shandy,* 1759). **—n.** recalcitrant person. 1865, from the adjective. **—recalcitrance** *n.* 1856, perhaps borrowed from French *récalcitrance,* or formed in English as a noun to *recalcitrant;* for suffix see -ANCE.

recall *v.* 1582, call back; formed from English *re-* + *call,* v. Formation in English of *recall* may, in some instances, have been a loan translation of Middle French *rappeler,* from Old French *rapeler;* see REPEAL; *or* especially in the political or legal sense a loan translation of Latin *revocāre;* see REVOKE. The sense of recollect or remember is first recorded in Locke's *Essay Concerning Human Understanding* (1690). **—n.** 1611, a calling back; from the noun. The sense of a recalling to the mind of something previously learned or experienced is first recorded in 1887, and that of the removal from office of an elected official by a system of petition and vote, in 1902 in American English.

recant *v.* withdraw or retract a statement, belief, etc. 1535, borrowed from Latin *recantāre* recall, revoke (*re-* back + *cantāre* to CHANT). **—recantation** *n.* 1545, formed from English *recant* + *-ation.*

recap[1] (rē′kap *or* rēkap′) *v.* put a strip of rubber on the tread of a tire. 1856, to cap again, formed from English *re-* again + *cap,* v. The specific sense relating to an automobile tire appeared before 1927 in American English.

recap[2] (rē′kap *or* rikap′) *v. Informal.* recapitulate. 1920's, American English; shortened form of *recapitulate.* **—n.** (rē′kap) *Informal.* recapitulation. 1930's, shortened form of *recapitulation.*

recapitulate *v.* go over and repeat again, restate briefly, summarize. 1570, back formation from *recapitulation,* and in some instances borrowed from Late Latin *recapitulātus,* past participle of *recapitulāre* recapitulate; for suffix see -ATE[1]. **—recapitulation** *n.* Before 1387 *recapitulacion* a summarizing of several events; also, a summing up, brief restatement (1392); borrowed through Old French *recapitulacion* and directly from Late Latin *recapitulātiōnem* (nominative *recapitulātiō*), from *recapitulāre* go over the main points of a thing again; literally, restate by heads or chapters (*re-* again + *capitulum* main part, CHAPTER); for suffix see -ATION.

recede *v.* go or move backward. Probably before 1425 *receden* to move backward, retreat, depart; borrowed from Middle French *receder,* and directly from Latin *recēdere* (*re-* back + *cēdere* to go; see CEDE).

receipt (risēt′) *n.* Before 1349 *resseite* the act of receiving; later *reseit* a sum of money received (1390), and *receit* a medicinal recipe (1392); borrowed from Anglo-French or Old North French *receite* receipt, recipe, alteration (under influence of *receit* he receives, from Vulgar Latin **recipit*) of Old French *recete,* from Latin *recepta* received, feminine past participle of *recipere* to RECEIVE.

The English spelling with *p* (in imitation of the Latin form) is first recorded in the late 1300's, but did not become the established form until the 1700's. The

meaning "written statement that something has been received" is first recorded in 1602.
—**v.** give a receipt. 1787, from the noun.

receive *v.* Probably before 1300 *resceiven* take something offered or sent, in *The Romance of Guy of Warwick;* later *receiven* (before 1325, in *Cursor Mundi*); borrowed from Old French *receivre, recevoir,* from Latin *recipere* (*re-* back + *-cipere,* combining form of *capere* to take; see CAPTIVE). —**receivable** *adj.* Before 1382, in the Wycliffe Bible; borrowed from Anglo-French *receivable,* Old French *recevable,* from *receivre* receive; for suffix see -ABLE. —**receivables** *n.pl.* debts owed to a business (1863). —**receiver** *n.* Before 1338, person who buys and sells stolen goods; also, a tax collector or rental agent, in Mannyng's *Chronicle of England;* earlier as a surname (1251); borrowed from Anglo-French *receivour, recevor,* Old French *recevëor,* from *recevoir;* for suffix see -ER[1]. Later meanings in English, such as a person appointed to administer property of a bankrupt (1793), and the part of a telephone held to the ear (1877), etc., were formed from English *receive* + *-er*[1]. —**receivership** *n.* (1485)

recent *adj.* Probably before 1425, borrowed from Latin *recentem* (nominative *recēns*) lately done or made, new, fresh. The Latin word is of uncertain origin but may be related to Greek *kainós* new, Gaulish *Cintu-* first, Welsh *cenedl* nation, Sanskrit *kanína-s* young, and Gothic *hindumists* hindmost, outermost, from Indo-European **ken-* spring up (Pok.563).

receptacle *n.* container. 1392, borrowed from Old French *receptacle,* and directly from Latin *receptāculum* place to receive and store things in, a receptacle, from *receptāre,* frequentative form of *recipere* to hold, contain; see RECEIVE.

reception *n.* Before 1393 *recepcion* the effect of two planets on each other, in Gower's *Confessio Amantis;* later, act of receiving, fact of being received (probably before 1425); borrowed from Old French *reception,* learned borrowing from Latin, and borrowed directly from Latin *receptiōnem* (nominative *receptiō*) a receiving, from *recipere* RECEIVE; for suffix see -TION.

The specific sense of a party to receive and welcome people is first recorded in 1842, and that of the quality of radio reception in 1907.
—**receptionist** *n.* 1867, one who accepts (a specific idea); later, person employed to receive callers (1901); formed from English *reception* + *-ist.* —**receptive** *adj.* Probably before 1425, capable of acting or serving as a receptacle, in a translation of Chauliac's *Grande Chirurgie;* later, able, quick, or ready to receive ideas, etc. (1817); borrowed from Medieval Latin *receptivus* able to receive, from Latin *receptus,* past participle of *recipere* RECEIVE; for suffix see -IVE. —**receptor** *n.* Before 1450 *receptour* one who receives, one who harbors criminals; borrowed through Anglo-French *receptour,* Old French *recepteur,* learned borrowing from Latin and borrowed directly from Latin *receptor,* from *receptus,* past participle of *recipere* RECEIVE; for suffix see -OR[2]. The meaning of a cell or organ that is sensitive to stimuli is first recorded in 1906.

recess (rē′ses) *n.* 1531, act of receding; borrowed in part from Middle French *reces, recez,* and directly from Latin *recessus* (genitive *recessūs*) a going back, a retreat, a retired place, from *recessum,* past participle of *recēdere* to RECEDE. The meaning of a hidden or remote part is first recorded in 1616, and that of an act of retiring for a time from some occupation, period of stopping from usual work or study, in 1620, perhaps both senses from French. —**v.** (rises′) 1809, put in a recess, from the noun. The meaning of take a recess or interval from work or study is first recorded in 1893 in American English. —**recession** *n.* act of receding. 1646; borrowed from Latin *recessiōnem* (nominative *recessiō*) a going back, receding, from *recēdere* to RECEDE; for suffix see -SION. The meaning of a period of temporary setback or decline in business activity is first recorded in 1929 in *The Economist.* —**recessional** *n.* hymn sung while the clergy and choir leave the church after a service. 1867, formed from English *recession* + *-al*[1]. —**recessive** *adj.* 1672-73, tending to recede; formed from English *recess* + *-ive* on the model of Latin *recessīvus,* from *recess-,* past participle stem of *recēdere* to recede; for suffix see -IVE. The meaning in genetics of pertaining to a characteristic that is latent in an animal or plant when contrasting characteristics are present is first recorded in English in 1900, after German *recessiv* (introduced by Gregor Mendel in 1865).

recharge *v.* Probably before 1430 (figurative) to restore; also, to reload a ship (1432); formed from English *re-* again + *charge* load, modeled on Middle French *rechargier, recharger.* The meaning of restore the electrical charge in a storage battery is first recorded in 1876.

recidivist (risid′əvist) *n.* person who relapses into a former state or way of acting, especially a habitual criminal. 1880, borrowed from French *récidiviste,* from *récidiver* to fall back or relapse, learned borrowing from Medieval Latin *recidivare* to relapse into sin, from Latin *recidivus* falling back, from *recidere* fall back (*re-* back + *-cidere,* combining form of *cadere* to fall; see CADENCE); for suffix see -IST. *Recidivist* replaced earlier *recidive,* n. (1854), and may have been influenced in its borrowing as a complement to earlier *recidivation* relapse into sin, crime, etc. (before 1415). —**recidivism** *n.* 1886, from *recidivist,* on the analogy of *baptist, baptism,* etc.; for suffix see -ISM.

recipe *n.* instructions for preparing anything. 1584, medical prescription, borrowed from Middle French *récipé,* or directly from Latin *recipe!* take!, imperative of *recipere* to take, RECEIVE. The transferred sense of a means for attaining or accomplishing something is first recorded before 1643, and that of instructions for preparing food is found in Walpole's *Letters* (1743). From the appearance of the translation of Lanfranc's *Science of Surgery* (before 1400) to about 1652 the word *recipe* was used as an imperative verb exactly as in Latin (and abbreviated R or Rx) as a directive in medical prescriptions. Now, only the abbreviation is retained in modern medicine.

Both *recipe* and *receipt* mean a formula, that is, a written set of directions for concocting something to eat. *Recipe* tends to be the general term, *receipt* the one confined to particular geographical areas or to people from those areas. While *recipe* is a borrowing directly from Latin, and *receipt* developed from a borrowing through Anglo-French and Continental Old French from Latin, the meaning is found in Middle English as early as 1392.

recipient *n.* person or thing that receives something. 1558, borrowed from Middle French *récipient,* and directly from Latin *recipientem* (nominative *recipiēns*), present participle of *recipere* to RECEIVE; for suffix see

-ENT. **—adj.** receiving, willing to receive. 1610, from the noun.

reciprocal *adj.* in return. 1570, inversely related; formed in English from Latin *reciprocus* returning the same way, alternating + English *-al*[1]. The standard etymology for Latin *reciprocus* refers to a pre-Latin form **reco-proco-* back and forth, said to derive from **recus* (*re-* back + *-cus* adjective formative) and **procus* (*pro-* forward + *-cus*). It has been extended further in reference to a possible Indo-European **re-kwe, *pro-kwe* both back and forth (containing **-kwe* and) but no convincing explanation has yet been produced.

It is possible that *reciprocal* was a deliberate borrowing from Latin to replace the older *reciproque* (1532, borrowed from Middle French), at a time when Latin replacements and adjustments in spelling of English words to Latinate forms was in full flower.

The sense of existing on both sides, mutual, is first recorded in 1579, and that of done (or felt, given, etc.) in return, in 1596.
—n. thing which is reciprocal to something. 1570, from the adjective. The mathematical meaning of a number so related to another that their product is one is first recorded in 1782, though the earliest attested uses of the adjective in English (1570) refer to similarity, oneness, or unity.

reciprocate *v.* give, do, feel, or show in return. 1611, in Cotgrave's *Dictionary;* probably a back formation from *reciprocation;* for suffix see -ATE[1]. **—reciprocation** *n.* 1561, act of reciprocating; earlier, reflexive mode of expression (1530); borrowed from Latin *reciprocātiōnem* (nominative *reciprocatiō*) the act or fact of going back upon itself, retrogression, alternation, ebb, from *reciprocāre* move back and forth, alternate, from *reciprocus* alternating, RECIPROCAL; for suffix see -ATION. **—reciprocity** *n.* 1766, condition of being reciprocal, borrowed from French *réciprocité,* from *réciproque* reciprocal, from Latin *reciprocus* + *-ité* -ity.

recite *v.* 1430 *reciten* to repeat aloud, relate in detail, in *Rolls of Parliament;* borrowed through Middle French *reciter,* or directly from Latin *recitāre* read aloud, recite, repeat from memory (*re-* back, again + *citāre* to summon; see CITE). **—recital** *n.* 1512, formal statement of relevant facts in a legal document, formed from English *recite* + *-al*[2]. The sense of an act of reciting is first recorded in 1612, and that of musical entertainment, especially one given by a single performer, is found in Busby's *Complete Dictionary of Music* (1811). **—recitation** *n.* 1484, act of detailing, in Caxton's translations; later, act of repeating aloud (1611); borrowed through Middle French *recitation,* and directly from Latin *recitātiōnem* (nominative *recitātiō*) a reading aloud, from *recitāre* read aloud, recite; for suffix see -ATION. **—recitative** *n.* style of singing, with the rhythm of ordinary speech. 1656, in Blount's *Glossographia;* borrowed from Italian *recitativo,* from *recitare* recite, from Latin *recitāre;* for suffix see -IVE.

reckless *adj.* Probably about 1200 *reckelaes* without care or heed, in *The Ormulum,* variant of earlier *recheles* (probably before 1200); developed from Old English *rēcelēas* careless, thoughtless, heedless (before 899, in Alfred's translation of Bede's *Ecclesiastical History*); earlier *reccilēas* (before 800); formed from **rēce, recce* care, heed (related to, if not developed from *rēcan, reccan* to care, heed) + *-lēas* -less, possibly on the model of an early compound formed outside of Old English as suggested by the variety of parallel Germanic formations found in Middle Dutch and modern Dutch *roekeloos,* Middle Low German *rōkelōs,* and Middle High German *ruochelōs* (modern German *ruchlos*) careless, untroubled, wicked. **—reck** *v. Archaic.* to care, heed. Probably about 1200 *rekken,* in *The Ormulum,* variant of earlier *recchen* (1123, in the *Peterborough Chronicle*); developed from Old English *rēcan* to care, heed (before 900); earlier *reccan* (about 725, in *Beowulf*); cognate with Old Saxon *rōkjan* to care, heed, Middle Dutch *roeken,* Old High German *ruohen, ruohhen,* and Old Icelandic *rœkja,* from Proto-Germanic **rōkijanan,* of obscure origin.

reckon *v.* Probably before 1200 *rikenin* to list, count up, consider, answer for, in *Ancrene Riwle;* variant of *recenen* (probably about 1200, in *The Ormulum*), and *rekenen* (about 1280); developed from Old English (before 1000) *gerecenian* to recount, relate; cognate with Old Frisian *rekenia* to reckon, Middle Low German *rekenen,* Middle Dutch and modern Dutch *rekenen,* Old High German *rehhanōn* (modern German *rechnen*), from Proto-Germanic **(ʒa-)rekenōjanan,* built on the adjective **rekenaz* ready, rapid, whence Old English *recen* ready, and Old Frisian *rekon* clear, open; and cognate probably with Old High German *reht* RIGHT. **—reckoning** *n.* Before 1325 *reckining* narrative account, in *Cursor Mundi;* also *recning;* later *rekening* an accounting, settling of an account (1340), and calculation (about 1380); formed from English *reckon* + *-ing*[1].

reclaim *v.* bring back to a useful, good condition. Before 1325 *reclaymen* call back, bring back, tame, exclaim, in *Cursor Mundi;* also *reclamen* (before 1393); borrowed from Old French *reclaimer, reclamer* to invoke or appeal, learned borrowing from Latin, and borrowed directly from Latin *reclāmāre* cry out against, appeal (*re-* opposite, against + *clāmāre* cry out; see LOW[2], v.).

The meaning of bring (waste or submerged land) to a state fit for use is first recorded in 1764, and the extended meaning of recover manufactured or raw materials for reuse (originally generally of rubber) is found as early as 1892.
—reclamation *n.* Before 1475 *reclamacion,* borrowed from Middle French *reclam,* learned borrowing from Latin, and borrowed directly from Latin *reclāmātiōnem* (nominative *reclāmātiō*) a cry of opposition, from *reclāmāre* cry out against, appeal; for suffix see -ATION.

recline *v.* Probably before 1425 *reclynen* lie or lay down; borrowed through Middle French *recliner,* and directly from Latin *reclīnāre* (*re-* back or against + *clīnāre* to bend, LEAN[1]).

recluse (riklüs′) *n.* Probably before 1200, person who lives withdrawn from the world, in *Ancrene Riwle;* borrowed from Old French *reclus* (feminine *recluse*), noun use of *reclus,* adj., shut up, from Late Latin *reclūsus,* past participle of *reclūdere* to shut up, enclose (Latin *re-* with intensive force + *claudere* to shut, CLOSE[1]). **—adj.** shut up or apart from the world. Probably before 1200 *reclus, reclused* living in seclusion, cloistered; originally past participle of *reclusen* to shut up, confine, influenced by, if not in some instances borrowed from, Old French *reclus,* past participle of *reclure,* from Latin *reclūdere* to shut up. **—reclusion** *n.* Before 1410, borrowed from Middle French *reclusion,* and directly from Medieval Latin *reclusionem* (nominative *reclusio*) enclosure, from Late Latin *reclūs-,* past participle stem of *reclūdere* to shut up; for suffix see -SION. **—reclusive** *adj.* 1599, in Shakespeare's *Much Ado About Nothing;* formed from earlier English *recluse,* v., seclude, borrowed from Late Latin *reclūsus,* past participle + *-ive.*

recognition *n.* About 1450 *recognycyon* knowledge of an event; *recognicion* acknowledgment of someone's right to property (about 1460); borrowed from Middle French *recognition,* and directly from Latin *recognitiōnem* (nominative *recognitiō*) act of recognizing, from *recognit-,* past participle stem of *recognōscere* to acknowledge, know again, examine; see RECOGNIZE; for suffix see -TION. The meaning of acknowledgment as true, valid, or an act of approval or sanction (as in *recognition of one's rights, receive recognition as an authority*) is first recorded in 1570, and that of an act or fact of identifying someone, is found in Wordsworth's *Tintern Abbey* (1798).

recognizance (rikog'nəzəns) *n.* obligation binding a person to perform some act or observe some condition. 1414 *recognisanze,* in *Rolls of Parliament;* borrowed from Old French *recognussance, recognuissance,* and eventually displacing earlier Middle English *reconisaunce* (recorded before 1325, but last found in the obsolete spelling *reconnoissance* with the sense of a binding obligation, in 1672); borrowed from Old French *reconissance, reconoissance* acknowledgment, recognition, from *reconoiss-,* stem of *reconoistre* RECOGNIZE; for suffix see -ANCE. Compare RECONNAISSANCE.

recognize *v.* 1414 *recognisen* resume possession of land; borrowed from Middle French *reconoiss-,* stem of *reconoistre* to know again, identify, recognize, from Old French, from Latin *recognōscere* acknowledge, recall to mind, know again, examine, certify (*re-* again + *cognōscere* know; see COGNIZANCE); for suffix see -IZE. Early variant forms of the word, such as *recunyse* and *racunnisen* were formed by direct borrowing from French, but fell away by influence of Medieval Latin *recognizare.* The meaning of perceive (someone or something) as already known, recognize, is first recorded in 1533 in the obsolete form *recognos* (*recognosce,* borrowed from Latin *recognōscere*), and the meaning of acknowledge by special notice or approval, treat as valid (as in *recognize a government*), is found in 1548-49.

recoil *v.* Probably before 1200 *reculen* force back, retreat, in *Ancrene Riwle;* later *recoilen* (before 1250); borrowed from Old French *reculer,* from Vulgar Latin **recūlāre* (Latin *re-* back + *cūlus* backside; see CUL-DE-SAC). The meaning of shrink back (as in fear, disgust, etc.) is first recorded in 1513, as a figurative use of draw back (probably before 1300, in *Arthour and Merlin*). The sense of rebound or spring back, in reference to firearms, is found in Palsgrave's *Lesclarcissement* (1530). **—n.** a recoiling. Probably before 1300, in *Arthour and Merlin;* in part from the verb in Middle English, and in part borrowed from Old French *recul* recoil, backward movement, from the verb in Old French. The noun is not recorded in common use until the late 1500's, and the sense of the rebound of a firearm is not found until 1575.

recommend *v.* About 1375 *recomenden* commit, dedicate, in Chaucer's *Canterbury Tales;* borrowed from Medieval Latin *recommendare* (Latin *re-* intensive + *commendāre* commit, COMMEND). The meaning of praise of present as worthy is first recorded in a version of *Piers Plowman* (about 1378). The forms *recommend* and the now obsolete *recommand* were identical in Middle English and early modern English, in the sense of commend (someone to another), convey regards of (someone to another), give one's regards to (another), and entrust, praise, extol, paralleling the indiscriminate use of *commend, command* in Middle English and reflecting the mixed use in Medieval Latin. Later, however, the original sense of *commend* in Latin was reborrowed from Latin *commendāre,* and English *command* in the sense of convey, entrust, fell out of use. **—recommendation** *n.* 1408, a greeting dedication; borrowed from Old French *recommendation,* and directly from Medieval Latin *recommendationem* (nominative *recommendatio*), from *recommendare;* for suffix see -ATION. The meaning of praise or commendation is first recorded in Middle English in 1433, and that of a presentation (of someone or something) as worthy, in 1457.

recompense *v.* Before 1400 *recompensen* to redress or remedy; later, to reward, repay, compensate (1422); borrowed from Middle French *recompenser,* learned borrowing from Late Latin, and borrowed directly from Late Latin *recompēnsāre* (Latin *re-* again + *compēnsāre* balance out; see COMPENSATE). **—n.** About 1420, payment, reward, amends; borrowed from Middle French *recompense,* from *recompenser* to recompense.

reconcile *v.* make friends again. Probably about 1350 *reconcylen;* borrowed through Old French *reconcilier,* and directly from Latin *reconciliāre* (*re-* again + *conciliāre* make friendly; see CONCILIATE). The extended meaning of make consistent or compatible, harmonize, is first recorded before 1398. **—reconciliation** *n.* About 1350 *reconsiliacioun;* later *reconciliacïon* (before 1398); borrowed through Old French *reconciliation,* and directly from Latin *reconciliātiōnem* (nominative *reconciliātiō*), from *reconciliāre* reconcile; for suffix see -ATION.

recondite (rek'əndīt) *adj.* hard to understand. 1649, hidden from view, kept out of sight; borrowed from Latin *reconditus,* past participle of *recondere* store away (*re-* away + *condere* to store; see ABSCOND). The figurative meaning of removed from ordinary comprehension, deep, profound, abstruse, is first recorded in English before 1652.

reconnaissance (rikon'əsəns) *n.* examination or survey, especially for military intelligence. 1810, Duke of Wellington in *Dispatches;* borrowing of French *reconnaissance* act or surveying; literally, recognition, from Old French.

The word was borrowed earlier as found in Middle English *reconisaunce* a legal inquiry (about 1460), and earlier, a bond acknowledging a debt (before 1325); from Old French *reconoissance* RECOGNIZANCE.

reconnoiter (rē'kənoi'tər) *v.* make a reconnaissance (of). 1707 *reconnoitre,* borrowing of obsolete French *reconnoître* (now *reconnaître*), from Old French *reconoistre* to take a precise view of, RECOGNIZE.

record (rikôrd') *v.* Probably before 1200 *recorden* to repeat, recite, in *Ancrene Riwle;* later, to set down in writing (1340, in *Ayenbite of Inwyt*); borrowed from Old French *recorder* repeat, recite, report, learned borrowing from Latin, and borrowed directly from Latin *recordārī* remember, call to mind (*re-* restore + *cor,* genitive *cordis* heart, understood by the ancients as the seat of judgment and memory; see HEART). The modern meaning of put (sounds or images) into a permanent form on disks, cylinders, or tape, is first attested in 1892, probably from the noun. **—n.** (rek′ərd) Probably before 1300 *rekord* testimony; later *record* state or fact of being recorded (before 1325, in *Cursor Mundi*), and an official written account (1399); borrowed from Old French *record,* from *recorder* to record. It is also probable that *record,* n. is, in part, from the verb in Middle English. The meaning of a disk, cylinder, or tape on which sounds or images have been recorded, is first attested in 1878, and that of the best known achievement in a sport or other endeavor is first found in 1883. **—recording** *n.* a phonograph record or other type of sound transcription is first found in 1932, though the act or process of making such a transcription is found as early as 1904. First use of *recording* in the sense of recollection is in *Ayenbite of Inwyt* (1340). **—record player** (1934)

recorder *n.* **1** person who is in charge of record keeping, especially the chief legal officer of a city. 1415 *recordour,* borrowed through Anglo-French *recordour,* Old French *recordëor* person who records, a witness, judge, from Medieval Latin *recordator,* from Latin *recordari* remember. **2** wooden musical wind instrument. Probably before 1425 *recordre,* in a translation of Higden's *Polychronicon;* probably formed from English *record,* v. + *-er*[1] and in part borrowed from Old French *recordëor.*

The musical instrument became very rare by the mid-1800's, as it lost popularity to the much-improved design of the flute, but a revival of interest in ancient instruments and early music popularized the easily-played recorder, which was reintroduced between 1911 and 1920 by the French-born expert in early music Arnold Dolmetsch.

recount *v.* tell in detail. 1456 *recounten;* borrowed from Middle French *reconter,* from Old French (*re-* again + *conter* to relate, reckon, COUNT[1]).

recoup (rikūp′) *v.* make up for, recompense. 1628, (in law) to deduct; borrowed from French *recouper* to cut back, from Old French (*re-* back + *couper* to cut, from *coup* a blow; see COUP). The sense of recompense for loss or outlay is first recorded in 1664. An earlier use in the sense of cut short, interrupt, is recorded once in Middle English (about 1450, but is essentially a different word).

recourse (rē′kôrs) *n.* a turning for help or protection. About 1380 *recours* course or movement, in Chaucer's translation of Boethius' *De Consolatione Philosophiae;* also, act of relying on for help or protection (about 1385, in Chaucer's *Troilus and Criseyde*); borrowed from Old French *recours, recors,* and directly from Latin *recursus* (genitive *recursūs*) return or retreat, from *recurs-,* stem of the past participle of *recurrere* run back; see RECUR.

recover *v.* Probably before 1300 *rekeveren, recoveren* get back something lost, etc., regain possession, return; also, to regain strength or health, get well again, recuperate, in *Arthour and Merlin;* borrowed through Anglo-French *rekeverer, recoverer,* Old French *recovrer,* from Latin *recuperāre* to recover. Doublet of RECUPERATE. **—recoverable** *adj.* Before 1471, formed from Middle English *recoveren,* v. + *-able.* **—recovery** *n.* Possibly about 1303 *recouere* help, in Mannyng's *Handlyng Synne;* later, a coming back to health or normal condition (before 1338, in Mannyng's *Chronicle of England*), and *recoveree* a gaining possession by legal action (1424); borrowed through Anglo-French *recoverie, recovery, rekevere,* Old French *recovree,* from past participle of *recovrer* recover.

recreant (rek′rēənt) *adj.* cowardly, false. Probably before 1300 *recreaunt* defeated, in *The Romance of Guy of Warwick;* later, *recreant* surrender, subdue (before 1338), and with the meaning of cowardly (probably about 1390); borrowed from Old French *recreant,* adj. and n., yielding or giving up his cause, present participle of *recroire* to yield in a trial by combat, surrender allegiance (*re-* with intensive force of again + *croire* entrust, believe, from Latin *crēdere;* see CREDIT); for suffix see -ANT. The extended sense of false, disloyal, is first recorded in Milton's *Doctrine and Discipline of Divorce* (1643). **—n.** Probably before 1400, coward, from the adjective. The extended sense of traitor, apostate, is first recorded in 1570.

recreation *n.* Before 1393, in Gower's *Confessio Amantis,* Middle English *recreacioun* refreshment or curing of a person, refreshment by eating food; borrowed from Old French *recrëacion,* learned borrowing from Latin, and borrowed directly from Latin *recreātiōnem* (nominative *recreātiō*) recovery from illness, from *recreāre* to refresh, restore, revive (*re-* again + *creāre* to CREATE); for suffix see -ATION. The meaning of the action of refreshing oneself by some pleasant occupation or amusement (as in *to read for recreation*) is first recorded in Middle English about 1400, and that of a means of refreshing oneself, a pleasurable occupation or pastime (as in *reading is her recreation*) in 1410. **—recreate** *v.* refresh or revive by recreation. About 1425 *recreaten* refresh (oneself); probably borrowed from Latin *recreātus,* past participle of *recreāre* refresh; and in part a later back formation from *recreation;* for suffix see -ATE[1]. The specific sense of refresh (oneself) with some pleasant occupation or amusement is first recorded in Palsgrave's *Lesclarcissement* (1530). **—recreational** *adj.* 1656, of or pertaining to recreation, formed from English *recreation* + *-al*[1].

recriminate *v.* accuse (someone) in return. 1603, in Florio's translation of Montaigne's *Essays;* borrowed, by influence of Middle French *récriminer,* from Medieval Latin *recriminatus,* past participle of *recriminari;* formed from Latin *re-* again or back + *crīminārī* to accuse, from *crīmen* (genitive *crīminis*) a charge, offense, CRIME; for suffix see -ATE[1]. **—recrimination** *n.* 1611, in Cotgrave's *Dictionary,* borrowed from French *récrimination* the making of a counter-accusation, from Medieval Latin *recriminationem* (nominative *recriminatio*), from *recriminari* recriminate; for suffix see -ATION. The meaning of a counter-accusation itself is first recorded in English in 1621 in the singular and as it is now usually in the plural in 1650.

recrudescence (rē′krūdes′əns) *n. Archaic or Literary.* a breaking out afresh. 1721, in Bailey's *Dictionary;* formed in English from Latin *recrūdēscere* (of wounds) become raw again, reopen, break out again + English *-ence.* Latin *recrūdēscere* is formed from *re-* again + *crūdēscere* become raw, from *crūdus* RAW. **—recrudescent** *adj. Archaic or Literary.* breaking out afresh. 1727, in the second volume of Bailey's *Dictionary;* borrowed from Latin *recrūdēscentem* (nominative *recrūdēscēns*), present participle of *recrūdēscere* break out again; for suffix see -ENT.

recruit *n.* newly enlisted soldier, sailor, etc. Before 1643, recovery or renewal; borrowed from obsolete French *recrute,* dialect variant of *recrue,* literally, new growth, from Old French *recreü,* past participle of *recreistre* grow or increase again (*re-* again + *creistre* to grow, from Latin *crēscere;* see CRESCENT). The form *recruit* is a replacement of earlier *recrew* a body of military reinforcements (1619).

The military meaning of a fresh or auxiliary body of troops, reinforcement, is first recorded in 1647. The plural form *recruits* is found in 1653; the singular *recruit,* in the sense of a newly enlisted soldier, sailor, etc., is first attested in 1844.
—v. 1635-56, to recover or renew; also, to enlist new soldiers (1655); borrowed from French *recruter,* from *recrute,* dialect variant of *recrue* recruit, n.
—**recruitment** *n.* 1824, a reinforcement; formed from English *recruit* + *-ment,* perhaps by influence of French *recrutement.* The meaning of the act of recruiting is first recorded in 1834.

rectangle *n.* 1571, borrowed from Middle French *rectangle* (*rect-,* combining form from Latin *rēctus* RIGHT + Old French *angle* ANGLE[1]). The form *rectangle* was also known from Medieval Latin *rectangulum* a triangle having a right angle, from *rectangulus* having a right angle (altered from Late Latin *rēctiangulus,* from Latin *rēctus* straight, right + *angulus* an angle). The Medieval Latin *rectangulus* was the source for the now obsolete *rectangle* and *rectangled,* adj., 1570, having a right angle. —**rectangular** *adj.* 1624, shaped like a rectangle with four sides and four right angles; borrowed from Middle French *rectangulaire* (*rect-* right + *angulaire* angular, from Latin *angulāris* ANGULAR); for suffix see -AR.

rectify *v.* make right, adjust, remedy. 1392 *rectifien;* borrowed from Old French *rectifier,* learned borrowing from Medieval Latin *rectificare* make right, from a lost adjective **rēctificus* (from Latin *rēctus* straight, RIGHT + the root of *facere* to make, perform, DO[1]); for suffix see -FY. The meaning of change (alternating current) into direct current is first recorded in 1892. —**rectification** *n.* Before 1400, borrowed through Middle or Old French *rectificacïon,* and directly from Medieval Latin *rectificationem* (nominative *rectificatio*) the act or fact of making right or remedying, from *rectificare* to rectify; for suffix see -FICATION.

rectitude *n.* upright conduct or character. Probably before 1425, straightness, in a translation of Higden's *Polychronicon;* borrowed from Middle French *rectitude,* learned borrowing from Late Latin, and borrowed directly from Late Latin *rēctitūdo* straightness, uprightness, from Latin *rēctus* straight, RIGHT; for suffix see -TUDE. The sense of moral straightness, upright conduct or character, is first recorded in English before 1533. —**rectitudinous** *adj.* characterized by rectitude. 1897, formed in English from Late Latin *rēctitūdo* (genitive *rēctitūdinis*) rectitude + English *-ous.*

rector *n.* Before 1387 *rector* ruler, head of a school, clergyman in charge of a parish, in Trevisa's translation of Higden's *Polychronicon;* borrowed from Old French *rector, rectour* and directly from Latin *rēctor* ruler, governor, guide, from *rēct-,* past participle stem of *regere* to rule, guide; see RIGHT; for suffix see -OR[2]. —**rectory** *n.* 1448, house of a rector, implied in *rectorybok* account book of a parish or of the house of a parish priest; later, educational establishment under the control of a rector (1536); borrowed from Middle French *rectorie,* and directly from Medieval Latin *rectoria* the office or rank of a rector, house of a rector, from Latin *rēctor* ruler; for suffix see -Y[3].

rectum *n.* lowest part of the large intestine. Probably before 1425, in a translation of Chauliac's *Grande Chirurgie,* borrowing of Latin *rēctum* in *intestīnum rēctum* straight intestine, with *rēctum,* n. from neuter past participle of *regere* to straighten, rule; see RIGHT. —**rectal** *adj.* of or belonging to the rectum. 1872, formed from English *rect(um)* + *-al*[1].

recumbent *adj.* lying down, reclining. 1705, borrowed from Latin *recumbentem* (nominative *recumbēns*), present participle of *recumbere* to recline (*re-* back + *-cumbere* to lie down, related to *cubāre* be lying; see HIP[1] haunch); for suffix see -ENT. Though the common form *recumbent* is not recorded until the beginning of the 1700's, related words were known much earlier, such as *recumbence* (1676), and *recumbency* (1642).

recuperate *v.* recover from sickness, exhaustion, loss, etc. 1542, get back, regain, recover; borrowed from Latin *recuperātus,* past participle of *recuperāre* to recover, related to *recipere* to RECEIVE; for suffix see -ATE[1]. Doublet of RECOVER. The intransitive meaning of recover from sickness, exhaustion, loss, etc. is first recorded in 1864. —**recuperation** *n.* 1481, recovery or regaining of things, in a translation of Caxton's; borrowed from Middle French *récupération,* and directly from Latin *recuperātiōnem* (nominative *recuperātiō*), from *recuperāre* recover; for suffix see -ATION. The sense of recovery from sickness, etc., is first recorded in 1865. —**recuperative** *adj.* 1861, having the ability or power to recover, in Emerson's writings; formed from English *recuperate* + *-ive;* earlier, recoverable (1623, borrowed from Late Latin *recuperātīvus,* from stem of Latin *recuperāre* recover; also found in earlier and now obsolete *recuperable,* probably before 1439, borrowed from Old French *recuperable* and Medieval Latin *recuperabilis*).

recur *v.* happen again. 1529, have recourse, resort; later, go back or return (1620); borrowed from Latin *recurrere* to return, recur, come back, run back (*re-* back, again + *currere* to run; see CURRENT). The meaning of happen again, occur repeatedly, is first recorded in 1673 but did not become common until the 1800's. —**recurrence** *n.* 1646, renewed, frequent, or periodical occurrence, formed from English *recur* + *-ence;* as a noun to *recurrent.* —**recurrent** *adj.* 1611, (of a nerve, etc.) turned back so as to run in the opposite direction; borrowed from Latin *recurrentem* (nominative *recurrēns*), present participle of *recurrere* to return, recur; for suffix see -ENT. The meaning of happening again is first recorded in 1666.

recycle *v.* 1926, implied in *recycling* reuse (of a material) in an industrial process; formed from English *re-* again + *cycle,* v. The specific application of convert (waste) into a usable form, is first recorded in 1960.

red *adj.* Probably before 1200 *red,* developed from Old English (about 700) *rēad* red; cognate with Old Frisian *rād* red, Old Saxon *rōd,* Middle Dutch and modern Dutch *rood,* Old High German *rōt* (modern German *rot*), Old Icelandic *raudhr* (Swedish *röd,* Danish and Norwegian *rød*), and Gothic *rauths,* from Proto-Germanic **rauđaz,* from Indo-European **roudh-,* found in the series **reudh-, roudh-, rudh-* (Pok.872). Cognates outside Germanic through Indo-European *roudh-* include Old Irish *rūad* red, and Lithuanian *raūdas.* The related Old English *rēod* red, cognate with Old Icelandic *rjōdhr* is from Indo-European **reudh-.* Sanskrit *róhita-s* red is derived from either Indo-European **reudh-* or **roudh-,* as are Latin *rūfus* (from Osco-Um brian territory), Welsh *rhudd* and Breton *ruz.* However, Sanskrit *rudhirá-s* red, bloody, Latin *ruber* Greek *erythrós,* Old English *rudu* red color, and possibly Tocharian A *rtär,* Tocharian B *rätre* red, are derived from Indo-European **rudh-.*

The original long vowel of Old and Middle English remains in the surnames *Read, Reade, Reed, Reid,* but was supplanted by a short vowel in the adjective which is phonetically parallel with the development of *lead, bread,* etc., that also had a long vowel in Middle and Old English. It may also be noted that from the English root are derived *ruddy* and *rust,* and that from Latin are derived English *ruby, rubric, russet.*

—n. About 1250 *rede,* in *The Story of Genesis and Exodus;* from the adjective. The sense of *red* as a noun and adjective referring to the revolutionary political movements in Europe, developed in part probably from the meaning of marked or characterized by blood or violence, found as early as 1297, and from reference to the red flag carried as a sign of defiance in battle (1602; later, as a symbol of radical forces, 1848). First specific political reference in English is recorded in 1848 in news reports about the Second French Republic, styled the *Red Republic* by the British press. Later popular reference came at the time of Louis Kossuth (1851) in Hungary and Cavour's and Garibaldi's activities in 1860 in Sicily and Italy when Garibaldi's groups of *Redshirts* (1864) were on the march. From these political developments journalists and other writers used such terms as *Red* (as in "England is not Red," 1864) and *Red Republicanism* (1850, 1858) in a general sense of radical and then specifically in the use of *red* (1878) to describe other radical political movements, particularly those based on the writings of Karl Marx. This later use is now better known by the term *communist* and the interesting formation *communist red.*

—redbird *n.* (1260, as a surname) **—red blood cell** (1910; earlier, *red corpuscle,* 1846) **—red-blooded** *adj.* (1802) **—redbreast** *n.* (before 1425) **—red carpet** (1948) **—red cent** a form of copper penny no longer circulated. 1839 (found especially in the phrase *not worth a red cent*).

—redden *v.* Before 1393 *reden,* in Gower's *Confessio Amantis,* developed from Old English (about 950) *rēadian.* **—reddish** *adj.* 1392, *redisch;* later *reddysch* (probably before 1450); formed from Middle English *rēd,* adj. + *-isch* -ish. **—red-faced** *adj.* embarrassed (1948; earlier, *red in the face,* about 1475; also, *having a red face,* 1579). **—red-handed** *adj.* in the very act of crime or mischief (1819, in Scott's *Ivanhoe*). **—redhead** *n.* (1256, as a surname) **—red herring** 1) 1884, something used to draw attention away from the real issue, referring to a herring (reddened by the smoking process, before 1333) supposedly used by fugitives to put bloodhounds off their trail; apparently from a method of training hunting dogs to follow a scent by dragging a smoked herring along a trail (1686). 2) About 1950, American English, a preliminary prospectus not intended as a legal offer (as for stocks, real estate, or other investment), referring perhaps to the cautionary statement printed in red on the cover or to red lines that originally ran down each page, but strongly influenced by the basic sense of *red herring* in that the prospectus is not the real issue or complete offer. **—red-hot** *adj.* probably before 1425) **—red lead** a red oxide of lead (1295). **—red-letter** *adj.* 1704 *red-letter day* memorable; originally, a saint's day or church festival, indicated on church calendars by red letters, or in reference to a letter colored in red (about 1385, in Chaucer's *Troilus and Criseyde*). **—red shift** a shift in the spectrum of a celestial body to the red end of the spectrum (1923). **—redstart** *n.* kind of songbird, so called from its conspicuous red tail. 1570, in Levins' *Dictionary;* a compound of English *red* + obsolete *start* a tail, developed from Old English (before 800) *steort* tail. Old English *steort* is cognate with Middle Low German and Middle Dutch *stert* tail (modern Dutch *staart*), Old High German *sterz* (modern German *Sterz*), and Old Icelandic *stertr* (Danish *stjert,* Swedish *stjärt*), from Proto-Germanic **stertaz,* cognate with Greek *stórthynx* point, spike, from Indo-European **sterd-, sterdh-/stordh-* (Pok.1023 f.) **—red tape** 1736, excessive bureaucratic routine; so called in allusion to the red-colored tape formerly used in Great Britain for tying up legal and official documents. **—red wine** (about 1150) **—redwood** *n.* very tall tree of the western U.S. 1832, American English; earlier, wood yielding red dye (1634).

red- a variant of the prefix *re-* before vowels in some words, such as *redaction, redeem, redolent, redundant.* Borrowed from Latin.

redeem *v.* About 1415 *redemen* buy back, pay off, free, deliver; in part possibly a back formation from *redemption,* or at least influenced by *redemption,* in the borrowing and alteration from Middle French *rédimer* buy back, learned borrowing from Latin *redimere* (*red-,* variant of *re-* back + *-imere,* combining form of *emere* to take, buy, gain, procure). Latin *emere* is cognate with Old Irish *em-* to take (as in *air-fo-emim* I seize), Lithuanian *im̃ti* to take, and Old Slavic *imǫ* I take away, from Indo-European **em-* (Pok.310). **—redeemer** *n.* Probably before 1425, a redeemer, but here used of Christ, though the conventional capitalized form is not recorded before 1500. **—redemption** *n.* About 1340 *redempcioun* act of redeeming, deliverance from sin, borrowed from Old French *redemption,* learned borrowing from Latin, and borrowed directly from Latin *redēmptiōnem* (nominative *redēmptiō*) a buying back, releasing, ransoming, from *redēmpt-,* past participle stem of *redimere* to redeem; for suffix see -TION. Doublet of RANSOM.

redingote (red′inggōt) *n.* outer coat with long skirts that overlap in front, formerly worn by men. 1793, borrowed from French *redingote* (1725), alteration of English *riding coat* long overcoat worn to protect a horseback rider from rain, mud, etc. *Riding coat* is first recorded in English as *riding cote* (1507).

redolent *adj.* having a pleasing or strong smell. Probably about 1400, borrowed from Middle or Old French *redolent* emitting an odor, learned borrowing from Latin, and borrowed directly from Latin *redolentem* (nominative *redolēns*), present participle of *redolēre* emit a scent (*red-,* variant of *re-* intensive form + *olēre* give off a smell; see ODOR); for suffix see -ENT. **—redolence** *n.* Probably before 1425, a pleasant or strong sweet smell, in a translation of Higden's *Polychronicon;* borrowed from Middle French *redolence,* from *redolent,* and probably directly from Medieval Latin *redolentia,* from Latin *redolēre;* for suffix see -ENCE. It is also possible that *redolence* was formed in Middle English as a noun to the earlier adjective *redolent.*

redouble *v.* double again, make or become twice as great or as much. About 1443 *redoublen;* borrowed from Middle French *redoubler, redobler,* from Old French (*re-* again + *doubler* to DOUBLE).

redoubt (ridout′) *n.* small fort standing alone. Before

1608, borrowed from French *redoute,* from Italian *ridotto,* from Medieval Latin *reductus* (genitive *reductus*) refuge, retreat, from Latin *reduct-*, stem of the past participle of Latin *redūcere* to lead or bring back, draw back, set back; see REDUCE.

The *b* in *redoubt* is probably due to association with the earlier verb *redoubten* to dread, fear (1417), itself an alteration (influenced by English *doubt*) of Middle English (about 1380) *redouten,* borrowed from Old French *redouter;* see REDOUBTABLE.

redoubtable *adj.* that should be feared or dreaded, commanding reverence or respect, formidable. About 1380 *redoutable* venerable, in Chaucer's translation of Boethius' *De Consolatione Philosophiae;* borrowed from Old French *redoutable,* from *redouter* to dread (*re-* intensive form for again + *douter* be afraid of, DOUBT) + *-able* -able.

The spelling with *b* is first recorded in 1421, probably by association with *doubt.*

redound *v.* come back as a result, contribute. 1382 *redounden* to overflow, flow back, come back as a result, in the Wycliffe Bible; borrowed from Old French *redonder* overflow, abound, learned borrowing from Latin *redundāre* to overflow; see REDUNDANT. The sense of contribute, as in the phrase *redound to* is first recorded in a translation of Higden's *Polychronicon* (probably before 1425).

redox (rē'doks) *n.* chemical reaction in which one reactant is oxidized (loses electrons) and another is reduced (gains electrons). 1928, acronym formed from *red(uction)* + *ox(idation).*

redress (ridres') *v.* set right. Probably before 1350 *redressen,* borrowed from Old French *redrecier, redresier* (*re-* again + *drecier, dresier* to straighten, arrange; see DRESS).

The senses of restore, correct, repair, remedy, are first recorded in 1375, and that of set right by making compensation for a wrong or loss, in 1395, in Chaucer's *Canterbury Tales.*

—n. (rē'dres) a setting right, reparation, compensation. About 1385, in Chaucer's *The Complaint of Mars;* borrowed from Old French *redrece, redresse,* from *redresser* to redress.

reduce *v.* About 1375 *redusen* bring or lead back, bring down; also, to trace to a source (probably about 1378, in Wycliffe's writings); borrowed from Old French *reducer, reducier,* and Latin *redūcere* (*re-* back + *dūcere* bring, lead; see TOW[1] pull). The meaning of diminish, lower, lessen, decrease, is first recorded in Middle English about 1380. **—reduction** *n.* Probably before 1425 *reduccioun* action of bringing back; borrowed from Middle French *réduction,* and directly from Latin *reductiōnem* (nominative *reductiō*) a leading back, restoration, from *reduct-*, past participle stem of *redūcere* to lead back, bring back; for suffix see -TION. The sense of diminution, decrease, lessening, is first recorded in English before 1676, probably from the earlier uses in mathematics (of reducing a fraction to its lowest terms, 1542), in logic (of reducing a syllogism to a clearer form, 1551), in chemistry (of reducing a substance to a simpler form, 1666).

redundant *adj.* extra, not needed. 1604, excessive, superfluous, in Cawdrey's *A Table Alphabeticall;* borrowed, perhaps by influence of French *redondant,* from Latin *redundantem* (nominative *redundāns*), present participle of *redundāre* to overflow, come back as a result, contribute (*red-*, variant of *re-* again + *undāre* rise in waves, from *unda* a wave; see UNDULATE); for suffix see -ANT. **—redundancy** *n.* 1601-02, state or quality of being redundant; borrowed from Latin *redundantia* an overflow, excess, superfluity, from *redundantem* (nominative *redundāns*), present participle of *redundāre;* for suffix see -ANCY.

reed *n.* kind of tall grass with a hollow jointed stalk. Before 1250 *red;* developed from Old English (about 700) *hrēod* reed; cognate with Old Frisian *hriād* reed, Old Saxon *hriod,* Middle Low German *rēt,* Middle Dutch *ried* (modern Dutch *riet*), and Old High German *hriot, riot* (modern German *Ried*), from Proto-Germanic **Hreuđán.* A cognate outside Germanic is seen in Lithuanian *krutù* I move, I stir, from Indo-European **kreut-/krut-* (Pok.623). The meaning of thin piece of cane, etc., in the mouthpiece of a musical instrument, is first recorded in Palsgrave's *Lesclarcissement* (1530), probably from the earlier meaning of a reed stem used as a musical instrument (about 1380, in Chaucer's *House of Fame*). **—reedy** *adj.* Before 1382, made of reeds, full of reeds, in the Wycliffe Bible; formed from English *reed* + *-y*[1]. The meaning of sounding like a reed instrument is first recorded in 1811.

reef[1] *n.* narrow ridge near the surface of the water. 1584 *riffe, riff,* probably borrowed from earlier Dutch *riffe,* from a Scandinavian source (compare Old Icelandic *rif* ridge, RIB; probably related to *reef*[2]).

For a similar semantic development of a word originally meaning rib, see COAST.

reef[2] *n.* section of a sail that can be taken in or let out. Before 1393 *riff,* in Gower's *Confessio Amantis;* earlier, in the compound *rifrope* rope used for tying down the reef (1336-37); ultimately from a Scandinavian source (compare Old Icelandic *rif* reef (of a sail), probably a transferred use of *rif* ridge, RIB and thereby probably related to *reef*[1]). The spelling *reef* is first recorded in the verb (1667), probably after *refe,* n. (1515, reshaped perhaps under influence of Middle English *ref* garment). **—v.** reduce the size of (a sail) by taking in a part. 1667, from the noun.

reefer[1] *n.* 1818, one who reefs, especially a midshipman; formed from English *reef*[2], v. + *-er*[1]. The transferred sense of a kind of short coat of thick cloth, worn originally by sailors and fishermen, is first recorded in 1878.

reefer[2] *n. Slang.* marijuana, especially a marijuana cigarette. 1931, American English, of uncertain origin (the OEDS conjectures that *reefer* is perhaps an alteration of Mexican Spanish *grifo* marijuana, drug addict; also, drunkard, cheap tavern, faucet + *-er*[1]. American dictionaries propose derivation from *reef*[2] a section of rolled sail + *-er*[1] in reference to the cigarette's resemblance to something rolled like a sail; both etymologies are unsupported and lack direct evidence).

reek *n.* About 1250 *reke,* smoke, vapor, mist, in *Genesis and Exodus;* later, *reche* (probably about 1380); developed from Old English (before 725) *rēc* (Anglian) and **rīec* (possibly West Saxon); and probably borrowed in part as a loan word from a Scandinavian source (compare Old Icelandic *reykr*), from Proto-Germanic **raukiz.* The Old English and Old Icelandic forms are cognate with Old Frisian *rēk* smoke, Old Saxon and Middle Low German *rōk,* Middle Dutch *rooc* (modern Dutch *rook*), and Old High German *rouh* (modern German *Rauch*). As the Anglian *rēc* would normally have developed into modern English *reech,* the *-k* can only be explained as showing influence of the Scandinavian form. The meaning of strong, unpleasant smell is first recorded in standard English in 1685. **—v.** send out a strong, unpleasant smell. About 1300 *reken* send out vapor or smoke; earlier (of smoke or stench) to rise (about 1250, in *Genesis and Exodus*); developed from Old English, (before 725) Anglian *rēcan,* (about 1000) West Saxon *rēocan.* Forms in Old English are cognate with Old Frisian *rēka* to smoke, Middle Low German *rēken* to smell, *rōken* to smoke, Middle Dutch *rūken, rieken* to smell (modern Dutch *ruiken, rieken*), Old High German *rouhhan, riohhan* to smoke, smell (modern German *rauchen* to smoke, *riechen* to smell), and Old Icelandic *rjūka* to smoke (Norwegian *ryke, røyke,* Swedish *ryka,* Danish *ryge*), from Proto-Germanic **reukanan,* cognate with Greek *ereúgesthai* belch out, and Latin *ē-rūgere* disgorge noisily, from Indo-European **reug-* (Pok.871).

reel[1] *n.* frame turning on an axis. Before 1325 *reel;* developed from Old English (about 1050) *hrēol* reel for winding thread (from Proto-Germanic **HreHulaz*); probably related to *hrægel, hrægl* garment, clothing, which are cognate with Old Icelandic *hræll* spindle, Old High German *hregil* garment, and Old Frisian *hreil.* Cognates outside Germanic include Greek *krékein* to strike, weave, *krókē* woof, and Latvian *krękls* shirt, from Indo-European **krek-/krok-* (Pok.618) **—v.** to wind on a reel. Probably before 1387 *reelen,* in *Piers Plowman;* from the noun in Middle English.

reel[2] *v.* to sway, swing, or rock. 1375 *relen* to whirl, rush about, sway; probably from *reel*[1], n., suggested by the spinning action of a *reel.* **—n.** reeling movement. 1572, from the verb.

reel[3] *n.* lively dance of the Scottish Highlanders. Before 1585, probably special use of REEL[2].

reentry *n.* 1443 *reentre,* formed from Middle English *re-* + *entre,* n., entry, probably independently of the earlier verb and therefore on the model of Middle French *rentree.* **—reenter** *v.* 1439 *reentren,* formed from Middle English *re-* + *entren,* probably on the model of Middle French *rentrer.*

refectory (rifek′tərē) *n.* room for meals, as in a monastery or convent. Probably before 1425, in a translation of Higden's *Polychronicon;* borrowed from Late Latin *refectōrium,* from Latin *refect-,* past participle stem of *reficere* to refresh (*re-* again + the root of *facere* make, perform, DO[1]); for suffix see -ORY.

refer *v.* About 1380 *referren* trace back, assign, or attribute (something) to a person or thing, in Chaucer's translation of Boethius' *De Consolatione Philosophiae;* borrowed from Old French *referer,* or directly from Latin *referre* (*re-* back + *ferre* take, carry, BEAR[2]). **—reference** *n.* act of referring or fact of being referred, in Puttenham's *The Arte of English Poesie;* formed from English *refer* + *-ence.* The meaning of a direction to a book, passage, etc., where certain information may be found, is first recorded in 1612. **—referent** *n.* 1844, person who is consulted, probably formed from English *refer* + *-ent.* The meaning of a person, thing, or idea that a word refers to, is first recorded in Ogden and Richards' *The Meaning of Meaning* (1923). **—referral** *n.* act of referring. 1920's, American English, formed from *refer* + *-al*[2].

referee (ref′ərē′) *n.* judge of play in games and sports. 1621, person appointed by Parliament to examine patent applications; formed from English *refer* + *-ee.* The meaning of a person to whom a dispute is referred is first recorded in 1670; the specific sense of a judge of play in games and sports is first found in 1840. **—v.** act as referee. 1889, from the noun.

referendum *n.* process of submitting a law to popular vote. 1847, in reference to the practice in Swiss politics, and therefore borrowed through both French *référendum* and German *Referendum,* from Latin *referendum* that which must be referred; literally, thing to be brought back, from neuter gerundive of *referre* to bring or take back, REFER.

refine *v.* make pure. 1582, but possibly implied earlier in *refined* as a past tense taking on past participial use, formed from English *re-* intensive form + earlier *fine,* v., make fine. **—refined** *adj.* 1574, subtle; either as a past tense of *refine* or as a past participle formed from English *refine* + *-ed*[2]. The sense of cultivated, elegant, is first recorded in Shakespeare's *Love's Labor's Lost* (1588). **—refinement** *n.* 1611, state of being refined, in Cotgrave's *Dictionary;* formed from English *refine* + *-ment.* The meaning of elegance of manners, polish, also the sense of a subtlety, and that of an advance or improvement, are first recorded between 1708 and 1710 in writings of Swift. **—refinery** *n.* place where refining (of sugar, petroleum, etc.) is carried out. 1727, in *Chambers Cyclopaedia;* formed from English *refine* + *-ery.*

reflation *n.* inflation designed to restore deflated prices. 1932, American English, formed from *re-* again + *(in)flation.* **—reflate** *v.* be subject to reflation. 1932, American English, formed from *re-* again + *(in)flate.*

reflect *v.* 1392 *reflecten* to turn or bend back; later, to deflect, divert (before 1420, in Lydgate's *Troy Book*); borrowed from Old French *reflecter,* and directly from Latin *reflectere* bend back (*re-* back + *flectere* to bend; see FLEXIBLE).

The meaning of turn back or throw back (light, etc.) is first recorded in 1429, probably from earlier use of this sense in *reflection.* The meaning of turn one's thoughts back on, meditate on, ponder, is first found before 1420.

—reflection *n.* About 1380 *reflexion* something that reflects a person's temperament; later, reflecting from a surface (1395), both senses in Chaucer's writings; borrowed from Old French *reflexion,* and directly from Late Latin *reflexiōnem* (nominative *reflexiō*), from Latin *reflex-,* past participle stem of *reflectere* reflect; for suffix see -ION. The spelling with *t* as in *reflection, reflectioun* (recorded before 1398) became the established form by the 1700's, influenced by the verb. **—reflector** *n.* 1665, one who reflects, in Robert Boyle's *Occasional Reflections Upon Several Subjects;* formed from English *reflect* + *-or*[2]. The sense of a thing that reflects is first recorded in 1767.

reflex (rē′fleks) *n.* 1508, reflected light, reflection of light, in Dunbar's *Poems;* from the verb in English, and in some instances, probably borrowed from Middle French *réflexe,* from Latin *reflexus,* from past participle of *reflectere.* The meaning of involuntary action in response to nerve cell stimulation is first recorded in 1877. **—adj.** 1649, directed back upon the mind; possibly from the noun, but more likely in early use borrowed from Latin *reflexus,* past participle of *reflectere.* The meaning of involuntary is first recorded in 1833. **—v.** (rifleks′) bend back, turn back. Before 1425 *reflexen* refract or deflect; borrowed from Latin *reflexus* a bending back, from past participle of *reflectere* to REFLECT. **—reflexive** *adj.* 1588, capable of bending back; borrowed from Medieval Latin *reflexivus,* from Latin *reflexus,* past participle; for suffix see -IVE. The meaning in grammar of expressing an action that refers to the subject is first recorded in 1837.

reform *v.* 1340 *reformen* make again, improve, in *Ayenbite of Inwyt;* borrowed from Old French *reformer,* from Latin *refōrmāre* (*re-* again + *fōrmāre* to FORM). **—n.** 1663, improvement, removal of some abuse or wrong, in Butler's *Hudibras;* from the verb. **—reformation** *n.* Before 1398 *reformacioun* restoration; later, improvement in form or quality (about 1440); borrowed from Old French *reformation,* from Latin *refōrmātiōnem* (nominative *refōrmātiō*) a reforming, amending, transformation, from *refōrmāre* to reform; for suffix see -ATION. The capitalized name *Reformation,* referring to the European religious movement of the 1500's that militated against many practices of the Roman Catholic Church, is first recorded in English as the Reformation in 1588 (*reformation* in 1563, and perhaps before 1548). **—reformatory** *n.* institution for reforming juvenile offenders. 1837, formed as if from Latin **refōrmātōrium,* from *refōrmāt-,* past participle stem of *refōrmāre* to reform; for suffix see -ORY.

refract *v.* bend (a ray) from a straight course. 1612, back formation from *refraction,* and possibly in some instances borrowed from Latin *refrāctus,* past participle of *refringere* break up (*re-* back + *-fringere,* combining form of *frangere* to BREAK). **—refraction** *n.* 1578, action of breaking up; later, process of bending a ray (1603); borrowed from Late Latin *refrāctiōnem* (nominative *refrāctiō*) a breaking up, from Latin *refrāct-,* past participle stem of *refringere* break up; for suffix see -TION. **—refractory** (rifrak′tərē) *adj.* stubborn, unmanageable. 1606, in Shakespeare's *Troylus and Cressida;* alteration (influenced by adjectives ending in *-ory*) of earlier *refractarie, refractary* (1604, in Cawdrey's *A Table Alphabeticall,* and earlier as a noun, 1599); borrowed, perhaps by influence of French *réfractaire,* from Latin *refrāctārius* obstinate, from *refrāct-,* past participle stem of *refringere;* for suffix see -ORY, -ARY.

refrain[1] *v.* hold oneself back. Probably about 1350 *refreynen* to hold back or restrain; borrowed from Old French *refrener, refreiner, refraigner* restrain, repress, learned borrowing from Late Latin *refrēnāre* bridle, hold in with a bit (*re-* back + *frēnāre* to restrain, furnish with a bridle, from *frēnum* a bridle, of uncertain origin).

refrain[2] *n.* verse repeated regularly in a song or poem. About 1385 *refrein,* in Chaucer's *Troilus and Criseyde;* borrowed from Old French *refrain,* alteration of *refrait,* from past participle of *refraindre* repeat; also, break off or modulate, from Vulgar Latin **refrangere* break off, from Late Latin *refrangere* lessen, alteration of Latin *refringere* break up, break off or back; see REFRACT.

refrangible (rifran′jəbəl) *adj.* capable of being refracted. 1673, in Newton's *Writings;* formed as if from Latin **refrangere* (alteration of *refringere* break up; see REFRACT) + English *-ible.*

refresh *v.* About 1380 *refresshen, refresschen* make fresh or fresher, restore, strengthen, in Chaucer's translation of Boethius' *De Consolatione Philosophiae;* borrowed from Old French *refrescher* (*re-* again + *fresche* fresh, from a Germanic source; compare Old High German *frisc* FRESH).

The meaning of freshen (the memory), make clear or distinct again, is first recorded in 1542. **—refresher** *n.* Before 1449, person or thing that refreshes; formed from English *refresh* + *-er*[1]. The meaning of reminder is first recorded in Dickens' *Pickwick Papers* (1837). **—refreshment** *n.* About 1385, borrowed from Old French *refreschement,* from *refrescher* to refresh; for suffix see -MENT. Use of *refreshments,* pl., food or drink, is first recorded in 1665.

refrigerate *v.* 1534, to cool, make cold, freeze, in Sir Thomas More's writings; in part perhaps a back formation from *refrigeration* and from earlier *refrigerate* (probably about 1440); borrowed from Latin *refrīgerātus,* past participle of *refrīgerāre* (*re-* again + *frīgerāre* make cool, from the lost stem **frīger-* of the noun *frīgus,* genitive *frīgoris,* cold; see FRIGID); for suffix see -ATE[1]. The meaning of preserve (food, etc.) by chilling is first recorded in 1875. **—refrigeration** *n.* 1471, Middle English *refrygeracion* act of cooling or freezing, borrowed from Latin *refrīgerātiōnem* (nominative *refrīgerātiō*) mitigation of heat, especially in a diseased condition, from *refrīgerāre* to cool; for suffix see -ATION. The meaning of cooling or freezing of food, etc., for storage, is first recorded in 1881. **—refrigerator** *n.* 1611, something that cools, in Cotgrave's *Dictionary;* formed from English *refrigerate* + *-or*[2]. The meaning of an apparatus or cabinet for keeping food or other items cool or cold is first recorded in 1824.

refuge *n.* shelter or protection. About 1385, in Chaucer's *Canterbury Tales;* borrowed from Old French *refuge,* learned borrowing from Latin *refugium* a taking refuge, place to flee back to (*re-* back + *fugere* to flee + *-ium* place for; see FUGITIVE). **—refugee** *n.* person who flees for refuge. 1685 *refugie;* later *refugee* (1687); borrowed from French *refugié,* past participle of *refugier* to take shelter, protect, either from the noun in Old French or from Latin *refugium* refuge.

refulgent *adj.* shining brightly, radiant. Before 1500, brilliant; borrowed from Middle French *refulgent,* or directly from Latin *refulgentem* (nominative *refulgēns*), present participle of *refulgēre* flash back, shine brilliantly (*re-* back + *fulgēre* to shine; see EFFULGENCE); for suffix see -ENT. **—refulgence** *n.* splendor, brightness, radiance. 1634, borrowed from Latin *refulgentia* reflected luster, splendor, from *refulgēns,* present participle of *refulgēre;* for suffix see -ENCE.

refund[1] (rifund′) *v.* pay back. Probably before 1425 *refunden* to transmit influence, restore, in a translatio of Higden's *Polychronicon;* borrowed from Old Frenc *refunder* restore, learned borrowing from Latin, an borrowed directly from Latin *refundere* pour back give back, restore (*re-* back + *fundere* to pour; se FOUND[2] cast). The word is recorded with an earlier dat (1386) in the OED, in the sense of pour back, but thi citation is not found in the MED. The meaning of han back, pay back, is first recorded in English in 1553. —r (rē′fund) return of money paid. 1866, from the ver (but the sense is found earlier in *refundment,* 1826 i Lamb's writings).

refund[2] (rēfund′) *v.* change debt into new form. 186 in Worcester's *Dictionary;* formed from *re-* again *fund,* v.

refurbish *v.* 1611, in Cotgrave's *Dictionary;* forme

from English from *re-* again + *furbish,* on the model of French *refourbir.*

refuse[1] (rifyüz′) *v.* say no to, decline to accept. Probably before 1300 *refusen* reject, decline, in *Kyng Alisaunder;* borrowed from Old French *refuser,* from Vulgar Latin **refūsāre,* frequentative form with past participle stem *refūs-* of Latin *refundere* pour back, give back; see REFUND[1]. It is also possible that Old French *refuser* was an alteration confused perhaps with *refuter* in borrowing of Latin *refūtāre* check, repress; see REFUTE. **—refusal** *n.* act of refusing. 1474, formed from English *refuse*[1] + *-al*[2].

refuse[2] (ref′yüs) *n.* useless stuff, waste. Before 1338 *refous* an outcast, in Mannyng's *Chronicle of England;* later, waste or trash (about 1390); borrowed from Old French *refus* waste product, rubbish, from *refuser* to REFUSE[1]. **—adj.** About 1385 *refus* despised, rejected, in Chaucer's *Troilus and Criseyde;* possibly borrowed from Old French *refuse,* past participle of *refuser* to refuse; also perhaps confused with Old French *refus* refugee, *refus* refuge. It is also likely that in some instances adjective use developed from the noun.

refusenik or **refusnik** (rifyüz′nik) *n.* Soviet citizen who has been refused permission to emigrate. 1975, formed from English *refuse*[1], v. + *-nik;* loan translation of Russian *otkáznik,* from *otkazát′* to refuse, *otkáz* refusal.

refute *v.* 1513, to refuse or reject; borrowed possibly from Middle French *réfuter,* and directly from Latin *refūtāre* drive back, repress, repel, rebut (*re-* back + *-fūtāre* to beat; see CONFUTE). The meaning of prove to be false or incorrect is first recorded in 1545. **—refutation** *n.* Before 1548, borrowed from Middle French *réfutation,* and directly from Latin *refūtātiōnem* (nominative *refūtātiō*) disproof of a claim or argument, from *refūtāre* to refute; for suffix see -ATION.

regal *adj.* About 1380, in Chaucer's translation of Boethius' *De Consolatione Philosophiae;* possibly, in some instances, adjective use developed from the now obsolete noun in the sense of sovereignty, royal person, borrowed from Old French *regal, regale,* from Latin; also borrowed from Latin *rēgālis* royal, kingly, from *rēx* (genitive *rēgis*) king; for suffix see -AL[1]. Latin *rēx* is cognate with Old Irish *rī* (genitive *rīg*) king, Sanskrit *rā́jan-,* and related to Latin *regere* to guide, rule; see RIGHT. Doublet of ROYAL.

regale (rigāl′) *v.* entertain agreeably. 1656, to feast or entertain sumptuously, in Blount's *Glossographia;* borrowed from French *régaler* to entertain or feast, from Old French *regale, rigale* feast, from *gale* merriment, from *galer* make merry, of uncertain origin. The Old French form *rigale* was influenced by the phrase *se rigoler* amuse oneself, rejoice, also of uncertain origin. Related to GALA and GALLANT.

regalia (rigāl′yə) *n.pl.* emblems of royalty. Before 1540, royal powers or privileges; later, emblems or insignia of royalty, such as the crown and scepter (1626); reborrowed from Latin *rēgālia* royal things, from neuter plural of *rēgālis* REGAL, and replacing earlier Middle English *regalie* royal powers or status (before 1393, in Gower's *Confessio Amantis*), emblems or insignia of royalty (before 1420, in Lydgate's *Troy Book*); borrowed from Latin *rēgālia,* possibly by influence of Old French *regale* royal powers, also from Latin *rēgālia.*

regard *n.* 1348, consideration, a paying attention to; later, aspect, appearance, look (about 1380); borrowed from Old French *regard,* from *regarder, reguarder* take notice of, look at, watch (*re-* intensive + *garder, guarder* look, heed, watch; see GUARD). Doublet of REWARD. The phrase *in regard to* is first recorded before 1438 and *as in regard of* about 1390, in Chaucer's writings. The meaning of esteem, affection, kindly feeling, is first found probably before 1396. The phrase *in this regard,* meaning in this respect, point, or particular, may be found before 1500, but is first recorded in 1602. **—v.** About 1348 *regarden* to consider; later, take notice of, look at (about 1430); borrowed from Old French *regarder, reguarder.* The meaning of pay attention to, take into account, probably appeared much earlier, but is first recorded in 1512-13. **—regardless** *adj.* 1591, without regard, indifferent, slighted. *—adv.* 1872, in spite of all, anyway, in Mark Twain's *Roughing It.*

regatta (rigat′ə) *n.* boat race. 1652, name of a boat race among gondoliers held on the Grand Canal in Venice; borrowing of Italian (Venetian dialect) *regatta* literally, a strife or contention for mastery, from *regattare* to compete, haggle, contend for mastery, sell at retail especially by haggling, possibly from *recatare, *recattare* buy and sell at retail especially to sell again and thereby increase the price, from Vulgar Latin **recaptāre* to capture (Latin *re-* intensive + *captāre* try to catch; see CATCH). The general meaning of a boat or yacht race, usually a series of races, is first recorded in English in 1775.

regenerate (rijen′ərāt) *v.* 1541, form or grow again, in Robert Copland's *Works;* probably in part a back formation from *regeneration,* and in part developed from adjective and past participle *regenerate;* replacing earlier *regeneren* to cause to grow again (before 1400, in a translation of Lanfranc's *Science of Surgery;* borrowed from Old French *regenerer,* and directly from Latin *regenerāre*) and *regenerativen* (probably before 1425, in a translation of Chauliac's *Grande Chirurgie,* from *regenerative*); for suffix see -ATE[1]. The meaning of cause to be spiritually reborn probably appeared much earlier (compare *regenerate,* adj. and *regeneration*) but is not recorded before 1557. The biological sense of reproduce is first recorded in 1597. **—adj.** (rijen′ərit) 1433, reborn, formed anew, borrowed from Latin *regenerātus,* past participle of *regenerāre.* **—regeneration** *n.* About 1350 *regeneraciun* spiritual rebirth; later, act of forming or growing again (probably before 1425); borrowed through Old French *regeneracion* and directly from Late Latin *regenerātiōnem* (nominative *regenerātiō*) a being born again, the act or fact of forming anew, from Latin *regenerāre* make over, generate again (*re-* again + *generāre* to produce, GENERATE); for suffix see -ATION. **—regenerative** *adj.* 1392, borrowed through Old French *regeneratif* (feminine *regenerative*), and directly from Medieval Latin *regenerativus,* from Latin *regenerāre.*

regent *n.* About 1400, one who rules or governs; earlier, member of a university faculty (before 1397, in the Wycliffe Bible); borrowed through Old French *regent,* and directly from Medieval Latin *regentem* (nominative *regens*), from Latin *regēns* ruler, governor; also present participle of *regere* to rule, direct; see RIGHT; for suffix see -ENT. It is probable that the earliest use referring to academic position was from the adjective in Middle English.

The meaning of a university official who rules or presides over disputations is first recorded before 1425; the related use of a member of the governing board of a State university is first recorded in 1813 in American

English. The familiar historical meaning of a person appointed to rule when the actual king is underage, absent, or incapacitated, is first recorded in Lydgate's *Troy Book* (before 1420).

—adj. Before 1387, acting as a university regent, in Trevisa's translation of Higden's *Polychronicon;* borrowed through Old French *regent,* and directly from Medieval Latin *regentem* (nominative *regens*) from Latin *regēns,* present participle of *regere;* for suffix see -ENT. The meaning of acting as the regent of a country, is first recorded about 1430; from the noun.

—regency *n.* Probably before 1430 *regencie* office or jurisdiction of a regent, sovereignty; borrowed from Medieval Latin *regentia;* from *regens* regent; for suffix see -CY.

reggae (reg′ā) *n.* kind of rock'n'roll music of Jamaican origin often with lyrics of social protest. 1968, Jamaican English, of uncertain origin (compare Jamaican English *rege-rege* a quarrel, row, protest; literally, rags, ragged clothes, variant form of *raga-raga,* alteration and reduplication of English *rag*).

regicide[1] (rej′əsīd) *n.* crime of killing a king. 1602, formed in English from Latin *rēx (*genitive *rēgis*) king + English suffix *-cide*[2].

regicide[2] *n.* person who kills a king. Before 1548; formed in English from Latin *rēx* (genitive *rēgis*) king + English suffix *-cide*[1].

regime or **régime** (rizhēm′ *or* rāzhēm′) *n.* About 1475, course of diet, exercise, etc., prescribed for healthful living; borrowed from Middle French *regime,* from Latin *regimen;* later, in the same meaning (1776), and system of government or rule (1792); borrowed from French *régime,* from Latin *regimen* rule, guidance, government. Doublet of REGIMEN.

regimen (rej′əmən) *n.* set of rules or habits. Before 1400, course of diet, exercise, etc., prescribed for healthful living, in a translation of Lanfranc's *Science of Surgery;* borrowed from Latin *regimen* rule, guidance, government, from *regere* to rule; see RIGHT. Doublet of REGIME. The transferred meaning of any set of rules or habits is first recorded in use by Johnson in 1791, in *The Rambler.*

regiment *n.* Before 1393, government, rule, control, in Gower's *Confessio Amantis;* borrowed from Old French *regiment* government, rule, learned borrowing from Late Latin *regimentum* rule, direction, from Latin *regere* to rule; see RIGHT; for suffix see -MENT. The meaning of a unit of an army or military force is first recorded in English in 1579, from the use in French. **—v.** form into a regiment or organized group. 1617, from the noun. The meaning of organize systematically is first recorded in 1698. **—regimental** *adj.* 1702, formed from English *regiment,* n. + *-al*[1]. **—regimentation** *n.* 1877, the act or process of regimenting, in Herbert Spencer's *The Principles of Sociology;* formed from English *regiment,* v. + *-ation.*

region *n.* Probably before 1300 *regioun* large tract of land, country, territory, kingdom, in *Kyng Alisaunder;* later *region* (before 1338); borrowed through Anglo-French *regioun,* Old French *region,* from Latin *regiōnem* (nominative *regiō*) direction, boundary, district, country, from *regere* to direct, rule; see RIGHT; for suffix see -ION. **—regional** *adj.* Probably before 1425 *regionale* that is special to a region or country; borrowed from Latin *regiōnālis* of or belonging to a region, from *regiō* region; for suffix see -AL[1].

register *n.* list or record. About 1378 *registre,* in a version of *Piers Plowman;* borrowed from Old French *regestre,* and directly from Medieval Latin *registrum,* alteration of Late Latin *regesta* list, matters recorded, from Latin *regesta,* neuter plural of *regestus,* past participle of *regerere* to record (*re-* back + *gerere* carry, bear; of uncertain origin).

The meaning of a set of pipes of an organ stop is first recorded in 1585, and the related sense of a compass of a voice or instrument (as in *upper, lower* or *middle register*) is first recorded in Busby's *Complete Dictionary of Music* (1811). The meaning of a registering device, apparatus by which data is automatically recorded, is first attested in 1830, this sense was later extended to a till (*cash register*) in 1875 in American English; these later senses from the verb.

—v. enter in a list or record. Before 1393 *registren,* in Gower's *Confessio Amantis;* borrowed from Old French *regestrer, registrer,* and directly from Medieval Latin *registrare,* from *registrum* register, n. The meaning of show or indicate an emotion, thought, etc. (as by the expression on one's face) is first recorded in 1901.

—registration *n.* Apparently 1566, act of registering; borrowed through Middle French *registration,* and directly from Medieval Latin *registrationem* (nominative *registratio*), from *registrare* to register; for suffix see -ATION. **—registry** *n.* 1483, perhaps in the sense of a record book; later, act of registering (1589), and place where registers are kept (1603); formed from English *register,* v. + *-ry.*

registrar (rej′əsträr) *n.* official recorder. 1675, shortened form of earlier *registrary* registrar (about 1541), and replacing *registerer* (about 1475), and *register, registere* (before 1443), both from the noun in Middle English. The form in modern English was borrowed from Medieval Latin *registrarius* one who keeps a record, from *registrum* REGISTER.

regnant (reg′nənt) *adj.* ruling, reigning. 1600, in William Watson's *Works;* perhaps from earlier noun in the sense of sovereign (before 1500); borrowed from Latin *rēgnantem* (nominative *rēgnāns*) reigning, present participle of *rēgnāre* to REIGN; for suffix see -ANT. The sense of predominant is first recorded in 1621, and that of widespread in 1625, in the writings of Charles I.

regress (rē′gres) *n.* About 1375 *regresse* a going back, return; borrowed from Latin *regressus* (genitive *regressūs*) a returning, return, from *regress-,* stem of the past participle of *regredī* to go back (*re-* back + *gradī* to step, walk; see GRADE). **—v.** (rigres′) 1552, to return to a former state; borrowed from Latin *regressus,* past participle of *regredī* to go back. The specific sense of move backward is first recorded in 1823. **—regression** *n.* Probably before 1425, repetition or returning to a subject; borrowed from Latin *regressiōnem* (nominative *regressiō*) a going back, return, from *regress-,* past participle stem of *regredī* go back; for suffix see -SION. The meaning of reversion to a less developed form or state, relapse, is first recorded in 1646. **—regressive** *adj.* 1634, showing regression, going backwards; formed from English *regress,* v. + *-ive.*

regret *v.* Probably about 1380 *regretten* feel sorry for or about, mourn or lament; borrowed from Old French *regreter* long after, bewail, lament, *regrater* (*re-* intensive + *-greter, -grater,* possibly from a Frankish form cognate with Gothic *grētan* weep, Old English *grǣtan* and Old Icelandic *grāta* to weep, groan; see GREET).

The weakened sense of feel distress on account of (as in *to regret causing trouble or inconvenience*) is first recorded in 1553.

—n. 1533, complaint, lament; borrowed from Middle French *regret,* from Old French, from *regreter* to regret. The meaning of sorrow, disappointment, is first recorded in Spenser's *Fairie Queene* (1590).

regular *adj.* Before 1387 *reguler* belonging to a religious order bound by certain rules, in Trevisa's translation of Higden's *Polychronicon;* borrowed from Old French *reguler,* learned borrowing from Late Latin, and borrowed directly from Late Latin *rēgulāris* containing rules for guidance, from Latin *rēgula* RULE. The English spelling was refashioned to *regular* after the Latin form and began to appear as early as 1398 (for suffix see -AR).

The meaning of following some rule or principle, symmetrical, is first recorded in 1584, and that of marked by steadiness or uniformity of occurrence or procedure, habitual, constant, in 1594 (but this latter sense is implied much earlier in the adverb *regularly* in order, systematically, 1392).

—n. About 1400, member of a religious order bound by certain rules, from the adjective. The meaning of a member of a standing army is first recorded in 1756-57. **—regularity** *n.* 1603, state or character of being regular; formed from English *regular* + *-ity,* perhaps on the model of French *régularité.*

regulate *v.* Probably before 1425, in a translation of Chauliac's *Grande Chirurgie;* borrowed from Late Latin *rēgulātus,* past participle of *rēgulāre* to control by rule, direct, from Latin *rēgula* RULE; for suffix see -ATE[1]. **—regulation** *n.* 1672, act of regulating; later, rule, law (before 1715); formed from English *regulate* + *-ation.* **—regulator** *n.* 1655, one that regulates; formed from English *regulate* + *-or*[2].

regurgitate (rēgėr′jətāt) *v.* Before 1640, to surge or flow back; possibly a back formation from *regurgitation,* and in part borrowed from Medieval Latin *regurgitatus,* past participle of *regurgitare* to overflow (Late Latin *re-* back + *gurgitāre* engulf, flood, found in Latin *ingurgitāre* to pour in, glut, gorge; *gurgitāre,* from *gurges* whirlpool, abyss; see GORGE); for suffix see -ATE[1].

The meaning of throw up, vomit, is first recorded in English in 1753.

—regurgitation *n.* 1601, act of regurgitating, in Holland's translation of Pliny's *Natural History;* probably in part borrowed from Middle French *régurgitation,* and directly from Medieval Latin *regurgitationem* (nominative *regurgitatio*), from *regurgitare* to overflow; for suffix see -ATION. It is also possible that *regurgitation, regurgitate* are formations in English from *gurgitation, gurgitate,* or at the least formed on partial abstraction of *gurgitate, gurgitation* from *ingurgitation,* as the forms were known in English considerably earlier than *regurgitation* (compare *gurgitation* 1542, *ingurgitation* 1530, *ingurgitate* 1570).

rehabilitate *v.* 1580-81, restore to a former rank, privilege, or reputation; possibly a back formation from *rehabilitation,* and in part borrowed from Medieval Latin *rehabilitatus,* past participle of *rehabilitare* (*re-* again + *habilitare* make fit, from Latin *habilis* easily managed, fit; see ABLE); for suffix see -ATE[1]. The meaning of restore to a good condition is first recorded in English in Carlyle's edition of Cromwell's letters and speeches (1845). **—rehabilitation** *n.* 1533-34, act of rehabilitating; borrowed from Middle French *réhabilitation,* and directly from Medieval Latin *rehabilitationem* (nominative *rehabilitatio*) restoration, from *rehabilitare;* for suffix see -ATION.

rehearse *v.* Probably before 1300 *rehercen* speak or write, utter, express, in *Kyng Alisaunder;* also, repeat, reiterate (before 1325, in *Cursor Mundi*), and in the spelling *rehersen* (about 1330); borrowed through Anglo-French *rehearser,* variant of Old French *rehercier, reherser* to rake over (*re-* again + *hercier* to rake, harrow, from *herce* harrow; see HEARSE). The meaning of practice a play, part, etc., for a public performance, is first recorded in English in 1579-80, from the earlier general sense of go over or through some subject matter (before 1376, in *Piers Plowman*). **—rehearsal** *n.* About 1395, act of recounting, recital, in Chaucer's *Canterbury Tales;* formed from Middle English *rehearse* + *-al*[2]. The meaning of a practicing of a play, part, etc., for a public performance, is first recorded in 1579-80, from the general sense of recounting, repetition (about 1443).

reify (rē′əfī) *v.* regard or treat (an idea, etc.) as a thing, materialize. 1854, probably a back formation from *reification* and perhaps separately formed from Latin *rē-* (stem of *rēs* thing or matter; see REAL[1]) + English connective *-i-* + English suffix *-fy,* as found in *deify.* **—reification** *n.* the act or fact of regarding or treating an idea, etc., as a thing. 1846, in Grote's *History of Greece;* formed from Latin *re-* (stem of *res* thing, matter) + English connective *-i-* + English suffix *-fication,* as found in *deification.*

reign *n.* period of power of a ruler. Probably about 1225 *rengne* kingdom, in *King Horn;* later *reyne* (before 1300), *regne* (about 1300); borrowed from Old French *reigne,* from Latin *rēgnum* dominion, rule, realm, from *rēg-* (found in *regere* to rule; *rēgis,* genitive of *rēx* king); see REGAL. The Old French spelling with *i* began to appear as early as sometime before 1387 (about 1380, for the verb) but did not prevail over the Latin spelling without *i* until well into the 1600's. The meaning "period of a sovereign's rule" is first recorded in Mannyng's *Chronicle of England* (before 1338). **—v.** be a ruler. Probably about 1280 *regnen,* borrowed from Old French *regner,* from Latin *rēgnāre,* from *rēgnum* reign, n.

reimburse *v.* pay back. 1611, in Cotgrave's *Dictionary,* formed from English *re-* back + obsolete *imburse* to pay, enrich, put in a purse (about 1530). English *imburse* was borrowed from Middle French *embourser* (Old French *em-* in + *borser* to get money, from *borse* purse, from Medieval Latin *bursa* PURSE). The form *reimburse* was probably influenced by French *rembourser* reimburse (*re-* back + Middle French *embourser* pay, put in a purse). **—reimbursement** *n.* 1611, formed from English *re-* back + (obsolete) *imburse* + *-ment.*

rein *n.* Probably before 1300 *rein* strap or line fastened to a bridle or bit; borrowed from Old French *reine, rene, resne,* probably from Vulgar Latin **retina* a bond, check (compare Italian *redine,* Portuguese *rédea,* Spanish *rienda,* also Latin *retināculum* tether, halter), from Latin *retinēre* hold back; see RETAIN.

The figurative meaning of control or means of guiding, a curb, check, or restraint, is first recorded about 1325.

—v. check or pull with reins. Probably about 1300 *reinen* tether; from the noun. The figurative meaning of put a check or restraint upon is first recorded in Shakespeare's *Love's Labour's Lost* (1588).

reindeer *n.* large deer with branching horns. Before 1400 *rayne-dere;* also *reyndere* (probably about 1408); borrowed from a Scandinavian source (compare Old Icelandic *hreindȳri* reindeer, formed of *hreinn* the usual name for the reindeer + *dȳr* animal; see DEER). Old Icelandic *hreinn* is cognate with Old English *hrān* reindeer, from Proto-Germanic **Hrainaz,* Indo-European **k̑roinos* (Pok.575), related to **ker-/kor-* HORN.

reinforce *v.* 1600, strengthen (a military force) with additional men; formed from English *re-* again + *inforce, enforce* strengthen (see ENFORCE). **—reinforcement** *n.* 1607, renewal of force, in Shakespeare's *Coriolanus;* later, act of reinforcing (1617); formed from English *reinforce* + *-ment.*

reiterate *v.* say or do several times. Probably before 1425, borrowed from Late Latin *reiterātus,* past participle of *reiterāre* to repeat (Latin *re-* again + *iterāre* to repeat, ITERATE); for suffix see -ATE[1]. **—reiteration** *n.* Probably before 1425, act of reiterating; borrowed through Middle French *réitération,* and directly from Medieval Latin *reiterationem* (nominative *reiteratio)* repetition, from Late Latin *reiterāre* repeat; for suffix see -ATION.

reject (rijekt′) *v.* About 1415 *rejecten* cast out, dismiss; later, refuse to recognize, submit to, adopt, etc. (1426); borrowed from Latin *rejectus,* past participle of *reicere* to throw back (*re-* back + *-icere,* combining form of *jacere* to throw; see JET[1] stream). **—n.** (rē′jekt) rejected person or thing. 1464, refusal; from the verb. **—rejection** *n.* Before 1464, act of rejecting, especially a setting aside in divorce; borrowed from Latin *rejectiōnem* (nominative *rejectiō*), from *reject-,* past participle stem of *reicere* to throw back; for suffix see -TION.

rejoice *v.* About 1303 *reioshen* to own, possess, in Mannyng's *Handlyng Synne;* later *rejoysen* to gladden, delight (about 1370), to delight in, be glad about (about 1380); borrowed from Old French *rejoiss-,* stem of *rejoissant,* present participle of *rejoir* gladden, rejoice (*re-* intensive + *joir* be glad, rejoice, from Latin *gaudēre;* see JOY).

rejoin[1] *v.* join or unite again. 1541, in Robert Copland's *Works;* formed from English *re-* again + *join,* perhaps influenced by Middle French *rejoin-,* stem of *rejoindre;* see REJOIN[2].

rejoin[2] *v.* to answer. 1447 *rejoinen* (in law) to answer the plaintiff's reply to the defendant's plea; borrowed from Middle French *rejoin-,* stem of *rejoindre* (Old French *re-* back + *joindre* to JOIN). The general use of say in answer is first recorded in 1637, preceded by the now obsolete sense of reply (1556). **—rejoinder** *n.* response, retort. 1447 *rejoynder* (in law) the defendant's answer; borrowed from Middle French *rejoindre,* infinitive used as a noun; for suffix see -ER[3].

rejuvenate *v.* make young or vigorous again. 1807, formed in English from *re-* again + Latin *juvenis* YOUNG + English *-ate*[1]. **—rejuvenation** *n.* 1834, restoration to youth, in Bulwer-Lytton's *The Last Days of Pompeii;* formed from English *rejuvenate* + *-ation.*

relapse (rilaps′) *v.* Before 1415 *relapsen* to renounce, in Wycliffe's writings; later, to fall back into a former state, as of illness, etc. (1568); borrowed from Latin *relāpsus,* past participle of *relābī* slip back (*re-* back + *lābī* to slip; see LAP[1], n.) **—n.** (rilaps′ *or* rē′laps) a relapsing. 1459, from the verb in English, and possibly from Medieval Latin *relapsus,* n., from Latin *relāpsus,* past participle of *relābī.*

relate *v.* 1530, to tell, in Palsgrave's *Lesclarcissement;* borrowed from Middle French *relater* refer, report, learned borrowing from Latin *relātus,* a form serving as the past participle of *referre* to tell of, to refer; for suffix see -ATE[1].

The meaning of have reference to is first recorded in Shakespeare's *Troylus and Cressida* (1606), and that of be connected to, in 1646.

—relation *n.* About 1378 *relacion* connection, association, correspondence, in a version of *Piers Plowman;* borrowed through Anglo-French *relacioun,* Old French *relacïon,* learned borrowing from Latin *relātiōnem* (nominative *relātiō*) a bringing back, restoring, a report, narration, association, reference, from *relāt-,* serving as the past participle stem of *referre* refer; for suffix see -TION. The meaning of a person related to one by blood or marriage, relative, is first recorded in Henry VII's *Letters* (1502). **—relationship** *n.* Before 1744, condition of being related, in Pope's *The Dunciad;* formed from English *relation* + *-ship.*

relative *n.* 1387 *relative* word that refers to an antecedent, in a version of *Piers Plowman;* later, person or thing that stands in a relation to another (probably before 1430); borrowed through Old French *relatif* (feminine *relative*), and directly from Late Latin *relātīvus* having reference or relation, from Latin *relātus,* a form serving as the past participle of *referre* to refer; for suffix see -IVE. The meaning of a person who belongs to the same family as another is first recorded in 1657. **—adj.** Probably before 1425, having reference; borrowed through Middle French *relatif* (feminine *relative*), and directly from Late Latin *relātīvus,* adj. and n. The sense of related or compared to each other is first recorded in 1594. **—relativity** *n.* Before 1834, condition of being relative, Coleridge in *Literary Remains;* probably borrowed from French *relativité,* from *relatif* (feminine *relative*) relative, adj.; for suffix see -ITY. The use of *relativity* in physics became current after 1905 when Einstein introduced his special theory of relativity, which dealt with the constancy of the speed of light and postulated the equivalence of mass and energy.

relax *v.* Before 1398 *relaxen* loosen, ease, in Trevisa's translation of Bartholomew's *De Proprietatibus Rerum;* borrowed from Old French *relaxer,* and directly from Latin *relaxāre* relax, loosen, open (*re-* back + *laxāre* loosen, from *laxus* loose, LAX[1]). Doublet of RELEASE. The sense of decrease tension is first recorded probably before 1425, and that of make less strict or severe, in 1662. **—relaxation** *n.* 1392 *relaxacioun* a rupture of some bodily part; later, reduction of a penalty (probably about 1425); borrowed through Old French *relaxacïon,* and directly from Latin *relaxātiōnem* (nominative *relaxātiō*), from *relaxāre* relax; for suffix see -ATION. The sense of relief from work, recreation is first recorded in 1548.

relay *n.* 1369 *relay* hounds placed along a line of chase in Chaucer's *Book of the Duchesse;* borrowed from Middle French *relai* reserve pack of hounds or other animals, from Old French *relaier* to exchange tired animals for fresh, leave behind (*re-* back + *laier* to leave; see DELAY). The meaning of an electromagnetic device with a weak current which acts as a switch for a circuit with a stronger current is first recorded in

1860. **—v.** Probably before 1400 *relayen* take a fresh horse, change horses, in *Morte Arthur;* borrowed from Middle French *relaier* to relay, leave behind. The meaning of provide or replace with a fresh supply, specifically of hunting hounds, is first recorded about 1410. The meaning of pass on or retransmit by electrical relays is found in 1878 used in reference to passing on (a message or information, especially by telegraph). **—relay race** race in which each contestant covers part of the distance and is then replaced (1898).

release *v.* About 1300 *relesen* revoke, relieve, surrender, discharge; borrowed from Old French *relaissier* relinquish, quit, let go, variant of *relacher* release, relax, from Latin *relaxāre* to RELAX. The meaning of set free, let go, is first recorded in Middle English about 1350, possibly developed as a weakened sense from earlier free from pain (about 1300). The spelling *release* is first recorded in 1464. **—n.** Before 1325 *reles* relief, surrender, discharge; borrowed from Old French *reles, relais,* n., from *relaissier* to release. The meaning of a setting free as from punishment is first recorded before 1376, and release from obligation, before 1387. A special sense of material released for publication is first recorded in 1907, in American English.

relegate *v.* Before 1420 *relegat,* past participle of *relegaten* to banish, send into exile, in Lydgate's *Troy Book;* borrowed from Latin *relēgātus,* past participle of *relēgāre* remove, dismiss, banish (*re-* back + *lēgāre* send with a commission; see LEGATE); for suffix see -ATE[1]. The extended meaning of send away or consign to another, especially to a lower, position, is first recorded in Burke's *Reflections on the Revolution in France* (1790). **—relegation** *n.* Before 1420, the action of banishing, in Lydgate's *Troy Book;* borrowed from Middle French *relégation,* and directly from Latin *relēgātiōnem* (nominative *relēgātiō*), from *relēgāre* remove; for suffix see -ATION. The extended meaning of a sending away or consignment to a place is first recorded in Southey's *Works* (1829, perhaps after Burke's use of the verb).

relent *v.* become less harsh. 1392 *relenten* to melt, soften, dissolve; perhaps formed in English from *re-* intensive + Latin *lentus* slow, supple; see LITHE. The transferred meaning of soften in temper, become less harsh or cruel, is first recorded in 1526. **—relentless** *adj.* harsh, without pity. 1592, formed from English *relent* + *-less.*

relevant *adj.* 1560, bearing upon, connected with, pertaining to (the matter at hand); borrowed from Medieval Latin *relevantem* (nominative *relevans*), from present participle of Latin *relevāre* to lessen, lighten, RELIEVE; for suffix see -ANT. *Relevant* and its related words did not come into general English use until after 1800, but *relevant* and *relevancy* did have earlier currency as Scottish legal terms referring to legal relevance or sufficiency. **—relevance** *n.* 1733, quality or condition of being relevant, formed from English *relevant* + *-ance,* or as a back formation from *relevancy.* **—relevancy** *n.* 1561, formed in English as if from Latin **relevantia* + English suffix *-cy.*

reliable *adj.* 1569 (Scottish) *raliabill;* later *reliable* trustworthy, safe, sure (1624); formed from English *rely* + *-able.* Before 1850 *reliable* was not in common use and thereafter was for some time considered a barbarism of American invention, though it occurs in the writings of Coleridge, Gladstone, and Trevelyan.

reliance *n.* trust or dependence. 1607, in Shakespeare's *Timon of Athens;* formed from English *rely* + *-ance.* **—reliant** *adj.* 1856, formed from English *rely* + *-ant.*

relic *n.* thing, custom, etc., that remains from the past. Probably before 1200 *relik* object, especially body part, belonging to a holy person, kept as a sacred memorial, in *Ancrene Riwle;* borrowed from Old French *relique,* from Late Latin *reliquiae,* pl., remains of a martyr, from Latin, remains or remnants, from *reliquus* remaining (*re-* back + root of *linquere* to leave; see LOAN). The plural *relics* in the sense of remains, ruins, is first recorded in Middle English about 1340, but is found in its religious reference in Old English *reliquias,* as a direct borrowing from Latin. The meaning of a trace of a past practice, fact, etc., is found before 1586, and that of an object having interest because of its age or association with the past, in 1596.

relict (rel'ikt) *n.* **1** widow. About 1460 *relicte,* borrowed from Medieval Latin *relicta* widow, noun use of feminine past participle of Latin *relinquere* to leave behind; see RELINQUISH. **2** Usually **relicts** *pl.* a surviving specimen or artifact of an earlier time. 1905, developed from the general sense of remains, remnants (1598); borrowed from Middle French *relict,* from Latin *relictus* that which is left behind, from masculine past participle of *relinquere* to leave behind.

relief[1] *n.* ease or alleviation. Before 1338 *releve* payment made to an overlord on taking possession of an estate, in Mannyng's *Chronicle of England;* borrowed from Anglo-French *relif,* from Old French *relief, relef* assistance, from *relever* to RELIEVE; or borrowed from Medieval Latin *relevium,* from past participle of Latin *relevāre* raise, lighten, RELIEVE. The spelling *relief* in English first began to appear about 1390. The meaning of ease or alleviation through the lessening of a burden, pain, etc., is first recorded probably about 1375, and that of aid or help given to poor people, about 1400, though the sense of a charitable donation is first recorded perhaps before 1200, certainly by about 1395.

relief[2] *n.* projection of a figure or design from a surface. 1606 *releve,* in Ben Jonson's *Hymenaei;* later *relief* (1662); borrowed through French *relief,* or directly from Italian *rilievo,* from *rilevare* to raise, from Latin *relevāre* to raise, lighten, RELIEVE.

relieve *v.* About 1370 *releeven* to raise out of trouble, ease, assist; borrowed from Old French *relever,* from Latin *relevāre* to raise, lift up, lighten, alleviate, mitigate (*re-* intensive + *levāre* to lift up, make light, free, from *levis* LIGHT[2] not heavy). The spelling *relieve* begins to appear before 1393. The meaning of release from a post or duty is first recorded in 1416, in the sense of release from duty as a juror.

religion *n.* Probably before 1200 *religiun* a religious order, community of monks or nuns, in *Ancrene Riwle;* borrowed from Old French *religion* religious community, learned borrowing from Latin, and borrowed directly from Latin *religiōnem* (nominative *religiō*) respect for what is sacred, probably with the original meaning of care (for worship and traditions); for suffix see -ION. The derivation of the Latin was in dispute even among ancient writers: Cicero derived it from *relegere* go through, or read again (*re-* again + *legere* read; see LEGEND) with later comparison of *religēns* revering the gods, pious, to *necligēns* negligent. If Cicero's derivation from *relegere* is correct, there is still little doubt that in popular etymology there existed a strong connection with the sense of binding obligation found in *religāre,* as attested among the Latin writers, such as Augustine; while Servius and Augustine derived Latin *religiōnem* (nominative *religiō*) from *religāre* to bind fast, in the sense of place an obligation on; see RELY. The spelling *religion* is first recorded about 1300.

The meaning of a particular system of faith and worship is first recorded before 1325, in *Cursor Mundi,* though reference to the Jewish ritual is found about 1275. The general sense of a belief in a divine power to be worshiped is also probably found in *Cursor Mundi.*

—religious *adj.* Probably before 1200, devout, pious, in *Ancrene Riwle;* borrowed from Old French *religious, religieus,* learned borrowing from Latin, and borrowed directly from Latin *religiōsus,* from *religiō* religion; for suffix see -OUS. —*n.* Probably before 1200, person bound by a religious vow, in *Ancrene Riwle;* borrowed from Old French *religious, religieus,* and directly from Latin *religiōsus* religious, adj.

The transferred sense of very careful, scrupulous, is first recorded in 1599.

—religiosity *n.* religious feeling or sentiment. 1382 *religiosite,* in the Wycliffe Bible; borrowed from Latin *religiōsitās* religiousness, from *religiōsus* religious; for suffix see -ITY.

relinquish *v.* 1454 *relinquisshen* to desert, abandon; borrowed from Middle French *relinquiss-,* extended stem of *relinquir,* from Latin *relinquere* leave behind, forsake, abandon, give up (*re-* back + *linquere* to leave; see LOAN); for suffix see -ISH². The sense of give up (an idea, etc.), desist from, is first recorded in 1497, and that of renounce or surrender (a right, etc.), in 1560.

reliquary (rel′əkwer′ē) *n.* container for a relic. 1656, in Blount's *Glossographia;* borrowed from French *reliquaire,* from Old French *relique* RELIC; for suffix see -ARY.

relish *n.* 1530, taste, flavor, in Palsgrave's *Lesclarcissement;* alteration of earlier (about 1320) *reles* scent, taste, aftertaste (probably before 1300); borrowed from Old French *reles* something remaining, RELEASE. The meaning of pleasure, enjoyment, zest is first recorded in 1649, and that of pleasant taste in 1665. The sense of something that adds flavor to food, savory, condiment, is not recorded before 1798. **—v.** 1586, give flavor to; from the noun. The meaning of care for or be pleased with, like, is first recorded in 1594, and that of enjoy, take pleasure in, in Shakespeare's *King Lear* (1605).

reluctance *n.* 1641, the act of struggling, resistance, opposition; probably formed from obsolete English *reluct* to struggle, strive, or rebel against (1526), from Latin *reluctārī* to struggle against (*re-* against, opposite + *luctārī* to struggle; see LOCK² tress of hair) + English *-ance.* The meaning of unwillingness or disinclination is first recorded in 1667. It is also possible that *reluctance* is in some instances a back formation from earlier *reluctancy* (1621, probably formed from English *reluct* + *-ancy*). **—reluctant** *adj.* 1667, struggling, in Milton's *Paradise Lost;* probably formed in English as an adjective to earlier *reluctance* or *reluctancy,* probably on the model of, if not in some instances borrowed from, Latin *reluctantem* (nominative *reluctāns*), present participle of *reluctārī* to struggle against; for suffix see -ANT. The extended meaning of unwilling, averse, disinclined, is first recorded in 1706.

rely *v.* Before 1338 *relien* to gather, assemble, rally, in Mannyng's *Chronicle of England;* borrowed from Old French *relier* fasten, attach, rally, bind together, oblige, from Latin *religāre* fasten, bind fast (*re-* intensive + *ligāre* to bind; see LIGAMENT). The meaning of put trust or confidence in a person or thing, depend, trust, is first recorded in 1574.

rem *n.* unit for measuring absorbed doses of radiation, equivalent to 1 roentgen of X rays or gamma rays. 1947, acronym formed from the initial letters of *r(oentgen) e(quivalent) m(an).*

REM *n.* rapid eye movement (associated with dreaming during sleep). 1957, acronym formed from the initial letters of *r(apid) e(ye) m(ovement).*

remain *v.* Before 1425 *remainen* to be left; borrowed from Old French *remain-,* stressed stem (as in *remainent* they remain) of *remanoir, remainer,* from Latin *remanēre* remain (*re-* back + *manēre* to stay, remain; see MANSION). **—n. remains** *pl.* what is left. 1456, remaining members of a group; possibly from the verb in English + *-s*¹ plural ending, probably influenced by Middle French *remain,* from Old French *remainer* to remain. It is also probable that *remain,* n. was in part influenced by earlier *remainder,* especially as *remainder* is the usual noun form in English, except in the plural *remains* and in the singular in the sense of a material relic of antiquity, an ancient building or other structure. The meaning of what is left, remaining parts, is first recorded in 1500-20, in Dunbar's *Poems.* The specific sense of a dead body, corpse, is not recorded before 1700. **—remainder** *n.* 1394, (in law) future estate to take effect after another has ended; borrowed from Anglo-French *remainder,* noun use of Old French *remaindre* to remain; for suffix see -ER³. The meaning of the part left over, the rest, is first recorded before 1547.

remand *v.* 1439 *remaunden* to send back, return; borrowed from Middle French *remander,* learned borrowing from Late Latin *remandāre* to send back word, repeat a command (Latin *re-* back + *mandāre* to consign, order, MANDATE). The meaning of send (a prisoner) back into custody is first recorded in 1643.**—n.** a remanding. 1771, from the verb.

remark *v.* 1633, to mark out or distinguish; also *remarque* (1675); in most instances re-formed in English from *re-* + *mark,* v. after borrowing of French *remarquer* to mark, note, heed, from Middle French (*re-* intensive form + *marquer* to mark, probably from a Germanic source; compare Old High German *marchōn, markōn* to delimit, MARK¹). The meaning of notice, observe, is first recorded in 1675, and that of make an observation, comment, is found in Locke's writings, before 1704. **—n.** a comment. 1654 *remarque* noteworthiness; later, remark (1663); re-formed like the verb from English *re-* + *mark,* n. as a borrowing of French *remarque,* from *remarquer* to remark. The meaning of observation, comment, is first recorded in 1673. It is quite possible that instances of *remarque* in English show only individual borrowings, and that the spelling *remark* was already standard in English as shown in the early spelling of *remarkable* in Cawdrey's dictionary. **—remarkable** *adj.* worthy of comment or notice, noteworthy. 1604, in Cawdrey's *A Table Alphabeticall;* re-formed in English from *re-* + *mark* + *-able* after borrowing of French *remarquable,* from *remarquer* to remark + *-able* -able.

remedy *n.* Probably before 1200 *remedie* way of avoid

ing vice or temptation, in *Ancrene Riwle;* later, cure, relief (about 1340); borrowed through Anglo-French *remedie,* Old French *remede,* learned borrowing from Latin, and borrowed directly from Latin *remedium* a cure, remedy (*re-* intensive + *mederī* to heal; see MEDICAL); for suffix see -Y[3]. **—v.** to cure. Probably about 1400 *remedien;* borrowed from Middle French *remedier,* from Latin *remediāre* to cure, remedy, from *remedium* remedy, n. **—remedial** *adj.* 1651, curing or relieving; borrowed from Late Latin *remediālis* healing, curing, from Latin *remedium* remedy; for suffix see -AL[1]. The meaning of intended to improve study habits and skills is first recorded in 1924.

remember *v.* Before 1338 *remembren,* in Mannyng's *Chronicle of England;* borrowed from Old French *remembrer,* from Latin *rememorārī* recall to mind, remember (*re-* again + *memorārī* be mindful of, from *memor* mindful; see MEMORY). **—remembrance** *n.* Probably before 1300 *remembraunce,* in *Arthour and Merlin;* borrowed from Old French *remembraunce,* from *remembrer* remember; for suffix see -ANCE.

remind *v.* 1645, to recall to mind, remember; formed from English *re-* again + *mind,* v. The meaning of put in mind of something, cause to remember, is first recorded in 1660. **—reminder** *n.* something to help one remember. 1653, formed from English *remind* + *-er*[1].

reminiscence *n.* 1589, act or process of remembering, in Puttenham's *The Art of English Poesie;* borrowed through Middle French *reminiscence,* or directly from Latin *reminīscentia* remembrance, from *reminīscentem* (nominative *reminīscēns*), present participle of *reminīscī* remember, recall to mind (*re-* again + *-minīscī,* from the root of *mēns* MIND); for suffix see -ENCE. **—reminiscent** *adj.* 1705, relating to or characterized by reminiscence; probably formed in English as an adjective to *reminiscence,* after Latin *reminīscentem,* present participle of *reminīscī* remember; for suffix see -ENT. The sense of bringing to mind something else, suggestive, is first recorded in 1880. **—reminisce** *v.* 1829, to remember; later, indulge in reminiscence (1882); back formation from *reminiscence.*

remiss *adj.* careless, neglectful. Probably before 1425 *remisse* weak, loose, slack, in a translation of Chauliac's *Grande Chirurgie;* borrowed from Latin *remissus,* past participle of *remittere* slacken, let go; see REMIT. The meaning of careless, negligent, lazy, is first recorded about 1450, in the spelling *remiss.*

remission *n.* Probably before 1200 *remissiun* forgiveness, in *Ancrene Riwle;* later, a lowering or decrease of intensity, force, etc. (before 1398); borrowed from Old French *remission,* from Latin *remissiōnem* (nominative *remissiō*) relaxation, a sending back, from *remiss-,* past participle stem of *remittere* send back, slacken, let go; see REMIT; for suffix see -SION. The sense of a temporary abatement of disease is first recorded probably before 1425, in Chauliac's *Grande Chirurgie.*

remit *v.* send money to a person or place. 1393-94 *remitten* forgive, give up, in *Rolls of Parliament;* later, refer (probably before 1400), and to send, send back (1414); borrowed from Latin *remittere* send back, slacken, let go (*re-* back + *mittere* to send; see MISSION). The meaning of send money to a person or place is first recorded in 1640. **—remittance** *n.* 1705, in Addison's *Remarks on Italy;* formed from English *remit* + *-ance.*

remittent *adj.* lessening for a time or at intervals. 1693, borrowed from Latin *remittentem* (nominative *remittēns*), present participle of *remittere* send back, slacken, let go; see REMIT; for suffix see -ENT.

remnant *n.* fragment, part remaining. Before 1375 *remnant,* contraction of earlier *remanant* (probably before 1300); borrowed from Old French *remanant,* present participle of *remanoir, remaindre* to REMAIN; for suffix see -ANT.

remonstrate (rimon′strāt) *v.* say in protest, object. 1599, demonstrate, show, in Ben Jonson's *Cynthia's Revels;* probably a back formation from *remonstration;* for suffix see -ATE[1]. The sense of say in protest, object, is first recorded in 1695. **—remonstrance** *n.* protest. About 1477, an appeal, request, in Caxton's translation of *The History of Jason;* borrowed from Middle French *remonstrance* to show, from Medieval Latin *remonstrantia,* from *remonstrans,* present participle of *remonstrare* point out, show (from Latin *re-* intensive + *mōnstrāre* to show, from *mōnstrum* evil omen, MONSTER); for suffix see -ANCE. The sense of an act of remonstrating, protest, is first recorded in 1603. **—remonstrant** *adj.* protesting. 1641, in Milton's *Animadversions;* borrowed from Medieval Latin *remonstrantem* (nominative *remonstrans*) a showing, present participle of *remonstrare;* for suffix see -ANT. **—remonstration** *n.* About 1489, borrowed through Middle French *remonstration,* from Medieval Latin *remonstrationem* (nominative *remonstratio*), from *remonstrare* point out, show; for suffix see -ATION.

remorse *n.* About 1385 *remors* feeling of deep regret for a sin or wrong, in Chaucer's *Troilus and Criseyde;* borrowed from Old French *remors,* learned borrowing from Medieval Latin *remorsum,* from neuter past participle of Latin *remordēre* to vex, disturb (*re-* again + *mordēre* to bite, of uncertain origin). **—remorseful** *adj.* 1591, compassionate, full of pity, in Shakespeare's *The Two Gentlemen of Verona;* formed from English *remorse* + *-ful.*

remote *adj.* About 1440, distant; borrowed from Middle French *remot* (feminine *remote*), or directly from Latin *remōtus,* past participle of *removēre* move back or away, REMOVE. **—remote control** (1904)

remove *v.* Probably before 1325 *removen* to move, take away, dismiss; borrowed from Old French *remouvoir,* from Latin *removēre* move back or away (*re-* back, away + *movēre* to MOVE). **—n.** 1553, act of removing; from the verb. The meaning of distance is first recorded in 1628. **—removal** *n.* 1597, formed from English *remove,* v. + *-al*[2].

remunerate *v.* to pay for work, services, trouble, etc. 1523, back formation from *remuneration,* perhaps influenced by Latin *remūnerātus,* past participle of *remūnerārī* to reward (*re-* back + *mūnerārī* to give); for suffix see -ATE[1]. Latin *mūnerārī* is derived from *mūnus* (genitive *mūneris*) gift, office, duty; see MEAN[2] inferior. **—remuneration** *n.* About 1400 *remuneracion* reward, recompense, payment; borrowed through Middle French *rémunération,* and directly from Latin *remūnerātiōnem* (nominative *remūnerātiō*), from *remūnerārī* to reward; for suffix see -ATION.

renaissance (ren′əsäns) *n.* 1872, a new birth or revival, especially in art, literature, or learning, in John Morley's *Voltaire;* earlier, in reference to the great revival of art and learning in Europe beginning in the 1300's, and specifically to the style of art and architecture developed in the period 1300-1500 (1840, in Thomas A.

Trollope's *A Summer in Brittany*), and in the spelling *Renaissance* (1845, in a travel book on Spain; 1851, in Ruskin's *The Stones of Venice*); borrowing of French *renaissance,* from Old French *renaissance* rebirth, from *renaître* be born again, from Vulgar Latin **renāscere,* from Latin *renāscī* be born again; see RENASCENT; for suffix see -ANCE. **—Renaissance man** (1906, humanist of the Renaissance, devoted to culture and the study of the classics; later, revived in the 1960's in the new sense of one who is knowledgeable in a wide variety of the arts and sciences, or, more loosely, interested or involved in many pursuits).

renal *adj.* of or pertaining to the kidneys. 1656, in Blount's *Glossographia;* borrowed through French *rénal,* and directly from Late Latin *rēnālis* of or belonging to the kidneys, from Latin *rēnēs* kidneys, of uncertain origin; for suffix see -AL[1].

renascent (rinā′sənt) *adj.* being born again, reviving. 1727, in Bailey's *Dictionary;* borrowed from Latin *renāscentem* (nominative *renāscēns*), present participle of *renāscī* be born again (*re-* again + *nāscī* be born; see NATIVE); for suffix see -ENT. **—renascence** *n.* rebirth, revival. 1727, formed from English *renascent* + *-ence.* The term was used in reference to, and as a variant of *Renaissance,* as early as 1869, in Matthew Arnold's *Culture and Anarchy.*

rend *v.* pull apart violently, split. Probably before 1200 *renden,* in Layamon's *Chronicle of Britain* and *Ancrene Riwle;* developed from Old English (about 950) *rendon* (from Proto-Germanic **randijanan*); cognate with Old Frisian *renda* to tear, Middle Low German *rende* broken things, and Old High German *rinda, rinta,* bark (modern German *Rinde* bark, crust). Related to RIND.

render *v.* Before 1376 *rendren* say over, recite, in *Piers Plowman;* later, hand over, deliver (probably before 1400); borrowed from Old French *rendre* give back, present, deliver, yield, from Vulgar Latin **rendere,* alteration (on the analogy of *prēndere* take hold of, grasp, contraction of *prehendere;* see PREHENSILE) of Latin *reddere* give back, return, restore, hand over (*red-,* variant of *re-* back + *-dere,* combining form of *dare* to give; see DATE[1] time). Retention in English of the infinitive ending *-er* from the French *-re* may be a deliberate form of differentiation from the earlier but unrelated verb *rend,* though there are several such verbs in English (*tender, reconnoiter, remainder, remember*), which leaves the problem unsolved.

A number of related meanings are first recorded in English in close sequence: cause to be or become, make (as in *The testimony was rendered invalid,* 1560); give (obedience), pay (honor), show (attention) (as in *render someone a service,* 1588); show or produce (artistically), reproduce, perform (as in *render a subject faithfully, render a difficult musical passage,* 1599, in Shakespeare's *Henry V*). Two much earlier, but still common, uses include that of translate, (as in *render a Latin word into English,* before 1376, in *Piers Plowman*), and melt (fat, etc.), clarify or extract by melting (before 1325), the latter of which may be the earliest use of this verb in English.

rendezvous (rän′dēvü) *n.* appointment to meet at a fixed place. 1591 *rendevous* place appointed for the assembling of troops; also, appointed meeting place (1594), and a meeting or appointment at a fixed place (1600); borrowed from Middle French *rendez-vous,* noun use of the phrase *rendez vous* present yourselves (*rendez,* second person plural present imperative of *rendre* present, from Old French; RENDER + *vous* you, from Latin *vōs* you, plural. The French spelling with *z* did not become the established form in English until the 1700's. **—v.** meet at a rendezvous. About 1645, from the noun.

rendition *n.* act of rendering. 1601, surrender of a place, possession, etc., Queen Elizabeth I quoted in Fynes Moryson's *An Itinerary* (1617); borrowed from obsolete French *rendition,* from Old French *rendre* to deliver or yield; see RENDER; for suffix see -TION. The meaning of a rendering in another language, translation, is first recorded in 1659. The sense of an act of giving out (a verdict or judgment) is first recorded in 1802, and that of a performance (of a dramatic or musical piece) in 1877; both of these latter senses first appeared in American English.

renegade *n.* deserter from a religious faith, political party, etc. 1583, probably borrowed from Spanish *renegado,* and replacing Middle English *renegat* (about 1390, in Chaucer's *Canterbury Tales*), *renegate* (about 1400); both the Middle English and Spanish forms borrowed from Medieval Latin *renegatus,* past participle of *renegare* to deny; see RENEGE; for suffix see -ADE.

renege (rinig′) *v.* 1548, deny, renounce, abandon, in Udall's translation of Erasmus' *Upon the New Testament;* borrowed from Medieval Latin *renegare* (Latin *re-* intensive form + *negāre* deny, NEGATE). Early forms of this word included *reneague, reneage,* and *renegue;* the latter form is still current in British use. The technical sense in cardplaying of refuse or fail to follow suit is first found in 1680. The informal sense of change one's mind, back out, is found in 1784, chiefly in American English.

renew *v.* Before 1382 *renewen* make like new, revive, restore, in the Wycliffe Bible; formed from Middle English *re-* again + *newen* resume, revive, renew, from *new* NEW. **—renewal** *n.* 1681-86, formed from English *renew* + *-al*[2].

rennet (ren′it) *n.* substance in an animal's stomach used to curdle milk. About 1450 *rennet* (originally a Kentish word; compare dialectal *runnet*); developed probably from Old English **rynet.* Middle English *rennet,* n. is related to **rennen* to coagulate or curdle, found in Old English *gerennan,* literally, cause to run together, because rennet makes milk run or curdle; cognate with Old Frisian *renna* coagulate, Old Saxon *rennian,* Old High German *rennen,* Old Icelandic *renna,* and Gothic *urrannjan* coagulate, from Proto-Germanic **rannjanan,* causative to **renwanan* RUN, v.

rennin *n.* enzyme in the gastric juice that curdles milk. 1897, in Thomas C. Allbutt's *A System of Medicine,* formed from English *rennet* + *-in*[2], chemical suffix.

renounce *v.* About 1380 *renouncen* give up, resign, in Chaucer's translation of Boethius' *De Consolatione Philosophiae;* borrowed from Old French *renoncer,* learned borrowing from Latin *renūntiāre* proclaim, protest against, renounce (*re-* opposite, against + *nūntiāre* to report, announce, from *nūntius* messenger, of uncertain origin).

renovate *v.* 1535, to renew, resume, either a back formation from the earlier *renovation,* or, more likely from the Middle English participial adjective *renovate* renewed (probably 1440); borrowed from Latin *renovātus,* past participle of *renovāre* renew, restore (*re-* again + *novāre* make new, from *novus* NEW); for suffix see -ATE[1].

The meaning of restore to good condition, repair, is first recorded before 1552.

—renovation *n.* act of renovating. Before 1400 *renovacyoun* spiritual rebirth, regeneration, borrowed through Middle French *renovation,* or directly from Latin *renovātiōnem* (nominative *renovātiō*), from *renovāre* renovate; for suffix see -ATION. The sense of rebuilding, reconstruction, appeared in Middle English probably before 1425, in a translation of Higden's *Polychronicon.*

renown *n.* Probably before 1300 *renoun* fame, in *Sir Tristrem;* borrowed through Anglo-French *renoun,* Old French *renon, renom,* from *renomer* make famous (*re-* repeatedly + *nomer* to name, from Latin *nōmināre;* see NOMINATE). **—renowned** *adj.* Probably before 1400 *renouned* celebrated, famous, in *Morte Arthur;* formed from *renoun* renown + *-ed*[2].

rent[1] *n.* payment for the use of property. 1137 *rente* source of income, revenue, in *Peterborough Chronicle;* borrowed from Old French *rente,* from Vulgar Latin **rendita,* from feminine past participle of *rendere* to RENDER. The sense of a payment made periodically by a tenant to a landlord, rent, is first recorded in Middle English about 1330. **—v.** Before 1376 *renten* provide with revenues, in *Piers Plowman;* from the noun. The meaning of rent out is found about 1447, and that of pay rent for is recorded in Palsgrave's *Lesclarcissement* (1530). **—rental** *n.* amount received or paid as rent. Before 1376, in *Piers Plowman,* record of the rents due; borrowed from Anglo-French *rental* register of income (1279) and Medieval Latin *rentale* rent book, both from Old French and Middle English *rente,* n.; for suffix see AL[2]. The meaning of an amount owed as rent appeared probably before 1461. The meaning in American English of something rented (as in *few rentals are available*) is first found in 1952.

rent[2] *n.* torn place. 1535, in the Coverdale Bible, noun use of earlier Middle English *renten* to tear, rend (before 1325), variant of *renden* to REND. The variant with *-t-* was influenced by *rent* (before 1420), past tense and past participle of *rend.* **—adj.** torn, split. Before 1420, from the past participle of *rend,* v.

renunciation *n.* act of renouncing. 1399, borrowed from Latin *renūntiātiōnem* (nominative *renūntiātiō*), from *renūntiāre* RENOUNCE; for suffix see -ATION.

reovirus (rē′ōvī′rəs) *n.* type of virus associated with respiratory and intestinal infections. 1959, acronym formed from *r(espiratory) e(nteric) o(rphan) virus;* called "orphan virus" because it is not known to cause any of the diseases it is associated with. Compare ECHOVIRUS.

rep *n. Informal.* repertory (company or theater). 1925, American English, shortened form of *repertory* or *repertoire.*

repair[1] *v.* put in good condition. Probably before 1350 *reparen* to restore; later *repairen* (probably before 1425, in a translation of Higden's *Polychronicon*); borrowed from Old French *reparer,* learned borrowing from Latin *reparāre* repair, restore, renew (*re-* again + *parāre* make ready, prepare; see PARE). **—n.** act or work of repairing. Probably before 1400, from the verb. **—repairable** *adj.* 1489, in Caxton's *Faytes of Armes,* formed from Middle English *repairen* repair + *-able.* **—repairman** *n.* (1871)

repair[2] *v.* go to a place. Probably before 1300 *repairen,* in *Sir Tristrem;* borrowed from Old French *repairer,* earlier *repairier,* from Late Latin *repatriāre* return to one's own country. Doublet of REPATRIATE.

reparable *adj.* capable of being repaired, repairable. 1570, borrowed from Middle French *reparable,* learned borrowing from Latin *reparābilis* able to be restored, from *reparāre* restore, REPAIR[1]; for suffix see -ABLE.

reparation *n.* compensation for wrong or injury done. About 1380 *reparacion* compensation, amends, recompense, in Chaucer's *House of Fame;* borrowed from Old French *reparacion,* learned borrowing from Late Latin, and borrowed directly from Late Latin *reparātiōnem* (nominative *reparātiō*) act of repairing, restoration, from Latin *reparāre* restore, REPAIR[1]; for suffix see -ATION.

repartee (rep′ərtē′) *n.* witty reply or replies. About 1645, borrowed from French *repartie,* noun use of the feminine past participle of Old French *repartir* to reply promptly, start out again (*re-* back, again + *partir* to PART).

repast (ripast′ *or* rē′past) *n.* meal, food. Before 1382, rest or repose, in the Wycliffe Bible; also, a meal (probably before 1387, in a version of *Piers Plowman*); borrowed from Old French *repast* a meal, from Late Latin *repāstus,* n., meal, from past participle stem of *repāscere* feed in turn (Latin *re-* repeatedly + *pāscere* to graze; see FOOD).

repatriate *v.* send back or go back to one's own country. 1611, in Cotgrave's *Dictionary;* borrowed from Late Latin *repatriātus,* past participle of *repatriāre* return to one's own country (Latin *re-* back + *patria* native land); see PATRIOT; for suffix see -ATE[1]. Doublet of REPAIR[2]. **—repatriation** *n.* 1592, borrowed from Medieval Latin *repatriationem* (nominative *repatriatio*), from Late Latin *repatriāre* repatriate; for suffix see -ATION.

repeal *v.* About 1385 *repealen* to do away with, revoke, recall, in Chaucer's *Troilus and Criseyde;* but generally found in the spelling *repelen;* borrowed from Anglo-French *repeler,* alteration of Old French *rapeler* call back, revoke, repeal (*re-* back + *apeler* to call, APPEAL). **—n.** 1483, a recall, summoning; borrowed from Anglo-French *repel,* from the verb in Anglo-French and Old French. The meaning of act of repealing is first recorded in 1503-04.

repeat *v.* Before 1382 *repeten* return, turn again, in the Wycliffe Bible; later, say again, reiterate (1427, in *Rolls of Parliament*); borrowed from Old French *repeter* say or do again, get back, demand the return of, learned borrowing of Latin *repetere* do or say again, attack again (*re-* again + *petere* go toward, seek, demand, attack; see FEATHER). The spelling with *ea* first began to appear in the very late 1500's. The meaning of do again is first recorded in English in 1560. **—n.** About 1450, repeated words, refrain; from the verb. The meaning of act of repeating, repetition, is first recorded in 1556. **—repeatedly** *adv.* again and again, frequently. Before 1718, formed from English *repeated,* adj. (1611, in Shakespeare) + *-ly*[1].

repel *v.* Probably about 1421 *repellen* drive away, repulse, in Lydgate's *Siege of Thebes;* also, drive or force back, repulse (probably before 1425); borrowed through Old French *repeller,* or directly from Latin *repellere* to drive back (*re-* back + *pellere* to drive, strike; see PULSE[1] beat). **—repellent** *adj.* 1643, (of medicine) serving to reduce tumors; borrowed from Latin *repellentem* (nominative *repellēns*), present participle of *repellere* repel. The meaning of repelling, distasteful, disagreeable, is first recorded in English in 1797. —*n.* anything that repels. 1661, medicine that reduces tumors; from the adjective. The meaning of repelling power or influence is first recorded in 1802, and that of a substance that repels insects, in 1908.

repent *v.* Probably before 1300, to regret, be sorry, in *Kyng Alisaunder;* also, feel sorrow or regret for sin (about 1300); borrowed from Old French *repentir* (*re-* intensive form + Vulgar Latin **paenitīre* to regret, from Latin *paenitēre* make sorry; see PENITENCE). **—repentance** *n.* About 1300 *repentaunce* act of repenting, contrition; probably formed in English as a noun to *repentant* and the model of (and in some instances probably borrowed directly from) Old French *repentaunce,* from *repentant,* present participle of *repentir* repent; for suffix see -ANCE. **—repentant** *adj.* repenting, penitent. About 1230, in *Ancrene Riwle;* borrowed from Old French *repentant,* past participle of *repentir* repent; for suffix see -ANT.

repercussion *n.* indirect influence or reaction from an event. Probably before 1425 *repercussioun* act of driving back, in a translation of Chauliac's *Grande Chirurgie;* borrowed from Middle French *répercussion,* from Latin *repercussiōnem* (nominative *repercussiō*), from *repercuss-,* past participle stem of *repercutere* to strike or beat back (*re-* back, again + *percutere* to strike or thrust through; see PERCUSSION); for suffix see -ION. The extended meaning of a return of a sound, reverberation, echo, is first recorded in 1595, and that of a blow or stroke given in return, in 1603. The figurative sense of an influence or reaction from an event, especially one that is indirect, is probably not recorded before the early 1600's.

repertoire (rep′ərtwär) *n.* the list of plays, ballets, operas, parts, pieces, etc., that a company, actor, musician, or singer is prepared to perform. 1847, borrowing of French *répertoire,* learned borrowing from Late Latin *repertōrium* inventory. Doublet of REPERTORY.

repertory (rep′ərtôr′ē) *n.* repertoire. 1552, index or list, catalogue; borrowed from Late Latin *repertōrium* inventory, list, from Latin *repertus,* past participle of *reperīre* to find, get, invent (*re-* intensive form + *parere* produce, bring forth; see PARENT); for suffix see -ORY. Doublet of REPERTOIRE. The meaning of a list of performances an actor, musician, etc., is prepared to make, repertoire, is first recorded in 1845. **—repertory company** (1909, in G.B. Shaw's letters)

repetition *n.* act of repeating. Probably before 1425 *repeticioun,* borrowed from Middle French *répétition,* learned borrowing from Latin, and directly borrowed from Latin *repetītiōnem* (nominative *repetītiō*), from *repetere* do or say again, REPEAT; for suffix see -TION. **—repetitious** *adj.* characterized by repetition; tiresome. 1675, in William Penn's writings; borrowed from Latin *repetītus,* past participle of *repetere* repeat. **—repetitive** *adj.* repetitious. 1839, formed from English *repetition* + *-ive.*

repine *v.* be discontented. 1449, to grieve; probably formed from English *re-* intensive + *pine*[2], v., yearn. The sense of long discontentedly for something is first recorded in 1742.

replenish *v.* About 1380 *replenishen* to fill or supply, in Chaucer's translation of Boethius' *De Consolatione Philosophiae;* borrowed from Old French *repleniss-,* extended stem of *replenir* (*re-* intensive form + *-plenir,* from Latin *plēnus* full, related to *plēre* to fill; see FULL); for suffix see -ISH[2]. The meaning of provide a new supply for is first recorded in Drayton's *Poly-Olbion* (1612). **—replenishment** *n.* 1526, formed from English *replenish* + *-ment.*

replete *adj.* abundantly supplied. 1384 *repleet,* in the Wycliffe Bible; later in the spelling *replete* (before 1398); borrowed from Old French *replet, replete* filled up, from Latin *replētus,* past participle of *replēre* to fill (*re-* intensive form + *plēre* to fill; see FULL). **—repletion** *n.* About 1390 *repleccioun* eating to excess, condition of being filled up, in Chaucer's *Canterbury Tales;* borrowed from Old French *repletion,* from Late Latin *replētiōnem* (nominative *replētiō*) a filling up, from Latin *replēre* to fill; for suffix see -TION.

replica (rep′ləkə) *n.* 1824, borrowed from Italian *rèplica* copy, reproduction, repetition, reply, from *replicàre* to repeat or reply, from Latin *replicāre* to repeat; see REPLY. **—replicate** *v.* Probably before 1425 *replecate* to repeat (found in the form *replecated*); borrowed from Latin *replicātus,* past participle of *replicāre* to repeat, reply; for suffix see -ATE[1]. Later use may also have developed as a back formation from *replication.* The meaning of copy or reproduce is first recorded in 1882. **—replication** *n.* About 1380 *replicacioun* legal reply, rejoinder, answer, in Chaucer's translation of Boethius' *De Consolatione Philosophiae;* borrowed probably through Anglo-French *replicacioun,* Old French *replication,* from Latin *replicātiōnem* (nominative *replicātiō*) a reply, repetition, a folding back, from *replicāre* to repeat, reply, reflect on, unroll, fold back; see REPLY; for suffix see -ATION. The meaning of a copy or reproduction is first recorded in 1692. The specific sense in biology of process of reproducing or duplicating genetic material in cells is first recorded in 1948.

reply *v.* Before 1382 *replien* to repeat, in the Wycliffe Bible; also, to answer (about 1386, in Chaucer's *Legend of Good Women*); borrowed from Old French *replier* to reply, turn back, fold again, from Latin *replicāre* to reply, repeat, reflect on, unroll, fold back (*re-* back + *plicāre* to fold; see PLY[2] fold). **—n.** 1560, answer; from the verb.

report *n.* About 1385, rumor, gossip, common talk, in Chaucer's *Troilus and Criseyde;* borrowed from Old French *report,* n., from *reporter* to tell, relate, report, learned borrowing from Latin *reportāre* carry back (*re-* back + *portāre* to carry; see PORT[4] bearing).

The sense of an account, especially of some matter being investigated, is first recorded about 1410. The extended sense of a resounding noise, especially one caused by the discharge of a firearm or explosive, is not recorded before 1590. The specific sense of a teacher's official statement in writing about the work and behavior of a pupil is recorded from about 1840 in American English, in Mary Terhune's *An Old-Field School-Girl,* since the 1920's, when it became customary to make such a statement on a suitably printed card, the statement has been called a *report card.*

—v. make a report of. About 1385 *reporten* to relate, repeat, give an account of, in Chaucer's *Troilus and Criseyde;* borrowed from Old French *reporter* to report.

—reportage *n.* 1612, repute; formed from English *report,* v. + *-age.* The meaning of reported matter or gossip is first recorded in 1881, possibly from the somewhat earlier French use (1878). The usual sense of act of reporting news or events is found in 1891. **—reporter** *n.* 1450, one who reports or relates; developed by alteration (in association with *-er*[1]) of Middle English *reportour* (about 1387-95, in Chaucer's *Prologue* to the *Canterbury Tales*); borrowed from Old French *reportour,* from *reporter* to report. The meaning of one who reports for a newspaper is first recorded in 1798 in American English. **—reportorial** *adj.* of or having to do with reporters. 1860, formed irregularly from English *reporter* + *-orial,* as in *professorial, dictatorial.*

repose[1] *v.* lie at rest. About 1450 *reposen;* borrowed from Middle French *reposer,* from Late Latin *repausāre* cause to rest (Latin *re-* intensive + Late Latin *pausāre* to stop; see PAUSE). **—n.** rest, sleep. 1509, in Stephen Hawes' *The Pastime of Pleasure;* either borrowed from Middle French *repos,* from *reposer* to repose; or developed from the verb in English.

repose[2] *v.* put, place. Probably 1440 *reposen* replace, put back; borrowed from Latin *repos-,* perfect stem of *repōnere* put back, put away (*re-* back, away + *pōnere* to put, place; see POSITION), on the pattern of other English verbs such as *dispose* and *depose.* The meaning of put down or deposit is first recorded in 1548, and the extended sense of place (confidence, trust, etc.) is found in 1560.

repository *n.* 1485, container where things are stored, in Caxton's *Charles the Great;* borrowed from Middle French *repositoire,* and directly from Late Latin *repositōrium* store, from Latin, a stand on which food is placed, from *reposit-,* past participle stem of *repōnere* put away, store, see REPOSE[2]; for suffix see -ORY. The sense of a place where things are kept is recorded in 1648.

reprehend *v.* reprove. Before 1340 *reprehenden* reprove; borrowed from Latin *reprehendere,* originally, pull back (*re-* back + *prehendere* to grasp, seize; see PREHENSILE). **—reprehensible** *adj.* deserving reproof. About 1384, in the Wycliffe Bible; borrowed perhaps through Old French *reprehensible,* or directly from Late Latin *reprehēnsibilis,* from Latin *reprehēnsus,* past participle of *reprehendere* to reprove, reprehend; for suffix see -IBLE. **—reprehension** *n.* reproof. About 1385 *reprehencioun,* in Chaucer's *Troilus and Criseyde;* borrowed perhaps through Old French *reprehension,* or directly from Latin *reprehēnsiōnem* (nominative *reprehēnsiō*), from *reprehendere* reprehend; for suffix see -SION.

represent *v.* 1375 *representen* to present, bring before the mind; borrowed from Old French *representer,* learned borrowing from Latin *repraesentāre* (*re-* intensive form + *praesentāre* place before; see PRESENT[2] gift).

The meaning of show, display, portray, depict, is first recorded in 1392. The meaning of act in place of, stand for, is found in Wycliffe's writings, in 1389.

—representation *n.* act of representing. Probably before 1400 *representacioun;* borrowed from Old French *representation,* learned borrowing from Latin, and borrowed directly from Latin *repraesentātiōnem* (nominative *repraesentātiō*) a showing, exhibiting, from *repraesentāre* represent; for suffix see -ATION. **—representative** *adj.* About 1385 *representative* serving to portray or represent, in Thomas Usk's *The Testament of Love;* borrowed from Old French *representatif* (feminine *representative*), from Medieval Latin *repraesentativus,* from Latin *repraesentāre* represent; for suffix see -ATIVE. The meaning of having its citizens represented by chosen persons is first recorded in 1628. *—n.* 1647, example type, from the adjective. The meaning of a person appointed or elected to represent others is first recorded in 1635, and the meaning of a legislative body, as found in *Representatives,* is first recorded in 1694.

repress *v.* About 1385 *repressen* to check, restrain, weaken, keep down, in Chaucer's *Troilus and Criseyde;* borrowed from Latin *repressus,* past participle of *reprimere* (*re-* back + *premere* to push, PRESS[1]). **—repression** *n.* act of repressing. About 1385 *repressioun* ability to repress, in Chaucer's *Troilus and Criseyde;* borrowed from Medieval Latin *repressionem* (nominative *repressio*) act of repressing, from Latin *repress-,* past participle stem of *reprimere;* for suffix see -ION. The meaning of act of repressing is first recorded in English in 1533. **—repressive** *adj.* tending or having power to repress. About 1425, borrowed from Middle French *répressif* (feminine *répressive*), from Latin *repress-,* past participle stem of Latin *reprimere* repress; for suffix see -IVE.

reprieve *v.* to delay the execution or punishment of a person. 1571 *reprive* take back to prison, remand; alteration (perhaps influenced by Middle English *repreven* contradict, refute, disapprove, blame, variant of *reproven* REPROVE) of Middle English *repryen* to remand, detain (1494); probably borrowed from Middle French *repris,* past participle of *reprendre* take back; see REPRISE.

The spelling *reprieve* first appeared in 1647, formed on analogy with *achieve* (acheve) and probably *chief* (chef). The current meaning is first found in Spenser's *Faerie Queene* (1596).

—n. delay in carrying out a punishment. 1598, in Shakespeare's *The Merry Wives of Windsor;* from the verb.

reprimand *n.* severe reproof. 1636, borrowed from French *réprimande,* from Middle French *reprimende* reproof, learned borrowing from Latin *reprimenda* that is to be repressed, feminine singular of *reprimendus,* gerundive form of *reprimere* reprove; see REPRESS. **—v.** reprove severely. 1681, either borrowed from French *réprimander,* from *réprimande,* n.; or from the noun in English.

reprisal *n.* injury done in return for injury. 1419 *reprisail* seizing of property or subjects of another nation in retaliation for injury or loss; borrowed from Middle French *reprisaille,* from earlier Italian *ripresaglia* (now *rappresaglia*), from *ripreso,* past participle of *riprendere* take back, from Latin *reprēndere,* earlier *reprehendere,* originally, pull back, REPREHEND.

The meaning of injury or assault in warfare done in return for injury or assault is first recorded in 1710.

reprise (rəprēz′) *n.* renewal or resumption of an action. Before 1393, in Gower's *Confessio Amantis, reprise* loss, expense, deduction; later, act of taking back (before 1475); borrowed from Old French *reprise* act of taking back, from feminine of *repris,* past participle of *reprendre* take back, from Latin *reprēndere,* earlier *reprehendere* recover, originally, pull back; see REPREHEND.

The meaning of a renewal or resumption of an action is first recorded in Dryden's *Albion and Albanius* (1685), and the sense in music of repetition or return to the first theme, subject or passage, is first recorded in Grove's *Dictionary of Music and Musicians* (1879).

—**v.** begin again, repeat. About 1410 *reprisen,* borrowed from Middle and Old French *repris,* past participle of *reprendre.*

reproach *n.* About 1350 *reproce* a rebuke, insult, object of scorn; later *reproche* a rebuking (about 1390, in Chaucer's *Canterbury Tales*); borrowed from Old French *reproche,* from *reprocher* to blame, bring up against, bring near, from Vulgar Latin **repropiāre* (Latin *re-* opposite + *prope* near; see APPROACH). —**v.** About 1350 *reprocen* to rebuke; later *reprochen* (about 1400); borrowed from Old French *reprocher.* —**reproachful** *adj.* 1548, in Elyot's *Dictionary;* formed from English *reproach,* n. + *-ful.*

reprobate *v.* disapprove, condemn, censure. Probably before 1425 *reprobaten,* in a translation of Higden's *Polychronicon;* either a back formation from *reprobation,* or borrowed from Late Latin *reprobātus,* past participle of *reprobāre* disapprove, reject, condemn (Latin *re-* opposite + *probāre* prove to be worthy; see PROVE); for suffix see -ATE[1]. The verb may, in some instances, have also developed from the adjective as a past participle in English. —**adj.** Probably before 1425, in a translation of Higden's *Polychronicon;* borrowed from Late Latin *reprobātus,* past participle of *reprobāre.* The meaning of unprincipled is first recorded in 1660. —**n.** 1545, person beyond salvation or one rejected by God; from the adjective, or possibly a noun use of Late Latin *reprobātus,* past participle of *reprobāre.* The meaning of an unprincipled scoundrel is first recorded in 1592. —**reprobation** *n.* disapproval, condemnation. Before 1400 *reprobacyoun* rejection; borrowed from Late Latin *reprobātiōnem* (nominative *reprobātiō*) blame, censure, rejection, from Latin *reprobāre* reject, condemn; for suffix see -ATION.

reproduce *v.* 1611, in Cotgrave's *Dictionary,* produce again, create anew; formed from English *re-* again + *produce,* v. The meaning of make a copy of is first recorded in 1850, and that of produce (offspring), multiply by generation, in 1894. —**reproduction** *n.* 1659, formed in English from *reproduce* + *-tion,* on the pattern of *produce, production.* —**reproductive** *adj.* of or concerned with reproduction. 1753, in *Chambers Cyclopaedia;* formed in English from *reproduce* + *-tive,* on the pattern of *produce, productive.*

reproof *n.* words of blame or disapproval. Before 1338, in Mannyng's *Chronicle of England, reprof, reprove, repreve;* borrowed from Old French *reprove, reprouve,* from *reprover* to blame, REPROVE.

The current English form was influenced by *proof.*

reprove *v.* to blame, scold. About 1303 *reproven* to accuse, in Mannyng's *Handlyng Synne;* later, to rebuke, scold (about 1350); borrowed from Old French *reprover,* learned borrowing from Late Latin *reprobāre* disapprove, reject, condemn; see REPROBATE.

reptile *n.* Before 1393 *reptil* creeping or crawling animal, in Gower's *Confessio Amantis;* borrowed through Old French *reptile,* or directly from Late Latin *rēptile,* from neuter of *rēptilis,* adj., creeping, crawling, from Latin *rēpt-,* past participle stem of *rēpere* to crawl, creep. The Latin *rēpere* is cognate with Lithuanian *rėplióti* to creep, and Old High German *rebo, reba* shoot, tendril (modern German *Rebe*). —**adj.** of or like a reptile, crawling, creeping. 1607, borrowed from Late Latin *rēptilis,* and especially in later use from the noun. —**reptilian** *adj.* of or having to do with reptiles. 1846, formed in English from New Latin *Reptilia* the class name of reptiles (from Late Latin *rēptilia,* plural of *rēptile* reptile) + English *-an.*

republic *n.* 1604, nation governed by elected representatives, commonwealth, in Cawdrey's *A Table Alphabeticall;* borrowed from French *république,* learned borrowing from Latin *rēs pūblica* public interest, the state (*rēs* affair, matter, thing, see REAL[1], adj.; and *pūblica,* feminine of *pūblicus* PUBLIC); for suffix see -IC. —**republican** *adj.* 1712, like that of a republic, Addison, in *The Spectator;* formed from English *republic* + *-an,* probably on the model of French *républicain.* The meaning of favoring a republic is first recorded in 1793. —*n.* 1697, one who favors a republic; from the adjective. The meaning in U.S. politics of a member of a Republican party is first recorded in John Adams' *Diary* (1782).

repudiate *v.* 1545, to cast off by divorce, from Middle English *repudiate* divorced, rejected, condemned (1464); borrowed from Latin *repudiātus,* past participle of *repudiāre* to divorce or reject, from *repudium* divorce, rejection (*re-* back or away + *-pudium,* probably related to *ped-, pēs* FOOT, and having originally the sense of "push away with the foot," but associated in popular etymology with *pudēre* cause shame to); for suffix see -ATE[1]. The meaning of refuse to accept, reject, is first recorded in English before 1548. —**repudiation** *n.* act of repudiating. 1545, divorce; borrowed from Middle French *répudiation,* from Latin *repudiātiōnem* (nominative *repudiātiō*), from *repudiāre* repudiate; for suffix see -ATION. The meaning of act of repudiating is first recorded in English in 1848-56.

repugnant *adj.* About 1385 *repugnaunt* contrary, contradictory, opposing, antagonistic, in Usk's *The Testament of Love;* borrowed through Old French *repugnant,* or directly from Latin *repugnantem* (nominative *repugnāns*), present participle of *repugnāre* to resist (*re-* back + *pugnāre* to fight; see PUGNACIOUS); for suffix see -ANT. The meaning of distasteful, disagreeable, offensive, is first recorded in English in 1777. —**repugnance** *n.* 1385 *repugnaunce* contradiction, opposition; borrowed through Old French *repugnance,* or directly from Latin *repugnantia* resistance, opposition, contradiction, from *repugnantem* (nominative *repugnāns*) resisting, opposing, present participle of *repugnāre;* for suffix see -ANCE. The meaning of a strong dislike, distaste, or aversion, is first recorded in 1643.

repulse *v.* drive back, repel. Probably before 1425 *repulsen,* in a translation of Higden's *Polychronicon;* borrowed from Latin *repulsus,* past participle of *repellere* REPEL. —**n.** 1533, refusal, rejection, denial; later act of repelling (about 1540); from the verb in English and in some instances possibly borrowed from Latin *repulsus* (genitive *repulsūs*), formed from *repellere* repel. —**repulsion** *n.* Before 1420, repudiation, divorce, in Lydgate's *Troy Book;* borrowed from Late Latin *repulsiōnem* (nominative *repulsiō*) act of repelling, from Latin *repuls-,* past participle stem of *repellere* repel; for suffix see -ION. The meaning of act of repelling is first recorded in English in 1547. The meaning of a strong dislike or aversion is found in 1751. —**repulsive** *adj.* Probably before 1425, able to dissipate or repel, repelling, in a translation of Chauliac's *Grande Chirurgie;* borrowed through Middle French *répulsif* (feminine *répulsive*), or directly from Medieval Latin *repulsivus,* from Latin *repuls-,* past participle stem of *repellere* repel; for suffix see -IVE. The meaning of causing disgust, strong dislike, or aversion, is first recorded in English in 1816.

repute *v.* suppose to be, consider, suppose. About 1399 *reputen* to believe; borrowed from Middle French *reputer,* learned borrowing from Latin *reputāre* reflect upon, reckon (*re-* repeatedly + *putāre* to reckon, consider; see PUTATIVE). The meaning of attribute, credit, is first recorded before 1400, and that of consider, in 1442. **—n.** distinction, credit, good reputation. 1551, opinion, estimate; from the verb. The meaning of good reputation, credit, is first recorded in 1615. **—reputable** *adj.* having a good reputation. 1674, formed from English *repute,* v. + *-able.* An earlier sense of capable of being regarded appeared in 1611. **—reputation** *n.* Probably about 1350 *reputacioun* distinction, credit, good reputation, borrowed from Latin *reputātiōnem* (nominative *reputātiō*) consideration, from *reputāre* reflect upon, reckon; for suffix see -ATION. **—reputed** *adj.* 1549, held in repute; later, accounted or supposed to be such (1576); replacing earlier *repute,* past participle (about 1375); from *repute,* v.

request *n.* Before 1338 *requeste* act of asking, in Mannyng's *Chronicle of England;* borrowed from Old French *requeste* a request, from Vulgar Latin **requaesita,* replacing Latin *requīsīta* a thing asked for, feminine of *requīsītus* requested, demanded, REQUISITE. **—v.** 1533, to ask (someone) to do something; from the noun in English, probably influenced by Middle French *requester,* from Old French *requeste,* n.

requiem (rek′wēəm) *n.* Mass for the dead. About 1303, in Mannyng's *Handlyng Synne;* borrowing of Latin *requiem,* accusative of *requiēs* rest, repose (*re-* intensive + *quiēs* quiet; see WHILE). *Requiem* is the first word of the beginning of the Mass for the dead in the Latin liturgy: "Requiem aeternam dona eis, Domine. . . (Eternal rest give to them, O Lord. . .)."

require *v.* About 1381 *requeren,* in Chaucer's translation of Boethius' *De Consolatione Philosophiae;* later *requiren* (before 1400); borrowed from Old French *requerre,* from Vulgar Latin **requaerere,* alteration (influenced by Latin *quaerere* ask) of Latin *requīrere* seek again, seek to know, ask or inquire (*re-* repeatedly + *quaerere* ask, seek; see QUERY). **—requirement** *n.* 1530, request; formed from English *require* + *-ment.* The meaning of a thing required or needed is first recorded in 1662.

requisite *adj.* required by circumstances, essential. 1442, borrowed from Latin *requīsītus,* from past participle of *requīrere* REQUIRE. **—requisition** *n.* act of requiring, request. Probably before 1402, borrowed through Middle French *réquisition,* and directly from Medieval Latin *requisitionem* (nominative *requisitio*), from Latin *requīsītiōnem* (nominative *requīsītiō*) a searching, investigation, from *requīsīt-,* past participle stem of *requīrere* require. The meaning of a formal written demand is first recorded in English in 1553 (originally a Scottish legal use). *—v.* make a requisition for. 1837, in Carlyle's *The French Revolution,* from the noun.

requite (rikwīt′) *v.* pay back, make return for. Probably before 1400 *requiten,* in *Morte Arthur;* formed from Middle English *re-* back + *quite* to discharge (as a debt), clear, pay up; variant of QUIT, v. **—requital** *n.* repayment, return. 1579, formed from English *requite* + *-al*[2].

reredos (rer′ədos) *n.* screen or a decorated part of the wall or screen behind an altar. 1372-73, borrowing of Anglo-French *reredos,* shortened variant of *areredos,* from Old French *arere, arrere, ariere* behind, backward (see ARREARS) + *dos* back, from Latin *dossum,* variant of *dorsum;* see DORSAL.

rescind *v.* deprive of force, repeal, cancel. 1637-50, borrowed through French *rescinder,* and directly from Latin *rescindere* (*re-* back + *scindere* to cut, split; see SHED[2] cast off). **—rescission** *n.* 1651, act of rescinding; borrowed from Late Latin *rescissiōnem* (nominative *rescissiō*), from Latin *resciss-,* past participle stem of *rescindere* rescind. An earlier meaning of act of cutting off is recorded in Cotgrave's *Dictionary* (1611).

rescue *v.* Probably about 1300 *rescouen, rescuwen* to save from captivity, some evil, or harm, in *The Romance of Guy of Warwick;* borrowed from Old French *rescou-,* stem of *rescourre* (*re-* intensive + *escourre* to shake out, cast off, discharge, from Latin *excutere,* from *ex-* out + *-cutere,* combining form of *quatere* to shake; see QUASH[1] crush). **—n.** Probably about 1380 *rescoghe* act of rescuing, deliverance; also *rescowe* (probably about 1390); later *rescu* (about 1425); from the verb.

Another form developed in Middle English became dominant in the 1400's, was retained in noun use in law until the 1760's, and thereafter disappeared. It is interesting to note that this variant *rescousen* (before 1338, in Mannyng's *Chronicle of England*), borrowed from Old French *rescosser, rescouser,* developed a verb form *rescous, rescus* (about 1385, in Chaucer's *Canterbury Tales*); borrowed from Old French *rescos, rescous,* at about the same time as the Middle English form that became present-day *rescue.*

research (risėrch′ *or* rē′sėrch) *n.* 1577, careful search; borrowed from Middle French *recerche,* from Old French *recercher* seek out, search closely (*re-* intensive form + *cercher* to seek for, SEARCH). The meaning of a careful hunting for facts is first recorded in English before 1639. —**v.** do research, investigate closely. 1593, borrowed from Middle French *recercher,* from Old French.

resemble *v.* 1340 *resemblen* be like or similar to, in *Ayenbite of Inwyt;* borrowed from Old French *resembler* (*re-* intensive form + *sembler* to appear, from Latin *simulāre* to copy, from *similis* like, SIMILAR). **—resemblance** *n.* Before 1393, likeness, similarity, in Gower's *Confessio Amantis;* borrowed from Anglo-French *resemblance,* from Old French *resembler* to resemble; for suffix see -ANCE.

resent *v.* 1605, to feel pain or distress; borrowed from French *ressentir* feel pain, regret, from Old French *resentir* (*re-* intensive + *sentir* to feel, from Latin *sentīre;* see SENSE). The meaning of feel injured and angry at (some wrong, insult, etc.) is first recorded in 1628-29. **—resentful** *adj.* 1654, formed from English *resent* + *-ful.* **—resentment** *n.* 1619, borrowed from French *ressentiment,* from *ressentir* to resent; for suffix see -MENT.

reserve *v.* 1357 *reserven* to retain (jurisdiction); later, keep back, store up, set apart (before 1382); borrowed from Old French *reserver,* learned borrowing from Latin, and borrowed directly from Latin *reservāre* keep back, save back (*re-* back + *servāre* to keep; see CONSERVE). **—n.** 1644, storage place; later something stored up, stock, store (before 1658); borrowed from French *réserve* a store, reserve, from Old French *re-*

server to reserve. The meaning of an imposing of some limit to one's own actions, self-restraint, self-control, is first recorded in 1655. The plural form *reserves,* used in the sense of soldiers who are not in active service, is first recorded in 1648. **—adj.** kept in reserve, forming a reserve. 1719, from the noun. **—reservation** *n.* 1377 *reservacioun* act of reserving; borrowed from Old French *reservation,* learned borrowing from Late Latin, and borrowed directly from Late Latin *reservātiōnem* (nominative *reservātiō*), from Latin *reservāre* to reserve; for suffix see -ATION. The meaning of a limiting condition or qualification is first recorded in English in 1606. The specialized meaning of public land set aside for an American Indian tribe is first recorded in American English in the *Annals of the First Congress* (1789). **—reservist** *n.* member of the military reserves. 1876, probably borrowed from French *réserviste,* from *réserve,* n., reserve + *-iste* -ist.

reservoir (rez′ərvwär) *n.* 1690, (figurative use) place where anything is stored or tends to collect; borrowing of French *réservoir* storehouse, from Old French *reserver* to RESERVE + suffix *-oir* (see -ORY). The sense of a place where water is collected and stored is first recorded in Addison's *Remarks on Italy* (1705).

reside *v.* Before 1475 *residen* to remain or settle in some place; borrowed through Middle French *resider,* and directly from Latin *residēre* remain behind (*re-* back + *sedēre* to SIT). It is also probable that in some instances *reside* is a back formation from *residence.*

The meaning of live (in or at), dwell, is first recorded in 1578, and that of be or exist in (as in *sovereignty resides in the people*), in 1607.

—residence *n.* Probably about 1378, act or fact of residing; also, a dwelling place, in Wycliffe's writings; borrowed from Old French *residence,* and directly from Medieval Latin *residentia,* from Latin *residentem* (nominative *residēns*) residing or dwelling, present participle of *residēre* reside; for suffix see -ENCE. **—residency** *n.* 1579, act or fact of residing; formed from English *resident* + *-cy.* The meaning of position of a doctor with advanced training is first recorded in 1924, in American English **—resident** *adj.* About 1384, residing or dwelling in a place, in the Wycliffe Bible; borrowed through Anglo-French and Old French *resident,* from Latin *residentem* (nominative *residēns*), present participle of *residēre* reside; for suffix see -ENT. *—n.* 1464, person who resides in a place, inhabitant, in *Rolls of Parliament;* from the adjective, probably influenced by Middle French *résident,* n. The meaning of a doctor with advanced training is first recorded in 1892 in American English. **—residential** *adj.* 1654, of or for residents of a place; formed from English *resident* + *-ial.*

residue *n.* what remains after a part is taken, remainder. Probably before 1350, borrowed from Old French *residu,* learned borrowing from Latin *residuum* a remainder, neuter of *residuus* remaining, left over, from *residēre* remain behind; see RESIDE. **—residual** *adj.* 1570, (of a quantity) left after subtraction; formed in English from Latin *residuum* remainder + English *-al*[1]. The general meaning of remaining, left over, is first recorded in 1609. *—n.* 1570, a residual quantity, probably from the adjective. The general meaning of remainder is first recorded in 1860. The specialized meaning of a fee or royalty paid to a performer, writer, etc. for each rerun of a taped or filmed performance, is first recorded about 1960 in American English.

resign *v.* About 1370 *resignen* give up, surrender, abandon, submit, in Chaucer's *An A.B.C.;* borrowed from Old French *resigner,* from Latin *resignāre* to check off, cancel, give up (*re-* opposite + *signāre* to make an entry in an account book, SIGN). In this use, *resignāre* denoted making an entry (by means of a mark, *signum*) opposite (on the credit side), balancing the former mark and thus canceling the claim for which it stood.

The common meaning of give up or relinquish an office or position is first recorded before 1387, in Trevisa's translation of Higden's *Polychronicon.*

—resignation *n.* Before 1387, in Trevisa's translation of Higden's *Polychronicon;* borrowed from Old French *resignation,* and directly from Medieval Latin *resignationem* (nominative *resignatio*), from Latin *resignāre* give up, resign; for suffix see -ATION.

resilient *adj.* springing back. 1644, formed in English as an adjective to earlier *resilience* on the model of Latin *resilientem* (nominative *resiliēns*), present participle of *resilīre* to rebound, recoil (*re-* back + *salīre* to jump, leap; see SALLY); for suffix see -ENT. **—resilience** *n.* 1626, in Bacon's *Sylva Sylvarum,* formed in English from Latin *resilīre* to rebound + English *-ence.*

resin (rez′ən) *n.* sticky substance that flows from certain plants and trees. Before 1382, in the Wycliffe Bible; borrowed from Old French *resine,* learned borrowing from Latin, and borrowed directly from Latin *rēsīna,* from an East Greek word **rhēsī́nā,* dialectal variant of Greek *rhētī́nē* resin, of non-Indo-European origin. **—resinous** *adj.* of or like resin. 1646, borrowed, perhaps through influence of French *résineux,* from Latin *rēsīnōsus,* from *rēsīna* resin; for suffix see -OUS.

resist *v.* About 1380 *resisten* stop or hinder, stand against, in Chaucer's translation of Boethius' *De Consolatione Philosophiae;* borrowed from Old French *resister,* learned borrowing from Latin, and borrowed directly from Latin *resistere* stand back or still, withstand, resist (*re-* opposite, against + *sistere* cause to stand, stand firm, related to *stāre* to STAND). **—resistance** *n.* Probably about 1350, act of resisting; borrowed from Old French *resistence,* from Late Latin *resistentia,* from Latin *resistentem* (nominative *resistēns*), present participle of *resistere* resist; for suffix see -ANCE. **—resistant** *adj.* 1410, resisting, opposed; borrowed from Middle French *résistant,* present participle of *résister* to resist, from Old French *resister;* for suffix see -ANT. **—resistor** *n.* device used to impede the flow of an electric current. 1905, formed from English *resist* + *-or*[2].

resolute *adj.* Probably before 1425, dissolved, softened, in a translation of Chauliac's *Grande Chirurgie;* also dissolute, in a translation of Higden's *Polychronicon,* later, from the sense of breaking into parts, final, absolute (1501) developed the meaning of resolved, firmly determined, first recorded in a translation of Livy's *History of Rome* (1533); borrowed from Latin *resolūtus* unrestrained, from past participle of *resolvere* to loosen, undo, settle, RESOLVE. **—resolution** *n.* Before 1397 *resolucion* a breaking up into parts, a resolving, in the Wycliffe Bible; borrowed through Old French *resolution,* or directly from Latin *resolūtiōnem* (nominative *resolūtiō*), from *resolūt-,* past participle stem of *resolvere* loosen, resolve. The meaning of a solving or answering is first recorded in 1548, probably from the sense of frame of mind, decision (1438) and resolution of doubt (before 1500), and the meaning of power of holding firmly to a purpose is later found in Shakespeare's *Titus Andronicus* (1588). The meaning of a formal or official expression of opinion by a deliberative body is first recorded in 1604.

resolve *v.* About 1380 *resolven* dissolve, break into parts, in Chaucer's translation of Boethius' *De Consolatione Philosophiae;* borrowed through Old French *resolver,* learned borrowing from Latin, or directly from Latin *resolvere* to loosen, undo, settle (*re-* intensive + *solvere* loosen; see SOLVE).

The meaning of untie or solve (a problem) especially by analyzing its parts is first recorded in English in 1577, and that of to decide, determine, or settle (a doubtful point), in 1612.

—n. 1591, determination, firmness of purpose, in Shakespeare's *1 Henry VI;* from the verb.

The meaning of a thing determined on is first recorded in Shakespeare's *Romeo and Juliet* (1592).

resonance *n.* resounding quality. Before 1460, reinforcement or prolongation of sound; borrowed from Middle French *resonance,* from Latin *resonantia* echo, from *resonāre* RESOUND; for suffix see -ANCE. The meaning of a resounding quality is first recorded in 1669. **—resonant** *adj.* resounding, echoing. 1592, borrowed perhaps through Middle French *résonnant,* from Latin *resonantem* (nominative *resonāns*), present participle of *resonāre* RESOUND; for suffix see -ANT. **—resonate** *v.* display resonance, resound. 1873, in Sedley Taylor's *Sound and Music;* borrowed from Latin *resonātum,* past participle of *resonāre* RESOUND; for suffix see -ATE[1].

resort *v.* go, turn to. About 1400 *resorten* to return, revert; also, turn for help (about 1410), go frequently (1432); borrowed from Middle French *resortir* go out again, resort (Old French *re-* again + *sortir* go out; see SORTIE). **—n.** About 1385 *resort* source of help, recourse, in Chaucer's *Troilus and Criseyde;* borrowed from Old French *resort* resource or help, from *resortir* to resort. The meaning of a coming or going to a place or person is first recorded before 1420, and its later concomitant meaning of a place people go to, especially for recreation or relief, in 1754.

resound *v.* About 1380 *resounen* to ring or reecho with some sound, in Chaucer's translation of Boethius' *De Consolatione Philosophiae;* borrowed from Old French *resoner,* from Latin *resonāre* sound again, resound, echo (*re-* back, again + *sonāre* to SOUND).

The current spelling (influenced by *sound*) began to appear probably about 1450.

resource *n.* 1611, stock or reserve available to meet a need, in Cotgrave's *Dictionary;* borrowed from French *resource;* earlier, *resourse,* from the feminine form of the past participle *resors,* *resours* of Old French *resourdre* to rally, rise again, from Latin *resurgere* rise again; see RESURGENT.

The meaning of a skill in meeting difficulties is first recorded in 1853. The plural form *resources,* used in the sense of a country's actual potential wealth or means, is first recorded in 1779.

—v. to supply with or draw upon resources. 1975, from the noun.

—resourceful *adj.* 1851, full of resource; formed from English *resource* + *-ful.*

respect *n.* Probably about 1380 *respecte* relation, reference, regard; borrowed from Old French *respect,* learned borrowing from Latin, and borrowed directly from Latin *respectus* (genitive *respectūs*) regard; literally, act of looking back at one, from *respect-,* past participle stem of *respicere* look back at, regard, consider (*re-* back + *specere* look at; see SPY). Doublet of RESPITE.

The meaning of high regard, honor, esteem, is first recorded in English in 1586, from the earlier sense of consideration (1483), and regard (probably about 1380).

—v. 1548, to regard, consider, take into account; probably from the noun reinforced by, or perhaps even borrowed from Middle French *respecter* look back, delay, respect, and Latin *respectāre,* frequentative form of *respicere* look back at, regard. The meaning of treat with deference, esteem, or honor, is first recorded in English in 1560.

—respectability *n.* 1785, formed as a noun to *respectable,* from English *respectable* after such pairs as *capable, capability.* **—respectable** *adj.* Before 1586, worthy of notice or consideration, in Sidney's *Arcadia;* probably formed from English *respect,* possibly by influence of Middle French *respectable.* The meaning of worthy of respect appeared in English in 1750, in Lord Chesterfield's correspondence. **—respectful** *adj.* 1598, mindful, heedful, in a translation of Homer's *Iliad;* formed from English *respect,* n. + *-ful.* The meaning of showing respect is first recorded in 1687.

respective *adj.* with respect to each, separate, particular, individual. About 1454, relating to, relative; borrowed perhaps through Middle French *respectif* (feminine *respective*) from Medieval Latin *respectivus* having regard for, from Latin *respectus,* past participle of *respicere* look back, have regard for, see RESPECT; for suffix see -IVE.

The meaning of with regard to each, particular, individual, is first recorded in English in 1646, probably from the earlier adverb use.

—respectively *adv.* About 1454, relatively; formed from English *respective* + *-ly*[1]. The sense of individually, separately, singly, is first recorded in Bacon's *Sylva Sylvarum* (1626).

respire *v.* 1385 *respiren* come up for breath, breathe again, in Usk's *The Testament of Love;* borrowed from Old French *respirer,* learned borrowing from Latin, and borrowed directly from Latin *respīrāre* breathe again, breathe in and out (*re-* again + *spīrāre* to breathe; see SPIRIT).

The general meaning of breathe, draw breath, inhale and exhale, is first recorded probably before 1425.

—respiration *n.* 1392 *respiracioun* physiological process analogous to breathing; later, act of breathing (probably before 1425); borrowed from Latin *respīrātiōnem* (nominative *respīrātiō*), from *respīrāre* breathe, respire; for suffix see -ATION. **—respirator** *n.* 1836, device worn over the mouth or nose to prevent inhalation of harmful substances; formed in English as if from Latin *respīrātor,* from *respīrāre* to breathe, respire; for suffix see -OR[2]. The modern sense of a device to help a person breathe, especially in giving artificial respiration, appeared in 1929, in the phrase *mechanical respirator.* **—respiratory** *adj.* of or used for respiration. 1790, borrowed from French *respiratoire,* learned borrowing from Late Latin *respīrātōrius* of or for breathing, from Latin *respīrāt-,* past participle stem of *respīrāre* breathe, respire; for suffix see -ORY.

respite (res′pit) *n.* time of relief and rest, lull. About 1250 *respit;* borrowed from Old French *respit* delay, respect, from Latin *respectus* consideration, act of looking back, recourse, regard. Doublet of RESPECT. **—v.** give a respite to. Before 1330, *respiten;* borrowed from Old French *respiter* postpone, respect, from *respit,* n.

resplendent *adj.* Probably 1440, brilliant; borrowed, perhaps through influence of Middle French *resplendant,* earlier *resplendent,* from Latin *resplendentem* (nominative *resplendēns*) brilliant, radiant, present participle of *resplendēre* to glitter, shine (*re-* intensive form + *splendēre* to shine; see SPLENDID); for suffix see -ENT. **—resplendence** *n.* Probably before 1425, in a translation of Higden's *Polychronicon;* borrowed from Late Latin *resplendentia* brilliance, radiance, from Latin *resplendentem;* see RESPLENDENT; for suffix see -ENCE.

respond *v.* About 1300 *responden* answer, reply; borrowed from Old French *respondre* respond or correspond, from Latin *respondēre* respond, answer to, promise in return (*re-* back + *spondēre* to promise; see SPOUSE). **—respondent** *adj.* 1533, correspondent (to something else); probably borrowed directly from Latin *respondentem* (nominative *respondēns*), present participle of *respondēre* respond; for suffix see -ENT. The meaning of answering or responding is first recorded in 1726, from *respondent,* n. *—n.* 1528, probably borrowed directly from Latin *respondentem* (nominative *respondēns*) a respondent, from present participle of *respondēre.* The noun meaning of a defendant, especially in a divorce case, is first recorded in 1562.

response *n.* About 1300 *respounse* an answer or reply; later in the spelling *respons* (before 1338); borrowed from Old French *respons* (feminine *response*), and directly from Latin *respōnsum* answer, from neuter past participle of *respondēre* to RESPOND. The sense of a part of the liturgy said or sung by the congregation in reply to the priest is first recorded before 1387. **—responsive** *adj.* 1419, responding, answering; borrowed through Middle French *responsif* (feminine *responsive*), and directly from Late Latin *respōnsīvus,* from Latin *respōnsus,* past participle of *respondēre* to respond; for suffix see -IVE. The meaning of responding readily to some influence, easily moved, is first recorded in 1762.

responsible *adj.* 1599, corresponding or answering to something, in Ben Jonson's *Every Man Out of His Humour;* borrowed from obsolete French *responsible,* from Latin *respōnsus,* past participle of *respondēre* to RESPOND; for suffix see -IBLE.

The meaning of answerable or accountable is first recorded in English in 1643, and that of trustworthy or reliable in 1691, in Locke's writings. The meaning of involving obligation or duties (as in *a responsible position*) is first recorded in 1855. **—responsibility** *n.* 1787, Hamilton, in *The Federalist;* formed from English *responsible* + *-ity.*

rest[1] *n.* sleep, stillness, ease. Before 1121 *reste* in the *Peterborough Chronicle;* developed from Old English *ræste, reste* rest, bed, forms found in both Anglian and West Saxon sources: *reste* (before 830, in the *Vespasian Psalter*), and *ræste, selereste* (about 725, in *Beowulf*). Old English *reste* (from Proto-Germanic **rastjō*) is cognate specifically with Old Frisian *rest* bed, Old Saxon *resta,* Old High German *resta;* Old English *ræsta* (from Proto-Germanic **rastō*) is cognate specifically with Old Saxon *rasta* bed, resting place, Old High German *rasta* league (measure of distance) (modern German *Rast* rest), Old Icelandic *rǫst* (Norwegian *rast,* Swedish *rast*) league, distance after which one rests, Gothic *rasta* mile, a stage of a journey. **—v.** be asleep or still. About 1175 *resten,* developed from Old English *ræstan, restan* to rest, *ræstan* (about 950, in the *Lindisfarne Gospels*), and *restan* (about 725, in *Beowulf*). Old English *restan* is cognate specifically with Old Frisian *resta* to rest, Old Saxon *restian;* Old English *ræstan* is cognate specifically with Old High German *rastōn* (modern German *rasten*) to rest, and the verb in Old English is related to, if not derived from *ræste, reste* rest, n. The Indo-European source of this word is the extended stem **rə-s-* of the root **erə-/rē-* to rest (Pok.338). **—restful** *adj.* 1340 *restevol, restvol* characterized by rest, contemplative; later *restful* quiet, peaceful (about 1395, in the Wycliffe Bible); formed from Middle English *reste* rest + *-ful.* **—restless** *adj.* Probably about 1380 *restlez* unceasing, endless; later *resteles* unable to rest, uneasy (about 1385, in Chaucer's *Troilus and Criseyde*); formed from Middle English *reste* rest + *-less.* **—rest room** (1899, American English)

rest[2] *n.* what is left, remainder. About 1440; borrowed from Middle French *reste* residue, remnant, from *rester* to remain, from Latin *restāre* stand back, be left (*re-* back + *stāre* to STAND).

restaurant *n.* 1827, a public dining room (such as those first found in Paris), in James Fenimore Cooper's *The Prairie;* borrowing of French *restaurant* a restaurant; originally, food that restores, noun use of present participle of *restaurer* to restore or refresh, from Old French *restorer* RESTORE.

The use of French *restaurant* in the sense of a public dining room is said to have originated in Paris in 1765, when an eating establishment was opened principally serving soup; previous to that the usual term for a public place to obtain a meal was *tavern* in English. **—restaurateur** (res′tərətėr′) *n.* owner of a restaurant. 1796, a French word used in Burke's writings; formed from *restaurer* to restore + *-eur,* on the model of Late Latin *restaurātor* restorer, from Latin *restaurāre* RESTORE.

restitution *n.* return of what has been lost. Before 1325 *restituciun* the act of restoring something to its owner, or of paying back a debt, etc., in *Cursor Mundi;* later *restitution* (1423); borrowed from Old French *restitucïon,* learned borrowing from Latin, and borrowed directly from Latin *restitūtiōnem* (nominative *restitūtiō*) a restoring, from past participle of *restituere* restore, rebuild, replace (*re-* again + *statuere* to set up; see STATUTE); for suffix see -TION.

restive *adj.* About 1410 *restif* not moving forward, stationary; later, (of a horse) refusing to go forward, unmanageable; borrowed from Middle French *restif* (feminine *restive*) motionless, from *rester* to remain, REST[2]; for suffix see -IVE. The extended sense of uncontrollable, restless, uneasy, fidgety, is not recorded in English before 1806-07.

restore *v.* About 1300 *restoren* give back, compensate for, rebuild, renew; borrowed from Old French *restorer,* from Latin *restaurāre* repair, rebuild, renew, restore (*re-* back, again + *-staurāre,* as in *īnstaurāre* restore; see STORE). **—restoration** *n.* Probably before 1500 *restoracion* renewal, alteration (influenced by *restore*) of earlier *restauracion* a restoring to health (before 1393, in Gower's *Confessio Amantis*); borrowed from Old French *restauration,* and perhaps directly from Latin *restaurātiōnem* (nominative *restaurātiō*), from *restaurāre* restore; for suffix see -ATION. —**restorative** *adj.* capable of restoring or renewing. Before 1398 *restoratif,* in Trevisa's translation of Bartholomew's *De Proprietatibus Rerum,* alteration (influenced by *restore*) of earlier *restauratif* (before 1393, in Gower's *Confessio Amantis*); borrowed from Old French *restauratif,* from Latin *restaurātus,* past participle of *restaurāre* restore; for suffix see -IVE. —*n.* a food, drink, or medicine that restores health or strength. Probably before 1435 *restoratif;* from the adjective.

restrain *v.* Before 1349 *restreynen* hold back, keep in check, stop; later, with the spelling of *restraynen* (about 1375); borrowed from Old French *restraindre, restreindre,* from Latin *restringere* draw back tightly, confine, check; see RESTRICT. —**restraint** *n.* About 1412, act of restraining, check, hindrance; borrowed from Middle French *restrainte,* noun use of feminine past participle of Old French *restraindre* to restrain. The meaning of a means of restraining or keeping under control is first recorded about 1422. The meaning of reserve, self-restraint, is first found in Shakespeare's *All's Well That Ends Well* (1601).

restrict *v.* 1535, keep within limits, confine; probably a back formation from the earlier *restriction;* but possibly in some instances borrowed from Latin *restrictus,* past participle of *restringere* bind fast, draw back tightly, confine, check, restrain (*re-* back + *stringere* draw tight; see STRAIN[1] stretch). —**restriction** *n.* About 1412 *restriccioun* a cessation, in Hoccleve's *Regement of Princes;* borrowed through Middle French *restriction,* and directly from Late Latin *restrictiōnem* (nominative *restrictiō*) limitation, from Latin *restrict-,* past participle stem of *restringere* restrict, restrain; for suffix see -TION. —**restrictive** *adj.* Probably before 1425, astringent, binding, in a translation of Chauliac's *Grande Chirurgie;* borrowed from Middle French *restrictif* (feminine *restrictive*), from Latin *restrictus,* past participle; for suffix see -IVE. The meaning of restricting or limiting, in relation to words or expressions, is first recorded in 1579.

result *v.* Probably before 1425 *resulten* follow as an outcome, in a translation of Higden's *Polychronicon;* borrowed from Latin *resultāre* to spring back, rebound, frequentative form derived from the past participle of *resilīre* to rebound; see RESILIENT. —**n.** 1626, in Bacon's *Sylva Sylvarum,* act of springing back; from the verb. The meaning of a consequence, outcome, is first recorded in 1651. —**resultant** *adj.* that results, resulting. 1639, possibly formed from English *result* + *-ant,* and perhaps borrowed from Latin *resultantem* (nominative *resultāns*), present participle of *resultāre* to rebound; for suffix see -ANT.

resume (rizüm′) *v.* 1404 *resumen* to get or take again, take back; later, renew (before 1420), and begin again (about 1450); borrowed from Middle French *resumer,* and directly from Latin *resūmere* take again, take up or assume again (*re-* again + *sūmere* take up; see ASSUME). —**resumption** *n.* act of resuming. 1443 *resumpcion* repossessing by grant; borrowed from Middle French *resumption,* and directly from Late Latin *resūmptiōnem* (nominative *resūmptiō*), from Latin *resūmpt-,* past participle stem of *resūmere* to resume; for suffix see -TION.

résumé (rez′əmā′) *n.* summary. 1804, borrowing of French *résumé,* noun use of past participle of Middle French *resumer* to sum up; originally, take back; see RESUME. The meaning of a biographical summary, especially of a person's career, is first recorded before 1960. Middle French *resumer* would seem to have been altered in its meaning by Old French *sommer* find the sum of, from Late Latin *summāre* sum up, from Latin *summa* SUM.

resurgent (risėr′jənt) *adj.* rising or tending to rise again. 1808, probably formed from English *resurge* rise again (1575, borrowed from Latin *resurgere* rise again; *re-* again + *surgere* to rise; see SURGE) + *-ent.* —**resurgence** *n.* a rising again. Before 1834, Coleridge quoted in *Literary Remains;* formed from English *resurgent* + *-ence.*

resurrection *n.* About 1300, church festival commemorating the rising again of Christ after His death and burial; borrowed from Anglo-French *resurrectiun* and from Old French *resurrection,* learned borrowing from Late Latin, and borrowed directly from Late Latin *resurrēctiōnem* (nominative *resurrēctiō*), from Latin *resurrēct-,* past participle stem of *resurgere* rise again; see RESURGENT; for suffix see -TION.

The figurative meaning of revival, restoration, as of from decay or disuse, is first recorded in 1649, from the earlier sense of rebirth, spiritual revival (about 1475). —**resurrect** *v.* raise from the dead. 1772, back formation from *resurrection.* The figurative sense of bring back to sight or into use is first recorded in 1852.

resuscitate (risus′ətāt) *v.* Probably about 1425, revive, restore to life or consciousness; borrowed from Latin *resuscitātus,* past participle of *resuscitāre* rouse again, revive (*re-* again + *suscitāre* to raise, revive, from *sus-,* variant of *sub-* from under + *citāre* to move, excite; see CITE); for suffix see -ATE[1].

After 1535 *resuscitate* displaced the variant Middle English verb *resusciten* (recorded probably about 1450); borrowed through Middle French *resusciter,* or directly from Latin *resuscitāre* resuscitate.

—**resuscitation** *n.* Probably about 1425 *resuscitacion* restoration to life or consciousness; borrowed from Middle French *ressuscitation,* learned borrowing from Late Latin, and borrowed directly from Late Latin *resuscitātiōnem* (nominative *resuscitātiō*), from Latin *resuscitāre* resuscitate; for suffix see -ATION. —**resuscitator** *n.* 1847, one who revives; formed from English *resuscitate* + *-or*[2]. The modern sense of a device used to revive a person overcome by gas, water in the lungs, etc., is first attested in 1929, in American English.

retail *n.* sale of goods in small quantities. 1413 *retayll,* 1417 *retaile;* borrowed from Middle French *retail* (feminine *retaille*) piece cut off, shred, scrap, paring (also found in Italian *ritaglio* a selling by the piece), from Old French *retaillier* to cut off, pare, clip, divide (*re-* back + *taillier* to cut, trim; see TAILOR). —**v.** 1419 *retaylen* sell in small quantities; borrowed from Middle French *retaillier* to cut off, divide. The extended meaning in English of recount or tell over again, relate in detail, is first recorded in Shakespeare's *Richard III* (1594). —**adj.** selling in small quantities. 1601, from the noun. —**retailer** *n.* retail merchant or dealer. Probably 1466, earlier *retaillour* (1444, in *Rolls of Parliament*); probably formed from Middle English *retailen* to retail + *-er*[1] or *-or*[2].

retain *v.* About 1386 *reteinen* hold back, restrain, in Chaucer's *Canterbury Tales;* later in the spelling *retaynen* (probably before 1400); borrowed from Old French *retenir,* from Latin *retinēre* hold back (*re-* back

+ *tenēre* to hold; see TENANT). The meaning of keep hold of, continue having or keeping, is first recorded about 1450. The specialized sense of employ by payment of a fee, secure the services of (a lawyer, etc.) by paying a retainer, is first attested in 1437.

retainer[1] *n.* fee paid to secure services. 1453 *reteignour* retention of revenue from customs; later *reteiner* engagement of a person as a servant or for some other position (1467-68, in the *Rolls of Parliament*); probably from *retain,* v. + *-er*[3], and perhaps influenced by noun use of Old French *retenir* to RETAIN. The meaning of a fee paid to a lawyer, etc., to secure services, engagement by a retaining fee, is first recorded in Byron's *Don Juan* (1818).

retainer[2] *n.* person who serves someone of rank, servant, attendant. 1540 *retaynour,* 1570 *reteyner;* probably formed from English *retain* + *-er*[1], on the model of Old French *reteneor,* from *retenir* to RETAIN. The meaning of a person who retains, maintains, or preserves, is recorded in Elyot's *Dictionary* (1548).

retaliate *v.* repay in kind, especially for wrong or injury, requite. 1611, probably a back formation from *retaliation;* for suffix see -ATE[1]. **—retaliation** *n.* repayment in kind, requital. 1581, formed in English from Latin *retāliāre* pay back in kind (*re-* back + *tāliō* exaction of payment in kind, retaliation, of uncertain origin) + English *-ation.* **—retaliatory** *adj.* of or characterized by retaliation. 1813, formed from English *retaliate* + *-ory.*

retard *v.* About 1477 *retarden* keep back, delay, hinder, impede the progress or accomplishment of; borrowed from Middle French *retarder,* learned borrowing from Latin *retardāre* to make slow, delay (*re-* intensive form + *tardāre* to slow, from *tardus* slow, TARDY). **—retardant** *adj.* tending to hinder or delay. 1642, formed from English *retard* + *-ant.* —*n.* substance that delays or hinders a process or effect (as in *fire-retardant*). 1952, from the adjective. **—retardate** *n.* mentally retarded person. 1956, American English (technical use in psychology); formed from English *retard(ed)* + *-ate*[3]. **—retardation** *n.* Probably before 1430, act of retarding, delay, in Lydgate's works; borrowed from Middle French *retardation,* and directly from Latin *retardātiōnem* (nominative *retardātiō*), from *retardāre* to retard; for suffix see -ATION. The meaning in psychology of mental backwardness or slowness is first recorded in English in 1914, in a translation of Binet and Simon's *Mentally Defective Children.* **—retarded** *adj.* slow in mental development. 1910, from the past participle of English *retard.*

retch *v.* make efforts to vomit. 1548, to clear the throat noisily, bring up phlegm (implied in *retching*), in Elyot's *Dictionary,* alteration (probably by influence of *retch* to stretch, draw out, expand) of Middle English *rechen* to belch, retch (1392); developed from Old English *hrǣcan* to cough up, spit (before 899, in Alfred's translation of St. Gregory's *Pastoral Care*), from Proto-Germanic **Hrǣkjanan,* and related to *hrāca* phlegm, from Proto-Germanic **Hrǣkōn.* Old English *hrǣcan* and *hrāca* are cognate with Old Icelandic *hrāki* spittle, Old High German *rāchisōn* to clear one's throat, hawk. Outside Germanic Old English *hrǣcan* is cognate with Lithuanian *krėgėti* to grunt, Sanskrit *kharjati* (he) rattles, and with Greek *krázein* to scream, shriek, *krṓzein* to croak, caw, from Indo-European **krēg-/krōg-* (Pok.569). The extended meaning of make efforts to vomit is first recorded in 1801.

retention *n.* 1392 *retencioun* power or capacity to retain; borrowed through Old French *retention,* and directly from Latin *retentiōnem* (nominative *retentiō*) a retaining, from *retent-,* past participle stem of *retinēre* RETAIN; for suffix see -ION, -TION. **—retentive** *adj.* About 1390 *retentif* able to hold or keep, in Chaucer's *Canterbury Tales;* borrowed from Old French *retentif* (feminine *retentive*), from Medieval Latin *retentivus* restraining, confining, from Latin *retent-,* past participle stem of *retinēre* retain; for suffix see -IVE. The sense of having a good memory, good at remembering, is first recorded in Lydgate's *Troy Book* (before 1420).

reticence *n.* tendency to be silent or say little. 1603, in Holland's translation of Plutarch's *Moralia;* borrowed from French *réticence,* from Latin *reticentia* silence, from *reticēre* keep silent (*re-* intensive form + *tacēre* be silent; see TACIT); for suffix see -ENCE. According to the OED *reticence* was not in common use in English until after 1830. **—reticent** *adj.* characterized by reticence. Before 1834, in Lamb's *Letters;* formed in English as an adjective to *reticence,* on the model of Latin *reticentem* (nominative *reticēns*), present participle of *reticēre* keep silent; for suffix see -ENT.

reticulate *adj.* covered with a network, netlike. 1658, borrowed from Latin *rēticulātus* having a netlike pattern, from *rēticulum* little net, diminutive of *rēte* net; see RETINA; for suffix see -ATE[1]. **—reticular** *adj.* netlike, reticulate. 1597, borrowed from New Latin *reticularis* of or formed like a network, from Latin *rēticulum* little net; for suffix see -AR. **—reticulation** *n.* netlike formation, network. 1671, in Nehemiah Grew's *The Anatomy of Plants;* formed from English *reticulate* + *-ion.*

retina (ret′ənə) *n.* layer of light-sensitive cells at the back of the eyeball which receives the images of things looked at. 1392, membrane at the back of the eyeball; borrowing of Medieval Latin *retina* membrane on the inside surface of the eyeball, from Latin *rēte* net; so called from the appearance of its blood vessels as a fine network. Latin *rēte* is cognate with Lithuanian *rẽtis* sieve, *ìrti* loosen, separate, from Indo-European **er, erə-* loose (Pok.332).

retinue *n.* About 1385, state of being in service, in Chaucer's *Canterbury Tales;* also, group of attendants or followers, in Usk's *Testament of Love;* borrowed from Old French *retenue* group of followers, state of service, from feminine past participle of *retenir* to employ, RETAIN.

retire *v.* 1533, to retreat, go back, in Bellenden's translation of Livy's *Roman History;* borrowed from Middle French *retirer* (*re-* back + Old French *tirer* to draw; see TIRADE.

The meaning of go away, as for seclusion or rest, is first recorded in 1538, and that of withdraw from an occupation, office, or business activity, in Pepys' *Diary* (1667), and withdraw from company and go to bed, in Dryden's *Conquest of Granada* (1670).

—retiree *n.* 1945, American English, formed from English *retire* + *-ee.* **—retirement** *n.* 1596, act of falling back or retreating, in Shakespeare's *1 Henry IV;* possibly formed from English *retire* + *-ment,* but also found in Middle French *retirement,* from *retirer* to retire; for suffix see -MENT. The meaning of the act of withdrawing into seclusion is also first recorded in Shakespeare's works (*Henry V,* 1599); the meaning of withdrawal from an occupation, office, or business activity, is first attested in 1648, in Oliver Cromwell's *Letters,* quoted by Carlyle.

retool *v.* 1866, to redo the tooling or ornamentation on stonework, a bookbinding, etc.; later, to redesign the dies and manufacturing tools of a factory (1940), and to reorganize something in general (1952); formed from English *re-* again + *tool,* n. and v.

retort[1] (ritôrt′) *v.* About 1557, to return (an insult, wrong, etc.), repay, retaliate; borrowed from Latin *retortus,* past participle of *retorquēre* turn back (*re-* back + *torquēre* to twist; see TORTURE). The extended meaning of answer in kind is first recorded in 1602, and that of say in sharp reply, in 1625. **—n.** sharp or witty reply. 1600, in Shakespeare's *As You Like It;* probably extended from the verb sense of retaliate.

retort[2] (rē′tôrt) *n.* container with a curved or slanting neck, used for distilling or decomposing substances. 1605, borrowed from French *retorte* a vessel with a curved neck, from Medieval Latin *retorta* thing with a twisted neck, from feminine past participle of Latin *retorquēre* turn or bend back (see RETORT[1]).

retrace *v.* 1697, trace the origin of, in Dryden's translation of Vergil's *Aeneid;* probably formed from English *re-* + *trace,* on the model of French *retracer* (*re-* back + Old French *tracier* to follow, TRACE[1]). The meaning of go back upon (one's steps, etc.) is first recorded in 1794. **—retraceable** *adj.* 1847, formed from English *retrace* + *-able.*

retract *v.* withdraw. Probably before 1425 *retracten* draw in or pull back, in a translation of Higden's *Polychronicon;* borrowed from Latin *retractus,* past participle of *retrahere* draw back (*re-* back + *trahere* to draw; see TRACT). The specific sense of draw back (claws, etc.) is first recorded in 1664.

The various and earlier discrete senses of *retract* (in general, draw in or back, as against withdraw or revoke) have become so confused in English that any distinction seems almost artificial, but etymologically the meanings represent distinct words and the sense of *retract* to withdraw (an opinion, declaration, etc.), revoke, recall (1545) was originally either a back formation from *retraction* or borrowed from Latin *retractāre* revoke or cancel (*re-* back + *tractāre* draw violently, frequentative form of *trahere* to draw; see TRACT). **—retraction** *n.* About 1390 *retraccioun* withdrawal of an opinion, etc., in Chaucer's *Canterbury Tales;* borrowed from Latin *retractiōnem* (nominative *retractiō*), from Latin *retrahere* draw back, revoke, cancel. The generalized sense of a drawing back, found later in Middle English (probably before 1425), was borrowed from *retract-,* past participle stem of *retrahere* draw back; for the suffix of both forms see -TION.

In the 1400's and 1500's *retraction* in the sense of withdrawal of an opinion, statement, etc., admission of error, gave way in large part to *retractation* (borrowed from Latin *retractātiōnem,* nominative *retractātiō,* from *retractāre*), possibly by influence of a book of that title written by St. Augustine revising theological matters treated in his previous works.

retreat *n.* Probably about 1300 *retret* a step backwards; later, signal for military withdrawal (1375, in John Barbour's *The Bruce*); borrowed from Old French *retret, retrait,* noun use of past participle of *retrere, retraire* draw back, from Latin *retrahere* draw back (*re-* back + *trahere* to draw; see TRACT). The meaning of an act of withdrawing is first recorded in Gower's *Confessio Amantis* (1393), and that of a safe, quiet place for seclusion or privacy probably before 1437. **—v.** withdraw. 1422 *retreten* draw back or in; later, to withdraw from battle (before 1460); probably from *retret,* n., but perhaps in some instances borrowed from Old French *retret, retrait,* past participle of *retrere, retraire* draw back.

retrench *v.* 1607, cut short, check, repress; later, cut down, reduce (1625); in some instances possibly a back formation from *retrenchment,* but in general probably borrowed from obsolete French *retrencher,* now *retrancher* (*re-* back + Old French *trenchier* to cut; see TRENCH). The extended meaning of reduce expenses, economize, is first recorded in 1663, in Pepys' *Diary.* **—retrenchment** *n.* About 1600, the act of cutting down or out, curtailment, reduction; borrowed from obsolete French *retrenchement* (now *retranchement*), from *retrencher* retrench + *-ment* -ment.

retribution *n.* About 1384 *retribucion* repayment, recompense, return, in the Wycliffe Bible; borrowed from Latin *retribūtiōnem* (nominative *retribūtiō*) recompense, repayment, from *retribuere* hand back, repay (*re-* back + *tribuere* to assign, allot; see TRIBUTE); for suffix see -TION. The meaning of deserved punishment, retaliation for evil done, first recorded in 1570, probably developed from the earlier meaning in theology of the dispensing of divine reward or punishment (1526). **—retributive** *adj.* of or characterized by retribution. 1678, formed from earlier English *retribute,* v., give in return (1575) + *-ive. Retribute* may have been a back formation from *retribution* or borrowed from Latin *retribūtus,* past participle of *retribuere* repay.

retrieve *v.* About 1410 *retreven* (of dogs) to find again (lost game); borrowed from Middle French *retruev-,* stem of *retrouver* find again (*re-* again + *trouver* to find, probably from Vulgar Latin **tropāre* to compose; see CONTRIVE). The extended meaning of recover, regain, restore (anything) is first recorded in English in 1567. **—n.** recovery. 1575, from the verb. **—retrieval** *n.* Before 1643, act of retrieving, recovery, in Cartwright's *Poems;* formed from English *retrieve,* v. + *-al*[2]. **—retriever** *n.* 1486, dog used for retrieving game; formed from Middle English *retreven,* v. + *-er*[1].

retro- a prefix meaning backward, back, behind, as in *retroactive, retrocede, retrogress.* Borrowed from Latin *retrō-,* from *retrō,* prep., adv., backward, back, behind, probably originally the ablative form of a lost contrastive adjective **reteros,* based on *re-* back, as Latin *intrō* inward is formed from a lost adjective **interos;* see RE- and INTRO-.

This combining form became especially productive in the 1950's and 1960's in the fields of astronautics in reference to a rocket's backward or opposing thrust during reentry into the earth's atmosphere, as in *retroengine* (1965), *retrofire* (1961), *retropackage* (1962), *retro-rocket* (1957), *retrosequence* (1962).

retroactive *adj.* 1611, acting back, having an effect on what is past, in Cotgrave's *Dictionary;* borrowed from French *rétroactif* (feminine *rétroactive*) casting, driving, or relating back, from Latin *retroāctus,* past participle of *retroagere* drive or turn back (*retrō-* back, retro- + *agere* to drive; see AGENT).

retrofit *v.* modify (a product) to include changes made in later models. 1954, American English; formed from *retro(active)* + *fit,* v. **—n.** act or process of retrofitting. 1956, from the verb.

retrograde *adj.* moving backward, retreating. 1392, (of a planet) appearing to move backward or contrary to the normal movement; borrowed from Latin *retrōgradus* going backward, from *retrōgradī* move backward (*retrō-* backward + *gradī* to go, step; see GRADE). The generalized meaning of moving backward, especially towards an inferior position is first recorded about 1530. —**v.** 1582, turn back, reverse, revert; borrowed from Latin *retrōgradī* move backward.

retrogress *v.* move backward, go back. 1819, probably a back formation from earlier *retrogression;* but perhaps borrowed (on the model of English *progress*) as if from Latin **retrōgressus,* past participle of *retrōgradī* move backward; see RETROGRADE. —**retrogression** *n.* 1646, apparent backward movement of a planet or other celestial body; formed (on the model of English *progression*) as if from Latin **retrōgressiōnem,* from **retrōgressus,* past participle of *retrōgradī* move backward; for suffix see -SION. The generalized meaning of the act or fact of moving backward in development, a return to a less advanced stage is first recorded in English about 1768.

retrospect *n.* survey of past time or events. 1602, reference to a precedent or authority; borrowed as if from Latin **retrōspectus,* past participle of *retrōspicere* look back (*retrō-* back, retro- + *specere* look at; see SPY). The meaning of a survey of past events is first recorded in Andrew Marvell's correspondence in 1663. —**retrospection** *n.* 1633, act of looking back; borrowed as if from Latin **retrōspectiōnem* (nominative **retrōspectiō*), from the past participle stem of *retrōspicere* look back; for suffix see -TION. —**retrospective** *adj.* 1664, looking back on things past; formed from English *retrospect,* n. + *-ive.* —*n.* exhibition reviewing an artist's work over a period. 1932, American English, from the adjective.

retrovirus *n.* kind of tumor-producing virus. 1977, formed from English *retro-* backward + *virus;* so called because it contains an enzyme (reverse transcriptase) that uses RNA instead of DNA to encode genetic information, and thereby reverses the usual pattern of encoding. The choice of *retro-* may also have been influenced by popular use of the prefix in aerospace terminology and by the initial letters of *re(verse) tr(anscriptase).*

return *v.* Before 1325 *retornen* come or go back; later *returnen* (about 1386, in Chaucer's *Legend of Good Women*); borrowed from Old French *retorner, retourner* turn back, return (*re-* back + *torner, tourner* to TURN). The meaning of to bring or send back is first recorded in Chaucer's translation of Boethius' *De Consolatione Philosophiae* (about 1380). —**n.** Before 1393 *retorn* act of returning, in Gower's *Confessio Amantis;* borrowed from Old French *retorn,* from *retorner* to return. —**returnable** *adj.* Probably before 1424; borrowed from Middle French *retornable, retournable,* from *retorner, retourner* return + *-able* -able; it is also probable that in some instances *returnable* was formed in English from *return* + *-able.* —**returnee** *n.* person who returns to his own country after capture or service abroad. 1944, American English; formed from *return,* n. + *-ee.*

reunite *v.* 1591, from earlier participial adjective *reunit* reunited (before 1500); borrowed from Medieval Latin *reunitus,* past participle of *reunire* unite again (Latin *re-* again + *ūnīre* join together, UNITE). —**reunion** *n.* 1610, in Donne's *Pseudo-Martyr;* borrowed from French *réunion* a reuniting (*re-* again + *union* UNION). The sense of a social gathering of friends or relatives after a separation is first recorded in English in 1820, in Byron's writings.

rev *n. Informal.* revolution (of an engine or motor). 1901, shortened form of *revolution.* —**v.** increase the revolutions or speed of (an engine or motor). 1920, from the noun.

revamp *v.* revise, renovate, repair. 1850, American English; formed from *re-* again + *vamp*[1] patch up.

revanchist (rəväɴ′shist) *n.* person advocating a policy aimed at recovering lost territory. 1926, formed in English from *revanche* revenge (1858, borrowed from French *revanche,* from Middle French *revenche, revenge* REVENGE) + *-ist.*

Revanchist was originally applied to any German nationalist who sought to avenge Germany's defeat in World War I by recovering lost territory. The word was probably modeled on French *revanchard* politician who advocates revenge against an enemy country, used in reference to the defeat of France by Germany in the Franco-Prussian War (1870-71).

reveal *v.* about 1400 *revelen* disclose, make known; borrowed from Old French *reveler,* learned borrowing from Latin *revēlāre* reveal, unveil, draw back a veil (*re-* back, opposite of + *vēlāre* to cover, veil, from *vēlum* a VEIL).

reveille (rev′əlē; *British* rival′ē) *n.* signal on a bugle to waken. 1644, borrowed from French *réveillez* awaken!, imperative plural of *réveiller* to awaken (Middle French *re-* again + *eveiller* to rouse, from Vulgar Latin **exvigilāre,* from Latin *ex-* out + *vigilāre* be awake, keep watch; see VIGILANT).

Early forms of this word included *revelly* and *revalley* (reflecting the British pronunciation); the current spelling appeared in 1700, preceded by *reveillee* (1651).

revel *v.* About 1390 *revelen* make merry; borrowed from Old French *reveler* be disorderly, make merry, from Latin *rebellāre* to rebel. Doublet of REBEL. The meaning of take great pleasure (in) is first recorded in 1754, in Gray's *The Progress of Poesy.* —**n.** merrymaking. Before 1375, earlier as a surname (1201); borrowed from Old French *revel,* from *reveler* to revel. —**revelry** *n.* About 1410, in Chaucer's *Canterbury Tales;* formed from Middle English *revel,* n. + *-ry.*

revelation *n.* act of revealing, thing revealed. About 1303 *revelacyun* disclosure or communication of divine knowledge to man, in Mannyng's *Handlyng Synne;* borrowed through Old French *revelation,* or directly from Late Latin *revēlātiōnem* (nominative *revēlātiō*), from Latin *revēlāre* to REVEAL; for suffix see -ATION.

Revelation as the name of the last book of the New Testament is first found in Middle English about 1384, in the Wycliffe Bible. The meaning of a revealing of something not previously known is first recorded probably about 1475.

revenge *v.* 1375 *revengen* take vengeance, in Barbour's *The Bruce;* borrowed from Old French *revengier,* variant of *revenchier* (*re-* intensive + *vengier* take revenge; see VENGEANCE). —**n.** 1547, in a translation of Vergil's *Aeneid;* borrowed from Middle French *revenge, revenche* revenge, from Old French *revengier, revenchier* to revenge.

revenue *n.* 1419, profit from property or other source of income; 1422, return, yield; borrowing of Middle French *revenue,* from Old French *revenue* a return, from feminine past participle of *revenir* come back, from Latin *revenīre* return, come back (*re-* back + *venīre* COME). The meaning of income from taxes, etc., that a government receives, is first recorded in English in 1690, in Locke's writings, and that of a government department that collects revenue, in 1700. **—revenuer** *n.* revenue agent, especially one enforcing the laws against illegal distilling of liquor. 1880, American English; formed from *revenue* + *-er*[1].

reverberate *v.* 1547, to beat, drive, or force back, probably a back formation from earlier *reverberation,* formed on the model of Latin *reverberātus,* past participle of *reverberāre* beat back (*re-* back + *verberāre* to beat, from *verber* whip, lash, rod; see WARP); for suffix see -ATE[1]. *Reverberate* replaced Middle English *reverberen* (recorded probably before 1425, in a translation of Chauliac's *Grande Chirurgie*); borrowed from Middle French *réverbérer,* from Latin *reverberāre.* As in English, so the Old French noun *réverbération* (1314) is recorded earlier than the verb *réverbérer* (late 1300's), suggesting that the French verb was probably a back formation from the agent noun.

The meaning of send back sound, reecho, is first recorded in English in 1591.

—reverberation *n.* About 1395 *reverberacioun* fact of being driven or forced back, in Chaucer's *Canterbury Tales;* later in the spelling *reverberation* (probably about 1425); borrowed from Old French *reverberation,* from Medieval Latin *reverberationem* (nominative *reverberatio*), from Latin *reverberāre* beat back; for suffix see -ATION. The meaning of a return of sounds, reechoing, is first recorded in English in Bacon's *Sylva Sylvarum* (1626).

revere *v.* 1661, to respect greatly, venerate, in Blount's *Glossographia;* possibly a back formation from *reverence,* reinforced by, and especially in Blount's dictionary, borrowed directly from French *révérer* revere, learned borrowing from Latin *reverērī* (*re-* intensive + *verērī* stand in awe of, fear; see WARY). **—reverence** *n.* About 1280, deep respect felt or shown towards a person; borrowing of Old French *reverence,* from Latin *reverentia* reverence, from *reverērī* to revere; for suffix see -ENCE. **—reverent** *adj.* About 1380, inspiring or worthy of reverence, in Chaucer's translation of Boethius' *De Consolatione Philosophiae;* probably formed in English as an adjective to the noun *reverence,* on the model of Latin *reverentem* (nominative *reverēns*), present participle of *reverērī* revere; for suffix see -ENT. The meaning of feeling or showing reverence, respectful, is first recorded about 1390. **—reverential** *adj.* About 1555, formed in English from Latin *reverentia* reverence + English *-al*[1].

reverend *adj.* worthy of great respect or reverence. 1428, borrowed from Middle French *reverend,* from Latin *reverendus* (he who is) to be respected, gerundive of *reverērī* to REVERE.

Reverend as a respectful form of address or epithet applied to a member of the clergy is first recorded in 1484. In 1642 the word appeared as a title prefixed to a clergyman's name (usually capitalized and often abbreviated as *Rev.*), as in *the Reverend Mr. Bear, the Reverend Dr. Atterbury.*

—n. one who is worthy of respect, especially a member of the clergy. Before 1500, from the adjective.

reverie *n.* About 1350 *ryvori* wild conduct, frolic, revelry; later *reverye* (about 1390, in Chaucer's *Canterbury Tales*); borrowed from Old French *reverie* revelry, raving, delirium, from *rever, resver* to dream, wander, rave, of uncertain origin (perhaps, according to Dauzat, from an Old French **esver* to wander, compare Old French *desver* lose one's mind, with a change in prefix, possibly from Gallo-Romance **esvo* vagabond, from Vulgar Latin **exvagus,* Latin *ex-* out, from + *vagus* roving); or according to others, related to the development of *rave.*

The meaning of dreamy thinking of pleasant things, daydream, is first recorded in English in 1657.

reverse *adj.* About 1303 *revers* opposite or contrary in character, order, etc., in Mannyng's *Handlyng Synne;* borrowed from Old French *revers* reverse, cross, from Latin *reversus,* past participle of *revertere* turn back; see REVERT.

—n. About 1350, in Chaucer's *Canterbury Tales, revers* the opposite or contrary of or to something specified; from the adjective.

—v. Before 1333 *reversen* change, alter; later, turn the other way (before 1393), and go backward (probably before 1425); borrowed from Old French *reverser* turn in an opposite direction, from Late Latin *reversāre* turn round, frequentative form of *revertere* turn back; see REVERT.

—reversal *n.* 1488, act of reversing a legal judgment; formed from English *reverse,* v. + *-al*[2]. The general meaning of the act or process of reversing is first recorded in 1698. **—reversible** *adj.* able to be reversed. 1648, formed from English *reverse,* v. + *-ible.* **—n.** 1863, a reversible garment; 1892, a reversible fabric; from the adjective. **—reversion** *n.* 1394, (in law) an estate that is returned to a donor; later, return of an estate to the grantor or his heirs (about 1436); borrowed from Old French *reversion,* learned borrowing from Latin, and borrowed directly from Latin *reversiōnem* (nominative *reversiō*) act of turning back, from *revers-,* past participle stem of *revertere* turn back; for suffix see -SION. The generalized meaning of a return to a former condition, practice, or belief is first recorded in 1582. The sense in biology of a reverting to a primitive or ancestral type is first recorded in Darwin's *Origin of Species* (1859).

revert *v.* Probably before 1300 *reverten* revive, recover consciousness; later, cause to return (probably before 1400), and return to a previous condition (about 1450); borrowed from Old French *revertir,* from Vulgar Latin **revertīre,* variant of Latin *revertere* turn back (*re-* back + *vertere* to turn; see VERTEX). The specific meaning of return to a custom, practice, idea, etc., is first recorded in Bacon's *Essays* (1612). The sense in biology of return to an earlier or primitive form is first recorded in Darwin's *Origin of Species* (1859).

review *n.* 1441 *review* an inspection of military forces; later, a looking over something with a view to correction or improvement, a revision, as of a book, etc. (1565); borrowed from Middle French *reveüe, revue* a reviewing or review, from feminine past participle of *reveeir* to see again, go to see again, from Latin *revidēre* (*re-* again + *vidēre* to see; see WIT[2] know).

The meaning of a general survey of a subject or thing is first recorded in 1604, that of inspection or examination in Cotgrave's *Dictionary* (1611), and account or criticism of a performance or literary work in 1649. The sense of a magazine devoted to book reviews and essays (as in a *literary review,* a *law review*) is first attested in 1705.

—**v.** 1576, to view or inspect again; formed from English *re-* again + *view,* v., probably influenced by, if not developed from, *review,* n. The meaning of examine again or survey (facts, one's lessons, etc.) is first recorded about 1600, in Shakespeare's *Sonnets.* The sense of write a review (as of new literary or dramatic works) is first cited in 1781.

revile *v.* About 1303 *revilen* to degrade, abuse, in Mannyng's *Handlyng Synne;* borrowed from Old French *reviler* consider vile, despise (*re-* intensive + *vil* VILE).

revise *v.* 1567, look again or back; borrowed from Middle French *reviser,* learned borrowing from Latin *revīsere* look at again, visit again, frequentative form of *revidēre* (*re-* again + *vidēre* to see; see WIT[2] know). The meaning of look over or read over carefully in order to correct or improve is first recorded in the King James Version of the Bible (1611). —**n.** 1591, act of revising or reviewing; from the verb. The meaning of a revised or corrected form is first recorded in 1612. —**revision** *n.* 1611, act or work of revising, review, in Cotgrave's *Dictionary;* borrowed from French, learned borrowing from Late Latin *revīsiōnem* (nominative *revīsiō*), from Latin *revīsere* look at again; for suffix see -SION. The meaning of a revised version is not recorded before 1845.

revive *v.* Probably before 1425 *reviven* return to consciousness; also, restore to health, bring to life again (about 1425); borrowed from Middle French *revivre,* from Latin *revīvere* to live again (*re-* again + *vīvere* to live; see VIVID). The meaning of bring back to notice, come back to use or fashion, return to memory, is first recorded in 1442; and the generalized sense of restore after decline or decay is first cited in 1631. —**revival** *n.* 1651, act of reviving; formed from English *revive* + *-al*[2]. The meaning of a bringing back to notice, such as a literary work or an old play is first recorded in 1664, and that of a general reawakening of religion in a community or in some part of a community is first found in Cotton Mather's writings, in 1702. Later, the sense of special services to awaken or increase interest in religion is recorded in 1799. —**revivalist** *n.* person who promotes or takes part in a religious revival. 1820, formed from English *revival* + *-ist.*

revivify *v.* restore to life; give new life to. 1675, borrowed from French *revivifier,* from Late Latin *revīvificāre* revivify (*re-* again + *vīvificāre* make alive; see VIVIFY). Earlier *revivification* (1638, of which obsolete *revivificate,* 1660, was probably a back formation, but *revivify* is not) was formed in English from Late Latin *revīvificāre* + English suffix *-ation,* as if from Latin **revīvificātiōnem* (nominative **revīvificātiō*).

revocation *n.* About 1410 *revocacioun* act of revoking, retraction (of an oath, vow, etc.); borrowed from Middle French *revocation,* learned borrowing from Latin, and borrowed directly from Latin *revocātiōnem* (nominative *revocātiō*), from *revocāre* REVOKE; for suffix see -ATION. —**revocable** *adj.* capable of being revoked. Before 1500, probably borrowed from Middle French *revocable,* from Old French *revoquer* revoke + *-able* -able, but later assimilated with *revokable* (1584), a formation in English of *revoke,* v. + *-able,* which appears to have dropped out of use in the latter half of the 1700's.

revoke *v.* About 1350 *revoken* make a retraction; later, to call back (about 1384), and rescind, repeal, annul (about 1400); borrowed from Old French *revoquer,* learned borrowing from Latin *revocāre* rescind, call back (*re-* back + *vocāre* to call, related to *vōx,* genitive *vōcis* VOICE). —**n.** (in cards) renege; failure to follow suit. 1709, from the verb.

revolt *v.* to rebel. 1548, in Elyot's *Dictionary;* borrowed from Middle French *revolter,* from Italian *rivoltare* to revolt, overthrow, overturn, from Vulgar Latin **revolvitāre* to overturn, overthrow, frequentative form of Latin *revolvere* turn, roll back; see REVOLVE. —**n.** rebellion. 1560, borrowed from Middle French *révolte,* from Italian *rivolta* a revolt, overthrow, turn, from *rivoltare* to revolt. —**revolting** *adj.* 1593, that revolts or rebels, in Shakespeare's *Richard II,* from the present participle of *revolt;* for suffix see -ING[2]. The sense of that repels, repulsive, disgusting, is first recorded in 1806.

revolution *n.* About 1385 *revolucioun* the revolving of a celestial body in an orbit or circle, in Chaucer's *The Complaint of Mars;* later, change of fortune (probably before 1400), and a turning of a wheel (before 1420); borrowed from Old French *revolution,* learned borrowing from Late Latin *revolūtiōnem* (nominative *revolūtiō*) a revolving, from Latin *revolūt-,* past participle stem of *revolvere* turn, roll back; see REVOLVE; for suffix see -TION.

The political meaning of revolution as an overthrow of an established government is first recorded in English in 1600 (possibly derived from the political use in French in 1559), and was initially reinforced in English in reference to the expulsion of the Stuart dynasty in 1688, and later particularly to the violent turmoil of the French Revolution (1789-95), which at that time seems to have had more effect on and caused much greater concern among the British than the American Revolution (1775-81).

—**revolutionary** *adj.* 1774, of or connected with a political revolution; formed from English *revolution* + *-ary.* The term was reinforced particularly in the phrase Revolutionary War, used widely in American English. —*n.* one who instigates or favors a political revolution. 1850, from the adjective. —**revolutionize** *v.* 1797, bring about a revolution in (a country); formed from English *revolution* + *-ize.* The generalized meaning of change over completely or fundamentally is first recorded shortly thereafter in 1799.

revolve *v.* About 1385 *revolven* to change, in Thomas Usk's *The Testament of Love;* turn around (about 1450); borrowed through Old French *revolver,* and directly from Latin *revolvere* turn, roll back (*re-* back, again + *volvere* to roll; see VOLUME). The specific meaning of cause to travel in an orbit around a central point, rotate on an axis, is first recorded in Milton's *Paradise Lost* (1667).

revolver *n.* pistol that can be fired several times without reloading. 1835, American English, from *revolve* + *-er*[1]; so called by its inventor, Samuel Colt, because it consists of a set of cartridge chambers which revolve in succession when the gun is fired.

revue *n.* theatrical entertainment. 1872, show presenting a humorous or satirical review of current events, fashions, etc.; borrowing of French *revue* from Middle French, survey; see REVIEW.

revulsion *n.* sudden violent change or reaction. 1541, a diverting of a disease or blood from one region of the body to another; borrowed from Latin *revulsiōnem* (nominative *revulsiō*) act of pulling away, from *revuls-,* past participle stem of *revellere* to pull away (*re-* away + *vellere* to tear, pull, pluck; see VULTURE); for suffix see -SION. The sense of a sudden violent change or reaction, especially of disgust, is first recorded in Scott's *Old Mortality* (1816).

reward *v.* Probably before 1300, to grant, bestow; later, to recompense or reward (about 1350); borrowed from Anglo-French and Old North French *rewarder,* variant of Old French *regarder, reguarder* take notice of, regard, watch over; see the doublet REGARD. **—n.** Before 1338, regard, consideration, in Mannyng's *Chronicle of England;* borrowed from Anglo-French and probably Old North French *reward,* from *rewarder* take notice of. The meaning of something given in return for a thing done, recompense, is first recorded in 1371.

rhapsody *n.* utterance or writing marked by extravagant enthusiasm. 1542, epic poem suitable for recitation at one time (especially in reference to parts of Homer's *Iliad* and *Odyssey* recited at one time), in Udall's translation of Erasmus' *Apothegms;* borrowed from Latin *rhapsōdia,* from Greek *rhapsōidiā* verse composition, a derivative of *rhapsōidós* reciter of epic poems (*rháptein* to stitch + *ōidḗ* song; see ODE). Greek *rháptein,* earlier **wrapye-,* is cognate with Lithuanian *virpěti* to tremble, quiver, and *veȓpti* to spin, from Indo-European **wer-p-/wr̥-p-* turn, twist (Pok.1156); see WARP.

The meaning of an utterance or writing marked by extravagant enthusiasm is first recorded in English in 1639, and the transferred sense in music of an instrumental composition of indefinite form marked by enthusiastic character is first recorded in English after 1851.

—rhapsodic *adj.* extravagantly enthusiastic. 1782, shortened form of earlier *rhapsodical* (1659, formed in English from Greek *rhapsōidikós,* from *rhapsōidiā* rhapsody + English suffix *-ical*). Later *rhapsodic* was a shortening influenced by Greek *rhapsōidikós;* for suffix see -IC. **—rhapsodize** *v.* 1607, formed from English *rhapsody* + *-ize.* The meaning of talk or relate rhapsodically is first recorded in 1806.

rhea (rē′ə) *n.* kind of large bird similar to the ostrich. 1801, New Latin *Rhea* the genus name, from Latin *Rhea* mother of Zeus, Hera, and other Greek gods and goddesses, from Greek *Rhéā.*

rhenium (rē′nēəm) *n.* metallic chemical element. 1925, New Latin, formed from Latin *Rhēnus* the Rhine River + New Latin *-ium* (chemical suffix). The term was coined by its discoverers, the German chemists Walter and Ida Noddack and their colleague, O. Berg.

rheo- a combining form meaning flow, stream, current, as in *rheology, rheostat;* borrowed from Greek *rhéos* a flowing, stream, from *rheîn* to flow; see STREAM.

rheology (rēol′əjē) *n.* science that deals with flow and alteration of form of matter. 1929, borrowed from French *rhéologie,* from *rheo-* flow + *-logie* study of, -logy. **—rheological** *adj.* 1930, formed from English *rheology* + *-ical.* **—rheologist** *n.* 1931, formed from English *rheology* + *-ist.*

rheostat (rē′əstat) *n.* instrument for regulating the strength of an electric current. 1843, formed from English *rheo-* (electric) flow or current + *-stat* (regulating device). The term was coined by the English physicist Sir Charles Wheatstone.

rhesus (rē′səs) *n.* kind of small monkey of India, often used in medical research. 1827, New Latin *Rhesus* the genus name of this monkey, said to be an arbitrary use of Latin *Rhēsus,* name of a legendary prince of Thrace, from Greek *Rhêsos.* Compare RH FACTOR.

rhetoric (ret′ərik) *n.* art of using language, especially to persuade or influence others. About 1330 *Rettorike,* later *rethoryk* (before 1382, in the Wycliffe Bible); borrowed from Old French *rethorique,* from Latin *rhētoricē,* from Greek *rhētorikḗ téchnē* art of an orator, from *rhḗtōr* (genitive *rhḗtoros*) orator; earlier **wrḗtōr,* see WORD; for suffix see -IC.

The spelling *rhetoric* (with *rh-*) is first recorded about 1475, in imitation of the Latin spelling. The extended sense of mastery of literary eloquence, elegance in writing or speech, appeared in Middle English in 1395, in Chaucer's *Canterbury Tales.* The depreciatory meaning of language characterized by artificial, ostentatious, or exaggerated expression, is first recorded in the 1500's.

—rhetorical *adj.* 1447 *rethorycal,* as an alternate to earlier *rethorik,* adj. (about 1385), and formed from Middle English *rethoryk,* n. + *-al*[1], partially on the model of Latin *rhētoricus,* from Greek *rhētorikós,* from *rhḗtōr* orator. The term *rhetorical question,* a question asked only for effect, not for information, is first recorded in 1843. **—rhetorician** *n.* person skilled in rhetoric. Before 1420 *rethoricyen,* in Lydgate's *Troy Book;* later *rethorician* (about 1450); borrowed from Middle French *rethoricien,* from Old French *rethorique* + *-ien* -ian. The spelling *rhetorician* (with *rh-*) is first recorded about 1450, in imitation of the Latin spelling.

rheum (rüm) *n.* watery discharge such as mucus, tears, or saliva. About 1373 *reame;* also *reume* (about 1378, 1392); borrowed from Old French *reume,* learned borrowing from Latin *rheuma,* from Greek *rheûma* a flowing, from *rhein* to flow; see STREAM. The spelling *rheum* (with *rh-*) is first recorded in English in 1591.

rheumatism (rü′mətizəm) *n.* disease of the joints. 1601 *rheumatisme* excessive flow of rheum; borrowed perhaps through Middle French *rhumatisme,* learned borrowing from Latin *rheumatismus* rheum, flux, from Greek *rheumatismós,* from *rheumatízein* suffer from a flux, from *rheûma* RHEUM.

In Middle English, *reumatisme* is recorded once as an adjective (probably about 1425, in a translation of Chauliac's *Grande Chirurgie*), with the sense of consisting of rheum; probably borrowed from a Medieval Latin form of Latin *rheumatismus.* The specific meaning of a disease of the joints is first recorded in 1688, because rheumatism was formerly thought to be caused by an excessive flow of rheum, as is attested in Chauliac's use of *reumatising* (about 1425) in reference to rheum flowing into a joint and thereby stretching ligaments.

—rheumatic *adj.* 1392 *reumatik* consisting of, or of the nature of rheum; borrowed through Old French *reumatique* (learned borrowing from Latin), and borrowed directly from Latin *rheumaticus* troubled with rheum, from Greek *rheumatikós,* from *rheûma* rheum; for suffix see -IC. The meaning of suffering from a disease caused by rheum is first recorded in Middle English probably about 1425, in a translation of Chauliac's *Grande Chirurgie.* The sense of having to do with or characterized by rheumatism is first recorded in 1704. **—rheumatoid** *adj.* 1859, in the phrase *rheumatoid arthritis,* resembling rheumatism; formed in English from Greek *rheúmat-,* stem of *rheûma* (genitive *rheúmatos*) rheum + English *-oid.*

Rh factor antigen found in the red blood cells. 1942, from *rh(esus);* so called because it was first discovered in the blood of the rhesus monkey.

rhin- a variant of the combining form *rhino-* before a vowel, as in *rhinal, rhinitis.*

rhinal (rī′nəl) *adj.* of or having to do with the nose, nasal. 1864, formed from English *rhin-* + *-al*[1].

rhinestone *n.* glass stone used in costume jewelry. 1888, formed in English from *Rhine* river in western Europe + *stone,* as a loan translation of French *caillou du Rhin* Rhine pebble; so called because rhinestones were originally made in Strasbourg, a city near the Rhine River in northeastern France.

rhinitis (rīnī′tis) *n.* inflammation of the nose or its mucous membrane. 1884, New Latin; formed from *rhin-* of the nose + *-itis* inflammation.

rhino (rī′nō) *n.* 1884, shortened form of *rhinoceros.*

rhino- a combining form meaning nose or of the nose, as in *rhinoceros, rhinoscope, rhinovirus.* Borrowed from Greek *rhīno-,* combining form of *rhī́s* (genitive *rhīnós*) nose, of uncertain origin.

rhinoceros (rīnos′ərəs) *n.* large, thick-skinned mammal. Probably before 1300 *rinoceros,* in *Kyng Alisaunder;* borrowed from Latin *rhīnocerōs,* from Greek *rhīnókerōs* (*rhīnós* nose; see RHINO- + *kéras* HORN); so called from the one or two upright horns on the rhinoceros' snout. The spelling *rhinoceros* is first recorded in English in 1553, in imitation of the Latin form.

rhinovirus (rī′nōvī′rəs) *n.* type of virus associated with the common cold. 1961, formed from English *rhino-* of the nose + *virus.*

rhizome (rī′zōm) *n.* rootlike stem. 1845, borrowed perhaps through French *rhizome* (1817), from New Latin *rhizoma,* from Greek *rhízōma* mass of tree roots, from *rhizoûn* cause to strike root, from *rhíza* ROOT, earlier **wridya* (Indo-European **wredyə*).

rhodium (rō′dēəm) *n.* metallic chemical element. 1804, New Latin; formed from Greek *rhódon* ROSE + New Latin *-ium* (chemical suffix); so called from the rosy color of the element's salts. The term was coined by its discoverer the English chemist and physicist William H. Wollaston.

rhododendron (rō′dəden′drən) *n.* kind of evergreen shrub of the heath family. 1601, oleander, in Holland's translation of Pliny's *Natural History;* borrowed through French, or directly from Latin *rhododendron,* from Greek *rhodódendron,* a compound of *rhódon* ROSE + *déndron* tree, related to *drŷs* TREE. The word in the sense of an evergreen shrub of the heath family is not recorded before 1664.

rhombus (rom′bəs) *n.* parallelogram with equal sides. 1567, borrowing of Late Latin *rhombus,* from Greek *rhómbos* rhombus, spinning top, from *rhémbesthai* to spin, whirl, of uncertain origin. **—rhomboid** *n.* parallelogram with equal opposite sides. 1570, borrowed from Middle French *rhomboïde,* from Late Latin *rhomboīdēs,* from Greek *rhomboeidḗs* shaped like a rhombus, from *rhómbos* rhombus + *-oeidḗs* -oid.

rhubarb (rü′bärb) *n.* kind of garden plant. About 1390, borrowed from Old French *rubarbe, reubarbe,* learned borrowing from Medieval Latin *rheubarbarum,* alteration of *rhabarbarum,* from Greek *rhâ bárbaron* foreign rhubarb (*rhâ* rhubarb, associated with *Rhâ,* ancient name of the Volga river; and *bárbaron* foreign, neuter of *bárbaros;* see BARBARIAN). The Medieval Latin variant *rheubarbarum* was probably influenced in form by Greek *rhêon* rhubarb, from Persian *rēwend.* The New Latin genus name of the rhubarb, *Rheum,* was coined by Linnaeus from Greek *rhêon.*

rhyme or **rime** (rīm) *n.* 1610 *rhyme* verse or poetry; a spelling alteration (influenced by *rhythm*) of Middle English (about 1200) *ryme, rime* measure, meter, rhythm (probably about 1200, in *The Ormulum*); later, rhymed verse (before 1250); borrowed from Old French *rime* (feminine), related to Old Provençal *rim* (masculine), both Old French and Old Provençal probably from a Germanic source (compare Old High German, Old Frisian and Old English *rīm* number, Old Icelandic *rīm* reckoning, computation, and Old English *rīman* to count, recount, enumerate, these Germanic words being cognate with Old Irish *rīm* number, Welsh *rhif,* and Greek *arithmós* number; see ARITHMETIC). All these are from Indo-European **ari-, rī-,* with extension *rīm-* (Pok.60).

The origin of Old French *rime* is uncertain. It was long thought that Old French *rime* developed from Latin *rhythmus* RHYTHM, but this assumption was later questioned on phonetic and semantic grounds. For instance, there is no evidence for intermediate forms in Old French, such as **ritme* or **ridme,* to justify Latin *rhythmus* as the source. Also, the sense of Old French *rime* rhymed verse differs substantially from the Latin *rhythmus* metrical movement. An assumed Germanic source presents its own obstacles, particularly in postulating an unrecorded sense of series or row in addition to the attested meanings of number or reckoning. (A case for the Germanic origin of Old French *rime* is presented in FEW 70, 1959).

Earliest English spelling *rime,* still found in Coleridge's *The Rime of the Ancient Mariner,* is now generally displaced by *rhyme.*

—v. 1660 *rhime* to make rhymes or verses; spelling alteration (influenced by *rhythm*) of Middle English *rymen, rimen* (about 1300), from *ryme, rime,* n.

—rhymester *n.* maker of rather poor verses. 1719 *rhimester,* alteration of earlier *rimester* (1589); formed from Middle English *rime,* n. + *-ster.*

rhythm (riᴛʜ′əm) *n.* About 1557, rhyming or rhymed verse; also, metrical movement with alternating long and short, or accented and unaccented syllables (1560); borrowed from Latin *rhythmus* movement in time, rhythm, from Greek *rhythmós* measured flow or movement, rhythm, related to *rheîn* to flow; see STREAM.

The meaning in music of repetition of beats, arrangement of recurring strong and weak accents, is first recorded in English in 1776. The generalized meaning of any movement with a regular succession of strong and weak elements (as in *the rhythm of the tides*) is not recorded in English until 1855).

—rhythmic *adj.* having rhythm. Before 1631 *rythmique,* in Donne's *Works;* shortened form of earlier *rhythmical;* formed from English *rhythm* + *-ic,* on the model of French *rhythmique,* from Latin *rhythmicus,* from Greek *rhythmikós,* from *rhythmós* rhythm. **—rhythmical** *adj.* 1567, rhyming; formed in English from Latin *rhythmicus* of rhythm + English *-al*[1]. The sense of having rhythm appeared in 1589.

rib *n.* Probably before 1200 *rib, ribbe,* in Layamon's *Chronicle of Britain;* later in the spelling *rib* (before 1325); developed from Old English (before 800) *ribb* rib; cognate with Old Frisian *ribb, rebbe* rib, Old Saxon *ribbi,* Middle Dutch and modern Dutch *ribbe,* Old High German *rippi, rippa* (modern German *Rippe*), and Old Icelandic *rif* (Norwegian *riv*), from Proto-Germanic **reƀja-.* Outside Germanic cognates are found in Old Slavic *rebró* rib, and Greek *eréphein* to roof over, from Indo-European **rebh-* (Pok.853). The meaning of cut of meat for food is first recorded before 1398, and that of a framework as for the hull of a boat, in 1378. **—v.** furnish or strengthen with ribs, enclose as with ribs. Before 1547, in a translation of Vergil's *Aeneid;* from the noun. The informal meaning of tease, fool, is first recorded in 1930 in American English, perhaps as a figurative use of the earlier sense of beat (one) on the ribs (1723).

ribald *n.* coarsely irreverent or wanton person. Before 1250 *ribaude* low, worthless fellow, rascal, scoundrel; later, a coarsely irreverent or wanton person (probably before 1300, in *Kyng Alisaunder*), and in the spelling *ribald* (before 1393); borrowed from Old French *ribalt, ribaut, ribaud,* from *riber* be wanton, from a Germanic source; compare Old High German *rīban* be wanton, literally, to rub, modern German *reiben* to rub, which are cognate with Middle Low German and Middle Dutch *wrīven* to rub (from Proto-Germanic **wrīƀanan*), and Greek *rhíptein* to throw, from Indo-European **wreip-/wrīp-* turn (Pok.1159). **—adj.** coarsely irreverent or wanton. 1500-20, in Dunbar's *Poems;* from the noun, and replacing *ribaudi.* **—ribaldry** *n.* Before 1325, in *Cursor Mundi, ribaudrie* ribald language, debauchery; later in the spelling *ribaldrie* (about 1450); borrowed from Old French *ribaulderie, ribauderie,* from *ribauld* ribald; for suffix see -RY.

ribbon *n.* Probably about 1325 *riban* strip or band of cloth; borrowed from Old French *riban* a ribbon, variant of *ruban,* of uncertain origin (possibly from a Germanic compound whose first element is uncertain and whose second element is related to *band,* as in early modern Dutch *ringhband* dog's collar).

The spelling *rybban* appeared in 1446, and *rybben* in 1545; the current spelling is first attested in Shakespeare's *A Winter's Tale* (1611), and with *-on* is reminiscent of the *-on* in *button.*

riboflavin (rī′bōflā′vin) *n.* a constituent of the vitamin B complex present in food. 1935, formed from English *ribo(se)* + *flavin,* from Latin *flāvus* yellow (see BLUE); so called because it is a yellowish pigment derived from ribose. The original name in Great Britain was *flavin* (1933).

ribonucleic acid (rī′bōnüklē′ik) acid found in the nuclei of all living cells, RNA. 1931, formed from English *ribo(se)* sugar component of this acid + *nucleic acid.*

ribose (rī′bōs) *n.* sugar present in the nucleic acid of cells. 1892, borrowing of German *Ribose,* shortened and altered form of earlier English *arabinose* a kind of sugar (about 1880); formed from *gum arabic,* a gum used in preparing arabinose + *-in*[2] + *-ose*[2].

ribosome (rī′bəsōm) *n.* cellular particle consisting largely of ribonucleic acid. 1958, formed from English *ribo-(nucleic acid)* + *-some*[3] body. **—ribosomal** *adj.* of or having to do with a ribosome. 1959, formed from English *ribosome* + *-al*[1].

rice *n.* 1234 *ris, rys;* later *ryce* (before 1475); borrowed from Old French *ris,* from Italian *riso,* learned borrowing from Latin *oriza, oryza,* from Greek *óryza* rice, from an Indo-Iranian form (compare Pashto *vrižē* and Sanskrit *vrīhí-s,* both meaning rice, of unknown origin). **—v.** reduce to a form like rice (as in *to rice vegetables*). 1923, from the noun.

rich *adj.* Before 1121 *riche,* probably a fusion of Old French *riche* wealthy, from a Germanic source; and Old English (before 900) *rīce* wealthy, powerful, mighty. Old English *rīce* (from Proto-Germanic **rīkjaz*) is cognate with Old Frisian *rīke* wealthy, mighty, Old Saxon *rīki,* Middle Low German and Middle Dutch *rīke* (modern Dutch *rijk* wealthy), Old High German *rīhhi* (modern German *reich*), Old Icelandic *rīkr* (Norwegian and Swedish *rik,* Danish *rig*), and Gothic *reiks* mighty, sovereign, *reiki* rule, realm, kingdom. The Germanic words were all borrowed from a Celtic word or group of words represented by Gaulish *Rīgo-* and *-rīx* (well attested in proper names) and by Old Irish *rī* (genitive *rīg*) king; see REGAL. **—riches** *n.pl.* Probably before 1200 *richesces* wealth, in *Ancrene Riwle,* variant of *richesse* (also probably before 1200, a singular form misunderstood as a plural); borrowed from Old French *richesse* wealth, opulence, from *riche* RICH. The Old French suffix *-esse* derives from Latin *-itia,* added to adjectives to form nouns of quality, found in *duresse, largesse.*

rick *n.* Before 1325 *reke* stack of hay, straw, etc.; later *reek* (1440), developed from Old English (900) *hrēac* rick. Old English *hrēac* is cognate with Middle Dutch *rooc* rick (modern Dutch *rook*), Old Icelandic *hraukr* rick (Norwegian *rauk*), from Proto-Germanic **Hraukaz,* Indo-European **kroug-* (Pok.938), and perhaps related to Old English *hrycg* RIDGE. **—v.** form into a rick or ricks. 1623, from the noun.

rickets *n.* disease of the bones due to lack of vitamin D. 1634, of uncertain origin. *Rickets* was originally a localism applied to the disease in Dorset and Somerset, southwestern England, where it was first recognized about 1620. In 1650 the New Latin technical name *rachitis* was adopted from Late Greek *rhachîtis* inflammation of the spine (from Greek *rháchis* spine), probably because of the resemblance of *rachitis* to the common English name *rickets.* **—rickety** *adj.* 1685, (figurative) liable to fall or break down; formed from English *rickets* + *-y*[1]. The rare literal meaning of having rickets is first recorded about 1720.

rickettsia (riket′sēə) *n.* kind of microorganism that causes typhus and other diseases. 1919, New Latin *Rickettsia* the genus name of this organism, formed in allusion to Howard Taylor's *Ricketts* (1871-1910, American pathologist, who first identified the microorganism in 1909 and died a year later from typhus contracted during his investigation of this disease in Mexico City).

rickey *n.* kind of alcoholic drink. 1895, American English, reputedly from the name of a Colonel *Rickey.*

rickshaw or **ricksha** (rik′shô) *n.* = jinrikisha. 1887, a shortened and altered form of JINRIKISHA.

ricochet (rik′əshā′) *n.* rebound. 1769, rebound (of a projectile along the ground); borrowing of French *ricochet,* from Old French, especially in *fable du ricochet* entertainment in which the teller of a tale skillfully evades questions, and *chanson du ricochet* a kind of repetitious song, of uncertain origin. **—v.** to rebound. 1828, from the noun.

rid *v.* Probably before 1200 *ruden, rudden* to clear (a way or space), set free, save; also *ridden* (before 1250); borrowed from a Scandinavian source (compare Old Icelandic *rydhja* to clear or free of obstructions, past tense *ruddi,* past participle *ruddr*); cognate with Old Frisian *rothia* to clear, Middle Low German and modern German *roden,* and Old High German *riuten* to clear land (modern dialectal German *reuten*), from Proto-Germanic **reuđijanan,* Indo-European **reudh-* (Pok.869).

The phrase *rid of* free from (a troublesome or useless thing or person) is first recorded probably before 1400. **—riddance** *n.* 1535, clearance, removal, in the Coverdale Bible; formed from English *rid* + *-ance.* The exclamation *good riddance,* in which *riddance* means deliverance or relief, is first found in 1782, preceded by *gentle riddance* (1596, in Shakespeare's *Merchant of Venice*).

riddle[1] *n.* puzzling question or statement. Probably about 1225 *redel, redels;* developed from Old English *rǣdels* opinion, counsel, conjecture, riddle (about 1000, in Ælfric's paraphrase of the book of *Numbers* in the Bible). Old English *rǣdels* (showing metathesis of *s* and *l*) is cognate with Old Frisian *riedsal* riddle, Old Saxon *rādisli,* Middle Dutch *raedsel* (modern Dutch *raadsel*), and Middle High German *rātsel* (modern German *Rätsel*),from Proto-Germanic **rǣđislijan,* and is related to Old English *rǣdan* to advise, READ. **—v.** speak in riddles. 1571, in Golding's translation of Calvin's *Commentaries on Psalms;* from the noun.

riddle[2] *n.* coarse sieve. About 1350 *ridelle;* later *riddil* (about 1395); developed from Late Old English (before 1100) *hriddel* sieve, alteration (by dissimilation of *l* to *r*) of Old English (before 800) *hridder, hrīder* sieve, cognate with Old High German *rītera, rītra* (modern German *Reiter*) a sieve, from Proto-Germanic **Hrīđran.* Outside Germanic cognates are found in Latin *crībrum* sieve, *cernere* to sift, Old Irish *crīathar* and Old Welsh *cruitr* sieve; see CERTAIN. **—v.** make many holes in. Probably before 1200 *ridlen* to sift, pass through a riddle, in *Ancrene Riwle;* later *riddlen* (about 1395), from *ridelle, riddil,* n. The meaning of make many holes in is first recorded in 1817, and the figurative sense of impair or weaken, as if by making many holes in, in 1888; an earlier figurative sense of shoot at, as if to pierce, is found in Mark Twain's writings in 1872.

ride *v.* 1123 *riden* to ride, travel; developed from Old English *rīdan* ride (as on horseback), move forward (as a ship or cloud), rock (as a ship at anchor), swing (about 725, in *Beowulf*); cognate with Old Frisian *rida* to ride, Old Saxon *rīdan,* Middle Low German and Middle Dutch *rīden* (modern Dutch *rijden*), Old High German *rītan* (modern German *reiten*), and Old Icelandic *rīdha* (Swedish *rida,* Norwegian and Danish *ride*), from Proto-Germanic **rīđanan.* Cognates outside Germanic include Old Irish *riadaim* I ride, Gaulish *rēda* wagon, and Latvian *raidīt* to rush, send quickly. Related to ROAD. **—n.** About 1250, in the phrase *wenden ride* make one's way; from the verb. The next appearance of the noun is in 1779, previous expression of the noun sense therefore found in the verbal noun *riding* a ride on horseback (probably before 1300), a path or way (probably about 1200), which is parallel to the development of *read* as a noun, replacing *reading* in many instances. **—rider** *n.* Probably before 1200, in Layamon's *Chronicle of Britain;* found in Old English *rīder, rīdere,* formed from *rīdan* + *-er*[1].

ridge *n.* Probably before 1200, in Layamon's *Chronicle of Britain, rugge* back, spine, ridge; also *rug,* in *Ancrene Riwle;* earlier as a surname *Rigge* (1166); developed from Old English *hrycg* back of a man or beast (about 725, in *Beowulf*); and probably reinforced by Old Icelandic *hryggr* back, ridge. Old English *hrycg* and Old Icelandic *hryggr* are cognate with Old Frisian *hregg* the back, Old Saxon *hruggi,* Middle Low German *rugge,* Middle Dutch *ruc* (modern Dutch *rug*), and Old High German *hrukki* (modern German *Rücken*), from Proto-Germanic **Hruȝjás.* Cognates outside Germanic include Middle Irish *crūach* heap, hill, Welsh *crug* heap, knoll, Latin *crux* CROSS, from Indo-European **krouk-/kruk-* (Pok.938). The spelling with *-dg-,* as in *rydge,* is first recorded before 1470; for a note on spelling see DRUDGE. **—v.** form or make into ridges. 1440 *riggen* put a ridgepole in a roof; from *rigge,* n. **—ridgepole** *n.* 1788, horizontal pole of a tent; 1814, horizontal timber into which rafters are fastened in a roof.

ridicule *n.* 1677, laughable or absurd thing; borrowed from French *ridicule,* and directly from Latin *rīdiculum* laughing matter, joke, from neuter of *rīdiculus* RIDICULOUS. It is probable that *ridicule* was borrowed into English by influence of earlier *ridiculous.*

The meaning of words or actions that make fun of something or someone is first recorded in 1690. **—v.** 1684, make ridiculous, probably from English *ridicule,* n., reinforced by earlier French *ridiculer* (now *ridiculiser*), from *ridicule,* n. The meaning of laugh at, make fun of, is first recorded in English before 1700. **—ridiculous** *adj.* 1550, borrowed from Latin *rīdiculōsus* laughable, from *rīdiculus,* from *rīdēre* to laugh, cognate with Sanskrit *vrīdate* is ashamed, from Indo-European **wrisd-* (Pok.1158); for suffix see -OUS.

rife *adj.* Probably before 1200 *rife* numerous, abundant, prevalent, widespread, in Layamon's *Chronicle of Britain;* developed from Old English *rīfe* abundant; cognate with Middle Low German *rive* abundant, Middle Dutch *rive, rijf,* and Old Icelandic *rīfr* agreeable, desired (modern Icelandic *rīfur* abundant, ample).

Throughout its history, *rife* has primarily functioned as a predicate adjective (*rumors were rife*). On rare occasions it has been used to modify a noun (*a rife phrase, rife flocks*).

riff *n.* recurring melodic phrase in jazz. 1935 (but according to jazzmen, current since about 1917), American English, of uncertain origin; perhaps a shortened form of RIFFLE, *n.* **—v.** to perform riffs. 1955, from the noun.

riffle *v.* to shuffle, skim. 1754, American English, to form rapids or a stretch of choppy water; perhaps variant of RUFFLE[1] make rough. The meaning of shuffle (cards) is first recorded in 1894. The extended sense of skim, leaf through quickly, is first cited in 1922. **—n.** 1785, American English, rapids, stretch of choppy water; from the verb. The meaning of act of riffling or shuffling (cards) is first recorded in 1894.

riffraff *n.* worthless people. About 1475, in Gregory's *Chronicle of London,* from earlier *rif and raf, riffe and raf* one and all, every scrap (before 1338, in Mannyng's *Chronicle of England*); borrowed from Old French *rif et raf,* and *rifle et rafle,* from *rifler* to spoil, strip, RIFLE[2] and *raffler* carry off, related to *rafle* plundering; see RAFFLE. **—adj.** worthless. About 1608, from the noun.

rifle[1] *n.* gun with spiral grooves in its barrel. Before 1751, noun use of earlier *rifled,* adj. (1689, as in *rifled pistol, rifled piece*); from the verb. **—v.** 1635, to cut spiral grooves in (a gun barrel); probably borrowed from French *rifler,* from Old French *rifler* to scratch or groove; see RIFLE[2].

rifle[2] *v.* search and rob. About 1333, and before 1338 *riflen;* borrowed from Old French *rifler* to graze, scratch; also, strip, plunder, probably from a Germanic source (compare obsolete Dutch *rijffelen* to scratch, modern German *riefeln* to groove, flute (from Low German), Old English *geriflian* to wrinkle, and probably Old Icelandic *rīfa* to tear, Danish *rifle,* Swedish *reffla* to groove, chamfer), of unknown origin.

rift *n.* Before 1325 *rift* a split, act of splitting or breaking, in *Cursor Mundi;* borrowed from a Scandinavian source (compare Old Icelandic *ript,* pronounced rift, and meaning breach, related to *rīfa* to tear, RIVE). **—v.** cause or form a rift. Before 1325 *riften,* in *Cursor Mundi;* borrowed from a Scandinavian source (compare Old Icelandic *ripta* to breach, related to *ript* a breach).

rig *v.* equip (a ship) with masts, sails, ropes, etc. About 1489 *riggen,* in Caxton's translation of *Blanchardyn and Eglantine;* probably borrowed from a Scandinavian source (compare Danish and Norwegian *rigge* to equip, rig, and Swedish *rigga* to rig). **—n.** arrangement of masts, sails, ropes, etc., on a ship. 1822, either from the verb or a shortened form of *rigging.* The sense of clothes, costume, is first recorded in Hughes' *Tom Brown's School Days* (1857). **—rigging** *n.* ropes, chains, etc., to work the sails and support the masts of a ship (1594).

right *adj.* Before 1121 *riht, rihte* straight, lawful, true, genuine; later, in the spelling *right* (about 1303); found in Old English (before 830) *riht* just, good, fair, proper, fitting, straight; cognate with Old Frisian *riucht* right, Old Saxon *reht,* Middle Dutch and modern Dutch *recht,* Old High German *reht* (modern German *recht*), Old Icelandic *rēttr* (Norwegian *rett,* Danish *ret,* Swedish *rät*), and Gothic *raíhts,* from Proto-Germanic **reHtaz.* Cognates outside Germanic include Old Irish *recht* law, Welsh *rhaith,* Latin *rēctus* straight, right, *rogāre* to ask, propose, request (from a lost noun **rogā́* an addressing, a question), *regere* keep straight, guide, rule, straighten, Greek *orektós* stretched out, upright, *orégein* to stretch out, and Sanskrit *ṛjyati, ṛñjáti* (he) stretches, hurries, directs, *rají-s* straight, from Indo-European **reĝ-/roĝ-/ṛĝ-* (Pok.854). The meaning right, as opposed to left, is first recorded in 1125.
—n. About 1121 *riht;* later in the spelling *right* (about 1303), found in Old English *riht* fairness, justice, just claim (about 725, in *Beowulf*); cognate with Old Frisian *riucht,* n., right, Old Saxon *reht,* Middle Dutch and modern Dutch *recht,* Old High German *reht* (modern German *Recht*), and Old Icelandic *rēttr* (Norwegian *rett,* Danish *ret,* Swedish *rätt*); related to Old English *riht,* adj. The meaning of right side or hand is first recorded probably about 1200. *Right,* in the sense of the conservative members of a legislative body (customarily assigned to the right side of the chamber in relation to the presiding officer) is first recorded in 1825, as a loan translation of French *Droite* (1791) the Right, Conservative Party. According to the OED, "This use originated in the French National Assembly of 1789, in which the nobles as a body took the position of honour on the President's right, and the Third Estate [persons not of the nobility or clergy] sat on his left. The significance of these positions, which was at first ceremonial, soon became political," and the right side of a legislative chamber was assigned by custom to those holding political views considered conservative in the 19th century.
—v. Probably about 1150 *rigten* to correct, amend; later *rihten* to straighten, set in order, govern, (probably before 1200, in Layamon's *Chronicle of Britain*), and in the spelling *right* (about 1300); developed from Old English *rihtan* to straighten, rule, set up, set right (before 899, in Alfred's translation of Boethius' *De Consolatione Philosophiae*); cognate with Old Frisian *riuchta* to right, Old Saxon *rihtian,* Middle Low German *richten, rechten,* Middle Dutch and modern Dutch *richten, rechten,* Old High German *rihten* (modern German *richten*), Old Icelandic *rētta* (Norwegian and Danish *rette,* Swedish *rätta*), and Gothic *garaíhtjan* to guide.
—right angle (about 1400, in Chaucer's *Treatise on the Astrolabe*) **—righteous** *adj.* 1526, alteration of earlier *rightuous* (before 1475), *rihtwise* (probably before 1200); developed from Old English (before 830) *rihtwīs* (*riht* right, adj. + *wīs* WISE). The suffix *-eous, -ous* was a substitution based on *courteous* and similar formations of the 1500's. **—right field** (1857, American English) **—rightful** *adj.* 1100 *rihtfullan* honorable; later, according to law (probably before 1300); developed from Old English *rihtfull* (found in *unrihtfull*). The spelling *rightful* is first recorded about 1370. **—rightist** *n.* 1937 *Rightist* person with conservative political ideas; formed from English *Right,* n. + *-ist.* **—right of way** (1768, in Blackstone's *Commentaries*) **—right triangle** (1903) **—right wing** (1905, in William James' *Meaning of Truth*) **—right-winger** *n.* (1928) **—righty** *n.* right-handed person (1949, American English).

rigid *adj.* Probably before 1425 *rigide* stiff, in a translation of Chauliac's *Grande Chirurgie;* borrowed from Latin *rigidus,* from *rigēre* be stiff, be stiff with cold (a sense influenced by Latin *frīgēre* be cold). Latin *rigēre* was probably altered from **regēre* by influence of *ērigere* raise up; see ERECT, from Indo-European **reĝ-* straight (Pok.855). **—rigidity** *n.* 1624, state of being rigid; borrowed from Latin *rigiditās,* from *rigidus* rigid; for suffix see -ITY.

rigmarole (rig′mərōl) *n.* 1736, a long, rambling discourse or story, long-winded harangue; alteration of earlier *ragman roll* long list or catalogue (1523), in Middle English *Ragmane Rolle* a roll of verses descriptive of personal character, used in a medieval game of chance called Rageman (about 1450); this name was perhaps derived from Anglo-French *Ragemon le bon* Ragemon the good, the heading of a set of the verses, written in French and referring to a character by that name. The transferred sense of a long succession of meaningless actions, lengthy and foolish activity or commotion, is first recorded about 1955 (but was known orally in the 1930's).

rigor *n.* 1392 *rigour* stiffness, numbness; also, harshness, severity (about 1395, in Chaucer's *Canterbury Tales*); borrowed from Old French *rigor, rigour,* learned borrowing from Latin, and borrowed directly from Latin *rigor* numbness, stiffness, rigor, from *rigēre* be stiff: see RIGID; for suffix see -OR[1]. **—rigorous** *adj.* Before 1425, harsh, severe, stern, strict, in Wycliffe's *Sermons* (implied earlier in *rigorously,* 1408); borrowed from Old French *rigoros, rigoureus,* and directly from Medieval Latin *rigorosus,* from Latin *rigor* rigor; for suffix see -OUS. **—rigor mortis** stiffening of the muscles after death. 1839-47, a Latinate form used in a reference book on anatomy; formed from *rigor* stiffness, RIGOR, and *mortis* (genitive of *mors* death); see MORTAL.

rile *v.* 1825, irritate, vex, in John Neal's *Brother Jonathan;* American English, spelling alteration of ROIL. The spelling alteration may have been from a dialectal or regional pronunciation of *roil,* as *heist* from *hoist.*

Riley (rī′lē) *n.* **the life of Riley,** *Slang.* a carefree, easy life. 1919, in the song *My Name is Kelly,* American English, from a common Irish surname. In the song, by H. Pease, the phrase appears as "I'm living the life of Reilly." The spelling *Riley* first appears in Elmer Rice's *The Adding Machine* (1923). Some possible explanations are given in "The Life of Riley" by Samuel J. Raff in American Speech 51, 1-2 (1976), pp. 94-101.

rill *n.* tiny stream. 1538, in John Leland's *The Itinerary;* borrowed from modern Dutch *ril* or Low German *rille* groove, furrow, forms cognate with Frisian *ril* narrow passage, and probably related to Middle Low German *rīde* brook, stream, Old Saxon *rīth,* and Old English *rīth, rīthe* brook, stream; probably also cognate with Latin *rīvus* stream, brook; see RIVULET.

rim *n.* Probably before 1200 *rieme* edge, border, margin; also, rim of a wheel (probably before 1400), and in the spelling *rim* (1440); developed from Old English *rima* edge, border (chiefly in compounds, such as *dægrima* rim of the day, dawn, and *sǣrima* rim of the sea, seashore, 897, in *Anglo-Saxon Chronicle*); cognate with Old Frisian *rim* edge, and Old Icelandic *rimi* raised strip of land, ridge, *rim* fence, of unknown origin. **—v.** to form or put a rim around. 1794, from the noun.

rime[1] *n.* white frost, frozen mist. Probably before 1200 *rim* (usually in the compound *rim frost*); developed from Old English (about 725) *hrīm;* cognate with Old Icelandic *hrīm, hrīmi* frost (Norwegian, Swedish, and Danish *rim* frost, rime), Middle Dutch and modern Dutch *rijm,* Middle High German *rīm,* from Proto-Germanic **Hrīma-,* related to the root **Hrī-p-an-,* the source of Old Saxon *hrīpo* rime, Middle Dutch *rijpe* (modern Dutch *rijp*), and Old High German *hrīffo, riffo* (modern German *Reif* hoarfrost). The two Proto-Germanic forms are traced back to the Indo-European root **krei-* (Pok.618), represented by Latvian *krèims* and Lithuanian *krėnà,* both meaning cream. **—v.** cover with rime. 1755, in Johnson's *Dictionary;* from the noun. **—rimy** *adj.* covered with rime, frosty. Probably before 1200 *rimie,* in Layamon's *Chronicle of Britain;* developed from Old English *hrīmig,* from *hrīm* rime + *-ig* -y[1].

rime[2] *n.* See RHYME.

rind *n.* Old English *rinde* bark, crust (before 899, in Alfred's translation of Boethius' *De Consolatione Philosophiae*); later, peel of a fruit or vegetable (about 1150); cognate with Old Saxon *rinda* bark, Middle Low German *rinde,* Middle Dutch *rinde, rende, runde* (modern Dutch *run* tanning bark), Old High German *rinda, rinta* bark, rind (modern German *Rinde*), from Proto-Germanic **rendō;* related to Old English *rendan* to REND; cognate with Sanskrit *rándhra-m* a hole, a split, from Indo-European **rendh-/rondh-/r̥ndh-* to tear (Pok.865).

ring[1] *n.* circle. Probably before 1200 *ring,* in Layamon's *Chronicle of Britain;* earlier in the surname *Ringstan* (1167); developed from Old English *hring* circular band (about 725, in *Beowulf*); also, circular group (about 900), rim of a circular object (about 1000); cognate with Old Frisian and Old Saxon *hring* ring, Middle Dutch *rinc* (modern Dutch *ring*), Old High German *hring* (modern German *Ring*), and Old Icelandic *hringr* ring (modern Icelandic *hringur,* Norwegian, Swedish, and Danish *ring*), from Proto-Germanic **Hrengaz.* Outside Germanic possible cognates are found in Old Slavic *krǫgŭ* circle, and Umbrian *krenkatrum, cringatro* belt, from Indo-European **krengh-/krongh-/kr̥ngh-* (Pok.936).
—v. Probably before 1387 *ringen* provide or attach a ring, from the noun. The meaning of put a ring around, encircle, is first recorded before 1500.
—ringleader *n.* 1503, from the phrase *lead the ring* be foremost in a group, (originally) lead the dance, from Middle English *leden the ring* (probably about 1343).
—ringlet *n.* (1555) **—ringside** *n.* (1866) **—ringworm** *n.* Before 1425 *rengworme* skin disease caused by fungi, earlier *rencgwirme* intestinal worm (about 1150).

ring[2] *v.* give forth a clear sound, as a bell does. About 1131 *ringen;* developed from Old English *hringan* (about 725, in *Beowulf*), from Proto-Germanic **Hrenȝanan;* cognate with Old Icelandic and modern Icelandic *hringja* to ring (Norwegian *ringe, ringje,* Swedish *ringa,* Danish *ringe*), Middle Dutch and modern Dutch *ringen* to ring, and Old Icelandic *hrang* noise, din. Outside Germanic cognates are found in Lithuanian *krañkti* to croak, rattle, and Tocharian B *kraṅko* cock, from Indo-European **krenk-/kronk-* (Pok.568). **—n.** 1549, peal or set of church bells, from the verb. The meaning of act of ringing appeared in 1727.

ringer[1] *n.* one who rings a bell. About 1425, earlier as a surname *Ringere* (1207); formed from Middle English *ringen,* v. + *-er*[1].

ringer[2] *n.* **be a (dead) ringer for,** *Informal.* have the exact image of, resemble very closely. 1891, American English, from *ringer,* a racing slang term for a horse entered fraudulently in a race, possibly derived from the British slang phrase *ring in* to substitute or exchange (coins, hats, etc.) fraudulently (1812), associated with the slang expression *ring the changes* to substitute counterfeit money in various ways, a pun on the phrase *ring the changes,* used in bell ringing in the sense of go through all the variations in ringing a peal of bells (1614).

rink *n.* 1375 (Scottish dialect) *renk, rinc* area marked out for a contest, in Barbour's *The Bruce,* perhaps derived from, and earlier confused with *ring* an area for sport or contest (1303, in Mannyng's *Handlyng Synne*); borrowed from Old French *renc, reng* row, line, from Frankish; see RANK[1] row.

The meaning of stretch of ice marked out for the game of curling is first recorded in Burns' *Tam Samson's Elegy* (1787), and the word was restricted to Scottish use until the later 1800's. First evidence of its general use in the sense of sheet of ice for skating is recorded in 1867. About 1879 *rink* was applied to an artificially prepared area for ice skating.

rinky-dink *n. Slang.* something cheap, tinny, or trite. 1912, American English, (said to be imitative of the sound of banjo music formerly played at parades, but of uncertain connection to the meaning). **—adj.** cheap, tinny, or trite. 1913, probably from the noun.

rinse *v.* Probably about 1300 *rincen* to cleanse with water; borrowed from Old French *rincier,* variant of *räincier* and perhaps a dissimilated form (with loss of *c*) of *recincier* cleanse, from Vulgar Latin **recentiāre* renew, refresh, from Latin *recēns* (genitive *recentis*) fresh; see RECENT. **—n.** a rinsing. 1837, in Dickens' *Pickwick Papers;* from the verb. An earlier sense of a bundle of twigs for cleaning vessels appeared in Scottish in 1800.

riot *n.* Probably before 1200 *riote* debauchery, extravagance, unrestrained revelry, in *Ancrene Riwle;* borrowed from Old French *riote* (masculine *riot*) dispute, quarrel, corresponding to Provençal *riota,* both of uncertain origin. Archaic Italian *riotta* was a borrowing from Old French. The extended meaning of disorder, confusion, public disturbance, is first recorded in Gower's *Confessio Amantis* (before 1393).

The phrase *run riot,* meaning "to act without restraint", appeared in 1523. This is a figurative use of the earlier (about 1410) meaning of *riot* "a hound's following of the wrong scent."

—v. About 1390 *rioten* to revel, live wantonly, in Chaucer's *Canterbury Tales;* from the noun. The meaning of take part in a public disturbance is first recorded in Johnson's *Dictionary* (1755), though the sense of ravage, harry, is recorded before 1400.

—riotous *adj.* 1340, troublesome, wanton, extravagant, in *Ayenbite of Inwyt;* formed from Middle English *riote,* n. + *-ous.* The meaning of characterized by riot, lawless, violent, is first recorded in 1433.

rip[1] *v.* tear apart. Before 1400 *rippen* to cut, pull out, or tear away (something) vigorously; cognate with Flemish *rippen* to strip off roughly, rip, Frisian *rippe* to tear, rip, and probably with Middle Low German *reppen* to move, touch; see RAFFLE.

The slang phrase *rip off* to steal or rob is first recorded about 1967 in American English, from earlier use in prison slang *rip* to steal (1904).

—n. torn place. 1711, Addison in *The Spectator;* from the verb.

—rip cord (1907) **—rip-off** *n. Slang.* theft, robbery, racket. 1970, American English. **—ripsaw** *n.* (1846, replacing earlier *ripping saw,* 1825)

rip[2] *n.* rough water made by cross currents meeting. 1775, American English; perhaps special use of *rip*[1], n. **—rip current** (1936, American English) **—riptide** *n.* (1862)

riparian (rīpãr′ēən) *adj.* of or on the bank of a river, lake, etc. 1849, formed in English from Latin *rīpārius* of a riverbank (see RIVER) + English *-an.*

ripe *adj.* Old English *rīpe* ready for reaping (before 899, in Alfred's translation of Boethius' *De Consolatione Philosophiae*); cognate with Old Saxon *rīpi* ripe, Middle Dutch *rīpe* (modern Dutch *rijp*), Old High German *rīfi* (modern German *reif*), from Proto-Germanic *rīpijaz;* compare Old English *repan, rīpan* to REAP.

The transferred sense of fully developed, mature, advanced (applied to people and things) is first recorded in Middle English about 1200 (in *Vices and Virtues*). The extended sense of fully prepared, ready or able, to do or undergo something is first cited before 1398 (in Trevisa's translation of Bartholomew's *De Proprietatibus Rerum*).

The expression "the time is ripe" reflects a semantic direction reminiscent of German *zeitig* timely, which, in Southern Germany, means "ripe" (i.e., when fruits and grains have reached their time). Comparable also is Latin *mātūrē* at the right (or early) time, from *mātūrus* ripe, mature.

—ripen *v.* 1561, grow ripe, come to maturity; formed from modern English *ripe* + *-en*[1], gradually replacing earlier *ripe,* v., about 1250, Middle English *ripen;* developed from Old English *rīpian,* presumably from *rīpe,* adj. Old English *rīpian* is cognate with Old Saxon *rīpōn* become ripe, Middle Dutch *rīpen* (modern Dutch *rijpen*), Old High German *rīfan, rīffen* (modern German *reifen*).

riposte (ripōst′) *n.* sharp reply, retort. 1707, (in fencing) a quick return thrust; borrowed from French *riposte,* dissimilated form (by omission of *-s-* in *ris-*) of earlier *risposte,* from Italian *risposta* a reply, from *rispondere* to respond, from Latin *resondēre* RESPOND.

The transferred sense of a counterstroke, sharp or effective reply, retort, is first recorded in English in 1865, from the earlier verb.

—v. 1707, (in fencing) to make a quick thrust; borrowed from French *riposter,* dissimilated form of earlier *risposter,* probably from the noun in French. The transferred sense of make a quick, sharp reply, is first recorded in 1851.

ripple *v.* Before 1425 *ripplen, riplen* to wrinkle, crease, of unknown origin; later, to form or have small waves (implied in *rippling,* n. formation or appearance of ripples, 1669); re-formed in English perhaps as a frequentative form of English RIP[1]; for suffix see -LE[3]. **—n.** 1755, American English, stretch of shallow water where rocks, etc., cause a rippling action; from the verb. The meaning of a very small wave is first found in Coleridge's *The Rime of the Ancient Mariner* (1798); its transferred sense of anything that seems like a small wave is first recorded in 1843.

riproaring *adj. Informal.* hilarious, uproarious, lively. 1834, American English, alteration of earlier *riproarious* (1830); formed from *rip*[1] tear apart + *-roarious,* as in *uproarious* (1819).

ripsnorter *n. Informal.* thing that is unusually violent. 1840, American English, perhaps formed from *rip*[1] tear apart + *snort,* v. + *-er*[1].

rise *v.* 1135 *risen* rebel, revolt; probably before 1200, get up, go up, ascend; developed from Old English *rīsan* (found usually in *ārīsan,* before 830). The Old English form is cognate with Old Frisian *rīsa* to rise, Old Saxon *rīsan,* Middle Dutch *rīsen* (modern Dutch *rijzen*), Old High German *rīsan* to rise, flow, Old Icelandic *rīsa* to rise (Norwegian *rise*), and Gothic *urreisan* (from Proto-Germanic **us-rīsanan*). Outside Germanic cognates may exist in Latin *orīrī* to rise, Greek *orínein* to set in motion, *óros* mountain, Old Slavic *rějati* to push, set in motion, Armenian *ari* rise!, Sanskrit *riṇā́ti* (he) causes to flow, *r̥svá-s* high, *árṇa-s* flowing, surging, Avestan *arənu-* struggle, and Hittite *arāi* he rises, from Indo-European **erei-* to flow, root **er-/or-/r̥-* (Pok.326-330). Related to RAISE. **—n.** About 1400, a rebellion; earlier in a surname *Dingelonyerise;* from the verb. The meaning of a piece of rising ground is first recorded about 1440, and that of upward movement, about 1573. **—riser** *n.* 1397, a rebel; later, one who rises from bed (before 1450); formed from Middle English *rīsen* + *-er*[1]. The sense of the upright part of a step is first recorded in 1771, and gradually replaced earlier *rise,* n. in the same sense (1711).

risible (riz′əbəl) *adj.* laughable. 1557, inclined or able to laugh, borrowed from Middle French *risible* (learned borrowing from Late Latin), and directly from Late Latin *rīsibilis* laughable, that can laugh, from Latin *rīsus,* past participle of *rīdēre* to laugh; see RIDICULOUS; for suffix see -IBLE. The meaning of capable of exciting laughter, laughable, comical, is first recorded in English in 1727.

risk *n.* 1661 *risque* hazard, danger; borrowing of French *risque,* from Italian *risco, rischio,* of uncertain origin. The Anglicized spelling *risk* is first recorded in 1741, probably influenced by the earlier spelling *risk* of the verb. The earlier form *risque* continued to be used in English alongside *risk* until the late 1800's. Compare RISQUÉ. **—v.** Before 1687 *risque* to expose to hazard or danger; borrowed from French *risquer,* from Italian *riscare, rischiare,* from the noun in Italian. The Anglicized spelling *risk* is first recorded in 1728, but did not displace the original form *risque* until the early 1800's. **—risky** *adj.* 1826-27, in James Fenimore Cooper's writings; venturesome, bold, in *The Last of the Mohicans;* full of risk, dangerous, hazardous, in *The Prairie;* formed from English *risk,* n. + *-y*[1].

risqué (riskā′) *adj.* bordering on indecent, off-color. 1867, in Ouida's *Under Two Flags;* borrowing of French *risqué,* past participle of *risquer* to RISK.

rite *n.* solemn ceremony. Before 1333, borrowed from Latin *rītus* (genitive *rītūs*) religious observance or ceremony, custom, usage, cognate with Greek *arithmós* number, and Old High German *rīm* row, sequence, number; see RHYME.

ritual *adj.* of rites, done as a rite. 1570, borrowed perhaps through Middle French *ritual* (1564, in Rabelais) or directly from Latin *rītuālis* relating to rites, from *rītus* (genitive *rītūs*) RITE; for suffix see -AL[1]. **—n.** form or system of rites. 1649, in Jeremy Taylor's *Works;* from the adjective. **—ritualism** *n.* 1843, excessive observance or practice of ritual; probably formed in English from *ritual* + *-ism,* as a noun to earlier *ritualist* one versed in ritual (1657), influenced by, if not in some instances borrowed from, French *ritualisme,* from Middle French *ritual* + *-isme* -ism. **—ritualistic** *adj.* 1850, having to do with ritual or ritualism; formed from earlier English *ritualist* one versed in ritual (1657) + *-ic.* **—ritualize** *v.* 1842, to practice ritualism, in Emerson's *The Transcendentalist;* formed from English *ritual* + *-ize.* The meaning of change into a ritual, make a ritual of, is first recorded in 1847.

ritzy *adj. Slang.* smart, stylish, classy. 1920, in P.G. Wodehouse's *Jill the Reckless;* formed from *Ritz,* name of a chain of palatial hotels in London, Paris, New York City, and elsewhere, founded by César Ritz, 1850-1918, a Swiss hotelier + *-y*[1].

rival *n.* 1577, competitor; borrowing of Middle French *rival,* and perhaps borrowed directly from Latin *rīvālis* a rival, especially in love; originally, a person who uses the same stream as another, from *rīvus* stream, brook; see RIVULET; for suffix see -AL[2]. **—adj.** competing. 1590, in Shakespeare's *Midsummer Night's Dream;* from the noun. **—v.** to compete. 1605, in Shakespeare's *King Lear;* from the noun. **—rivalry** *n.* competition. 1598, in John Marston's *The Scourge of Villainy;* formed from English *rival,* n. + *-ry.*

rive (rīv) *v.* tear apart, split, cleave. Probably before 1200 *riven,* in a version of Layamon's *Chronicle of Britain;* borrowed from a Scandinavian source (compare Old Icelandic *rīfa* to tear apart, Norwegian *rive, riva* to split, tear, cognate with Old Frisian *rīva* to tear). The Scandinavian forms derive from Proto-Germanic **rīfanan,* cognate with Greek *ereípein* plunge down, and Latin *rīpa* (steep) bank, from Indo-European **reip-/rip-* (Pok.858). Related to RIFT. **—riven** *adj.* torn apart, split. Probably before 1300, from the past participle of *rive.*

river *n.* Probably about 1225 *rivere,* in *King Horn;* earlier as a surname *Rivere* (1200); borrowed through Anglo-French *rivere,* Old French *riviere,* from Vulgar Latin **rīpāria* riverbank or seashore, river, noun use of feminine of Latin *rīpārius* of a riverbank, from *rīpa* (steep) bank of a river, shore, cognate with Greek *ereípein* plunge down, from Indo-European **reip-/rip-* (Pok.858). Apparently Old French *riviere* is the source of Middle Dutch *riviere* (modern Dutch *riviere*) and Middle High German *rivier* (modern German *Revier* district, region). **—riverbank** *n.* (1565) **—riverbed** *n.* (1833, in Tennyson's poetry). **—riverboat** *n.* (1851, American English) **—riverside** *n.* (Probably before 1400, in Chaucer's translation of *Roman de la Rose*)

rivet *n.* metal bolt with each end hammered into a head. 1358-59, borrowed from Anglo-Latin *rivettis,* and from Old French *rivet,* from *river* to fix or fasten; also perhaps, in part, from Middle Dutch *wrīven* turn, grind, from Indo-European **wreip-/wrīp-* (Pok.1159). **—v.** fasten with a rivet or rivets. Probably before 1430, from the noun. The figurative sense of fix firmly (as the eye or the mind) is first recorded in Shakespeare's *Hamlet* (1602). **—riveting** *adj.* that holds the attention, spellbinding. 1854, from the past participle of *rivet,* v.

rivulet *n.* very small stream. 1587, borrowed in part possibly from Italian *rivoletto,* diminutive of *rivolo,* but more likely directly from Latin *rīvulus,* diminutive of *rīvus* stream, brook; for suffix see -ET. Latin *rīvus* is cognate with Irish *rían* sea, Old Irish *riathor* waterfall, Old Welsh *reatir,* Old Slavic *rěka* river, and Sanskrit *rītí-s* stream, course, related to *riṇā́ti* (he) causes to flow; see RISE.

roach[1] *n.* cockroach. 1837, American English, shortened form of COCKROACH. The slang meaning of a butt of a (marijuana) cigarette is first recorded in 1938.

roach[2] *n.* kind of freshwater fish. Probably about 1200 *roche;* borrowed of Old French *roche,* of uncertain origin.

road *n.* Probably about 1200 *rade* a riding, journey; later, in the spelling *rode* (1250); developed from Old English *rād* (871, in *Anglo-Saxon Chronicle*). Old English *rād* (from Proto-Germanic **raidō*) is cognate with Old Frisian *rēd* ride, Old Saxon *rēda,* Middle Dutch *rede,* Old High German *reita, reiti* foray, raid, and Old Icelandic *reidh* a riding, vehicle; all derived from the Proto-Germanic root **rīđanan* that is the source of Old English *rīdan* to RIDE, from Indo-European **reidh-/roidh-* (Pok.861). Related to RAID. The spelling *road* did not begin to appear before the latter part of the 1500's and was not the established form until the 1700's.

The meaning of an open way for traveling between two places is first recorded late in English, in Shakespeare's *1 Henry IV* (1596-97).

—roadbed *n.* (1840, American English) **—roadblock** *n.* (1940) **—road hog** (1891) **—road map** (1883, American English) **—roadrunner** *n.* a long-tailed, fast-running American bird related to the cuckoo. (1856, American English) **—roadside** *n.* (1712, Steele, in *The Spectator*) **—roadster** *n.* 1744, ship lying at anchor near the shore; later, horse for riding on the road (1818, in Scott's *Rob Roy*); a light carriage (1892, American English); kind of automobile, especially an open two-seater (1908, American English); formed from English *road* + *-ster*

—**road test** (1906) —**roadway** *n.* (1600) —**roadworthy** *adj.* (1819)

roam *v.* About 1330 *romen* to wander about, earlier to walk or walk about (probably before 1300, in *Kyng Alisaunder*); probably an alteration of *ramen,* represented by earlier *rameden* (probably before 1200, in Layamon's *Chronicle of Britain*), of uncertain origin. The Middle English word possibly developed from Old English **rāmian,* from older **raiman;* cognate with Old Icelandic *reimudhr* act of wandering about, *reimast* to haunt, and probably related to Old English *ārǣman* arise, lift up, from the Indo-European root **erei-* (Pok.330); see RISE. —**n.** act of roaming. 1667, in Milton's *Paradise Lost;* from the verb.

roan (rōn) *adj.* yellowish- or reddish-brown sprinkled with gray or white. 1530, in Palsgrave's *Lesclarcissement;* borrowing of Middle French *roan,* from Spanish *roano,* probably from a Germanic source (compare Gothic *raudan,* accusative of *rauths* RED). —**n.** roan horse. 1580, from the adjective.

roar *v.* Probably about 1200 *rarin;* later *roren* (before 1225); developed from Old English (before 900) *rārian,* probably of imitative origin. Similar formations, if not cognates of Old English *rārian,* are found in Middle Dutch *reren* to roar, Middle Low German *rāren,* Old High German *rērēn* to bleat (modern German *röhren* to bellow), Lithuanian *ríeti* to scold, and Sanskrit *rā́yati* he barks. —**n.** Before 1393 *rore* the roar of a beast, in Gower's *Confessio Amantis,* from the verb in Middle English.

roast *v.* About 1280 *rosten* to cook by dry heat; borrowed from Old French *rostir,* from Frankish **raustjan* (compare Old High German *rōstan* to roast, and Middle Dutch *roosten*), cognate with Old English *geroscian* dry by the fire, and Old High German *rosc* crackling, from Indo-European **rous-/rus-* to crackle (Pok.868). The figurative sense of ridicule, criticize, denounce, is first recorded in 1710, probably developed from the earlier transferred sense of torture by exposure to flame, or fire (about 1290). —**adj.** roasted. Before 1338 *rost,* in Mannyng's *Chronicle of England;* from the past participle of *rosten* to roast. —**n.** Probably about 1300 *roste* piece of roasted meat; borrowing of Old French *rost,* from *rostir* to roast. The figurative sense of ridicule, criticism (1740) was derived from the verb. The meaning of an occasion at which someone is exposed to humorous banter, ridicule, or criticism, appears in American English about 1900.

rob *v.* Probably before 1200 *robben* to steal from, plunder, pillage, in *Ancrene Riwle;* borrowed from Old French *rober,* from a Germanic source (compare Old High German *roubōn* to rob, modern German *rauben,* Old Saxon *rōƀōn,* Middle Low German and Middle Dutch *roven,* modern Dutch *rooven,* Gothic *biraubōn,* Old English *rēafian,* from Proto-Germanic **rauƀōjanan,* which survives in the archaic modern English *reave* to rob, and Old Icelandic *raufa* to break up, open, *rjūfa* to tear, from Proto-Germanic **reuƀanan,* cognate with Sanskrit *ropayati* causes violent pain, from Indo-European **reup-/roup-/rup-,* Pok.870). —**robber** *n.* Probably before 1200 *robber, robbere;* borrowed from Old French *robere,* from *rober* to rob; for suffix see -ER[1]. —**robbery** *n.* Probably before 1200 *roberie,* borrowing of Old French *roberie,* from *rober* to rob; for suffix see -RY.

robe *n.* Probably about 1200, borrowing of Old French *robe* long, loose outer garment worn in the Middle Ages, gown; originally, plunder or booty (presumably as derived from the meaning "vestments," found in Old High German), from a Germanic source (compare Old High German *rouba* vestments, presumably taken from the enemy, spoils or booty; related to *roubōn* to ROB, from Proto-Germanic **rauƀṓ,* Indo-European **roupā́*). —**v.** put a robe on. About 1378 *roben,* in a version of *Piers Plowman;* from the noun in Middle English.

robin *n.* kind of large thrush. 1549, shortened form of earlier *Robin Redbreast* a small European thrush (about 1450); from *Robin,* a proper name (before 1376); borrowing of Old French *Robin,* diminutive of *Robert.* An earlier Middle English name for the European thrush was *robynet* (before 1425), borrowed from Old French *robinet,* diminutive of *Robin;* for suffix see -ET.

robot (rō′bət) *n.* mechanical device that does some of the work of a human being. 1923, in P. Selver's translation of Karel Čapek's play *R.U.R.* (1920); formed in Czech as the name for the mechanical men who were heroes of the play *R.U.R.* (Rossum's Universal Robots, the name of the firm manufacturing the robots). Czech *robot* is derived from *robota* work or labor, related to Old Slavic *rabŭ* slave, from Proto-Slavic **orb-,* cognate with Old High German *arabeit* work, from Indo-European **orbh-* (Pok.781). —**robotic** *adj.* of or pertaining to robots. 1941, coined by Isaac Asimov in *Astounding Science Fiction,* American English, from *robot* + *-ic.* —**robotics** *n.* science or technology dealing with robots. 1941, coined by Isaac Asimov in *Astounding Science Fiction,* American English, from *robot* + *-ics.*

robust *adj.* 1549, borrowed perhaps through Middle French *robuste,* or directly from Latin *rōbustus* strong and hardy; originally, oaken, from *rōbur,* earlier *rōbus* (genitive *rōboris*) oak tree, hard timber, strength, probably (from the color of the heart-wood) related to *ruber* RED, but with *rōbur* for **rūbur* by dialectal influence; from Indo-European **reudhos* (Pok.872).

roc (rok) *n.* 1579, legendary bird of enormous size; borrowed from Arabic *rukhkh,* from Persian *rukh.* Early forms of this word included *roche, roque,* and *ruc;* the spelling *roc* appeared in 1802 in a translation of the *Arabian Nights,* also in the writings of Thackeray and Charles Kingsley.

rock[1] *n.* large mass of stone. About 1250 *roc* cliff, outcropping of rock; also in the surname *Stanrok* (1241); later *rokke* (1369), and *rocke* (about 1384, in the Wycliffe Bible, also in the surname *Stonrocke,* 1265); found in, and probably in part developed from, Old English *rocc* (in *stānrocc* stone rock or obelisk); also, more immediately borrowed from Old North French *roque,* from Vulgar Latin **rocca,* of uncertain origin.

Middle English also had the form *roche* rock formation, cliff, at least by 1225, and in the meaning "rock, stone," probably before 1300. It is also found earlier in place names (1164) and surnames (1185). The term was borrowed from Old French *roche,* from Vulgar Latin **rocca.* Except in older terms, such as *roche alum* and *roche lime,* and in the term *roche* in geology (now only in *roche montonée* a glacially round bedrock) the word disappeared from the record of English in the early 1800's.

—**rock-bottom** *adj.* (1866, American English) —**rock candy** (1723) —**rock garden** (1836) —**rock-ribbed** *adj.* 1776, having ridges of rock; (figurative) American English, unyielding, inflexible (1887). —**rock salt** (1707)

—rock wool (1909, in *The Century Dictionary Supplement*) **—rocky** *adj.* Probably about 1475 *rokky,* formed from Middle English *rokke* rock[1] + *-y*[1].

rock[2] *v.* to sway from side to side. Probably before 1200 *rocken,* in *Ancrene Riwle;* developed from Late Old English (before 1100) *roccian;* cognate with Middle Low German and Middle Dutch *rucken* to sway (modern Dutch *rukken* to pull, tug), Old High German *rucken* cause to move (modern German *rücken* to move, push along), and Old Icelandic *rykkja* to pull, tug (Danish *rykke,* Swedish *rycka*), of unknown origin. **—n.** 1823, rocking movement, from the verb. *Rock* in the sense of musical rhythm marked by a strong beat is first recorded in 1946 in American English, and became the first element in *rock and roll* a kind of popular music characterized by a strong beat and simple melody (1954, now usually *rock'n'roll,* 1955, and later shortened to *rock,* 1957). **—rocker** *n.* Before 1325, one who rocks a cradle, nurse; also, rocking chair (1852); formed from English *rock,* v. + *-er*[1]. **—rocking chair** (1766, American English) **—rocking horse** (1724) **—rocky** *adj.* shaky. 1770, formed from English *rock*[2], v. + *-y*[1].

rocket[1] *n.* garden plant of the mustard family. Before 1500 *rokette;* borrowed from Middle French *roquette,* from earlier Italian *rochetta,* variant of *ruchetta,* diminutive of *ruca* a kind of cabbage, from Latin *ērūca,* of uncertain origin; for suffix see -ET.

rocket[2] *n.* self-propelling cylindrical device used to carry fireworks, signals, spacecraft, etc. 1611, rocket used for fireworks, in Florio's *New World of Words;* borrowed from Italian *rocchetto* a rocket; literally, a bobbin (so named from the similarity in shape; also found in Old Italian and in Medieval Latin *roccheta, rocheta*), diminutive of Italian *rocca* distaff, possibly from a Germanic source (compare Old High German *rocko* distaff, spinning wheel, modern German *Rocken*). Old High German *rocko* is cognate with Middle Low German and Middle Dutch *rocken* distaff (modern Dutch *rokken*), and Old Icelandic *rokkr* (modern Icelandic *rokkur* and Norwegian *rokk* spinning wheel), from Proto-Germanic **rukka-* (Pok.874), from Indo-European **ruknṓn;* for suffix see -ET.

The extended meaning of a device or craft carried or propelled by a rocket engine is first recorded in R.H. Goddard's *Method of Reaching Extreme Altitudes* (1919).

—v. 1803, bombard with rockets; from the noun. The extended meaning of fly like a rocket, travel or rise quickly, soar, is first recorded in 1924.

—rocketry *n.* science of rockets. 1930, American English; formed from *rocket,*[2] n. + *-ry.*

rococo (rōkō'kō) *adj.* 1836, old-fashioned, antiquated, particularly in reference to the rococo style; borrowed from French *rococo,* n. and adj. By the 1840's specific reference to this old-fashioned style took on the meaning of having to do with a style of meaninglessly lavish ornamentation, in art, music, architecture, etc. It flourished in the overdecoration at the end of the baroque period, from approximately 1720 to about 1780, or the beginning of the Classical period, in architecture referred to as the Classical Revival. **—n.** style of architecture, music, etc., with elaborate ornamentation. 1840, borrowing of French *rococo,* apparently alteration of *rocaille* shellwork, with a humorous substitution of suffixes (compare French *coco* peek-a-boo, *cocorico* cock-a-doodle-do, etc.). French *rocaille* derives from Middle French *roche* rock, from Vulgar Latin **rocca* stone, ROCK[1]; so called in reference to excessive use of shell designs in this style of architectural ornamentation.

rod *n.* thin, straight bar of metal or wood. About 1250 *rodde;* found in Old English *rodd* a rod, pole; probably cognate with Old Icelandic *rudda* club, and possibly related to *rydhja* to clear of obstructions (Norwegian *rydje, rydde,* Danish *rydde,* Swedish *röja*); see RID. The meaning of a measure of length is first recorded about 1380, though the sense was known in Old English *rōd* rood, which is a distinctly different form.

rodent *n.* kind of mammal with teeth adapted for gnawing. 1835, borrowed from Latin *rōdentem* (nominative *rōdēns*), present participle of *rōdere* to gnaw; see RAT. **—adj.** gnawing. 1833, borrowed from Latin *rōdentem* (nominative *rōdēns*), present participle.

rodeo (rō'dēō) *n.* 1834, the driving together of cattle, in Darwin's *Journal;* borrowing of Spanish *rodeo* pen for cattle at a fair or market; also, a going round, from *rodear* go around, surround (from Vulgar Latin **rotidiāre,* as if from a Latin **rotizāre*), related to *rodar* revolve, roll, from Latin *rotāre* go around; see ROTATE.

The meaning of a contest or exhibition of skill in bronco riding, cattle roping, etc., is first recorded in 1914 in American English.

roe[1] *n.* fish eggs. About 1450 *row, roof;* cognate with Middle Low German and Middle Dutch *roge* roe, Old High German *rogo, rogan* (modern German *Rogen*), and Old Icelandic *hrogn* (Norwegian and Danish *rogn,* Swedish *rom*), from Proto-Germanic **Hruȝná* or **Hruȝán-;* outside Germanic cognates are Lithuanian *kurkulaĩ* and Latvian *kur̃kulis* frog's eggs, from Indo-European **krek-/kr̥k-* (Pok.619).

roe[2] *n.* kind of small deer. Probably about 1200 *ro;* later *roo* (about 1325) and *roe* (before 1398); developed from Old English (about 700) *rā,* from earlier *rāha;* cognate with Old Saxon *rēho* roe, Middle Low German *rē,* Middle Dutch and modern Dutch *ree,* Old High German *rēh* (modern German *Reh*), and Old Icelandic *rā* (Danish, Norwegian *rå, rådyr,* Swedish *rådjur*), from Proto-Germanic **raiHōn,* Indo-European **roik̑-.* Possible cognates outside Germanic are found in Old Irish *rīabach* dappled, Lithuanian *raĩbas* and Latvian *raibs* mottled, dappled, checked, from Indo-European **rei-/roi-* variegated (Pok.859). **—roebuck** *n.* roe deer, especially a male. Before 1387 *roobukke,* in Trevisa's translation of Higden's *Polychronicon;* earlier, as a surname *Robucke* (1209); formed from Middle English *ro, roo* roe[2] + *bucke, bukke* buck[1].

roentgen or **Roentgen rays** (rent'gən) X rays. 1896 *Röntgen,* in allusion to Wilhelm K. *Röntgen,* the German physicist who discovered X rays. Röntgen himself called the rays *X-Strahlen* X rays; a colleague, the German anatomist Rudolf A. Kölliker, named them after the discoverer.

roger *interj. Informal.* O.K., message received and understood. 1941, American English, a radio communications word for the letter *r* (derived from the name *Roger*), used as an abbreviation for "received".

rogue (rōg) *n.* 1561 *roge* vagabond, perhaps a shortened form of earlier *roger* (pronounced with the *g* of *go*) a begging vagabond pretending to be a poor scholar from Oxford or Cambridge (about 1540); perhaps formed in English from Latin *rogāre* to ask (see RIGHT + English *-er*[1].

There is no evidence to connect this word with the French adjective *rogue* arrogant (from Old Icelandic *hrokr*). However, the spelling *rogue* of the English word might have been influenced by the French word.

The meaning of a tricky, dishonest, or worthless person, is first recorded in English in 1578. The spelling *rogue* is first recorded in 1591.

—roguery *n.* 1596, conduct of rogues, dishonest trickery, in Shakespeare's *1 Henry IV;* formed from English *rogue* + *-ery.* **—rogues' gallery** (1859, in American English) **—roguish** *adj.* 1572, having to do with rogues, dishonest, rascally; formed from English *rogue* + *-ish*[1]. The meaning of playfully mischievous is first recorded in 1681.

roil *v.* make (water, etc.) cloudy by stirring up sediment. 1590, probably borrowed from Middle French *rouiller* to rust; earlier, make muddy, from Old French *rouil, rouille* mud, rust, (compare Old Provençal *rovilh, rovilha*), from Vulgar Latin **rōbīcula,* alteration of Latin *rōbīgō* (genitive *rōbīginis*) rust, related to *ruber* RED.

The figurative sense of disturb, irritate, vex, is first recorded before 1734.

roister *v.* revel noisily. 1582, in a translation of Vergil's *Aeneid;* from the obsolete noun *roister* (1551, now replaced by *roisterer,* 1820); probably borrowed from Middle French *ruistre, rustre* a ruffian, from variant (with added *r*) of Old French *ruste* an awkward, rough country person, rustic, from Latin *rūsticus* RUSTIC.

role or **rôle** *n.* 1606 *rowle;* borrowed from French *rôle* part or character played by a person in society or life; literally, roll (of paper) on which an actor's part was written, from Old French *rolle* ROLL. The spelling *rôle,* in imitation of the French, does not appear before 1790-91, which is also the date when the word was first recorded as meaning an actor's part in a drama.

roll *n.* Probably before 1200 *rolle* scroll, list, rolled-up mass, in *Ancrene Riwle;* borrowed from Old French *rolle, roule,* from Latin *rotula* small wheel, diminutive of *rota* wheel. Latin *rota* is cognate with Old Irish *roth* wheel, Welsh *rhod,* Lithuanian *rãtas,* Latvian *rats,* and Sanskrit *rátha-s* wagon, from Indo-European **rot(h)-,* root **ret(h)-* to run (Pok.866). Germanic cognates are found in Old Icelandic *rǫdhull* halo, sun, Old High German *rad* wheel (modern German *Rad*), Middle Dutch and modern Dutch *rad,* Old Saxon *rath,* and Old Frisian *reth* wheel, from Proto-Germanic **ratha-.*

The meaning of dough which is rolled over before baking is first recorded before 1450. Later senses of *roll* which derive from the verb in English include that of a rapid, continuous beating of a drum (1688), a deep, loud sound, as of thunder (1818, in Keats' poetry), and act of rolling, motion from side to side (1743).

—v. About 1300 *rollen* turn over and over; borrowed from Old French *roller,* from Vulgar Latin **rotulāre,* from Latin *rotula* small wheel. Other meanings include that of move about from side to side (before 1325), specifically of the eyes (probably before 1400), consider or ponder (about 1380, in Chaucer), and make deep, loud sounds, as of thunder (1598).

—roll call (1779) **—roller** *n.* 1295 *rollere* thing that rolls; before 1399, a rolling pin; formed from Middle English *rollen* to roll + *-ere* -er[1]. **—roller coaster** 1888, kind of sled running on rollers; 1903, American English, amusement park railway that curves and dips as it rolls. **—roller skate** (1863, American English) **—rolling mill** (1787) **—rolling pin** (1589, but for earlier use see ROLLER) **—rolling stock** (1853)

rollicking *adj.* frolicking, jolly, lively. 1826, in William Hone's *The Every-day Book;* adjective use of the present participle of *rollick* to frolic, sport; perhaps a blend of *roll,* v. + *frolic,* v., or a shortened form of *frolic* in an altered spelling with *-k.*

roly-poly *adj.* short and plump. 1820, probably a varied reduplication of *roll;* probably influenced by earlier *roly-poly,* n., name of various games in which a ball is rolled (1713). The formation is found as early as 1601, in Ben Jonson's *Poetaster,* with the meaning of a rascal.

romaine (rōmān′) *n.* variety of lettuce. 1907, borrowing of French *romaine,* from feminine of Old French *romain* Roman, learned borrowing from Latin *Rōmānus* (see ROMANCE); according to Bloch and Wartburg, this lettuce was so called because it was first introduced into France by Bureau de la Rivière, chamberlain of Charles V and VI, at Avignon in the days of the Avignon papacy (1309-77).

Roman *adj.* Before 1325 *romain* of ancient Rome, the Roman Empire, its people, or their language, in *Cursor Mundi;* probably from the noun, reinforced by, if not in some instances borrowed directly from, Old French *romain, romein, roman,* from Latin *Rōmānus,* from *Rōma* Rome; for suffix see -AN. This later form of the adjective replaced *Romanisce* (probably before 1200), and *Romanisshe* (about 1200), developed from Old English *rōmānisc* (before 899; borrowed from Latin *Rōmānus* + *-isc* -ish). **—n.** About 1300 *romein,* borrowed from Old French *romain, romein,* adj. and n.; earlier as a surname *Roman* (1205); developed from Old English *romane* inhabitant of ancient Rome or of the Roman Empire (before 899, in Alfred's translation of Orosius' *Historiarum Adversus Paganos*); borrowed from Latin *Rōmānus,* adj. and n. **—Roman candle** (1834) **—Roman Catholic** 1605, member of the Church of Rome; 1614, of or belonging to the Church of Rome. **—Roman numeral** (1735)

roman[1] *adj.* of or in the upright style of type most used in printing, as distinguished from *italic.* 1519 *Romayne,* borrowed from Middle French *Romain,* literally, Roman, from Old French *romain;* see ROMAN. The spelling *Roman* appeared in 1598; in lower-case form it is first found in 1848. **—n.** the roman style of type. 1598, from the adjective.

roman[2] (rômäɴ′) *n.* a novel. 1889, borrowing of French *roman,* from Old French *romanz* verse narrative; see ROMANCE. The term *roman à clef* (rômäɴ à klā′), a novel in which the characters represent real persons; literally, novel with a key, is first found in English in 1893, in Henry James' correspondence.

romance *n.* Probably before 1300 *romaunce;* about 1300 *romance* story about the adventures of some hero in chivalry (written in the vernacular in *Arthour and Merlin*); later, the vernacular language of France, as opposed to Latin (before 1338, in Mannyng's *Chronicle of England*); borrowed from Old French *romans, romanz* verse narrative; originally, an adverb with the meaning of in the vernacular language, from Vulgar Latin **rōmānicē scrībere* to write in a Romance language (that is, one developed from Latin instead of Frankish), from Latin *Rōmānicus* of or in the Roman style, from *Rōmānus* Roman.

In English *Romance* originally referred to the vernacular language of France and was only later extended to include Spanish, Italian, etc., developed from Latin (1612). In areas of other language use, such as Spanish, the terms *Roman, Romanz* were used to mean

Castilian and were already found in the 1200's; in Italian Dante used *Romanzo* in the *Divine Comedy* to mean a prose composition in Provençal. The meaning of an adventurous or imaginative quality, character, or spirit, is first recorded in 1801, and that of a love affair, idealistic quality in a love affair, is found in George Bernard Shaw's *Overruled* (1916).
—v. About 1390, recite a narrative, give an account of; from the noun. The later meaning of exaggerate, make up romances, is first recorded in English in 1671, and that of court as a lover in Berrey and Van den Bark's *American Thesaurus of Slang* (1942).

Romanesque *adj.* 1715, descended from Latin, Romance; later, of the architectural style developed in Europe between the Roman and Gothic periods of architecture (1819); formed from English *Roman* + *-esque,* but probably influenced in form by French *romanesque* fabulous, romantic (1628).

romantic *adj.* characteristic of romances or romance. 1659, borrowed from French *romantique,* from Middle French *romant* a romance formed as an oblique case of the Old French noun *romanz* verse narrative, see ROMANCE; for suffix see -IC. The form *romantic* displaced earlier and rare *romancical* (1656, formed from English *romance* + *-ical*) which is found as late as 1825 in Lamb's letters.
—n. 1679, characteristic or idea suggestive of romance; from the adjective. The meaning of romantic person is first recorded in 1865.
—romanticism *n.* 1803, romantic idea; formed from English *romantic,* adj. + *-ism.* The meaning of a tendency toward romantic ideas is first recorded in 1840, and that of a romantic tendency in literature, music, or art, in 1844, a sense probably borrowed from French *romanticisme,* used by Stendhal in 1823 (later replaced in French by *romantisme*). **—romanticist** *n.* 1830, formed from English *romantic* + *-ist.* **—romanticize** *v.* 1818, in Coleridge's letters; formed from English *romantic* + *-ize.*

Romany (rom′ənē) *n.* the Indic language of the Gypsies. 1812, Romany *romani,* feminine of *romano,* adj., Gypsy, from *rom* man, husband, male Gypsy, plural *romá,* from Sanskrit (really Prākrit) *ḍomba-s, ḍoma-s* a male member of a low caste of musicians.

romp *v.* to play in a rough, boisterous way. 1709, Steele in *The Tatler,* perhaps variant of RAMP[2], v. **—n.** rough, boisterous play or frolic. 1734, in Fielding's *Universal Gallant;* from the verb. **—rompers** *n.pl.* one-piece garment for small children to play in. 1909, formed from English *romp,* v. + *-er*[1] + *-s,* modeled after trousers, pants, etc.

rondeau (ron′dō) *n.* 1525, short poem with thirteen lines; borrowing of Middle French *rondeau,* from Old French *rondel* RONDEL. The meaning of a musical composition, now spelled *rondo* is first recorded in English in 1773.

rondel (ron′dəl) *n.* short poem, usually with fourteen lines and two rhymes. About 1380 *roundel,* in Chaucer's *Parlement of Foules;* borrowed from Old French *rondel* short poem; literally, small circle, diminutive of *roont* (feminine *roonde*) circular, ROUND; so called because the initial couplet is repeated in the middle and at the end.

rondo (ron′dō) *n.* 1797, a musical composition having one principal theme; borrowing of Italian *rondo,* from French *rondeau, rondel,* from Old French *rondel* little round; see RONDEL.

rood *n.* Before 1121 *rode* the cross on which Christ died, (also) a representation of it, crucifix; later in the spelling *roode* (probably about 1350) and *rood* (before 1400); developed from Old English (before 830) *rōd* cross, pole, measure of land; cognate with Old Frisian *rōd, rōde* gallows, Old Saxon *rōda* pole, gallows, cross, Middle Low German *rōde* rod, stick, Middle Dutch *roede* (modern Dutch *roede, roe*), Old High German *ruota* (modern German *Rute*), and Old Icelandic *rōdha* rod, cross (influenced in meaning by Old English *rōd*), from Proto-Germanic **rōđṓ,* cognate with Old Slavic *ratište* shaft of a lance, from Indo-European **rōt-/rət-* (Pok.866).

roof *n.* About 1175 *rof;* later *roof* (1431); developed from Old English *hrōf* roof, ceiling, top (about 725, in *Beowulf*); cognate with Old Frisian *hrōf* roof, Middle Low German *rōf, rūf* roof, covering, Middle Dutch *roef* (modern Dutch *roef* deckhouse), Old Icelandic *hrōf* boat shed (from Proto-Germanic **Hrōfaz*), and probably with Old Slavic *stropŭ* roof (from **k̑rāpos*), from Indo-European **k̑rapos/krāpos* or **k̑rōpos* (Pok.616).
—v. to cover with a roof. Before 1420 *rofen,* in Lydgate's *Troy Book;* from the noun. **—roofer** *n.* (1855) **—roofless** *adj.* (1610)

rook[1] *n.* European crow. Probably about 1200 *roc;* later, *rook* (before 1325), developed from Old English (about 725) *hrōc;* cognate with Middle Low German *rōk* rook, Middle Dutch *roec* (modern Dutch *roek*), Old High German *hruoh, ruoho,* Old Icelandic *hrōkr* rook (modern Icelandic *hrōkur,* Swedish *råka,* Danish *råge*) (from Proto-Germanic **Hrōkaz*), and Gothic *hrukjan* to crow. Outside Germanic Old English *hrōc* is cognate with Greek *krōgmós* a croaking, *krṓzein* to croak, caw; see RETCH.

The word was figuratively applied to persons as an abusive or disparaging term as early as 1508. This was extended by 1577 to the meaning of a cheat, swindler, especially at cards or dice.
—v. to cheat. About 1590, from the noun.
—rookery *n.* colony of rooks. 1725, formed from English *rook* + *-ery.*

rook[2] *n.* chess piece often called castle (because of its appearance). Probably before 1300 *roke;* later *rok* (before 1338), and *rook* (probably before 1430); borrowed from Old French *roc,* from Arabic *rukhkh,* from Persian *rukh,* the original meaning of which is unknown, but in Middle English confused with ROC.

rookie *n.* 1892, inexperienced recruit, in Kipling's *Barrack-Room Ballads;* perhaps an alteration of *recruit,* influenced by *rook*[1] in the sense of a person easily duped, simpleton.

room *n.* Probably about 1200 *rum* space, sufficient space, in *The Ormulum;* later *roume* (probably before 1300, in *Arthour and Merlin*), *roum* (about 1330); developed from Old English *rūm* (about 725, in *Beowulf*) cognate with Old Frisian and Old Saxon *rūm* space room, Middle Dutch *ruum* (modern Dutch *ruim*), Old High German *rūm* (modern German *Raum*), Old Icelandic *rūm* (Swedish and Danish *rum,* Norwegian *rom*), and Gothic *rūm* (attested in genitive singular *rūmis*), from Proto-Germanic **rūman,* with corresponding adjectives in Old English *rūm* roomy, spacious, Middle Dutch *ruum,* Old High German *rūm,* Old Icelandic *rūmr,* and Gothic *rūms,* from Proto-Ger manic *rūmaz. Outside Germanic Old English *rūm* is cognate with Old Slavic *ravĭnŭ* even, level, Latin *rūs* (genitive *rūris*) open land, country (from earlier **rewos*), Middle Irish *rōe, rōi* level field, Avestan *ravah-* room, distance, and Tocharian A, Tocharian B *ru-* to open, from Indo-European **rewə-/rū-* space; broad (Pok.874). The sense of an interior part of a building divided off by walls, a chamber or cabin, appeared in Middle English in 1312-13 as a nautical term; it was first applied to dwellings or houses in the 1400's. **—v.** occupy a room or rooms. 1828, from the noun.

From the historical phonetic standpoint, modern English *room* is a curiosity in that it did not develop from Old English *rūm* into modern English **rowm,* as *cū* developed into *cow* and *dūn* developed into *down.* The failure to do so is probably due to the influence of Scandinavian forms (compare Old Icelandic *rūm* room, Swedish and Danish *rum*); this is similar to the case of English *give,* where the expected form **yive* was displaced by the Scandinavian forms with *g.* The spelling *room* appeared in the late 1400's.

—roomer *n.* (1871, American English) **—roomful** *adj.* (1710, in Swift's writings) **—roommate** *n.* (1789, American English) **—roomy** *adj.* having plenty of room. 1627, in Captain John Smith's *The Seaman's Grammar,* formed from English *room,* n. + *-y*[1].

roorback (rúr′bak) *n. Archaic or Occasional.* false story or slander about a political figure. 1844, American English in allusion to a Baron von *Roorback,* an imaginary author of a nonexistent travel book *A Tour Through the Western and Southern States.* During the campaign of 1844 a New York newspaper cited a part of this book (later found to be a forgery perpetrated by an abolitionist), which stated that James K. Polk, the Democratic Presidential candidate, had bought a number of slaves and branded them with his initials. The widespread circulation of this gossipy false story popularized the word, which occasionally reappears in the sense of political slander in United States election campaigns.

roost *n.* perch on which birds rest. Before 1398 *rooste* a chicken's perch, in Trevisa's translation of Bartholomew's *De Proprietatibus Rerum;* developed from Late Old English (before 1100) *hrōst;* cognate with Old Saxon *hrōst* framework of a roof, attic, Middle Dutch and modern Dutch *roest* roost, of unknown origin. The figurative sense of a resting place, lodging, bed, is first recorded in 1818. **—v.** sit as birds do on a roost. 1530, in Palsgrave's *Lesclarcissement;* from the noun. **—rooster** *n.* 1772, American English; formed from *roost,* n. + *-er*[1]; compare earlier *roost cock* (1606). The use of *rooster* came to be strongly favored in the United States over the use of *cock* probably for euphemistic reasons (*cock* being an English equivalent of penis, attested since 1618). Similar hypersensitive changes are found in *occupy* in the 1500's and 1600's, and in the pronunciation of *harass* and *Uranus* in contemporary English.

root[1] *n.* underground part of a plant. 1127 *rot,* also *rote* (probably before 1200); found in Late Old English *rōt;* both the Middle and Old English forms borrowed from a Scandinavian source (compare Old Icelandic *rōt* root, Norwegian and Swedish *rot,* with traditional loss of *w-* before *r*). Late Old English *rōt,* perhaps also represented in **wrōt,* is a collateral form of Old English *wyrt* root, herb, plant, which is related to Latin *rādīx* root; see WORT. **—v.** Probably before 1200 *roten* (in past participle *roted*) fix or establish firmly, in *Ancrene Riwle;* from the noun. The meaning of pull, dig, or take out by the roots, is first recorded before 1387, and that of the figurative sense (as in *to root out evil*) before 1500. **—root beer** (1843, American English) **—root canal** (1893) **—rootless** *adj.* (about 1385, in Chaucer's *Troilus and Criseyde*) **—rootstock** *n.* (1832)

root[2] *v.* dig with the snout. 1538, in John Leland's *The Itinerary;* alteration (influenced by *root*[1]) of Middle English *wroten* dig with the snoot (about 1200); developed from Old English (about 725) *wrōtan;* cognate with Middle Low German *wrōten* dig with the snout, Middle Dutch and modern Dutch *wroeten,* Old High German *ruozzen,* and Old Icelandic *rōta* (Norwegian *rote,* Swedish *rota,* Danish *rode*), from Proto-Germanic **wrōtanan.* Cognates outside Germanic are found in Albanian *varrë* wound, injury, Old Slavic *vrědŭ,* Old Prussian *redo* furrow, and Avestan *varədva-* soft, loose, from Indo-European **werd-/wrēd-/wrōd-* to tear up (Pok.1163). The figurative meaning of poke, pry, search is first recorded in 1831.

root[3] *v.* cheer or support a contestant, etc. 1889, American English; probably derived from earlier sense of *root*[2], v. to study or work hard (1856).

rope *n.* About 1200 *rope,* in *Vices and Virtues;* developed from Old English (about 725) *rāp;* cognate with Old Frisian *-rāp* in *silrāp* shoe thong, Middle Low German *rēp* rope, Middle Dutch and modern Dutch *reep,* Old High German *reif* hoop (modern German *Reifen*), Old Icelandic *reip* rope (Norwegian *reip,* Swedish *rep,* Danish *reb*), and Gothic *-raip* in *skaudaraip* shoe thong, from Proto-Germanic **raipaz,* of unknown origin. **—v.** to tie with a rope. About 1515, from the noun. The irregular form *raipen* is recorded once in Middle English before 1325, in *Cursor Mundi.* **—ropy** *adj.* forming sticky threads, stringy. 1480, in Caxton's translation of Higden's *Polychronicon;* formed from Middle English *rope,* n. + *-y*[1].

rorqual (rôr′kwəl) *n.* kind of whale. 1827, borrowing of French *rorqual,* from Norwegian *røyrkval,* from Old Icelandic *reydharhvalr* (*reydhr* rorqual, related to *raudhr* RED + *hvalr* WHALE); compare NARWHAL.

Rorschach test (rôr′shäk) psychological test based on the subject's response to inkblot designs. 1927, in allusion to Hermann *Rorschach,* 1884-1922, a Swiss psychiatrist who devised this test.

rosary *n.* About 1440 *rosarie* rose garden, borrowed from Latin *rosārium,* from neuter of *rosārius* of roses, from *rosa* ROSE; for suffix see -ARY. The sense of a series of prayers (1547) probably came from Middle French *rosaire* (1495), in which it probably developed as a figurative sense from the original meaning of a rose garden, conveying the idea of a "garden" of prayers; this corresponds with the Medieval use of the phrase *hortulus animae* little garden of the soul, as a term meaning prayerbook. The meaning of a string of beads used in counting these prayers appeared in English in 1597. Compare BEAD for sense development.

rose *n.* Old English *rose, rōse* (before 899, in Alfred's translation of Boethius' *De Consolatione Philosophiae*); borrowed from Latin *rosa;* later, in Middle English probably influenced by Old French *rose,* from Latin, which reinforced the spelling *rose.* The Latin word was borrowed by other Germanic languages: compare Middle Dutch *rōse* (modern Dutch *roos*), Old

High German *rōsa* (modern German *Rose*), Old Icelandic *rōsa* (Danish and Norwegian *rose,* Swedish *ros*).

Latin *rosa* was probably borrowed from Greek *rhódon* rose (compare Aeolic *wródon,* written *bródon* by later grammarians). The Aeolic forms are from Persian **vr̥da-* (represented by Iranian *gul,* from **wr̥d,* and by Armenian *vard* rose), originally from a non-Indo-European language.

—adj. pinkish-red. 1816, in Byron's *Childe Harold's Pilgrimage;* from the noun.

—roseate *adj.* rose-colored. 1449, formed in English from Latin *roseus* (from *rosa* rose) + English *-ate*[1]. The figurative sense of optimistic is first recorded in 1868. **—rosebud** *n.* (before 1500) **—rosebush** *n.* (1587)**—rosewood** *n.* (1660) **—rosy** *adj.* like a rose, pinkish-red. About 1381; formed from Middle English *rose* + *-y*[1], but probably modeled on Old French *rosé* pink, rosy, from *rose* rose (the flower). The figurative sense of bright, cheerful, is first recorded in English in 1775.

rosé (rōzā′) *n.* a pink wine. 1897, borrowing of French *rosé,* shortened form of *vin rosé* pink wine. **—adj.** pink or light red. 1959, from the noun, and probably in part borrowed from French *rosé,* adj. The wine was known in Middle English as *rosate* (probably in 1440, and in the Latin form *rosātum* before 1398).

rosemary *n.* plant used in making perfume and in seasoning food. 1373 *rosemarye,* borrowed from Latin *rōsmarīnus* the plant; literally, dew of the sea (*rōs* dew + *marīnus* MARINE). Middle English *rosmarine* was a literal translation of the Latin; the formation of *rosemary* was by association of the word in popular etymology with *rose* and the name *Mary.* Latin *rōs* is cognate with Lithuanian *rasà* dew, Old Slavic *rosa,* and Sanskrit *rása-s* juice, liquid, from Indo-European **res-/ros-/rōs-* to flow (Pok.336).

rosette (rōzet′) *n.* ornament, object, or arrangement shaped like a rose. 1790, borrowing of French *rosette,* from Old French *rosette,* diminutive of *rose* rose, from Latin *rosa* ROSE; for suffix see -ETTE.

rosin (roz′ən) *n.* substance that remains when turpentine is evaporated from pine resin. 1295 *rosyn;* before 1393 *rosine;* both forms borrowed as alterations of Old French *raisine, rousine,* variants of *résine* RESIN, and also borrowed through Anglo-Latin *rosina,* from Medieval Latin *rosina,* from Latin *rēsīna.* **—v.** cover or rub with rosin. 1356 (implied in *rosinyne* rosining); from the noun.

roster *n.* list giving names and often assigned living space, duties, etc. 1727, military roster; borrowed from Dutch *rooster* table, list; originally, gridiron, from Middle Dutch *roosten* to ROAST; so called from the parallel lines drawn on the paper in making a timetable or other list; for suffix see -ER[1].

rostrum (ros′trəm) *n.* platform for public speaking. 1542, rostrum in the Roman forum, in Nicholas Udall's translation of Erasmus' *Apothegms;* borrowing of Latin *rōstrum* platform in the Forum decorated with the beaks of ships taken in the first naval victory of the Republic; also, beak, muzzle, snout; originally, means of gnawing, instrument-noun to *rōdere* gnaw, from Indo-European **rōd-trom;* see RAT. The general sense of a platform for public speaking is first recorded in English in 1766.

rot *v.* Probably before 1200 *roten,* developed from Old English *rotian* (before 899, in Alfred's translation of Saint Gregory's *Pastoral Care*); cognate with Old Frisian *rotia* to rot, Old Saxon *rotōn,* Middle Low German and Middle Dutch *roten* (modern Dutch *rotten*), Old High German *rozzēn,* and Old Icelandic *rotna* to rot (Norwegian *rotne, råtne,* Swedish *ruttna,* Danish *raadne*), a weak verb formed from Proto-Germanic **rut-,* the same stem as is found in Old Icelandic *rotinn,* whence English *rotten.* The Indo-European root *reud-/rud-,* Pok.869, underlying this verb, seems to have meant to wet or allow to become soaked. **—n.** Before 1325, in *Cursor Mundi,* either from the verb or possibly borrowed from a Scandinavian source (compare modern Icelandic and Norwegian *rot* decay, corruption, related to Old Icelandic *rotna* to rot).

rotary *adj.* turning like a top or wheel, rotating. 1731, in Bailey's *Dictionary,* borrowed from Medieval Latin *rotarius* pertaining to wheels, from Latin *rota* wheel; see ROLL; for suffix see -ARY.

rotate *v.* move around a center or axis. 1808, probably a back formation from *rotation;* for suffix see -ATE[1]. **—rotation** *n.* act or process of rotating. 1555, borrowed possibly through Middle French *rotation,* and directly from Latin *rotātiōnem* (nominative *rotātiō*), from *rotāre* revolve, roll; for suffix see -ATION. *Rotation* is recorded in an isolated instance in Middle English *rotacion* (1471). **—rotator** *n.* 1676, muscle by which a limb is rotated, borrowed from Latin *rotātor* one that causes to rotate, a spinner, from *rotāre* to rotate; for suffix see -OR[2]. The meaning of a machine or device that has a rotating motion or action is first recorded in English in 1772. **—rotatory** *adj.* 1755, in Johnson's *Dictionary;* formed from English *rotator* + *-y*[1], or perhaps from Latin *rotator* + English *-y*[1].

rotavirus (rō′təvī′rəs) *n.* kind of wheel-shaped virus causing inflammation of the lining of the stomach and intestines. 1974, formed in English from Latin *rota* wheel + English *virus.*

rote (rōt) *n.* a set, mechanical way of doing things. Probably about 1300, in the phrase *bi rote* by heart, according to form; of uncertain origin. There is insufficient evidence to confirm the suggestions that *rote* was borrowed from Old French *rote, route* a way or route, or from Latin *rota* wheel.

rotisserie (rōtis′ərē) *n.* spit for roasting food. 1868, American English, restaurant where meat is roasted on a spit; borrowed from French *rotisserie* shop selling cooked foods; also, restaurant, from *rôtiss-,* stem of *rôtir* to roast, from Old French *rostir;* see ROAST. The meaning of a cooking appliance for roasting meat on a rotating spit is first recorded about 1953, also in American English.

rotogravure (rō′təgrəvyůr′) *n.* process of printing from an engraved copper cylinder. 1913 *Rotogravure* (altered in American English to the spelling of earlier *photogravure* with *-e*), American English; borrowed from German *Rotogravur,* in the name *Rotogravur Deutsche Tiefdruck Gesellschaft* German Rotogravure Company, said to be a blending of two company names *Roto(phot)* and *(Deutsche Photo)gravur* (*roto-* ultimately from Latin *rota* wheel + *gravur;* see GRAVURE).

rotor (rō′tər) *n.* rotating part of a machine or apparatus 1873, shortened form of ROTATOR, paralleling *vector* the sense of revolving curiously coming from mathematics in which the description of a quantity's magnitude, direction, and position is most simply given in velocity of rotation about an axis (called a rotor). Late application to the rotating part of a machine is first recorded in 1903.

rotten *adj.* Probably before 1300 *roten,* in *Arthour and Merlin;* borrowed from a Scandinavian source (compare Old Icelandic *rotinn* decayed, past participle of an old strong verb, related to the weak verb *rotna* to decay, ROT).

The figurative sense of morally, socially, or politically corrupt (as in "Something is rotten in the state of Denmark") is recorded from about 1380, in Wycliffe's writings. The weakened sense of bad, nasty, lousy (as in *rotten luck, shame,* etc.) appeared in 1881, in Robert Louis Stevenson's letters, and as an adverbial intensifier *(spoiled rotten)* in Mark Twain's *Tramp Abroad* (1881).

rotund *adj.* round, plump. 1705, in Addison's *Remarks on Italy;* borrowed from Latin *rotundus* round, circular, like a wheel, related to *rota* wheel. Doublet of ROUND. The form *rotund* replaced the earlier English *rotound* (1619), which developed from Middle English *rotounde* (probably before 1425, in a translation of Chauliac's *Grande Chirurgie*). The Middle English word was a borrowing of Italian *rotondo* round; see ROTUNDA. **—rotundity** *n.* 1597, roundness or plumpness; borrowed from Latin *rotunditās,* from *rotundus* round; for suffix see -ITY.

rotunda (rōtun′də) *n.* circular building, especially one with a dome. 1611, in Coryat's *Crudities;* alteration of Italian *rotonda* (originally feminine of *rotondo,* adj.), learned borrowing from Latin *rotunda,* feminine of *rotundus* ROUND. The association with Latin *rotundus* ROTUND influenced the alteration from Italian *rotonda.*

roué (rüā′) *n.* 1800, borrowing of French *roué* dissipated man, rake; originally, past participle of Old French *rouer* to break on the wheel, from Latin *rotāre* roll, ROTATE; said to be first applied in French about 1720 to a group of profligates, specifically companions of the Duc d'Orléans, Regent of France (1715-23), to suggest that they deserved to be broken on the wheel as torture or punishment for their behavior.

rouge (rüzh) *n.* coloring for cheeks or lips. 1753, in Lord Chesterfield's writings; borrowing of French *rouge* red coloring matter; also, as an adjective, red, from Old French *rouge* red, from Latin *rubeus* red; related to *ruber* RED. This was a reborrowing of a word that existed in Middle English as a noun meaning a clear bright red color (1437), and as an adjective meaning red (before 1425), both borrowed from Old French. It was also used in the Middle English period in various titles, such as *Rouge Cross* and *Rouge Dragon.* **—v.** color with rouge. 1777, in Frances Burney's *Early Diary;* from the noun.

The modern equivalent term for the cosmetic is *blush.*

rough *adj.* Probably before 1200 *ruhe* shaggy, hairy, in *Ancrene Riwle;* also *ruchʒe* rugged, uneven (probably about 1225); developed from Old English (about 1000) *rūh.* Old English *rūh* is cognate with Middle Low German *rū, rūch, rūw* shaggy, hairy, rough, Middle Dutch *ruuch* (modern Dutch *ruig*), and Old High German *rūh* (modern German *rauh* rough), from Proto-Germanic **rūHaz.* Cognates outside Germanic include Latin *runcāre* to weed, *rūga* a wrinkle, fold, Greek *orýssein* to dig, *órygma* ditch, trench, Lithuanian *raũkas* wrinkle, *raũkti* to wrinkle, and Sanskrit *rūkṣá-s* rough, from Indo-European **reuk-/ruk-/rūk-* pluck, tear away (Pok.869).

The original sound represented by *gh* in *rough,* and also in *cough, laugh,* etc., was a guttural *ch,* as in Scottish *loch* or German *ach.* As the pronunciation shifted to the sound of *f* in *off,* the spelling of many words also changed to reflect this process, as in *draft* for *draught,* etc.; but a group of spellings remained fixed.

—n. Probably before 1200 *ruhe* rough surface, in *Ancrene Riwle;* later *roughe* quality of being rough, coarseness (about 1353); probably from the adjective. The sense of a stretch of rough ground is first recorded in 1600. The phrase *in the rough,* meaning in a rough, imperfect state, appeared in 1823, and that of a coarse, rough person, a rowdy, in 1837.

—adv. in a rough manner, roughly, rudely. About 1300 *rowe* angrily, fiercely; later, *roghe* in a violent manner, roughly (probably about 1390); from the adjective.

—v. make rough; roughen. 1763, especially in the phrase *rough up* to make rough; from the adjective. The phrase *to rough it* to live without comforts and conveniences is first recorded in 1768.

—roughage *n.* 1883, rough grass or weeds, the less useful part of crops; formed from English *rough,* adj. + *-age.* The meaning of coarse, bulky kinds of food, such as bran, is first recorded about 1927. **—rough draft** (1699) **—roughen** *v.* 1582, formed from English *rough,* adj. + *-en*[1]. **—rough-house** *n.* disturbance, horseplay (1887, American English); *v.* (1900, American English). **—roughly** *adv.* About 1300 *rohly* violently; formed from Middle English *ruhe* rough + *-ly*[1]. The meaning of approximately is first recorded in 1841, from the sense of in an imperfect manner, without much care or skill (1607). **—roughneck** *n.* a rowdy (1836, American English). **—roughrider** *n.* one who rides unbroken horses (1733). **—roughshod** *adj.* (of horses) having shoes with projecting nailheads (1688). The phrase *ride roughshod over,* in the figurative sense of treat roughly, show no consideration for, is first recorded in 1861.

roulette (rület′) *n.* Before 1734, a small wheel; later, a gambling game played by betting on which numbered compartment of a revolving wheel a small ball will come to rest in (1745); borrowing of French *roulette* the gambling game, a small wheel, from Old French *roelete* little wheel (feminine diminutive of *roele, rouele* little wheel); formed on the model of Late Latin *rotella* (diminutive of Latin *rota* wheel); for suffix see -ETTE. Old French *roele, rouele* is a diminutive of *roue* wheel (altered by influence of *rouele, rouer* from expected **reue,* which is found in dialects), from Latin *rota.*

round *adj.* Probably before 1300 *round* circular or spherical, in *Kyng Alisaunder;* also *rowund, rount, roend;* borrowed through Anglo-French *röunde, röunt,* and directly from Old French *roont, roond* (feminine *roonde*), and *reont,* probably (with loss of the medial consonant) from **redond, *rodond,* from Vulgar Latin **retundus.* Formation of Vulgar Latin **retundus* (evidenced by existent Provençal *redon, redun,* Spanish and Portuguese *redondo,* Old Italian *ritondo*) is assumed by dissimilation of the "rounded" vowel sound represented by *o* and by *u* around *t* in Latin *rotundus* like a wheel, circular, round, related to *rota* wheel. Doublet of ROTUND.

—adv. About 1300 *rounde* in a ring or circle; from the adjective. The meaning of throughout, all through (as in *the year round*) is first recorded in 1753.

—v. About 1387 *rounden* be curved, make circular, in

Chaucer's *Prologue* to the *Canterbury Tales;* from the adjective.

—n. Before 1325 *round* a halo; later *rond* spherical body or form, round mass (about 1330); in part borrowed from Old French *rond* (originally an adjective and late variant of *roont* round) and in part noun use of Middle English *rounde,* adj. The meaning of a dance in which the performers move in a circle or ring is first recorded in 1513.

—prep. so as to encircle, on all sides of. 1602, in Shakespeare's *Hamlet;* in part from the adjective, but more commonly used as a shortened form of *around.*

—roundabout *adj.* 1608, from earlier noun, about 1535. **—roundhouse** *n.* About 1437, lockup, jail. The sense of a circular building for locomotives is first recorded in 1856, in American English. **—roundly** *adv.* Probably before 1425, in an arc; also, completely, fully, in a translation of Chauliac's *Grande Chirurgie;* formed from Middle English *round* + *-ly*[1]. **—round number** 1648, from earlier sense of full or complete, also used in reference to numbers (1340). **—round robin** 1546, a name of ridicule applied to one of the sacraments; later, a petition of protest signed in a circular pattern to hide the fact of who signed it first (1731), and a contest in which every player or team plays against every other player or team (1895). **—round-shouldered** *adj.* (1586) **—round table** Probably before 1300, the table at which King Arthur and his knights sat, in *Arthour and Merlin.* The meaning of an assembly or group in which all those present participate is first recorded in 1889. **—round trip** (1860, American English) **—roundup** *n.* (1873, American English)

roundelay (roun′dəlā) *n.* short simple song with a refrain. Probably before 1430, in Lydgate's writings; borrowed from Middle French *rondelet,* diminutive of *rondel* short poem with a refrain; literally, small circle, from Old French. The Old French *rondel* was itself a diminutive of *rond* circle, sphere; originally, an adjective and late variant of *roont, roond;* see ROUND. The spelling *roundelay* developed from an association with *lay*[3] (poem to be sung), probably confused with the French pronunciation of *-let* in *rondelet.*

rouse *v.* About 1460 *rowsen* (implied in *rowsyng* rising, in reference to a heraldic symbol); later, (of a hawk) to shake the feathers or the body (before 1475, technical term of falconry); probably borrowed from Anglo-French or Old French, but of uncertain origin (compare Old French *rëuser, ruser* repel, push back). The continued specialized use of *rouse* is found in the sense of cause game to break from cover, in 1531, followed by extended generalized senses of stir up (1582) and excite (1586). The meaning of start up from sleep or rest, awaken, is first recorded in 1590. The variant form *arouse* is first recorded in 1593 (in Shakespeare's *2 Henry VI*); formed from *rouse* on the pattern of such pairs as *rise, arise, wake, awake.*

roust *v.* rouse or stir up. 1658, usually considered a probable alteration of ROUSE. **—roustabout** *n.* unskilled laborer. 1868, a deck hand or wharf laborer, American English; formed from *roust* + *about.* The sense of a casual or unskilled laborer is first recorded in 1877. The specific sense of a worker in a circus is first found in 1931 in American English.

The word has a parallel form *rouseabout* (1746, a rough, drifter), which is almost certainly an independent formation from *rouse* + *about,* and is also known in Australian English with the meaning of a hired hand on a sheep station, from 1881, but compare the American use above for a laborer (1877).

rout[1] *n.* flight of a defeated army in disorder. 1598, in Robert Barret's *The Theory and Practice of Modern Wars;* borrowed from Middle French *route* disorderly flight of troops; literally, a breaking off or rupture, from Latin *rupta,* feminine past participle of *rumpere* to break; see RUPTURE. **—v.** put to flight. About 1600 (implied in *routing,* n.), to put (an army) to rout; from the noun.

Earlier use of the term is found in the neutral sense of a group of soldiers, an army (probably before 1225, in a version of *Ancrene Riwle*), any large group of people (about 1280), and later begins to take on a pejorative sense, as in a gang of outlaws or disorderly people, a mob (about 1300), and in the phrase *run in rout* (*rennen in rowte,* before 1400).

rout[2] *v.* poke about, rummage. 1547-64, (of swine) dig with the snout, root; irregular variant of ROOT[2]. The extended sense of poke about, rummage, is first recorded in Swift's *Journal to Stella* (1711), and that of search out, bring to light, uncover (1805). A transferred sense, used especially in carpentry, of hollow out, scoop out, gouge, is first recorded in 1726. **—router** *n.* (1818)

route (rüt *or* rout) *n.* way, road, or course. Probably before 1200 *rute* a way, road, in *Ancrene Riwle;* later *route* a course, progression (before 1333, in Shoreham's *Poems*); borrowed from Old French *rute,* from Latin *rupta via* a road opened up by force, from *rupta,* feminine past participle of *rumpere* to break; see RUPTURE. The meaning of a fixed or regular course for carrying things (as in *the overland mail route*) is first recorded in 1792, and that of a regular course of delivery or service (as in *a paper route*), in 1841, both extensions of a meaning found in Middle English, "a customary path of animals, game trail" (about 1410). **—v.** arrange a route for, send by a certain route. 1881, from the noun.

routine *n.* fixed, regular way of doing things. Before 1680, in Samuel Butler's *Remains;* borrowing of French *routine* usual course of action, beaten path, from *route* way, path, course; see ROUTE. The theatrical sense of a regularly performed sketch or skit is first recorded in 1926. The computer sense of a sequence of coded instructions for a specific task is recorded from 1945. **—adj.** 1817, following routine, mechanical, unvaried; from the noun. The extended sense of average or ordinary, usual, typical, commonplace (as in *a routine check* or *investigation*) is first recorded about 1940. **—v.** make routine, apply a routine (to). 1897, George Bernard Shaw in *Saturday Review;* from the noun and adjective.

rove *v.* 1536, wander about, roam; of uncertain origin. Early modern English *rove* may be a dialectal variant of earlier northern British English and Scottish dialect *rave* to wander, stray, rove; developed from Middle English *raven* (probably about 1380), probably borrowed from a Scandinavian source (compare Icelandic *rāfa* to wander, rove).

This word is connected by the OED with the verb *rove,* a term in archery meaning to shoot arrows at random marks, on the basis of an earlier (1474) citation for the archery term. However, the difference in meaning between the two words makes such a connection doubtful. A more plausible relationship may be found in the obsolete verb *rove* to sail as pirates, roam the seas as rovers (implied in *roving,* 1513), which was probably a back formation from ROVER.

rover *n.* sea robber, pirate. Before 1393 *rovere,* in Gower's *Confessio Amantis;* borrowed from Middle Dutch *rover, rovere* robber, predator, plunderer (especially in *zeerovere* sea robber, pirate), from *roven* to ROB; for suffix see -ER[1].

row[1] (rō) *n.* line of people or things. Probably before 1200 *rawe* order, succession, in *Ancrene Riwle;* also, a row or line of people or things (probably about 1200); developed from Old English *rǣw* a row, line (940, also probably *rāw,* and in Late Old English *rēawe, rēwe*). The Old English *rǣw* (from Proto-Germanic **raiwiz*) is probably cognate with Middle Dutch *rīe* line, row (modern Dutch *rij*), Middle High German *rīhe* (modern German *Reihe* line, row, series), Old High German *riga* line (modern German *Riege* squad, section), and dialectal Norwegian *reig* row. Outside Germanic cognates are found in Sanskrit *rekhā́* line, stroke (Indo-European **roik(h)ā́*) and *rikháti* he scratches, and in Greek *ereíkein* rend, from Indo-European **reik(h)-/roik(h)-/rik(h)-,* extended from root **rei-* (Pok.857).

row[2] (rō) *v.* propel a boat by using oars. Probably before 1200 *rouwen,* in Layamon's *Chronicle of Britain;* also, in the spelling *rowen* (probably about 1200); developed from Old English (about 950) *rōwan.* Old English *rōwan* is cognate with Middle Dutch *roeyen, royen* to row (modern Dutch *roeijen*), Middle Low German *rōien, rōen,* Middle High German *ruōn, rüejen,* and Old Icelandic *rōa* (Norwegian, Danish, and Swedish *ro*). Cognates outside Germanic include Old Irish *rā-* to row, *rāme* oar, Latin *rēmus* oar, Greek *eréssein, eréttein* to row, Lithuanian *ìrti* to row, and Sanskrit *arítra-s* oar, rudder, from Indo-European **(e)rē-/(e)rō-/erə-* (Pok.338). **—n.** act of rowing. 1832, American English; from the verb. **—rowboat** *n.* (1538)

row[3] (rou) *n.* noisy commotion or disturbance. 1746, originally a slang word, in common use in the early 1800's along with the derivative *rowdy;* of uncertain origin; (perhaps related to, if not a shortened form of, earlier *rouse* a carousal or bout of drinking (1602, in Shakespeare's *Hamlet*), also spelled *rowse* (1604, in *Othello*), a shortened form of *carouse*). **—v.** make a row. 1790, to tease or rough up (someone); later, to make a noisy commotion or disturbance (1797); from the noun.

rowdy *n.* rough, disorderly person. 1808, American English; probably formed on ROW[3], n. **—adj.** rough, disorderly. 1819, American English; from the noun.

rowel (rou′əl) *n.* small wheel with sharp points, attached to the end of a spur. 1344 *ruel* small wheel; later *rowel* small wheel with sharp points forming the end of a spur (about 1400); borrowed from Old French *roelle, ruele* little wheel; see ROULETTE. **—v.** use a rowel on. 1599, in Nashe's *Lenten Stuffe;* from the noun.

royal *adj.* About 1250 *royal* fit for a king, magnificent; later, of or pertaining to a monarch, majestic, regal (about 1375, in Chaucer's *Canterbury Tales*); borrowing of Old French *royal, roial,* from Latin *rēgālis,* from *rēx* (genitive *rēgis*) king; for suffix see -AL[1]. Doublet of REGAL.

French origin of several Middle English and early modern uses is evident in the position of the adjective after the noun, as in *blood royal, court royal.* The phrase *battle royal* (1672) is a modern example of this. **—n.** Before 1400 *royalle* a royal person, king or queen; from the adjective. The extended sense of any person of royal lineage, any member of the nobility, is found as early as 1410.

—royalist *n.* supporter of a king or of a royal government. 1643, formed from English *royal,* adj. + *-ist,* on the model of French *royaliste.* **—royalty** *n.* About 1390 *roialtee* magnificence, pomp, wealth, in Chaucer's *Canterbury Tales;* later *royalte* royal power or authority, in *Morte Arthur* (probably before 1400); probably formed from Middle English *royal* + *-te* -ty[2], on the model of Old French *roiauté,* from *roial* royal. The sense of royal persons collectively is first recorded in 1480, and that of a share of the earnings made from the use of land and mineral rights (1839), or from the sale of a publication, such as a book, musical composition, etc. (1857), derived from the earlier meaning of a royal prerogative or right granted to an individual or corporation (1483).

rub *v.* Before 1325 *robben* to rub, massage, *rubben* to scratch (before 1338, in Mannyng's *Chronicle of England*); later *rubben* to rub (about 1378, in a version of *Piers Plowman*); cognate with East Frisian *rubben* to scratch, rub, and Low German *rubbelig, rubberig* rough, uneven, and Danish and Norwegian *rubbe,* Swedish *rubba* to rub, scrub; ultimate origin unknown. **—n.** 1586, an obstacle in the game of bowls by which a bowl is hindered in its proper course; from the verb. The extended sense of any obstacle or hindrance (as in Hamlet's *there's the rub*) is first recorded in 1590. The general meaning of an act or spell of rubbing is not recorded before 1615.

rubber *n.* 1) a hard brush, cloth, or the like, used for rubbing. 1536, formed from English *rub,* v. + *-er*[1]. 2) India rubber (elastic substance obtained from the latex of tropical plants). 1788-89, called *rubber* from its use originally as an eraser. **—rubber band** (1895) **—rubberize** *v.* treat or coat with rubber (1912). **—rubberneck** *v.* to look around (1896, American English). **—rubbers** *n.pl.* (1842) **—rubber stamp** (1881) The figurative sense of a person or institution that endorses policies automatically, is first recorded in 1919. The verb meaning of mark with a rubber stamp is first recorded in 1922, and that of endorse automatically, in 1934. **—rubbery** *adj.* 1907, formed by English *rubber* + *-y*[1].

rubbish *n.* About 1400 *robous;* later *robys* (1429-30), and *robish* (1477), found in Anglo-French *robouses* (1419), and *rubouses* (1392-93); of uncertain origin (connection with Old French through a Late Middle English *robeux* considered a plural of *robel,* cannot be supported, as it is not possible to establish borrowing from Old French or, indeed, that any form existed in Old French); development with the suffix *-ish* may have been through some erroneous association with the verb *rub.* **—v.** treat with contempt, scorn, disparage. 1953, originally Australian and New Zealand figurative use; from the noun.

rubble *n.* waste fragments of stones, bricks, etc. 1376-77 *robeyl,* 1425 *rubyll,* probably related to *rubbous, robys* RUBBISH (rubble being considered the rubbish of demolished buildings); the suffix *-le* is unaccounted for.

rube *n.* unsophisticated countryman, bumpkin, yokel. 1899, American English; respelling of earlier *Reub* (1896, in George Ade's *Artie*), shortened form or nickname of *Reuben,* perhaps because it was considered a common name among countrymen.

Rube Goldberg (of an invention, device, or scheme)

ridiculously complicated. 1940's, American English, in allusion to *Rube Goldberg* an American cartoonist, 1883-1970, noted for a cartoon series depicting fantastically complicated mechanical inventions for performing the simplest tasks.

rubella (rübel′ə) *n.* German measles. 1883, New Latin *rubella* rash, from Latin, neuter plural of Latin *rubellus* reddish, a diminutive related to *ruber* RED; so called from the red rash characteristic of this disease.

rubicund *adj.* reddish, ruddy. Probably before 1425 *rubicunde* red, reddish, in a translation of Chauliac's *Grande Chirurgie;* borrowed from Latin *rubicundus* red, very red, related to *ruber* RED.

rubidium (rübid′ēəm) *n.* metallic chemical element. 1861, New Latin, from Latin *rubidus* red, from *rubēre* be red, related to *ruber* RED; so called in reference to the two red lines in the element's spectrum. The term was coined by the German chemist R.W. Bunsen, who, with the physicist G.R. Kirchhoff, discovered *rubidium* in 1860.

ruble (rü′bəl) *n.* unit of money of Russia or the Soviet Union. 1554, in Hakluyt's *Voyages;* borrowed from Russian *rubl'*, of uncertain origin. The connection with Old Russian *rublĭ* a cut piece of wood, block of wood (from *rubiti* to hew, cut), is disputed and considered very doubtful by Russian etymologists.

rubric (rüb′rik) *n.* descriptive heading or title, designation, name, category. Probably about 1300 *robryk* directions for participation in religious services included in a prayerbook, often in red writing or print; later *rubrice* any title or heading of a book (probably before 1425, in a translation of Chauliac's *Grande Chirurgie*); borrowed from Old French *rubrique,* learned borrowing from Latin, and borrowed directly from Latin *rubrica* red ochre, red coloring matter, from *ruber* RED.

ruby *n.* red precious stone. Probably about 1300 *ribe,* about 1325 *ruby;* borrowed from Old French *rubi,* probably from Medieval Latin *rubinus lapis* red stone, from Latin *rubeus* red, related to *ruber* RED. **—adj.** deep, glowing red. About 1477, of or like a ruby; from the noun. The sense of deep, glowing red (as in *ruby skies*) is first recorded in 1508.

rucksack *n.* kind of knapsack. 1866, borrowing of German *Rucksack;* dialectal (Alpine) German *Ruck,* corresponding to standard German *Rücken* the back + *Sack* bag, from Old High German, *sac* sack¹.

ruckus (ruk′əs) *n.* noisy disturbance or uproar. 1890 *rucus,* American English (originally dialectal); sometimes suggested as a blend of earlier *ruction* disturbance (1825, of uncertain origin) and *rumpus* (1764, also of uncertain origin), though not a very convincing supposition.

rudder *n.* 1377-78 *rother* device for steering a boat; also found as *roper* oar (about 1225); developed from Old English (about 725) *rōthor* paddle or oar; also found in such compounds as *rothres blæd* rudder blade, and *scip-rōthor* ship rudder. Old English *rōthor* is cognate with Old Frisian *rōther* rudder, Middle Dutch *roder, roeder* (modern Dutch *roer*), Old High German *ruodar* (modern German *Ruder*), and Old Icelandic *rōdhr* act of rowing (modern Icelandic *rōdhur,* Norwegian *ror* rudder), from Proto-Germanic **rōthru-;* these words are derived from the Germanic root (**ro-*) that is the source of Old English *rōwan* to ROW².

The spelling with *d* (for *th*) is first recorded in Middle English in 1440 and represents a change opposite to that which occurred in *father, mother, gather.* The spelling with *u* begins to appear as early as the late 1200's but did not become firmly established until the early 1600's, though *rudder* is found as early as 1526. **—v.** to steer. 1856, from the noun.

ruddy *adj.* red, reddish. Late Old English (before 1100) *rudi,* probably derived from *rudu* redness, red color or complexion, related (with different vowel grade) to *rēad* and *rēod* RED; for suffix see -Y¹. The spelling *ruddy* is first recorded in Middle English about 1410, in Chaucer's *Canterbury Tales.*

rude *adj.* Probably about 1280 *reud* (of a board) coarse, rough; later *rude* (of a writer or writing) artless, simple (before 1325, in *Cursor Mundi*), and ill-mannered (probably before 1350); borrowed from Old French *rude,* learned borrowing from Latin, and borrowed directly from Latin *rudis* rough, crude, unpolished, unrefined, unlearned; of unknown origin. Latin *rudis* is related to *rūdus* broken stones, rubble, which may be cognate with Middle Irish *rūad* ruin, Old Icelandic *reyta* to tear down, pluck out, and Middle Dutch *rūten* to tear, plunder.

rudiment *n.* part to be learned first, beginning. 1548, in Udall's translation of Erasmus' *Upon the New Testament;* borrowed from Middle French, or directly from Latin *rudīmentum* early training, first lesson or experience, from *rudis* unlearned, untrained, unrefined; see RUDE; for suffix see -MENT. **—rudimentary** *adj.* 1839, pertaining to the rudiments of knowledge; formed from English *rudiment* + *-ary,* perhaps by influence of French *rudimentaire,* and replacing earlier *rudimental* (1597).

rue¹ *v.* feel sorrow, regret, repent. Probably about 1150 *rewen;* later *reuwen* (about 1300), and *ruen* (about 1330); developed from a blend of: 1) Old English *hrēowan* make sorry, grieve (before 899, in Alfred's translation of Boethius' *De Consolatione Philosophiae*); cognate with Old Frisian *riowa* to affect with sorrow, rue, Middle Dutch and modern Dutch *rouwen* to mourn, lament, Old Saxon *hrewan* to regret, rue, Old High German *hriuwan* (modern German *reuen*), from Proto-Germanic **Hrewanan,* and Old Icelandic *hryggja* make sad, from Proto-Germanic **Hruwjanan,* from Indo-European **kreu-/kru-* hit hard (Pok.622); and of: 2) *hrēowian* feel pain or sorrow; cognate with Old Saxon *hriwōn* and Old High German *hriuwōn.* **—n.** sorrow, regret, Before 1325 *rewe;* developed from Old English *hrēow* (about 725, in *Beowulf*); cognate with Frisian *rou* sorrow, regret, Middle Dutch and modern Dutch *rouw* mourning, Old High German *hriuwa* sorrow, regret (modern German *Reue*), and related to Old English *hrēowan* to rue; see also RUTH.

rue² *n.* strong-smelling plant. Before 1300, borrowing of Old French *rue,* from Latin *rūta* rue (the plant), probably from Greek *rhȳté,* of uncertain origin.

ruff *n.* stiff frilled collar worn around the neck. 1523, ruffle on the sleeve of a garment; probably a shortened form of RUFFLE¹, v. The sense of a stiff frilled collar (worn around the neck in the 1500's and 1600's, said especially to disguise the swollen glands of scrofula) is first recorded in 1555. From this meaning developed the extended sense of a collar of feathers or hair around the neck of various birds and other animals (1698).

ruffian *n.* 1531, in Elyot's *The Boke Named the Governour;* borrowed from Middle French *rufian,* from Ital ian *ruffiano* a pander, pimp, of uncertain origin. The English meaning of a rough, brutal person, rowdy, may have been influenced by the similarity in sound with the word *rough* because earliest citations refer to rough behavior and thieves, not to the business of pimping. **—adj.** rough and brutal. 1533, from the noun.

ruffle[1] *v.* make rough or uneven, wrinkle. Before 1325 *ruffelen* stir up, poke about, in *Cursor Mundi;* cognate with Low German *ruffelen* to crumple, curl, Dutch *roffelen* work roughly, and perhaps Old Icelandic *hrufla* to scratch, of unknown origin.

The extended meaning of disarrange (hair or feathers) is first recorded about 1450, and that of make irregular, disorder, in 1528; the subsequent figurative sense of annoy, irritate, disconcert (a person, the mind, etc.), is found in 1658.

—n. 1533, disorder or confusion; from the verb. The literal meaning of a break in the evenness of a surface is first recorded in 1713. The specialized sense of a strip of fabric gathered at one edge and used as a frill appeared in 1707.

ruffle[2] *n.* low, steady drumbeat. 1802, in Charles James' *Military Dictionary,* noun use of earlier *ruffle,* v., to beat a drum with a low, steady beat (1721). The verb may be a frequentative form of earlier *roofe* (1688), *ruff* low steady drumbeat (1706); perhaps of imitative origin; for suffix see -LE[3].

rufous (rü′fəs) *adj.* reddish, ruddy. 1782, in John Latham's *A General History of Birds;* borrowed from Latin *rūfus* RED; for suffix see -OUS. The word is commonly used to describe the color of birds and sometimes of other animals, often becoming part of the animal's name, as in *rufous hummingbird, rufous lemur.*

rug *n.* 1551-52, coarse fabric; borrowed from a Scandinavian source (compare Norwegian dialect *rugga* coarse coverlet, Swedish *rugg* ruffled or coarse hair, and Old Icelandic *rǫgg* shaggy tuft); related to RAG. The extended meaning of a large piece of thick woolen stuff used as a coverlet or wrap is first recorded in English in 1591, and that of a mat for the floor, often of thick or shaggy stuff, in 1808, in Jane Austen's letters. The American slang sense of a wig is first found in John O'Hara's *Pal Joey* (1940).

Rugby *n.* English game somewhat like football. 1864, named after *Rugby,* a school for boys where the game was played, situated in *Rugby,* a city in Warwickshire, central England.

rugged (rug′id) *adj.* rough and uneven. Probably before 1300, rough with hair, shaggy, in *Arthour and Merlin;* borrowed from a Scandinavian source (compare Old Icelandic *rǫgg* shaggy tuft); see RUG; for suffix see -ED[2]. The sense of rough, uneven, suggests some relation to *rug,* especially by way of Old Icelandic *rǫgg,* and the similarity in form with *ragged,* besides the near coincidence of appearance in Middle English, also prompts a sense of relationship. It is reinforced by the shared meaning of tattered, torn, probably found before 1439. The sense of rough, uneven, is first recorded in 1548, and that of harsh, severe, in 1597. The sense of strong, hardy, robust, is first found in 1731 in American English.

ruin *n.* About 1375 *ruyne* a falling down or collapse of a building, etc.; also, a condition of ruin, degradation (about 1380, in Chaucer's *House of Fame*); borrowed from Old French *ruine* (learned borrowing from Latin), and borrowed directly from Latin *ruīna* a collapse, related to *ruere* to rush, fall, collapse, of obscure origin. The sense of devastation, wreckage, ruins, is found in Middle English before 1420. **—v.** bring to ruin, destroy, spoil. 1581, to destroy, eradicate, in Sidney's *Apology for Poetry;* borrowed through Middle French *ruiner,* or directly from Medieval Latin *ruinare,* from Latin *ruīna* ruin, n. **—ruination** *n.* 1664, ruin, destruction; derived from earlier English *ruinate* reduce to ruins (before 1548); borrowed from Medieval Latin *ruinatus,* past participle of *ruinare* to destroy, ruin; for suffix see -ATION. **—ruinous** *adj.* About 1384 *ruynouse* going to ruin, dilapidated, in the Wycliffe Bible; borrowed from Latin *ruīnōsus* fallen to ruin, from *ruīna* a collapse, ruin; for suffix see -OUS. The sense of causing ruin, destructive, disastrous, is found in Middle English probably before 1439.

rule *n.* Probably before 1200 *riwle* principle or regulation governing conduct, in *Ancrene Riwle;* also *reule* (before 1225), and *rule* (about 1378); borrowed from Old French *riule, reule,* from Vulgar Latin **regula* (altered by influence of *regere* to rule) of Latin *rēgula* straight stick, bar, ruler, pattern; related to *regere* to rule, straighten, guide; see RIGHT. **—v.** Probably before 1200 *riwlen* to direct, guide, regulate; borrowed from Old French *riuler, reuler,* from Vulgar Latin **regulāre* to regulate, from *regula* rule. **—rule of thumb** (1692) **—ruler** *n.* Before 1382 *rewlere* one who rules; also, straight edge, in the Wycliffe Bible; formed from Middle English *rewlen,* variant of *riwlen* to rule + *-er*[1].

rum[1] *n.* alcoholic liquor made from sugar cane or molasses. 1654, apparently shortened form of earlier *rumbullion* (about 1651), of uncertain origin. The form *rombostion,* with the same meaning, is recorded in 1652. English *rum* was borrowed into Dutch, Portuguese, Danish, and Italian as *rum,* into German as *Rum,* into Swedish and Russian as *rom,* into French as *rum,* (later) *rhum,* and Spanish as *ron.*

rum[2] *adj.* Before 1700, good, fine, excellent; alteration of earlier *rome* fine (1567); said to be borrowed from Romany *rom* male, husband (see ROMANY), but the semantic connection is not at all clear.

rumba (rum′bə) *n.* Latin-American dance. 1922, in Joseph Hergesheimer's *The Bright Shawl;* American English, borrowing of Cuban Spanish *rumba.* According to Corominas, *rumba* originally meant spree, carousal, party, from Spanish *rumbo* spree, party; earlier, pomp, ostentation, leadership; originally, the course of a ship. In its original sense, Spanish *rumbo* is an alteration of *rombo* rhombus, in reference to the compass marked with a rhombus, which sailors believed were magical symbols that helped a pilot guide the ship. **—v.** dance the rumba. 1938, in Graham Greene's *Brighton Rock;* from the noun.

rumble *v.* About 1375 *romblen* make noise, in Chaucer's *Canterbury Tales;* later *rumblen* move with a heavy continuous sound (about 1380, in Chaucer's *House of Fame*); of uncertain origin (compare Middle Dutch and modern Dutch *rommelen* to rumble, Middle High German and modern German *rummeln,* Old Swedish *rumbla,* Danish and Norwegian *rumle,* and Old Icelandic *rymja* to shout, roar; see RUMOR). **—n.** deep, heavy, continuous sound. About 1385 *rumbel,* in Chaucer's *Canterbury Tales;* probably from the verb. The sense of commotion, bustle, uproar, is also recorded in *Canterbury Tales.* The related sense of a street fight between teen-age gangs is first recorded as

American English slang in the 1940's. In this use, *rumble* is perhaps an Anglicization of Spanish *rumbo.* **—rumble seat** outside seat in the back of a coupe or roadster (1912, American English).

ruminant *n.* animal that chews the cud. 1661, in Robert Lowell's *A Complete History of Animals and Minerals;* borrowed from Latin *rūminantem* (nominative *rūminans*), present participle of *rūmināre* to chew the cud; see RUMINATE; for suffix see -ANT. **—adj.** of or belonging to the group of ruminants. 1679, from the noun.

ruminate *v.* 1533, turn over and over in the mind, muse or meditate on, in Elyot's *The Castel of Helth;* borrowed from Latin *rūminātus,* past participle of *rūmināre* chew the cud, chew over again, turn over again, turn over in the mind, meditate, from *rūmen* (genitive *rūminis*) gullet; for suffix see -ATE[1]. Latin *rūmen* is cognate with Sanskrit *romantha-s* chewing the cud, from Indo-European **reu-smen-* (root **reu-* to belch, Pok.873). The literal sense of chew the cud is first recorded in English in 1547. **—rumination** *n.* 1600, contemplation, meditation, in Shakespeare's *As You Like It;* probably formed in English from *ruminate* + *-ation,* on the model of Latin *rūminātiōnem* (nominative *rūminātiō*), from *rūmināre* chew the cud. The meaning of the action of chewing the cud is first recorded in Phillips' *Dictionary* (1658).

rummage *n.* thorough search. 1526 *romage* act of arranging cargo in the hold of a ship; shortened and altered form of Middle French *arrumage* arrangement of cargo, from *arrumer* to stow cargo (*a-* to, from Latin *ad-* + Middle French *-rumer,* probably from Germanic; compare Old Icelandic *rūm* compartment in a ship, space, room, and Gothic and Old High German *rūm* space, ROOM); for suffix see -AGE.

The sense of a thorough search is first recorded in Walpole's *Letters* (1753). The term *rummage sale* is first recorded in Simmond's *Dictionary of Trade Products* (1858) with the meaning of a clearance sale of unclaimed goods at the docks, or of odds and ends left in a warehouse.

—v. search thoroughly. 1544, to arrange (cargo) in the hold of a ship; from the noun. The meaning of search thoroughly is first recorded in Beaumont and Fletcher's *Wit Without Money* (before 1616).

rummy *n.* kind of card game. 1910 *rum, rhum, rhummy,* American English; of uncertain origin. The spelling *rummy* appeared in 1915. The name *gin rummy* for a kind of rummy game is first recorded in 1941, in Somerset Maugham's *A Writer's Notebook.*

rumor *n.* About 1380 *rumour* unsubstantiated report, hearsay, gossip, in Chaucer's translation of Boethius' *De Consolatione Philosophiae;* borrowed from Old French *rumour* widespread noise or report, learned borrowing from Latin, and borrowed directly from Latin *rūmor* noise, clamor, report, common talk, rumor, related to *ravus* hoarse. Latin *rūmor* is cognate with Old Slavic *ruti* to shout, roar, Greek *ōrýesthai* to howl, roar, and Sanskrit *rāúti, ravati* he shouts, roars. Cognates in Germanic include Middle High German *rienen* to moan, Old Icelandic *rymja* to shout, roar, *rymr* noise, roar, and Middle Low German *ruinen* to shout, from Indo-European **reu-/rēu-/ru-/rū-* (Pok. 867). **—v.** 1594, to circulate by way of rumor, in Shakespeare's *Richard III;* from the noun.

rump *n.* hind part of an animal. About 1410 *rumpe* rump of a quadruped animal, tail; earlier as a surname (about 1170); borrowed from a Scandinavian source (compare Swedish *rumpa* rump, buttocks, Danish and Norwegian *rumpe,* and Icelandic *rumpr,* which are cognate with Middle Dutch and modern Dutch *romp* trunk, torso, Middle Low German *rump,* and Middle High German *rumpe,* modern German *Rumpf*).

The figurative sense of a small, unimportant, or contemptible remnant of a group, legislative party, or convention (derived from the sense of a tail), is first recorded in English in 1649, in reference to English parliamentary history.

—adj. small, unimportant, inferior, as of a splinter group. 1605, in Shakespeare's *Macbeth;* from the noun. In English history the name *Rump Parliament* was given to the remaining members who sat after December 1648, when about one hundred supporters favoring a compromise with Charles I during the Civil War were excluded from Parliament.

rumple *v.* 1603, possibly a variant of earlier (and now dialectal) *rimple* to wrinkle (probably before 1400 *rimpled,* from *rimple,* n. + *-ed*[2], developed from Old English *hrympel*), influenced in alteration to *rumple* by Dutch *rompelen,* Middle Dutch *rumpelen.* It is also probable that in some instances *rumple,* v., is a direct borrowing from Dutch *rompelen,* Middle Dutch *rumpelen,* and that it may also be from the earlier noun in Middle English. **—n.** 1500-20, in Dunbar's *Poems;* possibly a variant of earlier (and now rare) *rimple* a wrinkle (1440), influenced in alteration to *rumple* by Middle Dutch *rumpel,* from the verb in Middle Dutch. It is also possible that in some instances English *rumple* is a direct borrowing of Middle Dutch *rumpel.*

rumpus *n.* noisy disturbance, row. 1764, in Samuel Foote's *The Mayor of Garet;* of uncertain origin (perhaps a fanciful alteration of *robustious* boisterous, noisy, before 1548).

run *v.* About 1325 *runnen,* in *Cursor Mundi,* representing originally distinct forms: a strong intransitive verb and a weak transitive verb, both of which were more commonly recorded in Middle and Old English with sounds of the initial syllable transposed. The strong intransitive verb, found in Middle English as *rinnen* and *irnen* (both probably before 1200), developed from Old English *rinnan, irnan,* past tense *ran,* past participle *runnen,* whose cognates include Old Frisian *rinna,* Old Saxon *rinnan,* Middle Dutch *rinnen,* Old High German *rinnan* (modern German *rinnen* to run, flow), Old Icelandic *rinna* (Norwegian *renne,* Swedish *rinna,* Danish *rinde*), and Gothic *rinnan,* from Proto-Germanic **renwanan.* The weak transitive verb, appearing in Middle English *rennen* (before 1121) and *ernen* (probably about 1200), developed from Old English *ærnan, earnan,* usually in the sense of to ride, and its cognates include Old Frisian *renna* to cause to run, Middle Dutch and modern Dutch *rennen,* Old Saxon *rennian,* Old High German *rennen,* Old Icelandic *renna* to cause to run (Norwegian *renne,* Swedish *ränna,* Danish *rende*), and Gothic *urranjan* let go up, a thoroughly secondary formation (**ranjanan*), a causative of what was treated as a Proto-Germanic root **ren-* (Pok.328) apparently related to Old English *rīsan* to RISE.

Rareness of Old English *rinnan* and absence of an Old English form **rennan* for the transitive verb make it probable that Middle English *rinnen* and *rennen* are mainly, if not entirely, due to the influence of Old Icelandic *rinna* and *renna,* especially since the Middle

English forms first appear in texts where the Scandinavian influence is prominent.
—n. act of running. About 1390 *ren* a running, a run, in Chaucer's *Canterbury Tales;* from the verb. The spelling *run* for the noun is not found before 1450. The use of *run* as a unit of scoring in various sports is first recorded in 1746 in cricket and in 1856 in baseball.
—runaway *n.* (1547); *adj.* (1548). **—rundown** *n.* 1945, brief account, summary of pertinent facts, American English; earlier, (in baseball) a tagging out of a runner caught between bases (1908, American English). **—run-down** *adj.* 1866, unwound, tired out, in writings of George Eliot; later, dilapidated (1896). **—run-in** *n.* 1857, act of running in; later, a quarrel (1905, American English). **—runner-up** *n.* (1842) **—running mate** 1868, horse entered in a race to set the pace for another horse, American English; later, vice-presidential candidate (1900, American English). **—run-off** *n.* 1873, final deciding contest; later, amount of water that flows off the land without soaking in (1892-93, American English). **—run-of-the-mill** *adj.* (1930) **—runway** *n.* 1833, track customarily followed by animals, American English; later, airstrip (1923).

runcible spoon (run′səbəl) kind of fork with three wide prongs curved like a spoon. 1871, in Edward Lear's *The Owl and the Pussy-Cat,* a nonsense phrase coined by Lear, of unknown origin; speculation among some dictionary etymologists has centered on the botanical term *runcinate* (1776) irregularly saw-toothed (formed from Latin *runcina* a plane, but taken to mean a saw) + the suffix *-ible;* however, this seems to be reaching as Lear used the term with indistinct meaning, applying *runcible* to a cat (1877), to a hat (1888), and to a goose and a wall (1895). About 1926 *runcible spoon* was adopted as the name of a spoonlike three-pronged fork used for eating pickles and various other foods.

rune (rün) *n.* letter of the earliest Germanic alphabet. 1685 (but implied in earlier *runic,* 1662); introduced into English by early Germanic philologists from a Scandinavian source, possibly Danish *rune* (but compare modern and Old Icelandic *rūn* rune). An obsolete parallel form was known in Middle English *rune, roune* utterance, whisper, murmur, message (probably about 1175); language, speech (probably before 1200); and song, poem (probably about 1200), and in Old English *rūn, rūne* a secret or mystery (about 950); a runic letter (before 899); and counsel or consultation (about 725); forms which are cognate with Old Saxon *rūna* a secret, mystery, counsel, rune, Middle Dutch *rune,* Old High German *rūna,* and Gothic *rūna,* from Proto-Germanic **rūnō;* see RUMOR.
—runic *adj.* 1662, consisting of runes, in John Evelyn's *Sculptura;* perhaps formed in English from *rune* + *-ic* (paralleling earlier Middle English *runisch,* 1380); or borrowed from New Latin *runicus,* formed from modern Icelandic *rūn* + Latin *-icus* -ic.

Runes are believed to be developed from an early contact with the Greek, and later Roman, alphabets (though prolonged contact with the Roman alphabet, especially in Christian texts, finally supplanted the runic forms by about 1100). The traditional reason given for formation of the straight lines of the runic forms, found as early as the 200's A.D., is that they were originally used as markings in hard surfaces such as stone, wood, and some metal coins, which made rounded characters difficult to use.

rung *n.* About 1300 *roungue* step of a ladder; earlier *runge* horizontal side rail of a cart; developed from Old English (before 1000) *hrung* a rod or bar; cognate with Middle Dutch *ronghe* spoke of a wheel (modern Dutch *rong*), Middle Low German and Middle High German *runge,* Old High German *runga* (modern German *Runge*), Gothic *hrunga* staff, from Proto-Germanic **Hrungō,* Indo-European **kr̥ngh-* (root **krengh-,* Pok.936), and perhaps cognate with Old Icelandic *hringr* RING.

runnel *n.* small stream or brook. 1577, in Hakluyt's *Diverse Voyages;* alteration (probably by association with *run*) of Middle English (about 1350) *ryneil;* developed from Old English (about 825) *rinelle,* related to *rinnan* to RUN.

runt *n.* 1501, an old or decayed stump of a tree; of uncertain origin. The meaning of an ox or cow of a small breed or size, is first recorded in 1549, and that of a stunted or undersized person or animal (before 1700).

rupee (rü′pē) *n.* unit of money of India, Pakistan, etc. 1612 *rupie,* 1615 rupee, probably borrowed through Anglo-Indian from Hindi *rūpyā,* from Sanskrit *rū́pya-s* wrought silver or gold; literally, beautiful or shapely, from *rūpá-m* form, shape, of unknown origin.

rupture *n.* 1392, the breaking of a vein; later (figurative) a violation of a treaty (1439, in *Proceedings of the Privy Council*); borrowing of Middle French *rupture* a breaking, breach, or directly from Latin *ruptūra* the breaking (of a limb), fracture, from *rupt-,* past participle stem of *rumpere* to break; for suffix see -URE. Latin *rumpere* is cognate with Sanskrit *ropáyati* he breaks off; see ROB. The specific sense of an abdominal hernia is first recorded probably before 1425, in a translation of Chauliac's *Grande Chirurgie.* **—v.** 1739, from the noun.

rural *adj.* Before 1420 *rual* common, lowly, unlearned, unskilled, in Lydgate's *Troy Book;* also, probably before 1425 *rural* of or having to do with farm work; borrowed from Middle French *rural,* from Latin *rūrālis* of the countryside, from *rūs* (genitive *rūris*) open land, country (earlier **rewos*); see ROOM; for suffix see -AL[1]. The sense of living in or being from the countryside, rustic, is recorded before 1465. **—rural free delivery** (*RFD,* 1916) free delivery of mail in rural districts (1892, American English).

rurban (rur′bən *or* ru̇r′bən) *adj.* of or characterized by both rural and urban features. 1918, in C.J. Galpin's *Rural Life;* a blend of *rural* and *urban.*

ruse (rüs) *n.* trick, stratagem. 1625, originally a hunting term for a game animal's dodging movements to elude pursuit (about 1410); borrowing of Old French *ruse, reüse,* noun of *ruser, reüser* to dodge, repel, retreat, from Latin *recūsāre* push back, deny, reject, oppose (*re-* intensive + *causārī* plead as an excuse or reason, object, allege, from *causa* reason, CAUSE).

rush[1] *v.* move with speed. 1375 *ruschen* to drive back, repel, in Barbour's *The Bruce;* later, move quickly, dash (about 1380, in *Sir Ferumbras*); borrowed from Anglo-French *russher,* variant of Old French *ruser, reüser* to dodge, repel; see RUSE. **—n.** act of rushing. About 1380 *russche* a charge, onslaught, in *Sir Ferumbras,* from *ruschen* to rush. **—adj.** requiring haste. 1879, from the noun. **—rush hour** (1898, American English)

rush[2] *n.* kind of grasslike plant with hollow stems. Before 1325 *ress,* about 1350 *ruch* (with several other variations in the vowel); developed from Old English *resc* (before 1100); earlier *risc* (about 725). The Old English forms are cognate with Middle Low German *risch, rusch* rush, Middle Dutch *rusch* (modern Dutch *rus*), Middle High German *rusch.* Outside Germanic cognates may exist in Latin *restis* rope or cord (from earlier **rezgtis*), Latvian *režģis* basketwork, and Sanskrit *rájju-s* rope or cord, from Indo-European **rezg-* (Pok.874).

rusk *n.* 1595, a hard, crisp bread used especially aboard ships; borrowed from Spanish or Portuguese *rosca* roll, twist of bread; literally, coil or spiral, of uncertain origin.

The meaning of a kind of bread hardened or browned by rebaking and sometimes sweetened is first recorded in 1759.

russet *n.* a reddish-brown color. About 1248, a coarse homespun cloth of a reddish-brown color; later, the color (1422); borrowed from Old French *rousset,* from *rosset, russet,* adj., reddish, diminutive of *ros, rous* red, from Latin *russus* (from Indo-European **rudh-tos* or **rudh-sos,* Pok.872), related to *ruber* RED; for suffix see -ET. **—adj.** 1390 *russet* (of cloth) reddish-brown; probably borrowed from Old French *rosset, russet* reddish, or possibly from the noun in English.

rust *n.* Old English *rūst* (about 725); cognate with Old Saxon *rost* rust, Old High German *rost* (modern German *Rost*), Swedish *rost,* Danish and Norwegian *rust,* and Middle Dutch and modern Dutch *roest;* all probably derived from the root represented by Old Icelandic *rydh, rydhr* rust, and Old English *rudu* redness; see RUDDY. The closest cognates outside Germanic are Lithuanian *rùstas* reddish-brown, and Latvian *rusta* brown color.

The length of the vowel in Old English *rūst* is confirmed by the modern dialectal forms *roust, rowst,* and Scottish *roost;* however, a form with short *u* may have existed at an early date.

As the name of a disease of plants characterized by reddish-brown or rusty spots, *rust* appeared in Middle English about 1340.

—v. Probably before 1200 *rusten* become covered with rust, in *Ancrene Riwle;* from the noun.

—rusty *adj.* Before 1225, developed from Old English *rūstig* (before 899, in Alfred's translation of Orosius' *Historiarum Adversus Paganos*); formed from *rūst* rust + *-ig* -y[1]. The figurative sense of impaired by neglect, requiring exercise or practice, is first recorded in 1508.

rustic *adj.* rural. Probably 1440, shortened form of Middle English *rustical* (probably before 1425); borrowed from Latin *rūsticus,* from *rūs* (genitive *rūris*) open land, country; see ROOM; for suffix see -IC, -ICAL. The sense of rough or awkward is first recorded in 1585, and that of simple or plain in Nashe's writings in 1594. **—n.** rural person. About 1550, countryman, peasant; from the adjective. **—rusticity** *n.* 1531, lack of breeding or culture, rustic manner or behavior, in Elyot's *The Boke Named the Governour;* probably formed from English *rustic* + *-ity* on the model of Middle French *rusticité,* from Latin *rūsticitātem* (nominative *rūsticitās*) state or character of being rustic, from *rūsticus* rustic.

rusticate *v.* go or stay in the country. 1660, probably a back formation from *rustication,* formed after Latin *rūsticātus,* past participle of *rūsticārī* live or stay in the country, from *rūsticus* RUSTIC; for suffix see -ATE[1]. **—rustication** *n.* 1623, borrowed from Latin *rūsticātiōnem* (nominative *rūsticātiō*) the act or fact of living or staying in the country, from *rūsticārī* live or stay in the country; for suffix see -ATION.

rustle *v.* Before 1387 (implied in *rustelyng*) making a sound of things rubbing together, in Trevisa's translation of Higden's *Polychronicon;* perhaps of imitative origin, also possibly influenced by Scandinavian words, such as Old Swedish *ruska* rustle, shake, and Icelandic *rȳsla* rattle and *hrista* shake, tremble; for suffix see -LE[3].

The informal meaning of move about vigorously, work with energy, hustle, is first recorded in 1844 in American English, and that of gather, round up (cattle, horses, etc.) in 1896. The specialized use of steal (cattle, etc.) however, is recorded earlier in 1893, perhaps just an accident of the record; or more likely from the earlier noun sense, which suggests that the generalized meaning in the noun of round up animals is simply a weakened sense of steal cattle.

—n. rustling sound. 1759, Johnson in *The Idler;* from the verb.

—rustler *n.* 1820, one that makes a rustling sound, formed from English *rustle,* v. + *-er*[1]. The meaning of cattle thief is first recorded in 1882 in American English.

rut[1] *n.* track made in the ground by the wheels of a vehicle. 1580, of uncertain origin; perhaps a variant of *route,* also found in Middle English *rute, route,* and according to the OED, in the compound *cart-rote.* The figurative meaning of a narrow, undeviating, and monotonous course of life or action, is first recorded in Carlyle's *Essay on Chartism* (1839). **—v.** make a rut in, furrow. 1607, from the noun.

rut[2] *n.* 1183 *ruyth* the rutting season, especially among deer; later *rutte* periodical sexual excitement of animals (about 1410); borrowed from Old French *rut, ruit,* from Vulgar Latin **rūgitus,* from Late Latin *rūgītus* a bellowing, from Latin, past participle of *rūgīre* to bellow. **—v.** be in rut. Before 1425, to beget; from the noun.

rutabaga (rü'təbā'gə) *n.* kind of large turnip. 1799, borrowing of dialectal Swedish *rotabagge* (*rot* root + *bagge* bag).

ruth (rüth) *n.* feeling of sorrow for another, pity, compassion. Probably before 1200 *reuthe,* in *Ancrene Riwle,* from *reowen, reuwen* to RUE[1]; for suffix see -TH[1]. **—ruthless** *adj.* having no pity. About 1330 *rewtheles;* formed from Middle English *reuthe* pity + *-les* -less.

ruthenium (ruthē'nēəm) *n.* metallic chemical element. 1848, New Latin, from Medieval Latin *Ruthenia* Russia; so called because the element was discovered in platinum ore from the Urals. The term was coined in 1828 for the platinum ore by its discoverer, G.W. Osann, but the word was first applied to the element itself in 1845 by the Russian chemist Karl K. Klaus, who isolated it from the crude ore.

-ry a suffix, a shortened form of *-ery,* forming especially abstract nouns with the meaning of act of, quality or condition of, as in *mimicry, ribaldry, wizardry,* and collective nouns, as in *citizenry, jewelry, peasantry.* Middle English *-rie,* borrowed from Old French *-rie,* shortened form of *-erie* -ERY.

rye *n.* Before 1325 *rie* cereal grass that yields rye grain; later, the grain itself (about 1333-52); developed from Old English (about 725) *ryge;* cognate with Old Icelandic *rugr* rye (Swedish *råg,* Danish and Norwegian *rug*), Old Frisian *rogga,* Old Saxon *roggo,* Middle Dutch and modern Dutch *rogge,* and Old High German *rocko* (modern German *Roggen*). Cognates outside Germanic include Lithuanian *rugỹs* rye grain, Old Slavic *rŭžĭ* rye grass, Russian *rozh',* from Indo-European **wrughyo-* (Pok.1183). As a shortened form of *rye whiskey* (1785), the word *rye* appeared in 1835 in American English. The form *rye bread* is first recorded about 1440.

S

-s[1] a suffix forming the plural of most nouns, as in *books, fathers, pilgrims.* Also *-es*[1] after nouns ending in *s, z, sh, ch,* etc. Middle English *-es, -s,* developed from Old English *-as,* nominative and accusative plural ending of certain masculine nouns.

-s[2] a suffix forming the third person singular (present indicative) of verbs, as in *knows, looks, runs.* Also *-es*[2] after forms ending in *s, z, sh, ch,* etc. Middle English *-es, -s,* developed from Old English *-es, -as,* of unknown origin.

-s[3] a suffix forming some adverbs, as in *needs, unawares.* Middle English *-es, -s,* developed from Old English *-es,* from the genitive singular ending of masculine and neuter nouns and adjectives.

-'s a suffix forming the possessive case of nouns, as in *boy's, cat's, England's, women's.* Also *-s'* for plural nouns, as in *customers' confidence,* and for proper names that normally end in *-s*[1], as *Jones' house.* Middle English *-es, -s,* developed from Old English *-es,* genitive singular ending of masculine and neuter nouns.

Sabbath *n.* Old English (about 950) *sabat* the seventh day of the week (Saturday) observed by Jews as a day of rest; borrowed from Latin *sabbatum,* from Greek *sábbaton,* from Hebrew *shabbāth,* from *shābath* he rested.

Sabbath was applied to the first day of the week (Sunday) about 1410. The spelling with double *b* is first recorded about 1280, and that with *th* though recorded before 1382, in the Wycliffe Bible, did not become widespread before the 1500's through the influence of the Hebrew form. The word began to be capitalized about 1400 by analogy with the names of the days of the week and of festivals.

sabbatical *adj.* 1645, of or suitable for the Sabbath, formed in English from Greek *sabbatikós* of the Sabbath (from *sábbaton* SABBATH) + English *-al*[1]. Alternatively, the first element may have been borrowed from French *sabbatique,* from Greek.

The use of *sabbatical* to designate a year or other period during which a leave of absence is granted teachers (originally every seven years to university professors) appeared in 1886 in American English. The phrase *sabbatical year* also appeared in 1886 in this sense, in allusion to the *sabbatical year* (1635-56) the seventh year, in which according to Mosaic law the land was to remain untilled and debtors and slaves were to be released.
—n. sabbatical year or leave. Before 1934, American English, shortened from *sabbatical year.*

saber *n.* 1680, borrowed from French *sabre* heavy, curved sword, alteration of earlier *sable,* from German *Sabel* (now *Säbel*), from a Slavic source (compare Russian *sáblya* and Polish *szabla* sword, saber). The ultimate source of the Slavic words (as of Hungarian *száblya* saber) is uncertain. **—v.** strike, wound, or kill with a saber. 1790, in Burke's *Reflections on the Revolution in France;* from the noun. The earlier *sabered* armed with a saber (1760), was formed from English *saber,* n. + *-ed*[2], not from the verb, which has never been recorded with the meaning of give a saber to.
—saber-toothed tiger (1849)

sable *n.* small mammal valued for its dark fur. Probably before 1422, in Lydgate's writings; borrowed from Middle French *sable* the mammal or its fur, from Old French, from a Germanic source (compare Middle Dutch *sabel,* Middle Low German *sabel,* and Middle High German *zabel, zobel*), ultimately from Russian *sóbol'.*

The word is recorded earlier in Middle English (probably before 1325) in the sense of black, as one of the heraldic colors, probably in reference to the color of the mammal's fur. This meaning passed into general use in the 1500's, but is now chiefly used as an adjective in poetic and rhetorical contexts. However, it is possible that this earlier use of *sable* may not be the same word as the name of the mammal, since the fur is generally brown, not black. This fact has led to the conjecture that it may have been customary to dye sable fur black, perhaps to heighten the contrast with ermine, with which it was often worn. If the heraldic term is a different word, its origin is unknown.

The term *sablefish* has been applied since the early 1800's to various fishes; in American English the term has been recorded since the 1930's to mean a black-skinned or gray-skinned North American food fish that is also called black cod or simply sable.
—adj. black, dark. Before 1400 *sabyll* (in heraldry) black; from the noun.

sabot (sab'ō) *n.* wooden shoe worn by peasants. 1607, borrowed from French *sabot,* alteration (by association with Old French *bot, bote* BOOT[1]) of Middle French *savate* old shoe, from the same indeterminate source as Catalan and Old Provençal *sabata* shoe, Portuguese *sapato,* Spanish *zapato,* Italian *ciabatta* old shoe, Basque *zapatu* shoe, and Arabic *sabbāṭ* sandal. An earlier word *sabaton* is recorded in 1388 with the meaning of a piece of armor to cover the foot, and later, a kind of shoe (1423). Both meanings are also found with the spelling *sabbatin* (1448) and *sabatin* (probably about 1475), but apparently these are different words, borrowed from Medieval Latin *sabbatum.*

sabotage (sab'ətäzh) *n.* damage done to hinder or subvert the plans of an employer, enemy, etc. 1910, borrowing of French *sabotage,* from *saboter* to sabotage, bungle, walk noisily, from *sabot* wooden shoe, SABOT; for suffix see -AGE. The word in French is traditionally said to have been used in reference to the action of striking workers who threw sabots into machinery to damage it, but this cannot be substantiated, and the verb in French carries the sense of bungle, execute poorly, which suggests a different semantic development indirectly associated with the wooden shoes and more closely associated with the noise they make in walking. **—v.** practice sabotage on. 1918, from the noun. **—saboteur** (sab'ətėr') *n.* person who practices sabotage. 1921, borrowing of French *saboteur,* from *saboter* to sabotage.

sac *n.* baglike part in an animal or plant. 1741, in a treatise on anatomy; borrowing of French *sac,* from Latin *saccus* bag, SACK[1]. The meaning was known earlier in Middle English (1340, in *Ayenbite of Inwyt*), but was just one of the meanings of *sak,* later *sack,* this sense not being recorded in the form *sac,* until the 18th century.

saccharin (sak′ərin) *n.* very sweet substance obtained from coal tar and used as a substitute for sugar. 1885 *saccharine,* said to be coined by the American chemist I. Remsen and the discoverer of the substance, the Russian-born chemist K. Fahlberg, from Latin *saccharon* (erroneously *saccharum*) + English *-ine*[2]. It is more likely that the name given to this synthetic sweetener is simply a transferred use of earlier *saccharine,* n., saccharine matter, sugar (1841), or other noun use of *saccharine,* adj. (1674). Formations in English based on Medieval Latin *saccharun* or Latin *saccharon* cane-sugar are commonly found in the vocabulary of science and technology in the 1700's and 1800's, so that it seems most unlikely a well-known form in English would have been overlooked for a reborrowing from Latin to come up with the same term.

saccharine (sak′ərin) *adj.* sugary, very sweet. 1674, of or like sugar, in Blount's *Glossographia;* formed in English from Medieval Latin *saccharum* sugar, from Latin *saccharon,* from Greek *sákcharon,* from Pali *sakkharā,* from Sanskrit *śárkarā* gravel, grit, SUGAR + English *-ine*[1]. The figurative sense of unpleasantly friendly, overly sweet, sugary, is first recorded in Emerson's *Essays* (1841-44).

sacerdotal (sas′ərdō′təl) *adj.* priestly. About 1400; borrowed from Old French *sacerdotal,* learned borrowing from Latin, and borrowed directly from Latin *sacerdōtālis* of or pertaining to a priest, from *sacerdōs* (genitive *sacerdōtis*) priest; literally, one who offers sacrifices; from **sacro-* holy, SACRED (the stem of *sacra* sacred rites; see SACRIFICE) + the stem *dō-* (see DO[1]) to perform, put, related to *-dere* to put, set, + the agent stem *t-;* for suffix see -AL[1].

sachem (sā′chəm) *n.* chief of an American Indian tribe. 1622, American English; borrowed from Algonquian (Narragansett) *sâchimau* chief, ruler. Narragansett *sâchimau* is cognate with Abnaki *sāngman* SAGAMORE. The transferred sense of political leader, chief, ruler, is first recorded in 1684 in American English. In 1786 the title of *sachem* was applied to any of the twelve high officials of the Tammany Society of New York (originally associated with the early Democratic-Republican party, later with the Democratic party); the *Grand Sachem* was the chief officer of the Tammany Society or one of its associated societies.

sachet (sashā′) *n.* small bag containing perfumed powder. 1838, borrowing of French *sachet,* diminutive of *sac* SAC. *Sachet* is recorded in Middle English in the sense of a small bag or wallet (1483), and is related to an earlier word *sacket* in the same sense (about 1450).

sack[1] *n.* large bag. Probably before 1200 *sac;* later in the spelling *sack* (1275-76); reinforced by Old French *sac,* Old Icelandic *sekkr,* and Latin *saccus,* but initially developed from Old English (about 1000, in West Saxon) *sacc* large cloth bag generally used for storage of produce, but also found in Mercian *sec,* and Old Kentish *sæc,* and in *sæce* sackcloth. The Old English *sacc* is an early borrowing of Latin *saccus,* from Greek *sákkos,* from Semitic (compare Hebrew *saq* sack), and is parallel to similar early borrowings from Latin *saccus,* found in Middle Dutch and Middle Low German *sak* sack, Old High German *sac,* Old Icelandic *sekkr,* and Gothic *sakkus* sackcloth. —**v.** put into a sack or sacks. 1303 *sekken,* in Mannyng's *Handlyng Synne;* later *sakken* (about 1390); from the noun in Middle English. The spellings of the noun and verb with *e* instead of *a* were probably directly influenced by Old Icelandic *sekkr* sack. **—sackcloth** *n.* (1297)

sack[2] *n.* act of plundering (a captured city). 1549, borrowed from Middle French *sac* (found in the phrase *mettre à sac* put into a bag, also Old French *a sac* a command authorizing the sack of a city or town), from, or at least parallel to, Italian *sacco* (found in *a sacco* to the plunder), from Latin *saccus* bag, SACK[1]; perhaps referring to the filling of sacks with plunder, as found in the verb of Vulgar Latin **saccāre* take by force, of uncertain origin. —**v.** plunder (a captured city). Before 1547, probably from the noun, although recorded somewhat earlier. *Sack* in the sense of *plunder,* v., is parallel in English to *bag* and *pocket.*

sack[3] *n.* sherry. 1531-32, alteration of French *vin sec* dry wine, from Latin *siccus* dry. The Latin word is semantically distant from cognates in Greek *ikmás* moisture, Old Slavic *sicati* urinate, and Sanskrit *sécate, siñcáti* (he) pours, from Indo-European **seikw-/sikw-* pour, drip (Pok.893).

sacrament *n.* religious act or ceremony. Probably before 1200 *sacrement,* in *Ancrene Riwle;* later *sacrament* (probably about 1300); borrowed from Old French *sacrement, sacrament,* and directly from Latin *sacrāmentum* a consecrating (usually an oath or surety), from *sacrāre* to consecrate, from *sacer* (genitive *sacrī*) holy, SACRED; for suffix see -MENT. **—sacramental** *adj.* 1382, borrowed from Middle French *sacramental,* and directly from Late Latin *sacrāmentālis,* from Latin *sacrāmentum* a consecrating; for suffix see -AL[1].

sacred *adj.* About 1380 *sacrid,* from past participle of earlier *sacren* to make holy, consecrate, sanctify (probably before 1200, in *Ancrene Riwle*); borrowed from Old French *sacrer,* or directly from Latin *sacrāre* to make sacred, consecrate, from *sacer* (genitive *sacrī*) sacred, related to *sancire* make sacred, confirm, ratify, ordain. Latin *sancīre* is cognate with Hittite *saklāis* rite, custom, law, from Indo-European **sak-* (Pok.878). **—sacred cow** person or thing held to be completely above criticism or opposition. 1910, American English (originally, among journalists) a person or company that may not be criticized in print; extended in the 1930's to any person or thing, as in Margaret Mitchell's *Gone With The Wind* (1936). The allusion is to earlier use of *sacred cow* meaning one of the animals regarded as sacred among the Hindus and an object of worship (1891).

sacrifice *n.* About 1275 *sacrefise;* later *sacrifice* (1340); borrowed from Old French *sacrifise, sacrefise,* and directly from Latin *sacrificium,* from *sacrificus* performing priestly functions or sacrifices (*sacra* sacred rites, from neuter plural of *sacer* SACRED + the root of *facere* to perform, DO[1]). The transferred sense of the act of giving up one thing for another is first found in Shakespeare's *Romeo and Juliet* (1592). —**v.** About 1300 *sacrifisen,* formed from Middle English *sacrefise, sacrifise,* n. The transferred sense of give up one thing for another is recorded in Kersey's edition of Phillips' *Dictionary*

(1706). —**sacrificial** *adj.* 1607, in Shakespeare's *Timon of Athens;* formed from Latin *sacrificium* sacrifice + English *-al*[1].

sacrilege (sak′rəlij) *n.* disrespectful treatment of anything sacred. About 1303 *sacrylage,* in Mannyng's *Handlyng Synne;* later *sacrilege* (before 1325, in *Cursor Mundi*); borrowed from Old French *sacrilege,* learned borrowing from Latin *sacrilegium* temple robbery, from *sacrilegus* robber of temples or altars (*sacrum* sacred object, from neuter singular of *sacer* SACRED + *legere* take, pick up; see LEGEND). —**sacrilegious** *adj.* committing or involving sacrilege. About 1449 *sacrilegiose;* later *sacrilegious* (1582); formed from Middle English *sacrilege* + *-iose* -ious.

sacristan (sak′ristən) *n.* person in charge of the sacred objects in a church, sexton. About 1375; earlier as a surname *Sacristain* (1199); borrowed from Medieval Latin *sacristanus,* from *sacrista* a sacristan, from Latin *sacer* (genitive *sacrī*) SACRED; for suffix see -AN. Middle English also had the form *segerstane* (1367); borrowed from Old French *segrestein, secrestein,* from Medieval Latin *sacristanus;* see the doublet in English SEXTON. A later form *sacrist* (1577-87) is recorded into the late 1800's, but is now largely of antiquated ecclesiastical vocabulary, or used in reference to a ceremonial officer of the University of Aberdeen.

sacristy (sak′ristē) *n.* place where the sacred objects of a church are kept. About 1450 *sacristie;* borrowed from Anglo-French *sacrestie, sacristie,* learned borrowing from Medieval Latin *sacristia;* later *sacristy* (1656, in Blount's *Glossographia*); probably reborrowed directly from Medieval Latin *sacristia,* from *sacrista* SACRISTAN; for suffix see -Y[3].

sacrosanct (sak′rōsangkt) *adj.* set apart as sacred, consecrated. Before 1500 *sacroseint* (reinforced by Middle English *seint* holy, sacred); borrowed from Latin *sacrōsānctus;* later *sacrosanct* (1601, in Holland's translation of Pliny's *Natural History*); reborrowed from Latin *sacrōsānctus* protected by religious sanction (*sacrō,* ablative of *sacrum* religious sanction, from neuter singular of *sacer* sacred + *sānctus,* past participle of *sancīre* make sacred; see SACRED).

sacrum (sā′krəm) *n.* bone at the lower end of the spine. 1753, in *Chambers Cyclopaedia;* borrowing of Late Latin *os sacrum* sacred bone, from Latin *os* bone, and *sacrum,* neuter of *sacer* SACRED; probably so called because the bone was thought to be offered in sacrifices. The Late Latin phrase is a translation of Greek *hieròn ostéon.* In Middle English texts the bone was referred to as *sacrum os* or *os sacrum* (probably before 1425), also a borrowing of Late Latin *os sacrum.* For etymology of Latin *os* bone, see OSSEOUS.

sad *adj.* Probably before 1200 *sad* sated, satisfied, weary or tired of, in Layamon's *Chronicle of Britain;* later, sorrowful, unhappy (before 1300); developed from Old English (before 1000) *sæd* sated. Old English *sæd* is cognate with Old Saxon *sad* sated, Middle Dutch *sat* (modern Dutch *zat*), Old High German *sat* (modern German *satt*), Old Icelandic *sadhr, saddr,* and Gothic *sads,* from Proto-Germanic **sađás.* Cognates outside Germanic include Latin *satis* enough, *satur* sated, Old Irish *sāith* satiety, Greek *hádēn* to satiety, enough, Lithuanian *sōtùs* sated, Armenian *atok'* full, and Sanskrit *asinvá-s* insatiable, from Indo-European **sā-/sə-* (Pok.876). Development of the meaning sorrowful, unhappy is unclear as the seemingly intervening senses of indifferent, resolute, serious, appear in the record of Middle English at least 75 to 100 years after the sense of unhappy. —**sadden** *v.* to make sad or sorrowful. 1628, formed from English *sad* + *-en*[1]; note, however, the verb use of Middle English *saden* to become sated, grow weary of (about 1390), and to become resolute, be serious (about 1378), developed from Old English *sadian,* and also from the adjective in Middle English; it is difficult to determine how indebted modern English *sad* sorrowful is to the Middle English verb, as there is a gap in the record of 150 years between the Middle English and modern English forms.

saddle *n.* Probably before 1200 *sadele,* in Layamon's *Chronicle of Britain;* later *sadle* (probably before 1300); developed from Old English *sadol* seat for a rider (about 725, in *Beowulf*). Old English *sadol* is cognate with Middle Dutch *sadel* saddle, Old High German *satul,* and Old Icelandic *sǫdhull,* from Proto-Germanic **sađulaz,* perhaps adopted, as suggested in the OED, from some other Indo-European language possessing a formation **sodulos,* derived from Indo-European **sed-* SIT. —*v.* put a saddle on. Probably before 1200 *sadelien,* in Layamon's *Chronicle of Britain;* later *sadelen* (probably about 1225), *sadlen* (probably about 1300); developed from Old English *sadolian* (about 1000), from *sadol,* n., saddle. —**saddle bag** (1773) —**saddle horse** (1662) —**saddle shoe** (1941)

sadism *n.* love of cruelty. 1888, borrowed from French *sadisme,* from the name of Count Donatien A.F. de *Sade* + *-isme* -ism. The "Marquis" de Sade (1740-1814) was notorious for cruel sexual practices and for his novels describing them. —**sadist** *n.* 1897, formed from English *sadism* + *-ist.* —**sadistic** *adj.* 1892, in C.D. Chaddock's translation of Krafft-Ebing's *Psychopathia Sexualis;* probably formed from English *sadist* + *-ic,* after German *sadistisch.*

sado- a combining form meaning sadistic, involving sadism, as in *sadomasochism* (1935, in L. Brink's translation of Wilhelm Stekel's *Sadismus und Masochismus*). Formed in English from *sadist* or *sadism* + connective *-o-,* on the pattern of *psycho-,* etc.

sad sack *Informal.* bewildered, inept soldier. 1943, American English (originally army slang); from the title and chief character of a comic strip drawn by the American cartoonist George Baker for Armed Services publications during World War II.

safari (səfä′rē) *n.* journey or hunting expedition. 1890 (also in earlier travel account, 1860); borrowed from Swahili *safari* journey, expedition, from Arabic *safar* journey.

safe *adj.* About 1280 *sauf* not damned, redeemed; later, uninjured, free from danger, secure (about 1300), healed, healthy (before 1325); and with the spellings *saf* (about 1330), *safe* (about 1343); borrowed from Old French *sauf, salf,* from Latin *salvus* uninjured, healthy, safe, related to *salūs* good health, safety, *salūber* healthful, and *solidus* solid. The Latin words are cognate with Welsh *holl* whole, Albanian *gjalë* strong, fat, vigorous, Greek *hólos* whole (earlier **hólwos*), Armenian *olj* healthy, whole, Sanskrit *sárva-s* unharmed, whole, all, and Tocharian A *salu* complete, whole, Tocharian B *solme* entire, from Indo-European **sol-/sel-* well-preserved, whole (Pok.979). —*n.* steel or iron box for valuables. 1440, *save* a chest or cupboard for keeping meats, etc., in *Promptorium Parvulorum;* noun use of *save,* v., but also found as a noun in the phrase *in saaf* in a safe place (about 1430, borrowed from Middle French *en sauf* in safety). The spelling *safe* is first recorded in 1688, influenced by the adjective. The sense of a burglarproof box for safekeeping of valuables is first found in 1838. **—safe-conduct** *n.* privilege of passing safely through a region (about 1300). **—safe-deposit box** (1882) **—safeguard** *n.* About 1385 *save-garde* promise of safety, in Chaucer's *Troilus and Criseyde;* later, protection, defense (1421). *—v.* protect. About 1445 (implied in *saaf gardyng*); from the noun in Middle English. **—safekeeping** *n.* (about 1410, in Lovelich's *Merlin*) **—safety** *n.* Before 1325 *sauvete* salvation, state of being spiritually safe, in *Cursor Mundi;* later *saufte* (before 1338), *safte* (about 1378); borrowed from Old French *sauveté, salveté,* from Medieval Latin *salvitatem,* from Latin *salvus* safe; for suffix see -TY². **—safety belt** (1858) **—safety glass** glass layered with plastic that resists shattering (1922). **—safety pin** (1857) **—safety valve** (1813). The figurative sense of a harmless way to get rid of frustration, anger, etc., is recorded in 1818.

safflower *n.* herb like a thistle. 1407 *saflour;* borrowed from Middle French *safleur,* from early Italian *saffiore, zaffrole,* from Arabic *aṣfar* a yellow plant, yellow. The spelling was influenced (in the 1600's) by *saffron* and *flower.*

saffron *n.* orange-yellow spice. Probably before 1200 *saffran;* later *saffron* (before 1398); borrowed from Old French *safran,* learned borrowing from Medieval Latin *safranum,* ultimately from Arabic *za'farān.* **—adj.** orange-yellow. Before 1398, in Trevisa's translation of Bartholomew's *De Proprietatibus Rerum;* from the noun.

sag *v.* sink under weight or pressure. 1392 *saggen;* possibly borrowed from a Scandinavian source (compare Norwegian *sakke* slow down, lag behind, and Swedish *sacka* settle, sink down; probably related to Old Icelandic *søkkva* to SINK) or from Middle Low German *sacken* to sink (as dregs do). **—n.** 1580, the drift of a ship from its course; from the verb. The sense of the act or fact of sagging is first recorded in 1861.

saga *n.* story of heroic deeds. 1709, Medieval Icelandic story of heroic deeds, in Pepys' *Diary;* borrowed from Old Icelandic *saga* saga, story; see SAW² proverb. The meaning of any story of heroic deeds is first recorded in 1857 in Longfellow's writings.

sagacious *adj.* wise, shrewd. 1607, acute in sensory perception; probably formed in English as an adjective to the earlier noun, on the model of Latin *sagāx* (genitive *sagācis*) of quick perception, acute, related to *sāgus* prophetic and *sāgīre* perceive quickly and keenly; see SEEK; for suffix see -OUS. The sense of wise, shrewd, is first recorded in 1650. **—sagacity** *n.* keen, sound judgment. Before 1500 *sagacite;* borrowed from Middle French *sagacité,* from Latin *sagācitātem* (nominative *sagācitās*) the quality of being acute or having quick perception, from *sagāx* (genitive *sagācis*) of quick perception, acute, sagacious; for suffix see -ITY.

sagamore (sag'əmôr) *n.* (among the Algonquian Indian tribes of New England) a chief or great man. 1613 *sagamo,* in *Purchas his Pilgrimage,* American English; borrowed from Algonquian (Abnaki) *sāngman* chief, ruler. Abnaki *sāngman* is cognate with Narragansett *sâchiman* SACHEM.

sage¹ *adj.* wise. About 1300; earlier as a surname (1179); borrowed from Old French *sage,* from Gallo-Romance **sabius,* alteration of Vulgar Latin **sapius,* from Latin *sapere* have a taste, have good taste or discernment, be wise. Latin *sapere* is cognate with Oscan *sipus* knowing, from earlier **sēpwōs,* an ancient perfect participle. Cognates in Germanic are found in Old High German *antseffen, intseffen* perceive, notice, Old Icelandic *sefi,* Old Saxon *sebo,* and Old English *sefa,* all meaning mind, sense, from Indo-European **sap-* taste, become aware (Pok.880). **—n.** wise man. Probably before 1350; from the adjective, perhaps influenced by Old French *sage* one who knows.

sage² *n.* plant whose leaves are used as seasoning and in medicine. Before 1325 *sage;* about 1325 *sauge;* borrowed from Old French *sauge,* from Latin *salvia,* from *salvus* healthy, SAFE; so called from the plant's supposed healing properties. Doublet of SALVIA. **—sagebrush** *n.* shrub of western North America that smells like sage (1852, American English).

sago (sā'gō) *n.* starchy food used in making puddings, etc. 1555, East Indian palm tree, in Eden's translation of Peter Martyr's *Decades of the New World or West India;* borrowed from Malay *sagu.* The meaning of starchy food obtained from the pith of the sago tree is first recorded about 1580.

sahib (sä'ib) *n.* sir, master (used especially by Hindus and Moslems in former British India when speaking to or of a European). 1673, in John Fryer's *A New Account of East India and Persia* (1698); borrowed from Hindi *ṣāhib* master, lord, from Arabic, (originally) friend.

sail *n.* Probably before 1200 *seil,* in Layamon's *Chronicle of Britain;* later *sayle* (1265), *sail* (probably before 1300); developed from Old English *segl* (before 899, in Alfred's translation of Boethius' *De Consolatione Philosophiae*). Old English *segl* is cognate with Old Frisian *seil* sail, Old Saxon *segel,* Middle Dutch *seil* (modern Dutch *zeil*), Old High German *segal* (modern German *Segel*), and Old Icelandic *segl* sail, probably originally a piece of cloth cut, from Proto-Germanic **seʒlan;* with distant semantic relationship to SAW¹ cutting tool. **—v.** Probably before 1200 *seilen* travel on a ship with sails, in Layamon's *Chronicle of Britain;* later *saylen* (about 1250); developed from Old English *segli-an, seglan* (before 899, in Alfred's translation of Orosius' *Historiarum Adversus Paganos*). The Old English forms are cognate with Middle High German *segelen, sigelen* (modern German *segeln*), and Old Icelandic *sigla,* all derived from the Germanic source of Old English *segl,* n. **—sailboat** *n.* (1798) **—sailcloth** *n.* (probably before 1200, in Layamon's *Chronicle of Britain*) **—sailfish** *n.* saltwater fish with a very large dorsal fin, related to the swordfish (1879, American English). The term was earlier applied to the basking shark (1591). **—sailor** *n.* Probably before 1400 *sailer* one who sails; later, professional seaman or mariner (before 1511); formed from *sailen* sail, v. + *-er*¹. The suffix was later changed to *-or*² (before 1642) perhaps on the model of *tailor, gaolor* (*jailor*), *bailor,* and more distantly *advisor,* etc.

saint *n.* About 1125 *seinte;* later *sainte* (before 1225), borrowed from Old French *saint, seinte,* from Latin; also Middle English *sont* (before 1200, in *Ancrene Riwle*) and *sannt* (about 1200, in *The Ormulum*), developed from Old English *sanct,* borrowed from Latin, and borrowed into Middle English directly from Latin *sānctus* holy, consecrated (in Late Latin found as a noun), past participle of *sancīre* make sacred, ordain; see SACRED. In Middle English first use of *saint* as a title in a name is found in *Seinte Marian Magdalene,* but earlier use is known by appearance of the abbreviated *S or St.,* at least by 1100, and in Old English by 963. —**v.** Probably before 1200 *sonten* to be or become a saint, in *Ancrene Riwle;* later *saynten* (before 1450); from the noun, probably influenced by Old French *saintir* through Anglo-French *santir.* The meaning of make a saint of is first recorded in 1375. —**sainthood** *n.* 1550, formed from English *saint,* n. + *-hood.* —**saintly** *adj.* of a saint, very holy. 1660, formed from English *saint,* n. + *-ly*[2], but found earlier as an adverb about 1460.

sake[1] *n.* purpose, cause, account. Probably about 1175 *sake* blame, guilt; later, strife, dispute, account, sake (probably before 1200); developed from Old English *sacu* a cause at law, crime, dispute (about 725, in *Beowulf*); cognate with Old Frisian *seke, sake* affair, thing, dispute, Old Saxon *saka* lawsuit, enmity, guilt, thing, Middle Dutch *sake* (modern Dutch *zaak*) lawsuit, cause, thing, Old High German *sahha* (modern German *Sache*) thing, matter, cause, Old Icelandic *sǫk* lawsuit, guilt, crime, cause, sake, (from Proto-Germanic **sakō*), Gothic *sakjō* quarrel, and *sakan* to quarrel; see SEEK. The phrases *for the sake of* (probably before 1200), and *for (someone's* or *something's) sake* (about 1325) were perhaps adopted from Old Icelandic.

sake[2] (sä'kē) *n.* Japanese fermented alcoholic beverage. 1687 *saque,* in a translation of Thevenot's *Travels into the Levant;* borrowed from Japanese *sake.* The spelling *sake* is first recorded in 1878.

sal *n.* salt (used especially in chemical and pharmaceutical terms). About 1395, in Chaucer's *Canterbury Tales;* earlier in combinations such as *salkemini* common salt, and in the place name *Salford* (about 1100); borrowed from Old French *sal* (variant of *sel*), and directly from Latin *sāl* SALT.

salaam (səläm') *n.* greeting in Moslem countries. 1613, in *Purchas his Pilgrimage,* borrowed from Arabic *salām* a greeting, literally, peace. Related to SHALOM. —**v.** greet with a salaam. 1693, from the noun.

salacious (səlā'shəs) *adj.* lustful, lewd. 1661, borrowed from Latin *salāx* (genitive *salācis*) lustful, probably originally meaning fond of leaping, as in animals' sexual advances, from *salīre* to leap; see SALLY; for suffix see -OUS.

salad *n.* Before 1399 *salat* raw vegetable dish, salad; later *salade* (1472); borrowed from Old French *salade,* and from Medieval Latin **salata;* both from Vulgar Latin **salāta* salted, feminine past participle of **salāre* to salt, from Latin *sāl* (genitive *salis*) SALT. The phrase *salad days,* meaning days of youthful inexperience in allusion to the figurative sense of *green,* is first recorded in Shakespeare's *Antony and Cleopatra* (1606).

salamander *n.* lizardlike amphibian. 1340 *salamandre* legendary lizardlike animal supposed to be able to endure fire, in *Ayenbite of Inwyt;* borrowed from Old French *salamandre,* and directly from Latin *salamandra,* from Greek *salamándra,* of unknown origin. The sense of a lizardlike amphibian is first recorded in Cotgrave's *Dictionary* (1611).

salami *n.* kind of sausage. 1852, borrowed from Italian *salami,* plural of *salame* spiced pork sausage, from Vulgar Latin **salāmen,* from **salāre* to salt, from Latin *sāl* (genitive *salis*) SALT.

salary *n.* Probably about 1280 *salerie* periodic payment for regular service; later *salarye* (about 1378); borrowed through Anglo-French *salarie,* Old French *salaire, salare, sallere,* learned borrowing from Latin, and borrowed in Middle English directly from Latin *salārium* soldier's allowance for the purchase of salt, hence, salary or stipend, from neuter of *salārius* pertaining to salt, from *sāl* (genitive *salis*) SALT. —**v.** About 1477 *salarien* to pay, reward; from the noun. The meaning of pay a salary to is recorded from 1837.

sale *n.* Probably before 1300 *sale;* developed from Late Old English (about 1050) *sala;* borrowed from a Scandinavian source (compare Old Icelandic *sala, sal* sale); cognate with Old High German *sala* sale, delivery of goods, and Old English *salu* sale (from Proto-Germanic **salō*), related to Old English *sellan* to SELL. —**salable** or **saleable** *adj.* that can be sold. 1530 *saleable,* in Palsgrave's *Lesclarcissement;* later *salable* (1579); formed from English *sale* + *-able.* —**salesman** *n.* (1523) —**sales tax** (1921)

salient *adj.* easily seen or noticed, prominent. 1646, leaping, jumping, replacing earlier *salience,* adj. (before 1393); borrowed from Latin *salientem* (nominative *saliēns*), present participle of *salīre* to leap; see SALLY. The sense of pointing outward (said of an angle) is first recorded in 1687. The sense of jutting out, prominent, is found in 1789, and the figurative sense of prominent, striking, easily seen or noticed, is first recorded in 1840.

The phrase *salient point* was originally a medical term referring to the heart of an embryo, which seems to leap as if alive, the term being a translation of New Latin *punctum saliens,* going back to Aristotle's writings. A transferred sense of beginning, starting point, is first recorded in 1672.

—**n.** 1828, a salient angle or part; from the adjective. The sense of a narrow projection of land, especially one held as a line of defense, is first recorded in 1864. —**salience** *n.* 1836, formed as a noun to *salient* + *-ence.*

saline (sā'līn *or* sā'lēn) *adj.* like salt, salty. Before 1500 *salyne* made of salt; probably borrowed from Latin **salīnus* (found only in the neuter form *salīnum* salt cellar, and in the feminine plural form *salīnae* salt pits), from *sāl* (genitive *salis*) SALT; for suffix see -INE[1]. —**salinity** *n.* saline quality or condition. 1658, formed from English *saline* + *-ity.*

saliva *n.* Probably before 1425 *salive,* in Chauliac's *Grande Chirurgie;* borrowing of Middle French *salive,* from Latin *salīva;* later *saliva* (1676, in Richard Wiseman's *Several Chirurgical Treatises*); reborrowed from Latin *salīva* spittle, of uncertain origin. —**salivary** *adj.* of or producing saliva. 1709, formed in English from *saliva* + *-ary* on the model of Latin *salīvārius* resembling saliva, slimy, from *salīva* saliva. —**salivate** *v.* produce saliva. 1657, back formation from *salivation,* possibly formed after Latin *salīvātus,* past participle of *salīvāre,* from *salīva* saliva; for suffix see -ATE[1]. —**salivation** *n.* 1598, borrowing of Middle French *salivation,* and borrowed directly from Late Latin *salīvātiōnem* (nominative *salīvātiō),* from Latin *salīvāre* to produce saliva; for suffix see -ATION.

sallow *adj.* having a sickly color or complexion. Probably before 1400 *salowe,* in Chaucer's translation of *Roman de la Rose;* developed from Old English *salo, salu* dusky, dark, sallow (before 1000), related to *sōl* dark, dirty. The Old English forms are cognate with Middle Dutch *salu* dirty, discolored, Old High German *salo* dirty gray, murky, and Old Icelandic *sǫlr* dirty, from Proto Germanic **salwa-* . Cognates outside Germanic include Old Irish *sal* dirt, *salach* dirty, Welsh *halog* polluted, defiled, and probably Russian *solovói* cream-colored, from Indo-European **sal-/sāl-* dirty gray (Pok.879). —**v.** make yellowish. 1831, in Peacock's *Crotchet Castle;* from the adjective.

sally *n.* sudden attack, sortie. 1542, place from which a sudden attack is launched; later, an attack (1560); borrowed from Middle French *saillie* a rushing forth, outrush, noun use of feminine past participle of *saillir* to leap, from Latin *salīre* to leap. Latin *salīre* is cognate with Lithuanian *sálti* to flow, and Greek *hállesthai* to leap, from Indo-European **sal-* to jump (not **sel-*, as cited in Pok.899). —**v.** make a sally. 1560, from the noun.

salmagundi (sal'məgun'dē) *n.* dish of chopped meat, anchovies, eggs, etc. 1674, in Blount's *Glossographia;* borrowed from French *salmigondis* of the same meaning; originally, seasoned salt meats (as in French *salmis* salted meats), from Middle French *salmigondin* (used by Rabelais), of uncertain origin (but probably related to *salomene* a hodge-podge of meats or fish cooked in wine, before 1325; borrowed from Old French *salemine*).

salmon (sam'ən) *n.* large fish. 1228 *salmon;* earlier as a surname *Salmun* (1205); borrowed from Old French *salmun, saumon, salmon,* from Latin *salmōnem* (nominative *salmō*) a salmon, of uncertain origin, but possibly in the literal sense of leaper, and if so, from *salīre* to leap. —**adj.** of the color of salmon, yellowish-pink. 1786, from the noun.

salmonella (sal'mənel'ə) *n.* kind of bacterium that causes food poisoning. 1913, New Latin *Salmonella* the genus name, formed from the name of Daniel Elmer *Salmon,* 1850-1914, an American veterinarian who isolated one type of these bacteria in 1885.

salon (səlon' *or French* sålôN') *n.* large, elegant reception room. 1699, in Martin Lister's *Journey to Paris;* borrowing of French *salon,* from Italian *salone* large hall, from *sala* hall, from a Germanic source; compare Old High German *sal* hall, house (from Proto-Germanic **salaz*), modern German *Saal* hall, Old Saxon *seli,* Middle Dutch *sāle,* modern Dutch *zaal,* Old English *sele* hall, (from Proto-Germanic **saliz*), Old Icelandic *salr* hall, house, and Gothic *salithwōs* inn, *saljan* stay at an inn. Cognates outside Germanic are found in Old Slavic *selo* estate, village, *selitva* dwelling, and Lithuanian *salà* village, from Indo-European **sel-/sol-* the one room that a house had (Pok.898). The transferred meaning of a gathering of distinguished or fashionable people in a salon is first recorded in English in 1888 (found in the form *saloon,* in 1838).

saloon *n.* 1728, a salon; Anglicized form of SALON; for ending see -OON. Between the early 1700's and the early 1800's *saloon* was used as a variant of *salon* and, by extension, developed the sense of any large apartment or hall, especially in a hotel or other public place, used for assemblies, entertainments, exhibitions, etc. The meaning of a place where alcoholic drinks are sold and drunk, a public bar, is first recorded in American English in 1841.

salsa (säl'sä) *n.* kind of popular music of Caribbean origin. 1975, borrowed from Spanish *salsa,* literally, sauce, from Vulgar Latin **salsa* condiment, see SAUCE.

salsify (sal'səfī) *n.* edible root with a flavor like an oyster. 1706, in Kersey's edition of Phillips' *Dictionary;* borrowed from French *salsifis,* from earlier Italian *erba salsifica,* of uncertain origin.

salt *n.* Probably about 1150 *salt* table salt; found in Old English *salt, sealt* (probably before 830, implied in *saltnisse* saltness); cognate with Old Frisian, Old Saxon, Old Icelandic, and Gothic *salt* salt, Middle Dutch *sout* (modern Dutch *zout*), and Old High German *salz* (modern German *Salz*), from Proto-Germanic **saltan,* Indo-European **sal-d-om.* Cognates outside Germanic include Latin *sāl* (genitive *salis*) salt, Old Irish *salann,* Welsh *halen,* Greek *háls* salt, sea, Latvian *sā̀ls* salt, Old Slavic *solĭ,* Armenian *ał,* Tocharian A *sāle,* Tocharian B *sālyiye* salt, and perhaps Sanskrit *sal-* in *salilá-m* sea, from Indo-European **sal-* (Pok.878).

The meaning of a chemical compound derived from an acid and a base is first recorded in English in 1790. —**adj.** Probably before 1200 *saltne,* in Layamon's *Chronicle of Britain;* probably about 1200 *salte;* earlier in the place name *Salteburnam* (1180-90); found in Old English (before 900) *salt, sealt;* from the noun in Old English.
—**v.** Probably before 1300 *salten* treat with salt, sprinkle salt on; found in Old English *saltan, sealtan,* also probably influenced by Old English **sieltan* (found in Northumbrian *selta*) and *seltan, syltan.* The Old English forms are cognate with Middle Low German *solten* to salt, Middle Dutch *souten* (modern Dutch *zouten*), Old High German *salzan* (modern German *salzen*), Old Icelandic *salta,* and Gothic *saltan;* all derived from the Germanic source of Old English *salt, sealt,* n.
—**saltbox** *n.* 1) 1611, box for keeping salt; earlier *saltark* (1348); 2) 1876, a style of building resembling a box for keeping salt. —**saltcellar** *n.* (1390) —**saltine** *n.* (1907) —**salt lick** deposit of salt that animals lick (1751, American English). —**saltpeter** (sôlt'pē'tər) *n.* potassium nitrate. Before 1400, alteration (by influence of *salt*) of Middle English *salpetre* (about 1330); borrowing of Old French *salpetre,* a learned borrowing from Medieval Latin; also borrowed directly from Medieval Latin *sal petrae* salt of rock (Latin *sāl* SALT + *petrae,* genitive of Latin *petra* rock; see PETRIFY); so called because it appears as a saltlike encrustation on rocks. —**salt pork** (1723) —**saltshaker** *n.* (1895) —**saltwater** *n.* (before 1225); *adj.* (before 1420 *water salt;* later *saltwater* 1528) —**salty** *adj.* 1440 *salti* containing salt, tasting of salt, in *Promptorium Parvulorum;* earlier, in the surname *Saltiland* (1286); formed from Middle English *salt,* n. + *-y*[1].

SALT (sôlt) *n.* 1968, American English, acronym formed from *S(trategic) A(rms) L(imitation) T(alks),* a round of talks between the Soviet Union and the United States to limit nuclear armaments, begun in Helsinki, Finland, on November 17, 1969.

salubrious (səlü'brēəs) *adj.* healthful. 1547, borrowed, perhaps by influence of Middle French *salubre,* from Latin *salūber* healthful; see SAFE; for suffix see -OUS.

salutary (sal'yəter'ē) *adj.* beneficial. 1490, in Caxton's translation of *The Book of Eneydos;* earlier as a noun with the meaning of remedy (1426); borrowed from Middle French *salutaire* beneficial, or directly from Latin *salūtāris* healthful, from *salūs* (genitive *salūtis*) good health; see SAFE; for suffix see -ARY.

salutatory *adj.* expressing greeting, welcoming. 1670, designating the welcoming address given at a college commencement, American English; borrowed from Latin *salūtātōrius* pertaining to visiting or greeting, from *salūtāt-*, past participle stem of *salūtāre* to greet,

SALUTE; for suffix see -ORY. The general sense of expressing welcome is first recorded in 1895. —**n.** 1779, welcoming address at a college commencement, American English; from the adjective. An earlier noun sense of a place for salutations is first recorded in 1641. —**salutatorian** *n.* student who delivers the salutatory. 1847, American English; formed from *salutatory,* adj. + *-an.*

salute *v.* Before 1382 *saluten* to greet, in the Wycliffe Bible; borrowed from Latin *salūtāre* to greet (wish health to), from *salūs* (genitive *salūtis*) greeting, good health; see SAFE. The meaning of greet with a gesture of respect is first recorded in Middle English about 1440. —**n.** Before 1400 *salut* act of saluting, borrowed from Old French *salut,* from Latin *salūtem* (nominative *salūs*) greeting. The military salute of a discharge of cannon or a dipping of a flag is first recorded in 1698, and that of a gesture of the hand in 1876, though the older form executed by a raising of the hat is recorded as early as 1779. —**salutation** *n.* greeting, saluting. About 1384 *salutacioun,* in the Wycliffe Bible; borrowed from Old French *salutacion,* or directly from Latin *salūtātiōnem* (nominative *salūtātiō*), from *salūtāre* to greet; for suffix see -ATION.

salvage *n.* 1645, payment for saving a ship from wreck or capture; borrowing of French *salvage,* from Old French *salver, sauver* to SAVE[1]; for suffix see -AGE. The meaning of the act of saving a ship is first recorded in 1713, and that of property saved in 1755. The sense of the saving of waste material for recycling (in wartime) is first recorded in 1918. —**v.** save from fire, shipwreck, etc. 1889, from the noun.

salvation *n.* a saving or a being saved. Probably before 1200 *salvatiun* deliverance from sin and damnation, in *Ancrene Riwle;* borrowed from Old French *salvaciun, salvation,* and directly from Late Latin *salvātiōnem* (nominative *salvātiō*), from *salvāre* to SAVE; for suffix see -ATION.

salve[1] (sav) *n.* soft, greasy healing ointment. Probably before 1200 *salve* (figuratively) spiritual remedy, in *Ancrene Riwle;* also, literally, healing ointment (probably about 1200, in *The Ormulum*); developed from Old English (about 700) *sealf* salve; cognate with Old Saxon *salƀa* salve, Middle Low German *salve,* Middle Dutch *salve* (modern Dutch *zalf*), and Old High German *salba* (modern German *Salbe*), from Proto-Germanic **salƀṓ.* Cognates outside Germanic include Albanian *gjalp* butter, Greek *élpos* oil, fat, Cyprian Greek *élphos* butter, *ólpē* oil flask, Sanskrit *sarpís* melted butter, and Tocharian A *ṣälyp,* Tocharian B *ṣalype* fat, butter, oil, from Indo-European **selp-/solp-* (Pok.901). —**v.** put salve on. Probably before 1200 *salven* (figuratively) to heal or treat spiritually; also, literally, to apply ointment (probably about 1200); developed from Old English (about 700) *sealfian* anoint (a wound) with salve; cognate with Old Saxon *salƀōn* to salve, anoint, Middle Low German *salven,* Middle Dutch *salven* (modern Dutch *zalven*), Old High German *salbōn* (modern German *salben*), and Gothic *salƀōn,* from Proto-Germanic **salƀōjanan;* all derived from Proto-Germanic **salƀṓ,* the source of Old English *sealf* salve, n. The figurative sense of soothe (one's conscience, wounded pride, etc.) is first recorded in 1825, in Lamb's writings.

salve[2] (salv) *v.* to salvage. 1706, in Kersey's edition of Phillips' *Dictionary;* back formation from SALVAGE or from SALVABLE. —**salvable** *adj.* that can be saved. 1667, (in theology) fit for salvation; later, that can be salvaged (1797); implied earlier in *salvability* (1654), but probably formed in English as if from Latin **salvābilis* of or pertaining to saving or salvation, or directly from Latin *salvāre* to save + English *-able.*

salver *n.* tray. 1661, in Blount's *Glossographia,* formed in English (on the model of *platter* or similar words) from French *salve* tray used for presenting certain objects to the king + English *-er*[1]. The French word was borrowed from Spanish *salva* a foretasting, as to a prince, a testing of food or drink; hence, a tray on which the cup or dish was placed to show that its contents were free of poison, from *salvar* to save, render safe, from Late Latin *salvāre* to SAVE[1].

salvo[1] (sal′vō) *n.* discharge of guns as a salute. 1719, alteration of earlier *salva* simultaneous discharge of firearms (1591); borrowed from Italian *salva,* from French *salve,* from Latin *salvē* (a Roman greeting) hail!, be in good health!, imperative of *salvēre* to be in good health, from *salvus* healthy, SAFE. —**v.** fire of a salvo. 1839, in Marryat's *The Phantom Ship;* from the noun.

salvo[2] *n.* reservation, proviso. 1642, borrowed from Medieval Latin *salvo* chiefly in the legal phrase *salvo jure* without prejudice to the right of (some person); literally, with a right being saved or reserved; Latin *salvō,* ablative singular of *salvus* intact, SAFE; and *jūre,* ablative singular of *jūs* right, law (see JUST). The extended sense of a quibbling evasion, bad excuse, is first recorded in Sir Thomas Herbert's *Travels* (1665), and a further extension of meaning, that of an expedient for saving a person's reputation, or for soothing offended pride or conscience, is found in 1754, in Richardson's writings.

samara (sam′ərə *or* səmăr′ə) *n.* dry fruit that has a winglike extension. 1577, originally New Latin *samara,* from Latin, variant of *samera* elm seed, of uncertain origin.

samarium (səmăr′ēəm) *n.* metallic chemical element. 1879; formed in English from *samarskite* a mineral (1849) + New Latin *-ium,* chemical suffix; so called because this element was first found in the mineral samarskite. The term was coined by its discoverer, the French chemist Lecoq de Boisbaudran. *Samarskite* was borrowed from German *Samarskit,* formed in allusion to Colonel *Samarski,* a Russian official in the 1800's + German *-it* -ite[1].

samba (sam′bə) *n.* Brazilian ballroom dance. 1885 *Zemba;* later *Samba* (1911); borrowed from Portuguese *samba, zamba.* According to Corominas, the Portuguese forms are shortened from *zambacueca* a type of dance, probably an alteration (influenced by *zamacueco* stupid), of *zambapalo* a grotesque dance, alteration of *zampapalo* stupid man, from *zamparse* to bump, crash.

same *adj.* Probably about 1200, in *The Ormulum;* probably abstracted from the adverbial use in Old English *swā same* the same as, likewise, in part by influence of Scandinavian use (compare Old Icelandic *samr, same, sama* same); cognate with Old Saxon *so sama* the same, Old High German and Gothic *sama* same, from Proto-Germanic **samōn.* Cognates outside Germanic include Old Irish *samail* likeness, Latin *similis* like, *simul* together, at the same time, Greek *homós* same, *heîs hén* one, *háma* together, Lithuanian *sam-, są-* with, Old Slavic *sǫ-* with, *samŭ* one, and Sanskrit *samá-s* level, equal, same, *-samá-m* together, from Indo-European **sem-/som-/sm̥-* (Pok.902). —**pron.** the same person or thing. About 1303, in Mannyng's *Handlyng Synne;* from the adjective.

samisen (sam′əsen) *n.* Japanese musical instrument with three strings, resembling a guitar. 1616 *shamshin,* borrowed from Japanese, from Chinese *san-hsien* (*san* three + *hsien* string). The spelling *samishen* is first recorded in 1840, and that of *samisen* in 1880.

samite (sam′īt *or* sā′mīt) *n.* heavy, rich silk fabric. Probably before 1300 *samyt,* in *Kyng Alisaunder;* borrowed from Old French *samit,* from Medieval Greek **hexámiton,* from neuter of Greek *hexámitos* six-threaded *(héx* SIX + *mítos* warp thread, of uncertain origin).

samizdat (säm′izdät′) *n.* practice of secretly reproducing and distributing banned literature. 1967, borrowing of Russian *samizdat,* literally, self-publishing; formed from *sam* self + *izdat(el′stvo)* publishing, probably as a word play on *Gosizdat* the State publishing house.

samovar (sam′əvär) *n.* metal urn of Russian origin, used for heating water, especially to make tea. 1830, borrowing of Russian *samovar,* literally, self-boiler; formed from *sam* self + *varit′* to boil, from Old Slavic *variti* to cook.

sampan (sam′pan) *n.* small boat used especially in China, and corresponding to the skiff of Europe and America. 1620, in Richard Cocks' *Diary in Japan;* borrowed from Chinese *san pan,* literally, three boards or planks (*san* three + *pan* board).

sample *n.* Probably about 1300 *saumpel* parable; also, about 1303 *sample* illustration, example; in part borrowed through Anglo-French *saumple, sample,* variants of Old French *essemple,* variant of *example* from Latin *exemplum* a sample; see EXAMPLE; and in part developed as a shortened form of earlier Middle English *ensample* a model, example (about 1275); also found in Anglo-French *ensample.* **—adj.** serving as a sample. 1820, from the noun. **—v.** take a sample of. 1592, to parallel, put in comparison with; from the noun. The meaning of take a sample of is first recorded in 1767. **—sampler** *n.* Before 1325 *samplere* pattern, model, example, in *Cursor Mundi;* earlier as a surname *Sampler* (1250); borrowed from Anglo-French *essampleire, essampler,* Old French *essamplaire,* from Latin *exemplārium* copy, from *exemplum* example. The meaning of a piece of cloth embroidered to show skill in needlework is first recorded in 1523.

samurai (sam′ùrī) *n.* member of a military class in feudal Japan. 1727, borrowing of Japanese *samurai* warrior, knight.

sanatorium (san′ətôr′ēəm) *n.* place for treatment of the sick and convalescent. 1839, New Latin *sanatorium,* from neuter of Late Latin *sānātōrius* health-giving, from Latin *sānāt-,* past participle stem of *sānāre* to heal, from *sānus* healthy, sane. Compare SANITARIUM.

sanctify *v.* make holy. Before 1400 *sanctifien,* in Lanfranc's *Science of Surgery,* alteration (influenced by the Latin form) of earlier *seintefien* consecrate, hallow (before 1393, in Gower's *Confessio Amantis*); borrowed from Old French *saintifier,* and directly from Late Latin *sānctificāre,* from *sānctificus* holy (*sānctus* holy; see SAINT + the root of *facere* make, perform, DO[1]); for suffix see -FY.

sanctimony (sangk′təmō′nē) *n.* a show of holiness. 1540-41, borrowed from Middle French *sanctimonie,* learned borrowing from Latin, and borrowed directly from Latin *sānctimōnia* holiness, virtuousness, from *sānctus* holy; see SAINT; for suffix see -Y[3]. **—sanctimonious** *adj.* making a show of holiness. 1603, in Shakespeare's *Measure for Measure;* formed in English from Latin *sānctimōnia* holiness + English *-ous.*

sanction *n.* permission with authority. Probably before 1425 *sanccion* confirmation or enactment of a law, in a translation of Higden's *Polychronicon;* later *sanction* (probably before 1475); borrowed through Middle French *sanction,* or directly from Latin *sānctiōnem* (nominative *sānctiō*), the act of decreeing or ordaining; also, a decree or ordinance, from *sancīre* to decree, confirm, ratify, make sacred; see SACRED; for suffix see -TION.

The meaning of a penalty enacted to enforce obedience to a law is first recorded before 1633, and the specific sense of economic or military pressure used against a nation to achieve a change in policy or action is first found in 1845. The sense of authoritative permission is first recorded in 1720, in Pope's translation of the *Iliad,* and the figurative sense of encouragement given by an authoritative person or by custom, in 1738, in Swift's writings.

—v. 1778, make valid or binding, in Thomas Jefferson's *Autobiography;* later, authorize, allow (1797); from the noun.

sanctity *n.* holiness. About 1390 *saunctite, sauntite;* borrowed from Old French *saínctité, saintité,* from Latin *sānctitātem* (nominative *sānctitās*) holiness, sacredness, from *sānctus* holy; see SAINT; for suffix see -ITY.

sanctuary *n.* sacred place. Before 1325 *santuare,* in *Cursor Mundi;* later *sanctuary* (about 1340); borrowed from Old French *saínctuarie,* and directly from Late Latin *sānctuārium* a sacred place, shrine; also, a private room, from Latin *sānctus* holy; see SAINT; for suffix see -ARY. The extended meaning of a place of refuge or protection, especially a church or building in which a fugitive could take refuge, immune from arrest, is first recorded in English about 1380, in Chaucer's translation of Boethius' *De Consolatione Philosophiae.*

sanctum (sangk′təm) *n.* sacred place. 1577, borrowing of Latin *sānctum,* as in Late Latin *sānctum sānctōrum* holy of holies, from neuter of *sānctus* holy; see SAINT. The sense of a private room or office where a person is free from intrusion, is first recorded in 1819.

sand *n.* Old English (before 830) *sand;* cognate with Old Frisian *sond* sand, Old Saxon *sand,* Middle Dutch *sand, sant* (modern Dutch *zand*), Old High German *sant* (modern German *Sand*), and Old Icelandic *sandr* (Swedish and Danish *sand*), from Proto-Germanic **sanda-,* earlier **sámaða-.* A cognate outside Germanic is found in Greek *ámathos,* earlier **hámathos,* from Indo-European **samədho-* (Pok.146). **—v.** sprinkle with sand. About 1385 *sonden,* in Chaucer's *Troilus and Criseyde;* later *sanden;* from the noun. The sense of polish with sand is recorded in 1858, and that of use sandpaper on, in 1928, though it was probably known much earlier. **—sandbag** *n.* (1590, earlier in *sandpoke,* 1415-16); *v.* hit with, or as if with a sandbag (1882, implied in *sandbagger*). **—sandbank** *n.* (1458-60) **—sandbar** *n.* (1766, American English) **—sandblast** *n.* blast of air or steam containing sand, used to clean, grind, or decorate hard surfaces (1871); *v.* use a sandblast on (1888). **—sandbox** *n.* 1572, box for sprinkling sand on the wet ink of a manuscript. The sense of a box filled with sand for children to play in is first recorded in 1937, replacing earlier *sandpit* (1898, in George Bernard Shaw's *Candide*). **—sand dollar** (1884) **—sander** *n.* 1627, one who spreads sand; 1881, one who or that which uses sandpaper to make something smooth. **—sandlot** *n.* vacant lot (1878, American English). In attributive use referring to sports played in sandlots, the word is recorded in 1890 in American English. **—sandman** *n.* fabled man said to make children sleepy by sprinkling sand in their eyes (1869, in a translation of Hans Christian Andersen's fairy tales). **—sandpaper** *n.* (1825); *v.* use sandpaper on (1846). **—sandpiper** *n.* (1674) **—sandstone** *n.* (1434-35) **—sandstorm** *n.* (1774) **—sandy** *adj.* 1384 *sandy,* in the Wycliffe Bible; developed from Old English (about 1000) *sandig,* formed from *sand* + *-ig* -y[1].

sandal *n.* open shoe with straps. 1382 *sandalie,* in the Wycliffe Bible; later *sandal* (about 1425); borrowed from Old French *sandale,* and directly from Latin *sandalium,* from Greek *sandálion,* diminutive of *sándalon* sandal, of unknown origin.

sandalwood *n.* About 1511, earlier *sandal* dish colored with sandalwood (1381); borrowed from Old French *sandale,* and directly from Medieval Latin *sandalum,* found also in Late Greek *sántalon (=sándalon),* from Sanskrit *çandana-m* the sandalwood tree.

sandwich *n.* 1762, said to be in allusion to the fourth Earl of *Sandwich,* John Montagu, 1718-1792, who on occasion is traditionally supposed to have spent long hours at the gaming tables without other refreshment than some slices of cold meat between slices of toast.

Other use of *sandwich* appears in the name of the islands of Hawaii, originally called the *Sandwich* Islands, given by Captain James Cook after the same Earl of Sandwich, who was first lord of the British admiralty in 1778, when Captain Cook landed in Hawaii.
—v. put or squeeze in (between). 1861, from the noun. An earlier rare sense of eat a light meal is recorded once in 1815.

sane *adj.* having a healthy mind. 1721, in Bailey's *Dictionary;* possibly formed in English as an adjective to earlier *sanity,* n. by back formation from *sanity* on the model of Latin *sānus* healthy, sane; of uncertain origin. It is also probable that in some instances *sane* was borrowed from Latin *sānus.*

Earlier use with the sense of sound, healthy, in the legal phrase *of sane memory,* is recorded as early as 1628, and according to the OED the use of *sane* has been largely restricted in English to reference relating to the mind in contrast to *insane* which always refers to mental condition, as was apparently the case with its Latin source *īnsānus.*

Sanforized (san′fərīzd) *adj.* trademark for cotton or linen cloth preshrunk by a patented process. 1930, American English, formed from the name of its inventor *Sanfor(d)* L. Cluett + *-ized,* as in *sterilized, oxidized,* etc.

sangfroid (säNfrwä′) *n.* coolness of mind, calmness, composure. 1750, in Lord Chesterfield's *Letters;* borrowing of French *sang froid,* literally, cool blood (*sang* blood, from Latin *sanguen,* variant of *sanguis* + *froid* cold, cool, from Vulgar Latin **frigidus,* altered by influence of *rigidus* stiff from Latin *frīgidus* FRIGID).

sangria (sanggrē′ə) *n.* Spanish drink made of red wine mixed with fruit juices. 1736 *sangre;* later *sangaree* (1785), *sangria* (1954); of uncertain origin. The word is attested in English nearly a century before it is recorded in Spanish, and Corominas considers it improbable that the word is derived from Spanish *sangría* bleeding.

sanguinary (sang′gwəner′ē) *adj.* with much blood or bloodshed. 1625, in Bacon's *Essays;* possibly formed from English *sanguine* + *-ary,* perhaps by influence of French *sanguinaire,* and on the model of Latin *sanguinārius* pertaining to blood, from *sanguis* (genitive *sanguinis*) blood; for suffix see -ARY. It is also probable that in some instances the word was borrowed into English directly from Latin.

sanguine (sang′gwin) *adj.* cheerful and hopeful. 1378 *sangueyn* blood-red; earlier as a surname *Sanguin* (1194); also *sanguine* (before 1398); borrowed from Old French *sanguin* (feminine *sanguine*), learned borrowing from Latin, and borrowed directly from Latin *sanguineus* of blood, bloody, bloodthirsty, from *sanguis* (genitive *sanguinis*) blood, of uncertain origin.

The meaning of having a ruddy complexion is first recorded in Chaucer's *Canterbury Tales* (about 1385); the extended sense of cheerful, hopeful, confident, is first found in 1509, and was formerly associated with a *sanguine* complexion which was thought to be an indication of the predominance of blood over the other humors (itself not recorded before 1392).

sanitarium (san′ətãr′ēəm) *n.* sanatorium. 1851, New Latin *sanitarium;* formed from Latin *sānitās* health (from *sānus* healthy, sane) + *-ārium* -ary.

sanitary *adj.* of or pertaining to health or hygiene, preventing disease. 1842, borrowed from French *sanitaire;* formed from Latin *sānitās* health, from *sānus* healthy, sane + French *-aire* -ary.

sanitation *n.* a making sanitary or hygienic. 1848, formed from English *sanit(ary)* + *-ation.* Use of the term *sanitation* to replace *garbage* in several compounds, such as *sanitation worker, sanitation truck,* and *sanitation department,* was coined as a euphemism in American English in 1939.

sanitize *v.* make sanitary or hygienic. 1836, formed from English *sanit(ary)* + *-ize.* The figurative sense of give a wholesome appearance to, make more palatable or otherwise acceptable by removing offensive aspects or confidential elements, is recorded in 1934 in American English, possibly first used by Leon Henderson, an economic adviser to President Franklin Roosevelt.

sanity *n.* condition of being sane. Probably before 1425 *sanite* health, healthy condition, in a translation of Higden's *Polychronicon;* borrowed from Middle French *sanité* health, from Latin *sānitās* health, sanity, from *sānus* healthy, sane; for suffix see -ITY. The meaning of the condition of being sane, soundness of mind, mental health, is first recorded in Shakespeare's *Hamlet* (1602).

sanserif or **sans-serif** (san′ser′if) *n.* style of printing type without serifs. 1830, possibly formed in English from French *sans* without + English *serif* from earlier *ceref, syrif* (1827, perhaps borrowed from Dutch *schreef* line). Early use of a *sanserif* face is found in a specimen page of type for setting Greek texts (developed by the amateur type designer John Hibbert, London 1827, from a comparison with Greek manuscripts).

Santa Claus 1773, American English; borrowed from dialectal Dutch *Sante Klaas* (modern Dutch *Sinterklaas*), from Middle Dutch *Sinter (Ni)klaas* Saint Nicholas, a bishop of Asia Minor who lived in the 300's A.D. and became a patron saint associated with children.

Saint Nicholas owes his position as Santa Claus to the legend that he provided three impoverished girls with dowries by throwing three purses of gold in their open window. From this legend is said to derive the custom of placing gifts in the stockings of children on Saint Nicholas' Eve (the night of December 6) and attributing the gifts to Santa Claus, a custom that in the United States and some other countries has been transferred to Christmas Eve.

sap[1] *n.* liquid that moves through a plant. 1340 *zep,* in *Ayenbite of Inwyt;* later *sap* (1377); developed from Old English (about 750) *sæp;* cognate with Middle Low German, Middle Dutch, and modern Dutch *sap* sap, juice, and Old High German *saf* (modern German *Saft*), from Proto-Germanic **sapan,* Indo-European **sab-* (Pok.880). Probable cognates outside Germanic are found in Latin *sapa* new wine boiled down, and Avestan *višāpa-* (earlier **viš-šāpa-*) whose juices are poison, (from Indo-European **sap-/sāp-,* Pok.880); see SAGE[1] wise. The meaning of a simpleton, fool, is first recorded in Scott's *Guy Mannering* (1815) and was possibly in part a back formation from *sappy,* and a shortened form of *sapskull* (1735). **—sappy** *adj.* full of sap. 1435; developed from Old English (before 1100) *sæpig;* formed from *sæp* sap[1] + *-ig* -y[1]. The extended meaning of wet, sodden, full of moisture, is first recorded about 1470; perhaps the figurative sense of foolish, especially in a silly, sentimental way (1670), developed from this meaning. **—sapsucker** *n.* kind of woodpecker (1804-06, in the *Journals* of Lewis and Clark, American English). **—sapwood** *n.* (1791, in Erasmus Darwin's *Botanic Garden*)

sap[2] *v.* dig under or wear away the foundation of. 1598, dig a trench to approach the enemy's position, in Florio's *A World of Words;* borrowed from Middle French *saper,* from *sappe* spade, (also found in Italian *zappare,* from *zappa* spade); both the Middle French and Italian forms derive from Late Latin *sappa,* of uncertain origin. The transferred meaning of dig under or wear away the foundation of is first recorded in 1652. The figurative sense of weaken, use up, is found in 1755, probably influenced by the sense of undermine (1711, Addison in *The Spectator*) and by *sap*[1], as if to drain the vital sap from. **—n.** 1591 *sappe, zappe* the digging of trenches; borrowed from Middle French *sappe* spade, and Italian *zappa* spade, both from Late Latin *sappa.* The extended meaning of a trench dug to approach the enemy's position is first recorded in 1642. **—sapper** *n.* soldier employed in the construction of trenches, fortifications, etc. 1626, formed from English *sap*[2] + *-er*[1]; patterned on Middle French *sappeur.*

sapient (sā′pēənt) *adj.* wise, sage. 1468; earlier, as a surname (1413); probably, in part, formed in Middle English as the adjective to earlier *sapience* (before 1376), influenced by Old French *sapient;* and, in part, borrowed directly from Old French *sapient,* and from Latin *sapientem* (nominative *sapiēns*), present participle of *sapere* be wise; see SAGE[1] wise; for suffix see -ENT.

sapling *n.* young tree. About 1330; earlier as a surname (about 1277); formed from English *sap*[1] liquid + *-ling.*

sapodilla (sap′ədil′ə) *n.* large evergreen tree of tropical America. 1697, in William Dampier's *A New Voyage Round the World;* borrowed from Spanish *zapotilla,* diminutive of *zapote* fruit of the sapodilla, from Nahuatl *tzapotl.*

saponaceous (sap′ənā′shəs) *adj.* soapy. 1710, borrowed from New Latin *saponaceus,* from Latin *sāpō* (genitive *sāpōnis*) hair dye, pomade (in Late Latin, soap), possibly from Celtic, but ultimately from the Germanic base **saipōn-* (compare Old English *sāp* resin, pomade, and *sāpe* SOAP); for suffix see -ACEOUS.

saponify (səpon′əfī) *v.* make (a fat or oil) into soap. 1821, in Andrew Ure's *Dictionary of Chemistry;* borrowed (probably after familiarity with *saponaceous* of the nature of soap, 1710) from French *saponifier,* from New Latin *saponificare,* formed as if from an adjective **saponificus* (Late Latin *sāpō,* genitive *sāpōnis* SOAP + the root of Latin *facere* to make, perform, DO[1]).

sapphire (saf′īr) *n.* bright-blue precious stone. About 1250 *saphir;* earlier as a surname *Safir* (1221); borrowed from Old French *saphir, safir,* and directly from Latin *sapphīrus,* from Greek *sáppheiros,* from a Semitic language, probably Hebrew *sappīr* sapphire. The spelling *sapphire* (*-pp-*) is first recorded in 1676, in imitation of the Latin. **—adj.** bright-blue. 1432 *saffir;* from the noun in Middle English.

saprophyte (sap′rəfīt) *n.* bacteria or fungi that live on decaying organic matter. 1875, formed in English from Greek *saprós* rotten + English *-phyte* plant.

sarcasm *n.* 1579 *sarcasmus* sharp, cutting remark; borrowed from Late Latin *sarcasmos;* later replaced by *sarcasm* (1619, borrowed from French *sarcasme,* also from Late Latin); from late Greek *sarkasmós* a sneer, from *sarkázein* to speak bitterly, sneer; literally, to strip off flesh, from *sárx* (genitive *sarkós*) flesh; probably cognate with Avestan *thwarəs-* to cut, from Indo-European **twerk-* (Pok.1102). **—sarcastic** *adj.* using sarcasm. 1695, derived from English *sarcasm,* on the pattern of *enthusiasm, enthusiastic;* for suffix see -IC.

sarcoma (särkō′mə) *n.* harmful tumor of the connective tissue. 1657, fleshy excrescence, New Latin *sarcoma,* from Greek *sárkōma,* from *sarkoûn* to produce flesh, grow fleshy, from *sárx* (genitive *sarkós*) flesh. The meaning of a harmful tumor of the connective tissue is first recorded in 1804.

sarcophagus (särkof′əgəs) *n.* stone coffin. 1601, in Holland's translation of Pliny's *Natural History;* borrowed from Latin *sarcophagus,* from Greek *sarkophágos* limestone used for coffins; literally, flesh-eating in reference to the supposed action of limestone on the body (*sárx,* genitive *sarkós* flesh + *phageîn* to eat); see SARCASM and ESOPHAGUS. The sense of a stone coffin is first recorded in English in 1705. An isolated instance is recorded in Middle English as *sartophagus* (probably about 1425).

sardine *n.* 1393 *sardyn;* later *sardeyne* (before 1450); borrowed from Middle French *sardine,* from Italian *sardina,* and borrowed directly from Latin *sardīna,* from Greek *sardī́nē,* possibly from *Sardṓ* Sardinia, an island in the Mediterranean sea, near which the fish was probably caught in great numbers and then exported. **—v.** *Informal.* to pack closely, crowd, cram. 1895, American English; from the noun, as used in the phrase *packed like sardines* (1911).

sardonic *adj.* bitter, scornful, mocking. 1638, in Sir Thomas Herbert's *Works;* probably borrowed from French *sardonique;* also found in Spanish *sardónico* and Italian *sardonico;* formed as if from Latin *sardon(ius)* + *-icus,* from Greek *sardónios* of bitter or scornful laughter; for suffix see -IC.

Greek *sardónios* was an alteration (influenced by *Sar-*

dónios Sardinian) of the earlier form *sardánios,* found in Homer; the reason for the alteration was the belief among the ancient Greeks that the word had a primary reference to a "Sardinian plant" called *sardónion* that when eaten produced facial convulsions resembling those accompanying bitter or scornful laughter.

The original Greek *sardánios* is from Indo-European **sward-,* represented in the Celtic languages by Welsh *chwardd* he will laugh (with infinitive *chwerthin,* Cornish *hwerthin,* and Middle Breton *huersin,* all meaning to laugh).

sargasso *n.* 1598, borrowed from Portuguese *sargasso, sargaço* seaweed, perhaps from *sarga* a type of grape (because of the berrylike air sacs on the seaweed), or perhaps from Latin *sargus* a kind of fish, of unknown origin.

sari (sä′rē) *n.* Hindu garment worn by women. 1785, borrowed from Hindi *sāṛī,* from Prakrit *sāḍī,* from Sanskrit *śāṭī* garment, petticoat, of unknown origin.

sarong (sərông′) *n.* rectangular piece of cloth worn as clothing. 1834, borrowed from Malay *sārung* sheath, covering.

sarsaparilla (sas′pəril′ə) *n.* tropical American plant or the drink made from its root. 1577, borrowed from Spanish *zarzaparrilla* (*zarza* bramble, from Arabic *šaraṣ* thorny plant + *parrilla,* diminutive of *parra* vine); so called because the sarsaparilla is a climbing plant with berries that resemble grapes.

sartorial (särtôr′ēəl) *adj.* of tailors or their work. 1823, in Sydney Smith's *Works;* formed in English as if from Late Latin **sartōrius,* from *sartor* patcher, mender + English *-al*[1]. Late Latin *sartor* is formed from Latin *sart-,* past participle stem of *sarcire* to patch, mend (see EXORCISE) + *-or* -or[2].

The word was popularized by Carlyle in his *Sartor Resartus* and other writings, but earlier forms derived from the Latin stem *sartor-* have appeared in English from time to time, including *sartor,* n. (1656), *sartorian,* adj. (1668), *sartry* (*sartre* 1448-49, *sarterie* 1275), and *sartin* (1199).

sash[1] *n.* strip of cloth. 1599 *shash* strip of cloth twisted into a turban, in Hakluyt's *Voyages;* borrowed from Arabic *shāsh* muslin cloth (worn as turbans). The spelling *sash* represents a differentiation or dissimilation of sound in the beginning and end of the word, and is first recorded in this form in 1687. An earlier dissimilated form that occurs terminally (*shass*) is found in 1617. The meaning of a strip of cloth worn around the waist or over the shoulder is first recorded in 1681.

sash[2] *n.* frame of a window or door. 1681 *sashes,* pl., alteration of French *châssis* frame, as of a window or door; see CHASSIS. The French word was apparently taken as a plural because of the *-s* ending and the singular *sash* was formed from it before 1704 by back formation. **—v.** furnish with sashes. 1796, in Burke's *Letters;* from the noun.

sashay *v.* perform a gliding step, especially in folk dancing. 1836, American English, alteration of earlier *chassé* gliding step (1867); borrowing of French *chassé* a gliding step; literally, chased, past participle of *chasser* to chase, from Old French *chacier* to hunt; see CHASE[1].

The sense of glide or move about usually with an affected casualness is first recorded in 1865.
—n. 1900, in George Ade's *More Fables,* (figurative) a short trip or excursion, American English, from the verb. The sense of a gliding step is first recorded about 1940.

sassafras (sas′əfras) *n.* slender American tree with fragrant, yellow flowers and bluish-black fruit. 1577, American English borrowed from Spanish *sasafrás,* from Late Latin *saxifragia* a kind of herb, variant of *saxifraga* SAXIFRAGE.

sassy *adj.* rude, impertinent, saucy. 1833, American English, alteration of SAUCY.

Satan *n.* the Devil. Old English (about 750) *Satan;* borrowed from Late Latin *Satān,* from Greek *Satanâs,* adapted from *Satân,* from Hebrew *śāṭān* adversary, one who plots against another, from *śāṭan* to oppose, plot against. **—satanic** *adj.* 1667, of Satan, in Milton's *Paradise Lost,* shortened form of earlier *Satanical* (before 1548) and in some instances probably independently formed in English from *Satan* + *-ic* on the model of French *satanique,* from Greek *Satanikós.* The meaning of like or characteristic of Satan, very wicked, is first recorded in 1793.

satchel *n.* small piece of luggage. About 1340 *sachel,* borrowing of Old French *sachel,* from Late Latin *saccellum* money bag, purse, diminutive of Latin *sacculus,* itself a diminutive of *saccus* bag, SACK[1].

sate *v.* satisfy fully. 1602, in Shakespeare's *Hamlet,* probably alteration (influenced by Latin *satiāre* SATIATE) of earlier *sade,* in Middle English *saden* become satiated, satiate (about 1390); developed from Old English *sadian* to satiate (before 899, in Alfred's translation of Boethius' *De Consolatione Philosophiae*). Old English *sadian* is cognate with Middle Low German *saden* sate, Middle Dutch *saden* (modern Dutch *verzaden*), and Old High German *satōn* (Middle High German *saten*), from Proto-Germanic **sađōjanan,* from the West Germanic source of Old English *sæd* sated; see SAD.

sateen (satēn′) *n.* cotton cloth with a shiny finish. 1878, variant of *satin,* perhaps influenced by *velveteen.*

satellite *n.* Before 1548, one who attends a person of importance; borrowing of Middle French *satellite,* learned borrowing from Latin, and borrowed directly from Latin *satellitem* (nominative *satelles*) attendant, perhaps from Etruscan.

The sense of a small planet that revolves around a larger one is first recorded in English in 1665; the Latin plural *satellites* was first applied in 1611 by Kepler to the secondary planets revolving around Jupiter, recently discovered by Galileo. The meaning of a man-made object launched into orbit around the earth is first recorded in English in 1936; reference to a similar, but imaginary, projectile is found earlier in a translation of Jules Verne's *Begum's Fortune* (1880). The figurative sense of a country under the control of another is first found in 1800, in John Adams' *Works.*

satiate *v.* satisfy fully. About 1450 *saciaten;* borrowed from Latin *satiātus,* past participle of *satiāre* fill full, fill enough, from *satis* enough; see SAD; for suffix see -ATE[1]. The spelling *satiate* is first found in 1611. **—adj.** filled to satiety. 1440 *saciate;* borrowed from Latin *satiātus,* past participle. **—satiation** *n.* state of being satiated. 1638, probably formed from English *satiate* + *-ion,* on the model of Latin **satiātiōnem* (nominative **satiātiō*), from *satiāre* satiate. **—satiety** (səti′ətē) *n.* satiated condition. 1590; earlier *saciety* (1533); borrowed from Middle French *satieté,* from Latin *satietātem* (nominative *satietās*) sufficiency, abundance, from *satis* enough; for suffix see -TY[2].

satin *n.* silk or rayon cloth with one very smooth, glossy side. 1369 *satyn,* in Chaucer's *Book of the Duchesse;* borrowed from Old French *satin, zatanin,* probably from Arabic (*aṭlas*) *zaitūnī* (satin) from *Zaitūn,* the name of a Chinese city identified with *Tsinkiang* (Chuanchow), a city in southern China used as a port in the Middle Ages. **—adj.** of or like satin, smooth and glossy. 1449 *satyn;* from the noun.

satire *n.* 1509, poem or prose work intended to ridicule vice or folly, in Barclay's *The Ship of Fools;* borrowing of Middle French *satire,* learned borrowing from Latin, and probably borrowed directly from Latin *satira* satire, poetic medley, from *lanx satura* mixed dish; literally, full dish, from feminine of *satur* full of food, sated; see SAD. The alteration of Latin *satura* to *satyra* and *satira* developed from the mistaken notion that this Roman genre derived from Greek *satyr* drama.

The meaning of a branch of literature ridiculing vice or folly is first recorded in 1589, and that of the use of sarcasm or irony to ridicule vice or folly about 1675. **—satiric** or **satirical** *adj.* of or containing satire. 1509 *satiric,* borrowed from Middle French *satirique,* from Late Latin *satiricus,* from Latin *satira* satire; before 1529 *satirical,* formed in English from Middle French *satirique* + English *-al*[1]. The form *satiric* appears in Middle English as a noun with the meaning of a writer of satires (before 1387), but was replaced by satirist in the 1600's. **—satirist** *n.* writer of satires, person who uses satire. 1589, in Puttenham's *The Art of English Poesie;* formed from English *satire* + *-ist.* **—satirize** *v.* attack with satire. 1601, in Ben Jonson's *Poetaster;* probably formed in English from *satire* + *-ize,* on the model of Middle French *satiriser,* from *satire* satire.

satisfaction *n.* Before 1325 *satisfacciun* performance of some act or duty set forth by a priest or other Church authority to make up for some wrong, sin, etc., atonement, in *Cursor Mundi;* borrowed from Old French *satisfaction,* and directly from Latin *satisfactiōnem* (nominative *satisfactiō*) a satisfying of a creditor, reparation, amends, apology, from *satisfacere* SATISFY; for suffix see -TION.

The general sense of contentment, appeasement, is found in the Wycliffe Bible (before 1382). **—satisfactory** *adj.* About 1443 *satisfactorie* capable of atoning for sin; borrowed from Late Latin *satisfactōrius* affording satisfaction, from Latin *satisfact-,* past participle stem of *satisfacere* satisfy; for suffix see -ORY. The general sense of adequate, good enough to satisfy, is first recorded in English in 1640.

satisfy *v.* About 1412 *satisfien* make amends, recompense, in Hoccleve's *Regement of Princes;* also, fulfill, assuage (1419); borrowed from Middle French *satisfier,* variant of *satisfaire,* from Old French, from Latin *satisfacere* discharge fully, comply with, make amends; literally, do enough (*satis* enough; see SAD + *facere* perform, DO[1]); for suffix see -FY.

satrap (sā'trap) *n.* subordinate ruler, often a tyrant. Probably about 1380 *sathrapas* (pl.) governor of a province of ancient Persia; also, governor or leader; before 1382 *satrape;* borrowed from Latin *satrapa, satrapēs* a provincial governor of ancient Persia, from Greek *satrápēs,* from Old Persian *xshathrapāvan-,* literally, guardian of the realm (*xshathra-* realm, related to *xshāyathiya-* king; see CHECK + *pāvan-* guardian). Old Persian *pāvan-* is cognate with Sanskrit *pāti* (he) guards; see FUR. **—satrapy** *n.* province or authority of a satrap. 1603, in Richard Knolles' *General History of the Turks;* borrowed from Middle French *satrapie,* from Latin *satrapīa, satrapēa,* from Greek *satrapeíā,* from *satrápēs* satrap; for suffix see -Y[3].

saturate *v.* 1538, to satisfy, satiate, in Elyot's *Dictionary,* probably developed as verb use of earlier *saturate,* adj., satisfied, satiated (before 1450); borrowed from Latin *saturātus,* past participle of *saturāre* to fill full, sate, drench, saturate, from *satur* sated, full; see SAD; for suffix see -ATE[1]. The meaning of soak thoroughly, drench, imbue, is first recorded in English in 1756 in figurative use and later in literal use, in 1764. **—saturation** *n.* Probably 1554, a being saturated, in Coverdale's *The Hope of the Faithful;* probably formed from English *saturate,* v. + *-ion,* on the model of Late Latin *saturātiōnem* (nominative *saturātiō*), from Latin *saturāre* saturate.

Saturday *n.* Probably before 1200 *Sætterdæi;* later *Saturday* (about 1300); developed from Old English *Sæterdæg* (before 899), also *Sæternesdæg,* literally, day of the planet Saturn (*Sæternes,* genitive of *Sæter, Sætern* Saturn, borrowed from Latin *Sāturnus* + *dæg* DAY). See SATURNINE. The Germanic compounds found in Old Frisian *Sāterdei* Saturday, Middle Low German *Sāterdach,* Middle Dutch *Saterdach,* and Dutch *Zaterdag,* are a partial loan translation of Latin *Sāturnī diēs* Saturn's day, which in turn was a translation of Greek *Krónou hēmérā* day of the god Cronus, who was identified by the Romans with the god *Sāturnus.*

Saturnalia (sat'ərnā'lēə) *n.pl.* 1591, borrowing of Latin *Sāturnālia* ancient Roman festival of Saturn, celebrated in December, from neuter plural of *Sāturnālis* pertaining to Saturn, from *Sāturnus* Saturn; see SATURNINE. The transferred sense of any period of unrestrained revelry is first found in 1782.

saturnine (sat'ərnīn) *adj.* About 1380 *saturnyn* having characteristics determined by influence of the planet Saturn, in Chaucer's *House of Fame;* later, with a more general application in the meaning of gloomy, grave, taciturn (about 1433, in Lydgate's writings); formed from Middle English *Saturne,* the planet (supposed to cause gloomy behavior in those born under its sign) + *-ine*[1]. The form with the suffix *-ine*[1] rather than *-ial* as in *Jovial, Mercurial,* was possibly influenced by the Roman surname *Sāturnīnus.* Latin *Sāturnus* the planet, originally the name of the Roman god of agriculture, is a word of Etruscan origin, though it was associated by folk etymology with Latin *satus,* past participle of *serere* to SOW[1].

satyr (sā'tər) *n.* deity of the woods, part man and part beast, in Greek mythology. Before 1398 *satire* a type of ape, in Trevisa's translation of Bartholomew's *De Proprietatibus Rerum;* earlier *satirus* (implied in the Latinate plural *satiry*) deity of the woods (about 1385, in Chaucer's *Troilus and Criseyde*); borrowed from Old French *satire,* and directly from Latin *satyrus,* from Greek *sátyros,* of uncertain origin.

sauce *n.* 1340 *sause* a liquid seasoning or condiment, in *Ayenbite of Inwyt;* later *sauce* (in the compound *sauce-maker,* 1353); borrowed from Old French *sause, sauce,* (earlier) *saulse,* from Vulgar Latin **salsa,* noun use of Latin *salsa,* feminine singular or neuter plural form of *salsus* salted, from past participle of *sallere* (earlier stem **sald-*) to salt, from *sāl* (genitive *salis*) SALT. The figurative sense of something which adds piquancy or zest to a thought, action, etc., is found in Dunbar's *Poems* (before 1500). The slang meaning of alcoholic liquor is first recorded in American English, in John O'Hara's *Pal Joey* (1940). **—v.** to season. Before 1438 *sawsen;* later *saucen* (1450); from the noun. **—saucepan** *n.* (1686)

saucer *n.* 1343 *saucer;* borrowed from Old French *saucer, saucier* sauce dish (from *sauce* SAUCE), and from Anglo-Latin *saucerium,* from Late Latin *salsārium,* neuter of *salsārius* of or for salted things, from Latin *salsus* salted; see SAUCE; for suffix see -ER[2]. Both *saucer* and *flying saucer,* referring to an unidentified saucer-shaped object reported in the sky, are first recorded in 1947.

saucy *adj.* 1508, resembling sauce, savory; later, impertinent, forward, cheeky (1530, in Palsgrave's *Lesclarcissement*); formed from English *sauce* + *-y*[1].

sauerkraut (sour′krout′) *n.* salted, fermented cabbage. 1617 *sower crawt;* later *sour-crout* (1775); borrowed from German *Sauerkraut* (*sauer* SOUR + *Kraut* vegetable, cabbage, from Old High German *krūt,* from Proto-Germanic **krūđán,* cognate with Greek *brýon* a marsh-plant, and *brýein* to sprout, Indo-European **gwrū-,* root **gweru-,* Pok.479). The spelling *sauerkraut* is first recorded in English in Charles Lamb's *Elia* (1823).

sauna (sô′nä) *n.* Finnish type of steam bath. 1881, bath-house with sauna; borrowing of Finnish *sauna.* Reference to the steam bath itself is first recorded in 1936. **—v.** take a bath in a sauna. 1966, from the noun.

saunter *v.* walk along slowly and aimlessly. Before 1667, probably developed from Middle English *santren* to muse, brood (before 1500), and perhaps, if not the same word as *saunteren* (found in *saunteryng* idle chattering, babbling, before 1450); of uncertain origin. **—n.** leisurely or careless gait. 1712, from the verb.

sausage *n.* About 1450 *sawsyge;* borrowed from Old North French *saussiche,* from Vulgar Latin **salsīcia* (also found in Medieval Latin *salsicia,* pl., sausages, salted or seasoned meats), from Latin *salsus* salted; see SAUCE. The spelling *sausage* (probably mistakenly influenced by the suffix *-age* in the sense of something that is the result of the verb; in this case "to salt") is first recorded in 1553.

sauté (sōtā′) *n.* dish fried quickly in a little fat. 1813, borrowing of French *sauté,* literally, jumped or bounced (in reference to the tossing action while cooking, so that the meat, or whatever is cooked does not lie on the surface of the pan continuously), from past participle of *sauter* to jump, from Latin *saltāre* to hop, dance, frequentative form of *salīre* to leap; see SALLY. **—v.** fry quickly in a little fat. 1859, from the noun. **—adj.** fried quickly in a little fat. 1869, from the noun.

sauterne (sōtėrn′) *n.* kind of French white wine. 1833, from earlier *Sauternes* (1711); named after *Sauternes,* a town in southwestern France, in the region where the grapes are grown.

savage *adj.* About 1250 *savage* fierce, ferocious; later, wild or untamed, bold, cruel (probably before 1300, in *Kyng Alisaunder*); borrowed from Old French *sauvage,* from Late Latin *salvāticus,* alteration by vowel assimilation of *i* to *a* of Latin *silvāticus* wild, of the woods, from *silva* forest, grove, of uncertain origin; for suffix see -AGE. The extended sense of uncivilized, barbarous, is first recorded in Middle English in Gower's *Confessio Amantis* (before 1393). **—n.** uncivilized person. Probably before 1400 *savagyus,* pl., in *The Wars of Alexander;* from the adjective. **—v.** attack savagely. 1563, from the adjective. **—savagery** *n.* 1595, in Shakespeare's *King John;* formed from English *savage,* adj. + *-ry.*

savanna or **savannah** (səvan′ə) *n.* treeless plain. 1555 *zavana,* in Eden's translation of Peter Martyr's *Decades of the New World or West India;* later *savana* (1604); borrowed from Spanish *sabana,* from earlier Spanish *zavana,* from Arawakan (Haiti).

savant (səvänt′) *n.* person of learning or science. 1719, borrowing of French *savant* a learned man, from *savant* learned, knowing, former present participle of *savoir* to know, from Old French, from Vulgar Latin **sapēre,* from Latin *sapere* be wise; see SAGE[1] wise.

save[1] *v.* make or keep safe. Probably before 1200 *sauven* rescue, bring to safety, in *Ancrene Riwle;* later *saven* (about 1250); borrowed from Old French *sauver, salver* save, from Late Latin *salvāre* make safe, secure, from Latin *salvus* SAFE. The meaning of store up, accumulate, is first recorded in Mannyng's *Handlyng Synne* (about 1303), and that of keep possession of, in *Piers Plowman* (before 1376). **—n.** an act of saving. 1890, (in sports) an act of preventing the opposite side from scoring. **—savings** *n.pl.* money saved. 1786; earlier *saving* (1737); formed from English *save* to reserve, store up + *ing*[1]. **—savings account** (1911) **—savings and loan association** (1887, American English) **—savings bank** (1817) **—savings bond** (1942)

save[2] *prep.* except, but. Probably about 1300 *save;* from the adjective *safe, saf, sauf* SAFE in the sense of keeping safe or intact, reserving, excepting (about 1300), on the pattern of the similar development in the use of the equivalent Old French *sauf* safe.

In Old French the adjective *sauf,* feminine *sauve,* following the pattern of similar Latin ablative absolute constructions, had already assumed a prepositional role in phrases such as *sauf votre respect* saving your reverence often with the sense of "being excepted," so that it eventually became (like the analogous *except,* past participle, in Middle English) functionally equivalent to a preposition.

—conj. excepting. Probably before 1325 *saf;* about 1325 *save;* from the adjective *safe, saf, sauf* SAFE, on the pattern of the similarly used Old French *sauf* safe.

saving *prep.* except, save. About 1375 *savyng,* in Chaucer's *Canterbury Tales;* from the present participle of *save*[1], v. The meaning of without prejudice or offense to _____ (as in *saving your reverence, saving your honor, grace,* etc.) is found in Middle English in Trevisa's translation of Higden's *Polychronicon* (before 1387).

savior or **saviour** *n.* Probably before 1300 *saveour* one who saves mankind from sin, a title of Jesus Christ, in *Arthour and Merlin;* borrowed from Old French *saveour,* from Late Latin *salvātōrem* (nominative *salvātor*) a saver, preserver, from *salvāre* to SAVE[1]; for suffix see -OR[2]. The word in Late Latin and especially in English was chiefly used in reference to Christ, as a translation of Greek *sōtḗr* savior, equivalent to *Iēsoûs* Jesus.

savoir-faire (sav′wärfär′) *n.* social grace, tact. 1815, French term used in Scott's *Guy Mannering;* literally, knowing how to act (*savoir* to know, from Old French; see SAVANT + *faire* to do, from Latin *facere* to make, perform, DO[1]).

savor *n.* taste or smell, flavor. Probably before 1200 *savur* agreeable flavor, taste, sweetness, in *Ancrene Riwle;* probably about 1200 *savour;* borrowed from Old French *savor, savour, savur,* from Latin *sapōrem* (nominative *sapor*) taste, flavor, related to *sapere* to have a flavor; see SAGE[1] wise. **—v.** Probably before 1250 *savouren* give pleasure to; later, give a taste or flavor to, season (about 1350), to relish, enjoy (probably 1382); borrowed from Old French *savourer, savorer,* from Late Latin *sapōrāre* give taste or flavor, from Latin *sapōrem* taste, savor, n.

savory[1] *adj.* pleasing in taste or smell. Probably about 1200 *savure* spiritually delightful; later *savery* flavorful (about 1300); borrowed from Old French *savouré,* past participle of *savourer* to taste, SAVOR. **—n.** *British.* savory dish served at the end of dinner. 1661, from the adjective.

savory[2] *n.* herb used for seasoning. 1373 *savory;* earlier as a surname *Sauvary* (1250); ultimately from Latin *satureja,* of uncertain origin. The history of this word in English is also uncertain. The Middle English word may be an alteration of Old English *sǣtherie* (about 1000), from Old French **sathereie,* from Latin, or it may be a borrowing from an Old French form with *v* (compare a modern French form *savorée),* perhaps influenced by *savour* SAVOR.

savvy (sav′ē) *v. Slang.* to know, understand. 1785, in Grose's *Classical Dictionary of the Vulgar Tongue;* borrowed from French *savez (-vous)?* do you know? and probably in part from Spanish *sabe (usted)* you know; both from Vulgar Latin **sapēre,* from Latin *sapere* be wise, be knowing; see SAGE[1] wise. **—n.** *Slang.* understanding, intelligence, sense. 1785, in Grose's *Classical Dictionary of the Vulgar Tongue,* from the same source as the verb. **—adj.** knowledgeable, experienced, wise. 1905, from the noun.

saw[1] *n.* cutting tool with sharp teeth. About 1350 *sawe;* earlier *sagen,* pl. (about 1125), and in dialect of northern England *sagh* (before 1335); developed from Old English *sagu* (about 1000, in Ælfric's *Glossary*); cognate with Middle Dutch *saghe* saw (modern Dutch *zaag*), Old High German *saga,* and Old Icelandic *sǫg* (Swedish *såg,* Danish *sav*), from Proto-Germanic **saʒō.* Cognates outside Germanic include Albanian *shatë* mattock, Latin *secūris* ax, *sēcula* sickle, and Old Slavic *sekyra* ax, *sěkǫ, sěšti* cut, from Indo-European **sek-/sēk-/sok-* (Pok. 895). **—v.** cut with a saw. About 1300 *sawien;* later *sawen* (about 1350); earlier *isahet,* past participle (probably about 1200); from the noun. **—sawbuck** *n.* frame or trestle with X-shaped ends for holding wood to be sawed. 1850, American English; formed from *saw*[1] + earlier *buck* sawbuck (1817); probably borrowed from Dutch *(zaag)bok (zaag* SAW[1] + *bok* trestle, vaulting frame; originally, male goat, cognate with English BUCK[1]). The American slang sense of ten dollars particularly in the form of paper currency, is found in 1850, probably from the similarity between *X* the Roman numeral (10) and the X-shaped ends of a sawbuck; perhaps later reinforced by the slang term *buck*[3] a dollar. **—sawdust** *n.* (1530, in Palsgrave's *Lesclarcissement*) **—sawhorse** *n.* (1778) **—sawmill** *n.* (1553, in Richard Eden's translation of *A Treatise of the New India*) **—sawyer** *n.* person who saws timber into planks. 1257 *sawer;* earlier as a surname *Saer* (1202); also *sawier* (1350); formed from Middle English *sawe* saw[1] + *-er*[1], *-ier.* The meaning of a kind of beetle whose larva bores holes in wood is first recorded in American English in 1789.

saw[2] *n.* wise saying, proverb. Probably about 1150 *sawe;* developed from Old English (before 1000) *sagu* saying, discourse, speech; related to *secgan* SAY. Old English *sagu* is cognate with Middle Low German and Middle Dutch *sage* story, account (modern Dutch *sage* legend, myth), Old High German *saga* story, account, (modern German *Sage* myth, rumor), Old Icelandic and Icelandic *saga* story, tale, saga, and Swedish *saga* fairy tale, from Proto-Germanic **saʒwṓ.*

saxifrage (sak′səfrij) *n.* low, spreading plant. 1373 *saxfrage;* later *saxifrage* (probably before 1425); borrowed from Old French *saxifrage, sassifrage,* from Late Latin *saxifraga* kind of herb, from Latin *saxifragus* stone-breaking (*saxum* stone, rock + *frag-,* root of *frangere* to break; see BREAK). The plant was probably so called because it was used medicinally to dissolve gallstones. Doublet of SASSAFRAS.

Saxon *adj., n.* Probably before 1200 *Sexun;* later *Saxon* (before 1338); borrowed from Late Latin *Saxonem* (nominative *Saxō,* usually found in the plural *Saxonēs*), from an old Germanic form represented by Old English *seaxe, seaxa;* cognate with Old High German *sahso* (modern German *Sachse*), Old Icelandic *saxi* (Swedish *Sachsare,* Danish *Sachser*), all with the possible literal sense of swordsmen, found in Old English *seax* a short sword or knife, cognate with Old High German *sahs,* from Proto-Germanic **saHsan;* see SAW[1]. Middle English *Saxon* replaced the Old English *seaxe* and for a time, in the 1300's and 1400's, was a parallel term to various spellings such as *sessoyn, sesson, sesiogn* that were Anglicized borrowings of Old French *saisoigne, sesne* and Anglo-French *sessoun,* ultimately borrowed from Germanic.

saxophone *n.* brass musical instrument with keys for the fingers. 1851, borrowing of French *saxophone* (after Antoine Joseph *Sax,* Belgian instrument maker + connecting *-o-* + French *-phone* sound). The saxophone was invented by Sax about 1840 from principles applied by his father, Charles Joseph, to create the earlier *saxhorn.* **—saxophonist** *n.* (1865)

say *v.* Before 1121 *seien, seggen,* in *Peterborough Chronicle;* developed from Old English *secgan* to utter, say (about 725, in *Beowulf*); also *sægen* (1070). The Old English is cognate with Old Frisian *sedza* to say, Old Saxon *seggian,* Middle Dutch *segghen,* Dutch *zeggen,* Old High German *sagēn,* modern German *sagen,* and Old Icelandic *segja* to say, from Proto-Germanic **saʒjanan* (earlier **saʒwjanan*). Outside Germanic cognates are found in Old Irish *insce* speech, Old Latin *inseque* (imperative) and Greek *énnepe* (imperative) tell! relate!, Lithuanian *sakýti* say, and Old Slavic *sočiti* announce, from Indo-European **sekw-/sokw-* (Pok. 897). The spelling of the past tense *said* developed through Middle English *seid, sǣde, seaide,* from Old English *segde, sǣde, sǣgde.* The spelling with *ai* of any form began to appear in Kentish dialect about 1250 and in *ay* between about 1300 and 1380, becoming frequent in the 1500's and the established spelling in the 1600's. **—n.** what one says. 1571, from the verb. The meaning of the right or authority to influence a decision (as in *have a say*) is first recorded in 1614. **—say-so** *n. Informal.* 1637, mere word; later, authority (1902).

sayonara (sä′yōnä′rə) *n.* goodbye, farewell. 1875, borrowing of Japanese *sayōnara* farewell; literally, since it must be so.

scab *n.* About 1275 *scab* skin disease forming pustules or scales; earlier as a surname *Skabbe* (1264); probably developed in part from Old English *sceabb* scab, itch, related to *scafan* to scratch; see SHAVE; but primarily borrowed from a Scandinavian source (compare Old Icelandic *skabb* scab, itch, Danish *skab,* Norwegian and Swedish *skabb*). Related to SHABBY.

The meaning of a crust that forms over a wound is found in Middle English in 1392, probably reinforced by Latin *scabiēs* scab, itch, mange, from *scabere* to scratch; see SHAVE. The slang sense of a mean, low, scurvy fellow, is found about 1590. The use of *scab* as a derogatory term for a person who refuses to join a trade union is first recorded in 1777, and the extended sense of a worker who refuses to join a strike, a strikebreaker, appeared in 1806.
—**v.** 1632, form a scab; later, become covered with scabs (1683); from the noun.
—**scabby** *adj.* Probably before 1425, in a translation of Chauliac's *Grande Chirurgie;* formed from Middle English *scab,* n. + *-y*[1].

scabbard *n.* sheath for a sword, dagger, etc. 1391 *scabard;* spelling alteration (perhaps influenced by *tabard* or a similar word) of earlier *sckauberk* (probably before 1300, in *The Romance of Guy of Warwick*); borrowed from Anglo-French **escauberc* sheath (implied in *escaubers,* pl.), *escauberge* (also Anglo-French *escalbert, eschaubert* and Anglo-Latin *scabergia, scaubergum*). These forms suggest a Germanic derivation, probably a compound (represented by known elements found in Old High German) whose literal meaning was blade protector, made up of Frankish **skār* blade (compare Old High German *skār;* see SHEARS) + **berg-* protect (compare Old High German *bergan* to protect; see BURY, and English HAUBERK).

scabies (skā′bēz) *n.* disease of the skin causing itching. Before 1400, in a translation of Lanfranc's *Science of Surgery;* borrowed from Latin *scabiēs* mange, itch, related to *scabere* to scratch; see SHAVE. —**scabious** *adj.* of the nature of or relating to scabies. 1603, in Florio's translation of Montaigne's *Essays;* borrowed through French *scabieux,* or directly from Latin *scabiōsus* mangy, rough, from *scabiēs* scabies; for suffix see -OUS.

scabrous (skā′brəs) *adj.* rough. Before 1585, harsh, unmusical; borrowed from Late Latin *scabrōsus* rough, from Latin *scaber* rough, scaly, related to *scabere* to scratch, scrape; see SHAVE; for suffix see -OUS. The extended sense of full of difficulties, thorny, is first recorded in 1646, and that of risqué, vulgar, indelicate, in 1881. A further extension is found in American English in the sense of begrimed, squalid, in 1939, and nasty, repulsive, obnoxious, about 1951.

scads *n.pl.* large quantity or number. 1869, American English, of uncertain origin. Other earlier meanings of dollar, money (1809), and gold left after panning (1863) are probably not of the same word, though according to E. G. Fichtner ("The origin of New English 'scads' and 'oodles'," in *Neuphilologische Mitteilungen* 84, 3: 387-95), *scads* may have originated (by way of Scotland and northern England) from a Scandinavian word related to Old Icelandic *skattr* tax, tribute, money, Danish *skat* and Swedish *skatt* treasure, tax. Cognates of the Scandinavian words include Old English *sceatt* treasure, money, Old Frisian *skett* money, livestock, Old Saxon *skat* coin, property, Middle Low German and Middle Dutch *schat* tax, value, Old High German *scaz* denarius, money (modern German *Schatz* treasure), and Gothic *skatts* money, coin, from Proto-Germanic **skattás* (Indo-European **skət-nós*) wealth (in domestic animals), cognate with Latin *scatere* gush, abound, and Lithuanian *skasti* to spring, from Indo-European **skēt-/skət-* (Pok.950).

scaffold *n.* temporary platform. About 1385 *scaffold* raised platform, in Chaucer's *Canterbury Tales;* earlier, in Latin context, *scaffote* (1349), *skaffald* (1354), and as a surname *Scaffol* (1299); borrowed from a dialect variant (compare Middle French *escharfault*) of Old French *eschafaut* scaffold, expanded (probably by influence of *eschace* a prop, support) from earlier *chaffaut,* from Vulgar Latin **catafalicum;* see CATAFALQUE.
—**v.** furnish or support with a scaffold. Before 1548, from the noun.

scalar (skā′lər) *adj. Mathematics.* having or indicating magnitude but no direction. 1656, resembling a ladder, in Blount's *Glossographia;* borrowed from Latin *scālāris* of or pertaining to a ladder or flight of steps, from *scālae,* pl., ladder, steps; see SCALE[3] flight of steps; for suffix see -AR. The extended sense in mathematics is found in 1846.

scalawag (skal′əwag) *n. Informal.* scamp, rascal, rogue. 1848, American English, of uncertain origin. The word may possibly be an alteration (influenced by *wag* habitual joker) of Scottish *scallag* farm servant, rustic, from Old Scottish *scoloc* bond servant, tenant of church land; originally, monastery student, scholar, from *scol* school, from Latin *schola;* see SCHOOL. *Scalawag* also appears as the name for an undersized or worthless animal. If this was the original sense of the word, then *scalawag* is perhaps an alteration of the name *Scalloway,* one of the Shetland Islands, undersized animals being so called in allusion to the small size of the Shetland ponies.

scald *v.* to burn with hot liquid or steam. Probably before 1200 *scalden* (implied in *scaldinge,* present participle), in *Ancrene Riwle;* borrowed from Old North French *escalder, escauder,* from Late Latin *excaldāre* bathe in hot water (Latin *ex-* off + *caldus, calidus* hot; see CALDRON). The sense in cookery of heat almost to the boiling point is found in Middle English in 1483.
—**n.** burn caused by hot liquid or steam. 1601, in Holland's translation of Pliny's *Natural History;* from the verb.

scale[1] *n.* thin, flat, hard plate on some fishes, snakes, etc. Probably about 1300, in *The Romance of Guy of Warwick;* borrowed from Old French *escale* scale, husk, from Frankish (compare Old High German *scala* SHELL). —**v.** remove scales from. Probably before 1425 *scalen* to scrape, remove infected parts; later, remove the scales from (1440, in *Promptorium Parvulorum*); from the noun. —**scale insect** (1840) —**scaly** *adj.* Before 1398 *skaly* covered with scales, in Trevisa's translation of Bartholomew's *De Proprietatibus Rerum;* formed from Middle English *scale*[1], n. + *-y*[1].

scale[2] *n.* dish or pan of a balance. Probably before 1200, drinking cup, bowl, in *Ancrene Riwle;* borrowed from a Scandinavian source (compare Old Icelandic *skāl* weighing scale, bowl, Swedish and Danish *skål* bowl, related to Old Icelandic *skel* SHELL). The Scandinavian words are cognate with Old Saxon *skāla* cup, bowl, Middle Dutch *scāle,* Dutch *schaal,* Old High German *skāla,* and modern German *Schale,* from Proto-Germanic **skǣlō.*

The meaning of a dish or pan of a balance is found in Middle English about 1390; this was followed by the meaning of a weighing instrument, balance (usually *scales*) in 1421-22.

—v. weigh. 1603 (figurative) to compare, estimate, in Shakespeare's *Measure for Measure;* from the noun. The meaning of weigh in scales is found in 1691.

scale[3] *n.* series of steps or degrees. 1391 *skale* series of marks along a line to use in measuring, in Chaucer's *Treatise on the Astrolabe;* borrowed from Latin *scālae,* pl., ladder, steps, (earlier **scandslai*), related to *scandere* to climb; see SCAN.

The meaning of a series of musical tones ascending or descending in pitch is found in 1597; the general sense of a series of steps or degrees is found in 1605. Another frequent meaning, that of the size of a map, etc., compared with what it represents, is first recorded in 1662. The figurative sense of a standard of measurement or estimation, especially in the phrase *on a large* (or *small*) *scale,* is found in Francis Bacon's *Sylva Sylvarum* (1626).

—v. Probably about 1380 *scathen* (error for *scalen*) climb up by means of a ladder; from the noun. The generalized sense of climb, ascend, mount, is found in Middle English before 1425. The technical sense of reduce according to a fixed scale is found in 1790, in American English.

scalene (skālēn′) *adj.* (of a triangle) having three unequal sides. 1684, (of a solid figure) having the axis inclined to the base; borrowed from Late Latin *scalēnus,* from Greek *skalēnós* uneven, unequal, rough, from *skállein* chop, hoe, related to *skélos* leg, and *skoliós* crooked, from Indo-European **skel-/skol-* bend (Pok.928). The meaning of having three unequal sides (referring to a triangle) is found in English in 1734.

scallion *n.* kind of onion. Before 1375 *scaloun* (figurative) something of little or no value; later *scalone* kind of onion (probably before 1387, in a version of *Piers Plowman*), and with the spelling *scalyon* (1483); borrowed from Anglo-French *scalun, escalone,* Old French *eschaloigne,* from Vulgar Latin **escalōnia,* from Latin *(caepa) Ascalōnia* (onion) from Ascalon a seaport in southwestern Palestine, on the Mediterranean (now Ashkelon, Israel). Compare SHALLOT.

scallop *n.* shellfish somewhat like a clam. Probably before 1400 *skalop* representation of a scallop shell; later *scalop* scallop, the shellfish (1440, in *Promptorium Parvulorum*); borrowed from Old French *escalope* variant of *eschalope,* probably from a Germanic source (compare Old Icelandic *skalpr* sheath, and Middle Dutch *schelpe* shell; see SCALP). The meaning of one of a series of curves along an edge is found in English in 1612, used in allusion to the edge of a scallop shell. **—v.** bake with sauce in a pan or scallop shell. 1737 (implied in *scollopt,* past participle); from the noun. The meaning of shape or cut out in the form of a scallop shell is first recorded in 1749.

scallopini (skal′əpē′nē) *n.pl.* thin slices of meat covered with flour and sautéed or broiled. 1957, alteration of earlier *scaloppine* (1950, in Hemingway's *Across the River and into the Trees*); borrowing of Italian *scaloppine,* plural of *scalopina* small thin slice, diminutive of *scaloppa* thin slice, from French *escalope,* from Middle French, shell (see SCALLOP); so called because the slices are often served curled up like shells.

scalp *n.* skin and hair on the head. About 1340 *skalp* top of the head; earlier as a surname (1201); borrowed from a Scandinavian source (compare Old Icelandic *skalpr* sheath, which is cognate with Middle Dutch *schelpe* shell, Dutch *schelp,* Middle Low German *schulpe,* and probably with Old High German *scala* husk, SHELL). The meaning of the skin and hair on the head is first recorded in 1601, in reference to the scalp cut off and used as a battle trophy or token of victory. **—v.** cut or tear the scalp from. 1676, from the noun. **—scalper** *n.* 1760, American English, Indian warrior who takes the scalp of an enemy; formed from English *scalp,* v. + *-er*[1]. The slang meaning of a person who obtains theater tickets, etc., and sells them at unauthorized prices, is found in 1869 in American English.

scalpel *n.* small knife used by surgeons. 1742, borrowed from Latin *scalpellum,* diminutive of *scalprum, scalper* (genitive *scalprī*) tool for scraping or cutting, knife, related to *scalpere* to carve, cut; see SHELF.

scam *n. Slang.* dishonest scheme, swindle. 1963, American English, a carnival term of unknown origin. **—v.** *Slang.* to cheat, defraud, swindle. 1963, American English, presumably from the same source as the noun.

scamp[1] *n.* worthless person, rascal, rogue. 1782, highway robber; probably from the earlier dialectal verb *scamp* to roam (1753), shortened from SCAMPER. The meaning of rascal, rogue, is first recorded in Jamieson's *Etymological Dictionary of the Scottish Language* (1808).

scamp[2] *v.* do in a hasty, careless manner. 1837, perhaps borrowed from a Scandinavian source (compare Old Icelandic *skemma* to shorten, from *skammr* short; see SCANT). The related meaning of be stingy, scrimp, is first recorded in 1894, in American English.

scamper *v.* run quickly. 1687, run away, flee; probably borrowed from Flemish *schampeeren,* a frequentative verb form of *schampen* run away, from Old French *escamper,* from Italian *scampare,* from Vulgar Latin **excampāre* decamp, leave the field, from the Latin phrase *ex campō* (*ex* out of; *campō,* ablative of *campus* field, CAMP[1]). The extended meaning of run quickly is first recorded in 1691 (implied in *scampering*). **—n.** quick run. 1697, from the verb.

scampi (skäm′pē) *n.pl.* shrimp dish. 1930, an Italian word used in Evelyn Waugh's *Labels;* plural of *scampo* a kind of lobster, of Venetian origin. The singular form *scampo* is first recorded in English in 1928.

scan *v.* look at closely. Before 1398 *scanden* to mark off (verse) into metric feet, in Trevisa's translation of Bartholomew's *De Proprietatibus Rerum;* later *scannen* (1440); borrowed from Latin *scandere* to scan verse; originally, to climb; cognate with Middle Irish *scendim* I leap, Greek *skándalon* stumbling block, trap, and Sanskrit *skāndati* he leaps, from Indo-European **skand-* (Walde-Hofmann, *Lateinisches Etymologisches Wörterbuch,* II 488).

The extended sense of look at closely, examine minutely, is first recorded in English in 1550. The opposite sense of look over quickly, skim, is found in 1926. **—n.** act or fact of scanning. 1706, from the verb.

scandal *n.* 1581, discredit to religion caused by irreligious conduct; borrowed from Middle French *scandale,* learned borrowing from Late Latin *scandalum* cause for offense, stumbling block, temptation, from Greek *skándalon* stumbling block; originally, trap with a springing device; see SCAN. Doublet of SLANDER. The meaning of damage to reputation is first recorded in Shakespeare's *Comedy of Errors* (1590), and that of a shameful action or event that brings disgrace is found in Shakespeare's *1 Henry VI* (1591).

The forms *scandle* and *schaundle* are recorded in Middle English, in manuscripts of *Ancrene Riwle* (probably about 1200), borrowed from Old French *escandele, escandle* scandal, from Late Latin *scandalum.* The current form is a reborrowing from Middle French.

—scandalize *v.* About 1489, make a public scandal of, in Caxton's translation of *Blanchardyn and Eglantine;* borrowed from Middle French *scandaliser,* from Late Latin *scandalizāre* tempt, cause to stumble, from Greek *skandalízein,* from *skándalon* stumbling block. The meaning of shock or horrify by doing something immoral or improper is first recorded in 1647. **—scandalous** *adj.* About 1475 *standalouse* (error for *scandalouse*) disgraceful, shameful; borrowed from Middle French *scandaleux,* from Late Latin *scandalum* temptation.

scandium (skan′dēəm) *n.* metallic chemical element. 1879, New Latin, formed from Latin *Scandia* Scandinavia + New Latin *-ium,* chemical suffix; so called because scandium is found in various minerals in Scandinavia. The term was coined by its discoverer, the Swedish physicist Lars F. Nilson.

scansion (skan′shən) *n.* the marking off of lines of poetry into feet. 1671, in Phillips' *Dictionary* (in 1654, act of climbing); borrowed from Late Latin *scānsiōnem* (nominative *scānsiō*), from Latin, act of climbing, from *scandere* to climb; see SCAN; for suffix see -SION.

scant *adj.* meager, poor. Probably before 1350, borrowed from a Scandinavian source (compare Old Icelandic *skamt,* neuter of *skammr* short, brief, Icelandic *skammur*). The Scandinavian words are cognate with Old English and Old High German *scamm* short, Old High German *hamm, hammēr* mutilated, Old English *hamola* mutilated man, and probably with Sanskrit *śámala-m* flaw, fault, injury, from Indo-European **(s)k̑em-/(s)k̑om-* curtailed (Pok.929). **—v.** About 1415 *scanten* become scant, in a version of Chaucer's *Canterbury Tales;* from the adjective. The meaning of limit the supply of, withhold, is found in 1573-80. **—scanty** *adj.* 1660, formed from English *scant,* adj. + *-y*[1]. *—n. Informal.* Usually **scanties** *pl.* underwear, panties. 1928, American English; from the adjective.

scantling *n.* small piece or portion, modicum. 1526, measured or prescribed size, as of timber or stone, dimension; alteration (by influence of words ending in *-ling*) of Middle English *scantiloun, scantlon* carpenter's or mason's tool for measuring thickness, gauge (about 1250); borrowed from Old French *escantillon, eschantillon,* alteration of **eschandillon* (compare Old Provençal *escandalh*) mason's gauge or measure, standard of measure, from Vulgar Latin **scandāculum* kind of measure, from Latin *scandere* to climb, scale, measure off (verse); see SCAN. The extended meaning of small measure, portion, or amount, modicum, is first recorded in 1585, followed by the sense of a small beam or piece of timber, in 1663.

-scape a combining form meaning scene, picture, view, as in *seascape, moonscape;* abstracted from LANDSCAPE. The first attested use of the combining form is in the compound *prison-scape,* which appeared in 1796, in Charlotte Smith's novel *Marchmont.*

scapegoat *n.* 1530, a goat chosen by lot to be sent into the wilderness on the Day of Atonement as the symbolic bearer of the sins of the people; literally, a goat that escapes, in the Tyndale Bible; formed from English *scape,* n., a shortened variant of ESCAPE + *goat.*

Scapegoat was coined by Tyndale to express what he believed to be the literal meaning of Hebrew *'azāzēl* (Leviticus 16:8, 10, 26), which he interpreted as *'ēz ōzēl* goat that departs; the same interpretation is found in the Vulgate's *caper emissarius* (translated into French as *bouc émissaire*) and in the rendering "the free goat" in the Coverdale Bible (1535). The Hebrew word is actually a proper name, perhaps a place name, of uncertain derivation; in Jewish tradition it is thought to be the name of a demon or devil, and some scholars have correlated the name with that of the Canaanite deity *Aziz.*

The transferred and now ordinary sense of one who is blamed or punished for the mistakes or sins of others is first recorded in 1824.

—v. make a scapegoat of. 1943 (technical term in psychology); from the noun.

scapegrace *n.* reckless, good-for-nothing person. 1809, formed from English *scape,* v., shortened variant of ESCAPE + *grace,* the literal sense being that of one who escapes the grace of God. Possibly influenced in formation by *scapegoat,* but compare the similar older formation *scapethryft* (before 1460) a spendthrift, and *want-grace* (1603) a reprobate or scoundrel.

scapula (skap′yələ) *n.* shoulder blade. 1578, in John Banister's *The History of Man;* New Latin, from Late Latin *scapula* shoulder, from Latin *scapulae,* pl., shoulders, shoulder blades; perhaps originally, spades, shovels; probably so called from the similarity in shape to a spade. Latin *scapulae* is perhaps cognate with Greek *skáptein* dig out; see CAPON.

scar *n.* About 1395 *scar* mark left by a healed wound, burn, etc., in the Wycliffe Bible; borrowed from Old French *escare* scab, and Medieval Latin *escara;* both from Late Latin *eschara,* from Greek *eschárā* scab formed after a burn, hearth, fireplace; of uncertain origin. **—v.** to mark with a scar. 1555, from the noun.

scarab (skar′əb) *n.* beetle, especially the sacred beetle of the ancient Egyptians. 1579, borrowed from Middle French *scarabée,* learned borrowing from Latin *scarabaeus* a beetle, from Greek *kárabos* beetle, crayfish, a word perhaps borrowed from Macedonian.

scaramouch or **scaramouche** (skar′əmüsh *or* skar′əmouch) *n.* cowardly braggart. 1662 *Scaramuzza;* later, *Scaramouch* (1677); name of a cowardly braggart in traditional Italian comedy; borrowed from French *Scaramouche,* from Italian *Scaramuccia,* from *scaramuccia* skirmish, from *schermire* to fence, from a Germanic source (compare Old High German *skirmen* defend; see SKIRMISH). Use of the name as a general term meaning cowardly braggart, rascal, scamp, is first recorded in English in 1676.

scarce *adj.* About 1300 *scars* not abundant, scant, meager; later *scarce* (probably before 1400); borrowed from Old North French *scars, escars,* Old French *eschars.* The Old North French and Old French forms developed from Vulgar Latin **excarpsus* made scant literally, plucked out, from past participle of **excarpere* pluck out, alteration of Latin *excerpere* pluck out select out, EXCERPT. **—adv.** Before 1325 *scarse;* from the adjective. **—scarcity** *n.* Probably before 1300 *scar* *sete;* borrowed from Old North French *escarseté,* from *escars* scarce, adj.; for suffix see -ITY.

scare *v.* 1591, in Shakespeare's *1 Henry VI;* alteration of Middle English *skerren* to frighten (probably about 1200, in *The Ormulum*); borrowed from a Scandinavian source (compare Old Icelandic *skirra* to frighten, from *skjarr* timid, shy, of uncertain origin).

The informal phrase *scare up,* originally meaning to frighten (game) out of cover, hence to bring to light, produce, procure, obtain, is first recorded in 1846, in American English.

—n. Before 1548; alteration of Middle English *sker* fear, dread (probably before 1400, in *The Wars of Alexander*); from the verb.

—scarecrow *n.* 1553, person employed in scaring birds; later, figure used to scare birds (1592). **—scary** *adj.* 1582, terrifying, frightful, in a translation of Vergil's *Aeneid;* formed from English *scare,* n. + *-y*[1].

scarf[1] *n.* strip of cloth worn about the neck. 1555, variant of *scarp* a kind of heraldic stripe; borrowed from Old North French *escarpe* sash, sling. The Old North French word is a dialect variant of Old French *escherpe* pilgrim's purse suspended from the neck, from Frankish **skirpja* little bag woven of rushes, from Latin *scirpus* rush, bulrush, of uncertain origin.

The original English plural form *scarfs* was altered from the beginning of the 1700's to *scarves* on the analogy of *halves,* etc. This is the only known noun of non-native origin that has undergone the change from *f* to *v* in the plural, though the original plural *scarfs* is still widely used.

scarf[2] *n.* joint connecting beams firmly. 1276, in the compound *scarfneil* nail for fastening a scarf joint; probably borrowed from a Scandinavian source (compare Swedish *skarv* scarf, seam, and Old Icelandic *skarfr).* The Scandinavian words are cognate with Old High German *scarbōn* cut into pieces, Middle Low German *scharven,* Old English *scearfian* scrape off, and *sceorfan* to gnaw, bite, from Proto-Germanic **skerf-/skarf-,* Indo-European **skerp-/skorp-* (Pok. 944). **—v.** joint with a scarf. 1627, in Captain John Smith's *The Seaman's Grammar;* from the noun.

scarify (skar′əfī) *v.* make scratches or cuts in the surface of the skin, etc. 1392 *scarifien;* borrowed from Middle French *scarifier,* learned borrowing from Late Latin *scarīficāre,* alteration (through influence of the suffix *-ficāre* -fy) of Latin *scarīfāre, scarīphāre* scratch open, from Greek *skarīphâsthai* to scratch an outline, sketch; see SCRIBE; for suffix see -FY. **—scarification** *n.* 1392 *scarificacioun;* borrowed from Late Latin *scarīficātiōnem* (nominative *scarīficātiō*) a scratching open, from *scarīficāre* scarify; for suffix see -ATION.

scarlet *n.* bright red color. About 1250 *scarlet* bright red cloth; later *scarlat* bright red color (about 1300); borrowed through Old French *escarlate,* or directly from Medieval Latin *scarlatum, scarlata* scarlet, a cloth of scarlet, from Persian *saqirlāt,* variant of *siqillāt* scarlet cloth, rich cloth, from Arabic *siqillāṭ* fine cloth. **—adj.** About 1300 *scarlat* of scarlet color; from the noun. **—scarlet fever** (1676)

scarp *n.* steep slope. 1589, inner slope of a ditch surrounding a fortification; borrowed from Italian *scarpa* slope, probably from a Germanic source (compare German *schroff* steep, Middle High German *schroffe* sharp rock, crag, and Old High German *screvōn* to cut into, which are cognate with Old Icelandic *skref* step, pace, Middle Low German *schreve* line, stroke, Middle Dutch *scrēve,* and Old English *scræf* cave, grave, related to *scearfian* scrape off; see SCARF[2] joint). **—v.** make into a scarp. 1803, in Wellington's *Letters;* from the noun.

scat[1] *interj., v. Informal.* go away! 1838 *'scat, scat,* American English, also earlier *s'cat* in the expression *quicker than s'cat* in a great hurry (1833), possibly representing a hiss followed by the word *cat,* used in driving away cats.

scat[2] *n.* nonsense chatter and sounds sung to jazz music. 1929, American English; probably of imitative origin. **—v.** to sing scat. 1935, American English; from the noun.

scathe *v.* Probably about 1200 *scathen* to hurt, damage, in *The Ormulum;* borrowed from a Scandinavian source (compare Old Icelandic *skadha* to hurt, injure, Swedish *skada,* and Danish *skade;* these forms are cognate with Old English *sceathian* to hurt, injure, Old Frisian *skethia,* Old Saxon *skathon,* Middle Dutch *scāden* (modern Dutch *schaden*), Old High German *scadōn* (modern German *schaden*), and Gothic *skathjan* (with past tense *skōth*), from Proto-Germanic **skath-,* which is cognate with Greek *a-skēthḗs* unharmed, from Indo-European **skēth-/skəth-/skōth-* (Pok.950).

The figurative meaning of blast or sear with abuse, invective, or satire, usually found now in the participial adjective *scathing,* is first recorded in English in 1852, from the earlier literal sense of scar, scorch, found in Milton's *Paradise Lost* (1667).

scatology *n.* obscene literature. 1876, formed in English from Greek *skat-,* stem of *skôr* (genitive *skatós,* earlier **skr̥tós*) excrement + connective *-o-* + English *-logy* treatise, study. Greek *skôr* is cognate with Old Slavic *skarędŭ* loathsome, Hittite *sakkar,* genitive *saknas* dung; also in Germanic with Old Icelandic *skarn,* Old Frisian *skern,* and Old English *scearn,* all meaning dung, from Indo-European **sker-/skor-/skōr-,* with alternate stem **sken-/skn-* (Pok.947). **—scatological** *adj.* 1924, formed from English *scatology* + *-ical.*

scatter *v.* Probably before 1160 *scateren* distribute, squander; later, disperse, separate (about 1300); possibly a northern English variant of Middle English *schateren* to SHATTER. **—n.** act or fact of scattering. 1642, from the verb. **—scatter-brain** *n.* (1790) **—scatter-brained** *adj.* (1804)

scavenger *n.* 1530, in Palsgrave's *Lesclarcissement,* person hired to remove refuse from streets, alteration of Middle English *scawageour* (1373), *scavager* (1477-79) an inspector in charge of collecting a toll or duty on goods for sale. Middle English *scawageour* was borrowed from Anglo-French *scawager,* from *scawage* toll or duty on goods, from Old North French *escauwage* inspection, from *escauwer* to inspect, from a Germanic source (compare Flemish *scauwen* to inspect, cognate with Old English *scēawian* to look at, examine, inspect; see SHOW).

In the 1500's a sound represented by *n* developed before the final syllable of scavenger as is found in some other words, including *harbinger* and *passenger* (compare MESSENGER).

The figurative sense of a person who collects or searches through refuse to collect things is found in 1562. By 1596 *scavenger* was applied to anyone who removed refuse or putrid matter, and especially to any animal feeding on decaying matter.

—scavenge *v.* Before 1644, to remove refuse; back formation from *scavenger.* The meaning of pick over (discarded objects) for things to use is first recorded in Joyce's *Ulysses* (1922). **—scavenger hunt** (1930's, American English)

scenario (sinãr′ēō) *n.* outline of a motion picture, play, etc. 1878, borrowing of Italian *scenario,* from *scena* scene, from Latin *scaena, scēna* SCENE. The figurative sense of an outline of an imagined situation or chain of events is first recorded in Herman Kahn's *Thinking About the Unthinkable* (1962). **—scenarist** *n.* one who writes motion-picture scenarios. 1920, American English; formed from English *scenario* + *-ist.*

scene *n.* 1540, part of an act of a play; also, stage scenery; borrowed from Middle French *scène,* learned borrowing from Latin, and borrowed directly from Latin *scaena, scēna* scene, stage, from Greek *skēnḗ* scene, stage; originally, tent or booth, which is cognate with Persian *sāya* shadow, protection, Sanskrit *chāyā́* shadow; see SHINE. **—scenery** *n.* 1748, dramatic action or display of feeling, in Richardson's *Clarissa;* alteration (influenced by words in *-ery*) of earlier *scenary* scenario (1695); borrowed from Italian *scenario* SCENARIO. The meaning of painted objects used on a stage to represent places is found in 1774, but first recorded in figurative use, 1770. The meaning of natural features of a landscape is first recorded in 1784. **—scenic** *adj.* 1623, dramatic, theatrical; borrowed from French *scénique,* and probably directly from Latin *scēnicus, scaenicus,* from Greek *skēnikós,* from *skēnḗ* scene; for suffix see -IC. The meaning of having to do with natural scenery is first recorded in Dickens' *American Notes* (1842).

scent *v.* find or detect by smell. Before 1398 *senten* to feel, in Trevisa's translation of Bartholomew's *De Proprietatibus Rerum;* later, perceive by smell (about 1410, in *The Master of Game*); borrowed from Old French *sentir* to feel, perceive, smell, from Latin *sentīre* to feel, perceive; see SENSE. **—n.** 1375, odor or smell as a means of pursuit by a hound, in John Barbour's *The Bruce;* probably from the verb, although attested somewhat earlier. The spelling *scent* (for both the verb and noun) did not appear until the 1600's, perhaps by mistaken analogy with *ascent, descent,* but compare the more closely related forms *assent, consent, dissent.*

scepter *n.* rod or staff carried by a ruler. Probably before 1300 *ceptre,* in *Kyng Alisaunder;* later *sceptre* (before 1393); borrowed from Old French *sceptre,* learned borrowing from Latin *scēptrum,* from Greek *skêptron* staff; see SHAFT. **—v.** furnish with a scepter. 1526, from the noun.

sceptic *n.* See SKEPTIC.

schedule *n.* 1397 *sedule* written document; later, appendix to a document (about 1420), and with the spelling *cedule* (1403-04); borrowed from Old French *cedule,* learned borrowing from Late Latin *schedula* strip of paper, diminutive of Latin *schida, scida* one of the strips forming a papyrus sheet, from Greek *schida* perhaps related to *schízein* to split; see SHED² cast off.

The spelling *schedule* was introduced in English in the 1400's, in imitation of the Latin form, and became established by the mid-1600's. The original pronunciation (sed′yül) remained in use long after the change in spelling, but during the 1800's the influence of the French pronunciation of certain words spelled *sch-* caused (shed′yül) to become the standard pronunciation in Great Britain. At the same time in the United States, the practice of Webster caused the pronunciation with *sk* (skej′ůl), patterned on that of *school, scheme,* etc., to become acceptable.

The specific sense of a printed timetable of arrivals and departures of trains, etc., is first recorded in 1863, in American English.
—v. 1855, file a schedule; later, enter in a schedule (1862); American English; from the noun.

schema (skē′mə) *n.* 1796, (in Kant's philosophy) representation produced by the imagination in the process of organizing experience, borrowing of Latin *schēma* shape, figure, form, from Greek *schêma;* see SCHEME. The meaning of a generalized outline, design, or diagram, is first recorded in 1890.

scheme *n.* 1553, figure of speech; borrowed from Latin *schēma* shape, figure, form, from Greek *schêma* (genitive *schḗmatos*) figure or appearance, related to *scheîn* to get, *échein* to have, hold. The Greek words are cognate with Sanskrit *sáhas* strength, victory, from Indo-European **seĝhos* (Pok.888), and in Germanic with Gothic *sigis* victory, Old Icelandic *sigr,* Old High German *sigu* (modern German *Sieg*), Middle Dutch *sēghe* (modern Dutch *zege*), Old Frisian *sī,* and Old English *sige* victory, from Proto-Germanic **seʒiz,* substituted for earlier **seʒaz.* The meaning of an astrological diagram is first recorded in 1610, and that of a program of action, plan, in 1647. **—v.** 1716, reduce to a scheme; later, devise a scheme (1767); from the noun. **—schematic** *adj.* having to do with or like a scheme. 1701, borrowed from New Latin *schematicus,* from Latin *schēma* (genitive *schēmatis*) shape, form.

scherzo (sker′tsō) *n.* fast, playful movement of a musical work. 1852, borrowed from Italian *scherzo,* literally, sport or joke, from *scherzare* to jest or joke, from a Germanic source (compare Middle High German *scherzen* to jump merrily, enjoy oneself, modern German *scherzen* to jest, related to Old High German *scern* to jest, joke; see SCORN).

Schick test (shik) test to determine susceptibility to diphtheria. 1916, from the name of the Hungarian-born American pediatrician Béla *Schick,* who developed the test.

schism (siz′əm *or* skiz′əm) *n.* division, cleavage, split. About 1384 *scisme* dissension within the church, in the Wycliffe Bible; borrowed from Old French *scisme* a cleft, split, learned borrowing from Late Latin *schisma,* from Greek *schísma* (genitive *schísmatos*) division, cleft, from *schízein* to split; see SHED² cast off. The spelling *schism* was a restoration of the Latin form appearing in the 1550's but not fully established until the late 1600's. **—schismatic** *adj.* 1456 *scismattike* guilty of participating in a religious schism; borrowed from Middle French *scismatique,* from Late Latin *schismaticus,* from Latin *schisma* schism; for suffix see -IC. **—n.** About 1378 *scismatik* person who participates in a religious schism, in a version of *Piers Plowman;* borrowed from Old French *scismatique,* from Late Latin *schismaticus* noun use of *schismaticus,* adj.

schist (shist) *n.* kind of metamorphic rock. 1795, borrowed from French *schiste,* learned borrowing from Latin *schistos lapis* stone that splits easily, from Greek *schistós* divided, separated, from *schízein* to split (see SHED² cast off); so called because schist splits easily into layers.

schistosome (shis′təsōm) *n.* kind of parasitic worm. 1905, borrowed from New Latin *Schistosoma* the genus name, from Greek *schistós* divided; see SCHIST + *sôma* body, -some[3]. **—schistosomiasis** (shis′təsōmī′əsis) *n.* disease caused by a schistosome. 1906, New Latin, from *Schistosoma* + *-iasis* diseased condition.

schizo (skit′sō *or* skiz′ō) *n. Informal.* a schizophrenic. 1945, shortened form of *schizophrenic.* **—adj.** *Informal.* schizophrenic. 1957, from the noun.

schizo- a combining form meaning split, division, cleavage, as in *schizogenesis* (reproduction by cleavage), *schizophrenia.* Also, *schiz-* before vowels. New Latin, from Greek *schizo-, schiz-* split, from *schízein* to split; see SHED[2] cast off.

schizoid (skit′soid *or* skiz′oid) *adj.* resembling or tending toward schizophrenia. 1925, borrowed from German *schizoid;* formed from German *Schizo(phrenie)* schizophrenia + *-oid* resembling, like; coined in 1921 by the German psychiatrist Ernst Kretschmer. **—n.** schizoid person. 1925, borrowed from German *Schizoid,* from the noun.

schizophrenia (skit′səfrē′nēə) *n.* form of psychosis characterized by dissociation from the environment, split personality. 1912, New Latin, from Greek *schizo-* split + *phrḗn* (genitive *phrenós*) mind; see FRENETIC + the New Latin suffix *-ia* disordered condition, disease. The word was coined in German in 1910 as *Schizophrenie* by the German psychiatrist Eugen Bleuler. **—schizophrenic** *adj.* 1912, of or having to do with schizophrenia, formed from English *schizophrenia* + *-ic.* **—n.** schizophrenic person. 1926, from the adjective.

schlemiel (shləmēl′) *n. Slang.* clumsy person, bungler. 1892, in Israel Zangwill's *Children of the Ghetto,* American English; borrowed from Yiddish *shlemiel,* probably from the Biblical name of *Shelumiel* chief of the tribe of Simeon (Numbers 7:36), identified in the Talmud with the Simeonite prince Zimri ben Salu, who was killed while committing adultery with a Midianite woman (Numbers 25:6-15).

schlepp or **schlep** (shlep) *v. Slang.* to move with difficulty, drag. 1922, in Joyce's *Ulysses;* borrowed from Yiddish *shlepn* to drag, from Middle High German *sleppen* (modern German *schleppen*), related to Old High German *sleifen* to drag, and *slīfan* to slide, SLIP[1]. **—n.** *Slang.* stupid, awkward, or slovenly person. 1939, American English; borrowed from Yiddish *shlep* a bore, a drag, from *shlepn* to drag.

schlock or **shlock** (shlok) *n. Slang.* cheap or inferior material, junk. 1915, American English; borrowed from American Yiddish *shlak,* possibly from Yiddish *shlak* a stroke, blow, curse (from Middle High German *slag,* from Old High German, from *slahan* to strike, SLAY), but more likely an American Yiddish borrowing of German *Schlacke* dregs, scum, dross, SLAG. **—adj.** *Slang.* cheap, inferior, junky. 1916, American English; from the noun.

schmaltz (shmälts) *n. Slang.* cloying sentimentality, especially in music, art, etc. 1935, American English; borrowed from Yiddish *shmalts,* literally, melted fat, from Middle High German *smalz,* from Old High German, related to *smelzan* to melt; see SMELT. Modern German *Schmalz* fat, grease, has the same figurative meaning. **—v.** *Slang.* make cloyingly sentimental. 1936, American English; from the noun. **—schmaltzy** *adj. Slang.* of or characterized by schmaltz. 1935, American English; formed from *schmaltz* + *-y*[1].

schmear (shmir) *n. Slang.* bribery, graft. 1961, American English (show business jargon); borrowed from Yiddish *shmir* spread, from *shmirn* to smear, grease, from Middle High German *smiren,* from Old High German *smirwen* to SMEAR. The slang phrase *the whole schmear,* meaning the whole business or affair, is found in 1962 in American English.

schmo (shmō) *n. Slang.* silly person, fool. 1948, American English; probably euphemistic alteration of Yiddish slang *shmok* fool, jerk, penis, probably from Polish *smok* grass snake.

schmooze or **schmoose** (shmüz) *v. Slang.* to talk idly, chat. 1897, American English; borrowed from Yiddish *shmuesn* to chat, from *shmues* idle talk, chat, from Hebrew *shĕmu'ōth* news, rumors, plural of *shĕmu'āh* report, rumor, from *shāmō'a* to listen, hear. **—n.** *Slang.* idle talk, chat. 1939, American English; borrowed from Yiddish *shmues* chat.

schnapps or **schnaps** (shnäps) *n.* alcoholic liquor. 1818, borrowing of German *Schnaps,* originally, a mouthful, gulp, from Low German *snaps,* from *snappen* to snap; see SNAP.

schnauzer (shnou′zər) *n.* wire-haired German terrier. 1923, borrowing of German *Schnauzer,* from *Schnauze* SNOUT.

schnitzel (shnit′səl) *n.* veal cutlet. 1854, American English; borrowing of German *Schnitzel* cutlet, slice, formed from *Schnitz* a cut, slice + *-el,* diminutive suffix. German *Schnitz* is from *schnitzen* to carve, a frequentative form of *schneiden* to cut, from Old High German *snīdan,* which is cognate with Gothic *sneithan* to cut, Old Icelandic *snīdha,* Middle Dutch *sniden* (modern Dutch *snijden*), Old Saxon *snīthan,* Old Frisian *snītha,* and Old English *snīthan* to cut, from Proto-Germanic **snīthanan,* Indo-European **sneit-* (Pok. 974).

schnook (shnu̇k) *n. Slang.* simple or stupid person. 1948, in Mencken's *The American Language,* American English; probably borrowed from Yiddish *shnuk* elephant's trunk, snout, of uncertain origin. It is also possible that the word was borrowed from or influenced by German *Schnucke* small sheep.

scholar *n.* About 1300 *scholer, scoler* learned person; developed from Old English (about 1000) *scolere, scoliere* student; borrowed from Medieval Latin *scholaris,* from Late Latin *scholāris* of a school, from Latin *schola* place of instruction; see SCHOOL[1]; for suffix see -AR. **—scholarship** *n.* 1535-36, status or position of a scholar, formed from English *scholar* + *-ship.* The meaning of learning, erudition, is first recorded in 1589.

scholastic (skəlas′tik) *adj.* of schools, scholars, or education, academic. 1596, of or relating to scholasticism; probably replacing earlier *scolasticalle* (probably before 1425); borrowed from Middle French *scholastique,* or directly from Medieval Latin *scholasticus,* from Latin *scholasticus* of a school, learned, from Greek *scholastikós* studious, learned, from *scholázein* be a scholar, devote one's leisure to learning, from *scholḗ* place of instruction, see SCHOOL[1]; for suffix see -IC. The meaning of having to do with schools, scholars, or education is first recorded in 1647. **—n.** Often, **Scholastic.** adherent of scholasticism. 1644, in Milton's *Doctrine and Discipline of Divorce;* borrowed from Medieval Latin *scholasticus* scholar, learned man, noun use of *scholasticus* of school, learned, adj. **—scholasticism** *n.* 1756-82, theological and philosophical teaching in the Middle Ages, based on the authority of the church fathers and of Aristotle; formed from English *scholastic* + *-ism.*

school[1] *n.* place of instruction. Probably before 1200 *scole,* in *Ancrene Riwle* and Layamon's *Chronicle of Britain;* developed from Old English *scōl* (before 899, in Alfred's translation of Bede's *Ecclesiastical History*); borrowed from Latin *schola,* from Greek *scholḗ* school, lecture, discussion, leisure; originally, a holding back, a keeping clear, formed from *scheîn* to get (*échein* to have, hold) by the addition of *-olḗ* through analogy with *bolḗ* a throw, *stolḗ* outfit, etc.; see SCHEME.

The sense of a group of people united by general similarity of principles and methods is first recorded in Bacon's *Essays* (1612).

—v. About 1425 *skolen* to study at a university, in a version of Chaucer's *Canterbury Tales;* later *scolen* to instruct, teach (about 1445); from the noun. An earlier Middle English verb *scoleyen* to study at school (about 1387-95, in Chaucer's *Canterbury Tales*) was probably borrowed from Anglo-French **escoleier,* from Old French *escole* school, from Latin *schola.*

—school board (1836) **—schoolbook** *n.* (1751) **—schoolboy** *n.* (1588, in Shakespeare's *Love's Labour's Lost*) **—school bus** (1908, American English) **—school district** (1809, American English) **—schoolgirl** *n.* (1809) **—schoolhouse** *n.* (1429) **—schooling** *n.* (about 1449) **—schoolroom** *n.* (1773) **—schoolteacher** *n.* (before 1847) **—schoolwork** *n.* (1857) **—schoolyard** *n.* (1870, in writings of Emerson) **—school year** (1857)

school[2] *n.* group of the same kind of fish. About 1400 *scole;* earlier *scoue* (1386); borrowed from Middle Dutch *schole* group of fish or other animals, multitude. Middle Dutch *schole* is cognate with Old English *scolu* band, troop, school of fish; see SHOAL[2] crowd.

schooner (skü'nər) *n.* ship with two or more masts. 1716 *skooner,* American English, of uncertain origin. The respelling of *schooner,* first recorded in 1721, was probably influenced by the spelling of Dutch words beginning with *sch.* Apparently first built in England in the 1600's, the ship became a popular working craft in American waters after early construction in the Gloucester area of Massachusetts about 1713. Since then, the word has passed from English into most of the European languages: Dutch *schoener,* German *Schoner,* French *schooner,* Swedish *skonare, skonert,* etc. Early association of the word with English words **scoon, *scun* to skim over the water, seems to have no basis in fact.

schottische (shot'ish) *n.* dance somewhat like the polka. 1849, borrowing of German *Schottische,* from *schottisch* Scottish, from *Schotte* a native of Scotland, from Old High German *Scotto,* from Late Latin *Scottus* member of an Irish tribe (one which invaded Scotland after the Romans left Britain in 423).

schtik *n.* See SHTICK.

schuss (shůs) *n.* (in skiing) fast run down a straight course. 1937, borrowing of German *Schuss,* literally, SHOT. **—v.** to make a schuss in skiing. 1937, from the noun.

schwa (shwä) *n.* unstressed vowel sound. 1818 *sheva;* earlier *Scheua* (1582); the modern form *schwa* is a borrowing of German *Schwa,* and both the German and earlier English forms are borrowed from Hebrew *shĕwā* emptiness, in reference to the lack of any vowel sound or to a neutral vowel quality.

sciatic (sīat'ik) *adj.* 1547, borrowed from Middle French *sciatique* of or affecting the hip, from Medieval Latin *sciaticus,* alteration of Latin *ischiadicus* of pain in the hip, from Greek *ischiadikós,* from *ischiás* (genitive *ischiádos*) pain in the hips, from *ischíon* hip joint, of uncertain origin; for suffix see -IC. **—sciatica** (sīat'əkə) *n.* pain in a sciatic nerve and its branches. Before 1400, in Lanfranc's *Science of Surgery;* borrowed from Medieval Latin *sciatica,* found in *sciatica passio* sciatic disease, feminine of *sciaticus* sciatic.

science *n.* About 1340 *science* knowledge, branch of learning, skill; borrowed from Old French *science,* learned borrowing from Latin *scientia* knowledge, from *sciēns* (genitive *scientis*), present participle of *scīre* to know, perhaps originally meaning to separate, divide, related to *scindere* to cut, split; see SHED[2] cast off; for suffix see -ENCE. The modern restricted sense of a branch of learning based on observation and tested truths, arranged in an orderly system, is first recorded in English in Isaac Watt's *Logic* (1725), developed from the sense of a particular branch of knowledge (logic, grammar, rhetoric, music, arithmetic, geometry, astronomy) as distinguished from art (1678, and related to the earlier sense of a recognized branch of learning, before 1376, in *Piers Plowman*). **—science fiction** (1851, though not in general use until the 1920's) **—science park** (1970, American English)

scientific *adj.* 1589, concerned with science or the sciences; borrowed from Middle French *scientifique,* or directly from Medieval Latin *scientificus,* from Latin *scientia* knowledge; see SCIENCE + *-ficus* making, from *facere* to make, perform, DO[1]. **—scientist** *n.* 1834, formed in English from Latin *scientia* knowledge + English *-ist.* The OED remarks on the late appearance of *scientific* in English in view of the fact that the Latin *scientificus* was used as early as the 1200's in a translation of Aristotle's *Ethics* and later by Aquinas, Dante (Italian *scientifico*) and Oresme, founder of French scientific terminology.

sci-fi (sī'fī') *n. Informal.* 1955, acronym formed from English *sci(ence*), *fi(ction),* patterned on *hi-fi.* **—adj.** of or relating to science fiction. 1957, from the noun.

scimitar (sim'ətər) *n.* Before 1548 *cimiterie* short, curved sword; borrowed from Middle French *cimeterre,* and from Italian *scimitarra,* of uncertain origin (perhaps from Persian *shimshīr*). The spelling *scimitar,* first found in 1562, was influenced by the Italian form of the word.

scintilla (sintil'ə) *n.* particle, trace. 1692, borrowing of Latin *scintilla* particle of fire, spark, glittering speck, of uncertain origin.

scintillate (sin'təlāt) *v.* to sparkle, flash, twinkle. 1623, in Cockeram's *Dictionary;* formed as if from Latin **scintillātum,* from past participle of *scintillāre* to sparkle, from *scintilla* spark; for suffix see -ATE[1]. **—scintillation** *n.* 1623, borrowed from French, or directly from Latin *scintillātiōnem* (nominative *scintillātiō*), from *scintillāre;* for suffix see -TION.

sciolism (sī'əliz'əm) *n.* superficial knowledge. 1816, in Coleridge's *The Statesman's Manual;* probably formed in English after *sciolist* with the English suffix *-ism.* **—sciolist** *n.* superficial pretender to knowledge. 1615 in Brathwait's *A Strappado for the Divell;* formed in English from Late Latin *sciolus* one who knows a little diminutive of *scius* knowing, from *scīre* to know; see SCIENCE + English suffix *-ist.*

scion (sī'ən) *n.* bud or branch cut for grafting. Before

1300 *sioun;* later *scyoun* (before 1398); borrowed from Old French *sion, cion,* of uncertain origin (attributed to sources of Germanic origin or an alteration from French *scier* to saw, none of which can fulfill the necessary shifts in form to be convincing sources). The transferred meaning of an heir or descendant appeared in 1814.

scissors *n.pl.* About 1380 *sisoures* cutting tool, in Chaucer's *House of Fame;* borrowed from Old French *cisoires,* pl., from Vulgar Latin **cīsōria,* pl., from **cīsus,* abstracted from such compounds as Latin *excīsus,* past participle of *excīdere* to cut out; see EXCISE² cut; for suffix see -OR². The spelling with *sc-* is first recorded in the 1500's, influenced by Medieval Latin *scissor* tailor, from Latin, carver, cutter, from *sciss-,* past participle stem of *scindere* to split; see SHED² cast off. **—scissor** *v.* to cut with scissors. 1612, back formation from *scissors.*

sclerosis (sklirō'sis) *n.* hardening of tissue. 1392 *scliro-sus;* before 1400 *sclirosis;* borrowed from Medieval Latin *sclirosis* a hardness, hard tumor, from Greek *sklḗrōsis* hardening, from *sklērós* hard; see SKELETON; for suffix see -OSIS. **—sclerotic** *adj.* Probably before 1425 *sclyrotyk* hard, in a translation of Chauliac's *Grande Chirurgie;* borrowed from Medieval Latin *scliroticus* hard, from Greek *sklēroûn* to harden, from *sklērós* hard; for suffix see -IC.

scoff *v.* make fun of, mock. Probably before 1300 *scoffen* jest, make light of something, in *Kyng Alisaunder;* later *skoffen* make fun of, mock (about 1450); from earlier *scof* something trivial or ridiculous (before 1300), a jibe, mockery (1340); perhaps borrowed from Scandinavian **skof* (compare Old Icelandic *skaup, skop* mockery, and early modern Danish *skuf, skof* jest, mockery, *skuffe* to deceive, frustrate, (earlier) to mock, ridicule). The Scandinavian words are cognate with Old High German *scopf, scof* mockery, (also) poet, Middle Dutch *schop* mockery, Old Saxon and Old English *scop* poet, of unknown origin. For another example of semantic connection between poetry and derision, see SCOLD.

scofflaw (skôf'lô') *n. Informal.* person who disregards or flouts the law. 1924, American English, formed from *scoff,* v. + *law.*

Scofflaw was the winning entry in a national contest held during Prohibition to coin a word characterizing a person who drinks illegally. It fell out of use after Prohibition, but was revived in the 1950's in its more general sense.

scold *n.* Probably about 1150 *scold* ribald or abusive person; later *skald* (before 1325); probably borrowed from a Scandinavian source (compare Old Icelandic *skāld* poet, SKALD, probably in the sense of one who lampoons, indicated in *skāldskapr* poetry, libel in verse). **—v.** About 1378 *scolden* quarrel noisily, use abusive language, in *Piers Plowman;* from the noun.

sconce *n.* wall bracket used to hold a light. About 1392, lantern or candlestick protected by a screen; borrowed from Old French *esconse* lantern, hiding place, from Medieval Latin *sconsa,* from Latin *abscōnsa,* feminine past participle of *abscondere* to hide; see ABSCOND. The meaning of a wall bracket used to hold a light is first recorded about 1450.

scone (skōn) *n.* thick, flat, round cake. 1513, in a Scottish translation of Vergil's *Aeneid;* probably borrowed from Dutch *schoon* bread, in *schoon brood* fine bread, from Middle Dutch *schoonbroot* (*schoon, scōne* bright, beautiful + *broot* bread; see SHEEN and BREAD).

scoop *n.* 1324-25 *scope* ladle for removing liquid; later, kind of shovel (1487); borrowed from Middle Dutch *schōpe, schoepe* bucket. The Middle Dutch forms are cognate with Middle Low German *schōpe* ladle, *schuppe* shovel, Middle High German *schuofe* ladle, bucket (from Proto-Germanic **skōp-*), and probably also with Old Saxon *sceppian* to draw water, Low German and Dutch *scheppen,* Old High German *scephan* (modern German *schöpfen*), from Proto-Germanic **skap-,* Indo-European **skab-/skāb-* to hew out (a vessel), Pok.930.

The informal sense of the publishing of a piece of news before a rival newspaper does is found in 1874 in American English, derived from an informal sense of the verb.

—v. take up or cut with a scoop. Before 1338 *scopen* to ladle or bail out water, in Mannyng's *Chronicle of England;* from the noun. The informal sense of appropriate (something) in large quantities or in advance so as to exclude competitors is found about 1850, in American English.

scoot *v. Informal.* go quickly, dart. 1758 *scout,* perhaps borrowed from a Scandinavian source (compare Old Icelandic *skjōta* to SHOOT). Another source might be *scud* to dart from place to place, but while the semantic connection is close, the phonetic connection is as weak as that of *scout* cited above. The spelling *scoot* apparently originated in American English. **—n.** act of scooting. 1864, from the verb. **—scooter** *n.* 1820, simple kind of plow used for marking furrows, etc., American English; formed from English *scoot,* v. + *-er*¹. The meaning of a child's vehicle propelled by pushing against the ground with one foot is first recorded in 1919.

scope¹ *n.* extent. 1534, range, space, extent; borrowed from Italian *scopo* aim, purpose, object, learned borrowing from Latin *scopus,* from Greek *skopós* aim, target, watcher, related to *skopeîn* behold, look, consider; see SPY. The meaning of the distance the mind can reach, extent of view, is first recorded in Shakespeare's *Sonnets* (about 1600).

scope² *n.* instrument for viewing, such as a microscope. 1872, in Oliver Wendell Holmes' *Poet at the Breakfast Table;* abstracted from *telescope, microscope,* etc.

-scope a combining form meaning an instrument for viewing, examining, or observing, as in *stethoscope, radarscope.* Borrowed from New Latin *-scopium* instrument for examination, from Greek *-skópion,* from *skopeîn* look at, examined; see SPY.

-scopy a combining form meaning viewing, examining, observation, as in *microscopy, rhinoscopy.* Borrowed from Greek *-skopíā* observation, from *skopeîn* look at, examine; see SPY.

scorbutic (skôrbyü'tik) *adj.* of or pertaining to scurvy. 1655, borrowed from New Latin *scorbuticus* pertaining to scurvy, from *scorbutus* scurvy, possibly from a Germanic source (compare Middle Dutch *scorft* small scales of dead skin, Old High German *scorf,* Old English *scurf,* and Icelandic *skurfa,* from Proto-Germanic **skurf-,* Indo-European **sk̥rp-,* root **skerp-,* Pok.944); for suffix see -IC.

scorch *v.* Before 1325 *scorchen* to burn on the surface, char, possibly an alteration of earlier *scorrcnenn* to make dry, parch (implied in *scorrcnedd,* past participle, probably about 1200, in *The Ormulum*); perhaps borrowed from a Scandinavian source (compare Old Icelandic *skorpna* to be shriveled, which is cognate with Old English *scrimman* to shrink, dry up; see SHRIMP). **—n.** 1611, in Cotgrave's *Dictionary;* from the verb. A single instance of *skorke* superficial burn, scorch, is found in Middle English (probably about 1450), from *scorchen, skorken* to scorch.

score *n.* About 1230 *score* financial record, in *Ancrene Riwle;* later, twenty (about 1250), limit, boundary (about 1303), reckoning, total amount (about 1330); developed from late Old English *scoru* twenty (before 1100); borrowed from a Scandinavian source (compare Old Icelandic *skor* mark, tally, twenty, related to *skera* to cut; see SHEAR).

The sense in sports and games of a record of points made is first recorded in Hoyle's *A Short Treatise on the Game of Whist* (1742), but probably occurred much earlier. The sense of a printed piece of music arranged for different instruments is first recorded in 1701, and developed from earlier use of the word in reference to the practice of connecting related staves by scores or lines continuing the bars.

—v. About 1390 *scoren* to notch, mark, record by notches, in Chaucer's *Canterbury Tales;* from the noun, perhaps reinforced by a Scandinavian word (compare Old Icelandic *skora* to notch, record, from *skor,* n.).

—scoreboard *n.* (1826) **—scorekeeper** *n.* (1880, American English)

scorn *n.* Probably before 1200 *scorne, scarn,* in *Ancrene Riwle;* possibly in part from the verb, and, in part, borrowed from Old French *escarn, escharn* mockery, derision, contempt, from a Germanic source (compare Old High German *skern* mockery, jest, sport). **—v.** Probably about 1150 *scarnen* to slander; later, to mock, ridicule, deride (probably before 1200, in *Ancrene Riwle*), and with the spelling *scornen* (about 1250); borrowed from Old French *escarnir, escharnir* mock, despise, from a Germanic source (compare Old High German *skernon* mock, deride). Probably influenced later in vowel color and meaning by Old French *escorner* insult, humiliate; originally, to dishorn, from Vulgar Latin **excornāre,* from Latin *ex-* without + *cornū* horn (compare Italian *scornare* treat with contempt). The shift in the vowel is said to derive from later confusion with Old French *escorner* disgrace. **—scornful** *adj.* Before 1400 *scornfull;* earlier *skornefulle* (about 1350); formed from Middle English *scorne* + *-full* -ful.

scorpion *n.* poisonous animal related to the spiders. Probably before 1200 *scorpiun,* in *Ancrene Riwle;* later *scorpion* (probably before 1300); borrowed from Old French *scorpion,* learned borrowing from Latin, and borrowed directly from Latin *scorpiōnem* (nominative *scorpiō*), from Greek *skorpíos* a scorpion, probably borrowed from some Mediterranean language.

Scot *n.* native or inhabitant of Scotland. Probably before 1200 *Scotte,* in Layamon's *Chronicle of Britain;* developed from Old English *Scottas, Sceottas* inhabitants of Ireland, Irishmen, a borrowing of Late Latin *Scottī,* of uncertain (perhaps Celtic) origin. Down to the reign of King Alfred (871-899), Old English *Scottas* was the ordinary word for the Irish of Ireland. After Alfred, the name began to be applied by the Anglo-Saxons to the Irish who had settled in the A.D. 500's in the northwest of Great Britain, and from that time onward the name was restricted to the kingdom of the Scots in Britain and only historically associated with Ireland. **—Scotch** *adj.* of or pertaining to Scotland. 1591, in Spenser's *Prosopopoia;* earlier, in the compound *Scotchman* (1570); contraction of *Scottish,* probably reflecting a much older colloquial pronunciation. **—Scotch tape** (1947, trademarked in 1945, but claiming use since 1928) **—Scotch terrier** (1810) **—Scotch whiskey** (1835, in Dickens' *Sketches by Boz*) **—Scotland** *n.* (before 1126 *Scotlande,* in *Peterborough Chronicle*) **—Scots** *adj.* About 1333 *Skottis,* also *Scottis* (probably before 1350), northern variant of *Scottish.* **—Scotsman** *n.* (1375 *Scottis man,* in John Barbour's *The Bruce*) **—Scottish** *adj.* Probably before 1200 *Scottisc,* in Layamon's *Chronicle of Britain;* formed from Middle English *Scotte* Scot + *-isc* -ish[1], probably by influence, or as an alteration, of Old English *Scyttisc* Scottish (before 899, in Alfred's translation of Bede's *Ecclesiastical History*), from *Scottas, Sceottas* + *-isc* -ish[1].

scotch *v.* make harmless, stamp out, crush. About 1412 *scocchen* to cut, score, gash, in Hoccleve's *Regement of Princes;* perhaps borrowed through Anglo-French *escocher,* Old French *cocher, cochier* to notch, nick, from *coche* a notch, groove, probably from Latin *coccum* berry of scarlet oak (notched or notchlike in appearance), from Greek *kókkos,* a loanword of unknown origin. The meaning of make harmless for a time is first recorded in 1798, derived from Lewis Theobald's conjectural reading of *scotched* in Shakespeare's *Macbeth:* "We have scotched the snake, not killed it." The extended sense of stamp out, crush, is first recorded in 1825.

scot-free *adj.* free from payment, exempt from obligation. Before 1066 *scotfre* exempt from royal tax; formed in late Old English from *scot* royal tax, in part borrowed from a Scandinavian source (compare Old Icelandic *skot* contribution, shot), and in part a transferred use of Old English *scot, sceot* SHOT + *fre* free.

scoundrel *n.* 1589 *skowndrell,* in William Warner's *Albions England;* of unknown origin. The spelling *scoundrel* is first recorded in Shakespeare's *Twelfth Night* (1601).

scour[1] *v.* clean or polish. Probably before 1200 *scuren,* in *Ancrene Riwle;* later *scouren* (about 1390); probably borrowed from Middle Dutch *scūren,* and perhaps in some early instances directly from Old French *escurer,* from Late Latin *excūrāre* clean off (Latin *ex-* out + *cūrāre* care for; see CURE). The borrowing from Middle Dutch suggests that the word was originally a technical term among the Flemish workmen in England. **—n.** 1619, apparatus for washing gold-bearing soil, from the verb. The meaning of a place in a river where the bottom is scoured by the current is first recorded in 1681.

scour[2] *v.* move quickly about, range about in search of something. Before 1425 *scouren, scuren* traverse in search or pursuit of enemies, in Wycliffe's sermons; perhaps borrowed from a Scandinavian source (compare Norwegian *skure* move quickly, related to Old Icelandic *skūr* rain; see SHOWER).

scourge *n.* cause of calamity. Probably before 1200 *scurge* whip, lash; later *scourge* (about 1250), and in the sense of affliction, calamity (before 1382, in the Wycliffe Bible); borrowed through Anglo-French *escorge,* back formation from Old French *escorgier* to whip from Vulgar Latin **excorrigiāre* (Latin *ex-* out, off + *corrigia* thong, shoelace, probably from a Gaulish word related to Old Irish *cuimrech* fetter). The figurative sense of a cause of calamity is first recorded in Chaucer's *Canterbury Tales* (probably about 1375-90). **—v.** to whip, punish. About 1300 *scourgen,* from the noun.

scout[1] *v.* to spy or hunt around. Probably about 1380 *scouten* to search, scout; borrowed from Old French *escouter* to listen, heed, variant of *ascouter,* from Vulgar Latin **ascultāre,* alteration (by dissimilation of vowel sounds represented by *au* and *u*) of Latin *auscultāre* to listen, give heed to. Latin *auscultāre* was probably formed by metathesis of *u* and *l* from **ausclutāre,* from pre-Latin **aus-clutos* heard with (one's own) ears (*aus-,* related to *auris* EAR + **clutos* heard, related to *cluēre* be called; see LOUD). **—n.** 1553, act of scouting; 1555, person who scouts; borrowed from Middle French *escoute* act of listening or scouting, surveillance, scout, sentinel, from the verb in Old French *escouter* to listen, heed. In the sense of a person who scouts, modern English *scout* may also be a shortened form of Middle English *scowte-wach* sentinel, guard (probably about 1380), formed in Middle English from the noun in Old French *escoute* act of listening, sentinel + Middle English *wacche* watch, sentinel. **—scoutmaster** *n.* (1579) The specific sense of a leader of boy scouts is first recorded in 1908.

scout[2] *v.* reject with scorn, dismiss scornfully. 1710; earlier, to mock (1605); borrowed from a Scandinavian source (compare Old Icelandic *skūta* to taunt).

scow *n.* large, flat-bottomed boat. 1780, in Thomas Jefferson's writings; American English; borrowed from Dutch *schouw* a ferry boat, punt, from Middle Dutch *scouwe, scoude.* The Dutch forms are cognate with Middle High German *schalte* barge, Old High German *scalta* pole to push or punt a boat, *scaltan* to push off, and Old Saxon *scaldan* push (a boat) from the shore.

scowl *v.* 1340 *skoulen* look angry or sullen by lowering the eyebrows, in Richard Rolle's *The Prick of Conscience;* later *scowlen* (about 1400); probably borrowed from a Scandinavian source (compare Norwegian *skule* look furtively, squint, look embarrassed). **—n.** angry, sullen look, frown. 1500-20, in Dunbar's *Poems;* from the verb.

scrabble *v.* scratch or scrape about with hands, claws, etc. 1537, to scrawl, scribble; borrowed from Dutch *schrabbelen,* frequentative form of *schrabben* to scratch, perhaps related to *schrapen* SCRAPE. The meaning of scratch or scrape about with hands, claws, etc., is first recorded in 1600, and that of struggle, scramble, in 1638. **—n.** 1794, a confused struggle, scramble, American English; from the verb. The meaning of a scrawled character, writing, etc., is first recorded in 1842. **—Scrabble** (*trademark* for a word game) 1950, probably abstracted from *scribble-scrabble* hasty writing (1760), a reduplicated formation on SCRIBBLE, n.

scrag *n.* lean, skinny person or animal. 1542, in Udall's translation of Erasmus' *Apothegms;* probably borrowed from a Scandinavian source (compare dialectal Swedish *skragge* old and torn thing, Danish and Norwegian *skrog* hull, carcass, and Icelandic *skröggur* decrepit person). **—scraggly** *adj.* 1879, formed as if from English *scrag* + *-ly*[2], but the appearance of *-gg* - implies a form **scraggle* (which is curiously recorded only in the forms *scraggled, scraggling* participial adjectives). **—scraggy** *adj.* lean. 1611, in Cotgrave's *Dictionary;* formed from English *scrag,* n. + *-y*[1].

scram *v. Slang.* go at once. 1928, American English; perhaps a shortened form of SCRAMBLE.

scramble *v.* Before 1586, make one's way by climbing, crawling, etc., in Sidney's *The Arcadia;* perhaps variant of SCRABBLE. The meaning of struggle with others for something is first recorded about 1590. **—n.** 1674, a confused struggle; from the verb. the meaning of an act of climbing or crawling is first recorded in Johnson's *Dictionary* (1755).

scrap[1] *n.* small piece. Before 1387 *scrappe* fragment of food, in Trevisa's translation of Higden's *Polychronicon;* borrowed from a Scandinavian source (compare Old Icelandic *skrap* scraps, trifles, related to *skrapa* SCRAPE). The general meaning of a small piece, remnant, is first recorded in English in 1583. **—v.** make into scraps, break up. 1891, from the noun. **—scrapbook** *n.* (1825) **—scrap iron** (1823) **—scrappy** *adj.* made up of odds and ends. 1837, formed from English *scrap*[1], n. + *-y*[1].

scrap[2] *n. Slang.* fight. 1846, possibly a variant of SCRAPE, n., in the extended sense of an abrasive encounter, from the meaning of embarrassing difficulty or predicament. An earlier sense of a villainous scheme is found in 1679-80. —**v.** *Slang.* to fight, quarrel. 1874, from the noun. **—scrappy** *adj. Slang.* inclined to fight or quarrel. 1895, American English; formed from English *scrap*[2], n. + *-y*[1].

scrape *v.* rub with something sharp or rough. Probably about 1225 *skrapen* erase with a knife; probably borrowed from a Scandinavian source (compare Old Icelandic *skrapa* to scrape, erase, Swedish *skrapa* and Danish *skrabe* to scrape, which are cognate with Old English *scrapian* to scrape, Middle High German *schreffen* to scratch, and Middle Low German, Middle Dutch, and modern Dutch *schrapen* to scrape), from Proto-Germanic **skrap-,* cognate with Latin *scrobis* hole, pit, from Indo-European **skreb-/skrob-* (Pok. 943). **—n.** About 1440, scraping tool; later, act of scraping (1483); from the verb. The figurative sense of a difficulty, predicament, is first recorded in 1709 (Steele and Swift, in the *Tatler*), probably from the notion of being "scraped" in going through a narrow passage.

scrapple *n.* scraps of pork boiled with corn meal. 1855, American English; probably a diminutive formation from *scrap*[1] piece.

scratch *v.* About 1400 *scracchen* to wound slightly with something sharp; probably a fusion of earlier Middle English *scratten* to scratch (before 1250; compare *scratlen* to scratch, probably before 1200); and of Middle English *crachen* to scratch (about 1330). Middle English *scratten* and *scratlen* are of uncertain origin; Middle English *crachen* was possibly borrowed from Middle Dutch *cratsen* to scratch (modern Dutch *krassen*), which is cognate with Old High German *krazzōn* to scratch (modern German *kratzen*), Old Swedish *kratta* (related to Old Icelandic *krota* engrave), and Albanian *gërrüej* I scratch, from Indo-European **gred-/grod-* (Pok.405).

The figurative sense of gather (money) by effort, scrape, is first recorded in English in 1509. The literal sense of rub or scrape to relieve itching is recorded in Palsgrave's *Lesclarcissement* (1530).

—n. 1586, a mark made by scratching, in Sidney's *The Arcadia;* from the verb. The meaning of a mark drawn at the starting point of a game is first recorded in 1778, and that of the starting point of a contestant with no odds, in 1867. From these earlier uses developed the meaning of the beginning, nothing (usually in the phrase *from scratch*) which is first recorded in Joyce's *Ulysses* (1922). The American slang sense of money, especially paper money, is first recorded in 1914, and may have derived from *scratch paper* paper to scribble on (1899).

—adj. 1853, collected or prepared hastily; from the noun.

—scratchy *adj.* 1710, affected with the scratches (a disease); formed from English *scratch,* n. + *-y*[1]. The meaning of tending to scratch or scrape is found in 1866.

scrawl *v.* write or draw poorly or carelessly. 1612 (implied in *scrawling*); perhaps developed from Middle English *scrawlen* spread out the limbs, sprawl, gesticulate (before 1425, in Wycliffe's sermons); possibly an altered form of *sprawlen* to SPRAWL by association with *crawlen* to CRAWL. **—n.** 1693, something scrawled, in Congreve's *The Old Bachelor;* from the verb.

scrawny *adj.* 1833, American English; apparently variant of earlier dialectal English *scranny* lean, thin (1820); of uncertain origin.

scream *v.* About 1225 *screamen* to utter a shrill, piercing cry; earlier *scræmen* (about 1175), *shreamen* (probably about 1200); of uncertain immediate origin (compare Old Icelandic *skræma* to scare away, terrify, and *skramsa* to scream; also Middle Dutch *schremen, scremen,* and *screuwen* to scream; Flemish *schreemen* and Frisian *skrieme* to scream; also Old Frisian *skrīa* to shout, scream, which may have been borrowed into Old English as a lost verb **scrǣman*). **—n.** shrill, piercing cry. Before 1460 *skreme;* from the verb.

scree *n.* a pile of rubble at the base of a cliff. 1781, probably a back formation from *screes,* pl., pebbles and small stones; borrowed from Old Icelandic *skridha* landslide (Swedish and Danish *skred*), from *skrīdha* to slide, glide; cognate with Old English *scrīthan* to go, glide, and Old High German *scrītan* (modern German *schreiten* to stride), from Proto-Germanic **skrīthanan,* Indo-European **skreit-* (Pok.937).

screech *v.* 1577 *skrech* utter a loud, piercing cry; later *screech* (1602), alteration of Middle English *skrichen* (before 1325), *schrichen* (about 1250); possibly of imitative origin in English and resembling similar formations in Old Saxon *skrikōn* and Old Icelandic *skrækja* to screech. Compare SHRIEK. **—n.** 1560 *skreeche;* alteration of earlier *scrich* (1513), from Middle English verb *skrichen* to screech. **—screech owl** 1593, in Shakespeare's *2 Henry VI;* alteration of earlier *scritch owl* (1530, in Palsgrave's *Lesclarcissement*).

screed *n.* long speech or writing. Before 1333 *screade* fragment, in Shoreham's poetry; later *screde* strip of cloth (before 1425); developed in northern dialect of England from Old English *scrēade* SHRED. The meaning of a long roll or list, lengthy speech or writing, is first recorded before 1789.

screen *n.* 1348 *skrene* covered frame for protection from the heat of a fire or from drafts; borrowed probably from Old North French *escren,* variant of Old French *escran* a screen against heat, the tester of a bed, from Middle Dutch *scherm, schirm* screen, cover; cognate with Middle Low German *scerm* and Old High German *skirm* screen, shield, (modern German *Schirm* umbrella, shade, shield). The sense of a surface on which images are shown is found in 1810, in reference to a magic lantern. The meaning of an open mesh for sifting grain, coal, dirt, etc., is first recorded in 1573, and that of a mesh on a frame to put up in a window or door to protect against insects, in 1840 (in *screen door*). **—v.** About 1485 *screanen* to shield or protect from danger, from the noun. **—screenplay** *n.* (1916, motion picture; 1938, motion picture script)

screw *n.* 1404 *scrwe* cylinder with a spiral groove or ridge, screw; later *skrewe* (1497); borrowed from Middle French *escroue* nut, cylindrical socket, hole in which a screw turns, probably from Gallo-Romance **scrōba,* altered from Latin *scrobis* hole, pit by influence of *scrōfa* breeding sow, of uncertain origin. Note that in Medieval Latin *scrofa* could mean female screw, and in South Italian *scrofula* means screw. Apparently the Germanic forms (Middle Dutch *schrūve,* Middle High German *schrūbe,* etc.) were all derived through Low German *schruve* from Old French. The spelling with *-ew* was influenced by *dew, flew,* etc. The figurative sense of a means of pressure or coercion is found in English in 1648-49. **—v.** to turn as one turns a screw, twist. 1599, in Ben Jonson's *Every Man in His Humour;* from the noun. **—screwdriver** *n.* (1779) **—screwy** *adj.* 1820, tipsy or slightly drunk; later, crazy, ridiculous (1887).

screwball *n. Slang.* eccentric person. 1866, (in cricket) ball bowled with a screw or twist; later, (in baseball) pitch that curves in an unexpected erratic way (1928); formed from English *screw,* n. + *ball*[1]. The figurative slang sense of an eccentric person is first recorded in 1933, in American English. Compare ODDBALL.

scribble *v.* About 1456 *scryblen* write carelessly or hastily; possibly borrowed from Medieval Latin *scribillare,* a diminutive form of Latin *scrībere* to write (see SCRIBE) + substitution of English *-le*[1], diminutive suffix or *-le*[3], frequentative suffix. **—n.** something scribbled. 1577, in Sidney's *Letters;* from the verb.

scribe *n.* Probably about 1200, a teacher of Jewish law, Pharisee, in *The Ormulum;* borrowed from Old French, or directly from Late Latin *scrība,* used in the Vulgate to render Greek *grammateús;* the corresponding Hebrew word is *sōphēr* writer, scholar. In Latin *scrība* meant a keeper of accounts, or secretary and was derived from the verb *scrībere* to write, cognate with Greek *skarīphâsthai* to scratch an outline, sketch, *skárīphos* stylus, from Indo-European **skrībh-* (Pok.946).

Scribe in the sense of a secretary or clerk is first recorded in Middle English, in the Wycliffe Bible (before 1382). The meaning of a person whose occupation is writing, especially copying manuscripts, is first recorded in George Joyce's *An Apology to Tindale* (1535).

—v. to act as a scribe, write. 1782, from the noun. An isolated example of a verb *scriben* to write, is found in Middle English, borrowed from Latin *scrībere.*

scrim *n.* kind of thin, loosely woven fabric. 1792, of unknown origin.

scrimmage *n.* rough fight or struggle. About 1470, skirmish, minor battle; alteration of SKIRMISH; for suffix see -AGE. The extended meaning of a confused struggle, noisy argument, is found in 1780. The meaning in Rugby and football of a play beginning when the ball is put into play is first recorded in 1857; a scrimmage originally involved a confused struggle between the players. **—v.** Before 1825, to skirmish or quarrel; later put a football in a scrimmage (1881); from the noun.

scrimp *v.* be sparing of, use too little of. Before 1774 treat stingily; developed from earlier *scrimp,* adj., scant, scanty, meager (1718); possibly borrowed from a Scandinavian source (compare Swedish *skrumpna* to shrink, shrivel up; see SHRIMP). The meaning of be niggardly, economize, is first recorded in James Russell Lowell's *Biglow Papers* (1848). **—scrimpy** *adj.* too small, scanty. 1855, formed from English *scrimp,* v. + *-y*[1].

scrimshaw *n.* articles made by carving designs on shells, whales' teeth, etc. 1864, American English, back formation of earlier *scrimshander* (1851, in Melville's *Moby Dick*), apparently derived from the verbal noun *scrimshonging* (1850), *scrimshonting* (1825-26) the making of scrimshaw work, of unknown origin.

scrip *n.* stock certificate, especially for a fraction of a share. 1762, receipt for a portion of a loan subscribed, probably shortened from *(sub)scrip(tion receipt)*. The meaning of a certificate issued as currency in place of money is first recorded in 1790 in American English. The related use of paper currency in denominations of less than a dollar is first attested in 1889.

script *n.* About 1385, piece of writing, text, in Chaucer's *Troilus and Criseyde,* alteration (influenced by the Latin form) of earlier *scrite* (probably before 1300, in *Sir Tristrem*); borrowed from Old French *escrit* a writing, a written paper, from Latin *scriptum* a writing, a book, treatise, law, line or mark, noun use of neuter past participle of *scrībere* to write; see SCRIBE. The meaning of handwriting is first recorded in 1860, and that of a system of written characters, a kind of writing, in 1883. The meaning of the manuscript of a play is first attested in 1897. **—v.** to write a script for. 1935, from the noun.

Scripture *n.* sacred writing. Before 1325 *scriptur* the sacred writings of the Bible, in *Cursor Mundi;* borrowed from Late Latin *scrīptūra* the writings contained in the Bible; also, a passage in the Bible, from Latin *scrīptūra* a writing, written character, composition, an inscription, from *scrīpt-,* past participle stem of *scrībere* write; see SCRIBE; for suffix see -URE.

scrivener (skriv′nər) *n.* clerk, notary. Before 1399 *scryvener* scribe; earlier as a surname *Scriviner* (about 1375); also with the meaning notary (1477-79); from earlier *scrivein* scribe (about 1303, in Mannyng's *Handlyng Synne*); borrowed from Old French *escrivain* a writer, notary, clerk, from Vulgar Latin **scrībānem,* accusative form of *scrība* a scribe, from Latin (modeled on such Latin accusatives as *fullōnem,* nominative *fullō*); see SCRIBE; for suffix see -ER[1].

scrod *n.* young fish. 1841, American English; possibly borrowed from earlier Dutch *schrood* piece cut off, from Middle Dutch *scrōde* SHRED; if so borrowed, then the name is probably associated with the fish because it is usually split or sliced into pieces for drying or cooking.

scrofula (skrof′yələ) *n.* tuberculosis of the lymph glands, especially of the neck. 1791 (but implied much earlier in *scrofulous*), in Boswell's *The Life of Samuel Johnson,* singular of Middle English *scrophulas* (before 1400, in Lanfranc's *Science of Surgery*); borrowed from Late Latin *scrōfulae,* pl., swelling of the glands of the neck, from Latin *scrōfa* breeding sow, of uncertain origin (sometimes suggested as so called because the swollen glands associated with this disease resemble the back of a hog, from a sense development seen in Greek *choirádes,* pl., scrofula and *choîros* young pig). **—scrofulous** *adj.* of or resembling scrofula. 1612, formed from Medieval Latin *scrofula* + English *-ous.* An isolated earlier instance is found in Middle English, in a translation of Chauliac's *Grande Chirurgie* (probably before 1425), borrowed from Medieval Latin *scrofulosus, scrophulosus.*

scroll *n.* 1405 *scrowell* roll of parchment or paper, written document; later *scrolle* (probably 1438); alteration (by association with *rolle* roll) of earlier *scrowe,* probably before 1200, in *Ancrene Riwle;* borrowed from Anglo-French *escrowe,* variant of Old French *escroe, escroue* scrap, roll of parchment, from Frankish **skrōda* (compare Old High German *scrōt* piece cut off, SHRED). **—v.** 1606, to write down in a scroll; from the noun. The meaning of form into a scroll is first found in 1868.

scrotum (skrō′təm) *n.* pouch containing the testicles. 1597, borrowing of Latin *scrōtum,* cognate with Old English *scrūd* garment (modern English *shroud*), from Indo-European **skreut-/skrōut-/skrūt-* (Pok.947).

scrounge *v.* search about for what one can find. 1915, alteration of earlier dialectal English *scrunge* to search about stealthily, rummage, pilfer (1909), of uncertain origin.

scrub[1] *v.* rub hard. Before 1425 *scrobben* curry a horse; earlier *shrubben* (probably before 1300, in *Kyng Alisaunder*); also, scratch or rub oneself (about 1303); borrowed either from Middle Dutch or Middle Low German *schrubben* to scrub, or from a Scandinavian source (compare Norwegian and Danish *skrubbe* to scrub, Swedish *skrubba*). **—n.** a scrubbing. 1621, from the verb.

scrub[2] *n.* brush, shrubs. Before 1398 *scrub* a low, stunted tree or shrub, in Trevisa's translation of Bartholomew's *De Proprietatibus Rerum;* variant of *shrobbe, shrub* SHRUB. The collective meaning of low, stunted trees or shrubs, land overgrown with scrub, is first recorded in 1809. **—adj.** small, poor, inferior. 1710-11, in Swift's *Journal to Stella;* from the noun. **—scrubby** *adj.* stunted. 1591, formed from *scrub*[2], n. + *-y*[1].

scruff *n.* back of the neck, nape. 1790, in Grose's *A Provincial Glossary;* alteration (influenced by *scruff* crust, scum) of *scuft* (1787), probably cognate with North Frisian *skuft* back of the neck of a horse, and Dutch *schoft* withers of a horse.

scruffy *adj.* 1660, scaly, covered with scurf, from earlier *scruff* dandruff, scurf (1526), variant of SCURF; for suffix see -Y[1]. The figurative sense of shabby or dirty, is first recorded in Mark Twain's *Screamers* (1871).

scrumptious (skrump′shəs) *adj. Informal.* delicious. 1830, stylish, splendid, first-rate; American English, probably alteration of SUMPTUOUS. The specific sense of delicious is first recorded in 1881.

scruple *n.* Before 1382 *scripil,* in the Wycliffe Bible; later *scrupul* (probably about 1425); borrowed from Latin *scrūpulus* and Old French *scrupule,* learned borrowing from Latin *scrūpulus* uneasiness, anxiety, pricking of conscience. Latin *scrūpulus* means literally a small sharp stone or pebble, and is the diminutive of *scrūpus* sharp stone or pebble, used figuratively by Cicero for a cause of uneasiness or anxiety, probably alluding to a pebble in one's shoe or sandal; from Indo-European **skreup-/skroup-* (Pok.947). The commonly used plural form *scruples* is recorded before 1500. **—v.** hesitate or be unwilling (to do something). 1627, from the noun. **—scrupulous** *adj.* About 1443, very careful to do what is right, borrowed from Middle French *scrupuleux,* or directly from Latin *scrūpulōsus,* from *scrūpulus* scruple; for suffix see -OUS.

scrutiny *n.* close examination, careful inspection. 1415 *scrutinie* the taking of a formal vote to choose someone or decide some question; borrowed from Latin *scrūtinium* a search, inquiry, from Latin *scrūtārī* to examine, investigate, search, rummage (as through trash), from *scrūta,* pl., trash, old things, rags, of uncertain origin. The meaning of close examination, careful inspection, is first recorded in 1604. **—scrutinize** *v.* subject to scrutiny. 1671, formed from English *scrutin(y)* + *-ize.*

scuba (skü′bə) *n.* underwater breathing equipment. 1952 *SCUBA;* American English, acronym formed from *S(elf)-C(ontained) U(nderwater) B(reathing) A(pparatus).* The lower-case spelling is first recorded in 1957. **—v.** 1964 *scuba-dive;* 1969 *scuba;* from the noun.

scud *v.* run or move swiftly. 1532, in Sir Thomas More's *The Confutation of Tyndale's Answer;* perhaps verb use of Middle English *scut* rabbit, rabbit's tail (1440); earlier *scot* (probably before 1300); of uncertain origin. The earliest instance of *scud* refers to the movement of a rabbit.

It has alternatively been suggested that *scud* was borrowed from a Scandinavian source (compare Danish *skyde* to shoot, fire, and Old Icelandic *skjōta* to throw, SHOOT).

—n. swift movement. 1609, in Ben Jonson's *Works;* from the verb.

scuff *v.* walk without lifting the feet, shuffle. 1595, to evade; Scottish, perhaps borrowed from a Scandinavian source (compare Swedish *skuffa* to shove, push, and Old Icelandic *skūfa, skȳfa* to SHOVE). The meaning of walk without lifting the feet, shuffle, is first recorded in 1847, and that of wear or injure the surface of, in 1897. **—n.** 1824, a glancing blow, Scottish; from the verb. The meaning of noise made by scuffing is first recorded in 1899. **—scuffle** *v.* struggle or fight in a rough, confused manner. 1579, probably a frequentative form of *scuff,* perhaps from the same source as SCUFF; for suffix see -LE³. *—n.* a confused, rough struggle or fight. 1606, in Shakespeare's *Antony and Cleopatra;* from the verb.

scull *n.* an oar worked with a side twist. 1345-46 *skulle;* later *sculle* (1486); of unknown origin. The word is occasionally associated with *skull* from the hollowed shape of the oar, but this is no evidence for a connection of this nature. **—v.** to row a boat with a scull, use a scull. 1624 (implied in *sculling*); from the noun.

scullery (skul′ərē) *n.* room near a kitchen where cleaning of dishes, etc. is done. 1445 *squillery* household department concerned with the care of kitchen utensils, in *Proceedings of the Privy Council;* earlier as a surname *Squillerye* (1330); also *sculerie* (1454), *scullery* (1474); borrowed from Middle French *escuelerie* office of the servant in charge of plates, etc., from *escuelle* dish, from Vulgar Latin **scūtella,* alteration (influenced by **scūtum* shield, and its resemblance to a platter, of Latin *scutella* serving platter, salver; see SCUTTLE¹ bucket; for suffix see -ERY.

scullion (skul′yən) *n.* kitchen helper, servant. Probably about 1475 *scwlioun;* later *scullian* (1515), *scullyon* (1531); borrowed from Middle French *escouillon, escouvillon* a swab, cloth, from *escouve* broom, twig, from Latin *scōpae,* pl., broom, related to *scāpus* stem, SHAFT.

sculpt *v. Informal.* to sculpture. 1864, in part borrowed from French *sculpter,* from Latin *sculpt-,* past participle stem of *sculpere* to carve; but also reinforced by back formation in English from *sculptor* or *sculpture,* n.

sculpture *n.* Before 1393, art of carving or engraving, in Gower's *Confessio Amantis;* borrowed from Latin *sculptūra* sculpture, from *sculpt-,* past participle stem of *sculpere* to carve, engrave, back formation from compounds (such as *exsculpere*) of *scalpere* to carve, cut; see SHELF; for suffix see -URE.

The Middle English word *sculpture* originally included the art of carving figures in relief, and also the art of intaglio. The sense of a work of sculpture, carved figure, is first recorded in 1616.

—v. carve or model. 1645, in John Evelyn's *Diary;* from the noun.

—sculptor *n.* 1634, borrowed from Latin *sculptor,* from *sculpere* carve; for suffix see -OR².

scum *n.* thin layer that rises to the top of a liquid. 1340 *scome* foam, froth, in *Ayenbite of Inwyt;* later, scum (1392); and with the spellings *scume* (before 1398), *scum* (1440); borrowed from Middle Dutch *scūme* (modern Dutch *schuim*) foam, froth. The Dutch words are cognate with Middle Low German *schūm* foam, and Old High German *scūm* (modern German *Schaum*), from Proto-Germanic **skūma-,* cognate with Sanskrit *skunóti* he covers, from Indo-European **skeu-/sku-/skewə-/skū-* (Pok.951). The transferred sense of the residue or dross of society, lowest class of people, is first recorded in Marlowe's *Tamburlane the Great* (1586). **—v.** 1373 *scomen* remove scum from; later *scumen* (before 1400); from the noun. **—scummy** *adj.* having the nature or appearance of scum. 1577, formed from English *scum,* n. + *-y*¹.

scupper *n.* opening in the side of a ship to let water run off the deck. 1422-27 *scoper,* implied in *scopernaill* scupper-nail; later *scupper,* implied in *scupper-hole* (about 1590); of uncertain origin (perhaps from Old French *escopir, escupir* to spit out; or possibly related to Middle English *scope* scoop).

scurf *n.* small scales of dead skin. Old English (before 1000) *scurf;* alteration (probably by Scandinavian influence) of *scorf, sceorf;* cognate with Middle Dutch *scorft* scurf (modern Dutch *schurft*), Old High German *scorf* (modern German *Schorf*), Danish *skurv,* and Icelandic *skurfa* scurf, from Proto-Germanic **skurf-,* Indo-European **skr̥p-,* root **skerp-* (Pok.944). **—scurfy** *adj.* 1483, covered with scurf, of the nature of scurf; formed from Middle English *scurf* + *-y*¹.

scurrilous (skėr′ələs) *adj.* coarsely joking. 1576, formed from English *scurrile* coarsely joking + *-ous.* English *scurrile* was borrowed from Middle French, or directly from Latin *scurrīlis* buffoonlike, from *scurra* fashionable city idler; later, buffoon, perhaps from Etruscan.

scurry *v.* 1810, to run quickly, scamper, in Southey's *The Curse of Kehama;* perhaps abstracted from *hurry-scurry* (adj. 1732, v. 1771), a reduplication of HURRY. An earlier sense of ride out as a scout is first recorded in 1580. **—n.** a scurrying. 1823, from the verb.

scurvy *n.* disease caused by lack of vitamin C. About 1565, R. Baker in Hakluyt's *Voyages;* noun use of Middle English *scurvy* covered with or suffering from scurf (probably about 1425, in a translation of Chauliac's *Grande Chirurgie*), formed from Middle English *scurf* SCURF + *-y*¹.

scuttle[1] *n.* bucket for holding or carrying coal. 1366-67 *scutel* basket; later *scutle* (1541); found in Old English (about 1050) *scutel* dish, platter; borrowed from Latin *scutella* serving platter, salver, diminutive of *scutra* flat tray, dish; perhaps related to *scūtum* shield; see SQUIRE. Latin *scutella* was borrowed into other Germanic languages as well; compare Old Icelandic *skutill,* Middle Dutch and modern Dutch *schotel,* Middle Low German *schötel,* and Old High German *scuzzila* (modern German *Schüssel*). The meaning of a bucket for holding or carrying coal is first recorded in 1849.

scuttle[2] *v.* scamper, scurry. Before 1450 *scottlen* (implied in *scottlynge*); later *scutlen* (1657); probably related to SCUD. **—n.** short, hurried run. 1623, from the verb.

scuttle[3] *n.* opening in a ship's deck. 1497 *skottell;* later *scuttle* (about 1595); borrowed from Middle French *escoutille,* or directly from Spanish *escotilla* hatchway, of uncertain origin. **—v.** cut a hole through the bottom or sides of (a ship) to sink it. 1642, from the noun. The figurative sense of undermine or destroy is first recorded in 1888.

scuttlebutt *n. Informal.* rumor, gossip. 1805 *scuttle-butt* water cask kept on a ship's deck, formed from English *scuttle*[3] opening, hole + *butt*[4] barrel, replacing earlier *scuttled cask* (1777). The meaning of rumor, gossip, is first recorded in 1901 in American English (originally nautical slang), traditionally said to be from the fact that sailors gathered around the scuttlebutt or water cask to gossip.

scuzzy *adj. Slang.* dirty, grimy. 1969, perhaps blend of *scummy* and *fuzzy.*

scythe (sīᴛʜ) *n.* tool used for cutting grass, etc. Probably before 1300 *sithe,* in *Kyng Alisaunder;* developed from Old English (about 700) *sīthe, sigthi;* cognate with Middle Low German *segede, sigde* scythe, Middle Dutch *sichte* (modern Dutch *zicht*), and Old Icelandic *sigdhr,* from Proto-Germanic **seȝíthō,* cognate with Latin *secāre* to cut and *secūris* ax, from Indo-European **sek-* (Pok.895). The spelling with *sc-* is first recorded in 1422-41, influenced by association with Latin *scissor* carver, cutter; see SCISSORS. **—v.** 1573-80, to use a scythe; from the noun.

sea *n.* Probably about 1150 *see;* later *sea* (probably before 1200); developed from Old English *sǣ* sea, lake (about 725, in *Beowulf*); cognate with Old Frisian *sē* sea, Old Saxon *sēo,* Middle Low German *sē,* Middle Dutch *see* (modern Dutch *zee*), Old High German *sē, sēo* sea, lake, pond (modern German *See* lake, sea), Old Icelandic *sær, sjōr, sjār* sea (Norwegian *sjø,* Swedish *sjö,* Danish *sø*), and Gothic *sáiws* sea, marsh, from Proto-Germanic **saiwiz.* No cognates are found outside of Germanic.

The figurative sense of a copious or overwhelming quantity or mass of something (as in *a sea of troubles*) is first recorded in Middle English, probably before 1200. The phrase *at sea* or *all at sea,* meaning in a state of uncertainty or perplexity, at a loss, is found in Blackstone's *Commentaries on the Laws of England* (1766). **—seaboard** *n.* 1788, land bordering the sea; earlier *see bord* seaward side of a ship (before 1490); formed from Middle English *see* sea + *bord* ship's side; see BOARD. **—sea change** transformation (1610, in Shakespeare's *The Tempest*). **—seacoast** *n.* (before 1400) **—seafarer** *n.* (1513) **—seafaring** *adj.* (probably before 1200); *n.* (1592) **—seafood** *n.* (1836, American English) **—sea gull** (1542) **—sea horse** (about 1475, walrus; 1587, fabled horselike sea monster; 1589, small fish with a horselike head) **—sea level** (1806) **—sea lion** (1601, kind of lobster or crab; 1661, fabled lionlike sea monster; 1697, large-eared seal) **—seaman** *n.* (about 725, in *Beowulf*) **—seaport** *n.* (1596) **—seashell** *n.* (before 900) **—seashore** *n.* (1526, in the Tyndale Bible) **—seasick** *adj.* (before 1566) **—sea wall** (about 725, cliff by the sea, in *Beowulf;* about 1450, wall or embankment to prevent encroachment of the sea) **—seawater** *n.* (about 1000) **—seaway** *n.* (before 1000, the sea as a means of travel; 1866, channel connecting two tracts of sea; 1921, deep inland waterway for ocean shipping) **—seaweed** *n.* (1577) **—seaworthy** *adj.* (1807)

Seabee *n.* member of the construction battalion of the U.S. Navy. 1942, American English; formed from the pronunciation of the initials *C.B.,* abbreviation of *Construction Battalion.*

seal[1] *n.* design stamped on a piece of wax, etc., to authenticate or confirm something. Probably about 1200 *seil* (figurative) something that joins two things; later *seel* official seal, authenticating mark (1258); and with the spelling *seal* (probably before 1300); borrowed from Old French *seel,* from Vulgar Latin **sigellum,* from Latin *sigillum* small picture, engraved figure, seal, diminutive of *signum* mark, token; see SIGN.

The Latin word *sigillum* was at various periods adopted into several Germanic languages: Gothic *sigljō,* Middle High German *sigel* (modern German *Siegel*), Old Frisian *sigel,* Middle Low German *segel,* Middle Dutch *segel* (modern Dutch *zegel*), Swedish *sigill,* Danish and Norwegian *segl.* A compound, or perhaps derivative form with the same meaning occurs in Old English *insegel,* which did not survive past early Middle English, but is also found in Old High German *insigili,* Old Frisian *insigel,* and Old Icelandic *innsigli.* The significance of the prefix *in-* is unknown as it is not found in Medieval or Late Latin (except in the Medieval Latin verb *insigillare*). It has been suggested that the form may have some relation to Latin *īnsigne* sign, mark.

—v. Probably before 1200 *sealen* attest by or fasten with a seal, in *Ancrene Riwle;* borrowed from Old French *seeler,* from *seel* seal, n.

—sealing wax (before 1400)

seal[2] *n.* mammal with large flippers. About 1300 *sele,* in *Havelok the Dane;* implied slightly earlier in the compound *selesmer,* probably meaning pieces of blubber (1293); developed from Old English *sēol-* (before 899, in Alfred's translation of Orosius' *Historiarum Adversus Paganos*), stem in the declension of *seolh* seal; cognate with Middle Low German *sel, sēl* seal, Middle Dutch *seel, sael,* Old High German *selah,* and Old Icelandic *selr,* (Norwegian *sel,* Swedish *säl,* Danish *sæl*), from Proto-Germanic **selHaz,* possibly cognate with Greek *hélkein* drag, *holkós* furrow, from Indo-European **selk-/solk-* (Pok.901). **—v.** hunt seals. 1828, from the noun.

seam *n.* About 1303 *seme* seam in a garment, hem, in Mannyng's *Handlyng Synne;* developed from Old English *sēam* (about 1000, in Ælfric's *Homilies*). Old English *sēam* is cognate with Old Frisian *sām* hem, seam, Middle Low German *sōm,* Middle Dutch *soom* (modern Dutch *zoom*), Old High German *soum* (modern German *Saum*), and Old Icelandic *saumr* (Swedish *söm,* Danish *søm*), from Proto-Germanic **saumaz;* ultimately derived from the same Germanic source as Old

English *sīwian* to SEW. Cognates outside Germanic are found in Greek *hymḗn* membrane and Old Prussian *schumeno* shoemaker's thread. —**v.** 1582, join with a seam; from the noun. —**seamstress** *n.* woman whose work is sewing. 1644 (before 1613 *sempstresse*); formed from Middle English *semster* person whose work is sewing (1379) + *-ess,* feminine suffix. Middle English *semster* developed from Old English (about 995) *sēamestre* seamstress, tailor (*sēam* seam + *-estre* -ster); *sēamestre* was originally the designation of a woman, but even in Old English it was applied to a man and the lack of a feminine form led to the formation of *seamstress.* —**seamy** *adj.* 1604, (figurative) least pleasant, worst, in Shakespeare's *Othello;* formed from English *seam,* n. + *-y*[1]. Shakespeare's figurative use alluded to the underside of a garment on which the rough edges of the seams are visible.

séance (sā'äns) *n.* spiritualistic session. 1789, a sitting or session, as of a learned society or other body of persons; borrowed from French *séance* a sitting, from archaic *seoir* (replaced by *asseoir*) to sit, from Latin *sedēre* SIT. The meaning of a spiritualistic session, meeting of people trying to communicate with spirits of the dead, is first recorded in Eliot Warburton's *The Crescent and the Cross* (1845).

sear *v.* burn or char the surface of. Before 1400 *seren* cauterize, burn; later, cause to wither (before 1420, in Lydgate's *Troy Book*); developed from Old English (probably about 890) *sēarian* dry up, wither, from *sēar* dried up, withered, SERE. The specific sense of burn or char the surface of is first recorded in Palsgrave's *Lesclarcissement* (1530). —**n.** mark made by searing. 1874, from the verb.

search *v.* Probably before 1300 *serchen* dig for, in *Arthour and Merlin;* also, overrun, occupy by force, in *Kyng Alisaunder;* later, go about trying to find something, explore (about 1330); borrowed from Old French *cerchier* to search, from Latin *circāre* go about, wander, traverse, from *circus* CIRCLE. —**n.** act of searching. Probably before 1400 *serche,* in *Destruction of Troy;* borrowed through Anglo-French *serche,* Old French *cerche,* from *cerchier* to search. —**searchlight** *n.* (1883) —**search warrant** (1818, in Scott's *Rob Roy*)

season *n.* Probably before 1300 *seysoun, seysyne* proper time, suitable occasion, time of the year characterized by some activity, in *Kyng Alisaunder;* later, time of year when a plant blooms, bears fruit, etc. (before 1325, in *Cursor Mundi*); also with the spelling *season* time of year characterized by a particular type of weather (about 1350); borrowed from Old French *saison, seison* a sowing, planting, from Latin *satiōnem* (nominative *satiō*) a sowing (in Vulgar Latin, time of sowing, seeding time), from *sat-,* past participle stem of *serere* to SOW. The meaning of one of the four periods of the year (often with defining word prefixed as *summer season*) is first found in *Piers Plowman* (before 1376). —**v.** Probably about 1390 *sesounen* improve the flavor of by adding spices or condiments, in *Sir Gawain and the Green Knight;* borrowed from Old French *assaisoner* to ripen, season (*a-* to + *saison, seison* season). This sense developed from the sense in Old French of ripen, make (fruit) more palatable by extending its growing season as long as possible. The sense of bring to maturity, ripen, and to dry or harden, in reference to timber, is not recorded in English before 1540. —**seasonable** *adj.* suitable to a season. About 1380 *sesounable,* in Wycliffe's writings; formed from Middle English *sesoun* season, n. + *-able.* —**seasonal** *adj.* of or depending on the seasons or a season. 1838, formed in English from *season,* n. + *-al*[1]. —**seasoning** *n.* 1511, act of adding something to food to improve its flavor; later, something added to improve flavor (1580); formed from English *season,* v. + *-ing*[1].

seat[1] *n.* thing to sit on. Probably before 1200 *sete,* in *Ancrene Riwle* and Layamon's *Chronicle of Britain;* borrowed from Old Icelandic *sǣti* seat, position, from Proto-Germanic **sǣt-,* Indo-European **sēd-* (Pok.884); related to SIT. It is also possible that Middle English *sete* was in part influenced by, if not a blend with, Old English *sǣt* a place where one sits in ambush, ambush; cognate with Old Icelandic *sāt* a sitting in ambush, ambush, both words related to Old Icelandic *sǣti* seat, and its cognates including Old High German *gisāzi* (modern German *Gesäss*) a seat, and Middle Dutch *gesaete.* The common word for seat in Old English was *setl;* see SETTLE[2]. —**v.** to set or place on a seat. 1589, from the noun. —**seat belt** (1932)

seat[2] *n.* established place, residence, location. About 1200 *sate;* later *sete* (about 1250); extended use of *sete* SEAT[1], influenced by Old French *siege* seat, established place, residence, and Latin *sēdēs* seat, resting place, residence, center of a particular activity.

The meaning of a location or site (as *the seat of a disease*) is found in Middle English before 1393, in Gower's *Confessio Amantis,* and that of the city or place in which a throne or government is established, about 1400. The related sense of the place where something occurs or is prevalent (as in *the seat of tyranny*) is first recorded about 1560, and that of an established place or center (as in *a seat of learning*), in 1585.
—**v.** 1577, be situated in a certain position, be located; later, to locate in a particular place (1603); from the noun.

sebaceous (sibā'shəs) *adj.* fatty, greasy. 1728, secreting a fatty or oily substance, in *Chambers Cyclopaedia;* later, fatty, oily (1783); formed in English from Latin *sēbum* tallow, grease + English *-aceous.* Latin *sēbum* is from Indo-European **sē(i)bom* liquid fat. From a variant **səibā* came the West Germanic **saipō,* the root of Old English *sāpe* SOAP and Latin *sāpō.*

sec (sek) *adj.* dry, not sweet (applied especially to champagne). 1863, borrowing of French *sec* not sweet, dry, from Latin *siccus* dry; see SACK[3] sherry.

secant (sē'kant) *n. Geometry.* line that intersects. 1593, borrowed from Latin *secantem* (nominative *secāns*) cutting, present participle of *secāre* to cut; see SECTION; for suffix see -ANT. The Latin form was known earlier in an English text (1583).

secede *v.* withdraw formally from an organization. 1702, withdraw, retire, in Cotton Mather's writings; formed as a verb to *secession,* n., by borrowing from Latin *sēcēdere* (*sē-* apart + *cēdere* to go; see CEDE). The meaning of withdraw formally from an organization or alliance is recorded in Johnson's *Dictionary* (1755). —**secession** *n.* 1533, withdrawal, retirement, in Bellenden's translation of Livy's *Roman History;* borrowed from Latin *sēcessiōnem* (nominative *sēcessiō*), from *sēcess-,* past participle stem of *sēcēdere* secede; for suffix see -ION. The meaning of withdrawal from an organization or alliance is first recorded in 1660; specific reference to proposals of withdrawal from the Union by one of the States composing it (after 1860 especially of one of the Southern States) is found in 1830, in

American English. **—secessionist** *n.* person who advocates secession. 1860, American English; formed from *secession* + *-ist.*

seclude *v.* 1451 *secluden* shut off, keep out, in Capgrave's *The Life of St. Gilbert;* borrowed from Latin *sēclūdere* shut off, confine (*sē-* apart + *claudere* to shut, CLOSE[1]). The meaning of withdraw or keep apart from company is first recorded in John Ford's *The Lovers Melancholy* (1628). **—seclusion** *n.* 1623, act of secluding, in Cockeram's *Dictionary;* borrowed from Medieval Latin *seclusionem* (nominative *seclusio*), from Latin *sēclūs-*, stem of the past participle of *sēclūdere* seclude; for suffix see -SION.

second[1] *adj.* next after the first. About 1300 *secunde;* borrowed from Old French *second,* and directly from Latin *secundus* following, next in order, second in sequence, hence (of wind) favorable, prosperous, from the root of *sequī* follow; see SEQUEL.

Since Old English had no ordinal number corresponding to two (this sense being expressed by *ōther* OTHER, which was indefinite in its reference and therefore ambiguous in its antecedent), the Old French word found early acceptance in Middle English.

—adv. in the second place. Before 1382, in the Wycliffe Bible; from the adjective.

—n. person or thing that is second. Probably before 1325, from the adjective. *Seconds,* in the sense of articles below first quality, is first recorded in Shakespeare's *Sonnets* (about 1600).

—v. to support, back up, assist. Before 1586, in Sidney's *The Arcadia;* borrowed from Middle French *seconder,* from Latin *secundāre* to assist, (of winds and currents) make conditions favorable, from *secundus* assisting, favorable, following, second.

—secondary *adj.* next after the first in order, place, time, or importance. Before 1382 *secoundarie,* in the Wycliffe Bible; borrowed from Latin *secundārius* of or belonging to the second class, second-class, inferior, from *secundus* second; for suffix see -ARY. **—secondary school** (1809) **—second-class** *adj.* (1837-38) **—second floor** (1821, in Coleridge) **—secondhand** *adj., adv.* (1654) **—second-rate** *adj.* (1669)

second[2] *n.* 1/60 of a minute. 1391 *secunde, seconde* 1/60 of a minute of time or of angular measurement, in Chaucer's *Treatise on the Astrolabe;* borrowed from Old French *seconde,* from Medieval Latin *secunda,* as in *secunda pars minuta* second diminished part (the result of the second division of the hour by sixty), from Latin *secunda,* feminine of *secundus* SECOND[1]. Medieval Latin *secunda* is also the source of German *Sekunde,* Swedish and Danish *sekund.* From the Medieval Latin neuter form *secundum minutum* second minute, came Spanish and Portuguese *segundo,* Italian *secondo.* **—second hand** (1759)

secrecy *n.* condition of being secret. 1573, alteration of Middle English *secretee* (about 1415, in a version of Chaucer's *Canterbury Tales*); formed from earlier *secre,* adj., secret (about 1375, borrowed from Old French *secré,* variant of *secret* SECRET) + *-tee* -ty[2]. Changing of Middle English *secretee* (representing the suffix *-ty*[2]) to *secrecy* (with suffix *-cy*) was common in early modern English.

secret *adj.* About 1378, hidden, concealed, private, in a version of *Piers Plowman;* borrowed from Old French *secret* concealed, private, learned borrowing from Latin, and borrowed into English directly from Latin *sēcrētus* set apart, withdrawn, hidden, originally past participle of *sēcernere* to set apart (*sē-* apart + *cernere* separate; see CERTAIN). **—n.** About 1380, something kept secret, mystery, in Chaucer's translation of Boethius' *De Consolatione Philosophiae;* borrowed from Old French *secret* a secret place, learned borrowing from Latin, and borrowed into English directly from Latin *sēcrētum* a secret,originally neuter of *sēcrētus,* past participle of *sēcernere* to set apart.

An earlier form *secre,* with the meaning of a prayer said in a low voice, is found in Middle English about 1300, borrowed from Old French *secré,* variant of *secret* secret, n.

—secretive *adj.* 1464 *secretife* secret, hidden, formed from Middle English *secret,* adj. + *-ive.* The current sense of having the habit of secrecy, not frank and open, is first recorded in Charlotte Brontë's novel *Villette* (1853). This sense is a back formation from earlier *secretiveness* (in phrenology) quality or state of being secretive (1815); formed from *secret* + *-ive* + *-ness,* patterned on French *secrétivité.*

secretary *n.* Before 1387 *secretarie* person entrusted with secrets, in Trevisa's translation of Higden's *Polychronicon;* borrowed from Medieval Latin *secretarius* clerk, notary, confidential officer, confidant, from Latin *sēcrētum* a SECRET; for suffix see -ARY. The meaning of a person who writes letters, keeps records, etc., is first recorded in Lydgate's writings, originally applied to a king's secretary (probably before 1430). *Secretary,* as the designation of an official presiding over a government department (Secretary of State) is first recorded in English in 1599. The transferred sense of a writing desk is found in 1833, patterned on French *secrétaire.* **—secretarial** *adj.* 1801, of or pertaining to a secretary, in Bentham's writings; probably formed in English from Medieval Latin *secretarius* secretary + English *-al*[1]. **—secretariat** *n.* 1811, office or position of secretary, in the correspondence of the Duke of Wellington; borrowing of French *secrétariat,* from Medieval Latin *secretariatum* office of secretary, from *secretarius* secretary.

secrete[1] (sikrēt′) *v.* to produce and discharge. 1707, in a physician's handbook; probably a back formation from *secretion.* **—secretion** *n.* production and discharge of a substance by a gland, etc. 1646, borrowed from French *sécrétion,* from Latin *sēcrētiōnem* (nominative *sēcrētiō*) separation, from *sēcrēt-*, stem of the past participle of *sēcernere* to separate, set apart; see SECRET; for suffix see -TION. **—secretory** *adj.* of or causing secretion. 1692, formed in English from Latin *sēcrētus,* past participle + English *-ory.*

secrete[2] (sikrēt′) *v.* to conceal, hide, keep secret. 1741, probably alteration of earlier *secret* to conceal (1595, from the noun), by influence of Latin *sēcrētus* set apart, hidden; see SECRET. The meaning of remove secretly, appropriate (someone's possessions) in a secret manner, is first recorded in Fielding's *Tom Jones* (1749).

sect *n.* Probably about 1350 *secte* a religious order or body, especially a heretical one; borrowed through Old French *secte,* and directly from Late Latin *secta* religious group or sect, from Latin *secta* following, line of teaching followed, school of thought; originally, a way, road, a noun made from the feminine of *sectus,* variant past participle of *sequī* to follow; see SEQUEL.

The transferred sense of a group of persons having similar opinions, beliefs, etc., is first recorded in Middle English in Chaucer's *Legend of Good Women* (about 1386). The sense of an organized religious body separated from an established church, denomination, is first attested in Holinshed's *Chronicles* (1577-87). **—sectarian** *adj.* 1649, of or having to do with a dissenting or nonconformist sect, in Milton's writings; formed from earlier *sectary* member of a sect (1556) + *-an. Sectary* was borrowed from Middle French *sectaire,* or directly from Medieval Latin *sectarius,* from Latin *secta* sect. The extended meaning of confined to a particular sect, partisan, is first recorded in 1796. —*n.* 1654, member of a nonconformist sect; from the adjective.

section *n.* About 1319 *seccion* a division, an intersection; borrowed from Middle French *section,* or directly from Latin *sectiōnem* (nominative *sectiō*) a cutting, or cutting off, division, part cut or separated, from *sect-,* stem of the past participle of *secāre* to cut; for suffix see -TION. Latin *secāre* is cognate with Lithuanian *išsėkti* to carve, and Old Slavic *sěšti* to cut; see SAW[1] tool. **—v.** cut into sections. 1819, in Keats' *The Cap and Bells;* from the noun. **—sectional** *adj.* 1806, of or having to do with a particular section, regional or local; formed from English *section,* n. + *-al*[1].

sector *n.* 1570, section of a circle between two radii; borrowed from Late Latin *sector* section of a circle, from Latin *sector* a cutter, from *sect-,* stem of the past participle of *secāre* to cut; see SECTION; for suffix see -OR[2].

The meaning of a part of a military front is first recorded in English in 1916, and that of an area, section, division, segment (as in *the public sector, the economic sector*), in the 1920's.

secular *adj.* worldly, not religious or sacred. About 1300 *seculer* living in the world, and not belonging to a religious order, belonging to the State; later *secular* (1402); borrowed from Old French *seculer,* learned borrowing from Late Latin, and borrowed into English directly from Late Latin *saeculāris* worldly, secular, from Latin *saeculāris* of an age, occurring once in an age, from *saeculum* age, span of time, generation; for suffix see -AR. **—secularism** *n.* skepticism in regard to religion. 1851, formed from English *secular* + *-ism.* **—secularize** *v.* make secular. 1611, in Cotgrave's *Dictionary;* borrowed from French *séculariser,* from Late Latin *saeculāris* secular; for suffix see -IZE.

secure *adj.* Probably 1533, without care or apprehension, careless, overconfident; borrowed from Latin *sēcūrus* without care, safe, from a lost prepositional phrase **sē cūrā; sē* free from, and *cūrā,* ablative of *cūra* care. The meaning of safe, free from danger, is first recorded in English in 1582. Doublet of SURE. **—v.** 1593, make secure, in Shakespeare's *2 Henry VI;* from the adjective. The meaning of get secure possession of is first recorded in 1743. **—security** *n.* Before 1425, freedom from anxiety; probably before 1425, condition of being secure, in a translation of Higden's *Polychronicon;* borrowed from Latin *sēcūritās,* from *sēcūrus* secure; for suffix see -ITY.

sedan (sidan′) *n.* 1635, covered chair carried on poles, of uncertain origin.

It has been suggested that this word was borrowed from a dialectal (southern) Italian derivative of *sede* chair, from Latin *sēdēs,* related to *sedēre* to SIT. This theory is based upon a statement by John Evelyn that the sedan was brought from Naples to England by Sir Sanders Duncombe, who was granted in 1634 the exclusive right of supplying "covered chairs (called sedans)." An alternative conjecture connecting the word with the name of Sedan, a town in northeastern France, lacks the specific connections of the story from Evelyn's diary.

The meaning of a closed automobile seating four or more persons is first recorded in 1915, in American English.

sedate[1] *adj.* quiet, calm, serious. 1663, probably a back formation from *sedation,* modeled on Latin *sēdātus,* past participle of *sēdāre* to settle, calm, causative of *sedēre* to SIT; for suffix see -ATE[1]. **—sedation** *n.* Probably before 1425 *sedacioun, sedacion* alleviation of pain, in a translation of Chauliac's *Grande Chirurgie;* borrowed through Middle French *sédation,* and directly from Latin *sēdātiōnem* (nominative *sēdātiō*), from *sēdāre;* for suffix see -ATION. The general sense of a making calm or quiet is first recorded in English in 1874. **—sedative** *adj.* Probably before 1425 *sedatif, sedatyve* tending to alleviate pain, soothing; borrowed through Middle French *sédatif* (feminine *sédative*), and directly from Medieval Latin *sedativus,* from Latin *sēdāt-,* stem of the past participle of *sēdāre;* for suffix see -IVE. The sense of calming, quieting, is first recorded in 1813. —*n.* 1785, sedative medicine; from the adjective, unless the noun use (first recorded in 1392) remained submerged in medical vocabulary until again recorded in 1785, in which case it may be that the adjective use derives from the noun in English.

sedate[2] *v.* treat with sedatives. 1945, back formation from SEDATION and SEDATIVE. (see SEDATE[1]).

sedentary *adj.* requiring one to sit still much of the time. 1598, remaining in one place, not migratory; borrowed from Middle French *sédentaire,* from Latin *sedentārius* sitting, remaining in one place, from *sedēns* (genitive *sedentis*), present participle of *sedēre* to SIT; for suffix see -ARY. The meaning of requiring one to sit still much of the time (said of habits, occupations, etc.) is first recorded in English in Florio's translation of Montaigne's *Essays* (1603).

sedge *n.* grasslike plant that grows in wet places. About 1250 *segge,* in *The Owl and the Nightingale;* developed from Old English (about 700) *secg,* from Proto-Germanic **sag̃jás,* Indo-European **sokyós;* cognate with Middle Low German *segge* sedge, and possibly with Welsh *hesg* sedge, Middle Irish *seisc* rush, reed, from Indo-European **sekskā,* formed from **sek-* to cut (Pok.895).

The form *sedge* is not recorded until the 1590's and did not generally displace the earlier *seg, segge* until the early 1900's; for a note on the later spelling see DRUDGE.

sediment *n.* matter that settles to the bottom of a liquid. 1547, borrowed from Middle French *sédiment,* learned borrowing from Latin, and probably borrowed into English directly from Latin *sedimentum* a settling, sinking down, from *sedēre* to settle, SIT. **—sedimentary** *adj.* 1830, formed by or from deposits of sediment, in Sir Charles Lyell's *Principles of Geology;* formed from English *sediment* + *-ary.* **—sedimentation** *n.* 1874, deposition of sediment, formed from English *sediment* + *-ation.*

sedition *n.* incitement to discontent or rebellion. Probably about 1350 *sediciun* violent strife between factions; later *sedicioun* (about 1384); borrowed from Old French *sedicion, sedition,* learned borrowing from Latin, and borrowed into English directly from Latin *sēditiōnem* (nominative *sēditiō*) civil disorder, dissension;

literally, a going apart, separation (*sēd-*, variant of *sē-* apart + *itiō* a going, from *it-*, past participle of *īre* to go; see EXIT); for suffix see -TION. The meaning of rebellion, mutiny, revolt is first recorded in Middle English in 1439; that of incitement to discontent or rebellion is first recorded in English in 1838. **—seditious** *adj.* stirring up discontent or rebellion. Probably 1435 *sedicious;* borrowed from Middle French *seditieux* (feminine *seditieuse*), from Latin *sēditiōsus* factious, from *sēditiōnem* (nominative *sēditiō*) sedition; for suffix see -OUS.

seduce *v.* 1526, to lead astray, tempt, entice; borrowed from Latin *sēdūcere* lead away, lead astray (*sē-* aside, away + *dūcere* to lead; see TOW[1] pull). The extended meaning of persuade or entice to have sexual intercourse is first recorded about 1560.

Seduce was again borrowed into English (from Latin) replacing the Middle English form *seduisen* (1477, in Caxton's translation of *The History of Jason*), borrowed from Middle French *séduis-*, stem of *séduire* seduce. This Middle French verb was an alteration of Old French *suduire* to corrupt, seduce, from Latin *subdūcere* draw away, withdraw, remove (*sub-* from under, further + *dūcere* to lead). Curiously, the Middle French verb was influenced in form by Medieval Latin *seducere* to seduce, from Latin *sēdūcere* lead away, lead astray, the Latin verb from which modern English *seduce* is borrowed.

—seduction *n.* 1526, borrowed from Middle French *séduction,* learned borrowing from Latin *sēductiōnem* (nominative *sēductiō*) a leading astray, from *sēduct-*, stem of the past participle of *sedūcere* lead away, lead astray; for suffix see -TION. **—seductive** *adj.* Before 1770, that tempts or entices; probably formed in English as an adjective to *seduction,* on the model of Medieval Latin *seductivus* deceiving, from Latin *sēduct-*, stem of the past participle + English suffix *-ive.*

sedulous (sej′ūləs) *adj.* hardworking, painstaking. 1540, constant, persistent; later, diligent, industrious (1593); borrowed from Latin *sēdulus* attentive or painstaking, probably evolved from the adverb *sēdulō* sincerely, painstakingly, diligently, representing earlier Latin *sē dolō* without deception or guile (*sē* without + *dolō,* ablative of *dolus* deception or guile, from or cognate with Greek *dólos;* see TALE); for suffix see -OUS. **—sedulity** *n.* 1542, diligence, industry; borrowed from Latin *sēdulitās* assiduity, from *sēdulus* painstaking; for suffix see -ITY.

see[1] *v.* look at. Before 1126 *seen;* earlier *sen* (1106); developed from Old English *sēon* (about 725, in *Beowulf*). The Old English word is cognate with Old Frisian *siā* to see, Old Saxon *sehan,* Middle Dutch *sien* (modern Dutch *zien*), Old High German *sehan* (modern German *sehen*), Old Icelandic *sjā* (Norwegian and Swedish *se*), and Gothic *saíhwan,* from Proto-Germanic **seHwanan* see. Cognates outside Germanic include Tocharian A *šotre,* Tocharian B *šotri* to show, and Hittite *sǎkwa,* pl., eyes, from Indo-European **sekw-* (Pok.898). It has often been claimed, but not accepted, that this is identical with the root **sekw-/sokw-* set up for English SAY (from the sense-development see: show: tell). Likewise, it has been asserted that **sekw-*, see, is only a special development of **sekw-* follow (as in Latin *sequī*). But this is all speculative.

Though the form *see* appeared before 1300 and occurs occasionally in the record of English thereafter, it did not become an established spelling until well into the 1600's. The form *saw* represented in the Old English past tense *seah,* is found as early as 1106 in the *Anglo-Saxon Chronicle,* but it did not become the established form until the late 1600's, the form *see* and *seen* also being used for the past tense. The past participle *seen* (Old English *sewen*) was spelled variously in Middle English (*seyen, seyn*), becoming established in its form about 1600.

—seer *n.* Before 1338, one to whom divine revelations are made in visions, in Mannyng's *Chronicle of England;* formed from Middle English *seen* to see + *-er*[1].

see[2] *n.* position or authority of a bishop. About 1300 *se* throne of a bishop or monarch; 1307 *see;* borrowed from Old French *sié,* from Gallo-Romance **sedem,* alteration (influenced by Latin *sedēre*) of Latin *sēdem* (nominative *sēdēs*) seat, abode, related to *sedēre* SIT. The extended meaning of the position or authority of a bishop is first recorded in Gower's *Confessio Amantis* (before 1393).

seed *n.* Before 1124 *sed* grain of a plant; later *sede* (probably about 1150), *seed* (before 1376); developed from Old English *sēd* (before 830), earlier *sǣd* (before 1050). The Old English forms are cognate with Old Frisian *sēd* seed, Old Saxon *sād,* Middle Dutch *saet* (modern Dutch *zaad*), Old High German *sāt* (modern German *Saat*), Old Icelandic *sādh,* and Gothic *manasēths* mankind, the world, from Proto-Germanic **sǣđís, *sǣđá-*, from the root **sǣ-* to SOW. Cognates outside Germanic include Latin *sēmen* seed, Old Prussian *semen,* Old Slavic *sěmę,* Welsh *had,* Cornish *has,* from Indo-European **sē-/sə-* throw, sow (Pok.890). **—v.** sow with seeds. About 1375 *seden, seeden* flower, flourish, in Chaucer's *Anelida and Arcite;* later, to produce seed (before 1398, in Trevisa's translation of Bartholomew's *De Proprietatibus Rerum*); from the noun. The meaning of sow seed is first recorded about 1440. **—seedling** *n.* 1660, formed from English *seed,* n. + *-ling*[1]. **—seedy** *adj.* 1440 *sedy* fruitful, abundant; formed from Middle English *sed* seed, n. + *-y*[1]. The meaning of shabby, no longer fresh, is first recorded in 1749, probably in allusion to the appearance of a flowering plant that has run to seed and is spent.

seek *v.* 1155 *sechan* require, demand; later *sechen* try to find, look for (probably about 1175), and *sekenn* (probably about 1200); developed from Old English *sēcan* visit, pursue (about 725, in *Beowulf*), and in the sense of try to find (before 899). Old English *sēcan* is cognate with Old Frisian *sēka* to seek, Old Saxon *sōkian,* Middle Dutch *soeken* (modern Dutch *zoeken*), Old High German *suohhan* (modern German *suchen*), Old Icelandic *sœkja,* and Gothic *sōkjan,* from Proto-Germanic **sōkjanan.* Cognates outside Germanic are found in Latin *sāgīre* perceive keenly, *sagāx* (genitive *sagācis*) keenly scenting, Old Irish *saigim* I seek, Greek *hēgeîsthai* to lead, guide, and Hittite *sǎk-*, *sǎkk-* to know, from Indo-European **sāg-/səg-* (Pok.876).

seem *v.* Probably before 1200 *semen* befit, be suitable to; probably about 1200, appear to be; later with the spelling *seemen* (probably about 1350); borrowed from a Scandinavian source (compare Old Icelandic *sœma* to befit, conform to, and *sœmr* fitting, seemly). These Scandinavian words are cognate with Old Saxon *sōmi* fitting, Old English *sōm* agreement, reconciliation, from Proto-Germanic **sōm-*, Indo-European **sōm-*, root **sem-* one (Pok.905). **—seemly** *adj.* suitable, proper. Probably before 1200 *semlich,* in *Ancrene Riwle;* later *semly* (probably before 1300), *seemly* (about 1380); borrowed from a Scandinavian source (compare Old Icelandic *sœmiligr,* from *sœmr* fitting); for suffix see -LY².

seep *v.* 1790, variant of earlier *sipe* to leak (1503); evidence for the word's occurrence in Middle English is uncertain. English *sipe* is probably related to Old English *sipian* to seep and cognate with Middle Low German *sīpen* to seep, Middle High German *sīfen,* dialectal Norwegian and Swedish *sipa,* Danish *sive,* from Proto-Germanic **sip-,* Indo-European **sib-,* root **seib-/sē(i)b-* (Pok.894). **—seepage** *n.* 1825, leakage, oozing, in Jamieson's *Etymological Dictionary of the Scottish Language;* formed from English *seep* + *-age.*

seersucker (sir′suk′ər) *n.* cloth with alternate stripes of plain and crinkled material. 1722 *sea sucker;* later, *seersucker* (1736); borrowed from Hindi *śīrśakar,* from Persian *shīr o shakkar* striped cloth; literally, milk and sugar. (Compare Sanskrit *kṣīrá-m* milk; *śarkara-m* sugar.)

The name evolved in allusion to the surface of the cotton cloth which originally had alternate smooth and puckered stripes, thereby producing the effect of the smooth surface of milk and the bumpy surface of sugar.

seesaw *n.* 1640, probably imitative of the motion of sawyers and the sound of the action of a two-man saw drawn over wood or stone. This notion is reinforced by the fact that *seesaw* was originally part of a rhythmical jingle imitating the back-and-forth motion of sawyers, as in *see saw sacke a downe* (1640), *see saw, Margery Daw* (1700's). The extended meaning of movement back and forth or up and down is first recorded in 1704. The meaning of a game in which children sit at opposite ends of a plank and move up and down is not found until 1821; and reference to the plank itself in 1824. **—v.** move up and down on a seesaw. 1712, in John Arbuthnot's writings; from the noun.

seethe *v.* About 1300 *sethen* boil; earlier *suden* (probably before 1200, in Layamon's *Chronicle of Britain*); developed from Old English *sēothan* (about 725, in *Beowulf*). Old English *sēothan* is cognate with Old Frisian *siātha* to boil, Middle Low German *sēden,* Middle Dutch *sieden* (modern Dutch *zieden*), Old High German *siodan* (modern German *sieden*), Old Icelandic *sjōdha* to boil (Norwegian and Danish *syde,* Swedish *sjuda*), from Proto-Germanic **seuthanan.* Cognates outside Germanic are found in Lithuanian *siaũsti* to rage, and Avestan *hāvayeiti* (he) stews, from Indo-European **seut-,* root **seu-* (Pok.914). The figurative sense of be disturbed, agitated, or excited, is first recorded in Shakespeare's *Troylus and Cressida* (1606).

segment *n.* 1570, (in geometry) part of a circle cut off by a line; borrowed from Latin *segmentum* a strip or piece cut off (in Medieval Latin a geometric segment), from earlier **sec-mentom,* from *secāre* to cut; see SECTION; for suffix see -MENT. The general sense of a division or section is first recorded in 1762. **—v.** divide into segments. 1859, from the noun. **—segmental** *adj.* 1816, having the form of a segment of a circle; later, of or composed of segments (1854); formed from English *segment,* n. + *-al*¹. **—segmentation** *n.* 1656, a cutting into small pieces, in Blount's *Glossographia;* formed from English *segment,* v. + *-ation.* The meaning of division into segments (specifically cell growth and division) is first recorded in 1851.

segregate *v.* 1542, borrowed from Latin *sēgregātus,* past participle of *sēgregāre* separate from the flock, isolate, divide, from a lost prepositional phrase **sē grege* (*sē* apart from; and *grege,* ablative of *grex* herd, flock; see GREGARIOUS); for suffix see -ATE¹. **—segregation** *n.* 1555, borrowed from Late Latin *sēgregātiōnem* (nominative *sēgregātiō*) a separating, dividing, from *sēgregāre;* for suffix see -ATION. **—segregationist** *n.* person who advocates racial segregation. 1920's American English, formed from *segregation* + *-ist.*

seigneur (sēnyėr′) *n.* feudal lord or landowner. 1592, borrowed from Middle French *seigneur,* from Old French *seignor* SEIGNIOR.

seignior (sēn′yər) *n.* lord, lord of a manor. Probably before 1300 *seygnour* ruler, in *Arthour and Merlin;* later *seygniour* (about 1400); borrowed from Old French *seignior, seignor,* learned borrowing from Latin *seniōrem,* accusative of *senior* older, SENIOR.

seine (sān) *n.* fishing net that hangs straight down in the water. About 1300 *seyne,* in *King Horn;* developed from Old English (about 950) *segne;* borrowed from Latin *sagēna,* from Greek *sagḗnē* a fishing net; also, a hunting net, of uncertain origin. Other Germanic words borrowed from the Latin include Old Saxon *segina* and Old High German *segina* seine, but the spelling in English, though from Latin, was later influenced by Old French *seine,* from Latin. **—v.** to fish with a seine. 1836 (implied in *seining*); from the noun.

seismic (sīz′mik) *adj.* of earthquakes or an earthquake. 1858, formed in English from Greek *seismós* earthquake + English *-ic.* **—seismograph** *n.* instrument for recording earthquakes. 1858, formed in English from Greek *seismós* earthquake + English *-graph.* **—seismology** *n.* study of earthquakes. 1858, formed in English from Greek *seismós* earthquake + English *-logy.* The identical dates for these words appear because the words were extracted from a single report of the British Association for the Advancement of Science describing the work of the great Italian physicist Luigi Palmieri (1807-96), who invented a seismograph while director of the meteorological observatory on Vesuvius.

seismo- a combining form meaning earthquake, as in *seismograph, seismology.* Borrowed from Greek *seismo-,* combining form of *seismós* earthquake, a shaking, from *seíein* to shake, cognate with Sanskrit *tvéṣati* is excited, from Indo-European **tweis-* to shake (Pok. 1099).

seize *v.* 1265 *saisen* take possession of; later *sesen, seisen* (probably before 1300), and *seizen* (before 1500); borrowed from Old French *seisir,* from Late Latin *sacīre,* perhaps from Frankish **sakjan* lay claim to, related to Old Saxon *saka* a case in court, and Gothic *sōkjan* to SEEK. **—seizure** *n.* 1482 *seisure* act of seizing; formed from *seisen* to seize + *-ure,* and replacing earlier Middle English *sesir* (1449), *seiser* (1451); borrowed from Old French *seisir* to seize; see -ER³.

seldom *adv.* Probably about 1150 *selden;* later *seldum* (before 1250), and *seldom* (probably before 1300); developed from Old English *seldum* (before 900), alteration of *seldan,* on the analogy of adverbial dative plurals ending in *-um,* like *whilom* at one time. Old English *seldan* is cognate with Old Frisian, Middle Low German, and Middle Dutch *selden* seldom, Old High German *seltan* (modern German *selten*), and *seltsāni* (modern German *seltsam* strange, odd), Old Icelandic *sjaldan* (Swedish *sällan,* Danish and Norwegian *sjelden*), and Gothic *sildaleiks* wonderful, astonishing, from Proto-Germanic **selda-*, a form perhaps cognate with Latin *sōlus* alone, and Latin *sēd, sē* apart from; see SELF.

select *v.* 1567, borrowed from Latin *sēlēctus,* past participle of *sēligere* choose out, select (*sē-* apart + *legere* gather, select; see LEGEND). **—adj.** chosen specially. 1565, in Cooper's *Thesaurus Linguae Romanae et Britannicae;* borrowed from Latin *sēlēctus,* past participle. **—selection** *n.* 1646-58, act of selecting; borrowed from Latin *sēlēctiōnem* (nominative *sēlēctiō*) a choosing out, selection, from *sēlēct-,* stem of the past participle of *sēligere;* for suffix see -TION. **—selective** *adj.* 1625, formed from English *select,* v. + *-ive.* **—selective service** military draft (1917, American English)

selenium (silē'nēəm) *n.* nonmetallic chemical element. 1818, New Latin; formed from Greek *selḗnē* moon (Doric *selā́nā*), from *sélas* light, brightness (of unknown origin) + New Latin *-ium,* chemical suffix. *Selenium* was named in reference to the moon by its discoverer, the Swedish chemist Berzelius, 1779-1848, in contradistinction to tellurium, an element with similar properties, named after the earth.

self *pron.* Old English *self, seolf, sylf* one's own person, not another, same (about 725, in *Beowulf*); cognate with Old Frisian and Old Saxon *self* self, same, Middle Dutch *selve, self* (modern Dutch *zelf*), Old High German *selb* (modern German *selbst*), Old Icelandic *sjālfr* self (Norwegian *sjøl,* Swedish *själv,* Danish *selv*), and Gothic *silba,* from Proto-Germanic **selƀa-*, **selban-*.

The ultimate etymology of this word is obscure; but many scholars regard it as a compound of the Indo-European pronominal stem **se-*, found in Latin *sē* self, Gothic *sik,* Old High German *sih* (modern German *sich*), etc.; see SUICIDE.

The pronoun *self* was originally used with a noun or pronoun, as in *the man self* and *the self deed;* this construction has been superseded by the use of intensive and reflexive pronouns such as *himself, myself,* as in *he can do it himself, I couldn't help myself. Self* is still sometimes used as an independent pronoun in expressions such as *make check payable to self, a room for self and wife,* a usage largely confined to commercial English.
—n. one's own person. Before 1325 *self,* in *Cursor Mundi;* from the pronoun.
—selfish *adj.* caring too much for oneself. 1640, formed from English *self,* n. + *-ish.* According to the OED *selfish* may have been coined during the Presbyterian upswelling of the mid-1600's, the term finally becoming the choice of established usage, as against *self-ended* and *self-ful.* **—selfsame** *adj.* very same (1408, in Lydgate's *Reson and Sensuallyte*).

self- a combining form meaning: **1** of or over oneself: *self-conscious = conscious of oneself; self-control = control over oneself.* **2** by or in oneself or itself, without outside aid: *self-inflicted = inflicted by oneself; self-evident = evident in itself.* **3** to or for oneself: *self-addressed = addressed to oneself; self-respect = respect for oneself.* **4** oneself (as object): *self-defeating = defeating oneself.* **5** automatic or automatically: *self-winding = winding automatically.* Developed from Old English *self-, sylf-,* combining form of *self, seolf, sylf* SELF, corresponding to Old Saxon and Middle Dutch *self-,* Old High German *selb-* (modern German *selb-,* also genitive *selbst-*), Old Icelandic *siālf-,* and Gothic *silba-,* with reflexive meaning "oneself," "itself."

sell *v.* Probably before 1200 *sellen;* developed from Old English *sellan* to give, sell (about 725, in *Beowulf*).

Old English *sellan* (past tense *sealde,* past participle *seald*) is cognate with Old Frisian *sella* to give, sell, Old Saxon *sellian* to give, Middle Low German *sellen* to sell by retail, Old High German *sellen* to deliver, Old Icelandic *selja* to hand over, sell (Norwegian *salge,* Swedish *sälja* to sell, Danish *sælge*), and Gothic *saljan* to offer (a sacrifice), from Proto-Germanic **saljanan.* It has been suggested that these words may be causative verb forms related to Old English *salu* sale, Old High German *sala* delivery of goods, Old Icelandic *sala* sale, Old Slavic *sŭlŭ* messenger, *sŭlati* to send, and perhaps Greek *heleîn* to take, seize, Latin **-selere* to take (in *cōnsulere* take counsel), and Old Irish *selb* and Welsh *helw* possession, from Indo-European **sel-/sol-* take (Pok.899).
—n. 1838, act of betraying, in Dickens' *Oliver Twist;* from the verb. The slang use of trick, hoax, is first recorded in 1853.
—seller *n.* (probably before 1200)

Seltzer *n.* carbonated mineral water. 1775, in Sheridan's *St. Patrick's Day;* alteration of earlier *Selters* (1741); borrowed from German *Selterser* a kind of mineral water; literally, of *Selters,* the name of a village in what is now western Germany, where the mineral water is found.

selvage or **selvedge** (sel'vij) *n.* edge of a fabric, border. Probably before 1425 *selfegge,* probably formed in English from *self* + *egge* edge, on the model of Middle Flemish *selfegghe* edge of a fabric; literally, self-edge; so called because the edge of such fabric so finished does not unravel and can therefore be its own edging. The Middle Flemish word is a compound of *self-* self + *egghe* edge.

semantic *adj.* of or having to do with the meaning of words. 1894, borrowed from French *sémantique* (coined in 1883 by the French linguist Michel J.A. Bréal, 1832-1915), from Greek *sēmantikós* significant, from *sēmaínein* to show, signify, indicate by a sign, from *sêma* sign (Doric *sâma*); for suffix see -IC. Greek *sêma* is probably cognate with Sacian (North Aryan) *śśāma* sign (in antiquity spoken in what is now Kirghiz), Pok.243. The word was recorded earlier in reference to its Greek sense of sign, or show by a sign, when used in English as the adjective sense "related to signs of the weather," a now obsolete meaning. **—semantics** *n.* study of meanings. 1893, borrowed from French *sémantique,* noun use of *sémantique,* adj.; for suffix see -ICS. The study of semantics as a branch of 19th century philology was known earlier in English as *semasiology* (1847, borrowed from German *Semasiologie,* from Greek *sēmasíā* signification, meaning, from *sēmaínein* signify + German *-logie* -logy, and was coined in German before 1829 by the philologist C.K. Reisig, 1792-1829).

semaphore (sem'əfôr) *n.* apparatus for signaling. 1816, probably borrowed from French *sémaphore;* ultimately formed from Greek *sêma* sign, signal + *-phóros* bearer, from *phérein* to carry, BEAR². **—v.** signal by semaphore. 1893, from the noun.

semblance *n.* Before 1325 *semblance* appearance, in *Cursor Mundi;* borrowed from Old French *semblance* likeness, appearance, from *sembler* to seem, appear, from Latin *simulāre, similāre* to resemble, imitate, from *similis* like; see SAME; for suffix see -ANCE. An earlier form *semblant* (probably before 1200, borrowed from Old French *semblant,* n., appearance, likeness, from *semblant,* adj., from *sembler*) was gradually replaced by *semblance* and is not recorded in English after the mid-1600's, except as an adjective (1843). The meaning of likeness, image or copy of something, is first recorded in Middle English in Chaucer's translation of Boethius' *De Consolatione Philosophiae* (about 1380). The meaning of false or deceiving appearance is first found in Shakespeare's *Henry V* (1599).

semen *n.* fluid containing the male sperm. Before 1398, in Trevisa's translation of Bartholomew's *De Proprietatibus Rerum;* borrowed from Latin *sēmen* SEED.

semester *n.* half of a school year. 1827, borrowed from German *Semester,* from Latin *sēmēstris* in *cursus sēmēstris* course of six months, from *sēmēstris* of six months (*sex* SIX + *mēnsis* month; see MOON).

semi- a prefix meaning: **1** exactly half: *semicircle = a half circle.* **2** about half, partly, incompletely: *semiskilled = incompletely skilled; semicivilized = partly civilized.* **3** half a (period of time), twice: *semiannually = every half year, twice a year.* Borrowed from Latin *sēmi-* half, cognate with Greek *hēmi-* half, HEMI-, and Sanskrit *sāmi-* half, incompletely, Old High German *sāmi-* and Old English *sām-* half, found in such formations as *sāmhāl* in poor health; literally, half-whole; *sāmsoden* half-cooked; figuratively, half-baked or stupid; and *sāmcucu* half-dead; literally, half-alive. The last survivor of this group is *sand-blind* dim-sighted, the perverted resultant of Old English **sāmblind.*

The prefix is used freely in English to form compounds with adjectives, participles, nouns, as found in Middle English words modeled on Latin: *semigod,* after Latin *sēmideus; semidouble,* after Medieval Latin *semiduplex;* or Middle English words borrowed from Latin or Old French: *semidiameter, semicircular;* or purely Middle English formations, such as *semibousi* half-drunk; or as in some of the newer formations: *semifinal,* n., adj. (1884, signifying one of two rounds or matches conducted to determine who will take part in the final one, which follows), *semitrailer,* n. (1919, type of truck and trailer that can be detached), *semidetached,* adj., n. (1859, signifying one house in a row of houses, each sharing a common or connecting wall with the next house). These latter examples have also produced a new clipped formation *semi,* n. with the meanings of: 1) semifinal, n., 2) semidetached house, 3) semitrailer truck.

seminal *adj.* of semen or seed. Before 1398, in Trevisa's translation of Bartholomew's *De Proprietatibus Rerum;* borrowed from Old French *seminal,* learned borrowing from Latin, and borrowed into English directly from Latin *sēminālis,* from *sēmen* (genitive *sēminis*) SEED; for suffix see -AL[1]. The figurative sense of containing the possibility of future development is first recorded in English in 1634, in the adverbial use *seminally.*

seminar *n.* group of college or university students doing research under direction. 1887, American English; borrowing of German *Seminar,* from Latin *sēminārium* breeding ground, plant nursery. Doublet of SEMINARY. The extended sense of any meeting or conference for discussion of a subject is first recorded in 1944, in American English.

seminary (sem′ənerʹē) *n.* About 1440, plot where plants are raised from seed; borrowed from Latin *sēminārium* plant nursery, (figurative) breeding ground, from *sēminārius* of seed, from *sēmen* (genitive *sēminis*) SEED; for suffix see -ARY. Doublet of SEMINAR. The meaning of a school or college for training students to be priests is first recorded in 1581; the sense of any school or college (as in *a ladies' seminary*) was current from 1585 to the early 1930's. **—seminarian** *n.* 1584, student at a seminary, formed from English *seminary* + *-an.*

semiotics *n.* science of signs or symbols. 1880, borrowed from Greek *sēmeiōtikós* observant of signs, adjective to *sēmeíōsis* indication (earlier **sēmeiōtis*), from *sēmeioûn* to signal, from *sēmeîon* sign, from *sêma* sign; see SEMANTIC; for suffix see -ICS. A form of the word closer to the Greek is known earlier in English *semeiotics* in the meaning of that branch of medicine dealing with the interpretation of symptoms (1670), and is referred to even earlier in the adjective *semeiotical* (1588).

In the general sense of signs or symbols and the study of their use in conveying meaning, the word is recorded as early as 1641 in the works of Bishop John Wilkins (first secretary of the Royal Society).

Semite *n.* member of an ancient group of people including the Hebrews, Arabs, Phoenicians, Assyrians, etc. 1847, probably a back formation from *Semitic,* perhaps formed by influence of French *Sémite* (1845), from Late Latin *Sēm* Shem, one of the three sons of Noah, regarded as the ancestor of the Semites, from Greek *Sēm,* from Hebrew *Shēm;* for suffix see -ITE[1]. **—Semitic** *adj.* of the Semites or their languages. 1813, borrowed from New Latin *Semiticus,* from *Semita* Semite; for suffix see -IC. —*n.* the Semitic family of languages. 1875, from the adjective.

semolina (sem′əlēʹnə) *n.* parts of hard wheat remaining after the flour has been sifted through. 1797, alteration of Italian *semolino,* diminutive of *semola* bran, from Latin *simila* the finest flour, probably from the same Semitic source as Greek *semídālis* the finest flour (compare Assyrian *samīdu* and Syrian *sĕmīdā* fine meal).

senate *n.* Probably before 1200 *senaht* Roman senate, in Layamon's *Chronicle of Britain;* later *senat* governing body of a city (about 1380, in Chaucer's translation of Boethius' *De Consolatione Philosophiae*); *senate* (about 1384); borrowed from Old French *senat,* learned borrowing from Latin, and borrowed into English directly from Latin *senātus* the highest council of state in ancient Rome; literally, council of elders, from *senex* (genitive *senis*) old man, old; see SENIOR; for suffix see -ATE[3]. The meaning of the upper and smaller branch of a legislature is first recorded in English in 1775, in the letters of Abigail Adams. **—senator** *n.* Probably before 1200 *senatur* Roman noble, in Layamon's *Chronicle of Britain;* borrowed from Old French *senateur,* learned borrowing from Latin, and borrowed directly into English from Latin *senātor,* from *senex* old man, old; for suffix see -OR[2]. The meaning of a member of the governing body of any state is first recorded in English before 1387, and is found earlier in a figurative sense in the Wycliffe Bible (before 1382). **—senatorial** *adj.* 1740, either formed from English *senator* + *-ial,* or borrowed from French *sénatorial,* from Latin *senātōrius* pertaining to a senator; for suffix see -IAL.

send *v.* Before 1121 *senden* cause or order to go; developed from Old English *sendan* (about 725, in *Beowulf*); cognate with Old Frisian *senda* to send, Old Saxon *sendian,* Middle Dutch *senden* (modern Dutch *zenden*), Old High German *senten* (modern German *senden*); Old Icelandic *senda* (Swedish *sända,* Danish and Norwegian *sende*), and Gothic *sandjan* from Proto-Germanic **sanđjanan,* related to **senth-* to go, found in Gothic *sinths* going, time, Old Icelandic *sinni* journey, Old High German *sind,* and Old Saxon, Old Frisian, and Old English *sīth* journey, from Proto-Germanic **senthaz.* Cognates outside Germanic are found in Old Irish *sēt* road, way (from earlier **sent-*), Welsh *hynt,* Armenian *ənt'aç,* Lithuanian *siųsti* to send, from Indo-European **sent-* take a direction, go (Pok.908). **—send-off** *n.* friendly demonstration in honor of a person setting out on a journey, career, etc. (1872, in Mark Twain's *Roughing It*).

seneschal (sen'əshəl) *n.* steward in charge of a royal palace or a nobleman's estate in the Middle Ages. Probably before 1378, in a version of *Piers Plowman;* borrowing of Old French *seneschal,* from Frankish **siniskalk,* a compound represented by Old High German *senescalh* eldest servant (*sene-* old; see SENIOR + *scalh, scalc* servant; see MARSHAL).

senile *adj.* 1661, of or belonging to old age, in Robert Boyle's writings; borrowed from French *sénile,* or directly from Latin *senīlis* of old age, from *senex* (genitive *senis*) old, old man; see SENIOR. The meaning of showing weakness often characteristic of old age is first recorded in Thackeray's *Vanity Fair* (1848). **—senility** *n.* 1791, in Boswell's *Life of Samuel Johnson;* formed from English *senile* + *-ity.*

senior *adj.* older. 1287-88 *seniore* the elder (as added to a personal name identical with a son's name); borrowed from Latin *senior* older, comparative of *senex* (genitive *senis*) old. Latin *senior, senis* is cognate with Old Irish *sen* old, Greek *hénos,* Lithuanian *sẽnas,* Armenian *hin,* Sanskrit *sána-s,* from Indo-European **sénos* (Pok.907), and in Germanic with Gothic *sineigs* old, *sinista* eldest, Old High German *sene-,* and Old Icelandic *sina* old grass; for suffix see -OR². The meaning of higher in rank or longer in service (as in *a senior officer*) is first recorded in 1513. **—n.** older person, elder. 1363 *senyour* person of authority; borrowed from Latin *senior,* noun use of *senior,* adj., older. The school and college sense of an advanced student is first recorded in 1612; the specialized U.S. sense of a student in the 4th year is attested since 1741. **—senior citizen** (1938, American English) **—seniority** *n.* Probably about 1450 *seniorite* priority or precedence in office or service; borrowed from Medieval Latin *senioritas,* from Latin *senior* senior; for suffix see -ITY.

senna (sen'ə) *n.* 1543, plant of the same genus as cassia, New Latin, from Arabic *sanā.* The meaning of a laxative extracted from the leaflets of the senna is first recorded in English in 1571.

sensate (sen'sāt) *adj.* Before 1450 *sensat* endowed with physical sensation; borrowed from Late Latin *sēnsātus* endowed with sense, sensible, from Latin *sēnsus* feeling, SENSE; for suffix see -ATE¹. The meaning of perceived by the senses was borrowed from Medieval Latin *sensatus* and is first recorded in English in 1847.

sensation *n.* 1615, the action of the senses, physical feeling, in Helkiah Crooke's *A Description of the Body of Man;* borrowed from French *sensation,* or directly from Medieval Latin *sensationem* (nominative *sensatio*), from Late Latin *sēnsātus* endowed with sense, sensible, see SENSATE; for suffix see -ATION. The meaning of a state of strong or excited feeling or impression produced in a community by some (shocking, surprising, etc.) event is first recorded in English in 1779. **—sensational** *adj.* 1840, of or pertaining to sensation or the senses; formed from English *sensation* + *-al*¹. The meaning of arousing strong or excited feeling, aiming at violent, exciting effects, occurs in 1854, specifically in reference to works of literature or art. **—sensationalism** *n.* 1865, (in literature, journalism, etc.) given or tending toward what is sensational; earlier, the philosophical theory that sensation is the only source of knowledge (1846); formed from English *sensational* + *-ism.*

sense *n.* Before 1382 *sense* meaning, in the Wycliffe Bible; borrowed from Old French *sens,* and directly from Latin *sēnsus* (genitive *sēnsūs*) perception, feeling, understanding, meaning, formed from *sentīre* perceive, know, feel. Latin *sentīre* is cognate with Lithuanian *sintė̃ti* to think, Old Slavic *sęštĭ* smart, Avestan *hant-* to reach, attain, Armenian *ənt'anam* I go, travel, hurry, and *ənt'ac* road, way; and in Germanic with Old High German *sinnan* to strive after, travel, *sin* mind, sense (in modern German *Sinn*); see SEND. The meaning of a faculty of perception or sensation (as in *a sense of touch*) is first recorded in English in 1526, and in the plural (*lull one's senses*), in 1597, in Shakespeare's *2 Henry IV.* The meaning of perception, understanding, appreciation (as in *a sense of humor*), before 1540. **—v.** be aware, feel. 1598, from the noun. **—senseless** *adj.* (1557) **—sense organ** (1854)

sensible *adj.* About 1380, perceptible by the senses, capable of being felt, in Chaucer's translation of Boethius' *De Consolatione Philosophiae;* borrowed from Old French *sensible,* and directly from Latin *sēnsibilis* having feeling, perceptible by the senses, from *sēnsus,* past participle of *sentīre* perceive, feel; see SENSE; for suffix see -IBLE.

The meaning of having good sense or judgment, reasonable, judicious, is first recorded in Middle English probably about 1400. Johnson in 1755 stigmatized this meaning as used only "in low conversation" despite its earlier use by Shakespeare, Bacon, Addison, and Walpole.

—sensibility *n.* About 1380 *sensibilitie* perceived image, in Chaucer's translation of Boethius' *De Consolatione Philosophiae;* later, ability to sense or perceive (1392); borrowed from Old French *sensibilité,* from Late Latin *sēnsibilitātem* (nominative *sēnsibilitās*) the sense or meaning of words, from Latin *sēnsibilis* sensible; for suffix see -ITY. The meaning of the quality of being easily and strongly affected by emotional influences (as in *sensibility to grief*) is first recorded in 1711, and that of fineness of feeling, delicate sensitiveness of taste (as in *sensibility for colors*) in 1756-82. The plural *sensibilities* sensitive feelings, is first recorded in 1634.

sensitive *adj.* 1392 *sensitif* having feeling or sensation; borrowed from Middle French *sensitif* (feminine *sensitive*), learned borrowing from Medieval Latin, and borrowed directly into English from Medieval Latin *sensitivus* capable of sensation, from Latin *sēnsus,* past participle of *sentīre* feel, perceive; see SENSE; for suffix see -IVE. The meaning of receiving impressions readily, easily affected (as in *to have a sensitive nature*), is first recorded in Scott's *Old Mortality* (1816). **—sensitivity** *n.* 1803, quality of being sensitive; formed from English *sensitive* + *-ity*. **—sensitize** *v.* 1856, make sensitive; formed from English *sensitive* + *-ize*.

sensor *n.* sensing device or organ. 1958, from an earlier adjective *sensor* sensory (1865), shortened from SENSORY, probably on the pattern of *motor*.

sensory *adj.* of or having to do with sensation or the senses. 1749, formed in English from Latin *sēnsus* (past participle of *sentīre* to perceive, feel; see SENSE) + English *-ory*.

sensual *adj.* Probably before 1425, carnal, unspiritual; later, pertaining to the physical senses (about 1443); borrowed from Middle French *sensuel*, learned borrowing from Latin, and borrowed into English directly from Latin *sēnsuālis* endowed with feeling, sensitive, from *sēnsus* (genitive *sēnsūs*) feeling, SENSE; for suffix see -AL[1]. **—sensuality** *n.* sensual nature. Before 1340 *sensualite*; borrowed from Old French *sensualité*, from Late Latin *sēnsuālitātem* (nominative *sēnsuālitās*) capacity for sensation, from *sēnsuālis* endowed with feeling; for suffix see -ITY. **—sensuous** *adj.* 1641, in Milton's writings; formed in English from Latin *sēnsus* sense + English *-ous*. *Sensuous* was probably coined by Milton to avoid the sense of voluptuous or lustful often connoted by *sensual;* Coleridge adopted *sensuous* from Milton.

sentence *n.* Probably before 1200, doctrine, authoritative teaching, in *Ancrene Riwle;* later, punishment imposed by a court (about 1300); borrowed from Old French *sentence*, learned borrowing from Latin, and borrowed into English directly from Latin *sententia* thought, meaning, judgment, opinion, alteration (by dissimilation in the second syllable from *-tien-* to *-ten-*) of **sentientia*, from *sentientem* (nominative *sentiēns*), present participle of *sentīre* be of opinion, feel, perceive; see SENSE; for suffix see -ENCE. The sense of an utterance, expression, statement, is first recorded in Middle English in the Wycliffe Bible (before 1382), and the specific sense in grammar of a statement with a subject and predicate, in Trevisa's translation of Bartholomew's *De Proprietatibus Rerum* (before 1398). **—v.** 1413 *sentensen* (implied in *sentesed*, error for *sentensed*) to pass judgment; borrowed from Old French *sentencier*, from *sentence* sentence, n. The specific meaning of pronounce punishment on is first recorded in 1592.

sententious *adj.* 1440, full of meaning, in *Promptorium Parvulorum;* borrowed from Middle French *sententieux*, and directly from Latin *sententiōsus* full of meaning, pithy, from *sententia* opinion, maxim; see SENTENCE; for suffix see -OUS. The meaning of given to uttering pointed sayings or maxims, addicted to pompous moralizing, is first recorded in Ben Jonson's writings in 1598-99.

sentient (sen′shənt) *adj.* that can feel, of or having feeling. 1632, borrowed from Latin *sentientem* (nominative *sentiēns*) feeling, present participle of *sentīre* to feel; see SENSE; for suffix see -ENT. **—sentience** *n.* quality or state of being sentient. 1839, in Poe's *The Fall of the House of Usher;* formed in English as a noun to *sentient;* for suffix see -ENCE.

sentiment *n.* 1639, what one feels about something, feeling, opinion; spelling alteration (influenced by modern French *sentiment*) of Middle English *sentement* (about 1385, in Chaucer's *Troilus and Criseyde*); borrowed from Old French *sentement*, learned borrowing from Medieval Latin, and borrowed into English directly from Medieval Latin *sentimentum* feeling, affection, opinion, from Latin *sentīre* to feel, see SENSE; for suffix see -MENT. **—sentimental** *adj.* characterized by sentiment. 1749, formed from English *sentiment* + *-al*[1]. The sense of appealing to sentiment, as of poetry or music, is first recorded in 1762, and that of having too much sentiment in 1827, perhaps implied earlier in *sentimentalist*, in 1783. **—sentimentalism** *n.* indulgence in sentiment. 1817, in writings of Byron; formed from English *sentimental* + *-ism*. **—sentimentality** *n.* quality of being sentimental. 1770, formed from English *sentimental* + *-ity*. **—sentimentalize** *v.* indulge in sentiment. 1788, formed from English *sentimental* + *-ize*.

sentinel *n.* 1579, armed soldier keeping watch, sentry; borrowed from Middle French *sentinelle*, from Italian *sentinella*, of unknown origin. —**v.** watch over as a sentinel does. 1593, in Shakespeare's *Lucrece;* from the noun.

sentry *n.* 1611, in Cotgrave's *Dictionary*, watchtower; 1632, sentinel; perhaps a shortening or back formation (taken as containing the suffix *-ry*) of earlier *centrinel* (1598), variant of SENTINEL.

sepal (sē′pəl) *n.* one of the leaflike divisions of the calyx of a flower. 1829, borrowed from New Latin *sepalum*, which was coined in 1790 by Noel J. de Necker, 1729-93, a Flemish physician and botanist. New Latin *sepalum* was formed from Latin *petalum* PETAL apparently by substitution of the first syllable of Latin *sēparāre* SEPARATE for the first syllable of *petalum*. However, H.C. Wyld maintains that *sepalum* is "said by inventor to have been formed from Greek *sképē* 'covering'," which, if true, fails to account for the disappearance of the *k* in the New Latin word.

separate *v.* Probably before 1425 *separaten* put apart, in a translation of Higden's *Polychronicon;* borrowed from Latin *sēparātus*, past participle of *sēparāre* (*sē-* apart + *parāre* make ready, prepare; see PARE); for suffix see -ATE[1]. Doublet of SEVER. **—adj.** disconnected. 1600, borrowed from Latin *sēparātus*, past participle. **—n.** 1612, person who favors separation from a church, separatist; from the adjective. The meaning of an article or document issued separately is first recorded in 1884, in American English. The plural *separates* women's sweaters, blouses, skirts, and slacks designed to be worn separately or as an ensemble, is first recorded in 1945. **—separation** *n.* Before 1400 *separacion;* borrowed from Old French *separation*, from Latin *sēparātiōnem* (nominative *sēparātiō*), from *sēparāre* separate, v.; for suffix see -ATION. **—separatism** *n.* principle or policy of maintaining separation, especially between Church and State. 1628, formed from English *separate*, adj. + *-ism*. **—separatist** *n.* person who favors separatism. 1608, formed from English *separate*, adj. + *-ist*.

sepia (sē′pēə) *n.* brown paint or ink prepared from the inky fluid of cuttlefish. 1821; in Middle English, cuttlefish (before 1398, in Trevisa's translation of Bartholomew's *De Proprietatibus Rerum*); borrowed from Latin *sēpia* cuttlefish, from Greek *sēpíā*, perhaps from *sḗpein* make foul, rot (see SEPSIS); so called from the inky fluid which the cuttlefish secretes. **—adj.** 1827, done in sepia; from the noun.

sepoy (sē′poi) *n.* (formerly) a native of India who was a soldier in the British army. 1717-18, borrowed from

Portuguese *sipae,* from Urdu *sipāhī,* from Persian *sipāhī* soldier, horseman, from *sipāh* army.

seppuku (sep′pü′kü) *n.* hara-kiri. 1871, borrowed from Japanese *seppuku,* from *setsu puku,* from Chinese *ts'et* to cut + *biuk* belly.

sepsis *n.* septic condition. 1876, New Latin *sepsis,* from Greek *sêpsis* putrefaction, from *sépein* to rot, of unknown origin.

September *n.* ninth month. Old English (about 1050) *september;* borrowed from Latin *September,* from *septem* SEVEN, this being originally the seventh month of the ancient Roman Calendar (which began with March); for the origin of the ending *-ber* see DECEMBER. The Julian calendar (46 B.C.) changed September to the ninth month.

A Middle English form (1114) *Septembre* (borrowed from Old French *Septembre,* from Latin *Septembrem,* accusative of *September*) was replaced in the 1500's by the current Latinized form.

septennial *adj.* 1640, in James Howell's *Dodona's Grove,* occurring every seven years; later, lasting seven years (1656, in Blount's *Glossographia*); formed in English from Latin *septennium* seven-year period (*septem* SEVEN + *-ennium,* from *annus* year) + English suffix *-al*[1].

septet or **septette** *n.* musical composition for seven voices or instruments. 1828, borrowed from German *Septett,* from Latin *septem* SEVEN; for suffix see -ET and -ETTE.

septi- a combining form meaning seven, as in *septisyllable, septivalent.* Borrowed from Latin *septi-,* combining form of *septem* SEVEN. Also spelled **sept-** before a vowel, as in *septennial.*

septic *adj.* causing infection or putrefaction. 1605, borrowed from Latin *sēpticus* of or pertaining to putrefaction, from Greek *sēptikós* characterized by putrefaction or rottenness, from *sépein* cause to rot; see SEPSIS; for suffix see -IC. **—septic tank** (1902)

septicemia or **septicaemia** (sep′təsē′mēə) *n.* blood poisoning. 1866, New Latin *septicaemia,* formed from Greek *sēptikós* SEPTIC + *haîma* blood; see HEMO-.

septuagenarian (sep′tyůəjənãr′ēən) *adj.* between 70 and 80 years old. 1793, formed in English from Latin *septuāgēnārius* containing seventy + English *-an.* Latin *septuāgēnārius* derives from *septuāgēnī* seventy each, from *septem* SEVEN. An earlier sense of English *septuagenarian,* pertaining to the number seventy, is first recorded in 1715, but is preceded by the earlier form *septuagenary* between 70 and 80 years old (1605), borrowed from French *septuagénaire,* and directly from Latin *septuāgēnārius.* **—n.** person between 70 and 80 years old. 1805, from the adjective.

Septuagint (septü′əjint) *n.* Greek translation of the Old Testament that was made before the time of Christ. 1633, borrowed from Late Latin *septuāgintā interpretēs* seventy interpreters, from Latin *septuāgintā* seventy (*septem* SEVEN + *-gintā* tens).

The Septuagint was so called because according to tradition the translation was made by seventy or seventy-two Jewish scholars brought to Alexandria by Ptolemy II of Egypt and completed by them in seclusion on the island of Pharos in seventy-two days.

An earlier English use of *Septuagint* (1577) refers to the translators of the Septuagint and appears both in the plural (1577) and in the singular (1589).

septum (sep′təm) *n.* dividing wall, partition. 1720, New Latin, from Latin *saeptum* a fence, from the neuter of the past participle of *saepīre* to hedge in, from *saepēs* hedge, fence; cognate with Greek *haimós* thicket (earlier **haipmós*), from Indo-European **saip-* (Pok.878).

In anatomical use, the nasal *septum,* a partition between the nostrils, appeared in English in 1726.

sepulcher (sep′əlkər) *n.* tomb. Probably before 1200 *sepulcre;* later *sepulchre* (before 1300); borrowed from Old French *sepulcre,* learned borrowing from Latin, and borrowed into English directly from Latin *sepulcrum, sepulchrum,* from the root of *sepelīre* to bury. Latin *sepelīre* is exactly cognate with Sanskrit *saparyáti* venerates, from Indo-European **sepelye-,* extended from **sep-* (Pok.909), whence Greek *hépein* perform, work, and Sanskrit *sápati* he courts, cares for. **—sepulchral** *adj.* of sepulchers or burial. 1615, in Chapman's translation of Homer's *Odyssey;* borrowed from Latin *sepulcrālis, sepulchrālis* of or belonging to a sepulcher, from *sepulcrum, sepulchrum* sepulcher; for suffix see -AL[1].

sequel *n.* 1439 *sequele* consequence, corollary; later, offspring, heirs, descendants (about 1450); borrowed from Middle French *sequelle,* learned borrowing from Late Latin, and borrowed into English directly from Late Latin *sequēla* that which follows, result, consequence, from *sequī* to follow. Latin *sequī* is cognate with Old Irish *sechem* a following, Greek *hépesthai* to follow, Lithuanian *sèkti* to follow, perceive, and Sanskrit *sácate* (he) accompanies, from Indo-European **sekw-* follow (Pok.896).

The sense of a story that continues an earlier story is first recorded in English before 1513.

sequence *n.* succession. Before 1398, hymn sung or recited after the Hallelujah and before the Gospel, in Trevisa's translation of Bartholomew's *De Proprietatibus Rerum;* borrowed perhaps through Old French *sequence* answering verses, a sequence at cards, and directly from Medieval Latin *sequentia* a following or succession, from Late Latin, from Latin *sequentem* (nominative *sequēns*), present participle of *sequī* to follow; see SEQUEL; for suffix see -ENCE.

Medieval Latin *sequentia* was in part also a loan translation of Greek *akolouthíā,* which denoted a prolonged succession of notes sung on the last syllable of the Hallelujah. In the Roman Catholic Church, these notes were sung as a separate hymn. Greek *akolouthíā* is derived from *akólouthos* following; see ACOLYTE. The general sense of a succession, order of succession, or connected series, is first recorded in English in 1575. **—sequent** *adj.* following, subsequent. Before 1560, borrowed from Latin *sequentem* (nominative *sequēns*), present participle of *sequī* to follow; for suffix see -ENT. **—sequential** *adj.* 1822-29, occurring as an aftereffect of disease or injury, formed in English from Medieval or Late Latin *sequentia* sequence + English *-al*[1]. The meaning of characterized by a regular sequence of occurrences is first recorded in 1844.

sequester *v.* About 1384 *sequestren* to remove, set aside, in the Wycliffe Bible; borrowed from Old French *sequestrer,* learned borrowing from Late Latin, and borrowed into English directly from Latin *sequestrāre* to place in safekeeping, from *sequester* trustee, mediator; originally, a follower, one who attends; related to *sequī* to follow; see SEQUEL. The meaning of seize by authority, confiscate, is first recorded in English before 1513. **—sequestrate** *v.* Probably before 1425 *seques-*

traten to isolate, segregate, in a translation of Chauliac's *Grande Chirurgie;* borrowed from Latin *sequestrātus,* past participle of *sequestrāre* sequester; for suffix see -ATE[1]. **—sequestration** *n.* Probably about 1400, act of sequestering; borrowed from Late Latin *sequestrātiōnem* (nominative *sequestrātiō*) separation, a laying aside, from Latin *sequestrāre* sequester; for suffix see -ATION.

sequin (sē′kwin) *n.* spangle used to ornament dresses, etc. 1617, a former Italian and Turkish gold coin; borrowed from French *sequin,* from Italian *zecchino,* from *zecca* a mint, from Arabic *sikkah* a minting die. The meaning of a spangle used to ornament dresses, etc., appeared in English in 1882, in reference to resemblance to the gold coins.

sequoia (sikwoi′ə) *n.* very tall evergreen tree. 1869, American English, borrowing of New Latin *Sequoia* the genus name of the tree, from *Sequoya,* in Muskogean (Cherokee) *Sikwayi,* the name of a Cherokee Indian who invented the Cherokee system of writing. Sequoya (about 1770-1843) began to devise the Cherokee catalogue of syllables in 1809, completing it in 1821. His syllabary helped to teach reading and writing to Cherokees. The New Latin name of the tree was given in 1847 by Stephan L. Endlicher, a Hungarian botanist and ethnologist who knew about Sequoya's achievement.

seraglio (səral′yō *or* seräl′yō) *n.* harem. 1581, borrowing of Italian *serraglio,* alteration of Turkish *saray* palace, court, from Persian *sarāī* palace, inn. The Italian word was probably influenced in form by *serraglio* enclosure, cage, from Medieval Latin *serraculum* bung, stopper, from Vulgar Latin **serrāre* to lock up, bolt; see SERRIED.

serape or **sarape** (sərä′pē) *n.* shawl or blanket worn over the shoulder. 1834 *zarape;* later *serape* (1853); American English, borrowing of Mexican Spanish *serape, sarape,* probably from Nahuatl. The precise origin of this word is difficult to determine because there is no *r-* sound in Nahuatl.

seraph (ser′əf) *n.* one of the highest order of angels. 1667, in Milton's *Paradise Lost;* new singular formed by back formation from Old English *seraphim, seraphin,* pl. (about 750, in Cynewulf's *Elene*); borrowed from Late Latin *seraphīm, seraphīn,* from Greek *seraphím, serapheím,* from Hebrew *sĕrāphīm,* plural of *sārā́ph,* probably from *sārā́ph* it burned, by unknown connection. The English singular *seraph* was probably formed on analogy with *cherub, cherubim.*

Traditionally seraphs have been regarded as burning or flaming angels. But some Bible authorities have identified them with the "burning serpents" of Numbers 21:6, in reference to the sting of the serpent's bite. There is further confusion with "flying," perhaps related to the root of Arabic *sharafa* be lofty.

sere (sir) *adj. Archaic.* dried up, withered. Probably before 1300 *sere,* in *Kyng Alisaunder,* developed from Old English *sēar* dried up, withered (824). The Old English word is cognate with Middle Low German *sōr* dry, Middle Dutch *soor* (modern Dutch *zoor*) from Proto-Germanic **sauzás,* and Old High German *sōrēn* to wither. Cognates outside Germanic are found in Albanian *thanj* I dry, Greek *haûos* dry, *haúein* to dry up, Lithuanian *saũsas* dry, Old Slavic *suchŭ* dry, Sanskrit *śúṣyati* (it) dries up, withers, and Latin *sūdus* (of weather) clear and bright (earlier **susdos*), (also) dry, from Indo-European **sauso-,* root **saus-/sus-* dry (Pok.880). Related to SEAR.

serenade *n.* music performed outdoors at night, especially by a lover. 1649, in Lovelace's *Lucasta;* borrowed from French *sérénade,* from Italian *serenata* an evening song, probably from *sereno* the open air, noun use of *sereno* clear, calm, from Latin *serēnus* peaceful, calm; see SERENE; for suffix see -ADE. Italian *serenata* was influenced in meaning by *sera* evening, from Late Latin *sēra* evening, from the feminine of Latin *sērus* late; see SINCE. **—v.** perform a serenade. 1668, in Dryden's *An Evening's Love;* from the noun. The transformed or figurative sense is first recorded in Fielding's *Tom Jones* (1749).

serendipity (ser′əndip′ətē) *n.* ability to make fortunate discoveries by accident. 1754, coined by the English author Horace Walpole, 1717-97, from the title of the Persian fairy tale "The Three Princes of *Serendip*" whose heroes "were always making discoveries, by accidents and sagacity, of things they were not in quest of" (Letter by Walpole, Jan. 28, 1754); for suffix see -ITY. *Serendip* was an old name of *Ceylon* (Sri Lanka), from Arabic *Sarandīb.* **—serendipitous** *adj.* Before 1950, formed from English *serendipity* + *-ous.*

serene *adj.* Probably 1440, (of the weather) clear, calm, in a translation of Palladius' *De Re Rustica;* borrowed from Latin *serēnus* peaceful, calm, clear. The Latin word is perhaps cognate with Greek *xērós* dry, Old High German *serawēn* become dry, and Tocharian A *ksär, ksärk* morning, from Indo-European **ḱsē̆-ro-* dry, clear (Pok.625).

English *serene* was applied to people, with the sense of calm, untroubled, before 1635, though it occurs earlier as an honorific epithet ("most serene") given to princes (1503, in Dunbar's *Poems*).

—serenity *n.* About 1450 *serenite* title of honor given to princes and other dignitaries; before 1460, fair weather, clearness; borrowed from Middle French *sérénité,* from Latin *serēnitātem* (nominative *serēnitās*) clearness, calmness, from *serēnus* serene; for suffix see -ITY.

serf *n.* 1483, a slave, in Caxton's version of *The Golden Legend;* borrowing of Middle French *serf,* from Latin *servus* slave; see SERVE.

The meaning of a member of the lower class of soil cultivators (as in Germany, Russia, etc.) is first recorded in English in 1611. Specific reference to a peasant in a feudal system, especially in medieval Europe, is found in Hume's *History of England* (1761).

—serfdom *n.* 1850, in Elizabeth Barrett Browning's writings; formed from English *serf* + *-dom.*

serge (sėrj) *n.* kind of cloth having slanting lines or ridges on its surface. Before 1382 *sarge;* borrowed from Old French *serge, sarge.* Old French *sarge* developed from Vulgar Latin **sārica* (in Medieval Latin, a silken tunic), variant of Latin *sērica vestis* silken garment. Old French *serge* developed from Medieval Latin *serga, sarga* cloth of wool mixed with silk or linen, from Latin *sērica,* from Greek *sērikḗ,* feminine of *sērikós* silken; see SILK.

The spelling *serge* is first recorded in English in 1599.

sergeant *n.* Probably before 1200 *sergante* servant later, officer of a city or royal household (about 1250) also, common soldier (about 1300); borrowed from Old French *sergent, serjent,* from Medieval Latin *servien* *tem* (nominative *serviens*) servant, vassal, soldier, (in Late Latin, public official), from Latin *servientem* (nominative *serviēns*) serving, present participle of *servīre* to SERVE; for suffix see -ANT. The meaning of a noncommissioned military officer is first found in English in 1548.

serial *adj.* 1840, arranged in a series; 1841, (of a story) published one part at a time; formed from English *series* + *-al*[1]. **—n.** serial story. 1846, from the adjective. **—serialize** *v.* publish in serial form. 1892, formed from English *serial,* adj. + *-ize.* **—serial number** (1935)

seriatim (sir′ēā′tim) *adv.* in a series, one after the other. Probably before 1500 *seratim;* borrowing of Medieval Latin *seriatim,* from Latin *seriēs* SERIES. Compare LITERATIM, VERBATIM. The spelling *seriatim* is first recorded in 1680.

series *n.* 1611, number of similar things in a row, in Coryat's *Crudities;* borrowed from Latin *seriēs* row, chain, series, from *serere* to join, link, bind together, put. Latin *serere* is cognate with Old Irish *sernaid* puts in a row, orders, Greek *eirein* fasten together in rows, *hérma* earring, *hórmos* necklace, Old Lithuanian *sėris* thread, and Sanskrit *sarat, sarit* thread, from Indo-European **ser-/sor-* fasten, join (Pok.911). An isolated instance occurs in Middle English as *serye* (about 1385, in Chaucer's *Canterbury Tales*).

serif (ser′if) *n.* thin line used to finish off a main stroke of a letter. 1841 *ceriph,* in William Savage's *A Dictionary of the Art of Printing;* earlier *ceref, syrif* (1827); perhaps borrowed from Dutch *schreef* line, stroke, from Middle Dutch *scrēve;* see SCARP.

seriocomic *adj.* partly serious and partly comic. 1783, formed from English *serio(us)* + *comic,* on the pattern of *tragicomic.*

serious *adj.* 1440 *seryows* earnest, solemn, in *Promptorium Parvulorum;* borrowed through Middle French *sérieux* grave, earnest, and directly from Late Latin *sēriōsus,* from Latin *sērius* weighty, important, grave; for suffix see -OUS. Latin *sērius* is probably cognate with Lithuanian *svarùs* heavy, and in Germanic with Old Icelandic *svārr* heavy, Old High German *swār, swāri* (modern German *schwer*), Middle Dutch *swaer, swāre* (modern Dutch *zwaar*), Old Saxon *swār,* Old Frisian *swēr,* Old English *swǣr* heavy, and Gothic *swērs* esteemed, from Proto-Germanic **swēraz* heavy; cognate also with Lithuanian *sver̃ti* to weigh, from Indo-European **swer-/swēr-* heavy (Pok.1151).

sermon *n.* Probably before 1200 *sarmun* public talk on religion, in *Ancrene Riwle;* about 1200 *sermun;* later, *sermon* (before 1325); borrowed through Anglo-French *sermun,* variant of Old French *sermon,* learned borrowing from Latin, and borrowed into English directly from Latin *sermōnem* (nominative *sermō*) discourse, speech, talk; originally, a stringing together of words, related to *serere* to join; see SERIES. **—sermonize** *v.* 1635 (implied in *sermonizing*); formed from English *sermon* + *-ize.*

serous (sir′əs) *adj.* of or having to do with serum. Probably before 1425 *serous, cerous* (of fluids in an infection) watery, wheylike, in a translation of Chauliac's *Grande Chirurgie;* later reinforced by Middle French *sereux,* but borrowed from Latin *serum* watery fluid, whey; see SERUM; for suffix see -OUS. The meaning of pertaining to serum is first recorded in 1594, even though *serum* itself is not recorded in English before 1672.

serpent *n.* Before 1300 *serpent,* borrowing of Old French *serpent, sarpent,* learned borrowing from Latin, and borrowed into English directly from Latin *serpentem* (nominative *serpēns*) snake, from present participle of *serpere* to creep. Latin *serpēns, serpere* is cognate with Albanian *gjarpën* serpent, Greek *hérpein* to creep, *herpetón* creeping animal, and Sanskrit *sárpati* (he) creeps, *sarpá-s* serpent, from Indo-European **serp-* (Pok.912).

serpentine (sėr′pəntēn *or* sėr′pəntīn) *adj.* of or like a serpent. Probably about 1408 *serpentyne,* in Lydgate's *Reson and Sensuallyte;* borrowed from Old French *serpentin* (feminine *serpentine*), learned borrowing from Late Latin, and borrowed into English directly from Late Latin *serpentīnus,* from Latin *serpentem* (nominative *serpēns*) snake; see SERPENT; for suffix see -INE[1]. The meaning of twisting or winding is first recorded in English in 1615. **—n.** (sėr′pəntēn) greenish mineral, sometimes spotted like a serpent's skin. 1408 *serpentyn;* borrowed from Medieval Latin *serpentinum* and *serpentina,* noun uses of the neuter and feminine singular respectively of Late Latin *serpentīnus* serpentine, adj.

serrate (ser′āt *or* ser′it) *adj.* notched like the edge of a saw. 1668, borrowed from Latin *serrātus* notched like a saw, sawlike, from *serra* a saw, of unknown origin; for suffix see -ATE[1]. An earlier form *serratic* is recorded in Middle English as *serratyk* (1392), formed from Latin *serrātus* + Middle English *-ic.* **—serrated** (ser′ātid) *adj.* serrate. 1703, formed in English from Latin *serrātus* notched like a saw + English *-ed*[2].

serried (ser′ed) *adj.* crowded closely together. 1667, in Milton's *Paradise Lost,* from past participle of an earlier verb *serry* to press close together (1581); borrowed from Middle French *serré* close, compact, past participle of *serrer* press close, fasten, from Vulgar Latin **serrāre* to bolt, lock up, variant of Latin *serāre,* from *sera* bolt, lock, of uncertain origin; for suffix see -ED[2].

serum (sir′əm) *n.* clear, pale-yellow, watery part of the blood. 1672, borrowed from Latin *serum* watery fluid, whey; cognate with Greek *orós* whey, *hormḗ* impulse, onset, and Sanskrit *sará-s* flowing, from Indo-European **sero-m* fluid, flow, root **ser-/sor-* to stream (Pok.909). The meaning of blood serum with specific antibodies used to prevent or cure disease, is first recorded in English in 1893, in *Lancet.*

servant *n.* Probably before 1200, one owing duty or service to a master or lord, in *Ancrene Riwle;* borrowed from Old French, an attendant, servant, noun use of *servant* serving, waiting, present participle of *servir* to attend, wait upon, see SERVE; for suffix see -ANT. The general sense of one who serves another for wages, as a butler, housekeeper, domestic, and the like, is probably first recorded about 1325, in *Cursor Mundi.* The specific sense of a government official, as in *public servant,* is first recorded in 1570.

serve *v.* About 1175 *serven* give service to, be useful to; borrowed from Old French *servir* to serve, from Latin *servīre* to serve; originally, be a slave, related to *servus* slave, perhaps from an Etruscan word (compare the Etruscan proper names *Servi, Serve*). The sense of take the place or meet the needs of (as in Shakespeare's *One turf shall serve as pillow for us both*) is first recorded in Trevisa's translation of Higden's *Polychronicon* (1387). **—n.** act or way of serving a ball in tennis, badminton, etc. 1688, from the verb.

service *n.* Probably before 1100 *serfise* religious ritual or ceremony; later *servise* the serving of God (about 1175), and performance of work or duties (probably before 1200, in *Ancrene Riwle*); and with the spelling *service* (probably before 1300); borrowed from Old French *servise, service,* from Latin *servitium* slavery, servitude, from *servus* slave; see SERVE. The sense of the duty or performance of a soldier or sailor is first recorded in 1590. The sense of a set of dishes or utensils (1669) developed from the earlier senses of provision of food by a servant, sequence of courses served in a meal (probably about 1300), and particular dish or kind of food (before 1536). **—v.** 1893, to supply with a service; from the noun. The sense of perform maintenance or repair work on is first recorded in American English in 1926. There was also a Middle English verb *servisen* serve as a retainer (about 1300); from the Middle English noun. **—serviceable** *adj.* Before 1375 *servisabul* willing to serve, ready to do service; later *servicable* suitable, useful (before 1393, in Gower's *Confessio Amantis*); borrowed from Old French *servicable, servisable,* from *service, servise* service, n. The spelling *serviceable* appeared in Middle English before 1450. **—service charge** (1929) **—serviceman** *n.* member of the armed forces (1899). **—service mark** (1945, American English) **—service road** (1921) **—service station** (1921, American English)

serviette (sėr′vēet′) *n.* napkin. 1818, borrowing of French *serviette* napkin, towel, perhaps from an earlier **servitette,* from *servit,* past participle of *servir* to SERVE, or perhaps directly from *servir;* for suffix see -ETTE. Earlier forms in English such as *serviot* (1489) and *serviat* (1560) were of Scottish use; the word was reintroduced into standard English in the 1800's.

servile (sėr′vil) *adj.* like that of slaves, mean, base. Before 1382, in the Wycliffe Bible; borrowed from Latin *servīlis* of a slave, servile, from *servus* slave; see SERVE. The earliest use of the word in English was in the phrase *servile work,* referring to work forbidden by the Bible to be done on the Sabbath and festivals. The sense of subject as a slave or serf to a master or owner is first recorded in 1565, and that of behaving like a slave, slavish, meanly submissive, cringing, fawning, is first recorded in Shakespeare's *King Lear* (1605).

servitude *n.* slavery. Before 1420, in Lydgate's *Troy Book;* borrowed from Middle French *servitude,* learned borrowing from Late Latin, and borrowed into English directly from Late Latin *servitūdō* slavery, from Latin *servus* a slave; see SERVE; for suffix see -TUDE.

servo *n.* 1910, a servomechanism or device; abstracted from *servo-motor* (1889, borrowing of French *servomoteur,* 1873).

servomechanism *n.* device used to maintain constant performance of some equipment. 1926, formed from English *servo-,* abstracted from *servo-motor* + *mechanism.* **—servomechanical** *adj.* (1947)

servomotor *n.* auxiliary motor to supplement the primary source of power. 1889, borrowed from French *servo-moteur,* formed from Latin *serv(us)* slave + French connective *-o-* + *moteur* motor, from Latin *mōtor* mover.

sesame *n.* East Indian plant with edible seeds. Probably about 1425 *sisamie,* in a translation of Chauliac's *Grande Chirurgie;* probably borrowed from Middle French *sisame* (though not found in records of Middle French until about 1500), and borrowed directly from Latin *sēsama, sēsamum,* from Greek *sḗsamon,* Doric *sā́samon,* from Late Babylonian **šawaš-šammu* (compare Assyrian *šamaš-šammu* sesame; literally, oil-seed, Aramaic *shūmshĕmā,* and Arabic *simsim*). The spelling *sesame* is found in translations of *The Arabian Nights* from French in the late 1700's. The word occurs in the tale of "Ali Baba and the Forty Thieves," where it is used as a magic password to open and shut the door of the thieves' den. The phrase *open sesame* has been used since about 1826 (in Scott's *Diary*) in the figurative sense of any marvelous or definite means of gaining immediate admission or reaching a desired goal.

sesquicentennial (ses′kwisenten′ēəl) *n.* 150th anniversary or its celebration. 1880, formed in American English from Latin *sēsqui-* one and a half + English *centennial.* Latin *sēsqui-* (compounding form of **sēsque*) literally means "and a half," compound of *sēmis* a half (formed from *sēmi-* half, by analogy with *bis* twice) + *-que* and. **—adj.** of a period or anniversary of a century and a half. 1888, American English; from the noun.

sessile (ses′əl) *adj.* 1725, adhering close to the surface; borrowed from Latin *sessilis* sitting, from *sessum,* past participle of *sedēre* to SIT. The botanical and zoological sense of attached at the base is found in 1753 and 1777 respectively. The more general meaning of sedentary, fixed to one spot, occurs in 1860.

session *n.* About 1387-95, the sitting together of a court, council, etc., in Chaucer's *Canterbury Tales;* borrowed from Latin *sessiōnem* (nominative *sessiō*) act of sitting, from *sess-,* past participle stem of *sedēre* to SIT; for suffix see -SION. The sense of a sitting together of officials, as of a legislative body, for the purpose of conducting business, is found in Middle English before 1425. The sense of a period of study into which the school day or year is divided is first recorded in 1714. The general sense of a period of time set aside for the pursuit of some activity is an Americanism originally occurring in the terms *bull session* (1920, in letters of Thomas Wolfe), *recording session* (of jazz musicians, 1927), and *jam session* (1933).

sestet (sestet′) *n.* = sextet.

set *v.* Before 1121 *setten,* developed from Old English *settan* cause to sit, put in some place, fix firmly (about 725, in *Beowulf*), causative verb form of *sittan* to SIT. Old English *settan* is cognate with Old Frisian *setta* to set, Old Saxon *settian,* Middle Dutch *setten* (modern Dutch *zetten*), Old High German *sezzen* (modern German *setzen*), Old Icelandic *setja* (Norwegian *sette,* Swedish *saeDtta,* Danish *sætte*), and Gothic *satjan,* from Proto-Germanic **satjanan.*

Many uses have become confused with *sit* since the early 1300's partly because of close similarity of past tense and past participial forms and partly because of a closeness of meaning in some uses (as in *to be set* meaning seated, and *to sit;* also *set down, sit down,* etc.). The phonetic similarity and close grammatical use when *set* is used reflexively or without an object has also contributed to this confusion.

—adj. fixed or appointed beforehand, established. Probably about 1200 *sett,* in *The Ormulum;* from past participle of *setten* to set.

—n. Before 1338 *set* act of setting, condition of being set, in Mannyng's *Chronicle of England;* from the verb or adjective. Middle English *sette,* meaning a number or collection of things, is first recorded in 1443, devel-

oped from an earlier sense of a number or group of persons, religious body (before 1387, in Trevisa's translation of Higden's *Polychronicon*). This use of the word was borrowed from Old French *sette* sequence, a learned borrowing from Medieval Latin *secta* retinue, suite, from Latin *secta* a following, SECT. Old English *set* seat, place of the setting sun, probably did not survive into Middle English.
—setback *n.* (1674) **—set theory** (1936) **—setup** *n.* (1841)

settee (setē′) *n.* sofa. 1716, perhaps variant of *settle*[2] bench; for suffix see -EE.

setter *n.* long-haired hunting dog. 1576, in a translation of Johannes Caius' *Of English Dogs;* formed from English *set,* v. + *-er*[1]; so called because the setter was originally "set" on game, or incited to attack or pursue it; now the setter is trained to point with the nose at its game.

settle[1] *v.* come to rest, fix. Probably about 1200 *settlen* to seat, place on a seat, in *The Ormulum;* developed from Old English *setlan* (about 1000), from *setl* a seat; see SETTLE[2]. The sense of come to rest, as after a flight, is first recorded before 1300. The sense of establish a permanent residence, especially in a foreign country, occurs in 1627, and that of decide, come to a fixed conclusion (on a question, dispute, etc.) appears in 1621, in Hobbes' *Leviathan.* **—settled** *adj.* 1556, from the verb. The sense of quiet, orderly, steady, is first recorded probably as early as 1557. **—settlement** *n.* 1626, the act of settling or becoming set, in Sir Francis Bacon's *Sylva Sylvarum;* formed from English *settle*[1] + *-ment.* The sense of a group of people settled in a new country, a colony, is first recorded in 1697, and the legal sense of a settling property arrangements (as in *marriage* or *divorce settlement*) in 1677.

settle[2] *n.* long bench. Before 1121 *setle* abode; later, seat or bench (probably before 1200, in Layamon's *Chronicle of Britain*); developed from Old English *setl* a seat, position, abode (about 725, in *Beowulf*), related to *sittan* SIT. Old English *setl* is cognate with Middle Low German and Middle Dutch *sētel* seat (modern Dutch *zetel*), Old High German *sezzal* (modern German *Sessel*), and Gothic *sitls* seat, from Proto-Germanic **setla-.* It is also cognate outside Germanic with Latin *sella* saddle, seat, Old Slavic *sedlo* saddle, and Armenian *etl* place, position.

seven *adj.* Probably about 1175 *sevene;* developed from Old English *seofon* (about 725, in *Beowulf*); cognate with Old Frisian *soven, sigun* seven, Old Saxon *siƀun,* Middle Dutch *seven* (modern Dutch *zeven*), Old High German *sibun* (modern German *sieben*), Old Icelandic *sjau* (Swedish and Norwegian *sju,* Danish *syv*), and Gothic *sibun,* from Proto-Germanic **seƀún.* Outside the Germanic languages cognates are found in Latin *septem* seven, Albanian *shtatë,* Greek *heptá,* Lithuanian *septyni,* Old Slavic *sedmĭ,* Sanskrit *saptá,* Tocharian A *ṣpät,* and Hittite *siptamya* (dative) seventh, from Indo-European **septṃ́* (Pok.909). **—seventeen** *adj.* Probably before 1200 *seoventene,* in Layamon's *Chronicle of Britain;* later *seventene* (probably before 1300); developed from Old English (about 900) *seofontȳne* (*seofon* seven + *-tēne* -teen, from *tēn* TEN) **—seventh** *adj.* About 1290 *seventhe,* a new formation from Middle English *sevene* + *-th*[2], replacing earlier *sefende* (probably about 1200); developed from Old English (Anglian) *seofunda;* cognate with Old Saxon *sivondo* seventh, Old High German *sibunto,* Old Icelandic *sjaunde,* etc., from Proto-Germanic **seƀundón.* **—seventy** *adj.* Before 1250 *seoventi,* in *Ancrene Riwle;* about 1250 *seventi;* developed from Old English *seofontig* (*seofon* seven + *-tig* group of ten, -TY[1]).

sever *v.* to part, separate, divide. Probably about 1300 *severen;* borrowed through Anglo-French *severer,* variant of Old French *sevrer,* from Vulgar Latin **sēperāre,* from Latin *sēparāre* SEPARATE. **—severance** *n.* 1422, act or fact of severing; borrowed through Anglo-French *severance,* variant of Old French *sevrance,* from *sevrer* to sever; for suffix see -ANCE.

several *adj.* Probably about 1421 *saverale* a number of, some; 1422 *severall* separate, individual; borrowing of Anglo-French *several,* from Medieval Latin *seperalis, separalis* separate, from Latin *sēpare, sēparī* (ablative of **sēpar*) distinct, back formation from *sēparāre* to SEPARATE; for suffix see -AL[1]. The legal sense of pertaining separately to each individual, not shared or joint, is first recorded in 1532.

severe *adj.* 1548, in Elyot's *Dictionary;* borrowed through Middle French *severe,* or directly from Latin *sevērus* stern, strict, serious, possibly formed from the phrase **sē vērō* without kindness (*sē* without + **vērō* kindness, neuter ablative of *vērus* true; see VERY). It is also possible that *severe* was in some instances formed in English by a back formation as an adjective to the noun *severity.* **—severity** *n.* strictness. 1481, borrowed through Middle French *severité,* or directly from Latin *sevēritātem* (nominative *sevēritās*) strictness, earnestness, from *sevērus* severe; for suffix see -ITY.

sew *v.* About 1290 *seuwen;* later *seuen* (before 1325); developed from Old English *siwian* to stitch with needle and thread (before 1050); earlier *siowian* (before 800); cognate with Old Frisian *sīa* to sew, Old High German *siuwen,* Old Icelandic *sȳja* (Swedish, Norwegian, and Danish *sy*), and Gothic *siujan,* from Proto-Germanic **siwjanan.* Outside Germanic cognates are found in Latin *suere* to sew, Lithuanian *siúti,* Old Slavic *šiti* to sew, Sanskrit *sī́vyati* (he) sews, *syū́man-* suture, and Hittite *sumanza* cord, rope, from Indo-European **syewā-, sewā-,* with many variants (Pok.915). The spelling *sew* (spelled in Wycliffe's works *sou-* and Chaucer's work *sow-*) began to appear in the late 1300's and became the established spelling. **—sewing machine** (1847)

sewage *n.* waste matter carried off in sewers. 1834, possibly formed in English from *sew* a sewer, drain (1475) + *-age. Sewage* is also analyzed as a formation of English *sewer,* n. + *-age.* This latter explanation assumes the noun *sewer* was interpreted as a derivation of *sew* to drain, draw off water from (before 1513, borrowed from Middle French *essewer, essever* make flow, from Old French; see SEWER) + *-er*[1]. However, it is interesting to note that both *sewage* and *sewerage* appear in the same government report on the sewer system of London (1834), but that *sewerage* is used to mean "drainage or system of drainage by sewers," and that it is not recorded in the meaning "sewage" before 1851. Since both *sewage* and *sewerage* were first used at the same time with different meanings, and derivation of *sewage* from *sewerage* would have necessitated dropping the medial syllable *-er-*, and since many words in *-age* (*postage, footage, shortage, roughage*) were formed on nouns, it is unlikely that *sewage* was derived from the verb.

sewer *n.* underground pipe. 1402-03 *seuer;* borrowed through Anglo-French *sewere,* corresponding to Old North French *sewiere* sluice from a pond; literally, something that makes water flow, from Gallo-Romance **exaquāria* (Latin *ex* out + *aquāria,* feminine of *aquārius* pertaining to water, from *aqua* water; see AQUATIC).

sex *n.* About 1380, either males or females collectively (as in *the male or female sex, both sexes*), in Chaucer's translation of Boethius' *De Consolatione Philosophiae;* borrowed from Latin *sexus* (genitive *sexūs*) state of being either male or female, gender, (also *secus,* probably only in the nominative and accusative), perhaps related to *secāre* to divide or cut; see SECTION. The meaning of the quality of being male or female (as in *the distinction of sexes*) is first recorded in 1526, and that of the distinction between male and female (as in *the organs of sex, sex in literature*), in Donne's *Songs and Sonnets* (1631). The meaning of sexual activity is attested in 1918, and that of sexual intercourse, in 1929, in the writings of D.H. Lawrence. **—sex appeal** (1924, American English) **—sex change** (1946) **—sex chromosome** (1906) **—sex discrimination** (1916) **—sex drive** (1918) **—sex education** (1920, American English) **—sex hormone** (1917) **—sex instinct** (1898) **—sexism** *n.* 1968, American English, patterned on *racism.* **—sexist** *adj., n.* 1965, patterned on *racist.* **—sex object** (1911) **—sexology** *n.* science dealing with sex. 1902, American English; formed from English *sex,* n. + *-ology.* **—sexploitation** *n.* exploitation of sex in the arts. 1942, American English, blend of *sex,* n. and *exploitation.* **—sex symbol** (before 1911) **—sex therapy** (1961) **—sexual** *adj.* 1651, borrowed from Late Latin *sexuālis* of or pertaining to sex or the sexes, from Latin *sexus* sex; for suffix see -AL[1]. **—sexuality** *n.* Before 1800, in Cowper's writings; formed from English *sexual* + *-ity.* **—sexy** *adj.* 1928, engrossed in or concerned with sex; 1932, sexually attractive; formed from English *sex,* n. + *-y*[1].

sex- a combining form meaning six, as in *sexennial, sextuplet.* Borrowed from Latin *sex* SIX. Also spelled *sexi-* in some compounds, as in *sexivalent.*

sexagenarian (sek′səjənãr′ēən) *n.* person between 60 and 70 years old. 1738, in *Chambers Cyclopaedia;* formed in English from Latin *sexāgēnārius* containing sixty + English *-an.* Latin *sexāgēnārius* derives from *sexāgēnī* sixty each, from *sex* SIX. **—adj.** between 60 and 70 years old. 1862, from the noun. An earlier adjective with the same meaning, *sexagenary,* is found in 1638, borrowed from French *sexagénaire,* or directly from Latin.

sextant *n.* instrument for measuring the angular distance between two objects. 1628, in Burton's *The Anatomy of Melancholy;* borrowed from New Latin *sextans* (genitive *sextantis*), from Latin *sextāns* a sixth, from *sex* SIX; so called because the sextant is furnished with a graduated arc equal to a sixth part of a circle; for suffix see -ANT. The New Latin name for the instrument was probably coined by the Danish astronomer Tycho Brahe, 1546-1601. An earlier meaning of *sextant,* one sixth of a circle, is found in English in 1596.

sextet or **sextette** (sekstet′) *n.* musical composition for six voices or instruments. 1841, alteration of earlier *sestet,* by influence of German *Sextett* and of Latin *sex* SIX; for suffixes see -ET and -ETTE. The earlier form *sestet* (sestet′), 1801, in Thomas Busby's *A Complete Dictionary of Music;* borrowed from Italian *sestetto,* diminutive of *sesto* sixth, from Latin *sextus,* from *sex* SIX. Between 1841 and 1859 *sestet* became differentiated from *sextet,* acquiring the meaning of the last six lines of a sonnet, especially an Italian sonnet, and also a poem or stanza of six lines.

sexton *n.* caretaker of a church. About 1303 *sekesteyn* person in charge of the sacred objects of a church, sacristan, in Mannyng's *Handlyng Synne;* later *sextein* (before 1325), and *sexten* (before 1450); borrowed from Old French *segrestein, secrestein,* learned borrowing from Medieval Latin *sacristanus* SACRISTAN. The extended sense of any custodian of a church, temple, synagogue, etc., is found in 1582.

sextuple (seks′tůpəl) *adj.* consisting of six parts, sixfold. 1626, in Bacon's *Sylva Sylvarum;* formed in English from Latin *sextus* sixth (from *sex* SIX), with the ending patterned on English *quadruple, quintuple,* etc. **—n.** sixfold number or amount. 1657, in Hobbes' *Stigmai;* from the adjective. **—v.** make or become sextuple. 1632, from the noun. **—sextuplet** *n.* group of six. 1852, formed from English *sextuple,* adj., on the pattern of *triplet, quadruplet,* etc. The meaning of one of six offspring born together is first recorded in 1894.

sh as the spelling used to represent the first consonant of *ship, shoe,* and similar native English words, did not exist in Old English. The sound of *sh* was represented in Old English by the digraph *sc,* as in Old English *fisc* fish, and *scearp* sharp; *sc* retained its original phonetic value (*sk*) only in words of foreign origin. After the 1100's the use of *sc* became rare, and scribes began using *ss* and sometimes *s* in its place. Since the sound of *sh* did not exist in early Old French, the early Middle English texts, written by French-educated scribes, show great diversity in representing the sound. In medial and final positions *ssh* was common, and Coverdale has frequently *szsh,* and sometimes *szh.* The prevailing form in initial position was *sch,* and most probably the digraph *sh* developed as a simplification of *sch. Sh* was the usual spelling in the manuscripts of Chaucer, and from the time of Caxton onwards it has been the standard spelling in all words except those which (as *machine, ratio,* the derivatives in *-tion,* etc.) are spelled on etymological grounds. See also CH, TH, WH.

shabby *adj.* 1669, poorly dressed, in a translation of Homer's *Odyssey,* derived from earlier *shab* scab (about 1300 *schabbe*); developed from Old English *sceabb* (before 899, in Alfred's translation of St. Gregory's *Pastoral Care*); see SCAB; for suffix see -Y[1]. The meaning of dingy and faded, much worn, is first recorded in 1685; the figurative sense of mean, low, ungenerous, is attested in 1679.

shack *n.* roughly built hut or cabin. 1878, American English, also *shackle* (1890); perhaps borrowed from Mexican Spanish *jacal,* from Nahuatl *xacalli* wooden hut.

Alternatively *shack* may be a back formation from dialectal English *shackly* shaky, rickety (1848), from dialectal *shackle* to shake, frequentative form of dialectal *shack,* alteration of SHAKE. It has also been suggested that *shack* is a back formation from RAMSHACKLE. **—v.** *Slang.* to live at a place, dwell. 1891, American English; from the noun. The slang sense of live with one's lover as if married, cohabit (usually in the phrase *shack up*) is first recorded in 1935, in American English.

shackle *n.* Probably before 1200 *schakel* metal fetter for ankle or wrist, in *Ancrene Riwle;* developed from

Old English *sceacel* (before 1000, in Ælfric's *Glossary*); cognate with Middle Dutch *scākel* link of a chain (modern Dutch *schakel*), and Old Icelandic *skǫkull* rope, carriage shaft (Swedish *skakel* shaft, Norwegian *skåk, skokle* shaft, Danish *skagle* trace of a horse), from Proto-Germanic **skakula-*. No connections are known outside Germanic. —**v.** put shackles on. 1440 *schaklen*, in *Promptorium Parvulorum;* from the noun.

shad *n.* kind of fish. 1538, in Elyot's *Dictionary;* developed from Old English *sceadd* (1002), of uncertain origin; possibly cognate with dialectal Norwegian *skadd* small whitefish.

shade *n.* About 1300 *ssade* partial darkness, shadow; later *schade* (before 1325), *shade* (about 1375); developed from Old English (before 900) *sceadu* from Proto-Germanic **skadwṓ*); cognate with Old Saxon *skado* shade, Middle Dutch *scāduwe, scāde* (modern Dutch *schaduw*), Old High German *scato,* genitive *scatawes,* (modern German *Schatten*), and Gothic *skadus,* from Proto-Germanic **skadwás.* Outside Germanic the word is cognate with Old Irish *scāth* shadow, Welsh *cysgod,* Cornish *scod,* and Greek *skótos* darkness, from Indo-European **skot-/skōt-* (Pok.957).

The meaning of degree of lightness or darkness of color is first recorded in Locke's *Essay Concerning Human Understanding* (1690).

—**v.** Probably about 1380 *schaden* protect from the sun; from the noun.

—**shady** *adj.* 1579, affording shade, in Spenser's *The Shepheardes Calender;* formed from English *shade,* n. + *-y*[1]. The informal sense "of doubtful honesty or character" is first recorded in 1862.

shadow *n.* Probably before 1200 *schadewe,* in *Ancrene Riwle;* later *schadowe* (probably before 1300), *shadow* (about 1340); developed from Old English *sceadwe, sceaduwe,* oblique case forms of Old English *sceadu* SHADE. —**v.** protect from light; shade. About 1350 *shadowen;* earlier *sseduyen* (1340); developed from Old English (about 1000) *sceadwian,* from *sceadu* shade, n. —**shadowy** *adj.* About 1380 *schadwy* resembling a shadow, unsubstantial, fleeting, in Chaucer's translation of Boethius' *De Consolatione Philosophiae;* later *schadowy* (before 1398); formed from Middle English *schadowe* shadow, n. + *-y*[1].

shaft *n.* Probably before 1200 *scaft,* in Layamon's *Chronicle of Britain;* later *shafte* (probably before 1300); developed from Old English *sceaft* long slender rod of a staff or lance, shaft, spear (about 1000, in Ælfric's *Glossary*); cognate with Old Frisian *skeft* shaft, spear, Old Saxon *skaft,* Middle Dutch *scacht, scaft* (modern Dutch *schacht, schaft*), Old High German *scaft* (modern German *Schaft*), and Old Icelandic *skapt* shaft, handle (Swedish, Norwegian, and Danish *skaft*), from Proto-Germanic **skaftaz.* Outside Germanic cognates are found in Latin *scāpus* shaft, stem, *scōpa* broom, Greek *skêptron* staff, scepter, Doric *skâpton* staff, from Indo-European **skap-/skāp-/skōp-* (Pok. 932).

shag *n.* rough, matted hair, wool, etc. 1592 *shage* a napped fabric, probably from Middle English **shagge;* developed from Old English (about 1050) *sceacga* hair (stem *sceacg-* from Indo-European **skok-n-*), cognate with Old Icelandic *skegg* beard, from Proto-Germanic **skaʒján,* Indo-European **skok-,* root **skek-* (Pok.923). Old English *sceagga* is related also to *sceaga* copse (modern English *-shaw*). —**v.** 1596, be shaggy, in Spenser's *Faerie Queene;* later, make shaggy (1612); from the noun. —**shaggy** *adj.* About 1590, in Marlowe's *The Jew of Malta;* formed from English *shag,* n. + *-y*[1].

shake *v.* Probably before 1200 *schaken;* developed from Old English *sceacan* to vibrate, make vibrate, move away (about 725, in *Beowulf*); cognate with Old Saxon *shakan* go away, Low German *schacken* to shake, Old Icelandic *skaka* to shake (Swedish *skaka*), from Proto-Germanic **skakanan,* Indo-European **skog-,* root *skeg-* (Pok.923). Outside Germanic there is no reliable cognate. —**n.** Probably before 1300 *shak* sudden movement; from the verb. The meaning of an act of shaking is first recorded in 1581. —**shaker** *n.* 1440 *schakare* person or thing that shakes; formed from Middle English *schaken* + *-are, -ere* -er[1]. The sense of something used for shaking (straw, hat, etc.) first occurred in 1812. —**shake-up** *n.* 1847, sudden, drastic change or rearrangement, in writings of John Stuart Mill. —**shaky** *adj.* 1703, (of timber) split, cracked; formed from English *shake,* v. + *-y*[1]. The meaning of shaking, tremulous, appeared in 1848, and that of liable to break down, not firm or solid, in 1850. The figurative sense of insecure or unreliable, is first recorded in 1841.

shako (shak′ō) *n.* high, stiff military hat. 1815, in writings of Scott; borrowed through French *schako,* or directly from Hungarian *csákó* peaked cap; originally, projecting point of a cow's horn, perhaps from Middle High German *zacke* peak, alteration of Middle Low German or Middle Dutch *tacke* TACK.

shale *n.* fine-grained rock formed from clay or mud. 1747, possibly a specialized use of earlier *shale* shell, husk, pod (about 1380, in Chaucer's *House of Fame*); developed from Old English (before 800) *scealu;* see SHELL.

There is surely some relationship between the meaning of rock formed in sheets of sediment and the previously known meanings of *shale,* including outer covering of a nut, scale of fish, and layers of rubble from a mine, all of which suggest the concept of thin layers of material, but the specific meaning in geology may have been reinforced by the German *Schal-* in *Schalstein* laminated limestone, and in *Schalgebirge* layer of stone in stratified rock.

shall *v.* Probably before 1200 *shal;* developed from Old English (about 725, in *Beowulf*) *sceal* I owe, he owes, will have to, ought to, must (infinitive *sculan,* past tense *sceolde*); cognate with Old Frisian *skel, skil* (infinitive *skilun,* past tense *scolde*), Old Saxon *skal* (infinitive *skulun,* past *skolda*), Middle Dutch *sal* (infinitive *sullen,* past *solde*), modern Dutch *zal* (infinitive *zullen,* past *zou*), Old High German *scal* (infinitive *scolan,* past *scolta*), modern German *soll* (infinitive *sollen,* past *sollte*), Old Icelandic *skal* (infinitive *skulu,* past *skylda*), Swedish *skall* (past *skulle*), Norwegian and Danish *skal* (past *skulle*), and Gothic *skal* (past *skulda*), Proto-Germanic **skal-/skul-.*

The sense of obligation in Old English *sceal* owe, ought, is found in the related Old English *scyld* debt, obligation, guilt, which is cognate with Old Frisian *skeld* debt, Old Saxon and Old High German *sculd* (modern German *Schuld*), and Old Icelandic *skuld;* with cognates outside Germanic found in Lithuanian *skolà* debt, guilt, *skìlti* get into debt, and Old Prussian *skellānts* guilty, *poskulīt* to admonish, from Indo-European **skel-/skol-/skl̥-* (Pok.927).

Old English *sceal,* while retaining its primary sense of obligation or necessity, functioned as a sign of tense announcing a future event that was certain to happen;

in the Middle English period, *shall* began to express simple futurity, but as a defective verb (in the class with *can, may,* and *will*) *shall* has no participles, no imperative, and no infinitive. A past tense, while found as *sceolde, scolden, scalde* in Old English, began to appear as *should* (with variants *shollde, shuld*) only in the 1200's, and is not found as an established form before the late 1500's.

The distinctions in use of *shall* and *will,* and *should* and *would* are so subtle and depend so much on the context or the subjective conditions that usage is haphazard even among writers of the highest rank. There is a tendency in informal English to the exclusive use of *will* and *would* (except in a conditional circumstance); this to some extent mirrors the situation in Old English in which the notion of the future tense was usually expressed by the present tense, and so in order to prevent ambiguity *wile* (will) was often used as a future auxiliary form. In Middle English *shall* and *will* were commonly used to express future action or condition, but usage varied between the two forms, and it was not until the 1650's that the idea of *shall* in the first person and *will* in the second and third persons, became the general rule. Now, at least in American English, all distinctions seem to be breaking down in speech and in writing.

shallot (shal′ət) *n.* small plant much like an onion. 1664, borrowed from French *échalote,* from Middle French *eschalotte,* alteration of Old French *eschaloigne,* from Vulgar Latin **escalōnia* SCALLION.

shallow *adj.* Before 1387 *schalowe* not deep, in Trevisa's translation of Higden's *Polychronicon;* earlier *shelowe* thin (1373); probably related to the synonymous *schald, schold* not deep (1375); developed from Old English (839) *sceald;* see SHOAL[1] shallow place. **—v.** 1510, to make shallow; from the adjective. **—n.** Usually **shallows** *pl.* shallow part of a stretch of water. 1571, from the adjective.

shalom (shälōm′) *n., interj.* Hebrew word meaning hello or good-by. 1941, earlier, in phrases such as *shalom aleikhem* peace be unto you (1881); borrowing of Hebrew *shālōm* peace, soundness, wholeness. Compare SALAAM.

sham *n.* 1677, in Wycherley's *The Plain-Dealer,* fraud, trick, perhaps dialectal variant of SHAME. The meaning of a counterfeit, an imitation, is first recorded in 1728. **—adj.** counterfeit, imitation. 1681, from the noun. **—v.** 1677, to trick, cheat, in Wycherley's *The Plain-Dealer;* presumably from the noun. The meaning of pretend to be is first recorded in 1698.

shaman (shä′mən) *n.* priest or medicine man with magic powers. 1698, in a journal of travel from Russia to China; borrowed probably from Russian *shamán,* from Tungus *šaman* Buddhist monk, from Prakrit *samaṇa-,* from Sanskrit *śramaṇá-s* Buddhist ascetic, from *śráma-s* exertion, religious exercise, related to *śrā́myati* becomes weary, probably cognate with Greek *krémasthai* to hang, and *krēmnós* cliff, from Indo-European **krem-/krēm-* (Pok.573).

shamble *v.* walk awkwardly or unsteadily. 1681 (implied in *shambling,* in Dryden's *The Spanish Friar*); probably from earlier *shamble,* adj., ungainly, awkward (1607, in the expression *shamble legs*), from shamble, n., table, bench, from Middle English *schamil;* see SHAMBLES; so called from the straddling legs of a bench. **—n.** shambling walk. 1828, in Disraeli's *Vivian Grey;* from the verb.

shambles *n.pl. or sing.* confusion, mess. 1477-78 *sheambles* meat or fish market, plural of earlier *schamil* table or stall for vending (probably before 1325); developed from Old English (before 830) *scomul, sceamel* stool, footstool, table for vending. Old English *sceamel* was an early borrowing of Latin *scamillus, scamillum* low stool, alteration (influenced by *scamnum*) of *scabillum,* diminutive of *scamnum* stool, bench; cognate with Sanskrit *skabhnā́ti* (he) supports, *skambhá-s* support, pillar, from Indo-European **skabh-/skambh-* to support (Pok.916). Other Germanic words borrowed from Latin *scamillus, scamillum* include Old Saxon *skamel* stool, Middle Dutch *scēmel* (modern Dutch *schemel*), Old High German *scamil* (modern German *Schemel*).

From the Middle English meaning of meat market, table on which meat was sold, there developed the sense of a slaughterhouse (1548); the figurative sense of a place of butchery or of great bloodshed (1593). The meaning of a confusion, mess, general disorder, is first recorded about 1901.

shame *n.* Probably before 1200 *shame, scheome;* developed from Old English (before 800) *sceamu, sceomu* feeling of guilt or disgrace; cognate with Old Frisian *skame* shame, Old Saxon *skama,* Middle Dutch *scāme* (modern Dutch *schaamte*), Old High German *scama* (modern German *Scham*), and Old Icelandic *skǫmm,* with unexplained doubling of the *m* (Norwegian, Swedish, and Danish *skam*), from Proto-Germanic **skamō.* Outside Germanic no root of corresponding form and sense has been found. **—v.** Probably before 1200 *shamen, scheomien* feel shame; developed from Old English *sceamian, sceomian* (about 725, in *Beowulf*), from *sceamu* shame. The Old English verb is cognate with Old Frisian *skamia* to shame, Old Saxon *skamon,* Middle Dutch *scāmen* (modern Dutch *schamen*), Old High German *scamōn* (modern German *schämen*), Old Icelandic *skemma* to shame, and Gothic *skaman* be ashamed. **—shame-faced** *adj.* bashful, ashamed. 1555 (implied in *shamefacedness*); alteration by popular etymology of earlier *shamefast* (about 1200); developed from Old English *scamfæst* bashful (before 899, in Alfred's translation of St. Gregory's *Pastoral Care*); formed from *sceamu, scamu* shame + *-fæst,* adjective suffix. **—shameful** *adj.* Probably before 1200 *scheomeful* modest, in *Ancrene Riwle;* later, causing shame, disgraceful (before 1250), and with the spelling *schameful* (probably before 1300), *shameful* (about 1390); developed from Old English (before 950) *sceomful* modest; formed from *sceamu, sceomu* shame + *-ful.*

shampoo *v.* 1762, to massage; Anglo-Indian *shampoo,* borrowed from Hindi *chāmpō,* imperative of *chāmpnā* to press, knead the muscles, perhaps from Sanskrit *capáyati* pounds, kneads, perhaps borrowed from the Munda (non-Indo-European) language-family of India. The meaning of wash the hair with some cleansing agent is first recorded in Worcester's *Dictionary* (1860). **—n.** 1838, act of shampooing; from the verb. The meaning of liquid soap used for shampooing is first recorded in 1866.

shamrock *n.* bright-green leaf composed of three parts. 1577, in Stanyhurst's *A Treatise containing a plain and perfect Description of Ireland;* earlier *shamrote* (1571, in Edmund Campion's *History of Ireland*); borrowed from Irish *seamrōg,* diminutive of *seamar* clover.

shamus (shā′məs) *n. Slang.* detective. 1925 *sharmus,*

American English; later, *shamus* (1930); perhaps a borrowing of Yiddish *shames* synagogue caretaker or watchman (from Hebrew *shāmmāsh* caretaker, servant, from *shammēsh* to serve), or from the Irish proper name *Seamus.* The word was popularized by the American writer of detective stories Raymond Chandler, 1888-1959.

shanghai (shanghī′) *v.* kidnap to serve as a sailor, usually by first making unconscious, and put on a ship. 1871, American English, nautical slang; so called from the former practice of kidnapping sailors to serve on extended voyages, as to the Chinese seaport of *Shanghai.*

Shangri-la (shang′rilä′) *n.* idyllic earthly paradise. 1938, American English, an allusion to the inaccessible land in the remote Himalayas in *Lost Horizon* (1933), a novel by the English novelist James Hilton, 1900-54.

shank *n.* the part of the leg between the knee and the ankle. Probably before 1200 *shonke;* later *shanke* (about 1300); earlier as a surname *Schanke* (1176); developed from Old English *sceanca* leg, shank (about 1000, in Ælfric's *Glossary*); earlier *scanca* (probably about 750); cognate with Middle Low German *schenke* leg, shank, Middle Dutch *scenkel* (modern Dutch *schenkel*), Middle High German *schenkel* thigh (modern German *Schenkel*), and probably with Old Icelandic *skakkr* askew, aslant, crooked (Norwegian *skonk* shank, Danish and Swedish *skank*); from Proto-Germanic **skanka-.* Old Icelandic *skakkr* is probably cognate with Greek *skázein* to limp, and Sanskrit *khañjati* (middle Indic for classical **skañjati*), from Indo-European **skang-* (H.Frisk, *Griechisches etymologisches Wörterbuch,* II,714).

shantung *n.* kind of fabric with a rough, uneven surface. 1882, from the name of *Shantung,* a province of northeastern China, where this fabric was manufactured.

shanty[1] *n.* roughly built hut or cabin. 1820, American English; borrowed from Canadian French *chantier* lumberjack's headquarters, from French, timber yard, dock, from Old French *chantier* gantry, from Latin *canthērius* rafter, frame; see GANTRY.

shanty[2] *n.* song sung by sailors. 1869, spelling alteration of CHANTEY.

shape *v.* Probably before 1200 *shapen,* in *Ancrene Riwle* and Layamon's *Chronicle of Britain,* a new present-stem form developed in Middle English from Old English (before 1000) *scapen,* past participle of *sceppan, scieppan* to create, form, destine. Old English *scieppan* is cognate with Old Frisian *skeppa* to create, form, Old Saxon *skeppian,* Middle Dutch *sceppen* (modern Dutch *scheppen*), Old High German *scepfen, scaffan* (modern German *schaffen*), Old Icelandic *skepja, skapa,* and Gothic *gaskapjan,* from Proto-Germanic *skapjanan* create, ordain, from Indo-European **skab-* shape by carving (Pok.931).

Old English *sceppan, scieppan* survived as a strong verb into the Middle English period as *sheppen, shippen,* but from the 1500's onwards *shape* has been a regular verb (with past tense and past participle *shaped*), though the old past participle form *shapen* still survives as an archaism and in the word *misshapen.*
—**n.** Probably before 1200 *shap,* in *Trinity Homilies;* developed from Old English (before 1000) *gesceap* creation, creature, structure, form, destiny, from *ge-* perfective prefix expressing completion (see ENOUGH) + *-sceap,* from the root of *sceppan, scieppan* to create, shape. —**shapely** *adj.* having a good shape; well-formed. Before 1382 *shaply,* in the Wycliffe Bible; formed from Middle English *shap* shape + *-ly*[2].

shard *n.* About 1300 *scherde;* later *sherd* (before 1382); earlier as a surname *Sharde* (1275); developed from Old English *sceard* fragment, gap (about 1000); cognate with Old Frisian *skerd* cut, notch, Middle Low German *skart* crack, chink, Middle Dutch *scaert, scart* fragment, notch (modern Dutch *schaard*), Middle High German *scharte* notch, gap (modern German *Scharte*), and Old Icelandic *skardh.* These cognates are noun uses of the older adjective forms Old English *sceard* cut, notched, Old Frisian *skerde,* Old Saxon *skard,* Old High German *scart,* Middle High German *schart,* and Old Icelandic *skardhr,* all from Proto-Germanic **skardás,* a past participle formation on the variant **skar-* of the root of Old English *sceran* to cut, SHEAR. The Middle English form is still seen in the word *potsherd.*

share[1] *n.* portion. 1372, duty levied on fishing boats; about 1375, a portion or share of something; before 1450 *schar* a part or piece of something; developed from Old English (about 1000) *scearu* a cutting, shearing, tonsure, division, also in such compounds as *land-scearu* division of land, boundary, and *folc-scearu* division of people, nation; related to *sceran, scieran* to cut, SHEAR.

Old English *scearu* is cognate with Old Frisian *skere* portion, share (in *hermskere* share of penalty), Old Saxon *scara* share in a common field, division, troop, Middle Low German *schāre* troop, share, Middle Dutch *scāre* troop, crowd (modern Dutch *schaar, schare*), Old High German *scara* troop, share of forced labor (modern German *Schar* troop, band, crowd), and Old Icelandic *skǫr* rim, edge, boundary, from Proto-Germanic **skarō,* Indo-European **skorā* (Pok.938).
—**v.** About 1586, to apportion, divide; from the noun. The meaning of use or enjoy together, have in common, is first recorded in Shakespeare's *Midsummer Night's Dream* (1590).
—**sharecropper** *n.* (1925, American English)—**shareholder** *n.* (1795, American English)

share[2] *n.* blade of a plow, plowshare. About 1300 *ssare;* later *schare* (about 1350), *share* (before 1382); developed from Old English (before 800) *scear, scær,* related to *sceran, scieran* to cut, SHEAR. Old English *scear* (from Proto-Germanic **skara-*) is cognate with Old Frisian *sker* plowshare, Middle Low German *schar* (feminine *schare*), Old High German *scaro* (feminine *scara*), and modern German *Schar* (feminine).

shark[1] *n.* large predatory fish. 1569, of uncertain origin. The word was apparently introduced by the sailors of Captain John Hawkins' 1567 expedition to Africa and the West Indies, who brought back a specimen which was exhibited in London in 1569.

shark[2] *n.* dishonest person who preys on others. 1599, a worthless sponger and petty swindler, in Ben Jonson's *Every Man Out of His Humour;* of uncertain origin, but possibly a borrowing of earlier German *Schorck,* variant of *Schurke* scoundrel, villain. In later uses (as in *loan shark,* 1905) the English word has been influenced in meaning by *shark*[1] predatory fish.

sharp *adj.* Probably before 1200 *scharp,* in *Ancrene Riwle;* developed from Old English (before 830) *scearp* cutting, keen, sharp; cognate with Old Frisian *skerp, skarp* sharp, Old Saxon *skarp,* Middle Dutch *scarp,* *scerp* (modern Dutch *scherp*), Old High German *scarf* (modern German *scharf*), and Old Icelandic *skarpr* withered, sharp (Norwegian, Swedish, and Danish *skarp* sharp), from Proto-Germanic **skarpaz.* Cognates outside Germanic include Middle Irish *cerb* sharp, cutting, and Latvian *skârbs* sharp, rough, *skrabt* to scrape, scratch, from Indo-European **skerb-/skorb-* (Pok.943). **—adv.** About 1250 *scharpe* loudly, shrilly, in *The Owl and the Nightingale;* later *sharpe* sharply, keenly (before 1420, in Lydgate's *Troy Book*); developed from Old English (about 1000) *scearpe,* from *scearp* sharp, adj. The meaning of promptly, exactly, is first recorded in 1840. **—n.** Before 1200 *scerpe* sharp weapon, sharp edge; later *sharp* (about 1350); from the adjective. The meaning of a musical tone one half step above a given tone, is first recorded in 1576. **—sharpen** *v.* Probably about 1395 *scharpenen* to make sharp or sharper; formed from Middle English *scharp,* adj., sharp + *-enen* -en[1]. **—sharpshooter** *n.* (1802)

shatter *v.* Probably before 1300 *schatren* to break apart, in *Arthour and Merlin;* later *schateren* disperse, scatter (before 1350); of uncertain origin (possibly a variant of Middle English *scateren* to SCATTER). Both *schateren* and *scateren* probably represent an unrecorded Old English form cognate with Middle Dutch *schateren, schatern* and Middle Low German *schateren* to resound, laugh uproariously, be shattered by an explosion. Outside Germanic cognates may exist in Greek *skedannýnai* to scatter, Lithuanian *skedervà* splinter, Armenian *šert* splinter, block of wood, Avestan *sčandayeiti* (he) broke, destroyed, and Middle Persian *škastan* to break, from Indo-European **sked-/skod-/skend-* to split, scatter (Pok.918).

shave *v.* Probably before 1200 *schaven* cut off (hair) with a razor, scrape off, in *Ancrene Riwle;* developed from Old English (before 800) *sceafan;* cognate with Middle Dutch *scāven* to shave, scrape (modern Dutch *schaven*), Old High German *skaban* (modern German *schaben*), Old Icelandic *skafa,* and Gothic *skaban,* from Proto-Germanic **skaƀanan,* Indo-European **skabh-.* Cognates outside Germanic are found in Latin *scabere* to scratch, scrape, Latvian *skabrs* splintery, sharp, Lithuanian *skabùs* sharp, cutting, and Old Slavic *skoblĭ* scraper, planing knife, from Indo-European **skab(h)-* (Pok.931). **—n.** 1352, instrument for cutting or scraping; developed from Old English *sceafa* (before 800). The meaning of an act of shaving the beard is first found in Southey's *The Doctor* (1838), and that of a narrow escape (as in *a close shave*) in 1856. **—shaving** *n.* About 1386, a thin slice, especially of wood, in Chaucer's *Canterbury Tales* (probably recorded chiefly in the plural by about 1440).

shawl *n.* 1662, kind of scarf or wrap worn in parts of Asia; borrowed through Urdu and other Indian languages from Persian *shāl.* The first record of *shawl* being applied to a piece of clothing worn in the West is found in Sterne's letters (1767), in reference to a covering about the shoulders or head worn chiefly by women. The equivalent French form *châle* (1666) was also borrowed from Persian *shāl,* and the word has spread into many European languages: Spanish *chal,* Italian *scialle,* Dutch *sjaal,* etc.

she *pron.* About 1250, in *The Story of Genesis and Exodus;* earlier *scæ* (probably before 1160); also later *sho* (about 1300); probably developed by alteration (influenced by Old Icelandic *sjā* this) of Old English *sēo, sīo* (accusative *sīe*), feminine of *sē,* demonstrative pronoun and adjective; see THE[1]. Old English *sīo,* like Old High German *siu,* was extended from earlier **si* (compare Old High German *si,* Gothic *si*), cognate with Old Irish *sī* she, and Greek *hī́,* from Indo-European **sī* (Pok.979).

The Old English word for *she* was *hēo, hīo,* feminine of *hē* HE. However, phonetic development in various Middle English dialects made *hēo* and *hē* almost or wholly indistinguishable in pronunciation; hence, the feminine demonstrative pronoun was probably used to replace the original feminine personal pronoun. Alternatively, some scholars have maintained that *she* descended directly from variant pronunciations (*hyē, hyō*) of the Old English feminine personal pronoun *hēo, hīo.* While this development did occur in some Scandinavian dialects, as shown by the proper name *Shetland* developing from Old Icelandic *Hjaltland,* no example of it is known in English.
—n. a female. Before 1325 *sco,* in *Cursor Mundi;* later *she* (about 1380); from the pronoun.

sheaf *n.* Probably about 1200 *shæf* bundle of reaped grain, in *The Ormulum;* later *sheve* (about 1250), *sheef* (about 1386); developed from Old English *scēaf* (about 1000, in Ælfric's version of *Genesis*); cognate with Middle Dutch *scoof* bundle, sheaf (modern Dutch *schoof*), Old High German *scoub* (modern German *Schaub*), and Old Icelandic *skauf* fox's tail, from Proto-Germanic **skauƀaz,* from Indo-European **skeup-/skoup-* or **skeubh-/skoubh-* (Pok.956).

The transferred sense of a bundle of iron or steel is found in Middle English in 1309-10; that of a bundle of arrows, in 1318. The generalized meaning of any bundle or cluster of things bound together is first recorded before 1728.

shear *v.* About 1250 *sheren* to cut with shears or scissors; developed from Old English *sceran, scieran* (about 725, in *Beowulf*); cognate with Old Frisian *skera* to shear, Middle Dutch *scēren* (modern Dutch *scheren*), Low German *scheren,* Old High German *sceran* (modern German *scheren*), and Old Icelandic *skera* (Norwegian *skjære,* Swedish *skära,* Danish *skære*), from Proto-Germanic **sker-* to cut, shear. Cognates outside Germanic are found in Old Irish *scaraim* I separate, cut, Albanian *shkjer* tear apart, Greek *keírein* to cut, Latin *curtus* cut short, mutilated, Lithuanian *skirti* to cut, divide, *kir̃vis* ax, Old Slavic *okrŭniti* amputate, Armenian *k'orem* I scratch, and Sanskrit *kṛṇā́ti, kṛṇóti* (he) hurts, wounds, kills, *kártati* (he) cuts, from Indo-European **(s)ker-/ (s)kor-/ (s)kr̥* to cut (Pok.938). Related to SHARD. **—n. shears** *pl.* About 1300 *shres* (error for *sheres*) large scissors, in *Havelok the Dane;* earlier in surname *Schersmyth* (1264); developed from Old English *scēara* pair of shears or scissors (before 899, in Alfred's translation of St. Gregory's *Pastoral Care*); related to *sceran* to cut, SHEAR. Old English *scēara,* pl., is cognate with Old Frisian *skēre* shears, Old High German *skār* blade, plural *skāri* (Middle High German *schære,* modern German *Schere*), and Old Icelandic *skǣri* shears, from Proto-Germanic **skǣr-,* Indo-European **skēr-* (Pok.938).

sheath *n.* About 1250 *sheeth* case for the blade of a sword, knife, etc.; earlier *shæthe* (probably about 1200, in *The Ormulum*); developed from Old English (about 950) *scēath, scǣth,* from Proto-Germanic **skaithiz;* cognate with Old Frisian *skēthe* sheath, Old Saxon *scēthia,* Middle Dutch *scēde* (modern Dutch *scheede*), Old High German *sceida* (modern German *Scheide*), from Proto-Germanic **skaithjō,* and Old Icelandic *skeidh* (Norwegian *skjede,* Swedish *skida,* Danish *skede*). The word may be from the same root as Old English *scēadan, scādan* to divide, separate; see SHED[2] (cast off), with an original sense of a stick split so as to receive a blade, as found in Swedish *skida* sheath, which may be related to Old Icelandic *skidh,* variant *skidha* block of wood. **—sheathe** (shēтн) *v.* Probably before 1400 *schethen* furnish with or put into a sheath, in *Morte Arthur;* from the noun in Middle English.

shebang (shəbang′) *n. Slang.* concern, affair, thing. 1862, a hut, shed, shelter; American English, of uncertain origin (perhaps alteration of SHEBEEN). The meaning of a matter of present concern, affair, thing, business (usually in the phrase *the whole shebang*) is first recorded in 1869, in writings of Mark Twain, but the relation of this meaning to that of the earlier hut, shelter, is obscure.

shebeen (shibēn′) *n.* (chiefly in Ireland and Scotland) place where alcoholic liquor is sold without a license. About 1787, borrowed from Irish *séibín* small mug, bad ale, diminutive of *séibe* mug, bottle, liquid measure.

shed[1] *n.* building used for shelter, storage, etc. 1481 *shadde,* in Caxton's translation of *The History of Reynard the Fox;* possibly a variant of SHADE.

shed[2] *v.* cast off. Probably before 1200 *sheden* to separate, divide; also *scheden* to pour out, spill, in *Ancrene Riwle;* developed from Old English (about 1000) *scēadan, scādan* to divide, separate; cognate with Old Frisian *skētha* to divide, separate, Old Saxon *skēthan,* Middle Dutch *sceiden* (modern Dutch *scheiden*), Old High German *sceidan* (modern German *scheiden* to part, depart, separate), and Gothic *skaidan,* from Proto-Germanic **skaithanan/skaiđanan,* Indo-European **skəi-t-,* extended from root **skēi-/skəi-* cut (Pok.919). By the form **skei-d-* also extended from root **skēi-/skəi-* cut, cognates are found outside Germanic in Greek *schízein* to split, Latin *scindere* (past participle *scissus*) to cut, split, cleave, Lithuanian *skíesti* to separate, Old Slavic *čistiti* purify, clean, and Sanskrit *chinátti* (he) splits. Related to SHEATH, SHIFT, SHIP.

sheen *n.* brightness, luster. 1602, in Shakespeare's *Hamlet,* noun use of an earlier adjective meaning beautiful, bright, found in Middle English *schene* (probably before 1200); developed from Old English *scēne, sciene* (about 725, in *Beowulf*); cognate with Old Frisian *skēne* beautiful, bright, Old Saxon *skōni,* Middle Dutch *scōne* (modern Dutch *schoon*), Old High German *skōni* (modern German *schön*), and Gothic *skáuns* beautiful, from Proto-Germanic **skauniz,* root **skau-* behold, SHOW.

sheep *n.* Probably before 1200 *scheap,* in Layamon's *Chronicle of Britain;* later *sheep* (about 1280); developed from Old English (before 830) *scēap, scēp;* cognate with Old Frisian *skēp* sheep, Old Saxon *scāp,* Middle Low German *schāp,* Middle Dutch *scaep* (modern Dutch *schaap*), and Old High German *scāf* (modern German *Schaf*), from Proto-West-Germanic **skǣpan.* The word is not found in Gothic or Scandinavian and no definite connections are known outside Germanic. **—sheep dog** (before 1774) **—sheepish** *adj.* (probably before 1200, sheeplike; 1693, bashful, in the writings of Locke).

sheer[1] *adj.* very thin, nearly transparent. 1565 *shere,* in Arthur Golding's translation of Ovid's *Metamorphoses;* probably developed from Middle English *schiere* thin, sparse (about 1400, in Sir John Maundeville's *Travels*). Middle English *schiere* was probably in part a borrowing from a Scandinavian source (compare Old Icelandic *skǣrr* bright, clean, pure, from Proto-Germanic **skairjaz,* Swedish *skär* clear, and Norwegian *skjær* pure, sheer), and in part developed from dialectal Middle English *shire, schir* clear, pure, thin; found in Old English *scīr* bright, clear, pure (about 725, in *Beowulf*). The two Middle English words are ultimately related to each other: Old Icelandic *skǣrr* is related to *skīrr,* meaning bright, clear, pure, which is cognate with Old English *scīr,* of the same meaning, and also with Old Frisian *skīre,* Old Saxon *skīri,* Middle Low German *schīre,* Middle High German *schīr* (modern German *schier*), and Gothic *skeirs* clear, from Proto-Germanic **skīraz,* from Indo-European **sḱī-* glimmer low; see SHINE.

Use of *sheer* with the extended meaning of complete, absolute, utter (as in *sheer nonsense*) is first recorded in 1583. The meaning of very steep (as in *a sheer drop*) is first found in Wordsworth's *Poems* (1800).

—adv. completely, quite. Before 1600, from the adjective.

sheer[2] *v.* turn aside, swerve. 1626, in Captain John Smith's *An Accidence;* probably borrowed from Low German or modern Dutch *scheren* to withdraw, depart, originally, divide, SHEAR. **—n.** a turning of a ship from its course. 1670, from the verb.

sheet[1] *n.* broad, thin piece of cloth, etc. About 1250 *shet;* later *shete* (about 1280), *sheet* (before 1382); developed from Old English *sciete* cloth, covering (about 900, West Saxon), *scēte* (before 800, Mercian), from Proto-Germanic **skautjōn;* related to *scēat* corner, region, lap, cloth. Old English *scēat* is cognate with Old Frisian *skāt* lap, lappet, Middle Low German *schōt,* Middle Dutch *scoot* (modern Dutch *schoot*), Old High German *scōz* (modern German *Schoss*), Old Icelandic *skaut* corner, lap, lappet (Norwegian *skaut* sheet, headdress, Danish *skød* lap, skirt), and Gothic *skaut* hem of a garment, from Proto-Germanic **skauta-,* Indo-European **skoudo-,* from root **skaut-* to project, SHOOT. The extended sense of a piece of paper is first recorded in English in 1510; and that of a broad, flat surface, in 1593. **—v.** furnish or cover with a sheet. 1606, in Shakespeare's *Antony and Cleopatra;* from the noun.

sheet[2] *n.* rope that controls a sail. 1294-95 *sheete;* developed from Old English *scēat-* (in the compound *scēatlīne* sheet-line), from *scēata* lower part of sail, piece of cloth, related to *scēat* corner, region, lap, cloth; see SHEET[1].

sheik or **sheikh** (shēk) *n.* Arab chief. 1577, borrowed from Arabic *shajkh* chief; literally, old man, from *shákha* he grew (or was) old.

shekel (shek′əl) *n.* ancient silver coin of the Hebrews. Before 1382, in the Wycliffe Bible; borrowed from Hebrew *sheqel,* from *shāqal* he weighed. The word was reborrowed in English from modern Hebrew in 1980 as the name of a new unit of money, equal to ten former Israeli pounds, introduced in Israel in that year.

sheldrake *n.* large duck of Europe and Asia. Before 1325 *shelderake, shelddrake;* earlier as a surname *Scheldrac* (1195) (*sheld-* variegated, piebald + *drake*). The first element of this compound is probably related to Middle Dutch *scillen* to make different.

shelf *n.* About 1390 *shelves,* pl., in Chaucer's *Canter-*

bury Tales; later *shelfs* (in 1422); earlier in surname *Shelvemel* (1241); probably borrowed from Middle Low German *schelf* shelf, set of shelves. Middle Low German *schelf* is cognate with Middle Dutch *scelf* haystack (modern Dutch *schelf*), Old English *scylfe, scilfe* shelf, ledge, floor, *scylf* peak, pinnacle, and possibly with Old Icelandic *-skjalf* bench, peak, from Proto-Germanic **skelf-/skalf-.* The Germanic words are also cognate with Latin *scalpere* to carve, cut, Greek *skálops* mole (animal), related to *skalís* hoe, and *skállein* to hoe, dig, from Indo-European **skel(e)p-/skol(e)p-* (Pok.926).

shell *n.* Probably before 1300 *shelle,* in *Kyng Alisaunder;* developed from Old English *sciell, scill* (before 1100); earlier *scel* (before 800); related to Old English *scealu* shell, husk. The Old English words are cognate with Middle Low German and Middle Dutch *schelle* shell, pod, rind, Old High German *scala* shell, husk (modern German *Schale*), Old Icelandic *skel* shell, and Gothic *skalja* tile, from Proto-Germanic **skaljō.* Cognates outside Germanic are found in Latin *silex* pebble, *siliqua* pod, Old Slavic *skala* rock, stone, and Sanskrit *kalā́* small part, from Indo-European **skel-/skol-* cut (Pok.923). —**v.** take out of a shell. 1562, from the noun. —**shellfish** *n.* (before 899, in Alfred's translation of Boethius' *De Consolatione Philosophiae*) —**shell shock** (1915)

shellac (shəlak′) *n.* refined lac, used as a varnish. 1713, formed from English *shell* + *lac;* translation of French *laque en écailles* lac in thin plates. —**v.** varnish or fasten with shellac. 1882, from the noun.

shelter *n.* 1585, something that covers or protects from weather; of uncertain origin, but possibly an altered form of Middle English *sheltron, sheltrun* roof or wall formed by locked shields (probably before 1400), earlier *sceldtrume* (probably before 1200); developed from Old English (about 1000) *scieldtruma* (*scield* SHIELD + *truma* troop); the original sense is that of a body of men protected by their shields locked to form a roof and wall. —**v.** 1590, in Spenser's *Faerie Queene;* from the noun.

shelve[1] *v.* put on a shelf. 1591, to overhang, project, in Shakespeare's *The Two Gentlemen of Verona;* back formation from *shelves,* plural of SHELF (also first recorded as a plural). The meaning of put on a shelf is first recorded in 1655. The figurative sense of lay aside, dismiss, is found in 1812.

shelve[2] *v.* to slope gradually. 1587 (implied in *shelving*), to tilt or tip up; later, to slope gradually (1614); perhaps a figurative use of SHELVE[1].

shenanigan *n. Informal.* mischief or trickery. 1855, American English, of uncertain origin. The term appears to have first come into use in California, and Spanish *chanada* (a shortened form of *charranada*), meaning trick or deceit, has been suggested as a possible source (see *American Speech* 2, p. 48, 1927). A less likely source is a German peddler's argot term *Schenigelei,* meaning work, craft, or the German slang verb *schinäglen* to toil (proposed in *American Speech* 23, pp. 210-213, 1948).

shepherd *n.* Probably about 1200 *shephirde* tender of sheep, in *The Ormulum;* later *shepherde* (about 1387-95); developed from Old English (before 1023) *scēaphierde* (*scēap* SHEEP + *hierde* herder, from *heord* a HERD). The figurative sense of a spiritual guardian or pastor is first recorded in Middle English about 1300, though it may have appeared much earlier in reference to Christ. —**v.** 1790 (implied in *shepherding*) to tend sheep; from the noun. The figurative sense of watch over, guide, direct, is found in Shelley's *Arethusa* (1820).

sherbet (shėr′bət) *n.* flavored ice. 1615 *sherbet* cooling drink made of fruit juice and sweetened water, popular in the Orient; earlier *zerbet* (1603); borrowed from Turkish *şerbet,* from Persian *sharbat,* from Arabic *sharbah* a drink, from *shariba* he drank. Compare SYRUP. The sense of flavored ice is first recorded in 1891, in the *Century Dictionary.*

sheriff *n.* 1100 *scirereve* law-enforcing officer of a shire or county; later *sherref* (about 1350), *sheryff* (before 1425); developed from Old English (about 1034) *scīrgerēfa* representative of the royal authority in a shire (*scīr* SHIRE + *gerēfa* chief official, reeve, of uncertain origin).

sherry (sher′ē) *n.* kind of strong wine, 1608, in Thomas Middleton's *A Mad World My Masters,* new singular formed from earlier *sherris* (1597, Shakespeare), which was taken as a plural. *Sherris* was a borrowing from Spanish *vino de Xeres* wine from Xeres, a town (now called *Jerez*), near the port of Cadiz, in southeastern Spain, where this wine was made.

shibboleth (shib′əlith) *n.* test word, watchword, or slogan of a political party, class, etc. Before 1382 *Sebolech,* in the Wycliffe Bible (Judges 12:4-6); later *Schiboleth* (1535, in the Coverdale Bible); borrowed from Hebrew *shibbōleth* flood, stream; said to have been used as a password by the Gileadites to distinguish their own men from the fleeing Ephraimites, because the Ephraimites could not pronounce the *sh* sound. The figurative sense of a test word, watchword, or slogan of a political party, class, etc., is first recorded in 1638.

shield *n.* Probably before 1200 *scheld* piece of armor, protection, in *Ancrene Riwle;* later *shild* (probably before 1400), *shielde* (about 1450); developed from Old English *scield, sceld, scild* (about 725, in *Beowulf*), related to *sciell* SHELL. The Old English forms are cognate with Old Saxon *skild* shield, Middle Dutch *scilt, scild* (modern Dutch *schild*), Old High German *scilt* (modern German *Schild*), Old Icelandic *skjǫldr* (Swedish *sköld,* Norwegian and Danish *skjold*), and Gothic *skildus,* from Proto-Germanic **skelđús,* Indo-European **skel-tús* (compare Lithuanian *skìltis* section cut off), Indo-European root **skel-* (Pok.924). —**v.** be a shield to, protect, defend. Probably before 1200 *schilden;* developed from Old English *scildan* (about 725, in *Beowulf*), from *scild* shield, n.

shift *v.* About 1250 *shiften* change, exchange, replace, in *The Story of Genesis and Exodus;* earlier *sciften* divide, distribute (about 1200); developed from Old English (about 1000) *sciftan* arrange, divide; related to *scēadan* divide, separate; see SHED[2] cast off. Old English *sciftan* is cognate with Old Frisian *skifta* determine, Middle Low German *schiften, schichten* arrange, divide, Middle Dutch *scichten* (modern Dutch *schiften* separate, sift), German *schichten* arrange in layers, and Old Icelandic *skipta* to share, divide, change (Swedish *skifta,* Norwegian and Danish *skifte*), from Proto-Germanic **skiftanan,* cognate with Lettish *šķibît* to hew, cut, from Indo-European **skēi-b-/ski-b-* (Pok.922).

The sense of move, transfer, and that of manage matters, are first recorded in Middle English before 1325

An extended sense of manage to get along is recorded before 1513.
—n. Before 1460 *shyft* effort; from the verb. The sense of a change, substitution, succession, is first recorded in 1580, and that of a change in position, in 1771.
—shiftless *adj.* 1562, helpless; later, not resourceful, lazy (1584); formed from earlier *shift* resourcefulness + *-less.* **—shifty** *adj.* 1570, able to manage for oneself, full of expedients; formed from English *shift,* n. + *-y*[1]. The sense of using dishonest methods, not straightforward, is first recorded in Carlyle's *The French Revolution* (1837).

shill *n. Slang.* one who acts as a decoy for a gambler, auctioneer, etc. 1916, American English (probably originally circus or carnival use); perhaps shortened from *shillaber* a shill (1913, American English), of unknown origin. **—v.** *Slang.* to act or entice as a shill. 1914, American English; related to the noun.

shillelagh or **shillalah** (shəlā'lē) *n.* cudgel. 1772; earlier, the oak wood used to make cudgels (1677); from *Shillelagh,* a town and barony of Ireland.

shilling *n.* former British unit of money. Probably before 1225 *shillinges,* in *Ancrene Riwle;* developed from Old English (about 900) *scilling;* cognate with Old Frisian and Old Saxon *skilling* coin used as unit of money, Middle Dutch *scellinc* (modern Dutch *schelling*), Old High German *skilling* (modern German *Schilling*), Old Icelandic *skillingr* (Norwegian, Swedish, and Danish *skilling*), and Gothic *skilliggs.* The Old English word and its cognates have been referred by some etymologists to Proto-Germanic **skell-* to resound, ring, and by others to Indo-European **skel-* to split, divide (see SHELL). Still others derive it from Proto-Germanic **skelđ-* SHIELD. The ending may represent the suffix *-ling.*

shilly-shally *adv.* in a vacillating or hesitating manner. 1703, in Steele's *The Tender Husband;* from earlier *shill I, shall I* (1700), varied reduplication of *shall I?,* reflected in and probably influenced by such formations as *dilly-dally,* and *wishy-washy.* **—adj.** vacillating, hesitating. 1734, from the adverb. **—v.** be undecided, vacillate, hesitate. 1782, from the adverb. **—n.** inability to decide, hesitation. 1755, from the adjective.

shimmer *v.* Before 1250 *schimeren,* gleam faintly; developed from Late Old English (before 1100) *scimerian;* related to *scīmian* to shine, grow dark, and *scīnan* to SHINE. Old English *scimerian* is cognate with Middle Low German *schēmeren* be shadowy, grow dark, shimmer, Middle Dutch *scēmeren* (modern Dutch *schemeren*), and modern German *schimmern* to shimmer. **—n.** faint gleam. 1821, in Scott's *Kenilworth;* from the verb.

shimmy *n.* 1918, a jazz dance with much shaking of the body; American English (originally in the phrase *shaking the shimmy* and *shimmy shake,* names of the dance); of uncertain origin (sometimes suggested as an extended sense of earlier *shimmey* a chemise (1837), alteration of CHEMISE, but this emphasizes a closeness in form and a disregard of meaning). The general sense of a shaking or vibration is first recorded in 1925. **—v.** 1919, to dance the shimmy, American English; from the noun. The general sense of shake, shiver, vibrate, is found in 1925.

shin *n.* front part of the leg from the knee to the ankle. About 1250 *shine,* in *The Owl and the Nightingale;* developed from Old English (before 1000) *scinu;* cognate with Middle Low German *schēne* shin, Middle Dutch *scēne* (modern Dutch *scheen*), Old High German *scina* shin, needle, modern German *Schienbein* shinbone, *Schiene* rail, band, Swedish *skena,* and dialectal Norwegian *skina* thin disc, from Proto-Germanic **skinō,* from Indo-European **skēi-/ski-* (Pok.920). **—v.** to climb. 1829, in Marryat's *Frank Mildmay;* from the noun. **—shinny** *v. Informal.* to shin, climb. 1888, American English; extended form of *shin,* v. + *-y*[3].

shindig *n. Informal.* merry or noisy dance, party, etc. 1871, American English; probably from earlier *shindy* a spree, merrymaking (1821), of unknown origin. An earlier noun *shindig* a blow on the shins (1859) was a literal use of the words *shin* and *dig* a blow, but any relation to the meaning of a noisy party is not apparent.

shine *v.* Probably before 1200 *schinen;* probably about 1200 *shinen;* developed from Old English (before 800) *scīnan* shed light, be radiant; cognate with Old Frisian *skīna* to shine, Old Saxon *skīnan,* Middle Dutch *scīnen* (modern Dutch *schijnen*), Old High German *skīnan* (modern German *scheinen*), Old Icelandic *skīna* (Norwegian and Danish *skinne,* Swedish *skina*), and Gothic *skeinan,* from Proto-Germanic **skīnanan.* Cognates outside Germanic are found in Old Slavic *sijati* to shine, grow bright, and Sanskrit *chāyā́* shadow, gleam, from Indo-European **sk̑āi-/sk̑əi, *sk̑ī-* glimmer low (Pok.917). **—n.** light, brightness. Before 1529, in Skelton's poetry; from the verb. **—shiny** *adj.* 1590, in Spenser's *Faerie Queene;* formed from English *shine* n. + *-y*[1].

shingle[1] *n.* thin piece of wood, etc., used to cover roofs, etc. About 1200 *scincle,* in *Vices and Virtues;* later *schingle* (before 1300), *shyngle* (1439); probably borrowed from Late Latin *scindula,* alteration (by influence of Greek *schídax* lath, or *schindalmós* splinter) of Latin *scandula* shingle, of uncertain origin. The informal sense of a small signboard is found in 1842, in American English. The meaning of a woman's short haircut is first attested in 1924. **—v.** cover with shingles. 1562, from the verb.

shingle[2] *n.* loose stones or pebbles, especially on the seashore. 1513, beach covered with pebbles; later, the pebbles themselves (1598); of uncertain origin (sometimes referred to Norwegian *singl* small stones, coarse sand).

shingles *n.sing. or pl.* disease that attacks certain nerves. Before 1398 *schingles,* in Trevisa's translation of Bartholomew's *De Proprietatibus Rerum;* borrowing of Medieval Latin *cingulus,* variant of Latin *cingulum* girdle, from *cingere* to gird (see CINCTURE); so called because shingles often causes inflammation that extends around the middle of the body. The Medieval Latin word is a loan translation of Greek *zōstḗr* girdle, shingles, related to *zṓnē* girdle; see ZONE.

ship *n.* Probably before 1200 *schip, shipe;* developed from Old English (before 800) *scip* ship, boat; cognate with Old Frisian and Old Saxon *skip* ship, Middle Dutch *scip* (modern Dutch *schip*), Middle Low German *schip, schêp* (modern Low German *schipp*), Old High German *scif, skef* (modern German *Schiff*), Old Icelandic *skip* (Swedish *skepp,* Norwegian *skip,* Danish *skib*), and Gothic *skip,* from Proto-Germanic **skipan.* The further origins of this word are uncertain; it has been conjectured that an original meaning of hollowed-out canoe would ultimately derive from Indo-European **skēi-* to cut, divide, and for instances of a *b*-formant comparison can be made to Lithuanian *skiẽbti* rip, rip apart, and Latvian *šķibît* cut, lop, from Indo-European **skēi-b-/ski-b-* (Pok.922). **—v.** Probably before 1300 *shippen* put or take on board a ship; developed from Old English (about 900) *gescipian* provide with ships; from *scip* ship, n. **—shipboard** *n.* (about 1200) **—shipmaster** *n.* (about 1375) **—shipmate** *n.* (1748) **—shipment** *n.* 1802, act of shipping goods, formed from English *ship,* v. + *-ment.* The meaning of something that is shipped, goods shipped, is found in 1861. **—shipper** *n.* (1075, a seaman; 1755 one who ships goods) **—shipshape** *adj.* in good order, trim, as things on board ship should be (1644 *ship shapen;* 1769 *ship shape*). **—shipwreck** *n.* (probably before 1100); *v.* (1589) **—shipyard** *n.* (before 1700)

-ship a suffix forming nouns meaning: **1** quality or condition, as in *partnership = the condition of being a partner.* **2** act, power, or skill, as in *workmanship = skill of a workman.* **3** relation between, as in *fellowship = relation between fellows.* **4** office, position, or occupation, as in *governorship= office of a governor.* **5** number, as in *readership= the number of readers.* Middle English *-schipe, -shipe, -ship;* developed from Old English *-scipe* state or condition of being, related to *sceppan, scieppan* to create, form, SHAPE. Old English *-scipe* is cognate with Old Frisian *-skip, -skipi* state or condition, -ship, Old Saxon *-skap, -skepi, -skipi,* Middle Dutch *-scap* (modern Dutch *-schap*), Old High German *-scaf, -scaft* (modern German *-schaft*), and Old Icelandic *-skapr* (Norwegian and Swedish *-skap,* Danish *-skab*), from Proto-Germanic **-skapaz.* The suffix has an ancient history in English and was added to numerous adjectives and past participles in Old English, a few of which survive today, such as in *worship.* Other formations from Old English are made from nouns, such as *friendship, lordship,* and *township.*

shire *n.* one of the counties into which Great Britain is divided as in *Yorkshire* and *Berkshire.* Probably before 1200 *schire;* developed from Old English (before 800) *scīr* administrative office or district. The only known Germanic cognate is Old High German *scīra* care, official charge (from Proto-Germanic **skīzṓ,* Indo-European *skeisā́;* a possible cognate outside Germanic may be found in Latin *cūra* care, earlier **coisā,* from Indo-European **kois-* (Pok.611); see CURE.

shirk *v.* 1633 *sherk,* 1634 *shirk* (implied in *shirking*) to practice fraud or trickery, prey on others, sponge; of unknown origin. The meaning of go evasively, sneak away, is first recorded in 1681; and that of evade one's work or duty, in Grose's *Classical Dictionary of the Vulgar Tounge* (1785).

shirr (shėr) *v.* draw up or gather (cloth) on parallel threads. 1847 (implied in *shirred*); American English, of unknown origin. **—shirred** *adj.* 1847, having elastic threads woven into the texture. **—shirred egg** (1883)

shirt *n.* Probably before 1200 *shurte;* later *schirt* (about 1300); developed from Old English (before 1000) *scyrte;* cognate with Middle Low German *schörte* apron, skirt, Middle Dutch *scorte* (modern Dutch *schort*), Middle High German *schurz* (modern German *Schurz* apron, *Schürze* apron, skirt), and Old Icelandic *skyrta* shirt, from Proto-Germanic **skurtjōn,* all perhaps originally meaning "a short garment," and derived from the same source as Old English *scort, sceort* SHORT. Doublet of SKIRT. **—shirtsleeve** *n.* Usually **shirtsleeves** *pl.* sleeves of a shirt (about 1566). *—adj.* informal, plainspoken (1924, perhaps 1908; earlier hardworking, 1864).

shish kebab (shish′ kəbob′) pieces of lamb or beef broiled on skewers or a spit. 1914, in Sinclair Lewis' *Our Mr. Wrenn,* American English; borrowing of Armenian *shish kabab,* from Turkish *şişkebabi* (*şiş* skewer + *kebap* roast mutton).

shivaree (shiv′ərē) *n.* mock serenade made by beating on pans, etc. 1843, American English, alteration of earlier *charivari, charivary* (1735); borrowed from French *charivari,* from Old French *chalivali* discordant noise made by pans, pots, etc., from Late Latin *carībaria, carēbaria* severe headache, from Greek *karēbariā* heaviness in head, headache (*kárē* head + *barýs* heavy).

shiver[1] *v.* shake with cold, fear, etc. Probably before 1405 *shyveren;* alteration of earlier *chiveren* (about 1200), of uncertain origin. **—n.** a shivering. 1727, from the verb. The alteration in spelling from *ch-* to *sh-* has been variously attributed to influence of *sh-* in *shake* and less plausibly to association with *shiveren* SHIVER[2].

shiver[2] *n.* small piece, splinter. Probably before 1200 *scifre,* in Layamon's *Chronicle of Britain;* later *schiver* (probably about 1300); probably cognate with Middle Low German *schēver, schiver* splinter, Old High German *scivaro,* modern German *Schiefer* slate, *Scheibe* slice, pane, and Old Icelandic *skīfa* a slice; see SKEWER. **—v.** to break into shivers. Probably before 1200 *shivren,* later *shiveren* (before 1338); from the noun.

shoal[1] *n.* place where water is shallow. About 1375 *schald;* later *sholde* (1414); noun use of adjective *shald* not deep, shallow (1375); earlier *schealde* (before 1333); developed from Old English (839) *sceald* shallow. The final *-d* gradually disappeared in the 1500's. Old English *sceald* is cognate with Middle Low German *schal* stale (modern Low German, dry), Middle High German and modern German *schal* stale, insipid; dialectal Swedish *skäll* thin, stale (from Proto-Germanic **skala-*), and possibly also with Greek *skéllein* to dry up (from Indo-European **skel-/skol-,* Pok.927), and Latvian *kàls* thin, *kàlst* become dried up. Related to SHALLOW. **—v.** become shallow. 1574 (implied in *shoaling*); from earlier *shoal,* adj., shallow (before 1554), alteration of Middle English *shald* (1375); developed from Old English *sceald* shallow.

shoal[2] *n.* large number, crowd. 1579 *shole,* in Spenser's *The Shepheardes Calender;* probably developed (through Middle English **shole*) from Old English *scolu* band, troop, school of fish; cognate with Old Saxon *scola* troop, multitude, Middle Dutch *schole* multitude, flock, school of fish, West Frisian *skoal.* It has been conjectured that these Germanic cognates had an original meaning of division and may have derived from Indo-European **(s)kel-* to divide, cut (Pok.923). **—v.** form into a shoal. 1610, from the noun.

shoat *n.* young pig that no longer suckles. 1408 *schote;* perhaps borrowed from a Low German word (compare Flemish *schote* shoat).

shock[1] *n.* sudden and violent shake, blow, or crash. 1565, encounter in a battle, joust, or charge; borrowed from Middle French *choc* violent attack, from Old French *choquer* strike against, probably borrowed from a Germanic source (compare Middle Dutch *schokken* to push, jolt, Middle Low German *schocken* to shake, tremble, and Middle High German *schocken* to swing, dance, all possibly cognate with Old High

German *scioban* to push, SHOVE). The sense of a sudden and violent shake, blow, or crash, is first recorded in English in 1614. **—v.** 1568, to shake or weaken by a shock; borrowed from Middle French *choquer* to strike against. The sense of offend, displease, astonish, is first recorded in Congreve's *Double Dealer* (1694). **—shock absorber** (1906) **—shocking** *adj.* (1691, with the French spelling *choquant;* 1697 *shocking,* in Dryden's writings; 1703, offensive) **—shock wave** (1907)

shock[2] *n.* bundles of grain set up on end together. Before 1325 *scholke* (probably an error for *schokke*); later *schocke* (about 1350); perhaps borrowed from Middle Low German *schok* shock of corn, group of sixty. Middle Low German *schok* is cognate with Dutch *schok* group of sixty, Middle High German *schoc* pile, group of sixty (modern German *Schock*), and Old Saxon *scok* group of sixty, from Proto-Germanic **skukka-,* Indo-European **skugná-,* root **skeu-g-/sku-g-* (Pok.589). **—v.** make into shocks. Before 1338 *schokken,* in Mannyng's *Chronicle of England;* from the noun.

shoddy *adj.* of inferior quality. 1862, adjective use of earlier *shoddy* inferior kind of wool made of woolen waste, old rags, etc. (1832), of uncertain origin. If, as some have proposed, the meaning of the smaller stones at a quarry (1880), is the original one, then the word may be from earlier *shoad* loose fragments of ore (1602), probably ultimately derived from Old English *scādan* to divide, separate; see SHED[2].

shoe *n.* Probably before 1200 *scheo, sho* covering for the foot; later *shoe* (about 1378); developed from Old English (about 950) *scoh;* cognate with Old Frisian *skōch* shoe, Old Saxon *skōh,* Middle Dutch *scoe, scoen* (modern Dutch *schoen*), Old High German *scuoh* (modern German *Schuh*), Old Icelandic *skōr* (Swedish, Danish, and Norwegian *sko*), and Gothic *skōhs,* from Proto-Germanic **skōHaz.* There is no known Indo-European source of these words. **—v.** furnish with shoes. Probably before 1200 *scheoien,* in *Ancrene Riwle;* later *shoen* (probably before 1300); developed from Old English *scōgan, scōgian* (before 899, in Alfred's translation of St. Gregory's *Pastoral Care*), from *scōh* shoe, n. **—shoehorn** *n.* (1589) **—shoelace** *n.* (1647) **—shoemaker** *n.* (1381) **—shoestring** *n.* (1616, but earlier *shoetie* 1599)

shogun (shō′gun) *n.* former hereditary commander in chief of the Japanese army. 1615, borrowing of Japanese *shōgun* general, from Chinese *chiang chün* leader of an army. **—shogunate** *n.* position or rule of a shogun. 1871, formed from English *shogun* + *-ate*[3].

shoji (shō′jē) *n.* paper screen used as a partition or sliding door. 1880, borrowing of Japanese *shōji.*

shoot *v.* Probably about 1200 *scheoten* move swiftly, rush, fly; later *shoten, schoten* (probably before 1300), *shooten* (before 1463); developed from Old English *scēotan* (before 899, in Alfred's translation of Orosius' *Historiarum Adversus Paganos*). Old English *scēotan* is cognate with Old Frisian *skiāta* to shoot, Old Saxon *skiotan,* Middle Dutch *scieten* (modern Dutch *schieten*), Old High German *skiozzan* (modern German *schiessen*), Old Icelandic *skjōta* (Norwegian *skyte,* Swedish *skjuta,* Danish *skyde*), and Crimean Gothic *schieten* to shoot, from Proto-Germanic **skeutanan.* Outside Germanic cognates are found in Albanian *heth* I throw, winnow, Lithuanian *skudrùs* quick, nimble, Russian *kidát'* to throw, and Sanskrit *skundate* (he) hurries, *códati* (he) incites, urges, from Indo-European **(s)keud-* (Pok.955). Such common meanings of *shoot* as that of send forth swiftly and suddenly and send forth or wound with missiles are recorded in Old English **—n.** About 1450 *schoyte* young branch, new growth, from the verb. The meaning of an act of shooting (with firearms, etc.) is first recorded in 1534. **—shooting star** (1593, in Shakespeare's *Richard II*)

shop *n.* About 1300 *ssope* place where goods are made for sale; later *schoppe* (before 1387), and as surname *Shoppe* (1301); developed from Old English (before 1050) *scoppa* booth or shed for trade or work. Old English *scoppa* is related to Old English *scypen, scipen* cowshed, and cognate with Middle Low German *schoppe* shed, and Old High German *scopf* porch, shed, from Proto-Germanic **skupp-,* Indo-European **skubn'-,* root **skeub-* (Pok.956). It is conjectured that the original meaning of these words was "roof thatched with straw," and that they may be cognate with Old English *scēaf* SHEAF. **—v.** 1583, to shut up in prison; from the noun. The meaning of visit shops is first recorded in 1764. **—shopkeeper** *n.* (1530) **—shoplift** *v.* steal goods from a store. 1820, in writings of Shelley; back formation from earlier *shoplifting* (1698, *shop* + slang *lifting* stealing, gerund of *lift*). **—shoplifter** *n.* 1680, formed from English *shop* + slang verb *lift* to steal (1595) + *-er*[1]. **—shopping center** (1898) **—shoptalk** *n.* talk about one's work (1881). **—shopworn** *adj.* soiled by being displayed or handled in a store (1838, American English).

shore[1] *n.* land at the edge of a sea, lake, etc. Probably about 1380 *schore,* of uncertain origin; possibly developed by shift in vowel grade from Old English *sceran* shear (as may be found in *scoren clif* shorn or sheared cliff, precipice); or perhaps borrowed from Middle Low German *schōr, schōre* shore, coast, headland, or from Middle Dutch *scorre* land washed by the sea (modern Dutch *schor*), which is cognate with Frisian *skoarre,* and Old High German *scorra* steep cliff). It is probable that all of these words had an original sense of division (between land and water), and derive from the same source as Old English *sceran, scieran* to cut, SHEAR. **—shorebird** *n.* 1874, American English, shore-dwelling bird; earlier, a kind of swallow (1672). **—shoreline** *n.* (1852)

shore[2] *v.* prop up, support. 1340 *ssoren,* in *Ayenbite of Inwyt;* later *schorien* (before 1425); probably from the noun, perhaps reinforced by Middle Dutch *scōren* (modern Dutch *schoren*) to prop up, support, which is cognate with Frisian *skoarje,* and Old Icelandic *skordha* (Norwegian *skorde*). **—n.** a prop, support. 1318 *shor;* probably borrowed from Middle Low German *schōre* a prop, stay, support, which is cognate with Middle Dutch *scōre* a prop, support (modern Dutch *schoor*), Frisian *skoarre,* and Old Icelandic *skordha* (Norwegian *skorde*). It is probable that all of these words are associated with the meaning of a split beam or stick, and derive from the same source as Old English *sceran, scieran* to cut, SHEAR.

short *adj.* Probably about 1200 *shorrt,* in *The Ormulum;* developed from Old English *sceort, scort* (before 899, in Alfred's translation of Boethius' *De Consolatione Philosophiae*); cognate with Old High German *scurz* short, and Old Icelandic *skort, skortr* lack, *skorta* to lack; probably from Proto-Germanic **skurtá-,* Indo-European **skr̥dó-,* root **skerd-* (Pok.941). **—adv.** Before 1325 *schort* in a short manner, in *Cursor Mundi;*

from the adjective. **—n.** Before 1586, summary, upshot, especially in the phrase *the short,* or *the short of it,* though an earlier use is found in the sense of briefly, concisely in the phrase *in short,* in Chaucer's *Canterbury Tales* (about 1386); later, something short (1591); from the adjective. *Shorts,* pl., in the sense of short trousers, is first recorded in Benjamin Disraeli's *Vivian Grey* (1826). The meaning of an electrical short circuit is first recorded in 1906. **—v.** 1904, to cause or experience an electrical short circuit. **—shortage** *n.* 1868, American English, formed from *short,* n. + *-age.* **—shortbread** *n.* 1801, formed from English *short* easily crumbled + *bread.* **—shortcake** *n.* (1594) **—shortchange** *v.* (1903, American English) **—short circuit** (1854) **—short-circuit** *v.* (1867, cause a short circuit in; 1902, fail as a result of a short circuit) **—shortcoming** *n.* (about 1680) **—shorten** *v.* 1513, in Thomas More's *History of King Richard III,* formed from English *short,* adj. + *-en*[1]. **—shortening** *n.* butter or other fat used in baking. 1823, formed from *shorten* make crumbly (from *short* in the sense of easily crumbled) + *-ing*[1]. **—shorthand** *n.* (1636) **—short-lived** *adj.* (1588, in Shakespeare's *Love's Labour's Lost*) **—shortly** *adv.* Probably before 1200 *shorrtlike* briefly, in *The Ormulum;* developed from Old English *scortlice* (before 899, in Alfred's translation of Orosius' *Historiarum Adversus Paganos*); formed from *sceort* short + *-lice* -ly[1]. The sense of "in a short time" is first recorded before 1050. **—short-range** *adj.* (1869) **—short run** (1830; later, a brief period of time, 1879, in George Eliot's letters) **—short shrift.** See under SHRIFT. **—short-sighted** *adj.* (1622) **—shortstop** *n.* (1857, American English) **—short story** (1877) **—short-tempered** *adj.* (1900) **—shortwave** *adj.* (1907)

shot[1] *n.* discharge of a gun. Probably about 1300 *schot* act of shooting, in *The Romance of Guy of Warwick;* developed from Old English *scot, sceot, gesceot* that which is discharged in shooting (before 899, in Alfred's writings), related to *scēotan* to SHOOT. Old English *scot, sceot* (from Proto-Germanic **skutan*) is cognate with Old Frisian *skot* missile, shot, Old Saxon *-scot,* Middle Low German *schot,* Middle Dutch *scot* (modern Dutch *schot*), Old High German *scoz, giscoz* missile (modern German *Geschoss*), *scuz* shot (modern German *Schuss*), and Old Icelandic *skot* (Norwegian *skot,* Swedish *skott,* Danish *skudd*).

The meaning of the discharge of a bow (later applied to a firearm) is first recorded in Old English (about 1000). The collective sense of balls, bullets, or other projectiles is first recorded in Middle English in Trevisa's translation of Higden's *Polychronicon* (before 1387).

—v. to load (a firearm) with shot. 1681, from the noun. **—shotgun** *n.* (1776, American English) **—shotput** *n.* (1898, American English)

shot[2] *adj.* woven so as to show a play of colors. 1763, adjective use of *shot,* past participle of SHOOT in the earlier sense of variegate by mixing in different colored threads in the woof (1532-33).

should *v.* past tense of SHALL. Probably about 1200 *shollde;* developed from Old English *sceolde, scolde* (about 725, in *Beowulf*), past tense of *sceal* SHALL.

shoulder *n.* Probably about 1200 *shulldre,* in *The Ormulum;* later *sholdre* (about 1300); developed from Old English (before 800) *sculdor;* cognate with Old Frisian *skuldere* shoulder, Middle Low German *schulder,* Middle Dutch *scouder* (modern Dutch *schouder*), and Old High German *scultra, sculterra* (modern German *Schulter*), from Proto-Germanic **skulđrō,* Indo-European **skl̥-dhrā* shoulder blade, conjectured as means of digging. The word is not found in Old Icelandic; Swedish *skuldra* and Danish *skulder* are probably early borrowings from Middle Low German. Outside Germanic the word may be cognate with Greek *skállein* hoe, stir up, *skalís* hoe, mattock, and Latin *culter* knife from Indo-European *(s)kel-/(s)kol-/(s)kl̥-* (Pok.925); for a similar semantic connection, compare SCAPULA. **—v.** About 1300 *shuldren* to push against with the shoulder, in *Havelok the Dane;* from the noun. The figurative sense of bear a burden, assume a responsibility or expense, is first recorded in Stanyhurst's translation of Vergil's *Aeneid* (1582). **—shoulder blade** (about 1300) **—shoulder holster** (1895) **—shoulder strap** (1688)

shout *v.* 1375 *schowten* to call or cry out loudly, in Barbour's *The Bruce;* of uncertain origin. According to the OED, derivation from the root of SHOOT, v., is probable. **—n.** loud call or cry. 1375 *schout,* from the same source as the verb. The noun corresponds formally to Old Icelandic *skūta* a taunt.

shove *v.* Probably before 1200 *scuven, shufen* to thrust away, push; later *shoven* (probably before 1300); developed from Old English *scūfan* (about 725, in *Beowulf*); cognate with Old Frisian *skūva* to push, shove, Middle Low German *schūven,* Middle Dutch *scūven* (modern Dutch *schuiven*), Old High German *scioban* (modern German *schieben*), Old Icelandic *skūfa, skȳfa* (Norwegian *skyve*), and Gothic *afskiuban* push away from Proto-Germanic **skeuƀ-/skūƀ-,* Indo-European **skeubh-/skūbh-* (Pok.955) **—n.** Before 1325 *scov* act of shoving, push, in *Cursor Mundi;* from the verb.

shovel *n.* About 1300 *schovele* spadelike digging tool; implied earlier in *soveltrowes* (1277); developed from Old English *scofl* (before 800, in *Corpus Glossary*), related to *scūfan* SHOVE. Old English *scofl* (from Proto-Germanic **skuƀlō*) is cognate with Old Saxon *skūfla* shovel, Middle Low German *schūfle, schuffele,* Middle Dutch *schuffel* (modern Dutch *schoffel*), Old High German *skūfla, scūvala* (modern German *Schaufel*), and Old Swedish *skofl* (Swedish *skovel*). **—v.** lift and throw with a shovel. 1440 *schovelen,* in *Promptorium Parvulorum;* from the noun.

show *v.* Probably before 1200 *shewen* let be seen, put in sight; later *showen* (before 1300); developed from Old English *scēawian* look at, see (about 725, in *Beowulf*); cognate with Old Frisian *skāwia, skōwia* look at, see, Old Saxon *skauwon,* Middle Dutch *scouwen* (modern Dutch *schouwen*), Old High German *scouwōn* (modern German *schauen*), from Proto-Germanic **skauwōjanan,* and Old Icelandic *skygn* sharp-sighted, *skygna* to spy (Norwegian *skygne*). Outside Germanic there is a cognate in Greek *thyo-skóos* sacrificing priest (earlier **thyo-skówos* watching the sacrifice); also in Sanskrit *kaví-s* seer, and Latin *cavēre* (earlier **covēre*) beware, from Indo-European **(s)keu-/ (s)kou-* (Pok. 587).

In all the Continental Germanic languages, as in Old English, the verb has the meaning of look at; the change to the causative sense of let be seen, exhibit, manifest, occurred in early Middle English, in the 1100's.

—n. Probably before 1300 *schewe* act of showing, in *Sir Tristrem;* from the verb. The meaning of an elaborate spectacle, large display, is first recorded in 1561. **—showboat** *n.* river steamer with a theater for plays (1869, American English). **—show business** (1850,

American English) **—showcase** *n.* (1835) **—showdown** *n.* (1892, American English, the act of laying down one's playing cards with their faces up; 1904, a final confrontation or reckoning) **—showman** *n.* (before 1734) **—showmanship** *n.* (1859) **—show-off** *n.* (1776, display, exhibition; 1856, ostentatious display; 1924, person given to showing off) **—showpiece** *n.* (1838) **—showroom** *n.* (1616) **—showy** *adj.* 1712, making a good display, Addison writing in *The Spectator;* formed from English *show,* n. + *-y*[1].

shower *n.* Probably about 1200 *shure;* later *shoure* (about 1325), *showre* (probably before 1425); developed from Old English *scūr* short fall of rain, fall of missiles or blows (about 950, in *Lindisfarne Gospels*). Old English *scūr* is cognate with Old Saxon *scūr* shower, Old Frisian *skūr* fit of illness, Middle Dutch *schuur* shower, Old High German *scūr* (modern German *Schauer*), from Proto-Germanic **skūraz;* Old Icelandic *skūr* shower, and Gothic *skūra* storm, from Proto-Germanic **skūrō.* Cognates outside Germanic include Latin *caurus, cōrus* northwest wind, Lithuanian *šiaurỹs* north wind, *šiáurė* north, Old Slavic *sěverŭ* north, and Armenian *çurt* cold, shower, from Indo-European **kēwero-/kōwero-/kəwero-, skūro-s, skūrdo-s* (Pok. 597).

The sense of a bath in which water pours down from above is first recorded in 1851 in American English, and that of a party for giving presents to a bride or a new baby appeared in 1904, also in American English, from the figurative sense of an abundant supply, as in *a shower of gifts, of plenty,* etc. (recorded since about 1325).

—v. to rain for a short time. 1573, from the noun.

shrapnel (shrap′nəl) *n.* artillery shell filled with pellets and powder. 1806, from the name of Henry *Shrapnel,* 1761-1842, a British army officer who invented this shell. The sense of shell fragments is first recorded in 1940.

shred *n.* Probably before 1200 *shrade* fragment, scrap, in *Ancrene Riwle;* later *schreade* (before 1250), *shrede* (about 1300); developed from Old English *scrēade* (about 1000, in Ælfric's *Glossary*); cognate with Old Frisian *skrēd* a cutting, clipping, Middle Low German *schrōt, schrāt* shred, piece cut off, Middle Dutch *scrōde,* Old High German *scrōt* (modern German *Schrot*), Old Icelandic *skrjōdhr* old book, from Proto-Germanic **skrauđás.* Outside Germanic cognates are found in Latin *scrūta* trash, and Middle Welsh *ysgrud* carcass, from Indo-European **skrout-,* root **skreut-,* (Pok.947). **—v.** Probably about 1200 *shrædenn* chop, cut up, in *The Ormulum;* later *shreden* (1373); developed from Old English *screādian* prune, cut (about 1000), related to *scrēade,* n. The Old English verb is cognate with Middle Low German *schrōden, schrāden* to shred, cut up, Middle Dutch *scrōden* (modern Dutch *schroeien*), and Old High German *scrōtan* (modern German *schroten*).

shrew[1] *n.* small insect-eating mammal. 1538, in Elyot's *Dictionary;* developed from Old English (before 800) *scrēawa.* The word is not found elsewhere in Germanic and its origin is uncertain.

shrew[2] *n.* bad-tempered, scolding woman. Probably about 1225 *schrewe* rascal, rogue, in *King Horn;* later, bad-tempered, scolding woman (about 1303, in Mannyng's *Handlyng Synne*). Traditionally the word is considered a figurative use of SHREW[1] in reference to various superstitions about the malignant influence of the animal, which was popularly held to be venomous and otherwise injurious. **—shrewish** *adj.* 1565, scolding, bad-tempered, formed from English *shrew*[2] + *-ish.* An earlier meaning of wicked or evil is found in Middle English about 1375.

shrewd *adj.* About 1280 *schrewede* wicked, evil, malicious; later *shrewde* (before 1382); formed from *shrewe, schrewe* SHREW[2] + *-ed*[2]. The sense of astute, clever, cunning, is first recorded in 1520.

shriek *v.* make a sharp, shrill sound. 1567 *shrick;* later *shreke* (1577); apparently a variant of earlier *skricke* (perhaps before 1500), *screak* (1565); borrowed from a Scandinavian source (compare Old Icelandic *skrǣkja* to SCREECH). **—n.** 1590, act of shrieking, in Spenser's *Faerie Queene;* from the verb.

shrift *n.* Probably before 1200, confession to a priest followed by penance and absolution; developed from Old English *scrift* (about 1030), verbal noun from *scrīfan* to SHRIVE. Old English *scrift* is an early borrowing of Latin *scrīptum* (see SCRIPT), corresponding to Old Frisian *skrift* letters, writing, Middle Low German *schrift,* Middle Dutch *scrift* (modern Dutch *schrift*), Old High German *scrift* (modern German *Schrift*), and Old Icelandic *skript* (Norwegian, Swedish, and Danish *skrift*).

The meanings of penance and confession are confined to Old English and Scandinavian, arising probably from an original meaning of prescribed penalty. The other languages cited have only the senses of writing, scripture, written characters. The expression *short shrift* originally had the meaning of a brief time allowed for a criminal to make his confession before execution (1594, in Shakespeare's *Richard III*). The figurative sense of little or no consideration, mercy, or delay in dealing with a person or problem (especially in the phrase *give short shrift to*) is first recorded in 1814, in the writings of Scott, who popularized this phrase as he did other archaisms.

shrike *n.* bird with a strong, hooked beak. 1544, perhaps developed from Old English *scrīc* a thrush, any bird with a shrill voice; cognate with Middle Low German *schrīk* moor hen, modern Icelandic *skrikja* crow, Swedish *skrika* jay, and possibly with Old Icelandic *skrǣkja* to SCREECH.

shrill *adj.* Probably about 1380 *schrylle* high and sharp in sound, piercing; later *shrille* (about 1390, in Chaucer's *Canterbury Tales*); probably related to Old English *scralletan* to sound loudly, and cognate with Low German *schrell* shrill (modern German *schrill*), Norwegian *skrelle* a rattle, Swedish *skrälla* to crack, clap, and Old Icelandic *skrölta* to rattle, clatter. **—v.** make a shrill sound. About 1250 *shrellen;* later *shrillen* (probably before 1300, in *Kyng Alisaunder*); related to the adjective. **—n.** shrill sound. 1591, in Spenser's *Ruins of Time;* from the verb.

shrimp *n.* 1327 *shrimpe* kind of slender shellfish; cognate (and having a shared sense of thin) with dialectal Danish *skrimpe* thin cattle, dialectal Norwegian *skrumpa* thin cow, and probably with standard Norwegian *skrumpe* to shrink up, shrivel, Swedish *skrumpna,* Middle High German *schrimpfen* (modern German *schrumpfen*), and Old Icelandic *skreppa* (n.) thin person, (v.) draw together, from Proto-Germanic **skrempanan,* Indo-European **skremb-/skrm̥b-* (Pok.948), related to *skarpr* wrinkled up, withered, SHARP. Compare SCRIMP. The meaning of a diminutive or puny person is first recorded in Middle English about 1390, in Chaucer's *Canterbury Tales,* and probably came directly from the etymological sense of a shrunken creature, though it is now felt to be a transferred sense of the shellfish or crustacean.

shrine *n.* About 1280 *schryne* case or box holding a holy object, especially a relic; developed from Old English (about 1000) *scrīn* ark of the covenant, case for relics, an early borrowing from Latin *scrīnium* case or box for keeping papers, of uncertain origin. The Latin word was borrowed by several other Germanic languages: Old Frisian *skrīn* shrine, Middle Low German *schrīn,* Middle Dutch *scrīne* (modern Dutch *schrijn*), and Old High German *scrīni* (modern German *Schrein*). The sense of a place of worship is first recorded in 1627, in Milton's works. **—v.** enclose in a shrine. About 1300 *schrinen;* from the noun.

shrink *v.* Before 1300 *schrinken* wither, shrivel; developed from Old English *scrincan* (before 899, in Alfred's translation of Orosius' *Historiarum Adversus Paganos*), from Proto-Germanic **skrenkanan;* cognate with Middle Dutch *schrinken* draw back, Old Swedish *skrunkin* shrunken, Swedish *skrynkla* to wrinkle, crease, Norwegian *skrukke* wrinkle, and Old Icelandic *skrukka* wrinkled old woman, from Indo-European **skreng-/skrn̥g-* (Pok.936).The meaning of draw back, recoil, is first recorded in English about 1325. The sense of make smaller is first recorded in English about 1380, in Chaucer's translation of Boethius' *De Consolatione Philosophiae.* **—n.** a shrinking. 1590, from the verb. The slang sense of psychiatrist is first recorded in 1966; compare earlier *headshrinker* (1950). **—shrinkage** *n.* 1800, formed from English *shrink,* v. + *-age.*

shrive *v. Archaic.* hear the confession of, impose penance on, and grant absolution to. Probably before 1200 *scriven, schrifen;* later *schriven* (about 1230); developed from Old English (before 776) *scrifan* assign, decree, impose penance, an early borrowing from Latin *scrībere* to write (see SCRIBE). The Latin word was borrowed into several other Germanic languages: Old Frisian *skrīva* to shrive, write, Old Saxon *skrīƀan* to write, Middle Low German *schrīven,* Middle Dutch *scrīven* (modern Dutch *schrijven*), Old High German *scrīban* (modern German *schreiben*), and Old Icelandic *skrifa* to draw, paint, write, depict. Related to SHRIFT.

shrivel *v.* 1568 (implied in *shriveled,* adj., contracted, wrinkled); later (as verb) 1608, in Shakespeare's *Pericles;* of unknown origin. Shakespeare's use was transitive and with *up* ("A fire from heaven came and shrivell'd up Their bodies"); the intransitive use, meaning to become wrinkled or curled up, is first recorded in 1612. A Swedish dialectal form *skryvla,* meaning to shrivel, has been cited as a possible cognate of the English word.

shroud *n.* cloth or garment in which a dead person is wrapped for burial. Probably before 1200 *shrud* garment; later *shroude* (about 1325); developed from Old English (about 1000) *scrūd* a garment, clothing (Proto-Germanic **skrūđán*), related to *scrēade* SHRED. Old English *scrūd* is cognate with Old Icelandic *skrūdh* shrouds of a ship, ornament, fabric, Middle Swedish *skruther* formal clothing, ornament, Norwegian and Swedish *skrud* attire, from Indo-European **skreut-/skrout-/skrūt-* (Pok.947). The specialized sense of a white cloth or sheet in which a corpse is wrapped for burial is first recorded in 1570, in Levins' *Dictionary.* The meaning of the *shroud,* usually *shrouds,* any of the ropes supporting the mast or masts of a ship, is sometimes treated as a separate term in standard dictionaries, but the development of this meaning seems a natural extension of the idea of clothe as supported by the use of the nautical phrase *clothe the mast with shrouds* and the application of the word *naked* to a mast or spar without its rigging, as explained in the OED. The same sense of development appears in Old Icelandic. **—v.** Probably before 1350 *schruden* to dress, clothe; later, to cover, veil (before 1420, in Lydgate's *Troy Book*); from the noun.

Shrovetide *n.* the three days before Ash Wednesday, the first day of Lent. Before 1400 *Schroftyde;* formed in Middle English from *Schrof-, Shrof-* (related to *schrifen* SHRIVE) + *tide* time, season; so called because Shrovetide is a time for confession and absolution. **—Shrove Tuesday,** the day before Ash Wednesday. About 1460 *Shrof Tuesday;* formed from Middle English *Schrof(tyde)* Shrovetide + *Tuesday.*

shrub *n.* Probably before 1387, developed from Old English (972) *scrybb* brushwood, shrubbery; possibly cognate with Middle Danish *skrubbe* thicket, shrub. Compare SCRUB², n. **—shrubbery** *n.* 1748, a plot of shrubs; formed from English *shrub* + *-ery.* **—shrubby** *adj.* 1581, resembling a shrub; formed from English *shrub* + *-y¹*. The sense of covered with shrubs is first recorded in 1598.

shrug *v.* 1440 *schruggen* to shiver, shudder, in *Promptorium Parvulorum* (possibly earlier in *schurgyng,* about 1400); also, about 1450, raise the shoulders as an expression of dislike, indifference, etc.; of uncertain origin. **—n.** 1594, in Nashe's *The Unfortunate Traveller;* from the verb.

shtick or **schtik** (shtik) *n. Slang.* act, routine, gimmick, or trick. 1959 *schtik;* American English, borrowed from Yiddish *shtik* an act, gimmick; literally, a piece, slice, from Middle High German *stücke,* from Old High German *stucki;* see STOCK.

shuck *n.* husk, pod, or shell. 1674, of unknown origin. The informal meaning of something valueless (as in *it isn't worth shucks*) is first recorded in 1847, in American English. The informal interjection *shucks,* used as a euphemistic exclamation of impatience or irritation, derives from this sense, and it also appeared in 1847, in American English. **—v.** to remove the husk, pod, or shell from. 1819, from the noun.

shudder *v.* Probably about 1200 *schuderen;* of uncertain origin (possibly borrowed from Middle Dutch *schūderen* to shudder, or Middle Low German *schōderen,* both frequentative forms derived from the source of Old High German *skutten* to shake), from Proto-Germanic **skuđ-,* cognate with Lithuanian *kutė̃ti* to shake up, from Indo-European **(s)kut-* shake (Pok.957). **—n.** a trembling, quivering. 1607, in Shakespeare's *Timon of Athens;* from the verb.

shuffle *v.* 1532 *shoffle* to put together hastily, in Sir Thomas More's *Confutation of Tyndale's Answer;* later *shuffle* to push or thrust in underhandedly, smuggle in (1565); probably from Middle English *shovelen* to move with dragging feet (before 1450, in a version of the Wycliffe Bible). Middle English *shovelen* is probably a frequentative form of *shoven* SHOVE; for suffix see -LE³. The sense of mix playing cards randomly is first recorded in 1570. Compare SHUFFLEBOARD. **—n.** 1628, evasive trick, subterfuge; from the verb. The sense of a dance done with dragging movement of the feet is found in 1659, and that of the act of shuffling playing cards, in 1651, in Hobbes' *Leviathan.* The sense of a dragging movement of the feet is first attested in 1847.

shuffleboard *n.* game played by pushing disks along a surface to certain spots. 1532 *shovillaborde;* later *shoofleboord* (1577-86); alterations of earlier *shovebord* (1522, *shove,* v. + *bord* board).

shun *v.* Probably before 1200 *schunen* keep away from, avoid, in *Ancrene Riwle;* developed from Old English *scunian* to shun, detest (before 950), of uncertain origin.

shunt *v.* Before 1250 *schunten* to shy or start, in *Ancrene Riwle;* later, turn away, withdraw (about 1390); perhaps derived from *shunen* to SHUN. The sense of move out of the way, push aside, is first recorded in 1706, in Kersey's edition of Phillips' *Dictionary.* The meaning of switch (a train) from one track to another is first recorded in 1849. **—n.** 1842, railroad switch; from the verb. The technical sense of an electric conductor providing an alternative path for part of the current is found in 1863. The medical sense of an artificial or natural channel for the passage of blood (also known as a *bypass*) is attested since 1923.

shut *v.* Probably before 1200 *schutten,* in *Ancrene Riwle;* developed from Old English *scyttan* to put (a lock, bar, or bolt) in place so as to fasten a door or gate (about 1000, in Ælfric's *Grammar*). Old English *scyttan* is cognate with Old Frisian *sketta* to shut up, obstruct, Middle Dutch *scutten* (modern Dutch *schutten*), and Middle Low German *schutten,* from Proto-Germanic **skutjanan,* cognate with Lithuanian *skudrùs* quick, nimble, from Indo-European **skud-* (root **skeud-*) throw, fling (Pok.955). **—adj.** closed. 1474, in Caxton's *The Game and Play of Chess;* from the past participle of *shut,* v. **—shutdown** *n.* (1884) **—shut-in** *n.* person confined by illness (1904). **—shutout** *n.* game in which one side scores no points (1889). **—shutter** *n.* 1542, person or thing that shuts; formed from English *shut,* v. + *-er*[1]. The sense of a movable cover for a window is first recorded in 1720. The sense of a device for opening and closing the aperture of a camera lens occurs in 1862. —*v.* close with a shutter. 1826, from the noun. **—shutterbug** *n. Slang.* devotee of photography (1940, American English).

shuttle *n.* weaver's instrument that throws the thread back and forth. 1338 *shittle;* later *shetel* (before 1425), *shootyll* (probably 1450), *shutylle* (probably about 1475), and in the surname *Shutelmaker* (1380); developed from Old English (before 850) *scytel* a dart, arrow, related to *scēotan* to SHOOT. The Old English noun is cognate with Old Icelandic *skutill* harpoon, Norwegian *skutel,* and Swedish *skyttel* shuttle, from Proto-Germanic **skutilaz.* The sense of a train that runs back and forth over a short distance is first recorded in 1895. A similar sense applied to aircraft is found in 1942. **—v.** move quickly to and fro. 1550, in Coverdale's writings; from the noun. **—shuttle diplomacy** (1974, American English) **—shuttle service** (1944)

shy[1] *adj.* bashful. 1440 *schey* easily frightened or startled, in *Promptorium Parvulorum;* developed from Old English (about 1000) *scēoh;* cognate with Middle Low German *schūw* shy, Middle Dutch *scū, scou* (modern Dutch *schuw*), Middle High German *schiech* shy (from Proto-Germanic **skeuH(w)az*), modern German *scheu* shy, Old High German *sciuhen* make fearful, frighten (modern German *scheuchen*), Norwegian and Swedish *skygg* shy (from Proto-Germanic **skuȝwás*); outside Germanic, cognate with Old Slavic *šĉuti* to hunt, hound, from Indo-European **skeu-k-/sku-k-,* root **skeu-/skou-/sku-* (Pok.955). The spelling *shy* is not recorded before the 1600's. The sense of cautious, suspicious, distrustful, is first recorded in 1600, and that of bashful, retiring, reserved, in 1672. **—v.** 1650, recoil, shrink; from the adjective. The meaning of start back or aside suddenly (said of horses) is first recorded in 1796. **—n.** 1791, sudden start to one side; from the verb.

shy[2] *v.* to throw, fling. 1787, in Bentham's *Defence of Usury;* of uncertain origin. The earliest uses refer to the game of throwing sticks at cocks, suggesting derivation from the earlier expression *shy cock* timid person (1768), perhaps suggesting an original meaning of a cock that refuses to fight or be caught; see SHY[1]. **—n.** a throw, fling. 1791, from the verb.

shyster (shī′stər) *n. Informal.* unscrupulous lawyer or other professional. 1843, unscrupulous lawyer; American English, alteration (influenced by *-ster,* as in *trickster*) of German *Scheisser* incompetent, worthless person, from *Scheisse* (vulgar) excrement. For a detailed study of this word's history, see Gerald L. Cohen's "Origin of the Term Shyster," *Forum Anglicum,* Vol. 12, Verlag Peter Lang, Bern, 1982.

si (sē) *n.* seventh note of the musical scale; ti. 1728, in *Chambers Cyclopaedia;* borrowed from Italian, from the initial letters of Latin *Sancte Iohannes* Saint John, the words sung to this note in the Hymn for St. John the Baptist's day; see GAMUT.

sib *adj.* related by blood, akin. Old English *sibb* (about 725, in *Beowulf*), related to *sibb,* n., kinship, relationship; cognate with Old Frisian *sibbe* kinship, *sib* akin, Old Saxon *sibbia* kinship, *sibbio* kinsman, Middle Dutch *sibbe* kinship, Old High German *sippea, sippa* (modern German *Sippe*), Old Icelandic *sifjar,* pl., and Gothic *sibja* kinship, from Proto-Germanic **seƀjō.* Another Germanic cognate is probably found in the Romanized North German tribal name *Semnonēs,* from **Seƀnanez* comrades in kinship. Cognates outside Germanic are probably found in Old Prussian *subs* self, and Old Slavic *sobĭstvo* character, demeanor, from Indo-European **s(w)e-bh(o)-/*s(w)o-bh(o)-* of one's own kind (Pok.883). **—n.** Old English (before 1000) *sibb* kinsfolk, relatives; later, a kinsman, relative (before 1023); from the adjective. **—sibling** *n.* one of two or more children of a family. 1903, modern revival (in anthropology) of Old English *sibling* relative, kinsman (about 1000, in Ælfric's various translations from the Bible); formed from *sib, sibb* sib, adj. + *-ling.*

sibilant *adj.* hissing. 1669, in William Holder's *Elements of Speech;* borrowed from Latin *sibilantem* (nominative *sībilāns*), present participle of *sībilāre* to hiss, whistle, possibly of imitative origin; for suffix see -ANT. **—n.** hissing sound, or a letter or symbol representing such a sound. 1822, from the adjective.

sibyl (sib′əl) *n.* prophetess. Probably before 1200 *sibeli* any of several prophetesses that the ancient Greeks and Romans consulted, in Layamon's *Chronicle of Britain;* later *sibil* (before 1325); borrowed from Old French *sibile, sebile,* learned borrowing from Latin, and borrowed into English from Medieval Latin *Sibilla,* from Latin *Sibylla,* from Greek *Síbylla,* of uncertain origin. The general sense of prophetess or fortuneteller is first recorded in 1589. **—sibylline** *adj.* 1579-80, said or written by a sibyl; later, prophetic, mysterious (1817, in Coleridge's *Sibylline Leaves*); formed in English from *sibyl* + *-ine* on the model of Latin *Sibyllīnus* of a sibyl, from *Sibylla* a sibyl.

sic[1] *adv.* so, thus (used to show that something has been copied as in the original). 1887, in Henry Sweet's *A Second Anglo-Saxon Reader;* borrowed, perhaps by influence of its use in French (1872), from Latin *sīc* so or thus, related to *sī* if.

sic[2] or **sick**[1] *v.* set upon or attack, in an order to one's dog, "Sick him!" 1845 *sick;* American English, dialectal variant of SEEK. The spelling *sic* is first recorded in 1890, also in American English.

sick[2] *adj.* ill, unwell, ailing. Probably about 1175 *sek;* later *sik* (probably about 1225), *sick* (about 1300); developed from Old English *sēoc* (before 899, in Alfred's translation of Boethius' *De Consolatione Philosophiae*); cognate with Old Frisian *siāk* sick, Old Saxon *siok,* Middle Dutch *siec* (modern Dutch *ziek*), Old High German *sioh, siuh* (modern German *siech*), Old Icelandic *sjūkr* (Norwegian and Swedish *sjuk,* Danish *syg*), and Gothic *siuks,* from Proto-Germanic **seukaz.* Possible cognates outside Germanic may be found in Middle Irish *socht* silence, depression, and Armenian *hiucanim* I languish, waste away, from Indo-European **seug-* troubled, sad, sick (Pok.915). For spelling see WICK. **—sick bay** infirmary on a ship (1813). **—sicken** *v.* Probably about 1200 *secnen* become sick, in *The Ormulum;* formed from Middle English *sek* sick + *-enen* -en[1]. The sense of make sick is first recorded in Shakespeare's *Henry VIII* (1613). **—sickly** *adj.* Before 1375 *sekly* ailing, often sick; formed from Middle English *sek* sick + *-ly*[2]; compare Middle Dutch *siekelic* (modern Dutch *ziekelijk*), Old Icelandic *sjúkligr* (Norwegian and Swedish *sjuklig,* Danish *sygelig*). **—v.** to cover with a sickly hue. 1602, in Shakespeare's *Hamlet;* from the adjective. **—sickness** *n.* Probably before 1200 *secnesse,* in *Ancrene Riwle;* developed from Old English (about 967) *sēocnesse,* formed from *sēoc* sick + *-nesse* -ness.

sickle *n.* tool used for cutting grass, etc. Probably before 1200 *sikel;* developed from Old English (about 1000) *sicol, sicel,* an early borrowing from Vulgar Latin **sicila,* from Latin *sēcula* sickle; see SAW[1] cutting tool. Other Germanic languages also borrowed the Latin word: Middle Dutch *sickele* (modern Dutch *sikkel*), and Old High German *sichila* (modern German *Sichel*). **—sickle cell anemia** (1922)

side *n.* Old English (before 800) *sīde;* cognate with Old Frisian *sīde* side, Old Saxon *sīda,* Middle Dutch *sīde* (modern Dutch *zijde*), Old High German *sīta* (modern German *Seite*), and Old Icelandic *sīdha* (Swedish *sida,* Danish and Norwegian *side*), from Proto-Germanic **sīđṓn,* originally denoting the long part or aspect of a thing, and connected with Old English *sīd* long, wide, Old Frisian *sīde* low, wide, Middle Dutch *sīde* low, Old High German *sīto,* adv., loose, and Old Icelandic *sīdhr* long (Norwegian and Danish *sid*), from Proto-Germanic **sīdás.* Outside Germanic cognates are found in Middle Irish *sith-* long-lasting, Welsh *hyd* length, duration, Lithuanian *sietuvà* deep place in a river, and Latin *saeculum* (earlier **saitlom*) an age, century, and Welsh *hoedl* lifetime, from Indo-European **sēit-/səit-/sīt-/sit-* (Pok.890,891).

The figurative sense of a position or attitude of a person in relation to another, interest, point of view, is first recorded in Middle English about 1250.

—adj. Before 1375, at or toward one side; from the noun.

—v. Before 1450 *syden* (implied in *syded,* past participle) to carve (an animal) into sides; from the noun. The sense of take the side of, favor, is found in 1591.

—side-effect *n.* (1884) **—sidekick** *n. Informal.* companion (1903) *side kicker,* American English, in writings of O. Henry; 1906, *side kick*) **—sidelight** *n.* (1610, light coming from the side; 1862, incidental information) **—sideline** *n.* (1862, line marking the limit of play in football, etc.; 1890, branch line of a railroad; 1890, American English, additional occupation or line of goods) **—sidelong** *adv.* (1580); *adj.* (1597) **—side-saddle** *n.* (about 1500); *adv.* (1885) **—sideshow** *n.* (1855, American English, in writings of P.T. Barnum) **—sidestep** *v.* 1900, from earlier *side step* a step to one side (1847). **—sideswipe** *v.* strike a glancing blow on the side (1904); *n.* (1917). **—sidetrack** *v.* (1880, American English, run a train onto a siding; 1887, American English, divert, cause to digress) **—sidewalk** *n.* (1739) **—sideways** *adv.* (1577) **—sidewise** *adv.* (1571) **—siding** *n.* 1825, short track parallel to a main railway; 1829, American English, boards, shingles, etc., forming the outside walls of a wooden building; formed from *side,* n. or v. + *-ing*[1].

sideburns *n.pl.* side whiskers. 1887, American English, alteration of earlier *burnsides* (1881, American English), from the name of General Ambrose E. *Burnside,* 1824-81, Union general in the Civil War, who popularized side whiskers.

sidereal (sīdir′ēəl) *adj.* of or pertaining to the stars. 1634, starlike; borrowed from French *sidereal,* formed from Latin *sīdereus* starry, astral + French *-al* -al[1]. Latin *sīdereus* derives from *sīdus* (genitive *sīderis*) star, constellation, which is cognate with Lithuanian *svidùs* shining, bright, Latvian *svīst* to dawn, and probably with Old High German *swīdan,* and Old Icelandic *svīdha* to burn, from Indo-European **sweid-/swid-* (Pok.1042).

sidle *v.* move sideways. 1697, probably a back formation from Middle English (before 1338) *sidlyng,* adv., obliquely, sideways (*side,* n. + *-ling*); formed on the analogy of verbs ending in *-le.* **—n.** movement sideways. 1853, from the verb.

siege *n.* Probably before 1200 *sege* seat, especially one used by a person of distinction, in *Ancrene Riwle;* later, act of besieging a city, castle, etc.; literally, the act of undertaking a seat or establishing forces to cut off a castle, town, etc., in order to capture it (probably before 1300); borrowed from Old French *sege, siege* seat, throne, from Vulgar Latin **sedicum* seat, from a lost verb **sedicāre,* from Latin *sedēre* to SIT. **—v.** lay siege to. Probably before 1300 *segen,* in *Kyng Alisaunder;* from the noun.

sienna (sēen′ə) *n.* yellowish-brown coloring matter. 1760 *terra sienna;* 1787 *sienna,* borrowing of Italian, short for *terra di Sienna* earth of Siena (ancient *Saena*), a city in central Italy, where the coloring matter was probably first produced.

sierra (sēer′ə) *n.* chain of hills or mountains with jagged peaks. 1613, in *Purchas his Pilgrimage;* borrowing of Spanish *sierra* mountain range; literally, a saw, from Latin *serra* a saw; see SERRATE.

siesta (sēes′tə) *n.* afternoon rest or nap. 1655, in James Howell's *Letters;* borrowing of Spanish *siesta,* from Latin *sexta hōra* sixth hour of the Roman day, midday, from *sexta,* feminine of *sextus* sixth, from *sex* SIX. The *siesta* was so called because it was customarily taken during the midday.

sieve *n.* Probably before 1300 *sive,* in *Sir Tristrem;* developed from Old English (before 800) *sife;* cognate with Middle Low German and Middle Dutch *sēve* sieve (modern Dutch *zeef*), Old High German *sib* (modern German *Sieb*), Old Icelandic *sef* rush (a plant used for making sieves), Norwegian *sev,* Swedish *säv,* Danish *siv,* from Proto-Germanic **sibí,* cognate with Serbian *sípiti* to trickle, drizzle, from Indo-European **sip-,* root **seip-* (Pok.894). **—v.** put through a sieve. Probably before 1475 *syffen,* in a version of *Promptorium Parvulorum;* later *syve* (1530); from the noun.

sift *v.* Before 1325 *siften* to pass (something) through a sieve, in *Cursor Mundi;* developed from Old English (before 800) *siftan,* related to *sife* SIEVE. Old English *siftan* is cognate with Middle Low German and Middle Dutch *siften* (modern Dutch *ziften*). The figurative sense of look carefully through is first recorded in 1535.

sigh *v.* About 1250 *sigen,* in *The Story of Genesis and Exodus;* later *syghen* (about 1303); probably a back formation from *sighte,* past tense of Old English *sīcan* to sigh (before 899, in Alfred's translation of Orosius' *Historiarum Adversus Paganos*); of unknown origin. **—n.** act or sound of sighing. Before 1325, in *Cursor Mundi;* from the verb.

sight *n.* Probably about 1175 *sihte* thing seen, power or act of seeing; later *syght* (about 1303); developed from Old English *gesiht, gesihth* (about 950, in the *Lindisfarne Gospels*). The Old English forms are cognate with Middle Low German and Middle Dutch *sicht* sight (modern Dutch *zicht*), and Old High German *siht* (modern German *Sicht*); all derived from Proto-Germanic **seH(w)-* , the stem of Old English *sēon* to SEE. **—v.** 1556, to look at, inspect; later, to see (1602); from the noun.

sign *n.* Probably before 1200 *sine,* in *Ancrene Riwle;* later *signe* (about 1280); borrowed from Old French *signe* sign, mark, signature, learned borrowing from Latin, and borrowed into English directly from Latin *signum* mark, token, indication, signal, of uncertain origin; possibly related to *secāre* to cut; see SECTION; or related to *sequī* to follow (see SEQUEL), perhaps with the original meaning of an object which one follows. **—v.** About 1300 *signen* to make the sign of the cross; later, to mark or stamp (about 1350); borrowed from Old French *signer,* from Latin *signāre,* from *signum,* n., sign. The sense of write one's name to show authority is first recorded in English in 1440. **—signboard** *n.* (1632) **—sign language** (1847) **—signpost** *n.* (1620)

signal *n.* About 1380, visible sign, indication, in Chaucer's *House of Fame;* borrowed from Old French *signal, seignal* signal, sign, from Medieval Latin *signale,* from Late Latin *signālis,* adj., used as a signal, from Latin *signum* signal; see SIGN; for suffix see -AL[2]. The sense of a sign agreed upon as the occasion of concerted action (as in *a signal to begin firing*) is first recorded in Shakespeare's *Richard II* (1593). **—v.** make a signal to. 1805, from the noun. **—adj.** 1641, striking, remarkable, notable (as in *a signal achievement*); borrowed from French *signalé,* past participle of *signaler* to distinguish, from Old French *signaler,* from *signal,* n.

signatory *adj.* signing. 1647, used in sealing; borrowed from Latin *signātōrius* of sealing, from *signāt-,* past participle stem of *signāre* to SIGN; for suffix see -ORY. The meaning of signing, sharing in a signature, is first recorded in 1870. **—n.** signer of a document. 1866, from the adjective.

signature *n.* 1534, (in Scottish law) a writing presented to be signed, as the ground of a royal grant; borrowed through Middle French *signature,* or directly from Medieval Latin *signatura* sign, from Latin *signātūra* the matrix of a seal, from *signāre* to mark, SIGN; for suffix see -URE. The meaning of a person's name written by himself is first recorded in 1580, and that of a distinctive mark (as in *a signature of divine power*) in 1613. The meaning of a number of folded and gathered sheets for binding in a book is first recorded in 1656, and the sense of a sign to show key and time of a piece of music, in 1806.

signet (sig′nit) *n.* small seal. Probably about 1380 *syngnette;* about 1384 *signet;* borrowing of Old French *signet,* diminutive form of *signe* SIGN; for suffix see -ET.

significant *adj.* 1579, full of meaning; formed in English as an adjective to *significance* on the model of Latin *significantem* (nominative *significāns*), present participle of *significāre* to indicate, mean; see SIGNIFY; for suffix see -ANT. The meaning of important or notable is first recorded before 1761. **—significance** *n.* Before 1400, the meaning of something; borrowed from Latin *significantia* meaning, force, energy, significance, from *significāns,* present participle of *significāre;* for suffix see -ANCE. The sense of importance or consequence, is first recorded in English in Defoe's *A New Voyage Around the World* (1725).

signify *v.* About 1275 *signefien* be a sign of, indicate, mean; probably before 1300 *signifien;* borrowed from Old French *signifier,* learned borrowing from Latin, and borrowed into English directly from Latin *significāre* to show by signs, mean, signify, from *significus,* adj. (not attested until Late Latin), from *signum* SIGN + the root of *facere* to make, perform, DO[1]; for suffix see -FY. **—signification** *n.* Before 1325 *significacioun* symbolization, representation, in *Cursor Mundi;* borrowed from Old French *signification,* learned borrowing from Latin, and borrowed directly into English from Latin *significātiōnem* (nominative *significātiō*) a signifying, indication, expression, sign, meaning, from *significāre* to signify, mean; for suffix see -ATION. The sense of meaning, significance, is found in Middle English probably before 1398.

silage (sī′lij) *n.* green fodder for winter feeding of livestock. 1884, alteration (probably influenced by *silo*) of earlier *ensilage* (1881); borrowing of French *ensilage,* from *ensiler* put in a silo, from Spanish *ensilar* (*en-* en-[1] + *silo* SILO); for suffix see -AGE.

silence *n.* Probably before 1200, in *Ancrene Riwle;* borrowed from Old French *silence* absence of sound, state of being silent, from Latin *silentium* a being silent, from *silēns,* present participle of *silēre* be quiet or still, be silent; cognate with Gothic *anasilan* (of wind) to quiet or calm down, based on an Indo-European adjective **silos* quiet; cognate also with Old English *sālness* (earlier **sail-*) quiet; from Indo-European **sēil-/səil-/sil-* let sink, release (Pok.891); for suffix see -ENCE. **—v.** 1560, to cease speaking, become silent or still; from the noun. The sense of make silent, reduce to silence, is first recorded in Shakespeare's *2 Henry IV* (1597). **—silencer** *n.* 1635, person or thing that silences; later, mechanism that quiets the sound of a motor, or of a pistol or rifle (1898). **—silent** *adj.* Before 1500, borrowed from Latin *silentem* (nominative *silēns*), present participle; for suffix see -ENT.

silhouette (sil'üet') *n.* outline portrait of one color. 1798, borrowing of French *silhouette,* formed in allusion to Étienne de *Silhouette,* 1709-1767, French minister of finance in 1759. The name (because it was an inexpensive way of making a likeness of someone, rather than paying for an artist's portrait) was probably intended to ridicule the petty economies introduced by Silhouette in 1759 to finance the Seven Years' War. Another explanation involves reference to Silhouette's brief (eight month) tenure in office, or to the amateurish outline portraits made by him to decorate the walls of his château at Bry-sur-Marne. **—v.** show in outline. 1876, from the noun.

silica (sil'əkə) *n.* hard, white or colorless mineral. 1801, New Latin, from Latin *silex* (genitive *silicis,* from earlier stem **scelic-*) flint, pebble; see SHELL. **—silicate** (sil'əkāt) *n.* compound containing silicon with oxygen and a metal. 1811, formed in English from New Latin *silica* + English suffix *-ate*[2].

silicon *n.* nonmetallic chemical element found chiefly in combination with oxygen in silica. 1817, in Thomas Thomson's *A System of Chemistry;* from New Latin *silica,* patterned on *boron, carbon,* etc.

silk *n.* Probably before 1200 *seolke,* in Layamon's *Chronicle of Britain;* later *selk* (about 1250), *silk* (about 1300); developed from Old English (before 899) *sioloc, seoloc, seolc* silk; cognate with Old Icelandic *silki* silk (modern Icelandic *silki,* Norwegian, Danish, and Swedish *silke*), and Old High German *silecho.*

The word is not found in the other Germanic languages, but is also represented in Baltic and Slavic by Old Prussian *silkas* silk, Lithuanian *šilkai,* and Old Slavic *šelkŭ.* The ultimate source is a Far Eastern word, which was also borrowed into Greek as *sērikós* silken, *sērikón* silk (which gave rise, according to Carl D. Buck, to the back formation *Sêres,* the Greek name of an Asian people who originated the making of silk, thought to be the Chinese). The use of *l* in Old English *sioloc,* and in the corresponding word in other languages along this northern route, may well reflect borrowing from a Chinese dialect that had *l* instead of *r.* Compare SERGE.

—adj. of, like, or pertaining to silk. Before 1375, from the noun.

—silken *adj.* Probably before 1200 *sulkene,* in Layamon's *Chronicle of Britain;* later *selkene* (probably before 1300), *silken* (about 1353); developed from Old English *seolcen* made of silk (before 899, in Alfred's translation of Boethius' *De Consolatione Philosophiae*); formed from *seolc* silk + *-en*[2]. **—silkworm** *n.* Old English *seolcwyrm* (about 1000, in Ælfric's *Glossary*). **—silky** *adj.* 1611, in Cotgrave's *Dictionary,* made of silk, formed from English *silk,* n. + *-y*[1].

sill *n.* piece of wood or stone across the bottom of a door, window, or house frame. Probably about 1390 *sille,* in *Sir Gawain and the Green Knight;* developed from Old English *syll* (about 725, in *Beowulf*), from Proto-Germanic **suljō;* cognate with Middle Low German and Middle Dutch *sulle, sille* beam, threshold, Old High German *swelli* (modern German *Schwelle*), from Proto-Germanic **swalja-,* Old Icelandic *svill* (from Proto-Germanic **swelja-*), also *syll* (Norwegian *svill,* Swedish *syll,* and Danish *syld*). Outside Germanic cognates may be found in Greek *selís* plank, thwart (of a boat), and *sélma* beam, framework, both from Indo-European **swel-,* whose other variants are **swol-/sul-* (Pok.898).

silly *adj.* Probably before 1200 *selie* spiritually favored, blessed, in *Ancrene Riwle;* developed from Old English *gesǣlig* happy (before 899, in writings of Alfred); cognate with Old Frisian *sēlich* happy, Old Saxon *sālig,* Middle Dutch *sālich* (modern Dutch *zalig*), and Old High German *sālīg* (modern German *selig*), from Proto-Germanic **sǣlīʒás;* for suffix see -Y[1]. Old English *gesǣlig* is derived from *sǣl* happiness, noun use of an adjective represented by Old Icelandic *sǣll* happy, Gothic *sēls* good, fit (from Proto-Germanic **sǣlaz*); and outside Germanic by Greek *hílaos* gracious, kindly (earlier **síslawos*), *hilarós* happy, cheerful (altered from earlier **helarós*), Latin *sōlārī* to console, soothe, and Old Irish *slān* healthy, sound, from Indo-European *sel-/sēl-/sōl-, selə-/slē-/slə-/sl̥-* (Pok.900).

Silly has undergone considerable sense development from the original meaning of happy. The sense of innocent is first recorded probably about 1200, that of weak about 1300, and that of unfortunate, pitiable, about 1280. From these senses developed the meaning of simple, rustic, ignorant, first recorded before 1547, and the sense of lacking in reason or sense, foolish, in 1576. **—n.** silly person. 1858, from the adjective.

silo (sī'lō) *n.* place where food for livestock is stored. 1835, borrowing of Spanish *silo,* probably of pre-Roman origin and from the same source as Basque *zilo, zulo* dugout, with the basic meaning of a cave or shelter for keeping grain.

Traditionally Spanish *silo* was said to have developed through Latin *sīrus* from Greek *sīrós, seirós* a pit for storing grain. However, Corominas points out various problems with this etymology, chiefly that the change from *r* to *l* in Spanish is phonetically abnormal and that Greek *sīrós* itself was a rare foreign term peculiar to Thrace, Phrygia, and other regions of Asia Minor and not likely to emerge in Castilian Spain.

The extended sense of a large bin used for storing loose materials, such as cement, is found in 1920. The military sense of an underground facility for housing and launching a guided missile appeared in 1958, in American English.

—v. preserve in a silo. 1883 from the noun.

silt *n.* very fine earth, sand, etc., carried by moving water. 1440 *cylte,* in *Promptorium Parvulorum;* later *silt* (before 1500); probably borrowed from Middle Low German or Middle Dutch *silte, sulte* salt marsh, brine (modern Dutch *zult*); cognate with Danish *syltlage* pickle, brine, Old High German *sulza* salt marsh, brine (modern German *Sülze* brine), and more distantly with Old English *sealt* SALT. **—v.** fill or choke up with silt. 1799, from the noun. **—silty** *adj.* 1658, formed from English *silt* + *-y*[1].

silver *n.* Before 1121 *silver, seolfre;* developed from Old English (before 830) *seolfor, siolfor;* cognate with Old Frisian *selover, silver* silver, Old Saxon *silubar,* Middle Dutch *silver* (modern Dutch *zilver*), Old High German *silabar, silbar* (modern German *Silber*), Old Icelandic *silfr* (Swedish *silver,* Icelandic *silfur,* Danish and Norwegian *sølv*), and Gothic *silubr,* from Proto-Germanic **silubra-.* The Germanic words are probably ultimately of Eastern origin, and related to, if not borrowed from, a source represented by Assyrian *ṣarpu* silver (from *ṣurrupu* purify, smelt), which also represents the source of Old Prussian *sirablan,* Lithuanian *sidabras,* Old Slavic *sŭrebro,* Russian *serebró,* all meaning silver. —**adj.** About 1303, made of silver, in Mannyng's *Handlyng Synne;* developed from Old English *seolfor* (1032); from the noun. —**v.** cover or coat with silver. About 1350 *selveren;* later *sylveren* (1440); from the noun. —**silversmith** *n.* Old English *seolforsmith* (before 1000, in Ælfric's *Colloquy*). —**silverware** *n.* (1860, in writings of Ruskin) —**silvery** *adj.* Before 1398, in Trevisa's translation of Bartholomew's *De Proprietatibus Rerum;* formed from Middle English *silver,* n. + *-y*[1].

simian *adj.* like or characteristic of an ape. 1607, formed in English from Latin *sīmia, sīmius* ape + English *-an.* Latin *sīmia, sīmius* derive from *sīmus* snub-nosed, from Greek *sīmós* snub-nosed, bent upwards; for suffix see -AN. The Greek form *sīmós* is ultimately derived from Indo-European **swi-mo-s* turning, root **swēi-/swī-/swi-* bend, turn (Pok.1041). —**n.** ape or monkey. 1880, in Wallace's *Ben Hur;* from the adjective.

similar *adj.* 1611, in Cotgrave's *Dictionary*); borrowed from French *similaire,* and perhaps directly from Medieval Latin **similaris* like, an extended form of Latin *similis* like (originally **semalis*); see SAME; for suffix see -AR. An earlier form *similarie* (1564), later spelled *similary,* was common in the 1600's. —**similarity** *n.* 1664, likeness, resemblance; formed from English *similar* + *-ity.*

simile (sim′əlē) *n.* comparison of two different things or ideas. Probably before 1387, in a version of *Piers Plowman;* borrowed from Latin *simile* a like thing, neuter of *similis* like; see SAME.

similitude (səmil′ətüd) *n.* similarity, likeness, resemblance. About 1380, a sign or symbol, in Chaucer's translation of Boethius' *De Consolatione Philosophiae;* later, similarity, likeness (about 1385, in Usk's *Testament of Love*); borrowed from Old French *similitude,* learned borrowing from Latin, and borrowed directly into English from Latin *similitūdō* likeness, from *similis* like; see SAME; for suffix see -TUDE.

simmer *v.* boil gently. 1653 *simber;* later *simmer* (1684); alteration of Middle English *simperen* to simmer (1477), possibly of imitative origin. The figurative sense of being on the point of becoming active or breaking out is first recorded before 1764. —**n.** 1809, condition of simmering; from the verb. The use of *simmer* in the opposite sense of cool off or calm down (as in *simmer down*) is first recorded in Mark Twain's correspondence, in 1871.

simonize *v.* to polish, especially with wax. 1934, American English, from *Simoniz* a trademark for a type of car polish.

simon-pure *adj.* real, genuine, authentic. 1840, American English; from an earlier phrase *the true Simon Pure* the real, genuine, or authentic person or thing (1795), from *Simon Pure,* the name of a Quaker who is impersonated by another character during part of the comedy *A Bold Stroke for a Wife* (1717) by Susannah Centlivre, about 1667-1723, English dramatist and actress.

simony (sī′mənē *or* sim′ənē) *n.* the making of money out of sacred things. Probably before 1200 *symonie* the sin of buying or selling an ecclesiastical office, in *Ancrene Riwle;* borrowed from Old French *simonie,* learned borrowing from Late Latin *simōnia,* from *Simon Magus,* a Samaritan who tried to buy the power of conferring the Holy Spirit (Acts 8:9-24); for suffix see -Y[3].

simp *n. Informal.* simpleton, fool. 1903, circus dialect, shortened from SIMPLETON.

simpatico (simpä′tikō) *adj.* arousing a sympathetic response, agreeable. 1888, borrowed from Spanish *simpático,* from *simpatía* sympathy, or borrowed from Italian *simpatico,* from *simpatia* sympathy; both ultimately from Latin *sympathīa* SYMPATHY. The feminine form *simpatica* is recorded earlier in English, in 1864; borrowed from Spanish *simpática,* feminine of *simpático,* or borrowed from Italian *simpatica,* feminine of *simpatico.*

simper *v.* to smile in a silly, affected way, smirk. About 1563, perhaps borrowed from a Scandinavian source; (compare Norwegian *semper* fine, smart, and dialectal Danish *semper, simper* affected, coy, prudish, both cognate with Middle Dutch *zimperlijk* affected, coy, prim). —**n.** silly, smiling look, smirk. 1599, in Ben Jonson's *Cynthia's Revels;* from the verb.

simple *adj.* Probably before 1200, humble, ignorant, in *Ancrene Riwle;* borrowed from Old French *simple,* from Latin *simplus* (in Classical Latin only in neuter *simplum*) or *simplex* (genitive *simplicis*). Latin *simplus* is probably directly inherited from Indo-European **sm̥-pl-o-s,* from the root of **sem-* one; see SAME + *-plus* -FOLD; Latin *simplex* is probably the resultant of a Proto-Italic compound **sm̥-plak-s,* cognate with Greek *pláx* flat surface, from Indo-European **plək-* (Pok.831). Doublet of SIMPLEX. The sense of lowly, common, impoverished, is first recorded in Middle English about 1280, and that of mere, pure, having nothing added, about 1303. The sense of single, not composite, is found before 1398, and that of not complicated, not difficult, about 1555. —**n.** Before 1375, person of humble birth, from the adjective. —**simple-minded** *adj.* (1744) —**simply** *adv.* About 1300 *simpleliche* sincerely, without duplicity; formed from Middle English *simple* + *-liche* -ly[2]. The form *simply* is found about 1380, in writings of Chaucer.

simpleton *n.* 1650, from *simple* + *-ton,* as in the surnames *Appleton, Chesterton,* and *Wellington.*

simplex *adj.* consisting of or characterized by a single part or structure. 1594, borrowed from Latin *simplex* single, SIMPLE. —**n.** 1892, a simple, uncompounded word; from the adjective. The mathematical sense of a figure having the minimum number of boundary points is recorded since 1914.

simplicity *n.* About 1380 *simplicite* singleness of nature, unity, in Chaucer's translation of Boethius' *De Consolatione Philosophiae;* borrowed from Old French *simplicité,* learned borrowing from Latin *simplicitātem* (nominative *simplicitās*) the state of being simple, from *simplex* (genitive *simplicis*) SIMPLE; for suffix see -ITY. The sense of lack of knowledge or judgment, ignorance, is first recorded in 1514, and that of plainness, artlessness, lack of artificiality, in 1526.

simplify *v.* 1653, borrowed from French *simplifier* to make simpler, from Medieval Latin *simplificare* to simplify, from a lost Latin adjective **simplificus,* formed from Latin *simplex* SIMPLE + the root of *facere* to make, perform, DO[1]; for suffix see -FY. —**simplification** *n.* 1688, borrowed from French *simplification* act or process of simplifying, from *simplifier* to simplify; for suffix see -FICATION.

simplistic *adj.* Before 1881, trying to explain everything, or too much, by a single principle; earlier, of or pertaining to simples (plants or herbs used in medicine) or to a simplist (one who studies such plants and herbs), 1860; formed from English *simplist* (1597) + *-ic.*

simulacrum (sim′yəlā′krəm) *n.* faint, shadowy, or unreal likeness, mere semblance. 1599, image, representation; borrowing of Latin *simulācrum* likeness, image, from *simulāre* to SIMULATE. The meaning of a faint, shadowy, or unreal likeness, mere semblance, is first recorded in 1805. An earlier, now archaic, doublet of this word, *simulacre,* existed since Middle English (about 1375) and was borrowed from Old French, in which it was a learned borrowing from Latin.

simulate *v.* 1652, developed from the earlier past participle *simulate* (1435), and probably as a back formation from earlier *simulation,* on the model of Latin *simulātus,* past participle of *simulāre* make like, imitate, formed from the earlier stem **semal-* of *similis* like; see SAME; for suffix see -ATE[1]. **—simulation** *n.* 1340 *simulacioun,* in *Ayenbite of Inwyt;* borrowed from Old French *simulation,* learned borrowing from Latin, and borrowed directly into English from Latin *simulātiōnem* (nominative *simulātiō*) an imitating, feigning, from *simulāre* imitate; for suffix see -ATION. Compare DISSIMULATION.

simulcast (sī′məlkast′) *v.* transmit a program over radio and television simultaneously. 1948, American English; formed in English from *simul(taneous)* + *(broad)cast.* **—n.** simulcast program. 1952, American English; from the verb.

simultaneous *adj.* Before 1660, probably formed in English from Latin *simul* at the same time (Old Latin *semol,* from earlier **semli,* from *similis* like; see SAME) + English *-taneous* as abstracted from *instantaneous, spontaneous.*

sin *n.* About 1125 *synne* sinfulness, wickedness; later *sinne* a wrongful act, sin (probably before 1160); developed from Old English (before 830) *synn* wrongdoing, offense, misdeed. Old English *synn* is cognate with several Germanic words that all have an extended form in *-d* or *-t,* including Old Frisian *sende* sin, Old Saxon *sundia,* Middle Dutch *sonde* (modern Dutch *zonde*), Old High German *sunta, suntea* (modern German *Sünde*), and Old Icelandic *synd,* from Proto-Germanic **sundjō.* A cognate outside Germanic is found in Latin *sōns* (genitive *sontis*) guilty, guilty person, a specialized use (as "the actual one") of the original present participle of *esse* to be (see IS). **—v.** Probably about 1175 *sungen;* probably before 1200 *sinen;* developed from Old English (before 830) *syngian* to commit sin; cognate with Old Frisian *sendigia* to sin, Old Saxon *sundion,* Middle Dutch *sondigen* (modern Dutch *zondigen*), Old High German *sunteōn* (modern German *sündigen),* all derived from the same Germanic source as Old English *synn,* n. **—sinful** *adj.* Probably about 1200 *sinnfull,* in *The Ormulum;* developed from Old English (before 830) *synnfull;* formed from *synn* sin + *-full* -ful. **—sinner** *n.* About 1350, formed from Middle English *sinne* sin + *-er*[1].

since *adv.* Before 1425 *synnes* afterwards, from then till now, before now, in a version of *Piers Plowman;* later *syns* (about 1450); reduced form of *sithenes* since (*sithen* since + the adverbial ending *-es*). The form *sithen* developed from Old English *siththan* then, later, after that (about 725, in *Beowulf*), a contraction of *sīth than* after that (*sīth* after + *than,* weakened form of *thām,* dative of *thæt* THAT), parallel to German *seitdem* since then, since. Old English *sīth* is cognate with Old Saxon *sīth* since, Old High German *sīd* (modern German *seit*), Old Icelandic *sīdhr* less, scarcely (from Proto-Germanic **sīthiz* later, after), and Gothic *seithus* late. Cognates outside Germanic include Old Irish *sīr* long-lasting, eternal, Latin *sērus* late, and Sanskrit *sáyā-m* evening, lodging, from Indo-European **sē(i)-/ sī-, sī-t-* (Pok.890,891).

The spelling *since* replaced the earlier *syns, synnes* in the 1500's to indicate that the final sound is a voiceless *s,* just as the form *ice* replaced *is, twice* replaced *twies,* etc.

—conj. Probably before 1387 *synnes* after the time that, in a version of *Piers Plowman;* from the adverb. The sense of because, inasmuch as, is first recorded in Middle English about 1450.

—prep. 1515, between (a specified time) and now; from the adverb.

sincere *adj.* 1533, honest, straightforward; borrowed from Middle French *sincere,* from Latin *sincērus* sound, whole, pure, genuine, perhaps originally "of one growth," not hybrid, unmixed (dissimilated by loss of *r* after *c* in earlier **sincrēros*), from *sem-, sin-* one (cognate with Greek *heîs, hén* one; see SAME) + the root of *crēscere* to grow; see CRESCENT. **—sincerity** *n.* Probably before 1425 *sinceritie* honesty, in a translation of Higden's *Polychronicon;* borrowed from Middle French *sincérité,* or directly from Latin *sincēritātem* (nominative *sincēritās*), from *sincērus* sincere; for suffix see -ITY.

sine (sīn) *n. Geometry.* the length of the side opposite an acute angle in a right triangle divided by the length of the hypotenuse. 1593, borrowed from Medieval Latin *sinus,* from Latin, fold in a garment, bend, curve, of unknown origin. The medieval translators of Arabic geometrical texts confused Arabic *jiba* chord of an arc, sine (borrowed from Sanskrit *jīvā* bowstring) with Arabic *jaib* bundle, bosom, fold in a garment; hence the use of Latin *sinus.* Sanskrit *jīvā* is an alteration (under the influence of *jīvá-s* alive) of *jyā́, jiā́,* cognate with Greek *biós* bow-string, from Indo-European **gwiyā́, *gwiyós* (Pok.481).

sinecure (sī′nəkyůr *or* sin′əkyůr) *n.* very easy job that pays well. 1662, a church benefice without parish duties; borrowed from Medieval Latin *beneficium sine cura* benefice without care (of souls); Latin *sine* without (see SUNDER) and *cūrā,* ablative singular of *cūra* care; see CURE. The extended sense of any paying job or position which has little or no work attached to it is first recorded in Wycherley's *The Plain-Dealer* (1676).

sine die (sī′nē dī′ē *or* sin′ā dē′ā) without a day fixed for future action. 1631, borrowed from Medieval Law Latin *sine die* without a day (being set); Latin *sine* without (see SUNDER) and *diē,* ablative singular of *diēs* day; see DEITY.

sinew *n.* tough, strong band that joins muscle to bone. Probably before 1200 *senuwe,* in Layamon's *Chronicle of Britain;* later *sinu* (before 1325), *synew* (before 1398); developed from Old English *seonowe, sionwe* (about 725, in *Beowulf*) oblique form from the nominative *sionu, sinu.* The Old English forms are cognate with Old Frisian *sine* sinew, Old Saxon *sinewa,* Middle Dutch *sēnuwe, sēnewe* (modern Dutch *zenuw*), Old High German *senawa* (modern German *Sehne*), and Old Icelandic *sin* (Swedish *sena,* Danish and Norwegian *sene*), from Proto-Germanic **senawō*. Cognates outside Germanic include Middle Irish *sīn* chain, necklace, Greek *himás* strap, thong, Latvian *pasainis* string, Lithuanian *síena* border, wall, Old Slavic *sětĭ* net, Sanskrit *sétu-s* band, fetter, *syáti, sinā́ti* (he) binds, straps, and Hittite *ishāi-* bind, from Indo-European **sēi-/səi-/sī-, sei-/si-* (Pok.891). —**v.** furnish with sinews. 1592, tie together, cover over with sinews, in Nashe's *Pierce Penilesse;* from the noun. —**sinewy** *adj.* Before 1382 *senewy* made of sinews, in the Wycliffe Bible; formed from *senewe, senuwe* sinew, n. + *-y*[1]. The meaning of tough, stringy, is first recorded in 1578.

sing *v.* Probably before 1200 *singen,* in Layamon's *Chronicle of Britain;* developed from Old English (about 725, in *Beowulf*) *singan* to chant, sing, tell in song (past tense *sang,* past participle *sungen*); cognate with Old Frisian *sionga, siunga* to sing, Old Saxon *singan,* Middle Dutch *singhen* (modern Dutch *zingen*), Old High German *singan* (modern German *singen*), Old Icelandic *syngva* (Norwegian and Danish *synge,* modern Icelandic *syngja,* and Swedish *sjunga*), Gothic *siggwan* (for **singwan*) to sing, from Proto-Germanic **sengwanan.* A cognate outside Germanic is found in Greek *omphḗ* voice, oracle (from Indo-European **songwhā́,* root **sengwh-,* Pok.906). —**n.** a singing. 1871, a ringing sound; 1884, act of singing; from the verb. —**singer** *n.* About 1303, in Mannyng's *Handlyng Synne;* earlier as a surname *Le Singere* (1268); formed from Middle English *singen* to sing + *-er*[1]. —**singsong** *n.* (1609, monotonous ballad; 1693, monotonous verse or rhyme; 1822, tone of voice with a monotonous up-and-down rhythm) —*adj.* (1734, of or like singsong; 1825, monotonous in rhythm)

singe (sinj) *v.* 1340 *zengen* to burn, scorch, in *Ayenbite of Inwyt;* later *sengen* (about 1350); developed from Old English (about 1000) *sengan* to burn lightly, burn the edges of (hair, wings, etc.). Old English *sengan* is cognate with Old Frisian *sandza, sendaza* to singe, Middle Low German *sengen,* Middle Dutch *senghen* (modern Dutch *zengen*), Old High German *bisengan* (modern German *sengen*), from Proto-Germanic **sangjanan,* Middle High German *senge* dryness, dialectal Swedish *sjängla* to singe, dialectal Norwegian *sengra,* modern Icelandic *sangur* singed, burnt, *sengja* singed taste, and outside Germanic probably with Old Slavic *prěsǫčiti, isǫčiti* to dry, from Indo-European **senk-/sonk-* (Pok.907). —**n.** light burn. 1658, from the verb.

single *adj.* Probably before 1300 *sengle* without armor, in *Kyng Alisaunder;* later, unmarried, celibate (about 1303, in Mannyng's *Handlyng Synne*); borrowed from Old French *sengle, single* being one, separate, from Latin *singulus* one, individual, separate (usually pl., *singulī* one by one), from Indo-European **sem-go-lo-s,* from **sem-* one; see SAME + *-golos* the suffix seen in Gothic *ainakls* single, from Indo-European **oino-golos.* The sense of individual, consisting of one unit, is first recorded in Middle English before 1387; the sense of one and no more, only one, is first recorded in Elyot's *Dictionary* (1538). —**n.** single thing or person. Before 1376 *sengle* unmarried person, in *Piers Plowman;* from the adjective. The sense of a single thing is first recorded in 1646. —**v.** 1570-76, to part, separate; from the adjective. The sense of pick from among others is first recorded in Shakespeare's *Love's Labour's Lost* (1588). —**single-handed** *adj.* (1709); *adv.* (1815, in writings of Jefferson) —**single-minded** *adj.* (1577, sincere; 1860, having a single aim or purpose) —**singly** *adv.* Before 1338 *senglely* separately, in Mannyng's *Chronicle of England;* later *sengly* (before 1400); formed from Middle English *sengle* single, adj. + *-ly*[1].

singleton *n.* something occurring singly. 1876, a playing card (in bridge or whist) that is the only one of a suit in a hand; a whimsical adoption of the surname *Singleton,* with the word *single* in mind; borrowed from English into French (1767 curiously not recorded in English until over 100 years later). The sense of something occurring singly, a single thing, is first recorded in English in 1892.

singular *adj.* About 1340 *syngulere, synguler* living alone, unique, special, unsurpassed; borrowed from Old French *singuler* single, separate, singular, learned borrowing from Latin, and borrowed directly into English from Latin *singulāris* single, solitary, singular, from *singulus* SINGLE. The formation of *singular* in English was probably influenced by earlier *singularity,* especially in the sense of unique. The sense in grammar of signifying only one person or thing is first recorded in Middle English before 1387, in Trevisa's translation of Higden's *Polychronicon.* The Middle English form *singuler* continued in use until the 1600's. —**n.** *Grammar.* form of a word indicating one in number. Probably about 1378 *synguler* particular thing, in Wycliffe's writings. The grammatical meaning in the noun is first recorded also in Trevisa's works (see adj.) in his translation of Bartholomew's *De Proprietatibus Rerum* (before 1398). —**singularity** *n.* About 1230 *singularite* unusual or exceptional behavior; borrowed from Old French *singularité,* learned borrowing from Late Latin *singulāritātem* (nominative *singulāritās*), from Latin *singulāris* singular; for suffix see -ITY.

sinister *adj.* 1411 *sinistre* deceptive, false, dishonest, in *Rolls of Parliament;* later, evil, corrupt (1474); borrowed through Old French *sinistre* contrary, unfavorable, on the left, or directly from Latin *sinister* left, on the left side, whose ending *-ter* (from earlier **-teros*) is the same contrastive suffix found in Latin *dexter,* meaning right, on the right; see DEXTER. The root of *sinister* is that found in Sanskrit *sánīyān* more profitable, more advantageous, related to *sanóti* he gains, cognate with Doric Greek *ánumes* we were reaching, from Indo-European **sen-/seneu-/senu-* achieve (Pok.906). Latin *sinister* was used in augury in the sense of lucky, favorable, presumably from the ancient Roman practice of facing south when taking auspices, so that the person's left side was to the East, considered to be a fortunate quarter. However, Latin also had the meaning of harmful, unfavorably situated, adverse, which came from Greek influence, reflecting the earlier Greek practice of facing north when observing omens. The sense of inauspicious, unfavorable, is first recorded in English in 1432, and that of suggestive of evil or being underhanded in 1474, though usage such as in *a sinister expression* is not recorded before 1797.

sink *v.* Probably before 1200 *sinken,* in Layamon's *Chronicle of Britain;* developed from Old English (about 950) *sincan* become submerged, go under (past tense *sanc,* past participle *suncen*); cognate with Old Saxon *sinkan* to sink, Middle Dutch *sinken* (modern Dutch *zinken*), Old High German *sinkan* (modern German *sinken*), Old Icelandic *søkkva,* (modern Icelandic *sökkva),* Norwegian *søkke,* Swedish *sjunka,* Danish *synke,* and Gothic *sinqan* to sink, from Proto-Germanic **senkwanan.* Outside Germanic a cognate is possibly found in Armenian *ankanim* I fall, give way, from Indo-European **sengw-* (Pok.906). —**n.** 1413-14, pool or pit for waste water or sewage; implied earlier in the compound *sincreste,* probably meaning the rim of a privy (1346); from the verb. The sense of a shallow basin or tub with a drainpipe is found in 1566. —**sinkhole** *n.* (1456, hole into which foul matter runs; 1780, American English, hole eroded in rock by running water)

Sino- a combining form meaning China or Chinese, as in *Sinology = the study of China or Chinese history, customs, etc.; Sino-Japanese = Chinese and Japanese.* Adapted from Late Latin *Sīnae,* pl., the Chinese, from Greek *Sînai,* from Arabic *Sīn* China, probably from Chinese *Ch'in,* name of the fourth dynasty in China, traditionally dated 221-207 B.C., under which all China was politically united for the first time.

sinuous (sin'yůəs) *adj.* winding. 1578, borrowed from Latin *sinuōsus* full of folds or bendings, from *sinus* curve, fold, bend; see SINUS; for suffix see -OUS. —**sinuosity** *n.* 1598, sinuous form of character, in Drayton's *England's Heroical Epistles;* borrowed from Medieval Latin **sinuositas* condition or quality of being sinuous, tortuousness, from Latin *sinuōsus* sinuous; for suffix see -ITY.

sinus (sī'nəs) *n.* cavity in a bone or other tissue. Probably before 1425, a hollow or cavity in the body, in a translation of Chauliac's *Grande Chirurgie;* Medieval Latin *sinus,* from Latin *sinus* bend, fold, or curve, is cognate with Albanian *ǵiri* (stem *ǵin*) bosom, lap, womb (Walde-Hofmann, *Lateinisches etymologisches Wörterbuch,* II 546). The specific sense of a natural cavity in a bone or other tissue, especially in the skull, is first recorded in 1704. —**sinusitis** (sī'nəsī'tis) *n.* inflammation of a sinus. 1896, New Latin, formed from *sinus* + *-itis* inflammation.

-sion a suffix found in some words of Latin origin as a form of *-tion* added to and fusing with a final *-d* or *-t* of a verb stem, as in *suspension* from *suspend* and *conversion* from *convert,* and occasionally elsewhere, as in *compulsion* from *compel.* In the Latin originals of these words the suffix is *-siō* (nominative), *-siōnem* (accusative), *-siōnis* (genitive).

sip *v.* About 1395 *sippen* take a small drink, in Chaucer's *Canterbury Tales;* of uncertain origin; probably cognate with Low German *sippen* to sip, and perhaps related to Old English *sūpan* to take into the mouth a little at a time, taste, sip, see SUP². It is unlikely that Middle English *sippen* is an alteration of *sipen* to leak, SEEP. —**n.** a sipping. Before 1500 *syppe* a small drink; from the verb.

siphon *n.* tube through which liquid can be drawn out. Before 1398, in Trevisa's translation of Bartholomew's *De Proprietatibus Rerum;* borrowed from Latin *sīphō* (genitive *sīphōnis*), from Greek *síphōn* pipe, of unknown origin. —**v.** draw off by means of a siphon. 1859, from the noun.

sir *n.* Probably before 1300, title of honor of a knight or baronet, placed before his name, in *Arthour and Merlin;* variant of SIRE. The reduced form probably resulted from the absence of stress before the following name. By about 1350 *sir* was used as a respectful form of address, and by 1425 as a salutation at the beginning of letters.

sire (sīr) *n.* Probably before 1200, a title of respect for a man, in Layamon's *Chronicle of Britain;* borrowed from Old French *sire,* from Vulgar Latin **seior,* reduced (not being in stressed position) from Latin *senior* older, elder; see SENIOR. The meaning of father or male forebear is first recorded in Middle English about 1250; the specific meaning of the male parent of an animal, especially a horse, is found in 1523. —**v.** 1611, be the father of (a person), in Shakespeare's *Cymbeline;* from the noun. The specific application of *sire,* v., to animals, especially horses, is first recorded in 1822-32.

siren *n.* Before 1393, female creature in Classical mythology (frequently confused with mermaid) who lured sailors to their destruction by her singing, in Gower's *Confessio Amantis;* borrowed from Old French *sereine,* learned borrowing from Late Latin *sīrēna,* from Latin, and borrowed into English directly from Latin *sīrēn,* from Greek *seirḗn,* of uncertain origin. An earlier sense of a mythical serpent is recorded in Middle English in 1340, in *Ayenbite of Inwyt.* The figurative sense of any woman who lures or entices is first recorded in Shakespeare's *Comedy of Errors* (1590). The transferred meaning of *siren* as a device that makes a loud sound or signal of warning (as from an ambulance, fire engine, and, originally, steamboat) is first recorded in 1879, and developed from an earlier sense of an acoustical device for producing musical tones (1820). The device was invented by a Frenchman in 1819; its name was borrowed from French *sirène* siren, from Old French *sereine.*

sirloin *n.* upper or choicer part of a loin of beef. Before 1425 *surloyne;* borrowed from Middle French **surloigne,* variant of *surlonge* (*sur* over, above + *longe* loin, from Old French *loigne* LOIN). The spelling with *sir-* first appeared in English in the 1600's, from an alleged connection to the fictitious story that this cut of beef was "knighted" by an English king because of its superiority; see SIR.

sirocco (sərok'ō) *n.* hot, dry, dust-laden wind. 1617, borrowing of Italian *sirocco, scirocco,* from Arabic *sharqī* east wind, from *sharaqa* it (the sun) rose. The forms *siroc, siroch* also occurred in English in the 1700's and 1800's, borrowed from earlier French *siroc, siroch* (now *sirocco, siroco*), from Italian *sirocco, scirocco.*

sisal (sis'əl) *n.* strong fiber used for making rope, twine, etc. 1843, in allusion to *Sisal,* a port in Yucatán, southeastern Mexico, from which the fiber was exported.

sissy *n. Informal.* effeminate man or boy. 1887, American English; extended sense of earlier American English *sissy* sister (1846), diminutive of earlier *sis* (1656), short for SISTER. —**adj.** effeminate. 1891, American English; from the noun. —**sissified** *adj. Informal.* effeminate. 1905, American English; formed from *sissy* + *-fied,* as in *cityfied, countryfied,* etc.

sister *n.* About 1250, in *The Story of Genesis and Exodus;* probably borrowed from a Scandinavian source; (compare Old Icelandic, modern Icelandic *systir,* and Swedish *syster,* and Danish and Norwegian *søster* sister). Middle English *sister* was a replacement of earlier *suster* (before 1121), developed from Old English (835) *sweostor, swuster,* cognate of Old Icelandic *systir;* other Germanic cognates are found in Old Frisian *swester, suster,* Old Saxon *swestar,* Middle Dutch *suster* (modern Dutch *zuster*), Old High German *swester* (modern German *Schwester*), and Gothic *swistar,* from Proto-Germanic **swestr-.* Cognates outside Germanic are found in Old Irish *siur* sister, Welsh *chwaer,* Latin *soror,* Old Prussian *swestro,* Lithuanian *sesuõ* (genitive *seseȓs*), Old Slavic *sestra* (Russian *sestrá*), Armenian *k'oir* Sanskrit *svásar-*, Tocharian A *ṣar*, Tocharian B *ṣer*, and Greek *éor* daughter, cousin, from Indo-European **swesor-* sister (Pok.1051). The sense of closely related or like another (as in *sister ships*) is first recorded in Milton's writings, in 1641. The meaning of a nun is first recorded in English before 899, in Alfred's translation of Bede's *Ecclesiastical History*. **—sisterhood** *n.* (before 1393, in Gower's *Confessio Amantis*) **—sister-in-law** *n.* (1440, in *Promptorium Parvulorum*) **—sisterly** *adj.* (1570)

sit *v.* About 1125 *sitten,* developed from Old English *sittan* (about 725, in *Beowulf*); cognate with Old Frisian *sitta* to sit, Old Saxon *sittian,* Middle Dutch *sitten* (modern Dutch *zitten*), Old High German *sizzen* (modern German *sitzen*), and Old Icelandic *sitja* (Swedish *sitta,* Danish *sidde,* Norwegian *sitte*), from Proto-Germanic **setjanan.* Outside Germanic a group of cognates are found in Latin *sedēre* to sit, *sēdēs* seat, Greek *hézesthai* to sit, *hédrā* seat, Lithuanian *sėdėti* to sit, Old Slavic *sěděti,* Armenian *nstim* I sit down, and Sanskrit *sī́dati* (he) sits, from Indo-European **sed-* sit (Pok.884). The forms of *sit,* partly by phonetic similarity and partly by mere confusion have been more or less mixed with those of *set*[1]. **—sit-down strike** (1936, American English) **—sit-in** *n.* demonstration or strike in which persons occupy a public building, etc. (1937, American English). **—sitter** *n.* Probably before 1300 *sittere* a hare; literally, one that sits; formed from Middle English *sitten* to sit + *-ere* -er[1]. The literal sense of one who sits is found in Middle English in 1440. Modern English *sitter,* meaning one who baby-sits (1943), is a shortening of *baby-sitter* (1937). **—sitting room** (1771) **—sit-up** *n.* (1843)

sitar (sitär′) *n.* guitarlike musical instrument of India. 1845, borrowing of Hindi *sitār,* from Persian *sitār* guitarlike instrument; literally, three-stringed (*si* three, from Old Persian *thri-,* + *tār* string).

sitcom *n.* type of television comedy series based on contrived situations. 1964, American English, acronym formed from *sit(uation) com(edy),* first recorded in 1953.

site *n.* About 1380, position or location (of a building), physical situation of a place, in Chaucer's *House of Fame* and in his translation of Boethius' *De Consolatione Philosophiae;* borrowed from Anglo-French *site,* and directly from Latin *situs* (genitive *sitūs*) place, position, from *si-,* root of *sinere* let, leave alone, let remain, permit, of unknown origin.

situate *v.* Probably before 1425 *situaten* put into proper position, set, in a translation of Chauliac's *Grande Chirurgie;* borrowed from Medieval Latin *situatus,* past participle of *situare* to place, locate, from Latin *situs* (genitive *sitūs*) place, position, SITE; for suffix see -ATE[1]. **—situation** *n.* Probably before 1425 *situacion* act of setting, position; borrowed through Middle French *situation,* or directly from Medieval Latin *situationem* (nominative *situatio*) position, location, situation, from *situare;* for suffix see -ATION. The extended sense of a state or condition (as in *an interesting situation, a situation of difficulty*) is first recorded in English in 1710, as is the related sense of a position in life, or in relation to others. The specific sense of a job or post is found in 1803.

six *adj.* Old English *siex, six* (before 899, in Alfred's translation of Orosius' *Historiarum Adversus Paganos*); earlier *sex* (835); cognate with Old Frisian *sex* six, Old Saxon *sehs,* Middle Dutch *ses* (modern Dutch *zes*), Old High German *sehs* (modern German *sechs*), Old Icelandic *sex* (modern Icelandic and Swedish *sex,* Danish and Norwegian *seks*), and Gothic *saíhs,* from Proto-Germanic **seHs.* Cognate forms outside Germanic are found in Old Irish *sē* six, Welsh *chwech,* Latin *sex,* Albanian *gaštë,* Greek *héx,* Lithuanian *šeši,* Old Slavic *šesti,* Armenian *veç,* Sanskrit *ṣáṣ-,* and Tocharian A *ṣäk,* Tocharian B *ṣkas,* from Indo-European **s(w)eks* (Pok.1044). **—sixteen** *adj.* Old English (before 900) *sixtȳne, sixtēne* (*six* six + *-tēne* -teen, from *tēn* TEN). **—sixth** *adj.* 1526, replacing earlier *sixte* (probably before 1200), developed from Old English *syxte* (before 899, in Alfred's writings); for suffix see -TH[2]. **—sixty** *adj.* Probably before 1200, in Layamon's *Chronicle of Britain;* developed from Old English (before 899, in Alfred's writings) *sixtig* (*six* six + *-tig* group of ten, -TY[1]).

size[1] *n.* extent, amount, magnitude. Probably before 1300 *sise* manner, style, in *Arthour and Merlin;* about 1300, ordinance, law; borrowed from Old French *sise,* shortened from *assise* session, assessment, regulation, manner, ASSIZE. The sense of extent, amount, magnitude (about 1303, in Mannyng's *Handlyng Synne*) developed by influence of *assize,* in the sense of an ordinance regulating weights and measures and the weight and price of articles for general consumption. The spelling *size* appeared in the 1600's, its currency possibly increased by *assize* being taken as *a size.* **—v.** Probably before 1400 *sysen* regulate according to a fixed standard, in *The Wars of Alexander;* from the noun. The meaning of adjust the size of (something) is first recorded in 1609, and that of arrange according to size, before 1635.

size[2] *n.* sticky substance. About 1325 *sise;* probably borrowed from Middle French *sise,* special use of Old French *sise* a setting, fixing, shortened from *assise* ASSIZE. **—v.** coat or treat with size. 1633 (figurative); from the noun. The literal sense is first found in 1667.

sizzle *v.* make a hissing sound as fat does when frying. 1603, to burn or scorch so as to produce a hissing sound; perhaps a frequentative verb form of Middle English *sissen* make a hissing sound, hiss, buzz (before 1300), of imitative origin like Middle Dutch *cissen,* modern Dutch and Low German *sissen* to hiss, (also) to sizzle; for suffix see -LE[3]. The sense of make a hissing sound as fat does when frying is first recorded in English before 1825. **—n.** 1823, in Edward Moor's *Suffolk Words and Phrases;* from the verb.

skald (skôld *or* skäld) *n.* Scandinavian poet and singer of medieval times. 1763, borrowed from a Scandinavian source (compare Old Icelandic *skāld,* modern Icelandic *skáld* skald, poet, Swedish and Norwegian *skald* poet, skald, and Danish *skjald* skald; compare SCOLD).

skate[1] *n.* kind of broad, flat fish. About 1340 *schat;* later *scate* (about 1375); earlier in the surname *Scate* (1202); borrowed from a Scandinavian source (compare Old Icelandic and modern Icelandic *skata,* Norwegian *skate,* Danish *skade,* and Faeroese *skøta*).

skate[2] *n.* ice skate or roller skate. 1662 *skeates* ice skates, in Pepys' *Diary;* borrowed from Dutch *schaats* (a singular taken in English as plural) skate, stilt, from Middle Dutch *schaetse,* from Old North French *escache* a stilt, trestle, variant of Old French *eschace* stilt, from Frankish **skakkja* thing that shakes or moves fast, perhaps related to the root of Old English *sceacan* to vibrate, SHAKE. The application of the word to roller skates is found in 1876. **—v.** glide on skates. 1696, from the noun. **—skateboard** *n.* (1964)

skein (skān) *n.* quantity of yarn. 1373 *skeyne;* borrowed from Middle French *escaigne* a hank of yarn, of uncertain origin (compare Medieval Latin *scagna* a skein).

skeleton *n.* 1578 *sceleton,* in John Banister's *The History of Man;* borrowed from New Latin *sceleton, skeleton* bones or bony framework of a body, from Greek *skeletón* dried-up in *skeletòn sôma* dried-up body, neuter of *skeletós* dried-up, from *skéllein* dry up; see SHOAL[1] shallow place. The figurative meaning of a bare outline or very thin object is first recorded in 1607, and formed the basis of such terms as *skeleton crew, skeleton key.* The phrase *skeleton in the closet,* meaning a secret source of shame to a family, etc., was popularized by Thackeray, who used it in 1845 and 1855. **—adj.** of or like a skeleton. 1778, from the noun. **—skeletal** *adj.* 1854, of or like a skeleton; formed from English *skeleton,* n. + *-al*[1].

skeptic or **sceptic** *n.* doubter. 1587, member of an ancient Greek school that doubted the possibility of real knowledge of any kind; borrowed through Middle French *sceptique* or Latin *scepticus* (plural *Scepticī* the Skeptics), from Greek *skeptikós* (plural *Skeptikoí*), literally, inquiring, reflective, assumed by the disciples of the ancient Greek philosopher Pyrrho as their distinctive name, from *sképtesthai* to reflect, look, view; see SPY; for suffix see -IC. The general meaning of one who maintains a doubting attitude, doubter, is first recorded in English in 1615.

The English spelling and pronunciation represented by *sk-* was influenced by the Greek form, which is first recorded in English before 1631, and was adopted by Johnson in his *Dictionary* (1755) and became the standard form in the United States. **—skeptical** *adj.* 1639, in Thomas Fuller's *History of the Holy War;* formed from English *skeptic* + *-al*[1]. **—skepticism** *n.* 1646, skeptical attitude, doubt; borrowed from New Latin *scepticismus,* from Latin *scepticus* skeptic; for suffix see -ISM.

sketch *n.* 1668 *scetch* rough drawing; borrowed from Dutch *schets,* from Italian *schizzo* sketch, drawing, special use of *schizzo* a splash, squirt, from *schizzare* to splash or squirt, of uncertain origin. The extended sense of a brief account or description is found in 1715. **—v.** make a sketch of. 1694, from the noun. **—sketchbook** *n.* (1820) **—sketchy** *adj.* 1805, giving only a rough outline or sketch; formed from English *sketch,* n. + *-y*[1].

skew *v.* to slant, twist. About 1470 *skewen* to turn aside, move sideways, twist; borrowed from Old North French *eskiuer, escuer* shy away from, avoid, corresponding to Old French *eschiver, eschever* to ESCHEW. The meaning of depict or represent unfairly (that is in a slanted or twisted way) is first recorded in 1872. **—adj.** slanting. 1609, from the verb. **—n.** slant. 1688, from the adjective or verb.

skewer *n.* long pin used to hold meat together while cooking. 1411 *skuer;* later *skeuier* (1458), *skewer* (1679); perhaps borrowed from a Scandinavian source (compare Old Icelandic *skīfa* disk, cut, slice, Swedish *skiva,* Danish *skive*). The Scandinavian words are cognate with Old High German *scība* disk, Latin *scīpiō* staff, Greek *skīpōn* staff, from Indo-European **skēip-/skīp-* (Pok.922). Related to SHIVER[2]. **—v.** 1701, fasten (meat) with a skewer. 1701, from the noun.

ski *n.* 1755, borrowing of Norwegian *ski,* also *skid,* related to Old Icelandic *skīd* snowshoe, stick of wood. Old Icelandic *skīdh* is cognate with Old High German *skīt* stick, block, board, plank (modern German *Scheit*), Old Frisian *skid,* and Old English *scīd,* from Proto-Germanic **skīđ-* to divide, split off, from Indo-European *skēi-t-* cut (Pok.921); see SHED[2]. The English (skē) is an Anglicized pronunciation, influenced by the spelling. In Norwegian *ski* is pronounced (shē). **—v.** glide over the snow on skis. 1893, from the noun. The sense of glide over water on skis, water-ski, is first recorded in 1947 in American English, though the sport was known before World War II.

skid *n.* 1609-10, beam or plank on which something rests; perhaps borrowed from a Scandinavian source (compare Old Icelandic *skīdh* stick of wood; see SKI). The sense of a piece of wood or metal attached to a wheel to keep it from turning is first recorded in 1766. The sense of a sliding along developed from the verb *skid* in the 1890's. **—v.** 1674, apply a skid to (a wheel); from the noun. The sense of slide along without turning, as a wheel does when held by a skid, is first recorded in 1838; the extended sense of slip sideways is first recorded in 1884.

skiff *n.* light rowboat. Before 1500 *skif;* borrowed from Middle French *esquif,* from Italian *schifo,* from a Germanic source (compare Old High German *skif* boat; see SHIP).

skill *n.* About 1175 *skil* that which is reasonable or right, differentiation, distinction; later, the faculty of reason (probably before 1200, in *Ancrene Riwle*); borrowed from a Scandinavian source (compare Old Icelandic *skil* distinction, discernment). The Old Icelandic noun is related to the verb *skilja* distinguish, separate, part, which is cognate with Middle Low German *schelen* distinguish, separate, and Lithuanian *skélti* to split; see SHELL. The extended sense of practical knowledge, ability, cleverness, expertness, is first recorded in Middle English before 1225. **—skillful** or **skilful** *adj.* Before 1325, having skill, knowledgeable, in *Cursor Mundi;* formed from Middle English *skil* skill + *-ful.*

skillet *n.* shallow frying pan. 1404 *skelett;* earlier as a surname *Skelete* (1332); of uncertain origin; perhaps borrowed from Middle French *esculette, escuelete* small plate, diminutive of *escuele* plate, from Latin *scutella* serving platter; see SCUTTLE[1] bucket; or formed in English from earlier *skele* a wooden bucket or pail (about 1330) + *-et.* Middle English *skele* was a borrowing from a Scandinavian source (compare Old and modern Icelandic *skjōla* pail, bucket).

skim *v.* clear (a liquid) of fat, scum or other floating matter. 1373 *skemmen* to froth; later *skymen* to remove (floating matter) from a liquid (before 1398, in Trevisa's translation of Bartholomew's *De Proprietatibus Rerum*); earlier as a surname *Skym* (1285); probably borrowed from Middle French *escumer* remove scum, from *escume* scum, from a Germanic source (compare Old High German *scūm* SCUM). The meaning of deal with or study in a superficial manner is first recorded in Sidney's *The Arcadia* (before 1586). **—n.** that which is skimmed off. Before 1398, frothing matter on the surface of a liquid; from the verb. **—skim milk** (1596, in Shakespeare's *1 Henry IV*); also **skimmed milk** (1623)

skimp *v.* be sparing of, stint, scrimp. 1879, possibly developed by a back formation from *skimpy* and perhaps influenced by SCRIMP. **—skimpy** *adj.* scanty, meager. 1842, derived from English *skimp,* adj., scanty, meager (1775), perhaps alteration of *scrimp,* adj. (1718), from the same source as *scrimp,* v.; for suffix see -Y[1].

skin *n.* Probably before 1200 *skinn* animal hide or pelt, in *The Ormulum;* later, skin of the body (probably before 1325); borrowed from a Scandinavian source (compare Old Icelandic *skinn* animal hide, Norwegian and Swedish *skinn,* Danish *skind,* from Proto-Germanic **skintha-,* Indo-European **sken-to-,* Pok.929). The Scandinavian words are cognate with Middle Low German *schin* scurf, Middle High German *schint* rind, Old High German *scinten* to flay, skin (modern German *schinden*), Middle Dutch and modern Dutch *schinden,* and outside Germanic probably also with Old Irish *ceinn* scale, Breton *scant* fish scales, and Welsh *cenn* scale. **—v.** 1392 (implied in the past participle *yskynned*) to circumcise; before 1400 (implied in the past participle *skynned*) remove the skin of; from the noun. **—skin diver** (1932) **—skin diving** (1938) **—skinner** *n.* (1398) **—skinny** *adj.* About 1400, having to do with outward appearance; formed from Middle English *skin,* n. + *-y*[1]. The meaning of very thin is first recorded in Shakespeare's *Macbeth* (1605).

skinflint *n.* mean, stingy person, miser. Before 1700, miser; literally, person who would skin a flint to save or gain something; formed from English *skin,* v. + *flint,* n.

skink *n.* smooth-scaled lizard with no legs or with short, weak legs. 1590 *scinc;* 1591 *skink;* borrowed through Middle French *scinc,* and probably directly from Latin *scincus,* from Greek *skínkos* a kind of lizard common in Asia, of uncertain origin.

skip *v.* Probably before 1300 *skippen* jump up, jump over, in *Kyng Alisaunder;* perhaps borrowed from a Scandinavian source (compare Old Icelandic *skopa* to skip, run, from Proto-Germanic **skupanan,* Indo-European **skub-* root **skeub-,* Pok.955). The meaning of pass from one thing to another, omitting intervening parts, is first recorded in English, in Chaucer's *Legend of Good Women* (about 1386). **—n.** light spring or leap. About 1422, from the verb.

skipper *n.* captain of a ship. 1391; earlier in the surname *Scipre* (1177); borrowed from Middle Dutch *scipper,* from *scip* SHIP; for suffix see -ER[1]. **—v.** act as a skipper. 1883, from the noun.

skirl (skėrl) *v.* (of bagpipes) sound loudly and shrilly. About 1450 *scrillen, skirlen* cry out shrilly, shriek; borrowed from a Scandinavian source (compare dialectal Norwegian *skryla, skrella* to shriek, or Swedish *skrälla* to crack, clap; see SHRILL). The word was used in reference to the sound of bagpipes before 1665. **—n.** 1513, shrill cry, shriek, in a translation of Vergil's *Aeneid;* from the verb.

skirmish *n.* minor fight, small, irregular combat. Probably about 1380 *skarmoch;* about 1385 *skarmyssh;* borrowed from Old French *escarmouche* skirmish, from Italian *scaramuccia.* The Italian word was borrowed from a Germanic source (compare Old High German *skirmen* to protect, defend, and *skirm* shield, SCREEN). The Middle English form *skyrmissh* (before 1400), from which the current spelling developed, was influenced by the verb *skirmysshen* to brandish a weapon; see the verb. **—v.** Probably before 1200 *sceremiggen* engage in a skirmish, in Layamon's *Chronicle of Britain;* borrowed from Old French *escarmouchier* to skirmish, from Italian *scaramucciare,* from *scaramuccia* skirmish, n. The later form *skirmysshen* (probably 1436) and late forms of the noun were influenced by a separate verb *skirmysshen,* meaning to brandish a weapon (1387, in Trevisa's translation of Higden's *Polychronicon*), which was borrowed from Old French *eskirmiss-,* stem of *eskirmir* to fence, ward off, from a Germanic source (compare Old High German *skirmen* to protect, defend); for suffix see -ISH[2].

The verb and noun forms *skyrmisshen* and *skyrmissh* were probably also influenced by Middle English *skirmen* to fence, skirmish (probably before 1200, in *Ancrene Riwle*); borrowed from Old French *eskirmir* to fence, ward off.

skirr *v.* go or move rapidly, scurry. Before 1548, of uncertain (perhaps imitative) origin. **—n.** grating, rasping, or whirring sound. About 1870, from the verb, or imitative of the grating, rasping, or whirring sound.

skirt *n.* Before 1325 *skirt* lower part of a woman's dress, in *Cursor Mundi;* earlier as a surname (1224); borrowed from a Scandinavian source (compare Old and modern Icelandic *skyrta* shirt, Swedish *skjorta,* Danish and Norwegian *skjorte;* see SHIRT). The development in English of the lower part of a woman's dress from the meaning "a shirt" is unclear, but the corresponding Middle Low German *schörte* had the meaning of apron, skirt, and the modern Low German *schört* has in some areas the sense of a woman's gown. From this similar development in German it is possible that the long shirt of peasant garb, known from ancient times, was the source of the meaning that later referred to the lower part of the shirt and thence a woman's dress. The figurative sense of a border or edge is first recorded in Middle English about 1470. **—v.** 1602, to border, edge; later, to pass along the border or edge (1623); from the noun.

skit *n.* short humorous or satiric play. 1820, from the earlier sense of whimsical notion or remark, caprice, whimsy (1727, in Bailey's *Dictionary*); perhaps noun use of an earlier verb *skit* be skittish, move lightly, caper or frolic (1611), probably a back formation from SKITTISH.

skitter *v.* move lightly or quickly, hurry about. 1845, a frequentative verb form of earlier *skite* to dart, run quickly (1721); perhaps borrowed from a Scandinavian source (compare modern Icelandic *skjóta,* Swedish *skjuta* to SHOOT, or dialectal Norwegian *skutla* glide rapidly); for suffix see -ER[4]. Compare SKITTISH. **—skittery** *adj.* 1905, frivolous; formed from English *skitter* + *-y*[1]. The sense of restless, skittish, is found in 1941.

skittish *adj.* About 1412, very lively, frivolous, in Hoccleve's *The Regement of Princes;* perhaps formed by influence of a Scandinavian base **skyt-* (represented by Old Icelandic *skýt-,* stem of *skjōta* to SHOOT) + English suffix *-ish*[1]. Compare SKITTER. The sense of apt to start, jump, or run, restive, is first recorded in English about 1510.

skittles *n.* game of ninepins. 1634, plural of *skittle* one of the pins used in the game, probably borrowed from a Scandinavian source (compare Norwegian and Swedish *skyttel* shuttle).

skoal (skōl) *n., interj.* toast to one's health. 1600 *scoll;* borrowed from Danish *skaal* (now *skål*) corresponding to Norwegian and Swedish *skål* a toast; literally, bowl, cup; see SCALE[2] dish. *Skoal* was originally only in Scottish use; it was perhaps introduced into English following the visit of King James VI to Denmark in 1589.

skua (skyü'ə) *n.* kind of sea bird related to the gulls. 1678, alteration of Faeroese *skūgvur* (earlier **skūvur*), related to Old Icelandic *skūfr* seagull, tuft, tassel, and possibly to *skauf* fox's tail; see SHEAF.

skulduggery *n. Informal.* trickery, dishonesty. 1867 *sculduggery;* earlier *schulduggy* (1856); American English, apparently alteration of Scottish *sculdudrie* fornication or adultery (1713), *sculduddery* obscenity (1821), a humorous euphemism of uncertain origin.

skulk *v.* Probably before 1200 *sculken* move stealthily, in *Ancrene Riwle;* borrowed from a Scandinavian source (compare Norwegian *skulke* to shirk, malinger, Danish *skulke* to spare oneself, shirk, and Swedish *skolka* play truant). There is a remarkable lack of evidence for the currency of this verb in English during the 1400's and 1500's, compared with its frequency in earlier and later use, suggesting that it may have become obsolete for 200 years and been reborrowed in the 17th century. **—n.** person who skulks. Probably before 1200 *scucke* (error for *sculcke*) creature that skulks, in Layamon's *Chronicle of Britain;* later *sculke* (about 1300); from the verb.

skull *n.* Probably before 1200 *sculle,* in *Ancrene Riwle;* of uncertain origin; probably borrowed from a Scandinavian source (compare Old Icelandic *skalli* bald head, skull, modern Icelandic *skalli* bald head, Norwegian and Swedish *skalle* skull). Old Icelandic *skalli* is probably related to Old English *scealu* husk, SHELL. **—skullcap** *n.* (1682)

skunk *n.* 1634 *squunck,* in William Wood's *New England's Prospect;* later *skunk* (1701); American English, borrowed from Algonquian (probably Abnaki) *seganku.* **—v.** *Slang.* to defeat or get the better of. 1843, American English; from the noun. A somewhat earlier sense, to fail (as in the game of checkers), is found in 1831 in American English (New England dialect). The sense of cheat or be cheated is first recorded in 1890.

sky *n.* Probably before 1200, in *Ancrene Riwle;* borrowed from a Scandinavian source (compare Old Icelandic *skȳ* cloud, modern Icelandic *ský,* Norwegian and Danish *sky* cloud, and Swedish *sky* heaven, sky, cloud). The Scandinavian words are cognate with Old Saxon *skion* cloud cover, probably with Old English *scēo* cloud, and perhaps more distantly with Old English *scua* shadow, shade, Old High German *scuwo,* Old Icelandic *skuggi* shadow, Gothic *skuggwa* mirror, Latin *obscūrus* dark, and Sanskrit *skunā́ti* (he) covers, from Indo-European **(s)keuə-/(s)kū-* to cover (Pok.951). **—v.** hit, throw, or raise high into the air, as in golf (to sky a ball). 1802, from the noun. **—skyjack** *v.* hijack (an aircraft). 1961, American English, formed from *sky* + *(hi)jack.* **—skylight** *n.* window in a ceiling (1690). **—skyline** *n.* (1824, line where earth and sky meet, horizon; 1896, outline of buildings against the sky, in writings of George Bernard Shaw) **—skyrocket** *n.* (1688); *v.* (1895) **—skyscraper** *n.* 1888, American English, a very tall building (in 1883, a tall ornament on top of a building; the phrase *skyscraping building* is recorded in 1884). *Skyscraper* was used earlier in various other senses: a baseball thrown high in the air (1866), a high hat or bonnet (1847), a high-flying bird (1840), and a light sail at the top of a mast (1794). The word is also found as the name of a horse, *Skyscraper,* that won the Epsom Derby in 1789. **—skywriting** *n.* (1923)

slab *n.* broad, thick piece of something. About 1300 *sclabbe;* later *slab* (before 1325); of unknown origin (sometimes suggested as borrowed from Old French *esclape* splinter, thin fragment of wood, itself of uncertain origin; or related to *slappel* a piece, portion, found in British English dialect; but these suggestions have only semantic connections and are too distant in form or in time to be relevant).

slack[1] *adj.* loose, careless. About 1250 *slac* lazy, lax, slow; later *slak* (about 1350); developed from Old English *slæc* (about 725, in *Beowulf*); cognate with Old Saxon and Middle Low German *slak* slack, Old High German *slah,* Old Icelandic *slakr* (modern Icelandic *slakur* loose, slack, Swedish *slak* and Norwegian *slakk* loose, slack), from Proto-Germanic **slakás,* Indo-European **sləgós,* root **slēg-* (Pok.959). Cognates outside Germanic include Latin *laxus* wide, open, loose; see LAX[1]. The sense of not tight, loose, is first recorded in Middle English probably before 1300. **—n.** Before 1325 *slak* cessation of pain or grieving, relief, in *Cursor Mundi;* from the adjective. The sense of a quiet period, lull, is first recorded in 1851. The nautical sense of a loose part or end (as of a rope or sail) is attested since 1794. The plural form *slacks,* meaning loose trousers, is first recorded in 1824. **—v.** 1520, to moderate, make slack; from the adjective. **—adv.** in a slack manner. 1392; from the adjective. **—slacken** *v.* Probably about 1425 *slakenen* to extinguish, abate; formed from Middle English *slac, slak,* adj. + *-enen* -en[1]. The sense of make slower, delay, retard, is first recorded in 1580, and that of to make slack, loosen, in 1611. **—slacker** *n. Informal.* person who shirks work (1898).

slack[2] *n.* dirt, dust, and small pieces left after coal is screened. About 1440 *sleck;* probably borrowed from Middle Dutch *slacke, slecke.* The Middle Dutch forms are cognate with Middle Low German *slecke* slack, slag, perhaps related to *slagge* SLAG. The modern English spelling *slack* is first found in Swift's *Works* (1729).

slag *n.* waste left after metal is separated from ore. 1552, borrowed from Middle Low German *slagge,* related to modern German *Schlacke* slag, from Middle High German *schlacken;* also related to Old High German *slahan* to strike, SLAY, with reference to the fragments produced by hammering or forging metal. **—v.** to free from or change into slag. 1824 (implied in *slagged,* participial adjective); from the noun.

slake *v.* satisfy (thirst, revenge, wrath, etc.). About 1175 *slakien* make slack or loose; later *slaken* (before 1250); developed from Old English (about 1000) *slacian* slacken an effort, from *slæc* lax, careless; see SLACK[1]. The sense of satisfy or allay (thirst, revenge, etc.) is first recorded in Middle English about 1325.

slalom (slä'ləm) *n.* skiing race over a downhill, twisting course. 1921, borrowed from Norwegian *slalåm* skiing race; literally, sloping track (*sla* slope, sloping + *låm* track, as made by skis).

slam[1] *v.* shut with force and noise. 1691, to beat or slap vigorously; probably borrowed from a Scandinavian source (compare dialectal Swedish *slämma* to slam, bang, Norwegian *slamre,* and Icelandic *slæma*). The sense of shut with force and noise is recorded as "a colloquial word" in John Ash's *Dictionary* (1775). **—n.** 1672, violent impact, severe blow, probably borrowed from the same (Scandinavian) source as *slam*[1], v. and probably only by accident of the record appearing before the verb in English. **—slambang** *v.* (1813, implied in *slambanging; adv.* (1840); *adj.* (1823) **—slammer** *n. Slang.* jail. 1952, American English; formed from *slam*¹, v. + *-er*¹; so called from the *slamming* of the prison cell door.

slam² *n.* winning of all the tricks in a card game. 1621, the card game of ruff and honors, in Jeremy Taylor's *Works;* later, a slam, especially in whist (1660); of unknown origin. Reference to the game of bridge (*grand slam*) is first recorded in 1892.

slander *n.* About 1280 *sclaundre* state of impaired reputation or disgrace; later, defamation (probably before 1300, in *Kyng Alisaunder*), and with the sense of the utterance of false statements meant to discredit (about 1300); borrowed from Anglo-French *esclaundre,* Old French *esclandre* scandalous report or statement, alteration of *escandle, escandele* scandal, from Latin *scandalum* cause of offense, stumbling block, temptation; see SCANDAL. The form *slaunder* (without *c*) is first recorded about 1340. **—v.** talk falsely about, defame. Probably about 1280 *sclaundren;* borrowed from Anglo-French *esclaundrer,* from *esclaundre* scandalous report or statement. The form *slaundren* (without *c*) is first recorded about 1415, but may have been in use much earlier (compare the verb spelling). **—slanderous** *adj.* 1397 *sclaunderous* insulting, in the *Rolls of Parliament;* later, calumnious, defamatory (about 1425); formed from Middle English *sclaundre* slander + *-ous.* The form *slaunderous* (without *c*) is found about 1410.

slang *n.* 1756, special vocabulary of tramps or thieves, in William Toldervy's *The History of Two Orphans;* later, the jargon of a particular profession (1801); of uncertain origin. It has been suggested that *slang* was borrowed from a Scandinavian word; parallel forms exist in Norwegian: *sleng* peculiarity of style in speech and writing; literally, fling, toss, *slengenavn* nickname, and *slengord* gibe, jeer, taunt, all derivatives related to Old Icelandic *slyngva* to SLING; even as persuasive as this may seem, the semantic connection is flawed and the remoteness of the borrowing is hard to overcome, so that perhaps both English and Scandinavian are from a different common source. The English sense of very informal language characterized by vividness and novelty is first recorded in 1818. **—adj.** of or like slang. 1758, from the noun. **—v.** 1812, to cheat, defraud, in Vaux's *A New and Comprehensive Vocabulary of the Flash Language;* from the noun. The sense of to utter or use slang or abusive language is found in 1828. **—slangy** *adj.* 1842, formed from English *slang,* n. + *-y*¹.

slant *v.* to slope. 1521, to strike obliquely, alteration of Middle English *slenten* to strike obliquely, slip sideways (probably about 1300), perhaps borrowed from a Scandinavian source (compare Swedish *slinta* to slip, from Proto-Germanic **slintanan,* from the Indo-European present **sli-n-donti* they slip, root **sleid-/slid-,* Pok.916, and more distantly related to Old Icelandic *sletta* to throw, spray from analogically created Proto-Germanic **slantjanan*). The sense of have to take an oblique direction, slope, is first recorded in 1698. **—n.** slope. 1655, from the verb. The word is also found as a noun in Middle English, in the phrase *on slent,* meaning at an angle, obliquely (probably before 1350). **—adj.** sloping. About 1618, from the verb. **—slantways** *adv.* (1826) **—slantwise** *adv.* (1573); *adj.* (1856, in writings of Hawthorne)

slap *n.* quick blow with the hand. About 1450 *slappe,* probably of imitative origin, as is the similarly formed Low German *slapp, slappe* a slap. **—v.** to strike with the hand. Before 1470 *slappen,* in writings of Malory; from the noun, or independently formed of imitative origin like the noun. **—adv.** 1672, quickly, suddenly, probably from the verb. The sense of straight, directly, is found in 1829. **—slapdash** *adv.* 1679, hastily, carelessly, in Dryden's *Limberham;* formed from English *slap,* adv. + *dash,* adv., quickly, with a dash. *—adj.* About 1792, from the adverb.

slapstick *n.* comedy full of rough play. 1926, American English, so called from the *slapstick,* a device consisting of two sticks fastened so as to slap together loudly when a clown or actor hits somebody with it (1896). *Slapstick* was formed from English *slap,* v. + *stick*¹ piece of wood.

slash *v.* to cut with a sweeping stroke of a sword, knife, etc. 1548, perhaps borrowed from Middle French *esclachier* to break, variant of *esclater* to break, splinter; see SLAT. Formerly this word was thought to have been used in Middle English on the basis of a citation from a version of the Wycliffe Bible in which the word *slascht* appeared; it has now been determined by the editors of the MED that the word was *flascht.* **—n.** slashing stroke. 1576, from the verb.

slat *n.* long, thin, narrow piece. 1302-03 *sclat* slate; later, tile used for covering roofs (before 1382, in the Wycliffe Bible); borrowed from Old French *esclat* split piece, splinter, from *esclater* to break, splinter, burst, probably from Frankish **slaitan* to tear, slit, related to Old High German *slīzan* to SLIT. Compare SLATE and ÉCLAT. The spelling *slat* appeared in Middle English before 1400. The sense of a long, thin, narrow piece of wood or metal, is found in 1764. **—v.** furnish with slats. About 1475 *slatten* to cover with roofing tiles; from the noun. The sense of furnish or make with slats is first recorded in 1886.

slate *n.* bluish-gray rock. About 1340 *sclate;* borrowed from Old French *esclate,* feminine of *esclat* split piece, splinter; see SLAT; so called because slate splits easily into thin layers. The sense of a writing tablet made of slate is found in Middle English in a supplement of Chaucer's *Treatise on the Astrolabe* (probably 1397); the extended sense of a list of candidates or officers is first recorded in American English, in 1842. **—v.** to cover with slate. 1530, in Palsgrave's *Lesclarcissement;* from the noun. The sense of nominate (a candidate) is found in American English in 1804, and that of propose or schedule (an event), in 1904. **—adj.** 1531, made of slate; later, of a slate color (1796); from the noun.

slather *n. Informal.* Usually **slathers** *pl.* large amount. 1857, American English, of uncertain (probably dialectal) origin. **—v.** *Informal.* to slop, spread liberally. 1866, in writings of Mark Twain; of uncertain origin.

slattern *n.* slovenly woman, slut. 1639 *slaterne,* of uncertain origin; probably cognate with Low German *Slattje* slovenly woman, slut, Dutch *slodder,* and dialectal Swedish *slåta;* see SLUT.

slaughter *n.* Probably before 1300 *slauȝter* killing of large numbers of people, massacre, in *Arthour and Merlin;* later *slaghter* (about 1303); borrowed from an early Scandinavian word **slahtr* (compare Old Icelandic *slātr* a butchering, butcher meat, *slātra* to slaughter, and *slāttr* a mowing, all related to *slā* SLAY). The Old Icelandic words are cognate with Gothic *slaúhts* slaughter from Proto-Germanic **sluHtis,* Indo-European *slek-tís*), Old High German *slahta* (modern German *Schlacht* battle), *slahtōn* to slaughter, butcher (modern German *schlachten*), Middle Dutch and modern Dutch *slacht* slaughter, *slachten* to kill, slaughter, Old Saxon *slahta* slaughter, and Old English *slieht, sleaht* slaughter, from Proto-Germanic **slaHtiz* from *slaHanan;* see SLAY. —**v.** to kill, butcher. 1535, in Coverdale's translation of the Bible; from the noun. —**slaughterhouse** *n.* (about 1374)

Slav *n.* member of a group of peoples chiefly of eastern Europe comprising the Russians, Poles, Czechs, Bulgarians, Serbo-Croats, etc. Before 1387 *Sclave,* in Trevisa's translation of Higden's *Polychronicon;* borrowed from Medieval Latin *Sclavus,* from late Greek *Sklábos,* alteration of Old Slavic *Slověninŭ* Slav, probably related to *slovo* word, speech, so that the name of the people meant originally a member of a single speech community. The spelling *Slav* appeared in English in 1866 (in 1788 *Slave*), influenced by French or German *Slave* Slav, from Medieval Latin *Sclavus.* See SLAVE.

slave *n.* About 1300 *sclave* servant, slave; borrowed from Old French *esclave,* from Medieval Latin *Sclavus* slave, originally, SLAV; so called because many Slavs were taken captive and sold into slavery by their conquerors. The spelling *slave* (without *c*) is first recorded in Middle English about 1385, and is a reduction normal in English and most Germanic languages. —**v.** work like a slave. 1559, to enslave (a person), bring into subjection; from the noun. The sense of work like a slave is found in 1719. —**slave driver** (1807) —**slavery** *n.* 1551, hard work, drudgery; formed from English *slave,* n. + *-ery.* The sense of the condition or fact of being a slave is first recorded in 1577. —**slave trade** (1734) —**slavish** *adj.* 1565, servile, characteristic of a slave; formed from English *slave,* n. + *-ish.* The figurative sense of lacking originality and independence is first recorded in 1753.

slaver *v.* let saliva run from the mouth. Before 1325 *slaveren;* borrowed from a Scandinavian source (compare Old Icelandic *slafra* to slaver, and Norwegian *slabbe* to slop, eat noisily). The Scandinavian words are cognate with Middle Low German and Middle Dutch *slabben* to eat or drink noisily. Compare SLOBBER. —**n.** saliva running from the mouth. Before 1325, probably from the verb.

slay *v.* kill. Probably about 1200 *slan;* probably before 1300 *slen;* 1307 *slayen* (past tense *slow, slew,* past participle *slawen, slain*), developed from Old English (about 725, in *Beowulf*) *slēan* to strike, slay (past tense *slōg, slōh,* past participle *slægen*); cognate with Old Frisian *slā* to strike, beat, slay, Old Saxon *slahan,* Middle Low German *slān,* Middle Dutch *slaen* (modern Dutch *slaan*), Old High German *slahan* (modern German *schlagen*), Old Icelandic *slā* (Swedish, Norwegian, and Danish *slå*), and Gothic *slahan,* from Proto-Germanic **slaHanan.* The word appears to be attested only in Germanic and a few Celtic languages: Gaelic *slachdaim* I strike with the hammer, Middle Irish *slachta* beaten, *slacc* sword, and modern Irish *slacaire* beater, bruiser, from Indo-European **slak-* to strike, beat (Pok.959).

sleazy *adj.* About 1645, flimsy, unsubstantial; of unknown origin. The word is found with the sense of hairy, fuzzy, in 1644. The sense of shoddy, sordid, squalid, is first recorded in 1941. —**sleaze** *n.* sordidness, squalor. 1961, American English; back formation from *sleazy.*

sled *n.* Probably before 1325 *sledde* vehicle for drawing loads over ground or ice; earlier as a surname (1286); borrowed from Middle Dutch *sledde* sled, variant of *slēde* (modern Dutch *slede, slee*), from Proto-Germanic **sliđō.* Middle Dutch *sledde* is cognate with Old Saxon *slido* sled, Old High German *slito, slita* (modern German *Schlitten*), and Old Icelandic *sledhi* (Swedish *släde,* Norwegian *slede,* Danish *slæde*), all from the same Germanic root as Old English *slīdan* SLIDE. —**v.** 1718, carry (something) on a sled; later, ride on a sled (1780); from the noun.

sledge[1] *n.* large, heavy hammer. 1336 *slegge;* developed from Old English (before 1000) *slecg* (from Proto-Germanic **slaȝj-*), related to *slēan* to strike, SLAY. Old English *slecg* is cognate with Middle Dutch and modern Dutch *slegge* sledge, Old Icelandic *sleggja,* and Swedish *slägga* sledge. —**v.** pound or strike with a sledge. 1654, from the noun. —**sledgehammer** *n.* (1495)

sledge[2] *n.* sled, sleigh. 1617, borrowed from dialectal Dutch *sleedse, sleeds,* related to modern Dutch *slede, slee* SLED. —**v.** carry on a sledge. 1708, from the noun.

sleek *v.* to make soft and glossy, smooth. 1440 *sleken,* in *Promptorium Parvulorum;* later variant form of *sliken* to SLICK. —**adj.** soft and glossy, smooth. 1589, in Puttenham's *The Arte of English Poesie;* later variant form of Middle English *slike* SLICK.

sleep *v.* 1137 *slepen* be or fall asleep; developed from Old English (before 830) *slǣpan;* cognate with Old Frisian *slēpa* to sleep, Old Saxon *slāpan,* Middle Dutch *slāpen* (modern Dutch *slapen*), Old High German *slāfan* (modern German *schlafen*), and Gothic *slēpan,* from Proto-Germanic **slǣpanan,* Indo-European **slēb-* (Pok.655). Outside Germanic cognates are found in Lithuanian *slōbti* become weak, Old Slavic *slabŭ* weak, and also in Latin *lābī* slip, glide, fall; see LAP[1]. The word, both verb and noun, is lacking in the Scandinavian languages. —**n.** 1135 *slep;* developed from Old English *slǣp* (about 725, in *Beowulf*), related to *slǣpan* to sleep. Old English *slǣp* is cognate with Old Frisian *slēp* sleep, Old Saxon *slāp,* Middle Dutch *slaep* (modern Dutch *slaap*), Old High German *slāf* (modern German *Schlaf*), and Gothic *slēps.* —**sleeper** *n.* Probably before 1200, one who sleeps; 1607, strong horizontal beam used for support; 1875, railroad sleeping car; 1892, something whose importance proves to be greater than expected. —**sleeping bag** (1850) —**sleeping car** (1839) —**sleeping sickness** 1551, disease characterized by sleeping, in Robinson's translation of Sir Thomas More's *Utopia;* 1875, specifically, a tropical disease transmitted by the tsetse fly. —**sleep-walker** *n.* (1747) —**sleepwalking** *n.* (1797) —**sleepy** *adj.* Probably before 1200 *slepi,* in *Ancrene Riwle;* formed from Middle English *slep,* n., sleep + *-y*[1].

sleet *n.* half-frozen rain. Before 1300 *slete;* later *sleet* (about 1395) from Proto-Germanic **slautjanan;* cognate with Middle High German *slōz, slōze* (modern German *Schlosse*) hailstone, Middle Low German *slōten,* pl., hail, *slōt* mud, puddle, pool, Middle Dutch and modern Dutch *sloot* ditch, and Old Frisian *slāt* ditch, from Proto-Germanic **slaut-,* Indo-European **sloud-,* root **sleud-* (Pok.963).

sleeve *n.* Probably before 1200 *sleve* garment, or part of a garment, which covers the arm, in *Ancrene Riwle;* developed from Old English *slīefe* (before 901, West Saxon), *slēfe* (before 971, Mercian), from Proto-Germanic **slaubjōn,* Indo-European **sloubh-,* root

sleubh-,* (Pok.963). Old English *slīefe, slēfe* are related to *slīefan* put on (clothes), and *slūpan* to slip, glide, which are cognate with Middle Low German and Middle Dutch *slūpen* to slip (modern Dutch *sluipen*), Old High German *sliofan* (modern German *schliefen*), Gothic *sliupan* to slip in, from Proto-Germanic **slūpanan,* Indo-European **sleub-/slūb-/slub-* (Pok.963). Outside Germanic the only known cognate is Latin *lūbricus* slippery (from Indo-European **slūbros*). **—v. furnish with sleeves. 1440 *sleven,* in *Promptorium Parvulorum;* from the noun.

sleigh *n.* 1703 *slay,* in Samuel Sewall's *Diary;* American English; borrowed from Dutch *slee,* variant of *slede* SLED. The spelling *sleigh* first appeared in 1768. An early form of this word is found in Middle English *scleye,* in Sir John Maundeville's *Travels* (about 1400), probably borrowed from a variant of Middle Dutch *slēde* sled. **—v.** travel on a sleigh. 1728 *slay,* in Sewall's *Letter-Book;* American English; from the noun. The spelling *sleigh* for the verb first occurs in 1868, in letters of Dickens (implied earlier in *sleigher* one who drives a sleigh, used by Southey in 1830).

sleight (slīt) *n.* skill, dexterity. Before 1325 *slight,* in *Cursor Mundi;* later *sleight* (before 1338); alteration of earlier *sleahthe, sleththe* strategy, wisdom, cleverness (probably before 1200, in Layamon's *Chronicle of Britain*); borrowed from a Scandinavian source (compare Old Icelandic *slœgdh* cleverness, cunning, slyness, from *slœgr* SLY). The term *sleight of hand* is first found before 1460 in the sense of dexterity or skill in using the hands for any purpose; in reference to juggling or magic it is first recorded in Fletcher's *The Beggar's Bush* (1622), as a more "English" equivalent of *legerdemain.*

slender *adj.* Probably before 1400 *slendre;* variant of earlier *sclendre* (about 1387-95, in Chaucer's *Canterbury Tales*); probably borrowed from Old French *esclendre* thin, slender, from Old Dutch *slinder,* of the same meaning. According to the *Französisches Etymologisches Wörterbuch* (17,1962, p. 147), it is unlikely that the Old French and Dutch words were borrowed from Middle English, as has been proposed, chiefly because the *scl-* cluster suggests a borrowing from French. **—slenderize** *v.* make or cause to look slender. 1923, formed from English *slender* + *-ize.*

sleuth *n. Informal.* detective. Probably about 1200 *sloth* track, trail of a person or animal, in *The Ormulum;* later *sleuth* (1375); borrowed from a Scandinavian source (compare Old Icelandic *slōdh* trail, of uncertain origin). *Sleuth* in the transferred sense of a detective is first recorded in 1872 in American English, probably as a shortened form of *sleuthhound* keen investigator, tracker (1856), itself a figurative use of the original meaning of a kind of bloodhound for tracking game or fugitives (1375, in Barbour's *The Bruce*). **—v.** be or act like a detective. 1900, American English; from the noun.

slew[1] (slü) *n.* swampy place. 1708, in Samuel Sewall's *Diary;* American English, spelling variant of SLOUGH[1] muddy place.

slew[2] *v.* to turn, swing, twist. 1834, in Michael Scott's *The Cruise of the Midge;* variant of earlier *slue* (1769), a nautical word of uncertain origin.

slew[3] *n. Informal.* large number or amount. 1840, in Daniel P. Thompson's *The Green Mountain Boys;* American English; borrowed from Irish *sluagh* a host, crowd, multitude, cognate with Welsh *llu* army, from Indo-European **slougos* (Pok.965).

slice *n.* Probably before 1300 *slice* splinter, sliver, in *Kyng Alisaunder;* borrowed from Old French *esclis* splinter, from *esclicier* to splinter, from Frankish **slītan* to split, related to Old High German *slīzan* to SLIT. The sense of a thin piece cut from something is first recorded before 1475. **—v.** cut into slices. Before 1475 *sklicen;* borrowed from Middle French *esclicier* to splinter. The spelling *slice* for the verb is first recorded about 1500.

slick *v.* make sleek or smooth. Probably about 1200 *sliken;* probably developed from Old English (before 900) *-slician* (attested in *nīgslicod* newly made sleek), from Proto-Germanic **slikōjanan;* cognate with Old High German *slīhhan* to glide (modern German *schleichen*), Middle Low German *slīk* mud, mire, Middle Dutch *slijc* (modern Dutch *slijk*), and Old Icelandic *slīkr* smooth, from Proto-Germanic **slīkaz.* Cognates outside Germanic are found in Old Irish *sligim* I smear, daub, *sliachtad* smoothing, leveling, Russian *slízkiĭ* slippery, and Greek *lígdēn* grazing the surface, from Indo-European **sleiĝ-/sliĝ-* smooth, slippery (Pok.663). Compare SLEEK. **—adj.** sleek, smooth. Before 1325 *slike,* in *Cursor Mundi;* earlier as an adverb, probably meaning smoothly, deceitfully (about 1300, in *Havelok the Dane*), and in the place name *Slickeburn* (1181); related to *sliken,* v. The figurative sense in the adjective of plausible, clever in deception, smooth, is first recorded in Ben Jonson's *Cynthia's Revels* (1599), probably from this sense in the earlier adverb. **—n.** 1626, a cosmetic, ointment, from the adjective or verb. The sense of a slick place or spot is first recorded in 1849 in American English. **—slicker** *n.* (1884, American English, waterproof raincoat; 1900, American English, sly, tricky person).

slide *v.* Probably about 1150 *sliden;* developed from Old English (before 950) *slīdan* move smoothly, glide; cognate with Middle High German *slīten* to slide, glide, and early Low German *slīden,* from Proto-Germanic **slīđanan.* Cognates outside Germanic include Greek *olisthánein* to slip, fall, Lithuanian *slidùs* smooth, *slýsti* to glide, and Sanskrit *srédhati* (he) glides off, goes astray, from Indo-European **(s)leidh-/(s)lidh-* slippery (Pok.960), root **lei-* (Pok.662). **—n.** act of sliding. 1570, from the verb. The sense of a smooth surface for sliding on (as at a playground) is first recorded in 1687. The sense of a slip of glass on which an object is mounted for examination under a microscope is first recorded in 1819, and that of a photographic transparency, in 1940. **—slide rule** (1663, in Pepys' *Diary*)

slight *adj.* Before 1325, smooth, plain, even, slender, flimsy, small, unimportant, in *Cursor Mundi;* probably developed from Old English *-sliht* level (attested in *eorthslihtes* level with the earth or ground). Old English *-sliht* is cognate with Old Frisian *sliucht* smooth, even, Old Saxon *sliht,* Old Icelandic *slēttr* (Norwegian *slett,* Swedish *slät*), Old High German *sleht* smooth, even (later senses "simple, plain, of little value, worthless," hence modern German *schlecht* bad), Middle Low German and Middle Dutch *slecht, slicht* smooth, simple, plain (modern Dutch *slecht* bad), Old High German *slihtan* make smooth or level (modern German *schlichten,* whence *schlicht* simple, plain, smooth), and Gothic *slaíhts* smooth, plain, from Proto-Germanic **sliHtaz,* Indo-European **slik̑-tos,* from **sleiĝ-/sliĝ-* slippery, smooth (Pok.663). Related to

SLICK. For a similar connection between the meanings "little" and "bad" in cognates, compare SLIM. —v. Before 1325 *slighten* make oneself appear sleek, in *Cursor Mundi;* from the noun. The sense of treat with contemptuous indifference or disrespect, disdain, ignore, is first recorded in Shakespeare's *2 Henry IV* (1597), and developed from or was influenced by the adjective sense of having little worth or value, mean, low, insignificant. —**n.** 1549-62, small amount, weight, or matter; from the adjective. The sense of a display of contemptuous indifference or disrespect is first recorded in 1701, in the writings of William Penn.

slim *adj.* 1657, thin or slight; later, sly or crafty (1674); borrowed from Dutch *slim* bad, sly, clever, from Middle Dutch *slim, slimp* bad, crooked. The Middle Dutch forms are cognate with Middle Low German *slim* bad, crooked, Middle High German *slimp* slanting, awry (modern German *schlimm* bad), from Proto-Germanic **slembaz,* cognate with Sanskrit *lambate* hangs down, from Indo-European **(s)lembh-, *(s)lemb-* (Pok.656). For similar semantic connections, compare SLIGHT. —**v.** 1808, to do little or no (work); from the adjective. The sense of make slim or slender is found in 1862.

slime *n.* About 1300 *slyme* soft, sticky mud; developed from Old English (before 1000) *slīm* slime, probably related to *līm* sticky substance; see LIME[1] calcium oxide. Old English *slīm* is cognate with Middle Low German *slīm* slime, Middle Dutch and Dutch *slijm,* Middle High German *slīm* (modern German *Schleim*), Old Icelandic *slīm* (Norwegian and Danish *slim*), from Proto-Germanic **slīmaz.* Cognates outside Germanic include Greek *leímāx* snail, Old Irish *slemun* smooth, slippery, Lithuanian *sliẽnas,* pl., spittle, saliva, Old Slavic *sliny* mucus, and Russian *slyuná* spittle, saliva, from Indo-European **slei-/sli-* (Pok.663). —**v.** cover or smear with or as with slime. 1628, from the noun. —**slimy** *adj.* Probably before 1387 *slymy* covered with slime, in a version of *Piers Plowman;* formed from Middle English *slyme* n., slime + *-y*[1].

sling *n.* Probably before 1300 *slynge* implement for throwing stones, in *Kyng Alisaunder;* probably borrowed from Middle Low German *slinge* sling, corresponding to Old Frisian *slinge* sling, loop, and Old High German *slinga* (modern German *Schlinge*). These nouns are cognate with Old English *slingan* to creep, twist, Middle Low German and Middle Dutch *slingen,* Old High German *slingan* (modern German *schlingen*), Old Icelandic *slyngva* to throw, sling (Norwegian *slengje,* Danish *slynge,* and Swedish *slunga*), from Proto-Germanic **slenȝanan.* Cognates outside Germanic are found in Lithuanian *sliñkti* to creep, and Latvian *slìkt* to settle, sink, from Indo-European **slenk-* (Pok.961).

The sense of a loop for lifting or carrying heavy objects is first recorded in 1323-24, and that of a hanging loop of cloth to support an injured arm occurs in Defoe's *Captain Singleton* (1720).
—**v.** Probably about 1200 *slingen* strike down using a sling; later, to throw, hurl (about 1250); probably borrowed from Old Icelandic *slyngva* to throw, sling; see *sling,* n. The sense of place (something) in a sling for lifting or carrying is first recorded in 1522.
—**slingshot** *n.* (1849, American English)

slink *v.* About 1385 *slinken* move in a sneaking, guilty manner, in Chaucer's *Troilus and Criseyde;* developed from Old English *slincan* to creep, crawl; cognate with Old Swedish *slinka* to creep, cling to, Middle Low German, Middle Dutch, and modern Dutch *slinken* to shrink, subside, from Proto-Germanic **slenkanan,* Indo-European **sleng-* (Pok.962). —**slinky** *adj.* 1921, sinuous, slender; American English, formed from *slink* + *-y*[1]. The sense of stealthy, furtive, is first recorded in 1944, also in American English.

slip[1] *v.* to glide, slide. Before 1325 *slippen* get away, escape, in *Cursor Mundi;* later, slide out of place (about 1340); probably borrowed from Middle Low German *slippen* to glide, slide. The Middle Low German word is cognate with Middle Dutch *slīpen* to glide, slide (modern Dutch *slijpen*), Old High German *slīfan* (modern German *schleifen* to slide, grind, polish), from Proto-Germanic **slīpanan* and Old Icelandic *slīpari* polisher, *sleipr* slippery (Norwegian *sleip*), from Indo-European **(s)leib-* slippery (Pok.663). The sense of cause to move with a sliding motion is first recorded in English in a translation of Vergil's *Aeneid* (1513). —**n.** 1455-56 *slype,* 1467 *slippe* landing place for ships; from the verb. The sense of an act of slipping is first recorded in Spenser's *Faerie Queene* (1596). The sense of a sleeveless garment worn by women is found in 1761.
—**slipknot** *n.* (1659) —**slipper** *n.* light, low shoe that is slipped on easily. Before 1475, formed from Middle English *slippen* slip, to slide + *-ere* -er[1]. The word may have also been influenced by an earlier form *slipper* readily slipping (1377); see SLIPPERY. —**slippery** *adj.* Probably before 1500 *slipperie* having a smooth or slimy surface; formed from Middle English *slipper* readily slipping + *-ie* -y[1], perhaps by influence of Low German *slipperig.* Middle English *slipper,* in the sense of readily slipping (1410; earlier *sliper,* 1377) developed from Old English (before 1050) *slipor* readily slipping, slippery; cognate with Middle Low German *slipper* slippery, Old High German *sleffar,* and Old Icelandic *sleipr;* see SLIP[1] to glide. The figurative sense of shifty, deceitful, is first recorded in English in 1555.
—**slip-up** *n. Informal.* mistake (1909, American English).

slip[2] *n.* narrow strip. 1440 *slyp* edge of a garment, in *Promptorium Parvulorum;* later *slippe* narrow piece or strip (1555); probably borrowed from Middle Low German or Middle Dutch *slippe* cut, slit, lappet (modern Dutch *slip*), related to Middle Low German *slippen* to cut. Middle Low German *slippen* may be cognate with Old English *-slīfan* (as in *tōslīfan*) to split; cleave; see SLIVER. The sense of a slender twig or sprig for grafting or planting is recorded in English in Palsgrave's *Lesclarcissement* (1530). The sense of a young slender person (especially in the phrase *a slip of a girl*) is found in 1582. The sense of a narrow piece of paper (as in *a citation slip*) first occurs in 1687. —**v.** 1498, to cut off; probably borrowed from Middle Dutch or Middle Low German *slippen* to cut. The sense of cut slips from (a plant) is recorded in Palsgrave's *Lesclarcissement* (1530).

slip[3] *n.* potter's clay. 1440 *slyp* mud, slime, in *Promptorium Parvulorum;* probably developed from Old English (about 1000) *slyppe* slime, slippery substance, related to *slūpan* to slip; see SLEEVE. The sense of potter's clay is first recorded in 1640, with the spelling *slip*

slipshod *adj.* 1580, wearing slippers or loose shoes, in Lyly's *Euphues;* formed from English *slip*[1] to slide + *shod* wearing shoes, from past participle of SHOE, v The figurative sense of slovenly, careless, is found in 1815, in Leigh Hunt's *Works.*

slit *v.* Probably before 1200 *slitten* cut, split, divide, in

Layamon's *Chronicle of Britain;* related to Old English *slītan* cut or tear up, slit (a form which developed into Middle English *sliten,* dialectal English *slite* to slit). Old English *slītan* is cognate with Old Frisian *slīta* to slit, tear, Old Saxon *slītan,* Middle Dutch *slīten* (modern Dutch *slijten*), Old High German *slīzan* split or tear off (modern German *schleissen*), and Old Icelandic *slīta* (Swedish *slita* pull, tear, rend, Norwegian *slite*), from Proto-Germanic **slītanan,* earlier **sklītanan.* Cognates outside Germanic include Middle Irish *scoiltim* I split, Lithuanian *skleidžiù, skleĩsti* open up what was folded together, *skeliù, skélti* to split, burst, from Indo-European **skleid-* (Pok.926). **—n.** straight and narrow cut, tear, or opening. About 1250 *slitte,* in *The Owl and the Nightingale;* from the verb.

slither *v.* Probably before 1200 *slethren* to fall; later, to slip, slide, or glide (probably before 1425, in a translation of Chauliac's *Grande Chirurgie*); a variant form of *slideren,* developed from Old English *slidrian, sliderian* (before 899, in Alfred's translation of St. Gregory's *Pastoral Care*), a frequentative verb form of *slīdan* to SLIDE; for suffix see -ER[4]. For the change in spelling from *d* to *th,* see the explanation under GATHER. **—n.** 1805 (plural) loose stones; from the verb. The sense of a slipping or sliding is first recorded in Trollope's *Tales of All Countries* (1861).

sliver *n.* About 1385 *slyvere* piece cut off, splinter, in Chaucer's *Troilus and Criseyde;* formed from earlier *sliven* to split, cleave (about 1300) + *-ere* -er[1]. Middle English *sliven* developed from Old English *-slīfan* as in *tō-slīfan*) to split, cleave, from Proto-Germanic **slīfanan,* Indo-European **skleip-* (Pok.926). **—v.** split or break into slivers. About 1385 *sleveren,* in Chaucer's *Canterbury Tales;* from the noun.

slob *n.* 1780, mud, muddy land, ooze, in Arthur Young's *A Tour in Ireland;* borrowed from Irish *slab* mud. The Irish word was probably borrowed from English *slab* muddy place, puddle (1610), which in turn was borrowed from a Scandinavian source (compare dialectal Swedish *slabb* slime, mud, and Icelandic *slabb* sludge). The informal sense of a stupid or untidy person, careless worker, is first recorded in Allen H. Clington's *Frank O'Donnell: A Tale of Irish Life* (1861).

slobber *v.* let saliva run from the mouth, slaver. Probably about 1380 *sloberen* (implied in *sloberande,* present participle); probably cognate with Frisian *slobberje* to slurp, Middle Low German *slubberen* slurp, Middle Dutch *ōverslubberen* wade through a ditch, modern Dutch *slobberen* to lap up, eat noisily, related to Middle Dutch *slabben* to eat or drink noisily; see SLAVER. **—n.** Probably before 1400 *slober* mud, slime; related to the verb. The sense of saliva running from the mouth is first recorded in Johnson's *Dictionary* (1755).

sloe *n.* plumlike fruit. Probably before 1300 *slo* (plural *slon*), in *Kyng Alisaunder;* developed from Old English (before 800) *slāh,* plural *slān;* cognate with Frisian *slē* sloe, Middle Dutch and modern Dutch *slee,* Old High German *slēha, slēwa* (modern German *Schlehe*), Old Swedish *slå* (modern Swedish *slån*), from Proto-Germanic **slaiHwōn,* Indo-European **slaikw-* (Pok.965).

slog *v.* 1824, to hit hard; probably a variant form of SLUG[3] to hit hard. The sense of walk heavily or doggedly, as through snow or mud, is first recorded in 1872, and that of work hard, plod, in 1888. **—n.** 1846, hard blow; later, hard, steady work (1888); from the verb.

slogan *n.* 1513 *slogorne* battle cry used by Irish or Scottish Highland clans; borrowed from Gaelic *sluaghghairm* (*sluagh* army, host; see SLEW[3] large number + *gairm* a cry; cognate with Greek *gêrys* voice; see CARE). The spelling *slogan* appeared in 1680, and the sense of a distinctive word or phrase used by a political or other group is first found in 1704. **—sloganeer** *n.* user of slogans. 1922, American English; formed from *slogan* + *-eer.* *—v.* make up or use slogans. 1941, from the noun.

sloop *n.* kind of sailboat having one mast. 1629, borrowed from Dutch *sloep* a sloop, earlier *sloepe,* probably from French *chaloupe,* from Old French *chalupe* any of various small sloop-rigged vessels, found also in English *shallop.* According to the OED the possible alteration of French *chaloupe* to Dutch *sloepe, sloep* is unexplained.

slop[1] *n.* weak liquid or semiliquid food. Probably before 1400 *sloppe* muddy place, mud hole, in *Morte Arthur;* probably developed from Old English *-sloppe* dung (attested in *cūsloppe* cow dung), related to *slyppe* slime; see SLIP[3] potter's clay. The sense of a weak liquid or semiliquid food (usually *slops*) is first recorded in 1657. The meaning of an act of spilling or splashing occurs in 1727, and that of mud, slush, in 1796. —**v.** 1557, to spill or splash; from the noun. **—sloppy** *adj.* 1727, very wet, muddy, in Bailey's *Dictionary;* formed from English *slop*[1], n. + *-y*[1]. The sense of loose or baggy, ill-fitting, is first recorded in 1825, influenced by SLOP[2].

slop[2] *n.* loose outer garment. 1376, probably borrowed from Middle Dutch *slop.* The Middle Dutch word is cognate with Old English *oferslop* a stole, cassock, Old Icelandic *sloppr* loose outer garment, and Old English *slūpan* to slip, glide; see SLEEVE. The plural form *slops,* meaning ready-made clothing supplied to seamen, is found in Pepys' *Diary* (1663), and the extended sense of ready-made, cheap, or inferior garments generally, is first recorded in 1799.

slope *v.* move in an oblique direction, slant. 1591, from earlier *slope,* adj., slanting (1502), probably derived from Middle English *aslope,* adv., on the incline, aslant, obliquely (before 1398), developed from Old English **āslopen,* past participle of *āslūpan* to slip away (*ā-* away + *slūpan* to slip; see SLEEVE). **—n.** line or surface that slopes. 1611, in Cotgrave's *Dictionary;* from the verb.

slosh *n.* slush, sludge. 1814, in Southey's *Letters,* probably a blend of *slop*[1] (in the sense of muddy place) and *slush.* —**v.** to splash about in slosh. 1844, from the noun.

slot *n.* narrow opening. Probably about 1390, the hollow at the base of the throat above the breastbone, in *Sir Gawain and the Green Knight;* borrowed from Old French *esclot,* of uncertain origin. The sense of a narrow opening or depression into which something can be fitted is first recorded in 1523. The specific sense of the opening of a slot machine for receiving a coin is found in 1888. The figurative sense of a position in a list, hierarchy, system, etc., such as a place in a timetable, is first recorded in 1942, in American English. —**v.** Probably before 1400 *slotten* stab (someone) through the hollow at the base of the throat, in *Morte Arthur;* later, cut a slot or slots in (1747); from the noun. **—slot machine** (1891)

sloth *n.* Before 1150 *slauthe* indolence, sluggishness; later *slouthe* (before 1300); formed from Middle English *slou, slowe* SLOW + *-th*[1]. The sense of slowness, tardiness, is first recorded about 1380, in Chaucer's *Canterbury Tales. Sloth* as the name of a very slow-moving mammal is found in *Purchas his Pilgrimage* (1613).

slouch *n.* 1515, awkward, slovenly, or lazy man; dialectal variant of *slouk* (1570). Perhaps these English forms were borrowed from a Scandinavian source (compare Old Icelandic *sloekr* lazy fellow, Swedish *slok,* probably related to *slakr* loose, careless, SLACK[1]). The meaning of a stooping of the head and shoulders, loose, ungainly bearing, is first recorded in 1725, in writings of Swift. **—v.** 1754, move or walk with a slouch, in writings of Henry Fielding; from the noun.

slough[1] (slou) *n.* muddy place, mud hole. Before 1250 *slo* degraded condition, in *The Owl and the Nightingale;* later, *sloghe* (about 1340), *slough* (about 1390); and as a surname *Slough* (1273); earlier in the place name *Polslewe* (1159); developed from Old English *slōh* muddy place (before 899, in Alfred's translation of Bede's *Ecclesiastical History*). Old English *slōh* is possibly cognate with Middle Low German *slōch* muddy place, and Middle High German *sluoche* ditch, from Proto-Germanic **slōHaz,* earlier **sklōHaz,* cognate with Lithuanian *šlākas* drop, spot, and *šlēkti* to spray, from Indo-European **sk̂lēk-/sk̂lōk-/sk̂lək-* (Pok.957). The phrase *slough of despond,* meaning deep despondence, hopeless dejection, appeared in 1776, in allusion to Bunyan's use in *Pilgrim's Progress* (1678) as the name of a place from which Christian cannot get out because of the heavy burden of sin he carries on his back.

slough[2] (sluf) *n.* cast-off skin of a snake or other animal. Before 1325 *slughe, in Cursor Mundi;* possibly cognate with Middle High German *slūch* snakeskin (modern German *Schlauch* tube, pipe), Middle Low German *slū* husk, peel, skin, modern Dutch *sluiken* to smuggle, from Proto-Germanic **slūk-;* and outside Germanic with Lithuanian *šliaũžti* to creep, crawl, and Latvian *šl'užât* to glide, slide, from Indo-European **sleuĝ-/slouĝ-/slūĝ-/sluĝ-* (Pok.964). **—v.** cast off, shed. 1720, from the noun.

sloven *n.* dirty, untidy, or careless person. Probably before 1475 *sloveyn* immoral woman; later *sloven* knave, rascal (before 1500); probably borrowed from Middle Flemish *sloovin* a gossip, scold, related to *sloef* dirty, untidy, shabby, Dutch *slof* careless, negligent, from Proto-Germanic **slup-,* Indo-European **slub-,* root **sleub-* hang down loosely (Pok.964); probably cognate with Lithuanian *slùbnas* slack, limp, from Indo-European **sleub(h)-/slub(h)-* (Pok.964). The meaning of a dirty, untidy, or careless person, is first recorded in English in Palsgrave's *Lesclarcissement* (1530) **—adj.** untidy, dirty, careless. 1815, from the noun. **—slovenly** *adj.* Before 1515, low, base, lewd; later, untidy, dirty (before 1568); formed from English *sloven,* n. + *-ly*[2].

slow *adj.* Probably before 1200 *slou, slowe;* developed from Old English *slāw* sluggish, not quick (before 899, in Alfred's translation of Boethius' *De Consolatione Philosophiae*); cognate with Old Saxon *slēu* blunt, dull, Middle Dutch and modern Dutch *slee,* Middle Low German *slē,* Old High German *slēo,* Old Icelandic *sljōr, slær* (Swedish *slö,* Danish and Norwegian *sløv*), from Proto-Germanic **slǣwaz,* of unknown origin. **—v.** Probably about 1175 *slawen* be slow; later *slouwen* (before 1425); from the adjective. The meaning of make slower is first found in 1557; the sense of go slower is found in 1594. **—adv.** in a slow manner. Before 1500, from the adjective. **—slowpoke** *n. Informal.* slow person. 1848, American English; formed from *slow,* adj. + *poke,* n., thrust, push, poke[1].

sludge *n.* muddy deposit or sediment, slush. 1649, of uncertain origin; possibly from earlier *slutch* mud, mire (1669; but recorded as a past participle in the 1300's); or perhaps a variant form of SLUSH. Other words for mud or mire, such as *slitch* (about 1400) and *sleech* (1587), also suggest possible sources for a variant form *sludge.* The earlier appearance in the record of English argues in their favor, but the sound changes do not. Therefore, *sludge* may be simply an independent formation generally accepted as quite descriptive of a deposit of mud or sediment. For a possible relationship similar to *slutch* and *sludge,* see SMUTCH and SMUDGE.

slug[1] *n.* slow-moving animal somewhat like a snail. 1408 *slogge* lazy person; later *slugge* (about 1425); borrowed, possibly by influence of earlier Middle English *sluggard* lazy, idle person, from a Scandinavian source (compare dialectal Swedish and dialectal Norwegian *slugga* be sluggish, and dialectal Norwegian *sluggje* a heavy slow person). The meaning of a slow-moving animal somewhat like a snail is first recorded in English in 1704.

slug[2] *n.* piece of lead for firing from a gun. 1622, of uncertain origin; perhaps special use of SLUG[1], with reference to its shape, suggesting that of the snail-like animal. The use of *slug* in the meaning of a round metal piece, either a token or a counterfeit coin, is first recorded in 1881, possibly developed from the meaning of a gold coin, privately minted in California (1851) or from the meaning in printing of a metal strip used to space lines of type (1871). The meaning of a drink, especially of strong alcohol, is first recorded in 1756. **—v.** to drink quickly, often in a single gulp. 1856, in the phrase *slug it up.*

slug[3] *n.* a hard blow. 1830, in Thomas Wilson's *The Pitman's Pay;* dialectal English, of uncertain origin. **—v.** to hit hard. 1862, in C. Clough Robinson's *The Dialect of Leeds;* probably from the noun. **—slugger** *n.* 1877, a boxer, American English; formed from *slug*[3], v. + *-er*[1]. The sense in baseball of a hard-hitting batter is found in 1877, in American English, and that of a baseball bat (as in *Louisville slugger*), in 1946.

sluggard *n.* Before 1398 *slogard* lazy, idle person, in Trevisa's translation of Bartholomew's *De Proprietatibus Rerum;* later *sluggart* (probably before 1437); earlier as a surname *Slogard* (1275); formed from earlier *sluggi, sloggi* sluggish, indolent (probably before 1200) + *-ard.* Middle English *sluggi, sloggi* was probably borrowed from a Scandinavian word related to the source of Middle English *slugge, slogge* lazy person; see SLUG[1]. It is also possible that *sluggard* is immediately a back formation from earlier *sluggardy* laziness, indolence (about 1386, in Chaucer's *Canterbury Tales*); but even if this is so, the derivation in English and the related borrowing process from Scandinavian would be the same as that of *sluggard.* **—adj.** lazy, idle. 1593, in Shakespeare's *Richard II;* from the noun.

sluggish *adj.* Before 1450 *sloggissh* lazy; about 1450 *slugissh* slow, dull; formed from Middle English *slugge* lazy person (see SLUG[1]) + *-issh* -ish[1].

sluice *n.* structure of gates or a single gate for regulating the flow of water. About 1400 *sluse,* alteration of earlier *scluse* (1340, in *Ayenbite of Inwyt*); borrowed from Old French *escluse* a sluice, floodgate, from Late Latin *exclūsa* barrier to shut out water, from feminine singular of Latin *exclūsus,* past participle of *exclūdere* shut out, EXCLUDE. The spelling *sluice,* paralleling *juice,* came into general use in the 1700's. **—v.** let out by or as if by opening a sluice. 1593, in Shakespeare's *Richard II* and Nashe's *Christ's Tears Over Jerusalem;* from the noun.

slum *n.* section in a city where the poorest people live. 1845, from earlier *back slum* back alley or street inhabited by poor people (1825), originally a cant or slang word meaning a room, especially a back room or parlor (1812); of unknown origin. **—v.** visit a slum or slums. 1884, from the noun. The meaning of live in or go about in a manner of indifference to one's personal appearance or surroundings is first recorded in 1928. **—slumlord** *n.* landlord of tenements in a slum. 1953, American English, contraction of earlier *slum landlord* (1893, in writings of George Bernard Shaw). **—slummy** *adj.* Before 1860, given to frequenting slums, in Oxford University slang; formed from English *slum,* n. + *-y*[1]. The meaning of characteristic of a slum is first recorded in 1873, and that of slovenly, careless, in 1881.

slumber *v.* Before 1376 *slumberen, slomberen* to sleep, especially to sleep lightly, in *Piers Plowman;* alteration (by influence of the earlier noun spelling *slomber*) of *slumeren* (before 1250), frequentative verb form of *slumen* to doze, probably derived from Old English (before 1000) *slūma* light sleep, doze; for suffix see -ER[4]. Old English *slūma* is cognate with Middle High German *slumen, slummern* to slumber (modern German *schlummern*), Middle Low German *slummeren,* Middle Dutch *slūmen, slūmeren* (modern Dutch *sluimeren*), and Norwegian *slumre,* from Indo-European **sleu-/slū-* hang down loosely (Pok.962). The appearance of *b* between *m* and *r* parallels such words as *number, lumber* (move heavily), *-cumber* (in *cucumber*), etc. **—n.** light sleep. Before 1338 *slomber,* in Mannyng's *Chronicle of England;* from the verb. **—slumberous** or **slumbrous** *adj.* Before 1398 *slombrous,* in Trevisa's translation of Bartholomew's *De Proprietatibus Rerum;* formed from Middle English *slomber,* n., slumber + *-ous.*

slump *v.* Before 1677, fall or sink into a muddy place; perhaps borrowed from a Scandinavian source (compare Norwegian and Danish *slumpe* fall upon, chance upon). The Scandinavian words are cognate with Middle Low German *slump* lucky accident (modern German *schlumpen* hang loosely, be slovenly). **—n.** heavy drop or sudden fall. 1888, heavy decline in prices on the stock exchange, American English; also 1888, (transferred sense) sudden fall, collapse; from the verb. The specific sense in economics of a general, sharp or sudden decline in trade or business, usually accompanied by a rise in unemployment, is attested since 1922.

slur *v.* 1602, to smear, stain, sully, in Marston's *Antonio's Revenge;* possibly verb use of dialectal English *slur* thin or fluid mud, variant of Middle English *sloor, slore* (1440, in *Promptorium Parvulorum*). The Middle English forms are cognate with Middle Low German *slūren,* Middle Dutch *sloren,* and Dutch *slouren* to drag, trail, and Middle High German *slier* mud. The transferred sense of insult, slight, disparage, is first recorded in 1660, as is the sense of pass over lightly without due consideration. The meaning of make confused or indistinct, blur, is first recorded in 1782, in Sir Joshua Reynold's writings, though the meaning is implied earlier in *slurred* (1746). **—n.** 1609, insult, slight, from the verb. The sense of a curved mark in music indicating a slurring of tones is first recorded in 1801, and that of a slurred utterance or sound, in 1861, in Reade's *The Cloister and the Hearth.*

slurp *v.* 1648, drink greedily or noisily; borrowed from Dutch *slurpen,* perhaps of imitative origin similar to Middle Low German *slorpen,* modern German *schlürfen,* and Norwegian *slurpe* to slurp. **—n.** a slurping sip or noise. 1949, from the verb.

slurry *n.* thin, watery mud or cement. Before 1438 *slory* mud, slime; probably related to Middle English *sloor, slore* thin or fluid mud; see SLUR. The spelling *slurry* is first recorded in 1825. **—v.** 1440 *sloryen* to dirty, soil, smear, in *Promptorium Parvulorum;* probably from the noun.

slush *n.* snow and water mixed. 1641, perhaps borrowed from a Scandinavian source (compare Norwegian and Swedish *slask* slushy ground or weather, obsolete Danish *slus* sleet, and modern Danish *slud*). The nautical sense of refuse fat from meat boiled on a ship (see *slush fund* below) is first recorded in 1756. The figurative sense of nonsense, drivel, sentimental rubbish, is found in American English, in Mark Twain's *Innocents Abroad* (1869). **—v.** splash or soak with slush. 1807, from the noun. **—slush fund** 1839, money obtained from the sale of a ship's slush (refuse fat) distributed among a ship's officers at the discretion of the commanding officer; later (transferred sense) money collected to spread influence, bribes, etc., especially to support a political candidate (1874, American English). **—slushy** *adj.* 1791, covered with or resembling slush; formed from English *slush,* n. + *-y*[1].

slut *n.* 1402 *slutte* slovenly woman, in Hoccleve's *Letter of Cupid;* later, woman of loose morals (probably before 1475), of uncertain origin; probably cognate with dialectal German *Schlutt, Schlutte* slovenly woman, dialectal Swedish *slåta* idle woman, slut, Dutch *slodde, slodder* slut, and more distantly with Old Icelandic *slodhra* drag oneself forward, Middle High German *slottern, sluttern* to hang loosely, dangle, flat (modern German *schlottern* dangle, tremble, shake), Dutch *slodderen* spatter, from Indo-European **sleu-* hang loosely (Pok.962). Gothic *afsláuthjan* to worry (originally, cause to tremble or shake), *afsláuthnan* become alarmed (originally, to tremble or shake), are built on a lost adjective **slauthaz* shaking, from Indo-European **slout-.*

sly *adj.* Probably about 1200 *sleh* clever, crafty, wily; later *slye* (about 1303); borrowed from a Scandinavian source; compare Old Icelandic *slœgr* (from Proto-Germanic **slōʒís,* Indo-European **slākís*), modern Icelandic *slægur,* Norwegian *sløg* cunning, crafty, sly; originally meaning able to strike, from *slōg-,* stem in the past-tense form of *slā* to strike, SLAY. **—n. on the sly,** in a sly way, secretly. 1812, in Vaux's *Vocabulary of the Flash Language;* from the adjective.

smack[1] *n.* taste or flavor. Probably about 1200 *smacc,* in *The Ormulum;* later *smak* (about 1250); developed from Old English (before 1000) *smæc;* cognate with Old Frisian *smek, smaka* taste or flavor, Middle Low German and Middle Dutch *smāke* (modern Dutch *smaak*), Old High German *smac, gismac* (modern German *Geschmack*), and Old Icelandic *smekkr* (Norwegian and Swedish *smak,* Danish *smag*), from Proto-Germanic **smak-,* Indo-European **smog-,* root **smeg-* (Pok.967). **—v.** Before 1250 *smaken* to smell (something); later, to taste (something), before 1333, and to have a taste (before 1398, in Trevisa's translation of Bartholomew's *De Proprietatibus Rerum*); from the noun. The figurative sense of have a trace or suggestion, be reminiscent, is found in Shakespeare's *King John* (1595).

smack[2] *v.* open (the lips) quickly so as to make a sharp sound. 1557, probably of imitative origin similar in formation to Middle Low German *smacken* to strike, throw, Low German and Dutch *smakken* to fling, dash, and German *schmatzen* to smack the lips, eat noisily. The meaning of kiss loudly is first recorded in 1570. The sense of strike with the open hand, slap, appears in Thackeray's *Shabby-Genteel Story* (1840). **—n.** 1570, sharp sound made by smacking the lips; from the noun.

smack[3] *n.* sailboat. 1611, in Cotgrave's *Dictionary;* probably borrowed from Dutch or Low German *smak* sailboat, from *smakken* to fling, dash (see SMACK[2]); perhaps so called from the slapping of the sails.

smack[4] *n. Slang.* heroin. 1960; earlier, a small packet of drugs (1942); American English, probably a variant of earlier *smeck* (1932) and *shmeck* (1941) narcotic drug, dope; borrowed from Yiddish *shmek* a sniff or smell, from *shmekn* to sniff or smell, from Middle High German *smecken, smacken* to smell or taste, from Old High German *smac* smell or taste; see SMACK[1].

small *adj.* Probably before 1200 *smal,* in Layamon's *Chronicle of Britain;* developed from Old English (before 800) *smæl* slender, narrow, small; cognate with Old Frisian *smel* narrow, Old Saxon, Middle Low German, Middle Dutch and modern Dutch *smal,* Old High German *smal* (modern German *schmal*), Old Icelandic *smalr* small (in compounds), *smali* small cattle, and Gothic *smalista* smallest, from Proto-Germanic **smalaz.* Cognates outside Germanic include Greek *mêlon* sheep, Old Irish *mīl* small animal, Latin *malus* bad (compare SLIGHT and SLIM), and Old Slavic *malŭ* small, from Indo-European **(s)mēl-/(s)mōl-/(s)məl-* (Pok.724). **—adv.** into small pieces. About 1375, developed from Old English *smale* (before 899, in Alfred's translation of Boethius' *De Consolatione Philosophiae*); from Old English *smæl,* adj. **—n.** something small. Probably before 1200, in *Ancrene Riwle;* from the adjective. **—small beer** (1568, weak beer; 1604, trifles, in Shakespeare's *Othello*) **—small fry** (1697, small fish; 1885, insignificant people) **—small intestine** (1767) **—smallish** *adj.* rather small. About 1370 *smalish,* in Chaucer's translation of *Roman de la Rose;* formed from Middle English *smal* + *-ish*[1]. **—smallpox** *n.* (1518) **—small talk** (1751)

smarmy (smär′mē) *adj. Informal.* offensively flattering or ingratiating. 1924, formed in English from earlier *smarm* to behave in a flattering way (1920), variant of *smalm* (1890) and *smawm* (1846) to smear, bedaub, of unknown origin; for suffix see -Y[1].

smart *v.* Probably about 1150 *smerten* cause (someone) to suffer grief or sorrow, distress; later *smearten* ache, be painful (probably before 1200), and with the spelling *smarten* (about 1303); developed from Old English *smeortan* be painful (before 899, in Alfred's translation of Orosius' *Historiarum Adversus Paganos*). Old English *smeortan* is cognate with Middle Low German *smerten* to be very painful, Middle Dutch *smerten, smarten* (modern Dutch *smarten*), and Old High German *smerzan* (modern German *schmerzen*), from Proto-Germanic **smertanan.* Cognates are found outside Germanic in Greek *smerdnós, smerdaléos* terrible, fearful, Latin *mordēre* to bite, and Sanskrit *mṛdnāti, márdati* (he) crushes, destroys, from Indo-European **smerd-/smord-* (Pok.737).

—adj. Probably before 1200 *smærte, smerte* sharp, severe, stinging; developed from Old English (before 1023) *smeart* (from Pre-Old-English **smartaz*), related to *smeortan* to smart. The extended meaning of quick, active, prompt, is first recorded about 1303; and that of quick at learning, clever, in 1628. Another meaning in modern English, that of stylish, neat and trim, is first recorded in 1716.

—n. sharp pain. Probably about 1175 *smirte;* later *smerte* (probably before 1300); cognate with Middle Dutch and Middle Low German *smerte, smarte* sharp pain, Old High German *smerza, smerzo* (modern German *Schmerz*), all derived from the same Germanic source as Old English *smeortan* to smart.

—adv. in a smart manner. About 1300 *smerte* sharply, severely, in *Havelok the Dane;* from the adjective.

—smarten *v.* 1815, make smart, spruce up, in Jane Austen's *Emma;* formed from English *smart,* adj. + *-en*[1]. **—smarts** *n.pl. Informal.* good sense, intelligence, brains. 1968, American and Canadian English; from *smart,* adj.; for suffix see -S[1]. **—smarty** *n.* (1861); *adj.* (1883, Mark Twain)

smart aleck (al′ik) *Informal.* conceited, obnoxious person. 1865 *smart Aleck,* American English; perhaps in allusion to *Aleck* Hoag, a notorious pimp, thief, and confidence man in New York City in the early 1840's. See "Origin of Smart Aleck," by Gerald L. Cohen, *Comments on Etymology,* Vol. VII, No. 4, 1977.

smash *v.* 1778, break to pieces, crush, shatter; earlier, to kick downstairs (before 1700); probably of imitative origin, similar to *clash, crash,* etc. The meaning in tennis of strike the ball swiftly in an overhand shot is first recorded in 1882. **—n.** 1725, hard blow; from the verb. The sense of a sound of smashing, crash, is first recorded in Jamieson's *Dictionary of the Scottish Language* (1808). The meaning of a success or hit in films or on stage is first recorded in 1930, as a shortened form of *smash hit* (1923). **—smashing** *adj. British.* very good, excellent, sensational, is first recorded before 1911.

smatter *v.* About 1410 *smateren* talk idly, chatter, prate; of uncertain (perhaps imitative) origin. Similar forms occur in Middle High German *smetern* to chatter (modern German *schmettern* to dash, resound), and Swedish *smattra* to patter, rattle. The meaning of have a slight or superficial knowledge of, dabble, is recorded in Palsgrave's *Lesclarcissement* (1530). An earlier sense of make dirty, defile, is found in Middle English about 1390. **—n.** 1668, superficial knowledge, smattering; from the verb. **—smattering** *n.* slight or superficial knowledge. 1538, formed from English *smatter,* v. + *-ing*[1].

smear *n.* Probably about 1200 *smere* fat, grease, ointment, in *The Ormulum;* developed from Old English (before 800) *smeoru* grease, from Proto-Germanic **smerwan;* cognate with Old Saxon *smero* fat, grease, Middle Dutch *smere* (modern Dutch *smeer*), Old High German *smero* (modern German *Schmer*), Old Icelandic *smjǫr, smǫr* butter (Swedish *smör,* Norwegian and Danish *smør*), and Gothic *smaírthr* fat, from Proto-Germanic **smerthran.* Cognates outside Germanic are found in Old Irish *smir, smiur* marrow (modern Irish *smior*), and Welsh *mer,* from Indo-European **smeru-* (Pok.970). The meaning of a mark or stain left by smearing is first recorded in Cotgrave's *Dictionary* (1611). **—v.** About 1125 *smeren* rub or daub with a greasy substance, anoint; developed from Old English (before 830) *smerian, smirian,* related to *smeoru* grease. The Old English verb is cognate with Middle Low German, Middle Dutch and Dutch *smeren* to smear, Old High German *smirwen* (modern German *schmieren*), and Old Icelandic *smyrva, smyrja* (Swedish *smörja,* Norwegian and Danish *smøre*).

smell *v.* About 1175 *smellen* emit or perceive an odor, perhaps cognate with Middle Dutch *smōlen, smölen* to SMOLDER. For a similar connection between the meanings "smoke" and "smell," compare REEK. The Old English equivalent is *stenc* STENCH. **—n.** About 1175 *smel;* related to the verb. **—smelling salts** (1840, in Dickens' *The Old Curiosity Shop*) **—smelly** *adj.* 1826, emitting a bad smell, formed from English *smell,* n. + *-y*[1]. An instance of this word is also found in Middle English as *smilly,* with the sense of having a strong odor.

smelt[1] *v.* melt (ore) to get the metal out of it. 1543; implied earlier in Middle English *smeltar* one who smelts ore (1455), and as a surname *Smelter* (probably about 1382); borrowed from Dutch or more probably Low German *smelten,* from Middle Dutch or Middle Low German; cognate with Old High German *smelzan* to melt (modern German *schmelzen*), Old Swedish *smælta* (modern Swedish *smälta*), Norwegian and Danish *smelte,* and Old English *meltan* to MELT.

smelt[2] *n.* small, edible sea fish. Old English (before 800) *smelt;* cognate with Dutch *smelt* sand eel, Norwegian *smelte,* and Danish *smelt.*

smidgen or **smidgeon** *n. Informal.* tiny bit, small amount. 1845 *smitchin;* later *smidgeon* (1878), and *smidgen* (1886), American English; perhaps formed from Scottish *smitch* very small amount, small insignificant person (1822) + *-in,* dialectal variant of *-ing*[1].

smile *v.* About 1303 (implied in *smylyng* pleasant), in Mannyng's *Handlyng Synne;* also as a surname *Smyles* (1301); of uncertain origin; perhaps borrowed from Middle Low German **smilen;* or from a Scandinavian source (compare Swedish *smila* smile). All of these forms have, at one time or another, been suggested as cognates with Old High German *smīlan* to smile, Middle High German *smielen,* and may be more remotely related to Greek *meidiân* to smile, Latin *mīrus* wonderful, and *mīrārī* to wonder, be surprised, Latvian *smiêt* to ridicule, Old Slavic *smijati (sę)* to laugh, Sanskrit *smita-s* smiling, *smáyate* he smiles, and Tocharian A *smi-* to smile, from Indo-European **smei-/smi-* (Pok. 967). **—n.** 1562, in John Heywood's *Epigrams and Proverbs;* from the verb.

smirch *v.* Before 1398 *smorchen* to discolor, soil, in Trevisa's translation of Bartholomew's *De Proprietatibus Rerum;* of uncertain origin; no satisfactory semantic connection can be made with the Old French *esmorcher* to torture, but the similarity in form with the Middle English *smorchen* suggests the Old French word may have had another meaning, such as befoul or stain (as also found later in English). Original formation of Old French *esmorcher* is from *es-* out (from Latin *ex-*) + Old French *morcher* to bite, from Late Latin *mordicāre,* from Latin *mordēre* to bite, sting; see SMART. Any connection with *smear* seems to be purely semantic. The altered spelling *smirch* is first recorded in Shakespeare's plays (1599, *Much Ado About Nothing,* 1600, *As You Like it,* etc.).

The figurative sense of dishonor, disgrace, discredit, is first recorded in Scott's *The Monastery* (1820). **—n.** dirty mark, blot. Before 1688, in John Bunyan's writings; from the verb.

smirk *v.* Probably about 1200 *smirken* to smile; later, to smile in an affected, silly way (before 1500); developed from Old English *smearcian* to smile (before 899, in Alfred's translation of Boethius' *De Consolatione Philosophiae*). Old English *smearcian* is related to *smerian* to laugh at, and to *gāl-smǣre* given to frivolous laughter. **—n.** affected, silly, self-satisfied smile. About 1560, from the verb.

smite *v.* Probably before 1200 *smiten* to strike or hit hard; developed from Old English (before 800) *smītan;* cognate with Old Frisian *smīta* to throw, Old Saxon *smītan,* Middle Low German and Middle Dutch *smīten* to throw, strike (modern Dutch *smijten*), Old High German *bismīzan* to soil, stain, Middle High German *smīzan* to smear, strike (modern German *schmeissen* to throw, fling), Norwegian and Swedish *smita,* Danish *smide,* and Gothic *bismeitan* anoint, from Proto-Germanic **smītanan.* Cognates outside Germanic include Old Slavic *smědŭ* dusky, dark, and Armenian *mic* dirt, from Indo-European **smeid-/smid-* (Pok.966). The sense of to kill, slay (originally a Biblical use) is found in Middle English before 1325, in *Cursor Mundi.* The sense of inspire or inflame with love (chiefly used in the past participle form *smitten*) occurs in 1663, in Pepys' *Diary.*

smith *n.* Old English *smith* one who makes or shapes things out of metal, blacksmith (about 725, in *Beowulf*); cognate with Old Frisian and Old Saxon *smith* blacksmith, Middle Dutch and modern Dutch *smid,* Old High German *smid* (modern German *Schmied,* and the surname *Schmidt*), Old Icelandic *smidhr* (Norwegian, Swedish, and Danish *smed*), and Gothic *-smitha* (in *aizasmitha* coppersmith), from Proto-Germanic **smithaz,* Indo-European **smitos;* also cognate outside Germanic with Greek *smílē* chisel, and possibly with Lithuanian *smailùs* pointed, from Indo-European **smēi-/sməi-/smī-/smi-* work with a sharp tool (Pok. 968). **—smithy** *n.* workshop of a smith, forge. Before 1250 *smithie,* in *Ancrene Riwle;* probably a formation in Middle English of *smith* + *-ie* -y[3]; influenced by Old Icelandic *smidhja* smithy, from *smidhr* SMITH, but based originally on Old English *smiththe;* cognate with Old High German *smitta* (modern German *Schmiede*) smithy, Middle Dutch *smisse* (modern Dutch *smidse*), and Old Frisian *smithe,* from Proto-Germanic **smithjōn.*

smithereens (smiᴛʜ′ərēnz′) *n.pl. Informal.* small pieces, bits. 1829 *smiddereens,* borrowed from Irish *smidirīn,* diminutive of *smiodar* fragment; for suffix see -S[1]. The spelling *smithereens* is first recorded in 1841.

smock *n.* About 1300 *smok,* before 1325 *smock* woman's undergarment, chemise; developed from Old English (before 1000) *smoc;* cognate with Old High German *smoccho* and Old Icelandic *smokkr* woman's garment, from Proto-Germanic **smukkaz,* earlier **smuȝnás,* Indo-European **smugh-nós;* also cognate with Middle High German *gesmuc* (modern German *Schmuck* adornment) and *smiegen* (modern German *schmiegen* creep close to, nestle against), Old English *smūgan* to creep, modern Dutch *smuigen* to sneak, and Old Icelandic *smjūga* creep into, put on a garment, from Indo-European *smeugh-/smūgh-/smugh- (F. Kluge, *Etymologisches Wörterbuch der deutschen Sprache,* 665, 667).

smog *n.* a heavy layer of air pollution, usually close to the ground. 1905, blend of *smoke* and *fog;* reportedly coined by H.A. Des Vœux, a representative of the Coal Smoke Abatement Society, in reference to the London fog, during a meeting of the Public Health Congress in London in 1905. **—v.** envelop in smog. 1966, from the noun. **—smoggy** *adj.* 1905, formed from English *smog,* n. + *-y*[1].

smoke *n.* 1137 *smoke,* developed from Old English (about 1000) *smoca,* related to *smēocan* give off smoke, from Proto-Germanic **smeukanan;* cognate with Middle Dutch *smieken* give off smoke, *smoock* smoke (modern Dutch *smook*), Middle Low German *smōk,* and Middle High German *smouch* smoke (modern German *Schmauch*). A cognate outside Germanic is found in Lithuanian *smáugti* to choke, from Indo-European **smeug-/smug-* (Pok.971). **—v.** 1137 *smoken* give off smoke, expose to smoke; developed from Old English (about 1000) *smocian,* from *smoca* smoke, n. The meaning of draw in and puff out the smoke of tobacco is first recorded in 1617. **—smoker** *n.* 1599, person who cures fish, bacon, etc., by means of smoke, in Nashe's *Lenten Stuffe;* formed from English *smoke,* v. + *-er*[1]. The meaning of a person who smokes tobacco is first recorded in 1617. The sense of a railroad car where smoking is allowed is first recorded in 1882, in American English. **—smoke screen** 1915, screen of smoke used to hide military forces from an enemy; 1926, something designed to conceal or mislead. **—smokestack** *n.* (1859, American English) **—smoky** *adj.* About 1300, give off smoke; formed from Middle English *smoke,* n. + *-y*[1].

smolder *v.* Probably about 1380 *smolderen* (implied in *smolderande,* present participle) to smother, suffocate; from *smolder,* n., smoke (about 1378). The Middle English forms are probably cognate with Middle Dutch *smōlen, smölen* to burn and smoke without flame, smolder (modern Dutch *smeulen*), Low German *smelen, smälen,* and Flemish *smoel* hot, from Proto-Germanic **smel-/smul-/smōl-.* The Germanic words are cognate with Middle Irish *smāl, smōl, smūal* fire, glow, Upper Wendish *smalić* to singe, and Lithuanian *smilkýti* to smoke, from Indo-European **smel-/sml̥-/smōl-* (Pok.969). The meaning of burn and smoke without flame is first recorded in English in 1529. During the 1600's and 1700's the verb fell into disuse, although it continued to appear in poetry in the participial adjective *smoldering.* The revival of the verb in the early 1800's was probably the result of Scott's use in *The Lady of the Lake.*

smooch *v., n. Slang.* kiss. 1932 v., 1942 n., American English; alteration of dialectal English *smouch,* attested as a noun since 1578 and as a verb since 1583, possibly imitative of the sound of kissing.

smooth *adj.* About 1330 *smothe* level, flat, in *Sir Orfeo;* developed from Old English (before 1050) *smōth* free from roughness, not harsh; cognate with Old Saxon *smōthi* smooth, and dialectal (Westphalian) German *smǫie* soft, supple, of unknown origin. The figurative sense of pleasant, polished, polite, seemingly friendly or sincere, is first recorded probably about 1390. **—v.** make smooth or smoother. 1340 *smothen,* in *Ayenbite of Inwyt;* from the adjective. **—smoothen** *v.* 1635, formed from English *smooth,* adj. + *-en*[1]. **—smoothie** *n. Informal.* smooth-tongued or suave person. 1929, American English; formed from *smooth,* adj. + *-ie.* **—smooth-tongued** *adj.* speaking smoothly; agreeable or flattering (1592, in Marlowe's *Edward II*).

smorgasbord (smôr′gəsbôrd) *n.* elaborate buffet of hors d'oeuvres. 1893, borrowing of Swedish *smörgåsbord,* formed from *smörgås* bread and butter (*smör* butter + dialectal Swedish *gås* lump of butter) + *bord* table; see SMEAR and BOARD. The figurative sense of a variety of things, principles, subjects, etc., is first recorded in English in 1948.

smother *v.* Probably about 1200 *smeorthren* (implied in *smeorthrinde,* present participle) suffocate with smoke, from *smorthre,* n., dense, stifling smoke (probably before 1200); developed from the stem of Old English (before 800) *smorian* to suffocate, choke; cognate with Middle Low German and Middle Dutch *smōren* to suffocate, stew (modern Dutch *smoren*), Flemish *smoren, smooren* to smoke, be smoky, and possibly with Middle Dutch *smōlen, smölen* to SMOLDER. The spelling *smother* (without the medial *r*) is recorded in Middle English about 1300. The loss of the r- sound may have been due either to a shortening of the initial vowel or to dissimilation. The general sense of suffocate, choke, kill by suffocation, is first recorded before 1548. The figurative sense of stifle, suppress, is first recorded in 1579.

smudge *v.* Probably before 1425 *smogen* (implied in *smoginge,* gerund) to soil, stain, blacken, smirch; of unknown origin. Variant spellings such as *smoog* (1604), *smodge* (1624), and *smoudge* (1565) show the development of the form from Middle English *smogen* to modern English *smudge;* see *drudge* for further explanation of this development. **—n.** dirty mark or stain. 1768-74, from the verb.

smug *adj.* 1551 *smugge* trim, neat, spruce, smart, in a translation of Sir Thomas More's *Utopia;* of uncertain origin, but possibly an alteration of **smucke,* borrowed from Low German *smuk* trim, neat, from Middle Low German *smucken* to adorn, related to Middle High German *smücken* to adorn, and *smiegen* press close; see SMOCK. The meaning of having a self-satisfied or conceited air is found in 1701, in writings of Sir Richard Steele, and is an extension of the earlier sense of smooth, sleek (1582).

smuggle *v.* Before 1687 *smuckle;* 1687 *smuggle;* borrowed from Low German *smukkeln, smuggeln* or Dutch *smokkelen* to bring in or take out (goods) illegally, apparently of a frequentative formation; compare modern Dutch *smuigen* (from Proto-Germanic **smūȝanan*) to sneak (see SMOCK); for suffix see -LE[3]. **—smuggler** *n.* 1661 *smuckellor,* borrowed from Low German *smukkeler* or Dutch *smokkelaar.* The later form *smugler,* recorded in Blount's *Glossographia* (1670), was probably borrowed from Low German *smuggeler,* variant of *smukkeler;* for suffix see -ER[1].

smut *v.* to stain, blacken. Probably before 1425 *smutten* debase, defile; probably a variant of earlier *smotten* (before 1387, in Trevisa's translation of Higden's *Polychronicon*). The Middle English forms are cognate with Middle High German *smotzen, smutzen* (modern German *schmutzen*) make dirty, from Proto-Germanic **smutt-* (earlier **smutn′-*), cognate with Greek *mýdos* wetness, rot, and Sanskrit *mudirá-s* a cloud, from Indo-European **mud-,* root **meud-* moist (Pok.741). The sense of stain with some black substance, blacken, is first recorded in English in 1587. **—n.** 1664, black mark or stain, in Henry More's *Mystery of Iniquity;* from the verb. *Smut* in the sense of a plant disease characterized by black spores is attested as early as 1665 (and implied in *smutty,* 1597). The sense of indecent or obscene language is first recorded in 1698. **—smutty** *adj.* 1597, affected by the plant disease smut; probably formed from English *smut,* n. + *-y*[1]. The meaning of soiled or dirty is recorded about 1645, and that of indecent or obscene in 1668, in Pepys' *Diary.*

snack *v.* to have a light meal. About 1300 *snaken* (of a dog) to bite or snap; probably borrowed from Middle Dutch *snacken* to snatch, chatter, prate; see SNATCH. The meaning of have a mere bite or morsel, eat a light meal, is first recorded in 1807 in a travel book; probably derived from the noun use. **—n.** light meal. 1402 *snak* a bite, taste; from the verb. The meaning of a mere bite or morsel, light meal, is recorded in 1757.

snaffle *n.* bit used on a bridle. 1533, perhaps borrowed from Dutch *snavel* beak, bill; see NIB. **—v.** put a snaffle on (a horse, etc.) 1559, from the noun.

snafu (snafü') *n. Slang.* disorder, confusion, snarl. 1941, American English (Army use), acronym formed from the initial letters of *situation normal - all fouled* (probably a euphemism for *fucked*) *up.* The general sense of confusion, muddle, mix-up, is recorded since 1943. **—adj.** *Slang.* confused, snarled. 1942, American English (Army use); from the noun or acronym. **—v.** *Slang.* put in disorder or chaotic state. 1943, American English (Army use); from the noun or acronym.

snag *n.* 1577-87, stump of a tree or of a branch, in Holinshed's *Chronicles;* borrowed from a Scandinavian source (compare dialectal Norwegian *snage* point of land, *snag* stump, spike, and Old Icelandic *snagi* clothes peg, *snaga* a kind of ax). The meaning of a sharp or jagged projection is first recorded in 1586. The meaning of a tree or branch held fast in a river or lake is found in 1804, in Clark's writings in *Journals of Lewis and Clark Expedition,* and the figurative sense of an obstacle, impediment, in 1829; both in American English. **—v.** 1807, be caught or damaged by a snag; from the noun (possibly influenced by *snagged* jagged, ragged, 1658, formed from *snag,* n. + *-ed*[2]).

snail *n.* Before 1250 *snaile,* in *The Owl and the Nightingale;* developed (with *i* from the earlier *g* as in *nail*) from Old English (before 800) *snægl,* a diminutive form (with *g* for *c*) of *snaca* a snake; literally, creeping thing. Old English *snægl* is cognate with Old Saxon *snegil* snail, Middle Low German *sneil,* Middle High German *snegel* (dialectal German *Schnegel*), from Proto-Germanic **snaȝilás,* Indo-European **snəkilós,* root **snēk-/snək-* (Walde-Pokorny II, 698); Old Icelandic *snigill* (Swedish *snigel,* Danish and Norwegian *snegl*), and Lithuanian *snãke* snail.

snake *n.* 1137 *snāke,* developed from Old English (about 1000) *snaca,* related to *snægl* SNAIL. Old English *snaca* (from Proto-Germanic **snakōn,* Indo-European **(s)nəg-*), translating Latin *scorpiō,* is cognate with Middle Low German *snake;* literally, creeper, Old Icelandic *snākr, snōkr* (modern Icelandic *snákur*) serpent, and possibly with Sanskrit *nagá-s* snake, from Indo-European **(s)nēgós/(s)nōgós/(s)nəg-* (Walde-Pokorny II, 698). The figurative sense of a treacherous person is first recorded in 1590. **—v.** 1653, to twist or wind hair; later, to twist or wind ropes (1815); and to move, wind, or curve like a snake (1848, in Bartlett's *Dictionary of Americanisms*); from the noun. **—snakeskin** *n.* (1825, in Scott's *The Talisman*) **—snaky** *adj.* 1567, snakelike; formed from English *snake,* n. + *-y*[1]. The meaning of winding or twisting, sinuous, tortuous, is first recorded in Shakespeare's *Merchant of Venice* (1596).

snap *n.* 1495 *snappe* a quick, sudden bite or cut; probably borrowed from Dutch or Low German *snappen* to snap, snatch. The Dutch and Low German form is cognate with Middle High German *snappen* to snap, snatch (modern German *schnappen*), Old Icelandic *snapa,* and probably related to Middle Low German and Middle Dutch *snāvel* beak, bill; see NIB. The sense of a quick movement or effort is found in 1631; that of something easily done is first recorded in 1877. **—v.** 1530 *snappe* to bite suddenly, in Palsgrave's *Lesclarcissement;* probably from the noun. The meaning of catch or seize suddenly (usually in the phrase *snap up*) appeared in 1550, followed by the sense of break suddenly or sharply, first recorded in 1602. The meaning of reply with a sharp remark is first recorded in 1647, but is implied earlier in *snappish.* **—adv.** 1583, quickly, smartly, with a snap; from the verb. **—adj.** 1790 (Scottish), quick, smart, sharp; from the verb. **—snapdragon** *n.* flowering garden plant (1573) **—snapping turtle** (1784, American English) **—snappish** *adj.* apt to snap, peevish. 1542, in Udall's translation of Erasmus' *Apothegms;* formed from English *snap,* v. + *-ish*[1]. **—snappy** *adj.* 1825, keen in business; formed from English *snap,* v. + *-y*[1]. The meaning of sharp, harsh, testy, is first recorded in 1834; the informal sense of having snap, crisp, brisk, lively, is first recorded in 1871, in the writings of Mark Twain, and that of stylish, elegant, smart, in 1881. **—snapshot** *n.* (1808, shot fired hastily at an animal; 1890, informal photograph)

snare[1] *n.* noose for catching small animals and birds. Before 1100 *snear;* later *snare* (before 1325); borrowed from a Scandinavian source (compare Old Icelandic *snara* noose, snare, related to *snœri* twisted rope; see NARROW). Old Icelandic *snara* is cognate with Old Saxon *snari* string, cord, Middle Low German and Middle Dutch *snāre* (modern Dutch *snaar*), and Old High German *snaraha, snarha* noose, snare, from Proto-Germanic **snarHō;* also cognate with Old High German *snerhan* to bind, Armenian *nergev* thin, graceful, and Greek *nárkē* numbness, from Indo-European **snerk-/snork-* (Pok.976). **—v.** catch with a snare. About 1395 *snaren,* in the Wycliffe Bible; from the noun.

snare[2] *n.* one of the strings of wire or gut stretched across a drum. 1688, probably borrowed from Dutch *snaar* string; see SNARE[1] noose. **—snare drum** (1873)

snarl[1] *v.* to growl and bare the teeth. 1589 *snarle,* frequentative verb formed with *le,* see -LE[3]; from earlier *snar* (1530, in Palsgrave's *Lesclarcissement*). Obsolete English *snar,* meaning to snarl or growl, was perhaps borrowed from Dutch or Low German *snarren* to rattle, probably of imitative origin, similar to Middle Dutch and Middle Low German *snorren* to whir, drone, hum; see SNORE. The figurative sense of speak in a harsh or rude manner is first recorded in 1693, from the earlier meaning of quarrel (1593, in Nashe's writings). **—n.** act of snarling. 1613, probably in the figurative sense of a harsh or rude answer or remark; from the verb.

snarl[2] *n.* tangle. Before 1387, moral snare, temptation, trap, in Trevisa's translation of Higden's *Polychronicon;* probably a diminutive formed from SNARE[1] noose, trap. The literal sense of a tangle or knot is first recorded in 1609. **—v.** to tangle or become tangled. Before

1387 *snarlen* to trick, deceive by guile, ensnare; from the noun. The literal sense of tangle, twist together, is first recorded in 1440.

snatch *v.* Probably before 1200 *snecchen* take a sudden snap or bite at something, in *Ancrene Riwle;* later *snacchen* (about 1225); perhaps borrowed from Middle Dutch *snacken* (modern Dutch *snakken*) to snatch, chatter, prate; cognate with Middle Low German and Middle High German *snacken* to chatter, prate, and Old Icelandic *snaka* to sniff about, smell. The meaning of grab or seize suddenly or unexpectedly is first recorded before 1338. **—n.** act of snatching. Probably before 1300 *snacche* trap, snare, in *Kyng Alisaunder;* from the verb. The meaning of a hasty catch, sudden grab, is first recorded in 1577.

snazzy *adj. Slang.* fancy, flashy. 1932, American English; of uncertain origin; sometimes thought of as a blend of *snappy* (in the sense of stylish, elegant) and *jazzy.*

sneak *v.* 1596, move in a stealthy, sly way, in Shakespeare's *1 Henry IV;* the stem *sneak-* is also found earlier in *sneakishly,* adv. (1560). *Sneak* is probably related to early Middle English *sniken* to creep, crawl (probably about 1200), developed from Old English **snician,* related to *snīcan* (before 899). The Old English form *snīcan* (Proto-Germanic **sneikanan*) is cognate with Old Icelandic *snīkja* to desire, reach for sneakily (Norwegian *snike,* Swedish *snika,* Danish *snige* to sneak), and with modern Irish *snighim* I creep, from Indo-European **sneig-/snig-* (Walde-Pokorny II, 698). **—n.** sneaking or contemptible person. Before 1643, in Cartwright's *The Ordinary;* from the verb. **—sneaky** *adj.* 1833, of or like a sneak; formed from English *sneak,* n. + *-y*[1].

sneaker *n.* light shoe with rubber sole. 1895, American English; altered (by influence of *sneaker* one who sneaks, 1598) from earlier *sneak* rubber-soled shoe (1883); so called because the shoe was noiseless and the wearer could sneak about unheard; for suffix see -ER[1].

sneer *v.* Before 1400 *sneren* mock, hold in derision, scoff; probably cognate with North Frisian *sneere* to scorn, and ultimately of imitative origin similar to Middle High German *snerren* to chatter, prate, *snarren* to rattle, and *snurren* to whir, drone, hum; see SNORE. **—n.** sneering look or words. 1707, from the verb.

sneeze *v.* Before 1333 *sniesen, snesen;* alteration of earlier *fnesan* to sneeze (about 1150). According to the OED, the change in form from *fn-* to *sn-* is attributed to a possible misreading or misspelling of *fnesen, fnesan* as *nesen* after the initial combination *fn-* became unfamiliar, but it seems more likely that the initial sound of *f* was gradually lost, producing *nesen* in the early 1300's, and that, influenced by words such as *snort* and *snore, s* began to appear (thus *sn-* replacing *fn-* and *n-*).

The original Middle English form *fnesan* developed from Old English (about 1000) *fnēosan* to snort, sneeze (Proto-Germanic **fneusanan*); cognate with Middle Dutch *fniesen* to sneeze, Old High German *fnehan* to breathe, Old Icelandic *fnȳsa* to snort, and Greek *pneîn* to breathe, *pneûma* breath, from Indo-European **pneu-* (Pok.838). The later Middle English *nesen* to sneeze (probably before 1325) is probably a reduced form of *fnesen* and may be only coincidentally associated with Old Icelandic *hnjōsa,* Swedish *nysa,* and Danish and Norwegian *nyse,* which are cognate with Old High German *niosan* (modern German *niesen*) to sneeze, and Middle Dutch *niesen* (modern Dutch *niezen*). **—n.** 1632, powder for inducing sneezing; from the verb. The meaning of an act of sneezing is recorded in 1646, the earlier form being *nesing* (1382, in the Wycliffe Bible), *neesing* (1609, in Ben Jonson's *The Silent Woman*).

snicker *v.* laugh in a half-suppressed manner; giggle. 1694, possibly of imitative origin, similar to Dutch *snikken* to gasp, sob, Low German *snucken* to sob; for suffix see -ER[4]. **—n.** half-suppressed laugh. 1836, American English; from the verb.

snide *adj.* 1859 (thieves' slang) counterfeit, sham; of unknown origin. The sense of bad, wretched, contemptible, is found in 1903, while that of sneering, insinuating, slyly derogatory, is first recorded in 1933.

sniff *v.* About 1350 *sniffen* draw air through the nose in short quick breaths; possibly related to *snyvelen* SNIVEL. The meaning of sniff in smelling, smell with a sniff or sniffs, is first recorded in 1788, but is probably earlier, as the sense of show contempt by sniffing is found in Swift's writings as early as 1729. **—n.** act or sound of sniffing. 1767, from the verb.

sniffle *v.* sniff again and again. 1819, in Scott's *The Legend of Montrose,* frequentative verb form of SNIFF; for suffix see -LE[3]. **—n.** 1880, sound of sniffling, from the verb. The plural form *sniffles,* meaning a slight head cold, is found earlier, in the Supplement to Jamieson's *Dictionary of the Scottish Language* (1825). The verbal noun and participial adjective *sniffling* are recorded much earlier, the noun in 1653, the adjective in 1631.

snip *v.* 1578 (implied in *snipped*), to snap, snatch; later, to cut, cut off (1593); probably borrowed from Dutch or Low German *snippen* to snip, shred, of unknown origin. **—n.** 1558, small piece cut off; probably borrowed from Dutch or Low German *snip* and *snippe* a small piece, related to *snippen* to snip. The meaning of an act of snipping is first recorded in English in 1676. **—snippers** *n.pl.* 1593, scissors. **—snippy** *adj.* 1727, mean, parsimonious, in Bailey's *Dictionary;* formed from English *snip,* v. + *-y*[1]. The meaning of fault-finding, snappy, sharp, is recorded in Bartlett's *Dictionary of Americanisms* (1848).

snipe *n.* marsh bird with a long bill. Probably before 1300, borrowed from a Scandinavian source (compare Old Icelandic *-snīpa* (in *mȳrisnīpa* marsh snipe), Norwegian *snipe, snipa.* The Scandinavian forms are cognate with Middle Low German and Middle Dutch *snippe* (modern Dutch *snip*), and Old High German *snepfa* (modern German *Schnepfe*) snipe, of unknown origin. **—v.** to shoot from a hidden place at an enemy. 1782, from the noun; so called in allusion to the hunting of the snipe as game. The figurative sense of criticize in a sudden, sharp attack is first recorded in 1892. **—sniper** *n.* 1824, one who snipes; formed from English *snipe,* v. + *-er*[1].

snippet *n.* small piece snipped off. 1664, in Butler's *Hudibras;* formed from English *snip,* v. + *-et.*

snitch[1] *n. Slang.* an informer. 1785, in Grose's *Classical Dictionary of the Vulgar Tongue;* of unknown origin. An earlier meaning "the nose" is recorded before 1700, preceded by the sense of a fillip on the nose (1676, in Elisha Coles' *Dictionary*). **—v.** *Slang.* be an informer. 1801, from the noun.

snitch² v. *Slang.* to snatch, steal. 1904, to take stealthily; perhaps variant of SNATCH, v.

snivel v. About 1300 *snyvelen* to run at the nose, sniffle; developed from Old English **snyflan* (implied in early Middle English *snyflung* sniveling, before 1100); related to Old English *snofl* nasal mucus. Old English *snofl* is cognate with Middle Low German *snuve* nasal mucus, Middle Dutch *snūven* to sniff (modern Dutch *snuiven*), Middle High German *snūben* to blow, snort (modern German *schnauben*), *snupfe* head cold (modern German *Schnupfen*), and probably Old Icelandic *snoppa* snout, Middle Low German *snoppe* nasal mucus. The meaning of make a sniffling sound expressive of real or affected emotion, cry with sniffling, is first recorded in 1690, in Dryden's writings, preceded by the sense of affect by sniveling (1668). —**n.** About 1440, mucus running from the nose; from the verb. The meaning of a sniveling or sniffling is first recorded in Dicken's *Dombey and Son* (1848).

snob n. one having pretensions to rank, wealth, etc. 1781, a slang word meaning a shoemaker or shoemaker's apprentice; of unknown origin. About 1796, in Cambridge University slang, *snob* was used in the extended sense of any townsman or local merchant, and by 1831 use was broadened to include any person of the ordinary or lower classes of society of nineteenth-century England. The now common meaning of a person who has pretensions to social importance, and wishes to associate with those who are socially prominent, was popularized by Thackeray in such works as *The Irish Sketch-Book* (1843), *The Snob Papers* (1846), and especially *The Book of Snobs* (1848), which consists of satirical pieces originally published in the magazine *Punch.* —**snobbery** n. 1833, the class of snobs (people belonging to ordinary classes of society); later, the character or quality of being a snob (people having social pretensions), snobbishness (1843); formed from English *snob* + *-ery.* —**snobbish** adj. of or like a snob. 1840, in Dickens' *The Old Curiosity Shop;* formed from English *snob* + *-ish¹*. —**snobbishness** n. 1846, in Thackeray's *Snob Papers;* formed from English *snobbish* + *-ness.*

snood n. net or bag worn over a woman's hair. Before 1225 *snod* ribbon for the hair; developed from Old English (before 800) *snōd,* from Proto-Germanic **snōđṓ,* Indo-European **snōtā́,* root **snē-/snō-* (Pok. 973); cognate with Breton *neud* thread, and Old Irish *snāth* thread, *snāthat* NEEDLE. The spelling *snood* is first recorded in English in 1643, preceded by *snude* (1535). The modern sense of a net or bag worn over a woman's hair is first recorded in 1938, in American English. —**v.** bind (hair) with a snood. 1725, from the noun.

snooker n. kind of pool game. 1889, of uncertain origin. An explanation found in the OED Supplement is that the word is an allusive use (with reference to the rawness of the play of a fellow officer) of earlier British slang *snooker* a newly joined cadet (1872). It was supposedly first applied to the game by a Colonel Chamberlain, while stationed with his regiment in Central India in 1875. —**v.** to block (a player) in snooker. 1889, from the noun. The figurative sense of baffle, stymie, fool, is first recorded in 1915.

snoop v. *Informal.* go about in a sneaking, prying way. 1832, American English (probably with an original meaning of take food on the sly); borrowed from Dutch *snoepen* eat in secret, eat sweets, sneak, steal (food), probably related to *snappen* to bite, snatch, SNAP. Dutch *snoepen* is cognate with East Frisian *snōpen* eat in secret, and Norwegian *snope* to chew, munch. —**n.** *Informal.* person who snoops. 1891, American English; from the verb. The sense of an act of snooping is first recorded in 1908. —**snoopy** *adj. Informal.* 1895, inclined to snoop; formed from English *snoop,* v. + *-y¹*.

snoot n. *Slang.* nose. 1861, originally a Scottish variant of SNOUT. —**v.** *Slang.* treat with contempt; look down the nose at. 1928, American English; from the noun. —**snooty** *adj. Informal.* acting haughtily, snobbish, conceited. 1919, in writings of Aldous Huxley; probably an alteration of earlier *snouty* (1858), formed from English *snout* + *-y¹*; from the idea of looking down the nose at someone.

snooze v. *Informal.* take a nap, doze. 1789, probably a cant or slang word, of unknown origin (possibly in part influenced by the form of *sneeze,* and more distantly, *doze*). —**n.** *Informal.* a nap. 1793, from the verb.

snore v. 1440 *snoren* to snore, in *Promptorium Parvulorum;* earlier, to snort (about 1400); probably related to SNORT, and both probably of imitative origin, similar to Middle Dutch and Middle Low German *snorren* to whir, drone, hum, Middle High German *snurren* (modern German *schnurren*) to rattle, *snarchen* (modern German *schnarchen*) to snore, from Proto-Germanic **snark-,* Indo-European **snorg-,* root **snerg-* (Pok.975). —**n.** sound of snoring. Before 1338, a snort, snorting, in Mannyng's *Chronicle of England;* probably of imitative origin, similar to the verb. The meaning of a sound of snoring is first recorded in Shakespeare's *Macbeth* (1605).

snorkel (snôr′kəl) n. 1944 *Schnorkel,* 1949 *snorkel* periscopelike intake and exhaust shaft of a submarine; borrowed from German navy slang *Schnorchel* nose, related to German *schnarchen* to SNORE; so called from the resemblance of the snorkel to a nose projecting from the submarine, and its noise, when in operation, to that of a snore. The transferred meaning of a curved tube used by a swimmer to breathe underwater is first recorded in 1953, in writings of Jacques Cousteau. —**v.** to travel or swim using a snorkel. About 1950, from the noun.

snort v. About 1410 *snorten* to snore, in Chaucer's *Canterbury Tales;* probably related to *snoren* to snort, SNORE. The meaning of force the breath through the nose with a loud, harsh sound, is first recorded in Palsgrave's *Lesclarcissement* (1530). An earlier sense of turn up (the nose) is found probably before 1400, in Chaucer's translation of *Roman de la Rose.* —**n.** 1619, a snore; from the verb. The meaning of an act of snorting is first recorded in Jamieson's *Dictionary of the Scottish Language* (1808).

snot n. *Slang.* About 1425 *snot* nasal mucus; earlier, *snotte* snuff of a candle (about 1395); probably developed from Old English *gesnot* nasal mucus, from Proto-Germanic **snuttán,* earlier **snutnán;* cognate with Old Frisian *snotta* nasal mucus, Middle Low German and Middle Dutch *snotte* (modern Dutch *snot*), Middle High German *snuz,* Old High German *snuzza,* Norwegian *snottet* snotty. A cognate outside Germanic is found in Middle Irish *snūad* river, from Indo-European **sneu-d-/snu-d-* (Pok.972). —**snotty** *adj.* 1570, foul with snot, in Levins' *Dictionary;* formed from English *snot* + *-y¹*. The meaning (originally dialectal) of impudent, curt, conceited, is found in 1870.

snout n. Probably about 1225 *snute* a person's nose

(used derisively), in *King Horn;* possibly borrowed from, or at least cognate with, Middle Low German and Middle Dutch *snūte* (modern Dutch *snuit*) snout, modern German *Schnauze,* Norwegian *snute* snout, from Proto-Germanic **snūt-* and related to Old English *gesnot* SNOT. Both the spelling *snout* and the sense of the projecting nose of an animal such as a dog or pig are found in Middle English in *Kyng Alisaunder* (probably before 1300), preceded by *snute* in the sense of an elephant's trunk (before 1250).

snow *n.* Probably before 1200, developed from Old English (before 830) *snāw;* cognate with Old Frisian *snē* snow, Old Saxon *snēo,* Middle Low German *snē,* Middle Dutch *snee* (modern Dutch *sneeuw*), Old High German *snēo* (modern German *Schnee*), Old Icelandic *snær, snjōr* (Norwegian *snø,* Swedish *snö,* Danish *sne*), and Gothic *snaiws,* from Proto-Germanic **snaiwaz.* Cognates outside Germanic include Old Irish *snechtae, snechte* (modern Irish *sneachta*) snow, Latin *nix* (genitive *nivis*), Greek (accusative) *nípha,* Lithuanian *sniẽgas,* Latvian *snìegs,* Old Prussian *snaygis,* Old Slavic *snĕgŭ* (Russian *sneg*), Avestan *snaēža-* to snow, and Prakrit *siṇeha-* snow, from Indo-European **sneigwh-/snoigwh-/snigwh-* (Pok.974). **—v.** Probably before 1300 *snowen,* in *Kyng Alisaunder;* from the noun. **—snowball** *n.* (probably before 1200, in Layamon's *Chronicle of Britain*); *v.* (1684, form snowballs; 1855, throw snowballs at; 1929, grow like a rolling snowball) **—snowbank** *n.* (1779) **—snowbound** *adj.* (1814, in writings of Byron) **—snowdrift** *n.* (before 1325, in *Cursor Mundi*) **—snowdrop** *n.* small plant with white flowers that blooms early in the spring. 1664, in Robert Boyle's *Experimental History of Colours.* **—snowfall** *n.* (1821, a fall of snow; 1875, amount of snow falling at a certain place) **—snowflake** *n.* (1734) **—snowman** *n.* (1827) **—snowmobile** *n.* 1931, formed from English *snow,* n. + *(auto)mobile.* **—snowplow** *n.* (1792, American English) **—snowshoe** *n.* (1674) **—snowstorm** *n.* (1771) **—snow-white** *adj.* About 1386, in Chaucer's *Canterbury Tales,* developed from Old English *snāwhwīt* (about 1000, in Ælfric's *Homilies*), formed from *snāw* snow + *hwīt* white. **—snowy** *adj.* 1600, having snow; developed from Old English *snāwig* (about 1000), formed from *snāw* snow + *-ig -y*[1]. The sense of covered with snow is first recorded in 1548; the sense of white as snow, in 1590.

snub *v.* Probably before 1250 *snibben* reprove, rebuke; later *snubben* (about 1340); borrowed from a Scandinavian source (compare Old Icelandic *snubba* to curse, scold, reprove, dialectal Norwegian and Swedish *snubba* to cut short, reprove). The meaning of treat coldly or with contempt appeared in the 1700's. An earlier literal meaning of shorten, cut, nip, or break off, is first recorded in 1615. **—n.** 1537, act or instance of snubbing, sharp rebuke; from the verb. Middle English *snibbe* (about 1350), with the same meaning, was derived from *snibben* to snub. The meaning of a cold or scornful treatment appeared in the 1700's. **—adj.** (of the nose) short and turned up at the tip. 1724, from the verb in the sense of shorten, cut, nip off. **—snub-nosed** *adj.* (1725)

snuff[1] *n.* burned part of a candlewick. Before 1382 *snoffe,* in the Wycliffe Bible; later *snuffe* (probably before 1475); of unknown origin. —**v.** Before 1450 *snuffen* to cut or pinch off the snuff; from the noun. The meaning of extinguish, put out (a candle), is recorded in Miege's *Dictionary* (1687); the figurative use, as in *to snuff out a life,* is first recorded in Byron's *Don Juan* (1818).

snuff[2] *v.* draw in through the nose. Before 1477 *snoffen* clear one's nose, sniffle, in Chaucer's *Canterbury Tales;* later *snuff* to draw in through the nose, inhale (1527); borrowed from Dutch or Flemish *snuffen* to sniff, snuff, related to Dutch *snuiven* to sniff; see SNIVEL. The meaning of inhale powdered tobacco, take snuff, first occurs in Scottish, in Allan Ramsay's *The Gentle Shepherd* (1725), and may have been introduced by Scottish soldiers stationed in the Low Countries during the 1600's. **—n.** powdered tobacco taken into the nose. 1683, borrowed from Dutch or Flemish *snuf,* shortened from *snuftabak* snuff tobacco, from *snuffen* to sniff, snuff. The practice of taking snuff became fashionable in England probably about 1680, but existed earlier in Ireland and Scotland. **—snuffbox** *n.* (1687)

snuffle *v.* breathe noisily through a partly clogged nose. 1583, to sniff at contemptuously; probably borrowed from Dutch or Flemish *snuffelen* to sniff about, pry, related to Dutch and Flemish *snuffen* to sniff, SNUFF[2]. The meaning of breathe noisily through a partly clogged nose is first recorded about 1600. **—n.** Before 1764, act or sound of snuffing; from the verb. An earlier sense of a surge (of the sea) is found in 1630, in writings of Captain John Smith.

snug *adj.* About 1595, (of a ship) compact, trim, well prepared, in Hakluyt's *Voyages;* perhaps borrowed from a Scandinavian source (compare Swedish *snygg* neat, trim, and Old Icelandic *snøggr* short-haired, related to *snaudhr* bare, poor). Old Icelandic *snaudhr* is cognate with Middle High German *snœde* contemptible, base (modern German *schnöde*), and Middle Dutch *snōde* (modern Dutch *snood*). The sense of in a state of ease or comfort is first recorded in 1630. The meaning of fitting closely is not found before 1838. **—v.** 1583, to nestle; later, to make comfortable and tidy, make snug (1787); probably from the adjective, although recorded earlier, probably by accident of the record.

snuggle *v.* lie or press closely, nestle. 1687, in Miege's *Dictionary;* frequentative form of SNUG, v.; for suffix see -LE[3].

so *adv., conj.* Probably about 1150, developed from Old English (about 700) *swā, swǣ;* cognate with Old Frisian *sā, sō* so, Old Saxon *sō,* Middle Dutch *sō* (modern Dutch *zoo*), Old High German *sō* (modern German *so*), Old Icelandic *svā,* and Gothic *swa* so, *swē* as. Cognates outside Germanic include Old Latin *suād* so, Latin *sī* if, and Greek *hōs* thus, earlier **swōs* (Pok.884). Compare AS and ALSO. **—so-and-so** *n.* (1596, something unspecified, in Spenser's *Faerie Queene;* 1897, a euphemistic term of abuse) **—so-called** *adj.* (1657, called by that name; 1837, incorrectly named, in Carlyle's *The French Revolution*) **—so-so** *adv.* tolerably, indifferently (1530, in Palsgrave's *Lesclarcissement*); *adj.* neither very good nor very bad (1542, in Udall's translation of Erasmus' *Apothegms*).

soak *v.* About 1340 *soken* wet through, saturate; developed from Old English (about 1000) *socian,* related to *sūcan* to SUCK. **—n.** act or process of soaking. About 1450 *soke;* from the verb.

soap *n.* Before 1250 *sope;* developed from Old English (about 1000) *sāpe;* cognate with Middle Low German and Middle Dutch *sēpe* (modern Dutch *zeep*) soap, Old High German *seifa* (modern German *Seife*), and probably Old Icelandic *sāpa* (Swedish *såpa*, Norwegian *såpe*, Danish *sæbe*), though the Old Icelandic word might have been borrowed from Old English *sāpe*, from West Germanic **saipō*. Late Latin *sāpō* soap, the source of French *savon*, Italian *sapone*, Spanish *jabón*, etc., is probably ultimately from Germanic; see SAPONACEOUS. **—v.** rub or treat with soap. 1585, from the noun. **—soapbox** *n.* (1660) **—soap opera** radio or television serial drama. 1939, American English; so called because early sponsors of the programs were soap manufacturers.

soar *v.* About 1380 *soren* fly high, in Chaucer's *House of Fame;* borrowed from Old French *essorer* fly up, soar, from Vulgar Latin **exaurāre* rise into the air (Latin *ex-* out + *aura* breeze; see AURA). **—n.** 1596, altitude attained in soaring; from the verb. The meaning of an act of soaring is first recorded in Coleridge's *Biographia Literaria* (1817).

sob *v.* Before 1200 *sobben* to cry with short, quick breaths, in *Vices and Virtues;* probably of imitative origin. **—n.** a sobbing. About 1385 *sobbe*, in Chaucer's *Troilus and Criseyde;* from the verb. **—sob sister** 1912, reporter who writes sentimental stories, American English; later, sentimental, impractical person (1913). **—sob story** overly sentimental story, hard-luck story (1913, American English).

sober *adj.* 1340 *sobre* moderate, temperate, in *Ayenbite of Inwyt;* borrowed from Old French *sobre*, learned borrowing from Latin, and possibly borrowed into English directly from Latin *sōbrius* not drunk, temperate (**sō-* variant of *sē-* apart from, without + *ēbrius* drunk, of uncertain origin). The sense of not drunk or intoxicated is first recorded in Middle English about 1384, in the Wycliffe Bible. The sense of serious, solemn, is first recorded before 1390. **—v.** make or become sober. About 1375 *sobren* to calm, appease; from the adjective. The sense of make sober is first recorded in Pope's translation of Homer's *Odyssey* (1726); the sense of become sober is first recorded in 1820. **—sobriety** *n.* 1402 *sobriete* quality of being temperate or sober; borrowed from Middle French *sobriété*, learned borrowing from Latin *sōbrietās*, from *sōbrius* sober, adj.; for suffix see -TY².

sobriquet (sō'brəkā) *n.* nickname. 1646, borrowing of French *sobriquet*, from Middle French *soubriquet* a chuck under the chin, of unknown origin.

soccer *n.* game played with a ball which is kicked between two teams of eleven players each. 1889 *socca;* later, *socker* (1891), *soccer* (1895); originally university slang, from a shortened form of *assoc.*, abbreviation of *association* (football); for suffix see -ER⁵.

sociable *adj.* 1553, liking society, friendly, in Thomas Wilson's *The Art of Rhetoric;* borrowing of Middle French *sociable*, and borrowed directly from Latin *sociābilis* easily joined in partnership, close, intimate, from *sociāre* to join, unite, join as a companion, from *socius* companion; see SOCIAL; for suffix see -ABLE. **—sociability** *n.* Before 1471 *socibbilitee* friendly discourse or expression, formed from Latin *sociābilis* close, intimate + Middle English *-itee, -ite* -ity.

social *adj.* Before 1387 *sociale* domestic, in Trevisa's translation of Higden's *Polychronicon;* borrowing of Middle French *social*, and borrowed directly from Latin *sociālis* united, living with others, from *socius* associate, companion, from earlier **soqwyos*, related to Latin *sequī* to follow, and cognate with Old Icelandic *seggr* companion, man, Old Saxon *segg*, Old English *secg*, and possibly Sanskrit *sákhā* companion, friend, from Indo-European **sekw-* (Pok.896); for suffix see -AL¹. The meaning of marked by companionship or friendliness is first recorded in Milton's *Paradise Lost* (1667), and that of living or liking to live with others, in 1722. **—n.** social gathering. 1870, from the adjective. An earlier sense of companion, associate, is found in 1632. **—socialization** *n.* 1841, process of making social; formed from English *socialize* + *-ation*. The sense of a process of making socialistic is first recorded in 1884. **—socialize** *v.* 1828, to make social, borrowed from French *socialiser*, formed from *social*, adj., social + *-iser* -ize. The meaning of make socialistic in nature (as in *to socialize medicine*) is first recorded in Worcester's *Dictionary* (1846). **—social science** (1785, in writings of John Adams) **—social security** (1908, in writings of Winston Churchill) **—social studies** (before 1854, in writings of John Stuart Mill) **—social work** (1890) **—social worker** (1904)

socialism *n.* social organization in which the means of production and distribution are collectively owned. 1837, formed from English *social* + *-ism*, perhaps after earlier *socialist*. Apparently *socialism* was first used in English with reference to Robert Owen's efforts to achieve social reform through small experimental communities. However, the French word *socialisme* was probably first used in 1831 with reference to the teachings of the French social scientist Comte de Saint-Simon (1760-1825), regarded as the founder of French socialism.**—socialist** *n.* 1827, supporter of socialism; borrowed from French *socialiste* or formed independently from English *social*, adj. + *-ist*. **—socialistic** *adj.* 1848, formed from English *socialist* + *-ic*.

socialite *n.* member of fashionable society. 1928, American English (probably a coinage among writers and editors at *Time* magazine); formed from *social*, adj. + *-ite*¹.

society *n.* 1531, companionship, fellowship, in Elyot's *The Boke Named the Governour;* borrowed from Middle French *societé*, learned borrowing from Latin, and probably borrowed into English directly from Latin *societās*, from *socius* companion; see SOCIAL; for suffix see -TY². The meaning of an organized group with a common interest or purpose, club, association, is first recorded before 1548, and that of a system or condition of living with others as a community, in 1553. The sense of fashionable people or their doings is first recorded in Byron's *Don Juan* (1823). The sense in ecology of a plant society is first recorded in 1899.

socio- a combining form meaning: **1** of society, social, as in *sociodrama* = *play involving social situations* (1943), *sociopath* = *person lacking social sense, antisocial person* (1930), *sociobiology* = *the study of the biological basis of social behavior* (1946), *sociolinguistics* = *the study of language in its social context* (1939). **2** social and _____, as in *socioeconomic* = *involving social and economic factors* (1883), *sociocultural* = *of or involving social and cultural aspect of society* (before 1930). **3** of or having to do with sociology, sociological, as in *sociography* = *sociological analysis or description* (1881). Borrowed from French *socio-*, combining form of Latin *socius* companion, associate, on the analogy of similar combining forms derived from Greek, such as *psycho-*.

sociology *n.* study of the nature, origin, and development of society. 1843, borrowed from French *sociologie*, from *socio-* (from Latin *socius* associate, companion; see SOCIAL) + *-logie* -logy. French *sociologie* was coined in 1830 by the French philosopher and social reformer Auguste Comte, 1798-1857. **—sociological** *adj.* 1843, formed from English *sociology* + *-ical.* A variant form *sociologic* (1861) was formed in English from *sociology* + *-ic* on the model of French *sociologique.* **—sociologist** *n.* 1843, formed from English *sociology* + *-ist.*

sock[1] *n.* short stocking. About 1330, developed from Old English (before 800) *socc* light slipper; an early borrowing from Latin *soccus* light low-heeled shoe. Also borrowed from Latin are Middle Dutch *socke, soc* (modern Dutch *sok*) sock, Old High German *soc* (modern German *Socke*), and Old Icelandic *sokkr.* Latin *soccus* is borrowed from Greek **sókchos,* variant of *sýkchos, sykchás* a kind of shoe, of Eastern origin; compare Avestan *haxa-* sole of the foot.

sock[2] *v. Slang.* strike or hit hard. Before 1700, of uncertain origin. **—n.** *Slang.* hard blow. Before 1700, from the same (uncertain) source as the verb.

sockdolager (sokdol′əjər) *n. Slang.* 1830, a decisive blow; American English, fanciful formation from SOCK[2] to hit hard. The extended sense of something unusual or exceptional is first recorded in 1838, also in American English.

socket *n.* Probably before 1300 *soket* spearhead (originally, such a weapon shaped like a plowshare), in *Arthour and Merlin;* borrowed from Anglo-French *soket,* diminutive formed from Old French *soc* plowshare, from Vulgar Latin **soccus,* probably from a Gaulish source (compare Welsh *swch* plowshare, Middle Irish *soc* plowshare, hog's snout, and Old Irish *socc* hog; see SOW[2]); for suffix see -ET. The meaning of a hollow part or piece for receiving and holding something is first recorded in Middle English before 1425, in a translation of Chauliac's *Grande Chirurgie.*

sod *n.* ground covered with grass, turf. Before 1450, probably borrowed from Middle Dutch *sode* (modern Dutch *zode*) turf, or Middle Low German *sode, sade,* corresponding to Old Frisian *sātha* sod, all of uncertain origin. Connection with *seethe* has been conjectured, on the supposition that the word may have originally denoted turf used as fuel, but evidence for this is lacking.**—v.** cover with pieces of sod. Probably about 1400 *sodden* bury, cover with sod (implied in *i-sod,* past participle); possibly from the noun, though recorded somewhat earlier.

soda *n.* 1471 *sode* alkaline substance containing sodium, sodium carbonate; later *soda* saltwort (before 1500); borrowed from Italian *soda* a kind of saltwort from which sodium is obtained, soda, from Arabic *suwwād* the name of a variety of saltwort, related to *sawād* black, the color of the plant. It was formerly widely believed that *soda* came into the various European languages from a Medieval Latin **soda* (the supposed source of *sodanum* a kind of saltwort), from Arabic *ṣudā'* headache, presumably because the plant was used to make a headache remedy. The modern scholars Steiger and Hess and Corominas have demonstrated, however, that the word most likely came into Italian directly from the Arabic *suwwād,* since that was the name of a variety of saltwort exported from North Africa to Sicily in the Middle Ages. Italian *soda* is indeed the earliest form documented (in the 1300's or early 1400's), followed by Middle English *sode,* Middle French *soude* (1527), and Spanish *soda* (1555). The meaning of carbonated water (originally, water containing a solution of sodium bicarbonate) is first recorded in English in 1834, shortened from the earlier term *soda water* (1802). **—soda fountain** (1824, American English)

sodality (sōdal′ətē) *n.* fellowship, friendship. 1600, borrowed from Middle French *sodalité,* or directly from Latin *sodālitātem* (nominative *sodālitās*) companionship, a brotherhood, from *sodālis* companion; see ETHNIC; for suffix see -ITY.

sodden *adj.* soaked through. About 1390 *soden* boiled, in Chaucer's *Canterbury Tales* (earlier *sothen,* alteration influenced by *sethen* to seethe, before 1325); developed from Old English *soden,* past participle of *sēothan* to cook, boil; see SEETHE. The meaning of soaked through is first recorded in Keats' *Hyperion* (1820), preceded by the transferred sense of resembling one that has been soaked or steeped in water, dull-looking or stupid from drunkenness (1599, in Ben Jonson's *Cynthia's Revels*).

sodium *n.* metallic chemical element. 1807, New Latin, from English *soda;* for suffix see -IUM. The name *sodium* was coined in 1807 by the English chemist Sir Humphry Davy, 1778-1829, because he isolated this element from caustic soda (sodium hydroxide).

sodomy *n.* unnatural sexual intercourse. Probably about 1280 *sodomye,* borrowed from Old French *sodomie,* from *Sodome* Sodom, from Latin *Sodoma,* ultimately from Hebrew *s'dōm,* a morally corrupt city in ancient Palestine which was destroyed, together with Gomorrah, by fire from heaven (in the Bible, Genesis 18 and 19); for suffix see -Y[3]. **—sodomite** *n.* one who practices sodomy. Before 1387, in Trevisa's translation of Higden's *Polychronicon;* borrowed from Old French *sodomite,* from Late Latin *sodomīta* inhabitant of Sodom, from Latin *Sodoma* Sodom. **—sodomize** *v.* commit sodomy on. 1868, formed from English *sodomy* + *-ize.*

sofa *n.* 1625, (in eastern countries) cushioned dais for reclining, in Purchas' *Pilgrims;* borrowed from Arabic *ṣuffah* bench. The sense of a long, upholstered seat or couch is first found in 1717.

soft *adj.* Before 1114 *softe* meek, mild; developed from Old English *sōfte* (about 1000, in Ælfric's *Homilies*); later, alteration (influenced by *sōfte,* adv., soft) of *sēfte* gentle, easy, comfortable, agreeable. Old English *sēfte* is cognate with Old Saxon *sāfti* soft, Middle Dutch *sachte* (modern Dutch *zacht*), Middle High German *senfte,* and Old High German *semfti* (modern German *sanft*),from Proto-Germanic **samthijaz,* cognate with Sanskrit *sant(i)ya-s* in fellowship, from Indo-European **som-tiyo-s.* These adjectives are probably cognate with Old Icelandic *semja* to arrange, settle, Gothic *samjan* to please, and outside Germanic with Sanskrit *samá-s* level, equal, SAME, the semantic connection between these words being (approximately): uniform, level even, smooth, gentle, easy, soft. The sense of yielding to the touch, not hard, is found in Middle English before 1200, in Layamon's *Chronicle of Britain.* **—adv** in a soft manner. Probably before 1200 *softe,* in Layamon's *Chronicle of Britain;* developed from Old English *sōfte* (before 1000); cognate with Old Saxon *sāfto,* Middle High German *sanfte,* and Old High German *samfto* (modern German *sanft*) in a soft manner **—softball** *n.* kind of baseball using a larger, softer ball (1926) **—soft drink** (1880) **—soften** *v.* About 1386 *softnen,* in Chaucer's *Legend of Good Women;* forme from Middle English *softe,* adj., soft + *-enen* -en[1]. **—soft-hearted** *adj.* (1593, in Shakespeare's *2 Henry VI*) **—soft-land** *v.* land (a spacecraft) slowly (1958). **—soft-pedal** *v.* tone down, play down (1915, American English). **—soft shoe** kind of dancing (1927, American English). **—soft soap** (1634, semiliquid soap; 1830, flattery, American English) **—soft-soap** *v.* (1840, to flatter, American English) **—soft-spoken** *adj.* (1609, in Ben Jonson's *The Silent Woman*) **—software** *n.* computer programs (1960, patterned on *hardware*) **—softy** *n. Informal.* 1863, weak or silly person, formed from English *soft,* adj. + *-y*[3]. The sense of a soft-hearted person is first recorded in 1886.

soggy *adj.* Before 1722, perhaps formed from earlier dialectal English *sog* bog, swamp (1538, of unknown origin) + *-y*[1]. Alternatively, *soggy* may have been formed from an earlier verb *sog* become soaked (1440 *soggon,* past participle; of unknown origin) + *-y*[1].

soil[1] *v.* make dirty. Before 1250 *soillen,* in *Ancrene Riwle;* borrowed from Old French *souillier* to soil, make dirty; originally, to wallow, from *soil, souil* tub, wild boar's wallow, pigsty, from Latin *solium* tub for bathing, seat, probably related to *sedēre to* SIT.

The original etymology of the Old French was given as being from Vulgar Latin **suculāre,* from Late Latin *suculus* little pig, but this has been superseded by von Wartburg's work in the FEW.

soil[2] *n.* ground, earth, dirt. Probably before 1300 *sol* land, area, place; later *soyle* dirt, the ground (probably about 1380); borrowed from Anglo-French *soil* piece of ground, place, from Latin *solium* seat (see SOIL[1]), influenced in meaning by Latin *solum* soil, ground; see SOLE[1] bottom of the foot.

soiree or **soirée** (swärā') *n.* evening party or social gathering. 1793, a French word used in the *Journals* of Fanny Burney, from French *soir* evening, from Old French *soir,* variant of *seir,* from Latin *sērō,* adv., late, at a late hour, from *sērum* late hour, neuter of *sērus* late; see SINCE.

sojourn (sō'jėrn) *v.* Probably before 1300 *soiournen* stay for a time, in *Arthour and Merlin;* borrowed from Old French *sojorner* stay or dwell for a time, from Vulgar Latin **subdiurnāre* to spend the day (Latin *sub-* under, until + *diurnus* of a day, DIURNAL). **—n.** brief stay. About 1250 *suriurn,* in *Genesis and Exodus;* later *soiourne* (probably before 1300); borrowed from Old French *sojorn,* from *sojorner* to sojourn.

sol[1] (sōl) *n.* fifth note of the musical scale. Before 1380, borrowed from Medieval Latin *sol,* from the initial syllable of Latin *solve* purge, the word sung to this note in the Hymn for St. John the Baptist's day; see GAMUT.

sol[2] (sol) *n.* colloidal solution. 1899, W.B. Hardy in *The Journal of Physiology;* shortened form of SOLUTION.

Sol (sol) *n.* sun. 1392, borrowed from Latin *sōl* the sun; see SOLAR.

solace (sol'is) *n.* Probably before 1300 *solas* joy, comfort, relief, in *Arthour and Merlin;* borrowed from Old French *solas,* from Latin *sōlācium,* from *sōlārī* to console, soothe; see SILLY. **—v.** to comfort, relieve. Probably about 1280 *solacen;* borrowed from Old French *solacier, solasier* to console, from *solas* solace, n.

solar *adj.* of the sun. About 1450, borrowed from Latin *sōlāris,* from *sōl* sun; for suffix see -AR. Latin *sōl* is cognate with Old Icelandic *sōl* (Norwegian, Swedish, and Danish *sol*) sun, Gothic *sauil,* Greek (Attic) *hḗlios,* (Homeric) *ēélios,* Welsh *haul,* Lithuanian and Latvian *sáulė,* and Sanskrit *sū́ra-s,* from Indo-European **sə̄wel-/sāwol-/sūl-* (Pok.881). **—solar cell** (1955) **—solar power** (1908) **—solar system** (before 1704, in Locke's *Elements of Natural Philosophy*)

solarium (səlãr'ēəm) *n.* room used for taking the sun. 1891, borrowing of Latin *sōlārium* sundial, solarium, from *sōl* sun; see SOLAR. An earlier sense of a sundial is found in English in 1842.

solder (sod'ər) *n.* metal or alloy that can be melted and used for joining metal surfaces. About 1320 *soudour;* borrowed from Old French *soldure,* from *solder* to join with solder, from Latin *solidāre* to make solid, from *solidus* SOLID. The spelling with *l* is first recorded in 1428 as Middle English *souldour,* in imitation of the Latin. The pronunciation without *l* (as represented in the earliest Middle English spelling) has been retained in the United States; in Great Britain the *l* is usually pronounced. **—v.** to join with solder. Before 1450 *soudren;* from the noun.

soldier *n.* Probably before 1300 *souder,* in *Arthour and Merlin;* borrowed from Old French *soudier, soldeer* one who serves in an army for pay, soldier, from Medieval Latin *soldarius* a soldier; literally, one having pay; also influenced by Old French *sout* pay, from Late Latin *soldum,* from the accusative of Latin *solidus* a Roman gold coin, SOLIDUS. The spelling with *l* is found in Middle English probably before 1350 as *soldeyour* in imitation of the Latin; the spelling *soldier* is first recorded about 1590. **—v.** act or serve as a soldier. 1647, from the noun.

sole[1] *n.* bottom of the foot. About 1325, borrowing of Old French *sole,* from Latin *solea* sandal, bottom of a shoe, from *solum* bottom, ground, soil, of uncertain origin. The sense of the bottom of a shoe or boot is found in Middle English in 1378-79. **—v.** put a sole on. 1570, in Levins' *Dictionary;* from the noun.

sole[2] *adj.* one and only, single. About 1395 *soul* single, unmarried, in Chaucer's *Canterbury Tales;* borrowed from Old French *soul, sol* (feminine *soule, sole*), from Latin *sōlus* alone, perhaps related to *sed, sēd, sē* without, and *suī* of oneself; see SUICIDE[1]. The sense of one and only (as in *one's sole support*) is found in Middle English in Trevisa's translation of Bartholomew's *De Proprietatibus Rerum* (before 1398).

sole[3] *n.* kind of flatfish. 1252, borrowed from Old French *sole,* from Latin *solea* a kind of flatfish; originally, sandal (see SOLE[1]); so called from the resemblance of the fish to a sandal.

solecism (sol'əsizəm) *n.* mistake in using words; violation of the rules of grammar. 1577, borrowed from Middle French *solécisme,* and directly from Latin *soloecismus* mistake in speaking or writing, from Greek *soloikismós,* from *sóloikos* speaking incorrectly, said by ancient writers to refer to *Sóloi,* an Athenian colony in Cilicia, whose form of the Attic dialect the Athenians considered barbarous; for suffix see -ISM. The extended sense of a breach of good manners or etiquette is found in 1599, and that of an error or impropriety of any kind, also in 1599, in Ben Jonson's *Cynthia's Revels.*

solemn (sol'əm) *adj.* Before 1333 *solempne* connected with religion, formal, ceremonial, in Shoreham's poetry; later *solemne* (1340); and in the sense of serious, grave, earnest (before 1375), borrowed from Old French *solempne, solemne,* learned borrowing from Latin *sollemnis* formal, ceremonial, traditional, of uncertain origin. The explanation, traced back to the Roman lexicographer Festus, that Latin *sollemnis* was formed from *sollus* whole + *annus* year (hence the original meaning, occurring annually) is not considered valid by modern scholars such as Ernout and Meillet. **—solemnity** *n.* About 1300 *solempnete;* about 1303 *solemnyte;* borrowed from Old French *solempnité,* learned borrowing from Latin, and borrowed into English directly from Latin *sollemnitās* a solemnity, from Latin *sollemnis* solemn; for suffix see -ITY. **—solemnize** *v.* Before 1382 *solempnysen,* in the Wycliffe Bible; borrowed from Old French *solempniser,* formed from *solempne* solemn + *-iser* -ize.

sol-fa (sōl′fä′) *n.* system of singing the syllables, *do, re, mi, fa, sol, la, ti, do* to tones of the scale; solmization. 1548, in writings of Bishop John Hooper; borrowed from Italian *solfa,* from Medieval Latin *solfa* (*sol* SOL¹ + *fa* FA). In Middle English there was a verb *solfen,* meaning to sing the notes of the scale, recorded about 1380. Middle English *solfen* was probably borrowed from Old French *solfier,* from *solfa* solfa, from Medieval Latin.

solicit *v.* About 1422 *soliciten* to disturb, trouble; 1450, to further (business affairs); borrowed from Middle French *soliciter, solliciter,* from Latin *sollicitāre* to disturb, rouse, bother, from *sollicitus* restless, uneasy; originally, all stirred up (*sollus* whole, entire, earlier **solnos,* related to *salvus* SAFE + *citus* aroused, past participle of *ciēre* shake, excite, set in motion; see CITE). The sense of make requests or appeals, beg, entreat, is first recorded in English in 1509. **—solicitation** *n.* 1492, management; later, act of soliciting (1500-20, in Dunbar's *Poems*); borrowed from Middle French *solicitation,* and directly from Latin *sollicitātiōnem* (nominative *sollicitātiō*) vexation, disturbance, from *sollicitāre* disturb; for suffix see -ATION. **—solicitor** *n.* Before 1420 *solicytour* instigator, in Lydgate's *Troy Book;* later, agent, representative (about 1449); borrowed from Middle French *soliciteur, solliciteur,* from *soliciter, solliciter* to solicit; for suffix see -OR². The specific meaning of lawyer or attorney is first recorded before 1577. *Solicitor* is still a general term for *lawyer* in Great Britain, though a *solicitor* is restricted in practice before certain courts of law.

solicitous *adj.* 1563, showing care or concern, borrowed from Latin *sollicitus* restless, uneasy, careful (see SOLICIT); for suffix see -OUS. **—solicitude** *n.* care, concern. Probably before 1425, in a translation of Chauliac's *Grande Chirurgie;* borrowed from Middle French *sollicitude,* and directly from Latin *sollicitūdō* anxiety, from *sollicitus* restless, uneasy; for suffix see -TUDE.

solid *adj.* 1391 *solide* not hollow, in Chaucer's *Treatise on the Astrolabe;* borrowed from Old French *solide* firm, dense, compact, learned borrowing from Latin, and borrowed into English directly from Latin *solidus* firm, unyielding, whole, entire, related to *salvus* SAFE. The meaning of dense, hard, compact, is first recorded in English about 1532, and that of firm, strong, substantial, in 1586. **—n.** Before 1398, a body that has length, breadth, and thickness, in Trevisa's translation of Bartholomew's *De Proprietatibus Rerum;* from the adjective. The sense of a solid substance, not a liquid or gas, is first recorded in 1698. **—solidify** *v.* 1799, to make solid; borrowed from French *solidifier,* from *solide* solid, from Old French; for suffix see -FY. **—solidity** *n.* 1392 *silidite* (error for *solidite*) quality of being solid; later *solidite* (probably before 1425); borrowed from Middle French *solidité,* from Latin *soliditās* solidness, from *solidus* solid; for suffix see -ITY.

solidarity *n.* unity or fellowship. 1841, borrowed from French *solidarité* joint liability, mutual responsibility, from *solidaire* interdependent, complete, entire, from *solide* SOLID; for suffix see -ITY.

solidus *n.* Roman gold coin, introduced by Constantine. Before 1387 *solidy,* in Trevisa's translation of Higden's *Polychronicon;* later *solidus* (before 1398); borrowed from Late Latin *solidus* an imperial Roman coin, Latin *solidus nummus* solid coin; see SOLID.

soliloquy (səlil′əkwē) *n.* 1604, a talking to oneself, monologue, in Cawdrey's *A Table Alphabeticall;* borrowed from Late Latin *sōliloquium* a talking to oneself (coined by Saint Augustine from Latin *sōlus* alone, SOLE² + *loquī* speak; see LOQUACITY). The word is also found in Middle English in the title *Bok Soliloquijs* (about 1380), translation of Latin *Liber Soliloquiorum,* a treatise written by Saint Augustine. The sense of a literary or dramatic monologue is first recorded in English in 1641. **—soliloquize** *v.* 1759, to talk to oneself; formed from English *soliloquy* + *-ize.*

solitaire (sol′ətãr) *n.* card game played by one person. Before 1500 *solitere* widow; later *solitaire* solitary person, recluse (1716, in Pope's *Letters*); borrowed from French *solitaire,* learned borrowing from Latin *sōlitārius* SOLITARY. The transferred sense of a diamond or other gem set by itself is first recorded in English before 1727 (in French since 1798). The sense of a card game played by one person is found in English in 1746, in Walpole's *Letters* (in French since 1765).

solitary *adj.* About 1340, alone; borrowed from Old French *solitaire,* and directly from Latin *sōlitārius* alone, lonely, from *sōlitās* loneliness, solitude, from *sōlus* alone, SOLE²; for suffix see -ARY. **—n.** person living alone, hermit, recluse. Before 1396, from the adjective.

solitude *n.* Probably 1348, state of being alone; borrowing of Old French *solitude* loneliness, learned borrowing from Latin, and probably borrowed into English directly from Latin *sōlitūdō* loneliness, from *sōlus* alone, SOLE²; for suffix see -TUDE.

solmization (sol′məzā′shən) *n.* = sol-fa. 1730 *solmisation,* borrowing of French *solmisation,* from *solmiser* to sing to the sol-fa syllables (*sol* SOL¹ + *mi* MI); for suffix see -ATION. The spelling *solmization* is first recorded in Grove's *Dictionary of Music and Musicians* (1879).

solo *n.* 1695, in Congreve's *Love for Love;* borrowed from Italian *solo* piece of music for one voice or instrument; literally, alone, from Latin *sōlus* alone, SOLE². The sense of a performance by a single person is found in 1779. **—adj.** arranged for and performed by one voice or instrument. 1776, in Charles Burney's *A General History of Music;* from the noun. The general sense of without a partner or companion, alone, unassisted (as in *a solo flight*) is first recorded in 1909. **—adv.** by oneself, alone. 1712, from the noun. **—v.** 1858, perform a musical solo; from the noun. The meaning of fly solo is found in 1917. **—soloist** *n.* person who performs a solo. 1864, formed from English *solo,* n. + *-ist.*

solstice (sol′stis) *n.* time in the year when the sun is at its greatest angular distance from the equator. About 1250, in *Genesis and Exodus;* borrowed from Old French *solstice,* learned borrowing from Latin *sōlstitium* a point at which the sun seems to stand still (*sōl* sun; see SOLAR + *-stitium,* from earlier **statyom,* as i formed from the past participle *statum* of *sistere* to come to a stop, make stand still, related to *stāre* to STAND). **—solstitial** *adj.* 1559, borrowed from Latin *sōlstitiālis,* from *sōlstitium* solstice; for suffix see -AL[1].

soluble *adj.* that can be dissolved or made into liquid. 1373 *solabill* relaxed, unconstipated; later *soluble* capable of being dissolved (probably before 1425, in a translation of Higden's *Polychronicon*); borrowed from Middle French *soluble,* from Late Latin *solūbilis* that may be loosened or dissolved, from Latin *solvere* loosen, dissolve; see SOLVE.

solution *n.* 1375, a solving or being solved, clarification, explanation, in Barbour's *The Bruce;* borrowed from Old French *solution,* learned borrowing from Latin *solūtiōnem* (nominative *solūtiō*) a loosing or unfastening, a solving, from *solūt-,* past participle stem of *solvere* loosen, untie, solve, dissolve; see SOLVE; for suffix see -TION. The meaning of the act or process of dissolving is first recorded in Middle English in Gower's *Confessio Amantis* (before 1393). The sense of a liquid containing a dissolved substance is found in 1594.

solve *v.* Before 1398 *solven* to disperse, dissipate, loosen, in Trevisa's translation of Bartholomew's *De Proprietatibus Rerum;* borrowed from Latin *solvere* to loosen, dissolve, from **se-luō* (*se-,* variant of *sē-* apart, aside, away + *luere* release, atone, expiate; originally, wash away; see LOSE). The meaning of clear up, explain, answer, is first recorded about 1533, though the corresponding noun sense of clarification, explanation, is the first attested meaning of *solution* (1375).

solvent *adj.* 1653, able to pay all one owes; borrowed from French *solvent,* learned borrowing from Latin *solventem* (nominative *solvēns*), present participle of *solvere* loosen, dissolve (used in *rem solvere* to free one's property and person from debt; compare also the legal Latin phrase *solvendō est* he is in a position to pay); see SOLVE; for suffix see -ENT. The meaning of able to dissolve substances is first recorded in 1686. **—n.** substance that can dissolve other substances. 1671, in writings of Robert Boyle; probably borrowed from Latin *solventem* (nominative *solvēns*), present participle of *solvere* to loosen, dissolve. **—solvency** *n.* ability to pay all one owes. 1717, in Bailey's *Dictionary;* formed from English *solvent,* adj. + *-ency.*

somatic *adj.* of or pertaining to the body. 1775, in Ash's *Dictionary;* borrowed from French *somatique,* and probably directly from Greek *sōmatikós* of the body, from *sôma* (genitive *sṓmatos*) body; see -SOME[3]; for suffix see -IC.

somber *adj.* 1760 *sombre,* in Horace Walpole's *Letters;* borrowed from French *sombre* dark, gloomy, from Old French *sombre,* from a lost verb **sombrer,* from Late Latin *subumbrāre* to shadow (from the phrase *sub umbrā;* Latin *sub* under; *umbrā,* ablative of *umbra* shade, shadow; see UMBRAGE). The spelling *somber* is an Americanism introduced by Noah Webster (1828) on the pattern of *center, theater,* etc.

sombrero (sombrãr′ō) *n.* 1770, borrowing of Spanish *sombrero* a broad-brimmed hat; originally, umbrella or parasol, from *sombra* shade, alteration of Latin *umbra* shade (see UMBRAGE) by influence of Spanish *sol* sun (from Latin *sōl;* see SOLAR); or more traditionally, from *sombrar* to shade, from Late Latin *subumbrāre* to shadow; see SOMBER. An earlier (now obsolete) meaning of an Oriental umbrella or parasol appeared in English in Hakluyt's *Voyages* (1598).

some *adj.,* 1106, *pron.* 1102 *sumne,* in *Peterborough Chronicle;* later *some* (adj. 1340, pron. about 1300); developed from Old English *sum* (about 725, in *Beowulf*); cognate with Old Frisian and Old Saxon *sum* some, Middle Low German and Middle Dutch *som,* Old High German *sum,* Old Icelandic *sumr,* and Gothic *sums,* from Proto-Germanic **sumás.* In some of the modern Germanic languages, this word is restricted to dialectal use, or represented only in derivatives or compounds, such as Dutch *sommige* some. Cognates outside Germanic include Greek *oud(h)amós* not any, *hamê* somehow, and Sanskrit *sama-s* any, related to *samá-s* level, equal, SAME. **—adv.** somewhat; to some degree. About 1280, from the adjective. **—somebody** *pron.* (about 1303, in Mannyng's *Handlyng Synne*) **—somehow** *adv.* (1664) **—someone** *pron.* (about 1305, as a phrase; 1848, as one word) **—something** *pron.* (about 1000, as an Old English phrase; before 1325, as one word) **—sometime** *adv., adj.* (1279, as two words) **—sometimes** *adv.* (1526 *some,* adj. + *times,* n.pl.) **—somewhat** *adv.* (probably about 1200, in *The Ormulum*) **—somewhere** *adv.* (probably about 1200, in *The Ormulum*)

-some[1] a suffix forming adjectives. **1** (added to verbs) tending to, as in *meddlesome = tending to meddle.* **2** (added to nouns) causing, as in *troublesome = causing trouble.* **3** (added to adjectives) to a considerable degree, as in *lonesome = lone to a considerable degree.* Middle English *-som,* developed from Old English *-sum;* cognate with Old Frisian *-sum* -some, Old Saxon *-sam,* Middle Dutch *-sam, -saem* (modern Dutch *-zaam*), Old High German and modern German *-sam,* Old Icelandic *-samr,* and Gothic *-sams* -some, related to *sama* SAME.

-some[2] a suffix added to a number, meaning a group of that number, as in *twosome = a group of two; foursome = a group of four.* Middle English *-sum,* developed from Old English *sum* SOME, pron. Old English *sum* was used after the genitive plural of a numeral as in *sixa sum* six-some; the inflection disappeared in Middle English and the pronoun was suffixed to the numeral.

-some[3] a combining form meaning body, as in *chromosome = color body; ribosome = ribose body; monosome = single body.* Borrowed from New Latin *-soma,* from Greek *sôma* body (from Indo-European **twōm̥*), related to *sōrós* heap, *sṓs* healthy, sound, and possibly cognate with Latin *tōmentum* stuffing (for cushions) and *tumēre* to swell, from Indo-European **twō-, towə-, tu-,* root **tēu-/təu-/tewə-/twō-/tu-/tū-* to swell; stout; strong (Pok.1080).

somersault *n.* 1530, in Palsgrave's *Lesclarcissement;* borrowed from Middle French *sombresault,* from Old Provençal *sobresaut* (*sobre* over, from Latin *suprā* over, above, SUPRA + *saut* a leaping, jump, from Latin *saltus* (genitive *saltūs*), from the root of *salīre* to leap; see SALLY). **—v.** perform a somersault. 1858, from the noun.

somnambulism (somnam′byəlizəm) *n.* sleepwalking. 1797, formed in English from New Latin *somnambulus* sleepwalker (Latin *somnus* sleep + *ambulāre* to walk; see SOMNOLENT and AMBLE) + English suffix *-ism.* **—somnambulant** *adj.* sleepwalking. 1866, formed from New Latin *somnambulus* + English suffix *-ant.* **—somnambulist** *n.* sleepwalker. 1794, in writings of Mary Wollstonecraft; formed from New Latin *somnambulus* + English suffix *-ist.*

somnolent (som′nələnt) *adj.* sleepy, drowsy. About 1460 *sompnolente;* later *somnolent* (1615); probably formed in English as an adjective to *somnolence* on the model of Middle French *sompnolent, somnolent,* learned borrowing from Latin *somnolentus,* from *somnus* sleep; for suffix see -ENT. Latin *somnus* is cognate with Old Irish *sūan* sleep, Welsh *hun,* Greek *hýpnos,* Lithuanian *sãpnas, sapnỹs* dream, Old Slavic *sŭnŭ* sleep, dream, Armenian *k'un,* Sanskrit *svápna-s,* Avestan *xvafna-,* Tocharian B *ṣpäne,* from Indo-European **swépnos/s(w)ópnos/súpnos* (Pok.1048), and Hittite *suppariya-* to sleep. Cognates in Germanic include Old Icelandic *svefn* dream, sleep (Danish and Norwegian *søvn,* Swedish *sömn*), Old English *swefn* sleep, dream, Old Saxon *swebbian* and Old High German *antswebben* put to sleep. **—somnolence** *n.* About 1390, *sompnolence,* in Chaucer's *Canterbury Tales;* borrowed from Old French *sompnolence, somnolence,* from Latin *somnolentia* sleepiness, from *somnolentus* somnolent; for suffix see -ENCE. The spelling *somnolence* is first recorded in Bailey's *Dictionary* (1721).

son *n.* Probably before 1150 *sone;* developed from Old English *sunu* (about 725, in *Beowulf*); cognate with Old Frisian and Old Saxon *sunu* son, Middle Low German and Middle Dutch *sone* (modern Dutch *zoon*), Old High German *sun* (modern German *Sohn*), Old Icelandic *sonr* (Norwegian *son, sønn,* Swedish *son,* Danish *søn*), and Gothic *sunus,* from Proto-Germanic **sunuz.* Outside Germanic similar forms appear in Lithuanian *sūnùs* son, Old Slavic *synŭ,* Sanskrit *sūnú-s* son, *sū́te* (he) begets, Old Irish *suth* birth, Greek *hyiós* son; earlier *hyiýs,* and Tocharian A *se,* Tocharian B *soyä* son, from Indo-European **seu-/sewə-/sū-/su-* (Pok.913). **—son-in-law** *n.* (before 1325, in *Cursor Mundi*)

sonant *adj.* sounded with voice, voiced. 1846, borrowed from Latin *sonantem* (nominative *sonāns*), present participle of *sonāre* make a noise, see SOUND[1]; for suffix see -ANT. **—n.** a voiced sound. 1849, from the adjective.

sonar (sō′när) *n.* device for detecting objects under water by the reflection of sound waves. 1946, American English; acronym formed from *so(und) na(vigation) r(anging),* on the pattern of *radar;* used to detect submarines, and as a navigation device.

sonata (sənä′tə) *n.* 1694, borrowing of Italian *sonata* piece of instrumental music having three or four movements; literally, sounded (played on an instrument, in contrast to *cantata* sung), feminine past participle of *sonare* to sound, from Latin *sonāre* to SOUND[1].

song *n.* Probably before 1200, in *Ancrene Riwle;* developed from Old English *sang* (about 725, in *Beowulf*); cognate with Old Frisian and Old Saxon *sang* song, Middle Dutch *sanc* (modern Dutch *gezang*), Old High German *sang* (modern German *Gesang*), Old Icelandic *sǫngr* (modern Icelandic *söngur,* Swedish *sång,* Danish and Norwegian *sang*), and Gothic *sangws;* from Proto-Germanic **sanȝwaz;* all from the root of the Germanic verb **singwan* to SING. **—song and dance** contrived story, fuss, outcry (1895, American English). **—songbird** *n.* (1774, in Goldsmith's *Natural History*) **—songbook** *n.* 1489, book of songs; earlier, book of prescribed services in the Anglo-Saxon church; found in Old English (about 1000) *sangbōc,* formed from *sang* song + *bōc* book. **—songfest** *n.* (1912, Canadian English) **—songsmith** *n.* composer of songs (1795). **—songster** *n.* 1382, singer, in the Wycliffe Bible; developed from Old English (about 1000) *sangystre,* formed from *sang* song + *-estre* -ster). **—songwriter** *n.* (1821)

sonic *adj.* of or having to do with sound waves. 1923, American English, formed from Latin *sonus* SOUND + English suffix *-ic;* perhaps patterned on *phonic,* and more remotely *conic, tonic.* **—sonic boom** (1952)

sonnet *n.* poem having 14 lines, usually with meter of five disyllabic words per line. 1557, borrowed from Middle French *sonnet,* and probably directly from Italian *sonetto,* from Old Provençal *sonet* song, diminutive of *son* song, sound, from Latin *sonus* SOUND; for suffix see -ET. **—sonneteer** *n.* writer of sonnets. 1665 *sonnettier,* in Dryden's *The Indian Emperor;* borrowed from Italian *sonettiere* writer or composer of sonnets, from *sonetto* sonnet. The spelling *sonneteer* (influenced by the suffix *-eer*) is first recorded in Wycherley's *The Plain-dealer* (1676).

sonorous (sənôr′əs) *adj.* giving out a deep, loud sound. 1611, in Cotgrave's *Dictionary;* borrowed from Latin *sonōrus,* from *sonor* (genitive *sonōris*) sound, noise, from *sonāre* to SOUND; for suffix see -OUS. The meaning of having a full, rich sound, is first recorded in Dryden's translations of Juvenal's poetry (1693). Modern English *sonorous* replaced earlier *sonouse* sonorous (before 1500; borrowed from Medieval Latin *sonosus,* from Latin *sonus* sound), and *sonoure* possessing a pleasant voice (probably about 1400; formed in Middle English from *sonōrus* + *-e* -y[3]). **—sonority** *n.* 1623, in Cockeram's *Dictionary;* borrowed from French *sonorité,* and directly from Latin *sonōritās,* from *sonōrus* sonorous; for suffix see -ITY.

soon *adv.* Before 1121 *sone;* later *soon* (about 1250); developed from Old English (before 830) *sōna* at once, immediately; cognate with Old Frisian *sōn* at once, Old Saxon *sān, sāna, sāno,* Middle Low German *sān,* Old High German *sān, sāno* (from Proto-Germanic **sǣnō*), and probably Gothic *suns.* The form is not represented in Scandinavian and is now obsolete in most other Germanic languages. Since Old English *sōna* had the sense of at once, immediately, it did not readily admit of comparison, and no Old English comparative or superlative forms are recorded. The appearance of the comparative *sonre* sooner, and the superlative *sonest* soonest, in early Middle English (by about 1200) resulted from the more extended senses (such as "before long, quickly, readily") which the word had acquired by that time.

soot *n.* black substance in the smoke from burning fuel. Before 1200 *sot;* later *soot* (about 1385); developed from Old English (before 800) *sōt;* cognate with Middle Low German *sōt* soot, Middle Dutch *soet,* and Old Icelandic *sōt* (Norwegian and Swedish *sot,* Danish *sod*), from Proto-Germanic **sōtan* what settles. A cognate outside Germanic is found in Lithuanian *súodžiai,* pl., soot, from Indo-European **sōd-,* root **sed-* to sit (Pok.884). **—v.** cover or blacken with soot. 1602, in Marston's *Antonio's Revenge;* from the noun. **—sooty** *adj.* Before 1250 *soti* covered or blackened with soot, in *The Owl and the Nightingale;* formed from Middle English *sot* soot + *-y*[1].

sooth (süth) *n. Archaic.* truth. About 1380, developed from Old English *sōth* (about 725, in *Beowulf*), noun use of *sōth,* adj., true; cognate with Old Saxon *sōth* true, Old High German *sand,* Old Icelandic *sannr* (Norwegian and Swedish *sann,* Danish *sand*), from Proto-Germanic **santhaz,* and Gothic *sunja* truth, **sunjis* true (Proto-Germanic **sunđjás*), all from the stem **sont-* or **sn̥t-* of the Indo-European present participle of the verb "to be," with corresponding forms outside Ger manic in Sanskrit *satyá-s* true, right (compare Sanskrit *sán,* genitive *satás* being), Avestan *haithya-* and Old Persian *hašiya-* true, real, genuine, from Indo-European **sn̥tyós* (Pok.341). Compare SIN. *Sooth* was in common use in English up to about 1650; after that it apparently became obsolete (except perhaps in the expression *by my sooth*) until it was revived as a literary archaism, chiefly by Scott and his contemporaries. **—soothsayer** *n.* 1340 *zoth ziggere* truth sayer, truthful person, in *Ayenbite of Inwyt;* later *sothseiere* (before 1393). The meaning of a person who makes prophecies or predictions, fortuneteller, prognosticator, is first recorded in Middle English in 1381.

soothe (süᴛʜ) *v.* to quiet, calm, comfort. Probably before 1200 *sothien* to prove to be true, verify; developed from Old English (about 950) *sōthian,* from *sōth* true, SOOTH. The modern sense of *soothe* developed from the meaning of uphold as truth, corroborate, support (before 1553); comfirm or encourage (a person) by assent or approval (1568); make calm or quiet, mollify, appease (1697, in Dryden's translation of *The Works of Virgil*).

sop *n.* piece of food dipped or soaked in a liquid. Before 1338, in Mannyng's *Chronicle of England;* developed from Old English (before 1000) *sopp-* (in *soppcuppe* sop-cup, cup into which sops are put), related to *sūpan* to suck up, drink (of animals), SUP², from Indo-European **seub-/sub-/sub-* (Pok.913). Old English *sopp* is cognate with Middle Low German *soppe* broth, Middle Dutch *sop,* Old High German *sopfa* sop, and Old Icelandic *soppa* soup, from Proto-Germanic **suppṓ,* earlier **supnṓ.* In Middle English the word was probably reinforced by the synonymous Old French *soupe* (see SOUP¹).

The meaning of something given to appease, a bribe, is first recorded in English in 1665, in allusion to the myth of a sop given by the Sibyl to Cerberus, the three-headed dog guarding the entrance to Hades, in Vergil's *Aeneid.*

—v. to dip or soak. Old English (about 1000) *soppian;* from the noun. This verb is not recorded in Middle English, but reappears in modern English before 1529 in Skelton's poetical works.

—sopping *adj.* soaking, drenched. 1877, from the past participle of *sop,* v. The use *sopping wet* is first recorded in 1897. **—soppy** *adj.* 1611, full of sops, in Cotgrave's *Dictionary;* formed from English *sop,* n. or v. + *-y*¹. The meaning of very wet, soaked, is first recorded in 1823. The figurative sense of mawkish, sentimental, is first recorded in H.G. Wells' *Joan and Peter* (1918).

sophism (sof'izəm) *n.* clever but misleading argument. Probably before 1430 *sophisme;* borrowed from Latin *sophisma;* replacement of earlier Middle English *sophyme* (about 1383); borrowed from Old French *sophime* a fallacy, false argument, from Latin *sophisma.* The Latin word was borrowed from Greek *sóphisma* sophism, clever device, from *sophízesthai* become wise, from *sophós* wise, clever, of uncertain origin; for suffix see -ISM. **—sophist** *n.* person who uses sophisms. 1440 *sophiste,* in *Promptorium Parvulorum;* borrowed from Late Latin *sophista* a sophist, from Greek *sophistḗs* a wise man, master of one's craft, teacher of arts, sciences, rhetoric, and reasoning, especially by disputation, from *sophízesthai* become wise; for suffix see -IST. **—sophistic** *adj.* 1549, shortened form of *sophistical* 1382 (implied in *sophistically*); borrowed from Latin *sophisticus* of sophists, from Greek *sophistikós* of or pertaining to a sophist, from *sophistḗs* SOPHIST; for suffix see -IC. **—sophistry** *n.* 1340, unsound and misleading reasoning, in *Ayenbite of Inwyt;* borrowed from Old French *sophistrie,* from *sophistre* sophist, from Latin *sophista;* for suffix see -RY.

sophisticate (səfis'təkāt) *v.* make experienced in worldly ways. About 1400 *sophisticaten* adulterate, make impure, in Sir John Maundeville's *Travels;* borrowed from Medieval Latin *sophisticatus,* past participle of *sophisticare* to adulterate, corrupt, cheat, quibble, from Latin *sophisticus* of sophists, from Greek *sophistikós* of or pertaining to a sophist, from *sophistḗs* SOPHIST; for suffix see -ATE¹. The meaning of make less genuine or honest, corrupt, is first recorded in 1604, and that of make artificial, deprive of simplicity, in 1796. **—n.** (səfis'təkit) sophisticated person. 1923, American English; from the verb. **—sophistication** *n.* Probably about 1400 *sophisticacioun* the use of sophistry, falsification; later, adulteration (1423); borrowed from Middle French *sophistication,* and directly from Medieval Latin *sophisticationem* (nominative *sophisticatio*), from *sophisticare* adulterate; for suffix see -ATION. The meaning of worldliness, urbanity, a lessening or loss of naturalness or simplicity, is first recorded in Leigh Hunt's *Autobiography* (1850).

sophomore (sof'môr *or* sof'əmôr) *n.* student in the second year of college or secondary school. 1688; earlier *sophumer* student in the second year of university study (1653); originally, one taking part in dialectic exercises; formed from earlier *sophom* (before 1603), variant of Middle English *sophime* SOPHISM + *-or*². The later spelling *sophomore* and its pronunciation were probably influenced by Greek *sophós* wise, and *mōrós* foolish, dull. **—sophomoric** *adj.* 1813, conceited and pretentious, but crude and ignorant; American English, formed from *sophomore* + *-ic.*

soporific (sop'ərif'ik) *adj.* causing or tending to cause sleep. 1690, in Locke's *Essay Concerning Human Understanding;* borrowed from French *soporifique,* formed from Latin *sopor* (genitive *sopōris*) deep sleep + French suffix *-fique* -fic. Latin *sopor* is related to *somnus* sleep; see SOMNOLENT. **—n.** drug that causes sleep. 1722-27, from the adjective.

soprano (səpran'ō *or* səprä'nō) *adj.* of or for the highest singing voice in women and boys. 1730, borrowing of Italian *soprano* the treble in music; literally, high, from *sopra* above, from Latin *suprā* SUPRA. **—n.** soprano voice. 1738, from the adjective.

sorb *v.* to absorb or adsorb. 1909, abstracted from *absorb* and *adsorb* on the pattern of *sorption.* **—sorption** *n.* absorption or adsorption. 1909, from the second element of *absorption* and *adsorption.* The term was coined by the British chemist J.W. McBain.

sorbet *n.* 1585, a cooling drink made of fruit juice, sugar, and water; later, a frozen dessert made of fruit juice, sugar, and water or milk, sherbet (1864); borrowed from French *sorbet,* probably from Italian *sorbetto,* from Turkish *şerbet,* from Arabic *sharbat* a drink.

sorcery *n.* witchcraft. Probably before 1300 *sorcerie,* in *Kyng Alisaunder;* borrowing of Old French *sorcerie,* from *sorcier* sorcerer, from Vulgar Latin **sortiārius,* literally, one who influences lot, fate, or fortune, from Latin *sors* (genitive *sortis*) lot, fate, fortune; see SORT; for suffix see -Y³. **—sorcerer** *n.* Probably about 1425 *sorcerour;* later *sorcerer* (probably before 1475); formed from earlier *sorser* sorcerer (probably about

1380) + *-our* -or², *-er* -er¹. Middle English *sorser* was borrowed from Old French *sorcier.* **—sorceress** *n.* About 1380 *sorceresse,* in Chaucer's *House of Fame;* formed from Middle English *sorser* sorcerer + *-esse* -ESS.

sordid *adj.* low, vile. Probably before 1425 *sordide* festering, in a translation of Chauliac's *Grande Chirurgie;* later, dirty, foul, low, mean (1611, in Cotgrave's *Dictionary*); borrowed from Latin *sordidus* dirty, from *sordēre* be dirty, be shabby, related to *sordēs* dirt; see SWART.

sore *adj.* Probably about 1175 *sare;* later *sore* (probably before 1200); developed from Old English *sār* painful, grievous, aching (before 899, in Alfred's translation of St. Gregory's *Pastoral Care*); cognate with Old Saxon *sēr* sore, Middle Low German *sēr,* Middle Dutch *seer* (modern Dutch *zeer*), Old High German *sēr* (modern German *sehr* very), and Old Icelandic *sārr* sore, wounded (modern Icelandic *sár,* Norwegian, Danish, and Swedish *sår*), from Proto-Germanic **sairaz.* Possible cognates outside Germanic are found in Old Irish *sāeth* pain, Latin *saevus* wild, terrible, and Lithuanian *šaižùs* rough, sharp, Latvian *sievs, sīvs* sharp, biting, from Indo-Euorpean **sāi-* (Pok.877). **—n.** About 1150 *sor;* developed from Old English *sār* pain, injury, suffering, grief (before 830, in the *Vespasian Psalter*), related to *sār,* adj., painful. The Old English noun is cognate with Old Saxon *sēr* pain, wound, Middle Dutch *seer* (modern Dutch *zeer*), Old High German *sēr,* Old Icelandic *sār,* and Gothic *sair.*

sorghum (sôr′gəm) *n.* tall cereal plant. 1597, borrowing of New Latin *Sorghum,* the genus name, from Italian *sorgo* one of the tall cereal grasses, probably from Medieval Latin *surgum,* perhaps a variant from Latin *syricum,* neuter adjective, Syrian, from (the Greek name) *Syríā* Syria, which may have been a source of this plant or its grain.

sorority (sərôr′ətē) *n.* sisterhood. 1532, a society of women, in the writings of Sir Thomas More; borrowed from Medieval Latin *sororitas* of or pertaining to sisters, from Latin *soror* SISTER; for suffix see -ITY. The meaning of a club or society of woman at a college is first recorded in 1900 in American English.

sorrel¹ (sôr′əl *or* sor′əl) *adj.* reddish-brown. 1397 *sorell;* earlier in *sorelborgh* as the name of a horse (1340); borrowed from Middle French *sorel,* from *sor* yellowish-brown, probably from a Frankish word (compare Middle Dutch *soor* and Middle Low German *sōr* dry; see SERE). If Middle French *sorel* is a diminutive form (unexplained) of *sor,* then the suffix is *-el,* form of -LE². **—n.** 1397 *sorell* horse of a sorrel color; borrowed from Middle French *sorel,* from *sorel,* adj.

sorrel² (sôr′əl *or* sor′əl) *n.* plant with sour leaves. 1373 *sorell;* borrowed from Old French *surele,* from *sur* sour, from a Frankish word (compare Old High German *sūr* SOUR); for suffix see -LE¹, form of Middle English *-el.*

sorrow *n.* Probably about 1150 *sorege* grief, emotional distress; later *sorwe* (probably before 1200), and *sorrowe* (about 1400); developed from Old English *sorg,* grief, regret, trouble, care (about 725, in *Beowulf*); cognate with Old Saxon *sorga* sorrow, care, Old Frankish *sworga,* Middle Dutch *sorghe* (modern Dutch *zorg*), Old High German *sorga* (modern German *Sorge*), Old Icelandic *sorg* (Swedish, Norwegian, and Danish *sorg*), and Gothic *saúrga,* from Proto-Germanic **surʒō.* Cognates outside Germanic are found in Old Irish *serg* sickness, Old Slavic *sraga,* Lithuanian *sirgti* to be sick, and Sanskrit *sū́rkṣati* he is concerned, from Indo-European **swergh-/surgh-* (Pok.1051). **—v.** Probably before 1200 *sorhin, sorgeden;* later *sorowen* (probably before 1300), developed from Old English *sorgian* to feel sorrow (about 725, in *Beowulf*), derived from *sorg,* n., sorrow. The Old English verb corresponds to Old Saxon *sorgōn* to sorrow, Middle Dutch *sorghen* (modern Dutch *zorgen*), Old High German *sorgēn* (modern German *sorgen*), Old Icelandic *syrgja* (Swedish *sörja,* Norwegian and Danish *sørge*), and Gothic *saúrgan.*

sorry *adj.* 1114 *sari;* later *sori* (probably before 1200); developed from Old English *sārig* distressed, full of sorrow (about 725, in *Beowulf*), from *sār* SORE; for suffix see -Y¹. The meaning of wretched, worthless, poor, is first recorded in Middle English about 1250. According to the OED the shift in spelling from *a* to *o* represents the semantic connection with *sorrow.*

sort *n.* About 1390, in Chaucer's *Canterbury Tales;* borrowed from Old French *sorte* class, kind; earlier *sort,* from Latin *sortem* (nominative *sors*) lot, fate, share, portion, rank, category, (from Indo-European **sr̥tís*), and perhaps related to *serere* to join (since, in ancient Italy, one drew a lot from objects lined up in a row); see SERIES. **—v.** arrange by kinds or classes. 1358 *sorten* (implied in *sortinge* verbal noun) to allot, arrange, sort, borrowed from Old French *sortir* allot, sort, assort, from Latin *sortīrī* draw lots, obtain by lot, receive as a portion, divide, distribute, choose, from *sors* lot, fate, share. Some senses of the English verb derive from the noun, and some senses are perhaps, in part, a shortened form of *assort,* though that word does not appear in the record of English until 1490.

sortie *n.* sudden attack by troops. 1778, in letters of Walpole; borrowing of French *sortie,* from feminine past participle of *sortir* to go out, from Old French, to go out, escape (compare Spanish *surtir* gush forth), from Vulgar Latin **surctīre,* from **surctum,* past participle (replacing *surrēctum*) of Latin *surgere* rise up; see SURGE.

SOS (es′ō′es′) *n.* the international radiotelegraph signal of distress used especially by ships. 1910, from the letters *s o s* of the International Morse code, consisting of three dots, three dashes, and three dots, arbitrarily chosen as being easy to transmit and distinguish, and not, as has been mistakenly averred, an acronym for "save our ship," "save our souls," etc. The signal was recommended at the Radio Telegraph Conference in 1906 and officially adopted two years later. Compare MAYDAY. **—v.** to give an SOS or other signal of distress. 1918, in Kipling's *Land and Sea Tales;* from the noun.

sot *n.* Old English (about 1000) *sott* stupid person, fool; borrowed from Old French *sot,* from Gallo-Romance **sott-,* an expressive word of uncertain origin, represented in the Romance languages also by Spanish and Portuguese *zote* fool, and Calabrian *ciotu* foolish, and recorded in Medieval Latin (about 800) as *sottua.* Besides Old English, the Old French word was borrowed by Middle Dutch *sot* (modern Dutch *zot*) fool, foolish, Middle High German *sot,* and Middle Low German *sot, sotte.*

The extended meaning of English *sot* one who is dulled or stupefied by drink, habitual drinker, drunkard, is first recorded in Nashe's *Pierce Penilesse* (1592). **—v.** Probably before 1200 *sotten* delude, confuse, in Layamon's *Chronicle of Britain;* later, become stupid or foolish (before 1415); from the noun. The more com mon intensive verb, *besot* (formed from *be-* + *sot,* v.) is first recorded in 1580 in the sense of affect with a foolish infatuation, and in the sense of make mentally or morally stupid or blind (1615). The meaning of make a sot of, intoxicate, muddle the brain of, is first recorded in 1672.

soufflé (süflā′) *n.* light baked dish. 1813, in Louis E. Ude's *The French Cook;* borrowing of French *soufflé,* from the past participle of *souffler* puff up, from Latin *sufflāre* (*suf-* under, up, variant of *sub-* before *f* + *flāre* to BLOW[2]).

sough (sou *or* suf) *v.* make a rustling or murmuring sound. About 1380 *souȝen;* earlier *swowen* (probably before 1300), and *suhhȝhenn* (probably before 1200, in *The Ormulum*); developed from Old English *swōgan* (about 750, in Cynewulf's *Christ*); cognate with Old Saxon *swōgan* to rustle, Old Icelandic *sœ̄gr* noise, commotion, and Gothic *gaswōgjan* to sigh, from Proto-Germanic **swōȝanan.* Probable cognates outside Germanic are found in Lithuanian *svagẽti* to sound, and Greek *ēchḗ* sound, noise, *ēchṓ* ECHO. **—n.** soughing sound. About 1380 *swogh, swough,* in Chaucer's *Parlement of Foules* and *House of Fame;* from the verb.

soul *n.* Before 1121 *sawle,* in *Peterborough Chronicle;* later *sowle, soule* (probably before 1200); developed from Old English *sāwol* the spiritual and emotional part of a person, animate existence (about 725, in *Beowulf*); cognate with Old Frisian *sēle* soul, Old Saxon *seola, siola,* Middle Low German *sēle,* Old Low Franconian *sēla, sīla,* Middle Dutch *siele* (modern Dutch *ziel*), Old High German *sēula, sēla* (modern German *Seele*), and Gothic *saiwala* (related to *saiws* sea, lake), from Proto-Germanic **saiwalō,* meaning "coming from the sea, belonging to the sea," because that was supposed to be a stopping place of the soul before birth and after death, according to F. Kluge's *Etymologisches Wörterbuch der deutschen Sprache.* No cognates are found outside Germanic. The meaning of a disembodied spirit of a (deceased) person is first recorded in Old English in 971, and that of a person, individual (as in *every living soul aboard ship*), about 1000.

sound[1] *n.* what is heard. About 1280 *soun,* borrowed from Old French *son,* from Latin *sonus* sound. Latin *sonus* is cognate with Old Irish *senim* playing, sounding, Sanskrit *svánati* (it) sounds, and Old English *swinsian* to sing, make music, *swinn* music, singing, from Indo-European **swen-/swon-* (Pok.1046). The spelling with final *-d* is first recorded in Middle English about 1350, but was not the established spelling until the 1500's. This spelling resulted from a tendency in dialectal English from the 1300's on to add the sound *d* after *n* (as is often heard in *drownd*). **—v.** make a sound. Probably about 1225 *sunen,* in *King Horn;* later *sownen* (probably about 1343); borrowed from Old French *soner,* from Latin *sonāre,* related to *sonus* sound, n. **—sound barrier** (1952) **—soundproof** *adj.* (1884) **—soundtrack** *n.* (1929).

sound[2] *adj.* free from injury or defect. Probably before 1200 *sund, sunde,* in Layamon's *Chronicle of Britain;* developed (with loss of the prefix) from Old English *gesund* sound, safe, healthy (about 725, in *Beowulf*). Old English *gesund* is cognate with Old Frisian *sund* healthy, sound, Old Saxon *gisund,* Middle Dutch *ghesont* (modern Dutch *gezond*), and Old High German *gisunt* (modern German *gesund*), from Proto-Germanic **sundás,* related to **swinthaz,* the source of Gothic *swinths* strong, Old English *swīth,* and Middle High German *swint* violent (modern German *geschwind* quick), from Indo-European **swentos/suntós* (Pok. 1048). There are no clear cognates outside Germanic. **—adv.** in a sound manner. About 1330 *sounde,* in *Sir Orfeo;* from the adjective.

sound[3] *v.* to measure the depth (of water), fathom, probe. About 1385 *sounden* sink in, penetrate, in Chaucer's *Troilus and Criseyde;* later, measure the depth of water (before 1460); borrowed from Old French *sonder,* from *sonde* sounding line, probably from a Germanic source (compare Old English *sund* water, sea, especially in the compounds *sundlīne* sounding line, *sundgyrd* sounding pole, *sundrāp* sounding rope, and Old Icelandic *sund* strait, SOUND[4]). This view is held by von Wartburg in FEW (17, pp. 270-272). Earlier scholars, such as Meyer-Lübke and Gamillscheg, held that Old French *sonder* developed from Vulgar Latin **subundāre* submerge (Latin *sub-* under + *unda* wave; see WATER). This point of view is somewhat weakened by the fact that Old French *sonder* is attested only since 1382, whereas the noun *sonde* is recorded much earlier, in 1220. The transferred meaning of try to find out the views or feelings of is first recorded in English in 1575. **—n.** 1584, act of sounding; borrowed from Middle French *sonde,* from Old French. The meaning of a long, slender instrument used in examining body cavities is first recorded in 1797.

sound[4] *n.* narrow channel of water, strait. Before 1300, in *King Horn;* in part developed from Old English *sund* power of swimming, water, sea, and probably in part influenced by, if not borrowed from, a Scandinavian cognate (compare Old Icelandic *sund* a strait, swimming, Norwegian, Swedish, and Danish *sund* channel, strait, sound, from Proto-Germanic **sumđán,* Indo-European **swm̥tóm;* related to Old Icelandic *svimma* to SWIM).

soup[1] *n.* liquid food made by boiling meat, fish, vegetables, etc. 1653, in Sir Thomas Urquhart's translations of works of Rabelais; borrowed from French *soupe* soup, broth, from Late Latin *suppa* bread or other food dipped or soaked in broth, from a Germanic source (compare Middle Dutch *sop* sop, broth, and Old High German *sopfa* SOP). The figurative sense of soup with the meaning of fog or thick mist is first recorded in 1901. **—soup kitchen** (1839) **—soupy** *adj.* (1869, in Dickens' writings)

soup[2] *v. Slang.* increase the horsepower of (an engine). 1921 *soup up,* probably from *soup*[1] in the slang sense of a narcotic injected into horses to make them run faster; perhaps also influenced by *sup(ercharge),* v., 1876.

soupçon or **soupcon** (süpsôn′ *or* süp′sôn) *n.* slight trace or flavor. 1766, in letters of Horace Walpole; borrowing of French *soupçon* suspicion, trace, from Old French *sospeçon,* from Late Latin *suspectiōnem* (nominative *suspectiō*) SUSPICION.

sour *adj.* Probably 1303 *sour* tart, acid, bitter (implied in *soure dogh* sourdough, fermented dough); developed from Old English (about 1000) *sūr;* cognate with Middle Dutch *suur* (modern Dutch *zuur*) sour, Old High German *sūr* (modern German *sauer*), and Old Icelandic *sūrr* (Norwegian, Swedish, and Danish *sur*), from Proto-Germanic **sūraz.* The Germanic forms are further cognate with Lithuanian *sū́ras* salty, Old Slavic *syrŭ* damp, and Russian *syrói* damp, moist, raw, from Indo-European **sūros* (Pok.1039). **—v.** make or become sour. Probably before 1300 *souren* to become sour, spoil, in *Kyng Alisaunder;* from the adjective. **—adv.** About 1300, bitterly or severely; later, crossly, disagreeably (as in *to look sour*), in Dunbar's poetry (1500-20); from the adjective. **—n.** something sour. Before 1325 *sure,* in *Cursor Mundi;* later *sowre* (about 1333-52); developed from Old English (about 1000) *sūr;* from the adjective. The sense in American English of a sour drink (as in *whiskey sour*) is first recorded in 1862. **—sourball** *n.* (1900, ill-tempered person; 1933, a kind of tart candy) **—sourpuss** *n.* (1937)

source *n.* 1346, a support or base; later *sours* main cause, orign (about 1385, in Chaucer's *Troilus and Criseyde*), and in the spelling *source* (before 1393, in Gower's *Confessio Amantis*); borrowed from Old French *sourse* rise, beginning, spring, feminine noun use of the past participle of *sourdre* to rise, spring up, from Latin *surgere* to rise, SURGE. The specific meaning of the beginning of a river or stream is first recorded in Middle English about 1395, in Chaucer's *Canterbury Tales.*

sourdough *n.* prospector or pioneer in Alaska or Canada. 1898; so called from the practice of the early prospectors in the Yukon of saving a lump of fermented dough as leaven for raising the bread baked during the winter. The compound *sourdough, sour dough,* meaning fermented dough used as leaven, is first recorded in Middle English probably in 1303, in Mannyng's *Handlyng Synne.* Compare similarly formed Middle High German *sūrteic* (modern German *Sauerteig*) sourdough.

souse *v.* Before 1387 *sousen* to pickle, steep in vinegar, in Trevisa's translation of Higden's *Polychronicon;* probably borrowed from Old French **souser,* from *sous, souci,* adj., preserved in salt and vinegar, pickled, from Frankish **sultja.* The Frankish word is cognate with Old High German *sulza* saltwater, pickled meat (modern German *Sülze* brine, jellied meat), and Old Saxon *sultia* saltwater, related to *salt* SALT. The general sense of plunge or immerse in liquid is first recorded in 1470-85. The participial adjective *soused,* meaning steeped in alcoholic liquor, drunk, is found in Beaumont and Fletcher's *The Captain* (1613). **—n.** 1391 *sows* liquid used for pickling; borrowed from Old French *sous,* variant of *souci* pickle. The meaning of an act of sousing or drenching with water (from the verb) is first recorded in 1741.

south *adv.* Before 1300, in a version of *The Owl and the Nightingale;* developed from Old English *sūth* southward, in the south (about 725, in *Beowulf*); cognate with Old Frisian and Old Saxon *sūthar* southward, south, Middle Low German *sūt,* Old High German *sund-* (modern German *süd*), and Old Icelandic *sudhr,* from Proto-Germanic **sunthaz.* These words are perhaps cognate with English SUN; hence *south* would mean "toward the region of the sun." **—adj.** Probably before 1300, in *Kyng Alisaunder;* developed from Old English (before 800) *sūth-* (as in *sūthdǣl* the southern region, the south), adjective use of *sūth,* adv. **—n.** Probably before 1300; from the adverb. **—southerly** *adj.* 1551, situated toward the south, formed from *south,* adj., on the pattern of *easterly,* + *-ly*². *—adv.* 1577, in a southern position or direction; for suffix see -LY¹. **—southern** *adj.* About 1300, developed from Old English (before 899) *sūtherne* (*sūth* south + *-erne,* suffix denoting direction); cognate with Old High German *sundrōni* and Old Icelandic *sudhrœnn* southern, from Proto-Germanic **sunthrōnjaz.* **—southward** *adj.* About 1290, developed from Old English (before 899) *sūthweard (sūth* south + *-weard* -ward). **—southwester** *n.* 1 1833, southwest wind. 2 1836, a waterproof hat with a broad brim, worn by seamen. Also **sou'wester** (1837).

souvenir (sü'vənir') *n.* 1775, remembrance, memory, in letters of Horace Walpole; borrowing of French *souvenir,* noun use of *souvenir,* v., to remember, come to mind, from Latin *subvenīre* come to mind (*sub-* up + *venīre* COME). The meaning of a token of remembrance, memento, keepsake, is first recorded in English in 1782.

sovereign (sov'rən) *n.* About 1280 *sovereyn* a superior, a ruler, governor, lord, or master; borrowed from Old French *soverain,* from Vulgar Latin **superānus,* from Latin *super* OVER. The spelling *sovereign* (with *g*) is found in Middle English about 1378, in a version of *Piers Plowman,* and earlier as *soveraigne* (1357), probably resulting from the influence of *reign.* **—adj.** Before 1338 *sovereyne* great, superior, supreme, in Mannyng's *Chronicle of England;* borrowed from Old French *soverain,* adj. and n. **—sovereignty** *n.* About 1340 *soveraynte;* later *sovereignete* (about 1385, in Chaucer's *Troilus and Criseyde*); borrowed through Anglo-French *sovereyneté, soverentee,* from Old French *soveraineté* quality or condition of being sovereign, from *soverain* sovereign; for suffix see -TY².

soviet (sō'vēet) *n.* governing council or assembly in the Soviet Union. 1917, borrowed from Russian *sovét* governing council; literally, council, from Old Russian *sŭvětŭ* (*sŭ* with, together + *větŭ* counsel, agreement); loan translation of Greek *symboúlion* council of advisors. *The Soviets,* meaning the government or people of the Soviet Union, is first recorded in 1920. **—adj.** of or pertaining to soviets. 1918, from the noun.

sow¹ (sō) *v.* to plant, seed. Probably about 1150 *sowen;* developed from Old English (before 830) *sāwan;* cognate with Old Saxon *sāian* to sow, Middle Dutch *sayen* (modern Dutch *zaaien*), Old High German *sāwen, sājen* (modern German *säen*), Old Icelandic *sá* (Norwegian, Swedish, and Danish *så*), and Gothic *saian,* from Proto-Germanic **sǣjanan.* Outside Germanic cognates are found in Lithuanian *sėti* to sow, Old Slavic *sějati,* Latin *sēvī* I have sown, and Sanskrit *síra-m* plow for sowing, from Indo-European **sēi-/sī-/sē-* sow (Pok. 890). Related to SEED.

sow² (sou) *n.* female pig. Probably before 1200 *suhe,* in *Ancrene Riwle;* later *souwe* (about 1300), *sowe* (before 1325); developed from Old English (before 800) *sugu,* related to *sū* sow, two words which gradually fell together. The Old English form *sugu* (from Proto-Germanic **suʒṓ,* Indo-European **sukā́,* is cognate with Old Saxon *suga* sow, Middle Low German *soge,* Middle Dutch *sōghe* (modern Dutch *zeug*), and outside Germanic with Sanskrit *sūkará-s* swine, boar, and (from Proto-Celtic **sukkos, *sokkā*) Old Irish *socc* hog, swine, Welsh *hwch* hog, sow, Cornish *hoch,* Breton *houc'h, hoc'h* swine. The Old English form *sū* sow, is cognate with Old High German *sū* (modern German *Sau*) and Old Icelandic *sýr,* accusative *sū* (Swedish and Danish *so*), and outside Germanic with Avestan *hū,* and Greek *hŷs,* from Indo-European **sūs* (Pok.1038). Related to SWINE.

soy *n.* brown sauce made from the fermented beans (soybeans) of an Asian plant of the pea family. 1696 *souy;* earlier *saio* (1679); borrowed from Dutch *soya* *soja,* from Japanese *sōyu,* variant of *shōyu* soy, from Chinese *shi-yu* (*shi* fermented soybeans + *yu* oil). Most etymologies of *soy* derive the English word directly from Japanese. This is open to doubt, since diplomatic ties between England and Japan had been cut off in 1624, and *soy* appeared in English more than fifty years later. It is much more likely that *soy* passed into English through Dutch, since, as the Dutch scholar J.F. Bense points out, the Dutch had trade relations with Japan before any other European nation and continued to trade with the Japanese throughout the period in which the English had no contact with Japan. It was not until 1868 that relations between Great Britain and Japan were resumed. **—soybean** *n.* (1795) **—soy sauce** (1795)

spa *n.* 1626, mineral spring, from earlier (1565) *Spa,* the name of a health resort in the province of Liège, in eastern Belgium, known for the curative properties of its mineral springs. The meaning of town or resort where there is a mineral spring is first recorded in 1777, in Sheridan's writings. The special sense of a hot tub is first recorded in 1974.

space *n.* Probably before 1300, an area, extent, expanse, in *Kyng Alisaunder;* borrowed from Old French *espace,* learned borrowing from Latin *spatium* room, area, distance, stretch of time. Latin *spatium* is probably cognate with Greek *spân* to draw, from Indo-European **spē-/spə-* (H. Frisk, *Griechisches etymologisches Wörterbuch,* II, 761). The sense of the great expanse in which the stars and planets are situated is first recorded in Milton's *Paradise Lost* (1667). **—v.** 1548, to separate by a space or spaces, from the noun. An earlier use, with the meaning of walk or pace, is found in Chaucer's *Troilus and Criseyde* (about 1385). **—adj.** 1600, of or involving space; from the noun. The meaning of having to do with travel in outer space appeared about 1894. Many of the commonly used compounds incorporating this sense first appeared in science fiction or other speculative writing: *spacecraft* (1930), *spaceman* (1942), *spaceship* (1894), *space station* (1936), *spacesuit* (1920), *space travel* (1931). Exceptions are *space age* (1946), *space capsule* (1959), *space medicine* (1949), *space vehicle* (1946), and *spacewalk* (1965). **—spacious** *adj.* Before 1382, wide, extensive, in the Wycliffe Bible; borrowed from Old French *spacieux,* and directly from Latin *spatiōsus,* from *spatium* space, n.; for suffix see -OUS.

spacy or **spacey** *adj. Slang.* dazed or stupefied; also eccentric. 1971, American English, formed from earlier *space(d)* or *space(d-out)* dazed or stupefied, especially by the use of narcotics (1965) + *-y*[1]; probably so called from the strangeness (as in *outer space*) or vacuousness (as in *empty space*) of the behavior of people under the influence of narcotic or hallucinogenic drugs.

spade[1] *n.* tool for digging. Probably before 1200, in *Ancrene Riwle;* developed from Old English (before 800) *spadu;* cognate with Old Frisian *spada* spade, shovel, Old Saxon *spado,* Middle Dutch and Dutch *spade,* Middle High German *spat, spate* (modern German *Spaten*), Icelandic *spadhi,* and Danish, Swedish, and Norwegian *spade,* from Proto-Germanic **spađōn.* Cognates outside Germanic include Greek *spáthē* broad blade (from Indo-European **spədhā*), and Hittite *ispă̄tar* eating implement, perhaps from Indo-European **sphē-* (Pok.980), the source of Old Icelandic *spānn* SPOON. **—v.** dig with a spade. 1594, in Nashe's *Terrors of the Night;* from the noun.

spade[2] *n.* leaf-shaped figure on playing cards. 1598, in Florio's *A World of Words;* probably a borrowing of Italian *spade,* plural of *spada* sword, spade[1], from Latin *spatha* broad, flat weapon or tool, from Greek *spáthē* broad blade; see SPADE[1] tool.

spadix (spā′diks) *n. Botany.* spike composed of minute flowers on a fleshy stem. 1760, New Latin, from Latin *spādīx* branch broken off a date-palm tree; from Greek *spádīx,* from *spân* tear away, pull; see SPASM.

spaghetti *n.* long, slender sticks of pasta. 1849 *sparghetti;* later *spaghetti* (1888); borrowing of Italian *spaghetti,* plural of *spaghetto* string, twine, diminutive of *spago* cord, of uncertain origin.

span[1] *n.* distance between two objects. Old English *span, spann* distance between the thumb and little finger of an extended hand (before 899, in Alfred's translation of Bede's *Ecclesiastical History*). Old English *span, spann* is cognate with Middle Dutch and modern Dutch *spanne* span, Old High German *spanna* (modern German *Spanne*), Old Icelandic *spǫnn* (Norwegian and Swedish *spann,* Danish *spand*), and is probably related to Old English *spannan* to join, fasten; see SPAN[2]. The meaning of a length of time is found in 1599. The usual sense of the distance or stretch between two objects, such as the supports of an arch, is first recorded in 1725. **—v.** Before 1398 *spannen* to twist around; later (about 1420) to grasp, take hold of; from the noun. The sense of measure by the outstretched hand is found in the Geneva Bible (1560). The transferred sense of reach or extend over (space or time) is first recorded in 1624, in the writings of Donne.

span[2] *n.* pair of animals driven together. 1769, American English; borrowed from Dutch *span,* from *spannen* to stretch or yoke, from Middle Dutch. Middle Dutch *spannen* is cognate with Old English *spannan* to join, fasten, clasp, Old Frisian *spanna,* Old Icelandic *spenna* to fasten (Norwegian and Swedish *spanna*), and Old High German *spannan* to fasten, yoke (modern German *spannen*), from Proto-Germanic **spanwanan* (cognate with Greek *spân* to draw), from Indo-European present stem **spə-nu-,* root **spē-* (Pok.982).

spangle *n.* 1440 *spangele, spangyl* small piece of glittering metal, in *Promptorium Parvulorum;* diminutive form of earlier *spang* glittering ornament, spangle (1406); probably borrowed from Middle Dutch *spange* brooch, clasp; for suffix see -LE[1]. Middle Dutch *spange* is cognate with Old English *spang* buckle, clasp, Old High German *spanga* (modern German *Spange*), and Old Icelandic *spǫng* (Norwegian *spong*), from Proto-Germanic **spanʒō,* from an extension of the root of SPAN[2]. **—v.** decorate with spangles. Probably before 1450 *spanglen* (implied in *spangled,* participial adjective); from the noun.

Spaniard *n.* native of Spain. Before 1400 *Spaynard,* in a translation of Lanfranc's *Science of Surgery;* later *Spaniard* (1443); earlier as surnames *Spaynard* (1318), *Spaniard* (1379); borrowed from Old French *Espaignart, Espaniard,* from *Espaigne* Spain, from Latin *Hispānia,* from Greek *Hispāníā;* for suffix see -ARD.

spaniel (span′yəl) *n.* breed of dog. About 1350 *spaynel;* earlier as a surname (with the original sense of Spaniard) *Spaynel* (1275); borrowed from Old French *espagneul,* literally, Spanish (dog), from Vulgar Latin **Hispāniōlus* of Spain, diminutive of Latin *Hispanus*

Spanish, Hispanic, from Greek *Hispānós,* from *Hispāníā* Spain.

Spanish *adj.* Probably before 1200 *Spainisc,* in Layamon's *Chronicle of Britain;* formed from *Spaine* Spain (borrowed from Anglo-French and Old French *Espaigne;* see SPANIARD) + *-isc* -ish[1]; replacing Old English *Speonisc.* The spelling *Spanish* appeared before 1533, indicating an alteration probably through influence of Latin *Hispānia* (compare SPANIARD and HISPANIC).

spank[1] *v.* to strike with the open hand. 1727, in Bailey's *Dictionary;* possibly imitative in origin, in reference to the sound of spanking. **—n.** a blow with the open hand, slap. 1785, in Grose's *Classical Dictionary of the Vulgar Tongue;* from the verb.

spank[2] *v. Informal.* to move quickly and vigorously. 1807-10, probably a back formation from SPANKING.

spanker *n.* fore-and-aft sail on the mast nearest the stern. 1794, in *The Elements and Practice of Rigging and Seamanship;* probably formed from English *spank(ing)* + *-er*[1]. An earlier sense of anything fine, large, or unusual for its kind is found in Smollett's *The Adventures of Peregrine Pickle* (1751).

spanking *adj.* Before 1666, very big or fine; later, moving at a quick lively pace (1738); perhaps borrowed from a Scandinavian source (compare Danish *spanke* to strut); for suffix see -ING[2]. The meaning of blowing briskly (said of a breeze) is first recorded in 1849, and that of rapid, smart, vigorous, in 1857, in Hughes' *Tom Brown's School Days.*

spar[1] *n.* stout pole. Before 1325 *sparr* rafter, beam, stout pole, in *Cursor Mundi;* cognate with Old Saxon *sparro* rafter, Middle Low German and Middle Dutch *sparre* (modern Dutch *spar*), Old High German *sparro* (modern German *Sparren*), Old Icelandic *sparri* (Danish, Swedish, and Norwegian *sparre*), from Proto-Germanic **sparrōn;* related to Old English *spere* SPEAR[1] lance. The sense of a stout pole used to support or extend a ship's sail is found in 1640, but is first recorded in the compound *cant spar* (1611), or perhaps *spar deck* (1570). —**v.** provide with spars. 1657-58; from the noun.

spar[2] *v.* to box. Probably before 1300 *sperden* go quickly, rush, in *Kyng Alisaunder;* later *sparren* (probably about 1380); perhaps borrowed from Middle French *esparer* to kick, from Italian *sparare* to fling (*s-* as an intensive form from Latin *ex-* + *parare* ward off, PARRY). The meaning of strike (with spurs) is found in Middle English, in *Sir Gawain and the Green Knight* (probably about 1390); the sense of fight, as roosters do, with the feet or spurs, is recorded in Levins' *Dictionary* (1570). The meaning of make motions of attack and defense with the arms and fists, box, is recorded in Johnson's *Dictionary* (1755), and the figurative sense of dispute, bandy words, in 1698. **—n.** Probably about 1400, a thrust or blow; from the verb. The sense of a boxing match is found in 1814.

spar[3] *n.* shiny mineral that splits easily. 1581, borrowed from Low German *Spar,* from Middle Low German *spar, sper.* Middle Low German *spar, sper* is cognate with Old English *spær-* (in *spærstān* spar-stone, gypsum), and *spæren,* adj., of gypsum or plaster. Compare FELDSPAR.

spare *v.* Probably about 1150 *sparen;* developed from Old English (before 830) *sparian* to refrain from harming, allow to escape, go free; cognate with Old Frisian *sparia* to spare, Old Saxon *sparon,* Middle Dutch and modern Dutch *sparen,* Old High German *sparōn, sparēn* (modern German *sparen*), and Old Icelandic *spara* (Norwegian and Danish *spare,* Swedish *spara*); all derived from the source of Old English *spær* sparing, frugal, Old High German *spar,* and Old Icelandic *sparr* sparing, frugal, from Proto-Germanic **sparaz,* Indo-European **sp(h)əros* (Pok.983). **—adj.** Probably about 1380, free for other use, additional, extra; related to Old English *spær* sparing, frugal, and *sparian* to spare. The sense of thin, not abundant, is first recorded before 1548. **—n.** Before 1325, a sparing, leniency, mercy, in *Cursor Mundi;* from the verb. The meaning of a spare thing or part is first recorded in 1642. The meaning of a single pin left standing in various bowling games is first recorded in 1879, in American English. **—spare ribs** (1596, in Nashe's *Have With You to Saffron-Walden*)

spark[1] *n.* a small bit of fire. Probably before 1200 *sperke, sparke, spærc,* in *Ancrene Riwle* and Layamon's *Chronicle of Britain;* developed from Old English (before 800) *spearca;* cognate with Middle Low German and Middle Dutch *sparke* spark, Old Icelandic *sparkr* lively, from Proto-Germanic **spark-,* and outside Germanic possibly with Latvian *spirgsti* glowing coals, Lithuanian *sprāgēti* to crackle; see SPEAK. **—v.** to produce sparks. Probably about 1200 *sparken;* cognate with or possibly borrowed from Middle Low German or Middle Dutch *sparken* to spark, related to the noun; also cognate with Old Icelandic *spraka* to crackle, spark (Norwegian *sprake,* Swedish *spraka,* Danish *sprage*). **—spark plug** (1903)

spark[2] *n.* beau, lover. 1575, woman of great beauty or wit, probably a figurative use of SPARK[1]. The extended sense of beau or lover is first recorded in Farquhar's *The Beaux' Stratagem* (1706-07) and is from the verb sense of court, woo. **—v.** be a beau or lover, court, woo. 1676, from the noun.

sparkle *v.* Probably before 1200 *sperclen, *sparklen* (not recorded before 1338) send out little sparks; frequentative verb form of Middle English *sparke,* v.; see SPARK[1]; for suffix see -LE[3]. **—n.** little spark. About 1300, either a diminutive form of Middle English *sparke* SPARK[1], n.; for suffix see -LE[1]; or from the verb *sparklen;* perhaps formed on the analogy of the verb.

sparrow *n.* kind of small finch. Probably before 1200 *sparewe, sparwe,* in Layamon's *Chronicle of Britain,* developed from Old English (before 800) *spearwa;* cognate with Gothic *sparwa,* Middle High German *sparwe,* and older Danish *sparwe* (Swedish *sparv,* Danish and Norwegian *spurv*), from Proto-Germanic **sparwōn.* The original *w* of the stem is reflected in the ending of Old High German *sparo* and in the vocalism of Old Icelandic *spǫrr* (from Proto-Germanic **sparwaz*). Outside of Germanic the stem probably occurs in Greek *sparásion* sparrowlike bird, Old Prussian *spurglis* sparrow, and Tocharian A *spārāñ* bird, from Indo-European **sper-/spor-/spr̥-* (Pok.991). **—sparrow hawk** (about 1450)

sparse *adj.* 1727, (of writing) widely spaced or spread out; borrowed from Latin *sparsus* scattered, past participle of *spargere* to scatter, spread. Latin *spargere* is possibly cognate with Greek *spargân* to swell, Lithuanian *sprógti* to germinate, *spùrga* sprout, and Sanskrit *sphūrjati* bursts forth, crackles, rattles; see SPEAK. The extended sense of thinly dispersed, and distributed at wide intervals, not crowded or close (as in *a sparse* *population*), is first recorded in English as an Americanism in Jefferson's writings (1801). The sense of scanty or meager is first recorded in 1871.

spasm *n.* sudden muscle contraction. 1373 *spasom, spasum;* later *spasme* (1392); borrowed from Old French *spasme,* and from Latin *spasmus* a spasm, from Greek *spasmós* a spasm, convulsion, from *spân* draw up, tear away, contract violently, pull. Greek *spân* is cognate with Old High German *spannan* to fasten, yoke; see SPAN[2] animals driven together. —**spasmodic** *adj.* 1681; earlier *spasmatic* (1603, perhaps borrowed from French *spasmatique*), of or characterized by spasms; borrowed from New Latin *spasmodicus* convulsive, from Greek *spasmṓdēs* of the nature of a spasm, from *spasmós* spasm, convulsion; for suffix see -IC.

spastic *adj.* of, having to do with, or characterized by spasms. 1753, in *Chambers Cyclopaedia;* borrowed from Latin *spasticus,* from Greek *spastikós* afflicted with spasms; literally, drawing, pulling, from *spân* draw up; see SPASM; for suffix see -IC. The term *spastic paralysis* a form of paralysis characterized by prolonged contraction of muscles with exaggerated reflexes, is first recorded in 1877. —**n.** person suffering from spastic paralysis. 1896, from the adjective.

spat[1] *n.* petty quarrel. 1804, American English; of unknown origin (sometimes said to be of imitative origin, though imitative of what is not indicated). —**v.** to quarrel pettily. 1809, American English; probably from the noun.

spat[2] *n.* short gaiter for covering the ankle. 1779 *spatts,* shortened spelling of earlier *spatterdash* long gaiter worn to keep the trousers or stockings from being spattered with mud (1687), formed from English *spatter,* v. + *dash,* v.

spate *n.* About 1425, flood, inundation; of unknown origin. The figurative sense of a sudden or violent outburst or outpouring (of words, anger, etc.) is first recorded about 1614.

spathe (spāᴛʜ) *n.* bract that encloses a flower cluster. 1785, borrowed from Latin *spatha* spathe of a palm tree, broad, flat weapon or tool, from Greek *spáthē* broad blade; see SPADE[1] tool.

spatial *adj.* 1847, occupying space; later, of or relating to space (1857); formed in English as an adjective to *space,* n., from Latin *spatium* SPACE + English *-al*[1].

spatio-temporal (spā′shēōtem′pərəl) *adj.* belonging to both space and time. 1900, in writings of Bertrand Russell; formed in English from Latin *spatium* SPACE + connective *-o-* + English *temporal.*

spatter *v.* 1582 (found earlier in *spattering,* participial adjective, 1576) to scatter in drops or particles; possibly a frequentative verb form of the stem *spat-,* found in Dutch or Low German *spatten* to spout, burst, or the extended form *spatter-,* in Frisian *spatterje* and *spetter-,* in Flemish *spetteren* to spatter; for suffix in English see -ER[4]. —**n.** a spattering. 1797, from the verb.

spatula (spach′ələ) *n.* broad, flat tool used for mixing. 1525, borrowing of Latin *spatula, spathula* broad piece, spatula, diminutive of *spatha* broad, flat tool or weapon, from Greek *spáthē* broad blade; see SPADE[1] tool. The Latin word was also borrowed into Middle English as *spatule* a medical instrument used to spread salve or clean wounds (about 1425).

spavin (spav′ən) *n.* disease of horses causing lameness. Probably before 1430 *spaven,* in Lydgate's translation of *Pilgrimage of the Life of Man;* borrowed from Middle French *espavain, esparvain,* probably from Frankish **sparwan* sparrow, related to Middle High German *sparwe* SPARROW. The disease was perhaps so called either from a comparison between a sparrow's ungainly gait and that of a horse affected with spavin, or between the sparrow's round body and the bony swelling of the horse's hock. —**spavined** *adj.* Probably before 1430 *spaveyned* affected with spavin; formed from Middle English *spaveyne,* variant of *spaven* spavin + *-ed*[2].

spawn *v.* bring forth, give birth to. 1413 *spawnen* (of fish) to reproduce; borrowed through Anglo-French *espaundre,* or Old French *espandre* to spread out, pour out, from Latin *expandere* EXPAND. The meaning of bring forth, give birth to, produce, is first recorded in Nashe's *The Unfortunate Traveller* (1594). —**n.** tiny eggs of fishes, frogs, etc., deposited in a mass. Before 1450 *spawne* the male reproductive glands of a fish; later, tiny eggs of fishes, etc. (1491); from the verb.

spay *v.* remove the ovaries of. About 1410 *spaien* stab with a sword, kill; also, remove the ovaries of; borrowed from Anglo-French *espeier* cut with a sword, from Middle French *espeer,* from Old French *espee* sword, from Latin *spatha* broad, flat weapon or tool, from Greek *spáthē* broad blade; see SPADE[1] tool.

speak *v.* Probably before 1200 *speken,* in Layamon's *Chronicle of Britain;* developed from Old English (about 1000) *specan,* variant of earlier *sprecan* to speak (about 725, in *Beowulf*). Old English *sprecan* is cognate with Old Frisian *spreka* to speak, Old Saxon *sprecan,* Middle Dutch *speken, spreken* (modern Dutch *spreken*), Old High German *spchhan, sprehhan* (modern German *sprechen*), from Proto-Germanic **sprekanan,* and probably Old Icelandic *spraka* to rattle, crackle (Swedish *spraka* to crackle, sparkle), *spraki* rumor, report; not recorded in Gothic. Cognates outside Germanic are found in Welsh *ffreg* chatter, gossip, Albanian *shpreh* I speak out, Greek *spharageîsthai* to crackle or hiss, Lithuanian *sprãgěti* to crackle or rattle, and Sanskrit *sphū́rjati* (it) bursts forth, crackles, rattles, from Indo-European **sp(h)reg-, *sp(h)erəg-/sp(h)rəg-/sp(h)r̥g-* (Pok.996).

In Old English the past tense form of *sprecan, specan* was *spræc, spæc,* which developed in Middle English into *spake,* now an archaism. The modern past tense form *spoke* replaced *spake,* probably by influence of the past participle *spoken.* The past participle followed a more direct course of development from Old English *(ge)sprecen, (ge)specen* to Middle English *(i-)speken, (i-)spoken,* to modern English *spoken.*

—**n.** *Scottish and dialectal English.* talk, speech. About 1300 *speke,* in *Havelok the Dane;* from the verb. In 1949, George Orwell used *speak* as a noun to form the compound *Newspeak,* meaning the official language of the fictitious country of Oceania in his novel *Nineteen Eighty-Four.* By 1950 *newspeak* was used to mean any type of distorted language or gobbledygook, a use that in the 1960's gave rise to the noun combining form *-speak,* with the meaning of the typical language or jargon of (a particular group, cause, discipline, etc.), and used informally to coin ad hoc compounds such as *artspeak, sportspeak, videospeak, warspeak,* etc.

—**speaker** *n.* 1303, a person who speaks, in Mannyng's *Handlyng Synne;* formed from English *speak,* v. + *-er*[1]. The word was first applied to a person who presides over a legislative assembly about 1400. The sense of a loudspeaker is first recorded in 1926.

speakeasy *n. Slang.* 1889, American English, an unlicensed saloon; formed from *speak,* v. + *easy* softly; so called from the practice of speaking quietly or sparingly about such an establishment in public, or speaking softly in such a place to avoid attracting undue attention, as by neighbors or the police. *Speakeasy* gained wide currency during the period of Prohibition (1920-1932), with which it is chiefly associated at present.

spear[1] *n.* long thrusting weapon, lance. Old English (before 800) *spere;* cognate with Old Frisian *spere, spiri* spear, Old Saxon *sper,* Middle Dutch and modern Dutch *speer,* Old High German *sper* (modern German *Speer*), and Old Icelandic *spjǫr,* pl., spears, from Proto-Germanic **speri.* A possible cognate outside Germanic is found in Latin *sparus* hunting spear, from Indo-European **speros,* root **sper-* (Pok.990). The Middle English form of the word was *spere,* as in Old English. The spelling *speare* is first recorded in 1524 (also in the name *Shakespeare,* originally, 1248, *Shakespere*); the modern *spear* occurs in 1539. **—v.** pierce with a spear. 1755, in Johnson's *Dictionary;* from the noun. **—spearhead** *n.* pointed head of a spear (about 1400); later, the leading part of an attack, undertaking, etc. (1929). *—v.* to lead. 1938, from the noun. **—spearmint** *n.* (1539, perhaps because of the shape of the flowers)

spear[2] *n.* sprout or shoot of a plant. 1509 *speere* church spire, variant of SPIRE. The transferred sense of the sprout or shoot of a plant is first recorded in 1647. **—v.** to sprout or shoot into a long stem. 1573 *speere,* variant of SPIRE, v.

special *adj.* Probably before 1200 *spetiale* uncommon, exceptional, in *Ancrene Riwle;* later *speciale* (probably before 1300); borrowed from Old French *especial,* and directly from Latin *speciālis* individual, particular, from *speciēs* appearance, kind, sort; see SPY; for suffix see -AL[1]. **—n.** Probably before 1300 *speciale* special person or thing, in *Kyng Alisaunder;* from the adjective. The specific sense of a special offer is first recorded in 1939. The sense of a special radio or television program is first recorded in American English in 1957. **—specialist** *n.* 1856, person who pursues a special branch of study, business, etc.; borrowed from French *spécialiste,* and formed in English from *special,* adj. + *-ist.* **—speciality** *n.* Probably before 1425 *specialite* special or unusual thing, in a translation of Higden's *Polychronicon;* borrowed from Middle French *especialité, specialité,* and probably directly from Late Latin *speciālitās* particularity, peculiarity, from Latin *speciālis* special, adj.; for suffix see -ITY. The meaning of special quality or characteristic is first recorded in 1625. **—specialize** *v.* 1613, to mention specially, formed from English *special,* adj. + *-ize.* The meaning of engage in a special study, some special line of business, etc., appeared in 1881. **—specially** *adv.* 1297, in a special manner; formed from English *special* + *-ly*[1]. The sense of for a special purpose, expressly, is first recorded about 1315. **—specialty** *n.* About 1303 *specialte* special affection, in Mannyng's *Handlyng Synne;* borrowed from Old French *especialté,* from Late Latin *speciālitās* speciality; for suffix see -TY[2]. The meaning of special line of work is first recorded in 1860.

specie (spē′shē) *n.* money in the form of coins. 1615, coin, money in the form of coins; from the earlier phrase *in specie* in the real or actual form (1551, in Bishop Cranmer's writings), from Latin *in speciē* in kind, ablative case of *speciēs* kind, form, sort; see SPY.

species (spē′shēz) *n.* Before 1398, a classification in logic, in Trevisa's translation of Bartholomew's *De Proprietatibus Rerum;* borrowed from Latin *speciēs* kind, sort; originally, appearance; see SPY. Doublet of SPICE. The sense of a distinct kind or sort (as in *a species of composition*) is first recorded in 1561. The sense in biology of a group of animals or plants that have common characteristics is first recorded in 1608. **—speciation** *n.* development of new species. 1906, formed from English *species* + *-ation.*

specific *adj.* Before 1631, having a special determining quality, in Donne's *Poems;* borrowed from French *spécifique,* learned borrowing from Late Latin, and borrowed directly into English from Late Latin *specificus* constituting a species, from Latin *speciēs* kind, sort, SPECIES; for suffix see -FIC. The meaning of definite, precise, explicit, is first recorded in English in 1740. **—n.** 1661, specific remedy or cure, in John Evelyn's *Fumifugium;* from the adjective. The sense of a specific quality, difference, detail, etc., (as in *the specifics of the accident*), is first recorded in 1697 and as a transferred sense of remedy, in 1662. **—specification** *n.* 1615, conversion to something specific; borrowed from Medieval Latin *specificationem* (nominative *specificatio*), from Late Latin *specificāre* to specify; for suffix see -ATION. The meaning of specific mention, detailed statement, is first recorded in 1642. **—specific gravity** a measure of density (1666, in writings of Robert Boyle) **—specificity** *n.* quality of being specific. 1876, borrowed from French *spécificité,* or formed from English *specific,* adj. + *-ity.* **—specify** *v.* Before 1325 *specifien* speak of something in detail, in *Cursor Mundi;* borrowed from Old French *specifier,* learned borrowing from Late Latin *specificāre* mention or note particularly, from *specificus* specific; for suffix see -FY.

specimen *n.* 1619, a pattern, model, borrowing of Latin *specimen* outward form, appearance, model, from *specere* to look at; see SPY. The meaning of a single thing regarded as typical of its kind is first recorded in English in 1654. An earlier sense of a means of finding out, experiment, is found in 1610.

specious (spē′shəs) *adj.* About 1390 *speciouse* pleasing to the sight, fair; borrowed from Latin *speciōsus,* from *speciēs* appearance; see SPY; for suffix see -IOUS. The meaning of seemingly desirable, reasonable, or probable, but not really so, deceptively attractive, is first found in John Speed's *History of Great Britain* (1611). The transition from the meaning of fair in appearance, lovely, attractive, to that of merely appearing to be fair, attractive, etc. (but not really so) is suggested by the transferred sense of having brilliant, gaudy, or showy coloring (applied to flowers, birds, etc., as in *specious feathers*), found in 1513, which implies mere superficial or outward show.

speck *n.* Before 1398 *speckke,* in Trevisa's translation of Bartholomew's *De Proprietatibus Rerum;* developed from Old English (before 800) *specca* small spot, stain; see SPECKLE. The sense of tiny bit, particle, is first recorded in the early 1400's. **—v.** to mark with specks 1580, from the noun.

speckle *n.* small spot or mark, speck. 1440 *spakle,* in *Promptorium Parvulorum;* later *speckle* (1495); probably related to Old English *specca* small spot, speck, and corresponding to Middle Dutch *speckel* speckle (modern Dutch *spikkel*), by loss of *r* from earlier **spreckel*, as found in Middle High German *spreckel* a spot or speck; originally, an eruption on the skin, from Indo-European **sp(h)reg-* break forth (Pok.997); see SPEAK. —**v.** 1570, in Levins' *Dictionary;* from the noun, or back formation from earlier *speckled*, adj., marked with speckles or specks (1440 *spaklyd;* before 1387 *splekked*), corresponding to Middle Dutch *spekelde* and *gespekeld* (modern Dutch *gespikkeld*) speckled, spotted, past participle of Middle Dutch *speckelen* to speckle (modern Dutch *spikkelen*).

spectacle *n.* About 1340 *spectakil* public entertainment or display; borrowed from Old French *spectacle*, from Latin *spectāculum* a show, spectacle, from *spectāre* to view, watch, frequentative verb form of *specere* to look at; see SPY. The sense of a glass lens to help a person's sight (usually in the plural *spectacles*) is first recorded in 1415, preceded by the figurative sense of a means through which anything is viewed (about 1395, in Chaucer's *Canterbury Tales*). —**spectacular** *adj.* 1682, striking or imposing as a display; formed in English from Latin *spectāculum* spectacle + English suffix *-ar.* —*n.* 1890, a spectacular show or display; from the adjective.

spectator *n.* Before 1586, onlooker, observer, in Sidney's *The Arcadia;* borrowed from Latin *spectātor* viewer, watcher, from *spectāt-*, past participle stem of *spectāre* to view, watch; see SPECTACLE; for suffix see -OR[2]. —**spectate** *v.* be a spectator. 1709, back formation from English *spectator.*

specter *n.* ghost. 1605, borrowed from French *spectre* an image, figure, ghost, from Latin *spectrum* appearance, vision, apparition; see SPECTRUM. The first spelling attested in English was *specter;* the variant spelling *spectre*, used chiefly in British English, appeared in 1703, in Pope's *Thebais*, and was modeled on the French form. —**spectral** *adj.* 1718, capable of seeing specters; later, of or like a specter (1815); formed in English from Latin *spectrum* appearance + English *-al*[1].

spectro- a combining form meaning having to do with the spectrum of colors, as in *spectroscope = an instrument for spectrum analysis; spectrogram = a photograph of a spectrum.* Formed by abstraction from such words as *spectrology, spectrological*, and from English *spectrum* + the connective vowel *-o-*.

spectroscope *n.* instrument for spectrum analysis. 1861, formed from English *spectro-* + *-scope.* —**spectroscopic** *adj.* 1864, performed by means of the spectroscope; formed from English *spectroscope* + *-ic.* —**spectroscopy** (spektros′kəpē) *n.* science of spectrum analysis. 1870, formed from English *spectroscope* + *-y*[3].

spectrum *n.* band of colors formed when a beam of light is broken up. 1611, apparition, specter, in John Speed's *The History of Great Britain;* borrowed from Latin *spectrum* appearance, image, apparition, from *specere* to look at, view; see SPY. The technical sense of a band of colors formed when a beam of light is broken up is first recorded in 1671, in Newton's writings. The figurative meaning of range, scope, compass, is first recorded in 1860.

speculate *v.* 1599, think carefully, consider, in Sir Edwin Sandys' *Europae Speculum;* back formation from *speculation* or *speculator*, modeled on Latin *speculātus*, past participle of *speculārī* to watch, examine, observe, from *specula* watchtower, from *specere* to look at; see SPY; for suffix see -ATE[1]. The extended meaning of conjecture or guess is first recorded in English before 1677, and the commercial sense of buy or sell when there is a great risk, hoping that one will profit from price changes in the market, is first recorded in 1785, in Jefferson's correspondence. —**speculation** *n.* About 1380 *speculacioun* serious study of some subject, careful thought, in Chaucer's translation of Boethius' *De Consolatione Philosophiae;* borrowed from Old French *speculation*, and directly from Late Latin *speculātiōnem* (nominative *speculātiō*) contemplation, observation, exploration, from Latin *speculārī* observe; for suffix see -ATION. The meaning of a buying or selling at great risk in order to profit by the rise or fall in the market value of commodities is first recorded in 1774, in letters of Horace Walpole. —**speculative** *adj.* About 1380 *speculatif*, in Wycliffe's writings; borrowed from Old French *speculatif* (feminine *speculative*), learned borrowing from Late Latin, and borrowed into English directly from Late Latin *speculātīvus*, from *speculāt-*, past participle stem of *speculārī* observe; for suffix see -IVE. —**speculator** *n.* 1555, person who engages in mental speculation, in Eden's translation of *Decades of the New World or West India;* borrowed from Latin *speculātor* scout, sentinel, from *speculāt-*, past participle stem of *speculārī* observe; for suffix see -OR[2]. The sense of a person who engages in financial speculation is first recorded in 1778, in the writings of Alexander Hamilton.

speculum (spek′yələm) *n.* mirror of polished metal. Probably before 1425, surgical instrument for enlarging a body cavity to examine it, in a translation of Chauliac's *Grande Chirurgie;* borrowed from Middle French *spéculum*, learned borrowing from Latin, and borrowed directly into English from Latin *speculum* mirror, from *specere* to view, look at; see SPY. The sense of a mirror or reflector of polished metal is first recorded in 1646.

speech *n.* Probably about 1150 *speche;* developed from Old English *spǣc* act of speaking, manner of speaking, utterance (before 1050, in *West Saxon Gospels*), variant of earlier *sprǣc* (before 800, in *Corpus Glossary*), related to *sprecan, specan* to SPEAK. Old English *sprǣc* is cognate with Old Frisian *sprēke, sprēze* speech, Old Saxon *sprāka*, Middle Low German and Middle Dutch *sprāke* (modern Dutch *spraak*), Old High German *sprāhha* (modern German *Sprache*), and Old Icelandic *spraki* rumor, report, from Proto-Germanic **sprǣkjō.* —**speechify** *v. Informal.* make a speech or speeches. 1723 (implied in *speechifying*); formed from English *speech* + *-ify*, as in *pacify, rectify*, etc.

speed *n.* Probably about 1200 *sped* swiftness, quickness, in *The Ormulum;* developed from Old English (before 800) *spēd* success, prosperity, advancement, swiftness; cognate with Old Saxon *spōd* success, prosperity, speed, Middle Dutch *spoed* (modern Dutch *spoed* speed), and Old High German *spuot*, from Proto-Germanic **spōđis*, Indo-European **sp(h)ōtis.* Cognates outside Germanic include Latin *spēs* hope, expectation, Lithuanian *spėti* have leisure, be quick enough, Old Slavic *spěti* be successful, Sanskrit *spháyate* (it) increases, becomes fat, *sphīti-s* prosperity, and Hittite *ispāi-* to sate oneself, from Indo-European **sp(h)ēi-/sp(h)ī-/sp(h)ē-* (Pok.983). —**v.** Probably before 1200 *speden* to travel swiftly, in Layamon's *Chronicle of Britain;* developed from Old English (993) *spēdan* to succeed, prosper, advance, from *spēd* success, speed. The Old English verb is cognate with Old Saxon *spōdian* to prosper, Middle Dutch and modern Dutch *spoeden* to speed, and Old High German *spuoten* to succeed, prosper (modern German *sputen* make haste, hurry). **—speedboat** *n.* (1911) **—speedometer** *n.* 1904, formed from English *speed* + *-o-* + *-meter.* **—speedway** *n.* (1894, American English, track for fast horse-driving; 1903, road on which cars can travel fast; 1925, race track for cars) **—speedy** *adj.* 1375 *spedy* moving with speed, swift, in Barbour's *The Bruce;* formed from Middle English *sped* speed, n. + *-y*[1].

speleology (spē'lēol'əjē) *n.* scientific study of caves. 1895, borrowed from French *spéléologie,* from Latin *spēlaeum* cave (from Greek *spḗlaion*) + French *-logie* -logy. Greek *spḗlaion* is related to *spéos* cave, grotto, and *spêlynx* (genitive *spḗlyngos*) cave, of unknown origin. Compare SPELUNKING.

spell[1] *v.* name the letters of. Before 1325 *spellen* to read letter by letter, read slowly or with difficulty, in *Cursor Mundi;* in part probably developed from Old English *spellian* to tell, declare, relate, speak, and in part borrowed from Old French *espeller* declare, spell, from a Germanic source (compare Old High German *spellōn* to tell, Old Icelandic *spjalla* to talk, converse, and Gothic *spillōn,* all derived from the same root as Old English *spell* story, discourse; see SPELL[2]). The common meaning of write or say the letters of a word is first recorded in Middle English probably before 1400. **—spelling bee** (1875)

spell[2] *n.* incantation, charm. Old English *spell* story, discourse, speech (about 725, in *Beowulf*); cognate with Old Saxon *spell* story, Old High German *spel,* Old Icelandic *spjall,* and Gothic *spill,* from Proto-Germanic **spellan,* earlier **spelnan.* Possible cognates outside Germanic include Armenian *aṙaspel* proverb, riddle, Greek *apeilḗ* threat, Latvian *pel̃t* to slander, and Tocharian A, Tocharian B *päl-, pāl-* to praise, from Indo-European **spel-* speak out loud (Pok.985). The meaning of a set of words supposed to have magical powers, incantation, charm, is first recorded in English in 1579; the word is also a part of the compound GOSPEL.

spell[3] *v.* work in place of (another) for a time. 1595, in Raleigh's *The Discovery of the Empire of Guiana;* developed from Old English (about 960) *spelian* to take the place of, represent, related to *gespelia, spala* substitute, of uncertain origin. **—n.** Before 1625, turn of work taken to relieve another; earlier, relief gang, relay, shift of workers (1593); related to the verb, and perhaps directly representing Old English *gespelia* substitute. The meaning of a continuous course or period of some work or occupation is first recorded in 1706, followed by the sense of an indefinite period of time, a while, in 1728.

spellbound *adj.* 1799, formed from English *spell*[2] charm + *bound*[1] fastened. **—spellbind** *v.* fascinate, enchant. 1808, in Southey's *Chronicle of the Cid;* formed from *spell*[2] charm + *bind,* as a verb to *spellbound.*

spelt *n.* species of wheat. Old English (before 1000) *spelt,* corresponding to Old Saxon *spelta* spelt, Middle Dutch *spelte, spelt* (modern Dutch *spelt*), Old High German *spelza* (modern German *Spelz, Spelt*); an early borrowing from Late Latin *spelta* spelt, from a Germanic source (compare Old High German *spaltan* to split, Middle High German *spelte* split piece of wood, splinter; see SPILL[1] let fall).

spelunking *n.* hobby of exploring and mapping caves. 1946, American English, formed from obsolete English *spelunk* cave or cavern + *-ing. Spelunk* is first recorded in Middle English (before 1382; earlier *spelonke,* about 1378), borrowed from Old French *spelunque,* from Latin *spēlunca* a cave, cavern, grotto, from Greek *spêlynx* (genitive *spḗlyngos*); see SPELEOLOGY. **—spelunker** *n.* person who engages in spelunking. 1942, American English; formed from obsolete English *spelunk,* n. + *-er*[1].

spend *v.* About 1175 *spenden* pay out, expend; developed from Old English *-spendan* (as in *forspendan* use up); borrowed from Latin *expendere* to EXPEND. Old English *-spendan* is cognate with Old High German *spendōn* (modern German *spenden*) to give, present, bestow, and Middle Low German and Middle Dutch *spenden,* also borrowed from Latin *expendere.* **—spendthrift** *n.* 1601, one who spends money profusely and wastefully, in Holland's translation of Pliny's *Natural History;* formed from English *spend,* v. + *thrift,* n. savings, profits, acquired wealth.

sperm[1] *n.* male reproductive cell. About 1375 *sperme* semen, in Chaucer's *Canterbury Tales;* borrowed probably from Old French *esperme,* learned borrowing from Late Latin, and borrowed into English directly from Late Latin *sperma* seed, semen, from Greek *spérma* seed, from *speírein* to sow, scatter; see SPRAY[1] sprinkle. The sense of a single male reproductive cell is first recorded in English in 1904. **—spermatic** *adj.* 1392 *spermatik* containing, conveying, or producing sperm; borrowed from Middle French *spermatique,* and directly from Late Latin *spermaticus* of sperm, from Greek *spermatikós,* from *spérma* (genitive *spérmatos*) seed; for suffix see -IC.

sperm[2] *n.* = spermaceti. 1839, shortened form of SPERMACETI. The term *sperm whale* also appeared in 1839 as a shortening of *spermaceti whale.* This whale was so called because the waxy substance found in its head was erroneously identified with animal sperm.

spermaceti (spėr'məsē'tē) *n.* waxy substance obtained from the sperm whale. Probably 1471, borrowed from Medieval Latin *sperma ceti* sperm of a whale (Late Latin *sperma* seed, SPERM[1]; and Medieval Latin *ceti,* genitive of Latin *cētus* large sea animal; see CETACEAN).

spermato- a combining form meaning seed, sperm, as in *spermatocyte = a germ cell that produces sperms.* Borrowing of Greek *spermato-,* combining form of *spérma* (genitive *spérmatos*) seed, semen, SPERM[1].

spermatozoon (spėr'mətəzō'ən) *n., pl.* **-zoa** (-zō'ə). male reproductive cell. 1836-39, New Latin, formed from *spermato-* + *-zoon,* from Greek *zôion* animal.

spew (spyü) *v.* throw out, vomit. Probably before 1200 *spewen;* developed from Old English *spīwan* (before 899, in Alfred's translation of St. Gregory's *Pastoral Care*); cognate with Old Frisian *spīa* to spew, spit, Old Saxon *spīwan,* Middle Dutch *spūwen* (modern Dutch *spuwen*), Old High German *spīwan* (modern German *speien*), Old Icelandic *spȳja* (Danish, Norwegian, and Swedish *spy*), and Gothic *speiwan,* from Proto-Germanic **spīwanan.* Cognates outside Germanic are found in Latin *spuere* to spit, Greek *ptýein,* Lithuanian *spiáuti,* Old Slavic *pljĭvati,* and Sanskrit *ṣṭhī́vati* (he) spits out, from Indo-European **(s)p(h)yēu-/(s)pyū-/(s)pīw-* (Pok.999).

sphagnum (sfag'nəm) *n.* kind of soft moss. 1741, New

Latin, from Latin *sphagnos* a kind of fragrant lichen, from Greek *sphágnos* a spiny shrub, of unknown origin.

sphere *n.* Before 1450 *sphere* (in ancient astronomy) hollow globe containing the stars and planets; alteration (influenced by Latin *sphaera*) of earlier *spere* the cosmos, composed of celestial spheres (probably before 1300, in *Arthour and Merlin*); borrowed from Old French *espere,* and probably directly from Latin *sphaera* globe, ball, celestial sphere, from Greek *sphaîra* globe, ball, possibly related to *spaírein* to quiver, move convulsively; see SPURN. The sense of a particular place or position occupied by the planets or stars is first recorded in Middle English about 1385 (in Chaucer's *Troilus and Criseyde*). From this meaning developed the senses of (a) a place, position, or station in society (1601, in Shakespeare's *All's Well That Ends Well*), and (b) the whole province, domain, or range of something (1602). The literal sense of a round body, globe, ball, is first recorded in Middle English before 1382. **—v.** 1605, make into a sphere, in Ben Jonson's *Masque of Blackness;* from the noun. **—spherical** *adj.* 1523, having the form of a sphere, in Skelton's writings, formed from English *sphere* + *-ical.* **—spheroid** *n.* thing shaped like a sphere. 1664, borrowed from Latin *sphaeroīdēs* spherical, from Greek *sphairoeidḗs,* from *sphaîra* ball; for suffix see -OID.

sphincter (sfingk′tər) *n.* ringlike muscle that can contract to close an opening or passage of the body. 1578; borrowed from Middle French *sphincter* (1548, in Rabelais), and directly from Late Latin *sphinctēr* contractile muscle, from Greek *sphinktḗr* band, anything that binds tight, from *sphíngein* to squeeze, bind; see SPHINX

sphinx (sfingks) *n.* Probably about 1421 *Spynx,* in Lydgate's *Siege of Thebes;* later *Sphinx* (1579-80); borrowed from Latin *Sphinx* monster having a lion's body with a woman's head, from Greek *Sphínx* (genitive *Sphingós*), back formation from *sphíngein* to squeeze, bind, perhaps cognate with Latvian *spaiglis, spaigle* fork for grasping crayfish, and Old Icelandic *spīkr* nail; see SPIKE[1] nail. The first reference in English was to the monster in Greek mythology that plagued Thebes by strangling everyone who could not solve the riddle it posed until Oedipus solved the riddle, and the Sphinx killed itself. The general sense of a figure or statue of a lion's body with a human head is first recorded in 1579-80, in a translation of Plutarch. The transferred meaning of a person with sphinxlike qualities, an enigmatic, inscrutable, or mysterious person, is first recorded in English in Ben Jonson's *Sejanus* (1603).

spice *n.* Probably before 1200, in *Ancrene Riwle;* borrowed from Old French *espice,* learned borrowing from Late Latin *speciēs* (plural) spices, goods, wares, from Latin, kind, sort; see the doublet SPECIES. **—v.** Before 1325 *spicen* (implied in *spiced,* participial adjective) prepare with a spice or spices, season; from the noun. **—spicy** *adj.* 1562, like a spice, sharp and fragrant, in William Turner's *A New Herbal;* formed from English *spice,* n. + *-y*[1]. The figurative sense of racy, piquant, salacious, is first recorded in 1844, from the earlier sense of spirited (1828).

spick-and-span or **spic-and-span** *adj.* neat and clean. 1665, in Pepys' *Diary;* shortened form of earlier *spick-and-span-new* new as a recently made spike and chip (1579-80, from *spick,* variant of SPIKE[1] nail + *span-new* very new, borrowed from Old Icelandic *spān-nýr,* from *spānn* chip, SPOON + *nýr* NEW).

spicule (spik′yül) *n.* small, slender, sharp-pointed piece. 1785, in a translation of Rousseau's *Letters on the Elements of Botany;* borrowed from Latin *spīculum,* diminutive of *spīca* ear of grain, SPIKE[2].

spider *n.* 1440 *spyde* (error for *spyder*), in *Promptorium Parvulorum;* alteration of earlier *spithre* (1340, in *Ayenbite of Inwyt*); developed from Old English *spīthra,* earlier **spinthra,* from Proto-Germanic **spenthrō,* formed from **spenwanan* to SPIN. **—spiderweb** *n.* (before 1649; earlier *spyders webbe,* in the Coverdale Bible, 1539) **—spidery** *adj.* 1825, like a spider, in letters of Coleridge; formed from English *spider* + *-y*[1].

spiel (spēl) *v. Slang.* to speak in a glib, wordy manner. 1894; earlier, to play circus music (1870); American English; borrowed from German *spielen* to play, from Old High German *spilōn;* cognate with Old English *spilian* to play, Old Frisian *spilia,* Old Saxon *spilōn,* Middle Dutch and modern Dutch *spelen.* **—n.** *Slang.* glib or persuasive speech or harangue, line, pitch. 1896, in George Ade's *Artie;* American English, probably from the verb, though with influence of German *Spiel* play, game.

spiffy *adj. Slang.* smart, neat, trim. 1853, of uncertain origin. The shorter form *spiff,* meaning fine or smart in dress or appearance, is recorded in dialectal English from 1862.

spigot *n.* Before 1382, plug used to stop the hole of a cask, in the Wycliffe Bible; probably borrowed from Old French **espigot,* represented by dialectal (Gascony) *espigot* core of a fruit, small ear of grain, Old French *espigeot* badly-threshed ear of grain, all diminutive forms derived from Old Provençal *espiga* ear of grain, from Latin *spīca;* see SPIKE[2] ear of grain. The extended sense of a valve for controlling the flow of a liquid, faucet, is first recorded in English about 1530.

spike[1] *n.* large, strong nail. 1345-46, probably borrowed from a Scandinavian source (compare Old Icelandic *spīk* splinter, *spīkr* nail, from Proto-Germanic **spīkaz,* and Middle Swedish *spīk, spijk* nail, Norwegian and Swedish *spik,* Danish *spig*). The Scandinavian forms are cognate with Middle Low German and Middle Dutch *spīker* nail (modern Dutch *spijker*), Middle High German *spīcher,* Old English *spīcing* large nail, and possibly with Lithuanian *speigliaĩ,* pl., thorns, from Indo-European **spei-g-* (Pok.981). **—v.** 1624, in writings of Captain John Smith; from the noun. **—spiky** *adj.* 1720, in Pope's translation of Homer's *Iliad;* formed from English *spike*[1], n. + *-y*[1].

spike[2] *n.* ear of grain. Probably before 1300 *spyc,* in *Kyng Alisaunder;* borrowed from Latin *spīca* ear of grain. Latin *spīca* is cognate with Dutch *spie* peg, pin, and Armenian *p'k'in* arrow, and possibly related to Latin *spīna* thorn, SPINE.

spikenard *n.* aromatic ointment used by the ancients. About 1280, borrowed from Old French *spicanarde,* and directly from Medieval Latin *spica nardi* ear of nard (Latin *spīca* SPIKE[2]; *nardī,* genitive of *nardus* spikenard, from Greek *nárdos,* from Semitic). The sense of aromatic plant yielding the ointment spikenard is first recorded in English in 1548.

spill[1] *v.* to let fall. Probably before 1200 *spillen* to waste; before 1325, to shed (blood), in *Cursor Mundi;* about 1340, let (liquid) fall or run out; developed from

Old English (about 950) *spillan* destroy, kill, variant of *spildan,* from Proto-Germanic **spelthjanan.*

The Old English forms correspond to Old Saxon *spildian* destroy, kill, Middle Low German and Middle Dutch *spilden, spillen* to waste, squander, spill (modern Dutch *spillen*), Old High German *spildan* destroy, waste, and Old Icelandic *spilla* destroy, kill (Swedish *spilla* to shed, waste, spill, Norwegian *spille,* Danish *spilde*). This group of words is further related to Middle Low German *spalden* to split, Middle Dutch *spouden* (modern Dutch *spouwen*), Old High German *spaltan* (modern German *spalten*), Middle High German *spelte* split piece of wood, splinter, Old English *speld,* Old Icelandic *spjald, speld* wooden tablet, beam, and Gothic *spilda* writing tablet, from Proto-Germanic **speldṓ,* Indo-European **sp(h)eltā́* (Pok.986).

—n. Before 1845, a fall or tumble; from the verb. The meaning of a spilling of liquid is first recorded about 1848.

—spillover *n.* (1940) **—spillway** *n.* (1889)

spill[2] *n.* splinter. About 1300 *spille* splinter, sliver; of uncertain origin; probably related to dialectal *spile* a stopper for a cask, splinter or sliver of wood (1513); borrowed from Middle Dutch *spīle* splinter, peg, which is cognate with Middle High German *spil* spearhead, and Old Icelandic *spila* narrow piece of wood (Danish and Norwegian *spile*), from Proto-Germanic **spīlō,* Indo-European **sp(h)ī-lo-s* (Pok.981). The sense of a thin piece of wood used to light a candle is first recorded in 1839.

spin *v.* Before 1250 *spinnen* (implied in *sponnen* spun, participial adjective); developed from Old English (before 800) *spinnan* draw out and twist fibers into thread; cognate with Middle Low German, Middle Dutch, and modern Dutch *spinnen* to spin, Old High German *spinnan* (modern German *spinnen*), Old Icelandic *spinna* (Swedish *spinna,* Norwegian *spinne,* Danish *spinde*), and Gothic *spinnan,* from Proto-Germanic **spenwanan,* from Indo-European **spen-* (Pok.988). The meaning of revolve, turn around rapidly, is first recorded in Milton's *Paradise Lost* (1667). **—n.** a spinning. 1831, from the verb. **—spinner** *n.* Before 1250 *spinnere;* probably formed in English from *spinnen* + *-ere* -er[1]. **—spinning jenny** (1783; the reason for the use of the personal name *Jenny* is uncertain) **—spinning wheel** (1404)

spinach *n.* Before 1399 *spynoche;* earlier as a surname *Spinach* (1267, but not found as a name for the vegetable in this spelling until sometime around 1425); borrowed from Old French *espinache,* from Old Provençal *espinarc, spinarch,* from Catalan *espinac* or Spanish *espinaca,* from Spanish-Arabic *ispinākh,* variant of Arabic *isbānakh, isfānākh,* from Persian *aspanākh* spinach.

spindle *n.* rod or pin used to twist, wind, or hold thread in spinning. Before 1225, alteration (with added *d* after *n,* as in *sound* and *thunder*) of Old English (before 800) *spinel,* related to *spinnan* to SPIN; for suffix see -LE[1]. Old English *spinel* is cognate with Old Frisian *spindel* spindle, Old Saxon *spinnila,* and Old High German *spinila* (modern German *Spindel*). **—v.** (of plants, etc.) grow tall and slender. 1577, (implied earlier in *spindling* 1441-42); from the noun in the sense of a stalk, stem, or shoot of a plant. **—spindly** *adj.* too tall and thin. 1651, formed from English *spindle,* n. + *-y*[1].

spindrift *n.* spray blown or dashed up from the waves. 1600 *spenedrift;* Scottish; formed from *spene,* alteration of earlier *spoon* to sail before the wind (1576, of uncertain origin) + *drift,* n. The spelling *spindrift* is first recorded in 1823.

spine *n.* About 1400, backbone, in a translation of Lanfranc's *Science of Surgery;* later, pointed, thornlike part (probably before 1422); borrowed from Old French *espine,* and directly from Latin *spīna* backbone; originally, thorn or prickle; cognate with Latvian *spina* twig, switch, Middle High German *spenel* pin, Sanskrit *sphyá-s* wood chip, stick, oar, and Tocharian A *spin-* hook, peg, from Indo-European **spīnā,* root **sp(h)ēi-/sp(h)ī-* (Pok.981). The sense of backbone, spinal column, was not common in English until the 1600's. **—spinal** *adj.* 1578, of or having to do with the backbone; borrowed from Late Latin *spīnālis* of or pertaining to the spine or a thorn, from Latin *spīna* spine; for suffix see -AL[1]. **—spinal column** (1836) **—spinal cord** (1836) **—spineless** *adj.* 1827, having no spine or backbone; formed from English *spine* + *-less.* The figurative sense of without courage, determination, or moral force, is first recorded in 1885, probably extended from the earlier sense of limp, destitute of force or vigor (1860, in Dickens' writings). **—spiny** *adj.* 1586, like a spine; later, covered with spines (1604); formed from English *spine* + *-y*[1].

spinet (spin′it) *n.* 1936, a small upright piano; earlier *spinette* musical instrument like a small harpsichord (1664, in Pepys' *Diary*); borrowed from earlier French *espinette* (now *épinette*), from Middle French, from Italian *spinetta,* perhaps diminutive of *spina* thorn, spine, from Latin *spīna* thorn, SPINE; so called because the strings of the spinet were plucked with quills; for suffix see -ET. The OED in commenting on this etymology says, "This would be an unusual application of *spīna,* and greater probability attaches to the explanation given by A(driano) Banchieri," an Italian musician who claimed to have seen the name of the inventor, Giovanni Spinetti, on a spinet dated 1503.

spinnaker (spin′əkər) *n.* large triangular sail. 1866 *spinniker,* of uncertain origin; perhaps derived from *spin* in the sense of go rapidly; see also the etymology of *spindrift* for a possible connection by phonetic alteration with *spoon* to sail before the wind. According to the OED, the word is said to be a fanciful formation of *spinx,* mispronunciation of *Sphinx,* the name of the first yacht known to carry this type of sail. The spelling *spinnaker* is found in 1869.

spinster *n.* unmarried woman. Before 1376 *spinstere* female spinner of thread, in *Piers Plowman;* formed from Middle English *spinnen* to SPIN + *-stere* -ster. Since spinning was commonly done by women in the Middle Ages, the term *spinster* was often appended in Middle English to names of women to denote their occupation, and was later used (from the 1600's to the early 1900's) as the legal designation for an unmarried woman. The generalized sense of a woman who has not married, especially one beyond the usual age for marriage, is first recorded in 1719.

spiracle (spir′əkəl) *n.* opening for breathing. Probably 1440, air hole, vent, in a translation of Palladius' *De Re Rustica;* borrowed from Latin *spīrāculum* air hole, from *spīrāre* to breathe; see SPIRIT. An earlier sense of breath, spirit, vitality, is recorded in Middle English probably before 1380.

spiral *adj.* 1551, borrowed from Middle French *spiral* (1534, in Rabelais), and directly from Medieval Latin *spiralis* winding, coiling, from Latin *spīra* coil, from Greek *speîra* coil, twist, wreath, related to *spártē* rope, and to Old Lithuanian *spartas* ribbon, band, and Latvian *sprangât* to lace up, from Indo-European **sper-/spor-* turn, wind (Pok.991); for suffix see -AL[1]. **—n.** continuous curve, coil. 1656, in a translation of Hobbes' *Elements of Philosophy;* from the adjective. **—v.** move in a spiral. 1834, from the noun.

spirant (spī′rənt) *n. Phonetics.* = fricative. 1862, borrowed from Latin *spirantem* (nominative *spirāns*) breathing, present participle of *spīrāre* to breathe; see SPIRIT; for suffix see -ANT.

spire *n.* About 1250, tapering stalk or blade of a plant, sprout, shoot, in *The Owl and the Nightingale;* developed from Old English (before 1000) *spīr;* cognate with Middle Low German *spir* small point or top, Middle Dutch and modern Dutch *spier* shoot, blade of grass, and Old Icelandic *spīra* reed, slender tree (Swedish *spira,* Norwegian and Danish *spire* sprout, spire), from Proto-Germanic **spīraz,* Indo-European **sp(h)īros,* root **sp(h)ēi-/sp(h)ī-* sharp point (Pok.981). The extended meaning of the tapering top part of a tower or steeple is first recorded in 1596, preceded by the sense of a tall, slender, sharp-pointed summit, peak, or column, found in 1586. **—v.** Before 1325 *spiren* to send forth or develop shoots, sprout; from the noun. The meaning of rise up into a spire is first recorded in 1591, in Spenser's writings.

spirit *n.* About 1250, animating or vital principle, breath of life, in *Genesis and Exodus;* borrowed from Old French *espirit,* learned borrowing from Latin, and borrowed into English directly from Latin *spīritus* (genitive *spīritūs*) soul, courage, vigor, breath, related to *spīrāre* to breathe. Latin *spīrāre* is possibly cognate with Lithuanian *pyškėti* to bang, Old Slavic *piskati* to play a pipe, and Sanskrit *picchorā* pipe, flute, from Indo-European **peis-/pis-, speis-* (Pok.796).

The original English uses of *spirit* are mainly derived from passages in the Vulgate, in which Latin *spīritus* is used to translate Greek *pneûma* and Hebrew *rūaḥ.* The extended meaning of a supernatural, incorporeal being, is first recorded in Middle English, probably before 1350, and the sense of the activating or essential principle of an emotion, etc. (as in *the spirit of independence*), before 1382 in Wycliffe's writings. The common meaning of brisk or lively quality is first recorded in 1588. The plural *spirits,* in the sense of an alcoholic solution of a volatile substance is first recorded in Ben Jonson's *The Alchemist* (1610); the meaning of strong alcoholic liquor first occurs in Bunyan's *Pilgrim's Progress* (1678, 1684).

—v. 1599, make (the blood, a liquor, etc.) more active or lively, in Shakespeare's *Henry V;* from the noun. The meaning of infuse with energy or ardor, animate, is first recorded in 1608. The sense of carry off or away secretly is first recorded in 1666.

—spiritual *adj.* About 1303 *spirituele* of, relating to, or consisting of spirit, relating to sacred or religious matters, in Mannyng's *Handlyng Synne;* borrowed from Old French *spirituel,* and directly from Medieval Latin *spiritualis* of or pertaining to breath, wind, air, or spirit, from Latin *spīritus* spirit; for suffix see -AL[1]. —*n.* Probably before 1400, the church; later, a spiritual person (1532); from the adjective. A *spiritual* (plural *spirituals*), a religious or spiritual song of a type that originated among American blacks, is first recorded in 1870. **—spiritualism** *n.* 1796, tendency towards a spiritual view of things; formed in English from *spiritual,* adj. + *-ism,* perhaps on the model of French *spiritualisme.* The sense of the belief that dead spirits communicate with the living is first recorded in 1855. **—spiritualist** *n.* 1649, formed from English *spiritual,* adj. + *-ist,* perhaps on the model of French *spiritualiste.* **—spiritualize** *v.* to make spiritual. 1631, formed from English *spiritual,* adj. + *-ize,* perhaps on the model of French *spiritualiser.* **—spirituous** *adj.* 1599, spirited, animated, in Ben Jonson's *Cynthia's Revels;* probably borrowed from Middle French *spiritueux,* or, less likely formed in English from Latin *spiritus* spirit + English *-ous.* The meaning of like, of, or containing alcohol, is first recorded in 1667.

spirochete or **spirochaete** (spī′rəkēt) *n.* spiral-shaped bacterium. 1877, in Huxley and Martin's *Elementary Biology;* borrowed from New Latin *Spirochaeta,* the genus name; formed from Greek *speîra* a coil; see SPIRAL + *chaítē* hair, cognate with Avestan *gaēsa-* curly hair (modern Persian *gēs* hair hanging down), and Middle Irish *gaiset* stiff hair, bristle, from Indo-European **ghait-, *ghait-s-* (Pok.410).

spit[1] *v.* expel saliva. Probably before 1200 *spitten,* in *Ancrene Riwle;* developed from Old English *spittan* (about 950, Anglian), probably a dialectal variant of *spǣtan* (West Saxon), of imitative origin in Proto-Germanic, and in dialectal German *spitzen* to spit, Danish and Norwegian *spytte,* Swedish *spotta,* and Icelandic *spýta.* Compare SPITTLE. **—n.** saliva. Before 1325, in *Cursor Mundi;* from the verb. **—spitball** *n.* (1846, wad of chewed paper, American English; 1905, baseball pitch using a moistened ball) **—spitfire** *n.* 1611, cannon, in Cotgrave's *Dictionary* (1600, as adjective, *fire-spitting*). The sense of a fiery-tempered person is first recorded in 1680. **—spitting image** exact likeness. 1901, alteration (by folk etymology) of earlier *spit and image* (1895). *Spit* has been recorded since 1825 as a noun meaning exact likeness.

spit[2] *n.* sharp-pointed rod on which meat is roasted. Probably before 1200, in Layamon's *Chronicle of Britain;* developed from Old English *spitu* (about 1000, in Ælfric's *Grammar*); cognate with Middle Dutch *spit, spet* spit (modern Dutch *spit),* Old High German *spiz* spit (modern German *Spiess*), *spizzi* pointed (modern German *spitz*), Swedish *spett* spit, and Danish *spid,* from Proto-Germanic **spituz,* Indo-European **spidus,* root **sp(h)ēi-/sp(h)ī-/*sp(h)i-* sharp (Pok.981) A probable cognate outside Germanic is found in Lithuanian *spitėlė, spitulė* needle, thorn. **—v.** Probably before 1200 *spiten* to put on a spit, thrust through with a spit, in Layamon's *Chronicle of Britain;* from the noun.

spite *n.* ill will, grudge. Probably before 1300, contempt, disdain, ill will, in *Arthour and Merlin;* shortened form of *despit* malice, DESPITE. **—v.** Probably before 1400 *spiten* to regard with spite; from the noun.

spittle *n.* saliva. 1481, in Caxton's *The Mirror of the World;* probably alteration (influenced by SPIT[1]) of earlier *spatel* saliva (before 1250); developed from Old English *spǣtl, spātl* (before 899, in Alfred's translation of St. Gregory's *Pastoral Care*), from Proto-Germanic **spǣtlan,* related to *spǣtan* to SPIT[1].

spittoon *n.* container to spit into. 1823, American English; formed from *spit*[1], v. + *-oon.*

spitz *n.* kind of dog with pointed nose and ears. 1842, borrowing of German *Spitz* (also, rarely, *Spitzhund*), from *spitz* pointed; see SPIT[2] rod.

splash *v.* cause (water, mud, etc.) to fly about. 1715, in Matthew Prior's *Poetical Works;* probably alteration of PLASH, with initial *s* regarded as intensive to the meaning. **—n.** a splashing. 1736, in Robert Ainsworth's *Thesaurus;* from the verb. **—splashdown** *n.* landing of a spacecraft in the ocean (1961, American English). **—splashy** *adj.* 1834, sounding like a splash; 1836, attracting attention, sensational; formed from English *splash* + *-y*[1].

splatter *v.* to splash, spatter thoroughly. 1784-85 (found earlier in *splatterdash,* 1772, variant of *spatterdash* leggings worn to protect clothing from mud, 1687), perhaps a blend of *spatter* and *splash.* **—n.** a splash, spatter. 1819, from the verb.

splay *v.* to spread out. Before 1338 *splayen* to unfold, unfurl, in Mannyng's *Chronicle of England;* shortened form of *desplayen* to DISPLAY. The meaning of spread out, expand, extend, is first recorded probably before 1405.

spleen *n.* ductless glandlike organ near the stomach. Probably before 1300 *splen;* borrowed through Old French *esplen, esplien,* or directly from Latin *splēn,* from Greek *splḗn.* Greek *splḗn,* earlier **splḗnch* (compare *splánchna* innards), is cognate with Latin *liēn* (genitive *liēnis*) spleen, Old Irish *selg,* Old Slavic *slězena,* Armenian *p'aicałn,* Sanskrit *plīhán-,* and Avestan *spərəzan-.* Distortions through taboos have made reconstructions of the Indo-European original wellnigh impossible: **sp(h)elĝhen, *splenĝh-, *spleĝh-, *splēĝh-* (Pok.987).

In the Middle Ages and even into the 1700's the spleen was commonly believed to be the seat of emotions, especially of low spirits, and of mirth or laughter; both senses found in Gower's *Confessio Amantis* (1393). The meaning of bad temper, which developed from the sense of low spirits, is found in Shakespeare's *Richard III* (1594), and in the phrase *vent one's spleen* (1885).

—splenetic (splinet'ik) *adj.* pertaining to the spleen. 1544, borrowed from Late Latin *splēnēticus,* from Latin *splēn* SPLEEN; for suffix see -IC. The word is also found in Middle English as a noun *splenetik,* meaning a person afflicted with a disorder of the spleen (before 1398). The meaning of bad-tempered, testy, irascible, is found in 1592.

splendid *adj.* 1624, sumptuous, grand, magnificent, in part, perhaps a shortened form of earlier *splendidious* (probably before 1425, in a translation of Higden's *Polychronicon*), on the model of, and probably in some instances borrowed directly from, French *splendide,* and directly from Latin *splendidus* resplendent, brilliant, from *splendēre* be bright, shine; cognate only with Old Lithuanian *splendėti* to shine, from Indo-European **splēnd-/slənd-* (Pok.987). **—splendiferous** *adj.* About 1460; borrowed from Medieval Latin **splendifer,* Late Latin *splendōrifer* (*splendor* + *ferre* to bear, carry); reborrowed 1843 from Medieval Latin **splendifer;* for suffix see -OUS. The latter formation is considered a jocular usage, similar to *splendacious* (1843, formed in English from *splend(id)* + *-acious*).

splendor *n.* Probably before 1475 *splendure* great brightness, brilliant light; borrowed perhaps through Anglo-French *esplendur,* or more likely from Middle French *esplendour,* and directly from Latin *splendor,* from *splendēre* be bright; see SPLENDID; for suffix see -OR[1]. **—splendorous** *adj.* 1591, formed from English *splendor* + -ous.

splice *v.* Before 1625 (nautical use) join together by weaving; back formation from earlier *splisyng* act of joining together ropes, etc., by weaving (1524-25); borrowed from Middle Dutch *splissinge,* verbal noun of *splissen* to splice, related to *splitten* to SPLIT. The general sense of fasten together (timber, girders, etc.) is first recorded in 1626. The word was first used in reference to a motion picture film in 1912, and to genetic materials, such as DNA, in 1975. The now somewhat archaic informal sense of marry is found as early as 1751, in Smollett's *Adventures of Peregrine Pickle.* **—n.** act or result of splicing. 1627, in Captain John Smith's *The Seaman's Grammar;* from the verb.

splint *n.* Probably before 1300 *splente* flexible strip of wood or metal, in *The Romance of Guy of Warwick,* earlier in *splenteware* strip of wood (1267), and later with the spelling *splynte* (1376-78); probably borrowed from Middle Low German *splinte, splente* thin piece of iron, related to Middle Dutch *splinte* splint (modern Dutch *splint*), and cognate with Norwegian and Swedish *splint* pin, wedge, splinter. These words are probably also cognate with Middle High German *spelte* splinter, and Old High German *spaltan* to split; see SPILL[1] to let fall. The meaning of a piece of wood, metal, etc., to hold a broken or dislocated bone in place, is first recorded before 1400. **—v.** put (a fractured bone) into splints, bind with a splint (1392); from the noun.

splinter *n.* thin, sharp piece of wood, bone, glass, etc. Before 1325 *splentre;* later *splintre* (before 1398); borrowed from Middle Dutch *splinter, splenter* a splinter, related to *splinte* SPLINT. **—adj.** separated from a larger unit or group, breakaway. 1935, (as in *splinter party*), from the noun. **—v.** split or break into splinters. 1582, in Stanyhurst's translation of Vergil's *Aeneid;* from the noun. **—splintery** *adj.* 1796, producing splinters; 1807, apt to splinter; formed from *splinter* + *-y*[1].

split *v.* 1590, to break up, in Shakespeare's *Comedy of Errors;* 1593, to divide, cleave, rend, in Shakespeare's *3 Henry VI;* borrowed from Dutch *splitten,* from Middle Dutch. Middle Dutch *splitten* is cognate with Middle Low German *splīten* to split, Middle High German *splīzen* (modern German *spleissen*), and Old Frisian *splīta* to split, from Proto-Germanic **spleit-/split-,* cognate with Old Irish *sliss* a slice, from Indo-European **spleid-/splid-* (Pok.1000).

The slang meaning of leave, depart, is first recorded in American English in 1954, and probably developed from the earlier meaning of separate, become divorced (1942).

—n. 1597, from the verb.

—adj. broken or cut from end to end, divided. 1648, from the past participle of the verb. **—split infinitive** (1897) **—split-level** *adj.* (1952) **—split personality** (1919) **—split second** (1912, in Chesterton's writings) **—split ticket** ballot cast for candidates of more than one political party (1836, American English).

splotch *n.* large, irregular spot. 1601, perhaps a blend of *spot, blot,* and *botch.* Compare later BLOTCH. **—v.** make splotches on. 1654, from the noun. **—splotchy** *adj.* covered with splotches. 1863, formed from English *splotch,* n. + *-y*[1].

Other formations of this type include *splash, splatter, splotty* (obsolete), all of which denote some kind of action that spreads a liquid or loose, watery mixture in small drops, and may be imitative of the sound of doing so, or in the case of nouns, such as *splotch,* denote the result of such action, in the form of spots of liquid that fall on some object, such as clothing.

splurge *n.* 1830, American English, ostentatious display; perhaps a blend of *splash* and *surge.* The sense of an extravagant indulgence in spending is found in 1928, also in American English. **—v.** 1843, to show off, American English; from the noun. The sense of spend extravagantly, indulge oneself lavishly, is first recorded in 1934.

splutter *n.* 1677, noise or fuss; later, violent and confused talk (1688); perhaps variant of SPUTTER, felt to be reinforced or intensified by substitution of the prefixal *spl-* as in *splash* and *splatter.* **—v.** to talk in a hasty, confused way. 1728, in Defoe's *The Memoirs of Captain Carleton;* from the noun.

spoil *v.* Probably about 1300 *spoulen* undress (someone), strip (an enemy) of arms and armor; later *spoilen* (about 1330), and with the meaning of pillage, loot (before 1382, in the Wycliffe Bible); borrowed from Old French *espoillier* to strip, plunder, from Latin *spoliāre* to strip of clothing, rob, from *spolium* armor stripped from an enemy, booty; cognate with Greek *spolás* leather garment, *sphállein* cause to fall, from Indo-European **sphel-* to split (Pok.986). Middle English *spoilen* may be in some uses a shortened form of *despoilen* DESPOIL. The ordinary meaning of damage or injure so as to make unfit or useless, is first recorded in English in 1563. The sense of damage in character by overindulgence (as in *spoil a child*) is first recorded in Congreve's *Double Dealer* (1694). **—n.** Often, **spoils.** plunder, loot. About 1340; borrowed from Old French *espoille, espuille,* from Latin *spolium* booty. **—spoilage** *n.* 1597, act of plundering or robbing; formed from English *spoil,* v. + *-age.* The meaning of a spoiling or being spoiled is first recorded in 1816 in Bentham's writings, and that of something spoiled, in 1888. **—spoilsport** *n.* person who spoils the sport or plans of others (1801, in Maria Edgeworth's *Belinda*). **—spoils system** system or practice of a successful political party giving public offices to its supporters (1838, American English).

spoke *n.* one of the bars from the center of a wheel to the rim. Probably before 1300, developed from Old English *spāca* spoke (before 899, in Alfred's translation of Boethius' *De Consolatione Philosophiae*), related to *spīcing* large nail, SPIKE[1]. Old English *spāca* is cognate with Old Frisian *spēke* spoke, Old Saxon *spēka,* Middle Dutch *speke, speec,* and Old High German *speicha* (modern German *Speiche*), from Proto-Germanic **spaikōn,* Indo-European **spoig-,* root **spei-g-* (Pok. 981). **—v.** furnish with spokes. 1720, in Pope's translation of Homer's *Iliad;* from the noun. **—spokeshave** *n.* 1510, a drawknife, originally used to fashion spokes.

spokesman *n.* 1519, an interpreter; later, a person who speaks for another or others (1540); irregularly formed from English *spoke* (past participle of *speak*) + *man,* on analogy of *craftsman, landsman,* etc. **—spokesperson** *n.* spokesman or spokeswoman. 1972, American English; coined to avoid reference to the subject's sex. **—spokeswoman** *n.* 1654, woman who speaks for another or others; formed from English *spokes(man)* + *woman.*

spoliation (spō'lēā'shən) *n.* a plundering or despoiling. Probably about 1400 *spoliacioun;* borrowed from Latin *spoliātiōnem* (nominative *spoliātiō*), from *spoliāre* to plunder, rob; see SPOIL; for suffix see -ATION.

spondee (spon'dē) *n.* foot or measure in poetry. Before 1382, in the Wycliffe Bible; borrowed from Old French *spondee,* learned borrowing from Latin *spondēus,* from Greek *spondeîos* the meter originally used in chants accompanying libations, from *spondḗ* libation, related to *spéndein* make a drink offering; see SPOUSE.

spondulicks (spondü'liks) *n. Slang.* money, cash. 1856, American English, of unknown origin. *Spondulicks* was used by Mark Twain in *The Adventures of Huckleberry Finn* (1884) and by O. Henry in *Cabbages and Kings* (1904); since then it has been adopted in British English, where it appears from time to time in periodicals such as the Daily Express (1959) and the Manchester Guardian (1970).

sponge *n.* Old English (about 1000) *sponge,* borrowed from Latin *spongia, spongea* a sponge or the sea animal from which it comes, from Greek *spongiá,* related to *spóngos* sponge. The Greek words are probably cognate with, or borrowed from the same source (a Mediterranean language) as Latin *fungus* mushroom, FUNGUS. Compare German *Schwamm,* meaning sponge or mushroom. The zoological sense of any of the sea animals with tough, porous skeletons from which sponges are obtained is first recorded in English in Elyot's *Dictionary* (1538). **—v.** 1393 *spongen* (implied in *spongyng,* verbal noun) wipe or rub with a wet sponge, clean with a sponge; from the noun. The figurative sense of clean out or deprive (a person) of money, etc., is first recorded in 1631, and the related meaning of live on others in a dependent or parasitic manner is found in 1673. The sense of get or profit from another in the manner of a dependent or parasite is first cited in 1676. **—sponge cake** (1808, in letters of Jane Austen) **—sponger** *n.* 1677, one who lives as a parasite. **—spongy** *adj.* 1539, in Elyot's *The Castel of Helth;* formed from English *sponge,* n. + *-y*[1].

sponson (spon'sən) *n.* structure built out from the side of a vessel for support or protection. 1835 *sponcing;* 1838 *sponson;* nautical use, of unknown origin.

sponsor *n.* 1651, godfather or godmother; borrowing of Late Latin *spōnsor* sponsor in baptism, Latin, a surety guaranty, from *spōns-,* past participle stem of *spondēre* give assurance, promise solemnly; see SPOUSE; for suffix see -OR[2]. The sense of a person who makes a formal promise or pledge on behalf of another, is first recorded in Miége's *French and English Dictionary* (1677). The modern sense of a person who pays for a radio (or, after 1947, television) program in order to advertise is first found in 1931. **—v.** support or assist as a sponsor. 1884, from the noun. The modern sense of act as a sponsor for (a radio or television program) is first recorded in 1931. **—sponsorship** *n.* 1809, formed from English *sponsor,* n. + *-ship.*

spontaneous *adj.* occurring or caused by natural impulse. Probably about 1200 *sponntaneuss* acting of one's own accord, in *The Ormulum;* borrowed from Late Latin *spontāneus* willing, from Latin *(suā) sponte* of one's own accord, willingly, of unknown origin; for suffix see -OUS. The sense of occurring by natural impulse, without external stimulus, is first recorded in 1656, in Hobbes' writings. **—spontaneity** (spon'tənē'-ətē) *n.* spontaneous quality, action, etc. 1651, formed as a noun to English *spontaneous;* for suffix see -ITY.

spoof *n.* 1889, a hoax, deception, humbug; extended sense of earlier *Spouf,* a game involving hoaxing (1884), invented and named by the British comedian Arthur

Roberts (1852-1933). The sense of a light satirical parody is probably first recorded in 1914. **—v.** 1889, to hoax or deceive, from the name of the hoaxing game. The extended sense of make fun of by parodying is found in 1927.

spook *n.* ghost, specter. 1801, American English; borrowed from Dutch *spook,* from Middle Dutch *spooc* spook, ghost, related to Middle Low German *spōk* spook, of unknown origin. The slang sense of a secret agent, spy, is first recorded in 1942, in American English. **—v.** 1867, walk as a ghost; haunt, scare; in Lowell's poetry; from the noun. **—spooky** *adj.* scary. 1854, American English; formed from *spook,* n. + *-y*[1].

spool *n.* cylinder on which thread, wire, etc., is wound. Before 1325, borrowed from Old North French *spole* a spool, and directly from Middle Dutch *spoele* a spool. Middle Dutch *spoele* is cognate with Middle Low German *spōle* and Old High German *spuola* spool (modern German *Spule*), from Proto-Germanic **spōlōn,* related to **speldǭ* splinter; see SPILL[1] let fall. **—v.** wind on a spool. 1603, from the noun.

spoon *n.* About 1350 *spon* eating utensil (but implied earlier in *sponeful* spoonful, about 1300); also earlier, chip of wood (probably before 1300); found in Old English (before 800) *spōn* chip, shaving; cognate with Middle Low German *spōn* wooden spatula, Middle Dutch *spaen* chip, splinter (modern Dutch *spaan*), Old High German *spān* (modern German *Span*), and Old Icelandic *spánn, spónn* chip, tile, spoon, from Proto-Germanic **spǣnuz.* A probable cognate outside Germanic is Greek *sphḗn* (genitive *sphēnós*) wedge, earlier **sphān-*, still earlier **sphans-*, from Indo-European **sphē-/sphə-* (Pok.980). The Middle English sense of an eating utensil was perhaps borrowed from Old Icelandic *spónn.* **—v.** take up in a spoon. 1715, from the noun. The meaning of court or flirt is first recorded in 1831, and with its implications of being foolishly sentimental, may have developed from the earlier sense of the noun "a foolish person, simpleton" (1799). **—spoonbill** *n.* bird with spoon-shaped bill (1678). **—spoonfeed** *v.* (1615, to teach in easy steps)

spoonerism *n.* accidental transposition of sounds of two or more words, such as "a well-boiled icicle" for "a well-oiled bicycle." 1900, formed from the name of the Reverend William A. *Spooner,* 1844-1930, of New College, Oxford, who was famous for such mistakes + English *-ism.* According to the OED, *spoonerism* was in informal use in Oxford from about 1885.

spoor *n.* trail of a wild animal. 1823, borrowed from Afrikaans *spoor,* from Middle Dutch *spor, spoor,* related to *spōre* SPUR. Middle Dutch *spor, spoor* is cognate with Old English, Old High German, and Old Icelandic *spor* footprint, track, trace, modern German *Spur,* Danish and Norwegian *spor,* and Swedish *spår.* **—v.** to track by a spoor. 1850, in R.G. Cumming's *Hunter's Life in South Africa;* borrowed from Afrikaans, from Middle Dutch *sporen,* from *spor, spoor,* n.

sporadic *adj.* Before 1689, (of diseases) occurring in scattered instances, not epidemic; shortened form of *sporadical* (1654); borrowed from Medieval Latin *sporadicus* scattered, from Greek *sporadikós* scattered, from *sporás* (genitive *sporádos*) scattered, from *sporá* a sowing; see SPORE; for suffix see -IC, -ICAL. The meaning of happening now and again or at intervals, occasional, is first recorded in 1847, but may have occurred earlier in the variant form *sporadical* (1654).

sporangium (spəran′jēəm) *n. Botany.* spore case. 1821, in Sir William J. Hooker's *Flora Scotica;* New Latin, formed from Greek *sporá* seed, SPORE + *angeîon* vessel, from *ángos* vessel, pail, of unknown origin.

spore *n.* cell capable of growing into a new organism. 1836, borrowed from New Latin *spora,* from Greek *sporá* seed, a sowing, related to *spóros* sowing, and *speírein* to sow; see SPRAY[1] sprinkle.

sporo- a combining form meaning spore, as in *sporogenesis = the formation of spores.* Formed in English from New Latin *spora* SPORE + English connective *-o-.*

sporran (spor′ən) *n.* purse or pouch worn in front of a kilt. 1818, in Scott's *Rob Roy;* borrowed from Gaelic *sporan,* Irish *sparan* purse, of uncertain origin. An earlier Scottish form *sparren* appeared in 1752.

sport *n.* About 1400 *sporte* pleasant pastime, amusement, diversion; shortened from earlier *dysporte* (about 1303); borrowed from Anglo-French *disport,* from Old French *desport* pastime, recreation, pleasure, sport, from *desporter* to divert, amuse (oneself), please, play; see DISPORT. The sense of a game, usually one involving physical exercise, is first recorded in English in 1523. The meaning of good fellow (as in *be a sport*) developed about 1905 from the earlier sense of one concerned with sports, sportsman (1861). The term *sport of nature* (1635) for a spontaneous mutation or variation in biology (shortened to *sport* in 1842) was a translation of Latin *lūsus nātūrae* a playing or freak of nature. **—v.** Probably before 1400 *sporten* to amuse (oneself); shortened from *disporten* to DISPORT. The meaning of display, show off, is found in 1712. **—adj.** of sports, suitable for sports. 1582, in Stanyhurst's translation of Vergil's *Aeneid;* from the noun. **—sporting** *adj.* 1653, engaged in sport; later, sportsmanlike (1867); formed from English *sport,* v. + *-ing*[2]. **—sportive** *adj.* playful, merry. 1590, in Shakespeare's *Comedy of Errors;* formed from English *sport,* n. or v. + *-ive.* **—sports** *adj.* of sports, suitable for sports (1897). *—n.* = athletics (1594). **—sports car** (1928) **—sportscaster** *n.* (1938) **—sports coat** (1914; also *sports jacket,* 1927) **—sportsman** *n.* (1706-07) **—sportsmanlike** *adj.* (1816, like a sportsman, in Scott's *The Antiquary;* 1853, fair, honorable) **—sportsmanship** *n.* (1745, in Fielding's *Tom Jones*) **—sporty** *adj.* sporting. 1889, formed from English *sport,* n. + *-y*[1].

spot *n.* Probably before 1200 *spot* (but usually *spotte*) small mark, blot, stain, in *Ancrene Riwle;* earlier as a surname *Spotte* (1194); perhaps, in part, developed from Old English *splot* a spot, and probably, in part, borrowed from the same Germanic source as the cognate forms Middle Dutch *spotte, spot* speck, spot, East Frisian *spot* speck, North Frisian *spōt* speck, piece of ground, and Old Icelandic *spotti* small piece, bit. The figurative sense of a stain or blot (of sin) is found in Middle English about 1200. The sense of a particular place, site, or location is first recorded in Middle English (probably about 1380) but did not come into general use until the late 1600's. **—v.** make spots on. About 1250 *spotten,* in *Genesis and Exodus;* from the noun. The sense of to mark or note, recognize or detect, was originally applied to a criminal or suspected person (1718), and later, used generally (1860). **—spot check** (1933) **—spotless** *adj.* (probably about 1380) **—spotlight** *n.* (1904); *v.* (1923) **—spotty** *adj.* 1340, blemished or speckled, in *Ayenbite of Inwyt;* formed from Middle English *spot, spotte,* n. + *-y*[1]. The sense of lacking in uniformity, patchy, is first recorded in 1812.

spouse *n.* Probably before 1200 *spuse* married woman, wife; later, a betrothed man, bridegroom (probably about 1225, in *King Horn*), and in the spelling *spouse* (about 1280); borrowed from Old French *spus* (feminine *spuse*), also *espus* (feminine *espuse*), and *espouse* from Latin *spōnsus* bridegroom (feminine *spōnsa* bride), from the masculine and feminine past participles of *spondēre* to bind oneself, promise solemnly; see ESPOUSE. Latin *spondēre* is cognate with Greek *spéndein* make a drink-offering, *spéndesthai* make a treaty, and Hittite *sipanti* he pours a libation, sacrifices, dedicates, from Indo-European **spend-* (Pok.989). **—n. spousals** *pl.* marriage ceremony. Probably about 1300 *spusaile;* later *sposailes* (before 1325); borrowed from Old French *espusailles, espousailles,* from Latin *spōnsālia* betrothal, neuter plural of *spōnsālis* pertaining to betrothal, from *spōnsus* (genitive *spōnsūs*) a betrothal (compare *spōnsus* bridegroom); see SPOUSE; also see ESPOUSAL.

spout *v.* Before 1325 *sputen* discharge (a liquid), gush with water, blood, etc.; later *spouten* (before 1338); cognate with Middle Dutch *spoiten* to spout (modern Dutch *spuiten*), North Frisian *spütji* spout, squirt, and probably with Middle Dutch *spūwen* to spit, SPEW. The figurative sense of speak at great length, declaim, is first recorded in English in 1756. **—n.** 1392-93 *spowte* pipe for carrying off water; earlier in the place name *Sputekelde* (about 1200); and later, a pipe to discharge water (1408), a tube or lip to help pour liquid (1444); cognate with Middle Dutch *spoite* spout, North Frisian *spüti* spout, squirt, and *spütji* to spout. The sense of a forceful discharge of water, stream, jet, is first recorded in English in Dunbar's *Poems* (1500-20).

sprain *n.* sudden twist of a joint causing injury. 1601, in Holland's translation of Pliny's *Natural History;* of uncertain origin. —**v.** to injure (a joint) by a sudden twist. 1622, probably from the noun. Connection of *sprain* with Old French *espraindre* to press, to squeeze out (from Latin *exprimere*) is doubtful, both on account of the late appearance of the English word and its special meaning. Note also that the noun occurs in English before its corresponding verb.

sprat *n.* small herring. 1469 *spratte,* variant of earlier *sprotte* (1309-10); developed from Old English (about 1000) *sprot,* perhaps related to Old English *-sprūtan* to SPROUT. Old English *sprot* is cognate with Middle Low German, Middle Dutch, and modern Dutch *sprot,* modern German *Sprotte,* all meaning a sprat.

sprawl *v.* About 1300 *spraulen* move convulsively, writhe, spread oneself out, in *Havelok the Dane;* developed from Old English (about 1000) *sprēawlian* move convulsively; of unknown origin. The sense of spread out in an irregular or awkward manner is found in English since the 1500's. **—n.** act or position of sprawling. 1719, from the verb.

spray[1] *n.* liquid scattered in drops, sprinkle. Before 1621, in George Sandys' translation of Ovid's *Metamorphoses;* noun use of obsolete *spray* to sprinkle (1527); borrowed from Middle Dutch *sprayen, spraeien,* from Proto-Germanic **sprǣwjanan.* The Middle Dutch verb is cognate with Middle High German *spræjen, spræwen* to squirt, spray, modern German *sprühen,* and modern Dutch *sproeien.* Cognates outside Germanic are found in Greek *speírein* to sow, scatter, Middle Irish *sreb* stream, *srāb* torrent, and Armenian *p'arat* scattered, from Indo-European **sp(h)er-, spreu-* (Pok.993). **—v.** to scatter in the form of spray. 1829, in Carlyle's writings; from the noun.

spray[2] *n.* small branch with leaves, flowers, or fruit. About 1250, leafy branches and twigs collectively; earlier as a place name *Spray* (1179); possibly related to Old English *spræc* shoot, twig; see SPRIG. The meaning of a small branch with leaves, flowers, or fruit, used for decoration, is first recorded in 1862.

spread *v.* Probably before 1200 *spreaden, spradden* extend over an area, in *Ancrene Riwle* and Layamon's *Chronicle of Britain;* developed from Old English *-sprǣdan,* especially in *tō-sprǣdan* to spread out, and *spraedung* spreading. Old English *sprǣdan* is cognate with Middle Low German and Middle Dutch *sprēden, spreiden* to spread (modern Dutch *spreiden*), Old High German and modern German *spreiten,* and Old Swedish *sprēdha,* from Proto-Germanic **spraiđjanan,* causative of **sprīđanan,* whence Old High German *sprītan* be extended, from Indo-European **spreit-/sproit-* (Pok.994). **—adj.** stretched out, expanded, extended. About 1511, from the past participle of the verb. **—n.** 1626, act of spreading, in Bacon's *Sylva Sylvarum;* from the verb. The meaning of the extent or expanse of something is found in 1691, and the informal concrete sense, as in a ranch, farm, or large house, in 1927, in American English. The meaning of an article of food suitable for spreading, as butter or jam, is recorded since 1812, and the informal sense of a feast, meal, or banquet is first recorded in 1822. **—spreadsheet** *n.* (1982)

spree *n.* lively frolic. 1804, perhaps alteration of French *esprit* lively wit, from Middle French; see ESPRIT.

sprig *n.* Before 1398 *sprigge* shoot, twig, or small branch, in Trevisa's translation of Bartholomew's *De Proprietatibus Rerum;* probably related to Old English *spræc* shoot, twig; cognate with Middle Low German *sprik, sprok* dry twig, Middle Dutch *sproc,* modern Dutch *sprokkel,* Old High German *sprahhula* splinter, chaff, and Old Icelandic *sprek* dry wood.

sprightly *adj.* lively. 1596, in Nashe's *Have With You to Saffron-Walden;* formed from earlier English *spright* (before 1533, variant of SPRITE, in the sense of spirit) + adjective suffix *-ly*[2]. **—adv.** in a lively manner. 1604, in Thomas Dekker's *Works;* from the adjective; for suffix see -LY[1].

spring *v.* Probably before 1200 *springen* move suddenly, leap, jump, in *Ancrene Riwle;* developed from Old English *springan* (about 725, in *Beowulf*); cognate with Old Frisian *springa* to spring, Middle Dutch *springhen* (modern Dutch *springen*), Old High German *springan* (modern German *springen*), and Old Icelandic *springa* spring up, burst through (Swedish *springa,* Danish and Norwegian *springe*), from Proto-Germanic **sprenȝanan,* cognate with Greek *spérchesthai* be in haste, and Sanskrit *spr̥hayati* is eager, from Indo-European **sperĝh-/spr̥ĝh-, *spreĝh-, *sprenĝh-* (Pok.998). **—n.** Old English (816) *spring* source of a stream or river, wellspring, related to *springan* to spring, and cognate with Middle Low German *sprink* spring, Old Frisian *spring* leap, Old Saxon and Old High German *gispring* spring. The meaning of a stream of water flowing from the earth, mineral spring, is first recorded about 1125. The sense of act of springing or leaping is first recorded probably about 1450; and the related sense of an elastic device that returns to its own shape, in 1428. The sense of the season of the year after winter (when plants spring up) is first recorded in *springtime* (before 1398, in Trevisa's translation of Bartholomew's *De Proprietatibus Rerum*), but is found in the form *spring* in 1547, possibly as a shortening of the earlier *spring of the leaf* (1538); compare this sense development with that of FALL (autumn). **—springboard** *n.* (1799) **—springy** *adj.* elastic (1660, in Robert Boyle's *New Experiments*).

springbok (spring′bok′) *n.* gazelle or small antelope. 1775, borrowed from Afrikaans, a compound of *spring* to leap (from Middle Dutch *springhen* to SPRING) + *bok* antelope, from Middle Dutch *boc* BUCK¹.

sprinkle *v.* Before 1382 *sprynkklen* (implied in *sprynkklyd,* participial adjective) mark with spots, scatter in drops, in the Wycliffe Bible; cognate with Dutch *sprenkelen* to sprinkle, Middle Low German, Middle Dutch, and Middle High German *sprenkel, sprinkel* spot, speck, Swedish *spräcklig* speckled, Old Icelandic *sprækr* lively, nimble, and *spraka* to rattle, crackle; see SPEAK. The meaning of rain lightly is first recorded in 1778. **—n.** Before 1382 *sprynkill* device for sprinkling holy water, in the Wycliffe Bible; related to the verb. The meaning of an act or instance of sprinkling is first recorded in 1641 in Milton's writings, and the specific meaning of light rain or snowfall in 1888, in Stevenson's *Black Arrow.* **—sprinkling** *n.* About 1450, action of someone who sprinkles; later, small amount (1594, in Nashe's *Terrors of the Night*); formed from English *sprinkle,* v. + *-ing*¹.

sprint *v.* 1566, to spring, dart; probably alteration of Middle English *sprenten* to leap, spring (before 1325, in *Cursor Mundi);* borrowed from a Scandinavian source (compare Old Icelandic *spretta* to jump up, and dialectal Swedish *sprinta* to jump, hop, related to Old Icelandic *spradhka* to wriggle). The Scandinavian words are cognate with Old English *spyrd,* Old High German *spurt,* and Gothic *spaúrds,* all meaning race course, and, outside Germanic, with Greek *spyrthízein* to jump up, Old Slavic *prędati* to jump, tremble, and Sanskrit *spárdhate* (he) contends, fights, from Indo-European **sp(h)erd(h)-, *(s)p(h)red(h)-, *sprend-* (Pok. 995).

The meaning in sports of run at full speed, especially for a short distance, is first recorded in English in 1871 (implied in *sprinting*).

—n. Before 1790, a spring, dart; later, short run at full speed (1865); from the verb.

sprit *n.* small pole that supports and stretches a sail. Probably before 1300 *spreet* pole used for propelling a boat, in *Kyng Alisaunder;* later *spryt* (probably before 1400); developed from Old English (before 800) *sprēot* pole; originally, a sprout, shoot, branch of a tree, related to *-sprūtan* SPROUT. Old English *sprēot* is cognate with Middle Low German *sprēt* pole, Middle Dutch and modern Dutch *spriet,* and North Frisian *sprit, spret.* The sense of a pole that supports and stretches a sail is first recorded in Middle English before 1400. **—spritsail** *n.* (1466)

sprite *n.* elf, fairy, goblin. About 1303 *spryt* spirit, sprite, in Mannyng's *Handlyng Synne;* before 1325 *spreit;* borrowed from Old French *esprit, espirit* spirit, learned borrowing from Latin *spīritus* SPIRIT.

sprocket *n.* 1536, a term in carpentry and building, meaning a piece of timber used in framing; of unknown origin. The extended sense of a projection from the rim of a wheel, engaging with the links of a chain, is first recorded in 1750.

sprout *v.* Probably before 1200 *spruten* to shoot forth, bud, in *Ancrene Riwle;* later *sprouten* (before 1400); developed from Old English *-sprūtan,* as in *āsprūtan* to sprout; cognate with Old Frisian *sprūta* to sprout, Middle Low German and Middle Dutch *sprūten* (modern Dutch *spruiten*), Old High German *spriozan* (modern German *spriessen*), (from Proto-Germanic **spreutanan*), Middle High German *sprützen* to squirt, sprout (modern German *spritzen* to squirt), and Gothic *sprautō,* adv., quickly, soon, from Indo-European **spreud-/sproud-/sprūd-* (Pok.994). **—n.** shoot of a plant. Before 1400 *sproute;* from the verb.

spruce¹ *n.* evergreen tree. 1670, in Evelyn's *Sylva;* from the earlier adjective *spruse* (1412), meaning made of spruce wood; literally, Prussian, from *Spruce, Sprws* Prussia (1378), variant of *Pruce* (about 1378); borrowed from Anglo-French *Pruz, Prus* Prussia; probably the tree was so called because it was grown widely in Prussia.

spruce² *adj.* neat, trim. 1589, brisk, smart, lively, perhaps a special use of earlier *Spruce* Prussian, as in (jerkins of) *spruce leather* (1466), a popular style in the 1400's made in Prussia and considered smart-looking; see SPRUCE¹. The meaning of neat, trim, is first recorded in Ben Jonson's *Every Man Out of His Humour* (1599). **—v.** make or become spruce. 1594, in Nashe's *Terrors of the Night;* from the adjective.

spry *adj.* full of health and spirits, lively. 1746, dialectal English, perhaps shortened and altered form of SPRIGHTLY. Alternatively, *spry* may have come into English from a Scandinavian source (compare dialectal Swedish *sprygg* lively, perhaps related to Old Icelandic *sprækr* lively, nimble, and *spraka* to rattle, crackle; see SPEAK).

spud *n.* tool with a narrow blade. 1440 *spudde* small or poor knife, in *Promptorium Parvulorum;* of uncertain origin. The sense of a digging tool resembling a spade is found in 1667, in Pepys' *Diary.* The slang sense of a potato is first recorded in 1845 as a New Zealand usage. **—v.** remove with a spud. 1652, from the noun.

spume (spyüm) *n.* Before 1393, foam, froth, in Gower's *Confessio Amantis;* borrowed from Old French *spume, espume,* from Latin *spūma* FOAM. **—v.** to foam. Probably about 1380 *spumen,* in *Cleanness;* borrowed from Old French *spumer, espumer,* from Latin *spūmāre,* from *spūma* foam.

spumone or **spumoni** (spəmō′nē) *n.* kind of Italian ice cream with layers of different colors and flavors. 1929, American English; borrowing of Italian *spumone* (singular), *spumoni* (plural), from *spuma* foam, from Latin *spūma* FOAM.

spunk *n.* 1536 *sponk* a spark, in Bellenden's translation of Hector Boece's *History and Chronicles of Scotland;* Scottish, from Gaelic *spong* tinder, pith, sponge; compare Middle Irish *spongc* tinder (modern Irish *sponnc* sponge, tinder, spark, courage, spunk). These Celtic words are borrowed from Latin *spongia* SPONGE. The spelling *spunk* appeared in English in 1596. The figurative sense of courage, pluck, mettle, first appeared in Goldsmith's *She Stoops to Conquer* (1773). **—spunky** *adj.* full of spunk or spirit. 1786, in Burns' *The Author's Earnest Cry and Prayer;* formed from English *spunk* + *-y*¹.

spur *n.* Probably before 1200 *spure* device for poking the side of a horse to urge it forward, in Layamon's *Chronicle of Britain;* developed from Old English *spura,* variant of *spora* (before 800, in *Corpus Glossary*), related to *spurnan* to kick, SPURN. Old English *spura, spora* (from Proto-Germanic **spurōn*) is cognate with Middle Dutch *spōre* spur (modern Dutch *spoor*), Old High German *sporo* (modern German *Sporn*), and Old Icelandic *spori* (Danish and Norwegian *spore,* Swedish *sporre*). The figurative sense of anything that urges on, stimulus, goad, incitement, is first recorded in Middle English about 1390, and is from the verb, in the figurative sense. **—v.** poke with spurs. Probably before 1200 *spuren,* in Layamon's *Chronicle of Britain;* from the noun. The figurative sense of urge, prompt, goad, incite, is first recorded in Middle English probably about 1200.

spurge *n.* plant with an acrid milky juice. 1373 *sporge;* later *spurge* (before 1400); borrowed from Old French *espurge,* from *espurgier* to purge, from Latin *expūrgāre* (*ex-* out + *pūrgāre* to PURGE); so called from the plant's purgative properties.

spurious *adj.* not genuine, false, sham. 1598, born out of wedlock, illegitimate; borrowed from Latin *spurius* illegitimate, from *spurius,* n., illegitimate child (often used among the ancient Romans as a praenomen or first of the usual three names), probably from Etruscan; for suffix see -IOUS. The sense of having an illegitimate or irregular origin, not properly qualified or constituted, is first recorded in Ben Jonson's *The Poetaster* (1601), and the extended sense of false, sham, counterfeit, in 1615.

spurn *v.* Probably before 1200 *spurnen* to kick, trip, stumble, in *Ancrene Riwle;* later, to reject, despise (before 1382, in the Wycliffe Bible); developed from Old English (about 1000) *spurnan* to kick, reject, scorn, despise; cognate with Old Frisian *spurna* to kick, Old Saxon and Old High German *spurnan,* and Old Icelandic *sporna, spyrna, sperna* (Swedish *spjärna* to spurn), from Proto-Germanic **spurnanan.* Cognates outside Germanic are found in Latin *spernere* to reject, disdain, spurn, Greek *spaírein* to move convulsively, Lithuanian *spìrti* to kick, force, Armenian *spaṙnal* threaten, and Sanskrit *sphuráti* (he) kicks, from Indo-European **sp(h)er-/sp(h)ṛ-* (Pok.992). Related to SPUR. **—n.** Before 1325, trip, stumble, kick, in *Cursor Mundi;* from the verb. The meaning of disdainful rejection is first recorded in Shakespeare's *Hamlet* (1602).

spurt[1] *v.* gush out, squirt. 1570, variant of *spirt* (recorded perhaps by accident of the record slightly later in 1582); perhaps cognate with Middle High German *spürzen, spirzen* to spit, and *sprützen* to squirt, SPROUT. **—n.** forceful stream of water. 1775, from the verb (also found as *spirt,* 1716, in Gay's writings) and probably in part from *spurt*[2] in the use *by spurts* flowing by intermittent activity (1644).

spurt[2] *n.* brief burst of effort or activity. Before 1566, a short spell or period of time, in Richard Edwards' *Damon and Pithias;* variant of earlier *spirt* brief period of time (about 1550); of uncertain origin. The sense of a brief burst of effort or activity is first recorded before 1591. **—v.** make a spurt. 1664, from the noun (found as *spirt,* 1599, in Nashe's writings).

sputnik (sput′nik) *n.* artificial earth satellite, especially one launched by the Soviet Union. 1957, borrowing of Russian *spútnik* satellite; literally, traveling companion, from Old Slavic *sŭpǫtĭnikŭ* (from *sŭ-,* prefix meaning together, with + *pǫtĭ* way, journey, from Indo-European **pont-;* see PATH + the personal suffix *-nik*). The first Soviet sputnik, officially referred to as *Iskússtvennyj Sputnik Zemli* Artificial Satellite of the Earth, was launched on October 4, 1957.

sputter *v.* 1598 (implied in *sputtering*), to spit out saliva, etc., with explosive sounds; cognate with Dutch *sputteren* to sputter, and *spuiten* to SPOUT; for suffix see -ER[4]. The meaning of utter hastily in a confused or explosive manner is found before 1677, and that of make spitting or popping sounds, as hot fat, etc., in 1692, in Dryden's plays. **—n.** confused talk. 1673, in Wycherley's *The Gentleman Dancing Master;* from the verb.

sputum (spyü′təm) *n.* saliva, spit. 1693, borrowing of Latin *spūtum,* noun use of neuter past participle of *spuere* to spit; see SPEW.

spy *v.* About 1250 *spien* to watch in a secret manner or with hostile intent, in *Genesis and Exodus;* borrowed from Old French *espier* to spy, from a probable Frankish word cognate with Old High German *spehōn* to look out for, pry into, scout, spy (modern German *spähen*), Middle Low German *spēen,* Middle Dutch *spien* (modern Dutch *spieden*), and Old Icelandic *spā* to foretell, predict (Norwegian and Swedish *spå,* Danish *spaa*), from Proto-Germanic **speH-.* The Germanic words are cognate with Latin *specere* to look at, *speciēs* appearance, kind, species, Greek *sképtesthai* (from **spéktesthai*) to look, view, reflect, *skopeîn* to look at, examine, Albanian *pashë* I saw, Avestan *spasyeiti* (he) spies, and Sanskrit *spáś-* a spy, *páśyati* (he) sees, from Indo-European **spek̂-/spok̂-* (Pok.984).

The general sense of look out for, catch sight of, notice, observe, is first recorded in Middle English probably before 1300, in *Kyng Alisaunder.*

—n. About 1250 *spie* one who spies on others, in *Genesis and Exodus;* borrowed from Old French *espie* a spy, from *espier* to spy. Already in Middle English (probably before 1300, in *Arthour and Merlin*) the word was used to refer to a person employed in wartime to obtain secret information about the enemy, and in early use, especially such a person venturing in disguise into the enemy's camp or territory.

—spyglass *n.* (1706)

squab *n.* 1682, very young bird (in 1640, unformed, lumpish person); perhaps borrowed from a Scandinavian word (compare dialectal Swedish *skvabb* loose or fat flesh, *skvabba* fat woman, and dialectal Norwegian *skvabb* soft wet mass), from Proto-Germanic **(s)kwab-.* These Scandinavian words are probably cognate with Old Saxon *quappa* eelpout (a fish), Old Prussian *gabawo* and Old Slavic *žaba,* both meaning a toad, from Indo-European **gwēb(h)-/gwəb(h)-* slimy, flabby; tadpole, toad (Pok.466). The specific sense of a very young pigeon is first recorded in English in 1694.

squabble *n.* petty quarrel. 1602, probably of imitative origin; similar to dialectal Swedish *skvabbel* quarrel, and dialectal German *schwabbeln* to babble, prattle. **—v.** take part in a squabble. 1604, in Shakespeare's *Othello;* probably from the noun.

squad *n.* small military unit. 1649, borrowed from earlier French *esquade,* from Middle French *escadre,* from Spanish *escuadra* or Italian *squadra* battalion; literally, square, both from Vulgar Latin **exquadra* SQUARE; so called because troops were commonly arranged in a square formation to repel cavalry or superior forces, especially prior to large-scale use of automatic weapons in the American Civil War. Development of the squad as a military unit was, however, a practice designed to improve discipline. **—squad car** police car (1938).

squadron *n.* 1562, a body of soldiers arranged in square formation, in John Shute's translation of Cambini's *Turkish War;* borrowed from Italian *squadrone,* augmentative form of *squadra* battalion, SQUAD. The sense of a relatively small body or detachment of soldiers is first recorded in English in 1579, and that of a division of naval fleet, in 1588. The modern sense of a tactical unit or division of an air force (originally, the British Royal Air Force) is first recorded in 1913.

squalid *adj.* 1591, filthy, degraded, in Spenser's *Virgils Gnat;* borrowed from Middle French *squalide,* and directly from Latin *squālidus* rough, coated with dirt, filthy, related to *squālēs* filth, *squālus* filthy, *squālēre* be covered with a rough or scaly layer, be coated with dirt, be filthy, of unknown origin.

squall[1] *n.* sudden, violent gust of wind. 1719, originally nautical use; probably borrowed from a Scandinavian source (compare Norwegian *skval* sudden rush of water, splash, and Swedish *skvala* to gush, pour down, perhaps related to Old Icelandic *skvaldra* to chatter loudly, and *skvala* to cry out, SQUEAL).

squall[2] *v.* cry out loudly. Before 1631, in Drayton's *Works;* probably borrowed from a Scandinavian source (compare Old Icelandic *skvala* to cry out, SQUEAL). **—n.** loud, harsh cry. 1709, from the verb.

squalor *n.* 1621, misery and dirt, filth, in Burton's *Anatomy of Melancholy;* borrowed from Latin *squālor,* related to *squālēre* be filthy; see SQUALID; for suffix see -OR[1].

squamous (skwā′məs) *adj.* covered with or formed of scales. 1547, borrowed from Latin *squāmōsus* covered with scales, scaly, from *squāma* scale, of unknown origin; for suffix see -OUS. An earlier English spelling *scamous* is recorded in 1541, probably borrowed from Middle French *scamoux* scaly, from Latin *squāmōsus.*

squander *v.* 1593, to spend (money, goods, etc.) recklessly or wastefully, in Nashe's *Christ's Tears Over Jerusalem;* of unknown origin. The earliest recorded use, by Nashe, is still the most common one, especially frequent since 1810. A less common meaning, to be scattered over a wide area, is found in Shakespeare's *Merchant of Venice* (1596). **—n.** act of squandering. 1709, from the verb.

square *n.* About 1250 *squire* tool for measuring right angles; later *square* rectangular area or shape (before 1382); borrowed from Old French *esquire, esquarre, esquerre* a square, squareness, from Vulgar Latin **exquadra,* from **exquadrāre* to square (Latin *ex-* out + *quadrāre* make square, from *quadrus* square, (in Late Latin, square, four-cornered); related to *quattuor* FOUR). The mathematical sense of a product obtained when a number is multiplied by itself is first recorded in English in 1557. The common meaning of an open space (approximately square in shape) in a town or city, used as a park, etc., is first recorded in 1687. **—adj.** Before 1325, in *Cursor Mundi;* borrowed from Old French *esquarré,* past participle of *esquarrer* to square, from Vulgar Latin **exquadrāre* to square; see the noun. The figurative sense of just, honest, fair, is first recorded in 1591, in the phrase *square play,* and the slang sense of being out-of-date, old-fashioned, or too conventional is found in 1946, in American English, originally as a jazz usage. The meaning of full, solid, substantial (said of meals) is first found about 1850, in American English. **—v.** Before 1382 *squaren* to make square or rectangular, in the Wycliffe Bible; borrowed from Old French *esquarrer,* from Vulgar Latin **exquadrāre* to square; see noun. **—adv.** 1557, so as to be squared (by multiplication); from the adjective. The meaning of in a square form or position is first recorded in 1631. **—square dance** (1870) **—square knot** (1867) **—squarely** *adv.* (1557, so as to be squared by multiplication; 1564, honestly; 1667, in a direct manner) **— square root** (1557)

squash[1] *v.* to crush. Before 1325 *squachen* annul, shoot, destroy, crush; borrowed from Old French *esquasser* to crush, from Vulgar Latin **exquassāre* (Latin *ex-* out + *quassāre* to shatter; see QUASH[1] to crush). **—n.** something squashed. 1590, unripe pod of a pea, in Shakespeare's *Midsummer Night's Dream;* from the verb. The sense of something squashed (as in *lemon squash*) is found in 1888. The sense of a soft rubber ball used in a form of the game of rackets is first recorded in 1886; hence **squash rackets** (1886), **squash tennis** (1901, American English). **—squashy** *adj.* soft. 1698, formed from English *squash*[1], v. or n. + *-y*[1].

squash[2] *n.* fruit of the gourd family. 1643, in Roger Williams' *A Key into the Language of America;* American English; shortened form of *isquoutersquash,* borrowed from Algonquian (Narraganset) *askūtasquash,* literally, the green things that may be eaten raw.

squat *v.* Before 1349 *squatten* to thrust, crush; borrowed from Old French *esquatir* press down, lay flat, crush, (*es-* out, from Latin *ex-* + Old French *quatir* press down, flatten, from Vulgar Latin **coāctīre* press together, force, from Latin *coāctus,* past participle of *cōgere* compel; see COGENT). The meaning of to crouch on the heels is first recorded in Middle English about 1410. The meaning of settle on another person's land is first recorded in 1800 (but implied earlier in 1788, in *squatter*), in American English, in the writings of Madison. **—adj.** About 1410, (of a hare or other animal) seated in a squatting posture, from the past participle of *squatten* to squat. The meaning of short and thick, like the figure of an animal squatting, is first recorded in 1630. **—n.** Before 1400, heavy fall or bump, severe or violent jar; from the verb. The meaning of an act of squatting is first recorded in 1584. **—squatter** *n.* settler who occupies land or property without legal title to it (1788, in Madison's writings, American English).

squaw *n.* 1634, American Indian woman or wife, in William Wood's *New England's Prospect;* American English; borrowed from Algonquian (Massachuset) *squa* woman (compare Narraganset *squaws* and related forms in other Algonquian languages).

squawk *v.* make a loud, harsh sound. 1821 (implied in *squawking*), probably of imitative origin. **—n.** loud, harsh sound. 1850, from the verb.

squeak *v.* Before 1387 *squeken* make a short, sharp, shrill sound, in Trevisa's translation of Higden's *Polychronicon;* probably of imitative origin, similar to Middle Swedish *skväka* to squeak, croak. **—n.** 1664, act of squeaking; from the verb. **—squeaky** *adj.* squeaking. 1862, formed from English *squeak* n. or v. + *-y*[1]

squeal *v.* make a long, sharp, shrill cry. About 1300 *suelen;* later *squelen* (before 1325); probably of imitative origin, similar to Old Icelandic *skvala* to cry out. The slang sense of inform on another is first recorded in Hotten's *Slang Dictionary* (1865). **—n.** long, sharp, shrill cry. 1747, from the verb.

squeamish *adj.* Before 1398 *squaymisch* readily affected with nausea, in Trevisa's translation of Bartholomew's *De Proprietatibus Rerum;* variant of earlier *squeymous* disdainful, fastidious (about 1330); borrowed from Anglo-French *escoymous,* of unknown origin; the suffix -OUS was replaced by -ISH[1]. The extended sense of easily shocked, prudish, is first recorded in 1567.

squeegee (skwē′jē) *n.* rubber blade or sponge attached to a handle, used for sweeping water or mud, or for cleaning windows. 1844, nautical use, perhaps formed from earlier *squeege* to press (1782, alteration of SQUEEZE, v.) + the suffix *-ee.*

squeeze *v.* Before 1601 *squease,* probably an alteration of earlier *quease* (about 1550), from Middle English *quysen* to squeeze (before 1450); developed from Old English *cwӯsan, cwīesan* to squeeze, of unknown origin. **—n.** 1611, act of squeezing, in Cotgrave's *Dictionary;* from the verb.

squelch *n.* 1620, a heavy, crushing fall or blow on a soft body, probably imitative of the sound made from such a fall or blow. The figurative sense of a squashing or crushing, complete suppression, is first recorded in 1685. **—v.** 1624, to press on or strike with crushing force; from the noun. The figurative sense of squash or crush, suppress completely, is first recorded in 1864.

squib *n.* short, witty, or satirical attack in speech or writing, lampoon. About 1525, of unknown origin. The sense of a small firework that burns with a hissing noise is found before 1530; if this is the earliest sense, the word is perhaps imitative of a fizzy explosive sound. **—v.** to say, write, or publish a squib. 1579-80, from the noun.

squid *n.* sea animal like an octopus. 1613, in *Purchas his Pilgrimage;* of unknown origin.

squiggle *v.* to make with twisting or curving lines. 1804 (implied in *squiggling*), suggesting a blend of *squirm,* v. and *wriggle,* v. The meaning of writhe, squirm, wriggle, is first recorded in 1816, and that of write or draw in a wavy or twisty manner in 1942, from the noun. **—n.** wriggly twist or curve. 1902, from the verb. The sense of a wavy or twisty drawing or writing is found in 1928. **—squiggly** *adj.* wavy, wriggly (1902, in Kipling's *Just So Stories*).

squint *v.* 1599, (figurative) have an indirect aim, reference, etc., in Nashe's *Lenten Stuffe;* shortened form of Middle English *asquint,* adv., obliquely, with a sidelong glance (probably before 1200, in *Ancrene Riwle*); probably formed from *a-*[1] + *-squint,* of unknown origin, but related to obsolete *squin, skwyn* (about 1440, found in *ofskwyn* obliquely, slantingly), though not to *askance* as previously held by the OED; see ASKANCE. The meaning of glance sideways, peep, is first recorded in 1610. **—n.** act of squinting. Before 1652, cross-eyed condition or tendency; from the verb. The meaning of a sidelong or hasty glance is first recorded in 1673.

squire *n.* Probably about 1225 *squier* young man who attended a knight, in *King Horn;* later, member of the landowning class ranking below a knight (about 1300); borrowed from Old French *esquier, escuier* squire; literally, shield carrier, from Late Latin *scūtārius* guardsman, from Latin *scūtum* shield, perhaps from earlier **scoitom.* The Latin word is possibly cognate with Old Irish *sciath* shield (earlier **skeito-*), Old Slavic *štitŭ,* and Old Prussian *scaytan,* from Indo-European **skeit-/skoit-* (Pok.921). Compare EQUERRY and ESQUIRE. The general sense of a country gentleman or landed proprietor is first recorded in English in 1645. **—v.** attend as a squire, escort. About 1395 *squieren,* in Chaucer's *Canterbury Tales;* from the noun. **—squirearchy** (skwīr′ärkē) *n.* collective body of squires or landed proprietors. 1796, formed from English *squir(e),* n. + *-archy,* probably patterned on *hierarchy, monarchy,* etc.

squirm *v.* to turn and twist, wriggle. 1691, dialectal English, originally used in reference to the movement of an eel; of unknown origin, sometimes associated with worm or swarm, and sometimes said to be of imitative origin, but imitating what and by what association is not stated.

squirrel *n.* 1327 *scurelle;* about 1330 *squirel;* borrowed through Anglo-French *esquirel,* Old French *escurel,* from Vulgar Latin **scūriólus,* diminutive form of **scūrius* squirrel, variant of Latin *sciūrus,* from Greek *skíouros* a squirrel; literally, shadow-tailed, (probably *skiá* shadow; see SHINE + *ourá* tail, related to *órrhos* buttocks).

squirt *v.* Before 1475 *squyrten* eject water in a jet, of uncertain origin (Low German *swirtjen* to squirt, dart). **—n.** Before 1398 *squirte* diarrhea, in Trevisa's translation of Bartholomew's *De Proprietatibus Rerum;* from the same source as the verb. The meaning of a jet of liquid is first recorded in Bacon's *Sylva Sylvarum* (1626). **—squirt gun** (before 1889)

squish *v.* 1647, to squeeze, squash; probably a variant of *squash,* perhaps formed by influence of earlier *squiss* to squeeze or crush (1558). The meaning of make a splashing sound when walked on (said of water, soft mud, etc.) appeared before 1825. **—n.** squishing sound. 1902, from the verb. An earlier sense of marmalade is recorded in Hotten's *Slang Dictionary* (1874). **—squishy** *adj.* 1847, formed from English *squish,* v. + *-y*[1].

stab *v.* 1375 *stabben* to thrust with a pointed weapon, in Barbour's *The Bruce;* Scottish, of uncertain origin. Connection with English dialectal and Scottish *stob* to stab, is doubtful, since *stob* is not attested before 1529. **—n.** 1440, wound produced by stabbing, in *Promptorium Parvulorum;* from the verb. The meaning of act of stabbing is first recorded in Palsgrave's *Lesclarcissement* (1530). The informal figurative sense of an attempt at something is first recorded in 1908 in American English.

stabile (stā′bəl) *adj.* having stability, stable. 1797, borrowed from Latin *stabilis* STABLE[2]. **—n.** (stā′bēl) sculpture like a mobile but stationary. 1943, borrowed from Latin *stabilis;* coined by the French sculptor Jan (or Hans) Arp on the model of *mobile* (sculpture).

stability *n.* Probably before 1349 *stabylte* firmness, steadfastness, permanence; probably about 1350 *stabilite;* borrowed from Old French *stableté, estableté,* from Latin *stabilitās* firmness, steadfastness, from *stabilis* steadfast, firm, STABLE[2]; for suffix see -ITY. **—stabilize** *v.* make stable. 1861, borrowed from French *stabiliser,* from Latin *stabilis* stable; for suffix see -IZE.

stable[1] *n.* building where horses or cattle are kept. Probably about 1225, in *King Horn;* borrowed from

Old French *estable* a stable, stall, from Latin *stabulum* a stall, fold, aviary, etc.; literally, a standing place, from *stāre* to STAND. —**v.** put, keep, or live in a stable. About 1330 *stablen,* from the noun.

stable[2] *adj.* steadfast, firm. Probably about 1150; borrowed from Old French *estable, stable,* from Latin *stabilis* firm, steadfast; literally, able to stand, from *stāre* to STAND.

staccato (stəkä′tō) *adj.* disconnected, abrupt. 1724, with breaks between successive tones or notes; borrowing of Italian *staccato,* literally, detached, from past participle of *staccare* to detach, shortened form of *distaccare* separate, detach, from Middle French *destacher,* from Old French *destachier* to DETACH. —**adv.** in a staccato manner. 1844, in writings of Thomas Hood; from the adjective.

stack *n.* About 1300 *stac* pile, heap, in *Havelok the Dane;* earlier as the surname *Stac* (1199); borrowed from a Scandinavian source (compare Old Icelandic *stakkr* haystack, Norwegian *stakk,* Danish *stak,* and Swedish *stack*). The Scandinavian words are cognate with Middle Low German *stak* barrier of stakes and twigs, and Old English *staca* stick, STAKE[1]. The sense of a number of chimneys, flues, or pipes standing together is first recorded in 1667, and that of a chimney or funnel of a factory, locomotive, or steamship, in 1825. —**v.** to pile or arrange in a stack. Before 1325 *stacken,* from the noun. The meaning of arrange unfairly (as in *stack the cards*) is first recorded in 1825.

stadium *n.* About 1380, a foot race, in Chaucer's translation of Boethius' *De Consolatione Philosophiae;* also before 1398, an ancient Greek and Roman measure of length, equal in Athens to 606 feet, 9 inches, in Trevisa's translation of Bartholomew's *De Proprietatibus Rerum;* borrowed from Latin *stadium* a measure of length, a race course, from Greek *stádion* a measure of length, a running track for footraces (a generic sense that developed because the most noted track or course, at Olympia, was one stadium in length). Greek *stádion* may be, literally, a fixed standard of length, or may be an altered form of earlier *spádion* (from *spân* to draw up, pull; see SPASM) by influence of Greek *stádios* firm, fixed, related to *statherós* standing fast, firm, and *stênai* come to a stand; see STAND.

The sense of a running track for footraces is first recorded in English in Holland's translation of Plutarch's *Moralia* (1603). Later the word was used to mean any place for athletic exercises, and by 1901 the current meaning of a large, open, oval structure with tiers of seats, used for sports events, had become the usual sense.

staff *n.* Before 1102 *staf* a bishop's staff; also, a stick carried in the hand as an aid in walking or climbing (probably before 1200); developed from Old English (before 800) *stæf* stick, staff; cognate with Old Frisian *stef* staff, Old Saxon, Middle Dutch, and modern Dutch *staf,* Old High German *stab* (modern German *Stab*), Old Icelandic *stafr* (Swedish, Danish, and Norwegian *stav*), from Proto-Germanic **staƀaz,* and Gothic *stabeis* (nominative plural). Cognates outside Germanic are found in Lithuanian *stābas* post, Old Slavic *stoborŭ* pillar, post, and Sanskrit *stabhnā́ti, stabhnóti* (he) supports, from Indo-European **stəbh-,* root **stēbh-* (Pok.1011). The sense of a group of military officers that assists a commanding officer is first recorded in 1779, probably from the now obsolete sense of a strong pole used to support something (about 1000). The generalized sense of any group of employees (as at an office or in a hospital) is first recorded in Carlyle's *The French Revolution* (1837). —**v.** provide with a staff of officers, teachers, servants, etc. 1859, from the noun. —**staffer** *n.* member of a staff. 1949, American English, formed from *staff,* n. + *-er*[1].

stag *n.* full-grown male deer. 1346 *stagge* (in 1318, young male horse); developed from Old English *stagga* stag, specifically, one in its 5th year; cognate with Old Icelandic *andarsteggi* drake (modern Icelandic *steggi* male bird), (earlier) tomcat, male fox, from Proto-Germanic **staȝ-,* cognate with Greek *stóchos* pillar, from Indo-European **stegh-/stogh-* to prick, drive in; post, pole, stalk (Pok.1014). The word probably originally meant a male animal in its prime. —**adj.** attended by, or for, men only. 1843, American English, from the earlier sense of male (1606), as in *stag bird, stag horse.*

stage *n.* About 1250, a story or floor of a building; later, raised platform for public performance, step in a sequence (before 1325, in *Cursor Mundi*); borrowed from Old French *estage* a story, floor, stage for performance, from Vulgar Latin **staticum* a place for standing, from Latin *statum,* past participle of *stāre* to STAND. The specific sense of the theater, the actor's profession, is found in 1589. The sense of period of development or time in life is first recorded in Shakespeare's *Pericles* (1608). —**v.** Before 1338 *stagen* to erect, build, in Mannyng's *Chronicle of England;* from the noun. The meaning of put into a play is first recorded in Ben Jonson's *The Poetaster* (1601), that of put (a play, etc.) on the stage in 1879, and the general sense of mount or put on (an action, spectacle, etc.) in 1924. —**stagecoach** *n.* (1658; from *stage* meaning a part of a journey, a section of road, 1603) —**stage fright** (1878) —**stagehand** *n.* (1885) —**stage-manage** *v.* (1906) —**stage manager** (1805) —**stage whisper** (1864) —**stagy** *adj.* of or pertaining to the stage, theatrical. 1860, formed from English *stage,* n. + *-y*[1].

stagger *v.* to sway or reel. About 1434 *stageren;* variant of Middle English *stakeren* to stagger (before 1325, in *Cursor Mundi*); borrowed from a Scandinavian source (compare Old Icelandic *stakra* to push, stagger, Old Danish *stagra,* modern Danish *stavre,* and Old Icelandic *staka* to push, stagger; cognate with Middle Low German and Middle Dutch *stāken* to push, fix in the ground, and *stāke* post, STAKE[1]). The transitive sense of bewilder, amaze, is first recorded in English in 1556. The sense of arrange in a zigzag pattern is first recorded in 1856, and that of schedule (holidays, working hours, etc.) for different times, in 1918 in American English. —**n.** 1577 *the staggers* disease of domestic animals marked by a staggering gait; from the verb. The meaning of an act of staggering appeared in 1600.

stagnant *adj.* not running or flowing. 1666, probably in part formed in English as an adjective to earlier *stagnancy,* n. (1659); and in part borrowed from French *stagnant,* and directly from Latin *stagnantem* (nominative *stagnāns*), present participle of *stagnāre* STAGNATE; for suffix see -ANT. The figurative sense of not active, dull, is first recorded in Samuel Johnson's *Irene* (1749).

stagnate *v.* be or become stagnant. 1669, probably in part formed in English as a verb to *stagnancy, stagnant,* and in part borrowed from Latin *stagnātum,* past participle of *stagnāre* to stagnate, from *stagnum* standing water. Latin *stagnum* is probably cognate with Old Breton *staer* river, brook, and Greek *stázein* to drip, *stagṓn* a drop, from Indo-European **stag-* trickle, drip (Pok.1010); for suffix see -ATE[1].

staid *adj.* sober, sedate. 1541, fixed, permanent, adjective use of *stayed,* past participle of STAY[1], in the sense of restrain. The meaning of sober, sedate, serious, is first recorded in 1557.

stain *v.* Before 1382 *steynen* to discolor or dye, in the Wycliffe Bible; probably shortened from Old French *desteign-,* stem of *desteindre* to remove the color (*des-,* from Latin *dis-* remove + Old French *teindre* to dye, from Latin *tingere* to TINGE). Middle English *steynen* may have been formed partly by fusion with a Scandinavian form (compare Old Icelandic *steina* to paint), and partly by shortening from Middle English *disteynen* to discolor or stain (before 1393), borrowed from Old French *desteign-, desteindre.* The figurative sense of taint with guilt or vice is found in Middle English in 1446, and the sense of blemish, soil (a person's name, reputation, etc.) in 1513. **—n.** 1563, act of staining; from the verb. **—stainless steel** (1917).

stair *n.* Probably before 1200 *steire* flight of steps; also, a single stair step; later *staire* (about 1385); developed from Old English *stǣger* (about 1000, in Ælfric's *Glossaries*), from Proto-Germanic **staiʒrī,* related to Old English *stīgan* to climb, go, and *stīg* narrow path; cognate with Old Frisian *stīga* to rise, climb, Old Saxon *stīgan,* Middle Dutch *stīghen* (modern Dutch *stijgen*), Old High German *stīgan* (modern German *steigen*), Old Icelandic *stiga,* and Gothic *steigan,* from Proto-Germanic **stīʒanan.* Outside Germanic the word is cognate with Greek *steíchein* to step, go, *stíchos* row, line of verse, Old Irish *tíagu* I step, go, Albanian *shtek, shtegu* passage, way, Lithuanian *steĩgtis* to hurry, try hard, Old Slavic *stignǫ* I come, and Sanskrit *stighnoti* (he) steps, mounts, from Indo-European **steigh-/stoigh-/stigh-* (Pok.1017). **—staircase** *n.* (1624) **—stairway** *n.* (1708)

stake[1] *n.* pointed stick or post. Probably before 1200, in Layamon's *Chronicle of Britain;* developed from Old English *staca* (before 899, in Alfred's translation of Orosius' *Historiarum Adversus Paganos*), from Proto-Germanic **stakōn;* cognate with Middle Low German and Middle Dutch *stāke* stake (modern Dutch *staak*), and Old Icelandic *lýsistaki* candlestick. Cognates outside Germanic include Latin *tignum* beam (earlier **tegnom),* Lithuanian *stãgaras, stegerỹs* dry, long stalk, Old Slavic *stěgŭ* banner, and Armenian *t'akn* cudgel, stake, from Indo-European **(s)teg-/(s)tog-* stake, pole (Pok.1014) **—v.** Before 1338 *staken* mark with stakes, in Mannyng's *Chronicle of England;* from the noun.

stake[2] *v.* to risk, wager. 1530, in Palsgrave's *Lesclarcissement;* probably from Middle English *stake* post on which a gambling wager was placed (probably before 1300, in *Kyng Alisaunder*); see STAKE[1]. **—n.** that which is placed at hazard, such as a sum of money. 1540, in Palsgrave's translation of Willem Fullonius' *Comedy of Acolastus;* from the verb, or from *stake* post on which a gambling wager is placed. The figurative sense of something to gain or lose, share, interest, is first recorded in 1784. The plural *stakes* as is often found in horse racing is first recorded in 1696.

stalactite (stəlak′tīt) *n.* icicle-shaped formation of lime hanging from the roof of a cave. 1677, borrowed from New Latin *stalactites,* from Greek *stalaktós* dripping, from *stalássein* to trickle; for suffix see -ITE[1]. Greek *stalássein* is cognate with Middle Low German *stallen* to urinate, from Indo-European **(s)tel-/stol-* let flow, urinate (Pok.1018). Compare STALAGMITE.

stalag (stä′läg) *n.* German camp for prisoners of war. 1940, borrowing of German *Stalag,* shortened form of *Stammlager* base camp (*Stamm* base, STEM + *Lager* camp; see LAIR).

stalagmite (stəlag′mīt) *n.* cone-shaped formation of lime built up on the floor of a cave. 1681, borrowed from New Latin *stalagmites,* from Greek *stalagmós* a dropping, or *stálagma* a drop, drip, from *stalássein* to trickle; see STALACTITE; for suffix see -ITE[1].

stale *adj.* Probably about 1225 (of ale, wine, etc.) that has stood long enough to clear, freed from dregs or lees, in *King Horn;* cognate with Middle Dutch *stel* (of beer, urine, etc.) stale, and probably ultimately from the same Germanic source as Old English *standan* to STAND. The meaning of not fresh is first recorded in Middle English in 1475. The figurative sense of lacking freshness, novelty, or interest, worn out, out-of-date, is first recorded in English in 1562. **—v.** make or become stale. 1440 *stalen,* in *Promptorium Parvulorum;* from the adjective.

stalemate *n.* 1765, position of complete standstill in chess; formed from earlier *stale* stalemate (in Middle English probably before 1437) + *mate*[2] checkmate. Middle English *stale* was probably borrowed from Anglo-French *estale* standstill, from Old French *estal* place, stand, stall, from a Frankish word (compare Old High German *stal* stand, place, STALL[1]). The figurative sense of a deadlock, impasse, is first recorded in 1885. **—v.** bring to a stalemate. 1765, from the noun. The figurative sense of bring to a stalemate is first recorded somewhat earlier than the noun, in Hughes' *Tom Brown at Oxford* (1861).

stalk[1] *n.* stem of a plant. Before 1325 *stalk* (but usually *stalke*), probably a diminutive with *k* suffix of earlier *stale* one of the uprights of a ladder, handle, stalk (probably before 1200); developed from Old English *stalu* wooden part (as of a harp), from Proto-Germanic **stalō,* related to *stela* stalk, support (from Proto-Germanic **stelōn*), and *steall* place, STALL[1]. Parallel formations are found in Swedish *stjälk* stalk, Norwegian and Danish *stilk.* Old English *stela* is cognate with Middle Dutch *stele* handle, and Old Icelandic *stjǫlr* rump, coccyx, *stāl* haystack, pile. Cognates outside Germanic are found in Greek *steleá, steleón* ax handle, *stélechos* trunk, stump, and Armenian *steln* trunk, stalk, twig, from Indo-European **stel-/stol-* to set up (Pok.1019).

stalk[2] *v.* pursue an animal stealthily. Probably before 1300 *stalken* to walk stealthily or cautiously, in *Sir Tristrem;* developed from Old English *-stealcian,* as in *bestealcian* to steal along (about 1000, from Proto-Germanic **stalkōjanan*), and developed from Old English *stealcung* a stalking, related to *stealc* steep, lofty. Cognates include Middle Low German *stolkeren* strut about, flaunt, Old Swedish *stjœlke* stalk, stem, Old Icelandic *stelkr* pewit (bird), and, outside Germanic, Middle Irish *tolg* strength, and Lithuanian *stalgùs* stiff, defiant, proud, from Indo-European **stelg-/(s)tolg-* (Pok.1020). The sense of pursue an animal stealthily is first recorded in Middle English, probably about 1450. The meaning of walk with slow, stiff, or haughty strides, is first recorded in Palsgrave's *Lesclarcissement* (1530). **—n.** Before 1470 *stalke* act of stalking game, in Malory's *Works;* from the verb. **—stalking horse** 1519, horse used for concealment in stalking game; later, anything used to hide plans or acts (1579); person used as a blind to conceal someone or something (1612).

stall[1] *n.* place in a stable for one animal. Probably before 1200 *stalle;* developed from Old English (before 800) *steall* place where cattle are kept, place, position; cognate with Old Frisian *stal* stall, Middle Dutch and modern Dutch *stal,* Old High German *stal* (modern German *Stall*), Old High German and modern German *stellen* to place, and Old Icelandic *stallr* pedestal, stall (Swedish and Norwegian *stall,* Danish *stald* stable), from Proto-Germanic **stallaz,* earlier **stalnaz.* Cognates outside Germanic include Old Prussian *stallīt* to stand, Greek *stéllein* make ready, send, Armenian *stełcanem* I accomplish, and possibly Latin *stolidus* slow, dull, *stultus* foolish, from Indo-European **stel-/stol-* to place, make to stand; standing, immovable (Pok.1019).

Several of the English meanings having to do with the sense of seat or chair (as a British theater stall) and the meaning of a stand for selling were probably influenced by Old French *estal* place, stand, stall, from a Germanic source related to English *stall*[1]. The meaning of a stand for selling things is first recorded in Middle English, probably before 1300.
—**v.** Before 1333 *stallen* be situated, dwell, in Shoreham's poetry; from the noun in English, and as a borrowing from Old French *estaller.* Meanings of *install* (now obsolete) and put in an animal stall, probably developed in part from Old English, and in part were influenced by Old French *estaler* to place, from *estal* place, stall. The meaning of become stuck, come to a (forced) stop, is first recorded in Middle English about 1410.

stall[2] *n.* pretense to avoid doing something. Probably before 1500, bird used as a decoy, variant of earlier *stale* decoy (in Middle English, probably before 1425); borrowed from Anglo-French *estale* decoy, probably from a Germanic source (compare Old English *stælhrān* decoy reindeer, related to *stæl* place, position, and *steall* place, STALL[1]; so called because the decoy was placed in a permanent spot). The meaning of a pickpocket's assistant who distracts the attention of the victim is first recorded in English in 1591. The extended sense of an evasive trick or story, pretext, excuse, is first recorded as slang in Vaux's *Flash Dictionary* (1812). —**v.** 1592, to screen (a pickpocket) from observation; from the noun. The meaning of put off or prevent by evasive tactics is first recorded as slang in Vaux's *Flash Dictionary* (1812).

stallion *n.* uncastrated male horse. 1440 *stalyone,* in *Promptorium Parvulorum;* alteration of earlier *staloun, stalun* (before 1300); earlier in the place name *Stalunesbusc* (1218); borrowed from Old French *estalon* a stallion, from Frankish **stal,* cognate with Old High German *stal* stable, STALL[1]. The meaning may have developed from stall, stable, because such horses were kept there to service mares.

stalwart *adj.* strongly built, resolute, determined. 1375, in Barbour's *The Bruce;* Scottish variant of earlier *stealewurthe* (probably before 1200); developed from Old English *stǣlwierthe, stǣlwyrthe* good, serviceable (896, in the *Anglo-Saxon Chronicle*), probably a contraction of **statholwierthe* steadfast, well-based; literally, having a worthy foundation (*stathol* foundation, support + *wierthe* good, excellent, worthy, WORTH). Old English *stathol* is related to *standan* to STAND, and cognate with Old Frisian *stathul* foundation, Old High German *stadal* barn, shed, and Old Icelandic *stǫdhull* milking shed, from Proto-Germanic **stathlaz,* Indo-European **stətlos,* from **stā-/stə-* to stand (Pok.1004). Alternatively, Old English *stǣlwierthe, stǣlwyrthe* good, serviceable; literally, worthy of place (*stǣl* place + *wierthe* worth, worthy). Old English *stǣl* derives from Proto-Germanic **stǣlaz,* Indo-European **stēlos,* from root **stel-* to place, make to stand (Pok.1019). —**n.** About 1470, stalwart person; from the adjective. The sense of loyal supporter of a political party is first recorded in 1879 in American English, with specific reference to conservative Republicans who opposed friendly relations with the South after Reconstruction.

stamen (stā′mən) *n.* part of a flower which contains the pollen. 1668, borrowed from Latin *stāmen* warp, thread, stamen, related to *stāre* to STAND. Latin *stāmen* is cognate with Greek *stḗmōn* warp, thread, Old Irish *sessam* act of standing, Lithuanian *stomuõ* stature, Russian *stamík* supporting beam, Sanskrit *sthā́man-* place for standing, station, Tocharian A *ṣtām,* Tocharian B *stām* tree, and probably with Gothic *stōma* foundation, material. An earlier sense of warp (of cloth) is first recorded in English in 1650.

stamina (stam′ənə) *n.* strength, endurance. Before 1676, rudiments or original elements of something; borrowed from Latin *stāmina* threads, plural of *stāmen* (genitive *stāminis*) thread, warp, STAMEN. The sense of power to resist or recover from that which weakens, strength, endurance, is first recorded in 1726, in Swift's writings. This sense derives partly from the Latin application of the word to the threads spun by the Fates at a person's birth to determine how long he or she will live. It is also partly a figurative use of Latin *stāmen,* which meant the warp (of cloth), since the warp provides the structure or underlying foundation of a fabric.

stammer *v.* Before 1200 *stameren* to falter in one's speech, stutter; developed from Old English (about 1000) *stamerian;* cognate with Old Saxon *stamarōn* to stammer, Middle Low German and Middle Dutch *stameren, stamelen* (modern Dutch *stamelen*), Old High German *stamalōn* (modern German *stammeln*), Old Icelandic adjective *stammr* stammering (Norwegian and Swedish *stamm,* Danish *stam*), and Gothic adjective *stamms* stammering. Cognates outside Germanic are found only in the Baltic languages: Latvian *stuomîtiês* to stammer, stumble, and Lithuanian *stùmti* to push, from Indo-European **stem-/stom-/stōm-/stm̥-* (Pok.1021). —**n.** a stammering. 1773, in Goldsmith's *She Stoops to Conquer;* from the verb.

stamp *v.* About 1200 *stampen* pound, beat, crush, mash, in *Vices and Virtues,* probably an alteration (by Scandinavian influence) of earlier **stempen;* developed from Old English *stempan* to pound in a mortar, stamp. Old English *stempan* is cognate with Middle Low German *stempen* to stamp, Middle Dutch and modern Dutch *stampen* to pound, Old High German *stampfōn* (modern German *stampfen* to stamp with the foot, pound), Old Icelandic *stappa,* Swedish *stampa,* Norwegian and Danish *stampe* to stamp, from Proto-Germanic **stampōjanan.* Outside Germanic a cognate may possibly be found in Greek *stémbein* to handle roughly, abuse, from Indo-European **stemb-/stomb-* (Pok.1011).

The specific sense of stamp with the foot is found in Middle English about 1340. The meaning of impress or mark (something) with a die or similar tool is first recorded in English in 1560. The Germanic root **stamp-* is the source of the verb in several Romance languages,

as represented by Italian *stampare* to stamp, press, print, Provençal, Spanish, and Portuguese *estampar*, Old French *estamper*. The OED states that the Old French word influenced sense development of English *stamp*, but this is not readily evident.
—n. 1465 *stampe* a stamping tool; from the verb. The sense of an official mark or imprint certifying the genuineness or validity of something is first recorded in 1542. This sense came to be used in various figurative applications, as in *the stamp of merit* (1596, in Shakespeare's *Merchant of Venice*). In 1694 *stamps* were marks impressed on paper by government officials to certify that duty on an item had been paid; in the early 1800's adhesive labels were issued by the government to serve the same purpose as impressed stamps. About 1840 adhesive *postage stamps* were introduced in Great Britain and these immediately became known as *stamps*.

stampede *n.* headlong flight of frightened animals. 1844 (in 1838 *stomped;* 1826 *stompado*); American English; borrowed from Mexican Spanish *estampida*, from Spanish, an uproar, from *estampar* to stamp, press, pound, from Germanic (see remarks about the Germanic root under STAMP). **—v.** 1823, American English; from the noun (though recorded somewhat earlier).

stance *n.* 1532, standing place, station, position, probably borrowed from Middle French *stance* resting place, harbor, from Italian *stanza* stopping place, station, from Vulgar Latin **stantia*, from Latin *stāns* (genitive *stantis*), present participle of *stāre* to STAND; for suffix see -ANCE. Doublet of STANZA. The sense of position of the feet when making a stroke in golf or other games is first recorded in 1897. The extended sense of a manner of standing, posture, is first recorded in 1929, and the figurative sense of attitude, intellectual position, point of view, in 1956.

stanch[1] (stônch *or* stänch) *v.* to stop or check the flow of (blood, etc.). Probably before 1325 *staunchen* to stanch, quench, allay; before 1333 *stanchen;* borrowed from Old French *estanchier* to stop, hinder, from Vulgar Latin **stanticāre*, probably from Latin *stāns* (genitive *stantis*), present participle of *stāre* to STAND.

stanch[2] *n.* See STAUNCH.

stanchion (stan′chən) *n.* upright bar, post, or support. 1321 *staunson;* later *stanchon* (1343); borrowed from Middle French *estanchon* prop, brace, support, probably from *estant* upright, from present participle of *ester* be upright, stand, from Latin *stāre* to STAND. The meaning of an upright head hold for cattle in stalls of a cattle barn is first recorded in 1875.

stand *v.* Before 1121 *standen*, in *Peterborough Chronicle;* developed from Old English *standan* (from Proto-Germanic present stem **sta-n-đ′-*, Indo-European **stə-t-*), with past tense *stōd* (from Proto-Germanic past stem **stōđ′-*, Indo-European **stā-t-*), past participle *gestanden* (about 725, in *Beowulf*). Old English *standan* is cognate with Old Frisian *standa, stān* to stand, Old Saxon *standan, stān*, Middle Dutch *standen, staen* (modern Dutch *staan*), Old High German *stantan, stān* (modern German *stehen*), Old Icelandic *standa*, and Gothic *standan*. Outside Germanic a cognate form exists in almost every branch of the Indo-European languages, including Latin *stāre* to stand, Greek *histánai* cause to stand, set, place, *stênai* come to a stand, Lithuanian *stóti* to tread, step, Old Slavic *stojati* to stand, Sanskrit *tíṣṭhati* (he) stands (from Indo-European **sthī-sth-eti*), and Tocharian B *ste* is, *stare* are, deriving ultimately from Indo-European **stā-/stə-/sth-* to stand (Pok.1004). **—n.** Before 1325, place, position, in *Cursor Mundi;* from the verb. The noun is recorded in Old English (about 950) in the sense of a pause or delay.
—standby *n.* person or thing that can be relied upon (1796). **—stand-in** *n.* 1935, substitute for a film star (1928 *stand-in man*); the general sense of a substitute is found in 1937. **—standing** *n.* 1382, act of a person who stands, in Wycliffe's writings; formed from English *stand*, v. + *-ing*[1]. The sense of rank or status is first recorded in 1580. **—standpoint** *n.* point of view (1829, in writings of John Stuart Mill). **—standstill** *n.* (1702)

standard *n.* 1138, a flag or banner raised on a pole to indicate the rallying point of an army, in *Peterborough Chronicle;* borrowed from Old French *estandart*. According to many contemporary scholars, including Corominas and von Wartburg (*Französisches Etymologisches Wörterbuch*, 17, 1962), Old French *estandart* probably developed from a Frankish compound **standhard*, literally, stand fast or firm! (represented by Old High German *stantan* and Gothic *standan* to STAND + Old High German *hart* and Gothic *hardus* HARD). Accordingly, the flag or banner was probably so called because the pole or spear bearing it was fixed in the ground or mounted on a wagon or the like so as to stand upright. Existence of a Middle High German form *stanthart* and Middle Dutch form *standaert*, in the same sense as the Old French word, is cited as evidence of the compound in Germanic. Others have maintained that Old French *estandart* was derived from the verb *estendre* to stretch out, from Latin *extendere* EXTEND, and that Middle High German *stanthart* and Middle Dutch *standaert* were borrowed from Old French *estandart*. Corominas and von Wartburg object by pointing out that where *-an-* and *-en-* represent different pronunciations, the form is always *estandart*, not *estendart* (the expected form to derive from the verb *estendre*). Additionally the French suffix *-art* (of a formation *estendre* + *-art*) is usually restricted to personal names or epithets; see -ARD.

Alternatively, Gamillscheg proposes that Old French *estandart* developed from a Frankish form **standord*, with **-ord* represented by Old High German *-ort* point (modern German *Ort* place; see ODD) and presupposes alteration of Old French **estandort* by influence of French *-art*. But these older points of view have been generally replaced by the belief that the origin of Old French *estandart* is Germanic rather than Latin.

The sense development of English *standard* is somewhat obscure. The meaning of an authorized unit of measure or weight, an official yardstick, is first recorded in 1327, though the same meaning is recorded in Anglo-French *estaundart* in the 1200's. The figurative sense of an authoritative or recognized model, as of correctness or quality, a criterion, measure, is first recorded about 1445.
—adj. 1538, upright, set up on end; later, serving as a standard of measure, weight, or value (1622); from the noun.
—standardize *v.* 1873, to bring to a standard or uniform size, strength, shape, etc.; formed from English *standard*, n. or adj. + *-ize*.

stannic *adj.* containing tin, especially with a valence of four. 1790, formed in English from New Latin *stannum*, Late Latin *stannum* tin; earlier, alloy of silver and lead, scribal alteration of Latin *stagnum*, probably from a Celtic source (compare Irish *stān* tin, Welsh *ystaen,* Cornish and Breton *stēn*) + English *-ic.* The Celtic words are cognate with Greek *stagṓn* drop, from Indo-European **stag-* to trickle, drip, so called from being easily fusible (Pok.1010). **—stannous** *adj.* containing tin, especially with a valence of two. 1849, formed in English from New Latin *stannum* + English *-ous.*

stanza *n.* 1588 *stanze,* in Shakespeare's *Love's Labour's Lost;* borrowed from Italian *stanza* verse of a poem; originally, standing, stopping place, from Vulgar Latin **stantia* a stanza of verse (so called from the stop at the end of it); also, dwelling, chamber, stance; from Latin *stāns* (genitive *stantis*), present participle of *stāre* to STAND; see the doublet STANCE. The spelling *stanza* is recorded in English in 1589.

stapes (stā′pēz) *n.* innermost bone of the middle ear. 1670, New Latin, special use of Medieval Latin *stapes* stirrup, probably an alteration of Late Latin *stapia* (so called because the bone is shaped like a stirrup), of uncertain origin; perhaps borrowed from a Germanic source (compare Old High German *stapf, stapfo* STEP).

staphylococcus (staf′ələkok′əs) *n.* spherical parasitic bacterium. 1887, New Latin *Staphylococcus,* the genus name, from Greek *staphylḗ* bunch of grapes + New Latin *coccus* spherical bacterium (from Greek *kókkos* berry, grain); so called because these bacteria usually bunch together in irregular masses. Greek *staphylḗ* is related to *stémphylon* olive pulp, originally, what has been shaken down from the tree, and *astemphḗs* unshakable, firm; see STAFF.

staple[1] *n.* U-shaped piece of metal with pointed ends, driven into a surface to hold a hook, wire, fencing, etc. 1289 *stapel* post, stake; 1295 *staple* fastener; developed from Old English *stapol* post, pillar, column (about 725, in *Beowulf*); cognate with Old Frisian *stapul, stapel* tooth stem, block for executions, Old Saxon *stapal, stapel* candle, small tub, Middle Low German *stāpel* pillar, platform, heap, Middle Dutch *stāpel* foundation, heap, market (modern Dutch *stapel* heap), Old High German *staffel* step (modern German *Staffel* rung), and Old Icelandic *stǫpull* post, tower, from Proto-Germanic **stapulaz,* from Indo-European **steb-/stob-* post (Pok.1011). The sense applied to lightweight wire staples for holding papers together is first recorded in 1895. **—v.** Probably about 1390 *staplen* to fasten with or as with a staple, in *Sir Gawain and the Green Knight;* from the noun. **—stapler** *n.* (1926)

staple[2] *n.* principal article grown or manufactured in a place. Before 1400, official market in which merchants were granted the exclusive right to buy certain goods for export; borrowed from Anglo-French *estaple,* Old French *estaple* market, from a Germanic source (compare Middle Dutch *stāpel* market, heap; see STAPLE[1]). The sense of a principal article grown or manufactured in a place is first recorded in 1616 as a shortened form of earlier *staple ware* (1432), *staple gude* (1455, Scottish), i.e., wares or goods from a staple (market). **—adj.** most important, principal. 1615, having a foremost place among exported products, in George Sandys' *Travels;* from the noun. The generalized sense of most important, chief, principal, is first recorded in 1715.

star *n.* 1135 *sterre,* in *Peterborough Chronicle;* developed from Old English (before 830) *steorra* (from Proto-Germanic **stersōn*); cognate with Old Frisian *stēra* star, Old Saxon *sterro,* Middle Low German and Middle Dutch *sterre* (modern Dutch *ster*), Old High German *sterro, sterno* (modern German *Stern*), Old Icelandic *stjarna* (Swedish *stjärna,* Danish and Norwegian *stjerne*), and Gothic *staírnō* (from Proto-Germanic **sternō,* Indo-European **sternā*). Cognates outside Germanic include Breton and Cornish *sterenn* star, Welsh *seren,* Latin *stēlla* (earlier **stērlā*), Greek *astḗr, ástron,* Armenian *astł,* Avestan *stārō* (genitive), and Sanskrit *tāras* (nominative plural) stars, *stṛ́bhis* (instrumental plural) by means of stars, from Indo-European **ster-/stēr-/stṛ-* (Pok.1027).

The figurative sense of a person of brilliant reputation or celebrity is first recorded in English in 1824, and was originally used in theatrical language in reference to a leading actor, singer, or other performer. The term *film star* appeared in 1914 and *movie star* in 1919. **—v.** 1592, to mark with a star; from the noun. The sense of appear as a star, perform the leading part (said of an actor, singer, etc.), is first recorded in Washington Irving's *Tales of a Traveller* (1824).

—stardom *n.* 1865, the world or status of a theatrical star; formed from English *star,* n. + *-dom.* **—starfish** *n.* (1538) **—starlight** *n.* (about 1380, in Chaucer's translation of Boethius' *De Consolatione Philosophiae*) **—starry** *adj.* About 1380 *sterry,* in Chaucer's translation of Boethius' *De Consolatione Philosphiae;* formed from Middle English *sterre* star + *-y*[1].

starboard (stär′bərd) *n.* right side of a ship, when facing forward. Probably before 1400 *stere-bourde,* in *Morte Arthur;* developed from Old English (before 899) *stēorbord* side on which a vessel was steered (*stēor-* rudder, steering paddle + *bord* ship's side; see STEER[1], v., and BOARD. **—adj.** 1495, on or at the starboard; from the noun.

starch *v.* 1402 *sterchen* (but found earlier in *starchying* 1390-91) to stiffen, make rigid; probably developed from Old English (Mercian) **stercan* make rigid; (West Saxon) **stiercan* (attested in the past participle form, found in *stercedferhth* fixed, hard, or resolute of mind from Proto-Germanic **starkjanan*), from *stearc* stiff, strong; see STARK. Cognates of the Old English verb include Old Frisian *sterka* to stiffen, strengthen, Old Saxon *sterkian,* Middle Dutch and Dutch *sterken,* Old High German *sterchan* (modern German *stärken*), and Swedish *stärka.* **—n.** 1440 *starche* pasty substance obtained from flour and used to stiffen cloth, in *Promptorium Parvulorum;* from the verb. The chemical sense of a white, tasteless carbohydrate found in plant cells is first attested in 1812-16. **—starchy** *adj.* 1802, like starch, in letters of Coleridge; formed from English *starch,* n. + *-y* [1]. The figurative sense of stiff in manner formal, is first recorded in 1828-32.

stare *v.* About 1250 *staren* to gaze fixedly, be wide-eyed, in *The Owl and the Nightingale;* developed from Old English *starian* (about 725, in *Beowulf*); cognate with Middle Low German and Middle Dutch *stāren* to stare (modern Dutch *staren*), Old High German *starēn* to stare, *starrēn,* be rigid (modern German *starren* to gaze fixedly, stare), and Old Icelandic *stara* to stare (Norwegian *stare*), from Proto-Germanic **star-.* Cognates found outside Germanic include Greek *stereós* solid, stiff, Lithuanian *starìnti* make stiff, and probably Old Slavic *stradati* to suffer, from Indo-European **ster-/stor-* be rigid, stiff (Pok.1022). **—n.** Probably about 1380, power of sight; from the verb. The sense of an act of gazing, fixed gaze, is first recorded in Dryden's *Palamon and Arcite* (1700).

stark *adj.* Probably before 1200 *stark, sterc* firm, steadfast, powerful, severe, in Layamon's *Chronicle of Britain;* developed from Old English *stearc* stiff, strong (about 750, in Cynewulf's *Elene*), from Proto-Germanic **starkuz,* and related to Old English *starian* to STARE. Old English *stearc* is cognate with Old Frisian *sterk* strong, Old Saxon and Middle Low German *stark,* Middle Dutch *starc, staerc* (modern Dutch *sterk*), Old High German *starc* (modern German *stark*), *gistorchanēn* become stiff, Old Icelandic *sterkr* strong, *storkna* coagulate, and Gothic *gastaúrknan* become stiff. Cognates outside Germanic include Latvian *terglis* obstinate person, and Lithuanian *strė̃gti* become stiff, freeze, from Indo-European **(s)terg-/(s)torg-/(s)tr̥g-, (s)treg-* (Pok.1023).

The meaning of utter, complete, sheer, absolute, is first recorded in Middle English, probably before 1400, and the extended sense of bare, barren, desolate, in 1833.

—adv. Probably before 1200, in a stark manner, firmly, strongly, in Layamon's *Chronicle of Britain;* from the adjective. The sense of utterly, quite (as in *stark mad*) is found in writings of Skelton (1489).

starling *n.* common European bird. Before 1325 *sterling;* earlier as the surname *Starling* (1165-66); developed from Old English (before 1050) *stærling* (*stær* starling + *-ling*). Old English (before 800) *stær* (from Proto-Germanic **staraz*) is related to *stearn* a kind of bird, and cognate with Old High German *stara* (modern German *Star* starling), from Proto-Germanic **starōn,* Old Icelandic *stari* (Norwegian and Danish *stær,* Swedish *stare*), Latin *sturnus,* and Old Prussian *starnite* gull, from Indo-European **storos, *stornos* (Pok.1036).

start *v.* Probably before 1200 *sterten* move or spring suddenly, in Layamon's *Chronicle of Britain;* later *starten* (before 1325); perhaps developed from Old English **steortian* or **stiertan,* variants of *styrtan* to leap up (about 1000); related to *starian* to STARE. Old English *styrtan* is cognate with Old Frisian *sterta* to overturn or overthrow, Middle Low German *storten* to overthrow or fall, Middle Dutch and Dutch *storten* to spill or throw, Old High German *sturzen* to fall or throw (modern German *stürzen*), Middle High German *sterzen* stand stiffly or move briskly, and Old Icelandic *sterta* to stiffen or strengthen, from Indo-European **(s)terd-/(s)tord-/(s)tr̥d-* (Pok.1023).

The sense of awaken suddenly is first recorded about 1386, and that of flinch or recoil in alarm, before 1325. The meaning of cause to begin acting or operating is first recorded in 1666, in Pepys' *Diary,* and the specific sense of begin to move, leave, depart, in Scott's *Kenilworth* (1821).

—n. Probably before 1200 *stert* sudden movement, short space of time, in *Ancrene Riwle;* from the verb. The sense of the act or fact of beginning to move, go, or act, is first recorded in 1566, and that of a sudden jump of the body in reaction to surprise, fear, etc., about 1385.

startle *v.* Probably before 1300 *startlen, stertlen* run to and fro; developed as a frequentative verb form of *sterten* to START; for suffix see -LE[3]. The sense of move suddenly in fear or surprise is first recorded in Palsgrave's *Lesclarcissement* (1530), and the meaning of frighten suddenly, cause to start, in Shakespeare's *King John* (1595). **—n.** sudden shock of surprise or fright. 1714, from the verb.

starve *v.* Before 1225 *sterven* to die, kill; developed from Old English *steorfan* to die (about 1000, in Ælfric's *Homilies*); cognate with Old Frisian *sterva* to die, Old Saxon *sterƀan,* Middle Dutch and Dutch *sterven,* Old High German *sterban* (modern German *sterben*), from Proto-Germanic **sterƀanan,* cognate with Russian *stérbnut'* become numb, die off, and Middle Irish *ussarb* death (from **ud-sterbhā*), from Indo-European **sterbh-* (Pok.1025). The specific meaning of kill with hunger is first recorded in English in Palsgrave's *Lesclarcissement* (1530). Compare DIE[1] stop living. **—starvation** *n.* 1778, act of starving; formed from English *starve* + *-ation.* This is one of the few instances in which the Latin-derived suffix *-ation* has been added to a native English word. **—starveling** *n.* 1546, starved person or animal; formed from English *starve* + *-ling.*

stash *v. Slang.* hide or put away for future use. 1797, of unknown origin. An earlier sense of stop, desist from, is found in 1794. **—n.** *Slang.* 1914, something hidden away, American English; from the verb.

stat *adv.* (in medicine) immediately. Before 1970, shortened form of Latin *statim,* an adverb originally meaning "to a standstill," a vestigial accusative of a lost noun **statis,* exactly cognate with Greek *stásis* a standing still, and Sanskrit *sthíti-s* a standing, abode; see STATION and STEAD.

-stat a combining form used in naming devices for stabilizing, regulating, or controlling, as in *gyrostat, rheostat, thermostat.* Borrowed from New Latin *-stata,* and French *-stat,* from Greek *statós* standing, stationary, or *-státēs,* suffix forming agent nouns, from *histánai* to cause to STAND. The first such name recorded in English was *heliostat* (1747, from New Latin *heliostata,* French *héliostat*), referring to a device in which a rotating mirror casts the sun's rays in a fixed direction.

state *n.* Probably before 1200 *stat* position in society, station, in *Ancrene Riwle;* later, condition or fact of being (about 1280); borrowed from Latin *status* (genitive *statūs*) manner of standing, position, condition, from *stāre* to STAND; common in the Latin phrase *status reī pūblicae* condition of the republic. Some of the senses in Middle English were borrowed from Old French *estat,* learned borrowing from Latin *status.* The sense of government of a people, nation, territory, etc., is found in Middle English probably about 1300. The sense of one of a number of governments united under one federal government is first recorded in Jefferson's writings (1774). Doublet of ESTATE and STATUS. **—v.** About 1590, to place, station, in Marlowe's *The Jew of Malta;* from the noun. The meaning of set forth in proper form is recorded before 1641, and the sense of declare in words, in 1647. **—statecraft** *n.* statesmanship (1642) **—statehood** *n.* (1868, American English) **—statehouse** *n.* (1593, house for state ceremonies; 1639, American English, building for colonial government; 1786, American English, state capitol) **—stately** *adj.* About 1386 *statly* befitting or indicating high estate, noble, in Chaucer's *Legend of Good Women;* formed from Middle English *stat,* n., state + *-ly*[2]. Compare Dutch *statelijk* stately. The meaning of magnificent, splendid, is first recorded before 1420. **—statement** *n.* 1775, something stated, allegation, declaration; formed from English *state,* v. + *-ment.* **—stateroom** *n.* (1660, officer's room on a ship, in Pepys' *Diary;* 1774, private room on a ship; 1853, American English, private room on a train) **—stateside** *adj. Informal.* of or in the continental United States (1944, American English). *—adv.* in or towards the continental United States (1945,

American English). **—statesman** *n.* (1592) **—statesmanship** *n.* (1764) **—states' rights** (1798 *state rights;* 1858 *states rights*) **—stateswoman** *n.* (1609, Ben Jonson)

static *adj.* 1638, relating to the effects or equilibrium of weight; shortened form of earlier *statical* (1570); from the noun and also possibly modeled on New Latin *staticus,* from Greek *statikós* causing to stand, skilled in weighing (*sta-,* stem of *histánai* to cause to stand, weigh; see STAND); for suffix see -IC. The sense of having to do with bodies at rest or with forces that balance each other is first recorded in 1839 (but found in the same sense in *statical* 1802). The generalized meaning of in a fixed or stable condition is first recorded in 1856 (but found in the same sense in *statical,* adj. 1855). The specific technical sense used in reference to electricity is first recorded in Faraday's writings 1839, and in 1837 in the form *statical.* **—n.** 1570, science relating to weight and its mechanical effects; probably influenced by, and perhaps borrowed from New Latin *statica,* from Greek *statikè* (*téchne*) (the art or science) of weighing. The sense of electrical disturbances in the air is first recorded in 1913 in American English. The slang sense of criticism, fuss, is first recorded in 1926, also in American English.

The plural form *statics* is first recorded in Blount's *Glossographia* (1656), in the sense of the science relating to weight. The modern sense of the branch of physics concerned with the action of forces in producing equilibrium or relative rest was established by 1867.

station *n.* About 1280 *stacioun* place which one normally occupies; borrowed from Old French *station,* from Latin *statiōnem* (nominative *statiō*) a standing, place of standing, post, dwelling, position, office, a pre-Latin extension of a lost noun **statis* (see STAT), from *stāre* to STAND; for suffix see -TION. The meaning of a place of special purpose usually with particular equipment (*police station, zoological station*) where people are assigned to work is first recorded in 1823; a special sense *radio station* appears in 1912. The meaning of a regular stopping place (as in *a bus station*) is first recorded in 1797, from the earlier sense of a stopping place on a journey 1585. The meaning of a person's rank or position in the world is first recorded in 1675. **—v.** assign a station to, assign to a station, 1748, in Smollett's *Adventures of Roderick Random;* from the noun. **—stationary** *adj.* Probably before 1430 *stacionarye* (of planets, etc.) having no apparent motion; borrowed through Middle French *stationnaire* motionless, and directly from Medieval Latin *stationarius,* from Latin *statiōnārius* of or belonging to a military station, from *statiōnem* (nominative *statiō*) station, post; for suffix see -ARY. The general meaning of having a fixed position, not movable, remaining unchanged, is first recorded in English in 1628. **—station wagon** (1894, kind of horse-drawn carriage; 1929, American English, kind of car with a rear door)

stationer *n.* person who sells paper, pens, pencils, etc. 1311 *stacioner* book dealer; earlier as a surname *Staciner* (1293-94); borrowed from Medieval Latin *stationarius,* originally, stationary seller, as distinct from a roving peddler, from Latin *statiōnem* (nominative *statiō*) STATION; for suffix see -ER[1]. The sale of writing materials was originally part of a book dealer's business. The distinction between a bookseller and a stationer was not established until the 1700's, (and very often books are still available at a stationer's) although the current sense of *stationer* is recorded in Blount's *Glossographia* (1656). **—stationery** *n.* 1727 *stationary,* in Bailey's *Dictionary;* earlier in *stationery wares* articles sold by a stationer (1679-88); formed from English *stationer* + *-y*[3].

statistics *n.* numerical facts or data collected and classified. 1770, science dealing with data about the condition of a state or community; borrowed from German *Statistik,* probably from New Latin *statisticum* (*collegium*) (lecture course on) state affairs, from Italian *statista* one skilled in statecraft, from Latin *status* STATE; for suffix see -ICS. The German word was coined in 1748 by Gottfried Achenwall, 1719-1772, a German scholar sometimes considered to be the founder of the science of statistics. The sense of numerical facts or data collected and classified is found in English in 1837, but the term is first recorded in *medical statistics* (1829). **—statistical** *adj.* 1787, of or relating to statistics; formed from English *statistics* + *-al*[1]. **—statistician** *n.* 1825, expert in statistics; formed from obsolete English *statistic* of or relating to statistics (1789, probably borrowed from German *statistisch,* from *Statistik*) + English *-ian.*

statue *n.* About 1375, statue, image, in Chaucer's *Canterbury Tales;* borrowed from Old French *statue,* learned borrowing from Latin *statua,* back formation from *statuere* to cause to stand, set up, from *status* (genitive *statūs*) a standing, position, from *stāre* to STAND. **—statuary** *n.* 1563, art of making statues, sculpture, borrowed from Middle French *statuaire,* and directly from Latin *statuāria,* noun use of feminine of *statuārius* of a statue, from *statua* statue; for suffix see -ARY. *—adj.* having to do with or suitable for statues. 1627, from the noun, possibly influenced by Latin *statuārius* of a statue. **—statuesque** *adj.* Before 1834, like a statue, in Coleridge's *Works;* formed from English *statue* + *-esque,* patterned on *picturesque.* **—statuette** *n.* 1843, small statue; borrowed from French *statuette,* diminutive of *statue* statue, from Old French; for suffix see -ETTE.

stature *n.* Before 1325 *statur* height, in *Cursor Mundi;* borrowed from Old French *stature, estature,* learned borrowing from *statūra* height or size of a body, size, growth, from *stāre* to STAND; for suffix see -URE. The figurative sense of quality, worth, status, is first recorded in English in 1834, in John Henry Newman's writings.

status *n.* 1671, as a Latin word used in the sense of height, in Evelyn's correspondence; later, legal standing of a person (1791, in Boswell's *Life of Samuel Johnson*); borrowing of Latin *status* (genitive *statūs*) condition, position, state, from *stāre* to STAND. Doublet of ESTATE and STATE. The sense of social or professional standing is first recorded in Scott's *The Monastery* (1820). **—status quo** (kwō) existing state of affairs. 1833, borrowing of Latin *status quō* the state in which; see STATE.

statute *n.* Probably before 1300 *statout* decree, in *Arthour and Merlin;* borrowed from Old French *statut, estatut,* learned borrowing from Late Latin *statūtum* a law, decree, noun use of neuter past participle of Latin *statuere* enact, establish, from *status* (genitive *statūs*) condition, position, from *stāre* to STAND. The sense of law of the land, law enacted by a legislative body, is found in Middle English about 1300. **—statute mile** (1862) **—statutory** *adj.* 1717, (of a clause in a statute) enacting; formed from English *statute* + *-ory.* The meaning of having to do with or consisting of statutes is first recorded in 1766 (Johnson quoted in Boswell's *Life of Samuel Johnson*).

staunch or **stanch** (stônch *or* stănch) *adj.* firm, strong, substantial. Before 1393 *staunche* firm, intact, certain, in Gower's *Confessio Amantis;* borrowed from Middle French *estanche* firm, watertight, feminine of *estanc,* from Old French, dried, exhausted, wearied, vanquished, from *estanchier* cause to cease flowing, stop; see STANCH[1]. The sense of strong, substantial, is first recorded in 1455-56.

stave *n.* one of the pieces of wood that form the sides of a barrel or other vessel. Before 1398 *staves,* plural of STAFF. The plural of *staff* is found earlier as *stafæ* rungs of a ladder (possibly Old English, but recorded about 1175), and *staves* (before 1325). The singular form *stave* is a back formation from the plural, first found in 1750. **—v.** 1542, to fit with staves, from the noun. The meaning of break up (a cask) into staves is first recorded about 1595.

stay[1] *v.* to remain. 1440 *steyen* to halt, come to a stop, in *Promptorium Parvulorum;* borrowed from Middle French *stai-, estai-,* and *stei-, estei-,* stem of *ester* to stay or stand, from Old French, from Latin *stāre* to STAND. The sense of continue or remain in a given condition is first recorded in 1573-80. **—n.** 1523-34, appliance for stopping; from the verb. The sense of a halt, a stop, is first recorded in 1537, and the specific sense of a suspension of a judicial proceeding in 1542. The meaning of an act or period of remaining in a place, sojourn, is first recorded in 1538. **—staying power** power to endure (1859).

stay[2] *n.* support, prop, brace. About 1515, borrowed from Middle French *estaie* piece of wood used as a support, from Frankish **staka* support (compare Middle Dutch *stāke* stick, STAKE[1]). **—v.** to support, prop. 1423 *staien;* borrowed from Middle French *estayer,* from *estaie* support, prop. **—stays** *n.pl.* 1608, a corset, especially a stiffened one; plural in use because stays were usually made in two pieces laced together.

stay[3] *n.* strong rope which supports a ship's mast. 1294-95 *stei;* developed from Late Old English (before 1100) *stæg;* cognate with Middle Low German *stach* stay, rope, Dutch *stag,* dialectal German *stagen* become stiff, and Old Icelandic *stag* stay, from Proto-Germanic **stuʒán.* These forms are cognate with Sanskrit *stákati* (he) resists, and probably with Old High German *stahal* steel, from Indo-European **stok-,* root **stek-* stand; firm, strong (Pok.1011). **—v.** Before 1613, (of a ship) to change to the other tack; from the noun. The meaning of secure or steady with stays is first recorded in 1627.

stead *n.* place or function (taken by a successor or substitute). About 1450 *steade;* developed from Old English *stede* place, position, standing, delay (before 899, in Alfred's translation of Boethius' *De Consolatione Philosophiae*), related to *standan* to STAND. Old English *stede* is cognate with Old Frisian *stede, stidi* stead, Old Saxon *stedi,* Middle Low German *stede* place, abode, Middle Dutch *stat, stēde* town (modern Dutch *stad*), Old High German *stat* place (modern German *Statt* stead, *Stätte* place, abode, *Stadt* town), Old Icelandic *stadhr* place, and Gothic *staths,* from Proto-Germanic **staðís,* cognate with Sanskrit *sthíti-s* a standing, abode, Greek *stásis,* and Latin *statiō,* from Indo-European **stətís,* root **stā-/stə-/sth-* (Pok.1006). **—steadfast** *adj.* Probably before 1200 *studevest* firmly fixed, unchangeable, loyal; also with the spelling *stedefast* (about 1200); developed from Old English (993, in *The Battle of Maldon*) *stedefæst* secure in position (*stede* stead + *fæst* firmly fixed; see FAST[1], adj.).

steady *adj.* Probably about 1200 *stidiʒ* stubborn, in *The Ormulum;* later *studi* not deviating from course (about 1300, in nautical use), and *stedye* fixed, immovable (1530); formed from Middle English *stude, stede* stead, place + *-y*[1]. The sense of regular, uniform, is recorded in Elyot's *Dictionary* (1548), and that of firm in standing or movement, not shaking, in 1574. **—adv.** in a steady manner, steadily. Before 1605, from the adjective. The idiom *go steady,* meaning to be regular sweethearts, is first recorded in 1905, in American English. **—v.** make or keep steady. 1530, in Palsgrave's *Lesclarcissement;* from the adjective. **—n.** *Informal.* a person's regular date or sweetheart. 1897, American English; from the adjective.

steak *n.* 1440 *steyke* thick slice of meat cut for roasting, in *Promptorium Parvulorum;* earlier in the surname *Laythstayk* (1313-17); probably borrowed from a Scandinavian source (compare Old Icelandic *steik* roast meat, related to *steikja* to roast, and *stik, stikka* piece of wood, STICK[1]).

steal *v.* Probably about 1150 *stelen* take dishonestly; later, to go away stealthily (probably before 1160); developed from Old English (before 800) *stelan* to commit theft (past tense *stæl,* past participle *stolen*); cognate with Old Frisian *stela* to steal, Old Saxon *stelan,* Middle Dutch *stēlen* (modern Dutch *stelen*), Old High German *stelan* (modern German *stehlen*), Old Icelandic *stela* (Swedish *stjäla,* Norwegian *stjele,* Danish *stjæle*), and Gothic *stilan,* from Proto-Germanic **stelanan.* Possible cognates outside Germanic may be found in Middle Irish *serbh* theft, and Greek *stereîn* to deprive of, if it is accepted that the Indo-European root **ster-* to rob or deprive (Pok.1028), was altered in Germanic to **stel-* by influence of forms of the verb-root **kel-* to hide (compare German *hehlen* to conceal). **—n.** 1825, a theft, the thing stolen, in Jamieson's *Dictionary of the Scottish Language;* from the verb. An earlier sense of an act of going secretly is found in 1590. A single instance of the noun is also found in Middle English as *stele* a theft, probably before 1200.

stealth *n.* secret or sly action. About 1250 *stalthe* theft, in *Genesis and Exodus;* later, secret action (about 1300), and with the spelling *stelth* (before 1325, from Old English **stǣlth,* Proto-Germanic **stǣlíthō*); related to *stelen* to STEAL; for suffix see -TH[1]. **—stealthy** *adj.* 1605, moving or acting by stealth, in Shakespeare's *Macbeth;* formed from English *stealth* + *-y*[1].

steam *n.* Old English (before 1000) *stēam* vapor, fume; cognate with West Frisian, Low German, and Dutch *stoom* steam (from Proto-Germanic **staumaz*); of unknown origin. **—v.** About 1387-95 *stemen* to emit flame, glow, in Chaucer's *Canterbury Tales;* developed from Old English (before 1000) *stēmen, stȳman* to emit a scent or odor, related to *stēam* vapor, fume. The meaning of emit steam or vapor is first recorded in 1614, influenced by the noun. **—steam bath** (1794) **—steamboat** *n.* (1787) **—steam engine** (1751) **—steamer** *n.* 1811, (*slang use*) a tobacco pipe; formed from English *steam,* v. and n. + *-er*[1]. The sense of an apparatus or vessel for steaming is first recorded in 1814, and that of a vessel propelled by steam, steamboat, in 1825.**—steam iron** (1951) **—steamroller** *n.* (1866) **—steam room** (1972) **—steamship** *n.* (1819, in Shelley's letters) **—steam shovel** (1879) **—steamy** *adj.* 1644, emitting steam; formed from English *steam,* n. + *-y*[1]. The figurative sense of erotic, sexy, is first recorded in 1952.

stearin (stir′in) *n.* chemical substance, the main constituent of many fats. 1817, in Thomas Thomson's *A System of Chemistry;* borrowed from French *stéarine,* formed from Greek *stéār* (genitive *stéātos*) tallow, fat (see STONE) + French *-ine* -INE[2] (chemical suffix). The word was coined in French by its discoverer the chemist M.E. Chevreul, 1786-1889. The extended sense of the solid portion of any oil or fat is first recorded in 1910. **—stearic acid** fatty acid obtained from tallow and other fats. 1831, partial translation of French *acide stéarique* (Greek *stéār* fat + French *-ique* -IC).

steed *n.* horse. Probably about 1150 *stede;* developed from Old English *stēda* stallion (before 899, in Alfred's translation of Bede's *Ecclesiastical History*), related to *stōd* STUD[2].

steel *n.* Probably before 1200 *stel, stele,* in *Ancrene Riwle;* developed from Old English *stȳle* (about 725, in *Beowulf*). Old English *stȳle* (Old Mercian dialect *stēle*) and Old Saxon *stehli* were derived from a Proto-Germanic adjective **staHlijan,* meaning "made of steel." The related noun is represented by Middle Low German *stāl* steel, Middle Dutch *stael* (modern Dutch *staal*), Old High German *stahal* (modern German *Stahl*), and Old Icelandic *stāl* (Swedish and Norwegian *stål,* Danish *staal*), from Proto-Germanic **staHla-* standing fast. Possible cognates outside Germanic include Sanskrit *stákati* (he) resists, and Avestan *staxra-* firm, strong, from Indo-European **stek-/stok-* stand; firm, strong (Pok.1011). **—adj.** made of steel. Probably before 1200 *stele,* in Layamon's *Chronicle of Britain;* from the noun. **—v.** to point, edge, or cover with steel. Probably about 1200 *stelen* harden (iron); developed from Old English *stȳlan* (about 750, in Cynewulf's *Christ*), from *stȳle,* n. The sense of point, edge, or cover with steel, is found in Middle English before 1240. The figurative sense of make hard or strong like steel is first recorded in 1581, in a translation of the *Iliad.* **—steel mill** (1647, machine for grinding and fashioning things made of steel; 1858, factory for the manufacture of steel) **—steel wool** (1896) **—steelworker** *n.* (1884) **—steelworks** *n.* (1842) **—steely** *adj.* 1509, hard as steel; 1586, made of steel; formed from English *steel,* n. + *-y*[1].

steenbok (stēn′bok′) *n.* small African antelope. 1775, borrowing of Afrikaans *steenbok,* from Middle Dutch *steenboc* (*steen* STONE + *boc* BUCK[1]). The Middle Dutch compound had cognates in Old English *stānbucca* mountain goat, and Old High German *steinboc* ibex (modern German *Steinbock*).

steep[1] *adj.* having a sharp slope. Probably about 1200 *stepe* high, elevated, in *The Ormulum;* developed from Old English *stēap* (about 725, in *Beowulf*); cognate with Old Frisian *stāp* high, lofty, Old High German *stouf* cliff, and Old Icelandic *staup* hole in a road, from Proto-Germanic **staupaz,* Indo-European **stoub-,* root **steub-* lop off (Pok.1034). Related to STOOP[1] bend. The sense of having a sharp slope, precipitous, is first recorded in Middle English probably before 1300, in *Kyng Alisaunder.* **—n.** steep slope. 1555; from the adjective.

steep[2] *v.* to soak in a liquid. Before 1325 *stepen;* of uncertain origin; probably cognate with Old Icelandic *steypa* to pour out, throw (from Proto-Germanic **staupjanan*), Norwegian *støypa* to pour, cast, and Swedish *stöpa.* These verb forms are perhaps derived from Proto-Germanic **staupaz,* the source of Old English *stēap* cup for liquor, bowl, Old Icelandic *staup* pothole, beaker, Middle Low German *stōp,* Middle Dutch *stoop,* and Old High German *stouf.* Related to STOUP. **—n.** a soaking. About 1430 *stipe;* later *stepe* (about 1450); from the verb.

steeple *n.* Before 1121 *stepel* high tower, usually with a spire, in *Peterborough Chronicle;* developed from Old English *stēpel* (Mercian), *stīepel* (West Saxon, before 1050), from Proto-Germanic **staupilaz,* related to *stēap* high, lofty; see STEEP[1]. **—steeplechase** *n.* horse race over a course having obstacles. 1793, formed from English *steeple* + *chase*[1] to hunt; so called because formerly it was a race with a church steeple in view as a goal. **—steeplejack** *n.* person who repairs steeples or tall chimneys (1881).

steer[1] *v.* guide the course of a vehicle, etc. Before 1150 *steren;* developed from Old English *stēran* (Mercian), *stīeran* (West Saxon, before 899, in Alfred's translation of St. Gregory's *Pastoral Care*). The Old English forms are cognate with Old Frisian *stiōra* to steer, Middle Low German and Middle Dutch *stūren* (modern Dutch *sturen*), Old High German *stiuren* (modern German *steuern*), Old Icelandic *stȳra* (Swedish *styra,* Norwegian and Danish *styre*), and probably Gothic *stiurjan* establish, affirm; all from the Proto-Germanic **steurijanan,* which probably derived from **steurō* rudder, represented by Old English *stēor* helm, rudder (as in *stēoresman* steersman), Old Frisian *stiure,* Old High German *stiura* (modern German *Steuer*), Middle Dutch *stūre* (modern Dutch *stuur*), and Old Icelandic *stȳri* rudder, from Indo-European **steu-* (Pok.1009). **—steerage** *n.* 1399-1401 *sterage* steering apparatus of a ship; formed from Middle English *steren* to steer + *-age.* The meaning of section of a ship with the cheapest accommodations is first recorded in Washington Irving's writings in 1804. **—steering wheel** (1750, wheel for steering a ship; 1907, wheel for steering a car) **—steersman** *n.* person who steers a boat or ship. About 1330 *steres man,* developed from Old English *stēoresman* (about 1000), formed from *stēores-,* genitive of *stēor* helm, rudder + *man* person; see MAN.

steer[2] *n.* young ox. About 1250 *stere* young bull; developed from Old English (before 800) *stēor;* cognate with Middle Low German *stēr* young ox, Middle Dutch and modern Dutch *stier,* Old High German *stior* (modern German *Stier*), Old Icelandic *stjōrr, thjōrr* (Swedish *tjur,* Norwegian *tjor, tyr,* Danish *tyr* bull), and Gothic *stiur,* from Proto-Germanic **steuraz.* Cognates outside Germanic are found in Middle Persian *stōr* draft animal, and Avestan *staora-* large cattle from Indo-European **steuros;* compare **stewəros,* the source of Sanskrit *sthávira-s* broad, stout (Pok.1009).

stein (stīn) *n.* beer mug. 1855, borrowing of German *Stein,* shortened form of *Steinkrug* stone jug (*Stein* STONE + *Krug* jug, pitcher; see CROCK).

stellar *adj.* of or like a star. 1656, in Blount's *Glossographia;* borrowed from Latin *stēllāris* pertaining to a star, starry, from *stēlla* STAR; for suffix see -AR.

stellate (stel′āt) *adj.* star-shaped. About 1500, starry; later, star-shaped (1661); borrowed from Latin *stēllātus* covered with stars, from *stēlla* STAR; for suffix see -ATE[1].

stem[1] *n.* main part of a plant above the ground. 1294-95 *stemme* sternpost of a ship; later *stem* trunk of a tree (before 1338); developed from Old English *stemn, stefn* stem of a plant, also either end of a ship (before 899, in Alfred's translation of Boethius' *De Consolatione Philosophiae*), from Proto-Germanic **stamniz;* cognate with Old Saxon *stamn* stem of a ship, Middle Low German and Middle Dutch *stēvene* (modern Dutch *steven*), Old High German *stam* stem of a plant (modern German *Stamm* trunk or stem of a tree), and Old Icelandic *stafn* stem of a ship, from Proto-Germanic **stamnaz.* Cognates outside Germanic are found in Old Irish *tamun* tree trunk, Greek *stámnos* pitcher, *stamînes* ribs of a ship, and Tocharian A *ṣtam,* Tocharian B *stām* tree, from Indo-European **stəmnos,* root **stā-/stə-/sth-* stand (Pok.1008). —**v.** 1577, to rise erect, mount upwards; from the noun. The meaning of remove the stem from is first recorded in 1724, in American English. The phrase *stem from,* meaning originate or develop from (as from a stem), spring from, is first recorded in 1932, also in American English, as a translation of scholarly German *stammen aus. . .*

stem² *v.* to stop, check, dam up. Before 1325 *stemmen* to delay, hesitate, stop, in *Cursor Mundi;* probably borrowed from a Scandinavian source (compare Old Icelandic *stemma* to stop, related to *stama* to STAMMER). Old Icelandic *stemma* is cognate with Middle Low German and Middle Dutch *stemmen* to stop, and Middle High German and German *stemmen.* The current sense of stop, check, dam up, is first recorded probably before 1350.

stench *n.* very bad smell. Probably before 1200, in *Ancrene Riwle;* developed from Old English *stenc* pleasant or unpleasant smell (before 899, in Alfred's translation of Orosius' *Historiarum Adversus Paganos*), related to *stincan* emit a smell, STINK. Old English *stenc* (from Proto-Germanic **stankwiz*) is cognate with Old Saxon *stank* stench, Middle Dutch *stanc* (modern Dutch *stank*), and Old High German *stank* (modern German *Gestank*).

stencil *n.* sheet of metal, paper, etc., having letters or designs cut through it. 1707 *stanesile;* later *stensil* (1816), *stencil* (1848); probably developed from Middle English *stencellen* to ornament, color (before 1400); borrowed from Middle French *estenceler* cover with sparkles or stars, powder with color, from *estencele* spark, spangle, from Vulgar Latin **stincilla,* alteration (by metathesis of *t* and *c*) of Latin *scintilla* spark; of uncertain origin. —**v.** Before 1400 *stencellen* to ornament, color; see noun; later, to produce (a design, etc.) with a stencil (1861); from the noun.

stenography (stənog′rəfē) *n.* method of rapid writing that uses symbols, shorthand. 1602, formed in English from Greek *stenós* narrow (of uncertain origin) + English *-graphy.* —**stenograph** *v.* write in shorthand. 1821, back formation from *stenographer.* —**stenographer** *n.* 1809, in Washington Irving's *Knickerbocker's History of New York,* a shorthand writer; formed from English *stenography* + *-er¹.* —**stenographic** *adj.* 1681, formed from English *stenography* + *-ic.*

stentorian (stentôr′ēən) *adj.* very loud or powerful in sound. 1605, formed in allusion to *Stentor* (1600, in Greek, *Sténtōr*), a legendary Greek herald in the Trojan War, whose voice (as described in the *Iliad*) was as loud as the voices of fifty men; for suffix see -IAN. An earlier form *stentorious* (formed from *Stentor* + *-ious*) appeared in the 1500's.

step *v.* Probably before 1200 *steppen* to walk, go, move, in Layamon's *Chronicle of Britain;* later, take a step, in *Bestiary* (before 1250); developed from Old English *steppan* (before 1000, Anglian), *stæppan* (before 899, West Saxon). The Old English forms are cognate with Old Frisian *stapa, steppa* to step, Middle Dutch and modern Dutch *stappen,* Old High German *stapfōn, stepfen* (modern German *stapfen*), and Old Icelandic *stappa* (Norwegian and Danish *stappe,* Swedish *stappa*); probably related to *stampfōn* to pound, STAMP. —**n.** Before 1225 *steepe;* developed from Old English *steppa* (Mercian), *stæpe, stepe* (before 830, West Saxon); cognate with Old Frisian *stap* step, pace, Middle Dutch and modern Dutch *stap,* and Old High German *stapf, stapfo* (modern German *Stapfen*); related to the verb. —**stepladder** *n.* (1751) —**stepping stone** (about 1325, stone used in crossing a stream; 1653, means of advancing)

step- a combining form meaning related by remarriage of a parent rather than by blood, as in *stepfather, stepsister.* Middle English, developed from Old English *stēop-;* cognate with Old Frisian *stiāp-* step-, Middle Low German *stēf-,* Middle Dutch and modern Dutch *stief-,* Old High German *stiof-* (modern German *stief-*), and Old Icelandic *stjūp-* (Swedish *styv-,* Old Danish *stiūp-,* Norwegian *ste-*). The original sense of the combining form is indicated by the use of Old English *stēopcild* stepchild, for "orphan," and by the cognates, Old English *āstīepan, bestīepan* to bereave, Old High German *arstiufen, bestiufen* to bereave. Etymologically, *stepfather* (before 800) or *stepmother* (before 800) would mean "one who becomes a father (or mother) to an orphan," and *stepson* (before 800) or *stepdaughter* (before 850) "an orphan who becomes a son (or daughter) by the remarriage of a parent." It is uncertain which of these two applications of the prefix came first; all branches of Germanic (except Gothic) have both uses, and also the extended use in *stepbrother* (1440), *stepsister* (1440). The sense of orphan still applies in that on remarriage the natural children of a spouse must be formally adopted by the other spouse for the law to recognize the new parent as a father or mother.

The combining form, going back to the Germanic base **steupa-,* is not recorded in Gothic and not found in Indo-European languages outside Germanic. In Middle Dutch and Middle Low German and in some later Scandinavian forms the *p* of Germanic **steupa-* is anomalously represented by *f.* This is probably from assimilation to the following *f*-sound in the compounds of *stepfather* (Middle Low German *stēfvadere,* Middle Dutch *stiefvader,* as well as the early Middle English variant *steffader*).

According to Johnson in 1755, *stepmother* was the only one of the compounds of *step-* that had survived in general use. By the late 1800's most of the present-day compounds, *stepfather, stepson, stepchild, stepsister,* etc., had been revived.

steppe (step) *n.* vast treeless plain. 1671 *step;* borrowed from Russian *step',* of uncertain origin. The form *steppe* (1762) was borrowed from German *Steppe,* from Russian *step'.*

-ster a suffix forming nouns meaning: **1** a person who _____s, as in *trickster = a person who tricks.* **2** a person who makes or handles, as in *rhymester = a person who makes rhymes.* **3** a person who is, as in *youngster = a person who is young.* **4** also with special meanings, as in *gangster, roadster, teamster.* Middle English *-estre, -ester, -ster,* developed from Old English *-istre, -estre,* a feminine agent suffix used exactly as *-ere* (-er[1]) was used to form masculine agent nouns; cognate with Middle Low German *-ester, -ster,* Middle Dutch and modern Dutch *-ster,* modern Frisian *-ster,* feminine agent nouns. The suffix was probably a derivative of an older Germanic suffix **-stra-* forming nouns of action, as represented for example in Old Icelandic *bakstr* act of baking, Old High German *galstar* incantation.

In Old English, *-estre* (from Proto-Germanic *-istrijōn* and *-astrijōn*) was used to form feminine agent nouns such as *lǣrestre* female teacher, *sangestre* female singer. In Middle English the suffix was broadened in use. In northern Middle English, perhaps due to the frequent adoption by men of trades like weaving, baking, etc., the suffix came to be used very early interchangeably with *-er*[1] as an agent-noun ending irrespective of gender. It is probable that *-ster* was often preferred to *-er* as more unambiguously referring to the holder of a job, trade, or occupation, as distinguished from the doer of an occasional act.

Though in the south of England the suffix continued to be predominantly feminine throughout the Middle English period, by the 1500's northern influence prevailed, and even older words in *-ster* (e.g. *seamster, tapster*) came to be regarded as masculines. Several of them then gave rise to feminines in *-ess: seamstress, songstress, huckstress.* In modern English the suffix became very productive in forming derivatives of existing nouns (rather than, as originally, of verbs), such as *gamester, rhymester, jokester, punster.* These formations imitated those of trade designations and hence often had a disparaging sense, as *jokester* compared with *joker.* A formation from an adjective was *youngster* (1589), suggested by the earlier *younker,* borrowed from Middle Dutch; *oldster* (1818) was patterned on *youngster.*

stere (stir) *n.* unit of volume equal to one cubic meter. 1798, borrowing of French *stère,* from Greek *stereós* solid; see STARE.

stereo (ster'ēō) *n.* 1823, shortened from *stereotype;* 1876, from *stereoscope;* 1954, from *stereophonic,* in phrases like *stereophonic sound, stereophonic system.*

stereo- a combining form meaning: **1** hard, firm, or solid, as in *stereotype* (a solid printing block). **2** three-dimensional, as in *stereoscope, stereophonic,* and *stereophotography.* Borrowed from Greek *stereo-,* combining form of *stereós* solid; see STARE.

stereophonic *adj.* of or giving the effect of lifelike or three-dimensional sound by using separately placed loudspeakers. 1927, formed from English *stereo-* + *-phonic.*

stereoscope *n.* optical instrument that blends two pictures into a single three-dimensional image. 1838, formed from English *stereo-* + *-scope.* The word was coined by the British physicist and inventor, Sir Charles Wheatstone, 1802-1875, who invented the device. **—stereoscopic** *adj.* of or relating to a stereoscope, three-dimensional. 1855, formed from English *stereoscope* + *-ic.*

stereotype *n.* 1798, method of printing in which a solid plate (originally of metal, now of paper or plastic) is formed from a mold of composed type; borrowed from French *stéréotype,* adj. (1797), printed by means of a solid plate of type (*stéréo-* stereo-, solid + *type* type). The figurative sense of an image, formula, phrase, etc., fixed or perpetuated without change, is first recorded in English in 1850, from the earlier use of *stereotype,* v., in this sense. —v. 1804, to print from stereotype plates; borrowed from French *stéréotyper* (1797), from *stéréotype,* adj. The figurative sense of fix or perpetuate in an unchanging form, cast in a rigid mold, standardize, is first recorded in English before 1819.

sterile *adj.* About 1450, (of a tree) producing no fruit, barren; borrowed from Middle French *stérile* not producing fruit or offspring, and directly from Latin *sterilis* barren, unproductive; cognate with Greek *stéresthai* be deprived of, *steîra* sterile, Armenian *sterj,* Sanskrit *starí-s* sterile cow, Old Icelandic *stirtla* sterile cow, and Gothic *staírō* sterile, from Indo-European **ster-* barren (Pok.1031). The figurative sense of mentally or spiritually barren or fruitless (as in *a sterile imagination*) is first recorded in 1642. The modern sense in biology of free from microorganisms, sterilized, is first recorded in 1877. **—sterility** *n.* Probably before 1425 *sterilitee* infertility, in a translation of Chauliac's *Grande Chirurgie;* borrowed from Middle French *sterilité,* from Latin *sterilitās* unfruitfulness, barrenness, from *sterilis* sterile, barren; for suffix see -ITY. The meaning of the state of being free from microorganisms is first recorded in 1877, and the figurative sense of mental or spiritual barrenness, in 1665. **—sterilize** *v.* 1695, destroy the fertility of; formed from English *sterile* + *-ize.* The meaning of make incapable of reproducing is first recorded in 1828. The biological sense of render free of microorganisms is first recorded in 1878, and the figurative sense of make mentally or spiritually barren, render unprofitable or useless, in 1880. The verb also may have been borrowed from, or influenced by, French *stériliser,* from Middle French *steriliser* to make or become impotent. **—sterilizer** *n.* 1839, substance that makes soil unproductive; later, an apparatus for destroying microorganisms (1891). All citations of first use pertaining to the control or destruction of microorganisms are found in the works of the British physicist John Tyndale (1820-93).

sterling *n.* 1299, the English silver penny; probably formed from Middle English *sterre* STAR (which appeared on certain early Norman coins) + *-ling* (but known earlier on the Continent in the Old French form *esterlin,* perhaps before 1104, later in Anglo-Latin *sterlingus* 1180, possibly from Old English **steorling* coin with a star, from *steorra* star). The sense of money having the quality of the sterling is first recorded in 1565, and the sense of English money as distinguished from foreign money, in 1601. **—adj.** 1425, of English money; from the noun. The sense of having a fixed standard of purity for silver (chiefly in the phrase *sterling silver*) is first recorded in 1551, and the figurative sense of excellent, dependable, sound, about 1645.

stern[1] *adj.* severe, strict. About 1250 *sterne,* in *The Owl and the Nightingale;* developed from Old English (before 1000) *styrne, stierne-* (as in *stiernlīce* sternly), from Proto-Germanic **sternijaz,* related to *starian* to STARE.

stern[2] *n.* hind part of a ship. Probably about 1225 *sterne,* in *King Horn;* probably borrowed from a Scandinavian source (compare Old Icelandic *stjōrn* a steering, related to *stȳra* to guide, STEER[1]); alternatively the word may have come into Middle English through Old Frisian *stiārne* rudder, related to *stiōra* to STEER[1].

sternum (stėr'nəm) *n.* breastbone. 1667, New Latin, from Greek *stérnon* man's chest, related to *stornýnai* to spread out, STREW, emphasizing the chest as broad and flat, as opposed to the neck.

steroid (ster′oid) *n. Biochemistry.* any of a class of compounds including the sterols and various hormones. 1936, formed from English *ster(ol)* + *-oid.*

sterol (ster′ōl) *n. Chemistry.* any of a group of solid, chiefly unsaturated alcohols. 1913, abstracted from *(chole)sterol.*

stet *n.* direction on printer's proof, etc., to restore deleted matter. 1821, borrowing of Latin *stet* let it stand, third person singular present subjunctive of *stāre* to STAND. **—v.** to mark with a stet. About 1875; from the noun.

stethoscope (steth′əskōp) *n.* instrument for listening to sounds in the lungs, heart, etc. 1820, borrowed from French *stéthoscope* (Greek *stêthos* chest, breast, of uncertain origin + French *-scope* -scope). The word was coined about 1819 by R.T.H. Laënnec, 1781-1826, the French physician who invented the device.

Stetson *n.* trademark of a type of high-crowned hat, worn especially in the western United States. 1902, American English; named after its designer, John B. *Stetson,* 1830-1906, an American hat manufacturer.

stevedore (stē′vədôr) *n.* person who loads and unloads ships. 1828 (in 1788 *stowadore*), American English; borrowed from Spanish *estibador* one who loads cargo, from *estibar* to stow cargo, from Latin *stīpāre* pack down, press; see STIFF. **—v.** 1862, American English, to load and unload a ship; from the noun.

stew *v.* to cook by slow boiling. Before 1399 *stewen* to stew; earlier *styven* bathe in a steam bath (1373); borrowed from Old French *estuver* bathe, stew; of uncertain origin, possibly from Vulgar Latin **extūfāre* evaporate (Latin *ex-* out + Vulgar Latin **tūfus* vapor, steam, from Greek *tŷphos;* see TYPHUS). See also STOVE for discussion of a possible relationship to Germanic forms. **—n.** Before 1300 *stu* caldron, cooking pot; borrowed from Old French *estuve* heated room, hothouse, bathing room; of uncertain origin, possibly from Vulgar Latin **extūfa,* from **extūfāre* evaporate. The sense of stewed meat and vegetables is first recorded in English in 1756, influenced in meaning by the verb.

steward *n.* Probably before 1300, manager of a household or estate, in *Sir Tristrem;* developed from Old English (probably about 900) *stīward, stigweard* house guardian (*stig* hall, pen, see STY[1] + *weard* guard, see WARD). The meaning of officer on a ship in charge of provisions and meals is first recorded about 1450. **—stewardess** *n.* 1631, woman steward; formed from English *steward* + *-ess.* The meaning of woman employed on a ship to wait on passengers is first recorded in 1837; by 1931 this use was extended to airplanes (but is now replaced by the universal term *flight attendant* 1956). **—stewardship** *n.* (1465, office of a steward; 1684, management)

stick[1] *n.* short piece of wood. Probably about 1150 *sticke;* developed from Old English (about 1000) *sticca* rod, twig, spoon; cognate with Middle Dutch *stecke* stick (modern Dutch *stek* slip, cutting), Old High German *stehho, stecko* stick (dialectal German *Stecken*), and Old Icelandic *stik, stika* stick, yardstick, from a Proto-Germanic form derived from the root **stik-* pierce, prick; see STICK[2].

stick[2] *v.* pierce with a pointed instrument, stab. Probably before 1200 *stiken,* in Layamon's *Chronicle of Britain;* later, to attach or fasten (about 1250); developed from Old English *stician* to pierce, stab; also, remain imbedded, be fastened (before 899, in Alfred's translation of Boethius' *De Consolatione Philosophiae*). Old English *stician* is cognate with Old Frisian *steka* to pierce, Old Saxon *stekan,* Middle Dutch *stēken* (modern Dutch *steken*), Old High German *stehhan* (modern German *stechen*), and Old Icelandic *stika* to dam, measure; all derived from Proto-Germanic **stik-* pierce, prick, be sharp, corresponding to Indo-European **stig-* (root **steig-,* Pok.1016), found in Latin *instīgāre* to prick or urge on, Greek *stízein* to mark, tattoo, *stígma* a mark, Latvian *stigt* to sink into, Avestan *ti ra-* sharp, and Sanskrit *tigmá-s* sharp. **—n.** 1633, a stab; from the verb. **—sticker** *n.* Before 1585, person who sticks or stabs; formed from English *stick[2]*, v. + *-er[1]*. The meaning of a gummed adhesive label is first recorded in De Vere's *Americanisms* (1871). **—stickpin** *n.* ornamental pin (1895, American English). **—sticky** *adj.* that sticks. 1735, formed from English *stick[2]*, v. + *-y[1]*

stickle *v.* make objections about trifles. 1530, act as umpire, mediate, in Palsgrave's *Lesclarcissement;* probably a variant of Middle English *stightelen, steghtilen* to regulate, control (before 1350), frequentative form of earlier *stihten* to set in order, arrange, place (before 1121); developed from Old English (before 830) *stihtan* to arrange, order; for suffix see -LE[3]. Old English *stihtan* is cognate with Old Icelandic *stētta* to support, establish, *stētt* stair, step, rank, and *stīga* to rise, climb; see STAIR. The meaning of make objections about trifles, insist stubbornly, is first recorded in Keats' *Otho the Great* (1819), influenced by *stickler.* **—stickleback** *n.* small spiny-finned fish (before 1500). **—stickler** *n.* 1538, moderator, umpire, in Elyot's *Dictionary;* formed from English *stickle* + *-er[1]*. The meaning of a person who contends or insists stubbornly is first recorded in 1644.

stiff *adj.* Probably before 1200 *stif* not flexible, rigid, in Layamon's *Chronicle of Britain;* developed from Old English (1000) *stīf* (from Proto-Germanic **stīfaz*), cognate with Middle Low German *stīf* stiff, Middle Dutch and modern Dutch *stijf,* and Old Icelandic *stīfla* to dam up. Middle High German *stif* (modern German *steif*) was probably borrowed from Middle Low German. Cognate with these Germanic words is Latin *stīpes* stake, from Indo-European **stīp-* (Pok.1015). The current spelling and pronunciation of the English word represents either an irregular shortening of the long vowel of Old English *stīf* or development from an Old English variant with a short vowel. **—n.** 1680, stiffened article of clothing; from the adjective. The slang sense of a corpse is first recorded in Bartlett's *Dictionary of Americanisms* (1859). **—stiffen** *v.* Probably before 1425 *styffnen* make more steadfast or unyielding; formed from Middle English *stif,* adj. + *-enen* -en[1]. **—stiff-necked** *adj.* obstinate (1526, in the Tyndale Bible).

stifle (stī′fəl) *v.* smother. Before 1387 *stuflen* to choke, suffocate by immersion, drown, in Trevisa's translation of Higden's *Polychronicon;* later *stifilen* (about 1495), of uncertain origin; possibly an alteration (influenced by Old Icelandic *stīfla* dam up) of Old French *estouffer* to stifle, smother, from a Germanic source (compare Old High German *stopfōn* to plug, stop up, stuff; see STOP). The extended sense of suppress or smother (a cry, sob, cough, etc.) is first recorded about 1495. The figurative sense of conceal or suppress (a fact, report, truth, etc.) is first recorded in 1577.

stigma *n.* mark of disgrace or shame. 1596, special mark burned on the skin of a slave, criminal, etc.; earlier in the Anglicized form *stigme* (probably about 1400); borrowed from Latin *stigma,* from Greek *stígma* (genitive *stígmatos*) mark, spot, puncture, brand, especially one made by a pointed instrument, from *stig-,* root of *stízein* to mark, tattoo; see STICK² pierce. The figurative sense of a mark of disgrace or shame is first recorded in English before 1619. The botanical sense of the part of the pistil in flowering plants that receives the pollen is first recorded in 1753. The plural form *stigmata,* in the sense of marks resembling the wounds on the crucified body of Christ, is recorded in English by 1632. **—stigmatize** *v.* 1585, to brand, tattoo; borrowed from Middle French *stigmatiser* (1532, in *Rabelais*), and directly from Medieval Latin *stigmatizare,* from Greek *stigmatízein* mark, brand, from *stígma* (genitive *stígmatos*) stigma; for suffix see -IZE. The figurative sense of set a mark of disgrace on, reproach is first recorded in 1619.

stile *n.* step or steps for getting over a fence or wall. About 1333-52, developed from Old English (about 779) *stigel;* cognate with Old High German *stigilla* stile, and related to Old English *stigen* to climb; see STAIR.

stiletto (stəlet′ō) *n.* dagger. 1611, in Coryat's *Crudities;* borrowing of Italian *stiletto,* diminutive of *stilo* dagger, from Latin *stilus* pointed writing instrument; see STYLE. **—v.** stab or kill with a stiletto. 1613-14, in Bacon's *Resuscitatio;* from the noun. **—adj.** daggerlike, sharply pointed. 1621, from the noun.

still¹ *adj.* without movement, quiet, tranquil. Old English *stille* motionless, stationary (about 725, in *Beowulf*); later, (before 1000) quiet, silent; related to Old English *steall* place, STALL¹. Old English *stille* is cognate with Old Frisian *stille* still, Old Saxon *stilli,* Middle Low German and Middle Dutch *stille* (modern Dutch *stil*), and Old High German *stilli* (modern German *still*), from Proto-Germanic **steljaz.* **—v.** make quiet. Probably before 1200 *stillen,* developed from Old English (before 900) *stillan* to make or become still, related to the adjective. Old English *stillan* is cognate with Old Saxon *stillian* to make quiet, Middle Dutch and modern Dutch *stillen,* Old High German and modern German *stillen,* and Old Icelandic *stilla.* **—n.** stillness. Probably before 1200, a calm, in *Ancrene Riwle;* from the adjective. The meaning of a photograph, as distinguished from a motion picture, is first recorded in 1916. **—adv.** Probably before 1200 *stille* without moving, quietly (as in *stand still*), in Layamon's *Chronicle of Britain;* found in Old English *stille* (from Proto-Germanic **steljai*), with cognates in Old Saxon and Old High German *stillo,* Middle Dutch and modern German *stille,* modern Dutch *stil,* Swedish *stilla,* and Danish *stille.* The meaning of even now or even then, yet (as in *to still smell of skunk*) is first found in 1535, and the more general sense of even, yet (as in *still more*) in 1730. **—conj.** nevertheless, notwithstanding. 1722, in Defoe's *A Journal of the Plague Year;* from the adjective. **—stillbirth** *n.* (1785, in letters of William Cowper) **—stillborn** *adj.* (1607) **—still life** inanimate objects portrayed in a picture (1695, loan translation of Dutch *stilleven;* probably applied originally to living things portrayed at rest).

still² *n.* apparatus for distilling. 1562, noun use of Middle English *stillen* to distill (probably about 1225, in *King Horn*), subsequently a variant of later *distillen* to DISTILL.

stilt *n.* Probably before 1300, crutch, in *Sir Tristrem;* later, one of two poles used in walking above the ground (before 1425); cognate with Middle Low German and Middle Dutch *stelte* stilt (modern Dutch *stelt*), Old High German *stelza* (modern German *Stelze*), Swedish *stylta,* and Danish *stylte,* from Proto-Germanic **steltjōn,* Indo-European **steld-,* extended from root **stel-* standing (Pok.1019). **—stilted** *adj.* 1615, furnished with or having stilts; formed from English *stilt* + *-ed²*. The figurative sense of pompous, stiffly dignified or formal, is first recorded in 1820, in Byron's works.

stimulate *v.* 1619, spur on, stir up; earlier, to prick, sting (before 1548); probably a back formation from *stimulation,* and perhaps in part borrowed from Latin *stimulātus,* past participle of *stimulāre* prick, goad, urge, from *stimulus* spur, goad, related to *stilus* pointed writing instrument, see STYLE; for suffix see -ATE¹. The meaning in physiology of quicken the action or function of is first recorded in 1662. **—stimulant** *n.* 1728, something, such as a drug or alcohol, that temporarily quickens a physiological activity, in *Chambers Cyclopaedia;* borrowed from Latin *stimulantem* (nominative *stimulāns*), present participle of *stimulāre* stimulate; for suffix see -ANT. **—stimulating** *adj.* 1684, that quickens the physiological activity or function of; later, that incites or spurs to action or thought (before 1727, in Gay's *Fables*). **—stimulation** *n.* 1526, act of pricking or spurring to action; borrowed from Latin *stimulātiōnem* (nominative *stimulātiō*), from *stimulāre* stimulate; for suffix see -ATION. The meaning in physiology of quickening the action or function of is first recorded in 1733, probably from the verb. **—stimulative** *adj.* 1791, formed from English *stimulate,* v. + *-ive.* **—stimulus** (stim′yələs) *n.* something that stirs to action or effort. 1684, borrowing of Latin *stimulus* spur, goad; see STIMULATE.

sting *v.* Probably before 1200 *stingen,* in *Ancrene Riwle* and Layamon's *Chronicle of Britain;* developed from Old English *stingan* to prick with a small point (before 899, in Alfred's translation of Boethius' *De Consolatione Philosophiae*), from Proto-Germanic **stenȝanan;* cognate with Old High German *stungen* to sting, Old Icelandic *stinga,* and Gothic *usstangan* to pluck out. Possible cognates outside Germanic are found in Greek *stáchys* ear of corn, scion, and *stóchos* target, aim, from Indo-European **stegh-/stogh-* prick; point (Pok.1014). **—n.** Old English *sting* act of stinging, wound (before 899, in Alfred's translation of Bede's *Ecclesiastical History*); from the verb in Old English. **—stinger** *n.* 1552, one who goads or instigates; later, part of an insect or animal that stings (before 1889, earlier *sting,* 1398), formed from English *sting,* v. + *-er¹*. **—stinging** *adj.* Probably before 1200, that causes hurt feelings or irritation, biting, in *Ancrene Riwle.* **—stingray** *n.* flat fish with a spine on its tail (1612, in Captain John Smith's writings).

stingy (stin′jē) *adj.* miserly, niggardly, close-fisted. 1659, of uncertain origin; possibly a dialectal use (with altered pronunciation and meaning) of earlier *stingy* (sting′ē) biting, sharp, stinging (about 1615), formed from English *sting,* n. or v. + adjective suffix *-y¹*.

stink *v.* Probably before 1200 *stinken* emit a strong offensive smell, in *Ancrene Riwle;* developed from Old English (before 800) *stincan* emit a smell of any kind;

cognate with Middle Dutch and modern Dutch *stinken* to stink, Old High German *stinkan* (modern German *stinken*), from Proto-Germanic **stenkwanan.* These words coincide in form with Old Icelandic *støkkva* to spring, leap, and Gothic *stinqan* to come into collision, but the disparities in meaning make the connection doubtful, nor are there any cognates outside Germanic. —**n.** About 1250 *stinc* offensive quality or odor, in *Genesis and Exodus;* from the verb. —**stinker** *n.* (1607, formed from English *stink,* v. + *-er*[1]). —**stinky** *adj.* 1888, in writings of Kipling; formed from English *stink,* n. + *-y*[1].

stint *v.* to limit in supply, be sparing. Probably about 1200 *stinten* to cease, cause to stop, in *The Ormulum;* developed from Old English *styntan* to blunt, make dull. Old English *styntan* is cognate with Old Icelandic *stytta* to shorten, and both verbs derive from Proto-Germanic **stuntjanan;* see STUNT[1], v. The meaning of limit or confine is first recorded in 1513, and that of limit to a certain share or allowance, in 1567. —**n.** Before 1325, cessation, in *Cursor Mundi;* from the verb. The meaning of an allotted amount, allowance, is found about 1485, and that of an allotted portion of work, before 1530.

stipend (stī'pend) *n.* fixed or regular pay, salary. 1444-46, shortened form of earlier *stipendy* (probably before 1425, in a translation of Higden's *Polychronicon*); borrowed from Latin *stipendium,* shortened form of **stipipendium* (*stips* alms, small payment, of unknown origin + *pendere* weigh; see PENDANT). —**stipendiary** *adj.* 1545, that receives a stipend; earlier, as a noun *stipendiarie* salaried cleric (1449); borrowed from Latin *stipendiārius* contribution, pay, from *stipendium* stipend; for suffix see -ARY.

stipple *v.* paint, draw, or engrave by dots. 1760-62, in Goldsmith's *Citizen of the World;* borrowed from Dutch *stippelen,* frequentative form of *stippen* to prick, speckle, from *stip* a point, perhaps related to *stijf* STIFF; for suffix see -LE[3]. —**n.** 1837, method of painting, etc., by dots; from the verb. The plural *stipples,* in the sense of dots used in shading a design, is recorded earlier (1669), probably borrowed from Dutch *stippel,* diminutive of *stip* a point.

stipulate *v.* Before 1624, make a bargain or contract; probably a back formation from earlier *stipulation,* and in part borrowed from Latin *stipulātus,* past participle of *stipulārī* to exact a promise, of uncertain origin. Traditionally it has been referred to Old Latin **stipulus* firm, related to Latin *stīpāre* pack down, press (see STIFF). Others derive Latin *stipulārī* from *stipula* a straw (see STIPULE), from the ancient custom of the two parties' breaking a straw together; for suffix see -ATE[1]. The meaning of demand as a condition of agreement is first recorded in English about 1645. —**stipulation** *n.* 1552, engagement or undertaking to do something, in Huloet's *Abecedarium Anglico Latinum;* borrowed from Latin *stipulātiōnem* (nominative *stipulātiō*), from *stipulārī* exact a promise; for suffix see -ATION. The sense of an act of specifying one of the terms of an agreement, condition in an agreement, is first recorded in 1750 (Samuel Johnson, in *The Rambler*).

stipule (stip'yül) *n.* small leaflike part of the base of a leaf stem. 1793, in Thomas Martyn's *The Language of Botany;* borrowed from French *stipule* (1749), learned borrowing from Latin *stipula* stalk (of hay), straw, related to *stīpes* tree trunk, log, and thence to *stīpāre* pack down, press; see STIFF; for suffix see -ULE. Doublet of STUBBLE.

stir *v.* to move. Probably before 1160 *styren* to trouble, disquiet, set in motion; developed from Old English *styrian* (about 725, in *Beowulf*), from Proto-Germanic **sturjanan;* cognate with Old Frisian *stēra* to disturb, Old Saxon *stōrian,* Middle Low German *storen,* Middle Dutch *stōren* (modern Dutch *storen*), Old High German *stōran, stōrren* (modern German *stören*), from Proto-Germanic **staurjanan,* Middle High German *stürn* to stir, poke, Old Icelandic *styrr* disturbance, tumult, struggle, and Norwegian *styrje* cause a disturbance. The word is without convincing cognates outside of Germanic. —**n.** movement. 1375 *steir* commotion, disturbance, tumult; about 1375 *stere;* probably borrowed from a Scandinavian source (compare Old Icelandic *styrr* disturbance, tumult). Later forms and senses, especially the sense of movement, bustle, activity (about 1586) represent noun uses of English *stir,* v.

stir-crazy *adj. Slang.* 1908, dazed, disturbed, or upset, usually because of long confinement; American English, formed with English *crazy,* from the slang word *stir* prison (1851, in Henry Mayhew's *London Labour and the London Poor;* probably an alteration of earlier thieves' slang *Start* a prison, especially Newgate, a prison in London, 1747; later *start* any prison, 1823; probably borrowed from Romany *stardo* imprisoned, related to *staripen* a prison).

stirrup *n.* About 1225 *stirope;* developed from Old English (about 1000) *stigrāp* support for a rider's foot, hung from a saddle; literally, climbing rope; formed from *stige* a climbing, ascent (from Proto-Germanic **stiȝiz*), related to *stīgan* to climb (see STAIR) + *rāp* ROPE. The Old English compound corresponds to Old Saxon *stigerēp* stirrup, Middle Dutch *stegereep,* Old High German *stegareif,* and Old Icelandic *stigreip.*

stitch *n.* Probably before 1200 *stiche* sudden stabbing pain in the side, in *Ancrene Riwle;* developed from Old English *stice* a prick, puncture (before 899, in Alfred's translation of St. Gregory's *Pastoral Care*); related to *stician* to pierce, STICK[2]. Old English *stice* is cognate with Old Frisian *steke* prick, stab, Old Saxon *stiki* point, thrust, Middle Low German *steke* prick, sting, stab, Old High German *stih* (modern German *Stich*), and Gothic *stiks* point of time, moment, from Proto-Germanic **stikiz.*

The senses of a complete movement of a threaded needle or awl in sewing or shoemaking and that of the loop of thread left by a complete stitch, are first recorded in Middle English about 1300. The sense of work of any kind (as in *not to do a stitch more than necessary*) is first recorded in 1581.

—**v.** Probably before 1200 *sticchen* fasten with stitches, in *Ancrene Riwle;* from the noun.

stoa (stō'ə) *n.* portico or roofed colonnade. 1603, in Holland's translation of Plutarch's *Moralia;* borrowed from Greek *stoá* portico; see STOIC.

stoat *n.* ermine in its summer coat of brown. Before 1475 *stote;* of uncertain origin.

stochastic (stōkas'tik) *adj.* random, involving chance or probability. 1662, pertaining to conjecture, in John Owen's writings; borrowed from Greek *stochastikós* able to hit or to guess, conjecturing, from *stocházesthai* aim at a mark, guess, from *stóchos* target, aim, guess, see STING; for suffix see -IC. The specific sense (in mathematics and statistics) of randomly determined involving chance or probability, is first recorded in English in 1934, borrowed through German *Stochastik.*

stock *n.* Probably before 1200 *stocke* tree trunk, in Layamon's *Chronicle of Britain;* developed from Old English *stocc* stump, post, stake; cognate with Old Frisian *stok* tree trunk, stump, Old Saxon *stok* stick, Middle Low German *stok* stick, stump, Middle Dutch *stoc* (modern Dutch *stok* stick, cane), Old High German *stoc* stick, stump (modern German *Stock* stick, cane), and Old Icelandic *stokkr* block of wood, tree trunk, from Proto-Germanic **stukkaz,* Indo-European **stugnós,* root **steug-* (Pok.1033); also cognate with Old High German *stuki* piece (modern German *Stück*), and Old Icelandic *stykki* piece. Most scholars doubt that there are cognates outside Germanic, though a possible connection may exist in Sanskrit *tujáti, tuñjáti* (he) pushes or thrusts. Words such as Old French and Provençal *estoc* trunk, stump, race, and Italian *stocco* rapier, trunk, are borrowings from Germanic.

The meaning of lineage, ancestry, family, is first recorded in Middle English, in *The Ormulum* (probably before 1200), probably as a figurative use based on the sense of tree trunk. The sense of the stem in which a graft is inserted is found probably as early as 1300. From this or the sense of a trunk or stump arose the meaning of the heavy part of a tool or utensil, which was extended to the part of a rifle or musket held against the shoulder (1541).

The plural *stocks* wooden frame with holes for feet, formerly used for punishment, is first recorded before 1325, probably as a special use of the meaning post, stake, found in Old English about 1000. The meaning of a supply accumulated for future use is found in 1428, and the related sense of a sum or fund of money (probably 1419) gave rise to that of a company's capital worth divided into shares, before 1692. These senses occur originally only in English and their ultimate origin is uncertain, but perhaps they are a blend of several different lines of development, in part involving the notion of a trunk or stem from which gains are an outgrowth, and partly that of a fixed basis or foundation.

—v. Before 1325 *stocken* to place in the stocks, imprison; from the noun. The meaning of furnish, supply, is first recorded in 1622.

—adj. Before 1625, kept regularly in stock; from the noun. The figurative sense of commonly used, conventional, trite, is first recorded in 1738, in Swift's writings. **—stockbroker** *n.* (1706, in Kersey's edition of Phillips' *Dictionary*) **—stock exchange** (1773) **—stockholder** *n.* (1753) **—stock market** (1809) **—stockpile** *n.* (1872, pile of coal or ore accumulated at the surface after mining, American English; 1942, store of goods held in reserve); *v.* (1921, to heap up in piles outside a mine; 1943, to accumulate a stock of) **—stockroom** *n.* (1825) **—stockstill** *adj.* completely still. About 1470, literally, as still as a tree trunk; formed from Middle English *stocke* tree trunk + *still* still. **—stocky** *adj.* About 1300 *stokki* made of wood; formed from Middle English *stocke* stock + *-y*[1]. The meaning of having a sturdy build, thick-set, is first recorded in 1676. **—stockyard** *n.* place for livestock, often connected with a slaughterhouse, railroad, or market (1802).

stockade *n.* defense made of large, strong posts. 1614 (in 1612, *staccado*); borrowed from Spanish *estacada,* from *estaca* stake, from a Germanic source (compare Old English *staca* STAKE[1]); for suffix see -ADE. The meaning of a place of confinement or prison, especially on a military post, is first recorded in 1882, in American English. **—v.** protect or fortify with a stockade. 1755, from the noun.

stocking *n.* covering for the leg. 1583, formed in English from *stock,* in the sense of a leg covering, sock, stocking (1457) + *-ing*[1]; probably called a *stock* in figurative reference to a log or trunk.

stodgy (stoj′ē) *adj.* 1823, of a thick, semi-solid consistency; formed from earlier English *stodge* to stuff (1674), of uncertain origin + *-y*[1]. The figurative meaning of dull, heavy, uninteresting, had developed by 1874 from the earlier senses of the noun *stodge* (1825) applied to food: heavy, solid, stiff food (1841), and of the adjective use thick, glutinous (1858).

stogie or **stogy** (stō′gē) *n.* 1847 *stoga* rough, heavy kind of shoe; later *stogie* long, cheap cigar (1873); both American English, shortened from *Conestoga,* a town in Pennsylvania (supposed to be so called because drivers of Conestoga covered wagons, first built in Conestoga, were associated with the use of such shoes and cigars).

Stoic or **stoic** *n.* About 1384, in the Wycliffe Bible; borrowed from Latin *stōicus,* from Greek *stōikós* of or pertaining to a member or the teachings of an ancient Greek school (founded by Zeno) characterized by austere ethical doctrines; literally, pertaining to a portico, from *stoá* portico, porch, specifically the portico in Athens where Zeno taught; for suffix see -IC. Greek *stoá* (earlier **stōwiyá*) is related to *stŷlos* pillar, from Indo-European **stāu-/stōu-/stū-* (Pok.1008). The general meaning of a person who represses feelings or shows indifference to pain, one who practices patient endurance, is first recorded in English in 1579. **—adj.** like a Stoic in character, showing indifference to pain, practicing patient endurance. 1596, in Spenser's *Faerie Queene;* borrowed from Latin *stōicus,* adj. and n. **—stoical** *adj.* = Stoic. Probably before 1425 *stoicalle;* formed from Latin *stōicus,* adj. and n. + Middle English *-al*[1]. **—stoicism** *n.* 1626, the philosophy of the Stoics; later, stoic attitude or conduct (1630); borrowed from New Latin *stoicismus,* from Latin *stōicus;* for suffix see -ISM.

stoke *v.* stir up and feed (a fire). 1683 (implied in *stoking-hole*), back formation from earlier English *stoker* person who tends a furnace (1660); borrowed from Dutch *stoker,* from *stoken* to stoke, from Middle Dutch *stōken* to poke, thrust, related to *stoc* stick, stump, STOCK. The figurative sense of stir up or excite (hate, lust, etc.) is found in 1837, in writings of Thomas Hood.

stole *n.* scarflike garment. Old English *stole* long robe, scarflike garment worn by clergymen (about 950, in *Lindisfarne Gospels*); an early borrowing from Latin *stola* robe, vestment, from Greek *stolḗ* a long robe; originally, garment, equipment, related to *stéllein* to array, make ready; see STALL[1] place. The extended sense of a scarflike garment worn by women is first recorded in 1889.

stolid *adj.* hard to arouse, not easily excited, seeming dull. About 1600, perhaps, in some instances, a back formation from earlier *stolidity;* also borrowed from Middle French *stolide,* and directly from Latin *stolidus* insensible, dull, unmovable, brutish; see STALL[1] stable. According to the record of the OED, *stolid* rarely occurred before the 1800's. **—stolidity** *n.* 1563-83, borrowed from Middle French *stoliditē,* and directly from

Latin *stoliditās* dullness, stupidity, from *stolidus* dull, stupid, stolid; for suffix see -ITY.

stolon *n.* slender branch of a root that grows into a new plant. 1601, borrowed from Latin *stolōnem* (nominative *stolō*) a shoot, branch, sucker; cognate with Armenian *steln* stem, from Indo-European **stel-* standing, trunk (Pok.1019).

stoma (stō′mə) *n.* small opening. 1684, New Latin, from Greek *stóma* mouth; see STOMACH.

stomach *n.* Before 1325 *stomak;* later *stomach* (before 1393, in Gower's *Confessio Amantis*); borrowed from Old French *estomac, stomaque,* learned borrowing from Latin *stomachus* stomach, throat, gullet; also, taste, liking, and distaste, irritation, from Greek *stómachos* throat, gullet, stomach; literally, mouth, opening, from *stóma* mouth. Greek *stóma* is cognate with Avestan *staman-* mouth of a dog, Old Cornish *stefinic* palate, Middle Breton *staffn* palate, and Welsh *safn* jawbone, from Indo-European **stomen-* mouth (Pok.1035). The figurative senses of Latin are first recorded in Middle English in the sense of appetite (about 1386), and in modern English in the sense of taste, liking (1513), and irritation (about 1540). **—v.** 1523, to be offended at, resent; from the noun. The sense of put up with, endure, is found in 1677. It is interesting to note that in spite of the spelling change to a Latinate form in Late Middle English, the pronunciation of the word in modern English retains that reflected in the earlier spelling of this word.

stomp *v.* 1803, variant of STAMP. **—n.** 1912, a social dance with heavy stamping; later, a heavy walking gait (1971). **—stomping** *n.* the action of stamping or treading heavily (1819).

stone *n.* Probably before 1200 *ston;* developed from Old English (before 830) *stān;* cognate with Old Frisian and Old Saxon *stēn* stone, Middle Dutch and modern Dutch *steen,* Old High German *stein* (modern German *Stein*), Old Icelandic *steinn,* and Gothic *stains,* from Proto-Germanic **stainaz.* Cognates outside Germanic may include Latin *stīria* frozen drop, icicle, Greek *stíā, stîon* pebble, *stéār* fat, tallow, Lithuanian *stingti* to curdle, coagulate, Old Slavic *stěna* wall, and Sanskrit *styā́yate* (it) coagulates, hardens, from Indo-European **stāi-/stəi-/stī-/sti-* (Pok.1010). **—v.** Probably about 1200 *stanen* to throw stones at, in *The Ormulum;* from the noun. **—adv.** totally, completely (as in *stone broke, stone deaf*). About 1290, from the noun, with reference to hardness, etc. **—adj.** complete, total (as in *stone madness, a stone intellectual*). 1928, from the adverb. **—Stone Age** (1864, early period of human culture, characterized by use of stone tools) **—stone-age** *adj. Informal.* old-fashioned (1937, in letters of F. Scott Fitzgerald). **—stonecutter** *n.* (1540) **—stoned** *adj. Slang.* intoxicated or drugged, stupefied or dazed by alcohol or narcotics. 1952, American English, formed from *stone,* v. + *-ed*². **—stonemason** *n.* (1809) **—stone's throw** short distance (1581). **—stonewall** *n.* 1876, also *stone wall* an act or instance of obstruction in Australian parliamentary procedure, especially by the lengthy speeches; later, in American politics, any obstructive or evasive action (1973-74); found in Old English (before 830), in the sense of a wall built of stone. *—v.* 1880, to adopt tactics of parliamentary obstruction; later, in American politics, to act in an obstructive or evasive way (1974). **—stoneware** *n.* hard pottery (1683). **—stony** *adj.* Probably about 1200 *stani* hard, insensible; developed from Old English (about 950) *stānig,* from *stān* stone + *-ig* -Y¹.

stooge *n. Informal.* 1913, stage assistant, in American English; of uncertain origin. The extended sense of an obsequious subordinate, lackey, or a person used for another person's purpose, is first recorded in 1937, in writings of H.G. Wells.

stool *n.* Old English *stōl* seat (before 899, in Alfred's translation of St. Gregory's *Pastoral Care*); cognate with Old Frisian and Old Saxon *stōl* seat, Middle Dutch and modern Dutch *stoel,* Old High German *stuol* (modern German *Stuhl*), Old Icelandic *stōll,* Gothic *stōls* throne (from Proto-Germanic **stōlaz*), and outside Germanic with Old Slavic *stolŭ,* ultimately from Indo-European **stā-/stə-/sth-* to place, stand; see STAND. The meaning of bowel movement, often used in medicine, is first recorded in 1533, from the earlier sense of privy (1410). The term *stool pigeon,* a pigeon fastened to a stool and used to lure other pigeons, is first recorded in 1836, and the extended slang use of a person exployed as a decoy in 1830, in American English, (the figurative or extended use of a term appearing often before the literal use in the record of English). The extended sense of police informer is first recorded in 1901, also in American English. **—stoolie** *n. Slang.* police informer. 1924, American English, formed from *stool* (*pigeon*) + *-ie.*

stoop¹ *v.* bend forward. Probably before 1200 *stupen,* in Layamon's *Chronicle of Britain;* later *stoupen* (about 1280); developed from Old English *stūpian* (before 899, in Alfred's translation of Orosius' *Historiarum Adversus Paganos*), related to *stēap* high, lofty; see STEEP¹, adj. Old English *stūpian* is cognate with Middle Dutch *stūpen* to bow, bend, and Old Icelandic *stūpa* to stand upright (Norwegian and Swedish *stupa* fall, plunge). **—n.** forward bend. About 1300 *stoupe;* from the verb.

stoop² *n.* porch. 1755, American English; borrowed from Dutch *stoep* flight of steps, doorstep, stoop, from Middle Dutch, related to *stap* STEP. Middle Dutch *stoep* (from Proto-Germanic **stopō*) is cognate with Middle Low German *stope* step, flight of steps, and Old High German *stuofa, stuoffa* step (modern German *Stufe*), from Indo-European **stēb-/stōb-* post, trunk (Pok.1011). **—stoopball** *n.* (1941, American English, in Budd Schulberg's *What Makes Sammy Run?*)

stop *v.* Probably before 1200 *stoppen* to plug or block, in *Ancrene Riwle;* developed from Old English *-stoppian* (in *forstoppian* to stop up, stifle). Old English *-stoppian* is cognate with Old Frisian *stoppia* to plug, stop up, stuff, Old Low Franconian *stuppōn,* Middle Low German, Middle Dutch and modern Dutch *stoppen,* and Old High German *stopfōn* (modern German *stopfen*).

The word is generally held to be a common West Germanic adoption of a Latin form, traditionally a borrowing of Vulgar Latin **stuppāre* to stop or stuff with tow or oakum, evidenced in Italian *stoppare,* Provençal and Spanish *estopar,* and Old French *estoper.* The Vulgar Latin verb developed from Latin *stuppa* coarse flax or hemp, tow, from Greek *stýppē,* of uncertain origin. However, the German scholar Kluge and some others derive the Germanic group of words from a Germanic base **stoppōn,* and by tracing Germanic *-pp-* (before an accented syllable) to Indo-European *-pn-,* relate the group to Latin *stupēre* to be stunned, dazed, paralyzed, cognate with Sanskrit *pra-stumpati* (he) pushes, shoves; see STUPID. These scholars acknowledge that Old High German *stopfōn* and its cognates were influenced by

Vulgar Latin **stuppāre* both in form and meaning. This influence spread from the Lower Rhine valley, where plugs made of tow were used from ancient times. Compare STUFF.

The common meaning of English *stop,* to bring or come to a halt, is first recorded in Middle English in 1440 and was a specially English development, though in marine, railway, and other transit use the English word has been widely adopted in other languages, as French *stopper,* German *stoppen,* etc.

—**n.** 1385-86, a plug, something that stops; from the verb. The sense of a cessation or stopping is first recorded in Middle English about 1450.

—**stopgap** *n.* something that fills a gap or temporarily supplies a need. 1684, formed from English *stop,* v. + *gap,* n. An earlier instance occurs in the sense of an argument in defense of a contested point (1533). —**stoplight** *n.* (1930, red light on the rear end of a vehicle; 1931, traffic light, in writings of Ogden Nash) —**stopover** *n.* a stopping over on a journey (1884, American English). —**stoppage** *n.* 1540, obstruction; formed from English *stop,* v. + *-age.* An earlier sense of deduction from payments is found in 1465; the general sense of an act of stopping is first recorded in 1657. —**stopper** *n.* (1480) —**stop sign** (1934, American English) —**stop street** street with a stop sign (1934, American English). —**stopwatch** *n.* (1737)

store *v.* 1264 *storen* to supply or stock; borrowed from Old French *estorer* erect, furnish, store, from Latin *īnstaurāre* restore (*in-* + *-staurāre;* cognate with Greek *staurós* pole, stake; see STEER[1], v.). The meaning of put away for future use is first recorded in Shakespeare's *As You Like It* (1600). —**n.** Probably before 1300, supply, stock, in *Arthour and Merlin;* borrowed from Old French *estor,* from *estorer* erect, furnish. The meaning of a place where goods are kept for sale is first recorded in 1721 in American English. —**storage** *n.* 1612-13, space for storing; formed from English *store,* v. + *-age.* The sense of an act of storing is first recorded in 1828. —**storehouse** *n.* (1348) —**storekeeper** *n.* (1618, an officer in charge of naval stores; 1741, American English, a shopkeeper) —**storeroom** *n.* (1746)

stork *n.* large wading bird. Old English (before 850) *storc,* related to *stearc* stiff, strong (see STARK); so called with reference to the bird's stiff or rigid posture. Old English *storc* is cognate with Middle Low German and Middle Dutch *storc* stork, Old High German *storah* (modern German *Storch*), and Old Icelandic *storkr* (Swedish, Norwegian, and Danish *stork*), from Proto-Germanic **sturkaz.*

storm *n.* Old English *storm* (about 725, in *Beowulf*); cognate with Old Saxon *storm* storm, Middle Low German, Middle Dutch, and modern Dutch *storm,* Old High German *sturm* (modern German *Sturm*), and Old Icelandic *stormr,* from Proto-Germanic **sturmaz.* These words are probably related to Old Icelandic *styrr* disturbance, and Old English *styrian* to move, STIR. —**v.** About 1380 *stormen* to rage, be violent, in Chaucer's translation of Boethius's *De Consolatione Philosophiae;* from the Middle English noun. —**storm cellar** (1920, American English) —**storm door** (1878, American English) —**storm window** (1824, window in a roof; 1933, outer window, American English) —**stormy** *adj.* Before 1325 *stormi* characterized by storm, subject to storms, in *Cursor Mundi;* developed from Late Old English *storemig* (before 1150); formed from Old English *storm,* n. + *-ig* -y[1].

story[1] *n.* account of some happening. Probably before 1200 *storie* historical narrative or writing, in *Ancrene Riwle;* borrowed from Old French *estorie,* from Late Latin *storia,* and as a learned borrowing in Old French from Latin *historia* history, account, tale, story, from Greek *historíā* history, record, inquiry, from *historeîn* inquire, from *hístōr* wise man, judge (Boeotian *wístōr*), related to *ideîn* to see; see WIT[2] know. Doublet of HISTORY. The meaning of a tale related for the entertainment of the hearer or reader is first recorded in English in William Dunbar's *Poems* (1500-20). —**storybook** *n.* (1711, in writings of Swift) —**storyteller** *n.* (1709, in writings of Steele)

story[2] *n.* floor of a building. Before 1384, borrowed from Anglo-Latin *historia* picture, floor of a building, from Latin *historia* HISTORY; perhaps so called because the front of buildings in the Middle Ages often were decorated with rows of painted windows. It is also noteworthy that *-story* is found in early use in the term *clerestory* (1412).

stoup (stüp) *n.* cup, flagon, tankard. 1397 *stowp* jug, jar borrowed from a Scandinavian source (compare Old Icelandic and modern Norwegian *staup* cup); see STEEP[2], v.

stout *adj.* Probably before 1300 *stout* proud, fierce brave, strong, defiant, in *Arthour and Merlin;* borrowed from Old French *estout,* earlier *estolt* strong from a Germanic source (compare Old Frisian *stult* proud, stately, arrogant, Middle Low German *stolt* Middle Dutch and modern Dutch *stout,* Middle High German and modern German *stolz,* and Norwegian *staut* stately, fine). Some scholars regard the Germanic words as related to STILT, from the notion of rising above the ground or above others. In Middle English *stout* also had the meaning of physically strong, having a powerful build, robust, and gradually developed the meaning of thick-bodied, corpulent, fat and large which is first recorded in 1804. —**n.** strong, dark-brown beer. 1677, from the adjective. —**stout-hearted** *adj* brave, bold (1552).

stove *n.* 1456, heated room, room filled with steam for sweating; probably borrowed from Middle Low German *stove* a heated room or Middle Dutch *stove* a heated room, a foot warmer (modern Dutch *stoof* stove, furnace). The Middle Low German and Middle Dutch words are cognate with Old English *stofa* steam bath, Old High German *stuba* heated room (modern German *Stube* room), Old Icelandic *stofa* house, bathing room with a stove, Norwegian *stove, stue* cottage cabin, Swedish *stuga* cottage, and Danish *stue* room and with rare Old English *stofa* a bathing room. The meaning of a device for heating is first recorded in English before 1618.

The relation between the West Germanic group of words listed above and Romance words, including Old French *estuve* heated room, hothouse, caldron (modern French *étuve* steam room), Spanish *estufa* stove and Italian *stufa* is uncertain. As the Germanic words are very old and have passed into other language families (Old Slavic *istŭba, izba,* Lithuanian *stubà,* Finnish *tupa,* and Hungarian *szoba*), it was traditionally held that the Romance words were also of Germanic origin But the German linguist Schuchardt felt the Romance words were indigenous, developing from Vulgar Latin **extūfa, *extūfāre,* which existed alongside **tūfō* vapor steam, as attested in various Italian dialects. Thereaf ter, resemblance between the Germanic and Romance forms and senses was often considered accidental.

Other modern scholars, however, including Kluge, Gamillscheg, and Corominas, maintain that the Germanic group is ultimately of Romance origin, and apparent phonetic discrepancies can be resolved (for example, Old Spanish and Catalan *estuba* a steam bath, can result from an original intervocalic *p* developed during the Latinization of the Greek *ph* of *týphos* from a Vulgar Latin form **extūphāre* to **extūfāre*). Further they refer to the cultural fact that the stove was an ancient Roman invention adopted by the Germanic peoples, who likely borrowed Vulgar Latin **extūfa* as their name for a steam bath or heated room.

stow *v.* Probably about 1380 *stowen* to put in a certain place or position, in *Cleanness;* verb use of earlier *stowe* a place (before 1200); developed from Old English *stōw* a place (about 725, in *Beowulf*). Old English *stōw* is cognate with Old Frisian *stō* a place, Middle Low German, Middle Dutch, and modern Dutch *stouwen* to stow, Middle High German *stouwen* (modern German *stauen*) to stow (from Proto-Germanic **stōwijanan*), and Old Icelandic *eldstō* fireplace; outside Germanic possible cognates may be found in Lithuanian *stovēti* and Old Slavic *staviti* to stand, from Indo-European **stāu-*, extended from **stā-* stand (Pok.1008).

The meaning of put away to be stored, pack, is first recorded in Middle English probably before 1400. The verb phrase *stow away,* meaning to put away in a secret or not readily accessible place, to conceal, is first found in 1795. **—stowage** *n.* 1391, act of packing cargo on board, formed from Middle English *stowen* to stow + *-age.* The sense of a place in which something is stowed occurs before 1641. **—stowaway** *n.* person who hides on a ship, train, etc. 1850, from the verb phrase *stow away.*

strabismus (strəbiz′məs) *n.* disorder of vision, squint. 1684, also Anglicized *strabism* (1656); New Latin *strabismus,* borrowed from Greek *strabismós,* from *strabízein* to squint, from *strabós* squinting, squint-eyed (from Indo-European **str̥bós*), related most closely to *streblós* twisted, and *stróbos* a whirling, also to *stréphein* to turn; see STROPHE; for suffix see -ISM.

straddle *v.* walk, stand, or sit with the legs wide apart. 1565, in Cooper's *Thesaurus Linguae Romanae et Britannicae,* probably an alteration of Middle English (about 1450) *stridlen,* frequentative form of *striden* to STRIDE; for suffix see -LE³. **—n.** a straddling. 1611, from the verb.

strafe (strāf) *v.* attack by air at low range. 1915, originally used by British soldiers in World War I in the sense of punish, attack; borrowed from the German slogan *Gott strafe England* may God punish England, current in Germany about 1914-16. Middle High German *strāfen* punish (modern German *strafen*) is from Proto-Germanic **strǣf-*, Indo-European **strēp-*, root **strep-* be stiff (Pok.1025). **—n.** a strafing. 1916 (in 1915, *straff*), from the same source as the verb.

straggle *v.* wander, stray. Before 1425 *straglen* move about aimlessly, wander; perhaps borrowed from a Scandinavian source (compare dialectal Norwegian *stragla* to walk laboriously). Alternatively, the Middle English word may be an altered frequentative form of Middle English *straken* to move, go (probably before 1325), related to *strecchen* to STRETCH; for suffix see -LE³. **—straggly** *adj.* 1862, formed from English *straggle* + *-y*¹.

straight *adj.* Probably before 1325 *streyt* not bent or curved; later *streight* (1369, in Chaucer's *Book of the Duchesse*); adjective use of Old English *streht* (altered, by analogy with *streccan,* from earlier *streaht*), past participle of *streccan* to STRETCH. **—adv.** Probably before 1300 *streyte* closely, carefully, in *Kyng Alisaunder;* later *streight* immediately, directly (probably before 1325); adverb use of Old English *streht,* past participle of *streccan* to STRETCH. **—n.** straight form, position, or line. 1645, from the adjective. **—straightaway** *n.* straight course (1878). **—straightedge** *n.* (1812) **—straighten** *v.* 1542, to make straight, in Udall's translation of Erasmus' *Apothegms;* formed from English *straight,* adj. + *-en*¹. **—straightforward** *adj.* frank, direct (1806).

strain¹ *v.* to stretch, draw tight. About 1300 *streinen* draw tight, stretch; later *strainen* (1432); borrowed from Old French *estreindre* bind tightly, clasp, squeeze, from Latin *stringere* bind or draw tight. Latin *stringere* is cognate with Old High German *stric* (modern German *Strick* rope), from Indo-European **streig-/strig-* draw together (Pok.1036). The sense of press through a filter is first recorded in Middle English before 1325. The sense of lay undue stress on, make a forced interpretation of, is first recorded (1449, and the more usually adjective form *strained,* about 1600, in Shakespeare's *Sonnets*). **—n.** 1432 *straine* filter, strainer, from the verb. The sense of injury caused by straining is probably first recorded about 1400 (implied in *straining*), and that of strong muscular effort, in 1590. The musical sense of a passage of song or music, tune, melody, probably developed from the Middle English verb meaning (before 1387) to tighten (the strings of a musical instrument) so as to raise the pitch. **—strainer** *n.* (1326-27)

strain² *n.* line of descent. Probably before 1200 *strene* offspring, line of descent, stock; developed from Old English (about 950) *strēon, strion* gain, begetting (from Proto-Germanic **streun-*); shortened form of *gestrēon, gestrīon,* related to *strīenan* to gain. The Old English forms are cognate with Old High German *striunan* to gain; originally, to pile up, and Latin *struere* to pile, build, from Indo-European **streu-/strou-* (Pok.1030). The sense of variety of an animal species is first recorded in 1607. The modern spelling of this word was probably influenced by association with *strain*¹, and begins to appear in the late 1500's.

strait *n.* Often, **straits.** narrow channel connecting two larger bodies of water. About 1390 *straite,* in Chaucer's *Canterbury Tales;* noun use of earlier adjective *strait* narrow, strict (probably before 1300, in *Arthour and Merlin*); borrowed from Old French *estreit* tight, close, narrow, from Latin *strictus,* past participle of *stringere* bind or draw tight; see STRAIN¹ stretch. The figurative sense of difficulty, need, plight (usually *straits*) is first recorded in 1544. Doublet of STRICT. **—straiten** *v.* 1523, to restrict, narrow; formed from English *strait,* adj. + *-en*¹. **—straitjacket** *n.* (1814, in Scott's letters) **—straight-laced** *adj.* rigid, strict, prudish (1554, perhaps from Coverdale's use in the sense of narrow in range, 1549). The original sense is probably that of wearing a tightly laced corset, first recorded in literal use in 1626.

strand¹ *n.* shore. Old English (about 1000) *strand;* cognate with Middle Low German and Middle Dutch *strant* shore, beach (modern Dutch *strand*), Old Icelandic *strǫnd* border, edge, coast (Swedish, Norwegian, and Danish *strand*), from Proto-Germanic **strandás,* cognate with Old Lithuanian *trenta* place, region, from Indo-European **strontós,* root **(s)tren-/(s)tron-* (Pok. 1030). **—v.** drive on the shore, run aground. 1621, from the noun. The figurative sense of leave in a helpless position is first recorded in Carlyle's *French Revolution* (1837).

strand[2] *n.* one of the fibers of a rope, string, etc. 1497 *strond;* perhaps cognate with Old High German *strēno* (modern German *Strähne*) lock, tress, strand of hair (compare dialectal English *stran*), of unknown origin. The spelling *strand* is found in 1644. The meaning of a string of beads, pearls, or the like is first recorded in 1825, in the supplement of Jamieson's *Dictionary of the Scottish Language.* **—v.** Before 1780, to break a strand or strands; from the noun. The sense of to form (a rope, etc.) by twisting strands is first recorded in 1886.

strange *adj.* About 1280 *strounge* from elsewhere, foreign, unknown, unfamiliar; later *straunge* (probably before 1300, in *Kyng Alisaunder*); borrowed from Old French *estrange* foreign, alien, from Latin *extrāneus* foreign, external, from *extrā* outside of, from feminine ablative singular of *exter* outward, outside, from *ex* out of; see EX-. Doublet of ESTRANGE and EXTRANEOUS. **—stranger** *n.* 1375, unknown person, foreigner, in Barbour's *The Bruce;* borrowed from Old French *estrangier* foreigner, alien, from *estrange* strange; for suffix see -ER[1].

strangle *v.* Probably about 1280 *stranglen* to kill; later, to choke, smother (about 1300, in *Havelok the Dane*); borrowed from Old French *estrangler,* from Latin *strangulāre* to choke, stifle, check, constrain, from Greek *straggalân* choke, twist, from *straggálē* a halter, cord, lace, related to *straggós* twisted, from Indo-European **strn̥gós;* see STRING.

strangulate *v.* 1665, to choke, stifle; probably a back formation from earlier *strangulation,* influenced by Latin *strangulātus,* past participle of *strangulāre* to choke; see STRANGLE; for suffix see -ATE[1]. The specific medical sense of constrict so as to prevent circulation is found in 1771 (implied in *strangulated,* as in *a strangulated hernia*). **—strangulation** *n.* act of strangling, 1542, and later in the specific medical sense in 1749; borrowed from Latin *strangulātiōnem* (nominative *strangulātiō*), from *strangulāre;* for suffix see -ATION.

strap *n.* 1620, loop or band for fastening things together, variant of Middle English *strope* loop or strap on a harness (1345-49); probably borrowed from Old French *estrop* strap, from Latin *stroppus* strap, band, perhaps from Etruscan, ultimately from Greek *stróphos* twisted band, from *stréphein* to turn; see STROPHE. *Strop* is recorded once in Late Old English about 1050, an early borrowing from Latin *stroppus;* however, this form is probably not continuous with the Middle English word. Other Germanic borrowings from the Latin include: Middle Low German and Middle Dutch *strop* band, and Old High German *strupf.* **—v.** to fasten or bind with a strap or as with a strap. 1711, from the noun. **—straphanger** *n.* (1905, passenger on a bus or train who cannot get a seat; also commuter) **—strapping** *adj. Informal.* robust, sturdy. 1657, tall and sturdy (applied originally to a woman), formed from English *strap,* v. + *-ing*[2].

stratagem *n.* trick, trickery. 1489, trick for deceiving an enemy, in Caxton's translation of *Faytes of Armes;* borrowed from Middle French *stratagème* trick, especially to outwit an enemy, borrowed from Italian *stratagemma* (with vowel assimilation of *e* to *a* of the first syllable), from Latin *stratēgēma,* from Greek *stratḗgēma* the act of a general, military stratagem, from *stratēgeîn* to be a general, command, from *stratēgós* general; see STRATEGY.

strategy *n.* clever or careful plan. 1810, art of planning military movements and operations, in Charles James' *Military Dictionary;* borrowed from French *stratégie,* and probably directly from Greek *stratēgiā́* office or command of a general, from *stratēgós* general (*stratós* army + *agós* leader, from *ágein* to lead; see AGENT); for suffix see -Y[3]. Greek *stratós* (perhaps with an original meaning "deployed") is related to *stornýnai* to spread out; see STREW. **—strategic** *adj.* 1825 (implied earlier in *strategically* 1810) of or belonging to strategy; borrowed from French *stratégique,* and probably directly from Greek *stratēgikós* of a general, from *stratēgós* general; for suffix see -IC. **—strategist** *n.* 1838, person skilled in strategy; borrowed from French *stratégiste,* from *stratégie* strategy; for suffix see -IST. **—strategize** *v.* to devise a strategy or strategies. 1943, American English, formed from English *strategy* + *-ize.*

stratify *v.* to arrange in layers or strata. 1661, back formation from earlier *stratification;* for suffix see -FY. **—stratification** *n.* act of stratifying. 1617, borrowed from New Latin *stratificationem* (nominative *stratificatio*), from *stratificare* (*stratum* thing spread out; see STRATUM + the root of Latin *facere* to make, perform, DO[1]); for suffix see -FICATION.

stratosphere *n.* upper region of the atmosphere. 1908, borrowed from French *stratosphère,* formed from Latin *strātus* (genitive *strātūs*) a spreading out (from the root of *sternere* to spread out; see STREW) + French *-sphère,* as in *atmosphère* ATMOSPHERE.

stratum (strā′təm *or* strat′əm) *n.* layer. 1599, New Latin, special use of Latin *strātum* thing spread out, coverlet, pavement, from neuter past participle of *sternere* to spread out; see STREW.

straw *n.* About 1200 *strawe* stalk or stem, piece of straw, in *Vices and Virtues;* developed from Old English (about 950) *strēaw,* related to *strēowian* to STREW. Old English *strēaw* is cognate with Old Frisian *strē* straw, Middle Low German and Middle Dutch *strō* (modern Dutch *stroo*), Old High German *strō* (modern German *Stroh*), and Old Icelandic *strā* (Norwegian, Danish, and Swedish *strå*), from Proto-Germanic **strāwan.* The meaning of a tube, originally of straw or glass for sucking up a drink, is first recorded in 1851. **—adj.** made of straw. 1442, from the noun. **—straw man** (1594, scarecrow; 1896, a person of little substance) **—straw vote** unofficial vote, poll (1866, American English).

strawberry *n.* Probably about 1200 *streaberie* the plant, 1328-29 the fruit; later *strawbery* (1373); developed from Old English (about 1000) *strēawberige* (*strēaw* STRAW + *berige, berie* BERRY). No corresponding compound is found in other Germanic languages and the reason for the name is uncertain. One explanation is that the fruit was so called from the resemblance of the seedlike achenes scattered over the surface to particles of straw, another is that *straw* refers to the slender runners of the strawberry plant which track on the ground.

stray *v.* About 1300 *strayen* wander from a path; borrowed from Old French *estraier* wander about; literally, go about the streets or highways, from *estree* route, highway, from Late Latin *via strāta* paved road; see STREET. **—n.** 1228 *strai* domestic animal found wandering; borrowed from Anglo-French *stray, estrai,* from Old French *estraié* strayed, past participle of *estraier* to stray. An earlier sense, act of straying, appeared in Middle English probably in 1404, derived from the verb.

streak *n.* Before 1387 *strike* line, mark, stroke, in Trevisa's translation of Higden's *Polychronicon;* later *streke* (1440, in *Promptorium Parvulorum*); developed from Old English *strica* (about 1000, in Ælfric's *Homilies*), from Proto-Germanic **strikōn,* related to *strīcan* pass over lightly; see STRIKE. Old English *strica* is cognate with Middle Low German and Middle Dutch *strēke* line, stroke (modern Dutch *streek*), Old High German *strich* (modern German *Strich*), and Gothic *striks.* The sense of thin irregular lines of contrasting color or texture is found in English in 1567. **—v.** put streaks on. 1440 *streken* to cancel by drawing a line or lines across; from the noun. The sense of put streaks on is found in 1595.

stream *n.* Old English (before 850) *strēam* a course of water forming a river, brook, etc.; cognate with Old Frisian *strām* stream, Old Saxon *strōm,* Middle Dutch and modern Dutch *stroom,* Old High German *stroum* (modern German *Strom*), and Old Icelandic *straumr* (Swedish *ström,* Norwegian *straum, strøm,* Danish *strøm*), from Proto-Germanic **straumaz,* Indo-European *sroumos.* Cognates outside Germanic are found in Old Irish *sruaimm* river, Lithuanian *sravěti* flow gently, trickle, Old Slavic *struja* flowing, Greek *rheîn* to flow, Avestan *raodhaiti,* and Sanskrit *srávati* (it) flows, from Indo-European **sreu-/srou-/sru-* (Pok.1003). **—v.** to flow. Probably before 1200 *stremen,* in *Ancrene Riwle;* from the noun. **—streamer** *n.* 1292 *stremer* flag floating or waving in the air; formed from Middle English *stremen* to stream + *-er*[1]. **—streamline** *adj.* 1898, free from turbulence; later, shaped so as to reduce air or water resistance (1907); from an earlier noun meaning the path traced by a flowing fluid (1868). *—v.* (1913, implied in *streamlined*) give a streamline form to; from the adjective. The figurative sense of make slim or slender is found in 1935, and that of simplify, organize, make more efficient, in 1936, both American English.

street *n.* Probably about 1175 *strate, stret;* later *strete* (probably before 1200, in Layamon's *Chronicle of Britain*); developed from Old English (Mercian) *strēt* paved road, highway, street, (West Saxon) *strǣt* (about 725, in *Beowulf*); an early borrowing from Late Latin *strāta,* used elliptically for *via strāta* paved road, from past participle of Latin *sternere* lay down, spread out, pave; see STREW. The borrowing of Late Latin *strāta* was common to many West Germanic languages including Old Frisian *strēte* street, Old Saxon *strāta,* Middle Dutch *strāte* (modern Dutch *straat*), Old High German *straza, strazza* (modern German *Strasse*), and in the Romance languages the word is represented by Provençal, Spanish, and Portuguese *estrada,* Old French *estree,* and Italian *strada.* **—streetcar** *n.* passenger car running on rails in the street (1862, American English). **—street light** (1906, earlier *street lamp,* 1799) **—street people** (1967) **—streetwalker** *n.* prostitute (1592). **—streetwise** *adj.* (1965)

strength *n.* 1106 *strengthe,* in *Peterborough Chronicle;* developed from Old English *strengthu* power, force, vigor, moral resistance (before 899, in Alfred's translation of Bede's *Ecclesiastical History*), from *strang* STRONG; for suffix see -TH[1]. Old English *strengthu* is cognate with Old High German *strengida* strength, from Proto-Germanic **stranzíthō.* **—strengthen** *v.* Probably about 1378 *strengthnen* give support to, abet, in Wycliffe's writings; formed from Middle English *strengthe* strength + *-nen* -en[1].

strenuous *adj.* Before 1460 (implied in *strenuously*) vigorous, energetic; borrowed from Latin *strēnuus* active, vigorous, keen; probably cognate with Greek *strēnés, strēnós* harsh, rough, and Old English *styrne, stierne-* harsh, strict, STERN[1]; for suffix see -OUS. The sense of requiring much energy, arduous, is first recorded in Milton's *Samson Agonistes* (1671).

strep *n. Informal.* streptococcus. 1927 *strep throat;* American English, shortened form of STREPTOCOCCUS.

streptococcus (strep′təkok′əs) *n.* kind of spherical bacterium that causes serious infections. 1877, New Latin; formed from Greek *streptós* twisted, twisted chain + New Latin *coccus* spherical bacterium, from Greek *kókkos* berry; so called because these bacteria usually form chains. Greek *streptós* is related to *stréphein* to turn; see STROPHE. The New Latin word was coined by the Austrian surgeon Theodor Billroth, 1829-1894.

streptomycin (strep′təmī′sin) *n.* antibiotic similar to penicillin. 1944, formed from New Latin *Streptomyces,* genus name of the soil bacterium from which the antibiotic was obtained, from Greek *streptós* twisted + *mýkēs* fungus (see MYCOLOGY); for suffix see -IN[2].

stress *n.* About 1303 *stres, stresse* hardship, coercion, pressure, in Mannyng's *Handlyng Synne;* in part developed as a shortened form of Middle English *destresse* DISTRESS, and in part borrowed from Old French *estrece* narrowness, oppression, from Vulgar Latin **strictia,* from Latin *strictus* compressed, past participle of *stringere* draw tight; see STRAIN[1] stretch. The sense of great strain, anguish, distress, is first recorded in Middle English probably about 1380, in *Pearl.* The phonetic sense of greater or lesser force in the pronunciation of certain syllables or words is first recorded in 1749. **—v.** put pressure upon. About 1303 *stressen* restrain, confine, in Mannyng's *Handlyng Synne;* borrowed from Old French *estrecier* straighten, contract, from Vulgar Latin **strictiāre,* from **strictia* narrowness, oppression. The sense of put emphasis on, attach importance to is first recorded in 1896, and derives from the meaning of pronounce with a stress (1859), which like other later senses of the verb, derive from the noun.

stretch *v.* Probably before 1200 *strechen* to extend, in *Ancrene Riwle;* developed from Old English *streccan* (before 899, in Alfred's translation of Bede's *Ecclesiastical History*); cognate with Old Frisian *strekka* to stretch, Middle Low German and Middle Dutch *strecken* (modern Dutch *strekken*), and Old High German *strecchan* (modern German *strecken*), from Proto-Germanic **strakjanan,* related to Middle High German *strac* (modern German *strack* tense, taut) and to Russian *strogij* strict, hard, from Indo-European **streg-/strog-* (Pok.1023). **—n.** Probably about 1175 *streche* expanse of land; from the verb. The sense of an act of stretching or straining is first recorded in 1541, and that of an unbroken or uninterrupted continuance (as in the phrase *at one stretch, a stretch of 100 miles*) is first recorded in 1661. The specific meaning of an act of extending the limbs to relieve weariness is first recorded in 1712, in Steele's writings. **—stretcher** *n.* (about 1420, person who stretches; 1845, canvas stretched on a frame for carrying the sick or wounded)

strew *v.* Probably before 1300 *strewen* to scatter, sprinkle, in *Sir Tristrem* and in *Arthour and Merlin;* developed from Old English (about 971) *strēowian;* cognate with Old Frisian *strēwa* to strew, Old Saxon *strōian,* Middle Dutch *strōien* (modern Dutch *strooien*), Old High German *strewen* (modern German *streuen*), Old Icelandic *strā* (Norwegian and Danish *strø,* Swedish *strö*), and Gothic *straujan,* from Proto-Germanic **straujanan,* connected with Indo-European **ster-* (Pok.1029), represented in Latin *sternere* to spread out (past participle *strātus*), Greek *stornýnai,* Sanskrit *stṛṇā́ti, stṛṇóti* (he) strews, and Old Irish *sernim* (I) spread out. Related to STRAW.

striated (strī′ātid) *adj.* striped, streaked. 1646, formed in English from New Latin *striatus* striped, streaked + English *-ed*[2]. New Latin *striatus* is a special use of Latin *striātus,* a participle-like formation, developed directly from the noun *stria* furrow, channel (earlier **strigyā*); see STRIKE; for suffix see -ATE[3]. **—striation** *n.* 1849, one of a number of parallel streaks, in James Dwight Dana's *Geology;* formed in English from New Latin *stria* stripe, streak (in Latin, furrow, channel) + English *-ation.*

stricken *adj.* hit, wounded, or affected (by a weapon, disease, trouble, etc.). 1513, in Douglas' translation of Vergil's *Aeneid,* adjective use of the past participle of STRIKE, v. An early adjective use of the past participle is found in Middle English in the phrases *striken on age* (about 1380), *striken in elde* (probably before 1300), with the meaning of advanced in years.

strict *adj.* Probably before 1425 *stricte* (of an opening) narrow, drawn in, small, in a translation of Chauliac's *Grande Chirurgie;* perhaps influenced in part by earlier English *stricture,* but primarily a borrowing from Latin *strictus* drawn together, tight, rigid, past participle of *stringere* draw or bind tight; see STRAIN[1] stretch. Doublet of STRAIT. The sense of rigorous and stringent (as a law, rule, etc.) is first recorded in English in 1578, as is the sense of austere or stern in matters of morality and conscience (implied in *strictness,* 1578). The meaning of characterized by close and unrelaxing effort (as in *a strict examination*) is first recorded in Shakespeare's *1 Henry IV* (1596).

stricture *n.* Before 1400, an abnormal narrowing or contraction in a bodily part, in Lanfranc's *Science of Surgery;* borrowed from Late Latin *strictūra* contraction, constriction, from *strict-,* past participle stem of *stringere* to bind or draw tight; see STRAIN[1] stretch; for suffix see -URE. The figurative sense of an unfavorable criticism, critical remark, is first recorded in English about 1779, in Johnson's writings, from the general sense of a remark or comment (1655).

stride *v.* Probably before 1200 *striden* to walk with long steps; developed from Old English (before 800) *strīdan* to straddle; cognate with Middle Low German *striden* to set the legs wide apart, straddle, take long steps. The verb is not found in other Germanic languages with a similar sense, but it is remarkably similar in form to a verb with the meaning of strive, quarrel, found in Old Saxon *strīdian* and Old Frisian *strīda,* Middle Dutch and modern Dutch *strijden* to fight, struggle, Old High German *strītan* (modern German *streiten*), and Old Icelandic *strīdha* (Swedish *strida,* Danish and Norwegian *stride*), from Proto-Germanic **strīđanan,* Indo-European **streidh-* (Pok.1026). Thus the primary meaning of Proto-Germanic **strīđ-* to strive, make a strong effort, might account for the development of the English and Low German sense of move or walk with long steps. See also STRIFE, STRIVE.

The past tense and past participle forms *strode, striden* developed through Middle English from Old English *strād* (as in *bestrād* bestrode) and **striden.* **—n.** long step. Old English (before 800) *stride* distance covered by a long step, related to *strīdan* to stride. The sense of the act of striding, long step taken in walking, is first recorded in Middle English, probably before 1200.

strident *adj.* harsh-sounding, shrill. 1656, in Blount's *Glossographia;* borrowed from French *strident,* and directly from Latin *strīdentem* (nominative *strīdēns*), present participle of *strīdere, strīdēre* utter an inarticulate sound, grate, screech; possibly of imitative origin and perhaps similar to Greek *stríx* (genitive **strigós*) a kind of owl, and *trízein* to utter a shrill cry, screech, from Indo-European **streid(h)-* (Pok.1036); for suffix see -ENT.

stridulous *adj.* strident. 1611, in Chapman's translation of Homer's *Iliad;* borrowed from Latin *strīdulus* giving a shrill sound, creaking, from *strīdere* to utter an inarticulate sound, grate, creak; see STRIDENT; for suffix see -OUS. **—stridulate** *v.* make a shrill sound. 1838, formed in English either from Latin *strīdulus* giving a shrill sound, creaking + English *-ate*[1] or by back formation from *stridulation.* **—stridulation** *n.* 1838, borrowed from French *stridulation,* or formed in English directly from Latin *strīdulus* giving a shrill sound, creaking + English *-ation.*

strife *n.* Probably before 1200 *strif* quarrel, fighting, discord, in *Ancrene Riwle;* borrowed from Old French *estrif,* accusative of **estris* (formed by analogy with such pairs as *baillif, baillis*), variant of *estrit* quarrel, dispute, impetuosity, from Frankish **strīd* (compare Old High German *strīt* quarrel, dispute, related to *strītan* to fight; see STRIDE). Related to STRIVE. The spelling *strife* is first recorded in Middle English about 1375.

strike *v.* Before 1325 *striken* to deal a blow, hit with force, in *Cursor Mundi* (past tense *strok, strak,* past participle *striken*); developed from Old English (before 1000) *strīcan* pass over lightly, stroke, smooth, rub, go, proceed (past tense *strāc,* past participle *stricen*). Old English *strīcan* is cognate with Old Frisian *strīka* pass over lightly, stroke, rub, move, go, Middle Low German and Middle Dutch *strīken* (modern Dutch *strijken*), and Old High German *strīhhan* (modern German *streichen*), from Proto-Germanic **strīk-* which corresponds to Indo-European **streig-* (Pok.1028), represented by Latin *striga* strip, row, *stria* furrow, channel (earlier **strigyā*), *stringere* graze, touch lightly (note that *stringere* in the sense of bind or draw tight, is a completely different word; see STRAIN[1]), Greek *strínx* row, line, Old Prussian *strigli* thistle, and Old Slavic *strigǫ* I shear, cut. Related to STREAK and STROKE in form and meaning by the Proto-Germanic forms **straik-* (stroke) and **strik-* (streak), and perhaps influenced in the development of the sense of stroke, rub; later, hit, by the Old Icelandic *striūka* (Swedish *stryka,* Danish *stryge*), from Proto-

Germanic **streuk-*, from Indo-European **streug-* (Pok.1029). It is interesting to note that most modern dictionaries consider *stroke* in the noun and the verb as separate developments in English.

The meaning of cancel or expunge with or as with the stroke of a pen is first recorded in Middle English about 1395, in Chaucer's *Canterbury Tales.* The modern sense of refuse to continue work as a group in order to force an employer to meet demands is first recorded in 1768, originating perhaps in the sailors' practice of *striking* or lowering a ship's sail or mast as a symbol of their refusal to go to sea or to prevent a ship from sailing, a sense also recorded in 1768. The meaning in baseball of fail to hit a ball pitched in the strike zone (*strike out*) is first recorded in 1853.
—n. 1587, act of striking, from the verb. Some Middle English uses of the noun *strike,* such as the sense of a bundle or hank of flax, hemp, etc., (in Chaucer's *Canterbury Tales*), were probably borrowed from Middle Low German derivatives of the same root as English *strike.* The meaning in baseball of failure of a batter to hit a ball pitched in the strike zone is first recorded in 1841, in American English.
—strikebreaker *n.* person who takes the job of a striking worker (1904). **—strike force** (1961, an armed force, equipped for attack) **—strikeout** *n.*(1887, an out made by pitching three strikes against a batter) **—striker** *n.* Probably before 1387, a vagrant; 1850, a worker on strike; formed from English *strike,* v. + *-er*[1]. **—striking** *adj.* About 1611, that strikes; formed from English *strike,* v. + *-ing*[2]. The sense of remarkable, impressive, is first recorded in 1752.

string *n.* About 1175 *stringe;* developed from Old English *streng* line, cord, thread (about 725, in *Beowulf,* from Proto-Germanic **stranȝiz,* Indo-European **strongh-,* Pok.1037); cognate with Middle Low German *strenk* string, Middle Dutch *strenc, strengh* (modern Dutch *streng*), Old High German *strang* (modern German *Strang*), and Old Icelandic *strengr* (Swedish *sträng,* Norwegian and Danish *streng*). Cognates outside Germanic include Greek *straggós* twisted, Middle Irish *sreng* cord, string, *srengim* I pull, draw, and Latvian *stringt* become tight, from Indo-European **streng-/strong-/strŋg-* (Pok.1036). The sense of a number of objects arranged in a line, series, file, is first recorded in Middle English in 1488-92. **—v.** About 1400 *strengen* to fit (a bow) with its string; from the noun. The sense of fit (a musical instrument) with strings is found in 1530, and that of thread or hang on a string, in 1612. The meaning of extend or stretch (as in *debris strung out along the shore*) is first recorded before 1670. **—string bean** (1759, American English) **—stringy** *adj.* 1669, resembling string or fiber, consisting of stringlike pieces; formed from English *string,* n. + *-y*[1].

stringent *adj.* strict, severe. 1605, astringent, constrictive; borrowed from Latin *stringentem* (nominative *stringēns*), present participle of *stringere* to compress, contract, bind or draw tight; see STRAIN[1] stretch; for suffix see -ENT. The extended sense of strict, rigorous, binding, severe, is first recorded in 1846. **—stringency** *n.* 1844, quality of being stringent; formed from English *stringent* + *cy.*

strip[1] *v.* make bare or naked. Probably about 1200 *strupen* remove the clothes of; later, remove the bark of a tree (probably about 1225), and with the spelling *stripen* (before 1387); developed from Old English *-strīepan, -strȳpan,* as in West Saxon *bestrȳpan* to plunder; cognate with Middle Low German and Middle Dutch *strōpen* to plunder, strip (modern Dutch *stroopen*), and Old High German *stroufen* to plunder (modern German *streifen* strip off), from Proto-Germanic **straupjanan,* Indo-European **stroub-,* root **streub-* (Pok.1029). **—strip lighting** (1934, earlier *strip light,* 1920) **—stripper** *n.* 1581, person who strips off something, as bark off a tree; 1835, machine or appliance for stripping; formed from English *strip*[1] + *-er*[1]. The informal sense of a woman who performs in a striptease act is first recorded in 1930, but is implied in *strip*[1], v. 1929, in American English. **—striptease** *n.* (1936, but found earlier as *strip teaser,* 1930, American English)

strip[2] *n.* long, narrow, flat piece. 1459, narrow piece of cloth; probably borrowed from Middle Low German *strippe* strap, thong, related to *strīpe* STRIPE[1]. The extended sense of a long narrow tract of land, piece of wood, etc., is first recorded in 1638, in American English. **—v.** cut into strips. 1885, from the noun.

stripe[1] *v.* to ornament or mark with long, narrow bands of color. 1415 *stripen;* probably borrowed from Middle Flemish *stripen* to form a narrow band; cognate with Middle Low German and Middle Dutch *strīpen* to strip off, *strīpe* stripe, streak (modern Dutch *streep*), Middle High German *strīfe* stripe (modern German *Streifen*), Norwegian *stripe,* Swedish *stripa,* and Danish *stribe,* from Proto-Germanic **strīpanan,* cognate with Old Irish *sríab* a stripe, from Indo-European **streib-* (Pok.1029). **—n.** long narrow band. 1415, a line or band in cloth, of different material, color, etc., from the rest; probably borrowed from Middle Dutch or Middle Low German *strīpe* stripe, streak; see the verb. The general sense of a long narrow band, strip, is first recorded in English in 1785. The figurative sense of a particular shade or variety of political or other doctrine, (broadly) a sort, class, or type, is found in 1853, in American English.

stripe[2] *n.* a stroke or lash. Before 1420 *strype* mark of a lash, scar, in Lydgate's *Troy Book;* later, a stroke or lash (before 1481); probably a special use of STRIPE[1], n.

stripling *n.* a youth, lad. Before 1398, in Trevisa's translation of Bartholomew's *De Proprietatibus Rerum;* of uncertain origin, but possibly formed from Middle English *strip*[2] long narrow piece (though unrecorded before 1459) + *-ling.* The underlying sense would be that of one who is slender as a strip, and therefore one whose figure is not yet filled out.

strive *v.* Probably before 1200 *striven* to quarrel, contend, in *Ancrene Riwle;* later, to try hard, endeavor (before 1325, in *Cursor Mundi*); borrowed from Old French *estriver* to quarrel, dispute, from *estrif, estrit* quarrel, STRIFE.

strobe (strōb) *n.* electronic flash gun for action photography. 1942, shortened form of earlier *stroboscope* instrument for studying periodic motion by means of periodically interrupted light (1896); formed in English from Greek *stróbos* act of whirling (see STROPHE) + English *-scope.*

stroke[1] *n.* act of striking, blow. Probably before 1300 *strok,* in *Sir Tristrem;* probably from Old English **strāc* (from Proto-Germanic **straikaz*), the source of the verb *strācian* STROKE[2], and cognate with Middle Low German *streke* blow, stroke, Middle High German *streich* (modern German *Streich*), and Old High German *strihhan* pass over lightly, stroke. Related to STREAK and STRIKE. The sense of a movement or mark made by a pen, etc., is first recorded in English in 1567. The meaning of the striking of a clock is first recorded in 1436; a feat or achievement (as in *a stroke of genius*) in 1672; a single pull of an oar, in 1583, and a single movement of a piece of machinery having a reciprocating motion (as in *the stroke of a piston*) in 1731. The phrase *stroke of luck* is first recorded in 1853. The sense of an apoplectic or paralytic seizure is first recorded in 1599. **—v.** 1597, to mark with strokes; from the noun.

stroke[2] *v.* pass the hand gently over. About 1300 *stroken;* developed from Old English *strācian* (before 899, in Alfred's translation of St. Gregory's *Pastoral Care*), formed from Old English **strāc* stroke; related to *strīcan* pass over lightly; see STRIKE; also related to STREAK. Old English *strācian* is cognate with Middle Low German and Middle Dutch *strēken* to stroke (modern Dutch *streeken*), and Old High German *streihhōn* (modern German *streichen*), from Proto-Germanic **straikōjanan.* **—n.** act of stroking. 1631, in Ben Jonson's *The New Inn,* from *stroke*[2], v. and related to *stroke*[1] v.

stroll *v.* 1603, to roam, wander, in Thomas Dekker's *The Wonderful Year;* perhaps borrowed from dialectal German *strollen,* variant of German *strolchen* to stroll, loaf, from *strolch* vagabond, vagrant; also fortuneteller; perhaps from Italian *astròlogo* astrologer. The meaning of take a quiet walk for pleasure is first recorded in English in 1680. **—n.** 1814, a leisurely walk, in Jane Austen's *Mansfield Park;* from the verb. An earlier sense of itinerant actor is found in 1623. **—stroller** *n.* 1608, itinerant actor, strolling player; formed from English *stroll,* v. + *-er*[1]. The sense of a kind of light carriage in which a baby can sit is first recorded in 1920, in American English.

strong *adj.* Probably before 1200, in Layamon's *Chronicle of Britain* and in *Ancrene Riwle;* developed from Old English *strang* (about 725, in *Beowulf,* from Proto-Germanic **stranȝaz*), cognate with Old Saxon *strang* strong, bold, severe, Middle Dutch *strenghe* (modern Dutch *streng* strict), Middle Low German *strenge,* Old High German *strango* strongly, severely, *strengi* strong, severe, strict (modern German *streng*), and Old Icelandic *strangr* strong, hard, severe; related to Old English *streng* cord, rope, sinew; see STRING. **—strong-arm** *adj.* 1901, using force or violence; *v.* 1903; from *strong arm* force 1606. **—strongbox** *n.* strong chest or safe for valuables (1684). **—stronghold** *n.* strongly fortified place. Before 1325, in *Cursor Mundi;* formed from Middle English *strong* strong + *hold* fortified place, refuge, possession. **—strongman** *n.* (1699) **—strong point** (1875, Max Müller) **—strong suit** (1865, Mark Twain)

strontium (stron′shēəm) *n.* metallic chemical element. 1808, New Latin, from *Strontian,* in allusion to a parish in Argyllshire, Scotland, location of the lead mines where strontium was first found; for suffix see -IUM. The New Latin word was coined by the English chemist Sir Humphry Davy, 1778-1829.

strop *n.* leather strap used for sharpening razors. 1345-49 *strope* loop or strap on a harness; probably borrowed from Old French *estrop;* see STRAP. The meaning of a leather strap used for sharpening razors is first recorded in 1702. —v. sharpen on a strop. 1841, in Dickens' *Barnaby Rudge;* from the noun.

strophe (strō′fē) *n.* group of lines of poetry, stanza. 1603, in Holland's translation of Plutarch's *Moralia;* borrowed from Greek *strophḗ* stanza; originally, a turning, from which developed the meaning of a section of an ancient Greek ode sung by the chorus while turning and moving in one direction, from *stréphein* to turn. Greek *stréphein* is related to *streblós* twisted, *strabós* squint-eyed, squinting, *stróphos* twisted cord, and *stróbos* act of whirling, from Indo-European **strebh-/strobh-; streb-/strob-/str̥b-* (Pok.1025).

structure *n.* Probably 1440, building or reinforcing materials; borrowed from Latin *strūctūra* a fitting together, adjustment, building, edifice, from *strūct-,* past participle stem of *struere* to pile, build, assemble, arrange, related to *struēs* heap, from Indo-European **streu-/strou-* (Pok.1030); for suffix see -URE. The sense of something built, a building, is first recorded in 1615, in Chapman's translation of the *Odyssey,* and that of the manner of construction, in 1650. **—v.** Before 1693, from the noun. **—structural** *adj.* 1835, of or having to do with organic structure; formed from English *structure,* n. + *-al*[1].

strudel (strü′dəl *or* shtrü′dəl) *n.* 1903, borrowing of German *Strudel* kind of pastry usually filled with fruit or cheese; literally, whirlpool, from Middle High German, related to Old High German *stredan* to bubble.

struggle *v.* About 1395 *struglen* to contend physically, grapple, in Chaucer's *Canterbury Tales;* probably a frequentative formation of uncertain origin, but similar to Middle High German *strūcheln* to stumble (modern German *straucheln*), frequentative of Old High German *strūhhēn, strūhhōn* lose footing, trip. The meaning of English *struggle* makes a connection unlikely with Middle High German *strūcheln* and the cognate Middle Dutch *strūkelen* (modern Dutch *struikelen*); for suffix see -LE[3]. **—n.** 1692, act of struggling, in John Locke's writings; from the verb.

strum *v.* 1775, play on a musical instrument carelessly, as by running the fingers across the strings or keys, in Ash's *Dictionary,* possibly imitative of the sound so made. **—n.** act of strumming. About 1793, in writings of Burns; from the verb.

strumpet *n.* prostitute. About 1325, of uncertain origin. A supposed connection (through Medieval Latin or Italian) with Latin *stuprāta,* feminine past participle of *stuprāre* have illicit sexual relations with, violate the chastity of, has not been established.

strut[1] *v.* walk in vain, important manner. Before 1300 *strouten* stick out, protrude; later, to bluster, threaten (about 1300), and with the spelling *struten* (before 1325); *struten* developed from Old English *strūtian* to stand out stiffly (about 1000, in Ælfric's *Lives of Saints,* from Proto-Germanic **strūt-*); cognate with Middle High German *striuzen* to contend, Middle High German and modern German *strotzen* to bulge, swell, Norwegian and Danish *strutte* to swell, and Swedish *strutta* to strut, trip. The word is probably also related to Old English *thrūtian* swell with pride or anger, cognate with Old Icelandic *thrūtna* swell, and, outside Germanic with Welsh *trythu* swell, from Indo-European **(s)treud-/strūd-/strud-* (Pok.1026). The sense of display one's clothes proudly or vainly is found in Middle English about 1399. The sense of walk in a vain, important manner is first recorded in English in 1518. —n. strutting walk. 1607, from the verb.

strut[2] *n.* supporting piece, brace. 1587, of uncertain origin; perhaps related to STRUT[1] (compare Old Icelandic *strūtr* hornlike headdress, Norwegian *strut* a spout, nozzle, Low German *strutt* stiff, rigid, ultimately from Proto-Germanic **strūt-* probably in the sense of to stand out, protrude).

strychnine (strik′nīn) *n.* poisonous drug. 1819, borrowing of French *strychnine,* from New Latin *Strychnos,* the genus name of a plant (nux vomica) from which the poison is obtained, from Greek *strýchnon* a kind of nightshade, also various poisonous or emetic plants, of uncertain origin; for suffix see -INE[2].

stub *n.* About 1250 *stubbe* stalk of grain or flax, in *The Owl and the Nightingale;* later, stump of a tree (1324); developed from Old English (967) *stybb* stump of a tree, from Proto-Germanic **stuƀjaz;* cognate with Middle Low German and Middle Dutch *stubbe* stump, and Old Icelandic *stūfr* stub, piece, *stubbi, stubbr* stump (Norwegian and Swedish *stubb, stubbe,* Danish *stub, stubbe*), from Proto-Germanic **stuƀƀaz,* Indo-European **stubh-,* root **steubh-* strike (Pok.1034). A cognate outside Germanic is found in Greek *stýpos* stem, stump, related to *týptein* to strike, beat; see TYPE. The meaning of remaining piece (of a pencil, cigarette, etc.) that has been broken or worn down is first recorded in English about 1530, from the sense of what remains after something is broken (about 1386). —**v.** About 1450 *stubben* to dig up by the roots, remove stumps and trees, in *Jacob's Well;* from the noun. The sense of strike (one's toe) against something is first recorded in Bartlett's *Dictionary of Americanisms* (1848). —**stubby** *adj.* short and thick or broad. 1572, earlier, ground covered with stubble (about 1410); formed from English *stub,* n. + *-y*[1].

stubble *n.* About 1300 *stouple* stalk of grain; later *stubil* the ends of grain stalks left in the ground after reaping (about 1340); borrowed from Old French *estuble* stubble, from Latin *stupla,* reduced form of *stupula,* variant of *stipula* stem, stalk (of hay), diminutive of *stipes* stalk; see STIPULE. The sense of any short, rough growth, bristle, is first recorded in English before 1596. The spelling *stuble* occurs in Middle English about 1350.

stubborn *adj.* About 1395 *stibourne* unyielding, obstinate, in Chaucer's *Canterbury Tales;* later *styborne, stuborn* (about 1449); of uncertain origin. A commonly suggested derivation from *stubbe* stump, STUB, presents no difficulty with regard to the sense, as if meaning "immovable or unyielding as a stub or stump," but it is difficult to justify as to form.

stucco (stuk′ō) *n.* plaster for covering exterior walls of buildings. 1598, borrowing of Italian *stucco,* from a Germanic source (compare Old High German *stukki* crust, piece, fragment; see STOCK). —**v.** cover with stucco. 1726, from the noun.

stuck *adj.* 1702, that has been stabbed (as in *a stuck pig*); from past participle of *stick*[2], v. —**stuck-up** *adj. Informal.* conceited. 1829, from past participle of *stick up* to project, protrude.

stud[1] *n.* nailhead, knob, etc. 1277 *stude* upright piece of timber (in *studewerk*); developed from Old English (about 850) *studu* pillar, prop, post, related to *stōw* a place; see STOW. Old English *studu* is cognate with Middle High German *stud* post, prop, and Old Icelandic *stodh* (Swedish *stöd*). In this old consonant-stem noun, the original Germanic nominative **stuss* had long been supplanted by the accusative form *studu,* representing the Proto-Germanic stem **stuđ-,* Indo-European **stu-t-,*root **stāu-* stand straight (Pok.1008). The sense of ornamental round knob is first recorded in Middle English in 1420. —**v.** set with studs. 1505-06, from the noun.

stud[2] *n.* horses used for breeding, racing, etc. Probably before 1200 *stod meare* mare kept for breeding, brood mare; later *stode* place where horses are kept for breeding (before 1250, in *The Owl and the Nightingale*); developed from Old English *stōd* place where horses are kept for breeding (about 1000, in Ælfric's *Glossary,* from Proto-Germanic **stōđō,* Indo-European **stā-,* Pok.1007); cognate with Middle Low German *stōt* collection of horses, Old High German *stuot* (modern German *Stute* mare), and Old Icelandic *stōdh* stud of mares (Danish *stod* stud of 12 horses); related to Old English *standan* STAND. Compare Old Slavic *stado,* Lithuanian *stódas* stud of horses. The spelling *stud* is found in Middle English in 1252-53. The sense of collection of horses kept for breeding, hunting, or racing, is first recorded in English before 1661. The sense of a male horse kept for breeding, stallion, is first recorded in American English in 1803. The informal sense of a man given to seducing women, a womanizer, is first found in dialectal English in 1895; the extended sense of any young man or fellow is first recorded in American English underworld slang in 1929.

student *n.* Probably before 1425, one who pursues knowledge, scholar, in a translation of Higden's *Polychronicon;* alteration (influenced by Latin *studēre* to study) of earlier *studient* (before 1398); borrowed from Old French *estudient, estudiant* one who is studying; also, present participle of *estudier* to study, learned borrowing from Medieval Latin *studiare* to study, from Latin *studium* STUDY; for suffix see -ENT.

studio *n.* workroom of a painter, sculptor, etc. 1819, borrowing of Italian *studio* room for study, study, learned borrowing from Latin *studium* STUDY. The meaning of a room or building for the filming of motion pictures is first recorded in 1911, and that of a place for radio broadcasting in 1922, for television broadcasting in 1938. The term *studio apartment* is first recorded in 1903, in American English; *studio couch,* meaning a couch that can be made into a bed, is first recorded in 1931, also in American English. Doublet of ÉTUDE and STUDY.

study *n.* About 1300 *studie* pursuit of knowledge, effort to learn; also, room in which to read or study (about 1303, in Mannyng's *Handlyng Synne*); borrowed from Old French *estudie* application to learn, study, learned borrowing from Latin *studium* study, application; originally, eagerness, related to *studēre* to study, be eager, apply oneself; for suffix see -Y[3]. Latin *studēre* apparently originally meant to beat toward, strike toward, related to *tundere* to beat, Sanskrit *tudáti* (he) pounds, and Gothic *stauti* smites, from Indo-European **(s)teud-/(s)toud-/(s)tud-* (Pok.1033). Doublet of ÉTUDE and STUDIO. The sense of a person's work as a student, a subject of study, is first recorded in 1477. The sense of a piece of writing devoted to a particular subject is first recorded in 1866, in writings of Carlyle. —**v.** About 1125 *studien* devote oneself to something; later, apply oneself to learning (about 1303, in Mannyng's *Handlyng Synne*); borrowed from Old French *estudier* to study, from Medieval Latin *studiare,* from Latin *studium* study. —**studied** *adj.* planned, deliberate. 1606, in Shakespeare's *Antony and Cleopatra;* earlier in the sense of skilled, learned (1530); formed from English *study,* v. + *-ed*[2]. —**studious** *adj.* Before 1349 *studiouse* zealous, later *studious* eager to learn (before 1382, in the Wycliffe Bible); borrowed from Latin *studiōsus* eager, assiduous, from *studium* eagerness, zeal, study; for suffix see -OUS.

stuff *n.* Before 1338 *stof* quilted material worn under chain mail, in Mannyng's *Chronicle of England;* later *stoffe* material, cloth (1345-49); household goods, equipment (1395); borrowed from Old French *estoffe* quilted material, furniture, provisions, from *estoffer* to equip or stock, probably from Old High German *stopfōn* to plug, stuff, or from a Frankish word related to Old High German *stopfōn;* see STOP. The spelling *stuffe* is first recorded in Middle English probably about 1390.

Earlier objections to derivation of Old French *estoffer* from Frankish or Old High German on the grounds that an Old French form (with *-ff-*) could not have developed from Frankish **stoppōn,* and that a common Romance word (Provençal, Spanish, Portuguese *estofa* cloth, quality, Italian *stoffa* stuff, fabric, cloth) would probably not have proceeded directly from Old High German *stopfōn,* have been refuted by contemporary scholars, who point out that all the Romance words except the French are very recent, all proceeding from Old French, where *estoffe* has been recorded since 1241 and *estoffer* since about 1190. Moreover, these words originated in northern France, where the Frankish forms closely approached those of High German, so that the Old French verb probably derived from a late (perhaps 9th century) form (with *-pf-*). See also STOP. **—v.** Probably about 1350 *stuffen* to furnish, supply, fill, cram; borrowed from Old French *estoffer* to equip, stock.

—stuffed shirt *Informal.* smug, pompous, conservative person (1913, American English). **—stuffing** *n.* (1530, material used to fill or pack something; 1538, seasoned mixture used to stuff fowl before cooking) **—stuffy** *adj.* 1551-52, full of stuff or substance; 1831, poorly ventilated, close (as in *a stuffy little room*); 1895, pompous, smug, in Kipling's writings; formed from English *stuff,* n. + *-y*[1].

stultify *v.* 1766, (in law) allege to be of unsound mind, in Blackstone's *Commentaries on the Laws of England;* borrowed from Late Latin *stultificāre* turn into foolishness, from a lost adjective **stultificus* rendering foolish, from Latin *stultus* foolish (see STALL[1] stable) + the root of *facere* to make, perform, DO[1]); for suffix see -FY. The meaning of cause to appear foolish or absurd, is first recorded in 1809, and that of make worthless, useless, or futile, in 1865. **—stultification** *n.* 1832, act of stultifying; formed from English *stultify,* on analogy of *mortify, mortification,* and similar pairs; for suffix see -FICATION.

stumble *v.* About 1303 *stomblen* to lose one's footing morally, in Mannyng's *Handlyng Synne;* in part possibly influenced by *stumpen* to stumble, but probably borrowed from a Scandinavian source (compare dialectal Norwegian *stumla,* dialectal Swedish *stambla* to stumble). The Scandinavian words probably derive from a variant of the Germanic base **stam-,* which is the source of Old English *stamerian* to STAMMER. The literal sense of miss one's footing, trip on some obstacle, is first recorded in Middle English about 1325. **—n.** a stumbling. 1547, from the verb. **—stumbling block** (1526, something likely to cause moral downfall, in the Tyndale Bible; before 1593, obstacle, hindrance, in Marlowe and Nashe's *The Tragedy of Dido*)

stump *n.* lower end of a tree or plant. Probably about 1350 *stompe* remaining part of a severed arm, leg, etc., stump of a limb; later *stumpe* tree stump (1440, in *Promptorium Parvulorum*); cognate with Middle Low German *stump* and Middle Dutch *stomp* stump, Old High German *stumpf* stump (modern German *Stumpf*), and Old High German *stumpf* mutilated (modern German *stumpf* blunt, dull), from Proto-Germanic **stump-,* Indo-European **stm̥b-,* root **stemb-* (Pok.1012). **—v.** Before 1250 *stumpen* to stumble over a tree stump or other obstacle, in *The Owl and the Nightingale;* usually said to be from the noun, but contradicted by the record of English in which the noun form appears about 100 years after the verb, which tends to support the idea that *stomp* is a variant of earlier *stamp.* The extended sense of walk clumsily or heavily is recorded in 1600. The informal figurative sense of cause to be at a loss, baffle, is first recorded in 1812 in American English. The meaning of make political speeches is recorded in 1838, also in American English (but the sense is alluded to earlier in *stump orator* in Jefferson's writings in 1813); often said to be from the use of a tree stump as a speaking platform. **—stumpy** *adj.* short and thick. 1600, formed from English *stump,* n. + *-y*[1]. The sense of full of stumps is first recorded in 1838, in Hawthorne's *American Notebooks.*

stun *v.* Before 1325 *stunen* to daze, knock unconscious, in *Cursor Mundi;* probably borrowed from Old French *estoner, estuner* to stun, see ASTONISH. **—n.** a stunning or being stunned. 1727, from the verb. **—stunning** *adj.* 1667, dazing, astounding, in Milton's *Paradise Lost;* later, first-rate, splendid (1849-50, in Dickens' *David Copperfield*); from the present participle of *stun.*

stunt[1] *v.* to check in growth, dwarf. 1659, extended meaning of the earlier sense of bring to an abrupt stand, nonplus (1603), and to irritate, provoke (1583); verb use of Middle English adjective *stunnt* foolish (probably about 1200, in *The Ormulum*); developed from Old English (about 960) *stunt* short-witted, stupid, foolish, from Proto-Germanic **stuntaz,* Indo-European **stn̥d-,* root **sten-d-.* The Old English word is cognate with Middle High German *stunz* short, blunt, Old Icelandic *stuttr* scanty, short, and more distantly with Old Icelandic *stinnr* stiff, hard, and Old English *stīth,* from Proto-Germanic **stenthaz,* Indo-European **sten-t-,* a different extension of the same root **sten-* as appears in Greek *stenós* (earlier **stenwós*) narrow (Pok.1021). **—n.** 1725, stunted animal; 1795, a stunting; from the verb.

stunt[2] *n. Informal.* feat to attract attention. 1878, American English, originally college athletics slang, of uncertain origin. **—v.** perform a stunt or stunts. 1914 (implied in *stunting*), from the noun.

stupefy *v.* make stupid, dull, or senseless. Probably before 1425 *stupifien* make senseless, deaden, in a translation of Chauliac's *Grande Chirurgie;* also with spelling *stupefien;* borrowed from Middle French *stupéfier,* learned borrowing from Latin *stupefacere* make stupid or senseless, from *stupēre* be stunned (see STUPID) + *facere* to make, perform, DO[1]; for suffix see -FY. The sense of stun with amazement, fear, etc., astound, is first recorded in English in 1596, in Spenser's *Faerie Queene.* **—stupefaction** *n.* Probably before 1425 *stupefaccioun* property of making senseless or stupefying; borrowed from French *stupéfaction* act of stupefying or condition of being stupefied, or directly from

New Latin *stupefactionem* (nominative *stupefactio*), from Latin *stupefact-*, past participle stem of *stupefacere* stupefy; for suffix see -TION. The sense of overwhelming astonishment is found in English in 1597.

stupendous *adj.* 1666, amazing, marvelous, in Pepys' *Diary,* from earlier *stupendious* (1547); borrowed from Late Latin *stupendus* to be wondered at, stunning, gerundive form of Latin *stupēre* be stunned; see STUPID; for suffix see -OUS, -IOUS.

stupid *adj.* 1541, slow or dull in thinking, not intelligent, in Copland's translation Galen's *Terapeutyke;* borrowed perhaps in part from Middle French *stupide* (1377), but more likely directly from Latin *stupidus* struck senseless, amazed, confounded, stupid, from *stupēre* be stunned, amazed, confounded, be struck senseless; cognate with Greek *týptein* to beat, strike; see TYPE; The sense of characterized by stupidity or dullness is first recorded in English in 1621. **—n.** *Informal.* stupid person. 1712, Steele, in the *Spectator;* from the adjective. **—stupidity** *n.* lack of intelligence. 1541, in Copland's translation of Galen's *Terapeutyke;* borrowed from Latin *stupiditās* senselessness, dullness, from *stupidus* stupid; for suffix see -ITY. The sense of a stupid idea or action is first recorded in 1633.

stupor *n.* dazed condition. Before 1398, in Trevisa's translation of Bartholomew's *De Proprietatibus Rerum;* borrowed from Latin *stupor* insensibility, numbness, dullness, from *stupēre* be stunned or dazed; see STUPID; for suffix see -OR[1].

sturdy *adj.* Probably before 1300 *stourdi* hard to manage, reckless, violent, in *Kyng Alisaunder;* borrowed from Old French *estourdi* violent; originally, dazed, past participle of *estourdir* to daze, from Vulgar Latin **exturdire,* from Latin *ex-* (involving conversion) + *turdus* a thrush, from Indo-European **tr̥zdos* (Pok.1078). As to the sense, in Romance languages the thrush is frequently characterized as dizzy: compare Italian *tordo* thrush, simpleton, or French *soûl comme une grive* drunk as a thrush. The sense of characterized by rough vigor, solidly built, strong, hardy, is first recorded in Middle English about 1386, in Chaucer's writings.

sturgeon *n.* large food fish. About 1300 *sturgiun,* in *Havelok the Dane;* borrowed through Anglo-French *sturgeon, esturgeoun,* from Old French *esturjon, esturgon, esturion,* from a Germanic source (compare Old High German *sturio* sturgeon, modern German *Stör,* modern Dutch *steur,* Old English *styria,* and Old Icelandic *styrja*). The Romance forms, as found in Provençal *esturjon,* Spanish *esturión,* Portuguese *esturião,* and Italian *storione,* all came from the same Germanic source.

stutter *v.* 1570, in Levins' *Dictionary,* frequentative verb form of earlier *stutt* (before 1500), from Middle English *stutten* to stutter, stammer (about 1395, in the Wycliffe Bible); cognate with Middle Low German *stōten* to knock, strike against, collide, Old High German *stōzan* to push, shove (modern German *stossen*), and Norwegian and dialectal Swedish *stotre* to stammer, from Proto-Germanic **staut-* push, thrust, Indo-European **(s)teud-/(s)toud-/(s)tud-* (Pok.1033). **—n.** act or habit of stuttering. 1854, in Robert Surtee's *Handley Cross;* from the verb.

sty[1] *n.* pen for pigs. Before 1200 *sti,* in *Ancrene Riwle;* developed from Old English *stī, stig* hall, pen, as in *stī-fearh* sty-pig (from Proto-Germanic **stijan*); cognate with Middle Low German *stege* and Middle Dutch *stije* sty (modern Dutch *stijg*), and Old Icelandic *-stī,* as in *svīn-stī* swine-sty, *stīa* pen, fold (Danish and Norwegian *sti,* Swedish *stia*), from Indo-European **stāy-/stiy-* press together (Pok.1010). Related to STEWARD.

sty[2] *n.* inflamed swelling on the eyelid. 1617 *stye,* in Fletcher's *The Mad Lover;* probably shortened from earlier (1601) *styan,* from Middle English (1440, in *styanye,* literally, sty-eye). Middle English *styan* developed from Old English *stīgend* sty; literally, riser, from present participle of *stīgan* go up, rise; see STAIR.

style *n.* Before 1325 *stile* designation, title, in *Cursor Mundi;* later, manner or mode of expression (before 1338, in Mannyng's *Chronicle of England*); borrowed from Old French *estile* a stake, pale, from Latin *stilus* stake, pointed instrument for writing on a wax tablet, manner of writing, mode of expression. Latin *stilus* is cognate with Avestan *staēra-,* probably from Indo-European **stoilo-,* and contains the same root element as Latin *stimulus* goad, from Indo-European **stei-/stoi-/sti-* pointed (Pok.1015).

The spelling *style* (with *y*), both in modern English and French, comes from association of this word with Greek *stŷlos* pillar (see STOIC). The meaning of mode or fashion of life, behavior, etc., is first recorded in 1770, and in reference to mode of dress, in 1814, in Jane Austen's *Mansfield Park.* The botanical sense of the stemlike part of a flower pistil is first recorded in 1682 and derived from Latin *stilus* in the sense of stake, pale. **—v.** 1508, to address with a title; 1563-83, give a name to; from the noun. The sense of design or arrange in a fashionable style is first recorded in 1934.
—stylish *adj.* 1797, fashionable, in Jane Austen's *Sense and Sensibility;* formed from English *style,* n. + *-ish.* **—stylist** *n.* 1795, writer as characterized by his style; formed from English *style,* n. + *-ist.* The sense of a person who styles hair is first recorded in 1937. **—stylize** *v.* 1898, conform to a conventional style; formed from English *style,* n. + *-ize.*

stylus (stī′ləs) *n.* pointed instrument for writing on wax. 1728, stemlike part of a flower pistil, style; New Latin, alteration of Latin *stilus* stake, stylus, STYLE. The New Latin spelling with *y* was influenced by Greek *stŷlos* pillar (see STOIC). The meaning of pointed instrument for writing on wax is first recorded in English in 1807; the extended sense of a phonograph needle is first cited in 1875.

stymie *n.* 1857, condition in which an opponent's golf ball lies between the player's ball and the hole; perhaps from earlier Scottish *stymie* person who sees poorly (1616); formed from Middle English *stime* the least bit (before 1325, in *Cursor Mundi*), of uncertain origin + the suffix *-ie.* **—v.** 1857, (in golf) to block with a stymie; from the same source as the noun. The generalized figurative sense of block, hinder, thwart, is first recorded in American English, in George Ade's *Girl Proposition* (1902).

styptic (stip′tik) *adj.* able to stop or check bleeding. Before 1400 *stiptik* astringent, acidic, styptic, in Lanfranc's *Science of Surgery;* borrowed from Old French *stiptique,* or directly from Latin *stȳpticus* astringent, from Greek *styptikós,* from *stýphein* to constrict, draw together; for suffix see -IC. The spelling *styptic* (with *y*) appeared in the 1600's by influence of the Latin and Greek forms. **—n.** styptic substance. 1392 *stiptice,* borrowed from Late Latin *stypticum* an astringent, from Greek *stȳptikón,* neuter of *stȳptikós,* adj.

su- a form of the prefix *sub-* before *sp-,* in some words of Latin origin, as in *suspect;* see SUB-.

suasion (swā′zhən) *n.* an advising or urging, persuasion. About 1380 *suasioun,* in Chaucer's translation of Boethius' *De Consolatione Philosophiae;* borrowed probably from Old French *suasion,* and directly from Latin *suāsiōnem* (nominative *suāsiō*) an advising, a counseling, from *suās-,* past participle stem of *suādēre* to urge, persuade; for suffix see -SION. Latin *suādēre* is cognate with Sanskrit *svádati* makes agreeable (cognate with Greek *hadeîn* to please, from Indo-European **swad-/ swād-,* M. Mayrhofer, *Kurzgefasstes etymologisches Wörterbuch des Altindischen,* III, 568), and related to Latin *suāvis* SWEET. **—suasive** *adj.* 1601, borrowed from Middle French *suasif* (feminine *suasive*), and perhaps formed in English from Latin *suāsus,* past participle + English *-ive.*

suave (swäv) *adj.* smoothly agreeable or polite. About 1501, gracious, kindly; borrowed from Middle French *suave,* learned borrowing from Latin *suāvis* agreeable; see SWEET. The sense of smoothly agreeable or polite is first recorded in 1831. **—suavity** *n.* Before 1500 *suavitee* sweetness or agreeableness to the senses; borrowed from Middle French *suavité,* learned borrowing from Latin *suāvitās* pleasantness, sweetness, from *suāvis* agreeable, sweet; for suffix see -ITY. The sense of quality of being suave in manner is first recorded in English in 1815.

sub¹ *prep.* the Latin preposition for "under," commonly used in various modern legal and other phrases, such as the following: **—sub judice** (sub jü′dəsē). 1613, judicially undecided, still under consideration; literally, under a judge. **—sub rosa** (sub rō′zə). 1654, in strict confidence, privately, secretly; literally, under the rose; so called because the rose was anciently regarded as a symbol of secrecy. **—sub verbo** or **sub voce** 1859, under the word or heading.

sub² *v.* substitute. 1853, in letters of Mark Twain, American English; shortened form of *substitute,* v. **—n.** a substitute. 1830, American English, originally applied to substitute printers; shortened form of *substitute,* n.

sub- a prefix acquired in numerous words of Latin origin and productive in English, meaning: **1** under, below, as in *subnormal = below normal* (1890), *subsoil = soil under the topsoil* (1799), *substandard = below standard* (1909). **2** down, further, again, as in *subdivide = divide again* (probably before 1425). **3a** near, nearly, less than, as in *subtropical = nearly tropical* (1842), *subhuman = less than human* (1793). **b** incompletely, partially, as in *subconscious = incompletely conscious* (1824). **4a** lower, subordinate, as in *subcommittee = a lower or subordinate committee* (1610), *sublease = subordinate lease* (1826). **b** resulting from further division, as in *subsection = a section resulting from further division of something* (1621). **5** slightly, somewhat, as in *subacid = slightly acid* (1669). Borrowed from Latin *sub-,* from *sub,* prep., under, up to, towards; see UP. Latin *sub* is cognate with Oscan *sup* and Umbrian *su* (and *sub-*), having picked up an initial *s-* in pre-Italic, from Indo-European **upo.* Assimilations or changes in the final consonant of the prefix that took place in Latin survive in English in the forms *suc-, suf-, sug-, sum-, sup-,* and *sur-;* an assumed early variant *sups-* remained in Latin and in English as *sus-* before some words beginning with the consonants *c, p,* or *t,* and simply *su-* before *sp-,* as in *suspect.*

subaltern (sub′əltərn) *adj.* subordinate. 1581, borrowed from Middle French *subalterne,* and probably directly from Late Latin *subalternus* (Latin *sub-* under + *alternus* every other, as in every other one; see ALTERNATE). An earlier adjective form, *subalterned* made subordinate, is found in Middle English in 1413. **—n.** subordinate officer. 1605, from the adjective.

subconscious *adj.* 1823, (implied in *subconsciously*) not wholly conscious, in De Quincey's writings; formed from English *sub-* incompletely + *conscious.* **—n. the subconscious.** subconscious thoughts or feelings. 1890, from the adjective.

subdivision *n.* 1553, one of the parts into which something is divided; formed from English *sub-* + *division.*

subdue *v.* Before 1387 *sodewen, sudewen* conquer, overcome, in Trevisa's translation of Higden's *Polychronicon;* later *subdewen* (probably before 1475); borrowed from Old French *souduire* deceive, seduce, from Latin *subdūcere* draw, lead away, withdraw (*sub-* from under + *dūcere* to lead; see TOW¹ pull). Old French *souduire* may have been influenced in meaning by Latin *sēdūcere* to SEDUCE. Further influence of Latin is probably found in the meaning in English, altered by Latin *subdere* to subdue (*sub-* under + *-dere* to put; see DO¹ perform). The form *subdew* is first recorded about 1420, and that of *subdue* about 1460.

subjacent (subjā′sənt) *adj.* situated below, underlying. 1597, borrowed from Middle French (1532, Rabelais), and directly from Latin *subjacentem* (nominative *subjacēns*), present participle of *subjacēre* to lie below (*sub-* below + *jacēre* to lie, related to *jacere* to throw; see JET¹ stream).

subject *n.* Before 1333 *sugge* person under the rule of another, subordinate, in Shoreham's *Poems;* later *subgit* (about 1380, in Chaucer's translation of Boethius' *De Consolatione Philosophiae*), *subiecte* (before 1398, in Trevisa's translation of Bartholomew's *De Proprietatibus Rerum*); borrowed from Old French *suget, subgect;* later *subject* a subject person or thing, representing various stages of borrowing from Latin *subjectus* lying under or near, adjacent, subject, exposed; also, an inferior, from the past participle of *subicere* to place under (*sub-* under + *-icere,* combining form of *jacere* to throw; see JET¹ stream).

Some of the specific senses in logic and philosophy derive in English from Latin *subjectum* foundation or subject of a proposition, from neuter of *subjectus,* past participle. The Latin is a loan translation of Greek *tò hypokeímenon,* literally, that which lies beneath. The sense of something thought about or studied is first recorded in English in 1586. Reference to the grammatical subject occurred before 1638.

—adj. Before 1338 *suget* owing allegiance or obedience (to), in Mannyng's *Chronicle of England;* later *subgit* (before 1393, in Gower's *Confessio Amantis*), and *subject* (about 1386, in Chaucer's *Canterbury Tales*); borrowed from Old French *suget, subgiet, subject,* learned borrowing from Latin *subjectus* inferior in status, subject, from past participle of *subicere* to place under. The meaning of prone (to), likely to have, is first recorded in Middle English about 1380.

—v. before 1382 *subjecten* to subjugate, in the Wycliffe Bible; borrowed from Old French *subjecter* to subject, subjugate, from Latin *subjectāre* throw under, subju-

gate, frequentative form of *subicere* to place under. The meaning of expose, lay open (to), is first recorded in 1549.
—subjection *n.* About 1375 *subieccioun* dominion, control, domination, in Chaucer's *Canterbury Tales;* borrowed from Old French *subjection,* learned borrowing of Latin *subjectiōnem* (nominative *subjectiō*) a placing under, reducing to obedience, from *subject-,* past participle stem of *subicere* to place under; for suffix see -TION. **—subjective** *adj.* Probably before 1450 *subiective* of or relating to a political subject, submissive, obedient; borrowed from Latin *subjectivus,* from *subjectus* subject, n.; for suffix see -IVE. The meaning of existing in the mind is first recorded in English in 1707.

subjugate *v.* subdue. Probably before 1425 *subiugaten,* in a translation of Higden's *Polychronicon;* possibly a back formation from earlier *subjugation* (Middle English *subiugacioun*), influenced by Latin *subjugātus,* past participle of *subjugāre* subdue; literally, bring under a yoke (*sub-* under + *jugum* YOKE); for suffix see -ATE[1]. **—subjugation** *n.* 1373 *subiugacion* act of subjugating, subjection; borrowed from Late Latin *subjugātiōnem* (nominative *subjugātiō*), from Latin *subjugāre;* for suffix see -ATION.

subjunctive *adj. Grammar.* of or designating the mood of a verb which expresses something as possible, conditional, or dependent. 1530, in Palsgrave's *Lesclarcissement;* borrowed from Late Latin *subjūnctīvus* serving to join, connecting, (in grammar) subjunctive, from Latin *subjūnct-,* past participle stem of *subjungere* to append, add at the end, place under (*sub-* under + *jungere* to join; see YOKE); for suffix see -IVE. Late Latin *subjūnctīvus* is probably a loan translation of Greek *hypotaktikós* subordinated, so called because in Greek the subjunctive mood is used almost exclusively in subordinate clauses. **—n.** subjunctive mood. 1622, from the adjective.

sublet *v.* 1766, to lease to a subtenant, in Smollett's writings; formed from English *sub-* + *let,* v.

sublimation *n.* process of converting a solid substance by heat into a vapor, which resolidifies on cooling. Before 1393 *sublimacion,* in Gower's *Confessio Amantis;* borrowed from Old French *sublimation,* or directly from Medieval Latin *sublimationem* (nominative *sublimatio*) refinement; literally, a lifting up, deliverance, from *sublimare* refine or purify by sublimation, from Latin *sublīmāre* to raise, elevate, from *sublīmis* lofty, SUBLIME; for suffix see -ATION. The transferred sense in psychology of an act of changing an undesirable impulse or trait into a form desirable or acceptable to the conscious mind, is first recorded in 1910, in A.A. Brill's translation of Freud's *Three Contributions to Sexual Theory;* probably influenced by earlier *subliminal.*
—sublimate (sub′ləmit *or* sub′ləmāt) *n.* mercuric chloride or other substance obtained by sublimation. 1543, borrowed from Medieval Latin *sublimatum,* from neuter past participle of *sublimare* refine or purify by sublimation. *—v.* (sub′ləmāt) purify, refine. 1591, from the earlier adjective (1562) with the meaning of purified or refined by sublimation; probably borrowed from Medieval Latin *sublimatus,* past participle of *sublimare.* Alternatively, the verb might be a back formation in English of the earlier noun *sublimation.* The earlier, now obsolete, senses of raised, elevated (1464) and to raise, elevate (about 1425), *sublimate,* adj. and v., were borrowed directly from Latin *sublīmātus,* past participle of *sublīmāre* to raise, elevate.

sublime *adj.* 1586, lofty, noble; borrowed from Middle French *sublime,* or directly from Latin *sublīmis* uplifted, high, lofty; possibly originally, sloping up to the lintel (*sub-* up to + *līmen* threshold; see LIMIT). **—v.** to subject (a substance) to sublimation. About 1395 *sublimen,* in Chaucer's *Canterbury Tales;* borrowed from Old French *sublimer,* from Medieval Latin *sublimare* refine or purify by sublimation; see SUBLIMATION. The sense of exalt or elevate is first recorded in 1609.
—sublimity *n.* Probably about 1425 *sublimitee* worthiness, nobility; borrowed from Latin *sublīmitās* loftiness, elevation, from *sublīmis* lofty, sublime; for suffix see -ITY.

subliminal *adj. Psychology.* below the threshold of consciousness. 1886, formed from English *sub-* + Latin *līmen* (genitive *līminis*) threshold (see LIMIT) + English *-al*[1], apparently as a loan translation of the German phrase *unter der Schwelle (des Bewusstseins*) beneath the threshold (of consciousness), used by the German philosopher, psychologist, and educator, J.F. Herbart, 1776-1841.

submachine gun 1920, Thompson *sub-machine gun* an automatic weapon, somewhat like a machine gun that can be fired from the shoulder or hip. Conceived of by an American general, J.T. Thompson (1860-1940), but designed and named after Thompson by O.V. Payne in 1919.

submarine *adj.* below the surface of the sea. 1648, formed from English *sub-* + *marine.* **—n.** 1703, organism that lives under water; from the adjective. The sense of a boat that can go under water is first found in 1648, later recorded as *submarine boat* (1807, in letters of Jefferson), and in the noun use *submarine* (1899).

submerge *v.* 1606, in Shakespeare's *Antony and Cleopatra;* borrowed from French *submerger,* or possibly directly from Latin *submergere* (*sub-* under + *mergere* to plunge, immerse; see MERGE). **—submergence** *n.* 1832, condition of being submerged; formed from English *submerge* + *-ence.*

submerse *v.* submerge. 1727, (implied in *submersed*), probably a back formation from earlier *submersion,* perhaps influenced by Latin *submersus,* past participle of *submergere* SUBMERGE. **—submersible** *adj.* 1866, that may be submerged, perhaps borrowed from French *submersible,* and, in part, formed from English *submerse* + *-ible.* —*n.* 1900, submersible boat, from the adjective. **—submersion** *n.* 1611, act of submerging, in Cotgrave's *Dictionary;* perhaps borrowed from French *submersion,* and directly from Late Latin *submersiōnem* (nominative *submersiō*), from Latin *submers-,* past participle stem of *submergere* to sink, SUBMERGE; for suffix see -SION.

submission *n.* About 1390 *submissioun* act of submitting, in Chaucer's *Canterbury Tales;* borrowed from Old French *submission,* learned borrowing from Latin, or borrowed into English directly from Latin *submissiōnem* (nominative *submissiō*) a letting down, lowering, sinking, yielding, from *submis-,* past participle stem of *submittere* put under, let down, lower, reduce, yield, surrender; see SUBMIT; for suffix see -SION. The sense of humble obedience, deferential conduct, is first recorded in Middle English about 1449. **—submissive** *adj.* Before 1586, yielding, obedient, in Sidney's *The Arcadia;* formed in English from Latin *submissus,* past participle + English *-ive.*

submit *v.* About 1380 *submitten* to yield or surrender, in Chaucer's translation of Boethius' *De Consolatione Philosophiae;* borrowed from Latin *submittere* to yield, lower, let down, put under, reduce (*sub-* under + *mittere* let go, send; see MISSION). The sense of refer or send to another for consideration, judgment, etc., is first recorded in English in 1560.

subordinate (səbôr′dənit) *adj.* About 1449 *subordinat* inferior, lower, secondary; borrowed from Medieval Latin *subordinatus* placed in a lower order, made subject, past participle of *subordinare* place in a lower order (Latin *sub-* under + *ōrdināre* arrange, ORDAIN); for suffix see -ATE[1]. **—n.** subordinate person or thing. 1640, in Sandys' *Christ's Passion;* from the adjective. **—v.** (səbôr′dənāt) make subordinate. 1597, in writings of Hooker; borrowed from Medieval Latin *subordinatus,* past participle of *subordinare* place in a lower order. Alternatively, the verb may be from the adjective. **—subordination** *n.* Before 1600, condition of being subordinate, in writings of Hooker; probably formed in English from *subordinate,* v. + *-ion,* on the model of Medieval Latin *subordinationem* (nominative *subordinatio*).

suborn (səbôrn′) *v.* persuade someone to do an illegal or evil deed. 1534, borrowed from Middle French *suborner,* or directly from Latin *subōrnāre* suborn; originally, equip (*sub-* under, secretly + *ōrnāre* equip, related to *ōrdō* ORDER*).* The specific legal sense of persuade or induce someone to commit perjury is first recorded in English in 1557.

subpoena *or* **subpena** (səpē′nə) *n.* writ commanding a person to appear in court. 1422-61 *sub pena;* borrowing of Medieval Latin *sub poena* under penalty, the first words of the writ (Latin *sub* under + *poenā,* ablative of *poena* penalty; see PAIN). **—v.** to summon with a subpoena. 1640, from the noun.

subscribe *v.* 1425 *subscriben* to sign at the bottom of a document, in *Rolls of Parliament;* borrowed from Latin *subscrībere* write underneath or below, sign one's name (*sub-* underneath + *scrībere* write; see SCRIBE). The meaning of give one's consent, approval, or support, agree to, is first recorded in English in 1549; the sense of contribute money to (a fund, society, etc.) is first recorded in 1640; the sense of put one's name down as a regular buyer of a periodical, newspaper, or other publication, is found in Swift's *Journal to Stella* (1711, from the noun *subscription*). **—subscriber** *n.* (1599)

subscript *n.* Before 1704, something written underneath, in writings of Thomas Brown; borrowed from Latin *subscrīptus,* past participle of *subscrībere* write underneath; see SUBSCRIBE. The specific sense of subscript letter or symbol appeared in 1901. **—adj.** written underneath. 1871, in Wordsworth's *Greek Primer;* from the noun.

subscription *n.* act or process of subscribing. 1409 *subscripcion;* borrowed from Middle French *subscription,* and directly from Latin *subscrīptiōnem* (nominative *subscrīptiō*) anything written underneath, a signature, from *subscrīpt-,* past participle stem of *subscrībere* SUBSCRIBE; for suffix see -TION. The sense of act of subscribing money to a fund or stock is first recorded in 1647, and that of a periodic contribution of money to a society, etc., in 1679. The specific meaning of subscribing to a periodic publication is first recorded in 1679.

subsequent *adj.* About 1450, coming after, following; borrowed from Middle French *subséquent,* and directly from Latin *subsequentem* (nominative *subsequēns*), present participle of *subsequī* to follow closely (*sub-* closely, up to + *sequī* follow; see SEQUEL); for suffix see -ENT.

subservient *adj.* 1632, useful, serviceable; borrowed from Latin *subservientem* (nominative *subserviēns*), present participle of *subservīre* assist, lend support (*sub-* under + *servīre* SERVE); for suffix see -ENT. The meaning of slavishly polite and obedient, servile, is first recorded in 1794, in Ann Radcliffe's *Mysteries of Udolpho.* **—subservience** *n.* Before 1676, condition of being serviceable; formed from English *subservient,* on the analogy of such pairs as *obedient, obedience;* for suffix see -ENCE.

subside *v.* 1681, to sink or fall to the bottom; possibly a back formation from *subsidence,* influenced by Latin *subsīdere* settle down, sink down, remain, sit down (*sub-* down + *sīdere* to settle, related to *sedēre* SIT). The meaning of abate, become less active, die down, is first recorded before 1700, in Evelyn's *Diary.* **—subsidence** *n.* 1646, sediment; later, a settling down or to the bottom (1656); borrowed possibly through French *subsidence,* and directly from Latin *subsīdentia* sediment, from *subsīdēns,* present participle of *subsīdere* settle or sink down; see SUBSIDE; for suffix see -ENCE. The sense of abatement is first recorded in 1731.

subsidiary *adj.* 1543, auxiliary, supplementary; borrowed, perhaps through Middle French *subsidiaire,* and directly from Latin *subsidiārius* serving to assist or supplement, from *subsidium* help, aid, assistance; see SUBSIDY; for suffix see -ARY. The sense of subordinate, secondary, is first recorded in Carlyle's *Sartor Resartus* (1831). **—n.** subsidiary thing or person. 1603, in Florio's translation of Montaigne's *Essays;* from the adjective. An earlier sense of the levy of a subsidy is recorded in 1592.

subsidy *n.* grant or contribution of money. Before 1387 *subsidie,* in Trevisa's translation of Higden's *Polychronicon;* borrowed through Anglo-French *subsidie, subside,* from Old French *subside* help, aid, contribution, learned borrowing from Latin *subsidium* help, aid, assistance, (military) reinforcements, from **subsidēre* (*sub-* behind, near + *sedēre* to SIT). Although the general sense of a grant or contribution of money is first recorded in Middle English in 1421, the word was then often specifically applied to money raised by special taxes and given by parliament to the sovereign. **—subsidize** *v.* to aid or assist with a subsidy. 1795, formed from English *subsidy* + *-ize.*

subsist *v.* 1549, to have real existence, exist as a substance, in *Book of Common Prayer;* borrowed probably from Middle French *subsister* continue to exist, and directly from Latin *subsistere* stand still or firm, take a stand or position, support, continue (*sub-* under, up to + *sistere* to assume a standing position, from *stāre* to STAND). In some senses the word is probably a back formation from English *subsistence,* but in the meaning of continue to exist, remain in use or force (first recorded about 1600 in Shakespeare's *Sonnets*), the word is most likely a borrowing from the French. The sense of maintain or support oneself, make a living, is first attested in 1646. **—subsistence** *n.* Probably before 1425, real existence, in a translation of Higden's *Polychronicon;* borrowed from Late Latin *subsistentia* substance, reality, from Latin *subsistēns,* present participle of *subsistere* stand still or firm; for suffix see -ENCE. Late Latin *subsistentia* is a loan translation of Greek *hypóstasis* substance, foundation, support. The sense of means of support or livelihood is first recorded in English in 1639. **—subsistence farming** (1949) **—subsistence wage** (1926)

subsonic *adj.* having to do with speeds less than the speed of sound. 1937, formed from English *sub-* below + *sonic.* Compare SUPERSONIC.

substance *n.* Probably before 1300 *substaunce* essential nature, matter, material, in *Arthour and Merlin;* borrowed from Old French *substance,* learned borrowing from Latin *substantia* being, essence, material, from *substāns,* present participle of *substāre* stand firm, be under or present (*sub-* up to, under + *stāre* to STAND); for suffix see -ANCE. The sense of possessions, means, wealth (as in *a person of substance*) is first recorded in *Cursor Mundi* (before 1325). The sense of any particular kind of matter is found before 1393, in Gower's *Confessio Amantis.*

substantial *adj.* 1340 *substanciel* ample, abundant, in *Ayenbite of Inwyt;* borrowed from Old French *substantiel,* and directly from Latin *substantiālis* having substance or reality, material, from *substantia* SUBSTANCE; for suffix see -AL[1].

substantiate *v.* 1657, give substance to, make real or substantial; borrowed from New Latin *substantiatus,* past participle of *substantiare,* from Latin *substantia* SUBSTANCE; for suffix see -ATE[1]. The sense of establish by evidence, prove, verify, is first recorded in English in Malthus' *An Essay on the Principle of Population* (1803). **—substantiation** *n.* 1760-72, embodiment; formed from English *substantiate* + *-ion.* The sense of act of substantiating or proving is first recorded in 1861.

substantive *n.* noun, word or phrase used as a noun. Probably before 1378 *substantif,* in a version of *Piers Plowman;* borrowed from Old French *substantif* (feminine *substantive*), from Late Latin *substantīvum,* as used in *nōmen substantīvum* name or word of substance, neuter of Latin *substantīvus* of substance or being, from *substantia* SUBSTANCE; for suffix see -IVE. **—adj.** About 1450, independent, self-sufficient, self-existent; borrowed from Middle French *substantif* (feminine *substantive*) expressing existence, from Latin *substantīvus* of substance. The meaning in grammar "denoting something substantial, acting as a noun" is first recorded in 1509 in the phrase *noun substantive,* translation of Late Latin *nōmen substantīvum.*

substitute *n.* 1413, person acting in place of another, deputy, in a translation of *The Pilgrimage of the Soul;* in part perhaps a back formation from *substitution,* and in part borrowed from Middle French *substitut,* and directly from Latin *substitūtus,* past participle of *substituere* put in place of another, place under or next to (*sub-* under + *statuere* set up; see STATUTE). The specific meaning in sports of one who takes the place of another after a game has started is first recorded in 1849. **—adj.** taking the place of another. Before 1425, in a translation of Higden's *Polychronicon;* borrowed from Latin *substitūtus,* past participle; see the noun above. **—v.** 1532, to put in place of another, appoint as a deputy or delegate; probably a verb use of *substitute,* n., modeled on Latin *substitūtus,* past participle. **—substitution** *n.* Before 1393 *substitucion* appointment of a deputy, delegation, in Gower's *Confessio Amantis;* borrowed from Old French *substitution,* from Late Latin *substitūtiōnem* (nominative *substitūtiō*) a putting in place of another, substitution, from Latin *substitūt-,* past participle stem of *substituere* put in place of another; for suffix see -TION. The sense of an act of substituting, a putting of a person or thing in place of another, is first recorded in English in 1612. The meaning in mathematics of a method of replacing or interchanging quantities is first recorded in English in 1710.

subsume *v.* 1535, bring under, append; borrowed from New Latin *subsumere* (Latin *sub-* under + *sūmere* to take; see ASSUME). The sense of bring under a larger classification is first recorded in 1812, in Coleridge's writings.

subtend *v.* extend under or be opposite to, stretch across. 1570, borrowed from Latin *subtendere* (*sub-* under + *tendere* to stretch; see TEND).

subter- a prefix meaning beneath, as in *subterposition,* or secretly, as in *subterfuge.* Borrowed from Latin *subter* beneath, secretly, related to *sub* under, beneath; see SUB-.

subterfuge *n.* trick, excuse, or expedient used to escape something unpleasant. 1573, borrowed from Middle French *subterfuge,* or directly from Late Latin *subterfugium* an evasion, from Latin *subterfugere* to evade, escape, flee by stealth (*subter-* beneath, secretly + *fugere* flee; see FUGITIVE).

subterranean *adj.* underground. 1603, in Holland's translation of Plutarch's *Moralia;* formed in English from Latin *subterrāneus* underground (*sub-* under + *terra* earth; see TERRACE) + English *-an.*

subtile (sut′əl) *adj.* About 1375 *subtile* delicate, elusive, crafty, in Chaucer's *Anelida and Arcite;* borrowed from Old French *subtil,* learned borrowing from Latin *subtīlis* fine, thin, delicate; see SUBTLE. The sense of not dense, thin, is first recorded in Middle English before 1393, in Gower's *Confessio Amantis.* **—subtility** *n.* 1375 *subtilite* skill, cleverness, cunning, in Barbour's *The Bruce;* borrowed from Old French *subtilite* skill, cleverness, *sutclite* acuteness, learned borrowing from Latin *subtīlitās* fineness, slenderness, acuteness, from *subtīlis* subtle; for suffix see -ITY. *Subtile* is a form that developed in Middle English and remained as a parallel form to *subtle* into the 1600's, and in some instances (such as fine, delicate, thin, and acute, keen) into the 20th century.

subtitle *n.* 1825, subordinate or additional title; formed from English *sub-* + *title.* The sense of a caption on a motion-picture screen is found in 1909. **—v.** provide with a subtitle. 1891, from the noun.

subtle (sut′əl) *adj.* Before 1325 *sutile* clever, ingenious, crafty, in *Cursor Mundi;* borrowed from Old French *soutil, sutil,* from Latin *subtīlis* fine, thin, delicate, finely woven (*sub-* under + *-tīlis,* from *tēla* web and *texere* to weave; see TEXT). The spelling *subtle* (with *b*) first began to appear in the 1500's, in imitation of the Latin form. **—subtlety** *n.* About 1330 *sutelte* subtle quality; borrowed from Old French *sutilté, soutilté,* from Latin *subtīlitās* fineness, slenderness, acuteness, from *subtīlis* subtle; for suffix see -TY[2]. The Middle English spelling was refashioned in the 1500's in imitation of the Latin form. **—subtly** *adv.* Before 1333, in a subtle manner; formed in Middle English from *sutile* + *-lich* -ly[1].

subtraction *n.* About 1400 *subtractioun* withdrawal, removal; borrowed from Late Latin *subtractiōnem* (nominative *subtractiō*) a drawing back, taking away, from *subtract-,* past participle stem of *subtrahere* take away, draw off (*sub-* from under + *trahere* to pull, draw; see TRACT); for suffix see -TION. The mathematical sense of the taking of one quantity from another is first recorded in Middle English, probably about 1425. **—subtract** *v.* 1533, withdraw, remove, in Bellenden's translation of Livy's *Roman History;* probably a back formation from earlier *subtraction,* formed by influence of Latin *subtract-,* past participle stem of *subtrahere* draw off. The mathematical sense of take away one number from another is first recorded in 1557 from the use in English of *subtraction.* **—subtractive** *adj.* 1690, formed from English *subtract* + *-ive.*

subtrahend (sub′trəhend) *n.* number or quantity to be subtracted. 1674, in Samuel Jeake's *Logisticelogia;* borrowed from Latin *subtrahendus numerus* number to be subtracted, gerundive form of *subtrahere* SUBTRACT.

suburb *n.* Before 1325 *suburbe* residential area just outside a town or city; borrowed from Old French *suburbe,* learned borrowing from Latin *suburbium* an outlying part of a city (*sub-* below, near + *urbs,* genitive *urbis,* city; see URBAN). **—suburban** *adj.* Before 1625, of, relating to, or in a suburb; borrowed from Latin *suburbānus* near a city (*sub-* + *urbānus* urban). **—suburbanite** *n.* 1890, suburban resident; formed from English *suburban* + *-ite*[1]. **—suburbia** (səbėr′bēə) *n.* the suburbs. 1896 (originally, the suburbs of London); formed from English *suburb* + Latin *-ia* -y[3]; probably influenced by *utopia.*

subvention *n.* subsidy. Probably before 1430 *subvencion* subsidy levied by the state; borrowed from Middle French *subvention,* or directly from Late Latin *subventiōnem* (nominative *subventiō*) a giving of aid, assistance, from Latin *subvent-,* past participle stem of *subvenīre* come to one's aid (*sub-* up to + *venīre* COME); for suffix see -TION. The sense of money granted to support an institution, cause, or undertaking, is found in 1851.

subversion *n.* Before 1382 *subversioun* overthrow, destruction, in the Wycliffe Bible; borrowed from Old French *subversion,* from Late Latin *subversiōnem* (nominative *subversiō*) an overthrow, ruin, destruction, from Latin *subvers-,* past participle stem of *subvertere* SUBVERT; for suffix see -SION. The sense of overthrow of a law, rule, system, etc., is found in Middle English in 1399, in *Rolls of Parliament.* **—subversive** *adj.* tending to overthrow or undermine; causing subversion. 1644, probably formed in English from Latin *subvers-,* past participle stem of *subvertere* overthrow, ruin; see SUBVERT + English *-ive.* Alternatively, the word may have been formed from English *subversion* + the suffix *-ive.* —*n.* person who advocates subversive acts. 1887, from the adjective.

subvert *v.* About 1375 *subverten* to overthrow, ruin, destroy, undermine; borrowed from Latin *subvertere* (*sub-* under + *vertere* to turn; see VERTEX).

subway *n.* 1825, underground passage; formed from English *sub-* + *way.* The sense of an underground railway in a city is first recorded in 1893, in American English.

suc- a form of the prefix *sub-* before *c* in some words of Latin origin, as in *succeed.* Formed in Latin by assimilation of *b* to the following consonant (*c*).

succeed *v.* 1375 *succeden* come next after, take the place of another, in Barbour's *The Bruce;* borrowed from Old French *succeder,* and directly from Latin *succēdere* come after, go near to (*suc-* up, near, variant of *sub-* before *c* + *cēdere* go; see CEDE). The sense of have a desired or fortunate outcome, turn out well, have a favorable result, is first recorded in Middle English before 1475.

success *n.* 1537, result, outcome; borrowed from Latin *successus* (genitive *successūs*) an advance, succession, happy outcome, from *succēdere* come after, SUCCEED. The meaning of accomplishment of a desired end is first recorded before 1586; the same sense with particular reference to the attainment of wealth or high position is first recorded in 1885, in writings of Oliver Wendell Holmes.

succession *n.* Before 1325, act, right, or process of succeeding to an office, property, or rank; borrowed through Old French *succession,* and directly from Latin *successiōnem* (nominative *successiō*) a following after, a coming into another's place, succession, result, from *success-,* past participle stem of *succēdere* come after, SUCCEED; for suffix see -SION. The sense of a regular sequence is first recorded in Middle English about 1449, and that of a series of persons or things in orderly sequence, in 1579. **—successive** *adj.* coming one after another. Before 1425, in a translation of Higden's *Polychronicon;* borrowed from Medieval Latin *successivus* coming one after another, from Latin *succēdere* come after; for suffix see -IVE. **—successor** *n.* About 1300 *successour* one who succeeds another; borrowed through Anglo-French *successor* and Old French *successour,* learned borrowings from Latin *successor* a follower, one who succeeds another, from *success-,* past participle stem of *succēdere* succeed; for suffix see -OR[2].

succinct *adj.* Probably before 1425 *succincte* girt, engirdled, in a translation of Higden's *Polychronicon;* borrowed from Middle French *succincte,* and probably directly from Latin *succīnctus,* past participle of *succingere* tuck up (clothes for action), gird from below (*suc-* up, variant of *sub-* before *c* + *cingere* to gird; see CINCTURE). The extended sense of compressed into small compass, expressed concisely, brief and concise, is first recorded in English in 1585, but implied earlier in *succinctly* (about 1537).

succor (suk′ər) *n.* help, relief, aid. Probably before 1200 *sucurs,* in *Ancrene Riwle;* borrowed through Anglo-French *succors* and Old French *sucurres, socorres, secors,* from Medieval Latin *succursus* help, assistance, from past participle of Latin *succurrere* run to help (*suc-* up to, variant of *sub-* before *c* + *currere* to run; see CURRENT). The final *-s* of Middle English *sucurs* was at an early date taken as a plural suffix and a new singular form *sucur* came into use by about 1290. —*v.* to help or aid. About 1275 *sucuren;* borrowed from Old French *sucurre,* from Latin *succurrere* run to help.

succotash (suk′ətash) *n.* corn and beans cooked together. 1751 *suckatash,* in James MacSparran's *Diary,* American English; borrowed from Algonquian (Narragansett) *misickqatash* ear of corn.

succulent *adj.* juicy. 1601, in Holland's translation of Pliny's *Natural History;* borrowed from French *succulent,* and directly from Latin *succulentus* having juice, from *succus, sūcus* juice, related to *sūgere* to SUCK. —*n.* plant with fleshy and juicy tissues. 1825, from the adjective. **—succulence** *n.* 1787, formed from English *succulent* + *-ence.*

succumb (səkum′) *v.* About 1489 *succomben* bring

down, overwhelm, in Caxton's translation of *Blanchardyn and Eglantine;* borrowed from Middle French *succomber,* and directly from Latin *succumbere* submit, yield, sink down, lie under (*sub-* down + *-cumbere* take a lying position, related to *cubāre* lie down; see HIP[1] joint). The sense of sink under pressure, give way, yield, is first recorded in 1604. The specific sense of yield to the attacks of a disease, the effects of wounds, etc., hence, to die, developed by 1849.

such *adj.* Probably about 1175 *swich* of that kind, of the same kind; probably before 1200 *swuch,* developed from Old English *swylc* (about 725, in *Beowulf*), *swilc* (before 800, in *Corpus Glossary*), *swelc* (before 900); cognate with Old Frisian *sēlik, selk* such, Old Saxon *sulīk,* Middle Dutch *sulc* (modern Dutch *zulk*), Old High German *sulīh, solīh* (modern German *solch*), Old Icelandic *slīkr* (Swedish and Norwegian *slik,* Danish *slig*), and Gothic *swaleiks.* These forms derive from a Proto-Germanic compound **swalīkaz,* meaning "so formed" (*swa* SO + **līkan* form, the source of Old English *gelic* similar, LIKE[1]).

The modern standard form *such* came about by a series of changes in the word's pronunciation between Old English and Middle English. From Old English *swilc* and *swylc* developed a sporadic form *swulc* from about 1000. *Swylc* and *swulc* became in Middle English *swulch,* which, by the absorption of *w* and loss of *l,* gave *such.* Certain dialectal forms, such as *sech* and *sich* resulted from the same process carried through the Old English forms *swelc* and *swilc.* Compare EACH and WHICH for parallel development of forms.
—pron. Probably before 1200 *swuch,* in *Ancrene Riwle;* developed from Old English *swylc* (about 725, in *Beowulf*); from the adjective in Old English.

suck *v.* Probably about 1150 *suken* to draw into the mouth (especially milk from the breast or udder); developed from Old English (before 830) *sūcan;* cognate with Latin *sugere* to suck, from Indo-European **sūg-,* root **sewəg-* (Pok.912). Other cognates include Old Prussian suge rain, Latvian *sùkt* to suck, and Tocharian B *swese* rain. A parallel Indo-European form **sūk-,* root **sewə-k-* (compare Latin *sūcus* juice) is represented by Old English and Old Saxon *sūgan* to suck, Middle Dutch *sūghen* (modern Dutch *zuigen*), Old High German *sūgan* (modern German *saugen*), and Old Icelandic *sūga.* This verb is related to English SOAK. **—n.** act of sucking. About 1300 *souke;* from the verb. **—sucker** *n.* About 1384 *souker* young mammal before it is weaned, in the Wycliffe Bible; formed from Middle English *suken, souken* to suck + *-er*[1]. The zoological meaning of an organ for adhering or holding fast is first recorded in 1681, and that of an organ adapted for sucking, in 1685. The botanical meaning of a shoot growing from a stem is found in 1577-82. The figurative slang sense of a person who is easily hoodwinked or deceived is first recorded in 1836 in American English; it is a figurative use of the sense of a young animal, hence a naive person. The sense of a lollipop is first recorded in 1907, also in American English. *—v.* 1661, to remove superfluous young shoots from; from the noun. The slang sense of hoodwink is first recorded in 1948, in American English. **—suckling** *n.* young animal or child not yet weaned. Before 1225 *suceling;* formed from Middle English *suken* to suck + *-ling.* Compare Middle Dutch *sōghelinc* (modern Dutch *zuigeling*), Middle High German *sūgelinc* (modern German *Säugling*).

suckle *v.* Before 1425 *suclen* to nurse at the breast or udder, in a version of the Wycliffe Bible; perhaps a causative form of *suken* to SUCK; or a back formation from earlier *suckling,* as the suffix -LE[3] does not fit with *suck* to make *suckle* semantically. Alternatively, *suckle* may be a back formation from the earlier SUCKING.

sucrose (sü′krōs) *n.* ordinary sugar obtained from sugar cane, etc. 1857, formed in English from French *sucre* SUGAR + English *-ose*[2].

suction *n.* 1626, act of sucking, in Francis Bacon's *Sylva Sylvarum;* borrowed from Late Latin *sūctiōnem* (nominative *sūctiō*), from Latin *sūct-,* past participle stem of *sūgere* to SUCK; for suffix see -TION. The sense of the drawing of a liquid, gas, etc., into a space by sucking out or removing air, is first recorded in 1658.

sudden *adj.* Probably about 1300 *soden* happening unexpectedly; borrowed through Anglo-French *sodein, sudein,* from Old French *subdain* immediate, sudden. The Old French word developed from Vulgar Latin **subitānus,* variant of Latin *subitāneus* sudden, from *subitus* appearing unexpectedly, sudden, from past participle of *subīre* come or go up stealthily (*sub-* up to + *īre* come, go; see EXIT). **—n.** 1558 *upon the soden* in a sudden manner; 1570 *of the sudein;* 1596 *of a sudayn,* in Shakespeare's *Taming of the Shrew;* all from Middle English *soden* sudden. The phrase *all of a sudden* is first found in 1681.

suds *n.pl.* soapy water. 1548 *suddes* dregs, leavings, muck, of uncertain origin; sometimes thought to be borrowed from Middle Dutch *sudse, sudde* (early modern Dutch *zudse*) marsh, bog, cognate with Old English *soden,* past participle of *sēothan* to SEETHE, but the semantics are very much against such a borrowing. The extended meaning of soapy water is found in 1581. **—sudser** *n. Slang.* soap opera. 1968, American English; formed from (soap) *suds* + *-er*[1], perhaps patterned on earlier slang *soaper* (1946). **—sudsy** *adj.* soapy. 1884, formed from English *suds* + *-y*[1].

sue *v.* start a lawsuit against. Probably before 1200 *sewen* continue, persevere; borrowed through Anglo-French *suer, siwer* follow after, continue, from Old French *sivre, siuvre,* later *suivre* pursue, follow after, from Vulgar Latin **sequere* follow, from Latin *sequī* follow; see SEQUEL. Compare PURSUE. The sense of prosecute (a legal action), start a lawsuit against, is first recorded in Middle English about 1300.

suede or **suède** (swād) *n.* leather with a velvety nap. 1884 *Suède gloves,* borrowing of French *Suède* Sweden, in the partial translation of the French phrase *gants de Suède* gloves of Sweden. The transferred sense of any material or color like that of Suède gloves is first recorded in 1888.

suet (sü′it) *n.* hard fat about the kidneys and loins of cattle or sheep. Before 1325 *swete;* later *suet* (1375); probably borrowed from Anglo-French **suet,* an accusative analogically formed to *sius,* the nominative of *sue, seu* tallow, grease, variant of Old French *sieu* tallow (modern French *suif*), from Latin *sēbum;* see SEBACEOUS.

suf- a form of the prefix *sub-* before *f* in some words of Latin origin, as in *suffix, suffuse.* Formed in Latin by assimilation of *b* to the following consonant (*f*).

suffer *v.* Probably before 1200 *suffren* to undergo or endure (pain, death, etc.), in *Ancrene Riwle;* borrowed through Anglo-French *suffrir,* from Old French *sufrir,* *soffrir,* from Vulgar Latin **sufferīre,* variant of Latin *sufferre* to bear, undergo, endure, carry or put under (*suf-* up, under, variant of *sub-* before *f* + *ferre* to carry, BEAR[2]). The sense of allow, permit, tolerate, is first recorded about 1300. **—sufferance** *n.* Probably before 1300 *suffraunce* patient endurance, forbearance, in *Kyng Alisaunder;* borrowed through Anglo-French *suffrance, soffrance,* from Old French *sufrance,* from Late Latin *sufferentia* endurance, toleration, from Latin *sufferēns,* present participle of *sufferre* to suffer; for suffix see -ANCE. The meaning of consent implied by lack of interference is recorded as early as 1303.

suffice *v.* Before 1325 *suffisen* to be enough or adequate; borrowed from Old French *suffis-,* stem of *suffire* be sufficient, from Latin *sufficere* supply, suffice (*suf-* up to, variant of *sub-* before *f* + the root of *facere* to make, perform, DO[1]). **—sufficiency** *n.* 1495, sufficient means or wealth; 1565, condition or fact of being sufficient; borrowed from Latin *sufficientia* adequacy, from *sufficiēns,* present participle of *sufficere* supply, be enough; see SUFFICE; for suffix see -ENCY. **—sufficient** *adj.* enough. 1322, legally satisfactory; later, enough for a purpose (about 1380); borrowed through Old French *sufficient,* and directly from Latin *sufficientem* (nominative *sufficiēns*), present participle of *sufficere* suffice; for suffix see -ENT.

suffix *n.* affix put at the end of a word. 1778, borrowed from New Latin *suffixum,* noun use of neuter of Latin *suffixus* fastened, past participle of *suffigere* fasten below, fasten, fix on (*suf-* upon, variant of *sub-* before *f* + *figere* fasten, fix; see DIKE). **—v.** 1604, to fix or place under, in Robert Cawdrey's *A Table Alphabeticall;* borrowed from Latin *suffixus,* past participle of *suffigere* fasten, fix on. The meaning of add as a suffix is first recorded in 1778; from the noun.

suffocate *v.* 1599, kill by stopping the breath, choke, stifle; probably a back formation from earlier *suffocation,* modeled on Latin *suffōcātus,* past participle of *suffōcāre,* originally, to narrow up (*suf-* up, variant of *sub-* before *f* + *faucēs,* pl., throat, narrow entrance, of uncertain origin); for suffix see -ATE[1]. **—suffocation** *n.* act of suffocating or condition of being suffocated. Before 1400 *suffocacioun,* in Lanfranc's *Science of Surgery;* borrowed from Old French *suffocation,* and directly from Latin *suffōcātiōnem* (nominative *suffōcātiō*) a choking, stifling, from *suffōcāre* suffocate; for suffix see -ATION.

suffragan (suf′rəgən) *n.* bishop consecrated to assist another bishop. Before 1387, in Trevisa's translation of Higden's *Polychronicon;* borrowed through Anglo-French and Old French *suffragan,* from Medieval Latin *suffraganeus* assisting, supporting, from Latin *suffrāgium* support, approval, SUFFRAGE; for suffix see -AN.

suffrage *n.* Probably before 1200 *suffragie* prayers or pleas on behalf of another, interceding prayers, in *Ancrene Riwle;* later *suffrage* (before 1400); borrowed from Old French *suffrage,* and directly from Medieval Latin *suffragium,* from Latin *suffrāgium* expression of support or approval, recommendation, vote, the right of voting, from *suffrāgārī* to express or lend support, vote for someone (*suf-* under, near, variant of *sub-* before *f* + *fragor* a noise of breaking, crash, din, outbreak of shouts, as of approval by a crowd, related to *frangere* to BREAK). Until the early 1500's, *suffrage* in English had the religious or liturgical meaning of prayers on behalf of another; then, by 1534, English acquired the classical Latin meaning of a vote of assent or approval, and later the sense of the collective vote of a body of persons (1610), especially in the phrase *universal suffrage* (1798). The meaning of the right of voting as a member of a body or as a citizen of a nation or state is first found in the United States Constitution (1787): "No State. . .shall be deprived of its equal Suffrage in the Senate." **—suffragette** *n.* woman supporter of the right of women to vote in elections. 1906, formed from English *suffrage* + *-ette.* **—suffragist** *n.* person who favors the extension of suffrage, especially (after 1885) to women. 1822, formed from English *suffrage* + *-ist.*

suffuse *v.* to overspread with a liquid, dye, etc. 1590, in Spenser's *Faerie Queene* (implied in *suffused*); probably, in part a back formation from earlier *suffusion,* and in part borrowed from Latin *suffūsus,* past participle of *suffundere* pour underneath or upon, overspread, suffuse (*suf-* under, variant of *sub-* before *f* + *fundere* pour, melt, cast, FOUND[2]). **—suffusion** *n.* act of suffusing or condition of being suffused. Before 1398 *suffusioun,* in Trevisa's translation of Bartholomew's *De Proprietatibus Rerum;* borrowed from Latin *suffūsiōnem* (nominative *suffūsiō*) a pouring out or over, spreading, from *suffūs-,* past participle stem of *suffundere* suffuse; for suffix see -SION.

sug- a form of the prefix *sub-* before *g* in some words of Latin origin, as in *suggest.* Formed in Latin by assimilation of *b* to the following consonant (*g*).

sugar *n.* About 1325 *sucre;* later *sugure* (1381), *sugre* (1393); borrowed from Old French *sucre, sukere* sugar, from Medieval Latin *succarum,* from Arabic *sukkar,* from Persian *shakar,* from Sanskrit *śárkarā* ground or candied sugar; originally, gravel, grit. Compare SACCHARINE and modern use in SUCROSE. The Arabic variant (with prefixed article) *assukar* gave Spanish *azúcar* and Portuguese *açúcar.* Variations of the word are found in most European languages: Middle Low German and Middle Dutch *sucker* (modern Dutch *suiker*), Old High German *zucura* (modern German *Zucker*), Norwegian and Danish *sukker,* Swedish *socker,* Polish *cukier,* Hungarian *cukor,* etc.

The sound represented by *g* in the spelling of *sugar* (Middle English *sugure, sugre*) cannot be accounted for by any known Old French form. However, a similar change shown in Old French *segrestein,* variant of *secrestein* (see SEXTON and SACRISTAN) and in Middle English *flagon* representing Middle and Old French *flacon* suggests that voiced and voiceless variants already existed in the pronunciation of the French words. The shift in the pronunciation of *sugar* (from a sound represented by *s* to *sh*) apparently resulted from an original initial long vowel sound *syü-* like that of the original vowel in *sure* and *assure,* with the shortening of the vowel from *ü* (as in *move*) to *u̇* (as in *put*) taking place after the change in the initial consonant sound. Thus syü′gər became shü′gər, and finally shu̇g′ər.

—v. sweeten with sugar. About 1385 *sugren,* (figurative) to make pleasing; from the noun. The literal sense of add sugar to a substance is found in Middle English before 1475.

—sugar beet (1817) **—sugar cane** (1568) **—sugar-coat** *v.* (1870, coat with sugar; 1910, make acceptable or palatable) **—sugarless** *adj.* (1785, in Cowper's writings) **—sugar maple** (1731, American English) **—sugarplum** *n.* piece of candy (before 1668). **—sugary** *adj.* 1591, deceitfully or flatteringly pleasant; 1597, full of sugar; formed from English *sugar,* n. + *-y*[1].

suggest *v.* 1526, bring to mind or prompt the thought of (originally, something bad or evil), put forward the notion, opinion, or proposition (followed by *that*); back formation from *suggestion,* modeled on Latin *suggestus,* past participle of *suggerere* suggest, supply, bring up (*sug-* up, variant of *sub-* before *g* + *gerere* bring, carry; see GESTURE). **—suggestible** *adj.* capable of being influenced by suggestion. 1890, formed from English *suggest* + *-ible.* **—suggestion** *n.* About 1340 *suggestyn* a prompting to evil; later *sugestyoun* act of prompting, proposal (before 1382, in the Wycliffe Bible); borrowed through Anglo-French and Old French *suggestioun,* learned borrowing from Latin, and borrowed into English directly from Latin *suggestiōnem* (nominative *suggestiō*) an addition, intimation, suggestion, from *suggerere* suggest, supply; for suffix see -TION. **—suggestive** *adj.* 1631, conveying a suggestion or hint; probably formed in English from *suggest* + *-ive.* The meaning of tending to suggest something improper or indecent is recorded only since 1889 but is reminiscent of the original pejorative sense of the verb *suggest.*

suicide[1] *n.* deliberate killing of oneself. 1651, borrowed from New Latin *suicidium* suicide (Latin *suī* of oneself, genitive of *sē* self + *-cīdium* a killing; see -CIDE[2]). Latin *sē* is related to *suus* his, and cognate with Greek (accusative) *he* himself, *heós* one's own, Sanskrit *svá-s* one's own, and Old Slavic *svojĭ* his, one's own. Germanic cognates are found in Gothic *swēs* one's own, *seins* his, *sik* oneself, Old English *swǣs* one's own, *sīn* his, Old High German *sih* oneself (modern German *sich*), *sīn* his (modern German *sein*), and Old Icelandic *sik* oneself (Swedish and Danish *sig,* Norwegian *seg*). **—suicidal** *adj.* 1777, formed from English *suicide*[1] + *-al*[1].

suicide[2] *n.* person who kills himself deliberately. 1728, borrowed from New Latin *suicida* a suicide (Latin *suī* of oneself + *-cīda* killer, -cide[1]); see SUICIDE[1].

suit (süt) *n.* Probably before 1300 *sout* attendance at a court or the company attending; also, their livery or uniform, in *Arthour and Merlin;* and in the spelling *siwte* (about 1300); borrowed through Anglo-French *siwte, suite,* from Old French *suitte, sieute* attendance, act of following, from Gallo-Romance **sequita,* feminine of **sequitus,* replacing Latin *secūtus,* past participle of *sequī* to attend, follow; see SEQUEL. The meaning of an application to a court for justice, lawsuit, is first recorded in Middle English about 1412. The sense of a set of clothes to be worn together is probably first recorded before 1400, developing from the earlier meaning of court clothes that are a livery or uniform; a related sense of a set of playing cards bearing the same symbol is first recorded in 1529, probably used figuratively in Latimer's sermons. The meaning of bathing suit is first attested in 1883. **—v.** Probably about 1450 *suyten* do attendance at court, from the noun. The meaning of be agreeable, convenient, or acceptable to, is first recorded before 1578, probably from the earlier sense of provide with a suit of clothes (1577, now found usually in *suit up*). **—suitable** *adj.* 1582, (but implied earlier in *suitably,* 1577) matching; formed from English *suit,* v. + *-able.* The meaning of fitting, appropriate, is first recorded in Shakespeare's *Timon of Athens* (1607). **—suitcase** *n.* (1902) **—suitor** *n.* About 1290 *syutor* frequent visitor; later *suter* adherent, follower (before 1382, in the Wycliffe Bible); borrowed from Anglo-French *seutor, suitour, suter,* from Latin *secūtōrem* (nominative *secūtor*) attendant, follower, from *secūt-,* past participle stem of *sequī* to attend, follow; for suffix see -OR[2]. The meaning of a man who is courting a woman is first recorded in Sidney's *The Arcadia* (before 1586).

suite (swēt) *n.* connected series of rooms. 1673, train of followers or attendants, in Dryden's *Marriage-à-la-Mode;* borrowing of French *suite,* from Old French *suitte,* earlier *sieute* act of following, attendance, SUIT. The pronunciation of this word in English is taken from the French. The meaning of a connected series of rooms is first recorded in English in letters of Lady Montagu (1716), borrowed from French. The meaning of a set of furniture of the same pattern is first recorded in 1805. The musical sense of a set of instrumental compositions to be played in succession is first attested in 1760; though the sense is recorded earlier in the form *suit* (1682).

sukiyaki (sůkēyä'kē) *n.* Japanese dish of thin strips of meat fried with vegetables. 1920, borrowing of Japanese *sukiyaki* (*suki* spade + *yaki* roasting).

sulfate or **sulphate** *n.* salt or ester of sulfuric acid. 1790 *sulphat,* borrowed from French *sulphate,* learned borrowing from New Latin *sulphatum acidum,* from Latin *sulpur, sulphur* SULFUR; for suffix see -ATE[2]. The spelling *sulphate* appeared in English in 1794 and *sulfate* in 1809.

sulfur or **sulphur** *n.* nonmetallic chemical element that burns with a blue flame and a stifling odor, brimstone. About 1380 *soulfre,* in Chaucer's *House of Fame,* later *sulfur* (probably before 1425); borrowed through Old French *soufre* and Anglo-French *sulfre,* from Late Latin *sulfur,* from Latin *sulpur, sulphur,* perhaps from a Mediterranean language. **—sulfuric** or **sulphuric** *adj.* 1790 *sulphuric* of or derived from sulfur; formed from English *sulphur* + *-ic,* after French *sulfurique,* from Late Latin *sulfur* + French *-ique* -ic. The spelling *sulfuric* is first recorded in 1893. **—sulfurous** or **sulphurous** *adj.* 1530 *sulpherus* of sulfur, in Palsgrave's *Lesclarcissement;* formed from English *sulphur* + *ous,* after Middle French *sulphureux,* or after Latin *sulphurōsus.* The sense of hellish is first recorded in Shakespeare's *Hamlet* (1602, *sulphurous*). The spelling *sulfurous* is first attested in 1635.

sulk *v.* be moody or sullen. 1781, back formation from SULKY[1]. **—n.** a sulking. 1792, from the verb.

sulky[1] *adj.* keeping aloof from others in moody silence, sullen. 1744, possibly an alteration of earlier *sulke* slow in going off, sluggish (1636); probably developed from Old English *āsolcen* idle, lazy, slow, from past participle of *āseolcan* become sluggish, be languid, weak, or idle; for suffix see -Y[1]. Old English *āseolcan* is related to *besylcan* be languid, and cognate with Middle High German *selken* to drip, drop, sink (from Proto-Germanic **selkanan*), and probably with Sanskrit *sṛjáti* (he) releases, shoots, pours (compare *sṛjáti śúnas* he releases the dogs), Old Irish *selg* hunt(ing), and Welsh *hela* hunting, from Indo-European **selĝ-* let loose, pour out (Pok.900).

sulky[2] *n.* light carriage with two wheels. 1756, apparently a noun use of SULKY[1]; so called because the carriage has room for only one person.

sullen *adj.* 1577, unsociable, gloomy, morose; earlier *sollen* (1573), alteration of Middle English *soleyn* unique, singular (1369, in Chaucer's *Dethe of Blaun-*

che); borrowed from Anglo-French **solein, *solain,* probably formed on the pattern of Old French *soltain, soutain* (Vulgar Latin **sōlitānus*) from Old French *soul, sol* single, SOLE[2] + *-ein, -ain* -an. In Chaucer's *Parlement of Foules* (about 1380) *soleyn* meant all alone, solitary, and by about 1399 it is recorded in the sense of averse to society, unfriendly, morose, sullen.

sully *v.* to soil, stain, tarnish. 1591, in Shakespeare's *1 Henry VI;* probably borrowed from Middle French *souiller,* from Old French *souillier* make dirty, SOIL[1].

sultan *n.* ruler of a Moslem country. 1555, borrowed from Middle French *sultan* ruler of Turkey, from Arabic *sulṭān* ruler, power, from Aramaic *šulṭāna,* from *šalaṭ* he ruled. **—sultanate** *n.* 1822 *sultanat* (1879 *sultanate*) territory ruled over by a sultan; later, office or authority of a sultan (1884); formed from English *sultan* + *-ate*[3].

sultry *adj.* 1594, oppressively hot, close, and moist; developed from earlier *sulter* to swelter (1581), alteration of SWELTER; for suffix see -Y[1]. The figurative sense of characterized by the heat of temper or passion, hot with anger or lust, is found in Milton's *Samson Agonistes* (1671).

sum *n.* About 1300 *summe* quantity, amount; borrowed through Anglo-French and Old French *summe, somme,* from Latin *summa* total number or amount, totality, whole, essence, gist, noun use of the feminine form of *summus* highest (earlier **supmos*), related to *super* OVER. *The use in Latin of a word meaning "highest" to mean "sum" probably derived from the Roman practice of writing the sum of a column of figures at the top rather than the bottom; compare the English expression the bottom line.* **—v.** Before 1325 *sumen* to count up, find the sum of, in *Cursor Mundi;* borrowed from Old French *summer, sommer,* from Late Latin *summāre* sum up, from Latin *summa* sum. The figurative sense of give the substance or gist of, summarize, epitomize, is found in Middle English before 1398, and the phrase *to sum up,* meaning to recapitulate (evidence) to a jury, is recorded before 1700, in Evelyn's *Diary.*

sum- a form of the prefix *sub-* before *m* in some words of Latin origin, as in *summon.* Formed in Latin by assimilation of *b* to the following consonant (*m*).

sumac or **sumach** (sü′mak) *n.* kind of shrub or small tree. Before 1400 *sumac* preparation made from the dried leaves and shoots of the sumac, in Lanfranc's *Science of Surgery;* borrowed from Old French *sumac,* from Medieval Latin *sumach,* from Arabic *summāq.* The shrub itself was first called *sumac* in 1548. The spelling *sumach* is also found in English in 1548. **—poison sumac** shrub that causes a rash like that of poison ivy (1817, American English).

summary *adj.* covering the main points. Probably before 1425, in a translation of Higden's *Polychronicon;* borrowed from Medieval Latin *summarius* of or pertaining to the sum or substance, from Latin *summa* whole, totality, gist, SUM; for suffix see -ARY. The sense of done without delay, direct, prompt, is first found in Swift's *Cadenus and Vanessa* (1713). **—n.** brief statement covering the main points. 1509, borrowed from Latin *summārium* an epitome, abstract, summary, from *summa* totality, gist, sum; for suffix see -ARY. **—summarize** *v.* 1871, formed from English *summary* + *-ize.*

summation *n.* 1760, process of finding the sum of a series; borrowed from New Latin *summationem* (nominative *summatio*) an adding up, from Late Latin *summāre* to sum up, from Latin *summa* SUM; for suffix see -ATION. The meaning of an adding up, recapitulating, or summing up is first recorded in English in Bulwer-Lytton's *Athens* (1836).

summer *n.* Before 1121 *sumer,* in *Peterborough Chronicle;* developed from Old English (before 830) *sumor;* cognate with Old Frisian *sumur* summer, Old Saxon *sumar, somer* (modern Dutch *zomer*), Old High German *sumar* (modern German *Sommer*), and Old Icelandic *sumar* (Swedish *sommar,* Norwegian and Danish *sommer*), from Proto-Germanic **sumur-.* Cognates outside Germanic are found in Old Irish *sam* summer, Welsh and Cornish *haf,* Armenian *am* year, *amaṙn* summer, Avestan *ham-* summer, and Sanskrit *sámā* half year, year, season, from Indo-European **semā, semer-* (Pok.905). **—v.** pass the summer. 1440 *somoren,* in *Promptorium Parvulorum;* from the noun. **—summerhouse** *n.* structure to provide shade in a garden or park (about 1440, in Palladius' *On Husbondrie*). **—summertime** *n.* (about 1378, in a version of *Piers Plowman*) **—summery** *adj.* like summer. 1824, in Lamb's *Letters;* formed from English *summer,* n. + *-y*[1].

summit *n.* Before 1400 *somet* highest point, peak; borrowed from Middle French *somete,* from Old French *sommette,* diminutive of *som, sum* highest part, top of a hill, from Latin *summum,* noun use of neuter of *summus* highest, related to *super* OVER. The sense of the highest political level is first recorded in 1950, followed by the sense of a meeting between heads of state, in 1955. **—adj.** of or designating a meeting between heads of state. 1955, from the noun. **—summiteer** *n.* participant in a summit meeting. 1957, formed from English *summit,* adj. or n. + *-eer.* **—summitry** *n.* the conducting of summit meetings. 1958, formed from English *summit,* adj. or n. + *-ry.*

summon *v.* to call with authority. Probably before 1200 *sumunen,* in Layamon's *Chronicle of Britain;* borrowed from Anglo-French and Old French *sumundre, somondre* summon, from Vulgar Latin **summonere* to call, cite, variant of Latin *summonēre* hint to (*sum-* under, variant of *sub-* before *m* + *monēre* warn, advise; see MONITOR). **—summons** *n.* an order to appear at a certain place, especially in a law court. Probably about 1280 *somnes;* later *somunce, somounz* (about 1300); borrowed from Anglo-French and Old French *sumunse, soumonse,* noun use of feminine past participle of *somondre* to SUMMON.

sumo (sü′mō) *n.* Japanese form of wrestling. 1893, borrowing of Japanese *sumō* wrestling.

sump *n.* pit or reservoir for collecting water, oil, etc. Before 1450 *sompe* marsh, morass; earlier in the place name *Brunes Sumpe* (1241); borrowed from Middle Dutch *somp* or Middle Low German *sump,* from Proto-Germanic **sumpaz.* These forms are cognate with Middle High German *sumpf* swamp (modern German *Sumpf*), from Indo-European **swm̥bos,* related to **swombu-* SWAMP. The sense of a pit sunk to collect water, especially one at the bottom of a mine shaft is found in English in 1653.

sumpter *n.* horse or mule for carrying baggage. Probably before 1300 *sumter* driver of a pack horse, in *Kyng Alisaunder;* earlier in the surname *Le Summeter* (1206); also, *sompterhors* (about 1450); borrowed from Old French *sommetier,* from Vulgar Latin **sagmatāri-*

us a pack horse driver, from Late Latin *sagmat-* a pack, burden, stem of *sagma* packsaddle, from Greek *ságma,* probably related to *sáttein* (earlier **twakye-*) to pack, press, stuff, cognate with Tocharian *twank-* to force together, from Indo-European **twak-* (Pok.1098); for suffix see -ER[1]. The sense of a horse or mule for carrying loads or packs is first recorded in English in 1570.

sumptuary *adj.* having to do with the spending of money, regulating expenses. 1600, borrowed from Latin *sūmptuārius* relating to expenses, from *sūmptus* expense; see SUMPTUOUS; for suffix see -ARY.

sumptuous *adj.* luxuriously fine or elegant. About 1410 *sumptous;* later *sumptuous* (1472-73); borrowed probably by influence of Middle French *sumptueux,* from Latin *sūmptuōsus* costly, expensive, from *sūmptus* (genitive *sūmptūs*) cost, expense, from *sūmere* spend, procure, take; see ASSUME; for suffix see -OUS.

sun *n.* Before 1325 *sun,* in *Cursor Mundi;* developed from Old English *sunne* (about 725, in *Beowulf*); cognate with Old Frisian *sunne, sonne* sun, Old Saxon *sunna,* Middle Dutch *sonne* (modern Dutch *zon*), Old High German *sunna* (modern German *Sonne*), Old Icelandic *sunna,* and Gothic *sunnō,* from Proto-Germanic **sunnōn.* A cognate outside Germanic is found in Avestan *xvəng* of the sun, though ultimately the word is also cognate with Latin *sōl* and related words; see SOLAR. Also possibly related to SOUTH. **—v.** expose to the sun's rays. 1519 (implied in *sunning*); from the noun. **—sunbath** *n.* exposure to the sun (1866). **—sunbathe** *v.* (1600, implied in *sunbathing*) **—sunbeam** *n.* (about 1000, in Ælfric's *Lives of Saints*) **—sunburn** *n.* (1652); *v.* 1530, in Palsgrave's *Lesclarcissement;* back formation from *sunburnt* (about 1400 *sunne y-brent*) **—sundeck** *n.* (1897, upper deck of a ship; 1950, terrace, porch, etc., used for sunbathing) **—sundial** *n.* (1599) **—sundown** *n.* (1620) **—sunfish** *n.* (1629, large, round marine fish; 1685, American English, small North American freshwater fish) **—sunflower** *n.* tall plant with large yellow flowers (1597). **—sunglasses** *n.pl.* (1927) **—sunlight** *n.* (probably before 1200, in Layamon's *Chronicle of Britain*) **—sunny** *adj.* Before 1325, in *Cursor Mundi;* formed from Middle English *sun,* n. + *-y*[1]. **—sunrise** *n.* (1440, in *Promptorium Parvulorum*) **—sunset** *n.* Before 1393, in Gower's *Confessio Amantis;* either formed from Middle English *sun* sun + *set,* n., or formed like *sunrise,* the element *set* being originally a verb in the subjunctive mood, as in a clause like *ere the sun set.* **—sunshine** *n.* (1535, in the Coverdale Bible; an isolated Middle English instance occurs in *Genesis and Exodus,* about 1250, as *sunnesine*) **—sunspot** *n.* dark patch on the surface of the sun (1868). **—sunstroke** *n.* (1851, translation of French *coup de soleil*) **—suntan** *n.* (1904) **—sunup** *n.* sunrise (1712, American English)

sundae (sun′dē) *n.* portion of ice cream covered with syrup, fruit, nuts, etc. 1897, American English, thought to be an alteration of SUNDAY; the reason for the name is uncertain. According to some accounts, it was so called because it was originally sold on Sunday only, and the spelling was altered out of deference to religious people's feelings about the word *Sunday.* For various possible explanations, see H.L. Mencken's *The American Language,* Supplement I (1945), pages 376-77.

Sunday *n.* About 1250 *sunedai,* in *Genesis and Exodus;* developed from Old English (before 700) *Sunnandæg,* literally, day of the sun (*sunnan,* oblique case of *sunne* SUN + *dæg* DAY). Old English *Sunnandæg* corresponds to Old Frisian *sunnandei* Sunday, Old Saxon *sunnundag,* Middle Dutch *sonnendach* (modern Dutch *zondag*), Old High German *sunnūn tag* (modern German *Sonntag*), and Old Icelandic *sunnudagr* (Norwegian and Danish *søndag,* Swedish *söndag*). The Germanic compounds are each a loan translation of Latin *diēs sōlis* day of the sun, which in turn was a loan translation of Greek *hēmérā hēlíou.* **—Sunday school** (1783)

sunder *v.* separate, sever, split. Probably before 1200 *sundren,* in *Ancrene Riwle;* developed from Old English *sundrian* (about 950, in *Lindisfarne Gospels*), earlier *āsyndrian, gesyndrian, āsundrian (ā-* intensive prefix, *ge-* perfective prefix + *sundor* separately, apart). Old English *sundor* is cognate with Old Frisian *sunder* apart, Old Saxon *sundar,* Middle Dutch and modern Dutch *zonder* without, Old High German *suntar* aside, apart (archaic German *sonder* without), Old Icelandic *sundr* (Danish *sønder,* Swedish *sönder,* Norwegian *sund*), from Proto-Germanic **sunđér,* and Gothic *sundrō.* Cognates outside Germanic include Aeolic Greek *áter* without, apart from (earlier **hatér*), from Indo-European **sn̥-tér,* Sanskrit *sanutár* far away, from Indo-European **senu-* by itself + suffix *-tér;* Latin *sine* without, from Indo-European **seni-,* source of Old Irish *sain* different; and Tocharian A *sne,* Tocharian B *snai* without (Pok.907). A similar development is found in Old High German *suntarōn* (modern German *sondern*) to sunder, from *suntar,* adj.

sundry *adj.* several, various. Probably before 1200 *sundri* distinct, separate, several, in Layamon's *Chronicle of Britain;* developed from Old English *syndrig* separate, special (before 899, in Alfred's translation of Bede's *Ecclesiastical History*), related to *sundor* separately, apart; see SUNDER; for suffix see -Y[1]. Old English *syndrig* corresponds to Middle Low German *sunderich* single, special, and Old High German *suntarig.* **—n.** About 1250 *sundri* various ones; from the adjective. The expression *all and sundry* everybody of all classes, one and all, is first recorded in Middle English in 1389. The plural *sundries* sundry things, odds and ends, is found in Henry Fielding's *Voyage to Lisbon* (1755); formed from English *sundry,* adj. (taken as a noun) + *-s*[1], plural suffix. Compare *odds* for a similar formation.

sup[1] *v.* eat the evening meal. About 1300 *supen, soupen,* in *Havelok the Dane;* borrowed from Old French *super, soper, souper,* from *soupe* broth, SOUP[1].

sup[2] *v.* to sip. Probably before 1300 *soupen;* later *suppen* (before 1325); developed from Old English *sūpan* to sip, swallow (West Saxon, before 899, in Alfred's translation of St. Gregory's *Pastoral Care*), *suppan, sūpian* (Northumbrian). Old English *sūpan* is cognate with Middle Low German *sūpen* to sup, Middle Dutch *zūpen* (modern Dutch *zuipen* drink too much), Old High German *sūfan* (modern German *saufen* drink like an animal), and Old Icelandic *sūpa* to drink, from Proto-Germanic **sūpanan,* from Indo-European **sūb-,* root **seub-* (Pok.913); compare also Sanskrit *sū́pa-s* broth, soup.

sup- a form of the prefix *sub-* before *p* in words of Latin origin, as in *suppress.* Formed in Latin by assimilation of *b* to the following consonant (*p*).

super[1] *n. Informal.* superintendent. 1857, shortened form of SUPERINTENDENT, in the sense of an overseer, especially on a sheep ranch or station in Australia.

super[2] *adj.* first-rate, excellent. 1842, of superlative quality (implied earlier in *extra-super,* 1837, in Dickens' *Pickwick Papers*); developed after SUPER-.

super- a prefix meaning: **1** over; above, as in *superimpose = impose over or above.* **2** besides; further, as in *superadd = to add besides or further.* **3** in high proportion; to excess; exceedingly, as in *superabundant = abundant to excess.* **4** surpassing, as in *supernatural = surpassing the natural.* Borrowed from Latin *super-,* from adverb and preposition *super* above, OVER.

superable *adj.* that can be overcome, surmountable. 1629, in Hobbes' translation of Thucydides' *Eight Books of the Peloponnesian War;* borrowed from Latin *superābilis* that may be surmounted, from *superāre* to overcome, from *super* OVER; for suffix see -ABLE. The word's use was probably influenced by, or perhaps even a back formation of, the earlier English adjective *insuperable* incapable of being surmounted, unconquerable, unsurpassing, found in Middle English before 1398, in Trevisa's translation of Bartholomew's *De Proprietatibus Rerum. Insuperable* was borrowed from Latin *īnsuperābilis* (*in-* not + *superābilis* surmountable).

superannuate (süpəran'yüāt) *v.* retire on a pension. 1649, render old or obsolete; back formation from earlier *superannuated* obsolete, out of date (before 1633), formed in English from Medieval Latin *superannuatus* (of cattle) more than a year old + English suffix *-ed*[2]. Medieval Latin *superannuatus* is formed from Latin *super* beyond, OVER + *annus* year (see ANNUAL); for suffix see -ATE[1]. The extended meaning of dismiss from an official position on account of age, cause to retire on a pension, is found in English in 1692. **—superannuation** *n.* 1658, condition of being obsolete, in Phillips' *Dictionary;* later, act of retiring an official (before 1704); formed from English *superannuate* + *-ation.*

superb *adj.* 1549, imposing, of magnificent proportions; borrowed from Latin *superbus* grand, proud, sumptuous, from *super* above, OVER. Latin *superbus* is from Indo-European **(s)uper-bhwos,* as Greek *hyperphyḗs* extraordinary is from **uper-bhuwḗs,* each compound containing Indo-European **bhu-/bhuw-,* root **bheu-* to BE (Pok.146). The sense of very fine, splendid, magnificent, is found in English before 1729, in Congreve's *An Impossible Thing.*

supercilious *adj.* haughty. Before 1529 (implied in *superciliously*); borrowed from Latin *superciliōsus* haughty, arrogant, from *supercilium* haughty demeanor, pride; originally, eyebrow, the eyebrow as used to express sternness or haughtiness (*super-* above + **celyom* a cover, related to *cēlāre* to cover, conceal, hide; see CELL); for suffix see -OUS.

superego *n. Psychoanalysis.* part of the psyche that determines right or wrong conduct. 1924 (in a translation of Freud's collected papers by J. Riviere and others); formed from English *super-* + *ego,* as a translation of German *Über-Ich,* coined by Sigmund Freud.

supererogation (sü'pərer'əgā'shən) *n.* the doing of more than duty requires. 1526, borrowed from Late Latin *superērogātiōnem* (nominative *superērogātiō*) a payment in addition, from *superērogāre* pay or do additionally, formed from Latin *super-* above, over + *ērogāre* pay out (*ē-* out, form of *ex-* before *r* + *rogāre* ask, request; see RIGHT); for suffix see -ATION.

superficial *adj.* 1392, of or relating to a surface, external; borrowed, perhaps by influence of Old French *superficiel,* from Latin *superficiālis* of or pertaining to the surface, from *superficiēs* surface (*super-* above, over + *faciēs* form, FACE); for suffix see -AL[1]. The meaning of concerned only with what is on the surface, not deep or thorough, is first recorded in Middle English about 1456. **—superficiality** *n.* 1530, superficial condition or quality, in Palsgrave's *Lesclarcissement;* formed from English *superficial* + *-ity.*

superfluous *adj.* exceeding what is needed, redundant. Before 1398 *superfluus,* in Trevisa's translation of Bartholomew's *De Proprietatibus Rerum;* later *superfluous* (in a translation of Higden's *Polychronicon*); borrowed, probably by influence of Old French *superflueux,* from Latin *superfluus* overflowing, unnecessary, from *superfluere* to overflow (*super-* over + *fluere* to flow; see FLUENT); for suffix see -OUS. **—superfluity** *n.* Before 1387 *superfluyte* excess, overflowing supply, in Trevisa's translation of Higden's *Polychronicon;* borrowed from Old French *superfluite,* and directly from Late Latin *superfluitās* that which is superfluous or unnecessary, from Latin *superfluus* superfluous; for suffix see -ITY.

superintend *v.* oversee, manage, supervise. About 1615, in writings of Francis Bacon; borrowed from Late Latin *superintendere* oversee (Latin *super-* above + *intendere* turn one's attention, direct, INTEND). It is also probable that in some instances *superintend* is a back formation of earlier *superintendent.* **—superintendent** *n.* person who superintends. 1554, bishop; 1560, Protestant minister who supervises churches within a district; borrowed from Medieval Latin *superintendentem* (nominative *superintendens*), from present participle of Late Latin *superintendere* to superintend; for suffix see -ENT. The ecclesiastical senses are a loan translation of Greek *epískopos* overseer; see BISHOP. The general sense of a person who superintends is first recorded in 1588. The specific meaning of the janitor or custodian of a building is first recorded about 1935 in American English, but the general sense of an overseer is found earlier in *super* (1857).

superior *adj.* higher in position or rank. Before 1393 *superiour,* in Gower's *Confessio Amantis;* borrowed from Old French *superior, superiour,* from Latin *superior* higher, comparative form of *superus* situated above, upper, from *super* above, OVER. **—n.** person who is superior. Probably before 1425, in a translation of Higden's *Polychronicon;* from the adjective. **—superiority** *n.* About 1475 *superioryte* superior rank, dignity, or status; probably formed in English from *superior* + *-ity,* and in some instances, borrowed from Middle French *superiorité,* from Medieval Latin *superioritas,* from Latin *superior* superior; for suffix see -ITY.

superlative *adj.* About 1395 *superlatyf* (in grammar) expressing the highest degree of the quality described, in Chaucer's *Canterbury Tales;* borrowed from Old French *superlatif* (feminine) *superlative,* learned borrowing from Late Latin, and probably borrowed directly into English from Late Latin *superlātīvus* exaggerated, superlative, from Latin *superlātus,* used as past participle of *superferre* carry over or beyond, or to extremes (*super-* beyond + *ferre* carry, BEAR[2]); for suffix see -IVE. The meaning of supreme, above all others, is first recorded in Middle English, probably about 1408. **—n.** 1530, an adjective or adverb in the superlative degree, in Palsgrave's *Lesclarcissement;* from the adjective.

superman *n.* 1903, in George Bernard Shaw's *Man and*

Superman; borrowed as a loan translation of German *Übermensch,* literally, overman, coined by the German philosopher Nietzsche, in *Thus Spake Zarathustra* (1883-91). Nietzsche regarded Western civilization as decadent, and conceived of an ideal superior man (evolved from the normal human type) who would control the masses and initiate a new morality. German *Übermensch* has also been translated into English as *overman* (1895). The general sense of a man of extraordinary power or ability is found in 1925. The capitalized name *Superman,* referring to an invincible hero with superhuman powers, including the ability to fly, was introduced in an American comic strip in 1938.

supermarket *n.* 1933, American English; formed from English *super-* + *market.*

supernal (sùpėr'nəl) *adj.* heavenly, divine. 1447, borrowing of Middle French *supernal,* formed from Latin *supernus* situated above, celestial (from *super* above, OVER) + *-al* -al[1]; formed to contrast with *infernal.*

supernatural *adj.* Probably before 1425 *supernaturel;* later *supernatural* (about 1443); borrowed from Medieval Latin *supernaturalis* above or beyond nature (Latin *super-* above + *nātūra* NATURE); for suffix see -AL[1]. The Medieval Latin word is thought to have been coined by Saint Thomas Aquinas.

supernumerary *adj.* beyond the usual or necessary number, additional, extra. 1605, in Bacon's *Of the Advancement of Learning;* borrowed from Late Latin *supernumerārius* excessive in number (of soldiers added to a full legion), from Latin *super numerum* beyond the number (*super-* beyond, over + *numerum,* accusative of *numerus* NUMBER); for suffix see -ARY. **—n.** 1639, supernumerary person or thing; from the adjective.

superpower *n.* 1922, superior or extraordinary power, in D.H. Lawrence's *Aaron's Rod;* formed from English *super-* + *power.* The sense of a nation having an extremely powerful or dominant position in world politics is first recorded in 1944, in W.T.R. Fox's *Super-Powers.*

superscript *n.* 1588, address or direction on a letter, in Shakespeare's *Love's Labour's Lost;* borrowed from Middle French *superscript,* and directly from Latin *superscrīptus,* past participle of *superscrībere* write over or above something, especially as a correction (*super-* above + *scrībere* write; see SCRIBE). The meaning of a number, letter, etc., written above something, is first recorded in 1901. **—adj.** written above a word, line of writing, etc. 1882, from the noun.

supersede *v.* 1456 *superceden* to postpone, defer; Scottish, borrowed from Middle French *superceder,* later *superseder* desist, delay, defer, learned borrowing from Latin *supersedēre* sit on top of, stay clear of, abstain from; also, forbear, refrain from (*super-* above + *sedēre* SIT). The extended meaning of displace, replace, supplant, is first recorded in English in 1642. The spelling *supersede* is first attested in 1527.

supersonic *adj.* 1919, of or having to do with sound waves beyond the limit of human hearing; formed from English *super-* + Latin *sonus* SOUND + English *-ic.* The sense of exceeding the speed of sound, especially as a measure of aircraft speed, is first recorded in 1945. **—n.** a supersonic aircraft. 1962, from the adjective. **—supersonics** *n.* science of supersonic phenomena. 1928, formed from English *supersonic* + *-s*[1]; see also -ICS.

superstition *n.* Probably before 1200 *supersticiun* a false or irrational religious belief or practice, in *Ancrene Riwle;* borrowed from Middle French *superstition,* from Latin *superstitiōnem* (nominative *superstitiō*) excessive fear of the gods, unreasoning religious belief or awe, perhaps originally meaning a state of religious exaltation; related to *superstes* (genitive *superstitis*), earlier **superstats,* standing over or above, as in triumph; also, standing by, being present; also, surviving, remaining, from *superstāre* stand on or over, survive (*super* above + *stāre* STAND); for suffix see -TION. **—superstitious** *adj.* About 1395 *supersticious* characterized by superstition, in Chaucer's *Canterbury Tales;* borrowed, probably by influence of Old French *superstitieux,* from Latin *superstitiōsus* full of superstition, from *superstitiō* superstition; for suffix see -OUS.

supervene *v.* come as something additional or extraneous. 1647-48, borrowed, perhaps by influence of French *survenir,* from Latin *supervenīre* come on top of (*super-* upon, over + *venīre* COME). **—supervention** *n.* act of supervening, a coming on in addition. 1649, borrowed from Late Latin *superventiōnem* (nominative *superventiō*) a coming up, from Latin *supervent-,* past participle stem of *supervenīre* supervene; for suffix see -TION.

supervise *v.* Probably before 1475 *supervisen* oversee, inspect (implied in *supervysinge,* verbal noun); possibly a back formation from earlier *supervisor,* and probably borrowed from Medieval Latin *supervis-,* past participle stem of *supervidēre* oversee, inspect (Latin *super-* over + *vidēre* see; see WIT[2] know). **—supervision** *n.* 1623, act or function of supervising, in Shakespeare's *Othello;* probably formed from English *supervise* + *-ion,* possibly in some instances, on the model of Medieval Latin *supervisionem* (nominative *supervisio*), from *supervis-,* past participle stem of *supervidere* oversee, supervise. **—supervisor** *n.* About 1454, person who supervises; borrowed from Medieval Latin *supervisor,* from *supervis-,* past participle stem of *supervidere* oversee, supervise; for suffix see -OR[2]. **—supervisory** *adj.* 1847, formed from English *supervise* + *-ory.*

supine (süpīn') *adj.* lying flat on the back. About 1500, borrowed from Latin *supīnus* turned or thrown backward, going backward or downward; also, inactive, indolent, careless, related to *sub* under; see UP. **—n.** Latin verbal noun formed from the past participle stem. About 1450 *suppyn, supyn;* borrowed from Late Latin *supīnum verbum* supine verb, noun use of neuter of *supīnus,* adj., supine. The word was used particularly in Late Latin in reference to either verbal noun, in *-um* or *-ū, that was called supīnum,* perhaps because, although furnished with a noun case-ending, it rests or falls back on the verb.

supper *n.* About 1250 *sopere* the evening meal; later *supere, sopper* (before 1300); borrowed from Old French *super, soper* supper, noun use of *super, soper* to eat the evening meal; see SUP[1]; for suffix see -ER[3]. **—suppertime** *n.* (before 1376, in *Piers Plowman*)

supplant *v.* displace or set aside. Before 1325 (implied in *supplanter*) *supplanten* to trip up, overthrow, defeat, dispossess; borrowed from Old French *supplanter* to trip up, overthrow, from Latin *supplantāre* trip up, overthrow (*sup-* under, variant of *sub-* before *p* + *planta* sole of the foot; see PLACE). The meaning of displace or set aside, replace one thing with another, is first recorded in English in 1671, but the sense is found as early as 1608 in *supplantation.*

supple *adj.* About 1300 *souple* soft, not rigid; later, flexible, bending easily (about 1387-95); borrowed from Old French *souple, suple* pliant, flexible, easily bent, from Gallo-Romance **supples,* from Latin *supplex* submissive, bending, thought to be an altered form of **supplacos* humbly pleading or appeasing (*sup-* under, variant of *sub-* before *p* + *plācāre* appease; see PLACATE). **—v.** make supple. Before 1349 *souplen* soften, cause to yield or be submissive; from the adjective.

supplement *n.* About 1384, that which is added, addition, in the Wycliffe Bible; borrowed from Old French *supplement,* and directly from Latin *supplēmentum* something added to supply a deficiency, from *supplēre* to SUPPLY; for suffix see -MENT. **—v.** 1829, furnish a supplement to; from the noun. **—supplemental** *adj.* 1605, additional, in Bacon's *Of the Advancement of Learning;* formed from English *supplement,* n. + *-al*[1]. **—supplementary** *adj.* 1667, additional; formed from English *supplement,* n. + *-ary.*

suppliant (sup'lēənt) *n.* person who asks humbly and earnestly. 1429 *suppliaunt* petitioner at law, one who applies to an officer in a formal petition, in *Rolls of Parliament;* borrowed from Middle French *suppliant,* originally, present participle of *supplier* to plead humbly, entreat, beg, pray, from Latin *supplicāre* beg, beseech; see SUPPLICATE; for suffix see -ANT. The sense of a humble petitioner is first recorded in English in 1549-62, in a translation of *Psalms.* **—adj.** supplicating, humbly petitioning. Before 1586, in Sidney's *The Arcadia;* borrowed from Middle French *suppliant,* present participle of *supplier* to plead humbly. **—suppliance** *n.* supplication. 1611, in Chapman's translation of the *Iliad;* formed from English *suppliant,* adj. + *-ance.*

supplicant (sup'ləkənt) *n.* a suppliant. 1597, in writings of Richard Hooker; borrowed from Latin *supplicantem* (nominative *supplicāns*), present participle of *supplicāre* plead humbly; see SUPPLICATE; for suffix see -ANT. **—adj.** suppliant. 1597, in Shakespeare's *A Lover's Complaint;* borrowed from Latin *supplicantem* (nominative *supplicāns*), present participle of *supplicāre* to plead humbly.

supplicate *v.* plead humbly. 1417, probably, in part, a back formation from earlier *supplication,* and in part borrowed from Latin *supplicātus,* past participle of *supplicāre* plead humbly, beseech, beg, from *supplex* (genitive *supplicis*) submissive, bending, kneeling down; see SUPPLE; for suffix see -ATE[1]. **—supplication** *n.* About 1380 *supplicacion* prayer, in Chaucer's translation of Boethius' *De Consolatione Philosophiae;* later, an entreaty, plea (before 1393, in Gower's *Confessio Amantis*); borrowed from Old French *supplication,* from Latin *supplicātiōnem* (nominative *supplicātiō*), from *supplicāre* plead humbly; see SUPPLE; for suffix see -ATION.

supply *v.* 1375 *supplien* to help, support, maintain, in Barbour's *The Bruce;* later, fill up, make up for (before 1398); borrowed from Old French *supplier, soupleier, supleer* fill up, make full, and directly from Latin *supplēre* fill up, complete (*sup-* up, variant of *sub-* before *p* + *plēre* to fill; see FULL). The meaning of furnish, provide, is first recorded in English in Skelton's *Magnificence* (about 1520). **—n.** quantity supplied, act of supplying. 1423 *supplye* support, assistance; from the verb. The sense of an act of fulfilling a need or demand is first recorded in Dunbar's *Poems* (1500-20). The concrete sense of a quantity or amount of something supplied is first found in Shakespeare's *Timon of Athens* (1607). **—supply and demand** (1843, in writings of Carlyle)

support *v.* About 1384 *supporten* (figurative) to put up with, tolerate, in the Wycliffe Bible; borrowed from Old French *supporter,* learned borrowing from Latin, and probably borrowed into English directly from Latin *supportāre* convey, carry, bring up (*sup-* up, variant of *sub-* before *p* + *portāre* carry; see PORT[4] bearing). The meaning of sustain, supply with food or other necessities of life, is first recorded in Middle English before 1393, and that of hold up, prop up, probably before 1396. **—n.** act of supporting, person or thing that supports. About 1391, from the verb. **—supporter** *n.* (probably before 1425) **—supportive** *adj.* supporting, sustaining. 1593, formed from English *support,* v. + *-ive.*

suppose *v.* About 1303 *supposen* hold an opinion, assume, incline to think, in Mannyng's *Handlyng Synne;* borrowed from Old French *supposer* to assume (from Medieval Latin, to assume), probably a replacement of **suppondre* (by influence of Old French *poser* put or place; see POSE[1]) from Latin *suppōnere* put or place under (*sup-* under, variant of *sub-* before *p* + *pōnere* put, place; see POSITION). **—supposedly** *adv.* according to what is or was supposed. 1611, formed from earlier *supposed,* adj. + *-ly*[1]. The adjective *supposed* (as in *The supposed beggar was really a prince*) is first recorded in 1582; formed from English *suppose* + *-ed*[2]. **—supposition** *n.* 1410 *supposicioun* assumption, hypothesis; borrowed probably from Middle French, and directly from Late Latin *suppositiōnem* (nominative *suppositiō*), from Latin, act of putting under, from *supposit-,* past participle stem of *suppōnere* put under; for suffix see -TION. The sense of Late Latin *suppositiō* assumption, hypothesis, was influenced by Greek *hypóthesis* HYPOTHESIS. An earlier Middle English meaning, inclusion in a higher entity, is recorded before 1398.

suppository *n.* medicine in the form of a cone or cylinder to be put into a body cavity. 1392, rectal suppository; borrowed perhaps by influence of Old French *suppositoire,* from Medieval Latin *suppositorium,* noun use of neuter of Late Latin *suppositōrius* placed underneath or up, from Latin *supposit-,* past participle stem of *suppōnere* put or place under; see SUPPOSE; for suffix see -ORY.

suppress *v.* Probably about 1400 *suppressen* be burdensome, oppress, in Wycliffe's writings; borrowed from Latin *suppress-,* past participle stem of *supprimere* press down, stop, check, stifle (*sup-* down, under, variant of *sub-* before *p* + *premere* push against, PRESS[1]). The meaning of subdue (as a feeling, thought, or habit) is first recorded in English in 1526. The meaning of keep secret is first recorded in Sir Thomas More's works, in 1533. **—suppression** *n.* 1528, act of suppressing, in Sir Thomas More's *A Dialogue Concerning Heresies;* borrowed perhaps from Middle French, and directly from Latin *suppressiōnem* (nominative *suppressiō*) a pressing down or keeping back, from *suppress-,* past participle stem of *supprimere* press down; for suffix see -SION.

suppurate (sup'yərāt) *v.* to form or discharge pus. Probably before 1425 *suppuraten,* in a translation of Chauliac's *Grande Chirurgie;* borrowed from Latin *suppūrātum,* past participle of *suppūrāre* form or discharge pus (*sup-* under, variant of *sub-* before *p* + *pūr-,* stem of *pūs* pus; see FOUL); for suffix see -ATE[1]. **—suppuration** *n.* Probably about 1425 *suppuracioun* process or condition of suppurating; borrowed from Latin *suppūrātiōnem* (nominative *suppūrātiō*) a suppurating, from *suppūrāre* suppurate; for suffix see -ATION.

supra (sü′prə) *adv.* above, before (in a book or writing). 1463, borrowing of Latin *suprā,* adv., above, before, beyond, old feminine ablative singular of *superus,* adj., above, related to *super* OVER.

supra- a prefix meaning above, over, beyond, as in *supranational = above or beyond national boundaries* (1908), *supramolecular = above a molecule in complexity* (1909). Borrowed from Latin *suprā* above, before, beyond, related to *super* above, OVER.

suprarenal (süprərē′nəl) *adj.* above the kidneys, adrenal. 1828, formed in English from *supra-* above + *renal,* after New Latin *suprarenalis* (Latin *suprā* above + Late Latin *rēnālis* renal), in reference to the adrenal or suprarenal capsules or glands (New Latin *capsulae suprarenales*).

supreme *adj.* 1523, highest, loftiest, topmost, in Skelton's *Poetical Works;* borrowed from Middle French *suprême,* and directly from Latin *suprēmus* highest, superlative of *superus* situated above, from *super* above, OVER. The meaning of highest in rank or authority is first recorded in English in 1532-33. **—supremacy** *n.* 1547, condition of being supreme; formed from English *supreme* + *-acy.* **—Supreme Being** (1699) **—Supreme Court** (1709, highest court in a colony, American English; the sense of the highest court in the United States is first recorded in 1787, in the United States Constitution)

sur-[1] a prefix meaning over, above, beyond, in addition, found particularly in words borrowed from older French (including some words from Anglo-French), such as *surcharge, surpass, surtax, survey.* The Old French forms were *sour-, sor-, sur-* (from Latin *super-* SUPER-), in Anglo-French, Middle French, and modern French *sur-.*

sur-[2] a form of the prefix *sus-* before *r* in words of Latin origin, as in *surreptitious, surrogate.* Formed in Latin by assimilation of *s* to the following consonant (*r*).

surcease *v.* to stop, cease. 1428 *surcesen,* borrowed through Anglo-French *surseser,* from Old French *sursis,* past participle of *surseoir* to refrain, put off, delay, from Latin *supersedēre;* see SUPERSEDE. The English spelling with *c* was influenced by the unrelated verb *cease.* **—n.** stop, cessation. 1586, from the verb.

surcharge (sėrchärj′) *v.* to charge extra. 1429 *surchargen* to subject to an additional tax, overtax, in *Rolls of Parliament;* borrowed from Middle French *surcharger,* from Old French (*sur-* over, sur-[1] + *chargier* to load, CHARGE). **—n.** (sėr′chärj). 1429, an additional tax; from the verb. The corresponding Middle French noun is attested only since about 1500.

surcingle (sėr′singgəl) *n.* strap or belt around a horse's body to keep a saddle, blanket, or pack in place. 1469 *sursengle;* borrowed from Middle French *surcengle,* from Old French (*sur-* over, sur-[1] + *cengle* a girdle, from Latin *cingulum, cingulus,* from *cingere* to gird; see CINCTURE).

surd (sėrd) *adj.* 1551, (of numbers) irrational; borrowed from Latin *surdus* deaf, unheard, silent, dull, possibly related to *susurrus* a muttering, whispering; see SWARM[1] group of bees. The sense in mathematics developed from the use of Latin *surdus* to translate Arabic (*jadhr*) *aṣamm* deaf (root), itself a loan translation of Greek (in Euclid) *álogos,* literally, speechless, without reason. The meaning in phonetics of voiceless is found in 1767. **—n.** 1557, an irrational number; later, a voiceless sound (1789); from the adjective.

sure *adj.* About 1250, safe, secure, in *The Owl and the Nightingale;* later, having certainty, certain (about 1330); borrowed from Old French *sur, seür* safe, secure, from Latin *sēcūrus* free from care, untroubled, heedless, free from danger, safe; see the doublet SECURE. For development of pronunciation see SUGAR. **—adv.** Before 1325, assuredly, undoubtedly, in *Cursor Mundi;* from the adjective. **—sure-fire** *adj. Informal.* certain to succeed (1909, American English).

surety *n.* Probably about 1300 *surte* guarantee, assurance, security against loss, damage, etc.; borrowed from Old French *seürté,* from Latin *sēcūritātem* (nominative *sēcūritās*) freedom from care or danger, safety, security, from *sēcūrus* SECURE; for suffix see -TY[2]. The sense of a person who makes himself responsible or liable for the default of another is first recorded in Middle English in 1428.

surf *n.* waves of the sea breaking on the shore. 1685, probably an alteration (with possible influence of *surge*) of earlier *suffe* (1599); of uncertain origin. Both *surf* and *suffe* (or *suff,* 1687) were originally used especially in reference to the coast of India, which suggests an Indic origin for the words. It has also been conjectured that *suff(e)* may have been a phonetic respelling of *sough,* originally a rushing sound. —**v.** ride on the crest of a wave. 1917, from the noun. An earlier sense of form surf or foam is recorded in 1831. **—surfboard** *n.* (about 1826)

surface *n.* 1611, in Cotgrave's *Dictionary;* borrowed from French *surface* outermost boundary of anything, outside part (Old French *sur-* above, sur-[1] + *face* FACE), patterned on Latin *superficiēs* surface; see SUPERFICIAL. **—adj.** of or on the surface. 1664, from the noun. —**v.** 1778, put a surface on, make smooth; from the noun. The meaning of bring to the surface is first recorded in 1885, and that of come to the surface, in 1898.

surfeit (sėr′fit) *n.* Before 1325 *surfait* too much, excess, in *Cursor Mundi;* borrowed from Old French *surfet, surfait* excess, noun use of past participle of *surfaire* overdo (*sur-* over, sur-[1] + *faire* do, from Latin *facere* make, perform, DO[1]). —**v.** Probably before 1387 *surfeten* indulge to excess, in a version of *Piers Plowman;* from the noun. The sense of eat or drink to excess, overfeed, is first recorded in Middle English in 1422. The figurative sense of fill or supply to excess (as in *surfeited with office work*) is first recorded in 1592.

surge *n.* 1490 *sourge* fountain, stream, in Caxton's translation of *The Book of Eneydos;* probably borrowed from Middle French *sourge-,* stem of *sourdre* to rise, swell, from Latin *surgere* to rise, contraction of *surrigere* to rise (*sus-* up + *-rigere,* from *regere* to keep straight, guide; see RIGHT). The earliest examples of the English word (in Caxton) were loan translations of Middle French *sourgon* current of water, source of a river, spring, derived from *sourge-,* stem of the verb in Middle French. The meaning of a high, rolling swell of water, is first recorded in Palsgrave's *Lesclarcissement* (1530), but is found earlier in the figurative sense of violent or excited rising up as of feelings or thoughts (1520). **—v.** 1511, toss or ride on the waves (as at anchor); borrowed from Middle French *surgir* to rise, ride (as a ship) near the shore, from Catalan *sorgir* or Spanish *surgir,* from Latin *surgere* to rise. Modern English *surge, sourge* was also borrowed, in part from Middle French *sourge-*, stem of *sourdre* to rise, swell, also from Latin *surgere* to rise; see SURGE, n. The meaning of rise in great waves is first recorded in English in 1566 (implied in *surging*), probably derived from the noun in English.

surgeon *n.* Probably about 1300 *sorgien* person who heals by manual operation, in *The Romance of Guy of Warwick;* later *surgen* (before 1375), *surgeon* (before 1400); borrowed through Anglo-French *surgien,* variant of Old French *serurgien, cirurgien,* from *cirurgie* surgery, learned borrowing from Latin, also borrowed directly into English from Latin *chirūrgia,* from Greek *cheirourgíā,* from *cheirourgós* (earlier **chesro-worgós*) working or doing by hand, practicing a handicraft (*cheír* hand + *érgon* WORK). **—surgery** *n.* Probably about 1300 *sirgirie* the surgeon's art; later *surgerye* (about 1387-95); borrowed from Old French *surgerie, cirurgerie,* from *cirurgie* surgery (also borrowed into English as *cirurgie*); for suffix see -Y[3]. **—surgical** *adj.* 1770, pertaining to surgery, used in surgery, in Captain James Cook's *Voyages;* formed from English *surgeon* + *-ical.* The early form *cirurgicale* is found in Middle English (probably before 1425), borrowed from Middle French, from *cirurgie* surgery.

surly *adj.* 1566, lordly, majestic, in a translation of Horace's *Satires;* later, imperious, haughty (about 1572); alteration of Middle English *sirly* lordly, imperious (before 1375), formed from *sir,* in the sense of lord + *-ly*[2]. The extended sense of bad-tempered, rude, gruff, is probably first recorded in 1670.

surmise *v.* Probably about 1400 *surmysen* to charge, allege; borrowed from Old French *surmis* (feminine *surmise*), past participle of *surmettre* to accuse (*sur-* upon, sur-[1] + *mettre* put, from Latin *mittere* send; see MISSION). The meaning of infer, form a conjecture, guess, is found in English in 1700, probably derived from the noun meaning. **—n.** 1419 *surmys* charge, accusation, in *Proceedings of the Privy Council;* borrowed from Anglo-French and Old French *surmise* accusation, from *surmettre* to accuse. The extended meaning of inference, conjecture, guess, is first recorded in 1590.

surmount *v.* Before 1325 *surmonten* rise above, rule or prevail over; later *surmount* be superior to, exceed, transcend (about 1380, in Chaucer's translation of Boethius' *De Consolatione Philosophiae*); borrowed from Old French *surmonter* rise above, surmount (*sur-* over, sur-[1] + *monter* to go up, MOUNT[1]).

surname *n.* last name, family name. Probably before 1300, a name, title, or epithet added to a person's name, in *Arthour and Merlin;* formed in Middle English from *sur-*[1] above + *name,* modeled on Anglo-French *surnoun* surname, variant of Old French *surnom* (*sur-* over, sur-[1] + *nom* name, from Latin *nōmen* NAME). The sense of family name, as distinguished from the first or Christian name, is found in Middle English in 1375, in Barbour's *The Bruce.* **—v.** call by a surname. Before 1400 *surnamen,* from the noun.

surpass *v.* 1555, do better than, excel; borrowed from Middle French *surpasser* go beyond, exceed, excel (Old French *sur-* beyond, sur-[1] + *passer* to go by, PASS[1]).

surplice (sėr′plis) *n.* broad-sleeved, white gown worn by clergymen and choir singers. Probably before 1200 *surpliz,* in *Ancrene Riwle;* borrowed from Old French *surpeliz,* from Medieval Latin *superpellicium* a surplice (Latin *super-* over + Medieval Latin *pellicium* fur garment, tunic of skins, from Latin *pellis* skin, FELL[3]); so called because the surplice was formerly put on over fur garments worn by clergymen to keep warm.

surplus *n.* About 1385, remainder or excess, in Chaucer's *Troilus and Criseyde;* borrowed from Old French *surplus,* from Medieval Latin *superplus* excess, surplus (Latin *super-* over + *plūs* more; see PLUS). **—adj.** Before 1382 *soyrpluse* more than is needed, excess, in the Wycliffe Bible; from the noun, though recorded slightly earlier.

surprise *n.* About 1457, sudden, unexpected attack or capture; differentiated in meaning from and eventually replacing by the early 1600's, earlier *supprise* (about 1425). Middle English *supprise,* (borrowed from Middle French *suprise,* variant of *surprise, sourprise*) and Middle English *suprise* (borrowed from Middle French *surprise* a taking unawares) are both from the noun use of the past participle of Old French *surprendre* to overtake (*sur-* over, sur-[1] + *prendre* to take, from Latin *prēndere,* contracted form of *prehendere* to grasp, seize; see PREHENSILE). It is also possible that the noun was in part from the verb in Middle English.

The meaning of something unexpected is first recorded in 1592, and that of a feeling caused by something unexpected, in Shakespeare's *Pericles* (1608).

—v. About 1390 *surprisen* overcome, overpower, take hold of, in Chaucer's *Canterbury Tales* (replacing earlier *supprisen,* 1375); borrowed from Old French *surprise,* feminine past participle of *surprendre* to overtake. The meaning of come upon unexpectedly, take unawares, is first recorded in 1592, and that of affect with surprise in 1655; both meanings probably from the noun in English.

surrealism *n.* representation of the distortions of dreams and the subconscious in art, literature, etc. 1927 *surrealisme;* later *surrealism* (1931); borrowed from French *surréalisme* (*sur-* beyond, sur-[1] + *réalisme* realism). The term was coined about 1917 by the French poet and apologist of the cubist school, Guillaume Apollinaire (1880-1918), and adopted about 1924 by the French poet André Breton, 1896-1966. Breton was originally a member of the Dada movement, from which he broke away in 1921. In 1924 he issued the *Manifeste du surréalisme,* which established him as leader of the surrealist movement. **—surreal** *adj.* of or characterized by surrealism. 1937, back formation from *surrealism.* **—surrealist** *adj., n.* 1918 *surrealiste;* later *surrealist* (1925); borrowed from French *surréaliste.* The history of this term parallels *surrealism,* being originally coined by Apollinaire, and later adopted by Breton. **—surrealistic** *adj.* 1930, formed from English *surrealist,* n. + *-ic.*

surrender *v.* 1441 *surrendouren* give up (something) to another; borrowed from Old French *surrendre* give up (*sur-* over, sur-[1] + *rendre* give back; see RENDER). The spelling *surrender* is first recorded in Middle English in 1473. **—n.** 1423 *surrendre* act of surrendering, borrowed from Old French *surrendre,* noun use of *surrendre* to surrender.

surreptitious *adj.* 1443 *surrepticious* fraudulently obtained; borrowed, perhaps by influence of Middle French *surreptice,* from Latin *surrepticius,* from *surreptus,* past participle of *surripere* seize secretly (*sur-*

from under, variant of *sus-* before *r* + *-ripere,* from *rapere* to snatch, seize; see RAPID); for suffix see -IOUS. The extended sense of acting by stealth or secretly, crafty, sly, is first recorded in Chapman's translation of Homer's *Odyssey* (1615),

surrey *n.* light, four-wheeled carriage having two seats. 1895, in writings of William Dean Howells; American English, from *Surrey cart* an English pleasure cart, named after *Surrey,* a county in southern England where the cart was first made. An adaptation of the English Surrey cart was introduced into the United States in 1872.

surrogate *n.* 1430 *surrogat* substitute, representative, in *Proceedings of the Privy Council;* later *surrogate* (1465); borrowed from Latin *surrogāt-,* past participle stem of *surrogāre* put in another's place, substitute (*sur-* in the place of, under, variant of *sus-* before *r* + *rogāre* to ask, propose; see RIGHT); for suffix see -ATE[1]. The recently developed sense of a woman who carries the surgically implanted fertilized egg or embryo of another woman is first recorded in 1978 (often as *surrogate mother*). This sense was extended about 1986 to that of a woman who gives birth to a child through artificial insemination by a man who is not her husband. **—v.** to substitute for another. 1533, in Bellenden's translation of Livy's *Roman History;* borrowed from Latin *surrogāt-,* past participle stem of *surrogāre* substitute. **—surrogacy** *n.* quality or condition of being a surrogate. 1811, formed from English *surrogate* + *-cy.*

surround *v.* 1423 *surounden* to flood, overflow; borrowed from Middle French *soronder, souronder* to overflow, abound, surpass, dominate, from Late Latin *superundāre* overflow (Latin *super-* over + *undāre* to flow in waves, from *unda* wave; see UNDULATE). The extended sense of shut in on all sides, enclose, encompass, is first recorded in Bullokar's *English Expositor* (1616), influenced by the figurative meaning in French of dominate, and association with the similarity in sound of the English word *round.* The modern English spelling (with *rr*) is also influenced by the English word *round.*

surtax *n.* additional or extra tax. 1881, borrowed from French *surtaxe* (Old French *sur-* over, sur-[1] + *taxe* tax, from *taxer* to TAX).

surtout (sėrtü′) *n.* man's overcoat. 1686, borrowing of archaic French *surtout* overcoat; literally, overall (*sur-* over, sur-[1] + *tout* all, from Vulgar Latin **tōttus,* from Latin *tōtus* all, entire; see TOTAL).

surveillance *n.* close watch kept over a person or thing. 1802, borrowed from French *surveillance* oversight, a watch, from *surveiller* oversee, watch (*sur-* over, sur-[1] + *veiller* to watch, from Latin *vigilāre,* from *vigil* watchful; see VIGIL); for suffix see -ANCE. **—surveil** or **surveille** (sərvāl′) *v.* keep under surveillance. 1960, American English; back formation from *surveillance.*

survey *v.* About 1400 *servayen* examine in detail, appraise; later *surveyen* (1439); borrowed from Old French *surveeir, sourveeir,* from Medieval Latin *supervidere* oversee, SUPERVISE. The sense of determine the form, extent, and position of (land), is first recorded in 1550. **—n.** 1535, supervision, from the verb. The sense of an act of surveying is first recorded in 1548. **—surveyor** *n.* About 1417 *surveour* overseer, supervisor; borrowed from Middle French *surveiour,* from Old French *surveeir* to survey; for suffix see -OR[2]. The meaning of a person who surveys land is first recorded in 1551.

survive *v.* 1473 *surviven* live on, remain alive, especially in the legal sense of a *survivor,* in *Rolls of Parliament;* perhaps, in part, a back formation from earlier *survivor,* in the legal sense, and later (1591 or 1593) as a borrowing from Middle French *survivre, sourvivre,* from Latin *supervīvere* live beyond, live longer than (*super-* over, beyond + *vīvere* to live; see QUICK). **—survival** *n.* 1598, in Chapman's translation of Homer's *Iliad;* formed from English *survive* + *-al*[2]. **—survivor** *n.* 1425 (in law) the surviving person of two or more persons with a joint interest; formed from English *survive* + *-or*[2], in place of Old French *survivant* in the same sense (1125). The general sense of a person or thing that survives is first recorded in 1624.

sus- a form of the prefix *sub-* before *c, p,* or *t* in some words of Latin origin, as in *susceptible, suspend, sustain.* Formed in Latin from an assumed early variant *sups-;* see SUB-.

susceptible *adj.* 1605, capable of receiving or undergoing, in Bacon's *Of the Advancement of Learning;* borrowed from French *susceptible,* and directly from Late Latin *susceptibilis* capable, sustainable, susceptible, from Latin *susceptus,* past participle of *suscipere* sustain, support, acknowledge, take on oneself (*sus-* up, variant of *sub-* before *c* + *-cipere,* from *capere* to take; see CAPTIVE); for suffix see -IBLE. The meaning of easily influenced or affected by feelings is first recorded in 1646. **—susceptibility** *n.* 1644, quality or condition of being susceptible; borrowed from Medieval Latin *susceptibilitas,* from Late Latin *susceptibilis* susceptible; for suffix see -ITY.

sushi (sü′shē) *n.* Japanese dish of cold cooked rice and raw fish. 1893, borrowing of Japanese *sushi.*

suspect (sus′pekt) *adj.* Before 1325, regarded with mistrust, in *Cursor Mundi;* borrowed from Old French *suspect* suspicious, from Latin *suspectus* suspected, suspicious, past participle of *suspicere* look up at, mistrust, suspect (*su-* up to, variant of *sub-* before *sp* + *specere* to look at; see SPY). **—v.** (səspekt′) Before 1450 *suspecten* believe guilty, false, etc., without proof; in part developed from the adjective in Middle English, and in part probably from Middle French *suspecter,* or directly borrowed from Latin *suspectāre* mistrust, be suspicious of, frequentative form of *suspicere* to look up at, suspect. **—n.** (sus′pekt) person suspected. 1591, from the adjective.

suspend *v.* About 1300 *suspenden* to stop or debar temporarily; borrowed from Old French *suspendre,* or directly from Latin *suspendere* to hang, stop (*sus-* up, variant of *sub-* before *p* + *pendere* cause to hang, weigh; see PENDANT). The sense of hang, hang up, is first recorded in Middle English about 1440. The sense of hold in suspension, keep (one's judgment, etc.) undetermined, is first recorded in 1553, in Bishop Latimer's sermons. **—suspenders** *n.pl.* straps for holding up trousers. 1810, American English; formed from *suspend* + *-er*[1] + plural suffix *-s*[1].

suspense *n.* 1402 *suspence* state of suspended action, abeyance, in writings of Hoccleve; later, state of uncertainty (about 1450); borrowed through Anglo-French *suspens* (in the phrase *en suspens* in abeyance), from Old French *suspens* (feminine *suspense*) act of suspending, from Latin *suspēnsus,* past participle of *suspendere* to hang, stop; see SUSPEND.

suspension *n.* act of suspending, condition of being suspended. 1421, borrowed from Latin *suspēnsiōnem* (nominative *suspēnsiō*) the act or state of hanging up, a vaulting, from *suspēns-*, past participle stem of *suspendere* to hang; see SUSPEND; for suffix see -SION. The meaning of a mixture in which very small particles of a solid remain suspended without dissolving is first recorded in English in 1707. **—suspension bridge** (1821)

suspicion *n.* 1375 *suspicioun* act of suspecting, in Barbour's *The Bruce;* alteration of earlier *suspecioun* (probably before 1300, in *Kyng Alisaunder*); borrowed through Anglo-French *suspecioun,* earlier *suspeziun,* from Old French *suspeçun, sospeçon* mistrust, suspicion, from Latin *suspectiōnem* (nominative *suspectiō*) mistrust, suspicion, fear, awe, from *suspect-*, past participle stem of *suspicere* look up at; see SUSPECT; for suffix see -ION. The modern spelling in English was influenced by Latin *suspīciōnem* (nominative *suspīciō*) suspicion, from *suspicere* to suspect. **—v.** *Dialect.* to suspect. Before 1820, American English; from the noun. **—suspicious** *adj.* 1340 *suspecious* open to, deserving of, or exciting suspicion, in *Ayenbite of Inwyt;* borrowed from Old French *suspecious, suspicieus,* from Latin *suspīciōsus* full of suspicion, from *suspīciō* suspicion; for suffix see -OUS.

sustain *v.* Probably before 1300 *sustenen* keep up, keep going, in *Arthour and Merlin;* about 1300 *susteynen;* borrowed from Old French *sustenir, soustenir* hold up, keep up, endure, from Latin *sustinēre* hold up, keep up, support, endure, sustain (*sus-* up, variant of *sub-* before *t* + *-tinēre,* from *tenēre* to hold; see TENANT). **—sustenance** *n.* Probably before 1300 *sustenaunce* means of sustaining life; borrowed from Old French *sustenance, soustenance* endurance, patience, a sustaining, from *soustenir, sostenir* sustain; for suffix see -ANCE.

sutler *n.* person who follows or camps near an army and sells provisions to the soldiers; later, one who establishes a store near an army post. 1590, borrowed from early modern Dutch *soeteler* (modern Dutch *zoetelaar*) small tradesman, sutler, from Middle Low German *suteler,* (with a *t* that is falsely imitative of High German), *sudeler* person who performs mean or dirty tasks, from Middle High German *sudelen* to dirty, modern German *Sudler* bungler, messy worker; ultimately related to Old High German *siodan* to SEETHE.

suttee (sutē′ *or* sut′ē) *n.* Hindu widow who throws herself on the burning funeral pyre of her husband. 1786, borrowed through Hindi from Sanskrit *satī́* faithful wife, feminine of *sát-, sánt-* good, wise; literally, being, related to *satyá-s* true, right; see SOOTH. The sense of immolation of such a Hindu widow is first recorded in English in 1813.

suture *n.* the sewing together of the two edges of a wound, stitch. Probably before 1425, in a translation of Chauliac's *Grande Chirurgie;* borrowed from Latin *sūtūra* a seam, from *sūt-*, past participle stem of *suere* to SEW; for suffix see -URE. **—v.** unite by suture or as if by a suture. 1777, from the noun.

suzerain (su′zərān) *n.* feudal lord. 1807, borrowed from French *suzerain;* earlier *suserain* lord who holds a fief (*sus* above, from Latin *sūsum, sūrsum* upward, from **subsvorsum* turned upward; formed from *subs-*, variant of *sub* from under + *vorsum* turned, from neuter of Old Latin *vorsus,* past participle of *vertere* to turn; see VERTEX + *-erain),* abstracted from the pattern represented in French *souverain,* from Old French *soverain* SOVEREIGN. **—suzerainty** *n.* position or authority of a suzerain. 1845; earlier *suzerainté* (1823); borrowed from French *suzeraineté* position of a suzerain, from *suzerain* suzerain; for suffix see -TY[2]. An earlier sense of supremacy is recorded in Middle English about 1470 with the form *suserente,* borrowed from Middle French *suserenete,* from *suserain* suzerain.

svelte (svelt) *adj.* slender, lithe. About 1817 *svelt;* later *svelte* (1838); borrowing of French *svelte* slim, slender, from Italian *svelto* slim, slender; originally, pulled out, lengthened, from past participle of *svellere* to pluck or root out, from Vulgar Latin **exvellere* a re-formation replacing Latin *ēvellere* pull out (*ē-* out, from *ex-* + *vellere* to pluck, pull, stretch; see VULTURE).

swab *n.* 1659, a reduced form of earlier English *swabber* (1607, in the sense of a mop for cleaning a ship's deck, etc.); borrowed from early modern Dutch **zwabber* a mop (compare Low German and West Frisian *swabber* mop), from obsolete early modern Dutch *zwabben* to mop, from Proto-Germanic **swab-*, perhaps cognate with Old Latin *supāre* to throw, fling, from Indo-European **swep-/swop-/sup-* (Pok.1049). It is also probable that modern English *swab,* in part, was reborrowed from early modern Dutch in the noun *swabbe* a mop, from Middle Dutch. The meaning of an absorbent piece of sponge, cloth, or cotton for cleaning, is found in English in 1787. **—v.** clean with a swab, apply a swab to. 1719, possibly from the noun, but also a back formation from earlier English *swabber* (1592, in the sense of one who swabs a ship's deck); borrowed from early modern Dutch **zwabber,* from obsolete early modern Dutch *zwabben* to swab.

swaddle *v.* bind (a baby) with strips of cloth. 1491 *swadlen,* in Caxton's translation of *Vitas Patrum;* probably a back formation from earlier *swadling band* swaddling cloth or band (before 1325), or *swathelbonde* (about 1200, in *Vices and Virtues*), from *swathel-*, probably a frequentative form of Late Old English *swathian* to SWATHE; for suffix see -LE[3]. **—n.** swaddling cloth. 1538, in Elyot's *Dictionary;* from the verb.

swag *v.* move unsteadily, lurch, sway. 1530, especially in Palsgrave's *Lesclarcissement;* probably borrowed from a Scandinavian source (compare Norwegian *svage, svaie* to sway, toss, and Old Icelandic *sveggja* to swing, sway; cognate with Old English *swingan* to SWING[1]). The meaning of hang loosely or heavily, sag, is found in English in 1621, but is implied earlier in *swag-bellied* (1604, in Shakespeare's *Othello*). **—n.** 1660, a lurching or swaying; from the verb. The meaning of ornamental festoon of flowers, leaves, or ribbons, is found in 1794. The slang sense of booty, plunder, is first recorded in Vaux's *Flash Dictionary* (1812). Earlier senses of *swag* (a bulky bag, 1303, and a big blustering fellow, 1588) are probably borrowed from a Scandinavian source (compare Norwegian dialect *svagg* big, strong person).

swagger *v.* strut about or show off in a vain or superior way. 1590, in Shakespeare's *Midsummer Night's Dream;* probably a frequentative form of SWAG to sway; for suffix see -ER[4]. **—n.** swaggering way of walking or acting. 1725, in writings of Swift; from the verb. **—adj.** *Informal.* showily fashionable. 1879, from the verb.

swain *n.* lover or wooer. Before 1160 *swein* young man, attendant, follower, in *Peterborough Chronicle;* borrowed from a Scandinavian source (compare Old Icelandic *sveinn* boy, servant, attendant, Danish *svend* servant, apprentice, Norwegian *svenn,* and Swedish *sven* apprentice). The Scandinavian words are from Proto-Germanic **swainaz,* Indo-European **swoinos* (Pok.884), and cognate with Old English *swān* shepherd, Old High German *swein* shepherd, *giswīo* brother-in-law, and outside Germanic with Lithuanian *sváinė* sister-in-law. The extended sense of a lover or wooer is first recorded in English about 1585.

swale *n.* low, wet piece of land. 1667, American English; special use of Scottish *swaill* low, hollow place (1584), or dialectal English (East Anglian) *swale, swell* shady place; developed from Middle English *swale* shade (1440, in *Promptorium Parvulorum*). The Middle English word was probably borrowed from a Scandinavian source (compare Old Icelandic *svalr* cool, from Proto-Germanic **swalaz,* and *svala* to cool, Danish, Norwegian, and Swedish *sval* cool; cognate with Old English *swelan* to burn; see SWELTER).

swallow[1] *v.* take in through the throat. Probably before 1200 *swelȝen, swolegen;* later *swolowen* (about 1380), *swallow* (1500-20); developed from Old English *swelgan* (about 1000); cognate with Old Saxon *farswelgan* to swallow, Middle Dutch *swelghen* (modern Dutch *zwelgen*), Old High German *swelahan, swëlgan* (modern German *schwelgen* to revel, feast), from Proto-Germanic **swelH-/swelȝ-,* Indo-European **swel-k-,* and Old Icelandic *svelgja* to swallow (Norwegian *svelgje,* Danish *svælge,* Swedish *svälja*). A cognate outside Germanic is found in Avestan *xvar-* enjoy, consume, from Indo-European **swel-* swallow, eat, drink (Pok.1045). The figurative sense of consume, destroy, devour, is first recorded in English before 1340. **—n.** Before 1338 *swelw* gulf, abyss; later *swalow* throat, gullet (before 1400); developed from late Old English *geswelg, swelh* gulf, abyss (before 1100); cognate with Middle Low German *swalch* throat, glutton, gluttony, Middle High German *swalch* gullet, gorge, abyss, and Old Icelandic *svelgr* whirlpool, devourer, swallower (Swedish *svalg* throat, Norwegian *svelg,* Danish *svælg*); related to the verb. The meaning of a swallowing, gulp, is first recorded in English in 1822.

swallow[2] *n.* small, swift-flying bird. Probably before 1300 *swalu,* in *Sir Tristrem,* and *swalewe,* in *Kyng Alisaunder;* developed from Old English (before 800) *swealwe,* from Proto-Germanic **swalwōn;* cognate with Old Saxon *swala* swallow, Middle Low German *swalewe, swalue,* Middle Dutch *swāluwe* (modern Dutch *zwaluw*), Old High German *swalawa, swalwa* (modern German *Schwalbe*), and Old Icelandic *svala* (Swedish *svala,* Norwegian and Danish *svale*). **—swallow-tailed** *adj.* 1697, having a pair of projections suggestive of a swallow's tail, as in *swallow-tailed* coat (1824); developed from earlier **swallowtail** *n.* (1545, object having a forked projection like a swallow's tail; 1819, butterfly having taillike extensions of the hind wings).

swami (swä'mē) *n.* Hindu religious teacher. 1773, an idol; later, a religious teacher (1901); borrowed from Hindi *swāmī* master (used as term of address), from Sanskrit *svāmí* (genitive *svāminas*) lord, master, from *svá-s* one's own, cognate with Greek *heós, hós* and Latin *suus,* from Indo-European **sewós/swós,* possessive adjective to **swe-* oneself (Pok.882).

swamp *n.* 1624, in Captain John Smith's *The Generall Historie of Virginia;* earlier in the Middle English compound *swamwatyr* swamp water (before 1500); perhaps representing an Old English **swamp,* which would be cognate with Old Icelandic *svǫppr* sponge, fungus (Swedish and Danish *svamp*), from Proto-Germanic **swampuz,* from Indo-European **swombu-* (Pok.1052). The variant Indo-European base **swombh-,* meaning spongy, porous, is represented by Old English *swamm* sponge, fungus, Old High German *swamp,* genitive *swambes* (modern German *Schwamm*), Gothic *swamms,* and perhaps Greek *somphós* spongy, porous. However, the traditional etymology compares modern English *sump* as a variant and refers to Middle English *sompe* morass, swamp (before 1450); probably borrowed from Middle Dutch *somp* or Middle Low German *sump* swamp; cognate with Middle High German *sumpf* swamp (modern German *Sumpf*). **—v.** 1772-84, fill with water, submerge; from the noun. The figurative sense of overwhelm, sink as if in a swamp or water, is first recorded in Todd's revision of Johnson's *Dictionary* (1818). An earlier sense of be entangled or lost in a swamp is recorded in 1688. **—swampland** *n.* (1663, American English) **—swampy** *adj.* 1697, in William Dampier's *A New Voyage Round the World;* formed from English *swamp,* n. + *-y*[1].

swan *n.* Old English *swan* (probably about 750, in *Phoenix*), from Proto-Germanic **swanaz;* cognate with Middle Low German *swan* swan, Middle Dutch *swāne* (modern Dutch *zwaan*), Middle High German *swan* (modern German *Schwan*), and Old Icelandic *svanr* (Swedish *svan,* Danish and Norwegian *svane*). These words are possibly derived from the same Germanic source as Old English *swinsian* to sing, make music; see SOUND[1], n. **—swan song** a person's last piece of work or performance, especially in literature, music, or art. 1831, in Carlyle's *Sartor Resartus,* and later in his *The French Revolution* (1837); so called in allusion to the fabled song of surpassing beauty which a swan sings before it dies, probably a loan translation of German *Schwanengesang* or *Schwanenlied.*

swank *v. Slang.* to show off, swagger. 1809, to strut, of uncertain origin; perhaps related to Middle High German *swanken* to sway, totter (modern German *schwanken*), and Old High German *swingan* to SWING[1]. *Swank* was originally a dialectal English word, taken into general slang use in the early 1900's. **—n.** a showing off, swaggering. 1854, from the verb. **—adj.** stylish. 1913, from the noun or verb. **—swanky** *adj.* 1842, swaggering, strutting, pretentiously grand; formed from English *swank,* n. or v. + *-y*[1].

swap *v. Informal.* to exchange, barter, or trade. Probably before 1200 *swappen* to strike, strike the hands together, in Layamon's *Chronicle of Britain;* of unknown origin. The sense of exchange, barter, or trade, is first recorded in 1594; possibly so called from the practice of striking hands as a sign of agreement in bargaining, perhaps alluded to in the phrase "to strike a bargain." **—n.** About 1250 *swop* a blow, a striking; later *swappe* (about 1380, in Chaucer's *House of Fame*). The meaning of an exchange, barter, or trade, is first recorded in 1625.

sward (swôrd) *n.* grassy surface, turf. Probably before 1300 *swerd* flesh or skin, in *Kyng Alisaunder;* about 1300, sod, turf; developed from Old English (before 800) *sweard* skin, rind; cognate with Old Frisian *swarde* skin of the head, scalp, Middle Dutch *swaerde* skin, hide (modern Dutch *zwoord* bacon rind), Middle Low German *swarde* hairy skin, scalp, Middle High German *swarte* (modern German *Schwarte* rind), and Old Icelandic *svǫrdhr* (genitive *svardhar*) skin, walrus hide (Norwegian *svor, svord* rind, Swedish *svål* pigskin, turf), from Proto-Germanic **swarđu-*, of unknown origin. **—v.** cover with or form a sward. 1610, from the noun.

swarm[1] *n.* group of bees or other insects. About 1350 *swarme;* developed from Old English (before 800) *swearm;* cognate with Old Saxon and Middle Low German *swarm* swarm, Middle Dutch *swarm, swerm* (modern Dutch *zwerm*), Old High German *swaram* (modern German *Schwarm*), and Old Icelandic *svarmr* tumult (Danish *sværm* swarm, Swedish *svärm,* Norwegian *sverm*), from Proto-Germanic **swarmaz.* These words are possibly related to Middle Low German *swirren* to whiz, whir, Old Icelandic *svarra;* and outside Germanic may be related to Latin *susurrus* a whispering, hum, Old Slavic *svirati* to whistle, Lithuanian *surmà* pipe, and Sanskrit *svárati* sounds, resounds, from Indo-European **swer-/swor-/sur-* (Pok.1049). **—v.** Probably about 1380 *swarmen* to leave a hive to start another; from the noun.

swarm[2] *v.* to climb, shin (as in *swarm up a tree*). 1500's, perhaps originally a sailor's term; also found in obsolete *swarve* (1500's); both words of uncertain origin.

swart (swôrt) *adj.* dark, swarthy. Before 1121 *swarte,* in *Peterborough Chronicle;* developed from Old English *sweart* (about 725, in *Beowulf*); cognate with Old Frisian and Old Saxon *swart* black, Middle Low German and Middle Dutch *swart* (modern Dutch *zwart*), Old High German *swarz* (modern German *schwarz*), Old Icelandic *svartr* (Norwegian and Swedish *svart,* Danish *sort* black), and Gothic *swarts* from Proto-Germanic **swartaz;* also cognate outside Germanic with Latin *sordēs* dirt, *sordēre* be dirty, from Indo-European **sword-* (Pok.1052).

swarthy (swôr′ᴛʜē) *adj.* dark-colored or having a dark skin. 1581, alteration of earlier *swarty* (1572), formed from English *swart* + *-y*[1]. A derivative form, *swarthiness,* is found as early as 1577. It is not clear why the *t* of *swarty* changed to *th* beginning in the latter 1500's; but the form *swarty* continued to be used sporadically until the late 1800's.

swash *n.* 1538, the fall of a heavy body or blow; earlier, swill (1528); possibly a formation on *wash* with *s-* added for emphasis, and reminiscent of *splash,* etc. The related meaning of a body of splashing water appeared in 1671, and running water in a channel (1670); the meaning of a dashing or splashing is first recorded in 1847-54. **—v.** 1556 (implied in *swashing*) to swagger, bluster; 1589, to splash; probably from the noun.

swashbuckler *n.* a swaggering or dashing bully, ruffian, adventurer, or the like. 1560, formed from English *swash,* v. + *buckler* shield; the original, literal sense of the compound may have been that of one who makes a noise by striking his own or his opponent's shield, a swordsman. **—swashbuckling** *adj.* characteristic of a swashbuckler, noisily swaggering or blustering. Before 1693, formed from English *swashbuckler* (interpreted as ending in *-er*[1]) + *-ing*[2].

swastika (swos′təkə) *n.* ancient symbol adopted as the emblem of the Nazi party and regime in Germany. 1871, borrowed from Sanskrit *svastika-s,* from *svasti-s* well-being, luck; formed from *su-* well (from Indo-European **su-* good, source of Greek *hy-* in *hygiḗs* healthy; see HYGIENE) + *as-,* root of *ásti* (he) IS; so called because swastikas were thought in early times to bring good luck. The use of *swastika* in reference to the Nazi emblem is first recorded in English in 1932.

swat *v.* 1615, to sit down, squat; probably a dialectal variant of SQUAT. The informal sense of hit sharply or violently is found before 1796, and may be of entirely different derivation (possibly alteration of *swap* to strike, smite, deal a blow, probably before 1400). **—n.** Before 1800, sharp or violent blow; probably from the verb.

SWAT or **S.W.A.T.** *n.* paramilitary police unit trained in the use of special weapons. 1968, American English, acronym formed from *S(pecial) W(eapons) a(nd) T(actics)* (squad or team) or *S(pecial) W(eapons) A(ttack) T(eam).*

swatch *n.* sample of cloth or other material. 1512 *swache* the countercheck of a tally (in Northumberland); later, a tally attached to cloth sent to be dyed (1612, in Yorkshire); 1647, a sample piece of cloth; of unknown origin. The figurative sense of a sample or specimen of anything is first recorded in 1697.

swath *n.* space covered by a single cut of scythe or mowing machine. About 1250 *swathe* track, trace, in *Genesis and Exodus;* developed from Old English *swæth, swathu* (about 725, in *Beowulf*). The Old English forms *swæth* (from Proto-Germanic **swathan*), and *swathu* (from Proto-Germanic **swathō*) are cognate with Old Frisian *swethe* limit, boundary, Middle Low German *swat, swāde* furrow, swath, Middle Dutch *swat* swath (modern Dutch *zwad, zwade*), Middle High German *swade* swath (modern German *Schwaden*), and Old Icelandic *svadh* slippery place (Norwegian *sva* bare cliff, Swedish *svad* bare cliff, clearing), from Indo-European **swē-/swə-* to bend, turn, swing (Pok.1041). The meaning of a space covered by a single cut of a scythe is found in Middle English, probably about 1475. The figurative sense of a strip, belt, or lengthwise extent (of something), is first recorded in Drayton's *Poems* (probably 1605).

swathe *v.* wrap up closely or fully. Probably before 1325 *swathen;* developed from Late Old English (1100's) *swathian* to swathe; cognate with Middle Low German *swede* bandage, and more distantly with Old Icelandic *sveigja* to bend; see SWAY. **—n.** 1565, infant's swaddling bands, in Cooper's *Thesaurus Linguae Romanae et Britannicae;* 1598, band of cloth, wrapping, in Florio's *A World of Words;* from the verb. An isolated instance of the noun is found in Late Old English *swathum,* dative plural, (about 1050).

sway *v.* About 1300 *swien, sweiȝen* go, glide, move; later *sweyen* sweep (probably about 1380); probably borrowed from a Scandinavian source (compare Old Icelandic *sveigja* to bend, swing, give way, from Proto-Germanic **swaiȝjanan,* related to *svigna* give way, from Indo-European **sweik-/swoik-/swik-,* Pok.1042). The Old Icelandic words are probably cognate with Middle Low German *swāien* to sway, modern Dutch *zwaaien* to swing, wave, Welsh *chwyf* motion, and Lithuanian *svaĩgti* become giddy or dizzy. The current sense of swing, wave, waver, is first recorded about 1500, but was not common until the 1800's. The figurative sense of vacillate is first recorded in 1563. **—n.** About 1175 *sweiȝe* motion, in *Body and Soul;* later *sway* (probably before 1300, in *Kyng Alisaunder*); probably from the same Scandinavian source as the verb (compare Old Icelandic *svigi* a bending switch, *svig* a bend, Norwegian *sveg* switch). The figurative meaning of prevailing or controlling influence (as in *to be under the sway of a leader*) is found before 1510. **—swaybacked** *adj.* having a sagging back, said of horses (1690).

swear *v.* 1123 *sweren* to take an oath, in *Peterborough Chronicle;* developed from Old English *swerian* (about 725, in *Beowulf,* from Proto-Germanic **swarjanan*); cognate with Old Frisian *swera* to swear, Old Saxon *swerian,* Middle Low German and Middle Dutch *sweren* (modern Dutch *zweren*), Old High German *swerien, swerren* (modern German *schwören*), Old Icelandic *sverja* to swear (Swedish *svärja,* Norwegian *sverge,* Danish *sværge),* and Gothic *swaran* to swear, from Proto-Germanic **swar-,* found also in Old Icelandic *svar* answer, *svara* to answer, and Old English *andswaru* ANSWER. Possible cognates outside Germanic include Oscan *sverrunei* (dative) speaker, and Old Slavic *svarŭ* quarrel, from Indo-European **swer-/sworspeak,* talk (Pok.1049).

sweat *v.* Probably before 1200 *sweten,* in *Ancrene Riwle* and Layamon's *Chronicle of Britain;* developed from Old English *swǣtan* perspire, work hard (before 899, in Alfred's translation of St. Gregory's *Pastoral Care*), from *swāt,* n., sweat. Old English *swāt,* n. (from Proto-Germanic **swaita-*), is cognate with Old Frisian and Old Saxon *swēt* sweat, Middle Dutch *sweet* (modern Dutch *zweet*), Old High German *sweiz* (modern German *Schweiss*), and Old Icelandic *sveiti* (Swedish *svett,* Norwegian and Danish *sved*). Cognates outside Germanic include Welsh *chwys* sweat, Latin *sūdor* sweat, *sūdāre* to sweat, Albanian *dirsë, djersë* sweat, Greek *hidrós,* Latvian *svîst* to sweat, Armenian *k'irtn* sweat, and Sanskrit *svidyati, svedate* (he) sweats, from Indo-European **sweid-/swoid-/swid-* (Pok.1043). **—n.** Probably before 1200 *swete* life blood; also, perspiration, dialectal (northern English) variant of earlier *swote* (probably about 1150); developed from Old English *swāt* sweat. The change to the form *swete* was influenced by the verb *sweten* to sweat. **—sweater** *n.* Before 1529, one who works hard, toiler, in Skelton's poetry; formed from English *sweat,* v. + *-er*[1]. The meaning of a woolen vest or jersey, originally worn in rowing or other athletic exercise is first recorded in 1882, from earlier *sweaters* clothing worn to produce sweating and reduce weight (1828). **—sweat shirt** (1929, American English) **—sweatshop** *n.* place where work is done for low wages under poor conditions (before 1889). **—sweaty** *adj.* About 1380 *swety* causing sweat, in Chaucer's *The Former Age;* formed from Middle English *swete* sweat + *-y*[1]. The sense of covered with sweat is first recorded in Spenser's *Faerie Queene* (1590).

sweep *v.* Probably before 1200 *swepen* to clear away with a brush or broom; also figurative, move swiftly and strongly, in Layamon's *Chronicle of Britain;* of uncertain origin, but replacing *swope* sweep (about 1200), developed from Old English *swāpan* to sweep; see SWOOP. **—n.** About 1250 *swep* stroke, force, in *Genesis and Exodus;* from the verb. The sense of an act of sweeping is first recorded in 1552. The figurative sense of scope, reach, compass of a sweeping movement, is first cited in 1679.

sweepstakes *n.* system of gambling on horses, races, or other contests. 1773, prize won in a race or contest, from Middle English *swepestake* one who sweeps or wins all the stakes in a game (1495); formed from Middle English *swepen,* v., sweep + *stake*[2], n. The plural form *sweepstakes,* meaning a betting or gambling system or transaction in which all the stakes are won by one or divided among several, is first cited in 1862.

sweet *adj.* About 1175 *swete;* developed from Old English (before 830) *swēte* pleasing to the senses, mind, or feelings (from Proto-Germanic **swōtjaz*); cognate with Old Frisian *swēt* sweet, Old Saxon *swōti, suoti,* Middle Low German *sote, sute,* Middle Dutch *soete* (modern Dutch *zoet*), Old High German *suozi* (modern German *süss*), and Old Icelandic *sœtr* (Swedish *söt,* Norwegian *søt,* Danish *sød*). Cognates outside Germanic include Latin *suāvis* sweet, Greek *hēdýs, hadeîn* to please, Sanskrit *svádati* makes agreeable, and *svādú-s* sweet, from Indo-European **swad-/swād-* (M. Mayrhofer, *Kurzgefasstes etymologisches Wörterbuch des Altindischen,* III, 568). **—n.** something sweet. Probably before 1200 *swete,* in *Ancrene Riwle;* from the adjective. **—sweetbread** *n.* gland (pancreas or thymus) used for food (1565). **—sweetbrier** *n.* kind of rose (1538). **—sweet corn** (1646, American English) **—sweeten** *v.* (1552, in Huloet's *Abecedarium Anglico Latinum;* formed from English *sweet,* adj. + *-en*[1]. **—sweetheart** *n.* (about 1290, as a term of address; 1576, loved one, lover) **—sweetmeats** *n.pl.* sweets (about 1480). **—sweet pea** climbing garden plant (1732). **—sweet potato** (1750) **—sweet tooth** fondness for sweets (before 1393, in Gower's *Confessio Amantis;* Middle English *tooth* taste, liking; compare TOOTHSOME).

swell *v.* Probably before 1200 *swellen,* in *Ancrene Riwle* and Layamon's *Chronicle of Britain;* developed from Old English (about 725, in *Beowulf*) *swellan* grow or make bigger (past tense *sweall,* past participle *swollen*); cognate with Middle Low German and Middle Dutch *swellen* to swell (modern Dutch *zwellen*), Old High German *swellan* (modern German *schwellen*), Old Icelandic *svella* swell (Swedish *svälla,* Norwegian *svelle*), from Proto-Germanic **swelnanan,* and Gothic *ufswalleinōs* (plural) pride, arrogance. Possibly related to WELL[2] to rise. **—n.** Probably before 1200 *swel* abnormal enlargement of some bodily part, swelling, in *Ancrene Riwle;* from the verb. The meaning of a rising or heaving of the sea in rolling waves is first recorded in Shakespeare's *Antony and Cleopatra* (1606). The figurative meaning of an inflated or proud air or behavior, swagger, is found in 1724, but the transferred use, originally slang, of a fashionably or dashingly dressed person is first recorded in 1811. **—adj.** 1810, fashionably dressed or equipped; from the noun. The extended informal sense of stylish is first recorded as a slang term in Vaux's *Flash Dictionary* (1812), and the general slang sense of good, excellent, first occurs in American English, in Stephen Crane's *Third Violet* (1897).

swelter *v.* About 1403 *swelteren* suffer from heat, sweat profusely, in Lydgate's *Temple of Glass;* frequentative form of earlier *swelten* be faint, especially with heat (before 1390); developed from Old English *sweltan* to die (about 725, in *Beowulf*). Old English *sweltan* is cognate with Old Saxon *sweltan* to die, Middle Dutch *swelten* to faint, die, Old High German *swelzan* burn away, languish, Old Icelandic *svelta* to die, starve (Swedish *svälta* starve, Danish and Norwegian *sulte* to hunger), and Gothic *swiltan* to die, Crimean Gothic *schuualth* death. These words are probably derived from Proto-Germanic **swel-* to burn slowly, found in Old English *swelan* to burn, Middle Low German *swelen* to smolder, with cognates outside Germanic found in Greek *heílē, eílē, hélē* sun's heat or warmth (earlier *(e)swélā*), Lithuanian *svìlti* to singe, and Sanskrit *svarati* (it) lights up, shines, from Indo-European **swel-* (Pok.1045).

The Indo-European base may have a "moveable *s*": **(s)wel-*, covering both senses of "burn" and "die." According to Roman Jakobson, Lithuanian *velỹs* deceased person, *vė̃lės* spirits, and a Baltic Apollo-like deity *Veles,* suggest a link between "die" and "burn." The connection between starve and die, seen for example in Scandinavian, leads to the inclusion of Armenian *k'ałc* hunger, *k'ałc-nu-m* starve, from Indo-European **swl̥-d-sk̑ō* (Robert A. Fowkes, *Gothic Etymological Studies,* 44-46).

swerve *v.* Probably about 1200 *swerfen* go off, turn aside; later *swerven* (before 1338); developed in form from Old English *sweorfan* to rub, scour, file, but unaccounted for in the sense of development. Old English *sweorfan,* from Proto-Germanic **swerƀanan,* is cognate with Old Frisian *swerva* to creep, Old Saxon *swerƀan* to wipe, Middle Dutch *swerven* to rove, stray (modern Dutch *zwerven*), Old High German *swerban* wipe, move back and forth, Old Icelandic *sverfa* to file, and Gothic *-swaírban* to wipe, from Indo-European **swerbh-* turn, wipe (Pok.1050). Middle Dutch *swerven* stray, suggests that the Middle English sense of go off, turn aside, may have come from influence outside of English, though some scholars believe the sense in Middle English was present, though unrecorded, in Old English. **—n.** a turning aside. 1741, from the verb.

swift *adj.* Old English *swift* moving quickly (about 725, in *Beowulf*), related to *swīfan* move in a course, sweep; see SWIVEL. **—adv.** in a swift manner. Probably about 1380, in *Patience;* from the adjective. **—n.** Probably before 1481 *swyfte* something swift; from the adjective. Reference to a kind of bird noted for its swift flight is first found in 1668.

swig *n.* 1548, drink or liquor, in Udall's translation of Erasmus' *Apothegms;* later, big or hearty drink of liquor (1621-23); of unknown origin. **—v.** *Informal.* drink heartily or greedily. About 1654, from the noun.

swill *v.* About 1250, *swilen* to wash, stir, pour, drink, in a version of *The Body and the Soul;* developed from Old English (before 800) *swilian, swillan* to wash, gargle, from Proto-Germanic **sweljanan,* cognate with Avestan *xwar-* enjoy, consume, from Indo-European **swel-* (Pok.1045). Compare SWALLOW[1]. The meaning of drink greedily or to excess is first recorded about 1530. **—n.** 1553, (in figurative use) partly liquid kitchen refuse fed to pigs; from the verb.

swim *v.* About 1175 *swimmen;* developed from Old English *swimman* to move in or on the water, float (about 725, in *Beowulf*); cognate with Old Frisian *swimma* to swim, Middle Low German and Middle Dutch *swemmen* (modern Dutch *zwemmen*), Old High German *swimman* (modern German *schwimmen*), Old Icelandic *svimma,* Swedish *simma,* Norwegian and Danish *svømme* to swim, from Proto-Germanic **swemjanan,* Indo-European **swem-/swom-/swm̥-* (Pok.1046). The figurative sense of seem to spin, reel, or move unsteadily, is first recorded in Dryden's *All for Love* (1678). **—n.** 1599, smooth gliding movement, in Ben Jonson's *Cynthia's Revels;* later, act of swimming (1764); from the verb. An earlier sense of the clear part of a liquid which floats above the sediment is found in 1547. **—swim bladder** (1837, the air bladder of a fish; earlier *swimming bladder,* 1713) **—swimming hole** (1867, American English) **—swimmingly** *adv.* with great ease or success (1622). **—swimming pool** (1899, earlier *swimming bath,* 1742) **—swimsuit** *n.* (1934)

swindle *v.* 1782, to cheat, defraud, in Bailey's *Dictionary;* back formation from SWINDLER. **—n.** act of swindling. 1852, from the verb. **—swindler** *n.* 1774, person who cheats or defrauds; borrowed from German *Schwindler* giddy person, extravagant speculator, especially in money matters, cheat, from *schwindeln* to be giddy, act thoughtlessly or extravagantly, swindle, from Old High German *swintilōn* be giddy, frequentative form of *swintan* to languish, disappear. Old High German *swintan* is cognate with Old English *swindan* to languish, disappear, and probably with Old English *swīma* dizziness, from Indo-European **swī-* pass away, become silent (Pok.1052).

swine *n.* Before 1325 *suine;* later *swyne* (about 1375) also earlier *swein* (1128); developed from Old English (before 800) *swīn* pig, hog; cognate with Old Frisian, Old Saxon, and Middle Low German *swīn* swine, Middle Dutch *swijn* (modern Dutch *zwijn*), Old High German *swīn* (modern German *Schwein*), Old Icelandic *svīn* (Norwegian, Swedish, and Danish *svin*), and Gothic *swein.* These words are from Proto-Germanic **swīnan,* noun use of a neuter adjective represented in Indo-European by Latin *suīnus* and Old Slavic *svinŭ* of swine (also attested as noun *svinija* pig), ultimately from the same Indo-European base as Old English *sugu* and *sū* female pig, SOW[2]. **—swineherd** *n.* (before 1100) **—swinish** *adj.* Before 1200 *swinisse,* formed from Middle English *swine* swine + *-isse* -ish[1].

swing *v.* About 1175 *swingen* to beat, strike, move violently; developed from Old English (before 800) *swingan;* also earlier, to rush, fling oneself (about 725, in *Beowulf*). Old English *swingan* is cognate with Old Frisian *swinga* to fling, besprinkle, Old Saxon *swingan* fling oneself, Middle Low German *swingen,* Old High German *swingan* to fling, beat, move rapidly (modern German *schwingen* to swing), from Proto-Germanic **swenȝanan* (Indo-European **swenk-*), and Gothic *af swaggwjan* make doubtful. Cognates outside Germanic are found in Avestan *pairišxvaxta-* encircled, and Sanskrit *svájate* (he) encircles, from Indo-European **swe(n)g-, swe(n)k-* bend, swing (Pok.1047). The meaning of hang or suspend so as to turn freely is first recorded in English in 1528, and that of move freely or regularly back and forth, in 1545. **—n.** Before 1325, a stroke with a weapon; developed from Old English *geswing* stroke (as in *sweordgeswing* sword stroke); related to *swingan* to beat, strike, move violently. The meaning of an act of swinging or oscillating is found in 1589, but the figurative sense of a course of a career, activity, etc., is recorded earlier, in 1570; both senses derive from the verb. The concrete meaning of a device or apparatus that swings is first recorded in 1687. Reference to a type of jazz music characterized by a lively, swinging rhythm, is first recorded in 1934, in American English, though the development of this sense has been traced as far back as 1888. See Robert S. Gold's *A Jazz Lexicon,* 1964, for citations since the 1800's. **—swinger** *n.* 1543, person or thing that swings; formed from English *swing,* v. + *-er*[1]. The sense of a person who is lively, especially in an unrestrained way is first recorded in 1965, but is found in the form *swinging,* adj. in 1958.

swipe *n.* a sweeping stroke, hard blow. Before 1807

possibly a dialectal variant of SWEEP, and in part, perhaps from obsolete English *swip* a stroke, blow (from Proto-Germanic **swip-*, Indo-European **sweib-/swib-* Pok.1041), though the word disappears from the record of English before 1300. **—v.** to strike with a sweeping blow. 1825, in Jamieson's *Dictionary of the Scottish Language;* possibly a variant of *sweep,* v., and in part a verb use of *swipe,* n., perhaps earlier influenced by or developing in part from obsolete *swip* to strike, move hastily, from Middle English *swippen,* from Old English **swippan, *swipian* (compare Old English *swipu* a stick, whip; also Old Icelandic *svipa* whip, *svipr* sudden sweeping movement, and Old High German *swipfen* move quickly in a curve, as a whip does); also connected by some to obsolete *swope* to sweep with broad movement, brandish, rush, dash, from Old English *swāpan* (compare Old Icelandic *sveipa* to sweep, wrap, swoop), or to obsolete *swaip* stroke, blow (compare Old Icelandic *sveipa*), or to obsolete *swape* oar, pole, etc., having a sweeping motion (compare Old Icelandic *sveipa*). The slang sense of to steal, pilfer, appeared in 1889 in American English, and is of uncertain connection, originally said to be theatrical slang, in reference to the practice of performers stealing jokes or appropriating stage routines from one another.

swirl *n.* About 1425 *swyrl* whirlpool, eddy, in a chronicle of Scotland; probably a formation similar in origin to dialectal Norwegian *svirla* and Dutch *zwirrelen* to whirl. The meaning of a whirling movement is first recorded in Scott's *The Bride of Lammermoor* (1818). **—v.** 1513, to give a whirling motion to, in Douglas' translation of Vergil's *Aeneid;* from the noun. An earlier instance of the verb is recorded before 1398.

swish *v.* move with a light, hissing or brushing sound. 1756, probably imitative of the sound made by a person, clothing, etc., brushing against or moving through something. **—n.** swishing movement or sound. 1820, in John Clare's *Poems;* from the verb.

Swiss *n.* native of Switzerland. 1515, borrowed from Middle French *Suisse,* from Middle High German *Suizer,* from *Suīz* Switzerland. **—adj.** 1530, in Palsgrave's *Lesclarcissement;* borrowed from Middle French *Suisse.* **—Swiss cheese** (1822)

switch *n.* 1592, slender riding whip, in Shakespeare's *Romeo and Juliet;* probably borrowed from a Flemish or Low German word similar in formation to Hanoverian *swutsche,* variant of Low German *zwukse* long thin stick, switch. The meaning of a device for changing the direction of something, making or breaking a connection, or other purposes, is found in 1797. **—v.** About 1611, to beat or whip with or as with a switch, in Chapman's translation of Homer's *Iliad;* from the noun. The meaning of turn off onto another track, in reference to a train, is first recorded in 1853 in American English. The figurative sense of to shift, divert, is also first recorded in American English, in 1860. **—switchblade** *n.* pocket knife with a blade that springs out (1932, in writings of Langston Hughes). **—switchboard** *n.* (1873) **—switch-hitter** *n. Baseball.* player who bats either right- or left-handed (1948).

swivel *n.* thing that turns freely on a pin or the like. 1307-08 *swyvel* coupling device; possibly a frequentative form derived from *swif-,* stem of Old English *swīfan* to move in a course, sweep, from Proto-Germanic **swīpanan,* cognate with Lettish *svàipīt* to whip, from Indo-European **sweip-/swoip-/swip-* (Pok.1042); for suffix see -LE[3] (compare Old Icelandic *sveifla* set in circular motion). Old English *swīfan* is cognate with Old Frisian *swīvia* wander, sway, Middle Low German and Middle Dutch *sweven* to float, hover (modern Dutch *zweven*), Old High German *swēben* (modern German *schweben*), Old High German *sweibōn* to sway, hover, and Old Icelandic *svīfa* to wander, drift. **—v.** turn on a swivel. 1794, from the noun. **—swivel chair** (1884)

swivet (swiv′it) *n. Informal.* great agitation or excitement. About 1880, American English (chiefly southern dialect); of uncertain origin.

swizzle *n.* mixed alcoholic drink. 1813, possibly a variant of earlier American English *switchel* a drink of molasses and water (1790), of uncertain origin. **—v.** *Informal.* to drink habitually and to excess. 1843, from the noun. **—swizzle stick** (1885)

swoon *v.* to faint. About 1250 *swounen;* earlier *iswoȝen* (probably before 1200, in Layamon's *Chronicle of Britain*); developed from Old English *geswōgen* in a faint (about 1000, in Ælfric's *Homilies*), past participle of **swōgan,* as in *āswōgan* to choke, of uncertain origin. **—n.** a faint. About 1250 *in sowne;* later *in swoun* (about 1303, in Mannyng's *Handlyng Synne*); alteration of *a swoun* in a faint (*a* in + *sowne, swoun* faint, from *swounen* to faint).

swoop *v.* 1566, move in a stately manner, variant of Middle English *swopen* to sweep (about 1175, in *The Body and Soul*); developed from Old English (before 1000) *swāpan* to sweep, brandish, dash. Old English *swāpan* is cognate with Old Saxon *swēpan* to clean, sweep, Old High German *sweifen* to coil, wind (modern German *schweifen* to curve, rove, ramble), and Old Icelandic *sveipa* to sling, throw, wrap (Norwegian *sveipe,* Swedish *svepe,* Danish *svøbe*), from Proto-Germanic **swaipanan,* Indo-European **sweib-/swoib-/swib-* (Pok.1041). The meaning of pounce upon or seize with a sweeping movement is first recorded in 1638. Development of the spelling with *-oo-* may have been influenced by Scottish and Northern English dialect *soop* to sweep (about 1480), borrowed from Old Icelandic *sōpa* to sweep. **—n.** 1605, rapid downward sweep, sudden descent or attack, in Shakespeare's *Macbeth;* from the verb. An earlier sense of a blow, stroke, is found in 1544-45; the source of this sense is unclear.

sword *n.* About 1250, in *Genesis and Exodus;* developed from Old English *sweord* (about 725, in *Beowulf*); cognate with Old Frisian and Old Saxon *swerd* sword, Middle Dutch *swaert* (modern Dutch *zwaard*), Old High German *swert* (modern German *Schwert*), and Old Icelandic *sverdh* (Swedish *svärd,* Danish and Norwegian *sverd*), from Proto-Germanic **swerđan;* related to Old High German *sweran* to hurt, from Proto-Germanic **swer-* to cut. Cognates outside Germanic include Welsh *chwerw* bitter, sharp, and Avestan *xvara* wound, from Indo-European **swer-* cut, pierce (Pok.1050). **—swordfish** *n.* (about 1400) **—swordplay** *n.* (1627, fencing; also found in Old English, before 1000, meaning battle) **—swordsman** *n.* Before 1680, in Samuel Butler's *Remains;* replacing earlier *swerdman* (before 1387, in Trevisa's translation of Higden's *Polychronicon*).

sy- a form of the prefix *syn-*[1] before *s* with a following consonant, or before *z* in words of Greek origin, as in *system, syzygy.*

sybarite (sib′ərit) *n.* person devoted to luxury and pleasure. 1598, inhabitant of *Sybaris,* an ancient Greek town in southern Italy known for its luxury; borrowed from Latin *Sybarīta,* from Greek *Sybarī́tēs,* from *Sýbaris* Sybaris; for suffix see -ITE[1]. The meaning of a person devoted to luxury and pleasure is first recorded in 1623. **—sybaritic** *adj.* (1619)

sycamore *n.* kind of tall shade tree. About 1350 *sicamour* a kind of fig tree; borrowed from Old French *sicamor,* from Latin *sȳcomorus,* from Greek *sýkómoros* (*sŷkon* FIG + *móron* MULBERRY); so called because the tree has leaves somewhat resembling those of the mulberry. The use of *sycamore* in the sense of a maple tree of Europe and Asia appeared in 1588, in Shakespeare's *Love's Labour's Lost;* application of the word to a North American shade tree is first recorded in 1814.

sycophant (sik′əfənt) *n.* servile flatterer. Before 1548, informer, talebearer, slanderer; borrowed from Middle French *sycophante,* and directly from Latin *sȳcophanta,* from Greek *sȳkophántēs,* originally, one who makes the insulting gesture of the "fig," that is, sticking the thumb between two fingers (*sŷkon* vulva, FIG + *-phántēs* one who shows, from *phaínein* to show; see FANTASY); it is not known why informers were called by this apparently derogatory name in ancient Greece. The extended sense of a mean, servile, cringing flatterer, is first recorded in English in 1575. **—sycophancy** *n.* 1622, trade or occupation of an informer; 1657, servile flattery; borrowed from Latin *sȳcophantia,* from Greek *sȳkophantíā* the conduct of a sycophant, from *sȳkophántēs* informer; for suffix see -ANCY. **—sycophantic** *adj.* 1676, borrowed from Greek *sȳkophantikós,* from *sȳkophántēs* sycophant; for suffix see -IC.

syl- a form of the prefix *syn-*[1] before *l* in words of Greek origin, as in *syllogism.* Formed in Greek by assimilation of *n* before the following consonant (*l*).

syllable *n.* About 1380 *sillable* part of a word pronounced as a unit, in Chaucer's *House of Fame;* borrowed through Anglo-French *sillable,* alteration with *l* of Old French *sillabe,* from Latin *syllaba,* from Greek *syllabḗ* a syllable, several sounds or letters taken or joined together; originally a taking together (*syl-* together, variant of *syn-*[1] before *l* + *lab-,* stem of *lambánein* to take; see DILEMMA). The alteration with *l* in Anglo-French and English apparently developed on the analogy of such words as *participle* and *principle.* **—syllabary** *n.* table of syllables. 1586, borrowed from New Latin *syllabarium,* from Latin *syllaba* syllable; for suffix see -ARY. **—syllabic** *adj.* 1728, forming a syllable, in *Chambers Cyclopaedia;* borrowed through French *syllabique,* and directly from New Latin *syllabicus,* from Greek *syllabikós* of or pertaining to a syllable, from *syllabḗ* syllable; for suffix see -IC. **—syllabicate** *v.* 1775, back formation from earlier *syllabication* formation of syllables (1631); for suffix see -ATE[1]. English *syllabication* was borrowed from Medieval Latin *syllabicationem* (nominative *syllabicatio*) formation of syllables, from *syllabicare* form into syllables, from Latin *syllaba* syllable; for suffix see -ATION. **—syllabify** *v.* 1864, back formation from earlier *syllabification* formation of syllables (1838); for suffix see -FY. English *syllabification* was formed from Latin *syllaba* syllable + English connective *-i-* + *-fication.*

syllabus (sil′əbəs) *n.* brief outline of a treatise, course of study, etc. 1656, in Blount's *Glossographia;* borrowed from Late Latin *syllabus,* a misreading of Greek *síllybos* parchment label, of uncertain origin. The Late Latin form probably originated from a misprint in early editions of Cicero's *Letters to Atticus.*

syllogism (sil′əjizəm) *n.* form of argument or reasoning, consisting of two premises and a conclusion. Before 1387 *silogisme,* in Trevisa's translation of Higden's *Polychronicon;* borrowed from Old French *silogisme* a syllogism, learned borrowing from Latin *syllogismus,* from Greek *syllogismós* a syllogism, originally, inference, conclusion, from *syllogízesthai* bring together, premise, infer, conclude, reckon up (*syl-* together, variant of *syn-*[1] before *l* + *logízesthai* to reason, reckon, count, from *lógos* a reckoning, reason; see LOGIC); for suffix see -ISM. **—syllogistic** *adj.* About 1449 *sillogistik,* borrowed from Latin *syllogisticus,* from Greek *syllogistikós* pertaining to syllogism, from *syllogízesthai* infer, conclude, reckon up; for suffix see -IC.

sylph (silf) *n.* 1657, an imaginary spirit of the air; borrowed from New Latin *sylphes,* pl., coined in the 1500's by Paracelsus. The original reference was to any of a race of beings or spirits inhabiting the air, described by Paracelsus as having mortality but lacking a soul. The transferred meaning of a slender, graceful girl or woman with light, airy movement is first recorded in English in Dickens' *Nicholas Nickleby* (1838).

sylvan *n.* one that inhabits or frequents the woods. 1565, a spirit of the woods, in Golding's translation of Ovid's *Metamorphoses;* borrowed from Middle French *sylvain,* and directly from Latin *silvānus* pertaining to wood or forest, from *silva* a wood, forest, grove, of uncertain origin. The spelling *sylvan* (with *y*) was introduced into English from French by influence of the synonymous Greek word *hȳ́lē* wood, forest. **—adj.** of or in the woods. 1580-83, in Robert Greene's *Mamillia,* from the noun.

sym- a form of the prefix *syn-*[1] before *b, m,* or *p* in words of Greek origin, as in *symbol, symmetry, sympathy, symphony.* Formed in Greek by assimilation of *n* before the following consonant.

symbiosis (sim′bīō′sis) *n.* close biological association of two unlike organisms. 1877, New Latin, from Greek *symbíōsis* a living together, from *symbioûn* live together, from *sýmbios* (one) living together (with another), partner (*sym-* together, variant of *syn-*[1] before *b* + *bíos* life; see QUICK); for suffix see -OSIS. An earlier sense of living together, communal or social life, is first recorded in 1622. **—symbiont** *n. Biology.* organism that lives in symbiosis. 1887, borrowed from Greek *symbiount-,* stem of *symbiôn,* present participle of *symbioûn* live together. **—symbiotic** *adj.* having to do with or living in symbiosis. 1882, formed from English *symbiosis,* on the analogy of such pairs of words as *neurosis, neurotic, osmosis, osmotic.* **—symbiotically** *adv.* (1888)

symbol *n.* About 1434 *simbal* creed, summary or religious belief; later *symbole* (1490); borrowed from Middle French *symbole,* and directly from Latin *symbolum* creed, token, mark, from Greek *sýmbolon* (*sym-* together, variant of *syn-*[1] before *b* + *bol-,* stem related to that of *bállein* to throw; see BALL[2] dancing party). Latin *symbolum* was used by Cyprian, bishop of Carthage, with reference to the baptismal creed, the mark or symbol of a Christian as distinguished from a heathen. The meaning of something that stands for something else, representative or typical figure, sign, or token, is first recorded in English in Spenser's *Faerie Queene* (1590). **—symbolic** *adj.* 1656, in Hobbes' *Six Lessons;* shortened form of *symbolical* (1607), perhaps by influence of French *symbolique;* borrowed from Late Latin *symbolicus,* from Greek *symbolikós* of or belonging to a symbol, from *sýmbolon* symbol; for suffix see -IC. —**symbolism** *n.* 1654, use of symbols; formed from English *symbol* + *-ism.* —**symbolize** *v.* 1590, unite (elements or substances of similar qualities), in Marlowe's *Tamburlane the Great;* formed from English *symbol* + *-ize* on the model of Middle French *symboliser* be alike, represent; from Latin *symbolum* symbol; for suffix see -IZE. The meaning of represent or stand for is first recorded in 1603, in Holland's translation of Plutarch's *Moralia.*

symmetry *n.* 1563, mutual relation of parts, proportion; borrowed from Middle French *symmétrie,* or directly from Latin *symmetria,* from Greek *symmetríā* agreement in dimensions, arrangement, from *sýmmetros* having a common measure, even, proportionate (*sym-* together, variant of *syn-*[1] before *m* + *métron* meter, see MEASURE). The meaning of well-balanced arrangement of parts, due proportion, harmony, is first recorded in 1599, in Ben Jonson's *Cynthia's Revels.* —**symmetrical** *adj.* 1751, characterized by symmetry, Samuel Johnson in *The Rambler;* formed from English *symmetry* + *-ical,* on the analogy of *geometry, geometrical.*

sympathy *n.* 1579, agreement in qualities, conformity, concord, in Lyly's *Euphues;* borrowed from Middle French *sympathie,* or directly from Late Latin *sympathīa* community of feeling, sympathy, from Greek *sympátheia,* from *sympathḗs* having a fellow-feeling, affected by like feelings (*sym-* together, variant of *syn-*[1] before *p* + *páthos* feeling; see PATHOS); for suffix see -Y[3]. The meaning of agreement in feelings or temperament is first recorded in English in 1596, in Spenser's writings, and that of compassion, commiseration, in 1600. —**sympathetic** *adj.* 1644, acting by a real or supposed affinity; shortened form of *sympathetical* (1639, also implied in *sympathetically*, 1621); borrowed from New Latin *sympatheticus,* from Greek *sympathētikós* having sympathy, from *sympathḗs* having a fellow feeling; patterned after *pathētikós* pathetic; for suffix see -IC, -ICAL. —**sympathize** *v.* 1597, feel or show sympathy; borrowed from French *sympathiser,* from *sympathie* sympathy; learned borrowing from Latin *sympathīa* sympathy; for suffix see -IZE.

symphony *n.* elaborate musical composition for an orchestra. About 1300 *symphonye* any of various musical instruments; later *simphonia* harmony (before 1398, in Trevisa's translation of Bartholomew's *De Proprietatibus Rerum*); borrowed from Old French *symphonie,* and directly from Latin *symphōnia* a unison of sounds, harmony, from Greek *symphōníā* harmony, concert, from *sýmphōnos* harmonious (*sym-* together, variant of *syn-*[1] before *p* + *phōnḗ* voice, sound; see -PHONE); for suffix see -Y[3]. The meaning of an instrumental passage in a vocal composition appeared in 1661, in Pepys' *Diary,* and that of an elaborate orchestral composition in 1789, in Charles Burney's *A General History of Music.* —**symphonic** *adj.* 1856, involving similarity of sound, borrowed from French *symphonique,* or formed in English from *symphony* + *-ic,* on the analogy of *harmony, harmonic.* The meaning of having to do with or like a symphony is first recorded in 1864. —**symphony orchestra** (1881)

symposium (simpō′zēəm) *n.* meeting or conference for discussion of some subject. Before 1586, account of a convivial party or gathering, specifically, the title of one of Plato's dialogues, in Sidney's *Apology for Poetry;* borrowed from Latin *symposium* drinking party, symposium, from Greek *sympósion* (*sym-* together, variant of *syn-*[1] before *p* + *pósis* a drinking, from *po-,* a stem related to that of *pínein* to drink, cognate with Latin *pōtāre* to drink; see POTION). The meaning of a convivial meeting for drinking, conversation, and intellectual entertainment is first recorded in English in 1711 (Addison in *The Spectator*). The transferred sense of a meeting or conference or of a collection of articles for discussion on some subject is first cited in 1784.

symptom *n.* 1541, indication or evidence of sickness, in Copland's translation of Galen's *Terapeutyke;* alteration (influenced by Middle French *symptome,* and Late Latin *symptōma*) of Middle English *sinthoma* (before 1398, in Trevisa's translation of Bartholomew's *De Proprietatibus Rerum*). The Middle English word was borrowed from Medieval Latin *sinthoma* symptom of a disease, from Late Latin *symptōma,* from Greek *sýmptōma* (genitive *symptṓmatos*) a happening, accident, disease, from a stem of *sympíptein* to befall (*sym-* together, variant of *syn-*[1] before *p* + *píptein* to fall; see FEATHER). The general sense of a sign, indication, is first recorded in English in 1611 (Ben Jonson, in Coryat's *Crudities*). —**symptomatic** *adj.* 1698, in Sir John Floyer's *A Treatise of the Asthma,* shortened form of *symptomatical* (1586); borrowed through French *symptomatique,* and directly from Late Latin *symptōmaticus,* from Greek *symptōmatikós,* from *sýmptōma* symptom; for suffix see -IC.

syn-[1] a prefix occurring in words of Greek origin and especially in many modern scientific and technical terms, meaning: with, together, jointly, at the same time, alike, as in *synchronous, syntax, synthesis;* or completely, thoroughly, as in *syncope.* Borrowed from Greek *syn-,* from the preposition *sýn,* earlier *xýn* with. Assimilations in Greek yielded variant forms that are seen in English as *syl-* before *l, sym-* before *b, m,* or *p,* and *sy-* before *s* followed by a consonant (as in *system*) and before *z;* before *s* followed by a vowel the assimilated form was *sys-* (an English example barely survives in the rare anatomical and medical term *syssarcosis*).

syn-[2] a combining form meaning synthetic, added to nouns, as in *synjet, synoil, synfuel.* 1971, abstracted in English from SYNTHETIC.

synagogue *n.* About 1175 *sinagoge* a Jewish house of worship; also, assembly or congregation of Jews; later *synagogue* (about 1300); borrowed from Old French *sinagoge,* learned borrowing from Late Latin *synagōga* congregation of Jews, from Greek *synagōgḗ* place of assembly, synagogue; literally, meeting, assembly, from *synágein* to gather, assemble (*syn-* together, syn-[1] + *ágein* bring, lead; see AGENT).

synapse (sin′aps) *n.* place where a nerve impulse passes from one nerve cell to another. 1899, borrowed from Greek *sýnapsis* conjunction, from *synáptein* to clasp (*syn-* together, syn-[1] + *háptein* to fasten, of uncertain origin). Related to APSE.

sync or **synch** *n. Informal.* synchronization of sound and action or of speech and lip movement. 1929, American English shortened form of SYNCHRONIZATION. The generalized figurative sense of be in agreement, happen or work at the same time, coincide, found in the phrase *in sync* is first recorded in John Steinbeck's *Winter of Our Discontent* (1961). —**v.** *Informal.* to synchronize. 1945, shortened form of SYNCHRONIZE.

synchronic *adj.* 1833, synchronous, simultaneous, in Lamb's *Essays;* probably a shortened form of earlier *synchronical* (1652, formed in English from Late Latin *synchronus* occurring at the same time, simultaneous + English *-ical*). The sense of dealing with a language only as it occurs at a given time, as opposed to historical or diachronic, is first recorded in English in 1922, in the writings of Leonard Bloomfield, and was probably a reborrowing into English from French *synchronique* (used by Ferdinand de Saussure before 1913).

synchronism *n.* occurrence at the same time. 1588, borrowed from New Latin *synchronismus,* from Greek *synchronismós,* from *sýnchronos* SYNCHRONOUS; for suffix see -ISM.

synchronize *v.* About 1624, to occur at the same time, be synchronous; borrowed from Greek *synchronízein* be of the same time, be contemporary, from *sýnchronos* happening at the same time; see SYNCHRONOUS; for suffix see -IZE. The sense of assign to the same time or period, make synchronous, is first recorded in 1806. **—synchronization** *n.* 1828, formed from English *synchronize* + *-ation.*

synchronous *adj.* occurring at the same time, simultaneous. 1669, borrowed from Late Latin *synchronus,* from Greek *sýnchronos* happening at the same time (*syn-* together, syn-[1] + *chrónos* time, of uncertain origin); for suffix see -OUS.

synchrotron (sing′krətron) *n.* high-energy particle accelerator. 1945, formed from English *synchro(nous)* + *-tron;* so called because the frequency of its electric field can be adjusted so that it is synchronous with the motion of the particles. Compare CYCLOTRON.

syncopate *v.* 1605, shorten (a word) by omitting sounds from the middle, in writings of William Camden; probably a back formation from *syncopation,* on the model of Medieval Latin *syncopatus,* past participle of *syncopare* to shorten, from Late Latin *syncopē* SYNCOPE; for suffix see -ATE[1]. The meaning in music of modify (rhythm) by shifting accents, is first recorded in 1667, implied in *syncopated,* from the earlier use in *syncopation.* **—syncopation** *n.* About 1532, contraction of a word; 1597, shifting of accents in music; borrowed from Medieval Latin *syncopationem* (nominative *syncopatio*) a shortening or contraction, from *syncopare* shorten; for suffix see -ATION.

syncope (sing′kəpē) *n.* contraction of a word by omitting sounds from the middle. 1530 *syncopa,* in Palsgrave's *Lesclarcissement;* later *syncope* (1579), alteration (influenced by Greek *synkopḗ*) of Middle English *sincopene* (1464); borrowed from Late Latin *syncopēn* contraction of a word, a swoon, accusative of *syncopē,* from Greek *synkopḗ* contraction of a word; originally, a cutting off, from *synkóptein* to cut up (*syn-* together, thoroughly + *kóptein* to cut; see CAPON).

syncretism *n.* union or reconciliation of diverse tenets or practices. 1618, borrowed from French *syncrétisme* (1611), or directly from New Latin *syncretismus* (1615), from Greek *synkrētismós* union or federation of communities, from *synkrētízein* to combine against a common enemy, of uncertain origin; for suffix see -ISM. Explained in the 1500's and 1600's as meaning originally "to form alliances in the manner of the Cretans," hence supposedly formed from Greek *syn-* together + *Krḗs* (genitive *Krētós*) Cretan; but this explanation is generally regarded as folk etymology. The linguistic sense of the merging of two or more inflectional categories, such as the falling together of cases in the history of a declension, is first recorded in English in 1909. **—syncretize** *v.* to practice syncretism. 1675, borrowed from New Latin *syncretizare,* from Greek *synkrētízein* to combine; for suffix see -IZE.

syndic *n.* representative of a university or other corporation. 1601, civil magistrate, especially in Geneva; borrowed from French *syndic* chief representative or delegate, learned borrowing from Late Latin, and borrowed into English directly from Late Latin *syndicus* representative of a group or town, from Greek *sýndikos* public advocate (*syn-* together, syn-[1] + *díkē* defendant's justice, judgment, usage; see DICTION). The meaning of representative of a university or other corporation is first found in English in 1607.

syndicalism *n.* plan to put industry and government under the control of labor unions. 1907, borrowed from French *syndicalisme,* from *syndical* of a labor union, from *syndic* chief representative or delegate; see SYNDIC; for suffix see -ISM.

syndicate (sin′dəkit) *n.* combination of persons or companies to carry out some undertaking. 1624, council or body of representatives; borrowed from French *syndicat,* from *syndic* representative of a corporation, SYNDIC; for suffix see -ATE[1]. The extended sense of a combination of persons or companies to carry out some commercial undertaking first occurs in 1865. **—v.** (sin′dəkāt) 1610, to judge, censure, in Donne's *Pseudo-Martyr;* borrowed from Medieval Latin *syndicatus,* past participle of *syndicare* to examine as a magistrate, judge, censure, from Late Latin *syndicus* chief delegate, SYNDIC. The sense of control or manage by a syndicate is first recorded in English in 1882, and those of combine into a syndicate and publish simultaneously in a number of periodicals, both in 1889.

syndrome *n.* signs and symptoms considered together as characteristic of a particular disease. 1541, in Copland's translation of Galen's *Terapeutyke;* borrowed from New Latin, from Greek *syndromḗ* concurrence of symptoms, concourse, from *sýndromos,* literally, running together (*syn-* with, syn-[1] + *drómos* running, course, see DROMEDARY). The current general sense of behavior pattern, attitude, is first recorded in 1955.

synecdoche (sinek′dəkē) *n.* figure of speech by which a part is put for the whole, or the whole for a part (as in *a fleet of ten sail*). 1483, in Caxton's version of *The Golden Legend;* alteration (influenced by Late Latin *synecdochē*) of Middle English *synodoches* (before 1397, in the Wycliffe Bible); borrowed from Medieval Latin *synodoche.* The Medieval Latin word was itself an alteration of Late Latin *synecdochē,* from Greek *synekdochḗ,* from *synekdéchesthai* supply a thought or word, take with something else (*syn-* with, syn-[1] + *ek-* out, from *ex-* + *déchesthai* to receive, related to *dokeîn* seem good; see DECENT).

synergism (sin′ərjizəm) *n.* 1764, theological doctrine that the human will cooperates with divine grace in regeneration; borrowed from New Latin *synergismus,* from Greek *synergós* working together; see SYNERGY; for suffix see -ISM. The sense of the combined activity of two drugs or other substances is first recorded in 1910, probably suggested by the earlier use of this sense in *synergistic* (1876), or in *synergy* (1847). The figurative sense of interactive or interdependent, mutually responsive, is first recorded in 1925. **—synergist** *n.* 1657, person who holds the doctrine of synergism; borrowed from New Latin *synergista,* from Greek *synergós* working together; for suffix see -IST.

The sense of a drug, organ, etc., that works together with another or others, is first recorded in English in 1876. **—synergistic** *adj.* 1818, of or pertaining to synergism or the synergists, in Todd's revision of Johnson's *Dictionary;* formed from English *synergist* + *-ic.* The sense of acting as a synergist in medicine and physiology is found in 1876.

synergy (sin′ərjē) *n.* combined action of a group of bodily organs, drugs, etc. 1660, cooperation; borrowed from New Latin *synergia,* from Greek *synergíā* joint work, assistance, help, from *synergós* working together, related to *synergeîn* work together, help another in work (*syn-* together, syn-[1] + *érgon* WORK); for suffix see -Y[3]. The modern scientific sense of the combined action of a group of bodily organs, mental faculties, drugs, etc., is first recorded in English in 1847.

synod (sin′əd) *n.* church council. Before 1121 *sinoth,* in *Peterborough Chronicle;* later *synod* (before 1382, in the Wycliffe Bible); borrowed from Late Latin *synodus,* from Greek *sýnodos* assembly, meeting, conjunction of planets (*syn-* together, syn-[1] + *hodós* a going, a way; see CEDE). **—synodic** *adj.* 1640, made by or proceeding from a synod; borrowed from Late Latin *synodicus,* from Greek *synodikós* of a meeting or conjunction, from *sýnodos* assembly, meeting, conjunction; for suffix see -IC.

synonym *n.* Probably before 1425 *sinonymes,* pl., a word having the same sense as another, in a translation of Higden's *Polychronicon;* borrowed from Middle French *synonyme,* and directly from Latin *synōnymum,* from Greek *synṓnymon,* noun use of neuter of *synṓnymos* having the same name as, synonymous (*syn-* together, same + *ónyma,* dialectal form of *ónoma* NAME). The earliest examples of this word are plural, with Latin *-a* or English *-es.* The Anglicized singular is rarely found before the late 1700's. **—synonymous** *adj.* having the same or nearly the same meaning. 1610, in Donne's *Pseudo-Martyr;* borrowed from Medieval Latin *synonymus,* from Greek *synṓnymos;* for suffix see -OUS. **—synonymy** *n.* use, set, or system of synonyms. 1657, borrowed from French *synonymie,* and directly from Late Latin *synōnymia,* from Greek *synōnymíā* likeness of name or meaning, from *synṓnymos* synonymous; for suffix see -Y[3]. An earlier sense "synonym" appeared in 1609.

synopsis (sinop′sis) *n.* 1611, condensed statement, summary, digest, in Coryat's *Crudities;* borrowed from Late Latin *synopsis* a synopsis, from Greek *sýnopsis* general view (see OPTIC), from a stem of *synorân* to see altogether, all at once (*syn-* together, syn-[1] + *horân* to see, view; see WARY). **—synoptic** *adj.* giving a synopsis. 1763, borrowed from New Latin *synopticus,* from Greek *synoptikós* seeing the whole together, from *sýnopsis* synopsis; for suffix see -IC.

syntax *n.* arrangement of words in a sentence. 1605, orderly arrangement of parts or elements, in Bacon's *Of the Advancement of Learning;* borrowed from French *syntaxe,* and directly from Late Latin *syntaxis,* from Greek *sýntaxis* a putting together or in order, arrangement, syntax, from stem of *syntássein* put in order (*syn-* together, syn-[1] + *tássein* arrange; see TACTICS). The grammatical sense of an arrangement of words in a sentence is first recorded in English in Cawdrey's *A Table Alphabeticall* (1613). **—syntactic** *adj.* 1807, belonging or relating to grammatical syntax; borrowed from New Latin *syntacticus,* from Greek *syntaktikós* a joining together or in order, from *syntássein* put in order; for suffix see -IC.

synthesis *n.* combination of parts or elements into a whole. 1611, deductive reasoning from causes or principles to effects or particular instances; borrowed from Latin *synthesis* collection, set, composition (of a medication), from Greek *sýnthesis* composition (logical, mathematical), from *syntithénai* put together, combine (*syn-* together, syn-[1] + *tithénai* put, place; see DO[1] perform). The meaning of formation of a compound by the chemical union of elements is first recorded in English in 1733. The general sense of a combination of parts of elements into a whole is first recorded in 1833. An isolated instance of the word occurs in Middle English (about 1450, in *Battlefield Grammar)* with the spelling *sintecis.* **—synthesize** *v.* combine into a complex whole. 1830; formed from English *synthesis* + *-ize.* **—synthetic** *adj.* 1697, deductive; borrowed through French *synthétique,* or directly from New Latin *syntheticus,* from Greek *synthetikós* skilled in putting together, from *synthetós* put together, combined, from *syntithénai* to combine; for suffix see -IC. The sense of made artificially by chemical synthesis is first recorded in 1874. *—n.* synthetic product. 1934, from the adjective.

syphilis (sif′əlis) *n.* contagious venereal disease. 1718, New Latin, originally the title of a poem (full name, *Syphilis, sive Morbus Gallicus* Syphilis, or the French Disease), published in 1530 by Cirolamo Fracastoro, 1483-1553, an Italian physician, astronomer, and poet. The poem told the story of the shepherd *Syphilus,* supposedly the first sufferer from the disease. His name is of uncertain origin; the spelling was altered to *Syphilis* by influence of *Aeneis, Thebais,* and similar names. In 1686 the poem was translated into English by Nahum Tate with the title "Syphilis: or, a Poetical History of the French Disease." **—syphilitic** *adj.* 1786, borrowed from New Latin *syphiliticus,* from *syphilis* syphilis; for suffix see -IC. *—n.* 1181, from the adjective.

syringe (sərinj′) *n.* device for injecting or withdrawing fluids. Before 1398 *suringa* a catheter or a tube used for irrigating wounds, etc., in Trevisa's translation of Bartholomew's *De Proprietatibus Rerum;* later *siringe* (probably before 1425), *syringe* (before 1475); borrowed from Late Latin *sȳringa* from Greek *sȳ́ringa,* accusative of *sŷrinx* tube, hole, channel, shepherd's pipe, of uncertain origin. The sense of a hypodermic syringe is known in English before 1889. **—v.** inject with a syringe. 1610, from the noun.

syrinx (sir′ingks) *n.* vocal organ of birds. 1606, a musical instrument known before 1387 in English; borrowed from Latin *syrinx,* from Greek *sŷrinx* shepherd's pipe; see SYRINGE. The meaning of a vocal organ of birds is first recorded in English in 1872.

syrup *n.* Before 1398 *suripe, sirupe, syrop* thick, sweet liquid, in Trevisa's translation of Bartholomew's *De Proprietatibus Rerum;* borrowed from Old French *sirop,* possibly also through Italian *siroppo,* from Arabic *sharāb* a drink, beverage, syrup, related to *shariba* he drank. Compare SHERBET. **—syrupy** *adj.* 1707, formed from English *syrup* + *-y*[1].

system *n.* 1619, the whole creation, the universe, in writings of John Selden; borrowed from Late Latin *systēma* an arrangement, system, from Greek *sýstēma* organized whole, body (*sy-* together, variant of *syn-*[1] before *s* + *stā-,* root of *histánai* cause to STAND). The meaning of a set of correlated principles, facts, ideas, etc., is first recorded in English before 1656. **—systematic** *adj.* Before 1680, according to a system; borrowed from French *systématique,* and directly from Late Latin *systēmaticus,* from Greek *systēmatikós* combined in one whole, systematic, from *sýstēma* (genitive *systḗmatos*) system; for suffix see -IC. **—systematize** *v.* 1764, to arrange according to a system; borrowed from French *systématiser,* or formed in English from Late Latin *systēma* (genitive *systēmatis*) system + English *-ize.* **—systemic** *adj.* 1803, belonging to, supplying, or affecting the body as a whole, in John Barclay's *A New Anatomical Nomenclature;* formed from English *system* + *-ic.*

systole (sis′təlē) *n.* normal, rhythmical contraction of the heart. 1578, in John Banister's *The History of Man;* borrowed from Greek *systolḗ* contraction (*sy-* together, variant of *syn-*[1] before *s* + *stol-,* stem related to that of *stéllein* to put, send; see STALL[1] place). Compare DIASTOLE.

syzygy (siz′əjē) *n. Astronomy.* conjunction or opposition of two celestial bodies. 1656, in Blount's *Glossographia;* borrowed from Late Latin *syzygia,* from Greek *syzygíā* yoke, pair, union of two, conjunction, from *syzygeîn* to yoke together (*sy-* together, variant of *syn-*[1] before *z* + *zygón* YOKE); for suffix see -Y[3].

T

-t¹ a suffix found in the past tense and the past participle of some verbs, as in *kept, thought, built, meant, dreamt, lost, sent.* The past tense form of the ending of such verbs in Old English was (in first and third persons singular) *-te,* a form of *-de* assimilated to a preceding voiceless consonant (see -ED¹). The past participle of these verbs in Old English had the ending *-t,* an assimilated form of *-d* (see -ED²). In Middle English the corresponding endings were *-te* in the past tense and *-t* in the participle.

-t² a variant form of the suffix *-th¹* (in *depth, length, strength,* etc.), often used after *h,* as in *height* (Middle English *hihthe*), *sleight* (Middle English *sleahthe*), but also in forms like *theft* (Old English *thēofth*), *drought* (Middle English *drouth*), and others.

tab¹ *n.* small flap, strap, loop, or piece. 1607, in Markham's *Cavelarice;* possibly a dialectal word of uncertain origin. **—v.** to put a tab on (something). 1872 (implied in *tabbed*); from the noun.

tab² *n.* account, bill or check. 1889, American English, probably shortened form of *tabulation* or *tablet,* in a sense extended from a sheet for writing upon.

tab³ *n. Informal.* tablet, pill. Before 1961, American English, shortened form of *tablet.*

tabard *n.* short, loose coat worn by heralds. 1253 *thabardo;* later *taberd* (1293), *tabart* (1295), *tabard* (probably before 1300); borrowed from early Spanish *tabardo* and Old French *tabart,* of unknown origin.

Tabasco *n.* trademark of a kind of peppery sauce. 1876 *tabasco,* American English; named after *Tabasco,* a state and river in Mexico, perhaps because it was first encountered there by American and European travelers.

tabby *n.* 1638, silk cloth with a striped pattern; borrowed from French *tabis* a rich, watered silk, from Middle French *atabis,* from Arabic *'attābīya,* from *'Attābiy,* a section of Baghdad where such cloth was first made. In the extended sense of a striped cat, *tabby* is first found in Goldsmith's writings in 1774, shortened from earlier *tabby cat* (1695, in Congreve's *Love for Love*). **—adj.** 1638, made of tabby cloth, from the noun.

tabernacle *n.* About 1250, portable sanctuary carried by the Israelites in the wilderness, in *Genesis and Exodus;* borrowing of Old French *tabernacle,* learned borrowing from Latin, and borrowed into English directly from Latin *tabernāculum* tent, especially a tent of an augur (for taking observations), diminutive of *taberna* hut, cabin, booth; see TAVERN. The general sense of a temporary dwelling, tent, is first recorded in Middle English about 1300. The specific sense of a house of worship, especially a large church, is first recorded in 1711.

table *n.* About 1175, board, slab, plate, tablet; in part borrowed from Old French *table,* and in part developed from Old English (about 1000) *tabele;* earlier *tabule* (before 899, in Alfred's translation of Bede's *Ecclesiastical History*). Both the Old French and the Old English words were borrowed from Latin *tabula* a board, plank, table, small flat slab or piece usually intended to receive an inscription, itself probably a borrowed word of uncertain origin. The meaning of piece of furniture having a flat top on legs is first recorded in Middle English, probably before 1300, in *Kyng Alisaunder.* The extended sense of an arrangement of numbers or other items for convenience of reference or calculation, is also found in *Kyng Alisaunder.* **—v.** About 1450 *tablen* enter in a table or list; later, provide with meals (1457-58); from the noun. The parliamentary meaning of postpone action on (a bill or motion) by voting to leave it on the presiding officer's table is first recorded in 1849, in American English. **—table book** (1845, later *coffee-table book,* 1962) **—tablecloth** *n.* (1467) **—table lamp** (about 1849) **—tableland** *n.* plateau (1697). **—tablespoon** *n.* (1763) **—tablespoonful** *n.* (1772) **—table talk** (before 1569) **—table tennis** (1887) **—tabletop** *n.* (1807) **—tableware** *n.* (1772)

tableau (tablō′) *n.* striking scene, picture. 1699, in Martin Lister's *Journey to Paris;* borrowing of French *tableau* picture, painting, diminutive of Old French *table* slab, writing tablet; see TABLE.

table d'hôte (tä′ bəl dōt′) meal served at a fixed time and price. Before 1617, communal table for hotel guests, a French phrase used in a book relating to travel in Continental Europe; literally, host's table. The meaning of a meal served (at a communal table) at a fixed time and price is first recorded in English in 1816.

tablet *n.* About 1300, slab or flat surface intended to bear an inscription; borrowed from Old French *tablete;* later *tablette,* both diminutive forms of *table* slab; see TABLE; for suffix see -ET. The meaning of a small flat or compressed piece of candy, drug, etc., lozenge, pill, is first recorded in English in 1582. The sense of a pad of writing paper is first recorded in 1880, in American English.

tabloid *n.* newspaper that has short articles, many pictures, and often sensational headlines. 1884 *Tabloid,* trademark for compressed or concentrated chemicals and drugs; formed from English *tablet* + *-oid.* The term was registered by Burroughs, Wellcome and Co., in London, but was soon (by 1898) applied figuratively and in lower-case form to a compressed form or dose of anything. The term *tabloid journalism* appeared in 1901; *tabloid* in the sense of a newspaper typifying tabloid (condensed) journalism by having short news articles, etc., is first recorded in 1918.

taboo or **tabu** *adj.* 1777, (among the Polynesians) consecrated, inviolable, forbidden, unclean, or cursed, in Captain James Cook's *A Voyage to the Pacific Ocean;* borrowed from Tongan (usually rendered *taboo*), the Polynesian language of the island country of Tonga, in the South Pacific. *Taboo, tabu* is the form of the Tongan word as well as of several languages of Melanesia and

Micronesia; the Maori form is *tapu* and in Hawaiian it is *kapu*. Some of the Melanesian languages, like Fiji, have the form *tambu*. The accentuation (tabü′) and the use of the word as a noun and verb are English innovations; in the Polynesian languages the word is stressed on the first syllable and is generally used only as an adjective. —**n.** 1777, the practice among the Polynesians of putting people or things under an inviolable ban, the act of setting a person or thing apart as sacred, unclean, or cursed; from the adjective in English. —**v.** 1777, to put under a taboo, ban, forbid; from the adjective in English.

tabor or **tabour** (tā′bər) *n.* small drum. Probably before 1300 *tabour,* in *Kyng Alisaunder;* borrowing of Old French *tabour, tabur,* probably from Persian *tabīr* drum. Related to TAMBOURINE.

tabular *adj.* 1656, having the form of a slab or tablet, in Blount's *Glossographia;* borrowed from Latin *tabulāris* of a slab or tablet, from *tabula* slab; see TABLE; for suffix see -AR. The meaning of entered in a table or list is first recorded in 1710.

tabulate *v.* arrange (facts, figures, etc.) in tables or lists. 1734, formed in English from Latin *tabula* TABLE + English *-ate*[1]. An earlier sense of lay a board, plank, floor, is first recorded in Blount's *Glossographia* (1656). —**tabulation** *n.* process of arranging in tables or lists. 1837, formed from English *tabulate* + *-ation.* An earlier sense of the making of a floor is first recorded in Phillips' *Dictionary* (1658) as a borrowing of Latin *tabulātiōnem* (nominative *tabulātiō*) a flooring over, a boarding, from *tabula* board + *-ātiōnem* -ation.

tachometer (təkom′ətər) *n.* instrument for measuring speed of rotation. 1810, formed in English from Greek *tacho-,* stem of *táchos* speed (related to *tachýs* swift, of unknown origin) + English *-meter,* as in *barometer.*

tachyon (tak′ēon) *n.* hypothetical elementary particle with a speed greater than that of light. 1967, formed in English from Greek *tachy-,* stem of *tachýs* swift (related to *táchos* speed) + English *-on,* as in *electron, proton,* etc. The word was coined by the American physicist Gerald Feinberg. —**tachyonic** *adj.* having to do with tachyons, being a tachyon. 1970, formed from English *tachyon* + *-ic.*

tacit *adj.* 1604, saying nothing, still, silent, in Cawdrey's *A Table Alphabeticall;* borrowed through French *tacite,* and directly from Latin *tacitus* that is passed over in silence, done without words, assumed, silent, from past participle of *tacērę* be silent. Latin *tacēre* is cognate with Old Saxon *thagōn, thagian* be silent, Old High German *dagēn,* Old Icelandic *thegja,* and Gothic *thahan,* from Indo-European **tak-/takē(i)-* (Pok. 1055). The meaning of implied or understood without being openly expressed is found in English in 1637-50.

taciturn *adj.* speaking very little. 1771, in Smollett's *The Expedition of Humphry Clinker;* probably a back formation from *taciturnity,* formed on the model of Latin *taciturnus* disposed to be silent, from *tacitus* silent; see TACIT. —**taciturnity** *n.* Before 1500, borrowed from Middle French *taciturnité,* and probably directly from Latin *taciturnitātem* (nominative *taciturnitās*) a being or keeping silent, from *taciturnus* taciturn; for suffix see -ITY.

tack *n.* 1296-97 *tacke* clasp, hook, fastener; later *tak* (about 1390); borrowed from Old North French *taque* nail, pin, peg, probably from a Germanic source (compare Middle Dutch *tacke* twig, spike, Low German *takk* tine, pointed thing, modern German *Zacke* spike, prong) of uncertain origin. The nautical meaning of a rope to hold the corner of a sail in place is first recorded in 1481-90. The meaning of a sharp-pointed nail with a flat head, is first recorded in 1463 in the compound *taknail.* —**v.** Probably about 1200 (possibly as *tac(k)en*) attach, fasten; later *takken* (before 1387); ultimately, probably borrowed from the same Germanic source as the noun. The nautical meaning of shift the tacks in order to sail into the wind is first recorded in 1557.

tackle *n.* About 1250 *takel* equipment, apparatus, gear, in *Genesis and Exodus;* earlier as a surname (1179); borrowed from Middle Dutch or Middle Low German *takel* the rigging of a ship, perhaps related to Middle Dutch *taken* grasp, seize, TAKE; for suffix see -LE[1]. The meaning of a device for lifting, lowering or moving heavy things is first recorded in English in 1539-40. —**v.** About 1340 *takilen* entangle, involve; from the noun. The meaning of grip physically, lay hold of, attack, is first recorded in 1828, and the figurative sense of try to deal with (a task or problem), in 1847.

tacky[1] *adj.* very sticky or gummy. 1788, formed from English *tack,* in the sense of an act of attaching lightly or temporarily (1705) + *-y*[1].

tacky[2] *adj. Informal.* in poor taste, cheap, vulgar. 1862, shabby, seedy, American English, adjective use of earlier *tackey* small or inferior horse (1800), also American English, of uncertain origin. The sense of vulgar, in poor taste, is first recorded in 1883.

taco (tä′kō) *n.* folded tortilla filled with chopped meat, etc. Before 1940, borrowing of Mexican Spanish *taco,* from Spanish *taco* wad, plug, stopper, bite, snack, of uncertain origin.

tact *n.* 1651, sense of touch or feeling; borrowed from Latin *tāctus* (genitive *tāctūs*) touch, feeling, handling, sense of touch, from *tag-* a root of *tangere* to touch; see TANGENT. The meaning of a delicate sense of fitness or propriety, discernment, diplomacy, is first recorded in English in 1804-06; earlier, in reference to the same meaning in French (1793); borrowing of French *tact* (Voltaire 1769), from Latin *tāctus.* An isolated instance of the word is found in Middle English as *tactthe* (about 1200, in *Vices and Virtues*).

tactics *n.* procedures to gain advantage. 1626, art or science of deploying military or naval forces in battle, in William Gouge's *The Dignity of Chivalry;* possibly in part a back formation from earlier *tactical* + *-s,* modeled on, and in part borrowed from New Latin *tactica* the art of deploying forces in war, neuter plural, from Greek *taktikḕ téchnē* art of arrangement, noun use of feminine of *taktikós* of or pertaining to arrangement or ordering, especially tactics in war, adjective to *táxis* order, verbal noun of *tássein* arrange; for suffix see -ICS. Greek *tássein* , related to *tāgós* leader, chief, is cognate with Lithuanian *patogùs* respectable, comfortable, *sutógti* to get married, and Tocharian A *tāśśi* (plural) leaders, commanders, from Indo-European **tāg-/təg-* (Pok.1055). The transferred meaning of methods or procedures to gain advantage or success is first recorded in English in 1763. —**tactical** *adj.* 1570, of or pertaining to military tactics; formed in English from Greek *taktikós* of tactics + English *-al*[1]. —**tactician** *n.* 1798, person skilled in tactics; borrowed from French *tacticien,* from *tactique* tactics, from Greek *taktikḕ téchnē* art of arrangement; for suffix see -IAN.

tactile *adj.* of or pertaining to touch. 1615, that can be felt by touch, tangible; borrowed from French *tactile,* and directly from Latin *tāctilis* tangible, that may be touched, from *tag-,* root of *tangere* to touch; see TANGENT.

tad *n.* 1877, American English, a young or small child, probably a shortened form of TADPOLE. The extended meaning of a small amount (as in *a tad of salt, feeling a tad better*) is first recorded in dialectal American English in 1915.

tadpole *n.* immature frog or toad. Probably before 1475 *taddepol* (*tadde* TOAD + *pol* head, roundhead; see POLL).

tael (tāl) *n.* unit of weight of eastern Asia. 1588, a former Chinese unit of money; originally a tael (in weight) of silver; borrowed from Portuguese *tael,* from Malay *tahil* weight, probably from Hindi *tolā,* from Sanskrit *tulā́* balance, weight. Sanskrit *tulā́* is cognate with Greek *talássai* to bear, endure, and Gothic *thulan* to endure, from Indo-European **tel-/telə-/tlā-* (Pok. 1060). The sense of a unit of weight of eastern Asia is first found in English in 1598.

taffeta *n.* 1345-49 *taffata* stiff silk cloth with a smooth, glossy surface; later *taffeta* (1393-94); borrowed from Old French *taffetas,* from Italian *taffetà,* ultimately from Persian *tāftah* silk or linen cloth, noun use of *tāftah,* past participle of *tāftan* to shine, twist, spin, from a lost verb **tāpayati* he spins, a causative of **tap-,* from Indo-European **tm̥p-,* root **temp-* (Pok.1064), the source of Latin *tempus* time, and Lithuanian *tem̃pti* to stretch by pulling.

taffrail *n.* rail around a ship's stern. 1814, alteration of earlier *tafferel* the upper panel on the stern of a sailing ship, often ornamented (1704); earlier, a carved panel (1622-23); borrowed from Dutch *tafereel* panel for painting or carving, formed by dissimilation of *l. . .l* to *r. . .l,* from **tafeleel,* diminutive of *tafel* table, from Latin *tabula* slab, board; see TABLE. Dutch *tafereel* developed from the practice of ornamenting the high, broad, and generally flattened sterns of sailing ships. The spelling with *-rail* in English is the result of association (by folk etymology) with *rail*[1], n.

taffy *n.* kind of chewy candy made of brown sugar or molasses boiled down. 1817, perhaps originally a dialectal term for *toffee,* found in North America, Scotland, and northern England; of uncertain origin (perhaps in North America associated with *tafia* 1777, a rumlike alcoholic liquor of the West Indies, written also *tafia* in a French source in 1722; or with *tafia* a similar liquor also distilled from molasses, brown sugar, etc., found in Malay dictionaries; the connection with the simple candy presumably arising from the syrupy mixture skimmed off the liquor during distillation, probably eaten in some more reduced or dried form as candy). This accounts for the term in North America, but it is difficult to see how *taffy* would arise in the northern areas of Great Britain without appearing in the great port cities of the south — a reason for more closely associating *taffy* with *toffee,* which is further reinforced by similarity of sound and form.

tag[1] *n.* small hanging piece. Before 1400 *tagge* small hanging piece of cloth; earlier as a surname (1195); perhaps borrowed from a Scandinavian source (compare Norwegian *tagg* point, prong, barb, and Swedish *tagg* prickle, thorn). The Scandinavian words are probably cognate with Middle Low German *tagge, tacke* branch, twig, spike, and Middle Dutch *tacke* (modern Dutch *tak*); see TACK. The meaning of a piece of strong paper or other material fastened to something as a label is first recorded in American English, in 1835. **—v.** 1436 *tagen* furnish with a tag (implied in *taging*); from the noun.

tag[2] *n.* children's game in which one player chases the others until he touches one. 1738, perhaps variant of earlier Scottish *tig* touch, tap (1721); probably an alteration of Middle English *tek* touch, tap; see TICK[2] sound. **—v.** to tap or touch with the hand. 1878, American English; from the noun.

t'ai chi (tī′ jē′), or more fully **t'ai chi ch'uan** (chwän′) Chinese system of exercise and self-defense. 1962, borrowing of Chinese (*t'ai* extreme + *chi* limit + *ch'uan* fist, boxing).

taiga (tī′gə) *n.* swampy evergreen forest land. 1888, borrowing of Russian *taigá,* of Mongolian origin.

tail *n.* Probably before 1200 *taile* animal's tail, in Layamon's *Chronicle of Britain;* developed from Old English (before 800) *tægl, tægel;* cognate with Middle Low German *tagel* end of a rope, Old High German *zagal* animal's tail (dialectal German *Zagel*), Old Icelandic *tagl* horse's tail, Gothic *tagl* hair, from Proto-Germanic **taȝlá-.* Cognates outside Germanic are found in Old Irish *dūal* lock of hair, and perhaps with Sanskrit *daśā* fringe, wick, from Indo-European **dek-/dok-* tear apart, fray out (Pok.191). **—v.** 1523, to attach to the tail or hind end; from the noun. The informal sense of follow as a detective or spy is first recorded in 1907, in American English. **—adj.** at the tail, back or rear. 1673, from the noun. **—tailgate** *n.* board at the back of a vehicle that can be let down for loading and unloading (1868, American English). —*v.* drive too close behind another vehicle. 1951 (implied in *tailgating*), American English, from the noun. **—taillight** *n.* warning light at the back end of a vehicle (1844). **—tailspin** *n.* (1917, spinning downward movement of an airplane; 1928, state of chaos or panic, uncontrollable decline) **—tail wind** (1897)

tailor *n.* About 1300; borrowed through Anglo-French *taillour,* variant of Old French *tailleor* a cutter, tailor, from *tailler* to cut, from Late Latin *tāliāre* to split, from Latin *tālea* a slender stick, rod, staff, a cutting, twig, cognate with Greek *tâlis* young marriageable girl, from Indo-European **tāl-* grow, be green (Pok.1055); for suffix see -OR[2]. **—v.** 1662 (implied in *tailoring*), to do tailor's work; 1856, to make by tailor's work; from the noun. The general sense of adjust or alter is first recorded in 1942, in American English.

taint *v.* 1591, to touch or tinge with something undesirable, in Shakespeare's *1 Henry VI;* a fusion of Middle English *teynten* to convict, prove guilty (about 1350), and early modern English *taynt* to color, dye, tinge (before 1533). The earlier verb *teynten* was borrowed from Old French *ataint,* past participle of *ataindre* to touch upon, seize; see ATTAIN. The later verb *taynt* was borrowed from Anglo-French *teinter* to color, dye, from Old French *teint,* past participle of *teindre, taindre* to dye, color, from Latin *tingere* to TINGE. **—n.** 1601, a stain or spot, in Shakespeare's *Twelfth Night;* a fusion of Middle English *taynte* a blow, hit (about 1400), and early modern English *tainte* color, dye, tinge (1567). The Middle English noun *taynte* was borrowed (with loss of initial vowel) from Middle French *ateinte, atainte* one who is blemished, noun use of feminine past participle of *ataindre* to touch upon, seize. Early modern English *tainte* was borrowed from Middle French *teint* color, dye, noun use of Old French *teint,* past participle.

take *v.* Probably before 1200 *taken,* in Layamon's *Chronicle of Britain;* developed from Late Old English *tacan* (about 1100, in the *Anglo-Saxon Chronicle,* perhaps before 1000 in the Danelaw); borrowed from a Scandinavian source (compare Old Icelandic *taka* take, grasp, lay hold, past tense *tōk,* past participle *tekinn*). Old Icelandic *taka* is cognate with Middle Low German *tacken* to take, Middle Dutch *taken,* and Gothic *tēkan* to touch, from Proto-Germanic **tǣkanan,* Indo-European **dēg-/dəg-* lay hold of (Pok.183). In Middle English, this verb gradually replaced *nimen* to take; see NUMB.

The basic senses are to lay hold of (about 1000, in Old English), to accept or receive (as in *take my advice,* about 1200); from these developed to absorb (as in *take a high polish,* before 1325); to choose, select (as in *take the shortest way,* about 1275); to make, obtain (as in *take a bath,* 1375); to become affected by (as in *take cold,* before 1325).

—n. 1511, a lease of land or of a farm; from the verb. The sense of the amount taken (as in *a great take of fish*), that which is taken or received in payment, is first recorded in 1654.

—takeoff *n.* (1826, something that detracts or diminishes; 1846, parody; 1869, act of leaping into the air; 1904, act of becoming airborne) **—takeover** *n.* (1917, American English)

talc (talk) *n.* soft, smooth mineral. 1582 *talke;* later *talc* (1601); borrowed from Middle French *talc,* probably from Spanish *talco,* and Medieval Latin *talcum* talc; both from Arabic *ṭalq,* from Persian *talk* talc. **—v.** treat or rub with talc. 1888, from the noun.

talcum (tal'kəm) *n.* talc, especially powdered talc used on the body. 1558, borrowed from Medieval Latin *talcum* any of various shiny minerals, from Arabic *ṭalq;* see TALC. **—talcum powder** (1901)

tale *n.* Probably about 1150 *tale* story, account, counting; developed from Old English *talu* (about 950, in *Lindisfarne Gospels*); cognate with Old Frisian *tale* number, speech, Old Saxon *tala* number, Middle Low German and Middle Dutch *tāle* speech, narrative (modern Dutch *taal*), Old High German *zala* number, Middle High German *zal* number, story (modern German *Zahl* number, *Erzählung* story),Old Icelandic *tala* speech, narrative, number (Swedish and Icelandic *tal*), from Proto-Germanic **talō,* and Gothic *talzjan* to teach; outside Germanic probably cognate with Greek *dólos* craftiness, from Indo-European **del-/dol-* aim at, calculate, lie in wait (Pok.193). For similar semantic connections compare COUNT and RECOUNT. Related to TALK and TELL.

talent *n.* Probably before 1300, inclination, disposition, will, desire, in *Arthour and Merlin* and *Kyng Alisaunder;* borrowed from Old French *talent,* learned borrowing from Medieval Latin *talentum* inclination, leaning, will, desire, from Latin *talentum* balance, weight, sum of money, from Greek *tálanton,* related to *tlênai* to bear, suffer; see TOLERATE. The meaning of an ancient unit of weight or money is found in Middle English before 1382, in the Wycliffe Bible, borrowed directly from Latin *talentum.* The meaning of a special natural ability, aptitude, is first found in Lydgate's *Minor Poems* (about 1430), and developed from a figurative use of the word in the sense of money, value, taken from the parable of the talents in the Bible (Matthew 25:14-30).

talesman (tālz'mən *or* tā'lēzmən) *n.* person chosen among bystanders in court to fill out a jury. 1679, formed from Middle English *tales* writ ordering bystanders to serve (1495) + *man.* Middle English *tales* was borrowed through Anglo-French from Latin *tālēs,* in the phrase *tālēs dē circumstantibus* such (or similar) persons from those standing about, used in the writ. Latin *tālēs* is a noun use of the plural of *tālis* such.

talisman (tal'isman *or* tal'izmən) *n.* amulet, charm. 1638, borrowed from French *talisman* (perhaps known earlier in Spanish *talismán*), in part from Arabic *ṭilsam,* both the Arabic and also in part the French from Late Greek *télesma* talisman, religious rite, payment, from Greek in the sense of consecration ceremony, payment; originally, completion, from *teleîn* perform (religious rites), pay (tax), fulfill, accomplish, from *télos* services due, completion, end, tax, cognate with Sanskrit *tulā́* weight, and Latin *tollere* to lift, from Indo-European **tel-/tol-/tḷ-* (Pok.1060). The earliest use in English referred to stone statues in Egypt and Greece, but by 1652 the reference was to astrological charms.

talk *v.* Probably before 1200 *talken,* in *Ancrene Riwle* and Layamon's *Chronicle of Britain;* related to Middle English *tale* story, account, TALE. A possible cognate may exist in East Frisian *talken* to talk, chatter, whisper. **—n.** Probably about 1380 *talke* speech, discourse; earlier as a surname (1328); from the noun. The meaning of an informal or short lecture is first recorded in 1900. **—talkative** *adj.* Before 1425, tending to talk, in a translation of Higden's *Polychronicon;* formed from Middle English *talken* to talk + *-ative.* **—talking-to** *n. Informal.* a scolding (about 1875).

talkie *n. Informal.* motion picture with a synchronized sound track. 1913, American English, shortened form of *talking picture* (1908); patterned after *movie;* for suffix see -IE.

tall *adj.* About 1385 *talle* quick, prompt, in Chaucer's *The Complaint of Mars;* probably before 1400, brave, valiant, seemly, proper; later, attractive, handsome (about 1450); probably developed from Old English (about 1000) *getæl* prompt, active. Old English *getæl* is cognate with Old Saxon *gital* quick, prompt, Old High German *gizal,* and Gothic *untals* disobedient, related to *talzjan* teach; see TALE. The sense of being of more than average height is first recorded in Palsgrave's *Lesclarcissement* (1530). Compare STOUT for sense development, further consider the reverse development *stand* or *walk tall,* originally, to walk with one's head high; later, to be proud, be brave, valiant.

tallow *n.* hard fat from sheep, cows, etc., used for making candles and soap. Before 1382 *talowȝ,* in the Wycliffe Bible, a later form of *talwȝ* (before 1325; earlier in a surname *Talghmongere,* 1294); cognate with Middle Low German *talg, talch* tallow, and Middle Dutch *talch* (modern Dutch *talk*), from Proto-Germanic **talȝa-,* cognate with Armenian *tel* heavy rain, from Indo-European **del-* to drip (Pok.196). **—v.** smear with tallow. Probably before 1400 *talowen;* from the noun.

tally *n.* 1440 *taly, talye* stick marked with notches to indicate amount owed or paid, in *Promptorium Parvulorum,* (but found as early as 1166 in Anglo-Latin *talli-,* in the *Pipe Rolls* of Henry II); borrowed through Anglo-French *tallie,* from Medieval Latin *tallia,* from Latin *tālea* a cutting, rod, stick; see TAILOR. The meaning of a thing that matches another, counterpart, is first recorded in 1651, said to be from the practice of splitting a tally lengthwise, the debtor and creditor each retaining one of the halves. —**v.** mark on a tally, count up. Probably about 1200 *talien* keep an account; probably borrowed from Medieval Latin *talliare* to tax, from *tallia* tally. The extended sense of correspond, match, agree, fit, is first recorded in 1705, probably from the noun.

tallyho *interj.* hunter's cry on catching sight of the fox. 1772 *tallio;* earlier, as the name of a roistering character, Sir Toby *Tallyho* (1756, in a play by Samuel Foote); possibly an alteration of French *taïaut* cry used in deer hunting (in Molière's *Les Fâcheux,* 1662), from Old French *taho, tielau.* The spelling *tally ho* (two words) appeared in English in 1815; *tallyho* in 1835. An earlier form is found in Middle English *taylia* (probably before 1300); borrowed from Old French.

talon (tal'ən) *n.* claw. Probably before 1400 *taloun* dragon's claw, in *Morte Arthur;* earlier as a surname *talun* (1180); probably originally borrowed from Old French *talon* heel or hinder part of the foot of a beast, from Medieval Latin *talonem* heel, from Latin *tālus* ankle, TALUS[1].

talus[1] (tā'ləs) *n.* anklebone. 1693, borrowed from Latin *tālus* ankle, anklebone, knucklebone, from earlier **taxlos;* compare Latin *taxillus* a small die, a cube; of unknown origin.

talus[2] (tā'ləs) *n.* slope. 1645, slope, especially the slope of a military earthwork; borrowing of French *talus,* from Old French *talu* slope, from Gallo-Romance **talūtum,* alteration of Latin *talūtium* a slope or outcrop of rock debris as a superficial sign of the presence of gold underneath, possibly of Celtic origin (compare Welsh, Breton, and Cornish *tal* forehead, brow, and Middle Irish *taul, tul*). The specific sense in geology of a sloping mass of rocky fragments that has fallen from a cliff is first recorded in English in Lyell's *Principles of Geology* (1830).

tamale (təmä'lē) *n.* Mexican food made of corn meal and minced meat. 1691 *tamales,* American English, borrowed from American Spanish *tamales,* plural of *tamal,* from Nahuatl *tamal, tamalli* a food made of Indian corn and meat, seasoned with red peppers. The singular form *tamale* was formed in American English about 1893 by dropping the final *-s,* which was taken as the English plural.

tamarack (tam'ərak) *n.* American larch tree. 1805, in the *Journals* of Lewis and Clark; American English, probably of Algonquian origin (compare the earlier synonym *hackmatack,* 1792, from an Algonquian source, such as Abnaki *akemantak* a kind of supple wood used for making snowshoes).

tamarind (tam'ərind) *n.* tropical tree grown for its wood and fruit. 1313, fruit of the tamarind; borrowed from Old French *tamarinde, tamarandi,* from Arabic *tamr hindī,* literally, date of India. Reference to the tree itself is first found in English in *Purchas his Pilgrimage* (1614).

tambourine (tam'bərēn') *n.* small drum with metal disks. 1782, apparently a transferred use of earlier *tamburin* a small drum (1579, in Spenser's *The Shepheardes Calender*); borrowed from French *tambourin,* diminutive of *tambour* drum. French *tambour* is an alteration (influenced by Arabic *ṭunbūr* lute; also, a drum) of Old French *tabour* TABOR.

tame *adj.* Probably about 1200 *tom* not wild, domesticated, in *Ancrene Riwle,* found in Old English *tom* (about 1000); also, about 1250 *tame,* in *Genesis and Exodus;* developed from Old English *tam* (before 899, in Alfred's translation of Boethius' *De Consolatione Philosophiae*). Old English *tam* and its variant *tom* are cognate with Old Frisian, Old Saxon, Middle Low German, Middle Dutch and modern Dutch *tam* tame, Old High German *zam* (modern German *zahm*), and Old Icelandic *tamr;* all derived from Proto-Germanic **tamaz,* found in Gothic *tamjan* to tame.
—**v.** make tame. Probably before 1200 *temen,* in *Ancrene Riwle;* developed from Old English *temian* make tame (about 1000, in Ælfric's *Grammar*), and *tamian* become or grow tame, from *temman* (before 899, in Alfred's translation of St. Gregory's *Pastoral Care*). Old English *temman, temian* are cognate with Middle Low German and Middle Dutch *temmen,* Old High German *zemmen* (modern German *zähmen*), Old Icelandic *temja,* and Gothic *gatamjan,* from Proto-Germanic **tamjanan.* The Germanic stem *tam-* is cognate with that of Latin *domāre, domitāre* to tame, Greek *damnánai,* Welsh *goddef* endure, suffer, Ossetic *domun* to tame, Persian *dām* tame animal, and Sanskrit *damáyati* (he) tames, from Indo-European **domə-/demə-* (Pok.199). The new form found in Middle English *tamen* (probably before 1300) developed from the reformed adjective in Middle English and gradually replaced older *temen* in the 1300's.

tam-o'-shanter (tam'əshan'tər) *n.* Scottish cap. 1840-50, from *Tam o' Shanter* (that is, Tom of Shanter), name of the hero of a poem by Robert Burns, written in 1790.

tamp *v.* pack down. 1819, to fill (a hole containing an explosive) with dirt or clay before blasting; perhaps a back formation from *tampin,* variant of TAMPION, taken as *tamping,* present participle or verbal noun; possibly influenced by *stamp.* The meaning of pack down by a series of light blows is first recorded in 1879.

tamper *v.* 1567 *temper* to meddle or interfere with improperly or underhandedly; later *tamper* (1610); both figurative uses of *tamper* to work in clay, etc., so as to mix it thoroughly (1573); for suffix see -ER[1]. Before about 1600 the word was generally spelled *temper,* and probably originated as a variant of TEMPER, v. The transitive use (as in *to temper clay*) shows evidence of having been reduced to *to temper* (without an object), and then to an intransitive form (as in *to temper in clay*), which developed figuratively into *to temper* (or *tamper*) *in* or *with* any business or matter. *Tamper* may have represented a dialectal or workman's pronunciation, which at length became established as a differentiation from *temper.* Compare MEDDLE for a similar sense development.

tampion *n.* wooden plug in the muzzle of a gun to keep out dampness and dust. 1430 *tampioun* piece of cloth; later *tampyne* plug, bung (about 1460), *tampyon* wooden plug for a gun (1485); borrowed from Middle French *tampon,* variant of Old French *tapon* piece of cloth to stop a hole, from Frankish **tappo* stopper, plug, related to Old High German *zapho* and Old English *tæppa* stopper, TAP[2].

tampon *n.* plug of cotton or other absorbent material. 1848; borrowed from French *tampon,* from Middle French *tampon* plug; see TAMPION. —**v.** fill or plug with a tampon. 1860, from the noun.

tan *v.* Before 1400 *tannen* make a hide into leather;

developed from Old English *tannian,* implied in *getanned,* past participle (about 1000, in Ælfric's *Glossaries*); borrowed from Medieval Latin *tannare* tan, dye a tawny color, from *tannum* crushed oak bark used in tanning, probably from a Celtic source (compare Breton *tann* oak tree). The meaning of make brown by exposure to the sun is first recorded in Palsgrave's *Lesclarcissement* (1530). **—n.** 1604 (implied in *tan-mill*), oak bark used in tanning; borrowed from French *tan,* from Old French, from Medieval Latin *tannum.* The word is also found in Middle English as *tanne* (1392, implied in *tannedust*), borrowed from Old French *tan* or Medieval Latin *tannum.* The meaning of the brown color of a person's skin after tanning in the sun is first recorded in English in 1749, in allusion to the color of raw, but tanned leather. **—adj.** yellowish-brown. 1630, in writings of Jeremy Taylor; from the noun. **—tanbark** *n.* bark used in tanning (1799). **—tannery** *n.* place where hides are tanned. 1736, formed from English *tanner* one who tans + *-y*[3].

tanager (tan′əjər) *n.* kind of small Central and South American bird. 1844; borrowed from New Latin *tanagra* (1758), alteration of Portuguese *tángara,* from Tupi (Brazil) *tangara.* Earlier in English the bird was called a *tangara* (1614), borrowed from Portuguese *tángara.*

tandem *n.* 1785, carriage pulled by horses harnessed one behind the other, a punning use of Latin *tandem* at length (of time), from *tam* so + demonstrative suffix *-dem.* The meaning of a bicycle for two riders is first recorded in 1884, probably short for *tandem bicycle* (which is found slightly later, in 1896). **—adv.** one behind the other. 1795, from the noun. **—adj.** arranged one behind the other. 1801, from the noun.

tang *n.* sharp taste or flavor. Before 1350 *tange* a serpent's tongue, thought to be the stinging organ; later, sharp extension of a metal blade (1440); borrowed from a Scandinavian source (compare Old Icelandic *tangi* spit of land, pointed projection on a metal tool, perhaps related to Old Icelandic *tunga* TONGUE). The transferred sense of a sharp, penetrating taste or flavor is first recorded in Middle English in *Promptorium Parvulorum* (1440), and the figurative sense of a slight touch or suggestion, trace, in 1593. **—tangy** *adj.* having a tang or sharp taste. 1875, formed from English *tang* + *-y*[1].

tangent *adj. Geometry.* touching a curve at one point only. 1594, borrowed from Latin *tangentem* (nominative *tangēns*), present participle of *tangere* to touch; for suffix see -ENT. Latin *tangere* (with perfect *tetigī*) is probably cognate with Greek *tetagṓn* having grasped, and perhaps to Old English *thaccian* to pat, stroke, from Indo-European **tag-* (Pok.1054). **—n.** 1594, one of the fundamental trigonometric functions; revived in New Latin *tangentem,* from Latin, present participle of *tangere* to touch. **—tangential** *adj.* 1630, of or pertaining to a tangent; formed from English *tangent,* n. + *-ial.* The figurative sense of slightly connected with a subject is first recorded in 1825, and that of wandering off suddenly, erratic, digressive, in 1867 (but is found in adjective use of *tangent* as early as 1787, in correspondence of Robert Burns).

tangerine *n.* kind of citrus fruit. 1842, abstracted from the phrase *tangerine orange* (1841), meaning an orange of or from *Tangier,* a seaport in northern Morocco on the Strait of Gibraltar. The adjective *tangerine* (1710, Addison, in *The Tatler*) was probably modeled on Spanish *Tangerino* of or from Tangier; for suffix see -INE[1].

tangible *adj.* 1589, capable of being touched, in Puttenham's *The Arte of English Poesie;* borrowed from Middle French *tangible,* and directly from Late Latin *tangibilis* that may be touched, from Latin *tangere* to touch; see TANGENT; for suffix see -IBLE. The transferred sense of material, objective (as in *a tangible reward*), is first recorded in 1620, and the figurative sense of capable of being realized or dealt with as a fact (as in *tangible ideas*), in 1709.

tangle *v.* Before 1340 *tangilen,* in Richard Rolle's *The Psalter,* variant (with added nasalization of *g* to *ng*) of *tagilen* to involve in a difficult situation, entangle (in modern Scottish *taigle*); probably from a Scandinavian source (compare dialectal Swedish *taggla* to disorder) of unknown origin. The meaning of twist together and entwine in a confused mass is first recorded in Palsgrave's *Lesclarcissement* (1530). **—n.** confused mass, snarl. 1615, from the verb.

tango *n.* kind of ballroom dance. 1913, borrowed from Argentine Spanish *tango,* originally, (in other parts of America) a dance to the sound of drums, of African origin, probably from a Niger-Congo language (compare Ibibio *tamgu* to dance). The word *tango* was used slightly earlier in English (1896) to refer to a Spanish flamenco dance. **—v.** dance the tango. 1913, from the noun.

tank *n.* About 1616, (in India) pool or lake for irrigation or drinking water, artificial reservoir; borrowed from Gujarati *tānkh* cistern, Marathi *tānken,* or *tānkā,* perhaps from Sanskrit *taḍāga-m* pond, lake, pool. In later use, in the sense of a container for large quantities of liquid, in Dryden's *Don Sebastian* (1690) the word was probably borrowed also from Portuguese *tanque* reservoir (itself perhaps reinforced by association with Gujarati *tānkh*), from *estancar* hold back a current of water, from Vulgar Latin **stanticāre* STANCH[1]. It is also possible that this later use of *tank* was associated with *tankard* by sound and meaning. The use of *tank* in the military sense of a heavily armored combat vehicle originated in 1915 in the British army, which introduced this weapon in World War I; the newly invented vehicle was code-named *tank* partly because it resembled a large water tank and partly to conceal its true nature while it was being shipped around the country under canvas by calling it a "portable water tank" supposedly designed to be used in desert warfare. **—v.** 1863, immerse in a tank; later, to store in a tank (1900); from the noun. **—tanker** *n.* 1900, ship for carrying oil or other liquid cargo, for earlier *tank steamer* (1889) and *tank vessel* (before 1889).

tankard *n.* About 1384, large tublike vessel, in the Wycliffe Bible; earlier as a surname *Tankart* (1202); corresponding to Middle Dutch *tanckaert,* of the same meaning but both of unknown origin. The extended meaning of a large drinking vessel is first recorded in Middle English in 1485.

tannin *n.* astringent vegetable substance used in tanning hides. 1802, borrowed from French *tannin, tanin* (1798), from *tan* crushed oak bark containing tannin (see TAN); for suffix see -IN[2]. **—tannic acid** type of tannin derived from oak galls. 1836, Anglicized borrowing of French *acide tannique* (1834), from *tannin, tanin* tannin; for suffix see -IC.

tansy *n.* coarse, strong-smelling plant. Before 1250

tanesie; later *tansy* (1373); borrowed from Old French *tanesie, tanase,* from Gallo-Romance **tanacēta,* from Late Latin *tanacētum* wormwood, probably of pre-Roman origin. It was formerly thought that the Old French forms were shortened borrowings from Medieval Latin *athanasia* a medicine to prolong life, also used as a name for the tansy, from Greek *athanasíā* elixir, originally, immortality (*a-* without + *thánatos* death). However, recent scholarship (see *Französisches Etymologisches Wörterbuch* Vol. 13, p. 80) rejects this derivation on historic and phonetic grounds.

tantalize *v.* 1597, to subject to a torture or teasing like that inflicted on Tantalus, in Robert Tofte's *Laura;* formed in English from Latin *Tantalus,* name of a character in Greek mythology (from Greek *Tántalos*) + English *-ize.* Tantalus was the son of Zeus whose punishment for betraying the god's secrets was to stand in a river up to his chin, under branches of fruit. Whenever he tried to drink or eat, the water or fruit withdrew from his reach.

tantalum (tan′təlam) *n.* grayish metallic chemical element that is very resistant to acids. 1809, New Latin, formed from Latin *Tantalus* (see TANTALIZE) + New Latin *-um,* variant of *-ium,* chemical suffix; so called because this element cannot absorb acid even when immersed in it. The New Latin word was coined in 1802 by the Swedish chemist Anders Gustaf Ekeberg.

tantamount *adj.* equivalent. 1641, from the obsolete noun *tantamount* something equivalent (1637); developed from an earlier verb phrase *tant amount* be equivalent (1628, in Edward Coke's *Institutes: a commentarie on Littleton*). The verb phrase was borrowed from Anglo-French *tant amunter* amount to as much (from Old French *tant* as much, from Latin *tantum* neuter of *tantus* so great, from *tam* as, so + *amonter* amount to, go up; see AMOUNT).

tantrum *n.* fit of bad temper or ill humor. 1748, in Samuel Foote's *The Knights;* of unknown origin.

Taoism (tou′izəm *or* dou′izəm) *n.* religion of China founded on the doctrines of the ancient philosopher Lao Tzu. 1838, borrowed from Chinese *tao* way, path, in the title *Tao te Ching* (The Way and Its Power), attributed to Lao Tzu; for suffix see -ISM. **—Taoist** *n.* 1838, formed from Chinese *tao* + English *-ist.*

tap[1] *v.* strike lightly. Probably before 1200 *tepen,* in *Ancrene Riwle;* later *tappen* (before 1450); probably borrowed from Old French *taper* tap, rap, strike, possibly from: 1) a northern Gallo-Romance stem **tapp-,* generally with the meaning of strike, hit, especially with something flat, as the palm of the hand, perhaps ultimately imitative of the sound of tapping or slapping; 2) a Germanic source (compare Middle Low German *tappen, tapen* grope, fumble, seemingly distant semantically); 3) Scandinavian (compare Old Icelandic *tapsa* tap). —**n.** act of tapping, light blow. 1340 *teppe,* in *Ayenbite of Inwyt;* later *tape, tappe* (probably about 1390); possibly from the verb in Middle English, but also perhaps influenced by Old Frisian *tap* slap. **—tap dance** (1929) **—tap-dance** *v.* (1927, implied in *tap-dancer*) **—taps** *n.pl.* signal on a bugle or drum to put out lights at night (1824, American English).

tap[2] *n.* stopper, faucet. 1340 *teppe,* in *Ayenbite of Inwyt;* later *tappe* (about 1390); developed from Old English (about 1050) *tæppa;* cognate with Middle Low German and Middle Dutch *tappe* tap (modern Dutch *tap*), Old High German *zapho* (modern German *Zapfen*), and Old Icelandic *tappi* (Norwegian and Swedish *tapp,* Danish *tap*), from Proto-Germanic **tappōn,* of unknown origin. **—v.** Before 1325 *tepen* draw (liquid) from a tap; later *tappen* (1402); developed from Old English (about 1050) *tæppian* provide with a tap, from *tæppa* tap[2], n. Old English *tæppian* is cognate with Middle Low German, Middle Dutch, and modern Dutch *tappen* to tap, Middle High German and modern German *zapfen.* The figurative sense of open up, penetrate, make use of, is first recorded in English in 1575. The extended meaning of attach an electronic device to a telephone in order to eavesdrop is first recorded in English in 1929 (implied in *wire tapper* and *wire tapping;* earlier use refers to telegraph operators). **—taproom** *n.* barroom (1807). **—taproot** *n.* main root growing downward (1601).

tape *n.* Probably before 1300 *tape,* in *Arthour and Merlin;* developed from Old English *tæppe* narrow strip of cloth used for tying, measuring, etc. (about 1000, in Ælfric's writings). The development of a lengthened vowel in Middle English is unexplained, but may be by mistaken analogy with earlier *taper.* Old English *tæppe* is probably cognate with Old Frisian *tapia* and Middle Low German *tapen* to pull, pluck, tear, of unknown origin. The meaning of a ticker tape (a paper strip or ribbon on which a telegraph records information) is first recorded in 1884. The meaning of a tape coated with magnetized iron oxide to record sound is first found in 1932. —**v.** furnish with tape or tapes. 1609, from the noun. The meaning of record on magnetic tape appeared in 1950, shortened from *tape-record.* **—tape measure** (1873) **—tape-record** *v.* (1950, back formation from earlier *tape recorder*) **—tape recorder** (1892, device for recording data on ticker tape; 1932, device for recording sound on magnetic tape) **—tape recording** (1940) **—tapeworm** *n.* long, flat parasitic worm (1752).

taper *n.* Probably before 1200 *taper* candle; developed from Old English *tapur, taper* (before 1000); earlier *tapor* (before 899, in Alfred's translation of St. Gregory's *Pastoral Care*); of uncertain origin, though according to Kluge, the Old English may be a dissimilated form (with *t. . .p* for *p. . .p*) of **papur,* borrowed from Latin *papyrus* PAPYRUS, which in Medieval Latin and some Romance forms has the sense of the wick of a candle, for which the pith of the papyrus was used. The sense of a gradual decrease in size, force, capacity, is first recorded in 1793. **—adj.** becoming smaller toward one end. Before 1450, from the noun. —**v.** 1589, to rise up like a flame or spire, in Puttenham's *The Arte of English Poesie;* from the noun. The meaning of become gradually smaller toward one end is first recorded in 1610, implied in *tapering.*

tapestry *n.* 1397 *tapiestre;* later *tapstry* (probably about 1400); alteration of earlier *tapicery* heavy fabric with pictures or designs woven into it (1388); borrowed from Middle French *tapisserie* tapestry, from *tapisser* to cover with heavy fabric, from *tapis, tapiz* heavy fabric, from Byzantine Greek *tapḗtion* (pronounced as if spelled *tapítion*), from Classical Greek *tapḗtion,* diminutive of *tápēs* (genitive *tápētos*) tapestry, heavy fabric, probably from an Iranian source (compare Persian *tāftan, tābīdan* to turn, twist); see TAFFETA. The figurative use is first recorded in Sidney's writings in 1581. —**v.** 1630, to cover, hang, or adorn with tapestry; from the noun. The meaning of portray in tapestry is first found in Scott's *Waverley* (1814).

tapioca (tap'iō'kə) *n.* starchy food obtained from the root of the cassava plant. 1648 *tipioja, tipiaca;* later *tipioca* (1707), *tapioca* (1792); borrowed from Portuguese or Spanish *tapioca,* from Tupi (Brazil) *tipioca.*

tapir (tā'pər) *n.* large animal resembling a pig. 1774, in Goldsmith's *A History of the Earth and Animated Nature,* perhaps borrowed through French *tapir,* ultimately from Tupi (Brazil) *tapira.*

tar[1] *n.* black sticky substance distilled from wood or coal. About 1250 *ter,* in *Genesis and Exodus;* later *tar* (before 1382, in the Wycliffe Bible); developed from Old English (before 700) *teoru, teru;* cognate with Old Frisian *tera* tar, Middle Low German *tere* (modern German *Teer*), Middle Dutch *tar, terre* (modern Dutch *teer*), and Old Icelandic *tjara* (Swedish *tjära,* Danish and Norwegian *tjære*). The word probably derives from Proto-Germanic **terwō,* related to **trewan,* the source of TREE. —**v.** cover or smear with tar. About 1250 *terren,* in *Genesis and Exodus;* later *tarren* (about 1400); from the noun.

tar[2] *n.* sailor. 1676, in Wycherley's *The Plain-Dealer,* special use of *tar*[1], or possibly a shortened form of *tarpaulin* (1647, nickname for a sailor).

tarantella (tar'əntel'ə) *n.* whirling southern Italian folk dance. 1782, borrowing of Italian *tarantella,* from *Tàranto* Taranto, a city in southern Italy, from Greek *Tárās* (genitive *Tárantos*), Latin *Tarentum.* The dance in Italian folklore was associated with the tarantula and its bite which was supposed to cause tarantism (a nervous disorder characterized by an impulse to dance or move about feverishly). The dance was considered a cure for tarantism.

tarantula (təran'chələ) *n.* large, hairy spider. 1561, borrowed from Medieval Latin *tarantula,* from Italian *tarantola,* from *Tàranto* Taranto, a city in southern Italy, near which such spiders are found.

tardy *adj.* 1530 *take tardy* to overtake, in Palsgrave's *Lesclarcissement;* alteration of Middle English *tardyve* slow (1483, in Caxton's version of *The Golden Legend*); borrowed from Middle French *tardif* (feminine *tardive*), from Vulgar Latin **tardīvus,* from Latin *tardus* slow, sluggish, dull, stupid; of uncertain origin; for suffix see -Y[1]. The earliest recorded sense in English is that of slow in motion or action; the meaning of behind time, late, is first recorded in Milton's *Paradise Lost* (1667).

tare[1] (tãr) *n.* kind of fodder plant, vetch. Probably before 1300, in *Arthour and Merlin* and *Kyng Alisaunder;* perhaps cognate with Middle Dutch *tarwe* wheat (from Proto-Germanic **tarwō,* Indo-European **dorəwā*), Greek *dáratos* a kind of Thessalian bread, Lithuanian *dirvà* wheat field, and Sanskrit *dū́rvā* millet, from Indo-European **dr̥̄wā* (Pok.209).

tare[2] (tãr) *n.* the difference between the gross weight and the net weight. 1486, borrowed from Middle French *tāre* wastage in goods, deficiency, imperfection, from Italian *tara* (also found in Medieval Latin *tara* deduction), from Arabic *ṭaraḥ,* literally, thing deducted or rejected, related to *ṭaraḥa* he rejected. —**v.** ascertain, note, or allow for the tare of. 1812, from the noun.

target *n.* Probably before 1300 *target* shield, in *Kyng Alisaunder;* diminutive of *targe* shield (1297), borrowed from Old French *targe* light shield; for suffix see -ET. Old French *targe* derives from Frankish **targa* shield, cognate with Old High German *zarga* edging, border (modern German *Zarge*), and Old Icelandic *targa* shield, from Proto-Germanic **tarʒō,* cognate with Greek *drachmḗ* DRACHMA. The meaning of an object, usually circular, to be aimed at in shooting practice, is first recorded in English in 1757. —**v.** 1611, to shield; from the noun. The meaning of make a target of is first recorded in 1837.

tariff *n.* 1591, an arithmetic table, as for multiplication; 1592 *tariffa* list of duties or taxes on imports or exports; borrowing of Italian *tariffa* (in Medieval Latin *tarifa* list of prices, book of rates), from Arabic *ta'rīf* information, notification, inventory of fees to be paid, related to *'arafa* he notified. The Anglicized spelling *tariff* is first recorded about 1700.

tarn *n.* small lake or pool in the mountains. Probably about 1380 *terne* lake; later *tarne* (probably about 1425); borrowed from a Scandinavian source (compare Old Icelandic *tjǫrn* inland sea, pool, Swedish *tjärn* tarn, and Norwegian *tjern*). Old Icelandic *tjǫrn* comes from Proto-Germanic **ternō,* perhaps originally a water hole, cognate with Sanskrit *dr̥ṇā́ti* it bursts, from Indo-European **der-/dor-/dr̥-* (Pok.206).

tarnish *v.* Probably before 1439 *ternysshen,* in Lydgate's *Falls of Princes;* later *tarnish* (1598); borrowed from Middle French *terniss-,* stem of Old French *ternir* dull the luster or brightness of, make dim, probably from the adjective *terne* dull, dark; for suffix see -ISH[2]. Old French *ternir* derives from a Frankish source cognate with Old High German *tarnan, tarnjan* to conceal, hide, modern German *tarnen,* Old Saxon *dernian,* and Old English *dyrnan;* all from a Germanic adjective represented by Old High German *tarni,* Old Saxon *derni,* and Old English *dyrne, dierne* hidden, secret, obscure, from Proto-Germanic **darnjaz,* cognate with Sanskrit *dhárman-* steadfast decree, and Latin *firmus* strong, FIRM. —**n.** loss of luster or brightness. 1713, from the verb.

taro (tä'rō) *n.* starchy root. 1779, in Captain James Cook's *A Voyage to the Pacific Ocean;* borrowed from Polynesian (compare Tahitian and Maori *taro*). The corresponding Hawaiian form is *kalo.*

tarpaulin (tärpô'lən) *n.* waterproof canvas or other coarse strong cloth. 1605 *tarpauling,* in Ben Jonson's *Volpone;* probably formed from English *tar*[1] + *pall*[1] heavy cloth covering + *-ing*[1] (as in *netting, grating,* etc.); probably so called because the canvas is sometimes coated in tar to make it waterproof. The present spelling *tarpaulin* is first found in Defoe's *Robinson Crusoe* (1719), but various similar spellings ending in *-in* are recorded earlier: *Tarpawlin* (1647) as the nickname of a sailor, and *tarpalin* (1652).

tarry *v.* Probably before 1300 *taryen* delay, retard, prolong, in *Kyng Alisaunder;* of uncertain origin. Traditional identification of this word with Middle English *tarien* to provoke, irritate, worry (probably before 1300), either developed from Old English *tergan, terwian* to provoke, or borrowed from Old French *tarier* to provoke, is difficult to accept, because the meaning is so distant from that of Middle English *taryen* to delay.

tarsus (tär'səs) *n. Anatomy.* the ankle. 1676, New Latin, from Greek *tarsós* ankle, sole of the foot, rim of the eyelid; originally, flat basket, flat surface, especially for drying; cognate with Sanskrit *tŕ̥syati* he is thirsty, Latin *torrēre* parch, from Indo-European **ters-/tors-/tr̥s-* to dry out (Pok.1078). An earlier borrowing of the Greek word is found in Middle English as *tharsum* (probably about 1425, in a translation of Chauliac's *Grande Chirurgie*). **—tarsal** *adj.* 1817, borrowed from New Latin *tarsalis* of or pertaining to the tarsus, from Latin *tarsus* tarsus; for suffix see -AL[1].

tart[1] *adj.* having a sharp taste. About 1387, in Chaucer's *Canterbury Tales;* developed from Old English *teart* painful, sharp, severe (about 1000, in Ælfric's *Homilies*); possibly related to TEAR[2] pull apart. Old English *teart* is cognate with Middle Low German *trot* spite, malice, defiance, Middle High German *traz, truz* (modern German *Trotz*), and Middle Dutch *torten* to challenge, defy (modern Dutch *tarten*). **—v.** 1616, to make tart, sour; from the adjective.

tart[2] *n.* small pie. Before 1399, borrowed from Old French *tarte,* possibly an alteration of *torte* (whence modern French *tourte*), from Late Latin *torta* round loaf of bread. The form found in Old French *tarte* was perhaps influenced by Medieval Latin *tarta* a cake, tart, and later in Middle English by *tart* having a sour taste associated with fruit often used in tarts. The informal meaning of a woman of loose morals, prostitute, is found in 1887, from earlier use as a term of endearment (1864). **—v.** 1938, to dress up (originally, like a prostitute); from the noun.

tartan *n.* plaid woolen cloth worn by Scottish Highlanders. 1454 *tartyn;* later *tartane* (probably before 1500); probably borrowed from Middle French *tiretaine* strong coarse fabric of linen and wool, from Old French *tiret* kind of cloth, from *tire* silk cloth, from Medieval Latin *tyrius* cloth from Tyre, from Latin *Tyrus* Tyre, ancient capital of Phoenicia. The spelling of *tartan* was influenced by Middle English *tartaryn* rich silk cloth (1343), borrowed from Old French *tartarin* Tartar cloth, from *Tartare* Tartar, member of a group inhabiting Central Asia eastward from the Caspian Sea.

tartar *n.* acid substance used in dyeing and to make baking powder. 1392 *tartre;* borrowed from Old French *tartre,* from Medieval Latin *tartarum,* from Late Greek *tártaron* tartar encrusting the sides of casks; sometimes said to be from Arabic *durd, durdīy* dregs, sediment, but difficult to account for its alteration in form to either Greek or Latin, especially since modern dictionaries of Arabic enter a form close to that found in Greek and Latin. The meaning referring to the encrustation that builds up on the teeth is first recorded in 1806. **—tartaric** *adj.* of, containing or obtained from tartar. 1790, formed from English *tartar* + *-ic.*

task *n.* Before 1325, piece of work imposed as a duty, in *Cursor Mundi;* later, impost, tax (about 1400); borrowed from Old North French *tasque* (in Old French *tasche*) duty, tax, from Vulgar Latin **tasca* a duty, assessment, alteration (by transposition of the sound *ks* associated with *x* to *sk* written *sc*) of **taxa,* from Latin *taxāre* to evaluate, estimate, assess; see TAX. **—v.** About 1405 *tasken* put a duty or tax on; from the noun. The meaning of assign a task to (a person) is first recorded in Palsgrave's *Lesclarcissement* (1530). **—task force** (1941, American English) **—taskmaster** *n.* (1530, in the Tyndale Bible)

tassel *n.* Probably about 1300 *tassel* mantle fastener, in *The Romance of Guy of Warwick;* borrowed from Old French *tassel* a fastening, clasp, from Vulgar Latin **tassellus* (in Italian, collar of a cloak, a square), alteration of Latin *taxillus* small die or cube, a diminutive form derived from *tālus* knucklebone used in a game, ankle; see TALUS[1]. The form of the Vulgar Latin word was influenced by Latin *tessella* small cube; see TESSELATE. The meaning of a hanging bunch of threads or small cords is first recorded in English in *Sir Gawain and the Green Knight* (about 1390). **—v.** About 1353 *tasselen* put tassels on; from the noun.

taste *v.* Probably before 1300 *tasten* try the flavor of, taste, in *Kyng Alisaunder;* borrowed from Old French *taster* to feel, taste, from Vulgar Latin **tastāre,* apparently alteration of **taxitāre, taxtāre,* a frequentative form of Latin *taxāre* evaluate, handle; see TAX. **—n.** Before 1325 *tast* touch, touching, taste, tasting, in *Cursor Mundi;* borrowed from Old French *tast* touching, touch, from *taster* to feel, taste. The sense of aesthetic judgment, a sense of what is appropriate, harmonious or beautiful, is first recorded in Milton's *Paradise Regained* (1671). **—taste bud** (1889) **—tasty** *adj.* 1617, pleasing to the taste, formed from English *taste,* n. + *-y*[1].

tat *v.* make a kind of lace by looping and knotting (threads) with a shuttle. 1882, back formation from earlier *tatting* king of knotted lace (1842), of uncertain origin.

tatami (tätä'mē) *n.* floor mat of straw used in a Japanese house. 1614, borrowing of Japanese *tatami.*

tatter *n.* torn piece, rag. Before 1400 *tatrys,* pl. (implied earlier in *tatrid* wearing ragged clothes, about 1340); borrowed from a Scandinavian source (compare Old Icelandic *tǫturr* rag, modern Icelandic *tötur,* plural *tötrar* rags). The Scandinavian forms are cognate with Old English *tættec, tætteca* rag, tatter, Old High German *zotta* tuft of hair, matted or shaggy hair (modern German *Zotte, Zottel* tuft of hair), modern Dutch *tod, todde* rag, and East Frisian *todde* bundle, pack. The Middle English word may have been influenced by Old French *taterele* (implied in *tatereles* rags), probably borrowed from a Germanic source. **—v.** tear or wear to pieces, make ragged. About 1380 *tateren* (implied in *tatering*); from the noun.

tattle *v.* 1481 *tatelen* to stammer, prattle, in Caxton's translation of *The History of Reynard the Fox;* probably borrowed from Middle Dutch *tatelen* to stutter, a parallel or variant form of the more usual Middle Dutch, Middle Low German, and East Frisian *tateren* to chatter, babble, talk nonsense; possibly of imitative origin. The extended meaning of tell tales or secrets is first recorded in English in 1581 (implied in *tattling*). **—n.** Before 1529, idle or foolish talk, gossip; from the verb. **—tattletale** *n.* person who tattles. 1888, American English; formed from English *tattle* + *tale,* patterned on *telltale* (before 1548).

tattoo[1] *n.* signal on a drum, bugle, etc. 1688, signal calling soldiers or sailors to their quarters at night, assimilated variant (by alteration of *tap-* to *tat-*) of earlier *tap-too* (1644); borrowed from Dutch *taptoe* (*tap* faucet of a cask, TAP[2] + *toe* shut; so called because the police used to visit taverns in the evening to shut off the taps of casks). **—v.** beat a tattoo. 1780, from the noun.

tattoo[2] *v.* mark the skin with pigments. 1769 *tattow,* in Captain James Cook's *Journal;* borrowed from a Polynesian source (compare Tahitian and Samoan *tatau,* and Marquesan *tatu*). The spelling *tattoo* is first recorded in English in 1774. **—n.** act of tattooing. 1777, from the verb.

tatty *adj.* ragged or shabby. 1513, (of hair) tangled or matted, in Douglas' translation of Vergil's *Aeneid;* Scottish, probably related to Old English *tættec* a rag, TATTER. The sense of tattered, ragged, shabby, is first recorded in Noel Coward's *Design for Living* (1933).

taunt *v.* 1438 *tanten* to mock, jeer at (implied in *tantingly*); possibly borrowed from Middle French *tanter, tenter* to try, tempt, provoke, variant form of *tempter* to try, TEMPT. **—n.** bitter or insulting remark. Before 1529 *taunte,* in Skelton's *The Bowge of Courte;* of uncertain origin; possibly from the verb.

taupe (tōp) *n.* Before 1889, a mole; later, the dark, brownish gray color of moleskin (1911); borrowed from French *taupe* the color; originally, a mole, from Latin *talpa* a mole, of uncertain origin. **—adj.** 1967, from the noun (but probably used almost simultaneously with the noun).

taut (tôt) *adj.* Before 1625 *taught* tightly drawn; later *tau't* (1727-41); found in Middle English as *tohte* (about 1250, in *The Owl and the Nightingale*); later *toȝte* (about 1300); possibly developed from *tog-,* past participle stem of Old English *tēon* to pull, drag; see TOW[1].

tautology (tôtol′əjē) *n.* useless repetition. 1579, borrowed from Late Latin *tautologia* repetition of the same thing, from Greek *tāutologiā,* from *tāutológos* repeating what has been said (*tāutó* the same + *-lógos* saying, related to *légein* to say; see LEGEND); for suffix see -LOGY. Greek *tāutó* is a contraction of *tò autó* the same (*tò,* neuter definite article + *autó,* neuter of *autós* same, self). **—tautological** *adj.* having to do with or characterized by tautology. 1620, formed from English *tautology* + *-ical.*

tavern *n.* About 1290 *taverne* wine shop; later, public house, inn (about 1440); borrowed from Old French *taverne,* from Latin *taberna* shop, inn, tavern; originally, hut, shed, dissimilated (by loss of first *r*) from **traberna,* from *trabs* (genitive *trabis*) beam, timber. Latin *trabs* is cognate with Lithuanian *trobà* house, building, Old Welsh and Old Breton *treb* dwelling, from Indo-European **trĕb-/trōb-/trəb-* building (Pok.1090). **—taverner** *n.* one who keeps a tavern. 1340, in *Ayenbite of Inwyt;* borrowed through Anglo-French *taverner,* Old French *tavernier,* from *taverne* + *-ier* -er[1], or from Late Latin *tabernārius* keeper of a tavern, shopkeeper, from the adjective, from Latin *taberna* tavern + *-ārius* -ious.

tawdry *adj.* showy and cheap, gaudy. 1676, adjective use (with a figurative sense) of earlier *tawdry* silk necktie for women (1612), shortened form of *tawdry lace* (1548). *Tawdry lace* is an alteration of *Saint Audrey's lace* a necktie or ribbon sold at the annual fair commemorating St. Audrey (1530). The association with St. Audrey (Etheldrida, queen of Northumbria and abbess of Ely, England, 630?-679) is traced to the story that St. Audrey died of a throat tumor, a punishment she considered retribution for her youthful fondness for showy necklaces.

tawny *adj.* brownish-yellow. Probably before 1387 *tauny,* in a version of *Piers Plowman;* borrowed through Anglo-French *tauné,* associated with the brownish-yellow of tanned leather, Old French *tané,* past participle of *taner* to tan hides, from Medieval Latin *tannare* to TAN. **—n.** a brownish yellow. Possibly before 1400, from the adjective.

tax *v.* About 1300 *taxen* to assess, put a tax on; borrowed from Old French *taxer,* learned borrowing from Medieval Latin *taxare,* from Latin, and borrowed directly into English from Latin *taxāre* evaluate, estimate, assess, handle, probably a frequentative form of *tangere* to touch; see TANGENT. The figurative sense of burden, put a strain on, is found in Middle English before 1327. **—n.** Before 1327, assessment, levy; from the verb. **—taxable** *adj.* subject to taxation. 1474, in the *Rolls of Parliament;* borrowed from Anglo-French, from Old French *taxer* to tax + *-able* -able. **—taxation** *n.* About 1325 *taxacioun* fixing of a tax, borrowed through Anglo-French *taxacioun,* Old French *taxation,* from Medieval Latin *taxationem* (nominative *taxatio*), from Latin, and borrowed directly into English from Latin *taxātiōnem* (nominative *taxātiō*) evaluation, from *taxāre* evaluate; for suffix see -ATION. **—tax deduction** (1942) **—taxpayer** *n.* (1816) **—tax return** (1870, in Mark Twain's writings) **—tax shelter** (1959, implied in *tax-sheltered*)

taxi *n.* 1907, probably a shortened form of TAXICAB. **—v.** 1911, (of an airplane or seaplane) to travel slowly before taking off; from the noun, perhaps in allusion to the way a taxi driver slowly cruises when looking for fares. The meaning of travel in a taxi is first recorded in 1918.

taxicab *n.* 1907, automobile for hire, probably contraction of *taximeter cab* a cab fitted with an automatic meter (*taximeter*) to record the distance and fare. *Taximeter* (1898) was borrowed from French *taximètre,* alteration of earlier *taxamètre,* from German *Taxameter* (from Medieval Latin *taxa* tax, from *taxare* to TAX + German *-meter* -meter). An earlier English form *taxameter* is found in 1894; borrowed directly from German *Taxameter,* originally applied to a meter used in horsedrawn cabs (1890).

taxidermy (tak′sədėr′mē) *n.* art of stuffing and mounting the skins of animals. 1820, formed in English from Greek *táxis* arrangement, from *tássein* arrange; see TACTICS + *dérma* skin, DERMA; for suffix see -Y[3]. **—taxidermist** *n.* 1828, formed from English *taxidermy* + *-ist.*

taxonomy (takson′əmē) *n.* classification, as of plants and animals. 1828, borrowed from French *taxonomie,* from Greek *táxis* arrangement; see TAXIDERMY + *-nomiā* method, from *-nómos* managing, from *némein* manage; see NIMBLE.

tea *n.* 1655 *tay* (but found earlier as *chaa,* 1598, from the Portuguese *chá*); borrowed through Malay *teh,* and directly from Chinese (Amoy dialect) *t'e,* in Mandarin *ch'a.* English *tea* derives from the same Amoy form as French *thé,* Spanish *té,* Italian *tè,* Dutch *thee,* German *Tee,* and Norwegian and Swedish *te.* Such forms as Portuguese *chá,* Russian *chaĭ,* Persian *chā,* modern Greek *tsai,* Arabic *šāy,* and Turkish *çay* were borrowed from the Mandarin Chinese form. According to the OED tea was introduced to England in 1650-55, perhaps by the Dutch, who imported it from about 1610, but may have come also by way of the Portuguese who knew the term as early as 1559.

The original English pronunciation (tā), sometimes indicated by the spelling *tay,* is found in rhymes down to 1762 and still occurs in British dialects; but the current pronunciation (tē) had appeared already in the 1600's, as shown in rhymes and by the spelling *tee.* **—tea bag** (1930) **—teacup** *n.* (1700, in Congreve's *The Way of the World*) **—teahouse** *n.* (1869) **—teakettle** *n.* (1705) **—tearoom** *n.* (about 1702) **—teaspoon** *n.* (1686) **—teaspoonful** *n.* (1731)

teach *v.* Probably before 1200 *teachen,* in Layamon's

Chronicle of Britain; developed from Old English *tǣcan* to show, teach (before 899, in Alfred's translation of Boethius' *De Consolatione Philosophiae*), from Proto-Germanic **taikjanan;* related to Old English *tācen, tācn* sign, mark, TOKEN. The Old English past tense and past participle *tǣht(e)* developed into early Middle English *tahte, taghte* with a short vowel, and eventually into the current *taught.* **—teacher** *n.* Probably before 1300 *techere* person who teaches, in *Kyng Alisaunder;* formed from Middle English *techen, teachen* to teach + *-ere* -er[1]. An earlier Middle English sense, that which shows or points out, indicator, index finger, is recorded about 1290.

teak *n.* large tree of the East Indies. 1698, in John Fryer's *A New Account of East India and Persia;* borrowed from Portuguese *teca,* from Malayalam *tēkka,* corresponding to Tamil *tēkku,* Telugu *tēku,* Kanarese *tēgu.*

teal *n.* kind of small duck. Probably about 1300 *tele;* cognate with Middle Dutch *tēling, teiling* teal (modern Dutch *taling*), and Middle Low German *tēlink.*

team *n.* Old English *tēam* set of draft animals yoked together (about 825); cognate with Old Frisian *tām* bridle, Old Saxon *tōm,* Middle Dutch and modern Dutch *toom* bridle, rein, Old High German *zoum* (modern German *Zaum*), and Old Icelandic *taumr* bridle, rein, rope (Swedish *töm*), from Proto-Germanic **taumaz,* probably from **tauȝmaz* action of drawing or pulling, from the series **tauH-/tuH-/tuȝ-* to draw, pull, represented by Old English *togian* to pull, drag, TOW[1].

The transferred meaning of a number of people working or acting together is found in English before 1529, but was also known in Old English in the restricted sense of a group of people acting together to bring suit, especially to recover stolen property (before 800, but known in verb use before 700). Other senses that are recorded in Old English and Middle English include that of the bringing forth of children or a brood or litter of animals (about 1000), offspring or line of descendants (902), and a chain or other apparatus to harness oxen or horses to a plow or other farm equipment (1350).

—v. join together in a team. 1552, in Huloet's *Abecedarium Anglico Latinum;* from the noun; the other senses (bear offspring, and vouch to warranty) that correspond to the Old English noun senses were also from the noun in Old English and Middle English. **—teammate** *n.* (1915) **—teamster** *n.* 1779, person who drives a team of horses, especially in the handling of freight; formed from English *team,* n. + *-ster.* The meaning was transferred from wagon driver to truck driver as early as 1907, in American English. **—teamwork** *n.* (1828, work done by a team of horses; 1887, combined action of a team of players)

tear[1] (tir) *n.* drop of water from the eye. Probably before 1200, in *Ancrene Riwle;* found in Old English *tēar;* developed from earlier *tēahor, tæhher* (about 725, in *Beowulf*). The Old English forms are cognate with Old Frisian *tār* tear, Old High German *zahor* (literary German *Zähre*), Old Icelandic *tār* (Swedish *tår,* Danish *tåre), and Gothic tagr,* from Proto-Germanic **táHr-/taȝr'-.* Cognates outside Germanic are found in Old Irish *dēr* tear, Welsh *deigr* (earlier **dagrī,* plural *dagrau*), Old Latin *dacruma,* Latin *lacruma, lacrima,* and Greek *dákry, dákryon,* from Indo-European **dakru* (Pok.179). **—v.** Before 1425 *teren* to shed tears; from the noun. A rare Old English verb *tæherian* (recorded only in the present participle about 950, in the *Lindisfarne Gospels*) apparently did not survive into Middle English. **—teardrop** *n.* (1799) **—tear gas** (1917)

tear[2] (tãr) *v.* pull apart by force. Probably before 1200 *teren;* found in Old English *teran* (about 1000); earlier *teoran* (before 850). The Old English forms are cognate with Old Saxon *terian* consume, destroy, Middle Low German, Middle Dutch, and modern Dutch *teren,* Old High German *zeran* (modern German *zehren, zerren*), and Gothic *-taíran* in *distaíran* destroy. Cognates outside Germanic are found in Greek *dérein* to flay, Lithuanian *dìrti,* Old Slavic *dĭrati* to tear, flay, and Sanskrit *dṛṇā́ti* (he) tears, bursts, from Indo-European **der-* (Pok.206).

The Old English past tense *tær* survived as *tare* to the 1600's, when it was replaced by English *tore,* with the *o* from the past participle *toren, torn.*

—n. torn place. 1611, in Cotgrave's *Dictionary;* from the verb.

tease *v.* About 1290 *tesien* separate the fibers of, shred or card (wool or flax); later *tesen* (before 1325); developed from Old English *tǣsan* pluck, pull apart (about 1000); cognate with Middle Low German and Middle Dutch *tēsen* to pluck, and Old High German *zeisan* to pluck wool, from Proto-Germanic **taisjanan;* and outside Germanic cognate with Sanskrit *dáyate* divides, and Greek *daíesthai* to divide, apportion, from Indo-European **dəi-,* root **dāi-* (Pok.175). The transferred sense of to vex or worry, annoy, appeared in 1619, and is comparable to a similar sense development found in *heckle,* both words in this sense referring to repeated action. **—n.** 1693, act of teasing, in Cotton Mather's *The Wonders of the Invisible World;* from the verb. The sense of one who teases is first recorded in Dickens' *Bleak House* (1852); but the sense is found earlier in *teaser,* n. (1659).

teasel (tē′zəl) *n.* plant with stiff, prickly flower heads. About 1265 *tesel,* developed from Old English (about 1000) *tǣsel,* probably from *tǣsan* to pluck, TEASE. Cognates of Old English *tǣsel* are found in Old High German *zeisala, zeisila,* Middle High German *zeisel* teasel, from Proto-Germanic **taisilō.* **—v.** raise a nap on cloth with teasels. 1543, from the noun, probably further associated with *tease,* v.

teat *n.* nipple on the breast or udder. About 1250 *teten,* pl., in *Genesis and Exodus;* borrowed from Old French *tete, tette* teat, from Proto-Germanic **titta* (the source of Middle Low German *titte* teat, Old English *titt,* Middle High German *zitze,* modern German *Zitze,* and modern Dutch *tit*); compare Greek *títthē* nurse, breast.

technetium (teknē′shēəm) *n.* radioactive metallic chemical element produced artificially. 1947, New Latin, formed from Greek *technētós* artificial (from *technâsthai* produce by art, from *téchnē* art, skill; see TEXT) + New Latin *-ium,* chemical suffix.

technical *adj.* 1617, skilled in a particular art or subject, in John Hales' *Sermons;* formed in English probably from Greek *technikós* of art, from *téchnē* art, skill, craft; see TEXT; for suffix see -AL[1]. It is also possible that in some instances *technical* is an extended form of older *technic,* adj. (1612), or may even be formed from English *technic,* n. + *-al*[1], but this latter formation is difficult to accept from available evidence which first records *technic* as a noun in English in 1798. Latin *technicus* + English *-al*[1] is a possible source, though *technicus* was known only as a noun in the sense of a teacher or skilled artisan. The meaning of having to do with an art, science, discipline, or profession, especially the mechanical arts, is first recorded in English in *Chambers Cyclopaedia* (1727-41). **—technicality** *n.* 1814, technical point, detail, term, or expression, in Scott's *Waverley;* formed from English *technical* + *-ity.*

technician *n.* person experienced in the technicalities of a subject. 1833, formed in English from earlier *technic* technical (1612, from Greek *technikós;* see TECHNICAL) + *-ian.*

technicolor *n.* bright, intense color. 1946, American English, transferred use of earlier trademark *Technicolor,* a special process of making colored motion pictures (1917); formed from *techni(cal)* + *color.* **—adj.** brightly colored, vivid. Before 1940, in F. Scott Fitzgerald's *The Last Tycoon;* from the trademark. **—technicolored** *adj.* 1947, American English, formed from *technicolor* + *-ed*[2].

technique (teknēk′) *n.* mechanical details or skill in an art. 1817, in Coleridge's *Biographia Literaria;* borrowing of French *technique* manner of artistic expression, noun use of adjective *technique* of art, technical, from Greek *technikós;* see TECHNICAL.

techno- a combining form meaning 1) art, craft, skill, especially mechanical or industrial crafts and systems, as in *technology.* 2) technical or technology, as in *technocracy = government by technical experts.* Borrowed from Greek *techno-,* combining form of *téchnē* art, skill, craft, method, system; see TEXT.

technocracy (teknok′rəsē) *n.* government by technical experts. 1919, American English, coined by William H. Smyth, American engineer and inventor, as the name for a new system and philosophy of government; formed from English *techno-* + *-cracy.*

technology *n.* 1615, discourse or treatise on the arts, borrowed from Greek *technologíā* systematic treatment of an art, craft or technique; originally referring to grammar (*techno-* combining form of *téchnē* art, craft + *-logíā* -logy). The transferred sense of science of the mechanical and industrial arts, practical arts collectively, is first recorded in English in 1859. **—technological** *adj.* 1627, of technical terminology, in Captain John Smith's *The Seaman's Grammar;* formed from English *technology* + *-ical.* The meaning "of or relating to technology" appeared in 1800. **—technologist** *n.* person skilled in technology. 1859, formed from English *technology* + *-ist.*

tectonic *adj.* of or dealing with geological structure, especially of the earth's crust. 1656, of or relating to building, in Blount's *Glossographia;* borrowed from Late Latin *tectonicus,* from Greek *tektonikós* pertaining to building, from *téktōn* (genitive *téktonos*) builder, carpenter, related to *téchnē* art, craft; see TEXT; for suffix see -IC. The specific sense in geology is first recorded in English in 1894, probably from *tectonics,* though recorded slightly earlier. **—tectonics** *n.pl.* science of geological structure. 1850, building or the constructive arts in general, especially ornamentation, from *tectonic;* for suffix see -ICS. The sense in geology is first recorded in English in 1899.

teddy bear furry toy bear. 1906, American English, from *Teddy,* nickname of President Theodore Roosevelt, famous as a big-game hunter. Roosevelt was shown sparing the life of a bear cub in an editorial cartoon, reputedly drawn by C.K. Berryman in 1902 as a spoof on the President in the role of an ardent conservationist. It is interesting to note that stuffed bears were known as toys before 1906.

Te Deum (tē dē′əm) Latin hymn of praise. 1131 *Te Deum laudamus,* in *Peterborough Chronicle;* later *Te Deum* (before 1200, in *Ancrene Riwle*); borrowing of Late Latin *Te Deum laudāmus* Thee God we praise, the first words of the hymn.

tedious *adj.* long and tiring. Before 1410 *tedyouse;* borrowed from Late Latin *taediōsus* wearisome, irksome, tedious, from Latin *taedium* TEDIUM; for suffix see -OUS.

tedium *n.* tediousness. 1662, borrowed from Latin *taedium* weariness, disgust, related to *taedet* it is wearisome, and *taedēre* to weary, of uncertain origin.

tee *n.* mark or place from which a player starts playing each hole in golf. 1721, back formation from earlier *teaz* (1673), taken as a plural (compare *pea, pease*); originally a Scottish word, of uncertain origin. **—v.** to set (a golf ball) on a tee. 1673, from *teaz,* n.; later with the spelling *tee* (1737, also after the noun).

teem[1] *v.* abound, swarm. Probably before 1200 *temen* give birth to, produce, in *Ancrene Riwle;* developed from Old English (about 1000), found in Old Mercian *tēman,* in Old West Saxon *tīeman* (from Proto-Germanic **taumjanan*), from *tēam* offspring; see TEAM. The meaning of be fertile, abound, swarm (as in *streams teeming with fish*), is first recorded in Shakespeare's *Richard II* (1593).

teem[2] *v.* to pour or flow copiously. Before 1325 *temen* to empty a vessel, in *Cursor Mundi;* later, to discharge, pour out (1482); borrowed from a Scandinavian source (compare Old Icelandic *tœma* to empty, from *tōmr* empty, cognate with Old English *tōm* empty, of unknown origin). The sense of pour of flow copiously (as in *teeming rain*) is first recorded in 1828.

-teen a combining form meaning ten more than, used in forming the cardinal numbers from thirteen to nineteen, as in *seventeen = ten more than seven.* Old English *-tēne, -tīene* (from Proto-Germanic **teHuniz*), an inflected form of *tēn, tīen* TEN. **-teenth** combining form of ordinal numerals, from *thirteenth* to *nineteenth,* formed from *-teen* + *-th*[2]. Middle English *-tenthe,* alteration (influenced by *ten*) of earlier *-tethe,* developed from Old English (West Saxon) *-tēotha, -tēothe,* corresponding to Anglian *teoȝotha* tenth; see TITHE.

teen-age *adj.* of or for a person in his or her teens. 1921, formed from English *-teen,* treated as a separate word + *age,* n. **—teen-aged** *adj.* 1952 (implied in *teen-agedness*), formed from English *teen-age* + *-ed*[2]. **—teen-ager** *n.* 1941, American English; formed from *teen-age* + *-er*[1].

teens *n.pl.* the years of life from 13 to 19 inclusive. 1673, in Wycherley's *The Gentleman Dancing Master;* formed from English *-teen,* treated as a separate word + plural suffix *-s*[1].

teeny *adj. Informal.* very small, tiny. 1825, in John Neal's *Brother Jonathan;* American English, alteration of TINY.

teepee *n.* See TEPEE.

teeter *v.* 1843, to seesaw; 1844, move unsteadily; American English, alteration of earlier *titter* move unsteadily, totter; developed from Middle English *titeren* (about 1385), probably borrowed from a Scandinavian source (compare Old Icelandic *titra* to shake, shiver, totter). The Old Icelandic word is cognate with Old High German *zittarōn* to tremble (modern German *zittern*). —**n.** seesaw. 1863, from the verb. —**teeter-totter** *n.* seesaw (1905, American English).

teetotal *adj.* abstaining completely from alcoholic liquor. 1834, possibly formed from English *total (abstinence*), with repetition of the initial *t* of *total.* Alternatively, *teetotal* may have been based on American English *teetotally,* adv., entirely, wholly (1832), emphatic or reduplicated form of *totally,* adv.

Two historical explanations for *teetotal* are sometimes given, and their closeness in origin from both sides of the Atlantic attest to the growing movement for regulation of the consumption of alcohol in the 19th century. Accordingly *teetotal* was supposedly coined or first used in 1833 by Richard Turner of Preston, England, in a speech advocating total abstinence from alcoholic liquor; or *teetotal* may have been introduced in a New York temperance society in 1827, as an indication (with "T") after the signature of one taking the pledge of total abstinence.

Connection of *teetotal* and *teetotally* with *teetotum,* meaning a spinning top, is probably merest coincidence.

—**teetotaler** *n.* person who abstains completely from alcoholic liquor. 1834, formed from English *teetotal* + *-er*[1].

Teflon *n. Trademark.* plastic resin used as a coating to prevent friction or sticking. 1945, American English, formed from *te(tra-)* + *fl(uor-*), from the chemical name *polytetrafluoroethylene* + *-on,* arbitrary ending, as in *rayon* and *nylon.*

tegument (teg′yəmənt) *n.* natural covering of an animal body. About 1440, borrowed from Latin *tegumentum* a cover or covering, from *tegere* to cover; see THATCH; for suffix see -MENT.

tektite *n. Geology.* rounded, glassy, meteoritic object. 1909, formed from Greek *tēktós* molten (from *tḗkein* to melt; see THAW) + English *-ite*[1].

tele- a combining form meaning: 1) far, far off, operating over a long distance, as in *telegraph, telephone, television;* 2) television, as in *telecast, telethon, televiewer.* Borrowed from Greek *tēle-,* combining form of *têle* far off, afar, at or to a distance (compare Aeolic *pḗlui*), related to Greek *pálai* long ago, and cognate with Sanskrit *caramá-s* farthest off, *cirás* long, and Welsh *pell* far, from Indo-European **kwel-/kwēl-* (Pok.640).

telecast *n.* television program or broadcast. 1937, American English; formed from *tele-* television + *(broad)cast.* —**v.** to broadcast by television. 1940, American English, from the noun.

telegram *n.* message sent by telegraph. 1852, American English; formed from English *tele(graph)* + *-gram.* This term met much opposition from scholars when first introduced, because it was not formed on Greek analogies, which would have given *telegrapheme,* as in modern Greek *tēlegráphēma.*

telegraph *n.* apparatus for transmitting messages a long distance. 1794, a semaphore apparatus; borrowed from French *télégraphe,* from *télé-* far (from Greek *tēle-*) + *-graphe* -graph. The French word was suggested in 1792 by the French diplomat Miot de Melito, to replace *tachygraphe,* the term proposed by the coinventor of this apparatus, Claude Chappe. The term was first applied in English to an experimental electric telegraph in 1797; a practical telegraph was developed in the 1830's by Samuel Morse and first used widely in the 1840's. —**telegraphic** *adj.* 1794, in reference to the semaphore apparatus; formed from English *telegraph* + *-ic.* —**telegraphy** *n.* 1795, formed from English *tele-* + *-graphy.*

telemeter *n.* Before 1889, device for measuring various conditions (heat, radiation, pressure, etc.) and transmitting the information to a distant receiving station; earlier, a rangefinder used in surveying and artillery bombardment (1860, *telometer*); borrowed from French *télémètre (télé-* far, from Greek *tēle-,* + *mètre* -meter) and formed from English *tele-, telo-* + *-meter.* —**telemetry** *n.* Before 1885, the use of a telemeter, or the art or practice of using such a device; formed from English *tele-* + *-metry* on the model of Greek *tēle-* far + *-metríā,* from *métron* measure.

teleology (tel′ēol′əjē) *n.* purpose or design in nature. 1740, borrowed from New Latin *teleologia,* coined in 1728 by the German philosopher Christian von Wolff (1679-1754), from Greek *téleos* (genitive of *télos* end, goal, result) + *-logíā* -logy.

telepathy (təlep′əthē) *n.* transference of feeling or thought, psychic communication. 1882, coined by the English poet, writer, and psychic researcher F.W.H. Myers (1843-1901), from English *tele-* far + *-pathy* feeling. —**telepathic** *adj.* of or having to do with telepathy. 1884, formed from English *telepathy* + *-ic.*

telephone *n.* 1844, instrument similar to a foghorn for conveying signals from a ship; probably borrowed from French *téléphone,* formed about 1830 from *télé-* tele- + *-phone* sound, -phone. In 1849 *telephone* was applied in English to a kind of megaphone or loudspeaker, and in 1876, the Scottish-American inventor Alexander Graham Bell (1847-1922) applied the term to the modern instrument which he developed between 1873 and 1876. —**v.** 1877, talk or communicate by Bell's telephone; from the noun. —**telephone book** (1915) —**telephone booth** (before 1895) —**telephone directory** (1907)

telephoto *adj.* 1898, in *tele-photo lens;* shortened form of *telephotographic* (1892); formed on earlier *telephotograph* (not recorded before 1900, but probably known by 1892, and found earlier in the meaning of a photograph transmitted over a distance, 1881).

Teleprompter (tel′əpromp′tər) *n. Trademark.* device that shows a prepared speech line for line to a speaker being televised. 1951, American English; formed from *tele(vision) prompter.*

telescope *n.* 1648 *telescopio,* in Boyle's *A Treatise of Seraphic Love;* later *telescope* (1656); borrowing of Italian *telescopio* (used by Galileo in 1611) and New Latin *telescopium* (used by Kepler in 1613); both from Greek *tēleskópos* far-seeing (*tēle-* far + *-skópos* seeing, from *skopein* to watch; see SPY). The first telescope was probably made in 1608 by the Dutch optician Hans Lippershey, but the name of the instrument is generally attributed to Prince Cesi, head of the Roman Academy of the Lincei, to which Galileo also belonged. Galileo built his own telescope in 1609 but called it *perspicillum* in 1610, before he adopted *telescopio* and *telescopium.* —**v.** to force together one inside another, like the sliding tubes of some telescopes. 1867, American English; from the noun. **—telescopic** *adj.* 1705, formed from English *telescope* + *-ic.*

teletype *n.* 1904, trademark for a communications system of typewriters connected electronically; shortened form of *teletypewriter,* formed from English *tele-* + *typewriter.* **—v.** 1904 (implied in *teletyping*); from the noun.

televise *v.* broadcast by television. 1927, in the *Glasgow Herald,* back formation from TELEVISION.

television *n.* 1907, viewing of a distant object or scene by means of an apparatus (not yet perfected) which electrically transmits and reproduces it; borrowed from French *télévision,* or formed from English *tele-* far + *vision.* The modern electronic television was developed in the 1920's and 1930's; the first regular television broadcast was established in the United States in 1939.

Telex *n.* 1932, a communications system of teletypewriters; formed from English *tele(type)* + *ex(change).*

tell *v.* Before 1121 *tellen,* in *Peterborough Chronicle;* found in Old English *tellan* (before 899, in Alfred's translation of Boethius' *De Consolatione Philosophiae*); cognate with Old Frisian *talja, tella,* Old Saxon *tęlljan* tell, Middle Dutch, modern Dutch, Middle Low German, and modern Low German *tellan* count, reckon, Old High German *zęllen* tell (modern German *zählen* reckon, count), and Old Icelandic *tęlja* tell, count (Swedish *tälja,* Danish *tælle* count, reckon), from Proto-Germanic **taljanan.* Related to TALE. The sense of recognize, distinguish, know (as in *tell one thing from another*), is first recorded about 1370. **—teller** *n.* Probably before 1300 *tellere* person who tells, in *Kyng Alisaunder;* formed from Middle English *tellen* to tell + *-ere* -er[1]. The meaning of a person who keeps accounts is first recorded in Middle English in 1475. **—telling** *adj.* 1852, having effect or force, striking. **—telltale** *n.* person who discloses secrets, tattler (before 1548, in Edward Hall's *Chronicle*). *—adj.* revealing (before 1577).

tellurium (telůr′ēəm) *n.* chemical element similar to sulfur. 1800, New Latin, from Latin *tellūs* (genitive *tellūris*) earth + New Latin *-ium,* chemical suffix. The New Latin word was coined in 1798 by the German chemist Martin Klaproth (1743-1817) probably in contrast to *uranium* (from Greek *ouranós* heaven), which he had discovered earlier. Latin *tellūs* is the word for the earth as a planet. It is related to *meditullium* the inland part of a country, the interior, the center. Though the *-ūs, -ūris* ending is virtually without parallel in Latin, the root would seem definitely cognate with Sanskrit *tala-m* surface, level, bottom, and with Old English *thel* plank, floor, and Old High German *dil(o),* from Indo-European **tel-/tol-* (Pok.1061).

temblor (tem′blər *or* tem′blôr) *n.* earthquake. 1876, in Bret Harte's *Gabriel Conroy;* American English, borrowed through American Spanish *temblor* earthquake, from Spanish *temblor,* literally, a trembling, from *temblar* to tremble, from Vulgar Latin **tremulāre* to TREMBLE.

temerity *n.* rashness, boldness. Before 1387 *temerite,* in Trevisa's translation of Higden's *Polychronicon;* borrowed from Middle French *témérité,* or directly from Latin *temeritātem* (nominative *temeritās*) blind chance, accident, rashness, from *temere* by chance, blindly, casually, rashly, corresponding exactly to the Sanskrit locative *támasi* in the dark; for suffix see -ITY. Latin *temere* is also cognate with Old Irish *temel* darkness, Lithuanian *témti* become dark, Old Slavic *tĭma* darkness, and Tocharian B *tamāsse* dark, from Indo-European **temes-,* root **tem-* dark (Pok.1063).

temp *n. Informal.* temporary employee, especially a typist or secretary. 1932, American English, shortened form of TEMPORARY. **—v.** work as a temp. 1973, from the noun.

temper *v.* tone down, moderate. About 1200 *tempren* to moderate, regulate, in *Vices and Virtues;* developed from Old English *temprian* (about 1000, in Ælfric's *Homilies*); borrowed from Latin *temperāre* to mix correctly, observe due measure, moderate, regulate, from *tempus* time, season, proper time or season; see TEMPORAL[1] of time. The technical sense of bring a substance, such as clay, paint (later steel), etc., to a proper condition for working by mixing or preparing is found probably before 1300, in *Kyng Alisaunder,* and may have been influenced by Old French *temprer* to temper, also from Latin *temperāre.* **—n.** Before 1387 *tempre* balance, due proportion, in Trevisa's translation of Higden's *Polychronicon;* from the verb. The sense of habitual disposition, characteristic state of mind, is first recorded in Shakespeare's *King John* (1595), that of calm state of mind, in Shakespeare's *Measure for Measure* (1603), and the related sense of an angry state of mind in 1828. The sense of the condition of a substance given by mixing or preparing is first found about 1470.

tempera (tem′pərə) *n.* method of painting in which colors are mixed with substances other than oil. 1832, borrowing of Italian *tempera,* from *temperare* to mix colors, temper, from Latin *temperāre* to mix, TEMPER.

temperament *n.* Before 1398, proportioned mixture of elements, in Trevisa's translation of Bartholomew's *De Proprietatibus Rerum;* borrowed from Latin *temperāmentum* due proportion, proper mixture, from *temperāre* to mix, TEMPER; for suffix see -MENT. In medieval alchemy and philosophy *temperament* developed the meaning of a combination of qualities, as hot or cold, moist or dry, that in a certain proportion determine the nature of an organism (1471), and was further extended in medieval physiology to refer to the combination of the four humors (sanguine, choleric, phlegmatic, and melancholic). Their relative proportion in the body supposedly determined physical and mental constitution and reference to them is still found in such allusions as *a phlegmatic temperament.* The general meaning of a person's natural habit of mind or characteristic disposition (as in *a poetic temperament*) is found in Byron's *Don Juan* (1821). **—temperamental** *adj.* 1646, of or relating to temperament; formed from English *temperament* + *-al*[1]. The meaning of having an erratic or neurotic temperament, subject to moods and whims, is first recorded in 1907.

temperance *n.* moderation in action, speech, habits, etc. About 1340, in *Ayenbite of Inwyt;* borrowed through Anglo-French *temperaunce,* learned borrowing from Latin *temperantia* moderation, from *temperāns,* present participle of *temperāre* to moderate, TEMPER; for suffix see -ANCE. Latin *temperantia* was used by Cicero to translate Greek *sōphrosýnē* moderation, soundmindedness, considered as one of the cardinal virtues. In early modern English, *temperance* was used to render Latin *continentia* CONTINENCE or *abstinentia* ABSTINENCE. In the 1600's it was specifically applied to moderation or abstinence in eating and especially in drinking alcohol, and by the early 1800's it referred to the practice or principle of total abstinence from alcoholic drink; hence often used attributively in *temperance society* (1831), *the temperance movement* (1855), etc.

temperate *adj.* moderate, mild. About 1310 *tempret* of mild temperature, not very hot or cold; later *temperat* (about 1380); borrowed from Latin *temperātus* restrained, duly regulated, from past participle of *temperāre* to moderate, regulate, TEMPER; for suffix see -ATE[1]. The general sense of mild, restrained, moderate (applied to persons, their conduct, etc.), is found in Middle English before 1382. **—temperate zone** (1551)

temperature *n.* About 1450, a tempered or temperate condition (as of the weather); borrowed from Latin *temperātūra* a tempering or temperateness, moderation, from *temperātus,* past participle of *temperāre* to moderate, TEMPER; for suffix see -URE. The sense of the degree of heat or cold is first recorded in Boyle's *Of the Temperature in Submarine Regions* (1670).

tempest *n.* About 1275 *tempeste* violent storm; borrowed from Old French *tempeste* violent storm, from Vulgar Latin **tempesta,* variant of Latin *tempestās* (genitive *tempestātis*) storm, weather, season; also, time with respect to physical conditions or weather, especially bad weather; also, commotion, disturbance; related to *tempus* time, season; see TEMPORAL[1] of time. The figurative sense of a violent commotion or disturbance is first recorded in Middle English before 1333. The phrase *tempest in a teapot* is first recorded in 1854. —v. raise a tempest. About 1380 *tempesten,* in Chaucer's translation of Boethius' *De Consolatione Philosophiae;* borrowed from Old French *tempester,* from *tempeste* tempest. **—tempestuous** *adj.* stormy, violent. About 1385, in Chaucer's *Troilus and Criseyde;* borrowed, perhaps by influence of Middle French *tempetueux,* from Late Latin *tempestuosus* stormy, turbulent, from *tempestās* tempest; for suffix see -OUS.

template (temp′lət) *n.* 1677 *templet* horizontal piece under a girder or beam to distribute downward thrust; probably borrowed from French *templet* weaver's stretcher for keeping cloth at the proper width on a loom, diminutive of *temple,* of similar meaning, learned borrowing from Latin *templum* plank, rafter, building for worship, TEMPLE[1]; for suffix see -ET. The meaning of a pattern, gauge, or mold used in shaping a piece of work is first recorded in 1819 (but is found earlier in the form *temple,* 1688). The biochemical sense of a molecule that serves as a mold or pattern for the synthesis of other molecules is first recorded in 1949. Alteration of the spelling to *template* is first recorded in 1844, probably influenced by PLATE; pronunciation, however, was not influenced by the spelling change, until recently.

temple[1] *n.* building for worship. Old English *temple* (before 899, in Alfred's translation of St. Gregory's *Pastoral Care*); also *templ* and *tempel* (before 830, in the *Vespasian Psalter*); borrowed from Latin *templum* piece of ground consecrated for the taking of auspices, building for worship. Latin *templum* is possibly cognate with Greek *témenos* divine or royal domain, related to *témnein* to cut; see TOME. Though said to be reinforced in Middle English by Old French *temple,* the word has a continuous history in this spelling and sense of a building for worship, right through the transition period from Old to Middle English.

temple[2] *n.* side of the forehead, usually found as a plural in early use. About 1340 *tempils;* later in the spelling *temples* (about 1430); borrowed from Old French *temple* side of the forehead, from Vulgar Latin **tempula,* feminine singular, alteration of Latin *tempora,* plural of *tempus* (genitive *temporis*) side of the forehead, probably originally meaning the thin stretch or span of skin at the side of the forehead and thus associated with *tempus* in the sense of span, as of time (compare Old English *thun-wang* and Old High German *dunn-wengi* side of the forehead, literally, thin place), from Indo-European **temp-* stretch, extend (Pok.1064). Compare TEMPORAL[1].

tempo *n.* 1724, time or rate of movement in music; borrowing of Italian *tempo,* literally, time, from Latin *tempus* (genitive *temporis*) time; see TEMPORAL[1] of time. Doublet of TENSE[2], n. The figurative sense of the rate of motion or activity of someone or something (as in *the fast tempo of modern life*) is first recorded in 1898, in George Bernard Shaw's *You Never Can Tell.*

temporal[1] *adj.* of time, lasting only for a time, temporary. About 1340 *temporalle* worldly, secular, in Richard Rolle's *English Prose Treatises;* later *temporale* of time, temporary (about 1375); borrowed from Old French *temporal,* and directly from Latin *temporālis* of time, temporary, from *tempus* (genitive *temporis*) time, season, proper time or season; for suffix see -AL[1]. Latin *tempus* is cognate with Lithuanian *tem̃pti* to stretch, Old Slavic *tętiva* tendon, sinew, Tocharian A *tampe* power, might; and in Germanic, Old Icelandic *thambr* swollen, thick, from Indo-European **temp-* stretch, extend (Pok.1064).

temporal[2] *adj.* of or situated at the sides of the forehead. 1597, borrowed from Late Latin *temporālis* of the temples, from Latin *tempora* the temples, from *tempus* (genitive *temporis*) side of the forehead; see TEMPLE[2]; for suffix see -AL[1].

temporary *adj.* 1547, borrowed from Latin *temporārius* of seasonal character, lasting a short time, from *tempus* (genitive *temporis*) time, season; see TEMPORAL[1] of time; for suffix see -ARY. The noun use, which comes from an absolute or truncated use of the adjective with the following noun understood is found in the sense of a temporary employee, in *Dombey and Son* (1846).

temporize (tem′pərīz) *v.* 1579, to fit one's acts to the time or occasion; borrowed from Middle French *temporiser* to pass one's time, wait one's time, learned borrowing from Medieval Latin *temporizare* pass time, perhaps through Vulgar Latin **temporāre* to delay, from Latin *tempus* (genitive *temporis*) time; see TEMPORAL[1] of time; for suffix see -IZE. The meaning of evade immediate action or decision is first recorded in English in 1579, and that of draw out discussions, negotiations, etc., in order to gain time, in 1586, in Hooker's writings.

tempt *v.* Probably before 1200 *tempten* try to attract, allure, entice, in *Ancrene Riwle;* borrowed from Old French *tempter,* learned borrowing from Latin, and borrowed directly into English from Latin *temptāre* to feel, try out, attempt to influence, test, a frequentative form of **tempere* (compare Lithuanian *tim̃pinti* move slowly, feel one's way), from Indo-European **temp-* stretch, extend (Pok.1064). The popular Old French form *tenter* was not adopted in English, but the noun form *tentation* is found in early modern English as a borrowing from Old French. **—temptation** *n.* Probably before 1200 *temptaciun,* in *Ancrene Riwle;* borrowed from Old French *temptation* enticement, allurement, attraction, learned borrowing from Latin *temptātiōnem* (nominative *temptātiō*) trial, feeling, from *temptāre* to feel, try, test; for suffix see -ATION.

tempura (tempůr′ə) *n.* dish of seafood or vegetables fried in batter. 1920, borrowing of Japanese *tempura.*

ten *adj.* 1311 *tenn;* developed from Old English *tēn* (Mercian), *tīen* (West Saxon, about 725, in *Beowulf*); cognate with Old Frisian *tiān* ten, Old Saxon *tehan,* Middle Dutch and modern Dutch *tien,* Middle Low German *tein,* Old High German *zehan* (modern German *zehn*), Old Icelandic *tiū* (Danish and Norwegian *ti,* Swedish *tio*), and Gothic *taíhun.* Cognates outside Germanic include Latin *decem* ten, Greek *déka,* Old Irish *deich,* Welsh *deg,* Lithuanian *dẽšimt,* Old Slavic *desęti,* Armenian *tasn,* Sanskrit *dáśa,* and Tocharian A *śäk,* Tocharian B *śak,* from Indo-European **deḱm̥* (Pok.191). **—tenfold** *adj., adv.* Probably before 1200; developed from Old English *tīenfeald* (*tīen* ten + *-feald* -fold). **—tenpins** *n.* bowling (1600). **—tenth** *adj., n.* Before 1150 *tenthe,* formed from Middle English *ten* ten + *-the* -th², replacing Old English *tēotha, teogotha;* see TITHE.

tenable *adj.* capable of being held, restrained, or defended. 1579, borrowed from Middle French, from Old French *tenir* to hold, from Latin *tenēre* hold, keep; see TENANT; for suffix see -ABLE. The figurative sense of capable of being maintained against objection is first recorded in Addison's writings in *The Spectator* (1711).

tenacious *adj.* 1607, holding fast, clinging, cohesive, tough; formed as an adjective to *tenacity* from English *tenac(ity)* + *-ous.* The figurative sense of persistent, stubborn, is recorded in Blount's *Glossographia* (1656). **—tenacity** *n.* Probably before 1425 *tenacite* persistence, obstinacy, in a translation of Chauliac's *Grande Chirurgie;* borrowed from Middle French *ténacité,* and directly from Latin *tenācitās* the act or fact of holding fast, from *tenāx* (genitive *tenācis*) tough, holding fast, from *tenēre* to hold; see TENANT; for suffix see -ITY.

tenant *n.* Before 1325 *tenaun* person who holds lands by title or by lease; later *tenant* (about 1340); borrowed from Anglo-French *tenaunt* and Old French *tenant,* noun use of present participle of *tenir* to hold, from Latin *tenēre* hold, keep, related to *tendere* to stretch, aim; see TEND¹ incline; for suffix see -ANT. The meaning of a person who occupies or uses a house or other property by lease is first recorded in Middle English in *Piers Plowman* (before 1376). **—v.** hold or occupy as a tenant. 1634, from the noun. **—tenancy** *n.* 1423, property held by a tenant; formed from English *tenant* + *-cy,* probably by influence of Old French *tenance* and Medieval Latin *tenantia* state or condition of being a tenant. The meaning of a holding or possession of lands is first recorded in Swinburne's *Testaments* (1590).

tend¹ *v.* incline. About 1330 *tenden* to move toward, incline; earlier *tenen* (probably before 1300), *tenten* (before 1325); borrowed from Old French *tendre* stretch, hold forth, offer, from Latin *tendere* to aim, stretch, extend. Latin *tendere* is cognate with Greek *teínein* to stretch, Lithuanian *tìnti* to swell, Old Slavic *teneto, tonoto* cord, string, and Sanskrit *tanóti* (he) stretches. Germanic cognates of *tendere* include Old English *thennan* stretch out, Old High German *dennen* to stretch (modern German *dehnen*), Old Icelandic *thenja,* and Gothic *ufthanjan;* see THIN.

tend² *v.* attend to. Probably before 1200 *tenden,* in *Ancrene Riwle;* shortened earlier variant of *atenden, attenden* ATTEND.

tendency *n.* 1628, in Thomas Spencer's *The Art of Logic;* borrowed from Medieval Latin *tendentia* inclination, leaning, from Latin *tendēns,* present participle of *tendere* to stretch, aim; see TEND¹ incline; for suffix see -ENCY. **—tendential** *adj.* 1889, having a tendency, tendentious; formed in English from Medieval Latin *tendentia* tendency + *-al¹*. **—tendentious** *adj.* 1900, having a particular tendency, tending to take sides; formed in English from Medieval Latin *tendentia* tendency + English *-ous,* by influence of German *tendenziös.*

tender¹ *adj.* soft. Probably before 1200 *tendre* soft, delicate, in *Ancrene Riwle;* borrowed from Old French *tendre,* earlier *tenre,* from Latin *tenerem* (nominative *tener*) soft, delicate, of tender age; probably cognate with Sabine (an Italic language) *tereno-* soft, Greek *térēn* (genitive *térenos*) delicate, tender, Armenian *tarm* young, fresh, Sanskrit *táruṇa-s* young, tender, and Gothic *tharihs* (of cloth) unfulled, from Indo-European **ter-, teru-* (Pok.1070). The meaning of kind, affectionate, loving, is first recorded in Middle English before 1325, in *Cursor Mundi.* **—tenderfoot** *n. Informal.* newcomer to pioneer life (1849, American English). **—tender-hearted** *adj.* (1539) **—tenderize** *v.* to make tender. 1733, formed from English *tender¹* + *-ize.*

tender² *v.* to offer formally. 1542-43 *tendre,* borrowing of Middle French *tendre* to offer, hold forth, from Latin *tendere* to stretch, extend; see TEND¹ incline. The retention of the ending of the Middle French infinitive is unusual; compare BATTER¹, RENDER. **—n.** a formal offer. 1542-43 *tendre;* from the verb. **—tender offer** public offer to buy up a company's stock (1964, American English, an interesting tautology).

tender³ *n.* person or thing that tends another. About 1470, probably formed from Middle English *tenden* attend to, TEND² + *-er¹*. The meaning of a small boat used to attend a larger one is first recorded in 1675, and that of a railroad car to carry fuel and water for a steam locomotive, in 1825.

tenderloin *n.* tender part of the loin of beef or pork. 1828, American English, formed from *tender¹*, adj. + *loin.* The slang meaning of a police district (originally in New York City) noted for vice is first recorded in 1887; it is said to have been so named because of the large amount of graft available in the district.

tendon *n.* sinew. 1543, borrowed from Medieval Latin *tendonem* (nominative *tendo*), alteration (influenced by Latin *tendere* to stretch) of Late Latin *tenōn,* from Greek *ténōn* (genitive *ténontos*) tendon, sinew, from *teínein* to stretch; see TEND¹ incline.

tendril *n.* twisting, threadlike part of a climbing plant. 1538, in Elyot's *Dictionary;* borrowed from Middle French *tendrillon* bud, shoot, cartilage, diminutive of *tendron* cartilage, from Old French *tendre* soft, TENDER¹.

tenebrous (ten′əbrəs) *adj.* full of darkness, dark. Probably before 1475, in *The Assembly of Gods;* borrowed from Middle French *tenebreus,* learned borrowing from Latin *tenebrōsus,* from *tenebrae* darkness; for suffix see -OUS. Latin *tenebrae* (dissimilated from earlier **temafrā-*) is exactly cognate with Sanskrit (plural) *támisrā-s* darkness, from Indo-European **teməsrās,* while Old High German *dinstar* dark is from **temesro-* (Pok.1064); see TEMERITY.

tenement *n.* About 1303, a holding of immovable property such as land or buildings, in Mannyng's *Handlyng Synne;* borrowed from Anglo-French and Old French *tenement,* learned borrowing from Medieval Latin *tenementum* a holding, fief, from Latin *tenēre* to hold; see TENANT; for suffix see -MENT. The general meaning of a dwelling place, habitation, residence, is found in Middle English, probably before 1400. The term *tenement house,* meaning an apartment building usually in a poor section of a city, is first recorded in 1858, in American English; in the 1930's the phrase was shortened to *tenement.*

tenet *n.* doctrine, principle. 1413, probably from Medieval Latin use (to introduce a statement of doctrine) of Latin *tenet* he holds, third person singular present indicative of *tenēre* to hold; see TENANT. Compare CARET and HABITAT for a similar formation.

tennis *n.* 1345-46 *tenyes* the game of tennis, of uncertain origin (not recorded in the modern spelling until the 1500's).

A widely held belief is that the word was borrowed through Anglo-French *tenetz* hold! receive! take!, from Old French *tenez* (imperative of *tenir* to hold, receive, take; see TENABLE), presumably used as a call from the server to his opponent, though no mention of this call has been found in French (in Old French the game itself was apparently called *la paulme, la paume,* literally, the palm, because it was played in a much simpler form, striking the ball with the palm of the hand). The server's call in some Latin sources of the 1500's is given as *accipe* and *excipe* accept! take!, which suggests that *tenez* or some equivalent call may have existed in Old French. However, the lack of attestation of the word in Old French, in addition to the fact that Middle English nouns were very rarely formed from Old French imperatives, argue strongly against this derivation.

tenon (ten′ən) *n.* end of a piece of wood cut to fit another piece to form a joint. Probably about 1380 *tenoun,* in *Pearl;* borrowed from Middle French *tenon* a tenon, from Old French *tenir* to hold; see TENABLE. **—v.** 1596, fasten securely; from the noun. The meaning of fix with a tenon and mortise is found in 1649.

tenor *n.* Probably before 1300 *tenour* general meaning, purport, drift, in *Kyng Alisaunder;* borrowed from Old French *tenour* substance, sense, learned borrowing from Latin *tenōrem* (nominative *tenor*) contents, course, originally a holding on, from *tenēre* to hold; see TENANT; for suffix see -OR[1]. The meaning of the general tendency, course, direction, is first recorded in Middle English before 1398, in Trevisa's translation of Bartholomew's *De Proprietatibus Rerum.* The sense in music of an adult male voice is also recorded in Middle English (probably 1388), so called because the melody was carried or held by the tenor's part.

tense[1] *adj.* stretched tight. 1670, borrowed from Latin *tēnsus,* past participle of *tendere* to stretch; see TEND[1] incline. The figurative sense of keyed up, in a state of nervous tension, is first recorded in 1821, in Coleridge's writings. **—v.** stretch tight, stiffen. 1676, from the adjective. The figurative sense of make or become nervous or fill with nervous tension (often in *tense up*) is first recorded in 1946.

tense[2] *n.* form of a verb showing time of an action or state. Before 1333 *tens* time, also tense of a verb, in William of Shoreham's *Poems;* borrowed from Old French *tens* time, from Latin *tempus;* see TEMPORAL[1] of time. Doublet of TEMPO.

tensile *adj.* 1626, that can be stretched, ductile, in Bacon's *Sylva Sylvarum;* borrowed from New Latin *tensilis* capable of being stretched, from Latin *tēnsus,* past participle of *tendere* to stretch; see TEND[1] incline. The meaning of pertaining to tension is first recorded in English in 1841. **—tensile strength** (1868)

tension *n.* 1533, a stretched condition, in Elyot's *The Castel of Helth;* borrowed through Middle French *tension,* or directly from Latin *tēnsiōnem* (nominative *tēnsiō*) a stretching (in Medieval Latin, a struggle, contest), from *tēnsus,* past participle of *tendere* to stretch; see TEND[1] incline; for suffix see -SION. The figurative sense of mental or nervous strain is first recorded in English before 1763. The meaning of electromotive force or voltage (as in *high-tension wires*) is first recorded in English in 1802, but *high tension* itself did not appear before 1889.

tensor (ten′sər *or* ten′sôr) *n.* muscle that stretches part of the body. 1704, New Latin, from Latin *tēnsus,* past participle of *tendere* to stretch; see TEND[1] incline; for suffix see -OR[2].

tent *n.* Probably before 1300, portable shelter of skins or cloth stretched over poles, in *Kyng Alisaunder;* borrowed from Old French *tente,* from Medieval Latin *tenta* a tent, noun use of feminine singular of Latin *tentus* stretched, variant past participle of *tendere* to stretch; see TEND[1] incline. Also compare Latin *tentōrium* tent; see TENTER. **—v.** 1553, to pitch a tent, in Douglas' translation of Vergil's *Aeneid;* from the noun. **—tent caterpillar** (1854, American English)

tentacle *n.* long, flexible growth on the head or around the mouth of an animal. 1762, borrowed from New Latin *tentaculum* feeler (Latin *tentāre* to feel, try; see TENTATIVE + *-culum* diminutive suffix).

tentative *adj.* done as a trial or experiment. 1588 (implied in *tentatively*); borrowed from Medieval Latin *tentativus* trying, testing, from Latin *tentātus,* past participle of *tentāre* to feel, try, test, variant of *temptāre;* see TEMPT; for suffix see -IVE.

tenter *n.* framework for stretching cloth. About 1300 *teyntur* frame; later *tentour* tent (before 1325); of uncertain origin, though almost certainly connected with Latin *tentōrium* tent made of stretched skins, from *tentus,* variant past participle of *tendere* to stretch; see TEND[1] incline. The form *tenter* became established in the 1500's. The compound *tenterhook* is not recorded in Middle English before 1480 with reference to one of the hooks that holds cloth on a tenter. The figurative phrase *on tenterhooks* in painful suspense, is first recorded in Smollett's *Adventures of Roderick Random* (1748). **—v.** stretch cloth on a tenter. 1437 *teynteren;* from the noun.

tenuous *adj.* thin, slender. 1597, formed in English from Latin *tenuis* THIN + English *-ous.* The figurative sense of having slight importance, not substantial, is found before 1817. **—tenuity** *n.* thinness. Probably before 1425 *tenuite,* in a translation of Chauliac's *Grande Chirurgie;* borrowed from Middle French *ténuité,* or directly from Latin *tenuitās* thinness, from *tenuis* THIN; for suffix see -ITY.

tenure *n.* a holding of property, position, etc. 1414, holding of a tenement, in *Rolls of Parliament;* borrowed from Anglo-French and Middle French *tenure* a tenure, estate in land, from Old French *tenir* to hold; see TENABLE; for suffix see -URE. The general sense of the condition or fact of holding a status, position, or occupation (as in *a tenure of office, a lifetime tenure*) is first recorded in 1599, in Ben Jonson's *Cynthia's Revels.*

tepee or **teepee** *n.* conical tent of American Indians. 1743 *ti pee,* American English; borrowed from Siouan (Dakota) *tipi* dwelling. The spelling *teepee* is first found in 1849.

tepid *adj.* lukewarm. Before 1400, in Lanfranc's *Science of Surgery;* borrowed from Latin *tepidus* lukewarm, from *tepēre* be warm. Latin *tepēre* is cognate with Old Irish *tess* heat, Old Slavic *toplŭ* warm, and Sanskrit *tápati* (it) makes warm, burns, *tápas* heat, from Indo-European **tep-* (Pok.1069).

tequila (təkē′lə) *n.* alcoholic liquor distilled from a Mexican agave. 1849, American English; borrowing of American Spanish *tequila,* from *Tequila,* name of a district in central Mexico noted for the superiority of its tequila.

tera- a combining form meaning one trillion, as in *teracycle* (1964), *terawatt* (1969), *terahertz* (1969). Adapted from Greek *téras* (genitive *téraos*) marvel, monster. Greek *téras* is cognate with Lithuanian *kẽras* spell, enchantment, Old Slavic *čarodějĭ* magician, sorcerer, Sanskrit *kṛtyā́* spell, enchantment, *karóti* he makes, performs, and Welsh *peri* to cause, from Indo-European **kwer-/kwṛ-* (Pok.641).

teratogenic (ter′ətəjen′ik) *adj.* having to do with or causing malformation of an embryo or fetus. 1879, formed in English from Hellenistic Greek *terat-,* stem of *téras* marvel, monster (see TERA-) + English connective *-o-* + *-genic.*

teratology *n. Biology.* study of misshapen formations in animals or plants. 1678, discourse on prodigies, marvelous tale, in Phillips' *Dictionary;* formed in English from Greek *terat-,* stem of *téras* marvel, monster (see TERA-) + English connective *-o-* + *-logy.* The sense used in biology is first recorded in 1842.

terbium (tėr′bēəm) *n.* metallic chemical element of the yttrium group. 1843, New Latin, from *(Yt)terby,* town in Sweden where the mineral gadolinite (which contains terbium) was found + *-ium,* chemical suffix. The New Latin word was coined by the Swedish chemist Carl Gustaf Mosander, 1797-1858, who discovered the element in 1843.

tercentenary (tėr′senten′ərē) *adj.* having to do with a 300th anniversary. 1844, formed in English from Latin *ter* three times + English *centenary.* Latin *ter* (cognate with Sanskrit *trís,* Greek *trís*) is related to *trēs* THREE. **—n.** 300th anniversary. 1855, from the adjective.

tercet (tėr′sit) *n.* group of three lines rhyming together. 1598 *terset,* in Florio's *A World of Words;* borrowed from Italian *terzetto,* diminutive of *terzo* third, from Latin *tertius* THIRD; for suffix see -ET. The spelling *tercet* was influenced by French *tercet,* from Italian *terzetto.*

tergiversate (tėr′jəvərsāt′) *v.* evade, equivocate, use subterfuge. 1654, probably a back formation from *tergiversation,* modeled on Latin *tergiversātus,* past participle of *tergiversārī* turn one's back, evade; for suffix see -ATE[1]. **—tergiversation** *n.* evasion. 1570, borrowed from Latin *tergiversātiōnem* (nominative *tergiversātiō*) a shifting, evasion, from *tergiversārī* turn one's back on, evade (*tergum* the back, of uncertain origin + *versāre* to spin, frequentative form of *vertere* to turn; see VERTEX); for suffix see -ATION.

term *n.* Probably before 1200 *terme* limit in time, set or appointed time or period, in *Ancrene Riwle;* later, period of time a law court or school is in session (1454); borrowed from Old French *terme* limit of time or place, from Latin *terminus* end, boundary line, related to *termen* boundary, end. Latin *termen* is cognate with Greek *térma* goal, final point, *térmōn* border, boundary, Armenian *tʻarm* end piece, Sanskrit *tárati* (he) overcomes, crosses, and Hittite *tarahzi, taruhzi* (he) is powerful, controls, conquers, from Indo-European **ter-* cross (Pok.1074). The meaning of a word or phrase used in a limited or precise sense is first recorded in Middle English in a version of *Piers Plowman* (about 1378). This sense of *term* was borrowed from Medieval Latin *terminus* word, expression, from Late Latin *terminus* member of a mathematical ratio (found in English in 1542), part of a logical proposition or syllogism (loan translation of Greek *hóros*), from Latin, end, boundary line. The plural *terms,* meaning limited conditions, stipulations, is first recorded in Middle English in Shoreham's *Poems* (before 1333). Doublet of TERMINUS. **—v.** to express or denote by a term, name, call, designate. 1549 (found in *terming*); from the noun. An earlier sense of terminate is recorded in Middle English about 1410 (also found in *terming*); borrowed from Middle French *termer* terminate, limit, from Old French *terme* limit. **—term paper** essay written for a course in a school term (1931, in American English).

termagant (tėr′məgənt) *n.* 1500-20, violent, overbearing person, in William Dunbar's *Poems;* found in Middle English *Termagaunt,* name of a fictitious Moslem deity appearing in medieval morality plays as a violent, overbearing personage (about 1303); earlier *Tervagant* (probably before 1200); borrowed from Old French *Tervagan, Tervagant,* of uncertain origin. English *termagant,* applied specifically to women, is first recorded in 1659. **—adj.** 1596, violent, overbearing, in Shakespeare's *1 Henry IV* and in Nashe's *Have With You to Saffron-Walden;* from the noun.

terminal *adj.* 1459, relating to or marking a boundary, limit, or end; borrowed from Latin *termināIis* pertaining to a boundary or end, terminal, final, from *terminus* end, boundary line; see TERM; for suffix see -AL[1]. The sense of situated at or forming the end or extremity of something (chiefly in scientific and technical use, as in *a terminal bud*) is first recorded in 1805, and that of concluding, final (as in *a terminal payment, a terminal syllable* or *sound*) in 1827. The application to the final stage of a disease, with the meaning of fatal, approaching death (as in *a terminal case*) is first recorded in 1891. **—n.** 1831, final syllable, letter, or word; from the adjective. The technical sense of an end point, such as a screw or post, for making an electrical connection, is first recorded in 1838; that of an end point of a railroad line in 1888, in American English; that of a device for communicating with a computer, in 1954.

terminate *v.* 1589, determine, state definitely, in Nashe's *The Anatomy of Absurdity;* probably a back formation from *termination,* modeled on Latin *terminātus,* past participle of *termināre* to limit, end; for suffix see -ATE[1]. The meaning of bring or come to an end is first recorded about 1613. **—termination** *n.* 1395 *terminacioun* determination, decision; borrowed from

Old French, and directly from Latin *terminātiōnem* (nominative *terminātiō*) a fixing of bounds, bounding, determining, from *termināre* to limit, end, from *terminus* end, boundary line; see TERM; for suffix see -ATION. The sense of an end, cessation, conclusion, is first recorded in English about 1500.

terminology *n.* the special terms of a science, art, etc. 1801, in *The Medical and Physical Journal;* borrowed from German *Terminologie* (Medieval Latin *terminus* word, expression, TERM + German *-ologie* -ology).

terminus *n.* Before 1617, goal, end, final point; borrowing of Latin *terminus* end, boundary line; see the doublet TERM. The meaning of either end of a transportation line is found in 1836. An earlier meaning of a member of a mathematical ratio or proportion is recorded in 1571.

termite *n.* insect destructive of wood. 1849, new singular formed in English by back formation from the earlier plural *termites* (1781); borrowed from New Latin *termites,* plural of *termes* (genitive *termitis*). New Latin *termes* is a special use of Late Latin *termes* woodworm, alteration of Latin *tarmes,* (from the Indo-European root **ter-* bore, rub, Pok.1071), related to *terere* to rub, wear, erode; see THROW. The singular form *termite* is recorded earlier in French (1795, Cuvier).

tern *n.* kind of sea bird. 1678, borrowed from a Scandinavian source (compare Old Icelandic *therna* tern, Norwegian *terne,* and Swedish *tärna*).

terrace *n.* 1515, gallery, portico, balcony; later, flat, raised place for walking (1575); borrowed from Middle French *terrace,* from Old French *terrace, terrasse* platform (built on or supported by a mound of earth), from Vulgar Latin **terrācea,* from Latin *terra;* see TERRAIN. The sense of a natural platform of earth with sloping sides is found in English in 1674, but refers to a mountain system; the specific use of this meaning is not recorded until 1753. —**v.** form into a terrace or terraces. 1615, furnish with a terrace; from the noun. The sense of form into a terrace, arrange in artificial terraces, is found in 1650.

terra cotta (ter′ə kot′ə) kind of hard, brownish-red earthenware. 1722, in Jonathan Richardson's *An Account of Some of the Statues in Italy;* borrowing of Italian *terra cotta* (*terra* earth, from Latin; see TERRAIN; and *cotta* baked; literally, cooked, from Latin *cocta,* feminine past participle of *coquere* to COOK).

terra firma (ter′ə fėr′mə) solid earth, dry land, mainland. 1605, in Ben Jonson's *Volpone;* New Latin *terra firma* the part of the Italian mainland ruled by Venice (from Latin *terra* earth, land; see TERRAIN; and *firma* firm, feminine of *firmus* FIRM[1], adj.).

terrain *n.* 1727, ground for training horses, in Bailey's *Dictionary;* later, any tract of land or ground (1766); borrowed from French *terrain* piece of earth, ground, land, from Old French, from Vulgar Latin **terrānum,* alteration of Latin *terrēnum* land, ground, from neuter of *terrēnus* of the earth, earthly, from *terra* earth, land. Latin *terra* (earlier **tersā*) is cognate with Oscan *teerúm* territory, Old Irish *tīr* territory, Cornish, Breton, and Old Welsh *tir* ground, earth. The sense of a tract of land considered with respect to its natural features is first recorded in English in 1766.

terrapin (ter′əpin) *n.* kind of North American turtle. 1672 *terrapine, tarapine;* earlier *torope* (1613); American English, borrowed from an Algonquian source (compare Abnaki *turepé,* and Delaware *turpa* turtle). The spelling *terrapin* is first recorded in 1722; the origin of the final *-in, -ine* is obscure.

terrarium (tərãr′ēəm) *n.* small indoor enclosure for plants or animals. 1890, small enclosure for land animals, vivarium without water; New Latin, formed from Latin *terra* land; see TERRAIN + *-ārium* -ary; patterned on *aquarium,* with which it was contrasted. In the 1920's *terrarium* acquired the extended sense of a glass container for growing small plants, a plant vivarium.

terrestrial *adj.* of the earth. Before 1387 *terrestrialle,* in Trevisa's translation of Higden's *Polychronicon;* formed in Middle English from Latin *terrestris* earthly (from *terra* earth; see TERRAIN) + Middle English *-al*[1].

terrible *adj.* Before 1387, causing terror, frightful, dreadful, in Trevisa's translation of Higden's *Polychronicon;* borrowed from Old French *terrible,* learned borrowing from Latin *terribilis* frightful, from *terrēre* fill with fear; see TERROR; for suffix see -IBLE. The generalized meaning of very bad, awful, is first recorded in English in 1596. —**terribly** *adv.* 1526, formed from English *terrible* + *-ly*[1]. The informal sense of extremely is first recorded in 1833, in letters of Charles Dickens.

terrier *n.* kind of small, active dog. About 1410; earlier in the surname *Terrier* (1166); borrowed from Old or Middle French *chien terrier* terrier dog, from Medieval Latin *terrarius* of earth, from Latin *terra* earth (see TERRAIN); so called because the terrier pursues its quarry (foxes, badgers, etc.) into their burrows.

terrific *adj.* 1667, causing terror, frightening, in Milton's *Paradise Lost;* borrowed from Latin *terrificus* causing terror or fear, from *terrēre* fill with fear (see TERROR); for suffix see -FIC. The informal sense of very great or severe (as in *a terrific headache*) is first recorded in English in 1809. *Terrific* as a generalized term of approval equivalent to wonderful, marvelous (as in *a terrific dancer*), is first recorded in 1930, in American English.

terrify *v.* 1575, fill with terror, frighten very much; borrowed from Latin *terrificāre* to frighten, from *terrificus* causing terror; see TERRIFIC; for suffix see -FY.

territory *n.* Before 1398 *territorie* land under the jurisdiction of a town, state, or ruler, in Trevisa's translation of Bartholomew's *De Proprietatibus Rerum;* borrowed from Latin *territōrium* land around a town, domain, district, from *terra* earth, land (see TERRAIN), patterned after words such as *dormītōrium* dormitory. The general sense of any tract of land, district, region, is first recorded in English in 1610. —**territorial** *adj.* 1625, of or pertaining to a particular territory; borrowed from Late Latin *territōriālis* of or belonging to a territory, from Latin *territōrium* territory; for suffix see -AL[1].

terror *n.* About 1375 *terroure* great fear; borrowed from Old French *terreur,* learned borrowing from Latin *terror* great fear, dread, from *terrēre* fill with fear, frighten, terrify; for suffix see -OR[1]. Latin *terrēre* is cognate with Old Irish *tarrach* timid, Greek *treîn* to tremble, flee, Lithuanian *trišù* I tremble, Latvian *trisêt* to tremble, and Sanskrit *trásati* (he) trembles, from Indo-European **ters-/tres-,* from original **teres-* (Pok.1095). —**terrorism** *n.* 1795, government by intimidation in the Reign of Terror (1793-94) during the French Revolution; borrowing of French *terrorisme* (Latin *terror* terror + French *-isme* -ism). The general sense of systematic use of terror as a policy is first recorded in English in 1798. **—terrorist** *n.* 1795, person connected with the Reign of Terror during the French Revolution, in the *Annual Register;* borrowing of French *terroriste* (Latin *terror* terror + French *-iste* -ist). The sense of one who furthers his cause by the use of terror is first recorded in English in 1866, in connection with the activities of extreme radical or revolutionary groups in Russia. **—terrorize** *v.* 1823, to coerce or deter by terror; borrowed from French *terroriser* (Latin *terror* terror + French *-iser* -ize), or formed from English *terror* + *-ize.*

terry *n.* rough cloth made of uncut looped yarn. 1784, of uncertain origin; possibly alteration of French *tiré* drawn, from past participle of *tirer* draw out; see TIRADE. Compare German *gezogener Sammet* drawn velvet. **—terrycloth** *n.* (1921, American English)

terse *adj.* 1599, clean-cut, burnished, neat, (implied in *tersely,* in Ben Jonson's *Every Man Out of His Humour*); borrowed from French *ters* clean, and directly from Latin *tersus* wiped off, clean, neat, pure, from past participle of *tergēre* to rub, polish, wipe; see DETERGENT. The sense of neatly concise, compact and pithy in style or language, is first recorded in 1777 as a specific application of an earlier (now obsolete) figurative sense of polished, refined, cultured, especially in language, found in Burton's *The Anatomy of Melancholy* (1621).

tertiary *adj.* of the third degree, order, etc. 1656, in Blount's *Glossographia;* borrowed from Latin *tertiārius* of or pertaining to a third, from *tertius* THIRD; for suffix see -ARY.

tesla (tes′lə) *n.* unit for measuring magnetic flux density. 1960, in allusion to Nikola *Tesla,* 1856-1943, a Croatian-born American electrical engineer.

tessellate (tes′əlāt) *v.* to form into a checkered pattern. 1791, in Erasmus Darwin's *Botanic Garden;* back formation from earlier *tessellated,* adj., made in a checkered pattern (1695); and in some instances possibly borrowed directly from Latin *tessellātus* made of small square stones or tiles, from *tessella* small square stone or tile, diminutive of *tessera* a cube or square of stone or wood, tile, often used in a mosaic; perhaps from Greek *téssera,* neuter of *tésseres,* Ionic variant of *téssares* FOUR (so called from its four corners); for suffix see -ATE[1]. **—adj.** (tes′əlit) made in a checkered pattern. 1826, possibly a shortened form of *tesselated,* adj., modeled on Latin *tessellātus.*

test *n.* About 1395 *teste* small vessel used in assaying or refining precious metals, in Chaucer's *Canterbury Tales;* borrowed from Old French *test,* from Latin *testum* earthen container or pot, related to *testa* piece of burned clay, earthen pot, shell, and *texere* to weave; see TEXT. The transferred sense of that by which the correctness or genuineness of something may be determined, means of trial or examination, is first recorded in Nashe's *The Unfortunate Traveller* (1594). **—v.** 1603, to assay or refine (gold or silver), in Shakespeare's *Measure for Measure;* from the noun. The sense of try, examine, put to a test, is first recorded in 1748, in Richardson's *Clarissa.* Before 1800, this verb is chiefly recorded in the past participle (*they will have the theory tested*); the simple verb (*thcy will test the theory*) was considered by Southey an Americanism. **—test ban** 1958, ban on testing nuclear weapons. **—test case** 1894, legal case to test a law. **—test-drive** *v.* (1954) **—test-fire** *v.* (1947) **—test-market** *v.* 1958, test the public reaction to a product. **—test pilot** (1917) **—test tube** (1846)

testament *n.* About 1290, last will disposing of property; borrowed from Latin *testāmentum* a will, publication of a will, from *testārī* make a will, be witness to, from *testis* witness; for suffix see -MENT. Latin *testis* is cognate with Oscan *trstus* witnesses, and is thought by most scholars to be a reduced form of **tri-stis,* a compound whose first element is related to *trēs* THREE and second element to *stāre* STAND, so that its original sense was that of one standing as a third, in reference to the witness standing as a third entity in a lawsuit. Late Latin *testāmentum* a covenant, is a loan translation of Greek *diathḗkē,* used in this sense in the account of the Last Supper and thus associated with the notion of a last will or testament. As the name of either of the two main divisions of the Bible (Old Testament and New Testament), the word is found in Middle English in *Cursor Mundi* (before 1325), translated from Late Latin *vetus testāmentum* old testament, and *novum testāmentum* new testament, themselves loan translations from Greek *palaià diathḗkē* and *kainḕ diathḗkē.*

testate *adj.* having left a valid will. About 1430, in Lydgate's *Minor Poems;* borrowed from Latin *testātus,* past participle of *testārī* make a will, be witness to, declare; see TESTAMENT; for suffix see -ATE[1]. **—testator** *n.* person who makes a will. Before 1400 *testatour,* borrowed from Anglo-French, learned borrowing from Latin *testātor* one who makes a will, from *testat-,* past participle stem of *testārī* make a will; for suffix see -OR[2].

tester[1] *n.* one who tests or proves something. 1661, in Robert Boyle's writings; formed from English *test,* v. + *-er*[1].

tester[2] *n.* a canopy over a bed. About 1380, in Wycliffe's writings; borrowed from Medieval Latin *testerium,* from *testera* head stall, from Late Latin *testa* (*capitis*) skull, from Latin, earthenware, pot; see TEST.

testicle *n.* male sex gland. Probably before 1425, in a translation of Chauliac's *Grande Chirurgie;* alteration of earlier *testicule* (1392); borrowed from Latin *testiculus,* diminutive of *testis* testicle; see TESTIS.

testify *v.* About 1387 *testifyen* give evidence, bear witness, in a version of *Piers Plowman;* borrowed from Latin *testificārī* bear witness, formed from a lost adjective **testificus* making a witness (*testis* witness; see TESTAMENT + the root of *facere* to make, perform, DO[1]); for suffix see -FY.

testimony *n.* Before 1382 *testymonye* the Ten Commandments as inscribed on the two tablets of stone, or the tablets of stone themselves, in the Wycliffe Bible; a literal translation (in Exodus 31:18), a borrowing representing Late Latin *testimōnium* in the Vulgate, and Greek *tò martýrion* in the Septuagint, of Hebrew *'ēdūth* attestation, testimony, from *'ēd* witness. The general meaning of evidence, statement of a witness under oath, is first recorded in Middle English in a translation of Higden's *Polychronicon* (probably before 1425), and was borrowed from Old French *testimonie,* and directly from Latin *testimōnium* evidence, proof, testimony (*testis* witness; see TESTAMENT + *-mōnium,* suffix signifying action, state, condition); for suffix see -Y[3]. **—testimonial** *adj.* About 1422, of or serving as testimony, in the phrase *lettres testimonials* credentials; borrowed from Middle French *testimonial,* in the phrase *lettres testimoniaulx,* and directly from Latin *testimōniālis,* in the phrase *litterae testimōniālēs,* from *testimōnium* evidence, proof; for suffix see -AL[1]. It is also probable that the adjective was, in part, derived from the earlier noun use in English. —*n.* Before 1387, verbal or documentary evidence, testimony, in Trevisa's translation of Higden's *Polychronicon;* borrowed from Late Latin *testimōniālis,* adj., testimonial. The current meaning of a certificate of character or qualifications, letter of recommendation, is first recorded in English in 1571.

testis *n., pl.* **testes** (tes′tēz). testicle. 1704, borrowed from Latin *testis* testicle, a special application of *testis* witness; presumably because it bears witness to male virility; compare a similar use of Greek *parastátēs,* literally, one that stands by, and French *témoins,* literally, witnesses.

testosterone (testos′tərōn) *n.* male sex hormone secreted by the testicles or produced synthetically. 1935, formed from English *testis* + connecting *-o-* + *ster(ol)* + *-one.*

testy *adj.* 1510 *testie;* alteration (with substitution of *-ie* -Y[1]) for Middle English *testif* headstrong (about 1385, in Chaucer's *Troilus and Criseyde*); borrowed from Anglo-French *testif,* from Old French *teste* head + *-if* -ive; see -IVE. Old French *teste* is from Late Latin *testa* skull, in Latin, pot, shell; see TEST. The sense of easily irritated, impatient, is first recorded in English in 1526.

tetanus (tet′ənəs) *n.* disease caused by bacilli entering the body through wounds. 1392, borrowed from Latin *tetanus,* from Greek *tétanos* muscular spasm; literally, a stretching, tension, from *teínein* to stretch (see TEND[1] incline); so called because the disease is characterized by violent spasms and stiffness of the muscles.

tête-à-tête (tāt′ətāt′) *adv.* in private (said of a conversation between two people). 1700, in Congreve's *The Way of the World;* borrowing of French *tête-à-tête,* literally, head to head; *tête* head, from Old French *teste;* see TESTY. —**n.** private conversation between two people. 1697, borrowed from French *tête-à-tête,* adv. and n. —**adj.** of or for two people in private. 1728, from the noun.

tether *n.* rope or chain for fastening an animal. 1376-77, probably borrowed from a Scandinavian source (compare Old Icelandic *tjōdhr* tether, Norwegian *tjor,* and Swedish *tjuder*). The Scandinavian words are cognate with Middle Low German and Middle Dutch *tūder* tether (modern Dutch *tuier*), and Old High German *zeotar* pole of a cart, from Proto-Germanic **teuđrán,* Indo-European **deutróm,* root **deu-* pull (Pok.221). —**v.** fasten with a tether. About 1450 *teduren;* implied earlier in *horsthetheringg* (before 1382); from the noun.

tetr- a variant form of *tetra-* in some instances before a vowel, as in *tetroxide.*

tetra- a combining form meaning four, as in *tetrameter* (1612), *tetravalent* (1868). Borrowed from Greek *tetra-* (from Indo-European **kwetwr̥-*), combining form of *téttares, téssares* FOUR.

tetragrammaton (tet′rəgram′əton) *n.* the Hebrew divine name transliterated as YHWH; vocalized as Jehovah or Yahweh. Probably before 1400 *tetragramaton;* borrowed from Greek (*tò*) *tetragrámmaton,* literally, (the word) of four letters (*tetra-* four + *grámma,* genitive *grámmatos* letter, something written; see GRAMMAR).

tetrahedron (tet′rəhē′drən) *n. Geometry.* a solid bounded by four plane sides. 1570, borrowed from Late Greek *tetráedron,* originally, neuter of *tetráedros,* adj., four-sided (*tetra-* four + *hédrā* seat, base; see SIT).

tetralogy (tetral′əjē) *n.* series of four connected dramas, operas, etc. 1656, borrowed from Greek *tetralogíā* group of four dramas (*tetra-* four + *-logíā* -logy).

tetrameter (tetram′ətər) *n.* line of verse consisting of four measures or feet. 1612, borrowed from Latin *tetrametrus,* from Greek *tetrámetron* verse of four measures, originally, neuter of *tetrámetros,* adj., having four measures (*tetra-* four + *métron* MEASURE). —**adj.** having four measures or feet. 1770, from the noun.

tetrarch (tet′rärk) *n.* ruler of a part (originally a fourth part) of an ancient Roman or Greek province. Before 1387, in Trevisa's translation of Higden's *Polychronicon;* borrowed from Late Latin *tetrarcha,* from Latin *tetrarchēs,* from Greek *tetrárchēs* leader of four companies, tetrarch (*tetra-* four + *árchein* to rule, of unknown origin).

text *n.* 1369, the wording of anything written, in Chaucer's *Book of the Duchesse;* borrowed from Old French *texte,* learned borrowing from Medieval Latin *textus* the Scriptures, text, treatise, in Late Latin, written account, content, characters used in a document, from Latin *textus* (genitive *textūs*) style or texture of a work; originally, thing woven, from *texere* to weave. Latin *texere* is cognate with Greek *téchnē* art, skill, craft, *téktōn* carpenter, builder, Old Irish *tāl* ax, Lithuanian *tašýti* to cut, carve, Old Slavic *tesati,* Avestan *tašaiti* (he) forms, constructs, Sanskrit *tákṣati* (he) forms, builds, *tákṣan-* carpenter, and Hittite *taks-, takkss-* to join, build, from Indo-European **teḱþ-* to plait, and **tōḱþ-* (Pok.1058). —**textual** *adj.* About 1390 *textuel* well-read, of or conforming to the text, in Chaucer's *Canterbury Tales;* borrowed from Anglo-French *textuel,* learned borrowing from Medieval Latin *textualis* of or pertaining to text or a text, from *textus* the Scriptures, text, treatise; for suffix see -AL[1]. The spelling *textual,* found in Middle English about 1470, was an alteration from *textuel* to conform to the Medieval Latin form *textualis.* —**textbook** *n.* (1730, book in which students copy a classic text; 1779, book used for study)

textile *n.* 1626, in Bacon's *Sylva Sylvarum;* borrowed from Latin *textilis* woven fabric, cloth, noun use of *textilis* woven, from *texere* to weave; see TEXT. —**adj.** woven. 1656, in Blount's *Glossographia;* borrowed from Latin *textilis* woven, from the verb in Latin.

texture *n.* Probably about 1425, network, structure, in a translation of Chauliac's *Grande Chirurgie;* borrowed from Middle French, and directly from Latin *textūra* web, texture, structure, from *text-,* a stem of *texere* to weave; see TEXT; for suffix see -URE. The sense of the nature or character of a woven fabric is first recorded in English in 1685, preceded in 1611 by the figurative sense of constitution, nature, or quality (as in *the texture of a fable*).

th is a spelling found chiefly in words of Old English or Old Icelandic origin and sometimes in words borrowed from Greek. The digraph *th* became common during the Middle English period, replacing the Old English and Old Icelandic letters thorn (þ) and edh (đ), to represent both the voiceless consonant found in *thing* (Old English *þing*) and the voiced consonant found in *heathen* (Old English *hǣđen*). The letter *edh* went out of use in the 1200's. The thorn continued to be used, but was more and more restricted to pronouns and demonstratives, such as *þat, þe, þey, þis,* (*that, the, they, this*), other words being spelled with *th.* With the advent of printing, using continental type which had no thorn, *th* came into general use in all positions, though for a long time *y* was sometimes used to approximate the thorn's shape, resulting in spellings such as *ye* for *the.* See also CH, SH, WH.

-th[1] a suffix forming nouns from verbs, as in *bath, growth, stealth,* or from adjectives (rarely from other nouns), as in *depth, length, strength, truth.* Old English *-thu, -tho, -th,* cognate with Gothic *-itha,* Old High German *-ida,* Old Icelandic *-th;* cognate outside Germanic with Sanskrit *-tā,* Greek *-tē,* Latin *-ta,* or in some cases of a derivative from a verb, with another Indo-European suffix in *-t* -. This suffix has a variant *-t,* as in *height* (Middle English *hihthe*) and *theft* (Old English *thēofth*); see -T[2].

-th[2] a suffix forming ordinal numerals, as in *fourth, tenth, twelfth. Sixth = number six in order or position.* Old English *-tha;* cognate with Gothic *-da, -ta,* Old High German *-do, -to,* Old Icelandic *-di, -ti,* Greek *-tos,* Latin *-tus,* Old Slavic *-tŭ.* See also the variant -ETH[1], and compare *fifth* a re-formation with *-th,* on analogy with *fourth, seventh* and *ninth.*

-th[3] a variant form of the archaic suffix *-eth*[2] forming the third person singular of the present tense, as in *doth, hath.* See -ES[2] and -S[2].

thalamus (thal′eməs) *n.* part of the forebrain. 1753, the receptacle of a flower; New Latin, special use of Latin *thalamus* inner chamber, from Greek *thálamos* inner chamber, bedroom, perhaps related to *thólos* round building; see DALE. The anatomical sense of part of the forebrain is first recorded in English in 1756, but is found earlier in Latinate plural form in 1704.

thallium (thal′ēəm) *n.* soft, malleable metallic chemical element. 1861, New Latin, from Greek *thallós* green shoot + New Latin *-ium,* chemical suffix; so called because its spectrum is marked by a green band. The word was coined by its discoverer, the English chemist and physicist, Sir William Crookes, 1832-1919. Greek *thallós* comes from *thállein* to bloom, cognate with Albanian *dal* to sprout, Armenian *dalar* green, fresh, and Welsh *dail* leaves, from Indo-European **dhal-* bloom (Pok.234).

thallophyte (thal′əfit) *n.* plantlike organism that has no leaves, stems, or roots, such as an alga or fungus. 1854, borrowed from New Latin *Thallophyta* former division of the plant kingdom, from Greek *thallós* green shoot; see THALLIUM + *phytón* plant; see NEOPHYTE.

than *conj.* Old English *than* (before 735, in Bede's *Death Song*), developed from *thanne, thænne, thonne* THEN. It is not clear how the conjunction (*than*) used in comparisons developed from the adverb (*then*) showing time, but *than* after a comparative ("bigger than") parallels the use of Latin *quam,* French *que,* and is a pre-English development, existing early in West Germanic: Old Frisian *than,* Old Saxon *thanna, thanne,* Middle Dutch *danne, dan,* and Old High German *thanna, thanne, denne,* all used after the comparative. The semantic development may have been directly from the demonstrative sense of *then,* thus: "John is smarter than Tom" = "John is smarter; then (= after that) Tom." It could also derive from the relative or conjunctive use of Old English *thonne* when, when as, thus: "When as (whereas) Tom is smart, John is more (so)." For a long time the English adverb and conjunction were treated as one word; they did not become fully differentiated in form until about 1700.

thanatology (than′ətol′əjē) *n.* scientific study of death and dying. 1842, in Dunglison's *Medical Lexicon;* formed in English from Greek *thánatos* death (see EUTHANASIA) + English *-logy* study of. **—thanatological** *adj.* 1862, formed from English *thanatology* + *-ical.* **—thanatologist** *n.* 1972, formed from English *thanatology* + *-ist.* A nonce use, meaning a student of dead animals, is recorded in 1901.

thane *n.* 1124 *thæin* servant, retainer, in *Peterborough Chronicle;* later *thein* (probably before 1200), *thane* (about 1200); developed from Old English *thegn* military follower (about 725, in *Beowulf*), *thegen* (before 800, in Alfred's writings). Old English *thegn, thegen* is cognate with Old Saxon *thegan* man, boy, Old High German *thegan* warrior, hero, boy, servant (modern German *Degen* warrior, soldier), and Old Icelandic *thegn* freeman, thane, from Proto-Germanic **theʒnás.* Cognates outside Germanic include Greek *téknon* child, *tíktein* to bring forth, beget (earlier **títkein*), and Sanskrit *tákman-* offspring, child, from Indo-European **tek-* beget, bear (Pok.1057).

The specific sense of a man who ranked between an earl and a freeman is found in Middle English about 1470. The spelling *thane* was Scottish; the regular modern representation of Old English *thegn, thegen* would have been *thain* (compare *rain* from Old English *regn*). *Thane* was the spelling used by Shakespeare (in *Macbeth*) and was adopted by historians of the 1600's to represent Old English *thegen,* so that this became the usual form in writings about English history.

thank *v.* Probably about 1175 *thanken* express gratitude to; developed from Old English *thancian* (about 725, in *Beowulf*), from *thanc, thonc* thought, good will, gratitude. Old English *thanc, thonc* is cognate with Old Frisian *thank, thonk* gratitude, Old Saxon *thank,* Middle Dutch *danc* (modern Dutch *dank*), Old High German *thank, dank* (modern German *Dank*), Gothic *thanks* thought, from Proto-Germanic *thankaz,* and Old Icelandic *thǫkk* (Danish *tak,* Norwegian *takk,* Swedish *tack*), related to the root of English THINK. **—thankful** *adj.* 1375, deserving thanks, feeling gratitude; developed from Old English *thancfulle, thoncfulle* grateful, content (before 900), formed from *thanc* gratitude, good will + *-full* -ful. **—thankless** *adj.* 1536, formed from English *thank,* n. + *-less.* **—thanks** *n.pl.* Before 1250 *thonkes;* plural of *thank, thonk,* developed from Old English *thanc, thonc* thought, good will, gratitude (about 725, in *Beowulf*). **—thanksgiving** *n.* (1533, giving of thanks, in Tyndale's *The Supper of the Lord;* 1632, = Thanksgiving Day) **—Thanksgiving Day** (1674)

that *pron.* Old English *thæt* (about 725, in *Beowulf*), neuter singular of the demonstrative pronoun and adjective *sē* (masculine), *sēo* (feminine); see THE[1] and the plural THOSE. Old English *thæt* is cognate with Old Frisian *thet,* neuter demonstrative pronoun, Old Saxon *that,* Middle Dutch and modern Dutch *dat,* Old High German *daz* (modern German *das*), Old Icelandic *that,* and Gothic *thata.* Cognates outside Germanic include Latin *istud,* neuter demonstrative pronoun (that of yours), Greek *tó,* Old Slavic *to,* and Sanskrit *tád,* from Indo-European **tod* (Pok.1086). **—adj.** indicating some person or thing already mentioned. Probably about 1200, in *The Ormulum;* from the pronoun. **—conj.** Old English *thæt,* before 899, in Alfred's translation of Boethius' *De Consolatione Philosophiae;* from the pronoun in Old English. **—adv.** to such an extent or degree, so. About 1450, from the adjective.

thatch *v.* to roof or cover with straw, etc. About 1378 *thecchen,* in a version of *Piers Plowman;* later *thacchen* (before 1398); developed from Old English *theccan* to cover (about 725, in *Beowulf*), related to *thæc* roof, thatching material, from Proto-Germanic **thakan.* Cognates of the verb and noun in Germanic are found in Old Frisian *thekka* to cover, *thek* roof, Old Saxon *thekkian* to cover, Middle Dutch *decken* to cover (modern Dutch *dekken*), *dak* roof (modern Dutch *dak*), Old High German *decchen* to cover (modern German *decken*), *dah* roof (modern German *Dach*), and Old Icelandic *thekja* to cover (from Proto-Germanic **thakjanan*), *thak* roof. Cognates outside Germanic are found in Latin *tegere* to cover, *tēgula* tile, Old Irish *tech* house, Greek *stégein* to cover, *stégos, tégos* roof, Lithuanian *stíegti* to roof, and Sanskrit *sthagayati* (he) covers, hides, from Indo-European **(s)teg-/(s)tog-/(s)tēg-* (Pok.1013). The Middle English spelling *thacchen,* with *a,* was probably influenced by earlier *thacken* (about 1350), developed from Old English *thacian* (before 1100), from *thæc* roof, thatching material. **—n.** thatching material. Before 1325 *thach;* probably an alteration (influenced by Old English *theccan,* pronounced thēchən) of Middle English *thak* thatching material; developed from Old English *thæc.*

thaw *v.* melt. Before 1325 *thowen, thouen;* developed from Old English *thawian* (about 1000); cognate with Middle Low German and Middle Dutch *douwen* to thaw (modern Dutch *dooien*), Old High German *douwen, dōan, dewen* (modern German *tauen*), from Proto-Germanic **thawōjanan,* and with Old Icelandic *theyja* (Swedish *töa,* Norwegian and Danish *tø*). Possible cognates outside Germanic include Welsh *tawdd* dripping, *toddi* to melt, Old Slavic *tajetŭ,* Ossetic *thayun* to melt, Latin *tābēre* waste away, melt, Greek *tḗkein* (Doric *tā́kein*) to melt, and Armenian *t'anam* I moisten, from Indo-European **tād(h)-, *tāi-, *tābh-, *tāk-, *təu-,* all extensions of **tā-/tə-* melt, rot (Pok.1053). **—n.** a thawing. About 1400 *thawe;* from the verb.

the[1] *definite article.* Old English (about 950) *thē,* developed from adjective use of *thē,* nominative masculine form of the demonstrative pronoun and adjective, and replacing earlier *sē* (masculine), *sēo* (feminine), *thæt* (neuter). The *s*-forms were superseded by forms in *th-,* influenced by the neuter *thæt* (the source of *that*), and by such oblique cases as *thæs,* genitive singular masculine and neuter. Old English *sē, sēo* is cognate with Old Frisian *thi,* masculine demonstrative pronoun and adjective, Old Saxon *se,* Middle Dutch and modern Dutch *de,* Old High German and modern German *der,* Old Icelandic *sā,* Gothic *sa,* and outside Germanic with Greek *ho* and Sanskrit *sá,* all from an Indo-European demonstrative ("this" or "that"), for the parent language had no definite (or indefinite) article.

the[2] *adv.* by how much . . .by that much, as in *the more the merrier, the sooner the better.* Old English *thē* (before 899, in Alfred's translation of St. Gregory's *Pastoral Care*), variant of *thȳ,* originally, instrumental case of the neuter demonstrative *thæt* THAT.

the- the form of *theo-* before a vowel, as in *theism, monotheism, pantheist.*

theater *n.* About 1380 *theatre* (in ancient Greece and Rome) an open-air place for viewing plays and other spectacles, in Chaucer's translation of Boethius' *De Consolatione Philosophiae;* borrowed from Old French *theatre,* learned borrowing from Latin, and borrowed directly into English from Latin *theātrum,* from Greek *théātron* a place for seeing shows, theater, from *theâsthai* to behold, from *théā* a view; related to *thaûma* a marvel, from Indo-European **dhāu-/dhəu-* (Pok.243). The modern use of the English word for a building where plays are shown dates from 1577. The transferred meaning of plays, writing, production, the stage, is first recorded in 1668, in Dryden's writings, and the figurative sense of a place of action, something representing a theater, is found as early as 1581.

The earliest recorded English forms were *theatre* and *teatre* (about 1384). From about 1550 to about 1700, the prevalent spelling was *theater,* a form retained in the United States.

—theatrical *adj.* 1558, of or connected with the theater; formed in English from Middle French *theatrique* or Late Latin *theātricus* of or pertaining to the theater + English *-al*[1]. Late Latin *theātricus* (the source of Middle French *theatrique*) is borrowed from Greek *theātrikós* of or pertaining to the theater, from *théātron* theater. *—n.* 1657-83, dramatic performance; from the adjective.

thee *pron.* objective case of *thou.* 1382, in the Wycliffe Bible; developed from Old English *the, thē* (before 830), dative singular of *thu* THOU.

theft *n.* act of stealing. About 1250 *theft, thefte,* in *Genesis and Exodus;* developed from Old English (about 695) *thēofth* (*thēof* THIEF + *-th* -th[1]). Old English *thēofth* is cognate with Old Frisian *thiufthe, thiufte* theft, Old Saxon *thiubda,* and Old Icelandic *thȳfth, thȳft,* from Proto-Germanic **theuƀíthō.*

their *adj.* Probably about 1200 *theȝȝre,* in *The Ormulum;* later *theyr* (about 1303); borrowed from a Scandinavian source (compare Old Icelandic *theirra, theira,* genitive plural of *their* THEY). **—theirs** *pron.* Before 1325 *thairs,* in *Cursor Mundi;* from *their,* adj.

theism (thē′izəm) *n.* belief in one God. 1678, formed in English from Greek *theós* god + English *-ism.* **—theistic** *adj.* 1780, of or pertaining to theists or theism; formed from earlier (1662) *theist* believer in theism (Greek *theós* god + English *-ist*) + *-ic.*

them *pron.* Probably about 1200 *theȝȝm,* in *The Ormulum;* later *them* (probably before 1300); borrowed from a Scandinavian source (compare Old Icelandic *theim,* dative plural of *their* THEY). **—themselves** *pron. pl.* 1502, alteration (influenced by *selves,* plural of *self*) of Middle English *tham-self, thaim-self* (before 1325, in *Cursor Mundi*), plural of *himself* (Old English *him selfum*), *herself* (Old English *hire selfre*), and *itself* (before 1121 *hit sylfe*).

theme *n.* Before 1325 *teme* topic, subject, in *Cursor Mundi;* later *theme* (before 1387); borrowed from Old French *tesme* (with silent *s*), from Latin *thema* a subject, thesis, from Greek *théma* a proposition, subject, deposit; literally, something set down, from *the-* root of *tithénai* put down, place; see DO[1] perform. The application to music is first recorded in 1674. **—thematic** *adj.* 1697, borrowed from Greek *thematikós* of or connected with a theme, from *théma* (genitive *thématos*) theme; for suffix see -IC. The meaning of pertaining to or constituting musical themes and their contrapuntal development is first recorded in 1864. **—theme song** (1929)

then *adv.* Probably about 1200 *thenne* at that time, then; developed from Old English *thanne, thænne, thonne* (about 725, in *Beowulf*); cognate with Old Frisian *thenne, thanne* then, Old Saxon *thanna, than,* Middle Dutch *danne, dan* (modern Dutch *dan*), Old High German *danne, denne* (modern German *dann*), Old Icelandic *thā,* and Gothic *than.* These adverbs are all derived from the same Indo-European demonstrative root as Old English *thæt* THAT. Compare the related form THAN. **—n.** that time. Before 1325 *than,* in *Cursor Mundi;* from the adverb. **—adj.** being at that time. 1584, in Sidney's works; from the adverb.

thence *adv.* from that place, from there. About 1300 *thannes;* later *thennes* (before 1325); formed from *thanne, thenne* thence + adverbial genitive *-es, -s;* see -S[3]. Middle English *thanne, thenne* developed from Old English *thanone, thanon* (about 725, in *Beowulf*), forms cognate with Old Frisian *thana* thence, Old Saxon *thanana, thanan,* Middle Dutch and modern Dutch *dan,* Old High German *thanana, thanān, danān* (modern German *dannen*), from early West Germanic **thanana,* and with Old Icelandic *thanan;* all formed by the addition of suffixes to the demonstrative stem *tha-* found in English THAT and its cognates. The spelling *thence* (with *c*) functioned to preserve the voiceless sound represented by *s.* Compare HENCE. **—thenceforth** *adv.* (about 1380, in Chaucer's translation of Boethius' *De Consolatione Philosophiae*) **—thenceforward** *adv.* (1457)

theo- a combining form meaning god, gods, or God, as in *theocentric* = *centered or centering in God* (1886), *theocracy, theology.* Borrowed from Greek *theo-,* combining form of *theós* god; see THEOLOGY.

theocracy *n.* government in which God or religion is supreme. Before 1652, borrowed from Greek *theokratíā* the rule of God (*theós* god; see THEOLOGY + *krátos* a rule, regime, strength; see HARD); for suffix see -CRACY and -CY. An earlier spelling *theocraty* is found in 1622, in Donne's *Sermons.* **—theocratic** *adj.* 1741, formed in English from *theocracy* on the pattern of such pairs as *democracy, democratic.*

theology *n.* study of God and his relations with man and the universe. Before 1376 *teologye,* in *Piers Plowman;* later *theologie* (before 1387); borrowed from Old French *theologie* philosophical treatment of Christian doctrine, learned borrowing from Latin *theologia,* from Greek *theologíā* an account of the gods, or of God, from *theológos* one discoursing on the gods (*theós* god + *-lógos* treating of; see -LOGY). Greek *theós* is related to *thés-phatos* announced by a god, and is cognate with Armenian *dik* gods, Latin *fēriae* holy day, *fēstus* festival, and *fānum* shrine, temple, from Indo-European **dhēs-/dhəs-* holy (Pok.259). The sense of a system of religious beliefs (as in *Calvinist theology*) is first recorded in 1669. **—theologian** *n.* 1483, in Caxton's translation of Cato's writings; borrowed from Middle French *théologien,* from *théologie;* for suffix see -AN. **—theological** *adj.* Before 1450 *theologicalle* of or pertaining to the word of God, Biblical, Scriptural; formed in English from Late Latin *theologicus* of or pertaining to theology (Latin *theologia* + *-icus* -ic) + English *-al*[1]. The sense of pertaining to or dealing with theology is first recorded in English in 1603.

theorem *n.* statement in mathematics to be proved. 1551, borrowed from Middle French *théorème,* and directly from Late Latin *theōrēma,* and from Greek *theṓrēma* spectacle, speculation, theorem, from *theōreîn* to consider; see THEORY.

theoretical *adj.* 1616, contemplative, in Bullokar's *English Expositor;* formed in English from Late Latin *theōrēticus* of or pertaining to theory + English *-al*[1]. Late Latin *theōrēticus* was borrowed from Greek *theōrētikós* contemplative, pertaining to theory, from *theōrētós* that may be seen or considered, from *theōreîn* to consider, look at; see THEORY. The meaning of having to do with theory is found in English before 1652. **—theoretician** *n.* person who knows much about the theory of an art, science, etc. 1886, formed in English from Late Latin *theōrēticus* theoretical + English *-ian.*

theory *n.* 1597, conception, mental scheme, in Hooker's *Ecclesiastical Polity;* borrowed from Late Latin *theōria,* from Greek *theōríā* contemplation, speculation, a looking at, thing looked at, from *theōreîn* to consider, speculate, look at, from *theōrós* spectator. Greek *theōrós* is formed from *théā* a view; see THEATER + *-horós* seeing, related to *horân* to see; see WARY; for suffix see -Y[3]. The sense of the principles or methods of a science or art rather than its practice is first recorded in Robert Cawdrey's *A Table Alphabeticall* (1613). The sense of an explanation based on observation and reasoning is first recorded in 1638. **—theorist** *n.* 1594, one who is adept in the theory of a subject; formed from English *theory* + *-ist.* **—theorize** *v.* 1638, to contemplate, construct theories; formed from English *theory* + *-ize.*

theosophy (thēos′əfē) *n.* 1650, knowledge about God and nature obtained through mystical study; borrowed from Medieval Latin *theosophia,* from Late Greek *theosophíā* wisdom concerning God or things divine, from Greek *theósophos* one wise about God (*theós* god; see THEOLOGY + *sophós* wise, learned, of uncertain origin); for suffix see -Y[3]. *Theosophy* is also the name of a modern philosophical system or movement founded in 1875 in the United States, which combines the teachings of various religions, especially Hinduism and Buddhism.

therapeutic *adj.* having to do with the treatment of disease. 1646, probably a shortened form of *therapeutical* (1605); modeled on New Latin *therapeuticus* curing, healing, from Greek *therapeutikós,* from *therapeutḗs* one ministering, from *therapeúein* to cure, treat, related to *therápōn* (genitive *therápontos*) attendant, of uncertain origin; for suffix see -IC, -ICAL.

therapy *n.* treatment of disease. 1846, borrowed from New Latin *therapia,* from Greek *therapeíā* curing, healing, from *therapeúein* to cure, treat; see THERAPEUTIC; for suffix see -Y[3]. **—therapist** *n.* 1886, formed from English *therapy* + *-ist.*

there *adv.* Probably before 1200 *ther, thare,* in Layamon's *Chronicle of Britain;* developed from Old English *thǣr* in or at that place (before 800, in the *Anglo-Saxon Chronicle*); cognate with Old Frisian *thēr* there, Old Saxon *thār,* Middle Dutch *daer* (modern Dutch *daar*), Old High German *dār* (modern German *da, darin, daraus*), from Proto-Germanic **thǣr,* Indo-European **tēr,* and with Old Icelandic *thar* (Danish and Norwegian *der,* Swedish *där*), Gothic *thar.* A cognate outside Germanic is found in Sanskrit *tar-hi* then, from Indo-European **tor.* Related to Old English *thæt*

THAT. **—n.** that place. 1588, from the adverb. **—thereabouts** *adv.* About 1400, in Maundeville's *Travels;* also *thereabout,* developed from Old English *thǣr onbutan* (before 925). **—thereafter** *adv.* Old English *thǣr æfter* (before 899, in Alfred's translation of St. Gregory's *Pastoral Care*). **—thereby** *adv.* Old English *thǣrbig* (before 899, in Alfred's translation of St. Gregory's *Pastoral Care*). **—therefore** *adv.* About 1175 *therfore* (Middle English *ther* there + *fore* for). **—therein** *adv.* Old English *thǣrin* (before 1000). **—thereupon** *adv.* About 1175, on that; before 1325, after that, then, in *Cursor Mundi.* **—therewith** *adv.* Old English *thærwith* (before 899, in Alfred's translation of Boethius' *De Consolatione Philosophiae*).

therm- the form of *thermo-* before a vowel, as in *thermanesthesia.*

thermal *adj.* 1756, of or having to do with hot springs; borrowed from French *thermal,* formed from Greek *thérmē* heat; see WARM + French *-al* -al[1]. The sense of having to do with heat is recorded in English in 1837.

thermo- a combining form meaning heat, temperature, as in *thermometer, thermonuclear, thermoplastic.* Borrowed from Greek *thermo-,* combining form of *thermós* hot, *thérmē* heat; see WARM.

thermometer *n.* 1633, borrowed from French *thermomètre* (1624), formed from Greek *thermós* hot; see WARM + *métron* MEASURE. An earlier form appeared in Latinate *thermoscopium* (1617, found in the writings of Bianconi, who worked from Galileo's invention of the first thermometer in 1597).

thermonuclear *adj.* of or having to do with the fusion of atoms through very high temperature. 1938, formed from English *thermo-* + *nuclear,* adj.

thermoplastic *adj.* becoming soft and capable of being molded when heated. 1883, formed from English *thermo-* + *plastic,* adj. **—n.** thermoplastic substance. 1929, from the adjective.

thermos *n.* bottle, flask, or jug made with a vacuum between the inner and outer walls. 1907 *thermos flask,* a trademark patented in 1904 but not named or recorded until 1907; borrowed from Greek *thermós* hot; see WARM. **—thermos bottle** (1909)

thermostat *n.* automatic apparatus for regulating temperature. 1831, formed from English *thermo-* + *-stat.*

thesaurus (thisôr′əs) *n.* 1823, a treasury, storehouse, in George Crabb's *Universal Technological Dictionary;* borrowed from Latin *thēsaurus* treasury, treasure, from Greek *thēsaurós* a treasure, treasury, storehouse, chest, of uncertain origin. The sense of a dictionary or encyclopedia filled with information is first recorded in John Stuart Mill's *Dissertations and Discussions* (1840, but the sense was known earlier in English *thesaurarie,* 1592; and in the Latin title of Cooper's *Thesaurus Linguae Romanae et Britannicae,* 1565). Peter Mark Roget's *Thesaurus of English Words and Phrases,* which popularized the word's use in modern times in this sense, was published in 1852. Doublet of TREASURE.

these *pron.* plural of *this.* About 1175 *thes;* probably before 1200 *these;* developed from Old English *thǣs,* variant of *thās,* plural of *thes, thēos, this* THIS. The Old English form *thās* remained *thas* in northern Middle English, but by regular phonetic development became *thos* in Midland and South, resulting in the modern THOSE, which came to be used as the plural of *that.* Old English *thǣs,* in turn, became Middle English *thes,* remaining in the South as plural of THIS. The two forms became differentiated in use after 1250-1300. The ending *-e* was apparently patterned in Middle English on the plural forms of adjectives (*alle* for *all, sume* for *sum,* etc.).

thesis *n.* Before 1398, unaccented (weak) syllable or note, in Trevisa's translation of Bartholomew's *De Proprietatibus Rerum;* borrowed from Latin *thesis* unaccented syllable in poetry, accompanied by a lowering of the voice; later, the stressed part of a metrical foot, from Greek *thésis* a proposition, the downbeat (in music); originally, any setting down or placing, from a root of *tithénai* to place, put, set; see DO[1] perform. Later use in English sense development shows a consciousness of the original meaning of stress or emphasis in Latin and Greek as found in the sense of a proposition or statement to be proved or defended, first recorded in English in 1579, and specific use with the meaning of a dissertation written by a candidate for a university degree, in 1653.

Thespian or **thespian** (thes′pēən) *adj.* of or having to do with the drama or tragedy. 1675, in Edward Cocker's *Morals;* formed in English from Greek *Théspis* Thespis + English *-an.* Thespis was a Greek poet of the 500's B.C., the traditional father of Greek tragedy. **—n.** actor or actress. 1827, from the adjective.

thews (thyüz *or* thüz) *n.pl.* muscles. 1566, bodily powers or parts indicating strength, good physique, transferred sense of Middle English *theweas, theauwes* good qualities, virtues (probably before 1200, in Layamon's *Chronicle of Britain* and in *Ancrene Riwle*); developed from Old English *thēawes* customs, manners, personal qualities, plural of *thēaw* habit, custom (about 725, in *Beowulf*). Old English *thēaw* is cognate with Old Saxon *thau* usage, habit, custom, and Old High German *thau* discipline, from Proto-Germanic **thawaz,* cognate with Latin *tuērī* pay heed to, observe, guard, from Indo-European **teu-/tou-/tu-* (Pok.1079). The modern English sense of muscles, muscular development, was popularized by Scott, who associated it with *sinews.*

they *pron.* Probably before 1200 *thei;* borrowed from a Scandinavian source (compare Old Icelandic *their,* originally masculine plural demonstrative pronoun corresponding to *that,* neuter singular; see THAT). The Scandinavian form gradually replaced Old English *hī, hīe,* plural of *hē, hēo, hit;* see HE, SHE, IT.

thick *adj.* Probably before 1200 *thikke, thicke,* in *Ancrene Riwle* and Layamon's *Chronicle of Britain;* developed from Old English *thicce* not thin, dense (before 899, in Alfred's translation of Boethius' *De Consolatione Philosophiae*); cognate with Old Frisian *thikki* numerous, Old Saxon *thikki* thick, Middle Dutch *dicke* (modern Dutch *dik*), Old High German *dicki* (modern German *dick*), Old Icelandic *thykkr* (Swedish *tjock,* Danish *tyk,* and Norwegian *tykk*), from Proto-Germanic **theku-, *thekwia-.* Cognates outside Germanic include Old Irish *tiug,* and Welsh *tew* thick, fat, from Indo-European **tegu-* (Pok.1057). **—adv.** in a thick manner. Before 1175 *thicke;* developed from Old English *thicce* (before 971), from the adjective in Old English. **—n.** that which is thick. About 1250 *thikke,* in *The Owl and the Nightingale;* from the adjective. **—thicken** *v.* Before 1398 *thickenen* make thick, in Trevisa's translation of Bartholomew's *De Proprietatibus Rerum;* formed from Middle English *thicke* thick, adj. + *-enen* -en[1]. **—thickheaded** *adj.* (1707, having a thick head; 1801, slow-witted) **—thickset** *adj.*

About 1370, set close together, in Chaucer's translation of *Roman de la Rose;* later, stocky (1724). —**thick-skinned** *adj.* 1545, having thick skin; later, not sensitive (1602).

thicket *n.* shrubs, bushes, or small trees growing close together. 1530, in Palsgrave's *Lesclarcissement;* developed from Old English *thiccet* (before 1000), formed from *thicce* THICK + *-et,* a denominative suffix. No record of a Middle English **thicket* has been found, which suggests that the word was revived in the early 1500's by Tyndale and others after several centuries of obsolescence.

thief *n.* 1124 *thef,* in *Peterborough Chronicle;* later *thief* (probably before 1200); developed from Old English (688-695) *thēof;* cognate with Old Frisian *thiāf* thief, Old Saxon *thiof,* Middle Low German, Middle Dutch, and modern Dutch *dief,* Old High German *diob* (modern German *Dieb*), Old Icelandic *thjōfr* (Danish and Norwegian *tyv,* Swedish *tjuv*), and Gothic *thiufs,* from Proto-Germanic **theubaz,* with no known cognates. —**thievish** *adj.* About 1450 (implied in *theveschely* thievishly); formed from Middle English *thef* thief + *-ish*[1].

thieve *v.* to steal. 1530 (implied in *thieving*); developed from Old English (about 920) *thēofian,* from *thēof* THIEF. The verb is rare in Old English, after which it does not appear until the 1600's. However, the verbal noun *thieving* is recorded since 1530. —**thievery** *n.* 1568, act of stealing, theft; probably formed from English *thieve,* v. + *-ery.*

thigh *n.* Probably before 1200 *thih,* in Layamon's *Chronicle of Britain;* developed from Old English (before 800) *thēoh, thēh;* cognate with Old Frisian *thiāch* thigh, Old Saxon *thioch,* Middle Dutch *die* (modern Dutch *dij*), Old High German *dioh,* Middle High German *diech,* and Old Icelandic *thjō* upper thigh, buttock, from Proto-Germanic **theuHaz.* Cognates outside Germanic include Lithuanian *táukas* fat, Old Slavic *tukŭ* fat, and Middle Irish *tōn* posteriors (earlier **tuknā*), from Indo-European **teuk-/touk-/tuk-* (Pok. 1081). —**thighbone** *n.* (about 1450)

thimble *n.* 1440 *thymbyl* covering for the finger, in *Promptorium Parvulorum;* alteration (with *b*) of Old English (about 1000) *thȳmel* sheath or covering for the thumb, from *thūma* THUMB; for suffix see -LE[1]. For the development of the *b* after *m,* see BRAMBLE and HUMBLE.

thin *adj.* Probably before 1200 *thunne;* later *thynne* (before 1225), *thin* (about 1250); developed from Old English (849) *thynne* narrow, lean, scanty; cognate with Middle Low German and Middle Dutch *dunne* thin (modern Dutch *dun*), Old High German *dunni* (modern German *dünn*), Old Icelandic *thunnr* (Swedish *tunn,* Norwegian *tynn,* Danish *tynd*), from Proto-Germanic **thunnuz, *thunw-,* and with Gothic *ufthanjan* to stretch. Cognates outside Germanic are found in Old Irish *tanae* thin, Latin *tenuis,* Greek *tany-* long, Lithuanian *tę́vas* thin, Latvian *tiêv-s,* Old Slavic *tĭnŭkŭ,* and Sanskrit *tanú-s* thin (feminine *tanví*), from Indo-European **tenús* (Pok.1069). —**adv.** in a thin manner. About 1250 *thunne,* in *The Owl and the Nightingale;* from the adjective. —**v.** make or become thin. About 1340 *thynnen;* developed from Old English (about 900) *thynnian;* from the adjective in Old English. —**thin-skinned** *adj.* 1598, having thin skin; later, sensitive to criticism (1680).

thine *pron.* belonging to thee, yours. Before 1175 *thine;* developed from Old English (before 830) *thīn,* possessive pronoun; originally, genitive of *thū* THOU. Old English *thīn* is cognate with Old Frisian and Old Saxon *thīn* thine, Middle Dutch and modern Dutch *dijn,* Old High German *dīn* (modern German *dein*), Old Icelandic *thīn* (Danish, Norwegian, and Swedish *din*), and Gothic *theina* (genitive), *theins* (possessive pronoun), from Proto-Germanic **thīnaz.* Compare THY.

thing *n.* Old English (685-86) *thing* meeting, assembly; later, entity, being, matter (before 899); also, act, deed, event (about 1000); cognate with Old Frisian and Old Saxon *thing* assembly, action, matter, thing, Middle Dutch *dinc* lawsuit, matter, thing (modern Dutch *ding* thing), Old High German *ding* assembly, lawsuit, thing (modern German *Ding* matter, affair, thing), Old Icelandic *thing* assembly, meeting, parliament, council (Norwegian *ting* assembly, being, creature, thing, Swedish *ting* court session, thing, and Danish *ting* court, law court, thing), from Proto-Germanic **thenʒán.* Gothic has the cognate *theis* time, appointed time (from Proto-Germanic **thénHaz*), suggesting that the original Germanic sense of *thing* may have been "day of assembly," ultimately from a base meaning "stretch or extent of time" (from Indo-European **tenk-* draw out, or draw together, Pok.1067) and related to the source of Old English *thennan* stretch out; see TEND[1] incline.

Similar semantic developments are found in the Romance languages, in which Latin *causa,* legal case, has given rise to French *chose,* Italian and Spanish *cosa,* all meaning "thing." The meaning of personal possessions, often in the plural (perhaps from Old Icelandic *things* objects, articles, valuables), is first recorded in Middle English about 1300, the specific use applied to clothes, in 1634, and with the sense of implements or equipment, in 1688.

Iceland's general assembly (parliament) is the Althing.

think *v.* Probably about 1175 *thenken, thenchen;* developed from Old English (about 725, in *Beowulf*) *thencan* conceive in the mind, think (past tense *thōhte,* past participle *gethōht*), probably originally meaning "cause to appear to oneself," and thus a causative of *thyncan* to seem or appear. Old English *thencan* is cognate with Old Frisian *thanka, thenka, thenza* to think, Old Saxon *thenkian,* Middle Dutch, modern Dutch, Old High German, and modern German *denken,* Old Icelandic *thekkja* to perceive, know (Norwegian *tenke,* Swedish *tänka,* Danish *tænke* to think), and Gothic *thankjan* consider, meditate, think, from Proto-Germanic **thankjanan.* Possible cognates outside Germanic are found in Old Latin *tongēre* to know, Albanian *tângë* resentment, and Tocharian A *tùnk-,* Tocharian B *taṅkw* love, from Indo-European **tong-* (Pok.1088). Compare archaic METHINKS, which is a relic of a different word *think,* from Middle English *thinken,* variant of *thinchen,* found in Old English *thyncan* it seems or it appears, now obsolete except in *methinks* (Old English *mē thyncth* it seems to me, used impersonally with an indirect object); cognate with Old Saxon *thunkian,* Old High German *dunchen* (modern German *dünken*), Old Icelandic *thykkja,* and Gothic *thunkjan,* from Proto-Germanic **thunkjanan,* Indo-European **tn̥g-,* root **tong-.*

Because of close semantic relationship and a sharing of forms (*thought* and *think*), these two different words, now both spelled *think,* became thoroughly

confused in early modern English, which has led to the complete submersion of the form *think* to seem, to appear.
—**n.** 1834, act of continued thinking, meditation; from the verb.
—**thinkable** *adj.* 1854, in writings of Herbert Spencer; formed from English *think,* v. + *-able.* —**thinker** *n.* 1440, one who thinks; formed from English *think,* v. + *-er*[1]. The sense of a person devoted to abstract thought, scholar, philosopher, etc., is first recorded in 1830. —**think tank** *Informal.* institute for theoretical studies or research (1959, American English).

third *adj., n.* Probably about 1175 *therdde,* alteration (by metathesis of *i* and *r*) of earlier *thridde* (before 1121); developed from Old English *thridda* (about 750, in Cynewulf's *Christ*), from *thrēo* THREE. Old English *thridda* is cognate with Old Frisian *thredda* third, Old Saxon *thriddio,* Middle Low German, Middle Dutch and modern Dutch *derde,* Old High German *dritto* (modern German *dritte*), Old Icelandic *thridhi* (Danish, Norwegian, and Swedish *tredje*), and Gothic *thridja,* from Proto-Germanic **thriđjás.* Cognates outside Germanic include Welsh *trydydd* third, Latin *tertius,* Umbrian *tertiu,* Albanian *tretë,* Greek *trítos,* Lithuanian *trẽčias,* Old Slavic *tretijĭ,* Sanskrit *tṛtíya-s,* Avestan *thritya-,* Old Persian *thritīya-,* and Tocharian B *trit,* from Indo-European **trityos* (Pok.1091), among other forms.

The metathesis of (*i* and *r*) *third* for *thrid-* in Old English is also found in English *bird.* See also THIRTEEN and THIRTY.
—**third degree** *Informal.* use of continuous questioning and often physical force to make a person confess or give information. 1900, American English, figurative use of earlier *Third Degree* the degree of master mason in Freemasonry (1772); probably so called with reference to the interrogation ceremony performed in conferring this degree in Freemasonry. —**third-rate** *adj.* of decidedly poor or inferior quality (1838). —**third world** the underdeveloped countries of the world, especially those of Africa, Asia, and Latin America (1963, translation of French *tiers monde*).

thirst *n.* Probably before 1200 *thirst;* developed from Old English (about 1000) *thurst;* cognate with Old Saxon *thurst* thirst, Middle Dutch and modern Dutch *dorst,* Old High German *durst* (modern German *Durst*), Old Icelandic *thorsti* (Swedish *törst,* Norwegian and Danish *tørst*), and Gothic *thaúrstei,* from Proto-Germanic **thurs-.* Cognates outside Germanic are found in Old Irish *tart* thirst, Old Latin *torrus* dry, Latin *torrēre* to parch, Albanian *ter* (it) dries in the air, Greek *térsesthai* become dry, Armenian *t'airamim* I wither, Sanskrit *tṛ́ṣyati* (he) thirsts, and Avestan *taršna-* thirst, from Indo-European **ters-/tors-/tr̥s-* (Pok.1078). The change from Old English *thurst* to Middle English *thirst* was probably influenced by the verb. —**v.** Probably about 1200 *thirrsten,* in *The Ormulum;* developed from Old English *thyrstan* (before 899, in Alfred's translation of St. Gregory's *Pastoral Care*); from the noun in Old English. Old English *thyrstan* is cognate with Old Saxon *thurstian* to thirst, Middle Dutch and modern Dutch *dorsten,* Old High German *dursten* (modern German *dürsten*), and Old Icelandic *thyrsta* (Swedish *törsta,* Norwegian and Danish *tørste*).
—**thirsty** *adj.* 1388 *thirsti;* developed from Old English *thyrstig, thurstig* (before 899, in Alfred's translation of Boethius' *De Consolatione Philosophiae*), from *thurst,* n. + *-ig* y[1]. Old English *thyrstig, thurstig* is cognate with Old Saxon *thurstig* thirsty, and Old High German *durstag* (modern German *durstig*).

thirteen *adj.* Before 1398 *thyrtene,* in Trevisa's translation of Bartholomew's *De Proprietatibus Rerum;* alteration (by metathesis of *r* and *i*) of earlier *thrittene* (probably about 1200); developed from Old English (before 900) Mercian *thrēotēne,* West Saxon *thrēotīene* (*thrēo* THREE + *-tēne, -tīene* -teen). The Old English adjective is cognate with Old Frisian *thretten* thirteen, Old Saxon *thriutein, thrutein,* Middle Low German *dertēn, druttēn,* Middle Dutch and modern Dutch *dertien,* Old High German *drīzehan* (modern German *dreizehn*), and Old Icelandic *threttān* (Norwegian and Danish *tretten,* Swedish *tretton*).

thirty *adj.* Probably before 1350 *thurtty;* later *thyrty* (1413); alteration (by metathesis of *r* and *i*) of earlier *thritti,* developed from Old English (about 725, in *Beowulf*) *thritig* (*thrī, thrēo* THREE + *-tig* group of ten, -TY[1]). Old English *thrītig* is cognate with Old Frisian *thrītig* thirty, Old Saxon *thrītig,* Middle Dutch *dertich* (modern Dutch *dertig*), Old High German *drīzzug* (modern German *dreissig*), Old Icelandic *thrjātigi, thrjātiu* (Swedish *trettio,* Norwegian *tretti,* Danish *tredive*), and Gothic (accusative) *thrins tiguns.*

this *pron.* Old English (probably 670) *this,* neuter demonstrative pronoun and adjective (masculine *thes,* feminine *thēos*). In Middle English, the various case and gender forms were gradually eliminated so that by the 1400's, *this* was the only singular form, with the plural THESE, representing Old English *thǣs,* the relationship with THOSE, representing Old English *thās,* now passing to a plural of *that.* Old English *this* is cognate with Old Frisian *this,* Old Saxon *these,* Middle Dutch *dese* (modern Dutch *deze*), Old High German *dese, desēr* (modern German *dieser*), and Old Icelandic *thessi;* all probably derived from a Germanic pronoun formed by combining the simple demonstratives represented by Old English *thæt* THAT and *sē* THE[1]. The earlier pronominal base **tha* of *the, that,* etc., combined with added *-s* (earlier *-se, -si*) which is probably identical with Old English *se* the, but has also been identified with Old English *sēo* imperative of *see,* v., behold. —**adj.** Old English (before 899, in Alfred's translation of Orosius' *Historiarum Adversus Paganos*); from the pronoun. —**adv.** About 1375, from the pronoun.

thistle (this'əl) *n.* plant with a prickly stalk and leaves. About 1325 *thystle;* developed from Old English *thistel* (about 700, in the earliest Old English glossaries); cognate with Middle Dutch and modern Dutch *distel,* Old High German *distil* (modern German *Distel*), and Old Icelandic *thistill* (Norwegian and Swedish *tistel,* Danish *tidsel*), from Proto-Germanic **thiīHstilaz,* probably cognate with Sanskrit *téjas* sharpness, and Greek *stízein* to prick, from Indo-European **(s)teig-/(s)tig-* (Pok.1016).

thither *adv.* to that place, there. Before 1325 *tethir, thither,* in *Cursor Mundi,* alteration of earlier *thider* (probably before 1200); found in Old English *thider* (about 725, in *Beowulf*), an alteration (by influence of its opposite *hider* HITHER) of earlier *thæder* to that place. Related to Old English *thæt* THAT, THIS. Old English *thæder* is cognate with Old Icelandic *thadhra* there (from Proto-Germanic **thađrá-*) and Sanskrit *tátra* there, from Indo-European **to-tro-* (Pok.1087). For the change of *d* to *th* see GATHER. —**adj.** on that side, farther. 1830, in Lamb's *Letters to Wordsworth;* from the adverb.

thole *n.* an early form of oarlock, consisting of a peg on a boat for pivoting an oar. 1440 *tholle* peg, in *Promptorium Parvulorum;* developed from Old English *tholl* thole (about 725, in *Beowulf*); cognate with Middle Low German and Middle Dutch *dolle* thole (modern Dutch *dol*), and Old Icelandic *thollr* tree, peg (Norwegian *tolle* peg), from Proto-Germanic **thulnaz.* Possible cognates outside Germanic are found in Greek *týlos* callus, knob, Lithuanian *tulžis* gall, and Russian *tólstyj* thick, from Indo-European **tu-l-,* root **tēu-/təu-/tū-/tu-* swell (Pok.1081).

-thon a combining form, variant of -ATHON, as in *telethon.*

thong *n.* narrow strip of leather, etc. Probably before 1200 *thong, thwong,* in Layamon's *Chronicle of Britain;* developed from Old English *thwong* (about 950), *thwang* (about 1000) thong; cognate with Old High German *dwang* rein, bridle (from Proto-Germanic **thwanȝaz,* Indo-European **twonĝh-,* root **twenĝh-* press hard, Pok.1099)., and with Old Icelandic *thvengr* thong.

thorax *n.* part of the body between the neck and the abdomen. 1392, borrowing of Latin *thōrāx,* from Greek *thṓrāx* (genitive *thṓrākos*) breastplate, chest. **—thoracic** *adj.* 1656, having to do with or in the region of the thorax, in Blount's *Glossographia;* borrowed from Medieval Latin *thoracicus* of or pertaining to the chest, from Greek *thorākikós,* from *thṓrāx* (genitive *thṓrākos*) chest; for suffix see -IC.

thorium (thôr′ēəm) *n.* radioactive metallic element. 1832, New Latin, formed from *Thor,* ancient Scandinavian god of thunder and war (Old Icelandic *thōrr,* see THUNDER) + New Latin *-ium,* chemical suffix. The New Latin word was coined by the Swedish chemist J.J. Berzelius, 1779-1848, who discovered this element.

thorn *n.* Old English *thorn* sharp point on a stem or branch (about 750, in Cynewulf's *Christ*); earlier, thorny tree or plant (about 700, implied in *hæguthorn* hawthorn); cognate with Old Frisian and Old Saxon *thorn* thorn, Middle Dutch and modern Dutch *doorn,* Old High German *dorn* (modern German *Dorn*), Old Icelandic *thorn* (Swedish, Norwegian, and Danish *torn*), and Gothic *thaúrnus,* from Proto-Germanic **thurnuz.* Cognates outside Germanic are found in Greek *térnaka* (accusative) artichoke or cactus stalk, Old Slavic *trŭnŭ* thorn, and Sanskrit *tṛ́ṇa-m* blade of grass, grass, from Indo-European **-tṛno-, tṛnu-, terno-* (Pok.1031). **—thorny** *adj.* Probably before 1200 *thorni,* in *Ancrene Riwle;* developed from Old English *thornig* (about 1000, in Ælfric's *Homilies*), from *thorn* thorn + *-ig* -y[1].

thorough *adj.* 1300 *thoro* fully done or carried out, complete; later *thoruȝ* (before 1420); adjective use of Old English (about 1000) *thuruh,* adv., from end to end, from side to side, stressed variant of *thurh,* adv., prep., THROUGH. **—thoroughbred** *adj.* (1701) **—thoroughfare** *n.* About 1385 *thurghfare,* in Chaucer's *Canterbury Tales;* formed from Middle English *thurh, thuruh* through + *fare* course, way, journey; see FARE[1]. **—thoroughgoing** *adj.* (1819, in Scott's *Legend of Montrose*)

those *pron.* plural of *that.* Probably before 1300 *thoos;* before 1325 *thos* (Midland and Southern England), with Northern variant *thas;* developed from Old English *thās,* plural of *thes, thēos, this* THIS. Middle English *thos* replaced an earlier form *tho,* which developed from Old English *thā,* nominative plural of *sē, sēo, thæt* THE[1]; see also THESE.

thou *pron.* you. Probably before 1200, in Layamon's *Chronicle of Britain;* developed from Old English *thū* (about 725, in *Beowulf*); cognate with Old Frisian and Old Saxon *thu* thou, Middle Low German and Middle Dutch *du,* Old High German *dū, du* (modern German *du*), Old Icelandic *thū* (Danish and Swedish *du*), and Gothic *thu,* from Proto-Germanic **thū/thu,* Indo-European **tū/tu* (Pok.1097). The word is widely represented in the Indo-European family, as in Latin *-tū* thou, Old Irish *tū,* Albanian *ti,* Greek *sý,* Doric Greek *tý,* Lithuanian *tù,* Old Slavic *ty,* Armenian *du,* Sanskrit *tvám,* Avestan *tū,* Old Persian *tuvam,* Tocharian A *tu,* Tocharian B *tuwe, twe,* and Hittite *zik.*

Thou and its cases *thee, thine, thy* were used in ordinary speech in Old English as their cognates are still used in modern Germanic and Romance languages (French, Italian and Portuguese *tu,* Spanish *tú*). However, in Middle English they were gradually superseded by the plural *ye, you, your, yours* in addressing a superior and, later, an equal, though they were long retained in addressing an inferior. In recent times, except for special uses (as among Quakers and in Scriptural, liturgical, and some poetic writing), *thou* and its cases have become archaic and obsolescent.

though *conj.* Probably about 1200 *thohh,* in *The Ormulum;* later *thowgh* (about 1378); in part developed from Old English *thēah, thāh* (before 899), and in part borrowed from a Scandinavian source (compare Old Icelandic *thō* though). Cognates of the Old English and Old Icelandic forms are found in Old Frisian *thāch* but, yet, still, though, Old Saxon *thoh,* Middle Dutch and modern Dutch *doch,* Old High German *doh* (modern German *doch*), and Gothic *thauh* in that case, from Proto-Germanic **thauH.* The Germanic word probably consists of two elements: **thau-* (Indo-European **tou*), cognate with Sanskrit *tu* yet, however, and **-h,* cognate with Latin *-que* also. Hence the original sense may have been "and yet." **—adv.** Probably about 1200 *thohh;* developed from Old English (971) *thēah, thāh;* from the conjunction in Old English.

thought *n.* Probably before 1200 *thouht* (in *Ancrene Riwle*), *thoht* (in *Trinity Homilies*); developed from Old English (before 839) *thōht, gethōht,* from the stem of *thencan* to conceive of in the mind, consider; see THINK. Cognates of the Old English forms are found in Old Saxon *githāht* thinking, belief, Dutch *gedachte* thought, Old High German *gidāht* (modern German *Bedacht* thoughtfulness, consideration), Old Icelandic *thōtti, thōttr* thought, and Gothic *thūhtus* thought. **—thoughtful** *adj.* Probably about 1200 *thohtfull* given to thought, contemplative, in *The Ormulum;* formed from Middle English *thoht* thought + *-full* -ful. The sense of considerate, kindly, is first recorded in 1851. **—thoughtless** *adj.* 1592, formed from English *thought* + *-less.*

thousand *n.* Probably before 1300, in *Kyng Alisaunder;* developed from Old English *thūsend* (about 725, in *Beowulf*); cognate with Old Frisian *thūsend* thousand, Old Saxon *thūsundig,* Middle Dutch *dūsent* (modern Dutch *duizend*), Old High German *thūsunt, dūsunt* (modern German *Tausend*), Old Icelandic *thūsund* (Norwegian and Swedish *tusen,* Danish *tusind, tusinde*), and Gothic *thūsundi.* Cognates outside Germanic are probably found in Lithuanian *túkstantis* thousand, Latvian *tūkstuots,* Old Prussian *tūsimtons* (accusative plural), Old Slavic *tysęšta,* Russian *tysyacha,* Polish *tysiac,* Czech *tisíc,* etc., which may suggest an original Balto-Slavic and Germanic compound meaning literally, "a great hundred," whose first element **tūs-* is cognate with Sanskrit *tavás-* strong, *tavīti* (he) is strong (from Indo-European **tēu-/təu-,* **tewə-/tū-,* Pok.1083), and whose second element **kmt-* is found as a separate word in Old English *hund;* see HUNDRED. **—thousandth** *adj.* 1552, in Huloet's *Abecedarium Anglico Latinum;* formed from English *thousand* + *-th*².

thrall *n.* Probably before 1200 *thralle* person in bondage, slave; developed from Old English *thrǣl* (about 950, in *Lindisfarne Gospels*), borrowed from a Scandinavian source (compare Old Icelandic *thrǣll* slave, servant, Danish *træl,* Norwegian *trell.* Swedish *träl*). Old Icelandic *thrHll* (from Proto-Germanic **thraHilaz*) is probably cognate with Old High German *dregil, drigil* servant, apparently in the sense of "runner," Gothic *thragjan* to run, from Proto-Germanic **thraʒjanan,* from Indo-European **trok-,* root **trek-* (Pok. 1092).

The meaning of condition of a slave, bondage, servitude, thralldom, is found in Middle English in *Cursor Mundi* (before 1325).

—thralldom or **thraldom** *n.* bondage, slavery. Probably before 1200 *thraldome,* in Layamon's *Chronicle of Britain;* formed from Middle English *thralle* thrall + *-dom.* It is interesting to note that in spite of the fact that the meaning of *thralldom* could be expressed by *thrall,* the word *thralldom* continues to exist in modern English.

thrash *v.* 1588, to separate grains from wheat, etc., by beating, in Shakespeare's *Titus Andronicus;* variant form of Middle English *threshen* to THRESH. The extended sense of beat, with or as if with a stick or cudgel, is first recorded in Fletcher's *The Nice Valour* (before 1625). **—n.** 1669, threshing implement, flail; later, a thrashing or beating (1840); from the verb.

thread *n.* About 1200 *threade,* in *Vices and Virtues;* later *threde* (about 1380); developed from Old English (before 800) *thrǣd* fine cord, especially when twisted, related to *thrāwan* to twist; see THROW. Old English *thrǣd* is cognate with Old Saxon *thrād* wire, thread, Middle Dutch *draet* (modern Dutch *draad*), Old High German *drāt* (modern German *Draht*), and Old Icelandic *thrādhr* (Danish, Norwegian, and Swedish *tråd*), from Proto-Germanic **thrǣđús,* Indo-European **trētús.* **—v.** pass a thread through. About 1350 *threden,* from *threde* thread. **—threadbare** *adj.* (before 1376 *thred-bare,* in *Piers Plowman*)

threat *n.* Old English *thrēat* crowd, troop, oppression, menace (about 725, in *Beowulf*), related to *thrēotan* to trouble, weary (from Proto-Germanic **threutanan*). These Old English words are cognate with Old High German *driozan* to vex, trouble, Middle High German *drōz* annoyance, *verdriezen* annoy (modern German *verdriessen*), Old Icelandic *thrust* struggle, labor, trouble, *thrjōta* to fail, lack, and Gothic *usthriutan* to trouble, threaten. Cognates outside Germanic are found in Latin *trūdere* to push, thrust, and Old Slavic *trudŭ* difficulty, trouble, *truditi* to vex, trouble, from Indo-European **treud-/troud-/trud-* (Pok.1095). **—threaten** *v.* Probably before 1200 *threatenen,* in *Ancrene Riwle;* developed from Old English *thrēatnian* to press, urge, force (about 1000, in Ælfric's *Homilies*); formed from *thrēat* + *-nian* -en¹.

three *adj.* 1123 *thre,* in *Peterborough Chronicle;* developed from Old English (before 830) *thrēo,* feminine and neuter, (masculine *thrī, thrie*) from Proto-Germanic **thrijiz,* Indo-European **tréyes* (Pok.1090). Old English *thrēo* is cognate with Old Frisian *thrē, thriā, thriū,* Old Saxon *thria, thriu,* Middle Dutch and modern Dutch *drie,* Old High German *drī, drīo, driu* (modern German *drei*), Old Icelandic *thrīr, thrjār, thrjū* (Danish, Swedish, and Norwegian *tre*), and Gothic *thrija.* Cognates outside Germanic are found in Latin *trēs, tria,* Old Irish *tri, tēoir,* Albanian *tre, tri,* Greek *treîs, tría,* Lithuanian *trỹs,* Old Slavic *trije, tri,* Sanskrit *tráyas, tisrás, trī́,* Tocharian A *tre, tri-,* Tocharian B *trai, tarya,* Hittite *tri-.* Compare THIRD. **—threefold** *adj.* About 1000, comprising three parts, kinds, etc.; later, three times as great or as many (about 1200); *adv.* (about 1020). **—threescore** *adj., n.* (About 1388, in the Wycliffe Bible) **—threesome** *n.* group of three (1375).

threnody (thren′ədē) *n.* song of lamentation, especially at a person's death. 1634, borrowed from Greek *thrēnōidíā* (*thrênos* dirge, lament; see DRONE + *ōidḗ* ODE); for suffix see -Y³.

thresh *v.* Probably about 1200 *thresshen,* in *The Ormulum;* developed from Old English *threscan, therscan* to beat, sift grain by trampling or beating (about 750, in Cynewulf's *Elene*), related to *thrāwan* to twist, turn; see THROW. Old English *threscan, therscan* is cognate with Middle Dutch *derscen, dorscen* to thresh (modern Dutch *dorsen*), Old High German *dreskan* (modern German *dreschen*), Old Icelandic *thriskja* (Danish *tærske,* Norwegian *treske,* and Swedish *tröska*), and Gothic *thriskan,* from Proto-Germanic **threskanan,* Indo-European present-stem **tre-sḱ-* (Pok. 1072).

threshold *n.* Before 1376 *thresshewold,* in *Piers Plowman;* found in the Old English compound *threscold, thærscwold* doorsill, point of entering (before 899, in Alfred's translation of Boethius' *De Consolatione Philosophiae*). The first element of the compound is related to Old English *threscan, therscan* to THRESH, perhaps originally to tread, trample; the second element has not been identified. The Old English forms for threshold, doorsill are cognate with Old Icelandic *threskjǫldr* threshold (Swedish *tröskel,* Norwegian *terskel,* Danish *tærskel*). The meaning in psychology of the point at which stimuli can be perceived or differentiated is first recorded in James Sully's *Sensation and Intuition* (1874).

thrice *adv.* three times. Probably before 1200 *thries,* in *Ancrene Riwle* (Middle English *thrie* thrice + *-es,* genitive singular ending used adverbially; see -S³). Middle English *thrie* developed from Old English (about 950) *thriga, thriwa* thrice, from *thrīe* THREE. Old English *thriga, thriwa* is cognate with Old Frisian *thria* thrice, and Old Saxon *thriio, thriwo.*

The final *-s* in *thries* was voiceless (not pronounced as *z*), and so about 1600 it began to be spelled *-ce,* as in *hence, pence, ice, mice,* to represent this pronunciation.

thrift *n.* Probably before 1300, prosperity, savings, profit, in *Sir Tristrem;* from *thriven* to THRIVE; probably influenced by Old Icelandic *thrift,* variant of *thrif* prosperity, from *thrīfask* to thrive. The sense of a habit of saving, economy, is first recorded in 1553. Compare

SPENDTHRIFT. **—thrift institution** (1963, American English) **—thrift shop** (1947, American English) **—thrifty** *adj.* About 1385 *thrifti* respectable, thriving, successful, fortunate, in Chaucer's *Troilus and Criseyde;* formed from Middle English *thrift* + *-i* -y[1]. The sense of economical, frugal, saving, appeared in 1526.

thrill *v.* Before 1325 *thrillen* to pierce, penetrate, in *Cursor Mundi;* alteration (by metathesis of *i* and *r*) of *thirlen,* earlier *thurlen* (probably before 1200, in Layamon's *Chronicle of Britain*); developed from Old English (before 1000) *thȳrlian,* from *thȳrel* (earlier **thyrhil*) hole, from *thurh* THROUGH. The figurative meaning of give a shivering, exciting feeling, is first recorded in 1592, in Shakespeare's *Romeo and Juliet.* **—n.** Before 1680, a shivering, exciting feeling; from the verb. **—thriller** *n. Informal.* exciting or suspenseful play or story. 1889, formed from English *thrill,* v. + *-er*[1].

thrive *v.* Probably about 1200 *thrifenn* to flourish, prosper, in *The Ormulum;* later *thriven* (probably before 1300); borrowed from a Scandinavian source; compare Old Icelandic *thrīfask* to thrive; originally, grasp to oneself (Swedish *trivas* thrive, Danish and Norwegian *trives*), probably derived from Old Icelandic *thrīfa* to clutch, grip, grasp (Norwegian *trive* to grab, seize, and Swedish *treva* to grope, grab); of unknown origin.

throat *n.* Old English (before 700) *throte* (implied in Old English *throtbolla* throat boll, the Adam's apple, larynx), related to *thrūtian* to swell, possibly with reference to the external appearance of the throat; cognate with Old High German *drozza* throat (modern German *Drossel*), and Old Icelandic *throti* a swelling, *thrūtna* to swell, from Proto-Germanic **thrut-,* from Indo-European **treud-* (Pok.1027). **—throaty** *adj.* About 1645, guttural, hoarse; formed from English *throat* + *-y*[1].

throb *v.* Before 1376 *throbben* beat rapidly or strongly (implied in *throbbant* throbbing), in *Piers Plowman;* of uncertain origin (possibly imitative in the sense of representing the pulsation of arteries, veins, and heart, as in *My heart throbbed exceedingly,* 1542, or *A thrilling throb from her heart,* 1579). No cognate form is found in the other Germanic languages. **—n.** rapid or strong beat. 1579, in Spenser's *The Shepheardes Calender;* from the verb.

throe *n.* Probably before 1200 *throwe* violent spasm, pain; of uncertain origin. The form suggests that it is an early derivative from the verb *throwen* (Old English *thrāwan*) in its early sense of twist, turn, writhe; see THROW. Another contention is that Middle English *throwe* is an altered form (influenced by *throwen* to suffer) of *thrawe,* developed from Old English *thrēa* (genitive *thrawe*) affliction, pang, evil, threat, oppression, punishment, related to *thrōwian* to suffer. Old English *thrēa* (from Proto-Germanic **thrawō*) is cognate with Middle Low German *drawe, drouwe* threat, Old High German *drawa, drōa,* Old Icelandic *thrā* longing, and possibly with Old Slavic *truti* wear out, consume, and Greek *trŷ́ein* to wear out, distress. The spelling *throe* is first recorded in 1615. The figurative sense (usually in the plural form *throes*) of a violent convulsion or struggle preceding or accompanying the bringing forth of something (as in *the throes of a revolution, the throes of composition*) is first recorded in 1698.

thrombosis (thrombō′sis) *n.* formation of a blood clot in a blood vessel. 1706, in Kersey's edition of Phillips' *Dictionary;* New Latin, from Greek *thrómbōsis* a clumping or curdling, from *thromboûsthai* become curdled or clotted, from *thrómbos* clot, curd, lump; for suffix see -OSIS. The sense was known somewhat earlier in the word *thrombus* a clot (1693, New Latin, from Greek *thrómbos*).

throne *n.* Probably before 1200 *trone,* in *Ancrene Riwle;* later *throne* (about 1300, after the Latin form); borrowed from Old French *trone,* learned borrowing from Latin *thronus,* from Greek *thrónos* seat, chair, throne, which is cognate with Sanskrit *dhárma-s* law; literally, that which is affirmed, *dhāráyati* (he) keeps, holds, affirms, from Indo-European **dher-, dherə-, dhere-/dhero-* (Pok.252). **—v.** put on a throne. Probably about 1378 *tronen,* in a version of *Piers Plowman;* later *thronen* (about 1400); from the noun.

throng *n.* Probably before 1300 *thronge* crowd, crowding, pressure, in *Kyng Alisaunder;* also *thrang,* in *Arthour and Merlin;* probably a shortened form of Old English (993) *gethrang,* related to *thringan* to push, crowd, press. Old English *gethrang* (from Proto-Germanic **thranȝán*) is cognate with Middle Dutch *dranc* throng, pressure, crowd (modern Dutch *drang*), Middle High German *gedranc, dranc* (modern German *Drang*), Old Icelandic *throng* throng, crowd, Gothic *threihan* to crowd, press (from Proto-Germanic **thren-Hanan*); and, outside Germanic, with Lithuanian *treñkti* to jolt, from Indo-European **trenk-/tronk-* (Pok.1093). **—v.** to crowd. Before 1325 *thrangen* to press, compress, squeeze, in *Cursor Mundi;* probably from the noun. The sense of to crowd, go in a crowd, is first recorded in the 1500's, probably before 1542.

throstle *n.* thrush. Old English (before 800) *throstle;* cognate with Old Saxon *throsla* thrush, Old High German *drōscala,* Middle High German (Bavarian) *drōschel* (modern German *Drossel*), and, outside Germanic, with Old Breton *trascl* thrush (modern Breton *trask*), and Welsh *tresglen;* see THRUSH. Old English *throstle* developed from Proto-Germanic **thrustalō,* altered from **thurstaz,* Indo-European **tr̥zdos.*

throttle *v.* to choke, suppress. Before 1387 *throtelen,* in Trevisa's translation of Higden's *Polychronicon;* probably formed from Middle English *throte* THROAT + the suffix -LE[3]. **—n.** valve in an engine. 1877 (in 1824 *throttle-valve*), from the earlier sense of the throat (before 1547); probably formed from Middle English *throte* throat + the suffix -LE[1].

through *prep., adv.* Before 1375 *throu,* in *Cursor Mundi,* alteration (by metathesis of *r* and *u*) of earlier *thurh* (about 1175, in *The Body and the Soul*); developed from Old English *thurh* (about 750, in Cynewulf's *Elene*), later also *thuruh* (about 1000). The Old English forms are cognate with Old Frisian *thruch* through, Old Saxon *thurh, thuru,* Middle Dutch *dore* (modern Dutch *door*), Old High German *durh, duruh* (from Proto-West-Germanic **thurH,* Indo-European **tr̥-k(w)e*), and with Gothic *thaírh;* not found in Scandinavian. Cognates outside Germanic include Old Irish *tre, tri* through, Latin *trāns* across, beyond, and Sanskrit *tirás* through, across, from the Indo-European root **ter-* (Pok.1074).

Old English *thuruh* developed into modern English *thorough* and became differentiated, being used chiefly as an adjective while *through* is used as the preposition and (less exclusively) as the adverb. Similar formation is found in *burh* which became *borough* and *furh, furrow.*

—throughout *adv., prep.* About 1066 *thurhūt,* in *Peter-*

borough Chronicle; found in *thurh ūt* through out (about 1000, in Ælfric's *Lives of Saints*).

throw *v.* Probably before 1200 *thrauwen* to twist, turn, in Layamon's *Chronicle of Britain;* later *throwen* to cast, hurl (probably before 1300, in *Kyng Alisaunder*); developed from Old English *thrāwan* to twist, turn, writhe (about 1000, in Ælfric's *Homilies*); cognate with Old Saxon *thrāian* to twist, turn, Middle Dutch *draeyen* (modern Dutch *draaien*), and Old High German *drāen* (modern German *drehen*), from Proto-Germanic **thrǣ-*. The word is not found in Scandinavian and Gothic but cognates outside Germanic are seen in Latin *terere* to rub, grind, Old Irish *tarathar* borer, Greek *tetraínein* to pierce, perforate, *trêma* hole, *teírein* to oppress, trouble, *trī́bein* to rub, grind, wear, Old Slavic *trěti* to rub, and Tocharian A, Tocharian B *trik-* go astray, from Indo-European **ter-* (Pok.1071).

The sense of put by force (as in *throw into prison*) is first recorded in 1560, and the meaning of lose deliberately, let win, in 1868, in American English. Another sense once particular to American English is the meaning of disconcert, confuse, upset (as in *thrown by the mix-up*), first recorded in 1844.
—n. a cast, toss. 1530, in Palsgrave's *Lesclarcissement;* from the verb.
—throwaway *n.* 1903, from the verb phrase *throw away* (before 1382). **—throwback** *n.* 1888, in writings of Kipling; from the verb phrase *throw back* (before 1822).

thrum *v.* play on a stringed instrument by plucking or strumming the strings. 1592, from the noun, or of imitative origin similar to that of the noun. **—n.** sound made by thrumming. Before 1553, of imitative origin.

thrush *n.* kind of songbird. About 1250 *thrusche,* in *The Owl and the Nightingale;* developed from Old English (about 1000) *thyrsce,* related to *throstle* THROSTLE. Old English *thyrsce* (from Proto-Germanic **thruskjōn*) is cognate with Old High German *drosca(la),* from Proto-Germanic **thrau(d)-sk-* and, outside Germanic, with Latin *turdus* thrush, Middle Irish *truit, druit* starling, Welsh *drudw, drudwy,* Old Prussian *tresde* thrush, and possibly with *s-* prefix in Lithuanian *strãzdas* and Latvian *strazds* thrush, from Indo-European **trozdo-, trozdi-, tr̥zdo-,* with some alterations influenced by the names and sounds of other birds (Pok.1096).

thrust *v.* Probably before 1200 *thrusten* push with force, in Layamon's *Chronicle of Britain;* borrowed from a Scandinavian source (compare Old Icelandic *thrȳsta* to thrust, force, from Proto-Germanic **thrūstjanan,* cognate with Latin *trūdere* push, shove, from Indo-European **treud-/trūd-,* Pok.1095). **—n.** 1513, act of pressing, pressure, in Douglas' translation of Vergil's *Aeneid;* from the verb. The sense of act of pushing with force is found in 1580-83, in Sidney's *The Arcadia.* The aeronautical sense of propulsive force (as by a jet engine) is first recorded in 1870. The figurative sense of principal theme or gist (of a remark, argument, etc.) is first found in 1963, in American English.

thud *v.* Probably before 1200 *thudden* to strike, thrust, in Layamon's *Chronicle of Britain;* developed from Old English *thyddan* (before 899, in Alfred's translation of St. Gregory's *Pastoral Care*), earlier **thudjanan;* of uncertain origin. The sense of hit, move, or strike with a dull, heavy sound, is found in 1796 (implied in *thudding*). **—n.** 1535 *thude* a loud sound, as of a thunderclap; Scottish, from the verb. The sense of a dull, heavy sound, is first recorded in 1825.

thug *n.* ruffian, cutthroat. 1810, member of a former gang of professional robbers and murderers in India who typically strangled their victims; borrowed from Hindi *ṭhag,* perhaps from Sanskrit *sthaga-s* cunning, fraudulent, possibly from *sthagayati* (he) covers, conceals; see THATCH. The general sense of ruffian or cutthroat is first recorded in Carlyle's *Essay on Chartism* (1839). **—thuggery** *n.* 1839, in Carlyle's *Essay on Chartism;* formed from English *thug* + *-ery.*

thulium (thü′lēəm) *n.* silver-white metallic chemical element. 1879, New Latin, from Latin *Thūlē* Thule (from Greek *Thoúlē*) the part of the world that the ancient Greeks and Romans regarded as farthest north + New Latin *-ium* (chemical suffix). The New Latin word was coined by its discoverer, the Swedish chemist Per Theodor Cleve.

thumb *n.* 1137 *thumbe,* in *Peterborough Chronicle;* developed from Old English (before 800) *thūma* thumb; cognate with Old Frisian *thūma, tūma* thumb, Old Saxon *thūmo,* Middle Low German and Middle Dutch *dūme* (modern Dutch *duim*), Old High German *thūmo* (modern German *Daumen*), and Old Icelandic *thumall* thumb of a glove (Danish and Norwegian *tommel,* Swedish *tumme*), from Proto-Germanic **thūman-* the stout or thick (finger). Cognates outside Germanic are found in Latin *tumēre* to swell, Middle Irish *tomm* mound, hill, Greek *týmbos* burial mound, Lithuanian *tumě̃ti* become thick, coagulate, and Sanskrit *túmra-s* strong, thick, from Indo-European **tu-m-/tū-m-* extensions of the root **tēu-/təu-/tū-/tu-* to swell (Pok.1082). For a note on the spelling with *b,* see under LIMB[1], n.
—v. 1593, to play (a musical instrument) with or as with the thumbs; from the noun. The meaning of feel with the thumb is found in 1623 (implied in *thumbing*), and that of go through, as if with the thumbs (as in *thumb through a book*) is found in Dashiell Hammet's *Maltese Falcon* (1930, though a related sense of soil or wear, by use or handling, especially in reference to a book, is found as early as 1644-47). The sense of signal with the thumb, as for (a ride), hitchhike, is attested since 1932, and as a sign of contempt (as in *thumb one's nose*) in 1903. **—thumbnail** *n.* (1604); *adj.* very small or brief, as in *a thumbnail sketch* (1852). **—thumbscrew** *n.* 1794, screw that can be turned with thumb and fingers; 1817, instrument of torture, in Scott's *Old Mortality.* **—thumbtack** *n.* (1884)

thump *v.* strike with something thick and heavy. About 1537 (implied in *thumper);* probably imitative of the sound made by hitting with a heavy object. **—n.** heavy blow or knock. 1552, in Huloet's *Abecedarium Anglico Latinum;* from the verb.

thunder *n.* About 1250 *thunder,* in *Genesis and Exodus;* earlier *thunre* (probably before 1200, in Layamon's *Chronicle of Britain*); developed from Old English *thunor* (before 899, in Alfred's writings); earlier *thuner* (before 800); cognate with Old Frisian *thuner* thunder, Old Saxon *thunar,* Middle Dutch and modern Dutch *donder,* Old High German *donar* (modern German *Donner*), and Old Icelandic *Thōrr* god of thunder (earlier poetic form *Thunarr),* from Proto-Germanic **thunraz,* Indo-European **tn̥ros.* Cognates outside Germanic are found in Latin *tonāre* to thunder, and probably Greek *sténein* to moan, groan, Lithuanian *stenė́ti,* Old Slavic *stenati,* and Sanskrit *stánati, stániti, stanáyati* (it) thunders, *tányati* (it) rushes, roars, resounds, from Indo-European **(s)ten-/(s)ton-/(s)tn̥-* (Pok.1021). The intrusive *d* in English *thunder* also appears in Dutch *donder;*

compare also Old Icelandic *Thundr* (genitive *Thundar*) one of the names of the god Odin. **—v.** Before 1338 *thundren,* in Mannyng's *Chronicle of England;* developed from Old English *thunrian* (before 899, in Alfred's translation of Boethius' *De Consolatione Philosophiae*); from the noun. **—thunderbolt** *n.* About 1440, formed from Middle English *thunder* + *bolt* arrow, projectile. **—thunderclap** *n.* (about 1390, in Chaucer's *Canterbury Tales*) **—thundercloud** *n.* (1697) **—thunderhead** *n.* rounded mass of clouds appearing before a thunderstorm (1861). **—thunderous** *adj.* 1582, full of thunder, in a translation of Vergil's *Aeneid;* formed from English *thunder* + *-ous.* The sense of loud as thunder is first recorded in 1606. **—thunderstorm** *n.* (1652) **—thunderstruck** *adj.* astonished (1613), replacing *thunderstricken* (before 1586).

Thursday *n.* Before 1250 *thursdei,* in *Ancrene Riwle;* developed from Old English *Thurresdæg* (about 1000, in Ælfric's *Lives of Saints*), perhaps a contraction (influenced by Old Icelandic *Thōrsdagr* Thursday) of *Thunresdæg;* literally, Thor's day (*Thunre,* genitive of *Thunor* Thor, the ancient Scandinavian god of thunder, from *thunor* THUNDER + *dæg* DAY). Old English *Thunresdæg* corresponds to Old Frisian *Thunresdei* Thursday, Middle Dutch *Donresdach* (modern Dutch *Donderdag*), Middle Low German *Donersdach,* and Old High German *Donares Tag* (modern German *Donnerstag*). The Germanic compounds are loan translations of Latin *Jovis diēs,* day of Jove or Jupiter, the Roman god of the sky.

thus *adv.* Old English *thus* in this way (about 725, in *Beowulf*), related to *thæt* THAT. Old English *thus* is cognate with Old Frisian and Old Saxon *thus* and Middle Dutch *dus, dos* (modern Dutch *dus*).

thwart *adv., prep.* across, crosswise. Probably before 1200 *thwert-* (in such compounds as *thwertover* athwart over), in *Ancrene Riwle;* later *thweart* (about 1200, in *The Ormulum*); borrowed from a Scandinavian source (compare Old Icelandic *thvert* across; originally neuter of *thverr,* adj., transverse, cross). Old Icelandic *thverr* is cognate with Old English *thweorh* transverse, perverse, angry, cross, Middle Low German and Middle Dutch *dwers, dwars* (modern Dutch *dwars*), Old High German *dwerah, twerh* (modern German *zwerch-* in compounds), Gothic *thwaírhs* angry, from Proto-Germanic **thwerHaz,* altered (under the influence of **thwer-* to turn) from **therH-,* Indo-European **terk-/tork-* (Pok.1077). A cognate outside Germanic is found in Latin *torquēre* to twist; see TORTURE. **—v.** About 1250 *thwerten* run counter to, oppose, hinder, in *Genesis and Exodus;* from *thwert-* across. **—adj.** Probably about 1200 *thwert,* about 1250 *thweart;* from the adverb. **—n.** 1611, act of thwarting, hindrance, obstruction, in Cotgrave's *Dictionary;* from the verb. The sense of a seat across a boat, especially a canoe, is first recorded in 1736, probably from the adverb or adjective.

thy *adj.* your. Probably before 1200 *thi,* in *Ancrene Riwle;* reduced form of *thin* THINE, used before consonants, except *h.*

thyme (tīm) *n.* small plant with a fragrance like mint. Before 1398 *thyme,* in Trevisa's translation of Bartholomew's *De Proprietatibus Rerum;* earlier as a surname *Thymme* (1266); borrowed from Old French *thym* the plant, learned borrowing from Latin, and borrowed into English directly from Latin *thymum,* from Greek *thýmon* possibly first used as incense, from *thýein* burn as a sacrifice, from Indo-European **dheu-/dhu-, *dhewə-/dhū-* (Pok.261).

thymus (thī′məs) *n.* ductless gland near base of the neck. 1693, New Latin, from Greek *thýmos,* originally a warty excrescence or glandular substance; also, sweetbread; probably so called because it was likened to a bunch of thyme, but otherwise of uncertain origin.

thyroid (thī′roid) *adj.* of the ductless gland in the neck. 1726-41, in Monro's *Anatomy of the Human Bones;* borrowed from Greek *thyreoeidḗs* shield-shaped, from *thyreós* oblong, door-shaped shield, from *thýrā* DOOR + *-eidḗs* in the form of, -oid. **—n.** 1840, principal cartilage of the larynx; 1849-52, thyroid gland; from the adjective.

ti (tē) *n.* seventh note of the musical scale. 1839 *te,* about 1845 *ti;* replacement of earlier SI, to avoid confusion with *so, sol.*

tiara (tēãr′ə) *n.* ornamental headband of gold, jewels, or flowers. 1555, principally, the headdress of the Persian kings, but also worn by men of rank and distinction; borrowed from Latin *tiāra,* from Greek *tiárā, tiárās,* possibly of oriental origin. The sense of ornamental headband of gold, jewels, or flowers worn by women, is first recorded in English in 1718, but was known in the Anglicized form *tiar* perhaps as early as 1660, though this use was more closely associated with the meaning of crown worn by a religious personage. The form *tiar* for the Persian headdress is found even earlier in 1513.

tibia (tib′ēə) *n.* shinbone. 1726-41, in Monro's *Anatomy of the Human Bones;* borrowed from Latin *tībia* shinbone; earlier, pipe or flute; of uncertain origin.

tic *n.* habitual, involuntary twitching of the muscles. 1822, in John Mason Good's *The Study of Medicine* (often shortened form of *tic douloureux,* 1800; a severe facial neuralgia; literally, painful twitch); borrowed from French *tic* a twitching disease of horses (1611); of unknown origin.

tick[1] *n.* tiny parasitic animal. About 1310 *tik,* perhaps developed from Old English **ticca* or **tīca,* recorded in Old English as *ticia* tick (before 850, in the *Erfurt Glossary*). Old English *ticia* is cognate with Middle Low German and Middle Dutch *tēke* tick (modern Dutch *teek*), Middle High German *zeche* (modern German *Zecke*), and probably with Middle Irish *dega* stag beetle, and Armenian *tiz* tick, from Indo-European **deiĝh-* sting (Pok.187).

tick[2] *n.* sound made by a clock or watch. 1440 *tek* light touch or tap, in *Promptorium Parvulorum;* later *tick* (1580); probably cognate with Dutch *tik* light touch or tap, Middle High German *zic,* and dialectal Norwegian *tikka* touch lightly. These may indicate a common Germanic source, or they may be of later imitative origin. The meaning of a sound made by a clock or watch is first recorded in English in 1680, but is found earlier, possibly in *tick-tack* (1549). **—v.** make a tick, as a clock. 1546, to touch lightly, tap; from the noun. The meaning of make a tick, as a clock, is found in 1721 (implied in *ticking* which also had an earlier sense of a repeating noise, in 1566). **—ticker** *n.* 1828, part of a clock or watch that ticks; formed from English *tick[2]*, v. + *-er[1]*. The sense of a telegraphic recording instrument is first recorded in 1883. The slang sense of the heart appeared in 1930, in American English. **—ticker tape** 1902, paper tape on which information is printed by a telegraphic ticker. **—tick-tock** *n.* (1848, in Thackeray's *Vanity Fair,* but found earlier as *tick-tick* 1774, and possibly in *tick-tack,* 1549)

tick[3] *n.* cloth covering of a mattress or pillow. 1342 *tyke,* probably borrowed from Middle Dutch *tīke, tēke* (cognate with Old High German *ziahha* tick, pillowcase, modern German *Zieche*), a West Germanic borrowing from Latin *thēca* case, from Greek *thḗkē* a case, box, cover, sheath, related to *tithénai* to put, place; see DO[1] act. **—ticking** *n.* 1649, cloth covering for mattresses and pillows.

ticket *n.* 1528, short note or document; borrowed from Middle French *etiquet* label, note, as that which indicates information in a book, from Old French *estiquette* label, note, especially one affixed to a gate or wall as a public notice, from *estiquer* to affix, stick, from Frankish **stikkan,* cognate with Old English *stician* to pierce, STICK[2]. Compare ETIQUETTE.

The meaning of a card or piece of paper that gives its holder a right or privilege is first recorded in English in 1673, probably developed from the earlier meaning of a certificate, license, permit (1529). The meaning of the list of candidates to be voted on is first recorded in American English in 1711, probably from the earlier meaning of a written public notice (1567). The sense of a summons to appear in court, given by a policeman for a violation, is first recorded in 1930.

—v. put a ticket on, mark with a ticket. 1611, in Cotgrave's *Dictionary;* from the noun. The meaning of provide with a ticket that gives a right or privilege, is first recorded in American English (1842, in Longfellow's writings).

tickle *v.* Before 1338 *tikellen,* in Mannyng's *Chronicle of England;* of uncertain origin. The Middle English word or even a remote form of it is not recorded in Old English, though the sense is found in Old English *tinclian* to tickle (cognate with dialectal German *zickeln* to tickle). Various possibilities have been suggested, the most plausible being that *tickle* is a frequentative form of *tick*[2] to touch lightly (with -LE[3]), although the chronology does not favor this theory. Another, yet more complex, possibility sometimes given is that Middle English *tikellen* represents an alteration (by metathesis of *k* and *t*) of *kittlen* (probably about 1475 *kytill*), implied in Late Old English in *kitelung* tickling; compare German *kitzeln* tickle and Old Icelandic *kitla* to tickle. **—n.** 1801, from the verb. **—ticklish** *adj.* 1581, (figurative) sensitive, touchy; later, delicate, critical, risky (1591); formed from English *tickle,* v. + *-ish*[1]. The literal sense of easily tickled is first recorded in 1598, in Florio's *A World of Words.*

tick-tack-toe *n.* 1884, probably an extension of earlier *tick-tack* a form of backgammon (1558, possibly borrowed from Middle French *trictrac*).

tidbit *n.* About 1640 (in 1649 *tit-bit*), probably formed from dialectal English *tid* fond, solicitous, tender, wanton + *bit* morsel, BIT[1].

tide *n.* Before 1121 *tide* a season of the year, in *Peterborough Chronicle;* developed from Old English *tīd* point or portion of time, due time (about 725, in *Beowulf*); cognate with Old Saxon *tīd* time, Middle Low German *tīt,* Middle Dutch and modern Dutch *tijt* time (modern Dutch *tij* tide of the sea), Old High German *zīt* time (modern German *Zeit*), and Old Icelandic *tīdh* (Danish, Swedish, and Norwegian *tid*), from Proto-Germanic **tīdís,* Indo-European **dītís.* Cognates outside Germanic include Armenian *ti* age, year, time, Greek *daíesthai* to divide, distribute, and Sanskrit *dáyate* (he) apportions, *dā́ti* (he) divides, from Indo-European **dā-, dāi-/dəi-/dī-* (Pok.175). Related to TIME. The meaning of rise and fall of the sea is first recorded in Middle English probably before 1400. **—v.** 1593 (implied in *tiding*), to flow or surge as the tide does; from the noun. **—tidal** *adj.* of, having, or caused by tides. 1807, formed from English *tide,* n. + *-al*[1]. **—tidal wave** 1830, the global undulation of ocean water that causes the tides, in Sir Charles Lyell's *Principles of Geology;* later, an extremely large ocean wave caused by an underwater earthquake (1878, in writings of Thomas Huxley). **—tideland** *n.* land flooded at high tide (1802). **—tidewater** *n.* water affected by the tide, American English (1772). *—adj.* on or along tidewater (1832).

tiding *n.* Usually **tidings** *pl.* news. Probably before 1200 *tidinge,* in Layamon's *Chronicle of Britain;* developed from Late Old English *tīdung* event, occurrence, piece of news (1069, in the *Anglo-Saxon Chronicle*); perhaps in part a verbal noun of Old English *tīdan* to happen, but more likely borrowed from a Scandinavian source (compare Old Icelandic *tidhendi,* pl., events, news, from *tīdhr,* adj., occurring, from *tīdh* time; see TIDE). Compare also German *Zeitung* newspaper; literally, tiding.

tidy *adj.* About 1250 *tidi* in good condition, fair, healthy, in *Genesis and Exodus;* originally, in season, timely, opportune, excellent (though not found recorded before about 1350); formed from Middle English *tide* season, time (see TIDE) + *-y*[1]. The sense of neat and in order is first recorded in Kersey's edition of Phillips' *Dictionary* (1706). **—v.** put in order, make tidy. 1821, from the adjective.

tie *n.* About 1300 *tie* cord, rope, band; earlier *teg* (probably before 1200, in Layamon's *Chronicle of Britain*); developed from Old English *tēag* (about 750, in Cynewulf's *Christ*), related to *tēon* to pull, TOW[1]. Old English *tēag* is cognate with Old Icelandic *taug* rope, from Proto-Germanic **tauʒṓ,* Indo-European **doukā́.* The sense of equality in points, votes, etc. between two or more competitors or sides, is found in 1680. The sense of a necktie or cravat is first recorded in 1761 (*necktie* itself occurs in 1838). **—v.** Probably before 1200 *teien* fasten, unite; developed from Old English *tīgan, tīegan* (about 1000, in Ælfric's *Grammar*), from *tēag,* n. The Old English verb is cognate with Old Icelandic *teygja* to draw.

tier (tir) *n.* row, rank. Probably before 1450 *tir, tire;* borrowed from Middle French *tire,* from Old French *tire* rank, sequence, order, from *tirer* to draw, draw out; see TIRADE. **—v.** arrange in tiers. 1888-89, from the noun.

tiff *n.* small quarrel. 1727, outburst of temper, in Bailey's *Dictionary;* later, small quarrel (1754); of uncertain origin. **—v.** be in a tiff, be quarrelsome. 1727, in Bailey's *Dictionary;* from the same source as the noun.

tiger *n.* Probably before 1300 *tigre,* in *Kyng Alisaunder;* in part developed from Old English *tigras,* pl. (before 1000), and in part borrowed from Old French *tigre;* both from Latin *tigris* tiger, from Greek *tígris,* possibly from an Iranian source (compare Avestan *tigri-* arrow, *tiγra-* pointed, sharp; see STICK[2] pierce), but also possibly an adaptation of a foreign word to an Iranian stem by folk etymology.

tight *adj.* Probably before 1400 *tyght* dense, solid; earlier *tigt* (about 1325); borrowed from a Scandinavian source (compare Old Icelandic *thēttr* watertight, close in texture, solid, Norwegian *tett,* Danish *tæt,* Swedish *tät* tight, close, compact). Old Icelandic *thēttr* is presumably (through earlier **thēhtr,* from Proto-Germanic **thenHtuz*), the source of Middle English *thight* close, dense, and it is probable that *tight* and *thight* (about 1375) were confused from time to time. However, both English words seem to have developed the specific sense of watertight independently by the early 1500's, and maintained their separate use into the 1800's, so that *tight* cannot truly be said to be the variant of *thight* as is often stated. Old Icelandic *thēttr* is cognate with Old English *-thīt* in *metethīht* stout from eating, and Middle High German *dīhte* dense, thick (modern German *dicht*). Cognates outside Germanic include Middle Irish *tēcht* coagulated, Lithuanian *tánkus* thick, and Sanskrit *tanákti* (it) coagulates, contracts, from Indo-European **tenk-* draw together; firm, thick (Pok.1068).

The meaning of not letting water, etc., out or in, is first recorded in English in 1507, that of fixed firmly in place, in 1513, and drawn or stretched, in 1576. The sense of fitting closely appeared in 1779.

—adv. firmly. 1680, from the adjective.

—tighten *v.* 1727, in Bailey's *Dictionary;* formed from English *tight* + *-en*[1]. **—tight-fisted** *adj.* stingy (1844, in Dickens' *A Christmas Carol*). **—tightrope** *n.* (1801) **—tights** *n.pl.* tight-fitting garment (1827). **—tightwad** *n.* 1906, American English, implied earlier in *tightest wad* (1900); formed from English *tight* + *wad* roll of bank notes.

tilde (til′də) *n.* diacritical mark (~). 1864, in Webster's *Dictionary;* borrowed from Spanish, alteration of Catalan *title* (later *titlla*), from Latin *titulus* inscription, heading, TITLE.

tile *n.* thin piece of clay, etc., for covering roofs, paving floors, etc. Before 1325 *tile,* in *Cursor Mundi,* developed as a contracted form of earlier *tigel,* from Old English (before 800) *tigele;* borrowed from Latin *tēgula* tile, from *tegere* roof, cover; see THATCH. Other Germanic borrowings from the Latin are found in Old Saxon *tiegla* tile, Middle Dutch *tiegel* (modern Dutch *tegel*), Old High German *ziagala, ziagal* (modern German *Ziegel*), and Old Icelandic *tigl* (Danish and Norwegian *tegl,* Swedish *tegel*). **—v.** put tiles on or in. About 1375 *tilen;* from the noun.

till[1] *prep.* until. About 1200, in *The Ormulum,* developed from Old English (before 800) Northumbrian *til;* borrowed from a Scandinavian source (compare Old Icelandic, Danish and Norwegian *til* to, until, Swedish *till;* cognate with Old Frisian *til* to, until). These words are common prepositions in Scandinavian, taking the place of *to* as used in English, and probably originally accusative of a lost noun (Proto-Germanic **tilan,* of uncertain origin), except as found in Icelandic *tili, tili* scope, the noun used to express aim, direction, purpose, as seen in Old Icelandic *aldrtili* end of life, death, and superseded in English by the compound *until.* **—conj.** until. 1137 *til,* in *Peterborough Chronicle;* from the preposition, in Old English.

till[2] *v.* cultivate (land), plow. 1137 *tilen,* developed from Old English (before 850) *tilian* cultivate, tend, work at; originally, strive after, related to *till* fixed point, goal, and *til* good, suitable; see TILL[1]. Old English *tilian* is cognate with Old Frisian *tilia* to get, cultivate, Old Saxon *tilian* to obtain, Middle Dutch and modern Dutch *telen* to breed, raise, cultivate, Old High German *zil* goal (modern German *Ziel*), Old High German *zilōn, zilēn* to strive (modern German *zielen* to aim, strive), from Proto-Germanic **tilōjanan,* and Gothic *gatils* suitable. **—tillage** *n.* 1488-89, state or condition of being tilled; formed from Middle English *tillen* to till + *-age.*

till[3] *n.* drawer for money, cashbox. Before 1450, borrowed from Anglo-French *tylle* compartment, Old French *tille* compartment or shelter on a ship, probably from a Scandinavian source (compare Old Icelandic *thilja* plank, floorboard, Shetland dialect *tilji, tilli* loose floorboard on a ship). Old Icelandic *thilja* is from Proto-Germanic **theljōn,* cognate with Sanskrit *tala-m* flat surface, and Latin *tellūs* earth, from Indo-European *tel-* (Pok.1061).

tiller *n.* bar or handle to turn the rudder of a boat. Before 1325 *tilier* stock of a crossbow; borrowed from Old French *telier* stock of a crossbow; originally, weaver's beam, learned borrowing from medieval Latin *telarium,* from Latin *tēla* web, loom, from earlier **texlā,* from *texere* to weave; see TEXT; for suffix see -ARY. The nautical sense of a bar or handle to turn the rudder of a boat is first recorded in English before 1625. This meaning is a development in English, since the French equivalent of a tiller is *barre (du gouvernail*).

tilt *v.* Probably about 1350 *tulten;* probably about 1380 *tylten* to push over, fall over, in *Patience;* developed from Old English **tyltan* for **tieltan,* from *tealt* unsteady, from Proto-Germanic **taltaz,* Indo-European **dold-,* root **del-* totter, waver (Pok.193). Old English *tealt,* and its corresponding verb *tealtian* be unsteady, are cognate with Middle Dutch *touteren* to tremble, and dialectal Norwegian *tylta* walk softly.

The sense of engage in a contest, joust, fight, is first recorded (figuratively) in Shakespeare's *Love's Labour's Lost* (1588); from the noun. The meaning of lean, tip, slope, is first recorded in 1594, extended from the earlier sense of the verb "push or fall over."

—n. Before 1510, place for holding jousts; 1511, joust, fight; from the verb, in the sense of push over, overthrow. The sense of a sloping position appeared in 1562. The figurative sense of an inclination, tendency, bias (as in *a pro-Republican tilt*), is first recorded in 1975, in American English.

timber *n.* Old English (before 750) *timber* building, structure; later, building material, trees suitable for building (before 899, in Alfred's writings); cognate with Old Frisian *timber* building, Old Saxon *timbar,* Middle Dutch *timmer* building, wood (modern Dutch *timmer* timber), Old High German *zimbar* dwelling, room, wood (modern German *Zimmer* room, *Zimmermann* carpenter), and Old Icelandic *timbr* timber (Swedish *timmer,* Norwegian and Danish *tømmer*), from Proto-Germanic **temran.* Outside Germanic cognates are found in Latin *domus,* Greek *dómos,* Old Slavic *domŭ,* and Sanskrit *dáma-s,* all meaning house, from Indo-European **dómos,* root **dem-* build (Pok.198). **—v.** Probably before 1200 *timbren* to build, construct, in *Ancrene Riwle;* developed from Old English (before 750) *timbran, timbrian,* derived from *timber,* n. The Old English verb is cognate with Old Frisian *timbria* to build, Old Saxon *timbrian,* Middle Dutch and modern Dutch *timmeren,* Old High German *zimbarōn* (modern German *zimmern* to carpenter, frame), Old Icelandic *timbra* (Swedish *timra,* Danish and Norwegian *tømre*), and Gothic *timrjan.* **—timberland** *n.* (1654) **—timberline** *n.* line beyond which no trees grow (1867).

timbre (tim′bər *or* tam′bər) *n.* the distinctive quality in sounds. 1849, in Charlotte Brontë's *Shirley;* borrowing of French *timbre* quality of a sound; earlier, sound of a bell, from Old French in the sense of hemispherical bell without a clapper (also, heraldic crest, seal or stamp); originally, a drum, probably through Medieval Greek **timbanon,* from Greek *týmpanon* kettledrum; see TYMPANUM.

time *n.* 1154, in *Peterborough Chronicle;* developed from Old English *tīma* (before 899, in Alfred's translation of Orosius' *Historiarum Adversus Paganos*), related (according to F. Kluge, *Etymologisches Wörterbuch der Deutschen Sprache,* p. 880) to *tīd* time; see TIDE. Old English *tīma* is cognate with Old Icelandic *tīmi* time, proper time, good time (Swedish *timme,* Norwegian and Danish *time* hour), from Proto-Germanic **tīmōn.*

Some extended meanings are original to Old English, such as that of an occasion (as in *This time we will succeed,* before 899), and the right time (as in *time to eat,* before 899); other meanings are developments in Middle English, such as that of leisure (as in *have time to read,* about 1220), or in modern English, such as that of an experience (as in *have a good time,* before 1529), and rhythm or measure of a piece of music (1531). The plural *times* multiplied by, is first recorded about 1380. **—v.** About 1250 *timen* fare well; later, arrange the time for an event (probably about 1390, in *Sir Gawain and the Green Knight*). The sense of measure or note the time, rate, or duration of, is first recorded in Milton's *History of Britain* (1670).

—time-honored *adj.* honored because old and established (1593, in Shakespeare's *Richard II*). **—timekeeper** *n.* (1686) **—timeless** *adj.* About 1560, untimely; formed from English *time* + *-less.* The meaning of not subject to time, eternal, is first recorded before 1628. **—timely** *adj.* occurring at the right time, early, opportune. 1382, in the Wycliffe Bible; formed from Middle English *time* + *-ly*[2]. **—timepiece** *n.* clock or watch (1765). **—timer** *n.* 1841, person who fixes the time for an event; 1884, watch or clock; formed from English *time,* v. + *-er*[1]. The meaning of a device for indicating when a certain period has elapsed is first recorded in 1908. A much earlier instance with the meaning of a person skilled in time or measure, musician, is recorded about 1500. **—timetable** *n.* (1820) **—timeworn** *adj.* (1729) **—time zone** geographical region with a single standard time (1892).

timid *adj.* 1549, borrowed from Middle French *timide* easily frightened, shy, and directly from Latin *timidus* fearful, from *timēre* to fear, of uncertain origin. **—timidity** *n.* 1598, quality of being timid, in Florio's *A World of Words;* borrowed from Latin *timiditās* fearfulness, from *timidus* fearful, timid; for suffix see -ITY.

timorous *adj.* timid. Probably before 1425, borrowed from Middle French *timoureus,* from Medieval Latin *timorosus* fearful, from Latin *timor* fear, from *timēre* to fear, of uncertain origin; for suffix see -OUS.

timpani (tim′pənē) *n.pl.* kettledrums. 1876 (1740 *timpano,* singular), borrowing of Italian *timpani* drums, plural of *timpano,* from Latin *tympanum* drum; see TYMPANUM. **—timpanist** *n.* 1939, formed from English *timpani* + *-ist.*

tin *n.* Old English (before 899, in Alfred's translation of St. Gregory's *Pastoral Care*); cognate with Middle Low German, Middle Dutch, and modern Dutch *tin* tin, Old High German *zin* (modern German *Zinn*), and Old Icelandic *tin* (Danish *tin,* Norwegian *tinn,* Swedish *tenn*), from Proto-Germanic **tinan.* The word is not known outside Germanic (Irish *tinne* is borrowed from English). **—v.** to cover with tin. Before 1398 *tinnen,* in Trevisa's translation of Bartholomew's *De Proprietatibus Rerum;* from the noun. **—tin can** (1770, in Washington's *Diaries*) **—tinfoil** *n.* (1467-68) **—tinhorn** *adj. Slang.* cheap and showy, noisy and pretentious. 1885, American English, originally applied to a gambler; formed from *tin,* n. + *horn.* **—tinny** *adj.* 1552, of, containing, or yielding tin; formed from English *tin,* n. + *-y*[1]. The generalized meaning of like tin is first recorded in 1877, with specific reference to insubstantial, and of cheap metallic sound, in 1884. **—Tin Pan Alley, tin pan alley** 1908, musicians, songwriters, and their publishers as a group or industry, especially in the United States; 1909, district frequented by musicians, songwriters, and song publishers; American English; formed from *tin pan* tinny piano (1882) + *alley;* so called with reference to the tinny quality of the cheap pianos used in music publishers' offices.

tincture *n.* solution of medicine in alcohol. 1400, pigment, dye, in Lanfranc's *Science of Surgery;* borrowed from Latin *tinctūra* act of dyeing or tingeing, from *tinctus* dye, past participle of *tingere* to TINGE; for suffix see -URE. Compare TINT. The modern pharmaceutical sense of a solution of medicine in a mixture containing alcohol is recorded before 1648. **—v.** 1616, to dye, color, tinge; from the noun.

tinder *n.* anything that catches fire easily. Probably before 1200, in Layamon's *Chronicle of Britain;* developed from Old English (before 800) *tynder, tyndre,* related to or derived from Old English *tendan* to kindle. Old English *tynder, tyndre* is cognate with Middle Low German *tunder* tinder, Dutch *tondel, tonder,* Old High German *zuntra* (modern German *Zunder*), Old Icelandic *tundr* (Danish and Norwegian *tønder,* Swedish *tunder*), Gothic *tundnan* to catch fire, and *tandjan* to kindle. The word is not known outside Germanic. **—tinderbox** *n.* 1530, in Palsgrave's *Lesclarcissement.* The figurative sense of a very excitable person is first found in Shakespeare's *The Merry Wives of Windsor* (1598).

tine *n.* sharp projecting point or prong, especially those of a fork. About 1350 *tyne,* a reduced form (with loss of *d*) of Old English (before 800) *tind;* cognate with Middle Low German *tind* tine, Middle High German *zinke, zint* point, spike, tine (modern German *Zinke*), Old Icelandic *tindr* tine (Danish and Norwegian *tind,* Swedish *tinne*), and probably with Old High German *zinna* pinnacle (modern German *Zinne*), of unknown origin.

tinge (tinj) *v.* color slightly. 1471 *tingen* to dye, color, in Ripley's *The Compend of Alchemy;* borrowed from Latin *tingere* to dye, color, moisten, which is cognate with Greek *téngein* to moisten, and Old High German *dunkōn, thunkōn* to dip (modern German *tunken*). Related to DUNK. **—n.** slight coloring or tint. 1752, from the verb.

tingle *v.* Before 1382 *tinglen* have a ringing sensation at hearing something, in the Wycliffe Bible; later, to have a stinging or thrilling feeling (before 1398, in Trevisa's translation of Bartholomew's *De Proprietatibus Rerum*); variant of *tinkelen* TINKLE. **—n.** Before 1700, a tinkling sound; later, a tingling sensation or action (1848); from the verb.

tinker *n.* one who mends pots, pans, etc. About 1378

tynkere, in a version of *Piers Plowman;* earlier as a surname *Tynker* (1252); of uncertain origin. From the evidence of its very early use, it is questionable whether the word was formed as traditionally given from *tinken* to ring, jingle; see TINKLE + *-ere* -er[1], with reference to the noise made in hammering metal. **—v.** 1592 (implied in *tinkering*), to mend, especially in a clumsy or unskilled way; from the noun. The figurative sense of work or keep busy in a rather useless way is found in 1658. The expression *not worth a tinker's damn* is first recorded in 1839, in Thoreau's writing.

tinkle *v.* Before 1382 *tinklen* to ring, jingle, in the Wycliffe Bible; possibly a frequentative form of *tinken* to ring, jingle (also before 1382), perhaps of imitative origin; for suffix see -LE[3]. **—n.** 1682, a tinkling sound; from the verb.

tinsel *n.* About 1448 *tyneseyle* shining metallic thread; borrowed from Middle French *estincelle, estencele* spark, spangle; see STENCIL. **—v.** to trim with tinsel. 1594, from the noun. **—adj.** of or like tinsel, showy but not worth much. 1595, from the noun, especially from the earlier attributive use (1502) in the sense of made to sparkle by interweaving with metallic thread or overlaying with a thin coating of gold or silver.

tint *n.* a color or variety of a color. 1717, in Pope's *Moral Essays;* alteration of earlier *tinct* (1602, in Shakespeare's *Hamlet*); borrowed from Latin *tīnctus* (genitive *tīnctūs*) a dyeing, from *tingere* to dye; see TINGE; influenced by Italian *tinta* tint, hue, from Latin *tīnctus.* Compare TINCTURE. **—v.** put a tint on, color slightly. 1791, from the noun.

tintinnabulation (tin′tənab′yəlā′shən) *n.* the ringing of bells. 1845, American English; formed from Latin *tintinnābulum* bell + English *-ation.* This word was popularized by Edgar Allan Poe in his poem *The Bells,* written in 1849 (not as often recorded in 1831). The forming of *tintinnabulation* was probably influenced by the numerous earlier related words in English: *tintinnabular* (1767), *tintinnabulary* (1787), *tintinnabulous* (1791), *tintinnabulant* (1812), *tintinnabulatory* (1827), and earliest of all, *tintinnabulum* a small bell (before 1398, in Trevisa's translation of Bartholomew's *De Proprietatibus Rerum*). Latin *tintinnābulum* derives from the verb *tintinnāre* to ring, jingle, a reduplicated form of *tinnīre* to ring, of imitative origin.

tiny *adj.* very small. 1598 *tynie,* 1599 *tiny,* formed from Middle English *tyne* very small (of unknown origin) + *-ie, -y*[1]. Middle English *tyne* is first recorded probably before 1400, in *The Wars of Alexander,* and is preceded by *little* (as in *a little tyne child*).

-tion a suffix forming nouns from verbs, and meaning act or process of _____ing, as in *addition;* condition or state of being _____ed, as in *exhaustion;* result of _____ing, as in *reflection.* Found especially in the form -ATION; see also -SION. English *-tion* was borrowed from Latin *-tiōnem* (accusative of noun suffix *-tiō,* a compound fusing *-t* of the ancient Indo-European abstract noun stem *-ti-* and *-iō,* accusative *-iōnem,* a suffix forming nouns of condition and action). Compare English *station,* from Latin *statiōnem* (nominative *statiō*), found in the past participle *statum* of *stāre* to stand + *-iōnem* (nominative *-iō*); see also -ATION. Often *-tion* is a spelling replacement of Middle English *-tioun,* borrowed from Old French *-tion, -cion,* from Latin *-tiōnem* (nominative *-tiō*), and forms words modeled on derivatives from Latin and French (*protect, protection* and *opt, option*).

tip[1] *v.* to slope, overturn. Probably about 1380 *typen* to overthrow, overturn, of uncertain origin (possibly from a Scandinavian source, and then later perhaps a special use of *tip*[2] end, point, top, suggested by use with up, over, down, etc.; the change in vowel length of the original argues against early association with *tip*[2]). The sense of to slope, tilt, is found in 1624. The spelling *type* (with a long vowel) was in literary use as late as 1632. *Tip* with a short vowel first appeared in 1581, perhaps influenced by the past tense form, *tipt.* **—n.** 1673, the upsetting of a bowling pin; from the verb. The sense of an act of sloping or tilting appeared in 1849. **—tipsy** *adj.* somewhat intoxicated, unsteady. 1577, probably formed from English *tip* + *-sy,* as in *drowsy.*

tip[2] *n.* end, point, top. Probably before 1200 *tippe;* cognate with, and perhaps derived from, Middle Low German, Middle Dutch, and modern Dutch *tip* utmost point, extremity, tip, and Middle High German *zipf* (modern German *Zipfel*); ultimately probably from the same root as Old English *tæppa* stopper, TAP[2]. **—v.** put a tip on. About 1395 *tippen,* in Chaucer's *Canterbury Tales;* from the noun. **—tiptoe** *n.* the tips of the toes (about 1390, in Chaucer's *Canterbury Tales*); *adv.* (1592); *adj.* (1593) on tiptoe; from the noun; *v.* 1632 (implied in *tiptoed*); from the noun. **—tiptop** *n.* very top (1702); *adj.* at the very top (1722); first-rate, superlative (1732).

tip[3] *v.* give a small present of money to. 1610, to give, hand, pass, originally thieves' cant; perhaps from TIP[4] to tap. The meaning of give a present or gratuity to is first found in 1706-07, in George Farquhar's *The Beaux Stratagem.* The extended sense of give confidential information to occurs in 1883 (implied in *tipping*), probably from the noun. **—n.** 1755, small present of money; from the verb. The extended sense of a piece of confidential information, helpful hint, is first recorded in 1845. **—tipster** *n. Informal.* person who furnishes confidential information for use in betting. 1862, formed from English *tip*[3] piece of confidential information + *-ster.*

tip[4] *n.* light, sharp blow or tap. About 1450 *tippe;* possibly cognate with, or even derived from, Low German *tippen* to poke, touch lightly, related to Middle Low German *tip* end, point, TIP[2]. **—v.** to hit lightly and sharply, tap. 1567, in Golding's translation of Ovid's *Metamorphoses;* from the noun.

tipple *v.* drink (alcoholic liquor) often. 1531 (implied in *tippling,* verbal noun) sell alcoholic liquor by retail, of uncertain origin (possibly of Scandinavian origin; compare Norwegian *tiple* to drip, tipple). Alternatively, the verb may be a back formation from earlier *tippler.* The meaning of drink (alcoholic liquor) often or too much is found in 1560. **—n.** an alcoholic liquor. 1581, in a translation of Homer's *Iliad;* from the verb. **—tippler** *n.* person who tipples. 1396 *tipeler* seller of ale and other alcoholic liquors; in form and meaning formed from *tipple,* v. + *-er*[1] but actually known almost 150 years before the verb form; earlier as a surname *Tipeler* (1275).

tirade (tī′rād) *n.* long, vehement speech. 1801, borrowing of French *tirade* speech, volley, shot, continuation, drawing out; formed from *tirer* draw out, endure, suffer, probably from a shortened form of Old French *martirer, martirier* endure martyrdom + *-ade.* The

Old French forms developed from *martyrie, martyre* martyrdom, suffering, from Late Latin *martyrium* martyrdom, witness, testimony, from Greek *martýrion,* from *mártyr* MARTYR.

See FEW (VI, 78, pp. 397-422) for development of French words through Gallo-Romance from Late Latin *martyrium.*

tire[1] *v.* to weary. Before 1460 *tyren,* developed from Old English *tēorian* (about 1000), in Kentish *tīorian* (before 800), of unknown origin. **—tireless** *adj.* 1608, formed from English *tire*[1] + *-less.* **—tiresome** *adj.* 1500-20, wearisome, tedious, in William Dunbar's *Poems;* formed from English *tire*[1] + *-some*[1].

tire[2] *n.* band around a wheel. 1485 *tyre* iron rim of a carriage wheel, probably from earlier *tire* equipment, dress, covering (about 1300); shortened form of ATTIRE. The sense of band of rubber on the rim of a wheel is first recorded in 1877. From the 1600's through the 1700's the standard British and American spelling was *tire.* But since the beginning of the 1800's the spelling *tyre* has been revived to become standard in Great Britain, while *tire* has continued in use in the United States. **—v.** furnish with a tire. Before 1899, from the noun.

tissue *n.* About 1385 *tyssew* band or belt of rich material, in Chaucer's *Troilus and Criseyde;* borrowed from Old French *tissu* a ribbon, headband, belt of woven material, noun use of *tissu* woven, interlaced, past participle of *tistre* to weave, from Latin *texere* weave; see TEXT. The meaning of any woven fabric is found in English in 1565. The sense (figurative) of network, web, is first recorded in 1711. The specific sense in biology of the masses of cells forming the "fabric" or parts of animals or plants is first recorded in 1831, in Carlyle's *Sartor Resartus.* **—tissue paper** (1777)

tit[1] *n.* titmouse or other small bird. 1706, in Kersey's edition of Phillips' *Dictionary;* shortened form of TITMOUSE. The word is also sometimes used as a shortening of *titlark* (1668).

tit[2] *n.* nipple, teat. Old English *titt* (about 950, in *Lindisfarne Gospels*); see TEAT. The vulgar slang sense of a woman's breast is first recorded in 1928, in American English.

tit[3] *n.* See TIT FOR TAT.

Titan *n.* one of a family of giants in Greek mythology. 1727-41 (in 1667, ancestor of the Titans), borrowed from Latin *Tītān,* from Greek *Tītā́n* member of the mythological race of giants. The transferred sense of a person or thing having enormous size, strength, or intellect, is first found in Scott's *The Fair Maid of Perth* (1828). A much earlier sense of the name of the sun god, Helios (Sol), son of the Titan Hyperion, is recorded in Middle English about 1385, in Chaucer's *Troilus and Criseyde;* also found as a surname in 1207. **—titanic** *adj.* gigantic, huge. 1656, of or belonging to the sun, in Blount's *Glossographia;* later, of or like the Titans, gigantic, colossal (1709); borrowed from Greek *Tītānikós* of the Titans, from *Tītā́n* Titan; for suffix see -IC.

titanium (tītā'nēəm *or* titā'nēəm) *n.* metallic chemical element. 1796, New Latin, formed from Latin *Tītān* TITAN + New Latin *-ium* (chemical suffix). The word was coined in 1795 by Martin Klaproth, a German chemist, on the analogy of *uranium.*

tit for tat blow for blow, like for like. 1556, in John Heywood's *The Spider and the Fly;* possibly an alteration of *tip for tap* blow for blow (*tip*[4] tap, *tap*[1] touch lightly).

tithe *n.* tenth part, one tenth. Before 1338 *tithe* tax of one tenth of a yearly produce paid for the support of the church, in Mannyng's *Chronicle of England;* earlier *tigthe* (about 1250), *tigethe* (probably before 1200, in *Trinity Homilies*); developed from Old English (about 737) Anglian *teogotha* tenth (earlier **teʒúnthōn*), West Saxon (854) *tēotha* (from Proto-Germanic **te-Húnthōn*). Old English *teogotha* is cognate with Old Frisian *tegotha* tenth, Old Saxon *tegotho,* Middle Low German *tegede,* Old High German *zehanto* (modern German *zehnte*), Old Icelandic *tīundi,* and Gothic *taíhunda,* from Proto-Germanic **teHunđṓn.* Cognates outside Germanic include Greek *dékatos,* Lithuanian *dešim̃tas,* Old Slavic *desętŭ,* and Tocharian A *śkänt,* Tocharian B *śkante, śkañce,* from Indo-European **deḱm̥-tos* (Pok.192), from **deḱm̥* TEN. Compare TENTH and -TEENTH (under -TEEN). **—v.** Probably before 1200 *tithen* put or pay a tithe on, in *Ancrene Riwle;* developed from Old English (854) *tēothian,* from *tēotha* tenth.

titillate *v.* excite pleasantly, stimulate agreeably. 1620, back formation from English *titillation,* modeled on Latin *tītillātus,* past participle of *tītillāre* to tickle, a verb of intensive pattern, but of unknown origin; for suffix see -ATE[1]. **—titillation** *n.* pleasant excitement, agreeable stimulation. About 1425 *titilacion;* borrowed from Latin *tītillātiōnem* (nominative *tītillātiō*) a tickling, from *tītillāre* tickle; for suffix see -ATION.

title *n.* About 1303 *tytyl* inscription, heading, in Mannyng's *Handlyng Synne,* in part a borrowing of Old French *title,* and in part developed from Old English *titul* (about 950, in *Lindisfarne Gospels*); both borrowed from Latin *titulus* inscription, heading, of uncertain origin. Doublet of TILDE and TITTLE. The sense of the name of a book, poem, play, etc., is first recorded in Middle English about 1340. The sense of evidence to the legal rights to property, title deeds, is first found probably about 1421. The meaning of an appellation or name showing a person's rank, occupation, etc. (as Dr., Esq., Reverend), is first recorded in Spenser's *Faerie Queene* (1590). The sports sense of championship (as in *the heavyweight title*) is first attested in 1922. **—v.** Before 1325 *titlen* give a title to, entitle; from the noun. **—titleholder** *n.* (1904) **—title page** (before 1613) **—title role** (1886)

titmouse *n.* kind of small bird with a short bill. About 1325 *titmose,* formed in Middle English probably from Old Icelandic *tittr* titmouse + Middle English *mose* titmouse (about 1250). Middle English *mose* developed from Old English *māse* (before 800), and was later influenced in spelling by *mouse.* Old English *māse* is cognate with Middle Dutch *mēse* titmouse (modern Dutch *mees*), Old High German *meisa* (modern German *Meise*), and Old Icelandic *meisingr.* Old High German *meisa* is from Proto-Germanic **maisōn,* built on an adjective **maisa-* little, tiny, whence Norwegian dialect *meis* a thin, weak person (Pok.36).

titter *v.* giggle. Before 1619, in Fletcher's *Wit Without Money;* probably of imitative origin. **—n.** stifled laugh. 1728, from the verb.

tittle *n.* very little bit, particle, whit. About 1384 *titil* small stroke or point in writing, (figurative) very little bit, in the Wycliffe Bible (said to be a rendering of *apex* in the Late Latin sense of accent mark over a vowel);

borrowed (perhaps by influence of Provençal *titule* the dot over *i*) from Latin *titulus* inscription, heading; see the doublet TITLE.

titular *adj.* in title or name only. 1591, formed in English, perhaps by influence of Middle French *titulaire,* from Latin *titulus* TITLE + English *-ar.*

tizzy *n. Slang.* a very excited state, dither. 1935, American English; of uncertain origin (perhaps somehow related to earlier *tizzy* a sixpence piece, 1804, as in "A man reads at *a tizzy* what he had not read when priced at twelve times the humble tanner," with a play on words for the sense "little" in amount of money and time).

to *prep., adv.* Old English *tō* in the direction of, for the purpose of, furthermore, until (about 725, in *Beowulf*); cognate with Old Frisian *tō,* adv., *to, te, ti,* prep.; Old Saxon *tō,* adv., *te,* prep.; Middle Dutch and modern Dutch *toe,* adv., *te,* prep.; Old High German *zuo,* adv., *za, zi, ze,* prep. (modern German *zu*). Outside Germanic cognates are found in Latin *dōnec* as long as, while, *quandō* when, Greek *-de* toward, Lithuanian *da-*to, until, and Old Slavic *do,* from Indo-European **de/do/dō* (Pok.181).

Already in Old English the preposition (go *to* London) had leveled with the adverb (slam the door *to*) into one form, as in German both are now *zu.* But while Old English *tō,* adverb, retained its stress so that it came at last to be written *too* (see TOO), the preposition, being usually stressless, remained as *to* in modern English.

Beside the simple infinitive ending *-an* (Middle English *-en*), as in *etan* to eat, Middle English *eten,* Old English had a dative form ending in *-anne* or *-enne,* which in Middle English eventually blended with the simple infinitive. This dative form was always preceded by the preposition *tō,* which originally had the same meaning and use as before ordinary nouns, expressing motion, direction, inclination, purpose, etc., as in "he came *to help* (i.e. to the help of) his friends," "he prepared *to depart* (i.e. for departure)." But in the course of time this obvious sense of the preposition became weakened and generalized, so that *tō* became an ordinary link expressing any prepositional relation between an infinitive and a preceding verb, adjective, or noun (wants *to go,* nice *to see,* a book *to read*). The use of the infinitive with *to* was further increased by the loss of inflectional endings in the early Middle English period and the resulting need of some mark to distinguish the infinitive from other parts of the verb. Thus in modern English the infinitive with *to* is the ordinary form, the simple infinitive (without *to*) surviving only in auxiliary verbs like *shall, may, can,* and after certain verbs (*make, let, hear, feel,* etc.). To a large extent, therefore, *to* has lost most of its meaning and has become a mere sign or prefix of the infinitive. But after an intransitive verb, or the passive voice, *to* is still the preposition, as in "She proceeded *to speak,*" "He is known *to many.*"

Although in Middle English *to* was fairly commonly used in combination with verbs, nouns, adjectives, and adverbs in the sense of motion, direction, or addition to (as in *to-cast* add, *to-hear* listen to, *to-tach* attach, *togainst* against), the only surviving uses of *to* in compounds are found in *to-do, together,* and in the expressions of time *today, tonight,* and *tomorrow.*

toad *n.* small tailless amphibian similar to a frog. Probably before 1300 *tode;* earlier *tadde* (probably before 1200); developed from Old English (about 1000) *tādige, tādie,* of unknown origin and unusual form, with no known cognates in other languages. Compare TADPOLE.

toadstool *n.* Before 1398 *tadstole* mushroom, in Trevisa's translation of Bartholomew's *De Proprietatibus Rerum;* apparently a fanciful name formed from Middle English *tadde* TOAD + *stole* STOOL. The specific sense of a poisonous mushroom is first recorded in 1607.

toady *n.* fawning flatterer. 1826, in Disraeli's *Vivian Grey;* apparently shortened from earlier *toad-eater* (1742, in Horace Walpole's letters, 1807-08, in Washington Irving's *Salmagundi*), with the same meaning; originally, according to the story, referring to the assistant of a charlatan, employed to eat (or pretend to eat) poisonous toads to enable his master to display his skill in expelling the poison (1629); for suffix see -Y[2]. —**v.** act like a toady. 1827, in Lady Granville's *Letters;* from the noun. —**toadyism** *n.* 1840, formed from English *toady,* n. + *-ism.*

toast[1] *v.* to brown by heat. Before 1398 *tosten,* in Trevisa's translation of Bartholomew's *De Proprietatibus Rerum;* borrowed from Old French *toster* to roast or grill, from Vulgar Latin **tostāre,* frequentative form of Latin *torrēre* to parch; see THIRST. —**n.** toasted bread. About 1400 *tost,* from *tosten* to toast. —**toaster** *n.* 1582, person who toasts something, in Stanyhurst's translation of Vergil's *Aeneid;* formed from English *toast*[1] + *-er*[1]. The sense of an electric appliance for toasting bread is first recorded in 1913.

toast[2] *n.* a call to drink to someone's health. Perhaps before 1684 (the year of Charles II of England's death), but first attested in 1700, a beautiful or popular woman whose health is proposed and drunk, often one who is the reigning belle of the season, in Congreve's *The Way of the World.* Origin of the term has been explained variously (originally by Steele in the *Tatler,* no. 24 of June 4, 1709) as referring to an incident at Bath, England in the time of Charles II, when a beauty of the time was found standing in a bath and admirers drank to her health from the water, one however, declining the water but desiring the *toast* (an allusion to TOAST[1], from the fact that spiced toast was used to flavor drinks) or (later, in the *Tatler,* no. 31 of June 18, 1709) "to make a Lady have the same Effect as Burridge (borage, a plant whose leaves were earlier much used in flavoring beverages) in a Glass when a Man is drinking." By 1746 the word was applied to any person whose health is proposed and drunk, and by 1831 to the act of proposing a drink in honor of any person, thing, or event. —**v.** Before 1700 *tost,* (1701 *toast*) to propose a toast, drink to someone's health; probably from the noun. —**toastmaster** *n.* 1749, person who proposes toasts, in Fielding's *Tom Jones;* formed from English *toast*[2], n. + *master.*

tobacco *n.* 1597, alteration of earlier *tobaco* (1588), borrowing of Spanish *tabaco.* Traditionally the Spanish word is thought to have come from an Arawakan (probably Taino) language of the Caribbean, in which it meant a roll of tobacco leaves or a kind of pipe for smoking tobacco. According to Corominas, however, while it is a fact that the tobacco plant and the custom of smoking its leaves (already observed by Columbus in 1492) did originate in the New World, the origin of the word *tabaco* is not so certain. In fact, Italian *tabacco,* Spanish *tabaco, atabaca,* and *tabaca,* and similar words, were used in Italy, Spain, and elsewhere about 1410 and long before the discovery of the New World as the names of the eupatorium and other medicinal herbs, including some that caused dizziness and drowsiness. This group of words came from Arabic *ṭabbâq* or *ṭubbâq,* attested since the 800's A.D. as the names of various herbs. Considering that other Indian names have been widely recorded for the tobacco plant, it is possible that the Spaniards transferred the European plant name to the American plant, just as *corn, turkey, robin,* and other European (English) names were often applied to plants and animals in North America. **—tobacconist** *n.* 1599, person addicted to tobacco, in Ben Jonson's *Every Man Out of His Humour;* formed from English *tobacco* + inserted *-n-* (perhaps suggested by such words as *Platonist,* 1549) + *-ist.* The meaning of dealer in tobacco is first found in 1657.

toboggan (tə bog′ən) *n.* long, narrow, flat sled. Before 1820 *tobogin;* Canadian English, borrowed from Canadian French *tabagane, tobagan* (in French, *toboggan*), from Algonquian (probably Micmac) *tobâkun* a sled. **—v.** slide downhill on such a sled. 1846, from the noun.

tocsin (tok′sən) *n.* alarm sounded on a bell, warning signal. 1586 *tocksaine,* borrowed from Middle French *toquassen* an alarm bell, the ringing of an alarm bell, from Old Provençal *tocasenh,* formed from *tocar* to strike (from Vulgar Latin **toccāre* strike a bell; see TOUCH) + *senh* bell, bell note, from Late Latin *signum* bell, ringing of a bell, in Latin, mark or signal; see SIGN. The meaning of an alarm bell is first recorded in 1842 in Longfellow's poetry. The spelling *tocsin* appeared in English in 1794, adopted from modern French.

today *adv.* Probably about 1200 *to dai,* in *Trinity Homilies;* developed from Old English (before 899) *tō dæge* on (the) day (*tō* at, on; see TO + *dæge,* dative of *dæg* DAY). *Today* was regularly written as two words until the 1500's, after which it was usually written with a hyphen as *to-day* until the present century. **—n.** 1535, in Coverdale's translation of the Bible, this day; from the adverb.

toddle *v.* walk with short, unsteady steps as a baby does. About 1600 *todle,* Scottish and Northern British English, of uncertain origin (not originally related to *toddle,* which does not appear in this sense before 1821, but perhaps somehow related to *totter,* 1534 in *tottering;* also not originally related to *doddle,* 1761). An earlier sense of to toy, play, is found in 1500-20 in Dunbar's *Poems.* **—n.** act of toddling. 1825, from the verb. **—toddler** *n.* child just learning to walk. 1793, formed from English *toddle,* v. + *-er*[1].

toddy *n.* 1620, in William Foster's *The English Factories in India;* alteration of earlier *taddy* (1611) and *tarrie* (1609-10) beverage made from fermented palm sap; borrowed from Hindi *tāṛī* palm sap, from *tāṛ* palm tree, from Sanskrit *tála-s,* perhaps of Dravidian origin. The current sense of a beverage made of alcoholic liquor with hot water, sugar, and spices, is first recorded in 1786, in Burns' *Holy Fair.*

to-do *n. Informal.* bustle, fuss, commotion. 1570-76, formed from the verb phrase *to do,* Old English *tō dōn* proper or necessary to be done (*tō,* prep., see TO + *dōn* DO[1] act). Compare ADO.

toe *n.* Probably before 1300 *to,* in *Arthour and Merlin;* developed from Old English (before 900) *tā,* in plural *tān,* contraction of **tāhe,* in Mercian *tāhae* (before 800); cognate with Middle Low German *tē* toe (Old Low German **tēha*), Middle Dutch *tee* (modern Dutch *teen*), Old High German *zēha* (modern German *Zehe*), and Old Icelandic *tā* (Danish, Norwegian, and Swedish *tå*), from Proto-Germanic **taiHwō* (probably formerly meaning "finger" as well); cognate with Latin *digitus* (earlier **dicitus* pointer), related to *dīcere* to tell; behind **taiHwō* lay Indo-European **doiḱwā,* root **deiḱ-/doiḱ-/diḱ-* point to, show (Pok.188). **—v.** 1607-08, to furnish with a toe or toes (as in *toeing a stocking*); from the noun. The meaning of touch or reach with the toes (as in *toe a line*) is found in Marryat's *Peter Simple* (1833). **—toenail** *n.* (1841)

toffee *n.* kind of chewy candy. Before 1825 *tuffy, toughy,* southern British English variant of TAFFY. The spelling *toffee* is first recorded in 1862, in Dickens' letters.

tog *n.* garment. 1708, any outer garment, shortened form of *togman* or *togeman* cloak or loose coat (1567), an obsolete thieves' cant word; formed in English from French *togue* cloak, from Latin *toga* TOGA + *-man,* a cant suffix. The word may have been influenced by Middle English *toge* a toga (probably before 1400), used before 1700 as a cant word for coat. The plural *togs,* in the sense of clothes, is first recorded in 1779. **—v.** clothe, dress. 1793, probably from the noun, though perhaps influenced by *toged* (1604, in Shakespeare's *Othello*). **—toggery** *n.* 1812, garments, clothes collectively; formed from English *tog,* n. + *-ery.*

toga (tō′gə) *n.* loose outer garment worn by men of ancient Rome. 1600, in Holland's translation of Livy's *Roman History;* borrowing of Latin *toga* cloak or mantle, related to *tegere* to cover; see THATCH. The figurative sense of a mantle of office is first recorded in 1855, though other transferred senses are recorded as early as 1738.

together *adv.* Before 1160 *togedere,* in *Peterborough Chronicle;* developed from Old English (707) *tōgædere* (*tō,* see TO + *gædere* together, adv., an apparent variant of the adverb *geador* together, related to *gadrian* to GATHER). Old English *geador* is cognate with Old Frisian *gader, gadur* together, Middle Low German *tōgadere,* and Middle High German *gater.* For the change of *d* to *th* in this word and in words like *father* (Middle English *fader*), see GATHER. **—adj.** *Slang.* self-assured, free of emotional difficulties. 1966, American English, from the adverb.

toggle *n.* pin or rod put through the eye of a rope or the link of a chain to keep it in place. 1769-76 *toggel,* in William Falconer's *A Universal Dictionary of the Marine;* of uncertain origin, perhaps a frequentative form of *tog* tug + *-le*[3], earlier confined to nautical use. **—v.** 1836, to furnish or fasten with a toggle; American English, from the noun. **—toggle bolt** (1794)

toil[1] *n.* hard work, labor. Probably before 1300 *toyle* turmoil, contention, dispute, in *Kyng Alisaunder;* borrowed from Anglo-French *toil,* from *toiler* agitate, stir up, entangle, variant of Old French *toeillier* drag about, make dirty, from Latin *tudiculāre* crush with a small hammer, from *tudicula* instrument for crushing, from the root *tud-* of *tundere* to pound; see STUDY. The sense of hard work, labor, is first recorded in 1594. —**v.** work hard. Probably before 1300 *toilen* to drag, struggle (implied in *toiling,* in *Arthour and Merlin*); borrowed from Anglo-French *toiler* agitate, stir up. The sense of work hard is first recorded before 1376, in

Piers Plowman. **—toilsome** *adj.* 1581, laborious, tiring; formed from English *toil*[1], n. + *-some*[1].

toil[2] *n.* net, snare. Before 1529, in Skelton's poetry; borrowed from Middle French *toile* hunting net, cloth, web, from Old French *teile,* from Latin *tēla* web, related to *texere* to weave; see TEXT. The word is now used largely in the plural, a form known as early as 1530 in Palsgrave's *Lesclarcissement.*

toilet *n.* 1540, cover or bag for clothes; borrowed from Middle French *toilette* a cloth, bag for clothes, diminutive of *toile* cloth, net, TOIL[2]; for suffix see -ET.

The extended sense of articles for a dressing table or dressing room is first recorded in Evelyn's *Diary* (1662), and that of act or process of dressing, in 1681. The sense of dressing room is first recorded in Byron's *Don Juan* (1819); the specific meaning of lavatory or porcelain plumbing fixture is first recorded in 1895, though a similarly functioning device, known as a *water closet,* is recorded as early as 1755.

—adj. of or for the toilet. 1721, from the noun.

—toilet paper (1884) **—toiletry** *n.* 1892 (as a collective), articles used in washing or grooming; 1927 *toiletries,* pl.; formed from English *toilet,* n. + *-ry.* An earlier instance with the meaning of an act of getting dressed is recorded in 1832. **—toilet water** perfumed liquid (1855, in writings of Dickens).

toke (tōk) *v. Slang.* to smoke marijuana. 1952, smoke a cigarette, American English; 1970, smoke marijuana; of unknown origin. **—n.** *Slang.* a puff on a marijuana cigarette. 1968, from the verb.

token *n.* About 1250, in *Genesis and Exodus;* developed from Old English *tācen* sign, symbol, evidence (about 725, in *Beowulf*), related to *tǣcan* show, explain, teach. Old English *tācen* is cognate with Old Frisian *tēken* token, Old Saxon *tēkan,* Middle Low German and Middle Dutch *tēken* (modern Dutch *teken*), Old High German *zeihhan* (modern German *Zeichen*), Old Icelandic *teikn* (Swedish *tecken,* Norwegian and Danish *tegn*), and Gothic *taikn* sign, wonder, miracle, from Proto-Germanic **taiknan,* Indo-European **doiĝnom.* The sense of a coinlike piece of stamped metal issued, especially by tradesmen, in place of scarce coinage or for some service, is first recorded in 1598, and that of a similar metal piece used to operate a machine or exchange for goods or services has been recorded since 1934. Before that, *token* was also used in the sense of a voucher exchangeable for goods or services (1908).

—adj. serving as a token, minimal, nominal. 1915, from the noun. **—tokenism** *n.* policy or practice of making token concessions to minority groups. 1962, American English; formed from *token,* n. + *-ism.*

tolerable *adj.* bearable. Probably about 1425, borrowed from Middle French *tolerable,* and directly from Latin *tolerābilis* that may be endured, from *tolerāre* to TOLERATE; for suffix see -ABLE.

tolerance *n.* Before 1420 *tolleraunce* endurance, fortitude, in Lydgate's *Troy Book;* borrowed from Middle French *tolérance,* learned borrowing from Latin, and borrowed directly from Latin *tolerantia* endurance, from *tolerāns,* present participle of *tolerāre* to bear, endure, TOLERATE; for suffix see -ANCE. The sense of an act of indulging, allowing, or tolerating, forbearance, is first recorded in English in 1765, and the technical sense of allowable amount of variation in size of machine parts is first recorded in 1909, from the earlier use of allowable variation in minting coinage, 1868.

—tolerant *adj.* 1784, probably formed in English as an adjective to the noun *tolerance,* and borrowed directly from French *tolérant,* present participle of *tolérer* tolerate, learned borrowing from Latin *tolerāre* to endure, bear, tolerate; for suffix see -ANT.

tolerate *v.* 1531, to endure, bear, in Sir Thomas Elyot's *The Boke Named the Governour;* 1533, to allow, permit; either a back formation from *toleration,* or formed in English by influence of earlier *tolerable* or *tolerance* on the model of Latin *tolerātus,* past participle of *tolerāre* to bear, endure, tolerate; related to *tollere* to bear, lift up, raise; for suffix see -ATE[1]. Latin *tollere* is cognate with Greek *tlênai* to bear, endure, Armenian *t'ołum* I tolerate, Sanskrit *tulā́* balance, weight, and Tocharian A, Tocharian B *täl-* bear, raise, from Indo-European **tel-/tol-, *telə-/tlā-* (Pok.1060). Cognates in Germanic include Old English *tholian,* Old High German *dolēn,* Old Icelandic *thola,* and Gothic *thulan,* all meaning to bear, endure. **—toleration** *n.* 1517-18, permission granted by authority, license; borrowed from Middle French *tolération,* learned borrowing from Latin, and probably borrowed directly into English from Latin *tolerātiōnem* (nominative *tolerātiō*), from *tolerāre* tolerate; for suffix see -ATION. The sense of an act of allowing, forbearance, appeared in 1582.

toll[1] *n.* tax or fee paid for a right or privilege. Old English (about 1000, perhaps 963) *toll,* variant of *toln* (1023); usually considered to be an early borrowing from Late Latin *tolōnium,* from Latin *telōnium, telōnēum* tollhouse, from Greek *telōneîon* tollhouse, from *telṓnēs* tax collector, from *télos* tax, related to *tlênai* to bear, endure; see TOLERATE. Other early Germanic borrowings from the Late Latin include Old Frisian *tolen, tolene* toll, Old Saxon *tolna,* Old High German *zol* (modern German *Zoll*), and Old Icelandic *tollr* (Danish *told,* Norwegian *toll,* and Swedish *tull*). **—v.** collect tolls from. Before 1350 (implied in *tolling*), from the noun. **—tollbooth** *n.* (before 1400)

toll[2] *v.* to sound with single strokes. 1452 *tollen* to ring a bell by pulling a rope; possibly special use of earlier *tollen* to draw, lure (probably before 1200, in *Ancrene Riwle*), variant of *tillen;* developed from Old English *-tyllan* in *betyllan* to lure, decoy, and *fortyllan* draw away, seduce. The origin of these Old English words is unknown. **—n.** stroke or sound of a bell. 1452, probably from the verb.

tom *n.* the male of various animals. 1762, in allusion to the nickname *Tom* for Thomas, used in Middle English as a type name for a common man, and about 1303 (in Mannyng's *Handlyng Synne*) applied to a male kitten; possibly influenced later by the name of a male cat ("Tom the Cat") that was the hero of a popular anonymous work entitled "The Life and Adventures of a Cat," published in 1760. **—tomboy** *n.* Before 1553, rude, boisterous boy; formed from English *Tom + boy.* In 1579 the word was applied to a bold or immodest woman (a use that became obsolete before 1700). By 1592, in Lyly's *Midas* the word is recorded in the sense of a girl who behaves like a spirited, boisterous boy.

—tomcat *n.* 1809, in Malkin's translation of Lesage's *History of Gil Blas;* formed from English *tom + cat;* probably influenced by *Tom the Cat* (see *tom,* n.).

—tomfool *n.* 1650, buffoon, clown; later, silly or stupid person; originally, *Tom Fool,* a personification of a mentally deficient man, from Middle English *Thome Fole* (1338-39); formed from *Thome* Tom + *fole* FOOL.

—tomfoolery *n.* silly, foolish, or absurd behavior. 1812, formed from English *tomfool* + *-ery.*

tomahawk *n.* light ax. 1612 *tamahaac,* also *tomahack;* later *Tomahawke* (1648), American English; borrowed from Algonquian (probably Powhatan) *tamahack* a striking instrument. **—v.** strike or kill with a tomahawk. 1711, American English; from the noun.

tomato *n.* 1753, in *Chambers Cyclopaedia,* alteration of earlier *tomate* (1604); borrowed from Spanish, and perhaps also from Portuguese, *tomate,* from Nahuatl *tomatl* a tomato. It is possible that the English spelling *tomato* was also influenced by earlier *potato* (1565).

tomb *n.* Probably before 1200 *tumbe,* in Layamon's *Chronicle of Britain;* later *tomb* (before 1325, in *Cursor Mundi*); borrowed from Anglo-French *tumbe,* and directly from its variant Old French *tombe,* from Late Latin *tumba,* from Greek *týmbos* burial mound, grave, tomb; see THUMB. With the shift in spelling to *tomb,* the *b* began to be silent in English. **—v.** put in a tomb. Probably about 1300 *toumben;* from the noun. **—tombstone** *n.* (1565)

tome *n.* 1519, single volume of a literary work; later, book (1573); borrowing of Middle French *tome,* learned borrowing from Latin *tomus* section of a book, tome, from Greek *tómos* volume, section of a book; originally, section, piece cut off, from *témnein* to cut, from Indo-European **tem-/tom-* cut (Pok.1062). Greek *témnein* is related to *téndein* to gnaw (from **tem-d-*); cognate with Middle Irish *tennaid* (he) splits, Latin *tondēre* to shear, and Lithuanian *tinti* to sharpen, whet.

tommy gun submachine gun. 1929 *Tommy gun,* possibly American English; application of the nickname for *Thomas* to the *Thompson submachine gun* (1920), named after General John T. *Thompson,* 1860-1940, who conceived of the idea for such an automatic weapon.

tommyrot *n. Slang.* nonsense, rubbish. 1884, in George Moore's *A Mummer's Wife;* formed from earlier *tommy* a simpleton (1829), diminutive of *Tom* (as in TOMFOOL) + *rot,* n.

tomorrow *adv.* About 1250 *to morwe,* developed from Old English (about 897) *tō morgenne* on (the) morrow (*tō* at, on; see TO + *morgenne, morgne,* dative of *morgen* morning, MORN). *Tomorrow* was regularly written as two words until the 1500's, after which it was usually written with a hyphen as *to-morrow* until this century. **—n.** About 1390, in Chaucer's *Canterbury Tales;* from the adverb.

tom-tom *n.* drum beaten with the hands. 1693, drum (originally used in India), in J.T. Wheeler's *Madras in the Olden Time;* borrowed from Hindi *tam-tam,* probably of imitative origin similar to Singhalese *tamaṭ ṭama,* and Malay *tong-tong.*

-tomy a combining form meaning: **1** surgical incision or operation, as in *tracheotomy, lobotomy.* **2** a cutting or casting off, as in *autotomy = a casting off of part of the body.* Borrowed from Greek *-tomíā* a cutting, from *-tómos* person cutting, related to *tómos* piece cut off; see TOME.

ton *n.* measure of weight. Probably before 1300 *tonne* unit for measuring the carrying capacity of a ship; originally, the space occupied by a tun or cask of wine, and the same word as *tonne, tunne* cask, TUN. *Ton* and *tun* were not differentiated in form and sense until about 1688. The strict sense of a measure of weight is first recorded in 1485. The spelling *ton* is found as early as 1538, though it did not become established until the 1700's. **—tonnage** *n.* 1422 *tonage* tax or duty levied on wine imported in tuns or casks, in *Rolls of Parliament;* borrowed from Middle French *tonnage* weight of goods, carrying capacity in tuns, from Old French *tonne* cask, tun; see TUNNEL; for suffix see -AGE. Later senses of the English word are derived from English *ton* + *-age.* The sense of carrying capacity expressed in tons is first recorded in 1718.

tone *n.* Before 1300 *ton* musical sound or note; later *toune* (before 1325); borrowing of Old French *ton,* and perhaps borrowed directly from Latin *tonus* a sound, tone, accent, stretching (in Medieval Latin, a term particular to music), from Greek *tónos* vocal pitch, raising of voice, accent, key in music; originally, a stretching, taut string, related to *teínein* to stretch; see TEND[1] incline.

The figurative sense of manner of speaking, vocal expressiveness, is recorded before 1610. The sense of degree of firmness or tension normal to the organs or tissues when healthy is first recorded in 1669. The spelling *tone* appeared in Middle English before 1400. **—v.** Before 1300 *tonen* to sound with the proper tone; from the noun. The sense of impart a tone to, modify the tone of, is first recorded in Shelley's *St. Irvyne* (1811).

—tonal *adj.* of a tone or tones. 1776, in Sir John Hawkins' *General History of the Science and Practice of Music;* formed from English *tone* + *-al*[1], perhaps on the model of Medieval Latin *tonalis* of or pertaining to tone, from Latin *tonus* tone. **—tonality** *n.* 1838, formed from English *tonal* + *-ity.* **—tone arm** arm holding the needle on a phonograph (1907). **—tone deaf** (1894, but implied earlier in *tone-deafness,* 1884) **—tone language** a language that distinguishes otherwise identical words solely by difference of tone or pitch (1930). **—tone poem** an orchestral piece (1889, but also found in the related form *tone poet* a composer, perhaps a loan translation of German *Tondichter,* as early as 1874).

tong *n.* secret Chinese organization. 1883, American English; borrowed from Chinese (Cantonese) *t'ong,* originally, meeting hall.

tongs *n.pl.* tool with two hinged or pivoted arms for seizing, holding, or lifting. About 1250 *tonges,* in *The Owl and the Nightingale,* plural of *tonge;* developed from Old English (before 800) *tange, tang* tongs (from Proto-Germanic **tanʒṓ,* Indo-European **donkā́*); cognate with Old Frisian *tange* tongs, Middle Dutch *tanghe* (modern Dutch *tang*), Old High German *zanga* (modern German *Zange*), and Old Icelandic *tǫng* (Danish and Norwegian *tang,* Swedish *tång*). Outside Germanic cognates are found in Albanian (Gheg dialect) *danë* tongs, Greek *dáknein* to bite, and Sanskrit *dáśati* (he) bites, from Indo-European **donḱ-/dn̥ḱ-* (Pok.201).

tongue *n.* Probably before 1300 *tong;* developed from Old English *tunge* organ of speech, speech, language (before 899, in Alfred's translation of Bede's *Ecclesiastical History*). Old English *tunge* is cognate with Old Frisian *tunge* tongue, Old Saxon *tunga,* Middle Dutch *tonghe* (modern Dutch *tong*), Old High German *zunga* (modern German *Zunge*), Old Icelandic *tunga* (Swedish *tunga,* Norwegian and Danish *tunge*), Gothic *tungō* (from Proto-Germanic **tunʒōn*). Outside Germanic cognates are found in Old Latin *dingua* tongue, Latin *lingua* (altered by influence of *lingere* to lick), and Old

Irish *teng,* from Indo-European **dn̥ĝhū/dn̥ĝhwā* (Pok.223).

The regular modern English form of Old English *tunge* would be *tung,* as in *lung, rung, sung,* representing the actual pronunciation of the word in modern English. But the Middle English practice of writing *on* for *un* brought in the form *tong* with variants *tonge, tounge.* These variants, finally developing into *tongue,* were apparently formed to show a pronunciation of *g* (as in *tang*), and to avoid confusion with *g* (as in *tangent*).

—v. About 1388 *tongen* to reproach, scold; earlier *tuingen* (about 1300); from the noun. The literal meaning of touch with the tongue is first recorded in 1687.

—tongue-and-groove *adj.* 1882, of a joint made by fitting a projecting piece of wood into another piece of wood. **—tongue-in-cheek** *adj.* 1933, mockingly ironical or satirical, from earlier *have one's tongue in one's cheek* (1784). **—tongue-tied** *adj.* unable to speak (1529, in Sir Thomas More's *A Dialogue Concerning Heresies*). **—tongue twister** (1904)

tonic *adj.* 1649, relating to or characterized by muscular tension; borrowed from Greek *tonikós* of stretching, from *tónos* a stretching, TONE; for suffix see -IC. The meaning of having to do with or maintaining the tone, or healthy degree of firmness, of the tissues or organs, is first recorded in English in 1684, with the related sense of having the property of restoring to health and vigor appearing in 1756. The musical sense of relating to or based on a keynote or fundamental tone is first recorded in 1760. **—n.** 1799, tonic medicine; from the adjective.

tonight *adv.* Before 1325 *to night* on this very night, in *Cursor Mundi;* developed from Old English (about 1000) *tōniht* tomorrow night (*tō* at, on; see TO + *niht,* dative of *niht* NIGHT).

Tonight was regularly written as two words until the 1700's, after which it was usually written with a hyphen as *to-night* until the present century.

—n. Before 1325 *to night,* in *Cursor Mundi;* from the adverb.

tonsil *n.* 1601, in Holland's translation of Pliny's *Natural History;* borrowed from Latin *tōnsillae,* pl., tonsils, of unknown origin. **—tonsillectomy** *n.* surgical removal of the tonsils. 1899, formed from English *tonsil* + *-ectomy.* **—tonsillitis** *n.* inflammation of the tonsils. 1801, in Erasmus Darwin's *Zoonomia;* formed from English *tonsil* + *-itis.*

tonsorial *adj.* of or pertaining to a barber or his work. 1813, formed in English from Latin *tōnsōrius* of or pertaining to shearing or shaving (from *tōnsor* a shaver or barber, from *tōnsus,* past participle of *tondēre* to shear, shave) + English *-al*[1].

tonsure *n.* a clipping of the hair or shaving of a part or the whole head. Before 1387, in Trevisa's translation of Higden's *Polychronicon;* borrowed from Old French *tonsure,* and directly from Latin *tōnsūra* a shearing, clipping, from *tōnsus,* past participle of *tondēre* to shear, shave, related to Greek *téndein* to gnaw (at); see TOME; for suffix see -URE. The sense of the part of a priest's or monk's head left bare by shaving the hair is recorded in Middle English probably before 1439 and found earlier in Anglo-French (1351, probably from the same sense in Medieval Latin *tonsura*). **—v.** shave the head of. 1793, from the noun.

too *adv.* About 1175 *to* in addition, moreover, in *The Body and the Soul;* developed as a stressed variant of *to* from Old English *tō* in the direction of, furthermore; see TO. The spelling *too* is first recorded in Shakespeare's *Comedy of Errors* (1590).

tool *n.* Before 1225 *tool;* earlier *tol* (probably before 1200, in Layamon's *Chronicle of Britain*); developed from Old English *tōl* instrument, implement (before 899, in Alfred's translation of Boethius' *De Consolatione Philosophiae*). Old English *tōl* (from Proto-Germanic **tōlan*) is cognate with Old Icelandic *tōl* tool, both derived from a Germanic verb stem represented by Old English *tawian* prepare, Old Saxon *tōgian,* Middle Low German, Middle Dutch and modern Dutch *touwen,* Old High German *zouwen,* Old Icelandic *tœja, tȳja* to help, and Gothic *taujan* to do, make, from Proto-Germanic **taujanan,* cognate with Sanskrit *dúvas* favor, honor, from Indo-European **dou-/dōu-/du-* (Pok.218). **—v.** 1812 (*slang*) to drive a vehicle, etc., pull (someone) in a vehicle; from the noun, in the sense of manipulating or managing skillfully, as one does a tool. The meaning of work or shape with a tool is first recorded in 1815 (implied in *tooling*). The expression *tool up,* meaning equip (a factory) with the machine tools necessary to make a certain product, is first recorded in 1927. **—toolbox** *n.* (1832) **—toolhouse** *n.* (1818)

toot *v.* to sound or blow a horn, etc. About 1510, perhaps originally imitative, but found also in Middle Low German and modern Low German *tuten* blow a horn, Middle Dutch *tuyten,* modern Dutch *toeten,* Norwegian *tute,* and Swedish *tuta* (the latter two perhaps influenced by Low German, which may also have been the immediate source of the English word).

tooth *n.* Probably before 1200 *toth;* later *tooth* (about 1385, in Chaucer's *Canterbury Tales*); developed from Old English (before 800) *tōth,* plural *tēth;* cognate with Old Frisian *tōth* tooth, plural *tēth,* Old Saxon and Middle Low German *tand,* Middle Low German plural *tene* (modern Low German *Tähne*), Middle Dutch *tant, tand* (modern Dutch *tand*), Old High German *zand,* plural *zeni* (modern German *Zahn,* plural *Zähne*), Old Icelandic *tǫnn* (Norwegian *tann,* Danish and Swedish *tand*), plural *tenn, tennr,* and Gothic *tunthus,* from Proto-Germanic **tanth-/tunth-.* Cognates outside Germanic include Latin *dēns* (genitive *dentis*) tooth, Old Irish *dēt,* Welsh *dant,* Greek *odṓn, odoús* (genitive *odóntos*), Lithuanian *dantìs,* Armenian *atamn,* and Sanskrit *dán,* with accusative *dántam,* genitive *datás;* from Indo-European **dont-/dn̥t-,* an ancient present participle of **ed-/ēd-/d-* EAT. The meaning of something like a tooth, as the projecting parts of a comb or saw, is first recorded in 1523, and that of the projecting parts of a gear, in 1611.

Figurative use is early and prominent as found in the phrases *in the teeth (of)* in opposition to (1297), *cast or throw something in one's teeth* (1535), *to the teeth* fully or completely (about 1380), *tooth and nail* vigorously, fiercely (1534), *to set one's teeth* be firm or fixed, resolute (1599), and continues in relatively new collocations such as *to put teeth into* to make effective (1955).

—v. About 1410 *tothen* develop or grow teeth; from the noun. The sense of furnish with teeth is first recorded in 1483.

—teethe (tēᴛʜ) *v.* develop teeth. About 1410 *tethen,* from Middle English *teth,* plural of *toth* tooth. **—toothache** *n.* (about 1378, in a version of *Piers Plowman*) **—toothbrush** *n.* (1690, earlier *teeth brush,* 1651)

—toothed *adj.* having teeth or notches. Probably before 1300 *tothed,* in *Kyng Alisaunder;* formed from Middle English *toth* tooth + *-ed*[2]. **—toothpaste** *n.* (1832) **—toothpick** *n.* (1488) **—toothsome** *adj.* 1551, pleasant to the taste, palatable (*tooth* taste, liking; compare SWEET TOOTH + *-some*[1]).

top[1] *n.* highest point or part. Old English *top* summit, crest, tuft, as of hair or feathers (about 1000, in Ælfric's *Grammar*); cognate with Old Frisian *topp* tuft, Middle Low German, Middle Dutch, and modern Dutch *top* summit, crest, Old High German *zopf* summit, crest, tuft (modern German *Zopf* pigtail, plait), and Old Icelandic *toppr* (Swedish and Norwegian *topp,* Danish *top*), from Proto-Germanic **tuppaz;* of unknown origin. **—adj.** of, at, or forming the top. 1593, in Shakespeare's *3 Henry VI;* from the noun. **—v.** Probably before 1300 *toppen* remove the top of, in *Arthour and Merlin;* from the noun. The meaning of put a top on is first recorded in 1581, and that of be higher or greater than, in 1582. **—topcoat** *n.* light overcoat (1804). **—top hat** tall silk hat (1881). **—top-heavy** *adj.* (before 1533) **—topknot** *n.* (about 1686-88) **—topmost** *adj.* (1697, in Dryden's translation of the works of Vergil) **—top-notch** *adj.* (1900) **—tops** *adj. Slang.* of the highest quality; first-rate. 1936, American English, from *tops,* plural of *top*[1], n. **—topsoil** *n.* (1836)

top[2] *n.* toy that spins on a point. Late Old English *top* (about 1060, in the Anglo-Saxon version of the story of Apollonius of Tyre, originally in Latin), probably a special use of *top* highest point, TOP[1]. There are words coinciding in meaning, and probably related in form, in other Germanic languages and dialects (for example Middle Dutch *dop, doppe,* and dialectal German *Topf*) but no direct connection between them and the Old English word has been found.

topaz *n.* crystalline mineral used as a gem. About 1250 *topace,* borrowed from Old French *topace, topaze,* learned borrowing from Latin *topazus,* from Greek *tópazos, topázion,* thought to be of Asian origin; according to Pliny, named for an island in the Red or Arabian Sea, where the mineral abounded. The spelling *topaz* is first recorded in English in 1645 through influence of modern French *topaze* and Latin *topazus.*

topiary *adj.* of or having to do with the trimming of shrubs into ornamental shapes. 1592, borrowed from Latin *topiārius* of or pertaining to ornamental gardening, from *topia* ornamental gardening, from Greek *tópia,* plural of *tópion,* originally, a field, diminutive of *tópos* place (see TOPIC); for suffix see -ARY. **—n.** topiary art. 1908, from the adjective.

topic *n.* 1634, a kind of argument suitable for debate, singular form of earlier *Topics* (before 1568), the name of a work by Aristotle on logical and rhetorical generalities or commonplaces (passages that serve as the basis of argument); borrowed from Latin *Topica,* from Greek (*Tà*) *Topiká,* literally, matters concerning *tópoi* commonplaces, neuter plural of *topikós* commonplace, of a place, from *tópos* place, related to *topázein* aim at; for suffix see -IC. Greek *topázein* is cognate with Lithuanian *tàpti* become, Latvian *tapt* become, reach, and Old English *thafian* to bear, tolerate, allow, sanction, agree to, make available, from Indo-European **top-* arrive at, meet with (Pok.1088).

The meaning of a matter treated in speech or writing, subject, theme, is first recorded in English in 1720, in the writings of Swift.

—topical *adj.* 1588, of or pertaining to a place; formed from English *topic* + *-al*[1]. The meaning of pertaining to a subject or theme is first attested in 1856, in David Masson's essays. The meaning of having to do with topics of the day is first found in *Punch* in 1873.

topography *n.* detailed description or drawing of the surface features of a place. Probably before 1425, in a translation of Higden's *Polychronicon;* borrowed from Late Latin *topographia,* from Greek *topographíā* a description of a place, from *topográphos* describing a place, as a noun meaning one who is skilled in topography (*tópos* place + *gráphein* to write; see TOPIC and CARVE); for suffix see -Y[3]. **—topographic** *adj.* 1632, a shortened form of earlier *topographical* (1570, formed from Greek *topographikós,* from *topographíā* topography + English *-al*[1]), perhaps modeled on French *topographique;* for suffix see -IC, -ICAL.

topple *v.* fall forward, tumble down. 1590, in Shakespeare's *A Midsummer Night's Dream;* earlier, to tumble or roll about (1542); frequentative form of TOP[1], v.; for suffix see -LE[3].

topsy-turvy *adv.* 1528 *topsy-tervy* in utter confusion; 1530 *topsy-tirvy* upside down; probably formed from *tops* (plural of TOP[1] highest point) + obsolete *terve, tirve* turn upside down, topple over, from Middle English *terven* (about 1400), from Proto-Germanic **terƀanan,* cognate with Sanskrit *dṛbháti* he strings together, and West Russian *dórob* basket, from Indo-European **derbh-/dorbh-/dṛbh-* wind, twist together (Pok.211). **—adj.** turned upside down. 1618, from the adverb.

toque (tōk) *n.* a woman's small hat without a brim. 1505 *towk* kind of small cap worn by men or women in various countries; borrowed from Middle French *toque,* from Spanish *toca* woman's headdress, possibly from Arabic **ṭâqa,* from Old Persian *ṭāq* veil, shawl. The spelling *toque* is first recorded in English in 1817, and the sense of a kind of small brimless hat worn by women, about 1880.

torah (tôr′ə *or* tōr′ə) *n.* body of Jewish teachings; also, the Pentateuch. 1577, the law of Moses, Mosaic law; borrowing of Hebrew *tōrāh,* literally, instruction, law, from *hōrāh* he taught, showed. The sense of the five books of Moses, Pentateuch, is first recorded in English in 1842, and that of the body of Jewish teachings, doctrine, and tradition, in 1890.

torch *n.* About 1250 *torche* burning stick, firebrand; borrowed from Old French *torche,* originally, twisted thing; hence, torch formed of twisted tow dipped in wax, probably from Vulgar Latin **torca,* alteration of Latin *torqua,* variant of *torquēs* collar of twisted metal, from *torquēre* to twist; see TORTURE. The British sense of a flashlight or "electric torch" is first recorded in 1901. **—v.** 1819 (implied in *torched*), to illuminate with a torch, in Keats' *Isabella;* from the noun. The meaning of set fire to is first recorded in 1931. **—torch-bearer** *n.* 1538; in the figurative sense of a leader of a cause (1847). **—torchlight** *n.* (about 1425)

toreador (tôr′ēədôr) *n.* bullfighter. 1618, borrowing of earlier Spanish *toreador* (now *torero*), from *torear* to fight in a bullfight, from *toro* bull, from Latin *taurus;* cognate with Greek *taûros,* Lithuanian *taũras* bison, and Welsh *tarw,* from Indo-European **təuros,* a derivative of **tēu-/təu-* to swell (Pok.1083).

torment (tôr′ment) *n.* Probably before 1300 *tourment* torture, pain, distress, in *Kyng Alisaunder;* borrowing of Old French *tourment, torment,* learned borrowing from Latin *tormentum* twisted sling, rack, related to *torquēre* to twist (see TORTURE); for suffix see -MENT. —**v.** (tôrment′) About 1300 *tormenten* cause torment to, inflict torture upon, distress, vex; borrowed from Old French *tourmenter, tormenter* torment, from *tourment, torment,* n. —**tormentor** *n.* About 1300, official torturer; borrowed from Old French *tormenteur,* from *tormenter* to torment + *-eur* -or². The sense of one who persistently inflicts suffering is first recorded in 1553.

tornado *n.* extremely violent and destructive whirlwind. 1556 *ternado* violent thunderstorm; borrowed probably as an imperfect alteration of Spanish *tronada* thunderstorm, from *tronar* to thunder, from Latin *tonāre* to THUNDER. The forms *turnado, tournado* and *tornado* are recorded in English from 1625 onward, influenced by Spanish *tornar* to twist, turn, from Latin *tornāre* to TURN, which may also account for metathesis of *o* and *r* of original Spanish *tronada.* The ending with *-o* is often said to come from an attempt to impart a "Spanish" look to the word. The meaning of an extremely violent and destructive whirlwind is first recorded in 1626.

torpedo *n.* About 1520, the electric ray (a fish); borrowing of Latin *torpēdō,* originally, numbness (from the effect of the ray's electric discharges), from *torpēre* be numb; see TORPID. The transferred sense of an explosive device used to blow up enemy ships is first recorded in 1776. It was so called because it was towed or propelled through water and resembled somewhat an electric ray. —**v.** attack or destroy with a torpedo. 1873, in Howells' *A Chance Acquaintance;* American English, from the noun. —**torpedo boat** (1810, American English)

torpid *adj.* sluggish. 1613, in *Purchas his Pilgrimage;* borrowed (by influence of earlier *torpor*) from Latin *torpidus* benumbed, from *torpēre* be numb or stiff, cognate with Lithuanian *tiȓpti* and Old Slavic *utrŭpěti* to become stiff, from Indo-European **terp-/torp-/tr̥p-* (Pok.1024). —**torpidity** *n.* torpid condition, torpor. 1614, formed from English *torpid* + *-ity.*

torpor *n.* torpid condition. 1607, borrowed from Latin *torpor* numbness, from *torpēre* be numb; see TORPID.

torque (tôrk) *n.* force causing rotation or torsion. 1884, borrowed from Latin *torquēre* to twist; see TORTURE. —**v.** apply torque to an axle, bolt, wheel, or the like. 1954 (implied in *torquing*); from the noun.

torrent *n.* rushing stream of water. 1601, in Shakespeare's *Julius Caesar;* borrowed from English *torrent,* learned borrowing from Latin, and borrowed directly into English from Latin *torrentem* (nominative *torrēns*) rushing stream; originally, roaring, boiling, burning, parching, present participle of *torrēre* to parch (see THIRST); for suffix see -ENT. The figurative sense of any violent flow or onrush (as of words or feelings) is first recorded in English in 1647. —**torrential** *adj.* 1849, like a torrent, rushing; formed perhaps by influence of French *torrentiel,* from English *torrent* + *-ial.*

torrid *adj.* very hot. 1586 *torrid zone* region of the earth between the tropics, in Marlowe's *Tamburlane the Great;* borrowed from Latin *torrida zōna,* from feminine of *torridus* dried with heat, scorching hot, from *torrēre* to parch; see THIRST. The use of *torrid* in English in the general sense of very hot, scorching, burning, is first recorded in Cotgrave's *Dictionary* (1611).

torsion *n.* act or process of twisting. Probably before 1425 *torcion, torcioun* wringing pain in the bowels, in a translation of Chauliac's *Grande Chirurgie;* borrowed from Middle French *torsion,* learned borrowing from Late Latin *torsiōnem* (nominative *torsiō*) a wringing or griping, variant of Latin *tortiōnem* (nominative *tortiō*) torture, torment, from *tortus,* past participle of *torquēre* to twist (see TORTURE); for suffix see -SION. The sense of the action or process of twisting as of some body or structure by opposing forces is first recorded in English in 1543.

torso *n.* trunk of a body. 1797, borrowing of Italian *torso* trunk of a statue; originally, stalk, stump, from Vulgar Latin **tursus,* from Latin *thyrsus* stalk, stem, from Greek *thýrsos,* of uncertain origin.

tort *n.* breach of civil law for which one may sue for damages. About 1250, injury, wrong, in *The Owl and the Nightingale;* borrowing of Old French *tort,* from Medieval Latin *tortum* injustice, noun use of the neuter of *tortus* wrung, twisted, past participle of Latin *torquēre* turn, turn awry, twist, wring, distort; see TORTURE. The specific legal sense of an injury or wrong for which one may sue in a civil action is first recorded in English in 1586.

torte *n.* a rich cake. 1555, borrowed from German *Torte;* also probably borrowed from Middle French *torte;* both ultimately from Late Latin *torta* flat cake; also, round loaf of bread; of uncertain origin, but probably related to TART.

tortilla (tortē′yə) *n.* thin, round corn cake. 1699 *tartillo;* later in the spelling *tortilla* (1828); borrowing of American Spanish *tortilla,* in Spanish, a tart, diminutive of *torta* cake, from Late Latin *torta* flat cake; also, round loaf of bread; of uncertain origin.

tortoise (tôr′təs) *n.* turtle living only on land. 1552 *tortoyse,* in Huloet's *Abecedarium Anglico Latinum;* alteration (perhaps, because of a weakening of the final vowel, influenced by the ending of *porpoise*) of Middle English *tortuse* (1495), probably a variant of earlier *tortuce* (1440); borrowed from Medieval Latin *tortuca,* alteration (by loss of *-ar-* before the last syllable) of Late Latin *tartarūchus* of the underworld; see TURTLE¹. The Medieval Latin spelling may have been influenced by Latin *tortus* twisted, because of the shape of the tortoise's feet. —**tortoise shell** mottled shell of certain turtles (1632); **tortoise-shell** *adj.* made of tortoise shell (1651).

tortuous *adj.* full of twists, turns, or bends. About 1390, in Chaucer's *Canterbury Tales;* borrowed from Anglo-French *tortuous,* learned borrowing from Latin *tortuōsus* full of twists, winding, tortuous, from *tortus* (genitive *tortūs*) a twisting, winding, from *tort-,* stem of *torquēre* to twist, wind, wring, distort; see TORTURE; for suffix see -OUS.

torture *n.* Probably before 1425, severe pain or suffering, in a translation of Chauliac's *Grande Chirurgie;* borrowed from Middle French *torture* infliction of great pain, great pain, agony, learned borrowing from Late Latin *tortūra* a twisting, writhing, torture, torment, from Latin *tort-,* stem of *torquēre* to twist, turn, wind, wring, distort; for suffix see -URE. Latin *torquēre* is cognate with Greek *átraktos* spindle, Old Prussian *tarkue* strap, thong, Old Slavic *trakŭ* band, girdle, Sanskrit *tarkú-s* spindle, Tocharian A and Tocharian B *tsärk-* to torment, and in Germanic with Old High German *drāhsil* turner, and modern German *drechseln* to turn, from Indo-European **terkw-/torkw-/ṭrkw-, *trekw-/trokw-/trēkw-* (H. Frisk, *Griechisches etymologisches Wörterbuch* I,180; Pok.1077). **—v.** cause severe pain to, torment. 1588 in Shakespeare's *Love's Labour's Lost;* from the noun, perhaps influenced by Middle French *torturer* to torture. **—torturous** *adj.* causing torture, tormenting. About 1495, borrowed from Anglo-French *torturous,* Old French *tortureus,* formed from Latin *tortūra* torture + Old French *-eus* -ous.

Tory *n.* 1566 *tory* an outlaw; specifically, a robber, in *Irish State Papers;* borrowed from *tōruighe* plunderer; originally, pursuer or searcher, from Old Irish *tōirighim* I pursue, related to *tōracht* pursuit.

In British history *Tory* began to figure with some prominence from 1646 as a derogatory term referring to those Irish Catholics who had been dispossessed of their land since 1641, or the Irish shippers excluded from the colonial trade and those farmers affected by the ban on Irish cattle in England. Some of these dispossessed Irishmen (like the original buccaneers of the Caribbean) turned to outlawry, attacking the new English landholders and soldiers, so that by 1679-80 *Tory* was extended to refer to anyone who supported the Catholic Duke of York (later James II) in his succession to the throne of England. Attachment of *Tory* to the name of the Catholic Duke of York developed (partly by the efforts of Titus Oates and his inflammatory accusations of the Popish Plot) from anticipated restoration of lost landholdings and privileges to the disenfranchised Irish Catholics and the association of York with a large number of men in his entourage who were Irish Catholics. From 1689 *Tory* became the name of a newly-formed British political party that later came to be identified with conservatism; this use of *Tory* developed because the party's membership at first consisted mainly of the Yorkist Tories of 1679-80. As a formal name, *Tory* was superseded about 1830 by *Conservative,* but members of this party are informally still called *Tories.* Compare WHIG.

In American history *Tory* was used, specifically from 1769, to refer to American colonists who opposed separation of the American colonies, and thus remained loyal to George III of England. Earlier use is not recorded in American sources but may have existed, referring to British use of *Tory* in the sense of those who favored upholding the authority and legal privileges of the Church of England and maintaining the authority and power of the king. Compare WHIG.
—Toryism *n.* (1682)

toss *v.* Before 1450 *tossen* pitch or throw about; of uncertain origin, possibly borrowed from a Scandinavian source (compare dialectal Swedish and Norwegian *tossa* to strew, spread). **—n.** 1634, act of tossing; from the verb. **—tossup** *n.* Before 1800, toss of a coin; later, even chance (1809).

tot *n.* little child. 1725, in Allan Ramsay's *The Gentle Shepherd,* a Scottish word of uncertain origin; perhaps a shortened form of TOTTER, or by some associated with Icelandic *tottr* (Danish *tot*) nickname of a dwarf, but the late date of appearance in English makes any connection obscure.

total *adj.* About 1390, in Chaucer's *Canterbury Tales;* borrowing of Old French *total,* learned borrowing from Medieval Latin, and probably borrowed directly into English from Medieval Latin *totalis* entire, total (as in *summa totalis* sum total, whole amount), from Latin *tōtus* all, whole, entire, of uncertain origin; for suffix see -AL[1]. **—n.** whole amount, sum. 1557, from the adjective. **—v.** find the sum of, add. 1716, from the noun. The slang sense of wreck beyond repair, destroy totally, is first recorded in 1954, in American English; a sense of kill or injure is recorded earlier in East Anglian dialect (1895, implied in *totald,* past participle). **—totality** *n.* 1598, in Florio's *Italian-English Dictionary;* borrowed from Middle French *totalité,* and directly from Medieval Latin *totalitas,* from *totalis* total; for suffix see -ITY.

totalitarian *adj.* of or having to do with a government which suppresses all opposition. 1926, formed from English *total* + *(author)itarian.* **—totalitarianism** *n.* 1926, formed from English *totalitarian* + *-ism.*

tote *v. Informal.* carry, haul. 1677 *toat,* American English, of uncertain origin; possibly borrowed from a West African language (compare Kikongo *tota* pick up, and Kimbundu *tuta* carry, load, related to Swahili *tuta* pile up, carry). The spelling *tote* is first recorded in 1803, also in American English. **—n.** *Informal.* load, burden. 1884, American English; from the verb. **—tote bag** large handbag (1900, American English).

totem *n.* object taken as the emblem of a tribe, clan, family, etc.; image of such an object carved and painted on a pole. 1760-76, in Alexander Henry's *Travels,* American English; borrowed from Algonquian (probably Ojibwa) *ototeman* his sibling kin. Much has been written about this word; little is conclusive. The word is recorded as early as 1609 in the form *aoutem* among the Indians of Nova Scotia (presumably the Micmacs). **—totem pole** 1880, American English, but earlier referred to in a description of west coast Canadian Indians in 1808.

totter *v.* About 1200 *toteren* swing to and fro, in *Vices and Virtues;* of uncertain origin; possibly borrowed from a Scandinavian source (compare dialectal Norwegian *totra* to quiver, shake, dialectal Swedish *tuttra*). The form in Middle English is associated with, but probably not developed from, Old English *tealtrian* to stagger, be unsteady, totter. The meaning of stand or walk with shaky, unsteady steps, is first recorded in 1602. **—n.** Before 1387, board suspended between two ropes, swing, in Trevisa's translation of Higden's *Polychronicon;* from the verb. The sense of the act of tottering is found in 1747.

toucan (tükan′) *n.* bright-colored bird of tropical America. 1568, in a translation of *Thevet's New Found World;* borrowed from Middle French *toucan,* and perhaps directly from Spanish *tucán,* from Tupi (Brazil) *tukã́, tukána.*

touch *v.* Probably before 1300 *touchen,* in *Kyng Alisaunder;* borrowed from Old French *touchier* to touch, hit, knock, from Vulgar Latin **toccāre* to knock, strike (as a bell); perhaps of imitative origin.

It is sometimes held that the Romance forms (Old French *touchier,* Old North French *toquer,* Provençal *toquar, tocar,* Spanish and Portuguese *tocar,* Italian *toccare,* all meaning to strike, hit, touch) are from Germanic (compare Middle Low German *tocken, tucken,* Old High German *zucchen, zocchōn,* Low German *tocken,* all meaning to draw, pull with force, twitch, pluck), but the semantic shift from "twitch, draw, pull, pluck" to "knock, hit, strike" is unexplained and very questionable, which leads most modern etymologists to

believe that the Romance forms are imitative in origin and probably from a syllable, such as *toc,* as found in Rumanian *tocà* to knock.
—n. About 1300, borrowed from Old French *touche* a touching, blow, hit, from *touchier* to touch, hit.
—touch-and-go *adj.* uncertain, risky. 1655, something done quickly, from the verb phrase *touch and go* to deal with something briefly and then move on (1549). The sense of uncertain, risky, is first recorded in 1815.
—touchdown *n.* 1879, American English, act of scoring in football; originally, act of touching the ball to the ground behind the goal line; later, landing of an aircraft (1935). **—touched** *adj.* 1340, stirred emotionally; later, deranged, somewhat crazy or mad (1704, but first suggested in Shakespeare's *Measure for Measure,* 1603); formed from Middle English *touchen* touch + *-ed*[2].
—touch football (1933, American English) **—touching** *adj.* affecting the emotions. 1601, in Shakespeare's *Julius Caesar;* formed from English *touch,* v. + *-ing*[2].
—prep. concerning, about. About 1395, in Chaucer's *Canterbury Tales;* formed (on the model of Old French *touchant*), from the present participle of Middle English *touchen* to touch. **—touchy** *adj.* too sensitive; irritable. 1605, formed from English *touch,* n. + *-y*[1].

touché (tüshā′) *interj.* exclamation acknowledging an effective point in an argument, etc. 1904, exclamation acknowledging a hit in fencing; borrowed from French *touché,* past participle of *toucher,* from Old French *touchier* to hit, TOUCH. The extended sense of an exclamation pleasantly acknowledging a valid point, justified accusation, etc., is first recorded in 1907.

tough *adj.* Probably before 1200 *toge,* in Layamon's *Chronicle of Britain;* later *toghe* (probably before 1325); developed from Old English (about 700) *tōh* strong and firm in texture (from Proto-Germanic **tanHuz,* Indo-European **donk̂us,* Pok.201); cognate with Middle Low German *tā, teie* tough, Middle Dutch *taey* (modern Dutch *taai*), Old High German *zāhi* (modern German *zäh*), and Old Icelandic *tā* trodden ground or path, related to *tǫng;* see TONGS. See ROUGH for spelling change. The figurative sense of hard to influence, firm, persistent, is first recorded in Middle English about 1400; the extended sense of stubborn, obstinate, hardened, is found in 1603, and that of hard, trying, laborious, in 1619. **—n.** rough person; rowdy. 1866, in Howells' *Venetian Life;* American English, from the adjective. **—toughen** *v.* 1582, in Stanyhurst's translation of Vergil's *Aeneid;* formed from English *tough,* adj. + *-en*[1].

toupee (tüpā′) *n.* wig. 1727, in poetry of Alexander Pope; respelled borrowing of French *toupet* tuft of hair, forelock, diminutive (with suffix *-et*) formed from Old French *toupe* tuft, from Frankish **top* (compare Middle Low German *top* and Old High German *zopf* crest, tuft, summit, modern German *Zopf* pigtail); see TOP[1] highest point.

tour *n.* About 1300, a turn, revolution; borrowed from Old French *tour, tourn* a turn, trick, round, circuit, circumference, from *torner, tourner* to turn, from Latin *tornāre* to polish, round off, fashion, turn on a lathe; see TURN. The sense of a traveling around, journey, is first recorded in 1643. **—v.** 1746, to travel around, make the rounds of; from the noun. **—tourism** *n.* 1811, the practice of touring, especially for pleasure; formed from English *tour,* n. + *-ism.* **—tourist** *n.* 1780, person who makes a tour; formed from English *tour,* n. + *-ist.*

tour de force feat of skill or ingenuity. 1802, borrowing of French *tour de force,* literally, feat of strength.

tournament *n.* contest in some sport or game. Probably before 1200 *turnement* medieval contest between groups of knights on horseback, in *Ancrene Riwle;* borrowed from Old French *torneiement* a tournament (in Medieval Latin *tornamentum*), from *torneier* to joust, tilt; see TOURNEY; for suffix see -MENT. The later spellings in English were probably influenced by the Medieval Latin form. The generalized sense of a contest in any game or sport in which competitors play a series of selective games (as in *a chess or tennis tournament*) is first recorded in 1761.

tourney (tėr′nē) *v.* take part in a tournament. Probably before 1300 *tourneyen,* in *Kyng Alisaunder;* borrowed from Old French *torneier* to joust, tilt, tourney; literally, turn around, from Vulgar Latin **tornizāre,* from Latin *tornāre* to TURN. **—n.** tournament. Probably before 1300, borrowed from Old French *tornei,* from *torneier* to tourney.

tourniquet (tür′nəket) *n.* device for stopping bleeding by compressing a blood vessel. 1695, borrowing of French *tourniquet* turnstile, surgical tourniquet (with diminutive suffix), from *torner* to turn, from Old French *tourner, torner* TURN.

tousle (tou′zəl) *v.* make untidy, disorder, dishevel, rumple. About 1440 *touselen,* frequentative form of earlier *-tousen* handle or push about roughly (about 1300), as in *totousen, betousen;* for suffix see -LE[3]. Middle English *-tousen* is cognate with East Frisian *tūsen* to pull about, treat roughly, Old High German *-zūsōn* in *zirzūsōn* pull to pieces (modern German *zausen* pull about, tousle), from Proto-Germanic **tūs-*. Cognates outside Germanic include Latin *dūmus,* Old Latin *dŭsmos* brier bush, and Old Irish *doss* bush, from Indo-European **dus-/dūs-* (Pok.178). **—n.** 1788, a struggle, tussle, in Robert Galloway's *Poems;* from the verb. The sense of a tousled or disordered mass is first recorded in 1880.

tout *v.* Before 1700 (as a slang word) to act as a lookout, spy on; developed from Middle English *tuten* to peep, peer (before 1400), probably related to Old English (before 899) *tōtian* to stick out, peep, peer. The extended informal sense of look out busily for, try to get (customers, jobs, votes, etc.), is first recorded in 1731. The sense of praise highly and insistently is first cited in 1920. **—n.** person who touts. 1718, slang word for thieves' scout or watchman; from the verb. The informal sense of a person who busily solicits customers, etc., is first recorded in 1853.

tow[1] *v.* pull by a rope, chain, etc. About 1300 *togen,* in a version of Layamon's *Chronicle of Britain;* later *towen* (probably about 1350); developed from Old English (about 1000) *togian* to drag, pull; cognate with Old Frisian *togia* to draw, tug, drag, Middle Low German *togen,* Old High German *zogōn,* Old Icelandic *toga* to draw, pull, from Proto-Germanic **tuȝōjanan;* related to Old English *tēon* to draw, Old Saxon *tiohan,* Old High German *ziohan* (modern German *ziehen*), and Gothic *tiuhan,* from Proto-Germanic **teuHanan.* Cognates outside Germanic include Latin *dux* leader, *ē-dūcāre* bring up, *dūcere* to lead, draw, Middle Welsh *dygaf* I bring, Albanian *nduk* I pull out, pluck, and the Greek intensive *daidýssesthai* be dragged, from Indo-European **deuk-/duk-* (Pok.220). The Middle English spelling with *-og-* quickly shifted to *-ow-* on the model of earlier shifting as found in *bow*[2] where Old English *o* in *-og-* became *ō* and *g* became *w*. **—n.** 1600, rope used for towing, in Hakluyt's *Voyages;* later, act of towing (1622); from the verb. **—towage** *n.* act of towing or charge for towing a vessel, vehicle, etc. 1562, formed from *tow,* v. + *-age.* The Medieval Latin form *towagium* (1286), found as *towage* once in Middle English (before 1327), may have been formed from Old English *togian* or Old Icelandic *toga.*

tow[2] *n.* coarse, broken fibers of flax, hemp, etc. Probably before 1387, in a version of *Piers Plowman;* developed from Old English *tōw-* spinning, as in *tōwlīc* fit for spinning; perhaps cognate with Old Icelandic *tō* unworked fiber, tuft of wool for spinning, and Gothic *taui* work, doing, *taujan* to do, make; see TOOL. **—adj.** made from tow. 1601, in Holland's translation of Pliny's *Natural History;* from the noun. **—towhead** *n.* person with white or pale yellow hair (1830, American English).

toward *prep.* Probably before 1200 *touward;* earlier *toweard* (1114); found in Old English (before 899, in Alfred's translation of Orosius' *Historiarum Adversus Paganos*) *tōweard* in the direction of, prepositional use of *tōweard,* adj., coming, approaching (*tō* TO + *-weard* -WARD), and perhaps a shortening both in Middle English and Old English of the synonymous *towards,* developed from Old English *tōweardes* (before 899, also in Alfred's writings); formed from *tōweard,* adj. + *-es, -s* adverbial genitive ending. **—adj.** About 1350 *toward* impending, about to happen, promising, hopeful; earlier *touward* (about 1290); developed from Old English *tōweard* coming to or toward, about to come, future (*tō* to + *-weard* tending or leading to, found in the modern adjective and adverb suffix *-ward*).

towel *n.* About 1250 *towaille* piece of cloth for wiping or drying something; borrowed from Old French *toaille,* from Frankish **thwahlja* (compare Old High German *dwahila, dwehila* towel, Middle Dutch *dwāle, dwēle,* modern Dutch *dwaal* altar cloth, and Old Saxon *thwahila, twahila* towel from Proto-Germanic **thwaHlijan*). In reconstructing the Frankish **thwahlja* it is also useful to compare Old English *thwēal* a washing, Old Icelandic *thvāl* soap, Gothic *thwahl* a washing, Germanic nouns derived from a Proto-Germanic verb **thwaHanan* represented by Old English *thwēan* to wash, Old Saxon *thwahan,* Old High German *dwahan,* Old Icelandic *thvā,* Gothic *thwahan,* and Old Prussian *twaxtan* bath mop, from Indo-European **twak-* bathe (Pok.1098). **—v.** 1836-39, to rub or dry with a towel, in Dickens' *Sketches by Boz;* from the noun.

tower *n.* Before 1121 *tur* high structure, in *Peterborough Chronicle;* developed from Old English *torr* (about 899, in Alfred's translation of St. Gregory's *Pastoral Care*); borrowed from Latin *turris* high structure, which, like Greek *týrris,* dialectal variant of *týrsis,* is a borrowing from some Mediterranean language. The word was also reborrowed in the Middle English period as *tour* (before 1300), from Old French *tur, tour,* from Latin *turris.* The present form *tower* (first recorded in 1526) is probably the result of a blend of Middle English *tur* and *tour,* with replacement of *ou* by *ow* in *towr* (first found in 1382). **—v.** to rise high. 1582, in a translation of Vergil's *Aeneid* (but found earlier as the past participle *towered,* before 1400, either implying a verb or formed from *tower,* n. + *-ed*[2]); from the noun.

town *n.* About 1330 *toun,* developed from Old English (601-04) *tūn* enclosure, enclosed land with its buildings; later, village (about 700); cognate with Old Frisian, Old Saxon, and Middle Low German *tūn* enclosure, fence, hedge, Middle Dutch *taun* (modern Dutch *tuin* garden), Old High German *zūn* (modern German *Zaun*), Old Icelandic *tūn,* from Proto-Germanic **tūnaz, tūnan,* borrowed extremely early from Celtic **dūnom* (compare Old Irish *dūn* fortress); see DOWN[3]. The modern sense in English of an inhabited place larger and more regularly built than a village is first recorded after the Norman Conquest, and corresponds to the French *ville* town, city, as similarly developed from Latin *vīlla* farm, country house. **—town crier** (in former times) person who made public announcements in a town (1602, in Shakespeare's *Hamlet*). **—town hall** (1481-90) **—townhouse** *n.* 1530, town hall; later a house in town (1771), and one of a row of attached houses (1965, earlier *terrace house* 1817, in Jane Austen's writings). **—town line** (1645, in American English) **—town meeting** (1636) **—townsfolk** *n.* (1737 *townsfolks;* 1866 *townsfolk*) **—township** *n.* 1414 *tounshipe,* developed from Old English *tūnscipe* (before 899, in Alfred's translation of Bede's *Ecclesiastical History*) inhabitants or population of a town (*tūn* village + *-scipe* -ship). **—townsman** *n.* 1433, developed from Old English (962-63) *tūnesman* villager, formed from *tūn* village + *-es,* genitive suffix + *man* person. **—townspeople** *n.* (1648, in letters of Cromwell)

toxic *adj.* poisonous. 1664, in Evelyn's *Sylva;* borrowed from French *toxique,* and directly from Late Latin *toxicus* poisoned, from Latin *toxicum* poison, from Greek *toxikòn (phármakon)* (poison) for use on arrows, from *toxikón,* neuter of *toxikós* pertaining to arrows or archery, and thus to a bow, from *tóxon* bow, from Scythian (ancient Iranian) *taHša-;* for suffix see -IC. **—toxicity** *n.* 1881, formed from English *toxic* + *-ity.* **—toxicologist** *n.* expert in toxicology. 1829-32, formed from English *toxicology* + *-ist.* **—toxicology** *n.* study of poisons. 1799, formed in English from Latin *toxicum* poison + English connective *-o-* + *-logy.*

toxin *n.* poisonous product of an animal or plant. 1886, formed in English from Latin *toxicum* poison; see TOXIC + English *-in*[2], chemical suffix.

toy *n.* About 1303 *toye* amorous playing, sport, in Mannyng's *Handlyng Synne;* later *toy* a piece of fun or entertainment (before 1500); then, a thing of little value, trifle (1530, in Palsgrave's *Lesclarcissement*); and a thing for a child to play with, plaything (before 1586, in Sidney's *The Arcadia*). The origin of the word is uncertain. If instead, the chronologically last and now most common meaning, thing to play with, plaything, represents a different word than the earlier meanings, it is possible that *toy* was borrowed from Dutch *tuig* tools, apparatus, stuff, trash, *speeltuig* play-tool, plaything, toy, cognate with German *Zeug* stuff, gear, *Spielzeug* plaything, toy, and Danish *tøi* stuff, gear, *legetøi* playthings, toys. **—v.** Before 1529, act idly or without seriousness, trifle, play, in Skelton's *The Bowge of Courte;* from the noun. **—toy dog** very small dog (1806, in the *Journals* of Lewis and Clark). This sense of *toy* a small article, is first recorded in Shakespeare's *The Taming of the Shrew* (1596).

trace[1] *v.* follow by means of marks, tracks, or signs. 1381 *tracen* traverse, pass over, tread, in Chaucer's *Parlement of Foules;* borrowed from Old French *trasser, tracier* delineate, score, trace, follow, pursue, from Vulgar Latin **tractiāre* delineate, score, trace, from Latin *tractus* (genitive *tractūs*) track, course; literally, a drawing out, from *trac-*, stem of *trahere* to pull, draw; see TRACT[1].

The sense of draw, draw an outline of, is first recorded in Middle English about 1393. The sense of follow the tracks or traces of is found in Middle English about 1450. The figurative sense of follow the course, development, or history of occurs in English in 1654.
—n. footprint or other mark left; track, trail. Probably before 1300, path, course, track, in *Kyng Alisaunder;* borrowed from Old French *trace,* from *tracier* to trace. The plural *traces,* in the sense of vestiges or indications, is first recorded in Middle English about 1400.
—tracer *n.* 1552, person who tracks or investigates, in Huloet's *Abecedarium Anglico Latinum;* formed from English *trace*[1] + *-er*[1]. The sense of a bullet that emits a visible trail is first recorded in 1910; the sense of a substance (such as a radioactive isotope) that can be observed as it passes through something, especially a system of the body, is first recorded in 1938. **—tracing** *n.* 1523, tracks of an animal; formed from English *trace*[1] + *-ing*[1]. The sense of a copy made by drawing over something is first recorded in 1811, though probably occurring much earlier, as the corresponding verb sense is found about 1393.

trace[2] *n.* either of the two straps, ropes, or chains by which an animal pulls a vehicle. About 1400 *trays,* new singular (1404, plural *trasys*), developed from earlier collective plural *trays* (about 1330); borrowed from Old French *traiz,* plural of *trait* strap for harnessing, act of drawing, from Latin *tractus* (genitive *tractūs*) a drawing, track, from *trac-*, stem of *trahere* to pull, draw; see TRACT[1].

tracery *n.* ornamental work of very fine lines, as in a large stained glass window. 1669, in writings of Sir Christopher Wren; formed from English *trace*[1], v. + *-ery.*

trachea (trā′kēə) *n.* windpipe. 1392, borrowing of Medieval Latin *trachea,* as in *trachea arteria,* from Late Latin *trāchīa,* from Greek *trācheîa,* in *trācheîa ārtēríā* windpipe; literally, rough artery (so called from the rings of cartilage forming the trachea), from feminine of *trāchýs* rough; see ARTERY for Greek use of the word for windpipe. Greek *trāchýs* is related to *thrā́ssein* make uneasy, and *tarássein* disturb, cognate with Old Icelandic *dregg* yeast, dregs, from Indo-European **dherəgh-/dhr̥gh-* (Pok.251).

trachoma (trəkō′mə) *n.* contagious inflammation of the eyelids. 1693, New Latin, from Greek *trā́chōma* roughness, from *trāchýs* rough.

track *n.* Before 1470, footprint, mark left by anything, in Malory's *Morte d'Arthur;* borrowed from Middle French *trac,* of uncertain origin; possibly from a Germanic source (compare Middle Low German and Middle Dutch *trek, treck,* and modern Dutch *trek* a drawing, pull, haul, TREK). The sense of a line of metal rails for wheeled vehicles to run on is first recorded in 1805. **—v.** 1565, follow the track of; from the noun.
—track and field (1905) **—trackless** *adj.* 1656, without tracks or paths; formed from English *track,* n. + *-less.*
—track record 1915, record of speed in a race; later, any record of achievement (1957).

tract[1] *n.* extent, region, area. 1441, period or lapse of time; borrowed from Latin *tractus* (genitive *tractūs*) track, course, space, duration; literally, a drawing out or pulling, from *trac-*, stem of *trahere* to pull, draw. Latin *trahere* is cognate with Old Irish *traig* foot, and Welsh *traed* feet, from Indo-European **tragh-* pull, move, run (Pok.1089). The sense of a stretch of land or water, extent, region, area, is first recorded in English in 1553.

tract[2] *n.* little book or pamphlet on a religious or political subject. Before 1398 *tracte,* in Trevisa's translation of Bartholomew's *De Proprietatibus Rerum;* probably a shortened form of Latin *tractātus* (genitive *tractātūs*) a handling, treatise, treatment, from *tractāre* to handle, TREAT.

tractable *adj.* easily managed or controlled, docile. Probably before 1425, in a translation of Chauliac's *Grande Chirurgie;* borrowed from Latin *tractābilis* that may be touched, handled, or managed, from *tractāre* to handle, manage; see TREAT; for suffix see -ABLE.

traction *n.* 1615, a drawing or pulling of a part or organ (as by a device); borrowed from Medieval Latin *tractionem* (nominative *tractio*) a drawing, from Latin *trac-*, stem of *trahere* to pull, draw; see TRACT[1]; for suffix see -TION. The sense of the rolling friction of a vehicle is not recorded until 1825.

tractor *n.* 1856, something that pulls; earlier, a quack device, consisting of two metal rods for relieving pain of rheumatism (1798); borrowed from Medieval Latin *tractor,* from Latin *trac-*, stem of *trahere* to pull, draw; see TRACT[1]; for suffix see -OR[2]. The sense of an engine or vehicle for pulling wagons or plows, or for excavating, grading, etc., is first recorded in 1901, the earlier term being *traction engine* (1859); the extended sense of a powerful truck for pulling a freight trailer is found in 1926.

trade *n.* About 1375, path, track, course of action; borrowed from Middle Dutch or Middle Low German *trade* track, course (probably originally, of a trading ship); cognate with Old Saxon *trada* footstep, track, Old High German *trata* track, way, passage, and Old English *tredan* to TREAD.

The sense of one's habitual business or occupation is first recorded in 1546, as a development from the earlier meaning of way, course, or manner of life; the sense developed by contextual additions, such as *trade* (i.e. practice) *of fishing, of husbandry, of merchandise,* etc. This was closely followed by the sense of buying and selling or exchange of commodities, commerce, traffic, first recorded in 1555.
—v. engage in trade. 1548, to tread, traverse, go through; from the noun. The sense of engage in trade, buy and sell, is first recorded in 1570.
—trademark *n.* (1838) **—trade name** (1861) **—trade school** (1898) **—tradesman** *n.* 1597, craftsman; later, trader, shopkeeper (1601). **—tradespeople** *n.* (1728) **—trade union** (1831) **—trade wind** (1650; *trade* in the obsolete sense of habitual or regular course) **—trading post** (1796, American English) **—trading stamp** stamp that can be exchanged in quantity for goods (1897).

tradition *n.* About 1382 *tradicion* a belief, practice, or custom handed down, in the Wycliffe Bible; borrowed from Old French *tradicion,* learned borrowing from Latin, and borrowed into English directly from Latin *trāditiōnem* (nominative *trāditiō*) delivery, surrender, a handing down, from *trādi-*, stem of *trādere* deliver, hand over (*trāns-* over + *dare* give; see DATE[1] time); for suffix see -TION. Doublet of TREASON. **—traditional** *adj.* 1594, observant or bound by tradition, in Shakespeare's *Richard III;* formed from English *tradition* + *-al*[1]. The sense of handed down by or derived from tradition is recorded before 1600.

traduce *v.* speak evil of (someone) falsely, slander. Before 1533, to alter, change over, transport, also, to translate; borrowed directly from Latin *trādūcere* change over, convert; originally, lead along or across, transfer (*trāns-* across; see TRANS- + *dūcere* lead; see TOW[1] pull). The sense of speak evil of, defame, malign, slander, first recorded in 1586-87, was probably borrowed from one of the senses of Latin *trādūcere* to lead along as a spectacle, exhibit or expose (especially captives, prisoners, etc.) to scorn or disgrace. **—traducer** *n.* slanderer. 1614, in Raleigh's *The History of the World;* formed from English *traduce* + *-er*[1].

traffic *n.* 1505 *traffikke* trade, commerce; borrowed from Middle French *trafique, trafficque;* later *traffic,* from Italian *traffico,* from *trafficare* carry on trade, of uncertain origin. Corominas, in an analysis similar to that of the OED, proposes as the source of the Italian verb a Vulgar Latin **trānsfricāre* to rub across (Latin *trāns-* across + *fricāre* to rub) with the original sense of the Italian verb being that of to touch repeatedly, handle. In the 1800's other suggestions included an origin in Arabic *taraffaga* seek profit, but modern scholars no longer accept this. The meaning of people or vehicles coming and going along a way of travel is first recorded in English before 1825. The spelling *traffic* became prevalent in the 1700's. —**v.** 1542, carry on trade; borrowed from Middle French *trafiquer,* from Italian *trafficare.* **—traffic circle** rotary intersection (1942, American English). **—traffic jam** (1917) **—traffic light** (1912, light for guiding aircraft; 1926, light for regulating road traffic)

tragedy *n.* About 1375 *tragedie* a play or other serious literary work having an unhappy ending, in Chaucer's *Canterbury Tales;* borrowed from Old French *tragedie,* learned borrowing from Latin *tragoedia* a tragedy (in Medieval Latin, lofty style; also, a great commotion or disturbance), from Greek *tragōidíā* a dramatic poem or play in formal or stately language and action having an unhappy resolution; literally, goat song (*trágos* goat; see TRAGIC + *ōidḗ* song, ODE); for suffix see -Y[2]. Several theories have been proposed to explain the connection with a goat, one being that the actors or singers in Greek tragedies were originally dressed in goatskins to represent satyrs, and thereby became actors in satyric drama from which tragedy was later developed; alternatively, a goat may have been the prize for the best performance.

The generalized sense of a part of drama that deals with or includes tragedies is first recorded in Middle English in 1412-20. The figurative sense of an unhappy event, calamity, or disaster, is found in 1509. **—tragedian** *n.* About 1380, writer of tragedies, in Chaucer's translation of Boethius' *De Consolatione Philosophiae;* borrowed from Old French *tragedian,* from *tragedie* tragedy; for suffix see -IAN. The sense of a tragic actor is first recorded in 1592.

tragic *adj.* 1545, calamitous, disastrous, fatal; shortened form of earlier *tragical* (1489); modeled on Latin *tragicus* of or pertaining to tragedy (as an art), from Greek *tragikós* of or pertaining to tragedy; literally, of or pertaining to a goat, and probably to a satyr impersonated by a goat singer or satyric actor, goatish, from *trágos* goat; literally, nibbler, from *trageîn,* single-act infinitive of *trṓgein* to gnaw, nibble; see DETERGENT; for suffix see -IC, -ICAL. The sense of pertaining to tragedy as a part of drama, of the nature of or acting in tragedies, is first recorded in English in 1563. The original meaning of this word in English was influenced by the figurative sense of *tragedy.*

tragicomedy *n.* play having both tragic and comic elements. 1579-80, in a translation of Plutarch's *Lives;* borrowed from Middle French *tragicomédie,* from Italian *tragicommedia,* from Latin *tragicōmoedia,* contraction of *tragicocōmoedia* (*tragicus* TRAGIC + *cōmoedia* COMEDY). **—tragicomic** *adj.* 1683, shortened form of earlier *tragicomical* (1567, formed from *tragi-* + *comical*); for suffix see -IC, -ICAL.

trail *v.* About 1303 *trailen* to drag or be drawn along behind, in Mannyng's *Handlyng Synne;* borrowed from Old French *trailler* to tow, from Vulgar Latin **trāgulāre* to drag, from Latin *trāgula* dragnet, probably related to *trahere* to pull, draw; see TRACT[1]. The meaning of follow the trail or track of is first recorded in English in 1590. **—n.** Probably before 1325, something that trails, in *Cursor Mundi;* from the verb. The sense of a track or smell left by a person or animal is first recorded in 1590. The chiefly American and Canadian sense of a path or track worn by the passage of persons across a wild or unsettled region is first recorded in 1807. **—trailblazer** *n.* 1908, person who blazes or marks a trail; later, pioneer, person who prepares the way to something new (1937). **—trailer** *n.* 1590, person that follows a trail, tracker; formed from English *trail,* v. + *-er*[1]. The sense of a vehicle to be pulled by another vehicle is first recorded in 1890. The transferred sense of an excerpt of a film, telecast, etc., used as advanced publicity, is first recorded in 1928, in American English.

train *n.* Before 1338 *trayne* a drawing out, delay, in Mannyng's *Chronicle of England;* later *trayn* trailing part, retinue, procession (about 1440); borrowed from Old French *traïn* (feminine *traïne*), from *traïner* to pull, draw, from Vulgar Latin **tragīnāre,* extended from **tragere* to pull, back formation (on the analogy of *agere, āctus*) from *tractus,* past participle of Latin *trahere* to pull, draw; see TRACT[1]. The sense of a connected line of railroad cars or wagons moving together is first recorded before 1824, originally used contextually in such phrases as *a train of wagons, a train of cars,* etc. **—v.** 1375 *traynen* to draw along, allure, in Barbour's *The Bruce;* borrowed from Old French *traïner* to pull, draw. The sense of instruct, discipline, teach, is first recorded in 1542, probably developed from the earlier meaning of draw by persuasion, persuade, induce, convert (1526), and to treat or manipulate in order to bring to a proper or desired form (about 1440). **—trainee** *n.* 1841, person or animal undergoing training, formed from English *train,* v. + *-ee.* **—training** *n.* 1440, a drawing out, trailing; formed from Middle English *traynen* draw along + *-ing*[1]. The sense of instruction, discipline, education, is first recorded in 1548. **—trainload** *n.* (1882) **—trainman** *n.* (1881, American English)

traipse *v.* walk about aimlessly. 1593 (implied in *trapesing*), of uncertain origin. The dialectal forms *trapass, traipass* strongly echo dialectal French *trapasser, trepasser* pass over or beyond (Old French *trespasser* TRESPASS), though the senses do not fit exactly.

trait *n.* characteristic. About 1477, shot, missiles, in Caxton's translation of *The History of Jason;* later, a stroke, short line (1589); borrowed from Middle French *trait,* from Latin *tractus* (genitive *tractūs*) draft, drawing,

drawing out; later, line drawn, feature, from *trac-*, stem of *trahere* to pull, draw; see TRACT[1]. The sense of a particular feature of mind or character, distinguishing quality, characteristic, is first recorded in English in 1752, in Walpole's *Letters;* this sense developed from the meaning of a line, streak, stroke, stripe, feature, found also in part, in earlier English, French, and Latin.

traitor *n.* Before 1300 *traitur* person who betrays a trust, betrayer, in *Cursor Mundi;* borrowed from Old French *traitor, traitur,* from Latin *trāditōrem* (nominative *trāditor*) one who betrays, a betrayer; literally, one who delivers, from *trādi-*, stem of *trādere* deliver, surrender, hand over; see TRADITION; for suffix see -OR[2]. An earlier Middle English form *treitre* (probably before 1200, in *Ancrene Riwle*) was borrowed from Old French *traitre,* from Latin *trāditor.*

In early use the word was often applied to Judas Iscariot. The extended sense of one who betrays his country, one guilty of treason, is first recorded in Middle English about 1300.

—traitorous *adj.* About 1380 *traytrous* having the character of a traitor, in *Sir Ferumbras;* borrowed from Old French *traitreux* (*traitre* traitor + *-eux* -ous).

trajectory *n.* curved path of a projectile, comet, etc. 1696, borrowed from New Latin *trajectoria,* from feminine of *trajectorius* of or for throwing across, from Latin *trājectus* thrown over or across, past participle of *trāicere* throw across (Latin *trā-*, variant of *trāns-* across + *-icere,* combining form of *jacere* to throw; see JET[1] stream); for suffix see -ORY. An isolated Middle English use of this word is found probably before 1425, in a translation of Chauliac's *Grande Chirurgie,* where *traiectorie* is used in the sense of a funnel, borrowed from Middle French *trajectoire* end of a funnel, and directly from Medieval Latin *trajectorium* a funnel (from Latin *trājectus,* past participle + *-ōrium* -ory).

tram *n.* streetcar. 1500-20, beam or shaft of a barrow or sledge, in William Dunbar's *Poems;* also, a barrow or truck body (1516-17); Scottish; borrowed probably from Middle Flemish *tram* beam, handle of a barrow, bar, rung, which is cognate with Middle Low German *trame,* modern Low German *Traam,* and Middle Dutch *trame,* of similar meaning, of unknown origin. The sense of a track for a barrow, sledge, etc., tramway, is first recorded in 1826. The sense of streetcar is first recorded in 1879, though its earlier use is implied in *tramway* (1860). **—tramway** *n.* 1825, track for a barrow, etc.; later, track for a streetcar (1860).

trammel *n.* anything that hinders or restrains. 1397 *trameyle* a net to catch fish; borrowed from Middle French *tramail,* from Late Latin *trimaculum, trēmaculum,* perhaps meaning a net made of three layers of different-sized meshes (Latin *tri-, trēs* three + *macula* a mesh; originally, a spot, mark, of uncertain origin). The transferred and figurative sense of anything that hinders or impedes free action is first recorded before 1653. —**v.** 1536, to bind up (a corpse); from the noun. The figurative sense of catch or entangle as if in a trammel is first found in Shakespeare's *Macbeth* (1605), and that of to hinder, restrain, in Pope's letters, in 1727.

tramp *v.* About 1395 *trampen* walk heavily, stamp, in the Wycliffe Bible; borrowed from Middle Low German *trampen* to stamp; cognate with Middle High German *trumpfen* to run, dialectal Norwegian *trumpa* to knock, push, and Gothic *anatrimpan* to tread or press upon, perhaps ultimately related to the same source as English TRAP. —**n.** 1664, person who wanders about, vagabond; from the verb. The sense of a long, steady walk, is first recorded in 1760.

trample *v.* Before 1382 *tramplen* to walk heavily, in the Wycliffe Bible; frequentative form of TRAMP; for suffix see -LE[3]. The transitive sense of tread heavily on, crush, is first recorded in Palsgrave's *Lesclarcissement* (1530). —**n.** act or sound of trampling. 1604, from the verb.

trampoline *n.* piece of fabric stretched on a metal frame, used for acrobatics. 1798 *trampolin,* 1799 *trampoline;* borrowed from Spanish *trampolín* springboard, and from Italian *trampolino,* from *tràmpoli* stilts, from a Germanic source (compare Low German *trampeln* trample, and Middle Low German *trampen* walk heavily, TRAMP). Earliest use in English refers to a springboard or canvas sheet (perhaps at first used to toss acrobats in the air, suggesting a similar use found in *canvas, canvass*) but slightly later use refers to stilts and suggests separate borrowing from Italian.

trance *n.* About 1385 *traunce* state of extreme dread or suspense, in Chaucer's *Troilus and Criseyde;* later, a dazed, unconscious, or insensible condition (about 1395, in Chaucer's *Canterbury Tales*); borrowed from Old French *transe* fear of coming evil; originally, passage (especially from life to death), from *transir* be numb with fear; originally, die, pass on, from Latin *trānsīre* cross over; see TRANSIENT. The meaning of a state of mental abstraction, exaltation, rapture, ecstasy, is recorded in Middle English in 1434. —**v.** 1350 *trauncen, transen* to die, faint, be in extreme dread, borrowed from Old French *transir;* see the noun. The sense of entrance, enrapture, is first recorded in 1597-98.

tranquil *adj.* calm. Before 1450 *tranquill,* probably a back formation from earlier *tranquility,* modeled on Latin *tranquillus* quiet, tranquil, of uncertain origin. It is also possible, that in some later instances, *tranquil* was borrowed from Middle French *tranquille.* Some scholars derive the Latin word from *trāns-* over, beyond (here apparently meaning exceedingly) + a root related to *quiēs* rest, QUIET. **—tranquility** or **tranquillity** *n.* About 1380 *tranquillite* quality or state of being tranquil, in Chaucer's translation of Boethius' *De Consolatione Philosophiae;* borrowed from Old French *tranquillité,* learned borrowing from Latin *tranquillitātem* (nominative *tranquillitās*) tranquilness, from *tranquillus* tranquil; for suffix see -ITY. **—tranquilize** *v.* 1623, make tranquil, in Cockeram's *Dictionary;* formed from English *tranquil* + *-ize.* **—tranquilizer** *n.* 1800, something that tranquilizes; formed from English *tranquilize* + *-er*[1]. The specific sense of a sedative is first recorded in 1824, but did not come into widespread use until the 1950's.

trans- a prefix meaning: **1** across, over, through, as in *transcontinental* = *across the continent* (1853), *transatlantic* = *across the Atlantic Ocean* (1779). **2** beyond, on the other side of, as in *transcend* = *to go beyond, transatlantic* = *on the other side of the Atlantic Ocean* (1782). **3** to go into a different place, condition, or thing, as in *transform* = *to form into another condition.* **4** (in chemistry) having certain atoms on the opposite side of a plane: *a trans-isomeric compound.* Borrowed from Latin *trāns-* (also reduced to *trā-*, as in *trādere* hand over, *trādūcere* lead across), from *trāns,* prep., across, over, beyond, thought to be originally the present participle of a verb (**trāre*) meaning to cross; see THROUGH.

transact *v.* attend to, manage, do. 1584-85, probably a back formation from *transaction,* modeled on Latin *trānsāctus,* past participle of *trānsigere* drive or carry through, accomplish, complete, finish, perform (*trāns-* through + *agere* to drive; see AGENT). **—transaction** *n.* About 1460, (in Roman and civil law) adjustment of a dispute by mutual concession; borrowed from Middle French *transaction,* and directly from Latin *trānsāctiōnem* (nominative *trānsāctiō*) an agreement, completion, accomplishment, from *trānsigere* accomplish; for suffix see -TION. The sense of a piece of business is first recorded in 1647.

transceiver *n.* a combined radio transmitter and receiver. 1934, formed from English *trans(mitter)* + *(re)ceiver.*

transcend *v.* go beyond the limits or powers of. About 1340 *transcenden;* borrowed from Old French *transcendre,* and directly from Latin *trānscendere* climb over or beyond, surmount (*trāns-* beyond + *scandere* to climb; see SCAN). **—transcendence** *n.* 1601, in Shakespeare's *All's Well That Ends Well;* formed in English as a noun to *transcendent,* possibly on the model of Late Latin *trānscendentia* character of being transcendent, elevation, loftiness, from Latin *trānscendēns* transcending, present participle of *trānscendere* climb over or beyond; for suffix see -ENCE. **—transcendent** *adj.* About 1450, borrowed from Latin *trānscendentem* (nominative *trānscendēns*) surmounting, rising above, present participle; for suffix see -ENT. **—transcendental** *adj.* 1668, (in Aristotelian philosophy) transcending the bounds of any category; borrowed from Medieval Latin *transcendentalis* in the same meaning, from Latin *trānscendēns* extending beyond, present participle of *trānscendere* climb over or beyond; for suffix see -AL[1]. The Kantian sense of not derived from experience, but concerned with the presuppositions of experience, is first recorded in 1798. **—transcendentalism** *n.* 1803, transcendental philosophy; formed from English *transcendental* + *-ism. Transcendentalism* as the name of the teachings and philosophy of Emerson and his followers appeared in 1827, in the writings of Emerson.

transcribe *v.* to copy in writing from an original. 1552, in Huloet's *Abecedarium Anglico Latinum;* borrowed from Latin *trānscrībere* to copy, write again in another place, write over, transfer (*trāns-* over + *scrībere* write; see SCRIBE). The biological sense of synthesize a nucleic acid on a template so that genetic information is copied, is first recorded in 1962. **—transcript** *n.* 1467, a written copy; borrowed from Medieval Latin *transcriptum* a copy, noun use of Latin *trānscrīptus* transcribed, copied, neuter past participle of *trānscrībere* transcribe. **—transcription** *n.* 1598, act or process of transcribing, in Florio's *A World of Words;* borrowed from Middle French *transcription,* and directly from Latin *trānscrīptiōnem* (nominative *trānscrīptiō*), from *trānscrīptus,* past participle of *trānscrībere* transcribe; for suffix see -TION. The sense of a recording of a broadcast for later rebroadcast is first recorded in 1932. The sense in biology of the process by which a nucleic acid is synthesized on a template is first recorded in 1961.

transducer *n.* any device which converts energy from one form to another, such as a microphone that converts sound to electricity. 1924, formed in English from Latin *trānsdūcere* lead across, transfer (*trāns-* across + *dūcere* to lead) + English suffix *-er*[1]. **—transduce** *v.* to convert from one form of energy to another. 1949, back formation from earlier *transducer.*

transept *n.* the shorter part of a cross-shaped church. 1538 *transsept,* borrowed from New Latin *transeptum;* later, in the 1700's, borrowed from French *transept;* both the New Latin and modern French words were formed from Latin *trāns-* across + *saeptum* fence, partition, enclosure; see SEPTUM.

transfer *v.* About 1380 *transferren* move from one place to another, convey, transmit, in Chaucer's translation of Boethius' *De Consolatione Philosophiae;* borrowed from Latin *trānsferre* bear across, carry over, transfer, translate (*trāns-* across + *ferre* to carry, BEAR[2]). **—n.** 1674, (in law) conveyance of property; from the verb. The general sense of a transferring or being transferred (as in *the transfer of authority*) is first recorded in 1785, in Burke's correspondence. **—transference** *n.* 1681, procedure for transferring a legal action; probably formed from English *transfer* + *-ence,* modeled on New Latin *transferentia* transference, from Latin *trānsferēns* transferring, present participle of *trānsferre* to transfer; for suffix see -ENCE. The meaning in psychoanalysis of a transfer of feelings and desires from one person to another is first recorded in 1911, as a loan translation of German *Übertragung.*

transfigure *v.* change in form or appearance. Before 1325 *transfiguren,* in *Cursor Mundi;* borrowed from Old French *transfigurer,* and directly from Latin *trānsfigūrāre* change the shape of (*trāns-* across + *figūra* FIGURE). **—transfiguration** *n.* About 1375, (in the Bible) the change in the appearance of Christ before his disciples, John, Peter, and James; borrowed from Old French *transfiguration,* and directly from Latin *trānsfigūrātiōnem* (nominative *trānsfigūrātiō*) a change in form, from *trānsfigūrāre* transfigure; for suffix see -ATION. The sense of the action of transfiguring or state of being transfigured (as in *the mythical transfiguration of men into animals*) is first recorded in English before 1548.

transfix *v.* 1590, pierce through, impale, in Spenser's *Faerie Queene;* borrowed from Middle French *transfixer,* and directly from Latin *trānsfixus* impaled, past participle of *trānsfigere* to impale, pierce through (*trāns-* through + *figere* to fix, fasten; see DIKE). The figurative sense of make motionless or helpless (as with amazement, terror, or grief) is first recorded in Lovelace's *Poems* (1649).

transform (transfôrm′) *v.* About 1340 *transformen* change the form of, in Richard Rolle's *English Prose Treatises;* borrowed from Old French *transformer,* and directly from Latin *trānsfōrmāre* change the shape or form of (*trāns-* across + *fōrmāre* to FORM). The meaning in mathematics of change (a figure, term, etc.) to a different form with the same value is first recorded in 1743. **—n.** (trans′fôrm) 1853, (in mathematics) the result of transforming; from the verb. **—transformation** *n.* 1410 *transformacioun* act of transforming; borrowed from Old French *transformation,* and directly from Late Latin *trānsfōrmātiōnem* (nominative *trānsfōrmātiō*) a change of shape, from *trānsfōrmāre* change the shape of, transform; for suffix see -ATION. **—transformational** *adj.* 1955, of or having to do with a system of grammar using rearrangement of structure of spoken and written forms for analysis. **—transformer** *n.* 1601, person who transforms; formed from English *transform* + *-er*[1]. The sense of a device which reduces (transforms) electric currents from one voltage to another is first recorded in 1883 as a translation of French *transformateur.*

transfuse *v.* to flow or pour from one to another. Probably before 1425 *transfusen,* in a translation of Chauliac's *Grande Chirurgie;* borrowed from Latin *trānsfūsus,* past participle of *trānsfundere* pour from one container to another (*trāns-* across + *fundere* to pour; see FOUND² cast metal). The medical sense of transfer (blood from one individual) into the veins of another is first recorded in English in 1666, probably as a back formation from *transfusion.* —**transfusion** *n.* 1578, act of pouring a liquid from one container into another; borrowed from Middle French *transfusion,* and directly from Latin *trānsfūsiōnem* (nominative *trānsfūsiō*) a pouring from one container to another, from *trānsfūsus,* past participle of *trānsfundere;* for suffix see -SION. The sense of a transfer of blood from one individual into the veins of another is first recorded in English in 1643.

transgress *v.* About 1475 *transgressen* go beyond the limits prescribed by law, break a law or command; borrowed from Middle French *transgresser,* and probably a back formation from earlier *transgression,* modeled on Latin *trānsgressus,* past participle of *trānsgredī* go beyond (*trāns-* across + *gradī* to walk, go; see GRADE). —**transgression** *n.* About 1415 *transgrescion* violation of law, duty, or command, disobedience, trespass; borrowed from Middle French *transgression,* from Late Latin *trānsgressiōnem* (nominative *trānsgressiō*) a transgression of the law, from Latin in the generalized sense of a going over, from *trānsgressus,* past participle of *trānsgredī* go beyond; for suffix see -SION.

transient (tran′shənt) *adj.* passing soon, fleeting, not lasting. 1612, borrowed from Latin *trānsiēns* (accusative *trānseuntem*) passing over or away, present participle of *trānsīre* cross over, pass away (*trāns-* across + *īre* go; see EXIT); for suffix see -ENT. —**n.** 1652, transient thing or being; from the adjective. The sense of a transient guest or boarder is first recorded in 1748, in American English. —**transience** *n.* 1745, formed from English *transient* + *-ence,* possibly as a shortened form of *transiency* (1652, formed from English *transient* + *-ency*).

transistor *n.* electronic device that controls the flow of electricity in computers, radios, and other electronic equipment. 1948, formed from English *tran(sfer)* + *(re)sistor;* so called because it transfers an electrical current across a resistor. The sense of a transistorized radio is first recorded in 1961, from the earlier *transistor radio* (1955). —**transistorize** *v.* equip with transistors. 1953, formed from English *transistor* + *-ize.*

transit *n.* a passing across or through. 1440 *transite;* borrowed from Latin *trānsitus* (genitive *trānsitūs*) passage, transition, a going over, from *trānsi-,* stem of *trānsīre* cross over, go across; see TRANSIENT. The astronomical sense of the passage of a celestial body across the disk of a larger one is first recorded in English in 1669. As an instrument used in surveying *transit* is first recorded in 1862. —**v.** pass across or through. 1440 *transiten;* borrowed from Latin *trānsitus,* past participle of *trānsīre.* —**transition** *n.* About 1450 *transicion* a change or passing from one condition, place, etc. to another; borrowed from Latin *trānsitiōnem* (nominative *trānsitiō*) a passing over or away, from *trānsi-,* stem of *trānsīre* go or cross over; see TRANSIENT; for suffix see -TION. —**transitional** *adj.* About 1810, in Coleridge's *Literary Remains;* formed from English *transition* + *-al*¹. —**transitive** *adj.* 1560, passing away, transient; later, of or pertaining to a verb taking a direct object (1571, also earlier *transitory,* 1560); borrowed from Middle French *transitif* (feminine *transitive*), and directly from Late Latin *trānsitīvus* passing over, transitive in reference to verbs, from Latin *trānsitus,* past participle of *trānsīre* cross over; see TRANSIENT; for suffix see -IVE. —**transitory** *adj.* About 1380 *transitorie* passing soon or quickly, lasting only a short time, in Chaucer's translation of Boethius' *De Consolatione Philosophiae;* borrowed from Old French *transitoire,* from Late Latin *trānsitōrius* passing, transient, from Latin in the sense of having or allowing a passage through, from *trānsitus,* past participle of *trānsīre* go or cross over; see TRANSIENT; for suffix see -ORY.

translate *v.* Before 1325 *translaten* to transfer, change from one language to another, in *Cursor Mundi;* borrowed from Old French *translater,* but probably at first from Latin *trānslātus,* a form serving as past participle to *trānsferre* to bring over, carry over; see TRANSFER; for suffix see -ATE¹. —**translation** *n.* About 1340 *translacioun* act or process of changing from one language into another; borrowed from Old French *translation,* and directly from Latin *trānslātiōnem* (nominative *trānslātiō*) transference, translation, from *trānslātus,* a form serving as past participle to *trānsferre;* for suffix see -ATION.

transliterate *v.* change (letters, words, etc.) into corresponding characters of another alphabet or language; compare TRANSLATE. 1861, in writings of Max Müller; formed from English *trans-* across + Latin *lītera* LETTER + English suffix *-ate*¹. —**transliteration** *n.* 1861, act or process of transliterating, in writings of Max Müller; formed from English *trans-* across + Latin *lītera* letter + English suffix *-ation.*

translucent *adj.* letting light through without being transparent. 1596, formed in English as an adjective to earlier *translucence,* on the model of Latin *trānslūcentem* (nominative *trānslūcēns*) shining through, present participle of *trānslūcēre* shine through (*trāns-* through + *lūcēre* to shine; see LIGHT¹ radiant energy); for suffix see -ENT. —**translucence** *n.* quality or condition of being translucent. Probably before 1425, in a translation of Chauliac's *Grande Chirurgie;* formed in English as if from Latin **trānslūcentia,* from *trānslūcēns* shining through, present participle of *trānslūcēre* shine through; for suffix see -ENCE.

transmigration *n.* 1297, migration; borrowed from Old French *transmigration,* and directly from Late Latin *trānsmigrātiōnem* change of country, from Latin *trānsmigrāre* to migrate (*trāns-* over + *migrāre* to migrate).

transmission *n.* act or fact of transmitting. 1611, in Florio's *Queen Anna's New World of Words;* borrowed from Old French *transmission,* and directly from Latin *trānsmissiōnem* (nominative *trānsmissiō*) a sending over or across, passage, from *trānsmissus,* past participle of *trānsmittere* send over or across; see TRANSMIT; for suffix see -SION. The meaning of the part of a motor vehicle that regulates the transmission of power from the engine to the axle is first recorded in 1894. The sense of broadcast transmission is found as early as 1907. —**transmission line** high-tension electrical wires (1906).

transmit *v.* Probably before 1400 *transmitten* convey, transfer; borrowed from Latin *trānsmittere* send across, transfer, pass on (*trāns-* across + *mittere* send; see MISSION). —**transmitter** *n.* 1727, one that transmits; formed from English *transmit* + *-er*¹. The sense of a telegraphic or telephonic transmitting apparatus is first recorded in 1844, and that of an apparatus for transmitting radio or television signals in 1934.

transmute *v.* change in nature, form, etc., transform. 1392 *transmuten,* perhaps in part a back formation from *transmutation,* but more likely borrowed from Latin *trānsmūtāre* change from one condition to another (*trāns-* thoroughly + *mūtāre* to change; see MISS[1], v.).—**transmutation** *n.* About 1380, in Wycliffe's writings; borrowed from Old French *transmutation,* and directly from Late Latin *trānsmūtātiōnem* (nominative *trānsmūtātiō*) a change, shift, from Latin *trānsmūtāre* transmute; for suffix see -ATION.

transom *n.* 1388 *transeyn* crossbeam spanning an opening, lintel; later *traunsom* (1462); probably alteration (by dissimilation of medial *-tr-*) of Latin *trānstrum* crossbeam, especially one spanning an opening, from *trāns* across; see THROUGH + *-trum* an instrumental suffix. Related to TRESTLE. The sense of a small window over a door or other window is first recorded in 1844, in American English.

transparent *adj.* Probably before 1425, in a translation of Higden's *Polychronicon;* borrowed from Middle French *transparent,* and directly from Medieval Latin *transparentem* (nominative *transparens*) seeing through distinctly, present participle of *transparere* show light through (Latin *trāns-* through + *pārēre* come in sight, appear); for suffix see -ENT. The figurative sense of easily seen through or detected is first recorded in Shakespeare's *Romeo and Juliet* (1592). —**transparency** *n.* 1615, condition of being transparent; borrowed from Medieval Latin *transparentia* transparent, from *transparens* seeing through distinctly, present participle of *transparere;* for suffix see -ENCY. The meaning of a picture made visible by shining light through from behind (as in *color transparencies*) is first recorded in 1785.

transpire *v.* 1597, pass off in the form of a vapor or liquid; back formation from earlier *transpiration,* and probably, in some instances, borrowed from Middle French *transpirer,* from Latin *trāns-* through + *spīrāre* breathe; see SPIRIT. The sense of take place, happen, is first recorded in 1755, in American English, probably from a misunderstanding of an earlier figurative sense of leak out, become known (1741-42). —**transpiration** *n.* Probably before 1425 *transpiracioun* a passing out, exhalation, in a translation of Chauliac's *Grande Chirurgie;* borrowed from Middle French *transpiration* (*transpirer* transpire + *-ation*).

transplant *v.* About 1440, in a translation of *Palladius on Husbondrie;* borrowed from Middle French *transplanter,* and directly from Late Latin *trānsplantāre* plant again in a different place (Latin *trāns-* across + *plantāre* to PLANT). The extended sense of convey or remove (people, a colony, etc.) from one place to another is first recorded in 1555. The medical sense of transfer an organ or portion of tissue from one person or animal to another is first recorded in 1786. —**n.** something transplanted. 1756, a transplanted seedling. The medical sense of a transfer of an organ or portion of tissue from one person or animal to another is first recorded in 1968, although *transplantation* has been used in this sense since at least 1813. —**transplantation** *n.* 1601, probably borrowed from French *transplantation,* from *transplanter* transplant + *-ation* -ation; however, it is also probable that in many instances *transplantation* is a formation in English of *transplant* + *-ation.*

transport (transpôrt′) *v.* About 1380 *transporten* carry or convey from one place to another, in Chaucer's translation of Boethius' *De Consolatione Philosophiae;* borrowed from Middle French *transporter* carry or convey across, learned borrowing from Latin, and borrowed into Middle English from Latin *trānsportāre* (*trāns-* across + *portāre* carry; see PORT[4] bearing). The figurative sense of carry away by strong feeling is first recorded in English in 1509. —**n.** (trans′pôrt) 1456, a transfer or conveyance of property; from the verb. The sense of a means of transportation or conveyance is first recorded in 1694. —**transportation** *n.* 1540, act or process of transporting; borrowed from Middle French *transportation,* and formed from English *transport,* v. + *-ation.* The sense of a means of conveyance is first recorded in 1853, in American English. —**transporter** *n.* 1535, one who transports; later, a heavy vehicle used to transport large pieces of machinery (1944); formed from English *transport,* v. + *-er*[1].

transpose *v.* About 1392 *transposen* transform, transmute, convert; borrowed from Old French *transposer* transpose (*trans-* across + *poser* to put, place, POSE). The sense of change the position or order of, interchange, is first recorded in English in Elyot's *Dictionary* (1538). The specific sense in algebra of transfer a quantity from one side of an equation to another is first recorded in 1810, while the sense in music of put into a different key is recorded as early as 1609. —**transposition** *n.* 1538, act of transposing, in Elyot's *Dictionary;* borrowed from Middle French *transposition,* and directly from Medieval Latin *transpositionem* (nominative *transpositio*) act of transposing, from Latin *trānspositus,* past participle of *trānspōnere* place over (*trāns-* over + *pōnere* put, place; see POSITION); for suffix see -TION. The sense in music of a piece transposed to a different key is first recorded in 1740.

transsexual *adj., n.* (person) desiring to belong to the opposite sex. 1957, formed from English *trans-* across + *sexual,* but found earlier in *transsexuality* (1941).

transubstantiation *n.* Before 1398, changing of one substance into another, probably especially in the religious sense of the Eucharist, in Trevisa's translation of Bartholomew's *De Proprietatibus Rerum;* borrowed from Old French *transsubstantiation,* and directly from Medieval Latin *transubstantiationem* (nominative *transubstantiatio*) particularly in the religious sense of the Eucharist, from *transubstantiare* to change from one substance into another (Latin *trāns-* + *substantia* substance); for suffix see -ATION. The sense of the association of the bread and wine of the Eucharist, with the body and blood of Christ is probably first recorded in English before 1398, but the actual concept of the transformation of these elements into the body and blood of Christ is perhaps not recorded before 1533, in Tyndale's *The Supper of the Lord.*

transverse *adj.* 1621, lying across, placed crosswise, in Burton's *The Anatomy of Melancholy;* borrowed from Middle French *transverse,* and directly from Latin *trānsversus* turned or directed across, past participle of *trānsvertere* turn across (*trāns-* across + *vertere* to turn; see VERTEX). —**n.** something transverse. Before 1633, from the adjective.

transvestite (transves′tit) *n.* person who habitually dresses in the clothing of the opposite sex. 1922, borrowed from German *Transvestit* (Latin *trāns-* across + *vestīre* to clothe; see VEST); for suffix see -ITE[1]. Compare TRAVESTY.

trap *n.* About 1200 *trapp* snare, pitfall, in *The Ormulum;* developed from Old English *træppe* device for catching animals, snare, trap (before 1000, in Ælfric's *Glossaries*); cognate with Middle Dutch *trappe* trap, snare; also, stair, step, tread, from Proto-Germanic **trap-*, cognate with Lithuanian *drebėti* to tremble, from Indo-European **dreb-/drob-* to run, step (on) (Pok.204). The sense of a deceitful practice, trickery, or fraud is first recorded in 1681. The specific sense of a police speed trap to arrest motorists who exceed the speed limit is recorded as early as 1906. **—v.** Before 1393 *trappen* to catch in a trap, ensnare, in Gower's *Confessio Amantis;* from the noun. **—trap door** (about 1385, in Chaucer's *Troilus and Criseyde*) **—trappings** *n.pl.* Before 1398 *trappinge,* sing., ornamental covering for a horse, in Trevisa's translation of Bartholomew's *De Proprietatibus Rerum;* later *trappings,* pl., ornaments, dress, embellishments, in Nashe's *Have With You to Saffron-Walden* (1596); formed from Middle English *trappe* cloth for a horse (alteration of French *drap* cloth, DRAPE) + *-ings,* plural of *-ing*[1]. **—traps** *n.pl.* 1925, drums, cymbals, bells, gongs, etc., often used in a jazz or dance band, from *trap drummer* (1903) street musician who plays a drum and usually several other instruments at once; from *traps* belongings (1813), as a shortened form of *trappings* ornaments, belongings. **—trapshooter** *n.* person who shoots clay pigeons thrown from a trap (1899). **—trapshooting** *n.* 1892, from earlier *trap* a clay pigeon, 1812 + *shooting.*

trapeze *n.* short horizontal bar used in gymnasiums and circuses. 1861, borrowing of French *trapèze,* from Late Latin *trapezium* TRAPEZIUM; probably originally applied to a kind of trapeze in which the ropes formed a trapezium with the crossbar and the roof.

trapezium (trəpē′zēəm) *n.* four-sided plane figure having no sides parallel. 1570, in a translation of Euclid's *Elements;* borrowed from Late Latin *trapezium,* from Greek *trapézion* irregular quadrilateral; originally, small table, diminutive of *trápeza* table (*tra-* four, related to TETRA- + *péza* foot, edge, related to *poús* FOOT).

trapezoid (trap′əzoid) *n.* four-sided plane figure having only two sides parallel. 1706, a trapezium, in Kersey's edition of Phillips' *Dictionary;* borrowed from New Latin *trapezoïdes,* from Late Greek, special use of Greek *trapezoeidḗs* trapezium-shaped, from *trápeza* table; see TRAPEZIUM + *-oeidḗs* -oid. The sense of a four-sided plane figure having only two sides parallel is first recorded in English in 1795.

trash *n.* About 1518, worthless stuff, rubbish, in Skelton's *Magnificence;* perhaps borrowed from a Scandinavian source (compare dialectal Norwegian *trask* lumber, trash, Old Icelandic *tros* rubbish, fallen leaves and twigs, and Swedish *trasa* rag), of unknown origin. The sense of worthless people, riffraff is first recorded in Shakespeare's *Othello* (1604). **—v.** treat as trash, discard as worthless. 1859, American English; from the noun. The sense of destroy, vandalize, is first recorded in 1970, and the extended sense of criticize severely in 1975. **—trashy** *adj.* of the nature of trash, worthless. Before 1620, formed from English *trash,* n. + *-y*[1].

trauma (trô′mə) *n.* physical or psychic wound. 1693, physical wound; borrowed from Greek *traûma* wound, related to *titrṓskein* to wound, *trýein* wear out, distress; see THROE.

The transferred sense of an unpleasant experience which causes an abnormal mental stress, psychic wound, is first recorded in 1894 (implied in *traumata,* pl.), in writings of William James, and is implied still earlier in use of *traumatic* in psychology (1889, in T. Savill's translation of J.M. Charcot's lectures on disorders of the nervous system).

—traumatic *adj.* 1656, of or caused by a trauma, in Blount's *Glossographia;* borrowed from French *traumatique,* and directly from Late Latin *traumaticus* of or pertaining to a wound, from Greek *traumatikós,* from *traûma* (genitive *traúmatos*) wound; for suffix see -IC.

travail (trav′āl) *n.* About 1275, toil, labor, trouble; borrowed from Old French *travail* suffering or painful effort, trouble, from *travailler* to toil, labor; originally, to trouble, afflict, vex, torture, from Vulgar Latin **tripāliāre* to torture, from **tripālium* (attested as Late Latin *trepālium*) instrument of torture, probably from Latin *tripālis* having three stakes (*tria, trēs* THREE + *pālus* stake, PALE[2]); possibly so called from the instrument's structure. **—v.** About 1275 *travailen* to toil, labor, trouble; borrowed from Old French *travailler.* Related to TRAVEL.

travel *v.* 1375 *travelen* to journey; the sense found earlier (1300) in *travailen,* the form developing from a shift of stress in *travailen,* originally meaning to toil, labor; see TRAVAIL. The semantic development of *travel* may have come from an original meaning "to go on a difficult journey" or may have referred to the hardships and difficulties of early travel. **—n.** About 1375, action of traveling; perhaps from the verb, or developed, as the verb did, from a specialized sense and form of *travail.* **—travel agency** (1927) **—travel agent** (1925, earlier *travelling agent,* 1902) **—traveled** *adj.* 1413, experienced in travel, from *travel,* v. + *-ed*[2]. **—traveler** *n.* 1375, possibly formed in Middle English from *travel* + *-er*[1], or from earlier *travailen* + *-er*[1], *-our* and then leveled in form to *traveler.* **—travelers check** (1891, as a trade name) **—traveling salesman** (1885, earlier *traveler,* 1790)

travelogue *n.* illustrated lecture describing travel. 1903, American English; formed from *trave(l)* + *-logue,* as in *dialogue.*

traverse (travėrs′) *v.* Before 1325 *traversen* pass across, over, or through; borrowed from Middle French *traverser* to cross, thwart, from Vulgar Latin **trāversāre,* from Latin *trānsversāre* to cross, throw across, from Latin *trānsversus* turned across, TRANSVERSE. **—n.** (trav′ərs) 1347 *travers* act of crossing, something put across, borrowed from Old French, in part from 1) *travers* passage, a lying across, transverse, from Latin *trānsversum,* neuter of *trānsversus* transverse, lying across; and in part from 2) *traverse* crosspiece, crossroad, from Latin *trānsversa,* feminine of *trānsversus* transverse, lying across. **—adj.** lying across, being across. 1415, borrowed from Middle French *travers,* from Latin *trānsversus* transverse.

travesty (trav′əstē) *n.* parody, mockery. 1674, developed from earlier adjective meaning dressed so as to be made ridiculous, parodied, burlesqued (about 1662); borrowed from French *travesti* dressed in disguise, past participle of *travestir* to disguise (Latin *trā-, trāns-* over + *vestīre* to clothe; see VEST); for suffix see -Y[3].

Compare TRANSVESTITE. —v. make a travesty of. 1673, borrowed from French *travesti,* past participle of *travestir.*

trawl *v.* to fish with a dragnet. 1561, in Eden's translation of Cortes' *Art of Navigation;* borrowed from earlier Dutch *tragelen,* from Middle Dutch *traghelen* to drag, from *traghel* dragnet, probably from Latin *trāgula* dragnet; see TRAIL. —**n.** dragnet. 1630, action of *trawling;* later, a dragnet (1759); from the verb. —**trawler** *n.* 1630, person (and probably also a ship) that trawls (implied earlier in *trawler boat,* 1599); formed from English *trawl* + *-er*[1].

tray *n.* 1270 *trey;* later *tray* (1350); developed from Old English *trēg, trīg* flat container with a low rim (from Proto-Germanic **traujan,* from Indo-European **drou-,* root **dreu-*), related to *trēow* wood, TREE, so that the primary sense may have been "wooden (vessel)." Old English *trēg, trīg* is probably cognate with Old Swedish *trø* corn measure.

treachery *n.* Probably before 1200 *tricherie* deceit, treason, in *Ancrene Riwle;* later *trecherie* (about 1300, in *Havelok the Dane*); borrowed from Old French *trecherie, tricherie* deceit, cheating, from *trechier, trichier* to cheat, deceive; see TRICK; for suffix see -ERY. —**treacherous** *adj.* Before 1338 *tricherous* characterized by treachery, in Mannyng's *Chronicle of England;* borrowed from Old French *trecheros, tricheros* deceitfulness, from *trecheur, tricheur* a deceiver, cheat, from *trechier, tricher* to cheat; for suffix see -OUS.

treacle (trē'kəl) *n.* something overly sweet. 1340 *triacle* medicinal compound, an antidote for poison, in *Ayenbite of Inwyt;* borrowed from Old French *triacle* antidote, from Latin *thēriaca,* from Greek *thēriakḗ* (*antídotos*) antidote against poisonous wild animals, especially the bite of reptiles, from feminine of *thēriakós* of a wild animal, from *thēríon* wild animal, diminutive of *thḗr* (genitive *thērós*) wild animal; see FIERCE. The transferred sense of molasses is first recorded in British English in 1694, and the figurative sense of something that is too sweet or sentimental, is cited in Smollett's writings, 1771. The connection between the meaning "molasses" and the earlier sense "medicinal compound" is said to have come from the supposed resemblance of treacle to the ancient medicinal compound; however, it is more likely that the transfer in meaning was much closer in that molasses was also considered a medicine in its use as a laxative.

tread *v.* Probably about 1200 *treden* to step, step heavily on, in *The Ormulum;* developed from Old English *tredan* (about 725, in *Beowulf*), from Proto-Germanic **tređanan;* cognate with Old Frisian *treda* to tread, Old Saxon *tredan,* Old High German *tretan* (modern German *treten*), Old Icelandic *trodha* (Swedish *tråda, träda,* Danish *træde,* and Norwegian *trå*), and Gothic *trudan,* from Proto-Germanic **truđanan,* as if from Indo-European **dredh-.* But no cognates are known outside Germanic. (F. Kluge, *Etymologisches Wörterbuch der Deutschen Sprache,* p.790). —**n.** Probably before 1200 *tred* mark made in treading, footprint, in *Ancrene Riwle;* presumably from the verb. —**treadmill** *n.* (1822)

treadle *n.* lever worked by the foot to operate a machine. About 1410 *tredel;* literally, step, stair; found in Old English (about 1000, in writings of Ælfric), from *tredan* to TREAD; for suffix see -LE[1]. —**v.** work a treadle. 1891, in Hardy's *Tess of the D'Urbervilles;* from the noun.

treason *n.* Probably before 1200 *treison* the action of betraying, treachery, in *Ancrene Riwle;* borrowed through Anglo-French *treson,* from Old French *traïson* (influenced by the verb *traïr* betray), from Latin *trāditiōnem* (nominative *trāditiō*) a handing over, delivery, surrender; see the doublet TRADITION. The spelling *treason* began to appear in Middle English in the mid- to late 1400's.

treasure *n.* 1137 *tresor* wealth or riches stored up, in *Peterborough Chronicle;* borrowed from Old French *tresor* treasury, treasure, from Latin *thēsaurus* treasury, treasure, from Greek *thēsaurós* treasure; of uncertain origin. The spelling *treasure* began to appear in English about 1530. Doublet of THESAURUS. —**v.** Before 1382 *tresoren* to hoard, store up, preserve in the memory, in the Wycliffe Bible; from *tresor,* n. —**treasurer** *n.* About 1290 *tresurer, tresourer* person in charge of treasure or money; borrowed through Anglo-French *tresorer,* from Old French *tresorier,* from *tresor* treasure; for suffix see -ER[1]. —**treasure-trove** *n.* money, jewels, or other treasure that a person finds. 1550, borrowed from Anglo-French *tresor trové* treasure found (Old French *trové,* past participle of *trover* to find, probably from Vulgar Latin **tropāre* to hit upon, compose, from Latin *tropus* figure of speech; see TROPE). —**treasury** *n.* About 1300 *tresorie* place where valuables are kept, in *Beket;* borrowed from Old French *tresorie,* from *tresor* treasure; for suffix see -Y[3]. The sense of a government department that controls public revenue and finances is first recorded in Middle English about 1383.

treat *v.* About 1300 *tretien* negotiate, bargain, deal with; borrowed from Old French *traitier,* from Latin *tractāre* manage, handle, deal with; originally, drag about, frequentative form of *trahere* to pull, draw; see TRACT[1]. The sense of handle or deal with in speech or writing, discuss, is first recorded in Middle English about 1325. The specific sense of handle or deal with medically is first recorded in English in 1781. —**n.** 1375 *trete* act of negotiating, in Barbour's *The Bruce;* from the verb. The sense of a treating with food and drink, a feast, is first recorded in 1651; the extended sense of anything that gives pleasure is first recorded in 1770. —**treatment** *n.* About 1560, act or way of treating; formed from English *treat,* v. + *-ment.* The sense of medical or surgical application or service is first recorded in 1744.

treatise (trē'tis) *n.* book or writing on some subject. Before 1325 *tretice,* in *Cursor Mundi;* borrowed from Anglo-French *tretiz,* contracted from **treteïz,* from Gallo-Romance **tractāticius,* from Latin *tractāre* to deal with; see TREAT.

treaty *n.* signed agreement between nations. Before 1382 *tretee* treatment, discussion, in the Wycliffe Bible; borrowed from Old French *traité, traitié* assembly, agreement, treaty, from Latin *tractātus* (genitive *tractātūs*) discussion, handling, from *tractāre* to handle, manage; see TREAT; for suffix see -Y[3]. The sense of a signed contract between two or more nations is first recorded in Middle English in 1430-31, in the *Rolls of Parliament,* from the sense of an agreement or arrangement arrived at by discussion or negotiation (1427). The spelling *treaty* is first attested in the mid-1500's.

treble *adj.* Probably before 1300, three times, triple, in *Kyng Alisaunder;* borrowed from Old French *treble,* from Latin *triplus* TRIPLE. **—v.** Before 1325 *treblen* make or become three times as much; borrowed from Old French *trebler,* from *treble,* adj. **—n.** Before 1338, highest part in music, soprano, in Mannyng's *Chronicle of England;* borrowed from Old French *treble,* n. and adj. The musical use perhaps arose from the fact that in early contrapuntal music the chief melody was given to the tenor, and the voice parts added above were the alto and the treble (third part).

tree *n.* Before 1250 *tre,* in *Bestiary;* later *tree* (before 1325, in *Cursor Mundi*); developed from Old English (before 830) *trēo, trēow* tree; cognate with Old Frisian *trē* tree, Old Saxon *trio, treo,* Old Icelandic *trē* (Swedish *trä* wood, *träd* tree, Danish *træ,* and Norwegian *tre*), and Gothic *triu* tree, wood, from Proto-Germanic **trewan.* Cognates outside Germanic include Old Irish *daur* oak, Welsh *derwen,* Albanian *dru* tree, wood, stick, Greek *drŷs* tree, oak, *dóry* spear, Old Slavic *drěvo* tree, *drŭva* wood, Lithuanian *dervà* resinous wood, pitch, tar, Armenian *tram* firm, Sanskrit *dā́ru* (genitive *drós*) wood, and Hittite *taru* tree, wood, from Indo-European **deru-/dŏru-,* **dreu-/drou-/dru-,* **drewə-/drū-* (Pok.214). **—v.** 1650, grow into a tree; from the noun. The sense of take or cause to take refuge in a tree is first recorded before 1700. **—tree frog** (1738) **—treetop** *n.* (1530, in Palsgrave's *Lesclarcissement*)

trefoil (trē′foil) *n.* plant having threefold leaves, as the common clover. 1384 *treyfoyle,* borrowed perhaps through Anglo-French *trifoil,* from Old French *trefeuil,* from Latin *trifolium* three-leaved plant (*tri-* three + *folium* leaf; see BLADE).

trek *v.* travel slowly, migrate. 1850, to travel or migrate by ox wagon, in R.G. Cumming's *Hunter's Life in South Africa;* borrowed from Afrikaans *trek,* from Dutch *trekken* to march, journey; originally, to draw, pull, from Middle Dutch *trecken;* cognate with Middle Low German *trecken* and Old High German *trechan* to pull. Compare TRACK. **—n.** 1849, a journey by ox wagon or a stage of such a journey, in Edward Napier's *Excursions in Southern Africa* (but implied earlier in *Trek Boor,* 1835, a migrating Boer); borrowed from Afrikaans *trek,* from Dutch *trek* a drawing, pull, haul, march, trek, from *trekken* to journey, trek. The transferred sense of a slow or difficult journey or migration is first recorded in English in 1895.

trellis *n.* lattice. 1380 *trelis,* borrowed from Old French *trelis,* from Vulgar Latin **trilīcius,* from Latin *trilīcis,* genitive of *trilīx* having three threads, triple-twilled, in reference to the number of threads of the warp gathered together in weaving (*tri-* three + *līcium* thread, of uncertain origin). The specific sense of a lattice used to support growing vines is first recorded in English in 1513.

Apparently the sense of a lattice or grill developed from French *treillis* applying to things woven of iron wire, gold, etc., from Old French *tresliz* applying to stout woven fabric, from an early confusion with the prefix *tres-* from Latin *trāns-.*

—v. furnish with a trellis. Probably before 1400 *trelesen;* from the noun.

tremble *v.* About 1303 *tremlen* shake from fear, cold, etc., in Mannyng's *Handlyng Synne;* later *tremblen* (reinforced by the spelling in Old French, about 1380, in Chaucer's translation of Boethius' *De Consolatione Philosophiae*); borrowed from Old French *trembler* tremble, fear, from Vulgar Latin **tremulāre,* from Latin *tremulus* trembling, tremulous, from *tremere* to tremble. Latin *tremere* is cognate with Greek *trémein* to tremble, Lithuanian *trìmti,* Old Slavic *tręsti* to shake, and Tocharian A *träm-* become angry, Tocharian B *tremi* anger, rage, from Indo-European **trem-, trems-* (Pok.1092). **—n.** a trembling. 1609, in the Douay Bible; from the verb. **—trembly** *adj.* 1848, in James Russell Lowell's *A Fable for Critics;* formed from English *tremble,* v. or n. + *-y*[1].

tremendous *adj.* 1632 *tremenduous* awful, dreadful, terrible; later in the spelling *tremendous* (1657-83); borrowed from Latin *tremendus* fearful, terrible; literally, to be trembled at, a gerundive form of *tremere* to TREMBLE; for suffix see -OUS. The generalized sense of extraordinarily great or good, immense, is first recorded in English in Southey's *Essays* (1812), and parallels such semantic changes as are found in *terrific,* and in the intensive use of *terribly, awfully,* etc.

tremolo (trem′əlō) *n.* trembling or vibrating quality in tones. 1801, in Busby's *A Complete Dictionary of Music;* borrowing of Italian *tremolo,* from Latin *tremulus* trembling; see TREMULOUS.

tremor *n.* a trembling. About 1385 *tremor, tremour* terror, in Chaucer's *Troilus and Criseyde;* borrowed from Old French *tremor, tremour,* from Latin *tremōrem* (nominative *tremor*) a trembling, terror, and borrowed into Middle English directly from Latin *tremor,* from *tremere* to TREMBLE. The sense of an involuntary shaking or trembling is first recorded in English in 1615.

tremulous *adj.* trembling, quivering. 1611, borrowed from Latin *tremulus* shaking, quivering, from *tremere* to TREMBLE; for suffix see -OUS. Doublet of TREMOLO.

trench *n.* long and narrow ditch. About 1395 *trench* track cut through a wood, in Chaucer's *Canterbury Tales;* later, long and narrow ditch (1489); borrowed from Old French *trenche* a slice, ditch, from *trenchier* to cut, possibly from Vulgar Latin **trincāre,* from Latin *truncāre* to cut or lop off; see TRUNCATE. Alternatively, the FEW editors give Old French *trenchier* as derived from Vulgar Latin **trinicāre* to divide in three parts, from Latin *trīnī* three each, from *tria, trēs* THREE, but the semantics are difficult to account for. The specific sense of a trench used for military protection is first recorded in English about 1500. **—v.** 1483 *trenchen* to cut, in Caxton's version of *The Golden Legend;* borrowed from Middle French *trenchier,* from Old French. Some senses of the English verb derive from the noun. The meaning of dig a trench or trenches in is first recorded in 1530, in Palsgrave's *Lesclarcissement;* that of surround or fortify with a trench is found before 1548. **—trench coat** (1916, waterproof overcoat originally worn by officers in the trenches)

trenchant *adj.* sharp, keen, cutting. Before 1325 *trenchaunt* (implied in *trenchauntliche* trenchantly) sharp, incisive; borrowed from Old French *trenchant* cutting, sharp, present participle of *trenchier* to cut; see TRENCH; for suffix see -ANT. **—trenchancy** *n.* 1866; formed from English *trenchant* + *-cy.*

trencher *n.* platter for serving food, usually meat. About 1308 *trenchur* wooden platter on which to cut meat; later *trenchour* (1360-70); also *trencheour* knife (before 1338); borrowed from Anglo-French *trenchour,* from Old French *trenchoir* a trencher; literally, a cutting place, from *trenchier* to cut; see TRENCH. **—trencher-**

man *n.* 1590, eater, person with a hearty appetite; 1599, parasite, hanger-on, in Nashe's *Lenten Stuffe.*

trend *v.* have a general direction, tend, run. 1598, in Hakluyt's *Voyages,* (of rivers, coasts, etc.) to run or bend in a certain direction; developed from Middle English *trenden* roll about, turn, revolve (probably before 1300), found in Old English (before 1000) *trendan* (from Proto-Germanic **trandijanan*), related to *trinda, trinde* round lump, ball, and *trendel* circle, ring, disk; cognate with Old Frisian *trind, trund* round, Middle Low German *trent* ring, boundary, and Middle High German *trendel* disk, spinning top (modern German *Trendel*). Related to TRUNDLE.

The figurative sense of have a general tendency (said of events, opinions, etc.) is first recorded in 1863.

—n. general direction, course, tendency. About 1630, a rounded bend or circuit of a stream; from the verb. The sense of a general direction of a river, coast, etc., is first recorded in 1777, and the figurative sense of a general course or tendency (of action, thought, etc.) is found in 1884.

—trendy *adj. Informal.* 1962, fashionable, stylish; formed from English *trend,* n. + *-y*[1].

trepidation *n.* nervous dread, fear. 1607-12, in Bacon's *Essays;* borrowed from French *trépidation,* and directly from Latin *trepidātiōnem* (nominative *trepidātiō*) agitation, alarm, trembling, from *trepidāre* to tremble, hurry, from *trepidus* alarmed, scared; for suffix see -ATION. Latin *trepidus* is cognate with Old Slavic *trepetati* to tremble, Lithuanian *trepsěti* to stamp with the foot, Greek *trapeîn* to tread grapes, and Sanskrit *tṛprá-s* hasty, restless, from Indo-European **trep-/tṛp-* (Pok.1094).

trespass *v.* About 1303 *trespassen* transgress, offend, sin, in Mannyng's *Handlyng Synne;* borrowed from Old French *trespasser* pass beyond or across (*tres-* beyond, from Latin *trāns-* + *passer* go by, PASS[1]). The meaning of enter unlawfully on the land or property of another is first recorded in Middle English about 1455 in forest laws of the Scottish Parliament. **—n.** About 1300 *trespas* transgression, offense, sin; borrowed from Old French *trespas* a passing across, transgression, from *trespasser* pass beyond or across. The noun sense of a trespassing onto land is first recorded from the same source as the verb.

tress *n.* About 1300 *tresse* lock, curl, or braid of hair; borrowed from Old French *tresse, tresce, trece* (also compare Italian *treccia*), perhaps from Vulgar Latin **trichia* braid, rope, from Greek *trichíā* rope, from *thríx* (genitive *trichós*) hair, from Indo-European **dhrigh-/dhreikh-* hair, bristle (Pok.276). **—tressed** *adj.* having tresses, arranged in tresses. Probably before 1300, in *Kyng Alisaunder;* formed from Middle English *tresse* + *-ed*[2], representing an earlier borrowing of *tresse,* n. than the record shows.

trestle *n.* frame used as a support. About 1330 *trestle,* borrowed from Old French *trestel* crossbeam, alteration (probably by influence of *tres-* beyond) of possible **trastel,* from Vulgar Latin **trāstellum, *trānstellum,* diminutive of Latin *trānstrum* beam, crossbar; see TRANSOM.

trey (trā) *n.* card, die, or domino with three spots. About 1390 *treye,* in Chaucer's *Canterbury Tales;* borrowed from Old French *treie* three (in games of dice), from Latin *tria* (neuter) THREE.

tri- a combining form meaning: **1** having three, as in *triangle* = *(a plane figure) having three angles.* **2** once every three, lasting for three, as in *trimonthly* = *occurring every three months.* **3** containing three atoms, radicals, or other constituents of the substance specified, as in *trioxide, trisulfate.* Borrowed from Latin or Greek *tri-,* combining forms of Latin *trēs* (neuter *tria*) or Greek *treîs* (neuter *tría*) THREE.

Latin and Greek *tri-* are cognate with Sanskrit and Lithuanian *tri-,* Avestan *thri-,* and Old English *thri-* (as in *thrifēte* three-footed), from Indo-European **tri-* (Pok.1091). The Indo-European combining form **ter-* would be expected before consonants in Latin compounds, but having remained *tri-* before vowels (as in *triennium* three-year period), evidently the prevocalic form was extended to all occurrences (*triplus* triple, *tripartītus* tripartite, etc.).

triad *n.* group of three. 1546, borrowed from Late Latin *trias* (genitive *triadis*), from Greek *triás* (genitive *triádos*), from *treîs* THREE.

triage (trē ăzh′) *n.* act of sorting, as according to kind or quality. 1727-41, in an edition of *Chambers Cyclopaedia;* borrowing of French *triage* a picking out, sorting, from Old French *trier* to pick, cull; see TRY. In World War I *triage* was adopted as a military term for the sorting of wounded soldiers into three groups according to the urgency of their injuries. By 1974 this usage was extended to refer to any system of allocating limited resources according to urgency or expediency, as in the distribution of food during a famine.

trial *n.* 1436 *triall* act or process of testing; borrowed from Anglo-French *trial,* from *trier* to TRY; for suffix see -AL[2]. The sense of the examining and deciding of a case in a court of law is first recorded before 1577. The generalized sense of an ordeal is first recorded in Shakespeare's *King John* (1595). **—trial and error** (1806)

triangle *n.* 1392, figure having three sides and three angles; borrowed from Old French *triangle,* and directly from Latin *triangulum* triangle, from neuter of *triangulus* three-cornered (*tri-* three + *angulus* corner, ANGLE). **—triangular** *adj.* Before 1400, in a translation of Lanfranc's *Science of Surgery;* borrowed from Late Latin *triangulāris* pertaining to a triangle, from Latin *triangulum* triangle; for suffix see -AR. **—triangulate** *v.* 1833, to measure or survey by dividing into triangles, or to calculate distance or angle by measuring something in the form of a triangle, in Herschel's *Treatise on Astronomy;* probably a back formation from *triangulation;* for suffix see -ATE[1]. **—triangulation** *n.* 1818, borrowed from Medieval Latin *triangulationem* (nominative *triangulatio*) calculation of distance or area by measuring in the form of triangles; formed as is from **triangulare* triangulate; for suffix see -ATION.

tribe *n.* About 1250 *tribu* one of the twelve divisions of the ancient Hebrews, in *Genesis and Exodus;* later *tribe* (about 1380, in Wycliffe's writings); borrowed from Old French *tribu,* learned borrowing from Latin *tribus* (cognate with Umbrian *trifu,* accusative) one of three ethnic divisions of the original Roman State; later, one of the 35 political divisions, perhaps from *tri-* three, TRI- + *bhu-,* from the root of the verb BE. The sense of any ethnic group or race of people, especially one under a headman or chief, is first recorded in Shakespeare's *Merchant of Venice* (1596). **—tribal** *adj.* 1632, in William Lithgow's *Travels;* formed from English *tribe* + *-al*[1]. **—tribesman** *n.* (1798, in writings of Southey)

tribology (trībol′əjē) *n.* study of friction, wear, and lubrication. 1965, coined by a group of British scientists in consultation with the editors of the *Oxford English Dictionary* from Greek *tríbos* rubbing (from *tríbein* to rub; see THROW) + English *-logy* study of.

tribulation *n.* severe trial, affliction. Before 1200 *tribulaciun,* in *Ancrene Riwle;* borrowed from Old French *tribulacion,* learned borrowing from Late Latin, and borrowed directly into Middle English from Late Latin *trībulātiōnem* (nominative *trībulātiō*) distress, trouble, affliction, from *trībulāre* to oppress, afflict, a figurative use of Latin *trībulāre* to press; also possibly, to thresh out grain, from *trībulum* threshing sledge, from stem *trī-* of *terere* to rub; see THROW + *-bulum* a suffix forming names of implements and tools; for suffix see -ATION.

tribunal *n.* court of justice. 1447 *trybunal,* borrowed from Old French *tribunal,* and directly from Latin *tribūnal* platform for the seats of magistrates, elevation, embankment, from *tribūnus* official in ancient Rome, magistrate; literally, head of a tribe; see TRIBUNE[1] and TRIBUNE[2]; for suffix see -AL[2].

tribune[1] *n.* official in ancient Rome. About 1375, borrowed from Old French *tribun,* and directly from Latin *tribūnus* magistrate, tribune; originally, head of a tribe, from *tribus* (genitive *tribūs*) TRIBE.

tribune[2] *n.* raised platform, rostrum. 1762-71 (in 1645, place name), borrowed from French *tribune,* from Italian *tribuna* raised platform, from Latin *tribūnal* platform for the seats of magistrates in ancient Rome and from which they pronounced judgment, (by extension) court of law, TRIBUNAL.

tributary *n.* stream that flows into a larger body of water. 1375, person who pays tribute; borrowed from Latin *tribūtārius* liable to tax or tribute (also used as a noun meaning one who pays tribute), from *tribūtum* TRIBUTE; for suffix *see* -ARY. The sense of a stream that flows into a larger body of water is a late development, first recorded in 1822, in American English, and developed from the earlier adjective sense of subsidiary, auxiliary, contributory, applied to a stream or river (1611). **—adj.** Before 1382, paying tribute, in the Wycliffe Bible; borrowed from Latin *tribūtārius* liable to tax or tribute. The sense of subsidiary, auxiliary, is first recorded in English in Shakespeare's *Cymbeline* (1611).

tribute *n.* About 1350 *tribit* tax or impost paid to a ruler or master for security and protection; later *tribute* (about 1380); borrowed from Old French *tribut,* and later directly from Latin *tribūtum* tribute; literally, a thing contributed or paid, noun use of *tribūtus,* neuter past participle of *tribuere* to pay, allot, assign, grant, from *tribus* (sometimes analyzed as meaning originally a part of); see TRIBE. Another conjecture about the relation of Latin *tribuere* to *tribus* is that *tribuere* also had the sense of allot among the tribes or to a tribe. The figurative sense of an offering, gift, or token showing respect or affection, is first recorded in English in 1585.

trice[1] *v. Nautical.* haul up and fasten with a rope. About 1375 *tricen,* in Chaucer's *Canterbury Tales;* borrowed from Middle Dutch *trīsen* hoist, from *trīse* pulley; cognate with Middle Low German *trītse* pulley, of unknown origin.

trice[2] *n.* very short time. About 1440 *tryse,* in the phrase *at a tryse,* or later *in a tryce* (1508) at a single pluck or pull, in an instant; *tryse, tryce, trice* a pull, from *tricen* to pull, TRICE[1].

triceps (trī′seps) *n.* large muscle at the back of the upper arm. 1704, borrowed from Latin *triceps* (genitive *tricipitis*) three-headed (*tri-* three + *-ceps, caput* HEAD); so called because the muscle has three heads or origins.

trichina (trikī′nə) *n., pl.* **trichinae** (trikī′nē). small worm infesting the intestines and muscles. 1835, New Latin, borrowed from Greek *trichínē,* feminine of *tríchinos* of or like hair, from *thríx* (genitive *trichós*) hair; see TRESS. **—trichinosis** (trik′ənō′sis) *n.* disease caused by trichinae. 1866, formed from English *trichina* trichina + *-osis.*

trick *n.* About 1412 *trik* thing done to deceive or cheat, ruse, wile, in Hoccleve's *Regement of Princes;* borrowed from Old North French *trique* trick, deceit, treachery, cheating, from *trikier* to deceive, cheat, variant of Old French *trichier,* probably from Vulgar Latin **triccāre,* from Latin *trīcārī* be evasive, shuffle, from *trīcae* trifles, nonsense, a tangle of difficulties, of uncertain origin. It is also possible that the French forms could have represented a borrowing from Middle Dutch *treck* a trick, cunning; originally, a pull, draft, but such conjecture is not accepted among Romance scholars.

Both German *Trick* and French *trick* (a term used in card games) were late borrowings from English. French *triche,* the normal development from Old French, has the meaning of trickery, deception.
—v. 1595, to deceive, cheat; from the noun. An earlier sense of to dress, adorn (found before 1500) is perhaps an unrelated word of different origin.
—trickery *n.* deception, cheating. 1800, formed from English *trick,* n. + *-ery.* **—trickster** *n.* 1711, rogue, cheat, knave; formed from English *trick,* n. or v. + *-ster.* **—tricky** *adj.* 1786, in prose writings of Burns; formed from English *trick,* n. + *-y*[1].

trickle *v.* About 1375 *triklen* flow or fall in drops, of uncertain origin; possibly a variant of *striklen* to trickle (also about 1375), a frequentative form of *striken* to flow, move, STRIKE; for suffix see -LE[3]. If the word is indeed an alteration of Middle English *striklen,* the loss of the initial *s-* may have resulted from a preceding word ending in *-s,* such as *tears.* **—n.** small flow. 1580, from the verb.

tricolor *n.* 1798, flag having three colors; borrowed from French *tricolore,* originally found in *drapeau tricolore* three-colored flag, from Late Latin *tricolor* (Latin *tri-* three + *color* COLOR). **—adj.** having three colors. 1815, Southey writing in *The Quarterly Review;* borrowed from French *tricolore.*

tricot (trē′kō) *n.* knitted fabric. 1859, borrowing of French *tricot,* from *tricoter* to knit, probably variant of Old French *estriquer* to smooth, from a Germanic source (compare Middle Low German and Middle Dutch *strīken* pass over lightly; see STRIKE).

tricycle *n.* 1828, three-wheeled carriage; borrowing of French *tricycle* (*tri-* three, from Latin *tri-* + *cycle,* from Greek *kýklos* ring, circle, WHEEL). The sense of the modern three-wheeled vehicle worked by pedals is first recorded in English in 1868.

trident *n.* About 1450 *trydent* three-pronged spear; borrowed from Middle French *trident,* or directly from Latin *tridēns* (genitive *tridentis*) three-pronged, three-toothed (*tri-* three + *dēns,* genitive *dentis,* TOOTH).

triennial (trīen′ēəl) *adj.* 1640, lasting three years; 1642, occurring every three years; formed in English from

Latin *triennium* three-year period (*tri-* three + *annus* year) + English suffix *-al*[1]; see ANNUAL. **—n.** 1640, event that occurs every three years; from the adjective.

trifle *n.* Probably before 1200 *trufle* false or idle tale, in *Ancrene Riwle;* later, a matter of little value or importance, trivial or paltry thing (about 1300); borrowed from Old French *trufle* mockery, diminutive of *truffe* deception, of uncertain origin. The spelling *trifle* developed in Middle English by about 1390 through earlier *tryfyl* (about 1303). **—v.** Probably before 1200 *truflen* to cheat, mock, jest, in *Ancrene Riwle;* borrowed from Old French *truffler,* related to *trufle,* n. The sense of treat lightly, not seriously, is first recorded in English in 1523. The spelling *trifle* for the verb is first found about 1460.

trigger *n.* 1660, small lever that releases a spring or other mechanism, spelling alteration of earlier *tricker* (1621); borrowed from Dutch *trekker* trigger, from *trekken* to pull; see TREK. *Tricker* remained the usual form in English until about 1750. **—v.** set off (an explosion, etc.). 1930, from the noun.

trigonometry (trig′ənom′ətrē) *n.* branch of mathematics dealing with the relations between the sides and angles of triangles. 1614, in a translation of B. Pitiscus' *The Doctrine of Triangles,* in which the earlier New Latin *trigonometria* is used in the title. The New Latin word was formed on the model of Greek *trígōnon* triangle (*tri-* three + *gonia* angle, from *góny* KNEE) + *métron* a MEASURE; for suffix see -Y[3]. **—trigonometric** *adj.* 1811, shortened form of earlier *trigonometrical* (1666), formed from English *trigonometry* + *-ical.*

trilby *n.* soft felt hat. 1897, in allusion to *Trilby,* the heroine of the novel of the same name by George du Maurier, published in 1894; so called because this kind of hat was originally worn in the stage version of the novel.

trill *v.* sing, play, sound, or speak with a tremulous, vibrating sound. 1666-67, in Pepys' *Diary;* borrowed from Italian *trillare* to quaver, trill, probably of imitative origin, but found in Medieval Latin *trillare* and in an unnamed German source (compare Middle Dutch *trillen* vibrate, move back and forth, vacillate). **—n.** act or sound of trilling. 1649, in Lovelace's *Poems;* borrowed from Italian *trillo* a quaver or warbling in singing, from *trillare* to trill.

trillion *n.* 1690, (in Great Britain) fourth power of a million (one million billion), in Locke's *An Essay Concerning Human Understanding;* borrowed from French *trillion,* formed from *tri-* three + *(m)illion,* from Old French *million* MILLION. In the United States, Canada, and France, trillion is the third power of a thousand (1,000,000,000,000, or one thousand billion). Compare BILLION.

trilobite (trī′ləbīt) *n.* extinct arthropod. 1832, borrowed from New Latin *Trilobites* former group name of these animals (from Greek *tri-* three + *lobós* LOBE); so called because the trilobite's body is divided lengthwise into three lobes; for suffix see -ITE[1].

trilogy *n.* series of three related novels, plays, etc. 1661, in Blount's *Glossographia;* borrowed from Greek *trilogíā* series of three related tragedies performed in ancient Athens at the festival of Dionysus (*tri-* three + *lógos* story, speech; see -LOGY).

trim *v.* put in good order, make neat. Before 1460 *trimmen* make firm, make fit; probably developed from Old English (before 800) *trymman* strengthen, make ready, from *trum* strong, stable, from Proto-Germanic **trumaz,* Indo-European **drumos* (Pok.216). Though Old English *trum* has no known relation among the other Germanic languages, yet outside Germanic, it is probably cognate with Old Irish *dron* firm, and Armenian *tram* firm.

The meaning of make neat by cutting is first recorded in English in 1530, and that of decorate, adorn, in 1547. The nautical meaning of adjust (the sails or yards) to fit the direction of the wind and the course of the ship is first recorded in 1624, and was probably influenced by the earlier adjective sense.

—adj. in good condition or order, neat. Probably about 1500 *trym* elegant; from the verb. The sense of in good condition, neat, fit, is first recorded in 1503-13 (implied in *trimly*).

—adv. in a trim manner. 1529, from the adjective.

—n. 1579-80, ornament, decoration, from the verb. The sense of readiness of a ship for sailing is first recorded in Shakespeare's *Comedy of Errors* (1590).

—trimmer *n.* 1518, possibly in the obsolete meaning of a canopy; later, one who trims, repairs, or adjusts (1555), and one who changes his opinions, actions, etc., to suit the circumstances (Dryden, 1682); formed from English *trim,* v. + *-er*[1]. **—trimming** *n.* 1519, making trim, putting in order; later *trimmings* any adornment or accessories (1612).

trimaran (trī′məran′) *n.* sailboat with three hulls side by side. 1949, American English; formed from *tri-* three + *(cata)maran.*

trimester *n.* period or term of three months. 1821, borrowed from French *trimestre,* learned borrowing from Latin *trimēstris* of three months (*tri-* three + *mēnsis* month; see MOON).

trimeter (trim′ətər) *n.* line of poetry having three metrical feet. 1567, in Thomas Drant's *Horace His Art of Poetry;* borrowed from Latin *trimetrus,* from Greek *trímetros* having three measures (*tri-* three + *métron* a MEASURE).

Trinity *n.* Probably before 1200 *Trinite* the Father, Son, and Holy Spirit as constituting one God in Christian doctrine, in *Ancrene Riwle;* borrowed from Old French *trinité,* learned borrowing from Latin *trīnitātem* (nominative *trīnitās*) Trinity, triad, from *trīnī* three at a time, threefold (earlier **trisnoi*), related to *trēs* (neuter *tria*) THREE; for suffix see -ITY. The general sense of any group of three is first recorded in English in 1542, with the lower-case spelling *trinity.* **—Trinitarian** *adj.* of or holding the doctrine of the Trinity. 1656, in Blount's *Glossographia;* formed in English from New Latin *trinitarius* of the Trinity (from Latin *trinitās* Trinity) + English *-an,* probably by influence of French *trinitarien* (Calvin, 1541).

trinket *n.* any small fancy article, bit of jewelry, or the like. Before 1533, of uncertain origin; sometimes associated with an alteration of Middle English *trenket* shoemaker's knife (1440); borrowed from Old North French *trenquet,* from *trenquer* to cut, variant of Old French *trenchier;* see TRENCH. This seems unlikely from the point of view of semantic development.

trinomial (trīnō′mēəl) *n.* expression or name consisting of three terms. 1674, formed from English *tri-* three + *-nomial,* patterned on *binomial.* **—adj.** consisting of three terms. 1704, from the noun.

trio *n.* piece of music for three voices or instruments.

1724, borrowing of Italian *trio,* from *tri-* three (from Latin), patterned on *duo* DUO. The extended sense of any group of three is first recorded in English in 1777.

trip *v.* About 1390 *trippen* tread or step lightly, skip, caper, in Chaucer's *Canterbury Tales;* borrowed from Old French *tripper* strike with the feet, from a Germanic source (compare Low German *trippen, trippeln,* Middle Dutch *trepelen,* and modern Dutch *trippelen* to trip, related to Middle Low German, Middle Dutch, and modern Dutch *trappen* to stamp, tread; see TRAP). The sense of strike with the foot so as to cause to stumble is first recorded in Middle English about 1425; the sense of stumble over an obstacle is found in 1440. **—n.** Before 1420, act of tripping, stumble, in Lydgate's *Troy Book;* from the verb. The sense of a short journey or voyage, a run, is first recorded in 1691, originally as a nautical term, possibly developed from the earlier meaning of an act of tripping or moving lightly and quickly (1600).

tripartite *adj.* divided into or composed of three parts, threefold, triple. Probably before 1425, in a translation of Higden's *Polychronicon;* borrowed from Latin *tripartītus,* variant of *tripertītus* divided into three parts (*tri-* three + *partītus,* past participle of *partīrī* to divide, PART).

tripe *n.* the walls of the first and second stomachs of an ox, steer, or cow. Probably before 1300, in *Kyng Alisaunder;* borrowed from Old French *tripe* entrails, of uncertain origin (perhaps ultimately through Spanish *tripa* from Arabic *therb* suet). The informal figurative sense of something worthless, foolish, or offensive, is first recorded in 1892, from earlier use applied contemptuously to a person (1595).

triple *v.* make or become three times as great. 1375 *triplen,* in John Barbour's *The Bruce;* borrowed from Medieval Latin *triplare* to triple, from Latin *triplus* threefold, triple (*tri-* three + *-plus* -FOLD). **—n.** triple number, amount, etc. About 1425, borrowed from Latin *triplus,* n. and adj. **—adj.** Probably before 1425, consisting of three things, threefold, in a translation of Chauliac's *Grande Chirurgie;* borrowed from Latin *triplus* threefold.

triplet *n.* 1656, three successive lines of poetry; formed in English from TRIPLE, perhaps patterned on *doublet;* for suffix see -ET. The general meaning of any set or group of three is first recorded in 1733 (in Swift's writings), and that of one of three children born at the same birth (usually in plural *triplets*) in 1787.

triplicate (trip′lәkit) *adj.* Probably before 1425, triple, threefold, in a translation of Higden's *Polychronicon;* borrowed from Latin *triplicātus,* past participle of *triplicāre* to triple (*tri-* three + *plicāre* to fold; see PLY[2] fold); for suffix see -ATE[1]. **—n.** one of three things exactly alike. 1762-71, in writings of Horace Walpole; from the adjective. **—v.** (trip′lәkāt) make threefold. 1623, in Cockeram's *Dictionary;* borrowed from Latin *triplicātus,* past participle of *triplicāre* to triple; for suffix see -ATE[1].

tripod (trī′pod) *n.* stand or stool with three legs. 1603, in Holland's translations of Plutarch's *Moralia;* borrowed from French *tripode,* and directly from Latin *tripūs* (genitive *tripodis*), from Greek *trípous* (genitive *trípodos*) a three-legged stool or table; literally, three-footed (*tri-* three + *poús,* genitive *podós* FOOT).

triptych (trip′tik) *n.* set of three panels with pictures or carvings. 1731, hinged, three-leaved writing tablet used in ancient Greece and Rome; borrowed from Greek *tríptychos* three-layered (*tri-* three + *ptychós,* genitive of *ptýx* fold, layer, related to *ptýssein* to fold, of unknown origin). The meaning of a set of three panels with pictures or carvings is first recorded in 1849.

trireme (trī′rēm) *n.* ancient ship with three rows of oars. 1601, in Holland's translation of Pliny's *Natural History;* borrowed from Latin *trirēmis* (*tri-* three + *rēmus* oar; see ROW[2], v.).

trisect (trīsekt′) *v.* divide into three parts. 1695, in William Alingham's *Geometry Epitomized;* formed in English from *tri-* three + Latin *sectus,* past participle of *secāre* to cut (see SECTION); probably patterned on *bisect.*

trite *adj.* commonplace. Before 1548, borrowed from Latin *trītus* worn, familiar, trite, from past participle of *terere* to rub, wear down, wear out; see THROW.

triturate (trich′әrāt) *v.* rub, crush, or grind into a very fine powder. 1755, in Johnson's *Dictionary;* borrowed from Late Latin *trītūrātus,* past participle of *trītūrāre* to thresh, from Latin *trītūra* a rubbing, from *trītus,* past participle of *terere* to rub, grind; see THROW; for suffix see -ATE[1].

triumph *n.* About 1375 *triumphe* procession in honor of a victorious general in ancient Rome, in Chaucer's *Anelida and Arcite;* borrowed from Old French *triumphe, triomphe* achievement, conquest, rejoicing for success, learned borrowing from Latin *triumphus* achievement, a success, a victory celebration, procession for a victorious general or admiral; earlier, *triumpus,* from Greek *thríambos* hymn to Dionysus, of uncertain origin. The sense of victory, conquest, is first recorded in Middle English about 1400; that of the exultation of victory or success, elation, is found in 1582. **—v.** Probably before 1450 *tryomfen* rejoice in victory, exult; borrowed from Middle French *triumpher,* from Latin *triumphāre* to achieve a notable success, triumph over, celebrate a triumph, from *triumphus* triumph. The sense of be victorious, gain mastery, prevail, is first recorded in English in Dunbar's *Poems* (1508). **—triumphal** *adj.* Probably before 1439, of a triumph, in Lydgate's *Falls of Princes;* borrowed from Latin *triumphālis,* from *triumphus* triumph; for suffix see -AL[1]. **—triumphant** *adj.* About 1410 *triumphaunt* conquering, victorious; borrowed from Middle French *triumphant, triomphant,* or directly from Latin *triumphantem* (nominative *triumphāns*) celebrating, exultant, present participle of *triumphāre* to triumph; for suffix see -ANT. The sense of rejoicing, exultant is first recorded in English in Shakespeare's *Richard III* (1594).

triumvir (trīum′vәr) *n.* one of three men who shared the same public office in ancient Rome. Probably before 1439 *tryumvir,* in Lydgate's *Falls of Princes;* borrowed from Latin *triumvir* (usually *triumvirī,* plural), abstracted from the Old Latin phrase *trium virum,* genitive plural of *trēs virī* three men (*trēs* THREE + *virī,* plural of *vir* man; see VIRILE). **—triumvirate** *n.* 1584, any association of three joint rulers or powers; borrowed from Middle French *triumvirat,* or directly from Latin *triumvirātus* office of a triumvir, from *triumvir* a triumvir; for suffix see -ATE[3].

trivia (triv′ēә) *n.pl.* things of little or no importance. 1902, borrowing of Latin *trivia,* neuter plural of *trivium* place where three roads meet, common place, gutter, a meaning reinforced by influence of English *trivial;* see TRIVIAL.

trivial *adj.* not important, insignificant. Before 1425 *trivialle* of the trivium, in a translation of Higden's *Polychronicon;* borrowed from Medieval Latin *trivialis,* from *trivium* first three of the seven liberal arts, in Latin from *trivium* place where three roads meet (*tri-* three + *via* road, way; see VIA); for suffix see -AL[1]. The meaning of commonplace, ordinary, is first recorded in English in 1589, and that of not important, insignificant, in Shakespeare's *2 Henry VI* (1593). In these senses English *trivial* was borrowed from Latin *triviālis* commonplace, vulgar; originally, of or belonging to the crossroads, from *trivium* place where three roads meet. **—triviality** *n.* 1598, trivial quality, in Florio's *A World of Words;* later, trivial matter, in Cotgrave's *Dictionary* (1611); formed from English *trivial* + *-ity.*

trivium *n.* grammar, rhetoric, and logic, the first three of the seven liberal arts in ancient Rome and in the Middle Ages. 1804, borrowed from Medieval Latin, from Latin *trivium* place where three roads meet; see TRIVIAL.

troche (trō'kē) *n.* small medicinal tablet or lozenge. 1597 *troschies,* plural, alteration of Middle English *trocisc* (1392); borrowed from Latin *trochiscus,* from Greek *trochískos* small wheel or globe, lozenge, diminutive of *trochós* wheel, from *tréchein* to run; see TROCHEE. Greek *trochós* is exactly cognate with Old Irish *droch* wheel, from Indo-European **dhrogho-* (Pok.273). The spelling *troche* is first recorded in English in 1769.

trochee (trō'kē) *n.* foot or measure in poetry consisting of two syllables. 1603 *trochie,* borrowed from French *trochée* a trochee, learned borrowing from Latin *trochaeus* a trochee, from Greek *trochaîos* a trochee; literally, running, as in *trochaîos poús* running foot, from *tróchos* a running, spinning, from *tréchein* to run, from Indo-European **dhregh-* (Pok.273). The Latinate form *trocheus* appeared earlier in English, in Puttenham's *The Arte of English Poesie* (1589). **—trochaic** *adj.* 1589, consisting of or characterized by trochees, in Puttenham's *The Arte of English Poesie;* borrowed from Middle French *trochaïque,* and directly from Latin *trochāicus,* from Greek *trochāikós,* from *trochaîos* trochee; for suffix see -IC.

troglodyte (trog'lədit) *n.* cave man. 1555, borrowed from Middle French *troglodyte* (1552, Rabelais), or directly from Latin *trōglodyta,* from Greek *trōglodýtēs* cave dweller; literally, one who creeps into holes (*trṓglē* hole + *dýein* go in, dive in). Greek *trṓglē* is formed from *trṓgein* to gnaw; see TROUT. Greek *dýein,* related to *dýsis* setting (of the sun), cognate with Sanskrit *doṣā́* evening, is from Indo-European **deu-/du-* sink into, slip into (Pok.217). The now somewhat archaic, figurative sense of a person who lives in seclusion or is extremely old-fashioned or conservative is first recorded in English in 1854. **—troglodytic** *adj.* having to do with or characteristic of a troglodyte. 1585, borrowed from Greek *trōglodytikós,* from *trōglodýtēs* cave dweller; for suffix see -IC.

troika *n.* Russian vehicle drawn by three horses abreast. 1842, in a translation of Kohl's *Russia and the Russians;* borrowed from Russian *troĭka* three-horse team, any group of three, from the collective numeral *tróe* three, cognate with Old Slavic *trije* THREE. The sense of a group of three administrators or rulers, triumvirate, is first recorded in 1945. This sense was popularized by the Soviet proposal in 1961 to replace the then vacant office of Secretary General of the United Nations with a "troika" of three persons representing the Communist, capitalist, and nonaligned member nations.

troll[1] *v.* sing in a full, rolling voice. Probably before 1387 *trollen* to go about, stroll, in a version of *Piers Plowman;* later (about 1425) roll about, trundle; borrowed from Old French *troller* wander, search for game, from a Germanic source (compare Middle High German *trollen* to walk with short steps). Middle High German *trollen* is from Proto-Germanic **truzlanan,* Indo-European **trus-,* cognate with Sanskrit *drávati* runs, from Indo-European **dreu-/dru-* (Pok.205). The sense of sing in a full, rolling voice is first recorded in English in 1575, and that of fish with a moving line in 1606. The meanings of *troll* are extended technical applications of the generalized sense of roll, trundle. Compare TROLLEY. **—n.** 1570, fishing reel; from the verb. The meaning of a song sung in parts, round, is first recorded in 1820.

troll[2] *n.* ugly dwarf or giant. 1616, Scottish; borrowed from a Scandinavian source (compare Old Icelandic *troll* giant, fiend, demon, Swedish and Norwegian *troll* hobgoblin, giant, Danish *trold*), perhaps originally a creature that walks clumsily (from Proto-Germanic **truzlán,* from **truzlanan*); see TROLL[1].

trolley *n.* 1823, a cart, especially (1858) with wheels flanged for running on a track, probably from *troll*[1] in the sense of to roll. The meaning of a pulley or other device used to receive and convey current to a streetcar motor is first recorded in 1890 in American English, followed by that of a streetcar drawing power by means of a trolley, in 1891, also in American English. **—trolley bus** (1921) **—trolley car** (1895, American English)

trollop *n.* untidy or slovenly woman. 1615, probably derived from *troll*[1] in the sense of roll about, wallow; for suffix compare *gallop, wallop.*

trombone *n.* large brass musical instrument. 1724, borrowed from French *trombone,* and directly from Italian *trombone,* augmentative form of *tromba* trumpet, from a Germanic source (compare Old High German *trumba, trumpa* trumpet); see TRUMPET. **—trombonist** *n.* 1889, formed from English *trombone* + *-ist.*

-tron a suffix meaning: **1** having to do with electrons, as in *magnetron* (1924) a device in which the flow of electrons is controlled by a magnetic field. **2** device for directing the movement of subatomic particles, as in *cyclotron, synchrotron.* **3** device or structure for controlling physical conditions, as in *phytotron* (1949) a structure where plants are studied under controlled conditions. Borrowed from Greek *-tron,* suffix used in names of means, devices, and tools, as in *árotron* plow. Greek *-tron* is cognate with Latin *-trum,* Middle Irish *-thar,* Sanskrit *-tra-m,* Old Icelandic *-thr,* and Old English *-thor,* all having a similar use.

troop *n.* 1545, body of soldiers; borrowed from Middle French *troupe,* from Old French *trope* band of people, company, troop, probably from Frankish **throp* assembly, gathering of people; compare Old High German *thorf, thorph* village (modern German *Dorf*), Old Frisian and Old Saxon *thorp,* Old English *thorp, throp,* Old Icelandic *thorp* village, and Gothic *thaúrp* field, from Proto-Germanic **thurpa-.* The Germanic forms are cognate with Latin *trabēs* beam, Oscan *trííbúm* building, Middle Irish *treb* house, Welsh *tref* home, town, and Lithuanian *trobà* house, from Indo-European **treb-/trōb-/tr̥b-/trēb-* (Pok.1090). The sense of a number of persons or things gathered together is first recorded in English in 1584. **—v.** gather in troops or bands. 1565, in Cooper's *Thesaurus Linguae Romanae et Britannicae;* from the noun. **—trooper** *n.* 1640, soldier in the cavalry; formed from English *troop,* n. + *-er*[1]. The meaning of mounted policeman is first recorded in 1858, in Australian English, while that of a mobile state policeman (in full, *a state trooper*) is found in American English in 1911. **—troopship** *n.* (1862, in writings of Thackeray)

trope *n.* figure of speech. 1533, in Tyndale's *The Supper of the Lord;* borrowed from Latin *tropus* a figure of speech, from Greek *trópos* turn, direction, turn or figure of speech, related to *tropḗ* a turning, and *trépein* to turn, from Indo-European **trep-* turn (Pok.1094).

trophy *n.* memorial of victory. 1513, a spoil or prize of war; borrowed from Middle French *trophée,* learned borrowing from Latin *trophaeum, tropaeum* a sign of victory, a victory, mark, monument, from Greek *trópaion* monument of an enemy's defeat, from neuter of the adjective *tropaîos* of defeat, from *tropḗ* a rout; originally, a turning (of the enemy); see TROPE. The figurative sense of any token or memorial of victory is first recorded in English in 1569, in poetry of Spenser.

tropic *n.* 1391, either of two circles in the celestial sphere, in Chaucer's *Treatise on the Astrolabe;* borrowed from Old French *tropique,* and directly from Late Latin *tropicus* of or pertaining to the solstice (as a noun, one of the tropics), from Latin *tropicus* pertaining to a turn, from Greek *tropikós* of or pertaining to a turn or change, or to the solstice (as a noun, the solstice), from *tropḗ* a turning (see TROPE); for suffix see -IC. The geographical sense of either of the two parallels of latitude on the earth's surface forming the boundaries of the torrid zone (usually in the plural *the tropics*) is first recorded in English in 1527. **—tropical** *adj.* of or belonging to the tropics or torrid zone of the earth. 1527, in Hakluyt's *Voyages;* formed from English *tropic,* n. + *-al*[1].

tropism (trō′pizəm) *n.* tendency of an animal or plant to turn or move in response to a stimulus. 1899, abstracted from GEOTROPISM.

troposphere *n.* lowest region of the atmosphere. 1914, borrowed from French *troposphère* (from Greek *trópos* a turn, change + *sphaîra* SPHERE).

trot *v.* go at a gait between a walk and a run. Before 1387 *trotten,* in a version of *Piers Plowman;* borrowed from Old French *troter* trot, go, from a Germanic source (compare Old High German *trottōn* to tread and Middle High German *trotten* to run, related to Old High German *tretan* to TREAD). **—n.** motion or gait of a trotting horse. Before 1325 *trott,* in *Cursor Mundi;* borrowed from Old French *trot,* from *troter* to trot.

troth *n.* faithfulness. Probably about 1150 *trowthe;* developed from Old English *trēowth* faithfulness, TRUTH. The word *troth* probably derives from a variant form of Old English *trēowth* in which the stress shifted from the *e* to the *o;* the form with stressed *e* gave rise to the modern word *truth.*

troubadour (trü′bədôr) *n.* one of the lyric poets mainly of southern France and northern Italy from the 1000's to the 1200's. 1727-41, in *Chambers Cyclopaedia;* borrowing of French *troubadour,* from Old Provençal *trobador,* from *trobar* to find; earlier, invent a song, compose in verse, probably from Vulgar Latin **tropāre* compose, sing, especially in the form of tropes, from Latin *tropus* a song; originally, a figure of speech; see TROPE.

trouble *v.* Probably before 1200 *trublen* disturb, agitate, injure, in *Ancrene Riwle;* borrowed from Old French *trubler, troubler* (formed by metathesis of *u, ou* and *r,* found in Old French *turbler, tourble*), from Vulgar Latin **turbulāre,* alteration of Late Latin *turbidāre* to trouble, make turbid, from Latin *turbidus* TURBID. Vulgar Latin **turbulāre* was influenced by Latin *turbula* small group, diminutive of *turba* turmoil, crowd; see TURBID. **—n.** Probably about 1200 *trubuil* worry, distress; borrowed from Old French *truble, trouble,* from *trubler, troubler* to trouble. **—troublemaker** *n.* (1923) **—troubleshooter** *n.* 1905, American English, person who corrects faults in machinery and equipment, originally on telegraph or telephone lines; 1927, person who specializes in solving problems, especially in diplomatic or industrial matters. **—troublesome** *adj.* Before 1548, formed from English *trouble,* n. + *-some*[1]. **—troublous** *adj.* Probably before 1425, borrowed from Middle French *troubleus, troubleux,* from *trouble* trouble, n.; for suffix see -OUS.

trough (trôf) *n.* long, narrow container for holding food or water. Before 1325 *trow;* later *trogh, trough* (about 1390); developed from Old English (about 700) *trog;* cognate with Old Frisian and Old Saxon *trog* trough, Middle Dutch *trog* (modern Dutch *troch*), Old High German *trog* (modern German *Trog*), and Old Icelandic *trog* (Danish *trug,* Norwegian *trau,* Swedish *tråg*), from Proto-Germanic **truʒá-,* Indo-European **drukó-* (perhaps with original sense of thing of wood, log hollowed out), extended from the root **deru/dru-* tree (Pok.214).

The original sound represented by *gh* in *trough,* as in *cough, laugh,* etc., was a guttural *ch,* as in Scottish *loch* or German *ach.* As the pronunciation shifted to the sound of *f* in *off,* the spelling of many words also changed to reflect this process, as in *draft* for *draught, dwarf,* etc.; but a group of spellings remained fixed.

trounce *v.* to beat or thrash. 1551, to trouble, afflict, harass; later, to beat, thrash (1568); of uncertain origin. The original English spelling was *trounse,* but *trounce* was also used by 1568, perhaps through influence of Middle French *troncer* to cut, cut off a piece from, from *tronce* piece of timber, from Old French *tronc* TRUNK.

troupe *n.* company, especially a group of entertainers. 1825, American English; borrowing of French *troupe,* from Middle French *troupe* company, TROOP. **—trouper** *n.* 1890, member of a theatrical troupe; formed from English *troupe* + *-er*[1].

trousers *n.pl.* 1612, in Beaumont and Fletcher's *The Coxcomb;* extended form (through apparently accidental intrusion of *r*) of earlier *trouzes* (1581); borrowed from Gaelic or late Middle Irish *triubhas* (pronounced trē′wəs or trē′vəs), of uncertain origin. As early as 1581 *trouzes* was taken as a plural (and may have been known much earlier, compare *trues,* 1306, Irish state papers), and a singular *trouze* was formed by back formation. The singular form *trouser* is first recorded in 1702, in writings of Addison, and with the special sense of a single leg of a pair of trousers, is found in 1893.

Originally *trousers* referred to a close-fitting garment for the buttocks and thighs, to the lower parts of which stockings could be attached. Later (1681) it was applied to a loose-fitting garment for men covering the loins and legs to the ankles, in early use worn especially by sailors, later by soldiers, and gradually becoming common in the form known today from about 1820.

trousseau (trü′sō) *n.* bride's outfit of clothes, linen, etc. 1817; later borrowing of French *trousseau,* originally, a bundle, diminutive of Old French *trousse* bundle; see TRUSS. Old French *trousse* was borrowed into Middle English in its original sense of bundle, by about 1200 and is found in *Ancrene Riwle.*

trout *n.* freshwater food and game fish. Before 1325 *trute,* in *Cursor Mundi;* in part developed from Old English *truht* trout (about 1050, borrowed from Late Latin *tructa* a kind of sea fish), and in part borrowed from Old French *truite, troite,* from Late Latin *tructa, trōcta,* perhaps from Greek *trṓktēs* a kind of sea fish; literally, nibbler, from *trṓgein* to nibble, gnaw, from Indo-European **trōĝ-/trəĝ-,* extensions of root **ter-* rub (Pok.1073).

trowel *n.* 1344, tool for spreading plaster or mortar; borrowed from Old French *troele, truele,* from Late Latin *truella* small ladle, dipper, diminutive of Latin *trua* a stirring spoon, ladle, skimmer. Probably related to *turbāre* stir up, agitate, and *turba* turmoil; see TURBID. The meaning of a small spade held in one hand and used in gardening is first recorded in 1796. **—v.** apply or smooth with a builder's trowel. About 1670, from the noun.

troy *adj.* of or in a standard system of weights for gems and precious metals. 1380-81 *troye,* probably from *Troyes,* a city in France (ancient *Trícasses*), former site of a fair at which this weight is said to have been used.

truant *n.* About 1300, beggar, vagabond; borrowed from Old French *truant* beggar, vagabond, rogue, from Gaulish **trougant-* (compare Breton **truan,* later *truant* vagabond, Middle Welsh *tru* miserable, Welsh *truan* miserable, as a noun meaning wretch, Old Irish *trōg* miserable, from Indo-European **troughos,* Pok.1073; also compare Gaelic *truagh* miserable, *truaghan* wretch). The meaning of a child who stays away from school is first recorded in Middle English about 1449. **—adj.** Before 1550, that is a truant, or plays truant; from the noun. **—truancy** *n.* 1784, formed from English *truant* + *-cy.*

truce *n.* Probably before 1200 *triws* a stopping of fighting, feuding, or quarreling, armistice, in *Ancrene Riwle;* variant of *trewes,* originally the plural of *trewe* faith, assurance of faith, covenant, treaty; developed from Old English *trēow* faith, treaty (from Proto-Germanic **trewwō*); related to *trēowe* faithful; see TRUE. Cognates of Old English *trēow* are found in Old Frisian *triūwe* faith, loyalty, Old Saxon *treuwa,* Middle Dutch *trouwe* (modern Dutch *trouw*), Old High German *triuwa* (modern German *Treue*), Old Icelandic *trū* (Danish and Swedish *tro,* Norwegian *tro, tru*), and Gothic *triggwa* covenant.

In Middle English the plural *trewes* gradually became a singular through the application of the word to the agreement or promise of good faith pledged by parties after a dispute.

—v. 1569, to make a truce; from the noun.

—trucial *adj.* pertaining to or bound by a truce (used especially in reference to a maritime truce made in 1835 between the British government and certain sheikdoms in southeastern Arabia). 1876, formed from English *truce* + *-ial.* The so-called *Trucial States* became the United Arab Emirates in 1971.

truck[1] *n.* vehicle for carrying heavy loads. 1611, small wheel, especially one on which carriages of a ship's guns were mounted, in Florio's *Queen Anna's New World of Words;* probably borrowed from Latin *trochus* iron hoop, from Greek *trochós* wheel, from *tréchein* to run. The extended sense of a cart for carrying heavy loads is first recorded in 1774, and that of a motor vehicle for carrying such loads is first recorded in 1930, in American English, as a shortened form of earlier *motor truck* (1916). **—v.** carry on a truck. 1809 (implied in *trucking*); from the noun. **—trucker** *n.* 1853, worker who moves loads using a cart, in the writings of Dickens; formed from English *truck* a cart + *-er*[1]. The sense of a person who drives a truck is first recorded in 1955, in American English; earlier, *truck driver* (probably before 1931).

truck[2] *v.* exchange, barter. Probably before 1200 *trukien,* in *Ancrene Riwle;* borrowed from Old North French *troquer* to barter, exchange, from Medieval Latin *trocare* barter, of unknown origin. The figurative sense of have dealings with, traffic, is first recorded in English in 1615. **—n.** 1533, barter, in Hakluyt's *Voyages;* from the verb. The figurative sense of dealings, communication, traffic (as in *to have no truck with loansharks*) is first recorded in English before 1625. The sense of vegetables raised for the market, market-garden produce, is an Americanism first recorded in 1784. **—truck farm** or **garden** 1866, farm where vegetables are raised for market.

truckle[1] *n.* small wheel or roller. 1397 *trokell,* borrowed from Anglo-French *trocle,* from Latin *trochlea* a small wheel, sheaf of a pulley, from Greek *trochileíā* a pulley, from *trochós* wheel, from *tréchein* to run. **—truckle bed** low bed moving on small wheels or casters (1459).

truckle[2] *v.* give up or submit tamely, be servile. 1612, sleep in a truckle bed, in Beaumont and Fletcher's *The Coxcomb;* later, to submit, give precedence (1667, in Pepys' *Diary*); abstracted from *truckle bed,* in allusion to its use by servants and inferiors.

truculent *adj.* fierce, savage, cruel. About 1540, borrowed from Latin *truculentus* fierce, savage, ferocious, from *trux* (genitive *trucis*) fierce, wild; for suffix see -ENT. Latin *trux, trucis,* perhaps originally meaning slashing, may have been an alteration (by metathesis of *u* and *r*) of earlier **turx,* from Indo-European **twr̥k-s,* root **twerḱ-* to cut (Pok.1102). **—truculence** *n.* 1727, fierceness, savageness, in Bailey's *Dictionary;* formed in English as a noun to *truculent,* or borrowed from French *truculence,* and directly from Latin *truculentia* savageness, ferocity, from *truculentus* truculent; for suffix see -ENCE.

trudge *v.* 1547, to walk wearily but persistently; of unknown origin. **—n.** 1748, person who trudges, in Smollett's *Adventures of Roderick Random;* 1835, act of trudging; from the verb.

true *adj.* Probably before 1200 *trewe, treowe* faithful, loyal, trustworthy, in *Ancrene Riwle* and Layamon's *Chronicle of Britain;* developed from Old English (about 725, in *Beowulf*) West Saxon *trīewe,* Mercian *trēowe* faithful, trustworthy; related to TRUCE. The sense of consistent with fact, agreeing with reality (as in *a true story*) is first recorded in Middle English probably before 1200. The meaning of agreeing with a standard or rule, exact, accurate, correct (as in *true north*) is first recorded about 1550.

Old English *trīewe, trēowe* (from Proto-Germanic **trewwjaz*) is cognate with Old Frisian and Old Saxon *triuwi* faithful, trustworthy, Middle Dutch *ghetrūwe* (modern Dutch *getrouw*), Old High German *gitriuwi* (modern German *treu*) faithful, Old Icelandic *tryggr* trustworthy, safe (Danish *tryg,* Swedish and Norwegian *trygg* safe, secure), and Gothic *triggws* faithful. Cognates outside Germanic are found in Old Irish *derb* sure, Old Prussian *druwis* faith, Lithuanian *drū́tas* strong, thick, and Sanskrit *dhruvá-s,* from Indo-European **dreu-/dru-, *drewə-/drū-* hard, firm (Pok.214). **—adv.** in a true manner. About 1303 *trew* faithfully; from the adjective. The sense of truthfully, rightly, is found in Middle English before 1325.

—n. Probably about 1390, faithful person; from the adjective. The meaning of that which is true (as in the phrase *the true*) is first recorded in 1812.

—v. 1647, to prove true; from the adjective. The meaning of make true is first recorded in 1841.

—true-blue *adj.* staunchly loyal. 1663 (referring to a member of the Scottish Presbyterian party, whose distinctive color was blue), in Samuel Butler's *Hudibras;* the color blue was regarded as symbolic of constancy since before 1500. **—truism** *n.* a self-evident or obvious truth. 1708, in Swift's writings; formed from English *true,* adj. + *-ism.* **—truly** *adv.* in a true manner. About 1303 *trewely;* earlier *trouliche* (probably before 1200); developed from Old English (before 1000) *trēowlīce* faithfully, loyally (*trēowe* faithful, TRUE + *-līce* -ly[1]).

truffle *n.* fungus that grows underground. 1591, borrowed from Middle French *trufle,* alteration of Old French *truffe,* from Old Provençal *trufa,* from Late Latin *tūfera,* pl., from Osco-Umbrian **tūfer,* cognate of Latin *tūber* edible root, lump, TUBER.

trump[1] *n.* playing card of a suit that for the time ranks higher than the other suits. 1529, in Latimer's *Sermons;* alteration of *triumph* name of a card game, trump in a card game (1529), probably a special use of English TRIUMPH. It is also possible that the word is further loosely associated with *trumpet,* in the sense of sound or blow a trumpet or with *trumper* a trumpeter, with reference to announcing what suit is "trump" in a game of cards. **—v.** (in cards) lay a trump upon, take with a trump. 1598, in Florio's *A World of Words;* from the noun. The figurative sense of surpass, beat, is attested earlier than the literal one, in 1586, preceded by the sense of put in one's way as an obstruction, in 1553, a meaning probably influenced by obsolete *trump[2]* to deceive, cheat.

trump[2] *v.* **trump up** fabricate, devise unscrupulously. 1695, from earlier *trump* deceive, cheat (1513); developed from Middle English *trumpen,* borrowed from Old French *tromper* deceive, of uncertain origin.

trumpery *n.* worthless stuff, nonsense, rubbish. 1456 *trompery* deceit, trickery; also, nonsense, rubbish; borrowed from Middle French *tromperie,* from *tromper* to deceive, of uncertain origin; for suffix see -ERY. The spelling with *u* was influenced by confusion with *trump[2]* deceive. The transferred sense of showy but worthless finery is first attested in Shakespeare's *The Tempest* (1610). **—adj.** showy but without value, trifling, worthless. 1576, from the noun.

trumpet *n.* musical wind instrument. Before 1393 *trompette,* in Gower's *Confessio Amantis;* borrowed from Old French *trompette* trumpet, diminutive (perhaps because of the shortening by bending over into curves) of *trompe* a musical wind instrument of a long tubelike form, trumpet, from a Germanic source (compare Old High German *trumba, trumpa* and Old Icelandic *trumba,* both meaning trumpet and both perhaps of imitative origin); for suffix see -ET. The spelling *trumpet* is first recorded in Middle English about 1447. **—v.** blow a trumpet. 1530, in Palsgrave's *Lesclarcissement;* from the noun.

truncate *v.* cut off a part of. 1486 (implied in *truncated*), borrowed from Latin *truncātus* cut off, past participle of *truncāre* to maim, cut off, from *truncus* mutilated, cut off; see TRUNK; for suffix see -ATE[1]. **—adj.** cut off, blunt, as if cut off. 1579 (implied in *truncately*), borrowed from Latin *truncātus,* past participle of *truncāre* cut off. **—truncation** *n.* action of truncating. Probably before 1425 *truncacioun,* in a translation of Chauliac's *Grande Chirurgie;* borrowed from Late Latin *truncātiōnem* (nominative *truncātiō*) a cutting off or maiming, from *truncāre* to maim, cut off; for suffix see -ATION.

truncheon *n.* stick, club. Probably before 1300 *tronchon* shaft of a spear, in *Kyng Alisaunder;* also, a short stick, club, cudgel (probably about 1300); borrowed from Old North French *tronchon,* Old French *tronçon* a piece cut off, thick stick, stump, from Vulgar Latin **trunciōnem* (nominative **trunciō*), from Latin *truncus* stem, stock; see TRUNK.

trundle *n.* small wheel or caster. 1564 (in *trundle bed* low bed on small wheels), possibly alteration of Middle English *trendle* wheel, suspended hoop (1324); developed from Old English *trendel* ring, disk (806, in *Anglo-Saxon Chronicle*); see TREND. **—v.** roll along. 1598, in Florio's *A World of Words;* from the noun.

trunk *n.* 1440 *trunke* box, case, in *Promptorium Parvulorum;* borrowed from Old French *tronc* alms box in a church; also, trunk of a tree, trunk of the human body, from Latin *truncus* trunk of a tree, trunk of a human body; originally adj., mutilated, cut off, of uncertain origin. The meaning of a box or case is said to derive from that of tree trunk, out of which they were originally made, but it is more likely a matter of simple resemblance. The meaning of the main stem of a tree is first recorded in Middle English in 1490, and that of the torso of a human body in 1494; both senses derived from earlier use in Old French. The meaning of the luggage compartment of a motor vehicle, first recorded in 1930 in American English, derives from the early use of a trunk fixed to the rear of some models. The use of *trunk* referring to an elephant's snout, is first recorded about 1565, from the generalized sense of pipe or tube (1548, found earlier in *trump* about 1440, of uncertain origin).

trunnion (trun′yən) *n.* either of the two round projections of a cannon. Before 1625, borrowed from French *trognon* core of fruit, stump, tree trunk, from Middle French *troignon,* from Latin *truncus* TRUNK, but influenced by Old French *moignon,* with the same meaning, from Gallo-Romance **moniōnem,* from Gaulish **moni-* neck; compare Old Irish *muin* neck, *muinēl* necklace, Middle Welsh *mwn* neck, Welsh *mwnwgl* neck, *mwng* MANE.

truss *v.* to tie, fasten. Probably before 1200 *trussen,* in *Ancrene Riwle;* borrowed from Old French *trusser, trousser* to load, pack, truss, of uncertain origin. **—n.** Probably before 1200, bundle, pack, in *Ancrene Riwle;*

borrowed from Old French *trousse,* from *trousser* to pack. The sense of a framework for supporting a roof or bridge is first recorded in English in 1654.

trust *n.* Probably before 1200 *truste* confidence, reliance, in *Ancrene Riwle;* borrowed from a Scandinavian source (compare Old Icelandic *traust* help, confidence, Swedish *tröst,* Danish and Norwegian *trøst* consolation, related to Old Icelandic *tryggr* faithful, TRUE). The Scandinavian words are cognate with Old Frisian *trāst* trust, Middle Dutch *troost* (modern Dutch *troost* consolation), Old High German *trōst* (modern German *Trost* consolation), and Gothic *trausti* agreement, covenant, from Proto-Germanic **traust-,* Indo-European **droust-* (Pok.216). **—v.** have trust. Probably before 1200 *trusten,* borrowed from a Scandinavian source (compare Old Icelandic *treysta* to trust, related to *traust,* n.). **—trustee** *n.* 1647, person who is trusted; formed from English *trust,* v. + *-ee.* The extended meaning of a person responsible for the property or affairs of another is first recorded in 1653. **—trust fund** (1780) **—trustworthy** *adj.* (1808, implied in *trustworthiness*) **—trusty** *adj.* Probably before 1200 *trusti* having trust, trusting, in *Ancrene Riwle;* formed from Middle English *trust,* adj. + *-i* -y[1]. The sense of trustworthy (as in *my trusty dog*) is found in Middle English before 1310. *—n.* 1573, trustworthy person; from the adjective.

truth *n.* 1137 *treuthe* quality of being true (as in *whispering tongues can poison truth*), faithfulness, in *Peterborough Chronicle;* developed from Old English (before 899), West Saxon *trīewth,* Mercian *trēowth* faithfulness, from *trīewe, trōowe* faithful, TRUE. The sense of something that is true, true statement or account (as in *tell us the truth*), is first recorded in Middle English about 1378, in a version of *Piers Plowman.* The sense of conformity with fact, accuracy, correctness (as in *There is some truth in what you say*), is first recorded in 1570. Compare TROTH.

try *v.* Before 1325 *trien* examine judicially, sit in judgment of; borrowed from Anglo-French *trier,* from Old French *trier* to pick out, cull (also found in Old Provençal and Catalan *triar*) all suggesting derivation from Gallo-Romance **triāre,* of unknown origin. The sense of put to the proof, test, is first recorded in Middle English probably about 1380, and that of test one's ability to deal with, attempt to do, perform, etc., is found before 1333. **—n.** Before 1400, an attempt, endeavor; from the verb.

tryst (trist) *n.* appointment to meet, especially by lovers. 1375, in Barbour's *The Bruce;* borrowed from Old French *tristre, triste* appointed station in hunting, possibly from a Scandinavian source (compare Old Icelandic *treysta* to TRUST).

tsetse fly or **tsetse** (tset'sē) *n.* African fly that transmits sleeping sickness. 1849 *tsetse,* in Edward Napier's *Excursions in Southern Africa;* borrowed from a Bantu language (compare Setswana *tsētsē,* Luyia *tsiisi* flies). The compound *tsetse fly* is first recorded in 1865.

T-shirt *n.* light, short-sleeved shirt. 1920, in F. Scott Fitzgerald's *This Side of Paradise;* American English, formed from the letter *T,* in allusion to the shape of the shirt when spread out flat + *shirt.*

tsunami (tsünä'mē) *n.* huge ocean wave, tidal wave. 1904, borrowing of Japanese *tsunami* (*tsu* harbor + *nami* wave).

tub *n.* 1384 *tobbe,* 1388 *tub;* borrowed from Middle Low German, Middle Dutch, or Middle Flemish *tubbe,* of uncertain origin. Connection with Old High German *zubar* (contraction of *zwibar,* vessel with two handles) is phonetically improbable. The sense of a bathtub is first recorded in English in 1594, and that of a washtub, in 1560. **—v.** 1610, bathe in a tub, in Ben Jonson's *The Alchemist;* from the noun. The sense of put in a tub is first recorded in 1828. **—tubby** *adj.* 1806-07, sounding like a tub when struck; formed from English *tub,* n. + *-y*[1]. The meaning of shaped like a tub, corpulent, is first recorded in 1835.

tuba (tü'bə) *n.* large brass instrument of the trumpet class. 1852, borrowed from French *tuba,* from Latin *tuba* war trumpet, related to *tubus* TUBE.

tube *n.* long pipe. 1611, in Cotgrave's *Dictionary;* borrowed from Latin *tubus* tube, pipe, of uncertain origin. **—tubular** *adj.* 1673, having the form of a tube or pipe; formed in English from Latin *tubulus* small tube (diminutive of *tubus* tube) + English *-ar.*

tuber (tü'bər) *n.* thick part of an underground stem. 1668, borrowed from Latin *tūber* lump, bump, perhaps related to *tumēre* to swell; see THUMB. Compare TUMOR. **—tuberous** *adj.* 1650, covered with tubers, knobby; later, of the nature of a tuber (1668), and bearing tubers (1664); borrowed from French *tubéreux* (feminine *tubéreuse*) knobby, from Middle French *tuberoux,* from Latin *tūberōsus* full of lumps or tubers, from *tūber* tuber; for suffix see -OUS. A parallel form *tuberose* knobby, is found in Middle English, probably before 1425, in a translation of Chauliac's *Grande Chirurgie;* borrowed from Latin *tūberōsus.* **—tuberosity** *n.* tuberous formation, swelling, protuberance. Probably before 1425 *tuberosite,* in a translation of Chauliac's *Grande Chirurgie;* probably borrowed from Middle French *tubérosité,* from *tuberoux* + *-ité* -ity.

tubercle (tü'bərkəl) *n.* small, rounded swelling or knob. 1578, borrowed from Latin *tūberculum* small swelling, pimple, diminutive of *tūber* lump; see TUBER. **—tubercular** *adj.* 1799, characterized by tubercles, having tuberculosis (1898); borrowed from New Latin **tubercularis* of or pertaining to tubercles, from Latin *tūberculum* tubercle; for suffix see -AR.

tuberculosis (tubėr'kyəlō'sis) *n.* infectious disease characterized by the formation of tubercles. 1860, in Thomas Tanner's *On the Signs and Diseases of Pregnancy;* New Latin, from Latin *tūberculum* TUBERCLE. **—tuberculous** *adj.* 1747, tubercular; borrowed from New Latin *tuberculosus* characterized by tubercles, from Latin *tūberculum* tubercle; for suffix see -OUS. The sense of having to do with tuberculosis is first recorded in 1891.

tuck *v.* 1440 *tukken* gather up in folds, in *Promptorium Parvulorum;* earlier, to pull or gather up (about 1385), and to pluck, stretch (probably before 1300, and implied earlier in *tucker* one who dresses or finishes cloth, 1273); probably borrowed from Middle Low German or Middle Dutch *tucken* pull up, draw up, tug. The Middle Low German and Middle Dutch forms are cognate with Old High German *zucchen, zucken* to jerk, tug (modern German *zucken*), and Old English *tūcian* mistreat, torment, related to *togian* to pull, TOW[1]. The sense of thrust into a snug place is first recorded in English in 1587, and that of turn in the edges of (a bed covering or the like), in 1635. **—n.** a fold or pleat. About 1385 *tucke,* in Thomas Usk's *The Testament of Love;* from the verb, probably in the earlier sense of gathering up.

tucker[1] *n.* piece of lace or the like worn by women around the neck. 1688, piece of lace worn around the top of the bodice, especially in the 1600's and 1700's; earlier, one who tucks in loose edges (1506); developed from Middle English *tokker* one who dresses or finishes cloth (before 1376) (*tukken* to TUCK + *-er* -er[1]).

tucker[2] *v. Informal.* to tire, weary. 1833, American English; of uncertain (probably dialectal) origin.

-tude a suffix forming abstract nouns from adjectives and participles, usually in words borrowed (often through French) from Latin (with French or English *-tude* replacing Latin *-tūdō*), as in *altitude, fortitude, solitude;* occasionally in words of later formation, as in *decrepitude, exactitude, platitude,* from French. Borrowed from French *-tude,* from Latin *-tūdō* (genitive *-tūdinis*). An occasional formation is found in English, such as *torpitude,* formed from English *torpid* + *-tude,* perhaps by analogy with a form such as *turpitude.*

Tuesday *n.* Probably before 1200 *tisdæi,* in Layamon's *Chronicle of Britain;* earlier *tywesdæi* (1122); developed from Old English (about 1050) *Tīwesdæg* (*Tīwes,* genitive of *Tīw* Tiu + *dæg* DAY). *Tiu* is derived in form from Proto-Germanic **Tīwaz* god of the sky; see DEITY, but is a differentiation in sense specifically alluding to *Tiu* ancient Germanic god of war.

tuff *n.* rock produced by the consolidation of volcanic fragments. 1569, borrowed from Middle French *tuf,* from Italian *tufo* tufa (a porous rock), from Latin *tōfus,* probably from an Osco-Umbrian source.

tuft *n.* About 1387, a bunch of feathers, hair, grass, etc., in Chaucer's *Canterbury Tales;* borrowed perhaps from Old French *touffe, toffe, tofe,* either from Late Latin *tufa* a kind of crest on a helmet, also found in Late Greek *toûpha;* or from a Germanic source (compare Old High German *zopf* and Old Icelandic *toppr* tuft, summit, TOP[1]). The unexplained spelling ending in *-t* is an innovation of English. **—v.** put tufts on. 1535, from the noun.

tug *v.* Probably before 1200 *toggen* pull playfully, in *Ancrene Riwle;* later *tuggen* pull with force (about 1303, in Mannyng's *Handlyng Synne*); related to Old English *togian* to pull, drag; see TOW[1]. **—n.** 1500-20, a hard pull, in Dunbar's *Poems;* from the verb. **—tugboat** *n.* (1832) **—tug-of-war** *n.* 1677, decisive contest; 1876, contest between two teams pulling opposite ends of a rope.

tuition *n.* About 1410 *tuicioun* protection, care, custody, looking after, taking care of; borrowed from Anglo-French *tuycioun,* from Old French *tuicion* guardianship, learned borrowing from Latin *tuitiōnem* (nominative *tuitiō*) guard, protection, defense, from *tui-,* stem of *tuērī* to look after, protect, watch over; for suffix see -TION. Latin *tuērī* is cognate with Old Irish *cumtūth* protection, and Middle Welsh *tudd* to cover, from Indo-European **teu-* (Pok.1079). The meaning of money paid for teaching or instruction is first recorded in 1828, in American English, probably shortening of *tuition money, tuition fees,* and derives from the earlier extended meaning of an act of teaching, instruction of a pupil or pupils (1582).

tulip *n.* 1578, borrowed from earlier Dutch *tulipa,* from French *tulipe* a tulip; earlier *tulipan,* from Turkish *tülbent* turban, gauze, muslin, tulle, from Persian *dulband* turban; so called from the fanciful resemblance of the plant's flower to a turban. Doublet of TURBAN.

tulle (tül) *n.* thin, fine silk net. About 1818, named after *Tulle,* a town in central France where the fabric was first manufactured.

tumble *v.* Probably before 1300 *tomblen* (in *Arthour and Merlin*), *tumblen* (in *Kyng Alisaunder*) to roll over, fall suddenly; later (about 1325), to dance like an acrobat; perhaps a frequentative form of Old English (about 1000) *tumbian* dance about; cognate with Old High German *tūmōn* turn round, reel, Middle High German *tūmeln,* modern German *taumeln* to turn, reel (all ultimately derived from a Low German source), and Old Icelandic *tumba* to tumble, of unknown origin. If *tumblen* is a frequentative form of Old English *tumbian,* see suffix -LE[3]. **—n.** 1634, disorder, confusion; from the verb. The meaning of a fall or falling down is first recorded in 1716. **—tumble-down** *adj.* 1791, habitually falling down, said of a horse; 1818, dilapidated, in Scott's *Bride of Lammermoor.* **—tumbler** *n.* Before 1340, person who dances or tumbles, acrobat; formed from Middle English *tumblen* dance, roll about + *-er*[1]. The sense of a drinking cup or glass is first recorded in 1664, in Pepys' *Diary;* tumblers originally had rounded or pointed bottoms so that they could not be set down until emptied. **—tumbleweed** *n.* (1887)

tumbrel or **tumbril** (tum′brəl) *n.* farmer's cart. 1383 *tomrell,* 1440 *tumrel,* 1481 *tomberel;* all forms borrowed from Old French *tumberel, tomberel* dump cart, from *tomber* (let) fall or tumble, of uncertain origin. Old French *tomber* may have come from an imitative Gallo-Romance stem *tumb-, tomb-;* alternatively the word may derive from a Germanic source (compare Old High German *tūmōn* turn round, reel, and Old Icelandic *tumba* to TUMBLE).

tumescence *n.* condition of swelling. 1859, borrowed from French *tumescence,* from Latin *tumēscentem* (nominative *tumēscēns*) swelling, present participle of *tumēscere* begin to swell, from *tumēre* to swell; see THUMB; for suffix see -ENCE, -ESCENCE. **—tumescent** *adj.* swollen. 1882, formed in English as an adjective to *tumescence* on the model of Latin *tumēscēns,* present participle of *tumēscere* begin to swell; for suffix see -ENT, -ESCENT. It is also possible that in some instances *tumescent* was a direct borrowing from French.

tumid *adj.* swollen. 1541, in Copland's translation of Galen's *Terapeutyke;* borrowed from Latin *tumidus* swollen, swelling, from *tumēre* to swell; see THUMB.

tumor *n.* Probably before 1425 *tumour* an abnormal growth or swelling, in a translation of Chauliac's *Grande Chirurgie;* borrowed from Latin *tumor* a swelling, condition of being swollen, from *tumēre* to swell; see THUMB; for suffix see -OR[1].

tumult *n.* About 1380 *tumolte* noise, uproar, in Chaucer's translation of Boethius' *De Consolatione Philosophiae;* borrowed from Old French *tumulte,* from Latin *tumultus* commotion, disturbance, related to *tumēre* to be excited, swell; see THUMB. **—tumultuous** *adj.* Before 1548, characterized by or causing tumult; borrowed from Middle French *tumultuous,* from Latin *tumultuōsus* full of tumult, from *tumultus* (genitive *tumultūs*) commotion, disturbance; see TUMULT; for suffix see -OUS.

tun *n.* large cask for liquids, former measure of capacity for liquids. Probably before 1200 *tunne,* in Layamon's *Chronicle of Britain;* also *tonne* (1340, in *Ayenbite of Inwyt*); developed from Old English (before 800) *tunne.* Corresponding forms are found in Old Frisian and Old Saxon *tunna* tun, Middle Dutch *tonne, tunne* (modern Dutch *ton*), and Old High German *tunna* (modern German *Tonne*); yet its late appearance in Germanic (after 700, in Old High German) and the existence of corresponding forms in Latin and Romance (Old French *tonne,* Provençal *tona,* Medieval Latin *tunna,* etc.) suggest a borrowing. Accordingly some have suggested a Celtic source (though it may be simply accidental occurrence, or that Celtic adopted from English), citing Middle Irish *tonn* hide, skin, Middle Welsh *ton,* so that the original sense would be "wine skin." Compare TON and TUNNEL.

tuna *n.* 1881, American English; borrowed from American Spanish *tuna* a large saltwater food fish, from Spanish *atún,* from Arabic *tun,* from Latin *thunnus* TUNNY. It is not surprising that the fish (*tunny*) is known in both Spanish and Arabic, as the fish has been harvested in the Mediterranean from Phoenician times, but it is curious that for such a common food fish with such an ancient history the Arabic word replaced (presumably during the occupation of southern Spain by the Arabs) an earlier Spanish form that must have existed as a descendant from Latin (compare Italian *tonno,* French *thon,* Provençal *ton*).

tundra *n.* level, treeless plain in the arctic regions. 1841, borrowed from Russian *túndra,* from Lappish *tundar* elevated wasteland.

tune *n.* Before 1325 *tune* musical sound or tone, unexplained variant of TONE. The sense of a succession of musical tones, an air, melody (now the chief meaning) is first recorded in Trevisa's translation of Higden's *Polychronicon* (before 1387). The sense of agreement in pitch, unison, or harmony (mostly in the phrase *in* or *out of tune*) is first recorded in Middle English about 1440; the figurative sense of this usage is found in 1535. The idiomatic phrase *to the tune of,* meaning to the amount or sum of, is first recorded in 1716. —**v.** About 1500, give forth a musical sound, sing; from the noun. The sense of put into correct musical pitch is first recorded in 1505. —**tuner** *n.* About 1580, musician or singer; formed from *tune,* v. + *-er*[1]. The meaning of a person who tunes a musical instrument is first recorded in 1801, and that of a device for varying the frequency received by a radio is first recorded in 1909. —**tune-up** *n.* (1933) —**tuning fork** (1799)

tungsten *n.* metallic chemical element. 1770, borrowing of Swedish *tungsten* (*tung* heavy + *sten* stone), coined by its discoverer, the Swedish chemist, Karl Wilhelm Scheele.

tunic *n.* garment like a shirt or gown. Before 1481 *tunyk,* borrowed from Middle French *tunique,* and directly from Latin *tunica,* probably from a Semitic source (compare Hebrew *kuttōneth* coat; see CHITIN), through metathesis of earlier Latin **cituna.*

tunnel *n.* Probably before 1425 *tonel* funnel-shaped net for catching birds; borrowed from Middle French *tonnelle* net, or *tonel* cask, diminutive of Old French *tonne* tun, cask for liquids, possibly from the same source as Old English *tunne* TUN. The meaning of an underground passage is attested since 1765, about five years after the first modern tunnel was built (on the Grand Trunk Canal, England). The earlier term for a passage dug in the earth was *mine,* first recorded as an excavation for digging out ore, coal, salt, etc. (1303), but found later in the specific sense of an underground passage for reaching a fortified wall, either to enter a castle or to weaken and destroy its walls (1483). The term in mining for natural resources is now *gallery* (but was earlier known in the military sense of a horizontal underground passage, 1631). Since none of these meanings are appropriate to the modern sense of *tunnel* it is fitting that this new usage should develop. —**v.** 1577, furnish with a net; from the noun. The meaning of excavate an underground passage is first recorded in 1795 (implied in *tunnelling*).

tunny *n.* tuna. 1530, in Palsgrave's *Lesclarcissement;* alteration of Middle French *thon,* from Old Provençal *ton,* from Latin *thunnus, thynnus* a tuna, tunny, from Greek *thýnnos* a tuna, tunny, possibly in the literal sense of darter, from *thýnein* dart along, or perhaps from Hebrew *tannin* serpent, sea monster. See also TUNA. The ending *-y* in English may have been influenced by the *-a* in tuna.

tupelo (tü'pəlō) *n.* large tree of the dogwood family. About 1730, American English, apparently borrowed from Algonquian (Cree) *ito opilwa* swamp tree.

turban (tėr'bən) *n.* scarf wound around the head or around a cap. 1561 *tolipane,* in Hakluyt's *Voyages;* later *torbant* (1588), and *turban* (1597); borrowed through Middle French *turbant* from Italian *turbante,* from Turkish *tülbent* gauze, muslin, tulle, from Persian *dulband* turban. Doublet of TULIP.

turbid *adj.* 1626, muddy, thick, in Sir Francis Bacon's *Sylva Sylvarum;* borrowed from Latin *turbidus* muddy, full of confusion, from *turba* turmoil, crowd, probably borrowed from Greek *týrbē* turmoil, which is cognate with Sanskrit *tvárate, turáti* (he) hurries, and Old English *styrian* STIR[1], from Indo-European **twr̥bā,* root **(s)twer-/(s)tur-* (Pok.1100).

turbine (tėr'bin) *n.* engine with a wheel of vanes that revolve by the force of a jet of water, steam, etc. 1838, borrowing of French *turbine,* from Latin *turbō* (genitive *turbinis*) spinning top, eddy, whirlwind, any whirling object or motion, related to *turba* turmoil, crowd; see TURBID.

turbo- a combining form meaning: **1** coupled to a turbine, as in *turbogenerator = a generator coupled to a turbine* (1902). **2** powered by or consisting of a turbine, as in *turbocar = an automobile powered by a gas turbine* (1956). The terms *turbojet* (a jet engine having a turbine-driven air compressor) and *turboprop* (a turbojet with a turbine-driven propeller) are first recorded in 1944. Formed about 1900 from English *turb(ine)* + connective *-o-*, but influenced by Latin *turbō* spinning top.

turbot *n.* large European flatfish. About 1300 *turbut,* in *Havelok the Dane;* borrowed from Old French *turbut, tourbout,* from a Scandinavian source (compare Old Swedish *törnbut* turbot, from *törn* thorn + *but* flatfish; see HALIBUT). The fish is so called from its "thorns" or spines.

turbulent *adj.* Probably before 1425, unruly, violent; borrowed from Middle French *turbulent,* and directly from Latin *turbulentus* full of disturbance or commotion, restless, from *turba* turmoil, crowd; see TURBID; for suffix see -ENT. —**turbulence** *n.* Before 1410, state or quality of being turbulent; borrowed from Middle French *turbulence,* and directly from Latin *turbulentia* trouble, disgust, from *turbulentus* turbulent; for suffix see -ENCE.

tureen (tərēn′) *n.* deep, covered dish for serving soup, etc. 1706, in Kersey's edition of Phillips' *Dictionary;* borrowed from French *terrine* earthen vessel, from Old French *terrin,* adj., earthen, from Gallo-Romance **terrīnus,* from Latin *terrēnus* of the earth; see TERRAIN. The spelling with *u* is probably an everyday equivalent to *e* before *r* and is said to have arisen in cookbooks.

turf *n.* grass with its matted roots, sod. Old English (before 800) *turf;* cognate with Old Frisian, Old Saxon, Middle Dutch, and modern Dutch *turf* turf, Middle Low German *torf* (modern German *Torf* peat, turf), Old High German *zurba,* Old Icelandic *torf* (Swedish and Norwegian *torv,* Danish *tørv*), from Proto-Germanic **turƀ-*. Outside Germanic a possible cognate is found in Sanskrit *darbhá-s* tuft of grass, from Indo-European **dorbh-/dr̥bh-* (Pok.211). **—v.** cover with turf. About 1430 *turfen,* in Lydgate's *Minor Poems;* from the noun.

turgid (tėr′jid) *adj.* swollen, bloated. 1620, borrowed from Latin *turgidus* swollen, inflated, from *turgēre* to swell, of uncertain origin. The figurative sense of using long words, bombastic, pompous, is first recorded in English in 1725.

turkey *n.* 1541 (in *turkey cock*) the guinea fowl, a domesticated fowl imported from Africa by way of *Turkey.* Later (in 1555) the word *turkey* was applied to the familiar large American bird because it was originally identified with or treated as a species of the guinea fowl. If the turkey found domesticated by the Spanish in their invasion of Mexico in 1518, and found domesticated in Europe by 1530, is also the bird reputed to have reached England in 1524, then the record of English is somewhat behind the actual facts of the matter. It is further interesting to note that within about 50 years of its introduction to Europe, the turkey became associated with Christmas festivities (1575). The *turkey,* generally thought of as less than intelligent, probably from its tendency to run in panic when disturbed, has been associated with a person who is inept or unable to cope (1951) and before that with theatrical productions or motion pictures that are failures (1927). However, conversely, in the idiom *to talk turkey* (1824) the meaning has a positive aspect of talk frankly and plainly with good sense.

turmeric (tėr′mərik) *n.* yellow powder from the root of a plant, used as a seasoning, etc. 1538, alteration of Middle English *turmeryte* (probably before 1425); borrowed from Middle French *terre-mérite* saffron, from Medieval Latin *terra merita,* literally, worthy earth (Latin *terra* earth + past participle of *merēre* to earn, deserve, be worth; see TERRAIN and MERIT). Sometimes considered an alteration of some native form. *Turmeric* was undoubtedly in part so called from its tuberous form, and thus growing underground was thought to have its essence imparted from the earth it grows in.

turmoil *n.* condition of agitation or commotion. 1526, of uncertain origin. Sometimes analyzed as an alteration (influenced by TURN and MOIL) of Middle French *tremouille* mill hopper, in reference to its constant motion to and fro, from Latin *trimodia* vessel containing three modii (*tri-* three + *modius* Roman dry measure, related to *modus* measure, manner, MODE[1]).

turn *v.* Probably before 1200 *turnen,* in *Trinity Homilies;* in part developed from Old English (about 1000) *turnian* to turn; and in part borrowed from Old French *torner* to turn, both the Old English and Old French borrowed from Latin *tornāre* turn on a lathe, from *tornus* lathe, from Greek *tórnos* lathe, tool for drawing circles, related to *toreúein* to work in relief, and *tetraínein* to pierce, perforate; see THROW. **—n.** Probably before 1200, in *Ancrene Riwle;* borrowed from Old French *torn* circuit, circumference, turn, lathe, from *torner* to turn. The English noun was also influenced in meaning by the verb. **—turnbuckle** *n.* (1703) **—turncoat** *n.* person who changes his party or principles, traitor (1557). **—turner** *n.* About 1400, one who fashions things on a lathe; later, in the generalized sense of one who or that which turns (1440). **—turnkey** *n.* person in charge of the keys of a prison (1654). **—turnoff** *n.* place where a road or path turns off to another (1881). **—turnout** *n.* 1688, a signal to rise, in military use; 1816, gathering of people, assemblage; 1824, place where vehicles can pass each other. **—turnover** *n.* 1611, part which is turned or folded over; 1798, kind of tart; 1879, amount of business done in a given time, rate at which things are dealt with or processed. **—turnpike** *n.* About 1420, spiked road barrier used for defense, and later to restrict access to a road; formed from Middle English *turnen* to turn + *pike*[2] sharp spike. The sense of a toll gate is recorded before 1678, followed by that of a road with toll gates, in 1748 (earlier *turnpike road,* 1745). **—turnstile** *n.* Before 1643, gateway with bars that turn. **—turntable** *n.* 1835, revolving platform for turning locomotives around; 1908, device that rotates phonograph records.

turnip *n.* Before 1500 *turnepe,* perhaps formed from *turn* (implying its rounded shape) + Middle English *nepe* turnip; developed from Old English *nǣp,* borrowed from Latin *nāpus* turnip, of uncertain origin. The first element of the word is also analyzed as a borrowing of French *tour* turning, round, reinforced by folk etymology from the initial elements in such forms as *turbo,* found in Latin *turbō* whirlwind, spinning top, and *turbot,* where in Medieval Latin the reference is to the rounded shape of the fish. In such an instance, *tur-* would be an intensive element for the sense of round, and introduced by analogy.

turpentine *n.* mixture of oil and resin obtained from various pine trees. About 1400 *turpentyne;* earlier *terebentyn* (1322); borrowed from Old French *terebentine,* from Latin *terebinthina* in *terebinthina rēsīna* resin of the terebinth tree, a small European tree related to the sumac, from Greek *terebinthínē* in *rhētínē terebinthínē,* feminine of *terebínthinos* of the terebinth, from *terébinthos,* earlier *términthos* terebinth tree, probably from a pre-Greek language.

turpitude *n.* 1490, shameful wickedness, baseness, in Caxton's translation of *The Book of Eneydos;* borrowed from Middle French *turpitude,* learned borrowing from Latin *turpitūdō* (accusative *turpitūdinem*) baseness, from *turpis* vile, of unknown origin; for suffix see -TUDE.

turquoise (tėr′kwoiz) *n.* sky-blue or greenish-blue precious stone. 1567, replacement (by influence of Middle French *turquoise*) of Middle English *turkeis* (before 1398, in Trevisa's translation of Bartholomew's *De Proprietatibus Rerum*); originally borrowed from Old French *turqueise,* feminine adj. Turkish, in *pierre turqueise* Turkish stone, from *Turc* Turk; so called because it was first found in Turkestan or the Turkish dominions. **—adj.** sky-blue, greenish-blue. 1573, from the noun.

turret *n.* Probably about 1300 *turet* small tower, in *The Romance of Guy of Warwick;* borrowed from Old French *touret,* diminutive of *tour* tower, from Latin *turris;* see TOWER; for suffix see -ET.

turtle[1] *n.* aquatic reptile. 1657, in a translation of Plutarch's *Lives;* borrowed as an alteration (influenced by *turtle*[2]) of French *tortue* turtle, tortoise.

In an effort to make a connection of form and meaning between "turtle" and its relation to "the underworld," it is suggested that French *tortue* (perhaps also earlier **tortūga*) was an alteration (influenced by *tortus* twisted, because of the shape of the feet) of still earlier **tartūca,* from Vulgar Latin **tartarūca* hellish beast of Tartarus (the infernal regions), from Late Latin *tartarūchus* of the underworld, from Late Greek *Tartaroûchos* occupying Tartarus (*Tartaro-,* stem of *Tártaros* Tartarus, the infernal regions + *-óchos* possessing, related to *échein* to hold). Further connection rests on the supposition that the turtle was probably so called because in St. Jerome's time it was a symbol of heresy, by its previous association with the underworld or the deep, and may have been a word of English sailors, who altered the French *tortue* by substituting the like-sounding, known word *turtle*[2] as indicated above.

—turtleneck *adj.* having a high, close-fitting collar (1895, American English).

turtle[2] *n. Rare or obsolete.* turtledove. Old English (about 1000) *turtle, turtla;* borrowed from Latin *turtur* turtledove, a reduplicated form probably imitative of the call of the dove.

turtledove *n.* kind of small, slender dove. About 1300, formed from *turtle*[2] turtledove + *dove.*

tusk *n.* very long, pointed, projecting tooth. Probably about 1200, possibly an alteration (by metathesis of the sounds *ks* to *sk,* represented by *-x*) of Old English (before 899) *tūx,* variant of *tūsc* tusk; cognate with Old Frisian *tusk* tooth, perhaps from Proto-Germanic **tunthskaz,* extended form of the root found in Gothic *tunthus* TOOTH. **—v.** 1486, to carve (a barbel); from the noun. The meaning of dig or tear with tusks is first recorded in 1629.

tussah or **tussore** *n.* kind of coarse tan silk made especially in India. 1619 *tessar,* in *The English Factories in India,* edited by William Foster; borrowed from Hindi *tasar* shuttle, from Prakrit *ṭasara-, tasara-,* from Sanskrit *tásara-m* shuttle, related to *taṅsayati* draws back and forth, from Indo-European **tens-/tṇs-* to stretch (Pok.1068). The form with *-ore* was probably influenced by Indian place names such as *Mysore.*

tussle *v.* About 1470 *tussillen* to wrestle, scuffle; originally Scottish and Northern British English variant of *touselen* to TOUSLE. **—n.** a wrestling or scuffling. 1629, from the verb.

tussock *n.* tuft of growing grass, sedge, or the like. 1550, tuft of hair, in Latimer's *Sermons;* of uncertain origin, but found with the same meaning of a tuft of hair in 1530. The connection, however, is unknown. The extended sense of tuft of grass, sedge, or the like, is first recorded in 1607.

tut *interj.* exclamation of impatience, contempt, or rebuke. Before 1529, in Skelton's writings, perhaps a later variation on *trut* (about 1330); or sometimes associated with the now archaic and more affected *tush* (about 1440).

tutelage *n.* 1605, office or function of a guardian; formed in English from Latin *tūtēla* a watching, protection (*tūt-,* variant past participle stem of *tuērī* watch over; see TUITION) + English *-age.* The meaning of condition of being in the charge of a guardian is first recorded in 1650, and that of instruction, tuition, in 1857.

tutelary (tü'tələr'ē) *adj.* protecting, guardian. 1611, borrowed from Latin *tūtēlārius* guardian, from *tūtēla* protection, watching; see TUTELAGE; for suffix see -ARY. **—n.** tutelary saint, spirit, divinity, etc. 1652, from the adjective.

tutor *n.* Before 1376 *tutour* guardian, private teacher, in *Piers Plowman;* borrowed from Old French *tutour* guardian, private teacher, from Latin *tūtor* guardian, watcher, from *tūt-,* variant past participle stem of *tuērī* watch over; see TUITION; for suffix see -OR[2]. **—v.** teach privately. 1592, in William Warner's *Albions England;* from the noun. **—tutorial** *adj.* 1742, formed in English from Latin *tūtōrius* of a tutor (from *tūtor* tutor) + English *-al*[1]. *—n.* period of individual instruction given by a college tutor. 1923, from the adjective.

tutti-frutti (tü'tē frü'tē) *n.* ice cream or confection with mixed fruit flavors. 1834, American English, borrowing of Italian *tutti frutti* all fruits; *tutti,* plural of *tutto* all, from Vulgar Latin **tōttus,* alteration of Latin *tōtus;* and *frutti,* plural of *frutto* fruit, from Latin *frūctus* FRUIT.

tutu (tü'tü) *n.* very short stiff skirt worn by a ballet dancer. 1910, borrowing of French *tutu,* an alteration of *cucu,* infantile reduplication of *cul* bottom, backside; see CUL-DE-SAC, CULOTTES.

tuxedo (tuksē'dō) *n.* man's jacket or suit for evening wear. 1889, American English; named after *Tuxedo* Park, N.Y., site of a country club where it was first worn in 1886.

twaddle *n.* silly, feeble, tiresome talk. 1782, probably an alteration of *twattle* (1556, in *twittle-twattle*), with *twattle* possibly an alteration of TATTLE. **—v.** 1825, talk or write in a silly, empty style; from the noun.

twain *adj. Archaic.* two. Probably before 1200 *tweien,* developed from Old English (about 725) *twēgen,* masculine, TWO.

twang *n.* Before 1553, ringing sound produced when a tense string is plucked, felt to be imitative of the sound of the vibrating string (in *-ang*), and also of the dull sound of the plucking itself (in *tw-*). The sense of a sharp, nasal vocal sound, is first recorded in 1661. **—v.** 1542, make a ringing sound, play on a stringed instrument; of imitative origin like the noun.

tweak *v.* seize and pull with a sharp jerk and twist. 1601, in Holland's translation of Pliny's *Natural History;* variant of *twick,* found in Middle English *twykken* (1440); developed from Old English (before 1000) *twiccian* to pluck; see TWITCH. **—n.** sharp pull and twist. 1609, in Ben Jonson's *Epicoene;* from the verb.

tweed *n.* cloth woven with two or more colors. 1847 (but said to be known about 1831), a trade name, developing reputedly from a misreading (by James Locke, the London hatter) of *tweel,* Scottish variant of TWILL, possibly influenced by the name of the river *Tweed* in Scotland. **—tweedy** *adj.* 1912, consisting of or relating to tweed, formed from English *tweed,* n. + *-y*[1]. The figurative sense of characteristic of the country or suburban set who consider it fashionable to wear tweed clothing, and thought of as exclusively clannish or heartily informal, is first recorded in 1912.

tweezers *n.pl.* small pincers. 1654, extended form (probably on the pattern of *scissors*) of *tweezes,* plural of earlier *tweeze* case for tweezers and other small instruments (1622), shortened from *etweese,* considered as singular and plural of *etwee* a small case (1611); borrowed from French *étui* small case; originally, a keeping safe, from Old French *estuier* to keep, shut up, imprison (compare Old Provençal *estojar, estujar* with the same meanings). Though the Old French form could be from Vulgar Latin **studiāre* be zealous, attend to (from Latin *studium* zeal, attentiveness; see STUDY), it does not fit too well semantically. **—tweeze** *v.* to use tweezers. 1932, in Virginia Woolf's *The Common Reader;* back formation from *tweezers* or *tweezer,* n., v. **—tweezer** *v.* to use tweezers, pull out with tweezers. 1806, back formation from *tweezers.* —*n.* tweezers. 1904, in H.G. Wells' *The Food of the Gods;* back formation from *tweezers.*

twelve *adj.* About 1175 *twelve,* developed from Old English *twelf;* literally, two left (over ten), before 899, in Alfred's translation of Boethius' *De Consolatione Philosophiae.* Old English *twelf* is cognate with Old Frisian *twelef, twelif* twelve, Old Saxon *twelif,* Middle Dutch *twalef* (modern Dutch *twaalf*), Old High German *zwelif* (modern German *zwölf*), Old Icelandic *tōlf* (Swedish, Danish, and Norwegian *tolv*), and Gothic *twalif;* all developed from a Germanic compound made up of the source of Old English *twēgen, twā* TWO, + the root *-lif-* of the verb LEAVE[1]; see ELEVEN. **—twelfth** *adj., n.* Before 1387 *twelfthe;* formed from Middle English *twelf* + *-the* -th[2]; replacing Old English *twelfta* (*twelf* twelve + *-ta* -th[2]; 878, in *twelftan niht*).

twenty *adj.* Old English (before 899) *twēntig* group of twenty (*twēgen* TWO + *-tig* group of ten, -TY[1]). Old English *twēntig* is cognate with Old Frisian *twintich, tweintich,* Old Saxon *twēntig,* Dutch *twintig,* Old High German *zweinzug.* **—twentieth** *n., adj.* Old English (before 900) *twēntigotha* (*twēntig* twenty + *-tha* -th[2]).

twerp *n. Slang.* stupid, undesirable or inferior person. 1925, of unknown origin.

twi- a prefix meaning two, in two ways, twice, double, of Old English origin but little used nowadays. It is the stem of such words as *twice, twig, twill,* and *twin,* and the first component of *twibill,* an old name for any of several two-bladed tools, and of *twilight.* Old English *twi-* (from Proto-Germanic **twi-*) is cognate with Old High German *zwi-* two, Old Icelandic *tvī-*, Sanskrit *dvi-*, Greek *di-*, and Latin *bi-* (Old Latin *dvi-*), from Indo-European **dwi-* (Pok.229). Related to TWO. Compare BI-, DI-.

twice *adv.* About 1250 *twies;* developed from Old English *twiga, twigea* twice (before 899; related to *twi-* two, TWI-) + *-es,* genitive singular ending used adverbially; see -S[3]. The Old English forms are cognate with Old Frisian *twia* twice, Old Saxon *twio,* and Middle Low German *twie.*

The final *-s* was voiceless and so began to be spelled *-ce,* as in *ice, mice,* to show this pronunciation.

twiddle *v.* cause to rotate lightly or delicately, twirl, as with the thumbs. About 1540, to trifle, of unknown origin (sometimes said to combine the idea of *twist,* or *twirl* and *fiddle*). The meaning of cause to rotate lightly or delicately is first recorded in 1676. **—n.** a twirl, twist. 1774, from the verb.

twig *n.* Old English (about 950) *twigge,* related to *twig* (plural *twigu*), from *twi-* two, TWI- (in the sense of "forked"; also found in obsolete *twisel* a fork or point of division, 931, Old English *twisla*). Old English *twig* is from Proto-Germanic **twiȝán,* cognate with Sanskrit *dvika-* consisting of two, from Indo-European **dwikós* (Pok.231). Neither Old English *twigge* nor *twig* correspond exactly to the usual Continental forms having the same sense of slender shoot, twig; compare Middle Low German *twich* twig, Middle Dutch *twijch* (modern Dutch *twijg*), and Old High German *zwīg* (modern German *Zweig*).

twilight *n.* faint light of the sun before rising or after setting. Before 1420, in Lydgate's *Troy Book,* formed in Middle English from *twi-* + *light*[1] radiant energy; compare Low German *Twelecht* twilight. The exact connotation of *twi-* is obscure but even though appearing twice in each day probably refers to half light (as *bi-* implies half in one of the senses of *bimonthly,* meaning each half of a month or twice a month). The figurative sense of the period just before or after full development is first recorded in Shakespeare's *Sonnets* (about 1600).

twill *n.* cloth woven in raised diagonal lines. 1329 *twyll,* Scottish and Northern British English variant of Middle English *twile;* developed from Old English (about 700) *twilī* woven with double thread, twilled, borrowed from Latin *bilīx* (with substitution of English *twi-* two for Latin *bi-*). Latin *bilīx* (genitive *bilīcis*) with a double thread is formed from *bi-* two + *licium* thread, which is of uncertain origin (compare German *Zwillich* twill). **—v.** weave (cloth) in this way. 1808-18, in Jamieson's *Dictionary of the Scottish Language;* from the noun.

twin *adj.* Old English (about 1000) *twinn* consisting of two, twofold, double, from **twi-* two, TWI-. Old English *twinn* (probably ultimately from Proto-Germanic **twinjaz*) is cognate with Middle Dutch *twēlinc* twin (modern Dutch *tweeling*), Old High German *zwinal* born a twin, *zwiniling* twin (modern German *Zwilling*), and Old Icelandic *tvinnr, tvennr* double, in pairs. The meaning of born at the same birth is first recorded in English in Shakespeare's *Comedy of Errors* (1590). The meaning of forming a pair is found in 1591. **—n.** Probably before 1300 *twyn* one of two children born at the same birth; earlier *itwinn* (probably before 1200); developed from Old English (before 900) *getwinn* double; related to *twinn,* adj. **—v.** Probably about 1395 *twinnen* give birth to twins, from *twin,* adj. or n.

twine *n.* thread or string made of two or more strands twisted together. Probably before 1200 *twin,* in Layamon's *Chronicle of Britain;* developed from Old English (about 700) *twīn* a double thread, from *twi-* two, TWI-. Old English *twīn* is cognate with Middle Dutch and modern Dutch *twijn* twine, Middle High German *zwirn* (modern German *Zwirn*), and Old Icelandic *tvinni,* from Proto-Germanic **twizna-*, Indo-European **dwisno-*, the source of Latin *bīnī* two by two. **—v.** twist together. Probably before 1200 *twinen,* in Layamon's *Chronicle of Britain;* from the noun.

twinge *v.* feel a sudden sharp pain. About 1250 *twengen* to pinch, tweak, twitch, in *The Owl and the Nightingale;* developed from Old English (about 1000) *twengan* to pinch, of uncertain origin. The meaning of feel a sudden sharp pain is first recorded in 1640 from the earlier noun sense. —**n.** sudden sharp pain. 1548, act of pinching; from the verb. The meaning of sudden sharp pain is first recorded in 1608, in Middleton's *A Mad World My Masters.*

twinkle *v.* About 1350 *twynkelen* to sparkle, glitter, wink; developed from Old English *twinclian* (before 899, in Alfred's translation of Boethius' *De Consolatione Philosophiae*), frequentative form of *twincan* to wink, blink (also found in Middle and modern English *twink,* about 1400); cognate with Middle High German *zwinken* to wink (modern German *zwinkern*); for suffix see -LE[3]. —**n.** 1548, a winking of the eye; later, a sparkle, gleam (1663); also found in Middle and modern English *twink* (1471); from the verb. —**twinkling** *n.* Before 1300, the act of winking; later, the action of shining with wavering light (1398), and time taken to wink, as in *the twinkling of an eye* (1303).

twirl *v.* 1598, to spin, whirl, in Florio's *A World of Words;* of uncertain origin (possibly a blend of *twist* and *whirl,* or an alteration of *tirl* to twirl, about 1500, or less likely, connected with Old English *thwirl* a stirrer). —**n.** a twirling, spin, whirl, turn. 1598, in Florio's *A World of Words;* from the verb.

twist *n.* 1350-51, a divided or branched object or part, especially the flat part of a hinge, in reference to what a door twists or turns on; developed from Old English *-twist,* as in *mæsttwist* mast rope, stay, from *twi-* two, TWI-. Old English *-twist* is cognate with Old Frisian and Middle Low German *twist* quarrel, Middle Low German, Middle Dutch, and modern Dutch *twist,* Middle High German *zwist* (modern German *Zwist*), and Old Icelandic *tvistra* divide. The sense of a thread or cord formed by twisting two or more separate strands together is first recorded in 1555. The meaning of act or process of twisting is found in 1576, with associated senses derived mainly from the verb. —**v.** Probably before 1200 *tweasten* to divide, branch, in *Ancrene Riwle;* later *twasten* to wring, wrench (about 1330), and in the spelling *twisten* (1340); from the noun, developing out of Old English. The sense of to branch or divide is now obsolete in English, but the sense of combine, unite, is found as early as 1471, with the figurative meaning of entangle, confuse (as in *twist up someone's story*) recorded by 1863. The sense of rotate, revolve, is first recorded in 1789, developing out of the earlier sense of combine. —**twister** *n.* Probably about 1475, one that twists; formed from *twist,* v. + *-er*[1]. The informal sense of a whirling windstorm, tornado, is first recorded in 1897 in American English, but this sense may be found earlier in the Middle English "twyster of trees" (probably about 1475).

twit *v.* jeer at, reproach, taunt, tease. 1573, from earlier *twite* (1530, in Palsgrave's *Lesclarcissement*); shortened form of Middle English *atwiten;* developed from Old English *ætwītan* to blame, reproach (*æt* AT + *wītan* to blame, related to *witan* to know, WIT[2]). Old English *wītan* is cognate with Old Frisian *wīta* to punish, blame, Old Saxon *wītan,* Old High German *wīzan,* Old Icelandic *vīta,* and Gothic *fraweitan* avenge, from Proto-Germanic **wītanan,* originally, take notice of. —**n.** reproach, taunt. 1664, from earlier *twite* (1528); from the verb. The sense of a stupid person, fool, is first recorded in 1934.

twitch *v.* move with a quick jerk. About 1175 *to-twicchen* pull apart with a quick jerk; later *tuicchen* (about 1300), related to Old English *twiccian* to pluck; cognate with Low German *twicken* to pinch, tweak, Dutch *twikken,* and Old High German *gizwickan* (modern German *zwicken*), from Proto-Germanic **twikjōnan.* The meaning of move with a quick jerk is first recorded in 1523. —**n.** quick jerky movement. 1523, from the verb.

twitter *v.* About 1380 *twiteren* utter a series of light sounds, chirp, in Chaucer's translation of Boethius' *De Consolatione Philosophiae;* of imitative origin like Old High German *zwizzirōn* to twitter (modern German *zwitschern*); for suffix see -ER[4]. The meaning of be in a flutter, tremble, is first recorded before 1616. —**n.** 1678, state of agitation, flutter, in Samuel Butler's *Hudibras;* from the verb. The meaning of the action of chirping is first recorded in 1842.

two *adj.* Probably before 1200 *two,* in *Ancrene Riwle;* developed from Old English *twā* (about 725, in *Beowulf*), feminine and neuter form of *twēgen* two; cognate with Old Frisian *twēne* (feminine and neuter *twā*), Old Saxon *twēne* (feminine *twā*), (neuter *twē*), Middle Dutch and modern Dutch *twee,* Old High German *zwēne* (feminine *zwō, zwā*), (neuter *zwei*), modern German *zwei,* Old Icelandic *tveir* (feminine *tvǣr*), (neuter *tvau*), and Gothic *twai* (feminine *twōs*), (neuter *twa*), from Proto-Germanic **twai.* Cognates outside Germanic are found in Latin *duo* two, Old Irish *dāu, dā,* Albanian *dü,* Greek *dýo,* Lithuanian *dù,* Old Slavic *dŭva,* Sanskrit *dvāú, dvā́,* Tocharian A *wu,* Tocharian B *wī,* and probably Hittite *tān* again; Indo-European masculine **duwō (u)/ dwō (u);* feminine, neuter **duwoi/ dwoi* (Pok.228).

The pronunciation (tü) developed by elimination of the sound represented by *w* in earlier (twü) which had developed from earlier Middle English (twō). —**two-by-four** *n.* piece of lumber originally two inches thick and four inches wide (1884, American English). The informal sense of small, insignificant, is first recorded in 1897. —**two-faced** *adj.* deceitful (before 1619). —**two-fisted** *adj. Informal.* tough, vigorous (1774, American English). —**twofold** *adj., adv.* About 1175 *twafalde;* later *twofolde* (about 1394); alteration of Old English *tweofeald* (about 890), *twyfeald* (before 899); formed from Old English *twi-* two, double + *-feald* -fold. —**two-time** *v. Slang.* betray, be unfaithful to (1924, American English). —**two-way** *adj.* (1571)

-ty[1] a suffix representing ten in forming the cardinal numbers that are multiples of ten, from *twenty* to *ninety,* as in *seventy = seven tens, or seven times ten.* Developed from Old English *-tig,* cognate with Old High German *-zug* and modern German *-zig,* with corresponding forms in other West Germanic languages; an older stage is represented in Gothic *tigjus* and Old Icelandic *tigir,* independent words meaning tens or decades; see TEN.

-ty[2] a suffix forming abstract nouns from adjectives, meaning the fact, quality, or condition of being ______, as in *safety = condition of being safe, cruelty = fact or quality of being cruel.* Middle English *-tie, -tee, -te,* from Old French *-té,* from Latin *-tātem* (*-tās,* genitive *-tātis*). See -ITY. In some words the suffix is not recognizable as such, as in *city.*

tycoon (tīkün′) *n.* important businessman or leader. 1857, title given by foreigners to the shogun of Japan; borrowed from Japanese *taikun* great lord or prince, from Chinese *tai* great + *kiun* lord. The spelling was influenced by the English suffixal ending -OON.

tyke *n.* About 1378, cur, mongrel; borrowed from a

Scandinavian source (compare Old Icelandic *tīk* bitch; cognate with Middle Low German *tīke* bitch). The meaning of a child is first recorded in 1902, in American English, though the sense of *tyke* in playful reproof to a child is recorded earlier, in 1894.

tympanum (tim′pənəm) *n.* eardrum. 1619, in Purchas' *Microcosmus;* borrowed from Medieval Latin *tympanum,* from Latin *tympanum* drum, from Greek *týmpanon* a drum, panel of a door, from root of *týptein* to beat, strike; see TYPE. Doublet of TIMBRE. Compare TIMPANI. **—tympanic** *adj.* 1808, of or having to do with the eardrum; formed from English *tympanum* + *-ic.*

type *n.* About 1470, symbol, emblem, in Robert Henryson's *The Moral Fable of Esop;* borrowed from Latin *typus* figure, image, form, kind, from Greek *týpos* dent, impression, mark, figure, something made of metal or stone, type, original form from root of *týptein* to strike, beat. Greek *týptein* is cognate with Sanskrit *tupáti, túmpati* (he) hurts, from Indo-European *(*s*)*tup-* hit (Pok.1034). The meaning of the general form or character of some kind, class, or group, is first recorded in English in 1843, in John Stuart Mill's *System of Logic,* and that of kind, class, or group having common characteristics, in 1854, both senses evolving from the original sense in English and also from the same senses in Latin and Greek. The technical meaning of a block having on its upper surface a raised letter for use in printing is curiously not recorded before 1713 (compare TYPOGRAPHY). **—v.** 1596, (in theology) to foreshadow as a type, prefigure (as in *a time typed by the Sabbath day*); from the noun. The meaning of be a type of, symbolize, is first recorded in 1836. The modern sense of to write with a typewriter is found in 1888, by shortening of *typewrite.* **—typescript** *n.* a typewritten manuscript (1893). **—typesetter** *n.* person or machine that sets type for printing (1867). **—typewrite** *v.* write with a typewriter. 1887, back formation from *typewriter.* **—typewriter** *n.* 1868, American English; formed from English *type,* n. + *writer.* **—typist** *n.* 1843, printer, compositor; formed from English *type,* n. + *-ist.* The meaning of a person who operates a typewriter is first recorded in 1885.

typhoid (tī′foid) *adj.* of or resembling typhus (applied to an infectious disease characterized by intestinal inflammation, now called typhoid fever, formerly thought to be a variety of typhus). 1800, formed from English *typhus* + *-oid.* **—n.** typhoid fever. 1861, shortened form of *typhoid fever* (1845, in the current sense).

typhoon (tīfün′) *n.* 1555 *tiphon* violent storm, hurricane; borrowed from Greek *tȳphôn;* later *touffon,* in Thomas Hickock's translation of *The Voyage and Travaile of M.C. Frederick into the East India* (1588); presumably borrowed from Chinese (Cantonese) *tai fung* a great wind; influenced in form by Greek *tȳphôn* whirlwind, and by the English ending -OON. It is also probable that the identical meanings of Arabic, Persian, and Hindi *tūfān* (from Greek *tȳphôn*) influenced the adoption and formation of this word in English. The spelling *typhoon* is not recorded before 1819, in Shelley's *Prometheus Unbound.*

typhus (tī′fəs) *n.* acute infectious disease caused by a rickettsia carried by fleas, lice, etc. 1785, New Latin, from Greek *tŷphos* stupor caused by fever; originally, smoke, from *tȳ́phein* to smoke, related to *typhlós* blind; see DEAF.

typical *adj.* 1612 (implied earlier in *typically* 1605), symbolical, emblematic; borrowed from Medieval Latin *typicalis* figurative, symbolic, from Late Latin *typicus* of or pertaining to a type, from Greek *typikós,* from *týpos* impression, TYPE; for suffix see -AL[1]. The sense of distinctive, characteristic, is first recorded in English in 1850.

typify *v.* be a symbol of. 1634, formed in English from Latin *typus* TYPE + English *-ify,* variant of *-fy.*

typography *n.* art, practice, or process of printing with type. 1641, in Evelyn's *Diary;* borrowed from French *typographie,* from Medieval Latin *typographia,* from Greek *týpos* TYPE + *-graphíā* writing, -GRAPHY. **—typographical** *adj.* of or having to do with printing. 1593, formed in English probably by influence of French *typographique,* from Medieval Latin *typographicus* (from *typographia* typography) + English *-al*[1].

tyrannical *adj.* of or like a tyrant. 1538, formed in English from Latin *tyrannicus* like a tyrant, despotic (from Greek *tyrannikós* of or pertaining to a tyrant, from *týrannos* TYRANT*)* + English *-al*[1]. **—tyrannize** *v.* 1494, to rule as a tyrant; borrowed from Middle French *tyranniser,* from Old French *tyran* TYRANT*;* for suffix see -IZE. Perhaps formed in Middle French on the model of Late Latin *tyrannizāre* to act the tyrant. **—tyranny** *n.* About 1370 *tyrannie* cruel or unjust use of power, in Chaucer's *Complaint Unto Pite;* borrowed from Old French *tyrannie,* from Late Latin *tyrannia* tyranny, from Greek *tyranníā,* from *týrannos* master, TYRANT; for suffix see -Y[3].

tyrannosaurus *n.* a huge flesh-eating dinosaur that walked erect. 1905, in New Latin the genus name, from Greek *týrannos* tyrant + *saûros* lizard.

tyrant *n.* Probably before 1300 *tyraunt* absolute ruler; borrowed from Old French *tyrant,* alteration (by influence of the present participle suffix *-ant*) of earlier *tyran,* learned borrowing from Latin *tyrannus* lord, master, tyrant, from Greek *týrannos* lord, master, sovereign, tyrant; probably a borrowed word.

tyro (tī′rō) *n.* beginner in learning anything, novice. 1611, in Coryat's *Crudities;* borrowed from Medieval Latin *tyro,* variant of Latin *tīrō* young soldier, recruit, beginner, of uncertain origin. The plural *tyrones* (after Latin *tīrōnēs*) is found down to 1824, although *tyroes* appeared in 1672, and *tyros* in 1690.

U

ubiquity (yübik′wətē) *n.* a being everywhere at the same time. 1579, borrowed from Middle French *ubiquité,* also possibly from New Latin *ubiquitas* that is everywhere, from Latin *ubīque* everywhere (*ubī* where + *-que,* an ending that can give universal meaning to the word it is attached to); for suffix see -ITY. Latin *ubī* (and note *-cubi* in *sī-cubi* if anywhere) is cognate with Umbrian *pufe* and Sanskrit *kúha* where?, from Indo-European **kwu-dhe* (Pok.647). Latin *-que* (as in *quisque* "everyone" beside *quis* who?) is cognate with Gothic *-h* in *hwaz-u-h* each, every (beside *hwas* who?), from Indo-European *-kwe* meaning and (Pok.635). **—ubiquitous** *adj.* present everywhere. 1837, formed from English *ubiquity* + *-ous.*

U-boat *n.* German submarine. 1916, partial translation of German *U-Boot,* shortened form of *Unterseeboot* submarine; literally, undersea boat.

udder *n.* 1398 *udder;* developed from Old English (before 1000) *ūder* milk gland of a cow, goat, etc.; cognate with Old Frisian and Old Saxon *ūder* udder, Middle Low German and Middle Dutch *ūder* (modern Dutch *uier*), Old High German *ūtar* (modern German *Euter*), and probably (by unexplained consonant change) Old Icelandic *jūgr* (Norwegian *jur,* Danish *yver,* Swedish *juver*). Cognates outside Germanic are found in Latin *ūber* udder, Greek *oûthar,* and Sanskrit *ū́dhar,* from Indo-European **ēudhr̥/ōudhr̥/ūdhr̥* (Pok.347).

The long vowel in Old English was shortened in early Middle English, a process that occurred regularly in closed syllables (syllables that end in a consonant sound). In this word the shortening probably occurred in an oblique case such as the genitive *udres* (from Old English *ūderes*), and then spread by analogy to the other cases. The same process occurred in *fodder* (Old English *fōdor*) and *ladder* (Old English *hlǣder*).

UFO (yü′ef′ō′) *n.* unidentified flying object, flying saucer. 1953, American English, acronym formed from the initial letters of *u(nidentified) f(lying) o(bject).*

ugly *adj.* Before 1325 *ugli* frightful or horrible in appearance, in *Cursor Mundi;* earlier (about 1250) *uglike,* in *Genesis and Exodus;* borrowed from a Scandinavian source (compare Old Icelandic *uggligr* dreadful, from *uggr* fear, perhaps related to *agg* strife, hate); for suffix see -LY². The meaning of very unpleasant to look at, unsightly, repulsive, is first recorded in Middle English about 1375. The figurative sense of morally offensive or repulsive, loathsome, vile (as in *an ugly deed*) is first recorded before 1325, in *Cursor Mundi.* **—ugliness** *n.* About 1390; formed from Middle English *ugli* + *-ness.*

ukase (yükās′) *n.* decree or edict. 1729, decree issued by a Russian emperor or government; borrowed from Russian *ukáz* edict, from *ukazát'* to show, decree, from Old Slavic *ukazati* (prefix *u-* + *kazati* to show, order, from Indo-European **kwōĝ-,* Pok.639).

ukulele (yü′kəlā′lē) *n.* small guitar with four strings. 1896, American English; borrowed from Hawaiian *'ukulele;* literally, leaping flea (*'uku* louse, flea + *lele* to fly, jump, leap); possibly so called from the Hawaiian nickname of Edward Purvis, a British army officer of the late 1800's noted for his smallness and quick movements, who popularized the instrument brought to Hawaii by the Portuguese about 1879. The ukulele became popular for a time in the United States, especially during the 1920's, and again in the late 1940's.

ulcer *n.* open sore on the surface of the body or on one of its internal organs that discharges pus. Before 1400, in Lanfranc's *Science of Surgery;* borrowed from Old French *ulcere,* and directly from Latin *ulcus* (genitive *ulceris*) ulcer. Latin *ulcus* is cognate with Greek *hélkos* wound, ulcer (alteration of **élkos* by influence of *hélkein* draw, pull), and Sanskrit *árśas* hemorrhoids, from Indo-European **élkos* (Pok.310). The figurative use of a corrupting influence is first recorded in English in 1592. **—ulcerate** *v.* About 1425 *ulceraten* to form an ulcer; possibly in part a back formation from earlier *ulceration* (about 1400, in Lanfranc); and in part borrowed from Latin *ulcerātus,* past participle of *ulcerāre,* from *ulcus* (genitive *ulceris*) ulcer; for suffix see -ATE¹. **—ulcerous** *adj.* Probably about 1425, like an ulcer; borrowed from Latin *ulcerōsus* full of ulcers, from *ulcus* (genitive *ulceris*) ulcer; for suffix see -OUS.

-ule a suffix meaning small, little, as in *capsule, globule, granule, module, nodule.* Borrowed from French *-ule,* learned borrowing from Latin *-ulus* (feminine *-ula*), (neuter *-ulum*), diminutive suffix.

ulterior *adj.* 1646, borrowed from Latin *ulterior* more distant, further, comparative of **ulter, *ulterus* beyond, ULTRA. Compare EXTERIOR. The sense of beyond what is stated or evident, intentionally concealed (as in *ulterior motives*) is first recorded in English in 1735.

ultimate *adj.* 1654, in writings of Jeremy Taylor; borrowed from Medieval Latin *ultimatum* last possible, final, from Latin *ultimātum,* past participle of *ultimāre* be final, come to an end, from *ultimus* last, final, superlative of **ulter, *ulterus* beyond, ULTRA; for suffix see -ATE¹. **—n.** ultimate point, result, fact, etc. 1681, from the adjective.

ultimatum (ul′təmā′təm) *n.* 1731, New Latin *ultimatum* the final terms presented by one power to another in international diplomacy, noun use of Medieval Latin *ultimatum* ULTIMATE. The general meaning of a final condition or stipulation, one's last word in the matter, is first recorded in English in 1733, in the letters of Swift.

ultra *adj.* beyond what is usual, very, excessive, extreme. 1817, borrowing of French *ultra,* especially as a shortening of *ultra-royaliste* extreme royalist, from Latin *ultrā,* adv. and prep., beyond, on the further side. Latin *ultrā* is cognate with Old Irish *oll* large, big; originally, extending beyond (the usual), and Welsh *oll, holl* all, entire, from Indo-European **olnos* (root **ol-,* Pok.24), source of Old Latin *olle* that (over there).

ultra- a prefix meaning: **1** beyond, as in *ultraviolet* = *beyond the violet color* (1840). **2** going beyond the limits of, as in *ultramundane* = *going beyond the limits of the mundane* (1656). **3** extremely, as in *ultramodern* = *extremely modern* (1843). Borrowed from Latin *ultrā-*, from *ultrā*, adv. and prep., beyond; see ULTRA. Compare EXTRA-.

ultrasonic *adj.* 1923, having a frequency beyond the audible range; formed from English *ultra-* beyond + *sonic.* Compare SUPERSONIC. **—ultrasonics** *n.* 1924, ultrasonic waves; later, science that deals with ultrasonic phenomena (1940); formed from English *ultrasonic* + *-s*[1]; see -ICS.

ululate (yül'yəlāt) *v.* howl, as a dog or wolf. 1623, in Cockeram's *Dictionary;* probably a back formation from earlier *ululation,* and a borrowing from Latin *ululātus,* past participle of *ululāre* to howl or wail, of imitative origin; for suffix see -ATE[1]. **—ululation** *n.* 1599, a howl or wail, cry of lamentation; borrowed from Latin *ululātiōnem* (nominative *ululātiō*) a howling or wailing, from *ululāre* ululate; for suffix see -ATION.

umber (um'bər) *n.* kind of earth used as a reddish-brown pigment. About 1568 (implied in *umber-color*); borrowed from Middle French *ombre* (also *terre d'ombre*) or from Italian *ombra* (also *terra di ombra*), the two words meaning either "shadow," from Latin *umbra* shadow, shade (see UMBRAGE), or "Umbria," from Latin *Umbra,* feminine of *Umber* belonging to Umbria, a region in central Italy, from which the coloring matter first came. **—adj.** brown or reddish-brown. 1802, from the noun.

umbilical *adj.* of the navel. 1541, borrowed from Medieval Latin *umbilicalis* of the umbilicus or navel, from Latin *umbilīcus* NAVEL; for suffix see -AL[1]. *Umbilical* replaced Middle English *umbilic,* adj. and n. (probably before 1425, in a translation of Chauliac's *Grande Chirurgie*); borrowed from Latin *umbilīcus* navel. **—umbilical cord** (1753)

umbrage *n.* 1426, a shadow; borrowed from Middle French *ombrage* shade, shadow, from Latin *umbrāticum,* neuter of *umbrāticus* of or pertaining to shade, from *umbra* shade, shadow, from earlier **unzrā,* from **unksrā,* cognate with Lithuanian *ùnksna* shadow, and *úkanas* cloudy, from Indo-European **uk-,* root **wek-* (Pok.1173). The meaning of shadowy appearance or indication, semblance, is first recorded in Shakespeare's *Hamlet* (1604), and that of suspicion that one has been slighted, annoyance, resentment, offense, in 1620; later, especially in the phrase *to take umbrage at* (1680).

umbrella *n.* 1610 *umbrello,* 1611 *umbrella;* borrowed from Italian *ombrello, ombrella,* from Late Latin *umbrella,* alteration (by influence of **umbra*) of Latin *umbella* sunshade, parasol, diminutive form of *umbra* shade, shadow; see UMBRAGE. The form *umbrello* was used in English as a common variant of *umbrella* until the mid-1700's. An earlier form *umbrel* is found in 1603, in Florio's translation of Montaigne's *Essays.* Though strictly a borrowing from French, the term is ultimately from Italian and semantically suggestive of Middle English and early modern English *umbrel* the visor on a helmet (about 1470); later, hat with a broad brim (1688), borrowed from Middle French *ombrel,* probably from Italian *ombrello, ombrella.*

umiak (ü'mēak) *n.* open Eskimo boat. About 1743 *oomiak,* Canadian English; later *umyak* (1863); borrowed from Eskimo *umiaq* an open skin boat.

umpire *n.* one who decides between contestants, arbitrator, mediator. About 1350 *noumper,* borrowed from Old French *nonper* odd or not even, in reference to a third person (*non-* not + *per* equal, from Latin *pār;* see PAIR). Later in Middle English (by about 1440), the initial *n* was lost through the mistaken division of *a noumpere* as *an oumpere.* Compare ADDER, APRON, and NICKNAME for similar misdivisions. **—v.** 1611, act as an umpire (in 1592, adjudge, appoint); from the noun.

umpty *adj. Informal.* of an indefinite number. 1905, from military slang for 'dash', used in reading the Morse code; influenced by association with numerals such as *twenty, thirty;* for suffix see -TY. **—umpteen** *adj. Informal.* of an indefinite number, many. 1918, formed from English *umpty* + *-teen.* **—umpteenth** *adj., n.* (1918)

un-[1] a prefix meaning not when used with adjectives and adverbs, as in *unlucky, unpopular, unfortunately;* also when used with nouns, as in *uncooperation,* but many nouns in *un-,* such as *ungodliness, unsociability* may be considered nouns simply formed on adjectives in *un-* (as *ungodly, unsociable*). Old English *un-* is cognate with Gothic *un-,* Old High German *un-,* Old Icelandic *ū-, ō-,* Latin *in-,* Greek *a-, an-,* Sanskrit *a-, an-,* from Indo-European **n̥* (Pok.757); related to Old English *ne* not; see NO. See also the synonymous prefixes A-[4], AN-[1], IN-[1].

It is with *in-* that variants are often in dispute: as between *inescapable* and *unescapable; inelastic* and *unelastic; indigestible* and *undigestible,* though many times points are raised only in particular usages. The prefix has been freely used (except for words such as *big, long, ugly,* where direct synonyms exist, as in *small* or *little* for *unbig,* and *pretty, handsome* for *unugly*) from Old English times, when "about 1250" such terms existed, according to the OED, many of long derivative or compound formations, such as *unbegrīpendlic* incomprehensible, or with a lost pejorative sense, as in *unǣt* excessive eating, *uncrǣft* an evil art. Middle English was apparently left with only a fraction of these terms (*unclear, unborn, unwounded*), but the native word stock began to build up again (*uncomely, untidy, undone*), also with Scandinavian and French words (*ungirth, unmeek, ungracious*) until we see the present-day list of unlimited coinages. It is interesting to note that like the case of *ir-* in *irregardless,* so *un-* in older compounds such as *unmerciless, unremorseless,* has the same (but heretofore uncomplained-of) redundant function.

The use of *un-* before past participles was common in Old English and revived in Middle English, but subsequently it was greatly extended to produce such words as *unspoiled, unbearded, unwanted, unwarranted.* When formed on the model of an earlier verb in *un-* (as *undone* from *un-*[1] + *done,* but also from the past participle of earlier *undo*), *un-*[1] became confused with *un-*[2], as in *unbent, undressed, unfastened,* modeled on earlier *unbend, undress, unfasten.* This participial use can be illustrated by *unlocked,* modeled on *unlock,* v., which has provided three separate senses: 1) not now locked: *un-*[1] not + *locked* participial adjective; 2) not yet locked: *un-*[1] not + *locked* past participle; 3) no longer locked: *unlock,* v. (*un-*[2] + *lock,* v.) + *-ed*[2] past participle suffix.

—**un-American** *adj.* (1818) —**unassuming** *adj.* (1726) —**unawares** *adv.* (1535; for suffix see -s³) —**unbearable** *adj.* (about 1449) —**unbecoming** *adj.* (1598) —**unbeknownst** *adj.* (1854) —**unbelievable** *adj.* (1548) —**uncalled-for** *adj.* (before 1610) —**uncanny** *adj.* (1596, mischievous; 1773, supernatural, weird) —**uncertain** *adj.* (1303) —**uncertainty** *n.* (about 1380) —**uncivilized** *adj.* (1607) —**unclear** *adj.* (possibly about 1300) —**uncomfortable** *adj.* (about 1425, implied in *uncomfortably*) —**uncommon** *adj.* (1548, not held in common; 1611, unusual) —**unconditional** *adj.* (before 1660, implied in *unconditionally*) —**unconstitutional** *adj.* (1765) —**uncontrollable** *adj.* (1577) —**uncontrolled** *adj.* (1513) —**undecided** *adj.* (1540) —**undetermined** *adj.* (1442) —**undignified** *adj.* (1689) —**undisciplined** *adj.* (1382) —**undivided** *adj.* (1412) —**undoubtedly** *adv.* (probably before 1500) —**undreamed-of** *adj.* (1636) —**undue** *adj.* (before 1387) —**unduly** *adv.* (1399) —**undying** *adj.* (before 1325) —**unearthly** *adj.* (1611, in Shakespeare) —**uneasy** *adj.* (about 1290) —**unemotional** *adj.* (1876, in George Eliot) —**unemployed** *adj.* (1600, unused; 1667, out of work) —**unemployment** *n.* (1888) —**unendowed** *adj.* (1647) —**unequalled** *adj.* (1622) —**unequivocal** *adj.* (1784) —**unerring** *adj.* (1621) —**uneven** *adj.* (before 900, Old English *unefen* unequal; about 1275 *unevene* not smooth) —**unfailing** *adj.* (1382) —**unfaithful** *adj.* (1340, implied in *unfaithfully*) —**unfashionable** *adj.* (1563) —**unfathomable** *adj.* (1617) —**unfavorable** *adj.* (1460, implied in *unfavorably*) —**unfeeling** *adj.* (about 1000, Old English *unfelende* having no feeling; 1596, uncompassionate, unsympathetic) —**unfit** *adj.* (1545) —**unflattering** *adj.* (1581) —**unformed** *adj.* (before 1325) —**unfortunate** *adj.* (1530) —**unfounded** *adj.* (1648) —**unfurnished** *adj.* (1541) —**ungainly** *adj.* (1611) —**ungodly** *adj.* (1526, irreligious; 1887, outrageous, dreadful) —**ungovernable** *adj.* (1673) —**ungoverned** *adj.* (1591, in Shakespeare) —**ungrateful** *adj.* (1553) —**unguarded** *adj.* (before 1593, in Marlowe) —**unguided** *adj.* (1585) —**unheard-of** *adj.* (1592) —**uninformed** *adj.* (1597) —**uninhabited** *adj.* (1571, replacing earlier *unhabited,* 1490, in Caxton) —**unintelligible** *adj.* (1616) —**unintentional** *adj.* (1769, implied in *unintentionally*) —**unjust** *adj.* (1382, but also in *unjustified* about 1340) —**unkind** *adj.* (about 1250) —**unknown** *adj.* (before 1325) —**unlawful** *adj.* (before 1310, implied in *unlawfully*) —**unlike** *adj.* (probably about 1200; corresponding to Old English *ungelic, uniliche,* before 899) —**unmentionable** *adj.* (1837, in Carlyle); *n.pl. unmentionables* underwear or drawers (1823). —**unmerciful** *adj.* (1481, in Caxton) —**unmindful** *adj.* (1382) —**unmistakably** *adv.* (1854) —**unmoved** *adj.* (about 1375) —**unnatural** *adj.* (before 1425) —**unnecessary** *adj.* (1548) —**unnoticed** *adj.* (1720) —**unoccupied** *adj.* (1380) —**unofficial** *adj.* (1798) —**unopened** *adj.* (1600) —**unorganized** *adj.* (1690, in Locke) —**unpaid** *adj.* (1375) —**unparalleled** *adj.* (1594) —**unpardonable** *adj.* (1525) —**unperturbed** *adj.* (1420) —**unpleasant** *adj.* (1535) —**unpracticed** *adj.* (1540) —**unprecedented** *adj.* (1623) —**unprepared** *adj.* (1549) —**unprincipled** *adj.* (1634, in Milton) —**unproductive** *adj.* (1756, in Burke) —**unprofitable** *adj.* (before 1325) —**unqualified** *adj.* (1556) —**unread** *adj.* (1456, not read; 1606, not instructed by reading) —**unrecognizable** *adj.* (1817, in Coleridge) —**unrelenting** *adj.* (1588, in Shakespeare) —**unremitting** *adj.* (1812, implied in *unremittingness,* in Shelley) —**unresolved** *adj.* (1577) —**unrest** *n.* (1340) —**unrestrained** *adj.* (before 1586) —**unrestricted** *adj.* (1766, in Smollett) —**unruly** *adj.* (1400) —**unsafe** *adj.* (1597) —**unsatisfied** *adj.* (1430) —**unsavory** *adj.* (about 1380) —**unscathed** *adj.* (1425; earlier *unschait,* about 1375) —**unschooled** *adj.* (1589) —**unseasonable** *adj.* (about 1448) —**unseasoned** *adj.* (1582) —**unseemly** *adj.* (before 1300) —**unsettled** *adj.* (1591) —**unshrinking** *adj.* (1605, in Shakespeare) —**unsightly** *adj.* (before 1325) —**unskilfully** *adv.* (1338) —**unskilled** *adj.* (1581) —**unsold** *adj.* (1376) —**unsophisticated** *adj.* (1630) —**unsound** *adj.* (probably before 1300) —**unspeakable** *adj.* (before 1400) —**unspoken** *adj.* (1375) —**unstable** *adj.* (before 1200) —**unsteady** *adj.* (1598) —**unsuitable** *adj.* (before 1586, implied in *unsuitableness*) —**unsung** *adj.* (1422-61, not sung; 1667, not honored) —**unsupportable** *adj.* (1586) —**unsure** *adj.* (before 1400) —**untenable** *adj.* (1647) —**unthinkable** *adj.* (about 1430) —**untimely** *adj.* (1535) —**untold** *adj.* (about 1000, Old English *unteald* uncounted) —**untoward** *adj.* (1526, perverse, stubborn; 1621, unfavorable) —**unutterable** *adj.* (before 1586) —**unvarying** *adj.* (1690, in Locke) —**unwary** *adj.* (1544, implied in *unwariness*) —**unwieldy** *adj.* (about 1386, weak; 1513 difficult to handle) —**unwise** *adj.* (Old English, about 830, *unwis*) —**unwittingly** *adv.* (1375) —**unworkable** *adj.* (1839) —**unworthy** *adj.* (before 1240); *adv.* (1661) —**unyielding** *adj.* (1613, implied in *unyieldingness*)

un-² a prefix added to verbs and meaning to do the reverse or opposite, as in *uncover, unfasten, unhitch, unlearn,* or to remove, release, deprive, as in *undress, unearth, unpeel.* Old English *un-, on-;* alteration (perhaps influenced by *un-*¹) of Old English *and-, an-* against, opposite, toward. Old English *and-, an-* is cognate with Gothic *and-,* Old High German *ant-* (modern German *ent-*), Latin *ante* before, Greek *antí* opposite, Sanskrit *ánti* opposite, before; see ANTI-.

In the 1500's and 1600's use of *un-* was greatly expanded to include numerous formations that are not generally found in current English, such as *uncompass, unhide, unflow, unsort.* These and later formations were added by the Anglo-Italian lexicographer Florio and others who so easily built new combinations on the earlier model of *unbend, unfasten, untie,* etc.
—**uncover** *v.* (before 1325) —**undo** *v.* (Old English, before 899 *andōn;* about 930 *undōn*) —**undoing** *n.* (before 1330, exposition; about 1375, act of unfastening; also, 1378 downfall, ruin) —**unfold** *v.* (Old English, about 890 to spread out; before 1050 to disclose) —**unfurl** *v.* (1641) —**unhand** *v.* (1602) —**unhinge** *v.* (1612) —**unleash** *v.* (1671) —**unload** *v.* (1523 remove a load of; 1870 get rid of) —**unnerve** *v.* (1621) —**unpack** *v.* (1472-75) —**unravel** *v.* (1603) —**unsettle** *v.* (1591, unfasten; 1651, disturb) —**untie** *v.* (Old English, about 1000 *untīgan*) —**unveil** *v.* (1599) —**unyoke** *v.* (Old English, about 1000 *ungeocian*)

unanimous *adj.* in complete accord or agreement. Before 1619 (implied in *unanimously*); borrowed from Latin *ūnanimus* of one mind (*ūnus* ONE + *animus* mind; see ANIMAL); for suffix see -OUS. —**unanimity** *n.* 1436 *unanimite;* later *unanimitie* (1579); borrowed from Middle French *unanimite,* learned borrowing from Latin *ūnanimitātem* (nominative *ūnanimitās*) the state of being unanimous, from *ūnanimus* unanimous; for suffix see -ITY.

uncle *n.* About 1300, brother of one's father or mother; borrowed through Anglo-French *uncle,* Old French *oncle,* from Latin *avunculus* mother's brother; literally, little grandfather, endearing diminutive of *avus* grandfather. Latin *avus* is cognate with Old Prussian *awis* uncle, Lithuanian *avýnas* mother's brother, and Armenian *hav* grandfather, from Indo-European **awos* maternal grandfather (Pok.89). Welsh *ewythr,* Breton *eontr* uncle are from Indo-European **awentros* (Pok.89). Cognates in the Germanic languages are found in Old English *ēam* uncle, mother's brother (which did not survive into late Middle English), Old Frisian *ēm,* Middle Low German and Middle Dutch *ōm* (modern Dutch *oom*), Old High German *ōheim* (modern German *Oheim*), Old Icelandic *afi* grandfather, and Gothic *awō* grandmother. Old High German *ōheim* derives either from Proto-Germanic **awun-Haimaz* the one living in the home of the grandfather, or through **auhaim* from Indo-European **awos k̑oimos* grandfather dear; see HOME).

Uncle Sam the government or people of the United States. 1813, American English; originally a humorous expansion of the initials *U.S.,* abbreviation of *United States.*

The name arose during the War of 1812, apparently suggested by the common sight of military vehicles marked with the initials U.S. for the United States government. As a figure in a high hat decorated with stars and stripes, Uncle Sam began to appear in political cartoons about 1850; by 1870, due chiefly to the popularization of the figure by the cartoonist Thomas Nast, this personification superseded the earlier nickname *Brother Jonathan* (1776), which had been widely used from the time of the American Revolution as the counterpart of *John Bull* (1772), nickname of a typical Englishman, and later (1778) as the personification of Great Britain. The frequently cited story that the name *Uncle Sam* originally referred to Samuel Wilson, an army yard inspector of Troy, N.Y., is without confirmation.

Uncle Tom servile black man. 1922, American English; from the name of the central character of Harriet Beecher Stowe's antislavery novel *Uncle Tom's Cabin* (1851-52), a humble, pious, long-suffering black slave.

unconscionable *adj.* not influenced or guided by conscience. 1565, formed from English *un-*[1] not + *conscionable* conscientious (1549). *Conscionable,* now rarely used, was formed from obsolete English (1541) *conscioned* having a conscience (substandard variant of *conscienced,* 1530) + English suffix *-able.*

unconscious *adj.* 1712, unaware, not marked by conscious thought; formed from English *un-*[1] not + *conscious.* The meaning of temporarily not in a conscious state, unable to feel or think, is first recorded in Oliver Wendell Holmes' *Elsie Venner* (1860). **—n.** Usually, **the unconscious.** one's unconscious thoughts, feelings, etc. Before 1884, from the adjective; loan translation of German *das Unbewusste.*

uncouth *adj.* Old English *uncūth* unknown, uncertain, unfamiliar (about 725, in *Beowulf*); formed from *un-*[1] not + *cūth* known, well-known, past participle of *cunnan* to know; see CAN[1]. The extended meaning of strange, crude, clumsy, is first recorded in 1513. Compare COUTH.

unction (ungk′shən) *n.* an anointing with oil, ointment, etc. Before 1387 *unccioun* action of anointing as a religious rite, in Trevisa's translation of Higden's *Polychronicon;* borrowed from Latin *ūnctiōnem* (nominative *ūnctiō*) anointing, from *ūnct-,* stem of *unguere* to anoint; see UNGUENT; for suffix see -ION. **—extreme unction** sacrament in which a very sick or dying person is anointed by a priest (1513, now called *anointing of the sick*).

unctuous (ungk′chůəs) *adj.* like an oil or ointment, oily, greasy. Before 1387, in Trevisa's translation of Higden's *Polychronicon;* borrowed from Old French *unctueus,* and directly from Medieval Latin *unctuosus,* from Latin *ūnctus* (genitive *ūnctūs*) act of anointing, from *ūnct-,* stem of *unguere* to anoint; see UNGUENT; for suffix see -OUS. The transferred sense of complacently agreeable or self-satisfied, blandly ingratiating, is first recorded in English in 1742.

under[1] *prep., adv.* below, beneath. Old English (about 725, in *Beowulf*); cognate with Old Frisian *under* under, Old Saxon *undar,* Middle Low German *under,* Middle Dutch and modern Dutch *onder,* Old High German *untar* (modern German *unter*), Old Icelandic *undir* (Danish, Norwegian, and Swedish *under*), and Gothic *undar,* from Proto-Germanic **unđer-.* Cognates outside Germanic are found in Latin *īnfrā* below, *īnferus* that is below, beneath, Sanskrit *adhás* below, *ádhara-s* lower (from Indo-European **n̥dheros*), Armenian *ənd* under, and Tocharian A *añč,* from Indo-European **n̥dhos, n̥dheri* under (Pok.771). **—adj.** Before 1325, lower, in *Cursor Mundi;* from the adverb.

under[2] *prep.* between, among. Old English (before 900, in Alfred's writings); cognate with Old High German *untar* between, among (modern German *unter*), Latin *inter* between, among, Oscan *anter,* Old Irish *eter,* and Sanskrit *antár,* from Indo-European **enter/n̥tér* (Pok.313). The preposition still functions in modern English in the sense of due to the influence or force of, because of, as in *under these circumstances* (= German *unter diesen Umständen*). See also UNDER-[2].

under-[1] a prefix meaning below, beneath, in various extended senses, paralleling the use of *under*[1]: **1** as preposition, as in *underground* = *beneath the ground, underweight* = *below the normal weight;* **2** as adverb, as in *underdeveloped* = *not sufficiently developed;* **3** as adjective, as in *underclothes* = *(clothes) beneath the outer clothes, undersecretary* = *lower* or *subordinate secretary.* Old English *under-* (like its cognates Old Saxon *undar-,* Old High German *untar-,* Old Icelandic *undir-,* etc.) was used to form words clearly suggested by Latin forms with *sub-;* the frequency of such forms helped establish the prefix in ordinary use. **—underbrush** *n.* (1775, American English) **—undercover** *adj.* 1854, sheltered; later, operating secretly, in 1920, in the writings of Upton Sinclair. **—undercurrent** *n.* 1683, current beneath a surface current; later, underlying tendency (1792). **—undercut** *v.* 1382, to cut off; later, to cut away beneath, in Florio's *Italian-English Dictionary* (1598); and to render unstable, undermine (1955). **—underdeveloped** *adj.* (1892) **—underdog** *n.* (1887, American English, originally in allusion to the beaten dog in a fight) **—underfoot** *adv.* (about 1200) **—undergarment** *n.* (1530) **—undergraduate** *n., adj.* (1630) **—underground** *adj.* 1610, beneath the surface of the ground; later, hidden or secret (1677); also, in or into hiding (1935). *—n.* 1590, region below the earth; later, secret organization (1939, implied in the adjective use, but preceded in U.S. history by the sense of a clandestine system for sending escaped slaves to free territory, established about 1832, but not recorded before 1842). **—underhand** *adj.* 1592, secret, surreptitious; later, with the hand below the level of the shoulder (1850). *—adv.* 1538, secretly; later, with the hand held below (1828); found in Old English before 900 as *under hand* in subjection, under rule. **—underhanded** *adj.* (1806, implied in *underhandedly*) **—underlie** *v.* Before 899 Old English *underlicgan* be subject to; 1856, be the basis of. **—underline** *v.* 1721, to draw a line under; later, to emphasize (1880). **—undermine** *v.* 1382, dig under; later, work secretly against (probably before 1439), and weaken (1569). **—underpants** (1931) **—underpass** *n.* (1904) **—underpinning** *n.* 1489, act of supporting from beneath; later, supporting material or structure (1538). **—underrate** *v.* (before 1623) **—underscore** *v.* (1771) **—undersell** *v.* (1622) **—undershirt** *n.* (1648) **—underside** *n.* (1680) **—understudy** *v.* (1874); *n.* (1882) **—undertake** *v.* (probably about 1200, entrap, seize upon; later, take upon oneself, before 1325) **—undertaker** *n.* 1382, helper; later, one who assumes a task (about 1400); also, one who carries out arrangements for burial (1698). **—undertone** *n.* (1806) **—underway** *adj., adv.* (1743) **—underwear** *n.* (1872) **—underwrite** *v.* About 1430, write below something; later, to sign (1557); and to accept insurance risk (1622).

under-[2] a prefix meaning between, among, in senses paralleling the use of *under*[2], represented in Old English by such verbs as *underniman* to receive, *undersēcan* to investigate, but surviving in modern English only in the verb UNDERSTAND.

undergo *v.* Probably about 1200 *unnderrgan* submit to, in *The Ormulum;* later *undergon* go under, deceive, investigate (about 1250, in *Genesis and Exodus*), and *undergan* endure, suffer, go through (before 1325, in *Cursor Mundi*); developed from Old English (about 1000) *undergān* undermine (*under-*[1] under- + *gān* GO). Old English *undergān* is cognate with Middle Dutch *ondergaen* (modern Dutch *ondergaan*), Old High German *untarkān* (modern German *untergehen*), and Danish and Swedish *undergå.*

underneath *adv., prep.* beneath. About 1375 *undernethe,* developed from Old English (before 899) *underneothan* (*under* UNDER[1] + *neothan* below; see BENEATH).

understand *v.* Old English (before 899) *understandan* comprehend, grasp the idea of; literally, stand in the midst of, stand between (*under-*[2] + *standan* STAND), corresponding to Old Frisian *understonda* and Middle Danish *understande,* both meaning to understand. Compare, with a different prefix, Old English *forstandan,* Middle High German *verstān, verstēn* (modern German *verstehen*) to understand; literally, to stand in front or on top of; compare also Ionic Greek *epí-stasthai* to understand; literally, to stand on top of, stand over. Various forms of the past participle were current in the 1500's and 1600's, such as *understanden, understande,* and *understanded;* the current form *understood* (conforming to the past tense and past participle of *stand*) was usual by 1600.

underworld *n.* 1608, the lower world, Hades; 1609, the earth as distinguished from heaven; formed from English *under-*[1] + *world.* The figurative meaning of a lower, or the lowest, level of society, etc., is first recorded in 1890, and the specific meaning of the world of criminals and organized crime, in 1900.

undies *n.pl. Informal.* articles of women's underclothing. 1906, in *Punch;* formed from English *under,* as in *undergarment, underwear,* etc. + suffix *-ies,* plural of *-ie.*

undulate (un′jəlāt *or* un′dyəlāt) *v.* move in waves. 1664, in Henry Power's *Experimental Philosophy;* back formation from earlier English *undulation,* or formed in English from Late Latin *undula* wavelet (diminutive of Latin *unda* wave) + English *-ate*[1]. Latin *unda* is cognate with Sanskrit *unátti, undati* (it) gushes, wets, *udán-* wave, WATER. **—adj.** (un′jəlit *or* un′jəlāt) wavy. 1658, in Phillips' *Dictionary;* borrowed from Latin *undulātus* having a wavy form, from *unda* wave; for suffix see -ATE[1]. **—undulant** *adj.* waving, wavy. 1830, formed from English *undulate* + *-ant.* **—undulation** *n.* 1646, formed in English from Late Latin *undula* wavelet + English *-ation.*

unguent (ung′gwənt) *n.* ointment, salve. Probably before 1425, in a translation of Chauliac's *Grande Chirurgie;* borrowed from Latin *unguentum* ointment, from *unguere* to anoint or smear with unguents. Latin *unguere* is cognate with Old Irish *imb* butter, Welsh *ymenyn,* Old Prussian *anctan,* Armenian *aucanem* I anoint, Sanskrit *anákti* (he) anoints, *añjánti* they anoint, from Indo-European **ongw-/n̥gw-* (Pok.779). In Germanic a cognate is found in Old High German *ancho, anko* butter.

uni- a prefix meaning one, a single, the same, as in *unicellular = having one or a single cell.* Borrowed from Latin *ūni-,* combining form of *ūnus* ONE. **—unidirectional** *adj.* (1883) **—unilateral** *adj.* (1802) **—unisex** *n., adj.* (condition of being) sexually indistinguishable or neutral (1968).

unicorn *n.* mythical animal with a single long horn in the middle of its forehead. Probably before 1200 *unicorne,* in *Ancrene Riwle;* borrowed from Old French *unicorne,* learned borrowing from Late Latin *ūnicornis,* noun use of Latin *ūnicornis,* adj., having one horn (*ūni-* one + *cornū* HORN).

uniform *adj.* 1540, of one form, character, or kind; borrowed from Middle French *uniforme,* learned borrowing from Latin *ūnifōrmis* having one form (*ūni-* one + *fōrma* FORM). **—n.** distinctive clothes worn by members of a group. 1748, from the adjective. An earlier sense of one body or flock is found in 1623. **—uniformity** *n.* Probably before 1425 *uniformite* uniform condition or character, in a translation of Higden's *Polychronicon;* borrowed through Middle French *uniformité,* or directly from Latin *ūnifōrmitātem* (nominative *ūnifōrmitās*) uniform in condition or character, from *ūnifōrmis* uniform; for suffix see -ITY.

unify *v.* 1502, borrowed from Middle French *unifier,* and perhaps directly from Late Latin *ūnificāre* make one, from a lost adjective **ūnificus* (Latin *ūni-* one + the root of *facere* to make, perform, DO[1]); for suffix see -FY. **—unification** *n.* 1851, borrowed from French *unification,* and probably formed from English *unify* on the pattern of such pairs as *mollify, mollification.*

union *n.* 1410 *unioun* a uniting or being united; borrowed from Middle French *union,* from Late Latin *ūniōnem* (nominative *ūniō*) oneness, unity, a uniting, found in Latin in the meaning of a single pearl or onion, from *ūnus* ONE; for suffix see -ION.

The meaning of a group, as of people or states, united for some special purpose, is first recorded in 1660, and that of a labor union, in 1833.

—unionize *v.* 1841, make into a union; formed from English *union* + *-ize.* The specific sense of bring under the rules of a labor union is first recorded in 1890. **—Union Jack** flag of the United Kingdom (1674).

unique *adj.* 1602, single or solitary; borrowing of French *unique,* learned borrowing from Latin and in early use in English borrowed directly from Latin *ūnicus* single, sole, from *ūnus* ONE; for suffix see English -IC, in relation to French *-que*. In the sense of having no like or equal, unrivaled, unparalleled, *unique* was reborrowed from the French in the late 1700's and regarded as a foreign word (usually italicized) down to the middle of the 1800's.

unison *n.* agreement, concord. 1410 *unisoun* tone of the same pitch as another; later, agreement in pitch (before 1475); borrowed from Middle French *unisson* unison, concord of sound, earlier *unison,* borrowing from Medieval Latin *unisonus* having one sound, sounding the same, from Late Latin *ūnisonus* in immediate sequence in the scale, monotonous (Latin *ūni-* one + *sonus* SOUND). The figurative sense of harmonious agreement, concord, accord, is first recorded in English in 1650.

unit *n.* 1570, single magnitude or number considered as the base of all numbers, in a treatise on mathematics by John Dee; formerly *unite,* alteration of earlier *unity,* on the pattern of *digit.* The meaning of a single thing or person regarded as a separable member of a group is first recorded in 1642. The scientific sense of a quantity adopted as a standard of measurement is found in 1738, in the spelling *unite.*

Unitarian *n.* Christian who believes that God exists in only one person. 1687, formed in English from New Latin *unitarius* (from Latin *ūnitās* UNITY) + English *-an.* Compare TRINITARIAN.

unite *v.* Probably before 1425 *uniten* join together, in a translation of Higden's *Polychronicon;* borrowed from Latin *ūnītus,* past participle of *ūnīre* join together, make one, from *ūnus* ONE. **—united** *adj.* combined, joined together (especially in names of leagues, confederations, associations, unions, etc.). 1552, from the past participle of *unite;* for suffix see -ED². **—United Kingdom** kingdom of Great Britain, or (especially after 1801) of Great Britain and Ireland (1737). **—United Nations** (1942) **—United States** (1617, kingdom or republic of Holland; 1776, the republic of North America; in full UNITED STATES OF AMERICA, also 1776). **—unity** *n.* Probably about 1300 *unite,* borrowed from Anglo-French and Old French *unité,* learned borrowing from Latin *ūnitātem* (nominative *ūnitās*) oneness, sameness, agreement, from *ūnus* one; for suffix see -ITY. The mathematical sense of a single magnitude or number considered as the base of all numbers is first recorded in Middle English about 1425.

universal *adj.* About 1380, in Chaucer's translation of Boethius' *De Consolatione Philosophiae;* borrowed from Old French *universel, universal,* learned borrowing from Latin, and borrowed directly from Latin *ūniversālis* of or belonging to all as to the whole, from *ūniversus* all together, whole, entire, collective, general; see UNIVERSE; for suffix see -AL¹. **—n.** 1553, universal proposition in logic; from the adjective. **—universality** *n.* About 1380 *universalite* the quality of being universal, in Chaucer's translation of Boethius' *De Consolatione Philosophiae;* borrowed from Middle French *universalité,* and directly from Late Latin *ūniversālitās* a being universal, from Latin *ūniversālis* universal; for suffix see -ITY.

universe *n.* 1589, the whole world, the cosmos, in Puttenham's *The Arte of English Poesie;* borrowed from Middle French *univers,* learned borrowing from Latin, and borrowed into English directly from Latin *ūniversum* the whole world, noun use of neuter of *ūniversus,* adj., whole, entire; originally, turned into one (*ūnus* ONE + *versus,* past participle of *vertere* to turn; see VERTEX). The word appeared earlier in Middle English in the phrase *in universe,* meaning universally, about 1385, in Chaucer's *Troilus and Criseyde.*

university *n.* About 1300 *universite* institution of higher learning; also, body of persons constituting a university; borrowed from Anglo-French and Old French *université,* learned borrowing from Medieval Latin *universitatem* (nominative *universitas*) university, from Late Latin *ūniversitātem* (nominative *ūniversitās*) corporation, society, from Latin, aggregate, whole, from *ūniversus* whole, entire; see UNIVERSE; for suffix see -ITY.

unkempt *adj.* 1579, (of language) unrefined or rude, in Spenser's *The Shepheardes Calender;* from earlier *unkemd* uncombed (before 1393, in Gower's *Confessio Amantis;* formed from *un-*¹ not + *kembed, kempt,* past participles of *kemben* to comb, developed from Old English *cemban*). Old English *cemban* is cognate with Old Saxon *kembian* to comb, Old High German *kemben,* and Old Icelandic *kemba* (from Proto-Germanic **kambjanan*), all derived from the Proto-Germanic source of Old English *camb, comb* COMB.

unless *conj., prep.* 1467 *unlesse,* earlier *onlesse* (1438); originally, *on lesse* (*than*) on a less condition (than), except (*on* ON + *lesse* LESS). The negative connotation of the word, as well as the lack of stress on the first syllable, led to association with the prefix UN-¹.

until *prep.* Probably about 1200 *untill,* in *The Ormulum;* formed in Middle English from *un-* as far as, up to (as in *unto;* from Scandinavian; compare Old Icelandic *und*) + *till* until, up to; see TILL¹. The two syllables of *until* are originally of the same meaning.

Old Icelandic *und* is cognate with Old English *oth* up to, as far as, until, Old Frisian, Old Saxon, and Gothic *und,* and outside Germanic with Oscan *ant* up to, from Indo-European **n̥t-,* also **n̥ti* (Pok.49).

—conj. About 1300 *untill,* from the preposition.

unto *prep.* to. About 1250, formed from *un-* up to, as far as (see UNTIL) + *to* TO.

up *adv.* Developed in part from Old English *ūp, upp* upward (about 725, in *Beowulf*), and in part from Old English *uppe* on high, aloft (before 899). Both of the Old English adverbs are cognate with Old Frisian *up* upward, up, Old Saxon *up,* Middle Low German *up, uppe,* Middle Dutch and modern Dutch *op,* Old High German *ūf,* Middle High German *uf, ouf* (modern German *auf*), Old Icelandic *upp* (Norwegian *opp,* Danish *op,* and Swedish *upp*), from Proto-Germanic **upp,* from Indo-European **upn-* (with accent on the following vowel), extended from the adverb **upo* under, from under, over (Pok.1106). Indo-European **upo* is represented outside Germanic by Latin *sub* under, Greek *hypó,* Sanskrit *úpa* towards, at, under, and Hittite *upzi* to rise. Related to OVER. **—adj.** Probably before 1300, dwelling inland, in *Kyng Alisaunder;* from the adverb. The meaning of going up, ascending, (as in *the up escalator*) is first recorded in 1869. The figurative sense of enthusiastic, optimistic (as in *to be up about a new job,* or *to look on the up side of things*), is first recorded in 1942, derived from the earlier sense of sparkling, excited (1815). **—prep.** 1509, to a higher place (as in *The cat ran up the tree*); later, along or through (as in *to walk up the street, sail up the river,*

1513); also, toward, in, into (as in *to walk up the country,* 1596); from the adverb, by taking the place of the adverb *up* + a preposition, as in *up against, up through.* **—n.** 1536, person or thing that is up (as in *the ups and downs of life*); from the adverb. The meaning of a period of prosperity, success, is first found in Dickens' *Martin Chuzzlewit* (1844). **—v.** 1560-61, to drive up and catch (swans) for marking; from the adverb. The meaning of get up, arise, (as in *to suddenly up and march off*) is first recorded in 1643, and that of raise to a higher level, increase, (as in *to up the price of wheat*) is found in American English in 1915. **—up-and-coming** *adj.* 1889, active, alert, American English; later, beginning to achieve success, American English (1926). **—up-to-date** *adj.* (1888)

up- a prefix forming compound words with *up* (adverb, preposition, or adjective) in its various senses, as in *upcoming, upgrade, uphill, upriver, upcurrent, upstroke.* Old English *ūp-, upp-,* is identical in meaning with the Old English adverb and corresponding to similar prefixes in other Germanic languages, including Old Frisian *op-, up-,* Old Saxon, Middle Low German, and Low German *up-,* Middle Dutch and modern Dutch *op-,* Old High German and Middle High German *ūf* (modern German *auf-*), and Old Icelandic and Swedish *upp-,* Norwegian *opp-,* and Danish *op-.* **—upbringing** *n.* (1520) **—upcoming** *adj.* 1848, rising; later, forthcoming, American English (1954). **—update** *v.* 1948, American English; earlier, in an isolated British instance in British English (1910); *n.* (1967, American English) **—upend** *v.* (1823) **—upgrade** *v.* (1920, implied in *upgrading*) **—upheaval** *n.* (1838) **—upheave** *v.* (before 1300) **—uphill** *adj., n.* (1548); *adv.* (1607) **—uphold** *v.* (probably before 1200) **—upkeep** *n.* (1884) **—upland** *n.* 1566, hilly country. *—adj.* 1575, inland, remote; later, of or living in hilly country (1610). **—uplift** *v.* (1338); *n.* (before 1845) **—upmost** *adj.* (1560) **—uprising** *n.* About 1250, resurrection; later, insurrection (1587). **—uproot** *v.* (before 1620) **—upset** *v.* About 1440, to set up, erect; later, overturn (1803). *—adj.* 1338, erected; later distressed (1805). *—n.* About 1425, an insurrection; later, an overturning of a vehicle or boat (1804); an unexpected defeat (1822). **—upshot** *n.* 1531, final shot in an archery match; later, result (1604). **—upside down** About 1490; earlier *upsadoun,* (1382), and *up so doun* (before 1400). The earlier forms were literally of the sense "up so down" (meaning to upset), but were eventually reduced to *upside down* probably in an attempt to make the sense more easily intelligible. Sir William Craigie, in the OED, suggests that the earliest form may have been *up to down.* The figurative sense of in complete disorder is found in the 1300's. **—upstage** *adv.* (1870); *adj.* (1918); *v.* (1921) **—upstairs** *adv.* (1596, in Shakespeare's *1 Henry IV*); *adj.* (1782); *n.* (1872) **—upstanding** *adj.* (Old English, about 1000); later, honest or straight forward (1863). **—upstart** *n.* (1555) **—upstream** *adv.* (1681); *adj.* (1826) **—upsurge** *n.* (1928) **—upswing** *n.* (1922, in Wodehouse) **—uptown** *adv.* (1802); *adj.* (1838) **—upturn** *v.* Before 1340, to overthrow; later, to turn over (1567). *—n.* 1864, a great turmoil; later, an improvement in conditions (1930). **—upward** *adv.* (before 900, Old English *upweard*); *adj.* (1603) **—upwards, upward** *adv.* Before 900, Old English *upweardes, upweard.* *—adj.* **upward** (1607, also found in Old English).

upbraid *v.* find fault with, scold. Probably about 1150 *upbreyden;* developed from Old English *ūpbregdan* (about 1000) bring forth as a ground for censure (*ūp-* up + *bregdan* move quickly, intertwine, BRAID). According to Skeat, the original sense of this verb was to lay hands on, lay hold of, hence to attack. The generalized meaning of find fault with, reproach, scold, is found in Middle English about 1300.

upholster *v.* provide (furniture) with coverings, cushions, springs, etc. 1853, American English; back formation from *upholsterer.* **—upholsterer** *n.* one who upholsters. 1613, formed from obsolete English *upholster,* n., dealer in small goods + English *-er*[1]. *Upholster,* n. developed from Middle English *upholdester* (1411, *uphold* + *-ster*), from *upholden* to repair, uphold (*up-* up + *holden* to HOLD[1]). **—upholstery** *n.* upholsterer's work or materials. 1649, formed from obsolete English *upholster,* n. + *-y*[3].

upon *prep.* 1121 *uppon,* in *Peterborough Chronicle;* a compound of UP, adv. + ON, prep. The formation of this word was probably influenced by Scandinavian (compare Old Icelandic *upp ā,* Middle Swedish *uppa, oppa*), with which the Middle English form agrees in placing the stress on the preposition and weakening the force of the adverb *up,* which is reinforced by the development of Swedish, Norwegian and Danish *på,* and found also in dialectal English *'pon.* The form *upon* is distinct from Old and early Middle English *uppon,* which was a variant of Old English *uppan* up (about 960).

upper *adj.* Probably before 1300, higher in position or location, in *Kyng Alisaunder;* originally comparative of UP (*up,* adj. + *-er*[2]), and replacing the earlier *over,* adj. **—n.** that part of a shoe or boot above the sole. 1789, from the adjective. Figurative use in *on one's uppers* having hard luck, in poor circumstances, is first recorded in 1886, and *down on one's uppers,* in 1903. The slang word *upper* (stimulant drug) in the drug culture is first recorded in 1968, in American English. **—upper crust** About 1460, top crust of a loaf of bread; 1836, the upper classes. **—uppercut** *n.* a swinging blow in boxing directed upward (1842). **—upper hand** advantage (1481). **—uppermost** *adj.* (1481)

uppish *adj. Informal.* somewhat conceited or arrogant. 1678, lavish, formed from English *up,* adj. + *-ish*[1]. The meaning of somewhat conceited or arrogant is first recorded in 1734.

uppity *adj. Informal.* uppish. 1880, American English; probably formed by influence of *uppish,* from English *up* + *-ty,* as in *haughty.*

upright *adj.* Probably before 1200 *upriht,* in *Ancrene Riwle;* later *upright* erect, vertical (before 1325, in *Cursor Mundi*); developed from Old English *ūpriht* (about 725, in *Beowulf*), a compound of *ūp* UP + *riht* RIGHT; cognate with Old Frisian *upriucht,* Middle Dutch and modern Dutch *oprecht,* Old High German *ūfrëht* (modern German *aufrecht*), and Old Icelandic *uprēttr* (Danish *opret,* Swedish *upprät*). The figurative sense of morally good, honest, righteous, is first recorded in English in Palsgrave's *Lesclarcissement* (1530). **—adv.** 1509, sincerely or justly; later, in an upright position (1590); from the adjective, in Middle English. **—n.** 1563, a vertical front, face, or plane; later, something standing erect, vertical stone, post, etc. (1742).

uproar *n.* 1526, in the Tyndale Bible; also 1535, in the Coverdale Bible, used by translators of both Bibles in passages where Luther's Bible has German *Aufruhr* an insurrection, outbreak of disorder, revolt, commotion. According to the OED, the word came into English through Dutch *oproer* or Middle Low German *uprōr,* but Bense in the *Dictionary of the Low-Dutch Element in the English Vocabulary* explains that the borrowing in Tyndale was most likely from Middle Low German *uprōr,* and maintains that Coverdale, who is said to have translated the Dutch Bible, may have taken the word from Dutch *oproer,* which was itself probably translated from German *Aufruhr* (*auf* UP + *ruhr* a stirring, motion, related to *rühren* to stir, move, and corresponding to Middle Low German *roren,* Middle Dutch *roeren*); see RARE² undercooked.

The general meaning of the noise of shouting, loud outcry, tumult, is first recorded in English in 1544, probably influenced by the word *roar,* as the spelling *uproar* is mistakenly associated with *roar.*
—uproarious *adj.* noisy, disorderly. 1819, formed from English *uproar* + *-ious.*

ur- a prefix meaning original, earliest, primitive; originally in words borrowed from German, and now used more or less freely in English, as in *ur-performance* and *urtext.* Borrowed from German *ur-* primitive, original. The prefix is also found in borrowings from German such as *Ursprache* primitive language, usually in reference to Proto-Germanic or Indo-European, as original or parent languages. This use of *ur-* seems to be an intensification of the meaning of *ur-* as found in such a compound as *Ursprung* source, origin (corresponding to the verb *erspringen* to leap up). Cognate with German *ur-* is Gothic *us-* as in *us-wakjan* to wake up, and *ūt* OUT.

uranium (yu̇rā′nēəm) *n.* radioactive chemical element. 1797, New Latin, formed from *Uranus,* the planet + New Latin *-ium,* chemical suffix. New Latin *uranium* was coined about 1790 by the German chemist Martin Klaproth, 1743-1817, in honor of the discovery (in 1781) of the planet Uranus. The planet itself was named after *Uranus,* a god in Greek and Roman mythology who represented heaven; borrowed from Latin *ūranus,* from Greek *Ouranós,* from *ouranós* heaven, sky, of uncertain origin. Compare TITANIUM.

urban *adj.* 1619, of or relating to cities or towns; borrowed from Latin *urbānus* of or pertaining to a city or city life; as a noun, a city dweller, from *urbs* (genitive *urbis*) city, of uncertain origin; for suffix see -AN; for semantic differentiation of the Latin meanings in English see URBANE. The word had only infrequent use before the 1800's. **—urbanize** *v.* 1642, render urbane or civil; formed from English *urban* or *urbane* + *-ize.* The meaning of make urban in character is first recorded in 1884, and that of to accustom to urban life, in 1948. **—urbanization** *n.* act or fact of making urban. 1888, formed from English *urbanize* + *-ation.*

urbane (ėrbān′) *adj.* courteous, refined, elegant. 1533, of or relating to cities or towns, in a translation of Livy's *Roman History;* borrowed from Middle French *urbain,* and more likely directly from Latin *urbānus* URBAN.

The meaning of having the manners thought to be characteristic of townspeople, courteous, refined, elegant, is first recorded in 1623, in Cockeram's *Dictionary;* Latin *urbānus* also had this sense of refined, polished, elegant. For the difference in form, stress, and meaning between *urbane* and *urban,* compare HUMANE and HUMAN.
—urbanity *n.* courtesy, refinement. 1535, borrowed through Middle French *urbanité,* or directly from Latin *urbānitātem* (nominative *urbānitās*) urban life, refinement, from *urbānus* refined, polite, elegant; see URBAN, URBANE; for suffix see -ITY.

urchin *n.* 1528, hunchback; about 1530, pert or mischievous child; developed from Middle English *urchoun* hedgehog (before 1325), earlier *yrichon* (about 1300); borrowed from Old French *erichon, herichon* hedgehog, from Gallo-Romance **ēriciōnem* (nominative **ēriciō*), from Latin *ēricius* hedgehog, from *ēr* (genitive *ēris*) hedgehog, dialectal variant of **hēr,* cognate with Greek *chḗr* (genitive *chērós*) hedgehog, from Indo-European **ĝhēr-s* spiny creature (Pok.445).

Throughout the 1500's the word was applied to persons who either by their ugly or ragged appearance, or by the sharpness of their wit, suggested a hedgehog. Thus, in addition to being applied to a hunchback and to a mischievous child, it was applied to an ill-tempered or roguish girl (1534), a goblin or elf (1584), and a poorly or raggedly clothed boy or youngster (1556).

-ure a suffix forming abstract nouns of action or the means or result of action, especially in words borrowed from Latin or French or formed in English from materials of Latin or French origin: **1** the act or fact of _____ing, as in *failure = the act of failing.* **2** the condition of being _____ed, as in *pleasure = the condition of being pleased.* **3** the result of being _____ed, as in *exposure = the result of being exposed.* **4** something that _____s, as in *legislature = something that legislates.* **5** a thing that is _____ed, as in *disclosure = a thing that is disclosed.* **6** other special meanings, as in *procedure, sculpture, denture.* Borrowed through Old French *-ure,* and directly from Latin *-ūra,* especially in the longer forms *-tūra* and *-sūra.* Many words in *-ure* were adopted from Old French, as *figure, feature, lecture, closure, pressure, tonsure, fissure,* etc.; while others, such as *aperture, investiture, scripture, censure,* and *juncture,* were directly borrowed from Latin. The suffix was also added to English stems of Latin origin, giving *composure, exposure, legislature,* etc., or to true Latin stems, yielding such words as *divestiture.*

urea (yu̇rē′ə) *n.* chief substance in the urine of mammals. 1806, borrowing of New Latin form of French *urée,* from Old French *urine* URINE.

ureter (yu̇r′ətər) *n.* duct that carries urine from a kidney to the bladder. 1578, borrowing of New Latin form of Greek *ourētḗr* one of the urinary ducts of the kidneys, from *oureîn* to urinate; see URINE.

urethra (yu̇rē′thrə) *n.* duct by which urine is discharged from the bladder. 1634, borrowed from Late Latin *ūrēthra,* from Greek *ouréthrā* the passage for urine, from *oureîn* to urinate; see URINE.

urge *v.* 1560, borrowed, by influence of earlier English *urgent,* from Latin *urgēre* to press, push, drive, compel; see WREAK. **—n.** driving force or impulse. Before 1618, from the verb. **—urgency** *n.* 1540, probably formed in English as a noun to *urgent,* modeled on Late Latin *urgentia* urgent character, from Latin *urgentem* (nominative *urgēns*) urging, present participle of *urgēre* to urge; for suffix see -ENCY. **—urgent** *adj.* pressing, important. 1456, borrowed from Middle French *urgent* pressing, impelling, from Latin *urgentem* (nominative *urgēns*) pressing, urging, present participle of *urgēre* to urge; for suffix see -ENT.

urine *n.* Probably before 1300, borrowed from Old French *urine,* learned borrowing from Latin, and borrowed into English directly from Latin *ūrīna* urine; with the verb found only in Medieval Latin, the noun was probably formed after the related verb *ūrīnārī* plunge into water or as if from **ūrīnus* of water, from **ūrum* water, urine. The Latin forms are cognate with Greek *oûron* urine, back formation from *oureîn* to urinate (earlier **worse-*), Old Prussian *wurs* pond, Latvian *jū'ra* (Baltic) sea, Armenian *gayṙ* swamp, mud, Sanskrit *vā́r* water, and *várṣati* it is raining, Tocharian A *wär,* Tocharian B *war* water, Old Icelandic *ūr* drizzle, and Old English *ūrig* damp, from Indo-European **wer-/ wēr-; *awer-/ūr-; *wers-/wors-* (Pok.80). **—urinal** *n.* Probably before 1200, container for urine, in Layamon's *Chronicle of Britain;* borrowed from Old French *urinal,* from the neuter of Late Latin *ūrīnālis* of or pertaining to urine, from Latin *ūrīna* urine; for suffix see -AL². The sense of a place for urinating is first recorded in 1851. **—urinalysis** *n.* 1889, American English; formed from *urin (e)* + *(an)alysis.* **—urinary** *adj.* of or relating to urine. 1578, borrowed from New Latin *urinarius* of or pertaining to urine, from Latin *ūrīna* urine; for suffix see -ARY. **—urinate** *v.* discharge urine. 1599, probably a back formation from *urination;* formed by influence of Medieval Latin *urinatum,* past participle of *urinare* to urinate, from Latin *ūrīna* urine; for suffix see -ATE¹. **—urination** *n.* action of urinating. Probably before 1425 *urinacioun,* formed as if from Medieval Latin **urinationem* (nominative **urinatio*) a urinating, from *urinare* urinate; for suffix see -ATION.

urn *n.* vase with a foot or pedestal. About 1385 *urne* vase used to preserve the ashes of the dead, in Chaucer's *Troilus and Criseyde;* borrowed from Latin *urna* a jar, vessel, vessel of burned clay, probably from earlier **urc-nā,* related to *urceus* pitcher, from the same source as Greek *hýrchē* earthen vessel. The generalized meaning of a vase with a circular base is recorded in English before 1639.

ursine (ėr'sīn) *adj.* of or relating to bears, bearlike. About 1550, borrowed from Latin *ursīnus* of, pertaining to, or resembling a bear, from *ursus* bear; see ARCTIC; for suffix see -INE¹.

us *pron.* objective case of *we.* Old English *ūs* (before 830), accusative and dative plural of *wē* we. Old English *ūs* is cognate with Old Frisian and Old Saxon *ūs* us, and Old Icelandic *oss* (Norwegian and Swedish *oss,* Danish *os*); these forms have lost an *n,* which appears in Middle Dutch and modern Dutch *ons,* Old High German and modern German *uns,* and Gothic *uns.* The stem of these words represents *n̥s,* the weak grade of Indo-European **nĕs-, *nŏs-* (Pok.758), retained in Welsh *ni, ny* we, Albanian *ne* us, *na* we, Latin *nōs* we, us, Old Prussian *nōuson* of us, Old Slavic *nasŭ,* Sanskrit *nas* us, Hittite *naš,* and Tocharian A *näš,* Tocharian B *ñäś* I.

usable *adj.* that can be used. Before 1382, in the Wycliffe Bible; borrowed from Old French *usable,* from *user* to USE; for suffix see -ABLE. It is also probable that the word was later independently re-formed in English in the 1800's. This word was not common before 1800 and is, as therefore expected, not recorded in Johnson's *Dictionary* (1755).

usage *n.* way or manner of using. Probably before 1300, established practice, custom, habit, in *Kyng Alisaunder* and in *Arthour and Merlin;* borrowed from Anglo-French and Old French *usage* custom, habit, experience, from *us,* learned borrowing from Latin *ūsus* use, custom; see USE, n.; for suffix see -AGE. The meaning of customary way of using words is first recorded in English in 1697 in Defoe's writings.

use (yüz) *v.* Probably before 1200 *usen* utilize or employ for a purpose, in Layamon's *Chronicle of Britain;* borrowed from Old French *user* use, employ, practice, from Vulgar Latin **ūsāre* use, frequentative form derived from Latin *ūs-,* past participle stem of *ūtī* to use, in Old Latin *oeti* use, employ, exercise, perform; of unknown origin. **—n.** (yüs) Probably before 1200 *us* act of utilizing or employing a thing, in *Ancrene Riwle;* borrowed from Anglo-French and Old French *us* (feminine *use,* 1368), learned borrowing from Latin *ūsus* (genitive *ūsūs*) use, custom, skill, habit, experience, from *ūs-,* past participle stem of *ūtī* to use. **—useful** *adj.* 1595, in Shakespeare's *King John;* formed from English *use,* n. + *-ful.* **—useless** *adj.* 1593, in Shakespeare's *The Rape of Lucrece;* formed from English *use,* n. + *-less.*

usher *n.* person who shows people to their seats. About 1280 *usschere* doorkeeper; borrowed from Anglo-French *usser,* from Old French *ussier,* from Vulgar Latin **ūstiārius* doorkeeper, from Late Latin *ūstium,* variant of Latin *ōstium* door, related to *ōs* mouth; see ORAL. The sense of a person who shows people to their seats is first recorded in English in 1868, in letters of Dickens. **—v.** to conduct, escort. 1594, (figurative) admit ceremoniously, introduce; 1596 (literal) act as an usher to, conduct or escort; from the noun. The figurative sense of lead up to, precede (as in *evening ushers night*) is first recorded in 1599.

usual *adj.* Before 1387 *usualle,* in Trevisa's translation of Higden's *Polychronicon;* borrowed through Old French *usuel,* and directly from Late Latin *ūsuālis* ordinary, customary, from Latin *ūsus* (genitive *ūsūs*) custom, USE; for suffix see -AL¹. **—usually** *adv.* 1477, customarily, commonly, ordinarily; formed from English *usual* + *-ly*¹.

usurer (yü'zhərər) *n.* person who lends money at an extremely high rate of interest, one who practices usury. About 1300, borrowed from Anglo-French *usurer,* variant of Old French *usurier,* from Late Latin *ūsūrārius* moneylender, from Latin *ūsūrārius,* adj., that pays int rest, for use, from *ūsūra* use, interest, usury, from *ūsus* (genitive *ūsūs*), from the stem of *ūtī* to USE; for suffix see -ER¹. **—usurious** (yüzhůr'ēəs) *adj.* of or practicing usury. 1610, formed from English *usury,* n. + *-ous.* **—usury** (yü'zhərē) *n.* the lending of money at an extremely high rate of interest. About 1303 *usery,* in Mannyng's *Handlyng Synne;* borrowed from Medieval Latin *usuria,* alteration of Latin *ūsūra* usury, interest, use; see USURER; for suffix see -Y³.

usurp (yüsėrp') *v.* seize and hold (power, authority, etc.) by force. Before 1325 *usurpen;* borrowed from Old French *usurper,* from Latin *ūsurpāre* make use of, seize for use, take possession of (formed from **ūsurapos,* from *ūsus* USE + *rapere* seize; see RAPID). **—usurpation** *n.* About 1385 *usurpacion* unwarranted claim, act of usurping, in Usk's *The Testament of Love;* borrowed from Old French and Anglo-French *usurpacion,* learned borrowing from Latin *ūsurpātiōnem* (nominative *ūsurpātiō*) a using, an appropriation, from *ūsurpāre* use, usurp; for suffix see -ATION.

utensil *n.* container or implement for household use. About 1375, borrowed from Old French *utensile* implement, learned borrowing from Latin *ūtēnsilia* things for use, utensils, noun use of neuter plural of *ūtēnsilis* usable, that may be used or is fit for use, from *ūtī* to USE.

uterus (yü'tərəs) *n.* womb. Before 1398, in Trevisa's

translation of Bartholomew's *De Proprietatibus Rerum;* borrowed from Latin *uterus* womb, belly, possibly cognate with Greek *hóderos* (perhaps to be read as *hýderos*) belly, Sanskrit *udára-m* belly, and Lettish *vêders* belly, from Indo-European **udero-/wēdero-* (Pok.1104). Latin *uterus* (for expected **uderus*) may have been influenced by *uter* (genitive *utris*) inflated bag (for holding liquids, etc.). **—uterine** *adj.* of the uterus. Probably before 1425, having the same mother but a different father, in a translation of Higden's *Polychronicon;* borrowed through Old French *uterin* (feminine *uterine*), and directly from Late Latin *uterīnus* born of the same mother, from Latin *uterus* uterus; for suffix see -INE[1]. The meaning of having to do with the uterus is first recorded in English in 1615.

utilitarian *n.* adherent of utilitarianism. 1781, in writings of Jeremy Bentham; formed from English *utility* + *-arian,* as in *Trinitarian,* etc. **—adj.** consisting of or based upon utility; also, regarding the greatest good of the greatest number as the chief purpose or rule of morality. 1802, in writings of Jeremy Bentham; from the noun. **—utilitarianism** *n.* utilitarian doctrine or principles. 1827, formed from English *utilitarian,* n. + *-ism.*

utility *n.* usefulness. 1391 *utilite,* in Chaucer's *Treatise on the Astrolabe;* borrowed from Old French *utilité* usefulness, learned borrowing from Latin *ūtilitātem* (nominative *ūtilitās*) usefulness, serviceableness, profit, from *ūtilis* usable, from *ūtī* to USE; for suffix see -ITY.

utilize *v.* make use of. 1807, borrowed from French *utiliser,* from Italian *utilizzare,* from *utile* usable (also found in obsolete English *utile* useful, 1484), from Latin *ūtilis* usable, from *ūtī* to use; for suffix see -IZE. **—utilization** *n.* act of utilizing. 1847, formed in English from *utilize* + *-ation,* perhaps by influence of French *utilisation.*

utmost *adj.* greatest possible, extreme. Old English (Anglian) *ūtmest* outermost (before 830, in the *Vespasian Psalter*); formed from *ūt* OUT + *-mest* -MOST, double superlative (compare *foremost, inmost*). The extended sense of being of the greatest or highest degree, extreme, is found in Middle English before 1325. Compare UTTERMOST.

Utopia or **utopia** (yü tō'pē ə) *n.* 1551, an imaginary island enjoying a perfect social, legal, and political system, in Ralph Robinson's translation of Sir Thomas More's *Utopia* (1516); coined by More, from Greek *ou* not (of unknown origin) + *tópos* place; see TOPIC. The transferred sense of any place, state, or condition where perfect justice and social conditions exist is first recorded in *Purchas his Pilgrimage* (1613).

Although *Utopia* means literally "no place," it is often believed to mean "good place," as though formed from Greek *eu-* good + *tópos* place. Modern coinages such as *dystopia* and *kakotopia* (where all is bad) as opposites of *utopia* reinforce this belief. More himself apparently coined the word *Eutopia* in 1516 as a play on *Utopia,* which led some later writers, such as Sidney in 1595, to use *Eutopia* as the title of More's book, imagining *Utopia* to be an incorrect spelling. The name *Utopia* inspired Samuel Butler to entitle his satirical novel about a utopia, *Erewhon* (1872), an anagram of "Nowhere," which is a free rendering of the literal meaning of *Utopia.*

—Utopian or **utopian** *adj.* 1551, of or like the imaginary island of Utopia; borrowed from New Latin *Utopianus,* from *Utopia* Utopia; for suffix see -AN. New Latin *Utopianus* appears in More's *Utopia.* The transferred sense of having to do with or resembling a utopia, having ideal conditions, is first recorded in English in 1613. **—*n.*** 1551, inhabitant of a utopia; borrowed from New Latin *Utopianus,* n., adj. The meaning of impractical reformer, visionary idealist, is first recorded in English before 1873.

utter[1] *adj.* complete, total. Probably before 1200 *uttre* outward, exterior, in *Ancrene Riwle;* developed from Old English (before 901) *ūtera, ūterra* outer, comparative adjective formed from *ūt* OUT, and corresponding to Old Frisian *ūtera, uttra,* Middle Low German *uter,* Middle Dutch *utere,* Old High German *ūzero* (modern German *ausser*), from Proto-Germanic **ūtizōn;* for suffix see -ER[2]. The extended meaning of going to the utmost point, extreme, complete, total, is found in Middle English before 1420 and came into frequent use after 1515. **—uttermost** *adj.* utmost. Probably before 1382 *uttermest* outermost, remotest, formed from *utter*[1], adj. + *-most.* The extended meaning of utmost is found in Middle English in 1429.

utter[2] *v.* speak, say, or pronounce. Probably before 1400 *utteren,* in *Morte d'Arthur;* in part borrowed from Middle Low German *uteren* to turn out, bring forth, show, speak, declare, from *uter* outer, comparative adjective formed from *ūt* OUT; and in part an alteration (influenced by *utter*[1]) of Middle English *outen* to make known, disclose (probably about 1350); later, to utter words, speak (about 1412); developed from Old English *ūtian* to put out, from *ūt* OUT. **—utterance** *n.* Probably before 1400 *utterans* words, speech, from *utteren* to speak, utter; for suffix see -ANCE.

uvula (yü'vyə lə) *n.* small piece of flesh hanging down from the soft palate. 1392, borrowed from Late Latin *ūvula,* from Latin *ūvola* small bunch of grapelike fruit, diminutive of *ūva* grape. **—uvular** *adj.* of or articulated near the uvula. 1843, formed in English from *uvula* + *-ar,* as if from New Latin *uvularis,* from Late Latin *ūvula.* An earlier sense of used in disorders of the uvula is found in English in 1710.

uxorious (ug zôr'ē əs) *adj.* excessively or foolishly fond of one's wife. 1598, in Bishop Joseph Hall's *Byting Satyres;* borrowed from Latin *uxōrius* of or pertaining to a wife, from *uxor* (genitive *uxōris*) wife; for suffix see -OUS. Latin *uxor, uxōris* derives from Indo-European **ukwsōr,* feminine counterpart to **ukwsén-* (the source of Sanskrit *ukṣa* and Old English *oxa* OX), root **wegw-/ugw-* damp, to sprinkle (Pok.1118).

V

vacant *adj.* About 1300 *vacaunt* not held or occupied, empty; borrowed from Old French *vacant,* from Latin *vacantem* (nominative *vacāns*) empty, vacant, present participle of *vacāre* be empty, free, or unoccupied; see VACUUM; for suffix see -ANT. The meaning of empty of thought or intelligence, expressionless, inane, is first recorded in English in 1712 (Steele, in *The Spectator*). **—vacancy** *n.* About 1580, vacation; formed from English *vacant* + *-cy.* The meaning of state of being vacant is first recorded in 1607, and that of vacant office or post in 1693.

vacate *v.* make vacant. 1643, borrowed from Latin *vacātum,* past participle of *vacāre* be empty, free; see VACANT; for suffix see -ATE[1]. **—vacation** *n.* About 1395 *vacacioun* rest and freedom from any activity, in Chaucer's *Canterbury Tales;* borrowed through Old French *vacation,* and directly from Latin *vacātiōnem* (nominative *vacātiō*) leisure, from *vacāre* be empty, free, or at leisure; for suffix see -ATION. —*v.* 1896, take a vacation; from the noun.

vaccine (vak'sēn) *n.* serum used to prevent or lessen the effects of disease. 1846, cowpox serum used in vaccinating against smallpox, developed from earlier *vaccine,* adj., relating to cowpox (1799); borrowed from Latin *vaccīnus* of or from cows (as in the New Latin phrase *variolae vaccinae* cowpox), from *vacca* cow, cognate with Sanskrit *vaśā́* cow, from Indo-European **wakā* (Pok.1111); for suffix see -INE[2]. The New Latin term was coined in 1798 by the English physician Edward Jenner, who refined the technique of vaccination, introduced earlier in 1718, from practices known much earlier in the Near East. **—vaccinate** *v.* inoculate with a vaccine. 1803, formed from English *vaccine* + *-ate*[1], or possibly a back formation of *vaccination.* **—vaccination** *n.* 1800, act or practice of vaccinating; formed from English *vaccine* + *-ation.*

vacillate *v.* waver. 1597, to sway unsteadily; probably a back formation from *vacillation,* perhaps influenced by Middle French *vaciller,* from Latin *vacillāre* to sway, from Indo-European **wək-,* root **wāk-* be bent (Pok.1135); for suffix see -ATE[1]. The meaning of waver between different opinions or courses of action is first recorded in Cockeram's *Dictionary* (1623), from the earlier sense in *vacillation* (about 1400). **—vacillation** *n.* About 1400, a wavering, hesitation, uncertainty, in a translation of Caxton's; borrowed from Latin *vacillātiōnem* (nominative *vacillātiō*) a reeling, wavering, from *vacillāre* sway to and from, of uncertain origin; for suffix see -ATION.

vacuity (vakyü'ətē) *n.* 1392 *vacuite* empty space; later, emptiness (1546); borrowed from Middle French *vacuité,* or directly from Latin *vacuitās* empty space, vacancy, freedom, from *vacuus* empty; see VACUUM; for suffix see -ITY. The meaning of emptiness of mind, lack of ideas, is first recorded in English in Hooker's *Ecclesiastical Polity* (1594).

vacuole (vak'yůōl) *n.* tiny cavity in a living cell. 1853, borrowed from French *vacuole,* formed from Latin *vacuus* empty; see VACUUM + French *-ole,* diminutive suffix, from Latin *-olus.*

vacuous (vak'yůəs) *adj.* showing no thought or intelligence. 1648 (implied in *vacuousness*), empty of matter; borrowed from Latin *vacuus* empty, void, free; see VACUUM; for suffix see -OUS. The meaning of showing no thought or intelligence is first found in Thackeray's *Book of Snobs* (1848).

vacuum *n.* empty space, emptiness. 1550, in writings of Thomas Cranmer; borrowed from Latin *vacuum* an empty space, a void, noun use of neuter of *vacuus* empty, related to *vacāre* be empty, perhaps related to *vāstus* desolate, bleak, and cognate with Umbrian *vasetom* impairment, *vas* defect. Umbrian *vas* is possibly cognate with Gothic *wans* lacking, wanting, from Indo-European **wā-/wə-, *wə-k-* (Pok.345). The meaning of an empty space without air is first recorded in 1652. The use of *vacuum* to mean vacuum cleaner is first recorded in American English in 1910, as a shortened form of *vacuum cleaner* (1903). **—v.** clean with a vacuum cleaner. 1922, from the noun. **—vacuum tube** (1784)

vagabond *adj.* wandering, roving. 1426 *vagabonde,* borrowed from Middle French *vagabonde,* learned borrowing from Late Latin *vagābundus* wandering, strolling about, from Latin *vagārī* wander; see VAGARY. **—n.** vagrant, tramp. Probably before 1425 *vagabunde,* in a translation of Higden's *Polychronicon;* from the adjective. An earlier Middle English form *vacabunde* (1402) was borrowed from a variant form of Middle French *vagabonde* and became obsolete in English in the late 1500's.

vagary (vā'gərē) *n.* odd fancy, extravagant notion. 1573-80, borrowed probably as a noun use of Latin *vagārī* to wander, from *vagus* roving, wandering, rambling, cognate with Old Irish *fān* slanting, sloping (from **wāg-no-*), Welsh *gwaun* lowland, meadow, from Indo-European *wəg-/wāg-* be curved, bent (Pok.1120).

vagina (vəjī'nə) *n.* passage from the uterus to the vulva. 1682, New Latin, from Latin *vāgīna* sheath, scabbard, perhaps cognate with Lithuanian *vóžti* cover with something hollow, and Latvian *vāst* put a cover on, from Indo-European **wāg-* sheath; cover protectively (Pok.1110). **—vaginal** *adj.* 1726, of, resembling, or serving as a sheath; formed from English *vagina* + *-al*[1]. The sense of having to do with, or affecting the vagina is first recorded in 1825.

vagrant *n.* idle wanderer, tramp. 1444 *vagraunt,* in *Rolls of Parliament;* perhaps alteration (by influence of Latin *vagārī* wander) of Anglo-French *wacrant,* present participle of Old French *wacrer, walcrer* to walk or wander, borrowed from a Germanic source (compare Old Icelandic *valka* wander; see WALK). Middle English *vagraunt* may have also been influenced in form by Middle French *vagant* wandering, present participle of *vaguer* wander, from Latin *vagārī;* see VAGARY. **—adj.**

wandering. 1461, from the same source as the noun. **—vagrancy** *n.* a wandering. 1642, formed from English *vagrant,* adj. + *-cy.*

vague *adj.* 1548, not definitely or precisely expressed; borrowed from Middle French *vague,* learned borrowing from Latin *vagus* wandering, rambling, vacillating, vague; see VAGARY. The sense of not precise or exact in meaning is first recorded in 1690, in Locke's *Essay Concerning Human Understanding,* and that of indefinite, indistinct (as in *vague ideas*) before 1704, also in Locke's writings.

vain *adj.* Probably before 1200 (implied in *veine gloire*), but not found again until about 1300 in the phrase *in veyn* uselessly, ineffectually, implying the sense of worthless, futile; borrowed from Old French *vein, vain,* from Latin *vānus* idle, empty; see WANE.

The separate sense of having too much pride, conceited, is first found in English in 1692, in Dryden's *Eleonora,* but is implied much earlier in *veine gloire.* **—vainglory** *n.* extreme pride in oneself. Probably before 1200 *veine gloire,* in *Ancrene Riwle;* borrowed from Old French *vaine gloire* and Medieval Latin *vana gloria,* literally, vain glory. The phrase is first spelled as one word *wayngIori,* in *Cursor Mundi* (before 1325), and as *vaynglorie* in 1387. **—vainglorious** *adj.* excessively proud. About 1430 *vayneglorious,* formed from Middle English *vaynglorie* vainglory + *-ous,* or borrowed from Old French *vaneglorios* and Medieval Latin *vaniglorius.*

valance (val′əns) *n.* short drapery over the top of a window. 1463 *valaunce,* about 1475 *valance;* of uncertain origin. The word may have been borrowed from an Anglo-French **valance,* from *valer* go down, variant of Old French *avaler;* see AVALANCHE. Alternatively, plural forms such as *valents* and *valandes* suggest a possible derivation from the plural of Old French *avalant,* from present participle of *avaler* go down. Another possibility is that *valance* came from the name *Valence,* a town in southern France, on the Rhone, noted for the fabrics made there.

vale *n.* valley. Before 1325 *wale,* in *Cursor Mundi;* later *vale* (about 1400); borrowed from Old French *val* valley, from Latin *vallem,* with nominative *vallis, vallēs* valley, related to *volvere* to roll; see VOLUME.

valediction *n.* a bidding farewell. 1614, in letters of Donne, formed as if from Latin **valedictiōnem,* from Latin *valedīcere* bid farewell (*valē,* imperative of *valēre* be well + *dīcere* to say; see VALUE and DICTION); for suffix see -TION. **—valedictorian** *n.* student who gives the valedictory address at graduation. 1759, American English; formed from *valedictory,* adj. + *-an.* **—valedictory** *adj.* bidding farewell. 1651, formed in English from Latin *valedictum,* past participle of *valedīcere* bid farewell + English *-ory.* —*n.* valedictory oration. 1779, American English; from the adjective.

valence (vā′ləns) *n.* combining capacity of an atom measured by a unit of hydrogen. 1884 (in 1869, *valency*); borrowed from Latin *valentia* strength, capacity, from *valentem* (nominative *valēns*), present participle of *valēre* be strong; see VALUE; for suffix see -ENCE.

valentine *n.* Before 1450 *Volontyn* sweetheart chosen on Saint Valentine's Day; later *valentyne* (about 1485); from Saint *Valentine,* a saint whose feast day falls on February 14, from Late Latin *Valentīnus* the name of two early Italian saints. The sense of a letter or card sent to a sweetheart on Saint Valentine's Day is first recorded in 1824. The origin of the custom of choosing a sweetheart on Saint Valentine's Day is obscure. The earliest sources refer it to an old belief that birds begin to mate on February 14. **—Valentine's Day** February 14 (about 1380 *Volantynys day,* in Chaucer's *Parlement of Foules*).

valet (valā′) *n.* servant who takes care of a man's clothes, etc. Before 1400 *valette,* borrowed from Old French *valet,* variant of *vaslet* man's servant; originally, squire or young man, from Gallo-Romance **vassellittus, vassallittus* young nobleman, squire, page, diminutive of Medieval Latin *vassallus,* from *vassus* servant, VASSAL; for suffix see -ET. Doublet of VARLET. **—v.** serve as a valet. 1840, from the noun.

valiant *adj.* brave. About 1303 *vailaunt,* in Mannyng's *Handlyng Synne;* later *valiant* (before 1338, in Mannyng's *Chronicle of England*); borrowed from Anglo-French and Old French *vaillant, valiant* stalwart, brave, from present participle of *valoir* be worthy; originally, be strong, from Latin *valēre;* see VALUE; for suffix see -ANT.

valid *adj.* sound, true. 1571, having force in law, legally binding; borrowed from Middle French *valide,* learned borrowing from Latin *validus* effective, strong, from *valēre* be strong; see VALUE. The meaning of supported by facts or authority, sound, true, is first recorded in English before 1648. **—validate** *v.* make valid, confirm. Before 1648, borrowed from Late Latin *validātus,* past participle of *validāre* make strong, make valid, from Latin *validus* strong, valid; for suffix see -ATE[1]. **—validity** *n.* truth, soundness. About 1550, legal soundness or force; borrowed from Middle French *validité,* or directly from Late Latin *validitātem* (nominative *validitās*) bodily strength, strength, from Latin *validus* strong, valid; for suffix see -ITY.

valise (vəlēs′) *n.* traveling bag. 1615, borrowed from French *valise,* from Italian *valigia;* of uncertain origin.

valley *n.* Probably before 1300 *valey,* in *Kyng Alisaunder;* borrowed from Old French *valee* a valley, earlier *vallede,* from Vulgar Latin **vallāta,* from Latin *vallis, vallēs* valley; see VALE.

valor *n.* bravery. Probably before 1300 *valour* value or worth, in *Arthour and Merlin;* borrowed from Old French *valour* strength, value, valor, from Late Latin *valōrem* (nominative *valor*) value, worth, from Latin *valēre* be worth, be strong; see VALUE. The meaning of courage or bravery is first recorded in 1581, borrowed from Italian *valore,* from Late Latin *valōrem* worth. **—valorous** *adj.* brave. 1475 *vaillerous,* in Caxton's translation of *The History of Jason;* borrowed from Middle French *valeureux* (*valeur* valor, from Late Latin *valōrem* + Middle French *-eux* -ous).

value *n.* worth. About 1303 *valeu,* in Mannyng's *Handlyng Synne;* later *value* (before 1376, in *Piers Plowman*); borrowed from Old French *value* worth, value, from feminine past participle of *valoir* be worth, from Latin *valēre* be strong, be well, be worth. Latin *valēre* is cognate with Old Irish *flaith* dominion, prince, Welsh *gwlad* country, Lithuanian *veldėti* to rule, Old Slavic *vlasti* govern, command, Tocharian A *wäl,* Tocharian B *walo* king, and Old English *wieldan* to WIELD. **—v.** Probably before 1400 *valuen* estimate the value of; from the noun. The sense of think highly of, regard highly, is found in Middle English in 1439. **—valuable** *adj.* having value. Probably before 1430, formed from Middle English *valuen* to value + *-able.* **—valuation** *n.*

estimation of value. 1529, borrowed from Middle French *valuation,* from *valuer* to value, from Old French *value* value, n.; for suffix see -ATION. **—value judgment** (1892, loan translation of German *Werturteil*) **—valueless** *adj.* worthless. 1595, in Shakespeare's *King John;* formed from English *value,* n. + *-less.*

valve *n.* Before 1387, one of the halves of a folding door, leaf of a door, in Trevisa's translation of Higden's *Polychronicon;* borrowed from Latin *valva* (usually *valvae,* pl., a folding door), related to *volvere* to roll; see VOLUME. The sense of a membranous fold which regulates the flow of body fluids is first recorded in English in 1615, and the sense of a mechanical device that works like a valve, in 1659. The application in zoology to one of the halves of a hinged shell is first recorded in 1661.

valvular *adj.* 1797, having the form or function of a valve; formed in English from *valvula* a small valve (1615; borrowing of New Latin *valvula,* diminutive of Latin *valva* VALVE) + *-ar.*

vamoose (vamüs′) *v. Slang.* go away quickly. 1834 *vamos;* later *vamoose* (1868); American English, borrowed from Spanish *vamos* let us go, from Latin *vādāmus,* from *vādere* to go; see WADE.

vamp[1] *n.* upper front part of a shoe or boot. Probably before 1200 *vaumpe* the part of hose or stockings which covers the foot, in *Ancrene Riwle;* borrowed from Old French *avanpié* (*avant* before, from Latin *abante* in front + Old French *pié* foot, from Latin *pedem,* accusative of *pēs* FOOT). The extended sense of the upper front part of a shoe or boot is first recorded in English in 1654. —v. 1599 (implied in *vamping*), furnish with a vamp; from the noun. The transferred sense of patch up, restore, repair, is first recorded in 1632; compare REVAMP in this sense.

vamp[2] *n.* woman who attracts and exploits men. Before 1911, in writings of Chesterton; shortened form of VAMPIRE. —v. act as a vamp towards. 1918, from the noun.

vampire *n.* corpse supposed to come to life at night and seek nourishment by sucking the blood of sleeping persons. 1734, borrowed from French *vampire* and German *Vampir,* from an old West or South Slavic form *vŭmpir,* from Old Slavic *ǫpirĭ;* compare Serbian *vampir.* The transferred sense of a person who preys ruthlessly upon others, a parasite or exploiter, is first recorded in 1741. **—vampire bat** (1790; earlier called simply *vampire,* 1774)

van[1] *n.* front part of an army or other advancing group. 1610, in Beaumont and Fletcher's *The Scornful Lady;* shortened form of VANGUARD.

van[2] *n.* covered truck or wagon. 1829, in Bulwer-Lytton's *The Disowned;* shortened form of CARAVAN.

vanadium (vənā′dēəm) *n.* metallic chemical element. 1835, New Latin, from Old Icelandic *Vanadīs,* a name of the Scandinavian goddess Freya of love and fertility + New Latin *-ium,* chemical suffix. The element was named in 1830 by the Swedish chemist Nils Sefström, 1787-1854, but was originally discovered in 1801 in a lead ore from Mexico and called *erythronium* because its salts become red when heated. Its discoverer Andrés de Río, and other chemists finally discarded the original name, after coming to the conclusion that the substance was an impure form of chromium.

vandal *n.* 1663, person who acts like a barbarian by willfully destroying beautiful or valuable things; transferred use of earlier (1555) *Vandal* member of a Germanic tribe that lived in ancient times south of the Baltic between the Vistula and the Oder, and that invaded western Europe in the 300's and 400's, sacking Rome in the year 455; borrowed from Latin *Vandalus* (plural *Vandalī*), a name of Germanic origin. **—vandalism** *n.* 1798, ruthless destruction, especially of beautiful or valuable things; borrowed from French *vandalisme* (first used by the French priest Henri Grégoire about 1793), from *vandale* vandal, from Latin *Vandalus* Vandal; for suffix see -ISM. **—vandalize** *v.* destroy willfully. 1800, formed in English from *vandal* + *-ize.*

Vandyke or **vandyke** *n.* 1755, collar with a deeply cut edge; named after Anthony *Vandyke* (Anglicized spelling of Anton *Van Dyck*), 1599-1641, the Flemish painter; so called from a style of dress frequently depicted in his portraits. The sense of a short pointed beard, like that found on the subjects in many of Vandyke's paintings, is first recorded in English in 1894 as *Vandyke beard,* and in the shortened form *Vandyke* (1909).

vane *n.* About 1395 *vane* device that shows wind direction, in Chaucer's *Canterbury Tales;* variant in southern Middle English of *fane;* developed from Old English (before 1000) *fana* banner, flag. Old English *fana* is cognate with Old Frisian *fana* piece of cloth, Old Saxon and Old High German *fano* (modern German *Fahne* flag), Gothic *fana* (from Proto-Germanic **fanōn*), and outside Germanic with Latin *pannus* piece of cloth, rag, and perhaps Greek *pḗnē* thread on a bobbin, woof, from Indo-European **pan-/pān-* (Pok.788).

vanguard *n.* troops marching ahead of any army. Probably about 1450 *vaunt garde;* later *vandgard* (1487) and *vanguarde* (1503); borrowed from Middle French *avant-garde* advance guard (*avant* forward, from Latin *abante* in ADVANCE + *garde* GUARD).

vanilla *n.* 1662 *vaynilla* bean of the vanilla plant; borrowed from Old Spanish *vaynilla;* later in the spelling *vanilla* (1673); borrowed from New Latin *Vanilla* the genus name, from Spanish *vainilla* (in Old Spanish *vaynilla*) vanilla plant, little pod, diminutive of *vaina* sheath, from Latin *vāgīna;* see VAGINA. The meaning of a flavoring extract from the vanilla bean is first recorded in English in 1728, but implied as early as 1662, in use of the vanilla pod for flavoring. **—vanilla bean** (1874)

vanish *v.* About 1303 *vanisshen,* in Mannyng's *Handlyng Synne;* borrowing (with loss of initial syllable) of Old French *esvaniss-,* stem of *esvanir,* from Vulgar Latin **exvanire,* from Latin *ēvānēscere* disappear, die out (*ex-* out + *vānēscere* vanish, from *vānus* empty; see WANE); for suffix see -ISH[2]. Doublet of EVANESCE. **—vanishing point** (1797)

vanity *n.* conceit. Probably about 1200 *vanite;* borrowed from Old French *vanité,* learned borrowing from Latin *vānitātem* (nominative *vānitās*) emptiness, foolish pride, from *vānus* empty, vane, idle; see WANE; for suffix see -ITY. **—vanity case** (about 1904) **—vanity fair** place or scene of frivolity. 1816, figurative use of *Vanity Fair,* a fair in the town of Vanity, in Bunyan's *Pilgrim's Progress* (1678). The term was popularized by Thackeray's novel *Vanity Fair* (1848).

vanquish *v.* conquer. Before 1338 *venquisen, vencusen,* in Mannyng's *Chronicle of England;* borrowed from Old French *venqui, venquis,* past tense and *ven-*

cus, past participle of *veintre* conquer, from Latin *vincere* conquer; see VICTOR. The late Middle English form *vainquisshen* (1474) was borrowed from Middle French *vainquiss-,* present stem of *vainquir* conquer, from Old French *vainkir,* alteration of *veintre* conquer; for suffix see -ISH². The generalized sense of overcome, put an end to, suppress (as in *to vanquish fear*) is first recorded in English about 1380.

vantage *n.* advantage. Before 1325, in *Cursor Mundi;* borrowed through Anglo-French *vantage,* from Old French *avantage* ADVANTAGE. **—vantage point** (1865)

vapid *adj.* tasteless, dull. 1656, (of drinks) flat, insipid, in Blount's *Glossographia;* borrowed from obsolete French *vapide,* or directly from Latin *vapidus* flat, insipid; literally, that has exhaled its vapor; related to *vappa* stale wine, and probably to *vapor;* see VAPOR. The figurative sense of dull, flat, lifeless (applied to talk, writings, etc.) is first recorded in English in 1758 (Johnson, in *The Idler*). **—vapidity** *n.* 1721, deadness, flatness, in Bailey's *Dictionary;* formed from English *vapid* + *-ity.*

vapor *n.* Before 1382 *vapour* steam, mist, in the Wycliffe Bible; borrowed from Anglo-French *vapour* (in Old French *vapeur*), learned borrowing from Latin, and borrowed into English directly from Latin *vapōrem* (nominative *vapor*) exhalation, vapor, of uncertain origin. The British spelling has always been *vapour;* the spelling *vapor* was established in American English by Noah Webster. **—v.** Probably about 1408 *vapouren* rise or cause to rise as vapor; from the noun. **—vaporize** *v.* 1634, change into smoke; later, change into vapor (1803); formed in English from Latin *vapor,* n., vapor + English *-ize.* **—vaporous** *adj.* full of vapor. Before 1400, in Lanfranc's *Science of Surgery;* borrowed perhaps from Old French *vaporeux,* and directly from Latin *vapōrōsus* full of steam or vapor, from *vapor,* n., vapor; for suffix see -OUS. **—vapory** *adj.* consisting of vapor. 1598, formed from English *vapor,* n. + *-y*¹.

variable *adj.* About 1387, apt to change, fickle, in Trevisa's translation of Higden's *Polychronicon;* borrowed from Old French *variable,* and directly from Latin *variābilis* changeable, from *variāre* to change; see VARY; for suffix see -ABLE. **—n.** 1816, quantity that can vary in value; from the adjective. The sense of a symbol (in logic, mathematics, etc.) representing a variable quantity is first recorded in 1910. **—variable star** (1788)

variant *adj.* About 1380 *variaunt* not constant or uniform, tending to vary or change, in Chaucer's translation of Boethius' *De Consolatione Philosophiae;* borrowed from Old French *variant,* learned borrowing from Latin, and borrowed into English directly from Latin *variantem* (nominative *variāns*) a changing, varying, present participle of *variāre* to change; see VARY; for suffix see -ANT. **—n.** 1848, a different form; from the adjective. **—variance** *n.* About 1385 *variaunce* the fact of varying, difference, divergence, in Chaucer's *Troilus and Criseyde;* borrowed from Old French *variance,* learned borrowing from Latin, and borrowed directly into English from Latin *variantia* a difference, diversity, from *variantem* (nominative *variāns*), present participle; for suffix see -ANCE.

variation *n.* About 1385 *variacioun* difference, divergence, in Chaucer's *Canterbury Tales;* borrowed from Old French *variation,* learned borrowing from Latin, and borrowed into English directly from Latin *variātiōnem* (nominative *variātiō*) a difference, variation change, from *variāre* to change; see VARY; for suffix see -ATION. The sense of the fact of varying, change, is first recorded in English in 1502.

varicolored *adj.* 1665, of various or different colors formed in English from Latin *varius* VARIOUS + English *colored.*

varicose (var′əkōs) *adj.* swollen or enlarged. Probably before 1425, in a translation of Chauliac's *Grande Chirurgie;* borrowed from Latin *varicōsus* full of dilated veins, from *varix* (genitive *varicis*) dilated vein, of unknown origin; for suffix see -OSE¹.

variegate (vār′ēəgāt) *v.* to mark, spot, or streak with different colors. 1653, give variety to, diversify; borrowed from Late Latin *variegātus* made of various sorts or colors, past participle of *variegāre* diversify with different colors, from a lost adjective **variegus* (*varius* spotted; see VARIOUS + the root of *agere* to drive, make; see AGENT); for suffix see -ATE¹. The specific sense of mark, spot, or streak with different colors, is first recorded in English before 1728 (though found earlier in the adjective *variegated*). **—variegated** *adj.* marked with spots or streaks of different colors. Before 1661, formed in English from Latin *variegātus* variegated (past participle of *variegāre*) + English *-ed*².

variety *n.* fact, quality, or condition of being varied. Before 1533, borrowed through Middle French *variété,* and directly from Latin *varietātem* (nominative *varietās*) difference, diversity, from *varius* VARIOUS; for suffix -TY². **—variety show** (1882)

various *adj.* diverse. Probably before 1425, in a translation of Chauliac's *Grande Chirurgie;* borrowed perhaps from Middle French *varieux,* and directly from Latin *varius* changing, different, diverse, of uncertain origin; for suffix see -OUS.

varlet *n.* rascal. 1456, servant, attendant on a knight; borrowed from Middle French *varlet,* variant of *vaslet;* originally, squire or young man; see the doublet VALET. The meaning of rascal, rogue, is first recorded in English before 1550, in Skelton's writings.

varmint *n. Dialect.* vermin. 1539 *varment;* later in the spelling *varmint* (1829); dialectal variant of VERMIN. Compare VARSITY.

varnish *n.* liquid that gives a smooth, glossy appearance to wood, metal, etc. 1358 *vernisshe;* borrowed from Old French *vernis, verniz* varnish, from Medieval Latin *vernix, vernica* odorous resin, from Late Greek *vereníkē,* from Greek *Bereníkē,* an ancient city in Libya. The figurative sense of a false appearance, pretense, is first recorded in 1565. **—v.** put varnish on. About 1390 *vernisshen,* in Chaucer's *Canterbury Tales;* borrowed from Old French *vernissier,* from *vernis* varnish, n.; or from Old French *verniss-,* stem of *vernir* to varnish, from *vernis* varnish; for suffix see -ISH². The figurative sense of give a false appearance to is first recorded in 1571.

varsity *n.* 1846, university, variant of earlier *versity* (about 1680), shortened form of UNIVERSITY. The specific meaning of the team representing a university, college, or school in a given sport developed from such phrases as *varsity captain, varsity race, varsity team,* first found in American English in 1891. For a similar change in the vowel pronunciation, compare *sergeant, varmint,* and the British pronunciation of *clerk.*

vary *v.* About 1350 *varien,* borrowed from Old French

varier, and directly from Latin *variāre* change, alter, make different, from *varius* varied, different, spotted; see VARIOUS. **—varied** *adj.* of different kinds. 1588, in Shakespeare's *Titus Andronicus* and *Love's Labour's Lost;* from the past participle of *vary;* for suffix see -ED².

vascular *adj.* made of or provided with vessels that carry blood, sap, etc. 1672-73, in Nehemiah Grew's *The Anatomy of Plants;* borrowed from New Latin *vascularis* of or pertaining to vessels or tubes, from Latin *vāsculum,* diminutive of *vās* vessel; see VASE; for suffix see -AR.

vase (vās *or* vāz) *n.* 1563, ornamental vessel on a pillar; later, ornamental container, as for flowers (1629); borrowed from Middle French *vase,* from Latin *vās* container, vessel, cognate with Umbrian *vasor,* pl., vessels; no certain cognates outside Italic have been found.

vasectomy (vasek'təmē) *n.* surgical removal of part or all of the vas deferens (duct that conveys semen). 1897, borrowed in English from New Latin *vas* (*deferens*) + English *-ectomy.*

Vaseline (vas'əlēn) *n.* trademark for an ointment made from petroleum. 1874, American English. According to H.L. Mencken, the term was coined about 1870 by Robert A. Chesebrough, of the Chesebrough Manufacturing Company, from German *Wasser* WATER + Greek *élaion* OIL + English *-ine*¹.

vassal *n.* person who in feudal times held land from a lord. 1325, borrowed from Old French *vassal,* from Medieval Latin *vassallus* manservant, domestic, retainer, from *vassus* servant, from a Celtic source (compare Old Irish *foss* servant, Welsh *gwas* young man, servant, and Breton *gwaz* servant, man, male), ultimately from Indo-European **upo-sthos,* from **upo* under + the root **stā-/stə-/sth-* of STAND. **—adj.** of or like a vassal. 1588, in Shakespeare's *Love's Labour's Lost;* from the noun.

vast *adj.* 1575-85, borrowed from Middle French *vaste,* and directly from Latin *vastus* immense, extensive, huge; desolate, unoccupied, empty; cognate with Old Irish *fot, fut* length, *fotae* long. According to some scholars, Latin *vastus* is distinct from *vāstus* desolate, but the two forms must have merged early in Latin, so that English *vast* is related to *waste,* Old English *wēste* desolate, cognate with Old Irish *fās* empty; see WASTE. Ernout-Meillet, however, treat the two Latin adjectives as one.

vat *n.* tank. Probably about 1200 *veat* tank, variant in Southern Middle English of *fat* container; developed from Old English *fæt* (about 725, in *Beowulf*); cognate with Old Frisian *fet* container, vat, Old Saxon *fat,* Middle Dutch and modern Dutch *vat,* Old High German *vaz* (modern German *Fass* barrel, vat), Old Icelandic *fat,* from Proto-Germanic **fatan,* and outside Germanic probably with Lithuanian *púodas* pot, from Indo-European **pod-/pōd-* (Pok.790). For a similar change of *f* to *v,* compare VIXEN.

vaudeville (vô'dəvil *or* vōd'vil) *n.* theatrical entertainment consisting of a variety of acts. 1739, light popular song, especially one sung on the stage, in letters of Horace Walpole; borrowed from French *vaudeville,* alteration (influenced by *ville* town) of Middle French *vaudevire.* Traditionally the French word has been derived from (*chanson du*) *Vau de Vire* (song of the) valley of Vire in Calvados, Normandy, said to have been first applied to the songs composed by Olivier Basselin, a poet of the 1400's who lived in Vire; however, this derivation is not accepted by Dauzat and others, who derive *vaudevire* from Middle French (dialectal) *vauder* to go + *virer* to turn. The extended meaning of a light and amusing theatrical entertainment interspersed with songs is first recorded in English in 1827; the French word corresponding to this meaning is *variété,* the source of British *variety* vaudeville (1904).

vault¹ *n.* arched roof or ceiling. Probably before 1300 *vaute,* borrowed from Old French *voute, vaute, vaulte* a vault, arch, vaulted roof, from Vulgar Latin **volta,* contraction of **volvita,* noun use of feminine of **volvitus,* alteration of Latin *volūtus* bowed, arched, past participle of *volvere* to turn, turn around, roll; see VOLUME. The spelling with *l* is first found in late Middle English (recorded once about 1400 and once before 1490), by influence of the Latin forms, and possibly the Old French variant *vaulte.* The shift in spelling eventually influenced the pronunciation of the word in English; compare FAULT. **—v.** make in the form of a vault. 1387 *vouten;* borrowed from Old French *vouter, vauter,* from *voute, vaute* vault¹, n.

vault² *v.* jump or leap over. 1538, borrowed from Middle French *volter* to gambol, leap, from Italian *voltare,* from Vulgar Latin **volvitāre* to turn, leap, vault, a frequentative form derived from Latin *volvere* to turn, turn around, roll; see VOLUME. **—n.** a jump, leap. 1576, from the verb. **—vaulting** *adj.* overly aggressive. 1605, in Shakespeare's *Macbeth,* formed from English *vault*², v. + *-ing*².

vaunt *v.* to boast. Before 1425 *vaunten,* borrowed from Middle French *vanter,* from Late Latin *vānitāre* to boast, a frequentative form derived from Latin *vānāre* to utter empty words, from *vānus* idle, empty; see WANE. **—n.** a boast. Probably before 1400 *vaunte,* shortened form of earlier *avaunt* a boast (about 1380), from *avaunten* to boast (1303), borrowed from Old French *avanter* (*a-* to + *vanter* to boast).

veal *n.* meat from a calf. About 1395, in Chaucer's *Canterbury Tales;* borrowed from Anglo-French *vel,* from Old French *veel, veal* a calf, earlier *vedel,* from Latin *vitellus* little calf, diminutive of *vitulus* calf; cognate with Sanskrit *vatsá-s* calf, perhaps a yearling; see WETHER.

vector *n.* quantity involving direction as well as magnitude. 1704, line joining a fixed point (the sun) and a variable point (a planet); borrowed from Latin *vector* one who carries or conveys, carrier, from past participle stem of *vehere* carry, convey; see WEIGH; for suffix see -OR². The meaning in mathematics of a quantity involving direction as well as magnitude is first recorded in 1846.

veer *v.* change in direction. 1582, borrowed from Middle French *virer* to turn, origin uncertain; perhaps from Vulgar Latin **vīrāre* to turn, sheer off, which has been referred to the stem *vir-* in *viriae,* pl., bracelets (also found in French *environ* where *viron* represents the sense of circle) and where the original sense is thought to be to wind around, twist. It is also possible that a relationship exists with Latin *viēre* to bend, plait, and thereby with Old English *wīr* wire, from Indo-European **wei-/wi-/wī-* (Pok.1120); see WITHY. Compare FERRULE; also more remotely and from a different point of view, see GYRATE. **—n.** a shift, turn. 1611, in Cotgrave's *Dictionary;* from the verb.

vegetable *adj.* Before 1398 *vegetabil* living and growing as a plant, in Trevisa's translation of Bartholomew's *De Proprietatibus Rerum;* borrowed from Old French *vegetable* living, fit to live, and directly from Medieval Latin *vegetabilis* growing, flourishing, from Late Latin *vegetābilis* animating, enlivening, from Latin *vegetāre* enliven; see VEGETATE; for suffix see -ABLE. **—n.** 1582, organism of the vegetable kingdom, any plant; from the adjective. The sense of a plant cultivated for food is not recorded in English before 1767.

vegetarian *n.* person who eats no meat. 1839, irregularly formed from English *veget(able)* + *-arian,* as in *agrarian, trinitarian.* **—vegetarianism** *n.* practice or principle of eating no meat. 1851, formed from English *vegetarian* + *-ism.*

vegetate *v.* 1605, grow as plants do; probably in part a back formation from *vegetation,* and in part developed from *vegetate,* adj., endowed with vegetable life, growing as a plant (1574); borrowed from Late Latin *vegetatum,* past participle of *vegetare* grow, flourish, enliven, from Latin *vegetāre* impart energy to, invigorate, enliven, from *vegetus* vigorous, energetic, lively, from *vegēre* to impart vigor, move, excite; see WAKE[1] awaken; for suffix see -ATE[1]. The figurative sense of live with very little action, thought, or feeling, lead a dull life, is first recorded in English in 1740. **—vegetation** *n.* 1564, act of vegetating; borrowed from Middle French *végétation,* and directly from Medieval Latin *vegetationem* (nominative *vegetatio*) a quickening, action of growing, from *vegetare* grow, quicken; for suffix see -ATION. The sense of plant life, growing plants, is first recorded in English in 1727-46. The sense of plant life, growing plants (as in *deserts have sparse vegetation*) is first recorded in English in 1727, and the figurative sense of dull, empty, or stagnant life, is first recorded in English in 1797. **—vegetative** *adj.* growing as plants do. Before 1398 *vegetatif,* in Trevisa's translation of Bartholomew's *De Proprietatibus Rerum;* borrowed from Old French *vegetatif* (feminine *vegetative*), from Medieval Latin *vegetativus* growing or having the power of physical growth, from *vegetatum,* past participle of *vegetare* grow, quicken; for suffix see -IVE. The figurative sense of having very little action, thought, or feeling, is first recorded in English in 1802, and the use in medicine to describe someone who is reduced to the state of having only physical function is not found before 1893.

vehement (vē′əmənt) *adj.* eager, passionate, forceful. Probably before 1425, intense, severe; borrowed from Middle French *vehement* (impetuous, ardent, from Latin *vehementem* (nominative *vehemēns*) impetuous, headlong, carried away, perhaps from earlier **wéhemènos* carrying oneself, rushing, lost present middle participle of *vehere* to carry; see WEIGH. The form of Latin *vehemēns* was influenced by *mēns* (genitive *mentis*) MIND. The extended sense of eager, passionate, forceful, is first recorded in English in 1526.

Until the 1800's the only pronunciation recognized by dictionaries for *vehement, vehemence,* and *vehicle* was with *h* (vē′hə-). But by that time this was unusual in Great Britain and becoming rarer in the United States. Note, however, the retention of *h* in the stressed position of the pronunciation of *vehicular.*

—vehemence *n.* 1402 *vehemens,* borrowed from Middle French *vehemence* vehement quality or nature, forcefulness, from Latin *vehementia* eagerness, strength, from *vehementem* (nominative *vehemēns*) eager, impetuous; for suffix see -ENCE.

vehicle (vē′əkəl) *n.* 1612, (in medical use) a medium through which a drug or medicine is administered; 1615, any means of conveying or transmitting; borrowed from French *véhicule,* and directly from Latin *vehiculum* means of transport, a vehicle, from *vehere* to carry; see WEIGH. The sense of carriage, cart, or other conveyance, is first recorded in English in Blount's *Glossographia* (1656). On the pronunciation of *vehicle,* see the note under VEHEMENT. **—vehicular** (vihik′yələr) *adj.* 1616, borrowed from Late Latin *vehiculāris* of or pertaining to a vehicle, from Latin *vehiculum* vehicle; for suffix see -AR.

veil *n.* Probably before 1200, head covering worn by nuns, in *Ancrene Riwle;* borrowed from Anglo-French and Old North French *veil* a headcovering; also, a sail, from Latin *vēla,* plural (taken as feminine singular) of *vēlum* sail, curtain, covering (earlier **vexlom*), of uncertain origin. Doublet of VELUM.

The expression *to take the veil,* meaning to become a nun, is found in Middle English about 1325. The general sense of a covering for the face is recorded from about 1250. The figurative sense of something that conceals or hides is first recorded in English in 1382, in the Wycliffe Bible.

—v. cover with a veil. Before 1382 *veilen,* in the Wycliffe Bible; from the noun. The figurative sense of conceal or hide is first recorded in English in 1538, in Bishop Latimer's writings.

vein *n.* Probably before 1300 *veine* blood vessel, in *Kyng Alisaunder;* borrowed from Old French *veine,* from Latin *vēna* a blood vessel; also, a water course, a vein of metal, a person's natural ability or interest, of uncertain origin. The botanical sense of a strand of vascular tissue in a leaf is first recorded in English in 1513. The mineralogical sense of an ore deposit, lode, is found in Middle English before 1387. The figurative sense of a distinctive thread or strain of some quality (as in *a sophisticated vein of humor*) is first recorded in English in 1565, preceded by the meaning of a distinctive style (1548).

velar *n.* See VELUM.

Velcro *n.* trademark for a nylon fabric with minute hooks, used as a fastener. 1960, borrowed from French *vel(ours) cro(ché)* hooked velvet; see VELOUR and CROCHET.

veld or **veldt** (velt) *n.* open country in South Africa. 1785 *veld,* borrowed from Afrikaans *veld,* from Dutch *veld* (Middle Dutch *velt, veld*) FIELD. The spelling *veldt* is first recorded in English in 1863.

vellum *n.* parchment used for writing, binding books, etc. About 1430 *velym;* borrowed from Middle French *velin* parchment made from calfskin, from Old French *vel, veel* calf; see VEAL.

The change in pronunciation from the Middle French represented by final *n* to a sound represented by *m* in Middle English resulted from the influence in pronunciation of such words as *venom* and *pilgrim* or influences similar to those that introduced the sound associated with *m* into such words. The spelling *velum* is found in Middle English in 1499; *vellum* is first recorded in 1636.

velocipede (vəlos′əpēd) *n.* child's tricycle. 1819, a wheeled vehicle propelled by the feet on the ground; borrowed from French *vélocipède,* from Latin *vēlōx* (genitive *vēlōcis*) swift; see VELOCITY + *pedem,* accusative of *pēs* FOOT. In 1849-50 the word was applied to a kind of early bicycle or tricycle with pedals.

velocity *n.* speed. Probably before 1425 *velocite,* in a translation of Chauliac's *Grande Chirurgie;* borrowed from Latin *vēlōcitās* swiftness, speed, from *vēlōx* (genitive *vēlōcis*) swift, perhaps related to *vehere* carry; see WEIGH; for suffix see -ITY.

velour or **velours** (vəlůr′) *n.* fabric like velvet. 1706 *velours* plush cushion used by hatters, in Kersey's edition of Phillips' *Dictionary;* borrowed from French *velours* velvet, from Old French *velour,* alteration (with introduction of *r*) of *velous,* from Old Provençal *velos,* from Latin *villōsus,* adj., shaggy (in Medieval Latin, velvet), from *villus* shaggy hair, tuft of hair; see VELVET. The meaning of a fabric like velvet is first recorded in English in 1858. The spelling *velour* is first found in English in 1875.

velum (vē′ləm) *n.* soft palate. 1753, New Latin, from Latin *vēlum* covering; see the doublet VEIL. **—velar** *adj.* pronounced by means of the soft palate as certain sounds represented by the letters *qu.* 1876, borrowed perhaps by influence of French *vélaire,* from Latin *vēlāris* of or pertaining to a veil or covering, from *vēlum* covering; for suffix see -AR. An earlier sense of resembling a sail is found in 1726.

velvet *n.* 1327 *veluett;* later in the spelling *velvet* (1351); probably borrowed from Old Provençal *veluet,* from Vulgar Latin **villūtittus,* diminutive of Vulgar Latin *villūtus* velvet; literally, shaggy cloth, from Latin *villus* shaggy hair, nap of cloth, tuft of hair, probably a dialectal variant of *vellus* fleece, from Indo-European **wel-, welə-* hair, wool (Pok.1139). **—velveteen** *n.* velvetlike fabric. 1776, formed from English *velvet* + *-een,* variant of *-ine*[1]. **—velvety** *adj.* smooth and soft like velvet. 1752, formed from English *velvet* + *-y*[1].

venal (vē′nəl) *adj.* willing to sell one's services or influence basely. 1652, borrowed from French *vénal,* and directly from Latin *vēnālis* that is for sale, from *vēnum* (nominative **vēnus*) for sale. Latin *vēnum* is cognate with Homeric Greek *ônos* price, Sanskrit *vasná-s,* from Indo-European **wesnos/wosnos/wōsnos* cost, price (Pok.1173); for suffix see -AL[1]. **—venality** *n.* 1611, state of being for sale, in Cotgrave's *Dictionary;* later, state of being venal, corruption (before 1683); borrowed from French *vénalité,* and directly from Late Latin *venalitās* capable of being bought, from *vēnālis* that is for sale; for suffix see -ITY.

vend *v.* 1622, sell, peddle; in some instances a possible back formation from *vendible* or *vendee,* modeled on Latin *vēndere,* and also borrowed from Latin *vēndere* to sell, praise, contraction of *vēnumdare* offer for sale (*vēnum* for sale; see VENAL + *dare* give; see DATE[1] time). **—vendee** *n.* buyer. 1547, probably formed in English from Latin *vēndere* to sell + English *-ee.* **—vendible** *adj.* salable. 1330, borrowed from Old French *vendible,* and directly from Latin *vēndibilis* that may be sold, salable, from *vēndere* to sell; for suffix see -IBLE. **—vending machine** (1895) **—vendor** *n.* seller. 1594, borrowed from late Anglo-French *vendor,* earlier *vendour,* from *vendre* to vend, from Latin *vēndere* to sell; for suffix see -OR[2].

vendetta *n.* 1855, borrowing of Italian *vendetta* a feud, blood feud, from Latin *vindicta* revenge; see VINDICATE.

veneer *n.* thin layer of fine wood or other material to give an appearance of superior quality. 1702, borrowed (with loss of *r* in the unstressed first syllable) from German *Furnier,* from *furnieren* to cover with a veneer, inlay, from French *fournir* to furnish, accomplish, from Middle French *fornir, furnir* to FURNISH. The figurative sense of a merely outward show or appearance of some desirable quality is first recorded in English in 1868. **—v.** to cover with a veneer. 1728, in *Chambers Cyclopaedia;* earlier *fineer* (1708); borrowed from German *furnieren* to cover with veneer.

venerate *v.* revere. 1623, in Cockeram's *Dictionary;* probably a back formation from *veneration,* and possibly also developed from *venerate,* adj., reverent (1592); modeled on Latin *venerātus* revered, past participle of *venerārī* to seek a deity's favor, worship, revere, related to *venus* (genitive *veneris*) love, desire; for suffix see -ATE[1]. Latin *venus* is cognate with Sanskrit *vánati* (he) loves, attains, and Gothic *wēns* expectation, hope, from Indo-European **wen-/wēn-* (Pok.1146). **—venerable** *adj.* worthy of reverence. About 1410, borrowed through Old French *venerable,* and directly from Latin *venerābilis* worthy of reverence, from *venerārī* venerate; for suffix see -ABLE. **—veneration** *n.* reverence. About 1410 *veneracioun;* borrowed from Middle French *veneration,* and directly from Latin *venerātiōnem* (nominative *venerātiō*) reverence, from *venerārī* venerate; for suffix see -ATION.

venereal (vənir′ēəl) *adj.* of or relating to sexual intercourse. Probably before 1425 *venerealle,* in a translation of Higden's *Polychronicon;* formed in Middle English from Latin *venereus* (from *venus,* genitive *veneris* love, sexual desire) + Middle English *-alle* -al[1]; see VENERATE.

venery (ven′ərē) *n.* gratification of sexual desire. Before 1450, borrowed from Medieval Latin *veneria* sexual intercourse, from Latin *venus* (genitive *veneris*) love, sexual desire; see VENERATE; for suffix see -Y[3].

vengeance *n.* Probably before 1300 *vengeaunce* act of avenging, revenge, in *Kyng Alisaunder;* borrowed from Anglo-French *vengeaunce,* variant of Old French *vengeance* revenge, from *vengier* take revenge, from Latin *vindicāre* to set free, claim, avenge, VINDICATE; for suffix see -ANCE. **—vengeful** *adj.* seeking or inflicting vengeance. Before 1586, formed from obsolete English *venge* take revenge (from Middle English *vengen,* borrowed from Old French *vengier*) + *-ful.*

venial (vē′nēəl) *adj.* forgivable. About 1303, in Mannyng's *Handlyng Synne;* borrowed from Old French *venial,* learned borrowing from Latin, and borrowed directly into English from Latin *veniālis* pardonable, from *venia* forgiveness, indulgence, pardon, related to *venus* love, desire; see VENERATE; for suffix see -AL[1].

venison *n.* deer meat. Probably before 1300 *venisoun,* in *Arthour and Merlin;* borrowed from Old French *venesoun* meat of large game, especially the deer or boar as principal animals of the hunt; also, a hunt, from Latin *vēnātiōnem* (nominative *vēnātiō*) a hunt; also, game as the product of the hunt, from *vēnārī* to hunt, pursue, related to *venus* love, desire; see VENERATE.

venom *n.* poison of snakes, spiders, etc. Before 1250 *venim,* in *Bestiary;* later *venom* (about 1440); borrowed from Anglo-French and Old French *venim,* variant (probably on the model of Vulgar Latin) of *venin* poison, from Vulgar Latin **venīmen,* from Latin *venēnum* poison, drug, potion, from earlier **venes-nom* love potion, from *venus* love; see VENERATE. The figurative sense of bitter or virulent feeling, language, etc., is found in Middle English before 1325. **—venomous** *adj.* About 1300 *venimous* pernicious; borrowed from Anglo-French *venimus, venimous,* from Old French *venim* venom; for suffix see -OUS. The sense of poisonous is found in Middle English before 1338, and that of virulent, embittered, about 1340.

venous *adj.* 1626, having veins, in Sir Francis Bacon's *Sylva Sylvarum;* later, of or having to do with a vein (1681); borrowed from Latin *vēnōsus* full of veins, from *vēna* VEIN; for suffix see -OUS.

vent *v.* Before 1382 *venten* emit from a confined space, in the Wycliffe Bible (implied in *venting,* verbal noun); probably borrowed (with loss of initial *e*) from Old French *eventer, esventer* let out, expose to the air, from Vulgar Latin **exventāre* (Latin *ex-* out + *ventus* WIND[1], n.). The figurative sense of let out, express freely, is first recorded in English in Shakespeare's *The Taming of the Shrew* (1596). **—n.** 1508, act of emitting or discharging; probably borrowed (with loss of initial *e*) from Middle French *event, esvent,* from Old French *eventer, esventer* let out. The sense of a hole or opening serving as an outlet is first recorded in 1570.

ventilate *v.* About 1425 *ventilatten* blow away; borrowed from Latin *ventilātus,* past participle of *ventilāre* to brandish, toss in the air, winnow, fan, agitate, set in motion, from *ventulus* a breeze, diminutive of *ventus* WIND[1], n.; for suffix see -ATE[1]. The figurative sense of examine and discuss in public is first recorded in English in 1527. The sense of aerate (the blood) is found in 1668, and that of to supply (a room, or closed space) with fresh air first occurs in 1743 (implied in *ventilating*). **—ventilation** *n.* 1456, current of air, breeze; borrowed from Middle French *ventilation,* and directly from Latin *ventilātiōnem* (nominative *ventilātiō*) an exposing to the air, from *ventilāre* ventilate; for suffix see -ATION. The sense of an act of supplying fresh air is first recorded in 1664. **—ventilator** *n.* 1743, apparatus for ventilating; formed from English *ventilate* + *-or*[2].

ventral *adj.* of the belly, abdominal. 1739, borrowed from French *ventral,* and directly from Late Latin *ventrālis* of or pertaining to the belly or stomach, from Latin *venter* (genitive *ventris*) belly, paunch, of unknown origin; for suffix see -AL[1].

ventricle *n.* chamber of the heart. 1392, borrowed from Latin *ventriculus* stomach, ventricle, diminutive of *venter* (genitive *ventris*) belly; see VENTRAL.

ventriloquism (ventril′əkwizəm) *n.* art of throwing one's voice so that it seems to come from some source other than the speaker. 1797, formed as a descriptive noun to *ventriloquist,* with substitution of the suffix *-ism.* The word has generally replaced the older *ventriloquy.* **—ventriloquist** *n.* an expert in ventriloquism. 1656, in Blount's *Glossographia;* formed from English *ventriloquy* + *-ist.* **—ventriloquy** *n.* ventriloquism. 1584, formed from Late Latin *ventriloquus* ventriloquist + English *-y*[3]. Late Latin *ventriloquus* (Latin *venter,* genitive *ventris,* belly + *loquī* speak) was patterned on Greek *engastrímȳthos,* literally, speaking in the belly; see VENTRAL and LOQUACITY.

venture *n.* risky undertaking. Probably before 1400, fortune, luck, chance, in *Morte Arthur;* shortened form of *aventure,* itself an earlier form of ADVENTURE. The sense of risky undertaking is first recorded before 1566. **—v.** expose to risk, dare. About 1430 *venteren,* shortened and altered form of earlier *aventuren* to chance, risk (probably before 1300); borrowed from Old French *aventurer,* from *aventure* adventure. **—venturesome** *adj.* daring, hazardous. 1661, formed from English *venture,* n. or v. + *-some*[1].

venue (ven′yü) *n. Law.* place or neighborhood of a crime or cause of action. Probably about 1300 *veneu* assault, attack; borrowed from Old French *venue* coming, from the feminine of the past participle of *venir* to come, from Latin *venire* to COME. The sense of a place where a case in law is tried is first recorded in 1531.

veracious (vərā′shəs) *adj.* truthful. Before 1677, formed in English from Latin *vērāx* (genitive *vērācis*) truthful, from *vērus* true; see VERY + English *-ous.* **—veracity** *n.* truthfulness. 1623, in Cockeram's *Dictionary;* formed in English from Latin *vērāx* (genitive *vērācis*) truthful + English *-ity.*

veranda (vəran′də) *n.* large porch. 1711, in Charles Lockyer's *An Account of the Trade in India;* borrowed from Hindi *varandā,* probably from Portuguese *varanda,* originally, long balcony or terrace, veranda, of uncertain origin, but also related to obsolete Spanish *baranda* railing, Catalan *barana* small railing or balustrade, and Old Provençal *baranda* defense, barricade. The ultimate origin of this word is most probably European, perhaps from Vulgar Latin **barra* barrier, BAR. The word is found in several Indic languages besides Hindi, as in Bengali *bārāndā,* but such words appear merely to be adoptions of the Portuguese or perhaps the somewhat older Spanish word, both of the 1400's.

verb *n.* Before 1397 *verbe,* in the Wycliffe Bible; borrowed from Old French *verbe* part of speech that expresses action or being, learned borrowing from Latin *verbum* a verb; originally, a word; see WORD.

verbal *adj.* in words, of words. Probably before 1425 *verbale;* borrowed from Middle French *verbal,* and directly from Latin *verbālis* consisting of words, relating to verbs, from *verbum* verb; see WORD; for suffix see -AL[1]. **—n.** noun, adjective, or other word derived from a verb. 1530, in Palsgrave's *Lesclarcissement;* from the adjective. **—verbalize** *v.* 1609, to use too many words; borrowed from French *verbaliser,* and formed from English *verbal,* adj. + *-ize.* The meaning of express in words is first recorded in English in 1875.

verbatim (vėrbā′tim) *adv.* word for word. 1481, borrowing of Medieval Latin *verbatim* word for word, from Latin *verbum* WORD. **—adj.** 1737, following an original source word for word; from the adverb. Compare LITERATIM, SERIATIM.

verbiage *n.* use of too many words. Before 1721, borrowed from French *verbiage* wordiness, from *verbier* to chatter, from Old French *verbe* word, learned borrowing from Latin *verbum* WORD; for suffix see -AGE.

verbose *adj.* wordy. Before 1400 (implied in *verbously*); borrowed from Latin *verbōsus* full of words, wordy, from *verbum* WORD; for suffix see -OSE[1]. **—verbosity** *n.* wordiness. 1542, in Udall's translation of Erasmus' *Apothegms;* borrowed from Middle French *verbosité,* or directly from Late Latin *verbōsitātem* (nominative *verbōsitās*) wordiness, from Latin *verbōsus* wordy, verbose; for suffix see -ITY.

verboten (vėrbō′tən, *sometimes* fėrbō′tən) *adj.* forbidden. 1912, borrowing of German *verboten* forbidden, from past participle of *verbieten* to forbid, from Old High German *farbiotan, firbiotan* (*far-* away, completely + *biotan* to offer; see BID).

verdant *adj.* green. 1581, green in color; borrowed from Middle French *virdeant, verdoyant* becoming green, present participle of Old French *verdeiier, verdoyer* become green, from Vulgar Latin **viridiāre* grow green, make green, from Latin *viridis* green, related to *virēre* be green, of uncertain origin; for suffix see -ANT. The meaning of green with vegetation is first recorded in Spenser's *Faerie Queene* (1596). **—verdancy** *n.* greenness. 1631, formed from English *verdant* + *-ancy.*

verdict *n.* decision of a jury. 1533, alteration of Middle English *verdit* (about 1300); borrowed from Anglo-French *verdit* (from Old French *ver* true + *dit,* past participle of *dire* to speak, from Latin *dicere;* see DICTION). The alteration of Middle English *verdit* to modern English *verdict* was influenced by Medieval Latin *veredictum, verdictum* a verdict; literally, a true saying or report, from Anglo-French.

verdigris (vėr′dəgrēs) *n.* green or bluish coating that forms on brass, copper, or bronze. 1336-37 *verdegrez,* alteration of earlier *vertegrez* (1300-01); borrowed from Old French *verte grez, verte de Grece;* literally, green of Greece. The spelling *verdigris* is first recorded in English in 1789, preceded by a variety of forms such as *verdegrease* (1626, Bacon), *verdegris* (1601, Holland), and *vert-greece, verd-grease* (1656, Blount); some of these forms have been influenced by various forms outside of English such as French *gris* gray, and Old French *Gris* Greeks, and in English with *-gris* as an element in *ambergris;* and with English *grease.*

verdure (vėr′jər) *n.* fresh greenness. Probably about 1390, in *Sir Gawain and the Green Knight;* borrowed from Old French *verdure* greenness, from *verd,* variant of *vert* green; see VERDANT; for suffix see -URE.

verge[1] *n.* edge, rim, brink. 1459, border or margin of some object; borrowed from Middle French *verge* rod or wand of office, scope or territory dominated, from Latin *virga* shoot, rod, stick, of uncertain origin. The meaning of outermost edge (of an extensive area) is first found in Shakespeare's *Richard II* (1593), and that of the point at which something begins or happens, brink (as in *be on the verge of*) in 1602. **—v.** 1605, provide with a border; from the noun. The meaning of be adjacent to, lie on the border of, is first recorded in 1787.

verge[2] *v.* tend, incline. 1610, borrowed from Latin *vergere* to bend, turn, incline; see WRENCH.

verify *v.* Before 1325 *verifien* (implied in *verifying*) prove to be true, confirm; borrowed from Old French *verifier,* learned borrowing from Medieval Latin *verificare* make true, from a lost adjective **vērificus* (Latin *vērus* true; see VERY + the root of *facere* to make, perform, DO[1]); for suffix see -FY. **—verifiable** *adj.* 1593, formed from English *verify* + *-able.* **—verification** *n.* 1523, act of verifying; borrowed from Middle French *verification,* from Medieval Latin *verificationem* (nominative *verificatio*) a verifying, from *verificare* verify; for suffix see -TION.

verily *adv.* really, truly, indeed. Before 1325 *verraily,* in *Cursor Mundi;* formed from Middle English *verray* true, real; see VERY + *-ly*[1].

verisimilitude (ver′əsəmil′ətüd) *n.* appearance of truth, probability. 1603, in Holland's translation of Plutarch's *Moralia;* borrowed from obsolete French *vérisimilitude,* and probably directly from Latin *vērisimilitūdo* likeness to truth, from *vērisimilis* like truth (*vērī,* genitive of *vērum,* neuter of *vērus* true; see VERY + *similis* like, similar; see SAME).

veritable *adj.* true, real, actual. Probably before 1425, borrowed from AngloFrench and Old French *veritable* true, from *verité* VERITY; for suffix see -ABLE. Judging by the citations given in the OED, this word and its derived and most of its related words became obsolete by the middle of the 1600's. Some were revived (or, as in the case of *verism, verist, veritism* and *veritist,* introduced) in the 1800's; revival of *veritable* was probably a borrowing of modern French *véritable.* Webster's *Dictionary* (1828-32) notes it as *little used.*

verity *n.* truth. About 1375, borrowed from Anglo-French and Old French *verité,* learned borrowing from Latin *vēritātem* (nominative *vēritās*) truth, truthfulness, from *vērus* true; see VERY; for suffix see -ITY.

vermeil (vėr′məl) *adj.* bright-red. Probably before 1400 *vermayle,* in Chaucer's translation of *Roman de la Rose;* borrowed from Anglo-French and Old French *vermeil* bright-red; see VERMILION. **—n.** vermilion. 1596, in Spenser's *Faerie Queene;* from the adjective. The meaning of bronze, copper, or silver coated with gilt, is first recorded in 1858.

vermiform *adj.* shaped like a worm. 1730, in Bailey's *Dictionarium Britannicum;* borrowed from New Latin *vermiformis* (Latin *vermis* WORM + *fōrma* FORM). The word is now usually found in the compound *vermiform appendix* (1778).

vermilion (vərmil′yən) *n.* a bright red. 1296 *vermelyon;* borrowed from Old French *vermeillon,* from *vermeil* bright-red, from Late Latin *vermiculus* a little worm; also, in reference to the cochineal insect from which the color crimson was obtained, from Latin, larva of an insect, grub, maggot, diminutive of *vermis* WORM. Compare CRIMSON. **—adj.** bright-red. 1589, from the noun.

vermin *n.pl. or sing.* Probably before 1300, noxious animals, in *Kyng Alisaunder;* borrowed from Anglo-French and Old French *vermin,* from Vulgar Latin **verminum* vermin, possibly including bothersome insects, from Latin *vermis* WORM. The extended sense of creeping insects and other minute animals is found in Middle English about 1340. The figurative sense of low, obnoxious people is first recorded in 1562. **—verminous** *adj.* About 1616, like vermin, vile; borrowed from French *vermineux,* and directly from Latin *verminōsus* full of worms, from **vermina* maggots, related to *vermis* worm; for suffix see -OUS. The meaning of infested with or full of vermin is first recorded in English in 1632.

vermouth (vərmüth′) *n.* white wine flavored with wormwood or other herbs. 1806, borrowed from French *vermouth, vermout,* from earlier German *Wermuth* (now *Wermut*) wormwood, from Middle High German *wermuot, wermuote,* from Old High German *wermuota* WORMWOOD. The English pronunciation with (th) at the end was influenced by the spelling; in French and German, the *th* is pronounced as (t), since the sound (th) is foreign to these languages.

vernacular (vərnak′yələr) *adj.* of or in the native language. 1601, formed in English from Latin *vernāculus* domestic, native (from *verna* home-born slave, native, perhaps from Etruscan) + English *-ar.* The Latin adjective occurs in a wide variety of applications, but the adjective in English is restricted to the use represented in Latin by *vernācula vocābula,* in reference to language. —**n.** native language. Before 1706, in Evelyn's *History of Religion;* from the adjective.

vernal *adj.* of spring. 1534, in writings of Sir Thomas More; borrowed from Latin *vērnālis* of the spring, from *vērnus* of spring, from *vēr* spring; for suffix see -AL[1]. Latin *vēr* (adj. *vērnus*) is cognate with Greek *éar* (adj. *earinós*) and is an alteration of earlier **wesr* (influenced by **yer* year) as Greek *éar* is an alteration of earlier **wésr̥*. Other cognates are found in Old Icelandic *vār* spring, and Sanskrit *vasantá-s,* from Indo-European **wésr̥* (genitive **wesnés*) (Pok.1174). The figurative sense of youthful, having the mildness or freshness of spring, is first recorded in the poetry of Coleridge.

versatile (vėr′sətəl) *adj.* able to do many things well. 1605, characterized by changeability, changeable, variable, in Sir Francis Bacon's *Of the Advancement of Learning;* borrowed from French *versatile,* and directly from Latin *versātilis* turning, revolving, movable, capable of turning to varied subjects or tasks, from *versāt-,* past participle stem of *versāre* keep turning, be engaged in something, turn over in the mind, frequentative form of *vertere* to turn; see VERTEX.

The meaning of able to turn from one subject or occupation to another, many-sided, is first recorded in English in 1656.

—versatility *n.* 1755, quality of being versatile, in Johnson's *Dictionary;* probably formed from English *versatile* + *-ity,* and perhaps borrowed from French *versatilité,* from *versatile* versatile.

verse *n.* Probably before 1200 *vers* line or section of a psalm or canticle, in *Ancrene Riwle;* later, line of poetry (about 1369, in Chaucer's *Dethe of Blaunche*); borrowed from Anglo-French and Old French *vers,* from Latin *versus* (genitive *versūs*) verse, line of writing, (apparently so named in allusion to plowing or turning to make another line, as the plowman turns to make another row or furrow), from *vertere* to turn; see VERTEX. The sense of a stanza is first recorded in Middle English about 1308, and the phrase *in verse,* meaning in metrical form, about 1315. Middle English *vers* replaced the Old English *fers* (first recorded about 737), itself an early borrowing (along with Old Frisian *fers,* Middle Dutch and Middle Low German *vers,* Old High German *vers, fers,* and Old Icelandic *vers*) from Latin *versus* line of writing.

versed *adj.* experienced, practiced, conversant. Before 1610, from the past participle of earlier (now obsolete) English *verse* to turn over (a book, subject, etc.) in study or investigation (1606); borrowed from Middle French *verser* to turn or revolve, as in meditation, from Latin *versāre* and *versārī* keep turning, be engaged in something, turn over in the mind; see VERSATILE; for suffix see -ED[2]. The meaning of *versed* was probably influenced by Middle French *versé* experienced, skilled, and possibly by Italian *versato* and Spanish *versado* experienced, skilled, all from Latin *versātus,* past participle of *versārī.*

versicle *n.* short verse. Before 1380, borrowed from Latin *versiculus,* diminutive of *versus* VERSE.

versify *v.* make or compose verses. Probably before 1387, in a version of *Piers Plowman;* borrowed from Old French *versifier* turn into verse, learned borrowing from Latin, and borrowed into English directly from Latin *versificāre* compare verse, from a lost adjective **versificus* (*versus* VERSE + the root of *facere* to make, perform, see DO[1]); for suffix see -FY. **—versification** *n.* 1603, in Holland's translation of Plutarch's *Moralia;* borrowed from Middle French *versification,* and directly from Latin *versificātiōnem* (nominative *versificātiō*), from *versificāre* to versify; for suffix see -ATION.

version *n.* 1582, a translation of some text or work; borrowed from Middle French *version,* from Medieval Latin *versionem* (nominative *versio*) a turning, from Latin *vers-,* past participle stem of *vertere* to turn; see VERTEX; for suffix see -ION. The meaning of the particular form of a statement, account, or description given by one person or source (as in *her version of the story*) is first recorded in English in 1788. The word is also recorded in Middle English in the specialized sense of an overturning, overthrow, destruction (before 1420, in Lydgate's *Troy Book*).

versus *prep.* against (used especially in law to denote an action by one party against another). 1447-48, borrowed from Latin *versus* turned toward or against, from past participle of *vertere* to turn; see VERTEX.

vertebra (vėr′təbrə) *n.* one of the bones of the backbone or spinal column. Probably before 1425, in a translation of Chauliac's *Grande Chirurgie;* borrowed from Latin *vertebra* joint or articulation of the body, joint of the spine, from *vertere* to turn; see VERTEX. **—vertebral** *adj.* of the backbone. 1681, borrowed from New Latin *vertebralis* of the spine or backbone, from Latin *vertebra* vertebra; for suffix see -AL[1]. **—vertebrate** *adj.* having a backbone. 1826, borrowed from Latin *vertebrātus* jointed, articulated, from *vertebra* vertebra; for suffix see -ATE[1]. —*n.* vertebrate animal. 1826, from the same source as the adjective.

vertex *n.* highest point, top. 1570, the point opposite to the base in geometry; borrowed from Latin *vertex* highest point; originally, a whirling column, whirlpool, whirl, from *vertere* to turn. Latin *vertere* is cognate with Lithuanian *veřsti* to turn, Sanskrit *vártate* it is turned, happens, and Tocharian A *wärt-* become, Tocharian B *wrattsai* against. Cognates in Germanic are found in Old English *weorthan* become, Old Frisian *wertha,* Old Saxon *werthan,* Middle Dutch and modern Dutch *worden,* Old High German *werdan* (modern German *werden*), Old Icelandic *verdha,* and Gothic *wairthan* become, from Proto-Germanic **werthanan,* Indo-European **wert-* turn (Pok.1156).

The meaning of the crown or top of the head is first recorded in English in 1638, followed by the sense of the highest point of anything, in 1641. Both meanings occur in Latin.

vertical *adj.* 1559, of or at the vertex, directly overhead; borrowed from Middle French *vertical,* and directly from Late Latin *verticālis* overhead, from Latin *vertex* (genitive *verticis*) highest point, VERTEX; for suffix see -AL[1]. The meaning of straight up and down, perpendicular, is first recorded in English in 1704.

vertiginous (vėrtij′ənəs) *adj.* whirling. 1608, of the nature of or characterized by vertigo or dizziness; borrowed from French *vertigineux,* and directly from Latin *vertīginōsus* suffering from dizziness, from *vertīgō* (genitive *vertīginis*) VERTIGO; for suffix see -OUS. The meaning of whirling, revolving, rotary, is first recorded in English in 1663.

vertigo (vėr′təgō) *n.* dizziness, giddiness. Probably before 1425, in a translation of Chauliac's *Grande Chirurgie;* borrowed from Latin *vertīgō* dizziness; originally, a whirling or spinning movement, from *vertere* to turn; see VERTEX.

verve *n.* vigorous spirit, enthusiasm. 1697, special bent or talent in writing, in Dryden's translation of Vergil's *Aeneid;* borrowed from French *verve* enthusiasm, especially in what pertains to the arts, in Old French, fancy, caprice, and odd humor, proverb, probably from Gallo-Romance **verva,* from Latin *verba* whimsical words, plural of *verbum* WORD. The meaning of mental or intellectual vigor, liveliness of ideas or expression, is first recorded in English in 1803, and the generalized meaning of energy, vigor, spirit, enthusiasm, in 1863.

very *adj.* About 1275 *verray* true, real, genuine; later, in the sense of actual, sheer, as in *the very air, the veriest truth* (about 1390, in Chaucer's *Canterbury Tales*); borrowed from Anglo-French *verrai,* Old French *verai* true, from Vulgar Latin **vērācus,* from Latin *vērāx* (genitive *vērācis*) truthful, from *vērus* true. Latin *vērus* is cognate with Old Irish *fīr* true, Welsh *gwir,* from Indo-European **wēros* trustworthy, true (Pok.1165). Cognates in Germanic are found in Old High German *wār* true (modern German *wahr*), Middle Dutch *waer* (modern Dutch *waar*), Old Saxon *wār,* Old Frisian *wēr,* and Old English *wǣr* true, which (if this is the meaning) did not survive into Middle English. **—adv.** Before 1325 *verray* truly, really, genuinely; from the adjective. The meaning of greatly, extremely, is first recorded in Middle English in 1448. The use of *very* as an intensive form emphasizing the quality or the identity of something is attributable to both the adjective (as in *to fly like the very wind, passing under our very eyes*) and the adverb (as in *the very best of us, the very opposite word*), and has been known since Middle English, naturally extending the sense of true and truly.

vesicle *n.* small bladder, cavity, sac, or cyst. Probably before 1425, in a translation of Chauliac's *Grande Chirurgie;* borrowed from Middle French *vesicule,* from Latin *vēsīcula* a small bladder or blister, diminutive of *vēsīca, vēssīca* bladder, blister, perhaps cognate with Sanskrit *vasti-s* bladder, from Indo-European **wes-/wēs-*. **—vesicular** *adj.* 1715, borrowed from New Latin *vesicularis* bladderlike, from Latin *vēsīcula* vesicle; for suffix see -AR.

vesper *n.* evening. Before 1393, the evening star, in Gower's *Confessio Amantis;* borrowed from Old French *vespre,* and directly from Latin *vesper* (masculine), *vespera* (feminine) evening star, evening, west, cognate with Greek *hésperos, hespérā* evening, from Indo-European **wesperos* (Pok.1173). The meaning of evening is first found in English in Shakespeare's *Antony and Cleopatra* (1606). **—adj.** of evening. 1791, in Erasmus Darwin's *Botanic Garden;* from the noun. **—vespers** *n.pl.* church service held in late afternoon or early evening. 1611, borrowed from Middle French *vespres,* from Old French, from Medieval Latin *vesperae,* from plural of Latin *vespera* evening. An earlier sense of public disputations and ceremonies preceding a university commencement is recorded in English in 1574.

vessel *n.* About 1303 *vessel* container, in Mannyng's *Handlyng Synne;* borrowed from Old French *vessel* (masculine), from Latin *vāscellum* small vase or urn; also, a ship, diminutive of *vāsculum,* itself a diminutive of *vās* vessel (see VASE); also borrowed from Old French *vesselle* (feminine), from Latin *vāscella,* neuter plural (taken as feminine singular) of *vāscellum.* The sense of a ship or boat is found in Middle English, in *Cursor Mundi* (before 1325).

vest *v.* About 1425 *westen,* to put in the possession of a person (as in *authority is vested in the trustees*); later *vesten* (1464); borrowed from Middle French *vestir,* from Medieval Latin *vestire* to put into possession, to invest, from Latin *vestīre* to clothe, from *vestis* garment, clothing; see WEAR. The meaning of invest (a person) with some quality (as in *to be vested with the office of chancellor*) is first recorded in 1674. The meaning of dress in vestments is first recorded in English in 1513. **—n.** short sleeveless garment. 1613, loose outer garment, robe, gown; borrowed from French *veste,* from Italian *vesta, veste* robe, gown, from Latin *vestis* garment, clothing, attire. The meaning of a sleeveless garment worn by men under a coat is first recorded in English in Pepys' *Diary* (1666, in which he attributes introduction of its use to Charles II of England, "to teach the nobility thrift"). **—vested** *adj.* 1671, clothed or dressed; later, established or settled in the hands of a person (1766); from *vest,* v. + *-ed*[2]. **—vested interest** (1818) **—vested right** (before 1797)

vestibule *n.* 1623 *vestible* a porch, in Cockeram's *Dictionary;* later, an antechamber, entrance hall, or lobby (1730, in Bailey's *Dictionarium Britannicum*); borrowed from earlier French *vestible* (now *vestibule*), from Latin *vestibulum* forecourt, entrance court, entrance, of uncertain origin. The spelling *vestibule* is first recorded in English before 1751, borrowed directly from Latin *vestibulum.*

vestige *n.* surviving trace or visible sign of something. 1602, borrowed from French *vestige* a mark, trace, sign, from Latin *vestīgium* footprint, trace, mark, of uncertain origin. English *vestige* replaced earlier *vestigy,* borrowed from Middle French *vestigie,* also borrowed from Latin *vestīgium.* **—vestigial** *adj.* 1877, of the nature of a vestige, no longer fully developed or useful; formed in English from Latin *vestīgium* vestige + English *-al*[1].

vestment *n.* garment worn by a clergyman or official on solemn occasions. Probably before 1300 *vestement,* in *Kyng Alisaunder;* borrowed from Old French *vestment,* alteration of Latin *vestīmentum* clothing, clothes, from Latin *vestīre* to clothe; see VEST.

vestry *n.* room or part of a church where vestments are kept. 1388 *westre;* later *vestrye* (1440); probably borrowed from Anglo-French **vesterie,* alteration of Old French *vestiaire, vestiarie* room for vestments, from Latin *vestiārium* wardrobe, noun use of neuter of *vestiārius* of clothes, from *vestis* garment; see WEAR.

vesture *n.* clothing, garments. About 1380, in *Pearl;* borrowed from Anglo-French and Old French *vesture,* from Vulgar Latin **vestītūra* vestments, clothing, from *vestīre* to clothe; see VEST; for suffix see -URE.

vet[1] *n. Informal.* veterinarian. 1862, shortened form of VETERINARIAN. **—v.** 1891, to submit to veterinary care; from the noun. The figurative sense of subject to careful examination, scrutinize, evaluate, is first recorded in Kipling's *Traffics and Discoveries* (1904).

vet[2] *n. Informal.* veteran. 1848, American English, shortened form of VETERAN.

vetch *n.* vine or plant of the pea family. About 1384 *vetche,* in the Wycliffe Bible; borrowed from Old North French *veche,* from Latin *vicia,* of uncertain origin. The spelling with *t* is a convention of spelling reflecting other spellings of the same pattern in English (*fetch, tetch, ketch, retch*), with *vetch* appearing generally in the 1500's.

veteran *n.* 1509, old, experienced soldier; borrowed from Latin *veterānus,* from *vetus* (genitive *veteris*) old, cognate with Greek *étos* year; see WETHER. The meaning of any former member of the armed forces, ex-serviceman (not necessarily old) is first recorded in 1798, in American English, but is alluded to earlier in reference to the same condition in the Roman army (1779, in British English). The extended sense of a person who has had long service in any office or position is first recorded in English in 1597. **—adj.** 1611, having had much experience in war; from the noun. The extended sense of grown old in service, experienced by long practice, is first recorded in 1728.

veterinary *adj.* having to do with the medical treatment of animals. 1791, borrowed (perhaps by influence of French *vétérinaire,* adj.) from Latin *veterīnārius* of or having to do with beasts of burden; also, cattle doctor, from *veterīnum* beast of burden, *veterīnus* belonging to beasts of burden, perhaps derived from *vetus* (genitive *veteris*) old; probably a beast at least one year old; possibly also, experienced, or used to work as a draft animal in plowing or pulling; see VETERAN; for suffix see -ARY. **—n.** veterinarian. 1861, from the adjective. **—veterinarian** *n.* doctor who treats animals. 1646, formed in English (perhaps by influence of French *vétérinaire,* n.) from Latin *veterīnārius,* adj. + English *-an.*

veto *n.* 1629, a person's power or right to forbid something, rejection, prohibition; borrowed from Latin *vetō* I forbid, first person singular present indicative of *vetāre* to forbid, of uncertain origin. Latin *vetō* was the word used by Roman tribunes of the people when they opposed measures of the Senate or actions of the magistrates. The political sense of the act or power of preventing legislative or other political action by the use of a prohibitory right is first recorded in English in 1792. **—v.** reject by veto. 1706, from the noun, though this sense in politics is recorded 86 years later in the noun, which is probably a defect in the record of English.

vex *v.* About 1415 *vexen* annoy, provoke; borrowed from Middle French *vexer,* learned borrowing from Latin, and probably borrowed directly into English from Latin *vexāre* to attack, harass, trouble, of uncertain origin. **—vexation** *n.* annoyance. About 1400 *vexacioun,* borrowed through Old French *vexation,* and directly from Latin *vexātiōnem* (nominative *vexātiō*) agitation, annoyance, from *vexāre* vex; for suffix see -ATION. **—vexatious** *adj.* vexing, annoying. 1534, formed from English *vexation* + *-ous.*

via (vī'ə) *prep.* by way of. 1779, borrowing of Latin *viā,* ablative form of *via* way, road, channel, course, cognate with Oscan *víú* way, road, Umbrian (ablative) *vea, via,* and probably with Sanskrit *véti* pursues, *váyas* vitality, strength; see VIM.

viable (vī'əbəl) *adj.* 1828-32, capable of living (applied to a newborn infant), in Webster's *Dictionary;* borrowed from French *viable* capable of life, from *vie* life, from Latin *vīta* life; see VITAL; for suffix see -ABLE. The figurative sense of surviving or existing independently is first recorded in English in 1848. The extended sense of workable, practicable, is first recorded in 1955. **—viability** *n.* 1843, probably formed from English *viable* + *-ity,* on the model of French *viabilité.*

viaduct (vī'ədukt) *n.* bridge for carrying a road or railroad over a valley, etc. 1816, formed in English from Latin *via* road + English *-duct,* as in *aqueduct.*

vial (vī'əl) *n.* small glass bottle. About 1384 *viole,* variant of *fyole* PHIAL.

viand (vī'ənd) *n.* article of food. Before 1399 *viaunde;* borrowed from Anglo-French *viaunde, viande,* Old French *viande* food, from Vulgar Latin **vīvanda,* alteration of Late Latin *vīvenda* things for living, in Latin with the sense of be lived, neuter plural gerundive of *vīvere* to live; see QUICK.

vibrant *adj.* About 1550, agitated; later, vibrating (1616); borrowed from Latin *vibrantem* (nominative *vibrāns*) swaying, present participle of *vibrāre* move to and fro; see WIPE; for suffix see -ANT. The figurative sense of vigorous, full of life, is first recorded in English in 1860.

vibrate *v.* 1616, move to and fro in a fight; later, swing to and fro, oscillate (1667); borrowed from Latin *vibrātus,* past participle of *vibrāre* move to and fro, set in tremulous motion, shake; see WIPE; for suffix see -ATE[1]. **—vibration** *n.* 1656, in Hobbes' translation of *Elements of Philosophy;* borrowed from French *vibration,* and directly from Latin *vibrātiōnem* (nominative *vibrātiō*) a shaking, from *vibrāre* to vibrate; for suffix see -ATION. **—vibratory** *adj.* 1728, formed from English *vibrate* + *-ory.*

vicar (vik'ər) *n.* Before 1325 *wicare;* later *vicar* an earthly representative of God or Christ (specifically applied to the Pope, 1340); borrowed from Anglo-French *vikere, vicare,* Old French *vicaire,* learned borrowing from Latin *vicārius* a substitute, delegate, deputy; noun use of past participle; see VICARIOUS. The sense of a person acting as priest in place of a parson or rector is first recorded in Middle English about 1325. **—vicarage** *n.* residence or position of a vicar. 1425, in *Rolls of Parliament;* formed from Middle English *vicar* + *-age.*

vicarious (vikãr'ēəs) *adj.* done in place of others. 1637, taking the place of another, substitute; borrowed from Latin *vicārius* substitute, deputy, from *vic-,* found only in oblique cases (genitive *vicis,* etc.) and plural *vicēs,* with the meaning of turn, change, exchange, substitution; for suffix see -OUS. The Latin forms are perhaps cognate with Old High German *wehsal* change, exchange (modern German *Wechsel*), Old Saxon *wehsal,* Old Frisian *wixle,* Old Icelandic *vīxl,* from Indo-European **weik-/wik-* bend; change off (Pok.1130).

The meaning of done, attained, or suffered for or in place of others is first recorded in English in 1692, but the specific sense of at second hand (as in *the vicarious pleasure of another's success*) is not found before 1925 (implied in *vicariously,* in F. Scott Fitzgerald's *The Great Gatsby*).

vice[1] (vīs) *n.* evil habit or tendency. About 1300, evil or wickedness; borrowed from Old French *vice,* learned borrowing from Latin *vitium* defect, fault, vice (in Medieval Latin *vicium*); of uncertain origin. The sense of an evil habit or tendency is first recorded in Middle English about 1325, and the weakened sense of a fault or bad habit in 1338.

vice[2] (vī'sē) *prep.* instead of, in the place of. 1770, borrowed from Latin *vice,* ablative form of *vicis* (genitive) a change, turn, place, substitution; see VICARIOUS. Compare VICE VERSA.

vice[3] (vīs) *n.* = vise (a device for holding things).

vice- a prefix meaning a deputy, assistant, substitute, rank next to the highest, as in *vice-chairman = person who acts in the place of a chairman* (1858), *vice-consul = a subordinate consul* (1559, Roman proconsul; 1601, assistant consul). Middle English *vice-,* borrowed through Old French *vice-,* and directly from Late Latin *vice-,* from Latin *vice* instead of, ablative form of *vicis* (genitive) a turn, change, substitution; see VICARIOUS; also compare VISCOUNT.

vice-president *n.* 1574 *vice-president* one who acts as representative or deputy for a president; later *Vice-President* official next in rank to the President of the U.S., in the *Constitution* of the U.S. (1787).

viceroy *n.* person ruling a country or province as deputy of the sovereign. 1524 *vice-roy,* borrowing of Middle French *vice-roy* (Old French *vice-* deputy + *roi* king, from Latin *rēgem,* accusative of *rēx* king; see REGAL).

vice versa the.other way round, conversely. 1601, borrowing of Latin *vice versā* (*vice,* ablative form of genitive *vicis* a turn, change; see VICARIOUS; and *versā,* feminine ablative singular of *versus,* past participle of *vertere* to turn, turn about; see VERTEX).

vicinity *n.* neighborhood, surrounding district. 1560, nearness in place, being close; borrowed from Middle French *vicinité,* and directly from Latin *vīcīnitās* of or pertaining to neighbors or a surrounding area, from *vīcīnus* neighbor, neighboring, from *vīcus* group of houses, village, habitation; for suffix see -ITY. Latin *vīcus* is cognate with Greek *oîkos* house, Old Slavic *vĭsĭ* village, Sanskrit *viś-* house, dwelling, settlement (plural *viśa-s* people, subjects), and Gothic *weihs* house, from Indo-European **weik-/woik-/wik-* dwell; house (Pok. 1131). The meaning of neighborhood, surrounding district, is first recorded in English in 1796.

vicious *adj.* About 1340 *vecious* of the nature of vice, wicked, immoral; later *vicious* (about 1374); borrowed from Anglo-French *vicious,* Old French *vicieus,* learned borrowing from Latin *vitiōsus* faulty, defective, corrupt (in Medieval Latin *viciosus*), from *vitium* fault; see VICE[1]; for suffix see -OUS. The meaning of inclined to be savage or dangerous, evil-tempered, is first recorded in English in 1711. The transferred sense of full of malice or spite, malignantly bitter or severe, is first found in 1825, and the figurative sense of severe, unpleasant, in 1882. **—vicious circle** About 1792, circular argument (translation of New Latin *circulus vitiosus*); later, worsening cycle of events (1839).

vicissitude (vəsis′ətüd) *n.* change in circumstances, fortune, etc. 1570-76, borrowing of Middle French *vicissitude,* from Latin *vicissitūdinem* (nominative *vicissitūdō*) change, from *vicissim* changeably, in turn, from *vicis* (genitive) a turn, change; see VICARIOUS; for suffix see -TUDE.

victim *n.* 1497, living creature killed and offered as a sacrifice to a god; borrowed from Middle French *victime,* and directly from Latin *victima* animal offered as a sacrifice, any sacrifice; of uncertain origin (perhaps formed from **vict-* something consecrated, from root **wīk-* sacred). If the hypothetical reconstruction is accurate, then Latin *victima* is possibly cognate with Gothic *weihs* holy (see WITCH) and Sanskrit *vikta-s* separated, consecrated, from Indo-European **weik-/wik-* set apart (Pok.1128).

The extended sense of a person who is hurt, tortured, or killed by another is first recorded in English in 1660. The much weakened sense of a person badly treated or taken advantage of (as in *the victim of a swindle*), is first recorded in Gibbon's *Decline and Fall of the Roman Empire* (1781).

—victimize *v.* 1830, make a victim of, cause to suffer, formed from English *victim* + *-ize.*

victor *n.* winner, conqueror. About 1340, borrowed from Anglo-French *victor, victour* (Old French *victeur*), and directly from Latin *victōrem* (nominative *victor*) a conqueror, from past participle stem of *vincere* to conquer; for suffix see -OR[2]. Latin *vincere* is cognate with Old Irish *fichid* he fights, Lithuanian *apveĩkti* to subdue, and in Germanic with Old English and Old High German *wīgan* to fight, Old Icelandic *vega* to fight, kill, and Gothic *weihan* to fight, from Indo-European **weik-/wik-* strive against a foe (Pok.1128). **—victorious** *adj.* triumphant. About 1390, borrowed from Anglo-French *victorious* (Old French *victorieux*), and directly from Latin *victōriōsus* having many victories, from *victōria* victory, from *victor* victor; for suffix see -OUS. **—victory** *n.* triumph. About 1340, borrowed from Anglo-French and Old French *victorie,* and directly from Latin *victōria* victory, from *victor* a conqueror, victor; for suffix see -Y[3].

victual (vit′əl, after the original form in Middle English) *n.* Usually, **victuals,** *pl.* food. 1523, spelling alteration (with c, imitating Latin *vīctuālia* food) of Middle English *vitaylle* (about 1303, in Mannyng's *Handlyng Synne*); borrowed from Anglo-French and Old French *vitaille,* from Late Latin *vīctuālia* provisions, nourishment, food, neuter plural of *vīctuālis* of food, from Latin *vīctus* (genitive *vīctūs*) food, sustenance, from *vīvere* to live; see QUICK; for suffix see -AL[2].

vicuña or **vicuna** (vikün′yə) *n.* South American animal somewhat like a camel. 1604, borrowing of Spanish *vicuña,* from Quechua (Peru) *wikúña.*

videlicet (vədel′əset) *adv.* that is to say, to wit, namely (usually *viz.*). Before 1456, borrowing of Latin *vidēlicet,* contraction of *vidēre licet* it is permissible to see (*vidēre* to see, and *licet* it is allowed, third person singular present indicative of *licēre* be allowed; see LICENSE). See also VIZ.

video *adj.* of or used in the transmission or reception of television images. 1935, borrowed from Latin *videō* I see, first person singular present indicative of *vidēre* to see; see WIT[2] know; probably influenced in its adoption into English by the pronunciation of the final syllable of *radio.* **—n.** television. 1935, either from the adjective in English or borrowed from Latin *videō.* **—videocassette** *n.* (1971) **—videocassette recorder** (1971, now usually *VCR* 1971) **—videotape** *n.* magnetized tape for recording and reproducing television pictures and sound. 1953, formed from English *video* + *tape,* n. **—*v.*** to record on videotape. 1959, from the noun.

vie (vī) *v.* contend in rivalry, compete. 1565, to hazard or bet, make a bid; later, contend, compete (1602); shortened form of Middle English *envien* contend, strive (about 1385), borrowed from Old French *envier* increase the stake, challenge, invite, from Latin *invītāre* INVITE.

view *n.* 1415-16 *vewe* formal inspection or survey (of land); later *vew* observation, notice (about 1450), and in the spelling *view* (1454); borrowed from Anglo-French *vewe* view, variant of Old French *veüe,* noun use of feminine past participle of Old French *veoir* to see, from Latin *vidēre;* see WIT[2] know. Both the meaning of an act of seeing and the figurative sense of a manner of regarding something, opinion, are first recorded in English in 1573. **—v.** 1525, to inspect, examine carefully; from the noun. The meaning of scrutinize, observe closely, is first recorded in 1548, and that of consider, regard, in 1591. **—viewer** *n.* 1415, an inspector, later, a device for viewing photographic film (1936), one who looks at television (1935). **—viewpoint** *n.* (1856)

vigil *n.* a watching, watch. Probably before 1200 *vigile* the eve of a religious festival as an occasion for devotional watching or observance, in *Ancrene Riwle;* later, the watch kept on the eve of a festival, nocturnal service (about 1395); borrowed from Anglo-French and Old French *vigile,* learned borrowing from Latin *vigilia* watch, watchfulness, wakefulness, from *vigil* watchful, awake, related to *vigēre* be lively, thrive, and *vegēre* to enliven; see WAKE[1], v.

The general sense of a staying awake for some purpose, a watch, is first recorded in English about 1695, though the sense of one of the four night watches which Roman soldiers maintained was known as early as about 1380, in Wycliffe's writings.

—vigilance *n.* watchfulness. 1570, borrowed from Middle French *vigilance,* and possibly directly from Latin *vigilantia* watchfulness, from *vigilantem* (nominative *vigilāns*) wakeful, watchful, present participle of *vigilāre* keep watch, from *vigil* watchful; for suffix see -ANCE. **—vigilant** *adj.* watchful, alert. About 1480, borrowed from Middle French *vigilant,* and possibly directly from Latin *vigilantem* (nominative *vigilāns*) wakeful, watchful, present participle of *vigilāre* keep watch; for suffix see -ANT.

vigilante (vij′əlan′tē) *n.* member of a self-appointed group of citizens organized to keep order and punish criminals. 1856, American English, borrowing of Spanish *vigilante,* literally, watchman, from Latin *vigilantem* (nominative *vigilāns*) wakeful, watchful, present participle of *vigilāre* keep watch, from *vigil* watchful; see VIGIL. **—vigilantism** *n.* the activities or practices of vigilantes. 1937, American English; formed from *vigilante* + *-ism.*

vignette (vinyet′) *n.* 1751, decorative design (often in the form of vine tendrils) on a page of a book, in Walpole's correspondence; borrowing of French *vignette,* from Old French, diminutive of *vigne* vineyard, VINE; for suffix see -ETTE. The form *vignette* replaced the Middle English form *vinette* (before 1420), meaning a trailing ornament in architecture or decorative work, an Anglicized borrowing (with loss of *g*) of Old French *vignette.* The transferred sense of a literary sketch, short verbal description, is first recorded in English in 1880, probably extended from the then very popular use of the word in photography in reference to small portraits made by blurring the edges, as if looking through vines (1853).

vigor *n.* active strength or force. Probably before 1300 *vigour,* in *Kyng Alisaunder* and *Arthour and Merlin;* borrowed from Anglo-French *vigour,* Old French *vigor,* learned borrowings from Latin, and probably borrowed into English directly from Latin *vigōrem* (nominative *vigor*) liveliness, activity, force, from *vigēre* be lively, flourish, thrive; see VIGIL. **—vigorous** *adj.* full of vigor. Probably before 1300 *vigourous,* in *Kyng Alisaunder;* borrowed from Anglo-French and Old French *vigorous,* from *vigor, vigour* vigor; for suffix see -OUS.

Viking or **viking** *n.* 1807 *vikingr* one of the Scandinavian pirates who raided the coasts of Europe from the 700's to the 900's; borrowed from Old Icelandic *víkingr* (possibly with the sense of one who came out of the inlets of the sea, and formed from Old Icelandic *vīk* creek, inlet, bay + *-ingr* -ing). The modern Icelandic form is *vīkingur.* The spelling *viking* is first recorded in English in 1840. The word is not found in Middle English, but came into use in modern historical writings. However, cognates of the Old Icelandic word are found in Old English *wīcing* (occurring in compounds as early as the 700's) and Old Frisian *wīzing, wīsing,* which, according to the OED, is "from a date so early as to make its (*viking*) Scandinavian origin doubtful . . . because evidence for *vīkingr* in . . . Old Icelandic is doubtful before the latter part of the 10th cent." Thus, Old English *wīcing* was probably derived from *wīc* village, camp, from Latin *vīcus;* see VICINITY.

vile *adj.* very bad. Probably before 1300 *vyle, vile* of poor quality, very bad or inferior, in *Kyng Alisaunder* and *Arthour and Merlin;* borrowed from Anglo-French and Old French *vile,* from Latin *vīlis* cheap, worthless, base, common, of uncertain origin. The sense of despicable, disgusting, base, is first recorded in Middle English about 1300.

vilify (vil′əfī) *v.* speak evil of, revile, slander. Before 1500 *vilifien* to lower in worth or value; borrowed from Late Latin *vīlificāre* to make cheap or base, regard as of little value, from a lost adjective **vīlificus* (Latin *vīlis* cheap, base; see VILE + the root of *facere* to make, perform, DO[1]); for suffix see -FY. The meaning of slander, speak evil of, is first recorded in English in 1598. **—vilification** *n.* 1630, act of making vile, degradation, in poetry of Donne; later, act of reviling (1653); borrowed from Medieval Latin *vilificationem* (nominative *vilificatio*) a vilifying, cheapening, from Late Latin *vīlificāre* vilify; for suffix see -ATION.

villa (vil′ə) *n.* house in the country or suburbs. 1611, borrowing of Italian *villa,* from Latin *vīlla* country house, farm (earlier **veixlā*), related to *vīcus* village; see VICINITY.

village *n.* About 1390, in Chaucer's *Canterbury Tales;* borrowing of Old French *village* houses and other buildings in a group, usually smaller than a town, from Latin *vīllāticum* farmstead (with its associated buildings), noun use of neuter singular of *vīllāticus* having to do with a farmstead or villa, from *vīlla* country house, VILLA. **—villager** *n.* 1570, person who lives in a village; formed from English *village* + *-er*[1].

villain *n.* About 1303 *vyleyn* base or low-born rustic, in Mannyng's *Handlyng Synne;* later *vilaine* (about 1330); borrowed from Anglo-French and Old French *villain, vilein,* from Medieval Latin *villanus* farmhand, from Latin *vīlla* country house, VILLA. The extended (and now usual) sense of an unprincipled scoundrel or knave, evil person, is implied in the earliest uses of this word. **—villainous** *adj.* vile, base, evil, offensive. Probably about 1390 *vilanous,* borrowed from Old French *vilenneus,* from *villain, vilein* villain; for suffix see -OUS. **—villainy** *n.* villainous act or behavior. Probably before 1200 *vileinie,* in *Ancrene Riwle;* borrowed from Anglo-French and Old French *villainie, vileinie,* from *villain, vilein* villain; for suffix see -Y[3]. This word probably influenced the borrowing of *villain,* but had little to do with the early formation of *villain.*

–ville a pejorative suffix sporadically in vogue in American slang, since about 1840 (often with *-s-,* as in *dullsville, dragsville,* but also *mediaville*). Adapted from *-ville* in place names, such as *Clarksville, Hicksville;* ultimately a borrowing from Old French *ville* town, from Latin *vīlla* VILLA.

villein (vil′ən) *n.* member of a class of half-free peasants in the Middle Ages. Before 1325 *vileyn,* variant of VILLAIN.

vim *n.* force, energy, vigor. 1843, American English; borrowed from Latin *vim,* accusative of *vīs* strength, force, power, energy. Latin *vīs* is cognate with Greek *ī́s* strength, *híesthai* to move forward, hasten, and Sanskrit *váyas* strength, vitality, from Indo-European **wei-/weyə/wī-* drive at (Pok.1123).

vincible (vin′səbəl) *adj.* conquerable. 1548, in Udall's translation of Erasmus' *Upon the New Testament;* borrowed from Middle French *vincible,* and directly from Latin *vincibilis* that can be easily gained or overcome, from *vincere* to conquer; see VICTOR; for suffix see -IBLE. The word occurs once in Middle English in a translation of Higden's *Polychronicon* (probably before 1425), but it is regarded as an error or misprint for *invincible* (recorded before 1420).

vindicate *v.* clear from suspicion, dishonor, etc. 1533, to exercise in revenge, in a translation of Livy's *Roman History;* borrowed from Latin *vindicātus,* past participle of *vindicāre* to set free, lay claim to, assert, avenge; related to *vindicta* revenge; for suffix see -ATE[1]. It is probable that Latin *vindicāre* was found originally in the phrase *vim dīcāre* to show authority, and *vindicta* was known from the accusative *vim dictam* ownership asserted, both formed from *vim,* accusative of *vīs* force (see VIM) and the root of *dīcere* to say (see DICTION). It is also possible that in some instances *vindicate* is a back formation in English from *vindication.* The sense of clear from suspicion, dishonor, etc., is first recorded in English before 1635. **—vindication** *n.* 1484, act of avenging, in Caxton's translation of *Fables of Aesop;* borrowed from Middle French *vindication,* and directly from Latin *vindicātiōnem* (nominative *vindicātiō*) act of claiming or avenging, from *vindicāre* to set free, lay claim to, assert, avenge; for suffix see -ATION. The meaning of act of clearing from suspicion, dishonor, etc., is first recorded in English in 1647.

vindictive *adj.* wanting revenge, bearing a grudge. 1616, in Bullokar's writings; formed in English from Latin *vindicta* revenge (see VINDICATE) + English *-ive.*

vine *n.* Probably before 1300 *vyne,* in *Kyng Alisaunder;* borrowed from Old French *vigne, vine,* from Latin *vīnea* vine, vineyard, from *vīnum* WINE. **—vineyard** *n.* About 1300 *vynȝord* plantation of vines; formed from Middle English *vyne* vine + *ȝord* enclosure, yard[1]. The figurative sense of a sphere of action or labor, especially of a spiritual character, is first recorded in Middle English about 1375, chiefly in allusion to passages in the New Testament, as Matthew 20:1.

vinegar *n.* Before 1325 *vinegre,* in *Cursor Mundi;* borrowed from Old French *vinaigre, vinagre* (*vin* wine, from Latin *vīnum* WINE + *aigre* sour, sharp; see EAGER). **—vinegary** *adj.* sour like vinegar. 1730, formed from English *vinegar* + *-y*[1]. Largely used in a figurative sense of sour or acid, it is distinct from *vinegarish* (1648), which is more often used in the literal sense of resembling vinegar in taste.

vintage *n.* Probably before 1425, the yield of grapes or wine from a vineyard; borrowed from Anglo-French *vintage,* alteration (influenced by Middle English *viniter* or Anglo-French *vineter* VINTNER) of Old French *vendange* yield from a vineyard, from Latin *vīndēmia* a gathering of grapes, yield of grapes (*vīnum* WINE + *dēmere* take off, from *dē* away + *emere,* originally, to take; see REDEEM). The meaning of age or year of a particular wine is first recorded in English in 1746. The transferred sense of age or year of origin or making is first found in 1929, from the sense of a being of an earlier time (as in *a man of ancient vintage,* 1883).

vintner *n.* dealer in wine. Probably before 1410 *vynteneer,* about 1460 *vyntnere;* alteration of earlier *viniter* (1300), borrowed from Anglo-French *vineter,* Old French *vinetier,* from Medieval Latin *vinetarius* a wine dealer, from Latin *vīnētum* vineyard, from *vīnum* WINE; for suffix see -ER[1].

vinyl (vī′nəl) *n.* 1863, a univalent radical derived from ethylene, in Henry Watts' *Dictionary of Chemistry;* formed in English from Latin *vīnum* WINE + English *-yl.* The connection with Latin *vīnum* wine is through *ethylene,* and *ethyl* ordinary alcohol (1840), of course also present in wine, Latin *vīnum.* The meaning of a plastic or synthetic resin made from a compound containing the vinyl radical is first recorded in 1939.

viol (vī′əl) *n.* stringed musical instrument played with a bow. 1542 *veol;* 1560 *viol,* variant of Middle English *viel* (1483); borrowed from Middle French *viole, vielle,* from Old French, from Old Provençal *viola* VIOLA.

viola (vēō′lə) *n.* musical instrument somewhat larger than a violin. 1797, in letters of Southey; borrowing of Italian *viola,* from Old Provençal *viola,* from Medieval Latin *vitula* stringed instrument; see FIDDLE.

violate *v.* Probably before 1425 *violaten* to break or transgress (an oath, promise, etc.), in a translation of Higden's *Polychronicon;* borrowed from Latin *violātus,* past participle of *violāre* treat with violence, outrage, dishonor, of uncertain origin; perhaps related to Latin *vīs* violence, strength (see VIM); for suffix see -ATE[1]. The sense of ravish or rape is first recorded in Middle English about 1450. The sense of break in upon, disturb, interfere with, is first found in 1667, in Milton's *Paradise Lost.* **—violation** *n.* Before 1400 *violacion;* borrowed from Old French *violacion,* and directly from Latin *violātiōnem* (nominative *violātiō*) an injury, irreverence, from *violāre* to violate; for suffix see -ATION. **—violator** *n.* Probably before 1425, in a translation of Higden's *Polychronicon;* borrowed from Latin *violātor,* from *violāt-,* past participle stem of *violāre* to violate + *-or* -or[2].

violent *adj.* About 1340, very strong or severe, in *The Prick of Conscience;* borrowed from Old French *violent,* from Latin *violentus* vehement, forcible, probably related to *violāre* VIOLATE. The sense of using strong or excessive physical force, especially to harm or frighten, is first recorded in Middle English about 1384. **—violence** *n.* About 1300, borrowed from Anglo-French and Old French *violence,* from Latin *violentia* vehemence, impetuosity, from *violentus* vehement, forcible, violent; for suffix see -ENCE.

violet *n.* Probably before 1300, in *Arthour and Merlin;* borrowed from Old French *violette,* diminutive of *viole* violet, from Latin *viola,* a borrowed word, possibly from the same Mediterranean source as Greek *íon* (earlier **wíon*) violet; for suffix see -ET.

violin *n.* 1579, in Spenser's *The Sheepheardes Calender;* borrowed from Italian *violino,* diminutive of *viola* VIOLA. —**violinist** *n.* About 1670, borrowed from Italian *violinista,* from *violino* violin; for suffix see -IST.

violoncello (vī′ələnchel′ō) *n.* cello. 1724, borrowing of Italian *violoncello,* diminutive of *violone* bass viol, augmentative form of *viola* VIOLA.

VIP (vē′ī′pē′) *n. Informal.* important or influential person. 1933, abbreviation of *v(ery) i(mportant) p(erson).*

viper *n.* thick-bodied poisonous snake. Probably before 1425 *vipere,* in a translation of Chauliac's *Grande Chirurgie;* borrowed from Middle French *vipere,* from Latin *vīpera* viper, snake, serpent, contraction of **vīvipera,* remade in Late Latin *vīviparus* bringing forth alive (Latin *vīvus* alive, living; see QUICK + *parere* bring forth, bear; see PARE); so called from the former belief that the viper does not lay eggs. Compare VIVIPAROUS. The figurative sense of a malignant or spiteful person, a villain or scoundrel, is first recorded in English in 1591, probably originally in allusion to Matthew 3:7 (*O generation of vipers*).

virago (vərā′gō) *n.* violent, bad-tempered, or scolding woman. Before 1387, vigorous, heroic woman, amazon, in Trevisa's translation of Higden's *Polychronicon;* 1390, bad-tempered or scolding woman (about 1390, in Chaucer's *Canterbury Tales*); borrowed from Latin *virāgō* a manlike (or warrior) woman, from *vir* man, male; see VIRILE.

vireo (vir′ēō) *n.* small American songbird. 1834, in Audubon's *Ornithological Biography;* American English, borrowed from Latin *vireō* kind of bird, perhaps the greenfinch, from *virēre* be green, of uncertain origin.

virescent (vīres′ənt) *adj.* turning green. 1826, borrowed from Latin *virēscentem* (nominative *virēscēns*) a greening, growing green, present participle of *virēscere* turn green, from *virēre* be green, of uncertain origin; for suffix see -ESCENT.

virgin *n.* Probably before 1200 *virgine* unmarried or chaste woman, in *Trinity Homilies;* borrowed from Old French *virgine,* learned borrowing from Latin *virginem* (nominative *virgō*) maiden, unwedded girl or woman; also *adj.* unwedded, fresh, unused; probably related to *virga* young shoot, cognate with Lithuanian *vizgěti* to tremble, from Indo-European **weis-g-* bending, pliant (Pok.1133). The word is applied in Latin and in English to both girls or women (in Middle English probably before 1200) and boys or men (about 1330), but slightly earlier in the plural to both sexes (before 1325). —**adj.** Probably before 1300 *virgine,* in *Arthour and Merlin;* from the noun in English and borrowed from adjective use in Latin. The figurative sense of unsullied, pure, is first recorded in English in the 1300's, and the extended sense of new, fresh, unused, is found in Shakespeare's *A Midsummer Night's Dream* (1590). —**virginal** *adj.* About 1412, of or characteristic of a virgin, in Hoccleve's *Regement of Princes;* borrowed from Middle French *virginal,* and directly from Latin *virginālis* maidenly, from *virgō* (genitive *virginis*) virgin; for suffix see -AL[1]. The figurative sense of fresh, pure, untouched is first recorded in English before 1659. —*v.* small harpsichord. 1530, used in the plural to refer to a single instrument, in Palsgrave's *Lesclarcissement;* probably from the adjective, but the association is unknown. The singular is first recorded in 1570.—**virginity** *n.* About 1303 *virginite,* in Mannyng's *Handlyng Synne;* borrowed from Anglo-French and Old French *virginité,* from Latin *virginitātem* (nominative *virginitās*) maidenhood, from *virgō* (genitive *virginis*) virgin; for suffix see -ITY.

Virginia *n.* 1609 *Virginia colony* an English settlement in North America that later became the state of Virginia, its name being an allusion to Queen Elizabeth I of England (known as the Virgin Queen). The name has been widely applied to numerous objects from forms of fencing, to birds, and plants, to political resolutions; the most notable of these are: —**Virginia creeper** 1704, an American wild vine that is a weed. —**Virginia reel** 1817, an American folk dance, in which two lines of partners swing and twirl with one another.

virgule (vėr′gyül) *n.* slanting stroke. 1837, borrowing of French *virgule,* learned borrowing from Latin *virgula* punctuation mark, twig, diminutive of *virga* shoot, rod, stick; see VIRGIN. The form *virgule* replaced *virgula* (borrowing of Latin *virgula*) recorded in 1728.

virile *adj.* manly, masculine. 1490, in Caxton's translation of *The Book of Eneydos;* borrowed from Middle French *viril,* and directly from Latin *virīlis* of a man, manly, from *vir* a man, a hero. Latin *vir* is cognate with Old Irish *fer* man, Welsh *gwr* (plural *gwyr*), Old Prussian *wijrs,* Lithuanian *výras,* Latvian *wîrs,* Sanskrit *vīrá-s* man, hero, and Tocharian A *wir* young. Cognates in Germanic are found in Gothic *waír* man, Old Icelandic *verr,* and Old High German, Old Saxon, Old Frisian, and Old English *wer* man (which survives in WEREWOLF); from Proto-Germanic **wiraz,* Indo-European **wiros/wīros* (Pok.1177). The extended sense of vigorous, forceful, is first recorded in 1572. —**virility** *n.* 1586, period of fully developed manhood; borrowed from Middle French *virilité,* and possibly directly from Latin *virīlitātem* (nominative *virīlitās*) manhood, from *virīlis* manly, virile; for suffix see -ITY. The meaning of manly strength, masculine vigor, is first recorded in English in 1603.

virology *n.* branch of medicine that deals with viruses and virus diseases. 1935, formed from English *vir(us)* + *-ology.*

virtu (vėrtü′) *n.* excellence in an object of art. 1722, in a critique on Italian statuary; borrowed from Italian *virtù* excellence, from Latin *virtūtem* (nominative *virtūs*) VIRTUE.

virtual *adj.* being something in effect, though not so in name. Before 1398 *vertual* capable of exerting influence by means of certain physical virtues or capacities, in Trevisa's translation of Bartholomew's *De Proprietatibus Rerum;* borrowed from Medieval Latin *virtualis,* from Latin *virtūs* excellence, potency, efficacy, VIRTUE; for suffix see -AL[1]. The meaning of being something in essence or effect, though not so formally or in name, is first recorded in English in 1654, in the writings of Jeremy Taylor. The Middle English spelling *vertual* was influenced by Middle English *vertu* virtue; the spelling *virtual,* in imitation of the Latin, is first recorded about 1400.

virtue *n.* Probably before 1200 *vertu* moral excellence; borrowed from Anglo-French and Old French *vertu,* from Latin *virtūtem* (nominative *virtūs*) moral strength, manliness, valor, excellence, worth, from *vir* man; see VIRILE. The meaning of superiority or excellence, unusual ability, is found in Middle English about

1384, and that of a particular power, efficacy, or inherent good quality, before 1387. The phrase *by virtue of* is first recorded probably before 1200, originally in the sense of by the power or efficacy of (something aiding or justifying). The variant Middle English spelling *virtu* (influenced by the Latin) is first recorded before 1325; *virtue* did not become established until the 1700's. **—virtuous** *adj.* Probably before 1300 *vertuous* valorous, valiant, in *Kyng Alisaunder;* borrowed from Anglo-French and Old French *vertuous* excellent, effective, from Late Latin *virtuōsus* good, excellent, from Latin *virtūs* virtue; for suffix see -OUS. The meaning of showing virtue, acting morally, being good, just, righteous, is first recorded in Middle English before 1439.

virtuoso (vėr'chů̇ō'sō) *n.* 1620, scholar, connoisseur; borrowing of Italian *virtuoso,* noun use of adjective meaning skilled, learned, of exceptional worth, from Late Latin *virtuōsus* VIRTUOUS. The meaning of a person with great technical skill, especially in performing music, is first recorded in English in 1743. **—virtuosity** *n.* 1673, the pursuits of a virtuoso, interest or taste in the fine arts; formed from English *virtuoso* + *-ity.* The meaning of the skill of a virtuoso, great knowledge of technique or the production of special effects, is first recorded in 1865. Earlier use in the sense of manly qualities or character, which echoes the use in French and Latin of *virtue* moral strength, manliness, is recorded before 1470, but are not found later in English, except for obscure reference in Bailey's *Dictionary.*

virulent *adj.* very poisonous or harmful. 1400, in Lanfranc's *Science of Surgery;* borrowed from Latin *vīrulentus* poisonous, from *vīrus* poison; see VIRUS; for suffix see -ENT.

virus *n.* 1392, venomous substance; borrowed from Latin *vīrus* poison, sap of plants, slimy liquid. Latin *vīrus* is cognate with Old Irish *fī* poison, Greek *iós* (earlier **wīsós*) poison, and Sanskrit *viṣá-m* poison, *veṣati* (it) dissolves. Related to OOZE² soft mud or slime. The meaning of a poisonous substance or agent that causes an infectious disease is first recorded in 1728, in *Chambers Cyclopaedia.* **—viral** *adj.* of or having to do with a virus. 1948, formed from English *virus* + *-al*¹.

visa (vē'zə) *n.* 1831, official signature or endorsement upon a passport; borrowing of French *visa,* learned borrowing from Latin *vīsa* in *carta vīsa* paper that has been verified; literally, seen, feminine past participle of *vidēre* to see; see WIT² know. A verb form *visa* and *visaed* existed as early as 1847 and paralled the French *visé* (Anglicized *viséd*), found as early as 1810, in reference to endorsement on a passport.

visage (viz'ij) *n.* face. Probably before 1300, in *Kyng Alisaunder;* borrowed from Old French *visage,* from *vis* face, appearance, from Latin *vīsus* (genitive *vīsūs*) a look, vision, from the past participle stem of *vidēre* to see (see WIT² know); for suffix see -AGE.

vis-à-vis (vē'zəvē') *prep.* in comparison with, face to face with. 1755, in letters of Horace Walpole; borrowing of French, prepositional use of the adjective *vis-à-vis* face to face, from Old French *vis* face; see VISAGE. **—adv.** opposite, face to face. 1807, in letters of Byron; from the preposition.

viscera (vis'ərə) *n.pl.* the soft inside parts of the body. 1651, from Latin *viscera,* plural of *vīscus* internal organ, of uncertain origin. **—visceral** *adj.* 1575, (figurative) affecting inward feelings; borrowed from Middle French *viscéral,* and directly from Medieval Latin *visceralis* internal, from Latin *vīscera* viscera; for suffix see -AL¹.

viscid (vis'id) *adj.* thick and sticky. 1635, borrowed from French *viscide,* or directly from Late Latin *viscidus* sticky, clammy, from Latin *viscum* anything sticky, birdlime made from mistletoe, mistletoe. Latin *viscum* is cognate with Greek *ixós* mistletoe, and Old High German *wīchsila* (modern German *Weichsel)* morello, a kind of sour cherry, from Indo-European **wiks-/wīks-* (Pok.1134).

viscount (vī'kount) *n.* nobleman ranking next below an earl or count. Before 1387, in Trevisa's translation of Higden's *Polychronicon;* borrowed from Anglo-French and Old French *visconte* (in which the *s* eventually ceased to be pronounced; compare modern French *vicomte*), learned borrowing from Medieval Latin *vicecomes* (genitive *vicecomitis*), formed from Late Latin *vice-* deputy, VICE- + Latin *comes* member of the imperial court, nobleman, COUNT². Of the early forms in Middle English the spelling *vis-,* borrowed from Old French, *viscount, viscountess,* and their associated forms (*viscountcy,* etc.) contain the only remaining form in English.

viscous (vis'kəs) *adj.* sticky, thick like syrup or glue. 1392, borrowed from Anglo-French *viscous,* and directly from Late Latin *viscōsus* sticky, from *viscum* anything sticky, birdlime (see VISCID); for suffix see -OUS.

vise (vīs) *n.* Probably before 1300 *vys* device like a screw or winch for bending a crossbow or catapult; borrowed from Old French *vis, viz* screw, nominative case to a lost oblique case **vit* (cognate with Italian *vite,* Spanish *vid* vine), from Latin *vītis* vine, tendril of a vine; literally, that which winds; see WITHY. (The process of formation in French is postulated on the similar French *fils* son, from Old French *fiz,* nominative to oblique case *fil.*) The sense of a tool having two jaws opened and closed by a screw is first recorded in English in 1500. **—v.** hold, press, or force with a vise. 1602, from the noun.

visible *adj.* Before 1340, borrowed from Old French *visible,* and directly from Late Latin *vīsibilis* that may be seen, from *vīsus,* past participle of *vidēre* to see (see WIT² know); for suffix see -IBLE. **—visibility** *n.* 1581, borrowed from Middle French *visibilité,* or directly perhaps from Late Latin *vīsibilitātem* (nominative *vīsibilitās*) the condition of being seen, conspicuousness, from *visibilis* visible; for suffix see -ITY.

vision *n.* About 1300 *visioun* something seen in the imagination, especially as a supernatural experience; borrowed from Anglo-French *visioun,* Old French *vision,* learned borrowing from Latin *vīsiōnem* (nominative *vīsiō*) the act of seeing, sight, thing seen, from *vīs-,* past participle stem of *vidēre* to see (see WIT² know); for suffix see -ION. The meaning of the power of seeing with the eyes, sense of sight, is first recorded in English about 1491, and that of a mental concept (as in *a statesman of great vision*) in 1904, but from earlier sense of a mental concept, scheme, in 1592. **—visionary** *adj.* 1648, perceived in a vision; also, able to see visions (1651); formed from English *vision* + *-ary.* **—n.** person given to imagining or dreaming. 1702, in Addison's *Dialogue Upon the Usefulness of Ancient Medals;* from the adjective.

visit *v.* Probably before 1200 *visiten* come to (a person) in order to comfort or benefit, in *Ancrene Riwle;* borrowed from Old French *visiter,* and directly from Latin *vīsitāre* to go to see, come to inspect, call on a person, a frequentative form of *vīsere* look at well, behold, visit (a person or place), from *vīs-,* past participle stem of *vidēre* to see, notice, observe, witness, have a mental picture of, consider; see WIT[2] know.

The meaning of go to see a person in distress or illness is first recorded in English about 1250, that of make a call on in a social manner, probably before 1300, and of visit for pleasure or on some errand, about 1400. The sense of come upon, afflict, is first recorded in English in 1424, though known earlier in *visitation.* **—n.** 1621, act of visiting, in George Sandys' translation of Ovid's *Metamorphoses;* from the verb, or probably in some instances, borrowed from French *visite,* from the verb in French.

—visitation *n.* About 1303 *visitacioun* official visit to inspect, in Mannyng's *Handlyng Synne;* borrowed from Anglo-French and Old French *visitation,* from Latin *vīsitātiōnem* (nominative *vīsitātiō*) a sight, appearance, from *vīsitāre* to visit; for suffix see -ATION.

The meaning of a coming by God or some supernatural agent or agency to a person is first recorded in Middle English about 1340, and such a visit in order to afflict with sickness or other trouble is first found about 1380.

—visitor *n.* About 1370 *visitour,* borrowed from Anglo-French *visitour,* Old French *visiteur,* from *visiter* to visit; for suffix see -OR[2].

visor *n.* movable front part of a helmet, covering the face. 1459 *vesour,* alteration of earlier *viser* (probably before 1300); borrowed from Anglo-French *viser,* in Old French *visiere,* from *vis* face; see VISAGE; for suffix see -OR[2]. The spelling *visour* is first recorded in Spenser's *Faerie Queene* (1590); *visor* is first found in Shakespeare's *Much Ado About Nothing* (1599). The meaning of a stiff brim projecting from the front of a cap is first recorded in American English in 1847, in Francis Parkman's writings.

vista *n.* view. 1644, borrowing of Italian *vista* sight, view, noun use of feminine past participle of *vedere* see, from Latin *vidēre;* see WIT[2] know.

visual *adj.* of sight. Before 1420, coming from the eye or sight (as a beam of light, thought of as emanating from the eye), in Lydgate's *Troy Book;* borrowed from Late Latin *vīsuālis* of sight, from Latin *vīsus* sight, from past participle of *vidēre* to see; see WIT[2] know; for suffix see -AL[1]. The meaning of relating to or connected with sight or vision is first recorded in English in 1603. **—n.** 1726, ray emanating from the eye; from the adjective. The meaning of a photograph, film, or other visual display (often, *visuals,* pl.) is first recorded in 1951. **—visualization** *n.* 1883, formed from English *visualize* + *-ation.* **—visualize** *v.* 1817 (implied in *visualized*), to form a mental picture of; formed from English *visual* + *-ize.*

vital *adj.* About 1385, of or manifesting life, in Chaucer's *Canterbury Tales;* borrowed from Latin *vītālis* of or belonging to life, from *vīta* life, related to *vīvere* to live; see QUICK; for suffix see -AL[1]. The figurative sense of very necessary or important is first recorded in English in 1619, from the earlier meaning of essential or necessary to life (1482). **—vitals** *n.pl.* part or organs necessary to life. Before 1610, probably borrowed from Latin *vītālia* vital force, life, neuter plural of *vītālis* vital, and in some instances probably from the adjective in English + *-s* plural. **—vitality** *n.* 1592, vital force, power, or principle as manifested by living things; borrowed from Latin *vītālitātem* (nominative *vītālitās*) vital force, life, from *vītālis* vital; for suffix see -ITY.

vitamin *n.* 1920 *vitamin,* alteration of earlier *vitamine* (1912); formed in English from Latin *vīta* life (see VITAL) + English *amine;* so called because vitamins were originally thought to be amine derivatives.

vitiate (vish′ēāt) *v.* impair the quality of, spoil. 1534, in writings of Sir Thomas More; borrowed from Latin *vitiātus* injured, spoiled, corrupted, past participle of *vitiāre* to vitiate, make faulty, injure, spoil, corrupt, from *vitium* fault; see VICE[1]; for suffix see -ATE[1]. **—vitiation** *n.* 1635, borrowed from Latin *vitiātiōnem* (nominative *vitiātiō*) violation, corruption, from *vitiāre* vitiate; for suffix see -ATION. In some instances the word was probably formed in English from *vitiate* + *-ation.*

viticulture *n.* the cultivation of grapes. 1872, formed in English from Latin *vītis* vine (see WITHY) + English *culture.*

vitreous (vit′rēəs) *adj.* glassy, made from glass. 1646, borrowed from Latin *vitreus* of glass, glassy, from *vitrum* glass, of uncertain origin; for suffix see -OUS. **—vitreous humor** the transparent substance that fills the eyeball (1663).

vitrify *v.* to change into glass or something like glass, especially by fusion through heat. 1594, borrowed from Middle French *vitrifier* (also found in Spanish and Portuguese *vitrificar,* Italian *vitrificare*) implying a Medieval Latin **vitrificare,* from Latin *vitrum* glass, of uncertain origin; for suffix see -FY. Modern English *vitrify* replaced *vitrificate* (recorded in 1471), a form which adds weight to the possible existence of a Medieval Latin **vitrificare* to vitrify. **—vitrification** *n.* 1612, borrowed from Middle French *vitrification* (also found in Spanish *vitrificación,* Portuguese *vitrificação,* Italian *vitrificazione*) implying a Medieval Latin **vitrificationem* (nominative *vitrificatio*), from **vitrificare;* for suffix see -ATION.

vitriol (vit′rēəl) *n.* sulfuric acid, or any of its compounds. 1392, borrowed from Old French *vitriol,* from Medieval Latin *vitriolum* vitriol, from neuter of *vitriolus,* variant of Late Latin *vitreolus* of glass, from Latin *vitreus* of glass, glassy, from *vitrum* glass; so called from the glassy appearance of vitriol in certain states. The figurative sense of bitterly severe or caustic feeling is first recorded in 1769, with reference to the corrosive properties of vitriol. **—vitriolic** *adj.* 1670, of or belonging to vitriol; borrowed from French *vitriolique,* or formed from English *vitriol* + *-ic.* The figurative sense of sharp, bitterly severe, is first recorded in English in 1841.

vituperate (vītü′pərāt) *v.* revile, abuse. 1542, probably a back formation from *vituperation,* modeled on Latin *vituperātus,* past participle of *vituperāre* blame, censure, find fault with, disparage, formed from a lost adjective **vituperos* having faults (*vitium* fault; see VICE[1] + *-paros,* from *parāre* prepare, make ready; see PARE); for suffix see -ATE[1]. **—vituperation** *n.* About 1449 *vituperacioun* act or fact of abusing or reviling; borrowed from Middle French *vituperation,* and directly from Latin *vituperātiōnem* (nominative *vituperātiō*) blame, censure, from *vituperāre* vituperate; for suffix see -ATION. **—vituperative** *adj.* 1727, formed from English *vituperate* + *-ive.*

viva (vē′və) *interj., n.* shout of applause or good will.

1644, borrowing of Italian *viva* (long) live, may he or she live, third person singular present subjunctive of *vivere* to live, from Latin *vīvere* to live; see QUICK. The word was probably reborrowed in American English (1836) from Spanish *viva,* from *vivir* to live, from Latin *vīvere* to live.

vivacious *adj.* lively, animated. About 1645, formed in English as an adjective to *vivacity,* from Latin *vīvāx* (genitive *vīvācis*) lively, long-lived, from *vīvere* to live; see QUICK + English *-ous.* **—vivacity** *n.* liveliness. Probably before 1425 *vivacite* mental acuteness, in a translation of Higden's *Polychronicon;* borrowed from Middle French *vivacité,* and possibly directly from Latin *vīvācitātem* (nominative *vīvācitās*) vital force, liveliness, from *vīvāx* (genitive *vīvācis*) vivacious; for suffix see -ITY. The meaning of liveliness, spriteliness, animation, is first recorded in English in 1647.

vive (vēv) *interj., n.* shout of approval. Probably 1592, in Marlowe's works; borrowing of French *vive* (long) live, may he or she live, third person singular present subjunctive of *vivre* to live, from Latin *vīvere* to live; see QUICK.

vivid *adj.* 1638, active, energetic, lively; borrowed from French *vivide,* and probably directly from Latin *vīvidus* spirited, animated, lively, from *vīvus* alive; see QUICK. The meaning of brilliant, strikingly bright (said of colors) is first recorded in 1665, that of strong and distinct (as in *a vivid memory of the fire*) in Locke's writings in 1690, and that of very active or intense (as in *a vivid interest* or *imagination*) in 1853, in Charlotte Brontë's writings.

vivify *v.* give life or vigor to. 1392 *vivifien;* borrowed from Old French *vivifier,* from Late Latin *vīvificāre* make alive, from *vīvificus* enlivening (Latin *vīvus* alive; see QUICK + the root of *facere* to make, perform, DO[1]); for suffix see -FY.

viviparous (vīvip′ərəs) *adj.* bringing forth living young, rather than eggs. 1646, borrowed from Late Latin *vīviparus* bringing forth alive, from Latin *vīvus* alive, living; see QUICK + *parere* bring forth, bear; see PARE; for suffix see -OUS. Compare VIPER.

vivisection (viv′əsek′shən) *n.* a performing of a dissection or other experiment on living animals under sedation for scientific study. 1707, formed in English from Latin *vīvus* alive; see QUICK + English *(dis)section;* compare obsolete English *vividissection* (before 1711). **—vivisect** *v.* practice vivisection. 1859, back formation from *vivisection.* **—vivisectionist** *n.* person who practices or defends vivisection. 1879, formed from English *vivisection* + *-ist.*

vixen (vik′sən) *n.* female fox. About 1150 *fixen;* developed from Old English **fyxen* (attested once in the oblique case *fyxan*), feminine of *fox* FOX, corresponding to Old High German *fuhsin* (modern German *Füchsin*). Alternatively, Middle English *fixen* may have developed from Old English *fyxen,* adj., of the fox, as in the phrase *fyxen hȳd* fox hide. The transferred meaning of an ill-tempered, quarrelsome woman, is first recorded in 1575. The form *vixen* is first found in the late 1500's, probably representing an unrecorded southern British English dialectal variant of Middle English *fixen.* For a similar change of *f* to *v,* compare VAT.

viz. *adv.* that is to say, namely. Before 1540, abbreviation of VIDELICET. The *z* represents the ordinary Medieval Latin symbol for the ending *-et.* Earlier (now obsolete) English forms of this abbreviation were *vidz.* and *vidzt.*

vizier or **vizir** (vizir′) *n.* high official in Moslem countries. 1562 *vesir,* borrowed from Turkish *vezir,* from Arabic *wazīr* one who bears the burden of office, viceroy, in reference to the original sense of a porter or carrier, from *wazara* he carried.

vocabulary *n.* stock of words. 1532, in writings of Sir Thomas More; borrowed (perhaps by influence of Middle French *vocabulaire*) from Medieval Latin *vocabularium* a list of words, from Latin *vocābulum* word, name, noun, from *vocāre* to name, call; see VOICE; for suffix see -ARY.

vocal *adj.* of the voice. Before 1396, uttered by the voice, spoken, oral; borrowed from Old French *vocal,* and directly from Latin *vōcālis* sounding, sonorous, speaking (as a noun, a vowel), from *vōx* (genitive *vōcis*) VOICE; for suffix see -AL[1]. Doublet of VOWEL.

The meaning of having a voice is first recorded in 1601, that of expressive, eloquent, in 1608, and that of having to do with or belonging to the voice in 1644. The meaning full of voice or sound is found in Milton's *Paradise Lost* (1667). The technical sense in phonetics of voiced is first recorded in 1688, and that of like a vowel, in 1589. The sense of readily or freely expressing one's views, outspoken, is first recorded in 1871. **—vocal cords** (1872) **—vocal folds** (1936) **—vocalic** *adj.* of a vowel. 1814, composed mainly or entirely of vowels, in Scott's *Waverley;* formed from English *vocal* + *-ic.* The technical sense in phonetics of consisting of a vowel is first recorded in 1852, and that of having a vowel sound, in 1861. **—vocalism** *n.* 1873, a vocal sound, also, the vowel system of a language, language group, or dialect. An earlier sense of exercise of the voice is recorded in 1864. **—vocalist** *n.* singer. 1834, formed from English *vocal* + *-ist.* An earlier (now obsolete) sense of speaker is found in 1613. **—vocalize** *v.* make vocal. 1669, in William Holder's *Elements of Speech;* formed from English *vocal* + *-ize.* The technical sense in phonetics of change into a vowel (as in *vocalize the r in four*) is first recorded in 1844, that of to voice, in 1836, and that of to insert vowels in, in 1845.

vocation *n.* occupation, profession. Probably before 1430 *vocacioun* spiritual calling; borrowed from Middle French *vocation,* or directly from Latin *vocātiōnem* (nominative *vocātiō*), literally, a calling, from *vocāre* to call; see VOICE; for suffix see -ATION. Compare AVOCATION. The sense of one's ordinary occupation or profession is first recorded in English in 1553, perhaps influenced by that meaning in Middle French. **—vocational** *adj.* 1652, of or having to do with a vocation; formed from English *vocation* + *-al*[1].

vocative (vok′ətiv) *adj. Grammar.* in reference to the vocative case of nouns, pronouns, and adjectives, showing the person or thing spoken to. About 1432 *vocatif,* borrowed from Middle French *vocatif* (feminine *vocative*), from Latin *vocātīvus* (*cāsus*) (case of) calling, from *vocātus,* past participle of *vocāre* to call (translation of Greek *klētikḕ ptôsis; klētikós* related to calling, from *klētós* called); see VOICE; for suffix see -IVE. **—n.** the vocative case. Before 1522, from the adjective.

vociferate (vōsif′ərāt) *v.* cry out loudly or noisily, shout. 1617 (implied in *vociferating*); in part borrowed from Latin, and in part, probably a back formation from *vociferation,* modeled on Latin *vōciferātus,* past participle of *vōciferārī* to shout, yell, from a lost adjective **vōcifer* lifting one's voice (*vōx,* genitive *vōcis* VOICE + the root of *ferre* to carry, BEAR[2]); for suffix see -ATE[1]. **—vociferation** *n.* loud outcry, clamor. About 1400, borrowed from Old French *vociferacion,* learned borrowing from Latin, and borrowed into English directly from Latin *vōciferātiōnem* (nominative *vōciferātiō*) clamor, outcry, from *vōciferārī* to shout, cry out, yell; for suffix see -ATION. **—vociferous** *adj.* loud and noisy. About 1611, in Chapman's translation of Homer's *Iliad;* formed in English from Latin *vōciferārī* vociferate + English *-ous.* It is also possible that *vociferous* was formed from earlier unrecorded instances of English *vociferate* + *-ous.*

vodka *n.* alcoholic liquor distilled from potatoes, rye, etc. 1802, borrowed from Russian *vódka,* formed from *vodá* WATER + endearing diminutive suffix *-ka.*

vogue (vōg) *n.* fashion. 1571, the leading place in popularity at a particular time, most pronounced success or general acceptance; borrowed from Middle French *vogue* fashion, success, course drift, swaying motion (of a boat); literally, a rowing, from Old French *voguer* to row, sway, set sail, probably from Old Low German **wōgōn,* variant of *wagōn* float, fluctuate; literally, to balance oneself. According to this view, Italian *vogare,* Spanish *bogar,* and Portuguese, Catalan, and Old Provençal *vogar,* all meaning to row, are borrowed from Old French.

The sense of popularity, general acceptance (without the article *the*) is first recorded in English in 1604. The sense of prevailing fashion or tendency (with *the*) is first recorded in 1648-49.

—voguish *adj.* fashionable. 1927, formed from English *vogue* + *-ish*[1].

voice *n.* Probably before 1300, sound made by the human mouth, in *Kyng Alisaunder* and *Arthour and Merlin;* borrowed from Old French *voiz, vois,* from Latin *vōcem,* accusative of *vōx* voice, sound, utterance, cry, call, speech, sentence, language, word, related to *vocāre* to call. The Latin words are cognate with Sanskrit *vā́k* voice, *vácas* speech, word, *vákti, vívakti* (he) says, speaks, Avestan *vāxš* voice, speech, word, Tocharian A *wak,* Tocharian B *wek* voice, Greek *épos* word, Old Prussian *wackis* outcry; and in Germanic with Old High German *giwahnen* (and modern German *erwähnen*) to mention, *giwaht* mention, renown, and Old Icelandic *vātta* to testify, *vāttr* witness, from Indo-European **wekw-/wokw-/wōkw-* (Pok.1135). The transferred meaning of anything like speech or sound (as in *the voice of the bells, the voice of conscience*) is first recorded before 1325, that of opinion or choice (as in *a voice for compromise*) in 1390, and the meaning of ability as a singer, in 1607. The meaning in grammar of the form of a verb showing whether its subject is active or passive is first recorded in English in 1382. **—v.** to utter, express. Before 1438 *voicen,* from the noun. The meaning in phonetics of utter with a sound made by vibration of the vocal cords or folds (as the sounds represented by *z* and *v*) is first recorded in 1867, implied in *voiced.* **—voiceless** *adj.* 1535, having no voice; 1867, not voiced (as the sounds represented by *f* and *p*).

void *adj.* About 1300 *voide* unoccupied, vacant; borrowed from Anglo-French and Old French *voide,* feminine of *voit* empty, vast, wide, hollow, waste, from Vulgar Latin **vocitus,* presumably replacing Latin *vocīvus, vacīvus* unoccupied, vacant, and thereby related to *vacuus* empty; see VACUUM. The extended sense of without legal force or effect is first recorded in Middle English in 1433-34. **—v.** Probably before 1300 *voiden* to empty, discharge; borrowed from Anglo-French and Old French *voider* make void or empty, from Vulgar Latin **vocitāre,* from **vocitus* empty. **—n.** 1616, unfilled space in a building; before 1618, emptiness, vacancy; from the adjective. An earlier sense of a person who is devoid of something is found in 1614.

voile (voil) *n.* very thin cloth with an open weave. 1889, borrowing of French *voile,* from Old French *veile,* originally veil, from Latin *vēla,* plural (taken as feminine singular) of *vēlum* covering, curtain, VEIL.

volatile (vol′ətəl) *adj.* evaporating rapidly, changing into vapor easily. 1597, fine or light; later, evaporating rapidly (1605); borrowed from Middle French *volatile,* learned borrowing from Latin *volātilis* fleeting, transitory, flying, from *volāt-,* past participle stem of *volāre* to fly. Latin *volāre* is possibly cognate with Sanskrit *garút* wing, and *garuḍá-s* the name of a mythical bird, a Prakritized form of Sanskrit **garutrá-,* corresponding to Latin *volucer* winged, from Indo-European **gwol-(u)-* (Ernout-Meillet, *Dictionnaire Etymologique de la Langue Latine,* p. 1327; Walde-Hofmann, *Lateinisches Etymologisches Wörterbuch,* II, p. 828). The figurative sense of readily changing, fickle, is first recorded in 1647, and the extended sense of quickly vanishing, transient, in 1665. **—volatility** *n.* 1626, readiness to vaporize or evaporate, in Sir Francis Bacon's *Sylva Sylvarum;* borrowed from New Latin *volatilitas,* from Latin *volātilis* volatile; for suffix see -ITY. **—volatilize** *v.* make volatile. 1657, formed from English *volatile* + *-ize,* and probably borrowed from French *volatiliser,* from Middle French *volatile* volatile + *-iser* -ize.

volcano *n.* opening in the earth through which steam, lava, flames, etc., are ejected. 1613 *vulcano;* later, in the spelling *volcano* (1690); borrowed from Italian *vulcano, volcano,* literally, burning mountain, from Latin *Vulcānus,* earlier *Volcānus* Vulcan, the Roman god of fire and metal working; also, fire, flames, volcano (first applied to Mt. Etna by the Romans, as the seat of Vulcan). The later borrowings from Italian replaced the earlier forms in English *volcan* (1577, borrowed from French and Spanish *volcan*), and *vulcan* (1578, borrowed from Latin *Vulcānus*), all meaning volcano. **—volcanic** *adj.* 1774, ejected by a volcano; borrowed from French *volcanique,* from *volcan* volcano, from Italian *vulcano, volcano;* for suffix see -IC. The figurative sense of violently explosive, full of latent or explosive violence, is first recorded in English in 1807, in Isaac D'Israeli's writings.

vole *n.* kind of rodent. 1805 *vole mouse;* later *vole* (1828); probably borrowed from a Scandinavian source (compare Norwegian *voll,* perhaps **vollmus* field mouse, Icelandic *völlur,* and Swedish *vall* field, from Proto-Germanic **walthuz*).

volition *n.* act of willing (as in *go away of one's own volition*). 1615, borrowing of French *volition,* learned borrowing from Medieval Latin *volitionem* (nominative *volitio*) will, volition, from Latin *vol-,* stem (as in *volō* I wish) of *velle* to wish, WILL[2]; for suffix see -TION. Compare VOLUNTARY. The sense of power of willing (as in *drug use weakens volition*) is not recorded before 1660.

volley *n.* shower of stones, bullets, arrows, words, oaths, etc. 1573, the discharge of a number of guns at once;

borrowed from Middle French *volee* flight, from Vulgar Latin **volāta* (feminine), from Latin *volātum*, past participle of *volāre* to fly; for suffix see -Y[3]; see VOLATILE. The meaning in tennis of the flight of the ball in play before it has touched the ground is first recorded in 1596. The figurative sense of an outpouring of words, oaths, shouts, etc., is first recorded in 1590, in Nashe's writings. **—v.** to discharge or be discharged in a volley. 1591, from the noun. **—volleyball** *n.* 1896, American English, formed from English *volley*, n. + *ball*[1].

volt *n.* unit of electromotive force. Before 1873, probably created by back formation from *voltaic*, in allusion to Alessandro *Volta*, 1745-1827, Italian physicist who perfected a chemical action used in the electric battery. **—voltage** *n.* electromotive force expressed in volts. 1890, formed from English *volt* + *-age*. **—voltaic** *adj.* producing electric current by chemical action. 1813, in Sir Humphry Davy's writings; formed from *volta* (in allusion to Alessandro *Volta*) + the English suffix *-ic*.

voluble *adj.* talkative. Probably before 1425, variable, moving easily; earlier *volible* turning (before 1382); borrowed from Old French *voluble*, from Latin *volūbilis* that turns around, rolling, flowing, fluent (of speech), from *volvere* to turn around or about, roll; see VOLUME. The meaning of fluent, glib, talkative, is first recorded in English in Shakespeare's *Love's Labour's Lost* (1588). **—volubility** *n.* 1579, versatility; later, talkativeness (1596, in Shakespeare's *The Taming of the Shrew*); borrowed from Middle French *volubilité*, and perhaps directly from Latin *volūbilitātem* (nominative *volūbilitās*) rotating motion, fluency, from *volūbilis* rolling, flowing, fluent.

volume *n.* Before 1382, roll of parchment containing writing, large book, in the Wycliffe Bible; borrowed from Old French *volume*, learned borrowing from Latin, and borrowed directly into English from Latin *volūmen* (genitive *volūminis*) roll (as of manuscript), coil, wreath, etc., from *volvere* to turn around or about, roll. Latin *volvere* is cognate with Sanskrit *varutra-m* covering, Greek *eilýein* enfold, wrap around, *élytron* cloak, and with Armenian *gelum* I turn, twist. Cognates found in Germanic include Gothic *-walwjan* and Old English *walwian, wealwian*, both meaning to roll, from Indo-European **welu-* (Pok.1140).

The meaning of a book forming part of a set is first recorded in English in 1523, borrowed from Middle French, and the sense of the bulk or size (of a book) in 1530 (in Palsgrave's *Lesclarcissement*); the generalized sense of bulk, mass, quantity, is first recorded in English in 1621, borrowed from French. The meaning of the amount of sound is first recorded in Byron's writings (1822).

—volumetric *adj.* having to do with measurement by volume. 1857, probably formed from earlier English *volumeter* instrument for measuring volume (1829) + suffix *-ic*, on analogy with *meter, metric*. **—voluminous** *adj.* 1611, full of turnings and windings, writing so much as to fill volumes; 1612, extending to many volumes; borrowed from Late Latin *volūminōsus* full of turnings, bendings, or folds, from Latin *volūmen* (genitive *volūminis*) volume; for suffix see -OUS.

voluntary *adj.* About 1385, in Usk's *The Testament of Love;* borrowed from Latin *voluntārius* of one's free will, from *voluntās* will, from earlier **voluntitās*, formed from the ancient accusative singular present participle **velontem* of *velle* to wish, WILL[2]; for suffix see -ARY. Compare VOLITION. Doublet of VOLUNTEER. The extended sense of deliberate, intentional, is first recorded in English in 1495.

volunteer *n.* About 1600, person who voluntarily enrolls for military service; borrowed from Middle French *voluntaire, volontaire*, noun use of adjective meaning voluntary, learned borrowing from Latin *voluntārius* voluntary, of one's free will; see the doublet VOLUNTARY. For suffix see -EER. The generalized meaning of one who voluntarily offers his services in any capacity is first recorded in 1638. **—v.** 1755, to enlist as a soldier, in Johnson's *Dictionary;* from the noun. The meaning of offer (one's services) for any purpose or enterprise is first recorded in 1800. The meaning of tell or say voluntarily (as in, *to volunteer information*) is first recorded in 1805, in Jane Austen's letters. **—adj.** 1649, serving as a volunteer in an army or navy; from the noun. The meaning of voluntarily performing any service is first recorded in 1661.

voluptuous (vəlupʹchůəs) *adj.* sensual. About 1380, in Chaucer's translation of Boethius' *De Consolatione Philosophiae;* borrowed probably from Old French *voluptueux*, and directly from Latin *voluptuōsus* full of pleasure, delightful, from *voluptās* pleasure, delight, from *volup* pleasurably, from **volupis* pleasant (cognate with Greek *elpís* hope), ultimately related to Latin *velle* to wish, WILL[2]; for suffix see -OUS. **—voluptuary** (vəlupʹchůerʹē) *n.* person who cares much for luxurious or sensual pleasures. Before 1610, borrowed perhaps from French *voluptuaire*, and directly from Medieval Latin *voluptuarius*, alteration of Latin *voluptārius* of or pertaining to pleasure, from *voluptās* pleasure; for suffix see -ARY.

volute (vəlütʹ) *n.* spiral or twisted thing or form. 1696, spiral ornament on an Ionic capital, in Phillips' *Dictionary;* borrowed from French *volute*, from Italian *voluta*, from Latin *volūta* a spiral scroll; originally feminine past participle of *volvere* to turn around or about, roll; see VOLUME. The generalized meaning of a thing or part having a spiral form is first recorded in English in 1756. **—adj.** rolled up, spiral. 1845, from the noun.

vomit *v.* 1422 *vomiten*, borrowed from Latin *vomitāre* to vomit often, frequentative form of *vomere* spew forth, discharge, vomit. Latin *vomere* is cognate with Greek *emeîn* to vomit, Lithuanian *vémti*, Sanskrit *vámiti, vamati* (he) vomits, and in Germanic with Old Icelandic *vāma* nausea, from Indo-European **wem-/wēm-*, **wemə-* (Pok.1146). Related to EMETIC. **—n.** 1737, borrowed from Anglo-French and Old French *vomite*, and directly from Latin *vomitus* (genitive *vomitūs*) vomit, a throwing up, from past participle of *vomere* spew forth, vomit.

voodoo *n.* religious rites and beliefs involving sorcery, practiced especially in the West Indies, but originating in Africa. 1850 *voudou* (influenced by the name of an African deity, *Vandoo*, 1820); American English, borrowed from Louisiana French *voudou*, from a West African language (compare Ewe and Fon *vodu* spirit, demon, deity). The variant form *vodun*, found occasionally in English since 1874, was originally borrowed directly, possibly also influenced by *Vandoo*, from a West African language spoken in Dahomey, but was probably later reborrowed (1920) from Haitian Creole *vodun, vodou*. **—voodooism** *n.* 1865, American English; formed from *voodoo* + *-ism*.

voracity (vərasʹətē) *n.* 1526, quality or character of

being greedy, especially in eating, voraciousness; borrowed from Middle French *voracité*, and probably directly from Latin *vorācitātem* (nominative *vorācitās*) greediness, ravenousness, from *vorāx* (genitive *vorācis*) greedy, from *vorāre* to devour; for suffix see -ITY. Latin *vorāre* is cognate with Greek *borá* food (of carnivores), Sanskrit *giráti* (he) swallows, *gará-s* drink, Lithuanian *gérti* to drink, and Old Slavic *žrěti* to swallow, devour, from Indo-European **gwer-/gwor-/gwr-* (Pok.474). The figurative sense of a being unable to be satisfied, eagerness, is first recorded in English in 1601. **—voracious** *adj.* greedy, ravenous. 1635, formed in English as an adjective to earlier *voracity*, from Latin *vorāx* (genitive *vorācis*) greedy + English *-ous*. The figurative sense of very eager, unable to be satisfied, is first recorded in English in Addison's writings in *The Spectator*, in 1712, possibly influenced by the earlier figurative use of *voracity* (1601).

vortex *n.* whirling mass of water, air, etc., whirlpool, whirlwind. 1652, borrowed from Latin *vortex*, variant of *vertex* an eddy of water, wind, or flame, whirlpool, whirlwind, from *vertere* to turn; see VERTEX.

votary *n.* person devoted to something, devotee. 1546, person bound by vows to a religious life; formed in English from Latin *vōtum* VOW + English *-ary*. The extended sense of a person who is devoted to a particular pursuit or interest is first recorded in Shakespeare's *The Two Gentlemen of Verona* (1591).

vote *n.* Probably before 1300, a vow, wish; borrowed from Latin *vōtum* a vow, wish, promise, dedication, noun use of neuter of *vōtus*, past participle of *vovēre* to promise, pledge, dedicate; see the doublet VOW. The sense of a formal expression of a wish or choice, as in accepting or rejecting a proposal, motion, candidate, etc., is first recorded in Middle English about 1460. **—v.** 1533 (originally Scottish), to vow (to do something); probably borrowed from Late Latin *vōtāre* to devote by a vow, from Latin *vōtum* VOW, n. The meaning of give or cast a vote is first recorded in English in 1552, and that of choose, enact, or establish by vote, in 1568. **—voter** *n.* person who votes or who has a right to vote. Before 1578, formed from English *vote* + *-er*[1]. **—voting machine** (1900)

votive *adj.* promised by a vow. 1593, carrying out a vow, devout; borrowed from Middle French *votif* (feminine *votive*), and directly from Latin *vōtīvus* of or pertaining to a vow, conforming to one's wishes, from *vōtum* VOW; for suffix see -IVE. The meaning of made up or expressive of a vow or wish is first recorded in English in 1597.

vouch *v.* Before 1325 *vochen* summon into court to prove a title; later, allege, affirm (probably about 1380); borrowed from Anglo-French *voucher*, Old French *vocher, vochier* to call, summon, invoke, claim, probably from Gallo-Romance **voticāre*, by metathesis (of *t* and *c*) from Latin *vocitāre* to call to, summon insistently, a frequentative form of Latin *vocāre* to call, call upon, summon; see VOICE. For the Latin sequence *-tica-* becoming Old French *-che-*, compare Old French *perche* perch, from Latin *pertica*. The meaning of guarantee to be true or accurate is first recorded in English in 1591. **—voucher** *n.* 1531, the summoning of a person into court to prove a title; borrowed from Anglo-French *voucher*, noun use of *voucher* to vouch. The sense of a receipt from a business transaction is first recorded in English in 1696.

vouchsafe *v.* be willing to grant or give. About 1303 *vouchen sauf* to vouch as safe (*vouchen* to VOUCH + *sauf* SAFE). The one-word form is first recorded in Middle English (as *fouchesaf*) about 1330.

vow *n.* solemn promise. About 1300 *vou*, borrowed from Anglo-French and Old French *vou*, from Latin *vōtum* a vow, wish, promise, dedication, noun use of neuter of *vōtus*, past participle of *vovēre* to promise solemnly, pledge, dedicate, vow. Latin *vovēre* is cognate with Umbrian *vufru* relating to a vow, Greek *eúchesthai* to pray, vow, Sanskrit *vāghát* person who prays or offers sacrifices, *óhate* praises, and Avestan *aogədā, aoxta* spoke, from Indo-European **wegwh-, *eugwh-*, root **ewegwh-* speak solemnly, promise solemnly (Pok.348). Doublet of VOTE. **—v.** make a vow. About 1303 *vowen;* borrowed from Old French *vouer, vower* make a vow, promise, from *vou* vow, n.

vowel *n.* sound or letter representing such a sound, as a, e, i, o, u. About 1308, borrowed from Old French *vouel*, from Latin *vōcālis* in *littera vōcālis* vowel; literally, vocal letter (referring to its voiced quality), from *vōx* (genitive *vōcis*) VOICE. Doublet of VOCAL.

voyage *n.* Probably before 1300 *viage* a traveling, journey; about 1300 *veyage;* borrowed from Old French *veiage, vayage, voiage, vaiage* travel, journey, voyage, from Late Latin *viāticum* a journey, in Latin meaning provisions for a journey, noun use of neuter of *viāticus* of or for a journey, from *via* road, journey, travel; see VIA. The spelling *voyage* is first recorded in English in 1527, probably influenced by the spelling of the verb. **—v.** 1475 *voyagen*, in Caxton's translation of *The History of Jason;* borrowed from Middle French *voyager*, from Old French *voyage*, n. **—voyager** *n.* 1477, in Caxton's translation of *The History of Jason;* borrowed from Old French *voyagier* (*voyage* + *-ier* -er[1]), and probably formed from English *voyage*, v. + *-er*[1].

voyeur (vwä'yœr') *n.* person who gets pleasure from secretly watching the private acts of others. About 1920, borrowing of French *voyeur* (1898), literally, one who views or inspects, from *voir* to view, see, from Latin *vidēre;* see WIT[2] know. **—voyeurism** *n.* 1924, formed from English *voyeur* + *-ism*.

vulcanite *n.* a hard vulcanized rubber. 1860, formed from English *Vulcan* (from Latin *Vulcānus*) the Roman god of fire and metalworking + *-ite*[1]. An earlier sense, pyroxene (a mineral), is found in English in 1836.

vulcanize *v.* treat (rubber) with sulfur and heat to make it more elastic and durable. 1827, burn up, in letters of Southey; formed from English *Vulcan* (from Latin *Vulcānus*) the Roman god of fire + *-ize*. The meaning of treat (rubber) with sulfur and heat is first recorded in 1846. **—vulcanization** *n.* process of vulcanizing rubber. 1846, formed from English *vulcanize* + *-ation*.

vulgar *adj.* coarse, low. 1391, common, ordinary, in Chaucer's *Treatise on the Astrolabe;* borrowed from Latin *vulgāris* of or pertaining to the common people, common, vulgar, from *vulgus* the common people multitude, crowd, throng; for suffix see -AR. Latin *vulgus*, earlier *volgus*, is cognate with Sanskrit *várga-s* group, and Welsh *gwala* plenty, sufficiency, from Indo-European **wolgos* (Pok.1138). The meaning of coarse, low, ill-bred, is first recorded in English in 1643. The sense of commonly or customarily used, vernacular (as in *Vulgar Latin*) is first recorded in English in 1483, in Caxton's translations. **—vulgarian** *adj.* 1650, vulgar, formed from English *vulgar* + *-ian; n.* 1804, vulgar person;

probably from the adjective, but also in part possibly re-formed from English *vulgar* + *-ian.* **—vulgarism** *n.* 1644, a common or ordinary expression; later, a colloquialism of speech (1746, in Walpole's letters), and the quality of being vulgar (1749, in Chesterfield's letters); formed from English *vulgar* + *-ism.* **—vulgarity** *n.* 1579, the common people; borrowed from Middle French *vulgarité,* and directly from Latin *vulgāritās* the multitude; literally, the quality of being common, from *vulgāris* common, vulgar; for suffix see -ITY. The meaning of coarseness, lack of good breeding, is recorded in English before 1774. **—vulgarize** *v.* 1605, act in a vulgar manner, perhaps borrowed from French *vulgariser,* or more likely formed from English *vulgar* + *-ize.* The meaning of make vulgar, coarsen, is first recorded in English in 1756.

Vulgate *n.* Latin translation of the Bible made by Saint Jerome. 1609 (as an attributive use), in the Douay Bible; borrowed from Medieval Latin *Vulgata* the Vulgate edition, from Late Latin *vulgāta* common, general, ordinary, popular, in *vulgāta ēditiō* popular edition, from Latin *vulgāta,* feminine past participle of *vulgāre* make common or public, from *vulgus* the common people; see VULGAR; for suffix see -ATE[1].

vulnerable *adj.* capable of being wounded or injured. 1605, in Shakespeare's *Macbeth;* borrowed from Late Latin *vulnerābilis* wounding, from Latin *vulnerāre* to wound, from *vulnus* (genitive *vulneris*) wound; for suffix see -ABLE. Latin *vulnus,* earlier *volnus,* contracted from **wolenos,* is probably related to *vellere* to pull, tear, and cognate with Greek *oulḗ* (from earlier **wolnā́* or **wolsā́*) a wound scarred over; in Germanic further cognates are found in Old High German *wal* battlefield, and Old Icelandic *Valkyrja* Valkyrie (handmaiden of Odin in Norse mythology who chooses the heroes who are to die in battle; literally, chooser of the slain); all from Indo-European **wel-/wol-* to tear, wound (Pok.1144). **—vulnerability** *n.* 1808, quality or state of being vulnerable; formed from English *vulnerable* + *-ity.*

vulpine (vul′pīn) *adj.* of or like a fox. 1628, borrowed from Latin *vulpīnus* of or pertaining to a fox, from *vulpēs,* earlier *volpēs* (genitive *vulpis, volpis*) fox, probably cognate with Greek *alṓpēx* fox, Lithuanian *vilpišỹs* wildcat, and Avestan *urupiš* dog, *raopiš* fox, jackal, from Indo-European **wl̥p-* or **lup-* (Pok.1179); actually, the original form cannot be satisfactorily reconstructed; for suffix see -INE[1].

vulture *n.* large bird of prey. About 1380 *voltor,* in Chaucer's translation of Boethius' *De Consolatione Philosophiae;* also, about 1385 *voltur,* in Chaucer's *Troilus and Criseyde;* borrowed from Anglo-French *vultur,* and Old French *voultour,* from Latin *vultur,* earlier *voltur,* probably related to *vellere* to pull, tear and to *vulnus* wound; see VULNERABLE.

vulva (vul′və) *n.* external genital organs of the female. 1392, borrowing of Latin *vulva;* earlier *volva* womb; female sexual organ, from *volvere* to turn around or about, roll; see VOLUME.

W

wabble *v.* See WOBBLE. **—wabbly** *adj.* See WOBBLY.

wacky *adj. Slang.* eccentric, crazy. 1935, American English, variant of *whacky;* probably formed from *whack,* n., a blow, stroke + *-y*[1].

wad *n.* 1540 *wadde* soft material for padding or stuffing; of uncertain origin and of undetermined relation to earlier Medieval Latin *wadda* (1380), and later Dutch *watten* (after 1599), German *Watte* (from Dutch), Swedish *vadd* (from English). Because first use of *wad* means material of cotton, flannel, etc., it is tempting to suppose that *wad* is a shortened form of earlier *wadmal* woolen cloth (1392; borrowed from Old Icelandic *vathmāl* a woolen fabric of Scandinavia and Iceland, probably from **vāthmāl,* from *vāth* cloth + *māl* measure).

The meaning of a small, soft mass, especially for use as a plug or pad (as in *a wad of cotton stuffed in each ear*) is first recorded in 1580. *Wad* in the generalized sense of any tightly rolled mass (as in, *to throw a wad of paper in the wastebasket*) is not recorded before 1899, but in the meaning of a roll of (dollar) bills is recorded as early as 1814 in American English; and is found also in *tightwad* a miser (1900, in American English).

—v. 1579, put a wad in (a gun or cartridge); from the noun. The sense of roll up into a compact mass is first recorded in 1896, in American English, but in the generalized sense of press anything together is found in 1675.

waddle *v.* 1592, in Shakespeare's *Romeo and Juliet;* frequentative form of WADE; for suffix see -LE[3]. The meaning of fall heavily is recorded in Middle English probably before 1400; however, this may not be connected with the modern use. **—n.** act of waddling. 1691, from the verb. An earlier dialectal sense of wane of the moon (1678) probably belongs to a different word (compare Middle High German *wadal,* Middle Low German *wadel* phases or changes of the moon).

wade *v.* walk through water, snow, etc. Before 1250 *waden;* developed from Old English *wadan* to go forward, proceed (about 725, in *Beowulf*), the use of *wade* in Old English being confined to poetical use, except for instances such as in *oferwadan* overwade, wade across (before 899, in Alfred's works). Old English *wadan* is cognate with Old Frisian *wada* to proceed, wade, Middle Low German, Middle Dutch, and modern Dutch *waden,* Old High German *watan* (modern German *waten*), Old Icelandic *vadha* (Swedish *vada,* Danish *vade,* Norwegian *va, vade*) to wade, and outside Germanic with Latin *vādere* to go, from Indo-European **wadh-/wādh-* (Pok.1109). Old English *wadan* is also related to Old English *wæd* shallow water, ford; cognate with Old Icelandic *vadh,* Middle Low German and Middle Dutch *wat* shallows, Old High German *wat* ford (from Proto-Germanic **wađan,* Indo-European **wadhom*), and outside Germanic with Latin *vadum* ford. **—n.** act of wading. 1665, from the verb. **—wader** *n.* 1673, one who wades; later, a long-legged bird that wades in shallow water to feed (1771), and *waders* pl. high waterproof boots (1841); formed from English *wade,* v. + *-er*[1].

wadi (wä′dē) *n.* valley or ravine in Arabia, northern Africa, etc., through which a stream flows during the rainy season. 1839, borrowed from Arabic *wādi* river valley, wadi.

wafer *n.* 1368 *waffre* very thin cake or biscuit; borrowed from Anglo-French *wafre,* Old North French *waufre,* perhaps from Frankish (compare earlier Flemish *wāfer,* with alteration of *l* to *r* from Middle Dutch *wāfel* honeycomb; see WAFFLE[1]). The meaning is also found in Old French *gaufre, gofre* wafer, waffle; compare GOPHER. The meaning of a thin piece of bread used in a religious service is first recorded in 1559.

waffle[1] *n.* batter cake cooked in a special griddle. 1744 (in *wafel-frolic* party at which waffles are served); American English, borrowed from Dutch *wafel* waffle, from Middle Dutch *wāfel,* perhaps from Middle Low German *wāfel* waffle (though it is more likely the Middle Low German form comes from the Middle Dutch); cognate with Old High German *waba* honeycomb (modern German *Wabe*), related to *weban* to WEAVE. **—waffle iron** 1794, borrowed from Dutch *wafel-ijzer,* and probably from German *Waffel-eisen* waffle iron. The sense of honeycomb, found in Old French *gaufre,* Old High German *waba,* etc., is preserved in English in *waffle pattern* (1948), *waffle piqué* (1949) and other combinations referring to a weave of cloth.

waffle[2] *v.* talk incessantly or foolishly. 1698, to yelp, bark, a frequentative form of obsolete *waff* to yelp (1610); possibly of imitative origin; for suffix see -LE[3]. The meaning of talk or write foolishly, engage in doubletalk, is first recorded in 1701; the extended sense of waver, vacillate is implied in *waffler* an unreliable person, equivocator (1803). **—n.** 1861, the bark of a small dog; from the verb. The meaning of foolish talk, gossip, doubletalk, is first recorded in 1888.

waft *v.* 1513, to escort or convoy (a ship); back formation from *wafter;* earlier *waughter* convoy ship (1484); borrowed from Middle Dutch (or Middle Low German) *wachter* a guard, from *wachten* to guard, related to *wāken* rouse from sleep; see WAKE[1]. The meaning of sail or cross over water is first recorded before 1562, and the meaning of pass through the air or through space, float, in 1664 (implied earlier in *waftage* passage through air or space, before 1658), the latter meaning of *waft* perhaps from the noun. **—n.** 1607, wafting movement, puff, gust; from the verb, and probably in the earliest recorded sense of a taste or flavor, especially of a foul or unsavory nature, developed from *wef, weffe* (before 1300).

wag[1] *v.* move rapidly from side to side or up and down. Probably before 1200 *waggen* to stir, move, in *Ancrene Riwle;* probably from a Scandinavian source (compare Old Swedish *wagga* fluctuate, wag, rock a cradle, also, Old Icelandic *vagga,* Danish *vugga* a cradle, and *vugge* rock a cradle). Also in part probably developed from Old English *wagian* move backwards and forwards, wag (or its root), from Proto-Germanic **waȝōjanan*. Old English *wagian* is related to *wegan* to bear, move, carry; see WEIGH. **—n.** 1589, act of wagging; from the verb.

wag² *n.* person fond of making jokes. Before 1553, mischievous boy; traditionally considered a shortened form of obsolete *waghalter* (recorded in 1570) gallows bird (person likely to swing in a noose or halter, and apparently applied humorously to a child); formed from *wag¹* + *halter*. It seems more likely from the evidence of the date, that *wag* in this sense developed from *wag¹*, v. perhaps with reference to moving the head in a playful or derisive manner. The meaning of a person fond of making jokes is first recorded in 1584. **—waggery** *n.* joking. 1594, formed from English *wag²* + *-ery*. **—waggish** *adj.* fond of joking. 1589, formed from English *wag²* + *-ish*.

wage *n.* Before 1338, pledge, security, amount paid for services or work, in Mannyng's *Chronicle of England;* later *wages,* pl. (1378, in a version of *Piers Plowman*); borrowed from Old North French *wage* pledge, from Frankish **wadja-* (compare Gothic *wadi* pledge); see WED. The form *gage,* (earlier *guage*) appears in standard Old French and thus GAGE is a doublet of WAGE. **—v.** Probably before 1200 *wagien* to pledge, in *Trinity Homilies;* later *wagen* (probably before 1300, in *Sir Tristrem*); borrowed from Old North French *wagier,* from *wage* pledge, n. The meaning of carry on (a war, etc.) is first recorded in 1456, developing from the sense of offer as a pledge to combat (about 1430), and to give as a pledge (1376, in *Piers Plowman*).

wager *n.* something staked on an uncertain event, bet. About 1303 *waiour,* in Mannyng's *Handlyng Synne;* later *wager* (about 1450); borrowed from Anglo-French *wageure* (compare modern French *gageure* a wager), from Old North French *wagier* to pledge; see WAGE. **—v.** to bet, gamble. 1602, in Shakespeare's *Hamlet;* from the noun. An earlier sense of contend for a prize is found once in 1574.

waggle *v.* wag repeatedly. 1440 *wagelen,* in *Promptorium Parvulorum;* a frequentative form of *wag¹*, v.; corresponding to Dutch *waggelen* to stagger, Middle Low German *waggeln,* and German *wackeln* to stagger, totter; for suffix see -LE³. **—n.** waggling motion. 1885, in Robert Louis and Fanny Stevenson's *The Dynamiter;* from the verb.

wagon *n.* Before 1475 *waggin* four-wheeled vehicle, especially for carrying heavy loads; borrowed from Middle Dutch *wagen, waghen* wagon, cart. Middle Dutch *wagen, waghen* are cognate with Old English *wægn, wǣn* wagon, Old Frisian *wein,* Old High German *wagan* (modern German *Wagen*), and Old Icelandic *vagn* (Swedish *vagn,* Danish and Norwegian *vogn*). Outside Germanic, cognates are found in Old Irish *fēn* type of carriage (Indo-European **weĝhno-s*), Greek *óchos* carriage (earlier **wócho-s*), Old Slavic *vozŭ* carriage, and Sanskrit *vāhana-m* carriage, ship, beast of burden. The word is ultimately derived from the Indo-European root **weĝh-/woĝh-/wēĝh-* to carry (Pok. 1118), the source of Old English *wegan* to carry; see WEIGH. Doublet of WAIN; which developed from Old English *wǣn* (earlier *wægn*). The same process in development of spelling (with loss of *g*) is found in the series *hail, nail, tail* and in *day* from Old English *dæg,* which shows that modern English *wagon* (in which *g* is found) could not have developed from Old English, but was a later borrowing, possibly, in part, the result of soldiers' contact, especially in the Continental wars, and through the Flemish immigrants and Dutch trade.

It is interesting to note in the borrowing process, as the OED points out, that though now obsolete in English, *wagon* in the sense of a railroad car, was adopted into French, German, Italian, Spanish, Russian, etc.

waif *n.* 1376, unclaimed property, flotsam; also, stray animal; borrowed from Anglo-French *weyf* lost property (1228), earlier *gwayf* (1223), corresponding to Old French *gaif,* probably from a Scandinavian source (compare Old Icelandic *veif* something waving or flapping, *veifan* a moving about uncertainly, *veifa* to wave; see WAIVE). The transferred meaning of a person without home or friends is first recorded in Cowper's *The Task* (1784), but is found earlier in the phrase *waif and stray* in 1624, in Donne's writings.

wail *v.* Probably before 1300 *wailen* cry loud and long because of grief or pain, in *Kyng Alisaunder* and *Arthour and Merlin;* borrowed from a Scandinavian source (compare Old Icelandic *væla, vāla* to wail, related to *vei* WOE). The meaning of grieve bitterly is first recorded in Chaucer's *Troilus and Criseyde* (about 1385). **—n.** About 1300, act of wailing, in *The Body and the Soul;* from the verb.

wain *n. Archaic.* wagon. About 1250, in *Genesis and Exodus;* developed from Old English *wægn, wǣn* (about 725, in *Beowulf*); see the doublet WAGON, especially for forms related to Old English *wægn, wǣn.*

wainscot (wān′skōt) *n.* paneling of wood on the walls of a room. 1352-53, an imported oak of superior quality; probably borrowed from Middle Dutch or Middle Flemish *waghenscote* superior quality oak wood, possibly in the sense of board used for paneling, but originally board suitable for wagon building and coachwork (*waghen* WAGON + *scote, scot* partition, crossbar; see SHOT¹, n.) The meaning of paneling of wood on the walls of a room is first recorded in English in 1548. **—v.** to line with wood. 1570, in part from the noun in English, and in part probably borrowed from early modern Dutch or Flemish *waeghen-schotten,* a term that, "may have been imported into England by the 1500's Flemish artisans who settled in England" (J.F. Bense, *A Dictionary of the Low-Dutch Element in the English Vocabulary*). **—wainscoting** *n.* wainscot. 1580, formed from English *wainscot,* v. + *-ing¹*.

waist *n.* Probably 1350-75 *wast* middle portion of the body; possibly developed from Old English **wæst,* **weahst* growth, size, related to Old English *waestm* growth, and cognate with Old Icelandic *vǫxtr* growth, stature (Swedish *växt,* Norwegian and Danish *vekst*), Gothic *wahstus* growth, size, stature; all derived from the same root as Old English *weaxan* to grow, WAX².

With regard to the sense development of "waist" from "growth," the OED cites French *taille,* where the sense "waist" appears to have developed from that of "size (of the body)."

—waistband *n.* (1584) **—waistcoat** *n.* (1519) **—waistline** *n.* (1897)

wait *v.* Probably before 1200 *waiten* to watch, spy, lie in wait, in *Ancrene Riwle;* borrowed from Old North French *waitier,* originally, to watch (but compare modern French *guetter* lie in wait for), from Frankish **wahtōn* (compare Old High German *wahta* watch, guard, and *wahhēn, wahhōn* to watch, be awake; see

WAKE[1], v.) The sense of stop doing something or stay until someone comes or something happens (as in *wait in the shade*) is first recorded in 1375, and that of look forward to (as in *wait for vacation*) before 1400. The sense of delay doing something (as in *it can wait until tomorrow*) is first recorded before 1633. The meaning of serve as an attendant at the table, hand food and drink to persons at a meal, is first recorded in English in 1568, from the generalized sense of act as a servant, attend (as in *wait on*) recorded in 1509-10. **—n.** act or time of waiting. About 1200 *waite* a watching, watchman; borrowed from Old North French *waite,* probably from *waitier* to watch. Other senses of the noun developed from the verb in English. **—waiter** *n.* Before 1382, attendant, watchman, in the Wycliffe Bible; probably borrowed through Anglo-French from Old North French *waitteor,* from *waitier* to wait, and in some instances formed in Middle English from *waiten* to wait + *-er*[1]. The meaning of a person who waits on tables is first recorded before 1663. **—waiting room** (1683) **—waitress** *n.* 1834, woman who waits on tables; formed from English *waiter* + *-ess.* An earlier sense of handmaid occurs once about 1586.

waive *v.* About 1300 *weiven* deprive of legal protection, outlaw; about 1469 *waiven* give up (a legal right, claim, etc.); borrowed from Anglo-French *weyver* to abandon, disclaim ownership, waive, Old French *weyver, guesver, guever* to refine, abandon, surrender, give back, resign, probably from a Scandinavian source (compare Old Icelandic *veifa* to swing about, move to and fro, wave). Old Icelandic *veifa* is cognate with Gothic *biwaibjan* wind around, Old High German *-weiben* disperse, and Old English *wǣfan* to clothe, from Proto-Germanic **waiƀjanan.* Cognates of Old Icelandic *veifa* are found outside Germanic in Welsh *gwisgi* restless (from pre-Celtic **wip-ski-mo-*), Old Prussian *wipis* branch, bough, Latvian *viept* to cover, mask, and Sanskrit *vépate* (he) trembles, shakes, from Indo-European **weip-/woip-/wip-* (Pok.1131). Compare WAIF. **—waiver** *n.* a giving up a right, claim, etc. 1628, probably formed in English from *waive,* v. + *-er*[1], perhaps modeled on some retained use in legal circles of Anglo-French *weyver,* noun use of *weyver* to abandon, waive.

wake[1] *v.* rouse from sleep. A fusion in early Middle English of two distinct but synonymous verbs from the same root: (1) Middle English (probably about 1200) *waken* (past tense *wok, wook,* past participle *waken*); developed from Old English *wacan,* a strong verb meaning to become awake, and (2) Middle English (probably before 1200) *wakien* (past tense and past participle *waked*); developed from Old English *wacian,* a weak verb meaning to be or remain awake. Both verbs are related to Old English *wæccan* be awake (see WATCH) and Old English *weccan* to cause to wake, rouse from sleep, which did not survive into modern English. Cognates of Old English *wacian* and *wæccan* are Old Frisian *wakia, waka* be awake, Old Saxon *wakōn,* Middle Dutch *wāken* (modern Dutch *waken*), Old High German *wahhēn, wahhōn* (modern German *wachen*), Old Icelandic *vaka* (Swedish *vaka,* Norwegian *vake,* Danish *vaage*), and Gothic *wakan;* cognates of Old English *weccan* are Old Saxon *wekkian* cause to wake up, Old High German *wecchen* (modern German *wecken*), Old Icelandic *vekja* (Norwegian *vekke,* Danish *vække,* Swedish *väcka*), and Gothic *uswakjan,* from Proto-Germanic **wak-.* Cognates of this group of words outside Germanic are found in Latin *vegēre* enliven, and probably *vigil* wakeful, watchful, Sanskrit *vája-s* strength, swiftness, *vājáyati* (he) rouses, and Tocharian A and Tocharian B *waśir* lightning, from Indo-European **weĝ-/woĝ-/wōĝ-* (Pok.1117). **—n.** a watching, vigil. About 1200, in *Vices and Virtues;* partly developed from Old English *-wacu* (found in *nihtwacu* night watch), related to WATCH, and partly borrowed from a Scandinavian source (compare Old Icelandic *vaka* vigil, eve before a feast, related to *vaka* be awake). See also WAKEN. **—wakeful** *adj.* keeping awake. 1549, from English *wake,* v. + *-ful.*

wake[2] *n.* track left behind a moving ship. Before 1500, track, trace, of uncertain origin; possibly borrowed from Middle Low German or Middle Dutch *wake* hole in the ice, from a Scandinavian source (compare Old Icelandic *vǫk* hole in the ice, Norwegian *våk,* Swedish *vak,* and Danish *vaage,* probably related to Old Icelandic *vǫkr* damp; see HUMOR). Old Icelandic *vǫk* is from Proto-Germanic **wakwō,* Indo-European **wogwā.*

The sense of a track left behind by a moving ship is recorded in English before 1547, especially in the phrase *in the wake of.* The transferred and figurative use of this phrase, in the sense of behind, following as a result or consequence, is first recorded in 1806.

waken *v.* Probably about 1200 *wakenen* be stirred up or aroused, rouse, wake up; developed from Old English *wæcnan, wæcnian* to rise, spring (about 725, in *Beowulf*); cognate with Old Icelandic *vakna* (Swedish *vakna,* Norwegian *vakne,* Danish *vaagne*), and Gothic *gawaknan,* all meaning to waken and derived from the same source as English WAKE; for suffix see -EN[1] (not to be confused with the medial *n* which is also a suffix of verbs with the sense of act of becoming or getting into a state; sometimes referred to as having inceptive or inchoative force).

wale *n.* streak or ridge made on the skin, weal, welt. Late Old English (1024) *wale* ridge, as of earth or stone; later, ridge made on flesh by a lash (before 1100), variant of *walu;* cognate with Low German *wale* weal, welt, and perhaps with Old Frisian *walu-* staff; see WALL. Related to WEAL[2]. Old English *walu* is from Proto-Germanic **walō,* cognate with Latin *vola* the hollow in the palm of the hand, from Indo-European **wel-/wol-* turn, round (Pok.1140) The sense of streak or ridge is now often used of fabric, especially corduroy in which it is designated wide wale or narrow wale (from 1583). **—v.** to mark (the skin or flesh) with wales. About 1430 *walen,* from the noun.

walk *v.* Probably before 1200 *walken, walkien* travel on foot, move about, a fusion (before 1000) of Old English *wealcan* to toss, roll, and of Old English *wealcian* to roll up, curl, muffle up.

The abrupt change in meaning from Old English "roll" to Middle English "walk" is explained in the OED as perhaps coming from a colloquial use in Old English that was adopted in Middle English when "people wrote as they spoke," the original meaning in Old English no longer being current in Middle English. Another factor may be apparent in the sense carried by some of the cognates, that is in thickening cloth, which is done not only by rolling it, but also by treading or trampling, which has an obvious semantic connection with "walk" and may point to an earlier sense especially as suggested in such a term as *walker* one who fulls or thickens cloth (about 1050).

The Old English verbs are cognate with Middle Low German and Middle Dutch *walken* to knead, press, thicken cloth (modern Dutch *walken* to thicken cloth),

Old High German *walchan* (modern German *walken* to thicken cloth), Old Icelandic *valka* drag or roll about, torment. Outside Germanic cognates are found in Latin *valgus* bow-legged, and possibly Sanskrit *válgati* (he) jumps, from Indo-European **walg-* (Walde-Pokorny, *Vergleichendes Wörterbuch der Indo-germanischen Sprachen* I 301, 304). The added senses in baseball, peculiar to American English, include that of go to first base after the pitcher has thrown four balls (1867), and allow a batter to reach first base by throwing four balls (1913).
—n. act of walking. Before 1250 *walke,* in *Bestiary;* from the verb. The development of meaning includes a place for walking (about 1386), specifically, a path (1530); way of living (1752, in Fielding); and the sense in American English of a going to first base after four balls are thrown by the pitcher (1934).
—walkie-talkie *n.* small portable receiving and transmitting radio set. 1939, American English, formed from *walk,* v. and *talk,* v. + *-ie.* **—walking stick** (1580) **—walkout** *n.* (1888, a strike, American English; 1927, act of leaving, especially in protest). **—walkover** *n.* easy victory (1838). **—walk-up** *n.* building with several stories and no elevator (1925). **—walkway** *n.* (1792, American English)

wall *n.* Probably about 1175 *walle,* developed from Old English *weall* rampart, wall of a city or building (about 725, in *Beowulf*). Old English *weall* was an early borrowing from Latin *vallum* wall, rampart, row or line of stakes, apparently a collective form of *vallus* stake, and cognate with Old Frisian, Old Saxon, Middle Low German, and Middle Dutch *wal,* Gothic *walus* stake, and Old Icelandic *vǫlr* round staff. Latin *vallus* is from earlier **valnos,* from Indo-European **welnós,* root **wel-/wol-* to turn (Pok.1142). —**v.** to enclose, divide, protect, or fill with a wall. About 1250 *wallen,* in *Genesis and Exodus;* from the noun. **—wallflower** *n.* 1578, flowering plant found growing on walls, cliffs, etc.; later, person who sits by the wall at a dance (1820). **—wallpaper** *n.* (1827); *v.* (1934)

wallaby (wol′əbē) *n.* kind of small kangaroo. 1826, borrowed from Australian *wolabā.*

wallaroo (wol′ərü′) *n.* kind of large kangaroo. 1826, borrowed from Australian *wolarū.*

wallet *n.* About 1385-95 *walet* bag, knapsack, in Chaucer's *Canterbury Tales;* of uncertain origin. The word's form and original pronunciation (walet′) suggest an Anglo-French or Old French source. The meaning of a flat case for carrying paper money is first recorded in 1834 in American English.

walleyed (wôl′id′) *adj.* having eyes that show much white and little color. Probably before 1400 *wawileghed,* borrowed from a Scandinavian source (compare Old Icelandic *vagl-eygr* having speckled eyes, from *vagl* speck in the eye, beam + *eygr* eyed, from *auga* EYE). Old Icelandic *vagl* is related to *vega* to move, carry, lift; see WEIGH. The meaning of having one or both eyes turned away from the nose and so showing much white of the eye is first recorded perhaps in Shakespeare's *Titus Andronicus* (1588).

wallop *v.* 1375 *wallopen* to gallop, in Barbour's *The Bruce;* of uncertain origin; possibly borrowed from Old French *galoper* to gallop (related to *galop* a gallop), but more likely originally borrowed from Old North French **waloper* (compare Flemish and Middle High German *walop,* n. and Middle High German *walopiren,* v.), probably from Frankish **walalaupan, walahlaupan* to run well (compare Old High German *wela* WELL[1] and Old Low Franconian *loupon,* Old Saxon *hlōpan* to run, LEAP). Doublet of GALLOP, which displaced *wallop* in the sense of to go at the fastest gait of a horse, in the 1500's.

The meaning of beat soundly, thrash, is first recorded in 1825, and may be partly of imitative origin, probably influenced to some degree by the earlier sense of boil rapidly with noisy bubbling motion (1579).
—n. Before 1375 *wallop* horse's gallop; probably borrowed from Old North French *walop,* from **waloper* to gallop. The meaning of a very hard blow is first recorded in 1823.

wallow *v.* Probably before 1200 *walewen* roll about, flounder, in *Trinity Homilies;* developed from Old English *wealwian, walwian* to roll, before 899, in Alfred's translation of Boethius' *De Consolatione Philosophiae;* see VOLUME. **—n.** act of wallowing. Before 1591, from the verb.

walnut *n.* 1358-59 *walnotte;* developed from Old English (about 1050) *walhnutu* nut of the walnut tree; literally, foreign nut (*walh, wealh* foreign, WELSH in the sense of referring to the Celts or non-Germanic neighbors of the Continental Germanic people + *hnutu* NUT); so called because this nut was introduced into the Germanic region from Gaul and Italy, and further, according to the OED, distinguishing it from the native hazel nut.

Corresponding forms are found in most Germanic languages (e.g. Middle Dutch *walnote,* modern Dutch *walnoot,* Middle Low German *wallnot,* modern German *Walnuss,* Old Icelandic *valhnot,* Norwegian *valnøtt*).

walrus *n.* 1728, borrowed from Dutch *walrus, walros,* probably an alteration (by folk etymology with influence of Dutch *walvis* whale, and *ros* horse) of a word from a Scandinavian source (compare Old Icelandic *rosmhvalr* walrus, *hrosshvalr* a kind of whale, *rostungr* walrus). The Old Icelandic form *hrosshvalr* means literally horse whale, which indicates that the folk-etymological process found in Dutch was already at work in Old Icelandic.

waltz *n.* ballroom dance in triple rhythm. 1781, borrowed from German *Walzer,* from *walzen* to roll, dance, from Old High German *walzan* to turn, roll; see WELTER. **—v.** dance a waltz. About 1794, from the noun. The sense of move nimbly or quickly, especially through some difficult situation, is first recorded in Carlyle's writings in 1862.

wampum (wom′pəm) *n.* beads formerly used by American Indians as money and ornament. 1636, in John Winthrop's *The History of New England,* American English, shortened form of *wampumpeag* (1627); borrowed from Algonquian (probably Narraganset) *wanpanpiak* string of white shell beads.

wan *adj.* pale, pallid. Probably about 1200 *won;* before 1325 *wane;* developed from Old English *wann* dark, lacking luster, leaden, pale gray (about 725, in *Beowulf*); of uncertain origin.

wand *n.* Probably about 1200 *wand* slender stick or rod, in *The Ormulum;* borrowed from a Scandinavian source (compare Old Icelandic *vǫndr* rod, switch, Danish and Norwegian *vånd,* all cognate with Gothic *wandus* rod, probably from the same root as Old English *windan* to turn, twist, WIND[2]). The meaning of a slender stick used by a fairy or magician is first recorded probably before 1400.

wander *v.* Before 1175 *wandren;* developed from Old English *wandrian* move about aimlessly, wander (before 899, in Alfred's translation of Boethius' *De Consolatione Philosophiae*); cognate with Old Frisian *wondria* to wander, Middle Low German and Middle Dutch *wanderen,* and Middle High German and modern German *wandern;* related to Old English *windan* to turn, twist, WIND², and to forms in *l,* such as Middle Dutch *wandelen* to wander about, change (modern Dutch, to walk), Old Saxon *wandlon* to change, Old High German *wantalōn.*

The sense of stray in reference to the mind is first recorded about 1400, and in reference to purpose is found in Old English before 899.

—wanderlust *n.* desire to travel. 1902, borrowed from German *Wanderlust* call of the outdoors, desire to travel (*wandern* to travel, WANDER + *Lust* desire, longing, LUST). The pronunciation and meaning have been influenced by the English words *wander* and *lust.*

wane *v.* Before 1122 *wanien,* in *Peterborough Chronicle;* found in Old English *wanian* make or become smaller gradually, to lessen (about 725, in *Beowulf*); cognate with Old Frisian *wania* lessen, Old Saxon *wanon,* Middle Dutch *waenen, wanen,* Old High German *wanōn,* and Old Icelandic *vana* make less, *vanask* become less. Old English *wanian* is from Proto-Germanic **wanōjanan.* These verbs are associated with a Germanic adjective **wanaz* represented by Old English, Old Frisian and Old High German *wan* wanting, deficient, Old Icelandic *vanr,* and Gothic *wans,* from the Indo-European base **eu-, ewə-,* **wā-/wə-/ū-* be lacking; empty (Pok.345), as also found in Latin *vānus* idle, empty, Greek *eûnis* bereft, lacking, Armenian *unain* empty, and Sanskrit *ūná-s* wanting, deficient. **—n.** Probably about 1300 *wane* lack, shortage; later, a waning (before 1325); in part developed from the Old English noun *wana* shortage (before 899), related to *wan* deficient, and in part from the verb *wanen* to wane.

wangle *v. Informal.* manage to get by schemes, tricks, persuasion, or the like. 1888, originally, printer's slang in the sense of fake by manipulation; perhaps alteration of WAGGLE. **—n.** act of wangling. 1915, from the verb.

want *v.* Probably about 1200 *wanten* be lacking, be without, need, in *The Ormulum;* borrowed from a Scandinavian source (compare Old Icelandic *vanta* to lack, want, related to *vanr* wanting, deficient; see WANE). The meaning of desire or wish for is first recorded in English in 1706. **—n.** Probably about 1200, lack, deficiency; from the verb in Middle English and probably also from, or at least influenced by, Old Icelandic *vant* lack, deficiency, neuter of *vanr* wanting, lacking; see WANE. The meaning of thing desired (as in *a man of few wants*) is first recorded in 1578. **—want ad** *Informal.* (1897) **—wanting** *adj.* missing, lacking, not found. Before 1325 *wantand,* formed from Middle English *wanten* to want + *-and* -ing².

wanton *adj.* Before 1325 *wantun* undisciplined, unruly, in *Cursor Mundi;* later *wantowen* unchaste, lascivious, lewd (before 1376, in *Piers Plowman*); formed from Middle English *wan-* not, lacking (from Old English *wan* wanting; see WANE) + *towen* trained, disciplined, (from Old English *togen,* past participle of *tēon* to train, discipline, draw, related to *togian* to draw, pull, TOW¹). The meaning of reckless of justice and humanity, merciless, is first recorded in 1513. **—n.** wanton person. 1526, spoiled or pampered person; from the adjective. The meaning of lascivious or lewd person is first found in 1540, in Palsgrave's translation of *Comedy of Acolastus.* **—v.** act in a wanton manner. 1582, to gambol, frolic, in Stanyhurst's translation of Vergil's *Aeneid;* from the adjective.

war *n.* Before 1121 *wyrre;* later *uuerre* (1140), and *werre* (probably about 1175); borrowed from Old North French *werre* war, from Frankish **werra* (compare Old High German *werra* confusion, contention, strife, from Proto-Germanic **wersō,* and related to *werran* to bring into confusion, modern German *wirren* confuse, bewilder). A cognate of the Old High German words is found in Old Saxon *werran* bring into confusion or discord, and (though Pokorny denies that the Germanic words are cognate) outside Germanic possibly in Latin *verrere,* earlier *vorrere* to trail, drag, sweep, Old Slavic *vrěšti* to thrash, and Hittite *warsiya-* thresh, pluck, wipe off, from Indo-European **wers-/wors-/wr̥s-* (Pok.1169).

No Germanic nation in earliest historic times had in living use any word properly meaning "war," though several words with that meaning are found in poetry and some proverbial phrases. As a result, the Romance-speaking peoples (avoiding the Latin *bellum,* meaning war, probably because of its formal coincidence with *bello-* beautiful) found no nearer equivalent in Germanic than **werra,* meaning confusion or discord; this produced Old French and modern French *guerre,* Provençal *guerra, gerra,* and Spanish, Portuguese, and Italian *guerra.* In Old English the usual translation of Latin *bellum* was *gewin* struggle, strife which (like the native form *orlege* hostility, strife, war; cognate with Old Saxon *orlegas,* Old Frisian *orloch,* Old High German *orloge*), did not survive into modern times. Speakers of the Continental Germanic languages later developed separate words for "war," some based on much older terms: German *Krieg* (borrowed into Swedish and Danish as *krig*), Dutch *oorlog,* Icelandic *ófridhur,* literally, un-peace.

—v. make war. Before 1160 *uuerrieu,* from *uuerre, werre* war.

—warfare *n.* 1456, a going to war; formed from English *war* + *fare*¹, n. **—warhead** *n.* part of a missile, torpedo, etc., containing an explosive charge (1898). **—war horse** 1653, a charger; later, person who has taken part in many battles, struggles, etc., veteran (1837, in American English). **—warlike** *adj.* (about 1420) **—warmonger** *n.* (1590, in Spenser's *Faerie Queene*) **—warpath** *n.* (1775, American English) **—warplane** *n.* (1911) **—warship** *n.* (1533) **—wartime** *n.* (before 1387, in Trevisa's translation of Higden's *Polychronicon*)

warble *v.* sing with trills, quavers, etc. Probably about 1390 *werbelen* to resound, sound, in *Sir Gawain and the Green Knight;* borrowed from Old North French *werbler* to sing with trills and quavers, from Frankish **werƀilōn* (compare Middle Dutch *wervelen* to turn, whirl, Middle High German *wirbel* whirl, spinning top, and Old High German *wirbil* whirlwind; see WHIRL). The meaning of sing with trills, quavers, or melodious turns, is first recorded in English in Palsgrave's *Lesclarcissement* (1530). **—n.** a warbling. About 1385 *werble,* in Usk's *The Testament of Love;* borrowed from Old North French *werble,* related to *werbler* to sing with trills and quavers.

ward *n.* Probably before 1200 *warde* act of guarding,

guardianship, in Layamon's *Chronicle of Britain;* developed from Old English *weard* a guarding, from Proto-Germanic **warđō,* Indo-European **wordhā,* or from Proto-Germanic **warđṓ,* Indo-European **wortā́.* Old English *weard* is cognate with Old High German *warta* a guarding, Middle High German *warte* watch, observation (modern German *Warte* watchtower), Middle Low German *warde,* related to Gothic *wars* alert, WARY.

The meaning of a person under the control of a guardian is first recorded in Middle English in 1433, in *Rolls of Parliament.* The meaning of an administrative division or district (originating in the sense of a place for guarding) is first recorded about 1378, though the usage occurs in Latin contexts as early as about 1130. The meaning of division of a hospital is first found in Smollett's *Gil Blas* (1749). Some of the senses in English were influenced by Old North French *warde* guard, from *warder* to guard; see WARDEN.

—v. Probably before 1200 *warden* to guard, defend, in *Ancrene Riwle;* developed from Old English *weardian* (before 1000); cognate with Frisian *wardia* to guard, watch, Old Saxon *wardōn,* Old High German *wartēn* (modern German *warten* look after), and Old Icelandic *vardha,* all derived from the same Germanic root as Old English *weard* a guarding, guard. Doublet of GUARD.

The sense of parry, turn aside in reference to a blow or weapon, is first recorded in Middle English, probably before 1387. Some of the senses of the English verb were influenced by Old North French *warder* to guard; see WARDEN.

-ward a suffix meaning in the direction of, toward, forming adjectives and adverbs, as in *backward = toward the back, homeward = toward home, northward = in the direction of north.* Developed from Old English *-weard,* from Proto-Germanic **-warđ,* variant of **werth-;* cognate with Old High German *-wart,* Old Icelandic *-verdhr,* and related to Old English *weorthan* to become; see VERTEX; also compare -WARDS.

warden *n.* Probably before 1200 *wardein* guardian, custodian, in *Ancrene Riwle;* later, person in charge of a prison (probably about 1300); borrowed from Old North French *wardein,* from Frankish **warding-* (compare early Old French *guardenc*), from **wardōn* to watch, guard (compare Old High German *wartēn* to watch, guard, WARD). Doublet of GUARDIAN. The peculiarly British *Warden of the Cinque Ports* (now an honorary title) is first recorded in 1435, in *Rolls of Parliament,* probably derived from the sense of the governor of a town or district (1297).

warder *n.* guard or watchman. Probably before 1400, borrowed from Anglo-French *wardere* and *wardour* guardian, from Old North French *warder* to guard; see WARDEN; for suffix see -ER[1].

wardrobe *n.* About 1325, a private chamber, especially one for sleeping, in *Cursor Mundi;* later, room in which wearing apparel is kept (1387, in Usk's *Testament of Love*), and a person's stock of clothes (before 1400); borrowed from Old North French *warderobe,* variant of Old French *garderobe* place where garments are kept; also, a privy (*warder* to keep + *robe* garment); also found in Middle English *garderobe* (1333-34, *garder* to keep + *robe* garment). The meaning of a piece of furniture for holding clothes is first recorded in Hepplewhite's *Cabinet Maker* (1794).

-wards a suffix meaning in the direction of, toward, forming adverbs, as in *backwards = in the direction of* or *toward the back.* Old English *-weardes,* genitive singular case form with *-es* (neuter) of adjectives in *-weard;* corresponding to Dutch *-waarts,* German *-wärts,* and Gothic *-waírths;* see -WARD and -S[3].

ware *n.* Usually, **wares.** manufactured thing. Probably about 1175, developed from Old English *waru* (about 1000, in Ælfric's *Homilies*), probably with an original meaning of object of care, and hence related to *wær* aware, cautious, WARY. Old English *waru* is cognate with Old Frisian *were* manufactured thing, Middle Dutch *were, ware* (modern Dutch *waar*), Middle High German *ware* (modern German *Ware*), and Old Icelandic *vara* (Swedish *vara,* Norwegian and Danish *vare*), from Proto-Germanic **warō,* Indo-European **worā́* (Pok.1164). **—warehouse** *n.* (1349)

warlock *n.* wizard, male witch. Before 1400 *warlag, warlau, warlo;* developed from Old English *wærloga* (before 900) demon, traitor, scoundrel, damned soul, monster; originally, oathbreaker (*wær* covenant, related to *wǣr* true; VERY + *-loga,* agent noun related to *lēogan* to speak falsely, LIE[1]; see also WEDLOCK). The modern spelling *warlock* is Scottish, first recorded in 1685 (also Scottish *warlok,* before 1585).

warm *adj.* Probably before 1200 *warme* having or giving out heat, in *Ancrene Riwle;* developed from Old English *wearm* (before 899, in Alfred's translation of Boethius' *De Consolatione Philosophiae*); cognate with Old Frisian, Middle Low German, Middle Dutch, modern Dutch, Old High German, and modern German *warm* warm, and Old Icelandic *varmr* (Danish, Swedish, and Norwegian *varm*), from Proto-Germanic **warmaz,* earlier **ȝwarmaz.* The Germanic word is now almost universally derived from Indo-European **gwher-,* found in Sanskrit *gharmá-s* heat (from Indo-European **gwhormós*), Avestan *garəmō* hot, Greek *thermós* hot, *thérmē* heat, Latin *formus* warm, Old Prussian *gorme* heat, Lithuanian *gãras* steam, Old Slavic *gorěti* to burn, Armenian *ǰerm* warm, and Old Irish *fogeir* warms, heats (Pok.493, 1166). **—v.** Probably before 1200 *warmen* make or become warm, in Layamon's *Chronicle of Britain;* developed partly from Old English *wyrman* make warm, and partly from Old English *wearmian* become warm. The Old English verbs are cognate with Old Saxon *wermian* to warm, Middle Low German, Middle Dutch, and modern Dutch *warmen,* Old High German *warmen, wermen* (modern German *wärmen*), Old Icelandic *verma,* and Gothic *warmjan,* all derived from the Germanic source of Old English *wearm* warm, adj. The figurative meaning of inspire affection (as in *his heart warmed towards the dog,* or *warm the heart*) is first recorded before 1400, and the extended sense of become eager, enthusiastic (as in *to warm* or *warm to a subject*) in about 1580. **—warm-blooded** *adj.* (1793) **—warm front** (1921) **—warm-hearted** *adj.* (1500-20, in Dunbar's *Poems*) **—warmth** *n.* About 1175 *wermthe,* in *Lambeth Homilies;* formed from Old English *wearm* warm + the suffix *-thu-* -TH[1]. The cognates, Middle Low German *warmede, warmte,* Middle Dutch *warmte,* and Middle High German *wermede,* suggest a Proto-Germanic **warmíthō.* **—warm-up** *n.* 1878, act of getting warm; later, act of getting ready for something (1915).

warn *v.* Probably before 1200 *warnen,* in Layamon's *Chronicle of Britain;* developed from Old English *warnian* to warn, take heed (before 1000, in Ælfric's *Homilies*), related to *wær* aware, cautious, WARY. Old

English *warnian* (from Proto-Germanic **warnōjanan*) is cognate with Middle Low German *warnen* to warn, inform, and Old High German *warnōn* (modern German *warnen*). **—warning** *n.* Probably before 1200, in *Ancrene Riwle;* developed from Old English *warnung, wearning* (before 800); formed from *warnian* to warn + *-ung* -ing[1].

warp *v.* twist out of shape. Probably about 1200 *warpen* to throw, cast; developed from Old English *weorpan* to throw, hit with a missile (about 725, in *Beowulf*); cognate with Old Frisian *werpa* to throw, Old Saxon *werpan,* Middle Low German, Middle Dutch, and modern Dutch *werpen,* Old High German *werpan* (modern German *werfen*), Old Icelandic *verpa,* and Gothic *waírpan,* from Proto-Germanic **werpanan;* possibly also cognate with Latin *verber* a whip, lash, rod, and Lithuanian *vir̃bas* twig, branch, from Indo-European **werb-* twist, bend (Pok.1153).

The meaning of twist out of shape is first recorded in Middle English probably before 1400. The figurative sense of distort (the mind, principles, etc.) is found in Ben Jonson's *Cynthia's Revels* (1599).

—n. 1346, threads running lengthwise in a fabric; developed from Old English *wearp* (about 725); cognate with Middle Low German *warp* warp, Old High German *warf,* and Old Icelandic *varp* cast of a net, related to *verpa* to throw. The meaning of a twist or bending, especially in wood, is first recorded in 1679, but the figurative sense of the underlying fabric or structure of something is found earlier in 1575.

warrant *n.* that which gives a right, authority. Probably about 1200 *warant* protector, protection, safeguard; later, authorization, sanction, authority (before 1325); borrowed from Old North French *warant,* in Old French *guarant, garant,* from Frankish **wārand* (compare Middle Low German *warend, warent* guarantee, warranty, Old High German *wēren* to authorize, warrant, Old Frisian *wēria* to confirm, prove, Old High German *gawarjān* to verify, Gothic *-wērjan* to ascertain, and Old High German *wār* true; see VERY). **—v.** authorize. 1275, *warantien,* borrowed from Old North French *warantir,* from *warant* authorization, warrant. The meaning of guarantee (as in *he warranted the quality of the produce*) is first recorded in 1387. **—warrant officer** officer in the armed forces who has received a certificate of appointment, but not a commission (1693).

warranty *n.* legal warrant. Before 1338 *warantie* covenant annexed to a deed, in Mannyng's *Chronicle of England;* borrowed from Anglo-French and Old North French *warantie,* from *warant* WARRANT; for suffix see -Y[3]. The meaning of a guarantee, assurance, is first recorded in English in 1555. Doublet of GUARANTY.

warren *n.* piece of ground filled with burrows, where rabbits live. About 1378 *wareine* a franchise or piece of land enclosed for breeding beasts and fowls or warren (rabbits, hares, partridge, pheasant, etc.), in *Piers Plowman;* later, such a piece of land used for breeding rabbits (about 1400); borrowed from Anglo-French and Old North French *warenne,* central Old French *garenna* game park, also found in Anglo-Latin and Medieval Latin *warenna* preserve for animals, and in Medieval Latin *varenna* of charters. This brings up the fundamental problem of whether the development of *warren* is based on the enclosure and its parts or the charter or franchise to enclose. But on the basis of existing forms it is possible that all of these forms are traceable to a Gaulish **warenna* enclosed area, and that this was built on **warros* post. It is also possible that the Old French forms represent a present participle of Old French *warir, warer* defend, keep, from some Germanic source with the root **war-* to protect, guard (compare Old High German *warjan, werjan* protect; also in Old English *warian* take care, guard, as found in modern English BEWARE). Another point of view, reflecting the charter or franchise as the central idea, traces development through a probably Frankish **wārjan, wērjan* (compare Old High German *wēren* to authorize, warrant). The sense of warrant and the guaranteeing of a charter or franchise allowing enclosure of land is found in the parallel development of *warrant* and *warranty,* as also shown at GUARANTY.

The suffix is of uncertain formation; it may represent the present participle ending of the verb either in Old French or perhaps in Germanic.

warrior *n.* Probably before 1300 *werreyoure,* in *Kyng Alisaunder;* borrowed from Old North French *werreieor* a warrior, one who wages war, from *werreier* wage war, cognate with Italian *guerreggiare* and Spanish *guerrear,* from Vulgar Latin **werrizāre,* from Frankish **werra* WAR; for suffix see -OR[2].

wart *n.* small, hard lump on the skin. Before 1325 *wert,* in *Cursor Mundi;* developed from Old English *wearte* (before 800); cognate with Old Frisian *warte* wart, Old Saxon *warta,* Middle Dutch *warte, wratte* (modern Dutch *wrat*), Old High German *warza* (modern German *Warze*), and Old Icelandic *varta* (Swedish *vårta,* Norwegian and Danish *vorte*), from Proto-Germanic **wartō,* Indo-European **wordā,* root **werd-* (Pok. 1151). The related Indo-European root **wers-/wr̥s-* is found in Latin *verrūca* growth on the skin, wart (from earlier **wersūcā* elevation), Lithuanian *viršùs* summit, Old Slavic *vrĭchŭ,* and Sanskrit *várṣman-* height, point, *várṣiṣṭha-s* the highest. **—wart hog** (1840) **—warty** *adj.* 1483, having warts; formed from Middle English *wart* + *-y*[1].

wary *adj.* 1552, in Huloet's *Abecedarium Anglico Latinum;* formed from Middle English (1140) *war, ware* alert, wise, prudent + *-y*[1]. Middle English *war, ware* developed from Old English (917) *wær* prudent, aware, alert, wary (compare modern English AWARE, from Old English *gewær,* and BEWARE); cognate with Old Saxon *giwar* aware, Middle Dutch *ghewāre,* Old High German *giwar* (modern German *gewahr*), Old High German *biwarōn* to preserve, protect (modern German *wahren, bewahren*), Old Icelandic *varr* aware, wary (Danish and Norwegian *var*), and Gothic *wars,* from Proto-Germanic **waraz.* Possible cognates outside Germanic are found in Latin *verērī* to view with fear or awe, Greek *horân* to see, view, *ṓrā* care, concern (earlier **wṓrā*), Latvian *vērt* to look, notice, and Tocharian A *wär-,* Tocharian B *wärsk-* to smell, from Indo-European **wer-/wor-/wōr-* watch, pay heed to (Pok.1164).

was *v.* form of the verb *be.* Old English (about 950) *wæs* first and third person singular past indicative of *wesan* to be.

In Old English *wesan* to remain (with the stem *wes-*) was a distinct verb, but came to supply the past tense to the verb *am,* which had only a present tense, and as the needs of usage developed, all other parts of that verb were supplied by *wes-,* so that the two verbs supplemented each other in Old English and constituted the verb **es-/wes-* (*am-was*) showing "existence." By the 1200's parts of *am-was* became obsolete, and corresponding parts of *be* took the place of the infinitive, participle, imperative, etc. See BE and AM.

Old English *wesan* is cognate with Old Frisian *wesa* to be (past indicative *was*), Old Saxon *wesan* (past indicative *was*), Middle Dutch *wesen* (modern Dutch *wezen,* past indicative *was*), Old High German *wesan* (past indicative *was*), modern German *gewesen* has been (past indicative *war*), Old Icelandic *vera, vesa* to be (past indicative *var*), and Gothic *wisan* to be, dwell, remain (past indicative *was*), from Proto-Germanic **wesanan.* These words derive ultimately from the Indo-European root **wes-/wos-* to stay or dwell (Pok.1170), and are cognate with Sanskrit *vásati* (he) dwells, stays, Tocharian A *wast,* Tocharian B *ost* house. See BE.

wash *v.* Probably before 1200 *waschen,* in *Ancrene Riwle;* developed from Old English (900) *wascan, wæscan;* cognate with Old Saxon and Old Low Franconian *wascan* to wash, Middle Dutch *wasscen* (modern Dutch *wassen*), Old High German *waskan* (modern German *waschen*), and Old Icelandic *vaska* (Swedish *vaska,* Danish and Norwegian *vaske*), from Proto-Germanic **wat-sk-anan,* from the Germanic stem **wat-* of WATER. Except for the sense of cleaning clothes, this verb was little used in Old English; the principal verb for washing the body, dishes, etc., was *thwēan.* **—n.** a washing or being washed. 1440 *wasche* land alternately covered and exposed by the sea, in *Promptorium Parvulorum;* earlier, act or process of washing (as in *a good wash,* about 1050); from the verb. The sense of a surge left by a passing ship is first recorded in American English in 1883, and that of a dry stream bed, in 1894, though any place or erosion is known from 1835. **—washable** *adj.* 1821, formed from English *wash* + *-able.* **—washbasin** *n.* (1812) **—wash basket** (1881) **—washboard** *n.* 1742, board on the side of a boat; later, board with ridges for washing clothes, American English (1845). **—washbowl** *n.* Before 1529, washtub; later, basin for washing one's face and hands, American English (1816). **—washcloth** *n.* (1915, American English) **—washed-out** *adj.* (1796) **—washer** *n.* 1450-1530, person who washes; 1808, machine that washes, formed from English *wash,* v. + *-er*[1]. The development of the earlier meaning of a flat ring used for sealing joints (1346) has not been accounted for. **—washerwoman** *n.* (1632) **—washing machine** (about 1754) **—wash-out** *n.* 1873, break in a road or railway caused by flood or erosion, American English; later, failure (1902). **—washroom** *n.* 1806, room for washing clothes, American English; later, lavatory, American English (1854). **—washstand** *n.* (1789) **—washtub** *n.* (1602)

wasp *n.* 1373, developed from Old English (about 700) *wæfs, wæps, wæsp.* The forms with *p* (as contrasted with those in *fs*) are probably the result of influence by Latin *vespa,* in English and other Germanic cognates, such as Old Saxon *waspa* wasp, Middle Low German and Middle Dutch *wespe* (modern Dutch *wesp*), contrasted with Old High German *wafsa, wefsa* (modern German *Wespe*), Old Danish *hwæfse* (modern Danish *hveps*), Norwegian *veps, kvefs,* dialectal Swedish *väfs.* Cognates outside Germanic are found in Latin *vespa,* earlier **vospā* (from pre-Latin **wopsā*), Lithuanian *vapsà* wasp, and Avestan *vawžaka-* scorpion. The word is believed to be ultimately derived from Indo-European **webh-,* the source of Old English *webb* WEB and *wefan* to WEAVE. **—waspish** *adj.* 1566, (figurative) irascible, spiteful; formed from English *wasp* + *-ish*[1].

Wasp or **WASP** *n.* white Anglo-Saxon Protestant. 1960, American English, originally an acronym used especially in statistical and sociological studies of American ethnic groups; formed from the initials of *W(hite), A(nglo)-S(axon), P(rotestant).* **—Waspish** or **WASPish** *adj.* 1965, American English; formed from *Wasp* or *WASP* + *-ish*[1]. **—Waspy** or **WASPy** *adj.* 1968, American English; formed from *Wasp* or *WASP* + *-y*[1].

wassail (wos′əl *or* wosāl′) *n.* About 1140 *wes heil;* later *wæshail* salutation used when drinking to someone's health, drinking party, revelry (probably before 1200, in Layamon's *Chronicle of Britain*); borrowed from a Scandinavian source (compare the Old Icelandic phrase *ves heill* be healthy, from *ves,* imperative of *vera* to be; see WAS in which the original form *wes* is the imperative form of *wesan* to be + *heill* healthy, WHOLE). A similar formation appears in Old English *wes hāl,* but according to the OED, does not appear as a salutation in drinking, which use Bradley writing in the OED says, "arose among the Danish-speaking inhabitants of England and became more or less common among the native population." The meaning of a revelry, carousal, is first recorded in Shakespeare's *Hamlet* (1602). **—v.** take part in a wassail. About 1300 *wesseylen,* in *Havelok the Dane;* from the noun.

waste *v.* Probably before 1200 *wasten* devastate, ravage, ruin, in Layamon's *Chronicle of Britain* (replacement of earlier Middle English *westen*); borrowed from Anglo-French and Old North French *waster* to spoil, ruin, alteration of Latin *vāstāre* lay waste, from *vastus* empty, desolate, waste. The Old North French *waster* was altered in its descent from Latin *vāstāre* by influence of Frankish **wōstjan* (compare Old High German *wuostan* lay waste). Latin *vāstus* is cognate with Old Irish *fās* empty, *fāsach* wilderness, desert, Old English *wēste* empty, desolate, Old Saxon *wōsti,* Middle Dutch and modern Dutch *woest,* and Old High German *wuosti* (modern German *wüst*). Compare VAST. The sense of spend or consume uselessly, squander, is first recorded in Middle English in 1340, in *Ayenbite of Inwyt.* The earlier Middle English *westen* to lay waste, also found in Layamon's *Chronicle of Britain* (probably before 1200); developed from Old English (before 899) *wēstan,* from the adjective *wēste,* and is cognate with Old Saxon *wōstian,* and Old High German *wuostan.*

—n. Probably before 1200, desert, wilderness; borrowed from Old North French *wast,* partly from Latin *vāstum* (from neuter of *vāstus* empty), and partly from *waster* to waste. The sense of useless spending or consumption, squandering, is first recorded in Middle English about 1300.

Middle English *waste,* n. is a replacement of earlier *weste;* from Old English *wēsten, wœsten* a desert, wilderness, from the adjective; cognate with Old Saxon *wōstun,* and Old High German *wuostī* a waste.

—adj. About 1290, uncultivated, uninhabited, barren; borrowed from Old North French *wast,* from Latin *vāstus* empty, desolate. Middle English *waste,* adj. replaced earlier *west* (about 1200); developed from Old English *wēste, wœste* (about 725, in *Beowulf*), from the stem **wōst-,* related to Latin *vāstus* empty, desolate; see WASTE, v.; cognate with Old Frisian *wōste* waste, desolate, Old Saxon *wōsti,* and Old High German *wōsti, wuosti.*

—**wastage** *n.* waste, amount wasted. 1756, formed from English *waste,* v. + *-age.* —**wastebasket** *n.* (1850) —**wasteful** *adj.* Before 1325, formed from Middle English *waste* + *-ful.* —**wasteland** *n.* (1887) —**wastepaper** *n.* (1585) —**waster** *n.* 1352, spendthrift, idler; borrowed from Anglo-French *wastere, wastour,* especially in reference to a class of thieves, from *waster,* v., and also in Middle English, formed from *waste,* v. + *-er*[1]. —**wastrel** *n.* 1589-90, tract of wasteland; formed from English *waste,* v. + *-rel,* as in *mongrel, scoundrel,* etc. The meaning of something useless or imperfect is first recorded in 1790, and the sense of spendthrift, idler, is first recorded in 1847.

watch *v.* About 1200 *wacchen,* in *Vices and Virtues;* developed from Old English *wæccan* keep watch, be awake (implied in *watching,* about 725, in *Beowulf*); related to *wacian* become awake, WAKE[1]. The spelling with *t* began to appear in the mid-1400's. —**n.** Probably before 1200 *wecche,* in *Trinity Homilies;* developed from Old English (971) *wæcce* a watching, vigil, from *wæccan* to watch. The meaning of a small timepiece is first recorded in Shakespeare's *Love's Labour's Lost* (1588); a related sense of an alarm attached to a clock to wake up sleepers, alarm clock, is recorded in Middle English, in *Promptorium Parvulorum* (1440). —**watchdog** *n.* (1610, in Shakespeare's *The Tempest*) —**watchful** *adj.* 1548, formed from English *watch,* n. + *-ful.* —**watchmaker** *n.* (1630) —**watchman** *n.* (about 1400) —**watchtower** *n.* (1544) —**watchword** *n.* About 1400, password; later, motto, slogan (1738).

water *n.* Old English *wæter* (before 899, in Alfred's translation of St. Gregory's *Pastoral Care*), from Proto-Germanic **watar;* cognate with Old Frisian *weter* water, Old Saxon *watar,* Middle Dutch and modern Dutch *water,* Old High German *wazzar* (modern German *Wasser*), Old Icelandic *vatn* (Norwegian *vatn,* Swedish *vatten,* Danish *vand*), and Gothic *watō* (dative plural *watnam*) water. These forms derive from the Indo-European root **wed-, *wod-, *ud-* (Pok.78), found with various suffixes in Old Irish *uisce* water (from pre-Celtic **udeskio-*), Albanian *ujë,* Umbrian *utur,* Greek *hýdōr,* Latin *unda* wave, Lithuanian *vanduõ* water, Old Slavic *voda* and Russian *vodá* water, Sanskrit *udaká-m* wave, water, and Hittite *wātar* water. Compare WET.

This word is an outstanding example of an r/n stem in Indo-European. The forms in *-r-* and the forms in *-n-* were found in the same paradigm, with a neuter noun having *r* in the nominative or accusative singular and *n* in the other cases. This is shown clearly by the Hittite nominative *wātar,* genitive *wetenas,* dative and locative *weteni,* ablative *wetenaz,* instrumental *wetenit,* and by the Umbrian nominative *utur* water, ablative *une.* In Germanic, two separate nouns developed from this stem, one with *r* (Old English *wæter,* etc.) and one with *n* (Old Icelandic *vatn,* etc.)

—**v.** Old English *wæterian* supply water to (before 899, in Alfred's translation of St. Gregory's *Pastoral Care*); from *wæter,* n.

—**waterbed** *n.* (1853) —**water buffalo** (1889) —**water closet** (1755) —**watercolor** *n.* (1596, in Shakespeare's *1 Henry IV*) —**water cooler** (1846) —**watercress** *n.* (probably before 1300, in *Kyng Alisaunder*) —**waterfall** *n.* Before 1500; found in Old English *waetergefeal* (998). —**waterfowl** *n.* (before 1325, in *Cursor Mundi*) —**waterfront** *n.* (1766, American English) —**waterline** *n.* (before 1625) —**water-logged** *adj.* (1769-76) —**watermark** *n.* 1678, line showing how far water has risen; later, faint distinguishing mark on paper (1708). —**watermelon** *n.* (1615) —**water moccasin** (1821, American English) —**water pistol** (1905) —**waterproof** *adj.* (1836); *v.* (1843) —**water ski** (1931) —**water-ski** *v.* (1953) —**waterspout** *n.* Before 1393, pipe for water, in Gower's *Confessio Amantis;* later, spinning column of water (1738). —**water table** 1428, sloping ledge for shedding rainfall; later, level below which the ground is saturated (1879). —**watertight** *adj.* (1387) —**waterway** *n.* 1440, channel for water, in *Promptorium Parvulorum;* 1797, route for ships; found in Old English *wæterweg.* —**water wheel** (1408) —**waterworks** *n.* (1443) —**watery** *adj.* Old English *wæterig* (about 1000, in Ælfric's *Homilies*) full of water, formed from *wæter* water + *-ig -y*[1].

watt *n.* unit of electric power. 1882, in allusion to James *Watt,* 1736-1819, Scottish engineer and inventor, a pioneer in the development of the steam engine. —**wattage** *n.* electric power expressed in watts. 1903, formed from English *watt* + *-age.* —**watt-hour** *n.* work done by one watt in one hour (1888).

wattle *n.* sticks interwoven with twigs or branches. 1382 *wattel,* developed from Old English *watol* hurdle; in plural, twigs, thatching, tiles (before 899, in Alfred's translation of Bede's *Ecclesiastical History*); related to *wætla* and *wethel* bandage, and cognate with Old High German *wadal* bandage, and with Gothic *gawidan* to bind, join, Old Irish *fedan* harness, *fedil* yoke, and Sanskrit *vivadhá-s* shoulder-yoke, from Indo-European **wedh-/wodh-* fasten (Pok.1116). The meaning of fleshy appendage below the head or neck of certain birds is first recorded in English in 1513, but its connection with the primary sense of something intertwined is obscure, suggesting the possibility that *wattle* in the sense of an appendage may be a different word of unknown origin.

wave *v.* 1375 *waven* move back and forth; probably developed from Old English *wafian* to wave with the hands, fluctuate; also, waver in mind (about 1000, in Ælfric's *Lives of Saints*); related to *wǣfre* wavering, restless; see WAVER. —**n.** 1526, a moving swell of water, in the Tyndale Bible; from the verb. *Wave* is a replacement for earlier *waw* a wave, probably before 1200; from Old English *wagian* to move to and fro (before 899; earlier, to shake, totter, before 800). The meaning of an act of waving is first recorded in 1688. —**wavelength** *n.* (1850) —**wavelet** *n.* small wave. 1813, formed from English *wave,* n. + *-let.* —**wavy** *adj.* 1562, having wavelike lines or bands; formed from English *wave,* n. or v. + *-y*[1]. Like *wave, wavy* is a replacement for earlier *wawy* (1412).

waver *v.* Probably about 1280 *weyveren* to show indecision, fluctuate, vacillate, related to Old English *wǣfre* restless, wavering (from Proto-Germanic **wǣbraz*); cognate with Middle High German and modern German *wabern* to waver, totter, move to and fro, and Old Icelandic *vafra* hover about, move unsteadily, flicker, *vafi* doubt, *vāfa* to swing, vibrate, from Indo-European **webh-/wobh-/wēbh-* move back and forth (Pok.1114). The meaning of sway, stagger, is first recorded in Middle English probably before 1400, and that of float, flutter, in 1440. —**n.** a wavering. 1519, from the verb.

wax[1] *n.* yellowish substance made by bees. Before 1325 *wax;* earlier *wex* (probably before 1200); developed from Old English *weax* (805-10); cognate with Old Frisian *wax* wax, Old Saxon *wahs,* Middle Dutch and modern Dutch *was,* Old High German *wahs* (modern

German *Wachs*), and Old Icelandic *vax* (Swedish *vax,* Norwegian and Danish *voks*), from Proto-Germanic **waHsan.* Cognates outside Germanic are found in Lithuanian *vãškas* wax, Latvian *vasks,* and Old Slavic *voskŭ,* from Indo-European **wokso-* (Pok.1180). According to Pokorny, connection with the root of English *wick* or the root of English *weave* is possible but uncertain. The sense of any substance resembling beeswax in appearance or use is first recorded in English in 1799. **—v.** About 1378 *wexen* cover with wax, dress with wax, in *Piers Plowman;* from the noun. **—wax bean** (1905, American English) **—waxen** *adj.* Probably about 1390, made of wax; formed from Middle English *wax,* n. + *-en²*, replacing Old English (about 1000) *wexen.* **—wax paper** (1844) **—waxwing** *n.* small crested bird (1817). **—waxwork** *n.* (1697) **—waxy** *adj.* Probably before 1425 *wexy* made of wax, in a translation of Chauliac's *Grande Chirurgie;* formed from Middle English *wex* wax + *-y¹*.

wax² *v.* grow bigger or greater, increase. Probably before 1200 *waxen;* earlier *wexen* (before 1123); developed from Old English *weaxan* to increase, grow (about 725, in *Beowulf*); cognate with Old Frisian *waxa* to increase, grow, Old Saxon *wahsan,* Middle Dutch and modern Dutch *wassen,* Old High German *wahsan* (modern German *wachsen*), Old Icelandic *vaxa* (Swedish *växa,* Norwegian and Danish *vokse*), from Proto-Germanic **waHsanan,* also cognate with Gothic *wahsjan.* Cognates outside Germanic are found in Latin *augēre* to increase, Greek *auxánein* grow, increase, Sanskrit *vakṣati, úkṣati* grows, and Tocharian *oksiš* grows, from Indo-European **weg-/wog-/ug-, *aug-,* root **aweg-* (Pok.84); ultimately related to Old English *ēcan, ēacian* EKE¹ increase.

way *n.* Probably about 1225 *way;* earlier *weie* (probably before 1200); developed from Old English *weg* road, path, course of travel (before 800); cognate with Old Frisian *wei* way, Old Saxon *weg,* Middle Dutch and modern Dutch *weg,* Old High German *weg* (modern German *Weg*), Old Icelandic *vegr* (Swedish *väg,* Norwegian *veg,* Danish *vei*), Gothic *wigs* (from Proto-Germanic **weʒaz*), from the Indo-European root **weĝh-/woĝh-* to move, carry, travel, found in Latin *vehere* to carry and Greek *óchos* wagon; see WEIGH for development outside Germanic. The shift in spelling from *-eg* to *-ay* is a matter of spelling convention, as the same sound with the same type of spelling pattern is found in modern English *weigh.*

The central meaning of path in concrete and figurative use remains the core sense with various specific meanings developing from it, some suggested by Latin *via* and French *voie,* and some idiomatic use coming from various translations of the Bible. The sense of *way* meaning direction (as in *look this way*) is found before 1325, in *Cursor Mundi;* that of distance (as in *a long way off*) before 899, in Alfred's translation of Bede's *Ecclesiastical History;* that of means (as in *ways of preventing disease*) in about 1175; and that of style or manner (as in *wear one's hair in a new way*) before 800. The plural *ways* timbers on which a ship is built and launched is found in 1639, from the earlier, and now obsolete, sense of a duct or channel in the body (about 1425; Latin *via*) and the meaning of habits or custom (as in *teasing ways*) in 1742, in Fielding's writings.

—wayfarer *n.* (1440, in *Promptorium Parvulorum*) **—wayfaring** *adj.* Old English *wegfarende* (about 1000, in Ælfric's *Lives of Saints*). **—waylay** *v.* lie in wait for, ambush. 1513, formed from English *way* road, path + *lay,* in the sense of lie in wait, set a trap; modeled on Middle Low German and Middle Dutch *wegelagen.* **—wayside** *n.* (probably before 1400, in *Morte Arthur*) **—wayward** *n.* About 1380, shortened form of earlier *aweiward* turned away (probably before 1200, in Layamon's *Chronicle of Britain).*

-ways a suffix forming adverbs indicating direction, as in *lengthways = in the direction of the length,* or manner, as in *anyways = in any manner.* Middle English *-ways,* genitive case form of *way;* see also etymology of suffix -S³.

we *pron.* Old English *wē* (about 725, in *Beowulf*); cognate with Old Frisian *wi* we, Old Saxon *wī, wē,* Middle Dutch *wī* (modern Dutch *wij*), Old High German and modern German *wir,* Old Icelandic *vēr* (Swedish, Norwegian, and Danish *vi*), and Gothic *weis,* from Proto-Germanic **wīz,* Indo-European **wei-* (Pok. 1114). These plural forms are further cognate with Sanskrit *vayám* we, Avestan *vaēm,* Tocharian A *was,* Tocharian B *wes,* and Hittite *wēs.* A related Indo-European dual form ("we two") is found in Old English (and very early in Middle English) *wit,* Old Frisian, Old Saxon, and Gothic *wit,* Old Icelandic *vit,* Lithuanian *vèdu,* Old Slavic *vě.*

The use of *we* by a single person to denote himself is recorded in about 725, in *Beowulf,* in reference to a sovereign or ruler, and before 899, in Alfred's translation of Orosius' *Historiarum Adversus Paganos,* as a reference to the author, now also extended to editorial use and unsigned articles.

weak *adj.* About 1300 *wayke,* in *Havelok the Dane;* later *weke* (before 1325, in *Cursor Mundi*); borrowed from a Scandinavian source (compare Old Icelandic *veikr* weak, Swedish *vek* soft, Danish *veg,* Norwegian *veik* weak, pliant). The Scandinavian forms are cognate with Old English *wāc* weak, pliant, soft (which did not survive beyond late Middle English), Old Saxon and Middle Low German *wēk,* Middle Dutch *weec* (modern Dutch *week*), and Old High German *weih* yielding, soft (modern German *weich*), from Proto-Germanic **waikaz.* These adjectives derive from a Germanic verb represented by Old Icelandic *víkja* to move, turn, Old High German *wīhhan* to yield, give way (modern German *weichen*), Middle Dutch *wīken,* Old Saxon *wīkan,* and Old English *wīcan,* from Proto-Germanic **wīkanan,* Indo-European **weig-/woig-* to bend (Pok.1130).

The sense of lacking power or authority is first recorded in 1423, that of lacking moral strength or mental power, in about 1375, and that of lacking in amount, intensity, etc., in about 1400. The meaning of deficient, as in some skill, is first recorded in *The Prick of Conscience* (1340).

—weaken *v.* Probably about 1380 *wayknen;* formed from Middle English *wayke* weak + *-nen* -en¹. It is interesting to note that *weak,* v. (recorded first in *Roman de la Rose,* 1400, but probably known also in Chaucer's translation, 1370), from the adjective, existed alongside *weaken* for about 275 years before becoming obsolete in English. **—weakling** *n.* 1526, in the Tyndale Bible; formed from English *weak* + *-ling.*

weal¹ *n.* well-being, prosperity, happiness. Probably before 1200 *wele,* in Layamon's *Chronicle of Britain;* developed from Old English *wela* wealth, welfare, well-being (before 899, in Alfred's translation of Boethius' *De Consolatione Philosophiae*), from Proto-Germanic **welōn;* related to *wel* WELL¹, adv. Old English *wela* is cognate with Old Saxon *welo,* of similar meaning.

weal[2] *n.* raised mark on the skin. 1821, alteration (influenced by *wheal*), of WALE.

wealth *n.* About 1250 *welthe* prosperity, riches, in *Genesis and Exodus;* formed from Middle English *wele* well-being; see WEAL[1] + *-the* -th[1]. **—wealthy** *adj.* About 1375 *welthi* happy, prosperous; formed from Middle English *welth (e)* prosperity, riches + *-i* -y[1]. The meaning of having wealth, rich, opulent, is first recorded in Middle English before 1430.

wean *v.* accustom (a child or young animal) to food other than its mother's milk. Probably about 1200 *wenen;* developed from Old English (about 960) *wenian* to accustom. The sense of wean (a child) was ordinarily expressed in Old English by *gewenian* or *āwenian.* Old English *wenian* is cognate with Old Frisian *wenna* accustom, Old Saxon *wennian,* Middle Dutch and modern Dutch *wennen,* Old High German *giwennen* (modern German *gewöhnen*), Old Icelandic *venja* (from Proto-Germanic **wanjanan,* formed from **wanaz* accustomed, whence Old Icelandic *vanr,* Pok.1147), and related to Old English *wunian* to dwell, be used to; see WONT. The figurative sense of accustom a person to do without something, cause to turn away, is first recorded in 1526, but the sense of accustom was known in Old English and its cognates, as evidenced above.

weapon *n.* Probably about 1175 *wepen;* developed from Old English *wǣpen* instrument used in fighting or defense (about 725, in *Beowulf*); cognate with Old Frisian *wēpin* weapon, Old Saxon *wāpan,* Middle Dutch *wāpen* (modern Dutch *wapen*), Old High German *wāffan* (modern German *Waffe* armorial bearings), Old Icelandic *vāpn* (Swedish *vapen,* Norwegian *våpen,* and Danish *våben*), and Gothic *wēpna,* plural, weapons, from Proto-Germanic **wǣpnan.* Outside Germanic no probable cognates have been found. **—weaponry** *n.* 1844, weapons collectively; formed from English *weapon* + *-ry.*

wear *v.* Before 1121 *weren* grow (hair, beard) in a certain way; later, carry (clothes) on the body, be dressed in (probably before 1200); use up, destroy by use (about 1275); developed from Old English *werian* to clothe, put on (before 899, in Alfred's translation of Orosius' *Historiarum Adversus Paganos*). Old English *werian* (from Proto-Germanic **wazjanan*), is cognate with Old High German *werien* to clothe, Old Icelandic *verja* to cover, keep (with *r* standing for *s* by Verner's Law). A further cognate is found in Gothic *wasjan* to clothe, and all forms are derived from Indo-European **wes-/wos-* (Pok.1172) which is also the source of Gothic *wasti* garment, Latin *vestis* clothing or garment, Greek *esthḗs* clothing, *héssai* to wear, Armenian *z-gest* clothing, Sanskrit *váste* (he) puts on, wears, Avestan *vaste,* Tocharian A *wsāl* and Tocharian B *wastsi* garment, and Hittite *wassiya-, wessiya-* clothe.

The shift of this verb from a form with weak conjugation (found in *wered* past tense and past participle) to a strong conjugation (found in *wore* past tense, *worn* past participle) seems to have taken place on the analogy of other strong verbs, such as *bear* and *tear,* from the 1300's on, accelerating in the 1500's. It is possible that this shift was also influenced by such a vestige of Old English as is found in the past participle *foreworen* worn out, decayed.

—n. action of wearing. 1464 *were,* from Middle English *weren* to wear. The sense of clothing (as in *men's wear, underwear*) is first recorded in 1570; that of gradual damage (in the expression *wear and tear*) is found in 1666, in Pepys' *Diary.* **—wear-dated** *adj.* 1968, guaranteeing the length of normal wear of a garment. **—wearing** *adj.* exhausting. 1811, formed from English *wear,* v. + *-ing*[2]. **—wear-resistant** *adj.* (1960, earlier *wear-resisting* 1897).**—worn-out** *adj.* (1612)

weary *adj.* Probably about 1175 *weri;* developed from Old English *wērig* tired (about 725, in *Beowulf*), related to *wōrian* to wander, totter; for suffix see -Y[1]. Old English *wērig* (from Proto-Germanic **wōrīʒaz*) is cognate with Old Saxon *wōrig* weary, Old High German *wuorag* drunk, and probably with Old Icelandic *ōrar* (plural) attacks of vertigo, confusion, madness; cognate also with Greek *hōrākiânto* fall into a faint, from Indo-European **wōrā* faintness (Pok.1180). **—v.** Probably before 1200 *werien* to grow or make weary, in Layamon's *Chronicle of Britain;* developed from Old English *wērigan* (about 725, in *Beowulf*); from *wērig* weary, adj. **—wearisome** *adj.* causing weariness. About 1450 *werisom,* formed from Middle English *werien* to weary + *-som* -some[1].

weasel *n.* Before 1325 *wesele;* developed from Old English (before 800) *weosule, wesle* weasel; cognate with Middle Low German, Middle Dutch and Dutch *wezel* weasel, Old High German *wisula* (modern German *Wiesel*), from Proto-Germanic **wisulōn.* Further cognates are found in Old Swedish *visla* (modern Swedish *vessla*), Norwegian *vesel,* and Danish *vaesel,* probably related (as they both have a foul musky smell) to Old Icelandic *visundr* BISON. **—v.** 1900, American English, to deprive (a word or phrase) of its meaning; from the noun; so used because the weasel sometimes sucks out the contents of an egg, leaving the shell intact. The sense of extricate oneself (from a difficult situation) in the manner of a weasel is first recorded in 1925.

weather *n.* Old English *weder* (about 725, in *Beowulf*); cognate with Old Frisian *weder* weather, Old Saxon *wedar,* Middle Dutch and modern Dutch *weder,* Old High German *wetar* (modern German *Wetter*), Old Icelandic *vedhr* (Swedish *väder,* Norwegian *vær, ver,* Danish *veir*), from Proto-Germanic **weđrán,* Indo-European **wetróm,* root **awe-/we-* to blow (Pok.81). Outside Germanic cognates may exist in Lithuanian *vėtra* storm, and Old Slavic *vĕtrŭ* wind.

The spelling with *th* instead of the earlier *d* first appeared in Middle English in the 1400's (though the pronunciation with *th* may well be much older), and became established before the end of the 1500's. For a parallel development; see FATHER, GATHER.

—v. 1440 *wederen* expose to the air, from *weder,* n. The figurative meaning of come through safely is first recorded in 1655. The sense of wear away by atmospheric action is first found in 1757.

—weather-beaten *adj.* (1530, in Palsgrave's *Lesclarcissement*) **—weathercock** *n.* (before 1300) **—weatherman** *n.* 1545, observer of weather; later, person who presents a weather forecast, American English 1859. **—weatherproof** *adj.* (about 1620) **—weather strip** (1847, American English) **—weather vane** (1721)

weave *v.* About 1200 *weven;* developed from Old English *wefan* form (a fabric) by interlacing yarns (about 899, in Alfred's translation of Bede's *Ecclesiastical History*); cognate with Middle Low German, Middle Dutch and modern Dutch *weven* to weave, Old High German *weban* (modern German *weben*), and

Old Icelandic *vefa* (Swedish *väva,* Norwegian *veve,* Danish *væve*), from Proto-Germanic **weƀanan.* Cognates outside Germanic are found in Greek *hýphos* web, *hyphaínein* to weave, and Sanskrit *ubhnā́ti* (he) laces up, *ūrṇa-vā́bhi-s* spider; literally, wool weaver; from Indo-European **webh-/wobh-/wēbh-/ubh-* (Pok.1114). See WEB. In Middle English the past participle *weved* (and later the past tense *wevede*) shifted in form to that of a strong verb, assuming the spellings *woven,* in the past participle and *wove* in the past tense, probably by influence of words such as *steal,* in which the stem ends with the sound represented by *l* or *r.*

The sense of combine into a whole (as in *to weave a story from several incidents*) is first recorded in 1545, but was surely earlier confused with the meaning of fabricate, contrive, found in 1380. The sense of go by twisting and turning (as in *to weave through traffic*) is found in 1650, and is sometimes mistakenly thought to be attributable to a different verb formation in Middle English.

—n. 1581, something woven, in a translation of Homer's *Iliad;* from the verb. The meaning of a method or pattern of weaving is first recorded in 1888.

—weaver *n.* Before 1387, in *Piers Plowman;* formed from Middle English *weven* + *-er*[1].

web *n.* something woven. Old English *webb* woven fabric (about 725, in *Beowulf*), related to *wefan* to WEAVE. Old English *webb* (from Proto-Germanic **waƀjan,* Indo-European **wobhyom*) is cognate with Old High German *weppi* web, and Old Icelandic *vefr* (Swedish *väv,* Norwegian *vev,* Danish *væv*). The meaning of a spider's web, cobweb, is first recorded in Middle English before 1250, in *Bestiary.* The meaning of the membrane or fold of skin that connects the toes of an aquatic bird or other animal is first found in English in 1576. The figurative sense of a snare or entanglement is first recorded in 1574, and that of something that is flimsy, unsubstantial, or fanciful, in Francis Bacon's *Of the Advancement of Learning* (1605). **—v.** 1440 *webben* to weave, in *Promptorium Parvulorum;* developed from Old English *webbian* to weave, devise, from *webb* web. Two verbs for making fabric *web* and *weave* existed side by side in Old and Middle English, which is a curiosity given that weaving was such a fundamental craft and so well-known in earlier times. Their coincidental existence suggests a distinction in meaning which cannot be discerned from the available evidence. It may be that *web* continued in existence because of the influence of *webster,* which was the earlier term for *weaver,* and enjoyed wide-spread use in Middle English. The meaning of join by a web is first recorded in 1774, but is known earlier in *webbed,* adj. (1664), and in the compound *web-footed* (1681). **—webster** *n. Archaic.* weaver. About 1100 *webbestre* female weaver; formed from Old English *webbian* to weave, devise + *-estre* -ster.

wed *v.* Probably before 1200 *wedden* to marry, in Layamon's *Chronicle of Britain* and *Ancrene Riwle;* developed from Old English (before 1000) *weddian* to covenant or engage to do something, pledge, marry (from Proto-Germanic **wađjōjanan*); cognate with Old Frisian *weddia* to pledge, Middle Low German, Middle Dutch, and modern Dutch *wedden,* Middle High German and modern German *wetten* to pledge, wager, Old Icelandic *vedhja* to pledge, and Gothic *gawadjōn* to marry, espouse. The verb may derive from the noun in Old English, or directly from a Proto-Germanic noun meaning a pledge or covenant, represented by Old English *wedd* (as in *to wedde* being pawned, mortgaged; about 725, in *Beowulf*), Old Frisian *wed,* Old Saxon *weddi,* Middle Low German *wedde* pledge, wager, Middle Dutch and modern Dutch *wedde* wages, salary, Old High German *wetti* pledge, wager (modern German *Wette* bet, wager), Old Icelandic *vedh* pledge (Swedish *vad* bet, wager), and Gothic *wadi* surety, pledge, from Proto-Germanic **wađjan.* The Proto-Germanic noun is cognate with Latin *vas* (genitive *vadis*) surety, security, bail, and Lithuanian *vãdas* surety, bail, *vadúoti* redeem a pledge or surety, from Indo-European **wadh-* (Pok.1109). **—wedding** *n.* Probably about 1225, ceremony of marriage, in *King Horn;* later, action of marrying, marriage (about 1250, in *Genesis and Exodus*); developed from Old English (about 1000) *weddung;* formed from *weddian* to marry + *-ung* -ing[1]. **—wedding ring** (about 1395) **—wedlock** *n.* marriage. Probably before 1200 *wedlake, wedlac,* in *Ancrene Riwle* and Layamon's *Chronicle of Britain;* developed from Old English (before 1100) *wedlāc* marriage vow (*wedd* pledge + *-lāc,* noun suffix). The original form of this word was changed by folk etymology through association of the word's second element with *lock.*

wedge *n.* piece of wood or metal used in splitting, separating, etc. Before 1250 *wedg;* developed from Old English (before 800) *wecg* a wedge; cognate with Old Saxon *weggi* wedge, Middle Low German *wegge,* Middle Dutch *wegghe* bread roll (modern Dutch *wegge*), Old High German *weggi, wecki* wedge (dialectal German *Weck* bread roll), and Old Icelandic *veggr* wedge (modern Icelandic *veggur,* Norwegian *vegg,* Swedish *vigg,* Danish *vægge* wedge), from Proto-Germanic **waȝjaz.* Cognates outside Germanic include Lithuanian *vãgis* wedge, peg, nail, Latvian *vadzis* wedge, and Old Prussian *wagnis* plowshare, from Indo-European **wogwh-* (Pok.1179). **—v.** Probably before 1425 *wegen* tighten by driving in a wedge, in a translation of Chauliac's *Grande Chirurgie;* from the noun.

Wednesday *n.* Probably about 1200 *Wednesdai, Wodnesdei;* developed from Old English (about 950) *Wōdnesdæg,* literally, Woden's day; corresponding to Old Frisian *Wōnsdei, Wēnsdei* Wednesday, Middle Low German *Wōdensdach,* Middle Dutch *Wudensdach, Woensdach* (modern Dutch *Woensdag*), and Old Icelandic *Ōdhinsdagr* (Danish, Norwegian, and Swedish *onsdag*), a loan translation of Latin *diēs Mercuriī* day of Mercury, the Roman God of commerce (in Vulgar Latin **Mercuris diēs,* the source of French *mercredi* Wednesday, Spanish *miércoles,* etc.).

wee *adj.* very small, tiny. Before 1449 *wei,* from earlier noun use in the sense of quantity, amount, as in the phrase *a littel wei* a little thing or amount (before 1325, in *Cursor Mundi*); developed from Old English *wǣge* weight; see WEIGH. The spelling *wee* is first recorded in 1598, and the adjective use *wee bit* apparently developed as a parallel to such forms as *a bit thing* a little thing, but was not in common use before the 1800's, though known in Scottish writings before 1725.

weed *n.* About 1200 *wede;* earlier *wiede* (probably before 1200); developed from Old English *wēod* grass, herb, weed (before 899, in Alfred's translation of Boethius' *De Consolatione Philosophiae*); and implied earlier in *ueodhoc* (before 800); see WEEDER below. Old English *wēod* is cognate with Old Saxon *wiod* weed, Middle Dutch *wiet,* and Old High German *wiota* fern, from Proto-Germanic **weuđ-,* of unknown origin. The specific sense of tobacco is first recorded in English in 1606. —v. take weeds out of. Before 1325 *weden,* developed from Old English *wēodian,* from *wēod,* n. Old English *wēodian* is cognate with Old Saxon *wiodōn* to weed, and Middle Dutch *wieden.* **—weeder** *n.* About 1400 *wedare* a tool to cut weeds, found specifically in *weedhook* (before 800, Old English *uuēodhōc,* from *uuēod, wēod* + *hōc* hook). **—weedy** *adj.* About 1420, full of weeds; formed from Middle English *wede* + *-y*[1].

weeds (wēdz) *n.pl.* mourning garments. 1595, plural of archaic *weed* garment; developed from Middle English *wede, weade* garment (probably before 1200) and Old English *wǣd, wǣde* garment (before 899, in Alfred's translation of Boethius' *De Consolatione Philosophiae*). The Old English forms are cognate with Old Frisian *wēde* garment, Old Saxon *wād, wādi,* Old High German *wāt,* and Old Icelandic *vādh,* from Proto-Germanic **ʒawǣđjan,* of uncertain origin.

week *n.* Probably before 1200 *wike,* in Layamon's *Chronicle of Britain* and *Ancrene Riwle;* developed from Old English *wice* (878, in the *Anglo-Saxon Chronicle*); probably originally (in Germanic) having the sense of turn or succession. Cognates of Old English *wice* are found in Old Frisian *wike* week, Old Saxon *wika,* Middle Dutch *weke* (modern Dutch *week*), Old High German *wehha, wohha* week (modern German *Woche*), Old Icelandic *vika* week (Norwegian *veke,* Swedish *vecka*), from Proto-Germanic **wikōn,* and in Old Icelandic *vikja* to move, turn, and Gothic *wikō* order, turn, from Indo-European **wig-* bend, turn (Pok.1131). Further cognates are found in Old High German *wehsal* change, turn (modern German *Wechsel*), and Latin *vicis* (genitive) turn, change; see VICARIOUS.

According to the OED, the wide variety of forms in English (*wice, weke, wucu,* and Scottish *ouk*) results from the effect of the initial sound (represented by *w*) on the following vowel sound. The spelling *week* began to appear in the mid-1500's.

The development of the meaning of week, as we know it, is a purely astrological convention, borrowed by the Europeans directly from the Romans, but by substitution of Germanic divinities for those of the Romans without regard to the planets, in the Germanic speaking areas. Where the names of the planets were adopted for names of the week (as in French *Mardi* Mars day) the practice maintains the tradition of considering each day as being under the influence of a particular planet, the succession governed by the order of distance of each planet from the earth.

—weekday *n.* 1477, day of the week other than Sunday; developed from Old English (about 900) *wicdæge* day of the week. **—weekend** *n.* (1638) **—weekly** *adv.* (1465); *adj.* (1489); formed from Middle English *weke* + *-ly*[1] (adv.) and *-ly*[2] (adj.)

ween *v. Archaic.* think, suppose, believe, expect. Probably about 1200 *wenen;* developed from Old English *wēnan* to think (about 725, in *Beowulf*); cognate with Old Frisian *wēna* to think, Old Saxon *wānian,* Middle Dutch and modern Dutch *wanen* to think, fancy, Old High German *wānen* to think (modern German *wähnen* suppose wrongly), Old Icelandic *væna* to hope, and Gothic *wēnjan* expect, hope, from Proto-Germanic **wǣnjanan,* formed from **wǣniz* expectation, from the Indo-European root **wen-* (Pok.1146), the source of Old High German *wunsc* wish, *wunsken* to WISH.

weep *v.* About 1300 *wepen;* earlier *weopen* (probably before 1200); developed from Old English *wēpan* shed tears, cry (before 899, in Alfred's translation of St. Gregory's *Pastoral Care*); cognate with Old Frisian *wēpa* to weep, Old Saxon *wōpian* bewail, Old High German *wuofan,* Old Icelandic *œ̄pa* to cry, shout, Gothic *wōpjan,* from Proto-Germanic **wōpjanan.* Cognates outside Germanic are found in Lithuanian *võbyti* to summon to court, and Old Slavic *vabiti* to summon, from Indo-European **wāb-* cry out (Pok.1109). **—weeping willow** (1731)

weevil *n.* small beetle. 1440 *wevyl,* in *Promptorium Parvulorum;* developed from Old English (before 800) *wifel* beetle; cognate with Old Saxon *wibil* beetle, Middle Low German *wevel,* Old High German *wibil* (modern German *Wiebel*), from Proto-Germanic **weƀilaz.* Cognates outside Germanic are found in Lithuanian *vãbalas,* and Latvian *vabuolis,* from Indo-European **webh-/wobh-* (Pok.1115); see WEAVE. For the shift in vowel from Old English to Middle English see the analogous change in BEETLE.

weft *n.* woof. Old English (before 800) *weft, wefta,* from *wefan* to WEAVE. Old English *weft, wefta* is cognate with Old Icelandic *veptr,* of similar meaning.

weigh *v.* Probably before 1200 *weien, weʒen,* in *Ancrene Riwle* and Layamon's *Chronicle of Britain;* developed from Old English *wegan* find the weight of, have weight, lift, carry (about 725, in *Beowulf*), related to *wǣge* weight; cognate with Old Frisian *wega* to weigh, Old Saxon *wegan,* Middle Dutch and modern Dutch *wegen,* Old High German *wegan* (modern German *wiegen, wägen* to weigh), Old Icelandic *vega* to lift, weigh (Swedish *väga,* Danish *veje,* Norwegian *veie*), and Gothic *gawigan* to move, shake, from Proto-Germanic **weʒanan.* The Germanic words are cognate with Latin *vehere* to carry, Greek *ocheîn,* Lithuanian *vèžti* to go, travel, Old Slavic *vesti* to carry, and Sanskrit *váhati* (he) carries, pulls, from Indo-European **weĝh-/woĝh-* move, carry (Pok.1118). See also WAY. The old sense of lift, carry, survives in *weigh anchor,* and indirectly in *fruit weighing heavily on the bough.* For development of the spelling with *gh* see FIGHT, the spelling with *-ei-* developed, by influence of the spirant *gh,* from the diphthong as pronounced in later Old English *wegan.*

weight *n.* Before 1123 *wihte,* in *Peterborough Chronicle;* later *wiʒte* (about 1250, in *Genesis and Exodus*); *weiʒte* (before 1398, in Trevisa's translation of Higden's *Polychronicon*); developed from Old English (before 1000) *gewiht,* from *wegan,* v. WEIGH. Old English *gewiht* is cognate with Old Frisian *wicht* weight, Middle Dutch *wicht, ghewichte* (modern Dutch *wicht, gewicht*), Middle High German *gewiht* (modern German *Gewicht*), and Old Icelandic *vætt* (Danish *vegt,* Norwegian *vekt,* Swedish *vikt*), from Proto-Germanic *(ʒa)weHtiz* and *(ʒa)weHtjan.*

For general development of spelling see WEIGH (except that the vowel which by pattern with *night, sight,* would be **wight* is *weight* by influence of *weigh,* v.; and final *-t* is a formative of nouns from verbs in Germanic, after *gh*).

—v. load down, burden. 1647, from the noun.

—weightless *adj.* Before 1547, in a translation of Vergil's *Aeneid;* formed from English *weight,* n. + *-less.* **—weighty** *adj.* highly important, serious. Before 1398, heavy; formed from Middle English *weiʒte* weight + *-y*[1].

weir (wir) *n.* small dam in a river. About 1121 *waere;*

developed from Old English (839) *wer* a dam, fence or enclosure, especially one for catching fish; related to *werian* dam up. Old English *wer* is cognate with Old Frisian *were* dam, *wera* defend, protect, Old Saxon *werr* dam, *werian* defend, Middle Low German and Middle Dutch *were* dam (modern Dutch *weer*), Old High German *werī* defense (modern German *Wehr*), *werien, werren* defend (modern German *wehren*), Old Icelandic *ver* fishing-place, *verja* defend, and Gothic *warjan* defend, from Proto-Germanic **warjanan.* Cognates outside Germanic are found in Old Irish *ferenn* belt, *feronn* field, Latin *aperīre* (from pre-Latin *ap-werī-*) to open, uncover, *operīre* (from pre-Latin *op-werī-*) to close, cover, Albanian *varr* grave, Greek *érysthai* protect, guard, rescue, Lithuanian *ùžvérti* to close, Old Slavic *vrěti,* Sanskrit *vṛṇóti* (he) covers, holds back, surrounds, *vāras* covering, Avestan *-vārō* covering, and Tocharian B *wärto, warto* garden, forest, from Indo-European **wer-/wor-* close up, cover, protect (Pok.1160).

The spelling with *-ei-* represents a shift in pronunciation with a raising of the vowel before *r* in early modern English.

weird *adj.* About 1400, having the power to control the fate of men, attributive use of earlier *wierd, werd,* n. fate, destiny; developed from Old English *wyrd* (about 725, in *Beowulf*) from Proto-Germanic **wurđís,* Indo-European **wr̥tís.* Old English *wyrd* is cognate with Old Saxon *wurd* fate, Old High German *wurt,* and Old Icelandic *urdhr,* and related to Old English *weorthan* to become; see WORTH. For development of spelling see WEIR.

The Middle English adjective was originally used in *weird sisters,* the three Fates or goddesses who controlled human destiny; *weird sisters* was also Shakespeare's term for the three witches in *Macbeth* (1605). The meaning of odd in appearance is first recorded in Shelley's *Alastor* (1815).

—weirdo (wir′dō) *n. Slang.* odd person. 1955, American English; formed from *weird,* adj. + the slang suffix *-o;* see WINO. The meaning in modern English expresses the felt need for a noun, such as existed in Old and Middle English with a variety of specific meanings including that of a witch, wizard, or soothsayer (1625).

welch *v.* See WELSH.

welcome *interj.* About 1150 *welcume;* later *wel come* (1297); alteration (influenced in part by *wel* WELL[1], adv.) of Old English (about 890) *wilcuma* exclamation of kindly greeting, from earlier *wilcuma,* n., welcome guest (about 725, in *Beowulf*); formed from *willa* pleasure, desire, choice; see WILL[2] + *cuma* guest, related to *cuman* to COME; corresponding to independently formed Old High German *willicomo,* Middle Low German *willekome.* The alteration of *wil-* to *wel-* was also in part possibly influenced by a Scandinavian word (compare Old Icelandic *velkominn*). **—v.** Probably before 1200 *welcumen,* in Layamon's *Chronicle of Britain;* alteration of Old English (about 1000) *wilcumian* greet kindly, from *wilcuma* welcome guest. **—adj.** Old English *wilcuma* acceptable, freely permitted (about 725, in *Beowulf*); presumably from *wilcuma,* n., welcome guest. **—n.** 1525, kindly greeting; from the adjective.

weld *v.* join together (metal, plastic, etc.). 1599, alteration of WELL[2] to boil, rise; influenced by *welled,* past participle. **—n.** welded joint. 1831, from the verb.

welfare *n.* About 1303, condition of being or doing well, in Mannyng's *Handlyng Synne;* from the phrase *wel faren* fare well; developed from Old English *wel faran* (wel WELL[1], adv. + *faran* get along, FARE[2]); a parallel formation is found in Middle High German *wolvarn.* The modern sense of social concern or provision for the well-being of children, unemployed workers, etc., is first recorded in 1904, originally in such phrases as *welfare work, welfare committee, welfare policy.* **—welfare state** (1941)

welkin (wel′kən) *n. Archaic.* sky. Before 1250 *welkne,* in *The Owl and the Nightingale;* developed from Old English *weolcen, wolcen* cloud (about 725, in *Beowulf*), from Proto-Germanic **welknan, *wolknan.* The Old English forms are cognate with Old Saxon *wolcan* cloud, Middle Low German *wolken,* Middle Dutch *wolcke* (modern Dutch *wolk*), Old High German *wolkan* (modern German *Wolke*), *welk* moist, and outside Germanic with Latvian *vęlgs* and Old Slavic *vlaga* moisture, and Old Irish *folc* flow of water, Welsh *golchi* to wash. The two Celtic words (Old Irish *folc* and Welsh *golchi*) suggest an Indo-European **wolk-,* root **welk-,* but the other cognates derive from Indo-European **welg-/wolg-/wl̥g-/wōlg-* (Pok.1145).

well[1] *adv.* in a satisfactory manner, satisfactory (as in *everything is going well*). Old English *wel* (about 725, in *Beowulf*); cognate with Old Frisian, Old Saxon, Middle Dutch, and modern Dutch *wel* well, Old High German *wela, wola* (modern German *wohl*), Old Icelandic *vel* (Swedish, Norwegian, and Danish *vel*), and Gothic *waila,* from the same source as Old English *willan* to wish, WILL[2]. **—adj.** (as in *all was not well*), Old English *wel* in a state of good fortune, welfare, or happiness (about 725, in *Beowulf*); probably from the adverb (of which many uses of the adjective may be classified as adverbs). The meaning of in good health is first recorded in 1555. **—interj.** (as in *Well, I'm not sure*), Old English *wel,* an introductory expletive (before 899, in Alfred's translation of Boethius' *De Consolatione Philosophiae*); and (as in *Well, well, here he is*) *wel* an expression of surprise, resignation, etc. **—well-balanced** *adj.* (1629, in Milton) **—well-behaved** *adj.* (1598, in Shakespeare's *Merry Wives of Windsor*) **—well-being** *n.* (before 1613) **—wellborn** *adj.* belonging to a good family. About 950, Old English *wel-boren.* **—well-bred** *adj.* (1597, in Shakespeare's *2 Henry IV*) **—well-defined** *adj.* (1704, in Newton's *Optics*) **—well-done** *adj.* About 1200, skillfully done; later, thoroughly cooked (1747). **—well-founded** *adj.* (1369) **—well-grounded** *adj.* (about 1369) **—well-informed** *adj.* (about 1440) **—well-known** *adj.* (about 1470) **—well-made** *adj.* (1297) **—well-mannered** *adj.* (about 1387) **—well-meaning** *adj.* (1387) **—well-nigh** *adv.* almost. Before 1122, Old English *welneah.* **—well-off** *adj., adv.* in a good position (1733). **—well-read** *adj.* (1596, in Shakespeare's *The Taming of the Shrew*) **—well-thought-of** *adj.* (1579) **—well-to-do** *adj.* (1825) **—well-wisher** *n.* (1590) **—well-worn** *adj.* (1621)

well[2] *v.* to spring, rise, gush. Probably before 1200 *wellen,* in *Ancrene Riwle;* in part replacing earlier *wall* (Old English *weallan* to boil, bubble up, about 725, in *Beowulf*), and in part developed from Old English, before 1000: (West Saxon) *wiellan,* (Anglian) *wellan* cause to boil, from *weallan* to boil. The Old English forms are cognate with Old Frisian *walla* to boil, Old Saxon *wallan,* Old High German *wallan* (modern German *wallen*), Old Icelandic *vella* (Swedish *välla,* Danish *vælde,* Norwegian *velle*), and related to Old English *walwian, wealwian* to roll; see VOLUME. Possibly related to SWELL.

The earlier intransitive verb *wall* is recorded as late as 1894 in the verbal noun *walling* the action of boiling brine in salt making.

—n. hole dug in the ground to get water, spring of water. Probably before 1200 *welle,* in Layamon's *Chronicle of Britain;* developed from Old English, before 830 (West Saxon) *wielle,* (Anglian) *welle,* from *wiellan, wellan* cause to boil. The Old English forms are cognate with Old Frisian *walla* spring, Middle Dutch *welle,* Old High German *wella* wave (modern German *Welle*), and Old Icelandic *vella* boiling heat.

Welsh *adj., n.* Probably before 1200 *Welisc,* in Layamon's *Chronicle of Britain;* developed from Old English, 668-95: (West Saxon) *Wīlisc, Wȳlisc,* (Anglian and Kentish) *Wēlisc, Wǣlisc,* from *Wealh, Walh* Celt, Briton, Welshman, non-Germanic foreigner, corresponding to Old High German *Walh, Walah* Celt, Roman, Gaulish, and Old Icelandic *Valir* Gauls, Frenchmen; all from a Celtic name represented also by Latin *Volcae* an ancient Celtic tribe in southern Gaul; for suffix see -ISH[1]. The Old English noun survives in the names *Wales, Cornwall,* and in *Walsh, Wallace* (as surnames); also compare WALNUT. The spelling *Welsh* begins to appear in the early 1500's.

The English adjective *Welsh* corresponds to Old High German *walhisc* (modern German *wälsch, welsch*) Celtic, Gaulish, Roman, Romanic; Dutch *waalsch* Walloon; and Old Icelandic *valskr* Gaulish, French (Swedish *välsk,* Danish *vælsk* "Italian, French, southern"), from Proto-Germanic **WalHiskaz.*

—Welsh rabbit (1725; originally, a humorous formation like *Cape Cod turkey* for codfish; also *Welsh rarebit,* 1785).

welsh or **welch** *v. Slang.* avoid payment, cheat, swindle. 1857 *welch,* 1867 *welsh* (racing slang) to refuse or avoid payment of money laid as a bet; of uncertain origin (some dictionaries associate this word with *Welsh,* suggesting a disparaging derivation; but there is no evidence to support this). **—welsher** *n.* (1860)

welt *n.* strip of leather between the upper part and the sole of a shoe. About 1425 *weltte,* of uncertain origin; perhaps related to Middle English *welten* to overturn, roll over (probably before 1400), borrowed from a Scandinavian source (compare Old Icelandic *velta* to roll; see WELTER). The meaning of ridge on the skin from a wound is first recorded in English in 1800. **—v.** 1483 *welten* furnish (shoes) with welts, from *welte,* n. The meaning of beat severely is first recorded in 1823.

welter *v.* roll or toss about, wallow. Before 1325 *weltren,* in *Cursor Mundi;* borrowed from Middle Dutch or Middle Low German *welteren* to roll. The Middle Dutch or Middle Low German form is cognate with Old English *weltan, wæltan* to roll, Old High German *walzan* (modern German *wälzen*), Old Icelandic *velta* (Swedish *välta,* Danish *vælte,* Norwegian *velte*), and Gothic *waltjan,* from Proto-Germanic **waltjanan,* Indo-European **wol-d-,* root **wel-* (Pok.1143). A further cognate is probably found in Old English *wealwian, walwian* to roll; see VOLUME. **—n.** 1596, confusion, upheaval; from the verb. The meaning of a confused or surging mass (as in *a welter of inconsistencies and errors*) is first recorded in 1851, in Carlyle's writings.

welterweight *n.* boxer weighing between 135 and 147 pounds. 1832, heavyweight horseman; later, boxer or wrestler of a certain weight (1896); formed from earlier *welter* heavyweight horseman or boxer (1804); probably formed from *welt* beat severely + *-er*[1] and *weight.*

wen *n.* harmless cyst of the skin. Old English (about 1000) *wenn;* cognate with Middle Low German *wene* a wen, wart, Middle Dutch *wan,* and modern Dutch *wen,* of uncertain origin.

wench *n.* About 1300 *wenche* girl or young woman, shortened form of earlier *wenchel* child (probably before 1200); developed from Old English (about 890) *wencel,* probably related to *wancol* unsteady, fickle, weak, and perhaps *wincian* nod; see WINK. The meaning of a wanton woman is recorded in Middle English before 1387; the meaning of maidservant, about 1380.

wend *v.* direct (one's way). Probably before 1200 *wenden,* found in Old English *wendan* to turn, go, wend (about 725, in *Beowulf*); cognate with Old Frisian *wenda* to turn, wend, Old Saxon *wendian,* Middle Dutch and modern Dutch *wenden,* Old High German *wenten* (modern German *wenden*), Old Icelandic *venda* (Danish and Norwegian *vende,* Swedish *vända*), and Gothic *wandjan* (from Proto-Germanic **wandjanan*), causative verb form of **windan,* found in Old English *windan* to turn, twist; see WIND[2]. Compare WANDER.

The original forms of the past tense were *wende, wended* and past participle *wend,* but variants *wente, went* developed from about 1200, becoming later the more usual forms. In certain senses *went* also replaced the older past tenses of *go,* and from about 1500 were regarded as the past tense of that verb, while *wend* was given the new past tense form *wended.*

went *v.* past tense of *go.* Originally a past tense (and past participle) of WEND.

were *v.* form of the verb *be.* Developed from two different past indicative forms of Old English *wesan* to be: *wǣron,* plural, and *wǣre,* second person singular, both recorded about 1000; see WAS. The second person singular form *wast* (formed in the 1500's from *was* on the analogy of *be, beest*) displaced the etymological *were* (from Old English *wǣre*) chiefly under the influence of Biblical translations such as Tyndale's; the intermediate form *wert* was used by Shakespeare and prevailed in literature during the 1600's and 1700's.

werewolf *n.* in folklore, a person who can change into a wolf. Old English (about 1000) *werewulf,* formed from *wer* man (see VIRILE) + *wulf* WOLF. Old English *werewulf* is cognate with Middle Dutch and modern Dutch *weerwolf* werewolf, and Old High German *werwolf* (modern German *Werwolf*); compare Greek *lykánthrōpos* werewolf (*lýkos* wolf + *ánthrōpos* man).

west *adv.* Old English *west* in or toward the west (886, in the *Anglo-Saxon Chronicle;* also about 725, in *Beowulf,* in the compound *West-Dene* West Danes); also *westan* from the west; cognate with Old Frisian, Middle Low German, Middle Dutch, and modern Dutch *west,* Old Saxon and Old High German *-west* (in compounds), modern German *west,* Old Icelandic *vestr* (Danish and Norwegian *vest,* Swedish *väst*), and Sanskrit *avás* downwards, from Indo-European **awés.* The Proto-German **wes-t-* is perhaps an extension of Indo-European **wes-* (Pok.73), found in Latin *vesper, vespera* evening, evening star, west, and Greek *hésperos, hespérā* evening; see VESPER. For a similar connection with evening, compare OCCIDENT. The words for *west* in the Romance languages were borrowed from English: French *ouest,* Italian *òvest,* Spanish and Portuguese *oeste.* **—adj.** About 1375, toward the west; from the adverb. **—n.** Probably before 1200, from the adverb. **—westerly** *adj.* Before 1470, formed from Middle English *wester, westir* (probably before 1350), developed from Old English (963) *westra* + *-ly*[1]. The adverb *westerly* appeared in 1625. **—western** *adj.* Late Old English *westerne* coming from the west (about 1050, in a version of Bede's *Ecclesiastical History*); formed from *west* west, adv. + *-erne,* suffix denoting direction; cognate with Old Saxon and Old High German *westrōni,* Old Icelandic *vestrœn.*—*n.* 1708, native of a western region, from *western,* adj. The meaning of a story, play, movie, etc., about cowboy life on the western plains of the United States, is first recorded in 1912, in American English. **—Westerner** *n.* 1837, person from the western United States; formed from English *western,* adj. + *-er*[1]. The sense of a person from the western world, an Occidental, is first recorded in 1880. **—westward** *adv.* 1297, developed from Old English (before 900) *westweard* (*west* west + *-weard* -ward).

wet *adj.* Probably before 1200, in Layamon's *Chronicle of Britain* and *Ancrene Riwle;* developed in part from: 1) the past participle use of the Middle English verb *weten* to wet, found in Old English (before 830) *wǣtan;* 2) Old English *wǣt* moist, liquid (before 899, in Alfred's translation of Boethius' *De Consolatione Philosophiae*), from Proto-Germanic **wǣtaz,* Indo-European **wēd-,* root **wed-/wod-/ud-* (Pok.78); and 3) a Scandinavian source represented by the stem **wāt-* (compare Old Icelandic *vātr,* modern Icelandic *votur,* Norwegian and Swedish *våt,* Danish *våd*); cognate with Old Frisian *wēt* moist, liquid, related to English WATER.

The meaning of rainy (as in *wet weather*) is first recorded in Old English before 899. The sense of permitting the sale of alcoholic liquor, opposed to prohibition, once peculiar to American English, is first recorded in 1870, and the Americanism *all wet* completely wrong, in 1923.

—v. make or become wet. Old English (before 830) *wǣtan,* from the adjective in Old English. In spite of the fact that the verb is recorded more than half a century before the adjective and the noun in Old English, both the verb and noun have traditionally been analyzed as developing from the adjective. While it makes sense in the case of the noun, it creates a seeming problem for the verb, unless one considers the extreme age of the record (over 1100 years) and the limited number of sources available to examine vocabulary. Therefore, most etymologists assume that because of the wide-spread use of the adjective in the major meanings in Old English at an earlier date than the verb, it is probable the verb was derived from the adjective use, and postulate the adjective on a Proto-Germanic **wǣt-,* thus relating *wet* and *water.*

—n. water or other liquid, moisture. Old English (before 899) *wǣt;* from the adjective in Old English, but also found in Old English (before 899) *wǣta* moisture.

—wet blanket 1810, something that dampens enthusiasm; later, person who has a depressing effect; in allusion to the use of wet blankets to put out fires (1857). **—wetland** *n.* 1743, marsh or swamp. **—wet nurse** 1620, woman employed to suckle the infant of another. **—wet suit** 1955, a tight rubber suit worn especially by skin divers.

wether (weᴛʜ′ər) *n.* castrated male sheep. Old English (about 890) *wether;* cognate with Old Saxon *withar* ram, Middle Low German and Middle Dutch *weder* (modern Dutch *weer*), Old High German *widar* (modern German *Widder*), Old Icelandic *vedhr* (Danish *væder,* Norwegian *vær,* Swedish *vädur*), and Gothic *withrus* lamb, from Proto-Germanic **wethruz.* Cognates outside Germanic are found in Latin *vitulus* calf, *vetus* old, Greek *étos* year, and Sanskrit *vatsá-s* year, calf, from Indo-European **wet-* year (Pok.1175), all revolving around the notion of "year," a *wether* presumably being a yearling.

wh as the spelling used to represent the first consonant of *whale, white* developed during the Middle English period as a respelling of words with initial *hw,* usually of Old English origin, such as in Middle English *what* (Old English *hwæt*) and Middle English *whisperen* (Old English *hwisprian*) to whisper. Words in *wh-* that were borrowed into English, such as *whisk* and *whelk,* were spelled by analogy with Old English words. It is uncertain how much the spelling affected the pronunciation of any of these words and sometimes *wh* varies with simple *h* or *w,* as in *whortleberry, hurtleberry, whiz*[1], *wiz(ard).*

As a further complication, early in the 1400's, words that had customarily been spelled with *ho-,* such as *home* and *hot,* began to appear with the spelling *who-.* The free-ranging influence of the digraph *wh* led to the current spellings *whole* (for Middle English *hol,* Old English *hāl*) *whom* (from Middle English *hōm,* Old English *hām*), and *whore* (Middle English *hore,* Old English *hōre*), which became common about 1600; but even in the time of Samuel Johnson (1755) and John Walker (1791, *Pronouncing Dictionary*) pronunciation of words spelled with *wh,* such as *whole* were much in dispute in educated speech. See also CH, SH, TH.

whack *n.* 1737, sharp, resounding blow, in Allan Ramsay's *A Collection of Scots Proverbs;* possibly of independent imitative origin, but more likely from the verb. **—v.** strike with a whack. 1719, in figurative sense; probably of imitative origin.

whale[1] (hwāl) *n.* fishlike mammal. Probably before 1300 *whal,* in *Arthour and Merlin;* developed from Old English *hwæl* (before 899, in Alfred's translation of Orosius' *Historiarum Adversus Paganos*). Old English *hwæl* (from Proto-Germanic **Hwalaz*) is cognate with Old Saxon *hwal* whale, Middle Dutch *wal, walvisc* (modern Dutch *walvis*), Old High German *wal, walfisc* (modern German *Wal, Walfisch*), Old Icelandic *hvalr, hvalfiskr* (modern Icelandic *hvalur,* Swedish *val,* Danish *hval,* Norwegian *kval, hval*), from Indo-European **kwalos* large sea-fish (Pok.958). Compare *walrus* in which the Old Icelandic and Dutch words figure by folk etymology. **—v.** hunt and catch whales. About 1700, from the noun. **—whalebone** *n.* elastic substance in the upper jaw of a whale, baleen (1601).

whale[2] (hwāl) *v.* beat, whip severely. 1790, in Grose's *A Provincial Glossary;* possibly variant of WALE, v.

wharf *n.* 1320 *warf,* in *Rolls of Parliament;* developed from Old English (probably after 1042) *hwearf* shore, bank where ships could tie up; earlier, a dam or embankment (1038), from Proto-Germanic **Hwarfaz;* cognate with Middle Low German *werf, warf* dam, wharf, and related in form (and in meaning by the sense of divert or change, as a dam does water) to Old English *hweorfan, hwearfian,* and *hwierfan* to turn, change, revolve (before 890). The Old English verb forms are cognate with Old Frisian *hwerva* to turn, Old

Saxon *hwerƀan,* Old High German *hwarb* turn, *hwerban, hwerfan* to turn, return, move (modern German *werben* enlist, solicit), Old Icelandic *hverfa* to turn, *hvarfa* turn around, Gothic *hwaírban* to go, *hwarbōn* to turn, from Indo-European **kwerp-* (Pok.631). Related to WHIRL.

The spelling *wharf* is first recorded in Middle English in 1442 (in form of the plural *wharves*); the plural *wharfs* is first found in 1485.

what *pron., adj., adv., interj.* Probably before 1200 *whæt,* in Layamon's *Chronicle of Britain,* or *whatt, watt* (about 1200, in *The Ormulum*); developed from Old English *hwæt* (about 725, in *Beowulf,* except *huæt,* pron., before 735, in Bede's *Death Song*). The Old English forms are cognate with Old Frisian *hwet, wet,* Old Saxon *huat,* Middle Low German, Middle Dutch, and modern Dutch *wat,* Old High German *hwaz, waz* (modern German *was*), Old Icelandic *hvat* (Swedish *vad,* Norwegian *hva,* Danish *hvad*), and Gothic *hwa;* derived from Proto-Germanic **Hwat,* Indo-European **kwod;* see WHO. **—whatever** *pron., adj.* (before 1325, in *Cursor Mundi*) **—whatnot** *pron.* various things. 1576, in Abraham Fleming's *A Panoply of Epistles;* from the earlier phrase *what not?* (1540). **—whatsoever** *pron., adj.* (about 1250, in *Genesis and Exodus*)

wheal *n.* wale, welt. 1808, probably alteration of WALE, possibly by confusion with *weal* welt, though not recorded before 1821, and probably also developed by association with obsolete English *wheal* pimple, pustule (1530), from Middle English *whelle* (about 1440); related to Old English *hwelian* to suppurate, form pus, bring to a head (before 899, in Alfred's translation of St. Gregory's *Pastoral Care*), from **hwele,* of uncertain origin.

wheat *n.* Probably about 1200 *whæte,* in *The Ormulum;* developed from Old English (before 830) *hwǣte* wheat; cognate with Old Frisian *hwēte* wheat, Middle Dutch and modern Dutch *weit,* Old High German *weizzi* (modern German *Weizen*), Old Icelandic *hveiti* (Danish *hvede,* Norwegian *hvete, kveite,* Swedish *hvete, vete*), and Gothic *hwaiteis;* derived from Proto-Germanic **Hwaitijaz* that which is white, from the source of Old English *hwīt* WHITE. **—wheaten** *adj.* 1340 *hueten,* in *Ayenbite of Inwyt;* developed from Old English *hwǣten* made of the grain or flour of wheat; formed from *hwǣte* wheat + *-en²*. **—wheat germ** (1897)

wheedle *v.* persuade by flattery, smooth words, etc., coax. 1661, in Blount's *Glossographia,* of uncertain origin. The OED suggests a distant connection with Old English *wǣdlian* to beg; others say perhaps borrowed by English soldiers as slang during their service in the German wars of the 1600's (compare German *wedeln* wag the tail, and thereby fawn, flatter, a sense found in Danish *logre* wag the tail, fawn, flatter; also in Icelandic *flathra* wag the tail, fawn upon).

wheel *n.* Probably about 1200 *whel,* in *The Ormulum;* developed from Old English *hwēol, hweogl* (before 899); cognate with Old Frisian *hwēl* wheel, Middle Low German *wēl,* Middle Dutch and modern Dutch *wiel,* and Old Icelandic *hvēl, hjōl* (Swedish, Norwegian, and Danish *hjul*), from Proto-Germanic **HwéHwlan, *Hweȝwlán.* The Proto-Germanic forms developed from Indo-European **kwekwlo-,* found in Sanskrit *čakrá-s* wheel, Avestan *čaHrō,* Greek *kýklos* ring, circle, wheel, cycle, Lithuanian *kāklas* neck (in the sense of that which turns), and Tocharian A *kükal,* Tocharian B *kokale* wheel, also possibly, wagon or chariot. The extended Indo-European **kwekwlo-* is a reduplication of **kwelo-, *kwolo-,* found in Old Prussian *kelan* wheel, Old Slavic *kolo* wheel, Greek *pólos* pivot, axis, pole, Aeolic Greek *pélesthai* to be in motion, Albanian *sjeł* I turn, Latin *colere* to till, cultivate, and Sanskrit *cárati* moves about, goes, from Indo-European **kwel-/kwol-/kwl-* (Pok.639). The figurative sense of a moving or propelling force (as in *the wheels of progress*) is first recorded before 1340, from the earlier sense of the wheel of fortune or chance (before 899, in Alfred's translation of Boethius' *De Consolatione Philosophiae*). **—v.** to turn. About 1385 *whielen,* in Chaucer's *Troilus and Crisyede;* probably before 1200 *hweolen,* in *Ancrene Riwle;* from the noun. **—wheelbarrow** *n.* (about 1340) **—wheelchair** *n.* (before 1700) **—wheelwright** *n.* (1281, as a surname)

wheeze *v.* breathe with difficulty and a whistling sound. Before 1460 *whesen,* probably borrowed from a Scandinavian source (compare Old Icelandic *hvǿsa* to hiss, Swedish *väsa,* Norwegian *hvese, kvese,* Danish *hvæse*). The Scandinavian words are cognate with Old English *hwǣst* act of blowing, and outside Germanic with Latin *querī* complain, and Sanskrit *śvasiti* (he) snorts, from Indo-European **k̑wes-* gasp (Pok.631). **—n.** a wheezing. 1834, from the verb.

whelk *n.* mollusk with a spiral shell. Before 1500, alteration of Middle English *welke, wilke* (about 1170); developed from Old English *weoloc, wioloc* (about 700); cognate with Middle Dutch *willoc, wilc, welc* whelk, modern Dutch *wulk.* The later spelling with *wh* was by analogy with words such as *whale* and *whelp;* see WH.

whelm *v.* overwhelm. Before 1325 *qhelmen* turn upside down, about 1350 *welmen;* probably an alteration (by association with *helmen* to cover, Old English *helmian*) of earlier *whelven* to turn, overturn, cover by something overturned (about 1275); developed from Old English (West Saxon) *-hwielfan,* (Mercian) *-hwelfan,* as in *āhwelfan* cover over; related to *hwealf* arch, vault; see GULF.

whelp *n.* puppy or cub. Probably before 1200, in Layamon's *Chronicle of Britain;* developed from Old English (before 830) *hwelp* whelp; cognate with Old Saxon *hwelp* whelp, Old High German *hwelf, welf* (modern German *Welf*), and Old Icelandic *hvelpr* (Swedish *valp,* Danish *hvalp,* Norwegian *hvalp, kvalp*). The figurative sense of a scamp, a good-for-nothing, is first recorded about 1330. **—v.** give birth to whelps. About 1200, in *The Ormulum;* from the noun.

when *adv., conj., pron.* Probably about 1200 *whanne,* in *The Ormulum;* later *when* (about 1320, in *whensoever*); developed from Old English *hwænne, hwenne, hwonne* (before 899, in Alfred's translation of Bede's *Ecclesiastical History*). The Old English forms are cognate with Old Frisian *hwenne* until, if, Old Saxon *hwan* when, Middle Low German and Middle Dutch *wan, wen* when (surviving in modern Dutch *wanneer* when), Old High German *wanne, wenni* (modern German *wann* when, *wenn* if, whenever), Gothic *hwan* when, how; derived from the Germanic pronominal stem **Hwa-.* **—whenever** *adv., conj.* (about 1380)

whence *adv.* from what place. Probably about 1225 *whannes,* in *King Horn;* also *whennes;* formed from *whenne* whence + adverbial genitive suffix *-es* -S³. The earlier forms *whanne, whenne* developed from Old English *hwanone* (about 725, in *Beowulf*); related to *hwænne* WHEN. The spelling with *-ce,* first recorded in the Tyndale Bible (1526), is a spelling convention to indicate the sound of an earlier voiceless *-s* (in *-es*), as found in *twice* and *pence.* Compare HENCE, THENCE.

where *adv., conj.* Probably about 1200 *whære,* in *The Ormulum;* developed from Old English *hwǣr, hwar* (before 830; also about 725, in *Beowulf* in *elles hwǣr* elsewhere). Old English *hwǣr* is cognate with Old Frisian *hwēr* where, Old Saxon *hwār,* Middle Low German *wār,* Middle Dutch and modern Dutch *waar,* Old High German *hwār, wā,* Middle High German *wā* (modern German *wo*), Old High German *wār* (modern German *warum* why), Old Icelandic *hvar* (Swedish *var,* Danish *hvor,* Norwegian *hvor, kvar*), and Gothic *hwar* where. Old High German *wār* is from Proto-Germanic **Hwǣr,* and Gothic *hwar* is from Proto-Germanic **Hwar,* from Indo-European **kwēr/kwor-* (Pok.646). Old English also had a form *hwāra* (pronounced in two syllables), found in Middle English *whāre;* of similar construction to *thāra* there. **—n.** what place. About 1445, from the adverb. **—whereabouts** *adv.* Before 1415; earlier *whereabout* (before 1325). *—n.* 1795; earlier *whereabout* (1605). **—whereas** *conj.* 1424; earlier with the meaning of where (about 1350). **—whereat** *adv., conj.* (about 1250) **—whereby** *adv., conj.* (about 1200) **—wherefore** *adv., conj.* (about 1200, in *Vices and Virtues*); *n.* reason (1590, in Shakespeare's *Comedy of Errors*). **—wherein** *adv.* (probably before 1200) **—whereof** *adv.* (probably about 1200, in *The Ormulum*) **—whereon** *adv., conj.* (probably before 1200, in Layamon's *Chronicle of Britain*) **—wheresoever** *adv., conj.* (before 1325, in *Cursor Mundi*) **—whereto** *adv., conj.* (probably about 1200) **—whereupon** *adv., conj.* (before 1325, in *Cursor Mundi*) **—wherever** *adv., conj.* (about 1450 *wherever;* earlier *hwar ǣfre,* 971) **—wherewith** *adv., conj.* (probably about 1200, in *The Ormulum*) **—wherewithal** *adv., conj.* with what, with which (1535); *n.* means, resources (1583).

wherry (hwer′ē) *n.* light, shallow rowboat. 1443 *whery,* of uncertain origin. Connection with English *whirr,* with suggestion of rapid movement, is extremely doubtful in light of the early forms of the word: *wherye* (about 1515), *wherie* (1534), and *where* (1536). The history of the spelling, from its earliest form, is suggestive of some association with *ferry* (earlier *fery*), and the association is reinforced even to the extent of having parallel derivative forms, such as *ferryboat, wherryboat* and *ferryman, wherryman,* but no known connection in derivation is recorded.

whet *v.* Probably before 1200 *whætten* sharpen, make more acute; developed from Old English *hwettan* (about 725, in *Beowulf*); cognate with Middle Low German, Middle Dutch and modern Dutch *wetten* to whet, Old High German *wezzan* (modern German *wetzen*), Old Icelandic *hvetja,* and Gothic *gahwatjan* incite, from Proto-Germanic *Hwatjanan.* These verbs are derived from an adjective represented by Old English *hwæt* brave, bold, Old Saxon *hwat* sharp, Old High German *waz,* and Old Icelandic *hvatr* bold, vigorous, from Proto-Germanic **Hwataz,* cognate with Latin *tri-quetrus* triangular, originally three-pointed, earlier **triquedros,* from Indo-European **kwed-/kwod-* prick (Pok.636). **—n.** act of whetting. Before 1628, from the verb. **—whetstone** *n.* Old English *hwetstān* (about 725).

whether *conj.* Probably before 1200 *whæther, whether,* in Layamon's *Chronicle of Britain;* developed from Old English *hwæther, hwether* which of two (before 830; found also as an adverb about 725, in *Beowulf*). The Old English conjunctive forms with the meaning of which of two are cognate with Old Frisian *hweder, hwedder* which of two, whether, Old Saxon *hwethar* which of two, whether, Old High German *hwedar, wedar* which of two, whether, either (surviving in modern German *weder* neither), Old Icelandic *hvadharr* which of two, each, whether (Swedish *var* each, Danish *hver,* Norwegian *hver, kvar*), and Gothic *hwathar* which of two; all from Proto-Germanic **Hwatharaz,* corresponding to Indo-European **kwoteros,* represented by Sanskrit *katará-s* which of two, whether, Avestan *katārō,* Greek *póteros* (Ionian Greek *kóteros*), Latin *uter,* and Lithuanian *katràs,* formed from Indo-European **kwo-* WHO + the contrastive suffix **-tero-,* as in English OTHER. Compare EITHER.

whey (hwā) *n.* watery part of milk that separates from the curd when milk sours. Before 1250 *wei,* in *The Owl and the Nightingale;* later *whey* (1400, in Lanfranc's *Science of Surgery*); developed from Old English (before 800) *hwæg* whey; cognate with Middle Dutch *wey* (modern Dutch *wei*) and Middle Low German *hoie,* from Proto-Germanic **Hwaja-,* Indo-European **k̂woyo-* (Pok.628).

which *adj., pron.* Probably before 1300 *whiche,* in *Arthour and Merlin;* earlier *hwich* and *whilch* (both about 1200); developed from Old English *hwilc* (before 899, in Alfred's translation of Boethius' *De Consolatione Philosophiae*); cognate with Old Saxon *hwilīk,* Old Icelandic *hvīlīkr* (Danish and Norwegian *hvilken,* Swedish *vilken*), and Gothic *hwileiks* which; all from Proto-Germanic **Hwi-līkaz, *Hwi-,* from Indo-European **kwi-;* see WHO + Proto-Germanic **līkan* body, form, found in Old English *līc* body; see LIKE[1] similar.

Though *hwilc* is the surviving form in modern English *which,* two other principal forms existed in Middle and Old English: *hwelc* (before 800 from Proto-Germanic **Hwa-līkaz*) and *hwylc* (871-889), developing into early Middle English **hwelch* and *hwülch,* which later became (by loss of *l*) *hwech* and *hwüch,* both of which disappeared in late Middle English.

—whichever *pron., adj.* (about 1395, in the Wycliffe Bible)

whiff *n., v.* puff, gust. 1591, in part perhaps an alteration of earlier *weffe* foul scent or odor (before 1300), now found chiefly in *waff* a puff, gust (1686), *waft* a blast, gust (1607, figurative), and *weft* bad taste or smell (1542); also in part a new formation, probably of imitative origin. It is also possible that *whiff* is connected with earlier *whiffle* (found in *whiffling* that blows in gusts or puffs, 1568).

Whig *n.* 1657, in James Campbell's *Balmerino and Its Abbey,* in part perhaps a disparaging use from *whigg* a country bumpkin (about 1645), and in particular a shortened form of earlier (1649) *Whiggamore* one of the adherents of the Presbyterian cause in western Scotland who marched on Edinburgh in 1648 to oppose the secret agreement of the Scots with Charles I against the followers of Oliver Cromwell; perhaps associated with dialectal *whig* to urge forward.

In 1689 the name is first recorded in reference to a member of the British political party that opposed the Tories and favored reforms and progress. Except as a historical term, *Whig* has been superseded by *Liberal* since the middle of the 1800's. During the American

Revolution a *Whig* was a colonist who opposed the measures of the Royal Governors (1711); later the name was applied to a political opponent of Andrew Jackson, a member of the Whig party (1825). In 1854, the Whigs re-formed to become the Republican party.

while *n.* Before 1175, developed from Old English *hwīl* a space of time (about 725, in *Beowulf*); cognate with Old Frisian *hwīle* while, Old Saxon *hwīl,* Old High German *hwīla* (modern German *Weile*), Old Icelandic *hvīla* bed (Danish *hvile,* Swedish *vila,* Norwegian *hvile, kvile* rest), and Gothic *hwīla* time, while, from Proto-Germanic **Hwīlō.* Cognates outside Germanic are found in Latin *quiēs* rest, quiet, Old Persian *šiyātiš* comfort, rest, and Old Slavic *pokojĭ* rest, from Indo-European **kweyə-/kwoyə-/kwiyē-/kwiyə-/kwī-* (Pok.638). **—conj.** 1137, during the time that (now expressed by *while* alone, but earlier found in Middle English with the noun in the phrase *the while that* and Old English *þā hwīle þe*). **—v.** pass or spend in some easy, pleasant manner. 1606, from the noun.

whilom (hwī′ləm) *adv. Archaic.* formerly. About 1200 *whilumm,* in *The Ormulum;* developed from Old English (before 900) *hwīlum* at times, sometimes; dative plural of *hwīl* time, point of time; see WHILE.

whim *n.* 1641, pun or play on words, in Richard Brome's play *A Jovial Crew;* shortened form of earlier *whim-wham* fanciful object (before 1590); of unknown origin. The meaning of a sudden notion, fancy, or idea, is first recorded in English in 1697, probably a shortened form of *whimsy.*

whimper *v.* low, broken cry. 1513, in a translation of Vergil's *Aeneid;* probably of imitative origin, but compare German *wimmern* to whimper, moan. **—n.** Before 1700, fretful cry; from the verb, (but the noun sense is found much earlier in *whimpering,* in writings of Sir Thomas More in 1522).

whimsy *n.* odd or fanciful notion. 1605, in Ben Jonson's *Volpone,* probably related to earlier *whim-wham* (with the ending *-sy,* perhaps patterned on such words as *dropsy, topsy*); see WHIM. **—whimsical** *adj.* full of whims. 1653, formed from English *whimsy* + *-ical.* **—whimsicality** *n.* 1760, in Sterne's *Tristram Shandy;* formed from English *whimsical* + *-ity.*

whine *v.* Probably before 1300 *whynen* make a low cry of pain or distress, in *Kyng Alisaunder;* developed from Old English *hwīnan* to whiz; cognate with Old Icelandic *hvīna* to whiz, whistle in the air (Swedish *vina,* Danish and Norwegian *hvine*), Old High German *weiōn, hweiōn* to cry, shout, *wihōn* to neigh, Middle High German *wihen* (modern German *wiehern*) to neigh; all ultimately of imitative origin, though the sound-imitation is also found in Indo-European **k̑wei-/k̑wi-* (Pok.628). The meaning of make a low or feeble complaining sound, complain in a feeble way, is first recorded in 1530, in the Tyndale Bible. **—n.** low, complaining cry or sound. 1633, from the verb.

whinny *v.* to neigh. 1530, in Palsgrave's *Lesclarcissement,* probably related to *whine* in the sense applied to animals of make a protracted sound or cry, neigh (probably before 1300). **—n.** a neighing. 1823, from the verb.

whip *v.* Before 1250 *wippen* flap violently, as with the wings, in *The Owl and the Nightingale;* later *whippen* to strike or beat with a whip, flog, lash (about 1386, in Chaucer's *Canterbury Tales,* probably developed from the earlier sense found in the noun). Middle English *wippen* (from Proto-Germanic **wippanan,* Indo-European **wib-n-,* root **weib-,* Pok.1132) is cognate with Middle Low German, Middle Dutch and modern Dutch *wippen* move up and down or to and fro, swing, whip, Middle High German *wipfen* to leap, dance, and Old High German *wipf* swing; see WIPE. **—n.** thing to flog with. About 1340 *wippe,* in part developed from *wippen* to whip, and probably in part borrowed from Middle Low German *wippe, wip* quick movement, leap. The meaning of a leader of the legislative members of a political party who directs them in voting is first recorded in the obsolete form *whipper-in* (1771). **—whipcord** *n.* 1318-19, a strong twisted cord. **—whip hand** 1809, the hand that holds the whip in riding a horse or driving a carriage; earlier, position of control or advantage (1680). **—whiplash** *n.* 1573-80, lash of a whip; 1955, injury to the neck or spine caused by the head being jerked violently backwards and forwards. **—whipping boy** 1647, a boy educated together with a young prince or royal personage, and flogged in his stead when he committed a fault that was considered to deserve flogging; later, a person or thing that is the target of criticism or of blame, scapegoat (1841). **—whipsaw** *n.* 1538, long, narrow saw, used for scrollwork. —*v.* 1881, cut with a whipsaw; later, to get the better of (1884, in American English).

whipper-snapper *n.* insignificant or impertinent person. 1674, perhaps an alteration of earlier *snipper-snapper* (about 1590, in Marlowe's *Dr. Faustus*).

whippet *n.* very swift dog resembling a small greyhound. Before 1610, probably formed from *whip* in the sense of move quickly + diminutive suffix *-et.* This word is recorded earlier in the sense of a brisk, nimble woman (1550).

whippoorwill (hwip′ərwil) *n.* nocturnal North American bird. 1709, American English, of imitative origin. The word was coined in imitation of the bird's call, but made up of common words (*whip* + *poor* + the name *Will,* also found in such formations as chuck-will's-widow, 1791).

whir or **whirr** *v.* move quickly with a vibrating sound. Probably before 1400 (Scottish), fling, hurl; probably borrowed from a Scandinavian source (compare Danish *hvirre* to whir, whirl, and Old Icelandic *hverfa* to turn; see WHARF). The word was probably also reinforced by association with *whirl.* **—n.** Probably before 1400 (Scottish), rush, hurry; from the verb. The meaning of a vibrating sound is first recorded in 1677.

whirl *v.* to spin. About 1300 *ȝwirlen,* about 1380 *whirlen;* probably borrowed from a Scandinavian source (compare Old Icelandic *hvirfla* to go round, spin, related to *hvirfill* circle, ring, crown). Old Icelandic *hvirfill* is cognate with Middle Low German and Middle Dutch *wervel* bolt, hinge, whirlwind (modern Dutch *wervel* vertebra), Middle Dutch and modern Dutch *wervelen* to turn, and Old High German *wirbil* whirlwind (modern German *Wirbel* whirl, eddy, whirlpool), related to Old High German *hwarb* turn; see WHARF. The meaning of move or go swiftly is first recorded about 1386, and the figurative sense of spin around (as in *the room whirled round and round*) about 1384. The sense of feel giddy or confused is first recorded in 1561. **—n.** whirling movement. 1411 *whirle* flywheel or pulley on a spindle; later, act of whirling (about 1480); from *whirlen* to whirl. **—whirligig** *n.* toy that whirls. 1440 *whyrlegyge;* later *whirlygigge* (1530); formed from *whirly-* (Middle English variant of *whirl*) + *gigge* spinning top; see GIG[1] carriage. **—whirlpool** *n.* (1529) **—whirlwind** *n.* (before 1340)

whisk *n.* 1375 *wisk, wysk* quick sweeping movement, in Barbour's *The Bruce;* probably borrowed from a Scandinavian source (compare Old Icelandic *visk* wisp, Danish, Norwegian, and Swedish *visk* broom). The Scandinavian words are cognate with Old English *granwisc* awn, Middle Low German and Middle Dutch *wisch* wisp (modern Dutch *wis*), and Old High German *wisc* (modern German *Wisch*). The meaning of an implement for beating eggs, cream, etc., is first recorded in 1666, and that of a bundle of twigs, hair, etc., used as a brush, in 1729. The spelling *whisk* is first found in 1577. **—v.** move with a quick sweeping movement. About 1410 *wysken,* borrowed from a Scandinavian source (compare Old Icelandic *viska* to wipe); cognate with Old English *wiscian* to plait, related to *granwisc* awn. **—whisk broom** (1857)

whisker *n.* Usually **whiskers,** *pl.* hair growing on a man's cheeks. Before 1600, from Middle English *wisker* anything that whisks or sweeps (about 1425); formed from *wisk,* v. + *-er*[1]). The meaning of a long, stiff hair growing near the mouth of a cat or certain other animals is first recorded in 1678.

whiskey *n.* 1715 *whiskie;* later, in the spelling *whisky* (1746) and *whiskey* (1753); originally Scottish, reputedly in a form such as *whiskybea* or *whisquy-beath,* but according to the record *usky* (about 1730), *usquebea* (1706), *usquebaugh* (1703; earlier *iskie bae,* 1583); borrowed from Gaelic *uisge beatha* whisky; literally, water of life (Old Irish *uisce* WATER + *bethu* life, cognate with Greek *bíos* life; see QUICK). The Gaelic word is probably a loan translation of Medieval Latin *aqua vitae* alcohol, spirits; literally, water of life; in English *aqua vitae* had been recorded as applying to intoxicating drinks since 1547. Compare also VODKA, and French *eau-de-vie* brandy, spirits; literally, water of life. Of the two spellings *whiskey* is found chiefly in the United States and Ireland (except for imitation Scotch, which is usually spelled *Scotch Whisky*), and *whisky* is found in England and Scotland.

whisper *v.* 1440 *whysperen,* in *Promptorium Parvulorum;* developed from Old English *hwisprian* speak very softly (about 950, in *Lindisfarne Gospels*); cognate with Middle Low German and Middle Dutch *wispelen* to whisper, Old High German *hwispalōn* (modern German *wispeln*), and Old Icelandic *hvīskra* (Swedish *viska,* Danish and Norwegian *hviske*); possibly related to Old English *hwistlian* to WHISTLE. **—n.** very soft, low spoken sound. 1599, in Shakespeare's *Henry V;* from the verb.

whist *n.* kind of card game, forerunner of bridge. 1663, in Butler's *Hudibras,* alteration of earlier *whisk* kind of card game (1621, but alluded to as early as 1529); perhaps so called from the act of *whisking* up the cards after each trick of the game is won. However, according to Charles Cotton's *The Complete Gamester* (1680), the game was called *whist* "from the silence that is to be observed in the play," and so it was associated with *whist* an exclamation to command silence (about 1374, in Chaucer's translation of Boethius' *De Consolatione Philosophiae*); of imitative origin.

whistle *v.* Before 1382 *whistlen,* in the Wycliffe Bible; developed from Old English (about 1000) *hwistlian* utter a shrill sound; cognate with Old Icelandic *hvīsla* to whisper, Middle Swedish *hvisla* and modern Swedish *vissla* to whistle, Danish *hvisle* to hiss, Norwegian *hvisle, kvisle,* and Old Icelandic *hvīna* to whistle in the air; see WHINE. **—n.** About 1340 *whistil,* developed from Old English (about 950) *hwistle* a whistling instrument, shrill-toned pipe; related to *hwistlian* to whistle. **—whistle stop** 1934, small town on a railroad line, at which a train stops only when signaled; later, a brief appearance chiefly for a political speech or the like (1949, in adjective use).

whit *n.* very small bit. Probably before 1200 *na whit* no amount, in Layamon's *Chronicle of Britain,* found in Old English *nān wiht* (971), from *wiht* amount (before 900); originally, person, human being; see WIGHT. The meaning of an amount in Old English may have been influenced by senses in cognate words: Old Saxon *wiht* thing, Old High German *wiht* creature, being, thing, etc.

white *adj.* Before 1325, in *Cursor Mundi;* developed from Old English *hwīt* (before 899, in Alfred's translation of Boethius' *De Consolatione Philosophiae*); cognate with Old Frisian and Old Saxon *hwīt* white, Middle Dutch and modern Dutch *wit,* Old High German *hwiz, wiz* (modern German *weiss*), Old Icelandic *hvītr* (Danish *hvid,* Norwegian *hvit, kvit,* Swedish *vit*), and Gothic *hweits,* from Proto-Germanic **Hwītaz.* A cognate outside Germanic is found in Sanskrit *śvindate* glistens, from Indo-European **k̑weid-/k̑wid-* (Pok.628). **—n.** Before 1300, developed from Old English (about 1000) *hwīt* fluid surrounding an egg yolk, from *hwīt,* adj. **—v.** About 1325, developed from Old English (before 1000) *hwītian,* from *hwīt,* adj. **—white blood cell** (1905; earlier *white corpuscle,* 1866) **—whitecap** *n.* wave with a foaming white crest (1773). **—white-collar** *adj.* of or pertaining to workers of a business or professional class (1921, American English). **—white elephant** something that is expensive and troublesome to take care of, 1928; so called in allusion to the story that the King of Siam gave sacred white elephants that could not be disposed of or used for work as gifts to obnoxious courtiers who would be sore pressed by their cost of maintenance. The generalized sense of a possession that is no longer wanted is first recorded in 1928, in Galsworthy's works. **—whitefish** *n.* kind of freshwater fish used for food (1709); earlier, any white fish (1461-62). **—white flag** plain white flag displayed as a sign of peaceful intention or truce (1600, earlier *flag,* in *flag of truce,* 1582). **—white-hot** *adj.* 1820, in Shelley's *Oedipus Tyrannus;* from earlier *white heat* (1710). **—White House** residence of the President of the United States (1811, American English). **—white lie** (1741) **—whiten** *v.* make white. Before 1300, formed from Middle English *white,* adj. + *-en*[1]. **—whitewash** *v.* to coat with a white liquid (1591, in Percival's Spanish *Dictionary*). The sense of conceal the faults of is first recorded in 1762. —*n.* liquid for whitening walls, etc. 1697 (earlier, a cosmetic, 1689); from the verb. The sense of something that conceals faults is first recorded in 1865. **—whiting**[1] *n.* European fish like the cod. About 1425, borrowed from Middle Dutch *witinc, wittinc,* from *wit* WHITE + *-inc* -ing[1]. **—whiting**[2] *n.* powdered white chalk. 1440, in *Promptorium Parvulorum;* formed from Middle English *white,* v. + *-ing*[1].

whither *adv.* to what place, where. Probably before 1200 *wider,* in *Trinity Homilies;* developed from Old English (before 830) *hwider;* formed from Proto-Germanic **Hwi-* (from Indo-European **kwi-;* see WHO) +

-der, as in Old English *hider* HITHER and *thider* THITHER.

whitlow (hwit′lō) *n.* abscess on a finger or toe. 1440, in *Promptorium Parvulorum,* alteration of earlier *whitflaw* (before 1400), possibly formed from *white* + *flaw*[1]; or perhaps borrowed in part from early modern Dutch *vijt, fijt,* Low German *fit* abscess, whitlow.

Whitsunday (hwit′səndā) *n.* the seventh Sunday after Easter, Pentecost. Probably before 1200 *White-sunedæie,* in Layamon's *Chronicle of Britain;* developed from Late Old English (1067) *Hwita Sunnandæg* white Sunday (*hwīt* WHITE + *Sunnandæg* SUNDAY); possibly so called from the custom of having the newly baptized wear white baptismal robes on this day.

whittle *v.* cut shavings or chips from (wood, etc.) with a knife. 1552, in Huloet's *Abecedarium Anglico Latinum,* verb use of Middle English *whittel* a knife (1404), variant of earlier *thwittle* (1390), from *thwiten* to cut (about 1370); developed from Old English *thwītan;* cognate with Old Icelandic *thveita* to hew, hurl, from Proto-Germanic **thwītanan,* Indo-European **tweid-* (Pok.1099); for suffix see -LE[3].

whiz[1] or **whizz** *v.* make or move with a humming or hissing sound. Before 1547, in a translation of Vergil's *Aeneid;* of imitative origin. **—n.** humming or hissing sound. 1620, from the verb.

whiz[2] *n. Slang.* very clever person, expert. 1914, American English, probably a special use of earlier *whiz* something remarkable (1908), transferred use of *whiz*[1]. Alternatively, it is perhaps an alteration (by influence of *whiz*[1]) of a shortened form of *wizard.*

who *pron.* About 1250 *hwo,* in *The Owl and the Nightingale;* later *who* (about 1303, in Mannyng's *Handlyng Synne*); developed from Old English *hwā* (about 725, in *Beowulf*); cognate with Old Frisian *hwā* who (interrogative pronoun), Old Saxon *hwē,* Middle Dutch and modern Dutch *wie,* Old High German *hwer, wer* (modern German *wer*), Old Icelandic *hverr,* Old Danish *hwa* (modern Danish *hvo*), Old Swedish *hvar,* and Gothic *hwas,* feminine *hwō;* all from Proto-Germanic **Hwas, *Hwes* (*Hwez*), **Hwō,* from Indo-European **kwos, *kwe-, kwā* (Pok.644). The Indo-European pronominal stem is found in Sanskrit *ká-s,* feminine *ká-* who (interrogative pronoun), Avestan *kō,* feminine *kā,* Lithuanian *kàs,* Slavic *kŭto* (Russian *kto*), and Latin *quī* (relative pronoun), feminine *quae.* A variant stem **kwi-* is found in Sanskrit *kí-s* who (interrogative pronoun), Greek *tís,* Latin *quis* (neuter *quid*), Old Irish *cē, cia* who, *cid* what, Welsh *pwy* who, Old Slavic *čito* (Russian *chto*), and Hittite *kuis, kuit* who, what (relative and interrogative pronouns).

The pronunciation (hü), like that of *two* (tü), from Old English *twā,* developed in the process of labialization of the vowel (influenced by the sound represented by *w*). This labialization or rounding of the vowel in the Middle English pronunciation (whō) resulted in a shift to (whü), and finally to (hü) when the sound represented by *w* disappeared before the related ü-sound.

The pronoun *whom* developed from Old English *hwām,* the dative form of *hwā* who. The pronoun *whose* developed from Old English *hwæs,* the genitive form of *hwā* who. The pronunciation of *whom* and *whose* pronounced with the vowel (ü) are the result of analogy with *who.*

—whodunit (hüdun′it) *n. Slang.* mystery or detective story. 1930, American English, noun use (with altered spelling) of the question *"Who done it?"* **—whoever** *pron.* (before 1225) **—whomever** *pron.* (probably before 1300, in *Arthour and Merlin*) **—whosoever** *pron.* (probably before 1200, in *Ancrene Riwle*)

whole *adj.* 1420 *wholle,* spelling alteration of earlier *hol* (probably before 1200); developed from Old English *hāl* entire, unhurt, healthy (about 725, in *Beowulf*); cognate with Old Frisian *hāl, hēl* whole, Old Saxon *hēl,* Middle Dutch and modern Dutch *heel,* Old High German and modern German *heil,* Old Icelandic *heill* (Danish, Norwegian, and Swedish *hel*), and Gothic *hails,* from Proto-Germanic **Hailaz.* Cognates outside Germanic are found in Welsh *coel* omen, Old Prussian *kailūstiskun* health, and Old Slavic *cělŭ* healthy, unhurt, from Indo-European **kailo-/kailu-* (Pok.520). Doublet of HALE[2].

For an explanation of the spelling with *wh-,* see WH. **—n.** all of a thing, the total. Before 1387, in Trevisa's translation of Higden's *Polychronicon;* from the adjective.

—whole-hearted *adj.* (1840, American English) **—whole milk** (1794) **—whole number** (1557) **—wholesale** *n.* (before 1417); the figurative sense of general, extensive, as in *a wholesale reform of taxes,* is first recorded in 1642). *—v.* to sell at wholesale (1800). **—wholesome** *adj.* (about 1200) **—whole-wheat** *adj.* (1903) **—wholly** *adv.* completely. Before 1338 *holy,* formed from Middle English *hol* whole, adj. + *-ly*[1].

whoop (hüp *or* hwüp) *v.* shout "whoop!" Probably about 1450 *whowpen,* alteration of earlier *houpen* (about 1376); in part of imitative origin in English (compare the interjection), and in part borrowed from Old French *houper* to cry out; also of imitative origin. For an explanation of the spelling with *wh-,* see WH. **—interj.** (before 1460 *whop*) **—n.** shout of "whoop!" 1600, alteration of Middle English *houp* (about 1350), probably from the interjection. **—whoopee** *interj.* 1862 *whoopee;* American English, from *whoop,* interj. + *-ee.* *—n.* (wu̇p′ē) noisy, unrestrained revelry. 1928, in the song *Makin' Whoopee* by Gus Kahn; American English, from the interjection. **—whooping cough** (1739)

whopper *n. Informal.* something very large or great. 1785, in Grose's *Classical Dictionary of the Vulgar Tongue;* formed in English as if from *whop,* v. + *-er*[1] (though *whop,* v. is not recorded in the sense of to surpass, be great, until 1836, but is found in earlier *whopping,* adj., before 1625, which was no doubt the immediate source for *whopper*). The English *whop,* v. in the sense of beat, overcome, of which the later sense surpass, excel is an extended sense, is first recorded in 1575, but is of uncertain origin. *Whopper* in the sense of a big lie is first recorded in 1791.

whore *n.* 1535, spelling alteration (with replacement by *wh-*) of Middle English *hore* (probably before 1200, in *Ancrene Riwle*); developed from Late Old English (before 1100) *hōre* prostitute, harlot (from Proto-Germanic **Hōrōn*). Old English *hōre* is cognate with Middle Dutch *hoere* (modern Dutch *hoer*), Old High German *huora* (modern German *Hure*), Old Icelandic *hōra* (Norwegian and Danish *hore,* Swedish *hora*) adulteress, *hōrr* adulterer, and Gothic *hōrs* adulterer. Outside Germanic cognates are found in Latin *cārus* dear, Old Irish *caraim* I love; see CHARITY. **—v.** consort with whores, fornicate. 1583, from the noun. The sense of act as a whore is first recorded in 1615.

whorl (hwėrl *or* hwôrl) *n.* circle of leaves or flowers round a stem of a plant. 1440 *whorlwyl, whorle* flywheel or pulley on a spindle, in *Promptorium Parvulorum;* possibly alteration of *whirle* WHIRL. The meaning of a circle of leaves or flowers round a stem of a plant is first recorded in 1551.

why *adv.* About 1200 *whi,* in *The Ormulum;* developed from Old English *hwī, hwȳ* (before 899, in Alfred's translation of Boethius' *De Consolatione Philosophiae*), instrumental case (showing for what purpose or by what means) of *hwæt* WHAT. Old English *hwȳ* is cognate with Old Saxon *hwī* why and Old Icelandic *hvī* why (Danish *hvi,* Norwegian *hvi, kvi*), from Proto-Germanic **Hwī,* cognate with Doric Greek *peî* where, from Indo-European **kwei* (Pok.646). **—n.** cause, reason, purpose. About 1303 *why,* in Mannyng's *Handlyng Synne,* from earlier (before 1200) *hwi,* adv. **—interj.** 1519, as an expression of surprise or to call attention to a statement; from the adverb.

wick *n.* bundle of fiber that is lighted in an oil lamp or candle. Probably before 1200 *wueke;* later *wicke* (before 1376); developed from Old English (about 1000) *wēoce,* from a reduplicated Proto-Germanic noun **weukōn,* from Indo-European **we-ug-* (Pok. 1117). Old English *wēoce* is related to *wōcig* noose, and cognate with Middle Dutch *wieke* wick (modern Dutch *wiek*), Old High German *wiohha* (dialectal German *Wieche*). Outside Germanic probable cognates may be found in Old Irish *figim* I weave, and Sanskrit *vāgurā́* net, noose, from Indo-European **weg-/-wōg-/ug-* weave, knit (Pok.1117). The formation with *-ick* showing the shortening of the vowel is found generally in the 1600's and began to replace the lengthened vowel sound inherited from Middle English.

wicked *adj.* Probably before 1200, in Layamon's *Chronicle of Britain;* formed from earlier *wicke* wicked, evil (1154, perhaps attributive use of Old English *wicca* wizard; see WITCH) + *-ed*[1].

wicker *n.* slender, easily bent branch or twig. 1336 *wekirr* wickerwork; later *wyker* pliant twig, withe (before 1398), and *wickir* (1508); borrowed from a Scandinavian source (compare dialectal Swedish *vikker* branch of willow, Swedish *vika* to bend, and Old Icelandic *vīkja* to move, turn; see WEEK). **—adj.** made of wicker. 1502, from the noun. **—wickerwork** *n.* (1719, in Defoe's *Robinson Crusoe*)

wicket *n.* Probably about 1225 *wiket* small door or gate, in *King Horn;* borrowed from Anglo-French *wiket,* from Old North French (compare modern French *guichet* ticket-window), from a Germanic source (compare Old Icelandic *vīk* nook, *vīkja* to move, turn; see WEEK). The meaning of a set of sticks at which the ball is aimed in cricket is first recorded in English in 1733. The sense of a window with a grill or grate is first recorded in 1813.

wide *adj.* Probably 1200, in *Ancrene Riwle* and Layamon's *Chronicle of Britain;* developed from Old English *wīd* (about 725, in *Beowulf*); cognate with Old Frisian, Old Saxon, and Middle Low German *wīd* wide, Middle Dutch *wijt* (modern Dutch *wijd*), Old High German *wīt* (modern German *weit*), and Old Icelandic *vīdhr* (Danish, Norwegian, and Swedish *vid*), from Proto-Germanic **wīđás,* cognate with Sanskrit *vīta-s* having gone apart, from Indo-European **wītós,* contracted from **wi-* apart + **itós* gone, root **ei-/i-* go (Pok.295). **—adv.** Probably before 1200, in Layamon's *Chronicle of Britain;* developed from Old English *wīde* (about 725, in *Beowulf*); from *wīd,* adj. **—wide-awake** *adj.* (1818, in Shelley's *Julian and Maddalo*) **—wide-eyed** *adj.* (1853, in writings of Tennyson) **—widen** *v.* 1607, in Shakespeare's *Coriolanus;* formed from English *wide,* adj. + *-en*[1]. **—widespread** *adj.* (1705, but the sense of extending over a wide area is found earlier in *widespreading,* adj., 1591) **—width** *n.* 1627, in Drayton's *Ballad of Agincourt;* formed from English *wide,* adj. + *-th*[1], a parallel to earlier *wideness,* formed on the analogy of *breadth.*

widow *n.* About 1386 *wydow* (see also verb for spelling); developed from Old English (about 830) *widewe, widuwe;* cognate with Old Frisian *widwe* widow, Old Saxon *widowa,* Middle Dutch and modern Dutch *weduwe,* Old High German *wituwa, witawa* (modern German *Witwe*), and Gothic *widuwō,* from Proto-Germanic **widewō.* Cognates outside Germanic are found in Latin *vidua* widow, Old Irish *fedb* widow, Welsh *gweddw* widower, Cornish *guedeu* widow, Old Prussian *widdewū,* Old Slavic *vĭdova* widow, Greek *ēítheos* unmarried youth, Sanskrit *vidhávā* widow, *vidhú-s* lonely, and Avestan *vidhavā* widow, from Indo-European **widhéwā* (Pok.1127). **—v.** make a widow of. Before 1325 *widowen,* in *Cursor Mundi;* from the noun. **—widower** *n.* About 1378, in *Piers Plowman;* formed from English *widow* + *-er*[1]. **—widowhood** *n.* About 1200 *widewehod,* formed from Middle English *widewe* widow + *-hod* -hood; replacing Old English *wuduwanhad* (before 899, in Alfred's translation of St. Gregory's *Pastoral Care*). **—widow's walk** 1939 (found earlier as *walk,* 1775), a balcony on the top of some New England houses, affording a view of a harbor or the seacoast, associated with the notion that such structures were built by ships' captains to give their wives a view of returning ships.

wield *v.* Probably about 1175 *welden* to rule, guide, decide, handle with skill; developed from Old English (Mercian) *weldan,* (West Saxon) *wieldan, wealdan* (about 725, in *Beowulf*). The Old English forms are cognate with Old Frisian *walda* to rule, Old Saxon *waldan,* Old High German *waltan* (modern German *walten*), Old Icelandic *valda* (Swedish *vålla,* Danish and Norwegian *volde* to cause, occasion), and Gothic *waldan* to rule, from Proto-Germanic **wal-t-,* found outside Germanic in Welsh *gwlad* country, Old Cornish *gulat,* Old Irish *flaith* to rule; from Indo-European **wal-dh-* come, Lithuanian *veldėti* to rule, Old Slavic *vlasti* to command, Old Prussian *wāldnikans* (accusative plural) kings. These forms appear to be extended from the Indo-European root **wal-* be strong (Pok.1111), found in Latin *valēre* be strong, be worth, and Tocharian A *wäl,* Tocharian B *walo* king.

wiener (wē′nər) *n.* frankfurter. 1904, American English; shortened form of *wienerwurst* (1889); borrowing of German *Wienerwurst,* from *Wiener* of Vienna (from *Wien* Vienna) + *Wurst* sausage. **—wienie** *n.* 1911 (but found earlier in the misspelling *winnies,* 1867); formed by clipping *wien(er)* + *-ie.*

wife *n.* 1483 *wife;* found in Old English (before 800) *wīf* woman, wife; cognate with Old Frisian and Old Saxon *wīf* woman, wife, Middle Dutch and modern Dutch *wijf,* Old High German *wīb* (modern German *Weib*), and Old Icelandic *vīf* (Danish, Norwegian, and Swedish *viv*), from Proto-Germanic **wīban;* of uncertain origin.

The Old English general sense of woman survives in *fishwife, midwife,* and *old wives' tale;* the Middle

English sense of the mistress of a household survives in *housewife;* compare WOMAN.
—wifely *adj.* About 1386, befitting a wife; developed from Old English *wīflic* womanly (before 899, in Alfred's translation of Orosius' *Historiarum Adversus Paganos*); formed from Old English *wīf* woman + *-lic* -ly[1].

wig *n.* 1675, shortened form of PERIWIG. **—v.** furnish with a wig or wigs. 1826, from the noun.

wiggle *v.* move with short, quick movements from side to side, wriggle. Probably before 1200 *wigelen,* in *Ancrene Riwle;* perhaps borrowed from Middle Dutch or Middle Flemish *wigelen,* frequentative form of *wiegen* to rock, from *wiege* cradle; cognate with Old High German *wiga* cradle (modern German *Wiege*), and Old English *wegan* to move; see WEIGH; for suffix see -LE[3]. **—n.** wiggling movement. 1894, from the verb. **—wiggly** *adj.* 1903, formed from English *wiggle,* v. or n. + *-y*[1].

wight (wīt) *n. Archaic.* person. Old English *wiht* living being, creature (about 725, in *Beowulf*); cognate with Old Saxon *wiht* thing (plural, demons), Middle Low German *wicht* thing, being, creature, demon, Middle Dutch and modern Dutch *wicht* little child, Old High German *wiht* creature, being, thing (modern German *Wicht* creature, being, infant), Old Icelandic *vēttr, vættr* creature, thing, and Gothic *waíhts* thing, from Proto-Germanic **weHtiz,* of unknown origin. Compare AUGHT, NAUGHT, and NIX[1]. See FIGHT for spelling.

The more restricted meaning of a human being, person, appeared in Middle English (probably about 1200, in *The Ormulum*) and was widely used with the spelling *wight* (see FIGHT) in literature from Chaucer onward through Crowley, Spenser, Shakespeare, Milton, Pope, Scott, and Wordsworth.

wigwam (wig′wom) *n.* hut of poles covered with bark, mats, or skins, used by certain Algonquian Indians. 1628, American English; borrowed from Algonquian (probably Abnaki) *wigwâm* a dwelling; also said to be found in such formations as *wikiwam* and specifically in (Ojibwa) *wigiwam,* (Delaware) *wiquoam* their house.

wild *adj.* Old English (before 800) *wilde* in the natural state, uncultivated, undomesticated; cognate with Old Frisian *wilde* wild, Old Saxon *wildi,* Middle Dutch *wilde, wilt* (modern Dutch *wild*), Old High German *wildi* (modern German *wild*), Old Icelandic *villr* (Danish and Swedish *vild,* Norwegian *vill*), and Gothic *wiltheis,* from Proto-Germanic **wilthijaz,* from Indo-European **weltiyos* grown with bushes and underbrush, root **wel-, welə-* in words for hair, wool, grass (Pok.1139). **—n.** Probably before 1200, wild animal, in Layamon's *Chronicle of Britain;* from the adjective. The meaning of an uncultivated or desolate region or tract is first recorded in 1637, but is found earlier in the phrase *the wilds* in Shakespeare's *Merchant of Venice* (1596). **—adv.** in a wild manner, to a wild degree. 1549, from the adjective. **—wildcat** *n.* (1418) **—wildfire** *n.* 1032, in the *Anglo-Saxon Chronicle;* later, violent force or excited feeling (before 1325, in *Cursor Mundi*), and in the phrase *like wildfire* swiftly or forcibly (1593). **—wildflower** *n.* (1797) **—wild-goose chase** (1592, in Shakespeare's *Romeo and Juliet*) **—wildlife** *n.* (1879) **—wild West** (1851)

wildebeest (wil′dəbēst′) *n.* gnu. 1838, borrowed from Afrikaans *wildebees;* literally, wild beast, plural *wildebeest* (from Dutch *wild* WILD + *bees* beast, ox, from Middle Dutch *beeste,* from Old French *beste* BEAST).

wilderness *n.* About 1200, in *Trinity Homilies;* formed from Old English *wildēoren* wild, savage, like wild beasts (*wilde* WILD + *dēor* animal; see DEER) + *-ness.*

wile *n.* trick to deceive, cunning way. Before 1160, in *Peterborough Chronicle;* developed from Late Old English *wīl* wile, trick; perhaps borrowed from Old North French, or more specifically Norman French **wile,* from a Scandinavian source (compare Old Icelandic *vēl* trick, craft, fraud, and *vēla* defraud); and in part possibly reinforcing Old English *wīgle* witchcraft, magic, divination (compare Old Frisian *wigila* sorcery, witchcraft). Old English *wīgle* is cognate with Gothic *weihs* holy, and Latin *victima* a sacrifice, from Indo-European **weik-/wik-* to separate, set apart (Pok.1128). Doublet of GUILE. **—v.** About 1375 *wilen* deceive by a wile, coax, lure; from the noun. The weakened sense of divert attention pleasantly from, pass easily or pleasantly, is first recorded in 1796, strongly influenced by *while,* v. **—wily** *adj.* Before 1325, in *Cursor Mundi;* formed from Middle English *wile* + *-y*[1].

will[1] *v.* be going to, be determined to. Before 1121 *wilen;* later *willen* (before 1225), past tense *wolde, wulde* would; developed from Old English (about 725, in *Beowulf*) *willan* to wish, desire, want (past tense *wolde*); cognate with Old Frisian *willa* to wish, desire, Old Saxon *willian, wellian* (past tense *welda, wolda*), Middle Dutch and modern Dutch *willen,* Old High German *wellan, wellen* (past *wolta*), modern German *wollen* (past *wollte*), Old Icelandic *vilja* (past *vilda*), Swedish *vilja,* Danish and Norwegian *ville,* and Gothic *wiljan* (earlier **weljan*) to will (past *wilda*), *waljan* to choose. Cognates outside Germanic are found in Latin *velle* to wish, Welsh *gwell* better, Lithuanian *vēlyti* to wish, Old Slavic *voliti* to will, *velěti* to command, Greek (Doric) *lên* (earlier stem **wlēi-*) to wish, and Sanskrit *vr̥nóti* (he) chooses, likes, *vára-s* a wish, from Indo-European **wel-/wol-/wl̥-, *wlei-/wlēi-* (Pok.1137).

The unusual feature of this verb is its use as a regular auxiliary of the future tense, with implications of intention or volition, and thus distinguished from *shall,* expressing or implying obligation or necessity; see SHALL for other distinctions. The use of *will* as a future auxiliary is already found in Old English (before 899, in Alfred's writings), and is paralleled in some other Germanic languages, such as Middle High German and Yiddish.

Contracted forms of the verb, especially after pronouns, began to appear in the 1500's (as in *sheele* = she'll, *youle* = you'll), the form with an apostrophe (as in *I'll, he'll, it'll*) occurring since the 1600's. The contraction *won't* for *will not* is first recorded in Middle English (before 1475) as *wynnot,* later (1584) *wonnot* (compare *cannot* and *can't*), the form *won't* being first recorded in 1667, in Pepys' *Diary.*

Most of the basic senses of *will* are found in Old English, including the meaning of choose or decide to do something (as in *God willed it*), found before 950, and the meaning of do often or habitually (that is, habitual action, as in *she will read for hours*), found before 899, in Alfred's writings.

The forms of the past tense (*would*) vary in the Germanic languages. Old Saxon *welda* may have preserved its *e* on account of the following *a,* but the *o* in Old English *wolde,* Old Saxon *wolda,* and Old High German *wolta* is not due to normal vowel gradation but rather to association with the past tense form of the functionally related verb *shall* (Old English *scolde, sceolde,* Old Saxon *skolda,* Old High German *scolta*). **—willing** *adj.* Before 1325, in *Cursor Mundi;* formed from Middle English *willen* will + *-ing*[2]. The word is also found in Old English as an element in compounds, such as *unwillende* unwilling, *willendliche* willingly.

will[2] *n.* power to choose, choice, wish. Old English *will, willa* (about 725, in *Beowulf*), related to *willan* to wish; see WILL[1]. Old English *will, willa* is cognate with Old Frisian *willa* will, Old Saxon *willio,* Middle Dutch *wille* (modern Dutch *wil*), Old High German *willo, willio* (modern German *Wille*), Old Icelandic *vili* (Danish *villie,* Norwegian *vilje,* Swedish *vilja*), and Gothic *wilja,* from Proto-Germanic **weljōn.* The meaning of a written document expressing a person's wishes about his disposition of property after death is first recorded about 1380, in Wycliffe's works. **—v.** to use the will. About 1100 *willen,* developed from Old English (before 830) *willian,* from *will, willa,* n. **—willful** *adj.* About 1200 (implied in Old English *wilfullice* willfully, before 1100); formed from Old English *will* will, n. + *-ful* -ful.

willies *n.pl. Informal.* spell of nervousness. 1896, American English, of uncertain origin.

will-o'-the-wisp *n.* moving light appearing at night over marshy places. 1661, in Blount's *Glossographia;* earlier *Will with the wisp* (1608); formed from *Will,* used widely in literature from the time of *Piers Plowman* through Chaucer and Shakespeare as a shortened form of *William* + *wisp* handful or twisted bundle of hay or straw used for burning as a torch.

willow *n.* About 1340 *welew;* earlier *wilwe* (about 1325), also *wilghe;* alteration of Old English (before 750) *welig;* cognate with Old Frisian *wilig* willow, Old Saxon *wilgia,* Middle Low German and Middle Dutch *wilge* (modern Dutch *wilg*), Middle High German *wilge,* and probably with Greek *helíkē* willow, from Indo-European **welikā* (Pok.1140). Note the name Helicon, seat of the Muses ("Mt. Willow"), called in Doric Greek *Welikṓn.* The history of the change in form to *-ow* is unknown but is probably parallel to that of *bellow* and *fellow.* **—willowy** *adj.* 1766, bordered or shaded with willows; formed from English *willow* + *-y*[1]. The meaning of like a willow, graceful, slender, is first recorded in 1791.

willy-nilly *adv.* willingly or not. 1608 *wille nille,* in Thomas Middleton's *A Trick to Catch the Old One;* contraction of *will I, nill I* or *will he, nill he,* or *will ye, nill ye;* literally, with or without the will of the person or persons concerned, willingly or unwillingly (compare Latin *nōlēns volēns*). The word *nill* not will, developed from Old English *nyllan* (*ne* NO + *willan* WILL[1]).

wilt *v.* become limp and drooping. 1691, in the writings of John Ray (the father of natural history in England), probably a dialectal alteration of *wilk, welk* to wilt, influenced by earlier *welter* to wilt (1645, with the ending perhaps parallel to *wither,* 1535). Modern English *welk* was probably borrowed from Middle Dutch or Middle Low German *welken* to wither; cognate with Old High German *irwelkēn* to wilt, *irwelhēn* become soft, and *wolkan* cloud; see WELKIN. **—n.** a wilting. 1855, from the verb.

wimp *n. Slang.* unathletic or unaggressive person, weakling. 1920, in George Ade's *Hand-made Fables;* American English, perhaps a clipped form from WHIMPER a fretful cry; compare earlier *whimp* (1549), *wimp* (1890) to whimper. See Reinhold Aman in *Maledicta* VIII (1984-85), p. 43, for a discussion of this word.

wimple *n.* cloth for the head. Late Old English (before 1100) *wimpel, wimple;* cognate with Old Frisian *wimpel* veil, banner, Old Saxon *wimpal,* Middle Dutch and modern Dutch *wimpel,* Low German *wimpelen,* and Old Icelandic *vimpill,* from Proto-Germanic **wimpilaz,* from Indo-European **wimb-,* nasalized variant of **wib-/weib-* (Pok.1132), as represented by Gothic *wipja* crown and Old Icelandic *veipr* kerchief. **—v.** cover or muffle with a wimple. Probably before 1200 *wimplen,* in *Ancrene Riwle;* from the noun.

win *v.* Probably about 1200 *winnen* strive, contend; later, be victorious, prevail, win (about 1300); fusion of Old English *winnan* struggle for, work at (about 725, in *Beowulf*), and Old English *gewinnan* to gain or succeed by struggling, to win (971), from Proto-Germanic **wenwanan.* The Old English forms are cognate with Old Frisian *winna* obtain, Old Saxon *winnan* suffer, win, *giwinnan* obtain, Middle Low German, Middle Dutch, and modern Dutch *winnen* gain, win, Old High German *winnan* to rage, contend, exert oneself, also *gawinnan* to gain by labor or exertion (modern German *gewinnen* earn, gain, win), Old Icelandic *vinna* to work, gain, win (Swedish *vinna,* Norwegian *vinne,* Danish *vinde*), and Gothic *gawinnan* suffer. Outside Germanic a cognate is found in Sanskrit *vanóti* strives for, obtains, from Indo-European **wen-* (Pok.1146). Related to WISH. **—n.** Probably before 1200 *winne* strife, conflict; also, gain, acquisition, profit (probably about 1200); fusion of Old English *winn* labor, strife, conflict (before 1000), and *gewinn* gain, profit (before 1000); related to *winnan* struggle for, and *gewinnan* gain, succeed. The meaning of a victory in a game or contest is first recorded in English in 1862. **—winner** *n.* About 1353, in *Winner and Waster;* formed from Middle English *winnen* win, v. + *-er*[1].

wince *v.* draw back suddenly, flinch slightly. About 1300 *wincen* to kick or move in impatience or pain, alteration of earlier *wenchen* (probably before 1200, in *Ancrene Riwle;* found also in later variant *winchen*); borrowed from Anglo-French or Old North French **wenchier, *wenchir* (in Old French *guenchir* to turn aside, avoid), from Frankish **wenkjan* (compare Old Saxon *wenkian* to turn, direct, Old High German and Middle High German *wenken;* see WINK). The specific use of make an involuntary shrinking movement in reaction to pain or the anticipation of it is first recorded before 1748. **—n.** a wincing. 1612, a kick; from the verb. The meaning of an involuntary recoiling movement, a flinching, is first recorded in 1865.

winch *n.* machine for lifting or pulling. 1295 *wenche* reel, roller, pulley, or other device for drawing or pulling; developed from Old English (about 1050) *wince;* related to *wincian* to blink, WINK. The meaning of a machine for pulling and hauling is first recorded in 1577. **—v.** to hoist or pull up. 1529, from the noun.

wind[1] (wind) *n.* air in motion. Old English *wind* (about 725, in *Beowulf*); cognate with Old Frisian, Old Saxon, Middle Dutch, and modern Dutch *wind* wind, Old High German *wind* (modern German *Wind*), Old Icelandic *vindr* (Danish, Norwegian, and Swedish *vind*), and Gothic *winds,* from Proto-Germanic **wendás.* Sharing with the Germanic a shortening of the long vowel before *-nt-* are Latin *ventus* and Welsh *gwynt,* from Indo-European **wēntós,* re-formed from an earlier present participle stem **wē-nt-;* compare Greek (nominative plural) *aéntes* blowing. Other cognates outside Germanic are found in Greek *áēsi* it blows, and *ātmós* (from pre-Greek **awetmós*), Lithuanian *vė̃jas,* Old Slavic *větrŭ,* Old Irish *feth* air, Sanskrit *vā́ta-s* wind, Tocharian A *want, wänt,* Tocharian B *yente,* and Hittite *huwantes* winds, from Indo-European **wē-/wə-* to blow (Pok.82), also found in Old English *wāwan* to blow, Old High German *wājan, wāen* (modern German *wehen*), Old Swedish *vīa,* and Gothic *waian.*

The short *i* in *wind*[1] preserves the distinction in pronunciation between this and *wind*[2], v., to move by turning and follows the rule from Old English times, except among those poets (most noticeably Chaucer and Shakespeare) and in some general and now archaic use, where the *i* was lengthened from the 1300's to the 1600's, presumably with some affectation among general users, and in search for rhyme among poets.

While most meanings of *wind* in the sense of air in motion are traceable to Old English, two very common extended senses are found only from Middle English times: power of breathing, breath, and air filled with some smell (as in *the deer caught the wind of the dogs*), both first recorded probably before 1300 in *Arthour and Merlin.* The common figurative phrase *in the wind* afoot, about to happen (as in *danger in the wind, ideas in the wind*) is first recorded in 1535.

—**v.** Probably before 1400 *winden* to follow by scent; from the noun. The meaning of tire, put out of breath, is first recorded in 1811.

—**windbag** *n. Informal.* overly talkative person (1827, in writings of Carlyle); earlier, the lungs (1552). —**windbreak** *n.* a shelter from the wind (1861, American English). —**windbreaker** *n.* jacket (1918, as a trademark, American English). —**windfall** *n.* 1464, something blown down by the wind; later, unexpected acquisition or advantage (1542). —**windmill** *n.* (1297) —**windpipe** *n.* (1530, in Palsgrave's *Lesclarcissement*) —**windshield** *n.* (1902) —**windstorm** *n.* (before 1398, in Trevisa's translation of Bartholomew's *De Proprietatibus Rerum*) —**wind tunnel** (1911) —**windward** *adj.* situated toward the wind (1549); formed from English *wind* + *-ward.* —**windy** *adj.* Probably about 1200 *windy,* developed from Old English (about 1000) *windig;* formed from *wind,* n. + *-ig* -y[1].

wind[2] (wīnd) *v.* move by turning and twisting. About 1175 *winden,* found in Old English *windan* to turn, twist, wind (about 725, in *Beowulf*). Old English *windan* is cognate with Old Frisian *winda* to wind, Old Saxon *windan,* Middle Low German, Middle Dutch, and modern Dutch *winden,* Old High German *wintan* (modern German *winden*), Old Icelandic *vinda* (Swedish *vinda,* Norwegian and Danish *vinde*), and Gothic *biwindan* wind around, wrap, from Proto-Germanic **wenđanan,* Indo-European **wendh-* (Pok.1148). Related to WANDER and to WEND, the causative form of *wind*[2].

The past tense and past participle *wound* (wound) developed from the earlier Middle English past tense *wand, wonde* and past participle *wunden, wonden;* the separate forms gradually coalescing, probably mostly by confusion of use, into a common form for past tense and past participle between the 1300's and 1500's, so that by the early 1600's *wound* was the established spelling, except for *winded* in the past tense, which appears to the end of the 1800's. The actual change in pronunciation is attributed to the sounds represented by *-nd* after the vowel sound in Old English *wunden,* and the confusion of Middle English *wonde, wonden.*

—**n.** a bend, turn, twist. 1399, apparatus for winding, winch or windlass; in part borrowed from Middle Low German *winde* windlass, and in part from the verb in English.

—**windup** *n.* 1665, end, conclusion, in Bunyan's *The Holy City;* earlier *windupal, windupall* (1573).

windlass (wind′ləs) *n.* machine for pulling or lifting things, winch. Before 1400 *wynlase,* probably an alteration of earlier *wyndase* (1293); borrowed through Anglo-French *windas,* and directly from a Scandinavian source (compare Old Icelandic *vindāss,* a compound of *vinda* to WIND[2] + *āss* pole, beam).

window *n.* Probably before 1200, in *Ancrene Riwle,* borrowed from a Scandinavian source; compare Old Icelandic *vindauga* (*vindr* WIND[1] + *auga* EYE), Norwegian and Danish *vindu.* The Scandinavian loanword replaced Old English *ēagthyrl* (before 899; literally, eye-hole) and *ēagduru* (literally, eye-door), but the Old French or Medieval Latin borrowing *fenester* (found in Old High German *fěnster*) was in concurrent use with *window* till the mid-1500's. —**v.** 1606, in Shakespeare's *Antony and Cleopatra,* to place in a window; from the noun. —**window box** (1895) —**windowpane** *n.* (1819, in writings of Keats) —**window-shop** *v.* (1922, implied in *window-shopping,* in Sinclair Lewis' *Babbitt*) —**windowsill** *n.* (1703)

wine *n.* Probably before 1200 *wine,* in Layamon's *Chronicle of Britain;* developed from Old English *wīn* (about 725, in *Beowulf*); an early borrowing from Latin *vīnum* wine. Old English *wīn* is cognate with Old Frisian, Old Saxon, Middle Low German, Middle Dutch *win* (modern Dutch *wijn*), Old High German *wīn* wine (modern German *Wein*), Old Icelandic *vīn,* Swedish, Norwegian, and Danish *vin,* and Gothic *wein;* also early borrowings from Latin *vīnum* wine. The Latin word is the source of the Balto-Slavic (Lithuanian *vỹnas* and Old Slavic *vino*) and Celtic words (Old Irish *fīn,* Welsh *gwin*), and is ultimately related to Greek *oînos* wine, Albanian *vēne,* and Armenian *gini,* which are probably from Indo-European **woinos,* a derivative (with *-no-* suffix) of the root **wei-/woi-/wi-* (Pok.1120), represented by Latin *vītis* vine.

It may be that the knowledge of winemaking came originally from non-Indo-European peoples, but the relationship of the Indo-European words with Arabic and Ethiopic *wain,* Hebrew *yayin,* and Assyrian *īnu* is not understood.

—**v.** entertain with wine. About 1624, to spend in drinking wine; from the noun. The meaning of entertain with wine is first recorded in 1862.

—**wine cellar** (1371) —**wineglass** *n.* (1709) —**wine press** (1526, in the Tyndale Bible)

wing *n.* About 1175 *wenge;* later *whing* (probably before 1200, in Layamon's *Chronicle of Britain*) and *winge* (1390); replacement of Old English *fethra,* pl., wings, and borrowed from a Scandinavian source (compare Old Icelandic *vængr* wing of a bird, aisle, etc., Norwegian and Danish *vinge, veng,* Swedish *vinge*), of unknown origin.

The meaning of either of two divisions of an army, political group, etc., is first recorded about 1400, and that of a subordinate part of a building on one side of the main part, in 1523.

—**v.** 1486, to carve (a quail or partridge), in the *Book of St. Albans;* from the noun. The meaning of take

flight, fly, is first recorded in Shakespeare's *King Lear* (1605).
—wingspread *n.* (1889)

wink *v.* Probably before 1200 *winken* to close one's eyes, in *Ancrene Riwle;* developed from Old English *wincian* to nod, wink (before 899, in Alfred's translation of St. Gregory's *Pastoral Care*); cognate with Middle Low German, Middle Dutch, and modern Dutch *winken* to wink, stagger, Old High German *winkan* move sideways, stagger, nod (Middle High German and modern German *winken* to wave, wink), Old High German *wankōn* to stagger, totter, and Old Icelandic *vakka* to stray, wander about. Old High German *winkan* is from Proto-Germanic **wenkanan,* cognate with Lithuanian *véngti* to avoid, originally bend out of the way of, from Indo-European **weng-* be bent (Pok.1148). The meaning of blink is first recorded in Middle English in *Cursor Mundi* (before 1325). The meaning of close an eye as a hint or signal is first recorded about 1100, and the figurative sense of close one's eyes to a fault, irregularity, etc., about 1480. **—n.** a winking. About 1303, a closing of the eyes for sleep, nap, in Mannyng's *Handlyng Synne;* from *winken* to close one's eyes.

winkle *n.* sea snail used for food. 1585, shortened form of PERIWINKLE[2]. **—v.** 1925, to extract, eject, get out (as a winkle from its shell); from the noun.

winnow *v.* blow off the chaff from (grain). Before 1382 *winnewen,* in the Wycliffe Bible; earlier *windwen* (probably before 1200); developed from Old English (before 830) *windwian,* from *wind* air in motion, paring down, WIND[1]. The figurative sense of sort out, separate, sift (as in *to winnow truth from lies*) is first recorded in the Wycliffe Bible (1382, but may possibly occur earlier in Old English; compare the literal sense of separating refuse particles, before 830, in the *Vespasian Psalter*). **—n.** a winnowing. 1580, device, such as a fan, for winnowing grain; from the verb. The meaning of the act of winnowing is first recorded in the writings of Coleridge, in 1802.

wino (wī′nō) *n. Slang.* destitute alcoholic who drinks wine. 1915, American English; formed from English *wine* + the slang suffix *-o,* as in *dipso* (1880, formed by George Bernard Shaw from *dipsomaniac*).

It is also possible the slang suffix was influenced by the *-o* in Anglo-Irish *boyo* (1870) and forms, such as *bucko* (1833) and *kiddo* (1896). This latter use of the suffix *-o* (except in clipped forms like *dipso, psycho,* and *schizo*) possibly derives from an exclamatory *O* added on to the rhyme word at the end of a line in ballads, as in *Nanny-O.* A similar formation *cheery-O* (before 1810) was later used as a greeting in Great Britain. Compare WEIRDO.

winsome (win′səm) *adj.* 1677, charming, attractive, pleasing; surviving for almost 400 years apparently only in northern British dialect from Old English *wynsum* agreeable, pleasant (about 725, in *Beowulf*). Old English *wynsum* is cognate with Old Saxon *wunsam* and Old High German *wunnisam,* and is a compound of *wynn* pleasure, delight + *-sum* -some[1]. Old English *wynn* is cognate with Old Saxon *wunnia* joy, bliss, delight, Old High German *wunna, wunnī* (modern German *Wonne*), from Proto-Germanic **wunjō,* and Old Icelandic *una* be content, dwell; see WONT.

winter *n.* Old English, the fourth season of the year; also, a year (about 725, in *Beowulf*); cognate with Old Frisian *winter* winter, Old Saxon *wintar,* Middle Low German, Middle Dutch, and modern Dutch *winter,* Old High German *wintar* (modern German *Winter*), Old Icelandic *vetr* (Norwegian *vetr*), and Gothic *wintrus,* from Proto-Germanic **wentruz;* from a nasalized form of Indo-European **wed-* to be wet (Pok.78), found in English WET and WATER. **—v.** pass the winter. 1382 *winternen,* in the Wycliffe Bible; from the noun. **—winterize** *v.* 1934, formed from English *winter,* n. + *-ize.* **—wintertime** *n.* (probably before 1387, in a version of *Piers Plowman*) **—wintry** *adj.* 1590, in Spenser's *Faerie Queene;* formed from English *winter* + *-y*[1]. A corresponding form existed in Old English *wintrig* (*winter* + *-ig* -y[1]), but the modern word appears to be a new formation.

wipe *v.* Probably before 1200 *wipen* to rub clean or dry, in *Ancrene Riwle;* developed from Old English (about 960) *wipian.* Old English *wipian* is cognate with (but distant in semantic connection) Old High German *wīfan* to wind around (modern German *weifen*), *wipf* impulse, movement, *weif* bandage, band, head covering, Old Icelandic *veipr* head covering, cloth for wiping the head, and Gothic *wipja* wreath, and *weipan* to crown with a garland, from Proto-Germanic **wīpanan,* Indo-European **weib-/wib-/wib-* sweep back and forth (Pok.1132). Cognates outside Germanic include Latin *vibrāre* move to and fro, wave, brandish, shake, Lithuanian *výburti* to wag, and Latvian *viebt* to turn. **—n.** act of wiping. 1550, from the verb.

wire *n.* Before 1376 *wyre,* in a version of *Piers Plowman;* developed from Old English *wīr* metal drawn out into a thread (about 725, in *Beowulf*). Old English *wīr,* from Proto-Germanic **wīraz,* is cognate with Middle Low German *wīre* wire, Old High German *wiara* finest gold, gold ornament, Old Icelandic *vīra-* in *vīravirki* filigree work. Possible cognates outside Germanic are found in Old Irish *fiar* bent, curved, Welsh *gŵyr,* and Latin *viēre* to bend, twist, plait; see WITHY. **—v.** furnish with wire. Probably before 1300 *wyren* to adorn with (gold) wire, in *Kyng Alisaunder;* from the noun. The meaning of furnish with a wire is first recorded in 1435. **—wire-haired** *adj.* 1801, having a rough coat. **—wireless** *adj.* 1894, using no wires, transmitting by radio waves; *n. Archaic.* 1903, sound broadcasting, radio. **—wiretapping** *n.* interception of telephone or telegraph messages. 1904, back formation from earlier *wiretapper* (1893); for suffix see -ING[1]. **—wiring** *n.* 1809, system of wires, as for a snare; later, system of wires to carry electric current (1887). **—wiry** *adj.* 1588, made of wire, formed from English *wire,* n. + *-y*[1]. The transferred meaning of lean, tough, sinewy, is first recorded in Sir Walter Scott's *Marmion* (1808).

wisdom *n.* Old English *wīsdōm* (about 725, in *Beowulf*); formed from *wīs* WISE[1] + *-dōm* condition; see -DOM, and cognate with Old Frisian and Old Saxon *wīsdōm,* Middle Dutch *wijsdom,* Old and Middle High German *wīstuom* (modern German *Weistum* legal sentence, precedent), and Old Icelandic *visdōmr* (Swedish and Danish *visdom*). **—wisdom teeth** 1848 (but *teeth of wisdom* since 1668), loan translation of Latin *dentēs sapientiae,* after Greek *sōphronistêres* (used by Hippocrates); so called because they ordinarily appear after a person has reached adulthood (usually between the ages 17 and 25), from *sṓphrōn* prudent; self-controlled.

wise[1] *adj.* sage, judicious. Probably before 1200, in *Ancrene Riwle;* developed from Old English *wīs* (about 725, in *Beowulf*); cognate with Old Frisian, Old Saxon, and Middle Low German *wīs* wise, Middle Dutch and modern Dutch *wijs,* Old High German *wīs, wīse* (modern German *weise*), Old Icelandic *vīss* (Danish, Norwegian, and Swedish *vis*), and Gothic *-weis* (in compounds); from Proto-Germanic **wīsaz,* earlier **wītsas,* from Indo-European **weid-s-os* (Pok.1127) and related to the source of Old English *witan* to know, WIT². **—wiseacre** (wīz′ā′kər) *n.* person who thinks that he knows everything. 1595, partial translation of Middle Dutch *wijssegger* soothsayer, by association with English *wise*¹ and a probable phonetic misunderstanding of then obsolete English *segger* sayer, braggart (about 1440). The Middle Dutch word was perhaps altered (by association with Middle Dutch *segger* sayer) from Old High German *wīzzago* prophet, from *wizzan* to know; see WIT² know. **—wisecrack** *n. Informal.* clever remark (1924, in letters of George Ade, American English); *v. Informal.* make wisecracks (1915, implied in *wisecrackin',* American English). **—wise guy** *Informal.* (1896, in George Ade's *Artie,* American English)

wise² *n.* way of proceeding, manner (as in *no wise bad, just mischievous*). Old English *wīse* (about 725, in *Beowulf*); cognate with Old Frisian *wīs* way, manner, Old Saxon *wīsa,* Middle Low German *wīse, wīs,* Middle Dutch *wīze, wijs* (modern Dutch *wijze*), Old High German *wīsa, wīs* (modern German *Weise*), Old Icelandic *vīsa* stanza, *-vīs* manner (in *ǫdhruvīs* otherwise), Danish, Norwegian, and Swedish *vis* way, manner; ultimately from the same source as WISE¹. Compare GUISE.

-wise a suffix forming adverbs meaning: **1a** in a ______manner, as in *likewise = in a like manner.* **b** in a _____ing manner, as in *slantwise = in a slanting manner.* **2** in the characteristic way of a _____; like a _____, as in *clockwise = in the way the hands of a clock go.* **3** in the direction of the _____, as in *lengthwise = in the direction of the length.* **4** in the _____ respect or case, as in *otherwise = in the other respect.* Middle English *-wise,* developed from Old English *-wīsan,* from *wīse* way, manner; see WISE².

wish *v.* Before 1325 *wichen* to desire; earlier *wusshen* (probably before 1200); developed from Old English *wȳscan* (before 899, in Alfred's translation of St. Gregory's *Pastoral Care*). Old English *wȳscan* (with loss of *n* before spirant *s*) is cognate with Middle Dutch *wonscen, wunscen, wenscen* (modern Dutch *wensen*) to wish, *wonsc, wunsc, wensc* a wish, Middle Low German *wunschen* to wish, Old High German *wunsken* to wish, *wunsc* a wish (modern German *wünschen, Wunsch*), Old Icelandic *øskja* to wish (Swedish *önska,* Norwegian and Danish *ønske*), *ōsk* a wish; from Proto-Germanic **wunskjanan.* Other Germanic cognates are Gothic *wēns* expectation, hope, and Old English *wine* friend. Outside Germanic cognates are found in Sanskrit *vā́ñchati* (he) wishes, *vāñchā* a wish, related to *vánati* (he) desires, and in Latin *Venus* (genitive *Veneris*) love, desire (personified as a goddess), from Indo-European **wen-/wēn-* (Pok.1146); see VENERATE. **—n.** Before 1325 *wiss* a wishing, before 1393 *wissh;* from the verb. **—wishbone** *n.* (1853, American English) **—wishful** *adj.* 1523, wished-for, desirable; later, wishing, desirous (1593, in Shakespeare's *2 Henry VI*); formed from English *wish,* n. + *-ful.*

wishy-washy *adj.* Before 1693, feeble or poor in quality, unsubstantial, trifling, inconclusive; reduplication of *washy* thin, watery, with alternating vowel (found in earlier *swish-swash,* 1547).

wisp *n.* small bundle, small bunch. Before 1325 *wispe,* cognate with Norwegian and Swedish *visp* wisp, of unknown origin, sometimes connected with WIPE, with alternation of *-sp* and *-ps;* also formerly connected with WHISK. Another connection may be with Middle Low German and Middle Dutch *wispel* a measure of grain, but whether *wispel* contains the same word as English *wisp* is not certain. **—wispy** *adj.* like a wisp, thin, slight. Before 1717, formed from English *wisp* + *-y*¹.

wisteria *or* **wistaria** (wistir′ēə) *n.* kind of climbing shrub. 1819 *wisteria* (apparently a misprint), New Latin; formed in allusion to Caspar *Wistar,* 1761-1818, an American anatomist. The word was coined by Thomas Nuttall, 1786-1859, an English botanist who came to the United States in 1808.

wistful *adj.* longing, yearning. 1613-16, closely attentive, intent; formed from obsolete English *wist(ly)* intently (before 1500, of uncertain origin) + *-ful.* The meaning of expectantly or yearningly eager, longing, is first recorded in Gay's *The Shepherd's Week* (1714).

wit¹ *n.* mental capacity, knowledge, intellect. Old English *wit,* more commonly *gewit* (about 725, in *Beowulf*); cognate with Old Frisian and Old Saxon *wit* knowledge, intellect, Old High German *wizzi* (modern German *Witz* joke, witticism), Old Icelandic *vit* wit, knowledge (Danish *vid,* Norwegian *vidd, vett,* Swedish *vett*), and Gothic *-witi,* from Proto-Germanic **witjan;* related to Old English *witan* to know; see WIT².

The meaning of ability to make clever remarks in an amusing way is first recorded in English in 1542, and that of a person of wit or learning, one who is clever or intellectual, is found in Middle English about 1470.

wit² *v. Archaic.* know. Before 1225 *witen,* developed from Old English *witan* to know (about 725, in *Beowulf*); cognate with Old Frisian *wita* to know, Old Saxon *witan,* Middle Dutch and modern Dutch *weten,* Old High German *wizzan* (modern German *wissen*), Old Icelandic *vita* (Norwegian *vite,* Danish *vide,* Swedish *veta*), and Gothic *witan,* from Proto-Germanic **witanan.* The Germanic words, meaning basically to have seen, hence to know, are cognate with Latin *vidēre* to see, Greek *eidénai* to know, *ideîn* to see (*oîda* I know), Old Prussian *waidima* we know, Old Slavic *viděti* to see, *věděti* to know, and Sanskrit *véda* I know, *véda-s* knowledge, from Indo-European **weid-/woid-/wid-* (Pok.1125).

The phrase *to wit,* with the meaning of that is to say, namely, is first recorded in 1577, from the earlier expression *that is to wit,* with the same meaning (1340, in *Ayenbite of Inwyt*), probably a loan translation of Anglo-French *cestasavoir.*

witch *n.* About 1250 *wiche,* in *Genesis and Exodus;* developed from Old English *wicce* female magician, sorceress (about 1000), feminine of *wicca* sorcerer, wizard (about 890). These words are related to, and probably derivatives of Old English *wiccian* to practice witchcraft, itself related to Old English *wīgle* divination, *wīglian* to divine, and *wīg* idol, all cognate with Old Frisian *wigila* sorcery, witchcraft, and probably with Middle Low German and Middle High German *wicken, wikken* to bewitch, divine, Old High German *wīh, wīhi* holy, Old Icelandic *vē* temple, and Gothic *weihs* holy.

—v. use the power of a witch on. Before 1200 *wicchen;* developed from Old English (about 1000) *wiccian* practice witchcraft.

—witchcraft *n.* Probably before 1200 *wicchecraft,* in *Ancrene Riwle;* developed from Old English (about

1000) *wiccecræft* (*wicce* witch, n. + *cræft* CRAFT). **—witch doctor** (1718) **—witchery** *n.* sorcery. 1546, formed from English *witch,* n. or v. + *-ery.* **—witch hunt** 1885, the action of hunting out and persecuting persons suspected of witchcraft; later, the action of persecuting persons who hold unacceptable views or engage in unacceptable practices (1938, in Orwell's writings). **—witch hunting** (1640)

witch hazel (1541) *wyche hasill,* probably from Old English *wice* wych-elm + *hæsel* any of a group of bushes of the pine family. The sense of a North American bush from which a soothing lotion is made is first recorded in 1671, and is so called from application of the name of the European plant to a new plant found by the colonists.

with *prep.* Old English *with* against, opposite, toward (about 725, in *Beowulf*); related to *wither* against; cognate with Old Frisian *with, wither* against, with, Old Saxon *with, withar,* Middle Dutch and modern Dutch *weder* again, Old High German *widar* against, back, again (modern German *wider*), Old Icelandic *vidh, vidhr* against, with (Swedish *vid,* Norwegian and Danish *ved*), and Gothic *withra* against; cognate also with Sanskrit *vi-* apart, away, from Indo-European **wi-* (Pok.1175).

The basic senses of this preposition in the earliest periods were those of opposition ("against") and of motion in proximity ("towards, away, alongside," still found in such compounds as *withdraw* and *withstand*). Later, a significant change in the sense development took place in Middle English with assimilation of senses denoting association, combination, and union, which in Old English were carried by *mid.* This development in the meaning of *with* resulted partly from influence of Old Icelandic *vidh* (found also in Old Frisian, and in Old Saxon) and may have been further enlarged by association with Latin *cum* with (as in *pugnāre cum* . . .to fight with).

—within *prep., adv.* inside (of). Old English *withinnan* (about 1000, in Ælfric's translation of *Genesis*); formed from Old English *with* toward + *innan* in. **—without** *prep., adv.* About 1290 *withoute;* alteration of Old English *withūtan* (before 899, in Alfred's translation of Orosius' *Historiarum Adversus Paganos*); formed from Old English *with* toward + *ūtan* from without, from *ūt* OUT.

with- a prefix meaning: **1** away, back, as in *withdraw = to draw back.* **2** against, opposing, as in *withstand = to stand against.* **3** along with, alongside, toward, as in *withal, without, within.* Middle English and Old English *with-,* related to WITH, prep.

withal *adv. Archaic.* with it all, as well, besides, also. Probably about 1200 *with alle,* in *The Ormulum;* later *wit-al* (before 1325, in *Cursor Mundi*); formed from *with* WITH, prep. + *al, all* ALL. **—prep.** *Archaic.* with. Before 1325; from the adverb.

withdraw *v.* draw back, draw away. Probably before 1200 *withdrawen,* in *Ancrene Riwle;* formed from Middle English *with* away; see WITH + *drawen* to DRAW, probably by influence of, if not a loan translation of, Latin *retrahere* to retract (compare German *zurückziehen,* a probable loan translation from Latin). **—withdrawal** *n.* a withdrawing or being withdrawn. 1824, formed from English *withdraw* + *-al*[2]. The meaning of discontinuation of the use of an addictive drug is first recorded in 1897.

withe (wīTH *or* wiTH) *n.* tough, flexible twig, as of a willow. Old English *withthe* (about 1000, in Ælfric's *Homilies*); cognate with Old High German *wid, widi* twisted cord, Old Icelandic *vidh* willow twig, *vīdhir* willow; see WITHY.

wither *v.* dry up, shrivel. 1535, alteration of Middle English *wydderen* dry up, shrivel (probably about 1380), apparently a differentiated or special use of *wederen* to expose to the weather; see WEATHER. For the change of *d* to *th,* see GATHER, WEATHER.

withers *n.pl.* ridge between the shoulder blades of a horse or other animal. 1580, probably formed from the obsolete or dialectal English (and Old English) *wither* against, contrary, opposite; see WITH + the plural suffix *-s*[1]; possibly so called because the withers are the parts that the animal opposes to its load. An earlier form *wydersome* (1541, spelled *wyder sone* in 1547), is probably a borrowed word; compare German *Widerrist* withers.

withhold *v.* refuse to give. Probably before 1200 *withholden* hold back, in *Ancrene Riwle;* formed from Middle English *with-* back, away + *holden* to HOLD; probably by influence of, if not a loan translation of, Latin *retinēre* to withhold (compare German *zurückhalten,* a probable loan translation from Latin).

withstand *v.* About 1200 *withstanden* stand against, resist, oppose, in *Vices and Virtues;* developed from Old English *withstandan* (before 899, in Alfred's translation of Boethius' *De Consolatione Philosophiae*); formed from *with-* against + *standan* to STAND; cognate with Old Frisian *withstonda* and Old Icelandic *vithstanda,* all perhaps influenced by, or loan translations of, Latin *resistere* to resist (compare also German *widerstehen,* a probable loan translation from Latin).

withy (wiTH′ē) *n.* willow twig, willow. Probably before 1200 *withi,* in *Ancrene Riwle;* developed from Old English (961) *wīthig;* cognate with Old High German *wīda* willow (modern German *Weide*), Old Icelandic *vīdhir* (Swedish *vide,* Norwegian *vidje, vie,* Danish *vidje*), and Gothic *wida* in *kunawida* chain. Cognates outside Germanic are found in Latin *vītis* vine, Greek *ītéā* willow (from earlier **wītéwā*), Lithuanian *výtis* willow twig, Old Slavic *vitĭ* twisted thing, *větvĭ* branch, Avestan *vaēiti* willow; all derived from Indo-European **wei-, weyə-/wī-* to twist, bend (Pok.1120), found in Latin *viēre* to bend, twist, plait, Lithuanian *výti* to turn, twist, and Sanskrit *váyati* (he) weaves, plaits. Compare VEER.

witness *n.* Old English *witnes* attestation of a fact, event, etc., from personal knowledge, testimony, evidence, one who testifies; originally, knowledge, wit (about 950, in *Lindisfarne Gospels*); formed from WIT[1] + *-nes* -ness. The meaning of something that serves as evidence or substantiation of a fact (often in the phrase *as witness*) is first recorded in Middle English, in *Cursor Mundi* (before 1325). **—v.** see, perceive. Probably about 1300 *wittnessen* bear witness to, testify to; from the noun. The meaning of be a spectator of, observe, see, is first recorded in 1582.

witting *adj.* done or acting consciously, intentional. About 1378, in a version of *Piers Plowman;* formed from WIT[2], v., know + *-ing*[1]. **—wittingly** *adv.* 1535, formed from Middle English *witting* + *-ly*[1]; replacing Middle English *witandly* (before 1340); formed from *witand,* present participle of *witen* to know, WIT[2] + *-ly*[1].

witty *adj.* full of wit. About 1340, in *The Prick of Conscience;* developed from Old English *wittig* wise, clever (about 725, in *Beowulf*); formed from *wit* intellect; see WIT[1] + *-ig* -y[1]; cognate with Old High German *wizzīg* wise, clever (modern German *witzig* witty), and Old Icelandic *vitugr* wise. **—witticism** *n.* witty remark. 1677, in the writings of Dryden; coined by him from *witty,* on the model of *criticism.*

wive *v.* marry a woman. Probably before 1200 *wiuen,* in *Ancrene Riwle;* developed from Old English *wifian* (before 899, in Alfred's translation of Boethius' *De Consolatione Philosophiae*), from *wīf* woman, WIFE.

wizard *n.* sorcerer. Probably before 1425 *wysard* wise man, sage, in *Promptorium Parvulorum;* formed from Middle English *wys, wise* WISE[1] + *-ard.* The meaning of one who is supposed to have magic power, sorcerer, is not recorded before about 1550. The spelling *wizard* is first recorded in Ben Jonson's *The Poetaster* (1601), though the spelling with *z* is found in the noun as early as 1579. **—wizardry** *n.* sorcery. 1583 *wisardrie,* in Golding's translation of Calvin's *Commentaries on Psalms;* formed from earlier English *wisard* wizard + *-rie* -ry.

wizen (wiz′ən) *v.* dry up, shrivel, wither. Before 1450 *wisenen;* developed from Old English (before 893) *wisnian, weosnian;* cognate with Old High German *wesanēn* to dry up, shrivel, wither (modern German *verwesen* to decay), Old Icelandic *visna* (Swedish *vissna,* Norwegian and Danish *visne*). Outside Germanic cognates are found in Lithuanian *výsti* to wither, and Latin *viēscere* to wither, related to *viēre* to bend, twist; see WITHY.

wobble *v.* move unsteadily. 1677 *wabble* (implied earlier in *wabling,* 1657); probably borrowed from Low German *wabbeln* to wobble; cognate with Middle High German *wabelen* to waver, Old Icelandic *vafla* hover about, totter, related to *vafra* move unsteadily; see WAVER. The spelling *wobble* is first recorded in the 1850's. **—n.** wobbling motion. 1699 *wabble,* from the verb. **—wobbly** *adj.* unsteady. 1851-61 *wabbly;* 1871 *wobbly;* formed from English *wabble, wobble,* v. + *-y*[1].

woe *interj.* Probably before 1200 *wo, wa,* in *Ancrene Riwle* and Layamon's *Chronicle of Britain;* developed from Old English *wā* (about 725, in *Beowulf*). The word is a common exclamation of lament developed in many languages, and Old English *wā* is cognate with Old Frisian, Old Saxon, and Middle Low German *wē* woe, Middle Dutch and modern Dutch *wee,* Old High German and Middle High German *wē* (modern German *weh*), Old Icelandic *vei, væ* (Swedish, Norwegian, and Danish *ve*), Gothic *wai* and is found further in Latin *vae,* Middle Irish *fāe,* Welsh *gwae,* Latvian *vaĩ,* and Avestan *vayōi, avōi* (from Indo-European **wai* (Pok.1110), though Armenian *vay* and Late Greek *oá, ouá* are new formations. **—n.** great grief. Probably about 1175 *wo;* developed from the interjection in Old English. **—woebegone** *adj.* beset with woe, oppressed with misfortune. Probably about 1300, in the phrase *(he, she) is wo bigon,* in *The Romance of Guy of Warwick.* Originally the common construction was *me is wo bigon* woe has beset me (Middle English *wo* + *begon,* past participle of *begon* to beset, happen to, Old English *begān,* from *be-* + *gān* go). Subsequently a change of construction took place, and *woe* and *begone* became so closely associated as to form a closed compound. **—woeful** *adj.* Before 1325 *waful* full of woe, in *Cursor Mundi,* from *wa* woe, n. + *-ful.*

wok *n.* frying pan with a round bottom, used in Chinese cooking. 1952, borrowed from Chinese (Cantonese) *wok.*

wold *n.* high, rolling country, bare of woods. About 1220 *wolde* open country; developed from Old English: (Anglian) *wald,* (West Saxon) *weald* forest, wooded upland (786). The Old English forms are cognate with Old Frisian and Old Saxon *wald* forest, Old High German *wald* forest, wilderness, Old Icelandic *völlr* untilled field, plain (Swedish *vall* pasture, Norwegian *voll* grassy plain), from Proto-Germanic **walthuz,* Indo-European **woltus* (Pok.1139).

It appears that the sense development from forested upland to rolling country vaguely follows the historical deforestation of Britain. Beyond an occasional "poetical" use the word survives in place names associated with rolling country, in such formations as *Cotswold, Stow-on-the-Wold,* and *the Wolds.*

wolf *n.* Probably before 1300 *wolf,* in *Arthour and Merlin;* developed from Old English (about 750) *wulf;* cognate with Old Frisian *wolf,* Old Saxon *wulf,* Middle Dutch and modern Dutch *wolf,* Old High German *wolf* (modern German *Wolf*), feminine *wulpa,* Old Icelandic *ulfr* (Swedish, Norwegian, and Danish *ulv*), and Gothic *wulfs,* from Proto-Germanic **wulfaz* (earlier **wulHwaz*). Cognates outside Germanic are found in Latin (really Sabine) *lupus* wolf, Greek *lýkos,* Lithuanian *vil̃kas,* Latvian *vìlks,* Old Slavic *vlŭkŭ,* Avestan *vəhrkō,* and Sanskrit *vṛ́ka-s,* from Indo-European *wḷkwos* (Pok.1178). **—v.** eat like a wolf, devour. 1862, in George A. Sala's *The Seven Sons of Mammon;* from the noun. **—wolfhound** *n.* (1823, in Scott's *Quentin Durward*) **—wolfish** *adj.* 1570, formed from English *wolf,* n. + *-ish*[1]. An earlier form *wolvish* was formed in Middle English (about 1430) from *wolv-,* inflectional stem form of *wolf* + *-ish*[1], but became obsolete in the early 1800's.

wolverine (wůl′vərēn′) *n.* animal related to the weasel. 1619, in writings of Thomas Middleton, alteration of earlier *wolvering* (1574), of uncertain origin; possibly from *wolv-,* inflectional stem form of *wolf* (as in the plural *wolves*) + *-ing*[1]; or perhaps from *wolver* one who behaves like a wolf, ravenous or savage animal (1593).

woman *n.* About 1250 *woman;* earlier *wumman* (probably before 1200, in *Ancrene Riwle*); developed from Old English (about 1000) *wimman,* plural *wimmen,* alteration (by assimilation of *f* to *m*) of *wīfman,* plural *wīfmen* (before 766), a compound of *wīf* woman, WIFE + *man* human being; see MAN.

The formation is peculiar to English, and not found before 766 in Old English, the more ancient word being *wīf* WIFE. From about 1400 *woman* and *women* became the regular spellings for the singular and plural (corresponding to *man* and *men*), but in the standard speech the pronunciation (wů-) was appropriated to the singular and (wi-) to the plural, possibly by influence of pairs such as *foot, feet.*

—womanhood *n.* About 1385, in Chaucer's *Troilus and Criseyde,* state or condition of being a woman, formed from English *woman* + *-hood.* **—womanish** *adj.* About 1385, proper to a woman, feminine, womanly, in Chaucer's *Troilus and Criseyde;* formed from Middle English *woman* + *-ish*[1]. The word was first used in its current derogatory sense, in Gower's *Confessio Amantis* (1393). **—womankind** *n.* Before 1325, the female sex, women in general, in *Cursor Mundi;* formed from

English *woman* + *kind*[2] sort. **—womanly** *adj.* Probably before 1200 *wummonlich* like a woman, womanish, as in reference to a man's behavior, in *Ancrene Riwle;* formed from Middle English *woman* + *-lich* -ly[2]. The sense of having qualities traditionally admired in women is first recorded about 1385, in Chaucer's *Troilus and Criseyde.* **—womenfolk** *n.pl.* (1833 *womenfolk;* 1851 *womenfolks*) **—women's liberation** (1966) **—women's rights** (1840 *woman's rights;* 1850 *women's rights;* an isolated early example is recorded in 1632)

womb *n.* Probably about 1175 *wombe;* developed from Old English *wamb, womb* belly, uterus (before 830, in the *Vespasian Psalter*). The Old English forms are cognate with Old Frisian *wambe, wamme* belly, Middle Dutch *wamme* (modern Dutch *wam*), Old High German *wamba* (modern German *Wamme* in animals), Old Icelandic *vǫmb* (Norwegian, Swedish, and Danish *vom*), and Gothic *wamba* belly, from Proto-Germanic **wambō;* of unknown origin.

wombat (wom′bat) *n.* Australian animal resembling a small bear. 1798, borrowed from an aboriginal Australian source.

wonder *n.* Before 1137 *wunder,* in *Peterborough Chronicle* (implied earlier in *wonderful,* before 1100); later, in the spelling *wonder* (about 1300); developed from Old English *wundor* marvelous thing, marvel (about 725, in *Beowulf*); cognate with Old Saxon *wundar* wonder, Middle Dutch and modern Dutch *wonder,* Old High German *wuntar* (modern German *Wunder*), and Old Icelandic *undr* (Danish, Norwegian, and Swedish *under*), from Proto-Germanic **wunđran;* of unknown origin. **—v.** feel wonder. Probably before 1200 *wundren,* in *Ancrene Riwle* and Layamon's *Chronicle of Britain;* developed from Old English (before 899) *wundrian;* related to *wundor,* n., in Old English. Old English *wundrian* is cognate with Old High German *wuntarōn* to wonder, and Old Icelandic *undra.* **—wonderful** *adj.* Before 1100 *wunderful* full of wonder, marvelous; formed from Middle English *wunder,* n. + *-ful.* **—wonderland** *n.* (1790) **—wonderment** *n.* wonder. 1535, formed from English *wonder,* v. + *-ment.* **—wondrous** *adj.* Before 1500, wonderful; alteration of Middle English *wonders,* adj., by substitution of suffix *-ous,* patterned after *marvelous.* Middle English *wonders,* adj., wonderful (before 1325, in *Cursor Mundi*), was originally the genitive of *wonder,* n., and was probably influenced in its formation by a Scandinavian source (compare Middle Swedish *unders,* genitive of *under* wonder).

wont *adj.* accustomed. Before 1325 *wont, wunt,* in *Cursor Mundi;* earlier *iwoned* (probably about 1175); from the past participle of *wonen, wunen* to dwell, be accustomed (compare German *gewohnt* accustomed); developed from Old English *wunian* (before 899, in Alfred's translation of Boethius' *De Consolatione Philosophiae*). Old English *wunian* is cognate with Old Frisian *wonia, wunia* to dwell, be accustomed, Old Saxon *wunon, wonon,* Middle Dutch and modern Dutch *wonen,* Old High German *wonēn* (modern German *wohnen* to dwell), Old Icelandic *una* to dwell, be content, and Gothic *-wunan* be content, from Proto-Germanic **wun-,* Indo-European **wen-,* root **wen-;* related to Old English *winnan, gewinnan* to WIN; see also WINSOME and WISH. **—v.** accustom. 1440 *wonten, wunten,* probably from *wont, wunt,* past participle of *wonen, wunen* be accustomed. **—n.** custom, habit. Before 1400, from the adjective. The noun disappeared from use during the 1700's but reappeared in the 1800's, perhaps from its use by Shelley and Scott. **—wonted** *adj.* accustomed. Before 1413, in a version of Chaucer's *Troilus and Criseyde;* extension of *wont,* past participle of *wonen;* for suffix see -ED[2]. The word was probably reinforced by later formation from *wont,* v. and n. + *-ed*[2].

woo *v.* seek to marry, court. Probably before 1200 *wowen,* in *Ancrene Riwle;* developed from Late Old English *wōgian* (before 1050, but found earlier in *wooer,* about 1000), of uncertain origin (possibly related to *wōh, wōg-* bent or inclined, as in affection toward oneself; found in Gothic *-wāhs* bent, in the compound *unwāhs* not crooked, blameless), from Proto-Germanic **wanHaz* (Indo-European **wonkos*), cognate with Sanskrit *váñcati* goes crooked, *vakrá-s* crooked, and Latin *con-vexus* arched, from Indo-European **we-n-k-/wonk-* bend, root **wek-* (Pok.1134).

wood *n.* Probably about 1225 *wode,* developed from Old English *wudu* (about 725, in *Beowulf*); earlier *widu* tree, trees collectively, the substance of which trees are made (probably before 700). Cognates with Old English are found in Old High German *witu* wood, and Old Icelandic *vidhr* (Danish, Norwegian, and Swedish *ved*), from Proto-Germanic **wiđuz.* Outside Germanic cognates are found in Celtic: Old Irish *fid* tree, wood, and Welsh *gwŷdd* trees, from Indo-European **widhus* (Pok.1177). **—v.** 1538, surround with trees; from the noun. The meaning of supply with wood, especially for fuel, is first recorded in 1628. **—woodbine** *n.* honeysuckle. Before 1387 *wodebinde,* developed from Old English (before 850) *wudubinde* a climbing plant (*wudu* wood + *binde* wreath, related to *bindan* to BIND). **—woodcock** *n.* game bird. Old English *wuducoc* (about 1050); formed from *wudu* wood + *cocc* COCK[1]. **—woodcut** *n.* design cut in wood (1662). **—wooded** *adj.* 1605, formed from English *wood,* n. or v. + *-ed*[2]. **—wooden** *adj.* 1538, formed from English *wood* + *-en*[2]. **—woodland** *n.* Old English (869) *wudulond* (*wudu* wood + *lond* LAND). **—woodpecker** *n.* (1530) **—woodpile** *n.* (1552) **—woodshed** *n.* (1844) **—woodsman** *n.* (1688, American English; largely replacing *woodman,* about 1410) **—woodsy** *adj.* 1860, American English; formed from *woods,* pl. of *wood* + *-y*[1]. **—woodwind** *n.* 1876, the wooden wind instruments in an orchestra; later, an individual instrument of this kind (1922). **—woodwork** *n.* (1650) **—woody** *adj.* 1375, wooded; later, made of wood (before 1540), like or forming wood (1578); formed from Middle English *wode* + *-y*[1].

woodchuck *n.* North American marmot, groundhog. 1674, American English, alteration (influenced by *wood*) of Algonquian (Cree) *otchek* or (Ojibwa) *otchig,* the name of the marten, transferred to the groundhog.

woof *n.* threads running from side to side across a woven fabric. 1540 *wofe,* alteration of *oof* (1382); developed from Old English (before 800) *ōwef* (*ō-* on + *wefan* to WEAVE). Middle English *oof* became *woof* partly by association with *warp,* as in the phrase *warp and woof.*

wool *n.* About 1300 *wolle,* developed from Old English (before 800) *wull;* cognate with Old Frisian *wolle, ulle* wool, Middle Low German and Middle Dutch *wolle, wulle* (modern Dutch *wol*), Old High German *wolla* (modern German *Wolle*), Old Icelandic *ull* (Swedish, Norwegian, and Danish *ull*), and Gothic *wulla,* from Proto-Germanic **wulnō.* Cognates outside Germanic are found in Latin *lāna,* Greek *lênos,* Lithuanian *vìlna,* Latvian *vilna,* Old Slavic *vlŭna,* Sanskrit *ū́rṇā,* and Avestan *varənā,* from Indo-European **wl̥nā.* **—woolen** *adj.* Probably before 1300 *wollen,* in *Kyng Alisaunder;* developed from Late Old English (1046) *wullen* (*wull* wool + *-en*²). **—woolgathering** *n.* daydreaming (1553). **—woolly** *adj.* 1578, formed from English *wool* + *-y*¹.

woozy *adj. Informal.* somewhat dizzy or weak. 1897, muddled or dazed, as with drink; American English, usually considered a variant of *oozy* muddy, but probably more likely an alteration of earlier *boozy* (1719, showing the effects of intoxication, formed from *booze* alcoholic liquor + *-y*¹). The meaning of somewhat dizzy or weak, slightly ill, is first recorded about 1940.

word *n.* Old English *word* speech, talk, utterance, word (about 725, in *Beowulf*); cognate with Old Frisian and Old Saxon *word* word, Middle Dutch *wort* (modern Dutch *woord*), Old High German *wort* (modern German *Wort*), Old Icelandic *ordh* (Danish, Norwegian, and Swedish *ord*), and Gothic *waúrd,* from Proto-Germanic **wurđan-.* Outside Germanic cognates are found in Latin *verbum,* Old Prussian *wirds* word, and Lithuanian *var̃das* name; all from Indo-European **werdh-/wordh-/wr̥dh-,* derivative forms of the base **wer-, *werə-* to speak, say (Pok.1163). The meaning of promise (as in *keep one's word*) is first recorded in Old English, in 971). **—v.** Probably before 1200 *worden* utter words, speak, in Layamon's *Chronicle of Britain;* from the noun. The meaning of put into words is first recorded in 1613. **—wordage** *n.* 1829, words collectively, verbiage; formed from English *word,* n. + *-age.* **—wordbook** *n.* (1598) **—wording** *n.* choice of words, phrasing. 1649, in Milton's *Eikonoklastes;* formed from English *word,* v. + *-ing*¹. **—word processor** (1970) **—wordy** *adj.* Before 1382 *wordi;* developed from Late Old English *wordig* verbose (about 1100); formed from *word,* n. + *-ig -y*¹.

work *n.* Probably before 1200 *work,* developed from Old English *weorc, worc* something done, deed, action, proceeding, business (about 725, in *Beowulf*); cognate with Old Frisian and Old Saxon *werk* work, Middle Low German, Middle Dutch, and modern Dutch *werk,* Old High German *werc, werah* (modern German *Werk*), Old Icelandic *verk* (Swedish and Norwegian *verk,* Danish *værk*), from Proto-Germanic **werkan,* Indo-European **werĝom.* Cognates outside Germanic are found in Greek *érgon* work, *órganon* tool, instrument, Armenian *gorc* work, Avestan *varəza-* activity, and Tocharian A *wark* wickerwork. **—v.** do, perform, or execute. Before 1250 *werken;* later *worken* (about 1300, past tense *wroghte,* past participle *wroght*); developed from a fusion of: 1) Old English *wyrcan* (about 725, in *Beowulf,* with past tense *worhte,* past participle *geworht*); cognate with Old Saxon *workian* to work, Old High German *wurchen,* Old Icelandic *yrkja,* and Gothic *waúrkjan,* from Proto-Germanic **wurkjanan,* from Indo-European **wr̥ĝ-;* and 2) Old English (Mercian) *wircan;* cognate with Old Frisian *werkia, werka* to work, Old Saxon *wirkian, -werkon,* Old High German *wirchen, werchon* (modern German *wirken* to work, operate, function), and Old Icelandic *verka,* formed relatively late from the Proto-Germanic noun **werkan.* Cognates outside Germanic are found in Old Irish *fairged* they made, Avestan *vərəzyeiti* (he) works, Greek *érdō* I do, perform (earlier **wergyō*), and Middle Welsh *gwreith* deed (Indo-European **wreĝtu-*); from Indo-European **werĝ-/worĝ-/wr̥ĝ-, *wreĝ-* (Pok.1168).

The normal representative of Old English *wyrcan* in Middle English would be *worchen;* the substitution of *k* for *ch,* producing the modern English verb form *work* instead of *worch,* was the result of influence of the noun *work,* with possible Scandinavian influence.

The new past tense and past participle *worked,* formed directly on the stem of the infinitive *to work,* became established in the 1400's. The older form *wrought* is now archaic, except in senses that denote fashioning, shaping, or decorating with the hand or an implement; see WROUGHT.

—workable *adj.* 1545, formed from English *work,* v. + *-able.* **—workaday** *adj.* characteristic of a workday, ordinary, humdrum. 1554, developed from attributive use of Middle English *werkedei* working day, workday (probably before 1200, in *Ancrene Riwle*); formed from *werk* work + *dei* day. **—workbench** *n.* (1781, in the writings of Jefferson) **—workbook** *n.* 1910, record of work; 1932, book of instructions to be written in. **—workday** *n.* (about 1430; earlier, with three syllables, *werkedei;* see WORKADAY) **—worker** *n.* About 1340, a maker, doer, or creator; formed from Middle English *worken* to work + *-er*¹. **—workhorse** *n.* 1543, horse used for labor; later, hard worker (1949). **—workhouse** *n.* Old English (before 1100) *weorchūs* workshop (*weorc* work + *hūs* HOUSE). The sense of a place where the poor or petty criminals are lodged and set to work is first recorded in 1652. **—working class** (1789) **—working-class** *adj.* (1839, in writings of John Stuart Mill) **—working man** (1638) **—workman** *n.* Old English *weorcman,* implied in *weorcmen* (before 899, in Alfred's translation of Boethius' *De Consolatione Philosophiae*). **—workmanship** *n.* Before 1325, in *Cursor Mundi;* formed from Middle English *werkmon* workman + *-ship.* **—workout** *n.* (1909) **—workroom** *n.* (1828) **—workshop** *n.* (1562)

workaholic *n.* a person addicted to work, compulsive worker. 1968, American English, coined on the analogy of *alcoholic* by Wayne Oates, an American pastoral counselor, from *work* + connective *-a-* + (*alco*)*holic.* See the combining form -AHOLIC.

world *n.* Probably before 1200, in *Ancrene Riwle;* developed from Old English *woruld, worold* human existence, the affairs of life (about 725, in *Beowulf*); also, the human race, mankind (about 750, in the poetry of Cynewulf); and the earth (before 900, in the writings of Alfred).

The word is peculiar to Germanic (though not found in Gothic), with cognates in Old Frisian *warld, wrald,* Old Saxon *werold,* Middle Dutch and modern Dutch *wereld,* Old High German *weralt, worolt* (modern German *Welt*), and Old Icelandic *verǫld* (Swedish *värld,* Danish and Norwegian *verden*). The original Germanic word was a compound, meaning literally "age of man," made up of **wer-* man (Old English *wer;* see VIRILE) + **ald-* age (Old English *ild* age, related to *eald, ald* OLD). A similar semantic connection between age and world is seen in Latin *saeculum* (see SECULAR). **—world-famous** *adj.* (1837, in Carlyle's *The French Revolution*) **—worldly** *adj.* of the world, earthly, mundane. Probably before 1200 *worldlich,* in *Ancrene Riwle;* developed from Old English (before 900) *woruldlic* (*woruld* world + *-lic* -ly²). **—World Series** (1889, *world's series,* 1913, *world-series*) **—world's fair** (1850) **—world war** (1909) **—worldwide** *adj.* 1632, as wide as the world; later, spread throughout the world (1842).

worm *n.* Probably before 1300 *worme,* in *Kyng Alisaunder;* developed from Late Old English (about 1000) *wurm,* variant of earlier *wyrm* serpent, dragon, worm (about 725, in *Beowulf*), from Proto-Germanic **wurmiz;* cognate with Old Frisian *wirm* serpent, worm, Old Saxon *wurm,* Middle Dutch and modern Dutch *worm,* Old High German *wurm* (modern German *Wurm*), Old Icelandic *ormr* (Danish *orm* worm, Norwegian and Swedish *orm* snake) (from Proto-Germanic **wurmaz*), and Gothic *waúrms.* Cognates outside Germanic are found in Latin *vermis* worm, Greek *rhómos* woodworm, Welsh *gwraint,* pl., worms in the skin, and Lithuanian *var̃mas* insect, gnat, from Indo-European **wr̥mis, wr̥mos* (Pok.1152). Related to VERMIN.

The alteration in spelling found in Middle English *worm* for Old English *wurm* reflects similar changes in *wolf, wonder, wort,* etc., and a generally prevailing tendency found in Low German *worm,* Dutch *worm,* and possibly Scandinavian influence of Old Icelandic *ormr,* with Danish, Norwegian, and Swedish *orm.*

—v. 1564-78 (figurative) clear out worms; from the noun. The meaning of creep or crawl like a worm is first recorded in 1610. The phrase *to worm out,* meaning to extract (information, etc.), is first recorded in the writings of Addison, in 1715.

—worm-eaten *adj.* (1398, in Trevisa's translation of Bartholomew's *De Proprietatibus Rerum*) **—wormy** *adj.* About 1450, attacked, gnawed, or bored by worms or grubs, worm-eaten; later, full of worms (1590, in Shakespeare's *A Midsummer Night's Dream*); formed from English *worm,* n. + *-y*[1].

wormwood *n.* bitter plant used in medicine, absinthe, etc. Before 1400 *wormwod,* alteration by folk etymology (as if from *worm* + *wood,* partly because of its use as a worm medicine) of earlier *wormod, wermod* (before 1382, in the Wycliffe Bible); developed from Old English (before 800) *wermōd* wormwood; cognate with Old Saxon *wermōda* wormwood, Middle Low German *wermōt, wermōde,* Dutch *wermoet,* and Old High German *wermuota* (modern German *Wermut*); the ultimate etymology is unknown. Related to VERMOUTH.

worry *v.* Probably before 1350 *worien* to strangle, choke, alteration (through influence of *wolf, wonder,* etc.) of earlier *werien, wirien* (before 1325); developed from Old English *wyrgan* to strangle (before 800), from Proto-Germanic **wurȝjanan;* cognate with Old Saxon *wurgil* rope, Middle Dutch *worghen, wurghen* to strangle (Dutch *worgen, wurgen*), Old High German *wurgen* (modern German *würgen*), Old Icelandic *virgill* rope, and outside Germanic with Lithuanian *ver̃žti* bind tightly, from Indo-European **wergh-/wr̥gh-* choke (Pok.1154).

The spelling change to *-or-* in Middle English is parallel to that of *wolf, worm, wort,* showing the influence of *r* on the preceding vowel.

The meaning of harass by rough or severe treatment, assail, is first recorded in English before 1553; from this developed the sense of annoy, bother, vex, first found in Milton's *Samson Agonistes* (1671).

—n. a worrying. 1804, troubled state of mind; from the verb.

—worrisome *adj.* 1845, apt to cause worry or distress; formed from English *worry,* n. or v. + *-some*[1].

worse *adj.* 1340 *worse* more bad or ill, less well, in *Ayenbite of Inwyt,* alteration of earlier *werse, wurse* (probably before 1200, in *Ancrene Riwle*); developed from Old English *wiersa, wyrsa* (about 725, in *Beowulf*); cognate with Old Frisian *wirra, werra* more evil or bad, worse, Old Saxon *wirs, wirsa,* Old High German *wirsiro,* Old Icelandic *verri* (Danish and Norwegian *værre,* Swedish *värre*), and Gothic *waírs,* perhaps cognate with Sanskrit *várṣīyas-* higher, and Lithuanian *viršùs* the highest point, from Indo-European **wers-/wr̥s-* (Pok.1152). These words derive from a Proto-Germanic comparative form whose comparative suffix **-izan-* was added to a root **wers-,* also found in Old Saxon and Old High German *werran* bring into confusion or discord; see WAR. For shift in spelling in English, see WORRY, WORM.

—adv. Probably before 1200 *wers* more badly; developed from Old English (before 900) *wyrs, wiers;* related to *wyrsa, wiersa,* adj. The Old English adverb is cognate with Old High German *wirs* worse, Old Icelandic *verr,* and Gothic *waírs.*

—n. that which is worse (especially in the phrase *to do worse*). Before 1137 *werse,* developed from Old English *wyrsa,* adj.

—worsen *v.* Probably before 1200 *wursnen* make worse, in *Ancrene Riwle;* formed from Middle English *wurse* worse + *-nen* (Old English *-nian*) -en[1].

worship *n.* Probably about 1200 *wurrshipe* condition of being worthy, distinction, honor, renown, in *The Ormulum;* later *worschipe* (before 1338); developed from Old English (Anglian) *worthscip, wurthscip* (about 950), and (West Saxon) *weorthscipe* (before 900, in Alfred's translation of Boethius' *De Consolatione Philosophiae*); formed from Old English *weorth* WORTH + *-scipe* -SHIP. The meaning of respect or honor shown to a person or thing is first recorded in Old English (about 1000) and that of reverence or veneration paid to a being regarded as supernatural or divine, in *Cursor Mundi* (before 1325). **—v.** revere, venerate, adore. Before 1390 *worschipen,* in Gower's *Confessio Amantis;* alteration of earlier *wurthsupen* (probably before 1200, in *Trinity Homilies*); from the noun. **—worshipful** *adj.* Before 1300, honorable; formed from Middle English *worschipe* worship + *-ful.* The sense of worshiping is first recorded in 1809.

worst *adj.* About 1300 *worste* most badly, alteration of earlier *wurste* (probably before 1200, in *Ancrene Riwle*), *wurst* (probably about 1175); developed from Old English *wyrresta* (before 899, in writings of Alfred); cognate with Old Frisian *werste,* Old Saxon *wirsista,* Old High German *wirsisto,* and Old Icelandic *verstr* (Norwegian *verst,* Swedish *värst,* Danish *værst*). These words derive from a Proto-Germanic comparative form with the root **wers-* (see WORSE) and the suffix **-istaz* (see -EST). For shift in spelling in English, see WORRY, WORM. **—adv.** Probably before 1200 *werst, wurst;* developed from Old English *wyrst, wierst* (before 900), superlative of *wyrs, wiers,* adv., worse. **—n.** that which is worst. About 1385 *worste,* in Chaucer's *Troilus and Criseyde;* from the adjective. **—v.** beat, defeat. 1602, to make worse, impair, damage, inflict loss upon; from the adjective.

worsted (wu̇r′stid *or* wu̇s′tid) *n.* firmly twisted woolen thread or yarn. About 1387 *worstede,* in Chaucer's *Canterbury Tales,* alteration of earlier *Worthstede* (1296; later *Worsted,* now *Worstead*), a town in northeastern Norfolk, England, where worsted was originally made.

wort[1] (wėrt) *n.* plant, herb, or root. About 1300 *wort,* alteration of earlier *wurt* (probably before 1200, in Layamon's *Chronicle of Britain*); developed from Old English *wyrt* (before 830, in the *Vespasian Psalter*); cognate with Old Saxon *wurt* root, herb, plant, Old High German *wurz, wurzala* (modern German *Wurzel* root), Old Icelandic *urt* herb (Norwegian *urt,* Swedish *ört*), and Gothic *waúrts* root, from Proto-Germanic **wurtiz.* Cognates outside Germanic are found in Latin *rādīx* root, Welsh *gwraidd* roots, Albanian *rrânzë* root, Greek *rhā́dīx* branch, *rhíza* root, and Tocharian B *witsako* root. Related to ROOT[1], of a plant, from Indo-European **wrād-/wrəd-/wr̥d-* (Pok.1167). For the shift in spelling, see WORRY, WORM.

wort[2] (wėrt) *n.* liquid made from malt. Before 1325, developed from Old English (about 1000) *wyrt;* related to *wyrt* herb, plant, WORT[1]. Old English *wyrt* is cognate with Old Saxon *wurtia* spice, and Middle High German *würze* spice, brewer's wort (modern German *Würze*). For shift in spelling, see WORRY, WORM.

worth *adj.* Probably before 1200 *wurth,* in *Trinity Homilies;* later *worth* (before 1325, in *Cursor Mundi*); developed from Old English (before 695) *weorth* equal in value to (something); cognate with Old Frisian and Old Saxon *werth* worth, worthy, Middle Dutch *wert, weert* (modern Dutch *waard*), Old High German *werd* (modern German *wert*), Old Icelandic *verdhr* (Danish *værd,* Swedish *värd,* Norwegian *verd*), and Gothic *waírths,* from Proto-Germanic **werthaz;* relations beyond Germanic are uncertain. **—n.** Probably before 1200 *wurth,* in *Ancrene Riwle;* later *worth* (before 1325, in *Cursor Mundi*); developed from Old English (before 830) *weorth* monetary value, price; cognate with Old Frisian and Old Saxon *worth,* Old High German *werd* (modern German *Wert* worth, value), Old Icelandic *verdh,* and Gothic *waírth;* from noun use of the adjective. **—worthless** *adj.* 1588, (of things) having no intrinsic value, in Shakespeare's *Titus Andronicus;* formed from English *worth,* n. + *-less.* The sense of lacking merit, contemptible, despicable, is found first in Shakespeare's *1 Henry VI* (1591). **—worthwhile** *adj.* (1884, implied in *worthwhileness*) **—worthy** *adj.* Probably about 1250 *wurrthi* having worth, good, excellent, in *The Ormulum;* formed from Middle English *wurth,* n., worth + *-y*[1]. *—n.* Probably about 1390, person of merit; from the adjective.

wot *v. Archaic.* know. Before 1325, in *Cursor Mundi,* developed from Old English *wāt,* first and third person singular present indicative of *witan* to know, WIT[2]. Old English *wāt* is cognate with Gothic *wait,* from Proto-Germanic **wait.*

would *v.* About 1380 *wulde, wolde,* in the Wycliffe Bible; developed from Old English *wolde,* past tense of *willan* to WILL[1]. Old English *wolde,* from **wilde,* was altered under influence of *sceolde.* **—would-be** *adj.* wishing or pretending to be (1300).

wound (wünd) *n.* About 1300 *wounde,* in *The Metrical Chronicle of Robert Gloucester;* developed from Old English *wund* hurt, injury (about 725, in *Beowulf*); cognate with Old Frisian *wunde* wound, Old Saxon *wunda,* Middle Dutch *wonde* (modern Dutch *wond*), Old High German *wunta, wunda* (modern German *Wunde*), and Old Icelandic *und;* relations beyond Germanic are uncertain. **—v.** About 1300 *wounden,* developed from Old English (about 760) *wundian* to inflict a wound on (a person, the body, etc.) by means of a weapon; from the noun. Old English *wundian* is cognate with Old Frisian *wundia* to wound, Middle Dutch and modern Dutch *wonden,* Old High German *wuntōn,* Middle High German *wunden* (modern German *verwunden*), Old Icelandic *unda,* and Gothic *gawundōn.*

wow *interj.* exclamation, as of surprise, joy, or dismay. Before 1500, Scottish, of imitative origin. **—n.** *Slang.* an unqualified success, hit. 1920, American English; from the interjection. **—v.** *Slang.* overwhelm with delight or amazement. 1924, American English; from the interjection.

wrack (rak) *n.* damage, disaster, ruin, wreckage. About 1390 *wrak* wrecked ship, in Chaucer's *Canterbury Tales;* probably borrowed from Middle Dutch *wrak* wreck; cognate with Old English *wræc* misery, punishment, *wreccan* to punish, drive out; see WREAK. The extended meaning of damage, disaster, destruction (often in the phrase *wrack and ruin*) appeared probably about 1408.

wraith (rāth) *n.* ghost. 1513, in a translation of Vergil's *Aeneid,* Scottish; of uncertain origin.

wrangle *v.* dispute noisily. Probably before 1387, in a version of *Piers Plowman;* cognate with Low German *wrangeln* to wrangle, related to Middle Low German *wrangen* to struggle, wrestle, and *wringen* to WRING. **—n.** noisy dispute. 1547, from the verb. **—wrangler** *n.* About 1515, person who wrangles; formed from English *wrangle* + *-er*[1]. The sense of a person in charge of horses or cattle, herder, is first recorded in American English, in writings of Theodore Roosevelt (1888).

wrap *v.* About 1320 *wrappen* to swathe, envelop, enfold, of uncertain origin. **—n.** About 1412 *wrappe* a wrapper or covering; from the verb. **—wrapper** *n.* About 1460 *wrappere,* formed from Middle English *wrappen* to wrap + *-ere* -er[1].

wrath *n.* rage. Before 1200 *wraththe,* in *Vices and Virtues;* later *wrath* (before 1300); developed from Old English *wrǣththu* (about 950, in *Lindisfarne Gospels*), derived from *wrāth* angry (from Proto-Germanic **wraithíthō*); see WROTH. **—wrathful** *adj.* Before 1300, formed from Middle English *wrath* + *-ful.*

wreak (rēk) *v.* Probably before 1200 *wreken* avenge, in Layamon's *Chronicle of Britain;* developed from Old English *wrecan* to drive, drive out, punish, avenge (about 725, in *Beowulf*); cognate with Old Frisian *wreka* to punish, avenge, Old Saxon *wrekan,* Middle Low German, Middle Dutch, and modern Dutch *wreken,* Old High German *rehhan* (modern German *rächen*), Old Icelandic *reka* (earlier *vreka*) to drive, push, avenge, and Gothic *wrikan* persecute, from Proto-Germanic **wrekanan.* Cognates outside Germanic are found in Latin *urgēre* to press, drive, urge, and Lithuanian *var̃gti* to suffer distress, from Indo-European **wreg-/wr̥g-* push, press, drive (Pok.1181).

The meaning of inflict or cause (damage, destruction, etc.) is first recorded in English in 1817, in the writings of Shelley; it developed from the earlier sense of inflict or take (vengeance), first recorded in Middle English about 1489.

wreath (rēth) *n.* ring of flowers. Probably before 1350 *wrethe* twisted or wreathed band, in *Kyng Alisaunder;* developed from Old English (about 1000) *writha* (from Proto-Germanic **writhōn*), related to *wrīthan* to twist, WRITHE. The meaning of ring or garland of flowers is first recorded in 1563. **—wreathe** (rēᴛʜ) *v.* make into a wreath. 1530, in Palsgrave's *Lesclarcissement;* in part a back formation from *wrethen,* past participle of *writhe* to twist or turn, and in part from *wreath,* n.

wreck *n.* destruction. 1228 *wrek* goods cast ashore after a shipwreck, flotsam; borrowed through Anglo-French *wrec,* from a Scandinavian source (compare Old Icelandic *rek* wreck, flotsam, from older **wrek,* related to *reka* to drive, push; see WREAK).

The meaning of a shipwreck is first recorded in 1463, and that of a wrecked ship, before 1500. The meaning of remains of a ruin, destruction, etc. (as in *the wreck of a name*) is first recorded in Addison's *Cato* (1713). **—v.** cause the wreck of, destroy, ruin. Before 1400 *wrekken* to cast ashore; from the noun. The meaning of destroy, ruin, is first recorded in 1510.
—wreckage *n.* 1837, in Carlyle's *The French Revolution;* formed from English *wreck,* v. + *-age.*

wren *n.* kind of small songbird. Old English (before 1100) *wrenna;* earlier with metathesis of *e* and *r werna* (before 800); of uncertain origin, but probably cognate with Old High German *rentilo* wren, and Icelandic *rindill.*

wrench *v.* twist or pull violently. Probably before 1200 *wrenchen,* in *Ancrene Riwle;* developed from Old English (about 1050) *wrencan* to twist; cognate with Old High German and modern German *renken* to twist (from Proto-Germanic **wrankjanan*); and outside Germanic with Latin *vergere* to bend, incline, Lithuanian *reñgtis* bend over heavily, twist oneself, and Sanskrit *vṛṇákti* (he) bends, turns, from Indo-European **werg-/wṛg-; *wreg-; *wreng-/wrong-* (Pok.1154). **—n.** violent twist or twisting pull. About 1460, apparently from the verb.

wrest *v.* twist, pull, or tear away with force, wrench away. Probably before 1200 *wresten,* in *Ancrene Riwle;* developed from Old English (before 1000) *wrǣstan* to twist, wrench (from Proto-Germanic **wraistjanan,* earlier **wraiHstjanan*); related to *wrist* WRIST, and Dutch *gewricht* joint. Old English *wrǣstan* is cognate with Old Icelandic *reista* to wring, wrest, and with Avestan *urvisyeiti* turns in a circle, and Greek *rhiknós* shriveled, crooked, from Indo-European **wreiḱ-/wroiḱ-/wriḱ-* (Pok.1158). **—n.** a wresting, forcible twist. Before 1325, in *Cursor Mundi;* from the verb.

wrestle *v.* Before 1250 *wrestlen,* in *Genesis and Exodus;* developed from Old English *wrǣstlian* (implied about 890 in *wrǣstlung* a contention); frequentative form of *wrǣstan* to WREST; for suffix compare -LE³. **—n.** a wrestling match. 1593, from the verb.

wretch *n.* very unfortunate person. Probably before 1200 *wrecche,* in *The Ormulum;* developed from Old English *wrecca* wretch, stranger, exile (about 725, in *Beowulf*); related to *wrecan* to drive out, punish; see WREAK. Old English *wrecca* is cognate with Old Saxon *wrekkio* exile, and Old High German *reccho, reckio* (modern German *Recke* warrior, hero), from Proto-Germanic **wrakjōn,* from Indo-European **wrog-,* root **wreg-.* The spelling with *t* began to appear in the 1400's. **—wretched** (rech′id) *adj.* very unfortunate. Probably before 1200 *wrecchede,* in *Trinity Homilies;* from Middle English *wrecche* wretch + *-ede* -ed².

wriggle *v.* to twist and turn. Before 1398 *wrigglen,* in Trevisa's translation of Bartholomew's *De Proprietatibus Rerum;* cognate with Middle Low German *wriggelen* to wriggle, West Frisian *wriggelje,* dialectal Norwegian *rigla,* and perhaps related to Old English *wrigian* to turn, incline, go forward; see WRY; for suffix see -LE³. **—n.** a wriggling. 1709, Steele in *The Tatler;* from the verb.

wright *n.* (now usually in combinations) a maker of something, as in *wheelwright, playwright.* Before 1200 *wrihte,* in *Vices and Virtues;* later *wright* (before 1325, in *Cursor Mundi*); developed from Old English (about 950) *wryhta,* variant of earlier *wyrhta* (perhaps before 695), from *wyrcan* to WORK. Old English *wyrhta* (from Proto-Germanic **wurHtjōn*) is cognate with Old Frisian *wrichta* and Old High German *wurhto,* both meaning worker.

wring *v.* to twist with force, squeeze hard. About 1300 *wringen,* in *Havelok the Dane* (past tense *wrang* or *wrong,* past participle *wrung*); developed from Old English (before 899) *wringan* press, strain, wring (past tense *wrang,* past participle *wrungen*); cognate with Old Frisian **wringa* to wring, Old Saxon *-wringan* in *ūtwringan,* Middle Low German *wringen,* Middle Dutch *wringhen* (modern Dutch *wringen*), and Old High German *ringan* struggle, wrestle, wrest, wring (modern German *ringen* to wrestle), from Proto-Germanic **wrenʒanan,* Indo-European **wrenĝh-* (Pok. 1155). Related to WRANGLE. **—n.** a twist, squeeze. Before 1425, from the verb. **—wringer** *n.* Before 1300, extortioner; formed from Middle English *wringen* + *-er*¹. The sense of a device for squeezing water from clothes is first recorded in 1799.

wrinkle *n.* 1392 *wrynkle* ridge, fold; probably developed from the stem of Old English *gewrinclod* wrinkled, crooked, winding, past participle of *gewrinclian* to wind, crease, formed from *ge-* perfective prefix + *-wrinclian* to wind (from Proto-Germanic **wreng-*), related to *wrencan* to twist, WRENCH; for suffix see -LE³. The figurative meaning of a clever expedient or trick, innovation, is first recorded in 1731-38, in Swift's writings, and the meaning of a piece of useful information, helpful hint, tip, in 1818. —v. make a wrinkle or wrinkles in. Probably about 1425 *wrynclen,* in a translation of Chauliac's *Grande Chirurgie;* from the noun.

wrist *n.* Old English (probably before 940) *wrist;* cognate with Old Frisian *wrist, wirst* wrist, Middle Dutch and Middle Low German *wrist,* Middle High German *rist* wrist, ankle (modern German *Rist* instep, wrist), and Old Icelandic *rist* instep (Norwegian *rist*), from Proto-Germanic **wristiz* (earlier **wriHstiz*); related to Dutch *gewricht* joint, and Old English *wrǣstan* to turn, twist; see WREST. **—wristband** *n.* (1571) **—wristwatch** *n.* (1896)

writ *n.* legal document. Old English (before 900) *writ* something written, piece of writing (corresponding to Proto-Germanic **writa-*), from the past participle stem of *wrītan* to WRITE. The meaning of a legal document or instrument is first recorded before 1121.

write *v.* About 1100 *writen;* developed from Old English *wrītan* to score, outline, draw the figure of (about 725, in *Beowulf*); later, to set down in writing (832); cognate with Old Frisian *wrīta* to write, Old Saxon *wrītan* to tear, scratch, write, Old High German *rīzan* to tear, draw (modern German *reissen* to tear), Old Icelandic *rīta* to score, write (Swedish *rita,* Norwegian *rite* draw, scratch), from Proto-Germanic **wrītanan* tear, scratch, Indo-European **wrei-d-/wrī-d-,* and cognate with Gothic *writs* stroke, letter. Outside Germanic a cognate is found in Greek *rhī́nē* file, rasp, from Indo-European **wrī-nā* (Pok.1163). **—writer** *n.* Old English *wrītere* (before 899, in Alfred's translation of St.

Gregory's *Pastoral Care*); formed from *wrītan* write + *-ere* -er[1]. **—write-up** *n. Informal.* written account (1885).

writhe (rīTH) *v.* to twist and turn. Probably before 1200 *writhen,* developed from Old English (about 1000) *wrīthan* to twist or bend; earlier, to bind or fetter (about 725, in *Beowulf*); cognate with Old High German *rīdan* to turn, twist, Old Icelandic *rīdha* (Swedish *vrida,* Danish *vride*), from Proto-Germanic **wrīthanan;* cognate with Lithuanian *rietěti* to creep out, from Indo-European **wreit-* turn, twist (Pok.1159). Related to WREATH, WRATH, WROTH. **—n.** a writhing movement. About 1350, from the verb.

wrong *adj.* Probably before 1200 *wrang* twisted, crooked, wry, in *The Ormulum;* later *wrong* (before 1250, in *Bestiary*), and before 1325 in the sense of not right, bad, immoral, unjust, in *Cursor Mundi;* borrowed from a Scandinavian source (compare Old Icelandic *rangr;* earlier **wrangr* crooked, wry, wrong, Danish and Norwegian *vrang,* Swedish *vrång*); cognate with Middle Dutch *wrangh, wranc* acid, tart, Middle Low German *wrange* sour, bitter, from Proto-Germanic **wranȝaz,* Indo-European **wronĝhos;* see WRING.

It is a curious fact that the adjective use is not recorded in Old English (except perhaps in a manuscript copy of the 1200's, supposedly attested to a document in 944). Though probably borrowed from Scandinavian, it is also probable that earlier noun use influenced the development of the adjective, possibly at first in attributive constructions, such as that of *on wrangan hylle* (cited in the Old English document of 944).

—adv. badly, wrongly. Probably about 1200 *wrang, wrong;* from the adjective.

—n. Probably about 1175 *wronge* that which is wrong; developed from Late Old English (1067) *wrange* a wrongful act; later, that which is unjust, unfair, or improper (before 1100); perhaps borrowed from a Scandinavian source; see the adjective.

—v. Before 1338 *wrangen* do wrong to, in Mannyng's *Chronicle of England;* later *wrongen* (before 1393, in Gower's *Confessio Amantis*); from the adjective. **—wrongdoer** *n.* (about 1385, in Usk's *The Testament of Love*) **—wrongdoing** *n.* (1480) **—wrongful** *adj.* About 1311; formed from Middle English *wrong* + *-ful.* **—wrongheaded** *adj.* (1732)

wroth (rôth) *adj.* angry. Probably before 1200, in *Trinity Homilies* and *Ancrene Riwle;* developed from Old English *wrāth* (about 725, in *Beowulf*), from Proto-Germanic **wraithaz;* cognate with Old Frisian and Old Saxon *wrēth* angry, Middle Low German and Middle Dutch *wrēt* (Dutch *wreed* cruel), Old High German *reid* twisted, and Old Icelandic *reidhr* (Danish, Norwegian, and Swedish *vred*); from the same stem as that of the past tense of Old English *wrīthan* to twist, WRITHE. Related to WRATH.

wrought *adj.* made, fashioned, formed. About 1250 *wroght,* in *Genesis and Exodus;* from past participle of Middle English *werken, worken* to WORK.

wry *adj.* turned to one side, twisted (as in *to make a wry face*). 1523, adjective use of Middle English *wrien* to turn, swerve; developed from Old English (before 899) *wrigian* to turn, bend, move, go; cognate with Old Frisian *wrigia* to bow, bend, stoop, Middle Low German *wrich* twisted, cranky; and possibly outside Germanic with Greek *rhoikós* crooked, Lithuanian *rišti* to bind, tie, and Avestan *urvisyeiti* (he) turns, revolves, from Indo-European **wreik̂-/wroik̂-/wrik̂-* (Pok.1158). The meaning of ironic, somewhat twisted (as in *wry humor*) is first recorded before 1586, in Sidney's *The Arcadia.* **—wry-necked** *adj.* 1596, having a wry or crooked neck, in Shakespeare's *Merchant of Venice;* later, afflicted with a stiff neck (1608). The meaning is also recorded somewhat earlier in *wryneck* (1586).

X

X, x *n.* a term used to designate a person, thing, agency, factor, etc., that has not been named, or is unknown or secret (as in *Mr. X, brand X*). 1797, probably from earlier use in mathematics, used as a symbol for an unknown quantity (1660, from use by Descartes, in *Géométrie,* 1637). The first recorded use is from the *XYZ Affair* in which French emissaries designated as *X, Y,* and *Z* negotiated with American representatives of the United States government.

xenon (zē′non) *n.* gaseous chemical element. 1898, borrowed from Greek *xénon,* neuter of *xénos* strange, of uncertain origin. The element's name was coined by its discoverers: Sir William Ramsay, 1852-1916, Scottish chemist, and Morris William Travers, 1872-1961, English chemist.

xenophobia (zen′əfō′bēə) *n.* hatred or fear of foreigners. 1919 (in 1909 *xenophoby*); formed from Greek *xénos* stranger, n. (strange, foreign, adj.); of uncertain origin + *-phobiā* fear, -PHOBIA. **—xenophobic** *adj.* (1912)

xerography (zirog′rəfē) *n.* dry printing process for making copies of letters, pictures, etc. 1948, formed in English from Greek *xērós* dry; see SERENE + English suffix *-graphy,* as in *photography.* **—xerographic** *adj.* 1948, formed on the model of English *xerography,* from *xero-* + *-graphic.*

xerophyte (zir′əfīt) *n.* plant that loses very little water and can grow in deserts. 1897, borrowed from French *xérophyte,* formed from Greek *xērós* dry; see SERENE + French *-phyte* plant; see -PHYTE.

Xerox (zir′oks) *n.* trademark for a xerographic process of photocopying and a machine for photocopying. 1952, formed in English from Greek *xērós* dry, with substitution of *-x* for *-s* (originally *xerox*). **—v. xerox** to make copies by a xerographic process. 1966, from the noun.

-xion a suffix used especially in British English for many words leveled in American English to the ending *-ction,* such as *connexion* (American English *connection*) and *inflexion* (American English *inflection*). In British English the use of *-xion* is modeled on the Latin original, as in *īnflexiō* (genitive *īnflexiōnis*), while use of the spelling *-ction,* as in *convection, inspection* follows the model of Latin in *-ctiō* (genitive *-ctiōnis*), and *īnspectiō* (genitive *īnspectiōnis*). *Fluxion* is a survival of what in Latin was one of the two variants (*flūxiō* and *flūctiō*), and *complexion* in American and British English, while true to its original form in Latin *complexiō* is reinforced by English *complex.* See -TION and -SION.

Xmas (eks′məs *or* kris′məs) *n.* Christmas. 1551, formed from *X,* an abbreviation for *Christ* (from the Greek letter *X* chi, representing the first letter of Greek *Christós* Christ) + (*Christ*)*mas.*

X ray electromagnetic ray that can pass through many solid substances. 1896, partial translation of obsolete German *X-Strahlen* (*X,* in the sense of unknown + *Strahlen,* plural of *Strahl* ray, beam). The German word was coined in 1895 by the chemist Wilhelm Roentgen, 1845-1923. **—v. X-ray** examine, photograph, or treat with X rays. 1899, from *X ray.*

xylem (zī′lem) *n.* woody part of plants. 1875, in Bennett and Dyer's translation of Sachs' *Textbook of Botany;* borrowing of German *Xylem,* from Greek *xýlon* wood (of uncertain origin) + *-em,* as in *phloem.*

xylophone (zī′ləfōn) *n.* musical instrument. 1866, formed in English from Greek *xýlon* wood + English *-phone* sound. **—xylophonist** *n.* 1927, formed from English *xylophone* + *-ist.*

Y

y Modern English *yard, yarn, yarrow,* etc., developed from Old English words with initial *g.* In Old English the graphic symbol *g* (often transcribed as *ȝ* or some variant of that symbol and known as yogh, especially in Middle English) stood both for our *g* in *got* and *finger* (fiŋgər) and for *y* in *yet* (sometimes now transcribed as *ġ*). Later in early Middle English the so-called continental form *g* was used (and reinforced by the French scribes) for the sounds represented by *g* and also by *dg* in *edge* (a complex sound that had already developed in Late Old English or early Middle English, often transcribed with the symbol ɣ for native words). Gradually this symbol took the form of *ȝ*, representing our sound of *y* in *year,* and from the 1200's on this symbol was by degrees, wholly or partially, replaced by *y* or *gh.* The sound represented by yogh in words such as *knight, night* died out in the 1700's, but was also earlier represented by *g* in Old English and mostly by *ȝ* in Middle English.

-y¹ a suffix of wide application, forming adjectives from nouns, with the meaning of full of or having (as in *bumpy, salty, cloudy*), characterized by (as in *funny, wintry, icy*), somewhat (as in *chilly*), resembling or suggesting (as in *sugary*); also forming adjectives with the meaning of inclined to (as in *curly, sleepy, squeaky, sticky*); and occasionally added to other adjectives without a change in meaning (as in *stilly, vasty*). Middle English *-y,* developed from Old English *-ig;* cognate with Gothic *-igs,* Old Icelandic *-igr,* and Old High German *-ig;* and outside Germanic with Latin *-icus,* Greek *-ikós,* Sanskrit *-ika-s.* See also -EY.

-y² a suffix forming pet names and diminutives, as in *Billy, Tommy, daddy, pussy,* also informal alterations such as *nighty* and the plural *undies;* frequently written *-ie* (see -IE, also -EY). Middle English *-ie, -y,* is first recorded (as *-ie*) in Scottish.

-y³ a suffix forming nouns of condition or quality from adjectives or other nouns (as in *victory, jealousy*); or nouns showing activity, occupation, place of work, as in *carpentry, chandlery, laundry;* or with a collective meaning as in *soldiery, stationery.* Middle English *-ie, -ye* usually borrowed through Old French *-ie,* from Latin *-ia;* cognate with Greek *-ia, -íā.* In some words, this *-y* can denote a single instance or act, as in *perjury, remedy, subsidy;* this is through Middle English *-ie,* Anglo-French *-ie,* from Latin *-ium.* See also -ACY, -CY, -ERY, -RY (and others), in which *-y³* forms the last part of a compound suffix.

-y⁴ a suffix surviving in words such as *army, assembly, delivery, deputy;* in Middle English it is *-e* or *-ee,* borrowed through Anglo-French and Old French *-é, -ée* perfect participle suffix, from Latin *-ātum* and *-āta.* Compare -ATE¹.

yacht (yot) *n.* 1557 *yeaghe* (in the phrase *Norway yeaghes*); 1565 *yaucht* (in the phrase *Norroway yaucht*) a light, fast-sailing ship; probably borrowed from earlier Norwegian *jagt* (now *jakt*), from Middle Low German *jacht,* shortened form of *jachtschip, jageschip,* literally, ship for chasing (*jacht, jage* chase, from *jagen* to chase, hunt, from Old High German *jagōn* + *schip* SHIP); Old High German *jagōn* is from Proto-Germanic **jaȝōjanan,* perhaps cognate with Sanskrit *yahú-s* restless, vigorous, from Indo-European **yagh-* to chase after (Pok.502) —**v.** to sail or race in a yacht. 1836, in Marryat's *Mr. Midshipman Easy;* from the noun.

yak *n.* long-haired ox of Tibet and central Asia. 1795, in *Asiatick Researches;* borrowed (with conventional Roman letters) from Tibetan *ɣag;* possibly connected with Tocharian B *yakwe* horse.

yam *n.* starchy root of a vine. 1697 *yam;* earlier in various spellings adapted from foreign languages (*inany, nname* 1588; *iniamo* 1598; *igname* 1600; *inhame* 1640); borrowed from earlier Portuguese *inhame* or Spanish *igname,* from a West African language (compare Fulani *nyami* to eat, Twi *ànyinam* species of yam). In American English, the word is possibly a direct borrowing from a West African language, as is probably the case in Caribbean English (Jamaican), in which *nyaams* exists for "yam" after earlier application in various forms *nyam* to eat, *ninyam* food, forms, or a form which probably contributed to American use, in spite of the late dates of sources cited in Cassidy and Le Page's *Dictionary of Jamaican English* (see also Holm's *Dictionary of Bahamian English*). Mathews, in the *Dictionary of Americanisms,* cites Gullah *jambi* a reddish sweet potato.

yammer *v.* to whine or whimper. 1481 *yameren* to lament, whine, whimper, in Caxton's translation of *The History of Reynard the Fox.* Late Middle English *yameren* was probably in part borrowed from Middle Dutch *jammeren* and may also be an alteration of Middle English *yeoumeren* to mourn, complain (probably before 1200); developed from Old English *geōmrian* to lament (about 725, in *Beowulf*), from *geōmor* sorrowful. Cognates of *geōmor* are found in Old Saxon and Old High German *jāmar* sorrowful, Middle Low German *jamer, jammer* sorrow, woe, Middle Dutch *jāmer, jammer,* and Old Frisian *jōmerlik* wretched, miserable, but with no connections outside Germanic. The meaning of howl, yell, is first recorded in English in 1513.

yank *v.* pull suddenly, jerk. 1822 (Scottish), of uncertain origin. —**n.** a sudden pull, tug, jerk. 1885, American English; earlier, sudden blow, cuff (1818); of uncertain origin.

Note that almost opposite meanings of the verb and noun are contemporary (that is, the sense of to pull toward, jerk, and that of casting outward, a blow) while the noun use of pulling toward is not recorded until more than half a century later. This may expose a defect in the record of English, or it may show a yet unknown difference in derivation of early noun and verb.

Yankee *n.* a nickname, as applied in early quotations: *Yankey Duch* (1683), *Captain Yankey* (1684), *John Wil-*

liams, Yankey (1687), all from the same source, and "one negroe man named *Yankee*" (1725), also used by General James Wolfe (1758) as a term of contempt and found later as a general term for a native or inhabitant of New England (1765). This record shows a thread of usage traceable to earliest occurrence through the various opprobrious uses and the later prideful adoptions by the New England colonists themselves. What the earliest associations were is undecipherable with present evidence, but the word almost certainly came from the Dutch, whether ultimately from the Flemings is questionable; certainly a parallel to the pseudoeponym *John Bull* is suggested in the explanation by the Dutch linguist Henri Logeman, in *Studies in English Philology* (Klaeber volume, Minneapolis, 1929, pp. 403-13), in which he postulates that the name may have been an alteration of Dutch *Jan Kees,* dialectal variant of *Jan Kaas,* literally, John Cheese, a nickname for Dutchmen used by Flemings.

By about 1784 *Yankee* was extended by British writers and speakers to apply to Americans in general; then from about 1812, and particularly since the Civil War, the name has been applied in the South to anyone from the northern states above the Mason-Dixon line. The informal clipped form *Yank* is recorded from 1778.

Any association with American Indian use, such as *Yankee* representing their pronunciation of the word "English," or *Yanke, Yankee, Yankoo* as a tribal name is not supported by convincing evidence.

yap *n.* 1603, a yelping dog; probably of imitative origin. The meaning of a snappish bark, yelp, is first recorded in 1826, from the verb. **—v.** bark snappishly, yelp. 1668 (implied in *yapping*), probably of imitative origin similar to that of the noun.

yard[1] *n.* piece of ground around a house. Before 1325, in *Cursor Mundi;* developed from Old English *geard* enclosure, garden, court, house, yard (about 725, in *Beowulf*); cognate with Old Saxon *gard* enclosure, field, house, Middle Dutch and modern Dutch *gaard* garden, Old High German *gart* circle, ring, Old Icelandic *gardhr* yard, court (Danish, Norwegian, and Swedish *gård*), and Gothic *gards* house, from Proto-Germanic **ʒardaz.* Corresponding related forms are found in Old Frisian *garda* garden, Old Saxon *gardo,* Old High German *garto* (Middle High German *garte,* modern German *Garten*) garden, and Gothic *garda* enclosure. Cognates outside Germanic include Lithuanian *gar̃das* pen, enclosure, Old Slavic *gradŭ* castle, town, Russian *górod* town, city, and Sanskrit *gṛhá-s* house, from Indo-European *ĝhordhos,* root **ĝher-* enclose (Pok.444).

It is equally possible to derive Old English *geard* yard and its closest Germanic cognates from Proto-Germanic **ʒardás,* cognate with Greek *chórtos* farmyard, Latin *hortus* garden, plot of ground, Welsh *garth* (court)yard (altered from **gorth* by influence of *gardd* which was borrowed from Old Icelandic *gardhr*), and Hittite *gurtan* (accusative) fortress, from Indo-European *ĝhortós* (Pok.442). Related to GARDEN.
—v. enclose in a yard. 1758, from the noun.

yard[2] *n.* measure of length. About 1385 *yerd,* in Chaucer's *Troilus and Criseyde,* developed from Old English (Old Mercian) *gerd,* (West Saxon) *gierd* rod, stick, measure of length (about 725); cognate with Old Frisian *ierde* rod, Old Saxon *gerdia,* Old High German *gertia* switch, twig (modern German *Gerte*), from Proto-Germanic **ʒazdijō,* formed from **ʒazdaz,* the source of Gothic *gazds* sting, and Old Icelandic *gaddr* spike; see GADFLY. The spelling *yard* is first recorded in Middle English in Lydgate's *Falls of Princes* (probably before 1439). For shift in spelling see YARD[1].
—yardage *n.* length in yards. 1877, the cutting of coal at a fixed rate per yard; formed from English *yard*[2] + *-age.* The meaning of length in yards is first recorded in 1900. **—yardstick** *n.* (1816, American English)

yarmulke (yär′məlkə) *n.* skullcap worn by Jewish males. 1903 *jarmulka;* later in the spelling *yarmelke* (1929); borrowed from Yiddish *yarmlke,* from Polish *jarmułka* skullcap, probably from Medieval Latin *almunicum, almucium* clergyman's cap or hood, of unknown origin.

yarn *n.* spun thread. Before 1325, developed from Old English (about 1000) *gearn* spun fiber; cognate with Middle Low German *garn* yarn, Middle Dutch *gaern* (modern Dutch *garen*), Old High German *garn* (modern German *Garn*), and Old Icelandic *garn* (Danish, Norwegian, and Swedish *garn*) yarn (from Proto-Germanic **ʒarnan,* Indo-European **ĝhornom*), *gǫrn* gut (from Proto-Germanic **ʒarnō,* Indo-European **ĝhornā*). Cognates outside Germanic include Latin *haruspex* interpreter of animal entrails, *hernia* rupture, *hīra* intestine, Greek *chordḗ* gut, string, Lithuanian *žarnà* intestine, and Sanskrit *híra-s* band, from Indo-European **ĝher-/ĝhor-/ĝhēr-* (Pok.443).

The figurative phrase *spin a yarn,* tell a long story, is first recorded in 1812, originally probably in nautical slang.
—v. tell stories. 1812, in Vaux's *Flash Dictionary;* from the noun.

yarrow *n.* common plant with finely divided leaves. 1373 *yarowe,* developed from Old English (before 800) *gearwe;* cognate with Middle Dutch *garwe, gerwe* (modern Dutch *gerwe*) yarrow, and Old High German *garwa, garawa* (modern German *Garbe*), perhaps from Proto-Germanic **ʒarwō,* of unknown origin.

yaw *n.* movement from a straight course. 1546, perhaps borrowed from a Scandinavian source (compare Old Icelandic *jaga* and Old Danish *jæge* to drive, chase, Swedish *jaga,* Norwegian and Danish *jage*). In the sense of chase, the Scandinavian word probably came from Middle Low German *jagen;* see YACHT. **—v.** turn from a straight course. 1584, probably from the noun.

yawl *n.* boat like a sloop. 1670 *yall, yale;* borrowed from Dutch *jol* a yawl, skiff (found in Middle Dutch *jolleken,* diminutive form, also Danish *jolle* and Swedish *julle* skiff, yawl), from Middle Low German *jolle* (also found in Low German); of uncertain origin.

yawn *v.* Probably before 1300 *yanen* open the mouth wide, gape; later, to yawn from sleepiness, fatigue, etc. (about 1430); alteration of earlier *yenen* (about 1300), *yonen* (probably before 1300), which developed from Old English (before 830) *ginian, gionian, geonian* open the mouth wide, gape (from Proto-Germanic **ʒin-*), and related to *gīnan* to yawn; cognate with Old Saxon *ginōn* to yawn, Middle Dutch *ghēnen* (modern Dutch *geeuwen*), Old High German *ginēn, geinōn* (modern German *gähnen*), and Old Icelandic *gīna.* Cognates outside Germanic are found in Latin *hiāre* to yawn, *hīscere* to gape, Greek *cháskein,* Lithuanian *žióti,* and Old Slavic *zijati,* from Indo-European **ĝhə-* (root *ĝhē-*), **ĝhēi-/ĝhī-/ĝhi-/ĝhiy-ā-* (Pok.419).

The Middle English forms *yenen* and *yonen* were altered to *yanen* probably by influence of the synony-

mous Middle English word *ganen,* which became obsolete in the 1500's. Middle English *ganen* developed from Old English *gānian* (from Proto-Germanic *ʒain-,* Indo-European **ĝhəi-n-*), which is related to Old English *gīnan* to yawn, and *ginian* to gape. The spelling *yawn,* first recorded in 1549, may have resulted from a local or dialectal development of Middle English *yane(n).*
—**n.** a yawning. 1602, gaping opening, in John Marston's *Antonio's Revenge;* from the verb. The meaning of a yawning is first recorded in 1697.

yaws *n.pl.* contagious disease characterized by sores on the skin. 1679, in Thomas Trapham's *A Discourse of the State of Health in the Island of Jamaica;* probably borrowed from Carib *yaya,* the native name for the disease.

yclept or **ycleped** (iklept′) *adj. Archaic.* called, named. Probably before 1300 *ycleped,* in *Arthour and Merlin;* developed from Old English (about 950) *geclipod* named, past participle of *geclipian, gecleopian* to speak, call (*ge-* with, together; see ENOUGH + *clipian, cleopian* call out, cry out, cognate with Middle Low German *kleperen* chatter, clatter; of imitative origin).

ye[1] (yē *or unstressed* yi) *pron. pl. Archaic.* you. About 1150, in *The Proverbs of Alfred;* developed from Old English *gē,* the nominative plural of *thū* THOU (about 725, in *Beowulf*). Old English *gē* was an alteration (by influence of the first person plural pronoun *wē* we) of an earlier form represented by Gothic *jūs* you (plural). Similarly modified forms are seen in other Germanic languages: Old Frisian *gī* ye, Old Saxon *gī, ge,* Middle Dutch *gi, ge* (modern Dutch *gij*), Old High German *ir,* by influence of *wir* we (modern German *ihr*), Old Icelandic *ēr,* by influence of *vēr* we, and Old Swedish *ir* (Swedish and Danish *I*). Gothic *jūs* you (plural) is cognate with Albanian *ju* you (plural), Lithuanian *yūs,* and Sanskrit *yūyám,* from Indo-European *yu-* (Pok.513). Compare YOU, YOUR.

ye[2] (ᴛʜē; *popularly* yē) an old way of writing the definite article *the* . Before 1568, in Ascham's *The Schoolmaster* ("Ye great ones in ye Court"), graphic alteration of *Þe,* the form in which *the* was written in Old and Middle English. Printers in the 1500's, who often did not have the runic consonant letter *þ* (called "thorn") in their fonts, substituted *y* for it, but this was not intended to be read with the sound associated with *y.* In modern times *ye* is frequently used as part of quaintly archaic names of stores, shops, etc.

yea (yā) *adv.* yes. Before 1325 *yai, yaa,* in *Cursor Mundi;* developed from Old English (West Saxon) *gēa,* (Anglian) *gē* so, yes (about 900), an affirmative word found in corresponding forms throughout the Germanic languages, including Old Frisian *jē* yes, Old Saxon *jā,* Middle Low German, Middle Dutch, and modern Dutch *ja,* Old High German *jā* (modern German *ja*), Old Icelandic *jā* (Danish, Norwegian, and Swedish *ja*), Gothic *ja, jai;* also cognate with Latin *jam* already, now, from Indo-European **yām* (Pok.285). Compare YES. The American spelling *yeah* is not recorded before 1905.
—**n.** 1228 *ya,* affirmative statement; from the adverb. The meaning of an affirmative vote or voter is first recorded in 1657.

yean *v.* give birth to (a lamb or kid). Before 1387 *i-yenen,* in Trevisa's translation of Higden's *Polychronicon;* developed from Old English **geēanian* (*ge-* with, together; see ENOUGH + *ēanian* to yean). Old English *ēanian* (from Proto-Germanic **aʒwnōjanan*) is cognate with dialectal Dutch *oonen* to yean, and possibly with Old Irish *ūan* lamb, Welsh *oen,* Latin *agnus,* and Old Slavic *agnę,* from Indo-European **agwhnos* (Pok.9).
—**yeanling** *n.* lamb or kid. 1637, in Ben Jonson's *The Sad Shepherd;* formed from English *yean* + *-ling.*

year *n.* Before 1325 *yeir, yeire,* in *Cursor Mundi;* developed from Old English (900-30) *gēar* year; cognate with Old Frisian *gēr* year, Old Saxon *jār,* Middle Dutch *jaer* (modern Dutch *jaar*), Old High German *jār* (modern German *Jahr*), Old Icelandic *ār* (Danish, Norwegian, and Swedish *år*), and Gothic *jēr,* from Proto-Germanic **jǣran.* Cognates outside Germanic include Greek *hôros* year, *hṓrā* season, time of day, hour, Latin *hōrnus* of this year (earlier **hō-yōr-inos*), Old Slavic *jarŭ* spring, and Avestan *yarə* year, from Indo-European **yēro-/yōro-* (Pok.296). —**yearbook** *n.* (1588, annual book of legal cases; 1710, book with information about a year; 1926, American English, school album) —**yearling** *n.* year-old animal. 1465; formed from Middle English *yeir* + *-ling.* —*adj.* one year old. 1528; from the noun. —**yearlong** *adj.* (1813, in letters of Coleridge) —**yearly** *adj.* Probably before 1400 *yerely;* developed from Old English (before 800) *gēarlic* every year, once a year, year by year; formed from *gēar* year + *-lic* -ly[2].
—**year-round** *adj.* (1939)

yearn *v.* feel a longing or desire. Before 1325 *yernen,* in *Cursor Mundi;* developed from Old English (Mercian) *geornan,* (West Saxon) *giernan* to yearn (before 899), from Proto-Germanic **ʒernjanan.* These Old English forms are related to Old English *georn* eager, desirous, (from Proto-Germanic **ʒernaz*) which is cognate with Old Saxon and Old High German *gern* eager, willing (modern German *gern* gladly), Old High German *gerōn* to desire (modern German *begehren*), Old Icelandic *gjarn* eager, willing, *girna* to desire, and Gothic *-gaírns* (as in *faíhu-gaírns* money-desiring, covetous), wish. The Germanic forms are all from Proto-Germanic **ʒer-,* corresponding to Indo-European **ĝher-/ĝhor-* to long for, desire (Pok.440), probably the source of Latin *horitur* urges, *hortārī* to urge, incite, encourage, cheer, Greek *chaírein* rejoice, enjoy, *cháris* favor, grace, and Sanskrit *háryati* (he) likes, yearns for.

yeast *n.* About 1430 *yest* froth of fermenting beer; developed from Late Old English (about 1000) *gist* yeast; cognate with Middle Low German *gest* dregs, dirt, Middle Dutch *ghist* yeast (modern Dutch *gist*), Middle High German *jest* foam (modern German *Gischt*), Old High German *jesan, gesan* to ferment (modern German *gären*), and Old Icelandic *jǫstr* yeast (Swedish *jäst*), from Indo-European **yes-* to foam, froth (Pok.506). —**yeasty** *adj.* 1598, (figurative) swelling, frothy; formed from English *yeast* + *-y*[1].

yell *v.* Probably about 1200 *yellen* to cry out loud, shout, in Chaucer's *Canterbury Tales;* developed from Old English (Mercian) *gellan,* (West Saxon) *giellan* (before 1000); cognate with Middle Low German *gellen, gillen* to yell, Middle Dutch *ghellen* (modern Dutch *gillen*), Old High German *gellan* (modern German *gellen*), and Old Icelandic *gjalla* (Norwegian *gjalle,* Danish *gjalde* resound, ring). The Germanic forms are all from Proto-Germanic **ʒelnanan,* an extended form of the root found in Old English *galan* to sing, modern English *-gale* in *nightingale,* Old Icelandic *-gal* in *hanagal* cockcrow, and Old Saxon, Middle Dutch, and Old High German *galm* outcry, from Indo-

European *ghel- (Pok.428). —**n.** strong, loud cry. About 1375, (Scottish); from Middle English *yellen* to yell.

yellow *adj.* having a yellow color. About 1380-85 *yelowe, yelwe,* in writings of Chaucer; developed from Old English *geolu, geolwe* (about 725, in *Beowulf*); cognate with Old Saxon *gelo* yellow, Middle Dutch *ghēle* (modern Dutch *geel*), Old High German *gelo* (modern German *gelb*), and Old Icelandic *gulr* (Swedish, Norwegian, and Danish *gul*), from Proto-Germanic **ʒelwaz.* Cognates outside Germanic are found in Latin *helvus* dull yellow, Greek *chlóos, chlōrós* greenish yellow, Lithuanian *žeĩvas, žaĩvas* greenish, Old Slavic *žlŭtŭ* yellow, Avestan *zari-* yellow, and Sanskrit *hári-s* yellowish, from Indo-European **ĝhel-, ĝhlō-* (Pok. 429). Related to GALL[1] (bile) and GOLD. —**n.** About 1390 *yelow,* in Chaucer's *Canterbury Tales;* from the adjective. —**v.** turn yellow. 1598, from the adjective. —**yellow fever** (1739, American English) —**yellowish** *adj.* 1379, formed from Middle English *yelow* yellow + *-ish*[1]. —**yellow jacket** kind of wasp (1796, American English). —**yellow pages** special section of a catalog or directory (1908).

yelp *v.* make a quick, sharp bark or cry. Probably before 1200 *yelpen* to boast, in *Ancrene Riwle;* developed from Old English (Anglian) *gelpan,* (West Saxon) *gielpan* to boast (about 725, in *Beowulf*), from Proto-Germanic **ʒelpanan.* The Old English forms are cognate with Old Saxon *galpōn* to cry aloud, boast, Old High German *gelph* outcry, revelry, Old Icelandic *gjalpa* to yelp, *gjalp* boasting, and related to Old English *gielp* pride, boasting. Outside Germanic, a cognate is found in Lithuanian *guĩbinti* celebrate, praise, from Indo-European **ghelb-* (Pok.428). The meaning of make a quick, sharp bark or cry, is first recorded in English in 1553, probably from the noun. —**n.** quick, sharp bark or cry. Probably about 1200 *yellp* a boasting, in *The Ormulum;* developed from Old English *gielp* pride, boasting (about 725, in *Beowulf*). The meaning of a quick, sharp bark or cry is first recorded in 1500-20, in poems of Dunbar.

yen[1] *n.* unit of money in Japan. 1875, in William S. Jevons' *Money and the Mechanism of Exchange;* borrowed from Japanese *yen,* from Chinese *yüan* round, round object, circle, dollar.

yen[2] *n. Informal.* sharp desire or hunger. 1906, American English; earlier *yin* intense craving for opium (1876); probably borrowed from Chinese (Cantonese) *yăn* craving. —**v.** have a yen. 1919, American English; from the noun.

For a discussion of the borrowing and development of the word in English see *American Speech* (1961), 36 pp. 175-80.

yeoman (yō′mən) *n.* Probably before 1300 *yoman* high-ranking servant or attendant, in *Kyng Alisaunder;* of uncertain origin. Traditional explanations suggest that Middle English *yoman* is: 1) perhaps a contraction of *youngman* person in early manhood (1052, also found in Old English *iunge men,* 963-84); later, a servant or attendant (before 1376); 2) a form developed from Old English *gingra* (modern English *younger,* n.) follower, disciple, vassal (before 899, in Alfred's translation of Bede's *Ecclesiastical History*); an easy semantic development, but difficult to explain phonetically; 3) a form developed from Old English **gēaman, geāman;* borrowed from Old Frisian *gāman* villager. This latter explanation for the development of Middle English *yoman* is plausible phonetically and provides support for the sense of a commoner or countryman who cultivates his own land (before 1387, in Trevisa's translation of Higden's *Polychronicon*). The connection between the Old Frisian and possible Old English forms is reinforced by comparing the first element of Old English **gēaman* with the second element of *Sūthri-gēa* Southern district, found in the *Anglo-Saxon Chronicle.* Old English *-gēa* district, village, is thus cognate with Old Frisian *gā, gē,* Old Saxon *gā, gō,* Old High German *gewi, gouwi* (modern German *Gau*), and Gothic *gawi* region, district, from Proto-Germanic **ʒaujan;* perhaps cognate also with Greek *cháos* empty space, from Indo-European **ĝhəu-,* root **ĝhōu-* (Pok.449).

The sense of a petty officer in the navy in charge of supplies appeared in 1669. The phrase *yeoman's service,* meaning good, efficient service, is first found in Shakespeare's *Hamlet* (1602).

yep *adv. Informal.* yes. 1897, in Kipling's *Captains Courageous,* alteration of *yes;* possibly by influence of earlier NOPE, or formed by parallel process of closing the lips emphatically.

-yer a variant form of -IER after a vowel or *w,* as in *lawyer, sawyer.*

yes *adv.* Probably before 1200, in *Ancrene Riwle;* developed from Old English (before 899) *gīse, gēse* so be it!, probably formed from *gēa, gē* so, see YEA + *sī* be it!, a form used as the third person singular imperative of *bēon* to BE; see IS. —**n.** 1712, from the adverb.

yesterday *adv.* About 1250 *yisterdai,* in *Genesis and Exodus;* developed from Old English (about 950) *geostran dæg,* a compound of *geostran* yesterday (about 725, in *Beowulf*) and *dæg* DAY, parallel to Gothic *gistradagis* tomorrow. Old English *geostran* is found by itself only once, but cognates of it are found in Middle Low German *gistern* yesterday, Middle Dutch *ghisteren* (modern Dutch *gister, gisteren*), Old High German *gestaron, gestren* (modern German *gestern*), from Proto-Germanic **ʒestra-.* Cognates outside Germanic are found in Sanskrit *hyá-s* yesterday, Avestan *zyō,* Greek *chthés,* Albanian *dje,* Latin *herī* yesterday, *hesternus* of yesterday, from Indo-European **ĝhdyés,* simplified to **ĝhdés, ĝhyés, ĝhés* (Pok.416). —**n.** Before 1300 *yistredai;* developed from Old English *geostran dæg* (about 1000). —**yesteryear** *n.* last year, in former times. 1870, in Dante Gabriel Rossetti's *Three Translations from François Villon;* coined by Rossetti to translate French *antan* (from Vulgar Latin **anteannum* the year before), in François Villon's *Grand Testament* (*Mais où sont les neiges d'antan?* But where are the snows of yesteryear?).

Yester- was apparently abstracted from *yesterday* as early as 1420 in compounds such as *yester euyn* yesterday evening, and used in later modern compounds such as Coleridge's *yester-afternoon,* and others that survive today, such as *yesteryear* (1870, see above) and *yestermorn* (1702). However, there are one or two forms (besides *yesterday*) that are found in Old English, which suggest a similar type of formation, though they are constructed on the words *geostran, gystran* and not on a word element: *gystran niht* yesterday night (about 725, in *Beowulf*), *gyrstanæfen* (with metathesis of *r* and *st*) yesterday evening (about 900), and the unusual *giestron* of yesterday (before 1000), found in English dialect before 1860 as *yestern.*

yet *adv.* Probably before 1200, in *Ancrene Riwle;* developed from Old English (about 1000) *gēt, gīeta* till now, thus far; earlier, at last, ultimately (before 899);

and besides, also (about 725, in *Beowulf*). The only known cognate of the Old English word is Old Frisian *ieta, eta, ita* yet. Meanings of *yet* in other Germanic languages, beyond English and Frisian, are usually found in forms such as Old Saxon and Old High German *noh* (modern German *noch*). **—conj.** Before 1200, nevertheless, though, but; from the adverb.

yeti (ye′tē) *n.* legendary apelike creature of the Himalayas, also known as *abominable snowman.* 1937, borrowed from Tibetan *yeh-teh* small manlike animal.

yew *n.* kind of evergreen tree. Before 1325 *ew,* about 1450 *yew;* developed from Old English (before 800) *īw, ēow* yew; cognate with Middle Low German and Middle Dutch *īwe, īewe* yew (modern Dutch *ijf,* influenced by French *if*), Old High German *īwa* (modern German *Eibe*), and Old Icelandic *ȳr* yew or bow, from Proto-Germanic **īwa-, īwō.* Possible cognates outside Germanic are found in Old Irish *eō* yew, Welsh *yw,* pl. yews, Middle Breton *yuin,* pl. yews, and Old Slavic *iva* willow, from Indo-European **eiwo-/iwo-,*eiwā/iwā* (Pok.297).

Yiddish *n.* Jewish language developed primarily from Middle High German dialects, but with significant elements from Slavic and Romance languages and a mixture of Hebrew and Aramaic, written in Hebrew characters. 1875, borrowed from Yiddish *yidish,* from Middle High German *jüdisch* Jewish, from *jude* Jew, from Old High German *judo,* from Latin *Jūdaeus* JEW; for suffix see -ISH[1].

yield *v.* Before 1325 *yelden, yeilden* to pay, repay, return, produce, surrender; developed from Old English (Anglian) *geldan* to pay, (West Saxon) *gieldan* (about 725, in *Beowulf*); cognate with Old Frisian *gelda* be worth, be valid, concern, Old Saxon *geldan,* Middle Dutch *ghelden* (modern Dutch *gelden*), Old High German *geltan* (modern German *gelten*), Old Icelandic *gjalda* (Norwegian *gjelde,* Swedish *gälda,* Danish *gælde*), and Gothic *-gildan* (in compounds *forgildan, usgildan* to compensate), from Proto-Germanic **ʒelđanan,* with no known relations outside Germanic. **—n.** Before 1121 *yild* payment; developed from Old English *gield,* from *gieldan* to pay. Old English *gield* is cognate with Old Frisian and Old Saxon *geld* payment, Middle Low German and Middle Dutch *gelt* (modern Dutch *geld* money), Old High German *gelt* (modern German *Geld* money), Old Icelandic *gjald,* and Gothic *gild* tax. The sense of the action of yielding or producing, production, produce, is first recorded in Middle English about 1450.

yip *v.* bark or yelp briskly. 1903, in Kate D. Wiggin's *Rebecca of Sunnybrook Farm;* American English, possibly from earlier dialectal English *yip* to cheep like a bird (before 1825), from Middle English *yippen* (1440, in *Promptorium Parvulorum*); of imitative origin. **—n.** sharp barking sound. 1911, from the verb.

-yl a suffix used in chemistry in naming radicals acting like a simple element, as in *ethyl, propyl.* Borrowed from French *-yle,* in *benzoyle* (1832, in *Annales de Chimie*), from Greek *hȳlē* wood, material, matter. The suffix was coined by F. Wöhler, who synthesized the first organic compounds from inorganic material and L. Liebig, whose work on mineral replacement in soil is the basis for modern agricultural fertilizer methods.

yodel *v.* sing with frequent changes from the ordinary voice to falsetto and back again. 1827, borrowed from German *jodeln,* from dialectal German *jo* an exclamation of joy; of imitative origin. **—n.** act or sound of yodeling. 1849, in Thackeray's *Pendennis;* from the verb.

yoga (yō′gə) *n.* system of Hindu ascetic philosophy and exercises that seeks union with the Supreme Spirit. 1820, in William Ward's *A View of the History, Literature, and Religion of the Hindoos;* borrowed from Hindi *yoga,* from Sanskrit *yóga-s,* literally, union, yoking, from Indo-European **yougos;* related to *yugá-m* YOKE. **—yogi** (yō′gē) *n.* person who practices yoga. 1619, in Purchas' *Microcosmus;* borrowed from Hindi *yogī,* from Sanskrit, from *yóga-s* yoga.

yogurt *n.* a thickened liquid food made from milk acted upon by bacteria. 1625 *yoghurd,* in *Purchas' Pilgrims;* later *yogourt* (1687); borrowed from Turkish *yoğurt* (with *g* unpronounced so that the English word constitutes a kind of spelling pronunciation).

yoke *n.* device to fasten two draft animals together. About 1325 *yock,* about 1340 *yoke;* developed from Old English (before 899) *geoc* yoke, (figurative) heavy burden, oppression, servitude; earlier *geoht* a pair of draft animals (688-95). The Old English forms are cognate with Old Saxon *juk* yoke, Middle Dutch *joc, juc* (modern Dutch *juk*), Old High German *joh* (modern German *Joch*), Old Icelandic *ok* (Swedish *ok,* Norwegian *åk,* Danish *åg*), and Gothic *juk,* from Proto-Germanic **jukan,* Indo-European **yugóm.* Cognates outside Germanic are found in Latin *jugum* yoke, *jungere* to join, Greek *zygón* yoke, *zeugnýnai* to yoke, join, Welsh *iau* yoke, Lithuanian *jùngas* yoke, *jùngti* to join, Old Slavic *igo* yoke, Sanskrit *yugá-m* yoke, *yunákti* (he) yokes, and Hittite *yukan, yugan* yoke, from Indo-European **yeug-/youg-/yug-* (Pok.508). **—v.** fasten by yoke or harness. Probably before 1200 *yeoken,* about 1400 *yoken;* developed from Old English *geocian* (before 1000), from *geoc* yoke, n.

yokel *n.* country fellow, bumpkin, rustic. 1812, in Vaux's *Flash Dictionary;* origin uncertain (perhaps borrowed from dialectal German *Jokel* disparaging name for a farmer; originally, diminutive of *Jakob;* compare *Rube* in English).

yolk *n.* yellow part of an egg. Before 1325 *yelke;* later in the spelling *yolke* (before 1398); developed from Old English (before 1000) *geolca, geoloca, geoleca* yolk; literally, the yellow part, from *geolu* YELLOW.

yon *adj., pron.* yonder. About 1325, in *Cursor Mundi;* developed from Old English (before 899) *geon,* adj., that (over there), perhaps from Proto-Germanic **jenaz;* cognate with Old Frisian *gēna, iēna* that (over there), Old High German *enēr, jenēr* (modern German *jener*), Old Icelandic *enn, inn* the (definite article), Gothic *jains* that (perhaps from Proto-Germanic **jainaz*). Outside Germanic cognate forms are found in Old Slavic *onŭ* he, that, Lithuanian *añs* he, and Sanskrit *anéna* (instrumental masculine) that (one), from Indo-European **eno-/ono-* that (Pok.319). The source of the prefixed *y*-element of the Germanic words is unknown. **—adv.** About 1475, shortened form of *yonder* and of *yond* (before 1122; developed from Old English, before 899, *geond;* see YONDER).

yonder *adv.* within sight, but not near, that over there. Before 1325, in *Cursor Mundi,* extended form of earlier *yond,* developed from Old English (before 899) *geond,* adv. and prep., beyond, yonder; cognate with Middle Low German *gint, genten* beyond, Dutch *ginds,* and

Gothic *jaind, jainar* yonder, there, related to *jains* that; see YON.

yore *n.* (in the phrase **of yore**), of long ago, in the past, formerly. Probably about 1350, from earlier *yore,* adv., of old, long ago (about 1250); developed from a variant *geāra* of Old English *gēara,* adv., of yore (about 725, in *Beowulf*); originally, in the meaning "of years," genitive plural of *gēar* YEAR.

you *pron. pl. or sing.* Before 1325 *yow,* in *Cursor Mundi;* developed from Old English (about 725, in *Beowulf*) *ēow,* the dative and accusative form of *gē* YE[1]. Old English *ēow* (from Proto-West Germanic **iuwiz*) is cognate with Old Frisian *iuwe, iwe* you (dative and accusative of *gī* ye), Old Saxon *iu,* Middle Dutch and modern Dutch *u,* and Old High German *iu* (dative of *ir* ye). A parallel formation is found in Old Icelandic *ydhr* (dative and accusative of *ēr* ye), and Gothic *izwis* (dative and accusative of *jūs* ye).

In Old English *ēow* was the dative and accusative plural form of the second person singular pronoun *thou.* Between 1300 and 1400 in the form *you,* it began to be used also for the nominative form *ye,* which it replaced in general before 1700. During the 1300's *you* also appeared as a substitute for the singular nominative *thou,* being originally used as a sign of respect in addressing a superior, but later *you* was also used in speaking to an equal, and ultimately it came to be used as the general form of address. Compare THOU.

young *adj.* Before 1325 *yong,* in *Cursor Mundi;* developed from Old English *geong* youthful, young (about 725, in *Beowulf*). Old English *geong* is cognate with Old Frisian and Old Saxon *jung* young, Middle Dutch *jonc* (modern Dutch *jong*), Old High German *junc, jung* (modern German *jung*), Old Icelandic *ungr* (Danish, Norwegian, and Swedish *ung*), and Gothic *jungs,* from Proto-Germanic **jūnȝás,* earlier **juwunȝás.* Cognates outside Germanic are found in Latin *juvencus* young bull, Umbrian *iuenga* young cow, Welsh *ieuanc* young, and Sanskrit *yuvaśá-s* youthful, young; all derived from Indo-European **yuwn̥ḱós,* found also without any velar suffix in Latin *juvenis* young, Lithuanian *jáunas,* Latvian *jaũns,* Old Slavic *junŭ* young, Old Irish *ōa, ōam* younger, youngest, Welsh *iau, ieuaf* younger, youngest, Avestan *yuvan-* (genitive *yūnō*) young man, and Sanskrit *yúvan-* (genitive *yū́nas*) young, from Indo-European **yuwen-,* root **yeu-* (Pok.510). **—youngster** *n.* 1589, formed from English *young,* adj. + *-ster.*

your *adj.* Probably before 1300, developed from Old English (about 725, in *Beowulf*) *ēower,* the genitive form of *gē* YE[1]. Old English *ēower* is cognate with Old Frisian *iuwer* your, Old Saxon *iuwar, iwar,* Old High German *iuwēr* (modern German *euer*), Old Icelandic *ydharr, ydhvarr,* and Gothic *izvar;* all derived from the Germanic base represented by Old English *ēow* YOU. **—yours** *pron.* Before 1325, in *Cursor Mundi;* from the adjective; formed from English *your* + *-s*[3], as in *hers, ours, theirs.* **—yourself** *pron.* Before 1325, in *Cursor Mundi.* The plural *yourselves* is first recorded in 1523, providing an unambiguous form for the plural use.

youth *n.* Probably about 1150 *youhthe;* developed from Old English *geoguth* youth (about 725, in *Beowulf*); related to *geong* YOUNG. Old English *geoguth* is cognate with Old Frisian *jogethe* youth, Old Saxon *juguth,* Middle Dutch *joghet, jöghet* (modern Dutch *jeugd*), and Old High German *jugund* (modern German *Jugend*).

The formation is analyzed as *young* + *-th*[1] (actually found in *youngth,* 1303), from Old English *geong(u)* + *-th*[1]. Old English *geoguth, iuguth,* earlier **iugūth,* is from Proto-West Germanic **juȝúnthiz,* altered by influence of **duȝunthiz* ability (Old English *duguth*) from Proto-Germanic **juwúnthiz,* Indo-European **yuwn̥tis* (Pok.511). Compare Gothic *junda,* from Proto-Germanic **juwunđṓ,* Indo-European **yuwn̥tā́,* the source of Latin *juventa* youth.

—youthful *adj.* 1561, of youth or the young, juvenile; formed from English *youth* + *-ful.* The figurative sense of early, new, is first recorded in Shakespeare's *Titus Andronicus* (1588), and that of characterized by youth, young, in Spenser's *Faerie Queene* (1590).

yowl *v.* to howl. Probably about 1200 *yuhelen;* later *youlen* (before 1382); perhaps of independent imitative origin, but also similar in form to Old Icelandic *gaula,* and more closely to English *yawl* to howl, cry out (probably about 1590). **—n.** a howl. About 1450 *yowle;* from the verb.

yo-yo *n.* disk-shaped toy that is spun out and reeled in on an attached string. 1915, probably borrowed from a language of the Philippines. Apparently an earlier name for the toy was *bandalore* (1824), but it was from American contact in the Philippines that first commercial development was established. The figurative sense of fluctuating or vacillating is first recorded in 1960, from the earlier sense of up-and-down movement (1932). The slang meaning of a stupid person is not found before 1970.

ytterbium (i tėr′bēəm) *n.* metallic chemical element. 1879, New Latin, coined by the Swedish chemist Carl Gustaf Mosander, 1797-1858, from *Ytterby,* a town in Sweden where the element was discovered, + *-ium.*

yttrium (it′rēəm) *n.* metallic chemical element. 1822, New Latin, coined by the Swedish chemist Carl Gustaf Mosander, 1797-1858, from earlier *yttria* (1800, a heavy white powder, the oxide of yttrium) + *-ium. Yttria* was a New Latin word formed from *Ytterby,* the Swedish town where the oxide was discovered.

yucca (yü′kə) *n.* plant with sword-shaped evergreen leaves. 1664, in Evelyn's *Kalendarium Hortense;* New Latin *Jucca* genus name of the plant, from Spanish *yuca,* of uncertain origin. The spelling *yucca* for this plant appeared in 1731.

Yule or **yule** *n.* Christmas. Probably about 1200 *yole,* in *The Ormulum;* later *yoole,* in *Merlin* (probably about 1450); developed from Old English *geōl, geōla* Christmas day or Christmastide (before 899), found also in the phrases *se ǣrra geōla* December, *se æftera geōla* January. The Old English word was probably borrowed from a Scandinavian source (compare Old Icelandic *jōl,* pl., a heathen feast lasting twelve days; later in the meaning of Christmas, Swedish, Norwegian, and Danish *jul* Christmas). An Old English (Anglian) *giuli* recorded by Bede (726) as the name of December and January corresponds to Old Icelandic *ȳlir* the Yule month (middle of November to middle of December), and Gothic *jiuleis,* in *fruma jiuleis* November. **—yuletide** *n.* (about 1475)

yuppie *n.* young professional. 1984, American English; formed from the initial letters of *y(oung) u(rban) p(rofessional)* + suffix *-ie;* influenced by earlier *yippie* a politically active hippie (1968, American English); formed from the initials of *Y(outh) I(nternational) P(arty)* + *-ie,* after *hippie.*

Z

zany *n.* fool. 1588, in Shakespeare's *Love's Labour's Lost;* borrowed from Middle French *zani,* from dialectal Italian (Venetian) *zanni,* familiar variant of *Giovanni* John. *Zanni* was the name for a stock character in Italian farce. **—adj.** ridiculous. 1616, from the noun.

zap *v. Slang.* kill, hit. 1942, American English, an onomatopoeic word suggestive of the destructive force of a ray gun, as used in the comic strip "Buck Rogers" or of a blow delivered by a heavy club as in the comic strip "B.C." Later meanings include to move fast (1968) and to erase electronically (1982).

zeal *n.* eager desire, earnest enthusiasm. Before 1382 *zeel, zele,* in the Wycliffe Bible; borrowed (probably with influence of earlier *zealot*) from Old French *zel,* and directly from Latin *zēlus* zeal, from Greek *zêlos* jealousy, fervor, zeal. **—zealot** *n.* Before 1325 *zelote* member of a militant Jewish sect which fiercely resisted the Romans in Palestine, in *Cursor Mundi;* borrowed from Late Latin *zēlōtēs,* from Greek *zēlōtēs* a zealot, from *zēloûn* be zealous, from *zêlos* zeal, earlier and dialectal *zâlos,* apparently related to *zēteîn* to search, seek, and *zēmíā* punishment, but otherwise of unknown origin. **—zealous** *adj.* 1526, full of zeal, in the Tyndale Bible; borrowed from Medieval Latin *zelosus* full of zeal, from Latin *zēlus* zeal; for suffix see -OUS.

zebra *n.* striped horselike animal of Africa. 1600, in a translation (from Italian) of Leo Africanus' *Geographical History of Africa;* borrowing of Italian *zebra* (1554), and perhaps reinforced by Spanish *zebra, zebro* (now *cebra*), found also in Portuguese as *zevra* (1166) and *zevro* (1179), originally in the sense of a wild ass. In the early 1500's the Portuguese applied the word to the African animal. The ultimate origin of the word is uncertain.

Sometimes attributed to a borrowing from an unidentified African word. Corominas suggests a possible Vulgar Latin ***eciferus,* corresponding to Latin *equiferus* (in Pliny's writings) a wild horse (*equus* horse + *ferus* wild), but evidence of such a development, especially from most Romance languages, is lacking, and the phonetic development is difficult to account for.

zebu (zē′byü) *n.* oxlike animal with a large hump. 1774, in Goldsmith's *Natural History;* borrowed from French *zébu,* of unknown origin. According to the French naturalist Buffon, the animal was first shown under this name at a fair in Paris in 1752.

Zen *n.* Japanese and Chinese form of Buddhism. 1727 *Sen;* later *Zen* (1834); borrowed from Japanese *zen,* and perhaps from Chinese *chán,* from Sanskrit *dhyāna-m* meditation, thought, sense; see SEMANTIC.

zenith *n.* point in the heavens directly overhead. Before 1387 *cinit,* in Trevisa's translation of Higden's *Polychronicon;* later in the spelling *senith* (1391), in Chaucer's *Treatise on the Astrolabe;* borrowed from Old French *cenit, cenith,* and directly from Medieval Latin *cenit,* possibly *cenith, zenith,* from Arabic, transliterated as *samt* in *samt ar-rās* zenith; literally, the way over the head. Compare AZIMUTH, which retained the *m* found in the transliteration from Arabic, therefore giving rise to the theory that the *-ni-* of *zenith* may have developed from a misreading of *m* in the transliteration of Arabic *samt,* with the addition of *-h* first found in Chaucer.

The spelling *zenith* is first recorded in English in 1549. The figurative sense of highest point or state, acme, is first recorded in English in Shakespeare's *The Tempest* (1610).

zephyr (zef′ər) *n.* the west wind. 1369 *Zephirus* (personification of the west wind), in Chaucer's *Book of the Duchesse;* found also in Old English (about 1000) as *zefferus;* borrowed from Latin *zephyrus,* from Greek *zéphyros* the west wind, probably related to *zóphos* the west, the dark region, darkness, gloom. The spelling *zephyr* is first recorded in English in Chapman's translation of Homer's *Iliad* (1598). The meaning of a mild breeze is first recorded in Shakespeare's *Cymbeline* (about 1610).

zeppelin (zep′ələn) *n.* large dirigible balloon. 1900, borrowing of German *Zeppelin,* shortened form of earlier *Zeppelinschiff* (Zeppelin ship) and *Zeppelinkreuzer* (Zeppelin cruiser), in allusion to Count Ferdinand von *Zeppelin,* 1838-1917, who perfected this type of airship.

zero *n.* 1604, borrowed from French *zéro* (1515), and directly from Italian *zero* (1466), alteration of Medieval Latin *zephirum* (1202), from Arabic, transliterated as *ṣifr* empty, null, cipher, translating Sanskrit *śūnya-m* empty place, desert, naught, a cipher, neuter of *śūnyá-s* empty; see the doublet CIPHER. It is interesting to note that Arabic numerals are written from left to right (contrary to the practice of Arabic writing) by influence of the Indian origins of our number system. **—adj.** of or at zero. 1810, from the noun. **—v.** to adjust (an instrument or device) to zero point, take aim on a target; now especially in the phrase *zero in on* (1950, from earlier *zero in,* 1944). 1925, from the noun. **—zero gravity** (1951, in science fiction writings of Arthur Clarke) **—zero hour** (1917)

zest *n.* 1674, orange or lemon peel, in Blount's *Glossographia;* borrowed from French *zeste,* of uncertain origin. The figurative sense of something that adds flavor or relish is first recorded in English in 1709; and the meaning of keen enjoyment, in Boswell's *The Life of Samuel Johnson* (1791). **—v.** 1704, in Colley Cibber's *The Husband;* from the noun in the literal sense of add flavoring to. The figurative sense of add a piquant quality to is first recorded in English in 1737. **—zestful** *adj.* 1850, formed from English *zest,* n. + *-ful.* **—zesty** *adj.* 1934, formed from English *zest,* n. + *-y*[1].

zigzag *n.* series of lines with short sharp turns. 1712, borrowing of French *zigzag,* from German *Zickzack,* possibly a reduplication of *Zacke* tooth, prong. First found in English in reference to the laying out of garden paths. **—adv.** in a zigzag line or course. About

1730, from the noun. —**v.** move in a zigzag way. 1777, from the noun.

zilch *n. Slang.* nil, nothing, zero. 1966, American English; earlier, meaningless speech, gibberish (1960); and found in *Mr. Zilch* an indefinite nickname (1931); possibly from association with earlier *zip*[2] and *nil.* Compare ZIP[2].

zinc *n.* metallic chemical element. 1651 *zinke;* 1813 *zinc;* borrowed from German *Zink,* related to *Zinke, Zinken* prong, point, from Old High German *zinko;* perhaps so called from the form which zinc assumes after cooling. The spelling with *-c* was influenced by French *zinc.* —**v.** coat or cover with zinc. 1841, from the noun.

zinnia (zin′ēə) *n.* showy garden plant. 1767, in John Abercrombie's *Every Man his Own Gardener;* formed in allusion to Johann Gottfried *Zinn,* 1727-1759, German botanist.

Zion *n.* hill in Jerusalem on which Solomon's temple stood. Old English (about 1000) *Sion;* borrowed from Late Latin *Siōn,* from Greek *Seṓn,* from Hebrew *ṣiyyōn,* originally, a hill. —**Zionism** *n.* 1896, movement to establish a Jewish national state in Palestine; formed from English *Zion* + *-ism.* —**Zionist** *n.* 1896, formed from English *Zion* + *-ist.*

zip[1] *v.* move rapidly. 1852, American English, imitative of the sound of an object passing rapidly through the air or of a fabric being torn. —**n.** the sound of a zipping movement. 1875, from the verb or of imitative origin similar to that of the verb. The figurative sense of energy, force, impetus, is first recorded in 1900. —**zippy** *adj.* lively. 1904, American English, in George Ade's *True Bills;* formed from English *zip,* n. or v. + *-y*[1].

zip[2] *n. Slang.* zero, nothing (often referring to a score in sports). About 1900, a mark or grade of zero (used among students), American English; of uncertain origin (perhaps an expressive alteration of *zero;* compare ZILCH).

zip[3] *v.* to fasten or unfasten with a zipper. 1932, in Aldous Huxley's *Brave New World;* back formation from *zipper.* —**zipper** *n.* sliding fastener. 1925, probably formed from English *zip*[1], v. + *-er*[1]. As a trademark *Zipper,* registered in 1925 for a kind of boot with such a closing, apparently not specifically for the fastener, is no longer in any sense a proprietary name.

zip code Post-Office numeral identifying each zone of mail delivery. 1963, American English, from *ZIP,* acronym for*Z(one) I(mprovement) P(lan),* the United States Postal Service system of numerical coding by zones for faster mail sorting and delivery.

zircon *n.* crystalline mineral. 1797, earlier *jargon, circon* (1794); probably borrowed from French *zircone, jargon,* and German *Zirkon,* from Arabic *zarqūn,* from Persian *zargūn;* literally, golden, from *zar* gold, from Avestan *zari-* gold-colored, cognate with Sanskrit *hári-s,* from Indo-European **ĝhel-* YELLOW.

zirconium *n.* metallic chemical element commonly obtained from zircon, which was first isolated by modern chemical analysis by the German chemist M.H. Klaproth. 1808, New Latin; formed from *zircon* + *-ium.*

zither (ziᴛʜ′ər *or* zith′ər) *n.* stringed musical instrument. 1850, borrowing of German *Zither,* from Latin *cithara,* from Greek *kithárā* lyrelike instrument. Doublet of CITHARA and GUITAR. Apparently the zither is a modification (known among the Tyrolese in the Austrian Alps) of the *cithara,* an ancient lyre of seven to eleven strings.

zo- the form of *zoo-* before vowels, as in *Paleozoic.*

zodiac *n.* imaginary belt of the heavens divided into twelve equal parts called signs. 1391 *zodiak,* in Chaucer's *Treatise on the Astrolabe;* borrowed from Old French *zodiaque,* and probably directly from Latin *zōdiacus* the zodiac, of the zodiac, from Greek *zōidiakós* the zodiac, of the zodiac, of the figures (in reference to the *zōidiakòs kýklos* circle of figures that make up the zodiacal signs), from *zṓidion* zodiacal sign; originally, sculptured figure (of an animal), diminutive of *zôion* animal, living being; related to *zōḗ* life; see QUICK. —**zodiacal** *adj.* 1576, formed from English *zodiac* + *-al*[1].

zombie *n.* in the voodoo cult, a corpse brought back to life by supernatural power. 1871, American English, borrowed from a Bantu language of West Africa; compare Kikongo, Kimbundu, and Tshiluba *nzambi* god, Kikongo *zumbi* fetish. The transferred sense of a stupefied, stupid, or lethargic person, is first recorded in 1946, in American English.

zone *n.* 1393-94, any of the five great divisions (torrid zone, frigid zone, etc.) of the earth's surface; borrowed from Latin *zōna* geographic belt, celestial zone or band, from Greek *zṓnē* (earlier **zṓsnā*), originally, girdle, belt, from *zōnnýnai* to gird. Greek *zōnnýnai* is related to *zōstós* girt, and cognate with Lithuanian *júosti* to gird, Old Slavic *pojasŭ* girdle, and Avestan *yāsta-* encircled, girt, from Indo-European **yōs-* (Pok.513). The extended meaning of any region or area set off from adjacent regions is first recorded in 1822, and the meaning in town planning of an area under special building restrictions, in 1909. —**v.** divide into zones. 1705 (implied in *zoned*), from the noun. The meaning in town planning of divide into zones of restricted building is first recorded in 1916. —**zonal** *adj.* 1867, borrowed from Late Latin *zōnālis* of a zone, from Latin *zōna* zone; for suffix see -AL[1]. —**zoning** *n.* 1820, division into particular times or areas, in Keats' *The Fall of Hyperion;* later, the regulation of land use in town planning (1912).

zoo *n.* About 1847, in writings of Macaulay; shortened form of *the Zoological* (1831), itself a shortened form of the *Zoological Gardens* of the London Zoological Society, established in 1828 in Regent's Park, London, to house the Society's collection of wild animals. The first zoo in the United States was the Philadelphia Zoological Garden, which opened in 1874.

zoo- a combining form meaning animal, living being, as in *zoology, zooplankton.* Borrowed from later Greek *zōo-,* from Greek *zōio-,* combining form of *zôion* animal; see ZODIAC.

zoology (zōol′əjē) *n.* 1669, borrowed from New Latin *zoologia* science and study of animals, from modern Greek *zōiología,* originally, science of pharmaceuticals derived from animals (Greek *zôion* animal + *-logíā* -logy). —**zoological** *adj.* of animals or animal life. 1807, formed from English *zoology* + *-ical.* —**zoologist** *n.* 1663, in writings of Robert Boyle; formed in English from New Latin *zoologia* zoology + English *-ist.*

zoom *v.* 1886, travel or move with a humming or buzzing sound; later, move speedily along (1924), often with an abrupt upward movement as by aircraft (1918, from the noun); imitative of the sound. The sense of moving quickly closer to something as an aircraft does when zooming down or up, is first recorded in 1918. —**n.** 1917, act of zooming; from the verb. The use in photography as in *zoom lens* (1936), which developed from the sense of zooming in an aircraft, is first recorded in 1934.

zori (zō′rē) *n.* flat sandal, usually made of woven straw, leather, or rubber. 1823 *sori,* 1884 *zori;* borrowed from Japanese *zōri* straw sandals (*sō* grass, straw + *ri* sole).

zounds *interj. Archaic.* mild oath expressing surprise or anger. 1600, reduction of obsolete *God's wounds!,* an oath. A similar formation is found in *zooks* (1634, shortened form of *God's sokings* 1577). While *God's sokings* is obsolete (the meaning of *sokings* is not even known today), its modern form *Gadzooks* (1694) was familiar up into the 1930's and 1940's, unlike *God's wounds* which dropped out of English by the 1600's, if indeed it was ever a common phrase except in the shortened form *wounds.*

zucchetto (züket′ō) *n.* small, round skullcap worn by Catholic clergymen. 1853, borrowed from Italian *zucchetta* cap, small gourd, from *zucca* gourd, head (compare Late Latin *cucutia* gourd), of uncertain origin.

zucchini (zükē′nē) *n.* kind of dark-green summer squash. 1929 *succini;* 1945 *zuchini;* American English, borrowed from Italian, plural of *zucchino,* diminutive of *zucca* squash, gourd; see ZUCCHETTO.

zwieback (zwē′bäk′) *n.* kind of bread baked and cut into slices which are then toasted brown and crisp. 1894, American English; borrowing of German *Zwieback* biscuit, from *zwie-*, combining form of *zwei* TWO + *backen* to BAKE; loan translation of Italian *biscotto* biscuit. A similar formation in English is found in *twice-baked potatoes.*

zygote (zī′gōt) *n. Biology.* cell formed by the union of two gametes. 1891, borrowed from Greek *zygōtós* yoked, from *zygoûn* to yoke, from *zygón* YOKE.

zymurgy (zī′mėrjē) *n.* branch of chemistry dealing with fermentation. 1868, formed in English from Greek *zýmē* leaven; see JUICE + *-ourgíā* a working, from *érgon* WORK.

Glossary of Language Names and Linguistic Terms

This glossary is a selected list of language names and linguistic terms that appear in the body of the Dictionary. The definitions identify a language or a language process to help the user more fully understand the borrowing process in the context of a given etymology.

ablative a case in Latin and some other inflected languages which expresses the source or place of an action or the instrument or means with which it is carried out.

ablaut a systematic vowel alternation occurring in the root of words, especially in Indo-European languages, usually with corresponding variation of meaning, as in English *ring, rang, rung.* Also called *gradation.*

Abnaki (abnä′kē) the Algonquian language of a North American Indian people that lived mostly in Maine, New Hampshire, Vermont, and eastern Canada.

absolute 1 (of a verb) used without an expressed object, as *give* in the sentence *Please give generously.* **2** (of an adjective or pronoun) having its noun understood, as *younger* in the sentence *Older pupils should help the younger,* and *ours* in *His house is larger than ours.*

abstracted (of a form) taken from all or part of an older form but used in a different or broader range of contexts, as *-aholic* (abstracted immediately from *workaholic* but ultimately from *alcoholic*), *-athon* (abstracted from *marathon*), *mini-* (abstracted from *miniature*), and *-burger* (abstracted from *hamburger*).

accent 1 = stress. **2** a designation of vowel stress, as in Spanish, vowel quality, as in French, or vowel quantity, as in Hungarian. **3a** a distinctive regional or national way of pronouncing a given language, as in an Irish accent. **b** a foreign accent, as in to have an accent. **4** the phonetic features of a language influencing a learner's second language, as in a French or Russian accent.

accusative a case in Latin, Greek, and many other inflected languages, used as the direct object of the verb, as the subject of an infinitive, or as the object of a preposition to indicate the goal of action or motion toward.

acronym a word formed from the first letters or syllables of other words, as *laser, quasar, radar,* and *scuba.*

active showing the subject of a verb as acting. *Example:* The verb *broke* in *He broke the dish* is in the active voice. Compare *passive.*

Afar (ä′fär) A Cushitic language spoken in Ethiopia.

affix a prefix, suffix, or infix.

Afghan = Pashto.

Afrikaans a Germanic language of South Africa, developed from the Dutch of the colonists who settled there in the 1600's, formerly called South African Dutch.

Afro-Asiatic a language family of northern Africa, extending into Saudi Arabia, Syria, and Iraq. Branches of Afro-Asiatic include Semitic, Berber, Cushitic, and Egyptian.

agglutinative language a language characterized by joining together into a single word various elements that retain their individual form and meaning within the word. Turkish and Hungarian are typical agglutinative languages. Compare *isolating language.*

Akan (ä′kän) a Kwa language spoken in Ghana and other parts of western Africa.

Akkadian (əkā′dēən) the eastern division of the Semitic languages, spoken in ancient Mesopotamia, and including Babylonian and Assyrian.

Albanian the Indo-European language of Albania, not closely related to other Indo-European languages. It has two dialects, Geg and Tosk, and a large number of loanwords from Latin, Greek, Slavic, and Turkish.

Aleut (al′ēüt) the language of a people inhabiting the Aleutian Islands and the Alaska Peninsula, distantly related to Eskimo, and a branch of the Eskimo-Aleut language family.

Algonquian or **Algonkian** (algong′kēən) the most widespread family of North American Indian languages, including Abnaki, Cheyenne, Micmac, and Ojibwa.

Altaic (altā′ik) a language family of the Turkic, Mongolian, and Tungusic groups, spoken over most of Asia, and often combined with Uralic to form a hypothetical Ural-Altaic family.

alteration a change in the form of a word or phrase, usually as a result of the influence of a phonetically or semantically similar word. *Example:* English *crayfish* is an alteration (influenced by *fish*) of Middle English *crevis,* borrowed from Middle French *crevice.*

American English the form of English spoken and written in the United States.

American Spanish the group of Spanish dialects spoken in South America, Central America, and some islands of the West Indies (Cuba, Puerto Rico, the Dominican Republic).

Amharic (amhar′ik, ämhär′-) a Semitic language of the Ethiopic branch; the official and literary language of Ethiopia since the 1300's.

analogy the process by which words or grammatical forms are made to conform to similar words or forms or to some regular pattern in the language. Analogy has led to the regularization of inflectional endings (such as *-ed* for the past and past participle of verbs) in English. New words are often formed by analogy, as *sexism* and *sexist* on the model of *racism* and *racist.*

analytic language a language characterized by the use of function words and word order rather than inflectional endings to express grammatical relationships. Modern English is an analytic language. Compare *synthetic language.*

Anatolian (an′ətō′lēən) an Indo-European language or group of languages spoken in ancient Anatolia, including Hittite.

Anglian the Old English dialect of the Angles, originally spoken in Mercia and Northumbria.

Anglicize to make into English in form or pronunciation, as *covet, buffoon,* and *jail,* originally French words. **—Anglicization.** See also *naturalize.*

Anglo-French the dialect of French introduced into England mainly by the Normans (French-speaking descendants of Scandinavians who settled in France in the 800's) following their conquest of England in 1066. Anglo-French was used chiefly by the governing classes through the 1300's. A number of Old French literary masterpieces are actually Anglo-French, including the works of the poetess, Marie de France. Also called *Anglo-Norman* and *Norman-French.*

Anglo-Indian a dialect of British English spoken in India, containing many words taken directly from the languages of India, especially Hindi.

Anglo-Latin the form of Medieval Latin used in England during the Middle English period.

Anglo-Norman = Anglo-French.

Anglo-Saxon = Old English.

Annamese (an′əmēs′) = Vietnamese.

aorist a verbal aspect in Greek and some other inflected languages showing that an action took place in the past without indicating whether the act was completed, repeated, or continued.

Apache the Athapascan language of a native American people living in the southwestern United States.

aphesis the loss of a short, unaccented vowel at the beginning of a word, as in *cute* for *acute, possum* for *opossum.* Aphesis is a specialized variety of a more general phonetic process, *apheresis,* which is the omission of one or more sounds or words from the beginning of an utterance, as in *'em* for *them* and *most* for *almost* ("*most* all of *'em* are here"). **—aphetic** having to do with or resulting from aphesis. Compare *apocope, syncope.*

apocope the loss of a sound or syllable at the end of a word, as in the pronunciation of *old* as (ōl) or *child* as (chīl.) Compare *syncope.*

Arabic the Semitic language of the Arabs, now spoken chiefly in the Arabian Peninsula, Iraq, Syria, Lebanon, Jordan, Egypt, and North Africa.

Aramaic (ar′əmā′ik) a Semitic language or group of dialects dominant in the Near East from the 300's B.C. through the 500's A.D. Aramaic includes Syriac and was the language spoken in Palestine at the time of Christ. It is still spoken in parts of Iraq, Iran, and Syria.

Arawakan (ä′räwä′kən) a family of South American Indian languages, including the Arawak language, now found in parts of northern South America (Colombia, Venezuela, Guyana, Brazil), but formerly spoken in the West Indies and a part of southern Florida.

Armenian the Indo-European language of Armenia and parts of Georgia, Azerbaijan, and Iran, not closely related to any of the other Indo-European languages.

aspect a category of verb forms which express action or state as beginning, ending, continuing, or repeating, rather than indicating time, as do tense forms. See, for example, *aorist, frequentative, inceptive, perfective.*

assimilation a change in a speech sound making it like a similar sound nearby. *Example:* The Latin prefix *ad-* becomes *ab-* before *b* by assimilation of the *d* to the following consonant, as in *abbreviāre* (*ad-* + *breviāre* shorten). Compare *dissimilation.*

Assyrian the ancient Semitic language of Assyria.

Athapascan or **Athapaskan** (ath′əpas′kən) a family of North American Indian languages extending from Alaska and Canada to Mexico, and including Navaho and Apache.

Attic the ancient Greek dialect of Attica, whose capital was Athens. Attic became the literary language of Greece.

attributive placed immediately before a noun and serving as a modifier. *Highway* in the phrase *highway patrol* is an attributive noun.

augmentative a form of a word expressing largeness or bigness, usually by the addition of a suffix. *Example:* Italian *trombone* (the musical instrument) is in origin an augmentative of *tromba* trumpet.

Australian a collective name for the aboriginal languages of Australia, especially Aranda (or Arunta) and Worora, having no known relationship to other languages.

Australian English the form of English spoken and written in Australia.

Austronesian a probable linguistic family of the Pacific, comprising the Indonesian, Polynesian, Melanesian, and Micronesian languages. Also called *Malayo-Polynesian.*

Avestan (əves′tən) the Iranian language in which the Avesta, the sacred book of the Zoroastrian religion, is written, closely related to Old Persian.

Aymara (ī′märä′) a group of South American Indian languages of Bolivia and Peru, related to Quechua.

back formation a new word formed by analogy from an older word on the mistaken assumption that the older word is a derivative of the new word, as in *escalate* formed from *escalator, burgle* from *burglar, typewrite* from *typewriter,* and *kudo* from *kudos.*

Baltic the Indo-European ancestor of the languages of the eastern Baltic region, including Lithuanian, Latvian, or Lettish, and Old Prussian (now extinct).

Bantu a major branch of the Niger-Congo language family, consisting of languages found through most of Africa south of the Equator, including Swahili, Mbundu, Sotho, Setswana, Xhosa, and Zulu.

base = root.

Basque the language of the Basques, an ancient people inhabiting the western Pyrenees, in southern France and northern Spain. Basque is not related to any other known language. Also called *Euskara* or *Euskera.* A feature of Basque is the lack of (f), and the Spanish loss of (f) in many Latin words has been attributed to Basque influence (compare Spanish *harina* 'flour' from Latin *farina*). Many Spanish names and some words are of Basque origin; the name *Xavier* of Basque origin became popular throughout Europe because of the Spanish Basque missionary St. Francis Xavier.

Belorussian (bel′ərush′ən) the Slavic language of the Belorussian republic of the Soviet Union. Also spelled *Byelorussian.*

Berber a Hamitic language spoken in North Africa, especially in Morocco and Algeria. Berber still has some words of Latin origin traced to the period of Roman domination of North Africa.

blend 1 a word made by combining elements of two words, often by fusion of a letter or syllable they have in common. *Examples: chortle,* a blend of *chuckle* and *snort; motel,* a blend of *motor* and *hotel; smog,* a blend of *smoke* and *fog.* Compare *fusion.* **2** a combination of consonant sounds represented by two or more letters, as *bl* in *blend.* Compare *digraph, diphthong.*

borrow to take (a word, phrase, meaning, etc.) from another language, as *basis* from Latin *basis, bassoon* from French *basson,* and *bas-relief* from Italian *basso-rilievo.* Compare *develop, Anglicize, naturalize.* **—borrowing** a word taken from another language. Borrowings may retain their original form (adoption) and retain their foreign spelling (as *coup d'état*) or retain only part of their original form (adaptation or derivation) and take on the characteristics of a native English word (as *cab, cabbage, coleslaw,* etc.). Also called *loan word.* Another form of borrowing is a translation of a foreign term into the borrowing language (as English *superman* translating German *übermensch*). Also called *loan translation.*

bound form or **morpheme** a form which never occurs alone but always as part of a larger unit. *Example:* The word *activation* has three bound forms in it — activate *-ion,* activ-*ate,* and act-*ive.* Compare *free form.*

Breton the language of Brittany, a Celtic language closely related to Welsh and Cornish, and the only Celtic language now spoken on the European continent. Breton is believed to have been introduced on the European continent by immigrants from Britain; the older Gaulish, also a Celtic language, did not survive in France.

British English the form of English spoken and written in Great Britain, and to some extent imitated in India, South Africa, and certain other former British colonies.

Brythonic (brithon′ik) a division of the Celtic languages comprising Welsh, Cornish, and Breton.

Bulgarian the Slavic language of Bulgaria.

Burmese the Tibeto-Burman language of Burma.

Bushman a Khoisan language spoken in Botswana, Southwest Africa (Namibia), and parts of South Africa.

Byelorussian (byel′ərush′ən) = Belorussian.

calque = loan translation.

Canadian English the form of English spoken and written by English-speaking Canadians.

Canadian French the form of French spoken and written by French-speaking Canadians. English influence is evident not only in borrowed words but also in loan translation; note the use of *bienvenu* 'welcome' as the answer to *merci* 'thanks' instead of standard French *de rien* 'don't mention it.'

Cantonese the dialect of Chinese spoken in the city of Canton and the southeastern province of Kwangtung (Guangdong), of which Canton is the capital.

Carib (kar′ib) a family of South American Indian languages found in northern South America (Colombia, Venezuela, Guyana, Suriname, and Brazil), in Honduras and Belize, and to a lesser extent the West Indies.

case one of the forms of a noun, pronoun, or adjective used to indicate its relation to other words, usually by the addition of inflectional endings. Latin has six case endings, seven if the locative is considered separately (nominative, genitive, dative, accusative, ablative, and vocative), Greek has five, German four, Old English four and Modern English only the possessive, except for some pronouns, which have three case forms (such as nominative *he,* objective *him,* and possessive *his*). Most syntactical relationships in English are indicated by word order alone.

Castilian = Spanish.

Catalan the Romance language of Catalonia, a region in northeastern Spain, closely related to Provençal. Catalan is also spoken in the Balearic Islands, the area around Perpignan in France, in Andorra, and in the Sardinian city of Alghero.

Caucasian a family of languages spoken in the region of the Caucasus Mountains, between the Black and Caspian seas.

causative a word or form indicating that the subject causes performance of an action. *Examples:* The prefix *en-* in *enrich* is a causative. English *lay,* v., is the causative of *lie,* v., to recline.

Celtic a branch of Indo-European that includes Irish, Gaelic, Welsh, Breton, and Manx, and is usually divided into Brythonic and Goidelic.

centum language any of the Indo-European languages in which the sound represented by *k,* as in *Kent,* is found as the initial consonant of Latin *centum* hundred and thereby remained distinct from the sound of *s,* as in *sat,* found as the initial consonant of Avestan *satem.* The centum languages include Hellenic, Italic, Celtic, Germanic, Tocharian, and Hittite. Compare *satem language.*

Cherokee (cher′əkē) the Iroquoian language of an American Indian people now living mostly in Oklahoma and North Carolina, but originally throughout the southern Appalachians. By 1821, Sequoya, a tribal member, had introduced a remarkable syllabary writing system of 85 characters which increased the power and stature of the Cherokee among other tribes.

Cheyenne (shī′an) the Algonquian language of an American Indian people now living mostly in Oklahoma and Montana, but originally in Minnesota.

Chinese the tonal language of China, comprising a large group of dialects (Cantonese, Fukienese, Hakka, etc.) of which the Beijing (Peking) dialect, Mandarin, is regarded as standard.

Chinook (chənük′) **1** the language of a North American Indian people living along the Columbia River in the Pacific Northwest. **2** = Chinook jargon.

Chinook jargon a pidgin language based on Chinook and Nootka, with additional English and French elements, used in trading in the Pacific Northwest.

click a speech sound consisting of a stop produced by a sucking action of the tongue against the gums, used especially in the Khoisan languages of southern Africa.

clipped form or **word** a form or word shortened by dropping syllables, as in *quote* from *quotation, bus* from *omnibus, deli* from *delicatessen.* Compare *back formation.*

cognate related by common origin; descended from the same original language, root, or source. English *mother,* German *Mutter,* and Dutch *moeder* are cognate because they are all descended from Proto-Germanic **mōdér,* which in turn is cognate with Latin *māter,* Greek *mḗtēr,* and Sanskrit *mātár-,* descended from Indo-European **mətér-.*

coinage an invented word or phrase, usually created for a specific purpose. *Jabberwocky* and *chortle* were two of Lewis Carroll's coinages. Compare *nonce word.* **—coined** (of a word or phrase) made up or invented for a specific purpose. *Nylon* was coined by the Du Pont Company.

collocation a group of words commonly used together, as *little girl, prevail upon, have a good time.* Compare *idiom.*

colloquialism a word, phrase, or other expression used in common, everyday, familiar talk.

combining form a form of a word which is used to combine with other words or other combining forms to make new words, such as *astro-, hydro-, multi-, paleo-, semi-,* and the like.

comparative the second degree of comparison of an adjective or adverb. *Examples: Better* is the comparative of *good, less* or *lesser* is the comparative of *little.* Compare *positive, superlative.*

compound two or more words combined to form a new word or term with a different meaning. *Examples: playground, bookkeeper, high school, post office, go-between, nevertheless, on-again off-again.*

conjugation a systematic arrangement of the forms of a verb. Latin verbs, for example, are grouped in four conjugations according to the ending of the infinitive: 1) *-āre,* 2) *-ēre,* 3) *-ere,* and 4) *-īre.*

contraction 1 a shortened form of a word or words, as English *can't* or *I've,* and French *des* (instead of *de les*). **2** the process of forming a contraction.

Coptic a Hamitic language developed from ancient Egyptian. The use of Coptic is now confined to rituals of the Coptic Church.

Cornish a Celtic language spoken by the people of Cornwall, England, until the late 1700's.

correlative having a mutual relation and commonly used together, as *either...or, not only...but, doctor and patient, husband and wife.*

creole a standard native language or primary language of a community, formed from a mixture of elements from several other languages with which there is intensive contact. A creole was originally a pidgin, often characterized by vocabulary of one language (as French or Portuguese) with simplified morphology and with the structure influenced by other languages (as for example African languages in the case of Haitian Creole and of Cape Verdean). Compare *pidgin.* **—creolization** the process by which a creole is created out of a pidgin or a mixture of languages in contact.

Creole (krē′ōl) **1** a dialect of French spoken in southern Louisiana. **2** = Haitian Creole.

Crimean Gothic a dialect of Gothic used in the Crimea into the 1500's, known from a small group of words and phrases recorded in the Crimea in 1560-62.

Croatian (krōā′shən) the form of Serbo-Croatian spoken by Croats and written in the Roman alphabet.

Cushitic (kəshit′ik) a group of Hamitic languages of Ethiopia and eastern Africa, including Somali and Afar.

Czech the West Slavic language of the Czechs, spoken in western and central Czechoslovakia.

Danish the Scandinavian language of Denmark.

dative a case in Latin and other inflected languages, showing the indirect object of the verb or preposition. The dative function in English is indicated by word order (as in *show* him *the painting*) or a prepositional phrase (as in *show the painting* to him).

declension the system in inflected languages for giving different forms or endings to nouns, pronouns, or adjectives to show their case, gender, and number.

derive to originate or form a word, especially by adding a prefix or suffix to another word. **—derivative** a word formed by adding a prefix or suffix to another word. *Unkindly* is a derivative of *unkind; kindly* is a derivative of *kind.*

develop (of a word or form) to be formed from earlier words or elements of the same language or evolve through internal changes from an earlier stage of the language, as a Middle English word from an Old English word. Words which develop within a language are often said to be *inherited,* as opposed to words *borrowed* from another language, which often become *naturalized.*

diachronic historical; of or having to do with the study of a language from a historical perspective, by investigating changes in its forms in the course of its development. Compare *synchronic.*

dialect a distinctive form or variety of a language, usually one spoken in a particular geographical area and differing in some way from the standard or literary form (itself a dialect) of the language. Scottish is a dialect of English. Creole is a dialect of French. **—dialectal** of or belonging to a dialect.

digraph a combination of two letters used to represent a single speech sound (phoneme). *Ch* in *chin, sh* in *shop, th* in *with,* and *ea* in *eat* are digraphs. Compare *diphthong, blend.*

diminutive a form of a word used to express smallness, usually by the addition of a suffix. *Examples: Droplet* is a diminutive of *drop.* Latin *capreolus* wild goat, roebuck, is a diminutive of *caprea* wild she-goat.

diphthong a vowel sound (phoneme) made up of two vowel sounds pronounced within a syllable, as the sound of English *ou* in *house, oi* in *noise,* and *i* in *ice.* Compare *digraph, blend.* **—diphthongize** to change (a vowel or vowels) into a diphthong. The Middle English phoneme /ū/ diphthongized to /ou/in *house.*

dissimilation a change in a speech sound in a word making it less like a similar sound in the same word. *Example:* Latin *peregrīnus* became *pelegrin(o)* in some of the Romance languages by dissimilation of the first *r* to *l.* Compare *assimilation.*

doublet one of two or more words derived ultimately from the same word but coming into the language by different routes. *Examples: abridge* and *abbreviate, frail* and *fragile; dish, disk, desk,* and *dais.*

Dravidian (drəvid′ēən) a family of languages found in southern India, Sri Lanka, and Pakistan, including Tamil and Telugu.

dual a number category indicating two persons or things, used in addition to the singular and plural in certain languages, such as Greek, Old Slavic, and Sanskrit. In grammatical systems having a dual, the plural applies to three or more.

Dutch the West Germanic language of the Netherlands, descended from the Low German dialects of Franks and Saxons.

echoic = imitative.

Egyptian the Hamitic language of the ancient Egyptians. Coptic developed from it.

ending a letter or letters attached to a word or stem to change its meaning, to indicate its grammatical relationship to other words, or to Anglicize a foreign ending in a borrowed word. The adverbial suffix *-ly*[1], the plural inflection *-s*[1], and the Anglicizations *-oon* and *-ish*[2] are common endings in English.

English the West Germanic language of England, including Old English (before 1100), Middle English (about 1100-1475 or 1500), and Modern English (from about 1475 or 1500). Modern English is also spoken in Australia, Canada, India, Ireland, New Zealand, the Republic of South Africa, the United States, and many other countries, partly as a result of English colonization begun in the 1600's, and later partly as a world language of commerce and technology.

eponym a person from whose name a nation, people, place, or institution derives its name. *Examples: Colombia* from *Colombus, Judea* from *Judah, Rome* from *Romulus, Rhodesia* from *Rhodes.* **—eponymous** giving one's name to a nation, people, place, or institution.

Eskimo the language of a people living in Greenland, northern Canada, Alaska, and eastern Siberia, distantly related to Aleut, and a branch of the Eskimo-Aleut family. The name *Inuit* or *Innuit* is now preferred by its speakers for the language and in referring to themselves.

Eskimo-Aleut a family of languages spoken in the most northerly areas of North America, from Greenland to Alaska and into Siberia, along the Arctic coast.

Estonian the Finno-Ugric language of Estonia, closely related to Finnish.

Ethiopic a branch of Semitic that includes Amharic.

Etruscan the language of an ancient people who inhabited Etruria (modern Tuscany) in central Italy and developed a flourishing civilization from about 600 B.C. to 100 B.C. Etruscan influenced Latin, though its origin and relationship to other languages is obscure.

etymon the form of a word from which another or other forms have developed. *Example:* the immediate etymon of English *azure* is Old French *azur;* the ultimate etymon is Persian *lāzward.*

euphemism a mild or indirect word or expression used as a substitute for one thought to be too direct, harsh, unpleasant, or offensive. *Example: Gosh!* for *God!* Compare *taboo.*

Euskara or **Euskera** (yüs′kərə) = Basque.

Ewe (ā′vā) a Kwa language of western Africa, spoken in Ghana and Togo.

extended widened in meaning as by figurative or transferred use.

eye dialect a written form suggesting dialectal or nonstandard speech, as *wanna* for *want to,* and *should of* for *should have.* Such spellings do not indicate pronunciation but rather the supposed misspellings of the uneducated.

Faeroese or **Faroese** (făr′ōēz′) the Scandinavian language of the Faeroe Islands, situated between Norway and Iceland.

family a group of related languages developed from a common language; language family. Some of the largest families of languages are the Indo-European, Afro-Asiatic, Austronesian, Niger-Congo, and Sino-Tibetan.

Farsi (fär′sē) = Persian.

figurative extended from the narrow or literal meaning of a word to a wider meaning; shifted from the concrete to the abstract, or from the physical to the mental; metaphorical. Many words in English are recorded in a figurative sense before they are found in their literal sense.

Finnish the Finno-Ugric language of Finland.

Finno-Ugric (fin′ōü′grik, -ōyü′-) a family of languages of eastern Europe and western Asia that includes Finnish, Estonian, Lapp, and Hungarian.

Flemish the West Germanic language of the people of Flanders, a form of Low German closely related to Dutch.

folk etymology the alteration of an unfamiliar word to make it sound like a familiar one, thus distorting or obscuring its real etymology. *Examples: Sparrow-grass,* alteration of *asparagus; female,* alteration of Old French *femelle* on the analogy of *male.* Also called *popular etymology.*

form any of the ways in which a word or morpheme is spelled, pronounced, or inflected.

formative a sound, syllable, or bound morpheme used to form words. Prefixes and suffixes are formatives.

Franconian the West German dialect or dialects spoken by the Franks who lived along the Rhine.

Frankish the West Germanic language spoken in northern Gaul in the 400's and 500's. Many French words derive from Frankish.

free form or **morpheme** a form which can be used alone as a word with a distinct meaning or meanings. *Example:* The compound *applecart* has two free forms, *apple* and *cart;* the derivative *boosterism* has one free form, *boost,* and two bound forms, boost-*er-ism.*

French the Romance language of France, including Old French (to 1350 or 1400), Middle French (to 1600), and Modern French (from about 1600).

frequentative (a verbal aspect) expressing habitual or repeated action, as English verbs in *-le*[3] (such as *babble* and *giggle*) and *-er*[4] (as *clatter* and *jabber*).

Frisian (frizh′ən) the West Germanic language of Friesland, in the northern Netherlands, and some nearby islands on the North Sea. Frisian is closely related to English.

Fulani (fülä′nē) a West Atlantic language spoken widely in western Africa, especially in northern Nigeria.

function the way in which a word or phrase is used in a sentence, whether as a noun or verb, adjective or adverb, and so on.

functional shift a change in the function of a word or phrase without a change in form, as from one part of speech to another. The nouns *author, chair,* and *elbow* became verbs by functional shift.

function word a word that expresses the function or grammatical relationship of the words in a sentence. Prepositions, articles, conjunctions, and auxiliary verbs are function words.

fusion the blending or combining of two sounds or

words so that the new sound or word often has a part common to the combined elements.

Gaelic the Celtic language of the Highlands of Scotland. Also called *Scottish Gaelic.* Compare *Irish.*

Gallo-Romance a Romance language of largely hypothetical forms, thought to be developed from Vulgar Latin and spoken in France from about 600 to 900 A.D.

Gaulish The Celtic language of the ancient Gauls. Many Latin and Old French words came from Gaulish.

gender a grammatical division of nouns, pronouns, adjectives, and articles into certain classes such as masculine and feminine (French, Hebrew), masculine, feminine, and neuter (Old English, German, animate and inanimate (American Indian languages). Gender may be shown by the form of the article (*el, la* in Spanish, *der, die, das* in German) or by the form of the noun and adjective (Hebrew, Latin, Russian). In modern English, gender is based chiefly on sex differentiation and indicated by the meaning of words (*man/woman, niece/nephew, hen/rooster*) and certain noun endings (*-ess* and *-or, -us* and *-a,* as in *actor/actress, alumnus/alumna*), except in pronouns, where the distinction is between *he/him/his, she/her,* and *it.*

genitive a case in Latin, Greek, and other inflected languages, used to show possession, source, or origin. In Modern English, the genitive relationship is shown in nouns by the ending *'s* as well as by the preposition *of* and in pronouns by the genitive forms *my, mine, her, hers,* etc.; in Latin words, where the full form of the stem is obscured by the nominative, the genitive form is frequently given, as in *rēx* (genitive *rēgis*) king.

German the West Germanic language of Germany, Austria, and parts of Switzerland, especially High German.

Germanic a branch of Indo-European customarily divided into East Germanic (Gothic), North Germanic (the Scandinavian languages), and West Germanic (English, Frisian, Dutch, German).

gerund 1 a verb form in English ending in *-ing* and used as a noun, as in *Dancing and acting are fine arts.* **2** a Latin verbal noun ending in *-andum* or *-endum,* used only in the singular number and in four cases (genitive, dative, accusative, and ablative).

gerundive (in Latin and certain other languages) a word functioning as an adjective but having characteristics of a verb; a verbal adjective. Unlike the gerund in Latin, a gerundive is used with both numbers and in all cases. *Example: cōnficiendās* for accomplishing (or to accomplish).

gloss a word or words inserted into a text to explain or translate a difficult or foreign word or phrase.

Goidelic (goi′THəlik, gaTH′ə-, goidel′ik) a division of the Celtic languages comprising Irish, Gaelic, and Manx.

Gothic the east Germanic language of the Goths who settled mainly in eastern and southern Europe and, with the Vandals, invaded the Roman Empire from about 200 to 400 A.D. The Gothic language essentially died out in Europe although it was reportedly still spoken in the Crimea into the 1500's (Crimean Gothic). Today Gothic is known chiefly from the translations of the Bible by Bishop Ulfilas in the 300's A.D.

gradation = ablaut.

grade the position occupied by the vowel in an ablaut series: **a** a change in the vowel to show a change in function or meaning, as in the principal parts of English strong verbs, such as *ring, rang, rung,* and *ride, rode, ridden.* **b** (as assigned to Indo-European roots) the position occupied by *e* or *o* in its original or earliest stage (*normal grade*), or when shortened (*reduced grade*) or omitted altogether (*zero grade*).

grapheme the smallest significant unit of a written language; any form of a letter or combination of letters that represents a speech sound. Compare *phoneme, morpheme.*

Great Vowel Shift a series of sound shifts which occurred in certain vowels during the Middle English period, resulting in the development of the Modern English vowel system. The two highest Middle English vowels, (ē), (ü), became diphthongs (ī) and (ou) respectively, while the long vowels shifted upwards: Middle English (ā) became (ē), (ä) became (ā), and (ō) became (ü).

Greek the Hellenic language of Greece, or a particular dialect or form of it, especially Attic. Classical Greek was the language until about 300 A.D., Late Greek until about 700 A.D., Medieval Greek until about 1500 A.D., and Modern Greek began to develop about 1500. The Greek of the New Testament represents a later stage of the language than that of the Classical writers.

Grimm's Law a phonetic law describing the systematic sound shift of certain Indo-European consonants that occurred in the Germanic languages: Indo-European *bh, dh, gh* became Germanic *b, d, g;* Indo-European *p, t, k* became Germanic *f, th, h;* Indo-European *b, d, g* became Germanic *p, t, k.* The law was described by the German linguist Jacob Grimm in 1822. Compare *Verner's law.*

Guarani (gwä′ränē′) a South American Indian language spoken mainly in Paraguay and constituting the southern branch of Tupi-Guarani.

Gujarati (gu̇j′rä′ tē) an Indic language spoken mainly in the state of Gujarat, western India.

Gullah (gul′ə) a dialect of English spoken by blacks living along the coast of South Carolina, Georgia, some offshore islands, and northeastern Florida, containing elements from African languages.

Gypsy = Romany.

Haitian Creole the dialect of French, with many structural elements from African languages, spoken in Haiti.

Hamitic (hamit′ik) the branch of Afro-Asiatic comprising ancient Egyptian, Berber, and Cushitic.

Hawaiian the Polynesian language of Hawaii.

Hebrew the ancient Semitic language of the Jews, a modern form of which is spoken in Israel.

Hellenic the branch of Indo-European that includes the various dialects of Greek.

High German the West Germanic dialect or dialects of central and southern Germany, from which the literary and official language of modern Germany developed.

Hindi an Indic language of northern India that is a literary and official language of the Republic of India. It is closely related to Urdu.

Hittite the Indo-European (Anatolian) language of the Hittites, an ancient people of Asia Minor and Syria whose civilization dates from about 1900 B.C. to about 1200 B.C. Hittite is preserved in both cuneiform and hieroglyphic writing.

homograph one of two or more words having the same spelling but a difference in meaning and origin, as *bow* (bou) bend, *bow* (bō) of an arrow or violin.

homonym 1 one of two or more words having the same pronunciation but a difference in meaning and origin, as *mail* letters, *male* masculine. **2** = homograph.

homophone one of two or more words having the same pronunciation but a difference in meaning and sometimes in spelling, as *eight* and *ate*.

Hottentot a Khoisan language spoken mainly in Southwest Africa (Namibia).

Hungarian the Finno-Ugric language of Hungary. Also called *Magyar*.

hypercorrection = overcorrection.

Ibo (ē′bō) a Kwa language spoken chiefly in Nigeria.

Icelandic the Scandinavian language of Iceland.

idiom a phrase or other expression whose meaning cannot be understood from the ordinary meanings of the words in it, as *go back on,* meaning to abandon or betray, or *fly in the face of,* meaning to disobey openly, defy. Many prepositional and adverbial phrases, such as *get along, get over with, come through, come up with,* are idioms.

imitative imitating or suggesting a sound. Words like *babble, bump, buzz, clash, dash, flick, bobolink, pewee,* and *pewit* are imitative or of imitative origin. Also called *echoic* and *onomatopoeic*.

imperative a verbal mood which expresses a command, request, warning, prohibition, etc. In English, a verb in the imperative mood has the form of the infinitive (Go! Look out! Let's begin. God bless you.), but in some languages it has a present, past, and future tense.

inceptive or **inchoative** a verbal aspect expressing the beginning of an action.

Indic the branch of Indo-European that includes Prakrit, Pali, and Sanskrit and its descendants, among which are Hindi, Urdu, Gujarati, and Marathi.

indicative a verbal mood which expresses a statement of fact or simple declaration, such as "I am leaving" or "It rained all night."

Indo-European the assumed prehistoric language family from which many of the languages spoken in India, western Asia, and Europe are derived. Branches of Indo-European include Indic, Iranian, Baltic, Slavic, Germanic, Italic, Hellenic, and Celtic. Such independent languages as Albanian, Armenian, Tocharian, and Hittite also belong to the Indo-European family. Indo-European languages are spoken over 60% of the world, partly as a result of European and American colonialism. Also called *Proto-Indo-European*.

Indo-Iranian a division of Indo-European comprising the Indic and Iranian branches.

Indonesian 1 a branch of Austronesian, including Malay, Indonesian, Tagalog, and Malagasy. **2** the official language of Indonesia, based chiefly on Malay with elements from other related languages of the area.

infinitive a form of the verb not inflected for person or number. In English, the infinitive form may or may not be preceded by *to* and can function as a noun (*To swim* across the lake is his goal), adjective (They had money *to burn*), or adverb (He went home *to rest*). In some languages, such as Hungarian, the infinitive has a personal ending which expresses person and number.

infix an element inserted within a word to change its meaning or to make another word. *Example:* In Tagalog, *-um-* and *-in-* are infixes.

inflected (of a form, word, or language) showing or characterized by inflection. **—inflection 1** the addition of an ending or suffix to the root of a word to show gender, number, case, person, tense, mood, voice, or comparison. **2** the inflected form of a word. **—inflectional** *adj.* of or involving inflection.

inflectional (or **inflected**) **language** = synthetic language.

inherited. See **develop.**

instrumental a grammatical case that indicates the instrument or means by which something is done. *Example:* Russian *stolom* by means of the table, from *stol* table.

intensive a word, prefix, or other morpheme that gives force or emphasis to the meaning of a word. *Example:* The prefix *re-* in *repine* and *replenish* is an intensive.

intonation the pattern produced in speaking by the rise and fall in pitch of the voice, especially when it conveys emotional, syntactical, or other significant information. There is usually rising intonation in questions and falling intonation in declarative statements. British and American English often use different intonations in otherwise identical sentences.

intransitive (of a verb) that does not take an object, such as *belong, lie,* and *seem*. Some verbs can be either intransitive or transitive: *I like to cook* (intransitive); *Cook the meat* (transitive).

intrusive a speech sound that develops between syllables or words, generally for easier pronunciation. *Example:* The *d* in English *thunder* is an intrusive, since in Old English the word was *thunor*.

Inuit or **Innuit** (in′yủit) = Eskimo.

Iranian the branch of Indo-European that includes Persian, Old Persian, and Avestan, Pashto, and Kurdish.

Irish the Celtic language of Ireland. Also called *Irish Gaelic*.

Iroquoian (ir′əkwoi′ən) a North American Indian language family including such languages as Cherokee, Mohawk, and Oneida.

irregular (of a word) not inflected in the usual way. *Examples: sing* and *lie* (recline) are verbs with the irregular conjugations *sang, sung* and *lay, lain; goose* and *man* are nouns with the irregular plural forms *geese* and *men*.

isolating language a language in which each element is an independent word, usually monosyllabic, and in which meaning is determined mainly by word order. Chinese is a typical isolating language. Compare *agglutinative language*.

Italian the Romance language of Italy and one of the official languages of Switzerland. Modern literary Italian is essentially Tuscan, one of many dialects of Italy. However, the development of the Florentine dialect with its own peculiar features in comparatively recent times has led some to characterize Italian as the Tuscan language as spoken by the Romans (*lingua toscana in bocca romana).*

Italic a branch of Indo-European including Latin and other ancient dialects of Italy, such as Oscan and Umbrian.

Japanese the language of Japan, having no definite relationship to any other language, written in a syllabic script, generally refashioned from Chinese characters (either *kana* and *katakana* or *hiragana*).

Javanese the Malayo-Polynesian language of Java.

juncture the way in which sounds and sound sequences are joined together in the stream of speech, often not corresponding with the conventional division between words. *Examples: not at all,* pronounced (no′tə tôl′); *nitrate* (nī′trāt) and *night rate* (nīt′ rāt′). Juncture has been responsible for such misdivisions as *an apron* (for *a napron*), *an adder* (for *a nadder*), and *a newt* (for *an ewt*).

Kentish the Old English dialect spoken originally by the Jutes who settled in the kingdom of Kent.

Khmer (kmer) the Mon-Khmer language of Cambodia.

Khoisan (koi′sän) a group of languages of southern Africa, including Bushman and Hottentot, characterized by the use of click consonants.

Kikuyu (kikü′yü) a Bantu language of Kenya.

Kirghiz (kirgēz′) the Turkic language of a Mongolian people living in the western part of central Asia.

Korean the language of Korea, having no definite relationship to any other language.

Kpelle (kəpel′ə) the Mande language of Liberia.

Kurdish an Iranian language spoken mainly in Turkey, Iran, Iraq, and Syria.

Kwa (kwä) a branch of Niger-Congo, spoken along the coast of the Gulf of Guinea, including the Ivory Coast and extending into Nigeria. Kwa includes Akan, Ewe, Ibo, Twi, and Yoruba.

Kwakiutl (kwä′kēü′təl) the Wakashan language of an Indian people of the northern Pacific coast.

language family = family.

langue (läɴg) language as a social or conventional system or code used by a speech community, as distinguished from *parole* (individual speech). The *langue/parole* distinction was formulated by Ferdinand de Saussure (1857–1913) and published posthumously by his students in the *Cours de linguistique générale* (1916).

Langue d'Oc (läɴg′dôk′), **Langue d'Oïl** (läɴg′dôēl′). See **Provençal.**

Lao (lä′ō) or **Laotian** (lāō′shən, lä-) the Sino-Tibetan language of Laos.

Lapp or **Lappish** the Finno-Ugric language of Lapland, a region in northern Norway, Sweden, Finland, and the northwestern Soviet Union.

Late Greek the Greek language from about 300 to 700 A.D.

Late Latin the Latin language from about 300 to 700 A.D.

Latin the Italic language of the ancient Romans and the ancestor of the Romance languages. See also *Old Latin, Late Latin, Medieval Latin, New Latin, Vulgar Latin.* The Latin translation of the Bible by St. Jerome, known as the *Vulgate,* represents a later stage of Latin than that of the Classical writers; there one finds Latin words with new meanings, such as *parabola* word, loans from Greek such as *cata* each, and loan translations from Greek such as *ut quid* why.

Latvian the Baltic language of Latvia. Also called *Lettish.*

learned borrowing 1 a Latin word or form borrowed by a Romance language, usually with slight phonetic alteration, as distinguished from a borrowing that has undergone changes in form according to the system of phonetic change in the borrowing language, or an inherited word or form. Learned borrowings come either from actual literary remains of Classical Latin or from the Latin of the learned classes of the middle ages (Medieval Latin). **2** the process by which such words were borrowed into French and other Romance languages.

letter a unit in an alphabetic writing system; a sign or symbol that is used arbitrarily to represent any of the sounds that make up words. Since in many languages, including English, the spelling of words is based on convention and historical accident rather than on actual pronunciation, the letters of the alphabet often do not correspond to the sounds they are supposed to represent. Moreover, letters of the same alphabet differ in phonetic value from language to language, and even in the same language a particular letter may represent different sounds in different periods of the language's development. Compare *grapheme.*

Lettish = Latvian.

lingua franca a language used as a medium of communication by people speaking different languages. Medieval Latin was a lingua franca. Swahili is the lingua franca of eastern Africa. Compare *creole, pidgin.*

Lithuanian the Baltic language of Lithuania.

loan translation a word or phrase that is a literal translation of a foreign expression. *Examples:* English *superman* is a loan translation of German *Übermensch. Marriage of convenience* is a loan translation of French *mariage de convenance.* Also called *calque.*

loan word = borrowing.

locative a grammatical case used to indicate location, as in Latin *domi* at home, *Rōmae* at Rome.

Low German the German dialect or group of dialects of northern Germany, often called Plattdeutsch, distinguished from High German.

Magyar (mag′yär) = Hungarian.

Mahratti (mərat′ē) = Marathi.

Malagasy (mal′əgas′ē) the Indonesian language of Madagascar.

Malay the Indonesian language of the Malay Peninsula and nearby islands.

Malayo-Polynesian = Austronesian.

Malinke (məling′kē, -kā) a Mande language spoken in Senegal, Gambia, Guinea, Guinea-Bissau, Mali, and Ivory Coast.

Maltese the Semitic language of Malta, developed from Arabic with an admixture of Romance elements.

Mandarin the dialect of Chinese regarded as standard, based on the pronunciation of Beijing (Peking).

Mande (män′dā) or **Mandingo** (manding′gō) a branch of Niger-Congo including several languages widely used in western Africa, such as Malinke and Kpelle.

Manx the Celtic language spoken on the Isle of Man until recently.

Maori (mä′ōrē, mou′rē) the Polynesian language of the native inhabitants of New Zealand.

Marathi (mərā′tē, -rat′ē) an Indic language spoken chiefly in western India. Also spelled *Mahratti.*

Mayan (mī′ən) or **Maya** (mī′ə) a language family descended from the language of the ancient Maya people, consisting of a number of languages spoken in Mexico and Central America, especially Guatemala and Belize.

Mbundu (em′bündü) the Bantu language of Angola, comprising Umbundu, spoken in the southern part of Angola, and Kimbundu, spoken in the north.

Medieval Greek the Greek language during the Middle Ages, from about 700 A.D. to about 1500.

Medieval Latin the Latin language, especially of European intellectuals during the Middle Ages, from about 700 A.D. to about 1500. During this period (perhaps by 900) Latin ceased to be anyone's mother tongue in the countries where the Romance languages developed; thus French *fragile* was borrowed from written Latin when no one spoke Latin any longer in France, whereas the earlier *frele* (the source of English *frail*) developed from the spoken Latin of France. The syntax and meanings of Medieval Latin were often much closer to modern languages (from which Medieval Latin borrowed liberally) than Classical Latin. Compare *Anglo-Latin.*

Melanesian (mel′ənē′zhən, -shən) a branch of Austronesian that includes the languages of Melanesia (the Solomon Islands, Fiji, New Caledonia, Vanuatu, etc.).

Mercian (mėr′shən, -shēən) the Old English dialect originally spoken by the Angles in the kingdom of Mercia in central England.

metathesis the transposition of sounds or letters in a word, especially one in which a vowel and a consonant exchange position, as in English *bird* from Old English *bridd, ask* from Old English *ācs(ian), burn* from Middle English *bren(nan).* The process is seen in modern speech in *"aks"* for *ask.*

Mexican Spanish the dialect of Spanish spoken and written in Mexico.

Micmac the Algonquian language of an American Indian people living in the Maritime Provinces of Canada.

Micronesian the branch of Austronesian that includes the languages of Micronesia (Guam, Kiribati, Nauru, etc.).

Middle Dutch the Dutch language from about 1100 to 1500.

Middle English the English language from about 1100 to 1475 or 1500. During the Middle English period there were extensive changes in pronunciation and many of the grammatical distinctions that had begun to disappear in late Old English became completely obsolete. The word stock was completely altered by the introduction of words borrowed from French that replaced Old English formations. Chaucer's works, including the *Canterbury Tales,* are outstanding examples of Middle English. Other important works from this period are the *Ancrene Riwle* and *The Ormulum.*

Middle Flemish the Flemish language from about 1100 to 1500.

Middle French the French language from about 1350 or 1400 to 1600. The poems of François Villon represent a well-known example of Middle French. The 16th century, now often studied as a separate period, is represented by such influential writers as Rabelais, Montaigne, and Calvin.

Middle High German the High German language spoken in central and southern Germany from about 1100 to 1450 or 1500. The *Nibelungenlied* (or Song of the Nibelungs), the inspiration for Wagner's Ring operas, and the works of Wolfram von Eschenbach, Hartmann von Aue, Gottfried von Strassburg, and Walther von der Vogelweide are in Middle High German.

Middle Indic = Prakrit.

Middle Irish the Irish language from about 900 to about 1400.

Middle Low German the Low German language spoken in Germany from about 1100 to 1450 or 1500.

Middle Welsh the Welsh language from about 1150 to about 1500.

misdivision a mistaken or incorrect division of a word, as *an adder* instead of *a nadder, a nickname* for Middle English *an eke name,* etc. See *juncture.* The process is found in French *lingot* (a contraction of the theoretical form *le ingot*) from English *ingot.*

Miskito (miskē′tō) American Indian language spoken on the eastern coast of Nicaragua and Honduras.

Modern Dutch the Dutch language from about 1500 to the present.

Modern English the English language from about 1475 or 1500 to the present. It is sometimes divided into Early Modern English (1500-1700) and Late Modern English (1700 to the present).

Modern French the French language from about 1600 to the present.

Modern German the German language from about 1450 or 1500 to the present, developed from High German and distinguished from Plattdeutsch.

modifier a word or group of words that limits or qualifies another word or group of words. *Examples:* a *tall* building (adjective modifier); *very* clever, drive *slowly* (adverb modifiers); *exchange* student (noun modifier).

Mon (mōn) the Mon-Khmer language of a people living in southeastern Burma, not culturally related to the native Burmese.

Mongolian 1 the Altaic language of Mongolia. **2** a branch of Altaic that includes the language of Mongolia and several closely related languages or dialects spoken in the Soviet Union and in northwestern China.

Mon-Khmer (mōn′kmer′) a language family of southeastern Asia that includes Khmer (Cambodian), Mon (spoken in Burma), and several other languages spoken in parts of China, India, Burma, and Vietnam.

mood the form of a verb which indicates the manner in which the act or state expressed by the verb is performed. See, for example, *indicative, imperative, subjunctive.*

morpheme a minimal meaningful form in a language. Morphemes may be words, affixes, or endings that show inflection. *Examples:* The word *books* has two morphemes, *book* and *-s* (book is a *free morpheme, -s* is a *bound morpheme* since it cannot occur as a separate word). Compare *phoneme.*

Munda (mun′dä) a group of languages spoken in scattered areas of northern and central India, of unknown relations but predating Indo-European and sometimes linked with Mon-Khmer.

Muskogean (muskō′gēən) a North American Indian language family originally of the southeastern United States, including the languages of the Choctaw, Chickasaw, Creek, and Seminole.

Nahuatl (nä′wätəl) the Uto-Aztecan language spoken by the Aztecs, Toltecs, and other American Indian peoples of central Mexico and parts of Central America, and their descendants. It is the chief Indian language of Mexico. A number of Nahuatl words, chiefly designating fauna and flora, were adopted by Spanish, and many of these passed into English (tomato, coyote, etc.).

nasalization the pronunciation of a consonant or vowel with the soft palate lowered to allow the air to escape through the nasal cavity. *Examples: M* and *n* are nasals. The final vowel in French *bon* (bôN) is a nasal. In some languages, presence of a nasal sound is phonemic, as in the nasal vowel of French *banc* bench and the nonnasalized form of the vowel in French *bas* low.

native (of a word, etc.) not a borrowing, but belonging to or developed from the earliest known elements of a language.

naturalize to adapt (a borrowed word, phrase, etc.), so that it conforms to the spelling patterns or phonetic system of the borrowing language; to integrate into the language.

Navaho or **Navajo** the Athapascan language of an American Indian people living in New Mexico, Arizona, and Utah.

neologism a newly formed or borrowed word, phrase, or meaning, usually not yet widely used or accepted.

Nepali (nepä′lē) the Indic language of Nepal, also spoken in the Indian states of West Bengal and Assam, and in Bhutan and Sikkim.

New Latin the Latin language after 1500, containing words formed from Greek, Latin, and other elements. New Latin was formerly used in the liturgy of the Roman Catholic Church, and is still used in supplying new words to the sciences, especially biology and medicine chiefly by combining existing forms but also by borrowing from other languages.

Niger-Congo the major language family in Africa, including Bantu, Kwa, and West Atlantic languages, and many other West African languages.

nominative a case in Latin, Greek, and other inflected languages, showing a noun or adjective as the subject of a sentence. The nominative is usually a primary form, without any inflection indicating syntactical relationship. Compare *oblique.*

nonce word a word coined specifically for an occasion, and often recorded in a single occurrence, as Coleridge's use of *mammonolatry* worship of money, formed by analogy with *idolatry.* A recent nonce word is *beautility,* a blend of *beauty* and *utility,* which has now become an accepted term.

nonstandard not conforming to the currently accepted pronunciation, grammar, or vocabulary of a language.

Nootka the Wakashan language of an American Indian people living on Vancouver Island and in northwestern Washington.

normal grade. See **grade.**

Norman-French = Anglo-French.

Northumbrian the Old English dialect spoken originally by the Angles in the kingdom of Northumbria.

Norwegian the Scandinavian language of Norway. There are two standard languages in Norway: *Bokmål,* or Dano-Norwegian, formerly called Riksmål 'state language,' the language used by Ibsen that developed from Danish and replaced Old Norse, and *Nynorsk* 'New Norwegian,' earlier known as Landsmål 'country language' that developed from the various dialects spoken in Norway. The two forms are gradually being introduced as a combined form called *Samnorsk.*

number a word form or ending that shows whether a word refers to one or more persons or things and thereby distinguishes between singular, plural, and, in some systems, dual. *Cow, house, foot* are singular in number; *cows, houses, feet* are plural in number. *Sheep* and *deer* are both singular and plural.

Collective nouns that designate a group are singular in form but plural in meaning: *troop, herd, team, people;* count nouns refer to something that can be counted: *toy, book, game;* mass nouns refer to something that cannot be counted: *health, filth.* Some plurals are without a corresponding plural: *scissors,* others have been given an artificial singular form: *pant* for *pants.*

object the word or group of words designating the person or thing at which the action of the verb is directed or to which a preposition expresses some relation. A *direct object* is found in 'The boy threw *the ball.'* An *indirect object* is found in 'The boy threw the ball *to me.'*

oblique of or in any grammatical case except the nominative and vocative. Oblique cases include the accusative, dative, genitive, ablative, etc. In Old French, the oblique case combined the function of all the non-nominative cases, so that Old French had only two cases, nominative and oblique. The Greek grammarians assumed that the nominative was the original form and that other cases had developed or "fallen away" from the nominative, thus becoming the *oblique* cases.

Occitan. See **Provençal.**

Ojibwa the Algonquian language of an American Indian people living in the area around Lake Superior.

Old Church Slavic or **Old Church Slavonic** = Old Slavic.

Old Dutch the Dutch language before 1100.

Old English the West Germanic language of the English people before 1100. It included four principal dialects: Mercian, Northumbrian, West Saxon, and Kentish. Mercian and Northumbrian are often grouped together as Anglian. Old English differed from Middle English and Modern English in some fundamental ways in that it had many inflections, four grammatical cases, seven groups of strong verbs, and grammatical gender. Old English words were generally stressed on the first syllable and thousands were derivatives or compounds that had been elaborated to provide equivalents for the scientific and philosophical concepts found in Latin. Most of these were replaced or swept away in Middle English times, as if they had never existed. The epic poem *Beowulf* and the works of Cynewulf, Alfred, and Ælfric were written in Old English. Also called *Anglo-Saxon.*

Old Flemish the Flemish language before 1100.

Old French the French language from about 800 A.D. to about 1350 or 1400. Old French literature had a great influence in medieval Europe. The *Roman de la Rose* was translated into Middle English by Chaucer; Dante makes it clear that he was familiar with Old French literature; the Tristan legend turns up in medieval German literature, and there were Old Norse adaptations of Old French works.

Old Frisian the Frisian language before 1500. Old Frisian texts date from the middle of the 1200's.

Old High German the form of the German language used in southern Germany before 1100 (or sometimes 1450). Modern standard German is descended from Old High German. The *Hilderbrandslied* (Lay of Hildebrand), the *Merseburger Zaubersprüche* (Merseburg Charms), which are magic formulas telling of the power of the gods, and the *Ludwigslied* (Song of Ludwig), found on the same manuscript and in the same hand as the Old French *Sequence of Saint Eulalia,* making it possible for Romanists to date the Old French text because of the German reference to a battle fought in 881 A.D., are among the works from the Old High German period.

Old Icelandic the Icelandic language before 1500. Because it is extensively recorded in notable literary works such as the two Eddas, one in poetry and one in prose, collected during the 1100's and 1200's, and the sagas of the Vikings, Old Icelandic is sometimes referred to as the literary language of the North.

Old Irish the Irish language before 1200.

Old Latin the Latin language before the 100's B.C. Early writers like Plautus, who died in 184 B.C., give evidence of the existence of Vulgar Latin alongside Classical Latin on the basis of some of their usage.

Old Low German the form of the German language found in northern Germany and the Netherlands before 1100.

Old Norse Old Icelandic and Old Norwegian collectively, especially as representing the North Germanic language of the Scandinavians before the 1300's.

Old North French the dialect of northern France before the 1500's, especially that of coastal Normandy and Picardy.

Old Norwegian the Norwegian language before the 1500's.

Old Persian the ancient Iranian language, recorded in cuneiform inscriptions.

Old Provençal the form of Provençal before the 1500's, widely known as one of the principal languages used by the troubadours. Old Provençal literature had a great influence in neighboring areas of northern France, Italy and Catalonia. French words such as *amour* 'love' and *jaloux* 'jealous' betray Provençal origin for phonetic reasons, and are traceable to the importance of Provençal love poems in French-speaking northern France.

Old Prussian an extinct Baltic language preserved in records of the 1400's and 1500's.

Old Saxon the form of Low German spoken by the Saxons in northwestern Germany before 1100.

Old Slavic a South Slavic language preserved in Eastern Orthodox religious texts of the 800's and 900's A.D., still used in the liturgy of some Orthodox Churches. It is also called *Old Church Slavic,* and *Old Church Slavonic.*

Old Spanish the Spanish language before the 1500's. The epic work, *The Poem of the Cid,* is one of the major works written in Old Spanish. A number of didactic works were written in the court of Alfonso X in the 1200's on such subjects as history, law, astronomy, falconry, etc., often making use of Arabic sources.

onomatopoeic = imitative.

Oscan (os′kən) the ancient Italic language of Campania, a region in southern Italy, closely related to Umbrian and more distantly to Latin.

overcorrection a change in pronunciation or grammar mistakenly introduced by a person in an effort to avoid supposedly "incorrect" forms of speech. The pronunciation of *chicken* as *chicking* on the analogy of the *-ing* in words like *something, foundling, king* is an example of overcorrection; so are the sentences *I feel badly, Be there at 8 sharply,* and the phrase *between you and I.* Also called *hypercorrection.*

palatalization the pronunciation of a consonant with the front or middle of the tongue near or touching the hard palate, as in pronouncing the initial vowel sound of *Tuesday* with a *y*-sound at the beginning. Palatalization explains the development of [ch] in Italian *cento* from [k] in Latin *centum* hundred.

Pali (päl′ē) an Indic language found in the sacred writings of Buddhism and still existing as a literary language in Sri Lanka, Burma, and Thailand.

Panjabi (panjä′bē) an Indic language of the Punjab region of northwestern India that is the major language of the Sikh religion. Also spelled *Punjabi.*

paradigm the set of all the inflectional forms of a word or class of words. *Examples: run, runs, ran, runner, running; walk, walks, walked, walking; dog, dog's, dogs, dogs', dogged, dogging,* etc.

parole (pərōl′) language as spoken and understood by an individual; individual speech, as distinguished from *langue* (language as a system or code).

partial translation a borrowed word or phrase, part of which is translated into the borrowing language. *Examples: Feldspar* is a partial translation of German *Feldspath; songfest* is a partial translation of German *Sängerfest.*

participle a verb form that has both the character of a verb and of an adjective. *Examples:* The present participle *walking* functions as an adjective in *a walking encyclopedia.* The past participle *broken* functions as an adjective in *a broken promise.*

Pashto (push′tō) the Iranian language of Afghanistan and of the Pathan tribes of Pakistan. Also called *Afghan.*

passive showing the subject of a verb as acted upon. *Example:* the verb *was broken* in *The dish was broken by him* is in the passive voice. Compare *active.*

pattern the manner in which the phonemes, morphemes, etc., of a language are arranged or fall into certain classes, groups, or units according to their regularities of form or function. Nouns, verbs, adjectives, etc., are classified by pattern.

pejorative (a word or phrase) having or showing a worsening of meaning, often becoming disparaging, depreciating, or derogatory. Some English words that acquired pejorative meanings are *knave, boor,* and *silly.*

Pennsylvania Dutch = Pennsylvania German.

Pennsylvania German a dialect of High German with a varied admixture of English, spoken in southeastern Pennsylvania by descendants of immigrants from southern Germany and Switzerland who settled there in the 1600's and 1700's. Also known as *Pennsylvania Dutch,* as a holdover of the German use *deutsch* meaning "German" but transformed to the known English word *Dutch.*

perfective a verbal aspect in some languages, such as ancient Greek, that expresses completion of action, whether in the past, present, or future.

Persian the Iranian language of Persia. Though an Indo-European language, Persian makes use of the Arabic alphabet. The *Rubaiyat* (or Quatrains) of Omar Khayyam, in the translation by Fitzgerald, is probably the best-known work in English-speaking countries translated from Old Persian. Also called *Farsi.*

Phoenician (fənish′ən, -nē′shən) the ancient Semitic language of Phoenicia, an ancient kingdom in the eastern Mediterranean. The unknown language of Carthage was probably related (compare the term *Punic Wars,* in which Latin *Pūnicus* is derived from *Poenus* meaning a Carthaginian, an inhabitant of the Phoenician colony of Carthage).

phoneme one of the distinctive sounds in a language that is the smallest meaningful unit of speech, such as the /*p*/ in *pit* and the /*b*/ in *bit.* Phonemes are comprised of slight variations called allophones, such as the *p* of *ship* and the *p* of *pin.* **—phonemic** being or representing a phoneme; phonologically distinctive. In English /*b*/ and /*p*/ are phonemic. Compare *morpheme.*

phonetic having to do with or representing the sounds of speech. A **phonetic alphabet** is a set of symbols used for transcribing speech sounds.

phonetic law a statement that explains a sound shift or other regular phonetic change in a language or group of languages. *Grimm's law* is an example of a phonetic law.

phonology 1 the system or a description of the speech sounds of a language. **2** the study of the speech sounds of a language, either historically or descriptively.

Phrygian (frij′ēən) the Indo-European language of Phrygia, an ancient country in central and northwestern Asia Minor.

pidgin a language with a reduced grammar and vocabulary, used as a trade or communications jargon between people not having a common language. Pidgins often become the native and sole language of a group, at which time they are known as *creoles.*

Pidgin English any of several varieties of English having a simplified grammatical structure and often a mixed vocabulary, used in western Africa, Australia, Melanesia, and formerly in China, as a language of trade or communication between natives and foreigners. *Pidgin* is also found in reference to a simplified form of French and in West African Pidgin and bêche-de-mer, a bartering language of the South Pacific.

Pilipino (pil′əpē′nō) the official language of the Philippines, based on Tagalog. Since there is no (f) in Tagalog, Spanish *Filipino* became *Pilipino.*

Piman (pē′mən) a branch of Uto-Aztecan that includes several languages spoken in southern Arizona and northern Mexico.

pitch the highness or lowness of a sound or tone; acoustically, it is a measure of the frequency of vibration of the vocal folds. Pitch is important in the study of intonation patterns and juncture.

Plattdeutsch (plät′doich′) the speech of northern Germany, now often considered a nonstandard dialect, and distinguished from Modern German.

Polabian (polā′bēən) a West Slavic language formerly spoken in the basin of the Elbe River and on the Baltic coast of northern Germany. It has been extinct since the mid-1700's.

Polish the West Slavic language of Poland.

Polynesian a branch of Austronesian that includes the languages of Polynesia, such as Hawaiian, Tahitian, Samoan, and Maori.

popular etymology = folk etymology.

portmanteau word = blend.

Portuguese the Romance language of Portugal. It is the chief language of Brazil, and also known in such former Portuguese colonies as Angola, Mozambique, Cape Verde, Timor and Goa (in India). A variety of Portuguese called Galician (or Gallego) is spoken in northwestern Spain; in medieval times Galician was an important literary language.

positive the basic form of an adjective or adverb as distinct from the comparative and superlative. *Example:* positive *quick,* comparative quicker, superlative *quickest.*

possessive a grammatical case indicating possession or origin, generally equivalent to the genitive.

Prakrit (prä′krit) any of the Indic languages or dialects spoken in ancient and medieval times in northern and central India, exclusive of Sanskrit. Also called *Middle Indic.*

predicate the word or words in a sentence expressing what is said about the subject. The predicate is usually a verb or verb phrase together with its modifiers, object, etc. The subject and predicate are the two main elements in a sentence. **—predicative** having the characteristics of a predicate.

prefix a syllable or syllables put at the beginning of a word to change its meaning or to make another word, as *pre-* in *prefabricate* and *un-* in *unlike.* Compare *infix, suffix.*

preterit a tense form that expresses occurrence in the past; past tense.

privative a prefix, suffix, or other word element expressing deprivation, denial, or absence of something. The prefixes *a-*[4] as used in *amoral, atonal,* and *un-* as in *unnatural, undone* are privative.

proper name the name of a particular person, place, or thing, written in English with an initial captial letter. English nouns derived from proper names include such common words as *sandwich, boycott, atlas, mentor, quixotic, bayonet, spartan,* and *hamburger.*

Proto-Germanic the hypothetical language that was the ancestor of the Germanic languages.

Proto-Indo-European = Indo-European.

Provençal (prō′vənsäl′) the Romance language of Provence, a region in southeastern France bordering on the Mediterranean. The name Provençal is also used as a synonym of *Occitan* or *Langue d'Oc* to designate the various Romance dialects and languages of southern France, as distinguished from *Langue d'Oïl* of northern France (*Oc* and *Oïl* being the word for "yes" in the two parts of France).

Punjabi = Panjabi.

quantity the length of a sound or syllable in speech, conventionally differentiated by *long,* as in the long *e* of *see,* and *short,* as in the short *e* of *let.*

Quechua (kech′wä, kəchü′ə) a South American Indian language spoken in Colombia, Peru, Bolivia, Ecuador, Argentina, and Chile. It was once the language of the Inca Empire.

reconstruction 1 the process of reconstructing or reforming (a word or other part of a prehistoric language) by comparing shared features of recorded languages that presumably descended from the hypothetical language. **2** a reconstructed form, usually indicated by an asterisk (*). All Proto-Germanic and Indo-European forms are reconstructions.

reduced form a word formed by shortening of a full or longer form, as *can't* from *cannot,* and *flu* from *influenza.* Also called *contraction.*

reduced grade. See **grade.**

reduction 1 the process of forming a contraction or reduced form. **2** = reduced form.

reduplication repetition of a syllable or the initial part of a syllable. Reduplication in some Indo-European languages is a means to indicate tense or to form plurals. In English, words like *chit-chat* and *razzle-dazzle* are reduplications.

reflex a word or form corresponding to and usually derived from another comparable form. *Example:* Italian *assenza* is a reflex of Latin *absentia; -enza* is the Italian reflex of the Latin suffix *-entia.*

reflexive a pronoun that refers back to the subject, or a verb that implies action by the subject on itself.

replacement 1 the deliberate alteration of a word or form to make it conform to its earliest or classical form, as in the Middle French period, when many old, regularly derived or inherited words of the language were refashioned to conform with their Classical Latin or Late Latin forms. The process of replacement continued in English with the Latinization of borrowed French words (see, for example, words in *ad-,* such as *advance*) even after the practice waned in French. **2** a word or form altered in this way.

Rhaeto-Romanic (rē′tōrōman′ik) or **Rhaeto-Romansh** (rē′tōrōmansh′) a group of Romance dialects spoken in the Rhaetian Alps of Switzerland and adjoining regions of the Tyrol and northern Italy.

rhotacism the use or substitution of [r] in place of some other speech sound, especially *s* [z]. The difference in such related pairs as English *was* and *were, lose* and for*lorn* is the result of rhotacism. Rhotacism also occurs in the substitution of [r] for [l] in Portuguese (compare *branco* for Spanish *blanco* white) and in the Japanese pronunciation of foreign words with [l] (compare *Buraziru* Brazil).

rhyming slang a type of slang in which a word is replaced by a phrase which rhymes with it, as "hit or miss" for *kiss,* "bread and honey" for *money,* etc. Rhyming slang is especially common in the cockney dialect.

Romance the group of European languages that developed from Vulgar Latin. French, Italian, Spanish, Portuguese, Romanian, Provençal, Rhaeto-Romanic, and Catalan are Romance languages. Another Romance language, Dalmatian, became extinct in the late 1800's. See also *Gallo-Romance.*

Romanian or **Rumanian** the Romance language of Romania. A variety of Romanian known as Moldavian is spoken in the Moldavian S.S.R. of the Soviet Union. Romanian used the Cyrillic alphabet until 1860, when the Roman alphabet was adopted.

Romany (rom′ənē) the Indic language of the Romany (Gypsy) people, containing loanwords from Persian, Greek, Armenian, and other languages.

root 1 = stem. **2** a reconstructed form, as in Proto-Germanic or Indo-European, from which words with similar structure or meaning in cognate languages are thought to have developed. Also called *base.*

Russian the East Slavic language of Russia, the most widely used Slavic language and the official language of the Soviet Union.

Samoan (səmō′ən) a Polynesian language spoken in Western Samoa (an island country) and American Samoa.

Samoyed (sam′əyed′) a branch of Uralic comprising several languages of northern Siberia and northeastern Russia.

Sanskrit the ancient sacred and literary language of India, important in the study of Indo-European. Its introduction to Western scholars in the late 1700's led to the development of modern comparative linguistics.

satem language any of the Indo-European languages in which the sound represented by *s* as in *sat* and found in Avestan *satem* hundred is distinct from the sound of *c,* as in *cat,* found in the initial consonant of Latin *centum* hundred. The satem languages include Indo-Iranian, Armenian, Balto-Slavic, and Albanian. Compare *centum language.*

Scandinavian the historical and modern North Germanic languages of Denmark, Iceland, Norway, Sweden, and the Faeroe Islands, such as Old Danish and modern Danish, Old Icelandic and modern Icelandic, etc.

Scottish a dialect of British English spoken in Scotland, especially in the Lowlands, familiar to many readers in the poetry of Robert Burns.

Scottish Gaelic = Gaelic.

Semitic the branch of Afro-Asiatic comprising Hebrew, Arabic, Aramaic, Syriac, Ethiopic, Phoenician, and Assyrian.

Serbian the form of Serbo-Croatian spoken by Serbs and written in the Cyrillic alphabet.

Serbo-Croatian a South Slavic language spoken by the Serbs and Croats in Yugoslavia.

Setswana (setswä′nə, sətswä′-) the Bantu language of Botswana, in southern Africa, closely related to Sotho.

shortening = clipped form.

Sindhi (sin′dē) an Indic language spoken in southern Pakistan and northwestern India.

Singhalese (sing′gəlēz′, -lēs′) or **Sinhalese** (sin′hə-) the Indic language of Sri Lanka (Ceylon).

Sino-Tibetan a linguistic family that includes Chinese, Tibeto-Burman, Thai, and Lao.

Siouan (sü′ən) a North American Indian language family of the northern Midwest, including the languages of the Sioux, Crow, Omaha, and Osage.

Slavic a branch of Indo-European customarily divided into West Slavic (Polish, Czech, Slovak, Wendish, and the extinct Polabian), East Slavic (Russian, Ukrainian), and South Slavic (Bulgarian, Serbo-Croatian, and Slovene).

Slovak the West Slavic language of Slovakia, spoken in eastern Czechoslovakia.

Slovene the South Slavic language of Slovenia, in northwestern Yugoslavia, closely related to Serbo-Croatian.

Somali the Cushitic language of Somalia.

Sotho (sō′thō) the Bantu language of Lesotho and the western border of Natal, closely related to Setswana.

sound shift a systematic change in the sounds of a language or a group of languages at a particular time, such as the *Great Vowel Shift* in English.

Spanish the Romance language of Spain, and the language of most Latin-American countries. Originally the language of Castile in central and northern Spain, the term *Castilian* has become synonymous with *Spanish.* Among the Spanish writers of the Golden Age were Cervantes, Lope de Vega, and Calderón de la Barca.

spelling pronunciation a pronunciation influenced by the written form of a word, as the pronunciation of *comptroller* as (kəmptrō′lər) and *often* as (of′tən).

stem the part of a word to which inflectional and other endings or prefixes are added and in which changes occur. *Examples:* In English *run* is the stem of *running* and *runner; want* is the stem of *unwanted.* The stem of Sanskrit *bhárati* he bears, *bháratha* you bear, and *bháranti* they bear, is *bhára-*. The corresponding stem in Gothic is *baíra-* and in Old English *bera-*.

stress a greater force or emphasis given to a sound, syllable, or word. Also called *accent.*

strong verb a verb inflected for tense by a vowel change within the stem rather than by adding inflectional endings. *Examples:* rise, rose, risen; ring, rang, rung. Compare *weak verb.*

subject the word or words about which something is said in a sentence. The subject is usually a noun or noun phrase, though it can be another part of speech acting as a noun, such as the infinitive in "To be or not to be." Compare *predicate.*

subjunctive a verbal mood which expresses a wish or a state or act as possible, conditional, hypothetical, or dependent, rather than as actual.

Sudanic a family of languages of northern Africa that are not related either to the Bantu or Hamitic languages. Sudanic languages are spoken chiefly in Sudan, Chad, Kenya, and Uganda.

suffix a syllable or syllables put at the end of a word to change its meaning, make another word, or indicate person, number, tense, or grammatical relationship to other words. Compare *infix, prefix.*

Sumerian a non-Semitic language of ancient Sumer (a region in the lower part of Mesopotamia), recorded in cuneiform inscriptions.

superlative the third and highest degree of comparison of an adjective or adverb. *Examples: Best* is the superlative of *good, least* is the superlative of *little.* Compare *positive, comparative.*

suppletive serving as a substitute for a form missing from a set of inflected forms. *Examples:* the past tense *went* is a suppletive form in the paradigm *go, went, gone.* Latin *lātus* is a suppletive past participle of the verb *ferre* to carry.

Swahili the Bantu language of eastern Africa that is the official language of Tanzania and Kenya, also spoken in Zaire, Uganda, Rwanda, and Burundi. Swahili has borrowed many Arabic and other foreign words and has developed an extensive body of literature.

Swedish the Scandinavian language of Sweden and part of Finland, where it is the second official language.

syllable a word or part of a word pronounced as a unit, usually consisting of a vowel or a vowel with one or more consonants. In some instances (though transcribed without an accompanying vowel) a consonant also functions as a syllable (for example, the final syllable in *bottle* and *hidden*).

synchronic of or having to do with the study of a language at a particular stage in its development, without direct reference to its features at any earlier or later point in its development. Compare *diachronic.*

syncope the loss of a weakly stressed sound or syllable from the middle of a word, as in *ne'er* for *never.* Compare *apocope, aphesis.*

synthetic language a language characterized by the use of inflections and affixes to express grammatical relationships. Latin is a typical synthetic language. Old English was a synthetic language. Also called *inflectional* (or *inflected*) *language.* Compare *analytic language.*

Syriac the ancient Semitic language of Syria, a dialect of Aramaic.

taboo avoidance of the use of a particular word (*taboo word*) regarded as extremely offensive to good taste or morality, often leading to the word's replacement by a euphemism. Words dealing with sexual and excretory functions are the commonest taboo words in English.

Tagalog (tägä′log, tag′ə-) the Indonesian language of

the Philippines. Pilipino, the official language of the Philippines, is a form of Tagalog.

Tahitian the Polynesian language of Tahiti.

Tai (tī) a branch of Sino-Tibetan that includes Lao, Thai, and several other languages spoken in Burma, China, and Vietnam.

Tamil (tam′əl) a Dravidian language spoken in southern India, Sri Lanka, Singapore, and Malaysia.

Tatar (tä′tər) or **Tartar** (tär′tər) a Turkic language, spoken in the Volga region of European Russia and in western Siberia.

Telugu (tel′əgü) a Dravidian language spoken in southeastern India.

Temne (tem′nā) the Niger-Congo language of Sierra Leone.

tense the form of a verb that shows the time of the action expressed by the verb. English has present, past, and future; present perfect, past perfect, and future perfect.

Thai (tī) the Sino-Tibetan language of Thailand.

thematic vowel a vowel occurring between the root and the inflectional ending of a word in Latin, Greek, and some other Indo-European languages.

Tibetan the Sino-Tibetan language of Tibet, closely related to Burmese.

Tibeto-Burman or **Tibeto-Burmese** a branch of Sino-Tibetan that includes Tibetan, Burmese, and a large number of unwritten languages of southeastern Asia.

Tocharian (tōkār′ēən, -kär′-) an extinct Indo-European language or group of languages of which records from the 500's A.D. were discovered in Chinese Turkestan. Only two varieties of Tocharian (A and B, or Agnaean and Kuchean) are known. Texts dating from the 800's A.D. suggest that Tocharian may have still been spoken at that time.

tone a speech sound of definite pitch and character, used in tone languages to distinguish words that are otherwise pronounced identically. Chinese has four tones: high level, rising, low, and falling.

tone language a language characterized by the use of several different tones to distinguish between words that are otherwise identical. Chinese and Thai are typical tone languages; Chinese has four tones, Thai has five.

transcription a representation of speech by means of phonetic or phonemic symbols.

transitive (of a verb) that takes an object, such as *bring* a book, *raise* the flag. Compare *intransitive*.

transliteration the representation of the letters, ideograms, or other symbols of one writing system by equivalents in another. Rendering Arabic or Greek characters in a system of approximately phonetically equivalent Roman letters is an example of transliteration.

Tshiluba (chilü′bə) a Bantu language used widely in Zaire as a lingua franca.

Tungusic (tu̇ngu̇z′ik) a branch of Altaic including several languages spoken in central and eastern Siberia and in northwestern China. It includes Manchu, the now almost extinct literary language of the Manchu Dynasty.

Tupi (tüpē′) a South American Indian language spoken in the Amazon Valley of Brazil. Tupi constitutes the northern branch of Tupi-Guarani.

Tupi-Guarani (tüpē′gwä′ränē′) an American Indian language family of central South America, found especially along the lower Amazon. Tupi is the principal language of the northern branch of the Amazon and Guarani of the southern branch.

Turkic a branch of the Altaic language family spoken in Turkey and south central Asia. Turkic includes such languages as Turkish, Tatar, Kirghiz, Uzbek, and Yakut.

Turkish the Turkic language of Turkey.

Twi (twē) the Kwa language of Ghana.

Ugric (ü′grik, yü′-) a division of Finno-Ugric that includes Hungarian and Vogul.

Ukrainian the East Slavic language of Ukraine, the second most widely spoken language (after Russian) in the Soviet Union.

Umbrian the ancient Italic language of Umbria, a region in central Italy, closely related to Oscan and more distantly to Latin.

umlaut a change in a vowel sound in the Germanic languages because of the influence of another vowel in the following syllable. Umlaut is responsible for such pairs in English as *man - men, foot - feet, gold - gild,* in which the vowels of *men, feet,* and *gild* are the result of umlaut caused by vowels which have since disappeared.

unvoiced uttered without vibration of the vocal chords or folds, as the *s* in *sit,* the *f* in *fit* and the *th* in *thin;* voiceless. Compare *voiced.*

Ural-Altaic (yu̇r′əlaltā′ik) a hypothetical language family comprising the Altaic and Uralic families, based chiefly on grammatical (not lexical) correspondences.

Uralic (yu̇ral′ik) a language family consisting of the Finno-Ugric and Samoyed languages.

Urdu (u̇r′dü, ėr′-) an Indic language, originally a dialect of Hindi, that is the official language of Pakistan. Urdu uses Persian and Arabic loanwords and the Arabic alphabet.

Uto-Aztecan (yü′tōaz′tekən) an American Indian language family of the southwestern United States that includes Piman and Nahuatl.

Uzbek (u̇z′bek) a Turkic language of central Asia that is the most widely used non-Slavic language in the Soviet Union.

verbal a verb form functioning as: a noun, as in *to paint* (infinitive) is enjoyable; *Painting* (gerund) is an enjoyable pastime; or an adjective, as in a *painting* class.

vernacular 1 a native or indigenous language; the language used by the people of a certain country or place. **2** the everyday and informal language of a speech community, as distinguished from its literary or formal language.

Verner's Law a phonetic law explaining certain apparent exceptions to Grimm's law: Proto-Germanic voiceless sounds such as *f, th,* and *s* became voiced *v,* TH, *z* when in contact with voiced consonants, unless the original Indo-European stress was on the immediately preceding syllable. The law was formulated by the Danish linguist Karl Verner in 1877.

Vietnamese the language of Vietnam, having no certain affiliation with any other language. Also called *Annamese.*

vocalism 1 the vowel system of a language or dialect. **2** the range of vowels in a particular context. **3** a vocal sound or articulation.

vocalization 1 the voicing of a previously unvoiced sound. **2** the changing of a consonant into a vowel. As *l* is a consonant close in quality to a vowel, it is frequently affected (for example in Italian *piazza* from Latin *platea,* or French *sauter* from Latin *saltare* to jump).

vocative a case in Latin and some other inflected languages, indicating the person or thing being spoken to, as in Latin *Et tū, Brūte?* You too, Brutus?

Vogul (vō'gůl) a Ugric language of western Siberia.

voice a verb form that shows whether its subject is active or passive. In English, the passive voice is made with the past participle and some form of the verb *be,* as in *was asked, were caught.* In Greek and some other languages there is a *middle voice* which is typically passive in form but active in meaning expressing reflexive action that affects the subject. *Example:* Greek *phainesthai* meaning I show myself, is middle voice to *phainein* to show.

voiced uttered with vibration of the vocal chords or folds, as any vowel or such consonants as *b, d, m,* and *g.* Compare *unvoiced.*

voiceless = unvoiced.

vowel gradation = ablaut.

Vulgar Latin the spoken or popular form of Latin used throughout the later period of the ancient Roman Empire, and the main source of French, Italian, Spanish, Portuguese, and other Romance languages. Gallo-Romance is considered a development of Vulgar Latin.

Wakashan (wäkash'ən) an American Indian language family of the northwest United States and British Columbia, including Nootka and Kwakiutl.

Walloon a French dialect of Belgium spoken by the Walloons, a group of people living chiefly in the southern and southeastern parts of Belgium and adjacent regions in France.

weak verb a verb inflected by the addition of regular endings to the stem, rather than by vowel change. In English, weak verbs form the past tense and past participle by the addition of *-d, -ed,* or *-t,* as in *dive/dived, work/worked, dream/dreamt.* Compare *strong verb.*

Welsh the Celtic language of Wales.

Wendish a West Slavic language spoken in Lusatia, a region in southeastern East Germany. The language has two distinct dialects, Upper Wendish (influenced by Czech) and Lower Wendish (influenced by Polish).

West Atlantic a branch of Niger-Congo that includes Fulani and other West African languages.

West Germanic the division of Germanic consisting chiefly of English, Frisian, Dutch, and German.

West Saxon the Old English dialect originally of the Saxons living in the kingdom of Wessex south of the Thames and westward from Surrey and Sussex. Most of the Old English manuscripts existing today are written in West Saxon, including the works of Ælfric and King Alfred.

word element a combining form, prefix, suffix, or other element that by addition to a word changes the meaning or use of the word.

word order the arrangement of words in a sentence, clause, or phrase to indicate the function of words and their relation to each other. English, with its relative absence of inflections, depends heavily on word order, although word order is used as a grammatical device in all languages.

Xhosa (kō'sə) the Bantu language of a people living mainly in the Transkei, east of Cape Province, in South Africa. Xhosa is closely related to Zulu.

Yakut (yäküt') a Turkic language of eastern Siberia.

Yiddish a West Germanic language spoken mainly by Jews of eastern and central Europe and their descendants. Yiddish developed from one or more dialects of Middle High German, contains many Hebrew and Slavic words, and some Romance words, and is often written in Hebrew characters.

Yoruba (yō'rủbä) a Kwa language of Nigeria.

zero grade. See **grade.**

Zulu (zü'lü) the Bantu language of a people of southeastern Africa, living chiefly in Natal. Compare *Xhosa.*

Glossary of Literary Works Cited in Etymologies

This short glossary of literary works is a list of manuscripts, books, and other writings in which various words first appeared in the record of English, together with some authors cited who are better known than the titles of their work or who are chiefly known for their translations. Most of the entries have to do with English before 1600, as references after that time can be found easily in most histories of English literature, such as the *Oxford Companion to English Literature* and the *New Century Handbook of English Literature.* Even so, many of the entries herein will be found with fuller articles in the books referred to above, for this glossary serves only as a brief identification of works that are not generally known to the casual student of English.

A.B.C., An a minor poem to Our Lady (about 1370) by Chaucer, each stanza beginning with a different letter in alphabetical order.

Ælfric (about 955 - about 1020) abbot of the Benedictine order at Eynsham, noted for his elaborate but controlled and fluent prose style, often rhythmical and alliterative, considered the highest achievement in the Old English period. He wrote homilies, a glossary, a grammar, and commentaries on the Old and New Testaments.

Albions England a history of England in verse by William Warner (1586).

Alfred (849-899) king of the West Saxons from 871 to 899, who united southern England by defeating the invading Danes. He encouraged and participated in assembling the first large body of English scholarly literature intended for English readers. The most important works with which his name is associated are the translations of Boethius' *De Consolatione Philosophiae,* Orosius' *Historiarum Adversus Paganos* (Epitome of Universal History), St. Gregory's *Pastoral Care,* and Bede's *Ecclesiastical History.* He also guided initial work on the *Anglo-Saxon Chronicle.*

Almond for a Parrot, An an essay probably written by Thomas Nashe (1589) in reply to the Martin Marprelate pamphlets, which were religious tracts written by defenders of the Puritan doctrines against practices of the Church of England.

Alphabet of Tales a collection of word tales, translated from Latin into English about 1440.

Ancrene Riwle a manual governing the rules and duties of monastic life, specifically written for a society of three anchoresses in Dorsetshire, and usually ascribed to Simon of Ghent, bishop of Salisbury. Though composed first in English, probably before 1200, many versions exist in French and Latin as well.

Anelida and Arcite an unfinished poem by Chaucer (about 1375).

Anglo-Saxon Chronicle a group of manuscripts giving the history of England from the time of Alfred the Great to about 1154. Begun under Alfred, possibly with his participation, to aid his educational program.

Apocrypha a collection of 14 books no longer included in the Septuagint and Vulgate versions of the Bible. Both the Protestants and the Jews exclude the *Apocrypha* as lacking proven, inspired authorship, though it is largely accepted in the Roman and Greek churches.

Apology Made by Him, The an autobiographical work by Sir Thomas More (1533), written in defense of himself, also known as *Apologie of Syr Thomas More, Knyght.*

Arcadia, The a pastoral prose romance in two versions (1580 and before 1586) by Sir Philip Sidney, concerning the trials of two pairs of lovers.

Ars grammatica a Latin grammar written in the 300's A.D. by Donatus, teacher of St. Jerome, and translated into Middle English in 1500.

Arte of English Poesie, The a manual discussing new forms and authors of Elizabethan poetry, written by George Puttenham, and published in 1589.

Art of Rhetoric, The an orator's handbook on the art of spoken English, written by Thomas Wilson in 1533. It attacks the use of extravagant euphemism and so-called inkhorn terms.

Arthour and Merlin a romance in verse, written probably before 1300 in the Arthurian tradition, based on a French version.

Ashby, George (died 1475) English poet and clerk of the Signet.

A View of the Present State of Ireland a political survey of Irish art and politics, by Spenser (1596), recommending harsh measures to enforce England's political control.

Ayenbite of Inwyt a moral treatise of French origin literally entitled the "again-biting of inner wit" (the remorse of conscience). It was translated about 1340 by Dan Michel, a monk living at Canterbury, from a French treatise on morality, and is believed to have been partly incorporated in Chaucer's *Parson's Tale.*

Bacon, Francis (1561-1626) English essayist, philosopher, jurist, and statesman, instrumental in implementing an inductive investigation of nature and a philosophical tradition in systematic thought based upon conclusions obtained from empirical science. In his *Essays* (1597 and following) Bacon developed the form into a short treatise of a single problem. He also wrote *Of the Advancement of Learning* (1605), *Henry VII* (1622), *Sylva Sylvarum* (1626).

Battlefield Grammar a short Latin grammar written in a dialect of Middle English by an unknown author. It was published (about 1450 with a fund established by the King) at Battlefield, scene of Henry IV's victory over Hotspur.

Bede (about 673 - 735) English monk, scientist, and scholar, first great English writer of prose, wrote *Ecclesiastical History* and other works in Latin.

Becon, Thomas (1512-67) ecclesiastic and writer, associate of Archbishop Cranmer and chaplain to Lady Jane Seymour, wrote *A New Catechism* (1560) and other Protestant religious writings.

Bellenden, John (about 1490-1550 or perhaps about 1587) Scottish poet and translator of Livy's *Roman History* (1533).

Beowulf an epic poem written by an unknown author about 725. One of the first records of early Old English, it is the greatest literary work of the period. The poet celebrates the Germanic heroes of the 5th and 6th centuries.

Bestiary a poem written before 1250, giving fantastic descriptions of specific animals, each followed by a Christian moral.

Bevis of Hampton a romance in verse written before 1300, by an unknown author.

Bible the collection of sacred writings comprising the Old and New Testaments, appearing in English in various versions.
—*Coverdale Bible* a translation into English of the Dutch and Latin Bibles by Miles Coverdale (1535). This translation was based on Tyndale's translations of the Old and New Testaments, the Vulgate, and Luther's German translation.
—*Douay Bible* a translation into English based on the Vulgate, and published at Douay. It is the work of a group of Catholic exiles from the Elizabethan Reformation.
—*Geneva Bible* a translation of the Bible into English published in Geneva (1557, 1560) to escape Queen Mary's persecution. It was the first edition to be written in verses and to exclude the Apocrypha; in common use until the King James Bible.
—*King James Bible* a version of the Bible in English (1611), largely taken from the work of Tyndale and Coverdale. This translation influenced later writing by its euphony and powerful style.
—*Tyndale Bible* a translation into English of the New Testament by William Tyndale (1525), and with that of Coverdale the first printed Bible in English.
—*Wycliffe Bible* a version of the Bible (about 1382), the first complete translation into English. It was made from the Vulgate and probably carried out under the supervision of John Wycliffe, though some of the work is his, including the Gospels.

Body and the Soul, The a poem (before 1200) that takes the form of a recriminative argument between a knight's body and his soul concerning their conflicting needs; probably based on a similar text in Latin of the same period. Versions also appeared about 1250 and in 1300.

Boke Named the Governour, The a treatise on education and politics by Sir Thomas Elyot (1531), showing the influence of the Classics on the evolution of English prose.

Book of Common Prayer a book containing the prayers and services of the Church of England or the Episcopal Church, originally written to standardize the form of worship and make it accessible in the vernacular. The original version (1549) is a testament to Archbishop Cranmer's command of language and the art of compromise.

Book of Martyrs or **Actes and Monuments** a work by John Foxe (editions 1563-87) recording the persecution of Protestant reformers in England; originally written in Latin and later translated into English by Foxe.

Book of the Duchese or **The Dethe of Blaunche** an early poem (1369) by Chaucer. It takes the form of an elegy on the wife of John of Gaunt.

Bruce, The a historical poem relating the story of the struggles of King Robert I of Scotland against the English, written by John Barbour (about 1375).

Byting Satyres a collection of satirical character sketches by Bishop Joseph Hall (1598). They may have been a source for Ben Jonson's *Every Man Out of His Humor.*

Caedmon (about 670) earliest poet of record in English, author, according to Bede, of metrical paraphrases of the Old Testament.

Canterbury Tales an unfinished work by Chaucer (about 1385-1395 or 1400) planned as a series of 120 tales to be told by a group of Pilgrims on their way to Canterbury. Only 22 stories were completed, but even these give us our most vivid examples of life in the 1300's. The idea of the separate tales was borrowed from Chaucer's knowledge of Boccaccio's *Decameron.*

Castel of Helth, The a popular medical guide for laymen, written by Sir Thomas Elyot (1533).

Castle of Knowledge, The a mathematical treatise on astronomy by Robert Recorde (1556).

Caxton, William (about 1422-91) the first English printer, he kept his presses profitable by his and others' translations of such works as: *The History of Jason* (1475), Ovid's *Metamorphoses* (1480, classical legends), *The Chronicles of England* (1480), *The History of Reynard the Fox* (1481, bestiaries), *The Mirror of the World* (1481, on medieval education), *The Golden Legend* (1483, biographies of saints), *Blanchardyn and Eglantine* (1489, a romance of rescue from an unwelcome suitor), *The Book of Eneydos* (1490, the story of Aeneas), and *Fierabras* (1491 or about 1489, the *Ferumbras* tale).

Chapman, George (about 1559-1634) English poet, dramatist, renowned translator of Homer's *Iliad* (1598) and *Odyssey* (1615).

Chaucer, Geoffrey (about 1344-1400) English poet, generally considered the greatest writer of the Middle English period, especially known as author of the *Canterbury Tales.* He also translated Boethius' *De Consolatione Philosophiae,* and passages from the French classic *Roman de la Rose.*

Christ a poem by Cynewulf (about 750) sometimes known as *The Ascension,* and taken from St. Gregory's homily on that subject. The title *Christ* is also used to refer to this poem and one found with it in a book of Old English poetry, but the distinction is now made between this later poem (*Christ A*) and Cynewulf's (*Christ B*).

Christ's Tears Over Jerusalem a prose religious tract written by Thomas Nashe (1593) decrying the sinful life led by citizens of London, and paralleling its downfall to that of Jerusalem prophesied by Christ.

Chronicle of Britain a poetic chronicle and legendary history of the kings of Britain from the founding by the mythical Brutus (which accounts for the sometime title *Brut*) to 689 A.D. Written by Layamon, an English priest (probably before 1200), it is a masterful story in English and French verse, especially in its delineation of the story of Arthur.

Chronicle of England a chronicle in verse relating in tales and anecdotes the history of pre-Chaucerian England. Written before 1338 and derived from earlier chronicles, Robert Mannyng's work is chiefly important for his use of the Midland dialect, which makes it a milestone in the history of the development of Modern English.

Chronicles or **Holinshed's Chronicles** a history of England, Scotland, and Ireland (1577-87) by Raphael Holinshed and William Harrison, Richard Stanyhurst, and Edward Campion. The Chronicles had an enormous influence on literature of the period, particularly the historical plays of Shakespeare.

Cleanness an alliterative poem by an unknown author, perhaps that of *The Pearl* and *Patience* (probably before 1380), which illustrates by Biblical allusion the Lord's sorrow over the unclean state of man, and asks for forgiveness.

Colloquy a catechism, written by Ælfric (before 1000), it describes the day of the novice in contrast to that of the plowman, shepherd, hunter, and merchant, and thereby affords a glimpse of the life of pre-Norman Britain and a broader than usual record of Old English vocabulary.

Confessio Amantis a poem written by John Gower (before 1393), explaining courtly love and revealing Gower's sins against Venus by illustrative stories taken from the Bible and mythological sources.

Confutation of Barnes, The an attack written in 1532 by Sir Thomas More upon Lutheran principles of the Reformation preached by Robert Barnes, prior of the Austin friars at Cambridge, who died a martyr (1540).

Confutation of Tyndale's Answer, The an answer to Tyndale's defense of the Lutheran tenets of the Reformation, growing out of an earlier controversy that arose from More's *Supplycacyon of Soulys.* More's answer to Tyndale was written in 1532-33.

Copland, Robert (died 1547) author and printer, who was, as a pupil of Wynkyn de Worde, a successor to Caxton, translating works from French and Latin. He was also a minor poet in his own right.

Coverdale Bible. See **Bible.**

Coverdale, Miles (1488-1568) English divine who translated the whole Bible into English (1535, though Wycliffe had participated in the first translation into English) and supervised a later translation known as the *Great Bible* and edited a second edition known as *Cranmer's Bible* (1540).

Crudities or **Coryat's Crudities** a narrative by Thomas Coryat (1611) of his travels on the Continent, where in Italy he saw the fork in use at the table and introduced its use into England.

Cursor Mundi an early religious poem, based on Caedmon's paraphrase of Genesis, relating the course of the world from the Creation. Many versions exist, probably attesting to its popularity; composition probably before 1325, by an unknown author.

Cynthia's Revels a comedy by Ben Jonson (1599) that dramatizes the relationship of Queen Elizabeth and Essex and of Elizabeth's court with satirical portraits of Marston and Dekker.

Death Song an Old English poem of five lines by Bede (before 735), emphasizing an honorable name after death, and showing an ideal of conduct in transition from non-Christian to Christian times.

De Consolatione Philosophiae (*On the Consolation of Philosophy*) a Latin work in prose and verse about the problem of moral responsibility, written by Boethius (about 525 A.D.). The work attracted much attention in the Middle Ages and was translated by King Alfred, Chaucer, Queen Elizabeth, and others.

Defence of Poesie an essay on poetry, by Sir Philip Sidney (1581), written in response to an attack on poetry on puritanical and dogmatic grounds.

Dekker, Thomas (about 1572-1632) English dramatist and poetical collaborator known for his ear for dialect, wrote *Satiro-mastix* (1602) as a reply to Jonson's *Poetaster.*

De Proprietatibus Rerum a translation by John Trevisa (before 1398) of the Medieval encyclopedia of the physical and natural sciences, written by Bartholomew (Bartholomaeus Anglicus, a Franciscan) between 1230 and 1250.

De Re Rustica a work on agriculture written in Latin by Palladius (300's or 400's A.D.) and translated into English probably about 1450.

Destruction of Troy a northern English poem recounting the history of Troy from Jason's quest of the Golden Fleece to the sacking of Troy by the Greeks and the wanderings of Ulysses. It was probably written about 1400. Compare *Troy Book.*

Dethe of Blaunche = Book of the Duchesse.

Dictionary, Glossary reference work developed to assist translation, as among students of Latin. Early glossaries, compiled from interlinear glosses of hard Latin words, gave Latin synonyms and Old English equivalents; synonym lists were arranged by category or alphabetically. Later, wordbooks defined hard words, sometimes with considerable attention to definitions of unfamiliar words. The following selected list is arranged alphabetically by author.

—*Ash, John* a general English dictionary (1775) which included cant. Ash gave credit to Elisha Coles as his source for the less common cant terms.

—*Bailey, Nathan* a general English work (*Dictionarium Britannicum,* 1730) made for the widest possible audience. Innovations, beyond its scope and treatment of technical and obsolete terms, include attention to accent, etymology, and related terms or synonyms. Bailey included encyclopedic material, and in his second edition based his expanded list of entries upon reading of standard and contemporary authors. Johnson used Bailey's *Dictionary* in compiling his great work. Bailey also wrote a dictionary of etymology (1721).

—*Blount, Thomas* a general English work (*Glossographia,* 1656) that includes technical and specialized terms from the arts and sciences, and is the first to include etymologies and to cite the authorities he had consulted. Blount, the first to consider the concept of neologisms, viewed language as a growing, ever-changing body, probably as the result of his own reading of current literature and his attention to spoken language.

—*Cawdrey, Robert* a dictionary of hard words (*A Table Alphabeticall, 1604*) with emphasis on the vernacular, and based on the English vocabulary of Edmund Coote (1590).

—*Cockeram, Henry* an English-Latin dictionary (1623) distinguished by the addition of vulgarisms and encyclopedic information.

—*Coles, Elisha* a general English dictionary (1676) including proper names (market towns and cities of England and the Continent), cant, dialect, and old words.

—*Cooper, Thomas* a Latin-English dictionary (1565) distinguished by the rendering of Latin vocabulary into contemporary English with etymologies and proper names included; entitled *Thesaurus Linguae Romanae et Britannicae,* it absorbed Elyot's *Dictionary.*

—*Cotgrave, Randle* a French-English work (1611), most famous of the early bilingual dictionaries, serving as a source for Blount.
—*Elyot, Sir Thomas* a dictionary (1538) compiled to define enlarging vocabulary of English, appearing in several editions, that of 1548 made with Cooper and thereafter absorbed into Cooper's *Thesaurus Linguae* (see COOPER above).
—*Florio, John* an Italian-English dictionary (1598) filled with Elizabethan idioms, colloquialisms, and slang; probably in the enlarged revision (1611) a source used by Shakespeare, Jonson, and others (see FLORIO in general list).
—*Greene, Robert* various pamphlets (1580-92) enumerating contemporary slang of the low elements of the streets.
—*Hexham, Henry* an English-Dutch dictionary (1647).
—*Huloet, Richard* a series of Latin-English word lists (1552, *Abecedarium Anglico-Latinum*) compiled as a school text, and arranged by categories of English words in columnar form with Latin synonyms.
—*Kersey, John* extensive revision (1706) of Phillips' *Dictionary* adding much new scientific and technical vocabulary, dialect, agricultural terms, hard words, and common vocabulary. Kersey also made the first abridged dictionary (1708) selecting the common vocabulary, dialect, legal, and scientific terms.
—*Levins, Peter* a Latin-English dictionary (1570).
—*Minsheu, John* a polyglot dictionary (1617, *Guide Into Tongues*) with English first and emphasis on etymology.
—*Old English glossaries* word lists probably extracted from interlinear Old English glosses in Latin texts, and derived from lists of easier Latin synonyms, some arranged in alphabetical order, including the *Epinal Glossary* (before 800), the *Erfurt Glossary* (before 850), the *Corpus Glossary* (before 800), perhaps derived from earlier unnamed glossaries developed about 700 A.D.
—*Phillips, Edward* a general dictionary (1658) with greatly extended word list, and labeling of specialized subject area of a word. Although there is no evidence that he carried out the idea, Phillips advanced the notion of using advice from a committee of specialists to assist him.
—*Sherwood, Robert* an English-French dictionary (1632) made from Cotgrave's *Dictionary of the French and English Tongues* (1611).

Doctor Faustus a tragedy in blank verse and prose of the classic Faust tale, written by Christopher Marlowe about 1590.

Douay Bible. See **Bible.**

Douglas, Gavin (about 1474-1522) Scottish poet and bishop, translator of Vergil's *Aeneid* (1513), the first translation (after Caxton's) of any Classical work into English.

Drayton, Michael (1563-1631), English poet who experimented with different verse forms and wrote *England's Heroical Epistles* (1598) and the *Ballad of Agincourt* (1627), in which he imitated Spenser's romantic patriotism.

Dunbar, William (about 1460-about 1525) Scottish poet of the Chaucerian school, his works cover a wide range of forms and are collected under the title *Poems* (1500-20).

Ecclesiastical History a history of the English people from the conquest of Britain by the Romans to 731 A.D. (the year Bede completed it). It is an invaluable record of events especially in the period 550-731 when England was developing from barbarism to civilization. A translation from Latin was made by King Alfred before 899.

Ecclesiastical Memorials a history of the Church of England from Henry VIII to Mary by John Strype (1721). The three volumes are heavily documented by a lengthy appendix.

Ecclesiastical Polity a philosophical and theological prose work by Richard Hooker (1593-97) defending the position of the Anglican Church against the Puritans.

Elene a poem by Cynewulf (about 750) relating Constantine's conversion and the legend of St. Helen's discovery of the true cross.

English Prose Treatises three treatises on mysticism and the contemplative life by Richard Rolle (about 1340).

Euphues a romance by John Lyly (1579), continued in *Euphues and His England* (1580), relating the extravagant life of Elizabeth's court and the adventures of a romantic youth, Euphues, in an affected jargon that came to be known as *euphuism*.

Every Man In His Humour a comedy by Ben Jonson (1598) satirizing the various London types of the day.

Every Man Out of His Humour a comedy by Ben Jonson (1599) ridiculing various characters and fashions of the day.

Exodus a poem (about 725) relating the Biblical story of Exodus, of uncertain authorship, perhaps Caedmon.

Faerie Queene a verse allegory by Spenser (published in two parts: 1590, 1596), written in a new stanza form, each of its twelve parts portraying a different virtue with Queen Elizabeth represented as the Faerie Queene.

Falls of Princes a long poem written by John Lydgate (probably before 1439) relating tragedies that have befallen the great, ultimately adapted from Boccaccio's *De Casibus Virorum Illustrium*.

Famous Chronicle of War, The a translation by Alexander Barclay (1520) of Sallust's *Bellum Juqurthinum*.

Florio, John (about 1553-1625) English lexicographer and author, compiled *A World of Words* (see DICTIONARY) and translated Montaigne's *Essays* (1603) which provided a rich source of ideas for Shakespeare, Raleigh, and other writers. Florio used the Elizabethan idiom, and helped popularize the essay form in England.

Four Letters Confuted a violent attack on Richard and Gabriel Harvey written by Thomas Nashe (1593) in defense of Greene's *Menaphon* and his own *Pierce Penilesse*.

Genesis a poem in Old English describing Satan's rebellion and the Creation, now considered to be two works: *Genesis A* (about 725), attributed to an unknown follower of Caedmon, and *Genesis B* (probably about 875), a translation of an earlier German poem. The book of *Genesis* was also translated by Ælfric (before 1000).

Genesis and Exodus or **The Story of Genesis and Exodus** a poem relating the Biblical stories of Genesis and of Exodus (about 1250, also before 1325) by an unknown Norfolk poet, who adapted his work from Petrus Comestor's *Historia Scholastica.*

Geneva Bible. See **Bible.**

Gesta Romanorum, The a collection of stories with morals, probably written in Latin by an Englishman in the 1200's; a number of translations into English were made during the 1400's, one by Hoccleve (1440).

Glossary a Latin-English vocabulary compiled by Ælfric (about 1000) and later with additions by his students and by others in the Middle English period (1200). It is arranged by subject and is based on work by Isidore of Seville. See also DICTIONARY.

Golding, Arthur (about 1536-about 1605) English writer and translator of Caesar's *Gallic Wars* (1563), Ovid's *Metamorphoses* (1565-67, used by Shakespeare), and Calvin's *Commentaries on Psalms* (1571-83).

Grammar a Latin grammar written by Ælfric (about 1000) and adapted from an earlier work, but advocating the study of English once Latin has been mastered.

Grande Chirurgie an anonymous translation (probably before 1425) of the treatise on surgery, written by Chauliac, the great French surgeon-physician in 1363.

Greene, Robert (about 1560-1592) English dramatist, novelist, poet, collector of cant, who exerted great influence on Nashe and Marlowe and attacked Shakespeare as an "upstart bumpkin" in the later 1500's (see DICTIONARY).

Guy of Warwick or **The Romance of Guy of Warwick** a romance in verse of the early 1300's, but written perhaps before 1300, by an unknown author.

Hakluyt, Richard (about 1552-1616) English geographer and cleric, who published many accounts of English mariners and explorers (see VOYAGES).

Handlyng Synne a translation of the Anglo-French *Manuel des Pechiez,* rendered by Robert Mannyng about 1303. It is a commentary on the vices of man, in tales and anecdotes, revealing much in detail about medieval life.

Harvey, Gabriel (about 1545-1630), satirist and sometime literary intimate of Edmund Spenser, also known for caustic satires of leading literary and political figures of the period. —*Richard* (died 1623, brother of Gabriel) astrologer whose predictions provoked ridicule, and in the Martin Marprelate controversy attracted the satirical scorn of Greene and of Nashe.

Havelok the Dane an Anglo-Danish story (about 1300) probably based on an original version in Old English, containing the legend of the founding of the town of Grimsby in Lincolnshire and the romance of Havelok, the abandoned child of a Danish king, who returns to Denmark as conqueror.

Have With You to Saffron-Walden a vicious attack on Richard and Gabriel Harvey written by Thomas Nashe (1596), in which he makes reference to their ordinary antecedents as sons of a rope maker at Saffron-Walden in contrast to their pedantic literary style.

Heywood, John (about 1497-about 1580), English courtier and dramatist, he wrote *Epigrams and Proverbs* (1562) and numerous plays including *The Play of the Wether* (1533).

Historiarum Adversus Paganos a book of history and geography written by Orosius and translated into English by King Alfred (before 899).

History of King Richard III a witty and eloquent dramatic work in English, probably by Sir Thomas More (1513), which was a source for Shakespeare's play.

Hoccleve, Thomas (about 1370-about 1450) English poet, admirer of Chaucer; chief among his works is the *Regement of Princes.*

Holland, Philemon (1552-1637) English writer and translator of Livy's *Roman History* (1600), Pliny's *Natural History* (1601), Plutarch's *Moralia* or *Morals* (1603), and Suetonius' *History of the Caesars* (1606), noted for his simple and realistic style.

Homilies writings on moral conduct and various religious subjects, some probably given, at least in part, as sermons, and often notable for their rhythm and prose style.
—*Ælfric's Homilies* two series of homilies attributed to Ælfric; the Old English is sometimes distinguished by an eloquent poetic character.
—*Lambeth Homilies* a collection of religious writings, chiefly homilies, three of which are at least partly by Ælfric.
—*Old English Homilies* a collection of Ælfric's Homilies with others, rendered in Middle English, before 1225.
—*Trinity Homilies* a collection of homilies probably based on older collections, such as those of Ælfric, and containing some of the earliest prose writing in Middle English, before 1200.

House of Fame an unfinished poem by Chaucer (about 1380) showing influence of such Italian poets as Dante and Latin poets such as Ovid and Vergil. Chaucer uses the device of a dream-vision to explain how fame is so haphazardly distributed.

Imitation of Christ translation by William Atkynson (1502) of a work traditionally ascribed to Thomas à Kempis (1441), which places the rule of life in seclusion and renunciation.

Juliana a poem by Cynewulf (about 750) on the persecution and martyrdom of St. Juliana.

King Horn the earliest existing romance in English verse, probably composed about 1225; various versions circulated in the 1300's, all by unknown authors.

King James Bible. See **Bible.**

Kyng Alisaunder a verse romance (probably before 1300) relating the life of Alexander the Great from his birth to his death and including descriptions of his conquests.

Lantern of Light, The a tract by an unknown author (before 1415) defending basic Wycliffe doctrines.

Latimer, Hugh (about 1485-1555) English bishop and religious reformer, noted for his clarity of style in sermons and writings.

Legend of Good Women an unfinished poem by Chaucer (about 1386), written to Queen Alceste as penance for having slighted women in his writings, with plans to relate 19 stories about famous women.

Leland, John (about 1506-1552) English antiquarian, wrote *The Itinerary* (1538) an account of his journeys through England with descriptions of routes and matters of antiquarian interest.

Lenten Stuffe a tongue-in-cheek praise of Yarmouth and the red herring written by Thomas Nashe (1599).

Lesclarcissement (in full, *Lesclarcissement de la langue françoyse*) a book (1530) containing a grammar, dictionary, and treatise on educational instruction by John Palsgrave (about 1480-1554). It is one of the earliest French grammars for English use and a record of French and English of this period.

Lindisfarne Gospels a remarkably beautiful illuminated Latin text of the Gospels, executed perhaps about 700 A.D., with an interlinear Old English gloss in Northumbrian dialect added about 950. The gloss contains many variant terms for the Latin text.

Marlowe, Christopher (1564-93) English poet and playwright, author of *Tamurlane* or *Tamburlaine* and *The Jew of Malta* (about 1590).

Marston, John (about 1575-1634) English dramatist and divine, who was the object of Ben Jonson's ridicule in *The Poetaster.*

Merlin a poem telling the Merlin legend, written by Henry Lovelich about 1410. It is probably based on a prose version (about 1300) of Robert de Boron's poem of the same subject composed about 1200.

Middle English Dictionary the great scholarly record of Middle English being compiled at the University of Michigan, in its immediate form by Hans Robert Lewis, and formerly by Sherman Kuhn and Hans Kurath, originally based on the collection of citations from the OED and readings of the Early English Texts Society, later by a very broad reading under the direction of the Dictionary's editors.

Mirror of Good Manners a translation by Alexander Barclay (about 1510) of a Latin poem by Dominicus Mancinus on the four cardinal virtues.

Morte Arthur an alliterative romance written before 1400, dealing with Arthur's later years and his death and burial at Glastonbury. It is noted for its vivid and detailed scenes and for its use by Malory in composing *Morte d'Arthur.*

Morte Arthure a poem written probably before 1400, based on the French *Le Morte Arthure,* dealing primarily with the romantic exploits of Sir Lancelot, his love for Queen Guinevere, and his death.

Morte d'Arthur a Middle English collection of prose romances on the life and death of King Arthur and the knights of the Round Table, compiled (1470-85) by Sir Thomas Malory. The book was written largely in imitation of the original French tales of King Arthur and was entitled by Caxton, who first printed Malory's work.

Mum, Sothseger and **Mum and the Sothsegger** an alliterative poem (about 1405) originally attributed to Langland as author of *Piers Plowman,* written in the form of a letter to Richard II criticizing him for poor admininstration. Because of differences in style and form, the work is considered two different poems, but probably of the same authorship. The title's meaning "Hush, Truth-teller" is fairly transparent if *soothsayer* is substituted.

North, Thomas (about 1535-1601) English translator of Plutarch's *Lives* (1579-80), used by Shakespeare for *Julius Caesar, Antony and Cleopatra,* and *Coriolanus.*

Of the Advancement of Learning a work by Francis Bacon (1605) examining the analytical, encyclopedic, and inductive methods of learning.

Ormulum, The an unrhymed poem paraphrasing passages of the Gospels by Orm, an Augustinian canon (probably about 1200). The author devised a phonetic system distinguishing short vowels by doubling the following consonant.

Owl and the Nightingale, The a poem written perhaps by Guildford of Portesham about 1250, debating the cause of the new lyric poetry and the secular world as against the older forms of religious poetry and the ascetic, monastic life.

Parlement of Foules a fanciful poem by Chaucer (about 1380) written around a theme of birds choosing their mates, perhaps as an allegory to the betrothal of Richard II to Anne of Bohemia.

Parsons, Robert (1546-1610) English divine, author of Roman Catholic tracts against Protestantism (1582).

Paston Letters a collection of letters, over three generations (1422-1509) of the Paston family, giving details of domestic life and public concerns of the English upper classes during this period.

Pastoral Care a translation by King Alfred (before 899) of a religious tract by St. Gregory (earlier Pope Gregory the Great).

Pathway to Knowledge, The a mathematical treatise on geometry (1551) by Robert Recorde.

Patience a poem perhaps written by the author of *The Pearl* and *Cleanness* (probably about 1380), counseling patience in the face of adversity on the theme of the Biblical story of Jonah and the whale.

Pearl, The a poem perhaps written by the author of *Patience* and *Cleanness* (probably about 1380), composed of an elegiac lament for the poet's two-year-old daughter. As an example of lyric poetry, it is a highlight in Middle English literature.

Peterborough Chronicle the longest of the English chronicles, extending to 1154. Based on the now lost Kentish chronicle, it relates in especially gloomy prose and verse of Latin and English the history of the Danish invasions, the conquest and subjugation of England under William the Conqueror, and the generally wretched state of the common folk.

Phoenix, The a poem sometimes attributed to Cynewulf (about 750), in which the first part describes the legend of the bird, and the second half presents the Phoenix as a symbol of Christ, the Christian life, and the Resurrection.

Pierce Penilesse a prose satire by Thomas Nashe (1592) attacking Richard and Gabriel Harvey and complaining about the evils of the time, especially drunkenness. There is also a curious defense of the theater in a section on sloth.

Piers Plowman an allegory in unrhymed verse by an unknown author, perhaps William Langland (before 1376, with two principal later versions, about 1378, before 1387). It is a vivid picture of the life of its time.

Pilgrimage of Man a translation by John Lydgate (probably before 1430) of the first of Guillame de Deguileville's *Pèlerinages.*

Polychronicon a history in the form of a chronicle to 1342, by Ranulf Higden, translated from Latin before 1387 by John Trevisa, and in a subsequent edition before 1425. The title refers to its broad or universal treatment of history.

Prick of Conscience, The a poem describing the misery of life and the glory of heaven, once attributed to Richard Rolle (about 1340).

Prologue to the Canterbury Tales the description of the plan for the Canterbury Tales by Chaucer (about 1387-95), describing the individual pilgrims ranging from an eminent jurist and a worthy knight to a plowman and a dishonest miller.

Promptorium Parvulorum a Latin-English dictionary (1440) compiled of words collected from various authors by Fratre Galfridus, called Grammaticus, and said to have been the first in use. Its title with *Promptorium* (properly *promptuarium* storehouse) included was introduced by Wynkyn de Worde in his edition (1510).

Proverbs of Alfred a collection of wise sayings from the Old English period, long associated with King Alfred. The work is generally of the period before 1250 and is also found in an earlier edition (1150).

Ralph Roister Doister the first full English comedy, by Udall (before 1553).

Regement of Princes a long poem by Hoccleve (about 1412) on the responsibilities of a prince, dedicated to Henry V as Prince of Wales.

Reson and Sensuallyte a poem by John Lydgate, composed in 1408.

Rolls of Parliament the record of proceedings of old Parliaments of England.

Roman de la Rose a French poem of the Middle Ages, written as two parts: the first by Guillaume de Lorris (about 1237) and the second by Jean de Meung (about 1247-1257). A fragmentary English translation is in part the work of Chaucer, whose own poetry reflects the strong influence of this poem.

Rosemounde a ballad by Chaucer (about 1380).

Schoolmaster, The a treatise on education by Roger Ascham (1568), advocating humane pedagogy rather than the rod and detailing a method of teaching Latin.

Science of Surgery or **Cirurgie** a translation done under Lanfranc's supervision of an earlier Latin work, possibly also incorporating discoveries of the Arab medical men, compiled probably for the benefit of personnel in the first English hospital established about 1084 by Lanfranc at Canterbury during his tenure as archbishop. The work is not found in published form until sometime before 1400.

Seven Sages, The a romance in verse (about 1425) based on a series of Eastern tales, adapted into English through French and Latin.

Shepheardes Calender, The a poem in twelve eclogues marking the twelve months of the year, by Spenser (1579), in which the poet discusses religion, contemporary mores, and the state of poetry.

Ship of Fools, The a translation by Alexander Barclay (1509) of the poem by Sebastian Brant *Das Narrenschiff.* Barclay's lengthened version satirizes various practices and life styles among the English.

Siege of Jerusalem a romance in verse (before 1400) by an unknown author, distinctive for its battle scenes.

Sir Amadas a romance (about 1420) by an unknown author that employs supernatural effects to convey a moral lesson of chivalry and kindness.

Sir Ferumbras a romance in English verse by an unknown author (about 1380) describing Charlemagne's conquests in recovering Christian relics taken in a sacking of Rome by Ferumbras and his Saracen father. Ferumbras and his conversion to Christianity was the most popular of the Charlemagne romances.

Sir Gawain and the Green Knight an Arthurian romance, written perhaps by the unknown author of *The Pearl* (probably about 1390), telling the story of an elaborate plot to test the honor and courage of Arthur's knights.

Sir Orfeo a poem by an unknown author (about 1330) retelling the myth of Orpheus and Eurydice with medieval characters.

Sir Tristrem a version of the Tristram legend, written by an unknown author (probably before 1300), possibly as a minstrel's version of a story already well known.

Skelton, John (about 1460-1529) a scholar and poet, author of *The Bowge of Courte* (a satire of Henry VII's court) and *Speke Parrot* (a satire of humanistic education). Other works include a morality play *Magnificence,* and the poems *Elinor Rummyng* and *The Boke of Phyllyp Sparowe.*

Smith, Captain John (1580-1631) English adventurer and president of the Virginia colony (1608-09), author of *The Generall Historie of Virginia* (1624), *Seamen's Glossary* (1627), etc.

Solomon and Saturn a dialogue in metrical verse, actually two separate works by different unknown authors (before 900), debating the Judeo-Christian wisdom as against the so-called heathen wisdom of the northern and eastern traditions.

Song of Roland a paraphrase by an unknown author (before 1200) of the French verse romance, *Chanson de Roland.*

Spenser, Edmund (about 1552-1599), an English poet whose works include the allegory *Faerie Queene, Muiopotomos* (a parable of politics), *The Shepheardes Calender,* sonnets including *Epithalamion,* the elegies *Daphnaïda* and *Ruins of Time,* a satire *Mother Hubbard's Tale,* and *A View of the Present State of Ireland.*

Stanyhurst, Richard (1547-1618) Irish author and translator of Vergil's *Aeneid* (1582), who also wrote the description of Ireland in Holinshed's *Chronicles.*

Supplycacyon of Soulys a work by Sir Thomas More (1529) in answer to the doctrine of purgatory which provoked a controversy with William Tyndale.

Surrey, Earl of a title of courtesy of Henry Howard (about 1517-1547), English poet and adventurer, who translated parts of Vergil's *Aeneid* into blank verse and was the first English writer to use unrhymed iambic pentameter. With Sir Thomas Wyatt, Sr. he wrote the first sonnets to appear in English.

Sylvester, Josuah (1563-1618) English poet who translated *Divine Weeks and Works* (1590-1606) of the French religious poet Guilaume Du Bartas, also *Triumph of Faith* and *Rescue.*

Terapeutyke a translation by Robert Copland (1541) of Galen's Classical work on medicine; Copland was one of three printers who took over from William Caxton.

Testament of Love, The a political allegory (about 1385) in which the author, Thomas Usk, attempts to justify his conduct of treachery.

Thrush and the Nightingale a poem in the form of a dialogue between a thrush and a nightingale by an unknown author (probably before 1300), and apparently not related to *The Owl and the Nightingale.*

Travels or **Travels of Sir John Maundeville** or **Maundeville's Travels** an account originally in French (1371) purported to be of travels to distant lands by an author whose identity is still in dispute, perhaps an English physician, living in exile in Liège. One of the best-known books of the Middle Ages, it was translated into English about 1400, certainly before 1425.

Treatise on the Astrolabe probably the oldest work in English about a scientific instrument, written by Chaucer (about 1391) for his son, and based on a work in Latin adapted from a treatise in Arabic (700's A.D.).

Trevisa, John (about 1326 - about 1412) English cleric and translator of Higden's *Polychronicon* and Bartholomew's *De Proprietatibus Rerum.*

Troilus and Criseyde a long poem of romance by Chaucer (about 1385) based on Boccaccio's *Il Filostrato,* but with Chaucer's own reshaping of Boccaccio's story, almost foreshadowing the psychological novel.

Troy Book a poem by Lydgate written before 1420, recounting the Latin history of the legend of Troy, and within the story of Troilus and Cressida giving grateful mention to Chaucer.

Turberville, George (about 1540 - about 1610) English poet, translator, and writer on hunting, author of *The Book of Falconry* (1575), *Tragical Tales* (1568, paraphrase in blank verse of Italian stories and poems, some from Boccaccio).

Turner, William (died 1568) English physician and botanist, whose works, *The Names of Herbs* (1548) and *A New Herbal* (1562), introduced the serious study of botany into England.

Tyndale Bible. See **Bible.**

Tyndale, William (about 1484-1536), English divine and reformer, translator of the Bible (see BIBLE), author of *Obedience of a Christian Man* (1528, setting forth the authority of Scripture and the supremacy of the king), *Exposition of the Epistles of St. John* (1531), *The Supper of the Lord* (1533, part of a treatise on the sacraments).

Udall, Nicholas (1505-56) English dramatist and Latin scholar, translated (1542) Erasmus' *Apothegms,* maxims collected by the Continental scholar and theologian, and *Upon the New Testament,* the first volume of Erasmus' paraphrase of the New Testament; also wrote *Ralph Roister Doister.*

Unfortunate Traveller, The a fictional tale by Thomas Nashe (1594); written in a bold and dashing style, it is a forerunner of the historical novel.

Utopia a political romance by Sir Thomas More, written in Latin (1516) and translated into English (1551). It deals with the evils of government, and describes the ideal (*Utopia* or "Nowhere") where people live by reason; based largely on Plato's *Republic.*

Vespasian Psalter a paraphrase in Latin of original Biblical text containing a number of Psalms in the form of hymns, with an Old English translation given in an interlinear text, thought to be rendered about 830.

Vices and Virtues a poem by an unknown author (before 1200) on the theme of *The Body and the Soul,* in which the soul and body appeal to reason to resolve their conflicting needs.

Voyages and **Voyages and Discoveries of the English Nation** a series of works by Richard Hakluyt, published from 1584 on, intended to stimulate interest in the achievements of English mariners and explorers and thereby give impetus to colonization. His *Voyages and Discoveries* is an invaluable source of information, used by Shakespeare, among others.

West Saxon Gospels a translation of the Four Gospels (before 1050). Later Middle English translations indicate that copying of the Old English texts continued after the Norman Conquest (1066).

William of Shoreham (1300's) a religious of the Leeds Priory and poet who translated the Psalms of David into English prose.

Winner and Waster a poem by an unknown author (about 1353) dealing with the social and economic problems of the period, perhaps one of the sources of *Piers Plowman.*

Wolsey, Thomas (probably 1475-1530) English statesman and cardinal.

Wyatt, Sir Thomas (1503-1542) English diplomat and poet who with the Earl of Surrey wrote the first English sonnets (1541).

Wycliffe Bible. See **Bible.**

Wycliffe, John (about 1324-1384) English divine and religious reformer, who participated in the first complete translation of the Bible into English (probably translating the *Gospels* himself about 1360 though the Bible did not appear until about 1382). Wycliffe also wrote fearless tracts criticizing the Church administration and advocating the supremacy of secular power of the State.

Wynkyn de Worde (originally *Jan van Wynkyn,* died about 1535) an Alsatian who immigrated to England as an assistant to Caxton and eventually became his successor (1491).

York Plays a cycle of 48 mystery plays covering Biblical history from the Creation to Judgment Day, performed by the crafts or mysteries of York, England, from the 1300's to the 1500's.

Ywain and Gawain a romance in verse (probably about 1350), condensed and adapted from Chrétien de Troyes' *Ywain,* a story of reconciliation between two knights with the aid of supernatural forces.

Bibliography

GENERAL WORKS

Avis, Walter S. *A Dictionary of Canadianisms on Historical Principles*. Toronto, 1967.

Bartholomae, Christian. *Altiranisches Wörterbuch*. Berlin, 1961.

Battisti, Carlo and Giovanni Alessio. *Dizionario Etimologico Italiano*. Florence, 1948–57.

Baxter, J. H. and Charles Johnson. *Medieval Latin Word-List*. London, 1934. Revised Edition by Ronald E. Lathom. Oxford, 1965.

Bense, J. F. *A Dictionary of the Low-Dutch Element in the English Vocabulary*. The Hague, 1939.

Berrey, Lester V. and Melvin Van Den Bark. *The American Thesaurus of Slang*. New York, 1942.

Bloch, Oscar and Walther von Wartburg. *Dictionnaire Étymologique de la Langue Française*. Second Edition, Paris, 1950.

Boisacq, Émile. *Dictionnaire Étymologique de la Langue Grecque*. Fourth Edition, Heidelberg, 1950.

Bosworth, Joseph and T. Northcote Toller. *An Anglo-Saxon Dictionary*. London, 1882–98. Supplement, 1921.

Branford, Jean. *A Dictionary of South African English*. Oxford, 1978.

Brugmann, Karl. *Kurze Vergleichende Grammatik der Indogermanischen Sprachen*. Berlin and Leipzig, 1933.

Burchfield, Robert W. A *Supplement to the Oxford English Dictionary* (OEDS). Volume I (A-G), Oxford 1972; Volume II (H-N), 1976; Volume III (O-Scz), 1982; Volume IV (Se-Z), 1985.

Cassidy, Frederic G. *Dictionary of American Regional English*, Volume I (A-C). Cambridge, England, 1985.

——— and R. B. Le Page. *Dictionary of Jamaican English*. Cambridge, England, 1967.

Collinder, Björn. *Fenno-Ugric Vocabulary*. Stockholm, 1955.

Corominas, Juan. *Diccionario Crítico Etimológico de la Lengua Castellana* (4 Volumes). Bern, 1954.

Craigie, William A. and James R. Hulbert. *A Dictionary of American English on Historical Principles* (4 Volumes). Chicago, 1938–44.

Dauzat, Albert. *Dictionnaire Étymologique de la Langue Française*. Seventh Edition, 1938.

——— Jean Dubois and Henri Mitterand. *Nouveau Dictionnaire Étymologique*. Paris, 1964.

Delbridge, Arthur. *The Macquarie Dictionary*. St. Leonards, New South Wales, 1981.

De Vries, Jan. *Altnordisches Etymologisches Wörterbuch*. Second Edition, Leiden, 1962.

Ernout, Alfred and Antoine Meillet. *Dictionnaire Étymologique de la Langue Latine*. Fourth Edition, Paris, 1959.

Farmer, J. S. and W. E. Henley. *Slang and its Analogues* (7 Volumes), 1890–1904. Reprint Edition, 1970.

Fennell, C. A. M. *The Stanford Dictionary of Anglicised Words and Phrases*. Cambridge, England, 1892.

Frisk, Hjalmar. *Griechisches Etymologisches Wörterbuch* (3 Volumes). 1955–72.

Gamillscheg, Ernest. *Etymologisches Wörterbuch der Französischen Sprache*. Heidelberg, 1928.

Glare, P. G. W. *Oxford Latin Dictionary*. Oxford, 1968–82.

Godefroy, F. *Dictionnaire de l'ancienne langue française*. Paris, 1880–92.

———, J. Bonnard and A. Salmon. *Lexique de l'ancien français*. Paris, 1901.

Gold, Robert, S. *A Jazz Lexicon*. New York, 1964.

Grant, William and David D. Murison. *The Scottish National Dictionary* (11 Volumes). Edinburgh, 1929–76.

Holthausen, Ferdinand. *Altenglisches Etymologisches Wörterbuch*. Second Edition, Heidelberg, 1963.

——— *Altfriesisches Wörterbuch*. Heidelberg, 1925.

——— *Altsächsisches Elementarbuch*. Heidelberg, 1921.

——— *Gotisches Etymologisches Wörterbuch*. Heidelberg, 1934.

——— *Wörterbuch des Altwestnordischen*. Göttingen, 1948.

Hofmann, J. B. *Etymologisches Wörterbuch des Griechischen*. München, 1950.

Karg-Gasterstädt, Elisabeth and Theodor Frings. *Althochdeutsches Wörterbuch*. Berlin, 1952 (completed through *Fe-* in 1979).

Kent, Roland G. *Old Persian*. New Haven, 1950.

Kluge, Friedrich and Alfred Götze. *Etymologisches Wörterbuch der Deutschen Sprache*. Sixteenth Edition, Berlin, 1953.

Kurath, Hans, Sherman Kuhn, and Robert E. Lewis. *Middle English Dictionary* (MED). Ann Arbor, 1954 (completed through *Set* in 1987).

Lewis, Charlton T. and Charles Short. *Harper's Latin Dictionary*. New York, 1907.

Liddell, Henry George and Robert Scott. *A Greek-English Lexicon* (2 Volumes). Ninth Edition, 1940. Reprinted, 1948.

Little, William, H. W. Fowler, and Jessie Coulson. *The Shorter Oxford English Dictionary*. Third Edition, Oxford, 1973.

Lokotsch, Karl. *Etymologisches Wörterbuch der Europäischen Wörter Orientalischen Ursprungs*. Heidelberg, 1927.

Lübben, August. *Mittelniederdeutsches Handwörterbuch*. Norden and Leipzig, 1888.

Mathews, Mitford M. *A Dictionary of Americanisms on Historical Principles*. Chicago, 1951.

Matsuda, Yutaka. *Cross-Over Languages: English and Japanese (I), Japanese and English (II)*. Nishinomiya, Japan, 1986.

Mayrhofer, Manfred. *Kurzgefasstes Etymologisches Wörterbuch des Altindischen* (Concise Etymological Sanskrit Dictionary). Heidelberg, 1956–.

Meyer-Lübke, Wilhelm. *Romanisches Etymologisches Wörterbuch*. Third Edition, Heidelberg, 1935.

Migliorini, Bruno and Aldo Duro. *Prontuario Etimologico della Lingua Italiana*. Torino, 1949.

Morris, Edward E. *A Dictionary of Austral English*. Sydney, 1898 (reprint, 1972).

Murray, James A. H., et al. *The Oxford English Dictionary* (OED). Thirteen Volumes (with Supplement and Bibliography). Oxford, 1933.

Partridge, Eric. *A Dictionary of Slang and Unconventional English*. Fifth Edition, New York, 1961.

Pokorny, Julius. *Indogermanisches Etymologisches Wörterbuch* (3 Volumes). Bern, 1948–59.

Prinz, Otto and Johannes Schneider. *Mittellateinisches Wörterbuch*. München, 1959 (completed through Comp- in 1976).

Prokosch, Edward. *A Comparative Germanic Grammar*. Philadelphia, 1939.

Quemada, Bernard. *Datations et Documents Lexicographiques*. Matériaux pour l'histoire du vocabulaire française, Paris, 1959.

Robert, Paul. *Dictionnaire Alphabétique & Analogique de la Langue Française*. Paris, 1978.

Senn, Alfred. *Middle High German*. New York, 1937.

Sophocles, E. A. *Greek Lexicon of the Roman and Byzantine Periods* (2 Volumes). Cambridge, Massachusetts, 1887.

Souter, Alexander. *A Glossary of Later Latin to 600 A.D.* Oxford, 1949.

Streitberg, Wilhelm. *Gotisches Elementarbuch*. Heidelberg, 1920.

Sturtevant, Edgar H. *A Hittite Glossary*. Second Edition, Philadelphia, 1936. Supplement, 1939.

Tobler, Adolf and Erhard Lommatzsch. *Altfranzösisches Wörterbuch* (4 Volumes). Berlin, 1925.

Van Wijk, N. *Franck's Etymologisch Woordenboek der Nederlandsche Taal*. 'S-Gravenhage, 1912–49. Supplement by C. B. Haeringen, 1936.

Vasmer, Max. *Russisches Etymologisches Wörterbuch* (3 Volumes). 1953–58.

Von Wartburg, Walther. *Französisches Etymologisches Wörterbuch* (FEW). Tübingen, 1948– Basel, 1973. Edited by Otto Jänicke, 1973–77, and Carl Theodor Gossen until 1983.

Walde, Alois. *Lateinisches Etymologisches Wörterbuch* (3 Volumes). Third Revised Edition by J. B. Hofmann, Heidelberg, 1938–56.

Wentworth, Harold. *American Dialect Dictionary*. New York, 1944.

——— and Stuart Berg Flexner. *Dictionary of American Slang*. New York, 1960. Supplement, 1967.

Whitney, William Dwight. *The Century Dictionary and Cyclopedia* (10 Volumes). New York, 1889. Supplement (Volumes 11 and 12, 1909–10), edited by Benjamin E. Smith.

OTHER ENGLISH ETYMOLOGICAL DICTIONARIES

Klein, Ernest. *A Comprehensive Etymological Dictionary of the English Language* (2 Volumes). Amsterdam, 1966.

Onions, C. T. *The Oxford Dictionary of English Etymology*. Oxford, 1966.

Skeat, Walter W. *An Etymological Dictionary of the English Language*. Oxford, 1879–82. Revised Edition, 1909.

Weekley, Ernest. *An Etymological Dictionary of Modern English* (2 Volumes). London, 1921. Reprint, New York, 1967.

OTHER REFERENCE BOOKS AND TEXTBOOKS FREQUENTLY CONSULTED

Barnhart, Clarence L. *The New Century Handbook of English Literature*. New York, 1956.

Baugh, Albert C. *A History of the English Language*. Second Edition, New York, 1963.

——— *A Literary History of the English Language*. New York, 1948.

Hockett, Charles F. *A Course in Modern Linguistics*. New York, 1958.

Hoenigswald, Henry M. *Language Change and Linguistic Reconstruction*. Chicago, 1960.

Pyles, Thomas and John Algeo. *The Origins and Development of the English Language*. Third Edition. New York, 1982.

Sturtevant, E. H. *Linguistic Change: an introduction to the historical study of language*. Chicago, 1917.

Wyld, Henry Cecil. *A Short History of English*. Third Edition. New York, 1927.